CHILTON'S

AIR CONDITIONING AND HEATING MANUAL

Publisher Kerry A. Freeman, S.A.E.
Editor-In-Chief Dean F. Morgantini, S.A.E. □ **Managing Editor** David H. Lee, A.S.E., S.A.E.
Senior Editor Richard J. Rivele, S.A.E. □ **Senior Editor** Nick D'Andrea □ **Senior Editor** Ron Webb
Project Manager Peter M. Conti, Jr. □ **Project Manager** Ken Grabowski, A.S.E., S.A.E.
Project Manager Richard T. Smith
Service Editors Lawrence C. Braun, S.A.E., A.S.C., Robert E. Doughten, Jacques Gordon
Michael L. Grady, Ben Greisler, Martin J. Gunther, Steve Horner, Neil Leonard, A.S.E.,
James R. Marotta, Robert McAnally, Steven Morgan, Don Schnell, James B. Steele,
Larry E. Stiles, Jim Taylor, Anthony Tortorici, A.S.E., S.A.E.
Editorial Consultants Edward K. Shea, S.A.E., Stan Stephenson

Manager of Manufacturing John J. Cantwell
Production Manager W. Calvin Settle, Jr., S.A.E
Assistant Production Manager Andrea Steiger
Mechanical Artist Marsha Park Herman
Mechanical Artist Lorraine Martinelli
Special Projects Peter Kaprielyan

Director, Sales & Marketing Donald A. Wright
National Sales Coordinator David H. Flaherty
Regional Sales Managers Joseph Andrews, Jr., Larry W. Marshall, Bruce McCorkle

OFFICERS
President Gary R. Ingersoll
Senior Vice President, Book Publishing & Research Ronald A. Hoxter

CHILTON BOOK COMPANY
*ONE OF THE **ABC PUBLISHING COMPANIES,***
*A PART OF **CAPITAL CITIES/ABC, INC.***

ISBN 0-8019-8151-4 1234567890 0987654321 ISSN 1053-1114

SAFETY NOTICE

Proper service and repair procedures are vital to the safe, reliable operation of all motor vehicles, as well as the personal safety of those performing repairs. This manual outlines procedures for servicing and repairing vehicles using safe, effective methods. The procedures contain many NOTES, CAUTIONS and WARNINGS which should be followed along with standard safety procedures to eliminate the possibilty of personal injury or improper service which could damage the vehicle or compromise its safety.

It is important to note that the repair procedures and techniques, tools and parts for servicng motor vehicles, as well as the skill and experience of the individual performing the work vary widely. It is not possible to anticipate all of the conceivable ways or conditions under which vehicles may be serviced, or to provide cautions as to all of the possible hazards that may result. Standard and accepted safety precautions and equipment should be used when handling toxic or flammable fluids, and safety goggles or other protection should be used during cutting, grinding, chiseling, prying, or any other process that can cause material removal or projectiles.

Some procedures require the use of tools specially designed for a specific purpose. Before substituting another tool or procedure, you must be completely satisfied that neither your personal safety, nor the performance of the vehicle will be endangered

---

PART NUMBERS

Part numbers listed in this reference are not recomendations by Chilton for any product by brand name. They are references that can be used with interchange manuals and aftermarket supplier catalogs to locate each brand supplier‘s discrete part number.

Although information in this manual is based on industry sources and is complete as possible at the time of publication, the possibilty exists that some car manufacturers made later changes which could not be included here. While striving for total accuracy, Chilton Book Company cannot assume responsibity for any errors, changes or omissions that may occur in the compilation of this data.

1 CHRYSLER/DODGE/PLYMOUTH 1

ACCLAIM • ARIES • DAYTONA • DYNASTY • HORIZON • IMPERIAL • LANCER • LE BARON • NEW YORKER • OMNI • RELIANT • SHADOW • SPIRIT • SUNDANCE • TC

SPECIFICATIONS

ENGINE IDENTIFICATION

Year	Model	Engine Displacement cu. in. (liter)	Engine Series Identification (VIN)	No. of Cylinders	Engine Type
1989	Horizon	135 (2.2)	D	4	OHC
	Omni	135 (2.2)	D	4	OHC
	Aries	135 (2.2)	D	4	OHC
	Aries	153 (2.5)	K	4	OHC
	Reliant	135 (2.2)	D	4	OHC
	Reliant	153 (2.5)	K	4	OHC
	Daytona	135 (2.2)	A	4	OHC
	Daytona	153 (2.5)	J	4	OHC
	Daytona	153 (2.5)	K	4	OHC
	LeBaron (J body)	135 (2.2)	A	4	OHC
	LeBaron (J body)	153 (2.5)	J	4	OHC
	LeBaron (J body)	153 (2.5)	K	4	OHC
	Lancer	135 (2.2)	D	4	OHC
	Lancer	135 (2.2)	A	4	OHC
	Lancer	153 (2.5)	J	4	OHC
	Lancer	153 (2.5)	K	4	OHC
	LeBaron GTS	135 (2.2)	D	4	OHC
	LeBaron GTS	135 (2.2)	A	4	OHC
	LeBaron GTS	153 (2.5)	J	4	OHC
	LeBaron GTS	153 (2.5)	K	4	OHC
	Shadow	135 (2.2)	D	4	OHC
	Shadow	135 (2.2)	A	4	OHC
	Shadow	153 (2.5)	J	4	OHC
	Shadow	153 (2.5)	K	4	OHC
	Sundance	135 (2.2)	D	4	OHC
	Sundance	153 (2.5)	J	4	OHC
	Sundance	153 (2.5)	K	4	OHC
	Spirit	153 (2.5)	J	4	OHC
	Spirit	153 (2.5)	K	4	OHC
	Spirit	181 (3.0)	3	6	OHC
	Acclaim	153 (2.5)	J	4	OHC
	Acclaim	153 (2.5)	K	4	OHC
	Acclaim	181 (3.0)	3	6	OHC
	TC	135 (2.2)	A	4	OHC
	TC	135 (2.2)	R	4	DOHC
	Dynasty	153 (2.5)	K	4	OHC
	Dynasty	181 (3.0)	3	6	OHC
	New Yorker Landau	181 (3.0)	3	6	OHC
1990	Horizon	135 (2.2)	D	4	OHC
	Omni	135 (2.2)	D	4	OHC
	Daytona	135 (2.2)	C	4	OHC
	Daytona	153 (2.5)	J	4	OHC

ENGINE IDENTIFICATION

Year	Model	Engine Displacement cu. in. (liter)	Engine Series Identification (VIN)	No. of Cylinders	Engine Type
1990	Daytona	181 (3.0)	3	6	OHC
	LeBaron	135 (2.2)	C	4	OHC
	LeBaron	153 (2.5)	K	4	OHC
	LeBaron	153 (2.5)	J	4	OHC
	LeBaron	181 (3.0)	3	6	OHC
	LeBaron Landau	181 (3.0)	3	6	OHC
	Shadow	135 (2.2)	D	4	OHC
	Shadow	135 (2.2)	C	4	OHC
	Shadow	153 (2.5)	K	4	OHC
	Shadow	153 (2.5)	J	4	OHC
	Sundance	135 (2.2)	D	4	OHC
	Sundance	153 (2.5)	K	4	OHC
	Sundance	153 (2.5)	J	4	OHC
	Spirit	153 (2.5)	K	4	OHC
	Spirit	153 (2.5)	J	4	OHC
	Spirit	181 (3.0)	3	6	OHC
	Acclaim	153 (2.5)	K	4	OHC
	Acclaim	153 (2.5)	J	4	OHC
	Acclaim	181 (3.0)	3	6	OHC
	TC	135 (2.2)	R	4	DOHC
	TC	181 (3.0)	S	6	OHC
	Dynasty	153 (2.5)	K	4	OHC
	Dynasty	181 (3.0)	3	6	OHC
	Dynasty	201 (3.3)	R	6	OHC
	New Yorker Landau	181 (3.0)	3	6	OHC
	New Yorker Landau	201 (3.3)	R	6	OHC
	New Yorker Salon	181 (3.0)	3	6	OHC
	New Yorker Salon	201 (3.3)	R	6	OHC
	New Yorker 5th Avenue	201 (3.3)	R	6	OHC
	Imperial	201 (3.3)	R	6	OHC
1991	Daytona	153 (2.5)	K	4	OHC
	Daytona	153 (2.5)	J	4	OHC
	Daytona	181 (3.0)	3	6	OHC
	LeBaron	153 (2.5)	K	4	OHC
	LeBaron	153 (2.5)	J	4	OHC
	LeBaron	181 (3.0)	3	6	OHC
	LeBaron Landau	181 (3.0)	3	6	OHC
	Shadow	135 (2.2)	D	4	OHC
	Shadow	153 (2.5)	K	4	OHC
	Shadow	153 (2.5)	J	4	OHC
	Sundance	135 (2.2)	D	4	OHC
	Sundance	153 (2.5)	K	4	OHC
	Spirit	153 (2.5)	K	4	OHC
	Spirit	153 (2.5)	J	4	OHC

ENGINE IDENTIFICATION

Year	Model	Engine Displacement cu. in. (liter)	Engine Series Identification (VIN)	No. of Cylinders	Engine Type
	Spirit	181 (3.0)	3	6	OHC
	Spirit	135 (2.2)	4	4	DOHC
	Acclaim	153 (2.5)	K	4	OHC
	Acclaim	153 (2.5)	J	4	OHC
	Acclaim	181 (3.0)	3	6	OHC
	TC	181 (3.0)	3	6	OHC
	Dynasty	153 (2.5)	K	4	OHC
	Dynasty	181 (3.0)	3	6	OHC
	Dynasty	201 (3.3)	R	6	OHC
	New Yorker Salon	201 (3.3)	R	6	OHC
	New Yorker 5th Avenue	201 (3.3)	R	6	OHC
	New Yorker 5th Avenue	231 (3.8)	L	6	OHC
	Imperial	231 (3.8)	L	6	OHC

REFRIGERANT CAPACITIES

Year	Model	Freon (oz.)	Oil (fl. oz.) ①	Compressor Type
1989	All	38	11¹/₄	Fixed Displacement
	All	38	12³/₄	Variable Displacement
1990	All	38	11¹/₄	Fixed Displacement
	All	38	12³/₄	Variable Displacement
1991	Shadow	32	11¹/₄	Fixed Displacement
	Sundance	32	11¹/₄	Fixed Displacement
	Spirit	32	11¹/₄	Fixed Displacement
	Spirit	32	12³/₄	Variable Displacement
	Acclaim	32	11¹/₄	Fixed Displacement
	Acclaim	32	12³/₄	Variable Displacement
	LeBaron Landau	32	12³/₄	Variable Displacement
	Daytona	32	11¹/₄	Fixed Displacement
	Daytona	32	12³/₄	Variable Displacement
	LeBaron	32	11¹/₄	Fixed Displacement
	LeBaron	32	12³/₄	Variable Displacement
	Dynasty	34	11¹/₄	Fixed Displacement
	Dynasty	34	12³/₄	Variable Displacement
	New Yorker	34	12³/₄	Variable Displacement
	Imperial	34	12³/₄	Variable Displacement
	TC	38	12³/₄	Variable Displacement

① System total capacity

AIR CONDITIONING BELT TENSION CHART

Year	Model	Engine (L)	Belt Type	Specification ① New	Specification ① Used
1989	All	2.2	V	5/16	7/16
	All	2.5	V	5/16	7/16
	All	3.0	V	5/16	5/16
1990	All	2.2	V	5/16	7/16
	All	2.5	V	5/16	7/16
	All	3.0	V	5/16	5/16
	All	3.3	Serpentine	②	②
1991	All	2.2③	V	5/16	7/16
	Spirit R/T	2.2④	Serpentine	②	②
	All	2.5	V	5/16	7/16
	All	3.0	V	5/16	5/16
	All	3.3	Serpentine	②	②
	All	3.8	Serpentine	②	②

① Inches of deflection at the midpoint of the belt, using 10 lbs. force
② Automatic dynamic tensioner
③ Except Turbo III
④ Turbo III

SYSTEM DESCRIPTION

General Information

Conventional System

The components used in vehicles with heater only are very similar to those in vehicles equipped with air conditioning. Heater-only vehicles do not have the recirculating air door used in the A/C-heater housing of air conditioned vehicles. Additionally, vehicles with Automatic Temperature Control (ATC) share many basic air conditioning components with vehicles equipped with a conventional system, for the most part, only the control system is different. All vehicles, except 1989 Omni and Horizon, are equipped with a common A/C-heater housing fitted with different internal components, depending on its application.

The air flow system pulls outside air through the cowl opening at the base of the windshield and into the plenum chamber above the A/C-heater housing. On air conditioned vehicles, the air passes through the evaporator, then is either directed through or around the heater core by adjusting the blend air door with the TEMP control on the control panel. The air flow can be directed from the panel, panel and floor (bi-level), or floor and defrost oulets. The velocity of the flow can be controlled with the blower speed switch on the control panel.

On air conditioned vehicles, the intake of outside air can be shut off by moving the TEMP control knob to the RECIRC position, which closes the recirculation door and recirculates air already inside the passenger compartment. Depressing the DEFROST or A/C button will engage the compressor and remove heat and humidity from the air before it is directed through or around the heater core. Forced ventilation is directed from the instrument panel and/or floor outlets when the selector on the control panel is on the panel or bi-level position. The temperature of the forced vent air can be regulated with the TEMP control knob.

The side window demisters receive air from the A/C-heater housing and direct the flow to the front windows. The outlets are located either on the top outer corners of the instrument panel or on the doors themselves. The side demisters operate when the A/C control mode selector is in the FLOOR or DEFROST setting.

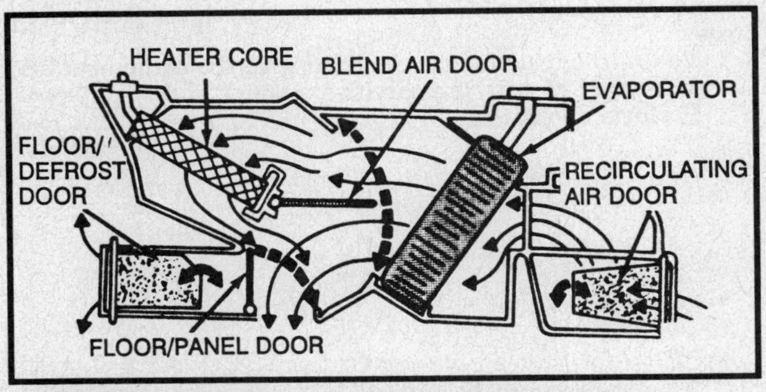
HEATER CORE
BLEND AIR DOOR
EVAPORATOR
FLOOR/
DEFROST
DOOR
RECIRCULATING
AIR DOOR
FLOOR/PANEL DOOR

Air conditioner/heater housing components

Automatic Temperature Control (ATC) System

The ATC system allows the operator to regulate the passenger compartment environment. A built-in computer regulates the desired temperature, air flow direction and blower speed. The operator may also select an AUTO mode feature, where the computer selects the variables.

The system goes into a maximum cool recirculted air lock-in mode when:

- A temperature setting of 65°F (18°C) is selected
- The compressor is turned on (snowflake illuminated)

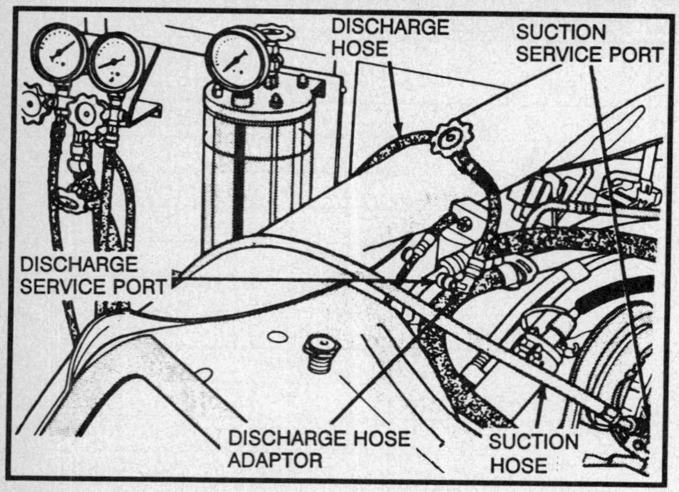
DISCHARGE HOSE
SUCTION SERVICE PORT
DISCHARGE SERVICE PORT
DISCHARGE HOSE ADAPTOR
SUCTION HOSE

Service valves—fixed displacement compressor

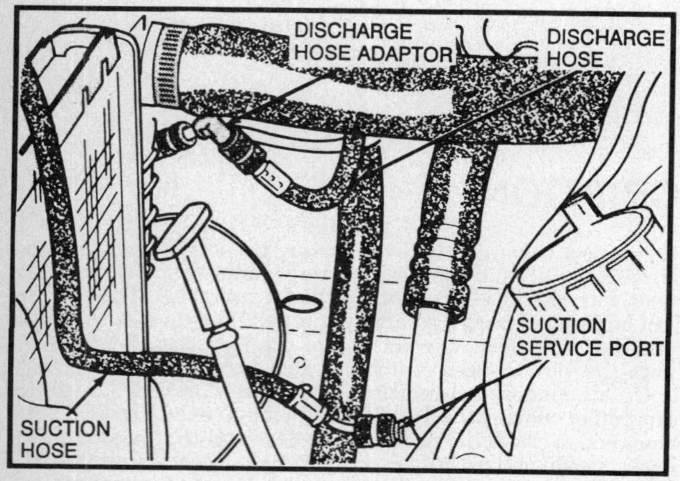
DISCHARGE HOSE ADAPTOR
DISCHARGE HOSE
SUCTION SERVICE PORT
SUCTION HOSE

Service valves—variable displacement compressor

- The system is not in the DEFROST mode
- The TEMP button is held in for 5 (1989–90) or 10 seconds (1991)

In the lock-in mode, the temperature will not be regulated until the system is turned off or the temperature setting is raised.

In 1989–90, vacuum is used to control the hot water valve, recirculation door, blend air door and defrost actuators. In 1991, vacuum is not used to control any of the ATC components. All items are driven or controlled electronically.

Service Valve Location

2.2L and 2.5L Engines

The discharge service port is located on the discharge line between the compressor and condenser. The suction service port is located on the compressor itself.

3.0L, 3.3L and 3.8L Engines

The discharge service port is located on the high pressure (liquid) line. The suction service port is located on the suction line between the compressor and the expansion valve.

System Discharging

R-12 refrigerant is a chloroflourocarbon which, when mishandled, can contribute to the depletion on the ozone layer in the upper atmosphere. Ozone filters out harmful radiation from the sun. In order to protect the ozone layer, an approved R-12 Recovery/Recycling machine that meets SAE standard J1991 should be employed when discharging the system. Follow the operating instructions provided with the approved equipment exactly to properly discharge the system.

System Evacuating

If the air conditioning system has been opened to the atmosphere, it should be air and moisture free before being recharged with refrigerant. Moisture and air mixed with refrigerant will raise the compressor head pressure, possibly damage the system's components and will reduce the performance of the system. Moisture will boil at normal room temperature when exposed to a vacuum. To evacuate, or rid the system of air and moisture:

1. Leak test the system and repair any leaks found.
2. Connect an approved charging station, Recovery/Recycling machine or manifold gauge set and vacuum pump to the discharge and suction ports. The red hose is normally connected to the discharge (high pressure) line, and the blue hose is connected to the suction (low pressure) line.
3. Open the discharge and suction ports and start the vacuum pump. If the pump is not able to pull at least 26 in. Hg, there is a leak that must be repaired before evacuation can occur.
4. Once the system has reached at least 26 in. Hg, allow the system to evacuate for at least 10 minutes. The longer the system is evacuated, the more contaminants will be removed.
5. Close all valves and turn the pump off. If the system loses more than 2 in. Hg after 15 minutes, there is a leak that should be repaired.

System Charging

1. Connect an approved charging station, Recovery/Recycling machine or manifold gauge set to the discharge and suction ports. The red hose is normally connected to the discharge (high pressure) line, and the blue hose is connected to the suction (low pressure) line.
2. Follow the instructions provided with the equipment and charge the system with the specified amount of refrigerant.
3. Perform a leak test.

SYSTEM COMPONENTS

Radiator

REMOVAL AND INSTALLATION

1. Disconnect the negative battery cable.
2. Drain the coolant.
3. Remove the upper hose and coolant reserve tank hose from the radiator.
4. Remove the electric cooling fan.
5. Raise the vehicle and support safely. Remove the lower hose from the radiator.
6. Disconnect the automatic transaxle cooler hoses, if equipped, and plug them. Lower the vehicle.
7. Remove the mounting brackets and carefully lift the radiator from the engine compartment.

To install:

8. Lower the radiator into position.
9. Install the mounting brackets.
10. Raise the vehicle, if necessary, and support safely. Connect the automatic transaxle cooler lines, if equipped.
11. Connect the lower hose and lower the vehicle.
12. Install the electric cooling fan.
13. Connect the upper hose and coolant reserve tank hose.
14. Fill the system with coolant.
15. Connect the negative battery cable, run the vehicle until the thermostat opens, fill the radiator completely and check the automatic transaxle fluid level, if equipped.
16. Once the vehicle has cooled, recheck the coolant level.

COOLING SYSTEM BLEEDING

To bleed air from the 2.2L and 2.5L engines, remove the hex-head plug on top of the thermostat housing. Fill the radiator with coolant until the coolant comes out the hole. Install the plug and continue to fill the radiator. This will vent all trapped air from the engine.

The thermostat in the 3.0L engine is equipped with a small air vent valve that allows trapped air to bleed from the system during refilling. This valve negates the need for cooling system bleeding in those engines.

On the 3.3L and 3.8L engines, remove the engine temperature sending unit. Fill the radiator with coolant until the coolant comes out the hole. Install the switch and continue to fill the radiator. This will vent all trapped air from the engine.

Cooling Fan

TESTING

CAUTION

Make sure the key is in the OFF position when checking the electric cooling fan. If not, the fan could turn ON at any time, causing serious personal injury.

1. Unplug the fan connector.
2. Using a jumper wire, connect the female terminal of the fan connector to the negative battery terminal.
3. The fan should turn ON when the male terminal is connected to the positive battery terminal.
4. If not, the fan is defective and should be replaced.

REMOVAL AND INSTALLATION

1. Disconnect the negative battery cable.
2. Unplug the connector.
3. Remove the mounting screws.
4. Remove the fan assembly from the vehicle.
5. The installation is the reverse of the removal procedure.
6. Connect the negative battery cable and check the fan for proper operation.

Condenser

REMOVAL AND INSTALLATION

1. Disconnect the negative battery cable.
2. Properly discharge the air conditioning system.
3. Remove the radiator assembly.
4. Remove the refrigerant lines attaching nut and separate the lines from the condenser sealing plate. Discard the gasket.
5. Cover the exposed ends of the lines to minimize contamination.
6. Remove the bolts that attach the condenser to the radiator support.
7. Lift the condenser and remove from the vehicle.

To install:

8. Position the condenser and install the bolts.
9. Coat the new gasket with wax-free refrigerant oil and install. Connect the lines to the condenser sealing plate and tighten the nut.
10. Install the radiator and fill with coolant.
11. Evacuate and recharge the air conditioning system. Add 1 oz. of refrigerant oil during the recharge. Check for leaks.

Compressor

REMOVAL AND INSTALLATION

1. Disconnect the negative battery cable.
2. Properly discharge the air conditioning system.
3. Remove the compressor drive belt. Disconnect the compressor lead.
4. Raise the vehicle if necessary. Remove the refrigerant lines from the compressor and discard the gaskets. Cover the exposed ends of the lines to minimize contamination.

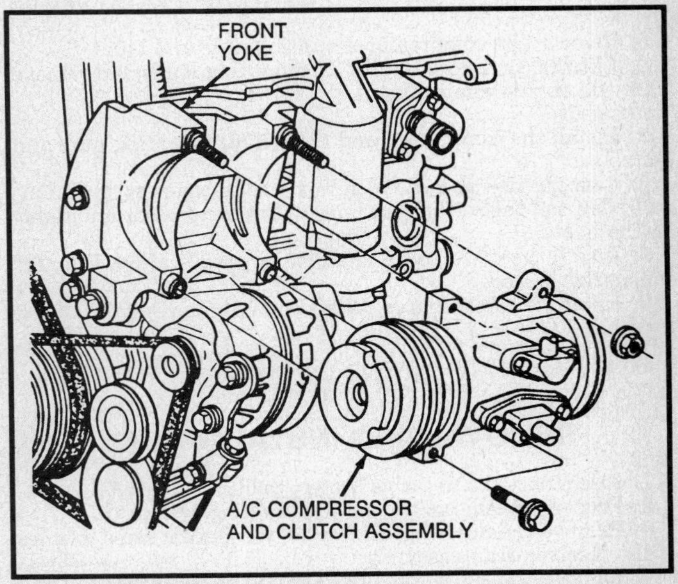
FRONT
YOKE
A/C COMPRESSOR
AND CLUTCH ASSEMBLY

Typical air conditioning compressor mounting—2.2L and 2.5L engines

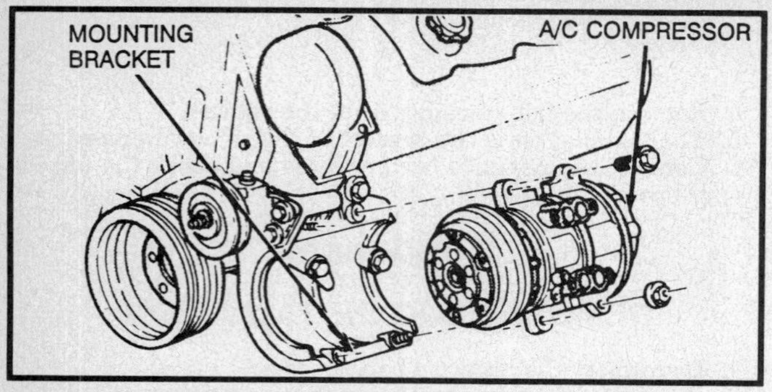
MOUNTING
BRACKET
A/C COMPRESSOR

Air conditioning compressor mounting — 3.0L engine

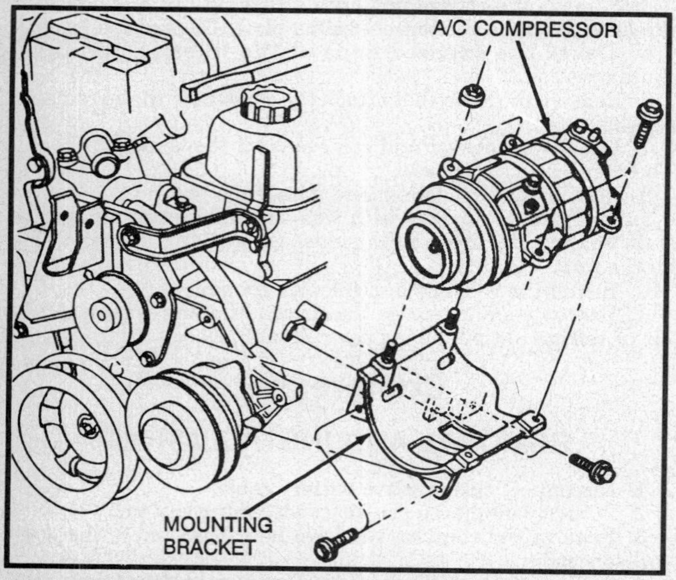
A/C COMPRESSOR
MOUNTING
BRACKET

Air conditioning compressor mounting — 3.3L and 3.8L engines

5. Remove the compressor mounting nuts and bolts.
6. Lift the compressor off of its mounting studs and remove from the engine compartment.

To install:

7. Install the compressor and tighten all mounting nuts and bolts.
8. Coat the new gaskets with wax-free refrigerant oil and install. Connect the refrigerant lines to the compressor and tighten the bolts.
9. Install the drive belt and adjust to specification. Connect the electrical lead.
10. Evacuate and recharge the air conditioning system. Check for leaks.

Receiver/Drier

REMOVAL AND INSTALLATION

1. Disconnect the negative battery cable.
2. Properly discharge the air conditioning system.
3. Remove the nuts that fasten the refrigerant lines to sides of the receiver/drier assembly.
4. Remove the refrigerant lines from the receiver/drier and discard the gaskets. Cover the exposed ends of the lines to minimize contamination.
5. Remove the mounting strap bolts and remove the receiver/drier from the engine compartment.

To install:

6. Transfer the mounting strap to the new receiver/drier.
7. Coat the new gaskets with wax-free refrigerant oil and install. Connect the refrigerant lines to the receiver/drier and tighten the nuts.
8. Evacuate and recharge the air conditioning system. Add 1 oz. of refrigerant oil during the recharge. Check for leaks.

Expansion Valve (H-Valve)

TESTING

1. Connect a manifold gauge set or charging station to the air conditioning system. Verify adequate refrigerant level.
2. On Omni and Horizon, disconnect and plug the water valve hose.
3. If the vehicle is not equipped with ATC, locate the recirculating door actuator on the right side of the A/C-heater housing. Switch the light green and dark green vacuum lines.
4. Bypass the clutch cycling switch by unplugging it and jumping the wires. If equipped with a fin-sensing cycling clutch switch, jump the outer wires in the connector.
5. Disconnect the low pressure or differential pressure cut off switch connector and jump the wires inside the boot.
6. Close all doors, windows and vents to the passenger compartment.
7. If equipped with ATC, set the automatic temperature control to A/C, 85°F, FLOOR and high blower speed.
8. If not equipped with ATC, set controls to A/C, full heat and high blower speed.
9. Start the engine and hold the idle speed at 1000 rpm. After the engine has reached normal operating temperature, allow the passenger compartment ot heat up to create the need for maximum refrigerant flow into the evaporator.
10. The discharge (high pressure) gauge should read 140–240 psi and suction (low pressure) gauge should read 20–30 psi, providing the refrigerant charge is sufficient.
11. If the suction side is within specifications, freeze the expansion valve control head using a very cold substance (liquid CO_2 or dry ice) for 30 seconds:
    a. If equipped with a silver H-valve used with fixed displacement compressor, the suction side pressure should drop to 15 in. Hg. If not, replace the expansion valve.
    b. If equipped with a black H-valve used with variable displacement compressor, the discharge pressure should drop about 15%. If not, replace the expansion valve.
12. Allow the expansion valve to thaw. As it thaws, the pressures should stabilize to the values in Step 10. If not, replace the expansion valve.
13. Once the test is complete, put the vacuum lines back in their original locations, and perform and overall performance test.

REMOVAL AND INSTALLATION

1. Disconnect the negative battery cable.
2. Properly discharge the air conditioning system.
3. Disconnect the low pressure cutoff switch.
4. Remove the attaching bolt at the center of the refrigerant plumbing sealing plate.
5. Pull the refrigerant lines assembly away from the expansion valve. Cover the exposed ends of the lines to minimize contamination.
6. Remove the 2 Torx® screws that mount the expansion valve to the evaporator sealing plate.
7. Remove the valve and discard the gaskets.

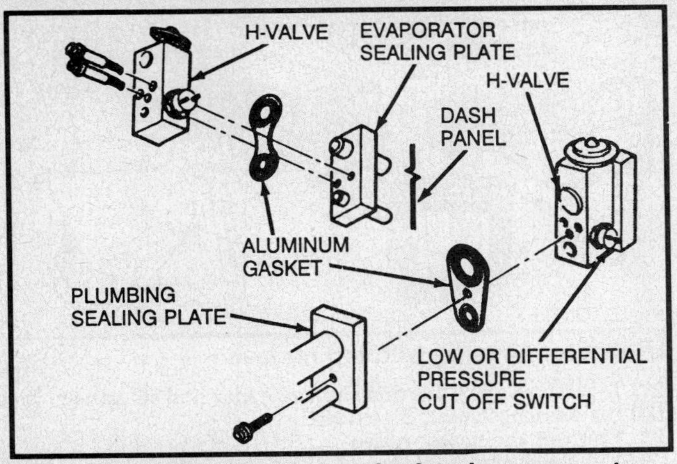
H-VALVE
EVAPORATOR SEALING PLATE
H-VALVE
DASH PANEL
ALUMINUM GASKET
PLUMBING SEALING PLATE
LOW OR DIFFERENTIAL PRESSURE CUT OFF SWITCH

Expansion valve (H-valve) and related components

To install:

8. Transfer the low pressure cutoff switch to the new valve, if necessary.
9. Coat the new "figure-8" gasket with wax-free refrigerant oil and install to the evaporator sealing plate.
10. Install the expansion valve and torque the Torx® screws to 100 inch lbs.
11. Lubricate the remaining gasket and install with the refrigerant plumbing to the expansion valve. Torque the attaching bolt to 200 inch lbs.
12. Connect the low pressure cutoff switch connector.
13. Evacuate and recharge the air conditioning system. Check for leaks.

Blower Motor

REMOVAL AND INSTALLATION

1. Disconnect the negative battery cable.
2. Remove the glove box assembly, lower right side instrument panel trim cover and right cowl trim panel, as required. Disconnect the blower lead wire connector.
3. If the vehicle is equipped with air conditioning, disconnect the 2 vacuum lines from the recirculating door actuator and position the actuator aside. On Omni and Horizon not equipped with air conditioning, remove the left side heater outlet duct.
4. Remove the 2 screws at the top of the blower housing that secure it to the unit cover.
5. Remove the 5 screws from around the blower housing and separate the blower housing from the unit.
6. Remove the 3 screws that secure the blower assembly to the heater or air conditioning housing and remove the assembly from the unit. Remove the fan from the blower motor.
7. The installation is the reverse of the removal procedure.
8. Connect the negative battery cable and check the blower motor for proper operation.

Blower Motor Resistor

REMOVAL AND INSTALLATION

Omni and Horizon Without Air Conditioning

1. Disconnect the negative battery cable.
2. Locate the resistor block at the right side of the heater housing.
3. Disconnect the wire harness.

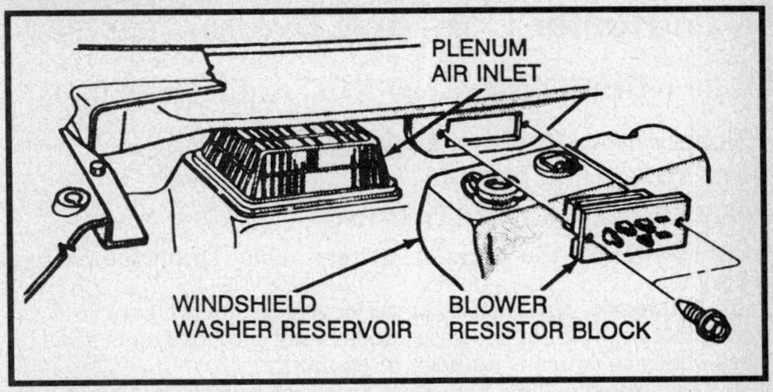
PLENUM AIR INLET
WINDSHIELD WASHER RESERVOIR
BLOWER RESISTOR BLOCK

Blower resistor location—Shadow, Sundance, Spirit, Acclaim, LeBaron Landau, Dynasty, New Yorker and Imperial

4. Remove the attaching screws and remove the resistor from the housing.
5. Make sure there is no contact between any of the coils before installing.
6. The installation is the reverse of the removal procedure.
7. Connect the negative battery cable and check the blower system for proper operation.

Aries, Reliant, Lancer, LeBaron GTS, Daytona, Maserati TC, LeBaron Without ATC, and Omni and Horizon with Air Conditioning

1. Disconnect the negative battery cable.
2. Remove the glove box assembly.
3. Remove the security and lamp outage modules, if equipped.
4. Locate the resistor block above and to the front of the glove box opening on the dash panel and disconnect the wire harness.
5. Remove the attaching screws and pull the resistor straight from the panel.
6. Make sure there is no contact between any of the coils before installing.
7. The installation is the reverse of the removal procedure.
8. Connect the negative battery cable and check the blower system for proper operation.

Shadow, Sundance, Spirit, Acclaim, LeBaron Landau, Dynasty, New Yorker and Imperial Without ATC

1. Disconnect the negative battery cable.
2. Raise the hood.
3. On Shadow and Sundance, remove the wiper arms and remove the cowl plenum grille.
4. Remove the 4 air intake shield attaching screws and remove the shield.
5. Disconnect the wire harness from the resistor, located behind the windshield washer reservoir.
6. Remove the attaching screws and pull the resistor straight from the panel.
7. Make sure there is no contact between any of the coils before installing.
8. The installation is the reverse of the removal procedure.
9. Connect the negative battery cable and check the blower system for proper operation.

Heater Core and Evaporator

REMOVAL AND INSTALLATION

Except Omni, Horizon, Dynasty, New Yorker and Imperial

WITHOUT AIR CONDITIONING

1. Disconnect the negative battery cable. Drain the cooling system.
2. Clamp off the heater hoses near the heater core and remove the hoses from the core tubes. Plug the hose ends and the core tubes to prevent spillage of coolant.
3. Remove the glove box, right side kick and sill panels and all modules, relay panels and computer components in the vacinity of the heater housing.
4. Remove the lower instrument panel silencers and reinforcements. Remove the radio and other dash-mounted optional equipment, as required.
5. Remove the floor console, if equipped. Remove the floor and defroster distribution ducts.
6. Remove the bolt holding the right side instrument panel to the right cowl.
7. Disconnect the blower motor wiring, antenna, resistor wiring and the temperature control cable.
8. On 1990–91 Daytona and LeBaron, using a suitable cutting device, cut the instrument panel along the indented line along the padded cover to the right of the glove box opening. Cut only plastic, not metal. Remove the reinforcement and the piece of instrument panel that is riveted to it.
9. Disconnect the demister hoses from the top of the housing, if equipped.
10. Disconnect the hanger strap from the package and rotate it aside.
11. Remove the retaining nuts from the package mounting studs at the firewall.
12. Fold the carpeting and insulation back to provide a little more working room and to prevent spillage from staining the carpeting. Pull the right side of the instrument panel out as far as possible.
13. Remove the heater housing from the dash panel and remove it from the passenger compartment. Remove the passenger seat, if it is preventing removal.
14. To disassemble the housing assembly, remove the retaining screws from the cover and remove the cover.
15. Remove the retaining screw from the heater core and remove the core from the housing assembly.

To install:

16. Remove the temperature control door from the housing and clean the unit out with solvent. Lubricate the lower pivot rod and its well and install. Wrap the heater core with foam tape and place it in position. Secure it with its screw.
17. Assemble the housing, making sure all cover screws were used.
18. Connect the demister hoses. Install the nuts to the firewall and connect the hanger strap inside the passenger compartment.
19. Fold the carpeting back into position.
20. Install the bolt that attaches the right side of the instrument panel to the cowl.
21. Connect the blower motor wiring, antenna, resistor wiring and the temperature control cable.
22. Install the air distribution ducts.
23. Install the floor console, if equipped.
24. Install the radio and all other dash mounted items that were removed during the disassembly procedure.
25. Install the lower instrument panel reinforcements and silencers.
26. Install all modules, relay panels and computer components that were removed during the disassembly procedure.

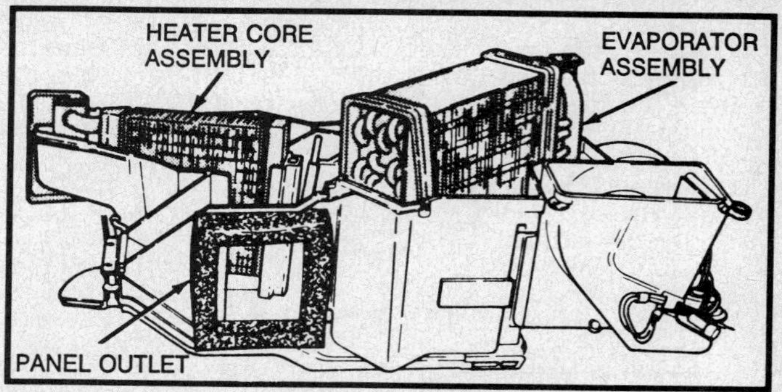
HEATER CORE
ASSEMBLY
EVAPORATOR
ASSEMBLY
PANEL OUTLET

A/C-heater housing with top removed

27. Install the glove box and right side kick and sill panels. Install the passenger seat, if removed.
28. Connect the heater hoses.
29. Fill the cooling system.
30. Connect the negative battery cable and check the entire climate control system for proper operation and leakage.

WITH AIR CONDITIONING

1. Disconnect the negative battery cable. Properly discharge the air conditioning system. Drain the cooling system.
2. Clamp off the heater hoses near the heater core and remove the hoses from the core tubes. Plug the hose ends and the core tubes to prevent spillage of coolant.
3. Disconnect the H-valve connection at the valve and remove the H-valve. Remove the condensation tube.
4. Disconnect the vacuum lines at the brake booster and water valve.
5. Remove the glove box, right side kick and sill panels and all modules, relay panels and computer components in the vacinity of the housing.
6. Remove the lower instrument panel silencers and reinforcements. Remove the radio and other dash-mounted optional equipment, as required.
7. Remove the floor console, if equipped. Remove the floor and center distribution ducts.
8. Remove the bolt holding the right side instrument panel to the right cowl.
9. Disconnect the blower motor wiring, antenna, resistor wiring and the temperature control cable. Disconnect the vacuum harness at the connection at the top of the housing. If equipped with Automatic Temperature Control (ATC), disconnect the instrument panel wiring from the rear of the ATC unit.
10. On 1990–91 Daytona and LeBaron, using a suitable cutting device, cut the instrument panel along the indented line along the padded cover to the right of the glove box opening. Cut only plastic, not metal. Remove the reinforcement and the piece of instrument panel that is riveted to it.
11. Disconnect the demister hoses from the top of the housing, if equipped.
12. Disconnect the hanger strap from the package and rotate it aside.
13. Remove the retaining nuts from the package mounting studs at the firewall.
14. Fold the carpeting and insulation back to provide a little more working room and to prevent spillage from staining the carpeting. Pull the right side of the instrument panel out as far as possible.
15. Remove the entire housing assembly from the dash panel and remove it from the passenger compartment. Remove the passenger seat, if it is preventing removal.
16. To disassemble the housing assembly, remove the vacuum diaphragm and retaining screws from the cover and remove the cover.
17. Remove the retaining screw from the heater core or evaporator and remove the unit from the housing assembly.

To install:

18. Remove the temperature control door from the housing and clean the unit out with solvent. Lubricate the lower pivot rod and its well and install. Wrap the heater core with foam tape and place it in position, if removed. Secure the core or evaporator with its screw.
19. Assemble the housing, making sure all vacuum tubing is properly routed.
20. Feed the vacuum lines through the hole in the firewall and install the assembly to the vehicle. Connect the vacuum harness and demister hoses. Install the nuts to the firewall and connect the hanger strap inside the passenger compartment. If equipped with Automatic Temperature Control (ATC), connect the instrument panel wiring to the rear of the ATC unit.
21. Fold the carpeting back into position.
22. Install the bolt that attaches the right side of the instrument panel to the cowl.
23. Connect the blower motor wiring, antenna, resistor wiring and the temperature control cable.
24. Install the center and floor distribution ducts.
25. Install the floor console, if equipped.
26. Install the radio and all other dash mounted items that were removed during the disassembly procedure.
27. Install the lower instrument panel reinforcements and silencers.
28. Install all modules, relay panels and computer components that were removed during the disassembly procedure.
29. Install the glove box and right side kick and sill panels. Install the passenger seat, if removed.
30. Connect the vacuum lines at the brake booster and water valve.
31. Using new gaskets, install the H-valve and condensation tube.
32. Connect the heater hoses.
33. Using the proper equipment, evacuate and recharge the air conditioning system. If the evaportor was replaced, add 2 oz. of refrigerant oil during the recharge.
34. Fill the cooling system.
35. Connect the negative battery cable and check the entire climate control system for proper operation and leakage.

Omni and Horizon

WITHOUT AIR CONDITIONING

1. Disconnect the negative battery cable.
2. Drain the coolant. Clamp off the heater hoses near the heater core and remove the hoses from the core tubes. Plug the hose ends and the core tubes to prevent spillage of coolant.
3. Disconnect the blower motor connector.
4. Remove the ash tray.
5. Depress the tab on the temperature control cable and pull the cable from its housing on the heater assembly.
6. Remove the glove box assembly and unplug the resistor block.
7. Remove the 2 nuts fastening the heater assembly to the firewall and remove the screw attaching the heater support brace to the instrument panel.
8. Remove the heater support bracket nut. Disconnect the strap from the plenum stud and lower the assembly from under the instrument panel.
9. Depress the tab on the flag and pull the mode door control cable from its housing on the heater assembly.
10. Move the assembly toward the right side of the vehicle and remove.
11. With the assembly on a workbench, remove the top cover and slide the heater from its cavity in the assembly.

To install:

12. Clean the inside of the assembly and assemble.
13. Connect the mode control cable to the mode door crank and position the heater assembly under the instrument panel. Slide the assembly forward so the mounting studs and heater core tubes project through their holes in the firewall. Install the support bracket and brace to hold the assembly in place.
14. From the engine compartment, install the 2 nuts on the firewall and connect the heater hoses.
15. Connect the temperature control cable, blower motor wiring and resistor block connector.
16. Install the defroster duct.
17. Install the ash tray and glove box.
18. Fill the cooling system.
19. Connect the negative battery cable and check the heater for proper operation and leaks.

WITH AIR CONDITIONING

1. Disconnect the negative battery cable. Properly discharge the air conditioning system. Drain the cooling system.
2. Clamp off the heater hoses near the heater core and remove the hoses from the core tubes. Plug the hose ends and the core tubes to prevent spillage of coolant.
3. Disconnect the H-valve connection at the valve and remove the H-valve. Remove the condensation tube. Disconnect the vacuum lines at the brake booster and water valve.
4. Disconnect the temperature door cable from evaporator/heater assembly.
5. Remove the glove box assembly.
6. On 1990–90 vehicles, remove the Air Bag Diagnostic Module (ABDM) from its mount and position aside. Remove the mounting bracket.
7. Disconnect the blower motor feed wire and vacuum harness.
8. Remove the central air duct cover from the central air distributor duct.
9. Remove the screws securing the central air conditioning air distributor duct. Remove the duct from under the dash panel.
10. From the engine compartment, remove the nuts that attach the unit to the firewall.
11. Remove the panel support bracket.
12. Remove the right side cowl lower panel and the top cover of the instrument panel.
13. Remove the instrument panel pivot bracket screw from the right side.
14. Remove the screws securing the lower instrument panel and steering column, if required.
15. Pull the carpet rearward as far as possible.
16. Remove the nut from the air conditioning to plenum mounting brace and blower motor ground cable. Support the unit and remove the brace from its stud.
17. Lift the unit and pull it rearward as far as possible to clear the dash panel and liner. Pull rearward on the lower instrument panel to gain enough clearance to remove the unit.
18. Slowly lower the unit to floor and slide out from the under dash panel.
19. With the unit on a workbench, remove the nut from the mode door actuator arm on the top cover. Remove the retaining clips from the front edge of the cover.
20. Remove the mode door actuator to cover screws and remove the actuator.
21. Remove the cover to heater evaporator assembly screws and remove the cover. Lift the mode door from the unit.
22. Remove the heater core or evaporator retaining bracket and screw. Lift the heater core or evaporator from the unit.

To install:

23. Remove the temperature control door from the housing and clean the unit out with solvent. Lubricate the lower pivot rod and its well and install. Wrap the heater core with foam tape and place it in position, if removed. Secure the unit with its screw.
24. Assemble the package, making sure all vacuum tubing is properly routed.

25. Feed the vacuum lines through the hole in the firewall and install the assembly to the vehicle. Connect the vacuum harness and defroster duct adaptor. Install the nuts to the firewall and connect the hanger strap inside the passenger compartment.
26. Fold the carpeting back into position. Connect the blower motor wiring and install the ABDM.
27. Install the center distribution and defroster adaptor ducts.
28. Secure the lower instrument panel and steering column, as required.
29. Install the instrument panel pivot bracket screw at the right side.
30. Install the right side cowl lower panel and the top cover of the instrument panel. Install the panel support bracket.
31. Connect the vacuum lines at the brake booster and water valve. Using new gaskets, install the H-valve and condensation tube.
32. Connect the heater hoses.
33. Using the proper equipment, evacuate and recharge the air conditioning system. If the evaporator was replaced, add 2 oz. of refrigerant oil during the recharge.
34. Fill the cooling system.
35. Connect the negative battery cable and check the entire climate control system for proper operation and leakage.

Dynasty, New Yorker and Imperial

WITH AIR CONDITIONING

1. Disconnect the negative battery cable. Properly discharge the air conditioning system. Drain the cooling system.
2. Clamp off the heater hoses near the heater core and remove the hoses from the core tubes. Plug the hose ends and the core tubes to prevent spillage of coolant.
3. Disconnect the H-valve connection at the valve and remove the H-valve. Remove the condensation tube.
4. Disconnect the vacuum lines at the brake booster and water valve, if equipped.
5. Remove the right upper and lower under-panel silencers.
6. Remove the steering column cover and the ash tray.
7. Remove the left side under-panel silencer.
8. Remove the right side cowl trim piece.
9. Remove the glove box assembly and the right side instrument panel reinforcement.
10. Remove the center distribution and defroster adaptor ducts.
11. Disconnect the relay module, blower motor wiring and 25-way connector bracket and fuse block from the panel.
12. Disconnect the demister hoses from the top of the package.
13. Disconnect the temperature control cable and vacuum harness, if equipped. If equipped with Automatic Temperature Control (ATC), disconnect the instrument panel wiring from the rear of the ATC unit.
14. Disconnect the hanger strap from the package and rotate it aside.
15. Remove the retaining nuts from the package mounting studs at the firewall.
16. Fold the carpeting and insulation back to provide a little more working room and to prevent spillage from staining the carpeting.
17. Move the package rearward to clear the mounting studs and lower.
18. Pull the right side of the instrument panel out as far as possible. Rotate the package while removing it from under the instrument panel.
19. To disassemble the housing assembly, remove the vacuum diaphragm, if equipped. Then remove the retaining screws from the cover and remove the cover.
20. Remove the retaining screw from the heater core or evaporator and remove the from the housing assembly.

To install:

21. Remove the temperature control door from the housing and clean the unit out with solvent. Lubricate the lower pivot rod and its well and install. Wrap the heater core with foam tape and place it in position, if removed. Secure the unit with its screw.
22. Assemble the package, making sure all vacuum tubing is properly routed.
23. If equipped, feed the vacuum lines through the hole in the firewall and install the assembly to the vehicle. Connect the vacuum harness and demister hoses. Install the nuts to the firewall and connect the hanger strap inside the passenger compartment.
24. Fold the carpeting back into position.
25. Connect the wiring to the ATC unit, if equipped.
26. Install the fuse block. Connect the 25-way connector, relay module and blower motor wiring.
27. Install the center distribution and defroster adaptor ducts.
28. Install the right side instrument panel reinforcement and the glove box assembly.
29. Install the right side cowl trim piece, left side under-panel silencer, steering column cover, ash tray and right side under-panel silencers.
30. Connect the vacuum lines at the brake booster and water valve.
31. Using new gaskets, install the H-valve and condensation tube.
32. Connect the heater hoses.
33. Using the proper equipment, evacuate and recharge the air conditioning system. If the evaporator was replaced, add 2 oz. of refrigerant oil during the recharge.
34. Fill the cooling system.
35. Connect the negative battery cable and check the entire climate control system for proper operation and leakage.

Refrigerant Lines

REMOVAL AND INSTALLATION

1. Disconnect the negative battery cable.
2. Properly discharge the air conditioning system.
3. Remove the nuts or bolts that attach the refrigerant lines sealing plates to the adjoining components.
4. Remove the lines and discard the gaskets.

To install:

5. Coat the new gaskets with wax-free refrigerant oil and install. Connect the refrigerant lines to the adjoining components and tighten the nuts or bolts.
6. Evacuate and recharge the air conditioning system. Check for leaks.

Manual Control Head

REMOVAL AND INSTALLATION

1. Disconnect the negative battery cable.
2. Remove the necessary bezel(s) in order to gain access to the control head.
3. Remove the screws that fasten the control head to the instrument panel.
4. Pull the unit out and unplug the electrical and vacuum connectors. Disconnect the temperature control cable by pushing the flag in and pulling the end from its seat.
5. Remove the control head from the instrument panel.
6. The installation is the reverse of the removal procedure.
7. Connect the negative battery cable and check the entire climate control system for proper operation.

Manual Control Cable

ADJUSTMENT

All control cables are self-adjusting. If the cable is not fuctioning properly, check for kinks and lubricate dry moving parts. The cable cannot be disassembled; replace if faulty.

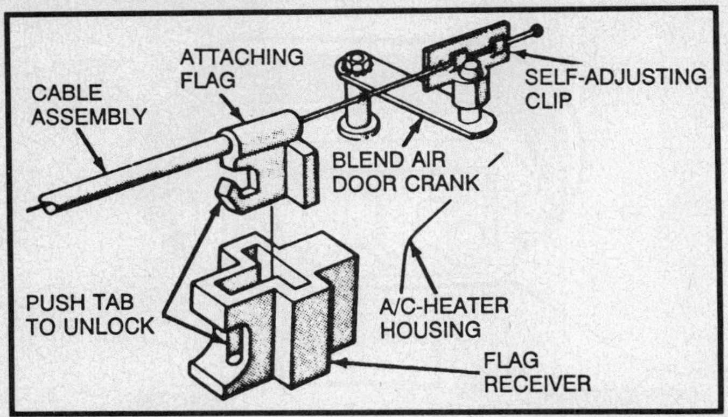
ATTACHING FLAG
CABLE ASSEMBLY
SELF-ADJUSTING CLIP
BLEND AIR DOOR CRANK
PUSH TAB TO UNLOCK
A/C-HEATER HOUSING
FLAG RECEIVER

Typical conventional cable attachment flag and door crank

REMOVAL AND INSTALLATION

1. Disconnect the negative battery cable.
2. Remove the necessary bezel(s) in order to gain access to the control head.
3. Remove the screws that fasten the control head to the instrument panel.
4. Pull the unit out and disconnect the temperature control cable by pushing the flag in and pulling the end from its seat.
5. The temperature control cable end is located at the bottom of the A/C-heater housing. On Omni and Horizon without A/C, the mode door cable end is accessed by removing the radio. Disconnect the cable end by pushing the flag in and pulling the end from its seat.
6. Disconnect the self-adjusting clip from the blend air or mode door crank.
7. Take note of the cable's routing and remove the from the vehicle.

To install:

8. Install the cable by routing it in exactly the same position as it was prior to removal.
9. Connect the self-adjusting clip to the door crank and click the flag into the seat.
10. Connect the upper end of the cable to the contol head.
11. Place the temperature lever on the COOL side of tis travel. Allowing the self-adjusting clip to slide on the cable, rotate the blend air door conterclockwise by hand until it stops.
12. Cycle the lever back and forth a few times to make sure the cable moves freely.
13. Connect the negative battery cable and check the entire climate control system for proper operation.

Electronic Control Head

REMOVAL AND INSTALLATION

1. Disconnect the negative battery cable.
2. Remove the necessary bezel(s) in order to gain access to the control head.
3. Remove the screws that fasten the control head to the instrument panel.
4. Pull the unit out and unplug the wire harness.
5. Remove the control head from the instrument panel.
6. The installation is the reverse of the removal procedure.
7. Connect the negative battery cable and check the entire climate control system for proper operation.

SENSORS AND SWITCHES

Compressor Clutch Coil Cycling Switches

NOTE: Vehicles equipped with a variable displacement compressor do not have clutch cycling switches. The compressor is designed to change displacement to match the vehicle's air conditioning demand without cycling. The variable displacement compressor can be identified by the location of the high pressure line mounted to the end of the compressor case.

OPERATION

Cycling Clutch Switch

OMNI AND HORIZON

On Omni and Horizon, the cycling clutch switch is located on the refrigerant plumbing sealing plate near the H-valve and is connected in series with the compressor clutch coil. It is a relay prevents evaporated freeze-up by cycling the compressor clutch coil depending on the temperature sensed by the freon-charged capillary tube, which is inserted in a well on the suction line. The tube must be lined with special grease required for proper switch sensing. The switch is a sealed and specially calibrated unit that should be replaced if found to be defective.

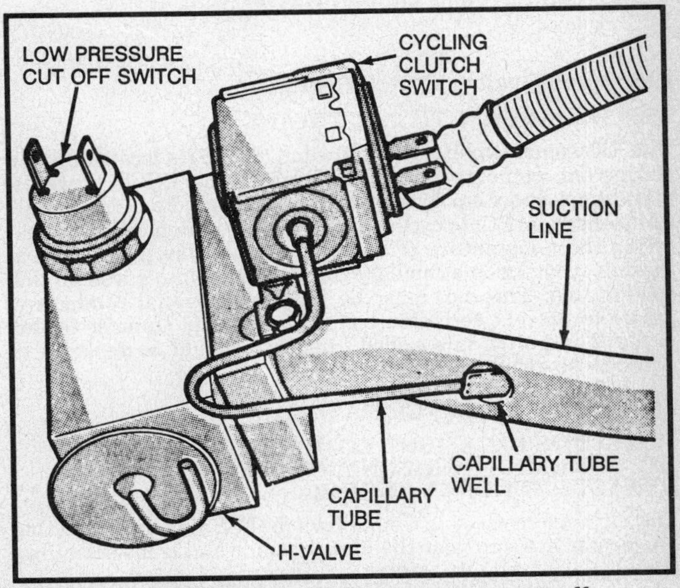
LOW PRESSURE CUT OFF SWITCH
CYCLING CLUTCH SWITCH
SUCTION LINE
CAPILLARY TUBE WELL
CAPILLARY TUBE
H-VALVE

Cycling clutch switch and low pressure cut off switch—Omni and Horizon

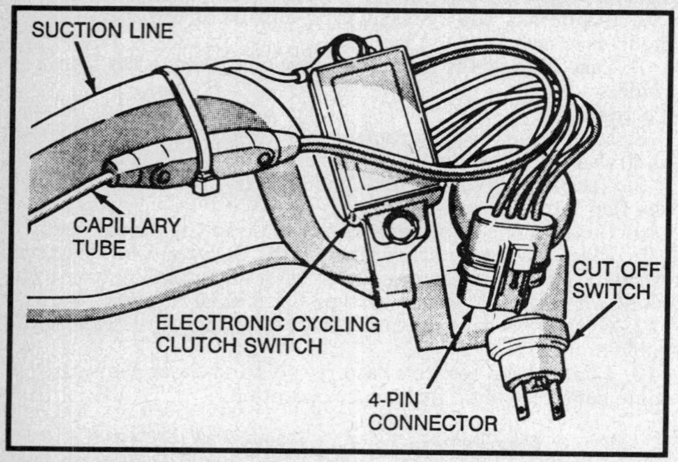
SUCTION LINE
CAPILLARY TUBE
ELECTRONIC CYCLING CLUTCH SWITCH
4-PIN CONNECTOR
CUT OFF SWITCH

Electronic cycling clutch switch—1989 Dynasty with 2.5L engine

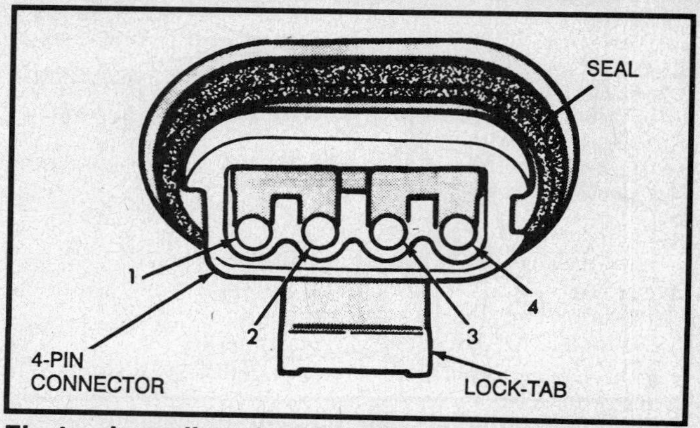
SEAL
1
2
3
4
4-PIN CONNECTOR
LOCK-TAB

Electronic cycling clutch switch connector, viewed from terminal end

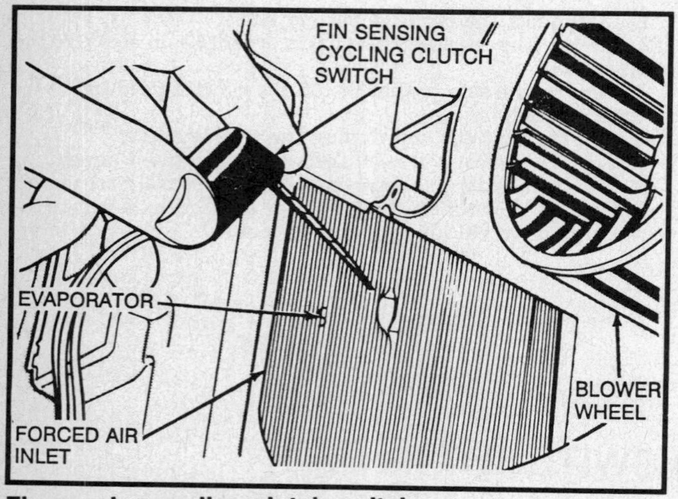
FIN SENSING CYCLING CLUTCH SWITCH
EVAPORATOR
BLOWER WHEEL
FORCED AIR INLET

Fin-sensing cycling clutch switch

Electronic Cycling Clutch Switch

1989 DYNASTY WITH 2.5L ENGINE

The Electronic Cycling Clutch Switch (ECCS) is located on the refrigerant pumbing near the H-valve. The ECCS prevents evaporator freeze-up by signaling the Single Module Engine Controller (SMEC) to cycle the compressor clutch coil by monitoring the temperature of the suction line. The ECCS uses a thermistor probe in a capillary tube, inserted into a well on the suction line. The well must be filled with special conductive grease to prevent corrosion and allow thermal transfer to the probe. The switch is a sealed unit that should be replaced if found to be defective.

Fin Sensing Cycling Clutch Switch

FIXED DISPLACEMENT COMPRESSOR EXCEPT OMNI, HORIZON AND 1989 DYNASTY WITH 2.5L ENGINE

The Fin Sensing Cycling Clutch Switch (FSSC) is located in the A/C-heater housing near the blower motor and is inserted into the evaporator fins. The FCCS prevents evaporator freeze-up by cycling the compressor clutch coil off when the evaporator temperature drops below freezing point. The coil will be cycled back on when the temperature rises above the freeze point. The FCCS uses a thermistor probe in a capillary tube inserted between the evaporator fins. The switch is a sealed unit that should be replaced if found to be defective.

TESTING

Cycling Clutch Switch

OMNI AND HORIZON

The compressor clutch coil should cycle 2–3 times per minute at ambient temperatures of 68–90°F (20–32°C). At temperatures above 90°F (32°C), the coil may not cycle at all.

1. Disconnect the wires from the switch.
2. Check for switch continuity. The switch should be closed at temperatures above 45°F (7°C).
3. If contacts are closed, reconnect the switch, set the temperature control lever to the full COOL position, turn the blower on low speed and operate the engine at 1000 rpm for 5 minutes to allow the air conditioning system to stabilize.
4. If the cycling clutch switch is good and the clutch does not engage properly, inspect the rest of the system for an open circuit.

Electronic Cycling Clutch Switch

DYNASTY WITH 2.5L ENGINE

The compressor clutch coil should cycle 2–3 times per minute at ambient temperatures of 68–90°F (20–32°C). At temperatures above 90°F (32°C), the coil may not cycle at all.

1. Test the switch in an area with ambient temperature of at least 70°F (21°C).
2. Disconnect the switch connector. Supply 12 volts to pin 2, and ground pin 4 of the ECCS connector.
3. Check for continuity between pins 1 and 3.
4. If coninuity is not detected, the switch is faulty and should be replaced.
5. If there is continuity, inspect the rest of the system for an open circuit.

Fin Sensing Cycling Clutch Switch

EXCEPT OMNI, HORIZON AND 1989 DYNASTY WITH 2.5L ENGINE

The compressor clutch coil should cycle 2–3 times per minute at ambient temperatures of 68°–90°F (20–32°C). At temperatures above 90°F (32°C), the coil may not cycle at all.

1. Test the switch in an area with ambient temperature of at least 70°F (21°C).

2. Disconnect the switch connector, located behind the glove box. Use a suitable jumper wire to jump between the outer wires of the harness connector.
3. If the compressor clutch engages, check for continuity between pins 1 and 3 of the FSSC connector. If there is no continuity, replace the switch.
4. If the compressor clutch did not engage, inspect the rest of the system for an open circuit.

REMOVAL AND INSTALLATION

Cycling Clutch Switch

OMNI AND HORIZON

1. Disconnect the negative battery cable.
2. Disconnect the switch connectors.
3. Remove the mounting screws from the refrigerant line manifold plate at the H-valve.
4. Separate the switch from the refrigerant manifold and pull the capillary tube out of the capillary tube well on the suction line.

NOTE: The capillary tube well is filled with special temperature conductive grease. If reusing the switch, try to save all the grease. If replacing the switch, new grease will be supplied in the replacement switch package.

To install:

5. Fill the well with the special grease and insert the capillary tube.
6. Mount the switch to the refrigerant manifold. Make sure the ground wire is in place.
7. Connect the connectors.
8. Connect the negative battery cable and check the entire climate control system for proper operation.

Electronic Cycling Clutch Switch

1989 DYNASTY WITH 2.5L ENGINE

1. Disconnect the negative battery cable.
2. Disconnect the ECCS connector.
3. Remove the plastic wire tie holding the bulb against the suction line.
4. Remove the mounting screw on the refrigerant line manifold plate at the H-valve.
5. Separate the switch from the refrigerant manifold and pull the capillary tube out of the capillary tube well on the suction line.

NOTE: The capillary tube well is filled with special temperature conductive grease. If reusing the switch, try to save all the grease. If replacing the switch, new grease will be supplied in the replacement switch package.

To install:

6. Fill the well with the special grease and insert the capillary tube.
7. Mount the switch to the refrigerant manifold.
8. Tie the bulb with a new wire tie.
9. Connect the ECCS connector.
10. Connect the negative battery cable and check the entire climate control system for proper operation.

Fin Sensing Cycling Clutch Switch

FIXED DISPLACEMENT COMPRESSOR EXCEPT OMNI, HORIZON AND 1989 DYNASTY WITH 2.5L ENGINE

1. Remove the heater-A/C housing.

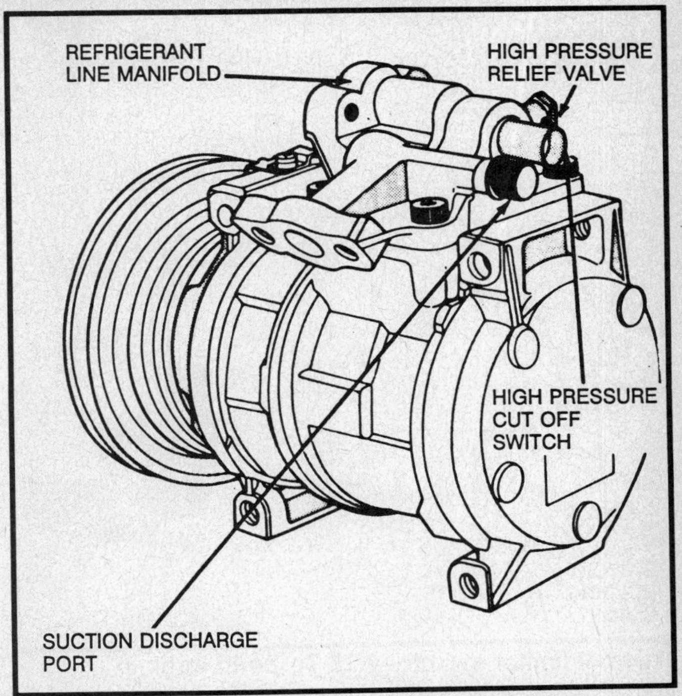
REFRIGERANT
LINE MANIFOLD
HIGH PRESSURE
RELIEF VALVE
HIGH PRESSURE
CUT OFF
SWITCH
SUCTION DISCHARGE
PORT

High pressure cut off switch – fixed displacement compressor model 10PA17

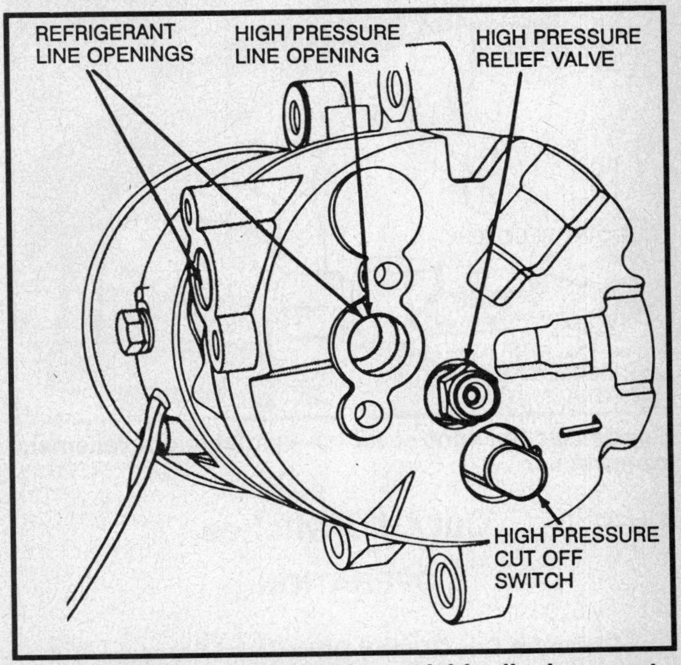
REFRIGERANT
LINE OPENINGS
HIGH PRESSURE
LINE OPENING
HIGH PRESSURE
RELIEF VALVE
HIGH PRESSURE
CUT OFF
SWITCH

High pressure cut off switch – variable displacement compressor

2. Disconnect the connector, push the wire grommet through the housing and feed the connector through the air inlet opening to the left of the blower wheel.
3. Remove the switch from the evaporator.
4. The installation is the reverse of the removal procedure.
5. Connect the negative battery cable and check the entire climate control system for proper operation.

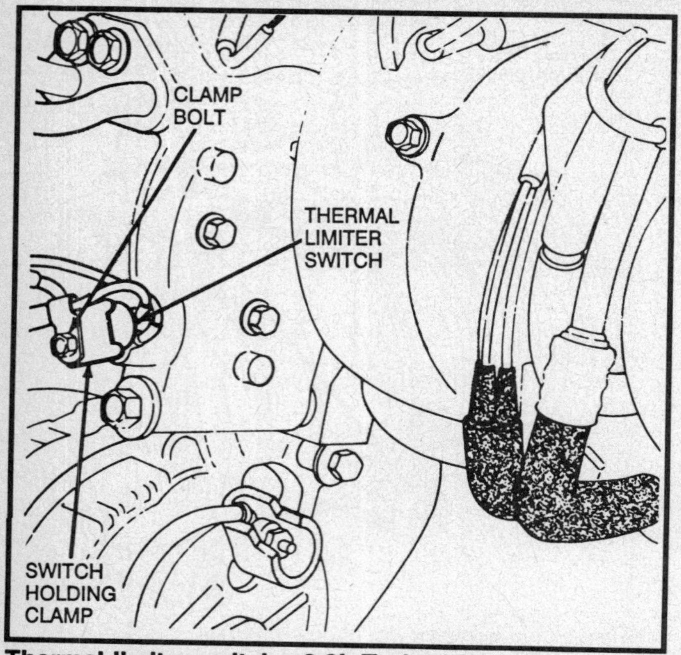
CLAMP
BOLT
THERMAL
LIMITER
SWITCH
SWITCH
HOLDING
CLAMP
Thermal limiter switch—2.2L Turbo III engine

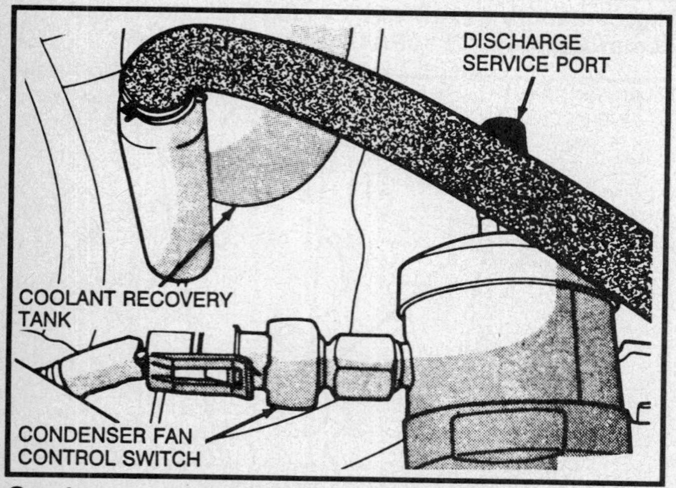
DISCHARGE
SERVICE PORT
COOLANT RECOVERY
TANK
CONDENSER FAN
CONTROL SWITCH
Condenser fan control switch—variable displacement compressor

Cut Off Switches

OPERATION

Low Pressure Cut Off and Differential Pressure Cut Off Switches

The low pressure cut off switch monitors the refrigerant gas pressure on the suction side of the system and is only used with fixed displacement compressors. The Differential pressure cut off switch monitors the liquid refrigerant pressure on the liquid side of the system and is only used with variable displacement compressors. The switches operate similarly in that they turn off voltage to the compressor clutch coil when the monitored pressure drops to levels that could damage the compressor. The switches are sealed units that must be replaced if faulty.

High Pressure Cut Off Switch

The high pressure cut off switch is located on the near the high pressure relief valve. The function of the switch is to disengage the compressor clutch by monitoring the discharge pressure when levels reach dangerously high levels. This switch is on the same circuit as the differential pressure cut off switch and the ambient sensor.

Thermal Limiter Switch

The thermal limiter switch is used only on the Spirit R/T with 2.2L Turbo III engine and is located on the side of the compressor case. It measures compressor surface temperature and is used as a safety device to cut battery voltage to the compressor clutch coil if the case temperature exceeds safe levels. Once the compressor has cooled to its normal temperature, the switch closes and allows voltage to energize the clutch coil. It is not used to cycle the clutch coil.

Ambient Temperature Switch

The ambient switch is used in vehicles equipped with a variable displacement compressor and is located behind the grille and in front of condenser. The ambient sensor prevents the compressor clutch from engaging when the ambient temperature is below 50°F (10°C). The ambient switch is a sealed unit and should be replaced if defective.

Condenser Fan Control Switch

The condenser fan control switch is used in vehicles with a variable displacement compressor and is located on the discharge line at the compressor. The fan control switch turns the radiator/condenser fan on and off by monitoring the compressor discharge pressure. The radiator top tank sensor can override this switch and cycle the fan any time the engine temperature gets too high.

TESTING

Low Pressure Cut Off and Differential Pressure Cut Off Switches

1. Start the engine and allow to idle. Turn the air conditioner ON.
2. Disconnect the switch connector and use a jumper wire to jump between terminals inside the connector boot.
3. If the compressor clutch does not engage, inspect the system for an open circuit.
4. If the clutch engages, connect an air conditioning manifold gauge to the system.
5. Read the low pressure gauge. The low pressure cut off switch should complete the circuit at pressures of at least 14 psi. The differential pressure switch will complete the circuit at pressure of at least 41 psi. Check the system for leaks if the pressures are too low.
6. If the pressures are nominal and the system works when the terminals are jumped, the cut off switch is faulty and should be replaced.

High Pressure Cut Off Switch

1. Start the engine and allow to idle. Turn the air conditioner ON.
2. Connect an air conditioning manifold gauge to the system. The system should operate at high gauge pressure below 430 psi.
3. Without allowing the engine to overheat, block the flow of air to the condenser with a cover. When the high pressure reaches 450 psi, the clutch should disengage.
4. Remove the cover. When the gauge reading falls below 265 psi, the clutch should cycle back on.
5. Replace the switch if it does not operate properly.

Thermal Limiter Switch

1. Disconnect the connector from the thermal limiter switch.
2. Check for continuity between the 2 leads. If no continuity is detected, replace the switch.
3. The switch should open when the temperature reaches 255°F (125°C). If this occurs, check the system for causes of overheating.
4. The switch should close when the temperature comes down to 230°F (110°C).

Ambient Temperature Switch

1. Disconnect the ambient switch connector.
2. Check the continuity across the switch terminals. At ambient tempeatures above 50°F (10°C), the circuit should be complete.
3. Chill the switch to below 50°F (10°C) and recheck for continuity. The switch should be open at below the specified temperature.
4. Replace the switch if it is found to be defective.

Condenser Fan Control Switch

1. Disconnect the fan control switch connector.
2. Connect an air conditioning manifold gauge to the system.
3. Jump across the terminals in the wire connector with a jumper wire.
4. Connect an ohmmeter to the switch terminals.
5. Start the engine and allow to idle at 1300 rpm. The radiator fan should run constantly.
6. Turn the air conditioner ON.
7. If the high pressure reads below 160 psi, the switch should be open.
8. Without allowing the engine to overheat, block the flow of air to the condenser with a cover. When the high pressure reaches 230 psi, the switch should close.
9. Remove the cover. When the pressure drops to below 160 psi, the switch should open again.
10. Replace the switch if it is defective.

REMOVAL AND INSTALLATION

Low Pressure Cut Off and Differential Pressure Cut Off Switches

1. Disconnect the negative battery cable.
2. Properly discharge the air conditioning system.
3. Unplug the boot connector from the switch.
4. Using an oil pressure sending unit socket, remove the switch from the H-valve.

To install:

5. Seal the threads of the new switch with teflon tape.
6. Install the switch to the H-valve and connect the boot connector.
7. Evacuate and recharge the system. Check for leaks.
8. Check the switch for proper operation.

High Pressure Cut Off Switch

1. Disconnect the negative battery cable.
2. Properly discharge the air conditioning system.
3. Disconnect the connector from the switch.
4. Remove the snapring that retains the switch in the compressor.
5. Pull the switch straight from the compressor and discard the O-ring.

To install:

6. Replace the O-ring and lubricate with refrigerant oil before installing.
7. Install the switch to the compressor and secure with a new snapring.
8. Evacuate and recharge the system. Check for leaks.
9. Check the switch for proper operation.

Thermal Limiter Switch

1. Disconnect the negative battery cable.
2. Disconnect the connector from the switch.
3. Remove the bolt retaining the hold-down clamp and switch at the side of the compressor.
4. Using a small prying tool, remove the switch from from the compressor.
5. Thoroughly clean the old silicone sealer from the case.

To install:

6. Apply silicone sealer to the copper surface of the switch.
7. Install the switch to the compressor case and connect the connector.
8. Check the switch for proper operation.

Ambient Temperature Switch

1. Disconnect the switch connector.
2. Check the continuity across the terminals. The switch should be closed at temperatures above 50°F (10°C). If not, replace the switch.
3. Cool the switch with crushed ice. The switch should open shortly after the cool down. If not, replace the switch.

Condenser Fan Control Switch

NOTE: System discharging is not necessary to remove the condenser fan conrol switch; only a small amount of freon will escape as the switch is being rotated. Take the proper precautions.

1. Disconnect the negative battery cable.
2. Disconnect the connector from the switch.
3. Loosen and quickly rotate the switch counterclockwise.
4. Remove the switch from the high pressure line.
5. The installation is the reverse of the removal procedure.
6. Check the switch for proper operation.

Automatic Temperature Control (ATC) System Components

OPERATION

Computer Controller

The ATC computer controller, which is actually the control head in the instrument panel, manages all of the system's elec-

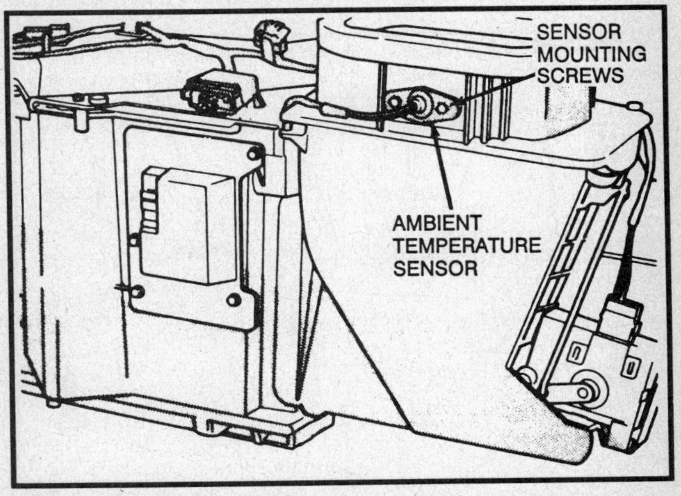
SENSOR
MOUNTING
SCREWS
AMBIENT
TEMPERATURE
SENSOR

ATC system ambient temperature sensor location

tronic functions. It provides power to operate the power module and various door actuators. It all retains the operator's selected settings when the vehicle is not running and measures return inputs from the sensors. After measuring all input information, the computer will fround the output circuits to provide logic signals for automatic system regulation.

Power Module

This module received signals from the computer controller (control head). It then supplies varied voltage to the blower motor ground circuit for different blower speeds. In 1989–90, the power module, also called the power/vacuum module, also controls various vacuum-operated actuators, which were replaced by motorized versions in 1991.

Ambient Temperature Sensor

The ambient temperature sensor is located on the A/C-heater housing above the glove box. It is a thermistor that will react to the environmental ambient temperature. The computer controller uses the information provided by the ambient sensor to regulate the low blower speed, temperature offsets and mode control. In 1989–90, its information is also used in determining cold lockout time.

In-Car Temperature Sensor/Aspirator Assembly

A small fan in the aspirator draws air through an intake on the instrument panel. The air flows over the temperature sensor's thermistor, which detects temperature variations. The computer controller then make adjustments to maintain a constant passenger compartment temperature. This is an assembly that is not separately serviceable.

Water Temperature Sensor (1991)

The water temperature sensor is located on the heater core mounting plate. Its function is to detect the engine coolant temperature. The computer controller uses this information to determine the cold engine lockout time.

Sun Sensor (1991)

The sun sensor is mounted on the top of the dirver's side of the instrument panel and is a light-sensitive photo diode. The sun sensor responds to sun light intensity and not temperature. It is used to aid in determining proper mode door position.

Blend Air Door Actuator

The blend air door actuator is an electric servo motor which mechanically positions the A/C unit temperature door. Actuation of the servo motor will occur when the drive signals are supplied to the actuator from the computer controller. A feedback strip in the actuator allows the computer controller to know the exact position of the door at all times.

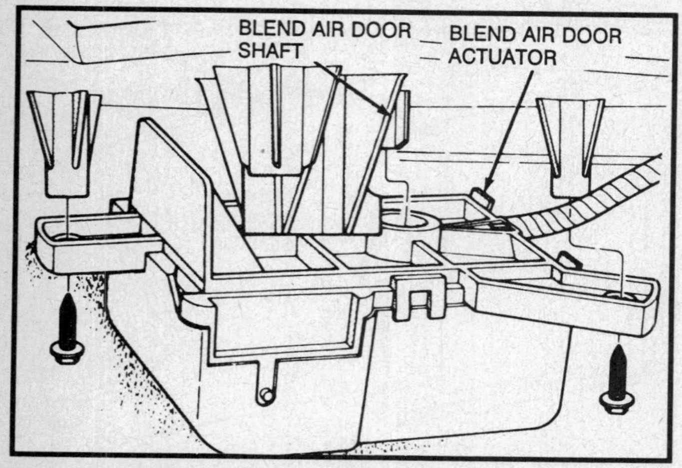
BLEND AIR DOOR
SHAFT
BLEND AIR DOOR
ACTUATOR

ATC system blend air door actuator

Fresh/Recirc Door Actuator

In 1989–90, this actuator is vacuum operated and is fed vacuum according to signals received by the power/vacuum module. In 1991, the actuator is an electric servo motor which positions the A/C unit door in the open or closed position by way of linkages. Actuation of the servo motor will occur when the drive signals are supplied to the actuator from the computer controller. This actuator does not have a feedback strip in the actuator, so the computer controller does not know the exact position of the door.

Mode Door Actuator

In 1989–90, this actuator is vacuum operated and is fed vacuum according to signals received by the power/vacuum module. In 1991, the actuator is an electric servo motor which positions the A/C unit panel/bi-level door and the floor/defrost door by way of linkages. Actuation of the servo motor will occur when the drive signals are supplied to the actuator from the computer controller. A feedback strip in the actuator allows the computer controller to know the exact position of the door at all times.

REMOVAL AND INSTALLATION

Computer Controller

1. Disconnect the negative battery cable.
2. Remove the necessary bezel(s) in order to gain access to the control head.
3. Remove the screws that fasten the control head to the instrument panel.
4. Pull the unit out and unplug the wire harness.
5. Remove the control head from the instrument panel.
6. The installation is the reverse of the removal procedure.
7. Connect the negative battery cable and check the entire climate control system for proper operation.

Power Module

1. Disconnect the negative battery cable.
2. Remove the glove box and ash tray assembly.
3. Remove the 4 mouning screws.
4. Disconnect the electrical and vacuum connectors, as required.
5. Remove the module from the A/C-heater housing and remove from the vehicle.
6. The installation is the reverse of the removal installation.
7. Connect the negative battery cable and check the entire climate control system for proper operation.

Ambient Temperature Sensor

1. Disconnect the negative battery cable.
2. Remove the glove box and ash tray assembly.
3. Disconnect the connector.

NOTE: When removing the sensor from the A/C-heater housing, pull it straight out slowly or the sensor may hang up on the plastic housing. This may cause the sensor to disengage from the receptacle and possibly fall in to the housing.

4. Remove the mounting screws and carefully remove the assembly from the housing.
5. Separate the sensor from the receptacle.
6. The installation is the reverse of the removal installation.
7. Connect the negative battery cable and check the entire climate control system for proper operation.

In-Car Temperature Sensor/Aspirator Assembly

The in-car temperature sensor and aspirator assembly is located in the instrument panel to the right of the steering column. They are wired together and must be replaced as an assembly.

1989–90 LEBARON

1. Disconnect the negative battery cable.
2. Remove the lower steering column cover.
3. Remove the 2 screws which attach the assembly to the instrument panel.
4. Unplug the connector and remove the assembly from the vehicle.
5. The installation is the reverse of the removal installation.
6. Connect the negative battery cable and check the entire climate control system for proper operation.

EXCEPT 1989–90 LEBARON

1. Disconnect the negative battery cable.
2. Remove the instrument cluster assembly.
3. Unsnap the sensor from the instrument panel.
4. Remove the 2 aspirator mounting screws.
5. Disconnect the aspirator intake hose.
6. Disconnect the connector and remove the assembly from the vehicle.
7. The installation is the reverse of the removal installation.
8. Connect the negative battery cable and check the entire climate control system for proper operation.

Water Temperature Sensor (1991)

1. Disconnect the negative battery cable.
2. Remove the A/C-heater housing.
3. Remove the sensor mounting screw.
4. Disconnect the pigtail connector and remove the sensor from the vehicle.
5. The installation is the reverse of the removal installation.
6. Connect the negative battery cable and check the entire climate control system for proper operation.

Sun Sensor

1. Disconnect the negative battery cable.
2. Using a suitable small prying tool and a clean rag to prevent damage to the top of the instrument panel, pry the sensor from the panel.
3. Pull up and disconnect the connector.
4. The installation is the reverse of the removal installation. Make sure the sensor is securely snapped in place
5. Connect the negative battery cable and check the entire climate control system for proper operation.

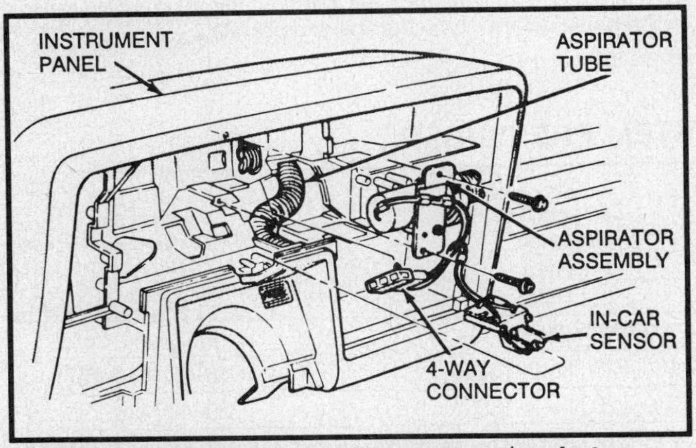
INSTRUMENT PANEL
ASPIRATOR TUBE
ASPIRATOR ASSEMBLY
IN-CAR SENSOR
4-WAY CONNECTOR

ATC system in-car temperature sensor/aspirator assembly—Dynasty, New Yorker and Imperial

Blend Air Door Actuator

NOTE: Removing an electronic actuator with power applied can damage the unit. The actuators do not have built-in mechanical stops and if the actuator rotates while disconnected from the assembly, it will become uncalibrated.

The blend air actuator is located on the A/C-heater housing above the floor hump.

1. Disconnect the negative battery cable.
2. Remove the under panel silencers.
3. Remove the carpeted cover over the air bag module.
4. Remove the floor air distribution duct.
5. Remove the actuator attaching screws.
6. Lower the actuator from the housing and disengage from the blend air door shaft.
7. Disconnect the connector to the actuator.
8. Remove the actuator from the vehicle.

To install:

9. Align the blend air door shaft with the slot in the actuator. Make sure the shaft is properly engaged to prevent damage when tightening the screws.
10. Install and tighten the attaching screws.
11. Connect the connector.
12. Connect the negative battery cable and check the entire climate control system for proper operation. If everything functions properly, disconnect the battery again and continue.
13. Install the floor air duct.
14. Install the carpeted cover over the air bag module and the under panel silencers.
15. Connect the negative battery cable.

Fresh/Recirc Door Actuator

NOTE: Removing an electronic actuator with power applied can damage the unit. The actuators do not have built-in mechanical stops and if the actuator rotates while disconnected from the assembly, it will become uncalibrated.

The fresh/recirc door actuator is located on the passenger side of the A/C-heater housing.

1. Disconnect the negative battery cable.
2. Remove the glove box and ash tray assembly.
3. Remove the under panel silencer pad.
4. Remove the carpeted cover over the air bag module.
5. Remove the right front kick panel.
6. Remove the metal instrument panel brace.
7. Remove the screws that attach the actuator mounting bracket to the A/C-heater housing.
8. Remove the screws that attach the actuator to the bracket. Make sure the innermost screw does not fall into the case.
9. Disconnect the electrical or vacuum connector from the actuator.
10. Tilt the actuator to release it from the actuating linkage and remove from the vehicle.

To install:

11. Attach the actuator and bracket assembly to the linkage and intall to the housing. Connect the connector to the actuator.
12. Connect the negative battery cable and check the entire climate control system for proper operation. If everything functions properly, disconnect the battery again and continue.
13. Install the metal brace and kick panel.
14. Install the carpeted cover over the air bag module and the under panel silencer pad.
15. Install the glove box and ash tray assembly.
16. Connect the negative battery cable.

Mode Door Actuator

NOTE: Removing an electronic actuator with power applied can damage the unit. The actuators do not have

built-in mechanical stops and if the actuator rotates while disconnected from the assembly, it will become uncalibrated.

The mode door actuator is located on the side of the A/C-heater case near the accelerator pedal.

1. Disconnect the negative battery cable.
2. Remove the under panel silencer.
3. Disconnect the electrical or vacuum connector from the actuator.
4. Pinch and remove the lower plastic clip from the actuator arm.
5. Remove the 3 actuator bracket mounting screws.
6. Rotate the actuator to gain access to the upper plastic clip. Pinch and remove the clip.
7. Remove the actuator to mounting bracket screws.
8. Remove the actuator from the mounting bracket and remove from the vehicle.

To install:

9. Install the actuator and mounting bracket assembly.
10. Attach the upper and lower plastic clips.
11. Connect the coonector to the actuator.
12. Connect the negative battery cable and check the entire climate control system for proper operation. If everything functions properly, disconnect the battery again and continue.
13. Install the under panel silencer.
14. Connect the negative battery cable.

SYSTEM DIAGNOSIS

Air Conditioning Performance

OVERALL PERFORMANCE TEST

Air temperature in the testing area must be at least 70°F (21°C) to ensure the accuracy of this test.

1. Connect a manifold gauge set the the system.
2. Set the controls to A/C RECIRC, PANEL or MAX A/C, temperature control level on full COOL and the blower on high.
3. Start the engine and adjust the idle speed to 1000 rpm with the compressor clutch engaged.
4. Allow the engine come to normal operating temperature and keep doors and windows closed.
5. Insert a thermometer in the left center A/C outlet and operate the engine for 5 minutes. The A/C clutch may cycle depending on the ambient conditions.
6. With the clutch engaged, compare the discharge air temperature to the performance chart.
7. Disconnect and plug the gray vacuum line going to the heater water control valve. Observe the valve arm for movement as the line is disconnected. If there is no movement, check the valve for sticking.
8. Operate the A/C for 2 additional minutes and observe the discharge air temperature again. If the discharge air temperature increased by more than 5°F, check the blend air door for proper operation. If not, compare the the temperature, suction and discharge pressures to the chart. Reconnect the gary vacuum line.
9. If the values do not meet specifications, check system components for proper operation.

Vacuum Actuating System

INSPECTION

Check the system for proper operation. Air should come from the appropriate vents when the corresponding mode is selected under all driving conditions. If a problem is detected use the flow-charts to check the flow of vacuum.

1. Check the engine for sufficient vacuum and the main supplier hose at the brake booster for leaks or kinks.
3. Check the check valve under the instrument panel for proper operation. It should not hold vacuum when vacuum is applied from the engine side, but should when appied from the system side.
4. Check all interior vacuum lines, especially the 7-way connection behind the instrument panel for leaks or kinks.
5. Check the control head for leaky ports or damaged parts.
6. Check all actuators for ability to hold vacuum.

Air Conditioning Compressor

COMPRESSOR NOISE

Noises that develop during air conditioning operation can be misleading. A noise that sounds like serious compressor damage may only be a loose belt, mounting bolt or clutch assembly. Improper belt tension can also emit a noise that can be mistaken for more serious problems. Check and adjust all possible causes of the noise before replacing the compressor.

AIR CONDITIONING SYSTEM PRESSURES

Ambient Temperature °F (°C)	Air Temperature at Center Panel Vent °F (°C)	Compressor Discharge Pressure PSI (kPa)	Evaporator Suction Pressure Psi (kPa)
70 (21)	35–46 (2–8)	140–210 (965–1448)	10–35 (69–241)
80 (27)	39–50 (4–10)	180–235 (1240–1620)	16–38 (110–262)
90 (32)	44–55 (7–13)	210–270 (1448–1860)	20–42 (138–290)
100 (38)	50–62 (10–17)	240–310 (1655–2137)	25–48 (172–331)
110 (43)	56–70 (13–21)	280–350 (1930–2413)	30–55 (207–379)

A/C SYSTEM DIAGNOSIS—FIXED DISPLACEMENT COMPRESSOR

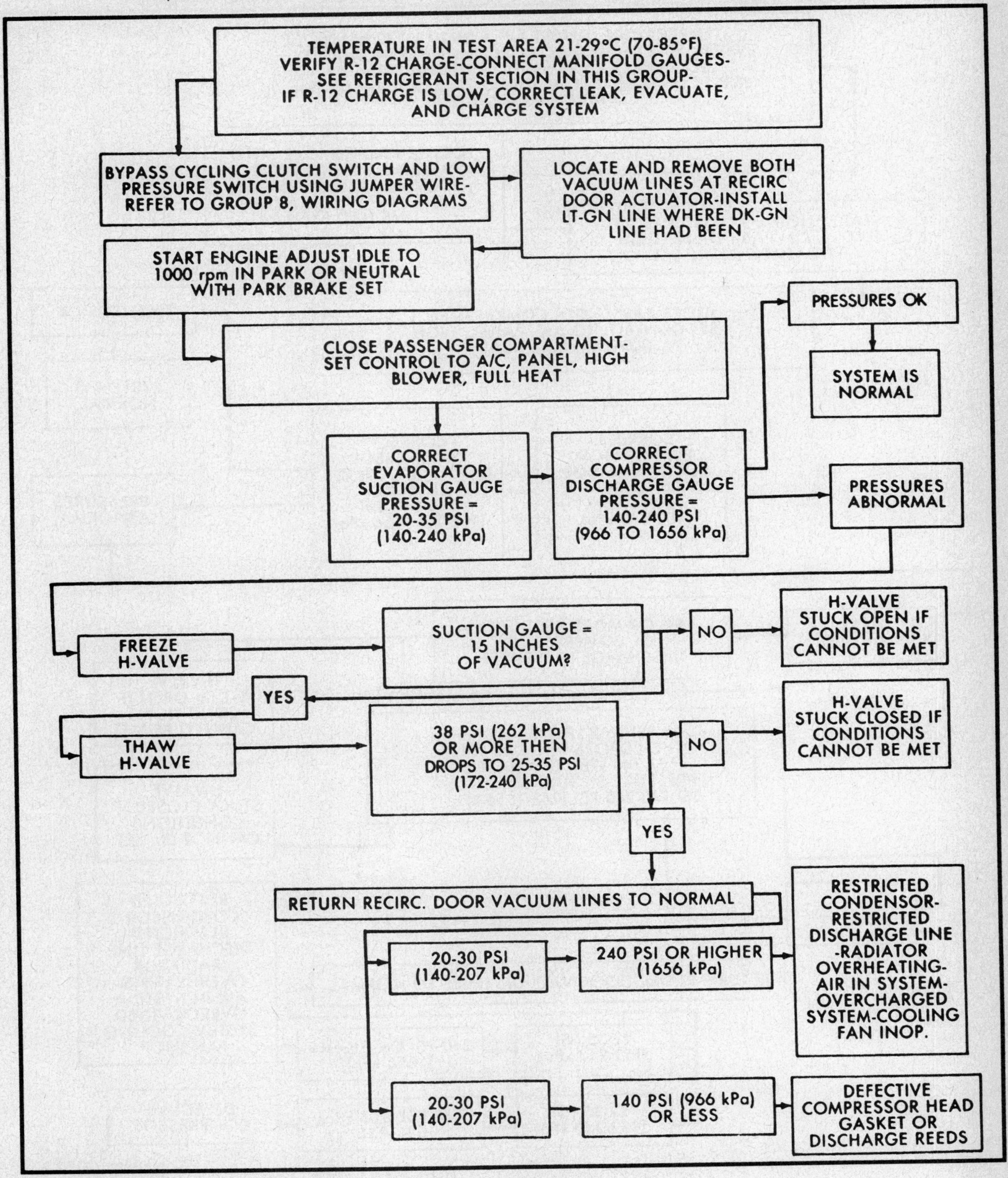
TEMPERATURE IN TEST AREA 21-29°C (70-85°F) VERIFY R-12 CHARGE-CONNECT MANIFOLD GAUGES-SEE REFRIGERANT SECTION IN THIS GROUP-IF R-12 CHARGE IS LOW, CORRECT LEAK, EVACUATE, AND CHARGE SYSTEM
BYPASS CYCLING CLUTCH SWITCH AND LOW PRESSURE SWITCH USING JUMPER WIRE-REFER TO GROUP 8, WIRING DIAGRAMS
LOCATE AND REMOVE BOTH VACUUM LINES AT RECIRC DOOR ACTUATOR-INSTALL LT-GN LINE WHERE DK-GN LINE HAD BEEN
START ENGINE ADJUST IDLE TO 1000 rpm IN PARK OR NEUTRAL WITH PARK BRAKE SET
CLOSE PASSENGER COMPARTMENT-SET CONTROL TO A/C, PANEL, HIGH BLOWER, FULL HEAT
CORRECT EVAPORATOR SUCTION GAUGE PRESSURE = 20-35 PSI (140-240 kPa)
CORRECT COMPRESSOR DISCHARGE GAUGE PRESSURE = 140-240 PSI (966 TO 1656 kPa)
PRESSURES OK
SYSTEM IS NORMAL
PRESSURES ABNORMAL
FREEZE H-VALVE
SUCTION GAUGE = 15 INCHES OF VACUUM?
NO
H-VALVE STUCK OPEN IF CONDITIONS CANNOT BE MET
YES
THAW H-VALVE
38 PSI (262 kPa) OR MORE THEN DROPS TO 25-35 PSI (172-240 kPa)
NO
H-VALVE STUCK CLOSED IF CONDITIONS CANNOT BE MET
YES
RETURN RECIRC. DOOR VACUUM LINES TO NORMAL
20-30 PSI (140-207 kPa)
240 PSI OR HIGHER (1656 kPa)
RESTRICTED CONDENSOR-RESTRICTED DISCHARGE LINE -RADIATOR OVERHEATING-AIR IN SYSTEM-OVERCHARGED SYSTEM-COOLING FAN INOP.
20-30 PSI (140-207 kPa)
140 PSI (966 kPa) OR LESS
DEFECTIVE COMPRESSOR HEAD GASKET OR DISCHARGE REEDS

A/C SYSTEM DIAGNOSIS—VARIABLE DISPLACEMENT COMPRESSOR

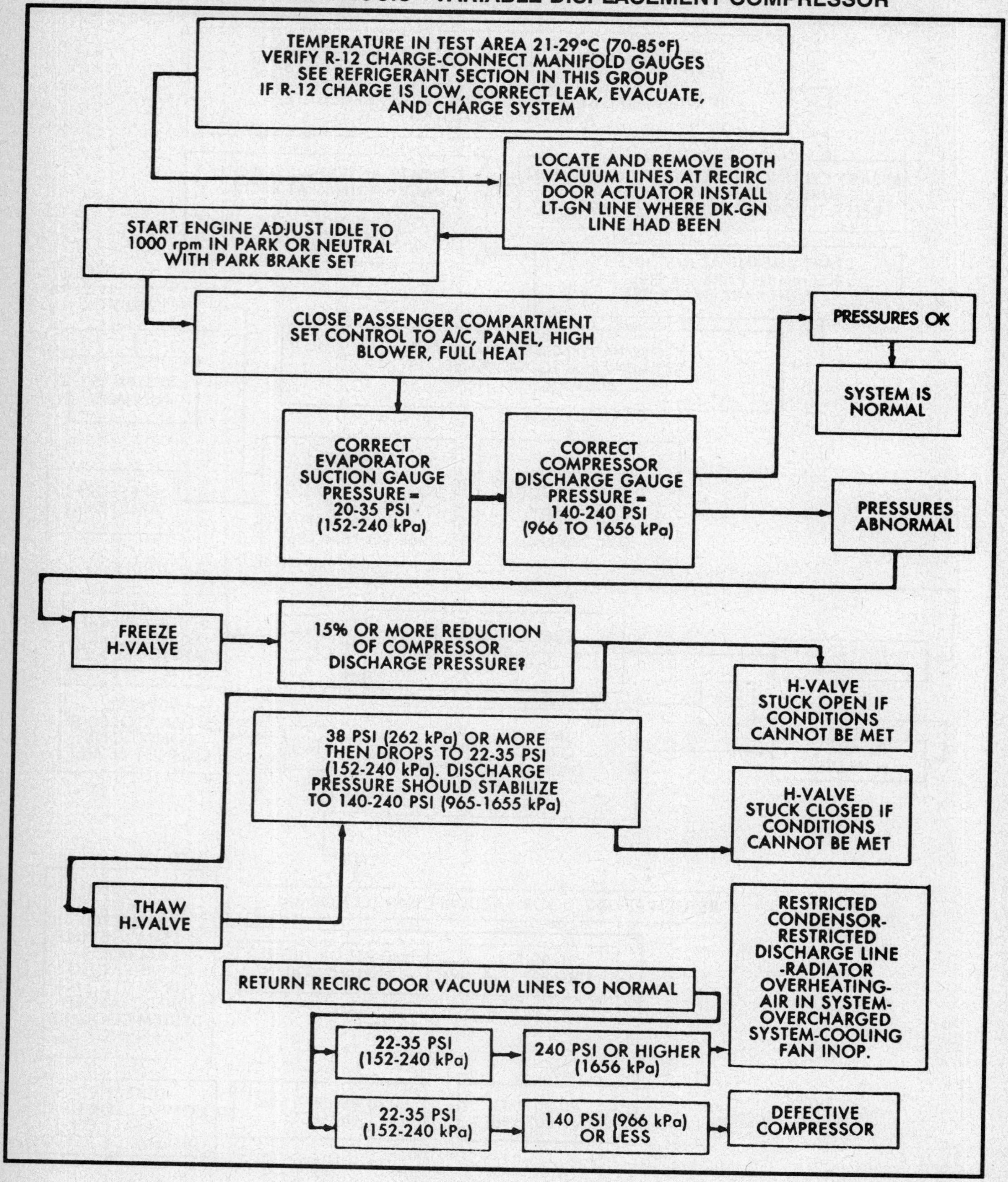
TEMPERATURE IN TEST AREA 21-29°C (70-85°F)
VERIFY R-12 CHARGE-CONNECT MANIFOLD GAUGES
SEE REFRIGERANT SECTION IN THIS GROUP
IF R-12 CHARGE IS LOW, CORRECT LEAK, EVACUATE, AND CHARGE SYSTEM
LOCATE AND REMOVE BOTH VACUUM LINES AT RECIRC DOOR ACTUATOR INSTALL LT-GN LINE WHERE DK-GN LINE HAD BEEN
START ENGINE ADJUST IDLE TO 1000 rpm IN PARK OR NEUTRAL WITH PARK BRAKE SET
CLOSE PASSENGER COMPARTMENT SET CONTROL TO A/C, PANEL, HIGH BLOWER, FULL HEAT
CORRECT EVAPORATOR SUCTION GAUGE PRESSURE = 20-35 PSI (152-240 kPa)
CORRECT COMPRESSOR DISCHARGE GAUGE PRESSURE = 140-240 PSI (966 TO 1656 kPa)
PRESSURES OK
SYSTEM IS NORMAL
PRESSURES ABNORMAL
FREEZE H-VALVE
15% OR MORE REDUCTION OF COMPRESSOR DISCHARGE PRESSURE?
H-VALVE STUCK OPEN IF CONDITIONS CANNOT BE MET
38 PSI (262 kPa) OR MORE THEN DROPS TO 22-35 PSI (152-240 kPa). DISCHARGE PRESSURE SHOULD STABILIZE TO 140-240 PSI (965-1655 kPa)
H-VALVE STUCK CLOSED IF CONDITIONS CANNOT BE MET
THAW H-VALVE
RESTRICTED CONDENSOR-RESTRICTED DISCHARGE LINE -RADIATOR OVERHEATING-AIR IN SYSTEM-OVERCHARGED SYSTEM-COOLING FAN INOP.
RETURN RECIRC DOOR VACUUM LINES TO NORMAL
22-35 PSI (152-240 kPa)
240 PSI OR HIGHER (1656 kPa)
22-35 PSI (152-240 kPa)
140 PSI (966 kPa) OR LESS
DEFECTIVE COMPRESSOR

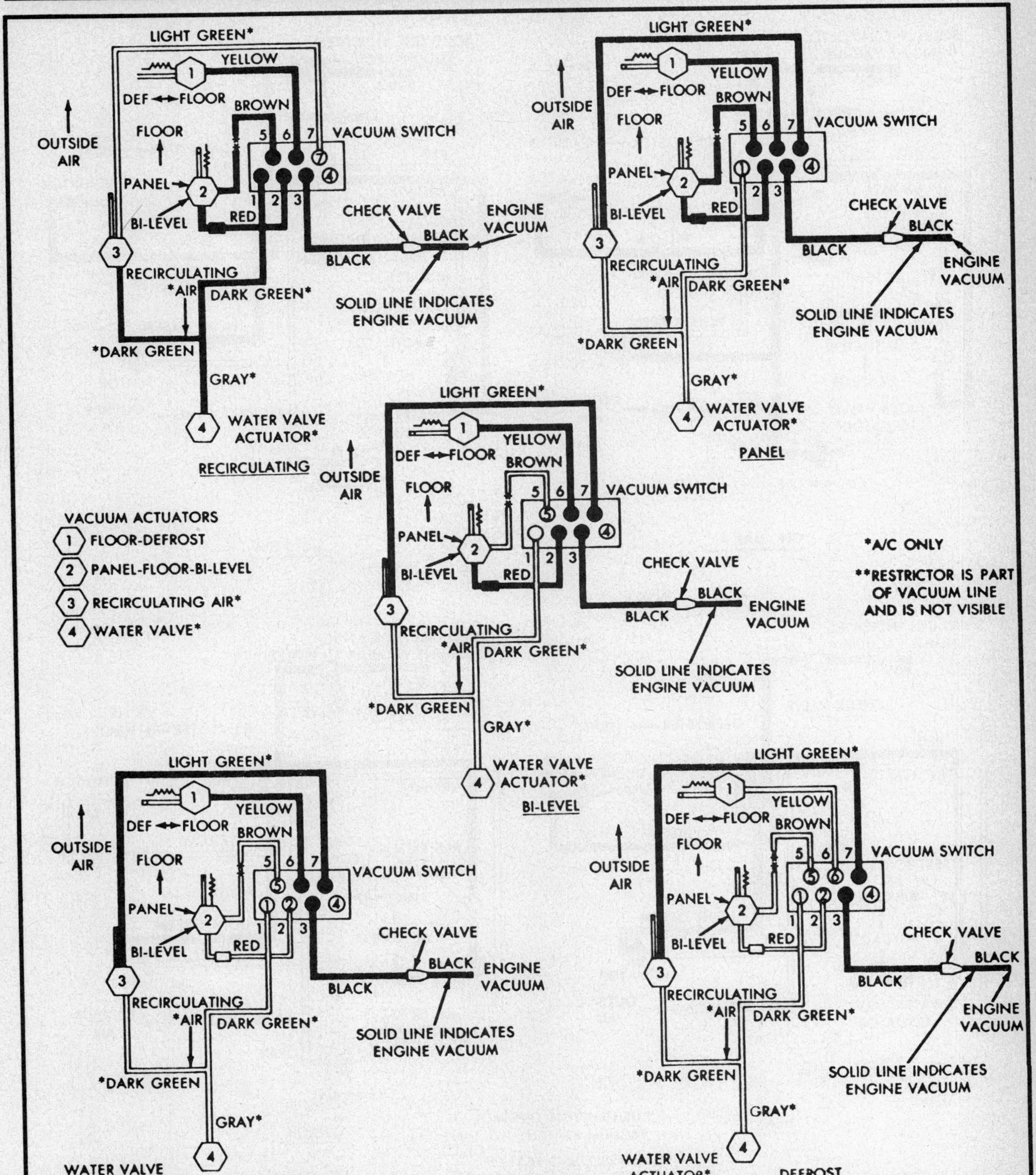
LIGHT GREEN*
YELLOW
DEF ↔ FLOOR
BROWN
OUTSIDE AIR
FLOOR
VACUUM SWITCH
PANEL
BI-LEVEL
RED
CHECK VALVE
ENGINE VACUUM
BLACK
BLACK
RECIRCULATING *AIR
DARK GREEN*
SOLID LINE INDICATES ENGINE VACUUM
*DARK GREEN
GRAY*
WATER VALVE ACTUATOR*
RECIRCULATING
LIGHT GREEN*
YELLOW
DEF ↔ FLOOR
BROWN
OUTSIDE AIR
FLOOR
VACUUM SWITCH
PANEL
BI-LEVEL
RED
CHECK VALVE
BLACK
BLACK
ENGINE VACUUM
RECIRCULATING *AIR
DARK GREEN*
SOLID LINE INDICATES ENGINE VACUUM
*DARK GREEN
GRAY*
WATER VALVE ACTUATOR*
PANEL
LIGHT GREEN*
YELLOW
DEF ↔ FLOOR
BROWN
OUTSIDE AIR
FLOOR
VACUUM SWITCH
PANEL
BI-LEVEL
RED
CHECK VALVE
BLACK
BLACK
ENGINE VACUUM
RECIRCULATING *AIR
DARK GREEN*
SOLID LINE INDICATES ENGINE VACUUM
*DARK GREEN
GRAY*
WATER VALVE ACTUATOR*
BI-LEVEL
VACUUM ACTUATORS
1 FLOOR-DEFROST
2 PANEL-FLOOR-BI-LEVEL
3 RECIRCULATING AIR*
4 WATER VALVE*
*A/C ONLY
**RESTRICTOR IS PART OF VACUUM LINE AND IS NOT VISIBLE
LIGHT GREEN*
YELLOW
DEF ↔ FLOOR
BROWN
OUTSIDE AIR
FLOOR
VACUUM SWITCH
PANEL
BI-LEVEL
RED
CHECK VALVE
BLACK
ENGINE VACUUM
BLACK
RECIRCULATING *AIR
DARK GREEN*
SOLID LINE INDICATES ENGINE VACUUM
*DARK GREEN
GRAY*
WATER VALVE ACTUATOR*
FLOOR
LIGHT GREEN*
YELLOW
DEF ↔ FLOOR
BROWN
OUTSIDE AIR
FLOOR
VACUUM SWITCH
PANEL
BI-LEVEL
RED
CHECK VALVE
BLACK
BLACK
ENGINE VACUUM
RECIRCULATING *AIR
DARK GREEN*
SOLID LINE INDICATES ENGINE VACUUM
*DARK GREEN
GRAY*
WATER VALVE ACTUATOR*
DEFROST

Heating and air conditioning system vacuum control circuits—without ATC, except Omni and Horizon

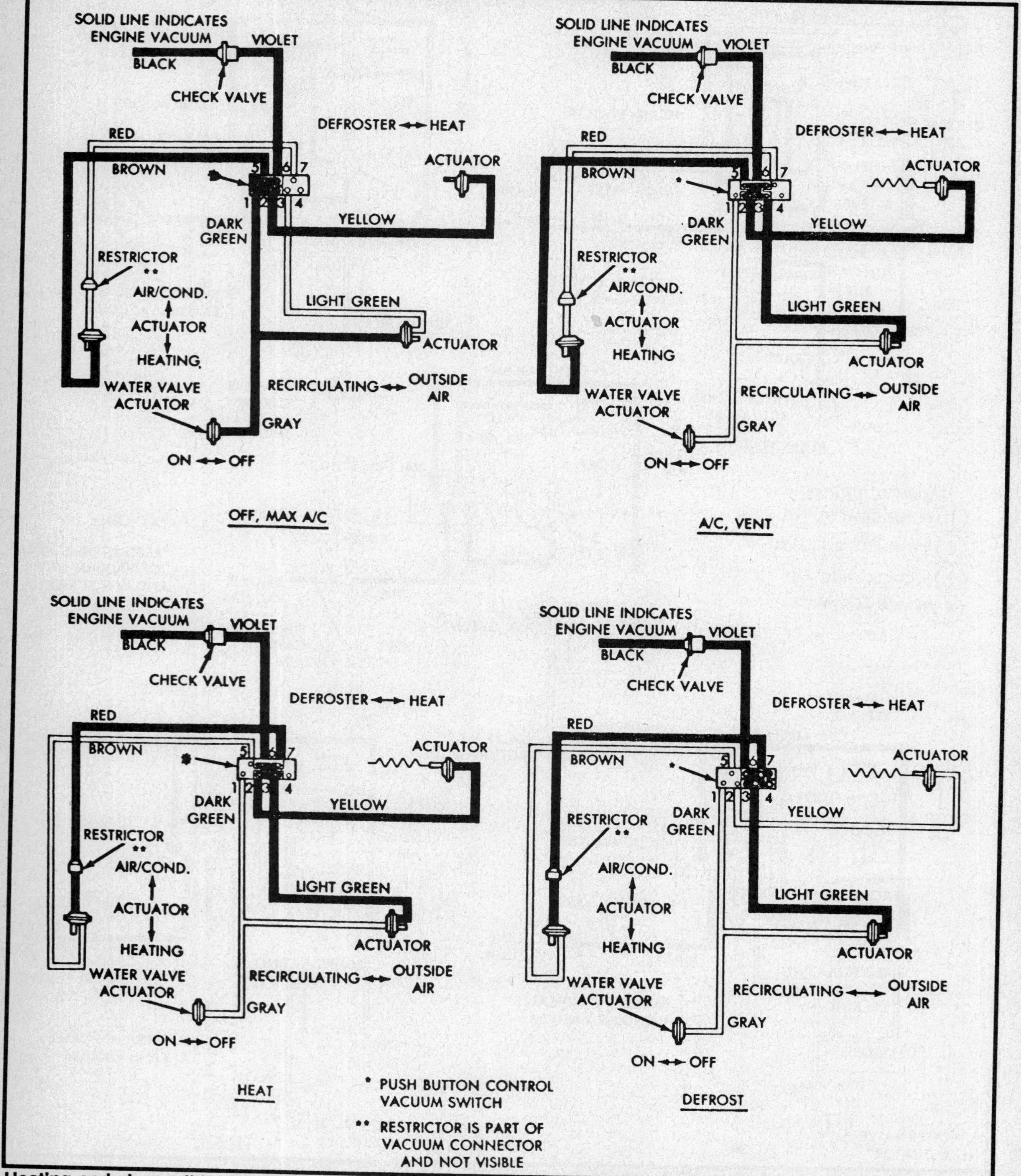
SOLID LINE INDICATES ENGINE VACUUM
VIOLET
BLACK
CHECK VALVE
DEFROSTER ↔ HEAT
RED
BROWN
ACTUATOR
5 6 7
1 2 3 4
DARK GREEN
YELLOW
RESTRICTOR **
AIR/COND.
ACTUATOR
HEATING
LIGHT GREEN
ACTUATOR
WATER VALVE ACTUATOR
RECIRCULATING ↔ OUTSIDE AIR
GRAY
ON ↔ OFF
OFF, MAX A/C
SOLID LINE INDICATES ENGINE VACUUM
VIOLET
BLACK
CHECK VALVE
DEFROSTER ↔ HEAT
RED
BROWN
ACTUATOR
*
5 6 7
1 2 3 4
DARK GREEN
YELLOW
RESTRICTOR **
AIR/COND.
ACTUATOR
HEATING
LIGHT GREEN
ACTUATOR
WATER VALVE ACTUATOR
RECIRCULATING ↔ OUTSIDE AIR
GRAY
ON ↔ OFF
A/C, VENT
SOLID LINE INDICATES ENGINE VACUUM
VIOLET
BLACK
CHECK VALVE
DEFROSTER ↔ HEAT
RED
BROWN
ACTUATOR
5 6 7
1 2 3 4
DARK GREEN
YELLOW
RESTRICTOR **
AIR/COND.
ACTUATOR
HEATING
LIGHT GREEN
ACTUATOR
WATER VALVE ACTUATOR
RECIRCULATING ↔ OUTSIDE AIR
GRAY
ON ↔ OFF
HEAT
SOLID LINE INDICATES ENGINE VACUUM
VIOLET
BLACK
CHECK VALVE
DEFROSTER ↔ HEAT
RED
BROWN
ACTUATOR
*
5 6 7
1 2 3 4
DARK GREEN
YELLOW
RESTRICTOR **
AIR/COND.
ACTUATOR
HEATING
LIGHT GREEN
ACTUATOR
WATER VALVE ACTUATOR
RECIRCULATING ↔ OUTSIDE AIR
GRAY
ON ↔ OFF
DEFROST
* PUSH BUTTON CONTROL VACUUM SWITCH
** RESTRICTOR IS PART OF VACUUM CONNECTOR AND NOT VISIBLE

Heating and air conditioning system vacuum control circuits—Omni and Horizon

COMPRESSOR AND CLUTCH DIAGNOSIS

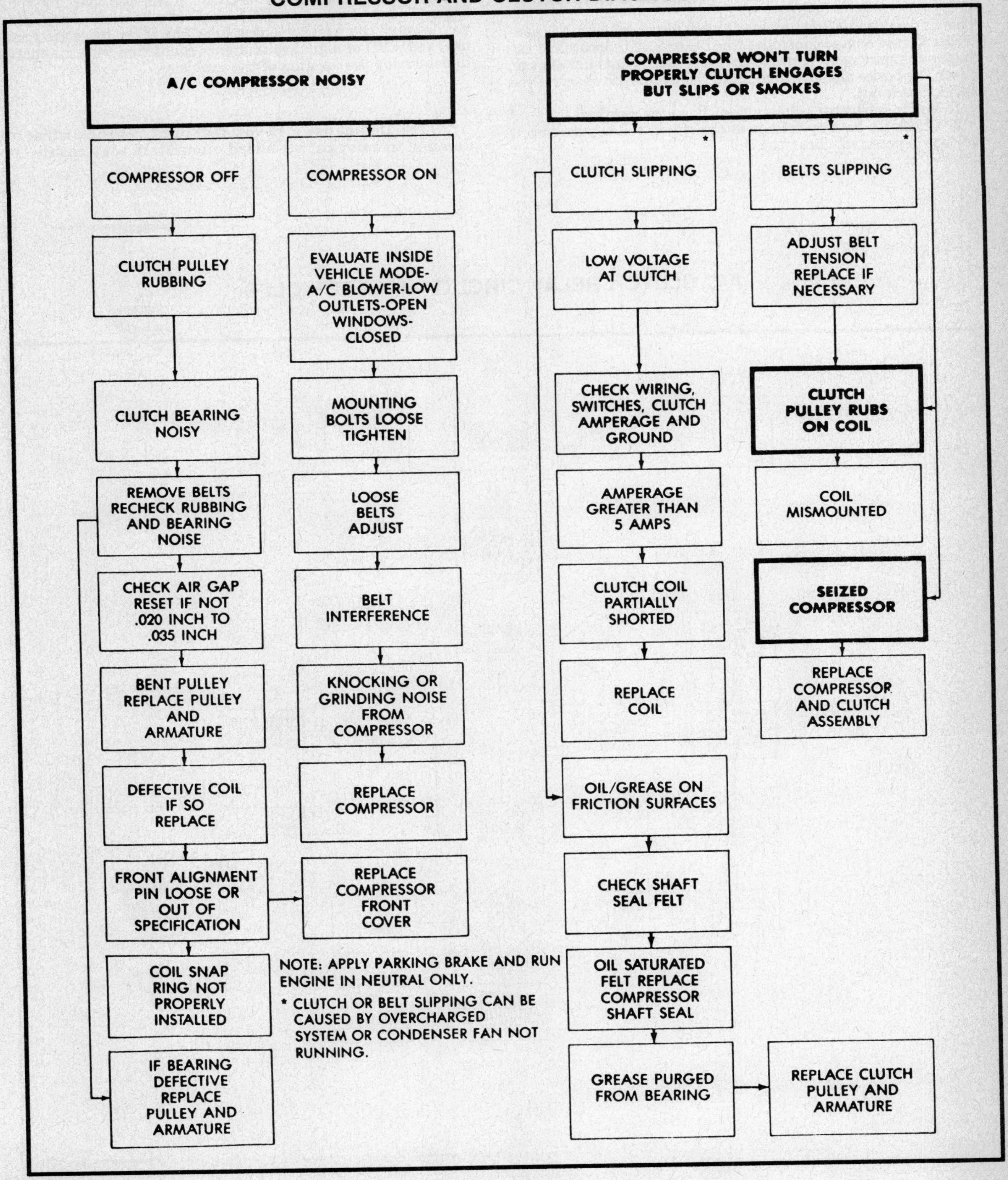
A/C COMPRESSOR NOISY
COMPRESSOR OFF
CLUTCH PULLEY RUBBING
CLUTCH BEARING NOISY
REMOVE BELTS RECHECK RUBBING AND BEARING NOISE
CHECK AIR GAP RESET IF NOT .020 INCH TO .035 INCH
BENT PULLEY REPLACE PULLEY AND ARMATURE
DEFECTIVE COIL IF SO REPLACE
FRONT ALIGNMENT PIN LOOSE OR OUT OF SPECIFICATION
COIL SNAP RING NOT PROPERLY INSTALLED
IF BEARING DEFECTIVE REPLACE PULLEY AND ARMATURE
COMPRESSOR ON
EVALUATE INSIDE VEHICLE MODE-A/C BLOWER-LOW OUTLETS-OPEN WINDOWS-CLOSED
MOUNTING BOLTS LOOSE TIGHTEN
LOOSE BELTS ADJUST
BELT INTERFERENCE
KNOCKING OR GRINDING NOISE FROM COMPRESSOR
REPLACE COMPRESSOR
REPLACE COMPRESSOR FRONT COVER
COMPRESSOR WON'T TURN PROPERLY CLUTCH ENGAGES BUT SLIPS OR SMOKES
CLUTCH SLIPPING *
LOW VOLTAGE AT CLUTCH
CHECK WIRING, SWITCHES, CLUTCH AMPERAGE AND GROUND
AMPERAGE GREATER THAN 5 AMPS
CLUTCH COIL PARTIALLY SHORTED
REPLACE COIL
OIL/GREASE ON FRICTION SURFACES
CHECK SHAFT SEAL FELT
OIL SATURATED FELT REPLACE COMPRESSOR SHAFT SEAL
GREASE PURGED FROM BEARING
REPLACE CLUTCH PULLEY AND ARMATURE
BELTS SLIPPING *
ADJUST BELT TENSION REPLACE IF NECESSARY
CLUTCH PULLEY RUBS ON COIL
COIL MISMOUNTED
SEIZED COMPRESSOR
REPLACE COMPRESSOR AND CLUTCH ASSEMBLY
NOTE: APPLY PARKING BRAKE AND RUN ENGINE IN NEUTRAL ONLY.
* CLUTCH OR BELT SLIPPING CAN BE CAUSED BY OVERCHARGED SYSTEM OR CONDENSER FAN NOT RUNNING.

COMPRESSOR CLUTCH INOPERATIVE

The air conditioning compressor clutch electrical circuit is controlled by the engine controller (SMEC or SBEC) located in the engine compartment. If the compressor clutch does not engage, check the basics and continue on to the diagnostic charts if the basics check out.

1. Verify refrigerant charge and charge as required.
2. Check for battery voltage at the clutch coil connection. If voltage is detected, check the coil.
3. If battery voltage is not detected at the coil, check for voltage at the low pressure or differential cut off switch. If voltage is not detected there either, check fuses etc. If the fuses are good, use the DRBII or digital voltmeter in conjuction with the charts to determine the location of the problem.

NOTE: Do not use a 12 volt test light to probe wires or damage to relevant on-board computers may result.

A/C CLUTCH RELAY CIRCUIT—1989 VEHICLES

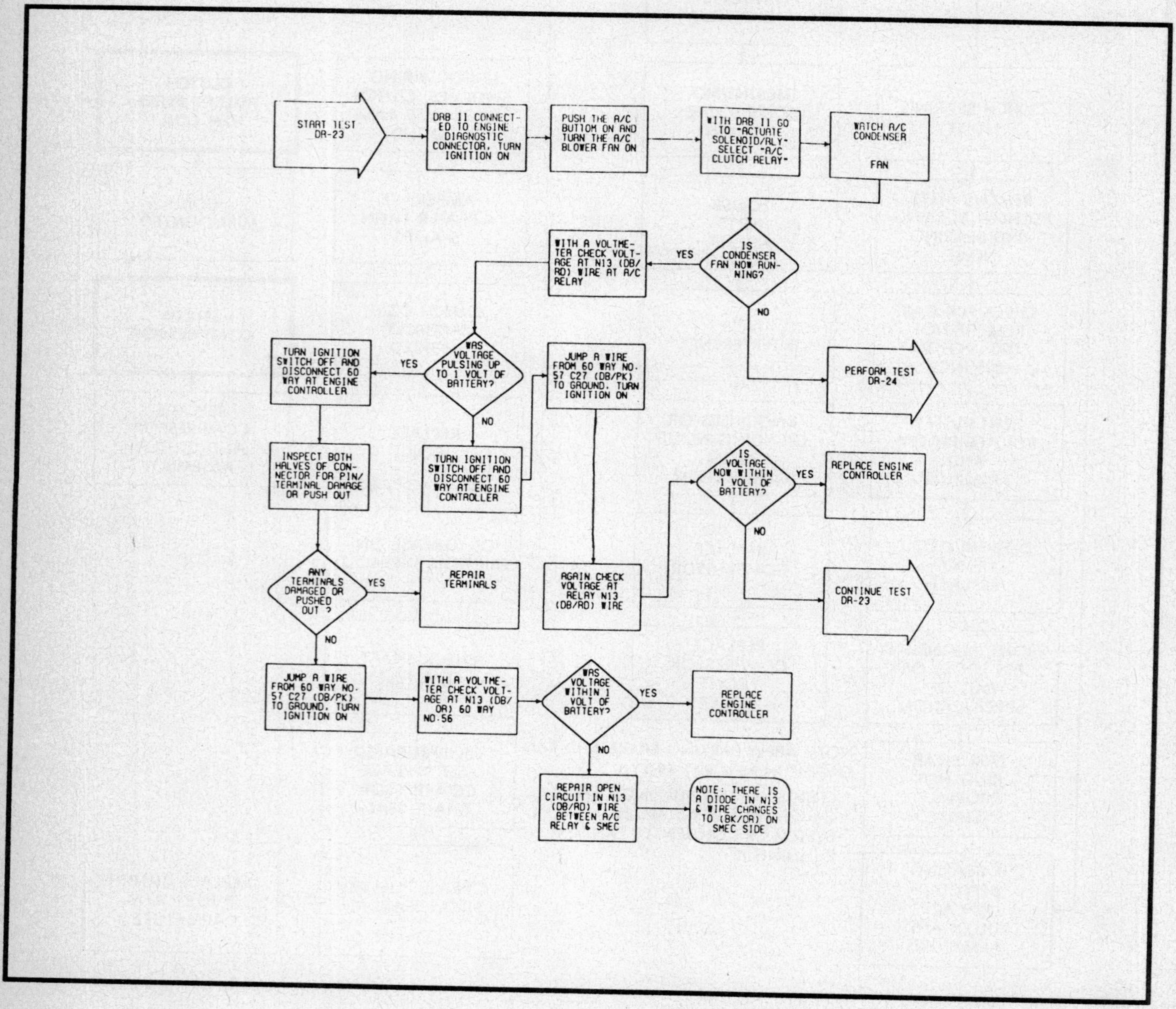
START TEST DR-23
DRB II CONNECTED TO ENGINE DIAGNOSTIC CONNECTOR, TURN IGNITION ON
PUSH THE A/C BUTTON ON AND TURN THE A/C BLOWER FAN ON
WITH DRB II GO TO "ACTUATE SOLENOID/RLY" SELECT "A/C CLUTCH RELAY"
WATCH A/C CONDENSER FAN
IS CONDENSER FAN NOW RUNNING?
YES
NO
WITH A VOLTMETER CHECK VOLTAGE AT N13 (DB/RD) WIRE AT A/C RELAY
PERFORM TEST DR-24
WAS VOLTAGE PULSING UP TO 1 VOLT OF BATTERY?
YES
NO
TURN IGNITION SWITCH OFF AND DISCONNECT 60 WAY AT ENGINE CONTROLLER
TURN IGNITION SWITCH OFF AND DISCONNECT 60 WAY AT ENGINE CONTROLLER
JUMP A WIRE FROM 60 WAY NO. 57 C27 (DB/PK) TO GROUND, TURN IGNITION ON
IS VOLTAGE NOW WITHIN 1 VOLT OF BATTERY?
YES
NO
REPLACE ENGINE CONTROLLER
INSPECT BOTH HALVES OF CONNECTOR FOR PIN/TERMINAL DAMAGE OR PUSH OUT
ANY TERMINALS DAMAGED OR PUSHED OUT ?
YES
NO
REPAIR TERMINALS
AGAIN CHECK VOLTAGE AT RELAY N13 (DB/RD) WIRE
CONTINUE TEST DR-23
JUMP A WIRE FROM 60 WAY NO. 57 C27 (DB/PK) TO GROUND, TURN IGNITION ON
WITH A VOLTMETER CHECK VOLTAGE AT N13 (DB/OR) 60 WAY NO. 56
WAS VOLTAGE WITHIN 1 VOLT OF BATTERY?
YES
NO
REPLACE ENGINE CONTROLLER
REPAIR OPEN CIRCUIT IN N13 (DB/RD) WIRE BETWEEN A/C RELAY & SMEC
NOTE: THERE IS A DIODE IN N13 & WIRE CHANGES TO (BK/OR) ON SMEC SIDE

A/C CLUTCH RELAY CIRCUIT—1989 VEHICLES

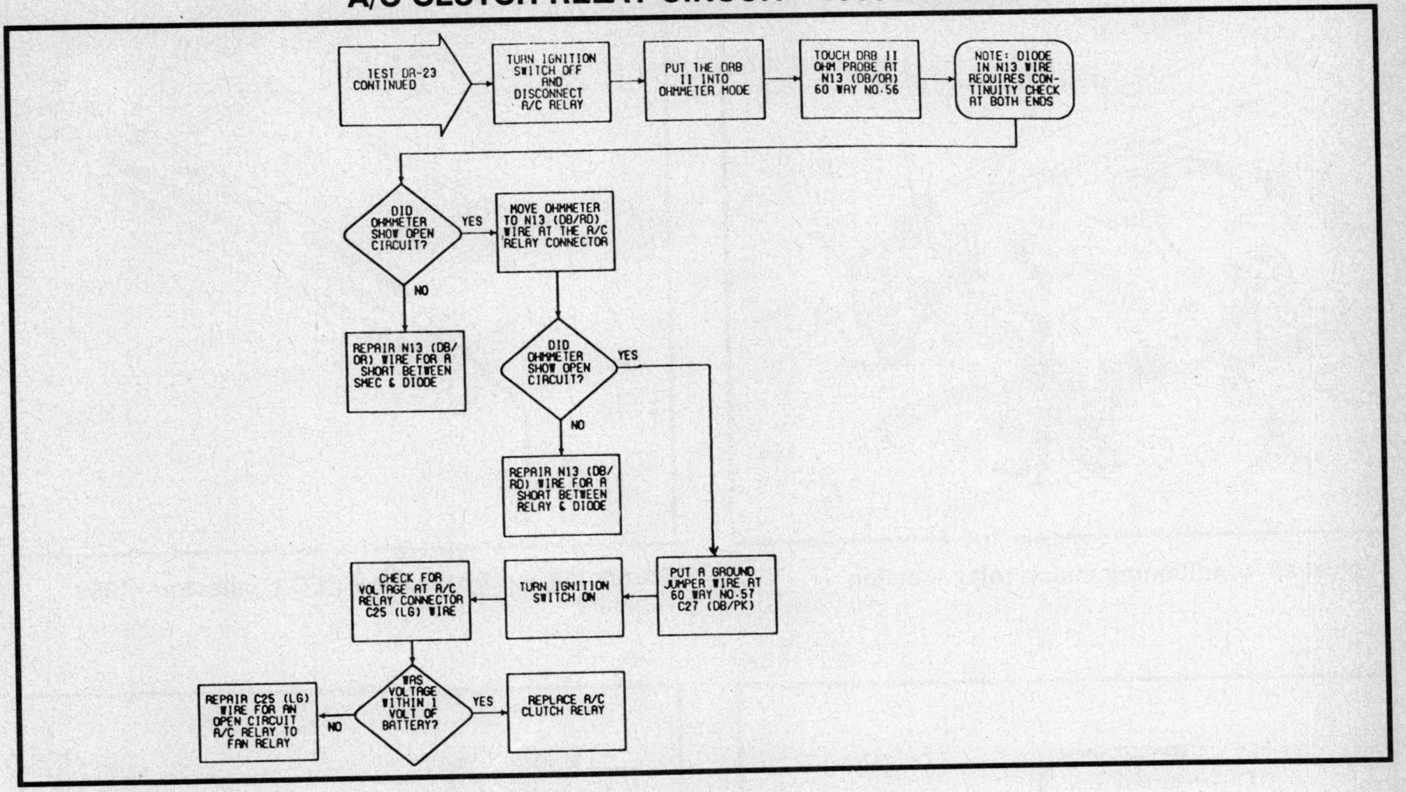
TEST DR-23 CONTINUED
TURN IGNITION SWITCH OFF AND DISCONNECT A/C RELAY
PUT THE DRB II INTO OHMMETER MODE
TOUCH DRB II OHM PROBE AT N13 (DB/OR) 60 WAY NO-56
NOTE: DIODE IN N13 WIRE REQUIRES CONTINUITY CHECK AT BOTH ENDS
DID OHMMETER SHOW OPEN CIRCUIT?
YES
MOVE OHMMETER TO N13 (DB/RD) WIRE AT THE A/C RELAY CONNECTOR
NO
REPAIR N13 (DB/OR) WIRE FOR A SHORT BETWEEN SMEC & DIODE
DID OHMMETER SHOW OPEN CIRCUIT?
YES
NO
REPAIR N13 (DB/RD) WIRE FOR A SHORT BETWEEN RELAY & DIODE
PUT A GROUND JUMPER WIRE AT 60 WAY NO-57 C27 (DB/PK)
TURN IGNITION SWITCH ON
CHECK FOR VOLTAGE AT A/C RELAY CONNECTOR C25 (LG) WIRE
WAS VOLTAGE WITHIN 1 VOLT OF BATTERY?
YES
REPLACE A/C CLUTCH RELAY
NO
REPAIR C25 (LG) WIRE FOR AN OPEN CIRCUIT A/C RELAY TO FAN RELAY

A/C CLUTCH RELAY CIRCUIT—1989 VEHICLES

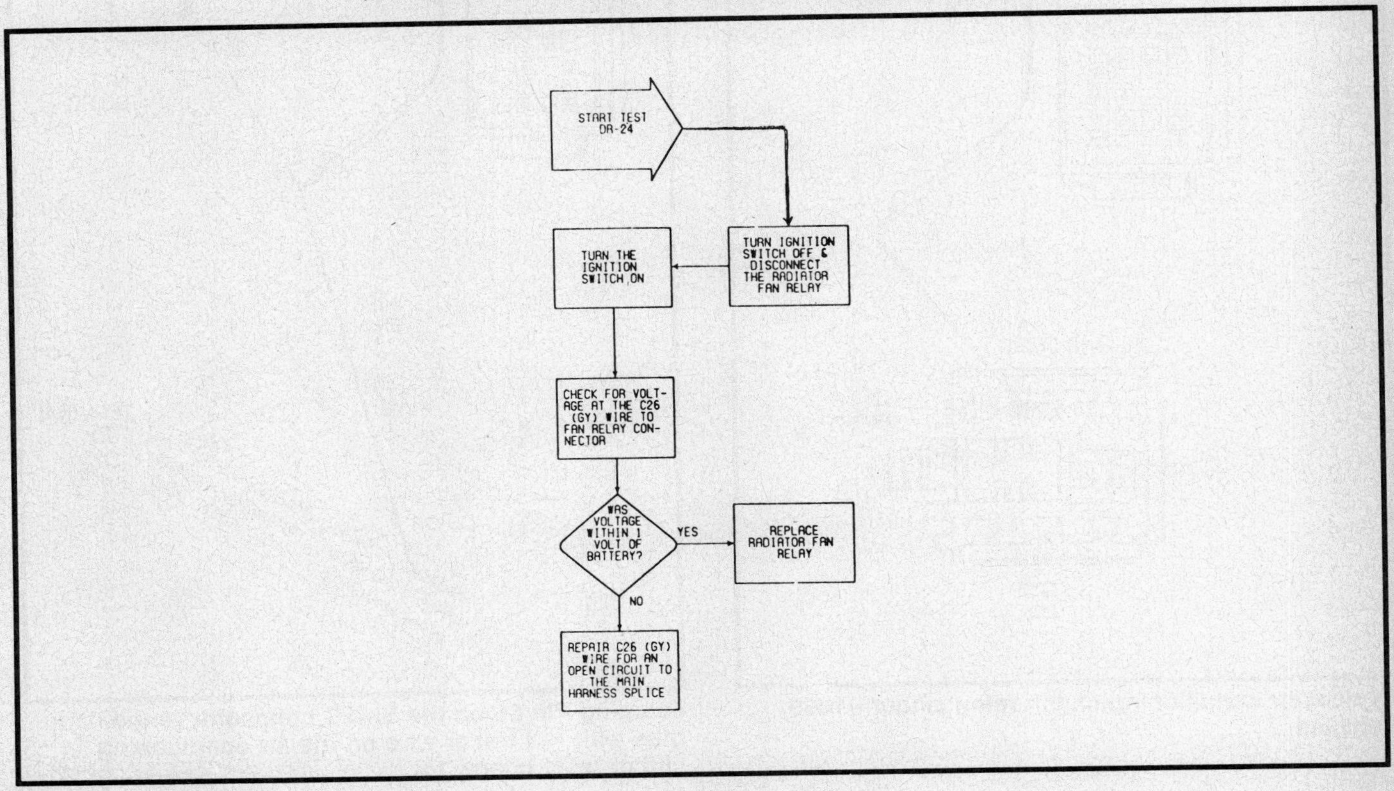
START TEST DR-24
TURN IGNITION SWITCH OFF & DISCONNECT THE RADIATOR FAN RELAY
TURN THE IGNITION SWITCH ON
CHECK FOR VOLTAGE AT THE C26 (GY) WIRE TO FAN RELAY CONNECTOR
WAS VOLTAGE WITHIN 1 VOLT OF BATTERY?
YES
REPLACE RADIATOR FAN RELAY
NO
REPAIR C26 (GY) WIRE FOR AN OPEN CIRCUIT TO THE MAIN HARNESS SPLICE

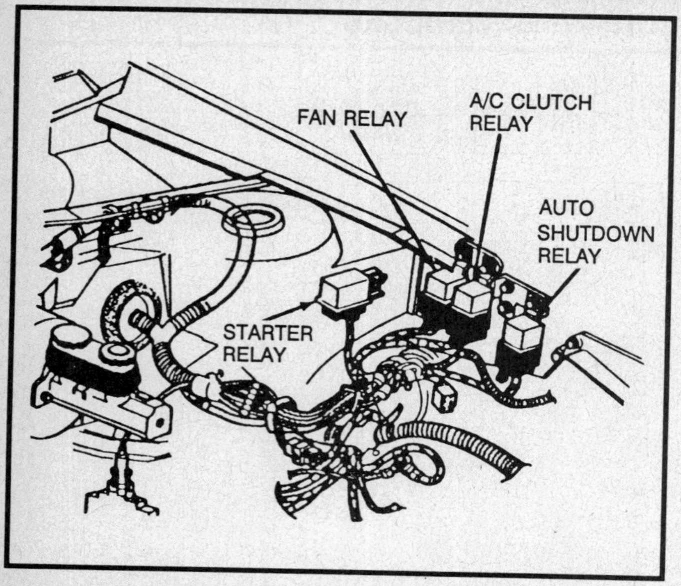
FAN RELAY
A/C CLUTCH
RELAY
AUTO
SHUTDOWN
RELAY
STARTER
RELAY

Typical air conditioning clutch relay location

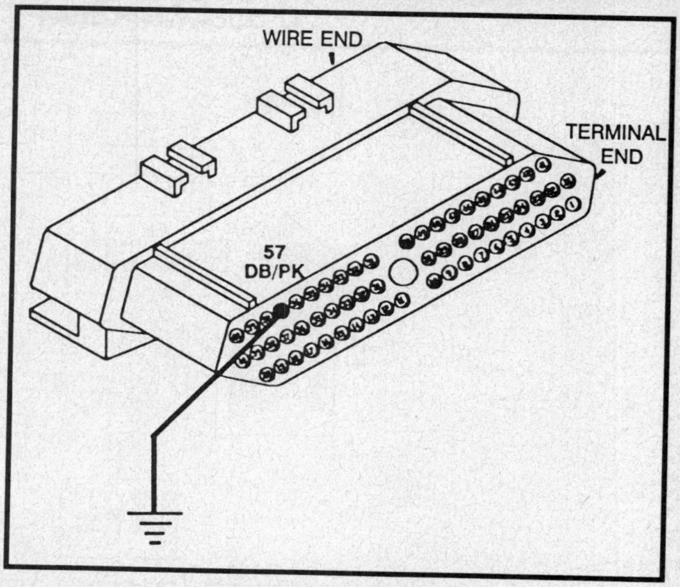
WIRE END
TERMINAL
END
57
DB/PK

Grounding Pin 57 on the SMEC connector—1989 vehicles

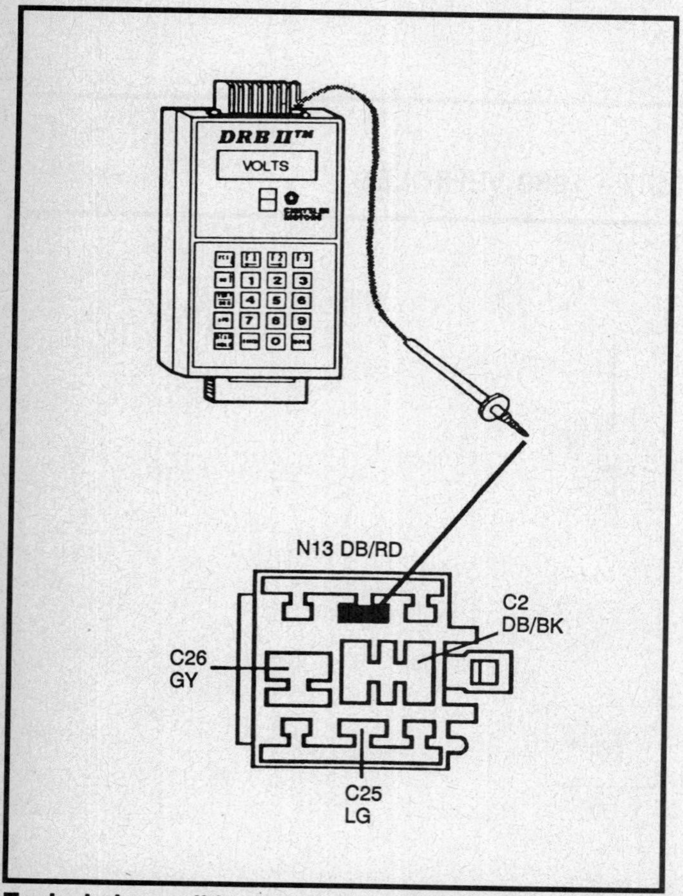
DRB II™
VOLTS
N13 DB/RD
C2
DB/BK
C26
GY
C25
LG

Typical air conditioning clutch relay pinout—1989 vehicles

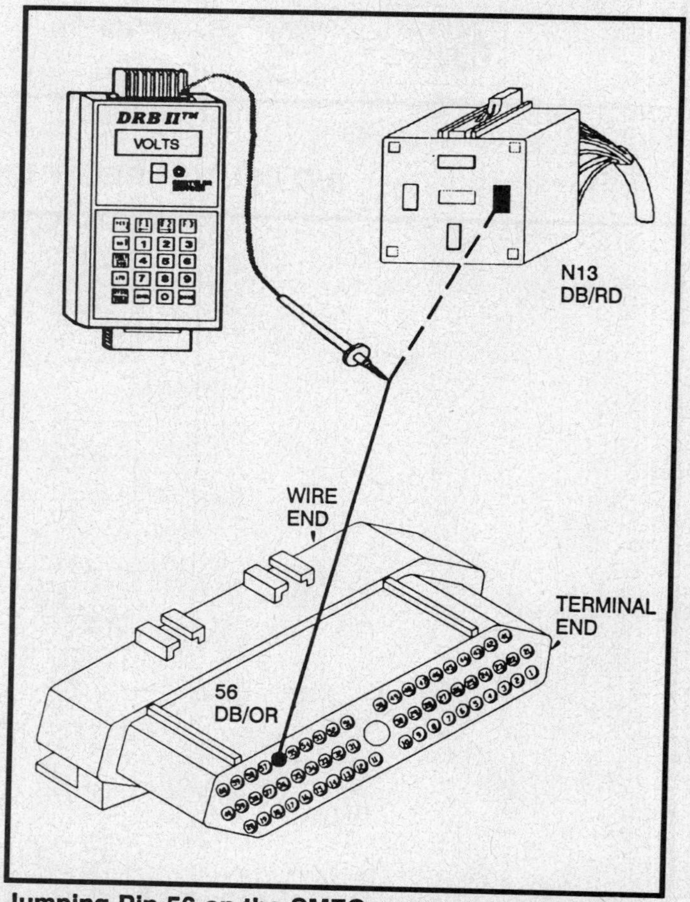
DRB II™
VOLTS
N13
DB/RD
WIRE
END
TERMINAL
END
56
DB/OR

Jumping Pin 56 on the SMEC connector to the dark blue with red tracer wire on the air conditioning clutch relay connector.

A/C CLUTCH RELAY CIRCUIT—1990–91 VEHICLES EXCEPT DYNASTY, NEW YORKER, IMPERIAL AND 1991 DAYTONA AND LEBARON

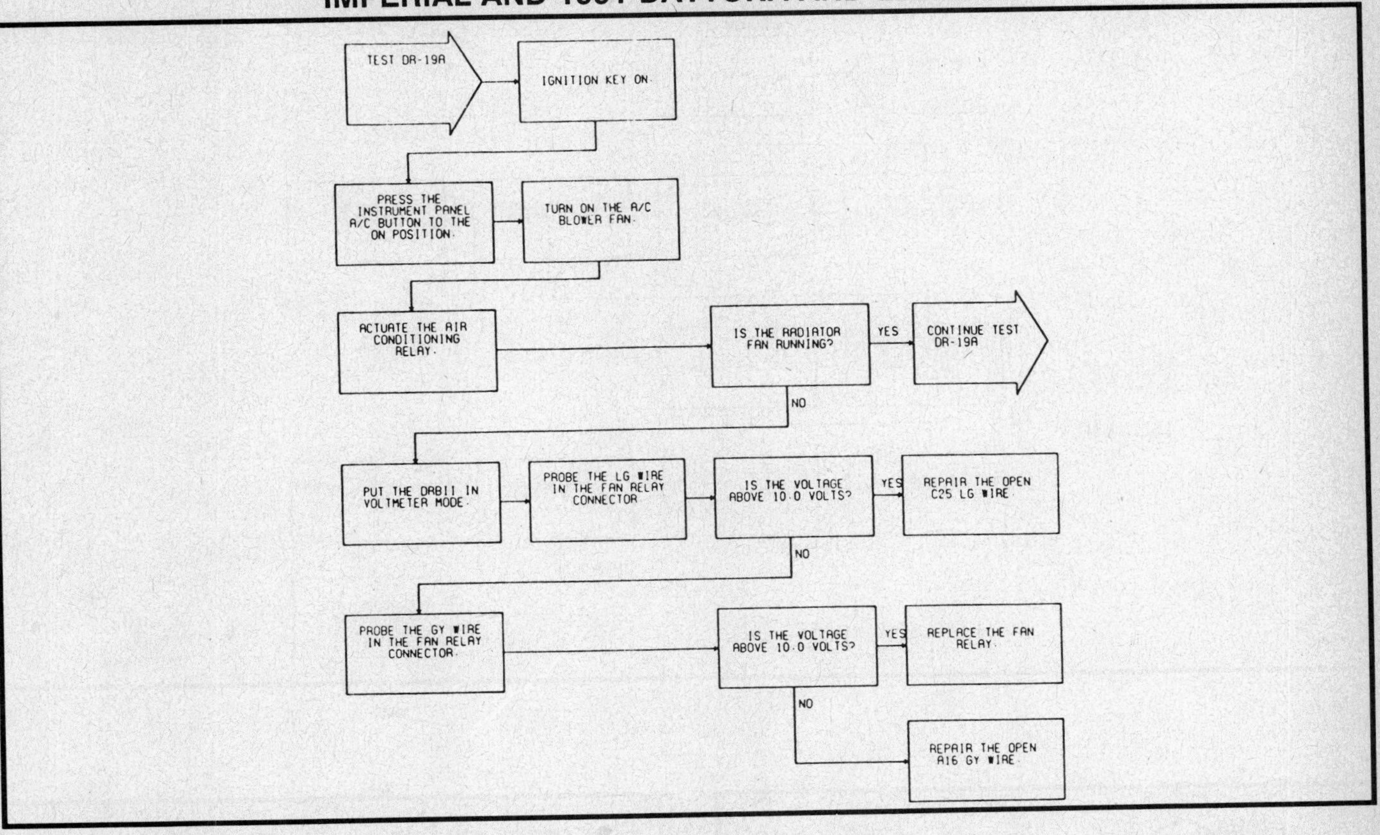
TEST DR-19A
IGNITION KEY ON.
PRESS THE INSTRUMENT PANEL A/C BUTTON TO THE ON POSITION.
TURN ON THE A/C BLOWER FAN.
ACTUATE THE AIR CONDITIONING RELAY.
IS THE RADIATOR FAN RUNNING?
YES
CONTINUE TEST DR-19A
NO
PUT THE DRBII IN VOLTMETER MODE.
PROBE THE LG WIRE IN THE FAN RELAY CONNECTOR
IS THE VOLTAGE ABOVE 10.0 VOLTS?
YES
REPAIR THE OPEN C25 LG WIRE.
NO
PROBE THE GY WIRE IN THE FAN RELAY CONNECTOR.
IS THE VOLTAGE ABOVE 10.0 VOLTS?
YES
REPLACE THE FAN RELAY.
NO
REPAIR THE OPEN A16 GY WIRE.

A/C CLUTCH RELAY CIRCUIT—1990–91 VEHICLES EXCEPT DYNASTY, NEW YORKER, IMPERIAL AND 1991 DAYTONA AND LEBARON

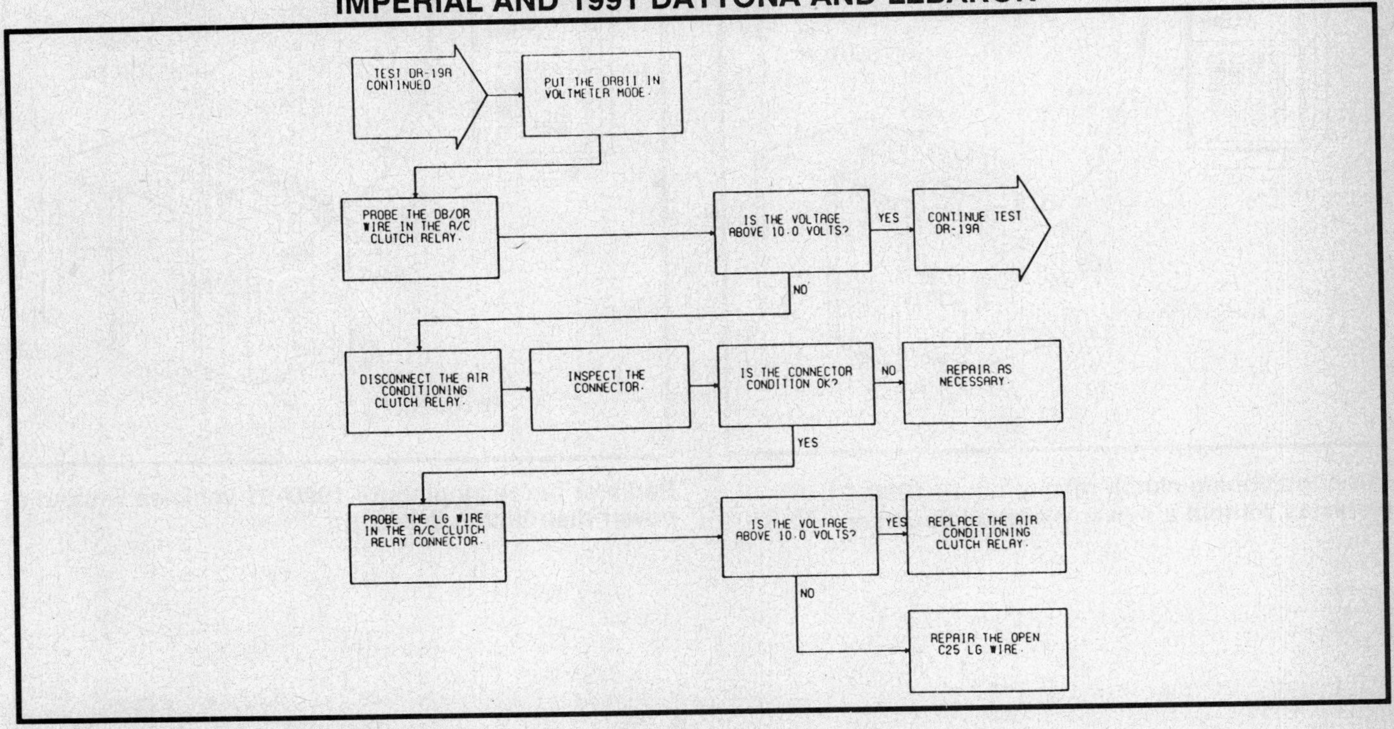
TEST DR-19A CONTINUED
PUT THE DRBII IN VOLTMETER MODE.
PROBE THE DB/OR WIRE IN THE A/C CLUTCH RELAY.
IS THE VOLTAGE ABOVE 10.0 VOLTS?
YES
CONTINUE TEST DR-19A
NO
DISCONNECT THE AIR CONDITIONING CLUTCH RELAY.
INSPECT THE CONNECTOR.
IS THE CONNECTOR CONDITION OK?
NO
REPAIR AS NECESSARY.
YES
PROBE THE LG WIRE IN THE A/C CLUTCH RELAY CONNECTOR.
IS THE VOLTAGE ABOVE 10.0 VOLTS?
YES
REPLACE THE AIR CONDITIONING CLUTCH RELAY.
NO
REPAIR THE OPEN C25 LG WIRE.

A/C CLUTCH RELAY CIRCUIT—1990–91 VEHICLES EXCEPT DYNASTY, NEW YORKER, IMPERIAL AND 1991 DAYTONA AND LEBARON

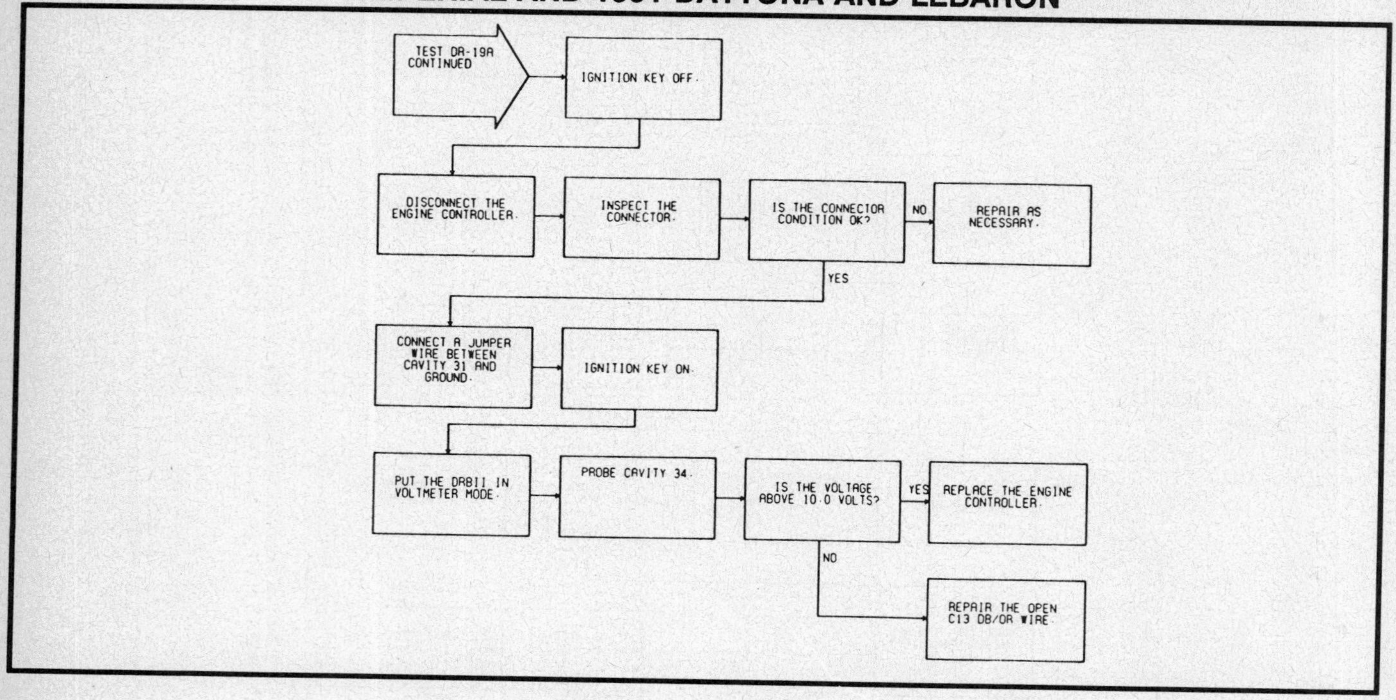
TEST DR-19A CONTINUED
IGNITION KEY OFF.
DISCONNECT THE ENGINE CONTROLLER.
INSPECT THE CONNECTOR.
IS THE CONNECTOR CONDITION OK?
NO
REPAIR AS NECESSARY.
YES
CONNECT A JUMPER WIRE BETWEEN CAVITY 31 AND GROUND.
IGNITION KEY ON.
PUT THE DRBII IN VOLTMETER MODE.
PROBE CAVITY 34.
IS THE VOLTAGE ABOVE 10.0 VOLTS?
YES
REPLACE THE ENGINE CONTROLLER.
NO
REPAIR THE OPEN C13 DB/OR WIRE.

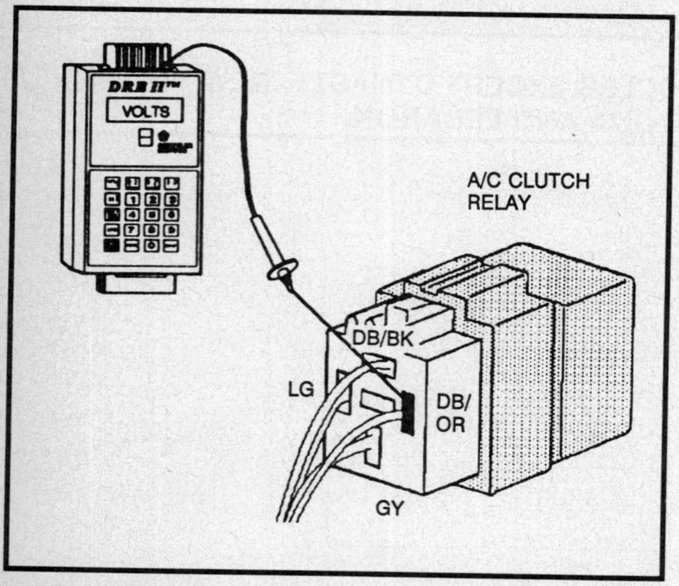
DRB II™
VOLTS
A/C CLUTCH RELAY
DB/BK
LG
DB/ OR
GY

Air conditioning clutch relay pinout—1990–91 vehicles without a power distribution center

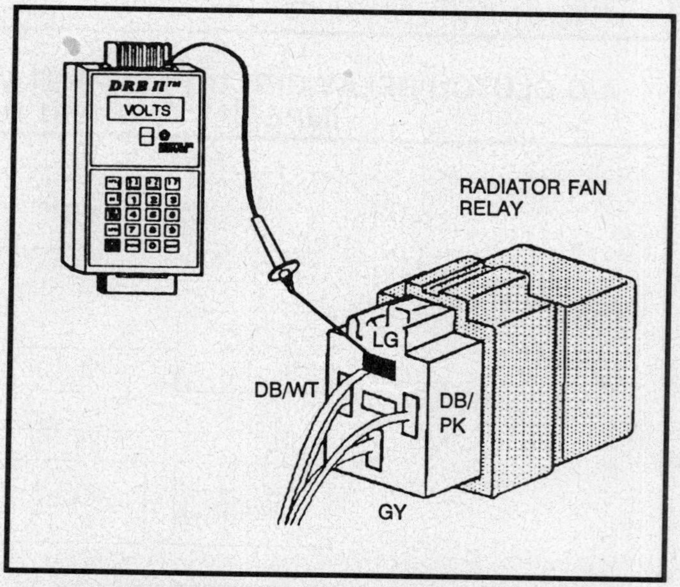
DRB II™
VOLTS
RADIATOR FAN RELAY
LG
DB/WT
DB/ PK
GY

Radiator fan relay pinout—1990–91 vehicles without a power distribution center

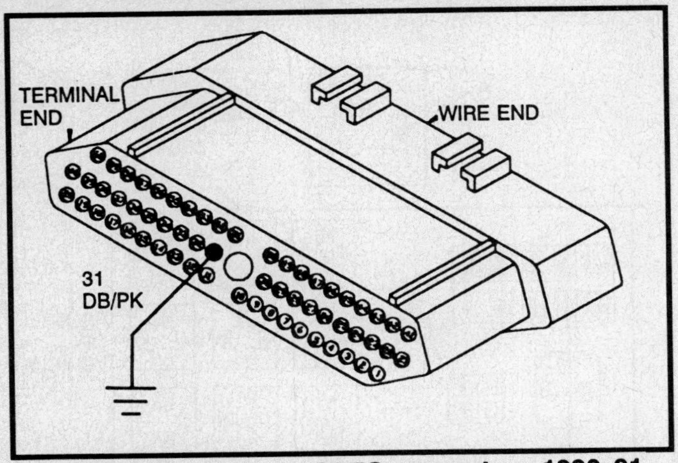
TERMINAL END
WIRE END
31
DB/PK

Grounding Pin 31 of the SBEC connector—1990–91 vehicles

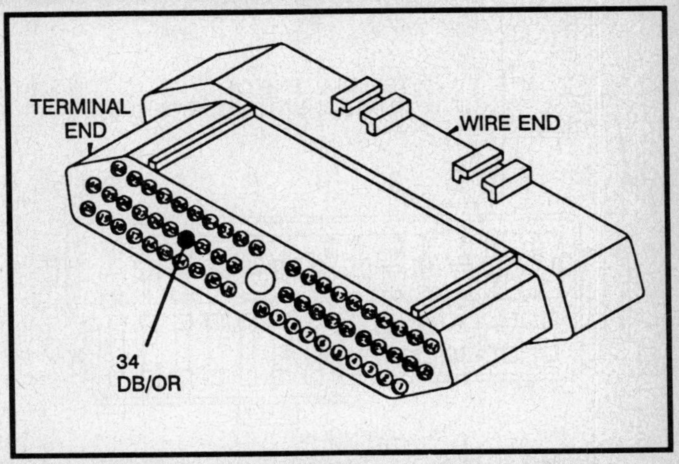
TERMINAL END
WIRE END
34
DB/OR

Pin 34 location on the SBEC connector—1990–91 vehicles

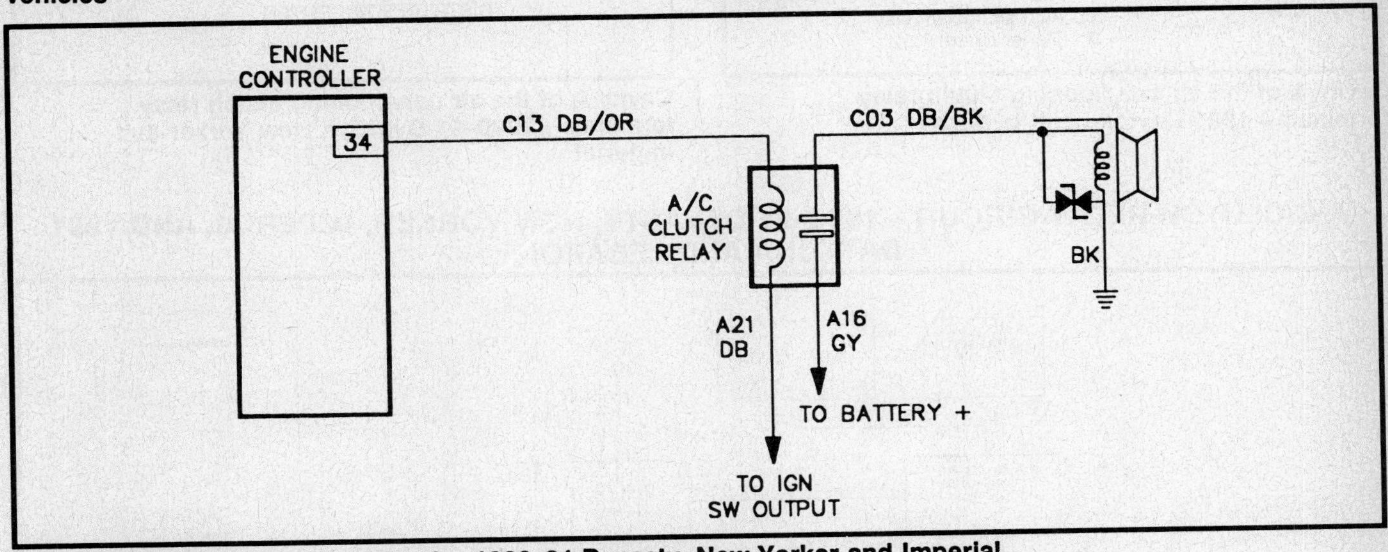
ENGINE CONTROLLER
34
C13 DB/OR
C03 DB/BK
A/C CLUTCH RELAY
BK
A21 DB
A16 GY
TO BATTERY +
TO IGN SW OUTPUT

Air conditioning clutch relay circuit—1990–91 Dynasty, New Yorker and Imperial

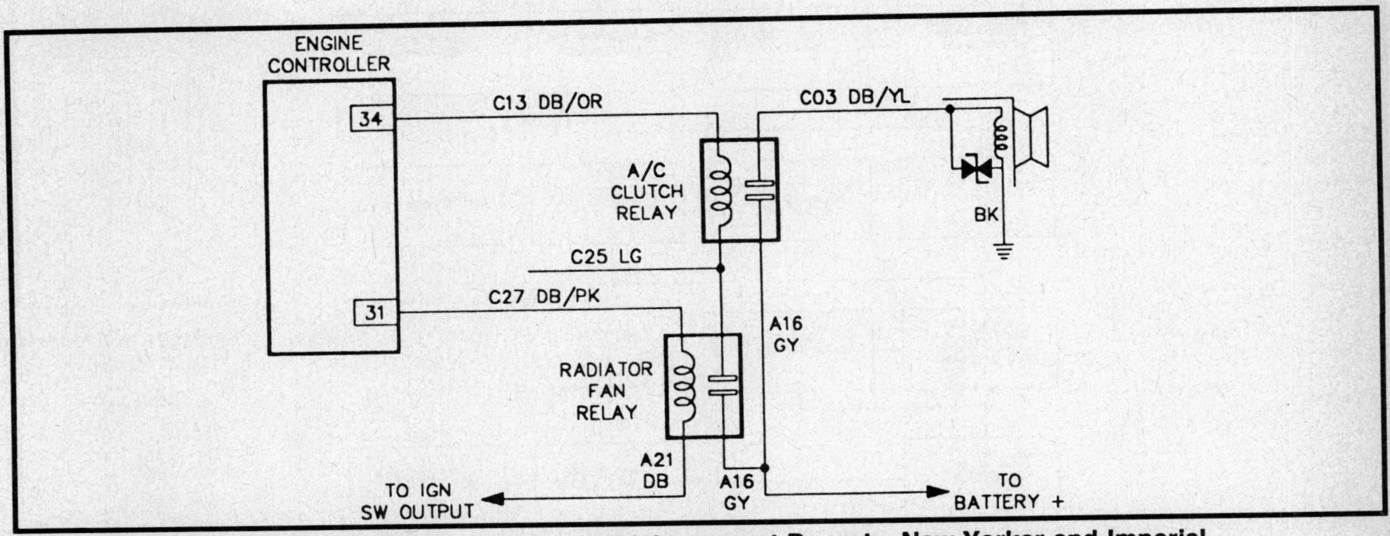
ENGINE CONTROLLER
34
C13 DB/OR
C03 DB/YL
A/C CLUTCH RELAY
BK
C25 LG
31
C27 DB/PK
A16 GY
RADIATOR FAN RELAY
A21 DB
A16 GY
TO IGN SW OUTPUT
TO BATTERY +

Air conditioning clutch relay circuit—1990–91 vehicles except Dynasty, New Yorker and Imperial

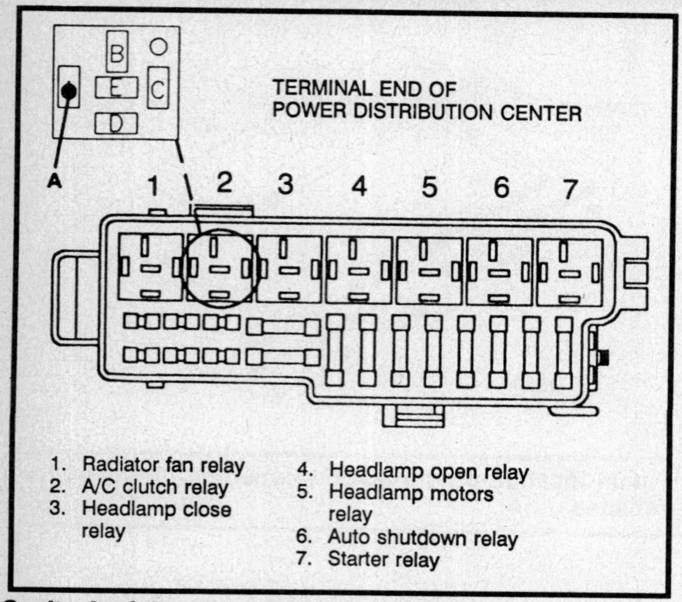
B
E
C
D
A
TERMINAL END OF
POWER DISTRIBUTION CENTER
1 2 3 4 5 6 7
1. Radiator fan relay
2. A/C clutch relay
3. Headlamp close relay
4. Headlamp open relay
5. Headlamp motors relay
6. Auto shutdown relay
7. Starter relay

Cavity A of the air conditioning clutch relay terminals—1991 Daytona and LeBaron

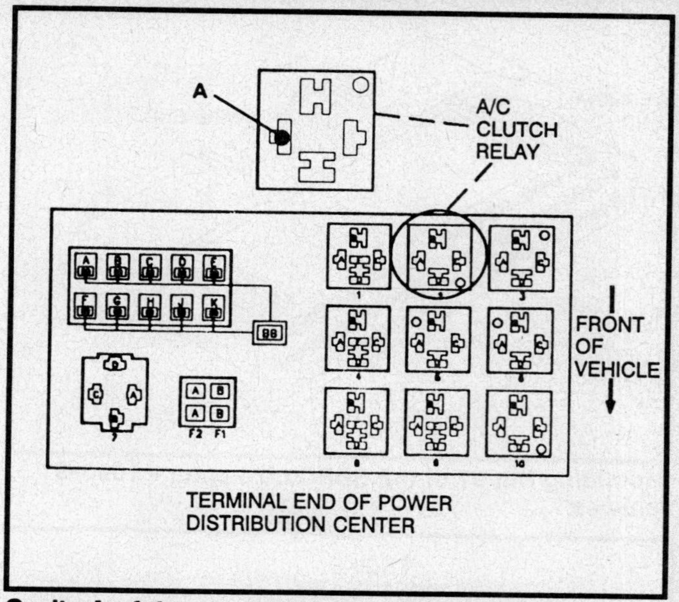
A
A/C
CLUTCH
RELAY
FRONT
OF
VEHICLE
F2 F1
TERMINAL END OF POWER
DISTRIBUTION CENTER

Cavity A of the air conditioning clutch relay terminals—1990–91 Dynasty, New Yorker and Imperial

A/C CLUTCH RELAY CIRCUIT—1990–91 DYNASTY, NEW YORKER, IMPERIAL AND 1991 DAYTONA AND LEBARON

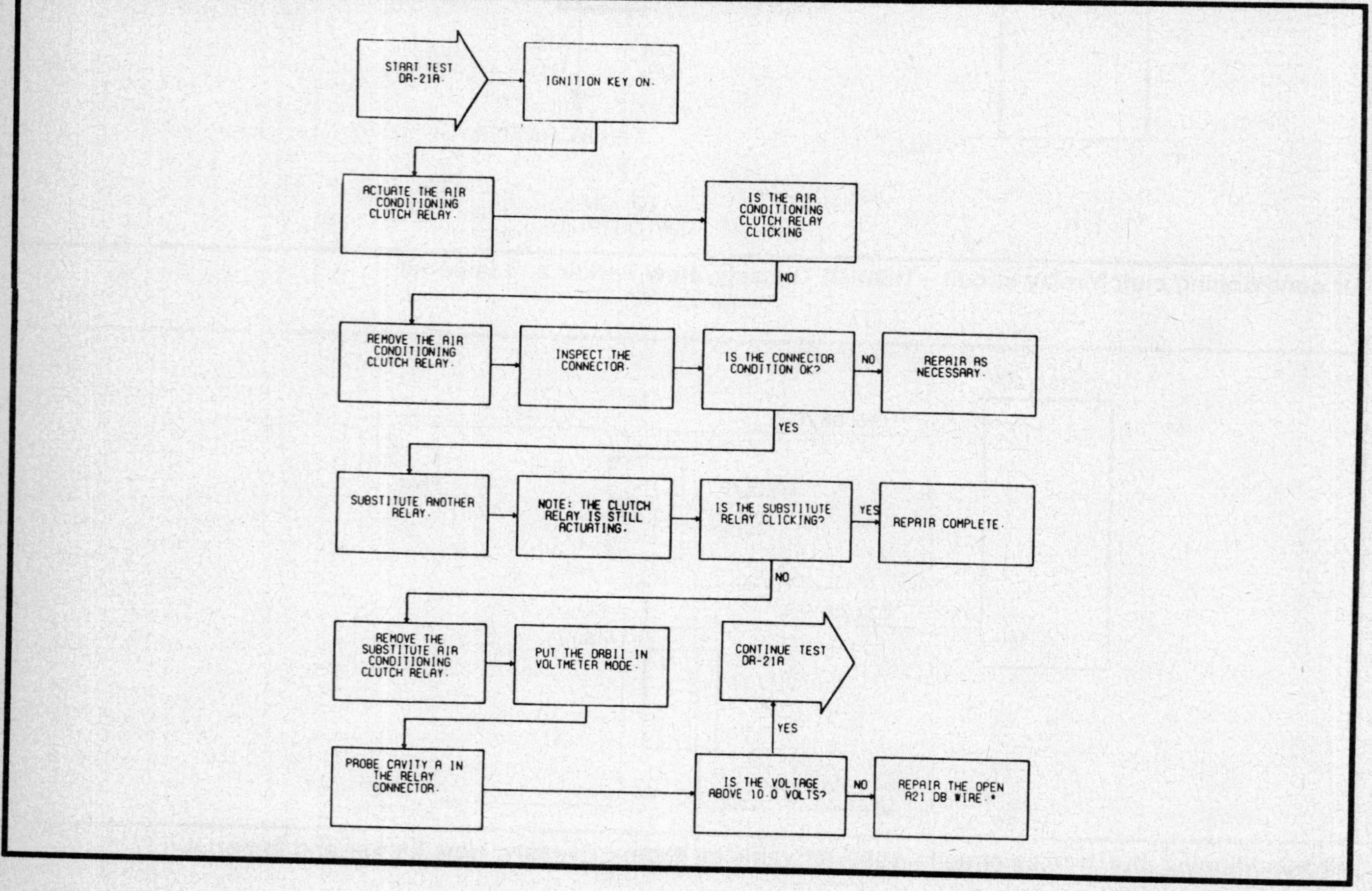
START TEST
DR-21A.
IGNITION KEY ON.
ACTUATE THE AIR CONDITIONING CLUTCH RELAY.
IS THE AIR CONDITIONING CLUTCH RELAY CLICKING
NO
REMOVE THE AIR CONDITIONING CLUTCH RELAY.
INSPECT THE CONNECTOR.
IS THE CONNECTOR CONDITION OK?
NO
REPAIR AS NECESSARY.
YES
SUBSTITUTE ANOTHER RELAY.
NOTE: THE CLUTCH RELAY IS STILL ACTUATING.
IS THE SUBSTITUTE RELAY CLICKING?
YES
REPAIR COMPLETE.
NO
REMOVE THE SUBSTITUTE AIR CONDITIONING CLUTCH RELAY.
PUT THE DRBII IN VOLTMETER MODE.
CONTINUE TEST
DR-21A
YES
PROBE CAVITY A IN THE RELAY CONNECTOR.
IS THE VOLTAGE ABOVE 10.0 VOLTS?
NO
REPAIR THE OPEN A21 DB WIRE.

A/C CLUTCH RELAY CIRCUIT—1990–91 DYNASTY, NEW YORKER, IMPERIAL AND 1991 DAYTONA AND LEBARON

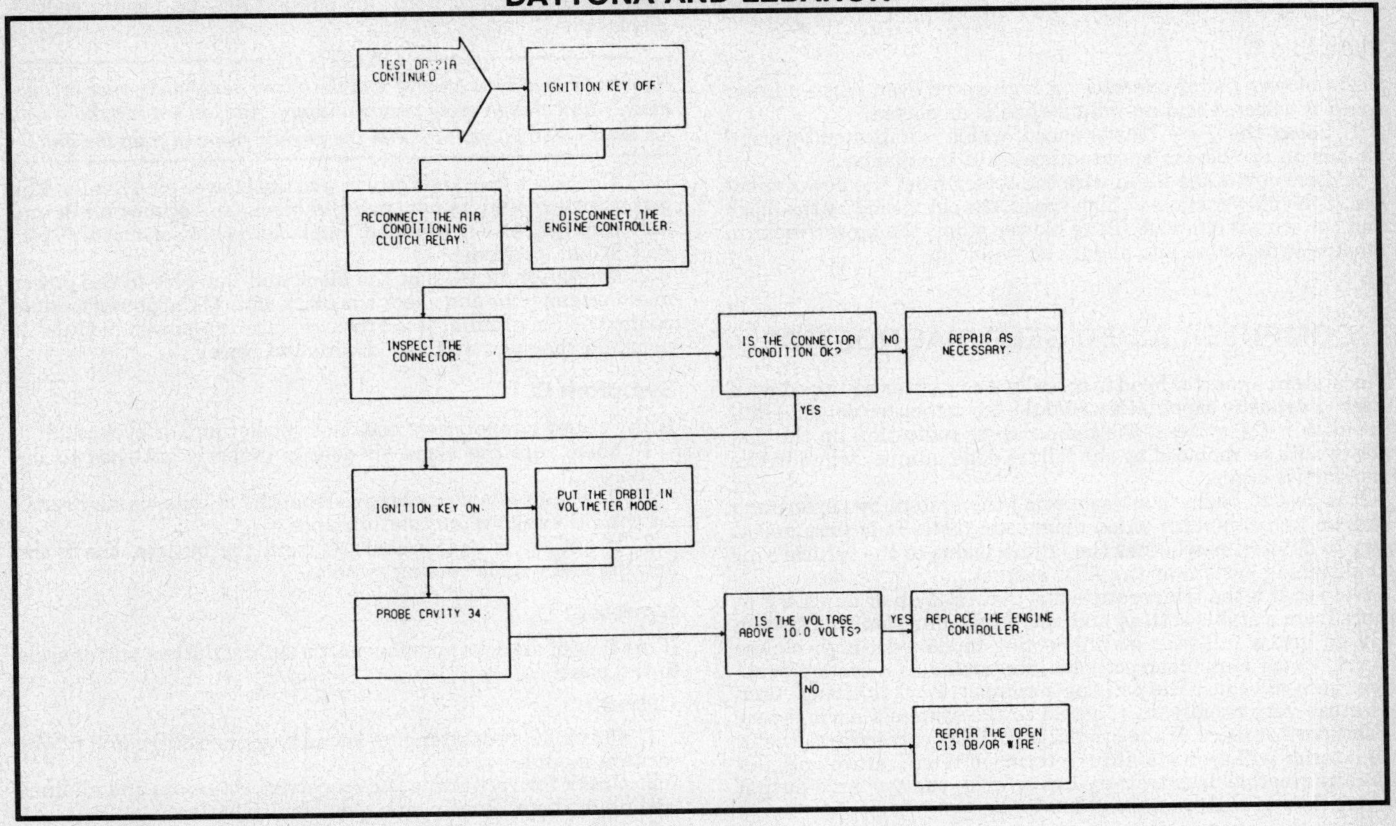
TEST DR-21A CONTINUED
IGNITION KEY OFF.
RECONNECT THE AIR CONDITIONING CLUTCH RELAY.
DISCONNECT THE ENGINE CONTROLLER.
INSPECT THE CONNECTOR.
IS THE CONNECTOR CONDITION OK?
NO
REPAIR AS NECESSARY.
YES
IGNITION KEY ON.
PUT THE DRBII IN VOLTMETER MODE.
PROBE CAVITY 34.
IS THE VOLTAGE ABOVE 10.0 VOLTS?
YES
REPLACE THE ENGINE CONTROLLER.
NO
REPAIR THE OPEN C13 DB/OR WIRE.

CLUTCH COIL TESTING

1. Verify the battery state of charge; the indicator should be green.
2. Connect a 0–10 scale ammeter in series with the clutch coil terminal. Use a volt meter with clips to measure the voltage across the battery and clutch coil.
3. Turn the A/C on and switch the blower to LOW speed. Start the engine and run at normal idle.
4. The A/C clutch should engage immediately and the clutch voltage should be within 2 volts of battery voltage.
5. The clutch coil is considered good if the current draw is 2.0–3.7 amperes at 12 volts at the clutch coil. If the voltage is more than 12.5 volts, add loads by turning on accessories until the voltage drops below 12.5 volts.
6. If the coil current reads 0, the coil is open and should be replaced.
7. If the ammeter reading is 4 or more amps, then the coil is shorted and should be replaced.
8. If the coil voltage is not within 2 volts of battery voltage, test the clutch coil feed circuit for excessive voltage drop.

Automatic Temperature Control (ATC) System

NON-COMPUTER AIDED DIAGNOSTICS

Symptom 1

If the ATC computer display does not dim when the headlight switch is turned ON, and other displays dim as they should:

1. Remove the ATC computer control panel from the instrument panel, keeping the wiring connected.
2. Test for voltage at pins 10 and 21 while rotating the headlight rheostat to regulate instrument display illumination voltage. Voltage should vary from 2–12 volts.
3. If the voltage supply is not satisfactory, repair the voltage supply circuit. If these checks are satisfactory and the other displays are normal, replace the ATC computer control head.

Symptom 2

If the computer does not remember settings after the key is turned OFF or displays an incomplete test display, replace the computer control panel and recheck system operation.

Symptom 3

If the ATC computer control panel push buttons stick, do not function properly, or the panel display figures are only partly illuminated, replace the computer control panel and recheck system operation.

Symptom 4

The ATC system output is inadequate in either the heating or cooling mode and no code is displayed:

1. Inspect the blend-air door shaft. Make sure it engages properly with its actuator. If the shaft engages properly, check the in-car sensor aspirator while the system is in operation. This may be done by placing a small piece of paper over the sensor intake in the instrument panel. If this does not resolve the problem, continue.
2. With the system operating, place a small piece of paper over the intake grille for the temperature sensor in the instru-

ment panel and release it. If the suction from the blower holds the paper in place, the system is operating. If not, the aspirator fan is inoperative.

Symptom 5

If the blower motor operates on high speed even when a lower speed is selected and no failure code is displayed:

1. Select the lower blower speed, which is indicated by a single bar on the blower speed indicator of the display.
2. Disconnect the 2-pin wire connector from the power module. If the blower stays at high speed, the circuit fed by the black and tan wire is shorted. If the blower stops, the power/vacuum module is defective and should be replaced.

COMPUTER AIDED SELF-DIAGNOSTICS

The system's control head is actually a computer equipped with a self-diagnostic capabilities. Should the computer detect a failure within the system, the temperature indication on the display would be replaced by the failure code number when in the diagnostics mode.

It is best to begin troubleshooting the system by performing various non-computer-aided diagnostic tests. It is first necessary to determine whether the failure is due to the vehicle's air conditioning system or the ATC system.

Note that if the temperature dial is turned up or down 4°F or more from a stable setting and operating condition, the system will go into a full-heat or full-cooling mode with high blower speed, which may incorrectly be interpreted as a system problem. This will cause the passenger compartment to change temperature very rapidly, in contrast to the system's normal very stable performance. If the system is working correctly, the vehicle interior will soon stabilize in terms of temperature and, unless the weather is extremely hot or cold, the system's output will reduce to a more normal level.

First, check the basics:

- Fuses, fusible links, cartridge fuses and relays
- Coolant level
- Heater core water valve operation
- Refrigerant charge and compressor operation
- Tension of compressor drive belt
- Tightness of vacuum line connections
- Radiator air flow and coolant flow through thermostat
- Radiator fan operation
- In-car sensor air intake is clear and air is drawn in

Procedure

1. Start the engine and allow to come to normal operating temperature.
2. Simultaneously depress the **AUTO**, **FLOOR** and **DEFROST** buttons. The display should flashing on and off.
3. During the test, check for the following symptoms:
   a. Any or all display symbols and indicators do not illuminate.
   b. The blower does not operate at its highest speed.
   c. Outlet temperature does not get hot and/or cycle cold.
   d. Flow of air does not start at the defrost outlets and/or cycle to the panel outlets.

If none of these symptoms are present and no codes are shown, the system will return to normal operation. If any of the symptoms are present, continue.

Symptom A

If any or all display symbols and indicators do not illuminate:

1. After self-diagnostics are complete, select the function that should display the malfunctioning symbol.
2. If the system operates properly and the display does not, replace the control head.

Symptom B

If the blower motor does not operate and no failure code is displayed:

CAUTION

Keep hands and arms clear of both the blower motor and power vacuum module heat sink to avoid personal injury. Also, do not run the system for longer than 10 minutes with the module removed from the unit.

1. Check the fuse and the wires to the blower for 12 volts. The green wire should be hot, and the black (sometimes black and tan) wire should be grounded. Replace the blower motor if correct. If not, continue.
2. Check for 12 volts at the black and tan wire in the power module connector and check the black wire at the power module connector for ground. If correct, replace the power module. If not, find the open or shorted wire and repair.

Symptom C

If the outlet temperature does not get hot and/or cycle cold:

1. Make sure the blend air door is properly attached to the actuator.
2. If cold air is not discharged from the outlets, check overall air conditioning system performance.
3. If hot air is not discharged from the outlets, check the heating and engine cooling system.

Symptom D

If the flow of air does not start at the defrost outlets and/or cycle to the panel oulets.

1989–90

1. Check for proper engine vacuum at the source and power vacuum module.
2. Check for vacuum to the respective actuators and all lines leading to them. Repair or replace faulty parts.
3. If the power vacuum module fails to redirect vacuum properly, replace it.

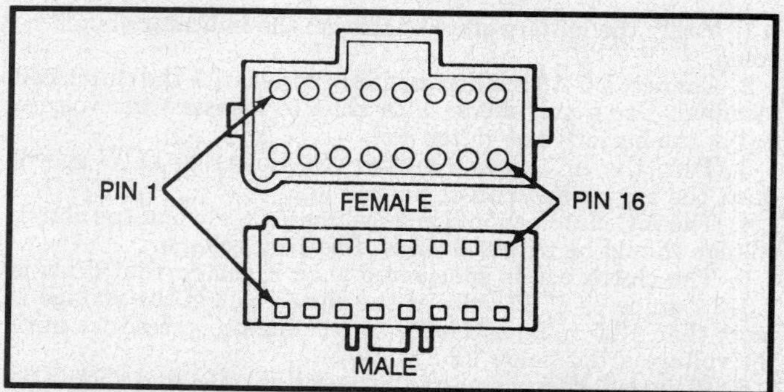
PIN 1
FEMALE
PIN 16
MALE

16-way connector above the power/vacum module pinout—1989–90 vehicles

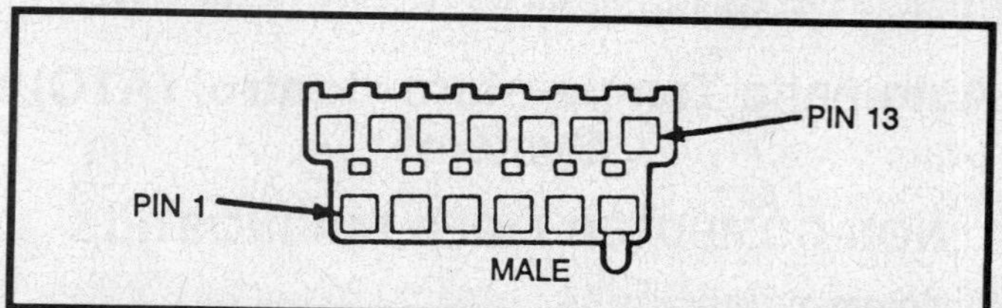
PIN 13
PIN 1
MALE

13-way power/vacuum module pinout—1989–90 vehicles

1991

1. Check the linkages from the mode door actuators for binding.
2. Check for proper door travel in the housiong.

If there are no codes stored in the system, it will resume normal operation. If there are any failure codes present, the blower will stop and each code can be displayed; after each failure code appears, push the **PANEL** button to display the next code. At the end of the cycle (after all codes have been shown), the display will return to its normal readout.

Failure Codes

1989–90

Failure Codes 1, 2 or 3—ATC Control Head, Blend Air Door Actuator and Wiring

NOTE: If Codes 12 or 13 appear in any combination with these codes, repair Codes 12 or 13 first and retest. If the failure Code is 3, skip Step 1.

1. Remove the blend air door actuator with the wire connector still connected and retest the system. If the failure code has disappeared, check the door for binding; if the code still exists, continue.
2. Disconnect the 21-way connector from the control head and the 5-way connector from the blend air door actuator. Check the following circuits for continuity:
   a. Pin No. 17 of control head connector to pin No. 3 of actuator connector (via pin No. 11 of 16-way connector above power vacuum module)
   b. Pin No. 18 of control head connector to pin No. 1 of actuator connector (via pin No. 13 of 16-way connector above power vacuum module)
   c. Pin No. 8 of control head connector to pin No. 4 of actuator connector (via pin No. 15 of 16-way connector above power vacuum module)
   d. Pin No. 7 of control head connector to pin No. 5 of actuator connector (via pin No. 14 of 16-way connector above power vacuum module)
   e. If any of the above circuits are open, repair the wire and retest.
   f. If all circuits are complete, plug the connectors back in and proceed to the next Step for Code 1, or Step 4 for Code 2.

If the failure Code is 3, replace the blend air door actuator and retest. If the code still exists, replace the ATC control head and retest.

3. Set the system at 65°F and wait for at least 30 seconds. Connect a voltmeter to pin No. 8 of the control head connector. Adjust the temperature setting to 85°F and monitor the voltage. The voltage should have increased to at least 4 volts, then stopped. If the test was satisfactory, replace the ATC control head. If not, replace the blend air door actuator. Retest the system in either case.
4. Set the system at 85°F and wait for at least 30 seconds. Connect a voltmeter to pin No. 8 of the control head connector. Adjust the temperature setting to 65°F and monitor the voltage. The voltage should have decreased to less than 1 volt. If the test was satisfactory, replace the ATC control head. If not, replace the blend air door actuator. Retest the system in either case.

Failure Code 4—ATC Control Head, Power/Vacuum Module and A/C Logic Circuit

1. Manually increase the the blower speed from the 1st to the 8th bar segment. If the blower goes to high speed, proceed to Step 2 If not, proceed as follows:
   a. Remove the control head and disconnect its connector. Measure the resistance between pins No. 2 and 12. The specification is 2600–2800 ohms. If within specification, replace the ATC control head. If not, continue.
   b. Check for continuity between pin No. 2 of the control head connector and pin No. 13 of the power/vacuum module. If the circuit is complete, replace the power/vacuum module. If the circuit was open, repair the wire and retest.
2. Check to see if the compressor turns on and off by pushing the A/C button on and off while not in the DEFROST mode. If the compressor turns on and off, replace the ATC control head. If not, continue.
   a. Unplug the low pressure cut off switch on Dynasty, New Yorker and Imperial or the electronic cycling clutch switch on LeBaron and perform diagnostics again. If the code disappeared, the problem is between the A/C switch and the engine controller. If Code 4 still exists, continue.
   b. Check for continuity between pin No. 5 of the ATC control head connector on Dynasty, New Yorker and Imperial, or pin No. 13 of the connector on LeBaron, and the unplugged switch connector. If open, repair the wire and retsest. If complete, replace the ATC control head and retest.

Failure Code 5—ATC Control Head, A/C Switches, Engine Controller and Wiring

1. Unplug the low pressure cut off switch on Dynasty, New Yorker and Imperial or the electronic cycling clutch switch on LeBaron and perform diagnostics again. If the code disappeared, the problem is between the unplugged switch and the engine controller. If Code 5 still exists, continue.
2. Check for continuity between pin No. 5 of the ATC control head connector on Dynasty, New Yorker and Imperial, or pin No. 13 of the connector on LeBaron, and the unplugged switch connector. If open, repair the wire and retsest. If complete, replace the ATC control head and retest.

Failure Code 6—ATC Control Head, Power/Vacuum Module and Wiring

1. Remove the ATC control head and disconnect its connector. Measure the resistance between pins No. 2 and 12. The specification is 2600–2800 ohms. If within specification, replace the ATC control head. If not, continue.
2. Check for continuity between pin No. 2 of the control head connector and pin No. 13 of the power/vacuum module. If the circuit is complete, replace the power/vacuum module. If the circuit was open, repair the wire and retest.

Failure Code 7—ATC Control Head, Power/Vacuum Module and Wiring

1. Set the ATC system to the **OFF** mode. Remove the control head and measure the voltage at pin No. 4 of the connector. If the voltage is more than 4 volts or 0.4–0.8 volts, replace the ATC control head. If the voltage is not within either specification, continue.
2. Disconnect the 13-way connector from the power/vacuum module. Check for continuity between pin No. 4 of the ATC control head connector and pin No. 6 of the power/vacuum module. If the circuit is complete, replace the power/vacuum module. If the circuit was open, repair the wire and retest.

Failure Code 8—ATC Control Head, Power/Vacuum Module and Wiring

1. Set the ATC system to the defrost mode. Remove the control head and measure the voltage at pin No. 5 of the connector. If the voltage is more than 4 volts or 0.4–0.8 volts, replace the ATC control head. If the voltage is not within either specification, continue.
2. Disconnect the 13-way connector from the power/vacuum module. Check for continuity between pin No. 5 of the ATC control head connector and pin No. 5 of the power/vacuum module.

If the circuit is complete, replace the power/vacuum module. If the circuit was open, repair the wire and retest.

Failure Code 9—ATC Control Head, Power/Vacuum Module and Wiring

1. Set the ATC system to the **OFF** mode. Remove the control head and measure the voltage at pin No. 6 of the connector. If the voltage is more than 4 volts or 0.4–0.8 volts, replace the ATC control head. If the voltage is not within either specification, continue.

2. Disconnect the 13-way connector from the power/vacuum module. Check for continuity between pin No. 6 of the ATC control head connector and pin No. 4 of the power/vacuum module. If the circuit is complete, replace the power/vacuum module. If the circuit was open, repair the wire and retest.

Failure Code 10—ATC Control Head, Power/Vacuum Module and Wiring

1. Set the ATC system to the **OFF** mode. Remove the control head and measure the voltage at pin No. 15 of the connector. If the voltage is more than 4 volts or 0.4–0.8 volts, replace the ATC control head. If the voltage is not within either specification, continue.

2. Disconnect the 13-way connector from the power/vacuum module. Check for continuity between pin No. 15 of the ATC control head connector and pin No. 2 of the power/vacuum module. If the circuit is complete, replace the power/vacuum module. If the circuit was open, repair the wire and retest.

Failure Code 11—ATC Control Head, Power/Vacuum Module and Wiring

1. Set the ATC system to the **OFF** mode. Remove the control head and measure the voltage at pin No. 16 of the connector. If the voltage is more than 4 volts or 0.4–0.8 volts, replace the ATC control head. If the voltage is not within either specification, continue.

2. Disconnect the 13-way connector from the power/vacuum module. Check for continuity between pin No. 16 of the ATC control head connector and pin No. 1 of the power/vacuum module. If the circuit is complete, replace the power/vacuum module. If the circuit was open, repair the wire and retest.

Failure Code 12 and/or 13—Control Head, Blend Air Door Actuator and Wiring

1. Disconnect the 21-way connector from the control head and the 5-way connector from the blend air door actuator. Check the following circuits for continuity:

a. Pin No. 12 of control head connector to pin No. 2 of actuator connector (via pin No. 11 of 16-way connector above power vacuum module)

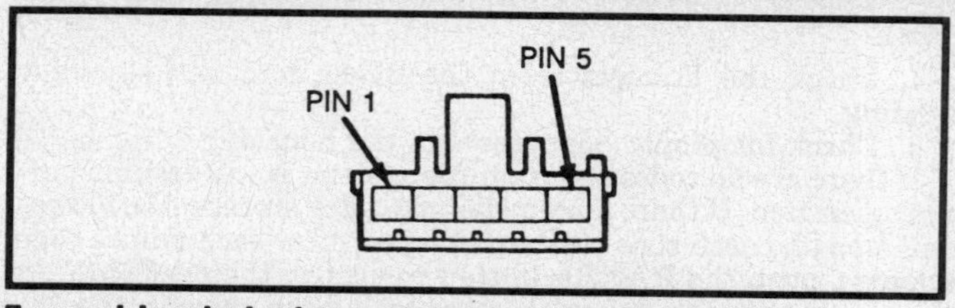
PIN 5
PIN 1

5-way blend-air door actuator way connector

b. Pin No. 17 of control head connector to pin No. 3 of actuator connector (via pin No. 13 of 16-way connector above power vacuum module)

c. Pin No. 18 of control head connector to pin No. 1 of actuator connector (via pin No. 15 of 16-way connector above power vacuum module)

d. If any of the above circuits are open, repair the wire and retest.

e. If all circuits are complete, replace the blend air door actuator and retest the system. If the code still exists, replace the ATC control head and retest.

Failure Code 14—ATC Control Head, Ambient Sensor and Wiring

NOTE: The resistance specification for the following checks is 2,000–350,000 ohms.

1. Remove the ATC control head and test the resistance between pins No. 7 and 9 of the connector. If within specification, replace the ATC control head. If not, continue.

2. Disconnect the 16-way connector, located above the power/vacuum module. Check the resistance between pins No. 10 and 14 of the female connector that is held in place with a metal bracket. If the resistance is within specification, repair the wire between the control head and 16-way connector. If not, continue.

3. Check the resistance of the ambient sensor itself. If the resistance is within specification, repair the wire between the 16-way connector and the sensor. If not within specifications, replace the ambient sensor.

Failure Code 15—ATC Control Head, In-Car Sensor and Wiring

NOTE: The resistance specification for the following checks is 2,000–350,000 ohms.

1. Remove the ATC control head and test the resistance between pins No. 7 and 20 of the connector. If within specification, replace the ATC control head. If not, continue.

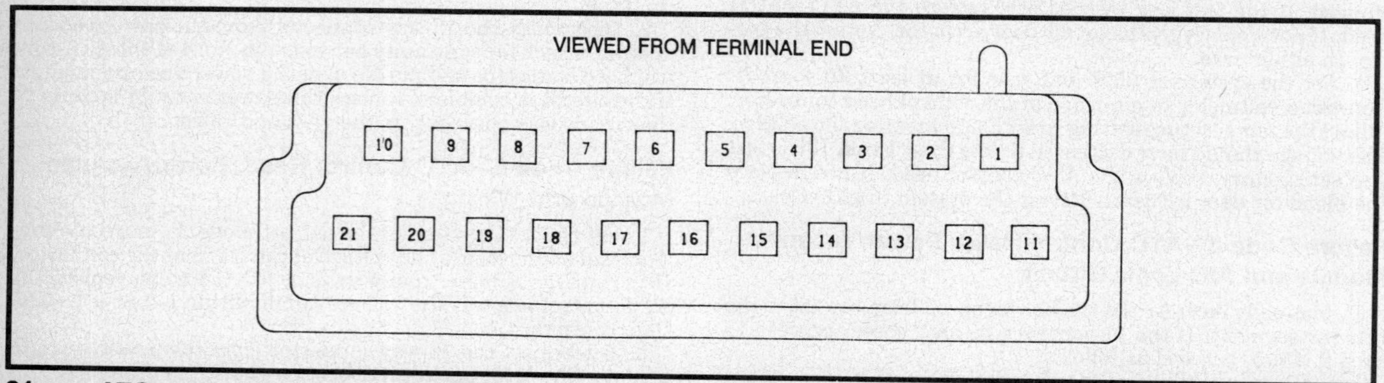
VIEWED FROM TERMINAL END
10
9
8
7
6
5
4
3
2
1
21
20
19
18
17
16
15
14
13
12
11

21-way ATC control head way connector

2. Check the resistance of the outer pins of the in-car sensor connector. If not within specifications, replace the ambient sensor. If the resistance is within specification, continue.
3. Check for continuity between pin No. 20 of the control head connector and pin No. 1 of the in-car sensor and pin No. 7 of the control head connector and pin No. 4 of the in-car sensor. Repair any open circuit(s) found.

Failure Codes 16, 17 and 18—ATC Control Head

These codes all indicate a faulty control head. Replace the unit and retest the system.

1991

Failure Code 1—Output Failure With All Outputs Low

1. Remove pin No. 2 from the 21-way control head connector and retest the system. If Code 1 still exists, replace the control head and retest the system. If the code disappears, continue.
2. Disconnect the 21-way connector from the control head. Measure the resistance between pins No. 2 and 12 of the control head connector. The specification is 2600–2800 ohms. If within specification, the source of the voltage at pin No. 2 is in the wiring; repair and retest the system. If not within specification, replace the power module. Retest; if the code still exists, continue.
3. Remove pin No. 13 from the control head connector and retest the system. If Code 1 still exists, replace the control head and retest the system. If the Code disappears, locate and repair the source of the voltage on pin No. 13. Retest; if the code still exists, continue.
4. Remove pin No. 5 from the control head connector and retest the system. If Code 1 still exists, replace the control head and retest the system. If the code disappears, locate and repair the source of the voltage on pin No. 5. Retest; if the code still exists, continue.
5. Remove pin No. 6 from the control head connector and retest the system. If Code 1 still exists, replace the control head and retest the system. If the code disappears, locate and repair the source of the voltage on pin No. 6. Retest; if the code still exists, continue.
6. Remove pin No. 15 from the control head connector and retest the system. If Code 1 still exists, replace the control head and retest the system. If the code disappears, locate and repair the source of the voltage on pin No. 15 and retest.

Failure Code 2—Blend Air Door Actuator Drive Signal Not High

NOTE: If both failure Codes 2 and 3 occur simultaneously, perform both check procedures. Normally, there is only 1 actual failure.

1. Remove pin No. 6 from the 21-way control head connector and retest the system. Note that removing this pin may generate additional codes which may be disregarded at this time. If Code 2 still exists, replace the control head. If not, the problem is a shorted blend door actuator motor or short to ground in the circuit involving pin No. 6.
2. Remove the 21-way control head connector and check pin No. 6 for continuity to chassis ground. If there is continuity, repair the wiring and retest. If not, continue.
3. Check the resistance across pins No. 4 and 6 of the 21-way connector for a shorted actuator motor. The specification is 20–50 ohms. If out of specification, replace the actuator and retest.

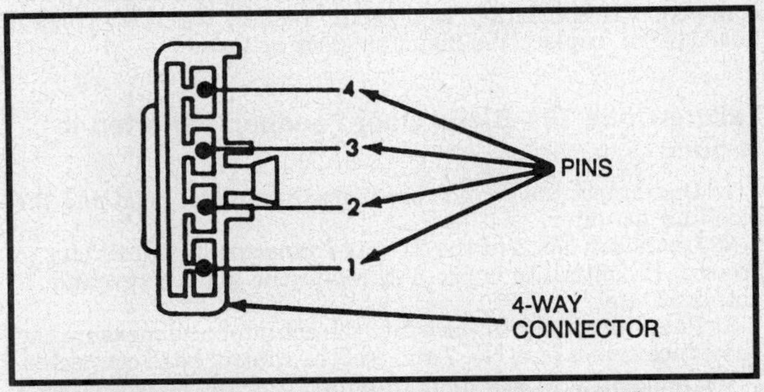
4
3
2
1
PINS
4-WAY
CONNECTOR

4-way power module connector—1991 vehicles

Failure Code 3—Mode Door Actuator Signal Not High

NOTE: If both failure Codes 3 and 2 occur simultaneously, perform both check procedures. Normally, there is only 1 actual failure.

1. Remove pin No. 6 from the 21-way control head connector and retest the system. Note that removing this pin may generate additional codes which may be disregarded at this time. If Code 3 still exists, replace the control head. If not, the problem is a shorted mode door actuator motor or short to ground in the circuit involving pin No. 5.
2. Remove the 21-way control head connector and check pin No. 5 for continuity to chassis ground. If there is continuity, repair the wiring and retest. If not, continue.
3. Check the resistance across pins No. 4 and 5 of the 21-way connector for a shorted actuator motor. The specification is 20–50 ohms. If out of specification, replace the actuator and retest.

Failure Code 4—Actuator Drive Common Signal Not High

NOTE: If both failure Codes 4 and 5 occur simultaneously, perform both check procedures. Normally, there is only 1 actual failure.

1. Remove pin No. 4 from the 21-way control head connector and retest the system. Note that removing this pin may generate additional Codes which may be disregarded at this time. If Code 4 still exists, replace the control head. If not, the problem is a shorted actuator motor or short to ground in the circuit involving pin No. 4.
2. Remove the 21-way control head connector and check pin No. 4 for continuity to chassis ground. If there is continuity, repair the wiring and retest. If not, continue.
3. Check the resistance across pins No. 4 and 5; 4 and 6; and 4 and 15 of the 21-way connector for a shorted actuator motor. The specification is 20–50 ohms. If out of specification, replace the appropriate actuator and retest.

Failure Code 5—Fresh/Recirc Actuator Drive Signal Not High

NOTE: If both failure Codes 5 and 4 occur simultaneously, perform both check procedures. Normally, there is only 1 actual failure.

1. Remove pin No. 15 from the 21-way control head connector and retest the system. Note that removing this pin may generate additional codes which may be disregarded at this time. If Code 5 still exists, replace the control head. If not, the problem is a shorted actuator motor or short to ground in the circuit involving pin No. 15.
2. Remove the 21-way control head connector and check pin No. 15 for continuity to chassis ground. If there is continuity, repair the wiring and retest. If not, continue.
3. Check the resistance across pins No. 4 and 15 of the 21-way connector for a shorted actuator motor. The specification is 20–50 ohms. If out of specification, replace the actuator motor and retest.

Failure Code 6 – Compressor Drive Signal Not High

1. Disconnect the low pressure cut off switch and perform retest.
2. If Code 6 disappears, check the wiring between the low pressure cut out switch and the engine controller. If all wiring is satisfactory, replace the engine controller.
3. If Code 6 still exists, disconnect the 21-way connector from the control head and check pin No. 13 for continuity to chassis ground. If continuity exists, repair the wire from the low pressure cut off switch. If there is no continuity, replace the control head and retest.

Failure Code 7 – Blower Drive Signal Not High

1. Turn the ignition ON and check for ignition voltage at pin No. 1 of the power module. If ignition is present at the power module, proceed to Step 3. If not, continue.
2. Check for power module ignition feed at pin No. 12 of the control head connector. If there is no voltage, replace the control head. If voltage is present, repair the open wire between the 2 pins checked.
3. Turn the ignition OFF and disconnect the control head 21-way connector. Measure the resistance between pins No. 2 and 12. The specification is 2600–2800 ohms. If within specification, replace the control head. If not, continue.
4. Disconnect the 4-way connector from the power module. Check for continuity between pin No. 2 of the control head connector and pin No. 2 of the power module connector. If the circuit is complete, replace the power module and retest. If the circuit is open, repair the wire and retest.

Failure Code 8 – A/D Convertor Internal Failure

Failure Code 8 will be displayed when the internal reference voltage of the A/D convertor is not correct, a condition which is not serviceable. In this case, the control head must be replaced.

Failure Code 9 – Sun Sensor

1. Disconnect the control head 21-way connector and check pin No. 19 for continuity to ground. If continuity is present, repair the shorted wire. If not, continue.
2. Remove pin No. 19 from the connector, plug it back in and perform diagnostics again. If Code 9 is still present, replace the control head. If not, replace the sun sensor.

Failure Code 10 – Water Temperature Sensor

1. Disconnect the control head 21-way connector. Measure the resistance between pins No. 7 and 17. The value should change according to the water temperature/resistance relationships below:
   20°F – 136,050 ohms
   40°F – 77,250 ohms
   60°F – 45,700 ohms
   80°F – 27,900 ohms
   100°F – 17,550 ohms
   150°F – 6,150 ohms
   200°F – 2,500 ohms
2. Replace the water temperature sensor if the resistance does not approximately match the figures.
3. If the values agree, check pin No. 17 for continuity to ground. If continuity is present, repair the short to ground and retest.

Failure Code 11 – Ambient Temperature Sensor

1. Disconnect the control head 21-way connector. Measure the resistance between pins No. 7 and 9. The value should change according to the ambient temperature/resistance relationships below:
   20°F – 52,500 ohms
   40°F – 38,000 ohms
   60°F – 12,670 ohms
   80°F – 9,310 ohms
   100°F – 5,730 ohms
   120°F – 3,550 ohms
2. Replace the ambient temperature sensor if the resistance does not approximately match the figures.
3. If the values agree, check pin No. 9 for continuity to ground. If continuity is present, repair the short to ground and retest.

Failure Code 12 – In-Car Temperature Sensor/Aspirator

1. Disconnect the control head 21-way connector. Measure the resistance between pins No. 7 and 20. The value should change according to the ambient temperature/resistance relationships shown above for Failure Code 11.
2. Replace the assembly if the resistance does not approximately match the figures.
3. If the values agree, check pin No. 20 for continuity to ground. If continuity is present, repair the short to ground and retest.

Failure Code 13 – Blend Door Failed to Drive to Heat Position

1. Check the door and linkage for binding or other mechanical problems.
2. Disconnect the control head 21-way connector and the blend air door actuator 5-way connector. Check for continuity between pin No. 6 of the 21-way connector and pin No. 5 of the 5-way connector. If the circuit is open, repair the wire and retest. If the circuit is complete, continue.
3. Plug the 5-way connector back in and check the resistance between pins No. 4 and 6 of the 21-way connector. A resistance of 20–50 ohms should be detected. If not, replace the actuator. If the resistance is within specification, replace the ATC control head.

Failure Code 14 – Blend Door Failed to Drive to Cold Position

1. Check the door and linkage for binding or other mechanical problems.
2. Disconnect the control head 21-way connector. Turn the ignition ON and check for ignition voltage between pin No. 8 and chassis ground. If voltage is present, repair the circuit for a short to ignition voltage. If not, continue.
3. Turn ignition OFF and disconnect the 5-way connector from the blend air door actuator. Check for continuity between pin No. 8 of the 21-way connector and pin No. 1 of the 5-way connector. If the circuit is open, repair the wire and retest. If the circuit is complete, continue.
4. Plug the connector back into the blend air door actuator and check for continuity between pins No. 7 and 8 of the 21 way connector. If continuity is present, replace the ATC control head. If not, replace the blend air door actuator.

Failure Code 15 – Blend Door Feedback Shorted to Ground

1. Disconnect the connectors from the control head and the blend air actuator.
2. Check pin No. 8 of the 21-way connector for continuity to ground. If continuity is present, repair the short to ground. If not, continue.
3. Plug the connector back into the actuator and measure the resistance across pins No. 7 and 8 of the control head connector. If the resistance is less than 10 ohms, replace the actuator. If not, replace the control head.

Failure Code 16—Mode Door Moved During Blend Air Door Test

1. Disconnect the connectors from the control head and all actuators.
2. Check for continuity between pin No. 4 of the control head connector and pin No. 4 of each actuator connector. Repair any open circuit found. If continuity is found in all circuits, continue.
3. Plug the connectors back into the actuators and check for resistance between pins No. 4 and 6 (blend air actuator) and pins No. 4 and 5 (mode actuator). The resistance should be 20–50 ohms. Replace the actuator corresponding to the failed resistance check. If both were within specification, replace the ATC control head.

Failure Code 17—Mode Door Failed to Drive to Defrost

1. Disconnect the control head 21-way connector and the blend air door actuator 5-way connectors. Check for continuity between pin No. 5 of the 21-way connector and pin No. 5 of the 5-way connector. If the circuit is open, repair the wire and retest. If not, continue.
2. Plug the 5-way connector back in and check for resistance between pins No. 4 and 5 of the 21-way connector. The resistance should be 20–50 ohms. If not within specification, replace the actuator. If both were within specification, replace the ATC control head.

Failure Code 18—Mode Door Failed to Drive to Panel

1. Check the door and linkage for binding or other mechanical problems.
2. Disconnect the control head 21-way connector. Turn the ignition ON and check for ignition voltage between pin No. 16 and chassis ground. If voltage is present, repair the circuit for a short to ignition voltage. If not, continue.
3. Turn the ignition OFF and disconnect the 5-way connector from the mode door actuator. Check for continuity between pin No. 16 of the 21-way connector and pin No. 1 of the 5-way connector. If the circuit is open, repair the wire and retest. If the circuit is complete, continue.
4. Plug the connector back into the mode door actuator and check for continuity between pins No. 7 and 16 of the 21 way connector. If continuity is present, replace the ATC control head. If not, replace the mode door actuator.

Failure Code 19—Mode Door Feedback Shorted to Ground

1. Disconnect the connectors from the control head and the mode door actuator.
2. Check pin No. 6 of the 21-way connector for continuity to ground. If continuity is present, repair the short to ground. If not, continue.
3. Plug the connector back into the actuator and measure the resistance across pins No. 7 and 16 of the control head connector. If the resistance is less than 10 ohms, replace the actuator. If not, replace the control head.

Failure Code 20—Blend Door Moved During Mode Door Test

1. Disconnect the connectors from the control head and all actuators.
2. Check for continuity between pin No. 4 of the control head connector and pin No. 4 of each actuator connector. Repair any open circuit found. If continuity is found in all circuits, continue.
3. Plug the connectors back into the actuators and check for resistance between pins No. 4 and 6 (blend air actuator) and pins No. 4 and 5 (mode actuator). The resistance should be 20–50 ohms. Replace the actuator corresponding to the failed resistance check. If both were within specification, replace the ATC control head.

Failure Code 21—ROM Checksum Error

During diagnostics, the computer control head will verify its own internal program. If it finds any faulty part, it will set a Code 21, a condition which is not serviceable. In this case, the control head must be replaced.

Failure Code 22—Computer Error

If incorrect data is detected within the computer control head, it will set a Code 22, a condition which is not serviceable. In this case, the control head must be replaced.

Failure Code 23–28

Codes 23–28 are set during normal ATC operation. The failure code will be set only after the system has been in operation for 15 minutes. The control head will compensate for the feedback failure immediately upon power up, thus the failure code will not be set until the time limit has been met.

- For Code 23—Blend Door Feedback, follow the repair procedure for Codes 14 and 15 when repairing.
- For Code 24—Mode Door Feedback, follow the repair procedure for Codes 18 and 19 when repairing.
- For Code 25—Ambient Temperature Sensor, follow the repair procedure for Code 11 when repairing.
- For Code 26—In-Car Temperature Sensor/Aspirator, follow the repair procedure for Code 12 when repairing.
- For Code 27—Sun Sensor, follow the repair procedure for Code 12 when repairing.
- For Code 28—Water Temperature Sensor, follow the repair procedure for Code 10 when repairing.

All codes will stored within the ATC control head and must be erased after the failure has been repaired. Intermittent Codes 23–28 will be stored for 60 ignition ON/OFF cycles.

ERASING FAILURE CODES

1. Run the diagnostic test.
2. Depress the **PANEL** button to access all failure codes. When the display starts flashing alternating zeros, any of the following 3 options can be performed:
   a. Do nothing. In 5 seconds the system will return to normal ATC operation and all codes will remain in memory.
   b. Depress any button (except the **AC** button) within 5 seconds and stop the test, in which case the system will return to normal ATC operation and all codes will remain in memory.
   c. Depress the **AC** button within 5 seconds and proceed to the erasing procedure (Step 3). Depressing the **AC** button will not erase any codes, but it will access the next part of the procedure.
3. After the **AC** button has been depressed, the display should begin flashing the letter **E** for ERASE. Now 2 options exist:
   a. Do nothing. In 5 seconds all failure Codes 23–28 will be erased from memory.
   b. Depress any button within 5 seconds and the codes will not be erased.
4. The ATC system should automatically return to normal operation after the above steps have been completed.

WIRING SCHEMATICS

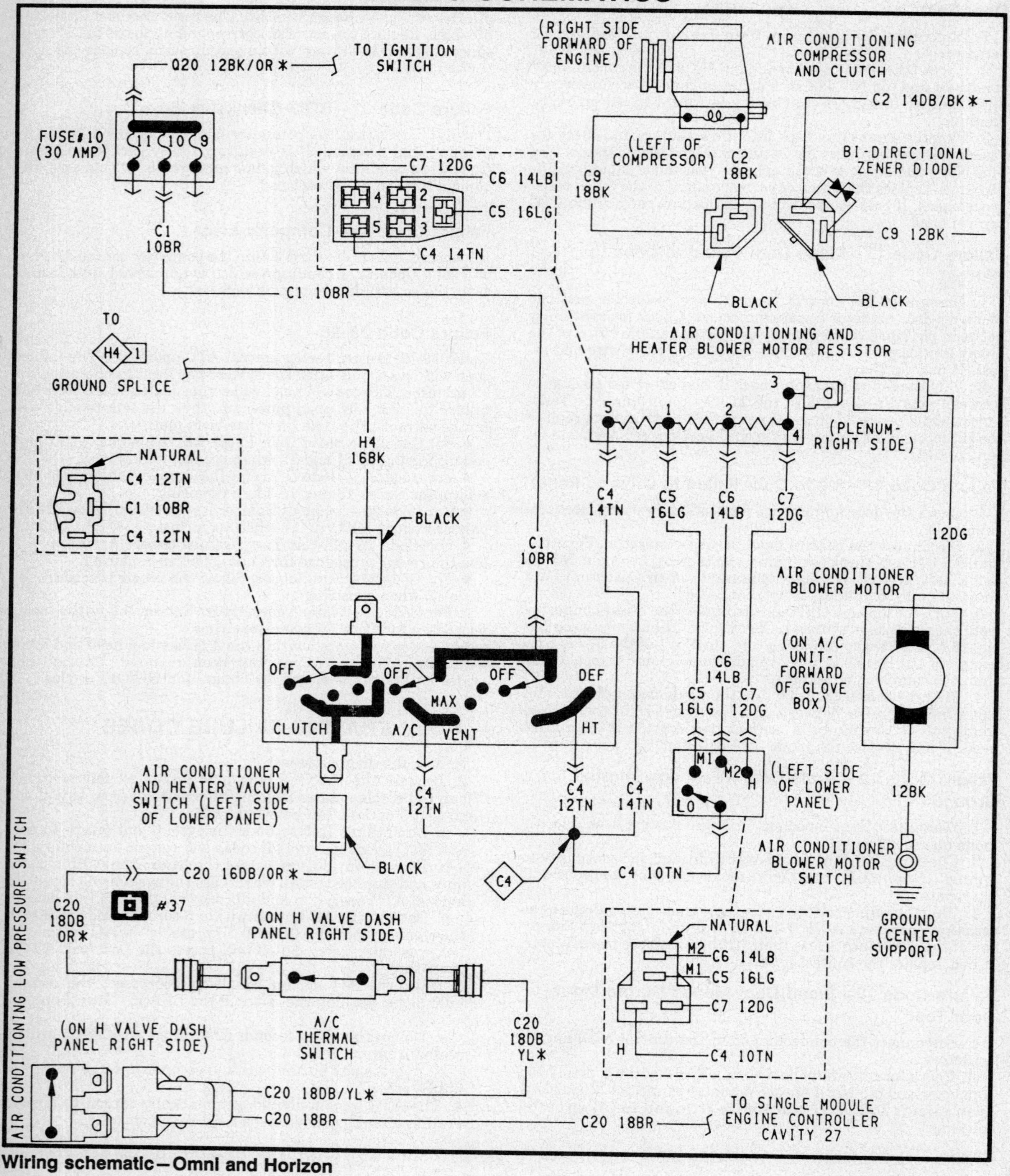
Q20 12BK/OR*
TO IGNITION SWITCH
FUSE#10 (30 AMP)
11 10 9
C1 10BR
C7 12DG
C6 14LB
C5 16LG
C4 14TN
(RIGHT SIDE FORWARD OF ENGINE)
AIR CONDITIONING COMPRESSOR AND CLUTCH
C2 14DB/BK*
(LEFT OF COMPRESSOR)
C9 18BK
C2 18BK
BI-DIRECTIONAL ZENER DIODE
C9 12BK
BLACK
BLACK
TO
H4 1
GROUND SPLICE
AIR CONDITIONING AND HEATER BLOWER MOTOR RESISTOR
(PLENUM-RIGHT SIDE)
NATURAL
C4 12TN
C1 10BR
C4 12TN
H4 16BK
BLACK
C1 10BR
C4 14TN
C5 16LG
C6 14LB
C7 12DG
12DG
AIR CONDITIONER BLOWER MOTOR
(ON A/C UNIT-FORWARD OF GLOVE BOX)
OFF OFF OFF DEF
MAX
CLUTCH A/C VENT HT
AIR CONDITIONER AND HEATER VACUUM SWITCH (LEFT SIDE OF LOWER PANEL)
C4 12TN
C4 12TN
C4 14TN
C6 14LB
C5 16LG
C7 12DG
M1 M2 H
LO
(LEFT SIDE OF LOWER PANEL)
12BK
AIR CONDITIONER BLOWER MOTOR SWITCH
GROUND (CENTER SUPPORT)
BLACK
C20 16DB/OR*
C4
C4 10TN
C20 18DB OR*
#37
(ON H VALVE DASH PANEL RIGHT SIDE)
NATURAL
M2 C6 14LB
M1 C5 16LG
C7 12DG
H
C4 10TN
AIR CONDITIONING LOW PRESSURE SWITCH
(ON H VALVE DASH PANEL RIGHT SIDE)
A/C THERMAL SWITCH
C20 18DB YL*
C20 18DB/YL*
C20 18BR
C20 18BR
TO SINGLE MODULE ENGINE CONTROLLER CAVITY 27

Wiring schematic—Omni and Horizon

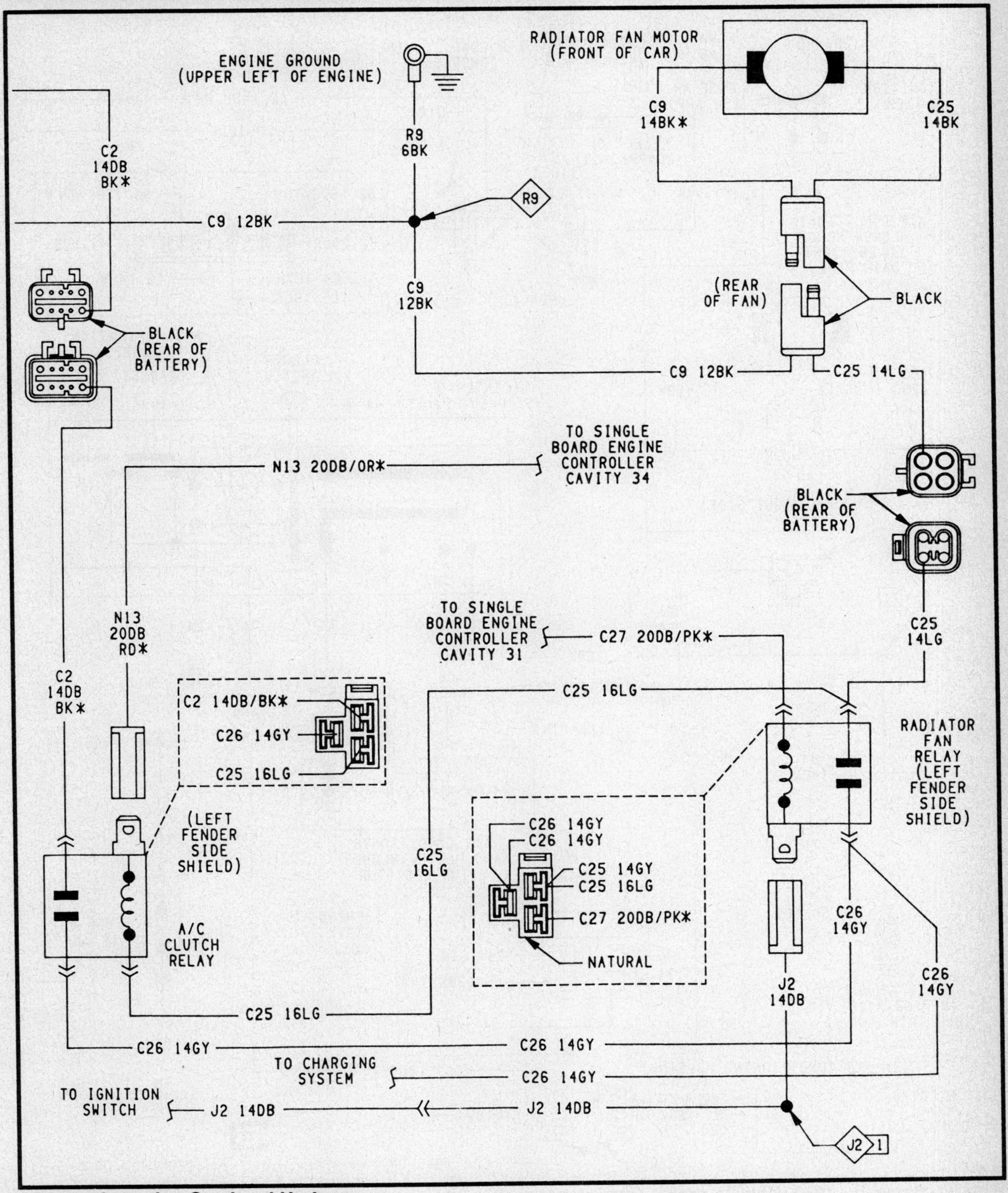
ENGINE GROUND
(UPPER LEFT OF ENGINE)
RADIATOR FAN MOTOR
(FRONT OF CAR)
C9
14BK*
C25
14BK
C2
14DB
BK*
R9
6BK
R9
C9 12BK
C9
12BK
(REAR
OF FAN)
BLACK
BLACK
(REAR OF
BATTERY)
C9 12BK
C25 14LG
TO SINGLE
BOARD ENGINE
CONTROLLER
CAVITY 34
N13 20DB/OR*
BLACK
(REAR OF
BATTERY)
N13
20DB
RD*
TO SINGLE
BOARD ENGINE
CONTROLLER
CAVITY 31
C27 20DB/PK*
C25
14LG
C2
14DB
BK*
C25 16LG
C2 14DB/BK*
C26 14GY
C25 16LG
RADIATOR
FAN
RELAY
(LEFT
FENDER
SIDE
SHIELD)
(LEFT
FENDER
SIDE
SHIELD)
C25
16LG
C26 14GY
C26 14GY
C25 14GY
C25 16LG
C27 20DB/PK*
NATURAL
A/C
CLUTCH
RELAY
C26
14GY
J2
14DB
C26
14GY
C25 16LG
C26 14GY
C26 14GY
TO CHARGING
SYSTEM
C26 14GY
TO IGNITION
SWITCH
J2 14DB
J2 14DB
J2
1

Wiring schematic—Omni and Horizon

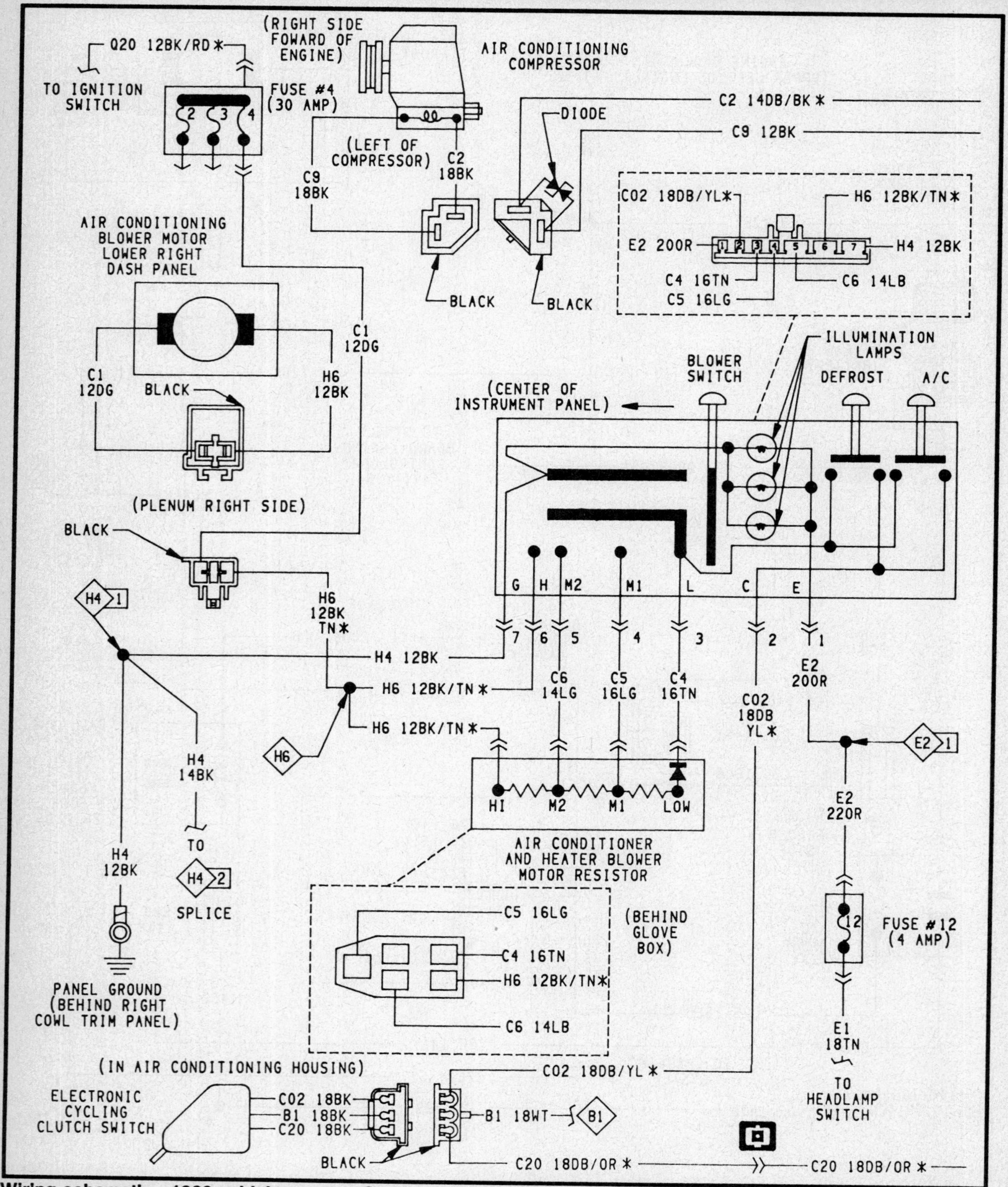
Q20 12BK/RD*
TO IGNITION SWITCH
FUSE #4 (30 AMP)
(RIGHT SIDE FOWARD OF ENGINE)
AIR CONDITIONING COMPRESSOR
(LEFT OF COMPRESSOR)
C9 18BK
C2 18BK
BLACK
DIODE
BLACK
C2 14DB/BK*
C9 12BK
C02 18DB/YL*
H6 12BK/TN*
E2 20OR
H4 12BK
C4 16TN
C6 14LB
C5 16LG
AIR CONDITIONING BLOWER MOTOR LOWER RIGHT DASH PANEL
C1 12DG
C1 12DG
H6 12BK
BLACK
(PLENUM RIGHT SIDE)
BLACK
ILLUMINATION LAMPS
BLOWER SWITCH
DEFROST
A/C
(CENTER OF INSTRUMENT PANEL)
G H M2 M1 L C E
7 6 5 4 3 2 1
H4
1
H6 12BK TN*
H4 12BK
H6 12BK/TN*
H6 12BK/TN*
C6 14LG
C5 16LG
C4 16TN
C02 18DB YL*
E2 20OR
E2
1
H6
H4 14BK
TO
H4
2
SPLICE
H4 12BK
HI M2 M1 LOW
AIR CONDITIONER AND HEATER BLOWER MOTOR RESISTOR
E2 22OR
FUSE #12 (4 AMP)
12
C5 16LG
C4 16TN
H6 12BK/TN*
C6 14LB
(BEHIND GLOVE BOX)
E1 18TN
TO HEADLAMP SWITCH
PANEL GROUND (BEHIND RIGHT COWL TRIM PANEL)
(IN AIR CONDITIONING HOUSING)
C02 18DB/YL*
ELECTRONIC CYCLING CLUTCH SWITCH
C02 18BK
B1 18BK
C20 18BK
B1 18WT
B1
BLACK
C20 18DB/OR*
C20 18DB/OR*

Wiring schematic—1989 vehicles except Omni, Horizon, Dynasty and New Yorker

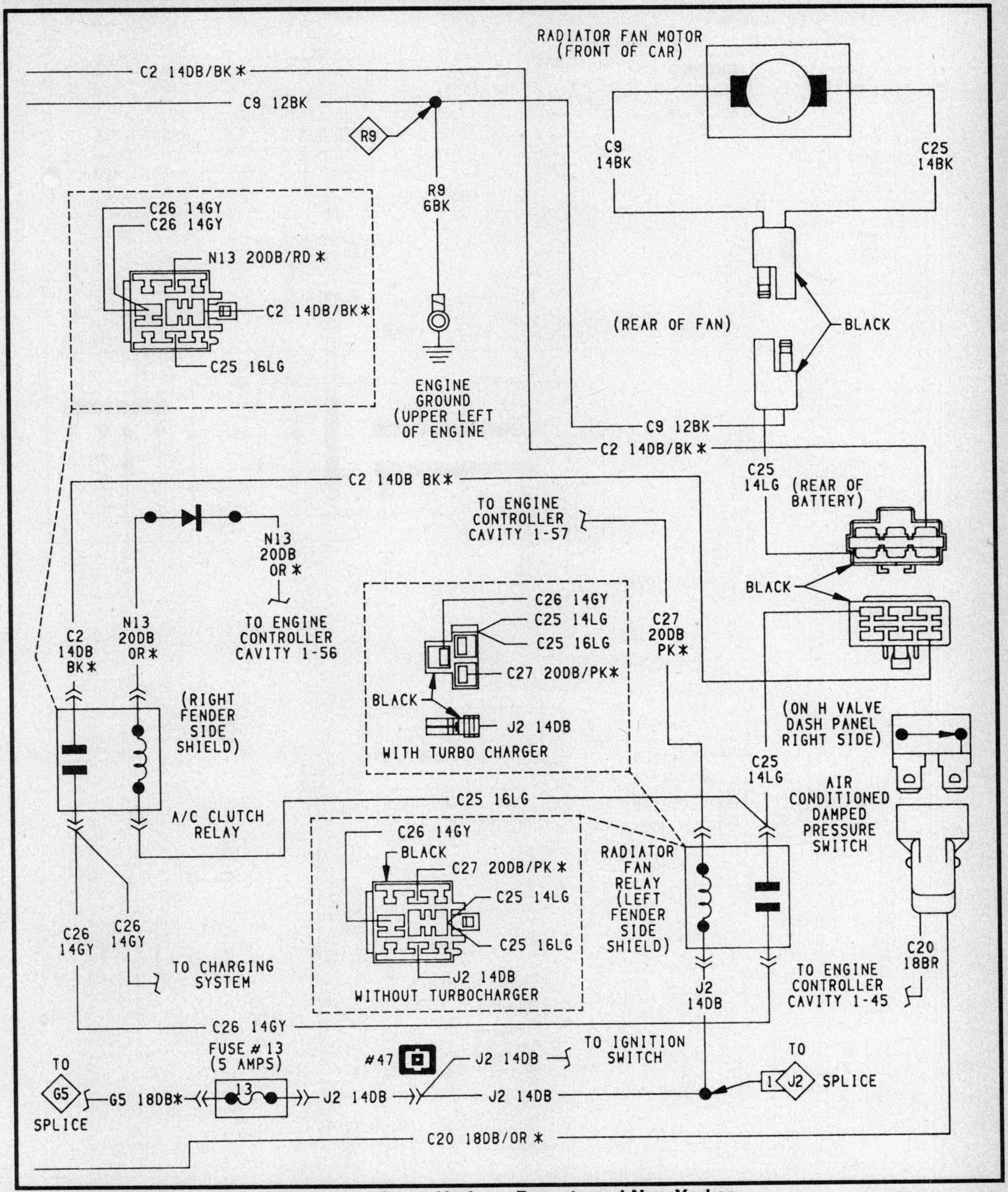
RADIATOR FAN MOTOR (FRONT OF CAR)
C2 14DB/BK*
C9 12BK
R9
R9 6BK
C9 14BK
C25 14BK
C26 14GY
C26 14GY
N13 20DB/RD*
C2 14DB/BK*
C25 16LG
(REAR OF FAN)
BLACK
ENGINE GROUND (UPPER LEFT OF ENGINE
C9 12BK
C2 14DB/BK*
C2 14DB BK*
C25 14LG
(REAR OF BATTERY)
TO ENGINE CONTROLLER CAVITY 1-57
N13 20DB OR*
BLACK
C2 14DB BK*
N13 20DB OR*
TO ENGINE CONTROLLER CAVITY 1-56
C26 14GY
C25 14LG
C25 16LG
C27 20DB/PK*
C27 20DB PK*
BLACK
J2 14DB
WITH TURBO CHARGER
(RIGHT FENDER SIDE SHIELD)
(ON H VALVE DASH PANEL RIGHT SIDE)
C25 14LG
AIR CONDITIONED DAMPED PRESSURE SWITCH
C25 16LG
A/C CLUTCH RELAY
C26 14GY
BLACK
C27 20DB/PK*
C25 14LG
C25 16LG
J2 14DB
WITHOUT TURBOCHARGER
RADIATOR FAN RELAY (LEFT FENDER SIDE SHIELD)
C26 14GY
C26 14GY
TO CHARGING SYSTEM
J2 14DB
TO ENGINE CONTROLLER CAVITY 1-45
C20 18BR
C26 14GY
FUSE # 13 (5 AMPS)
13
#47
J2 14DB
TO IGNITION SWITCH
TO
G5
SPLICE
G5 18DB*
J2 14DB
J2 14DB
TO
J2
SPLICE
C20 18DB/OR *

Wiring schematic—1989 vehicles except Omni, Horizon, Dynasty and New Yorker

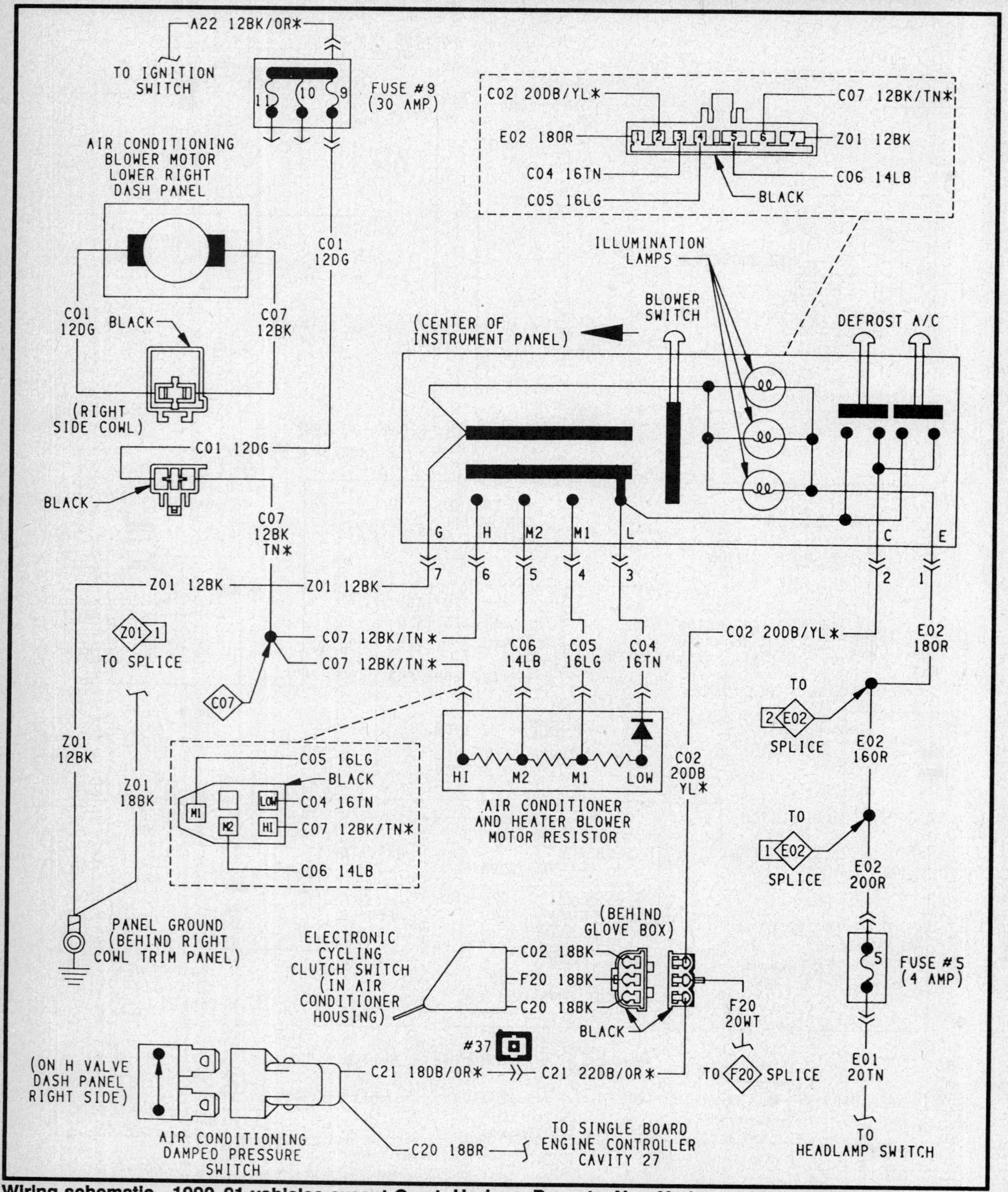
A22 12BK/OR*
TO IGNITION SWITCH
11
10
9
FUSE #9 (30 AMP)
C02 20DB/YL*
C07 12BK/TN*
E02 18OR
Z01 12BK
C04 16TN
C06 14LB
BLACK
C05 16LG
AIR CONDITIONING BLOWER MOTOR LOWER RIGHT DASH PANEL
C01 12DG
C01 12DG
BLACK
C07 12BK
(RIGHT SIDE COWL)
ILLUMINATION LAMPS
BLOWER SWITCH
(CENTER OF INSTRUMENT PANEL)
DEFROST A/C
C01 12DG
BLACK
C07 12BK TN*
G
H
M2
M1
L
C
E
7
6
5
4
3
2
1
Z01 12BK
Z01 12BK
Z01
TO SPLICE
C07 12BK/TN*
C07 12BK/TN*
C07
C02 20DB/YL*
E02 18OR
C06 14LB
C05 16LG
C04 16TN
TO
E02
SPLICE
Z01 12BK
Z01 18BK
C05 16LG
BLACK
M1
LOW
C04 16TN
M2
HI
C07 12BK/TN*
C06 14LB
HI
M2
M1
LOW
AIR CONDITIONER AND HEATER BLOWER MOTOR RESISTOR
C02 20DB YL*
E02 16OR
TO
E02
SPLICE
E02 20OR
PANEL GROUND (BEHIND RIGHT COWL TRIM PANEL)
ELECTRONIC CYCLING CLUTCH SWITCH (IN AIR CONDITIONER HOUSING)
(BEHIND GLOVE BOX)
C02 18BK
F20 18BK
C20 18BK
BLACK
F20 20WT
5
FUSE #5 (4 AMP)
#37
(ON H VALVE DASH PANEL RIGHT SIDE)
C21 18DB/OR*
C21 22DB/OR*
TO
F20
SPLICE
E01 20TN
AIR CONDITIONING DAMPED PRESSURE SWITCH
C20 18BR
TO SINGLE BOARD ENGINE CONTROLLER CAVITY 27
TO HEADLAMP SWITCH

Wiring schematic—1990–91 vehicles except Omni, Horizon, Dynasty, New Yorker and Imperial

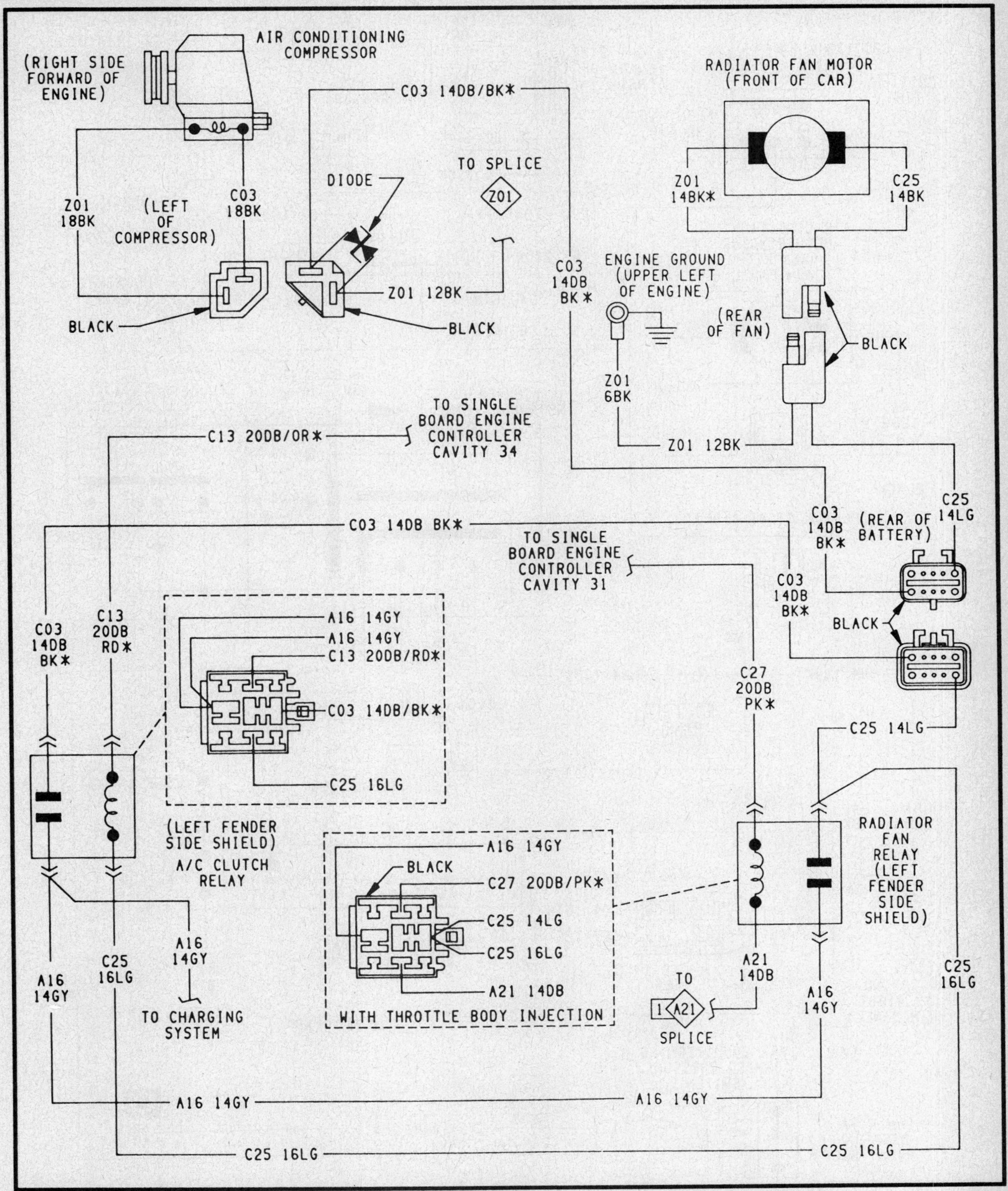
AIR CONDITIONING COMPRESSOR
(RIGHT SIDE FORWARD OF ENGINE)
C03 14DB/BK*
RADIATOR FAN MOTOR (FRONT OF CAR)
TO SPLICE
Z01
DIODE
Z01 18BK
(LEFT OF COMPRESSOR)
C03 18BK
Z01 14BK*
C25 14BK
Z01 12BK
BLACK
BLACK
C03 14DB BK*
ENGINE GROUND (UPPER LEFT OF ENGINE)
(REAR OF FAN)
BLACK
Z01 6BK
Z01 12BK
TO SINGLE BOARD ENGINE CONTROLLER CAVITY 34
C13 20DB/OR*
C03 14DB BK*
C03 14DB BK*
C25 14LG
(REAR OF BATTERY)
TO SINGLE BOARD ENGINE CONTROLLER CAVITY 31
C03 14DB BK*
BLACK
C03 14DB BK*
C13 20DB RD*
A16 14GY
A16 14GY
C13 20DB/RD*
C03 14DB/BK*
C25 16LG
C27 20DB PK*
C25 14LG
(LEFT FENDER SIDE SHIELD)
A/C CLUTCH RELAY
A16 14GY
BLACK
C27 20DB/PK*
C25 14LG
C25 16LG
A21 14DB
WITH THROTTLE BODY INJECTION
RADIATOR FAN RELAY (LEFT FENDER SIDE SHIELD)
A16 14GY
C25 16LG
A16 14GY
A16 14GY
TO CHARGING SYSTEM
TO
1 A21
SPLICE
A21 14DB
A16 14GY
C25 16LG
A16 14GY
A16 14GY
C25 16LG
C25 16LG

Wiring schematic—1990–91 vehicles except Omni, Horizon, Dynasty, New Yorker and Imperial

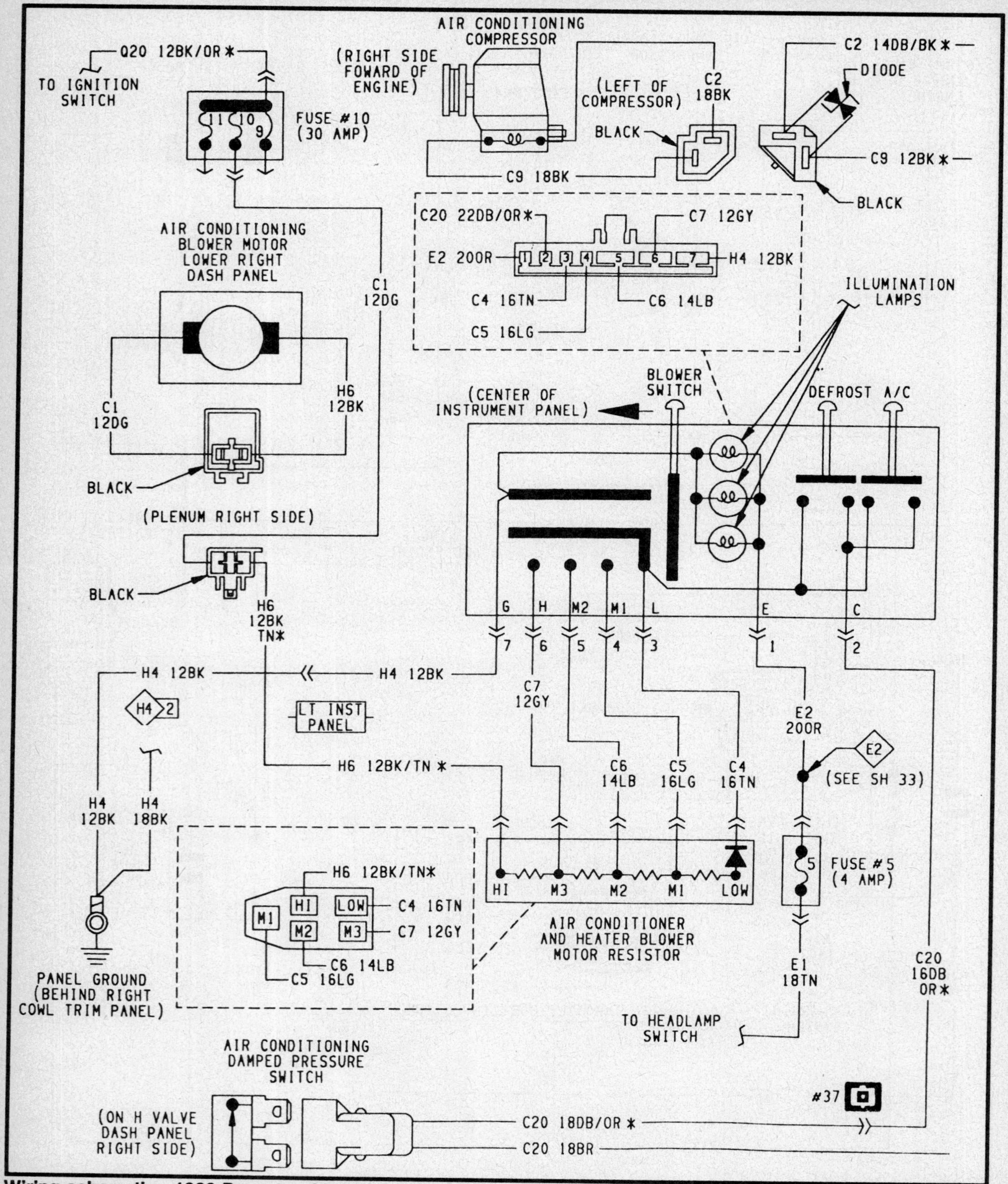
Q20 12BK/OR *
TO IGNITION SWITCH
FUSE #10 (30 AMP)
AIR CONDITIONING COMPRESSOR
(RIGHT SIDE FOWARD OF ENGINE)
(LEFT OF COMPRESSOR)
C2 18BK
BLACK
C9 18BK
C2 14DB/BK *
DIODE
C9 12BK *
BLACK
C20 22DB/OR *
C7 12GY
E2 20OR
H4 12BK
C4 16TN
C6 14LB
C5 16LG
AIR CONDITIONING BLOWER MOTOR LOWER RIGHT DASH PANEL
C1 12DG
H6 12BK
C1 12DG
BLACK
(PLENUM RIGHT SIDE)
BLACK
H6 12BK TN*
ILLUMINATION LAMPS
BLOWER SWITCH
(CENTER OF INSTRUMENT PANEL)
DEFROST A/C
G H M2 M1 L E C
7 6 5 4 3 1 2
H4 12BK
H4 12BK
H4 2
LT INST PANEL
C7 12GY
E2 20OR
E2
(SEE SH 33)
H6 12BK/TN *
C6 14LB
C5 16LG
C4 16TN
H4 12BK
H4 18BK
HI M3 M2 M1 LOW
FUSE #5 (4 AMP)
H6 12BK/TN*
HI LOW C4 16TN
M1
M2 M3 C7 12GY
C6 14LB
C5 16LG
AIR CONDITIONER AND HEATER BLOWER MOTOR RESISTOR
PANEL GROUND (BEHIND RIGHT COWL TRIM PANEL)
E1 18TN
C20 16DB OR *
TO HEADLAMP SWITCH
AIR CONDITIONING DAMPED PRESSURE SWITCH
#37
(ON H VALVE DASH PANEL RIGHT SIDE)
C20 18DB/OR *
C20 18BR

Wiring schematic—1989 Dynasty with 2.5L engine

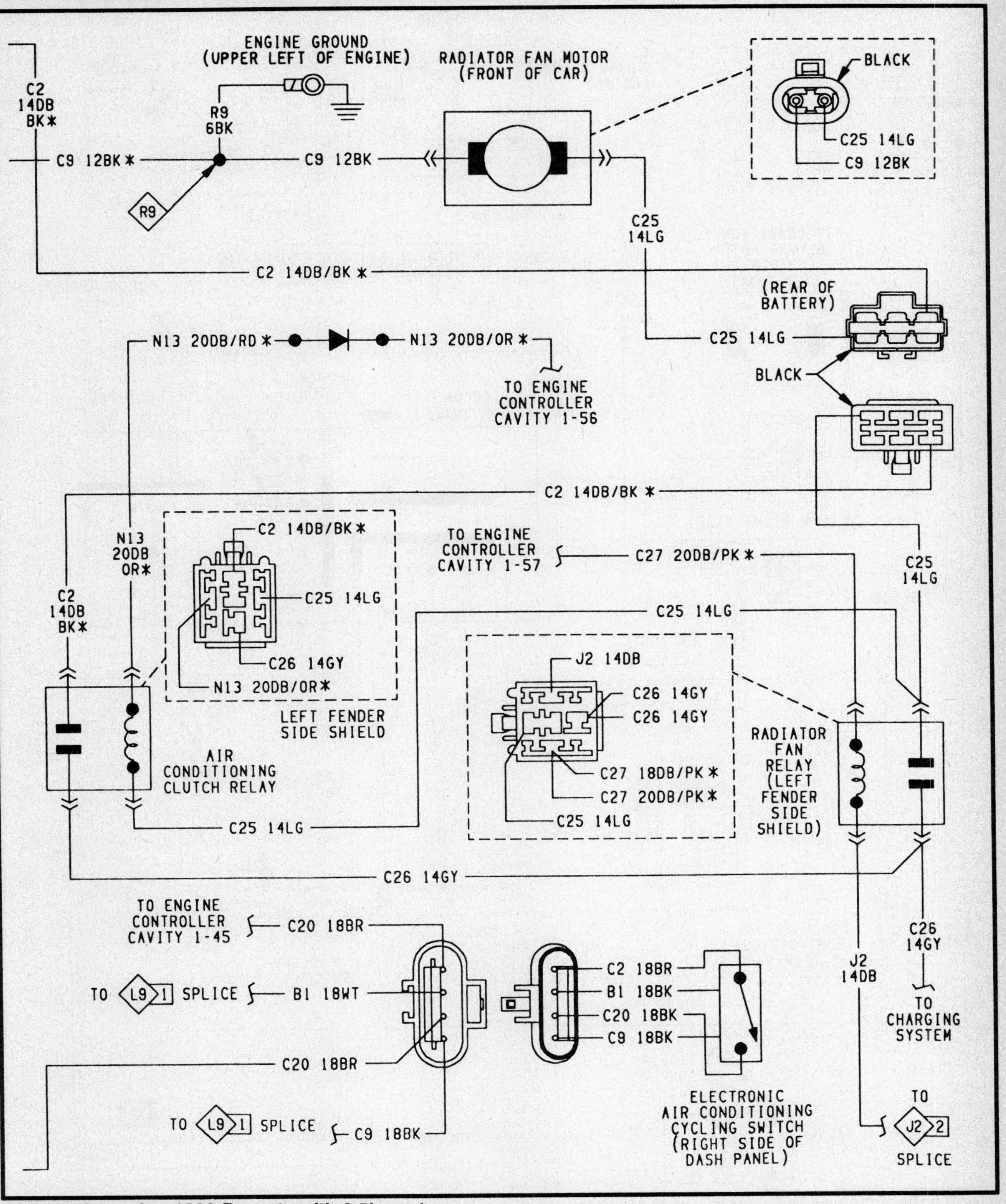
ENGINE GROUND
(UPPER LEFT OF ENGINE)
RADIATOR FAN MOTOR
(FRONT OF CAR)
BLACK
C2 14DB BK*
R9 6BK
C9 12BK*
C9 12BK
R9
C25 14LG
C9 12BK
C25 14LG
C2 14DB/BK*
(REAR OF BATTERY)
N13 20DB/RD*
N13 20DB/OR*
TO ENGINE CONTROLLER CAVITY 1-56
C25 14LG
BLACK
C2 14DB/BK*
C2 14DB/BK*
N13 20DB OR*
C2 14DB BK*
C25 14LG
C26 14GY
N13 20DB/OR*
TO ENGINE CONTROLLER CAVITY 1-57
C27 20DB/PK*
C25 14LG
C25 14LG
LEFT FENDER SIDE SHIELD
J2 14DB
C26 14GY
C26 14GY
C27 18DB/PK*
C27 20DB/PK*
C25 14LG
AIR CONDITIONING CLUTCH RELAY
C25 14LG
RADIATOR FAN RELAY (LEFT FENDER SIDE SHIELD)
C26 14GY
TO ENGINE CONTROLLER CAVITY 1-45
C20 18BR
TO L9 1 SPLICE
B1 18WT
C2 18BR
B1 18BK
C20 18BK
C9 18BK
C26 14GY
J2 14DB
TO CHARGING SYSTEM
C20 18BR
TO L9 1 SPLICE
C9 18BK
ELECTRONIC AIR CONDITIONING CYCLING SWITCH (RIGHT SIDE OF DASH PANEL)
TO J2 2 SPLICE

Wiring schematic—1989 Dynasty with 2.5L engine

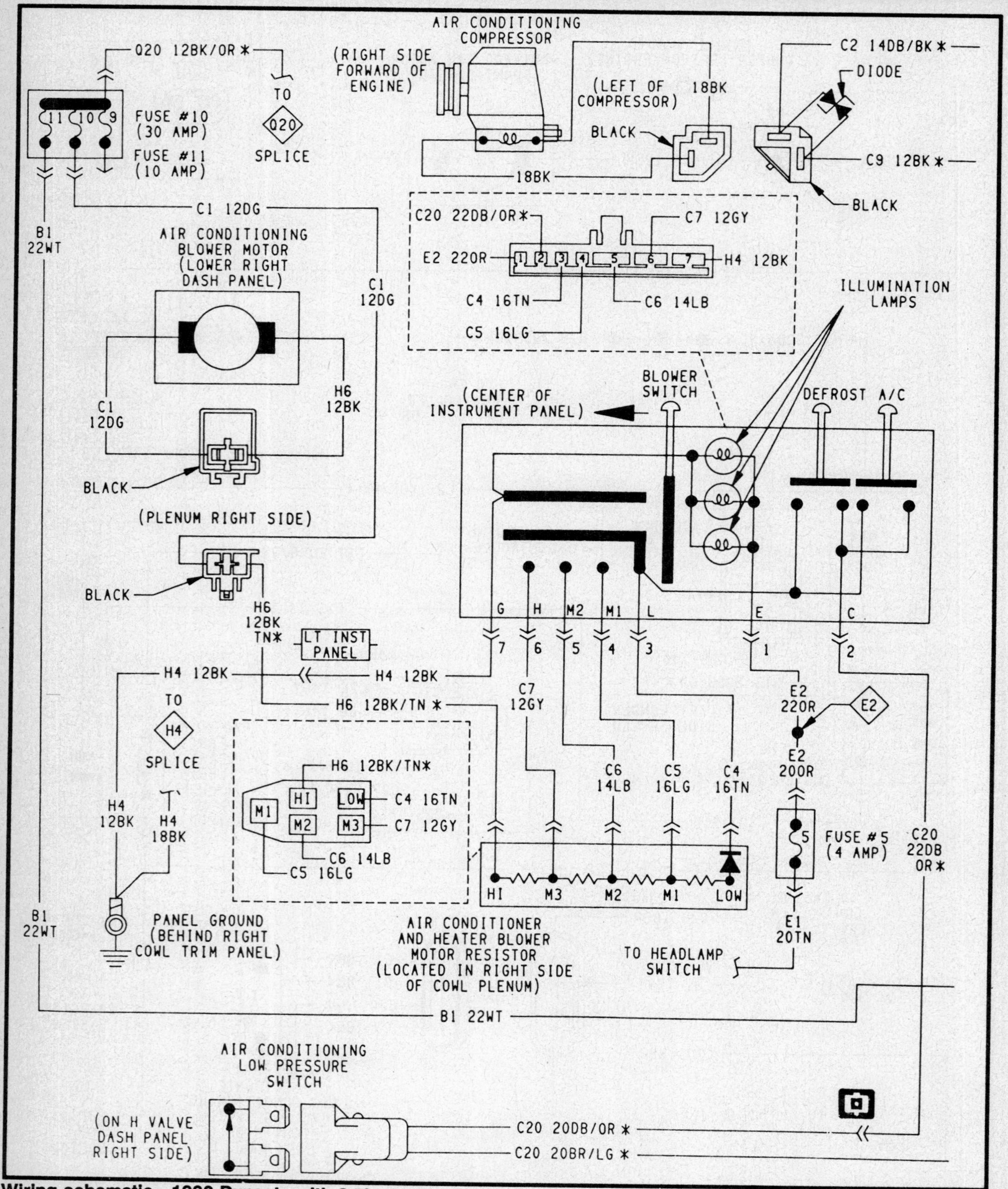
Q20 12BK/OR*
TO
Q20
SPLICE
11 10 9
FUSE #10
(30 AMP)
FUSE #11
(10 AMP)
B1
22WT
C1 12DG
AIR CONDITIONING
BLOWER MOTOR
(LOWER RIGHT
DASH PANEL)
C1
12DG
H6
12BK
C1
12DG
BLACK
(PLENUM RIGHT SIDE)
BLACK
H6
12BK
TN*
LT INST
PANEL
H4 12BK
H4 12BK
H6 12BK/TN*
TO
H4
SPLICE
H4
12BK
H4
18BK
B1
22WT
PANEL GROUND
(BEHIND RIGHT
COWL TRIM PANEL)
AIR CONDITIONING
COMPRESSOR
(RIGHT SIDE
FORWARD OF
ENGINE)
(LEFT OF
COMPRESSOR)
18BK
BLACK
18BK
C2 14DB/BK*
DIODE
C9 12BK*
BLACK
C20 22DB/OR*
C7 12GY
E2 22OR
1 2 3 4 5 6 7
H4 12BK
C4 16TN
C6 14LB
C5 16LG
ILLUMINATION
LAMPS
BLOWER
SWITCH
(CENTER OF
INSTRUMENT PANEL)
DEFROST A/C
G H M2 M1 L E C
7 6 5 4 3 1 2
C7
12GY
E2
22OR
E2
E2
20OR
H6 12BK/TN*
HI LOW
M1
M2 M3
C4 16TN
C7 12GY
C6 14LB
C5 16LG
C6
14LB
C5
16LG
C4
16TN
HI M3 M2 M1 LOW
AIR CONDITIONER
AND HEATER BLOWER
MOTOR RESISTOR
(LOCATED IN RIGHT SIDE
OF COWL PLENUM)
5
FUSE #5
(4 AMP)
C20
22DB
OR*
E1
20TN
TO HEADLAMP
SWITCH
B1 22WT
AIR CONDITIONING
LOW PRESSURE
SWITCH
(ON H VALVE
DASH PANEL
RIGHT SIDE)
C20 20DB/OR*
C20 20BR/LG*

Wiring schematic—1990 Dynasty with 2.5L engine

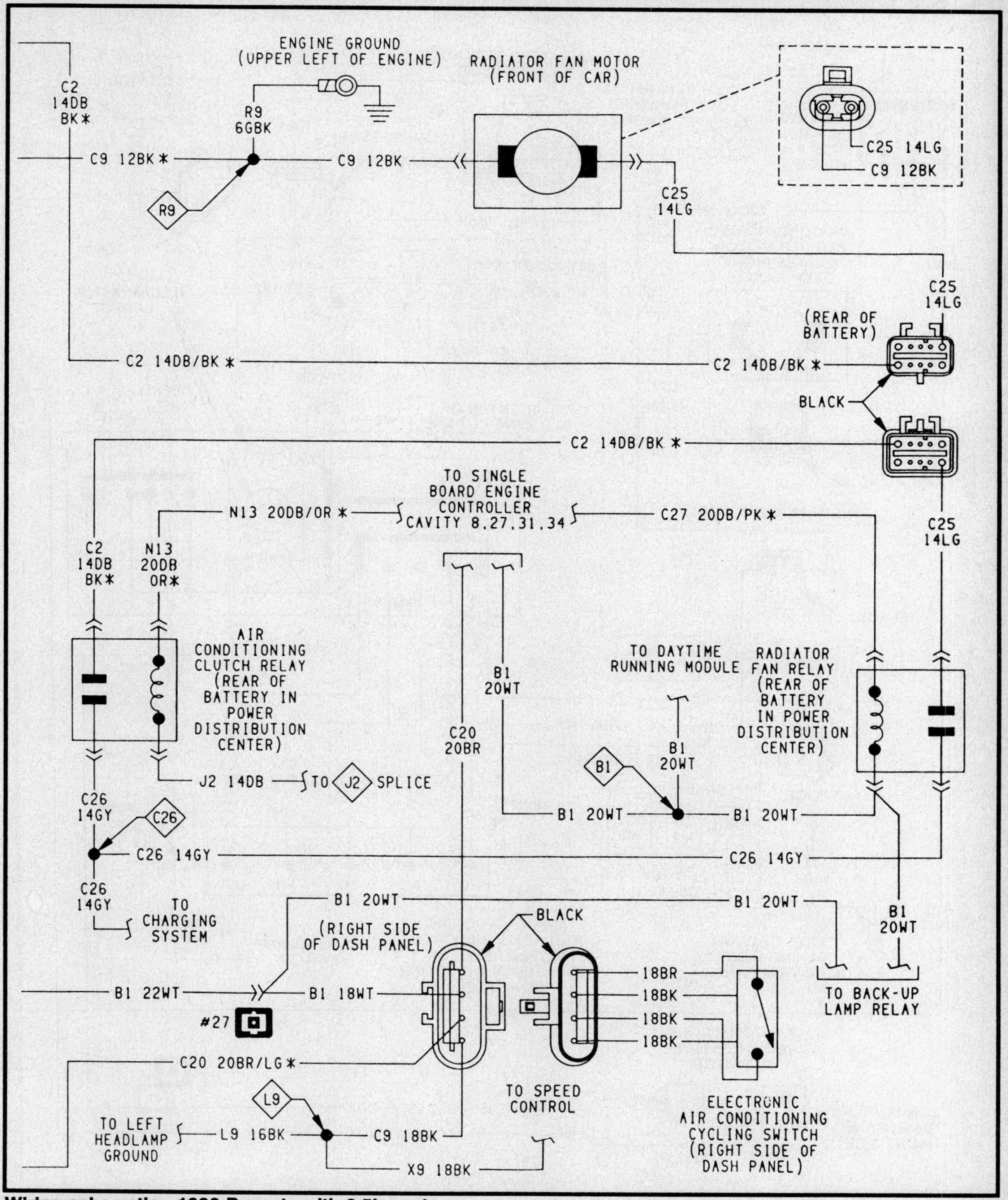
ENGINE GROUND
(UPPER LEFT OF ENGINE)
RADIATOR FAN MOTOR
(FRONT OF CAR)
C2
14DB
BK*
R9
6GBK
C9 12BK*
C9 12BK
R9
C25 14LG
C9 12BK
C25
14LG
C25
14LG
(REAR OF
BATTERY)
C2 14DB/BK*
C2 14DB/BK*
BLACK
C2 14DB/BK*
TO SINGLE
BOARD ENGINE
CONTROLLER
CAVITY 8,27,31,34
N13 20DB/OR*
C27 20DB/PK*
C25
14LG
C2
14DB
BK*
N13
20DB
OR*
AIR
CONDITIONING
CLUTCH RELAY
(REAR OF
BATTERY IN
POWER
DISTRIBUTION
CENTER)
B1
20WT
C20
20BR
TO DAYTIME
RUNNING MODULE
RADIATOR
FAN RELAY
(REAR OF
BATTERY
IN POWER
DISTRIBUTION
CENTER)
B1
20WT
B1
J2 14DB
TO
J2
SPLICE
C26
14GY
C26
B1 20WT
B1 20WT
C26 14GY
C26 14GY
C26
14GY
TO
CHARGING
SYSTEM
B1 20WT
B1 20WT
B1
20WT
BLACK
(RIGHT SIDE
OF DASH PANEL)
B1 22WT
B1 18WT
#27
18BR
18BK
18BK
18BK
TO BACK-UP
LAMP RELAY
C20 20BR/LG*
L9
TO SPEED
CONTROL
ELECTRONIC
AIR CONDITIONING
CYCLING SWITCH
(RIGHT SIDE OF
DASH PANEL)
TO LEFT
HEADLAMP
GROUND
L9 16BK
C9 18BK
X9 18BK

Wiring schematic—1990 Dynasty with 2.5L engine

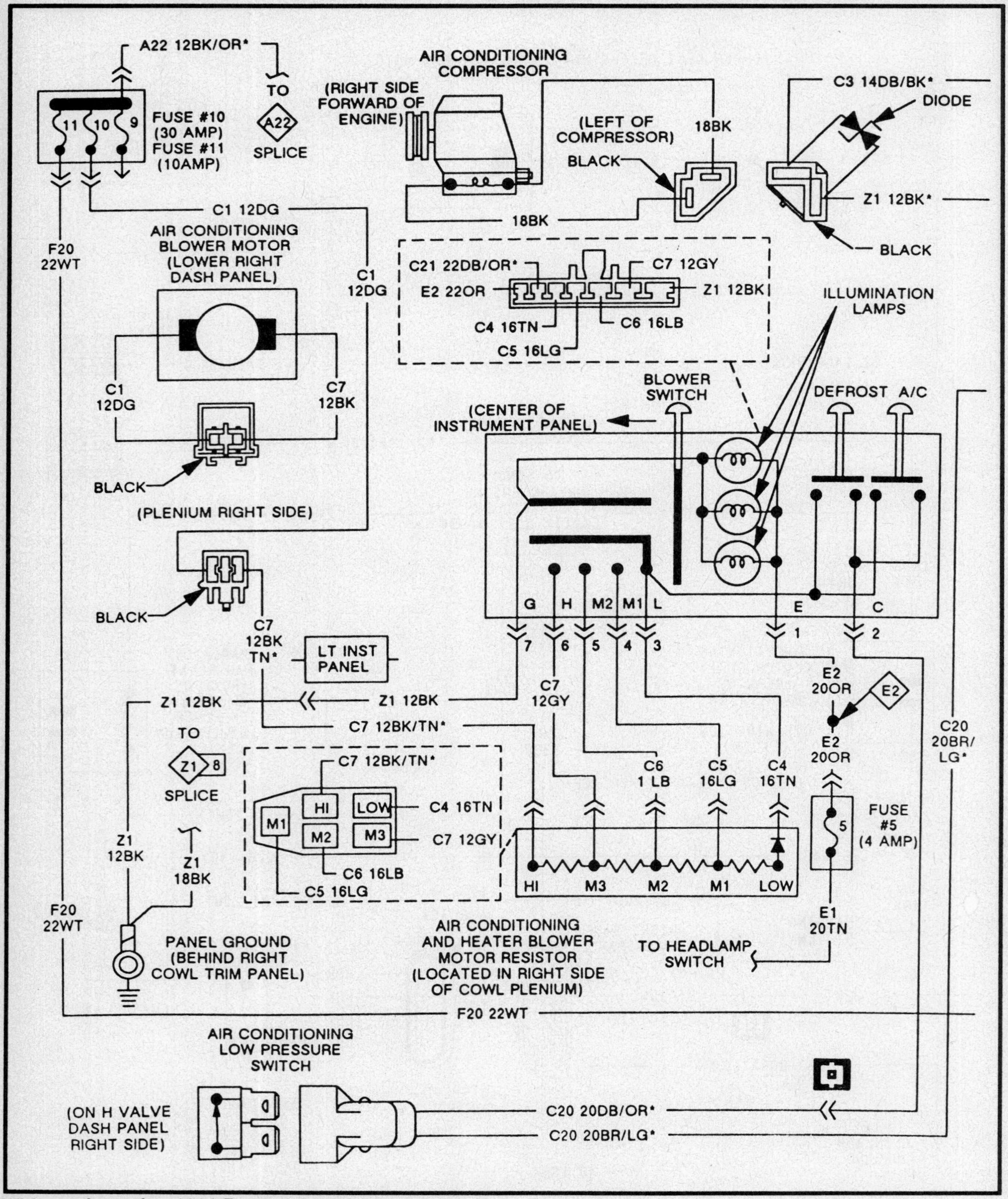
A22 12BK/OR*
TO
A22
SPLICE
11
10
9
FUSE #10
(30 AMP)
FUSE #11
(10AMP)
AIR CONDITIONING
COMPRESSOR
(RIGHT SIDE
FORWARD OF
ENGINE)
(LEFT OF
COMPRESSOR)
18BK
BLACK
18BK
C3 14DB/BK*
DIODE
Z1 12BK*
BLACK
C1 12DG
F20
22WT
AIR CONDITIONING
BLOWER MOTOR
(LOWER RIGHT
DASH PANEL)
C1
12DG
C21 22DB/OR*
C7 12GY
E2 22OR
Z1 12BK
C4 16TN
C6 16LB
C5 16LG
ILLUMINATION
LAMPS
C1
12DG
C7
12BK
BLACK
(PLENIUM RIGHT SIDE)
BLOWER
SWITCH
(CENTER OF
INSTRUMENT PANEL)
DEFROST
A/C
G
H
M2
M1
L
E
C
7
6
5
4
3
1
2
BLACK
C7
12BK
TN*
LT INST
PANEL
Z1 12BK
Z1 12BK
C7
12GY
E2
20OR
E2
E2
20OR
C20
20BR/
LG*
C7 12BK/TN*
TO
Z1
8
SPLICE
C7 12BK/TN*
HI
LOW
M1
M2
M3
C4 16TN
C7 12GY
C6 16LB
C5 16LG
C6
1 LB
C5
16LG
C4
16TN
FUSE
#5
(4 AMP)
5
Z1
12BK
Z1
18BK
F20
22WT
HI
M3
M2
M1
LOW
E1
20TN
PANEL GROUND
(BEHIND RIGHT
COWL TRIM PANEL)
AIR CONDITIONING
AND HEATER BLOWER
MOTOR RESISTOR
(LOCATED IN RIGHT SIDE
OF COWL PLENIUM)
TO HEADLAMP
SWITCH
F20 22WT
AIR CONDITIONING
LOW PRESSURE
SWITCH
(ON H VALVE
DASH PANEL
RIGHT SIDE)
C20 20DB/OR*
C20 20BR/LG*

Wiring schematic – 1991 Dynasty with 2.5L engine

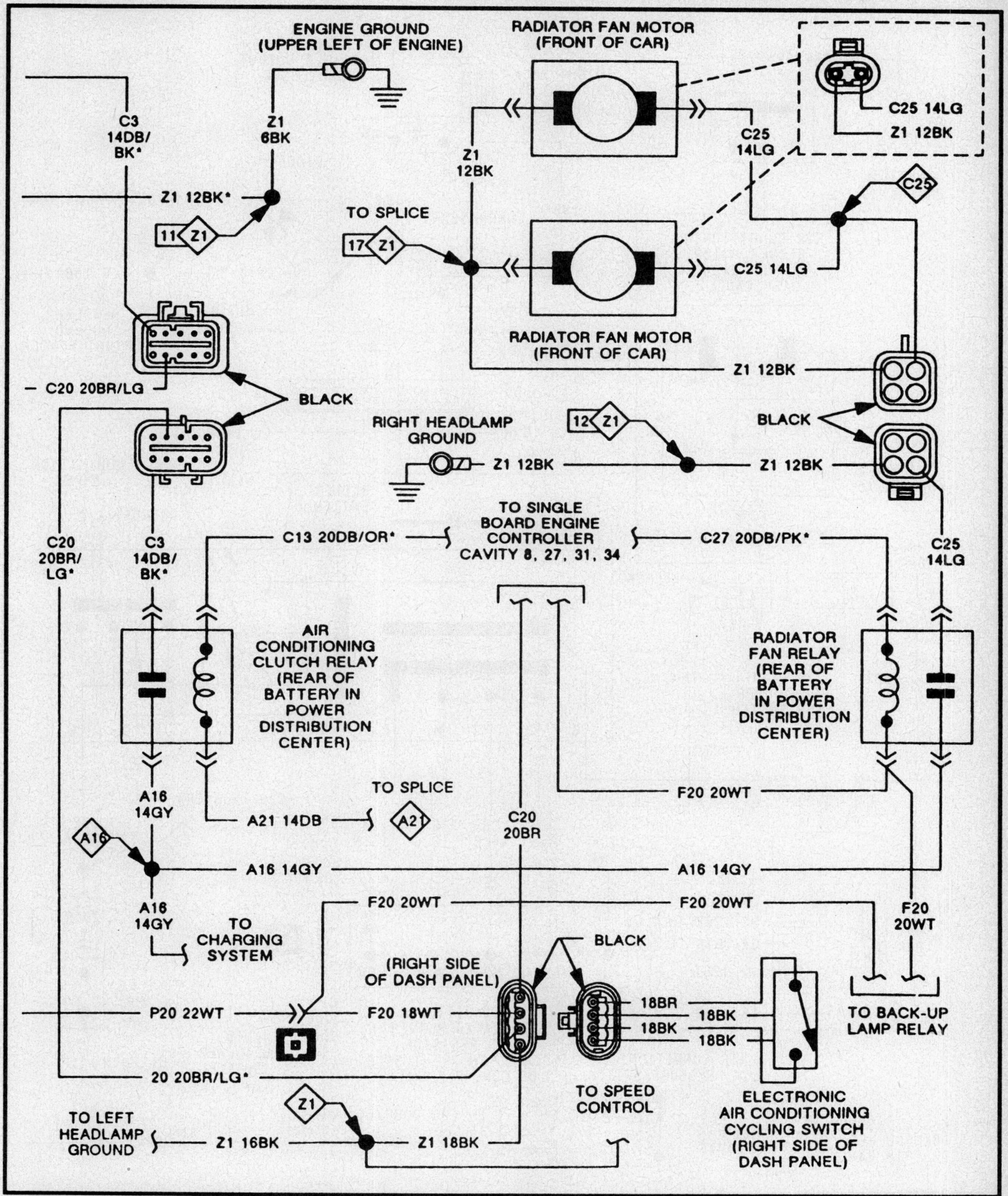
ENGINE GROUND (UPPER LEFT OF ENGINE)
RADIATOR FAN MOTOR (FRONT OF CAR)
C3 14DB/BK*
Z1 6BK
Z1 12BK*
11 Z1
C25 14LG
Z1 12BK
Z1 12BK
C25 14LG
C25
TO SPLICE
17 Z1
C25 14LG
RADIATOR FAN MOTOR (FRONT OF CAR)
Z1 12BK
C20 20BR/LG
BLACK
RIGHT HEADLAMP GROUND
12 Z1
BLACK
Z1 12BK
Z1 12BK
TO SINGLE BOARD ENGINE CONTROLLER CAVITY 8, 27, 31, 34
C13 20DB/OR*
C27 20DB/PK*
C20 20BR/LG*
C3 14DB/BK*
C25 14LG
AIR CONDITIONING CLUTCH RELAY (REAR OF BATTERY IN POWER DISTRIBUTION CENTER)
RADIATOR FAN RELAY (REAR OF BATTERY IN POWER DISTRIBUTION CENTER)
F20 20WT
TO SPLICE
A16 14GY
A21 14DB
A21
C20 20BR
A16
A16 14GY
A16 14GY
F20 20WT
F20 20WT
F20 20WT
A16 14GY
TO CHARGING SYSTEM
BLACK
(RIGHT SIDE OF DASH PANEL)
P20 22WT
F20 18WT
18BR
18BK
18BK
18BK
TO BACK-UP LAMP RELAY
20 20BR/LG*
Z1
TO SPEED CONTROL
ELECTRONIC AIR CONDITIONING CYCLING SWITCH (RIGHT SIDE OF DASH PANEL)
TO LEFT HEADLAMP GROUND
Z1 16BK
Z1 18BK

Wiring schematic—1991 Dynasty with 2.5L engine

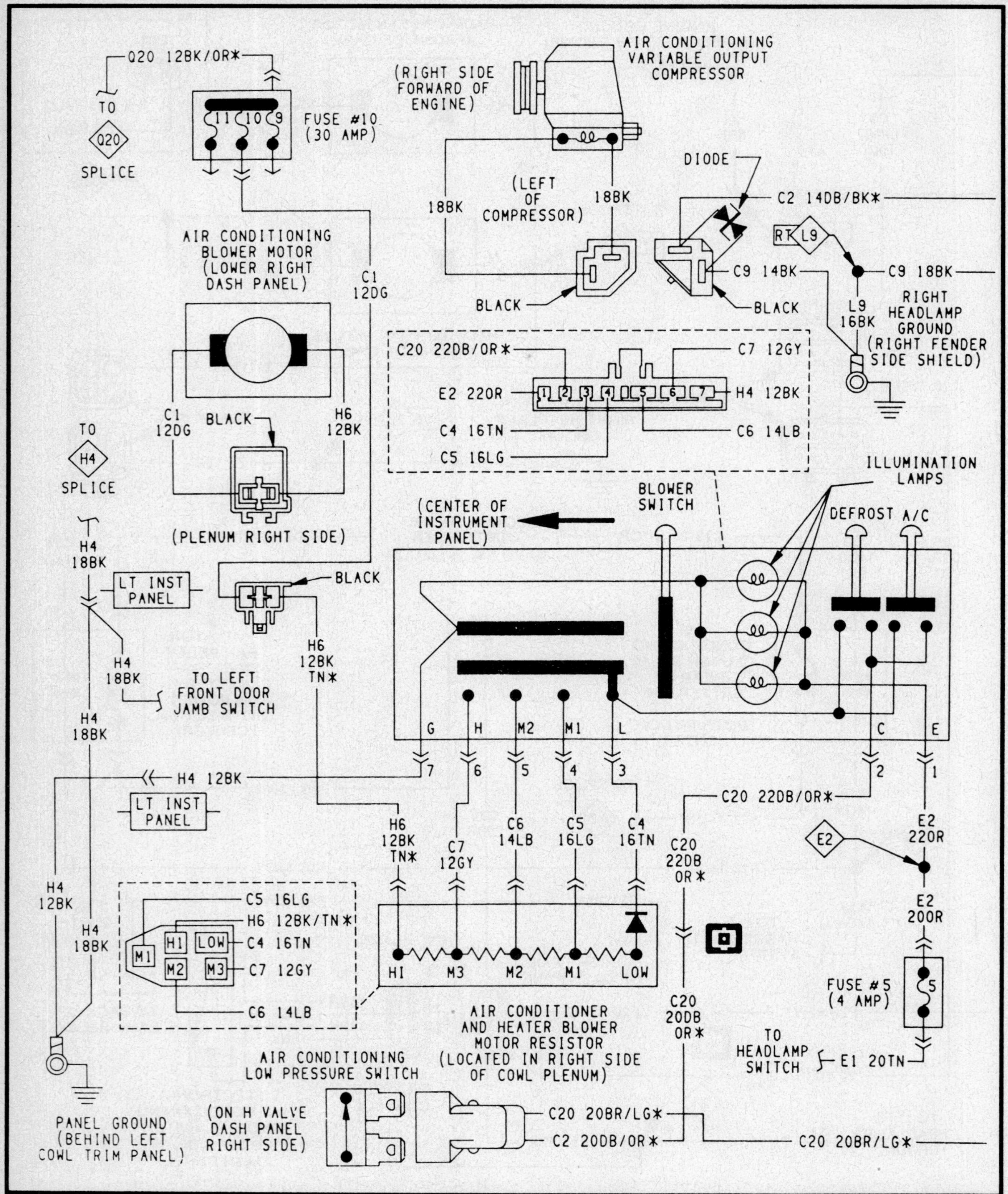
Q20 12BK/OR*
TO
Q20
SPLICE
11 10 9
FUSE #10
(30 AMP)
(RIGHT SIDE
FORWARD OF
ENGINE)
AIR CONDITIONING
VARIABLE OUTPUT
COMPRESSOR
DIODE
(LEFT
OF
COMPRESSOR)
18BK
18BK
C2 14DB/BK*
RT L9
C9 14BK
C9 18BK
BLACK
BLACK
L9
16BK
RIGHT
HEADLAMP
GROUND
(RIGHT FENDER
SIDE SHIELD)
AIR CONDITIONING
BLOWER MOTOR
(LOWER RIGHT
DASH PANEL)
C1
12DG
C20 22DB/OR*
C7 12GY
E2 22OR
H4 12BK
C4 16TN
C6 14LB
C5 16LG
1 2 3 4 5 6 7
C1
12DG
BLACK
H6
12BK
TO
H4
SPLICE
(PLENUM RIGHT SIDE)
ILLUMINATION
LAMPS
BLOWER
SWITCH
(CENTER OF
INSTRUMENT
PANEL)
DEFROST A/C
H4
18BK
LT INST
PANEL
BLACK
H4
18BK
TO LEFT
FRONT DOOR
JAMB SWITCH
H6
12BK
TN*
H4
18BK
G H M2 M1 L C E
7 6 5 4 3 2 1
H4 12BK
LT INST
PANEL
C20 22DB/OR*
H6
12BK
TN*
C7
12GY
C6
14LB
C5
16LG
C4
16TN
C20
22DB
OR*
E2
E2
22OR
H4
12BK
H4
18BK
C5 16LG
H6 12BK/TN*
M1
H1
LOW
C4 16TN
M2
M3
C7 12GY
C6 14LB
HI M3 M2 M1 LOW
E2
20OR
FUSE #5
(4 AMP)
5
AIR CONDITIONER
AND HEATER BLOWER
MOTOR RESISTOR
(LOCATED IN RIGHT SIDE
OF COWL PLENUM)
C20
20DB
OR*
TO
HEADLAMP
SWITCH
E1 20TN
AIR CONDITIONING
LOW PRESSURE SWITCH
(ON H VALVE
DASH PANEL
RIGHT SIDE)
C20 20BR/LG*
C2 20DB/OR*
C20 20BR/LG*
PANEL GROUND
(BEHIND LEFT
COWL TRIM PANEL)

Wiring schematic—1989–91 Dynasty, New Yorker and Imperial with 3.0L, 3.3L and 3.8L engines

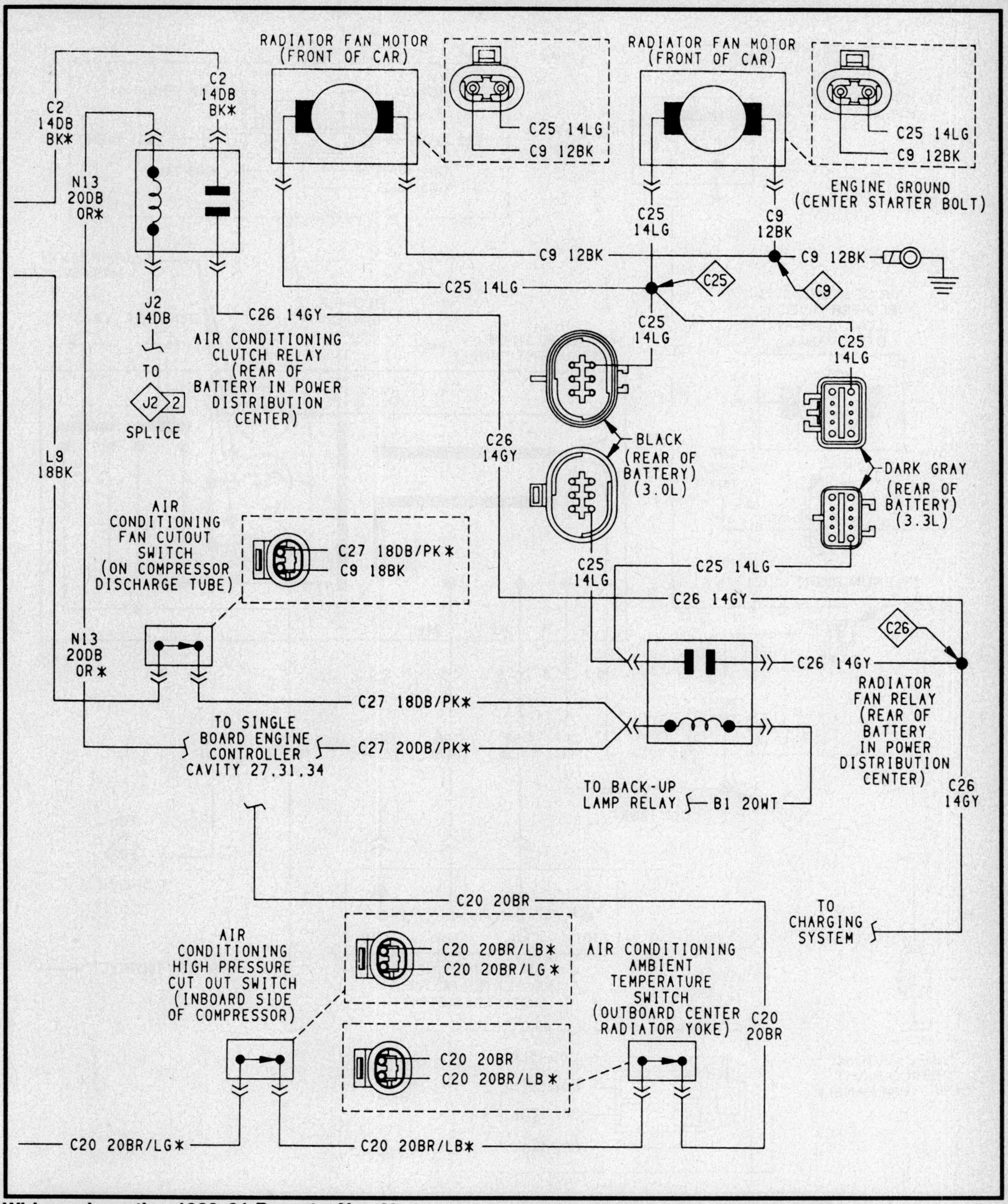
RADIATOR FAN MOTOR (FRONT OF CAR)
C25 14LG
C9 12BK
RADIATOR FAN MOTOR (FRONT OF CAR)
C25 14LG
C9 12BK
ENGINE GROUND (CENTER STARTER BOLT)
C2 14DB BK*
C2 14DB BK*
N13 20DB OR*
C25 14LG
C9 12BK
C9 12BK
C9 12BK
C25 14LG
C25
C9
J2 14DB
C26 14GY
C25 14LG
C25 14LG
AIR CONDITIONING CLUTCH RELAY (REAR OF BATTERY IN POWER DISTRIBUTION CENTER)
TO
J2 2
SPLICE
BLACK (REAR OF BATTERY) (3.0L)
DARK GRAY (REAR OF BATTERY) (3.3L)
C26 14GY
L9 18BK
AIR CONDITIONING FAN CUTOUT SWITCH (ON COMPRESSOR DISCHARGE TUBE)
C27 18DB/PK*
C9 18BK
C25 14LG
C25 14LG
C26 14GY
C26
N13 20DB OR*
C26 14GY
C27 18DB/PK*
RADIATOR FAN RELAY (REAR OF BATTERY IN POWER DISTRIBUTION CENTER)
TO SINGLE BOARD ENGINE CONTROLLER CAVITY 27.31.34
C27 20DB/PK*
TO BACK-UP LAMP RELAY
B1 20WT
C26 14GY
C20 20BR
TO CHARGING SYSTEM
AIR CONDITIONING HIGH PRESSURE CUT OUT SWITCH (INBOARD SIDE OF COMPRESSOR)
C20 20BR/LB*
C20 20BR/LG*
AIR CONDITIONING AMBIENT TEMPERATURE SWITCH (OUTBOARD CENTER RADIATOR YOKE)
C20 20BR
C20 20BR
C20 20BR/LB*
C20 20BR/LG*
C20 20BR/LB*

Wiring schematic—1989–91 Dynasty, New Yorker and Imperial with 3.0L, 3.3L and 3.8L engines

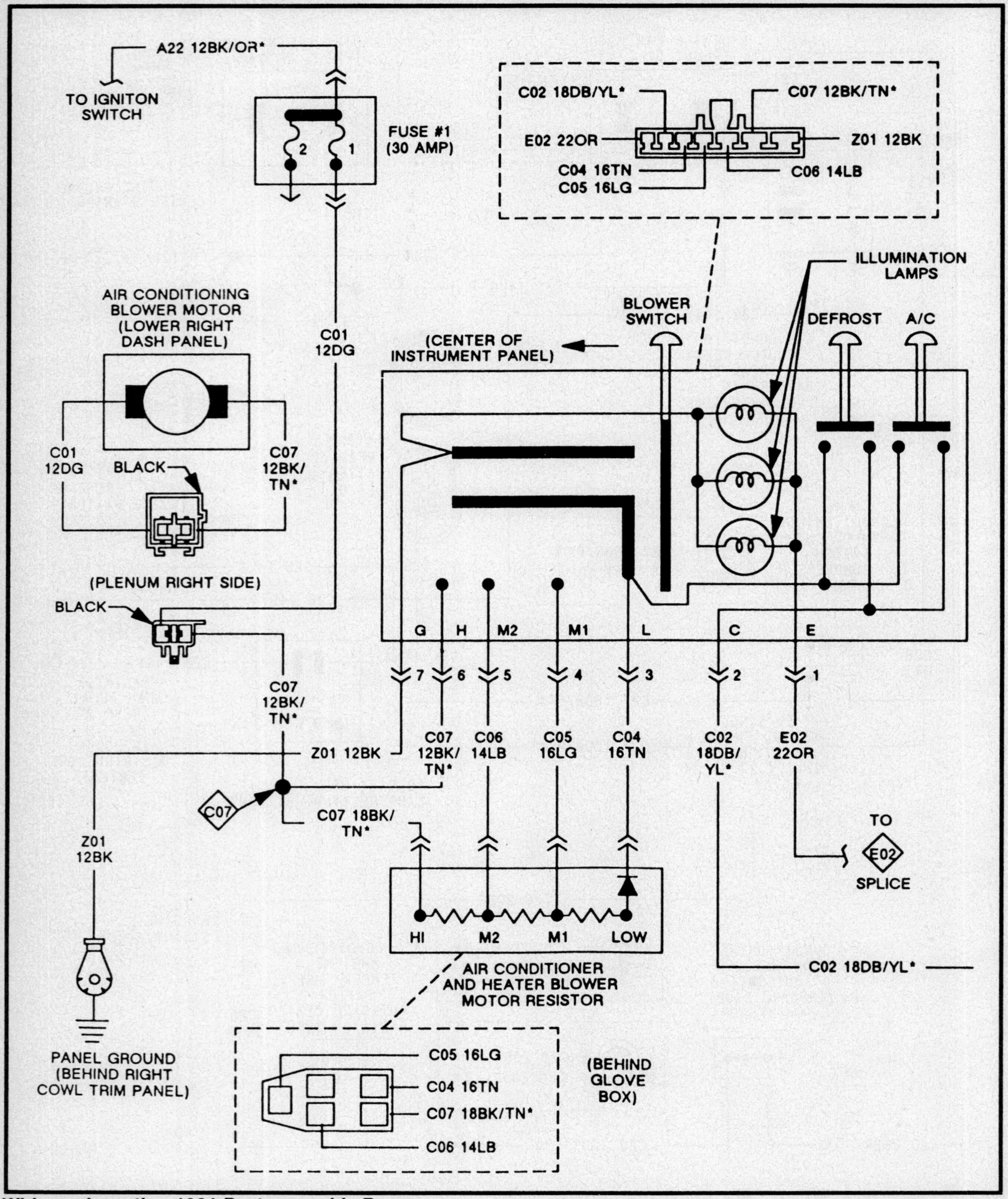
A22 12BK/OR*
TO IGNITON SWITCH
FUSE #1 (30 AMP)
C02 18DB/YL*
C07 12BK/TN*
E02 22OR
Z01 12BK
C04 16TN
C05 16LG
C06 14LB
ILLUMINATION LAMPS
AIR CONDITIONING BLOWER MOTOR (LOWER RIGHT DASH PANEL)
C01 12DG
BLOWER SWITCH
DEFROST
A/C
(CENTER OF INSTRUMENT PANEL)
BLACK
C07 12BK/TN*
(PLENUM RIGHT SIDE)
G H M2 M1 L C E
7 6 5 4 3 2 1
Z01 12BK
C07 12BK/TN*
C06 14LB
C05 16LG
C04 16TN
C02 18DB/YL*
E02 22OR
C07
C07 18BK/TN*
TO E02 SPLICE
HI M2 M1 LOW
AIR CONDITIONER AND HEATER BLOWER MOTOR RESISTOR
PANEL GROUND (BEHIND RIGHT COWL TRIM PANEL)
C05 16LG
C04 16TN
C07 18BK/TN*
C06 14LB
(BEHIND GLOVE BOX)

Wiring schematic—1991 Daytona and LeBaron

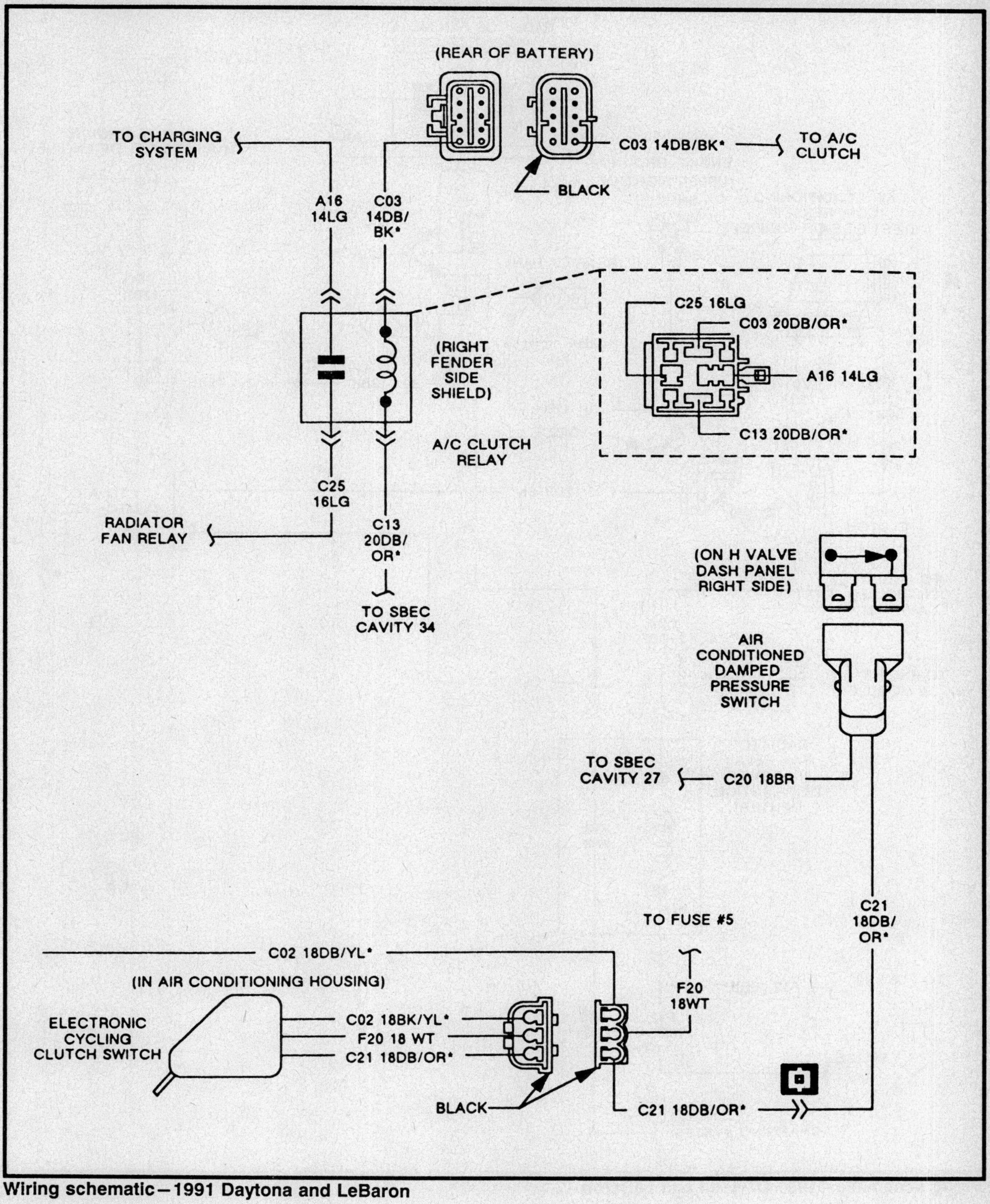
(REAR OF BATTERY)
TO CHARGING SYSTEM
C03 14DB/BK*
TO A/C CLUTCH
BLACK
A16 14LG
C03 14DB/BK*
C25 16LG
C03 20DB/OR*
A16 14LG
C13 20DB/OR*
(RIGHT FENDER SIDE SHIELD)
A/C CLUTCH RELAY
C25 16LG
RADIATOR FAN RELAY
C13 20DB/OR*
TO SBEC CAVITY 34
(ON H VALVE DASH PANEL RIGHT SIDE)
AIR CONDITIONED DAMPED PRESSURE SWITCH
TO SBEC CAVITY 27
C20 18BR
C21 18DB/OR*
TO FUSE #5
C02 18DB/YL*
(IN AIR CONDITIONING HOUSING)
F20 18WT
ELECTRONIC CYCLING CLUTCH SWITCH
C02 18BK/YL*
F20 18 WT
C21 18DB/OR*
BLACK
C21 18DB/OR*

Wiring schematic—1991 Daytona and LeBaron

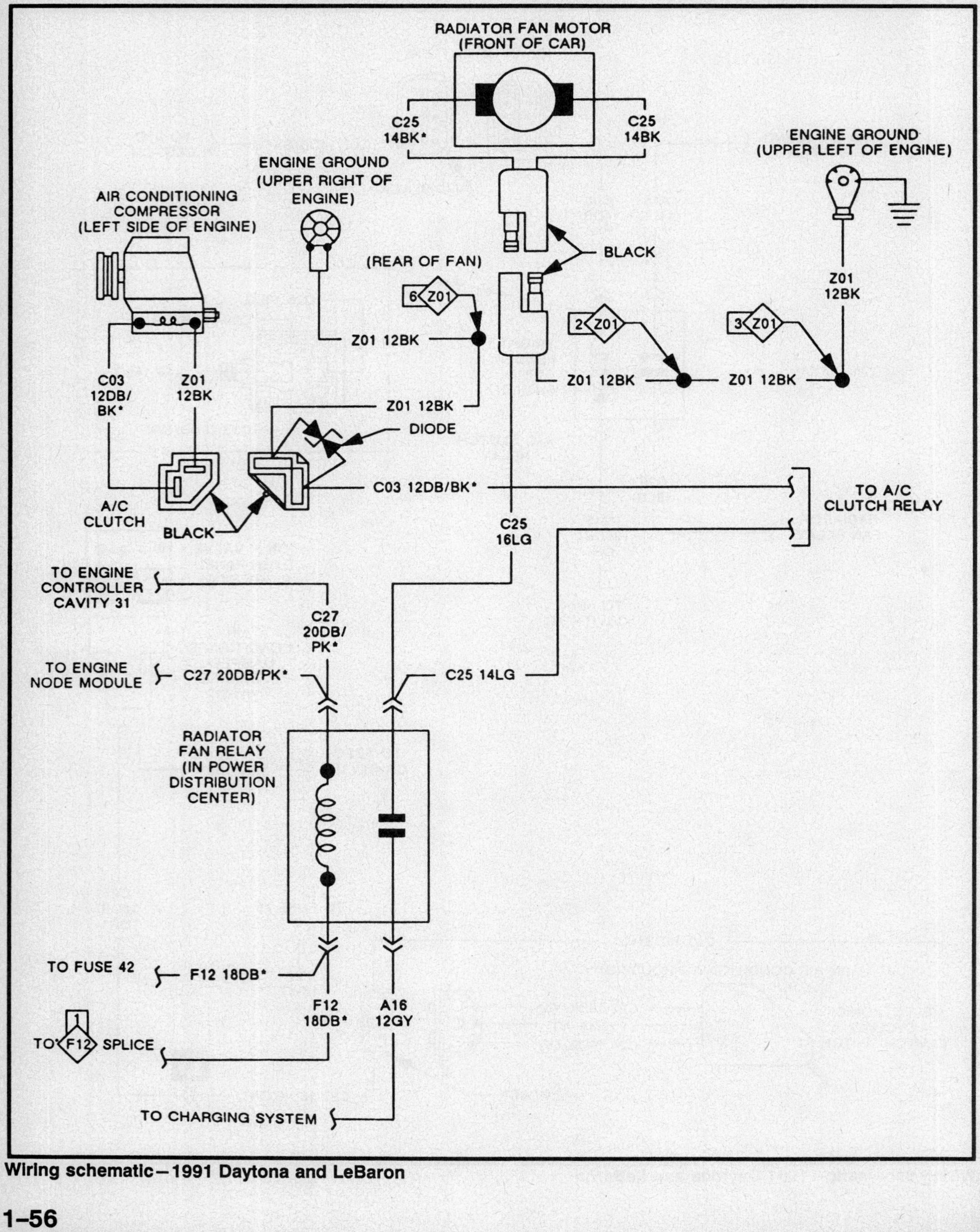
RADIATOR FAN MOTOR
(FRONT OF CAR)
C25
14BK*
C25
14BK
ENGINE GROUND
(UPPER LEFT OF ENGINE)
ENGINE GROUND
(UPPER RIGHT OF
ENGINE)
AIR CONDITIONING
COMPRESSOR
(LEFT SIDE OF ENGINE)
BLACK
(REAR OF FAN)
6 Z01
Z01
12BK
2 Z01
3 Z01
Z01 12BK
Z01 12BK
Z01 12BK
C03
12DB/
BK*
Z01
12BK
Z01 12BK
DIODE
C03 12DB/BK*
TO A/C
CLUTCH RELAY
A/C
CLUTCH
BLACK
C25
16LG
TO ENGINE
CONTROLLER
CAVITY 31
C27
20DB/
PK*
TO ENGINE
NODE MODULE
C27 20DB/PK*
C25 14LG
RADIATOR
FAN RELAY
(IN POWER
DISTRIBUTION
CENTER)
TO FUSE 42
F12 18DB*
F12
18DB*
A16
12GY
TO 1 F12 SPLICE
TO CHARGING SYSTEM

Wiring schematic—1991 Daytona and LeBaron

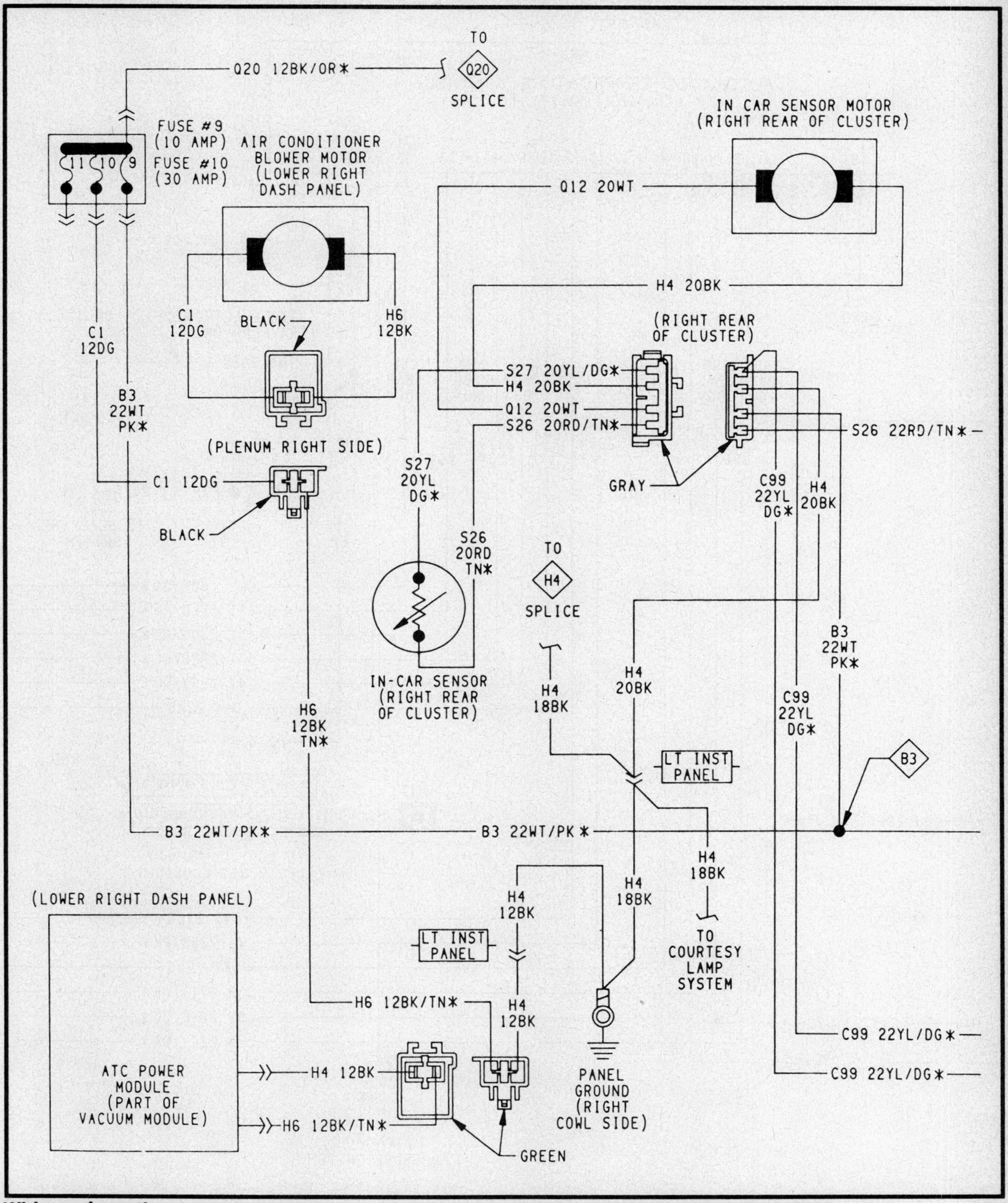
TO
Q20 12BK/OR*
Q20
SPLICE
FUSE #9
(10 AMP)
11 10 9
FUSE #10
(30 AMP)
AIR CONDITIONER
BLOWER MOTOR
(LOWER RIGHT
DASH PANEL)
IN CAR SENSOR MOTOR
(RIGHT REAR OF CLUSTER)
Q12 20WT
H4 20BK
C1
12DG
BLACK
H6
12BK
C1
12DG
B3
22WT
PK*
(RIGHT REAR
OF CLUSTER)
S27 20YL/DG*
H4 20BK
Q12 20WT
S26 20RD/TN*
S26 22RD/TN*
(PLENUM RIGHT SIDE)
C1 12DG
BLACK
S27
20YL
DG*
GRAY
C99
22YL
DG*
H4
20BK
S26
20RD
TN*
TO
H4
SPLICE
B3
22WT
PK*
IN-CAR SENSOR
(RIGHT REAR
OF CLUSTER)
H6
12BK
TN*
H4
18BK
H4
20BK
C99
22YL
DG*
LT INST
PANEL
B3
B3 22WT/PK*
B3 22WT/PK*
H4
18BK
(LOWER RIGHT DASH PANEL)
H4
12BK
H4
18BK
TO
COURTESY
LAMP
SYSTEM
LT INST
PANEL
H6 12BK/TN*
H4
12BK
C99 22YL/DG*
ATC POWER
MODULE
(PART OF
VACUUM MODULE)
H4 12BK
H6 12BK/TN*
PANEL
GROUND
(RIGHT
COWL SIDE)
C99 22YL/DG*
GREEN

Wiring schematic—1989–90 Dynasty, New Yorker and Imperial with Automatic Temperature Control

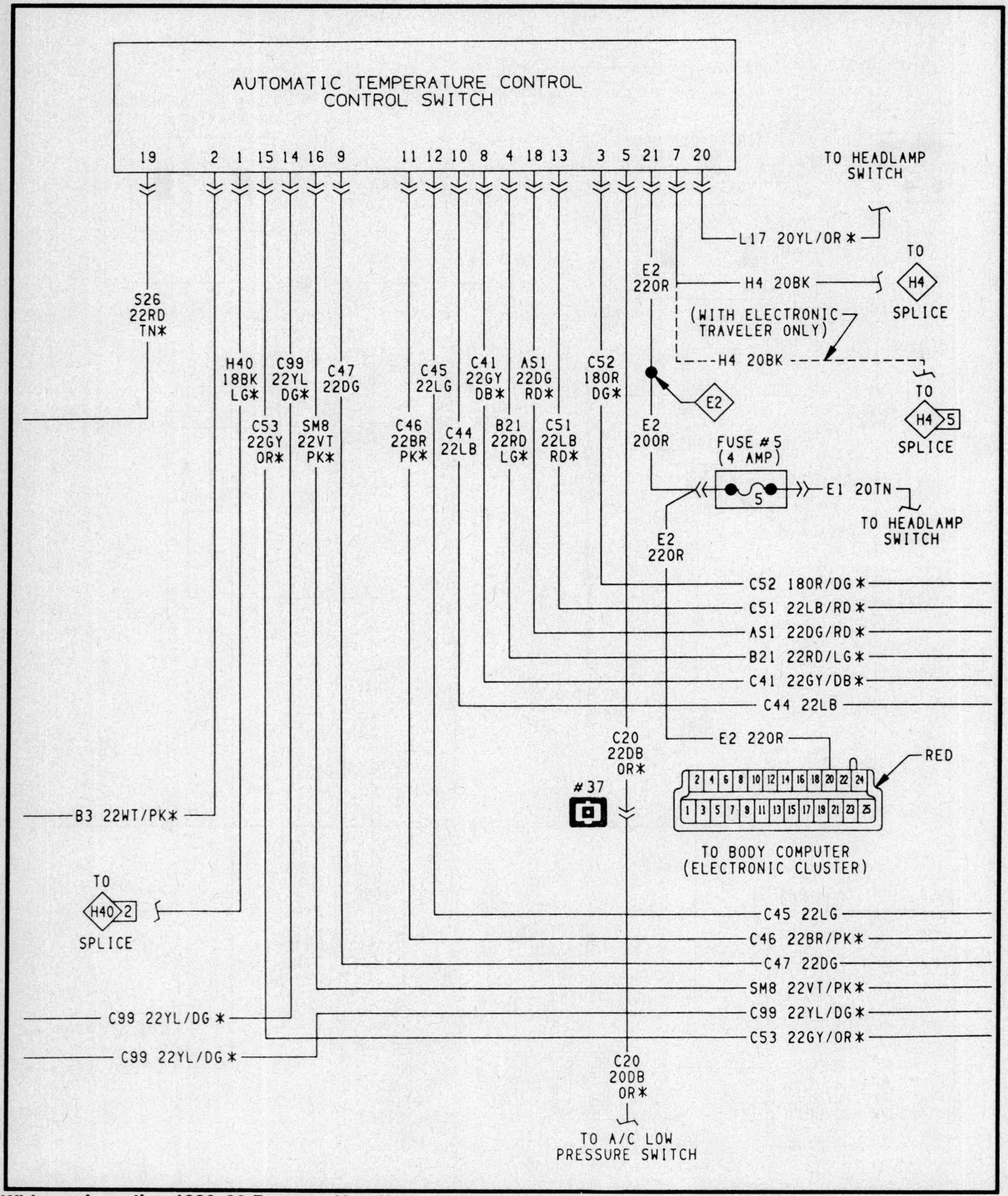
AUTOMATIC TEMPERATURE CONTROL
CONTROL SWITCH
19 2 1 15 14 16 9 11 12 10 8 4 18 13 3 5 21 7 20
TO HEADLAMP SWITCH
L17 20YL/OR*
E2 220R
H4 20BK
TO
H4
SPLICE
(WITH ELECTRONIC TRAVELER ONLY)
H4 20BK
TO
H4 5
SPLICE
S26 22RD TN*
H40 18BK LG*
C99 22YL DG*
C47 22DG
C45 22LG
C41 22GY DB*
AS1 22DG RD*
C52 18OR DG*
E2
E2 20OR
C53 22GY OR*
SM8 22VT PK*
C46 22BR PK*
C44 22LB
B21 22RD LG*
C51 22LB RD*
FUSE #5 (4 AMP)
5
E1 20TN
TO HEADLAMP SWITCH
E2 22OR
C52 18OR/DG*
C51 22LB/RD*
AS1 22DG/RD*
B21 22RD/LG*
C41 22GY/DB*
C44 22LB
C20 22DB OR*
E2 22OR
RED
#37
B3 22WT/PK*
TO BODY COMPUTER (ELECTRONIC CLUSTER)
TO
H40 2
SPLICE
C45 22LG
C46 22BR/PK*
C47 22DG
SM8 22VT/PK*
C99 22YL/DG*
C99 22YL/DG*
C53 22GY/OR*
C99 22YL/DG*
C20 20DB OR*
TO A/C LOW PRESSURE SWITCH

Wiring schematic—1989–90 Dynasty, New Yorker and Imperial with Automatic Temperature Control

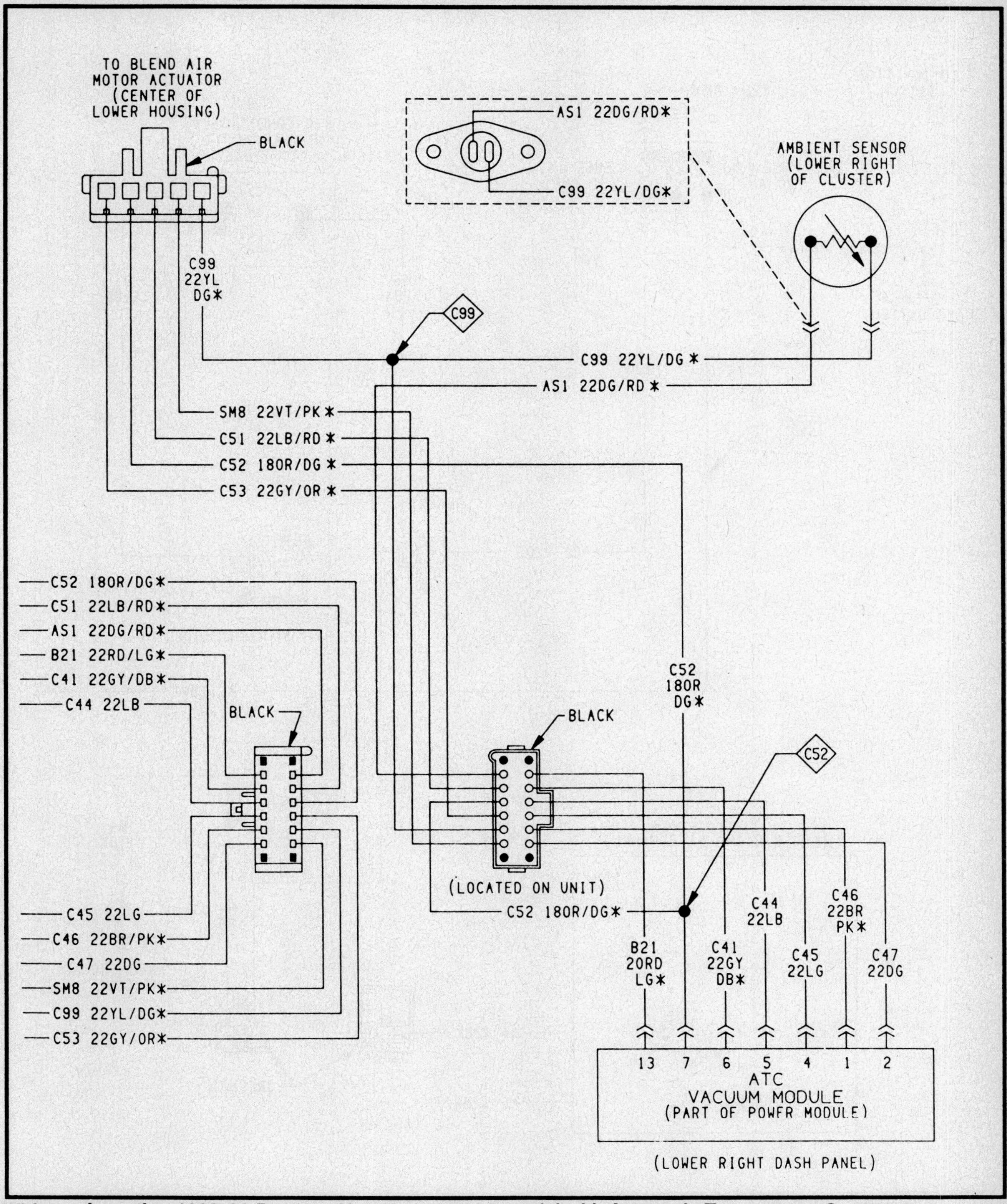
TO BLEND AIR MOTOR ACTUATOR (CENTER OF LOWER HOUSING)
BLACK
AS1 22DG/RD*
C99 22YL/DG*
AMBIENT SENSOR (LOWER RIGHT OF CLUSTER)
C99 22YL DG*
C99
C99 22YL/DG*
AS1 22DG/RD*
SM8 22VT/PK*
C51 22LB/RD*
C52 18OR/DG*
C53 22GY/OR*
C52 18OR/DG*
C51 22LB/RD*
AS1 22DG/RD*
B21 22RD/LG*
C41 22GY/DB*
C44 22LB
BLACK
BLACK
C52 18OR DG*
C52
(LOCATED ON UNIT)
C52 18OR/DG*
C45 22LG
C46 22BR/PK*
C47 22DG
SM8 22VT/PK*
C99 22YL/DG*
C53 22GY/OR*
B21 20RD LG*
C41 22GY DB*
C44 22LB
C45 22LG
C46 22BR PK*
C47 22DG
13 7 6 5 4 1 2
ATC VACUUM MODULE (PART OF POWER MODULE)
(LOWER RIGHT DASH PANEL)

Wiring schematic—1989–90 Dynasty, New Yorker and Imperial with Automatic Temperature Control

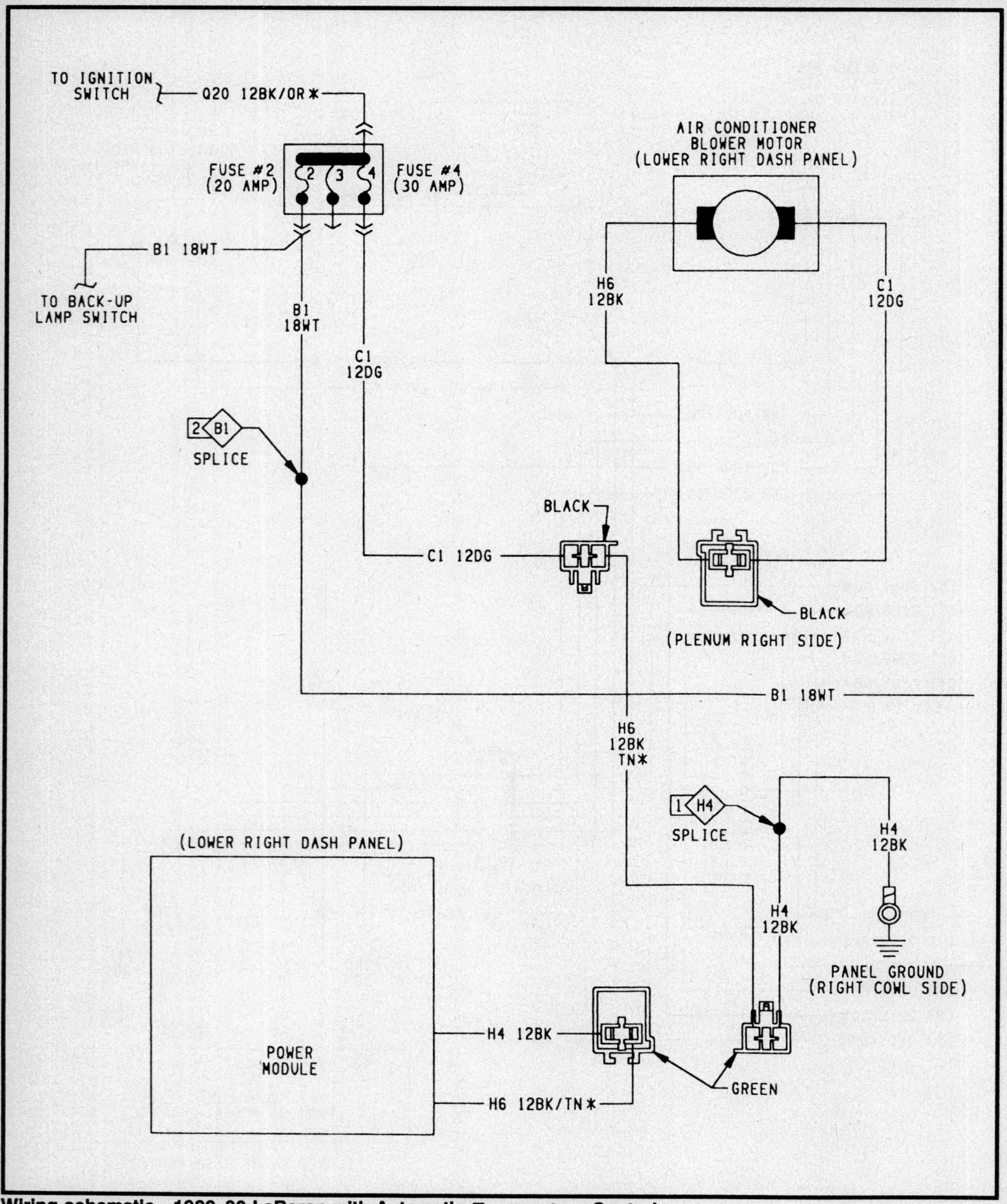
TO IGNITION SWITCH
Q20 12BK/OR*
FUSE #2 (20 AMP)
2
3
4
FUSE #4 (30 AMP)
B1 18WT
TO BACK-UP LAMP SWITCH
B1 18WT
C1 12DG
2 B1
SPLICE
AIR CONDITIONER BLOWER MOTOR (LOWER RIGHT DASH PANEL)
H6 12BK
C1 12DG
BLACK
C1 12DG
BLACK
(PLENUM RIGHT SIDE)
B1 18WT
H6 12BK TN*
1 H4
SPLICE
H4 12BK
H4 12BK
PANEL GROUND (RIGHT COWL SIDE)
(LOWER RIGHT DASH PANEL)
POWER MODULE
H4 12BK
H6 12BK/TN*
GREEN

Wiring schematic—1989–90 LeBaron with Automatic Temperature Control

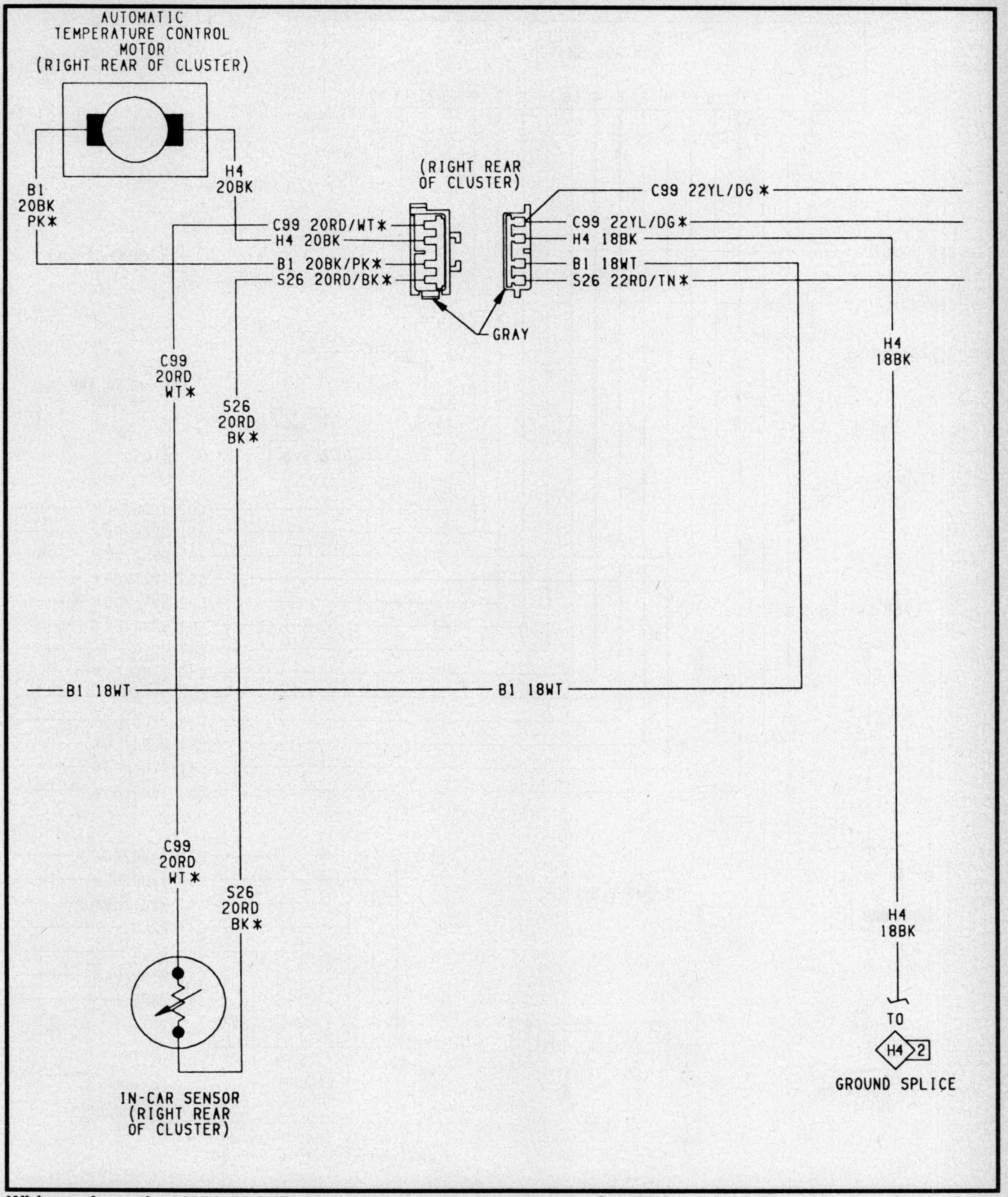
AUTOMATIC TEMPERATURE CONTROL MOTOR (RIGHT REAR OF CLUSTER)
B1 20BK PK*
H4 20BK
(RIGHT REAR OF CLUSTER)
C99 20RD/WT*
H4 20BK
B1 20BK/PK*
S26 20RD/BK*
C99 22YL/DG*
C99 22YL/DG*
H4 18BK
B1 18WT
S26 22RD/TN*
GRAY
H4 18BK
C99 20RD WT*
S26 20RD BK*
B1 18WT
B1 18WT
C99 20RD WT*
S26 20RD BK*
H4 18BK
TO
H4 2
GROUND SPLICE
IN-CAR SENSOR (RIGHT REAR OF CLUSTER)

Wiring schematic—1989–90 LeBaron with Automatic Temperature Control

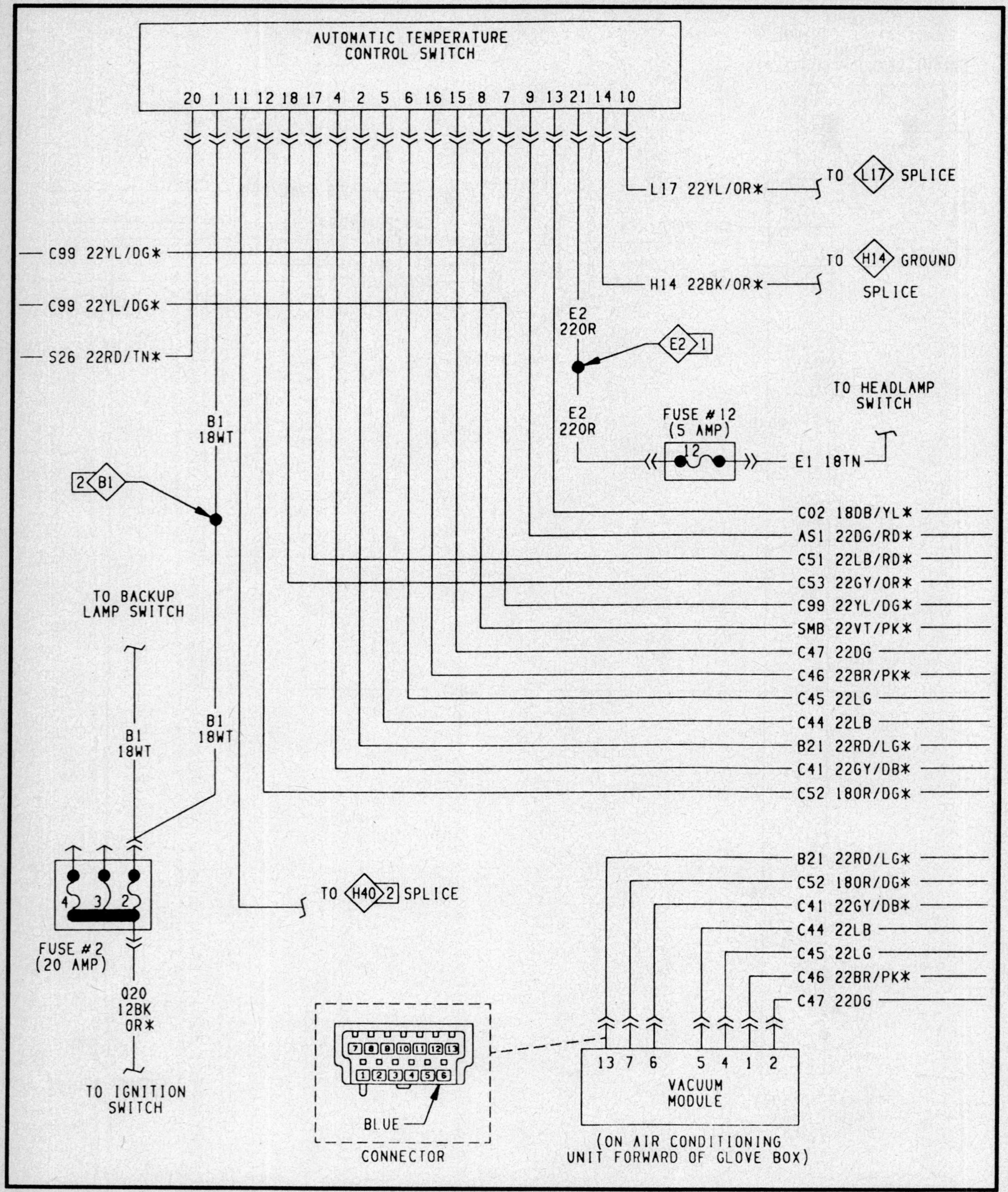
AUTOMATIC TEMPERATURE CONTROL SWITCH
20 1 11 12 18 17 4 2 5 6 16 15 8 7 9 13 21 14 10
L17 22YL/OR*
TO L17 SPLICE
C99 22YL/DG*
C99 22YL/DG*
S26 22RD/TN*
TO H14 GROUND SPLICE
H14 22BK/OR*
E2 22OR
E2 1
TO HEADLAMP SWITCH
E2 22OR
FUSE #12 (5 AMP)
12
E1 18TN
B1 18WT
2 B1
C02 18DB/YL*
AS1 22DG/RD*
C51 22LB/RD*
C53 22GY/OR*
C99 22YL/DG*
SMB 22VT/PK*
C47 22DG
C46 22BR/PK*
C45 22LG
C44 22LB
B21 22RD/LG*
C41 22GY/DB*
C52 18OR/DG*
TO BACKUP LAMP SWITCH
B1 18WT
B1 18WT
4 3 2
FUSE #2 (20 AMP)
Q20 12BK OR*
TO IGNITION SWITCH
TO H40 2 SPLICE
B21 22RD/LG*
C52 18OR/DG*
C41 22GY/DB*
C44 22LB
C45 22LG
C46 22BR/PK*
C47 22DG
7 8 9 10 11 12 13
1 2 3 4 5 6
BLUE
CONNECTOR
13 7 6 5 4 1 2
VACUUM MODULE
(ON AIR CONDITIONING UNIT FORWARD OF GLOVE BOX)

Wiring schematic – 1989–90 LeBaron with Automatic Temperature Control

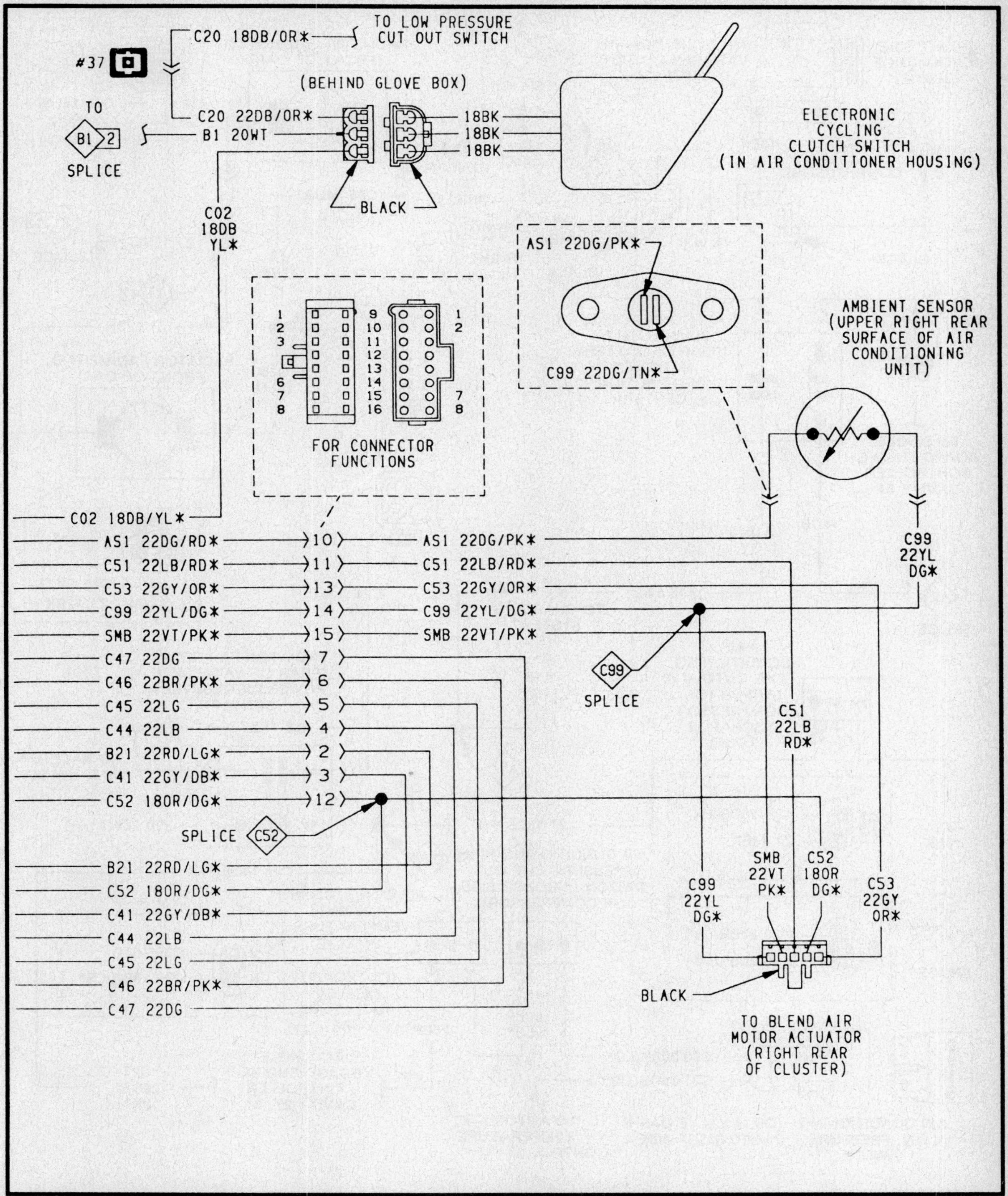
C20 18DB/OR*
TO LOW PRESSURE CUT OUT SWITCH
#37
(BEHIND GLOVE BOX)
TO
B1
2
SPLICE
C20 22DB/OR*
B1 20WT
18BK
18BK
18BK
ELECTRONIC CYCLING CLUTCH SWITCH (IN AIR CONDITIONER HOUSING)
BLACK
C02 18DB YL*
AS1 22DG/PK*
C99 22DG/TN*
AMBIENT SENSOR (UPPER RIGHT REAR SURFACE OF AIR CONDITIONING UNIT)
FOR CONNECTOR FUNCTIONS
C02 18DB/YL*
AS1 22DG/RD*
C51 22LB/RD*
C53 22GY/OR*
C99 22YL/DG*
SMB 22VT/PK*
C47 22DG
C46 22BR/PK*
C45 22LG
C44 22LB
B21 22RD/LG*
C41 22GY/DB*
C52 18OR/DG*
AS1 22DG/PK*
C51 22LB/RD*
C53 22GY/OR*
C99 22YL/DG*
SMB 22VT/PK*
C99 22YL DG*
C99 SPLICE
C51 22LB RD*
SPLICE C52
B21 22RD/LG*
C52 18OR/DG*
C41 22GY/DB*
C44 22LB
C45 22LG
C46 22BR/PK*
C47 22DG
C99 22YL DG*
SMB 22VT PK*
C52 18OR DG*
C53 22GY OR*
BLACK
TO BLEND AIR MOTOR ACTUATOR (RIGHT REAR OF CLUSTER)

Wiring schematic—1989–90 LeBaron with Automatic Temperature Control

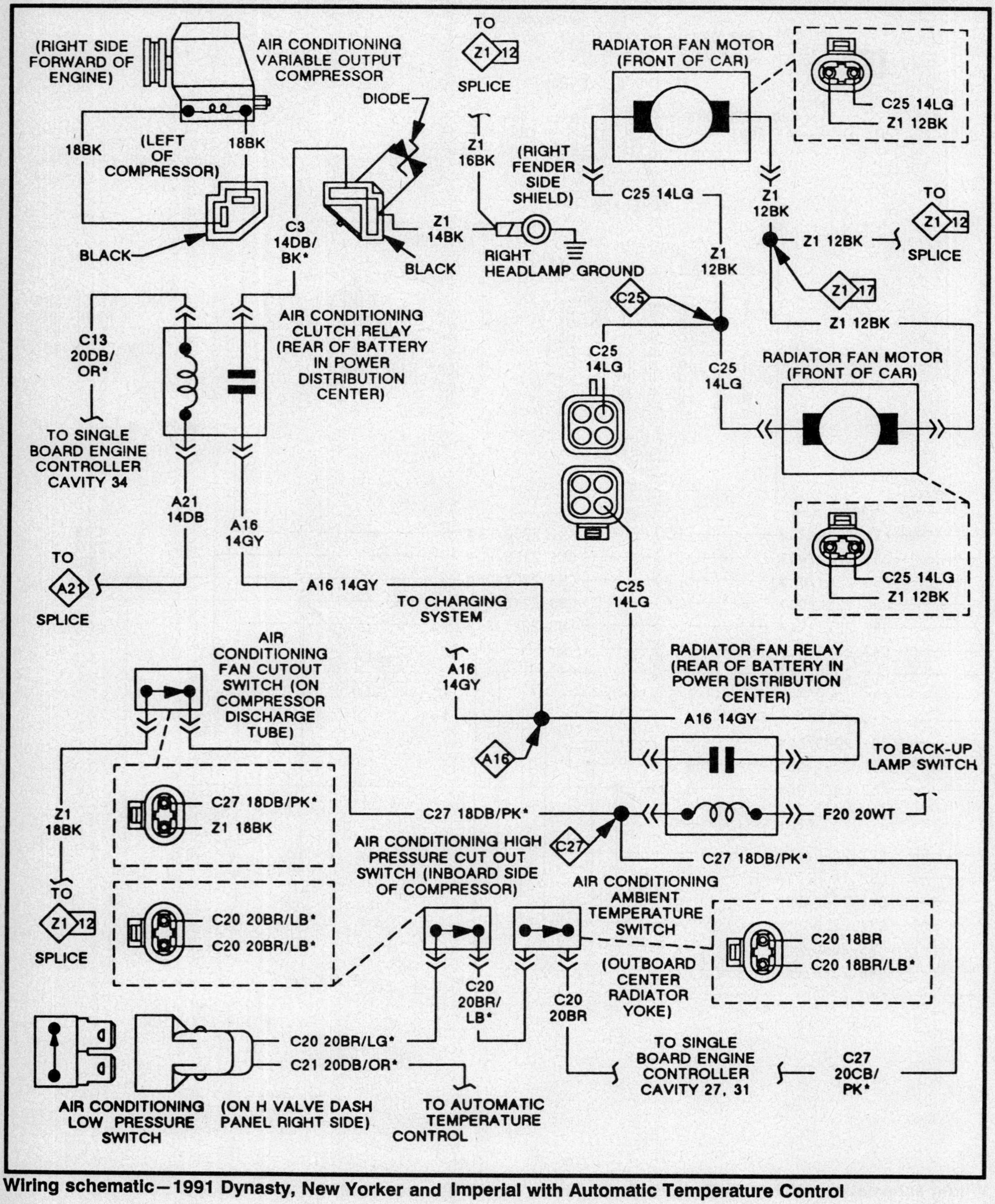
(RIGHT SIDE FORWARD OF ENGINE)
AIR CONDITIONING VARIABLE OUTPUT COMPRESSOR
TO
Z1 12
SPLICE
RADIATOR FAN MOTOR (FRONT OF CAR)
C25 14LG
Z1 12BK
DIODE
18BK
(LEFT OF COMPRESSOR)
18BK
Z1 16BK
(RIGHT FENDER SIDE SHIELD)
C25 14LG
Z1 12BK
TO
Z1 12
Z1 12BK
SPLICE
BLACK
C3 14DB/BK*
BLACK
Z1 14BK
RIGHT HEADLAMP GROUND
Z1 12BK
C25
Z1 17
Z1 12BK
AIR CONDITIONING CLUTCH RELAY (REAR OF BATTERY IN POWER DISTRIBUTION CENTER)
C13 20DB/OR*
C25 14LG
C25 14LG
RADIATOR FAN MOTOR (FRONT OF CAR)
TO SINGLE BOARD ENGINE CONTROLLER CAVITY 34
A21 14DB
A16 14GY
TO
A21
SPLICE
A16 14GY
TO CHARGING SYSTEM
C25 14LG
C25 14LG
Z1 12BK
AIR CONDITIONING FAN CUTOUT SWITCH (ON COMPRESSOR DISCHARGE TUBE)
A16 14GY
RADIATOR FAN RELAY (REAR OF BATTERY IN POWER DISTRIBUTION CENTER)
A16 14GY
A16
TO BACK-UP LAMP SWITCH
Z1 18BK
C27 18DB/PK*
Z1 18BK
C27 18DB/PK*
F20 20WT
C27
AIR CONDITIONING HIGH PRESSURE CUT OUT SWITCH (INBOARD SIDE OF COMPRESSOR)
C27 18DB/PK*
TO
Z1 12
SPLICE
C20 20BR/LB*
C20 20BR/LB*
AIR CONDITIONING AMBIENT TEMPERATURE SWITCH
C20 18BR
C20 18BR/LB*
(OUTBOARD CENTER RADIATOR YOKE)
C20 20BR/LB*
C20 20BR
C20 20BR/LG*
C21 20DB/OR*
TO SINGLE BOARD ENGINE CONTROLLER CAVITY 27, 31
C27 20CB/PK*
AIR CONDITIONING LOW PRESSURE SWITCH
(ON H VALVE DASH PANEL RIGHT SIDE)
TO AUTOMATIC TEMPERATURE CONTROL

Wiring schematic—1991 Dynasty, New Yorker and Imperial with Automatic Temperature Control

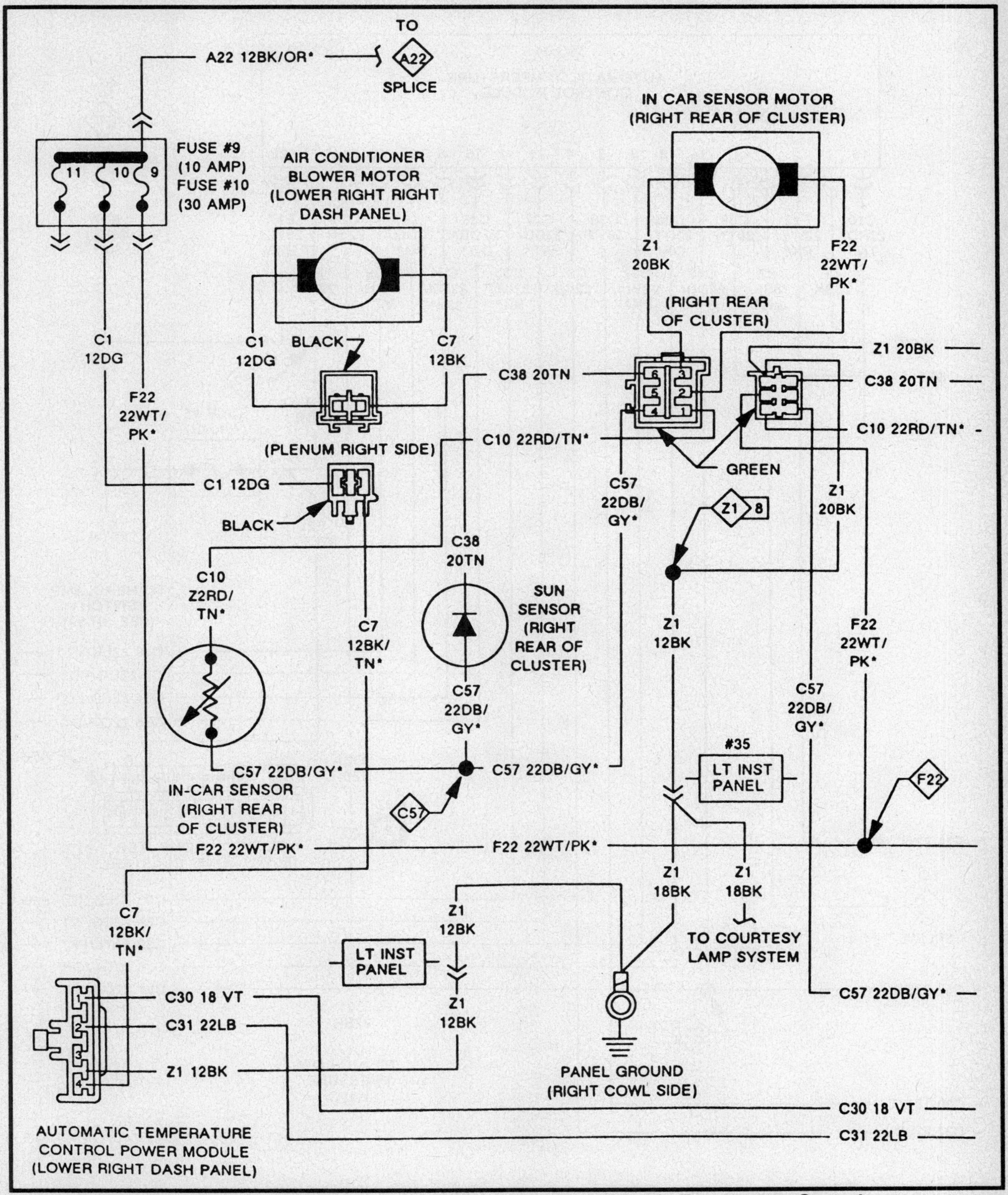
TO
A22 12BK/OR*
A22
SPLICE
FUSE #9
(10 AMP)
FUSE #10
(30 AMP)
11 10 9
AIR CONDITIONER
BLOWER MOTOR
(LOWER RIGHT RIGHT
DASH PANEL)
IN CAR SENSOR MOTOR
(RIGHT REAR OF CLUSTER)
Z1
20BK
F22
22WT/
PK*
(RIGHT REAR
OF CLUSTER)
C1
12DG
C1
12DG
BLACK
C7
12BK
C38 20TN
Z1 20BK
C38 20TN
F22
22WT/
PK*
C10 22RD/TN*
C10 22RD/TN*
(PLENUM RIGHT SIDE)
GREEN
C1 12DG
C57
22DB/
GY*
Z1
8
Z1
20BK
BLACK
C38
20TN
C10
Z2RD/
TN*
SUN
SENSOR
(RIGHT
REAR OF
CLUSTER)
C7
12BK/
TN*
Z1
12BK
F22
22WT/
PK*
C57
22DB/
GY*
C57
22DB/
GY*
#35
LT INST
PANEL
C57 22DB/GY*
C57 22DB/GY*
IN-CAR SENSOR
(RIGHT REAR
OF CLUSTER)
C57
F22
F22 22WT/PK*
F22 22WT/PK*
Z1
18BK
Z1
18BK
C7
12BK/
TN*
Z1
12BK
TO COURTESY
LAMP SYSTEM
LT INST
PANEL
Z1
12BK
C30 18 VT
C31 22LB
Z1 12BK
C57 22DB/GY*
PANEL GROUND
(RIGHT COWL SIDE)
C30 18 VT
C31 22LB
AUTOMATIC TEMPERATURE
CONTROL POWER MODULE
(LOWER RIGHT DASH PANEL)

Wiring schematic—1991 Dynasty, New Yorker and Imperial with Automatic Temperature Control

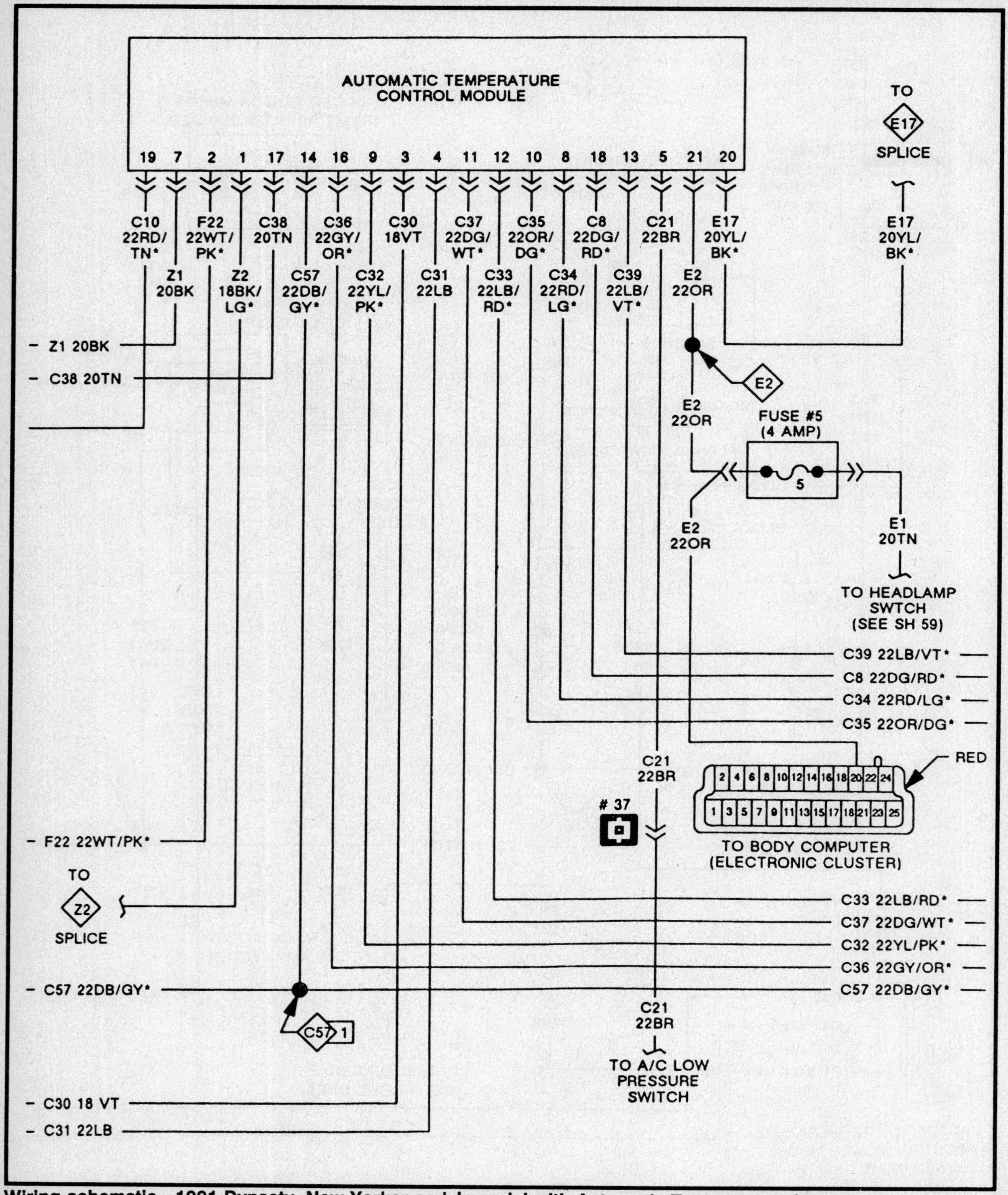
AUTOMATIC TEMPERATURE CONTROL MODULE
19 7 2 1 17 14 16 9 3 4 11 12 10 8 18 13 5 21 20
C10 22RD/TN*
F22 22WT/PK*
C38 20TN
C36 22GY/OR*
C30 18VT
C37 22DG/WT*
C35 22OR/DG*
C8 22DG/RD*
C21 22BR
E17 20YL/BK*
Z1 20BK
Z2 18BK/LG*
C57 22DB/GY*
C32 22YL/PK*
C31 22LB
C33 22LB/RD*
C34 22RD/LG*
C39 22LB/VT*
E2 22OR
TO E17 SPLICE
E17 20YL/BK*
– Z1 20BK
– C38 20TN
E2
E2 22OR
FUSE #5 (4 AMP)
5
E2 22OR
E1 20TN
TO HEADLAMP SWTCH (SEE SH 59)
C39 22LB/VT* –
C8 22DG/RD* –
C34 22RD/LG* –
C35 22OR/DG* –
C21 22BR
RED
37
TO BODY COMPUTER (ELECTRONIC CLUSTER)
– F22 22WT/PK*
TO Z2 SPLICE
C33 22LB/RD* –
C37 22DG/WT* –
C32 22YL/PK* –
C36 22GY/OR* –
– C57 22DB/GY*
C57 22DB/GY* –
C57 1
C21 22BR
TO A/C LOW PRESSURE SWITCH
– C30 18 VT
– C31 22LB

Wiring schematic—1991 Dynasty, New Yorker and Imperial with Automatic Temperature Control

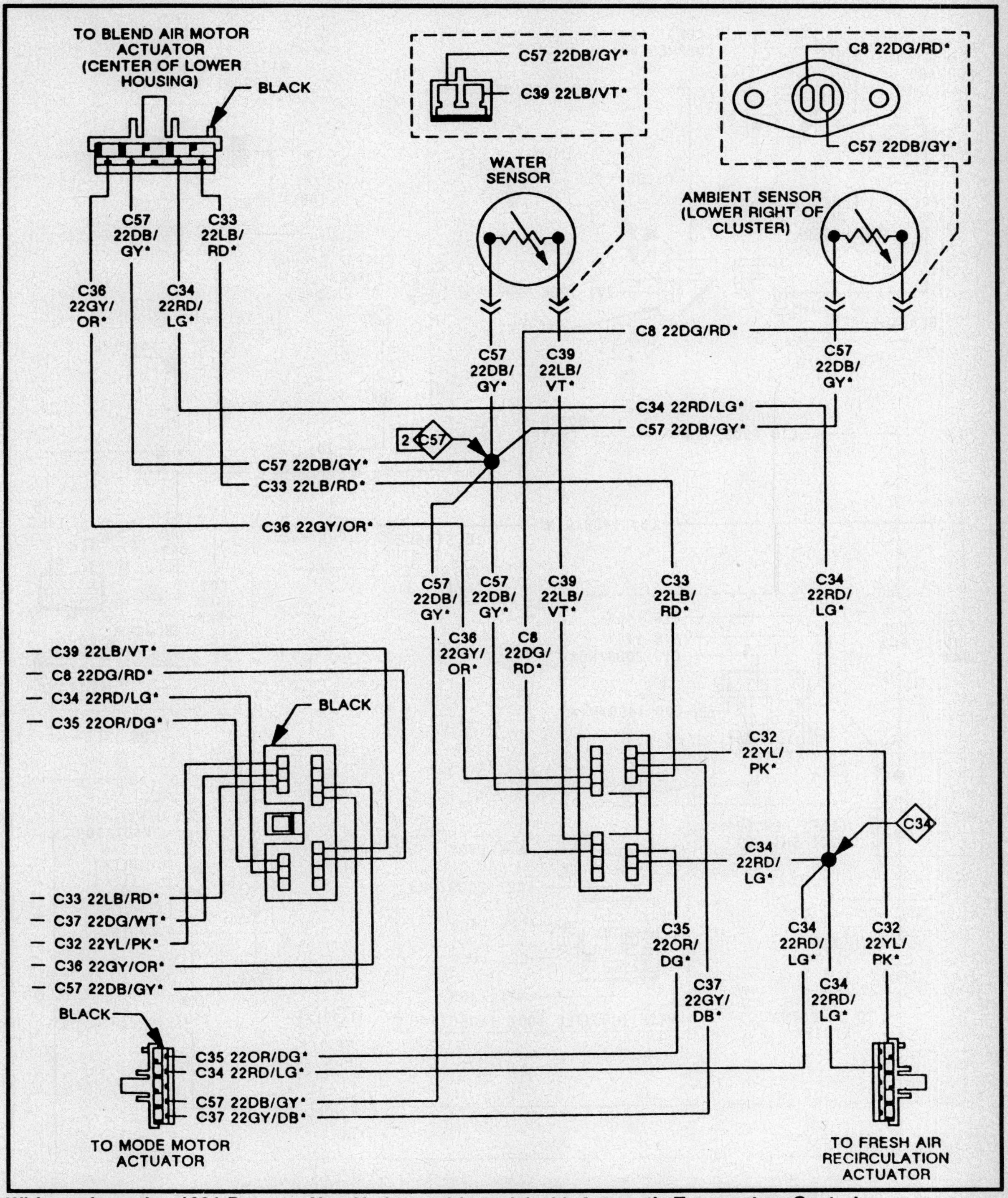
TO BLEND AIR MOTOR ACTUATOR (CENTER OF LOWER HOUSING)
BLACK
C57 22DB/GY*
C39 22LB/VT*
C8 22DG/RD*
C57 22DB/GY*
WATER SENSOR
AMBIENT SENSOR (LOWER RIGHT OF CLUSTER)
C57 22DB/GY*
C33 22LB/RD*
C36 22GY/OR*
C34 22RD/LG*
C8 22DG/RD*
C57 22DB/GY*
C39 22LB/VT*
C57 22DB/GY*
C34 22RD/LG*
C57 22DB/GY*
2 C57
C57 22DB/GY*
C33 22LB/RD*
C36 22GY/OR*
C57 22DB/GY*
C57 22DB/GY*
C39 22LB/VT*
C33 22LB/RD*
C34 22RD/LG*
C36 22GY/OR*
C8 22DG/RD*
C39 22LB/VT*
C8 22DG/RD*
C34 22RD/LG*
C35 22OR/DG*
BLACK
C32 22YL/PK*
C34
C34 22RD/LG*
C33 22LB/RD*
C37 22DG/WT*
C32 22YL/PK*
C36 22GY/OR*
C57 22DB/GY*
C35 22OR/DG*
C34 22RD/LG*
C32 22YL/PK*
C37 22GY/DB*
C34 22RD/LG*
BLACK
C35 22OR/DG*
C34 22RD/LG*
C57 22DB/GY*
C37 22GY/DB*
TO MODE MOTOR ACTUATOR
TO FRESH AIR RECIRCULATION ACTUATOR

Wiring schematic—1991 Dynasty, New Yorker and Imperial with Automatic Temperature Control

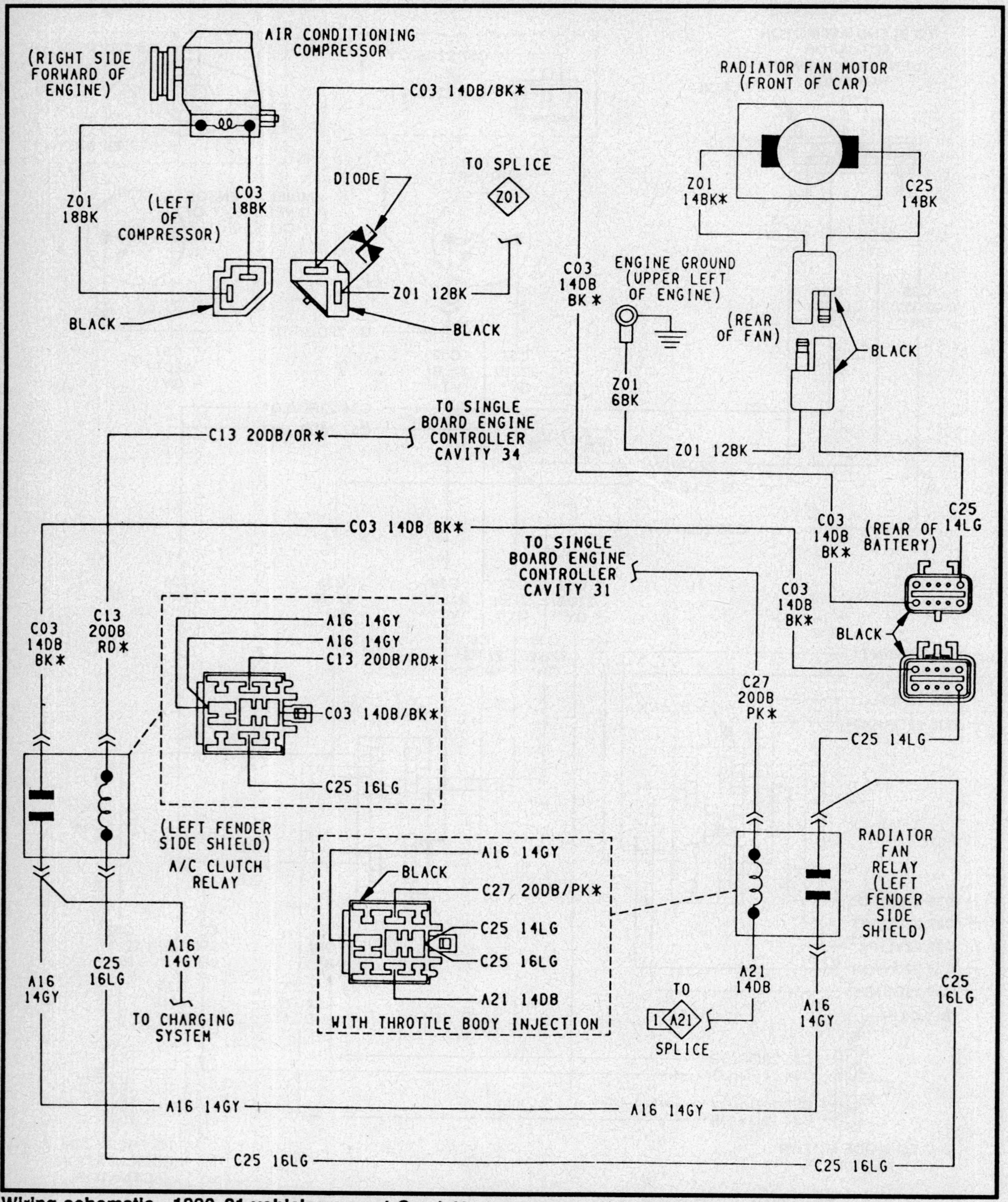
AIR CONDITIONING COMPRESSOR
(RIGHT SIDE FORWARD OF ENGINE)
C03 14DB/BK*
RADIATOR FAN MOTOR (FRONT OF CAR)
Z01 18BK
(LEFT OF COMPRESSOR)
C03 18BK
DIODE
TO SPLICE
Z01
Z01 14BK*
C25 14BK
Z01 12BK
BLACK
BLACK
C03 14DB BK*
ENGINE GROUND (UPPER LEFT OF ENGINE)
(REAR OF FAN)
BLACK
Z01 6BK
TO SINGLE BOARD ENGINE CONTROLLER CAVITY 34
C13 20DB/OR*
Z01 12BK
C03 14DB BK*
C03 14DB BK*
(REAR OF BATTERY)
C25 14LG
TO SINGLE BOARD ENGINE CONTROLLER CAVITY 31
C03 14DB BK*
BLACK
C03 14DB BK*
C13 20DB RD*
A16 14GY
A16 14GY
C13 20DB/RD*
C03 14DB/BK*
C25 16LG
C27 20DB PK*
C25 14LG
(LEFT FENDER SIDE SHIELD)
A/C CLUTCH RELAY
A16 14GY
BLACK
C27 20DB/PK*
C25 14LG
C25 16LG
A21 14DB
WITH THROTTLE BODY INJECTION
RADIATOR FAN RELAY (LEFT FENDER SIDE SHIELD)
A16 14GY
C25 16LG
A16 14GY
TO CHARGING SYSTEM
A16 14GY
TO
1 A21
SPLICE
A21 14DB
A16 14GY
C25 16LG
A16 14GY
A16 14GY
C25 16LG
C25 16LG

Wiring schematic—1990–91 vehicles except Omni, Horizon, Dynasty, New Yorker and Imperial

2 CHRYSLER/DODGE/PLYMOUTH 2

CARAVELLE • DIPLOMAT • FIFTH AVENUE • NEWPORT

SPECIFICATIONS

ENGINE IDENTIFICATION

Year	Model	Engine Displacement cu. in. (liter)	Engine Series Identification (VIN)	No. of Cylinders	Engine Type
1989	All	318 (5.2)	P①	8	OHV
		318 (5.2)	S②	8	OHV
		318 (5.2)	4③	8	OHV

① 2 BBL
② 4 BBL, Heavy duty
③ 4 BBL

REFRIGERANT CAPACITIES

Year	Model	Freon (oz.)	Oil (fl. oz.)	Type
1989	All	41	$11^1/_4$	Fixed Displacement

AIR CONDITIONING BELT TENSION CHART

Year	Model	Engine (liter)	Belt Type	New	Used
1989	All	5.2	V	$^1/_4$–$^1/_2$①	—

① Inches of deflection at the midpoint of the belt using 10 lbs. force

SYSTEM DESCRIPTION

General Information

Heater-Only

This heater system is a bi-level, or modified blend-air type heater. The heater assembly housing used for this bi-level system is the same housing used with air conditioned vehicles. When the vehicle has only a heater system, the evaporator and recirculating air door is omitted from the unit housing assembly. All air ducts and panel outlets are used in addition to the heater outlets for distribution of both heated and outside air. There is also a push button heater control used. The system provides increased air flow capacity, better air distribution and better side window defrost and defogging capability in the passenger compartment.

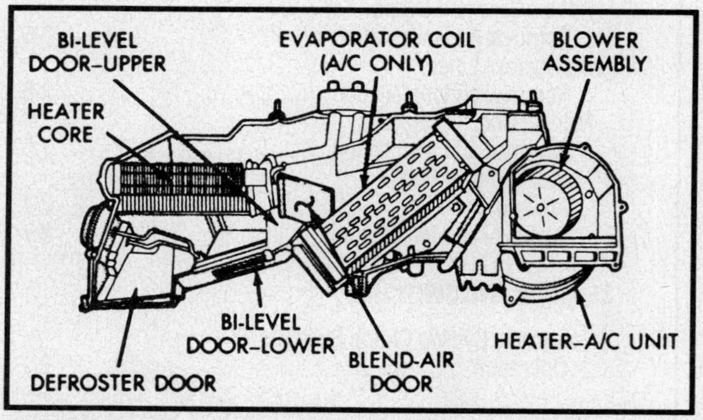
BI-LEVEL DOOR–UPPER
EVAPORATOR COIL (A/C ONLY)
BLOWER ASSEMBLY
HEATER CORE
BI-LEVEL DOOR–LOWER
HEATER–A/C UNIT
BLEND-AIR DOOR
DEFROSTER DOOR

Air conditioning/heater housing components

VACUUM CONTROL MODES

Vacuum determined by the 4 button switch controls the shut-off water valve and positions all the doors in the unit except the blend air door. The following is a breakdown of the vacuum logic for each mode.

OFF POSITION

The inlet door is closed to the outside air. The heat bi-level door is in the bi-level position. The heat defrost door is in the heat position and the blower is off. The water valve is controlled by the temperature level and may either be on or off, depending on the position of the lever.

BI-LEVEL POSITION

The doors are in the same position as the they were in the OFF position except for the inlet door which is open to outside air. The blower is on and may be operated in any of the 4 speeds available. The water valve is controlled by the temperature lever and is shut off only when the lever is in the full cool position. A blend air door, operated by the temperature lever, controls the temperature of the air coming from the unit.

HEAT POSITION

This mode operates the same as the BI-LEVEL mode, except the heat/bi-level door is in the heat position.

DEFROST POSITION

This mode is the same as the HEAT mode, except the heat-defrost door is in the defrost position.

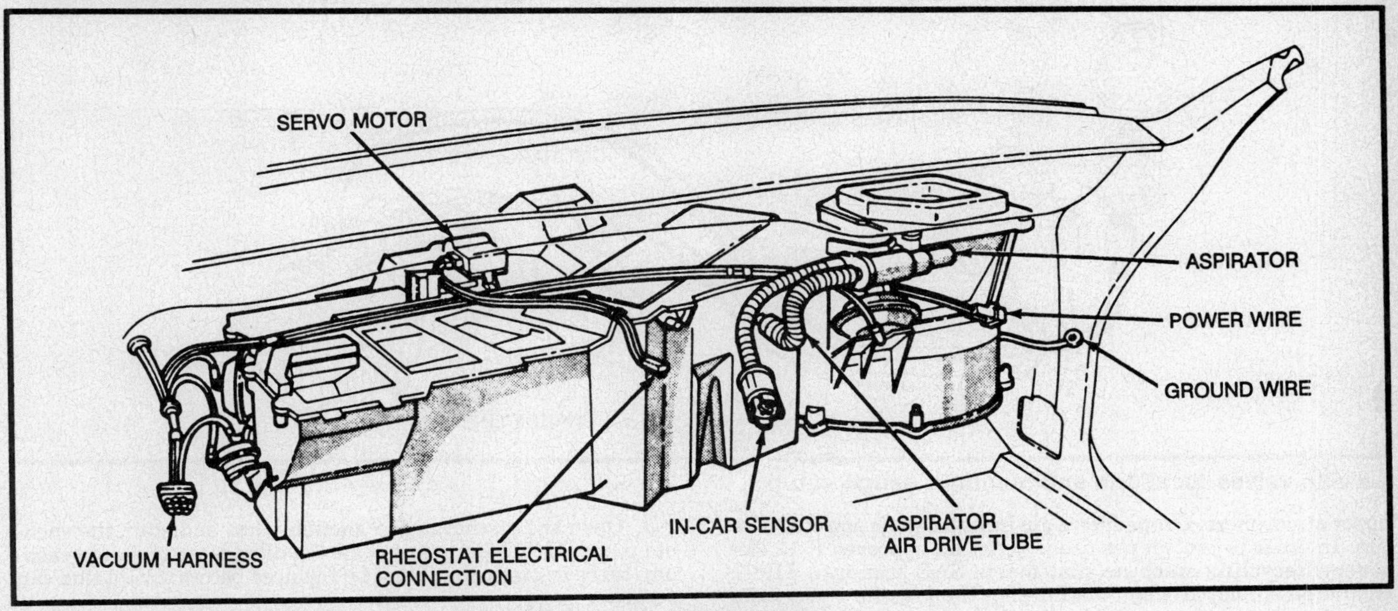
SERVO MOTOR
ASPIRATOR
POWER WIRE
GROUND WIRE
VACUUM HARNESS
RHEOSTAT ELECTRICAL CONNECTION
IN-CAR SENSOR
ASPIRATOR AIR DRIVE TUBE

Semi-Automatic Temperature Control (SATC) system components

Air Conditioning System

The operation of the system is controlled by either a manual control head or a Semi-Automatic Temperature Control (SATC) head, located on the instrument panel. These control heads regulate the control cables and vacuum supply to the evaporative housing to move the varied doors within the housing as required. An electric fan motor is used to regulate the air flow into the passenger compartment as required to maintain passenger comfort. A reed valve type compressor is used and is dual-belt driven from the engine crankshaft. The system is equipped with a high pressure relief valve on the receiver/drier, which will open automatically if the system pressure becomes excessive, preventing system damage.

Semi-Automatic Temperature Control (SATC) System

The SATC system maintains a selected confort level within the vehicle while allowing the selection of various modes of operation. After selecting the desired comfort setting and push-button mode, the SATC system will heat or cool, in varying degrees, depending on interior temperature, ambient temperature and the temperature control setting. The SATC system is made up of 2 temperature sensors, a lever-operated sliding resistor, an electronic servo motor and connecting wiring. These components constantly monitor and control vehicle interior air temperature when the system is operating.

The SATC push-button switch has 6 modes which controls the shut-off water valve and positions all the doors in the unit except the blend air door. The following is a breakdown of operations for each mode.

OFF POSITION

The inlet door is closed to the outside air. The heat bi-level door is in the bi-level position. The heat defrost door is in the heat position and the blower is off. The heater core coolant flow is shut off. The compressor and the SATC electronics are off because the blower and compressor clutch circuits are open.

MAX AIR CONDITIONING POSITION

All doors are in the same position as they are in off. **MAX A/C** mode closes the electrical circuits to the blower motor, SATC electronics and the compressor clutch. The heater core coolant flow is shut off.

AIR CONDITIONING NORM POSITION

The air conditioning system is on. The air inlet door is closed to inside and open to outside air flow. If this button is depressed and then pulled out fully, the compressor will not operate and no cooling will occur.

BI-LEVEL POSITION

The system will operate similar to the **NORM A/C** mode, except the air now flows between the upper and lower outlets. It also provides side window clearing when the instrument panel outlets are directed toward the sides and rear. If this button is depressed and then pulled out fully, the compressor will not operate and no cooling will occur.

HEAT POSITION

The outside air door is open as in the **A/C** mode. Vacuum is applied to the Bi-Level door actuator, closing off the passage to the air conditioning distribution duct and open the passage to the heater-defroster duct. The heated air passes through the heater outlet and a small amount bleeds through the defroster outlets.

DEFROST POSITION

This mode is the same as the HEAT mode, except the heat-defrost door is in the defrost position. The defroster door will be open to outside air. A small amount of heat will flow through the heater outlets. A built-in time delay will direct air to the panel outlets for 5–10 seconds after changing the settings from OFF to HEAT or DEFROST. The compressor clutch will be engaged if the ambient temperature is above 10°F (−12°C), but can be shut off by pulling the button back out.

Service Valve Location

The discharge (high pressure) service port is located on the discharge line muffler near the compressor. The suction (low pressure) service port is located on the compressor.

System Discharging

R-12 refrigerant is a chloroflourocarbon which, when mishandled, can contribute to the depletion on the ozone layer in the

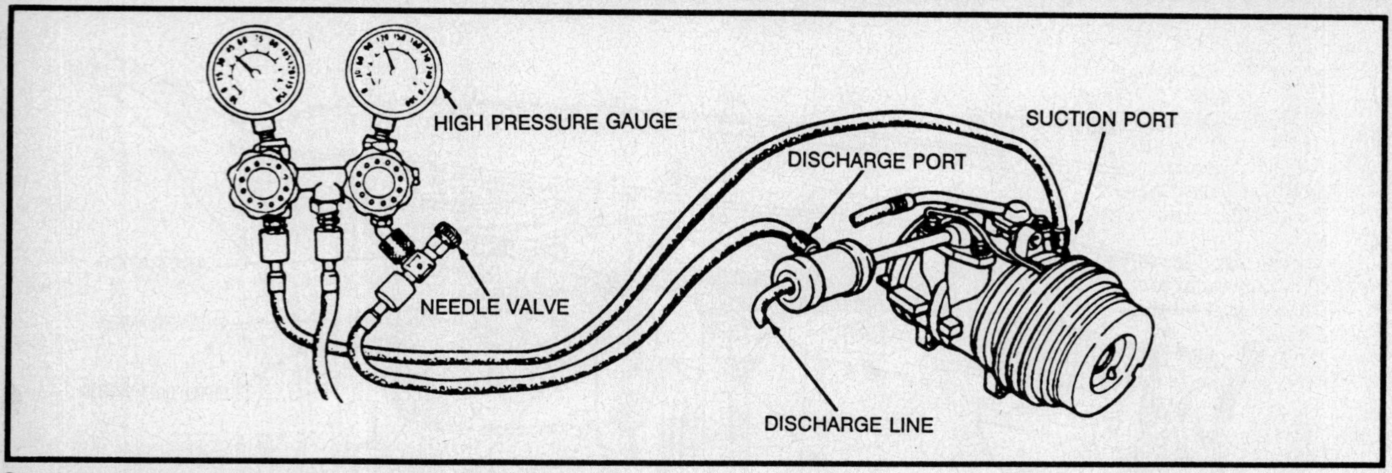
HIGH PRESSURE GAUGE
SUCTION PORT
DISCHARGE PORT
NEEDLE VALVE
DISCHARGE LINE

Service valves locations and manifold gauge setup

upper atmosphere. Ozone filters out harmful radiation from the sun. In order to protect the ozone layer, an approved R-12 Recovery/Recycling machine that meets SAE standard J1991 should be employed when discharging the system. Follow the operating instructions provided with the approved equipment exactly to properly discharge the system.

System Evacuating

If the air conditioning system has been opened to the atmosphere, it should be air and moisture free before being recharged with refrigerant. Moisture and air mixed with refrigerant will raise the compressor head pressure, possibly damage the system's components and will reduce the performance of the system. Moisture will boil at normal room temperature when exposed to a vacuum. To evacuate, or rid the system of air and moisture:

1. Leak test the system and repair any leaks found.
2. Connect an approved charging station, Recovery/Recycling machine or manifold gauge set and vacuum pump to the discharge and suction ports. The red hose is normally connected to the discharge (high pressure) line, and the blue hose is connected to the suction (low pressure) line.
3. Open the discharge and suction ports and start the vacuum pump. If the pump is not able to pull at least 26 in. Hg vacuum, there is a leak that must be repaired before evacuation can occur.
4. Once the system has reached at least 26 in. Hg vacuum, allow the system to evacuate for at least 10 minutes. The longer the system is evacuated, the more contaminants will be removed.
5. Close all valves and turn the pump off. If the system loses more than 2 in. Hg vacuum after 15 minutes, there is a leak that should be repaired.

System Charging

1. Connect an approved charging station, Recovery/Recycling machine or manifold gauge set to the discharge and suction ports. The red hose is normally connected to the discharge (high pressure) line, and the blue hose is connected to the suction (low pressure) line.
2. Follow the instructions provided with the equipment and charge the system with the specified amount of refrigerant.
3. Perform a leak test.

SYSTEM COMPONENTS

Radiator

REMOVAL AND INSTALLATION

1. Disconnect the negative battery cable.
2. Place the heater temperature selector to its hottest position and drain the coolant.
3. Remove the upper hose and coolant reserve tank hose from the radiator.
3. Remove the transmission oil cooler lines from the radiator.
4. Remove the lower hose clamp and hose from the radiator.
5. Remove the shroud mounting screws and position the shroud over the fan to provide maximum clearance.
6. Loosen the retaining screws at the bottom of the radiator and remove the screws at the top.
7. Lift the radiator from the engine compartment and remove from the vehicle.
8. The installation is the reverse order of the removal procedure.
9. Fill the system with coolant.
10. Connect the negative battery cable, run the vehicle until the thermostat opens, fill the radiator completely and check the automatic transmission fluid level.
11. Once the vehicle has cooled, recheck the coolant level.

CONDENSER

REMOVAL AND INSTALLATION

1. Disconnect the negative battery cable.
2. Properly discharge the air conditioning system.
3. Matchmark and remove the hood latch support assembly.
4. Remove the refrigerant line attaching nut and separate the lines from the sealing plate. Discard the gasket.

5. Cover the exposed ends of the lines to minimize contamination.
6. Remove the 2 bolts and 2 nuts securing the condenser to the radiator support yoke and remove the condenser from the vehicle.

To install:

7. Position the condenser and install the nuts and bolts.
8. Coat the new gasket with wax-free refrigerant oil and install. Connect the lines to the condenser sealing plate and tighten the nut.
9. Install the hood latch support assembly and adjust.
10. Evacuate and recharge the air conditioning system. Add 1 oz. of refrigerant oil during the recharge. Check for leaks.

Compressor

REMOVAL AND INSTALLATION

1. Disconnect the negative battery cable.
2. Properly discharge the air conditioning system.
3. Loosen the alternator adjusting bolt and remove the compressor drive belts. Disconnect the compressor lead.
4. Remove the refrigerant lines from the compressor and discard the gaskets. Cover the exposed ends of the lines and compressor to minimize contamination.
5. Remove the compressor mounting nuts and bolts.
6. Lift the compressor off the engine and remove from the vehicle.

To install:

7. Install the compressor and tighten all mounting nuts and bolts.
8. Coat the new gaskets with wax-free refrigerant oil and install. Connect the refrigerant lines to the compressor and tighten the bolts.
9. Install the drive belts and adjust to specification. Connect the electrical lead.
10. Evacuate and recharge the air conditioning system. Check for leaks.

Receiver/Drier

REMOVAL AND INSTALLATION

1. Disconnect the negative battery cable.
2. Properly discharge the air conditioning system.
3. Remove the nuts that fasten the refrigerant lines to sides of the receiver/drier assembly.
4. Remove the refrigerant lines from the receiver/drier and discard the gaskets. Cover the exposed ends of the lines to minimize contamination.
5. Remove the mounting strap bolts and remove the receiver/drier from the engine compartment.

To install:

6. Transfer the mounting strap to the new receiver/drier.
7. Coat the new gaskets with wax-free refrigerant oil and install. Connect the refrigerant lines to the receiver/drier and tighten the nuts.
8. Evacuate and recharge the air conditioning system. Add 1 oz. of refrigerant oil during the recharge. Check for leaks.

Expansion Valve (H-Valve)

TESTING

1. Connect a manifold gauge set or charging station to the air conditioning system. Verify adequate refrigerant level.
2. Disconnect and plug the water valve vacuum hose.
3. Disconnect the low pressure cut off switch connector and jump the wires inside the boot.
4. Close all doors, windows and vents to the passenger compartment.
5. Set the air conditioning controls to **MAX A/C**, full heat and high blower speed. If equipped with SATC, unplug the in-car sensor connector to lock the blend air door actuator in the full heat position.
6. Start the engine and hold the idle speed at 1000 rpm. After the engine has reached normal operating temperature, allow the passenger compartment to heat up to create the need for maximum refrigerant flow into the evaporator.
7. The discharge (high pressure) gauge should read 140–240 psi and suction (low pressure) gauge should read 20–30 psi, providing the refrigerant charge is sufficient.
8. If the suction side is within specifications, freeze the expansion valve control head using a very cold substance (liquid CO_2 or dry ice) for 30 seconds. The suction side pressure should drop to 15 in. Hg of vacuum. If not, replace the expansion valve.
9. Allow the expansion valve to thaw. As it thaws, the pressures should stabilize to the values in Step 7. If not, replace the expansion valve.
10. Once the test is complete, put the vacuum lines back in their original locations, connect the in-car sensor if disconnected, and perform and overall performance test.

REMOVAL AND INSTALLATION

1. Disconnect the negative battery cable.
2. Properly discharge the air conditioning system.
3. Disconnect the low pressure cutoff switch.
4. Remove the attaching bolt at the center of the refrigerant plumbing sealing plate.
5. Pull the refrigerant lines assembly away from the expansion valve. Cover the exposed ends of the lines to minimize contamination.
6. Remove the 2 Torx® screws that mount the expansion valve to the evaporator sealing plate.
7. Remove the valve and discard the gaskets.

To install:

8. Transfer the low pressure cutoff switch to the new valve, if necessary.
9. Coat the new "figure-8" gasket with wax-free refrigerant oil and install to the evaporator sealing plate.
10. Install the expansion valve and torque the Torx® screws to 100 inch lbs.

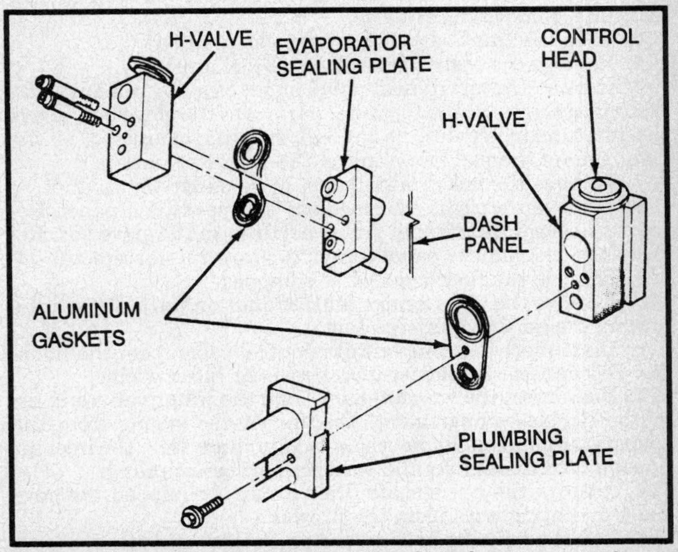
H-VALVE
EVAPORATOR SEALING PLATE
CONTROL HEAD
H-VALVE
DASH PANEL
ALUMINUM GASKETS
PLUMBING SEALING PLATE

Expansion valve (H-valve) and related components

11. Lubricate the remaining gasket and install with the refrigerant plumbing to the expansion valve. Torque the attaching bolt to 200 inch lbs.
12. Connect the low pressure cut off switch connector.
13. Evacuate and recharge the air conditioning system. Check for leaks.

Blower Motor

REMOVAL AND INSTALLATION

1. Disconnect the negative battery cable.
2. Disconnect the blower connector under the passenger's side of the instrument panel.
3. Remove the 5 screws that attach the blower to the air conditioning-heater housing.
4. Lower the blower assembly downward until it clears the lower portion of the instrument panel and remove from the vehicle.
5. The installation is the reverse of the removal procedure.
6. Connect the negative battery cable and check the blower for proper operation.

Blower Motor Resistor

REMOVAL AND INSTALLATION

1. Disconnect the negative battery cable.
2. Disconnect the resistor harness behind the glove box.
3. Working from behind the instrument panel, remove the 2 resistor mounting screws.
4. Remove the resistor from the vehicle.
5. Reshape or repair the seal before installing.
6. Connect the negative battery cable and check the blower speeds.

Heater Core and Evaporator

REMOVAL AND INSTALLATION

1. Disconnect the negative battery cable.
2. Drain the coolant and properly discharge the air conditioning system, if equipped.
3. Remove the air cleaner and disconnect the heater hoses. Plug the core tubes to prevent spillage. If equipped with air conditioning, remove the H-valve.
4. Slide the front seat to its rearmost position.
5. Remove the instrument cluster bezel assembly.
6. Remove the instrument panel upper cover by removing the mounting screws at the top inner surface of the glove box, above the instrument cluster, at the left end cap mounting, at the right side of the pad brow and in the defroster outlets.
7. Remove the instrument panel piece under the column.
8. Remove the right intermediate side cowl trim panel. Remove the lower instrument panel, partly with the glove box. Remove the instrument panel center to lower reinforcement.
9. Remove the floor console, if equipped.
10. Remove the right center air distribution duct. Detach the locking tab on the defroster duct.
11. Disconnect the temperature control cable from the housing. Disconnect the blower motor resistor block wiring.
12. Disconnect the vacuum lines from the water valve and tee in the engine compartment. Disconnect the wiring from the evaporator housing. Remove the vacuum lines from the inlet air housing and disconnect the vacuum harness coupling.
13. Remove the condensate drain tube, if equipped. Remove the 4 mounting nuts from the firewall.
14. Roll the housing back so the pipes clear and remove from the vehicle.
15. Remove the blend air door lever from the shaft. Remove the screws and lift off the top cover. Lift the heater core and/or evaporator out.

To install:

16. Remove the temperature control door from the housing and clean the unit out with solvent. Lubricate the lower pivot rod and its well and install. Wrap the heater core and/or evaporator with insulation and place in position. Secure with mounting screws.
17. Assemble the housing, making sure all cover screws were used.
18. Tip the housing up under instrument panel and press the mounting studs through the dash panel, making sure the defroster duct is properly seated on unit and gasket is installed properly. Connect the locking tab on the defroster duct.
19. While holding the housing in position, place the mounting bracket in position to the plenum stud and install the nut. Install the retaining nuts and tighten securely. Install the condensate drain tube.
20. Connect the electrical connectors to the resistor block and connect the control cable.
21. Connect the vacuum lines in the engine compartment, making sure the grommet is seated. Connect the vacuum lines to inlet air housing and vacuum harness coupling.
22. Install the right center air distribution duct.
23. Install the instrument panel center to the lower reinforcement.
24. Install the lower instrument panel, right intermediate side cowl trim panel and steering column cover.
25. Install instrument panel upper cover and cluster bezel assembly.
26. Connect the heater hoses to the heater core. Install the H-valve using new gaskets, if equipped.
27. Using the proper equipment, evacuate and recharge the air conditioning system. If the evaporator was replaced, add 2 oz. of refrigerant oil during the recharge.
28. Fill the cooling system.
29. Connect the negative battery cable and check the entire climate control system for proper operation and leakage.

Refrigerant Lines

REMOVAL AND INSTALLATION

1. Disconnect the negative battery cable.
2. Properly discharge the air conditioning system.
3. Remove the nuts or bolts that attach the refrigerant lines sealing plates to the adjoining components.
4. Remove the lines and discard the gaskets.

To install:

5. Coat the new gaskets with wax-free refrigerant oil and install. Connect the refrigerant lines to the adjoining components, and tighten the nuts or bolts.
6. Evacuate and recharge the air conditioning system. Check for leaks.

Manual or SATC Control Head

REMOVAL AND INSTALLATION

1. Disconnect the negative battery cable.
2. Remove the instrument panel center bezel in order to gain access to the control head.
3. Remove the screws that fasten the control head to the instrument panel.
4. Pull the unit out and unplug the electrical and vacuum connectors. Disconnect the temperature control cable, if equipped, by pushing the flag in and pulling the end from its seat.

5. Remove the control head from the instrument panel and disassemble as required.
6. The installation is the reverse of the removal procedure.
7. Connect the negative battery cable and check the entire climate control system for proper operation.

Manual Control Cable

ADJUSTMENT

The temperature control cable is self-adjusting. If the cable is not functioning properly, check for kinks and lubricate dry moving parts. The cable cannot be disassembled; replace if faulty.

REMOVAL AND INSTALLATION

1. Disconnect the negative battery cable.
2. Remove the dash bezel in order to gain access to the control head.
3. Remove the screws that fasten the control head to the instrument panel.
4. Pull the unit out and disconnect the temperature control cable by pushing the flag in and pulling the end from its seat.
5. The temperature control cable end is located at the top of the air conditioning-heater housing. Remove the instrument panel top cover and top right air distribution duct. Disconnect the cable end by pushing the flag in and pulling the end from its seat.
6. Disconnect the self-adjusting clip from the blend air or mode door crank.
7. Take note of the cable's routing and remove the from the vehicle. It is imperative that the cable is installed its original position or it will kink and make moving the temperature control lever very difficult.

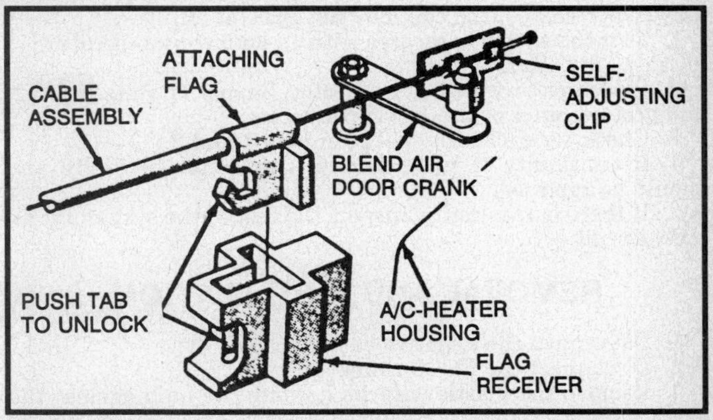
ATTACHING FLAG
CABLE ASSEMBLY
SELF-ADJUSTING CLIP
BLEND AIR DOOR CRANK
PUSH TAB TO UNLOCK
A/C-HEATER HOUSING
FLAG RECEIVER

Conventional temperature control cable attachment flag and door crank

To install:

8. Install the cable by routing it in exactly the same position as it was prior to removal.
9. Connect the self-adjusting clip to the door crank and click the flag into the seat.
10. Connect the upper end of the cable to the control head.
11. Place the temperature lever on the COOL side of its travel. Allowing the self-adjusting clip to slide on the cable, rotate the blend air door conterclockwise by hand until it stops.
12. Cycle the lever back and forth a few times to make sure the cable moves freely.
13. Connect the negative battery cable and check the entire climate control system for proper operation.

SENSORS AND SWITCHES

Electronic Cycling Clutch Switch

OPERATION

The Electronic Cycling Clutch Switch (ECCS) is located on the refrigerant plumbing near the H-valve. The ECCS prevents evaporator freeze-up by cycling the compressor clutch coil by monitoring the temperature of the suction line. The ECCS uses a thermistor probe in a capillary tube, inserted into a well on the suction line. The well must be filled with special conductive grease to prevent corrosion and allow thermal transfer to the probe. The switch is a sealed unit that should be replaced if found to be defective.

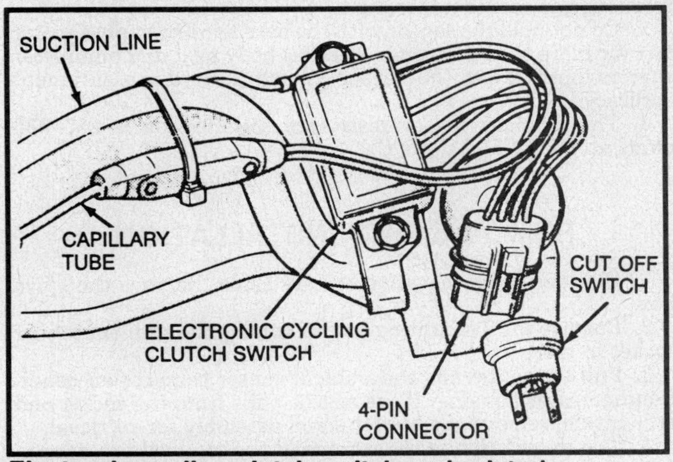
SUCTION LINE
CAPILLARY TUBE
ELECTRONIC CYCLING CLUTCH SWITCH
CUT OFF SWITCH
4-PIN CONNECTOR

Electronic cycling clutch switch and related components

TESTING

The compressor clutch coil should cycle 2–3 times per minute at ambient temperatures of 68–90°F (20–32°C). At temperatures

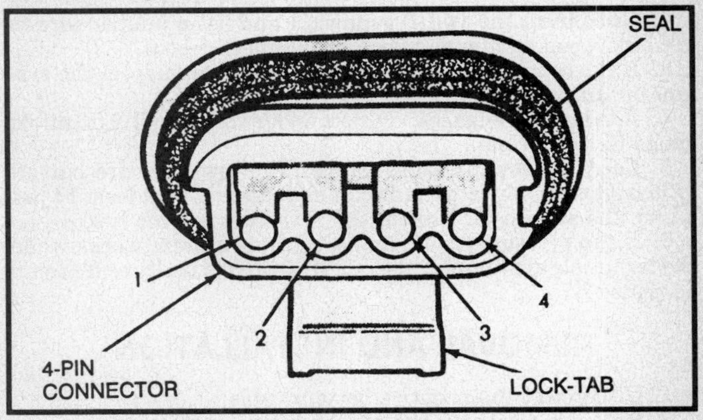
SEAL
1
2
3
4
4-PIN CONNECTOR
LOCK-TAB

Electronic cycling clutch switch connector terminals

above 90°F (32°C), the coil may not cycle at all.

1. Test the switch in an area with an ambient temperature of at least 70°F (21°C).
2. Disconnect the switch connector. Supply 12 volts to pin 2, and ground pin 4 of the ECCS connector.
3. Check for continuity between pins 1 and 3.
4. If continuity is not detected, the switch is faulty and should be replaced.
5. If there is continuity, inspect the rest of the system for an open circuit.

REMOVAL AND INSTALLATION

1. Disconnect the negative battery cable.
2. Disconnect the ECCS connector.
3. Remove the plastic wire tie holding the bulb against the suction line.
4. Remove the mounting screw on the refrigerant line manifold plate at the H-valve.
5. Separate the switch from the refrigerant manifold and pull the capillary tube from the capillary tube well on the suction line.

NOTE: The capillary tube well is filled with special temperature conductive grease. If reusing the switch, try to save all the grease. If replacing the switch, new grease will be supplied in the replacement switch package.

To install:

6. Fill the well with the special grease and insert the capillary tube.
7. Mount the switch to the refrigerant manifold.
8. Tie the bulb with a new wire tie.
9. Connect the ECCS connector.
10. Connect the negative battery cable and check the entire climate control system for proper operation.

Low Pressure Cut Off Switch

OPERATION

The low pressure cut off switch monitors the refrigerant gas pressure on the suction side of the system. The switch turns off voltage to the compressor clutch coil when the monitored pressure drops to levels that could damage the compressor. The switches are sealed units that must be replaced if faulty.

TESTING

1. Start the engine and allow to idle. Turn the air conditioner ON.
2. Disconnect the switch connector and use a jumper wire to jump between terminals inside the connector boot.
3. If the compressor clutch does not engage, inspect the system for an open circuit.
4. If the clutch engages, connect an air conditioning manifold gauge to the system.
5. Read the low pressure gauge. The low pressure cut off switch should complete the circuit at pressures of at least 14 psi. Check the system for leaks if the pressures are too low.
6. If the pressures are nominal and the system works when the terminals are jumped, the cut off switch is faulty and should be replaced.

REMOVAL AND INSTALLATION

1. Disconnect the negative battery cable.
2. Properly discharge the air conditioning system.
3. Unplug the boot connector from the switch.

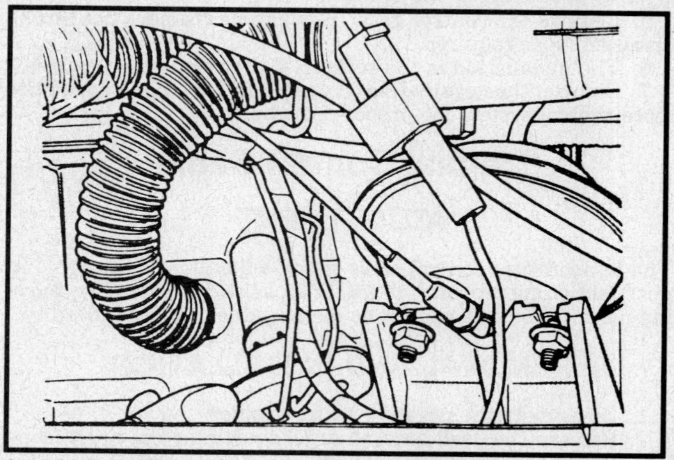

Ambient sensor and related components

4. Using an oil pressure sending unit socket, remove the switch from the H-valve.

To install:

5. Seal the threads of the new switch with teflon tape.
6. Install the switch to the H-valve and connect the boot connector.
7. Evacuate and recharge the system. Check for leaks.
8. Check the switch for proper operation.

Ambient Sensor

OPERATION

The ambient sensor is located inside the rear surface of the evaporator heater assembly. Outside air is drawn into the ventilation system plenum and blown across the ambient sensor. The sensor's electrical resistance increases with a decrease in ambient air temperature and visa versa, a reaction which allows the system to detect the outside air temperature.

TESTING

1. Pull the ambient sensor from the socket and measure its resistance at room temperature.
2. Do not hold the sensor with the bare hand or apply a meter test for more than 5 seconds, because body heat and ohmmeter current both affect the sensor resistance and measurement accuracy.
3. The ambient sensor resistance specification is 255–335 ohms at 70°–80°F (21°–27°C).

REMOVAL AND INSTALLATION

1. Disconnect the negative battery cable. Remove the glove box.
2. Remove the 2 mounting screws holding the ambient sensor socket in place.
3. Pull the socket and the ambient sensor from the air conditioning-heater housing. If the sensor pulls from the socket and falls inside, remove the blower scroll assembly for retrieval.
4. The installation is the reverse of the removal procedure.
5. Connect the negative battery cable and check the entire climate control system for proper operation.

ASPIRATOR SYSTEM DIAGNOSIS

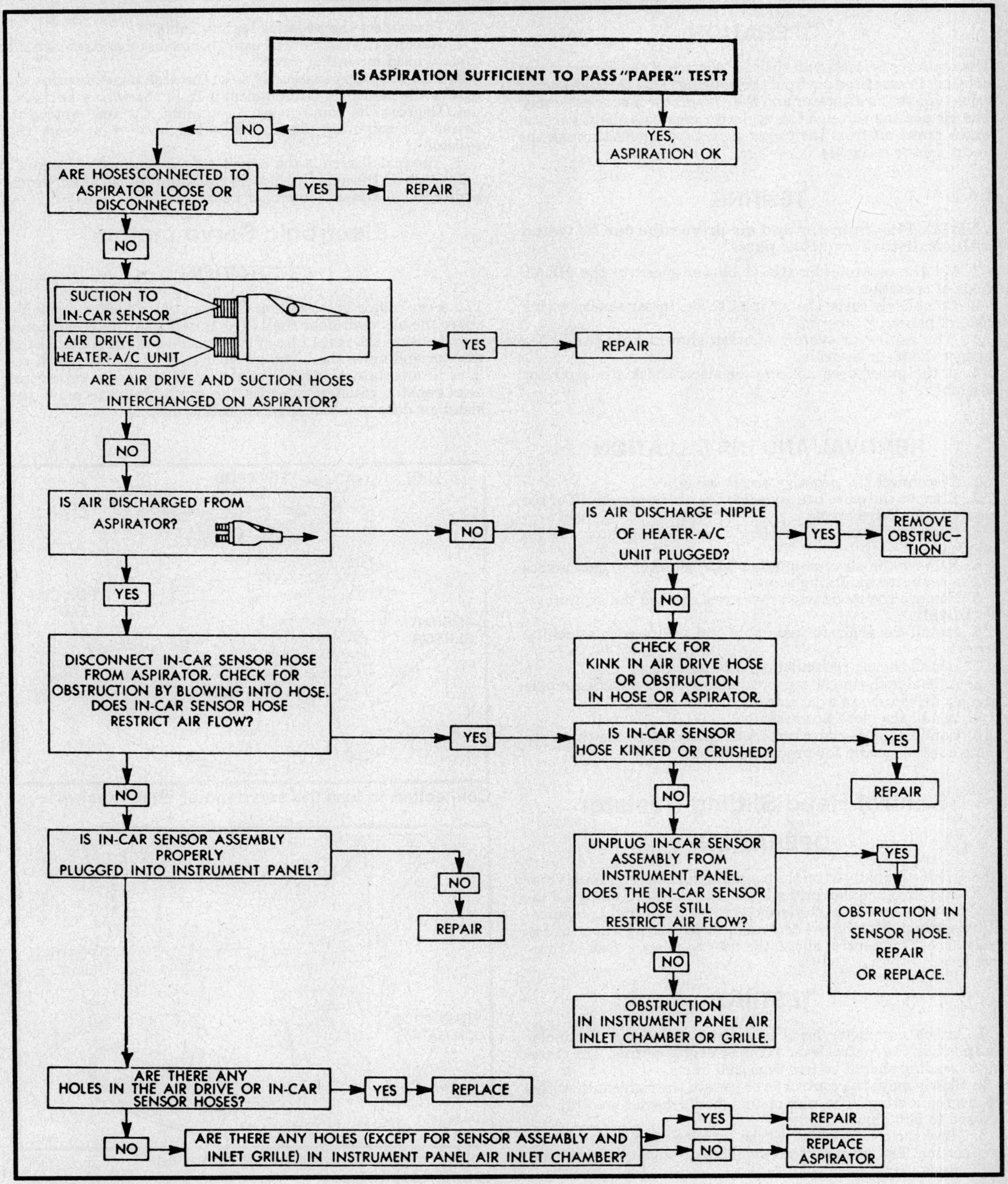
IS ASPIRATION SUFFICIENT TO PASS "PAPER" TEST?
NO
YES, ASPIRATION OK
ARE HOSES CONNECTED TO ASPIRATOR LOOSE OR DISCONNECTED?
YES
REPAIR
NO
SUCTION TO IN-CAR SENSOR
AIR DRIVE TO HEATER-A/C UNIT
ARE AIR DRIVE AND SUCTION HOSES INTERCHANGED ON ASPIRATOR?
YES
REPAIR
NO
IS AIR DISCHARGED FROM ASPIRATOR?
NO
IS AIR DISCHARGE NIPPLE OF HEATER-A/C UNIT PLUGGED?
YES
REMOVE OBSTRUCTION
NO
CHECK FOR KINK IN AIR DRIVE HOSE OR OBSTRUCTION IN HOSE OR ASPIRATOR.
YES
DISCONNECT IN-CAR SENSOR HOSE FROM ASPIRATOR. CHECK FOR OBSTRUCTION BY BLOWING INTO HOSE. DOES IN-CAR SENSOR HOSE RESTRICT AIR FLOW?
YES
IS IN-CAR SENSOR HOSE KINKED OR CRUSHED?
YES
REPAIR
NO
UNPLUG IN-CAR SENSOR ASSEMBLY FROM INSTRUMENT PANEL. DOES THE IN-CAR SENSOR HOSE STILL RESTRICT AIR FLOW?
YES
OBSTRUCTION IN SENSOR HOSE. REPAIR OR REPLACE.
NO
OBSTRUCTION IN INSTRUMENT PANEL AIR INLET CHAMBER OR GRILLE.
NO
IS IN-CAR SENSOR ASSEMBLY PROPERLY PLUGGED INTO INSTRUMENT PANEL?
NO
REPAIR
ARE THERE ANY HOLES IN THE AIR DRIVE OR IN-CAR SENSOR HOSES?
YES
REPLACE
NO
ARE THERE ANY HOLES (EXCEPT FOR SENSOR ASSEMBLY AND INLET GRILLE) IN INSTRUMENT PANEL AIR INLET CHAMBER?
YES
REPAIR
NO
REPLACE ASPIRATOR

Aspirator Assembly

OPERATION

The aspirator is located on the rear surface of the blower motor housing. Pressurized air from the housing is fed through the air drive tube to the aspirator and the evaporator heater assembly. The air passing through the aspirator creates a slight vacuum which draws air from the passenger compartment through the in-car sensor assembly.

TESTING

NOTE: The aspirator and air drive tube can be tested without disturbing other parts.

1. Set the controls for **HIGH** blower speed in the **HEAT** mode of operation.
2. Completely cover the air inlet to the in-car sensor with a piece of paper.
3. The aspirator system suction should hold the paper against the air inlet grille.
4. If the paper does not stay in place, check the aspirator assembly.

REMOVAL AND INSTALLATION

1. Disconnect the negative batery cable.
2. Remove the glove box and slide the air drive tube off of the aspirator air drive nipple.
3. Slide the in-car sensor tube off of the aspirator suction nipple.
4. Remove the air recirculation door actuator to gain access to the aspirator mounting screws.
5. Remove the mounting screws and remove the aspirator.

To install:

6. Install the aspirator assembly and secure with attaching screws.
7. Install the air recirculation door actuator.
8. Assemble the in-car sensor tube to aspirator suction nipple and air drive tube to aspirator air drive nipple.
9. Install the glove box assembly.
10. Connect the negative battery cable and check the entire climate control system for proper operation.

Control Head Sliding Resistor

OPERATION

The resistor is mounted on the control head assembly and is mechanically linked to the control lever. The resistor's electrical resistance increases when the lever is moved to the higher temperature settings. Moving the control lever to the left will decrease resistance. This control allows the user to select a desired comfort level.

TESTING

1. Attach ohmmeter leads to resistor connector terminals, and position the control lever at the 65 degree setting. The resistance reading should be less than 390 ohms.
2. Slowly move the control lever toward the right until at the 75 degree setting. The ohmmeter should have smoothly increased to 930 ohms.
3. Move the comfort lever to the extreme right at the 85 degree setting. The resistance should increase smoothly to at least 1500 ohms.

REMOVAL AND INSTALLATION

1. Disconnect the negative battery cable.
2. Remove the instrument panel center bezel and remove the control head mounting screws.
3. Pull the control assembly from the dash panel towards the rear of the vehicle and disconnect it from the wiring harness.
4. Depress the comfort lever retaining clip and remove it. Lower the retaining pin and slide the lever away from the resistor.
5. The installation is the reverse of the removal procedure.
6. Connect the negative battery cable and check the entire climate control system for proper operation.

Electronic Servo motor

OPERATION

The servo motor is located on the evaporator heater assembly above the blend air door shaft. The function of the servo motor is to measure the resistance of the sensors and the control head resistor and move the blend air door to the position which relates to a certain electrical resistance. High sensor or control head resistor resistances cause the servo motor to move the blend air door to a higher position (more heat).

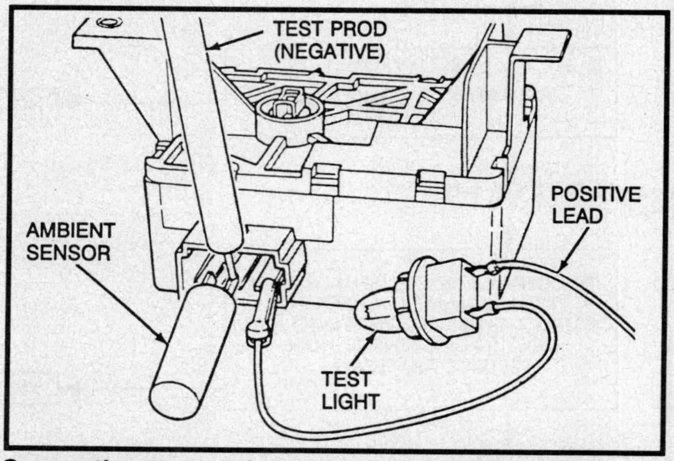
TEST PROD
(NEGATIVE)
POSITIVE
LEAD
AMBIENT
SENSOR
TEST
LIGHT

Connection to turn the servo motor shaft clockwise

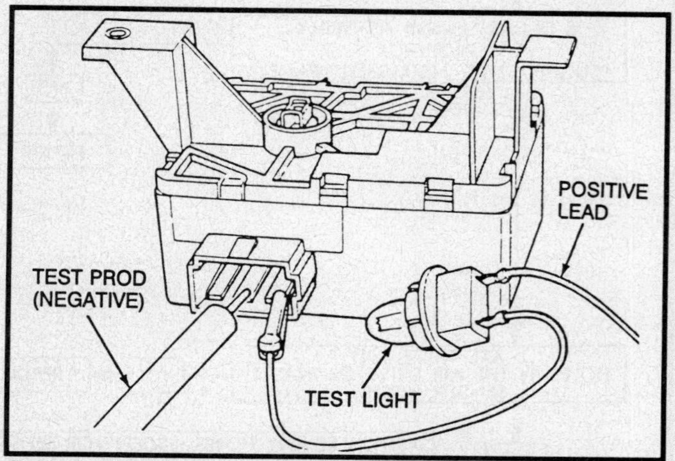
POSITIVE
LEAD
TEST PROD
(NEGATIVE)
TEST LIGHT

Connection to turn the servo motor shaft counterclockwise

TESTING

1. Remove the servo motor. Using a blend air door operating crank from a manual air conditioning-heater unit, check the door for free movement.
2. Connect the instrument panel lamp assembly in series with the motor (to show current flow), using a 12 volt battery for power.
3. Check for proper servo motor operation in both clockwise and conterclockwise directions.
4. With the test leads connected, the motor should run smoothly as it approach the internal stop. The test lamp will glow dimly as the shaft turns and should brighten when the internal stops of the motor are reached.

NOTE: The test lamp will also glow brightly if the motor jams between stops.

5. If the motor shaft does not turn, check the battery connections and make sure all connections are secure.
6. Check the ambient sensor if the motor only moves to the counterclockwise position. The motor must move to the full clockwise position and full counterclockwise position to be acceptable.

REMOVAL AND INSTALLATION

1. Disconnect the negative battery cable.
2. Remove the right side air distribution duct and remove the sound pad.
3. Disconnect the wiring harness connector from the servo motor and remove the mounting screws.
4. Rotate the servo motor until the forward tab on the motor housing clears the retaining clip on the air conditioning-heater unit cover.
5. Lift the servo motor off of the blend air door shaft and remove it from the vehicle.

To install:

6. Properly position the motor shaft by checking the alignment of the shaft flats. When using a straight-edge held against the shaft flat side, the straight-edge should lie within the molded sector lines so the motor can be installed. It may be necessary to move the motor shaft to the proper position using the procedure described in the servo motor test section.
7. When installing the servo motor, align the key on the end of the blend air door shaft with the slot in the motor shaft.
8. Gently press down on the servo motor until both motor housing legs touch the air conditioning-heater unit cover. The 2 shafts should engage without excessive force.

NOTE: If there is a need for excessive force to install the servo motor, check the length of the blend air door shaft. The shaft should extend less than 1 in. above the air conditioning-heater unit. Repair the shaft if necessary. Excessive force can damage the servo motor.

9. After the blend air and the servo motor shafts are engaged, rotate the motor until the tab fits under the retaining clip and the mounting screw holes align.
10. Install the attaching screws and connect the wiring harness.
11. Install the sound pad.
12. Connect the negative battery cable and check the entire climate control system for proper operation.
13. Install the air distribution duct.

In-car Sensor

OPERATION

The in-car sensor assembly is connected to the aspirator suction nipple and the instrument panel. Air from the passenger compartment is drawn through the instrument panel opening past a temperature sensing thermistor located in the sensor assembly. The electrical resistance of the thermistor increases when in car air temperature decreases. The electrical resistance decreases when the in-car temperature increases, enabling the system to detect temperature changes within the passenger compartment.

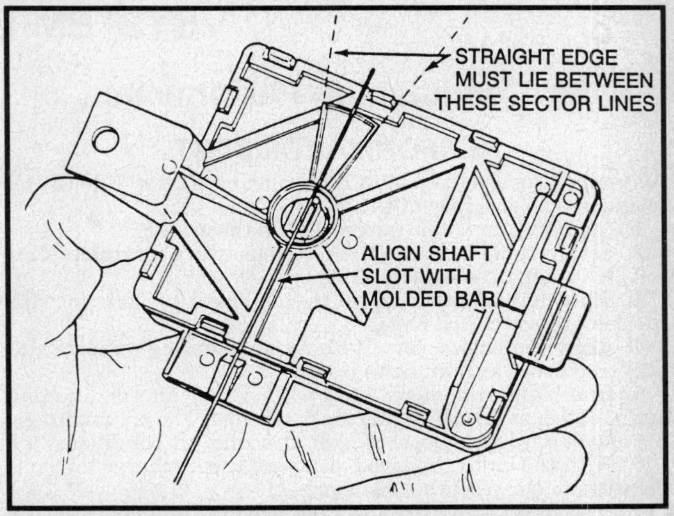
STRAIGHT EDGE MUST LIE BETWEEN THESE SECTOR LINES
ALIGN SHAFT SLOT WITH MOLDED BAR
Aligning the servo motor shaft for installation

TESTING

1. Remove the glove box and disconnect the in-car sensor wiring connector from the harness connector. Be sure not to disconnect the aspirator tubes or remove the sensor from the instrument panel.
2. Perform the aspirator paper test as performed in the aspirator sensor test.
3. Place the entire stem of a test thermometer into the air inlet grille near the in-car sensor.
4. Set the blower motor speed on the second notch, depress and then pull out the **MAX A/C** button to turn off the compressor and close the water valve.
5. Operate the blower and connect the ohmmeter leads to the sensor wiring terminals, and quickly measure the in-car sensor resistance.

NOTE: Do not leave the ohmmeter connected for more than 5 seconds, because the ohmmeter current can affect resistance and measurement accuracy.

6. The resistance specification of the in-car sensor is 1100–1800 ohms when the at 70°–80°F (21°–27°C).

REMOVAL AND INSTALLATION

1. Disconnect the negative battery cable.
2. Remove the glove box and disconnect the in-car sensor assembly from instrument panel by pulling and slowly rotating the sensor assembly plastic housing to unsnap it from the panel.

NOTE: Do not pull on the tube to remove the sensor.

3. Disconnect the in-car sensor assembly from the aspirator tube.
4. Separate the sensor wiring connector from the harness connector and remove the sensor.
5. The installation is the reverse of the removal procedure.
6. Connect the negative battery cable and check the entire climate control system for proper operation.

SYSTEM DIAGNOSIS

Air Conditioning Performance

PERFORMANCE TEST

Air temperature in the testing area must be at least 70°F (21°C) to ensure the accuracy of this test.

1. Connect a manifold gauge set the the system.
2. Set the controls to **MAX A/C**, temperature control level on full **COOL** and the blower on its highest setting.
3. Start the engine and adjust the idle speed to 1000 rpm with the compressor clutch engaged.
4. Allow the engine come to normal operating temperature and keep doors and windows closed.
5. Insert a thermometer in the left center air conditioning outlet and operate the engine for 5 minutes. The air conditioning clutch may cycle depending on the ambient conditions.
6. With the clutch engaged, compare the discharge air temperature to the performance chart.
7. Disconnect and plug the gray vacuum line going to the heater water control valve. Observe the valve arm for movement as the line is disconnected. If there is no movement, check the valve for sticking.
8. Operate the air conditioning for 2 additional minutes and observe the discharge air temperature again. If the discharge air temperature increased by more than 5°F, check the blend air door for proper operation. If not, compare the the temperature, suction and discharge pressures to the chart. Reconnect the gary vacuum line.
9. If the values do not meet specifications, check system components for proper operation.

Vacuum Actuating System

INSPECTION

Check the system for proper operation. Air should come from the appropriate vents when the corresponding mode is selected under all driving conditions. If a problem is detected use the flow-charts to check the flow of vacuum.

1. Check the engine for sufficient vacuum and the main suplier hose at the brake booster for leaks or kinks.
2. Check the check valve under the instrument panel for proper operation. It should not hold vacuum when vacuum is applied from the engine side, but should when appied from the system side.
3. Check all interior vacuum lines, especially the 7-way connection behind the instrument panel for leaks or kinks.
4. Check the control head for leaky ports or damaged parts.
5. Check all actuators for ability to hold vacuum.

Air Conditioning Compressor

COMPRESSOR NOISE

Noises that develop during air conditioning operation can be misleading. A noise that sounds like serious compressor damage may only be a loose belt, mounting bolt or clutch assembly. Improper belt tension can also emit a noise that can be mistaken for more serious problems. Check and adjust all possible causes of the noise before replacing the compressor.

COMPRESSOR CLUTCH INOPERATIVE

If the compressor clutch does not engage, check fuses and fusible links and continue on to the diagnostic charts if the basics check out.

1. Verify refrigerant charge, and charge as required.
2. Check for battery voltage at the clutch coil connection. If voltage is detected, check the coil.
3. If battery voltage is not detected at the coil, check for voltage at the low pressure cut off switch and cycling switch. If voltage is not detected there either, check fuses etc. If the fuses, etc. are good, check the control head switches and related wiring in conjunction with the charts to determine the location of the problem.

CLUTCH COIL TESTING

1. Verify the battery state of charge; the indicator should be green.
2. Connect a 0–10 scale ammeter in series with the clutch coil terminal. Use a volt meter with clips to measure the voltage across the battery and clutch coil.
3. Turn the air conditioning on and switch the blower to LOW speed. Start the engine and run at normal idle.
4. The air conditioning clutch should engage immediately and the clutch voltage should be within 2 volts of battery voltage.
5. The clutch coil is considered good if the current draw is 2.0–3.7 amperes at 12 volts at the clutch coil. If the voltage is more than 12.5 volts, add loads by turning on accessories until the voltage drops below 12.5 volts.
6. If the coil current reads 0, the coil is open and should be replaced.
7. If the ammeter reading is 4 or more amps, then the coil is shorted and should be replaced.
8. If the coil voltage is not within 2 volts of battery voltage, test the clutch coil feed circuit for excessive voltage drop.

AIR CONDITIONING PERFORMANCE CHART

Ambient Temperature °F (°C)	Air Temperature at Center Panel Vent °F (°C)	Compressor Discharge Pressure PSI (kPa)	Evaporator Suction Pressure PSI (kPa)
70 (21)	35–46 (2–8)	140–210 (965–1448)	10–35 (69–241)
80 (27)	39–50 (4–10)	180–235 (1240–1620)	16–38 (110–262)
90 (32)	44–55 (7–13)	210–270 (1448–1860)	20–42 (138–290)
100 (38)	50–62 (10–17)	240–310 (1655–2137)	25–48 (172–331)
110 (43)	56–70 (13–21)	280–350 (1930–2413)	30–55 (207–379)

AIR CONDITIONING REFRIGERATION SYSTEM DIAGNOSIS

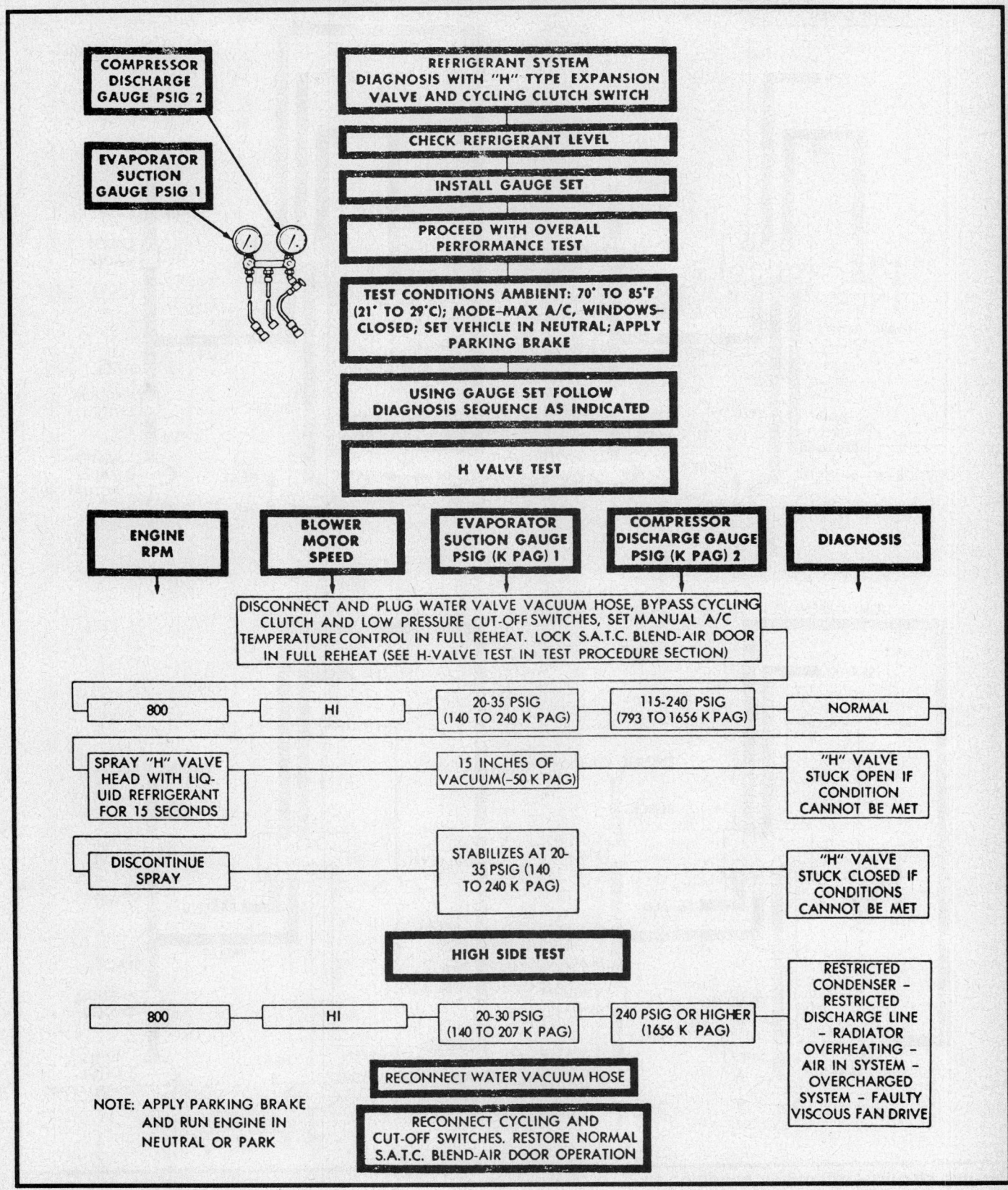

COMPRESSOR DISCHARGE GAUGE PSIG 2

EVAPORATOR SUCTION GAUGE PSIG 1

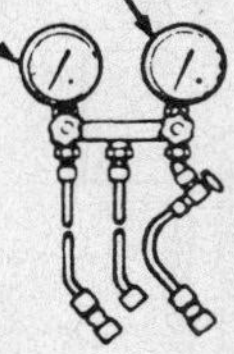

REFRIGERANT SYSTEM DIAGNOSIS WITH "H" TYPE EXPANSION VALVE AND CYCLING CLUTCH SWITCH

CHECK REFRIGERANT LEVEL

INSTALL GAUGE SET

PROCEED WITH OVERALL PERFORMANCE TEST

TEST CONDITIONS AMBIENT: 70° TO 85°F (21° TO 29°C); MODE–MAX A/C, WINDOWS–CLOSED; SET VEHICLE IN NEUTRAL; APPLY PARKING BRAKE

USING GAUGE SET FOLLOW DIAGNOSIS SEQUENCE AS INDICATED

H VALVE TEST

DISCONNECT AND PLUG WATER VALVE VACUUM HOSE, BYPASS CYCLING CLUTCH AND LOW PRESSURE CUT-OFF SWITCHES, SET MANUAL A/C TEMPERATURE CONTROL IN FULL REHEAT. LOCK S.A.T.C. BLEND-AIR DOOR IN FULL REHEAT (SEE H-VALVE TEST IN TEST PROCEDURE SECTION)

ENGINE RPM	BLOWER MOTOR SPEED	EVAPORATOR SUCTION GAUGE PSIG (K PAG) 1	COMPRESSOR DISCHARGE GAUGE PSIG (K PAG) 2	DIAGNOSIS
800	HI	20-35 PSIG (140 TO 240 K PAG)	115-240 PSIG (793 TO 1656 K PAG)	NORMAL
SPRAY "H" VALVE HEAD WITH LIQUID REFRIGERANT FOR 15 SECONDS		15 INCHES OF VACUUM(–50 K PAG)		"H" VALVE STUCK OPEN IF CONDITION CANNOT BE MET
DISCONTINUE SPRAY		STABILIZES AT 20-35 PSIG (140 TO 240 K PAG)		"H" VALVE STUCK CLOSED IF CONDITIONS CANNOT BE MET

HIGH SIDE TEST

ENGINE RPM	BLOWER MOTOR SPEED	EVAPORATOR SUCTION GAUGE PSIG (K PAG) 1	COMPRESSOR DISCHARGE GAUGE PSIG (K PAG) 2	DIAGNOSIS
800	HI	20-30 PSIG (140 TO 207 K PAG)	240 PSIG OR HIGHER (1656 K PAG)	RESTRICTED CONDENSER – RESTRICTED DISCHARGE LINE – RADIATOR OVERHEATING – AIR IN SYSTEM – OVERCHARGED SYSTEM – FAULTY VISCOUS FAN DRIVE

RECONNECT WATER VACUUM HOSE

RECONNECT CYCLING AND CUT-OFF SWITCHES. RESTORE NORMAL S.A.T.C. BLEND-AIR DOOR OPERATION

NOTE: APPLY PARKING BRAKE AND RUN ENGINE IN NEUTRAL OR PARK

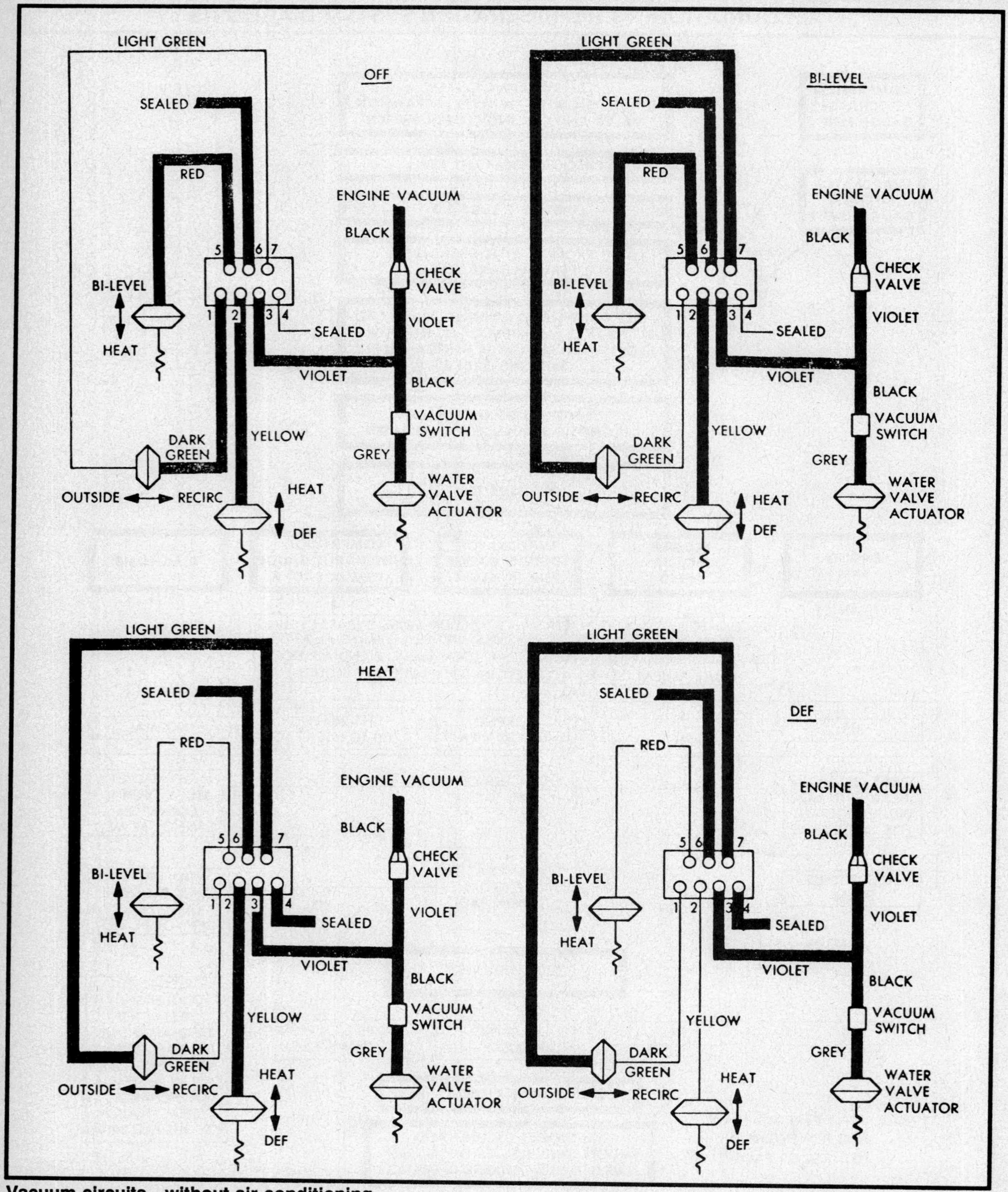
OFF
LIGHT GREEN
SEALED
RED
ENGINE VACUUM
BLACK
5 6 7
CHECK VALVE
BI-LEVEL
1 2 3 4
SEALED
VIOLET
HEAT
VIOLET
BLACK
VACUUM SWITCH
DARK GREEN
YELLOW
GREY
WATER VALVE ACTUATOR
OUTSIDE
RECIRC
HEAT
DEF
BI-LEVEL
LIGHT GREEN
SEALED
RED
ENGINE VACUUM
BLACK
CHECK VALVE
BI-LEVEL
SEALED
VIOLET
HEAT
VIOLET
BLACK
VACUUM SWITCH
DARK GREEN
YELLOW
GREY
WATER VALVE ACTUATOR
OUTSIDE
RECIRC
HEAT
DEF
HEAT
LIGHT GREEN
SEALED
RED
ENGINE VACUUM
BLACK
CHECK VALVE
BI-LEVEL
SEALED
VIOLET
HEAT
VIOLET
BLACK
YELLOW
VACUUM SWITCH
DARK GREEN
GREY
WATER VALVE ACTUATOR
OUTSIDE
RECIRC
HEAT
DEF
DEF
LIGHT GREEN
SEALED
RED
ENGINE VACUUM
BLACK
CHECK VALVE
BI-LEVEL
SEALED
VIOLET
HEAT
VIOLET
BLACK
YELLOW
VACUUM SWITCH
DARK GREEN
GREY
WATER VALVE ACTUATOR
OUTSIDE
RECIRC
HEAT
DEF

Vacuum circuits—without air conditioning

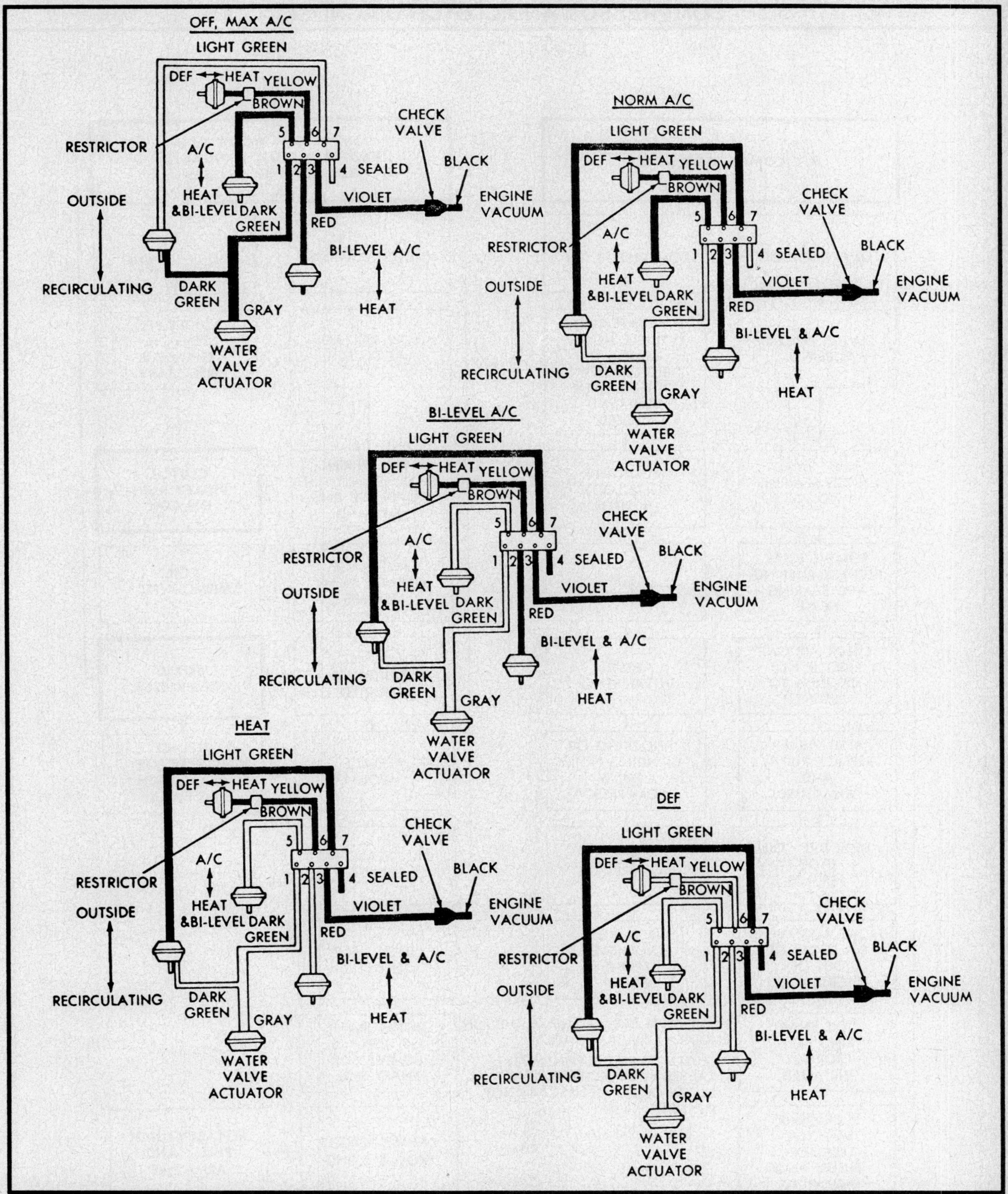
OFF, MAX A/C
LIGHT GREEN
DEF HEAT
YELLOW
BROWN
RESTRICTOR
A/C
HEAT &BI-LEVEL
DARK GREEN
5 6 7
1 2 3 4 SEALED
CHECK VALVE
BLACK
VIOLET
ENGINE VACUUM
RED
BI-LEVEL A/C
HEAT
OUTSIDE
RECIRCULATING
DARK GREEN
GRAY
WATER VALVE ACTUATOR
NORM A/C
LIGHT GREEN
DEF HEAT
YELLOW
BROWN
RESTRICTOR
A/C
HEAT &BI-LEVEL
DARK GREEN
5 6 7
1 2 3 4 SEALED
CHECK VALVE
BLACK
VIOLET
ENGINE VACUUM
RED
BI-LEVEL & A/C
HEAT
OUTSIDE
RECIRCULATING
DARK GREEN
GRAY
WATER VALVE ACTUATOR
BI-LEVEL A/C
LIGHT GREEN
DEF HEAT
YELLOW
BROWN
RESTRICTOR
A/C
HEAT &BI-LEVEL
DARK GREEN
5 6 7
1 2 3 4 SEALED
CHECK VALVE
BLACK
VIOLET
ENGINE VACUUM
RED
BI-LEVEL & A/C
HEAT
OUTSIDE
RECIRCULATING
DARK GREEN
GRAY
WATER VALVE ACTUATOR
HEAT
LIGHT GREEN
DEF HEAT
YELLOW
BROWN
RESTRICTOR
A/C
HEAT &BI-LEVEL
DARK GREEN
5 6 7
1 2 3 4 SEALED
CHECK VALVE
BLACK
VIOLET
ENGINE VACUUM
RED
BI-LEVEL & A/C
HEAT
OUTSIDE
RECIRCULATING
DARK GREEN
GRAY
WATER VALVE ACTUATOR
DEF
LIGHT GREEN
DEF HEAT
YELLOW
BROWN
RESTRICTOR
A/C
HEAT &BI-LEVEL
DARK GREEN
5 6 7
1 2 3 4 SEALED
CHECK VALVE
BLACK
VIOLET
ENGINE VACUUM
RED
BI-LEVEL & A/C
HEAT
OUTSIDE
RECIRCULATING
DARK GREEN
GRAY
WATER VALVE ACTUATOR

Vacuum circuits—with air conditioning

COMPRESSOR AND CLUTCH DIAGNOSIS

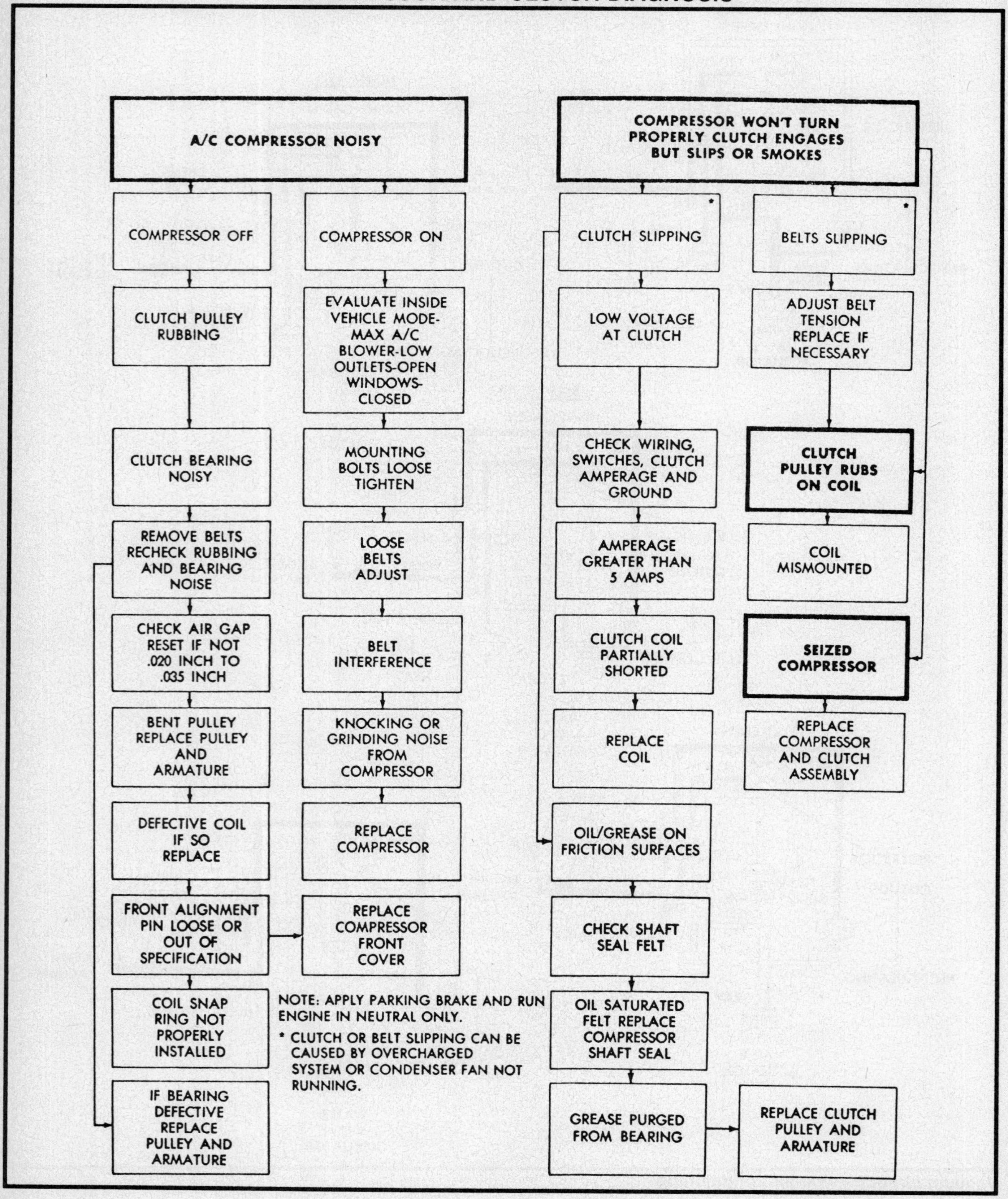
A/C COMPRESSOR NOISY
COMPRESSOR OFF
CLUTCH PULLEY RUBBING
CLUTCH BEARING NOISY
REMOVE BELTS RECHECK RUBBING AND BEARING NOISE
CHECK AIR GAP RESET IF NOT .020 INCH TO .035 INCH
BENT PULLEY REPLACE PULLEY AND ARMATURE
DEFECTIVE COIL IF SO REPLACE
FRONT ALIGNMENT PIN LOOSE OR OUT OF SPECIFICATION
COIL SNAP RING NOT PROPERLY INSTALLED
IF BEARING DEFECTIVE REPLACE PULLEY AND ARMATURE
COMPRESSOR ON
EVALUATE INSIDE VEHICLE MODE-MAX A/C BLOWER-LOW OUTLETS-OPEN WINDOWS-CLOSED
MOUNTING BOLTS LOOSE TIGHTEN
LOOSE BELTS ADJUST
BELT INTERFERENCE
KNOCKING OR GRINDING NOISE FROM COMPRESSOR
REPLACE COMPRESSOR
REPLACE COMPRESSOR FRONT COVER
NOTE: APPLY PARKING BRAKE AND RUN ENGINE IN NEUTRAL ONLY.
* CLUTCH OR BELT SLIPPING CAN BE CAUSED BY OVERCHARGED SYSTEM OR CONDENSER FAN NOT RUNNING.
COMPRESSOR WON'T TURN PROPERLY CLUTCH ENGAGES BUT SLIPS OR SMOKES
CLUTCH SLIPPING *
LOW VOLTAGE AT CLUTCH
CHECK WIRING, SWITCHES, CLUTCH AMPERAGE AND GROUND
AMPERAGE GREATER THAN 5 AMPS
CLUTCH COIL PARTIALLY SHORTED
REPLACE COIL
OIL/GREASE ON FRICTION SURFACES
CHECK SHAFT SEAL FELT
OIL SATURATED FELT REPLACE COMPRESSOR SHAFT SEAL
GREASE PURGED FROM BEARING
REPLACE CLUTCH PULLEY AND ARMATURE
BELTS SLIPPING *
ADJUST BELT TENSION REPLACE IF NECESSARY
CLUTCH PULLEY RUBS ON COIL
COIL MISMOUNTED
SEIZED COMPRESSOR
REPLACE COMPRESSOR AND CLUTCH ASSEMBLY

COMPRESSOR AND CLUTCH DIAGNOSIS

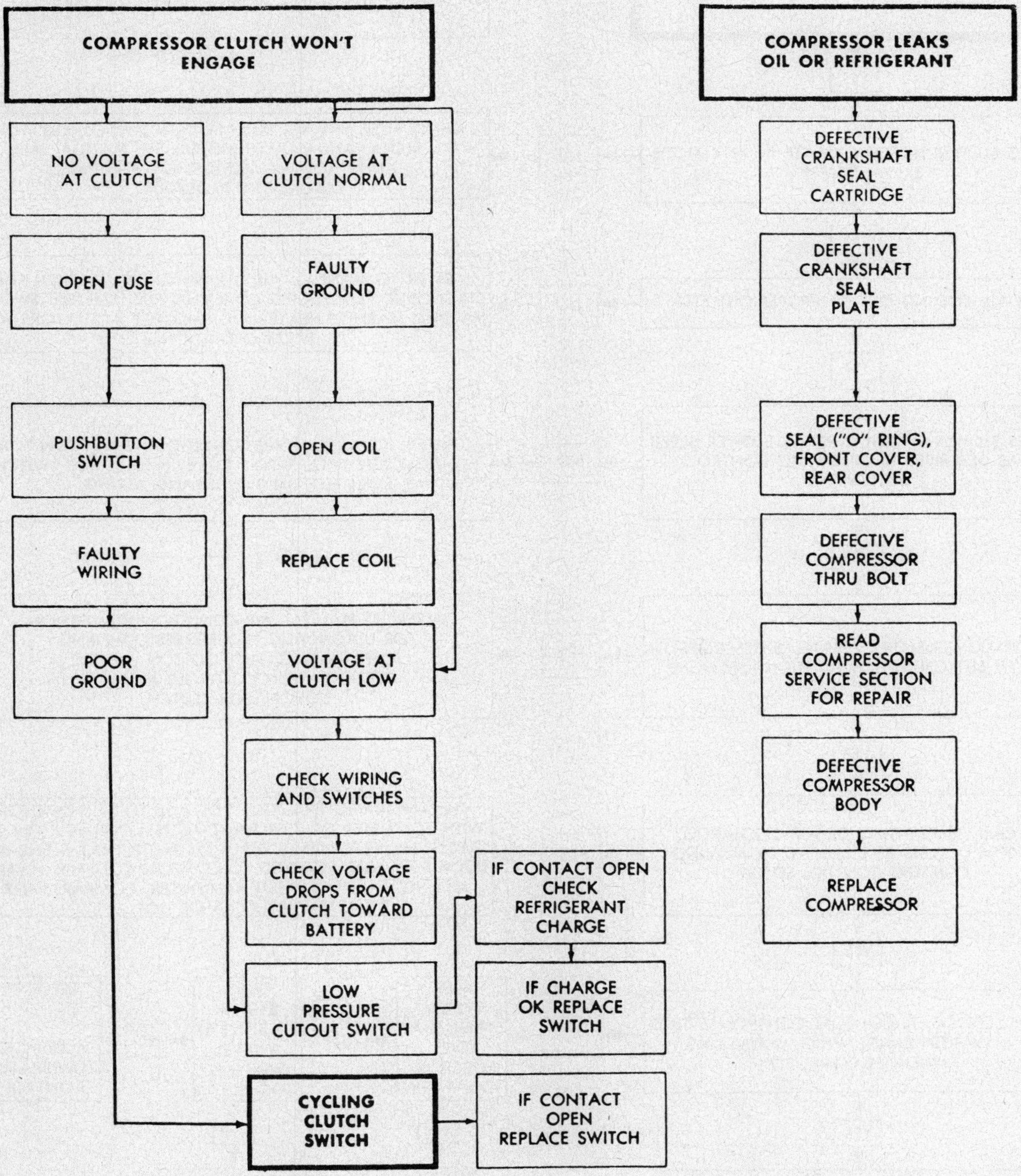
COMPRESSOR CLUTCH WON'T ENGAGE
NO VOLTAGE AT CLUTCH
VOLTAGE AT CLUTCH NORMAL
OPEN FUSE
FAULTY GROUND
PUSHBUTTON SWITCH
OPEN COIL
FAULTY WIRING
REPLACE COIL
POOR GROUND
VOLTAGE AT CLUTCH LOW
CHECK WIRING AND SWITCHES
CHECK VOLTAGE DROPS FROM CLUTCH TOWARD BATTERY
IF CONTACT OPEN CHECK REFRIGERANT CHARGE
LOW PRESSURE CUTOUT SWITCH
IF CHARGE OK REPLACE SWITCH
CYCLING CLUTCH SWITCH
IF CONTACT OPEN REPLACE SWITCH
COMPRESSOR LEAKS OIL OR REFRIGERANT
DEFECTIVE CRANKSHAFT SEAL CARTRIDGE
DEFECTIVE CRANKSHAFT SEAL PLATE
DEFECTIVE SEAL ("O" RING), FRONT COVER, REAR COVER
DEFECTIVE COMPRESSOR THRU BOLT
READ COMPRESSOR SERVICE SECTION FOR REPAIR
DEFECTIVE COMPRESSOR BODY
REPLACE COMPRESSOR

SATC SYSTEM DIAGNOSIS

SATC SYSTEM GENERAL DIAGNOSIS

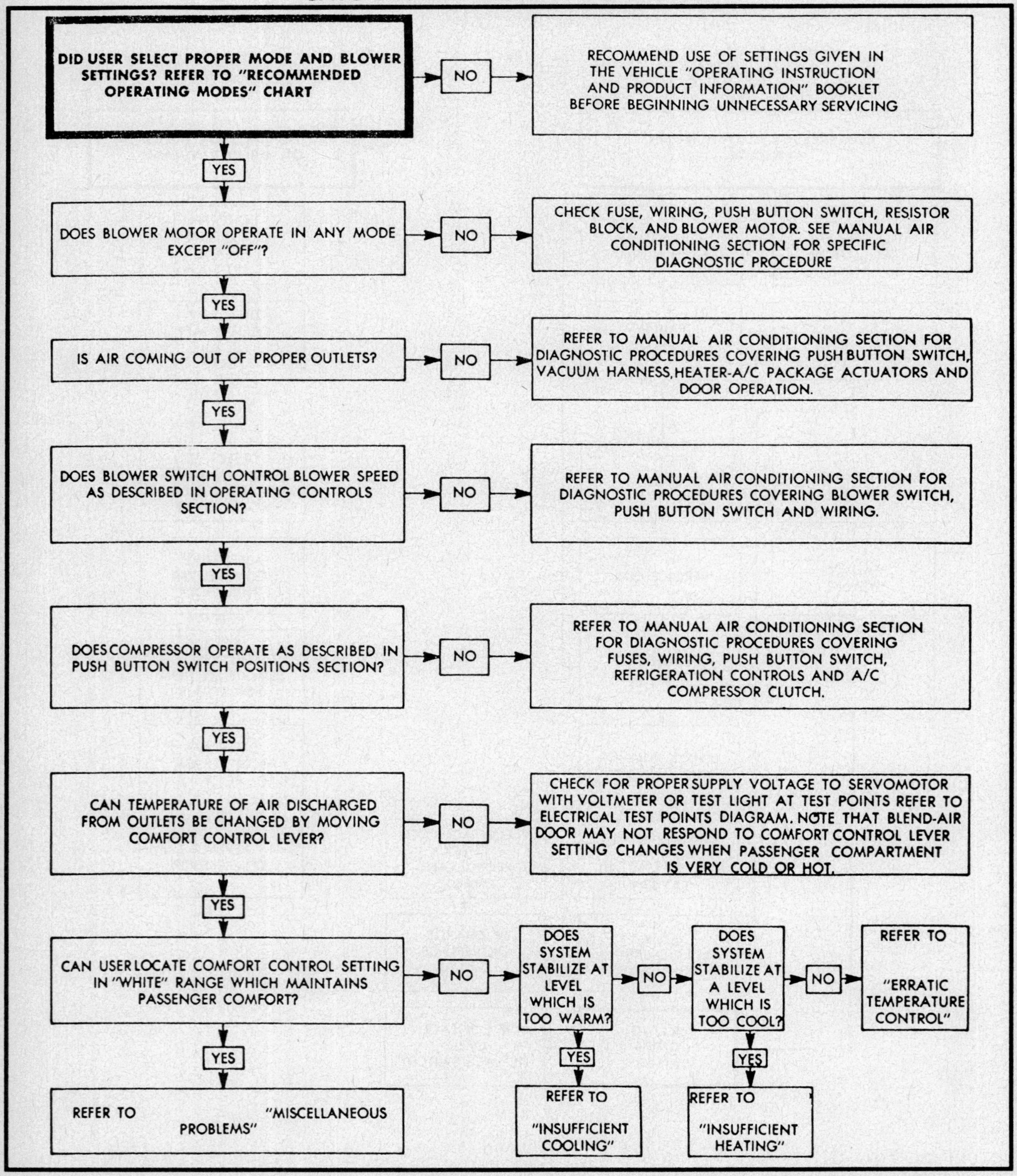
DID USER SELECT PROPER MODE AND BLOWER SETTINGS? REFER TO "RECOMMENDED OPERATING MODES" CHART
NO
RECOMMEND USE OF SETTINGS GIVEN IN THE VEHICLE "OPERATING INSTRUCTION AND PRODUCT INFORMATION" BOOKLET BEFORE BEGINNING UNNECESSARY SERVICING
YES
DOES BLOWER MOTOR OPERATE IN ANY MODE EXCEPT "OFF"?
NO
CHECK FUSE, WIRING, PUSH BUTTON SWITCH, RESISTOR BLOCK, AND BLOWER MOTOR. SEE MANUAL AIR CONDITIONING SECTION FOR SPECIFIC DIAGNOSTIC PROCEDURE
YES
IS AIR COMING OUT OF PROPER OUTLETS?
NO
REFER TO MANUAL AIR CONDITIONING SECTION FOR DIAGNOSTIC PROCEDURES COVERING PUSH BUTTON SWITCH, VACUUM HARNESS, HEATER-A/C PACKAGE ACTUATORS AND DOOR OPERATION.
YES
DOES BLOWER SWITCH CONTROL BLOWER SPEED AS DESCRIBED IN OPERATING CONTROLS SECTION?
NO
REFER TO MANUAL AIR CONDITIONING SECTION FOR DIAGNOSTIC PROCEDURES COVERING BLOWER SWITCH, PUSH BUTTON SWITCH AND WIRING.
YES
DOES COMPRESSOR OPERATE AS DESCRIBED IN PUSH BUTTON SWITCH POSITIONS SECTION?
NO
REFER TO MANUAL AIR CONDITIONING SECTION FOR DIAGNOSTIC PROCEDURES COVERING FUSES, WIRING, PUSH BUTTON SWITCH, REFRIGERATION CONTROLS AND A/C COMPRESSOR CLUTCH.
YES
CAN TEMPERATURE OF AIR DISCHARGED FROM OUTLETS BE CHANGED BY MOVING COMFORT CONTROL LEVER?
NO
CHECK FOR PROPER SUPPLY VOLTAGE TO SERVOMOTOR WITH VOLTMETER OR TEST LIGHT AT TEST POINTS REFER TO ELECTRICAL TEST POINTS DIAGRAM. NOTE THAT BLEND-AIR DOOR MAY NOT RESPOND TO COMFORT CONTROL LEVER SETTING CHANGES WHEN PASSENGER COMPARTMENT IS VERY COLD OR HOT.
YES
CAN USER LOCATE COMFORT CONTROL SETTING IN "WHITE" RANGE WHICH MAINTAINS PASSENGER COMFORT?
NO
DOES SYSTEM STABILIZE AT LEVEL WHICH IS TOO WARM?
NO
DOES SYSTEM STABILIZE AT A LEVEL WHICH IS TOO COOL?
NO
REFER TO "ERRATIC TEMPERATURE CONTROL"
YES
REFER TO "MISCELLANEOUS PROBLEMS"
YES
REFER TO "INSUFFICIENT COOLING"
YES
REFER TO "INSUFFICIENT HEATING"

INSUFFICIENT HEATING DIAGNOSIS

OUTPUT CAPACITY (AT DEFROSTER OUTLET)	
AMBIENT TEMPERATURE	MINIMUM DEFROSTER OUTLET TEMPERATURE WITH ENGINE WARMED UP AND IDLING
60°F (16°C)	142°F (60°C)
70°F (21°C)	146°F (61°C)
80°F (27°C)	150°F (63°C)
90°F (32°C)	154°F (64°C)

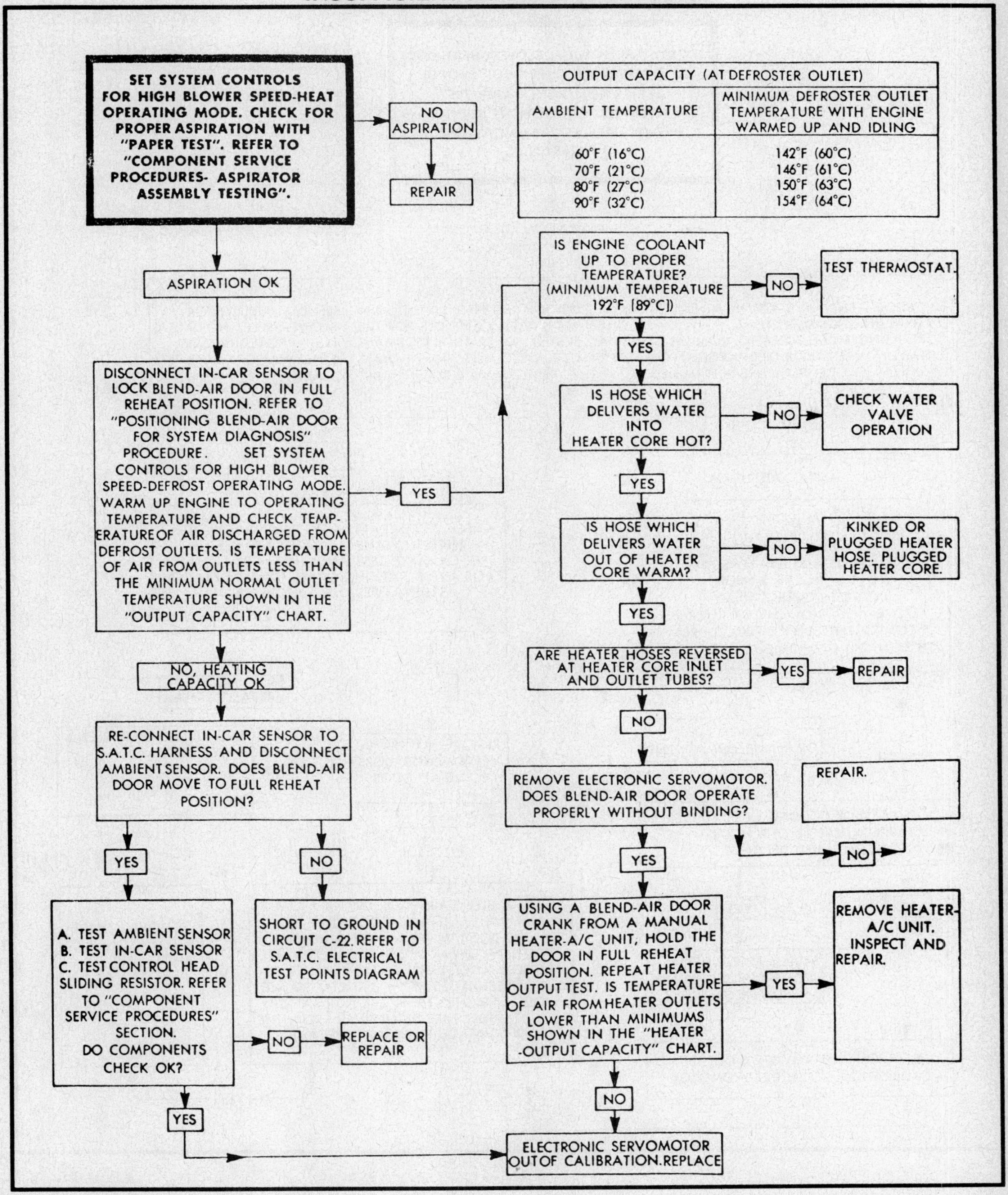
SET SYSTEM CONTROLS FOR HIGH BLOWER SPEED-HEAT OPERATING MODE. CHECK FOR PROPER ASPIRATION WITH "PAPER TEST". REFER TO "COMPONENT SERVICE PROCEDURES- ASPIRATOR ASSEMBLY TESTING".
NO ASPIRATION
REPAIR
ASPIRATION OK
DISCONNECT IN-CAR SENSOR TO LOCK BLEND-AIR DOOR IN FULL REHEAT POSITION. REFER TO "POSITIONING BLEND-AIR DOOR FOR SYSTEM DIAGNOSIS" PROCEDURE. SET SYSTEM CONTROLS FOR HIGH BLOWER SPEED-DEFROST OPERATING MODE. WARM UP ENGINE TO OPERATING TEMPERATURE AND CHECK TEMPERATURE OF AIR DISCHARGED FROM DEFROST OUTLETS. IS TEMPERATURE OF AIR FROM OUTLETS LESS THAN THE MINIMUM NORMAL OUTLET TEMPERATURE SHOWN IN THE "OUTPUT CAPACITY" CHART.
YES
NO, HEATING CAPACITY OK
RE-CONNECT IN-CAR SENSOR TO S.A.T.C. HARNESS AND DISCONNECT AMBIENT SENSOR. DOES BLEND-AIR DOOR MOVE TO FULL REHEAT POSITION?
YES
NO
A. TEST AMBIENT SENSOR
B. TEST IN-CAR SENSOR
C. TEST CONTROL HEAD SLIDING RESISTOR. REFER TO "COMPONENT SERVICE PROCEDURES" SECTION.
DO COMPONENTS CHECK OK?
SHORT TO GROUND IN CIRCUIT C-22. REFER TO S.A.T.C. ELECTRICAL TEST POINTS DIAGRAM
NO
REPLACE OR REPAIR
YES
IS ENGINE COOLANT UP TO PROPER TEMPERATURE? (MINIMUM TEMPERATURE 192°F [89°C])
NO
TEST THERMOSTAT.
YES
IS HOSE WHICH DELIVERS WATER INTO HEATER CORE HOT?
NO
CHECK WATER VALVE OPERATION
YES
IS HOSE WHICH DELIVERS WATER OUT OF HEATER CORE WARM?
NO
KINKED OR PLUGGED HEATER HOSE. PLUGGED HEATER CORE.
YES
ARE HEATER HOSES REVERSED AT HEATER CORE INLET AND OUTLET TUBES?
YES
REPAIR
NO
REMOVE ELECTRONIC SERVOMOTOR. DOES BLEND-AIR DOOR OPERATE PROPERLY WITHOUT BINDING?
NO
REPAIR.
YES
USING A BLEND-AIR DOOR CRANK FROM A MANUAL HEATER-A/C UNIT, HOLD THE DOOR IN FULL REHEAT POSITION. REPEAT HEATER OUTPUT TEST. IS TEMPERATURE OF AIR FROM HEATER OUTLETS LOWER THAN MINIMUMS SHOWN IN THE "HEATER-OUTPUT CAPACITY" CHART.
YES
REMOVE HEATER-A/C UNIT. INSPECT AND REPAIR.
NO
ELECTRONIC SERVOMOTOR OUT OF CALIBRATION. REPLACE

INSUFFICIENT COOLING DIAGNOSIS

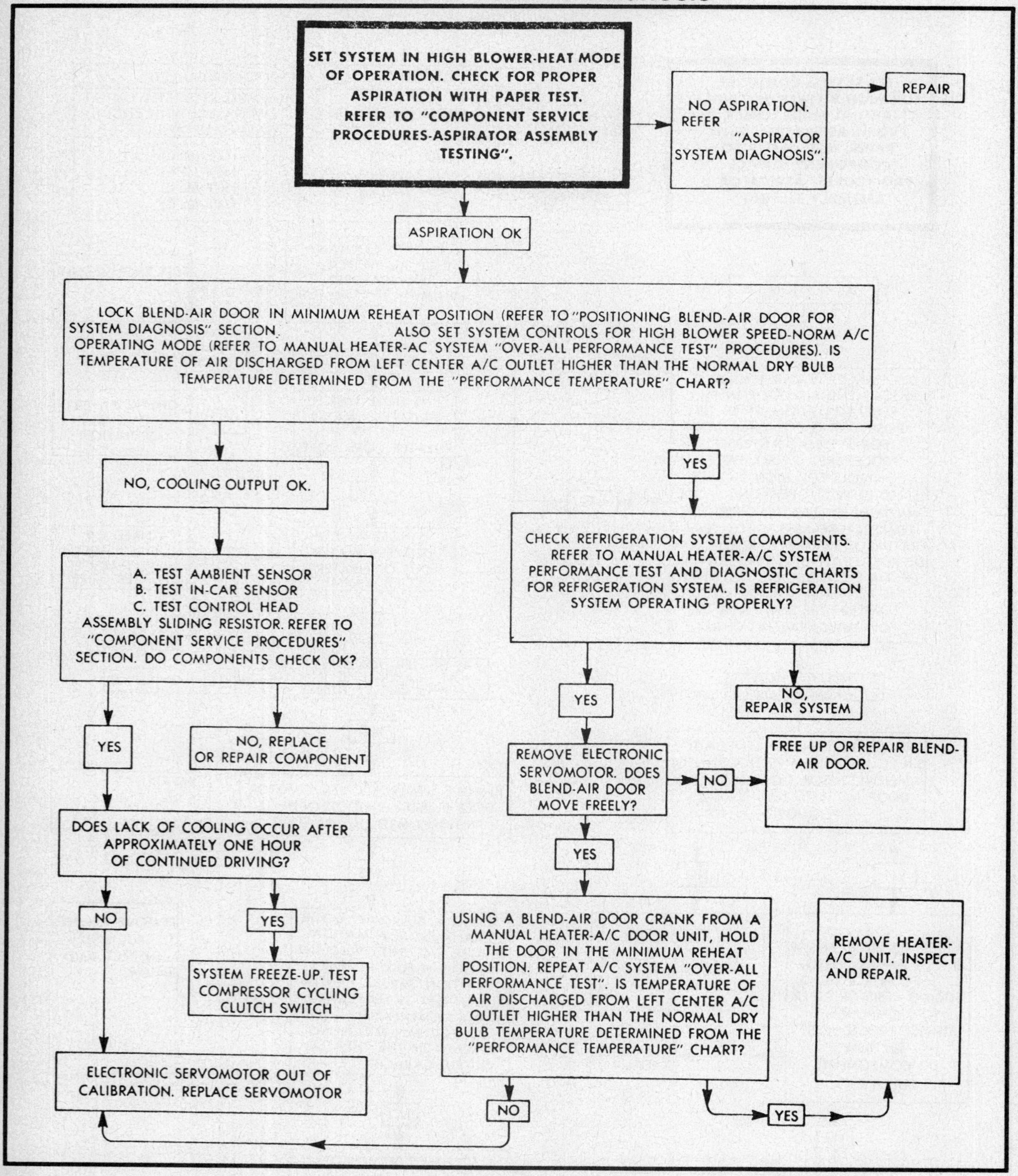
SET SYSTEM IN HIGH BLOWER-HEAT MODE OF OPERATION. CHECK FOR PROPER ASPIRATION WITH PAPER TEST. REFER TO "COMPONENT SERVICE PROCEDURES-ASPIRATOR ASSEMBLY TESTING".
NO ASPIRATION. REFER "ASPIRATOR SYSTEM DIAGNOSIS".
REPAIR
ASPIRATION OK
LOCK BLEND-AIR DOOR IN MINIMUM REHEAT POSITION (REFER TO "POSITIONING BLEND-AIR DOOR FOR SYSTEM DIAGNOSIS" SECTION. ALSO SET SYSTEM CONTROLS FOR HIGH BLOWER SPEED-NORM A/C OPERATING MODE (REFER TO MANUAL HEATER-AC SYSTEM "OVER-ALL PERFORMANCE TEST" PROCEDURES). IS TEMPERATURE OF AIR DISCHARGED FROM LEFT CENTER A/C OUTLET HIGHER THAN THE NORMAL DRY BULB TEMPERATURE DETERMINED FROM THE "PERFORMANCE TEMPERATURE" CHART?
NO, COOLING OUTPUT OK.
YES
A. TEST AMBIENT SENSOR
B. TEST IN-CAR SENSOR
C. TEST CONTROL HEAD ASSEMBLY SLIDING RESISTOR. REFER TO "COMPONENT SERVICE PROCEDURES" SECTION. DO COMPONENTS CHECK OK?
CHECK REFRIGERATION SYSTEM COMPONENTS. REFER TO MANUAL HEATER-A/C SYSTEM PERFORMANCE TEST AND DIAGNOSTIC CHARTS FOR REFRIGERATION SYSTEM. IS REFRIGERATION SYSTEM OPERATING PROPERLY?
YES
NO, REPAIR SYSTEM
YES
NO, REPLACE OR REPAIR COMPONENT
REMOVE ELECTRONIC SERVOMOTOR. DOES BLEND-AIR DOOR MOVE FREELY?
NO
FREE UP OR REPAIR BLEND-AIR DOOR.
DOES LACK OF COOLING OCCUR AFTER APPROXIMATELY ONE HOUR OF CONTINUED DRIVING?
YES
NO
YES
USING A BLEND-AIR DOOR CRANK FROM A MANUAL HEATER-A/C DOOR UNIT, HOLD THE DOOR IN THE MINIMUM REHEAT POSITION. REPEAT A/C SYSTEM "OVER-ALL PERFORMANCE TEST". IS TEMPERATURE OF AIR DISCHARGED FROM LEFT CENTER A/C OUTLET HIGHER THAN THE NORMAL DRY BULB TEMPERATURE DETERMINED FROM THE "PERFORMANCE TEMPERATURE" CHART?
REMOVE HEATER-A/C UNIT. INSPECT AND REPAIR.
SYSTEM FREEZE-UP. TEST COMPRESSOR CYCLING CLUTCH SWITCH
ELECTRONIC SERVOMOTOR OUT OF CALIBRATION. REPLACE SERVOMOTOR
NO
YES

ERRATIC TEMPERATURE CONTROL DIAGNOSIS

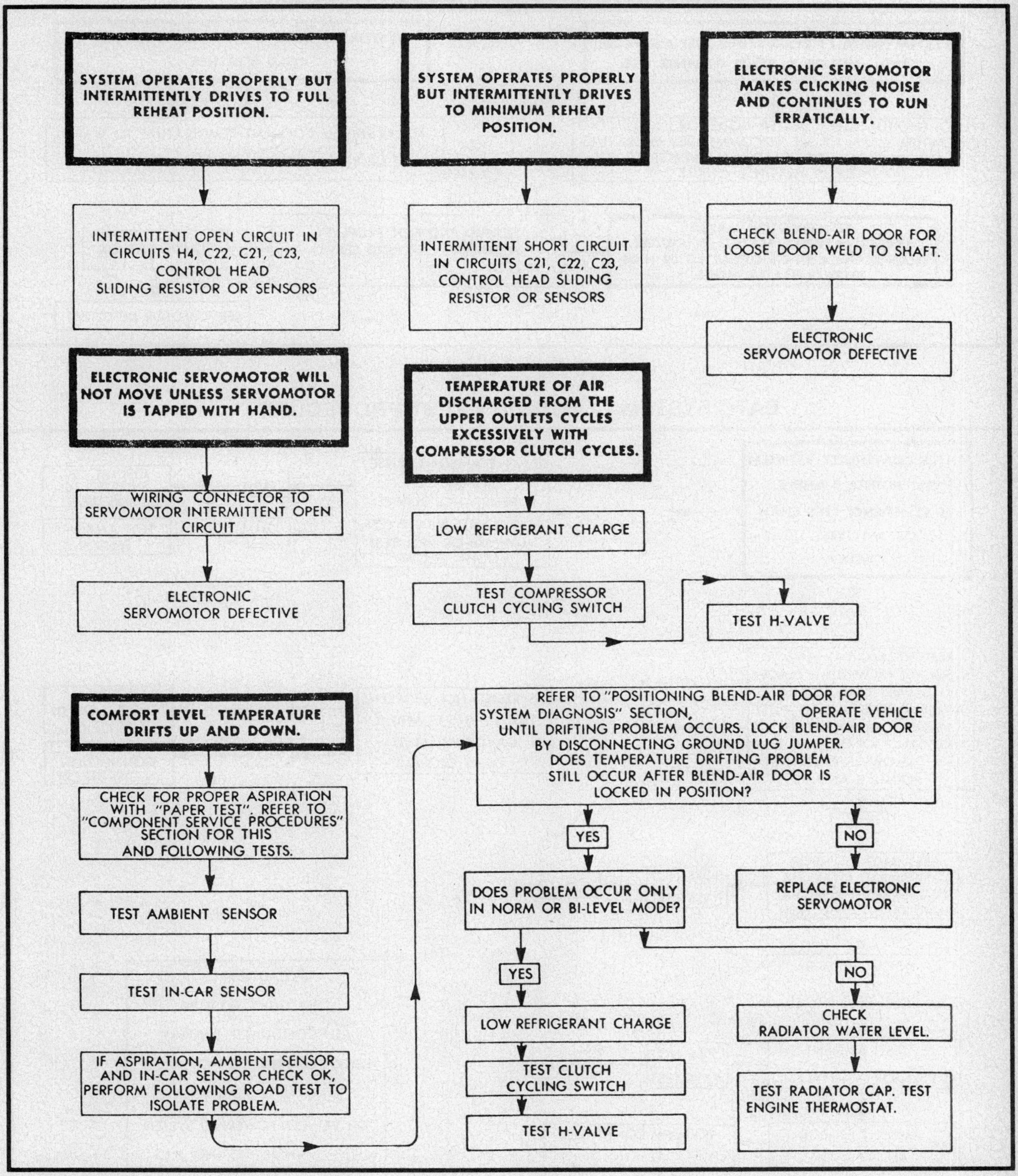
SYSTEM OPERATES PROPERLY BUT INTERMITTENTLY DRIVES TO FULL REHEAT POSITION.
INTERMITTENT OPEN CIRCUIT IN CIRCUITS H4, C22, C21, C23, CONTROL HEAD SLIDING RESISTOR OR SENSORS
SYSTEM OPERATES PROPERLY BUT INTERMITTENTLY DRIVES TO MINIMUM REHEAT POSITION.
INTERMITTENT SHORT CIRCUIT IN CIRCUITS C21, C22, C23, CONTROL HEAD SLIDING RESISTOR OR SENSORS
ELECTRONIC SERVOMOTOR MAKES CLICKING NOISE AND CONTINUES TO RUN ERRATICALLY.
CHECK BLEND-AIR DOOR FOR LOOSE DOOR WELD TO SHAFT.
ELECTRONIC SERVOMOTOR DEFECTIVE
ELECTRONIC SERVOMOTOR WILL NOT MOVE UNLESS SERVOMOTOR IS TAPPED WITH HAND.
WIRING CONNECTOR TO SERVOMOTOR INTERMITTENT OPEN CIRCUIT
ELECTRONIC SERVOMOTOR DEFECTIVE
TEMPERATURE OF AIR DISCHARGED FROM THE UPPER OUTLETS CYCLES EXCESSIVELY WITH COMPRESSOR CLUTCH CYCLES.
LOW REFRIGERANT CHARGE
TEST COMPRESSOR CLUTCH CYCLING SWITCH
TEST H-VALVE
COMFORT LEVEL TEMPERATURE DRIFTS UP AND DOWN.
CHECK FOR PROPER ASPIRATION WITH "PAPER TEST". REFER TO "COMPONENT SERVICE PROCEDURES" SECTION FOR THIS AND FOLLOWING TESTS.
TEST AMBIENT SENSOR
TEST IN-CAR SENSOR
IF ASPIRATION, AMBIENT SENSOR AND IN-CAR SENSOR CHECK OK, PERFORM FOLLOWING ROAD TEST TO ISOLATE PROBLEM.
REFER TO "POSITIONING BLEND-AIR DOOR FOR SYSTEM DIAGNOSIS" SECTION, OPERATE VEHICLE UNTIL DRIFTING PROBLEM OCCURS. LOCK BLEND-AIR DOOR BY DISCONNECTING GROUND LUG JUMPER. DOES TEMPERATURE DRIFTING PROBLEM STILL OCCUR AFTER BLEND-AIR DOOR IS LOCKED IN POSITION?
YES
NO
DOES PROBLEM OCCUR ONLY IN NORM OR BI-LEVEL MODE?
REPLACE ELECTRONIC SERVOMOTOR
YES
NO
LOW REFRIGERANT CHARGE
TEST CLUTCH CYCLING SWITCH
TEST H-VALVE
CHECK RADIATOR WATER LEVEL.
TEST RADIATOR CAP. TEST ENGINE THERMOSTAT.

DIAGNOSING MISCELLANEOUS PROBLEMS

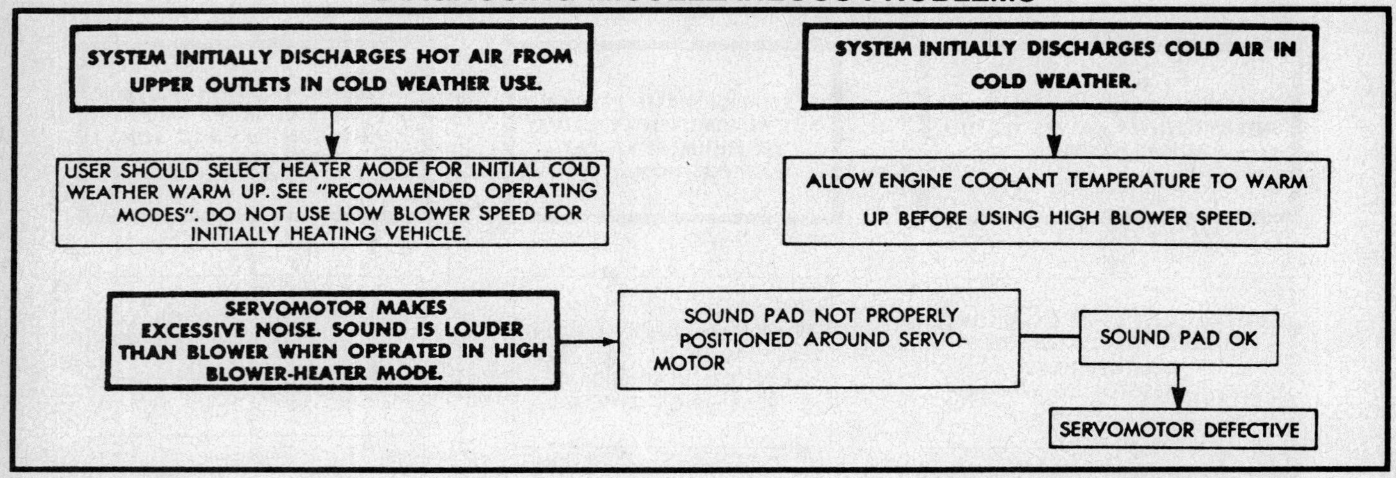
SYSTEM INITIALLY DISCHARGES HOT AIR FROM UPPER OUTLETS IN COLD WEATHER USE.
USER SHOULD SELECT HEATER MODE FOR INITIAL COLD WEATHER WARM UP. SEE "RECOMMENDED OPERATING MODES". DO NOT USE LOW BLOWER SPEED FOR INITIALLY HEATING VEHICLE.
SYSTEM INITIALLY DISCHARGES COLD AIR IN COLD WEATHER.
ALLOW ENGINE COOLANT TEMPERATURE TO WARM UP BEFORE USING HIGH BLOWER SPEED.
SERVOMOTOR MAKES EXCESSIVE NOISE. SOUND IS LOUDER THAN BLOWER WHEN OPERATED IN HIGH BLOWER-HEATER MODE.
SOUND PAD NOT PROPERLY POSITIONED AROUND SERVO-MOTOR
SOUND PAD OK
SERVOMOTOR DEFECTIVE

SATC SYSTEM CONTINUITY TEST PROCEDURE I

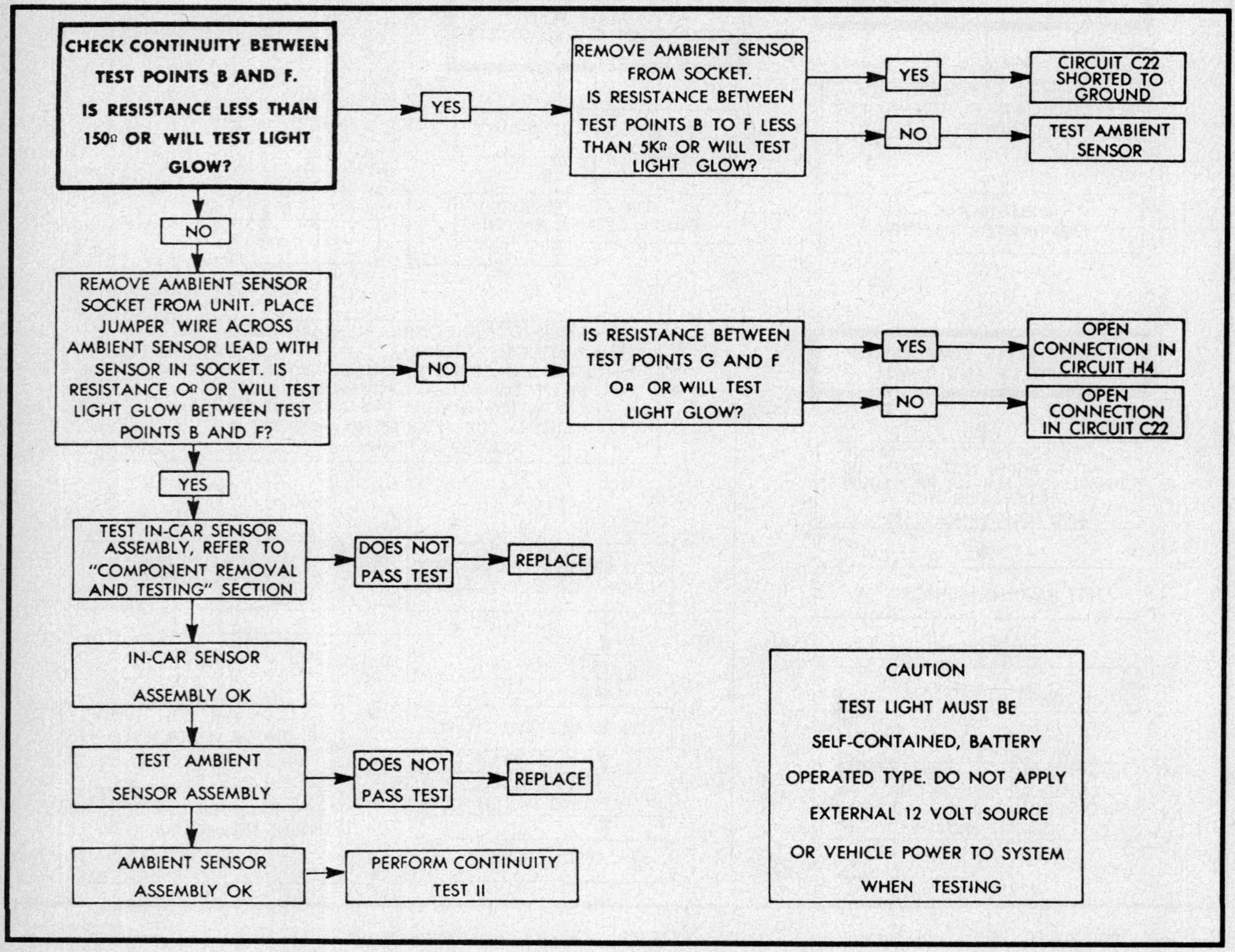
CHECK CONTINUITY BETWEEN TEST POINTS B AND F. IS RESISTANCE LESS THAN 150Ω OR WILL TEST LIGHT GLOW?
YES
REMOVE AMBIENT SENSOR FROM SOCKET. IS RESISTANCE BETWEEN TEST POINTS B TO F LESS THAN 5KΩ OR WILL TEST LIGHT GLOW?
YES
CIRCUIT C22 SHORTED TO GROUND
NO
TEST AMBIENT SENSOR
NO
REMOVE AMBIENT SENSOR SOCKET FROM UNIT. PLACE JUMPER WIRE ACROSS AMBIENT SENSOR LEAD WITH SENSOR IN SOCKET. IS RESISTANCE 0Ω OR WILL TEST LIGHT GLOW BETWEEN TEST POINTS B AND F?
NO
IS RESISTANCE BETWEEN TEST POINTS G AND F 0Ω OR WILL TEST LIGHT GLOW?
YES
OPEN CONNECTION IN CIRCUIT H4
NO
OPEN CONNECTION IN CIRCUIT C22
YES
TEST IN-CAR SENSOR ASSEMBLY, REFER TO "COMPONENT REMOVAL AND TESTING" SECTION
DOES NOT PASS TEST
REPLACE
IN-CAR SENSOR ASSEMBLY OK
TEST AMBIENT SENSOR ASSEMBLY
DOES NOT PASS TEST
REPLACE
AMBIENT SENSOR ASSEMBLY OK
PERFORM CONTINUITY TEST II
CAUTION
TEST LIGHT MUST BE SELF-CONTAINED, BATTERY OPERATED TYPE. DO NOT APPLY EXTERNAL 12 VOLT SOURCE OR VEHICLE POWER TO SYSTEM WHEN TESTING

SATC SYSTEM CONTINUITY TEST PROCEDURE II

REFER TO "COMPONENT SERVICE PROCEDURES" SECTION FOR DETAILS ON SERVOMOTOR AND CONTROL HEAD ASSEMBLY SLIDING RESISTOR. DISCONNECT S.A.T.C. ELECTRICAL HARNESS BETWEEN CONTROL HEAD SLIDING RESISTOR AND ELECTRONIC SERVOMOTOR.

↓

REFER TO SCHEMATIC FOR S.A.T.C. ELECTRICAL HARNESS CHECK CONTINUITY BETWEEN TEST POINTS A TO I, K TO C, D TO E, F TO G, H TO J AND J TO B. → OPEN CIRCUIT → REPAIR HARNESS

↓

CONTINUITY OK

↓

CHECK FOR SHORT CIRCUIT BETWEEN POINTS I TO J, J TO K, D TO C AND E TO F → SHORT CIRCUIT → REPAIR HARNESS

↓

NO SHORT CIRCUITS

SATC ELECTRICAL HARNESS TEST POINTS

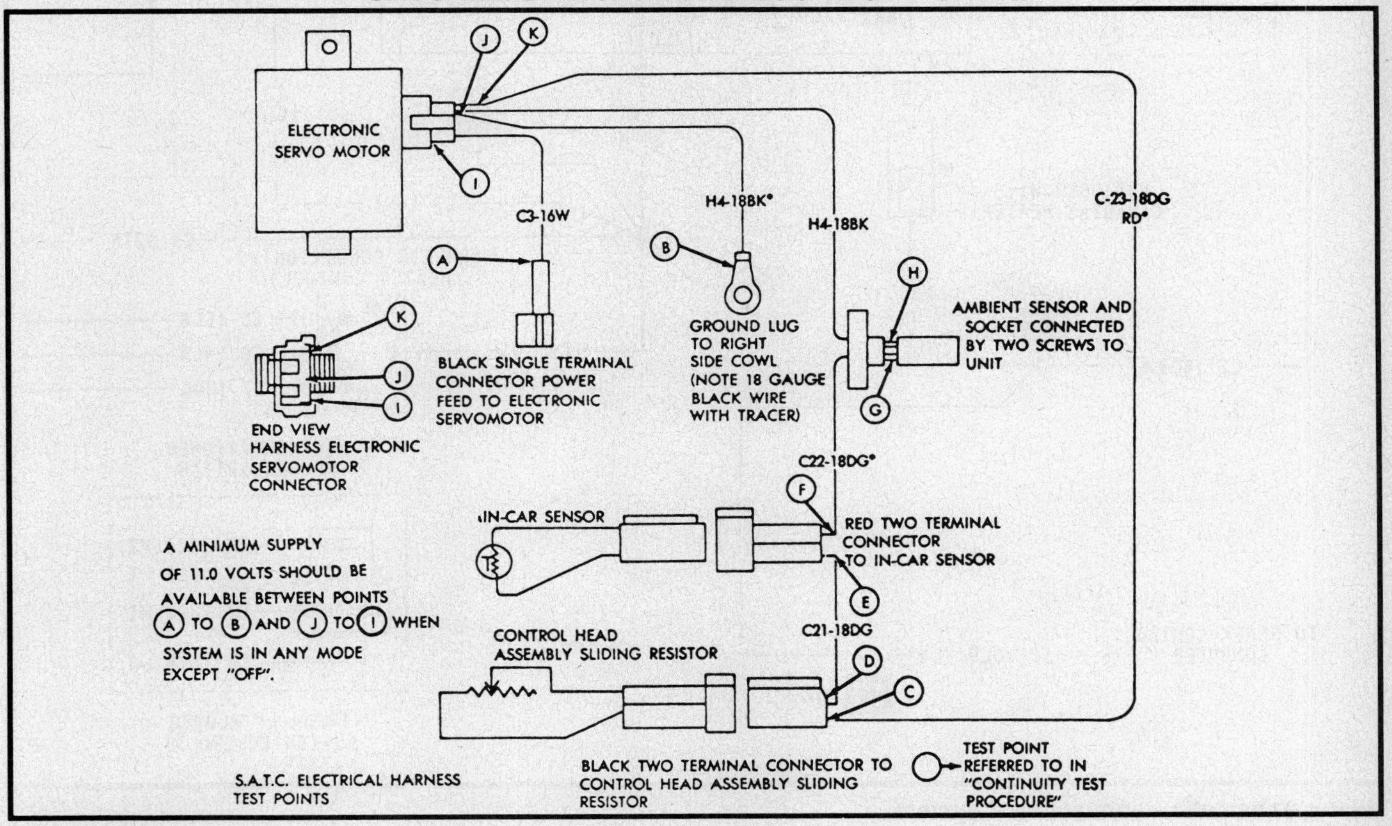
J
K
ELECTRONIC SERVO MOTOR
I
C3-16W
H4-18BK*
H4-18BK
C-23-18DG RD*
A
B
H
AMBIENT SENSOR AND SOCKET CONNECTED BY TWO SCREWS TO UNIT
G
K
J
I
END VIEW HARNESS ELECTRONIC SERVOMOTOR CONNECTOR
BLACK SINGLE TERMINAL CONNECTOR POWER FEED TO ELECTRONIC SERVOMOTOR
GROUND LUG TO RIGHT SIDE COWL (NOTE 18 GAUGE BLACK WIRE WITH TRACER)
C22-18DG*
F
IN-CAR SENSOR
RED TWO TERMINAL CONNECTOR TO IN-CAR SENSOR
E
A MINIMUM SUPPLY OF 11.0 VOLTS SHOULD BE AVAILABLE BETWEEN POINTS A TO B AND J TO I WHEN SYSTEM IS IN ANY MODE EXCEPT "OFF".
C21-18DG
CONTROL HEAD ASSEMBLY SLIDING RESISTOR
D
C
S.A.T.C. ELECTRICAL HARNESS TEST POINTS
BLACK TWO TERMINAL CONNECTOR TO CONTROL HEAD ASSEMBLY SLIDING RESISTOR
TEST POINT REFERRED TO IN "CONTINUITY TEST PROCEDURE"

WIRING SCHEMATICS

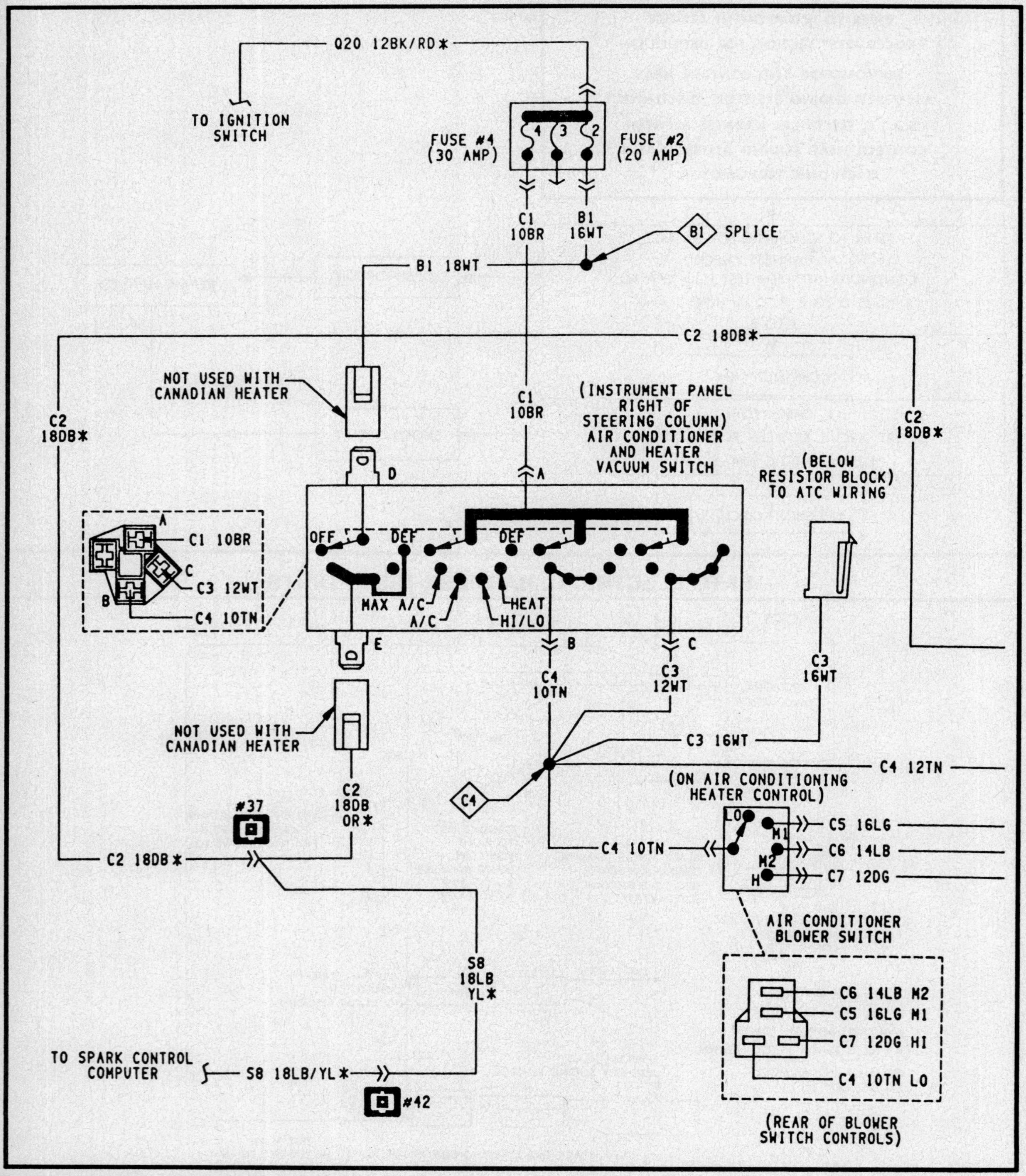
Q20 12BK/RD*
TO IGNITION SWITCH
FUSE #4 (30 AMP)
FUSE #2 (20 AMP)
4
3
2
C1 10BR
B1 16WT
B1
SPLICE
B1 18WT
C2 18DB*
NOT USED WITH CANADIAN HEATER
C2 18DB*
C1 10BR
(INSTRUMENT PANEL RIGHT OF STEERING COLUMN) AIR CONDITIONER AND HEATER VACUUM SWITCH
C2 18DB*
(BELOW RESISTOR BLOCK) TO ATC WIRING
D
A
A
C1 10BR
C
C3 12WT
B
C4 10TN
OFF
DEF
DEF
MAX A/C
A/C
HEAT
HI/LO
E
B
C
C4 10TN
C3 12WT
C3 16WT
NOT USED WITH CANADIAN HEATER
C3 16WT
C4 12TN
C4
(ON AIR CONDITIONING HEATER CONTROL)
#37
C2 18DB OR*
LO
M1
M2
H
C5 16LG
C6 14LB
C7 12DG
C4 10TN
C2 18DB*
AIR CONDITIONER BLOWER SWITCH
S8 18LB YL*
C6 14LB M2
C5 16LG M1
C7 12DG HI
C4 10TN LO
TO SPARK CONTROL COMPUTER
S8 18LB/YL*
#42
(REAR OF BLOWER SWITCH CONTROLS)

Wiring schematic—conventional system

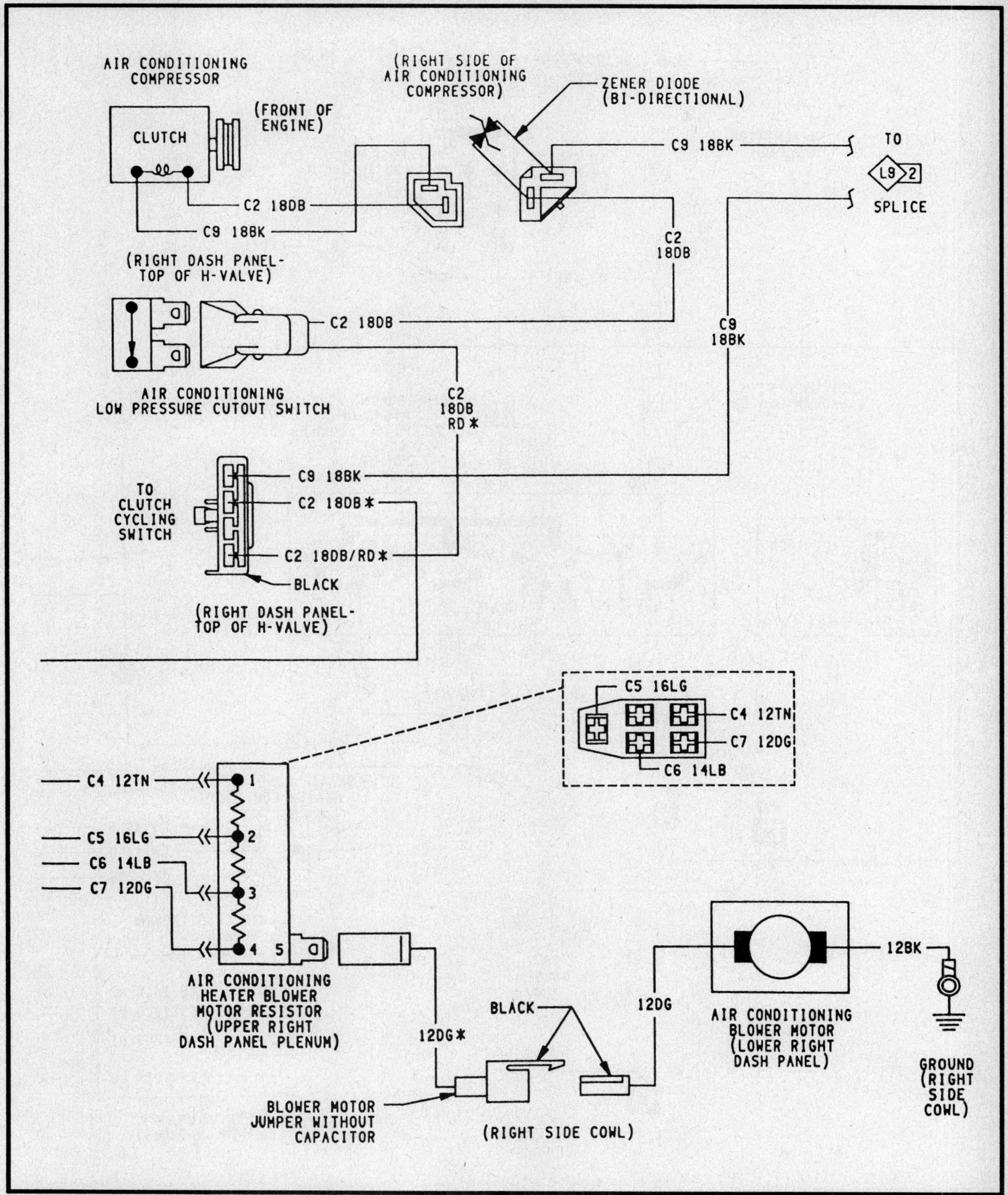
AIR CONDITIONING COMPRESSOR
CLUTCH
(FRONT OF ENGINE)
(RIGHT SIDE OF AIR CONDITIONING COMPRESSOR)
ZENER DIODE (BI-DIRECTIONAL)
C9 18BK
TO
L9 2
SPLICE
C2 18DB
C9 18BK
(RIGHT DASH PANEL-TOP OF H-VALVE)
C2 18DB
C2 18DB
C9 18BK
AIR CONDITIONING LOW PRESSURE CUTOUT SWITCH
C2 18DB RD*
TO CLUTCH CYCLING SWITCH
C9 18BK
C2 18DB*
C2 18DB/RD*
BLACK
(RIGHT DASH PANEL-TOP OF H-VALVE)
C5 16LG
C4 12TN
C7 12DG
C6 14LB
C4 12TN
C5 16LG
C6 14LB
C7 12DG
1
2
3
4
5
AIR CONDITIONING HEATER BLOWER MOTOR RESISTOR (UPPER RIGHT DASH PANEL PLENUM)
12DG*
BLACK
12DG
12BK
AIR CONDITIONING BLOWER MOTOR (LOWER RIGHT DASH PANEL)
GROUND (RIGHT SIDE COWL)
BLOWER MOTOR JUMPER WITHOUT CAPACITOR
(RIGHT SIDE COWL)

Wiring schematic—conventional system

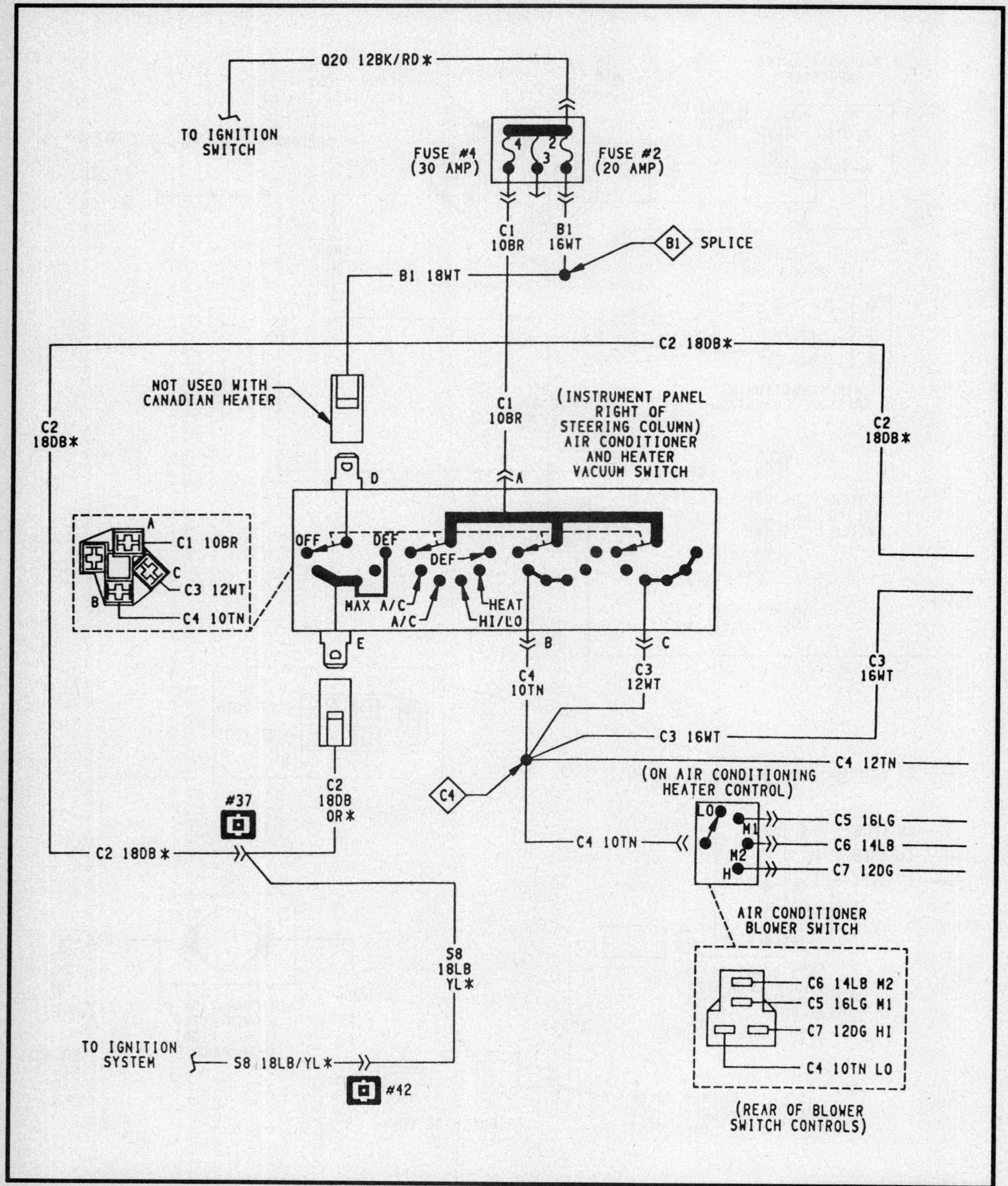
Q20 12BK/RD*
TO IGNITION SWITCH
FUSE #4 (30 AMP)
FUSE #2 (20 AMP)
C1 10BR
B1 16WT
B1 SPLICE
B1 18WT
C2 18DB*
NOT USED WITH CANADIAN HEATER
(INSTRUMENT PANEL RIGHT OF STEERING COLUMN) AIR CONDITIONER AND HEATER VACUUM SWITCH
C1 10BR
C3 12WT
C4 10TN
OFF
DEF
MAX A/C
A/C
HEAT
HI/LO
C4 10TN
C3 12WT
C3 16WT
C2 18DB OR*
#37
C4 12TN
(ON AIR CONDITIONING HEATER CONTROL)
LO
M1
M2
H
C5 16LG
C6 14LB
C7 12DG
C2 18DB*
C4 10TN
AIR CONDITIONER BLOWER SWITCH
S8 18LB YL*
C6 14LB M2
C5 16LG M1
C7 12DG HI
C4 10TN LO
TO IGNITION SYSTEM
S8 18LB/YL*
#42
(REAR OF BLOWER SWITCH CONTROLS)

Wiring schematic—Semi-Automatic Temperature Control (SATC) system

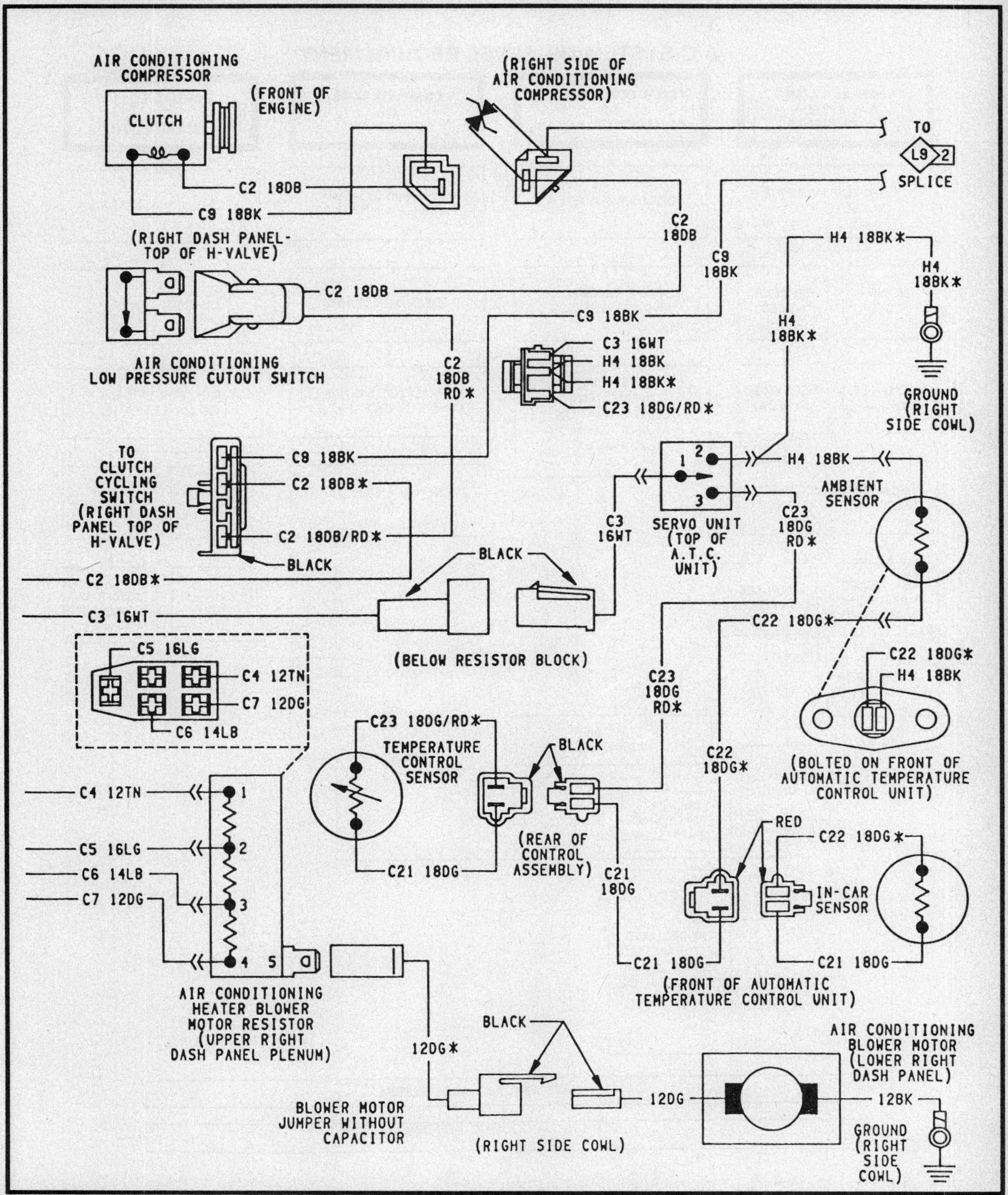
AIR CONDITIONING COMPRESSOR
CLUTCH
(FRONT OF ENGINE)
(RIGHT SIDE OF AIR CONDITIONING COMPRESSOR)
TO
L9 2
SPLICE
C2 18DB
C9 18BK
(RIGHT DASH PANEL-TOP OF H-VALVE)
C2 18DB
C9 18BK
H4 18BK*
AIR CONDITIONING LOW PRESSURE CUTOUT SWITCH
C2 18DB RD*
C3 16WT
H4 18BK
H4 18BK*
C23 18DG/RD*
GROUND (RIGHT SIDE COWL)
TO CLUTCH CYCLING SWITCH (RIGHT DASH PANEL TOP OF H-VALVE)
C8 18BK
C2 18DB*
C2 18DB/RD*
BLACK
SERVO UNIT (TOP OF A.T.C. UNIT)
C3 16WT
H4 18BK
AMBIENT SENSOR
C23 18DG RD*
C2 18DB*
C3 16WT
(BELOW RESISTOR BLOCK)
C22 18DG*
C5 16LG
C4 12TN
C7 12DG
C6 14LB
C22 18DG*
H4 18BK
C23 18DG RD*
C23 18DG/RD*
TEMPERATURE CONTROL SENSOR
(BOLTED ON FRONT OF AUTOMATIC TEMPERATURE CONTROL UNIT)
C4 12TN
C5 16LG
C6 14LB
C7 12DG
1 2 3 4 5
C21 18DG
(REAR OF CONTROL ASSEMBLY)
RED
C22 18DG*
IN-CAR SENSOR
C21 18DG
C21 18DG
(FRONT OF AUTOMATIC TEMPERATURE CONTROL UNIT)
AIR CONDITIONING HEATER BLOWER MOTOR RESISTOR (UPPER RIGHT DASH PANEL PLENUM)
12DG*
BLACK
AIR CONDITIONING BLOWER MOTOR (LOWER RIGHT DASH PANEL)
12DG
12BK
BLOWER MOTOR JUMPER WITHOUT CAPACITOR
(RIGHT SIDE COWL)
GROUND (RIGHT SIDE COWL)

Wiring schematic—Semi-Automatic Temperature Control (SATC) system

A/C SYSTEM OIL LEVEL REQUIREMENT

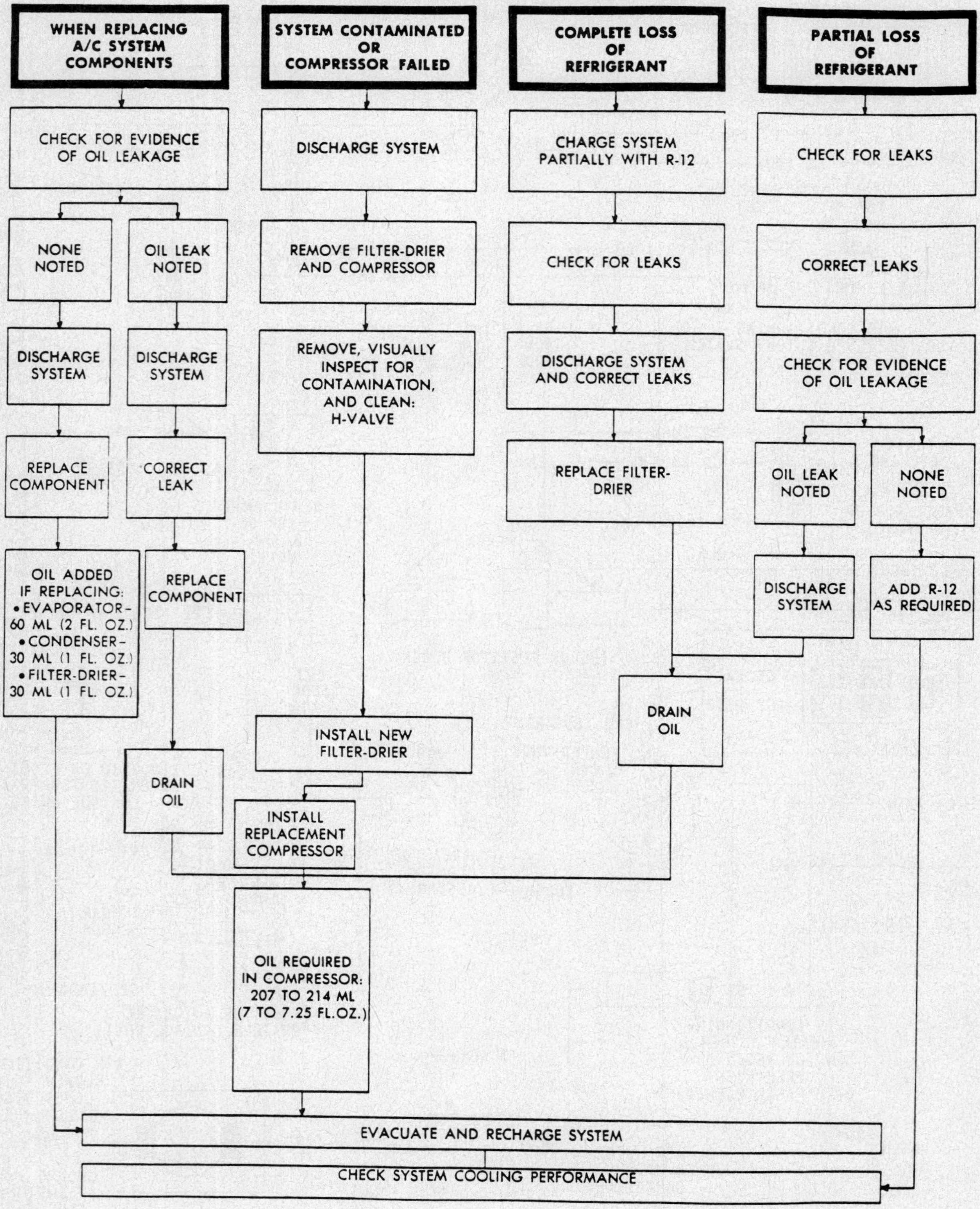
WHEN REPLACING A/C SYSTEM COMPONENTS
SYSTEM CONTAMINATED OR COMPRESSOR FAILED
COMPLETE LOSS OF REFRIGERANT
PARTIAL LOSS OF REFRIGERANT
CHECK FOR EVIDENCE OF OIL LEAKAGE
DISCHARGE SYSTEM
CHARGE SYSTEM PARTIALLY WITH R-12
CHECK FOR LEAKS
NONE NOTED
OIL LEAK NOTED
REMOVE FILTER-DRIER AND COMPRESSOR
CHECK FOR LEAKS
CORRECT LEAKS
DISCHARGE SYSTEM
DISCHARGE SYSTEM
REMOVE, VISUALLY INSPECT FOR CONTAMINATION, AND CLEAN: H-VALVE
DISCHARGE SYSTEM AND CORRECT LEAKS
CHECK FOR EVIDENCE OF OIL LEAKAGE
REPLACE COMPONENT
CORRECT LEAK
REPLACE FILTER-DRIER
OIL LEAK NOTED
NONE NOTED
OIL ADDED IF REPLACING: • EVAPORATOR - 60 ML (2 FL. OZ.) • CONDENSER - 30 ML (1 FL. OZ.) • FILTER-DRIER - 30 ML (1 FL. OZ.)
REPLACE COMPONENT
DISCHARGE SYSTEM
ADD R-12 AS REQUIRED
DRAIN OIL
INSTALL NEW FILTER-DRIER
DRAIN OIL
INSTALL REPLACEMENT COMPRESSOR
OIL REQUIRED IN COMPRESSOR: 207 TO 214 ML (7 TO 7.25 FL.OZ.)
EVACUATE AND RECHARGE SYSTEM
CHECK SYSTEM COOLING PERFORMANCE

3 CHRYSLER/DODGE/PLYMOUTH/EAGLE 3

LASER • MONACO • MEDALLION • PREMIER • SUMMIT • TALON

SPECIFICATIONS

ENGINE IDENTIFICATION

Year	Model	Engine Displacement cu. in. (liter)	Engine Series Identification (VIN)	No. of Cylinders	Engine Type
1989	Medallion	132 (2.2)	F	4	SOHC
	Summit	92 (1.5)	X	4	SOHC
	Summit	98 (1.6)	Y	4	DOHC
	Premier	150 (2.5)	H	4	OHV
	Premier	182 (3.0)	U	6	SOHC
1990	Summit	92 (1.5)	X	4	SOHC
	Summit	98 (1.6)	Y	4	DOHC
	Laser	107 (1.8)	T	4	SOHC
	Laser	122 (2.0)	R	4	DOHC
	Laser	122 (2.0)	U	4	DOHC w/Turbo
	Talon	122 (2.0)	R	4	DOHC
	Talon	122 (2.0)	U	4	DOHC w/Turbo
	Monaco	150 (2.5)	H	4	OHV
	Monaco	182 (3.0)	U	6	SOHC
	Premier	150 (2.5)	H	4	OHV
	Premier	182 (3.0)	U	6	SOHC
1991	Summit	92 (1.5)	A	4	SOHC
	Laser	107 (1.8)	T	4	SOHC
	Laser	122 (2.0)	R	4	DOHC
	Laser	122 (2.0)	U	4	DOHC w/Turbo
	Talon	122 (2.0)	R	4	DOHC
	Talon	122 (2.0)	U	4	DOHC w/Turbo
	Monaco	182 (3.0)	U	6	SOHC
	Premier	182 (3.0)	U	6	SOHC

REFRIGERANT CAPACITIES

Year	Model	Freon (oz.)	Oil	Type
1989	Medallion	29	①	R-12
	Summit	36	9.8 ②	R-12
	Premier	36	③	R-12
1990	Summit	36	9.8 ②	R-12
	Laser	32	6 ②	R-12
	Talon	32	6 ②	R-12
	Monaco	32	③	R-12
	Premier	36	③	R-12
1991	Summit	36	9.8 ②	R-12
	Laser	32	6 ②	R-12
	Talon	32	6 ②	R-12
	Monaco	36	③	R-12
	Premier	36	③	R-12

① 4–6 increments on dipstick
② Cubic inches
③ See oil checking procedure

AIR CONDITIONING BELT TENSION CHART

Year	Model	Engine (L)	Belt Type	New ①	Used ①
1989	Medallion	2.2	Serpentine	190	150
	Summit	1.5	V-belt	0.23	0.25
	Summit	1.6	V-belt	0.21	0.25
	Premier	2.5	Serpentine	190	150
	Premier	3.0	Serpentine	190	150
1990	Summit	1.5	V-belt	0.23	0.25
	Summit	1.6	V-belt	0.21	0.25
	Laser	1.8	V-belt	0.18	0.23
	Laser	2.0	V-belt	0.20	0.23
	Talon	2.0	V-belt	0.20	0.23
	Monaco	2.5	Serpentine	190	150
	Monaco	3.0	Serpentine	190	150
	Premier	2.5	Serpentine	190	150
	Premier	3.0	Serpentine	190	150
1991	Summit	1.5	V-belt	0.23	0.25
	Laser	1.8	V-belt	0.18	0.23
	Laser	2.0	V-belt	0.20	0.23
	Talon	2.0	V-belt	0.20	0.23
	Monaco	3.0	Serpentine	190	150
	Premier	3.0	Serpentine	190	150

① Serpentine belt: lbs. of belt tension
V-belt: Inches of deflection with 22 lbs. force applied at mid-point of belt between the tension pulley and compressor pulley.

SYSTEM DESCRIPTION

General Information

Medallion

MANUAL SYSTEM

The Medallion uses a conventional air conditioning system, consisting of all basic air conditioning components plus a vacuum-motor-operated fresh air door at the right side of the vehicle. Slide controls are used to regulate the temperature, air distribution and fan speed.

When the temperature control slide is pushed to the extreme left (cold air position) it operates the hot air/cold air door. When the temperature slide control is pushed to the extreme right (hot air position) there is constant water flow through the heater core and the temperatures are controlled by the positions of the hot air/cold air door and the up/down distribution doors.

The 4-position slide switch at the bottom of the control panel controls the distribution of the air flow through the vents. The first position on the extreme left controls the up/down distribution door (ventilation). In this position airflow only passes to the instrument panel vents. In the second position (heat/ventilation), airflow is distributed between the instrument panel vents, the lower vents and on some models the rear vents. Heating of the air is controlled by the temperature slide control. In the third position (heat/defrost), airflow is distributed between all the vents. The instrument panel vents may be closed with their own on-off controls. In the fourth position (defrost), air flows through the windshield vent and the instrument panel vents.

When the air conditioning switch is in the **NORM** position, airflow passes through the center vents from the evaporator, which receives air from both inside and outside the vehicle, and the air conditioning compressor clutch will be energized. When the switch is the in the **MAX** position, conditions are the same as above, except that a vacuum solenoid is activated and operates the vacuum motor to close the fresh air door. In this case, only inside air is circulated through the evaporator.

HEAVAC SYSTEM

The HEAVAC control panel receives voltage at all times from the DOME-CLK fuse. When the ignition switch is in the **RUN** or **ACCY** position, voltage comes from the BLWR fuse. When the HEAVAC contro panel energizes the blower motor power supply relay, voltage is applied to the blower motor.

The blower motor speed is controlled by the air flow control slide switch. The speed of the blower motor increases as the switch is moved from left to right. The temperature is controlled by the temperature control slide switch. The temperature increses as the switch is moved from left to right. The mode selection control buttoms operate in a conventional manner, directing air to the appropriate vents according to the mode. The HEAVAC control panel operates the motoros, relays, blower motor control module and air conditioning compressor clutch coil.

When the ignition switch is turned **OFF**, the last selection used is memorized and restored with a 2-second delay when the ignition is turned to the **RUN** position again. If the battery is disconnected, 15 seconds should elapse before reconnecing it to allow for system reinitialization, during which time the defrosting light will be on.

Summit, Laser and Talon

The heater unit is located in the center of the vehicle with the blower housing and blend-air system. In the blend-air system, hot air and cool air are controlled by blend-air damper to make a fine adjustment of the temperature. The heater system is also designed as a bi-level heater in which a separator directs warm air to the windshield or to the floor and cool air through the panel outlet.

The temperature inside the car is controlled by means of the temperature control lever, the position of which determines the opening of the blend-air damper and the resulting mixing ratio of cool and hot air is used to control the outlet temperature.

The air conditioning compressor coil will be energized when all of the following conditions are met:

1. The air conditioner switch is depressed in either the **ECONO** or **A/C** position.
2. The blower motor switch is not in the **OFF** position.
3. The evaporator outlet air temperature sensor is reading at least 39°F (4°C).
4. The evaporator inlet air temperature sensor is reading at least 39°F (4°C).
5. On Summit, the compressor discharge side refrigerant temperature must be less than 347°F (175°C).

Monaco and Premier

HEATER SYSTEM

The heater assembly is a blend air system, receiving outside air through the blower inlet, which is connected directly to an opening in the upper cowl, through the blower inlet and into the blower housing. It is forced through and/ or around the heater core, mixed and then discharged through the floor, instrument panel or defroster outlets.

The control switch assembly is located in a pod on the right side of the steering column. The control assembly contains the mode selection switch, which controls the mode of operation for the heating system. Also located on the control switch assembly is the blower speed selection switch, which controls the volume of air movement and the defroster push-button which can be activated to override the normal mode selection switch for immediate front windshield defroster activation.

Another control incorporated in the power ventilation system is the temperature control lever. The system utilizes a temperature blend method to provide controlled temperature to the vehicle interior. All air flow from the blower passes through the heater housing to the plenum assembly. Temperature is then regulated by heating a portion of the outside air and blending it with the remaining cooler air to the desired temperature. Temperature blending is varied by means of the temperature lever which activates the blend door to control the amount of air that flows through or around the heater core, where it is mixed and directed into the distribution plenum. The blended air is then directed to the selected mode of operation.

SEMI-AUTOMATIC CLIMATE CONTROL SYSTEM

An optional semi-automatic climate control system is also available. With the use of a microcomputer, the Air Conditioning Control Module (ACM) analyzes inputs from the following sources:

- Control pod
- Interior temperature sensor
- Ambient temperature sensor
- Blend door module
- Engine Control Unit (ECU)
- Headlight switch
- Cycling pressure switch
- English/metric switch

Using these inputs, the microcomputer determines the correct conditions for the following outputs:

- Display module
- Blend door module
- Relay control module
- Recirculation door vacuum motor
- Defrost door vacuum motor
- Mode door vacuum motor
- Compressor clutch engagement
- Rear defroster relay
- Engine Control Unit (ECU)

A small electric motor is used to operate the temperature blend door. A feedback circuit is used in the blend door actuator to supply the control with blend door position information. Vacuum actuators are used to control each of the 3 remaining air distribution doors.

The heater assembly on these vehicles is a blend air system, receiving outside air through the blower inlet, which is connected directly to an opening in the upper cowl, through the blower inlet into the blower housing. It is forced through and/or around the heater core, mixed and then discharged through the floor, instrument panel or defroster outlets.

The electronic climate control system automatically maintains the temperature selected for driving comfort and regulates the air flow between the instrument panel registers, floor ducts, windshield defroster nozzle and side window demisters selected by the driver.

Control of the passenger compartment temperature may be maintained in all function control settings, except when the system is turned off. In hot weather, it will cool the vehicle to a comfortable level and maintain that level automatically. The reverse will happen in cold weather conditions.

The electronic automatic temperature control module is located on the steering column pod. The module consists of 5 switches which control system operation. The select switch controls the selection of the various operating modes and indicator display on the instrument panel. The blower motor speed switch controls the blower motor speed with current speed setting indicated on the display panel. The 4-speed blower operates in every mode except off. The set temperature can be raised or lowered in 1 degree increments between 65–85°F through the use of the temperature control switch. There is also a 60°F setting for

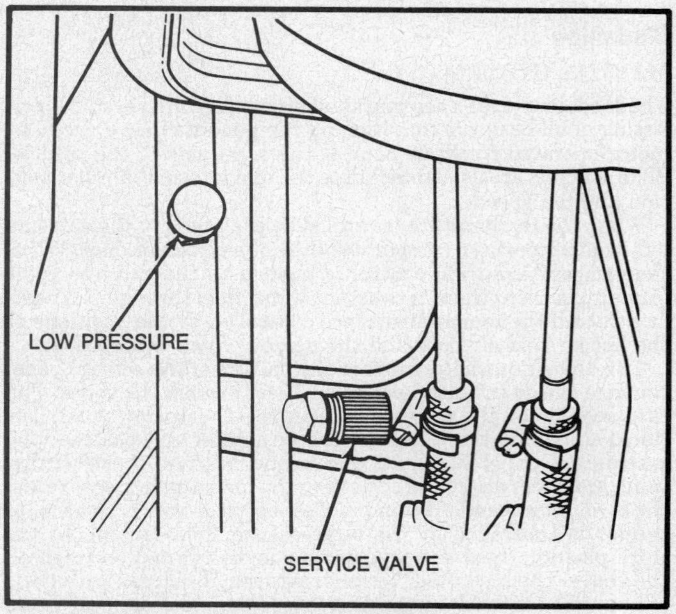
LOW PRESSURE
SERVICE VALVE

Service valve locations—Medallion

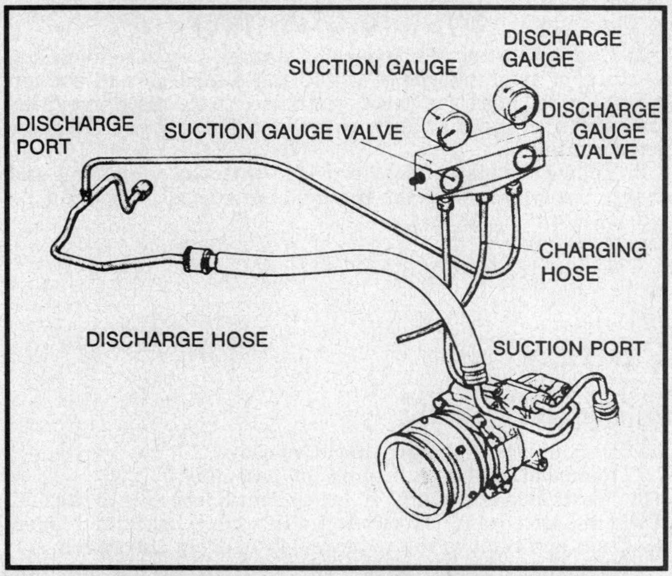
DISCHARGE GAUGE
SUCTION GAUGE
DISCHARGE PORT
SUCTION GAUGE VALVE
DISCHARGE GAUGE VALVE
CHARGING HOSE
DISCHARGE HOSE
SUCTION PORT

Service valve locations—Summit, Laser and Talon similar

maximum cooling and a 90°F setting for maximum heat. The currently set temperature is displayed on the display panel.

Service Valve Location

Medallion

The service valves are are located under the coolant expansion bottle. Be careful: the valves are the same size and could be connected backwards. The low pressure fitting is always located on the larger diameter line.

Summit, Laser and Talon

The suction (low pressure) port is located on the compressor itself. The discharge (high pressure) port is located on the discharge line at the left front corner of the engine compartment.

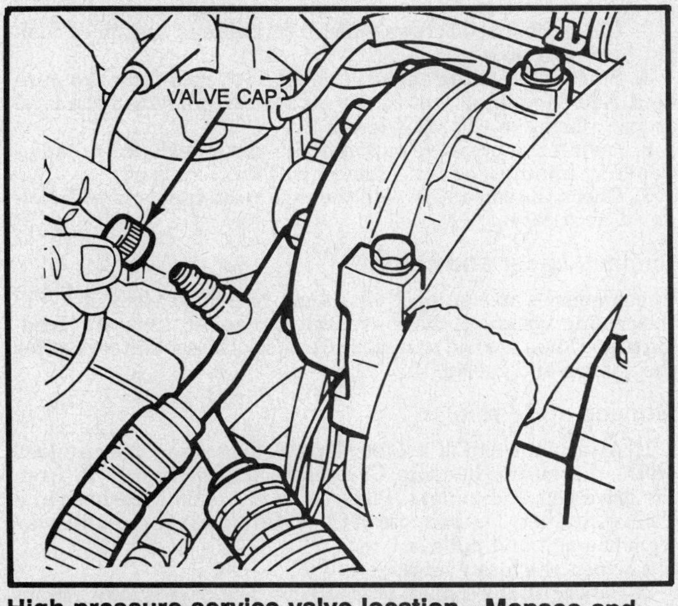
VALVE CAP

High pressure service valve location—Monaco and Premier

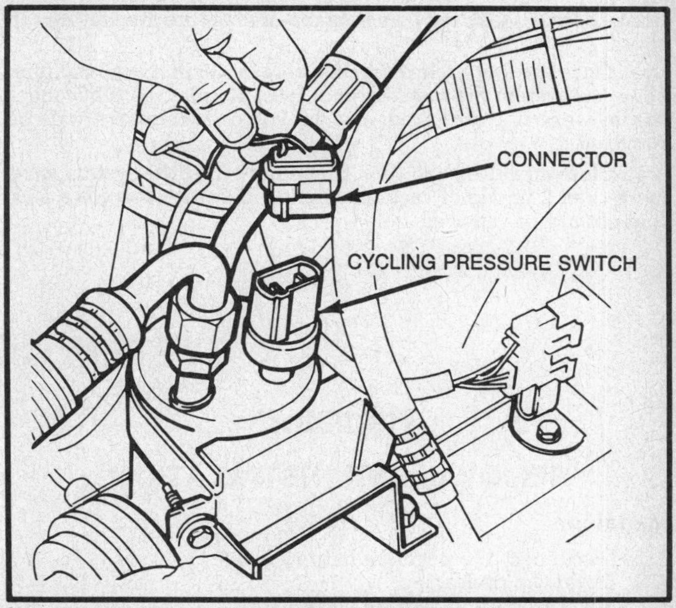
CONNECTOR
CYCLING PRESSURE SWITCH

Low pressure service valve location—Monaco and Premier

Monaco and Premier

The high pressure service port is located on the high pressure line near the compressor. The low pressure service port is located on the accumulator, under the cycling pressure switch.

System Discharging

R-12 refrigerant is a chloroflourocarbon which, when mishandled, can contribute to the depletion on the ozone layer in the upper atmosphere. Ozone filters out harmful radiation from the sun. In order to protect the ozone layer, an approved R-12 Recovery/Recycling machine that meets SAE standard J1991 should be employed when discharging the system. Follow the operating instructions provided with the approved equipment exactly to properly discharge the system.

NOTE: To access the low pressure service port on Monaco and Premier, disconnect the cycling pressure switch connector and unscrew the switch from the port.

System Evacuating

If the air conditioning system has been opened to the atmosphere, it should be air and moisture free before being recharged with refrigerant. Moisture and air mixed with refrigerant will raise the compressor head pressure, possibly damage the system's components and will reduce the performance of the system. Moisture will boil at normal room temperature when exposed to a vacuum. To evacuate, or rid the system of air and moisture:

1. Leak test the system and repair any leaks found.
2. Connect an approved charging station, Recovery/Recycling machine or manifold gauge set and vacuum pump to the discharge and suction ports. The red hose is normally connected to the discharge (high pressure) line, and the blue hose is connected to the suction (low pressure) line.
3. Open the discharge and suction ports and start the vacuum pump. If the pump is not able to pull at least 26 in. Hg of vac-

uum, there is a leak that must be repaired before evacuation can occur.

4. Once the system has reached at least 26 in. Hg of vacuum, allow the system to evacuate for at least 15 minutes. The longer the system is evacuated, the more contaminants will be removed.

5. Close all valves and turn the pump off. If the system loses more than 2 in. Hg of vacuum after 10 minutes, there is a leak that should be repaired.

System Charging

1. Connect an approved charging station, Recovery/Recycling machine or manifold gauge set to the discharge and suction ports. The red hose is normally connected to the discharge (high pressure) line, and the blue hose is connected to the suction (low pressure) line.
2. Follow the instructions provided with the equipment and charge the system with the specified amount of refrigerant.
3. Perform a leak test.

SYSTEM COMPONENTS

Radiator

REMOVAL AND INSTALLATION

Medallion

1. Disconnect the negative battery cable.
2. Drain the coolant.
3. Matchmark and remove the hood.
4. If equipped with air conditioning, properly discharge the system.
5. Remove the 5 grille mounting screws and remove the grille.
6. Remove the radiator support and facia panel.
7. Disconnect hoses from the radiator.
8. Disconnect the connectors from the cooling fans and thermo switch.
9. If equipped with air conditioning, disconnect the refrigerant lines from the condenser. Cover the exposed ends of the lines to minimize contamination.
10. Remove any remaining mounting hardware and lift the radiator, condenser and cooling fans from the engine compartment as an assembly. Separate the components as required.

To install:

11. Assemble the components and position in the engine compartment. Install mounting hardware.
12. Replace the O-rings and connect the refrigerant lines to the condenser, if equipped.
13. Connect the electrical connectors.
14. Connect the hoses to the radiator.
15. Install the facia panel, radiator support, grille and hood.
16. Fill the radiator with coolant and bleed the system.
17. Evacuate and recharge the air conditioning system.
18. Connect the negative battery cable and check the entire climate control system for proper operation.

Summit, Laser and Talon

1. Disconnect the negative battery cable.
2. Drain the cooling system.
3. Disconnect the overflow tube. If necessary, remove the overflow tank.
4. Disconnect upper and lower radiator hoses.
5. Disconnect the electrical connectors for the cooling fan and air conditioning condenser fan, if equipped.
6. Disconnect thermo sensor wires.
7. Disconnect and plug automatic transmission cooler lines, if equipped.
8. Remove the upper radiator mounts and lift out the radiator/fan assembly.
9. The installation is the reverse of the removal installation.
10. Fill the radiator with coolant.
11. Connect the negative battery cable and check for leaks.

Monaco and Premier

1. Disconnect the battery negative cable.
2. Remove the electric cooling fan assembly.
3. Attach one end of a ¼ in. hose about 3 feet long to the end of the radiator drain, the other end in a clean container. Open the drain and remove the radiator cap to drain the system.
4. Disconnect upper and lower hoses from the radiator.
5. Remove the front grille then disconnect the radiator from the air conditioning condenser by removing the top and bottom attaching screws. Lift out the radiator.
6. The installation is the reverse of the removal installation. Note that the radiator is equipped with alignment dowels on the bottom that fit into holes in the body crossmembers. Align these dowels when at installing.
7. Fill the radiator with coolant and bleed the sytem.
8. Connect the negative battery cable and check for leaks.

COOLING SYSTEM BLEEDING

Medallion

1. Open the cooling system bleed screws, located in the upper radiator hose and heater core inlet line. If equipped with an automatic transaxle, a third bleed screw is located on the automatic transaxle oiler cooler upper water line.
2. Remove the pressure cap from the expansion tank and fill the system through the tank; do not reinstall the cap.
3. Close the bleed screws when a continuous stream of coolant begins to flow.
4. Start and run the engne at about 1500 rpm for a few minutes. Add enough coolant to the expansion tank when the level drops to bring to the MAX level.
5. Install the pressure cap and run the vehicle for an additional 10 minutes, or until the coolant fan comes on.
6. Check the coolant level in the expansion tank and add coolant if necessary.

Summit, Laser and Talon

These vehicles are equipped with a self-bleeding thermostat. Fill the cooling system in the conventional manner; separate bleeding procedures are not necessary. Recheck the coolant level after the vehicle and cooled.

Monaco and Premier

1. Attach one end of a 4 foot long ¼ in. hose to the air bleed on the thermostat housing. Carefully route the hose away from the drive belt and pulleys. Place the other end of the hose in a clean container. The purpose of this hose is to keep coolant away from the belt and pulleys.
2. Open the bleed valve.
3. Slowly fill the coolant pressure bottle until a steady stream of coolant flows from the hose attached to the bleed valve. Close the bleed valve and continue filling to the full mark on the bot-

tle. The full mark is the top of the post inside the bottle. Install the cap tightly on the coolant pressure bottle.

4. Remove the hose from the bleed valve, start and run the engine until the upper radiator hose is warm to the touch.

5. Turn the engine off and reattach the drain hose to the bleed valve. Be sure to route the hose away from the belt and pulleys. Open the bleed valve until a steady stream of coolant flows from the hose. Close the bleed valve and remove the hose.

6. Check that the coolant pressure bottle is at or slightly above the full mark, at the top of the post inside the coolant pressure bottle. The full mark on the coolant pressure bottle is the correct coolant level for a cold engine. A hot engine may have a coolant level slightly higher than the full mark.

Cooling Fan

TESTING

CAUTION

Make sure the key is in the OFF position when checking the electric cooling fan. If not, the fan could turn ON at any time, causing serious personal injury.

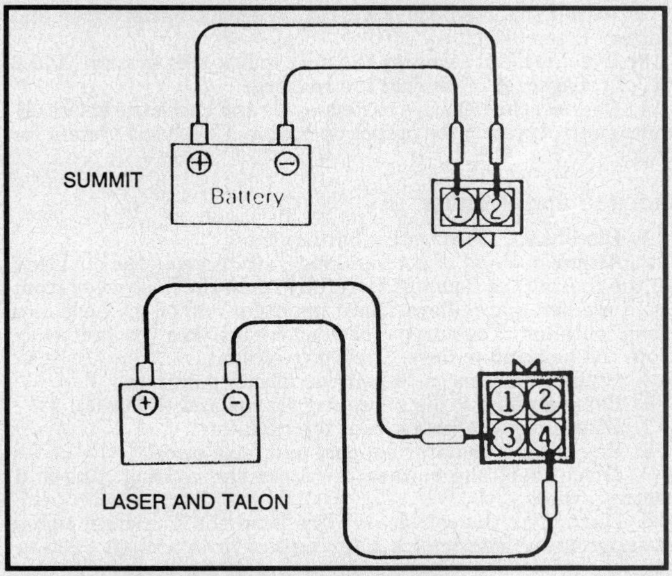
SUMMIT
Battery
1
2
1
2
3
4
LASER AND TALON

Condenser fan connector terminals

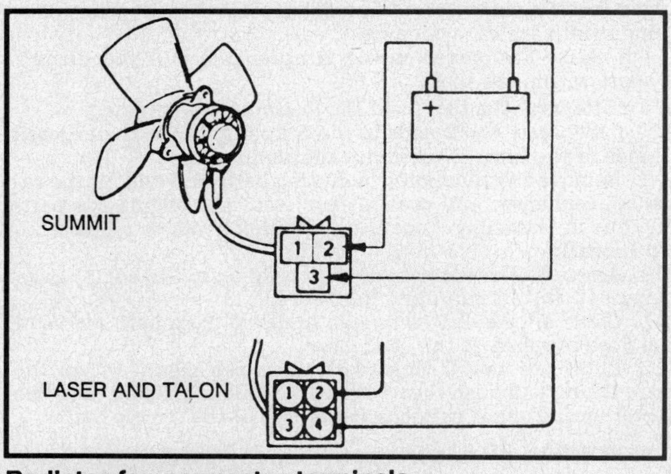
SUMMIT
1
2
3
LASER AND TALON
1
2
3
4

Radiator fan connector terminals

Medallion

1. Unplug the fan connector.
2. Using a jumper wire, connect the ground terminal of the fan connector to the negative battery terminal.
3. The fan should turn ON when the hot terminal is connected to the positive battery terminal.
4. If not, the fan is defective and should be replaced.

Summit, Laser and Talon

1. Disconnect the negative battery cable.
2. Disconnect the electrical plug from the fan motor harness.
3. On Summit, the radiator cooling fan connector has 2 terminals and the condenser cooling fan has 3 terminals. Laser and Talon connectors have 4 terminals. Connect the appropriate terminals and make sure the fan runs smoothly, without abnormal noise or vibration.
4. Reconnect the negative battery cable.

Monaco and Premier

All vehicles are equipped with an electric cooling fan systems designed to operate automatically under different conditions. The system reacts with the changes in engine temperature. When the engine coolant temperature reaches 198°F for 1989 models or 188°F for 1990–91 models, but below 212°F, the cooling fan switch low speed contacts close. This activates the cooling fan in low speed operation. When the coolant temperature exceeds 212°F, the fan switch activates the fan in high speed operation. If equipped with air conditioning, the coolant fan switch automatically turns the cooling fan **ON** while the air conditioning is activated.

If the cooling fan does not operate with the air conditioning on but the compressor operates, repair an open between terminal 5 of the cooling fan relay connector and the compressor clutch relay.

COOLING FAN TEMPERATURE SWITCH

1. Turn ignition switch to **RUN**. Connect a jumper wire between coolant temperature switch terminals **A** and **B**. The cooling fan should operate.
2. If the cooling fan operates, replace the cooling fan temperature switch.
3. If the cooling fan does not operate, check the cooling fan relay.

COOLING FAN RELAY

1. Turn ignition switch to **RUN**, with the relay plugged in. Note that the cooling fan relay can be found in the relay panel in the engine compartment. Look for a panel on the driver's side fender wall area, with 4 relays. The front one should be the starter relay, next behind it is the ignition relay, then the radiator fan relay, with the back relay the air conditioning clutch relay. Connect a jumper wire between coolant temperature switch terminals **A** and **B**. Check for voltage at the cooling fan relay connector terminal 5. If no voltage is present, repair an open between terminal 5 and the ignition switch.
2. If 12 volts is present, test for voltage at the cooling fan relay connector terminal 4. If no voltage is present, repair an open between terminal 4 and fusible link **G**. The multiple fusible link connection is the main electrical feed near the battery positive cable.
3. If 12 volts is present at terminal 4, check for voltage at the cooling fan relay connector terminal 2. If voltage is present, some power is getting through, repair an open to ground since the system is trying to ground through the test meter. If zero voltage is indicated, check for voltage at connector terminal 1.
4. If no voltage is present at connector terminal 1, replace the cooling fan relay. If 12 volts is present, check and clean the connections at the cooling fan motor. If connections are okay, replace the cooling fan.

REMOVAL AND INSTALLATION

Medallion

1. Disconnect the negative battery cable.
2. Unplug the connector.
3. Remove the mounting screws.
4. Remove the fan assembly.
5. The installation is the reverse of the removal procedure.
6. Connect the negative battery cable and check the fan for proper operation.

Summit, Laser and Talon

1. Disconnect the negative battery cable.
2. Unplug the connector. Remove the upper radiator hose if necessary.
3. Remove the mounting screws. The radiator and condenser cooling fans are separately removeable.
4. Remove the fan assembly.
5. The installation is the reverse of the removal procedure.
6. Check the coolant level and refill as required.
7. Connect the negative battery cable and check the fan for proper operation.

Monaco and Premier

1. Disconnect the negative battery cable.
2. Remove the radiator support bracket screws. Remove the vibration cushion nuts.
3. Remove the upper radiator crossmember mounting screws and the crossmember.
4. Disconnect the electrical connectors from the fan. Remove the cooling fan and shroud mounting bolts and the fan by lifting upwards.

To install:

5. Install the fan into position and install the mounting bolts.
6. Install the radiator crossmember and support bracket.
7. Connect the negative battery cable and check the fan for proper operation.

Condenser

REMOVAL AND INSTALLATION

Medallion

1. Disconnect the negative battery cable.
2. Drain the coolant.
3. Matchmark and remove the hood.
4. Properly discharge the system.
5. Remove the 5 grille mounting screws and the grille.
6. Remove the radiator support and facia panel.
7. Disconnect hoses from the radiator.
8. Disconnect the connectors from the cooling fans and thermo switch.
9. Disconnect the refrigerant lines from the condenser. Cover the exposed ends of the lines to minimize contamination.
10. Remove any remaining mounting hardware and lift the radiator, condenser and cooling fans from the engine compartment as an assembly. Separate the components as required.

To install:

11. Assemble the components and position in the engine compartment. Install mounting hardware.
12. Replace the O-rings and connect the refrigerant lines to the condenser.
13. Connect the electrical connectors.
14. Connect the hoses to the radiator.
15. Install the facia panel, radiator support, grille and hood.
16. Fill the radiator with coolant and bleed the system.
17. Evacuate and recharge the air conditioning system. Add 2 oz. of refrigerant oil during the recharge.
18. Connect the negative battery cable and check the entire climate control system for proper operation. Check the system for leaks.

Summit, Laser and Talon

1. Disconnect the negative battery cable. On Summit, remove the battery and battery tray.
2. Properly discharge the air conditioning system.
3. On Summit, remove the windshield washer reservoir.
4. Remove the radiator and condenser fans.
5. Remove the upper radiator mounts to allow the radiator to be moved toward the engine.
6. Disconnect the refrigerant lines from the condenser. Cover the exposed ends of the lines to minimize contamination.
7. Remove the condenser mounting bolts.
8. Move the radiator toward the engine and lift the condenser from the vehicle. Inspect the lower rubber mounting insulators and replace if necessary.

To install:

9. Lower the condenser into position and align the dowels with the lower mounting insulators. Install the bolts.
10. Replace the O-rings and connect the refrigerant lines.
11. Install the radiator mounts and cooling fans.
12. Install the windshield washer reservoir, battery tray and battery if removed.
13. Evacuate and recharge the air conditioning system. Add 2 oz. of refrigerant oil during the recharge.
14. Connect the negative battery cable and check the entire climate control system for proper operation. Check the system for leaks.

Monaco and Premier

1. Disconnect the negative battery cable.
2. Attach one end of a 4 foot long ¼ in. hose to the air bleed on the thermostat housing. Carefully route the hose away from the drive belt and pulleys. Place the other end of the hose in a clean container. The purpose of this hose is to keep coolant away from the belt and pulleys. Drain the coolant.
3. Properly discharge the air conditioning system.
4. Remove the 5 grille mounting screws and the grille.
5. Disconnect the hoses from the radiator.
6. Remove the radiator support and facia panel.
7. Disconnect the connectors from the cooling fans and thermo switch.
8. Disconnect the refrigerant line from the condenser using the appropriate spring lock coupling tool from tool kit 6125 or equivalent:
    a. Close the tool and push into the open side of the cage to expand the garter spring and release the female fitting. The garter spring may not release if the tool is cocked while pushing it into the cage opening.
    b. After the garter spring is expanded, pull the fittings apart within the tool.
    c. Remove the tool from the disconnected coupling.
    d. Separate the 2 ends of the coupling. Cover the exposed ends of the lines to minimize contamination.
9. Remove any remaining mounting hardware and lift the radiator, condenser and cooling fans from the engine compartment as an assembly. Separate the components as required.

To install:

10. Assemble the components and position in the engine compartment. Install mounting hardware.
11. Clean all the dirt or foreign material from both pieces of the hose coupling at the condenser.
12. Lubricate new O-rings with clean refrigerant oil on the male fitting and push together with the female fitting until the garter spring snaps over the flared end of the female fitting.

NOTE: If a plastic indicator ring is used, it will snap from the cage opening when the coupling is connected,

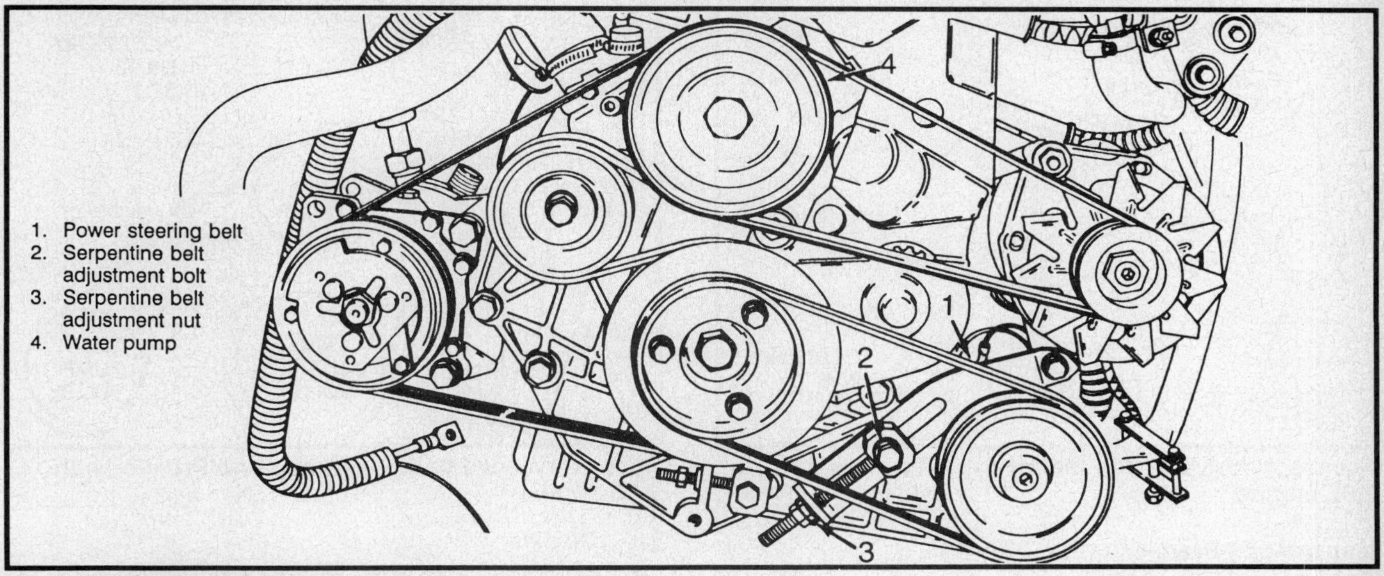
1. Power steering belt
2. Serpentine belt adjustment bolt
3. Serpentine belt adjustment nut
4. Water pump
1
2
3
4

Accessory belts—Medallion

indicating positive engagement. If the indicator ring is not used, verify coupling engagement by visually checking to make sure the garter spring is over the flared end of the female fitting.

13. Connect the electrical connectors.
14. Connect the hoses to the radiator.
15. Install the facia panel, radiator support, grille and hood.
16. Fill the radiator with coolant and bleed the system. Evacuate and recharge the air conditioning system. Add 2 oz. of refrigerant oil during the recharge.
17. Connect the negative battery cable and check the entire climate control system for proper operation. Check the system for leaks.

Compressor

REMOVAL AND INSTALLATION

Medallion

1. Disconnect the negative battery cable.
2. Properly discharge the air conditioning system.
3. Raise and support the vehicle. Remove the splash shield.
4. Loosen the serpentine belt tensioner and remove the belt from the compressor.
5. Lower the vehicle.
6. Remove the suction and discharge hoses from the compressor. Cover the exposed ends of the lines to minimize contamination.
7. Disconnect the compressor clutch wire.
8. Remove the 4 compressor bolts and the compressor.

To install:

9. If a replacement compressor is being installed, the correct amount of oil should be installed along with the new compressor. Drain and measure the old amount of oil in the old compressor. Drain the oil from the new compressor and install the same amount of oil that was in the old compressor plus 1 oz.
10. Place the compressor into position and install the 4 compressor mounting bolts.
11. Connect the compressor clutch wire.
12. Install the suction and discharge hoses to the compressor.
13. Raise and support the vehicle safely.
14. Install the drive belt and adjust the tension.
15. Install the splash shield and lower the vehicle.
16. Evacuate and recharge the air conditioning system.
17. Connect the negative battery cable and check the entire climate control system for proper operation. Check the system for leaks.

Summit, Laser and Talon

1. Disconnect the negative battery cable.
2. Properly discharge the air conditioning system.
3. Remove the distributor cap and wires so the compressor may be lifted from the engine compartment.
5. On Laser and Talon with turbocharged engine, remove the VSV bracket on the cowl top.
6. On Talon with AWD, remove the center bearing bracket mounting bolts.
7. If the alternator is in front of the compressor belt, remove it.
8. If equipped with 1.6L or 2.0L engine, remove the tensioner pulley assembly.
9. Remove the compressor drive belt. Disconnect the clutch coil connector.
10. Disconnect the refrigerant lines from the compressor and discard the O-rings. Cover the exposed ends of the lines to minimize contamination.
11. Remove the compressor mounting bolts and the compressor.

To install:

12. Install the compressor and torque the mounting bolts to 18 ft. lbs. (25 Nm). Connect the clutch coil connector.
13. Using new lubricated O-rings, connect the refrigerant lines to the compressor.
14. Install the belt and tensioner pulley, if removed. Adjust the belt to specifications.
15. Install and adjust the alternator belt, if removed.
16. Install the center bearing bracket mounting bolts and VSV bracket, if removed. Torque the center bearing bracket mounting bolts to 30 ft. lbs. (41 Nm).
17. Install the distributor cap and wires.
18. Evacuate and recharge the air conditioning system.
19. Connect the negative battery cable and check the entire climate control system for proper operation. Check the system for leaks.

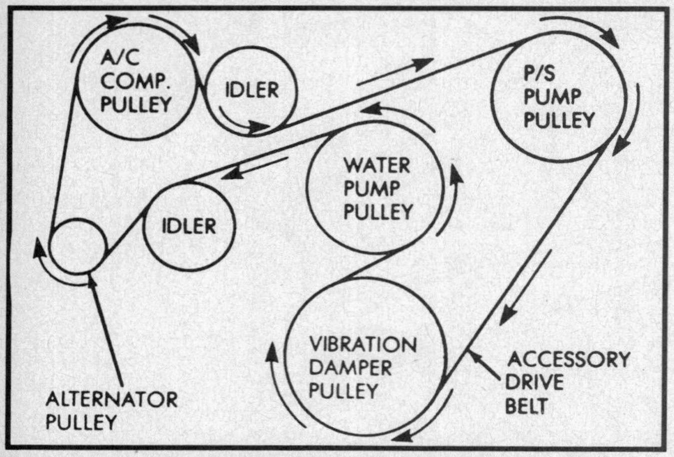
A/C COMP. PULLEY
IDLER
P/S PUMP PULLEY
WATER PUMP PULLEY
IDLER
VIBRATION DAMPER PULLEY
ACCESSORY DRIVE BELT
ALTERNATOR PULLEY

Accessory drive belts—Monaco and Premier with 2.5L engine

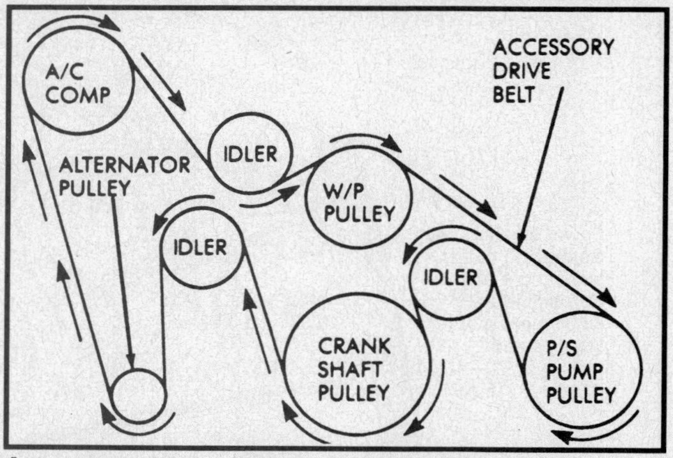
A/C COMP
ACCESSORY DRIVE BELT
ALTERNATOR PULLEY
IDLER
W/P PULLEY
IDLER
IDLER
CRANK SHAFT PULLEY
P/S PUMP PULLEY

Accessory drive belts—Monaco and Premier with 3.0L engine

Monaco and Premier

2.5L ENGINE

1. Disconnect the negative battery cable.
2. Properly discharge the air conditioning system.
3. Loosen the power steering pump locking nut, pivot bolt, the 2 bolts at the rear of the power steering pump, and the adjusting bolt, then remove the accessory drive belt.
4. Disconnect the compressor clutch coil electrical connector.
5. Remove the manifold attaching bolt and separate the manifold from the compressor. Disconnect the refrigerant lines from the compressor. Cover the exposed ends of the lines to minimize contamination.
6. Remove the compressor mounting bolts and the compressor.

To install:

7. If a replacement compressor is being installed, the correct amount of oil should be installed along with the new compressor. Drain and measure the old amount of oil in the old compressor. Drain the oil from the new compressor and install the amount of oil from the old compressor plus 1 oz.
8. Place the compressor into position and install the 4 compressor mounting bolts and tighten to 20 ft. lbs.
9. Install the drive belt on the pulleys.

NOTE: Make sure the drive belt is routed correctly. It is possible to install the belt incorrectly and turn the water pump in the wrong direction causing engine overheating.

10. Tighten the rear power steering pump mounting bolts finger tight.
11. Tighten the adjusting bolt until the specified belt tension is obtained.
12. Torque in the following order to 20 ft. lbs: the rear power steering pump mounting bolts, the pivot bolt and the locking nut.
13. Lubricate new O-rings with clean refrigerant oil and position them in the grooves of the manifold.
14. Position the manifold and hose assembly with new O-rings to the compressor and install the attaching bolts. Torque the bolts to 28 ft. lbs.
15. Connect the compressor electrical connector.
16. Evacuate and recharge the air conditioning system.
17. Connect the negative battery cable and check the entire climate control system for proper operation. Check the system for leaks.

3.0L ENGINE

1. Disconnect the negative battery cable.
2. Properly discharge the air conditioning system.
3. Disconnect the compressor clutch coil electrical connector.
4. Raise the vehicle and support safely.
5. Remove the lower splash shield retaining bolts and the lower splash shield.
6. Relieve the tension on the drive belt by turning the adjusting bolt on the alternator. Loosen the pivot bolts and remove the accessory belt.
7. Remove the manifold attaching bolt and separate the manifold from the compressor.
8. Remove the compressor mounting bolts and the compressor.

To install:

9. If a replacement compressor is being installed, the correct amount of oil should be installed along with the new compressor. Drain and measure the amount of oil in the old compressor. Drain the oil from the new compressor and install the same amount of oil that was in the old compressor plus 1 oz.
10. Place the compressor into position and install the 4 compressor mounting bolts and tighten to 20 ft. lbs.
11. Install the drive belt over the alternator pulley.
12. Torque the alternator pivot bolt to 30 ft. lbs.
13. Tighten the adjusting bolt until the specified belt tension is obtained.
14. Torque the remaining alternator bolt to 20 ft. lbs.
15. Install the splash shield and lower the vehicle.
16. Lubricate new O-rings with clean refrigerant oil and position them in the grooves of the manifold.
17. Position the manifold and hose assembly with new O-rings to the compressor and install the attaching bolts. Torque the bolts to 28 ft. lbs.
18. Connect the compressor electrical connector.
19. Evacuate and recharge the air conditioning system. Add 2 oz. of refrigerant oil during the recharge.
20. Connect the negative battery cable and check the entire climate control system for proper operation. Check the system for leaks.

Receiver/Drier

REMOVAL AND INSTALLATION

Except Monaco and Premier

The receiver/drier is located in the lower right area of the engine compartment on Medallion, to the rear of the left side wheel housing on Summit, and forward of the condenser on the Laser and Talon.

1. Disconnect the negative battery cable.
2. Properly discharge the air conditioning system.
3. Disconnect the electrical connector from the switch on the receiver/drier, if equipped.
4. Disconnect the refrigerant lines from the receiver/drier assembly.
5. Discard the O-rings. Cover the exposed ends of the lines to minimize contamination.
6. Remove the mounting strap and the receiver/drier from its bracket.
7. The installation is the reverse of the removal installation. Use new lubricated O-rings when assembling.
8. Evacuate and recharge the air conditioning system. Add 1 oz. of refrigerant oil during the recharge.
9. Connect the negative battery cable and check the entire climate control system for proper operation. Check the system for leaks.

Accumulator/Drier

REMOVAL AND INSTALLATION

Monaco and Premier

1. Disconnect the negative battery cable.
2. Properly discharge the air conditioning system.
3. Unplug the pressure switch.
4. Loosen the refrigerant line locknut located on the accumulator/drier.
5. Disconnect the refrigerant line at the dash panel using the appropriate spring lock coupling tool from tool kit 6125 or equivalent.
   a. Close the tool and push into the open side of the cage to expand the garter spring and release the female fitting. The garter spring may not release if the tool is cocked while pushing it into the cage opening.
   b. After the garter spring is expanded, pull the fittings apart within the tool.
   c. Remove the tool from the disconnected coupling.
   d. Separate the 2 ends of the coupling.
6. Remove the accumulator/drier mounting bolts, the accumulator/drier and bracket.
7. Loosen the securing bolt and separate the bracket and accumulator.

To install:

8. Whenever the accumulator is replaced, the oil trapped inside must be replaced. Drain and measure the amount of oil inside. Add the amount of oil removed plus 1 oz. of clean refrigerant to the new accumulator prior to installation.
9. Position the accumulator in the bracket and tighten the securing bolt.
10. Position the accumulator/drier and secure with bolts.
11. Clean all the dirt or foreign material from both pieces of the hose coupling at the dash panel.
12. Lubricate new O-rings with clean refrigerant oil on the male fitting and push together with the female fitting until the garter spring snaps over the flared end of the female fitting.

NOTE: If a plastic indicator ring is used, it will snap from the cage opening when the coupling is connected, indicating positive engagement. If the indicator ring is not used, verify coupling engagement by visually checking to make sure the garter spring is over the flared end of the female fitting.

13. Install the accumulator/drier hose and secure the locknut.
14. Connect the pressure switch. Evacuate and recharge the air conditioning system.
15. Connect the negative battery cable and check the entire climate control system for proper operation. Check the system for leaks.

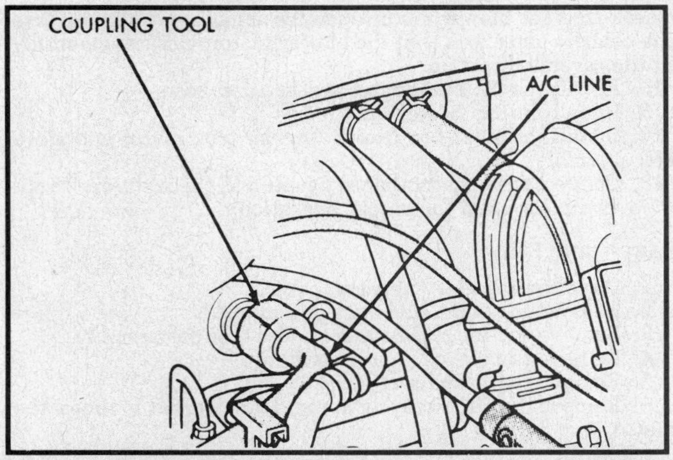
COUPLING TOOL
A/C LINE
Removing the refrigerant line with the coupling tool—Monaco and Premier

Expansion Valve

REMOVAL AND INSTALLATION

Medallion

1. Disconnect the negative battery cable.
2. Properly discharge the air conditioning system.
3. Disconnect the refrigerant lines from the expansion valve, located on the dash panel. Cover the exposed ends of the lines to minimize contamination.
4. Remove the expansion valve from the evaporator fittings.
5. The installation is the reverse of the removal installation. Use new lubricated O-rings when assembling.
6. Evacuate and recharge the air conditioning system.
7. Connect the negative battery cable and check the entire climate control system for proper operation. Check the system for leaks.

Summit, Laser and Talon

1. Disconnect the negative battery cable.
2. Properly discharge the air conditioning system.
3. Remove the evaporator housing and separate the upper and lower cases.
4. Remove the expansion valve from the evaporator lines.
5. The installation is the reverse of the removal installation. Use new lubricated O-rings when assembling.
6. Evacuate and recharge the air conditioning system.
7. Connect the negative battery cable and check the entire climate control system for proper operation. Check the system for leaks.

Fixed Orifice Tube

REMOVAL AND INSTALLATION

Monaco and Premier

1. Disconnect the negative battery cable.
2. Properly discharge the air conditioning system.
3. Disconnect the refrigerant line from the condenser and evaporator at the dash panel using the appropriate spring lock coupling tool from tool kit 6125 or equivalent:
   a. Close the tool and push into the open side of the cage to expand the garter spring and release the female fitting. The

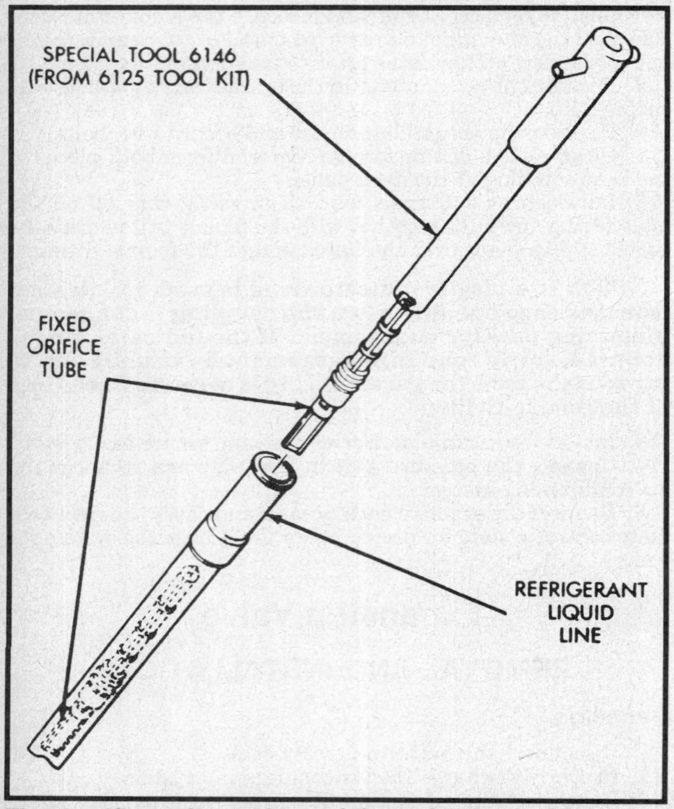
SPECIAL TOOL 6146
(FROM 6125 TOOL KIT)
FIXED
ORIFICE
TUBE
REFRIGERANT
LIQUID
LINE

Fixed orifice tube and special service tool—Monaco and Premier

garter spring may not release if the tool is cocked while pushing it into the cage opening.

b. After the garter spring is expanded, pull the fittings apart within the tool.

c. Remove the tool from the disconnected coupling.

d. Separate the 2 ends of the coupling. Cover the exposed ends of the lines to minimize contamination.

4. Insert the fixed orifice tube removal tool 6146 into the liquid line.
5. Turn the tool clockwise to engage the tabs on the fixed orifice tube.
6. Remove the tool and the fixed orifice tube from the liquid line.
7. If tool 6146 will not remove the tube, the tube may be broken. If this is the case, screw the threaded T-handle tool 6147 into the fixed orifice tube clockwise and pull the tube from the liquid line.

To install:

8. Position the fixed orifice tube tabs into the installation tool 6145.
9. Slide the orifice/tool assembly into the liquid line until the fixed orifice tube contacts the indents in the liquid line and bottoms.
10. Remove the tool.
11. Clean all the dirt or foreign material from both pieces of the hose coupling at the condenser and evaporator.
12. Lubricate new O-rings with clean refrigerant oil on the male fitting and push together with the female fitting until the garter spring snaps over the flared end of the female fitting.
13. Evacuate and recharge the air conditioning system.
14. Connect the negative battery cable and check the entire climate control system for proper operation. Check the system for leaks.

Blower Motor

REMOVAL AND INSTALLATION

Medallion

1. Disconnect the negative battery cable.
2. Remove the glove box door straps and the glove box door. Remove the inner glove box.
3. Unclip the ventilator outlet from the right side of the blower housing. Disconnect the electrical connector from the blower motor.
4. Remove the blower housing retaining screws and the housing.
5. Remove the fan assembly from the blower housing.

To install:

6. Install the fan assembly into the blower housing and install the retaining screws. Connect the electrical connector and the ventilator outlet.
7. Install the inner glove box and the glove box door.
8. Connect the negative battery cable and check the entire climate control system for proper operation.

Summit

1. Disconnect the negative battery cable.
2. Remove the glove box assembly and pry off the speaker cover to the lower right of the glove box.
3. Remove the passenger side lower cowl side trim kick panel.
4. Remove the passenger side knee protector, the panel surrounding in the glove box opening.
5. Remove the glove frame along the top of glove box opening.
6. Remove the lap heater duct. This is a small piece on vehicles without a rear heater, much larger on vehicles with a rear heater.
7. Remove the electrical connector from the blower motor.
8. Remove the molded hose from the blower assembly.
9. Remove the MPI computer from the lower side of the cowl.
10. Remove the blower motor assembly.
11. Separate the blower assembly case and packing seal from the blower motor flange.
12. Remove the fan retaining nut and fan in order to replace the motor.

To install:

13. Check that the blower motor shaft is not bent and that the packing and blower case are in good condition. Check the operation of the inside/outside air selection damper. Clean all parts of dust, etc.
14. Assemble the motor and fan. Install the blower motor assembly, then connect the motor terminals to battery voltage. Check that the blower motor operates smoothly. Then, reverse the polarity and check that the blower motor operates smoothly in the reverse direction.
15. Install the MPI computer and molded hose.
16. Install the lap heater duct.
17. Install the glove box frame, interior trim pieces and glove box assembly.
18. Connect the negative battery cable and check the entire climate control system for proper operation.

Laser and Talon

1. Disconnect battery negative cable.
2. Remove the right side duct, if equipped.
3. Remove the molded hose from the blower assembly.
4. Remove the blower motor assembly.
5. Remove the packing seal.
6. Remove the fan retaining nut and fan in order to renew the motor.

To install:

7. Check that the blower motor shaft is not bent and that the packing is in good condition. Clean all parts of dust, etc.

8. Assemble the motor and fan. Install the blower motor then connect the motor terminals to battery voltage. Check that the blower motor operates smoothly. Then, reverse the polarity and check that the blower motor operates smoothly in the reverse direction.
9. Install the molded hose and duct, if removed.
10. Connect the negative battery cable and check the entire climate control system for proper operation.

Monaco and Premier

1. Disconnect the negative battery cable.
2. Disconnect the electrical connector from the coolant reservoir.
3. Remove the coolant reservoir retaining strap and move the reservoir aside.
4. Remove the coolant reservoir mounting bracket. Disconnect the electrical wires from the blower motor.
5. Remove the blower motor mounting bolts and the blower motor.
6. The installation is the reverse of the removal installation.
7. Connect the negative battery cable and check the entire climate control system for proper operation.

Blower Motor Resistor

REMOVAL AND INSTALLATION

Medallion

WITHOUT HEAVAC

1. Disconnect the negative battery cable.
2. Remove the glove box door straps.
3. Lower the glove box door and release the 3 retaining clips along the back edge of the door and remove the door.
4. Remove the inner glove box.
5. Remove the blower motor retaining screws and the blower motor.
6. Remove the resister assembly retaining screws and disconnect the electrical connections at the resisters.
7. The installation is the reverse of the removal installation.
8. Connect the negative battery cable and check the entire climate control system for proper operation.

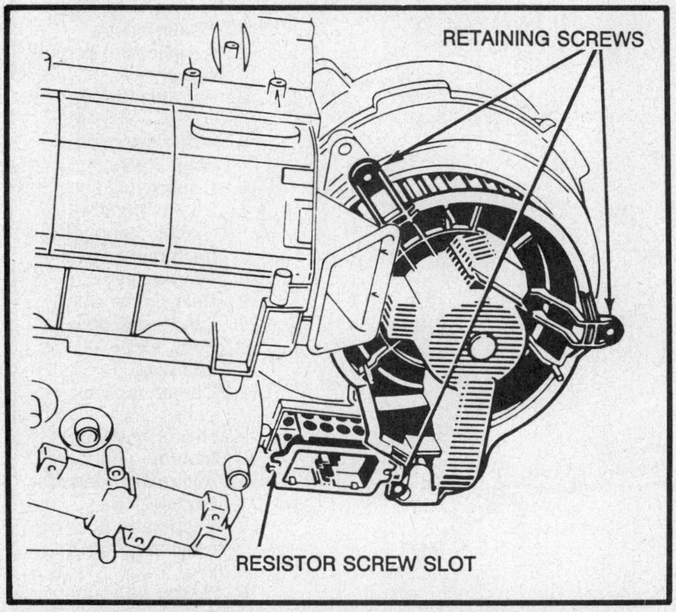
RETAINING SCREWS
RESISTOR SCREW SLOT

Blower motor resistor location—Medallion without HEAVAC

Summit, Laser and Talon

1. Disconnect the negative battery cable.
2. Remove the glove box assembly. The resistor is mounted on the left side of the glove box opening.
3. Disconnect the wire harness from the resistor.
4. Remove the mounting screws and the resistor.
5. The installation is the reverse of the removal installation.
6. Connect the negative battery cable and check the entire climate control system for proper operation.

Monaco and Premier

1. Disconnect the negative battery cable.
2. Remove the ECU mounting screws, located on the bottom of the air heater/air conditioning housing on the passenger side of the vehicle, and lower the ECU.
3. Remove the resistor board mounting screws and disconnect the wiring harness connector(s).
4. Remove the resistors.
5. The installation is the reverse of the removal installation.
6. Connect the negative battery cable and check the entire climate control system for proper operation.

Heater Core and Evaporator

REMOVAL AND INSTALLATION

Medallion

1. Disconnect the negative battery cable.
2. Drain the cooling system. If equipped with air conditioning, properly discharge the system.
3. Remove the left and right rocker trim panels.
4. Disconnect the instrument panel wiring at the A-pillars.
5. Disconnect the ground cables at the rocker sills.
6. Disconnect the fuse panel and door buzzer.
7. Remove the lower instrument panel cover.
8. Open the glove box door and pull the edge of the console out to free it from the instrument panel.
9. On manual transmission equipped vehicles, pry off the boot shifter cover.
10. If equipped with automatic transmission remove the following:
    a. Remove the shift indicator plate by prying off with a suitable tool.
    b. Remove the shift lever knob by pulling straight off.
    c. Remove the shift indicator cover plate.
11. Remove the screws to free the console from the support. Pull the lower section of the console straight back and lift it up to remove it. Pull the upper section down and from the instrument panel.
12. Remove the radio bezel retaining screws.
13. Drill out the rivets that retain the radio.
14. Remove the radio bracket.
15. Remove the retaining screw from the heater control.
16. Remove the heater control knobs by pulling straight up.
17. Lower the heater control panel and disconnect the 2 cables and all the electrical connections.
18. Remove the upper and lower steering column covers.
19. Remove the bolt and nut at the steering joint connection under the dash.
20. Remove the 4 hex head bolts and 1 large torx head bolt holding the steering column in place.
21. Pull the steering column forward slightly and it will drop down. Disconnect the instrument panel wiring and remove the steering column.
22. Remove the speaker covers at the upper corners of the dash.
23. Remove the dash attaching bolts at each corner and remove the dash assembly.

24. Disconnect all electrical connections.
25. Disconnect and plug the heater hoses from the core.
26. On vehicles without air conditioning, remove the 3 remaining screws which retain the heater blower housing to the cowl panel and the housing by pulling it rearward.
27. On vehicles with air conditioning, perform the following:
a. Disconnect the refrigerant lines from the expansion valve.
b. Remove the heater evaporator housing retaining screws from inside the passenger compartment.
c. Remove the vacuum reservoir from the bracket on the engine compartment side of the dash panel.
d. Remove the 2 heater evaporator housing retaining nuts in the engine compartment and the housing assembly.
28. Remove the screws that retain the heater core or evaporator to the blower housing.
29. Spread the 4 retaining clips.
30. Remove the heater core or evaporator by pulling straight up. Be careful of the capillary tube.

To install:

31. Install the heater core or evaporator with foam strips in place into the blower housing.
32. Make sure the 4 tabs clip into place.
33. Install the retaining screws.
34. On vehicles without air conditioning, position the heater housing against the cowl panel with the seals in place, then install the 3 heater housing retaining screws. On vehicles with air conditioning, mount and install the heater/evaporator housing into the vehicle and connect the heater hoses to the core and the air conditioning hoses to the evaporator.
35. Position the dashboard on the centering device and install the bolts in the corner of the dash.
36. Connect the wiring at the A-pillars.
37. Install the ground cables at the rocker sills.
38. Connect and adjust the heater control cables.
39. Install the control panel with the retaining screw.
40. Install the heater control knobs into the control panel.
41. Install the radio bracket, then secure the radio with rivets.
42. Install the lower console assembly.
43. Install the radio bezel and retaining screws.
44. Assemble the steering joint on the steering column.
45. Connect the speedometer cable.
46. Install the lower instrument panel cover.
47. Install the fuse panel and door buzzer.
48. Install the rocker trim panels.
49. On the vehicles without air conditioning, connect the heater hoses to the heater core.
50. Fill and bleed the cooling system.
51. Evacuate and recharge the air conditioning system, if equipped.
52. Connect the negative battery cable and check the entire climate control system for proper operation. Check the system for leaks.

Summit

HEATER CORE

1. Disconnect the negative battery cable.
2. Drain the cooling system and disconnect the heater hoses.
3. Remove the front seats by removing the covers over the anchor bolts, the underseat tray, the seat belt guide ring, the seat mounting nuts and bolts and disconnect the seat belt switch wiring harness from under the seat. Then lift out the seats.
4. Remove the floor console by first taking out the coin holder and the console box tray. Remove the remote control mirror switch or cover. All of these items require only a plastic trim tool to carefully pry them out.
5. Remove the rear half of the console.

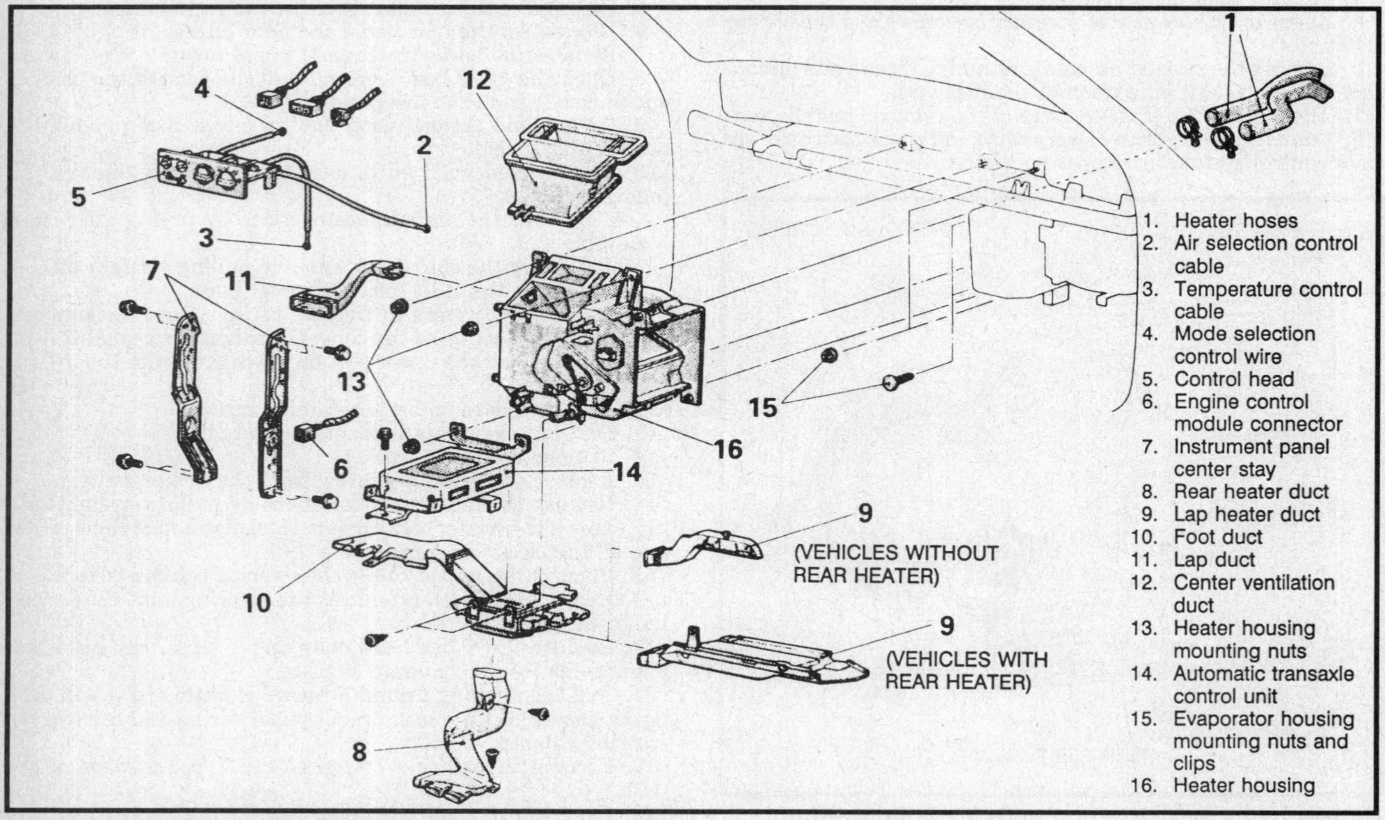
1
2
3
4
5
6
7
8
9
(VEHICLES WITHOUT REAR HEATER)
9
(VEHICLES WITH REAR HEATER)
10
11
12
13
14
15
16
1. Heater hoses
2. Air selection control cable
3. Temperature control cable
4. Mode selection control wire
5. Control head
6. Engine control module connector
7. Instrument panel center stay
8. Rear heater duct
9. Lap heater duct
10. Foot duct
11. Lap duct
12. Center ventilation duct
13. Heater housing mounting nuts
14. Automatic transaxle control unit
15. Evaporator housing mounting nuts and clips
16. Heater housing

Heater core housing and related parts—Summit

6. Remove the shift lever knob on manual transmission vehicles.
7. Remove the front console box assembly.
8. A number of the instrument panel pieces may be retained by pin type fasteners. They may be removed using the following procedure:
   a. This type of clip is removed by pressing down on the center pin with a suitable blunt pointed tool. Press down a little more than 1/16 in. (2mm). This releases the clip. Pull the clip outward to remove it.
   b. Do not push the pin inward more than necessary because it may damage the grommet, or the pin may fall in if pushed in too far. Once the clips are removed, use a plastic trim stick to pry the piece loose.
9. Remove the instrument panel assembly by performing the following:
   a. Remove both lower cowl trim panels (kick panels).
   b. Remove the ashtray and center panel around the radio.
   c. Remove the sunglass pocket at the upper left side of panel and the side panel into which it mounts.
   d. Remove the driver's side knee protector and the hood release handle.
   e. Remove the steering column top and bottom covers.
   f. Remove the radio.
   g. Remove the glove box striker and box assembly.
   h. Remove the instrument panel lower cover, 2 small pieces in the center, by pulling forward.
   i. Remove the heater control assembly screw.
   j. Remove the instrument cluster bezel and pull out the gauge assembly.
   k. Remove the speedometer adapter by disconnecting the speedometer cable at the transaxle pulling the cable sightly towards the vehicle interior, and giving a slight twist on the adapter to release it.
   l. Insert a small flat-tipped tool to open the tab on the gauge cluster connector, and remove the harness connectors.
   m. Remove, by prying with a plastic trim tool, the right side speaker cover and the speaker, the upper side defroster grilles and the clock or plug to gain access to some of the instrument panel mounting bolts.
   n. Drop the steering column by removing the bolt and nut.
   o. Remove the instrument panel bolts and the instrument panel.
10. Disconnect the heater hoses. Disconnect the air selection, temperature and mode selection control cables from the heater box and remove the heater control assembly.
11. Remove the connector for the ECI control relay.
12. Remove both stamped steel instrument panel supports.
13. Remove the heater ductwork.
14. Remove the heater box mounting nuts.
15. Remove the automatic transmission ELC control box.
16. Remove the evaporator mounting nuts and clips.
17. With the evaporator pulled outward, toward the vehicle interior, remove the heater unit. Be careful not to damage the heater tubes or to spill coolant.
18. Remove the cover plate around the heater tubes and the core fastener clips. Pull the heater core from the heater box, being careful not to damage the fins or tank ends.

To install:

19. Install the heater core to the heater box. Install the clips and cover.
20. Install the evaporator and the automatic transmission ELC box.
21. Install the heater box and connect the duct work.
22. Connect all wires and control cables.
23. Install the instrument panel assembly and the console by reversing their removal procedures.
24. Install the seats.
25. Refill the cooling system.

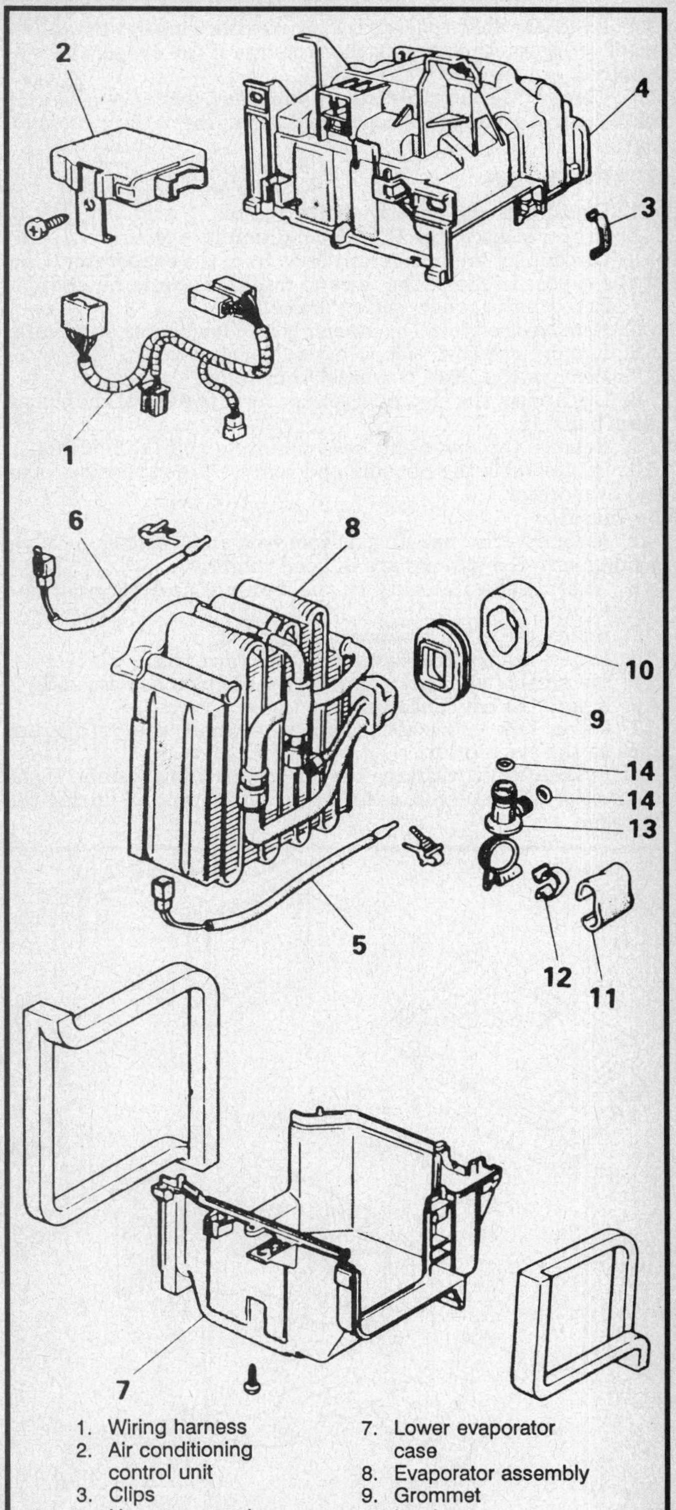
1
2
3
4
5
6
7
8
9
10
11
12
13
14
14

1. Wiring harness
2. Air conditioning control unit
3. Clips
4. Upper evaporator case
5. Air inlet sensor
6. Air thermo sensor
7. Lower evaporator case
8. Evaporator assembly
9. Grommet
10. Insulator
11. Rubber insulator
12. Clip
13. Expansion valve
14. O-ring

Exploded view of the evaporator and related parts—Laser and Talon, Summit similar

26. Evacuate and recharge the air conditioning system. Add 2 oz. of refrigerant oil during the recharge if the evaporator was replaced.
27. Connect the negative battery cable and check the entire climate control system for proper operation. Check the system for leaks.

EVAPORATOR

1. Disconnect the negative battery cable.
2. Properly discharge the air conditioning system.
3. Disconnect the refrigerant lines from the evaporator. Cover the exposed ends of the lines to minimize contamination.
4. Remove the condensation drain hose.
5. Remove the glove box assembly and lap heater duct work.
6. Remove the cowl side trim and speaker cover.
7. Remove the glove box bezel and frame.
8. Disconnect the electrical connector at the top of the evaporator housing.
9. Remove the mounting bolts and nuts and the housing.
10. Disassemble the housing and remove the expansion valve and evaporator.

To install:

11. Assemble the housing, evaporator and expansion valve, making sure the gaskets are in good condition.
12. Install the housing to the vehicle and connect the connector.
13. Install the glove box frame and bezel.
14. Install the speaker cover and side cowl trim.
15. Install the lap heater ductwork and glove box assembly.
16. Install the condensation drain hose.
17. Using new lubricated O-rings, connect the refrigerant lines to the evaporator.
18. Evacuate and recharge the air conditioning system. If the evaporator was replaced, add 2 oz. of refrigerant oil during the recharge.
19. Connect the negative battery cable and check the entire climate control system for proper operation. Check the system for leaks.

Laser and Talon

NOTE: The evaporator housing can be removed by itself, without removing the console, instrument panel or heater core. The heater core, though, cannot be removed without removing the evaporator.

1. Disconnect the negative battery cable.
2. Drain the cooling system and properly discharge the air conditioning system and disconnect the refrigerant lines from the evaporator, if equipped. Cover the exposed ends of the lines to minimize contamination.
3. Remove the floor console by first removing the plugs, then the screws retaining the side covers and the small cover piece in front of the shifter. Remove the shifter knob, manual transmission, and the cup holder. Remove both small pieces of upholstery to gain access to retainer screws. Disconnect both electrical connectors at the front of the console. Remove the shoulder harness guide plates and the console assembly.
4. Remove the instrument panel assembly by performing the following:
   a. Locate the rectangular plugs in the knee protector on either side of the steering column. Pry these plugs out, remove the screws. Remove the screws from the hood lock release lever and the knee protector.
   b. Remove the upper and lower column covers.
   c. Remove the narrow panel covering the instrument cluster cover screws, and remove the cover.
   d. Remove the radio panel and remove the radio.
   e. Remove the center air outlet assembly by reaching

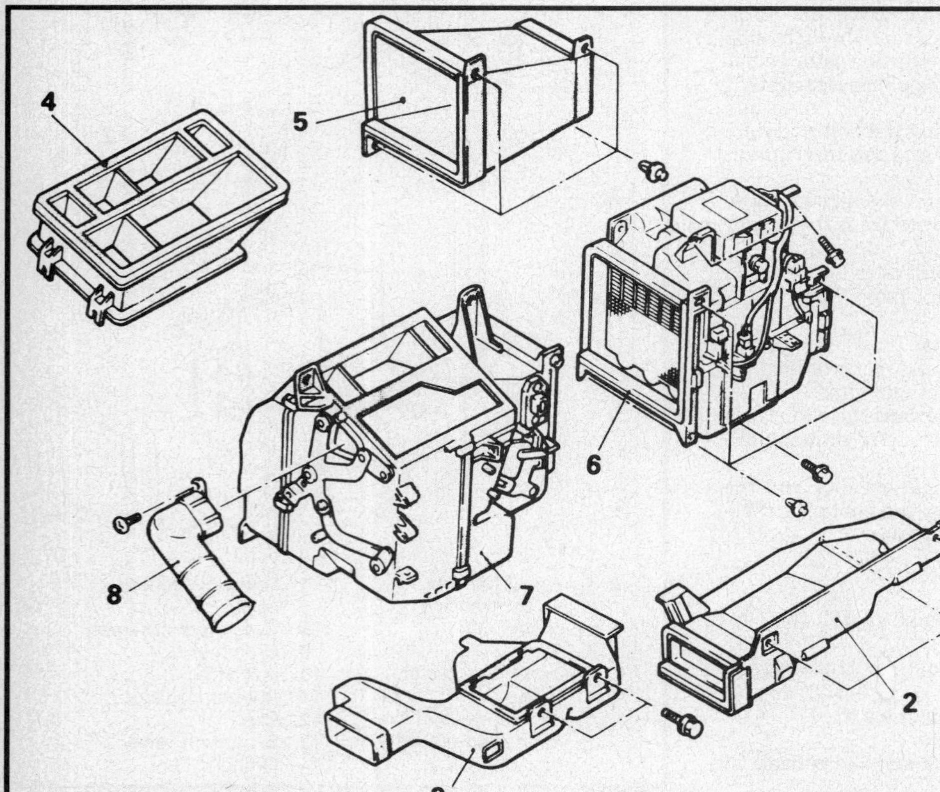
4
5
6
7
8
2
1
3

1. Center reinforcement
2. Right side shower duct
3. Foot duct
4. Center ductwork
5. Duct (vehicles without air conditioning)
6. Evaporator assembly
7. Heater assembly
8. Lap cooler duct

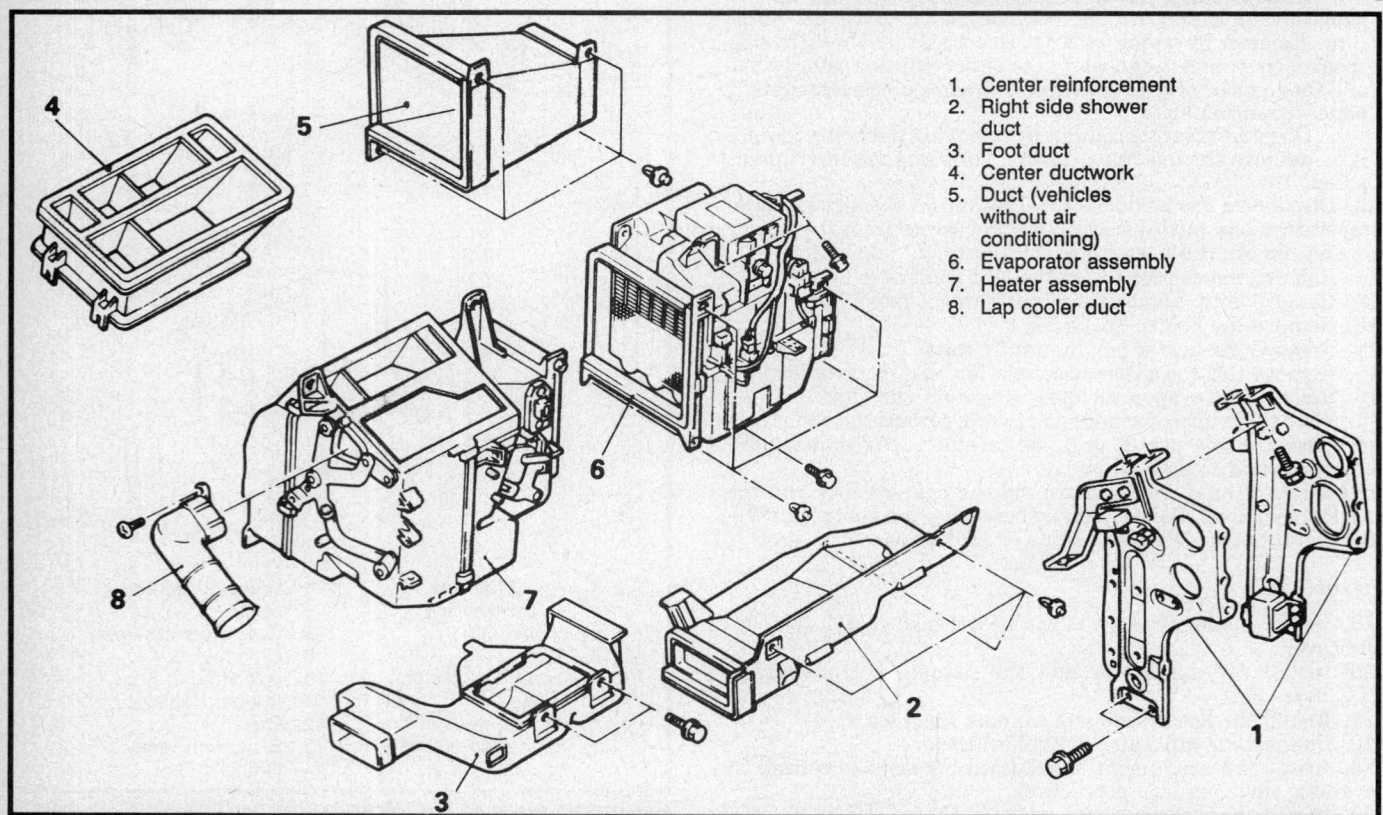

Heater and air conditioning housings—Laser and Talon

through the grille and pushing the side clips out with a small flat-tipped tool while carefully prying the outlet free.

f. Pull the heater control knobs off and remove the heater control panel assembly.

g. Open the glove box, remove the plugs from the sides and the glove box assembly.

h. Remove the instrument gauge cluster and the speedometer adapter by disconnecting the speedometer cable at the transaxle, pulling the cable sightly towards the vehicle interior, then giving a slight twist on the adapter to release it.

i. Remove the left and right speaker covers from the top of the instrument panel.

j. Remove the center plate below the heater controls.

k. Remove the heater control assembly installation screws.

l. Remove the lower air ducts.

m. Drop the steering column by removing the bolts.

n. Remove the instrument panel mounting screws, bolts and the instrument panel assembly.

5. Remove both stamped steel reinforcement pieces.
6. Remove the lower ductwork from the heater box.
7. Remove the upper center duct.
8. Vehicles without air conditioning will have a square duct in place of the evaporator. Remove this duct if present. If the vehicle is equipped with air conditioning, remove the evaporator assembly:

a. Remove the wiring harness connectors and the electronic control unit.

b. Remove the drain hose and lift out the evaporator unit.

c. If servicing the assembly, disassemble the housing and remove the expansion valve and evaporator.

9. With the evaporator removed, remove the heater unit. To prevent bolts from falling inside the blower assembly, set the inside/outside air-selection damper to the position that permits outside air introduction.
10. Remove the cover plate around the heater tubes and remove the core fastener clips. Pull the heater core from the heater box, being careful not to damage the fins or tank ends.

To install:

11. Install the heater core to the heater box. Install the clips and cover.
12. Install the heater box and connect the duct work.
13. Assemble the housing, evaporator and expansion valve, making sure the gaskets are in good condition. Install the evaporator housing.
14. Using new lubricated O-rings, connect the refrigerant lines to the evaporator.
15. Install the electronic transmission ELC box. Connect all wires and control cables.
16. Install the instrument panel assembly and the console by reversing their removal procedures.
17. Evacuate and recharge the air conditioning system. If the evaporator was replaced, add 2 oz. of refrigerant oil during the recharge.
18. Connect the negative battery cable and check the entire cli-

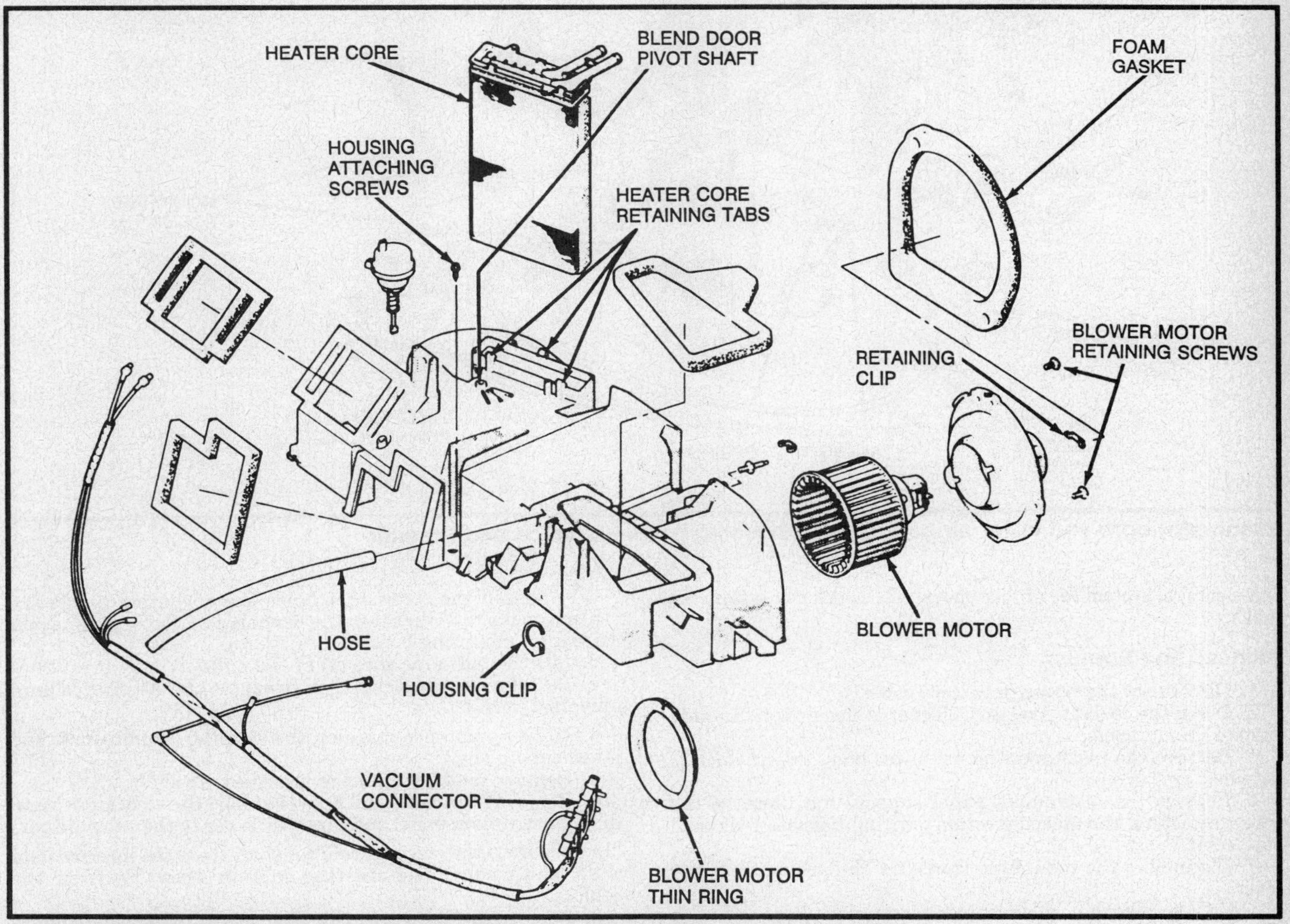
HEATER CORE
BLEND DOOR PIVOT SHAFT
FOAM GASKET
HOUSING ATTACHING SCREWS
HEATER CORE RETAINING TABS
RETAINING CLIP
BLOWER MOTOR RETAINING SCREWS
HOSE
BLOWER MOTOR
HOUSING CLIP
VACUUM CONNECTOR
BLOWER MOTOR THIN RING

Heater core and upper air conditioning housing parts—Monaco and Premier

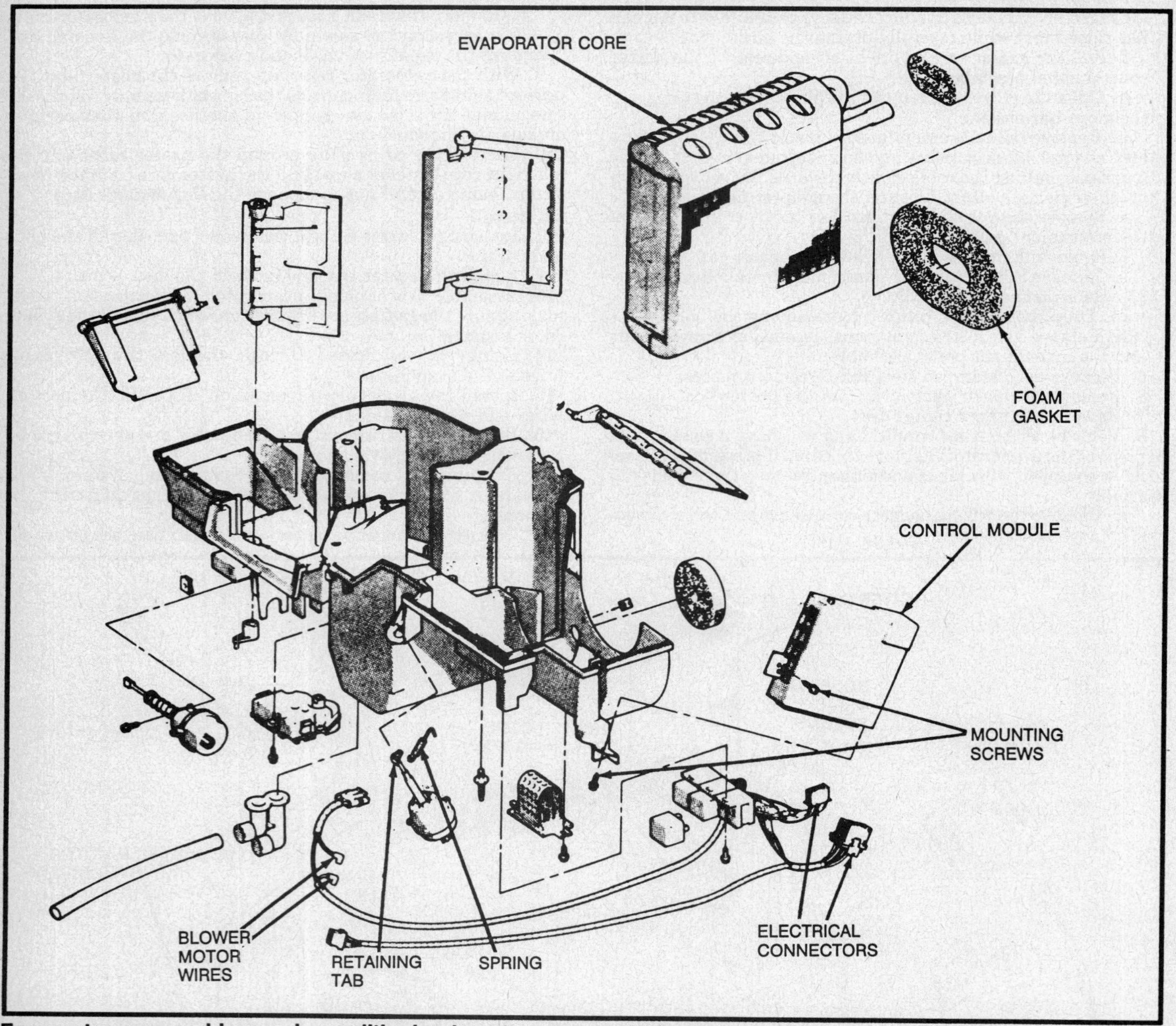
EVAPORATOR CORE
FOAM GASKET
CONTROL MODULE
MOUNTING SCREWS
ELECTRICAL CONNECTORS
BLOWER MOTOR WIRES
RETAINING TAB
SPRING

Evaporator core and lower air conditioning housing parts—Monaco and Premier

mate control system for proper operation. Check the system for leaks.

Monaco and Premier

1. Disconnect the negative battery cable.
2. Drain the coolant. Properly discharge the air conditioning system, if equipped.
3. Remove the instrument panel lower trim cover, which is retained by 3 screws.
4. Remove the instrument panel support rod. Remove the screw attaching the steering column wiring harness bulkhead connector.
5. Disconnect the automatic transaxle shift cable from the lever.
   a. Compress the cable retainer tangs with pliers and slide the cable from the column mounting bracket.
   b. Loosen the screw that holds the anchoring bracket in place, move the bracket to the keyhole position and remove it from its mounting bracket.
6. Lift the indicator wire off of the pulley.
7. Pull the plastic sleeve down to expose the steering column universal joint.
8. Make a reference mark on the steering column shaft and intermediate shaft.
9. Remove the bolt from the intermediate shaft.
10. Remove the 4 bolts and nuts that hold the steering column to the instrument panel and carefully lower to the vehicle floor.
11. Separate the steering column shaft from the intermediate shaft and remove the steering column assembly from the vehicle.
12. Remove the defroster grille from the top of the instrument panel.

13. Loosen but do not remove the nut located near the parking brake release handle and the nut which is located on the passenger side kick panel.
14. Remove the screws and lower the parking brake release handle.
15. Remove the ashtray.
16. Disconnect the cigarette lighter connectors.
17. Remove the screw from the ashtray cavity.
18. Disconnect all electrical connections.
19. Remove the bolts that hold the instrument panel to the center floor bracket.
20. Disconnect the interior temperature sensor.
21. Remove the floor duct extension.

NOTE: The heater core inlet and outlet tubes are made of plastic and may break if too much pressure is applied.

22. Remove the heater hoses from the heater core spouts.
23. Disconnect the coolant level switch connector.
24. Remove the coolant reservoir.
25. Disconnect the blower motor connector.
26. Disconnect the vacuum hoses.
27. Disconnect the refrigerant lines at the dash panel, if equipped.
28. Remove the retaining nuts from inside and outside of the vehicle and carefully pull the heater/air conditioning housing rearward to remove it.
29. Release the plastic tabs and remove the heater core from the housing.

To install:

30. Carefully insert the heater core into the housing and push until it snaps in place.
31. Before installing the housing, make sure the housing seals are in place and in good condition.
32. Position the heater/air conditioning housing to the dash panel. Make sure the drain tube extends through its opening in the upper floor and the blower motor connector and the vacuum line extends through the dash panel. Ensure that the ECU connectors are to the right of the drain tube.
33. Install new housing retaining nuts. Install the floor duct extension.
34. Install new O-rings on the refrigerant lines and lubricate with clean refrigerant oil. Press each line into its connector until it snaps into place.
35. Connect the vacuum hose and the blower electrical connector.
36. Install the coolant reservoir bracket and reservoir.
37. Reconnect the coolant level switch connector.
38. Carefully reconnect the heater hoses to the core.
39. Place the instrument panel into position so the mounting brackets engage the studs on the kick panels. Make sure the wiring harness is behind the center mounting bracket and connect all electrical connections.
40. Install the bolt to the brake support.
41. Install the screw into the ashtray cavity.
42. Install the 2 bolts to the center support bracket.
43. Connect the cigarette lighter connectors and the ashtray.
44. Tighten the nut located near the parking brake release handle and the nut located on the passenger side kick panel.
45. Install the parking brake release handle.
46. Install the bolts under the defroster grille, then install the grille.
47. Position and install the steering column shaft in the intermediate steering shaft U-joint. Align the 2 shafts using the reference marks made during removal. Install but do not tighten the U-joint bolt.
48. Attach the steering column to the instrument panel and tighten the bolts/nuts to 35 ft. lbs.
49. Tighten the bolt in the intermediate steering shaft U-joint and move the plastic sleeve into position.
50. Snap the shift cable into the mounting bracket.
51. Snap the shift cable head onto the mounting ball in the shift arm.
52. Loop the shift indicator wire over the pulley. Position the anchoring bracket over the screw.
53. Move the gearshift lever into **N** and check the position of the shift indicator. If the pointer is not aligned with the **N** mark on the display, slide the bracket forward/rearward to align the indicator. Tighten the screw.
54. Install the bulkhead connector and install the connector attaching screw.
55. Install the instrument panel support rod securely.
56. Install the instrument panel lower trim cover.
57. Evacuate and recharge the air conditioning system, if equipped.
58. Connect the negative battery cable and check the entire climate control system for proper operation. Check the system for leaks.

Refrigerant Lines

REMOVAL AND INSTALLATION

Medallion

1. Disconnect the negative battery cable.
2. Properly discharge the air conditioning system.
3. Separate the flare connections.
4. Remove the lines and discard the O-rings.

To install:

5. Coat the new O-rings with refrigerant oil and install.
6. Connect the refrigerant lines to the adjoining components and tighten the flare connections.
7. Evacuate and recharge the air conditioning system.
8. Connect the negative battery cable and check the entire climate control system for proper operation. Check the system for leaks.

Summit, Laser and Talon

1. Disconnect the negative battery cable.
2. Properly discharge the air conditioning system.
3. Remove the nuts or bolts that attach the refrigerant lines sealing plates to the adjoining components. If the line is not equipped with a sealing plate, separate the flare connection.
4. Remove the line and discard the O-rings.

To install:

5. Coat the new O-rings refrigerant oil and install. Connect the refrigerant lines to the adjoining components and tighten the nuts, bolts or flare connections.
6. Evacuate and recharge the air conditioning system.
7. Connect the negative battery cable and check the entire climate control system for proper operation. Check the system for leaks.

Monaco and Premier

1. Disconnect the negative battery cable.
2. Properly discharge the air conditioning system.
3. To disconnect coupled refrigerant line, use the appropriate spring lock coupling tool from tool kit 6125 or equivalent:
   a. Close the tool and push into the open side of the cage to expand the garter spring and release the female fitting. The garter spring may not release if the tool is cocked while pushing it into the cage opening.
   b. After the garter spring is expanded, pull the fittings apart within the tool.
   c. Remove the tool from the disconnected coupling.
   d. Separate the 2 ends of the coupling. Cover the exposed ends of the lines to minimize contamination.

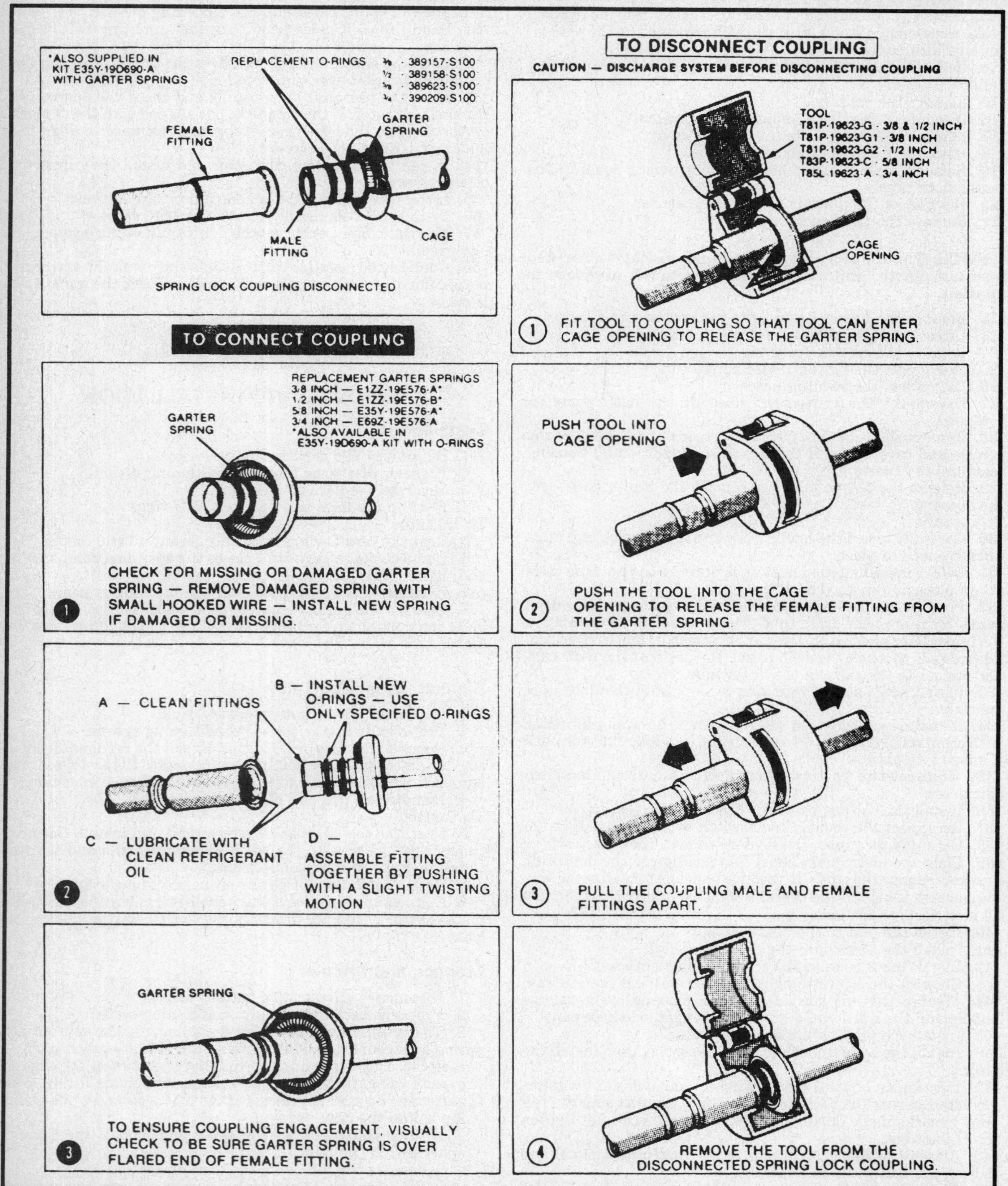
*ALSO SUPPLIED IN
KIT E35Y-19D690-A
WITH GARTER SPRINGS
REPLACEMENT O-RINGS
3/8 · 389157-S100
1/2 · 389158-S100
5/8 · 389623-S100
3/4 · 390209-S100
FEMALE FITTING
GARTER SPRING
MALE FITTING
CAGE
SPRING LOCK COUPLING DISCONNECTED
TO CONNECT COUPLING
REPLACEMENT GARTER SPRINGS
3/8 INCH — E1ZZ-19E576-A*
1/2 INCH — E1ZZ-19E576-B*
5/8 INCH — E35Y-19E576-A*
3/4 INCH — E69Z-19E576-A
*ALSO AVAILABLE IN
E35Y-19D690-A KIT WITH O-RINGS
GARTER SPRING
1 CHECK FOR MISSING OR DAMAGED GARTER SPRING — REMOVE DAMAGED SPRING WITH SMALL HOOKED WIRE — INSTALL NEW SPRING IF DAMAGED OR MISSING.
A — CLEAN FITTINGS
B — INSTALL NEW O-RINGS — USE ONLY SPECIFIED O-RINGS
C — LUBRICATE WITH CLEAN REFRIGERANT OIL
D — ASSEMBLE FITTING TOGETHER BY PUSHING WITH A SLIGHT TWISTING MOTION
2
GARTER SPRING
3 TO ENSURE COUPLING ENGAGEMENT, VISUALLY CHECK TO BE SURE GARTER SPRING IS OVER FLARED END OF FEMALE FITTING.
TO DISCONNECT COUPLING
CAUTION — DISCHARGE SYSTEM BEFORE DISCONNECTING COUPLING
TOOL
T81P-19623-G · 3/8 & 1/2 INCH
T81P-19623-G1 · 3/8 INCH
T81P-19623-G2 · 1/2 INCH
T83P-19623-C · 5/8 INCH
T85L-19623-A · 3/4 INCH
CAGE OPENING
1 FIT TOOL TO COUPLING SO THAT TOOL CAN ENTER CAGE OPENING TO RELEASE THE GARTER SPRING.
PUSH TOOL INTO CAGE OPENING
2 PUSH THE TOOL INTO THE CAGE OPENING TO RELEASE THE FEMALE FITTING FROM THE GARTER SPRING.
3 PULL THE COUPLING MALE AND FEMALE FITTINGS APART.
4 REMOVE THE TOOL FROM THE DISCONNECTED SPRING LOCK COUPLING.

Spring lock coupling usage

To install:

4. Clean all the dirt or foreign material from both pieces of the hose coupling.
5. Lubricate new O-rings with clean refrigerant oil on the male fitting and push together with the female fitting until the garter spring snaps over the flared end of the female fitting.

NOTE: If a plastic indicator ring is used, it will snap from the cage opening when the coupling is connected, indicating positive engagement. If the indicator ring is not used, verify coupling engagement by visually checking to make sure the garter spring is over the flared end of the female fitting.

6. Evacuate and recharge the air conditioning system.
7. Connect the negative battery cable and check the entire climate control system for proper operation. Check the system for leaks.

Manual Control Head

REMOVAL AND INSTALLATION

Medallion

1. Disconnect the negative battery cable.
2. Remove the radio bezel.
3. Drill out the 6 rivets that fasten the radio to its mounting brackets.
4. Remove the lower console.
5. Remove the radio bracket and radio.
6. Pull the control knobs off of the levers.
7. Remove the control panel retaining screws.
8. Lower the control panel, disconnect the 2 cables and electrical connections and remove the control head.
9. The installation is the reverse of the removal installation.
10. Connect the negative battery cable and check the entire climate control system for proper operation.

Summit

1. Disconnect the negative battery cable.
2. Remove the glove box and ashtray assembly.
3. Remove the heater control/radio bezel.
4. Remove the radio assembly.
5. Disconnect the air, temperature and mode selection control cables from the heater housing.
6. Remove the 3 control head mounting screws.
7. Separate the control head from the left side first, then press out the lower and upper mounting brackets from behind the instrument panel.
8. Pull the control head out and disconnect the 3 connectors. Remove the control head assembly.

To install:

9. Feed the control cable through the instrument panel, connect the connectors, install the control head assembly and secure with the screws.
10. Install the radio and bezel.
11. Move the mode selection lever to the **PANEL** position. Move the mode selection damper lever fully forward and connect the cable to the lever. Install the clip.
12. Move the temperature control lever to its leftmost (coolest) position. Move the blend air damper lever fully downward and connect the cable to the lever. Install the clip.
13. Move the air selection control lever to the **RECIRC** position. Move the air selection damper fully inward and connect the cable to the lever. Install the clip.
14. Connect the negative battery cable and check the entire climate control system for proper operation.
15. If everything is satisfactory, install the ashtray and glove box.

Laser and Talon

1. Disconnect the negative battery cable.
2. Remove the glove box assembly.
3. Remove the dial control knobs from the control head.
4. Remove the center air outlet by disengaging the tabs with a flat blade tool and carefully prying out.
5. Remove the instrument cluster bezel and radio bezel.
6. Remove the knee protector and lower the hood lock release handle.
7. Remove the left side lower duct work.
8. Disconnect the air, temperature and mode selection control cables from the heater housing.

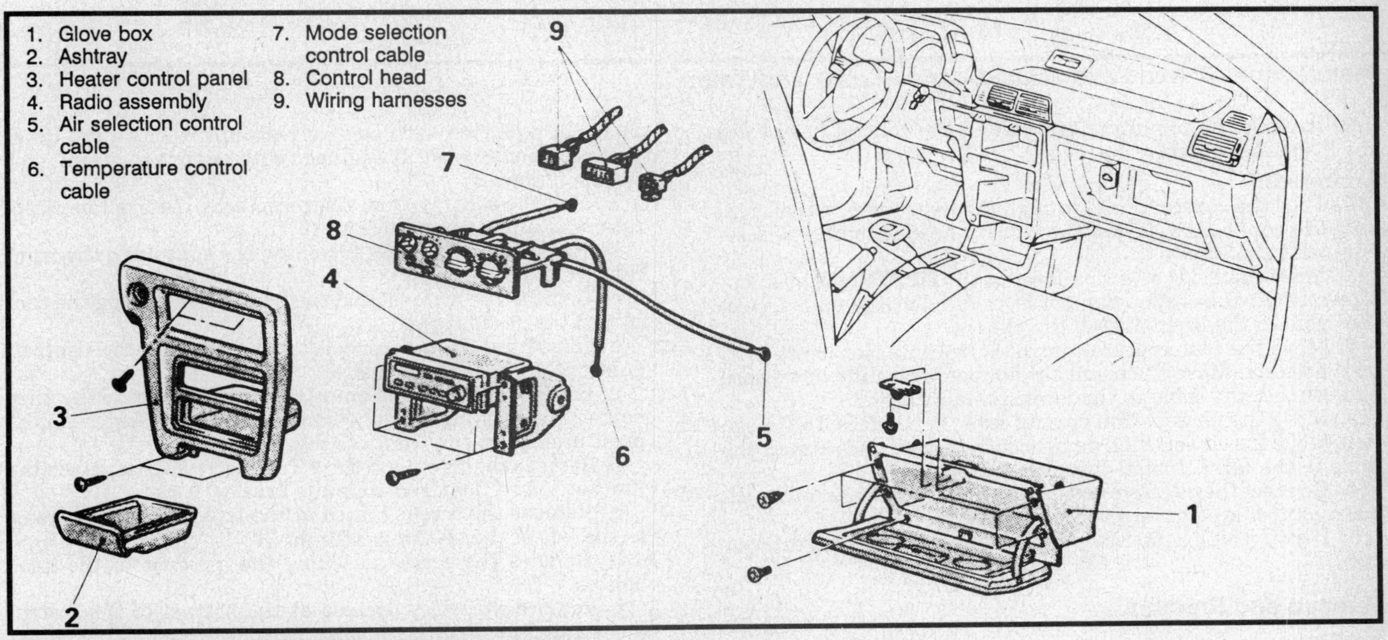
1. Glove box
2. Ashtray
3. Heater control panel
4. Radio assembly
5. Air selection control cable
6. Temperature control cable
7. Mode selection control cable
8. Control head
9. Wiring harnesses
9
7
8
4
3
6
5
1
2

Manual control head and related parts—Summit

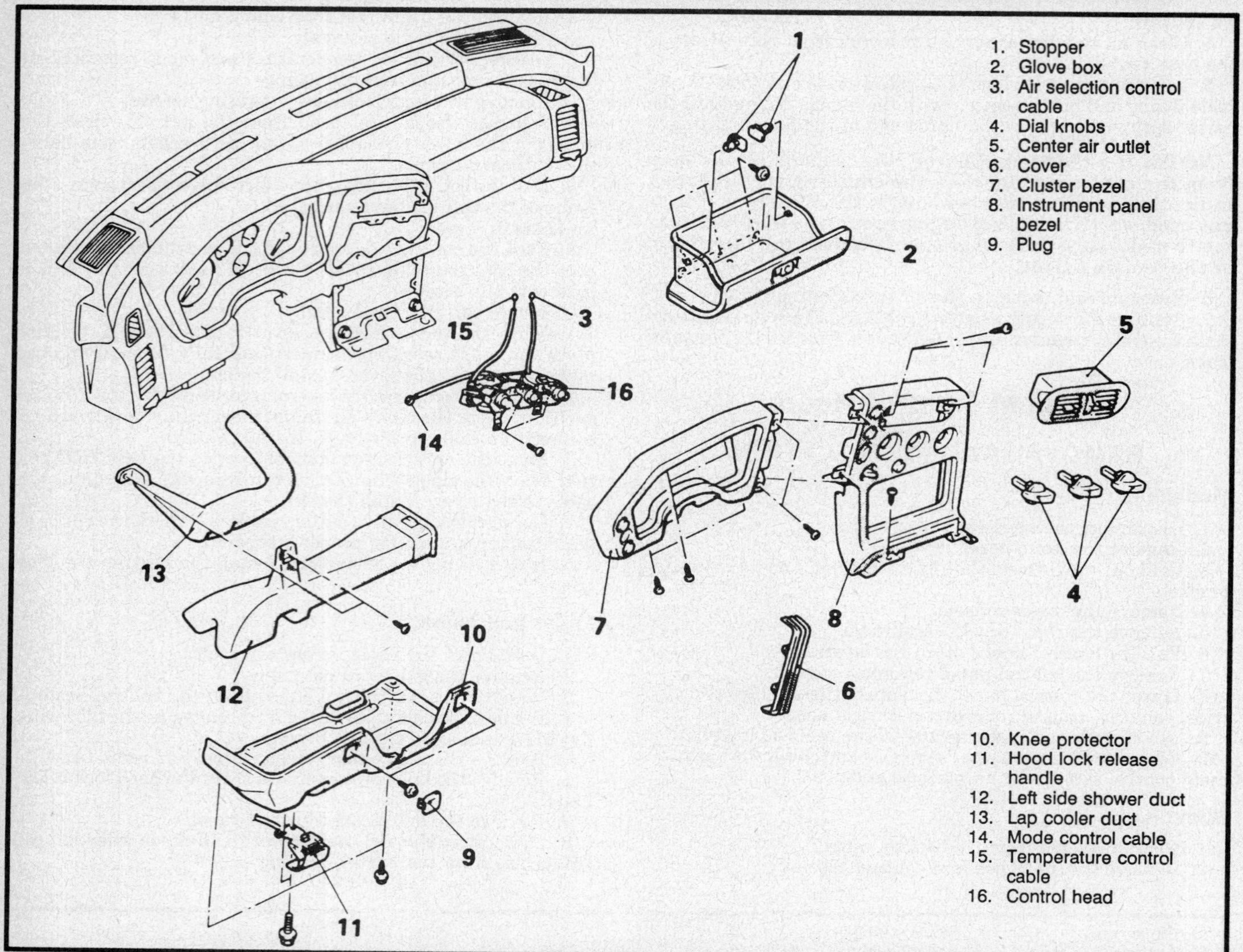
1
2
3
4
5
6
7
8
9
10
11
12
13
14
15
16
1. Stopper
2. Glove box
3. Air selection control cable
4. Dial knobs
5. Center air outlet
6. Cover
7. Cluster bezel
8. Instrument panel bezel
9. Plug
10. Knee protector
11. Hood lock release handle
12. Left side shower duct
13. Lap cooler duct
14. Mode control cable
15. Temperature control cable
16. Control head

Manual control head and related parts—Laser and Talon

9. Remove the mounting screws and the control head from the instrument panel.

To install:

10. Feed the control cable through the instrument panel, connect the connectors, install the control head assembly and secure with the screws.
11. Move the mode selection lever to the **DEFROST** position. Move the mode selection damper lever fully inward and connect the cable to the lever. Install the clip.
12. Move the temperature control lever to its rightmost (hottest) position. Move the blend air damper lever fully downward and connect the cable to the lever. Install the clip.
13. Move the air selection control lever to the **RECIRC** position. Move the air selection damper fully inward and connect the cable to the lever. Install the clip.
14. Connect the negative battery cable and check the entire climate control system for proper operation.
15. If everything is satisfactory, install the remaining interior pieces.

Monaco and Premier

1. Disconnect the negative battery cable.
2. If not equipped with passive restraint, remove the lower instrument panel cover. If equipped with passive restraint, perform the following:
   a. Pull the ashtray from the receptacle, remove the receptacle and unplug the lighter.
   b. Remove the 2 screws fastening the console to the front bracket.
   c. Remove the armrest and the 2 screws fastening the console to the rear bracket.
   d. Reach inside the console and push out the seatbelt guides. Remove the console.
   e. Remove the bolts fastening the pivot bracket to the knee bolster. Loosen, but do not remove, the 2 bolts fastening the pivot bracket to the front console bracket.
   f. Remove the screw and the 2 Torx® screws that attach the bracket to the floor and slide the bracket back.
   g. Remove the screw located at the top of the knee bolster to the left of the steering column.
   h. Remove the screw attaching the air duct to the knee bolster.
   i. Remove the screw located at the bottom of the instrument panel holding the garnish penal.
   j. Remove both bolster end caps and the revealed nuts.

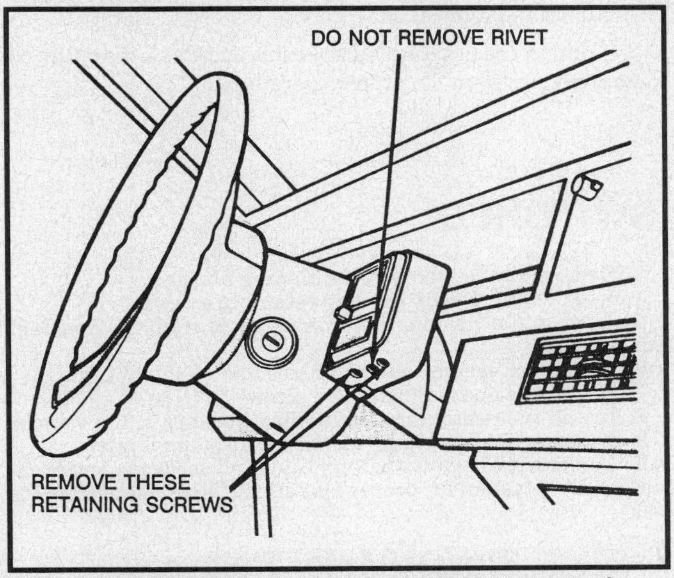
DO NOT REMOVE RIVET
REMOVE THESE
RETAINING SCREWS

Climate control system switch pod—Monaco and Premier

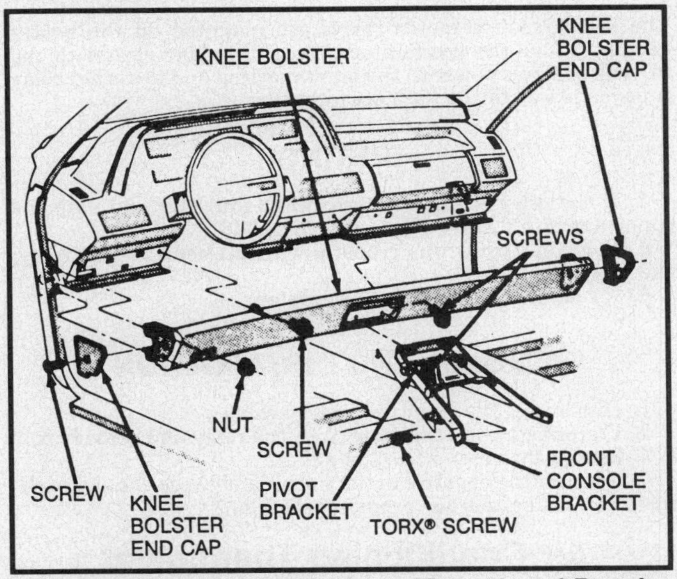
KNEE BOLSTER
KNEE
BOLSTER
END CAP
SCREWS
NUT
SCREW
SCREW
KNEE
BOLSTER
END CAP
PIVOT
BRACKET
TORX® SCREW
FRONT
CONSOLE
BRACKET

Knee bolster and related parts—Monaco and Premier

k. Move the knee bolster toward the rear of the vehicle enough to gain access to the 2 screws holding the parking brake handle, then lower the handle.

l. Remove the knee bolster.

3. Remove the instrument panel support rod.
4. Remove the air duct.
5. Remove the tie straps, loosen the hold-down nut in the center of the steering column connector and separate the steering column connector.
6. Disconnect the control head connector from the steering column connector.
7. Remove the 2 heater/air conditioning control head retaining screws from below the pod. Do not remove the center rivet.
8. Remove the lower steering column shroud.
9. Pull the control head wires through the housing and remove the control head. It may be necessary to remove the 2 screws inside the housing in order to remove the connector.

To install:

10. Route the control head connector through the opening in the housing and along the underside of the steering column.
11. Temporarily connect the harnesses, connect the negative battery cable and check the entire climate control system for proper operation.
12. If everything is satisfactory, disconnect the negative battery cable and continue.
13. Install the lower steering column shroud and install the control head retaining screws.
14. Install the steering column hold-down nut and install new tie straps.
15. Install the air duct and instrument panel support rod.
16. Install the knee bolster and console by reversing their removal procedure, if equipped, or install the lower instrument cover.
17. Connect the negative battery cable and recheck the entire climate control system for proper operation.

Manual Control Cables

ADJUSTMENT

Medallion

1. Disconnect the negative battery cable.
2. Move the temperature control lever to its hottest position and air distribution lever in the **PANEL** position.
3. Observe the air mixing door drive gear. The aligning marks on the gear should be aligned with the marks on the control drives. Adjust the cable as required.
4. Observe the air distribution door drive gear. The aligning marks on the gear should be aligned with the marks on the control drives. Adjust the cable as required.

Summit

1. Disconnect the negative battery cable. Remove the glove box, if necessary.
2. Move the mode selection lever to the **PANEL** position. Move the mode selection damper lever fully forward and connect the cable to the lever. Adjust as required.
3. Move the temperature control lever to its leftmost (coolest) position. Move the blend air damper lever fully downward and connect the cable to the lever. Adjust as required.
4. Move the air selection control lever to the **RECIRC** position. Move the air selection damper fully inward and connect the cable to the lever. Adjust as required.

Laser and Talon

1. Disconnect the negative battery cable. Remove the glove box, if necessary.
2. Move the mode selection lever to the **DEFROST** position. Move the mode selection damper lever fully inward and connect the cable to the lever. Adjust as required.
3. Move the temperature control lever to its rightmost (hottest) postion. Move the blend air damper lever fully downward and connect the cable to the lever. Adjust as required.
4. Move the air selection control lever to the **RECIRC** position. Move the air selection damper fully inward and connect the cable to the lever. Adjust as required.

REMOVAL AND INSTALLATION

1. Disconnect the negative battery cable.
2. Remove the manual control head and disconnect the cable(s) from it.
3. Remove the glove box to access the cable being removed, if necessary.
4. Disconnect the cable from the heater/air conditioning unit and remove the clip.

5. Take note of the cable's routing and remove it.
6. The installation is the reverse of the removal installation. Make sure the cable is routed in exactly the same position as it was prior to removal.
7. Adjust the cable(s) as required.
8. Connect the negative battery cable and check the entire climate control system for proper operation.

SENSORS AND SWITCHES

Vacuum Motor and Solenoid

OPERATION

If not equipped with HEAVAC, the Medallion is equipped with a vacuum motor operated by an electric solenoid. The vacuum motor operates the fresh air door at the right side of the vehicle.

When the key is in the **ON** position, and the climate control system is **OFF**, the solenoid is energized causing the motor to close off the door and block the entrance of fresh air.

When the blower is **ON** and the air conditioning is in the **NORM** position, the solenoid is de-energized causing the motor to open the door and allow the entrance of fresh air.

When the blower is **ON** and the air conditioning is in the **MAX** position, the solenoid is energized causing the motor to close the door and open the recirculating vents to quickly cool the interior.

TESTING

1. Check all vacuum hoses for dry rotting and leakage.
2. Check for voltage at the solenoid when the system is **OFF** and in the **MAX** position. Check for no voltage when the system is in the **NORM** position.
3. Switch the system between modes and watch the motor for corresponding movement.

REMOVAL AND INSTALLATION

1. Disconnect the negative battery cable.
2. Properly discharge the air conditioning system.

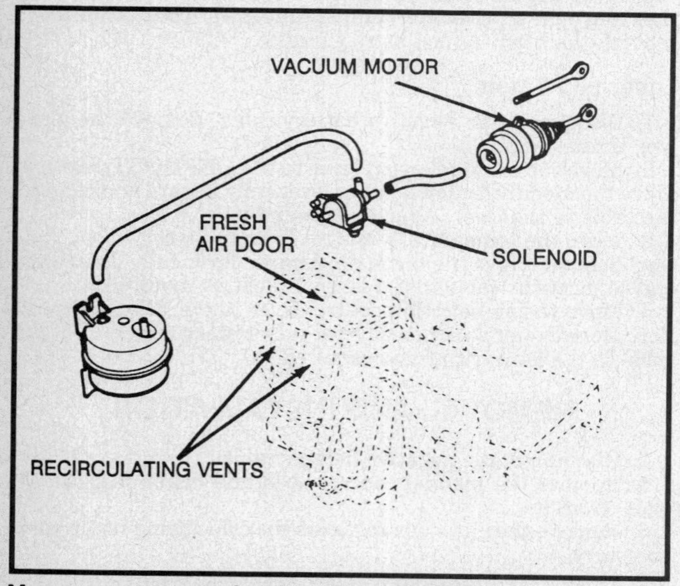
VACUUM MOTOR
FRESH AIR DOOR
SOLENOID
RECIRCULATING VENTS

Vacuum motor and solenoid—Medallion

3. Remove the heater/air conditioning housing.
4. Remove the 4 door housing retaining screws.
5. Remove the vacuum motor or solenoid from the housing.

To install:

6. Install the vacuum motor or solenoid to the housing.
7. Install the door housing and screws.
8. Install the heater/air conditioning housing to the vehicle.
9. Evacuate and recharge the air conditioning system.
10. Connect the negative battery cable and check the entire climate control system for proper operation. Check the system for leaks.

Blower Motor Relays

OPERATION

The heater blower motor relays are mounted on the heater housing above the accelerator pedal. The relay closest to the firewall controls power to the blower switch and the other relay controls power to the high speed blower.

TESTING

1. If the relay is suspect, disconnect the relay and plug the connector into a known good relay.
2. If the system works properly with the replacement relay, the relay was faulty.
3. If not, check the rest of the system.

REMOVAL AND INSTALLATION

1. Disconnect the negative battery cable.
2. Disconnect the connector from the relay and remove it.
3. Secure the relay when installing.
4. Connect the negative battery cable and check the entire climate control system for proper operation.

Air Conditioning Thermostat

OPERATION

To prevent evaporator freeze-up, the Medallion uses a thermostat, located behind the glove box on the evaporator housing, with a capillary tube inserted into the evaporator fins. When the temperature of the evaporator becomes cold enough to open the thermostat contacts, the compressor cycles, cutting off the flow of freon to the evaporator. When the evaporator warms up, the contacts close and compressor coil is energized.

TESTING

The compressor clutch coil should cycle 2–3 times per minute at ambient temperatures of 68–90°F (20–32°C). At temperatures above 90°F (32°C), the coil may not cycle at all.

1. Disconnect the wires from the switch.
2. Check for switch continuity. The switch should be closed at temperatures above 45°F (7°C) and open at cooler temperatures.

3. If the contacts are closed, reconnect the switch, set the temperature control lever to the coolest position, turn the blower on low speed and operate the engine for 5 minutes to allow the air conditioning system to stabilize.
4. If the cycling clutch switch is good and the clutch does not engage properly, inspect the rest of the system for an open circuit.

REMOVAL AND INSTALLATION

1. Disconnect the negative battery cable.
2. Remove the glove box door and the inner glove box.
3. Remove the screw that retains the thermostat to the housing.
4. Disconnect the thermostat wires.
5. Carefully pull the capillary tube from the evaporator housing.

To install:

6. Insert the capillary tube into the grommet in the housing and carefully push the capillary tube into the evaporator housing until the covered part of the tube contacts the grommet.
7. Connect the thermostat wires.
8. Install the thermostat to the housing with the retaining screw.
9. Install the inner glove box housing and the glove box door.
10. Connect the negative battery cable.

Dual Pressure Switch

OPERATION

The Summit, Laser and Talon use a dual pressure switch, which is a combination of a low pressure cut off switch and high pressure cut off switch. These functions will prevent the operation of the compressor in the event of either high of low refrigerant charge, preventing damage to the system. The switch is located on the receiver/drier on Summit and near the sight glass on the refrigerant line on Laser and Talon.

The dual pressure switch is designed to cut off voltage to the compressor coil when the pressure either drops below 30 psi or rises above 384 psi.

TESTING

1. Check for continuity through the switch. Under all normal conditions.
2. If the switch is open, check for insufficient refrigerant charge or excessive pressures.
3. If neither of the above conditions exist and the switch is open, replace the switch.

REMOVAL AND INSTALLATION

1. Disconnect the negative battery cable.
2. Properly discharge the air conditioning system.
3. Remove the switch from the refrigerant line or receiver/drier.
4. The installation is the reverse of the removal installation.
5. Evacuate and recharge the air conditioning system.
6. Connect the negative battery cable and check the entire climate control system for proper operation. Check the system for leaks.

Pressure Switch

OPERATION

The pressure switch, used on Summit with 1.6L engine, is used to control the condenser and radiator fans. The switch is located on the high pressure line near the left front of the engine compartment.

TESTING

1. Install a manifold gauge set to the air conditioning system.
2. Check the continuity of the switch at different pressures. The switch should be open a pressures below 213 psi and closed at 256 psi or higher.
3. For the purpose of testing, the pressures can be lowered by using an auxiliary fan to cool the condenser and raised by placing a cover over the condenser to prevent air flow.
4. Replace the switch if faulty.

REMOVAL AND INSTALLATION

1. Disconnect the negative battery cable.
2. Properly discharge the air conditioning system.
3. Remove the switch from the refrigerant line.
4. The installation is the reverse of the removal installation.
5. Evacuate and recharge the air conditioning system.
6. Connect the negative battery cable and check the entire climate control system for proper operation. Check the system for leaks.

Refrigerant Temperature Sensor

OPERATION

Located on the rear of the compressor on Summit, the refrigerant temperature sensor detects the temperature of the refrigerant delivered from the compressor during operation. The switch is designed to cut off the compressor when the temperature of the refrigerant exceeds 347°F (175°C), preventing overheating.

TESTING

1. Measure the resistance between the yellow-with-green-tracer wire and the black-with-yellow-tracer wire.
2. At 75–80°F, the resistance specification is about 80 kilo ohms.
3. If the reading deviates greatly from the specification, replace the sensor.

REMOVAL AND INSTALLATION

1. Disconnect the negative battery cable.
2. Properly discharge the air conditioning system.
3. Disconnect the connector.
4. Remove the mounting screws and the sensor from the compressor.
5. The installation is the reverse of the removal installation. Use a new lubricated O-ring when installing.
6. Evacuate and recharge the air conditioning system.
7. Connect the negative battery cable and check the entire climate control system for proper operation. Check the system for leaks.

Engine Coolant Temperature Switch

OPERATION

The engine coolant temperature switch, located on the thermostat housing, is connected in series with the compressor clutch relay on Summit with 1.6L engine and Laser and Talon with 2.0L engine. The switch is designed to cut off the compressor when the engine coolant temperature rises above 239°F (115°C), preventing engine overheating when cooling air is not sufficient for both the radiator and condenser.

TESTING

1. Remove the switch from the engine. The switch should be closed at room temperature.
2. Place the switch in an oil bath and heat to at least 222°F (108°C).
3. The switch should open when it reaches the above temperature.
4. Replace if faulty.

REMOVAL AND INSTALLATION

1. Disconnect the negative battery cable. Drain out some of the coolant.
2. Unplug the connector.
3. Unscrew the switch from the thermostat housing.
4. The installation is the reverse of the removal installation. Use sealant on the threads when installing.
5. Refill the cooling system.
6. Connect the negative battery cable and check the entire climate control system for proper operation.

Air Thermo and Air Inlet Sensors

OPERATION

These sensors function as cycling switches on Summit, Laser and Talon. Both sensors are located inside the evaporator housing; the air inlet sensor is normally on the right side of the housing and the air thermo sensor is normally on the left side.

The air thermo sensor detects the temperature of the air in the passenger compartment and the air inlet sensor detects the temperature of the air coming into the cooling unit. The information is input to the auto compressor control unit and the information is processed, causing the compressor clutch to cycle.

TESTING

1. Disconnect the sensor connector near the evaporator case.
2. Measure the resistance across the wires of the sensor that is suspect.
3. The resistance specifications for the air thermo sensor at different temperatures are:
   32°F (0°C)—11.4 kilo ohms
   50°F (10°C)—7.32 kilo ohms
   68°F (20°C)—4.86 kilo ohms
   86°F (30°C)—3.31 kilo ohms
   104°F (40°C)—2.32 kilo ohms
4. The resistance specifications for the air inlet sensor at different temperatures are:
   32°F (0°C)—3.31 kilo ohms
   50°F (10°C)—2.00 kilo ohms
   68°F (20°C)—1.25 kilo ohms
   86°F (30°C)—0.81 kilo ohms
   104°F (40°C)—0.53 kilo ohms
5. Replace the sensor if not within specifications.

REMOVAL AND INSTALLATION

1. Disconnect the negative battery cable.
2. Properly discharge the air conditioning system.
3. Remove the evaporator housing and the covers.
4. Unclip the sensor wires from the housing and remove the sensor(s).
5. The installation is the reverse of the removal installation.
6. Evacuate and recharge the air conditioning system.
7. Connect the negative battery cable and check the entire climate control system for proper operation. Check the system for leaks.

Power Relays

OPERATION

The Summit, Laser and Talon use relays to control the compressor clutch coil, heater, condenser fan and speed of the condenser fan.

On Summit, the compressor coil, condenser fan and condenser fan speed relays are in a small relay block located in the left front of the engine compartment next to the power steering fluid reservoir. The heater relay is located in an interior relay block under the left side of the instrument panel.

On Laser and Talon, the compressor coil, condenser fan and condenser fan speed relays are in a small relay block located in the left rear corner of the engine compartment. The heater relay is located on top of the interior junction block under the left side of the instrument panel.

TESTING

Compressor Coil, Heater and Condenser Fan Relays

1. Remove the relay.

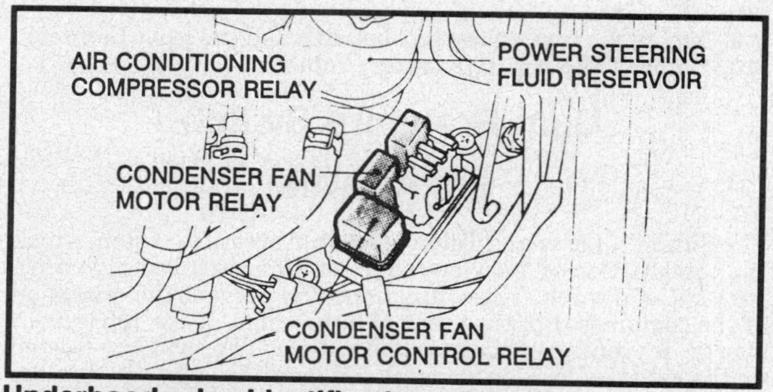
AIR CONDITIONING COMPRESSOR RELAY
POWER STEERING FLUID RESERVOIR
CONDENSER FAN MOTOR RELAY
CONDENSER FAN MOTOR CONTROL RELAY
Underhood relay identification—Summit

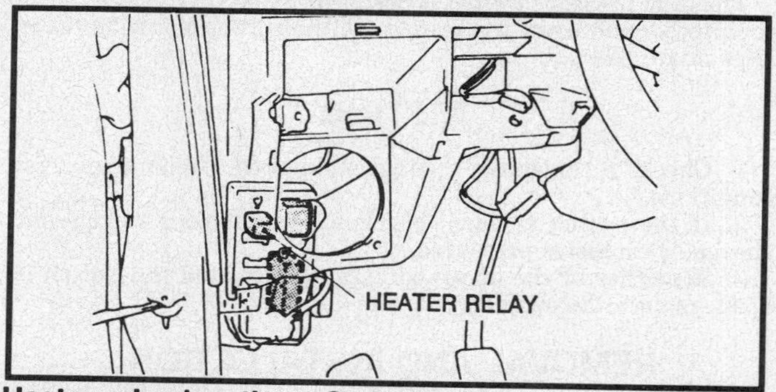
HEATER RELAY
Heater relay location—Summit

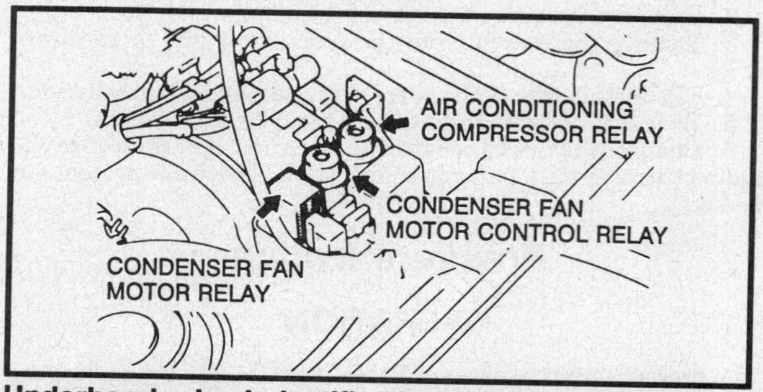
AIR CONDITIONING COMPRESSOR RELAY
CONDENSER FAN MOTOR CONTROL RELAY
CONDENSER FAN MOTOR RELAY
Underhood relay indentification—Laser and Talon

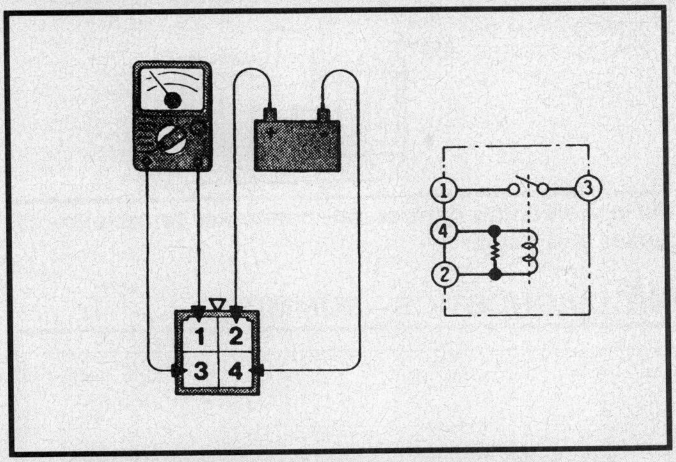
1
2
3
4

Compressor coil, heater and condenser fan relay check—Summit, Laser and Talon

2. Use jumper wires to connect the positive battery terminal to terminal 2 of the relay and the negative terminal to terminal 4.
3. With 12 volts applied, there should be continuity across terminals 1 and 3.
4. When the voltage is disconnected:
   a. Terminals 1 and 3 should be open.
   b. Terminals 2 and 4 should have continuity.
5. Replace the relay if faulty.

Condenser Fan Control Relay

SUMMIT

1. Remove the relay from the relay block.
2. Use jumper wires to connect the positive battery terminal to terminal 2 of the relay and the negative terminal to terminal 5.
3. With 12 volts applied:
   a. Terminals 1 and 3 should be open.
   b. Terminals 3 and 6 should have continuity.

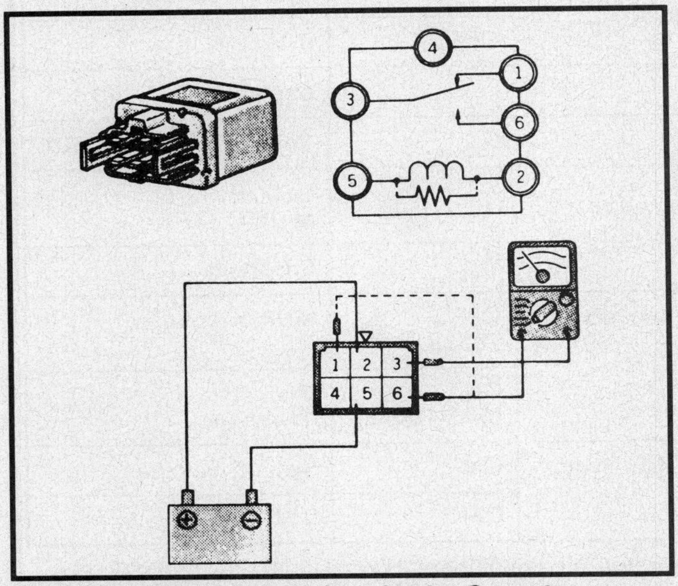
1
2
3
4
5
6

Condenser fan control relay check—Summit

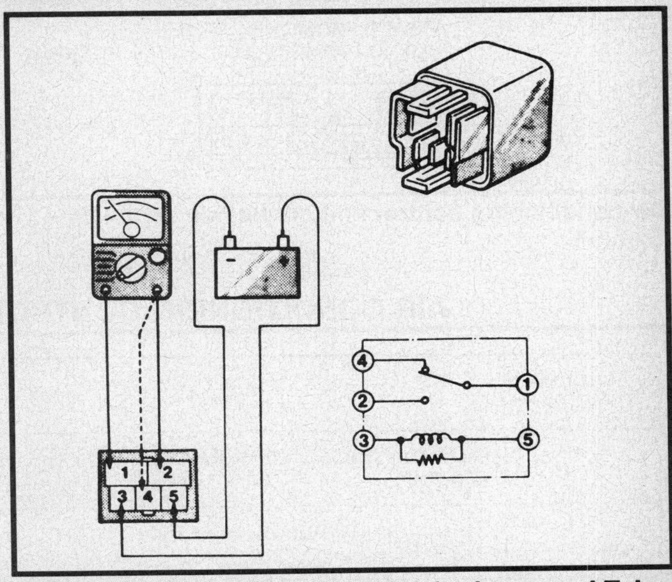
1
2
3
4
5

Condenser fan control relay check—Laser and Talon

4. When the voltage is disconnected:
   a. Terminals 1 and 3 should have continuity.
   b. Terminals 3 and 6 should be open.
   c. Terminals 2 and 5 should have continuity.
5. Replace the relay if faulty.

LASER AND TALON

1. Remove the relay.
2. Use jumper wires to connect the positive battery terminal to terminal 3 of the relay and the negative terminal to terminal 5.
3. With 12 volts applied, there should be continuity across terminals 1 and 2.
4. When the voltage is disconnected:
   a. Terminals 1 and 4 should have continuity.
   b. Terminals 3 and 5 should have continuity.
   c. Terminals 1 and 2 should be open.
5. Replace the relay if faulty.

REMOVAL AND INSTALLATION

1. Disconnect the negative battery cable.
2. Remove the relay block cover.
3. Remove the relay from the block by pulling it straight out.
4. The installation is the reverse of the removal installation.
5. Connect the negative battery cable and check the entire climate control system for proper operation.

Air Conditioning Control Unit

OPERATION

On the Summit, Laser and Talon, an electronic control unit is used to process information received from various sensors and switches to control the air conditioning compressor. The unit is located behind the glove box on top of the evaporator housing. The function of the control unit is to send current to the dual pressure switch when the following conditions are met:

1. The air conditioning switch is in either the **ECONO** or **A/C** mode.
2. The refrigerant temperature sensor, if equipped, is reading 347°F (175°C) or less.

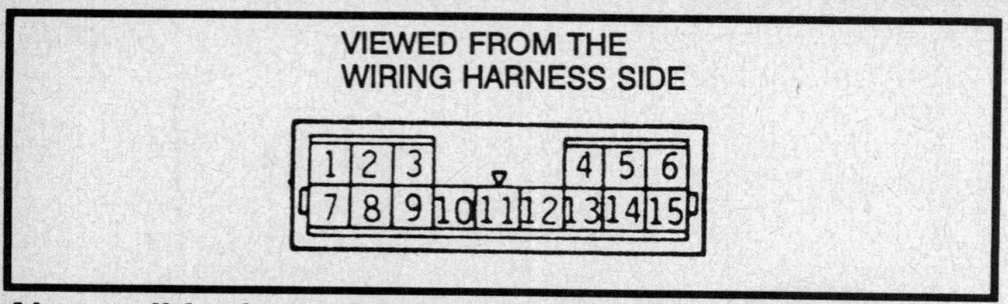
VIEWED FROM THE
WIRING HARNESS SIDE
1 2 3 4 5 6
7 8 9 10 11 12 13 14 15

Air conditioning control unit connector terminals—Summit

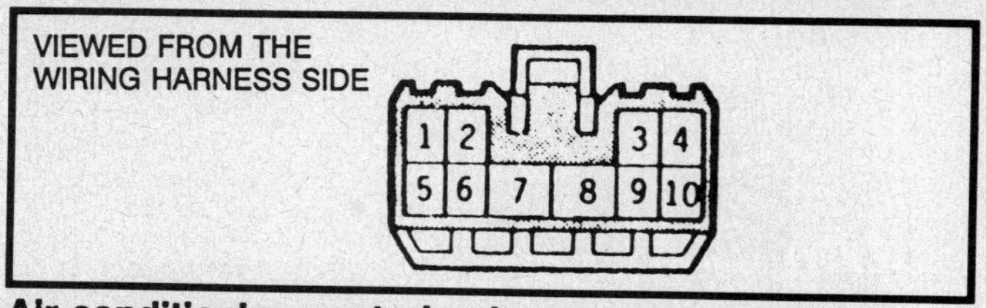
VIEWED FROM THE
WIRING HARNESS SIDE
1 2 3 4
5 6 7 8 9 10

Air conditioning control unit connector terminals—Laser and Talon

AIR CONDITIONING CONTROL UNIT DIAGNOSTICS—SUMMIT

Terminal No.	Signal	Conditions	Terminal voltage
1	Auto compressor control unit power supply	When ignition switch is ON	System voltage
5	Refrigerant temperature sensor ⊖	When air conditioner switch is OFF [Sensor temperature 25°C (77°F)]	0.15V
6	Air conditioner compressor relay	When all conditions for switch-ON of the compressor are satisfied	System voltage
8	Auto compressor control unit ground	At all times	0V
12	Refrigerant temperature sensor ⊕	At all times	5V

AIR CONDITIONING CONTROL UNIT DIAGNOSTICS—LASER AND TALON

Terminal	Measurement item	Tester connection	Conditions		Specified value
1	Resistance	1–6	—		1,500±150 Ω at 25°C (77°F)
2	Voltage	2–3 2–8	Air conditioner switch	ON	System voltage
				OFF	0 V
3	Continuity	3-Ground	—		Continuity
4	Continuity	4-Ground	—		Continuity
5	Resistance	5–7	—		1,500±150 Ω at 25°C (77°F)
8	Continuity	8-Ground	—		Continuity
9	Voltage	9–3 9–8	Thermo sensor	OFF 78°C (172°F)	System voltage
				ON 85°C (185°F)	0 V
10	Voltage	10–3 10–8	ECONO switch	ON	System voltage
				OFF	0 V

If the connector on the wire harness side is correct, replace the air conditioner control unit.

3. The air thermo and air inlet sensors are both reading at least 39°F (4°C).

TESTING

1. Disconnect the control unit connector.
2. Turn the ignition switch **ON**.
3. Turn the air conditioning switch **ON**.
4. Turn the temperature control lever too its coolest position.
5. Turn the blower switch to its highest position.
6. Follow the chart and probe the various terminals of the control unit connector under the the specified conditions. This will rule out all possible faulty components in the system.
7. If all checks are satisfactory, replace the control unit. If not, check the faulty system or component.

REMOVAL AND INSTALLATION

1. Disconnect the negative battery cable.
2. Remove the glove box and locate the control module.
3. Disconnect the connector to the module and remove the mounting screws.
4. Remove the module from the evaporator housing.
5. The installation is the reverse of the removal installation.
6. Connect the negative battery cable and check the entire climate control system for proper operation.

Temperature Sensors

OPERATION

The Monaco and Premier Semi-Automatic climate control system uses an outside and interior temperature sensors as input to the control module. The control module will process the information and may cut off voltage to the blower or compressor clutch coil according to the information received from the sensors.

REMOVAL AND INSTALLATION

Outside Air Temperature Sensor

1. Disconnect the negative battery cable.
2. Raise the vehicle and support safely. The sensor is located on the right side of the vehicle under the front bumper.
3. Disconnect the temperature sensor electrical connector and remove the retaining screws.
4. The installation is the reverse of the removal installation.
5. Connect the negative battery cable and check the entire climate control system for proper operation.

Interior Temperature Sensor

1. Disconnect the negative battery cable.
2. Remove the glove box liner.
3. Reach inside the glove box cavity and disconnect the air temperature sensor connector.
4. Pull the hose off of the air temperature sensor.
5. Pry the sensor grille from the instrument panel.
6. Use a small flat-bladed prying tool to unlock the tabs, then pull the sensor rearward to remove.
7. The installation is the reverse of the removal procedure.
8. Connect the negative battery cable and check the entire climate control system for proper operation.

System Door Vacuum Motors

OPERATION

The climate control system is a blend air system, receiving outside air through the blower inlet when in the FRESH AIR mode, or recirculated interior air when in the RECIRC mode. The air is forced through and/or around the heater core and evaporator, mixed and then discharged through the floor, instrument panel or defroster outlets.

Vacuum actuators are used to control each of the air distribution doors. Vacuum is delivered to the actuator via the control module.

TESTING

Check the system for proper operation. Air should come from the appropriate vents when the corresponding mode is selected under all driving conditions.

1. Check the engine for sufficient vacuum and the main supplier hose to the control module for leaks or kinks.
2. Check all interior vacuum lines, especially connections behind the instrument panel for leaks or kinks.
3. Check all actuators for their ability to hold vacuum and the linkages and doors for freedom and smoothness of movement.

REMOVAL AND INSTALLATION

Recirculation Door Vacuum Motor

1. Disconnect the negative battery cable.
2. Open the glove box and remove the glove box liner.
3. Reach inside the glove box cavity, disengage the locking tab, and remove the arm from the pivot shaft.
4. Remove the spring and the clear vacuum line.
5. Twist the motor in a counterclockwise direction and pull downward to remove the vacuum motor from the mounting bracket.

To install:

6. Position the motor to the vacuum bracket and press together until the locking tabs snap in place.
7. Connect the motor arm to the pivot shaft and press together until the locking tab snaps in place.
8. Install the spring and the clear vacuum line.
9. Install the glove box liner.
10. Connect the negative battery cable and check the entire climate control system for proper operation.

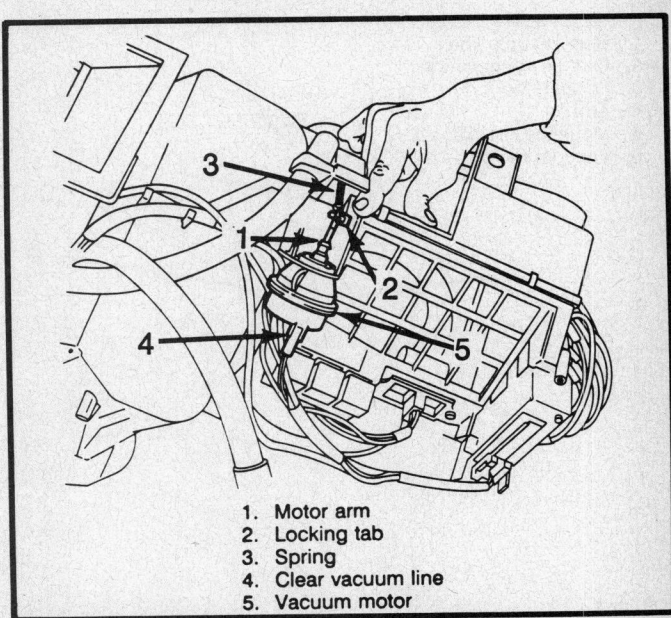

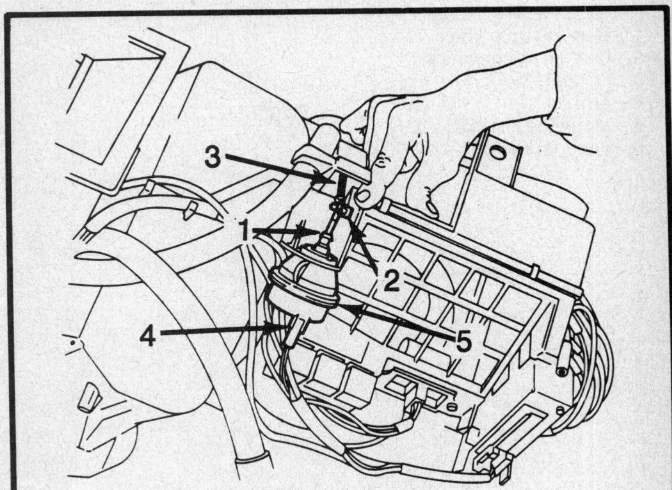
3
1
2
4
5
1. Motor arm
2. Locking tab
3. Spring
4. Clear vacuum line
5. Vacuum motor

Recirculation door vacuum motor—Monaco and Premier

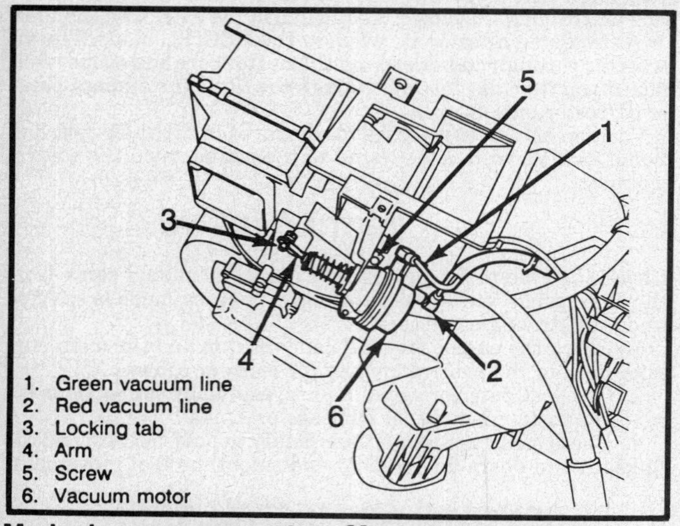
5
1
3
4
2
6
1. Green vacuum line
2. Red vacuum line
3. Locking tab
4. Arm
5. Screw
6. Vacuum motor

Mode door vacuum motor—Monaco and Premier

Mode Door Vacuum Motor

1. Disconnect the negative battery cable.
2. Matchmark and disconnect the green and red vacuum lines from the motor.
3. Disengaging the locking tab and remove the arm from the pivot shaft.
4. Remove the retaining screw. Twist the motor in a counterclockwise direction and pull downward to remove the vacuum motor from the mounting bracket.

To install:

5. Position the vacuum motor in the mounting bracket and make sure the locking tabs snap in place.
6. Install the retaining screw.
7. Position the motor arm to the pivot shaft and press together until the locking tab snaps in place.
8. Reconnect the vacuum lines.

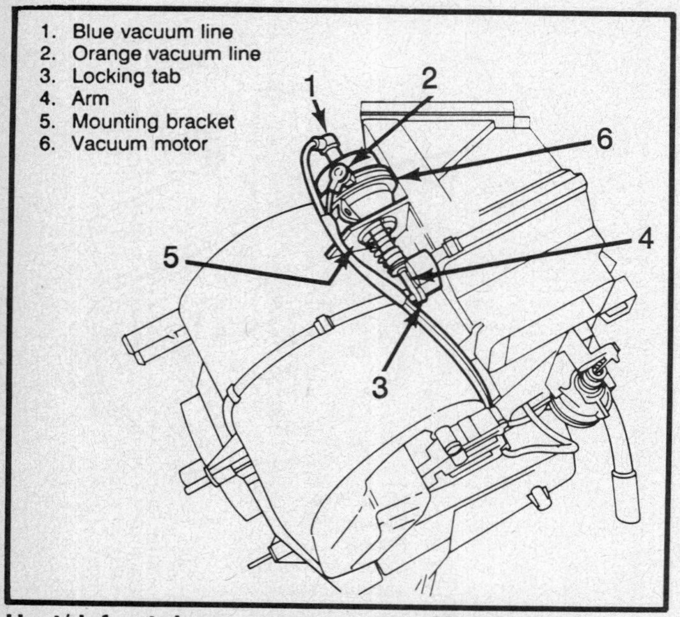
1. Blue vacuum line
2. Orange vacuum line
3. Locking tab
4. Arm
5. Mounting bracket
6. Vacuum motor
1
2
6
4
5
3

Heat/defrost door vacuum motor—Monaco and Premier

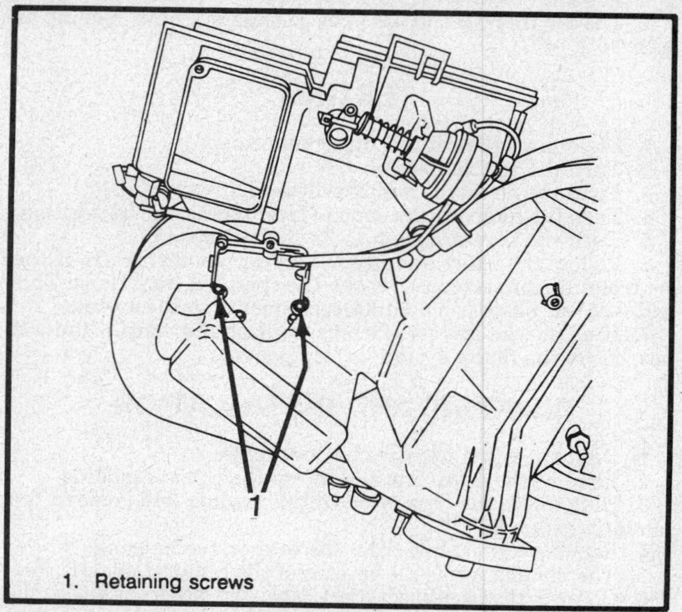
1
1. Retaining screws

Blend door motor—Monaco and Premier

9. Connect the negative battery cable and check the entire climate control system for proper operation.

Heat/Defrost Door Vacuum Motor

1. Disconnect the negative battery cable.
2. Matchmark and disconnect the blue and orange vacuum lines from the motor.
3. Disengaging the locking tab and remove the arm from the pivot shaft.
4. Place a small flat-bladed tool into the opening in the mounting bracket and apply slight pressure to the locking tab. With pressure on the tab, twist the motor in a counterclockwise direction and pull upward to remove the vacuum motor from the mounting bracket.

To install:

5. Position the vacuum motor in the mounting bracket and press together until the locking tabs snap in place.
6. Connect the vacuum lines to the motor.
7. Connect the negative battery cable and check the entire climate control system for proper operation.

Blend Door Module

OPERATION

The blend door module is a small electric motor used to directly operate the temperature blend door. A feedback circuit is used in the blend door actuator to supply the control module with blend door position information.

REMOVAL AND INSTALLATION

1. Disconnect the negative battery cable.
2. Remove the center console, if equipped.
3. Remove the floor duct.
4. Move the carpeting and padding aside and disconnect the electrical connector.
5. Remove the screws and the blend door module.
6. The installation is the reverse of the removal procedure.
7. Connect the negative battery cable and check the entire climate control system for proper operation.

Air Conditioning Control Module (ACM)

REMOVAL AND INSTALLATION

1. Disconnect the negative battery cable.
2. Remove the glove box liner.
3. Reach inside the glove box cavity and disconnect the vacuum and electrical connectors.
4. Remove the screws and the ACM.
5. The installation is the reverse of the removal procedure.
6. Connect the negative battery cable and check the entire climate control system for proper operation.

SYSTEM DIAGNOSIS

Air Conditioning Performance

PERFORMANCE TEST

Air temperature in the testing area must be at least 70°F (21°C) to ensure the accuracy of this test.

1. Connect a manifold gauge set the the system.
2. Set the controls to **RECIRC** or **MAX**, the mode lever to the **PANEL** position, temperature control level to the coolest position and the blower on its highest position.
3. Start the engine and adjust the idle speed to 1000 rpm with the compressor clutch engaged.
4. Allow the engine come to normal operating temperature and keep doors and windows closed.
5. Insert a thermometer in the left center panel outlet and operate the engine for 10 minutes. The clutch may cycle depending on the ambient conditions.
6. With the clutch engaged, compare the discharge air temperature to the performance chart.
7. If the values do not meet specifications, check system components for proper operation.

Air Conditioning Compressor

COMPRESSOR NOISE

Noises that develop during air conditioning operation can be misleading. A noise that sounds like serious compressor damage may only be a loose belt, mounting bolt or clutch assembly. Improper belt tension can also emit a noise that can be mistaken for more serious problems. Check and adjust all possible causes of the noise, including oil level, before replacing the compressor.

COMPRESSOR OIL LEVEL CHECK

Medallion

1. Remove the oil filler plug.
2. Look through the oil filter plug hole and rotate the clutch front plate to position the piston connecting rod on the center of the oil filler plug hole.
3. Insert the dipstick tool J-29642-12 or equivalent, through the oil fill plug hole to the right of the piston connecting rod, until the dipstick stop contacts the compressor housing.

AIR CONDITIONING PERFORMANCE CHART—SUMMIT, LASER AND TALON

Ambient Temperature °F (°C)	Air Temperature at Center Panel Vent °F (°C)	Compressor Discharge Pressure PSI (kPa)	Compressor Suction Pressure PSI (kPa)
70 (21)	35–45 (2–8)	130–188 (896–1295)	10–21 (69–145)
80 (27)	35–45 (2–8)	145–210 (1000–1447)	13–25 (90–172)
90 (32)	35–45 (2–8)	165–245 (1140–1688)	15–30 (103–207)
100 (38)	37–50 (3–10)	190–270 (1336–1860)	20–33 (138–227)
110 (43)	39–55 (4–13)	200–300 (1406–2109)	20–35 (138–241)

AIR CONDITIONING PERFORMANCE CHART—MONACO AND PREMIER

Ambient Temperature °F (°C)	Air Temperature at Center Panel Vent °F (°C)	Compressor Discharge Pressure PSI (kPa)	Compressor Suction Pressure PSI (kPa)
70 (21)	34–46 (2-8)	100–200 (689–1378)	22–45 (150–300)
80 (27)	34–46 (2–8)	125–225 (861–1550)	22–45 (150–300)
90 (32)	34–46 (2–8)	150–260 (1034–1791)	22–45 (150–300)
100 (38)	38–51 (4–10)	180–300 (1240–2067)	30–55 (207–379)
110 (43)	41–55 (5–12)	200–300 (1378–2250)	32–60 (220–400)

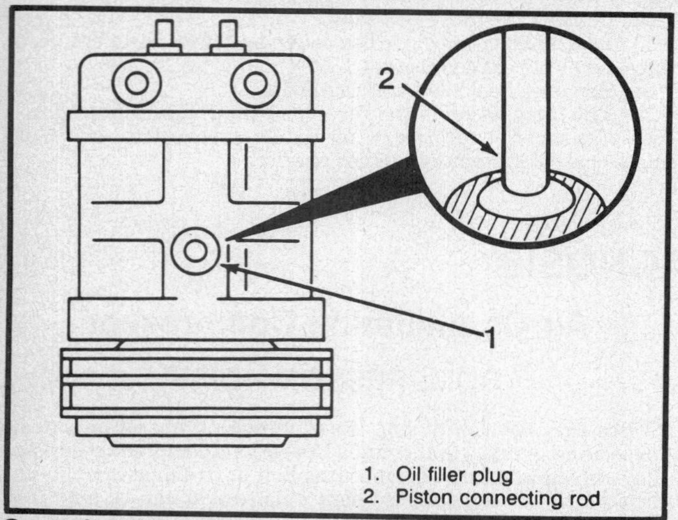
2
1
1. Oil filler plug
2. Piston connecting rod

Centering the piston connecting rod in the oil filler hole—Medallion

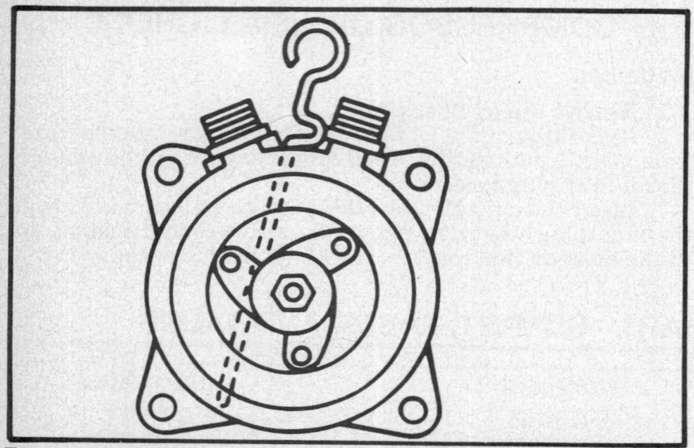

Proper positioning of the dipstick for reading oil level—Medallion

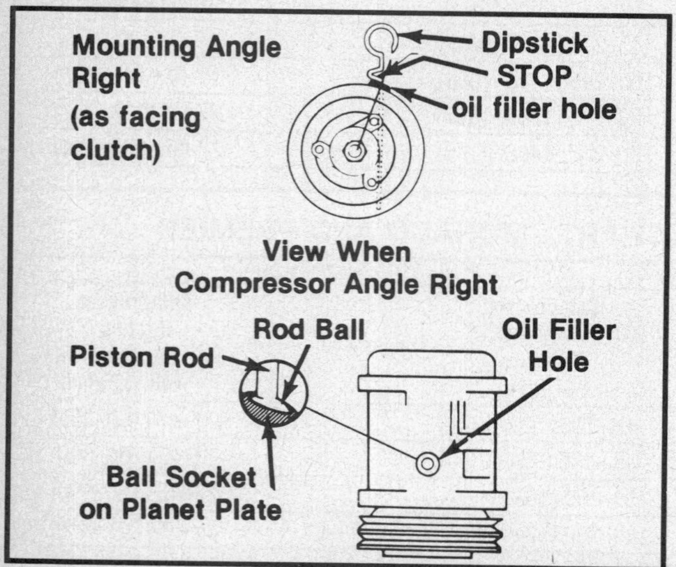
Mounting Angle Right
(as facing clutch)
Dipstick
STOP
oil filler hole
View When Compressor Angle Right
Rod Ball
Oil Filler Hole
Piston Rod
Ball Socket on Planet Plate

Positioning the connecting rod in the oil filler hole—Monaco and Premier

MOUNTING ANGLE/OIL LEVEL CHART MONACO AND PREMIER

Mounting Angle/Degree	Acceptable Oil Level In Increments
0	6-8
10	7-8
20	8-10
30	9-10
40	11-12
50	12-13
60	13-14
90	15-16

4. Remove the dipstick and count the number of increments (grooves) covered with oil. When properly filled, the compressor should contain between 4–6 increments of oil.
5. Add or remove oil as necessary, and install the plug.

Premier

The preferred method to check the oil level is to remove the compressor and check the oil level at the bench. On-vehicle checking is possible, but is not the most accurate.

1. Determine the mounting angle by positioning an angle gauge across the flat surfaces of the 2 front mounting ears. Center the bubble and read the mounting angle to the closest degree.
2. Remove the oil filler plug.
3. Look through the oil filter plug hole and rotate the clutch front plate to position the piston connecting rod on the center of the oil filler plug hole.
4. Insert the dipstick to the stop position. The stop is the angle near the top of the dipstick. The bottom surface of the angle must be flush with the surface of the filler hole.
5. Remove the dipstick and count the number of increments (grooves) covered with oil and refer to the oil level chart.
6. Add or remove oil as necessary and install the plug.

COMPRESSOR CLUTCH INOPERATIVE

1. Verify refrigerant charge, and charge as required.
2. Check for 12 volts at the clutch coil connection. If voltage is detected, check the coil.
3. If no voltage is detected at the coil, check the fuse or fusible link. If the fuse is not blown, check for voltage at the clutch relay. If voltage is not detected there, continue working backwards through the system's switches, etc. until an open circuit is detected.
4. Inspect all suspect parts and replace as required.
5. When the repair is complete, perform a complete system performance test.

CLUTCH COIL TESTING

Summit, Laser and Talon

1. Disconnect the negative battery cable.
2. Disconnect the compressor clutch connector.
3. Apply 12 volts to the wire leading to the clutch coil. If the clutch is operating properly, an audible click will occur when the clutch is magnetically pulled into the coil. If no click is heard, inspect the coil.

HEAVAC SYSTEM DIAGNOSTICS INDEX MEDALLION

CHART NO.	SYMPTOM
1	No Heating or Air Conditioning
2	Blower Motor does not operate correctly
3	A/C Compressor Clutch does not engage
4	Air Distribution does not operate correctly
5	Both Engine Cooling Fans inoperative at low speed
6	Engine Cooling Fans inoperative at high speed
7	No. 1 Engine Cooling Fan does not operate at high speed
8	No. 2 Engine Cooling Fan does not operate at high speed

4. Check the resistance across the coil lead wire and ground. The specification is 3.4–3.8 ohms at approximately 70°F (20°C).
5. Replace the clutch coil if not within specification.

HEAVAC System

Semi-Automatic Temperature Control System

ON-BOARD DIAGNOSTICS

The on-board diagnostic tests consist of 4 individual diagnostic modes – low, M1, M2 and high. The mode is selected by using the blower speed button and are displayed on the blower segment portion of the display. While in the diagnostic mode, the air distribution system will continue to operate in the mode that was selected prior to entering the diagnostic mode. When the mode indicator lights show a fault, the fault is already preset or has occurred within the last 60 key on/off cycles. Corrected faults can be erased by pressing the FRONT DEFROST button for 5 seconds. During this 5 seconds interval, the illuminated fault segment will flash, warning that the fault code is about to be erased.

DIAGNOSTIC CHART NO. 1 – MEDALLION

Connector C273 Disconnected and Ignition Switch in RUN

TEST	OK	NOT OK
Blwr and Dome-Clk fuse	Not blown	Replace fuse
Connector C273 Terminals A1 and A5	Battery voltage	Repair open to fuse
Connector C273 Terminals A4 and B1 to ground	Zero ohms, if ok replace Heavac Control Panel	Repair open to G103 or G105

DIAGNOSTIC CHART NO. 2 – MEDALLION

Ignition in RUN and Any Mode Selected on HEAVAC Control Panel

TEST	OK	NOT OK
Heater-A/C Fuse	Not blown	Replace fuse
Disconnect Blower Motor Power Supply Relay. Insert voltmeter between Terminals 5 and 1 of C459, then between Terminals 1 and 2 of C459	Battery voltage	Repair open in wires. If wire are ok replace Heavac Control Panel
Disconnect the Blower Motor Control Module. Jumper Terminals A4 and B4 of C452 to ground, then Jumper Terminals 5 and 3 of C459.	Blower Motor runs	Replace Blower Motor
Check wires to Heavac Control Panel and to the Blower Motor Control Module	Wires are good.	Repair wire(s)
Substitute a known good Blower Motor Control Module into connector C452	If Blower Motor runs, replace the Blower Motor Control Module	If blower Motor does not run replace the Heavac Control Panel

DIAGNOSTIC CHART NO. 3—MEDALLION

TEST	OK	NOT OK
Jumper Terminals A1 and B3 of C273	Compressor runs	Repair open to the Air Compressor Clutch. If wires are good replacce the Air Compressor Clutch
Reconnect the Heavac Module and Select A/C Max. Connector C487 Terminal B4	Battery voltage If OK replace Heavac Control Panel	Jumper Terminal 2 of C455 to ground. If battery voltage is now present, check wire to Heavac Module for an open. If wire is good replace Heavac Control Panel. If no battery voltage is present go to next step.
Terminals 1 and 3 of C457	Battery voltage If OK replace Compressor Clutch Control Relay	Check wire to Thermostat Switch. If wires are OK go to next step.
Terminals 3 of C457 and 4 of C458	Battery voltage	If no battery voltage at Terminal 3, replace the Thermostat Switch. If no battery voltage on Terminal 4 check wire to A/C Cut-Out Relay. If wire is good go to next step.
Terminals 5 and 3 of C426	Battery voltage If OK replace the Heavac Control Panel	If battery voltage is present at Terminal 3 but not Terminal 5, replace the A/C Cut-Out Relay. If battery voltage is not present at Terminal 3 repair open in wire.

DIAGNOSTIC CHART NO. 4—MEDALLION

TEST	OK	NOT OK
Check the wires between the Suspected bad motor and the Heavac Control Panel	Wires are good. If wires are good replace the motor with a known good one. If motor does not work, replace the Heavac Control Panel.	Repair wire(s)

DIAGNOSTIC CHART NO. 5—MEDALLION

COOLING FANS: Ignition Switch in RUN

TEST	OK	NOT OK
Connector C115 — Terminal 2* (connector C115 disconnected)	Zero ohms	Repair open to G101
Connector C295 — Terminal A1	Battery voltage	Repair open from ignition switch
Jumper Connector C295 — Terminals A1 and C1	Fans operate. If ok, replace temperature switch (ensure engine is cool).	Leave jumper connected. Go to next step.
Connector C247 — Terminal 1	Battery voltage	Repair open from temperature switch (if fans do not operate in AC mode, repair open from C104, terminal B2)

DIAGNOSTIC CHART NO. 5—MEDALLION

COOLING FANS: Ignition Switch in RUN

TEST	OK	NOT OK
Connector C247 — Terminal 2*	Zero ohms	Repair open to ground
Jumper C247 — Terminals 3 and 5	Fans operate. If ok, replace cooling fan control relay.	Go to next step
Connector C116 — Terminal 2	Battery voltage	Check circuit breaker. If ok, repair open from main fuse.
Connector C248 — Terminal 3	Battery voltage	Repair open from circuit break (includes cooling fan motor no. 1).
Connector C247 — Terminal 3	Battery voltage	Check wiring from cooling fan relay no. 1. If ok, replace cooling fan relay no. 1.
Connector C244 — Terminal 4	Battery voltage	Repair open from cooling fan control relay
Connector C244 — Terminal 3	Battery voltage. If ok, repair open to C115 terminal 2 (includes cooling fan motor no. 2).	Replace cooling fan relay no. 2

*Ignition switch off

DIAGNOSTIC CHART NO. 6—MEDALLION

COOLING FAN TEMPERATURE SWITCH: Ignition Switch in RUN

TEST	OK	NOT OK
Jumper Connector C295 — Terminals A1 and B1	Cooling fans operate. If ok, replace temperature switch (ensure engine is cool)	Leave jumper connected. Go to next step.
Connector C244 and Connector C248 — Terminal 1*	Battery voltage	Repair open from cooling fan temperature switch
Connector C244 and Connector C248 — Terminal 2**	Zero ohms. If ok, replace engine cooling fan relays no. 1 and no. 2	Repair open to splice B

*Remove jumper after this step **Ignition switch off

DIAGNOSTIC CHART NO. 7—MEDALLION

CIRCUIT CHECK: Ignition Switch in RUN, Connector C295 Disconnected

TEST	OK	NOT OK
Connector C248 — Terminals 2 and 5	Zero ohms	Repair open to splice B
Connector C248 — Terminal 1 with Connector C295 Terminals A1 and B1 jumpered*	Battery voltage. If ok, replace cooling fan no. 1 relay.	Repair connection at C248 — Terminal 1

*Remove jumper after this test step, connect C295

DIAGNOSTIC CHART NO. 8—MEDALLION

CIRCUIT CHECK: Ignition Switch in RUN, Connector C295 Disconnected

TEST	OK	NOT OK
Connector C244 — Terminal 2	Zero ohms	Repair open to splice B
Connector C244 — Terminal 1 with Connector C295 —Terminals A1 and B1 jumpered*	Battery voltage	Repair open from cooling fan relay no. 1.
Connector C244 — Terminal 5	Battery voltage. If ok, replace cooling fan relay no. 2	Repair open from main fuse

SEMI-AUTOMATIC TEMPERATURE CONTROL SYSTEM DIAGNOSTICS INDEX—MONACO AND PREMIER

CHART NO.	SYMPTOM
1	When the ignition is turned to RUN, the mode indicator (with heater only) or Er with heater-A/C) flashes for 5 seconds
2	No heating or air conditioning at all
3	Heating or air conditioning operates correctly, but climate display is inoperative
4	Control keys do not operate correctly
5	Blower motor does not operate correctly
6	A/C compressor clutch does not engage
1	Any other symptom not listed above

Low Mode

To enter into on-board diagnostics, press the blower speed select UP, mode select LEFT, and FRONT DEFROST buttons simultaneously for 3 seconds. When all segments on the display are illuminated, release the buttons. This will put the system in the low mode. Observe which segments are lit and perform the appropriate action.

When the problem is repaired, cycle the ignition switch from **OFF** to **RUN** and re-enter into on-board diagnostics. Erase the fault from memory. If the indicator did not go out, the problem is not fixed. To exit the diagnostic mode press the blower speed select up, mode select left, and front defrost buttons simultaneously.

NOTE: When diagnosing the blend-air door motor, keep the motor connected to the door. Use only on-board computer control module diagnostics with this motor and do not use jumper wires. Failure to use these cautions will cause the potentiometer inside the motor to lose memory with the control module and reference to the blend-air door will be lost. The control module will not be able to determine the position of the blend-air door.

LOW MODE DIAGNOSTICS—MONACO AND PREMIER

SEGMENT LIT	ACTION
OFF	None of the seven faults are now present or stored in memory. Press the blower speed select up button once, go to the M1 mode chart.
BI/LEV	Check wires to terminals 5 and 6 at air mixture door control for opens. If wires are ok, and no other indicators are lit, replace air mixture door control.
VENT	Airmix door travel range too small. Go to M2 mode chart.
HEAT	Airmix door travel range too large. Go to M2 mode chart.
HEAT/DEF	Check terminals 9 and 10 at air mixture door control for 5 volts. If ok, replace air mixture door control.
DEF	Check wire to terminal 9 of air mixture door control for a short to ground. If ok, replace air mixture door control.
MAX (A/C only)	Repair open in wires to terminals C13 and D5 (outside temp. sensor) of the ACM. If ok, replace outside temp. sensor.
NORM (A/C only)	Repair short to ground in wire to terminal C13 of the ACM. If ok, replace outside temp. sensor.

M1 MODE DIAGNOSTICS—MONACO AND PREMIER

SEGMENT LIT	ACTION
OFF	No faults are currently found by the on-board diagnostics
HEAT/DEF (heater only)	Repair open in wire to terminal E12 (temp. select potentiometer) of the Air Control Module
DEF (heater only)	Repair short to ground in wire to terminal E12 (temp. select potentiometer) of the Air Control Module
MAX (A/C only)	Repair open in wires to in car temp. sensor. If ok, replace the in car temp. sensor
NORM (A/C only)	Repair short to ground in wires to in car temp. sensor. If ok, replace the in car temp. sensor

M1 MODE DISPLAY—MONACO AND PREMIER

DISPLAY	MEANING	CLUTCH STATUS
ON	A/C clutch ON	ON
OP	Open A/C low pressure cut out switch	OFF
HL	Heavy load	OFF
NC	No clutch (OFF, VENT or HEAT mode active)	OFF

M1 Mode

The set temperature digits display the air conditioning clutch status while in this mode.

M2 Mode

In this mode, the 4 air mix doors can be manually selected by using the SELECT button. The operations are:

• BI/LEV—The air mix door is positioned in response to the automatic temperature calculations or manual temperature potentiometer. The set temperature digits display the current voltage on the air mix door feedback wires in tenths of volts, ±0.3 volts.

• VENT—The air mix door is moved toward the full hot position. The motor will stop when the door has stopped against the full hot stop or a position 45 degrees from center of travel has been reached. While the door is moving, and fro up to 5 seconds after the door has stopped, the air control selection buttons are deactivated. The VENT mode segment flashes at a 2 Hz rate while the motor is being driven. The set temperatures digits display the current voltage on the air mix door feedback wire in tenths of volts, ±0.3 volts.

• HEAT—The air mix door is moved toward the full cold position. The motor will stop when the door has stopped against the full cold stop, or when a position of 45 degrees from center has been reached. While the door is moving, and for up to 5 seconds after the door has stopped, the air selection control buttons are deactivated. The HEAT mode segment flashes at a 2 Hz rate while the motor is being driven. The set temperatures digits display the current voltage on the air mix door feedback wire in tenths of volts, ±0.3 volts.

• HEAT/DEF—The air mix door is positioned in response to the automatic temperature calculations. The set temperatures digits display the range of air mix door travel as determined in the previous 2 modes in degrees, ±3 degrees.

If the feedback wire for the air mix door is open or shorted to ground, the air mix door will not move. None of the 4 modes can be entered (the mode segments are blank) and the set temperature digits will display **?**.

High Mode

Both temperature sensor inputs can be read on the display by using the SELECT button to manually select either NORM (outside temperature) or BI/LEV (interior temperature).

The display range for the outside temperature reading is −40°–140°F and −40°–185°F for the in-car sensor. If a sensor line is open or shorted to ground, the set temperature digits will display **?** when the sensor is selected.

DIAGNOSTICS BY SYMPTOM

1. If there is no heating or air conditioning at all, use Diagnostic Chart 1 with the ignition key in the **RUN** position.
2. If the climate display is inoperative, use Diagnostic Chart 2 with the ignition key in the **RUN** position.
3. If the control keys or slider do not operate properly, first check the wires and connectors from the control module to the

HIGH MODE DIAGNOSTICS—MONACO AND PREMIER

TEMPERATURE IN °F	SET TEMPERATURE DISPLAY	SEGMENT "OFF" INDICATOR
Temperature below 0°F	Flasing Temperature	OFF
0°F through 99°F	Temperature displayed	OFF
Temperature above 100°F	Temperature displayed	ON

control switch pod for damage. If wires are satisfactory, replace the control module with a known good unit. If the problem still exists, replace the switch pod.

4. If there is a problem with the blower motor, use Diagnostic Chart 3 first, then continue to the appropriate chart from there.

5. If the air conditioning compressor does not engage, use Diagnostic Chart 8 with the ignition key in the **RUN** position, climate control system in **NORM** and the temperature setting at 65°F.

DIAGNOSTICS CHART NO. 1—MONACO AND PREMIER

TEST	OK
Check Fuse 2	Not blown
Air Control Module connector – Terminal D13	Battery voltage
Air Control Module connector – Terminal D3	Battery voltage
Air Control Module connector – Terminal D3 to Terminal D7	Battery voltage
Control Switch module connector – Terminal E3	5 volts

DIAGNOSTICS CHART NO. 2—MONACO AND PREMIER

TEST	OK	NOT OK
Instrument Cluster Climate Display connector – Terminal E	Battery voltage	Repair open from fuse
Instrument Cluster Climate Display connector – Terminal E to Terminal F	Battery voltage	Repair open to I/P harness splice
Instrument Cluster Climate Display connector – Terminal E to Terminal C	Battery voltage	Repair open to ACM

*If voltages are correct, check that the wires from the climate display connector terminals A and B are not open or shorted.

DIAGNOSTICS CHART NO. 3—MONACO AND PREMIER

SYMPTOM	ACTION
Blower motor does not operate in any mode	Go to chart 5A
Blower motor only operates in HI mode	Go to chart 5B
Blower motor does not operate in M1 mode and operates at M2 in LO mode	Check wire from M1 speed relay connector – terminal 5 for an open. If ok, replace M1 speed relay
Blower motor does not operate in M2 mode and operates incorrectly in M1 or LO mode	Go to chart 5C
Blower motor does not operate in M2 mode only	Check wire from M1 Speed Relay connector – terminal 3 for an open
Blower motor does not operate in LO mode only	Check wire from Blower Resistor Block connector – terminal 5 for an open. If ok, replace blower resistor block
Blower motor does not operate in M1 and LO modes only	Check wire from M1 Speed Relay connector – terminal 4 for an open. If ok, replace blower resistor block
Blower motor does not operate at LO in M2 mode	Check wire from M1 Speed Relay connector – terminal 5 for a short to ground. If ok, replace M1 speed relay
Blower motor does not operate at LO in M1 mode	Go to chart 5D
Blower motor always runs or other symptoms	Check for shorts to ground

DIAGNOSTICS CHART NO. 4—MONACO AND PREMIER

TEST	OK	NOT OK
Blower motor Connector A – Terminal S	Battery voltage	Repair open from Fuse Link
Blower motor Connector A – Terminal S to blower motor Connector B terminal S	Battery voltage. If ok, replace blower motor	Check for open to Hi speed relay connector terminal 1. If ok, continue test
Hi speed relay connector – Terminal 2	Battery voltage	Check for open to ACM connector terminal A12. If ok, replace ACM
Hi speed relay connector – Terminal 2 to terminal 5	Battery voltage	Check for open to ACM connector terminal A3. If ok, replace ACM
Hi speed relay connector – Terminal 1 to terminal 4	Battery voltage. If ok, replace the Hi speed relay	Repair open to ground

DIAGNOSTICS CHART NO. 5—MONACO AND PREMIER

TEST	OK	NOT OK
Blower resistor block connector – Terminal 1	Battery voltage	Repair open to Hi speed relay connector terminal 1
M1 speed relay connector – Terminal 2	Battery voltage	Repair open to Hi speed relay connector terminal 2
M1 speed relay connector – Terminal 1	Battery voltage. If ok, replace M1 speed relay	Check for open to blower resistor block connector terminal 2. If ok, replace blower resistor block
M2 speed relay connector – Terminal 1	Battery voltage	Check circuits attached to terminals 3 and 4 of blower resistor block for an open. If wires are good, replace the blower resistor block.
M2 speed relay connector – Terminal 1 to Terminal 3	Battery voltage. If ok, replace M2 speed relay	Check wire at terminal 3 of M2 speed relay for an open

DIAGNOSTICS CHART NO. 6—MONACO AND PREMIER

TEST	OK	NOT OK
M2 speed relay connector – Terminal 2	Battery voltage	Repair open to M1 speed relay connector terminal 2
M2 speed relay connector – Terminal 2 to terminal 5	Battery voltage	Check for open ACM connector terminal A1. If ok, replace ACM
M2 speed relay connector – Terminal 2 to terminal 3	Battery voltage. If ok, replace M2 speed relay	Check for open in harness to splice

DIAGNOSTICS CHART NO. 7—MONACO AND PREMIER

TEST	OK	NOT OK
M2 speed relay connector – Terminal 1	Battery voltage	Repair open to Blower resistor block connector terminal 4
M2 speed relay connector – Terminal 2 to terminal 5	0 volts. If ok, replace M2 speed relay	Check for a short to ground at ACM connector terminal A1. If ok, replace ACM

DIAGNOSTICS CHART NO. 8—MONACO AND PREMIER

TEST	OK	NOT OK
ACM connector terminal C8 to D5 Ignition switch OFF	Zero ohms	Check for normal refrigerant level. If ok, replace A/C low pressure cut out switch
A/C clutch relay connector – terminal 5	Battery voltage	Check Fuse 8. If ok, check for open to Fuse 8
A/C clutch relay connector – terminal 4	Battery voltage	Check fuse link. If ok, check for open to fuse link
A/C clutch relay connector – terminal 5 to terminal 2	Battery voltage	Check for open to ACM connector terminal C5, if ok, replace ACM
A/C clutch relay connector – terminal 4 to terminal 1	A/C compressor clutch engages. If ok, replace A/C clutch relay	Check for open to A/C compressor clutch connector terminal S. If ok, replace the air compressor clutch

WIRING SCHEMATICS

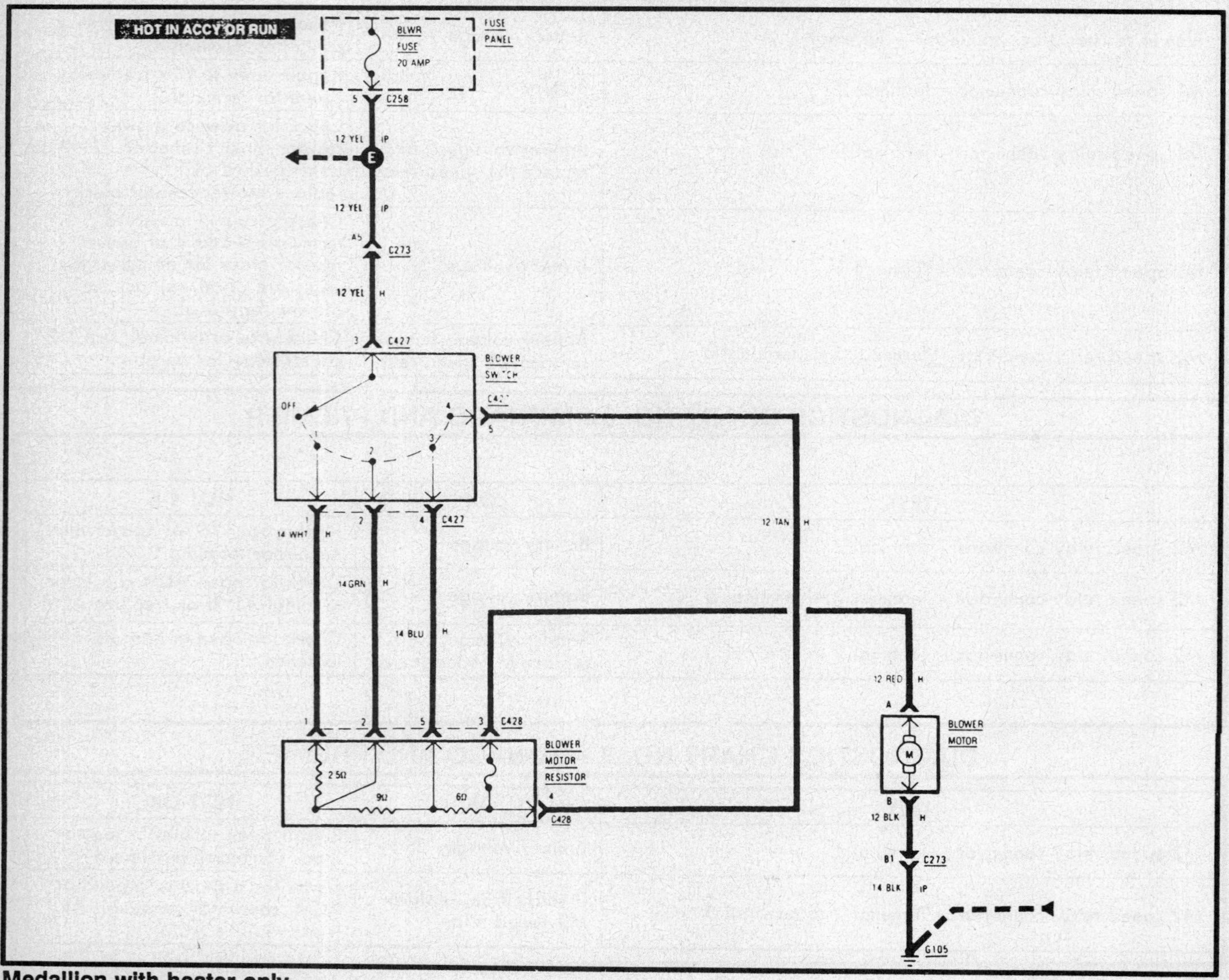
HOT IN ACCY OR RUN
BLWR FUSE 20 AMP
FUSE PANEL
C258
12 YEL IP
E
A5
C273
12 YEL H
C427
BLOWER SWITCH
OFF
14 WHT H
14 GRN H
14 BLU H
12 TAN H
C428
BLOWER MOTOR RESISTOR
2.5Ω
9Ω
6Ω
12 RED H
BLOWER MOTOR
M
12 BLK H
B1
14 BLK IP
G105

Medallion with heater only

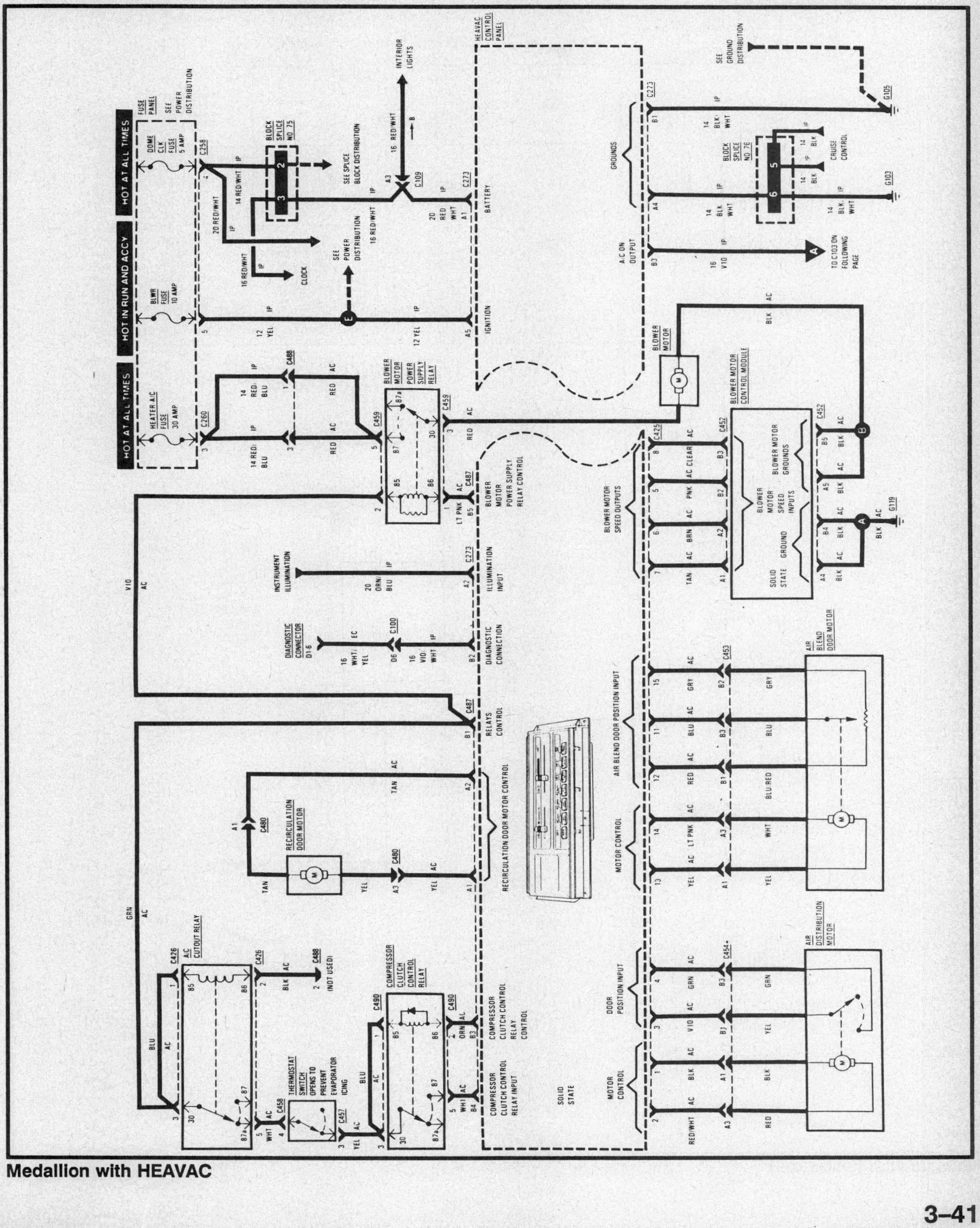
HOT AT ALL TIMES
HOT IN RUN AND ACCY
HOT AT ALL TIMES
FUSE PANEL
SEE POWER DISTRIBUTION
DOME CLK FUSE 5 AMP
BLWR FUSE 10 AMP
HEATER A/C FUSE 30 AMP
BLOCK SPLICE NO 75
SEE SPLICE BLOCK DISTRIBUTION
INTERIOR LIGHTS
CLOCK
SEE POWER DISTRIBUTION
HEAVAC CONTROL PANEL
BATTERY
IGNITION
BLOWER MOTOR POWER SUPPLY RELAY
BLOWER MOTOR POWER SUPPLY RELAY CONTROL
INSTRUMENT ILLUMINATION
ILLUMINATION INPUT
DIAGNOSTIC CONNECTOR D1 6
DIAGNOSTIC CONNECTION
RELAYS CONTROL
RECIRCULATION DOOR MOTOR
RECIRCULATION DOOR MOTOR CONTROL
A/C CUTOUT RELAY
(NOT USED)
THERMOSTAT SWITCH OPENS TO PREVENT EVAPORATOR ICING
COMPRESSOR CLUTCH CONTROL RELAY
COMPRESSOR CLUTCH CONTROL RELAY CONTROL
COMPRESSOR CLUTCH CONTROL RELAY INPUT
SOLID STATE
SEE GROUND DISTRIBUTION
GROUNDS
BLOCK SPLICE NO 76
CRUISE CONTROL
A/C ON OUTPUT
TO C103 ON FOLLOWING PAGE
BLOWER MOTOR
BLOWER MOTOR CONTROL MODULE
BLOWER MOTOR SPEED OUTPUTS
BLOWER MOTOR SPEED INPUTS
BLOWER MOTOR GROUNDS
SOLID STATE GROUND
AIR BLEND DOOR POSITION INPUT
AIR BLEND DOOR MOTOR
MOTOR CONTROL
DOOR POSITION INPUT
AIR DISTRIBUTION MOTOR

Medallion with HEAVAC

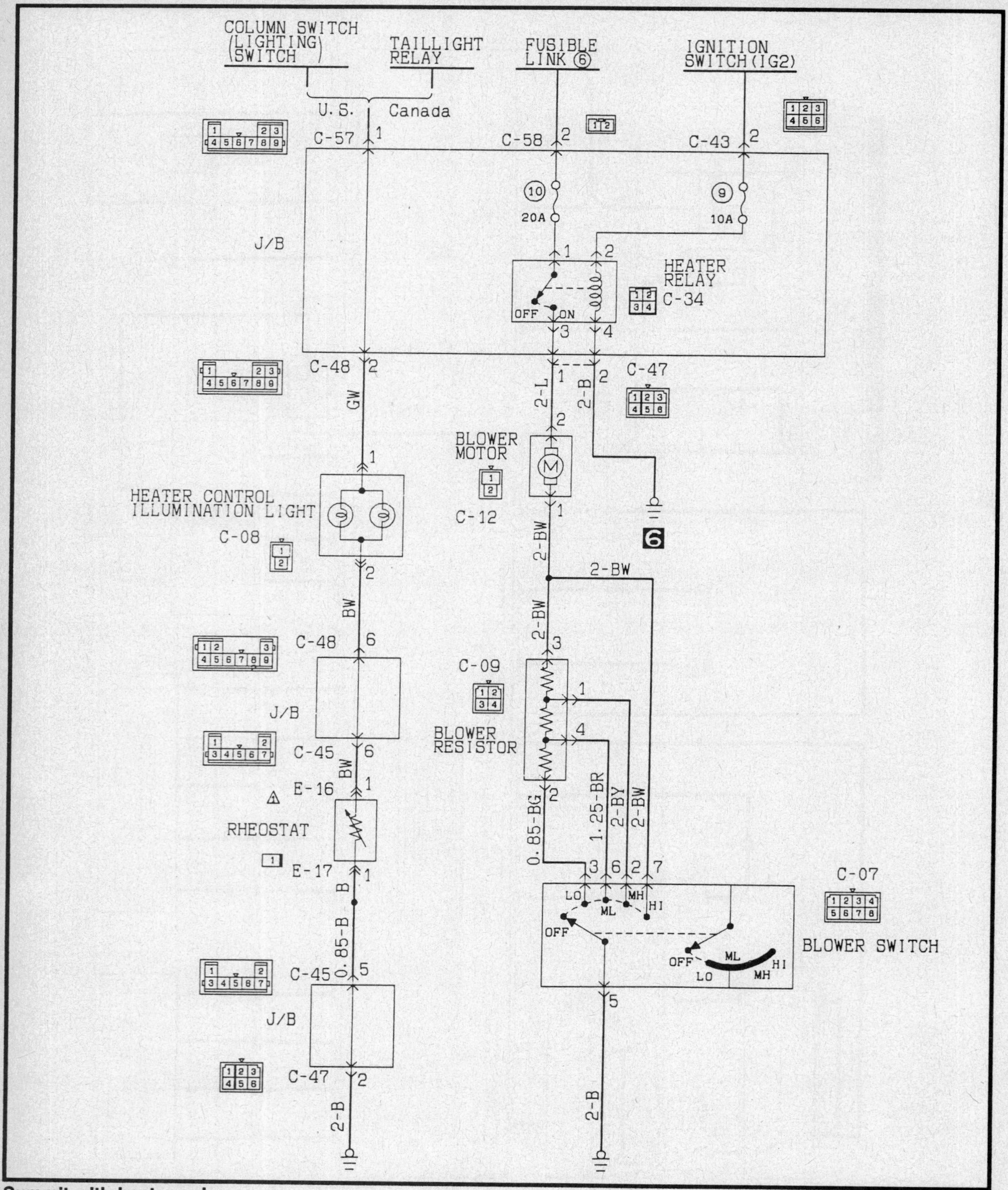
COLUMN SWITCH (LIGHTING SWITCH)
TAILLIGHT RELAY
FUSIBLE LINK ⑥
IGNITION SWITCH (IG2)
U.S.
Canada
C-57
C-58
C-43
J/B
20A
10A
HEATER RELAY
C-34
OFF
ON
C-48
C-47
GW
2-L
2-B
BLOWER MOTOR
C-12
HEATER CONTROL ILLUMINATION LIGHT
C-08
6
2-BW
BW
C-48
J/B
C-09
BLOWER RESISTOR
C-45
E-16
RHEOSTAT
E-17
0.85-BG
1.25-BR
2-BY
2-BW
B
0.85-B
C-45
J/B
C-47
2-B
LO
ML
MH
HI
OFF
C-07
BLOWER SWITCH
2-B

Summit with heater only

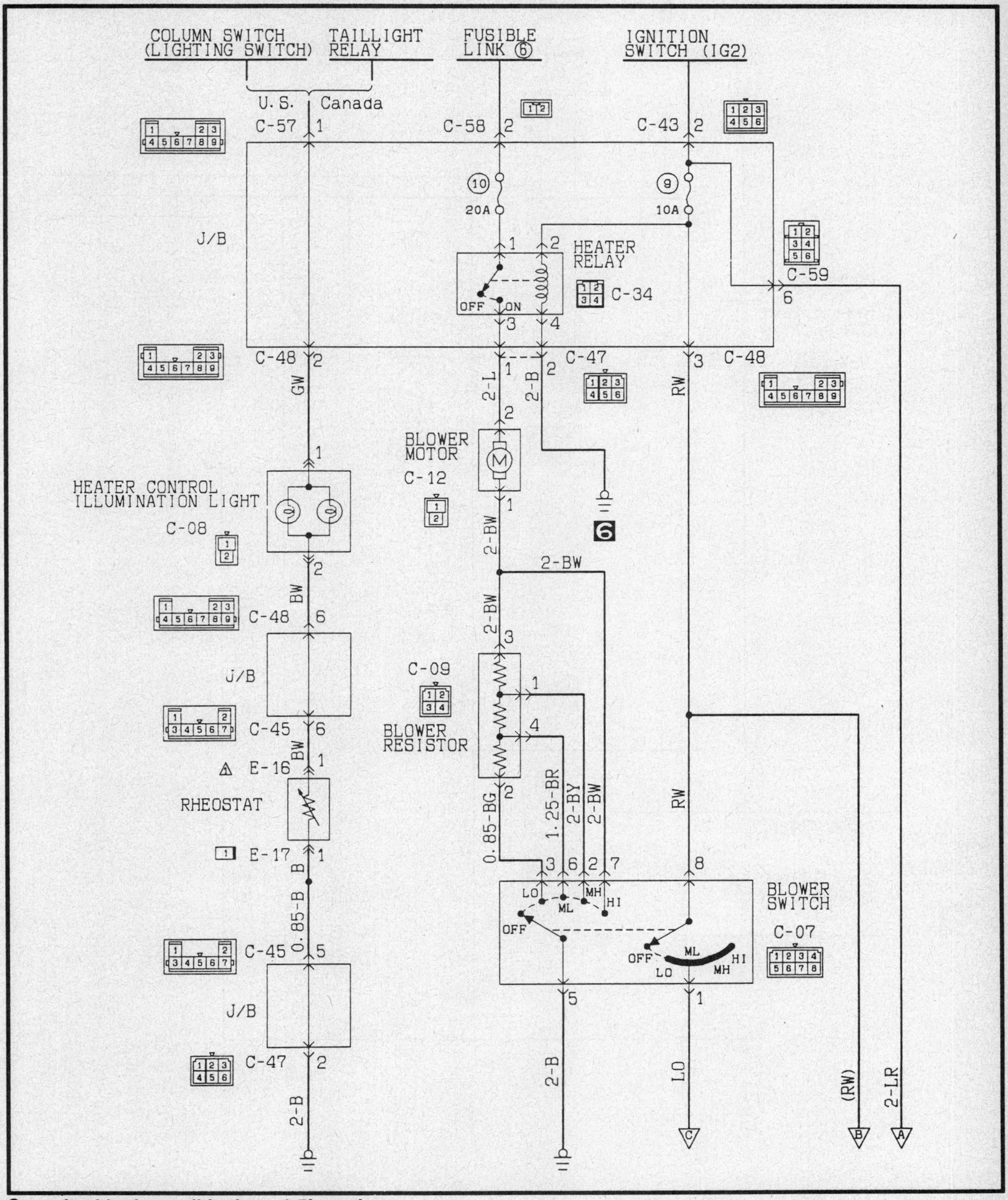
COLUMN SWITCH (LIGHTING SWITCH)
TAILLIGHT RELAY
FUSIBLE LINK ⑥
IGNITION SWITCH (IG2)
U.S.
Canada
C-57
C-58
C-43
J/B
10
20A
9
10A
HEATER RELAY
OFF
ON
C-34
C-59
C-48
C-47
GW
2-L
2-B
RW
BLOWER MOTOR
C-12
HEATER CONTROL ILLUMINATION LIGHT
C-08
6
2-BW
BW
C-09
BLOWER RESISTOR
C-45
E-16
RHEOSTAT
E-17
B
0.85-B
0.85-BG
1.25-BR
2-BY
LO
ML
MH
HI
BLOWER SWITCH
C-07
OFF
(RW)
2-LR
C
B
A

Summit with air conditioning—1.5L engine

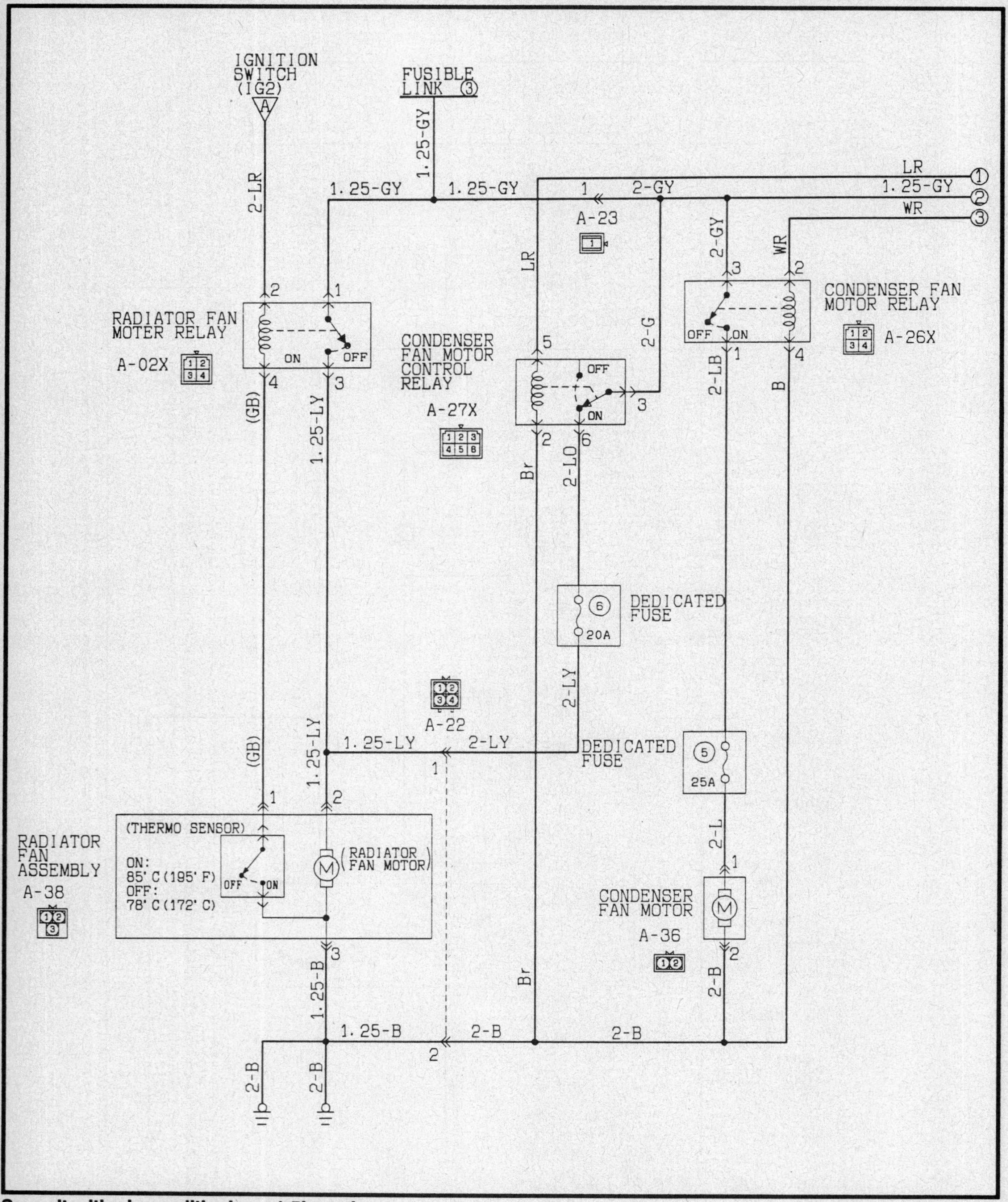
IGNITION SWITCH (IG2)
A
FUSIBLE LINK ③
1.25-GY
2-LR
1.25-GY
1.25-GY
LR
1.25-GY
WR
①
②
③
2-GY
A-23
LR
2-GY
WR
RADIATOR FAN MOTER RELAY
A-02X
ON
OFF
CONDENSER FAN MOTOR CONTROL RELAY
A-27X
OFF
ON
2-G
CONDENSER FAN MOTOR RELAY
A-26X
OFF
ON
(GB)
1.25-LY
Br
2-LO
2-LB
B
DEDICATED FUSE
⑥
20A
2-LY
A-22
1.25-LY
2-LY
DEDICATED FUSE
⑤
25A
(GB)
1.25-LY
2-L
RADIATOR FAN ASSEMBLY
A-38
(THERMO SENSOR)
ON: 85° C (195° F)
OFF: 78° C (172° C)
OFF
ON
(RADIATOR FAN MOTOR)
CONDENSER FAN MOTOR
A-36
1.25-B
Br
2-B
1.25-B
2-B
2-B
2-B
2-B

Summit with air conditioning—1.5L engine

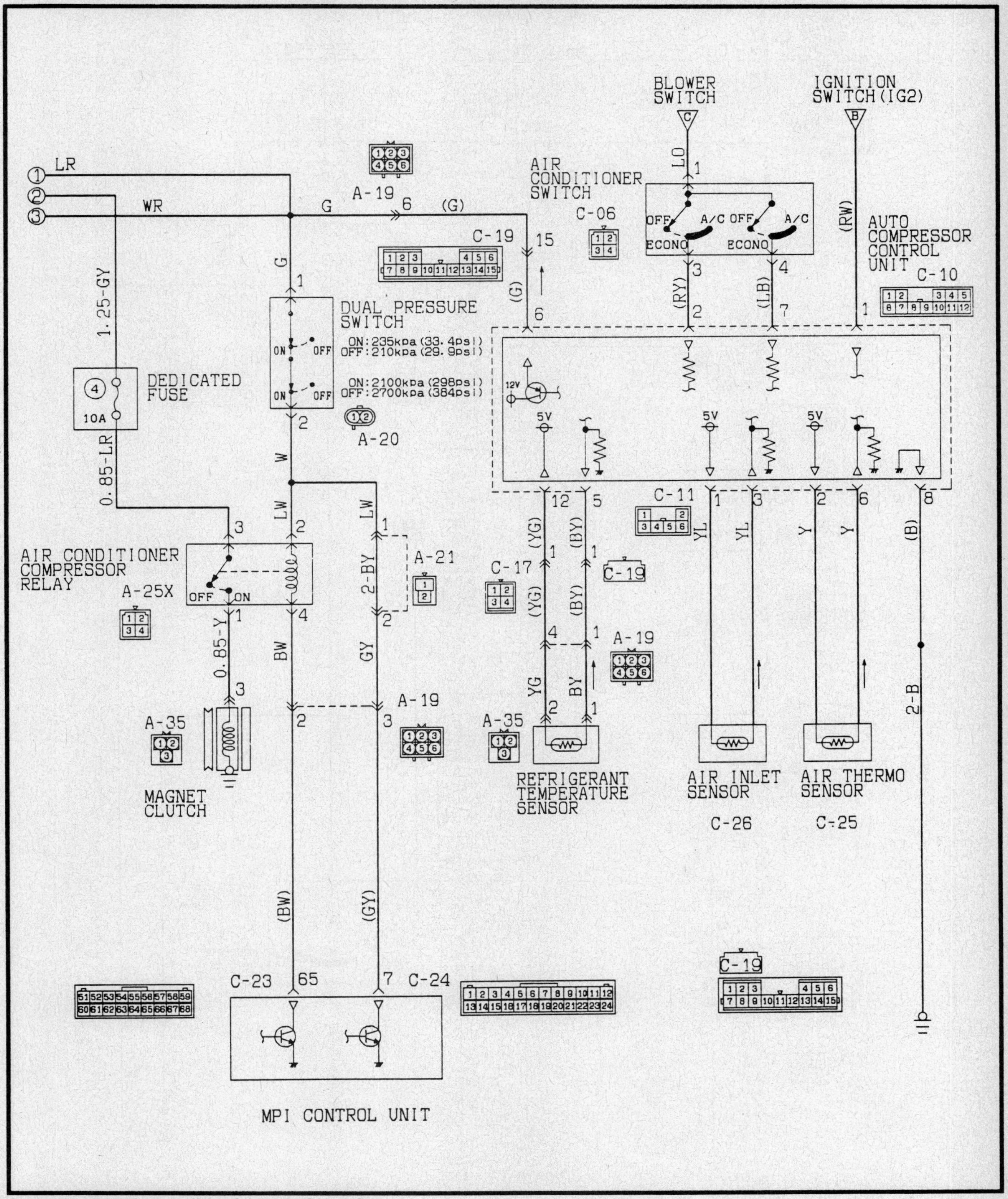
BLOWER SWITCH
IGNITION SWITCH (IG2)
AIR CONDITIONER SWITCH
A-19
C-06
C-19
AUTO COMPRESSOR CONTROL UNIT
C-10
DUAL PRESSURE SWITCH
ON:235kpa (33.4psi)
OFF:210kpa (29.9psi)
ON:2100kpa (298psi)
OFF:2700kpa (384psi)
A-20
DEDICATED FUSE
10A
C-11
AIR CONDITIONER COMPRESSOR RELAY
A-25X
A-21
C-17
MAGNET CLUTCH
A-35
REFRIGERANT TEMPERATURE SENSOR
AIR INLET SENSOR
AIR THERMO SENSOR
C-26
C-25
C-23
C-24
MPI CONTROL UNIT

Summit with air conditioning—1.5L engine

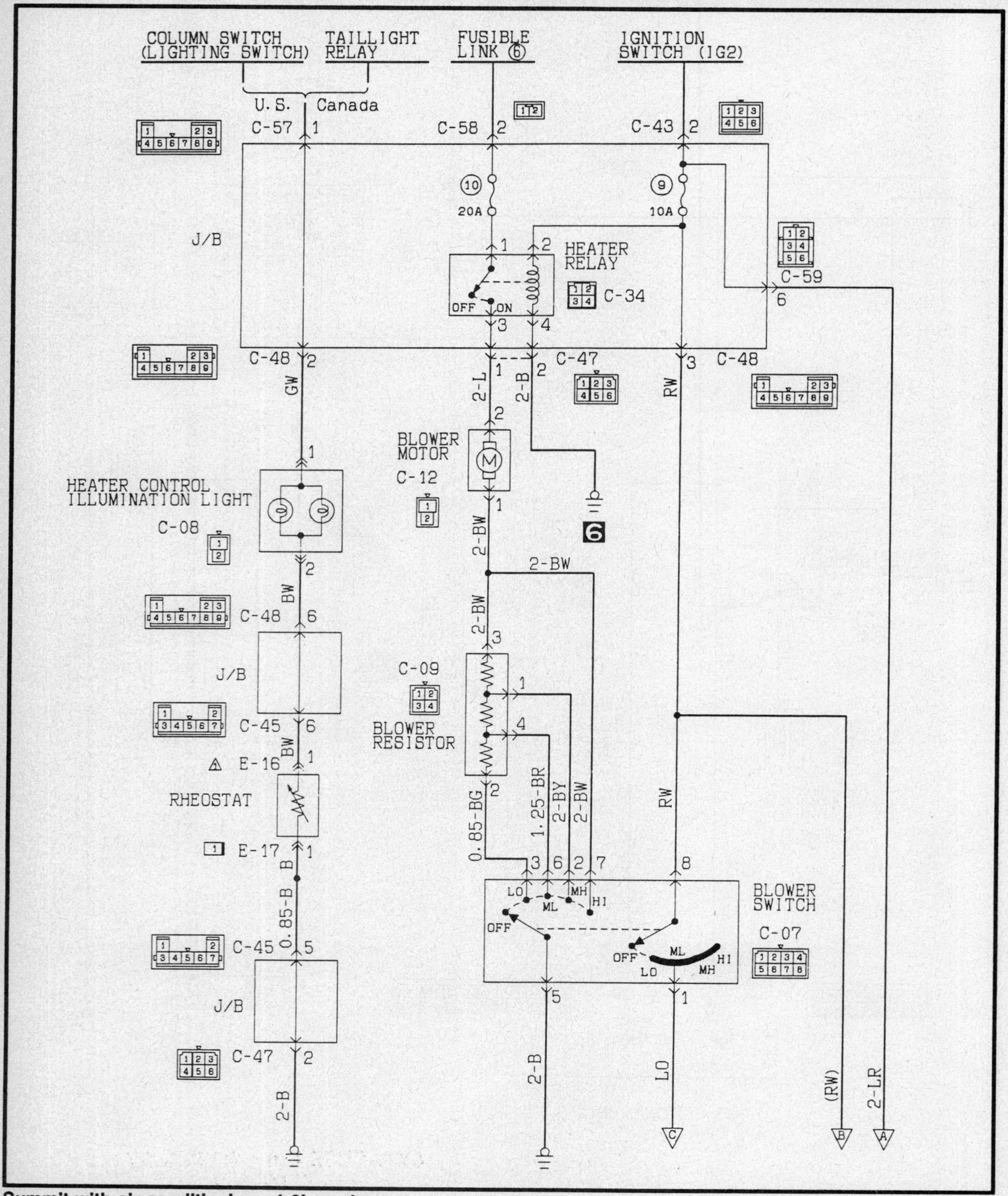
COLUMN SWITCH (LIGHTING SWITCH)
TAILLIGHT RELAY
FUSIBLE LINK ⑥
IGNITION SWITCH (IG2)
U.S.
Canada
C-57
C-58
C-43
J/B
20A
10A
HEATER RELAY
OFF
ON
C-34
C-59
C-48
C-47
GW
2-L
2-B
RW
BLOWER MOTOR
C-12
6
HEATER CONTROL ILLUMINATION LIGHT
C-08
2-BW
BW
C-45
C-09
BLOWER RESISTOR
E-16
RHEOSTAT
E-17
0.85-BG
1.25-BR
2-BY
B
0.85-B
LO
ML
MH
HI
BLOWER SWITCH
C-07
2-B
LO
(RW)
2-LR

Summit with air conditioning—1.6L engine

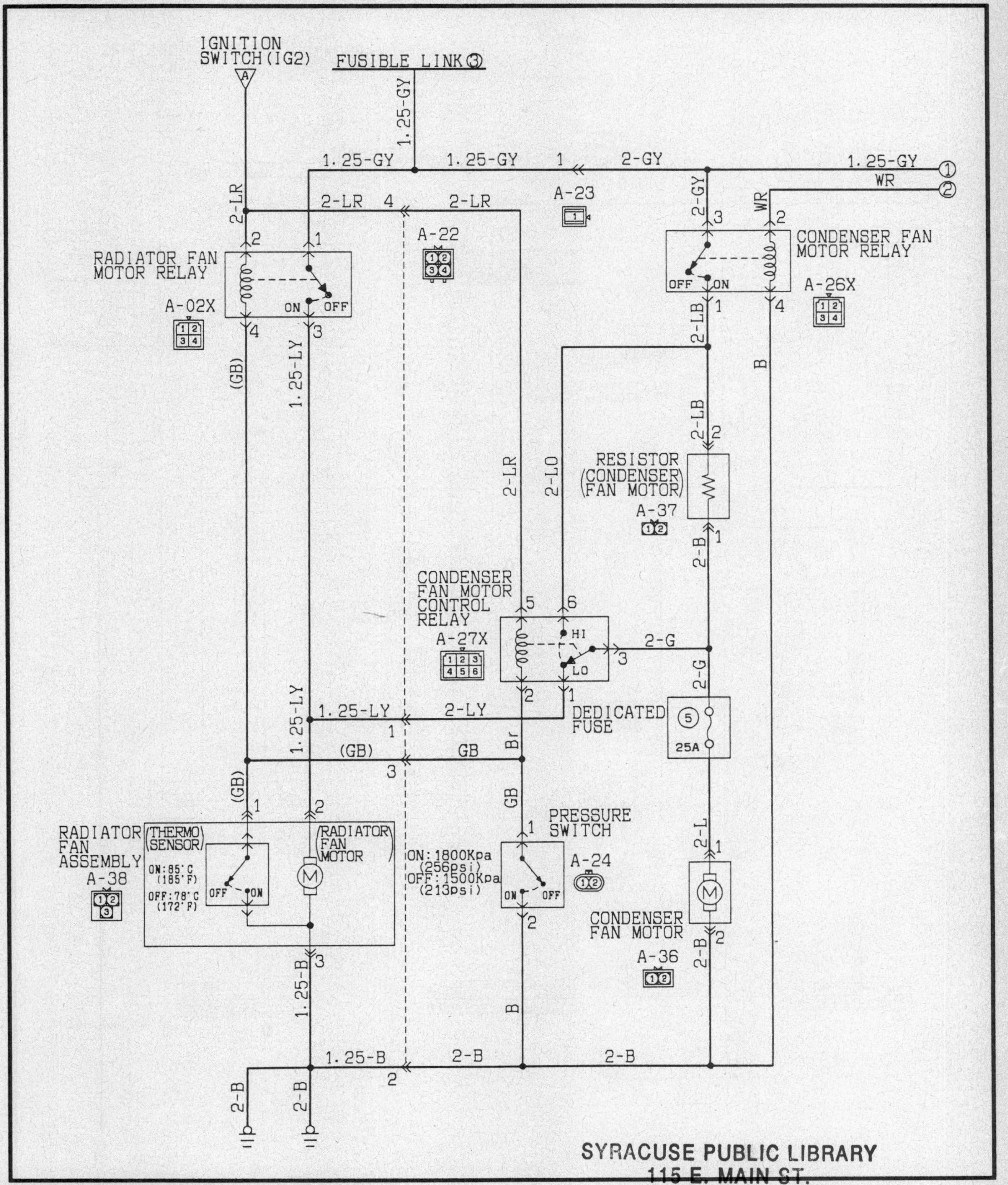
IGNITION SWITCH (IG2)
FUSIBLE LINK ③
1.25-GY
2-GY
WR
2-LR
A-23
A-22
RADIATOR FAN MOTOR RELAY
A-02X
ON
OFF
CONDENSER FAN MOTOR RELAY
A-26X
(GB)
1.25-LY
2-LB
B
RESISTOR (CONDENSER FAN MOTOR)
A-37
2-LO
2-B
CONDENSER FAN MOTOR CONTROL RELAY
A-27X
HI
LO
2-G
2-LY
DEDICATED FUSE
25A
GB
Br
RADIATOR FAN ASSEMBLY
A-38
THERMO SENSOR
ON: 85°C (185°F)
OFF: 78°C (172°F)
RADIATOR FAN MOTOR
PRESSURE SWITCH
ON: 1800Kpa (256psi)
OFF: 1500Kpa (213psi)
A-24
2-L
CONDENSER FAN MOTOR
A-36
1.25-B

Summit with air conditioning—1.6L engine

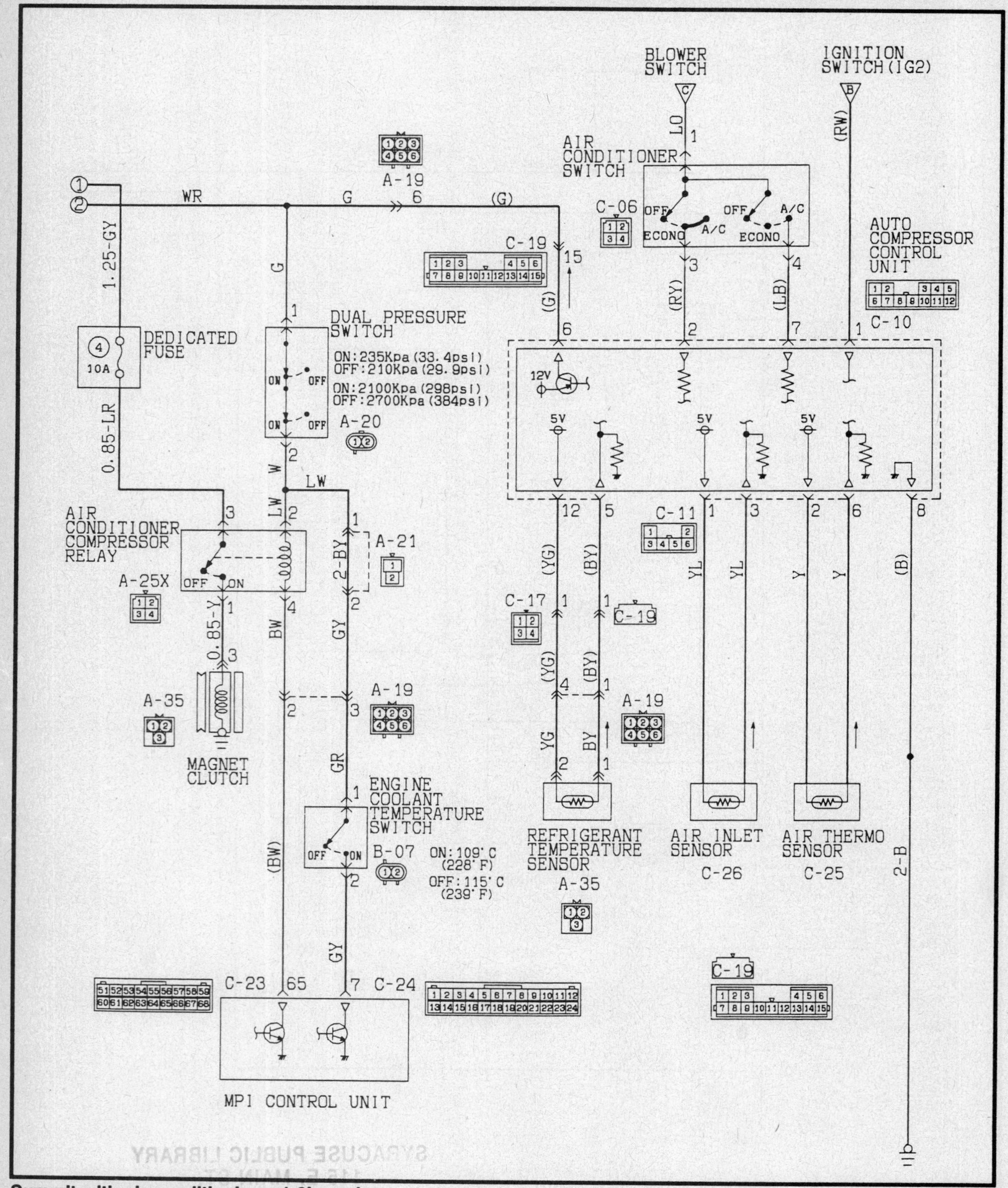
BLOWER SWITCH
IGNITION SWITCH (IG2)
AIR CONDITIONER SWITCH
OFF
A/C
ECONO
C-06
AUTO COMPRESSOR CONTROL UNIT
C-10
C-11
C-19
A-19
WR
G
(G)
1.25-GY
DEDICATED FUSE
10A
0.85-LR
DUAL PRESSURE SWITCH
ON:235Kpa (33.4psi)
OFF:210Kpa (29.9psi)
ON:2100Kpa (298psi)
OFF:2700Kpa (384psi)
A-20
W
LW
AIR CONDITIONER COMPRESSOR RELAY
A-25X
A-21
2-BY
0.85-Y
BW
GY
A-35
MAGNET CLUTCH
GR
ENGINE COOLANT TEMPERATURE SWITCH
B-07
ON:109°C (228°F)
OFF:115°C (239°F)
(BW)
C-23
C-24
MPI CONTROL UNIT
(RY)
(LB)
(RW)
LO
12V
5V
(YG)
(BY)
C-17
YG
BY
YL
Y
(B)
2-B
REFRIGERANT TEMPERATURE SENSOR
AIR INLET SENSOR
C-26
AIR THERMO SENSOR
C-25

Summit with air conditioning—1.6L engine

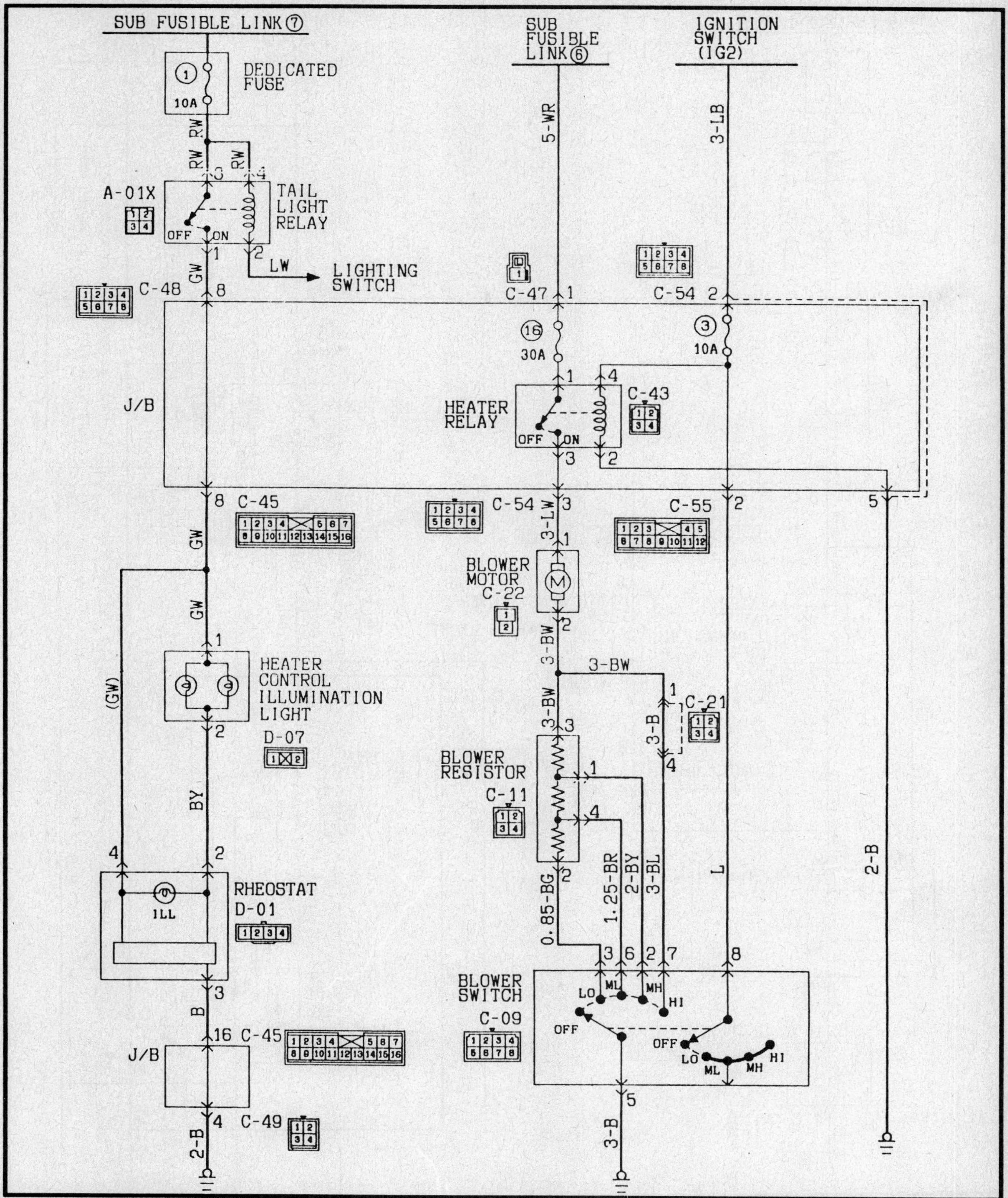
SUB FUSIBLE LINK ⑦
DEDICATED FUSE
10A
A-01X
TAIL LIGHT RELAY
OFF
ON
LW
LIGHTING SWITCH
C-48
J/B
SUB FUSIBLE LINK ⑥
5-WR
IGNITION SWITCH (IG2)
3-LB
C-47
C-54
30A
10A
HEATER RELAY
C-43
C-45
C-55
3-LW
BLOWER MOTOR
C-22
3-BW
HEATER CONTROL ILLUMINATION LIGHT
D-07
(GW)
GW
BY
C-21
3-B
BLOWER RESISTOR
C-11
RHEOSTAT
D-01
ILL
0.85-BG
1.25-BR
2-BY
3-BL
L
2-B
BLOWER SWITCH
C-09
LO
ML
MH
HI
OFF
C-49
B

Laser and Talon with heater only

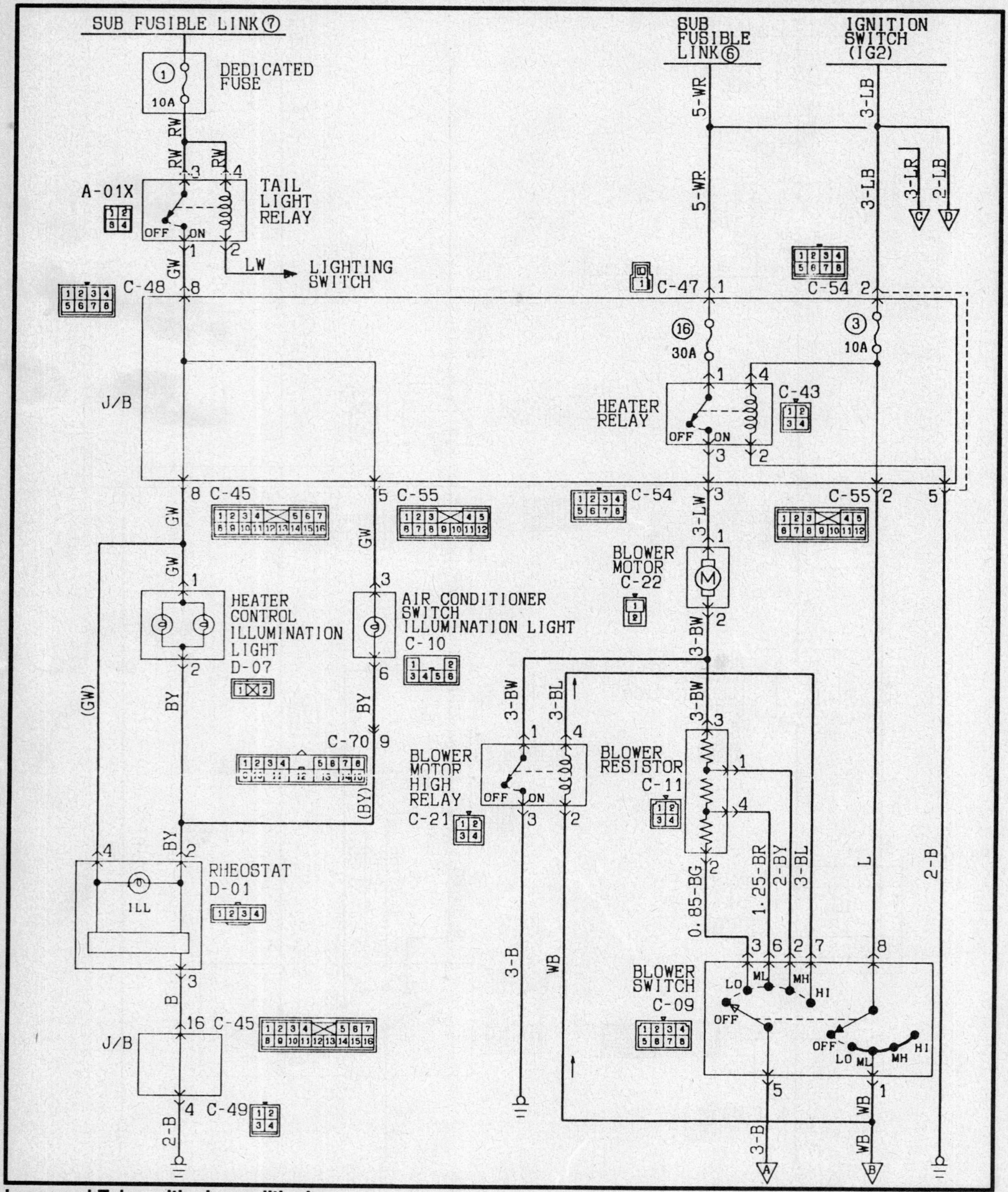
SUB FUSIBLE LINK ⑦
DEDICATED FUSE
10A
A-01X
TAIL LIGHT RELAY
OFF
ON
LW
LIGHTING SWITCH
C-48
J/B
SUB FUSIBLE LINK ⑥
IGNITION SWITCH (IG2)
5-WR
3-LB
3-LR
2-LB
C-47
C-54
30A
10A
HEATER RELAY
C-43
C-45
C-55
3-LW
BLOWER MOTOR C-22
3-BW
GW
HEATER CONTROL ILLUMINATION LIGHT D-07
AIR CONDITIONER SWITCH ILLUMINATION LIGHT C-10
BY
(BY)
(GW)
C-70
3-BL
BLOWER MOTOR HIGH RELAY C-21
BLOWER RESISTOR C-11
RHEOSTAT D-01
ILL
0.85-BG
1.25-BR
2-BY
L
2-B
3-B
WB
BLOWER SWITCH C-09
LO
ML
MH
HI
OFF
C-49

Laser and Talon with air conditioning

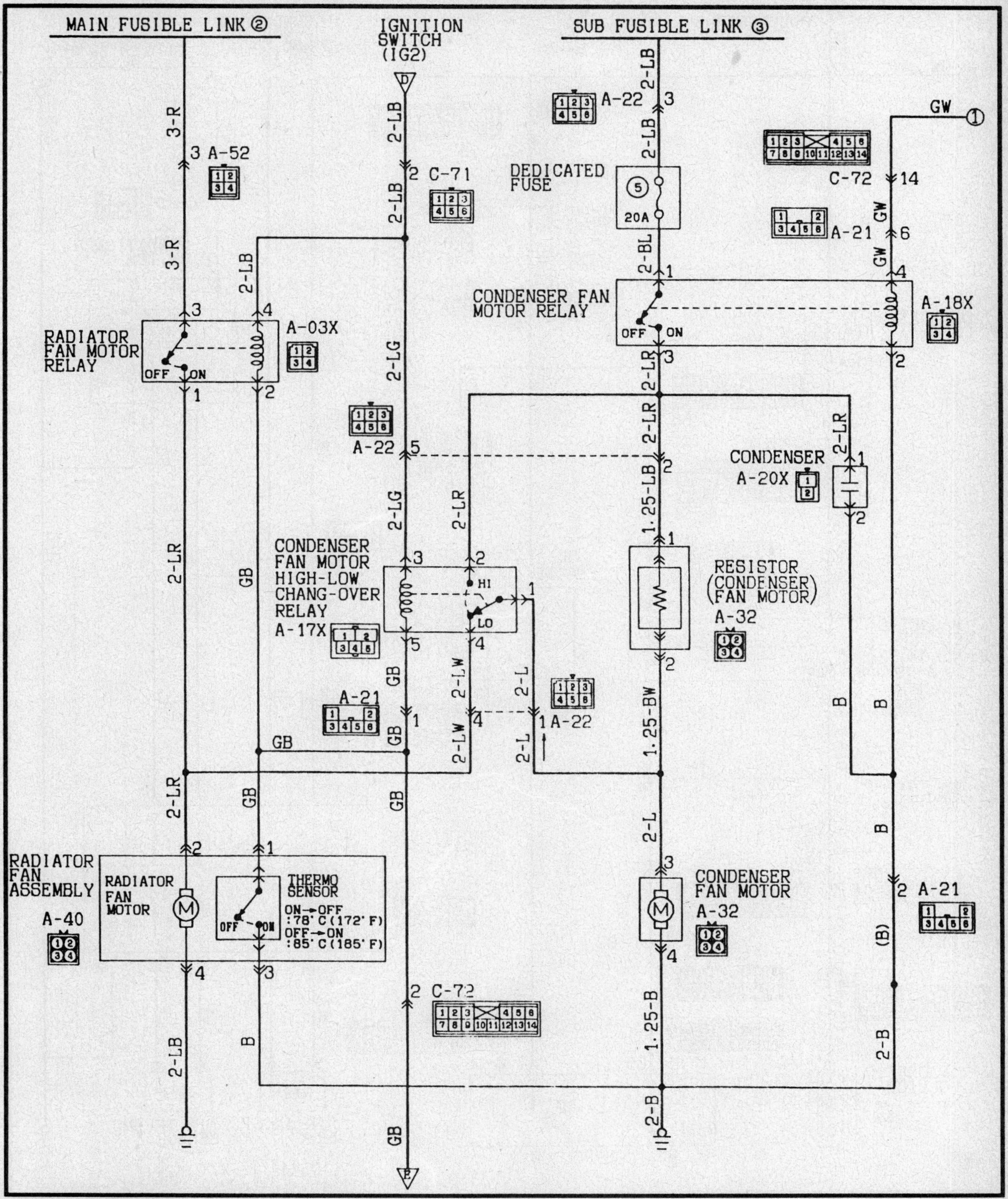
MAIN FUSIBLE LINK ②
IGNITION SWITCH (IG2)
SUB FUSIBLE LINK ③
A-22
A-52
C-71
DEDICATED FUSE
20A
C-72
A-21
GW
CONDENSER FAN MOTOR RELAY
A-18X
RADIATOR FAN MOTOR RELAY
A-03X
OFF
ON
CONDENSER
A-20X
CONDENSER FAN MOTOR HIGH-LOW CHANG-OVER RELAY
A-17X
HI
LO
RESISTOR (CONDENSER) FAN MOTOR)
A-32
RADIATOR FAN ASSEMBLY
A-40
RADIATOR FAN MOTOR
THERMO SENSOR
ON→OFF :78°C (172°F)
OFF→ON :85°C (185°F)
CONDENSER FAN MOTOR
3-R
2-LB
2-LG
2-LR
GB
2-BL
1.25-LB
1.25-BW
2-LW
2-L
B
2-B
1.25-B

Laser and Talon with air conditioning

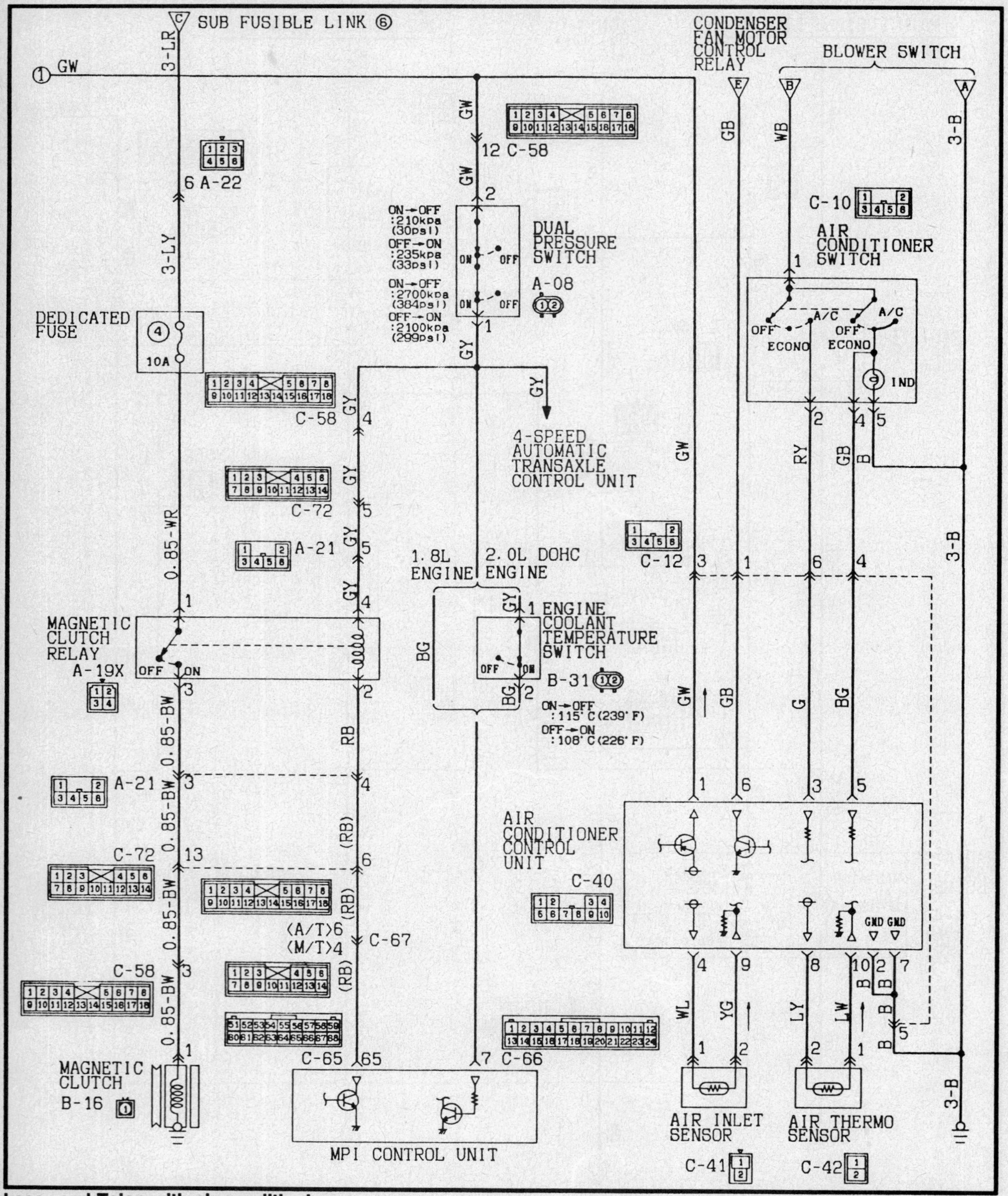
SUB FUSIBLE LINK ⑥
CONDENSER FAN MOTOR CONTROL RELAY
BLOWER SWITCH
DUAL PRESSURE SWITCH
A-08
ON→OFF :210kpa (30psi)
OFF→ON :235kpa (33psi)
ON→OFF :2700kpa (384psi)
OFF→ON :2100kpa (299psi)
AIR CONDITIONER SWITCH
C-10
DEDICATED FUSE
10A
4-SPEED AUTOMATIC TRANSAXLE CONTROL UNIT
1.8L ENGINE
2.0L DOHC ENGINE
ENGINE COOLANT TEMPERATURE SWITCH
B-31
ON→OFF :115°C (239°F)
OFF→ON :108°C (226°F)
MAGNETIC CLUTCH RELAY
A-19X
AIR CONDITIONER CONTROL UNIT
C-40
MAGNETIC CLUTCH
B-16
MPI CONTROL UNIT
C-65
C-66
C-67
AIR INLET SENSOR
C-41
AIR THERMO SENSOR
C-42
ECONO
IND
GND

Laser and Talon with air conditioning

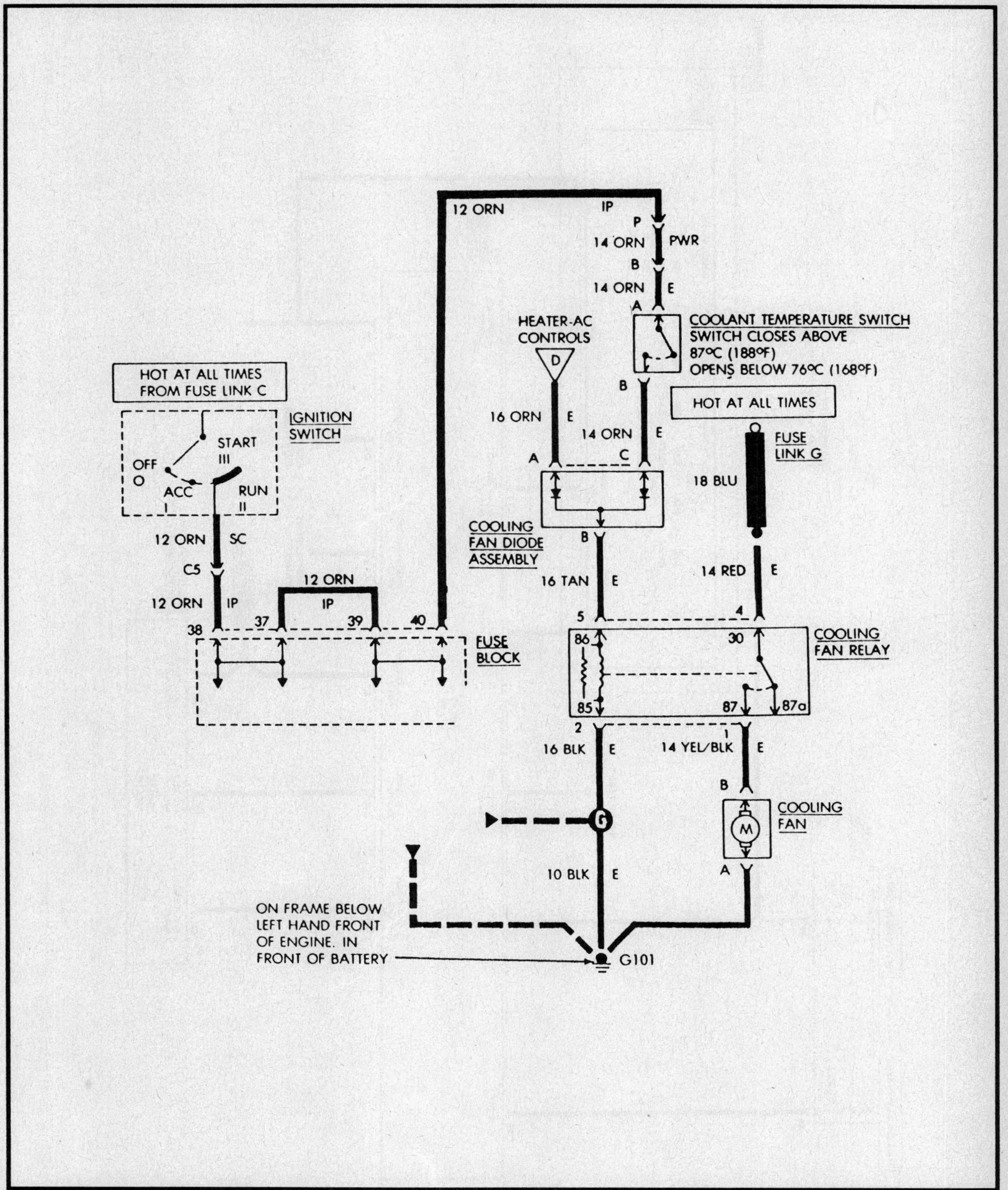
12 ORN
IP
P
14 ORN
PWR
B
14 ORN
E
A
HEATER-AC CONTROLS
D
COOLANT TEMPERATURE SWITCH
SWITCH CLOSES ABOVE 87°C (188°F)
OPENS BELOW 76°C (168°F)
B
HOT AT ALL TIMES FROM FUSE LINK C
IGNITION SWITCH
START III
OFF O
ACC I
RUN II
16 ORN
E
14 ORN
E
HOT AT ALL TIMES
FUSE LINK G
A
C
18 BLU
12 ORN
SC
C5
COOLING FAN DIODE ASSEMBLY
B
16 TAN
E
14 RED
E
12 ORN
IP
12 ORN
IP
38
37
39
40
FUSE BLOCK
5
4
86
30
COOLING FAN RELAY
85
87
87a
2
1
16 BLK
E
14 YEL/BLK
E
B
COOLING FAN
M
G
10 BLK
E
A
ON FRAME BELOW LEFT HAND FRONT OF ENGINE. IN FRONT OF BATTERY
G101

Monaco and Premier cooling fan

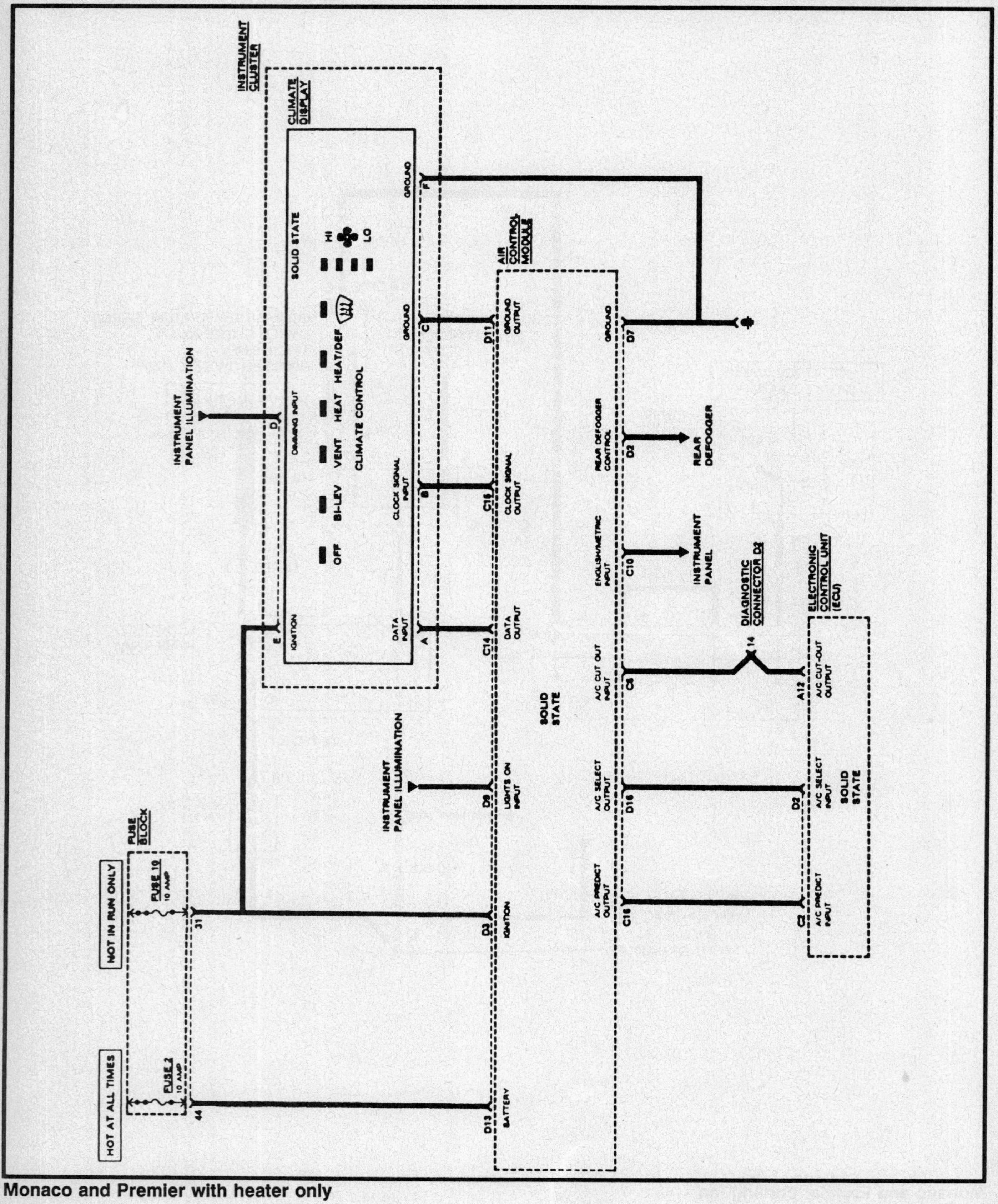
INSTRUMENT CLUSTER
CLIMATE DISPLAY
SOLID STATE
HI
LO
OFF
BI-LEV
VENT
HEAT
HEAT/DEF
CLIMATE CONTROL
GROUND
CLOCK SIGNAL INPUT
DATA INPUT
IGNITION
DIMMING INPUT
INSTRUMENT PANEL ILLUMINATION
AIR CONTROL MODULE
GROUND OUTPUT
CLOCK SIGNAL OUTPUT
DATA OUTPUT
LIGHTS ON INPUT
IGNITION
BATTERY
SOLID STATE
REAR DEFOGGER CONTROL
ENGLISH/METRIC INPUT
A/C CUT OUT INPUT
A/C SELECT OUTPUT
A/C PREDICT OUTPUT
REAR DEFOGGER
INSTRUMENT PANEL
DIAGNOSTIC CONNECTOR D2
ELECTRONIC CONTROL UNIT (ECU)
A/C CUT-OUT OUTPUT
A/C SELECT INPUT
A/C PREDICT INPUT
FUSE BLOCK
FUSE 10 10 AMP
FUSE 2 10 AMP
HOT IN RUN ONLY
HOT AT ALL TIMES

Monaco and Premier with heater only

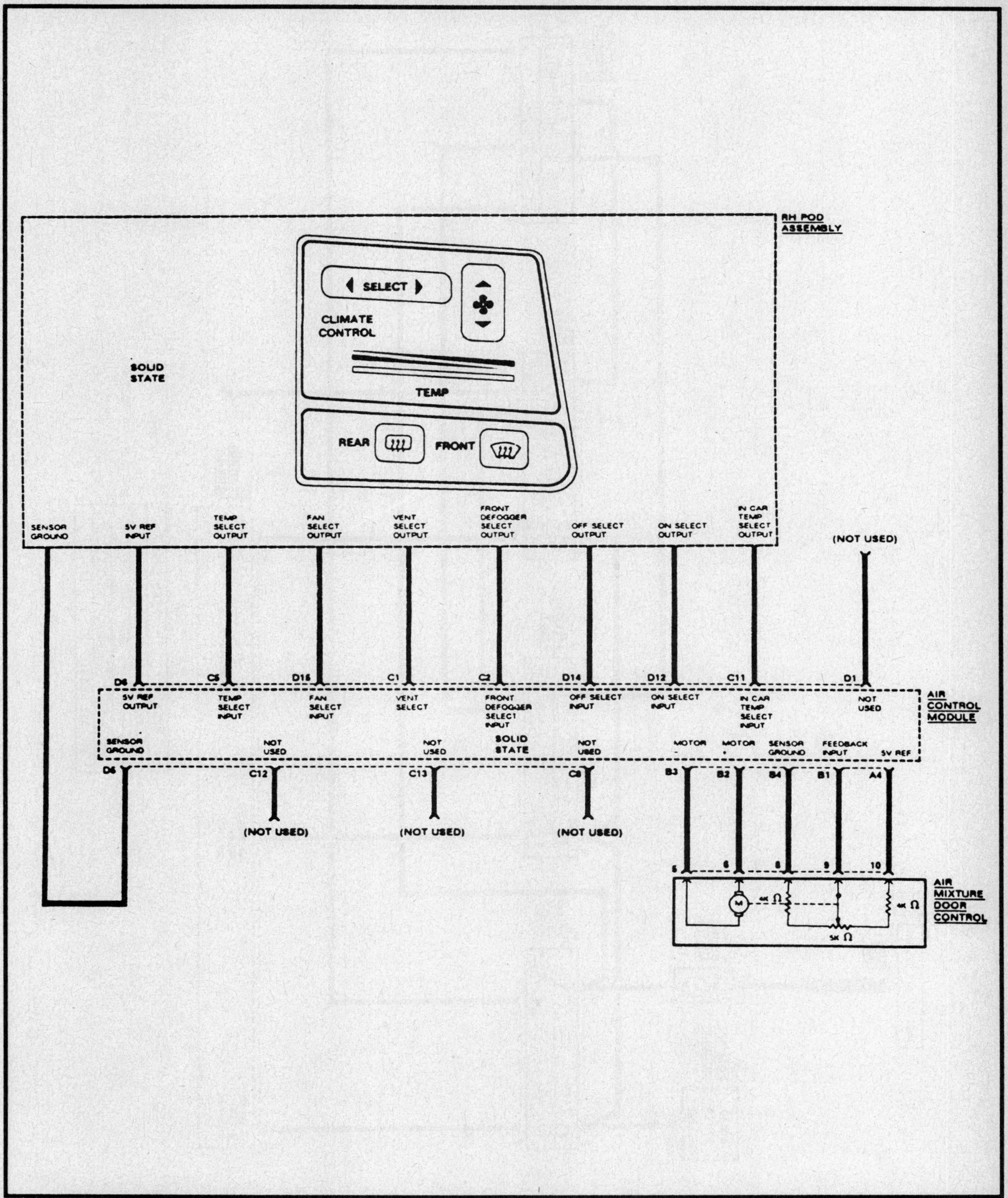
RH POD ASSEMBLY
SELECT
CLIMATE CONTROL
TEMP
REAR
FRONT
SOLID STATE
SENSOR GROUND
5V REF INPUT
TEMP SELECT OUTPUT
FAN SELECT OUTPUT
VENT SELECT OUTPUT
FRONT DEFOGGER SELECT OUTPUT
OFF SELECT OUTPUT
ON SELECT OUTPUT
IN CAR TEMP SELECT OUTPUT
(NOT USED)
D6
C5
D15
C1
C2
D14
D12
C11
D1
5V REF OUTPUT
TEMP SELECT INPUT
FAN SELECT INPUT
VENT SELECT
FRONT DEFOGGER SELECT INPUT
OFF SELECT INPUT
ON SELECT INPUT
IN CAR TEMP SELECT INPUT
NOT USED
AIR CONTROL MODULE
SENSOR GROUND
NOT USED
NOT USED
SOLID STATE
NOT USED
MOTOR -
MOTOR +
SENSOR GROUND
FEEDBACK INPUT
5V REF
D6
C12
C13
C8
B3
B2
B4
B1
A4
(NOT USED)
(NOT USED)
(NOT USED)
5
6
8
9
10
M
4K Ω
4K Ω
5K Ω
AIR MIXTURE DOOR CONTROL

Monaco and Premier with heater only

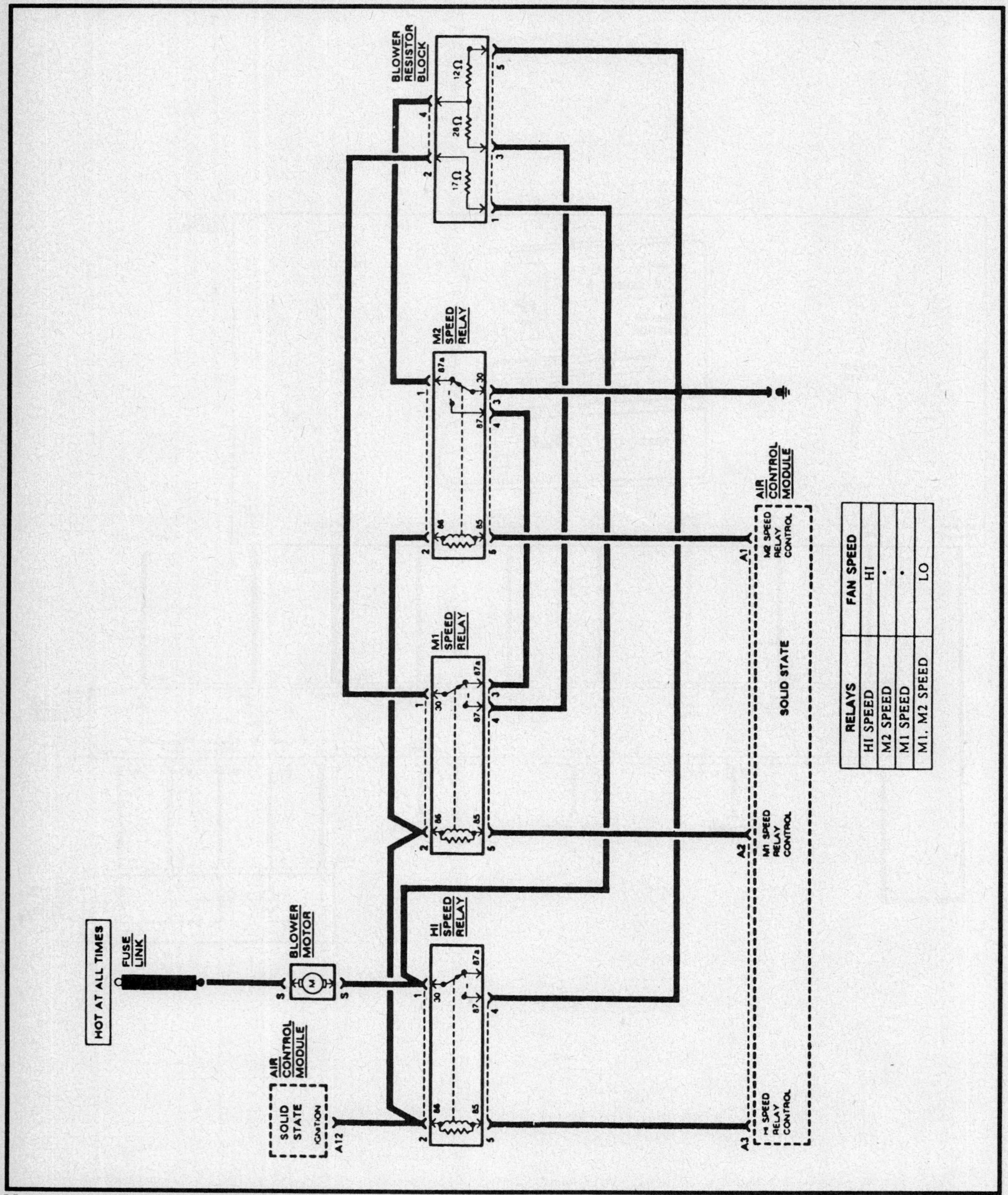
BLOWER RESISTOR BLOCK
12 Ω
28 Ω
17 Ω
M2 SPEED RELAY
M1 SPEED RELAY
HI SPEED RELAY
HOT AT ALL TIMES
FUSE LINK
BLOWER MOTOR
AIR CONTROL MODULE
SOLID STATE IGNITION
A12
M2 SPEED RELAY CONTROL
M1 SPEED RELAY CONTROL
HI SPEED RELAY CONTROL
A1
A2
A3
SOLID STATE
RELAYS
FAN SPEED
HI SPEED
M2 SPEED
M1 SPEED
M1, M2 SPEED
HI
LO

Monaco and Premier with heater only

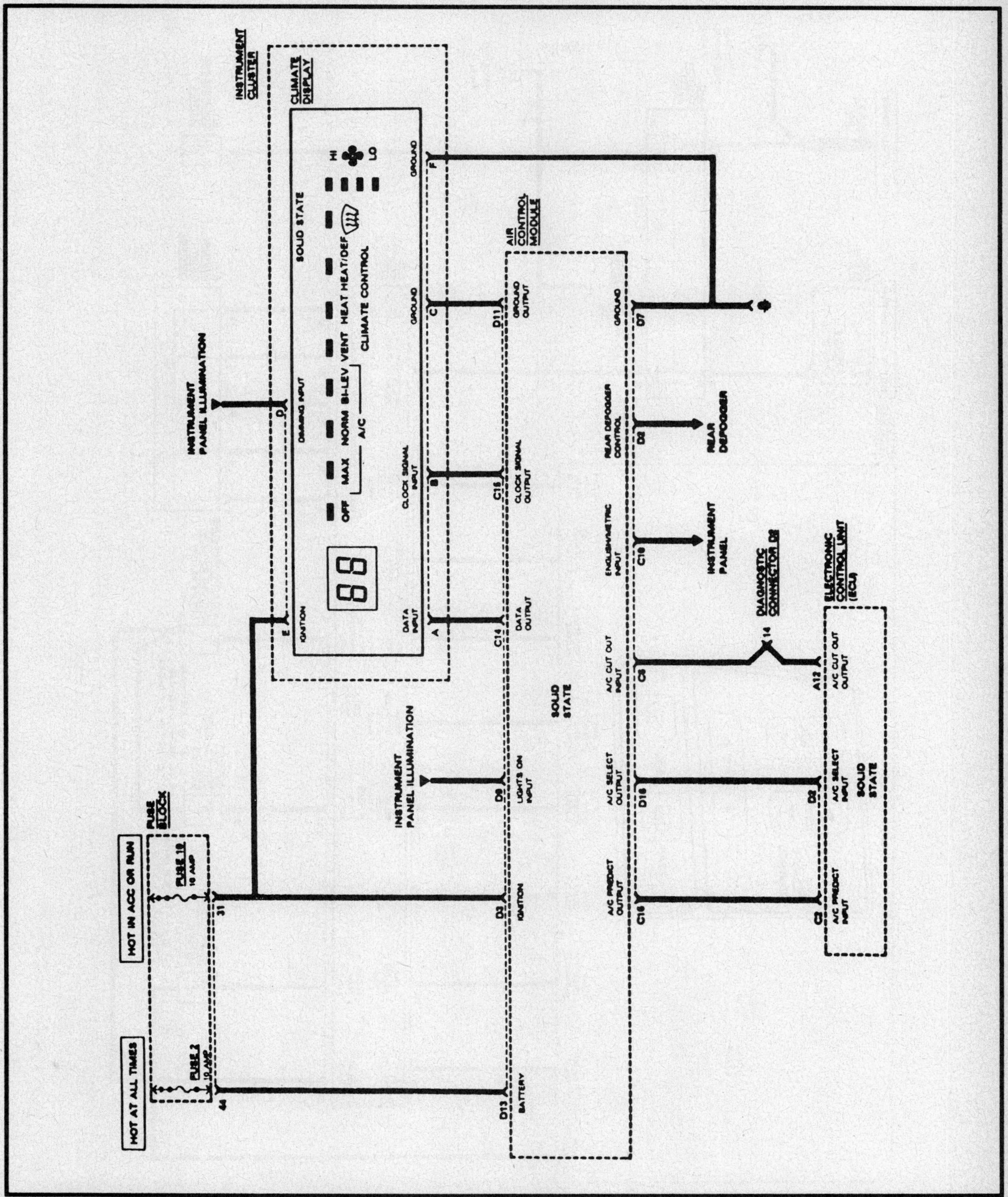
HOT AT ALL TIMES
HOT IN ACC OR RUN
FUSE BLOCK
FUSE 2 10 AMP
FUSE 18 10 AMP
44
31
INSTRUMENT CLUSTER
CLIMATE DISPLAY
SOLID STATE
OFF
MAX
NORM
BI-LEV
VENT
HEAT
HEAT/DEF
A/C
CLIMATE CONTROL
HI
LO
INSTRUMENT PANEL ILLUMINATION
AIR CONTROL MODULE
REAR DEFOGGER
INSTRUMENT PANEL
DIAGNOSTIC CONNECTOR D2
ELECTRONIC CONTROL UNIT (ECU)

Monaco and Premier with semi-automatic temperature control

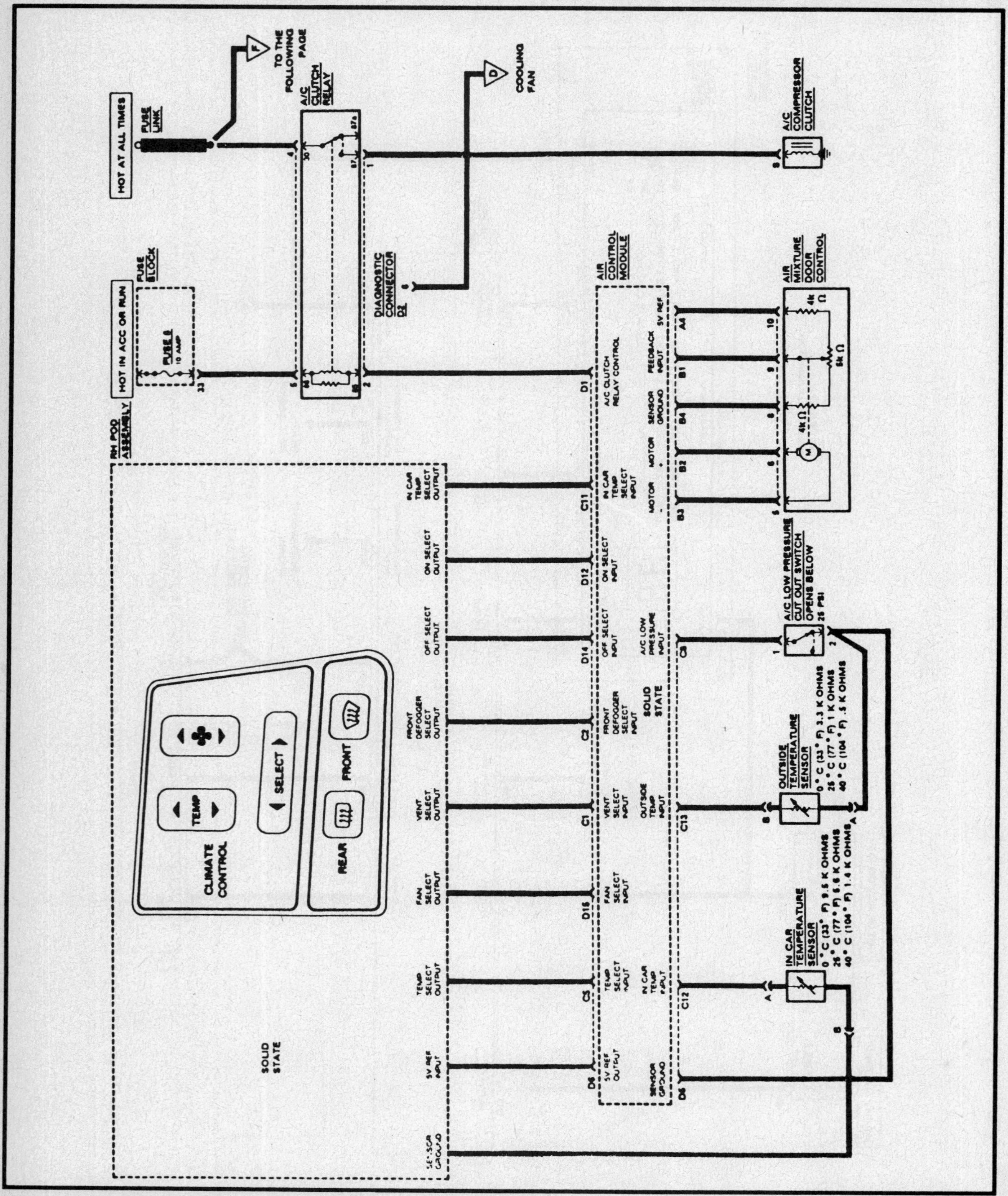
HOT AT ALL TIMES
FUSE LINK
A/C CLUTCH RELAY
TO THE FOLLOWING PAGE
COOLING FAN
A/C COMPRESSOR CLUTCH
DIAGNOSTIC CONNECTOR D2
FUSE BLOCK
HOT IN ACC OR RUN
RH POD ASSEMBLY
AIR CONTROL MODULE
AIR MIXTURE DOOR CONTROL
A/C LOW PRESSURE CUT OUT SWITCH OPENS BELOW 25 PSI
OUTSIDE TEMPERATURE SENSOR
IN CAR TEMPERATURE SENSOR
CLIMATE CONTROL
TEMP
SELECT
FRONT
REAR
SOLID STATE

Monaco and Premier with semi-automatic temperature control

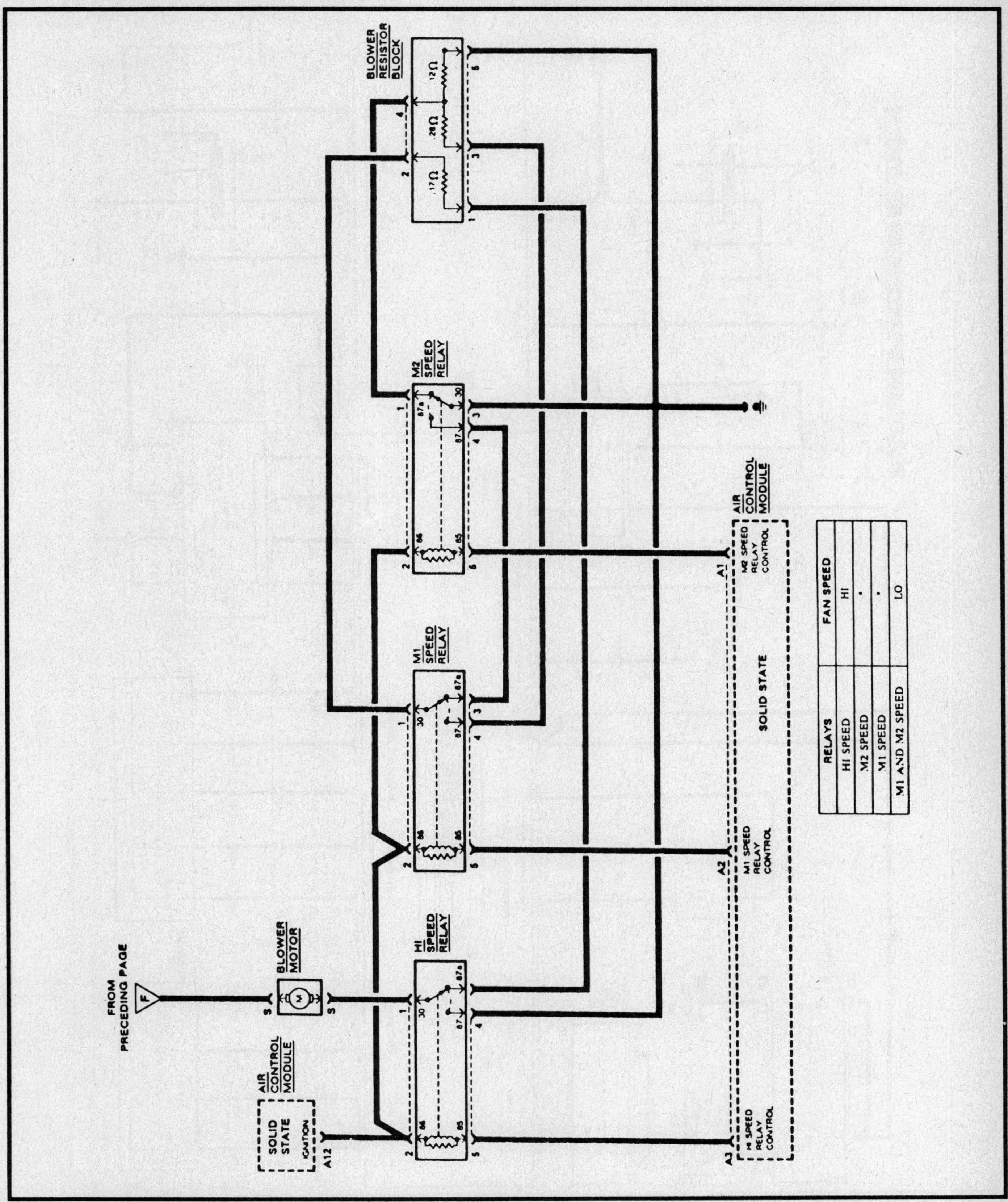
BLOWER RESISTOR BLOCK
.12 Ω
.28 Ω
.17 Ω
M2 SPEED RELAY
M1 SPEED RELAY
HI SPEED RELAY
BLOWER MOTOR
FROM PRECEDING PAGE
F
AIR CONTROL MODULE
SOLID STATE
IGNITION
A12
A1
M2 SPEED RELAY CONTROL
A2
M1 SPEED RELAY CONTROL
A3
HI SPEED RELAY CONTROL
SOLID STATE
AIR CONTROL MODULE
RELAYS
HI SPEED
M2 SPEED
M1 SPEED
M1 AND M2 SPEED
FAN SPEED
HI
LO

Monaco and Premier with semi-automatic temperature control

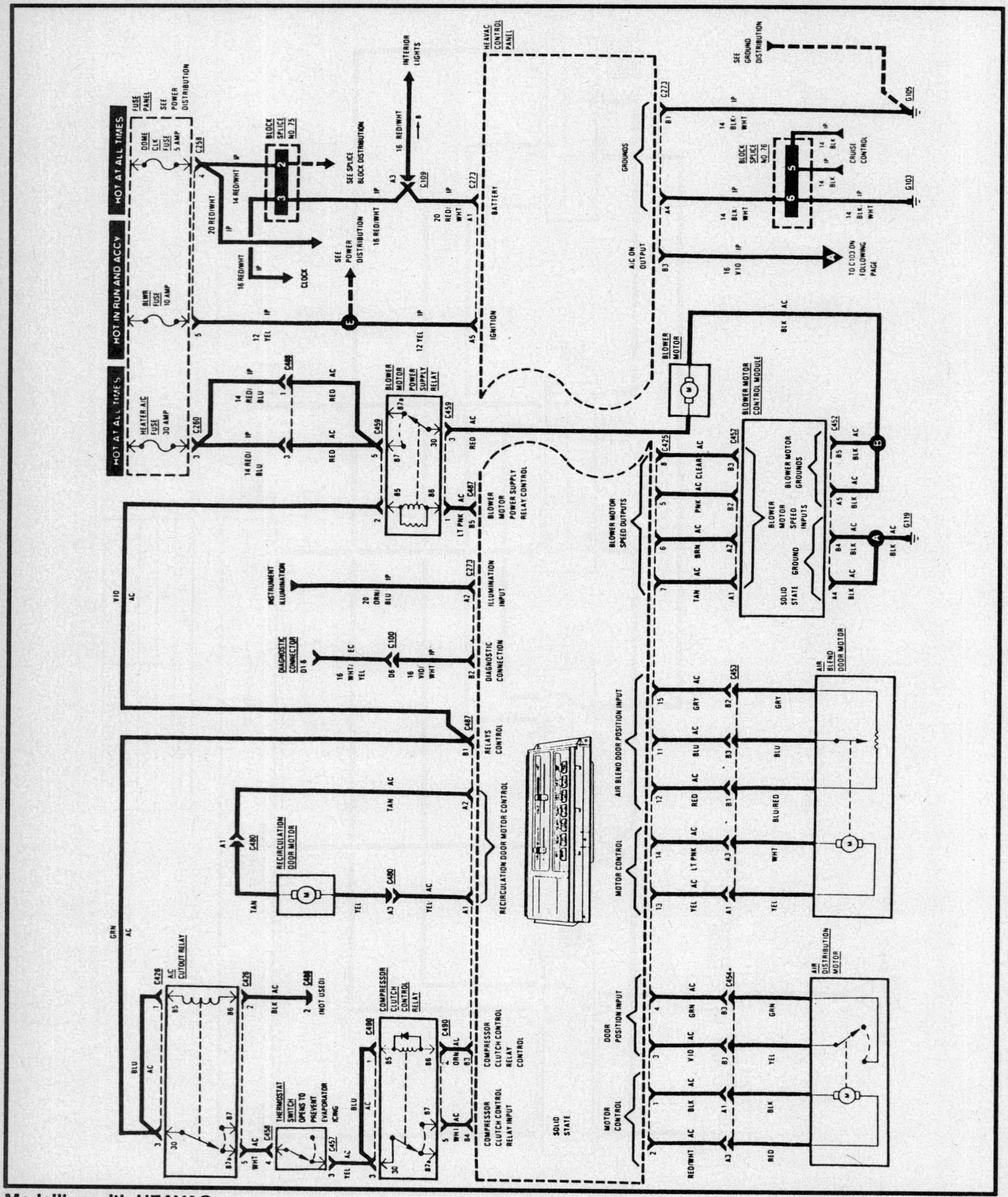
HOT AT ALL TIMES
HOT IN RUN AND ACCY
HOT AT ALL TIMES
FUSE PANEL
SEE POWER DISTRIBUTION
DOME CLK FUSE 5 AMP
BLWR FUSE 10 AMP
HEATER A/C FUSE 30 AMP
BLOCK SPLICE NO 75
SEE SPLICE BLOCK DISTRIBUTION
INTERIOR LIGHTS
CLOCK
HEAVAC CONTROL PANEL
BLOWER MOTOR POWER SUPPLY RELAY
BLOWER MOTOR
BLOWER MOTOR CONTROL MODULE
BLOCK SPLICE NO 76
CRUISE CONTROL
SEE GROUND DISTRIBUTION
TO C103 ON FOLLOWING PAGE
INSTRUMENT ILLUMINATION
DIAGNOSTIC CONNECTOR
RECIRCULATION DOOR MOTOR
AIR BLEND DOOR MOTOR
AIR DISTRIBUTION MOTOR
A/C CUTOUT RELAY
COMPRESSOR CLUTCH CONTROL RELAY
THERMOSTAT SWITCH OPENS TO PREVENT EVAPORATOR ICING
(NOT USED)
SOLID STATE

Medallion with HEAVAC

4 FORD/LINCOLN/MERCURY 4

CAPRI • CONTINENTAL • ESCORT • FESTIVA • PROBE • SABLE • TAURUS • TEMPO • TOPAZ • TRACER

SPECIFICATIONS

ENGINE IDENTIFICATION

Year	Model	Engine Displacement cu. in. (cc/liter)	Engine Series Identification (VIN)	No. of Cylinders	Engine Type
1989	Festiva	81 (1.3)	K	4	OHC
	Festiva	81 (1.3)	H	4	OHC
	Tracer	98 (1.6)	7	4	OHC
	Tracer	98 (1.6)	5	4	OHC
	Escort	116 (1.9)	9	4	OHC
	Escort	116 (1.9)	J	4	OHC
	Probe	133 (2.2)	C	4	OHC
	Probe	133 (2.2)	L	4	OHC
	Tempo	140 (2.3)	X	4	OHV
	Tempo	140 (2.3)	S	4	OHV
	Topaz	140 (2.3)	X	4	OHV
	Topaz	140 (2.3)	S	4	OHV
	Taurus	153 (2.5)	D	4	OHV
	Sable	153 (2.5)	D	4	OHV
	Taurus	182 (3.0)	U	6	OHV
	Sable	182 (3.0)	U	6	OHV
	Taurus SHO	182 (3.0)	Y	6	DOHC
	Taurus	232 (3.8)	4	6	OHV
	Sable	232 (3.8)	4	6	OHV
	Continental	232 (3.8)	4	6	OHV
1990	Festiva	81 (1.3)	H	4	OHC
	Tracer	98 (1.6)	5	4	OHC
	Escort	116 (1.9)	9	4	OHC
	Escort	116 (1.9)	J	4	OHC
	Probe	133 (2.2)	C	4	OHC
	Probe	133 (2.2)	L	4	OHC
	Tempo	140 (2.3)	X	4	OHV
	Tempo	140 (2.3)	S	4	OHV
	Topaz	140 (2.3)	X	4	OHV
	Topaz	140 (2.3)	S	4	OHV
	Taurus	153 (2.5)	D	4	OHV
	Probe	182 (3.0)	U	6	OHV
	Taurus	182 (3.0)	U	6	OHV
	Sable	182 (3.0)	U	6	OHV
	Taurus SHO	182 (3.0)	Y	6	DOHC
	Taurus	232 (3.8)	4	6	OHV
	Sable	232 (3.8)	4	6	OHV
	Continental	232 (3.8)	4	6	OHV
1991	Festiva	81 (1.3)	H	4	OHC
	Capri	98 (1.6)	Z	4	DOHC
	Capri	98 (1.6)	6	4	DOHC
	Escort	109 (1.8)	8	4	DOHC

ENGINE IDENTIFICATION

Year	Model	Engine Displacement cu. in. (cc/liter)	Engine Series Identification (VIN)	No. of Cylinders	Engine Type
1991	Tracer	109 (1.8)	8	4	DOHC
	Escort	116 (1.9)	J	4	OHC
	Tracer	116 (1.9)	J	4	OHC
	Probe	133 (2.2)	C	4	OHC
	Probe	133 (2.2)	L	4	OHC
	Tempo	140 (2.3)	X	4	OHV
	Tempo	140 (2.3)	S	4	OHV
	Topaz	140 (2.3)	X	4	OHV
	Topaz	140 (2.3)	S	4	OHV
	Taurus	153 (2.5)	D	4	OHV
	Probe	182 (3.0)	U	6	OHV
	Taurus	182 (3.0)	U	6	OHV
	Sable	182 (3.0)	U	6	OHV
	Taurus SHO	182 (3.0)	Y	6	DOHC
	Taurus	232 (3.8)	4	6	OHV
	Sable	232 (3.8)	4	6	OHV
	Continental	232 (3.8)	4	6	OHV

REFRIGERANT CAPACITIES

Year	Model	Freon (oz.)	Oil (fl. oz.)	Type
1989	Festiva	25	10	N/A
	Tracer	24.8	10	N/A
	Probe	40	8	10P15A
	Escort	35–37	10	10P15
	Tempo	35–37	10	10P15
	Topaz	35–37	10	10P15
	Taurus	①	②	③
	Sable	①	②	③
	Continental	38–42	8	10P15C
1990	Festiva	25	10	N/A
	Tracer	24.8	10	N/A
	Probe	40	8	④
	Escort	35–37	10	10P15
	Tempo	35–37	10	10P15
	Topaz	35–37	10	10P15
	Taurus	①	②	③
	Sable	①	②	③
	Continental	38–42	8	10P15C
1991	Festiva	25	10	N/A
	Capri	22.4	10	N/A
	Escort	N/A	7.75	10P13
	Tracer	N/A	7.75	10P13
	Probe	40	8	④

REFRIGERANT CAPACITIES

Year	Model	Freon (oz.)	Oil (fl. oz.)	Type
1991	Tempo	35–37	10	10P15
	Topaz	35–37	10	10P15
	Taurus	①	②	③
	Sable	①	②	③
	Continental	38–42	8	10P15C

① 2.5L and 3.0L Engines
42–46 oz.
3.8L Engine—38–42 oz.
② 2.5L Engine—10 oz.
3.0L Engine—7 oz.
3.0L SHO and 3.8L Engines—8 oz.
③ 2.5L Engine—FS-6
3.0L Engine—FX-15
3.0L SHO Engine—10P15F
3.8L Engine—10P15C
④ 2.2L Engine—10P15A
3.0L Engine—10P15
⑤ Compressor name

AIR CONDITIONING BELT TENSION CHART

Year	Model	Engine (L)	Belt Type	Specification New	Specification Used
1989	Festiva	1.3	V-Ribbed	110–125	92–110
	Tracer	1.6	V	110–132	110–132
	Probe	2.2	V-Ribbed	154–198	132–176
	Escort	1.9	V-Ribbed	140–180	120–140
	Tempo	2.3	V-Ribbed	①	①
	Topaz	2.3	V-Ribbed	①	①
	Taurus	2.5	V-Ribbed	①	①
	Taurus	3.0	V-Ribbed	①	①
	Taurus	3.0 SHO	V-Ribbed	220–265	148–192
	Taurus	3.8	V-Ribbed	①	①
	Sable	2.5	V-Ribbed	①	①
	Sable	3.0	V-Ribbed	①	①
	Sable	3.8	V-Ribbed	①	①
	Continental	3.8	V-Ribbed	①	①
1990	Festiva	1.3	V-Ribbed	110–125	92–110
	Tracer	1.6	V	110–132	110–132
	Probe	2.2	V-Ribbed	154–198	132–176
	Probe	3.0	V-Ribbed	①	①
	Escort	1.9	V-Ribbed	140–180	120–140
	Tempo	2.3	V-Ribbed	①	①
	Topaz	2.3	V-Ribbed	①	①
	Taurus	2.5	V-Ribbed	①	①
	Taurus	3.0	V-Ribbed	①	①
	Taurus	3.0 SHO	V-Ribbed	220–265	148–192
	Taurus	3.8	V-Ribbed	①	①
	Sable	3.0	V-Ribbed	①	①
	Sable	3.8	V-Ribbed	①	①
	Continental	3.8	V-Ribbed	①	①

AIR CONDITIONING BELT TENSION CHART

Year	Model	Engine (L)	Belt Type	Specification New	Specification Used
1991	Festiva	1.3	V-Ribbed	110–125	92–110
	Capri	1.6	V-Ribbed	110–132	110–132
	Escort	1.8	V-Ribbed	110–132	110–132
	Escort	1.9	V-Ribbed	②	②
	Tracer	1.8	V-Ribbed	110–132	110–132
	Tracer	1.9	V-Ribbed	②	②
	Probe	2.2	V-Ribbed	154–198	132–176
	Probe	3.0	V-Ribbed	①	①
	Tempo	2.3	V-Ribbed	①	①
	Topaz	2.3	V-Ribbed	①	①
	Taurus	2.5	V-Ribbed	①	①
	Taurus	3.0	V-Ribbed	①	①
	Taurus	3.0 SHO	V-Ribbed	220–265	148–192
	Taurus	3.8	V-Ribbed	①	①
	Sable	3.0	V-Ribbed	①	①
	Sable	3.8	V-Ribbed	①	①
	Continental	3.8	V-Ribbed	①	①

① Automatic tensioner
② Belt tension in Lbs.

SYSTEM DESCRIPTION

General Information

There are 2 different air conditioning systems used on Ford front wheel drive vehicles. The main difference between the systems is the component used to meter the flow of liquid refrigerant between the condenser and the evaporator. All Capri, Festiva and 1989–90 Tracer vehicles use a thermostatic expansion valve to meter the flow of refrigerant, while all other Ford front wheel drive vehicles use a fixed orifice tube.

Capri, Festiva and 1989–90 Tracer vehicles also feature a receiver/drier connected in line between the condenser and the expansion valve. All other Ford front wheel drive vehicles are equipped with a suction accumulator/drier connected between the evaporator and the compressor.

The remaining components of the air conditioning systems, the compressor, condenser and evaporator, are common to all Ford front wheel drive vehicles.

Service Valve Location

The air conditioning system has a high pressure (discharge) and a low pressure (suction) gauge port valve. These are Schrader valves which provide access to both the high and low pressure sides of the system for service hoses and a manifold gauge set so that system pressures can be read. The high pressure gauge port valve is located between the compressor and the condenser, in the high pressure vapor (discharge) line. The low pressure gauge port valve is located between the suction accumulator/drier and the compressor on fixed orifice tube systems and between the evaporator and the compressor on expansion valve systems, in the low pressure vapor (suction) line.

High side adapter set D81L–19703–A or tool YT-354, YT-355 or equivalent is required to connect a manifold gauge set or charging station to the high pressure gauge port valve. Service tee fitting D87P–19703–A, which may be mounted on the clutch cycling pressure switch fitting, is available for use in the low pressure side of fixed orifice tube systems, to be used in place of the low pressure gauge port valve.

System Discharging

WITHOUT RECOVERY SYSTEM

1. Connect a manifold gauge set as follows:
   a. Turn both manifold gauge set valves fully to the right, to close the high and low pressure hoses to the center manifold and hose.
   b. Remove the caps from the high and low pressure service gauge port valves.
   c. If the manifold gauge set hoses do not have valve depressing pins in them, install fitting adapters T71P–19703–S and R or equivalent, which have pins, on the low and high pressure hoses.
   d. Connect the high and low pressure hoses or adapters, to the respective high and low pressure service gauge port valves. High side adapter set D81L–19703–A or tool YT-354 or 355 or equivalent is required to connect a manifold gauge set or charging station to the high pressure gauge port valve.

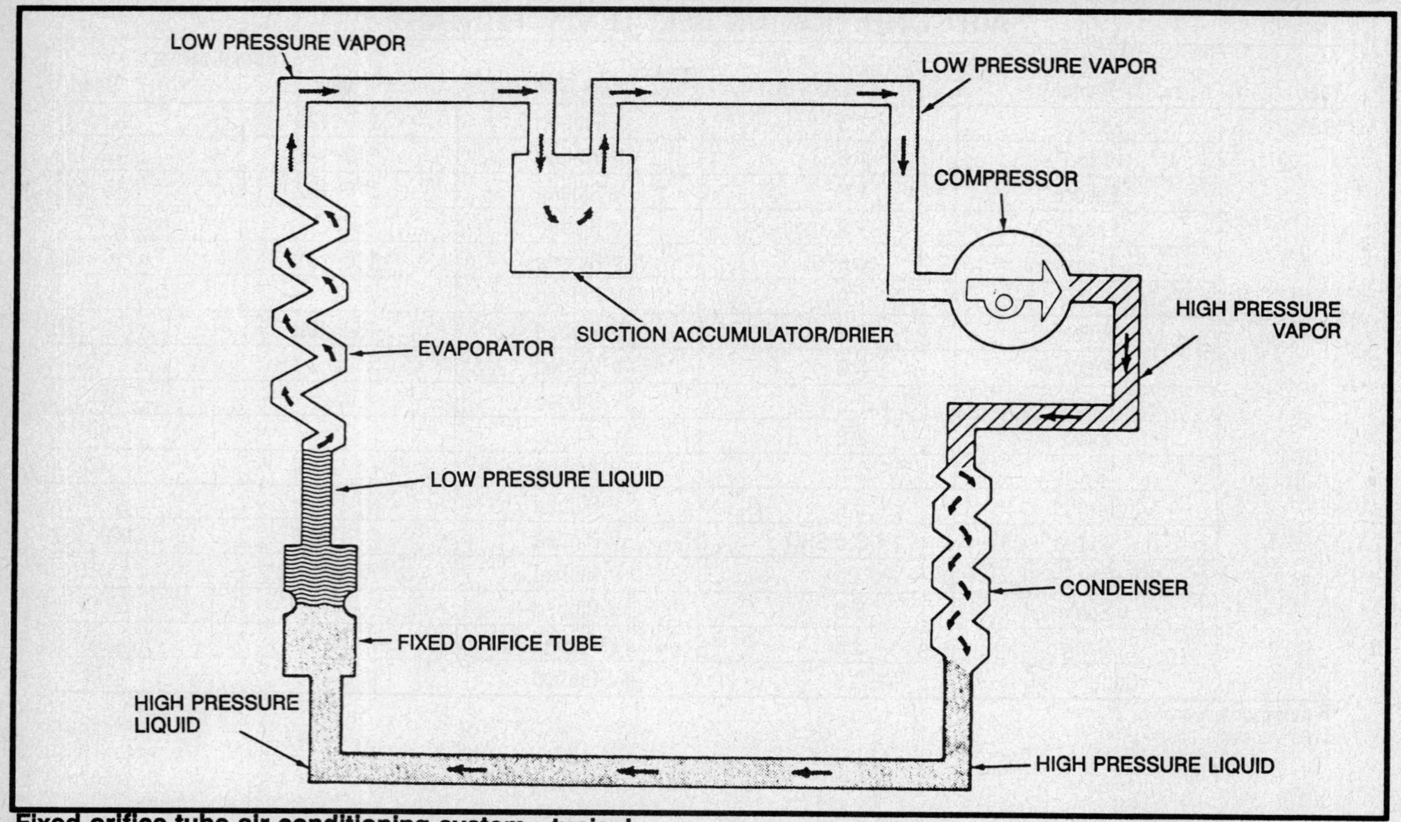
LOW PRESSURE VAPOR
LOW PRESSURE VAPOR
COMPRESSOR
HIGH PRESSURE VAPOR
SUCTION ACCUMULATOR/DRIER
EVAPORATOR
LOW PRESSURE LIQUID
CONDENSER
FIXED ORIFICE TUBE
HIGH PRESSURE LIQUID
HIGH PRESSURE LIQUID

Fixed orifice tube air conditioning system—typical

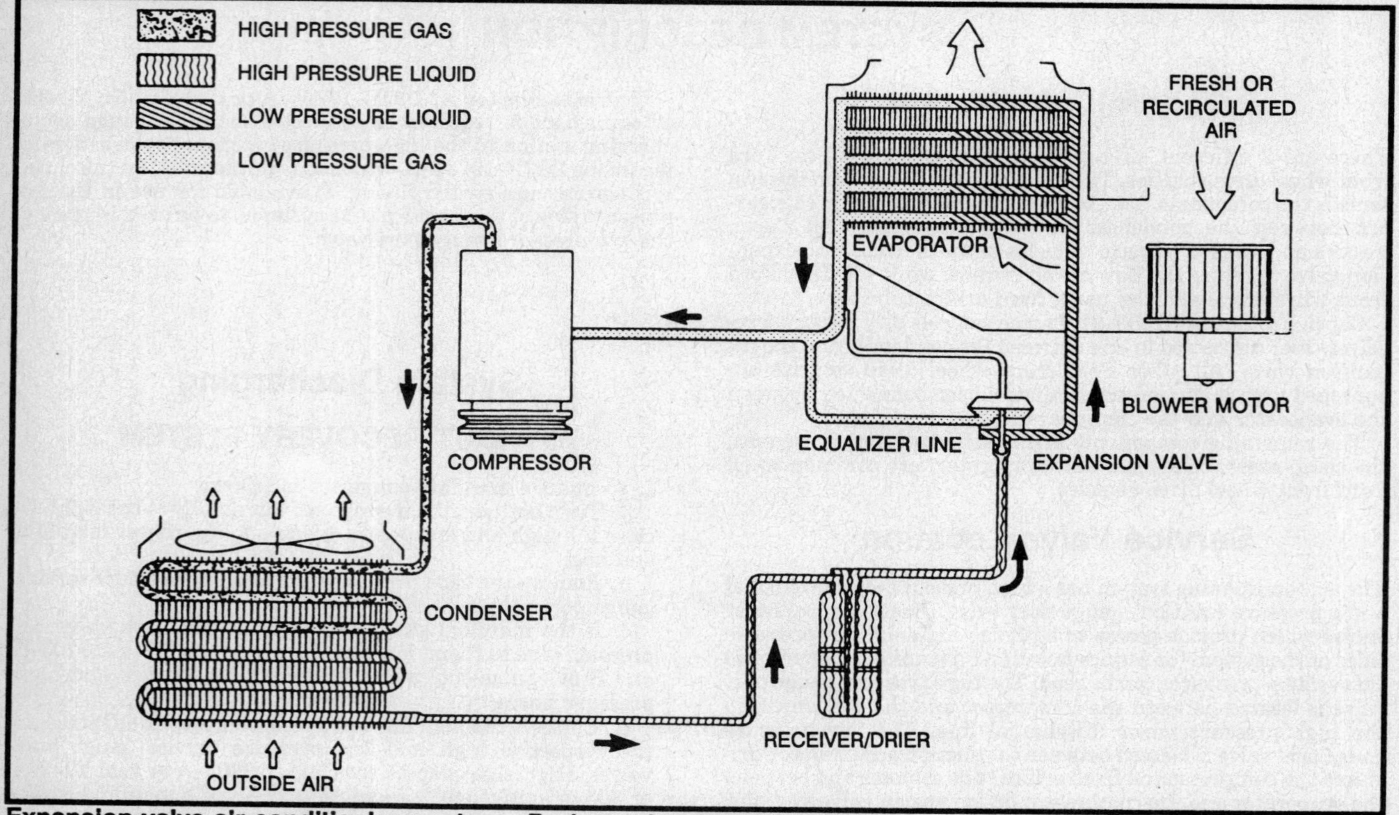
HIGH PRESSURE GAS
HIGH PRESSURE LIQUID
LOW PRESSURE LIQUID
LOW PRESSURE GAS
FRESH OR RECIRCULATED AIR
EVAPORATOR
COMPRESSOR
BLOWER MOTOR
EQUALIZER LINE
EXPANSION VALVE
CONDENSER
RECEIVER/DRIER
OUTSIDE AIR

Expansion valve air conditioning system—Probe and 1989–90 Tracer

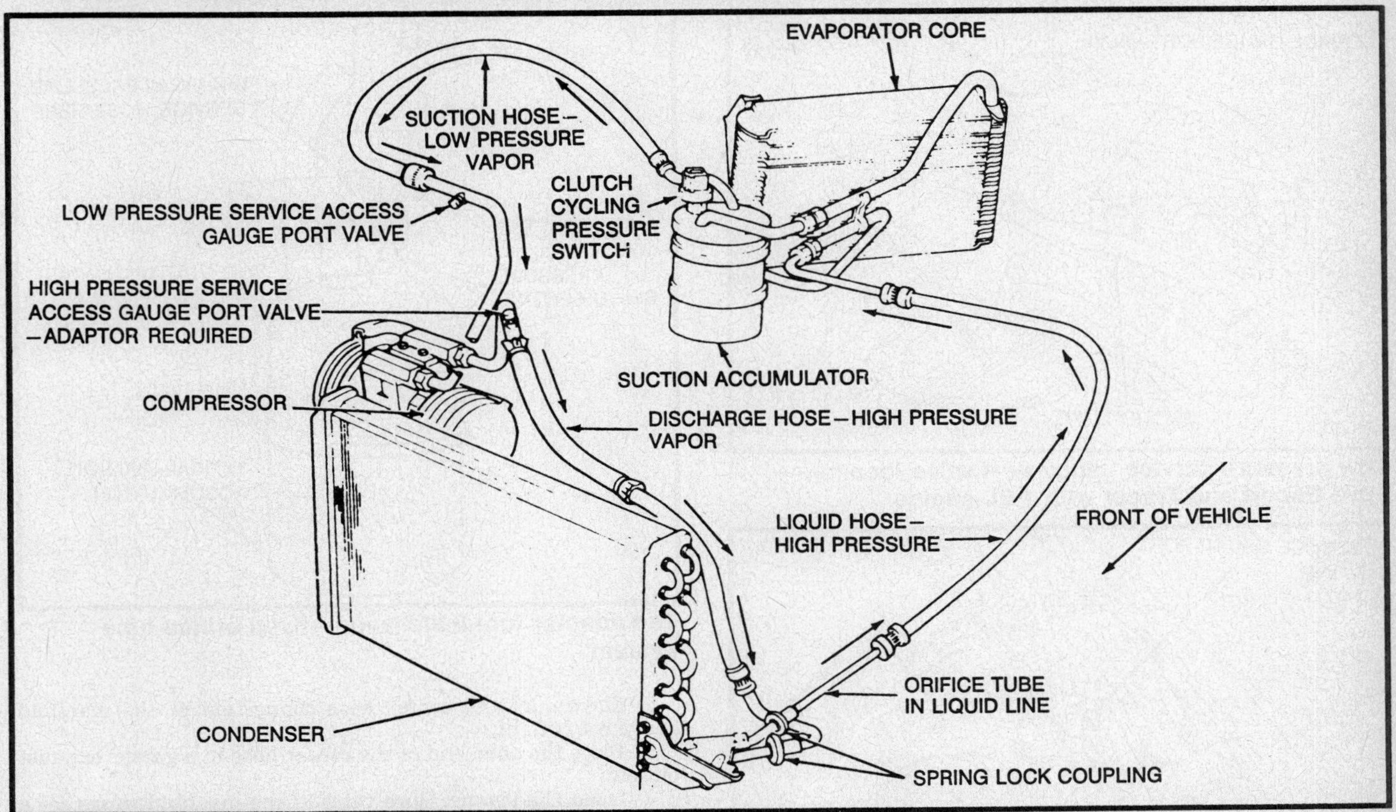
EVAPORATOR CORE
SUCTION HOSE—
LOW PRESSURE
VAPOR
CLUTCH
CYCLING
PRESSURE
SWITCH
LOW PRESSURE SERVICE ACCESS
GAUGE PORT VALVE
HIGH PRESSURE SERVICE
ACCESS GAUGE PORT VALVE
—ADAPTOR REQUIRED
SUCTION ACCUMULATOR
COMPRESSOR
DISCHARGE HOSE—HIGH PRESSURE
VAPOR
LIQUID HOSE—
HIGH PRESSURE
FRONT OF VEHICLE
ORIFICE TUBE
IN LIQUID LINE
CONDENSER
SPRING LOCK COUPLING

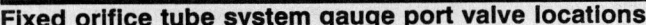

Fixed orifice tube system gauge port valve locations

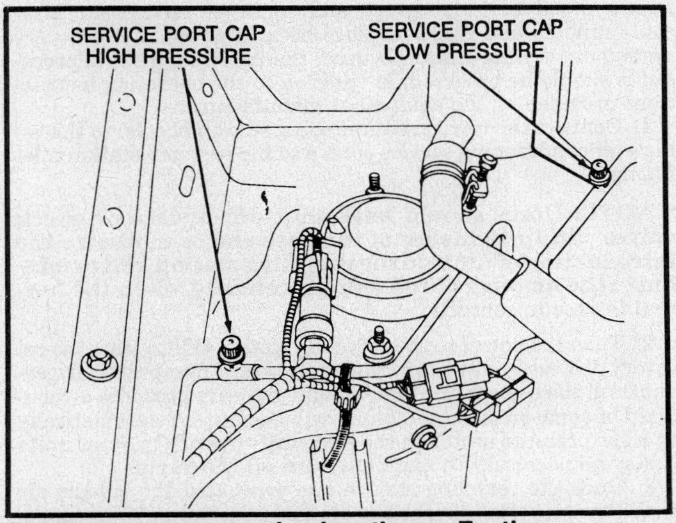
SERVICE PORT CAP
HIGH PRESSURE
SERVICE PORT CAP
LOW PRESSURE

Service gauge port valve locations—Festiva

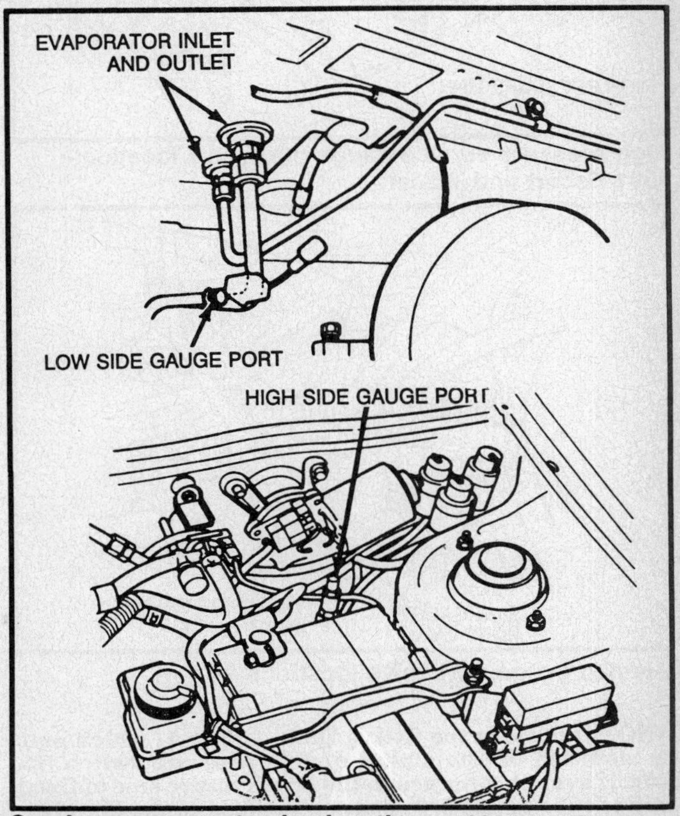
EVAPORATOR INLET
AND OUTLET
LOW SIDE GAUGE PORT
HIGH SIDE GAUGE PORT

Service gauge port valve locations—1989–90 Tracer

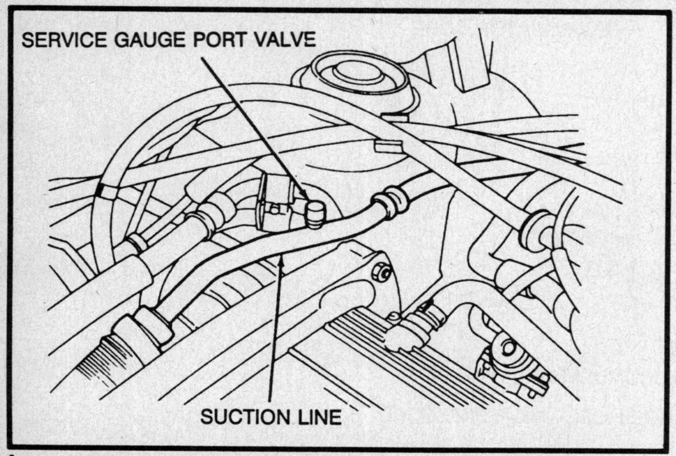
SERVICE GAUGE PORT VALVE
SUCTION LINE

Low pressure service gauge port valve location—1991 Escort and Tracer with 1.8L engine

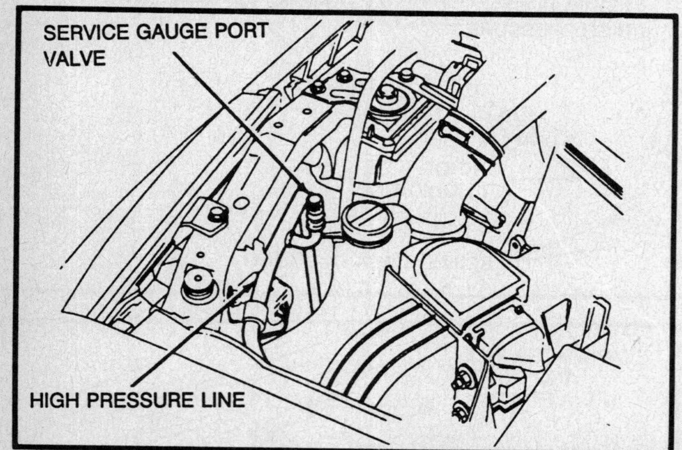
SERVICE GAUGE PORT VALVE
HIGH PRESSURE LINE

High pressure service gauge port valve location—1991 Escort and Tracer

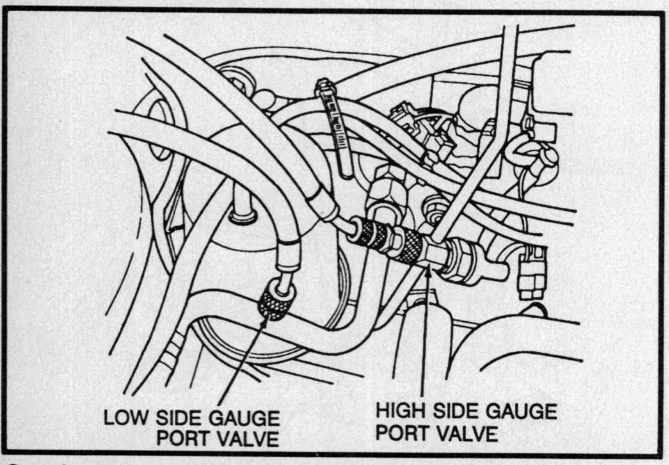
LOW SIDE GAUGE PORT VALVE
HIGH SIDE GAUGE PORT VALVE

Service gauge port valve locations—Capri

NOTE: Service tee fitting D87P–19703–A, which may be mounted on the clutch cycling pressure switch fitting, is available for use in the low pressure side of fixed orifice tube systems, to be used in place of the low pressure gauge port valve.

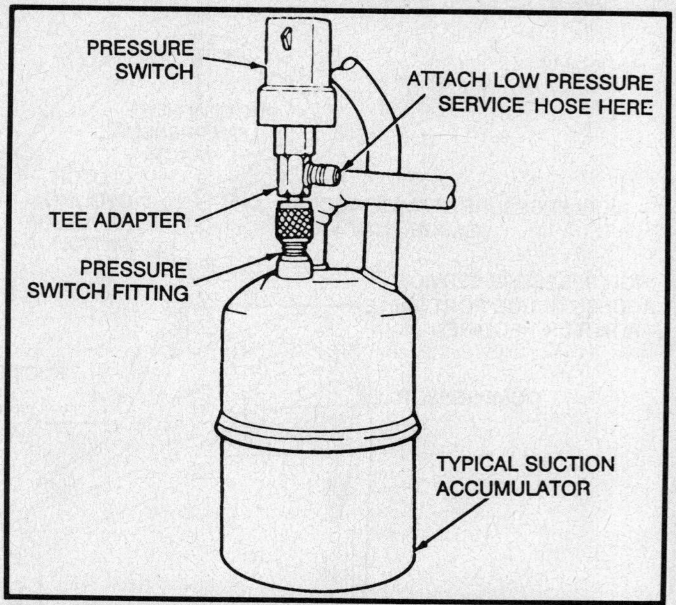
PRESSURE SWITCH
ATTACH LOW PRESSURE SERVICE HOSE HERE
TEE ADAPTER
PRESSURE SWITCH FITTING
TYPICAL SUCTION ACCUMULATOR

Tee adapter tool installation—fixed orifice tube system

2. Make sure the center hose connection at the manifold gauge set is tight.

3. Place the open end of the center hose in a garage exhaust outlet.

4. Open the low pressure valve of the manifold gauge set a slight amount and let the refrigerant slowly discharge from the system.

5. When the system is nearly discharged, open the high pressure gauge valve slowly, to avoid refrigerant oil loss. This will allow any refrigerant trapped in the compressor and high pressure discharge line to discharge.

6. As soon as the system is completely discharged, close both the high and low pressure valves to prevent moisture from entering the system.

WITH RECOVERY SYSTEM

The use of refrigerant recovery systems and recycling stations makes possible the recovery and reuse of refrigerant after contaminents and moisture have been removed. If a recovery system or recyling station is used, the following general procedures should be observed, in addition to the operating instructions provided by the equipment manufacturer.

1. Connect the refrigerant recycling station hose(s) to the vehicle air conditioning service ports and the recovery station inlet fitting.

NOTE: Hoses should have shut off devices or check valves within 12 inches of the hose end to minimize the introduction of air into the recycling station and to minimize the amount of refrigerant released when the hose(s) is disconnected.

2. Turn the power to the recycling station **ON** to start the recovery process. Allow the recycling station to pump the refrigerant from the system until the station pressure goes into a vacuum. On some stations the pump will be shut off automatically by a low pressure switch in the electrical system. On other units it may be necessary to manually turn off the pump.

3. Once the recycling station has evacuated the vehicle air conditioning system, close the station inlet valve, if equipped. Then switch **OFF** the electrical power.

4. Allow the vehicle air conditioning system to remain closed for about 2 minutes. Observe the system vacuum level as shown on the gauge. If the pressure does not rise, disconnect the recycling station hose(s).

5. If the system pressure rises, repeat Steps 2, 3 and 4 until the vacuum level remains stable for 2 minutes.

System Flushing

A refrigerant system can become badly contaminated for a number of reasons:

- The compressor may have failed due to damage or wear.
- The compressor may have been run for some time with a severe leak or an opening in the system.
- The system may have been damaged by a collision and left open for some time.
- The system may not have been cleaned properly after a previous failure.
- The system may have been operated for a time with water or moisture in it.

A badly contaminated system contains water, carbon and other decomposition products. When this condition exists, the system must be flushed with a special flushing agent using equipment designed specially for this purpose.

FLUSHING AGENTS

To be suitable as a flushing agent, a refrigerant must remain in liquid state during the flushing operation in order to wash the inside surfaces of the system components. Refrigerant vapor will not remove contaminent particles. They must be flushed with a liquid.

Some refrigerants are better suited to flushing than others. Neither Refrigerant-12 (R-12) nor Refrigerant-114 (R-114) is suitable for flushing a system because of low vaporization (boiling) points: −21.6°F (−29.8°C) for R-12 and 38.4°F (3.5°C) for R-114. Both these refrigerants would be difficult to use and would not do a sufficient job because of the tendency to vaporize rather than remain in a liquid state, especially in high ambient temperatures.

Refrigerant-11 (R-11) and Refrigerant-113 (R-113) are much better suited for use with special flushing equipment. Both have rather high vaporization points: 74.7°F (23.7°C) for R-11 and 117.6°F (47.5°C) for R-113. Both refrigerants also have low closed container pressures. This reduces the danger of an accidental system discharge due to a ruptured hose or fitting. R-113 will do the best job amd is recommended as a flushing refrigerant. Both R-11 and R-113 require a propellant or pump type flushing equipment due to their low closed container pressures. R-12 can be used as a propellant with either flushing refrigerant. R-11 is available in pressurized containers. Although not recommended for regular use, it may become necessary to use R-11 if special flushing equipment is not available. R-11 is more toxic than other refrigerants and should be handled with extra care.

SPECIAL FLUSHING EQUIPMENT

Special refrigerant system flushing equipment is available from a number of air conditioning equipment and usually comes in kit form. A flushing kit, such as model 015–00205, or equivalent, consists of a cylinder for the flushing agent, a nozzle to introduce the flushing agent into the system and a connecting hose.

A second type of equipment, which must be connected into the system, allows for the continuous circulation of the flushing agent through the system. Contaminents are trapped by an external filter/drier. If this equipment is used, follow the manufacturer's instructions and observe all safety precautions.

SYSTEM CLEANING AND FLUSHING

NOTE: Use extreme care and adhere to all safety precautions related to the use of refrigerants when flushing a system.

When it is necessary to flush a refrigerant system, the accumulator/drier or receiver/drier must be removed and replaced, because it is impossible to clean. On fixed orifice tube systems, remove the tube and replace it. If a new tube is not available, carefully wash the contaminated tube in flushing refrigerant or mineral spirits and blow it dry. If the tube does not show signs of damage or deterioration, it may be reused. Install new O-rings.

Any moisture in the evaporator core will be removed during leak testing and system evacuation following the cleaning job. Perorm the cleaning procedure carefully as follows:

1. Check the hose connections at the flushing cylinder outlet and flushing nozzle, to make sure they are secure.

2. Make sure the flushing cylinder is filled with approximately 1 pint of R-113 and the valve assembly on top of the cylinder is tightened securely.

3. Connect a can of R-12 to the Schrader valve at the top of the charging cylinder. A refrigerant hose and a special safety-type refrigerant dispensing valve, such as YT–280 refrigerant

REFRIGERANT FLUSHING INFORMATION CHART

Refrigerant	Vaporizes °C(°F) ①	APPROXIMATE CLOSED CONTAINER PRESSURE ① kPa (psi) ② 15.57°C (60°F)	21.13°C (70°F)	26.69°C (80°F)	32.25°C (90°F)	37.81°C (100°F)	Adaptability
R-12	−29.80(−21.6)	393 (57)	483 (70)	579 (84)	689 (100)	807 (117)	Self Propelling
F-114	3.56 (38.4)	55.16 (8)	89.63 (13)	131 (19)	172 (25)	221 (32)	
F-11 ③	23.74 (74.7)	27 (8 in Hg)	10 (3 in Hg)	7 (1)	34 (5)	62 (9)	
F-113	47.59 (117.6)	74 (22 in Hg)	64 (19 in Hg)	54 (16 in Hg)	44 (13 in Hg)	27 (8 in Hg)	Pump Required

① At sea level atmospheric pressure.
② kPa (psi) unless otherwise noted.
③ F-11 also available in pressurized containers. This makes it suitable for usage when special flushng equipment is not available. However, it is more toxic than R-12 and F-114.

dispensing valve or equivalent, and a valve retainer are required for connecting the small can to the cylinder. Make sure all connections are secure.

4. Connect a gauge manifold and discharge the system. Disconnect the gauge manifold.

5. Remove and discard the accumulator/drier or receiver/drier. Install a new accumulator/drier or receiver/drier and connect it to the evaporator. Do not connect it to the suction line from the compressor. Make sure the protective cap is in place on the suction line connection.

6. On fixed orifice tube systems, replace the tube. Install the protective cap on the evaporator inlet tube as soon as the new orifice tube is in place. The liquid line will be connected later.

7. Remove the compressor from the vehicle for cleaning and service or replacement, whichever is required. If the compressor is cleaned and serviced, add the specified amount of refrigerant oil prior to installing in the vehicle. Place protective caps on the compressor inlet and outlet connections and install it on the mounting brackets in the vehicle. If the compressor is replaced, adjust the oil level. Install the shipping caps on the compressor connections and install the new compressor on the mounting brackets in the vehicle.

8. Back-flush the condenser and liquid line as follows:

a. Remove the discharge hose from the condenser and clamp a piece of ½ in. I.D. heater hose to the condenser inlet line. Make sure the hose is long enough so the free end can be inserted into a suitable waste container to catch the flushing refrigerant.

b. Move the flushing equipment into position and open the valve on the can of R-12 (fully counterclockwise).

c. Back-flush the condenser and liquid line by introducing the flushing refrigerant into the supported end of the liquid line with the flushing nozzle. Hold the nozzle firmly against the open end of the liquid line.

d. After the liquid line and condenser have been flushed, lay the charging cylinder on it's side so that the R-12 will not force more flushing refrigerant into the liquid line. Press the nozzle firmly to the liquid line and admit R-12 to force all flushing refrigerant from the liquid line and condenser.

e. Remove the heater hose and clamp from the condenser inlet connection.

f. Stand the flushing cylinder upright and flush the compressor discharge hose. Secure it so the flushing refrigerant goes into the waste container.

g. Close the dispensing valve of the R-12 can (full clockwise). If there is any flushing refrigerant in the cylinder, it may be left there until the next flushing job. Put the flushing kit and R-12 can in a suitable storage location.

9. Connect all refrigerant lines. All connections should be cleaned and new O-rings should be used. Lubricate new O-rings with clean refrigerant oil.

10. Connect a charging station or manifold gauge set and charge the system with 1 lb. of R-12. Do not evacuate the system until after it has been leak tested.

11. Leak test all connections and components with flame-type leak detector 023–00006 or equivalent, or electronic leak detector 055–00014, 055–00015 or equivalent. If no leaks are found, proceed to Step 12. If leaks are found, service as necessary, check the system and then go to Step 12.

CAUTION

Fumes from flame-type leak detectors are noxious, avoid inhaling fumes or personal injury may result.

NOTE: Good ventilation is necessary in the area where air conditioning leak testing is to be done. If the surrounding air is contaminated with refrigerant gas, the leak detector will indicate this gas all the time. Odors from other chemicals such as anti-freeze, diesel fuel, disc brake cleaner or other cleaning solvents can cause the same problem. A fan, even in a well ventilated area, is very helpful in removing small traces of air contamination that might affect the leak detector.

12. Evacuate and charge the system with the specified amount of R-12. Operate the system to make sure it is cooling properly.

System Evacuating

1. Connect a manifold gauge set as follows:

a. Turn both manifold gauge set valves fully to the right, to close the high and low pressure hoses to the center manifold and hose.

b. Remove the caps from the high and low pressure service gauge port valves.

c. If the manifold gauge set hoses do not have valve depressing pins in them, install fitting adapters T71P–19703–S and R or equivalent, which have pins, on the low and high pressure hoses.

d. Connect the high and low pressure hoses, or adapters, to the respective high and low pressure service gauge port valves. High side adapter set D81L–19703–A or tool YT-354 or 355 or equivalent is required to connect a manifold gauge set or charging station to the high pressure gauge port valve.

NOTE: Service tee fitting D87P–19703–A, which may be mounted on the clutch cycling pressure switch fitting, is available for use in the low pressure side of fixed orifice tube systems, to be used in place of the low pressure gauge port valve.

2. Leak test all connections and components with flame-type leak detector 023–00006 or equivalent, or electronic leak detector 055–00014, 055–00015 or equivalent.

CAUTION

Fumes from flame-type leak detectors are noxious, avoid inhaling fumes or personal injury may result.

NOTE: Good ventilation is necessary in the area where air conditioning leak testing is to be done. If the surrounding air is contaminated with refrigerant gas, the leak detector will indicate this gas all the time. Odors from other chemicals such as anti-freeze, diesel fuel, disc brake cleaner or other cleaning solvents can cause the same problem. A fan, even in a well ventilated area, is very helpful in removing small traces of air contamination that might affect the leak detector.

3. Properly discharge the refrigerant system.

4. Make sure both manifold gauge valves are turned fully to the right. Make sure the center hose connection at the manifold gauge is tight.

5. Connect the manifold gauge set center hose to a vacuum pump.

6. Open the manifold gauge set valves and start the vacuum pump.

7. Evacuate the system with the vacuum pump until the low pressure gauge reads at least 25 in. Hg or as close to 30 in. Hg as possible. Continue to operate the vacuum pump for 15 minutes. If a part of the system has been replaced, continue to operate the vacuum pump for another 20–30 minutes.

8. When evacuation of the system is complete, close the manifold gauge set valves and turn the vacuum pump **OFF**.

9. Observe the low pressure gauge for 5 minutes to ensure that system vacuum is held. If vacuum is held, charge the system. If vacuum is not held for 5 minutes, leak test the system, service the leaks and evacuate the system again.

System Charging

1. Connect a manifold gauge set according to the proper procedure. Properly discharge and evacuate the system.
2. With the manifold gauge set valves closed to the center hose, disconnect the vacuum pump from the manifold gauge set.
3. Connect the center hose of the manifold gauge set to a refrigerant drum or a small can refrigerant dispensing valve tool YT-280, YT-1034 or equivalent. If a small can dispensing valve is used, install the small can(s) on the dispensing valve.

NOTE: Use only a safety type dispensing valve.

4. Loosen the center hose at the manifold gauge set and open the refrigerant drum valve or small can dispensing valve. Allow the refrigerant to escape to purge air and moisture from the center hose. Then, tighten the center hose connection at the manifold gauge set.
5. Disconnect the wire harness snap lock connector from the clutch cycling or low pressure switch and install a jumper wire across the 2 terminals of the connector.
6. Open the manifold gauge set low side valve to allow refrigerant to enter the system. Keep the refrigerant can in an upright position.

CAUTION

Do not open the manifold gauge set high pressure (discharge) gauge valve when charging with a small container. Opening the valve can cause the small refrigerant container to explode, which can result in personal injury.

7. When no more refrigerant is being drawn into the system, start the engine and set the control assembly for MAX cold and HI blower to draw the remaining refrigerant intyo the system. If equipped, press the air conditioning switch. Continue to add refrigerant to the system until the specified weight of R-12 is in the system. Then close the manifold gauge set low pressure valve and the refrigerant supply valve.
8. Remove the jumper wire from the clutch cycling or low pressure switch snap lock connector. Connect the connector to the pressure switch.
9. Operate the system until pressures stabilize to verify normal operation and system pressures.
10. In high ambient temperatures, it may be necessary to operate a high volume fan positioned to blow air through the radiator and condenser to aid in cooling the engine and prevent excessive refrigerant system pressures.
11. When charging is completed and system operating pressures are normal, disconnect the manifold gauge set from the vehicle. Install the protective caps on the service gauge port valves.

SYSTEM COMPONENTS

Radiator

REMOVAL AND INSTALLATION

Taurus, Sable and Continental

1. Disconnect the negative battery cable.
2. Drain the cooling system by removing the radiator cap and opening the draincock located at the lower rear corner of the radiator inlet tank.
3. Remove the rubber overflow tube from the coolant recovery bottle and detach it from the radiator. On Taurus SHO, disconnect the tube from the radiator and remove the recovery bottle.
4. Remove 2 upper shroud retaining screws and lift the shroud from the lower retaining clips.
5. Disconnect the electric cooling fan motor wires and remove the fan and shroud assembly.
6. Loosen the upper and lower hose clamps at the radiator and remove the hoses from the radiator connectors.
7. If equipped with an automatic transaxle, disconnect the transmission oil cooling lines from the radiator fittings using disconnect tool T82L-9500-AH or equivalent.
8. If equipped with 3.0L and SHO engines, remove 2 radiator upper retaining screws. If equipped with the 3.8L engine, remove 2 hex nuts from the right radiator support bracket and 2 screws from the left radiator support bracket and remove the brackets.
9. Tilt the radiator rearward approximately 1 in. and lift it directly upward, clear of the radiator support.
10. Remove the radiator lower support rubber pads, if pad replacement is necessary.

To install:

11. Position the radiator lower support rubber pads to the lower support, if previously removed.
12. Position the radiator into the engine compartment and to the radiator support. Insert the moulded pins at the bottom of each tank through the slotted holes in the lower support rubber pads.
13. Make sure the plastic pads on the bottom of the radiator tanks are resting on the rubber pads. Install 2 upper retaining bolts to attach the radiator to the radiator support. Tighten the bolts to 46–60 inch lbs. (5–7 Nm). If equipped with the 3.8L engine, tighten the bolts to 13–20 ft. lbs. (17–27 Nm).
14. If equipped with the 3.8L engine, fasten the left radiator support bracket to the radiator support with 2 screws. Tighten the screws to 8.7–17.7 ft. lbs. (11.8–24 Nm). Attach the right support bracket to the radiator support with 2 hex nuts. Tighten the nuts to 8.7–17.7 ft. lbs. (11.8–24 Nm).
15. Attach the radiator upper and lower hoses to the radiator. Position the hose on the radiator connector so the index arrow on the hose is in line with the mark on the connector. Tighten the clamps to 20–30 inch lbs. (2.3–3.4 Nm) if equipped with the 2.5L engine. If equipped with the 3.8L engine, install constant tension hose clamps between the alignment marks on the hoses.
16. If equipped with automatic transaxles, connect the transmission cooler lines using oil resistant pipe sealer.
17. Install the fan and shroud assembly by connecting the fan motor wiring and positioning the assembly on the lower retainer clips. Attach the top of the shroud to the radiator with 2 screw, nut and washer assemblies. Tighten to 35 inch lbs. (4 Nm).
18. Attach the rubber overflow tube to the radiator filler neck overflow nipple and coolant recovery bottle. On Taurus SHO, install the coolant recovery bottle and connect the overflow hose.
19. Refill the cooling system. If the coolant is being replaced, refill with a 50/50 mixture of water and anti-freeze. Connect the negative battery cable. Operate the engine for 15 minutes and check for leaks. Check the coolant level and add, as required.

Tempo, Topaz and 1989–90 Escort

1. Remove the negative battery cable.
2. Drain coolant from cooling system. Retain coolant in a suitable container for reuse.

3. On the Escort, remove air intake tube from radiator support.
4. Remove upper hose from radiator.
5. Remove 2 fasteners retaining upper end of fan shroud to radiator, and sight shield.

NOTE: If equipped with air conditioning, remove nut and screw retaining upper end of fan shroud to radiator at cross support, and nut and screw at inlet end of tank.

6. Disconnect electric cooling fan motor wires and air conditioning discharge line, if equipped, from shroud and remove fan shroud from vehicle.
7. Loosen hose clamp and disconnect radiator lower hose from radiator.
8. Disconnect overflow hose from radiator filler neck.
9. If equipped with an automatic transaxle, disconnect oil cooler hoses at transaxle using a quick-disconnect tool. Cap oil tubes and plug oil cooler hoses.
10. Remove 2 nuts retaining top of radiator to radiator support. If stud loosens, ensure it is tightened before radiator is installed. Tilt the top of radiator rearward to allow clearance with upper mounting stud and lift radiator from vehicle. Ensure mounts do not stick to radiator lower mounting brackets.

To install:

11. Ensure that lower radiator isomounts are installed over bolts on the radiator support.
12. Position radiator to radiator support making sure radiator lower brackets are positioned properly on lower mounts.
13. Position top of radiator to mounting studs on radiator support and install 2 retaining nuts. Tighten to 5–7 ft. lbs. (7–9.5 Nm).
14. Connect radiator lower hose to engine water pump inlet tube. Install constant tension hose clamp between alignment marks on the hose.
15. Check to ensure radiator lower hose is properly positioned on outlet tank and install constant tension hose clamp. The stripe on lower hose should be indexed with rib on tank outlet.
16. Connect oil cooler hoses to automatic transaxle oil cooler lines, if equipped. Use an appropriate oil resistant sealer.
17. Position fan shroud to radiator lower mounting bosses. If with air conditioning, insert lower edge of shroud into clip at lower center of radiator. Install 2 nuts and bolts retaining upper end of fan shroud to radiator. Tighten nuts on Tempo/Topaz to 35–41 inch lbs. (3.9–4.6 Nm). On Escort, tighten nut to 23–33 inch lbs. (2.6–3.7 Nm). Do not overtighten.
18. Connect electric cooling fan motor wires to wire harness.
19. Connect upper hose to radiator inlet tank fitting and install constant tension hose clamp.
20. Connect overflow hose to nipple just below radiator filler neck.
21. Install air intake tube or sight shield.
22. Connect negative battery cable.
23. Refill cooling system. Start engine and allow to come to normal operating temperature. Check for leaks. Confirm operation of electric cooling fan.

1991 Escort and Tracer

1. Disconnect the negative battery cable.
2. Raise and safely support the vehicle. Drain the cooling system.
3. Remove the right side and front splash shields and remove the lower radiator hose.
4. If equipped with automatic transaxle, remove the lower oil cooler line from the radiator. Remove the oil cooler line brackets from the bottom of the radiator.
5. Lower the vehicle.
6. If equipped with automatic transaxle and air conditioning, remove the seal located between the radiator and fan shroud.
7. If equipped with automatic transaxle, remove the upper oil cooler line from the radiator.
8. If equipped with 1.8L engine, remove the resonance duct from the radiator isomounts.
9. Disconnect the cooling fan motor electrical connector and the cooling fan thermoswitch electrical connector.
10. Remove the 3 fan shroud attaching bolts and remove the shroud assembly by pulling it straight up.
11. Remove the upper radiator hose and the 2 upper radiator isomounts. Remove the radiator by lifting it straight up.

To install:

12. Make sure the radiator lower isomounts are installed over the bolts on the radiator support.
13. Position the radiator to the radiator support, making sure the radiator lower brackets are positioned properly on the lower isomounts.
14. Install the radiator upper isomounts, making sure the radiator locating pegs are positioned correctly. Install the upper radiator hose.
15. Lower the cooling fan shroud assembly into place and install the 3 shroud attaching bolts.
16. Connect the cooling fan motor electrical connector and thermoswitch electrical connector.
17. If equipped with 1.8L engine, install the resonance duct on the radiator isomounts.
18. Install the upper oil cooler line on the radiator.
19. If equipped with automatic transaxle and air conditioning, install the seal between the radiator and fan shroud.
20. Raise and safely support the vehicle. Install the lower oil cooler line on the radiator.
21. Install the lower radiator hose and install the right side and front splash shields.
22. Lower the vehicle and fill the cooling system.
23. Connect the negative battery cable, start the engine and check for coolant leaks.

Probe

1. Disconnect the negative battery cable and the cooling fan wiring harness connectors.
2. Remove the radiator pressure cap from the filler neck.

NOTE. If the system is hot and pressurized, be careful to release the pressure before removing the cap fully.

3. Disconnect the overflow tube from the filler neck.
4. Drain the cooling system. The drain valve is located at the bottom of the radiator on the right side.
5. Disconnect the upper and lower radiator hoses.
6. Disconnect and plug the cooler lines, if equipped with an automatic transaxle.
7. Disconnect the coolant temperature sensor wires on the 2.2L engine.
8. Remove the radiator mounting bolts.
9. Remove the radiator and the cooling fan as a complete assembly.
10. Remove the fan shroud mounting bolts.
11. Remove the fan and shroud assembly from the radiator.

To install:

12. Install the fan and shroud assembly. Tighten the mounting bolts to 61–87 inch lbs. (7–10 Nm).
13. Install the radiator, making sure the lower tank engages the insulators.
14. Install the upper radiator insulators and tighten the retaining bolts to 69–95 inch lbs. (8–11 Nm).
15. Unplug and connect the cooler lines, if required.
16. Reattach the wiring harness and install the upper and lower radiator hoses to the radiator.
17. Connect the overflow tube to the radiator and connect the cooling fan wiring connectors.
18. Close the radiator drain valve and fill the system with coolant.
19. Warm the engine to pressurize the system and check for leaks.

20. Recheck the coolant level and refill if neccessary.

Capri

1. Disconnect the negative battery cable and the cooling fan wire harness connector.
2. Remove the radiator pressure cap from the filler neck. If the system is hot and pressurized, be careful to release the pressure before fully opening. Drain the cooling system at the draincock, located at the bottom left end of the radiator.
3. Disconnect the radiator upper and lower hoses from the radiator inlet and outlet.
4. Disconnect the overflow tube from the filler neck and disengage the wiring harness from the routing clips attached to the cooling fan shroud.
5. If equipped with automatic transaxle, disconnect and plug the cooler lines.
6. Remove the 6 bolts retaining the radiator upper tank brackets to the radiator core support. Remove the radiator and cooling fan as an assembly.
7. Remove the 4 bolts attaching the fan shroud assembly and remove the fan and shroud assembly.

To install:

8. Place the fan and shroud assembly against the rear of the radiator and secure with the 4 bolts. Tighten the bolts to 23–33 ft. lbs. 31–46 Nm.
9. Make sure the radiator insulators are positioned on the radiator supports. Position the radiator, making sure the lower tank engages the insulators.
10. Install the 6 radiator retaining bolts through the top tank mounting brackets into the core support. Make sure the insulators are aligned.
11. Unplug and connect the automatic transaxle oil cooler lines, if equipped.
12. Secure the wire harness in the routing clips.
13. Connect the upper and lower hoses to the radiator inlet and outlet. Connect the overflow tube to the radiator filler neck.
14. Close the radiator draincock and fill the cooling system. Install the pressure cap.
15. Connect the cooling fan harness connector and the negative battery cable. Start the engine and check for leaks.
16. Check the coolant level and fill as necessary.

Festiva

1. Disconnect the negative battery cable.
2. Disconnect the coolant recovery hose from the filler neck.
3. Loosen the retaining clamp and disconnect the upper radiator hose from the radiator.
4. Disconnect the cooling fan wiring harness connector. Disengage the wiring harness from the routing clamp on the cooling fan shroud.
5. Remove the radiator cap from the filler neck. Raise the vehicle and support safely.
6. Position a fluid catch pan under the radiator. Open the drain valve and drain the cooling system.
7. Disconnect the radiator temperature switch wires.
8. Loosen the retaining clamp and disconnect the lower radiator hose.
9. Lower the vehicle.
10. Support the radiator by hand and remove the 4 bolts attaching the radiator support brackets to the vehicle body. Raise the radiator/cooling fan/shroud assembly from the crossmember mounting insulator supports and remove from vehicle. Disconnect the cooling fan and shroud from the radiator as required.

To install:

11. Lower the radiator into the normal operating position making certain the mounting insualators engage with their supports. Attach the radiator to the support brackets with the 4 bolts.
12. Connect the upper radiator hose. Raise the vehicle and connect the lower radiator hose and temperature switch wires.
13. Close the drain valve and lower the vehicle. Connect the negative battery cable. Fill the cooling system to the proper level.
14. Start the engine and allow to reach normal operating temperature. Inspect for coolant leaks and correct as required.

1989–90 Tracer

1. Disconnect the negative battery cable.
2. Disconnect the coolant recovery hose from the filler neck.
3. Loosen the retaining clamp and disconnect the upper radiator hose from the radiator.
4. Disconnect the cooling fan wiring harness connector. Disengage the wiring harness from the routing clamp on the cooling fan shroud.
5. Remove the radiator cap from the filler neck. Raise the vehicle and support safely.
6. Position a fluid catch pan under the radiator. Open the drain valve and drain the cooling system.
7. Disconnect the radiator temperature switch wires.
8. Loosen the retaining clamp and disconnect the lower radiator hose.
9. Lower the vehicle.
10. Support the radiator by hand and remove the 4 bolts attaching the radiator support brackets to the vehicle body. Raise the radiator/cooling fan/shroud assembly from the crossmember mounting insulator supports and remove from vehicle. Disconnect the cooling fan and shroud from the radiator as required.

To install:

11. Lower the radiator into the normal operating position making certain the mounting insulators engage with their supports. Attach the radiator to the support brackets with the 4 bolts.
12. Connect the upper radiator hose. Raise the vehicle and connect the lower radiator hose and temperature switch wires.
13. Close the drain valve and lower the vehicle. Connect the negative battery cable. Fill the cooling system to the proper level.
14. Start the engine and allow to reach normal operating temperature. Inspect for coolant leaks and correct as required.

COOLING SYSTEM BLEEDING

When the entire cooling system is drained, the following procedure should be used to ensure a complete fill.

1. Install the block drain plug, if removed and close the draincock. With the engine off, add anti-freeze to the radiator to a level of 50% of the total cooling system capacity. Then add water until it reaches the radiator filler neck seat.

NOTE: On Taurus and Sable with the 2.5L engine, remove the vent plug on the water connection outlet. The vent plug must be removed before the radiator is filled or the engine may not fill completely. Do not turn the plastic cap under the vent plug or the gasket may be damaged. Do not try to add coolant through the vent plug hole. Install the vent plug after filling the radiator and before starting the engine.

2. Install the radiator cap to the first notch to keep spillage to a minimum.
3. Start the engine and let it idle until the upper radiator hose is warm. This indicates that the thermostat is open and coolant is flowing through the entire system.
4. Carefully remove the radiator cap and top off the radiator with water. Install the cap on the radiator securely.
5. Fill the coolant recovery reservoir to the FULL COLD mark with anti-freeze, then add water to the FULL HOT mark.

This will ensure that a proper mixture is in the coolant recovery bottle.

6. Check for leaks at the draincock, block plug and at the vent plug on 2.5L engines.

Cooling Fan

TESTING

Taurus, Sable and Continental

1. Disconnect the wiring connector from the fan motor.
2. Connect a jumper wire from the positive terminal of the battery to one of the terminals in the cooling fan electrical connector.
3. Ground the other connector terminal.
4. If the cooling fan does not function, it must be replaced.
5. If the cooling fan functions but does not run during normal engine operation, check the cooling fan temperature sensor and the integrated relay control assembly.

Tempo, Topaz and 1989–90 Escort

1. Check fuse or circuit breaker for power to cooling fan motor.
2. Remove connector(s) at cooling fan motor(s). Connect jumper wire and apply battery voltage to the positive terminal of the cooling fan motor.
3. Using an ohmmeter, check for continuity in cooling fan motor.

NOTE: Remove the cooling fan connector at the fan motor before performing continuity checks. Perform continuity check of the motor windings only. The cooling fan control circuit is connected electrically to the ECM through the cooling fan relay center. Ohmmeter battery voltage must not be applied to the ECM.

4. Ensure proper continuity of cooling fan motor ground circuit at chassis ground connector.

1991 Escort and Tracer

1. Make sure the ignition key is **OFF**.
2. Apply 12 volts to the **Y** wire at the cooling fan motor on all except 1.8L vehicles equipped with 4EAT automatic transaxle or 1.9L vehicles equipped with air conditioning. Replace the motor if it does not run.
3. On 1.8L vehicles equipped with 4EAT automatic transaxle or 1.9L vehicles equipped with air conditioning, apply 12 volts to the **BL** wire (1.8L) or the **LG/Y** wire (1.9L) at the cooling fan motor. Replace the motor if it does not run.

Probe

With the key **ON** and the engine warmed, disconnect the coolant temperature switch and ground the connector BK/GRN terminal. The fan should operate, if not, check the motor.

Capri

1. Make sure the ignition switch is **OFF**.
2. Locate the cooling fan motor connector and ground the **Y/GN** wire at the connector.
3. If the cooling fan motor does not turn on, replace it.

Festiva

RADIATOR FAN SWITCH

The cooling fan temperature switch is threaded into the front side of the thermostat housing. The themoswitch continuity test should be conducted when the coolant temperature is above and below the normal cut-in point of the switch (207°F).

CAUTION

To avoid the possibly of personal injury or damage to the vehicle, make certain that the ignition switch is in the OFF position before disconnecting the wire from the cooling fan temperature switch. If the wire is disconnected from the switch with the ignition switch in the ON position, the cooling fan may turn on. The maximum amount of time the engine is allowed to operate with the thermo switch disconnected is 2 minutes.

1. Turn the ignition switch to the **OFF** position. With the engine coolant below 207°F, disconnect the thermo switch connector.
2. Using a test meter, check for continuity across the green wire terminal of the switch and ground. At this temperature, continuity should be read across the switch.
3. Connect the thermo switch connector. Start the engine and allow the coolant to reach normal operating temperature (above 207°F).
4. Disconnnect the thermo switch connector and check for continuity across the switch as described in Step 2. At this temperature, there should be no continuity across the switch.
5. Secure the engine and connect the thermo switch connector. Replace the thermo switch as required.

COOLING FAN RELAY

The cooling fan relay is located in the left front corner of the engine compartment between the battery and the headlight. The relay is surrounded by a protective boot and is secured to the inner fender panel.

1. Turn the ignition switch to the **OFF** position.
2. Using a test meter, check for continuity across the green/yellow and black/red wire terminals. If continuity is not present, replace the cooling fan relay.

1989–90 Tracer

1. Disconnect the negative battery cable. Disconnect the fan electrical connector.
2. Using a 12 volt DC power supply, connect it to the electrical connector (fan side); the fan should operate.
3. If the fan does not operate, inspect the temperature coolant switch and/or the fan relay.

REMOVAL AND INSTALLATION

Taurus, Sable and Continental

1. Disconnect negative battery cable.
2. Disconnect the wiring connector from the fan motor. Remove the integrated relay control assembly from the radiator support.
3. Remove the nuts retaining the fan motor and shroud assembly and remove the component. Rotate the fan and shroud assembly and remove upwards past the radiator.
4. Remove the retaining clip from the motor shaft and remove the fan.

NOTE: A metal burr may be present on the motor shaft after the retaining clip has been removed. If necessary, remove the burr to facilitate fan removal.

5. Unbolt and withdraw the fan motor from the shroud.
6. Install in the reverse order of removal.

Tempo, Topaz and 1989–90 Escort

1. Disconnect negative battery cable.
2. Disconnect the wiring connector from the fan motor. Disconnect the wire loom from the clip on the shroud by pushing down on the lock fingers and pulling the connector from the motor end.
3. Remove the nuts retaining the fan motor and shroud assembly and remove the component.

4. Remove the retaining clip from the motor shaft and remove the fan.

NOTE: A metal burr may be present on the motor shaft after the retaining clip has been removed. If necessary, remove burr to facilitate fan removal.

5. Unbolt and withdraw the fan motor from the shroud.

To install:

6. Install the fan motor in position in the fan shroud. Install the retaining nuts and washers and tighten to 44–66 inch lbs.
7. Position the fan assembly on the motor shaft and install the retaining clip.
8. Position the fan, motor and shroud as an assembly in the vehicle. Install the retaining nuts and tighten to 35–45 inch lbs. on Escort and Lynx; 23–33 inch lbs. on Tempo and Topaz.
9. Install the fan motor wire loom in the clip provided on the fan shroud. Connect the wiring connector to the fan motor. Be sure the lock fingers on the connector snap firmly into place.
10. Reconnect battery cable.
11. Check the fan for proper operation.

1991 Escort and Tracer

1. Disconnect the negative battery cable.
2. On 1.8L engine equipped vehicles, remove the resonance duct from the radiator isomounts.
3. Disconnect the cooling fan motor electrical connector.
4. Remove the 3 shroud attaching bolts and remove the cooling fan shroud assembly by pulling it straight up.
5. Working on a bench, remove the cooling fan retainer clip. Remove the cooling fan from the motor shaft.
6. Unclip the cooling fan motor electrical harness retainers and remove the harness from the retainers.
7. Remove the cooling fan motor attaching screws and remove the cooling fan motor from the shroud assembly.

To install:

8. Position the cooling fan motor on the shroud assembly and install the attaching screws.
9. Position the cooling fan motor electrical harness in the harness retainers and clip the retainers shut.
10. Install the cooling fan on the cooling motor shaft and install the retainer clip.
11. Carefully lower the cooling fan shroud assembly into place and install the attaching bolts. Connect the cooling fan motor electrical connector.
12. If equipped with 1.8L engine, install the resonance duct on the radiator isomounts.
13. Connect the negative battery cable.

Probe

1. Disconnect the negative battery cable.
2. Disconnect the cooling fan electrical connectors.
3. Remove the fan shroud-to-radiator screws and the fan/shroud assembly.
4. If removing the fan motor from the shroud, perform the following:
   a. Remove the fan blade-to-motor nut and washer.
   b. Remove the fan motor-to-shroud bolts and the motor.
5. To install, reverse the removal procedures.

Capri

1. Disconnect the negative battery cable.
2. Disengage the fan wiring harness from the routing clamps and separate the cooling fan wiring connector.
3. Remove the 4 screws retaining the fan shroud to the radiator and remove the fan and shroud.
4. Remove the retaining nut and washer and remove the fan from the motor shaft.
5. Remove the 3 retaining screws and washers and separate the fan motor from the shroud.

To install:

6. Position the cooling fan on the shroud and install the 3 retaining screws and washers. Tighten to 3–4 ft. lbs. (4–6 Nm).
7. Install the fan on the motor shaft and install the retaining washer and nut.
8. Position the fan and shroud and install the 4 retaining screws. Tighten to 23–34 ft. lbs. (31–46 Nm).
9. Connect the cooling fan wiring. Position the wiring and secure in place using the routing clamps.
10. Connect the negative battery cable.

Festiva

1. Disconnect the negative battery cable.
2. Loosen the retaining clamp and disconnect the upper radiator hose at the radiator.
3. Disconnect the cooling fan wiring harness connector and disengage the wiring harness from the routing clamp on the cooling fan shroud.
4. Remove the bolts attaching the top of the fan shroud to the radiator.
5. Support the fan shroud assembly and remove the bolts attaching the bottom of the fan shroud to the radiator. Remove the fan shroud assembly from the vehicle.
6. Complete the assembly by reversing the removal procedure.
7. Reconnect the negative battery cable and fill the cooling system to the proper level.
8. Start the engine and allow it to reach normal operating temperature. Check for cooling leaks.

1989–90 Tracer

1. Disconnect the negative battery cable.
2. Disconnect the fan electrical wiring harnesses from the clamps.
3. Disconnect the electrical connector from the cooling fan.
4. Remove the fan shroud-to-radiator screws and the shroud/fan assembly from the vehicle.
5. Remove the fan from the shroud.
6. To install, reverse the removal procedures. Start the engine, allow it to reach normal operating temperature and the system operation.

Condenser

REMOVAL AND INSTALLATION

Taurus, Sable and Continental

NOTE: Whenever a condenser is replaced, it will be necessary to replace the suction accumulator/drier.

1. Disconnect the negative battery cable and properly discharge the refrigerant from the air conditioning system. Observe all safety precautions.
2. Disconnect the 2 refrigerant lines at the fittings on the right side of the radiator. Perform the spring-lock coupling disconnect procedure.
3. Remove the 4 bolts attaching the condenser to the radiator support and remove the condenser from the vehicle.

To install:

4. Add 1 oz. (30 ml) of clean refrigerant oil to a new replacement condenser.
5. Position the condenser assembly to the radiator support brackets and install the attaching bolts.
6. Connect the refrigerant lines to the condenser assembly. Perform the spring-lock coupling connection procedure.
7. Leak test, evacuate and charge the refrigerant system following the proper procedures. Observe all safety precautions.

SPRING-LOCK COUPLING PROCEDURE

TO CONNECT COUPLING

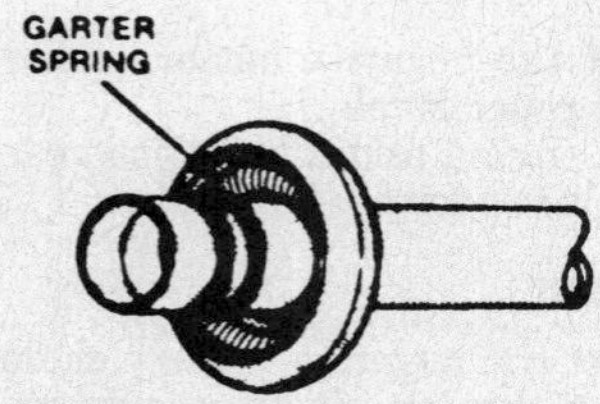
GARTER SPRING

1 CHECK FOR MISSING OR DAMAGED GARTER SPRING — REMOVE DAMAGED SPRING WITH SMALL HOOKED WIRE — INSTALL NEW SPRING IF DAMAGED OR MISSING.

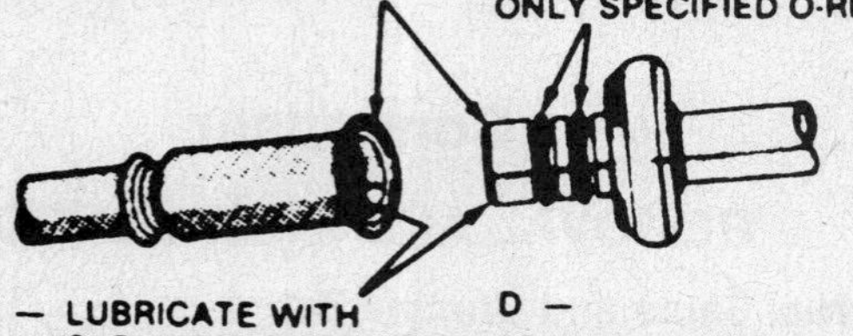
A — CLEAN FITTINGS
B — INSTALL NEW O-RINGS — USE ONLY SPECIFIED O-RINGS
C — LUBRICATE WITH CLEAN REFRIGERANT OIL
D — ASSEMBLE FITTING TOGETHER BY PUSHING WITH A SLIGHT TWISTING MOTION

2

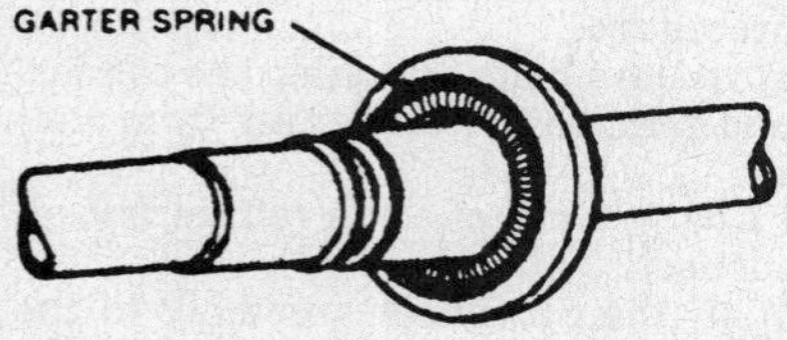
GARTER SPRING

3 TO ENSURE COUPLING ENGAGEMENT, VISUALLY CHECK TO BE SURE GARTER SPRING IS OVER FLARED END OF FEMALE FITTING.

TO DISCONNECT COUPLING

CAUTION — DISCHARGE SYSTEM BEFORE DISCONNECTING COUPLING

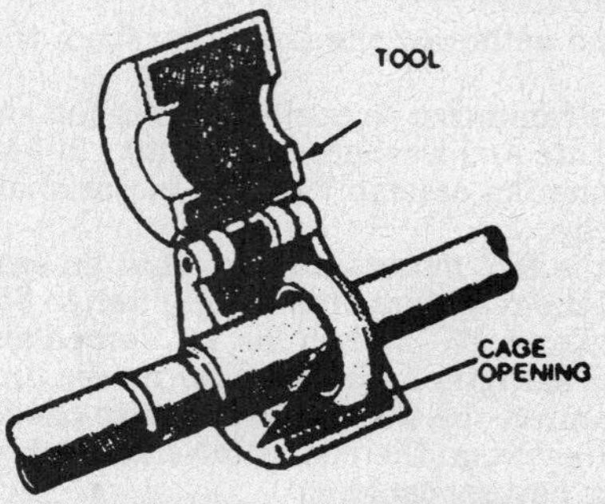
TOOL
CAGE OPENING

(1) FIT TOOL TO COUPLING SO THAT TOOL CAN ENTER CAGE OPENING TO RELEASE THE GARTER SPRING.

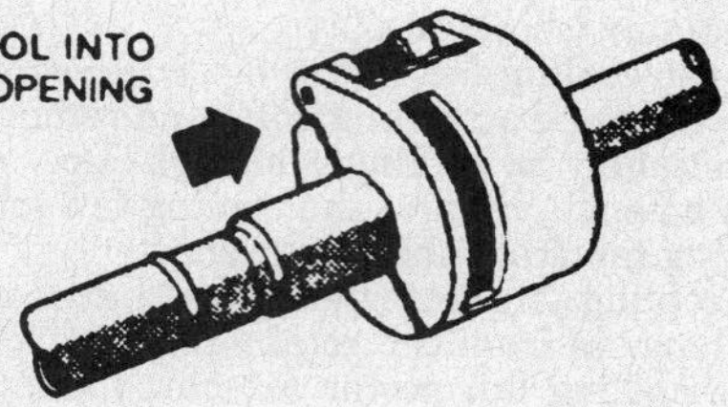
PUSH TOOL INTO CAGE OPENING

(2) PUSH THE TOOL INTO THE CAGE OPENING TO RELEASE THE FEMALE FITTING FROM THE GARTER SPRING.

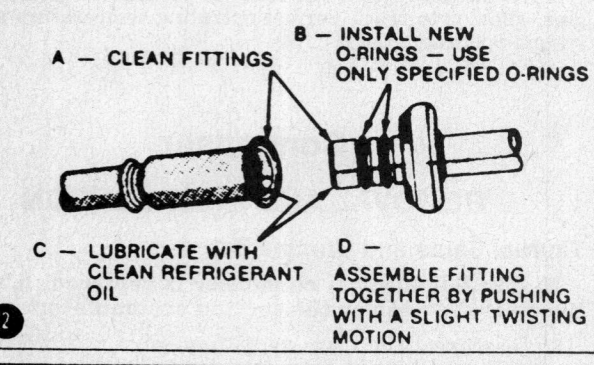

(3) PULL THE COUPLING MALE AND FEMALE FITTINGS APART.

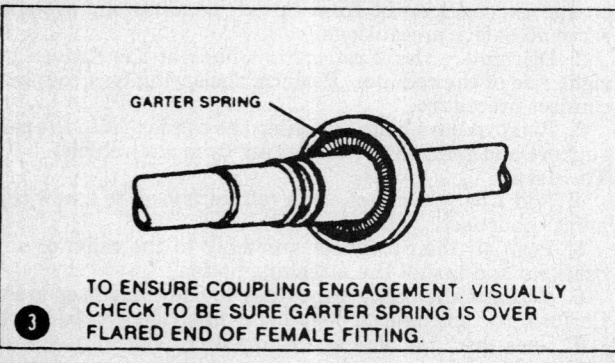

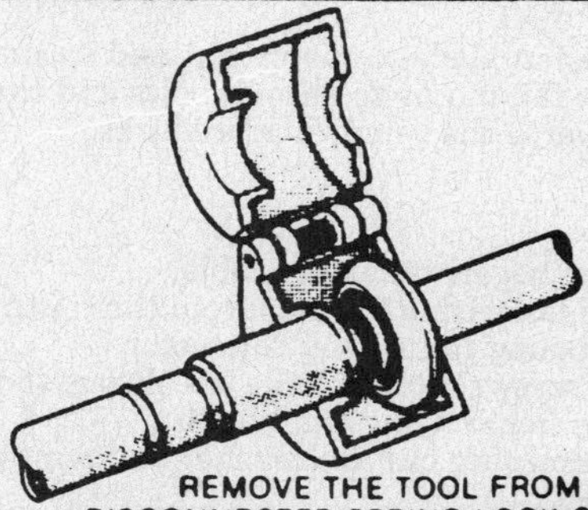

(4) REMOVE THE TOOL FROM THE DISCONNECTED SPRING LOCK COUPLING.

Tempo, Topaz and 1989–90 Escort

NOTE: Whenever a condenser is replaced, it will be necessary to replace the suction accumulator/drier.

1. Disconnect the negative battery cable and properly discharge the refrigerant system. Observe all safety precautions.
2. Place a drain pan under the radiator and drain the cooling system.
3. Remove the ignition coil from the engine.
4. Remove the radiator from the vehicle.
5. Disconnect the liquid line and compressor discharge line. Perform the spring-lock coupling disconnect procedure.
6. Remove the condenser upper bracket attaching screws and remove the condenser from the vehicle.

To install:

7. Add 1 oz. (30 ml) of clean refrigerant oil to a new replacement condenser.
8. Position the condenser to the lower mounts. Move the top of the condenser forward and push the condenser into the radiator opening. Install the upper mounting brackets.
9. Using new special O-rings E1ZZ–19B596–A or E35Y–19D690–A or equivalent, lubricated with clean refrigerant oil, connect the liquid line and the compressor discharge line to the condenser. Perform the spring-lock coupling connection procedure.
10. Install the radiator.
11. Install the ignition coil on the engine.
12. Fill the cooling system to the correct level according to the proper procedure.
13. Leak test, evacuate and charge the refrigerant system according to the proper procedure. Observe all safety precautions.

1991 Escort and Tracer

NOTE: If the condenser is replaced, it will be necessary to replace the suction accumulator/drier.

1. Disconnect the negative battery cable. Discharge the refrigerant from the air conditioning system according to the proper procedure.
2. Drain the cooling system and remove the radiator. Remove the radiator grille.
3. Disconnect the refrigerant lines from the condenser using the spring-lock coupling disconnect procedure. Plug all ports to prevent the entrance of dirt and moisture.
4. Remove the condenser mounting nuts from the mounting bracket and remove the condenser.

To install:

5. Add 1 oz. (30ml) of clean refrigerant oil to a new replacement condenser.
6. Position the condenser and install the mounting nuts.
7. Using new O-rings lubricated with clean refrigerant oil, connect the refrigerant lines to the condenser using the spring-lock coupling connect procedure.
8. Install the radiator grille. Install the radiator and fill the cooling system.
9. Connect the negative battery cable. Leak test, evacuate and charge the system according to the proper procedure. Observe all safety precautions.

Probe

NOTE: Replacing the condenser will also make it necessary to replace the suction accumulator/drier

1. Disconnect the negative battery cable and properly discharge the refrigerant from the air conditioning system. Observe all safety precautions.
2. Disconnect the 2 refrigerant lines from the fittings on the right side of the radiator. Perform the spring-lock coupling disconnect procedure.
3. Drain the cooling system and remove the radiator from the vehicle.
4. Remove the 4 bolts and 2 nuts attaching the condenser to the radiator support. Remove the condenser from the vehicle.

To install:

5. Add 1 oz. (30 ml) of clean refrigerant oil to a new replacement condenser.
6. Position the condenser assembly into it's mounting position and install the attaching bolts and nuts.
7. Connect the refrigerant lines to the condenser assembly. Perform the spring-lock coupling connection procedure.
8. Install the radiator and fill the cooling system according to the proper procedure.
9. Leak test, evacuate and charge the refrigerant system according to the proper procedure. Observe all safety precautions.

Capri

1. Disconnect the negative battery cable and drain the cooling system.
2. Discharge the refrigerant from the air conditioning system according to the proper procedure.
3. Disconnect the upper and lower radiator hoses from the radiator and remove the upper radiator mounts.
4. Disconnect the cooling fan connector and release the harness retainer.
5. Disconnect the coolant overflow hose and remove the radiator and fan assembly.
6. Disconnect the air conditioning lines and plug them to prevent moisture from entering the system.
7. Position the wiring harness aside.
8. Remove the condenser retaining bolts and carefully remove the condenser.

To install:

9. Add 0.845–1.014 oz. (25–30ml) of clean compressor oil to a new replacement compressor to maintain the total system oil requirements.
10. Carefully install the condenser and install the retaining bolts.
11. Connect the air conditioning lines. Tighten the discharge line fitting to 15–18 ft. lbs. (20–25 Nm) and the liquid line fitting to 9–11 ft. lbs. (12–15 Nm).
12. Install the radiator and fan assembly. Connect the electrical connector and install the harness retainer.
13. Connect the radiator hoses and fill the cooling system.
14. Connect the negative battery cable. Leak test, evacuate and charge the refrigerant system according to the proper procedure. Observe all safety precautions.

Festiva

1. Disconnect the negative battery cable and properly discharge the air conditioning system.
2. Remove the radiator grille.
3. Remove the sight glass cover and disconnect the high pressure hose fitting at the receiver/drier.
4. Remove the routing clamp bolt securing the high pressure hose to the condenser bracket.
5. Remove the 2 bolts securing the top of the hood latch and center brace. Remove the bolt securing the bottom of the hood latch center brace.
6. Lift the hood latch from the grille area and lay it back across the engine.
7. Remove the 2 nuts attching the condenser to the radiator core support. Lift the condenser to allow the mounting grommets to clear their mounts and remove the condenser.
8. If necessary, remove the condenser fan on automatic transaxle equipped vehicles. If necessary, remove the receiver/drier.

To install:

9. Add 1 fluid oz. (30 ml) of clean refrigerant oil to a new replacement condenser.
10. If removed, install the receiver/drier. If removed, install the condenser fan on automatic transaxle equipped vehicles.

11. Make sure the mounting grommets are in position and install the condenser. Make sure the mounting insulators are properly seated in the radiator core support crossmember.
12. Make sure the upper rubber mounts are secure on the condenser mounting studs.
13. Install and tighten the 2 nuts to secure the condenser to the radiator core support.
14. Position the center brace and hood latch and install the center brace attaching bolts.
15. Install a new O-ring on the compressor discharge hose fitting and connect it to the condenser.
16. Install and tighten the routing clamp attaching bolt.
17. Install a new O-ring and connect the high pressure hose fitting to the receiver/drier.
18. Install the radiator grille, evacuate, charge and test the system.

1989–90 Tracer

1. Disconnect the negative battery cable and properly discharge the air conditioning system.
2. Remove the front grille, center brace and hood lock.
3. Disconnect the air conditioning lines. Plug the lines to prevent moisture from entering the system.
4. Disconnect the auxiliary cooling fan connector, remove the fan mount bolts and remove the auxiliary fan.
5. Remove the condenser mount bolts and carefully remove the condenser.

To install:

6. Add 0.845–1.014 oz. (25–30 ml) of compressor oil to the condenser if it is being replaced.
7. Carefully position the condenser and secure with the mount bolts.

NOTE: Be careful not to damage the fins of the condenser. Straighten any bent fins.

8. Install the auxiliary fan and connect the fan connector.
9. Remove the plugs from the air conditioning lines and install them to the condenser. Tighten the discharge line to 15–18 ft. lbs. (20–25 Nm) and the liquid line to 9–11 ft. lbs. (12–15 Nm).
10. Install the center hood lock and brace.
11. Install the front grille and connect the negative battery cable.
12. Evacuate and recharge the air conditioning system.

Compressor

REMOVAL AND INSTALLATION

Taurus, Sable and Continental

EXCEPT 3.8L ENGINE

NOTE: Whenever a compressor is replaced, it will be necessary to replace the suction accumulator/drier.

1. Disconnect the negative battery cable and properly discharge the system.
2. Disconnect the compressor clutch wires at the field coil connector on the compressor.
3. Loosen the drive belt and disconnect the hose assemblies from the condenser and suction line.
4. Remove the mounting bolts and remove the compressor and manifold and tube assembly from the vehicle as a unit. The assembly will not clear the sub-frame and radio support if an attempt is made to remove the unit from the bottom. It must be removed from the top.
5. Remove the manifold and tube assembly as an on-bench operation.
6. If the compressor is to be replaced, remove the clutch and field coil assembly.

To install:

NOTE: New service replacement FS-6 compressors contain 10 oz. (300 ml) of refrigerant oil. Before replacement compressor installation, drain 4 oz. (120 ml) of refrigerant oil from the compressor. This will maintain the total system oil charge within the specified limits. New service replacement 10P15F compressors contain 8 oz. (240 ml) of refrigerant oil and new service replacement FX-15 compressors contain 7 oz. (207 ml) of refrigerant oil. Prior to installing either type replacement compressor, drain the refrigerant oil from the removed compressor into a calibrated container. Then, drain the refrigerant oil from the new compressor into a clean calibrated container. If the amount of oil drained from the removed compressor was between 3–5 oz. (90–148 ml), pour the same amount of clean refrigerant oil into the new compressor. If the amount of oil that was removed from the old compressor is greater than 5 oz. (148 ml), pour 5 oz. (148 ml) of clean refrigerant oil into the new compressor. If the amount of refrigerant oil that was removed from the old compressor is less than 3 oz. (90 ml), pour 3 oz. (90 ml) of clean refrigerant oil into the new compressor.

7. Install the manifold and tube assembly on the air conditioning compressor.
8. Install the compressor and manifold and tube assembly on the air conditioning mounting bracket.
9. Using new O-rings lubricated with clean refrigerant oil, connect the suction line to the compressor manifold and tube assembly. Attach the discharge line to the air conditioning condenser.
10. Connect the clutch wires to the field coil connector.
11. Install the drive belt.
12. Leak test, evacuate and charge the system according to the proper procedure. Observe all safety precautions.
13. Check the system for proper operation.

3.8L ENGINE

NOTE: Whenever a compressor is replaced, it will be necessary to replace the suction accumulator/drier.

1. Disconnect the negative battery cable and properly discharge the air conditioning system.
2. Position a suitable clean drain pan under the radiator and drain the coolant. Save the coolant for reuse.
3. Disconnect and remove the integrated relay controller.
4. Disconnect and remove the fan and shroud assembly.
5. Disconnect the upper and lower radiator hoses and remove the radiator.
6. Disconnect the air conditioning compressor magnetic clutch wire at the field coil connector on the compressor.
7. Remove the top 2 compressor mounting bolts.
8. Raise and safely support the vehicle.
9. Loosen and remove the compressor drive belt.
10. Disconnect the HEGO sensor wire connector and remove the air conditioning muffler supporting strap bolt from the subframe.
11. Disconnect the air conditioning system hose from the condenser and suction accumulator/drier using the spring-lock coupling tool or equivalent. Immediately install protective caps on the open lines.
12. Remove the bottom 2 compressor mounting bolts. Make sure the compressor is properly supported as the bolts are removed.
13. Remove the compressor, manifold and tube assemblies from the vehicle as a unit. The assembly can be removed from the bottom using care not to scrape against the condenser.
14. Remove the manifold and tube assemblies from the compressor.

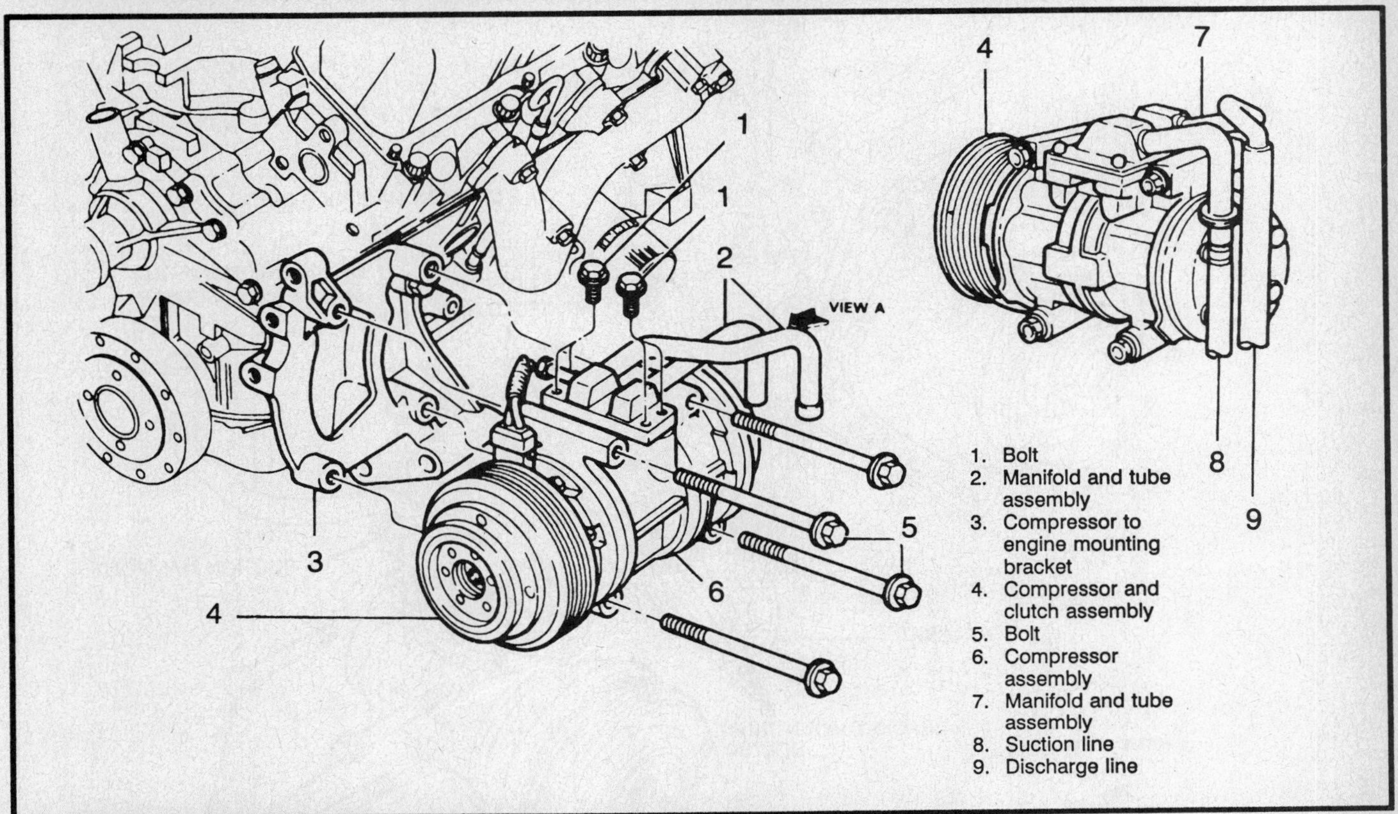
1
1
2
VIEW A
3
4
5
6
4
7
8
9
1. Bolt
2. Manifold and tube assembly
3. Compressor to engine mounting bracket
4. Compressor and clutch assembly
5. Bolt
6. Compressor assembly
7. Manifold and tube assembly
8. Suction line
9. Discharge line

Compressor installation—3.8L engine

15. If the compressor is to be replaced, remove the clutch and field coil assembly.

To install:

NOTE: A new service replacement 10P15C compressor contains 8 oz. (240 ml) of refrigerant oil. Before installing a new compressor, drain 4 oz. (120 ml) of refrigerant oil from the compressor. This will maintain total system oil charge within specified limits.

16. Using new O-rings, lubricated with clean refrigerant oil, install the manifold and tube assemblies onto the new compressor.
17. Install the compressor, manifold and tube assemblies onto the compressor mounting bracket.
18. Using new O-rings lubricated with clean refrigerant oil, connect the suction line to the compressor and manifold assembly.
19. Using new O-rings lubricated with clean refrigerant oil, connect the discharge line to the compressor and manifold assembly.
20. Install the muffler support onto the sub-frame and connect the HEGO sensor wire connector.
21. Install the compressor drive belt and lower the vehicle.
22. Install the radiator and connect the radiator hoses.
23. Install the fan and shroud assembly and connect the integrated relay connector.
24. Connect the negative battery cable and fill the radiator with the coolant that was saved.
25. Leak test, evacuate and charge the system according to the proper procedure. Check the system for proper operation.

Tempo and Topaz

NOTE: Whenever a compressor is replaced, it will be necessary to replace the suction accumulator/drier.

1. Disconnect the negative battery cable and properly discharge the refrigerant system.
2. Disconnect the compressor clutch wires at the field coil connector on the compressor.
3. Remove the discharge line from the manifold and tube assembly using the spring-lock coupling disconnect procedure.
4. Remove the suction line from the suction manifold using a backup wrench on each fitting.
5. Loosen 2 idler attaching screws and release the compressor belt tension.
6. Raise and safely support the vehicle. Remove the 4 bolts attaching the compressor to the mounting bracket.
7. Remove the 2 screws attaching the heater water return tube to the underside of the engine supports.
8. Remove the compressor from the underside of the vehicle.

To install:

NOTE: A new service replacement compressor contains 8 oz. (240 ml) of refrigerant oil. Prior to installing the replacement compressor, drain the refrigerant oil from the removed compressor into a calibrated container. Then, drain the refrigerant oil from the new compressor into a clean calibrated container. If the amount of oil drained from the removed compressor was between 3–5 oz. (90–148 ml), pour the same amount of clean refrigerant oil into the new compressor. If the amount of oil that was removed from the old compressor is greater than 5 oz. (148 ml), pour 5 oz. (148 ml) of clean refrigerant oil into the new compressor. If the amount of refrigerant oil that was removed from the old compressor is less than 3 oz. (90 ml), pour 3 oz. (90 ml) of clean refrigerant oil into the new compressor.

9. Position the compressor to the compressor bracket and install the 4 bolts.

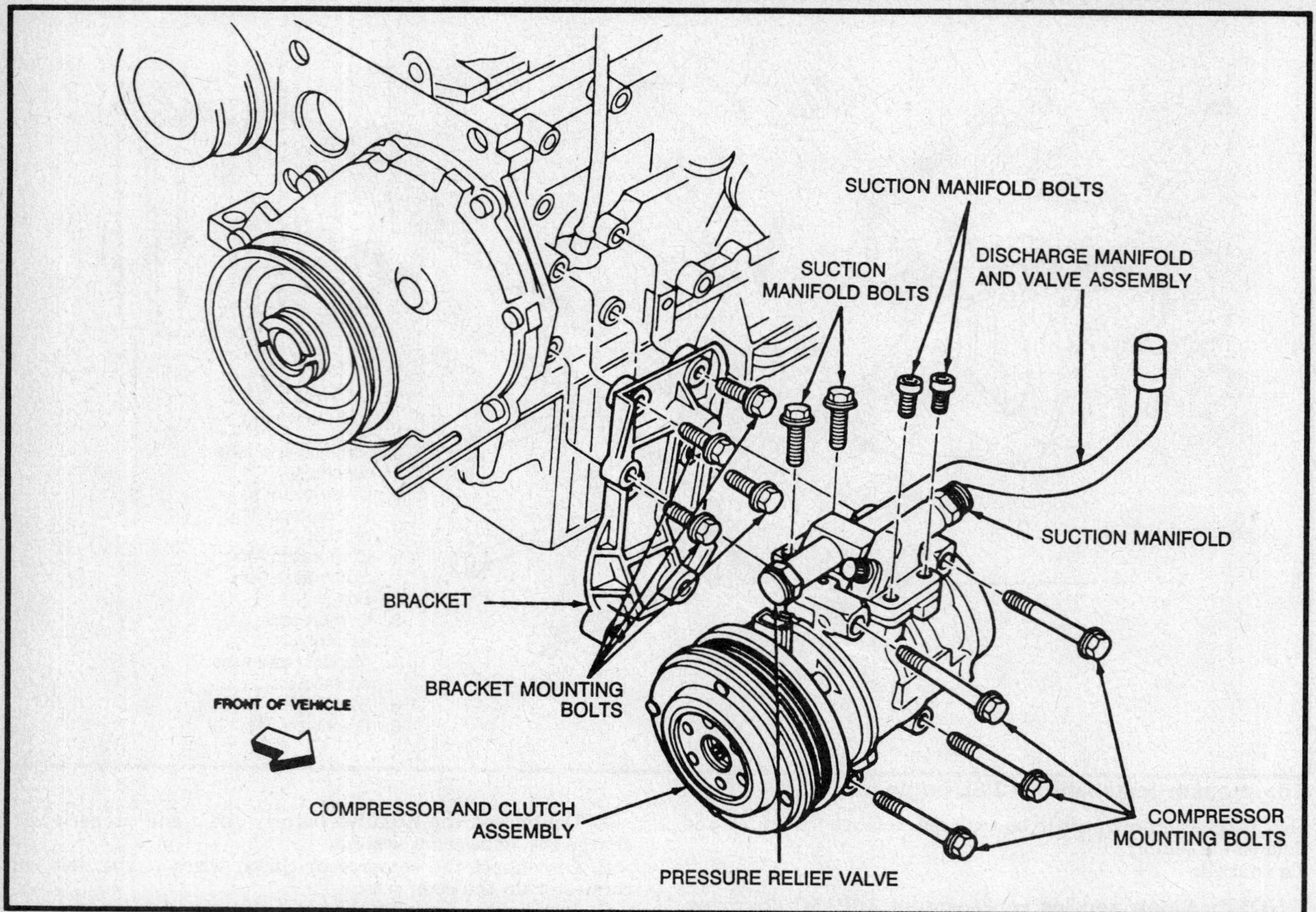
SUCTION MANIFOLD BOLTS
SUCTION
MANIFOLD BOLTS
DISCHARGE MANIFOLD
AND VALVE ASSEMBLY
SUCTION MANIFOLD
BRACKET
BRACKET MOUNTING
BOLTS
FRONT OF VEHICLE
COMPRESSOR AND CLUTCH
ASSEMBLY
COMPRESSOR
MOUNTING BOLTS
PRESSURE RELIEF VALVE

Compressor installation—2.3L engine

10. Attach 2 screws attaching the heater water return tube to the underside of the engine supports.
11. Attach the compressor belt and tighten the 2 idler screws.
12. Install the suction line to the suction manifold using a backup wrench on each fitting. Use new O-rings lubricated with clean refrigerant oil.
13. Install the discharge line spring lock fitting to the manifold and tube assembly. Use new O-rings lubricated with clean refrigerant oil.
14. Connect the compressor clutch wire connector to the field coil connector at the compressor.
15. Leak test, evacuate and charge the system according to the proper procedure. Check the system for proper operation.

1989–90 Escort

NOTE: Whenever a compressor is replaced, it will be necessary to replace the suction accumulator/drier.

1. Disconnect the negative battery cable.
2. Disconnect the alternator wires at the multiple connector and remove the alternator from the engine.
3. Properly discharge the refrigerant system.
4. Disconnect the compressor clutch wires at the field coil connector on the compressor.
5. Remove the discharge hose at the compressor manifold using a backup wrench at each fitting.
6. The suction hose of the CFI engine has a tube "O" fitting and must be removed with backup wrenches. On EFI engines, the suction hose has a spring-lock coupling and must be removed using the spring-lock coupling disconnect procedure.
7. Remove the 4 retaining bolts attaching the compressor to the compressor bracket, then lift the compressor from the engine compartment.

To install:

NOTE: A new service replacement compressor contains 8 oz. (240 ml) of refrigerant oil. Prior to installing the replacement compressor, drain the refrigerant oil from the removed compressor into a calibrated container. Then, drain the refrigerant oil from the new compressor into a clean calibrated container. If the amount of oil drained from the removed compressor was between 3–5 oz. (90–148 ml), pour the same amount of clean refrigerant oil into the new compressor. If the amount of oil that was removed from the old compressor is greater than 5 oz. (148 ml), pour 5 oz. (148 ml) of clean refrigerant oil into the new compressor. If the amount of refrigerant oil that was removed from the old compressor is less than 3 oz. (90 ml), pour 3 oz. (90 ml) of clean refrigerant oil into the new compressor.

8. Position the compressor to the compressor bracket and install the 4 bolts.
9. Connect the discharge and suction lines to the manifold and tube assembly. For threaded fittings, use new O-rings lubricated with clean refrigerant oil. Also, use a backup wrench when

tightening threaded fittings. Connect the suction line for spring-lock couplings according to the spring-lock coupling connect procedure.

10. Connect the clutch wires to the field coil connector.
11. Install the alternator and connect the multiple connector to the alternator.
12. Install the drive belt on the pulleys and adjust according to specification.
13. Leak test, evacuate and charge the system according to the proper procedure. Check the system for proper operation.

1991 Escort and Tracer

NOTE: Whenever the compressor is replaced, replace the suction accumulator/drier and the fixed orifice tube.

1. Disconnect the negative battery cable.
2. Discharge the refrigerant from the air conditioning system according to the proper procedure.
3. Raise and safely support the vehicle.
4. Remove the undercover and splash shield and disconnect the accessory drive belt from the compressor pulley.
5. Remove the manifold attaching bolts. Immediately plug all compressor and manifold openings to keep moisture out of the system.
6. Disconnect the field coil electrical connector and remove the compressor mounting bolts. Remove the compressor.

To install:

NOTE: A new service replacement compressor contains 7.75 oz. (230ml) of refrigerant oil. Prior to installing the replacement compressor, drain the oil from the old compressor into a clean calibrated container. Then drain the oil from the new compressor into a clean calibrated container. If the amount of oil removed from the old compressor is less than 3 oz. (90ml), pour 3 oz. (90ml) of clean refrigerant oil into the new compressor. If the amount of oil drained from the old compressor was between 3–5 oz. (90–150ml), pour the same amount of clean refrigerant oil into the new compressor. If the amount of oil removed from the old compressor is greater than 5 oz. (150ml), pour 5 oz. (150ml) of clean oil into the new compressor. This will maintain the total system oil charge requirements.

7. Position the compressor and install the mounting bolts. Tighten the bolts to 15–22 ft. lbs. (20–30 Nm).
8. Connect the field coil electrical connector.
9. Remove all plugs, then install new O-rings lubricated with clean refrigerant oil on the manifolds. Position the manifolds and install the attaching bolts. Tighten the bolts to 13–17 ft. lbs. (18–23 Nm).
10. Attach the accessory drive belt to the compressor pulley and install the splash shield and undercover.
11. Lower the vehicle. Check the accessory drive belt for proper tension.

NOTE: The air conditioning system should be flushed whenever a compressor is replaced.

12. Connect the negative battery cable. Leak test, evacuate and charge the system according to the proper procedure. Observe all safety precautions.

Probe

2.2L ENGINE

NOTE: The suction accumulator/drier and orifice tube (liquid line) should also be replaced whenever the compressor is replaced.

1. Disconnect the negative battery cable and properly discharge the refrigerant system.
2. Remove the suction and discharge manifold assembly from the compressor.
3. Remove the 2 attaching bolts at the upper compressor mounting bracket from the compressor to engine mounting bracket.
4. Remove the belt tension adjusting bolt from the belt tension fitting.
5. Remove the attaching nut from the compressor at the upper compressor mounting bracket.
6. Remove the upper through bolt from the compressor and remove the upper compressor mounting bracket.
7. Disconnect the clutch field coil electrical connector.
8. Remove the lower through bolt from the compressor at the chassis-to-compressor mounting bracket.
9. Remove the compressor, front compressor mounting bracket and rear compressor mounting bracket as an assembly.
10. Remove the through bolt from the compressor at the rear compressor mounting bracket and remove the rear bracket, spacer and front bracket from the compressor.

To install:

NOTE: A service replacement compressor should be emptied of any oil it contains from the factory. Add 3.3 oz. (100 ml) of the specified refrigerant oil. This will maintain the total system oil charge within the specified limits.

11. Position the rear compressor mounting bracket, front mounting bracket and spacer to the compressor and install the through bolt.
12. Position the compressor and bracket assembly into the vehicle and install the through bolt into the chassis-to-compressor mounting bracket.
13. Connect the clutch field coil electrical connector.
14. Position the upper compressor mounting bracket onto the compressor and install the upper through bolt.
15. Install the attaching bolts at the upper compressor mounting bracket into the compressor-to-engine mounting bracket.
16. Install the belt tension fitting into the upper compressor mounting bracket and install the attaching nut. Install the belt tension adjusting bolt.
17. Install the suction and discharge manifold hose assembly.
18. Adjust the belt tension to specification.
19. Leak test, evacuate and charge the system according to the proper procedure. Check the operation of the system.

3.0L ENGINE

NOTE: The suction accumulator/drier and orifice tube (liquid line) should also be replaced whenever the compressor is replaced.

1. Disconnect the negative battery cable and properly discharge the refrigerant system.
2. Remove the alternator/accessory support bracket and disconnect the clutch field coil electrical connector.
3. Remove the 4 compressor mounting bolts.

NOTE: Remove the brace with the 2 upper mounting bolts.

4. Lift the compressor, with the air conditioning hoses still attached, from the engine compartment and set it down carefully on the radiator core support.
5. Remove the 4 hose manifold bolts and pull the hose assemblies aside. Remove the compressor.

To install:

NOTE: A service replacement compressor should be emptied of any oil it contains from the factory. Add 3.3 oz. (100 ml) of the specified refrigerant oil. This will maintain the total system oil charge within the specified limits.

6. Position the hose assemblies on the compressor and install the manifold attaching bolts.
7. Position the compressor assembly on the mounting bracket and install the 4 mounting bolts and brace.
8. Connect the clutch field coil electrical connector and install the alternator/accessory support bracket.
9. Connect the negative battery cable and properly evacuate and recharge the system.

Capri

1. Run the engine at fast idle with the air conditioner **ON** for 10 minutes, then shut the engine **OFF**.
2. Disconnect the negative battery cable.
3. Discharge the refrigerant from the air conditioning system according to the proper procedure.
4. Remove the compressor drive belt.
5. Raise and safely support the vehicle.
6. Remove the underbody covers and disconnect the magnetic clutch electrical connector.
7. Disconnect the suction and discharge hose assembly from the compressor. Cap the open fittings to keep moisture and dirt out of the system.
8. Remove the compressor mounting bolts and remove the compressor.

To install:

9. Add 2.05–3.38 oz. (61–100ml) of clean refrigerant oil to a new replacement compressor to maintain total system oil requirements.
10. Position the compressor and install the retaining bolts. Tighten to 30–40 ft. lbs. (39–54 Nm).
11. Connect the suction and discharge hose assembly to the compressor.
12. Connect the magnetic clutch electrical connector and install the underbody covers.
13. Lower the vehicle.
14. Install the compressor drive belt and connect the negative battery cable.
15. Leak test, evacuate and charge the system according to the proper procedure. Observe all safety precautions.

Festiva

1. Disconnect the negative battery cable and properly discharge the refrigerant system.
2. Remove the compressor drive belt and disconnect the clutch coil wire.
3. Disconnect the suction and discharge fittings from the compressor. Cap the open fittings immediately to keep moisture from the system.
4. Remove the mounting bolts and the compressor.

To install:

NOTE: A new service replacement compressor contains 2.1–3.5 oz. (60–100 ml) of the specified refrigerant oil. Prior to installing the replacement compressor, drain 1.2 oz. (30 ml) of refrigerant oil from the compressor. This will maintain the system total oil charge within the specified limits.

5. Position the compressor on the mounting bracket and start the bolts.
6. Connect the refrigerant hoses and the clutch wire.
7. Tighten the bolts to 30–40 ft. lbs. (39–54 Nm) and adjust the tension of the drive belt.
8. Connect the negative battery cable and properly leak test, evacuate and charge the system.

1989–90 Tracer

1. Run the engine at fast idle with the air conditioner **ON** for 10 minutes, then shut the engine **OFF**.
2. Disconnect the negative battery cable.
3. If equipped with power steering, remove the power steer-

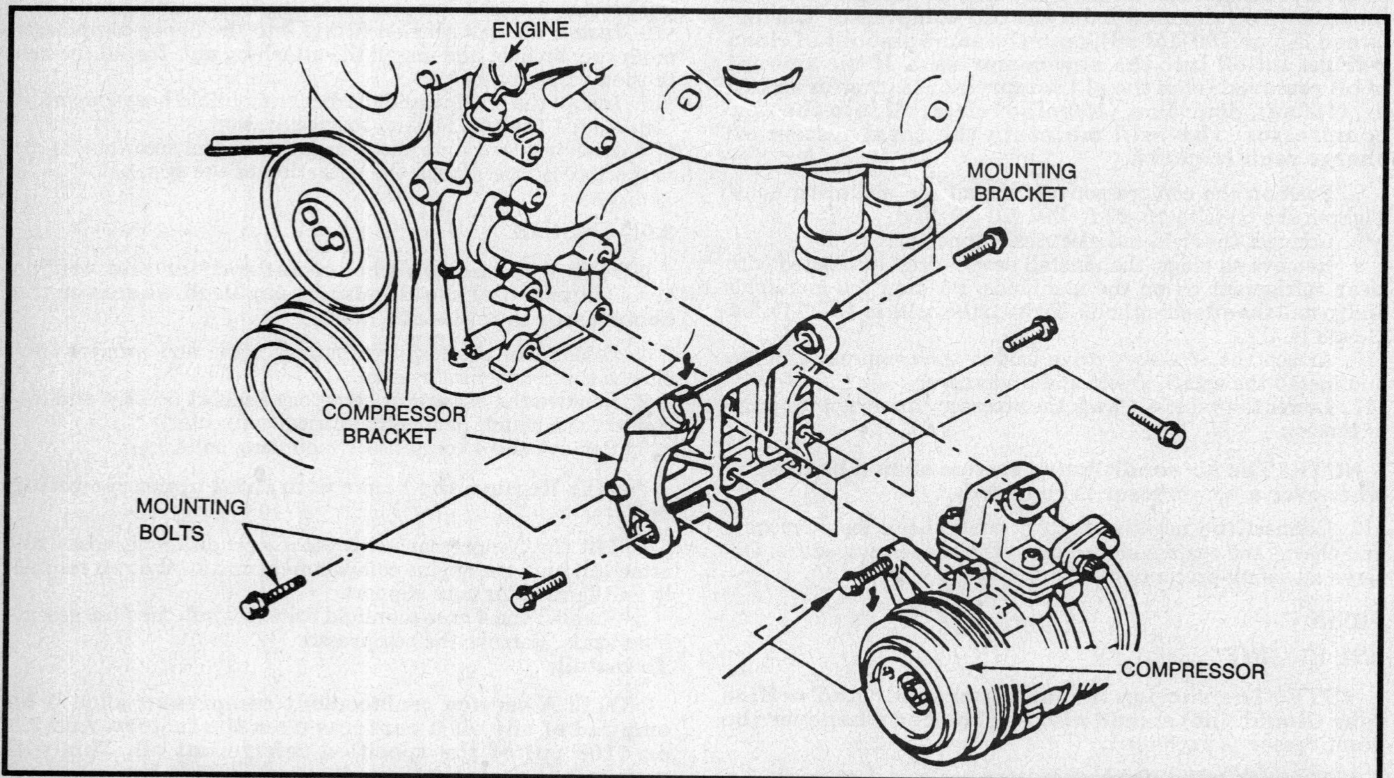
ENGINE
MOUNTING
BRACKET
COMPRESSOR
BRACKET
MOUNTING
BOLTS
COMPRESSOR

Compressor installation – 1.3L engine

ing pump.

4. Disconnect the electrical connector for the magnetic clutch.

5. Properly discharge the refrigerant from the air conditioning system.

6. Disconnect the suction and discharge hoses from the compressor. Immediately cap the open fittings to keep moisture and dirt from the system.

7. Loosen the compressor drive belt, remove the compressor mounting bolts and remove the compressor.

To install:

NOTE: Add 2.05–3.38 oz. (61–100 ml) of refrigerant oil to the compressor, if the compressor was replaced.

8. Position the compressor and install the mounting bolts. Tighten the bolts to 30–40 ft. lbs. (39–54 Nm).

9. Install the compressor drive belt.

10. Connect the suction and discharge hoses to the compressor. Tighten the fittings to 15–22 ft. lbs. (20–25 Nm).

11. Connect the magnetic clutch electrical connector.

12. Install the power steering pump, if removed.

13. Connect the negative batttery cable and properly evacuate and recharge the system.

Accumulator/Drier

REMOVAL AND INSTALLATION

Taurus, Sable and Continental

1. Disconnect the negative battery cable and discharge the refrigerant from the air conditioning system according to the proper procedure. Observe all safety precautions.

2. Disconnect the suction hose at the compressor. Cap the suction hose and the compressor to prevent entrance of dirt and moisture.

3. Disconnect the accumulator/drier inlet tube from the evaporator core outlet. Perform the spring-lock coupling disconnect procedure.

4. Disconnect the wire harness connector from the pressure switch on top of the accumulator/drier.

5. Remove the screw holding the accumulator/drier in the accumulator bracket and remove the accumulator/drier.

To install:

6. On Taurus SHO and Taurus, Sable and Continental equipped with the 3.8L engine, drill a ½ in. hole in the removed accumulator/drier body and drain the refrigerant oil through the hole. Add the same amount of oil removed, plus 2 oz. (60 ml) of clean refrigerant oil to the new accumulator/drier. On all other vehicles, drain the oil from the removed accumulator/drier. Add the same amount plus 2 oz. (60 ml) of clean refrigerant oil to 3.0L engine equipped vehicles and the same amount plus 1 oz. (30 ml) to 2.5L engine equipped vehicles.

7. Position the accumulator/drier on the vehicle and route the suction hose to the compressor.

8. Using a new O-ring lubricated with clean refrigerant oil, connect the accumulator/drier inlet tube to the evaporator core outlet.

9. Install the screw in the accumulator/drier bracket.

10. Using a new O-ring lubricated with clean refrigerant oil, connect the suction hose to the compressor.

11. Leak test, evacuate and charge the system according to the proper procedure. Check the system for proper operation.

Tempo and Topaz

1. Disconnect the negative battery cable. Properly discharge the refrigerant from the air conditioning system, observing all safety precautions.

2. Disconnect the suction hose at the accumulator.

3. Disconnect the accumulator/drier inlet tube from the evaporator core outlet by performing the spring-lock coupling disconnect procedure.

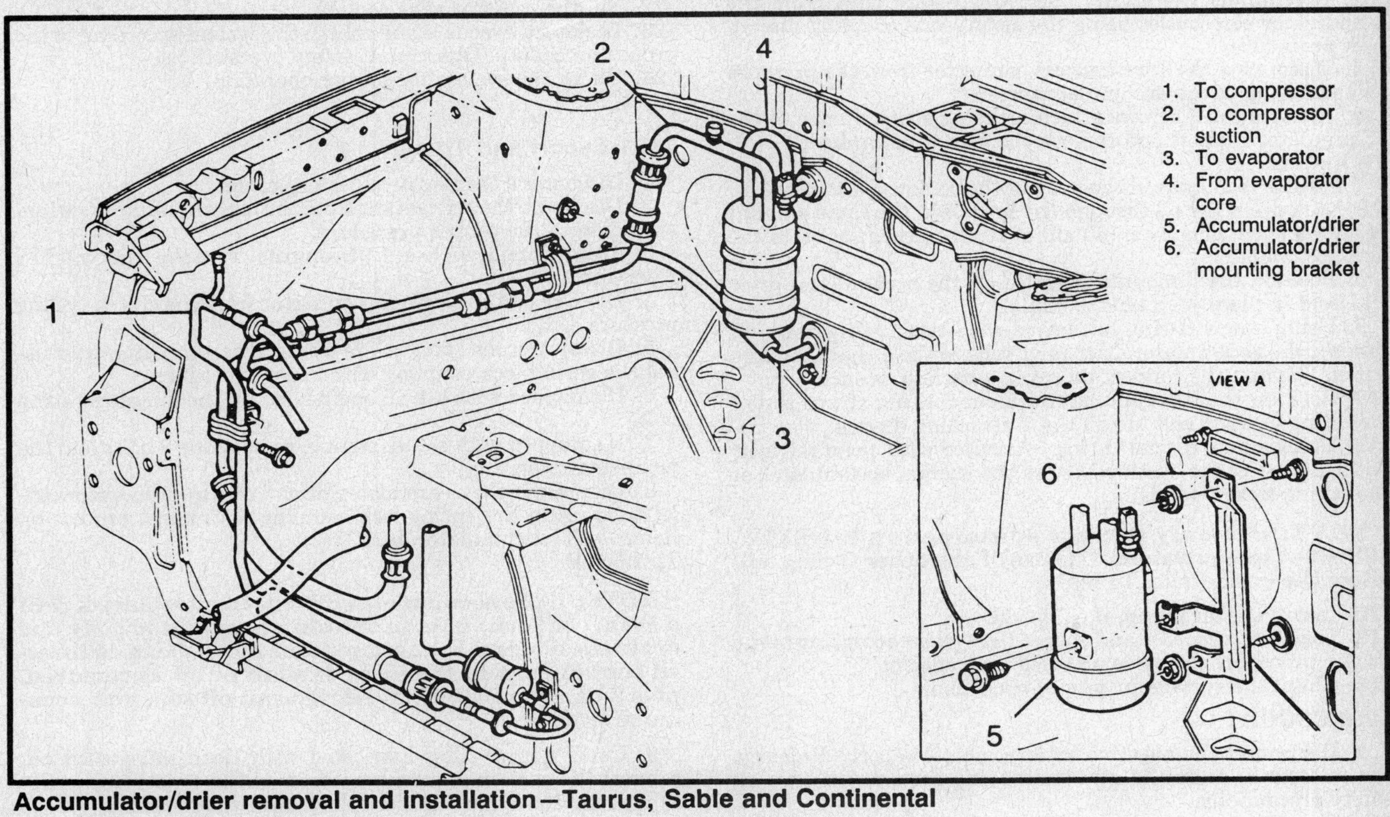
2
4
1
3
VIEW A
6
5
1. To compressor
2. To compressor suction
3. To evaporator
4. From evaporator core
5. Accumulator/drier
6. Accumulator/drier mounting bracket

Accumulator/drier removal and installation—Taurus, Sable and Continental

4. Disconnect the wire harness connector from the pressure switch on top of the accumulator/drier.
5. Remove the nut and screw that retain the accumulator/drier to the dash panel and remove the assembly.

To install:

6. Drill a ½ in. hole in the body of the removed accumulator/drier and drain the oil through the hole. Add the same amount of oil removed, plus 2 oz. (60 ml) of clean refrigerant oil to the new accumulator.
7. Position the accumulator/drier in the mounting bracket.
8. Using new O-rings lubricated with clean refrigerant oil, connect the accumulator/drier inlet tube to the evaporator core outlet.
9. Position the accumulator/drier mounting bracket over the evapoarator case stud and secure with the retaining nut. Install the screw through the slot in the lower leg of the mounting bracket.
10. Using a new special O-ring lubricated with clean refrigerant oil, connect the suction hose to the suction accumulator at the spring-lock coupling.

NOTE: Use only O-rings contained in kit E35Y–19D690–A or equivalent. The use of any other O-ring will allow the connection to leak.

11. Leak test, evacuate and charge the system according to the proper procedure. Observe all safety precautions.
12. Check the system for proper operation.

1989–90 Escort

EXCEPT 1990 ESCORT GT

1. Disconnect the negative battery cable. Properly discharge the refrigerant from the air conditioning system. Observe all safety precautions.
2. If equipped, remove the air pump from the engine.
3. Disconnect the suction hose.
4. Disconnect the accumulator/drier inlet tube from the evapoarator core outlet using the spring-lock coupling disconnect procedure.
5. Disconnect the wire harness connector from the pressure switch on top of the accumulator/drier.
6. Remove the 2 screws attaching the 2 strap clamps to the accumulator bracket and remove the accumulator/drier.

To install:

7. Drill a ½ in. hole in the body of the removed accumulator/drier and drain the oil through the hole. Add the same amount of oil removed, plus 2 oz. (60 ml) of clean refrigerant oil to the new accumulator.
8. Position the 2 mounting straps on the accumulator/drier and hold in place with tape or caulk.
9. Using a new O-ring lubricated with clean refrigerant oil, connect the accumulator/drier inlet tube to the evaporator core outlet. Tighten the connection using a backup wrench.
10. Position the 2 accumulator/drier mounting straps to the mounting bracket and install the 2 attaching screws.
11. Using a new special O-ring lubricated with clean refrigerant oil, connect the suction hose to the suction accumulator at the spring-lock coupling.

NOTE: Use only O-rings contained in kit E35Y–19D690–A or equivalent. The use of any other O-ring will allow the connection to leak.

12. Install the air pump, if equipped.
13. Leak test, evacuate and charge the system according to the proper procedure. Observe all safety precautions.
14. Check the system for proper operation.

1990 ESCORT GT

1. Disconnect the negative battery cable. Properly discharge the refrigerant from the air conditioning system. Observe all safety precautions.
2. Remove the fuel filter bracket and move the fuel filter aside. Do not disconnect the fuel lines.
3. Disconnect the accumulator/drier and hose assembly from the evaporator core and air conditioning compressor manifold using the spring-lock coupling disconnect procedure.
4. Disconnect the liquid line from the evaporator core using the spring-lock coupling disconnect procedure.
5. Remove the accumulator/drier top retaining nut.
6. Raise and safely support the vehicle.
7. Disconnect the catalytic converter and backfire hose and move it aside.
8. Drain the engine coolant and disconnect the lower heater hose.
9. Loosen the steel heater tube bracket.
10. Remove the accumulator/drier mounting bracket lower retaining screw and remove the bracket.
11. Remove the accumulator/drier and hose assembly from the vehicle.

To install:

12. Drill a ½ in. hole in the body of the removed accumulator/drier and drain the oil through the hole. Add the same amount of oil removed, plus 2 oz. (60 ml) of clean refrigerant oil to the new accumulator.
13. Position the accumulator/drier and mounting bracket in the vehicle and install the mounting bracket lower retaining screw.
14. Tighten the steel heater tube bracket.
15. Connect the lower heater hose.
16. Connect the catalytic converter and backfire hose.
17. Lower the vehicle.
18. Install the accumulator/drier retaining nut.
19. Connect the liquid line to the evaporator core.
20. Connect the accumulator/drier and hose assembly to the evaporator core and air conditioning compressor manifold.
21. Move the fuel filter into position and install the fuel filter bracket.
22. Fill the radiator with coolant.
23. Leak test, evacuate and charge the system according to the proper procedure. Observe all safety precautions.
24. Check the system for proper operation.

1991 Escort and Tracer

1. Disconnect the negative battery cable.
2. Discharge the refrigerant from the air conditioning system according to the proper procedure.
3. If equipped with a 1.9L engine, remove the washer reservoir.
4. Disconnect the electrical connector from the clutch cycling pressure switch.
5. Disconnect the suction line from the accumulator/drier using the spring-lock coupling disconnect procedure.
6. If equipped with a 1.8L engine, loosen the mounting strap bolt.
7. If equipped with a 1.9L engine, remove the 2 bolts and the mounting strap.
8. Disconnect the accumulator/drier from the evaporator outlet tube using the spring-lock coupling disconnect procedure. Remove the accumulator/drier.

To install:

NOTE: If the accumulator/drier is to be replaced, drill a ½ in. (12.7mm) hole in the old accumulator body and drain the oil from the accumulator into a clean calibrated container. Add the same amount of oil as removed, plus 2 oz. (60ml) of clean refrigerant oil to a new accumulator/drier.

9. Using new O-rings lubricated with clean refrigerant oil, connect the suction accumulator/drier to the evaporator outlet tube using the spring-lock coupling connect procedure.

10. If equipped with a 1.8L engine, tighten the mounting strap bolt.
11. If equipped with a 1.9L engine, position the mounting strap and install the 2 mounting bolts.
12. Using new O-rings lubricated with clean refrigerant oil, connect the suction line to the accumulator/drier using the spring-lock coupling connect procedure.
13. Connect the electrical connector to the clutch cycling pressure switch.
14. If equipped with a 1.9L engine, install the washer reservoir.
15. Connect the negative battery cable. Leak test, evacuate and charge the system according to the proper procedure. Observe all safety precautions.

Probe

1. Disconnect the negative battery cable. Properly discharge the refrigerant from the air conditioning system. Observe all safety precautions.
2. Remove the carbon canister.
3. Disconnect the accumulator/drier suction line at the bulkhead and the compressor suction line from the accumulator/drier. Cap the suction line and the evaporator core outlet to prevent entrance of dirt and excess moisture.
4. Disconnect the clutch cycling pressure switch electrical connector from the switch.
5. Remove the 2 mounting bolts from the accumulator/drier mounting bracket and carefully remove the accumulator/drier from the vehicle.

To install:

6. Drain the oil from the removed accumulator/drier. Add the same amount plus 1 oz. (30 ml) of clean refrigerant oil to the new accumulator.
7. Position the accumulator/drier onto the mounting bracket and install the mounting bolts.
8. Connect the suction line spring-lock coupling to the evaporator core according to the spring-lock coupling connect procedure.
9. Connect the compressor suction line to the accumulator/drier assembly.
10. Connect the clutch cycling pressure switch electrical connector and install the carbon canister.
11. Connect the negative battery cable. Leak test, evacuate and charge the refrigerant system according to the proper procedure. Observe all safety precautions.

Receiver/Drier

REMOVAL AND INSTALLATION

Capri

1. Disconnect the negative battery cable.
2. Discharge the refrigerant from the air conditioning system according to the proper procedure.
3. Remove the air cleaner assembly and front mounting bracket.
4. Disconnect the air conditioning lines and plug the ends to prevent dirt and moisture from entering the system.
5. Loosen the bracket and remove the receiver/drier.

To install:

6. Add 0.507–0.676 oz. (15–20ml) of clean refrigerant oil to a new replacement receiver/drier to maintain total system oil requirements.
7. Install the receiver/drier into the bracket.
8. Connect the air conditioning lines making sure to connect the line coming from the condenser to the port marked **IN**. Tighten the line connection retaining screws to 9–11 ft. lbs. (12–15 Nm).
9. Install the air cleaner assembly and mounting bracket.

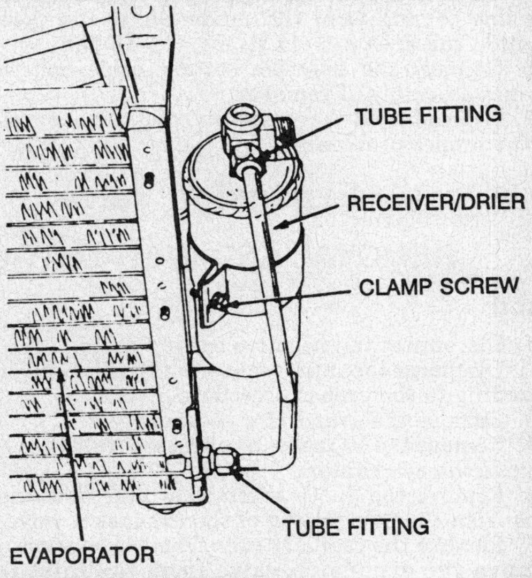
TUBE FITTING
RECEIVER/DRIER
CLAMP SCREW
TUBE FITTING
EVAPORATOR

Receiver/drier location — Festiva

10. Connect the negative battery cable. Leak test, evacuate and charge the system according to the proper procedure. Observe all safety precautions.

Festiva

1. Disconnect the negative battery cable. Properly discharge the refrigerant from the air conditioning system. Observe all safety precautions.
2. Remove the condenser.
3. Disconnect the condenser outlet tube from the receiver/drier.
4. Loosen the mounting clamp screw and remove the receiver/drier.

To install:

5. Drain the oil from the removed receiver/drier through the inlet fitting. Drain the oil into a calibrated measuring container. Add the same amount of clean refrigerant oil plus 1 oz. (29.5 ml) to the new accumulator drier.

NOTE: If more than 5 oz. (147 ml) of refrigerant oil is removed from a receiver/drier, it is an indication that the oil drain hole in the receiver/drier is plugged. Always check the receiver/drier for excessive oil if the compressor has been replaced for lack of performance.

6. Position the receiver/drier in the mounting clamp.
7. Install a new O-ring, lubricated with clean refrigerant oil and connect the condenser tube to the receiver/drier.
8. Tighten the mounting clamp screw.
9. Install the condenser.
10. Leak test, evacuate and recharge the system according to the proper procedure.

1989–90 Tracer

1. Disconnect the negative battery cable. Properly discharge the refrigerant system.
2. If equipped with EFI, remove the air cleaner assembly.
3. Disconnect the air conditioning lines and plug the ends to prevent dirt and moisture from entering the system.
4. Loosen the bracket and remove the receiver/drier.

To install:

5. Add 0.507–0.676 oz. (15–20 ml) of compressor oil to the receiver/drier if it was replaced.
6. Install the receiver/drier into the bracket.

7. Connect the air conditioning lines, making sure to connect the line coming from the condenser to the port marked **IN**. Tighten the lines to 9–11 ft. lbs. (12–15 Nm).
8. Connect the negative battery cable and install the air cleaner assembly, if removed.
9. Evacuate and charge the air conditioning system according to the proper procedure.

Expansion Valve

REMOVAL AND INSTALLATION

Capri

1. Disconnect the negative battery cable.
2. Discharge the refrigerant from the air conditioning system according to the proper procedure.
3. Remove the evaporator assembly.
4. Remove the 10 retaining clips, separate the case halves and remove the evaporator.
5. Remove the de-ice thermostat and disconnect the liquid tube from the inlet fitting of the expansion valve.
6. Remove the capillary tube from the evaporator outlet and remove the expansion valve from the inlet fitting of the evaporator.

To install:

7. Install the expansion valve to the inlet fitting of the evaporator. Tighten the fitting to 9–11 ft. lbs. (12–15 Nm).
8. Connect the liquid tube to the inlet fitting of the expansion valve. Tighten the fitting to 9–11 ft. lbs. (12–15 Nm).
9. Install the packing to fix the capillary tube of the expansion valve to the outlet of the evaporator.
10. Install the de-ice switch and assemble the case halves with the 10 retaining clips.
11. Install the evaporator assembly.
12. Connect the negative battery cable. Leak test, evacuate and charge the system according to the proper procedure. Observe all safety precautions.

Festiva

1. Disconnect the negative battery cable. Properly discharge the refrigerant from the air conditioning system.
2. Remove the evaporator housing.
3. Remove the air inlet duct.
4. Remove the staples and the capillary tube insulation. Remove the capillary tube clamp.
5. Disconnect the expansion valve at the evaporator tube fitting and inlet tube fitting and remove the expansion valve.

To install:

6. Install new O-rings on the evaporator and inlet tube fittings.
7. Connect the evaporator tube and inlet tube fittings.
8. Install the capillary tube and clamp, then install the insulation and staple it into position.
9. Install the air inlet duct and install the evaporator housing.
10. Leak test, evacuate and recharge the system according to the proper procedure.

1989–90 Tracer

1. Disconnect the negative battery cable. Properly discharge the refrigerant from the air conditioning system.
2. Disconnect the air conditioning lines from the evaporator and plug the ends to prevent dirt and moisture from entering the system.
3. Remove the evaporator tube grommets from the bulkhead.
4. Remove the glove box and disconnect the electrical connectors.
5. Remove the air duct bands and the drain hose.
6. Remove the evaporator housing mount bolts and nuts and carefully remove the evaporator housing.

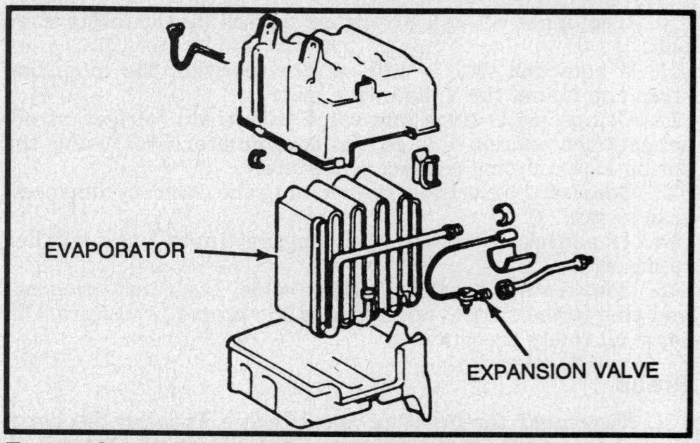
EVAPORATOR
EXPANSION VALVE

Expansion valve location – 1989–90 Tracer

7. Remove the 10 retaining clips from around the evaporator housing, separate the case halves and remove the evaporator.
8. Disconnect the liquid tube from the inlet fitting of the expansion valve. Remove the capillary tube from the evaporator outlet and remove the expansion valve from the inlet fitting of the evaporator.

To install:

9. Install the expansion valve to the inlet fitting of the evaporator. Tighten the fitting to 9–11 ft. lbs. (12–15 Nm).
10. Connect the liquid tube to the inlet fitting of the expansion valve. Tighten the fitting to 9–11 ft. lbs. (12–15 Nm).
11. Install packing to fix the capillary tube of the expansion valve to the outlet of the evaporator.
12. Assemble the case halves with the 10 retaining clips.
13. Add 0.845–1.014 oz. (25–30 ml) of compressor oil to the evaporator if the evaporator was replaced.
14. Carefully position the evaporator housing and install the mount bolts and nuts.
15. Install the air ducts and secure with bands.
16. Connect the electrical connectors and install the glove box.
17. Install the evaporator grommets at the bulkhead.
18. Unplug the liquid line and install to the evaporator inlet. Tighten the fitting to 9–11 ft. lbs. (12–15 Nm).
19. Unplug the suction line and install to the evaporator outlet. Tighten the fitting to 22–25 ft. lbs. (30–35 Nm).
20. Connect the negative battery cable. Evacuate and recharge the air conditioning system according to the proper procedure.

Fixed Orifice Tube

The fixed orifice tube is located in the liquid line near the condenser and is an integral part of the liquid line. If it is necessary to replace the orifice tube, the liquid line must be replaced or fixed orifice tube replacement kit E5VY–190695–A or equivalent, installed on all except 1991 Escort and Tracer. On 1991 Escort and Tracer, the fixed orifice tube is removed and installed using fixed orifice tube remover/replacer T83L–19990–A or equivalent.

The fixed orifice tube should be replaced whenever a compressor is replaced. If high pressure reads extremely high and low pressure is almost a vacuum, the fixed orifice is plugged and must be replaced.

REMOVAL AND INSTALLATION

Except 1991 Escort and Tracer

LIQUID LINE

NOTE: Whenever a refrigerant line is replaced, it will be necessary to replace the accumulator/drier.

1. Disconnect the negative battery cable. Properly discharge the refrigerant from the air conditioning system. Observe all safety precautions.
2. Disconnect and remove the refrigerant line using a wrench on each side of the tube O-fittings. If the refrigerant line has a spring-lock coupling, disconnect according to the spring-lock coupling disconnect procedure.

To install:

3. Route the new refrigerant line with the protective caps installed.
4. Connect the new refrigerant line into the system using new O-rings lubricated with clean refrigerant oil. Use 2 wrenches when tightening tube O-fittings or perform the spring-lock coupling connect procedure, as necessary.
5. Leak test, evacuate and charge the refrigerant system according to the proper procedure. Observe all safety precautions.

FIXED ORIFICE TUBE REPLACEMENT KIT

1. Disconnect the negative battery cable.
2. Discharge the refrigerant from the air conditioning system according to the proper procedure.
3. Remove the liquid line from the vehicle.
4. Locate the orifice tube by 3 indented notches or a circular depression in the metal portion of the liquid line. Note the angular position of the ends of the liquid line so that it can be reassembled in the correct position.
5. Cut a 2½ in. (63.5mm) section from the tube at the orifice tube location. Do not cut closer than 1 in. (25.4mm) from the start of the bend in the tube.
6. Remove the orifice tube from the housing using pliers. An orifice tube removal tool cannot be used.
7. Flush the 2 pieces of liquid line to remove any contaminants.
8. Lubricate the O-rings with clean refrigerant oil and assemble the orifice tube kit, with the orifice tube installed, to the liquid line. Make sure the flow direction arrow is pointing toward the evaporator end of the liquid line and the taper of each compressor ring is toward the compressor nut.

NOTE: The inlet tube will be positioned against the orifice tube tabs when correctly assembled.

9. While holding the hex of the tube in a vise, tighten each compression nut to 65–70 ft. lbs. (88–94 Nm) with a crow foot wrench.
10. Assemble the liquid line to the vehicle using new O-rings lubricated with clean refrigerant oil.
11. Leak test, evacuate and charge the system according to the proper procedure. Observe all safety precautions.
12. Check the system for proper operation.

1991 Escort and Tracer

1. Disconnect the negative battery cable.
2. Discharge the refrigerant from the air conditioning system according to the proper procedure.
3. Disconnect the spring-lock coupling next to the fixed orifice tube according to the spring-lock coupling disconnect procedure.
4. Remove as many refrigerant line retaining nuts and bolts as necessary to permit access to the open end of the refrigerant line.
5. Using fixed orifice tube remover/replacer T83L–19990–A or equivalent, remove the fixed orifice tube from the refrigerant line.

To install:

6. Install the fixed orifice tube using the orifice tube remover/replacer.
7. Install the refrigerant line retaining nuts and bolts.
8. Using new O-rings lubricated with clean refrigerant oil, connect the spring-lock coupling using the spring-lock coupling connection procedure.

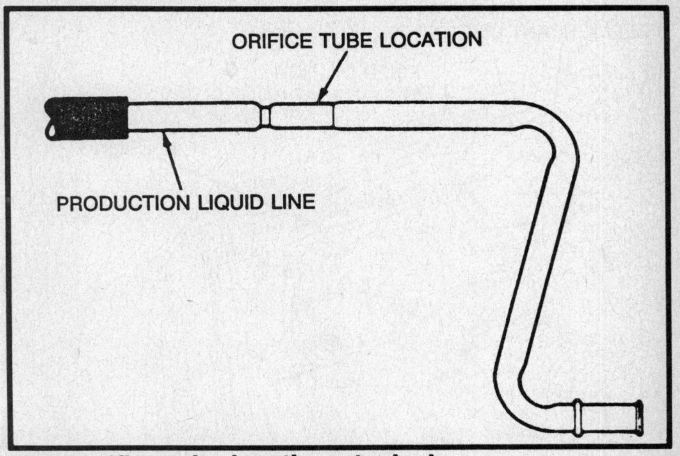
ORIFICE TUBE LOCATION
PRODUCTION LIQUID LINE
Fixed orifice tube location—typical

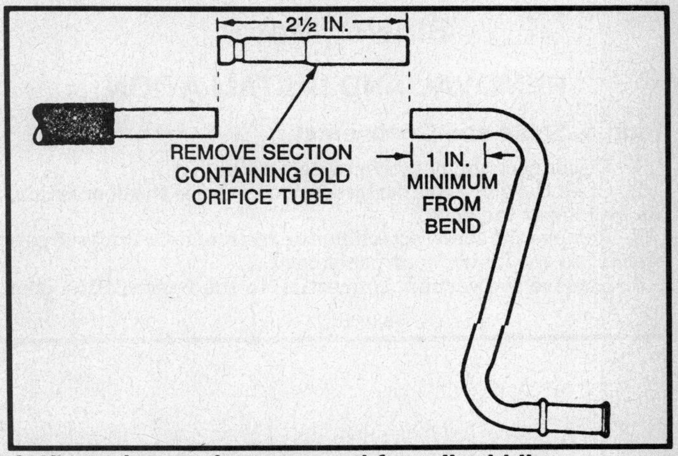
2½ IN.
REMOVE SECTION CONTAINING OLD ORIFICE TUBE
1 IN. MINIMUM FROM BEND
Orifice tube section removed from liquid line

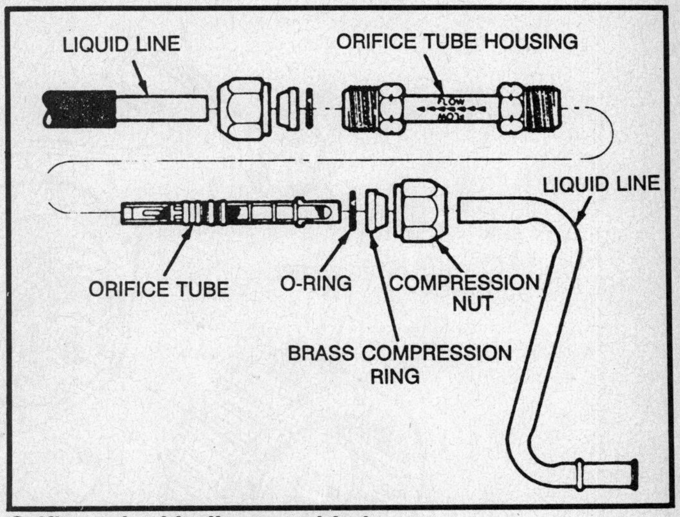
LIQUID LINE
ORIFICE TUBE HOUSING
FLOW
LIQUID LINE
ORIFICE TUBE
O-RING
COMPRESSION NUT
BRASS COMPRESSION RING
Orifice tube kit disassembled

9. Connect the negative battery cable. Leak test, evacuate and charge the system according to the proper procedure. Observe all safety precautions.

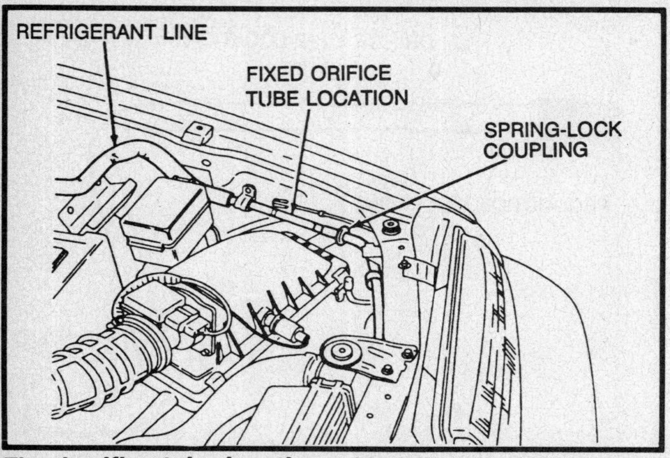
REFRIGERANT LINE
FIXED ORIFICE TUBE LOCATION
SPRING-LOCK COUPLING

Fixed orifice tube location—1991 Escort and Tracer

Blower Motor

REMOVAL AND INSTALLATION

Taurus, Sable and Continental

1. Disconnect the negative battery cable.
2. Open the glove compartment door, release the door retainers and lower the door.
3. Remove the screw attaching the recirculation duct support bracket to the instrument panel cowl.
4. Remove the vacuum connection to the recirculation door vacuum motor. Remove the screws attaching the recirculation duct to the heater assembly.
5. Remove the recirculation duct from the heater assembly, lowering the duct from between the instrument panel and the heater case.
6. Disconnect the blower motor electrical lead. Remove the blower motor wheel clip and remove the blower motor wheel.
7. Remove the blower motor mounting plate screws and remove the blower motor from the evaporator case.
8. Complete the installation of the blower motor by reversing the removal procedure.

Tempo, Topaz and 1989–90 Escort

WITHOUT AIR CONDITIONING

1. Disconnect the negative battery cable.
2. On Escort, remove the air inlet duct assembly. On Tempo and Topaz, remove the right ventilator assembly.
3. Remove the hub clamp spring from the blower wheel hub. Pull the blower wheel from the blower motor shaft.
4. Remove the blower motor flange attaching screws located inside the blower housing.
5. Pull the blower motor out from the blower housing (heater case) and disconnect the blower motor wires from the motor.
6. Connect the wires to the blower motor and position the motor in the blower housing.
7. Install the blower motor attaching screws.
8. Position the blower wheel on the motor shaft and install the hub clamp spring.
9. Install the air inlet duct assembly and the right ventilator assembly.
10. Connect negative battery cable.
11. Check the system for proper operation.

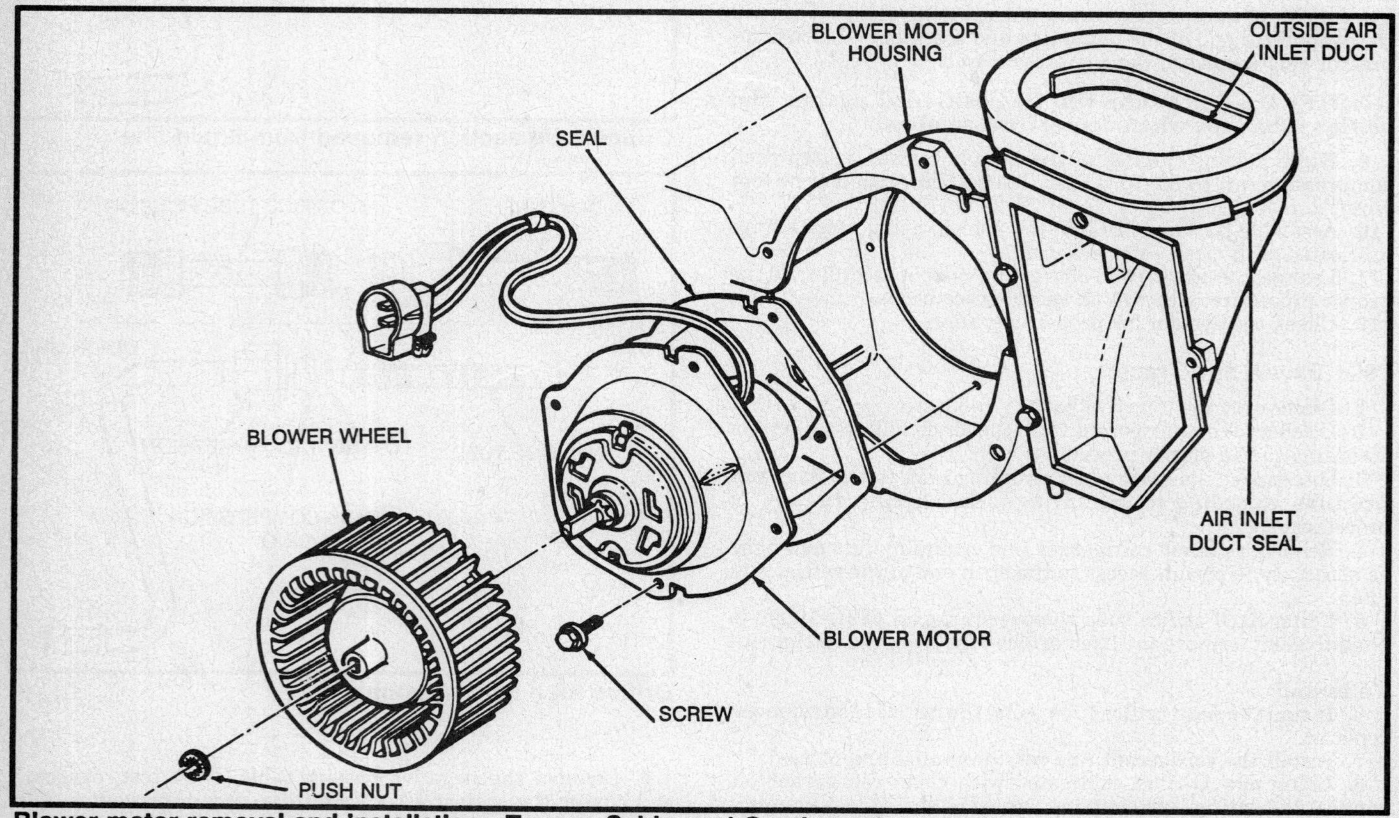
BLOWER MOTOR HOUSING
OUTSIDE AIR INLET DUCT
SEAL
BLOWER WHEEL
AIR INLET DUCT SEAL
BLOWER MOTOR
SCREW
PUSH NUT

Blower motor removal and installation—Taurus, Sable and Continental

WITH AIR CONDITIONING

1. Disconnect the negative battery cable.
2. Remove the glove compartment door and glove compartment.
3. Disconnect the blower motor wires from the blower motor resistor.
4. Loosen the instrument panel at the lower right side prior to removing the motor through the glove compartment opening.
5. Remove the blower motor and mounting plate from the evaporator case.
6. Rotate the motor until the mounting plate flat clears the edge of the glove compartment opening and remove the motor.
7. Remove the hub clamp spring from the blower wheel hub. Then, remove the blower wheel from the motor shaft.
8. Complete the installation of the blower motor by reversing the removal procedure.

1991 Escort and Tracer

1. Disconnect the negative battery cable.
2. Remove the trim panel below the glove compartment.
3. Remove the wiring bracket and bolt and disconnect the blower motor electrical connector.
4. Remove the 3 blower motor mounting bolts and remove the blower motor.
5. Remove the blower wheel retaining clip and remove the blower wheel from the blower motor.

To install:

6. Install the blower wheel and the retaining clip.
7. Position the blower motor and install the mounting bolts.
8. Connect the electrical connector and install the wiring bracket and bolt.
9. Install the trim panel and connect the negative battery cable.

Probe

1. Disconnect the negative battery cable.
2. Remove the sound deadening panel from the passenger side.
3. Remove the glove box assembly and the brace.
4. Remove the cooling hose from the blower motor assembly.
5. Disconnect the electrical connector from the blower motor.
6. Remove the blower motor-to-blower motor housing screws and blower motor.
7. If necessary, remove the blower wheel-to-blower motor clip and the wheel.
8. To install, reverse the removal procedures and check the blower motor operation.

Capri

1. Disconnect the negative battery cable.
2. Disconnect the electrical connector at the blower motor and remove the 3 screws retaining the motor and cover to the blower case.
3. Remove the cover, cooling tube and blower motor.
4. Remove the nut retaining the blower wheel to the blower motor and remove the blower wheel.
5. Remove the gasket from the blower motor.

To install:

6. Position the gasket onto the blower motor and install the blower wheel onto the blower motor. Install the attaching nut.
7. Position the blower motor, cooling tube and cover into the blower case. Install the 3 screws.
8. Connect the electrical connector to the blower motor and connect the negative battery cable. Check the operation of the blower motor.

Festiva

1. Disconnect the negative battery cable.

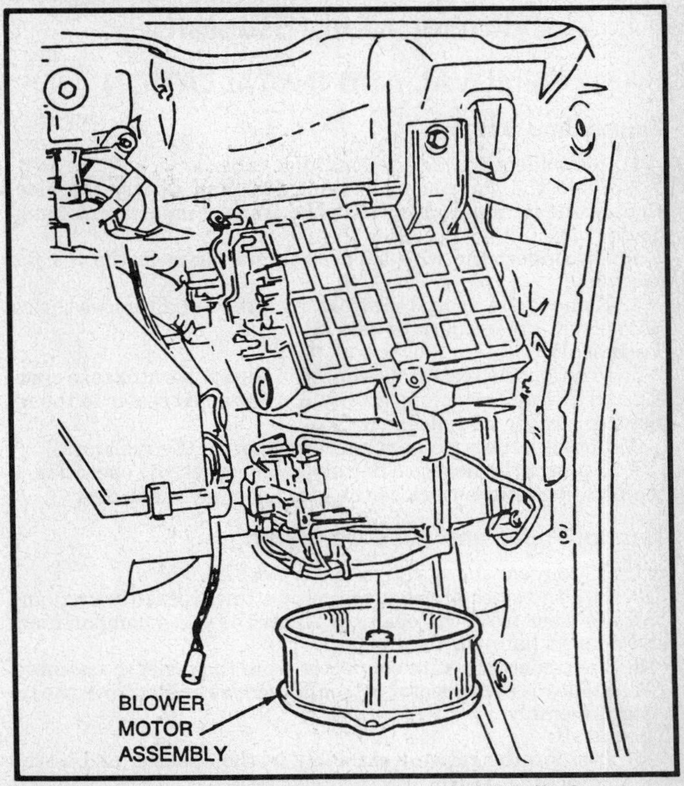
BLOWER
MOTOR
ASSEMBLY

Blower motor assembly removal and installation—Probe

2. Locate the instrument panel spacer brace below the steering column and remove it.
3. Disconnect and lower the length of flexible air discharge hose from below the steering column.
4. Disconnect the blower motor wiring.
5. Remove the blower motor-to-air distribution plenum attaching screws and pull the blower motor with blower wheel away from the heater housing.
6. Remove the blower wheel retaining nut from the motor shaft and remove the blower wheel. Remove the washer from the motor shaft.

To install:

7. Assemble the blower wheel to the new blower motor by reversing the removal procedure.
8. Position the blower assembly onto the air distribution plenum and install the attaching screws. Connect the blower wiring.
9. Raise and connect the length of flexible hose. Install the support brace.
10. Connect the negative battery cable. Check the blower operation.

1989–90 Tracer

1. Disconnect the negative battery cable.
2. From the passenger's side, remove the sound deadening panel.
3. Disconnect the electrical connector from the blower motor assembly.
4. Remove the blower motor-to-blower case screws, the cover, the cooling tube and the motor.
5. Remove the blower wheel-to-motor nut and pull the wheel straight off the motor. Remove the gasket from the motor.
6. To install, reverse the removal procedures. Check the blower motor operation.

Blower Motor Resistor

REMOVAL AND INSTALLATION

Taurus and Sable

1. Disconnect the negative battery cable.
2. Open the glove compartment door and release the glove compartment retainers so that the glove compartment hangs down.
3. Disconnect the wire harness connector from the resistor assembly.
4. Remove the 2 resistor attaching screws and remove the resistor from the evaporator case.

To install:

5. Position the resistor assembly in the evaporator case opening and install 2 attaching screws. Do not apply sealer to the resistor assembly mounting surface.
6. Connect the wire harness connector to the resistor.
7. Connect the negative battery cable, check the operation of the blower motor and close the glove compartment door.

Tempo, Topaz and 1989–90 Escort

1. Disconnect the negative battery cable.
2. Pull the sides of the glove compartment liner inward and pull the liner from the opening. Allow the glove compartment and door to hang on the hinges.
3. Disconnect the wire connector from the resistor assembly.
4. Remove the 2 resistor attaching screws and remove the resistor assembly.

To install:

5. Position the resistor assembly in the opening and install the 2 attaching screws.
6. Connect the wire harness connectors to the resistor assembly.
7. Connect the negative battery cable and check for proper operation of the blower motor in all blower speeds.
8. Install the glove compartment in the glove compartment opening.

1991 Escort and Tracer

1. Disconnect the negative battery cable.
2. Disconnect the 2 resistor assembly electrical connectors.
3. Remove the 2 attaching bolts and remove the resistor assembly.
4. Installation is the reverse of the removal procedure.

Probe

1. Disconnect the negative battery cable.
2. Remove the passenger side sound deadening panel.
3. Remove the 2 attching screws from the blower resistor assembly at the bottom of the blower case and remove the assembly from the blower case.
4. Disconnect the 2 electrical connectors from the blower resistor assembly.

To install:

5. Connect both electrical connectors to the blower resistor assembly.
6. Position the resistor into the blower case and install the 2 attaching screws.
7. Install the passenger side sound deadening panel.
8. Connect the negative battery cable and check the blower motor for proper operation.

Capri

1. Disconnect the negative battery cable.
2. Disconnect the electrical connectors at the resistor and blower motor and remove the 2 screws and resistor from the blower case.

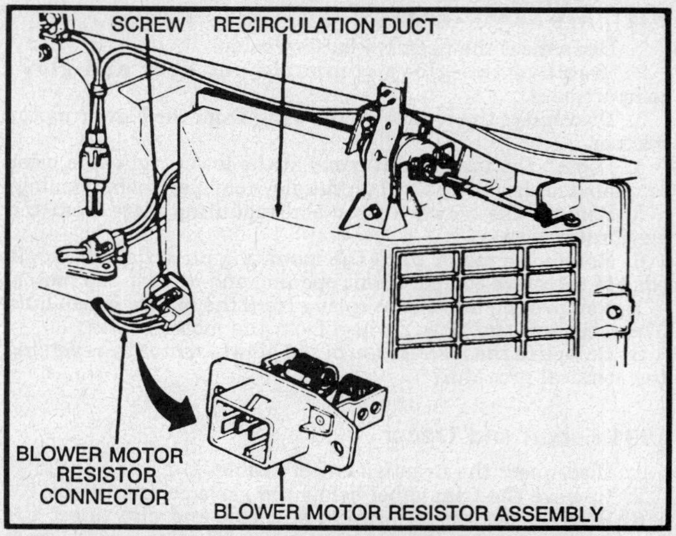
SCREW
RECIRCULATION DUCT
BLOWER MOTOR RESISTOR CONNECTOR
BLOWER MOTOR RESISTOR ASSEMBLY

Blower motor resistor location—Taurus and Sable with manual air conditioning

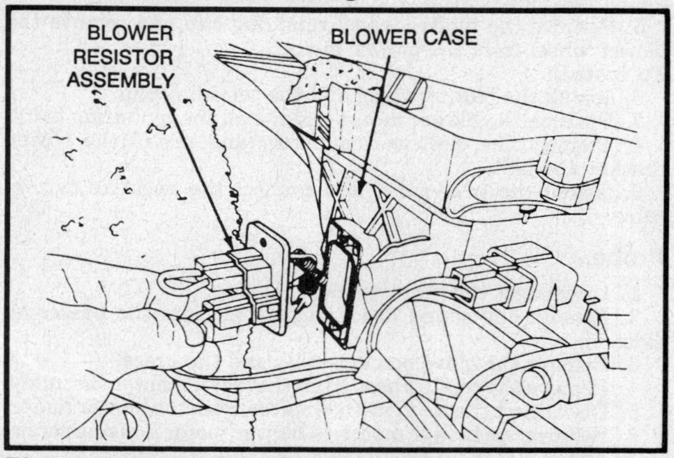
BLOWER RESISTOR ASSEMBLY
BLOWER CASE

Blower motor resistor location—Probe

3. Lower the glove compartment below the stops and disconnect the blower feed connector.
4. Installation is the reverse of the removal procedure.

Festiva

1. Disconnect the negative battery cable.
2. Remove the airflow duct located below the steering column.
3. Disconnect the blower resistor wiring.
4. Remove the attaching screws and the blower resistor.

NOTE: Do not remove the screw in front of the blower resistor. This screw attaches the blower resistor mounting plate to the air distribution plenum. Removal of this screw and the blower resistor attaching screws will allow the plate to fall into the air distribution plenum. Once in the plenum, the plate can be retrieved only by removal of the instrument panel.

To install:

5. Position the resistor on the plenum and install the attaching screws.
6. Connect the blower resistor wiring and install the airflow duct.

7. Connect the negative battery cable and check the blower motor operation.

1989–90 Tracer

1. Disconnect the negative battery cable.
2. Remove the passenger side sound deadening panel.
3. Disconnect the electrical connectors at the resistor and blower motor at the bottom of the blower case.
4. Remove the 2 attaching screws and the resistor from the blower case.
5. Disconnect the blower feed connector.

To install:

6. Connect the blower feed connector and position the resistor into the blower case.
7. Install the 2 attaching screws and connect the electrical connector at the resistor and blower motor.
8. Install the passenger side sound deadening panel.
9. Connect the negative battery cable and check the blower motor operation.

Heater Core

REMOVAL AND INSTALLATION

Taurus, Sable and Continental

1. Disconnect the negative battery cable.

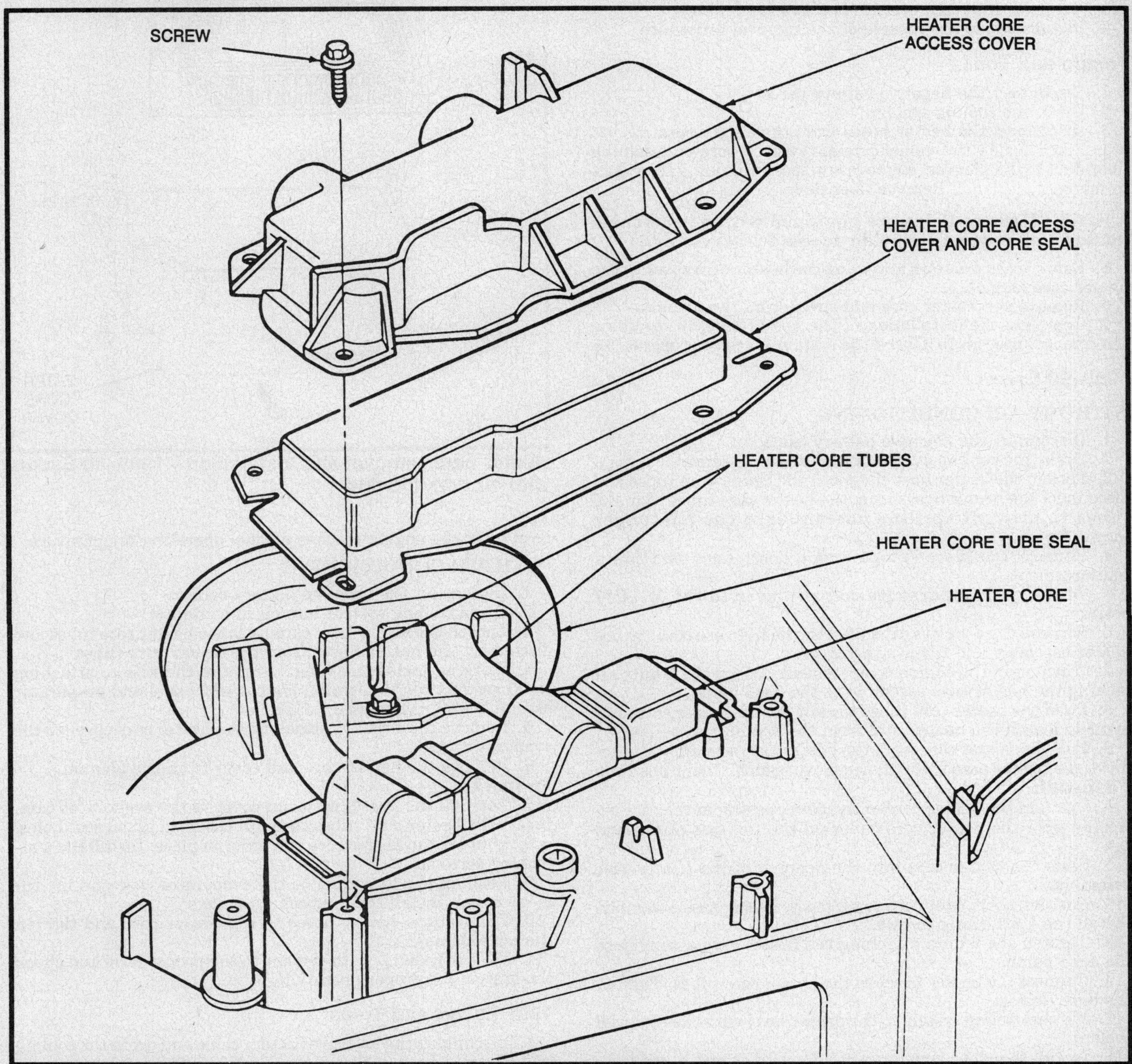
SCREW
HEATER CORE ACCESS COVER
HEATER CORE ACCESS COVER AND CORE SEAL
HEATER CORE TUBES
HEATER CORE TUBE SEAL
HEATER CORE

Heater core access cover removal—Taurus, Sable and Continental

2. Drain the cooling system.
3. Disconnect the heater hoses from the heater core.
4. Remove the instrument panel assembly and lay it on the front seat.
5. Remove the evaporator case.
6. Remove the vacuum source line from the heater core tube seal.
7. Remove the seal from the heater core tubes.
8. On Continental, remove the screws attaching the blend door actuator to the door shaft on the evaporator case. Remove the actuator from the case.
9. Remove the heater core access cover and foam seal from the evaporator case.
10. Lift the heater core with 3 foam seals from the evaporator case. Transfer the foam seals to the new heater core.
11. Installation is the reverse of the removal procedure.

Tempo and Topaz

1. Disconnect the negative battery cable.
2. Drain the cooling system.
3. Disconnect the heater hoses from the heater core.
4. From inside the vehicle, remove the 2 screws retaining floor duct to the plenum. Remove one screw retaining floor duct to instrument panel. Remove floor duct.

NOTE: Most vehicles are equipped with a removable heater core cover to provide access for servicing.

5. Remove the 4 screws attaching the heater core cover to the heater case assembly.
6. Remove the heater core and cover from the plenum.
7. Complete the installation of the heater core by reversing the removal procedure. Check the system for proper operation.

1989–90 Escort

WITHOUT AIR CONDITIONING

1. Disconnect the negative battery cable.
2. Drain the cooling system into a clean container.
3. Loosen the heater hose clamps at the heater core tubes and disconnect the heater hoses from the heater core tubes. Cap the tubes to prevent spilling coolant into the passenger compartment.
4. Remove the glove compartment door, liner and lower reinforcement.
5. Move the temperature control lever to the **WARM** position.
6. Remove the 4 screws attaching the heater core cover to the heater assembly and remove the cover.
7. Working in the engine compartment, loosen the 2 nuts attaching the heater case assembly to the dash panel.
8. Push the heater core tubes toward the passenger compartment to loosen the heater core from the heater case assembly.
9. Pull the heater core from the heater case assembly and remove the heater core through the glove compartment opening.

To install:

10. Position the heater core in the core opening in the case assembly with the heater core tubes on the top side of the end tank.
11. Slide the heater core into the opening of the heater case assembly.
12. Position the heater core cover to the heater case assembly. Install the 4 attaching screws.
13. Tighten the 2 nuts attaching the heater case assembly to the dash panel.
14. Connect the heater hoses to the heater core tubes. Tighten the hose clamps.
15. Fill the cooling system to the proper level with the removed coolant.
16. Install the glove compartment door, liner and hinge bar.
17. Check the heater for proper operation. Check the coolant level after the engine reaches normal operating temperature.

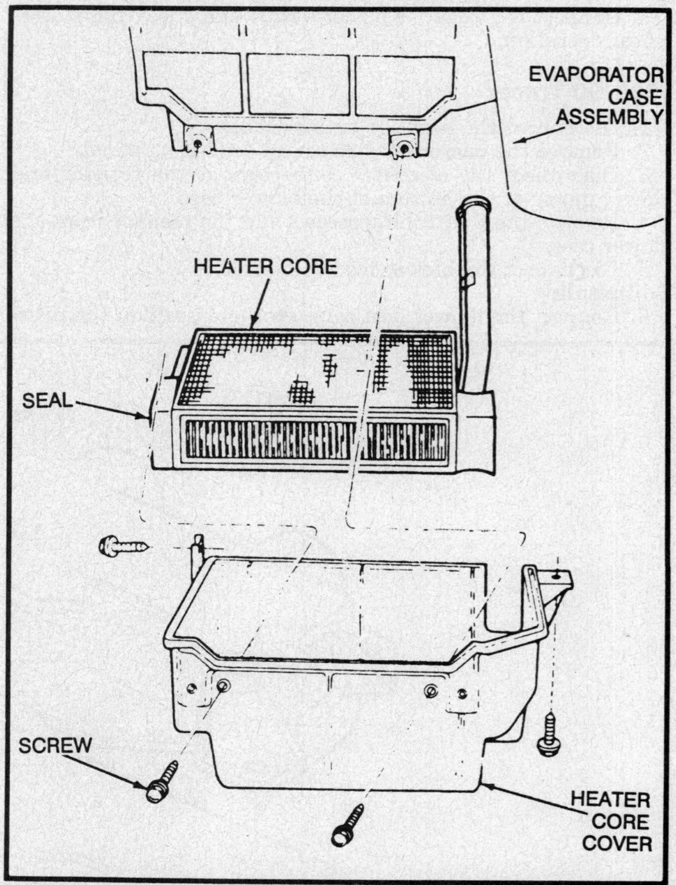
EVAPORATOR CASE ASSEMBLY
HEATER CORE
SEAL
SCREW
HEATER CORE COVER

Heater core removal and installation – 1989–90 Escort with air conditioning

WITH AIR CONDITIONING

1. Disconnect the negative battery cable.
2. Drain cooling system into clean container.
3. Loosen the heater hose clamps at the heater core tubes and disconnect the heater hoses from the heater core tubes.
4. Working inside the vehicle, remove the screws attaching the floor duct to the plenum, instrument panel and evaporator assembly and remove the floor duct.
5. Remove the 4 screws attaching the heater core cover to the evaporator case.
6. Remove the heater core and cover from the plenum.

To install:

7. Position the heater core and cover to the evaporator case. Insert the heater core tubes through the dash panel seal holes.
8. Support the heater core and cover in place. Install the 4 attaching screws.
9. Position the floor duct to the evaporator case and instrument panel. Install the 4 attaching screws.
10. Connect the heater hoses to the heater core and tighten the hose clamps.
11. Fill the radiator with coolant to the proper level and check the system for proper operation.

1991 Escort and Tracer

1. Disconnect the negative battery cable and drain the cooling system.
2. Disconnect the heater hoses at the bulkhead.

3. Remove the instrument panel as follows:

a. Remove the 4 bolts securing the steering column to the instrument panel frame. Lower the steering column.

b. Remove the cap screws securing the instrument cluster bezel to the instrument panel and remove the instrument cluster bezel.

c. Disconnect the speedometer cable at the transaxle by pulling the cable out of the vehicle speed sensor.

d. Remove the screws and bolts securing the instrument cluster to the instrument panel. Pull the instrument cluster out slightly and disconnect the electrical connectors from the rear of the instrument cluster.

e. Disconnect the speedometer cable from the instrument cluster. Remove the instrument cluster from the instrument panel.

f. Detach the hood release cable from the left lower dash trim panel. Carefully pry out both dash side panels.

g. Remove the 4 retaining screws and the left lower dash trim panel. Disconnect all necessary electrical connectors.

h. Remove the 2 hinge-to-instrument panel retaining screws and remove the glove compartment.

i. Remove the climate control assembly and the ash tray.

j. Remove the 7 accessory console retaining screws. Disconnect the radio antenna, radio wire connectors and cigarette lighter connector.

k. Remove the retaining screws and the right lower dash trim panel. Disconnect the 3 amplifier wire connectors.

l. Remove the 4 bolts attaching the instrument panel frame to the floor pan. Remove the bolt from both of the lower instrument panel mounts.

m. Remove the 2 bolts from both of the upper instrument panel mounts. Remove the retaining screw and the defroster duct bezel.

n. Remove the 3 mounting bolts that attach the upper instrument panel to the cowl and remove the instrument panel from the vehicle.

NOTE: Use care to prevent any damage to the instrument panel or the surrounding interior trim.

4. Disconnect the mode selector and temperature control cables from the cams and retaining clips.

5. Remove the necessary defroster duct screws and loosen the capscrew that secures the heater-to-blower clamp.

6. Remove the 3 heater unit mounting nuts and disconnect the antenna lead from the retaining clip. Remove the heater unit.

7. Remove the insulator and the 4 brace capscrews. Remove the brace.

8. Remove the heater core from the heater unit.

To install:

9. Install the heater core into the heater unit and install the brace.

10. Install the brace capscrews and the insulator.

NOTE: If a new heater unit is being installed, save the keys that are found on the new unit for mode selector and temperature control cable adjustment.

11. Position the heater unit and attach the defroster and floor ducting. Install the heater unit mounting nuts.

12. Tighten the heater-to-blower clamp capscrew and install the defroster duct screws. Connect the antenna lead to the retaining clip.

13. Install the instrument panel by reversing the removal procedure.

14. Connect and adjust the mode selector and temperature control cables. Connect the heater hoses at the bulkhead.

15. Fill the cooling system and connect the negative battery cable. Start the engine and check for leaks. Check the coolant level and fill as necessary.

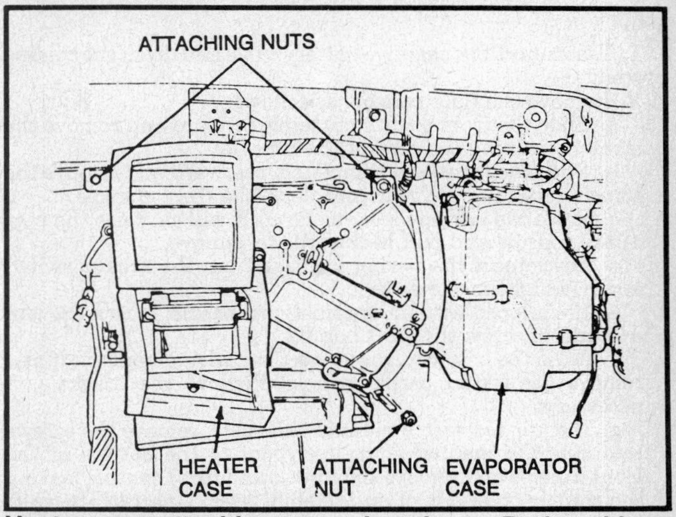
ATTACHING NUTS
HEATER CASE
ATTACHING NUT
EVAPORATOR CASE

Heater case attaching screw locations—Probe with air conditioning

Probe

WITHOUT AIR CONDITIONING

1. Disconnect the negative battery cable. Remove the instrument panel.

2. Drain the cooling system to a level below the heater core.

3. Disconnect and plug the hoses from the heater core.

4. Remove the main air duct from the heater case.

5. Remove the heater case-to-chassis screws and pull the heater case straight out; be careful not to damage the heater core extension tubes.

6. Remove the heater core tube braces-to-heater case screws and the tube braces.

7. Lift the heater core straight up and from the heater case.

8. To install, reverse the removal procedures. Refill the cooling system. Start the engine, allow it to reach normal operating temperatures and check the heater operation and leaks.

WITH AIR CONDITIONING

1. Disconnect the negative battery cable. Remove the instrument panel.

2. Drain the cooling system to a level below the heater core.

3. Properly discharge the air conditioning system. Disconnect and plug the refrigerant lines from the evaporator case.

4. Disconnect the electrical connectors from the air conditioning relays at the top of the evaporator case.

5. Remove the charcoal canister from the vehicle.

6. From both ends of the evaporator case, remove the air duct bands. Remove the drain hose from the evaporator case.

7. Remove the evaporator case-to-chassis nuts and the case from the vehicle.

8. Disconnect and plug the hoses from the heater core.

9. Remove the heater case-to-chassis bolts and pull the heater case straight; be careful not to damage the heater core extension tubes.

10. Remove the heater core tube braces-to-heater case screws and the tube braces.

11. Lift the heater core straight up and from the heater case.

12. To install, reverse the removal procedures. Refill the cooling system. Evacuate and charge the air conditioning system according to the proper procedure.

13. Start the engine, allow it to reach normal operating temperatures and check the heater and air conditioning system for proper operation and leaks.

Capri

1. Disconnect the negative battery cable and drain the cooling system.
2. Remove the floor console as follows:
   a. Slide the front seats completely forward and remove the screws retaining the rear of the console.
   b. Slide the front seat completely rearward and remove the screws retaining the rear console to the front console.
   c. Raise the parking lever as far as it will go, raise the rear of the console and pull backwards to remove.
   d. Disconnect the wiring harness from the mirror switch and headlight motor switch.
   e. If equipped with an automatic transaxle, loosen the jam nut and unscrew the shift handle.
   f. Raise the ash tray, disconnect the wiring beneath it and remove the center carpet panels. Remove the brackets, if necessary.
   g. If equipped with a manual transaxle, remove the screws retaining the manual shift lever boot to the bottom of the front console and remove the screws and front console leaving the shift knob and boot on the shift lever. Unscrew the shift knob with the boot and remove from the shift lever, if necessary.
   h. If equipped with an automatic transaxle, remove the screws and shift quadrant. Disconnect the shift quadrant light connector.
3. Remove the instrument panel as follows:
   a. Remove the left and right lower cowl trim panels.
   b. Remove the heater/radio bezel, trim covers, instrument cluster bezel and storage compartment.
   c. Remove the instrument cluster and the steering column.
   d. Loosen the nut retaining the hood release cable to the lower instrument panel and position the cable aside.
   e. Remove the radio and the heater control panel.
   f. Tag and remove all wiring harness retainers and connectors from the instrument panel.
   g. Remove the 3 screws, lockwashers and plain washers located near the base of the windshield. Remove the 2 bolts and washers from each side of the instrument panel. An access panel is provided for the upper bolts.
   h. Remove the 2 screws and lockwashers retaining the instrument panel to the center floor bracket. Remove the 2 screws retaining the instrument panel to the steering column support.
   i. With the help of an assistant, gently slide the instrument panel outward. Disconnect the ducts and wiring during removal.
4. Disconnect and plug the heater hoses at the extension tubes.
5. Remove the plastic rivets and both defroster hoses. Remove the main air duct connecting the heater case to the blower case or air conditioning unit, if equipped.
6. Roll back the carpet to gain access to the lower duct and lower mounting bolts. It may be necessary to remove the carpet fasteners.
7. Disconnect the lower duct for the rear seat supply from the heater case.
8. Remove the cable ends from the heater case, if still connected and remove the wiring harness.
9. Remove the 2 lower bolts, 2 upper nuts and 1 center retaining nut from the blower case and remove the heater case.
10. Remove the 3 screws attaching the heater core cover to the heater case and remove the cover. Remove the screws securing the tube braces.
11. Loosen the clamps and remove the extension tubes from the heater core. Remove the O-ring from the outlet tube.
12. Remove the heater core by pulling it straight out. Remove the extension tubes and grommets, if necessary.

To install:

13. Install the grommets and extension tubes, if removed. Make sure the grommets are flush with the engine compartment wall.
14. Install the heater core into the heater case and install a new O-ring onto the outlet extension tube. Connect the extension tubes to the heater core and tighten the clamps.
15. Secure the extension tube braces with the screws and install the heater core cover with the 3 screws.
16. Position the heater case onto the mounting studs and guide the extension tubes through the dash panel. Make sure the grommets are sealed around the extension tubes.
17. Install 2 upper nuts, 1 center retaining nut and 2 lower bolts. Tighten all fasteners to 5–7 ft. lbs. (7–10 Nm).
18. Install the lower duct onto the heater case. Reposition the carpet and install the fasteners, if removed.
19. Attach the wiring harness and connect the defroster hoses and main air duct to the heater case. Install the plastic retaining rivets.
20. Connect the heater hoses and tighten the clamps to 3–4 ft. lbs. (4–6 Nm).
21. Install the instrument panel by reversing the removal procedure. Connect the control cable to the heater case and adjust the cable.
22. Install the floor console by reversing the removal procedure.
23. Fill the cooling system and connect the negative battery cable. Operate the heater and check for leaks.

Festiva

1. Disconnect the negative battery cable. Drain the cooling system.
2. Remove the instrument panel.
3. Remove the air distribution plenum by performing the following steps:
   a. Disconnect the heater hoses from inside the engine compartment.
   b. Disconnect the blower motor and blower resistor wiring.
   c. Disengage the wiring harness and antenna lead from the routing bracket on the front of the air distribution housing.
   d. Loosen the clamp screw securing the connector duct to the air inlet housing.
   e. Remove the upper and lower plenum attaching nuts. Disengage the plenum from the defroster ducts and remove from the vehicle.
4. Disconnect the link from the 2 defroster doors.
5. Locate and remove the screws just above and to the right of the blower resistor. Turn the plenum around and remove the screw located to the left of the blower motor opening.
6. Remove the retaining clips that secure the the plenum halves. Separate the plenum halves.
7. Remove the heater core and tube insert/stiffener. Remove the tube insert/stiffener from the heater core and transfer to the new unit. Install the new heater core.
8. Complete the assembly and installation of the heater core and distribution plenum by reversing the disassembly and removal procedures.
9. Install the instrument panel.
10. Connect the negative battery cable. Refill and bleed the cooling system.

1989–90 Tracer

1. Disconnect the negative battery cable.
2. From under the instrument panel, remove both sound deadening panels and the lap duct register panel.
3. From the blower motor case and heater case, disconnect the 3 air door control cables.
4. From behind the instrument cluster, depress the speedometer lock tab and pull the speedometer cable from the cluster.
5. From behind the instrument cluster, depress the lock tab, located in the center of the connector, of the 3 electrical harness connectors and pull the connectors from the cluster.

6. From under the steering column, remove the lap duct brace-to-instrument panel screws, the brace, the lap duct and the driver's demister tube.
7. Remove the lower cover-to-steering column screws and the lower cover.
8. Remove the steering column-to-instrument panel bolts and lower the steering column.
9. Remove the glove box-to-instrument panel screws and the glove box.
10. Remove the hood release-to-instrument panel nut and move the release cable aside.
11. Remove the center floor console-to-chassis screws and the cover.
12. From below the radio, remove the lower trim panel-to-instrument panel screws and the lower panel.
13. Using a small prybar, pry the instrument panel-to-chassis bolt covers from the perimeter of the instrument panel. Remove the instrument panel-to-chassis nuts/bolts. Lift and pull the panel out slightly.
14. Disconnect the electrical connector from the blower motor assembly.
15. From the rear of the radio, disconnect the antenna cable.
16. From the left corner of the instrument panel, disconnect the 3 instrument panel harness connectors and remove the instrument panel.
17. Using a clean drain pan, place it under the radiator, open the radiator drain cock, remove the radiator cap and drain the cooling system to a level below the heater case.
18. Disconnect and plug the heater hoses from the heater case.
19. Remove the defroster tubes-to-heater case push pins and the defroster tubes from the heater case. Remove the main air duct-to-heater case push pins and the main air duct.
20. From under the heater case, remove the lower carpet panel push pins, screw and the panel.
21. From the heater case, disconnect the electrical harness braces and remove the lower brace screws and brace.
22. Remove the heater case-to-chassis nut and bolts. Remove the lower duct-to-heater case push pins and lower duct. Remove the heater case by pulling it straight out; be careful not to damage the extension tubes.
23. Remove the heater core cover-to-heater case screws and the cover. Remove the tube braces and pull the heater core straight out.
24. Remove the outlet extension tube clip and tube. Loosen the inlet extension tube clamp and the extension tube.

To install:

25. To install, use a new O-ring (outlet extension tube) and reverse the removal procedures.
26. Refill the cooling system.
27. Start the engine, allow it to reach normal operating temperature and turn the heater control to full heat. Inspect the system for leakage and operation.
28. Connect the negative battery cable.

Evaporator

REMOVAL AND INSTALLATION

Taurus, Sable and Continental

NOTE: Whenever an evaporator is removed, it will be necessary to replace the accumulator/drier.

1. Disconnect the negative battery cable.
2. Drain the coolant from the radiator into a clean container.
3. Properly discharge the refrigerant from the air conditioning system.
4. Disconnect the heater hoses from the heater core. Plug the heater core tubes.
5. Disconnect the vacuum supply hose from the in-line vacuum check valve in the engine compartment.

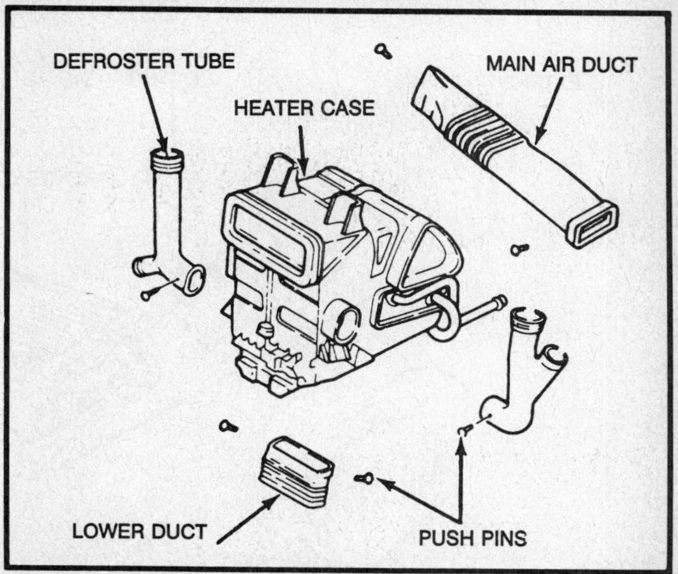
DEFROSTER TUBE
MAIN AIR DUCT
HEATER CASE
LOWER DUCT
PUSH PINS

Heater case and duct assembly – 1989–90 Tracer

6. Disconnect the liquid line and the accumulator from the evaporator core at the dash panel. Cap the refrigerant lines and evaporator core to prevent entrance of dirt and moisture.
7. Remove the instrument panel and place it on the front seat.
8. Remove the screw holding the instrument panel shake brace to the evaporator case and remove the instrument panel shake brace.
9. Remove the 2 screws attaching the floor register and rear seat duct to the bottom of the evaporator case.
10. Disconnect the vacuum line, electrical connections and aspirator hose from the evaporator case.
11. Remove the 3 nuts attaching the evaporator case to the dash panel in the engine compartment. Remove the 2 screws attaching the support brackets to the cowl top panel.
12. Carefully pull the evaporator assembly away from the dash panel and remove the evaporator case from the vehicle.
13. Disconnect and remove the vacuum harness.
14. Remove the 6 screws attaching the recirculation duct and remove the duct from the evaporator case.
15. Remove the 2 screws from the air inlet duct and remove the duct from the evaporator case.
16. Remove the support bracket from the evaporator case.
17. If equipped with automatic temperature control, remove the screws holding the electronic connector bracket to the recirculation duct and remove the blend door actuator and cold engine lock out switch, which is held on by spring tension at the outermost heater core tube.
18. Remove the moulded seals from the evaporator core tubes.
19. Drill a $^{3}/_{16}$ in. (4.75mm) hole in both upright tabs on top of the evaporator case.
20. Using a suitable tool, cut the top of the evaporator case between the raised outline. Fold the cutout cover back from the opening and lift the evaporator core from the case.

To install:

NOTE: Add 3 oz. (90 ml) of clean refrigerant oil to a new replacement evaporator core to maintain total system refrigerant oil requirements.

21. Transfer the foam core seals to the new evaporator core.
22. Position the evaporator core in the case and close the cutout cover.
23. Install a spring nut on each of the 2 upright tabs with 2 holes drilled in the front flange. Make sure the holes in the

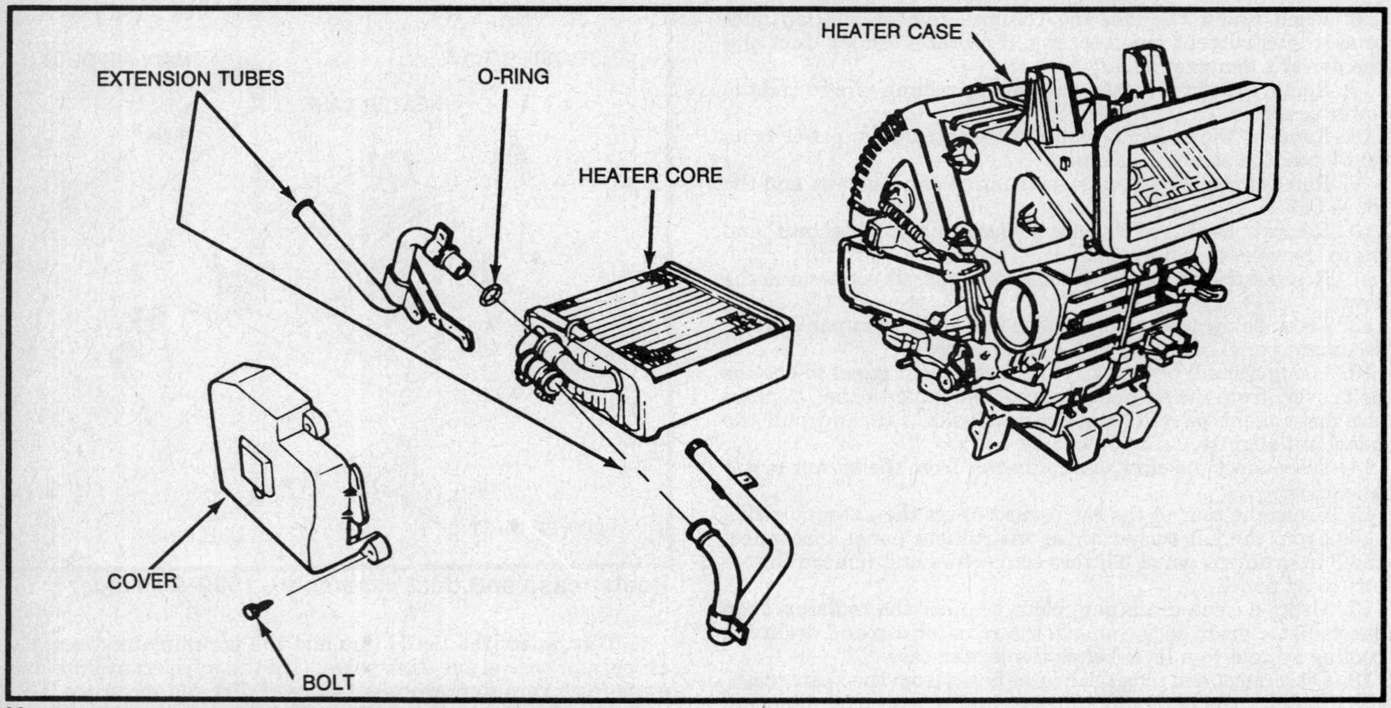
HEATER CASE
EXTENSION TUBES
O-RING
HEATER CORE
COVER
BOLT

Heater core removal and installation—1989–90 Tracer

spring nuts are aligned with the $^3/_{16}$ in. (4.75mm) holes drilled in the tab and flange. Install and tighten the screw in each spring nut to secure the cutout cover in the closed position.

24. Install caulking cord to seal the evaporator case against leakage along the cut line.
25. Install the air inlet duct to the evaporator case and tighten the 2 screws. Install the recirculation duct to the evaporator case and tighten 6 screws.
26. If equipped with automatic temperature control, install the electrical connector bracket to the recirculation duct, install the speed controller connector to the bracket and attach the blend door actuator to the evaporator case. Install the electrical connector to the bracket. Attach the cold engine lock out switch by snapping the spring clip in place on the outermost heater core tube.
27. Install the vacuum harness to the evaporator case and install the foam seals over the evaporator tubes. Assemble the support bracket to the evaporator case.
28. Position the evaporator case assembly to the dash panel and cowl top panel at the air inlet opening. Install the 2 screws attaching the support brackets to the top cowl panel.
29. Install the 3 nuts in the engine compartment attaching the evaporator case to the dash panel.
30. Connect the vacuum line, electrical connections and aspirator hose at the evaporator case.
31. Install the floor register and rear seat duct to the evaporator case and tighten the 2 attaching screws.
32. Install the instrument panel shake brace and screw to the evaporator case.
33. Install the instrument panel.
34. Connect the liquid line and accumulator/drier to the evaporator core and connect the heater hoses to the heater core.
35. Connect the black vacuum supply hose to the vacuum check valve in the engine compartment.
36. Fill the radiator to the correct level with the previously removed coolant.
37. Connect the negative battery cable and leak test, evacuate and charge the air conditioning system according to the proper procedure.
38. Check the system for proper operation.

Tempo, Topaz and 1989–90 Escort

NOTE: Whenever an evaporator is removed, it will be necessary to replace the accumulator/drier.

1. Disconnect the negative battery cable.
2. Drain the coolant from the radiator into a clean container.
3. Properly discharge the refrigerant from the air conditioning system.
4. Disconnect the heater hoses from the heater core. Plug the heater core tubes.
5. Disconnect the liquid line and the accumulator/drier inlet tube from the evaporator core at the dash panel. Cap the refrigerant lines and evaporator core to prevent the entrance of dirt and excess moisture.
6. Remove the instrument panel and lay it on the front seat.
7. Disconnect the wire harness connector from the blower motor resistor.
8. Remove 1 screw attaching the bottom of the evaporator case to the dash panel and remove the instrument panel brace from the cowl top panel.
9. Remove the 2 nuts attaching the evaporator case to the dash panel in the engine compartment.
10. Loosen the sound insulation from the cowl top panel in the area around the air inlet opening.
11. Remove the 2 screws attaching the support bracket and the brace to the cowl top panel.
12. Remove the 4 screws attaching the air inlet duct to the evaporator case and remove the air inlet duct.
13. Remove the evaporator-to-cowl seals from the evaporator tubes.
14. On Tempo and Topaz, perform the following procedure:
    a. Using a suitable tool, cut the top from the evaporator case completely.
    b. Remove the cover from the case and lift the evaporator core from the case.
    c. Use a suitable tool to remove any rough edges from the case that may have been caused by the cutting.

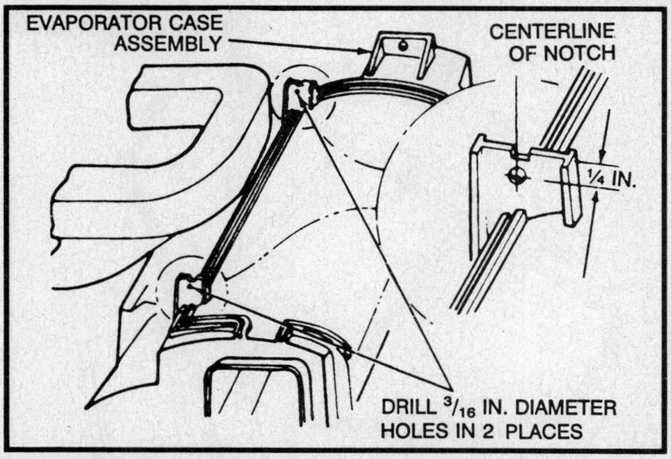
EVAPORATOR CASE ASSEMBLY
CENTERLINE OF NOTCH
¼ IN.
DRILL ³/₁₆ IN. DIAMETER HOLES IN 2 PLACES

Drilling holes in evaporator case tabs—Taurus, Sable and Continental

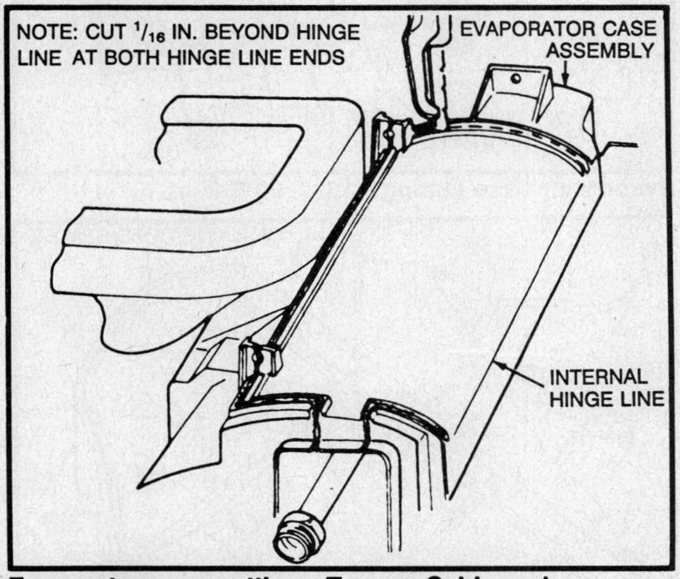
NOTE: CUT ¹/₁₆ IN. BEYOND HINGE LINE AT BOTH HINGE LINE ENDS
EVAPORATOR CASE ASSEMBLY
INTERNAL HINGE LINE

Evaporator case cutting—Taurus, Sable and Continental

15. On Escort, perform the following procedure:

a. Drill a $^{3}/_{16}$ in. hole in both upright tabs on top of the evaporator case.

b. Using a suitable tool, cut the top of the evaporator case between the raised outlines.

c. Remove the blower motor resistor from the evaporator case.

d. Fold the cutout cover back from the opening and lift the evaporator core from the case.

To install:

NOTE: Add 3 oz. (90 ml) of clean refrigerant oil to a new replacement evaporator core to maintain total system refrigerant oil requirements.

16. On Tempo and Topaz, install the new evaporator core and cover according to the instructions in the new evaporator core kit, E83H–19850–BB or equivalent.

17. On Escort, perform the following procedure:

a. Transfer the foam core seals to the new evaporator core.

b. Position the evaporator core in the case and close the cutout cover.

c. Install a spring nut on each of the 2 upright tabs and with the 2 holes drilled in the front flange. Make sure the holes in the spring nuts are aligned with the $^{3}/_{16}$ in. holes drilled in the tab and flange. Install and tighten the screw in each spring nut to secure the cutout cover in the closed position.

d. Install caulking cord to seal the evaporator case against leakage along the cut line.

e. Using new caulking cord, assemble the air inlet duct to the evaporator case.

f. Install the blower motor resistor and install the foam seal over the evaporator core and heater core tubes.

18. On all vehicles, position the evaporator case assembly to the dash panel and the cowl top panel at the air inlet opening. Install the 2 screws to attach the support bracket and brace to the cowl top panel.

19. Install the 2 nuts in the engine compartment to attach the evaporator case to the dash panel. Inspect the evaporator drain

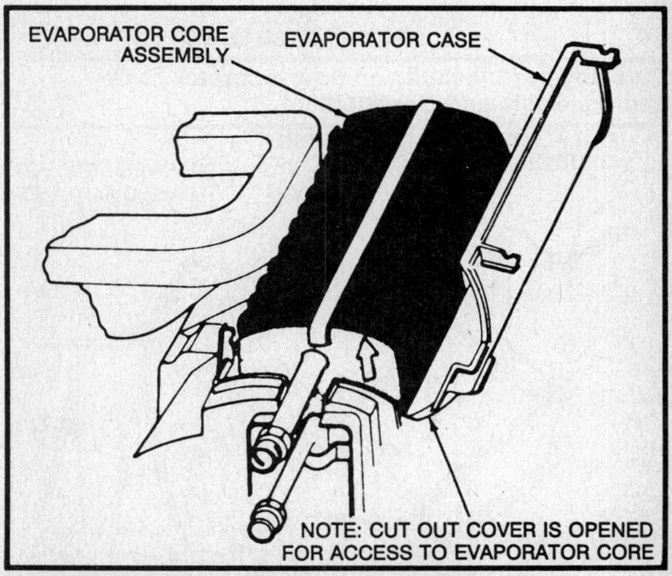
EVAPORATOR CORE ASSEMBLY
EVAPORATOR CASE
NOTE: CUT OUT COVER IS OPENED FOR ACCESS TO EVAPORATOR CORE

Evaporator core removal—Taurus, Sable and Continental

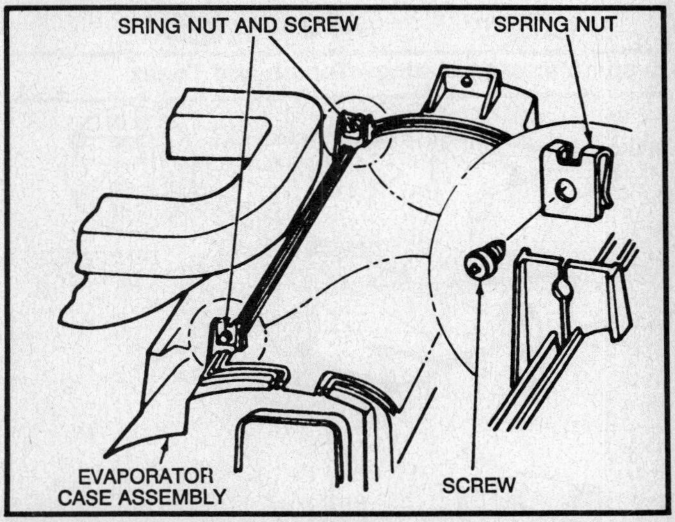
SRING NUT AND SCREW
SPRING NUT
EVAPORATOR CASE ASSEMBLY
SCREW

Securing cutout evaporator case cover in closed position—Taurus, Sable and Continental

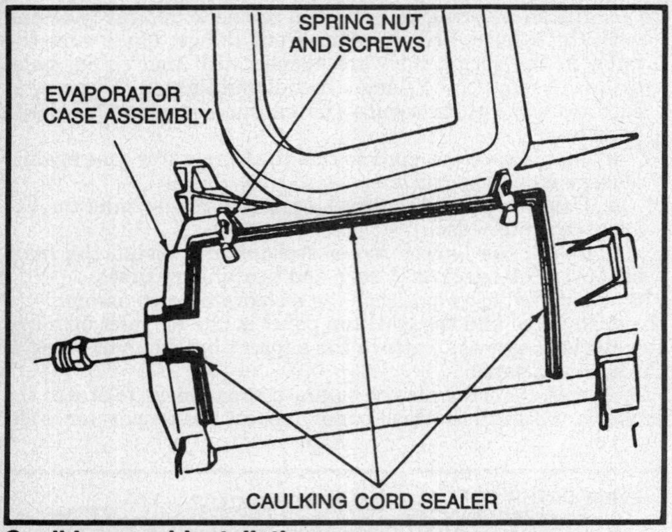
SPRING NUT AND SCREWS
EVAPORATOR CASE ASSEMBLY
CAULKING CORD SEALER

Caulking cord installation on evaporator case—Taurus, Sable and Continental

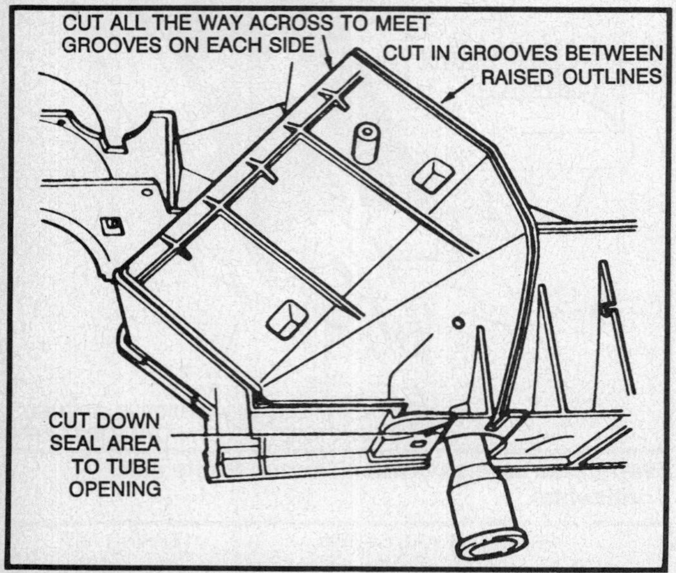
CUT ALL THE WAY ACROSS TO MEET GROOVES ON EACH SIDE
CUT IN GROOVES BETWEEN RAISED OUTLINES
CUT DOWN SEAL AREA TO TUBE OPENING

Evaporator case cutting—Tempo and Topaz

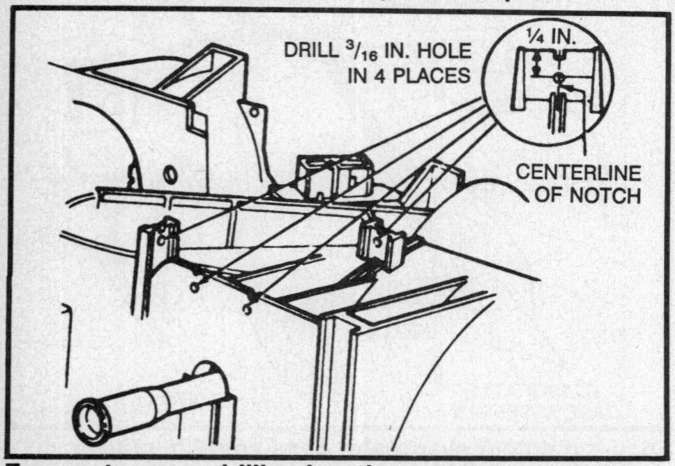
DRILL 3/16 IN. HOLE IN 4 PLACES
1/4 IN.
CENTERLINE OF NOTCH

Evaporator case drilling locations—1989–90 Escort

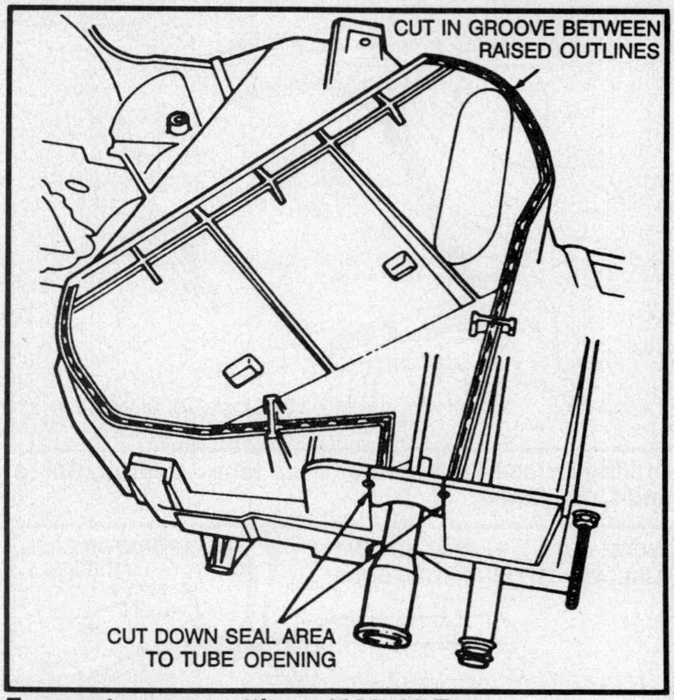
CUT IN GROOVE BETWEEN RAISED OUTLINES
CUT DOWN SEAL AREA TO TUBE OPENING

Evaporator case cutting—1989–90 Escort

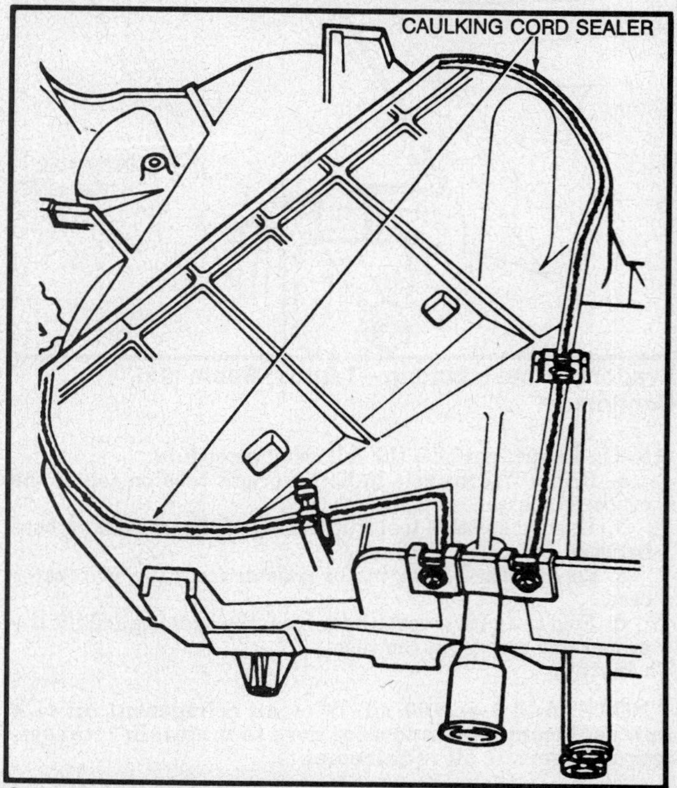
CAULKING CORD SEALER

Caulking cord installation—1989–90 Escort

tube for a good seal and that the drain tube is through the opening and not obstructed.

20. Position the sound insulation around the air inlet duct on the cowl top panel.
21. Install the instrument panel.

22. Install 1 screw to attach the bottom of the evaporator assembly to the dash panel.
23. Connect the heater hoses to the heater core.
24. Using new O-rings lubricated with clean refrigerant oil, connect the liquid line and the accumulator/drier inlet tube to the evaporator core. Tighten each connection using a backup wrench to prevent component damage.
25. Fill the radiator to the correct level with the removed coolant and connect the negative battery cable.
26. Leak test, evacuate and charge the air conditioning system according to the proper procedure. Check the system for proper operation.

1991 Escort and Tracer

NOTE: Do not disassemble the evaporator/blower unit. If the evaporator core needs to be replaced, replace the evaporator/blower unit as an assembly. If the evaporator/blower unit is replaced, it will also be necessary to replace the accumulator/drier.

1. Disconnect the negative battery cable.
2. Discharge the refrigerant from the air conditioning system according to the proper procedure.
3. Disconnect the high pressure line and the accumulator/drier inlet tube from the evaporator core at the bulkhead, using the spring-lock coupling disconnect procedure. Plug all ports to prevent the entrance of dirt and moisture.
4. Remove the glove comparment. If necessary, remove the trim panel below the glove compartment.
5. Disconnect the 2 electrical connectors from the resistor assembly and the electrical connector from the blower motor.
6. Remove the right dash side panel and the right lower dash trim panel and capscrews.
7. Remove the support bar and the support plate.
8. Disconnect the cable from the recirc/fresh air cam and retaining clip. Loosen the capscrew that secures the evaporator-to-heater clamp.
9. Remove the 4 mounting nuts from the evaporator/blower unit and remove the evaporator/blower unit.

To install:

NOTE: Make sure 3 oz. (90ml) of clean refrigerant oil is contained in the evaporator core of the replacement evaporator/blower unit.

10. Position the evaporator/blower unit and install the mounting nuts.
11. Tighten the capscrew that secures the evaporator-to-heater clamp. Connect the cable to the recirc/fresh air cam and adjust the cable.
12. Install the support plate and the support bar.
13. Install the right lower dash trim panel and the 3 capscrews. Install the right dash side panel.
14. Connect the blower motor electrical connector and the 2 resistor assembly electrical connectors.
15. If necessary, install the trim panel below the glove compartment. Install the glove compartment.
16. Using new O-rings lubricated with clean refrigerant oil, connect the high pressure line and the accumulator/drier inlet tube to the evaporator core at the bulkhead.
17. Connect the negative battery cable. Leak test, evacuate and charge the system according to the proper procedure. Observe all safety precautions.

Probe

1. Disconnect the negative battery cable.
2. Properly discharge the refrigerant from the air conditioning system.
3. Remove the carbon canister.
4. Disconnect the air conditioning lines from the evaporator using the spring-lock coupling disconnect procedure. Plug the lines to prevent dirt and moisture from entering the system.
5. Remove the instrument panel.
6. Disconnect the electrical connectors from the air conditioning relays at the top of the evaporator case.
7. Remove the air duct bands and remove the drain hose.
8. Remove the evaporator case attaching nuts and carefully remove the case from the vehicle.
9. Remove the foam seals at the inlet and outlet of the evaporator by peeling them away from the evaporator case.
10. Remove the 7 retaining clips from the housing, separate the case halves and remove the evaporator.

To install:

NOTE: Add 0.845–1.014 oz. (25–30 ml) of clean refrigerant oil to a new replacement evaporator core to maintain total system refrigerant oil requirements.

11. Install the evaporator core into the evaporator case.
12. Assemble the case halves with the 7 retaining clips and install the foam seals.
13. Carefully position the evaporator case into the vehicle and install the attaching nuts.
14. Install the drain hose to the evaporator case.

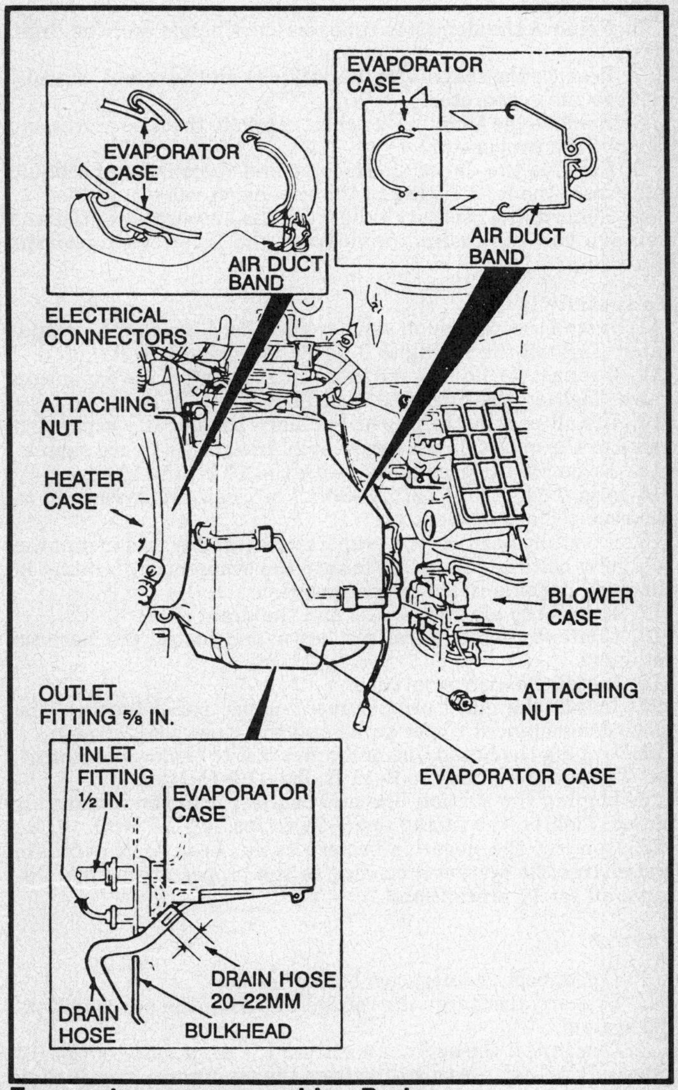
EVAPORATOR CASE
EVAPORATOR CASE
AIR DUCT BAND
AIR DUCT BAND
ELECTRICAL CONNECTORS
ATTACHING NUT
HEATER CASE
BLOWER CASE
ATTACHING NUT
OUTLET FITTING 5/8 IN.
EVAPORATOR CASE
INLET FITTING 1/2 IN.
EVAPORATOR CASE
DRAIN HOSE 20–22MM
DRAIN HOSE
BULKHEAD
Evaporator case assembly—Probe

15. Install and secure the air duct bands and connect the electrical connectors.
16. Install the instrument panel into the vehicle.
17. Unplug the liquid line and install it into the evaporator inlet by performing the spring-lock coupling connect procedure.
18. Unplug the suction line and install it into the evaporator outlet by performing the spring-lock coupling connect procedure.
19. Install the carbon canister and connect the negative battery cable.
20. Leak test, evacuate and recharge the air conditioning system. Check the system for proper operation.

Capri

1. Disconnect the negative battery cable.
2. Discharge the refrigerant from the air conditioning system according to the proper procedure.
3. Disconnect the air conditioning lines from the evaporator in the engine compartment and plug the ends to prevent dirt and moisture from entering the system.
4. Remove the glove compartment and the glove compartment upper panel. Remove the upper panel bracket.
5. Disconnect the electrical connectors and release the harness retainers.
6. Remove the defroster tube, air duct bands and the drain hose.
7. Remove the evaporator mount bolts and nuts and carefully remove the evaporator.
8. Remove the 10 retaining clips, separate the case halves and remove the evaporator.
9. Remove the de-ice thermostat and disconnect the liquid tube from the inlet fitting of the expansion valve.
10. Remove the capillary tube from the evaporator outlet and remove the expansion valve from the inlet fitting of the evaporator.

To install:

11. Install the expansion valve to the inlet fitting of the evaporator. Tighten the fitting to 9–11 ft. lbs. (12–15 Nm).
12. Connect the liquid tube to the inlet fitting of the expansion valve. Tighten the fitting to 9–11 ft. lbs. (12–15 Nm).
13. Install packing to fix the capillary tube of the expansion valve to the outlet of the evaporator. Install the de-ice switch.
14. Assemble the case halves with the 10 retaining clips.
15. Add 0.845–1.014 oz. (25–30ml) of clean refrigerant oil to the replacement evaporator.
16. Carefully position the evaporator assembly and install the retaining bolts and nuts. Make sure the evaporator grommet in the dash panel is in the proper position.
17. Install the air duct bands and the drain hose.
18. Connect the electrical connector and install the harness retainers.
19. Install the defroster tube.
20. Install the glove compartment upper panel bracket, the glove compartment upper panel and the glove compartment.
21. Unplug the liquid line and connect it to the evaporator inlet. Tighten the fitting to 9–11 ft. lbs. (12–15 Nm).
22. Unplug the suction line and connect it to the evaporator outlet. Tighten the fitting to 22–25 ft. lbs. (30–35 Nm).
23. Connect the negative battery cable. Leak test, evacuate and charge the system according to the proper procedure. Observe all safety precautions.

Festiva

1. Disconnect the negative battery cable.
2. Properly discharge the refrigerant from the air conditioning system.
3. Disconnect the suction line from the evaporator outlet fitting and the high pressure line from the evaporator inlet fitting.
4. Remove the attaching screws and the glove box.
5. Disconnect the 2 electrical connectors and the cable from the thermostat.
6. Disengage the wiring harness routing clamps from the evaporator housing.
7. Loosen the clamp screw securing the connector duct to the evaporator housing.
8. Disconnect the drain hose from the evaporator housing and remove the air inlet duct attaching bolt.
9. Remove the bolt attaching the base of the evaporator housing to the dash panel.
10. Remove the nuts attaching the top of the evaporator housing to the dash panel and remove the evaporator housing.
11. Remove the 10 clips securing the upper evaporator housing to the lower evaporator housing and remove the upper evaporator housing.
12. Remove the attaching screws and the thermostat. Pull the sensing tube from between the evaporator core fins as the thermostat is removed.
13. Remove the evaporator from the lower housing and remove the tube insert from between the inlet and outlet tubes.
14. Remove the staples securing the capillary tube insulator over the expansion valve capillary tube and suction tube.
15. Remove the clamp securing the expansion valve capillary tube to the suction tube.
16. Disconnect the evaporator tube fitting and remove the expansion valve.

To install:

NOTE: Add 3 oz. (90 ml) of clean refrigerant oil to a new replacement evaporator core to maintain total system refrigerant oil requirements.

17. Install a new O-ring on the evaporator tube fittings, then install the expansion valve.
18. Position the capillary tube and install the clamp. Install the capillary tube insulation and staple it in position.
19. Install the tube insert between the inlet and outlet tubes and position the evaporator in the lower evaporator housing.
20. Carefully push the thermostat sensing tube into position between the evaporator core fins.
21. Place the upper evaporator housing onto the lower evaporator housing and install the 10 clips.
22. Position the evaporator housing under the instrument panel.
23. Install and tighten the 2 nuts securing the top of the evaporator housing to the dash panel and the bolt securing the base of the evaporator housing to the dash panel.
24. Install the air inlet duct attaching bolt and connect the drain hose to the evaporator housing.
25. Tighten the connecting duct clamp screw and attach the wiring harness routing clamps to the evaporator housing.
26. Connect the cable and the 2 electrical connectors to the thermostat.
27. Position the glove box and install the attaching screws.
28. Slide the suction and liquid tube grommets onto their tubes.
29. Install a new O-ring, lubricated with clean refrigerant oil and connect the suction line to the evaporator outlet. Install a new O-ring, lubricated with clean refrigerant oil and connect the high pressure hose to the evaporator inlet fitting.
30. Connect the negative battery cable. Evacuate, charge and test the system according to the proper procedure.

1989–90 Tracer

1. Disconnect the negative battery cable.
2. Properly discharge the refrigerant from the air conditioning system.
3. Disconnect the air conditioning lines from the evaporator and plug the ends to prevent dirt and moisture from entering the system.
4. Remove the evaporator tube grommets from the bulkhead.

5. Remove the glove box and disconnect the electrical connectors.
6. Remove the air duct bands and the drain hose.
7. Remove the evaporator case mount bolts and nuts and remove the evaporator case.
8. Remove the 10 retaining clips, separate the case halves and remove the evaporator.
9. Remove the de-ice thermostat and disconnect the liquid tube from the inlet fitting of the expansion valve.
10. Remove the capillary tube from the evaporator outlet and remove the expansion valve from the inlet fitting of the evaporator.

To install:

NOTE: Add 0.845–1.014 oz. (25–30 ml) of clean refrigerant oil to a new replacement evaporator core to maintain total system refrigerant oil requirements.

11. Install the expansion valve to the inlet fitting of the evaporator. Tighten the fitting to 9–11 ft. lbs. (12–15 Nm).
12. Connect the liquid tube to the inlet fitting of the expansion valve. Tighten the fitting to 9–11 ft. lbs. (12–15 Nm).
13. Install the packing to fix the capillary tube of the expansion valve to the outlet of the evaporator.
14. Install the de-ice switch and assemble the case halves with the 10 retaining clips.
15. Carefully position the evaporator case and install the mount bolts and nuts.
16. Install the air ducts and secure with the bands.
17. Connect the electrical connectors and install the glove box.
18. Install the evaporator grommets at the bulkhead.
19. Unplug the liquid line and install to the evaporator inlet. Tighten the fitting to 9–11 ft. lbs. (12–15 Nm). Unplug the suction line and install to the evaporator outlet. Tighten the fitting to 22–25 ft. lbs. (30–35 Nm).
20. Connect the negative battery cable. Evacuate and charge the air conditioning system according to the proper procedure.
21. Check the system for proper operation.

Refrigerant Lines

REMOVAL AND INSTALLATION

NOTE: Whenever a refrigerant line is replaced, it will be necessary to replace the accumulator/drier on fixed orifice tube systems.

1. Disconnect the negative battery cable.
2. Properly discharge the refrigerant from the air conditioning system.
3. Disconnect and remove the refrigerant line using a wrench on each side of the tube O-fittings. If the refrigerant line has a spring-lock coupling, disconnect the fitting using the spring-lock coupling disconnect procedure.
4. Route the new refrigerant line with the protective caps installed.
5. Connect the new refrigerant line into the system using new O-rings lubricated with clean refrigerant oil. Use 2 wrenches when tightening the tube O-fittings or perform the spring-lock coupling connect procedure.
6. Connect the negative battery cable. Leak test, evacuate and charge the refrigerant system according to the proper procedure.

Manual Control Head

REMOVAL AND INSTALLATION

Taurus and Sable

1. Disconnect the negative battery cable.

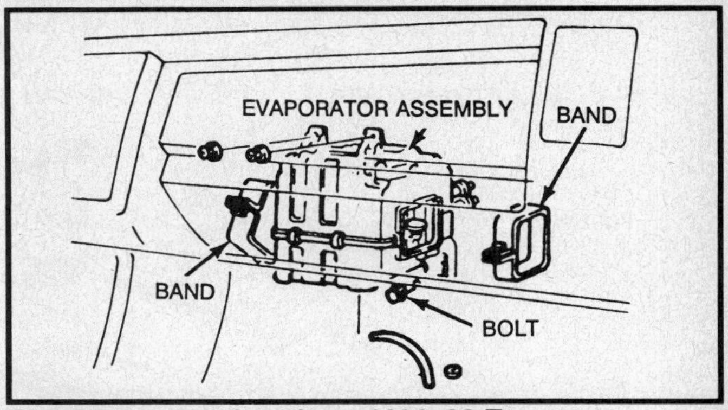
EVAPORATOR ASSEMBLY
BAND
BAND
BOLT
Evaporator case location—1989–90 Tracer

2. Remove the instrument panel finish applique.
3. Remove the 4 screws attaching the control assembly to the instrument panel.
4. Pull the control assembly from the instrument panel opening and disconnect the wire connectors from the control assembly.
5. Disconnect the vacuum harness and temperature control cable from the control assembly. Discard the used pushnut from the vacuum harness.

To install:

6. Connect the temperature cable to the control assembly.
7. Connect the wire connectors and vacuum harness to the control assembly using new pushnuts.

NOTE: Push on the vacuum harness retaining nuts. Do not attempt to screw them onto the post.

8. Position the control assembly to the instrument panel opening and install 4 attaching screws.
9. Install the instrument panel finish applique.
10. Connect the negative battery cable and check the system for proper operation.

Tempo and Topaz

1. Disconnect the negative battery cable.
2. Move the temperature control lever to the **COOL** position. Disconnect the temperature control cable housing end retainer from the air conditioning case bracket using control cable removal tool T83P–18532–AH or equivalent. Disconnect the cable from the temperature door crank arm.
3. Insert 2 suitable tools into the 3.5mm holes provided in the bezel. Apply a light inboard force at each side of the control. The spring clips will become depressed, releasing the air conditioner control from the register housing.
4. Pull the control assembly out from the register housing. Disconnect the temperature cable housing from the control mounting bracket using the control cable removal tool.
5. Remove the twist off cap from the temperature control lever and remove the temperature control cable.
6. Remove the temperature cable wire from the control lever and disconnect the electrical connectors from the control assembly.
7. Remove the 2 spring nuts that attach the vacuum harness assembly to the control assembly and remove the assembly.

To install:

8. Position the control assembly near the instrument panel opening. Connect the vacuum harness to the control assembly. Install the 2 spring nuts. Connect the electrical connectors to the control assembly.
9. Move the temperature control lever to the **COOL** position.
10. Connect the temperature control cable to the control.
11. Position the control assembly to the register housing. Align the locking tabs on the control bracket with the metal

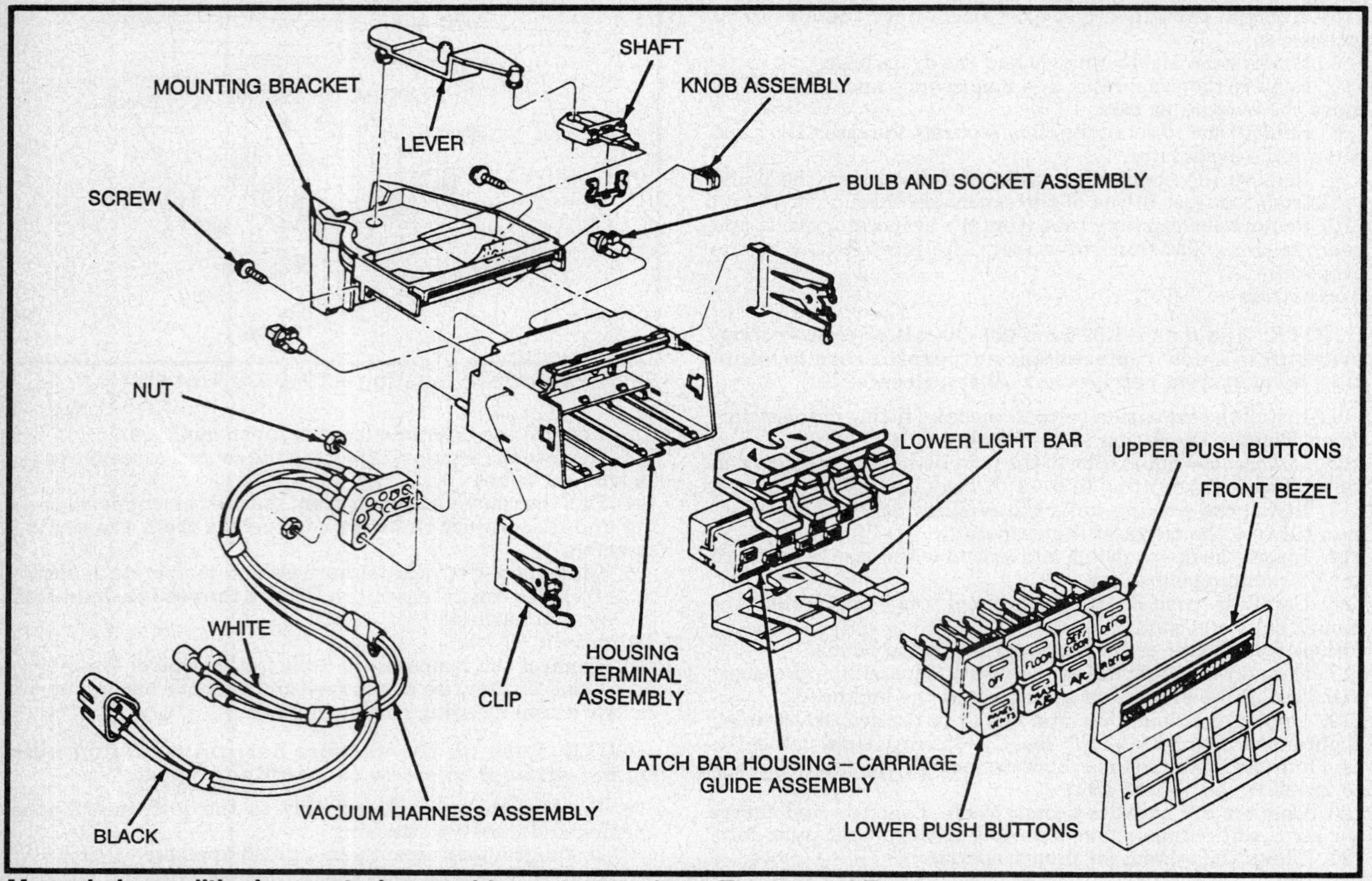
SHAFT
MOUNTING BRACKET
KNOB ASSEMBLY
LEVER
SCREW
BULB AND SOCKET ASSEMBLY
NUT
LOWER LIGHT BAR
UPPER PUSH BUTTONS
FRONT BEZEL
WHITE
HOUSING
TERMINAL
ASSEMBLY
CLIP
LATCH BAR HOUSING—CARRIAGE
GUIDE ASSEMBLY
VACUUM HARNESS ASSEMBLY
BLACK
LOWER PUSH BUTTONS

Manual air conditioning control assembly exploded view—Tempo and Topaz

slide track in the instrument panel.

12. Slide the aligned control assembly down the metal track until the spring clips on the control have snapped in, indicating that the control is locked in the register housing.
13. Move the temperature control lever to the **COOL** position.
14. Connect the self-adjusting clip of the temperature control cable to the temperature door crank arm.
15. Slide the cable housing end retainer into the evaporator case bracket and engage the tabs of the cable and retainer with the bracket.
16. Move the temperature control lever to the **WARM** position to adjust the cable assembly.
17. Check for proper operation of the temperature control lever.

1989–90 Escort

1. Disconnect the negative battery cable.
2. Move the Max A/C Norm selector lever to the **MAX A/C** position and disconnect the air inlet cable housing end retainer from the air conditioning case bracket using control cable removal tool T83P–18532–AH or equivalent. Disconnect the cable from the inlet door cam.
3. Move the temperature control lever to the **COOL** position and disconnect the temperature control cable housing and retainer from the air conditioning case bracket using the control cable removal tool. Disconnect the cable from the temperature door crank arm.
4. Move the function selector lever to the **PANEL** position and disconnect the function selector cable housing end retainer from the air conditioning case bracket, using the control cable removal tool. Disconnect the cable self-adjust clip from the cam pin.
5. Remove the instrument panel finish center panel.
6. Remove the 4 screws attaching the control assembly to the instrument panel.
7. Pull the control assembly out from the instrument panel. Move the temperature, function and outside/recirculate control levers to **COOL**, **PANEL** and **RECIRC**, respectively.
8. Disconnect the temperature cable housing from the control mounting bracket using the control cable removal tool.
9. Disconnect the temperature cable wire from the control lever.
10. Disconnect the outside/recirculate cable and the function cable from the control in the same way that the temperature cable was removed.
11. Disconnect the electrical connectors from the control assembly and remove the assembly.

To install:

12. Position the control assembly near the instrument panel opening. Connect the electrical connectors to the control assembly.
13. Move the temperature, function and outside/recirculate control levers to **COOL**, **PANEL** and **RECIRC**, respectively.
14. Connect the function cable wire and then the cable housing to the control assembly.
15. Connect the outside/recirculate and the temperature cable wire and then their respective cable housings to the control assembly.
16. Position the control assembly to the instrument panel and

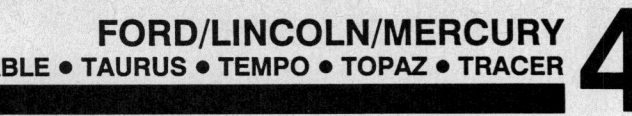

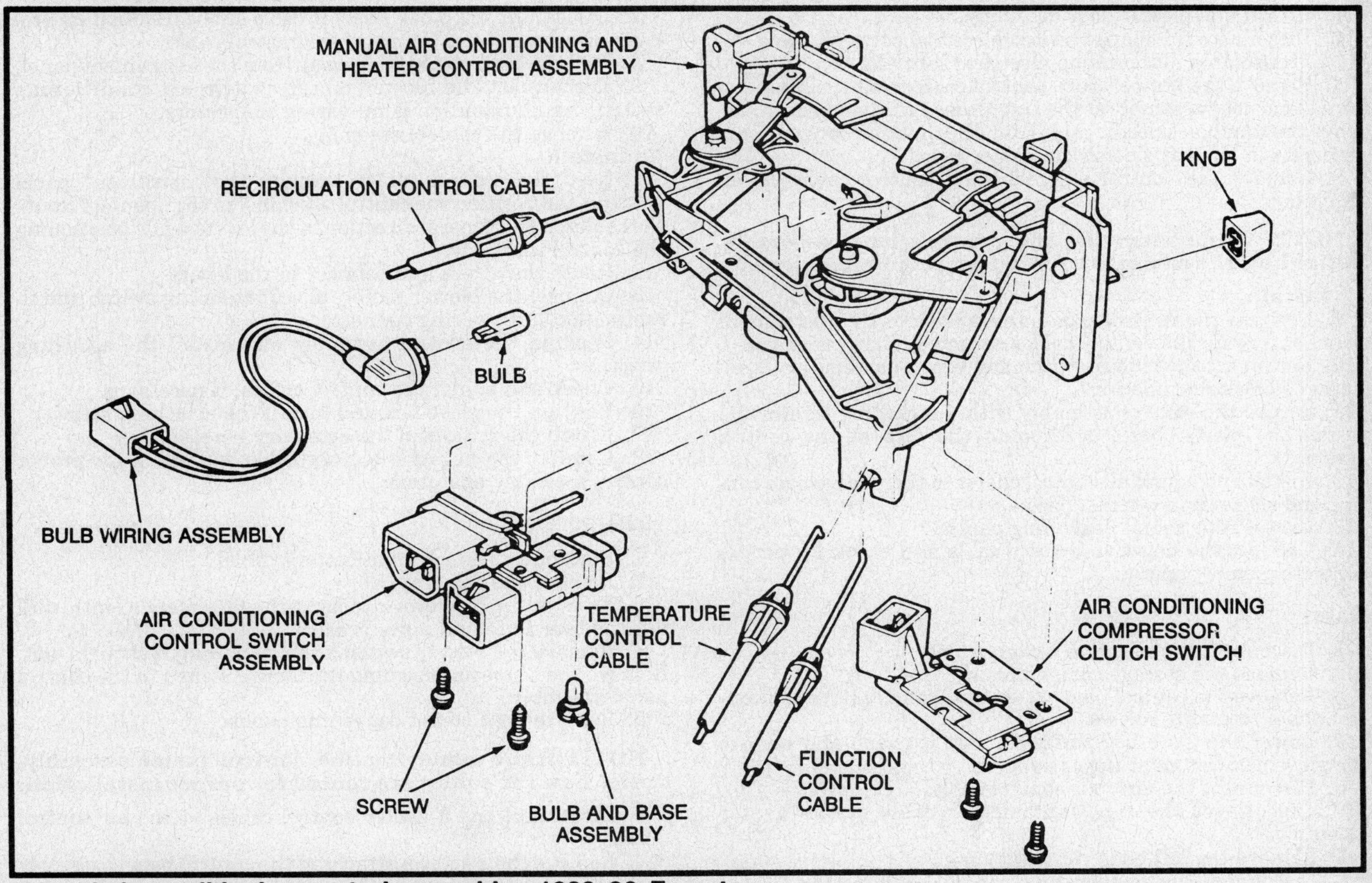
MANUAL AIR CONDITIONING AND HEATER CONTROL ASSEMBLY
RECIRCULATION CONTROL CABLE
KNOB
BULB
BULB WIRING ASSEMBLY
AIR CONDITIONING CONTROL SWITCH ASSEMBLY
TEMPERATURE CONTROL CABLE
AIR CONDITIONING COMPRESSOR CLUTCH SWITCH
FUNCTION CONTROL CABLE
SCREW
BULB AND BASE ASSEMBLY

Manual air conditioning control assembly—1989–90 Escort

install the 4 attaching screws. Install the instrument panel finish center.

17. Move the Max A/C Norm door lever to the **MAX A/C** position. Place the cable end loop over the pin on the air door cam and position the wire under the tab on the cam. Slide the cable housing end retainer into the plenum cable bracket to secure the cable housing to the evaporator.
18. Move the temperature control lever to the **COOL** position.
19. Connect the self-adjusting clip of the temperature control cable to the temperature door crank arm. Slide the cable housing end retainer into the evaporator case bracket and engage the tabs of the cable and retainer with the bracket.
20. Move the temperature control lever to the **WARM** position to adjust the cable assembly. Move the function selector lever to the **PANEL** position.
21. Connect the self-adjusting clip of the function cable to the cam pin on the side of the plenum.
22. Slide the cable housing end retainer into the plenum cable bracket and push to engage the tabs of the cable end retainer with the bracket.
23. Move the function selector lever to the **DEFROST** position to adjust the cable assembly.
24. Check for proper operation of the temperature control, function and Max A/C Norm levers.

1991 Escort and Tracer

1. Disconnect the negative battery cable.
2. Remove the glove compartment.
3. Disconnect the cable from the recirc/fresh air cam and the retaining clip.
4. Disconnect the cable from the mode selector cam and the retaining clip.
5. Disconnect the cable from the temperature control cam and the retaining clip.
6. Remove the trim bezel and remove the 4 retaining screws from the control assembly. Carefully pull the control assembly out of the accessory console.
7. Disconnect the blower and air conditioning switch electrical connector and disconnect the illumination light electrical connector.
8. Remove the control assembly.

To install:

9. Route each control cable to it's appropriate cam.
10. Connect the illumination light electrical connector and the blower and air conditioning switch electrical connector.
11. Position the control assembly and install the 4 retaining screws. Install the trim bezel.
12. Adjust the temperature control cable, the mode selector cable and the recirc/fresh air cable.
13. Install the glove compartment and connect the negative battery cable.

Probe

1. Disconnect the negative battery cable.
2. Remove the bezel cover from the control assembly face.
3. Remove the 4 attaching screws from the control assembly housing.
4. Remove the passenger and driver side sound deadening panels.
5. Remove the recirculate/fresh air control cable at the recir-

culate/fresh air selector door assembly.
6. Disconnect the blower switch electrical connector and the control assembly illumination electrical connector.
7. Remove the temperature control cable from the temperature blend door assembly at the right side of the heater case. Remove the function selector cable from the function control doors assembly at the left side of the heater case.
8. Remove the control assembly and control cables as an assembly.

NOTE: While removing the control panel assembly, notice how the cables are routed for proper installation.

To install:
9. Position the control panel assembly into the instrument panel and route the control cables as noted during removal.
10. Reconnect the blower switch and control assembly illumination electrical connectors.
11. Secure the control assembly with 4 attaching screws and install the plastic bezel cover onto the face of the control assembly.
12. Install and adjust all control cables to their respective control and selector door assemblies.
13. Install both sound deadening panels.
14. Connect the negative battery cable and check for proper control assembly operation.

Capri

1. Disconnect the negative battery cable.
2. Remove the storage compartment.
3. Remove the control panel/radio bezel and remove the control panel retaining screws.
4. Lower the glove compartment past it's stop and remove the glove compartment upper support.
5. Disconnect the air door control cable.
6. Disconnect the function selector cable at the heater assembly.
7. Remove the left center carpet panel.
8. Disconnect the temperature control cable at the heater assembly.
9. Pull the control panel from the instrument panel far enough to gain access to the electrical connectors and disconnect. Use caution so as not to damage the control cables.
10. Remove the 2 screws and the control panel assembly with the cables attached.

To install:
11. Route the cables into the instrument panel and position the control panel in the instrument panel. Connect the electrical connectors.
12. Install the control panel with the retaining screws.
13. Connect the temperature control cable, function selector cable and air door control cable. Check and adjust the control cables.
14. Install the left center carpet panel.
15. Install the glove compartment upper support and return the glove compartment to the closed position.
16. Install the control panel/radio trim bezel and storage compartment.
17. Connect the negative battery cable and check for proper operation.

Festiva

1. Disconnect the negative battery cable.
2. Remove the bezel screws and accessory bezel.
3. Remove the radio.
4. Remove the 4 screws securing the control assembly to the instrument panel.
5. Remove the attaching screws and the glove box.
6. Remove the retaining clip and disconnect the recirculate/fresh air door cable at the door operating lever. The cable end is accessible through the glove box opening.
7. Disconnect the mode selector cable at the function control lever. Disconnect the temperature control cable.
8. Pull the control assembly away from the instrument panel.
9. Disconnect the blower motor switch, air conditioning switch and illumination lamp wiring connectors.
10. Remove the control assembly.

To install:
11. Feed the control cables through the instrument panel opening and position the control assembly in the opening. Route the cables in the general direction of the levers while positioning the control assembly.
12. Route the cables and connect to the levers.
13. Connect the blower motor, air conditioning switch and illumination lamp wiring connectors.
14. Position the control assembly and install the attaching screws.
15. Check and adjust the control cables, if necessary.
16. Position the glove box and install the attaching screws.
17. Install the radio and the accessory bezel.
18. Connect the negative battery cable and check for proper control assembly operation.

1989–90 Tracer

1. Disconnect the negative battery cable.
2. Remove the ash tray.
3. Remove the 5 screws attaching the face plate. Gently pull out the face plate and move it aside.
4. Remove the blower switch knob by pulling it straight-out. Remove the 2 screws attaching the blower switch to the control panel assembly.
5. Remove both sound deadening panels.

NOTE: While removing the control panel assembly, notice how the cables are routed for proper installation.

6. Disconnect the 3 heater control cables at the air control doors.
7. Remove the 2 screws attaching the control panel assembly and remove the control panel assembly.

To install:
8. Position the control panel assembly into the instrument panel, while routing the control cables as noted during removal. Secure the control assembly with 2 attaching screws.
9. Install and adjust the control cables. Install both sound deadening panels.
10. Install the blower switch with the 2 attaching screws. Push the knob on the blower switch.
11. Install the face plate and the 5 attaching screws. Install the ash tray.
12. Connect the negative battery cable and check the operation of the control panel assembly.

Manual Control Cables

ADJUSTMENT

Taurus and Sable

The temperature control cable is self-adjusting when the temperature selector knob is rotated to it's fully clockwise (red) position, as marked on the face of the control assembly. A preset adjustment should be made before attempting to perform the self-adjustment operation, to prevent kinking the control wire. The preset adjustment can be performed either with the cable installed in the vehicle or before cable installation.

BEFORE CABLE INSTALLATION

1. Insert the end of a suitable tool in the end loop of the temperature control cable.
2. Slide the self-adjusting clip down the control wire, away from the loop, approximately 1 in. (25.4mm).

3. Install the cable assembly.
4. Rotate the temperature selector knob to the clockwise (red) position marked on the control assembly face to position the self-adjusting clip.
5. Check for proper control operation.

AFTER CABLE INSTALLATION

1. Move the selector knob clockwise to the **COOL** position.
2. Hold the crank arm firmly in position and insert a suitable tool into the wire loop. Pull the cable wire through the self-adjusting clip until there is a space of approximately 1 in. (25.4mm) between the clip and the wire end loop.
3. Rotate the selector knob clockwise to allow positioning of the self-adjusting clip.
4. Check for proper control operation.

Tempo and Topaz

The temperature control cable is self-adjusting with the movement of the temperature lever to the end of the slot in the bezel face of the control assembly. A preset adjustment must be made before attempting to perform the self-adjustment operation, to prevent kinking of the control wire during cable installation. The preset adjustment may be performed either with the cable installed at the control assembly or before cable installation.

1. Grasp the temperature control cable and the adjusting clip with suitable tools.
2. Slide the self-adjusting clip down the control wire, away from the end, approximately 1 in. (25mm).
3. With the selector lever in the maximum down position, insert the cable housing into the mounting bracket hole and push to snap into place. Attach the self-adjusting clip to the door crank arm.
4. Move the selector lever to the end of the slot in the bezel face of the control assembly to position the self-adjusting clip.
5. Check for proper control operation.

1989–90 Escort

The outside air door cable is not adjustable. The temperature and function control cables are self-adjusting with the movement of the temperature or function selector lever to the right of the slot in the bezel face of the control assembly. To prevent kinking of the control wire during cable installation, a preset adjustment must be made before attempting to perform the self-adjustment operation. The preset adjustment may be performed either with the cable installed at the control assembly or before cable installation.

1. Insert the end of a suitable tool in the wire end loop of the control cable, at the door crank arm end.
2. Slide the self-adjusting clip down the control wire, away from the end loop, approximately 1 in. (25mm).
3. With the selector lever in the far left position, insert the cable housing into the mounting bracket hole and push to snap into place. Attach the self-adjusting clip to the door crank arm.
4. Move the selector lever to the right side of the slot in the bezel face of the control assembly to position the self-adjusting clip.
5. Check for proper operation.

1991 Escort and Tracer

TEMPERATURE CONTROL CABLE

1. Move the temperature control lever to the **COLD** position on the control assembly.
2. To secure the cam in the proper position, insert cable locating key PNE7GH–18C408–A or equivalent, through the cam key slot to the heater case key boss opening.
3. Disconnect the cable from the retaining clip next to the temperature control cam.

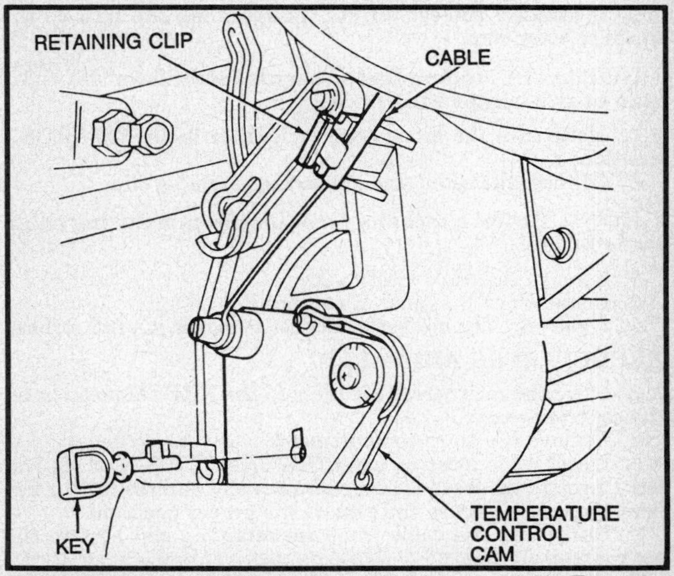
RETAINING CLIP
CABLE
KEY
TEMPERATURE
CONTROL
CAM

Temperature control cable adjustment—1991 Escort and Tracer

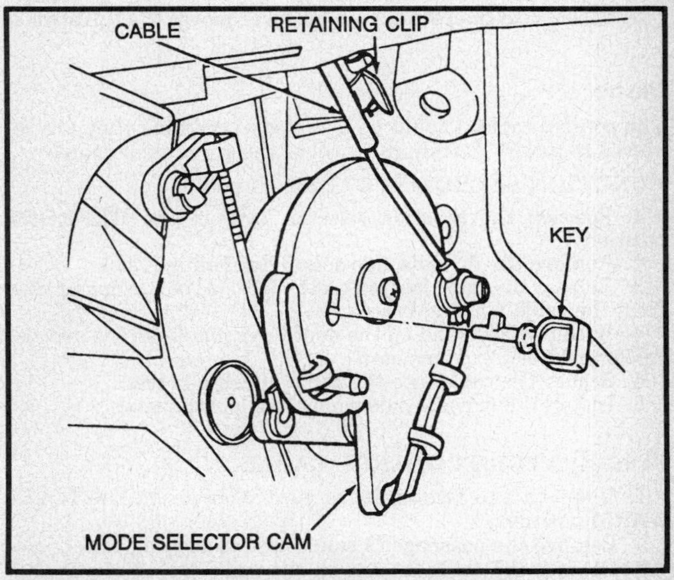
CABLE
RETAINING CLIP
KEY
MODE SELECTOR CAM

Mode selector cable adjustment—1991 Escort and Tracer

NOTE: The temperature control cam is located on the left side of the heater unit.

4. Connect the cable to the retaining clip and remove the cable locating key.
5. Make sure the temperature control lever moves it's full stroke.

MODE SELECTOR CABLE

1. Move the mode selector lever to the **DEFROST** position on the control assembly.
2. Insert cable locating key PNE7GH–18C408–A or equivalent, through the mode cam key slot and heater case key boss opening, to secure the cam in the proper position.
3. Remove the trim panel below the glove compartment, if equipped.

4. Disconnect the cable from the retaining clip next to the mode selector cam.

NOTE: The mode selector cam is located on the right side of the heater unit.

5. Make sure the mode selector lever is in the **DEFROST** position.
6. Connect the cable straight to the retaining clip.

NOTE: Do not exert any force on the cam during cable installation.

7. Remove the cable locating key.
8. Install the trim panel, if equipped.
9. Make sure the mode selector lever moves it's full stroke.

RECIRC/FRESH AIR CABLE

1. Move the recirc/fresh air lever to the **FRESH** position on the control assembly.
2. Remove the glove compartment.
3. Insert cable locating key PNE7GH–18C408–A or equivalent, through the fresh air door cam key slot and recirc door key boss opening to secure the cam in the proper position.
4. Disconnect the cable from the retaining clip next to the recirc/fresh air cam.
5. Connect the cable to the retaining clip and remove the cable locating key.
6. Install the glove compartment.
7. Make sure the recirc/fresh air lever moves it's full stroke.

Probe

The control cables should be adjusted every time they are removed to assure maximum travel of the air control doors.

FUNCTION SELECTOR CABLE

1. Position the function selector lever in the **DEFROST** position.
2. Remove the driver's side sound deadening panel.
3. Release the cable located on the left side of the heater case from the cable housing brace.
4. With the cable end on the door lever pin, push the door lever down to it's extreme stop.
5. Secure the cable into the cable housing brace.
6. Install the driver's side sound deadening panel.

TEMPERATURE CONTROL CABLE

1. Position the temperature control lever in the **MAX-WARM** position.
2. Remove the passenger's side sound deadening panel.
3. Remove the cable located on the right side of the heater case from the cable housing brace.
4. With the cable end on the door lever pin, push the door lever down to it's extreme stop.
5. Secure the cable into the cable housing brace.
6. Check the temperature control lever for proper operation.
7. Install the passenger's side sound deadening panel.

REC/FRESH CONTROL CABLE

1. Position the REC/FRESH control lever in the **FRESH** position.
2. Remove the passenger's side sound deadening panel.
3. Remove the cable located on the left side of the blower case from the cable housing brace.
4. With the cable end on the door lever pin, push the door lever forward to it's extreme stop.
5. Secure the cable into the cable housing brace.
6. Check the air door control lever for proper operation.
7. Install the passenger's side sound deadening panel.

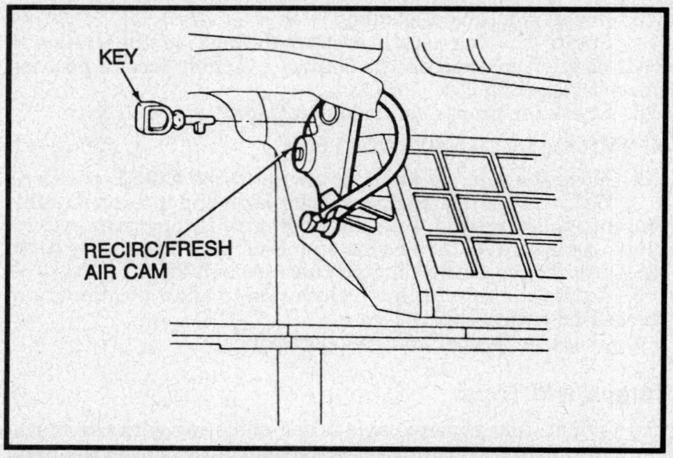
KEY
RECIRC/FRESH
AIR CAM

Recirc/fresh air air cable adjustment – 1991 Escort and Tracer

Capri

FUNCTION SELECTOR CABLE

1. Remove the right center carpet panel.
2. Position the function selector lever in the **DEFROST** position.
3. Release the cable from the housing brace located on the side of the heater case.
4. With the cable end on the door lever pin, push the door lever down to it's extreme stop.
5. Secure the cable into the cable housing brace and adjust the function selector rod as follows:
   a. Remove the rod from the retaining clip at the heater case.
   b. Push the door lever downward to it's extreme stop.
   c. Adjust the rod to align with the clip in the heater case lever and secure the rod into the retaining clip.
   d. Check the lever for proper operation and install the right center carpet panel.

TEMPERATURE CONTROL CABLE

1. Remove the left center carpet panel.
2. Position the temperature control lever in the **MAX-COLD** position.
3. Remove the cable from the housing brace on the side of the heater case.
4. With the cable end on the door lever pin, push the door lever down to it's extreme stop.
5. Secure the cable into the housing brace.
6. Check the temperature control lever for proper operation and install the left center carpet panel.

AIR DOOR CONTROL CABLE

1. Remove the right center carpet panel.
2. Position the air door control lever in the **FRESH AIR** position.
3. Remove the cable from the housing brace on the side of the blower case.
4. With the cable end on the door lever pin, push the door lever forward to it's extreme stop.
5. Secure the cable into the housing brace.
6. Check the air door control lever for proper operation and install the right center carpet panel.

Festiva

RECIRC/FRESH AIR DOOR CABLE

1. Remove the attaching screws and the glove box door.

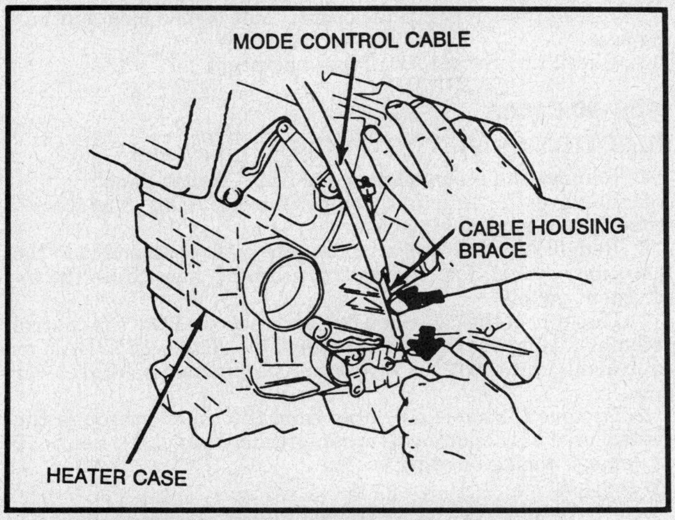
MODE CONTROL CABLE
CABLE HOUSING BRACE
HEATER CASE

Function selector cable adjustment—Capri

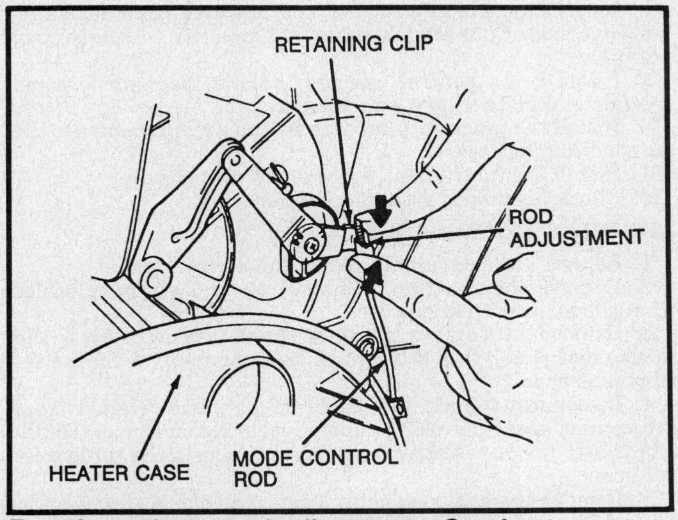
RETAINING CLIP
ROD ADJUSTMENT
HEATER CASE
MODE CONTROL ROD

Function selector rod adjustment—Capri

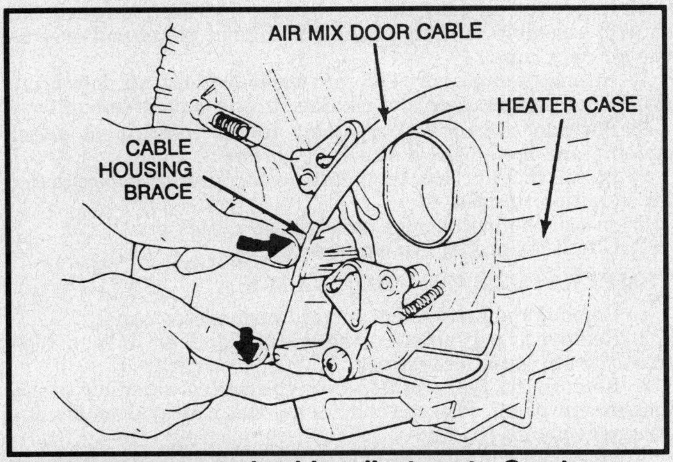
AIR MIX DOOR CABLE
HEATER CASE
CABLE HOUSING BRACE

Temperature control cable adjustment—Capri

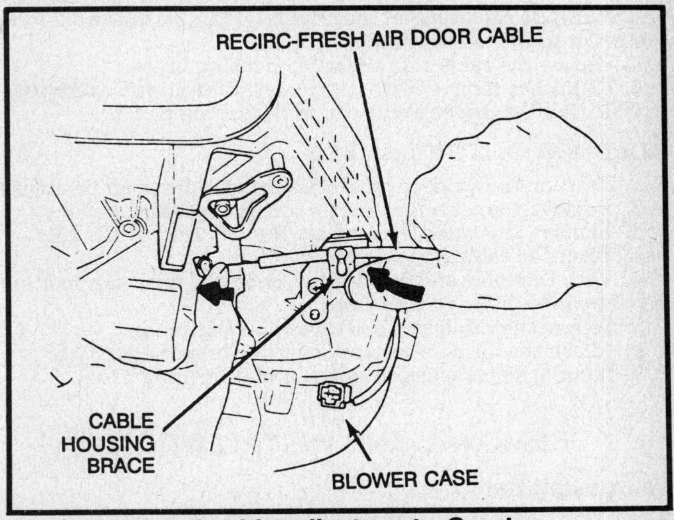
RECIRC-FRESH AIR DOOR CABLE
CABLE HOUSING BRACE
BLOWER CASE

Air door control cable adjustment—Capri

2. Release the cable retaining clip.
3. Move the control lever to the recirculation position.
4. While holding the door lever in the recirculation position, secure the cable casing with the retaining clip.
5. Position the glove box and install the attaching screws.

MODE SELECTOR CABLE

1. Release the cable retaining clip.
2. Move the control knob to the vent position.
3. While holding the function control lever downward against it's stop, secure the cable casing with the retaining clip.

TEMPERATURE CONTROL CABLE

1. Release the cable from the retaining clip.
2. Move the temperature control lever to the **MAX-COLD** position.
3. While holding the temperature control lever upward against it's stop, secure the linkage to the retaining clip.

1989–90 Tracer

The control cables should be adjusted every time they are removed to assure maximum travel of the air control doors.

FUNCTION SELECTOR CABLE

1. Position the function selector lever in the **DEFROST** position.
2. Remove the passenger's side sound deadening panel.
3. Release the cable, located on the right side of the heater case, from the cable housing brace.
4. With the cable end on the door lever pin, push the door lever down to it's extreme stop.
5. Secure the cable into the cable housing brace.
6. Adjust the function selector rod.

FUNCTION SELECTOR ROD

1. Remove the connecting rod from the retaining clip.
2. Push the door lever downward to it's extreme stop.
3. Secure the connecting rod into the retaining clip.
4. Check the function selector lever for proper operation.
5. Install the passenger's side sound deadening panel.

TEMPERATURE CONTROL CABLE

1. Position the temperature control lever in the **MAX-COLD** position.
2. Remove the driver's side sound deadening panel.
3. Remove the cable, located on the left side of the heater case, from the cable housing brace.

4. With the cable end on the door lever pin, push the door lever down to it's extreme stop.
5. Secure the cable into the cable housing brace.
6. Check the temperature control lever for proper operation.
7. Install the driver's side sound deadening panel.

AIR DOOR CONTROL CABLE

1. Position the air door control lever in the fresh air position.
2. Remove the passenger's side sound deadening panel.
3. Remove the cable, located on the left side of the blower case, from the cable housing brace.
4. With the cable end on the door lever pin, push the door lever forward to it's extreme stop.
5. Secure the cable into the cable housing brace.
6. Check the air door control lever for proper operation.
7. Install the passenger's side sound deadening panel.

REMOVAL AND INSTALLATION

Taurus and Sable

TEMPERATURE CONTROL CABLE

1. Remove the control assembly from the instrument panel.
2. Disconnect the cable retainer and wire from the control assembly.
3. Disconnect the temperature cable from the plenum temperature blend door crank arm and cable mounting bracket.

To install:

4. Check to make sure the self-adjusting clip is at least 1 in. (25.4mm) from the end loop of the control cable.
5. Route the cable behind the instrument panel and connect the control cable to the mounting bracket on the plenum.
6. Install the self-adjusting clip on the temperature blend door crank arm.
7. Snap the cable housing into place at the control assembly. Connect the "S" bend end of the control cable to the temperature lever arm on the control assembly.
8. Install the control assembly into the instrument panel.

Tempo and Topaz

TEMPERATURE CONTROL CABLE

1. Move the temperature control lever to the **COOL** position. Disconnect the temperature control cable housing and retainer from the air conditioning bracket using control cable removal tool T83P–18532–AH or equivalent. Disconnect the cable from the temperature door crank arm.
2. Insert 2 suitable tools into the 3.5mm holes provided in the bezel. Apply a light inboard force at each side of the control to depress the spring clips and release the air conditioning control from the register housing.
3. Pull the control assembly from the register housing. Move the temperature control lever to **COOL**.
4. Disconnect the temperature cable housing from the control mounting bracket using the control cable removal tool.
5. Remove the twist-off cap from the temperature control lever and remove the temperature control cable.

To install:

6. Position the self-adjusting clip on the control cable.
7. Insert the self-adjusting clip end of the temperature control cable through the control assembly opening of the instrument panel and down to the left side of the evaporator case.
8. Connect the cable wire and housing to the control assembly.
9. Install the twist-off cap by pushing it on.
10. Align the locking tabs of the control bracket with the metal slide track on the instrument panel.
11. Slide the aligned control assembly down the metal track until the metal clips on the control have snapped in, indicating that the control is locked in the register housing.
12. Install the temperature control cable on the air conditioning case.
13. Check the system for proper operation.

1989–90 Escort

FUNCTION SELECTOR CABLE

1. Remove the instrument panel finish center panel.
2. Remove the function, temperature and air inlet cables from the air conditioning case.
3. Remove the 4 screws attaching the control assembly to the instrument panel. Pull the control assembly away from the instrument panel.
4. Disconnect the cable housing end retainer from the control assembly, using control cable removal tool T83P–18532–AH or equivalent, and the cable wire from the function selector lever arm.
5. Remove the cable assembly from the vehicle through the control assembly opening in the instrument panel. Do not hook or damage wiring or other cables.

To install:

6. Position the self-adjusting clip on the control cable.
7. Insert the self-adjusting clip end of the function cable through the control assembly opening of the instrument panel and down to the left side of the plenum.
8. Insert the cable wire end into the hole in the function selector lever arm. Connect the cable end retainer to the control assembly.
9. Position the control assembly to the instrument panel opening and install the 4 attaching screws.
10. Install the function, temperature and air inlet cables to the air conditioning case.
11. Install the instrument panel finish center panel.
12. Check for proper system operation.

AIR INLET DOOR CABLE

1. Remove the instrument panel finish center panel.
2. Remove the function, temperature and air inlet cables from the air conditioning case.
3. Remove the 4 screws attaching the control assembly to the instrument panel. Pull the control assembly away from the instrument panel.
4. Disconnect the air inlet cable housing end retainer from the control assembly using control cable removal tool T83P–18532–AH or equivalent, and the cable wire from the air door lever arm.
5. Remove the cable assembly from the vehicle through the control assembly opening in the instrument panel. Do not hook or damage wiring or other cables.

To install:

6. Insert the air inlet door cable, loop end first, through the control assembly opening of the instrument panel and over to the air door cam.
7. Insert the cable wire end into the hole in the air door lever arm. Connect the cable and retainer to the control assembly.
8. Position the control assembly to the instrument panel opening and install the 4 attaching screws.
9. Install the function, temperature and air inlet cables to the air conditioning case.
10. Install the instrument panel finish center panel.
11. Check for proper system operation.

TEMPERATURE CONTROL CABLE

1. Remove the instrument panel finish center panel.
2. Remove the function, temperature and air inlet cables from the air conditioning case.
3. Remove the 4 screws attaching the control assembly to the instrument panel. Pull the control assembly away from the instrument panel.
4. Move the temperature control lever to the **COOL** position and remove the temperature cable housing/end retainer from

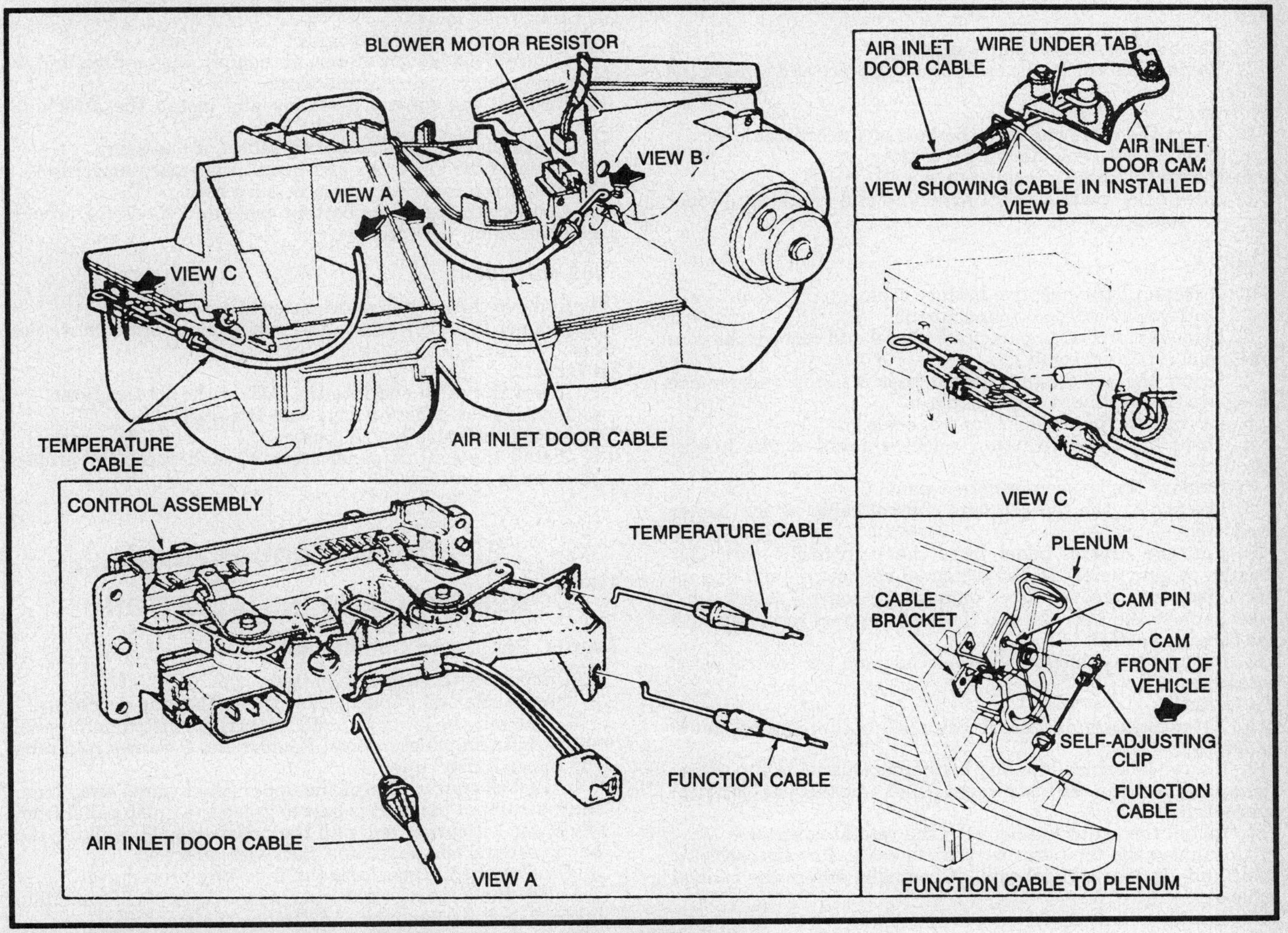
BLOWER MOTOR RESISTOR
VIEW B
VIEW A
VIEW C
TEMPERATURE CABLE
AIR INLET DOOR CABLE
AIR INLET DOOR CABLE
WIRE UNDER TAB
AIR INLET DOOR CAM
VIEW SHOWING CABLE IN INSTALLED
VIEW B
VIEW C
CONTROL ASSEMBLY
TEMPERATURE CABLE
FUNCTION CABLE
AIR INLET DOOR CABLE
VIEW A
PLENUM
CABLE BRACKET
CAM PIN
CAM
FRONT OF VEHICLE
SELF-ADJUSTING CLIP
FUNCTION CABLE
FUNCTION CABLE TO PLENUM

Air conditioning-heater system control cables—1989–90 Escort

the control assembly with control cable removal tool T83P–18532–AH or equivalent. Disconnect the cable wire from the temperature control lever.

5. Remove the cable assembly from the vehicle through the control assembly opening in the instrument panel. Do not hook or damage wiring or other cables.

To install:

6. Position the self-adjusting clip on the control cable.
7. Insert the self-adjusting clip end of the temperature control cable through the control assembly opening of the instrument panel and down to the left-hand side of the evaporator case.
8. Position the control assembly to the instrument panel opening and install the 4 attaching screws.
9. Install the function, temperature and air inlet cables to the air conditioning case.
10. Install the instrument panel finish center panel.
11. Check for proper system operation.

1991 Escort and Tracer

1. Disconnect the negative battery cable.
2. Remove the glove compartment.
3. Disconnect the cable from the recirc/fresh air cam and the retaining clip.
4. Disconnect the cable from the mode selector cam and the retaining clip.
5. Disconnect the cable from the temperature control cam and the retaining clip.
6. Remove the trim bezel and remove the 4 retaining screws from the control assembly. Carefully pull the control assembly out of the accessory console.
7. Disconnect the blower and air conditioning switch electrical connector and disconnect the illumination light electrical connector.
8. Remove the control assembly.
9. Disconnect the cable(s) to be replaced from the control assembly.

To install:

10. Attach the replacement cable(s) to the control assembly.
11. Route each control cable to it's appropriate cam.
12. Connect the illumination light electrical connector and the blower and air conditioning switch electrical connector.
13. Position the control assembly and install the 4 retaining screws. Install the trim bezel.
14. Adjust the temperature control cable, the mode selector cable and the recirc/fresh air cable.
15. Install the glove compartment and connect the negative battery cable.

Probe

1. Remove the control panel assembly.
2. Remove the applicable cable housing brace and remove the cable.

To install:

3. Insert the cable end into the hole of the control lever.
4. Position the cable housing into it's seat.
5. Install the cable housing brace.
6. Install the control panel assembly and check for proper control cable operation.

Capri

1. Disconnect the negative battery cable.
2. Remove the storage compartment.
3. Remove the control panel/radio bezel and remove the control panel retaining screws.
4. Lower the glove compartment past it's stop and remove the glove compartment upper support.
5. Disconnect the air door control cable.
6. Disconnect the function selector cable at the heater assembly.
7. Remove the left center carpet panel.
8. Disconnect the temperature control cable at the heater assembly.
9. Pull the control panel from the instrument panel far enough to gain access to the electrical connectors and disconnect. Use caution so as not to damage the control cables.
10. Remove the 2 screws and the control panel assembly with the cables attached.
11. Remove the cable(s) to be replaced from the control panel assembly.

To install:

12. Attach the replacement cable(s) to the control panel assembly.
13. Route the cables into the instrument panel and position the control panel in the instrument panel. Connect the electrical connectors.
14. Install the control panel with the retaining screws.
15. Connect the temperature control cable, function selector cable and air door control cable. Check and adjust the control cables.
16. Install the left center carpet panel.
17. Install the glove compartment upper support and return the glove compartment to the closed position.
18. Install the control panel/radio trim bezel and storage compartment.
19. Connect the negative battery cable and check for proper operation.

Festiva

1. Disconnect the negative battery cable.
2. Remove the bezel screws and accessory bezel.
3. Remove the radio.
4. Remove the 4 screws securing the control assembly to the instrument panel.
5. Remove the attaching screws and the glove box.
6. Remove the retaining clip and disconnect the recirculate/fresh air door cable at the door operating lever. The cable end is accessible through the glove box opening.
7. Disconnect the mode selector cable at the function control lever. Disconnect the temperature control cable.
8. Pull the control assembly away from the instrument panel.
9. Disconnect the blower motor switch, air conditioning switch and illumination lamp wiring connectors.
10. Remove the control assembly with the control cables.

To install:

11. Feed the control cables through the instrument panel opening and position the control assembly in the opening. Route the cables in the general direction of the levers while positioning the control assembly.
12. Route the cables and connect to the levers.
13. Connect the blower motor, air conditioning switch and illumination lamp wiring connectors.
14. Position the control assembly and install the attaching screws.
15. Check and adjust the control cables, if necessary.
16. Position the glove box and install the attaching screws.
17. Install the radio and the accessory bezel.
18. Connect the negative battery cable and check for proper control assembly operation.

1989–90 Tracer

1. Remove the control panel assembly.
2. Remove the applicable cable housing brace and remove the cable.

To install:

3. Insert the cable end into the hole of the control lever.
4. Position the cable housing into it's seat.
5. Install the cable housing brace.
6. Install the control panel assembly and check for proper control cable operation.

Electronic Control Head

REMOVAL AND INSTALLATION

Taurus, Sable and Continental

1. Disconnect the negative battery cable.
2. On Taurus and Sable, perform the following procedure:
   a. Pull out the lower left and lower right instrument panel snap-on finish panel inserts. Remove the 8 screws retaining the upper finish panel.
   b. Pull the lower edge of the upper finish panel away from the instrument panel. It is best to grasp the finish panel from the lower left corner and pull the panel away by walking the hands around the panel in a clockwise direction.
3. On Continental, perform the following procedure:
   a. Pry the left and right instrument panel shelf moulding up to disengage the clips and remove the mouldings.
   b. Remove the instrument panel cluster opening finish panel retaining screws and remove the panel.
4. On all vehicles, remove the 4 Torx® head screws retaining the control assembly. Pull the control assembly away from the instrument panel into a position which provides access to the rear connections.
5. Disconnect the 2 harness connectors from the control assembly by depressing the latches at the top of the connectors and pulling.
6. Remove the nuts retaining the vacuum harness to the control assembly.

To install:

7. Connect the 2 electrical harness connectors to the control assembly. Push the keyed connectors in until a click is heard.
8. Attach the vacuum harness to the vacuum port assembly. Secure the harness by tightening the 2 nuts.
9. Position the control assembly into the instrument panel opening and install the 4 attaching Torx® head screws. Make sure, as the control is positioned, the locating posts are correctly aligned with their respective holes.
10. Carefully place the instrument panel applique into it's assembly position. Make sure the spring clips are aligned with their proper holes. Press the applique into place. Make sure all spring clips and screws are secure.
11. On Taurus and Sable, install the 8 screws retaining the upper finish panel. Insert the lower left and lower right instrument panel snap-on finish panel inserts.
12. On Continental, install the left and right shelf mouldings.

13. Connect the negative battery cable and check the system operation.

Probe

1. Disconnect the negative battery cable.
2. Remove the bezel cover from the control assembly face.
3. Remove the 4 attaching screws from the control assembly housing.
4. Disconnect the 2 electrical connectors from the control assembly and remove the assembly.

To install:

5. Position the control panel assembly into the instrument panel.
6. Connect the electrical connectors to the control assembly and secure the control assembly with the 4 attaching screws.
7. Install the plastic bezel cover onto the face of the control assembly.
8. Connect the negative battery cable and check for proper control assembly operation.

SENSORS AND SWITCHES

Clutch Cycling Pressure Switch

OPERATION

The clutch cycling pressure switch is a safety device that opens and closes on pressure changes in the refrigerant. The switch shuts the compressor off when refrigerant pressure is not within the range specified for the vehicle. The clutch cycling pressure switch is located on top of the accumulator/drier on fixed orifice tube systems and in the liquid line between the evaporator and receiver/drier on expansion valve systems.

REMOVAL AND INSTALLATION

Except Capri, Festiva and 1989–90 Tracer

1. Disconnect the negative battery cable.
2. Disconnect the wire harness connector from the pressure switch.
3. Unscrew the pressure switch from the accumulator/drier.

To install:

4. Lubricate the O-ring on the accumulator nipple with clean refrigerant oil.
5. Screw the pressure switch on the accumulator nipple.
6. Connect the wire connector to the pressure switch.
7. Check the pressure switch installation for refrigerant leaks.
8. Connect the negative battery cable and check the system for proper operation.

Capri, Festiva and 1989–90 Tracer

1. Disconnect the negative battery cable.
2. Properly discharge the refrigerant system.
3. Disconnect the electrical connector from the pressure switch.
4. Remove the switch and remove and discard the O-ring.

To install:

5. Make sure a new O-ring is installed on the switch base.
6. Install the switch and connect the switch wiring.
7. Connect the negative battery cable. Evacuate, charge and test the system according to the proper procedure.

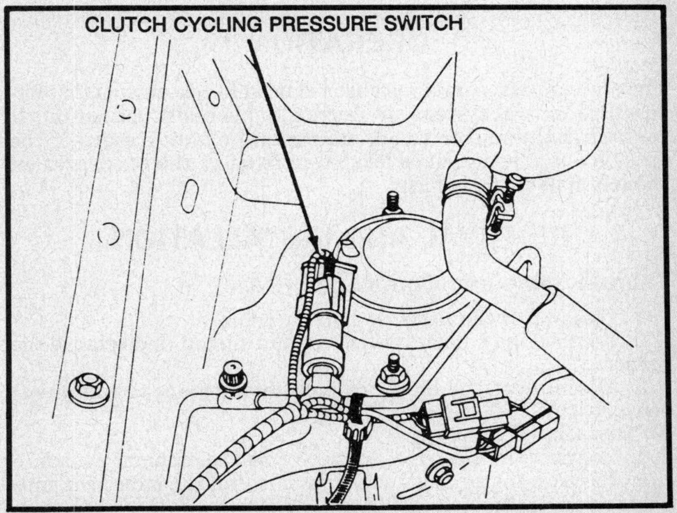
CLUTCH CYCLING PRESSURE SWITCH

Clutch cycling pressure switch location—Festiva

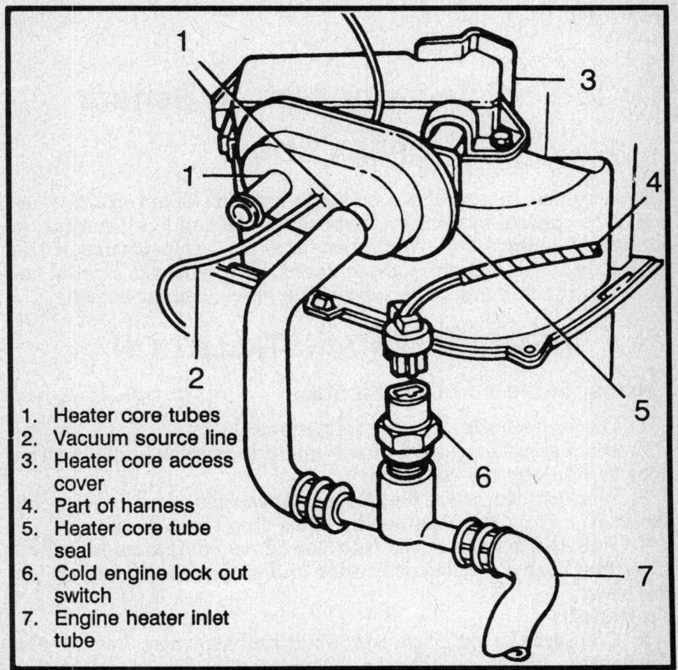
1
3
1
4
2
5
6
7
1. Heater core tubes
2. Vacuum source line
3. Heater core access cover
4. Part of harness
5. Heater core tube seal
6. Cold engine lock out switch
7. Engine heater inlet tube

Cold engine lock out switch location—Taurus, Sable and Continental

Cold Engine Lock Out Switch

OPERATION

The cold engine lock out switch is used in the automatic temperature control system on Taurus, Sable and Continental. It prevents the air conditioning compressor from running when the engine is cold. The switch is located in the heater core inlet tube in the engine compartment.

REMOVAL AND INSTALLATION

Taurus, Sable and Continental

1. Disconnect the negative battery cable.
2. Disconnect the 2 wire connector from the switch.
3. Partially drain the coolant from the radiator.
4. Remove the threaded switch from the heater tube.

To install:

5. Apply sealer to the switch threads and install it into the fitting in the heater tube. Tighten to 8–14 ft. lbs. (11–19 Nm).
6. Attach the electrical connector to the top of the switch.
7. Refill the radiator with the removed coolant to the proper level.
8. Connect the negative battery cable.

Ambient Temperature Sensor

OPERATION

The ambient temperature sensor is used in the automatic temperature control system on Taurus, Sable and Continental. It contains a thermistor which measures the temperature of the outside air. The sensor is located in front of the condenser on the left side of the vehicle.

REMOVAL AND INSTALLATION

Taurus, Sable and Continental

1. Disconnect the negative battery cable.
2. Remove the ambient sensor mounting nut and remove the sensor.
3. Disconnect the electrical connector from the ambient sensor.

To install:

4. Connect the electrical connector to the ambient sensor.
5. Position the ambient sensor and install the mounting nut. Tighten to 55–65 inch lbs. (6.2–7.3 Nm).
6. Connect the negative battery cable and check the system for proper operation.

In-Vehicle Temperature Sensor

OPERATION

The in-vehicle temperature sensor is used in the automatic temperature control system on Taurus, Sable and Continental. It contains a thermistor which measures the temperature of the air inside the passenger compartment. The sensor is located behind the instrument panel above the glove compartment.

REMOVAL AND INSTALLATION

Taurus, Sable and Continental

1. Disconnect the negative battery cable.
2. Disengage the glove compartment door stops and allow the door to hang by the hinge.
3. Working through the glove compartment opening, unclip the sensor from the retainer by squeezing the side tabs.
4. Pull the sensor down into the glove compartment, then disconnect the electrical connector and aspirator flex hose from the sensor.

To install:

5. Connect the electrical connector and aspirator flex hose to the sensor.
6. Working through the glove compartment opening, attach the sensor to the retaining clip.

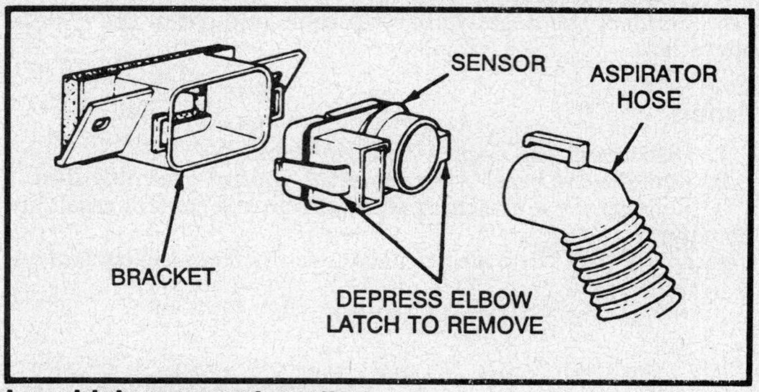
SENSOR
ASPIRATOR HOSE
BRACKET
DEPRESS ELBOW LATCH TO REMOVE

In-vehicle sensor installation

7. Engage the glove compartment door stops and close the door.
8. Connect the negative battery cable.

Sunload Sensor

OPERATION

The sunload sensor is used in the automatic temperature control system on Taurus, Sable and Continental. It contains a photovoltaic (sensitive to sunlight) diode that provides input to the system microcomputer. The sensor is located in the left radio speaker grille assembly on Taurus and Sable and in the right speaker grille assembly on Continental.

REMOVAL AND INSTALLATION

Taurus, Sable and Continental

1. Disconnect the negative battery cable.
2. On Taurus and Sable, remove the left-hand speaker grille assembly. On Continental, remove the right-hand speaker grille assembly.
3. Remove the sunload sensor assembly from the 2 mounting studs and disconnect the electrical connector.

To install:

4. Connect the electrical connector to the sunload sensor.
5. Install the sensor to the speaker grille by pushing the sensor firmly over the 2 mounting studs.
6. Install the speaker grille assembly and connect the negative battery cable.

Blower Speed Controller

OPERATION

The blower speed controller is used on Taurus, Sable, Continental and Probe with automatic temperature control. It converts the base current received from the electronic control assembly into high current, variable ground feed to the blower motor. The blower fan speed is therefore infinitely variable. The blower speed controller is located in the evaporator case, upstream of the evaporator core on Taurus, Sable and Continental. On Probe, the blower speed controller is known as the power transistor and is located under the instrument panel in the blower case.

REMOVAL AND INSTALLATION

Taurus, Sable and Continental

1. Disconnect the negative battery cable.
2. Disengage the glove compartment door stops and allow the door to hang by the hinge.

3. Working through the glove compartment opening, disconnect the electrical snap-lock connector and aspirator hose at the blower motor controller. Also, disconnect the snap-lock connector from it's mounting bracket.
4. Remove the 2 screws attaching the blower controller to the evaporator case and remove the controller. Do not touch the fins of the controller until it has had a sufficient time to cool.

To install:

5. Position the blower controller on the evaporator case and install the 2 attaching screws.
6. Connect the wire connector and aspirator hose to the blower controller. Install the connector on the mounting bracket.
7. Close the glove compartment door, connect the negative battery cable and check the system for proper operation.

Probe

1. Disconnect the negative battery cable.
2. Remove the instrument panel.
3. Remove the blower case assembly.
4. Disconnect the power transistor electrical connector and remove the power transistor assembly from the blower case air outlet.

To install:

5. Install the power transistor assembly into the blower case and connect the electrical connector.
6. Install the blower case assembly.
7. Install the instrument panel.
8. Connect the negative battery cable and check for proper blower motor operation.

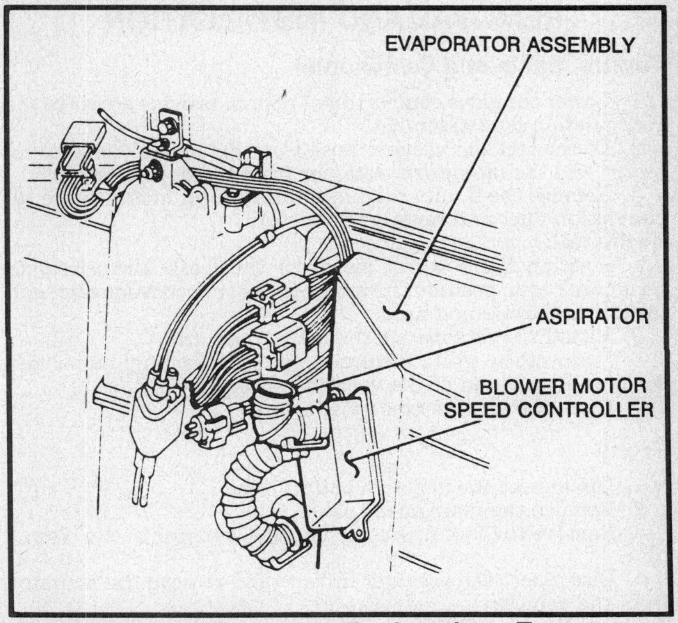
EVAPORATOR ASSEMBLY
ASPIRATOR
BLOWER MOTOR
SPEED CONTROLLER

Blower motor speed controller location—Taurus, Sable and Continental

NOTE: After replacement of the blend door actuator, the system must be recalibrated for proper operation. To recalibrate, disconnect the positive battery cable from the battery, wait 30 seconds and reconnect the battery cable. Calibration will be performed automatically when the automatic temperature control electronic control assembly is energized.

Probe

1. Disconnect the negative battery cable.
2. Remove the instrument panel.
3. Disconnect the temperature blend door actuator motor electrical connector.
4. Remove the 2 screws attaching the actuator to the heater case and remove the motor linkage from the heater case.
5. Remove the attaching screw from the actuator electrical connector retaining bracket and remove the actuator.

To install:

6. Position the electrical connector retaining bracket onto the heater case and install the attaching screw.
7. Position the function control actuator motor onto the heater case and reconnect the motor linkage.
8. Install the attaching screws to the actuator at the heater case and connect the actuator electrical connector.
9. Install the instrument panel.
10. Connect the negative battery cable and check for proper actuator motor operation.

Temperature Blend Door Actuator Motor

OPERATION

The temperature blend door actuator is used on Taurus, Sable, Continental and Probe with automatic temperature control. The actuator controls blend door movement on command from the control assembly. The blend door actuator is located on top of the evaporator assembly on Taurus, Sable and Continental and on the heater case on Probe.

REMOVAL AND INSTALLATION

Taurus, Sable and Continental

1. Disconnect the negative battery cable.
2. Loosen the instrument panel and pull back from the cowl.
3. Remove the blend door actuator electrical connector and plastic clamp from the bracket on the evaporator case. Remove the 3 actuator attaching screws.
4. Lift the actuator vertically for a distance of approximately ½ in. (12mm) to disengage it from the bracket and blend door shaft. Pull the actuator back toward the passenger compartment.

NOTE: The mounting bracket remains in place on the evaporator case.

To install:

5. Insert the blend door actuator horizontally over the actuator bracket on the evaporator case.

6 Insert the actuator shaft into the blend door. Manually moving the door will help engage the shaft.

7. Attach the actuator bracket with the 3 attaching screws.
8. Attach the actuator electrical connector and plastic clamp to the bracket on the evaporator case.
9. Install the instrument panel and connect the negative battery cable.

Recirculate/Fresh Air Selector Door Actuator Motor

OPERATION

The recirculate/fresh air selector door actuator motor is used on Taurus, Sable, Continental and Probe with automatic temperature control. The motor controls the position of the door which allows fresh air or recirculated air, or a combination of the two, into the vehicle. On Taurus, Sable and Continental, the motor is mounted on the recirculate/fresh air duct. On Probe, the motor is mounted on the blower case.

REMOVAL AND INSTALLATION

Taurus, Sable and Continental

1. Lower the glove compartment door to provide access to the recirculation duct assembly.
2. Disconnect the vacuum hose from the end of the vacuum motor and the motor arm retainer from the door crank arm.
3. Remove the 2 nuts retaining the vacuum motor to the recirculation duct and remove the motor.

To install:

4. Position the vacuum motor to the fresh air/recirculate door crank arm, position the motor to the recirculation duct and install the 2 retaining nuts.
5. Install the retainer on the door crank arm.
6. Connect the white vacuum hose to the vacuum motor and check the operation of the vacuum motor.
7. Close the glove compartment door.

Probe

1. Disconnect the negative battery cable.
2. Remove the instrument panel.
3. Remove the 2 screws attaching the actuator to the blower case.
4. Disconnect the actuator linkage and remove the actuator from the vehicle.

To install:

5. Position the recirculate/fresh air selector door actuator motor on the blower case and reconnect the motor linkage.
6. Install the attaching screws.
7. Install the instrument panel.
8. Connect the negative battery cable and check for proper actuator motor operation.

Function Control Actuator Motor

OPERATION

The function control actuator motor is used on Taurus, Sable, Continental and Probe with automatic temperature control. The motor controls the door which directs the flow of air to the defroster ducts, instrument panel ducts or floor ducts. On Taurus, Sable and Continental, 2 motors are used to perform the control function and they are both located on the plenum. On Probe the motor is located on the heater case.

REMOVAL AND INSTALLATION

Continental

1. Disconnect the negative battery cable.
2. Remove the steering column and the instrument panel assemblies.

NOTE: The plenum assembly will be attached to the instrument panel. The vacuum line connector will be disconnected from it's mating connector from the vacuum control valve.

3. If the panel-defrost door motor is being removed, perform the following procedure:
   a. Disconnect the vacuum hose from the motor.
   b. Remove the 2 nuts attaching the motor to it's mounting bracket.
   c. Compress the end of the pin on the door crank and lift the motor arm off the crank. This will release the motor assembly from the plenum.
4. If the panel-floor door vacuum motor is being removed. perform the following procedure:
   a. Disconnect both vacuum hoses from the motor.
   b. Remove the 2 screws which attach the motor arm shield to the plenum and remove the shield.
   c. Remove the 2 nuts securing the motor to it's mounting bracket.
   d. Compress the end of the pin on the door crank and lift the motor arm off the crank. This will release the motor assembly from the plenum.
5. Installation is the reverse of the removal procedure. Check the operation of the vacuum motors.

Taurus and Sable

PANEL/FLOOR DOOR VACUUM MOTOR

1. Disconnect the negative battery cable.
2. Remove the instrument panel.
3. Depress the tabs and disconnect the vacuum motor arm from the door shaft.
4. Remove the 2 screws retaining the vacuum motor to the mounting bracket.
5. Remove the vacuum motor from the mounting bracket and disconnect the vacuum hose.

To install:

6. Position the vacuum motor on the mounting bracket and door shaft.
7. Install the 2 screws attaching the vacuum motor to the mounting bracket.
8. Connect the vacuum hose to the vacuum motor and check the operation of the motor.
9. Install the instrument panel and connect the negative battery cable.

PANEL/DEFROST DOOR VACUUM MOTOR

1. Disconnect the negative battery cable.
2. Remove the instrument panel.
3. Remove the panel-defrost door vacuum motor arm to door shaft.
4. Remove the 2 nuts retaining the vacuum motor to the mounting bracket.
5. Remove the vacuum motor from the mounting bracket and disconnect the vacuum hose.

To install:

6. Position the vacuum motor to the mounting bracket and door shaft.
7. Install the 2 nuts attaching the vacuum motor to the mounting bracket and connect the vacuum hose. Check the operation of the motor.
8. Install the instrument panel and connect the negative battery cable.

Probe

1. Disconnect the negative battery cable.
2. Remove the instrument panel.
3. Disconnect the function control actuator motor electrical connector.
4. Remove the 3 screws attaching the actuator to the heater case.
5. Remove the motor linkage from the heater case assembly and remove the actuator.

To install:

6. Position the function control actuator motor onto the heater case and reconnect the motor linkage.
7. Install the attaching screws to the actuator at the heater case and connect the actuator electrical connector.
8. Install the instrument panel and connect the negative battery cable.
9. Check for proper actuator motor operation.

Relays

OPERATION

Relays are used in the air conditioning electrical circuits on Capri, Probe, Festiva, Tracer and 1991 Escort. Capri vehicles are equipped with an air conditioning relay, a cooling fan relay and a condenser fan relay. The relays are mounted on a bracket behind the left strut tower.

Probe vehicles equipped with manual air conditioning use a blower motor relay. Probe vehicles equipped with automatic temperature control have a blower motor OFF relay and a blower motor MAX relay. When the blower switch is moved from the **OFF** position, the OFF relay is energized and the contacts close. This allows the circuitry within the control amplifier to flow base current to the blower speed controller (power transistor) so the blower operates. When the blower switch is placed in the **MAX** position, the MAX relay is energized and the contacts within the relay close. This relay then creates a short circuit between the collector and emitter of the blower speed controller (power transistor), thereby bypassing the transistor and the blower motor will operate at maximum speed. Power is supplied to the OFF and MAX relays by the blower motor relay. The OFF and MAX relays are attached to the blower case.

Festiva vehicles equipped with automatic transaxle have 3 air conditioning relays, while manual transaxle vehicles are equipped with 2 relays. The main air conditioning relay is used on all Festiva vehicles. It grounds the engine cooling fan motor so that it will operate constantly with the air conditioning **ON**. It also sends a signal to the electronic control unit indicating the additional alternator load caused by the fan operation. The air conditioning relay is closed whenever the air conditioning is on and the blower is on. The Wide Open Throttle Air Conditioning Cut-Off Relay (WAC) is used on all Festiva vehicles. It supplies power to the compressor clutch and the condenser fan relay on automatic transaxle equipped vehicles. It is controlled by the electronic control unit and operates to cut off the air conditioning during wide open throttle driving or to cycle the compressor clutch. The condenser fan relay is used on Festiva vehicles with automatic transaxle only. When refrigerant pressure is high in the condenser and the pressure switch is closed, the relay contacts close and the condenser fan motor runs. All Festiva air conditioning relays are located in the left front corner of the engine compartment between the battery and the radiator core support near the rear of the left headlight.

1989–90 Tracer vehicles use 4 air conditioning relays. When the air conditioning system is operating, it is necessary for the cooling fan to operate full time. Cooling fan operation is controlled by a coolant temperature sensor at the thermostat housing. Whenever the air conditioning switch is turned **ON**, the sensor circuit is overridden by the 3 relays. Relay 3 will close and supply power to relays 1 and 2. Relay 1 will then close turning on the cooling fan. Relay 2 will also close turning on the auxiliary condenser fan for added cooling system efficiency. As soon as the air conditioning switch is turned **OFF**, the cooling fan circuit will revert back to temperature sensor control. There is also an air conditioning cut relay which is wired in circuit with the refrigerant pressure switch, which protects the compressor if the refrigerant pressure becomes too low. The air conditioning relays are located on the left side of the engine compartment.

1991 Escort and Tracer vehicles are equipped with an air conditioning relay. When the air conditioning switch is pressed, the air conditioning relay closes. The relay energizes the magnetic clutch allowing the engine to drive the compressor. Also at this time, the cooling fan relay is closed and the cooling fan is energized. 1991 Escort and Tracer equipped with the 1.9L engine are equipped with a WAC relay. This relay is controlled by the electronic control unit and prevents the air conditioning system from operating when the vehicle is operated at full throttle. The air conditioning relay and WAC relay are both located in the right rear corner of the engine compartment.

REMOVAL AND INSTALLATION

1991 Escort and Tracer

AIR CONDITIONING RELAY

1. Disconnect the negative battery cable.
2. Disconnect the electrical connector from the air conditioning relay.
3. Remove the relay mounting nut and remove the air conditioning relay.
4. Installation is the reverse of the removal procedure.

WAC RELAY

1. Disconnect the negative battery cable.
2. Disconnect the electrical connector from the relay.
3. Remove the relay mounting nut and remove the WAC relay.
4. Installation is the reverse of the removal procedure.

Capri

1. Disconnect the negative battery cable.
2. Lift the relay to be replaced and it's rubber retaining boot from the bracket.
3. Disconnect the relay electrical connector and remove the relay from the retaining boot.
4. Installation is the reverse of the removal procedure.

Probe

BLOWER MOTOR OFF RELAY

1. Disconnect the negative battery cable.
2. Remove the instrument panel.
3. Disconnect the OFF relay electrical connector and remove the screw attaching the relay to the blower case. Remove the relay.
4. Installation is the reverse of the removal procedure.

BLOWER MOTOR MAX RELAY

1. Disconnect the negative battery cable.
2. Remove the instrument panel.
3. Disconnect the MAX relay electrical connector and remove the screw attaching the relay to the blower case. Remove the relay.
4. Installation is the reverse of the removal procedure.

Festiva

The removal and installation procedure is the same for 1 or all relays.

1. Disconnect the negative battery cable.
2. Unclip the relay holder from it's mounting bracket.
3. Disconnect the relay wiring. Do not pull on the wiring connector to remove the relay from the holder.
4. Pull the relay from the holder.
5. Installation is the reverse of the removal procedure. A small amount of silicone spray on the rubber holder will make installation of the relay easier.

1989–90 Tracer

1. Disconnect the negative battery cable.
2. Disconnect the relay from the wiring connector.
3. Installation is the reverse of the removal procedure.

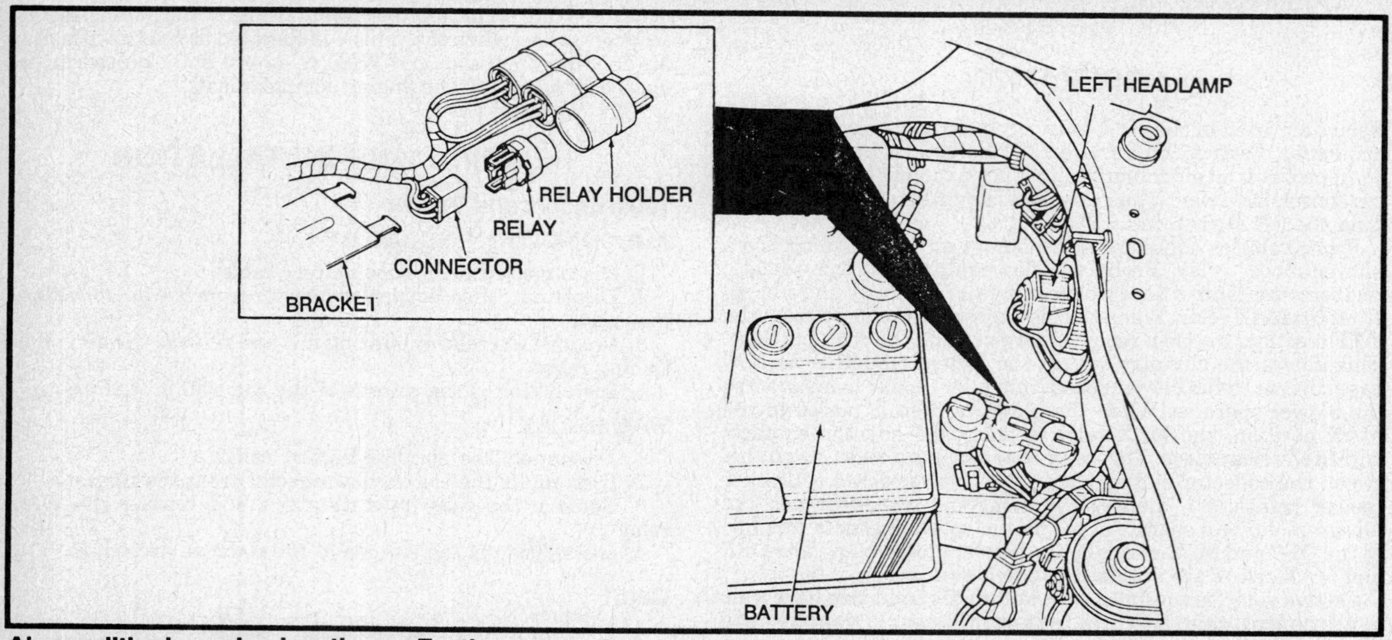
LEFT HEADLAMP
RELAY HOLDER
RELAY
CONNECTOR
BRACKET
BATTERY

Air conditioning relay locations—Festiva

SYSTEM DIAGNOSIS

Automatic Temperature Control System

DIAGNOSTIC PROCEDURE

Taurus, Sable and Continental

1. Perform the Self Diagnostic Test. Record all error codes displayed during the test.
2. If error codes appear during the Self Diagnostic Test, follow the diagnostic procedures indicated in the Error Code Key.
3. If a malfunction exists but no error code appears during the Self Diagnostic Test, perform the Functional Test and consult the No Error Code Found Diagnosis and Testing chart.

SELF DIAGNOSTIC TEST

The control assembly will detect electrical malfunctions occuring during the self test.

1. Make sure the coolant temperature is at least 120°F (49°C).
2. To display error codes, push the OFF and FLOOR buttons simultaneously and then the AUTOMATIC button within 2 seconds. The test may run as long as 20 seconds, during which time the display will be blank. If the display is blank for more than 20 seconds, consult the No Error Code Found Diagnosis and Testing chart.
3. The Self Diagnostic Test can be initiated at any time with the resulting error codes being displayed. Normal operation of the system stops when the Self Diagnostic Test is activated. To exit the self test and restart the system, push the COOLER button. The self test should be deactivated before powering the system down.

FUNCTIONAL TEST

The Functional Test is designed to catch those system failures that the self test is unable to test.

1. Make sure the engine is cold.
2. The in-vehicle temperature should be greater than 50°F (10°C) for proper evaluation of system response.
3. Follow the instructions in each step of the Functional Test.

VACUUM SYSTEM DIAGNOSIS

To test the automatic temperature control vacuum system, start the engine and depress the function buttons slowly from 1 position to another. A momentary hiss should be heard as each button is depressed from 1 position to another, indicating that vacuum is available at the control assembly. A continuous hiss at the control assembly indicates a major leak somewhere in the system. It does not necessarily indicate that the leak is at the control assembly.

If a momentary hiss cannot be heard as each function button is depressed from 1 position to another, check for a kinked, pinched or disconnected vacuum supply hose. Also, inspect the check valve between the vacuum intake manifold and the vacuum reservoir to ensure it is working properly.

If a momentary hiss can be heard as each function button is depressed from 1 position to another, vacuum is available at the control assembly. Cycle the function buttons through each position with the blower on HI and check the location(s) of the discharge air. The airflow schematic and vacuum control chart shows the vacuum motors applied for each function selection along with an airflow diagram of the system. The airflow diagram shows the position of each door when vacuum is applied and their no-vacuum position. With this chart, airflow for each position of the control assembly can be determined. If a vacuum motor fails to operate, the motor can readily be found because the airflow will be incorrect.

If a vacuum motor is inoperative, check the operation of the motor with a vacuum tester. If the vacuum motor operates properly, the vacuum hose is probably kinked, pinched, disconnected or has a leak.

If the function system functions normally at idle, but goes to defrost during acceleration, a small leak exists in the system. The leak can best be located by shutting **OFF** the engine and using a gauge to check for vacuum loss while selectively blocking off vacuum hoses.

HEATING SYSTEM DIAGNOSIS—TAURUS, SABLE, TEMPO, TOPAZ AND 1989–90 ESCORT

INSUFFICIENT, ERRATIC, OR NO HEAT OR DEFROST

Possible Source	Action
Low radiator coolant due to:	Fill to level. Pressure test for engine cooling system and heater system leaks. Service as required.
• Coolant leaks • Engine overheating	Remove bugs, leaves, etc. from radiator and/or condenser fins. Check for: Sticking thermostat Incorrect ignition timing Water pump impeller damage Restricted cooling system Slipping belt Cooling fan inoperative Service as required.
Plugged or partially plugged heater core	Clean and backflush engine cooling system and heater core separately.
Improperly adjusted control cables	Readjust as specified.
Airflow control doors sticking or binding	Check to see if cable operated doors respond properly to movements of the Control Levers. If hesitation in movement is noticed, determine cause and service sticking or binding door as required.
Kinked, clogged, collapsed, soft, swollen, or decomposed engine cooling system or heater system hoses	Replace damaged hoses and backflush engine cooling system, then heater core, until all particles have been removed.
Blocked air inlet	Check cowl air inlet for leaves, foreign material, etc. Remove as required.

NO HI-OUTPUT HEATING

Possible Source	Action
Fuse (Hi-Output Switch)	Replace if required.
Water Valve	Check if sticking — closed — service as required.
Vacuum Line Leak	Check vacuum lines to and from solenoid.
Hi-Output Switch	Check for power and continuity.
Open Circuit at Electro/Vacuum Solenoid	Check for voltage at Hi-output solenoid. Also check for a good circuit to ground at solenoid.

BLOWER MOTOR INOPERATIVE

Possible Source	Action
Blown fuse	Check fuse for continuity. Replace fuse as necessary.
Thermal limiter	Check thermal limiter for an open condition.
Open circuit	Check for voltage at blower motor. Also check for a good circuit to ground at the blower motor.
Blower motor	Check blower motor operation by grounding ground side lead to a good ground.
Blower switch	Perform a continuity check on the blower switch.

BLOWER MOTOR OPERATES ON HIGH SPEED ONLY

Possible Source	Action
Blower motor resistor	a. Check resistor for open circuit with a self-powered test lamp. Replace if open. b. Check to be sure wire harness connector makes good contact with resistor spade terminals. Service as required.
Blower motor wire harness	Check wire harness from resistor assembly to blower switch for a short to ground. Service as necessary.

HEATING SYSTEM DIAGNOSIS AND TESTING—FESTIVA

SYMPTOM	POSSIBLE CAUSE	ACTION TO TAKE
Improper blower motor operation (motor runs but at wrong speed or only at certain speeds)	• Wiring Harness • Blower Motor • Resistor • Blower Switch • Blower Fan Condition	Go to BM1
Intermittent blower motor operation	• Wiring Harness • Connections • Resistor • Blower Switch	Go to BM1
Blower runs constantly	• Resistor • Blower Switch • Shorted Wire(s)	Go to BN1
No blower motor operation	• Blown Fuse(s) • Open Fusible Link • Resistor • Blower Switch • Blower Motor • Grounds • Ignition Relay	Go to BM1
Improper air circulation (air comes out of wrong duct)	• Control Levers • Air Distribution Door(s) Adjustment • Cable(s) • Ducts Blocked or Leaky	Inspect, adjust or repair if necessary Clear blockage or repair leaks
No air circulation or insufficient air circulation (blower motor OK)	• Blower Motor Inlet Blocked • Ducts Blocked or Leaky	Clear blockage Repair leaks or damaged gaskets

SYMPTOM	POSSIBLE CAUSE	ACTION TO TAKE
No temperature control (no heating or cooling of air, heater core and refrigerant system OK)	• Temperature Blend Door Adjustment • Cable(s) • Ducts Blocked or Leaky • Damaged Control Levers	Inspect, adjust if necessary Clear blockage, repair leaks or damaged gaskets Inspect, repair as required
Recirc.-Fresh control malfunction (will not switch)	• Recirc.-Fresh Door Adjustment • Cable(s) • Ducts Blocked or Leaky • Control Levers	Inspect, adjust or repair if necessary Clear blockage, repair leaks or damaged gaskets Inspect, repair as required

HEATING SYSTEM DIAGNOSIS AND TESTING – FESTIVA

TEST STEP	RESULT ▶	ACTION TO TAKE
BM1 SYSTEM INTEGRITY CHECK		
• Check for fully charged battery. • Check for blown fuses, corrosion, poor electrical connections, signs of opens, shorts or damaged to the wiring harness. • Check ventilation system ductwork for obvious signs of cracks, leaks, blockage, separations or other damage. • Key on. • Blower on. • Shake the wiring harness vigorously from the blower motor to the ignition relay; look for signs of opens or shorts. • Tap each connector, ignition relay, 15 amp HEATER fuse and look for signs of bad connections, bad crimps or loose wires. • Does the system appear to be in good condition?	Yes ▶ No ▶	GO to BM2. REPAIR or REPLACE faulty components as required. **NOTE: If a blown fuse is replaced and fails immediately, there is a short to ground in the circuit.**

TEST STEP	RESULT ▶	ACTION TO TAKE
BM2 CHECK POWER AT BLOWER		
• Key on. • Measure voltage at blower motor BL/Y terminal. • Is voltage greater than 10V?	Yes ▶ No ▶	GO to BM3. SERVICE BL/Y wire from 15 amp HEATER fuse to blower motor.

TEST STEP	RESULT ▶	ACTION TO TAKE
BM3 GROUND BLOWER		
• Disconnect blower motor. • Jump battery power to blower motor BL/Y terminal. • Ground blower motor BL/R terminal with jumper wire. • Does motor run?	Yes ▶ No ▶	RECONNECT blower motor. GO to BM4. REPLACE blower motor.

TEST STEP	RESULT ▶	ACTION TO TAKE
BM4 CHECK POWER TO RESISTOR		
• Key on. • Blower off. • Disconnect resistor. • Measure voltage at resistor BL/R terminal. • Is reading greater than 10V?	Yes ▶ No ▶	RECONNECT resistor. GO to BM5. SERVICE BL/R wire from blower motor to resistor.

TEST STEP	RESULT ▶	ACTION TO TAKE
BM5 GROUND RESISTOR		
• Key on. • Leave resistor connected. • Ground BL/BK, BL/Y and BL/W leads of resistor, one at a time, with a jumper wire. • Does blower run at three different speeds?	Yes ▶ No ▶	GO to BM6. REPLACE Resistor.

TEST STEP	RESULT ▶	ACTION TO TAKE
BM6 GROUND BLOWER SWITCH		
• Key on. • Blower switch off. • Ground BL/BK, BL/Y and BL/W terminals of blower switch connector one at a time with a jumper wire. • Does motor run at three different speeds?	Yes ▶ No ▶	GO to BM7. SERVICE wire in question for opens.

HEATING SYSTEM DIAGNOSIS AND TESTING – FESTIVA

TEST STEP	RESULT ►	ACTION TO TAKE
BM7 CHECK BLOWER SWITCH CONTINUITY		
• Key off. • Disconnect blower switch. • Measure resistance between terminals on blower switch connector (switch side). (see table below) • Are all resistances less than 4 ohms?	Yes ► No ►	SERVICE blower switch ground connection (BK wire). SERVICE wires on switch side of connector; if all OK, REPLACE blower switch.

Terminals	Switch Position
BK–BL/W	1
BK–BL/Y	2
BK–BL/BK	3
BL/Y–BL/R	2
BL/BK–BL/R	3

TEST STEP	RESULT ►	ACTION TO TAKE
BN1 SYSTEM INTEGRITY CHECK		
• Check for poor electrical connections, signs of opens, short, corrosion or damage to the wiring harness. • Key on. • Blower on. • Shake the wiring harness vigorously from blower motor to blower switch and ignition relay; look for signs of opens or shorts. • Tap each connector and the blower switch; look for signs of bad connections, bad crimps or loose wires. • Does the system appear to be in good condition?	Yes ► No ►	GO to **BN2**. REPAIR or REPLACE faulty component as required.

TEST STEP	RESULT ►	ACTION TO TAKE
BN2 RESISTOR CHECK		
• Key on. • Blower switch off. • Disconnect resistor. • Does blower stop?	Yes ► No ►	GO to **BN3**. SERVICE BL/R wire from blower motor to resistor for short(s) to ground. If all OK, REPLACE blower motor (internal short).

TEST STEP	RESULT ►	ACTION TO TAKE
BN3 CHECK FOR SHORT		
• Key off. • A/C switch off. • Disconnect blower switch. • Measure resistance between resistor connector BL/Y, BL/BK, BL/W terminals and ground. • Are all resistances greater than 10,000 ohms?	Yes ► No ►	RECONNECT resistor. GO to **BN4**. SERVICE wire in question for short(s) to ground.

TEST STEP	RESULT ►	ACTION TO TAKE
BN4 CHECK BLOWER SWITCH		
• Disconnect blower switch. • Blower switch off. • Measure resistance from BL/R, BL/W, BL/Y and BL/BK terminals to BK terminal (switch side). • Are all resistances greater than 10,000 ohms?	Yes ► No ►	REPLACE blower motor (internal short). REPLACE blower switch.

AIR CONDITIONING DIAGNOSIS AND TESTING—EXCEPT PROBE, FESTIVA, TRACER AND 1991 ESCORT

INSUFFICIENT OR NO A/C COOLING — FIXED ORIFICE TUBE CYCLING CLUTCH SYSTEM

TEST STEP		RESULT ▶	ACTION TO TAKE
A1	VERIFY THE CONDITION		
	• Check system operation	System cooling properly ▶	INSTRUCT vehicle owner on proper use of the system.
		System not cooling properly ▶	GO to **A2**.
A2	CHECK COOLING FAN		
	• Does vehicle have an electro-drive cooling fan?	Yes ▶	GO to **A3**.
		No ▶	GO to **A5**.
A3	CHECK A C COMPRESSOR CLUTCH		
	• Does the A C compressor clutch engage?	Yes ▶	GO to **A4**
		No ▶	REFER to clutch circuit diagnosis in this section.
A4	CHECK OPERATION OF COOLING FAN		
	• Check to ensure electro-drive cooling fan runs when the A C compressor clutch is engaged.	Yes ▶	GO to **A5**
		No ▶	REFER to engine cooling fan circuit diagnosis. Section 27-10.
A5	COMPONENT CHECK		
	Under-hood check of the following: • Loose, missing or damaged compressor drive belt. • Loose or disconnected A C clutch or clutch cycling pressure switch wires connectors. • Disconnected resistor assembly. • Loose vacuum lines or misadjusted control cables. Inside vehicle check for: • Blown fuse proper blower motor operation. • Vacuum motors temperature door movement — full travel. • Control electrical and vacuum connections.	OK but still not cooling ▶	GO to **A7**.
		Not OK ▶	REPAIR and GO to **A6**.
A6	CHECK SYSTEM		
	• Check system operation.	(OK) ▶	Condition Corrected. GO to **A1**.
		(~~OK~~) ▶	GO to **A7**.

INSUFFICIENT OR NO A/C COOLING — FIXED ORIFICE TUBE CYCLING CLUTCH SYSTEM — Continued

TEST STEP		RESULT ▶	ACTION TO TAKE
A7	CHECK COMPRESSOR CLUTCH		
	• Use refrigerant system pressure/clutch cycle rate and timing evaluation charts. After preparing vehicle as follows: 1. Hook up manifold gauge set. 2. Set function control at max. A/C 3. Set blower switch on high. 4. Set temperature lever full cold. 5. Close doors and windows. 6. Use a thermometer to check temperature at center discharge register, record outside temperature. 7. Run engine at approximately 1500 rpm with compressor clutch engaged. 8. Stabilize with above conditions for 10-15 minutes. • Check compressor clutch off/on time with watch. Refer to charts for normal clutch cycle timing rates.	Compressor cycles very rapidly (1 second on) (1 second off) ▶	GO to **A8**.
		Compressor runs continuously (normal operation in ambient temperature above 27°C (80°F) depending on humidity conditions) ▶	GO to **A9**.
		Compressor cycles slow ▶	GO to **A8**.
A8	CHECK CLUTCH CYCLING PRESSURE SWITCH		
	• Bypass clutch cycling pressure switch with jumper wire. Compressor on continuously. • Hand feel evaporator inlet and outlet tubes.	Outlet tube same temperature approximately −2°C - 4°C (28°F - 40°F) or slightly colder than inlet tube (after fixed orifice) ▶	REPLACE clutch cycling pressure switch. Do not discharge system. Switch fitting has Schrader Valve. GO to **A9**.
		Inlet tube warm or (after fixed orifice) colder than outlet tube ▶	GO to **A10**.
A9	CHECK SYSTEM PRESSURES		
	• Compare readings with normal system pressure ranges.	Clutch cycles within limits, system pressure within limits ▶	System OK. GO to **A1**.
		Compressor runs continuously (normal operation in ambient temperature above 27°C (80°F) depending on humidity conditions) ▶	GO to **A11**.
		Compressor cycles high or low ON above 259 kPa (52 psi) OFF below 144 kPa (20 psi) ▶	REPLACE clutch cycling pressure switch. Do not discharge system. Switch fitting has Schrader valve. CHECK system. OK — GO to **A1**. NOT OK — REINSTALL original switch. GO to **A10**.

AIR CONDITIONING DIAGNOSIS AND TESTING—EXCEPT PROBE, FESTIVA, TRACER AND 1991 ESCORT

INSUFFICIENT OR NO A/C COOLING — FIXED ORIFICE TUBE CYCLING CLUTCH SYSTEM — Continued

TEST STEP	RESULT ▶	ACTION TO TAKE
A10 CHECK SYSTEM		
• Leak check system.	Leak found ▶	SERVICE, discharge, evacuate and charge system. System OK, GO to **A1**.
	No leak found ▶	Low refrigerant charge or moisture in system. Discharge, evacuate and charge system. System OK.
A11 CHECK CLUTCH CYCLING		
• Disconnect blower motor wire and check for clutch cycling off at 144 kPa (20 psi) (suction pressure).	Clutch cycles OFF at 144-179 kPa (20-26 psi) ▶	CONNECT blower motor wire. System OK, GO to **A1**.
	Pressure falls below 144 kPa (20 psi) ▶	REPLACE clutch cycling pressure switch. Do not discharge system. Switch fitting has Schrader valve. System OK, GO to **A1**.

COMPRESSOR CLUTCH CIRCUIT DIAGNOSIS

TEST STEP	RESULT ▶	ACTION TO TAKE
B1 CHECK SYSTEM OPERATION		
• Turn blower switch On. • Depress A/C push-button. • Turn ignition switch to Run position. • Compressor clutch should engage and engine cooling fan should operate.	Clutch and fan operate ▶	System OK.
	Clutch and fan do not operate ▶	GO to **B2**.
	Only clutch operates ▶	REFER to Section 27-10.
	Only fan operates ▶	GO to **B5**.
B2 CHECK FOR VOLTAGE		
• Check for voltage at circuit 348 (LG/P) wire at the clutch cycling pressure switch connector.	Voltage present ▶	GO to **B3**.
	No voltage ▶	GO to **B8**.
B3 BY-PASS PRESSURE SWITCH		
• Disconnect connector at clutch cycling pressure switch. • Jumper connector pins. • Clutch should engage.	OK ▶	GO to **B4**.
	NOT OK ▶	GO to **B5**.
B4 CHECK SYSTEM PRESSURE		
• Connect manifold gauge set and check system pressure.	Pressure above 55 psi. ▶	REPLACE clutch cycling pressure switch. GO to **A1**.
	Pressure below 55 psi (ambient temperature above 50°F) ▶	CHECK refrigerant system for leaks. SERVICE and CHARGE system as necessary. GO to **A1**.
B5 CHECK VOLTAGE AT CLUTCH		
• Check for voltage at clutch field coil.	Voltage present ▶	GO to **B7**.
	No voltage ▶	GO to **B6**.
B6 CHECK VOLTAGE AT CONTROLLER		
• Check for voltage at Pin 23 at cooling fan controller.	Voltage present ▶	CHECK for open in circuit 347 (BK/Y H). SERVICE as necessary. GO to **A1**.
	No voltage ▶	GO to **B7**.

COMPRESSOR CIRCUIT CLUTCH DIAGNOSIS — Continued

TEST STEP	RESULT	▶ ACTION TO TAKE
B7 CHECK VOLTAGE		
• Check for voltage at pin 16 of cooling fan controller.	Voltage present ▶	GO to **B9**.
	No voltage ▶	REPLACE clutch field coil. GO to **B1**.
B8 CHECK FUSE		
• Check Fuse 17 in fuse panel for continuity.	(OK) ▶	GO to **B9**.
	(NOT OK) ▶	CHECK for short. SERVICE as necessary. REPLACE fuse. GO to **B1**.
B9 CHECK A/C CONTROLS		
• Move Function selector lever to DEFROST postion. • Check for voltage at circuit 348 (LG/P) wire at the clutch cycling pressure switch connector.	Voltage present ▶	GO to **B11**.
	No voltage ▶	GO to **B10**.
B10 CHECK CIRCUIT 296		
• Remove connector from A/C push-button switch. • Check for voltage at circuit 296 (W/LB).	Voltage present ▶	GO to **B11**.
	No voltage ▶	CHECK for open in Circuit 296. SERVICE as necessary. GO to **B1**.
B11 CHECK A/C CONTROLS		
• Check A/C push button switch and Function switch for continuity. **NOTE: A/C push-button switch must be depressed. Function switch must be in DEFROST position.**	No continuity through function switch ▶	REPLACE Function switch. GO to **B1**.
	Continuity through function switch ▶	CHECK for open in circuit 348 (LG/P) between control assembly and clutch cycling pressure switch. SERVICE as necessary. GO to **B1**.

NORMAL FIXED ORIFICE TUBE REFRIGERANT SYSTEM PRESSURE/TEMPERATURE RELATIONSHIPS EXCEPT 1991 ESCORT AND TRACER

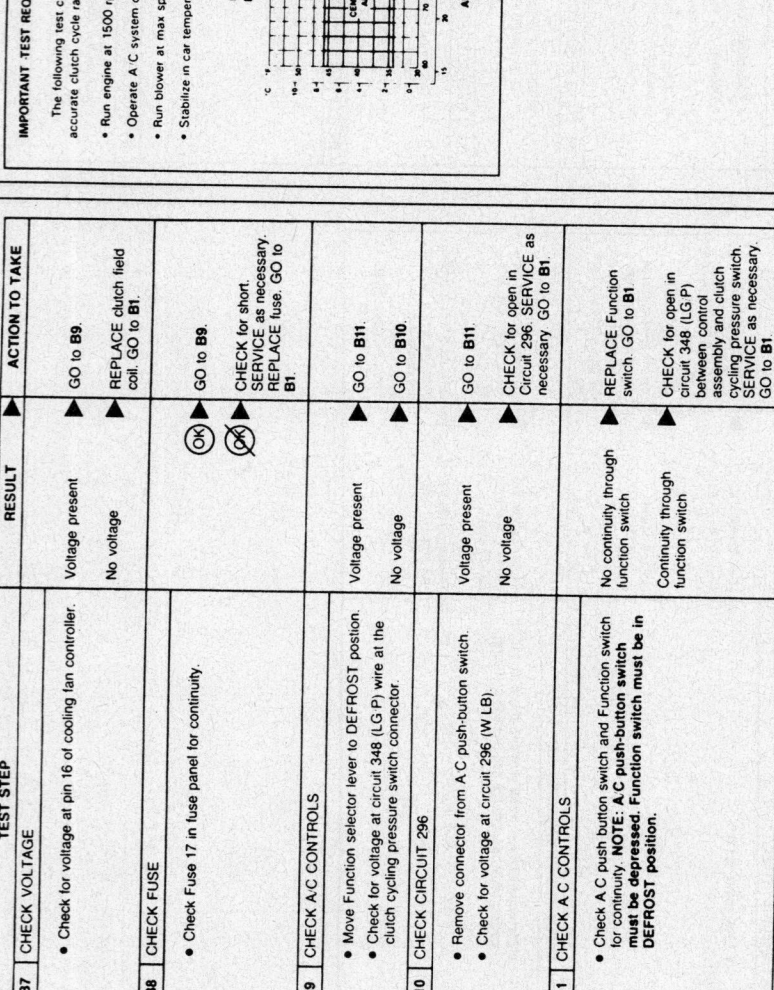

IMPORTANT TEST REQUIREMENTS

The following test conditions must be established to obtain accurate clutch cycle rate and cycle time readings:

- Run engine at 1500 rpm for 10 minutes.
- Operate A/C system on max A/C (recirculating air).
- Run blower at max speed.
- Stabilize in car temperature * 70° F. to 80° F. (21° C. to 22° C.).

NORMAL CENTER REGISTER DISCHARGE TEMPERATURES

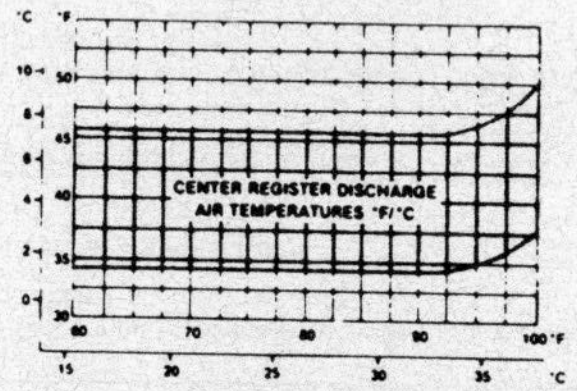
°C °F
CENTER REGISTER DISCHARGE AIR TEMPERATURES °F/°C
60 70 80 90 100 °F
15 20 25 30 35 °C
AMBIENT TEMPERATURES

NORMAL FIXED ORIFICE TUBE CYCLING CLUTCH REFRIGERANT SYSTEM PRESSURES

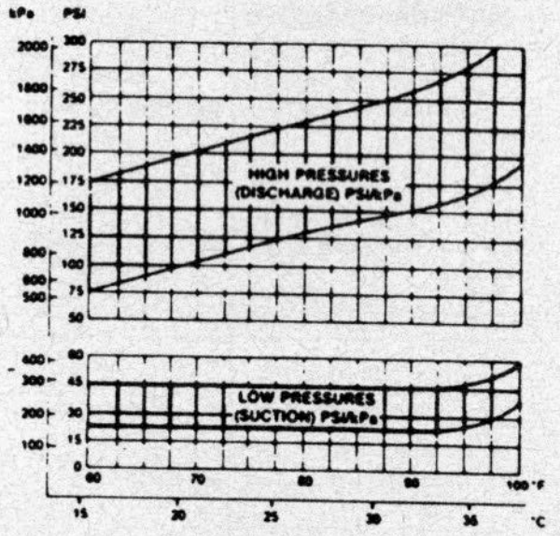
kPa PSI
HIGH PRESSURES (DISCHARGE) PSI/kPa
LOW PRESSURES (SUCTION) PSI/kPa
60 70 80 90 100 °F
15 20 25 30 35 °C
AMBIENT TEMPERATURES

NORMAL FIXED ORIFICE TUBE REFRIGERANT SYSTEM CLUTCH CYCLING TIMING RATES EXCEPT 1991 ESCORT AND TRACER

IMPORTANT — TEST REQUIREMENTS

The following test conditions must be established to obtain accurate clutch cycle rate and cycle time readings:

- Run engine at 1500 rpm for 10 minutes.
- Operate A/C system on max A/C (recirculating air).
- Run blower at max speed.
- Stabilize in car temperature @ 70°F to 80°F (21°C to 22°C).

SECONDS — TOTAL CLUTCH CYCLE TIME — SECONDS

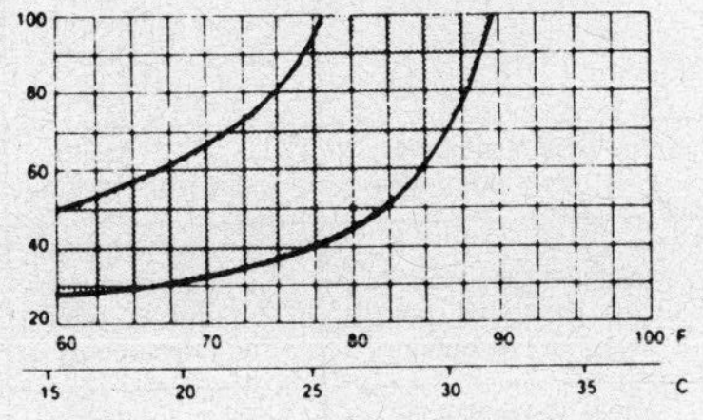
100
80
60
40
20
60
70
80
90
100 F
15
20
25
30
35
C

AMBIENT TEMPERATURES

SECONDS — NORMAL CLUTCH OFF TIME — SECONDS

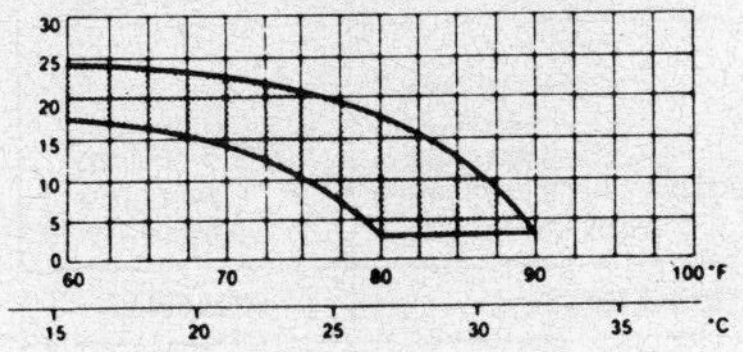
30
25
20
15
10
5
0
60
70
80
90
100°F
15
20
25
30
35
°C

AMBIENT TEMPERATURES

NORMAL CLUTCH CYCLE RATE PER MINUTE

CYCLES/MINUTE

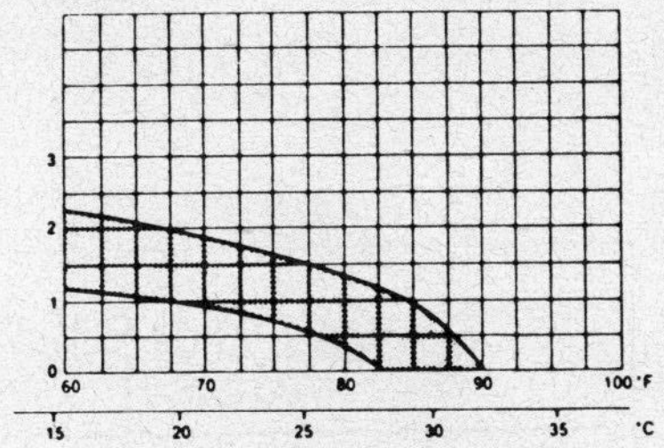
3
2
1
0
60
70
80
90
100°F
15
20
25
30
35
°C

AMBIENT TEMPERATURES

SECONDS — NORMAL CLUTCH ON TIME — SECONDS

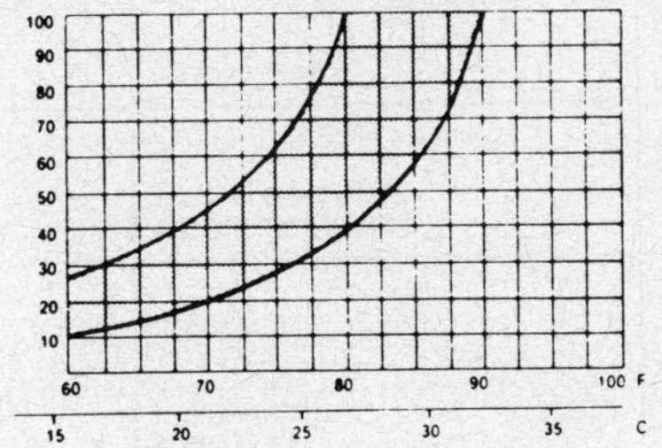
100
90
80
70
60
50
40
30
20
10
60
70
80
90
100 F
15
20
25
30
35
C

AMBIENT TEMPERATURES

FIXED ORIFICE TUBE REFRIGERANT SYSTEM PRESSURE AND CLUTCH CYCLE TIMING EVALUATION CHART—EXCEPT 1991 ESCORT AND TRACER

REFRIGERANT SYSTEM PRESSURE AND CLUTCH CYCLE TIMING EVALUATION CHART FOR FIXED ORIFICE TUBE CYCLING CLUTCH SYSTEMS

NOTE: System test requirements must be met to obtain accurate test readings for evaluation. Refer to the normal refrigerant system pressure/temperature and the normal clutch cycle rate and times charts.

HIGH (DISCHARGE) PRESSURE	LOW (SUCTION) PRESSURE	CLUTCH CYCLE TIME RATE	CLUTCH CYCLE TIME ON	CLUTCH CYCLE TIME OFF	COMPONENT — CAUSES
HIGH	HIGH	CONTINUOUS RUN			CONDENSER — Inadequate Airflow
HIGH	NORMAL TO HIGH	CONTINUOUS RUN			ENGINE OVERHEATING
NORMAL TO HIGH	NORMAL	CONTINUOUS RUN			REFRIGERANT OVERCHARGE (a) AIR IN REFRIGERANT HUMIDITY OR AMBIENT TEMP VERY HIGH (b)
NORMAL	HIGH	CONTINUOUS RUN			FIXED ORIFICE TUBE — Missing O Rings Leaking/Missing
NORMAL	NORMAL	SLOW OR NO CYCLE	LONG OR CONTINUOUS	NORMAL OR NO CYCLE	MOISTURE IN REFRIGERANT SYSTEM EXCESSIVE REFRIGERANT OIL
NORMAL	LOW	SLOW	LONG	LONG	CLUTCH CYCLING SWITCH — Low Cut Out
NORMAL TO LOW	HIGH	CONTINUOUS RUN			Compressor — Low Performance
NORMAL TO LOW	NORMAL TO HIGH	CONTINUOUS RUN			A/C SUCTION LINE — Partially Restricted or Plugged (c)
NORMAL TO LOW	NORMAL	FAST	SHORT	NORMAL	EVAPORATOR - Low or Restricted Airflow
			SHORT TO VERY SHORT	NORMAL TO LONG	CONDENSER FIXED ORIFICE TUBE OR A/C LIQUID LINE — Partially Restricted or Plugged
			SHORT TO VERY SHORT	SHORT TO VERY SHORT	LOW REFRIGERANT CHARGE
			SHORT TO VERY SHORT	LONG	EVAPORATOR CORE — Partially Restricted or Plugged
NORMAL TO LOW	LOW	CONTINUOUS RUN			A/C SUCTION LINE — Partially Restricted or Plugged (d) CLUTCH CYCLING SWITCH — Sticking Closed
ERRATIC OPERATION OR COMPRESSOR NOT RUNNING		—	—	—	CLUTCH CYCLING SWITCH — Dirty Contacts or Sticking Open POOR CONNECTION AT A/C CLUTCH CONNECTOR OR CLUTCH CYCLING SWITCH CONNECTOR A/C ELECTRICAL CIRCUIT ERRATIC — See A/C Electrical Circuit Wiring Diagram
ADDITIONAL POSSIBLE CAUSE COMPONENTS ASSOCIATED WITH INADEQUATE COMPRESSOR OPERATION					
• COMPRESSOR DRIVE BELT — Loose • COMPRESSOR CLUTCH — Slipping • CLUTCH COIL Open — Shorted, or Loose Mounting • CONTROL ASSEMBLY SWITCH — Dirty Contacts or Sticking Open • CLUTCH WIRING CIRCUIT — High Resistance, Open or Blown Fuse • COMPRESSOR OPERATION INTERRUPTED BY ENGINE COMPUTER					
ADDITIONAL POSSIBLE CAUSE COMPONENTS ASSOCIATED WITH A DAMAGED COMPRESSOR					
• CLUTCH CYCLING SWITCH - Sticking Closed or Compressor Clutch Seized • SUCTION ACCUMULATOR DRIER — Refrigerant Oil Bleed Hole Plugged • REFRIGERANT LEAKS					

(a) Compressor may make noise on initial run. This is slugging condition caused by excessive liquid refrigerant
(b) Compressor clutch may not cycle in ambient temperatures above 80°F depending on humidity conditions
(c) Low pressure reading will be normal to high if pressure is taken at accumulator and if restriction is downstream of service access valve
(d) Low pressure reading will be low if pressure is taken near the compressor and restriction is upstream of service access valve

AIR CONDITIONING DIAGNOSIS AND TESTING—PROBE

SYMPTOM	POSSIBLE CAUSE	ACTION TO TAKE
• No cooling or insufficient cooling.	• Compressor Clutch • Refrigerant level and condition • Electrical Circuit • Drive Belt • WAC Relay (2.2L) • A/C Relay (3.0L)	• GO to A1 • GO to CC1
• Compressor always runs (engine warm or cold).	• Pressure Switch • WAC Relay (2.2L) • A/C Relay (3.0L)	• GO to CC3 (2.2L) • GO to CC10 (3.0L)
• Condenser Fan never runs.	• Condenser Fan Relay • Electrical Circuit • Condenser Fan Motor	• GO to CFM1
• Condenser Fan always runs (engine warm or cold).	• Condenser Fan Relay • Electrical Circuit • Condenser Fan Motor	• GO to CFM1
• Blows frost out ducts.	• Evaporator Drain • Compressor always runs	• CLEAR any blockage • SEE Direction above
• Conderser Fan & Compressor run constantly **with warm engine** (2.2L engine only).	• WAC Relay	• REPLACE

TEST STEP	RESULT ►	ACTION TO TAKE
A1 STEP 1 CHECK SYSTEM PRESSURES		
• Connect manifold gauge set. • Engine running at 2,000 rpm. • Blower motor on high. • Temperature control at cool. • If compressor clutch does not engage, jump battery power to GN/BK wire at clutch connector. • Wait until air conditioning system stabilizes and check readings of hi and lo gauges. Normal HI: 199–220 psi (1373–1520 kPa) (14.0–15.5 kg/cm²) LO: 19–21 psi (131–145 kPa) (1.34–1.48 kg/cm²) • Is pressure normal?	Yes ► No ►	GO to CC1. GO to A2.

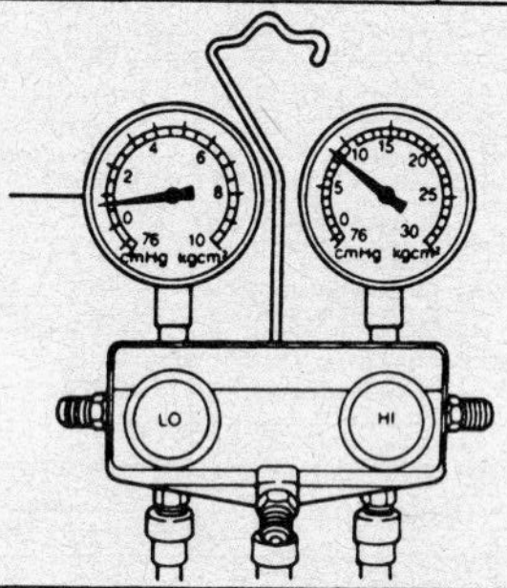
LO
HI

MANIFOLD GAUGE SET
063-00010

AIR CONDITIONING DIAGNOSIS AND TESTING—PROBE

TEST STEP	RESULT ►	ACTION TO TAKE
A2 CHECK FOR SUFFICIENT REFRIGERANT		
• Read hi and lo gauges on manifold set. • Check for low pressure on both hi and lo gauges. Hi: 114–128 psi (785–883 kPa) (8–9 kg/cm²) Lo: 0–11.4 psi (0–78 kPa) (0–0.8 kg/cm²) • Are both pressures low?	Yes ► No ►	LEAK check system and recharge with proper amount of refrigerant. GO to **A3**.

TEST STEP	RESULT ►	ACTION TO TAKE
A3 CHECK FOR EXCESSIVE REFRIGERANT		
• Read hi and lo gauges on manifold set. • Check for high pressure on both hi and lo gauges. Hi: 284 psi or greater (1965 kPa or greater) (20 kg/cm² or greater) Lo: 35.6 psi or greater (245 kPa or greater) (2.5 kg/cm² or greater) • Are both pressures high?	Yes ► No ►	RECHARGE system with proper amount of oil and refrigerant. GO to **A4**.

TEST STEP	RESULT ►	ACTION TO TAKE
A4 CHECK FOR AIR IN SYSTEM		
• Read hi and lo gauges on manifold set. • Check for warm low-pressure piping during operation. • Check for high pressure on both hi and lo gauges. Hi: 327 psi or greater (2257 kPa or greater) (23 kg/cm² or greater) Lo: 35 psi or greater (245 kPa or greater) (2.5 kg/cm² or greater) • Is low side piping warm and both pressures high?	Yes ► No ►	EVACUATE and recharge system. Check compressor oil for contamination. REPLACE receiver/drier. GO to **A5**.

TEST STEP	RESULT ►	ACTION TO TAKE
A5 CHECK FOR MOISTURE IN SYSTEM		
• Read hi and lo gauges on manifold set. • Check for fluctuating high-pressure side and low-pressure side becoming vacuum and pressure. • Are pressures fluctuating?	Yes ► No ►	EVACUATE system. REPLACE receiver/drier. RECHARGE system. GO to **A6**.

TEST STEP	RESULT ►	ACTION TO TAKE
A6 CHECK FOR POOR CIRCULATION		
• Read hi and lo gauges on manifold set. • Check for frost buildup on piping near receiver and fixed orifice tube. • Check for low pressure on hi gauge and very low pressure on lo gauge. Hi: 85–95 psi (586–655 kPa) (5.97–6.67 kg/cm²) Lo: 26 in-Hg vacuum (660 mm-Hg vacuum) • Is frost buildup present and are both pressures low?	Yes ► No ►	EVACUATE system. REPLACE receiver/drier. CLEAN or REPLACE fixed orifice tube as required; recharge system. GO to **A7**.

AIR CONDITIONING DIAGNOSIS AND TESTING – PROBE

TEST STEP	RESULT ►	ACTION TO TAKE
A7 CHECK FOR FAULTY COMPRESSOR		
• Read hi and lo gauges on manifold set. • Check for hi pressure gauge too low and lo pressure gauge too high. Hi: 99–143 psi (686–981 kPa) (7–10 kg/cm²) Lo: 57–86 psi (392–588 kPa) (4–6 kg/cm²) • Is hi gauge too high and lo gauge too low?	Yes ► No ►	SERVICE compressor as required. OPERATE system for longer 15–20 minute period, CYCLE temperature control from cold to hot, back to cold and RE-CHECK pressures.
NOTE: To prevent the replacement of good components, be aware that the following components may be at fault: – Compressor Clutch Circuit – Ventilation System (blockage) – Air Ducting – Manual Controls		

TEST STEP	RESULT ►	ACTION TO TAKE
CC1 CHECK POWER TO CLUTCH		
• Key on, engine idling. • A/C on. • Blower on. • Temperature on "low." • Measure voltage at Compressor Clutch GN/BK. • Is voltage greater than 10V?	Yes ► No 2.2L ► No 3.0L ►	INSPECT ground of Clutch, and condition of Drive Belt and Clutch material. GO to CC2. GO to CC5.

TEST STEP	RESULT ►	ACTION TO TAKE
CC2 CHECK GN/BK FOR OPENS		
• Key off. • Disconnect WAC relay. • Disconnect Condenser Fan Motor. • Measure resistance between Compressor Clutch GN/BK terminal and WAC Relay GN/BK terminal. • Is resistance less than 5 ohms?	Yes ► No ►	GO to CC3. SERVICE GN/BK for opens.

TEST STEP	RESULT ►	ACTION TO TAKE
CC3 CHECK GN/BK FOR SHORTS		
• Key off. • Disconnect Compressor Clutch. • Disconnect WAC Relay. • Disconnect Condenser Fan Motor. • Measure resistance between WAC Relay GN/BK terminal and ground. • Measure resistance between WAC Relay GN/BK terminal and BK/W terminal. • Are both resistances greater than 10,000 ohms?	Yes ► No ►	RECONNECT Compressor Clutch and Condenser Fan Motor. GO to CC4. SERVICE GN/BK for shorts to ground or key power.

TEST STEP	RESULT ►	ACTION TO TAKE
CC4 CHECK WAC RELAY GROUND		
• Key off. • Disconnect WAC Relay. • Measure resistance between WAC Relay BK terminal and ground. • Is resistance less than 5 ohms?	Yes ► No ►	GO to CC9. SERVICE BK wire for open.

AIR CONDITIONING DIAGNOSIS AND TESTING—PROBE

TEST STEP	RESULT ►	ACTION TO TAKE
CC5 CHECK COMPRESSOR CONNECTION		
• Key off. • Disconnect Integral Relay Controller. • Disconnect Compressor Clutch. • Measure resistance.	Yes ►	LEAVE Clutch and Integral Relay Controller disconnected. GO to CC6 .
	No ►	SERVICE wire in question.

From	To	Resistance
Compressor Clutch GN/BK	Integral Relay Controller GN/BK	0-5 ohms
Compressor Clutch GN/BL	Integral Relay Controller GN/BL	0-5 ohms

• Are resistances OK?

TEST STEP	RESULT ►	ACTION TO TAKE
CC6 CHECK FOR SHORTS		
• Key off. • Measure resistance from Compressor Clutch GN/BK and GN/BL to ground. • Are both resistances greater than 10,000 ohms?	Yes ►	RECONNECT Compressor Clutch. GO to CC7 .
	No ►	SERVICE wire in question.

TEST STEP	RESULT ►	ACTION TO TAKE
CC7 CHECK POWER TO RELAY		
• Key on. • A/C on, Blower on. • Measure voltage at Integral Relay Connector PK/BK terminal. • Is voltage greater than 10V?	Yes ►	REFER to NAAO Engine/Emissions Diagnosis Manual.
	No ►	RECONNECT Integral Relay Controller. GO to CC8 .

TEST STEP	RESULT ►	ACTION TO TAKE
CC8 CHECK POWER TO CCPS		
• Key on. • A/C on, Blower on. • Disconnect Clutch Cycling Pressure Switch (CCPS). • Measure voltage at CCPS Connector BL/BK terminal. • Is voltage greater than 10V?	Yes ►	GO to CC15 .
	No ►	Reconnect CCPS. GO to CC7 .

TEST STEP	RESULT ►	ACTION TO TAKE
CC9 RELAY POWER CHECK		
• Disconnect A/C Relay (3.0L). • Disconnect WAC Relay (2.2L). • Key on. • A/C on. • Blower on. • Measure voltage at relay BK/W and GN terminals. • Is voltage greater than 10V?	Yes ►	Reconnect WAC Relay. GO to CC10 .
	No ►	SERVICE wire in question.

AIR CONDITIONING DIAGNOSIS AND TESTING—PROBE

TEST STEP	RESULT ►	ACTION TO TAKE
CC10 CHECK WAC RELAY		
• Key on. • Blower on. • Measure voltage at: Engine 3.0L — Terminal BL/BK; Engine 2.2L — Terminal GN/BK • Ground: Engine 3.0L — Terminal BL/GN; Engine 2.2L — Terminal BL/BK • Is voltage greater than 10V with terminal grounded and less than 1V with terminal open?	Yes 3.0L ►	GO to CC11 .
	Yes. 2.2L ►	GO to CC12 .
	No ►	REPLACE Relay.

Measure voltage at:

Engine	Terminal
3.0L	BL/BK
2.2L	GN/BK

Ground:

Engine	Terminal
3.0L	BL/GN
2.2L	BL/BK

TEST STEP	RESULT ►	ACTION TO TAKE
CC11 CHECK VOLTAGE AT BLOWER SWITCH		
• Key on. • Switch A/C on and off. • Measure voltage at Blower Control Switch BL/BK. • Does voltage jump between OV and 10-12V?	Yes ►	SERVICE BL/BK between A/C Relay and Cycling Clutch Pressure Switch.
	No Conventional ►	GO to CC12 .
	No Electronic ►	GO to H.V.A.C. Control Unit Diagnosis.

TEST STEP	RESULT ►	ACTION TO TAKE
CC12 CHECK BLOWER SWITCH		
• Key off. • Blower on. • Turn A/C on and off. • Measure resistance between BL/GN and BK terminals on Blower Control Switch. • Does resistance jump from 0-5 ohms to 10,000 ohms?	Yes ►	GO to CC13 .
	No ►	REPLACE Blower Control Switch.

TEST STEP	RESULT ►	ACTION TO TAKE
CC13 CHECK SWITCH GROUND		
• Key off. • Measure resistance between Blower Control Switch BK terminal and ground. • Is resistance less than 5 ohms?	Yes 3.0L ►	SERVICE BL/GN from A/C Relay to Blower Ground Switch.
	Yes 2.2L ►	GO to CC14 .
	No ►	SERVICE ground.

TEST STEP	RESULT ►	ACTION TO TAKE
CC14 CHECK CCPS CONNECTION		
• Key off. • A/C off. • Measure resistance from Blower Control Switch BL/GN terminal and Clutch Cycling Pressure Switch BL/GN terminal. • Is resistance less than 5 ohms? • Measure resistance from Blower Control Switch BL/GN terminal to ground. • In resistance greater than 10,000 ohms?	Yes to both ►	GO to CC15 .
	No to either ►	SERVICE BL/GN for opens or shorts.

AIR CONDITIONING DIAGNOSIS AND TESTING – PROBE

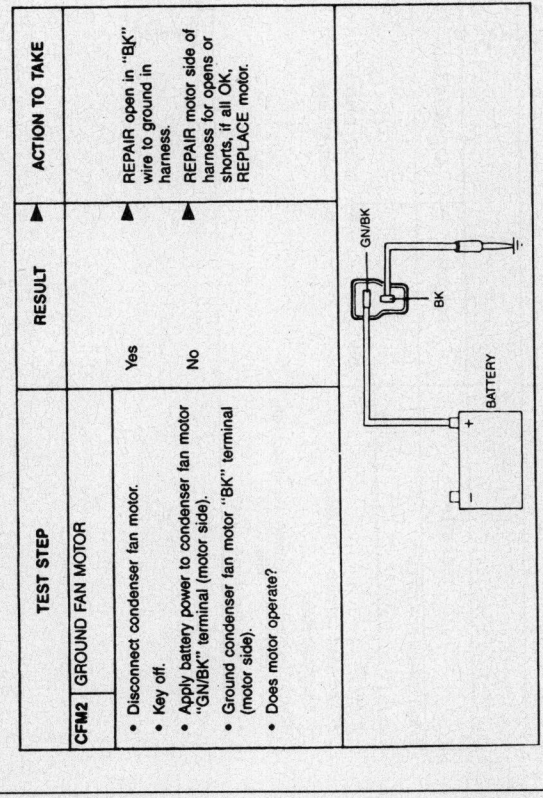

TEST STEP	RESULT ►	ACTION TO TAKE
CC15 CHECK CCPS OPERATION		
• Key on, engine idling. • A/C on, Blower on. • Disconnect Clutch Cycling Pressure Switch (CCPS). • Jump terminals of CCPS connector together. • Does the compressor operate with the terminals jumped and stop with the terminals open?	Yes ►	REPLACE Clutch Cycling Pressure Switch.
	No 2.2L ►	REFER to Non-NAAO Engine/Emissions Diagnosis Manual **Section 16.**
	No 3.0L ►	SERVICE PK/BK wire from CCPS to Integral Relay Controller.

TEST STEP	RESULT ►	ACTION TO TAKE
CFM1 JUMP POWER TO MOTOR		
• Key off. • Condenser fan motor connected. • Apply battery power to condenser fan motor connector "GN/BK" terminal. • Does motor operate?	Yes ►	GO to **CFM3** .
	No ►	GO to **CFM2** .

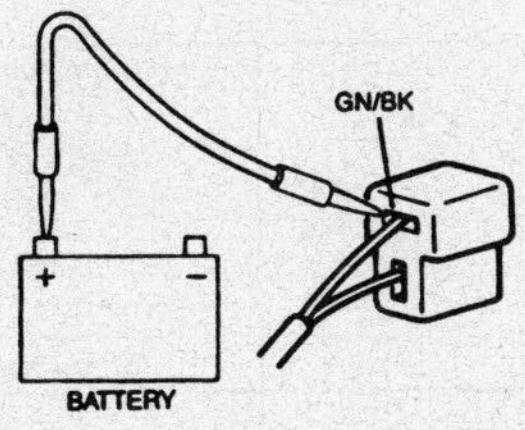
GN/BK
BATTERY

TEST STEP	RESULT ►	ACTION TO TAKE
CFM2 GROUND FAN MOTOR		
• Disconnect condenser fan motor. • Key off. • Apply battery power to condenser fan motor "GN/BK" terminal (motor side). • Ground condenser fan motor "BK" terminal (motor side). • Does motor operate?	Yes ►	REPAIR open in "BK" wire to ground in harness.
	No ►	REPAIR motor side of harness for opens or shorts, if all OK, REPLACE motor.

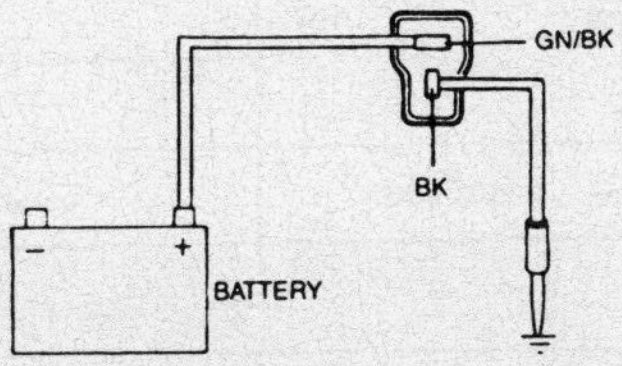
GN/BK
BK
BATTERY

TEST STEP	RESULT ►	ACTION TO TAKE
CFM3 CHECK VOLTAGE AT WAC RELAY		
• Key on. • VOM on 20 volt scale. • Measure voltage at relay GN and BK/W terminals. • Are both readings greater than 10 volts?	Yes ► No ►	GO to CFM4 . REPAIR wire in question (GN or BK/W to fuse panel).

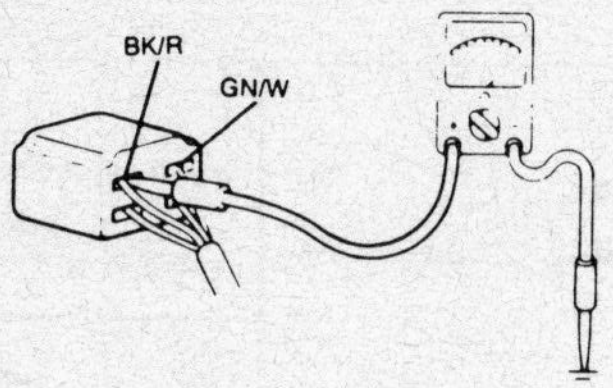
BK/R
GN/W

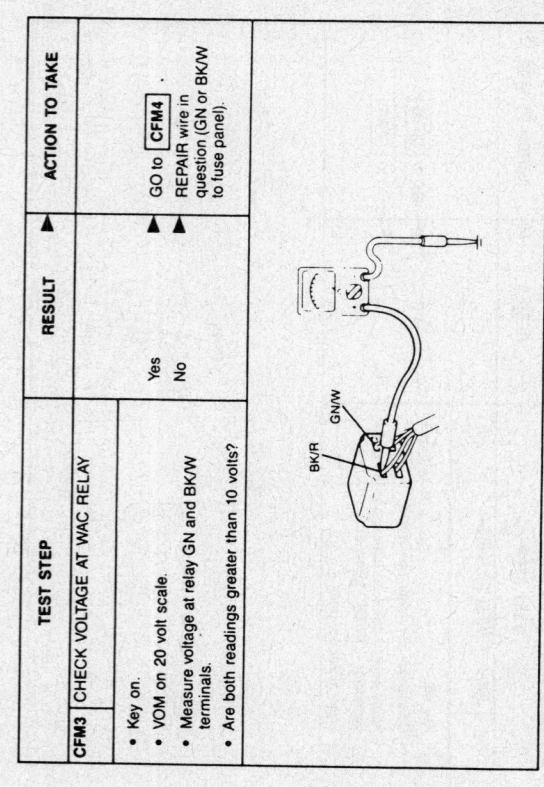

TEST STEP	RESULT ►	ACTION TO TAKE
CFM4 CHECK RELAY OPERATION		
• Key on. • Measure voltage at:	Yes 3.0L ► Yes 2.2L ► No ►	GO to CFM6 . GO to CFM5 . REPLACE Relay.

Engine	Relay	Terminal
3.0L	Condenser Fan	BL/BK
2.2L	WAC	GN/BK

• Ground:

Engine	Relay	Terminal
3.0L	Condenser Fan	BL/Y
2.2L	WAC	BL/BK

• Does voltage jump up to 10-12V when terminal is grounded?

TEST STEP	RESULT ►	ACTION TO TAKE
CFM5 CHECK WAC RELAY GROUND		
• Key off. • Disconnect Battery. • Measure resistance at WAC Relay.	Yes ► No ►	GO to CFM6 . SERVICE wire in question.

Voltmeter (+)	Voltmeter (−)	Resistance
BK	Ground	0-5 ohms
BK	BK/W	Over 10,000 ohms
BK	GN	Over 10,000 ohms

• Are resistances OK?

TEST STEP	RESULT ►	ACTION TO TAKE
CFM6 CHECK FOR OPENS		
• Key off. • Disconnect Condenser Fan Motor. • Disconnect Relay. • Measure resistance between Condenser Fan Motor GN/BK and Relay GN/BK. • Is resistance less than 5 ohms?	Yes ► No ►	GO to CFM7 . SERVICE wire.

AIR CONDITIONING AND HEATING SYSTEM DIAGNOSIS AND TESTING—FESTIVA

SYMPTOM	POSSIBLE CAUSE	ACTION TO TAKE
No heating or insufficient heating	• Coolant level and condition • Thermostat • Heater core	Go to AH1
Coolant odor in passenger compartment	• Heater core	Go to AH1
Intermittent Heating	• Coolant level	Check coolant level, go to AH1
No cooling or insufficient cooling	• Clutch condition • Drive belt tension and condition • Moisture, air, excessive oil or refrigerant in system • Compressor • Thermostatic expansion valve • Insufficient refrigerant • Leaks • Clogged refrigerant circulation system • Blocked evaporator or condensor • Circuit	Inspect, repair as required Go to A1 Go to CC1
Intermittent cooling	• Clutch slipping • Drive belt tension and condition • Thermostatic expansion valve • Excessive moisture in system • Insufficient refrigerant • Compressor clutch circuit	Inspect, repair as required Go to A1 Go to CC1
No compressor clutch operation	• Accelerator switch • Circuit • Fuses • Refrigerant pressure switch • Clutch condition • Belt tension and condition • Thermostatic switch	Go to CC1
Blows frost out of ducts (after several minutes of operation)	• Plugged evaporator drain line • Excessive refrigerant • Thermostatic switch	Clear blockage Go to A1 Go to CC8
Compressor clutch runs constantly (no cycling)	• Thermostatic switch • Circuit	Go to CC7
Improper blower motor operation	• Motor • Circuit • Resistor • Switch	Go to section 36-11
Condenser fan runs constantly	• Condenser fan relay • Circuit • Condenser fan motor	Go to CF1
Condenser fan never runs	• Fuse • Circuit • Condenser fan relay • Condenser fan motor	Go to CF1

TEST STEP	RESULT ▶	ACTION TO TAKE
AH1 SYSTEM INTEGRITY CHECK		
• Visually inspect the heater core, heater hoses and cooling system for evidence of leaks, separated connections, cracked hoses or any other damage. • Check for blocked heater inlet or outlet ducts. • Check for blown fuses, poor electrical connections, signs of opens, shorts or damage to the wiring harness. • Check passenger compartment for signs of coolant odor and wetness in carpeting or upholstery. • Does the system appear to be in good condition?	Yes ▶ No ▶	GO to AH2. REPAIR or REPLACE as required.

TEST STEP	RESULT ▶	ACTION TO TAKE
AH2 INSPECT COOLING SYSTEM		
• Check general condition of cooling system components for obvious signs of leaks or damage. • Check coolant level and condition. • Check radiator cap for proper pressure retention. • Check for proper cooling system hose routing. • Check condition of water pump and drive belt. • Check for proper thermostat operation. • Does the cooling system appear to be in good condition?	Yes ▶ No ▶	GO to AH3. REPAIR or REPLACE damaged component(s) as required.

AIR CONDITIONING AND HEATING SYSTEM DIAGNOSIS AND TESTING – FESTIVA

TEST STEP	RESULT ►	ACTION TO TAKE
AH3 HEATER CORE PRESSURE CHECK		
• Drain the cooling system. • Disconnect supply and return hoses to the heater core. • Attach short pieces of hose (about 4 inches long) to both the inlet and outlet of the heater core. • Plug the outlet side hose. • Fill heater core with water. • Apply 30 psi to the inlet side of the heater core with a radiator pressure tester. • Observe pressure gauge on pressure tester for 3 minutes. • Does heater core hold steady pressure for 3 minutes?	Yes ►	REMOVE pressure tester. Replace hoses. GO to **AH4**.
	No ►	REPAIR or REPLACE heater core as required.

NOTE: A leaky heater core connection can cause coolant to run into heater core and appear to be a heater core leak.

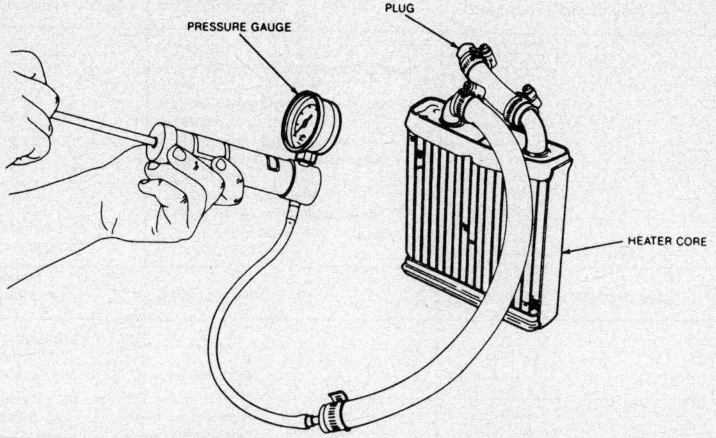
PLUG
PRESSURE GAUGE
HEATER CORE

TEST STEP	RESULT ►	ACTION TO TAKE
AH4 CHECK SYSTEM CIRCULATION		
• Let engine cool completely. • Start the engine. • Temporarily remove the outlet hose from the heater core at the firewall and direct coolant into a catch vessel. • Does coolant flow steadily from the heater core?	Yes ►	Shut engine off. Reconnect heater hose. System OK, problem may be located in cooling system or ventilation system.
	No ►	Check heater hoses and heater core for blockage; repair or replace as required.

Testing A/C Performance

1. Connect the manifold gauge set.
2. Run the engine at 2000 rpm.
3. Turn the A/C on.
4. Turn the blower on high.
5. Recirc/fresh air lever on recirculation.
6. Open windows.
7. Place a thermometer in the center console duct.
8. Place a thermometer in the blower inlet under the right-hand side of the dash.
9. Measure the relative humidity at the blower inlet using a psycrometer.
10. Wait 5-10 minutes for the A/C system to stabilize.
11. The high-pressure gauge should read 1372-1517kPa (199-220 psi) (if too low, cover the condenser; if too high, spray water through the condenser).

    If the pressure cannot be brought within specification, record the pressure once it stabilizes and proceed to the Symptom chart.
12. Determine the temperture difference between the air inlet and the center console duct.
13. Compare the temperature difference to the relative humidity on the chart; if the intersection of the temperature difference and the relative humidity is between the two hatched lines, the cooling performance is satisfactory.

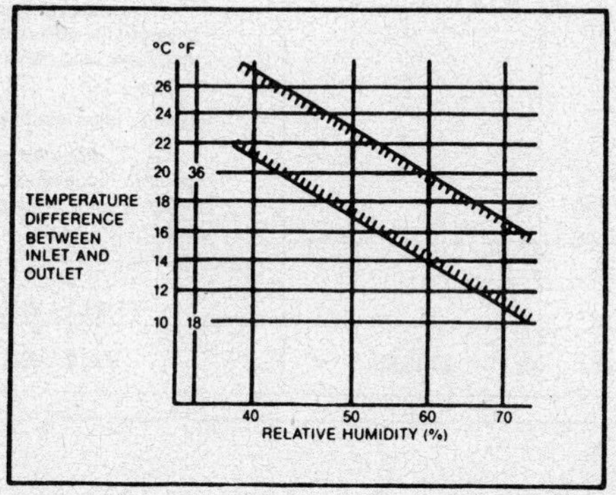
°C °F
26
24
22
20 36
18
16
14
12
10 18
TEMPERATURE DIFFERENCE BETWEEN INLET AND OUTLET
40
50
60
70
RELATIVE HUMIDITY (%)

AIR CONDITIONING AND HEATING SYSTEM DIAGNOSIS AND TESTING—FESTIVA

TEST STEP	RESULT ►	ACTION TO TAKE
A1 SYSTEM INTEGRITY CHECK		
• Inspect A/C system hoses and plumbing for signs of wear, leaks, cracks, loose connectors or other damage. • Inspect compressor clutch for signs of leaks (oil or refrigerant residue present on compressor case). • Inspect drive belt for proper tension condition and signs of wear. • Does the system appear to be in good condition?	Yes ► No ►	GO to A2 . REPAIR or REPLACE faulty components as required.

TEST STEP	RESULT ►	ACTION TO TAKE
A2 CHECK SYSTEM PRESSURES		
• Connect a manifold set to the A/C system. • Key on, engine idling at 2000 rpm. • Blower on high. • A/C on, temperature blend lever to extreme left (cool position). • Wait 5 minutes for system to stabilize. • Observe the gauges and feel the temperatures of the suction and pressure lines near the compressor. • Look for built up condensation on the A/C plumbing near the compressor and receiver/dryer. • Turn A/C off and observe sight glass, then turn A/C back on. • Compare gauge readings and system temperatures to the following chart.		

A2 CHECK SYSTEM PRESSURES (Continued)

GAUGE READING	PRESSURE SIDE PLUMBING	SUCTION SIDE PLUMBING	SIGHT GLASS	POSSIBLE CAUSE	ACTION TO TAKE
HI: 199-220 psi LO: 19-25 psi	Warm and dry	Cool and dry	Bubbles only after shut-off	Normal operation	Return to symptom chart.
HI: 114-128 psi LO: 0-12 psi (too low)	Warm and dry	Warm and dry	Bubbles all the time Never bubbles	• Insufficient refrigerant • Empty system	Test for leaks. Evacuate & recharge system.
HI: 235-280 psi LO: 34-44 psi (too high)	Warm and dry	Cool and dry	No bubbles after shut-off	• Excessive refrigerant • System oil level too low • Condenser obstruction • Condenser fan not operating	• Evacuate & recharge. • Put in proper amount of oil. • Clear obstruction. • Return to symptom chart.
HI: 260-290 psi (too high) LO: 25-35 psi (too high)	Warm	Heavy dew or frost build-up	No bubbles after shut-off	• Expansion valve stuck open • Heat sensing bulb improperly installed	• Repair or replace expansion valve as required. • Reinstall properly.
HI: 270-330 psi (too high) LO: 25-35 psi	Warm	Warm	–	• Air in system • Oil contamination	• Evacuate & recharge, if same symptom is present after recharge, repair or replace receiver dryer
HI: Fluctuates LO: Fluctuates between vacuum & normal pressure	Warm	Fluctuates between cool and warm	–	Moisture in system	Evacuate, repair or replace receiver dryer and recharge
HI: 70-150 psi (too low) LO: Vacuum (too low)	Warm	Frost or dew near expansion valve	–	Dirt or moisture in system is blocking expansion valve or equalizer tube	Evacuate, repair or replace expansion valve and receiver dryer, recharge.
HI: 70-150 psi (too low) LO: 25-35 psi (too high)	Warm	Warm	–	Faulty compressor	Repair or replace compressor

TEST STEP	RESULT ►	ACTION TO TAKE
CC1 SYSTEM INTEGRITY CHECK		
• Check for fully charged battery. • Check for blown fuses, corrosion, poor electrical connections, signs of opens, shorts or damage to the wiring harness. • Key on, engine idling. • A/C on. • Blower on. • Shake the wiring harness vigorously and look for signs of opens or shorts. • Tap each connector and look for signs of bad connections. • Does the system appear to be in good condition?	Yes ► No ►	GO to CC2 . REPAIR or REPLACE faulty components as required. **NOTE: If a blown fuse is replaced and fails immediately, there is a short to ground in the system.**

AIR CONDITIONING AND HEATING SYSTEM DIAGNOSIS AND TESTING—FESTIVA

TEST STEP	RESULT ►	ACTION TO TAKE
CC2 CHECK FOR POWER CLUTCH		
• Key on, engine off. • A/C on, blower on. • Measure voltage at compressor clutch electrical connector (BK/W terminal). • Is reading greater than 10V?	Yes ►	Turn key off. GO to CC3 .
	No ►	GO to CC4 .

TEST STEP	RESULT ►	ACTION TO TAKE
CC3 CHECK CLUTCH RESISTANCE		
• Key off, A/C off. • Allow engine to cool. • Disconnect compressor clutch electrical connector. • Measure resistance between compressor clutch connector (clutch side) and compressor clutch case. • Is reading between 2.7 and 3.1 ohms?	Yes ►	Check condition of drive belt, clutch material and compressor; service as required.
	No ►	Service ground of compressor clutch. If all OK, replace clutch.

TEST STEP	RESULT ►	ACTION TO TAKE
CC4 CHECK FOR SHORT IN CLUTCH LEAD		
• Key off. • Disconnect compressor clutch. • Disconnect condenser fan relay. • Disconnect WAC relay. • Measure resistance between WAC relay connect BK/W terminal and ground. • Is resistance less than 10,000 ohms?	Yes ►	Service shorts in BK/W wire from WAC relay to compressor clutch or Condenser Fan Relay
	No ►	Reconnect Condenser Fan Relay WAC relay, and compressor clutch. GO to CC5 .

TEST STEP	RESULT ►	ACTION TO TAKE
CC5 CHECK FOR POWER FROM RELAY		
• Key on, engine idling. • A/C on, blower on. • Measure voltage at WAC relay BK/W terminal. • Is reading greater than 10V?	Yes ►	SERVICE BK/W from WAC relay to compressor clutch and condenser fan relay for opens.
	No ►	TURN engine off. GO to CC6 .

TEST STEP	RESULT ►	ACTION TO TAKE
CC6 CHECK POWER TO RELAY		
• Key on. • A/C on, blower on. • Measure voltage at WAC relay BL/R and Y terminals. • Are both readings greater than 10V?	Yes ►	GO to CC7 .
	No BL/R ►	SERVICE BL/R wire as required.
	No Yellow ►	SERVICE Y wire or 20 amp "FAN" fuse as required.

TEST STEP	RESULT ►	ACTION TO TAKE
CC7 CHECK WAC RELAY OPERATION		
• Key on. • Measure voltage at WAC relay BK/W terminal. • Ground WAC relay GN/Y terminal with a jumper wire. • Is reading greater than 10V with GN/Y grounded and less than 1V with GN/Y open?	Yes ►	TURN key off. GO to CC8 .
	No ►	REPLACE WAC relay.

AIR CONDITIONING AND HEATING SYSTEM DIAGNOSIS AND TESTING – FESTIVA

TEST STEP	RESULT ►	ACTION TO TAKE
CC8 CHECK GROUND AT THERMOSTATIC SWITCH		
• Key off. • A/C on, blower on. • Measure resistance between thermostatic switch GN terminal and ground. • Is reading greater than 10,000 ohms with A/C off and less than 5 ohms with A/C on?	Yes ►	SERVICE GN/Y wire from WAC Relay to ECA.
	No ►	CHECK GN wire for open or shorts if all OK GO to CC9 .

TEST STEP	RESULT ►	ACTION TO TAKE
CC9 CHECK THERMOSTATIC SWITCH		
• Remove thermostatic switch. • Measure resistance between terminals on thermostatic switch. • Apply liquid freon or other cooling liquid to sensing bulb on switch to bring temperature of the sensing bulb below 32°F. • Is resistance greater than 10,000 ohms with sensing bulb warm (above 77°F) and less than 5 ohms with sensing bulb cold?	Yes ►	REINSTALL switch. GO to CC10 .
	No ►	REPLACE thermostatic switch.

TEST STEP	RESULT ►	ACTION TO TAKE
CC10 MEASURE VOLTAGE TO REFRIGERANT PRESSURE SWITCH		
• Key on. • A/C off. • Measure voltage at refrigerant pressure switch BK/W terminal. • Is reading greater tnan 10V?	Yes ►	GO to CC13 .
	No ►	SERVICE BK/W wire from thermostatic switch to refrigerant pressure switch.

TEST STEP	RESULT ►	ACTION TO TAKE
CC11 CHECK REFRIGERANT PRESSURE SWITCH		
• Connect a manifold set to the service gauge port valves.	Yes ►	SERVICE BK/W from refrigerant pressure switch to compressor clutch.
• Disconnect the refrigerant pressure switch electrical connector. • Measure resistance between BK/W and Y/GN terminals of the refrigerant pressure switch. • Is reading less than 5 ohms when the system high side pressure is above 206±20 kPa (30±3 psi)?	Yes ►	GO to CC12 .
	No ►	REPLACE refrigerant pressure switch. **NOTE: If high side pressure is below 206±20 kPa (30±3 psi) check refrigerant system, refer to test step A1.**

TEST STEP	RESULT ►	ACTION TO TAKE
CC12 CHECK A/C SWITCH POWER		
• Key on. • A/C off. • Measure voltage at A/C switch Y/GN terminal. • Is reading greater than 10V?	Yes ►	GO to CC13 .
	No ►	SERVICE Y/GN wire from refrigerant pressure switch to A/C switch.

TEST STEP	RESULT ►	ACTION TO TAKE
CC13 CHECK A/C SWITCH OPERATION		
• Key off. • Measure resistance between A/C switch Y/GN and BL/W terminals. • Is resistance greater than 10,000 ohms with switch off and less than 5 ohms with switch on?	Yes ►	GO to CC14 .
	No ►	REPLACE A/C switch.

AIR CONDITIONING AND HEATING SYSTEM DIAGNOSIS AND TESTING—FESTIVA

TEST STEP	RESULT ▶	ACTION TO TAKE
CC14 CHECK VOLTAGE AT BLOWER SWITCH		
• Key on. • A/C switch on. • Blower off. • Disconnect blower motor. • Measure voltage at blower control switch BL/W terminal. • is voltage greater than 10V?	Yes ▶ No ▶	RECONNECT blower motor, Go to step BM1. SERVICE BL/W wire from A/C switch to blower control switch and resistor.

TEST STEP	RESULT ▶	ACTION TO TAKE
CF1 SYSTEM INTEGRITY CHECK		
• Check for fully charged battery. • Check for blown fuses, corrosion, poor electrical connections, signs of opens, shorts or damage to the wiring harness. • Key on, engine idling. • A/C on. • Blower on. • Shake the wiring harness vigorously from the condenser fan motor to the condenser fan relay and the refrigerant pressure switch. Look for signs of opens or shorts. • Tap each connector and look for signs of bad connections. • Does the system appear to be in good condition?	Yes ▶ No ▶	GO to CF2 . REPAIR or REPLACE faulty components, as required. **NOTE: If a blown fuse is replaced and fails immediately there is a short to ground in the circuit.**

TEST STEP	RESULT ▶	ACTION TO TAKE
CF2 CHECK VOLTAGE AT MOTOR		
• Insert jumper wire at refrigerant pressure switch between W and BK wires. • Key on, engine idling. • A/C on. • Blower on. • Measure voltage at condenser fan motor Y terminal. • Is voltage greater than 10V?	Yes ▶ No ▶	GO to CF3 . SERVICE Y wire from main fuse panel to condenser fan for opens or shorts.

TEST STEP	RESULT ▶	ACTION TO TAKE
CF3 MOTOR OPERATION CHECK		
• Key off. • Disconnect condenser fan motor. • Jump battery power to condenser fan motor Y terminal. • Ground condenser fan GN/R terminal. • Does fan motor run?	Yes ▶ No ▶	GO to CF4 . SERVICE motor side of harness for opens or shorts. If all OK, replace condenser fan motor.

GN/R
Y

TEST STEP	RESULT ▶	ACTION TO TAKE
CF4 CHECK VOLTAGE FROM MOTOR		
• Key on. • Disconnect condenser fan relay. • Measure voltage at condenser fan relay GN/R terminal. • Is voltage greater than 10V?	Yes ▶ No ▶	GO to CF5 . SERVICE GN/R wire from condenser fan motor to condenser fan relay.

AIR CONDITIONING AND HEATING SYSTEM DIAGNOSIS AND TESTING—FESTIVA

TEST STEP	RESULT ►	ACTION TO TAKE
CF5 CHECK VOLTAGE TO RELAY		
• Key on, engine idling. • A/C on. • Blower on. • Disconnect condenser fan relay. • Measure voltage at condenser fan motor GN/R terminal. • Is voltage greater than 10V?	Yes ► No ►	RECONNECT condenser fan relay. GO to **CF6**. Go to **CF7**.

TEST STEP	RESULT ►	ACTION TO TAKE
CF6 CHECK RELAY OPERATION		
• Remove condenser fan relay. • Jump battery power to relay "A" terminal. • Measure resistance between relay "B" and "C" terminals. • Ground relay "D" terminal with a jumper wire. • Is reading greater than 10,000 ohms with "D" terminal open and less than 5 ohms with relay terminal grounded?	Yes ► No ►	SERVICE relay grounds (BK wires). REPLACE condenser fan relay.

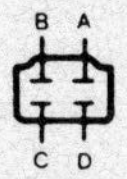
B
A
C
D

TEST STEP	RESULT ►	ACTION TO TAKE
CF7 CHECK VOLTAGE AT REFRIGERANT PRESSURE SWITCH		
• Key on, engine idling. • A/C on. • Blower on. • Measure voltage at Refrigerant Pressure Switch BK terminal. • Is voltage greater than 10 volts?	Yes ► No ►	GO to **CF8**. GO to **CC4**.

TEST STEP	RESULT ►	ACTION TO TAKE
CF8 CHECK REFRIGERANT PRESSURE SWITCH OPERATION		
• Install Manifold Gauge Set. • Key on, engine idling. • A/C on. • Blower on. • Verify that the pressure in the discharge line is below 1965 kPa (285 psi). • Measure voltage at refrigerant pressure switch W terminal. • Is the voltage greater than 10 V?	Yes ► No ►	REPLACE refrigerant pressure switch. GO to **CF9**.

AIR CONDITIONING AND HEATING SYSTEM DIAGNOSIS AND TESTING—FESTIVA

TEST STEP	RESULT ►	ACTION TO TAKE
CF9 CHECK REFRIGERANT PRESSURE SWITCH OPERATION		
• Install Manifold Gauge Set. • Key on, engine idling. • A/C on. • Blower on. • Run A/C system until high pressure gauge reads above 2350 kPa (340 psi). • Measure voltage at refrigerant pressure switch W terminal. • Is the voltage greater than 10 V?	Yes ► No ►	Service W wire between refrigerant pressure switch and cooling fan relay. Replace refrigerant pressure switch.

AIR CONDITIONING AND HEATING SYSTEM DIAGNOSIS AND TESTING—1989–90 TRACER

SYMPTOM	TEST STEP
A/C SYSTEM	
Insufficient cooling or no cooling	A1
No condenser fan operation	B1
Improper cooling fan operation	C1
HEATING SYSTEM	
Insufficient heating or no heating	D1
Coolant odor in passenger compartment	E1
AIR DUCTING SYSTEM	
No blower operation	F1
Improper air distribution	G1

A1 INTEGRITY CHECK

TEST STEP	RESULT	ACTION TO TAKE
• Visually inspect all A/C lines, compressor, condensor, evaporator, receiver and all connections for signs of leaks, poor connections or other damage, check compressor belt tension. • Inspect compressor clutch circuit for pinched wires, blown fuses, opens, shorts, bad connections or other damage. • Are any concerns evident?	Yes No	Repair or replace as required. Go to A-2.

A2 COMPRESSOR CLUTCH OPERATION CHECK

TEST STEP	RESULT	ACTION TO TAKE
• A/C on. • Engine running at idle. • Blower on. • Connect and disconnect compressor clutch electrical connector. • Does compressor clutch engage when connector is connected?	Yes No	Confirm belt tension and condition. Go to A3a. Go to A4.

A3a CHECK SYSTEM PRESSURES

TEST STEP	RESULT	ACTION TO TAKE
• Connect manifold set to system. • Close Hi and Lo valves. • Connect hi-pressure hose to the discharge service valve of the compressor. • Connect the low-pressure hose to the suction service valve of the compressor. • Engine running at idle. • A/C on, full cold. • Blower motor on high. • Check readings of Hi and Lo gauges: Normal Hi: 199-220 psi (1373-1520 KPa) (14.0-15.5 Kg cm^2) Lo: 19-21 psi (131-145 KPa) (1.34-1.48 Kg cm^2) • Is pressure normal?	Yes No	Check evaporator drain for possible blockage. Go to A3b. **NOTE:** Read step A3b through A3h before performing repairs to confirm failure.

A3b CHECK FOR SUFFICIENT REFRIGERANT

TEST STEP	RESULT	ACTION TO TAKE
• Read Hi and Lo gauges on manifold set. • Check for bubbles in sight glass. • Check for low pressures on both Hi and Lo gauges: Hi: 144-128 psi (992-882 KPa) (10-8.99 Kg/cm²) Lo: 0-11.4 psi (0-78.6 KPa) (0-.80 Kg/cm²) • Are bubbles present in sight glass and both pressures low?	Yes	Leak check system and recharge with proper amount of refrigerant.
	No	Go to A3c.

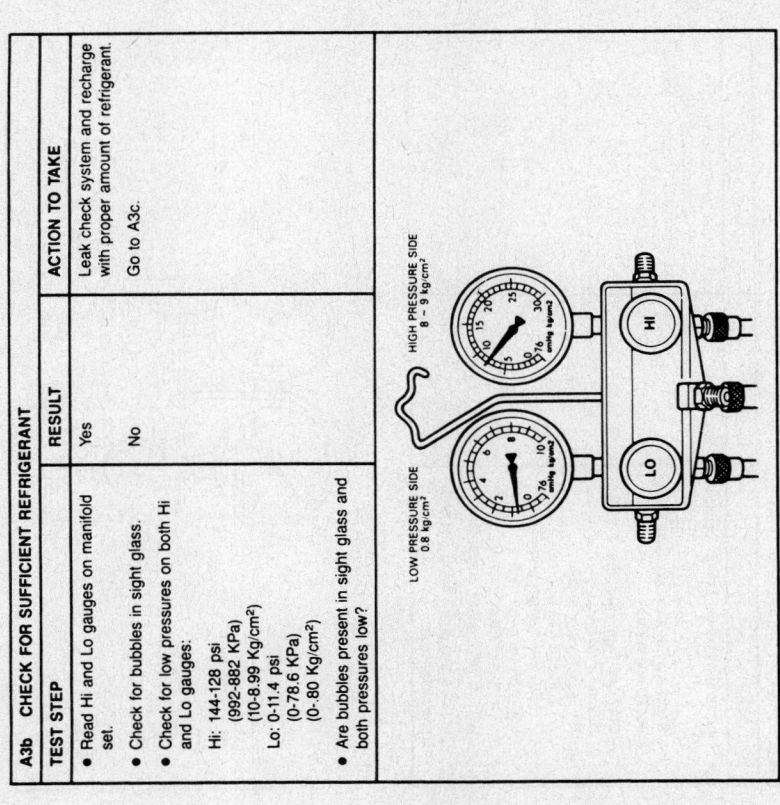

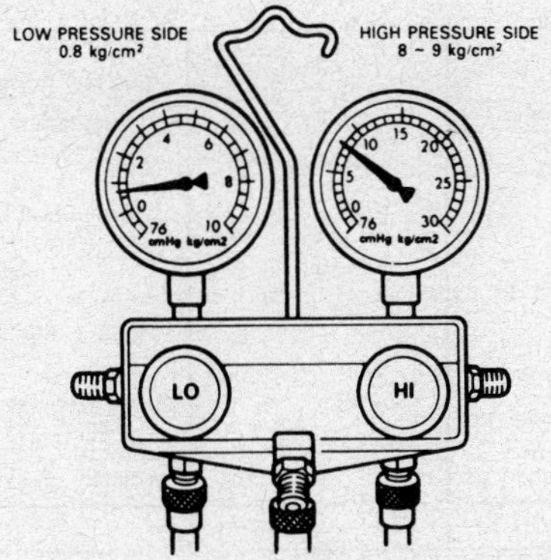
LOW PRESSURE SIDE
0.8 kg/cm²
HIGH PRESSURE SIDE
8 – 9 kg/cm²
LO
HI

A3c CHECK FOR EXCESSIVE REFRIGERANT

TEST STEP	RESULT	ACTION TO TAKE
• Read Hi and Lo gauges on manifold set. • Check for high pressure on both Hi and Lo gauges: Hi: 285 psi or greater (1965 KPa or greater) (20 Kg/cm² or greater) Lo: 25 psi or greater (172 KPa or greater) (1.75 Kg/cm² or greater) — Are both pressures high?	Yes	Recharge system with proper amount of oil and refrigerant.
	No	Go to A3d.

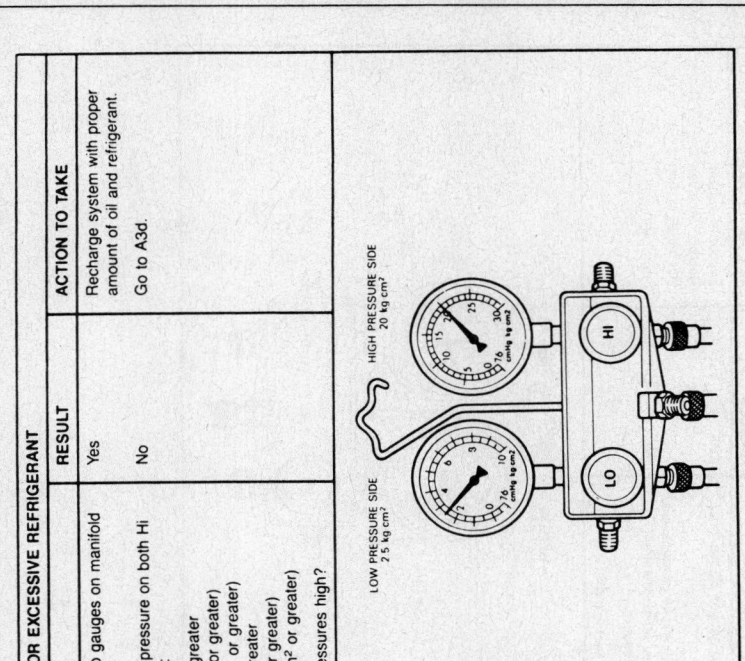

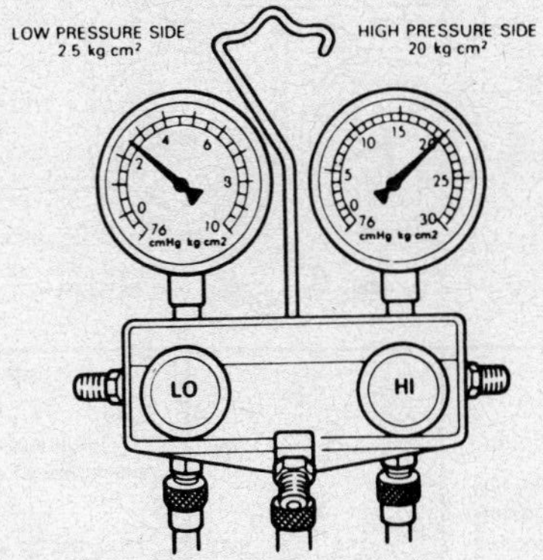
LOW PRESSURE SIDE
2.5 kg cm²
HIGH PRESSURE SIDE
20 kg cm²
LO
HI

A3d CHECK FOR AIR IN SYSTEM

TEST STEP	RESULT	ACTION TO TAKE
• Read Hi and Low gauges on manifold set. — Check for warm low pressure piping during operation. — Check for high pressures on both Hi and Lo gauges: Hi: 327 psi or greater (2250 KPa or greater) (22.94 Kg/cm² or greater) Lo: 35 psi or greater (241 KPa or greater) (2.46 Kg/cm² or greater) — Is low siding piping warm and both pressures high?	Yes No	Evacuate and recharge system. Check compressor oil for contamination. Replace receiver. Go to A3e.

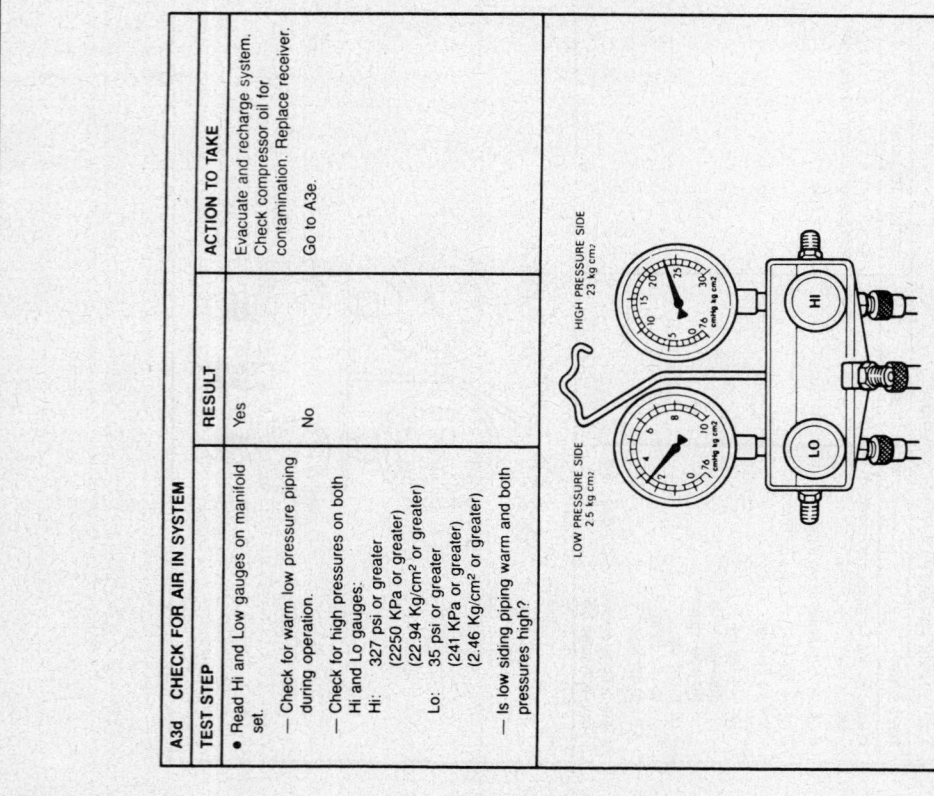

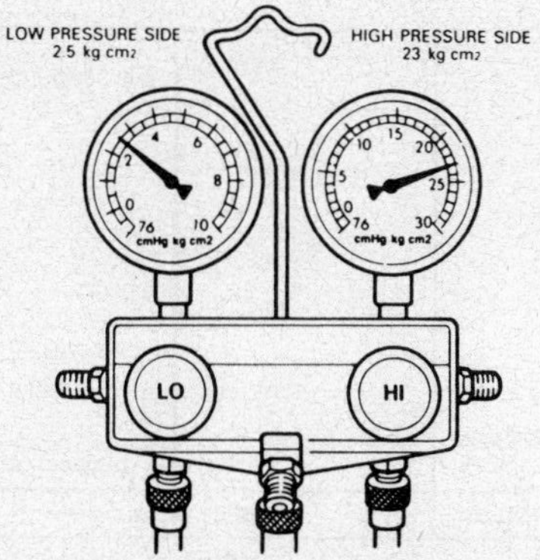
LOW PRESSURE SIDE
2.5 kg cm2
HIGH PRESSURE SIDE
23 kg cm2
LO
HI

A3e CHECK FOR MOISTURE IN SYSTEM

TEST STEP	RESULT	ACTION TO TAKE
• Read Hi and Lo gauges on manifold set. • Check for fluctuating Hi pressure side and Lo pressure side becoming vacuum and pressure. • Are pressures fluctuating?	Yes No	Evacuate system. Replace receiver. Recharge system. Go to A3F.

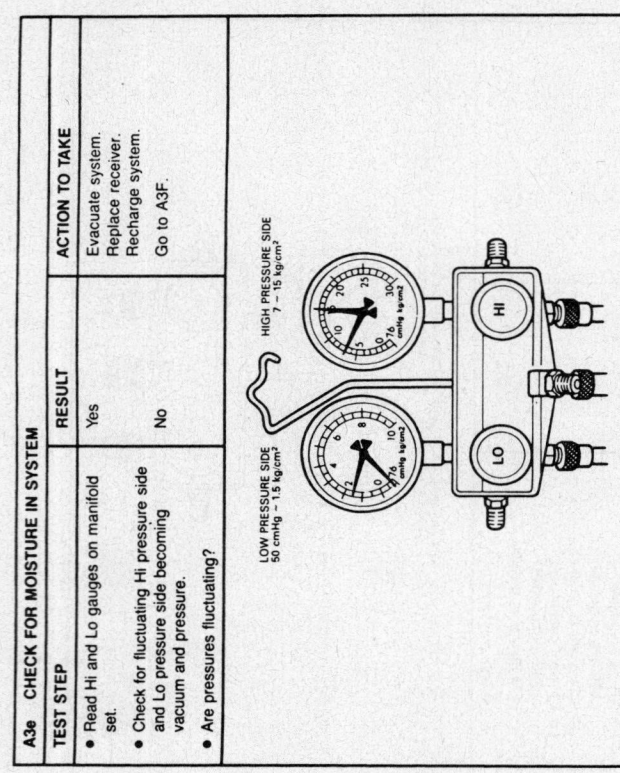

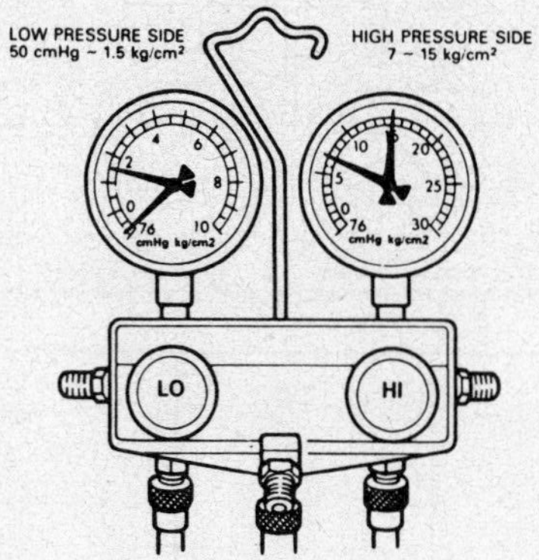
LOW PRESSURE SIDE
50 cmHg ~ 1.5 kg/cm²
HIGH PRESSURE SIDE
7 ~ 15 kg/cm²
LO
HI

A3f CHECK FOR POOR CIRCULATION

TEST STEP	RESULT	ACTION TO TAKE
• Read Hi and Lo gauges on manifold set • Check for frost build-up on piping near receiver and expansion valve • Check for low pressure on Hi gauge and very low pressure on Lo gauge: Hi: 85-95 psi (586-655 KPa) (5.97-6.67 Kg cm²) Lo: 26 in.Hg. vacuum (660 mmHg. vacuum) • Is frost build-up present and are both pressures low?	Yes No	Evacuate system. Replace receiver. Clean or replace expansion valve as required. Recharge system. Go to A3g.

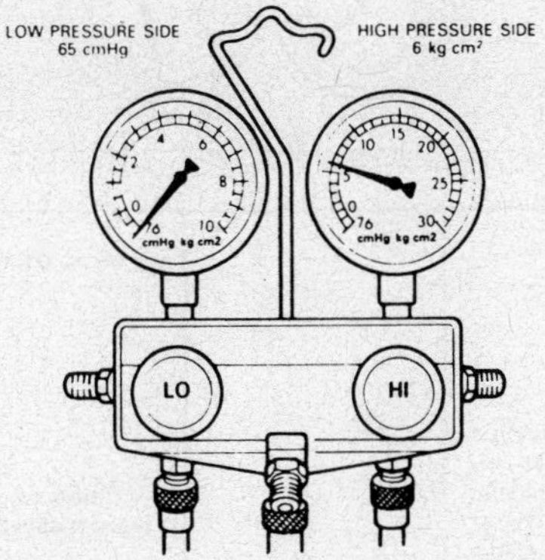
LOW PRESSURE SIDE
65 cmHg
HIGH PRESSURE SIDE
6 kg cm²
LO
HI

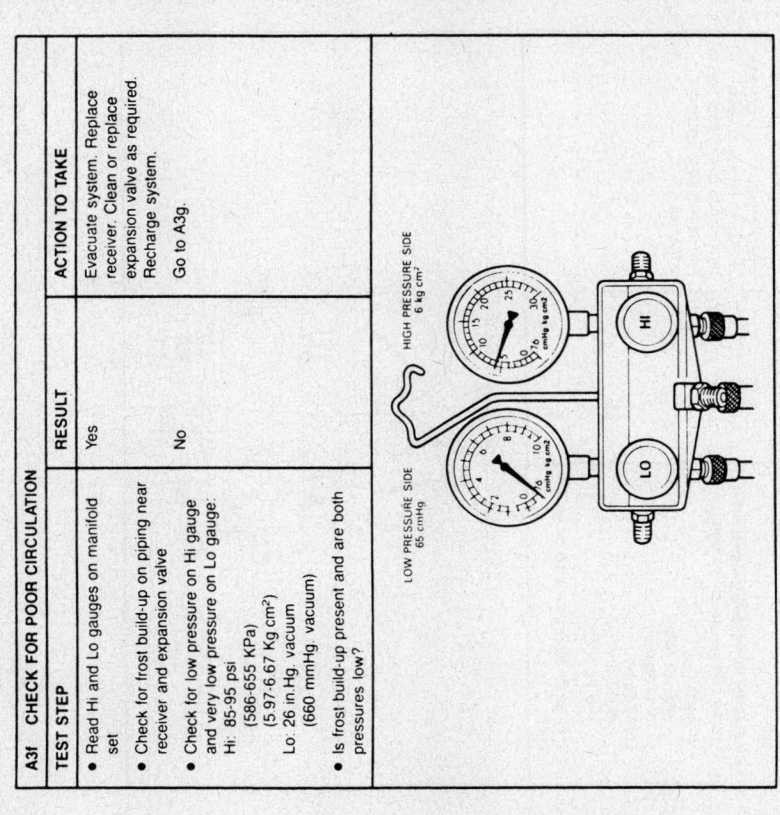

A3g CHECK FOR EXPANSION VALVE OPERATION

TEST STEP	RESULT	ACTION TO TAKE
• Read Hi and Lo gauges on manifold set. • Check for build-up of moisture (dew) on low side piping. • Check for high pressure on Hi gauge and Lo gauge: Hi: 270 psi or greater (1861 KPa or greater) (18.97 Kg/cm² or greater) Lo: 36 psi or greater (248 KPa or greater) (2.5 Kg/cm² or greater) • Is pressure high on both gauges and moisture build-up present on low side piping?	Yes No	Evacuate system. Replace expansion valve. Recharge system. Go to A3h.

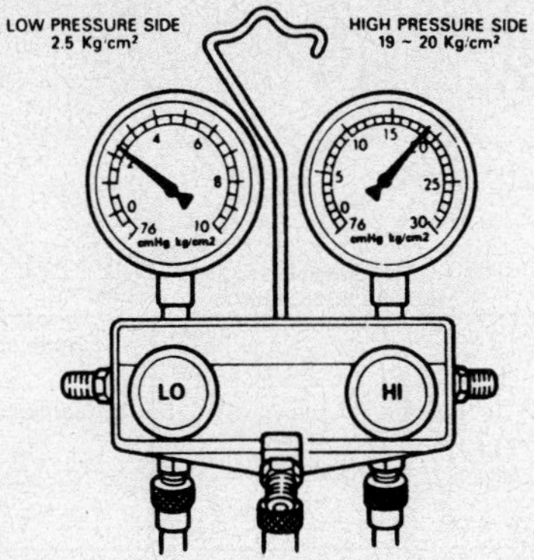
LOW PRESSURE SIDE
2.5 Kg/cm²
HIGH PRESSURE SIDE
19 ~ 20 Kg/cm²
LO
HI

A3h CHECK FOR FAULTY COMPRESSOR

TEST STEP	RESULT	ACTION TO TAKE
• Read Hi and Lo gauges on manifold set. • Check for Hi pressure gauge too low and Lo pressure gauge too high: Hi: 99-143 psi (686-981 KPa) (7-10 Kg/cm²) Lo: 57-86 psi (392-588 KPa) (4-6 Kg/cm²) • Is Hi gauge too high and Lo gauge too low?	Yes	Service compressor as required.
	No	Operate system for longer than 15-20 minute period. Cycle temperature control from cold to hot, back to cold. Recheck pressures.

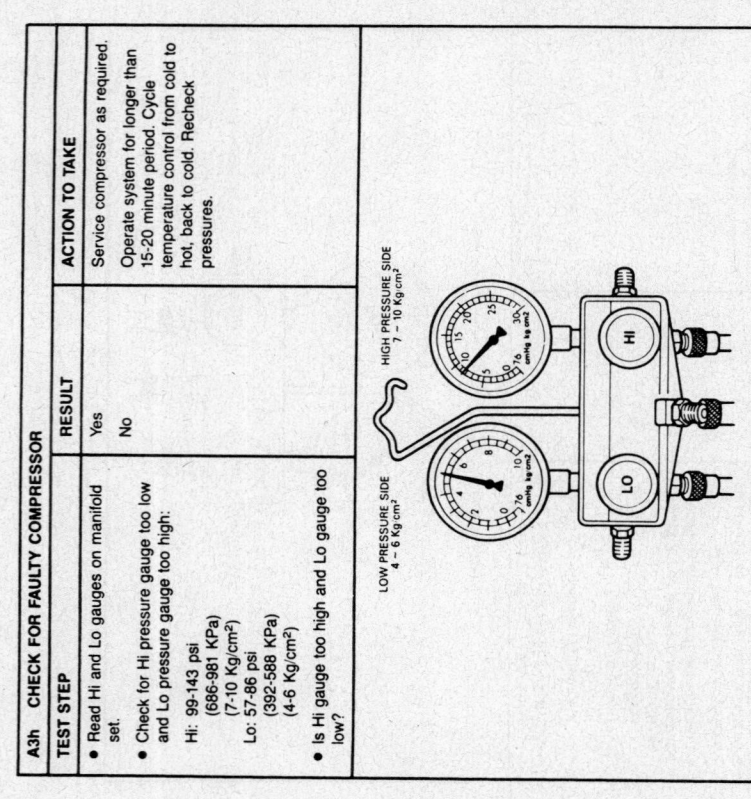

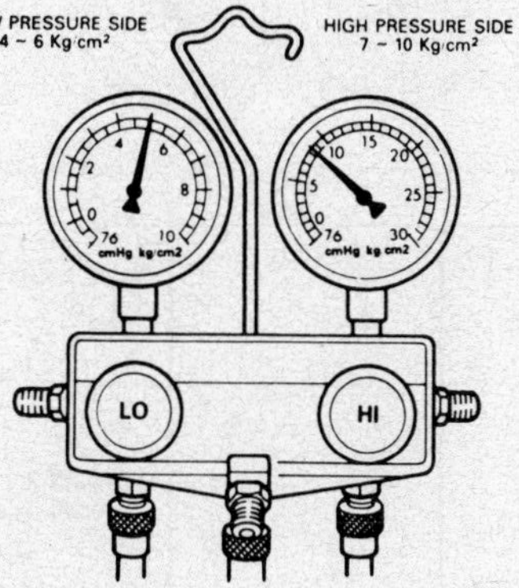
LOW PRESSURE SIDE
4 ~ 6 Kg/cm²
HIGH PRESSURE SIDE
7 ~ 10 Kg/cm²
LO
HI

A4 JUMP POWER TO COMPRESSOR CLUTCH

TEST STEP	RESULT	ACTION TO TAKE
• A/C on. • Engine running. • Blower on • Jump battery voltage to compressor clutch black/white terminal. • Does compressor clutch operate?	Yes	Go to A 5.
	No	Service or replace compressor clutch.

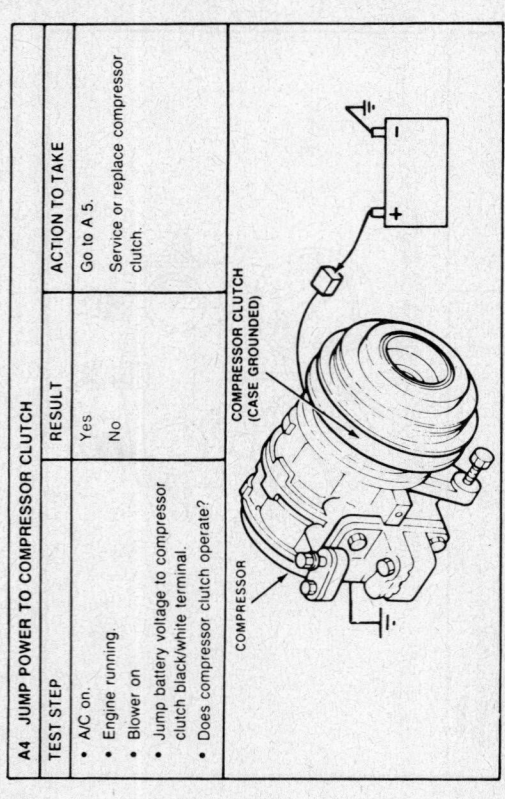

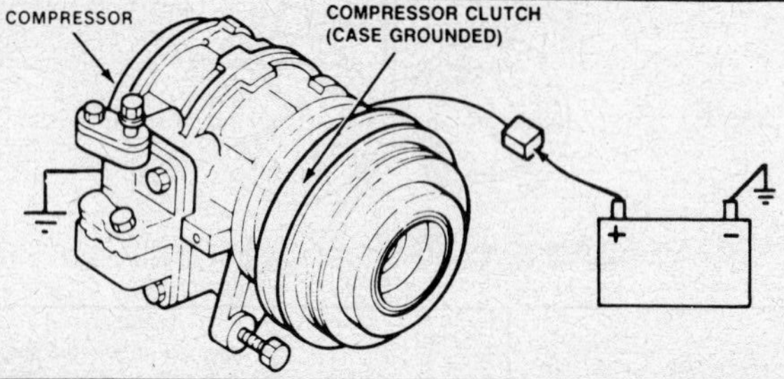
COMPRESSOR
COMPRESSOR CLUTCH
(CASE GROUNDED)

A5 CIRCUIT CHECK

TEST STEP	RESULT	ACTION TO TAKE
• Key on, engine off. • A/C pressure switch connected. • VOM on 20v scale. • A/C on. • Measure voltage at A/C pressure switch BK/W terminal. • Is reading greater than 10v?	Yes	Service BK/W wire from A/C pressure switch to compressor clutch for opens or shorts.
	No	Go to A6.

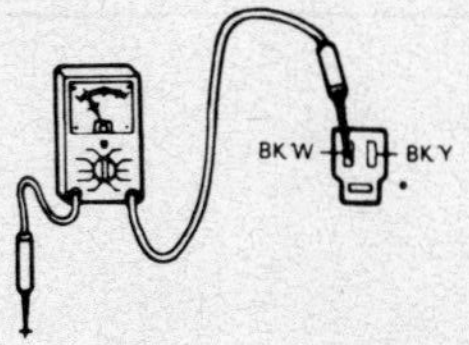
PROBE THROUGH
BACK OF
CONNECTOR
BK/W
BK/Y
CONNECTOR C264

AIR CONDITIONING AND HEATING SYSTEM DIAGNOSIS AND TESTING—1989–90 TRACER

A6 PRESSURE SWITCH VOLTAGE SUPPLY CHECK

TEST STEP	RESULT	ACTION TO TAKE
• Key on, engine off. • A/C on. • A/C pressure switch disconnected. • VOM on 20v scale. • Blower on. • Measure voltage at A/C pressure switch BK/Y terminal. • Is reading greater than 10v?	Yes No	Replace A/C pressure switch. Go to A7.

A7 CHECK VOLTAGE FROM RELAY

TEST STEP	RESULT	ACTION TO TAKE
• Key on, engine off. • Cold engine. • A/C on. • Blower on. • VOM on 20 v scale. • Measure voltage at A/C relay No. 1 BK/Y terminal (relay connected). • Is reading greater than 10v?	Yes No	Service BK/Y wire from A/C relay No. 1 to A/C pressure switch for opens or shorts. Go to A8.

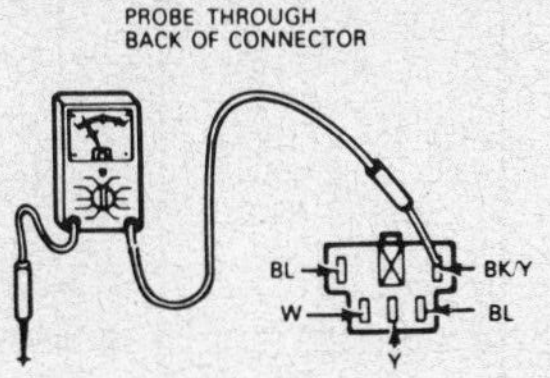
PROBE THROUGH
BACK OF CONNECTOR
BL
BK/Y
W
BL
Y
CONNECTOR C262

A8 A/C RELAY VOLTAGE SUPPLY CHECK

TEST STEP	RESULT	ACTION TO TAKE
• Key on, engine off. • A/C on. • Blower on. • VOM on 20v scale. • A/C relay No. 1 disconnected. • Measure voltage at A/C relay No. 1 connector blue terminals. • Are readings greater than 10v?	Yes No — C terminal No — A terminal	Go to A9. Service blue wire from ignition relay to A/C relay No. 1, or 30 amp circuit breaker for opens or shorts. Service blue wire from ignition switch to A/C relay for opens or shorts.

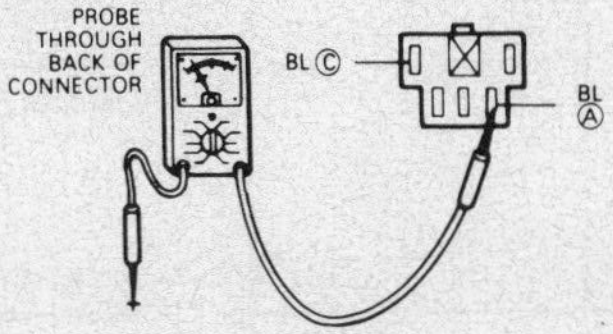
PROBE
THROUGH
BACK OF
CONNECTOR
BL Ⓒ
BL
Ⓐ
CONNECTOR C262

A9 No. 1 RELAY OPERATION TEST

TEST STEP	RESULT	ACTION TO TAKE
• Remove A/C relay No. 1. • Ground white terminal of A/C relay. • Jump battery power to BL terminal of A/C relay (pin "A"). • VOM on 200 ohm scale. • Measure resistance at A/C relay.	Yes No	Go to A10. Replace A/C relay No. 1.

Measure	Voltage to pin "A"	Resistance
BL ("C") and Y	Yes	0-5 ohms
BL ("C") and BK/Y	Yes	Infinite

• Are resistances OK?

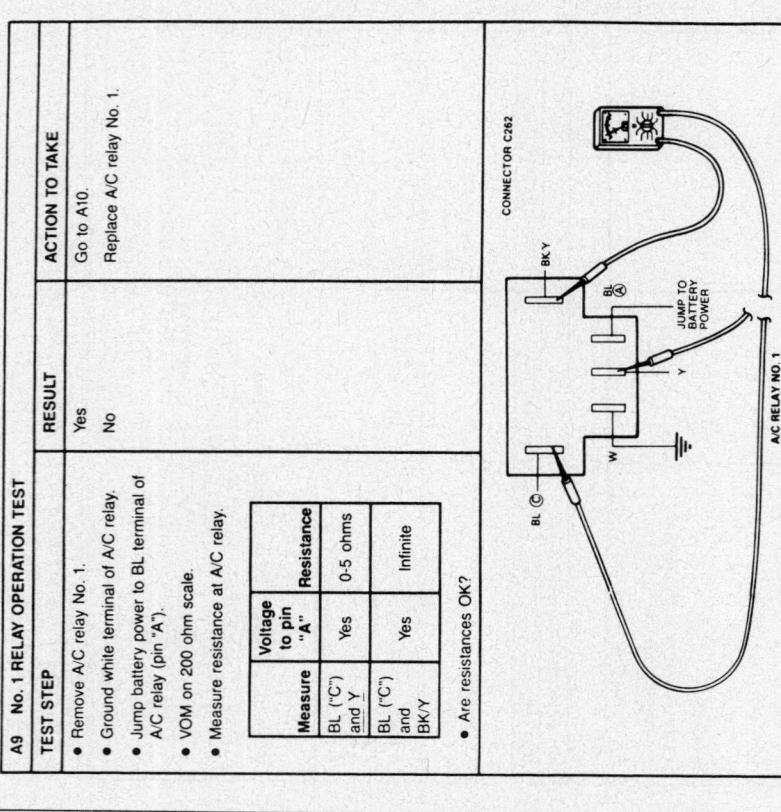

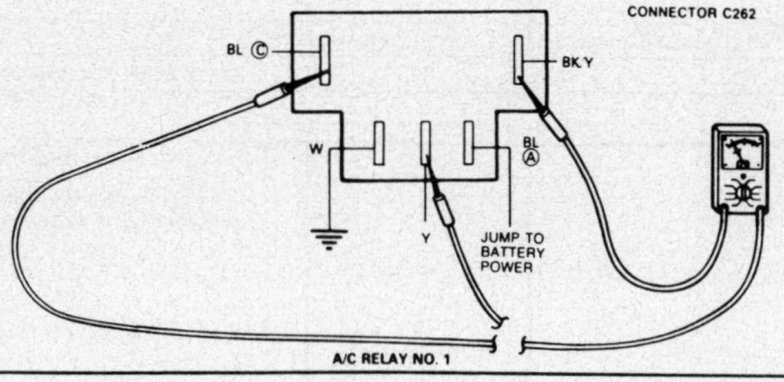
CONNECTOR C262
BL Ⓒ
BK Y
W
BL Ⓐ
Y
JUMP TO BATTERY POWER
A/C RELAY NO. 1

A10 CHECK CIRCUIT TO ECA

TEST STEP	RESULT	ACTION TO TAKE
• A/C relay No. 1 connected. • ECA disconnected. • VOM on 20v scale. • Key on, engine off. • A/C on. • Blower on. • Measure voltage at ECA connector 1F terminal white wire. • Is reading above 10v?	Yes No	Reconnect ECA. Reconnect A/C relay No. 1. Go to A11. Service white wire from A/C relay No. 1 to ECA for opens or shorts.

A11 CHECK SIGNAL FROM ECA

TEST STEP	RESULT	ACTION TO TAKE
• A/C control amp disconnected. • Key on, engine off. • VOM on 20v scale. • Measure voltage at A/C control amp connector red terminal. • Is reading greater than 10v?	Yes No	Go to A12. Service red wire from ECA 1L to A/C control amp for opens or shorts.

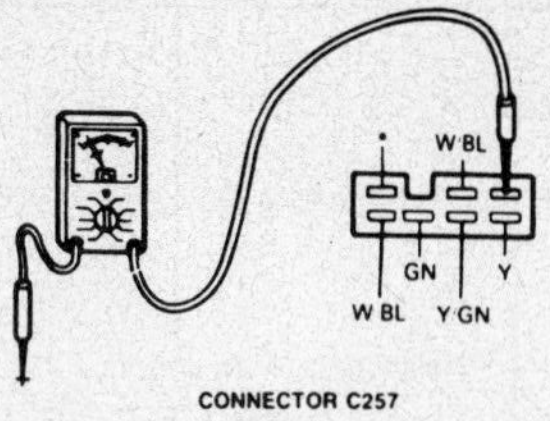
W BL
GN
Y
W BL
Y GN
CONNECTOR C257

A12 A/C CONTROL AMP VOLTAGE CHECK

TEST STEP	RESULT	ACTION TO TAKE
• A/C control amp disconnected • Key on, engine off • VOM on 20v scale • Measure voltage at A/C control amp connector yellow terminal • Is reading greater than 10v?	Yes No	Go to A14. Service Y wire from ignition switch to A/C control amp for opens or shorts.

A13 A/C CIRCUIT RESISTANCE TEST

TEST STEP	RESULT	ACTION TO TAKE
• A/C control amp disconnected. • VOM on 20v scale. • Check for continuity between Y/GN terminal and both W/BL terminals on A/C control and connector. • Is continuity OK?	Yes	Reconnect A/C control amp. Go to A14.
	No	Service circuit in question for opens.

A14 BLOWER SWITCH VOLTAGE CHECK

TEST STEP	RESULT	ACTION TO TAKE
• Blower switch disconnected. • A/C on. • Key on, engine off. • VOM on 20v scale. • Measure voltage at blower switch connector BL/Y terminal. • Is reading greater than 10v?	Yes	Reconnect blower switch. Go to A16.
	No	Reconnect blower switch. Go to A15.

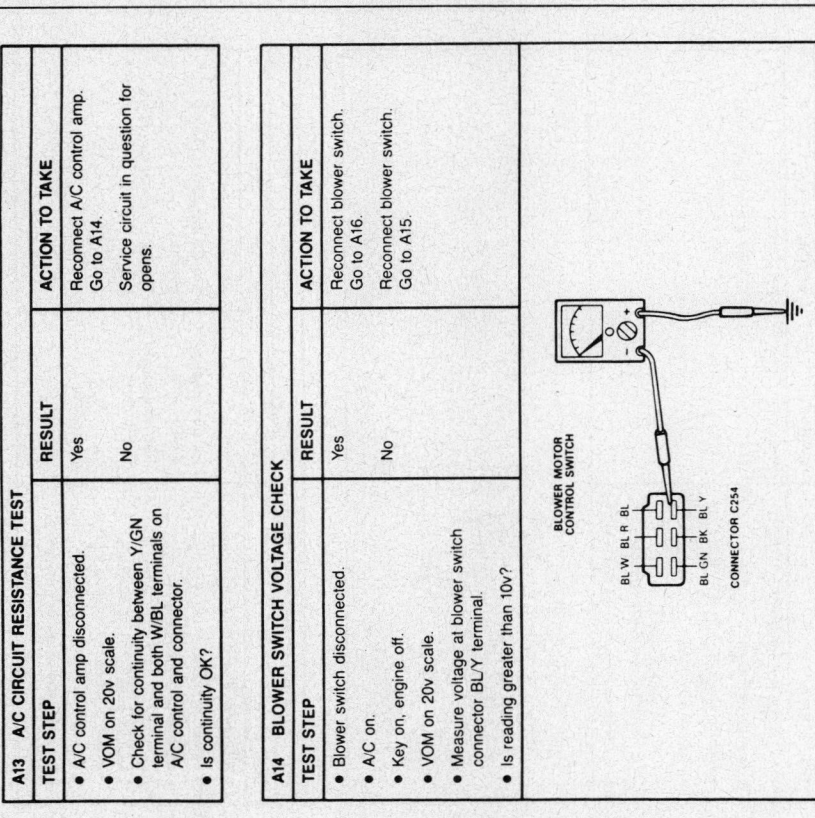

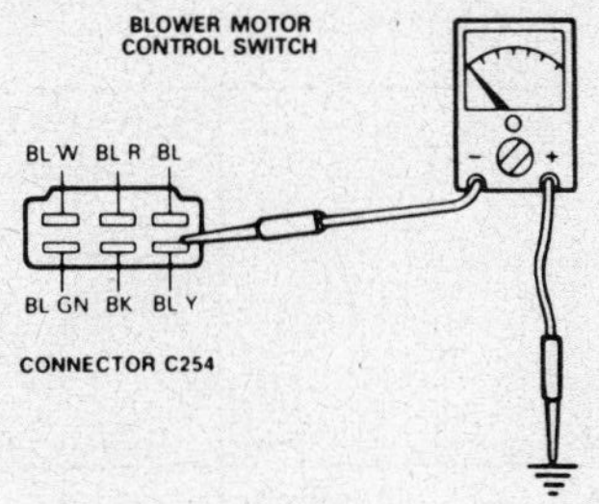
BLOWER MOTOR CONTROL SWITCH
BL W BL R BL
BL GN BK BL Y
CONNECTOR C254

A15 CONTROL AMP VOLTAGE CHECK

TEST STEP	RESULT	ACTION TO TAKE
• A/C control amp connected. • A/C on. • Blower on. • Key on, engine off. • VOM on 20v scale. • Measure voltage at A/C control amp GN terminal. • Is reading greater than 10v?	Yes	Service green wire from A/C control amp to blower switch for opens or shorts.
	No	Replace A/C control amp.

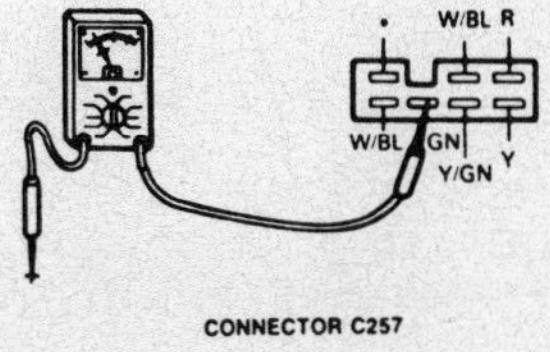
W/BL R
W/BL GN
Y/GN Y
CONNECTOR C257

A16 A/C SWITCH VOLTAGE CHECK

TEST STEP	RESULT	ACTION TO TAKE
• A/C switch disconnected. • Key on, engine off. • Headlights on. • VOM on 20v scale. • Measure voltage at A/C switch connector BL and R/GN terminals. • Are both readings greater than 10v?	Yes No	Go to A17. Service wire in question for opens or shorts.

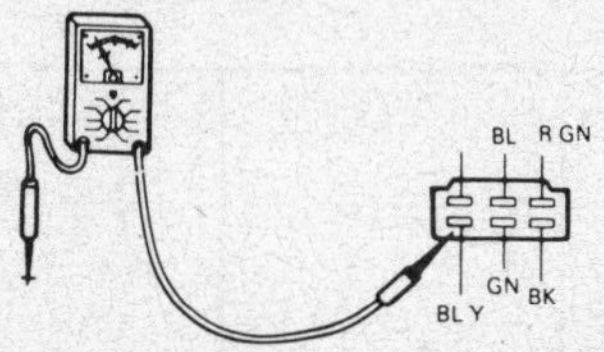
BL
R GN
GN
BK
BL Y

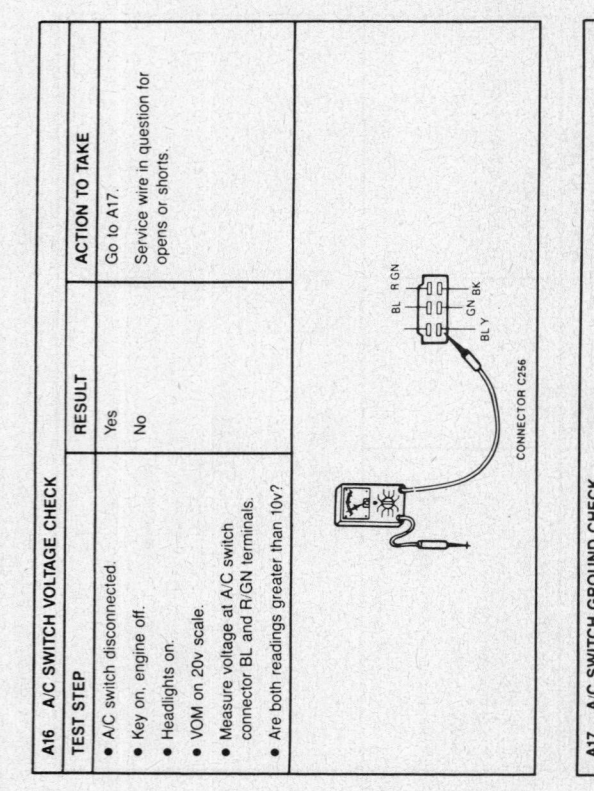

CONNECTOR C256

A17 A/C SWITCH GROUND CHECK

TEST STEP	RESULT	ACTION TO TAKE
• A/C switch disconnected. • Blower on LOW. • VOM on 200 ohm scale. • Measure resistance between A/C switch connector BK terminal and ground and between BL/Y terminal and ground. • Are both resistances less than 5 ohms?	Yes BK wire greater than 5 ohms BL/Y wire greater than 5 ohms	Replace A/C switch. Service BK wire for open to ground. Service BL/Y wire for open to ground. If all OK, reconnect A/C switch and Go to F6.

B1 CONDENSER FAN MOTOR SYSTEM INTEGRITY CHECK

TEST STEP	RESULT	ACTION TO TAKE
• Visually check condenser fan motor integrity (opens, shorts, bad fuses, bad connections.) • Are any concerns evident?	Yes No	Repair as required. Go to B2.

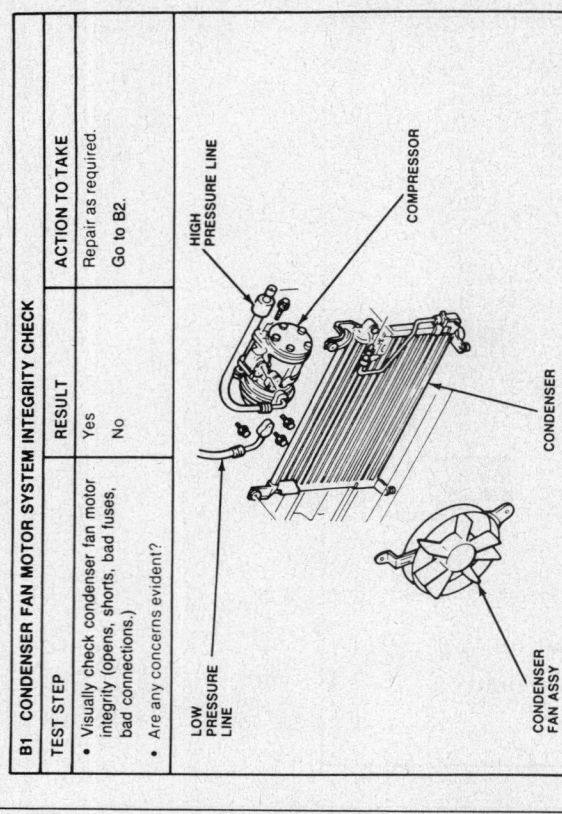

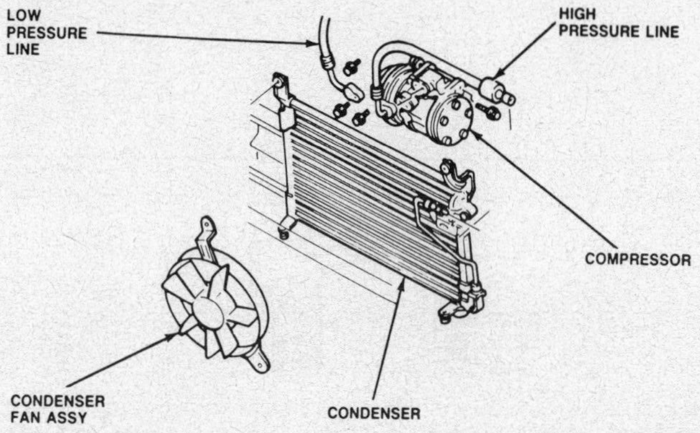
LOW PRESSURE LINE
HIGH PRESSURE LINE
COMPRESSOR
CONDENSER FAN ASSY
CONDENSER

B2 CONFIRM CONDENSOR FAN MOTOR OPERATION

TEST STEP	RESULT	ACTION TO TAKE
• Engine running at idle. • A/C on. • Blower on. • Jump battery power to condensor fan motor blue wire (fan motor connected). • Does condensor fan motor operate?	Yes No	Go to B-3. Go to B-4.

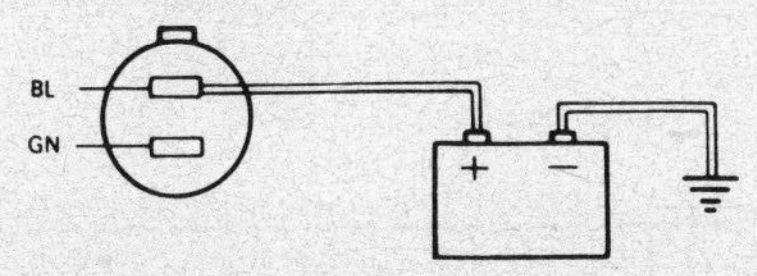
C259 CONNECTOR
BL
GN
+
−

B3 CHECK VOLTAGE AT IGNITION SWITCH

TEST STEP	RESULT	ACTION TO TAKE
• Key on, engine off. • Ignition switch connected. • VOM on 10v scale. • Do not pierce wire. • Measure voltage between BK/R wire and ground. • Is voltage reading less than 10v?	Yes No	Go to Group 31. Service BL wire from ignition switch to condensor fan motor for opens or shorts.

B4 CHECK CONDENSOR FAN MOTOR GROUND

TEST STEP	RESULT	ACTION TO TAKE
• Key off. • Jump battery power to condensor fan motor BL wire (refer to Test Step B-2). • With a jumper wire jump condensor fan motor GN wire to ground. • Does condensor fan motor operate?	Yes No	Go to B-5. Replace condensor fan motor.

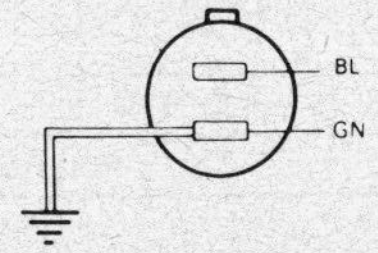
C259 CONNECTOR
BL
GN

B5 CHECK VOLTAGE AT A/C RELAY NO. 2

TEST STEP	RESULT	ACTION TO TAKE
• Engine running at idle. • A C on. • Blower on. • Disconnect A C relay No. 2 connector. • VOM on 20v scale. • Measure voltage between GN R wire and ground and BK Y wire and ground. • Are voltage readings less than 10v?	Yes No	GN R: Service wire between condensor fan motor and A C relay no. 2. BK Y: Go to B-6. Go to B-7.

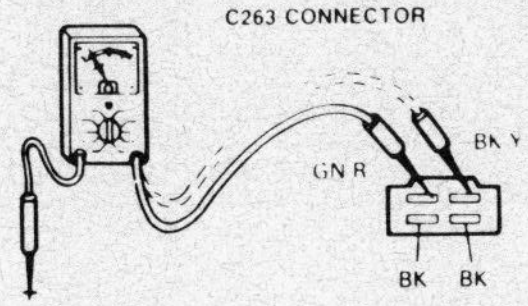
C263 CONNECTOR
GN R
BK Y
BK
BK

B6 CHECK VOLTAGE AT A/C RELAY NO. 1

TEST STEP	RESULT	ACTION TO TAKE
• Engine running at idle. • A/C on. • Blower on. • VOM on 20v scale. • Measure voltage at A/C relay No. 1 BK/Y wire (relay connected). • Is voltage reading less than 10v?	Yes No	Go to Test Step A-8. Service BK/Y wire from A/C relay No. 1 to A/C relay No. 2.

B7 CHECK A/C RELAY NO. 2 FOR CONTINUITY TO GROUND

TEST STEP	RESULT	ACTION TO TAKE
• Key off. • Disconnect A/C relay No. 2 connector. • VOM on 200 ohm scale. • Check continuity between A/C relay No. 2 BK wire and ground. • Are resistance readings greater than 5 ohms?	Yes No	Service wire in question. Replace A/C relay No. 2.

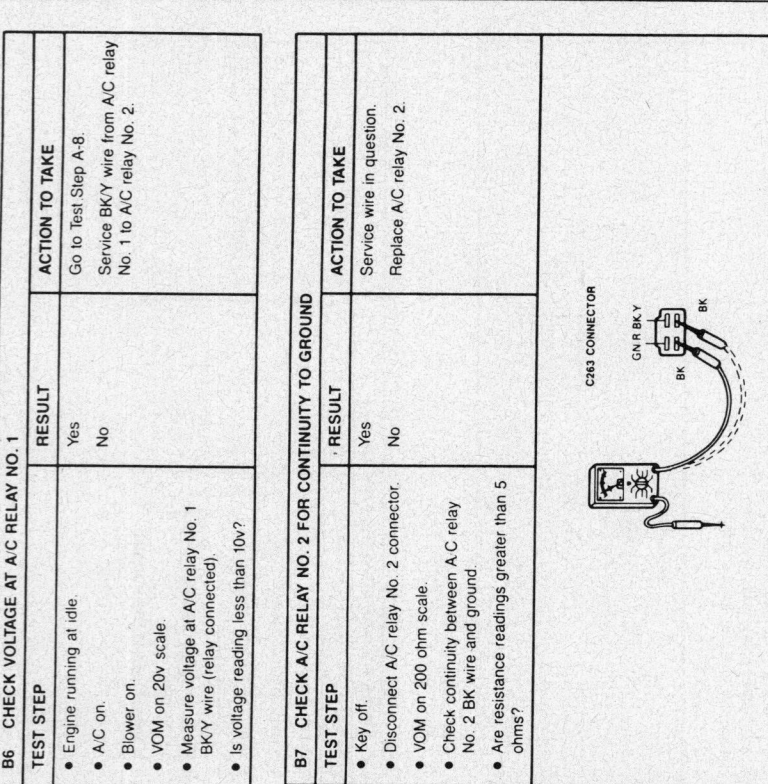

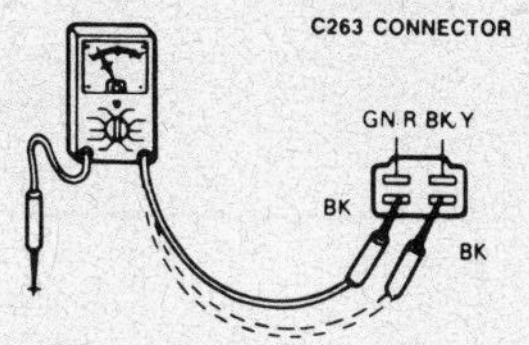
C263 CONNECTOR
GN R BK Y
BK
BK

C1 COOLING FAN MOTOR INTEGRITY CHECK

TEST STEP	RESULT	ACTION TO TAKE
• Visually check cooling fan system integrity. • Are there any concerns?	Yes No	Repair or replace as required. Go to C2.

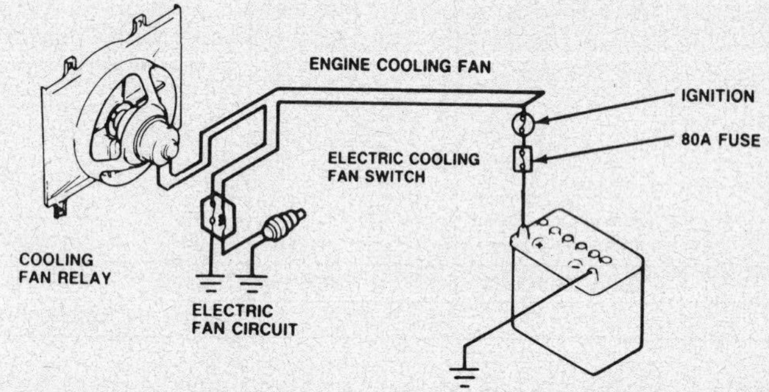
ENGINE COOLING FAN
IGNITION
80A FUSE
ELECTRIC COOLING FAN SWITCH
COOLING FAN RELAY
ELECTRIC FAN CIRCUIT

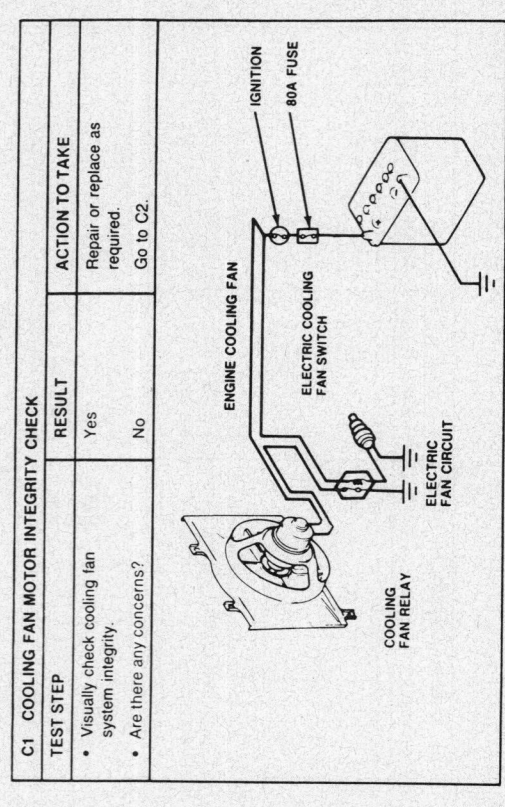

C2 CONFIRM COOLING FAN OPERATION

TEST STEP	RESULT	ACTION TO TAKE
• Key on, engine off. • Disconnect engine coolant temperature (ECT) switch. • Jump battery power to cooling fan motor yellow wire (fan motor connected). • Does cooling fan motor operate?	Yes No	Go to C-3. Go to C-4.

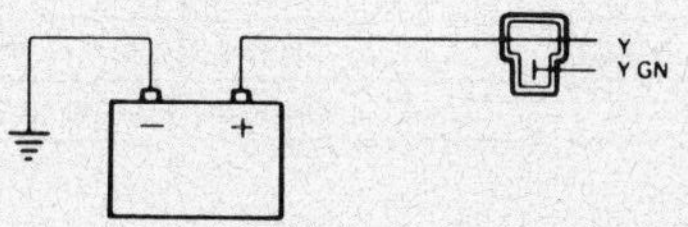
C112 CONNECTOR
Y
Y GN

AIR CONDITIONING AND HEATING SYSTEM DIAGNOSIS AND TESTING – 1989–90 TRACER

C3 CHECK VOLTAGE AT IGNITION SWITCH

TEST STEP	RESULT	ACTION TO TAKE
• Key on, engine off. • Ignition switch connected. • VOM on 20v scale. • Do not pierce wire. • Measure voltage between ignition switch BK/R wire and ground. • Is voltage reading less than 10v?	Yes No	Go to Group 31. Service Y wire from ignition switch to cooling fan motor.

C4 CHECK COOLING FAN MOTOR GROUND

TEST STEP	RESULT	ACTION TO TAKE
• Key off. • Jump battery power to cooling fan motor connector R/GR wire (fan motor connected). • With a jumper wire jump cooling fan motor connector BK/GR wire to ground. • Does cooling fan motor operate?	Yes No	Go to C-5. Service open or short in R/GR or BK/GR wire on cooling fan motor as required. If all OK replace cooling fan motor.

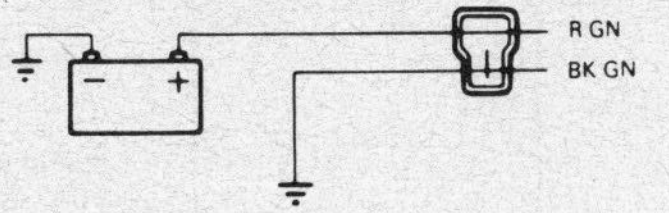
APPLY BATTERY POWER
R GN
BK GN

C5 CHECK VOLTAGE AT COOLING FAN RELAY

TEST STEP	RESULT	ACTION TO TAKE
• Key on, engine off. • Disconnect cooling fan relay connector. • VOM on 20v scale. • Measure voltage between Y/GR wire and ground and Y wire and ground. • Are voltage readings less than 10v?	Yes No	Y/GN: Service wire between cooling fan motor and cooling fan relay. Y: Go to C-6. Go to C-7.

C113 CONNECTOR

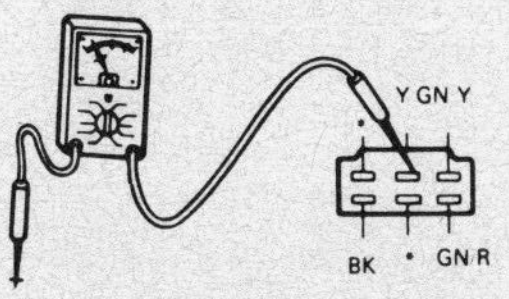
Y GN Y
BK
GN R

C6 CHECK VOLTAGE AT A/C RELAY NO. 1

TEST STEP	RESULT	ACTION TO TAKE
• Key on, engine off. • VOM on 20v scale. • A/C equipped: measure voltage at A/C Relay No. 1 Y wire (relay connected). • Non A/C equipped: measure voltage at short connector yellow wire. • Is voltage reading less than 10v?	Yes A/C equipped Yes Non A/C equipped No	Go to Test Step A-8. Service short connector as required. Service yellow wire from A/C relay No. 1 or short connector to cooling fan relay.

NON A/C EQUIPPED SHORT CONNECTOR C255

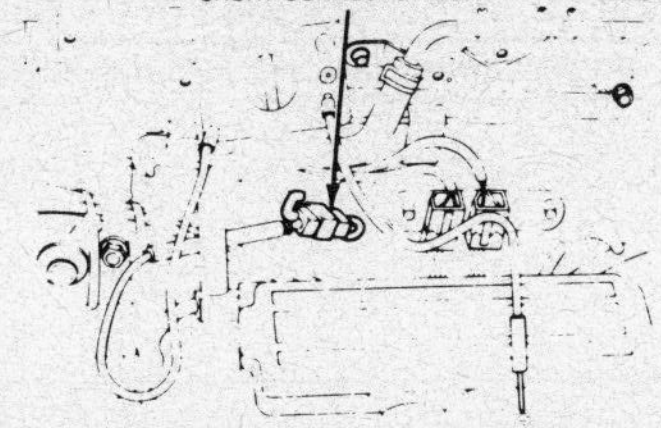

A/C RELAY NO. 1 CONNECTOR C262

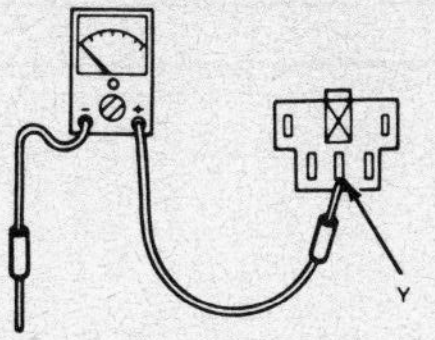
Y

C7 CHECK COOLING FAN RELAY GROUND CIRCUIT

TEST STEP	RESULT	ACTION TO TAKE
• Key off. • Disconnect cooling fan relay connector. • VOM on 200 ohm scale. • Measure resistance between cooling fan relay connector BK wire and ground. • Is resistance reading greater than 5 ohms?	Yes No	Service BK wire from cooling fan relay to ground. Go to C-8.

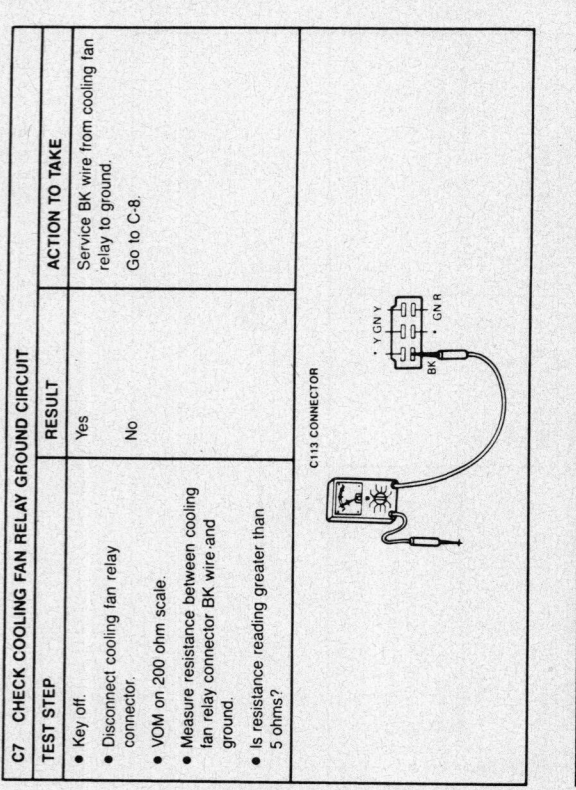

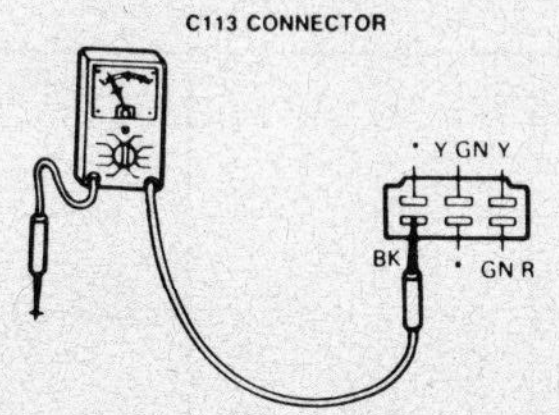
C113 CONNECTOR
Y GN Y
BK
GN R

C8 CHECK CONTINUITY FROM COOLING FAN RELAY TO COOLING FAN SWITCH

TEST STEP	RESULT	ACTION TO TAKE
• Key off. • Disconnect cooling fan relay and cooling fan switch connectors. • VOM on 200 ohm scale. • Measure resistance between cooling fan relay GN/R wire and cooling fan switch GN/R wire. • Is resistance greater than 5 ohms?	Yes No	Service GN/R wire between cooling fan relay and cooling fan switch. Reconnect cooling fan relay. Go to C9.

C9 CHECK COOLING FAN SWITCH OPERATION

TEST STEP	RESULT	ACTION TO TAKE
• Engine cool below 97°C (176°F). • Verify cooling fan switch for continuity between GN/R wire and ground. • Engine hot above 97°C (176°F). • Verify cooling fan switch is open between GN/R wire and ground. • Is cooling fan switch operation OK?	Yes No	Replace cooling fan relay. Replace cooling fan switch.

D1 HEATER SYSTEM INTEGRITY CHECK

TEST STEP	RESULT	ACTION TO TAKE
• Visually inspect heater system for obvious signs of leaks, pinched hoses, blockage, or damaged components. • Are any concerns evident?	Yes No	Repair or replace as required. Go to D-2.

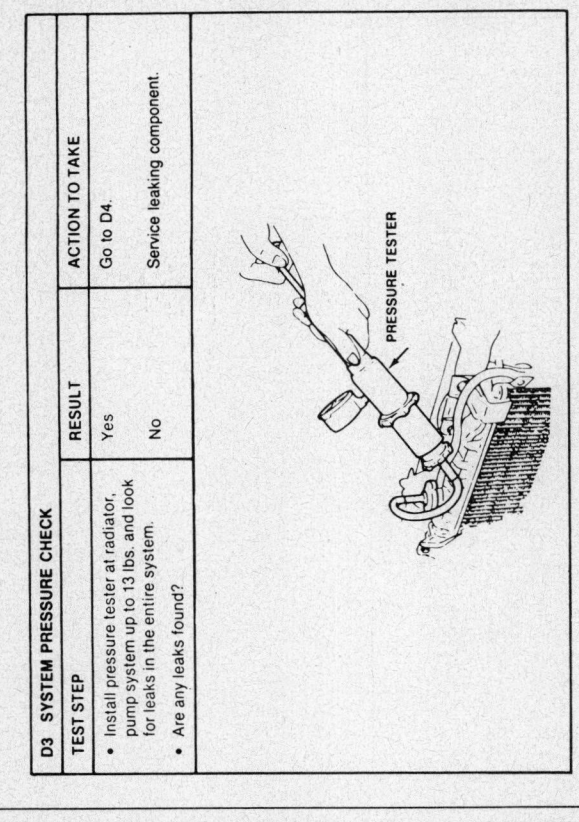

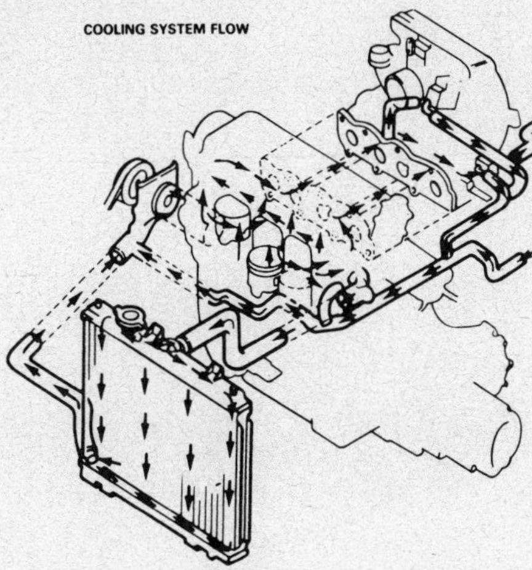
COOLING SYSTEM FLOW
TO HEATER
FROM HEATER

D2 COOLING SYSTEM CHECK

TEST STEP	RESULT	ACTION TO TAKE
• Inspect components and operation of the cooling system in the following areas: • Radiator condition • Thermostat condition • Coolant level and condition • Belt tension and condition • Water pump operation • Heater and radiator hose condition • Run coolant system pressure check • Are any components damaged, or not functioning properly?	Yes No	Repair or replace as required. Go to D-3.

D3 SYSTEM PRESSURE CHECK

TEST STEP	RESULT	ACTION TO TAKE
• Install pressure tester at radiator, pump system up to 13 lbs. and look for leaks in the entire system. • Are any leaks found?	Yes No	Go to D4. Service leaking component.

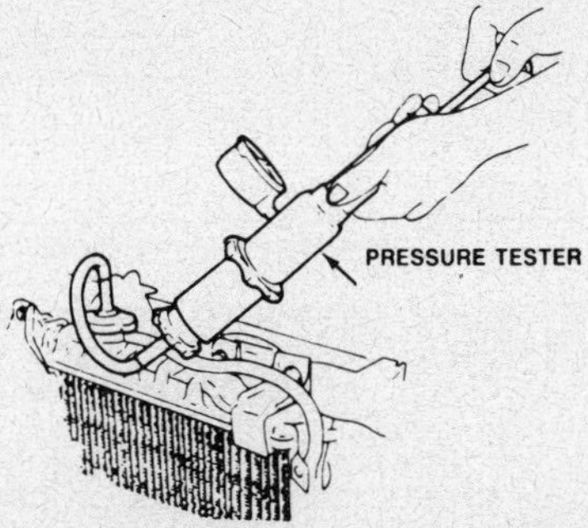
PRESSURE TESTER

D4 HEATER DUCT INSPECTION

TEST STEP	RESULT	ACTION TO TAKE
• Check for a restriction or damage in the ventilation air duct assembly. • Are there any restrictions or damage?	Yes	Repair as necessary.
	No	Go to Heating System Test G-1.

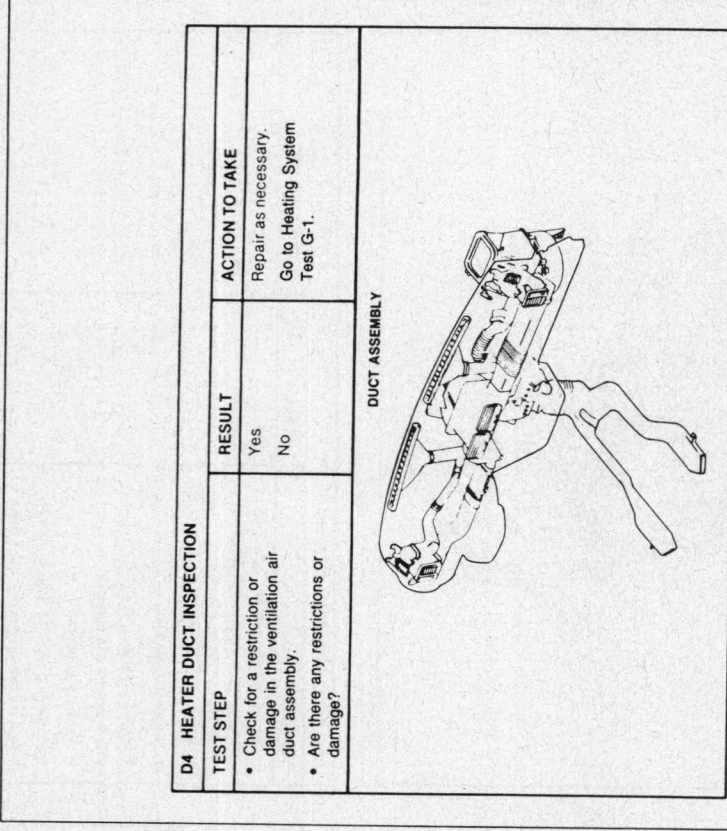

DUCT ASSEMBLY

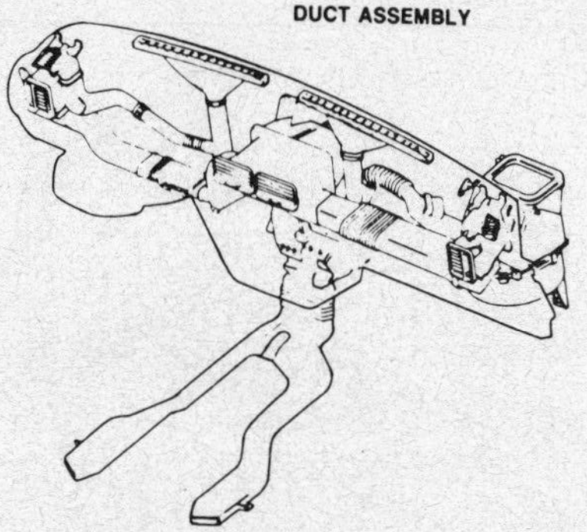

E 1 SYSTEM INTEGRITY CHECK

TEST STEP	RESULT	ACTION TO TAKE
• Inspect the passenger compartment carpeting for wetness and/or engine coolant odor. • Are any concerns evident?	Yes	Replace heater core.
	No	Warm up engine and recheck symptom. Go to E-2.

AREAS OF CONCERN WHEN CHECKING FOR LEAKS

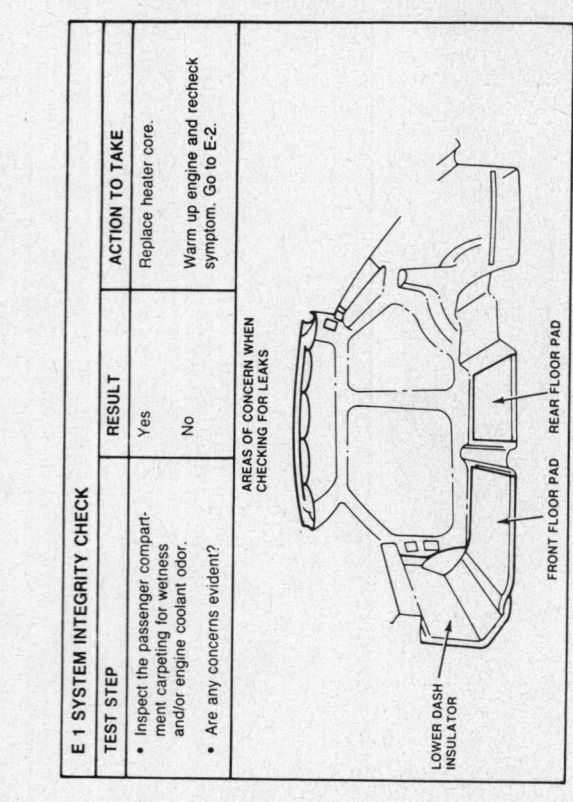

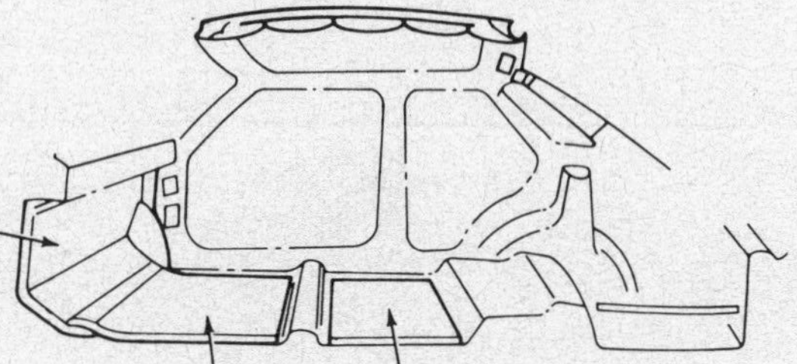
LOWER DASH INSULATOR
FRONT FLOOR PAD
REAR FLOOR PAD

AIR CONDITIONING AND HEATING SYSTEM DIAGNOSIS AND TESTING – 1989–90 TRACER

E2 SYSTEM PRESSURE CHECK

TEST STEP	RESULT	ACTION TO TAKE
• Install pressure tester at radiator, pump system up to 13 lbs. and look for leaks in the entire system. • Are any leaks found?	Yes	Check for other possible sources of leaks; doors, window gaskets, floor plugs, cracks in sheet metal, etc..
	No	Service leaking components.

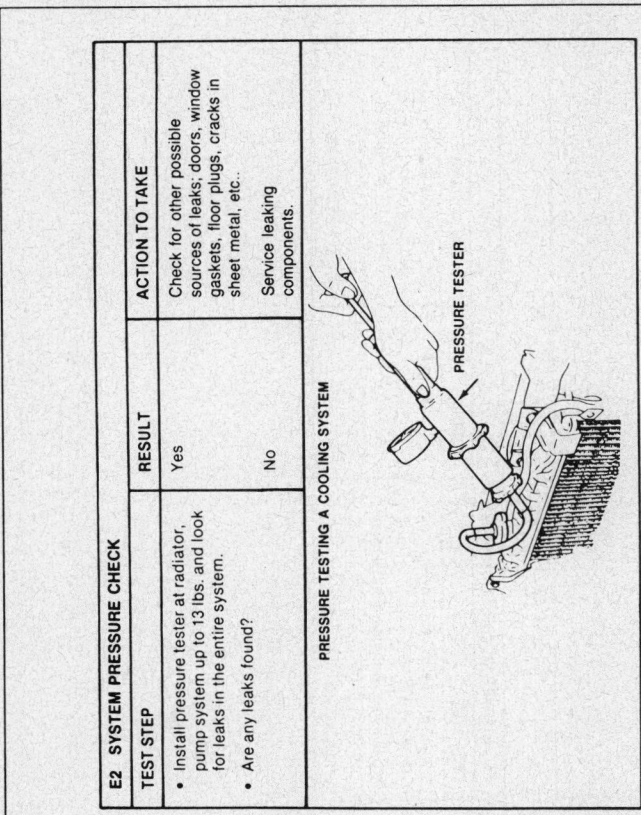

PRESSURE TESTING A COOLING SYSTEM

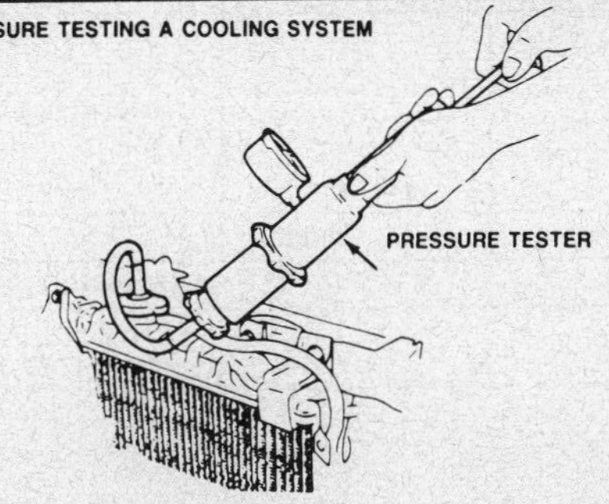
PRESSURE TESTER

F1 SYSTEM INTEGRITY CHECK

TEST STEP	RESULT	ACTION TO TAKE
• Visually inspect blower motor and circuit for blown fuses, open wires, shorts, bad connections and obvious damage. • Are any concerns evident?	Yes	Repair or replace as required.
	No	Go to F2.

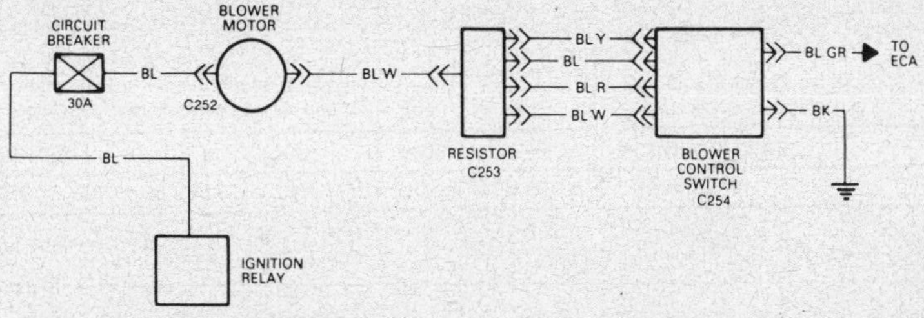
CIRCUIT BREAKER
30A
BL
C252
BLOWER MOTOR
BL W
BL Y
BL
BL R
BL W
RESISTOR C253
BLOWER CONTROL SWITCH C254
BL GR
TO ECA
BK
BL
IGNITION RELAY

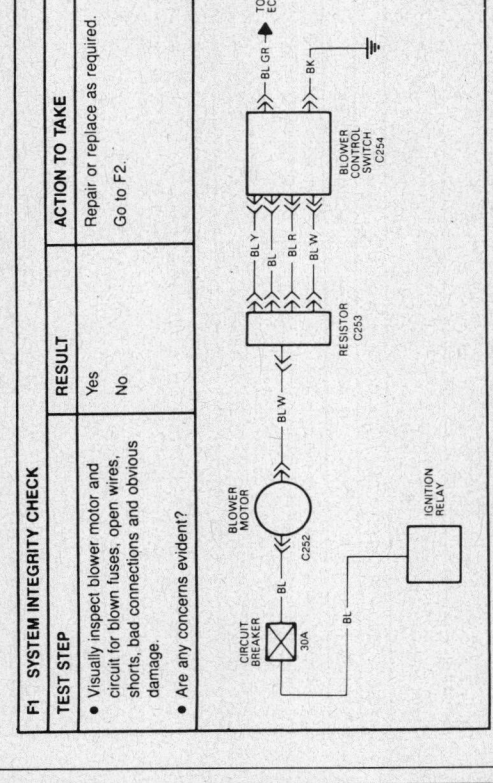

F2 BLOWER MOTOR OPERATION CHECK

TEST STEP	RESULT	ACTION TO TAKE
• Disconnect 1-pin power connector at blower motor (blue wire). • Blower switch on. • Jump battery power to motor side of connector. • Does blower motor run?	Yes	Service blue wire from ignition relay to blower motor for opens, shorts, or open circuit breaker.
	No	Go to F3.

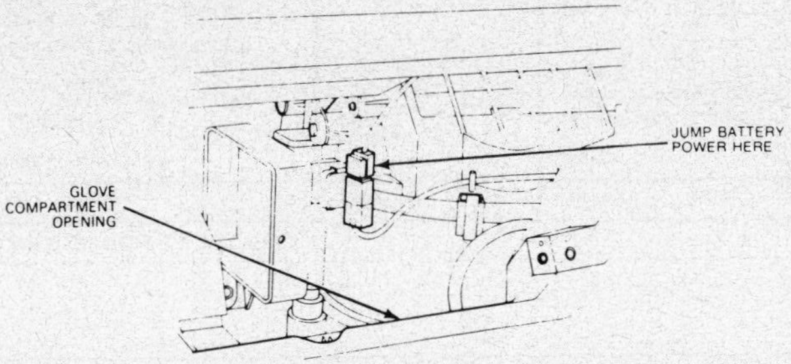
GLOVE COMPARTMENT OPENING
JUMP BATTERY POWER HERE

F3 BLOWER MOTOR GROUND CHECK

TEST STEP	RESULT	ACTION TO TAKE
• Blower motor resistor disconnected. • Jump all 4 terminals on resistor to ground, one at a time. • Battery power connected to blue wire at blower motor. • Does blower motor run with each terminal grounded?	Yes No	Reconnect resistor. Go to F5 Go to F4.

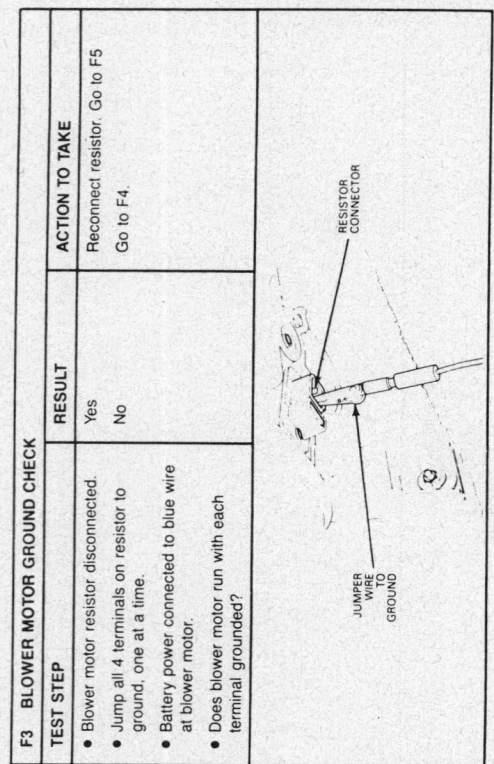

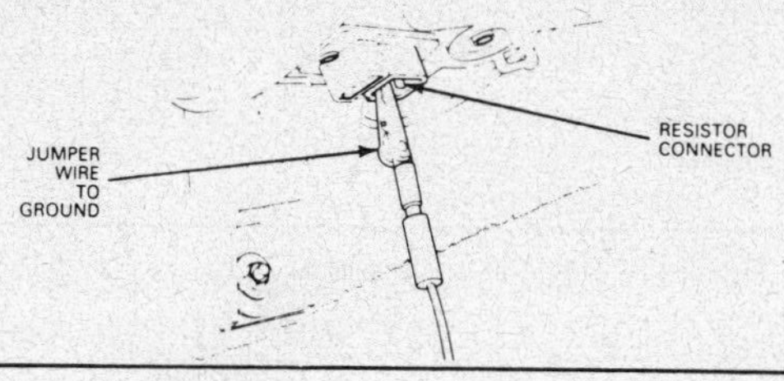
JUMPER WIRE TO GROUND
RESISTOR CONNECTOR

F4 BLOWER MOTOR GROUND CHECK

TEST STEP	RESULT	ACTION TO TAKE
• Jump BL/W wire from blower motor directly to ground. • Battery power connected to blower motor BL wire. • Does blower motor run?	Yes No	Service BL/W wire from opens or shorts from blower motor to resistor. If all OK, replace resistor. Replace blower motor.

F5 BLOWER SWITCH CIRCUIT TEST

TEST STEP	RESULT	ACTION TO TAKE
• Disconnect blower switch. • Key on, engine off. • VOM on 20v scale. • Measure voltage at blower switch connector BL/Y, BL, BL/R and BL/W terminals. • Are all measurements greater than 10v?	Yes No	Go to F6. Service wire in question for opens or shorts from blower.

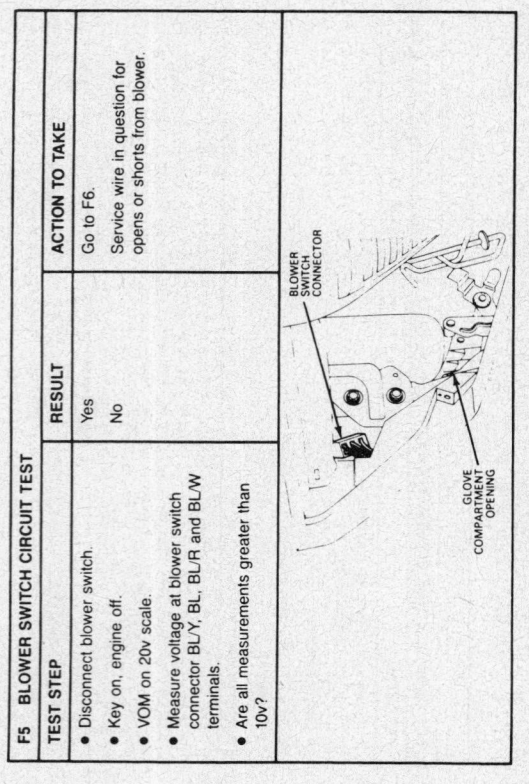

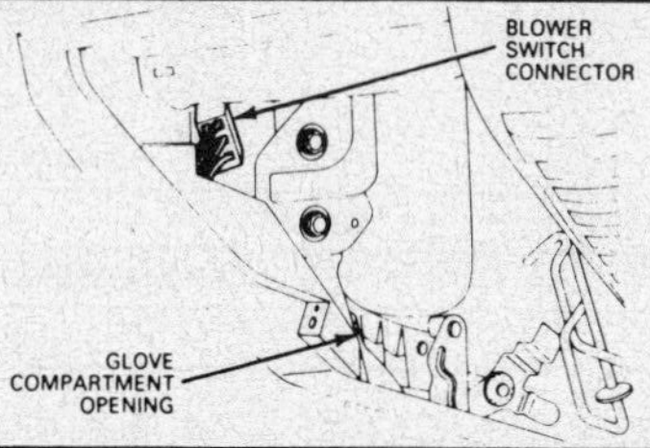
BLOWER SWITCH CONNECTOR
GLOVE COMPARTMENT OPENING

NHB 4 BLOWER SWITCH CONTINUITY (NO HEATER BLOWER OPERATION)

TEST STEP	RESULT	ACTION TO TAKE
• Check for continuity across blower motor control switch connector G-03, all positions, ignition off. • Is there continuity?	Yes No	Service open in black wire from blower switch to ground. Replace blower motor control switch.

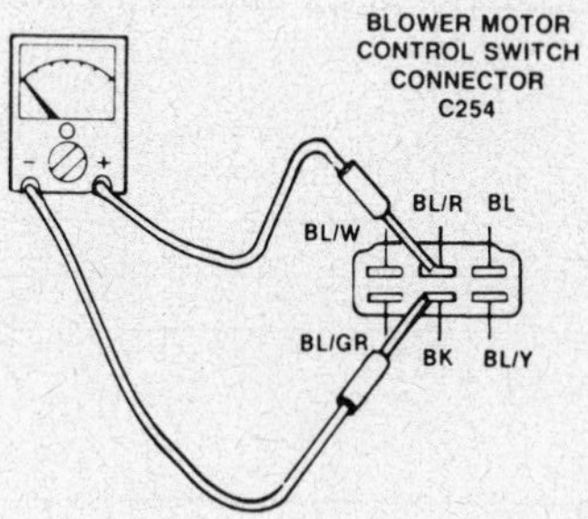
BLOWER MOTOR CONTROL SWITCH CONNECTOR C254
BL/R
BL
BL/W
BL/GR
BK
BL/Y

AIR CONDITIONING AND HEATING SYSTEM DIAGNOSIS AND TESTING – 1989–90 TRACER

G1 SYSTEM INTEGRITY CHECK

TEST STEP	RESULT	ACTION TO TAKE
• Check for a restriction in the ventilation air duct assembly. • **Are any concerns evident?**	Yes No	Repair as necessary. Go to G-2.

DUCT ASSEMBLY

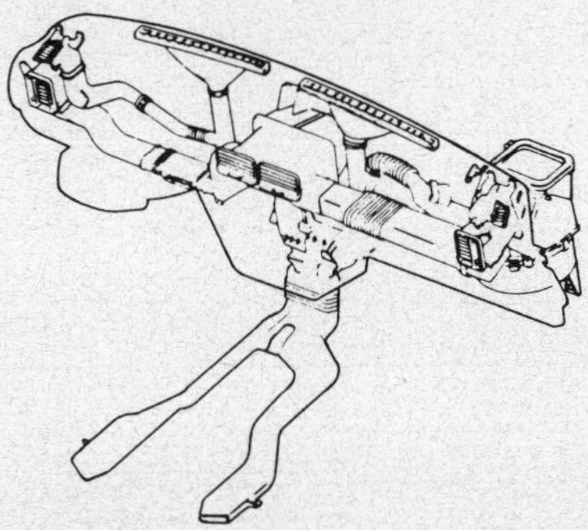

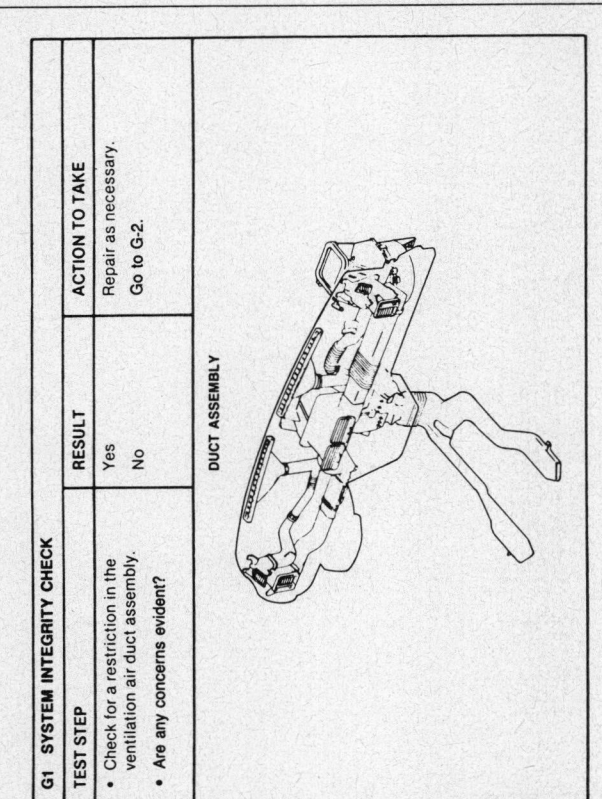

G2 FUNCTION CONTROL DOOR CHECK

TEST STEP	RESULT	ACTION TO TAKE
• Check function control door position. • Is function control door positioned correctly so as to send heat out the floor vents, when in "floor" position.	Yes No	Go to G3. Adjust cable. Refer to Section 36-02.

HEATER UNIT ASSEMBLY

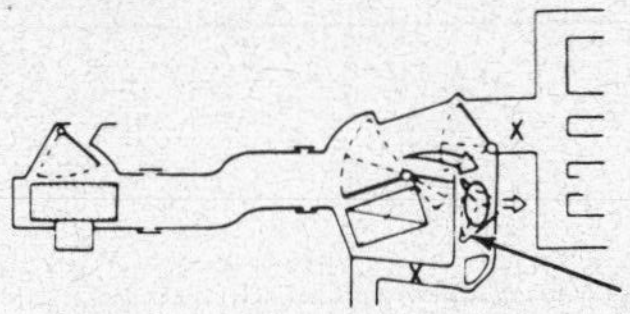
FUNCTION
CONTROL
DOOR

G3 FRESH AIR DOOR OPERATION

TEST STEP	RESULT	ACTION TO TAKE
• Set selector lever to recirc. air position. • Disconnect air door cable. • Push lever forward to stop. • Is cable in position to allow fresh air door to travel fully open (forward)?	Yes No	Go to G4. Service fresh air door cable for travel, binding and adjustment.

BLOWER UNIT

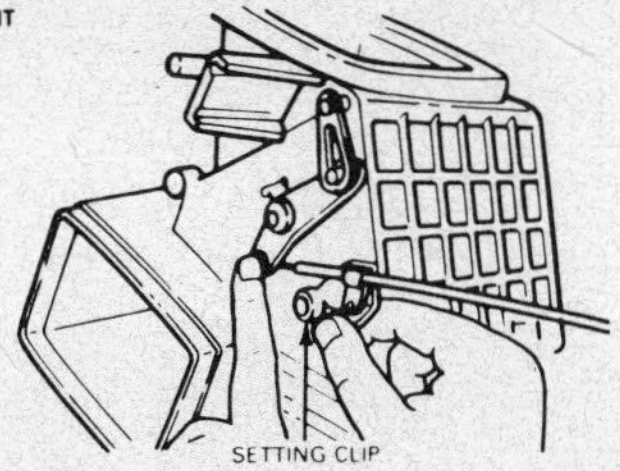
SETTING CLIP

G4 AIR MIX DOOR CHECK

TEST STEP	RESULT	ACTION TO TAKE
• Check air mix door position. • Is the air mix door positioned correctly to allow air to pass through the heater core?	Yes No	Go to G5. Adjust cable.

HEATER UNIT ASSEMBLY

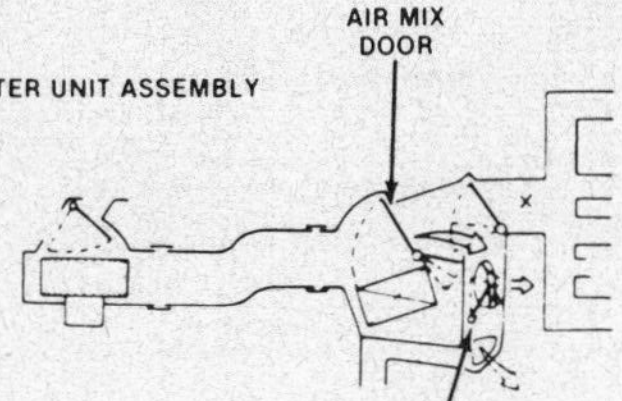
AIR MIX
DOOR
FUNCTION
CONTROL
DOOR

AIR CONDITIONING AND HEATING SYSTEM DIAGNOSIS AND TESTING—1989–90 TRACER

G5 CIRCULATION CHECK

TEST STEP	RESULT	ACTION TO TAKE
• Blower on high. • Key on, engine off. • Test circulation by placing function control levers on each position and checking if air circulation through proper ductwork. • Does air circulate properly?	Yes No	Inspect blower motor for correct operation. Go to F1. Check ductwork in question for cracks, damage, blockage or leaks, repair as required.

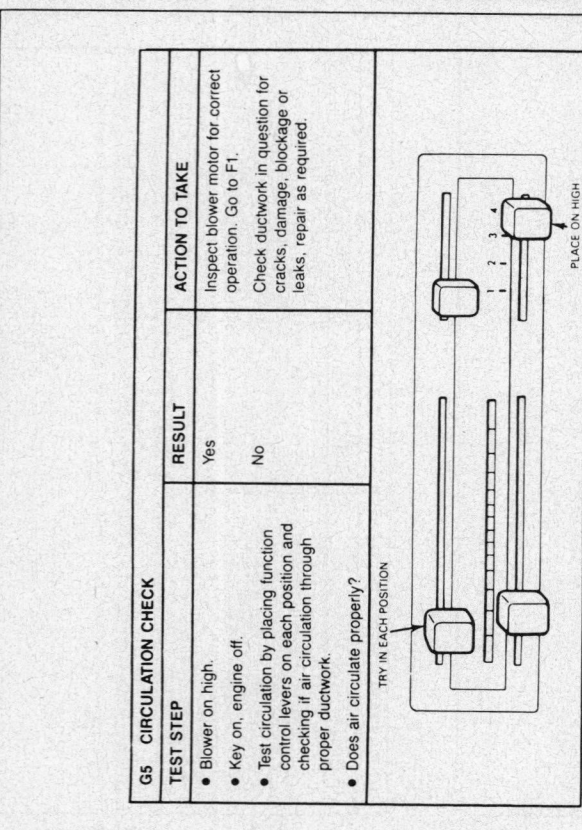

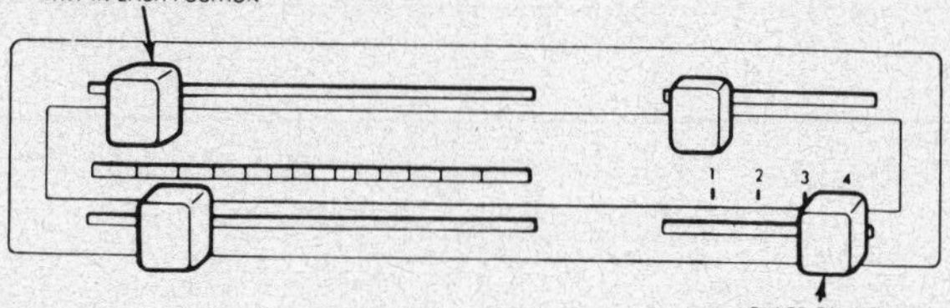
TRY IN EACH POSITION
1
2
3
4
PLACE ON HIGH

HEATING SYSTEM DIAGNOSIS AND TESTING 1991 ESCORT AND TRACER

CONDITION	POSSIBLE SOURCE	ACTION
• Blower Motor does not Operate	• "Main" fuse. • Resistor. • Blower Motor. • Blower motor control switch. • Circuit.	• GO to HP1. • GO to HP7. • GO to HP5. • GO to HP10. • GO to HP4.
• Blower Motor Runs Constantly	• Resistor. • Blower motor control switch. • Circuit.	• GO to HP7. • GO to HP10. • GO to HP4.
• Blower Motor does not Run in All Speeds	• Resistor. • Blower motor control switch. • Circuit.	• GO to HP7. • GO to HP10. • GO to HP4.
• Intermittent Blower Motor Operation	• Resistor. • Blower motor control switch. • Circuit.	• GO to HP10. • GO to HP10. • GO to HP4.
• Improper Air Circulation (air comes out of wrong duct)	• Temperature control cables. • Air distribution doors.	• GO to V1. • GO to V1.
• No Heat (Blower motor functioning properly)	• Coolant lever. • Heater hoses. • Engine thermostat. • Heater core. • Temperature blend cable.	• VISUAL inspection. • VISUAL inspection. • GO to NH1. • GO to NH2. • GO to NH4.

HEATING SYSTEM DIAGNOSIS AND TESTING—1991 ESCORT AND TRACER

TEST STEP	RESULT ►	ACTION TO TAKE
NH1 ENGINE THERMOSTAT FUNCTION		
• If engine overheating is reported or is present, refer to the cooling system diagnostics for servicing the engine thermostat. • If failure to reach normal operating temperature is a reported symptom, start and warm up the engine until the coolant temperature stabilizes. • Verify the reported symptom by checking the heater for adequate heat output (temperature control lever to the extreme right, mode selector lever at panel, blower at Position 4). • If the heater output is inadequate, remove the engine thermostat and check it for "start to open" temperature setting. • Is the "start to open" temperature setting within specification? • Specification: "start-to-open" temperature setting: 83.5-86.5°C (182-188°F)	Yes ► No ►	GO to NH2 . REPLACE the engine thermostat.

TEST STEP	RESULT ►	ACTION TO TAKE
NH2 HEATER CORE — CHECK FOR AIR FLOW BLOCKAGE		
• Check the heater core and connecting air passages for blockage, such as leaves, paper, etc. • Remove the blockage as required. • Are the heater core and its connecting air passages free of blockage?	Yes ► No ►	GO to NH3 . CLEAN, REPAIR or REPLACE components as required.

TEST STEP	RESULT ►	ACTION TO TAKE
NH3 HEATER CORE — CHECK FOR COOLANT BLOCKAGE		
• Refer to the engine cooling system diagnostics for the correct heater core block flush procedure. • Back flush the heater core to remove core sand, etc., following cooling system diagnostics. • Reassemble the cooling system components using "Installation" instructions. • Is the heater core free of blockage to coolant flow?	Yes ► No ►	GO to NH4 . REPLACE the heater core.

TEST STEP	RESULT ►	ACTION TO TAKE
NH4 TEMPERATURE CONTROL AND CABLES FUNCTION		
• Start and warm up the engine to its normal operating temperature. • Set the blower switch to Position 4. • Set the mode selector lever to panel. • Move the temperature control lever gradually from the extreme left to the extreme right and verify that the air temperature gradually increases from cold to hot. • Is the temperature control lever functioning properly and is the air hot when the lever is at the extreme right?	Yes ► No ►	RETURN to symptom chart. ADJUST the temperature control cable to close off all bypass air around the heater core when the temperature control lever is set to the extreme right.

TEST STEP	RESULT ►	ACTION TO TAKE
HP1 CHECK FUSE		
• Check the 30 amp "Heater" fuse. • Is the fuse good?	Yes ► No ►	GO to HP4 . GO to HP2 .

HEATING SYSTEM DIAGNOSIS AND TESTING – 1991 ESCORT AND TRACER

TEST STEP	RESULT ►	ACTION TO TAKE
HP2 CHECK SYSTEM		
• Replace the blown 30 amp "Heater" fuse. • Key ON. • Did the fuse blow again?	Yes ► No ►	GO to HP3. GO to HP4.

TEST STEP	RESULT ►	ACTION TO TAKE
HP3 CHECK FOR SHORT TO GROUND		
• Key OFF. • Disconnect the "BL/W" wire from the "Heater" fuse. • Measure the resistance of the "BL/W" wire between the fuse panel and ground. • Is the resistance less than 5 ohms?	Yes ► No ►	SERVICE the "BL/W" wire. GO to HP4.

TEST STEP	RESULT ►	ACTION TO TAKE
HP4 CHECK SUPPLY TO BLOWER MOTOR		
• Disconnect the blower motor connector. • Key ON. • Measure the voltage on the "BL/W" wire at the connector. • Reconnect the blower motor connector. • Is the voltage greater than 10 volts?	Yes ► No ►	GO to HP5. SERVICE the "BL/W" wire.

TEST STEP	RESULT ►	ACTION TO TAKE
HP5 CHECK BLOWER MOTOR		
• Key OFF. • Disconnect the blower motor connector. • Apply 12 volts to the "BL/W" terminal. • Ground the "BL/BK" terminal. • Reconnect the blower motor. • Did the blower motor run?	Yes ► No ►	GO to HP6. SERVICE/REPLACE the blower motor.

TEST STEP	RESULT ►	ACTION TO TAKE
HP6 CHECK LEAD TO RESISTOR		
• Locate the resistor connector. • Measure the resistance of the "BL/BK" wire between the motor and the resistor. • Is the resistance less than 5 ohms?	Yes ► No ►	GO to HP7. SERVICE the "BL/BK" wire.

TEST STEP	RESULT ►	ACTION TO TAKE
HP7 CHECK RESISTOR		
• Measure the resistance from the "BL/BK" wire at the connector to the following wires at the connector. Wire / Resistance: "BL/Y" — 2.6 ohms "BL" — 1.2 ohms "BL/R" — .6 ohm "BL/W" — .1 ohm • Are the resistances correct?	Yes ► No ►	GO to HP8. REPLACE the resistor.

HEATING SYSTEM DIAGNOSIS AND TESTING—1991 ESCORT AND TRACER

TEST STEP	RESULT ►	ACTION TO TAKE
HP8 CHECK LEADS TO BLOWER MOTOR CONTROL SWITCH		
• Locate the blower motor control switch connector. • Measure the resistance of the following wires between the resistor and the blower motor control switch. **Wire** "BL/Y" "BL" "BL/R" "BL/W" • Are the resistances less than 5 ohms?	Yes ► No ►	GO to HP9. SERVICE the wire in question.

TEST STEP	RESULT ►	ACTION TO TAKE
HP9 CHECK THE BLOWER MOTOR CONTROL SWITCH GROUND		
• Measure the resistance of the "BK" wire between the blower motor control switch and ground. • Is the resistance less than 5 ohms?	Yes ► No ►	GO to HP10. SERVICE the "BK" wire.

TEST STEP	RESULT ►	ACTION TO TAKE
HP10 CHECK THE BLOWER MOTOR CONTROL SWITCH		
• Disconnect the blower motor control switch. • Measure the resistance between ground and the wire colors listed below at the following switch positions. (see table below) • Reconnect the blower motor control switch. • Are the resistances correct?	Yes ► No ►	RETURN to the Symptom Chart. SERVICE/REPLACE the blower motor control switch.

Switch Position	Wire Color	Resistance
OFF	All Colors	Greater than 10,000 ohms
1	"BL/Y"	Less than 5 ohms
	All Others	Greater than 10,000 ohms
2	"BL"	Less than 5 ohms
	All Others	Greater than 10,000 ohms
3	"BL/R"	Less than 5 ohms
	All Others	Greater than 10,000 ohms
4	"BL/W"	Less than 5 ohms
	All Others	Greater than 10,000 ohms

TEST STEP	RESULT ▶	ACTION TO TAKE
V1 AIR FLOW SELECTOR SYSTEM FUNCTION		
• With the ignition switch ON and the blower switch set to Position 4 for maximum air flow, check the air flow patterns resulting from the following position settings of the mode selector. Verify that they conform to the specified air flow patterns as listed:	Yes ▶	GO to V2.
	No ▶	REPAIR, ADJUST or REPLACE the heater or its outlet door or components as required.

Air Flow Selector Position	Specified Air Flow Pattern (Exit Locations Shown)
PANEL	Ventilator outlets
HI-LO	Ventilator and floor outlets
FLOOR	Floor outlets and small amount to the defroster outlets
MIX	Floor and defroster outlets
DEF	Defroster outlets

• Do the air flow patterns conform to the specified patterns for each of the tested selector positions?

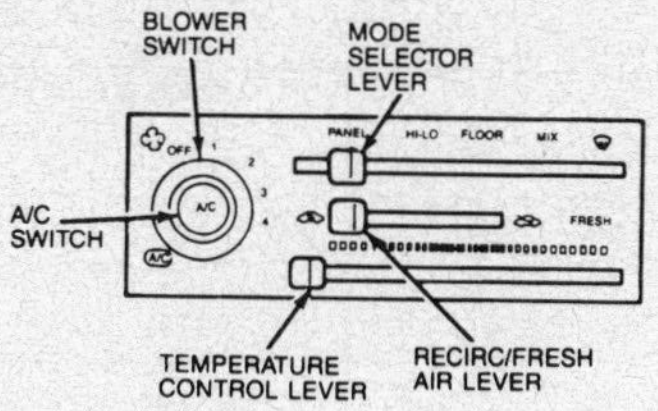
BLOWER SWITCH
MODE SELECTOR LEVER
A/C SWITCH
TEMPERATURE CONTROL LEVER
RECIRC/FRESH AIR LEVER
OFF
PANEL
HI-LO
FLOOR
MIX
FRESH
A/C

TEST STEP	RESULT ▶	ACTION TO TAKE
V1 AIR FLOW SELECTOR SYSTEM FUNCTION — CONTINUED		

PANEL MODE

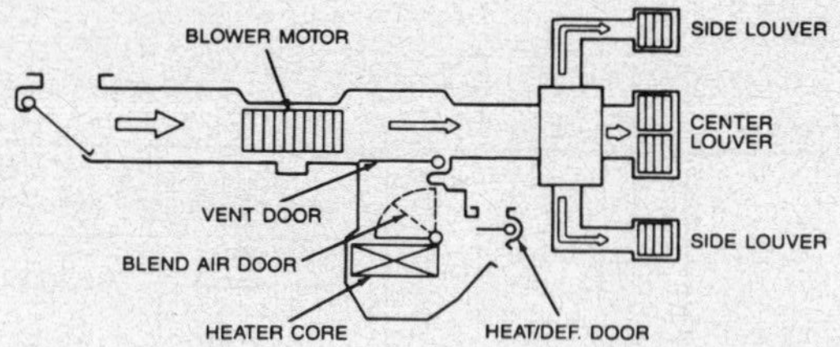
BLOWER MOTOR
SIDE LOUVER
CENTER LOUVER
SIDE LOUVER
VENT DOOR
BLEND AIR DOOR
HEATER CORE
HEAT/DEF. DOOR

HI-LO MODE

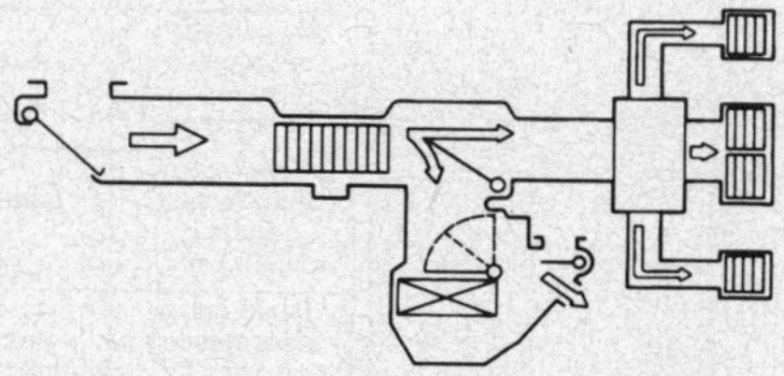

FLOOR MODE

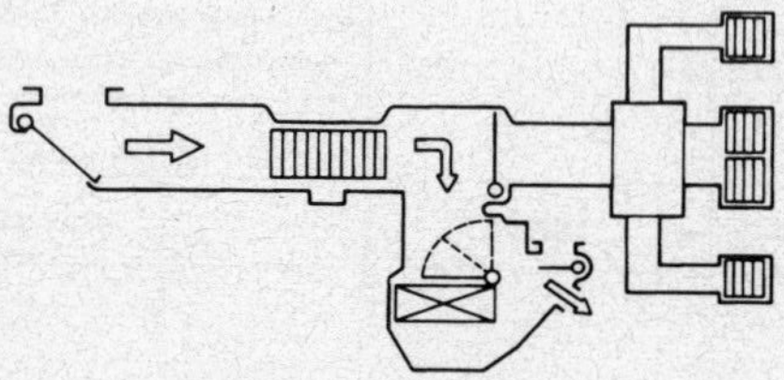

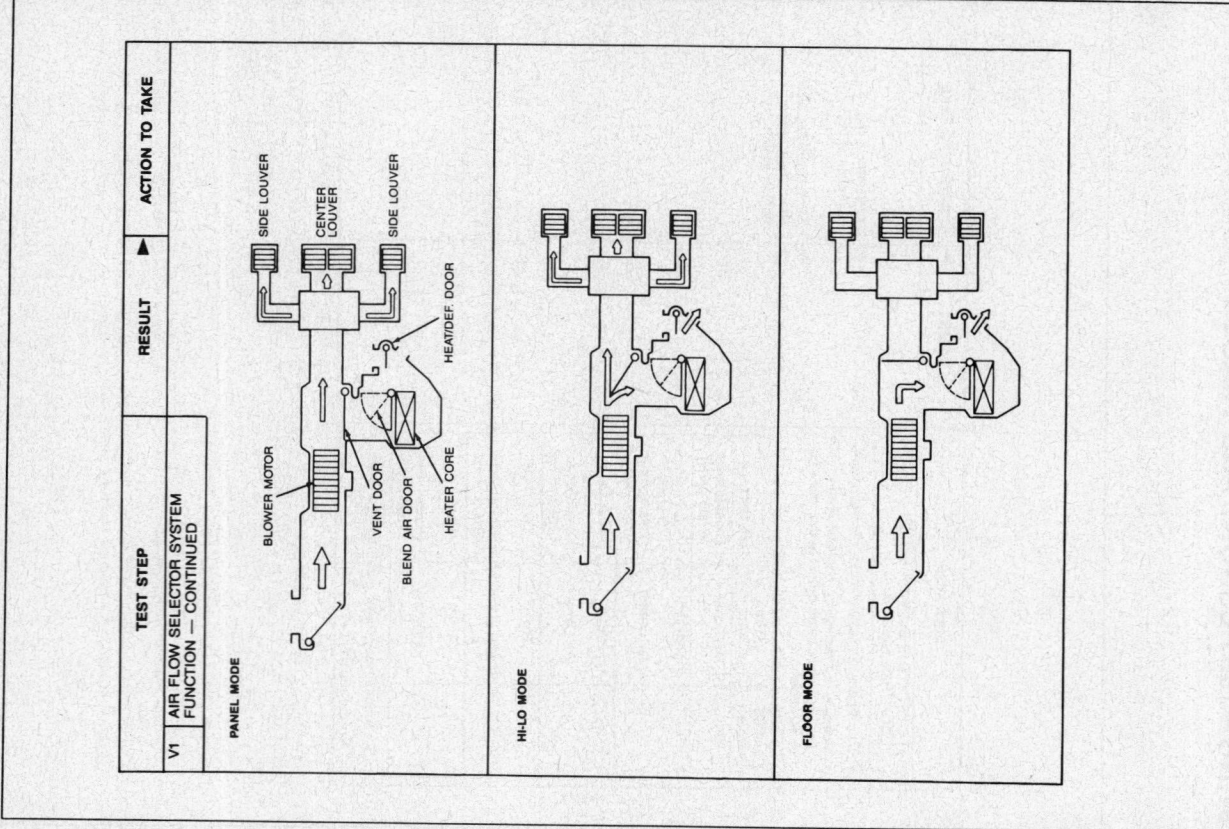

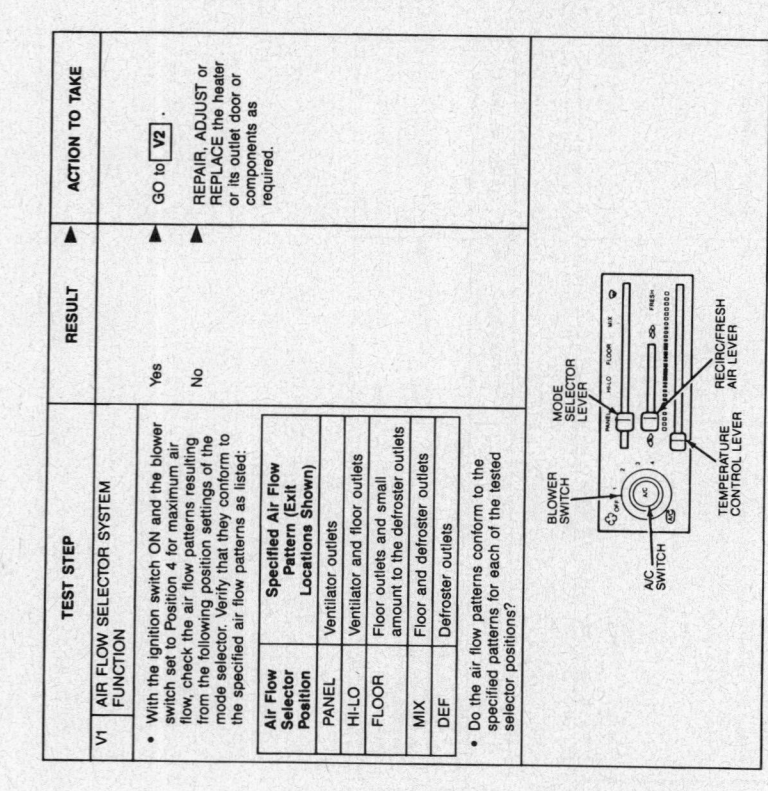

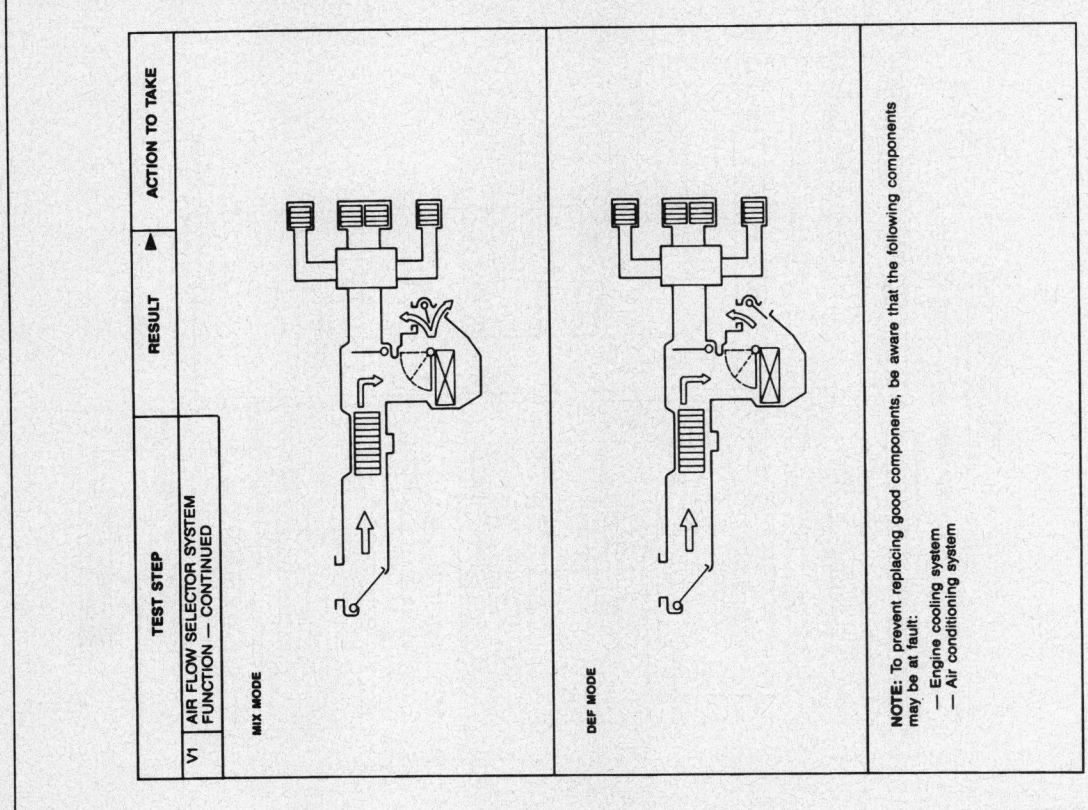

TEST STEP		RESULT ►	ACTION TO TAKE
V1	AIR FLOW SELECTOR SYSTEM FUNCTION — CONTINUED		

MIX MODE

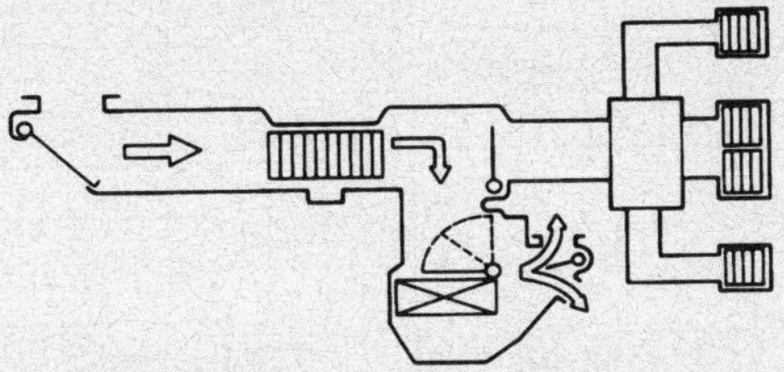

DEF MODE

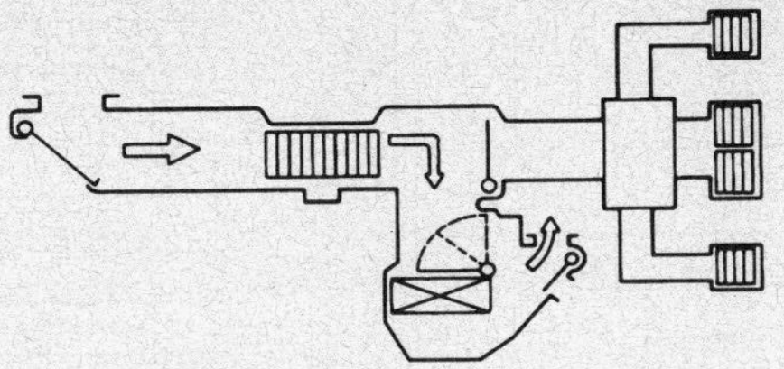

NOTE: To prevent replacing good components, be aware that the following components may be at fault:

— Engine cooling system
— Air conditioning system

TEST STEP		RESULT ►	ACTION TO TAKE
V2	RECIRCULATION — FRESH AIR SELECTOR FUNCTION		
	• With the ignition switch ON and the blower fan speed control set to Position 4 for maximum air flow, change the selector setting from RECIRCULATION (REC) to FRESH AIR. Verify that the air movement conforms to the specified patterns as listed:	Yes ►	GO to V3 .
		No ►	REPAIR, ADJUST or REPLACE the blower unit or the rec-fresh selector door or linkage as required.

Recirc/Fresh Air Lever Position	Specified Air Flow Movement (Air Intake)
Extreme Left (Recirc)	Air flow at REC air inlet openings under the instrument panel can be felt and heard (whistling).
Extreme Right (Fresh)	No air flow at the instrument panel REC air inlet openings, at instrument panel openings; no whistling-type air noise.

• Does the air flow conform to the specified patterns for each of the tested selector lever positions?

TEST STEP		RESULT ►	ACTION TO TAKE
V3	VENTILATION SYSTEM — CHECK FOR BLOCKAGE		
	• Disassemble the following components of the ventilation system for inspection as required, and remove any foreign material causing air flow blockage: Blower motor Blower housing Recirculation inlet (paper, etc.) Fresh inlet (leaves, etc.) Main air duct (no A/C) Evaporator (with A/C) Heater core inlet side Air outlets at floor, panel and defroster • Is the air flow adequate in all selector modes for both recirculation and fresh air modes?	Yes ►	RETURN to symptom chart. System OK.
		No ►	ADJUST recirculation-fresh air door, heat door, defroster door or vent door as required. REFER to "Adjustment" in this section.

AIR CONDITIONING SYSTEM DIAGNOSIS AND TESTING – 1991 ESCORT AND TRACER

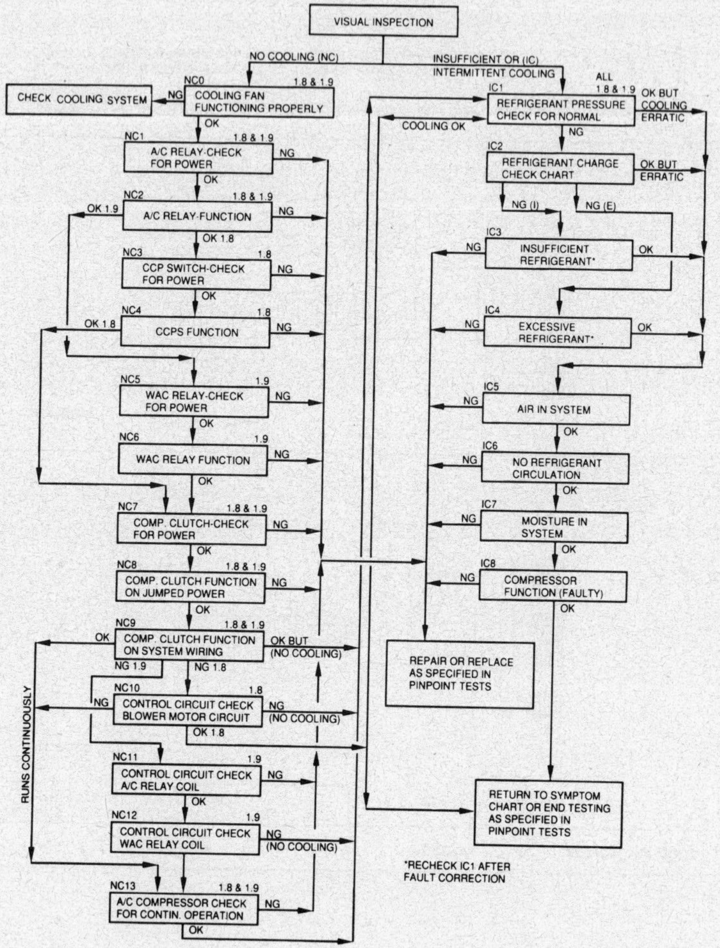
VISUAL INSPECTION
NO COOLING (NC)
INSUFFICIENT OR (IC) INTERMITTENT COOLING
CHECK COOLING SYSTEM
NC0 COOLING FAN FUNCTIONING PROPERLY 1.8 & 1.9
NC1 A/C RELAY-CHECK FOR POWER 1.8 & 1.9
NC2 A/C RELAY-FUNCTION 1.8 & 1.9
OK 1.9
OK 1.8
NC3 CCP SWITCH-CHECK FOR POWER 1.8
NC4 CCPS FUNCTION 1.8
NC5 WAC RELAY-CHECK FOR POWER 1.9
NC6 WAC RELAY FUNCTION 1.9
NC7 COMP. CLUTCH-CHECK FOR POWER 1.8 & 1.9
NC8 COMP. CLUTCH FUNCTION ON JUMPED POWER 1.8 & 1.9
NC9 COMP. CLUTCH FUNCTION ON SYSTEM WIRING 1.8 & 1.9
OK BUT (NO COOLING)
NG 1.9
NG 1.8
NC10 CONTROL CIRCUIT CHECK BLOWER MOTOR CIRCUIT 1.8
NG (NO COOLING)
OK 1.8
NC11 CONTROL CIRCUIT CHECK A/C RELAY COIL 1.9
NC12 CONTROL CIRCUIT CHECK WAC RELAY COIL 1.9
NG (NO COOLING)
NC13 A/C COMPRESSOR CHECK FOR CONTIN. OPERATION 1.8 & 1.9
RUNS CONTINUOUSLY
IC1 REFRIGERANT PRESSURE CHECK FOR NORMAL
ALL 1.8 & 1.9
OK BUT COOLING ERRATIC
COOLING OK
IC2 REFRIGERANT CHARGE CHECK CHART
OK BUT ERRATIC
NG (I)
NG (E)
IC3 INSUFFICIENT REFRIGERANT*
IC4 EXCESSIVE REFRIGERANT*
IC5 AIR IN SYSTEM
IC6 NO REFRIGERANT CIRCULATION
IC7 MOISTURE IN SYSTEM
IC8 COMPRESSOR FUNCTION (FAULTY)
REPAIR OR REPLACE AS SPECIFIED IN PINPOINT TESTS
RETURN TO SYMPTOM CHART OR END TESTING AS SPECIFIED IN PINPOINT TESTS
OK
NG

*RECHECK IC1 AFTER FAULT CORRECTION

TEST STEP		RESULT ►	ACTION TO TAKE
NC1	A/C RELAY — CHECK FOR POWER		
• Disconnect the A/C relay connector. • Using a VOM, check the voltage to ground at the connector terminals. • Key ON. • "BL/GN" for relay coil and "BL/Y" for relay contacts. • Is the voltage approximately 12 volts at both terminals?		Yes ► No ►	GO to NC2. REPLACE the "BL/GN" or "BL/Y" wire(s) or wiring harnesses as required.

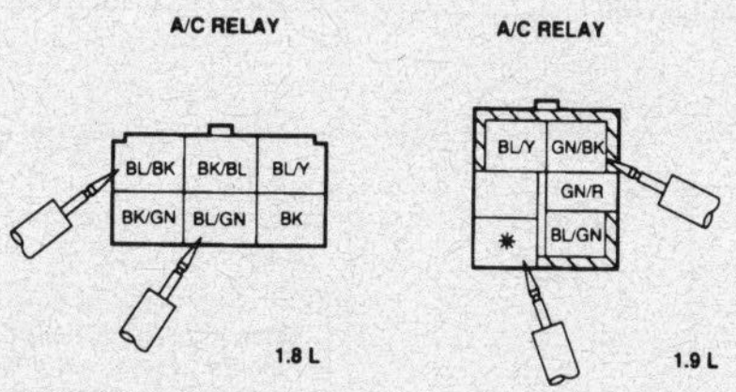
A/C RELAY
BL/BK
BK/BL
BL/Y
BK/GN
BL/GN
BK
1.8 L
A/C RELAY
BL/Y
GN/BK
GN/R
BL/GN
1.9 L

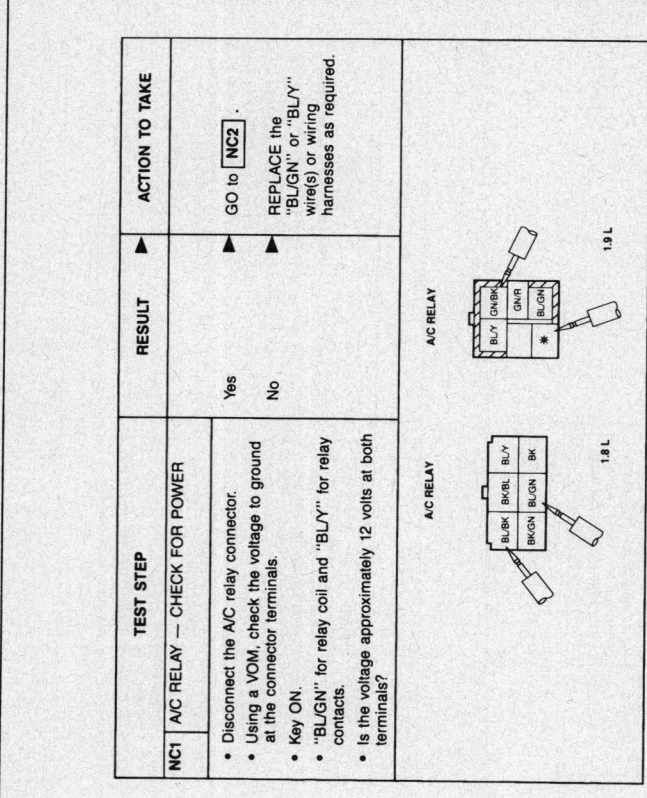

AIR CONDITIONING SYSTEM DIAGNOSIS AND TESTING—1991 ESCORT AND TRACER

TEST STEP	RESULT ►	ACTION TO TAKE
NC2 A/C RELAY FUNCTION		
• Disconnect the A/C relay connector. • Jump 12 volts from the battery to relay coil terminal "BL/GN" and to contact terminal "BL/Y." • Ground relay terminal "BL/BK" for 1.8L or "GN/R" for 1.9L. • Using a VOM, check the voltage to ground at relay terminals: "BK/BL" for 1.8L "GN/BK" for 1.9L • Is the voltage approximately 12 volts at terminal?	Yes ► No ►	GO to NC3 for 1.8L. GO to NC5 for 1.9L. REPLACE the A/C relay.

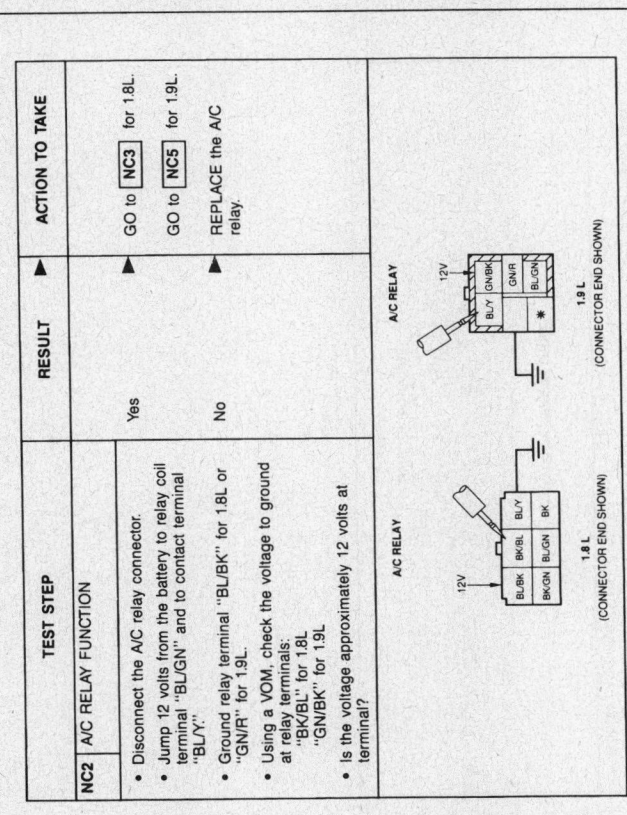

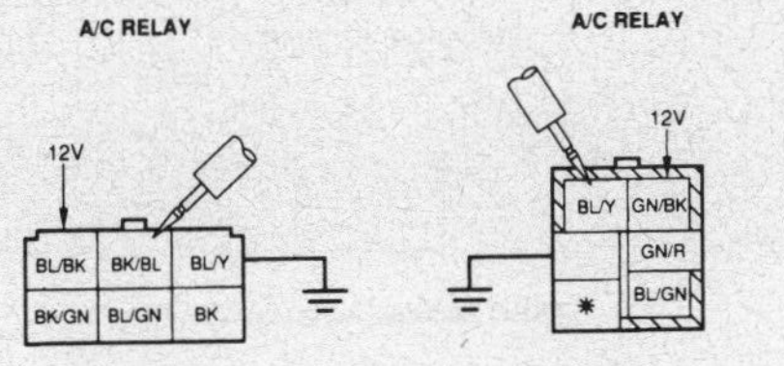
A/C RELAY
12V
BL/BK
BK/BL
BL/Y
BK/GN
BL/GN
BK
A/C RELAY
12V
BL/Y
GN/BK
GN/R
BL/GN

1.8 L
(CONNECTOR END SHOWN)

1.9 L
(CONNECTOR END SHOWN)

1.8L Engine

TEST STEP	RESULT ►	ACTION TO TAKE
NC3 CLUTCH CYCLING PRESSURE SWITCH (CCPS) CHECK FOR POWER		
• Disconnect the CCPS connector. • Leaving the A/C relay jumped as instructed in Test NC2, use a VOM to check voltage to ground at CCPS connector terminal "BK/BL." • Is the voltage approximately 12 volts at the connector terminal?	Yes ► No ►	GO to NC4 . REPLACE the "BK/BL" wire or the wiring harness as required.

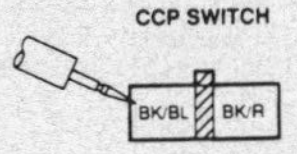
CCP SWITCH
BK/BL
BK/R

TEST STEP	RESULT ►	ACTION TO TAKE
NC4 CLUTCH CYCLING PRESSURE SWITCH (CCPS) FUNCTION		
• Disconnect the CCPS connector. • With the evaporator warmed up (system shut down), check continuity across the two terminals of the switch ("BK/R" to "BK/BL"). • Is there continuity?	Yes ► No ►	GO to **NC7**. REPLACE the CCPS (switch stuck open).

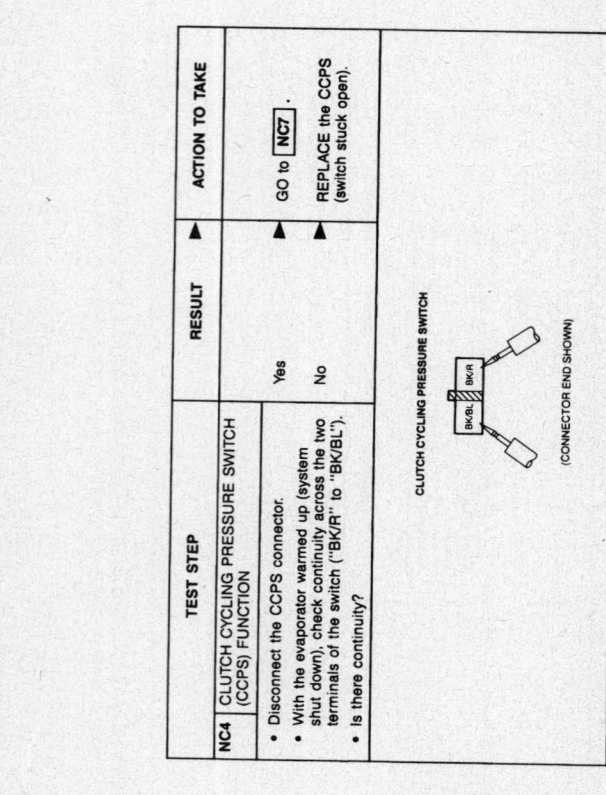

CLUTCH CYCLING PRESSURE SWITCH

BK/BL
BK/R

(CONNECTOR END SHOWN)

1.9L Engine

TEST STEP	RESULT ►	ACTION TO TAKE
NC5 WIDE OPEN THROTTLE A/C (WAC) RELAY — CHECK FOR POWER		
• Disconnect the WAC relay connector. • Key must be ON. • Using a VOM, verify that the voltage to ground at the connector terminal "BL/GN" is approximately 12 volts before going further. If it is not, replace the "BL/GN" wire or harness as required before proceeding. • Disconnect the A/C relay connector. • Jump 12 volts to the A/C relay terminals "BL/GN" and "BL/Y" and ground relay terminal "GN/R." • Using a VOM, check the voltage to ground at the WAC relay connector terminal "GN/BK." • Is the voltage at the "GN/BK" connector terminal approximately 12 volts?	Yes ► No ►	GO to **NC6**. REPLACE the "GN/BK" wire or wiring harness as required.

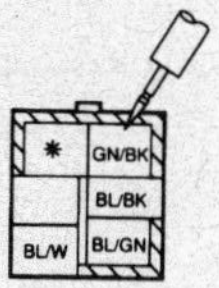
*
GN/BK
BL/BK
BL/W
BL/GN

AIR CONDITIONING SYSTEM DIAGNOSIS AND TESTING—1991 ESCORT AND TRACER

TEST STEP	RESULT ►	ACTION TO TAKE
NC6 WAC RELAY FUNCTION (1.9L ONLY)		
• Disconnect the WAC relay connector. • Jump 12 volts from the battery to the WAC relay terminal "BL/GN" and ground the "BL/BK" terminal to open the relay. • Apply 12 volts to "GN/BK" terminal. • Using a VOM, check the voltage at the WAC relay terminal "BL/W." • Is the voltage zero at WAC relay terminal "BL/W"?	Yes ► No ►	GO to NC7 . REPLACE the WAC relay.

WAC RELAY
GN/BK
BL/BK
BL/GN
BL/W
(CONNECTOR END SHOWN)

1.8L, 1.9L Engines

TEST STEP	RESULT ►	ACTION TO TAKE
NC7 COMPRESSOR CLUTCH — CHECK FOR POWER		
• Disconnect the A/C relay connector. • Jump 12 volts from the battery to the A/C relay terminals "BL/GN" and "BL/Y" and ground relay terminal "BL/BK" for 1.8L or terminal "GN/R" for 1.9L, to close the relay. • Verify that the CCPS for 1.8L is closed (A/C system shut down and warmed up). • Jump the A/C relay terminal "BK/BL" to the relay connector "BK/BL" (1.8L). • Disconnect the compressor clutch connector. • Using a VOM, measure the voltage to ground at the compressor clutch connector terminal "BK/R" for 1.8L, or "BL/W" for 1.9L. • Is the voltage approximately 12 volts at the clutch connector?	Yes ► No ►	GO to NC8 . REPLACE the wire "BK/R" for 1.8L or "BL/W" for 1.9L, or the wiring harness as required.

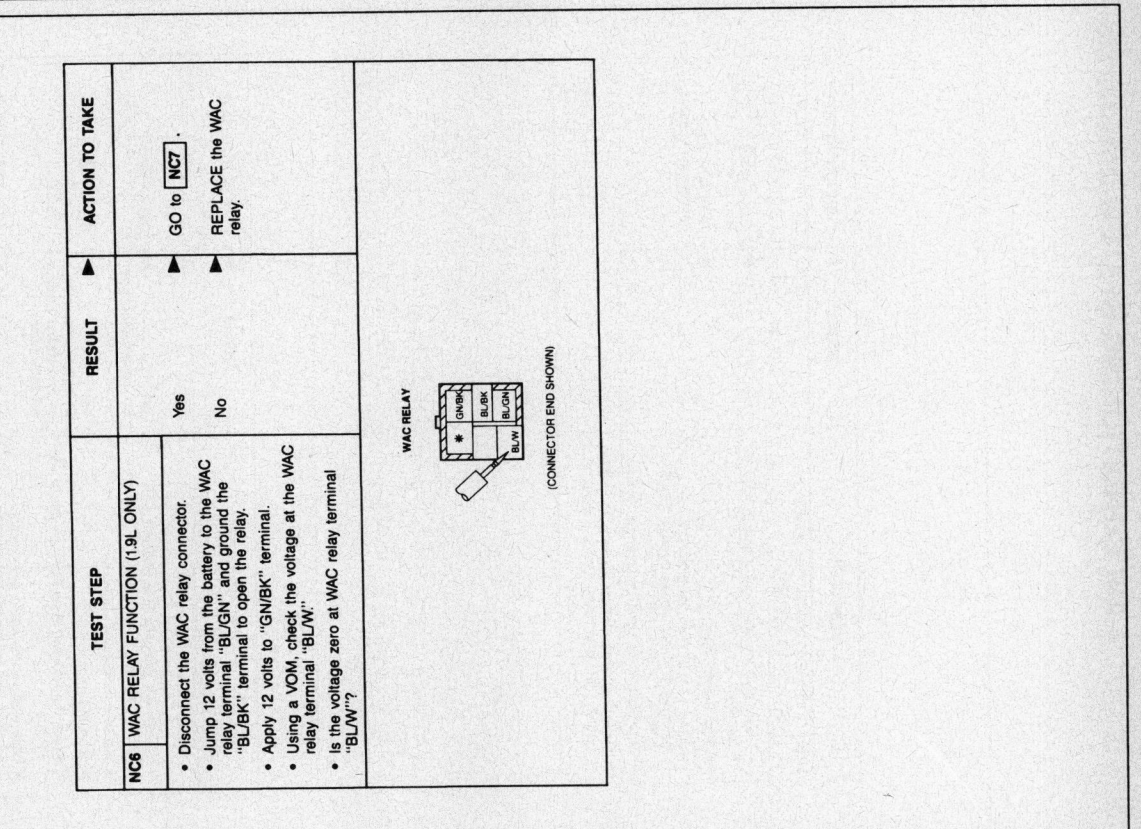

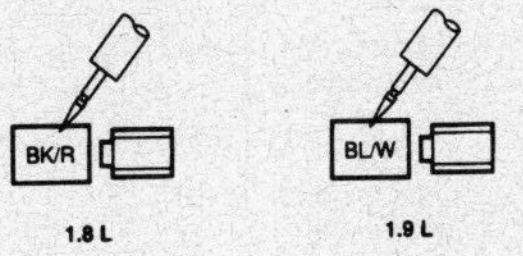
BK/R
1.8 L
BL/W
1.9 L

TEST STEP	RESULT ►	ACTION TO TAKE
NC8 COMPRESSOR CLUTCH FUNCTION ON JUMPED POWER		
• Disconnect the compressor clutch connector. • Start the engine. • Jump 12 volts from the battery to the compressor clutch power terminal "BK/R" (1.8L) or "BL/W" (1.9L) with the engine running and note the clutch engagement. • Does the clutch engage instantly and pick up the compressor very rapidly without screeching or squealing?	Yes ► No ►	GO to **NC9**. REPLACE the compressor clutch.

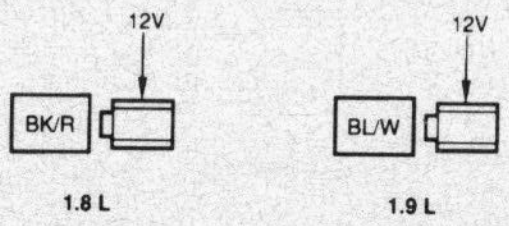
12V
BK/R
1.8 L
12V
BL/W
1.9 L

TEST STEP	RESULT ►	ACTION TO TAKE
NC9 COMPRESSOR CLUTCH FUNCTION ON SYSTEM WIRING		
• Reconnect all connectors previously disconnected. • Remove all jumper wiring. • Start the engine. • Press the A/C switch and turn on the blower control. • Note whether the compressor clutch engages and drives the compressor. • Does the compressor clutch operate on system wiring satisfactorily?	Yes But compressor runs continuously ► Yes Compressor cycles on and off but cooling not satisfactory ► No ►	GO to **NC13**. GO to **IC1**. GO to **NC10** for 1.8L GO to **NC11** for 1.9L (control circuit malfunction).

1.8L Engine

TEST STEP	RESULT ►	ACTION TO TAKE
NC10 CONTROL CIRCUIT CHECKS BLOWER MOTOR CIRCUIT		
• Blower motor switch ON (position 1, 2, 3, or 4). • A/C switch depressed (ON). • Key OFF. • Using a VOM, check continuity from the "BL/W" wire at ignition to the "GN/BK" wire at the ECA. • Check the continuity from the "BL/BK" wire at the ECA to the "BL/GN" terminal at the A/C relay. • If any of the above checks show no continuity, repair or replace the wires, wiring harnesses or connectors as required before proceeding. • If the above checks meet the specification for continuity, attempt to operate the A/C with the engine running. • Does the A/C system operate and is it cooling satisfactorily?	Yes ► No System operates but cooling not satisfactory ► No Compressor runs continuously ►	End of testing. GO to **IC1**. GO to **NC13**. (Shorted control circuit)

1.9L Engine

TEST STEP	RESULT ►	ACTION TO TAKE
NC11 CONTROL CIRCUIT CHECKS A/C RELAY COIL CIRCUIT		
• Blower motor switch ON. • Key OFF. • A/C switch depressed (ON). • Using a VOM, check continuity from the "BL/GN" terminal on the A/C relay through the "GN/R" wire to the CCPS, the "R/Y" wire to the A/C switch, and through the A/C and blower switches to the ground wire "BK." • Is there continuity?	Yes ► No ►	GO to **NC12**. REPAIR or REPLACE the wire, wires or harness as required, including connectors.

AIR CONDITIONING SYSTEM DIAGNOSIS AND TESTING—1991 ESCORT AND TRACER

TEST STEP	RESULT ►	ACTION TO TAKE
NC12 CONTROL CIRCUIT CHECKS — WAC RELAY COIL CIRCUIT		
• Using a VOM, check continuity from the "BL/GN" terminal at the WAC relay to the "BL/BK" terminal at the ECA. Also check the continuity from the "GN/BK" terminal on the WAC relay to the "GN/BK" terminal on the ECA. • If any of these checks show no continuity, repair or replace the wires, wiring harnesses or connectors as required before proceeding. • If the above checks meet the specification for continuity, attempt to operate the A/C system with the engine running. • Does the A/C system operate and is it cooling satisfactorily?	Yes ► No System operates but cooling not satisfactory ► No Compressor runs continuously ►	End of testing. GO to IC1. GO to NC13. (Shorted control circuit)

1.8L, 1.9L Engines

TEST STEP	RESULT ►	ACTION TO TAKE
NC13 A/C COMPRESSOR — CHECK		
• Using a VOM, check for shorts to ground in each control circuit wire as follows, referring as required to the 1.8L or 1.9L wiring diagram: **1.8L and 1.9L:** BL/Y," "BL," "BL/R," "BL/W" (blower switch to resistor), "BL/BK" (resistor to blower motor). **1.8L only:** "BL/BK" (A/C relay to ECA), "GN/BK" and "R/Y" (ECA to A/C switch), "O/BL" (blower switch to ECA). **1.9L only:** "GN/R" (A/C relay to CCPS), "R/Y" (CCPS to A/C switch). • Check for stuck closed contact points by testing for continuity as follows: 1.8L A/C relay — "BL/Y" to "BK/BL" 1.9L A/C relay — "BL/Y" to "GN/BK" 1.9L CCP switch — "GN/R" to "R/Y" Remove the CCPS from the suction accumulator to obtain sufficiently low pressure to open the switch. • Is the cause of continuous compressor operation corrected?	Yes ► No ►	GO to IC1. REPAIR or REPLACE any damaged or shorted wiring, wiring harnesses, connectors or components as required. RETEST after repairs.

TEST STEP	RESULT ►	ACTION TO TAKE
IC1 REFRIGERANT PRESSURE — CHECK FOR NORMAL PRESSURES		
• Connect the A/C manifold gauge set. • Measure the low-and high-pressure sides. • Compare the observed pressures with the specified normal pressures (see specifications). • Are the pressures within specified normal pressure limits?	Yes But cooling is still erratic ►	GO to **IC5**.
	No ►	GO to **IC2**.

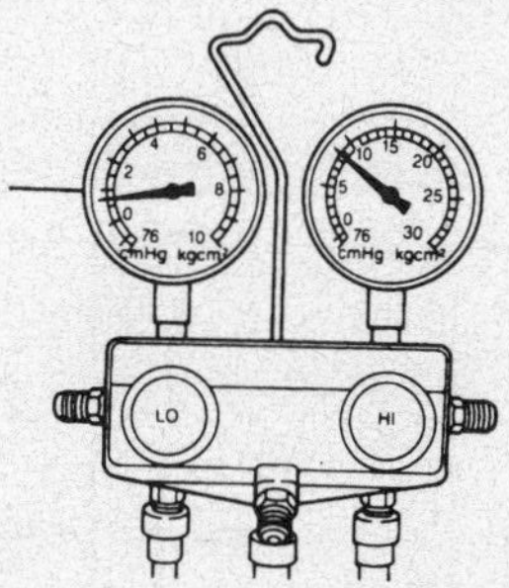

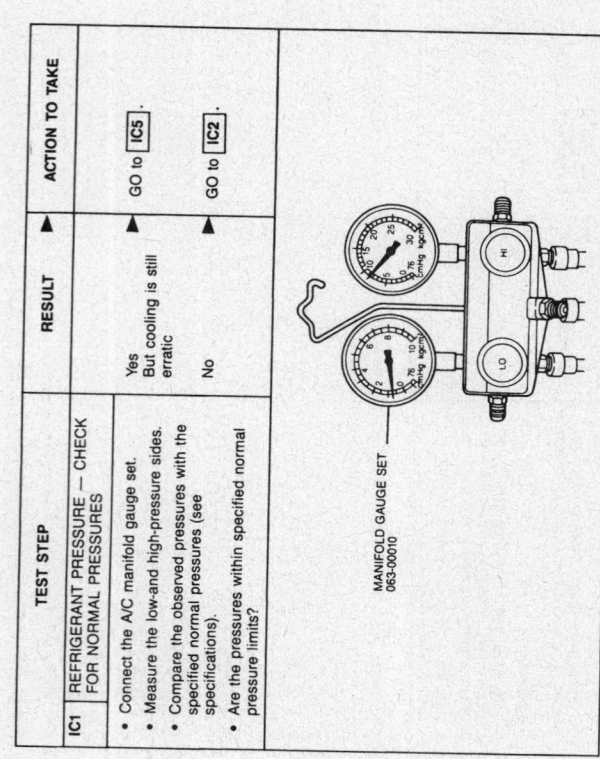

MANIFOLD GAUGE SET
063-00010

TEST STEP	RESULT ►	ACTION TO TAKE
IC2 REFRIGERANT CHARGE CHECK CHART		
• Manifold gauge still connected. • Run the engine at fast idle. • Operate the A/C at maximum cooling for a few minutes with blower on speed III. • Observe A/C system pressure on the high and low sides of the gauge. • Compare the gauge readings to the pressure specifications listed below.	Yes But cooling is still erratic ►	GO to **IC5**.
	No Insufficient ►	GO to **IC3**.
	No Excessive ►	GO to **IC4**.

Description	Specification
Normal Refrigerant Pressure Low Pressure Side	147-294 kPa (1.5-3.0 kg/cm², 21-23 psi)
High Pressure Side	1,177-1,619 kPa (12.0-16.5 kg/cm², 171-235 psi)

• Is the A/C pressure reading OK?

AIR CONDITIONING SYSTEM DIAGNOSIS AND TESTING—1991 ESCORT AND TRACER

TEST STEP	RESULT ►	ACTION TO TAKE
IC3 REFRIGERANT CHARGE — CHECK FOR INSUFFICIENT REFRIGERANT		
• Connect the manifold gauge set. • Operate the engine at 2000 rpm and set the A/C to maximum cooling. • Measure the low- and high-side pressures. • If insufficient refrigerant, the pressures should be: Low-side: Below 7.85 kPa (0.8 kg/cm², 11.4 psi) High-side: 785-883 kPa (8-9 kg/cm², 114-128 psi) • If the pressure is low, check for leakage as evidenced by oil stains at connections. • If no oil stains are evident, check for leakage at the following connections using a gas leak detector (observe warning and safety precautions): Inlet and outlet of; condenser, suction accumulator/drier, compressor, sight glass, cooling unit. • Is the refrigerant pressure low and is leakage present?	Yes (And leakage present) ►	REPLACE O-rings at leaking connectors and RETORQUE, then EVACUATE the system, RECHARGE and RETEST.
	Yes (No leaks present) ►	EVACUATE, RECHARGE, and RETEST the system. (Leakage occurred slowly over a long time.)
	No (But cooling is erratic) ►	GO to IC5.

TEST STEP	RESULT ►	ACTION TO TAKE
IC4 REFRIGERANT CHARGE — CHECK FOR EXCESSIVE REFRIGERANT		
• Connect the manifold gauge set. • Operate the engine at 2000 rpm and set the A/C to maximum cooling. • Measure the low-and high-side pressures. • If excessive refrigerant, the pressures should be: Low-side: Above 245 kPa (2.5 kg/cm², 35.6 psi) High-side: Above 1,962 kPa (20 kg/cm², 284 psi) • If the pressure is high, check the condenser for bent fins or other damage. • Is the refrigerant pressure high?	Yes ►	REPAIR condenser fins or other damage, DISCHARGE the excess refrigerant, until RETEST shows the low and high sides to be within normal specification.
	No (But cooling is erratic) ►	GO to IC5.

TEST STEP	RESULT ►	ACTION TO TAKE
IC5 REFRIGERANT CHARGE — CHECK FOR AIR IN SYSTEM		
• Connect the manifold gauge set. • Operate the engine at 2000 rpm and set the A/C to maximum cooling. • Measure the low-and high-side pressures. • If air is in the refrigerant, the pressures should be: Low-side: Above 245 kPa (2.5 kg/cm², 35.6 psi) High-side: Above 2256 kPa (23 kg/cm², 327 psi) • Do the pressures indicate air in the refrigerant charge?	Yes ►	DISCHARGE, EVACUATE and RECHARGE the system with fresh refrigerant R-12 to the correct amount GO to IC2. RECHECK the low- and high-side pressures, and if they are still too high, REPLACE the suction accumulator/drier, RECHARGE and RECHECK pressures.
	No (But cooling still erratic) ►	GO to IC6.

TEST STEP	RESULT ►	ACTION TO TAKE
IC6 REFRIGERANT CHARGE — CHECK FOR REFRIGERANT CIRCULATION		
• Connect the manifold gauge set. • Operate the engine at 2000 rpm and set the A/C to maximum cooling. • Measure the low-and high-side pressures. • If there is no circulation of refrigerant in the system, the pressures should be: Low-side: 76 cm-Hg (3.0 in-Hg) vacuum. High-side: Below 589 kPa (kg/cm², 85 psi) of pressure. • If the pressures indicate no refrigerant circulation, turn the A/C OFF for 10 minutes. • Turn the A/C ON to determine whether the blockage is due to moisture or solid material. • After turning the system ON, does it operate normally?	Yes (But cooling is erratic) ►	GO to IC7. (Moisture in system freezes, then melts and relieves blockage.)
	No ►	REPLACE the fixed orifice, EVACUATE the system and RECHARGE the system with fresh refrigerant R-12 to the correct amount GO to IC2. RECHECK the low-and high-side pressures.

AIR CONDITIONING SYSTEM DIAGNOSIS AND TESTING 1991 ESCORT AND TRACER

TEST STEP	RESULT ►	ACTION TO TAKE
IC7 REFRIGERANT CHARGE — CHECK FOR MOISTURE IN SYSTEM		
• Connect the manifold gauge set. • Operate the engine at 2000 rpm and set the A/C to maximum cooling. • Measure the low-and high-side pressures. • If moisture is in the refrigerant, the pressures should be: Low-side: 50 cm-Hg (2.0 in-Hg) of vacuum to 147 kPa (1.5 kg/cm², 21.3 psi) of pressure. High-side: 687-1,472 kPa (7-15 Kg/cm², 100-213 psi) • Do the pressures indicate moisture in the refrigerant system?	Yes ►	DISCHARGE, EVACUATE and RECHARGE the system with fresh refrigerant R-12 to the correct amount GO to IC2. RECHECK the low-and high-side pressures and if still too high, REPLACE the suction accumulator/drier, RECHARGE and RECHECK pressures.
	No ►	GO to IC8.

TEST STEP	RESULT ►	ACTION TO TAKE
IC8 A/C COMPRESSOR — CHECK FOR MALFUNCTION		
• Connect the manifold gauge set. • Operate the engine at 2000 rpm and set the A/C to maximum cooling. • Measure the low-and high-side pressures. • If the A/C compressor is malfunctioning (not pumping properly) the pressures should be: Low-side: 392-589 kPa (4-6 kg/cm², 57-85 psi) High-side: 687-981 kPa (7-10 kg/cm², 100-142 psi) • If the pressures indicate a faulty compressor or slipping clutch, operate the system for 20 minutes, cycling the temperature control from hot to cold to hot several times. • Recheck the pressures. • Do the pressures indicate a faulty compressor or clutch?	Yes Clutch slipping ►	GO to NC8 (clutch function) or REPLACE the clutch as required.
	Yes Clutch not slipping ►	REPLACE the A/C compressor, EVACUATE the system and RECHARGE with R-12 refrigerant to the correct amount GO to IC2. RECHECK the low-and high-side pressures.
	No ►	

HEATING SYSTEM DIAGNOSIS AND TESTING—CAPRI

CONDITION	POSSIBLE SOURCE	ACTION
• Insufficient, Erratic, or No Heat or Defrost	• Low coolant due to coolant leaks.	• Fill system to proper level. Pressure test system and radiator cap. Service as required.
	• Engine overheating.	• Check water pump drive belt. • Remove debris from radiator and/or condenser cooling fins. • Check electric cooling fan for proper operation. • Check thermostat for proper operation. • Check water pump for damage or restricted cooling system or heater core
	• Blocked air inlet.	• Check air inlet for leaves, etc. Clean as required.
	• Heater flaps sticking or inoperative.	• Check heater control unit operation. Service as required. • Check cable operation. Service as required. • Disconnect cable(s). Check control unit and flap operation. Service as required.
• Air Comes Out Defroster Outlet Only, or Air Distribution Not Controllable	• Cables disconnected or out of adjustment.	• Inspect control unit and cables. Service as required.

CONDITION	POSSIBLE SOURCE	ACTION
• Vent System Leaks Air When in OFF Position	• Vent / Recirc. door not sealing.	• Check door for obstructions, damaged seal. Service as required. • Check control cable for proper adjustment and operation. Service as required.
Blower Motor Does Not Run, or Blower Motor Does Not Run at Selected Speed	• No power to blower motor, blower motor switch.	• Check blower circuit breaker, fuse, wiring. Service as required.
	• No ground to blower motor.	• Check ground circuit. Service as required.
	• Blower switch worn or damaged.	• Check Blower switch. Service as required.
	• Blower resistor damaged.	• Check blower resistor. Bypass resistor with jumper wire. If blower runs, replace resistor.
	• Blower motor damaged.	• Connect fused jumper lead to power and "hot" side of blower motor. If motor does not run, connect jumper from ground to ground of blower motor. If blower does not run with both jumpers connected, replace blower motor.

HEATING SYSTEM DIAGNOSIS AND TESTING—CAPRI

CONDITION	POSSIBLE SOURCE	ACTION
• Blower Motor Does Not Operate	• Main fuse. • Resistor. • Blower motor. • Blower motor control switch. • Circuit.	• Go to **HP1.** • Go to **HP7.** • Go to **HP5.** • Go to **HP12.** • Go to **HP4.**
• Blower Motor Runs Constantly	• Resistor. • Blower motor control switch. • Circuit.	• Go to **HP7.** • Go to **HP12.** • Go to **HP4.**
• Blower Motor Does Not Run in All Speeds	• Resistor. • Blower motor control switch. • Circuit.	• Go to **HP7.** • Go to **HP12.** • Go to **HP4.**

CONDITION	POSSIBLE SOURCE	ACTION
• Intermittent Blower Motor Operation	• Resistor • Blower motor control switch. • Circuit	• Go to **HP12.** • Go to **HP12.** • Go to **HP4.**
• Improper Air Circulation (Air Comes Out of Wrong Duct)	• Temperature control levers. • Temperature control cables. • Air distribution doors.	• Go to **V2.** • Go to **V1.** • Go to **V2.**
• No Heat (Blower Motor Functioning Properly)	• Coolant level. • Heater hoses. • Engine thermostat. • Heater core. • Temperature blend cable.	• Visually inspect level. • Visually inspect hoses. • Go to **NH1.** • Go to **NH2.** • Go to **NH4.**

TEST STEP	RESULT ▶	ACTION TO TAKE
HP1 CHECK FUSE		
• Access main fuse panel. • Check the 60 amp main fuse. • Is the fuse good?	Yes ▶ No ▶	GO to **HP4.** GO to **HP2.**
HP2 CHECK SYSTEM		
• Replace blown 60 amp main fuse. • Key ON. • Did the fuse blow again?	Yes ▶ No ▶	GO to **HP3.** GO to **HP4.**
HP3 CHECK FOR SHORT TO GROUND		
• Key OFF. • Disconnect the BL wire from the main fuse. • Measure the resistance of the BL wire between the fuse panel and ground. • Is resistance less than 5 ohms?	Yes ▶ No ▶	SERVICE BL wire. GO to **HP4.**
HP4 CHECK SUPPLY TO BLOWER MOTOR		
• Disconnect the blower motor connector. • Key ON. • Measure the voltage on the BL wire at the connector. • Reconnect the blower motor connector. • Is the voltage greater than 10 volts?	Yes ▶ No ▶	GO to **HP5.** SERVICE BL wire.
HP5 CHECK BLOWER MOTOR		
• Key OFF. • Disconnect blower motor connector. • Apply 12 volts to the BL terminal. • Ground the BL/W terminal. • Reconnect blower motor. • Does the blower motor run?	Yes ▶ No ▶	GO to **HP6.** SERVICE/REPLACE blower motor.

HEATING SYSTEM DIAGNOSIS AND TESTING—CAPRI

TEST STEP	RESULT ▶	ACTION TO TAKE
HP6 CHECK LEAD TO RESISTOR		
• Locate the resistor connector. • Measure the resistance of the BL/W wire between the motor and the resistor. • Is the resistance less than 5 ohms?	Yes ▶ No ▶	GO to **HP7.** SERVICE the BL/W wire.
HP7 CHECK RESISTOR		
• Measure the resistance from the BL/W wire at the connector to the following wires at the connector: **WIRE** — **RESISTANCE** BL/Y — 2.6 ohms BL — 1.2 ohms BL/R — .6 ohms BL/W — .1 ohms • Are the resistances correct?	Yes ▶ No ▶	GO to **HP8.** REPLACE resistor.
HP8 CHECK LEADS TO BLOWER MOTOR CONTROL SWITCH		
• Locate the blower motor control switch connector. • Measure the resistance of the following wires between the resistor and the blower motor control switch: **WIRE** BL/Y BL BL/R BL/W • Are the resistances less than 5 ohms?	Yes ▶ No ▶	GO to **HP9.** SERVICE wire in question.
HP9 CHECK LEAD TO A/C SWITCH		
• Locate the A/C switch connector. • Measure the resistance of the BL/Y wire between the A/C switch and the blower motor control switch. • Is the resistance less than 5 ohms?	Yes ▶ No ▶	GO to **HP10.** SERVICE the BL/Y wire.

TEST STEP	RESULT ▶	ACTION TO TAKE
HP10 CHECK LEAD TO ELECTRICAL LOAD CONTROL SWITCH		
• Measure the resistance of the BL/GN wire between blower motor control switch and the electrical load control switch. • Is the resistance less than 5 ohms?	Yes ▶ No ▶	GO to **HP11.** SERVICE BL/GN wire.
HP11 CHECK BLOWER MOTOR CONTROL SWITCH GROUND		
• Measure the resistance of the BK wire between the blower motor control switch and ground. • Is the resistance less than 5 ohms?	Yes ▶ No ▶	GO to **HP12.** SERVICE BK wire.
HP12 CHECK BLOWER MOTOR CONTROL SWITCH		
• Disconnect the blower motor control switch. • Measure the resistance between ground and the wire colors listed below at the following switch positions: **SWITCH POSITION** — **WIRE COLOR** — **RESISTANCE** OFF — All Colors — Greater than 10,000 ohms 1 — BL/Y — Less than 5 ohms All Others — Greater than 10,000 ohms 2 — BL — Less than 5 ohms All Others — Greater than 10,000 ohms 3 — BL/R — Less than 5 ohms All Others — Greater than 10,000 ohms 4 — BL/W — Less than 5 ohms All Others — Greater than 10,000 ohms • Reconnect the blower motor control switch. • Are the resistances correct?	Yes ▶ No ▶	RETURN to condition chart. SERVICE/REPLACE blower motor control switch.

HEATING SYSTEM DIAGNOSIS AND TESTING—CAPRI

TEST STEP	RESULT ▶	ACTION TO TAKE
V1 CHECK CABLE OPERATION		
• Access the control panel. • Slide the temperature control lever, air intake control lever and the airflow control lever back and forth. • Do the levers slide smoothly?	Yes ▶ No ▶	GO to **V2.** CHECK control panel and cables for damage, SERVICE/REPLACE as required.
V2 AIRFLOW SELECTOR SYSTEM FUNCTION		
• With the ignition switch ON and the blower control switch set to position 4 for maximum airflow, change the position settings of the airflow selector. Verify that they conform to the specified airflow patterns as listed. **Airflow Selector Position** — **Specified Airflow Pattern (Exit Locations Shown)** Panel — Ventilator outlets Hi-Lo — Ventilator and floor outlets Floor — Floor outlets and small amount to defroster outlets Mix — Floor and defroster outlets Def — Defroster outlets • Do the airflow patterns conform to the specified patterns for each of the tested selector positions?	Yes ▶ No ▶	GO to **V3.** SERVICE, ADJUST, or REPLACE the heater or its outlet door or components as required.

Panel

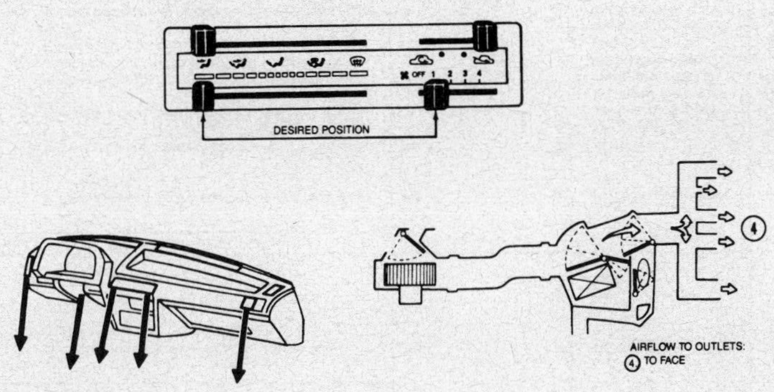
DESIRED POSITION
OFF 1 2 3 4
AIRFLOW TO OUTLETS:
4 TO FACE

Hi-Lo

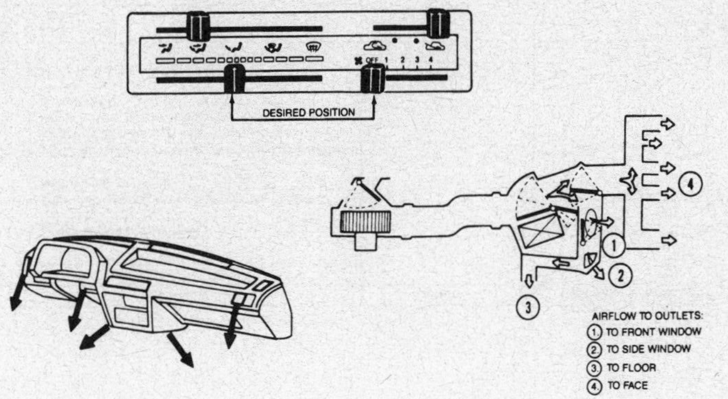
DESIRED POSITION
OFF 1 2 3 4
AIRFLOW TO OUTLETS:
1 TO FRONT WINDOW
2 TO SIDE WINDOW
3 TO FLOOR
4 TO FACE

HEATING SYSTEM DIAGNOSIS AND TESTING—CAPRI

Def

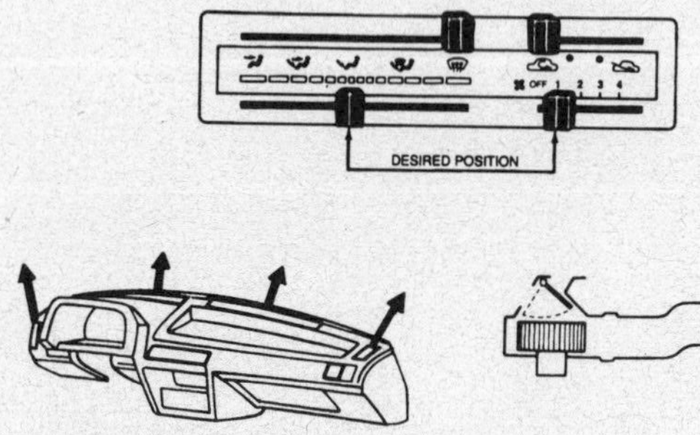
DESIRED POSITION
OFF 1 2 3 4

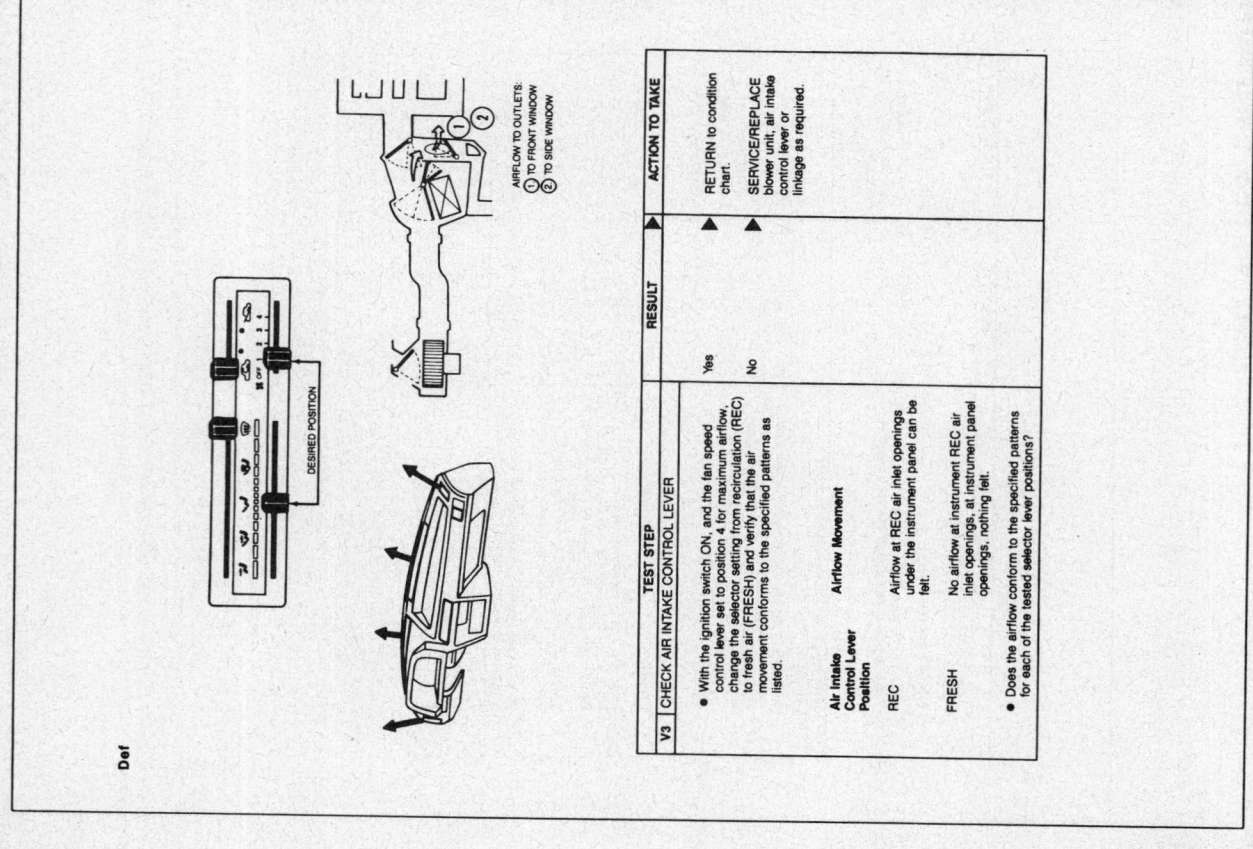

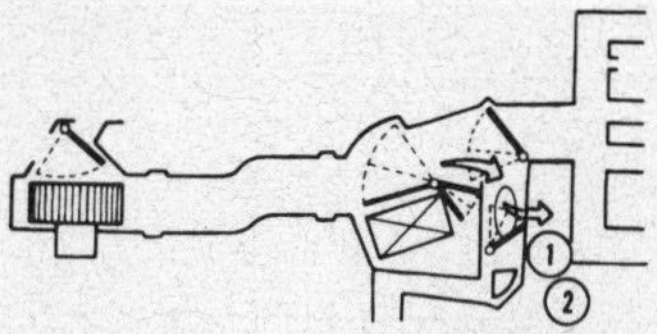
AIRFLOW TO OUTLETS:
1 TO FRONT WINDOW
2 TO SIDE WINDOW

TEST STEP	RESULT	▶	ACTION TO TAKE
V3 CHECK AIR INTAKE CONTROL LEVER			
• With the ignition switch ON, and the fan speed control lever set to position 4 for maximum airflow, change the selector setting from recirculation (REC) to fresh air (FRESH) and verify that the air movement conforms to the specified patterns as listed. **Air Intake Control Lever Position** — **Airflow Movement** REC — Airflow at REC air inlet openings under the instrument panel can be felt. FRESH — No airflow at instrument REC air inlet openings, at instrument panel openings, nothing felt. • Does the airflow conform to the specified patterns for each of the tested selector lever positions?	Yes	▶	RETURN to condition chart.
	No	▶	SERVICE/REPLACE blower unit, air intake control lever or linkage as required.

TEST STEP	RESULT	▶	ACTION TO TAKE
NH1 ENGINE THERMOSTAT FUNCTION			
• Check engine coolant level. • Start and warm up the engine until the coolant temperature stabilizes. • Verify the reported condition by checking the heater for adequate heat output (temperature blend lever to extreme right, airflow selector lever at panel, blower at position 4). • Is the heat output inadequate?	Yes	▶	GO to **NH2.**
	No	▶	Check cooling system
NH2 HEATER CORE — CHECK FOR AIRFLOW BLOCKAGE			
• Check the heater core blower motor housing and connecting air passages for blockage (such as leaves, paper, etc). • Is the heater core and its connecting air passages free of blockage?	Yes	▶	GO to **NH3.**
	No	▶	REMOVE components and clean as required.
NH3 HEATER CORE — CHECK FOR COOLANT BLOCKAGE			
• Back flush the heater core to remove core sand, etc. • Is the heater core free of blockage to coolant flow?	Yes	▶	GO to **NH4.**
	No	▶	REPLACE heater core.
NH4 TEMPERATURE BLEND FUNCTION			
• Start and warm up the engine to normal operating temperature. • Set the blower control to position 4. • Set the airflow selector lever to panel. • Move the temperature blend lever gradually from extreme left to extreme right and verify that the air temperature gradually increases from cold to hot. • Does the temperature blend function properly and is the air hot with the lever at its extreme right?	Yes	▶	RETURN to condition chart.
	No	▶	ADJUST the temperature blend cable to close off all bypass air around the heater core when the temperature blend lever is set to the extreme right. REFER to adjustments.

AIR CONDITIONING SYSTEM DIAGNOSIS AND TESTING—CAPRI

CONDITION	POSSIBLE SOURCE	ACTION
• No Cooling or Insufficient Cooling	• Clutch condition. • Drive belt tension and condition. • Moisture, air, excessive oil or refrigerant in system. • Compressor. • Thermostatic expansion valve. • Insufficient refrigerant. • Leaks. • Clogged refrigerant circulation system. • Blocked evaporator or condenser. • Circuit.	• Inspect, repair as required. Go to **A2.**
• Intermittent Cooling	• Clutch slipping. • Drive belt tension and condition. • Thermostatic expansion valve. • Excessive moisture in system. • Insufficient refrigerant. • Compressor clutch circuit.	• Inspect, repair as required. Go to **A2.** • Go to **CC2.**

CONDITION	POSSIBLE SOURCE	ACTION
• No Compressor Clutch Operation	• Circuit. • Fuses. • Refrigerant pressure switch. • Clutch condition. • Belt tension and condition. • Thermostatic switch.	• Go to **CC2.**
• Blows Frost Out of Ducts (After Several Minutes of Operation)	• Plugged evaporator drain. • Excessive refrigerant. • Thermostatic switch.	• Clear blockage. • Go to **A2.** • Go to **CC20.**
• Compressor Engaged, Compressor Runs Constantly (No Cycling)	• A/C relay. • Circuit. • Thermostat.	• Go to **CC13.** • Go to **CC20.**
• Improper Blower Motor Operation	• Motor • Circuit. • Resistor. • Switch.	• Check Blower Motor
• Condenser Fan Runs Constantly	• Condenser fan relay. • Circuit. • Condenser fan motor.	• Go to **CF2.**
• Condenser Fan Never Runs	• Fuse. • Circuit. • Condenser fan relay. • Condenser fan motor.	• Go to **CF2.**

TEST STEP	RESULT ▶	ACTION TO TAKE
A1 SYSTEM INTEGRITY CHECK		
• Inspect A/C system hoses and plumbing for signs of wear, leaks, cracks, loose connectors or other damage. • Inspect compressor clutch for signs of leaks (oil or refrigerant residue present on compressor case). • Inspect drive belt for proper tension condition and signs of wear. • Does the system appear to be in good condition?	Yes ▶ No ▶	GO to **A2**. SERVICE or REPLACE damaged components as required.
A2 CHECK SYSTEM PRESSURES		
• Connect a manifold set to the A/C system. • Key ON, engine idling at 2000 rpm. • Blower on high. • A/C ON, temperature blend lever to extreme left (cool position). • Wait 5 minutes for system to stabilize. • Observe the gauges and feel the temperatures of the suction and pressure lines near the compressor. • Look for built up condensation on the A/C plumbing near the compressor and receiver/drier. • Compare gauge readings and system temperatures to the following chart.		

AIR CONDITIONING SYSTEM DIAGNOSIS AND TESTING—CAPRI

CHECK SYSTEM PRESSURES — Continued

Gauge Reading	Pressure Side Plumbing (High)	Suction Side Plumbing (Low)	Sight Glass	Possible Source	Action To Take
HI: 199-220 psi LO: 19-25 psi	Warm and dry	Cool and dry	Bubbles only after shut-off	Normal operation.	RETURN to condition chart.
HI: 114-128 psi LO: 0-12 psi (too low)	Warm and dry	Warm and dry	Bubbles all the time Never bubbles	Insufficient refrigerant. Empty system.	TEST for leaks. EVACUATE and RECHARGE system.
HI: 235-280 psi LO: 34-44 psi (too high)	Warm and dry	Cool and dry	No bubbles after shut-off	Excessive refrigerant. System oil level too low. Condenser obstruction. Condenser fan not operating.	EVACUATE and RECHARGE. Put in proper amount of oil. Clear obstruction. RETURN to condition chart.
HI: 260-290 psi (too high) LO: 25-35 psi (too high)	Warm	Heavy dew or frost build-up	No bubbles after shut-off	Expansion valve stuck open. Heat sensing bulb improperly installed.	SERVICE or REPLACE expansion valve as required. Reinstall properly.
HI: 270-330 psi (too high) LO: 25-35 psi	Warm	Warm		Air in system. Oil contamination.	EVACUATE and RECHARGE, if same symptom is present after recharge, SERVICE or REPLACE receiver/drier.

CHECK SYSTEM PRESSURES — Continued

Gauge Reading	Pressure Side Plumbing	Suction Side Plumbing	Possible Source	Action To Take
HI: Fluctuates LO: Fluctuates between vacuum and normal pressure	Warm	Fluctuates between cool and warm	Moisture in system	EVACUATE, SERVICE or REPLACE receiver/drier and recharge.
HI: 70-150 psi (too low) LO: Vacuum (too low)	Warm	Frost or dew on new expansion valve	Dirt or moisture in system is blocking expansion valve or equalizer tube.	EVACUATE, SERVICE or REPLACE expansion valve and receiver/drier, recharge.
HI: 70-150 psi (too low) LO: 25-35 psi (too high)	Warm	Warm	Damaged compressor.	SERVICE or REPLACE compressor

	TEST STEP	RESULT ▶	ACTION TO TAKE
CC1	**SYSTEM INTEGRITY CHECK**		
	• Check for fully charged battery. • Check for blown fuses, corrosion, poor electrical connections, signs of opens, shorts or damage to the wiring harness. **NOTE: If a blown fuse is replaced and fails immediately, there is a short to ground in the system.** • Key ON, engine idling. • A/C ON. • Blower ON. • Shake the wiring harness vigorously and look for signs of opens or shorts. • Tap each connector and look for signs of bad connections. • Does the system appear to be in good condition?	Yes ▶ No ▶	GO to **CC2.** SERVICE or REPLACE damaged components as required.
CC2	**CHECK FOR CLUTCH VOLTAGE**		
	• Engine ON. • A/C ON, blower ON. • Measure voltage at compressor clutch electrical connector (BK/W terminal). • Is voltage greater than 10 volts?	Yes ▶ No ▶	GO to **CC3.** GO to **CC4.**
CC3	**CHECK CLUTCH RESISTANCE**		
	• Key OFF, A/C OFF. • Allow engine to cool. • Disconnect compressor clutch electrical connector. • Measure resistance between compressor clutch connector (clutch side) and compressor clutch case. • Is resistance between 2.7 and 3.1 ohms?	Yes ▶ No ▶	CHECK condition of drive belt, clutch material and compressor. SERVICE as required. SERVICE ground compressor clutch. If all OK, REPLACE clutch.
CC4	**CHECK FOR SHORT IN CLUTCH LEAD**		
	• Key OFF. • Disconnect compressor clutch. • Disconnect refrigerant pressure switch. • Measure resistance between refrigerant pressure switch connector BK/W terminal and ground. • Is resistance less than 5 ohms?	Yes ▶ No ▶	SERVICE shorts in BK/W wire from refrigerant pressure switch to compressor clutch. RECONNECT refrigerant pressure switch and compressor clutch. GO to **CC5.**

AIR CONDITIONING SYSTEM DIAGNOSIS AND TESTING—CAPRI

	TEST STEP	RESULT	▶	ACTION TO TAKE
CC5	CHECK FOR VOLTAGE FROM A/C RELAY			
	• Engine idling. • A/C ON, blower ON. • Measure voltage at A/C relay BK/Y terminal. • Is voltage greater than 10 volts?	Yes No	▶ ▶	GO to **CC7.** TURN engine off. GO to **CC6.**
CC6	CHECK 30 AMP CIRCUIT BREAKER			
	• Key ON. • Measure voltage at 30 amp circuit breaker BL terminal. • Is reading greater than 10 volts?	Yes No	▶ ▶	GO to **CC7.** REPLACE 30 amp circuit breaker.
CC7	CHECK 15 AMP (AIR COND.) FUSE			
	• Check 15 amp (air cond.) fuse. • Is fuse OK?	Yes No	▶ ▶	GO to **CC9.** GO to **CC8.**
CC8	15 AMP (AIR COND.) FUSE SUPPLY CHECK			
	• Replace 15 amp (air cond.) fuse. • Check fuse. • Is fuse OK?	Yes No	▶ ▶	GO to **CC9.** SERVICE BL wire between fuse and 30 amp circuit breaker.
CC9	CHECK FOR VOLTAGE TO A/C RELAY			
	• Key ON. • Measure voltage at A/C relay BL terminal from wire side of A/C relay connector. • Is reading greater than 10 volts?	Yes No	▶ ▶	GO to **CC10.** SERVICE BL wire.
CC10	CHECK 15 AMP COOLER FUSE			
	• Key ON. • Check 15 amp cooler fuse by measuring voltage at BL wire terminal of cooler fuse connector. • Is reading greater than 10 volts?	Yes No	▶ ▶	GO to **CC12.** GO to **CC11.**
CC11	15 AMP COOLER FUSE SUPPLY CHECK			
	• Replace 15 amp cooler fuse. • Key ON. • Measure voltage at BL wire terminal of cooler fuse connector. • Is reading greater than 10 volts?	Yes No	▶ ▶	GO to **CC12.** SERVICE BK/R wire between fuse and ignition switch.
CC12	CHECK LEAD BETWEEN 15 AMP COOLER FUSE AND A/C RELAY			
	• Key ON. • Measure voltage at LB wire side of A/C relay connector. • Is reading greater than 10 volts?	Yes No	▶ ▶	GO to **CC13.** SERVICE LB wire.

	TEST STEP	RESULT	▶	ACTION TO TAKE
CC13	CHECK A/C RELAY OPERATION			
	• Key ON. • Ground A/C relay W terminal with a jumper wire. • Measure voltage at A/C relay BK/Y terminal. • Is reading greater than 10 volts with W grounded and less than 1 volt with W open?	Yes No	▶ ▶	TURN key off. GO to **CC14.** REPLACE A/C relay.
CC14	CHECK VOLTAGE TO ECA			
	• Disconnect W wire connector from ECA. • Key ON. • Measure voltage at ECA connector W wire terminal. • Is reading greater than 10 volts?	Yes No	▶ ▶	GO to **CC15.** SERVICE W wire between A/C relay and ECA.
CC15	CHECK 20 AMP COOLING FAN FUSE			
	• Check 20 amp cooling fan fuse. • Is fuse OK?	Yes No	▶ ▶	GO to **CC17.** GO to **CC16.**
CC16	CHECK 20 AMP COOLING FUSE SUPPLY			
	• Replace 20 amp cooling fan fuse. • Key ON. • Check fuse. • Is fuse OK?	Yes No	▶ ▶	GO to **CC17.** SERVICE BK/R wire between ignition switch and fuse.

AIR CONDITIONING SYSTEM DIAGNOSIS AND TESTING—CAPRI

TEST STEP	RESULT ▶	ACTION TO TAKE
CC17 CHECK FOR VOLTAGE TO A/C CONTROL AMPLIFIER		
• Disconnect A/C control amplifier connector. • Key ON, A/C OFF. • Measure voltage at Y wire of A/C control amplifier connector. • Is reading greater than 10 volts?	Yes ▶ No ▶	GO to **CC18**. SERVICE Y wire between 20 amp fuse and A/C control amplifier.
CC18 CHECK A/C CONTROL AMPLIFIER OPERATION		
• Checks are made at harness side of amplifier connector with amplifier connected. • Check A/C control amplifier voltages as listed below with: **Key ON, A/C OFF: Blower OFF:** / **Eng ON, A/C ON: Blower ON:** R: Greater than 10V / 2.2V Y: Greater than 10V / Greater than 10V GN: Greater than 10V / 1.5V W/BL: Greater than 10V / 3.3V W/BL: Greater than 10V / 3.3V Y/GN: Greater than 10V / 1.5V • Are measured voltages the same?	Yes ▶ No ▶	GO to **CC19**. REPLACE A/C control amplifier.
CC19 CHECK A/C CONTROL AMPLIFIER LEAD TO A/C SWITCH AND CONDENSER FAN RELAY		
• Key OFF. • Disconnect A/C switch and condenser fan relay. • Measure resistance between GN wire at A/C control amplifier to A/C switch and condenser fan relay. • Is resistance less than 5 ohms?	Yes ▶ No ▶	GO to **CC20**. SERVICE GN wire between A/C control amplifier and A/C switch or A/C condenser fan relay.
CC20 CHECK THERMOSTAT CIRCUIT		
• Key OFF. • Disconnect A/C control amplifier and thermostat. • Measure resistance of each wire between A/C control amplifier and thermostat. Two W/BL wires. One Y/GN wire. • Is resistance less than 5 ohms on each wire?	Yes ▶ No ▶	GO to **CC21**. SERVICE each wire between A/C control amplifier and thermostat as required.

TEST STEP	RESULT ▶	ACTION TO TAKE
CC21 CHECK THERMOSTAT		
• Remove thermostat. • Measure resistance between W/BL and Y/GN wire terminals on thermostat. • Apply liquid freon or other cooling liquid to sensing bulb on switch to bring temperature of the sensing bulb below 32°F. • Is resistance less than 1,500 ohms with sensing bulb warm (above 77°F) and more than 4,500 ohms with sensing bulb cold (32°F or below)?	Yes ▶ No ▶	Install thermostat. GO to **CC22**. REPLACE thermostat.
CC22 CHECK VOLTAGE TO A/C SWITCH		
• Disconnect A/C switch. • Key ON. • Measure voltage on BL wire at A/C switch connector. • Is reading greater than 10 volts?	Yes ▶ No ▶	GO to **CC23**. SERVICE BL wire.
CC23 CHECK A/C SWITCH OPERATION		
• Engine ON, A/C ON. • Check A/C switch voltages at harness side of connector with: **Eng ON, A/C ON: Blower ON:** / **Eng ON, A/C OFF: Blower OFF:** GN: Less than 2V / Greater than 10V BL: Greater than 10V / Greater than 10V BL/Y: Less than 1V / Less than 1V • Are measured voltages the same?	Yes ▶ No ▶	GO to **CC24**. REPLACE A/C switch.
CC24 CHECK LEAD BETWEEN A/C SWITCH AND BLOWER SWITCH		
• Key OFF. • Measure resistance of BL/Y wire between A/C switch and blower control switch. • Is reading greater than 10 volts?	Yes ▶ No ▶	REFER to Blower Motor test step HP1. GO to **CC25**. SERVICE BL/Y wire from A/C switch to blower control switch and resistor.

AIR CONDITIONING SYSTEM DIAGNOSIS AND TESTING—CAPRI

TEST STEP	RESULT ▶	ACTION TO TAKE
CC25 CHECK LEAD BETWEEN A/C RELAY AND REFRIGERANT PRESSURE SWITCH		
• Key OFF. • Disconnect BK/Y connector from refrigerant pressure switch. • Measure resistance of BK/Y wire between refrigerant pressure switch connector and ground. • Is resistance greater than 10,000 ohms?	Yes ▶ No ▶	RECONNECT BK/Y wire connector to refrigerant pressure switch. GO to **CC26.** SERVICE BK/Y wire between refrigerant pressure switch and A/C relay.
CC26 CHECK REFRIGERANT PRESSURE SWITCH		
• Connect a manifold set to the service gauge port valves. • Disconnect the refrigerant pressure switch electrical connector. • Measure resistance between BK/W and BK/Y terminals of the refrigerant pressure switch. • Is reading less than 5 ohms when the system high side pressure is above 206 ± 20 kPa (30 ± 3 psi)?	Yes ▶ No ▶	GO to **CC27.** REPLACE refrigerant pressure switch. NOTE: If high side pressure is below 206 ± 20 kPa (30 ± 3 psi) check refrigerant system, refer to test step **A1.**
CC27 CHECK LEAD BETWEEN A/C CONTROL AMPLIFIER AND ECA		
• Key OFF. • ECA and A/C control amplifier disconnected. • Measure resistance of R wire between A/C control amplifier and ECA. • Is resistance less than 5 ohms?	Yes ▶ No ▶	Check ECA and A/C control amplifier SERVICE R wire between A/C control amplifier and ECA.

TEST STEP	RESULT ▶	ACTION TO TAKE
CF1 SYSTEM INTEGRITY CHECK		
• Check for fully charged battery. • Check for blown fuses, corrosion, poor electrical connections, signs of opens, shorts or damage to the wiring harness. • **NOTE: If a blown fuse is replaced and fails immediately there is a short to ground in the circuit.** • Key ON, engine idling. • A/C ON. • Blower ON. • Shake the wiring harness vigorously from the condenser fan motor to the condensor fan relay and the refrigerant pressure switch. Look for signs of opens or shorts. • Tap each connector and look for signs of bad connections. • Does the system appear to be in good condition?	Yes ▶ No ▶	GO to **CF2.** REPAIR or REPLACE damaged components, as required.
CF2 CHECK 15 AMP COOLER FUSE		
• Key ON. • Check 15 amp cooler fuse by measuring voltage at BL wire terminal of cooler fuse connector. • Is reading greater than 10 volts?	Yes ▶ No ▶	GO to **CF4.** GO to **CF3.**
CF3 15 AMP COOLER FUSE SUPPLY CHECK		
• Replace 15 amp cooler fuse. • Key ON. • Measure voltage at BL wire terminal of cooler fuse connector. • Is reading greater than 10 volts?	Yes ▶ No ▶	GO to **CF4.** SERVICE BK/R wire between fuse and ignition switch.
CF4 CHECK 20 AMP COOLING FAN FUSE		
• Check 20 amp cooling fan fuse. • Is fuse OK?	Yes ▶ No ▶	GO to **CF6.** GO to **CF5.**
CF5 CHECK 20 AMP COOLING FUSE SUPPLY		
• Replace 20 amp cooling fan fuse. • Key ON. • Check fuse. • Is fuse OK?	Yes ▶ No ▶	GO to **CF6.** SERVICE BK/R wire between ignition switch and fuse.
CF6 CHECK VOLTAGE TO CONDENSER FAN MOTOR		
• Key ON. • Measure voltage at condenser fan motor. • Is reading greater than 10 volts?	Yes ▶ No ▶	GO to **CF7.** SERVICE BL wire between condenser fan motor and 15 amp cooler fuse.

AIR CONDITIONING SYSTEM DIAGNOSIS AND TESTING—CAPRI

	TEST STEP	RESULT	►	ACTION TO TAKE
CF7	CHECK FOR VOLTAGE TO CONDENSER FAN RELAY			
	• Key ON. • Measure voltage at LB wire terminal of condenser fan relay connector. • Is reading greater than 10 volts?	Yes No	► ►	GO to **CF8**. SERVICE LB wire.
CF8	CHECK CONDENSER FAN RELAY CONTROL CIRCUIT			
	• Key OFF. • Disconnect A/C control amplifier condenser fan relay and A/C switch. • Measure resistance of GN wire between each of the above components. • Is resistance less than 5 ohms?	Yes No	► ►	GO to **CF9**. SERVICE GN wire between condenser fan relay: A/C control amplifier and A/C switch.
CF9	MOTOR OPERATION CHECK			
	• Key OFF. • Disconnect condenser fan motor. • Ground GN/R terminal of condenser fan motor connector. • Does fan motor run?	Yes No	► ►	GO to **CF10**. REPLACE condenser fan motor.
CF10	CHECK RESISTANCE BETWEEN MOTOR AND CONDENSER FAN RELAY			
	• Key ON. • Disconnect condenser fan relay. • Measure resistance between condenser fan relay GN/R terminal and motor. • Is resistance less than 5 ohms?	Yes No	► ►	Go to **CF11**. SERVICE GN/R wire from condenser fan motor to condenser fan relay.
CF11	CHECK CONDENSER FAN RELAY GROUND (CONDENSER FAN MOTOR)			
	• Disconnect condenser fan relay. • Measure resistance of BK wire between condenser fan relay and ground. • Is resistance less than 5 ohms?	Yes No	► ►	GO to **CF12**. SERVICE BK wire between condenser fan relay and ground.
CF12	CHECK CONDENSER FAN RELAY			
	• Disconnect condenser fan relay. • Measure resistance between GN/R terminal and BK terminal of relay. • Is resistance greater than 10,000 ohms? • Apply 12 volts to LB terminal and ground GN terminal. • Measure resistance between GN/R terminal and BK terminal. • Is resistance less than 5 ohms?	Yes No	► ►	RETURN to condition chart. REPLACE relay.

AUTOMATIC TEMPERATURE CONTROL ERROR CODE KEY—TAURUS, SABLE AND CONTINENTAL

ERROR CODE KEY

Error Code	Detected Condition	Troubleshooting/Repair Procedure
01	Replace control head	
02	Blend door problem	• Refer to Blend Door Actuator Diagnosis
03	In-car temp sensor open or short	• Refer to In-Car Temp Sensor Diagnosis
04	Ambient temp sensor open or short	• Refer to Ambient Temp Sensor Diagnosis
05	Sunload sensor short	• Refer to Sunload Sensor Diagnosis
888	Testing complete — no test failure (all segments on)	• Refer to EATC System Functional Check

	TEST STEP	RESULT	►	ACTION TO TAKE
1	Turn ignition switch to the RUN position. Press the AUTO button. Set control at 90°F setting.	Control powers up Control does not light	► ►	GO to 2. REFER to Diagnosis When Self-Test And Functional Test Indicate No Errors Found.
2	Verify that the blower does not come on. (Engine coolant temp. < 120°F)	Blower off Blower on	► ►	GO to 3. REFER to CELO Inoperative.
3	Ensure that engine is warm (coolant temp. > 120°F). Set control at 75 setting.	Blower on Blower off	► ►	GO to 4. REFER to Blower Speed Controller Diagnosis-No Blower.
4	Rotate blower thumbwheel fully down.	Blower goes to low blower Blower does not go to low blower	► ► ►	GO to 5. CHECK battery voltage. If voltage is below 10 volts, refer to Charging System Diagnosis. REFER to Blower Speed Controller Diagnosis.
5	Rotate blower thumbwheel fully up.	Blower goes to high blower Blower does not go to high blower	► ►	GO to 6. REFER to Blower Speed Controller Diagnosis.
6	Press the DEFROST button.	Verify that air is discharged from defroster nozzle with small bleed through the side window demistors. Verify that the outside air/recirc door is in the outside air position. Air is not discharged through the defroster or side window demistors.	► ►	GO to 7. REFER to Vacuum System Diagnosis.

AUTOMATIC TEMPERATURE CONTROL FUNCTIONAL TEST—TAURUS, SABLE AND CONTINENTAL

	TEST STEP	RESULT ▶	ACTION TO TAKE
7	Press the FLOOR button.	Verify that the air is discharged through the floor ducts. ▶	GO to **8**.
		Air is not discharged through the floor ducts. ▶	REFER to Vacuum System Diagnosis.
8	Press the VENT button.	Verify that the air is discharged through the panel ducts. ▶	GO to **9**.
		Air is not discharged through the panel ducts. ▶	REFER to Vacuum System Diagnosis.
9	Make sure that the ambient temperature is greater than 40°F. Press the MAX A/C button.	Verify that the outside air/recirc door is in the recirc position. ▶	GO to **10**.
		Outside air/Recirc door is not in the recirc position. ▶	REFER to Vacuum System Diagnosis.
10	Press the VENT button.	Verify that the VENT display is lit. Verify that the clutch is off. ▶	GO to **11**.
		A/C clutch is still on. ▶	REFER to Clutch Does Not Disengage When In OFF Diagnosis.
11	Press the MAX A/C button again.	Verify that the MAX A/C display is lit and that the clutch is on. ▶	GO to **12**.
		A/C clutch is off. ▶	REFER to No Clutch Operation Diagnosis.
12	Press the AUTO button.	Verify that the AUTO display is lit. ▶	REFER to Diagnosis When Self-Test And Functional Test Indicate No Errors Found.

AUTOMATIC TEMPERATURE CONTROL NO ERROR CODE FOUND DIAGNOSIS AND TESTING TAURUS, SABLE AND CONTINENTAL

CONDITION	POSSIBLE SOURCE	ACTION
• Cool Discharge Air When System is Set to Auto/90°F	• Heater system malfunction. • Blend door not in max. heat.	• REFER to heater system operating principles • CHECK position of blend door. • CHECK coolant level. • CHECK shaft attachment. • TEST per Blend Door Actuator Diagnosis (assume 2 was displayed in the Self-Test).
• Warm Discharge Air in Auto/60°F	• Clutch circuit malfunction. • Check refrigerant. • Blend door not in max. A/C position. • Outside/Recirc door not in recirc.	• TEST clutch circuit per No Clutch Operation Diagnosis. • REFER to Section 36-32. • CHECK position of blend door. • CHECK shaft attachment. • TEST per Blend Door Actuator Diagnosis (assume 2 was displayed in the Self-Test). • TEST per Vacuum System Diagnosis.
• Cool Air in 85°F, Max. Heat in 90°F	• Sensor shorted.	• TROUBLESHOOT according to Sensor Diagnosis.
• Heat in 65°F Max. Cool in 60°F	• Sensor open.	• TROUBLESHOOT according to Sensor Diagnosis.
• No Blower	• Damaged CELO switch/wiring. • Damaged blower controller. • Damaged control head. • Damaged blower motor. • Damaged wiring.	• TEST per No Blower Section of Blower Speed Controller.
• High Blower Only	• Damaged control head. • Damaged blower controller. • Damaged wiring.	• TEST per High Blower Only Section of Blower Speed Controller.
• Clutch is On in Off Mode	• Damaged control head. • Damaged wiring or interface components.	• TEST according to "Clutch does not Disengage when in OFF mode".

AUTOMATIC TEMPERATURE CONTROL NO ERROR CODE FOUND DIAGNOSIS AND TESTING TAURUS, SABLE AND CONTINENTAL

CONDITION	POSSIBLE SOURCE	ACTION
• Control Assembly Digits and VFD Do Not Light Up Blower Off	• Fuse. • Ignition Circuit No. 298 open. • Ignition Circuit No. 797 open. • Ground Circuit No. 57A open. • Damaged control head.	• Replace fuse. • Check Circuit No. 298. • Check Circuit No. 797. • Check Circuit No. 57A. • Change control assembly.
• Cold Air is Delivered During Heating when Engine is Cold.	• Damaged wiring. • Damaged or inoperative engine temperature switch.	• Place system at 90°F/Auto. With ignition off, (ignition must be off when grounding Circuit No. 244 for valid results) ground Circuit No. 244 at engine temp. switch. Start vehicle. If blower is off, replace cold engine lockout (CELO). If blower is on, check wiring. If OK, replace control assembly. • Replace engine temperature switch.
• Temperature Set Point Does Not Repeat After Turning Off Ignition	• Circuit No. 797 not connected to control head. • Damaged or inoperative control assembly.	• Remove control assembly connector. With ignition off, check for 12 volts at Pin 12 (Driver's side connector VA). • If no voltage, check fuse/wiring. If voltage, replace control head.
• Control Head Temperature Display Will Not Switch From Fahrenheit To Centigrade When the E/M Trip Computer Button is Pushed	• Damaged or inoperative wiring, trip minder or control head.	• **CAUTION: ACCIDENTAL SHORTING OF THE WRONG PIN COULD DESTROY THE CONTROL HEAD.** Short Pin 20 of connector VA (Circuit No. 506) to ground. Turn on ignition. If the display does not switch from F to C, Circuit No. 506 is open at the control assembly and the control assembly is damaged. Otherwise check the wiring and the trip minder.
• System Does Not Control Temperature	• Sensor hose not connected to aspirator or sensor. • Aspirator not secured to evaporator case. • Sensor seal(s) missing or not installed properly. • Aspirator or sensor hose blocked with foreign material or kinked. • Damaged aspirator hose.	• Inspect and service. • Inspect and service. • Inspect and service. • Inspect and service. • Inspect and service.
• EATC Control Head Turns On and Off Erratically. No Control of System.	• Damaged charging system. EATC will not function with too low or too high battery voltage.	• Check battery voltage. If battery voltage is less than 10 volts or greater than 16 volts, ~~refer to charging system diagnosis~~. Do not replace EATC control head.

AUTOMATIC TEMPERATURE CONTROL IN-CAR TEMPERATURE SENSOR DIAGNOSIS AND TESTING TAURUS, SABLE AND CONTINENTAL

CONDITION	POSSIBLE SOURCE	ACTION
• Self-Diagnostics Error Code 03 (Warm Air Discharge at 65°F or Cool Air Discharge at 85°F)	1. Sensor open or shorted.	• Disconnect wire harness connector at sensor. Measure resistance across sensor terminals and compare with Sensor Resistance Table below. • If resistance is out of specifications shown in Table, replace sensor. If sensor is okay, go to Step 2.
	2. Wire harness open or shorted.	• Disconnect battery cables. Disconnect wire harness connector from sensor and disconnect both connectors from control head. • Check for continuity and for possible shorting between the two wires (pin 2 and pin 17). Repair if necessary. Reconnect wire harness and battery cables.

SENSOR RESISTANCE TABLE

APPROXIMATE TEMPERATURE	SENSOR RESISTANCE ACCEPTABLE RANGE
10°C to 20°C (50°F to 68°F)	37K to 58K ohms
20°C to 30°C (68°F to 86°F)	24K to 37K ohms
30°C to 40°C (86°F to 104°F)	16K to 24K ohms

AUTOMATIC TEMPERATURE CONTROL AMBIENT SENSOR DIAGNOSIS AND TESTING— TAURUS, SABLE AND CONTINENTAL

CONDITION	POSSIBLE SOURCE	ACTION
• Self-Diagnostics Error Code 04 and Outside Temperature Display is Reading −40°F or 140°F (Warm Air Discharge at 65°F or Cool Air Discharge at 85°F)	1. Sensor open or shorted.	• Disconnect battery cables (this is necessary to reset outside temperature display memory). Disconnect the wire harness connector at sensor. Measure resistance across sensor terminal and compare with Sensor Resistance Table in In-Car Temperature Sensor Diagnosis Chart. • If resistance is out of specifications shown in Sensor Resistance Table, replace sensor. If sensor is okay, go to Step 2. Reconnect battery cables. NOTE: Install sensor and electrical connections before battery is reconnected.
• Intermittent Heating and Cooling. Outside Temperature Display Sometimes Inaccurate	2. Sensor wire harness open or shorted.	• Disconnect battery cables. Disconnect wire harness connector from sensor and disconnect both connectors from the control head. • Inspect for crimped terminals. • Check for continuity and for possible shorting between the two wires (pins 1 and 2). Service if necessary. Reconnect wire harness and battery cables.

AUTOMATIC TEMPERATURE CONTROL SUNLOAD SENSOR DIAGNOSIS AND TESTING— TAURUS, SABLE AND CONTINENTAL

CONDITION	POSSIBLE SOURCE	ACTION
• Self-Diagnostics Error Code 05	1. Sensor shorted.	• Disconnect battery cables. Disconnect wire harness connector at sensor and disconnect both connectors from control head.* Check for continuity and for possible shorting between the two wires (pin 3 and pin 16). Repeat if necessary. Reconnect battery cables.

* NOTE: Check the sensor for a short using an ohmmeter. Since the sensor is a Photodiode, there should be some unspecified resistance across the terminals dependent upon the available light in the area. The only test that should be made is for a short circuit (zero resistance). If resistance is zero ohms, replace the sensor.

AUTOMATIC TEMPERATURE CONTROL NO CLUTCH DIAGNOSIS AND TESTING TAURUS, SABLE AND CONTINENTAL

	TEST STEP	RESULT	ACTION TO TAKE
A	Jump the LB/PK and LG/P wires Pin 26 and Pin 25 of driver side connector VA.	Clutch engages ▶	REPLACE control assembly.
		Clutch does not engage ▶	(Damaged wiring, integrated controller or EEC-IV module, damaged pressure switch.)
		15A fuse blows ▶	Clutch is shorted. CHECK diode in wiring harness across clutch in particular. Service short, then test to see if the control head will turn the clutch off and on. If not, replace control assembly.

AUTOMATIC TEMPERATURE CONTROL CLUTCH DOES NOT ENGAGE WHEN IN OFF POSITION DIAGNOSIS AND TESTING—TAURUS, SABLE AND CONTINENTAL

	TEST STEP	RESULT	ACTION TO TAKE
A	Disconnect connector VA (driver's side) from control assembly.	Clutch disengages ▶	CHANGE control assembly.
		Clutch stays on ▶	(Faulty wiring, faulty integrated controller or EEC-IV module, faulty pressure switch.)

AUTOMATIC TEMPERATURE CONTROL BLOWER SPEED CONTROLLER TEST CONDITION 1—NO BLOWER, IGNITION IN RUN, AUTO FUNCTION, 90°F (32°C) TAURUS, SABLE AND CONTINENTAL

	TEST STEP (CELO TEST)	RESULT		ACTION TO TAKE
A	Change temp. setting to 60° Auto.	Blower On	▶	GO to B.
		No blower	▶	GO to C.
B	Disconnect cold engine lockout (CELO) switch and change temp. to 90° setting Auto.	Blower On	▶	Faulty CELO switch.
		No blower	▶	CELO wire grounded.
C	Connect voltmeter between BSC ignition Pin 3 and ground Pin 4.	0 volts	▶	CHECK V ignition circuit fuse, continuity in wiring.
		More than 10 volts	▶	GO to D.
D	Connect voltmeter between BSC input Pin 2 and ground Pin 4.	Fluctuating voltage less than 3 volts	▶	GO to E.
		More than 3 volts	▶	GO to F.
E	Connect voltmeter between BSC output Pin 1 and ground Pin 4.	Less than 1 volt	▶	Damaged motor, B+ feed to motor.
		More than 1 volt	▶	REPLACE BSC.
F	Connect voltmeter between control head Pin 23 and Pin 24.	More than 3 volts	▶	REPLACE control assembly.
		Less than 3 volts	▶	CHECK circuit continuity.

AUTOMATIC TEMPERATURE CONTROL BLOWER SPEED CONTROLLER TEST CONDITION 2—HIGH ONLY, NO AUTO FUNCTION, THUMBWHEEL TO LOW POSITION TAURUS, SABLE AND CONTINENTAL

	TEST STEP (Voltmeter Connections)	RESULT		ACTION TO TAKE
A	Disconnect HBR and BSC electronic connections.	Blower in high	▶	Faulty blower motor or blower wire circuit.
		Blower OFF	▶	GO to B.
B	Reconnect BSC and connect voltmeter between BSC input Pin 2 and ground Pin 4 (auto function). Rotate blower switch from high to low blower.	Less than 7 volts fluctuating	▶	REPLACE control assembly.
		More than 7 volts fluctuating	▶	REPLACE BSC.

AUTOMATIC TEMPERATURE CONTROL BLOWER SPEED CONTROLLER TEST CONDITION 3—BLOWER OPERATES BUT DOES NOT VARY WITH TAURUS, SABLE AND CONTINENTAL

	TEST STEP (Voltmeter Connection)	RESULT	ACTION TO TAKE
A	Connect voltmeter between BSC input Pin 2 and ground Pin 4 (Auto mode). Rotate blower switch from min. to max. then back to min.	Voltage fluctuation from below 7 volts to above 7 volts then back below 7 volts ▶	GO to **B**.
		No change in voltage ▶	Replace control head assy.
B	Connect voltmeter between BSC output Pin 1 and ground Pin 4 (Auto mode). Rotate blower switch from min. to max.	Voltage changes from less than 1 volt to 7 volts ▶	Faulty blower motor, or B+ feed to motor.
		No change in voltage ▶	Replace BSC.

AUTOMATIC TEMPERATURE CONTROL BLOWER SPEED CONTROLLER TEST CONDITION 4—COLD ENGINE LOCK OUT (CELO) INOPERATIVE: BLOWER TURNS ON IN AUTO, —TAURUS, SABLE AND CONTINENTAL

	TEST STEP	RESULT	ACTION TO TAKE
A	Cold engine (engine coolant temp. below 120°) control set at auto 90°.	Blower on ▶	CHECK coolant and retest. If blower turns on again with a cold engine, REPLACE CELO.
		Blower off ▶	CELO OK.

AUTOMATIC TEMPERATURE CONTROL BLEND DOOR ACTUATOR DIAGNOSIS AND TESTING TAURUS, SABLE AND CONTINENTAL

	TEST STEP	RESULT	ACTION TO TAKE
	Letters in parentheses indicate (wire color, circuit no.). See Fig. 11 for wiring schematic and connector pin diagrams.		
A	Check error code during EATC functional test.	02 ▶ Any other number	GO to **B**. REVIEW error code key
B	Disconnect both connectors from EATC control head and drive actuator in both directions using any 9-12 volt battery. The following pins can be jumped to utilize the vehicle battery. Insure the ignition is in the RUN position. All pins are located on the LEFT connector (E6DB-14489-VA). Trial 1: Pin 24 (BK, 57) to Pin 22 (DB/LG, 249) Trial 2: Pin 24 (BK, 57) to Pin 21 (0,250)	Actuator drives both directions ▶ Actuator does not drive both directions ▶	GO to **C**. GO to **F**.
C	Reconnect control head and test according to EATC functional test.	Test successful ▶ Test fails	Done GO to **D**.
D	Disconnect both connectors from EATC control assembly. Measure resistance as shown below at the control assembly connector with the connector disconnected. All pins are located on the RIGHT connector (E6DB-14489-UA). Pin 15 (LG/O, 243) to Pin 6 (O/BK, 776) 5000-7000 ohms Pin 5 (O/W, 351) to Pin 6 (O/BK, 776) 300-7300 ohms Pin 5 (O/W, 351) to Pin 15 (LG/O, 243) 300-7300 ohms	All resistances OK ▶ Any resistance not OK ▶	GO to **E**. GO to **F**.
E	Change control head and test according to EATC functional test.	Test successful ▶ Test fails	Done GO to **A**.
F	Check vehicle wiring harness and connector continuity as shown below. Disconnect connectors from both control assembly and blend door actuator. Blend door actuator connector is accessible through glove compartment. PIN — COLOR/CIRCUIT — FUNCTION 1 — (DB/LG, 249) — Motor CCW 2 — (LG/O, 243) — Feedback Pot. (−) 3 — (O/W, 351) — Feedback Pot. (Wiper) 4 — (O/BK, 776) — Feedback Pot. (+) 5 — (O, 250) — Motor CW 6 — (BK, 57) — Ground 7 — — — No Connection 8 — (LB/PK, 295) — Voltage In Reconnect all three connectors at end of this test.	Continuity bad ▶ Continuity good ▶	GO to **H**. GO to **G**.
G	Change blend door actuator and test according to EATC functional test.	Test successful ▶ Test fails	Done GO to **A**.
H	Fix/replace wiring harness, connect and test according to EATC functional test.	Test successful ▶ Test fails	Done GO to **A**.

AUTOMATIC TEMPERATURE CONTROL DIAGNOSIS AND TESTING—PROBE

SYMPTOM	POSSIBLE CAUSE	ACTION TO TAKE
No blower operation.	• Fuses • Circuit • Motor • Relays • H.V.A.C. Control Amplifier • Transistor • Control Amplifier Ground	INSPECT and REPLACE. GO to **BM1**.
Blower only runs at low or medium speed.	• Transistor • Control Amplifier • BL/O wire from Transistor to Control Amplifier	GO to **BM14**.
No high speed	• Relay #3 • Control Amplifier • Circuit	GO to **BM10**.
Blower only runs at high speed.	• Relay #3 • Control Amplifier • Circuit	GO to **BM11**.
Recirc.-Fresh Malfunction.	• Servo Motor • Control Amplifier • Circuit	GO to **REC1**.
Temperature never changes	• Heating System • A/C System • Servo Motor • Control Amplifier • Circuit	GO to **36-11**. GO to **36-01**. GO to **MIX1**.
"Panel" doesn't work.	• Servo Motor • Control Amplifier • Circuit	GO to **MODE 2**.
"Hi-Lo" doesn't work.	• Servo Motor • Control Amplifier • Circuit	GO to **MODE 4**.
"Floor" doesn't work.	• Servo Motor • Control Amplifier • Circuit	Go to **MODE 6**.
"Heater-Defrost" doesn't work.	• Servo Motor • Control Amplifier • Circuit	GO to **MODE 8**.
"Defroster" doesn't work	• Servo Motor • Control Amplifier • Circuit	GO to **MODE 10**.
No operation of any modes	• Servo Motor • Control Amplifier • Circuit	GO to **MODE 12**.

TEST STEP	RESULT ►	ACTION TO TAKE
BME1 GROUND BLOWER MOTOR		
• Key on. • Blower on "MAX." • Leave motor connected. • Ground "BL/BK" terminal at blower motor. • Does motor operate?	Yes ► No ►	REPAIR ground connection ("BL/BK" wire). GO to BME2 .

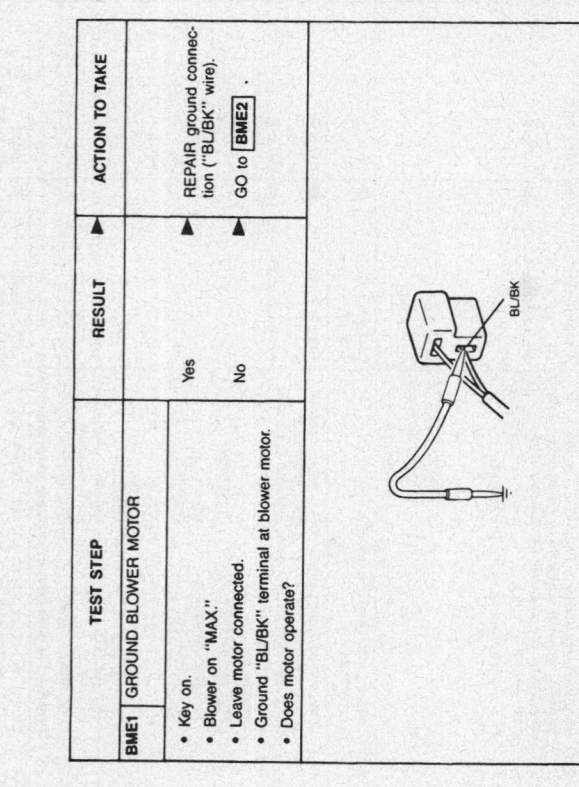

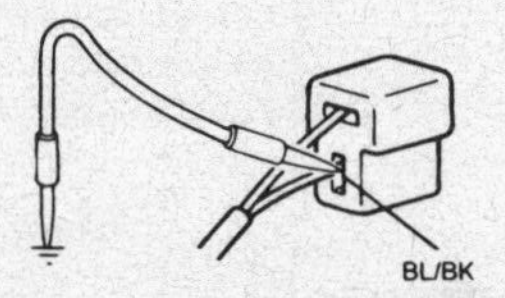
BL/BK

TEST STEP	RESULT ►	ACTION TO TAKE
BME2 APPLY POWER TO MOTOR		
• Key off. • Disconnect motor. • Apply battery power to blower motor "BL/W" terminal. • Ground blower motor "BL/BK" terminal. • Does motor operate?	Yes ► No ►	GO to BME3 . REPLACE blower motor.

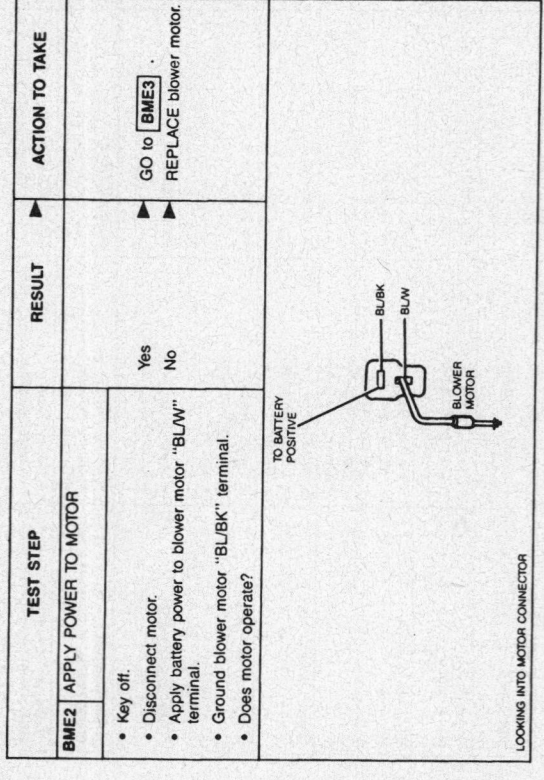

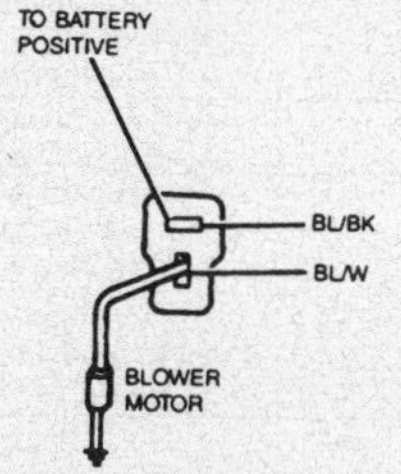
TO BATTERY POSITIVE
BL/BK
BL/W
BLOWER MOTOR

LOOKING INTO MOTOR CONNECTOR

TEST STEP	RESULT ►	ACTION TO TAKE
BME3 CHECK VOLTAGE AT TRANSISTOR		
• Key on. • Blower at middle setting. • Disconnect Relay #3. • Transistor disconnected. • VOM on 20 volt scale. • Measure voltage at transistor "R/Y" terminal. • Is reading greater than 10 volts?	Yes ► No ►	GO to BME14 . GO to BME4 .

AUTOMATIC TEMPERATURE CONTROL DIAGNOSIS AND TESTING – PROBE

TEST STEP	RESULT ►	ACTION TO TAKE
BME4 CHECK BLOWER RELAY NO. 2 SUPPLY VOLTAGE		
• Key on. • Blower off. • VOM on 20 volt scale. • Disconnect REC-FRESH Servo Motor. • Disconnect #3 relay. • Measure voltage at blower relay no. 2 "BL" and "BK/Y" terminals. • Are both readings greater than 10 volts?	Yes ► No "BL" ► No "BK/Y" ►	GO to BME5 . GO to BME8 . REPAIR "BK/Y" wire.

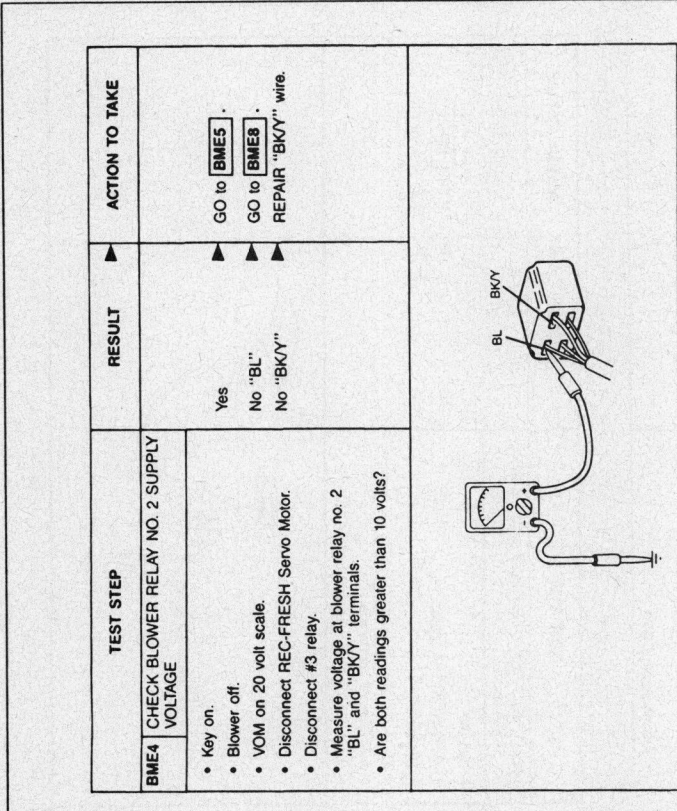

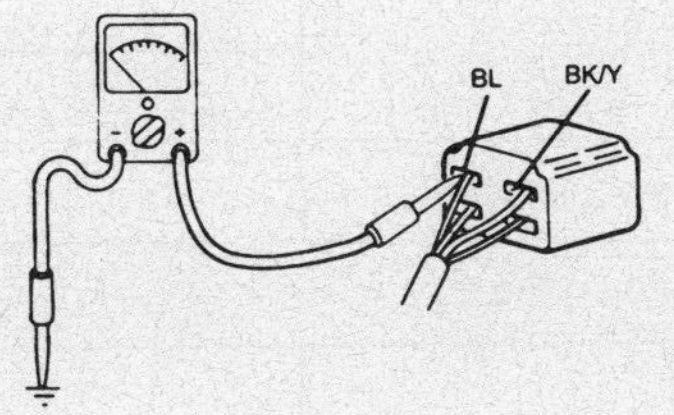
BL
BK/Y

TEST STEP	RESULT ►	ACTION TO TAKE
BME5 BLOWER RELAY NO. 2 OPERATION CHECK		
• Key on. • Blower off. • VOM on 20 volt scale. • Leave relay connected. • Ground blower relay no. 2 "BL/R" terminal. • Measure voltage at blower relay no. 2 "R/Y" terminal. • Is reading greater than 10 volts with BL/R Grounded, and 0 volts with BL/R open?	Yes ► No ►	GO to BME6 . REPLACE relay.

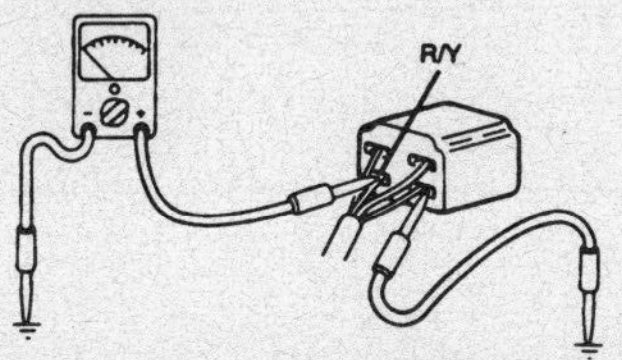
R/Y

TEST STEP	RESULT ►	ACTION TO TAKE
BME6 CHECK R/Y WIRE (BLOWER RELAY #2)		
• Key off. • Disconnect Battery. • Disconnect #2 Relay. • Disconnect #3 Relay. • Disconnect Transistor. • Measure resistance. • Are resistances OK?	Yes ► No ►	RECONNECT Transistor. GO to BME7 . SERVICE R/Y Wire.

From	To	Resistance (OHMS)
#2 Relay connector R/Y	Battery +	Over 10,000
	Ground	Over 10,000
	Transistor R/Y	0-5
	#3 Relay R/Y	0-5

AUTOMATIC TEMPERATURE CONTROL DIAGNOSIS AND TESTING—PROBE

TEST STEP	RESULT ►	ACTION TO TAKE
BME7 CHECK BL/R WIRE		
• Key off. • Disconnect Battery. • Disconnect H.V.A.C. Control Amplifier. • Disconnect #2 Relay. • Measure resistance.		
(see table below) • Are resistances OK?	Yes ► No ►	GO to **BME18**. SERVICE wire in question.

From	To	Resistance (OHMS)
H.V.A.C. Control Amplifier BL/R	Battery +	Over 10,000
	Ground	Over 10,000
	#2 Relay BL/R	0-5

TEST STEP	RESULT ►	ACTION TO TAKE
BME8 CHECK BLOWER RELAY NO. 1 SUPPLY VOLTAGE		
• Key on. • VOM on 20 volt scale. • Blower off. • Measure voltage at blower relay no. 1 "BL" and "BK/W" terminals. • Are both readings greater than 10 volts?	Yes ► No ►	GO to **BME9**. REPAIR wire in question.

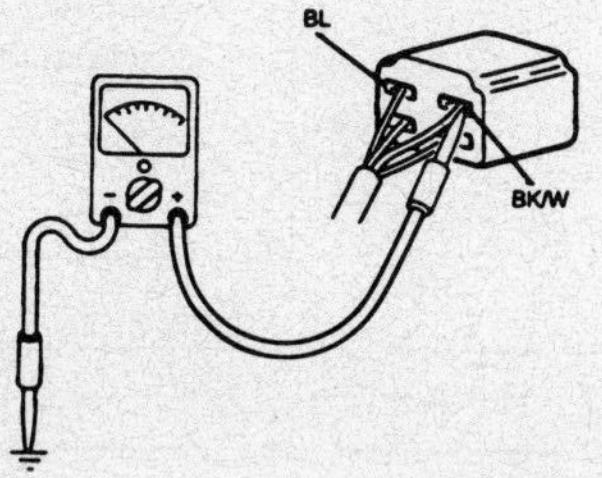
BL
BK/W

TEST STEP	RESULT ►	ACTION TO TAKE
BME9 BLOWER RELAY NO. 1 OPERATION CHECK		
• Key on. • VOM on 20 volt scale. • Leave relay connected. • Ground "BK" terminal of blower relay no. 1 with jumper wire. • Measure voltage at blower relay no. 1 "BL/R" terminal. • Is reading greater than 10 volts with "BK" grounded, and 0V with "BK" open?	Yes ► No ►	Service "BL/R-BL" wire from Relay #1 to Relay #2. REPLACE relay.

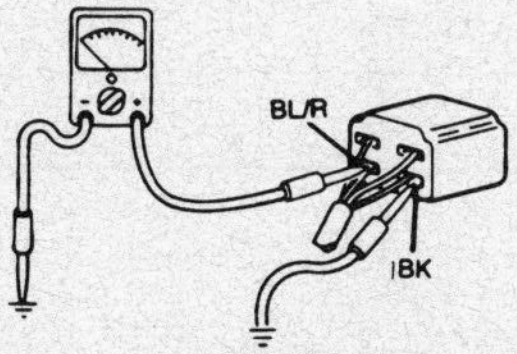
BL/R
BK

TEST STEP	RESULT ►	ACTION TO TAKE
BME10 CHECK BLOWER RELAY NO. 3 SUPPLY VOLTAGE		
• Key on. • Blower on "MAX." • VOM on 20 volt scale. • Measure voltage at blower relay no. 3 "BK/Y" and "R/Y" terminals. • Are both readings greater than 10 volts?	Yes ► No ►	GO to **BME11**. REPAIR wire in question.

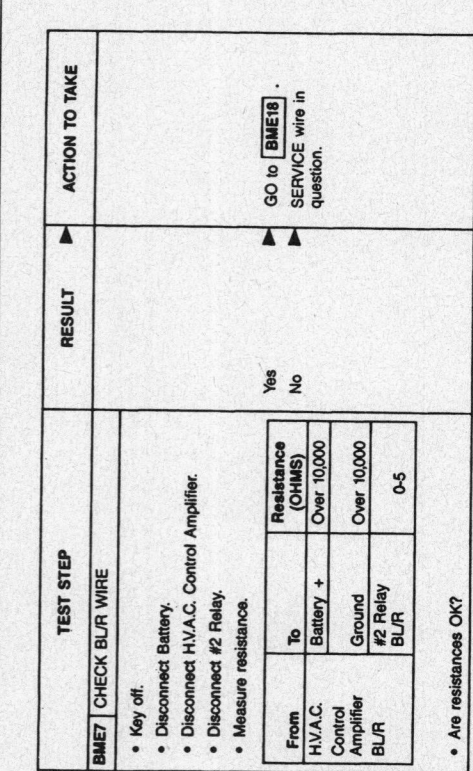

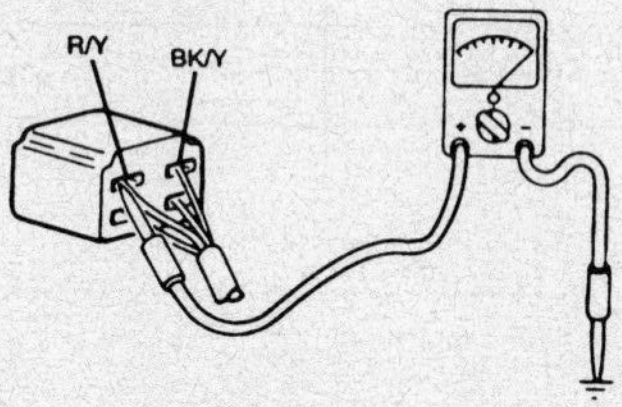
R/Y
BK/Y

TEST STEP	RESULT ►	ACTION TO TAKE
BME11 BLOWER RELAY NO. 3 OPERATION CHECK		
• Key on. • VOM on 20 volt scale. • Blower off. • Leave relay #3 connected. • Disconnect Relay #2. • Disconnect Transistor. • Ground "BL" terminal of blower relay no. 3 with jumper wire. • Measure voltage at blower relay no. 3 "BL/W" terminal. • Is reading greater than 10 volts?	Yes ► No ►	GO to BME12. REPLACE relay.

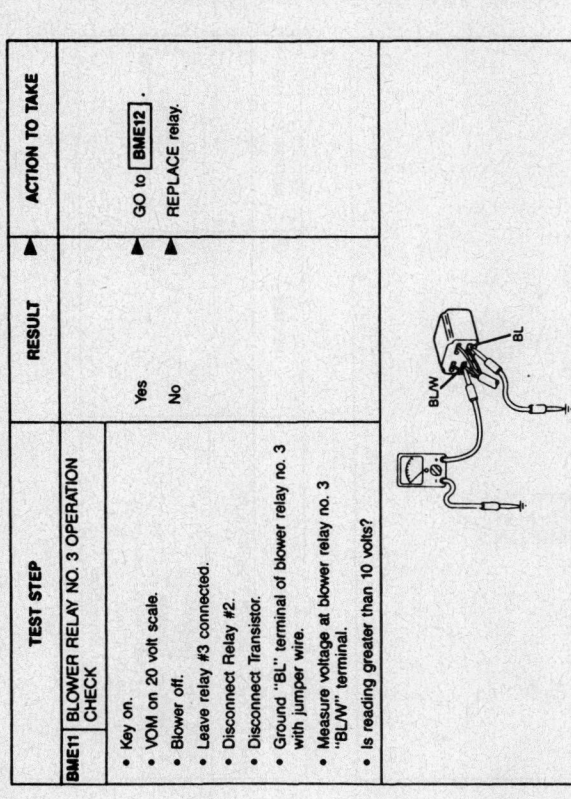

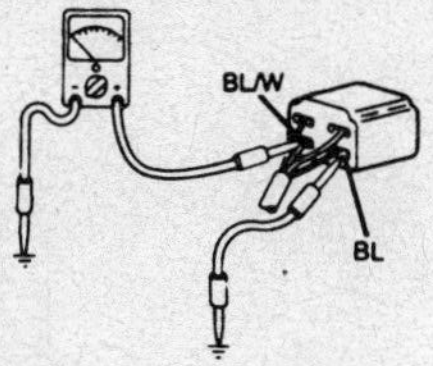
BL/W
BL

TEST STEP	RESULT ►	ACTION TO TAKE
BME12 CHECK WIRES TO TRANSISTOR		
• Disconnect Transistor. • Disconnect Battery. • Disconnect Relay #3. • Disconnect Relay #4. • Measure resistance. • Are resistances OK?	Yes ► No ►	RECONNECT Transistor. RECONNECT Relay #2. GO to BME13. SERVICE wire in question.

From	To	Resistance (OHMS)
Relay #2 R/Y	Battery +	Over 10,000
	Ground	Over 10,000
	Transistor R/Y	0-5
Relay #3 BL/W	Battery +	Over 10,000
	Ground	Over 10,000
	Transistor BL/W	0-5

TEST STEP	RESULT ►	ACTION TO TAKE
BME13 CHECK BL WIRE		
• Key off. • Disconnect Battery. • Disconnect H.V.A.C. Control Amplifier. • Disconnect #3 Relay. • Measure resistance. • Are resistances OK?	Yes ► No ►	GO to BME18. SERVICE "BL" wire.

From	To	Resistance (OHMS)
H.V.A.C. Control Amplifier BL	Battery +	Over 10,000
	Ground	Over 10,000
	#3 Relay BL	0-5

TEST STEP	RESULT ►	ACTION TO TAKE
BME14 CHECK TRANSISTOR CONTINUITY		
• Key off. • VOM on 200 ohm scale. • Leave transistor connected. • Measure resistance between transistor "BL/O" and "BL/W" terminals. • Is resistance less than 2,500 ohms?	Yes ► No ►	GO to BME15 . REPLACE transistor.

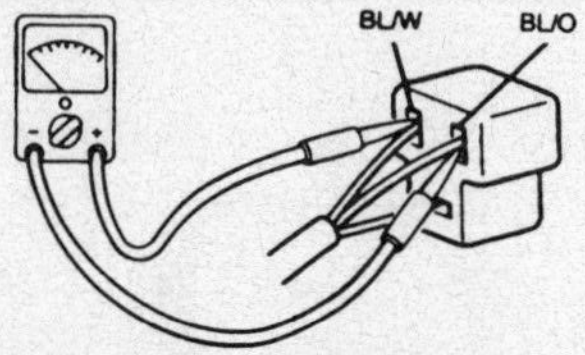
BL/W
BL/O

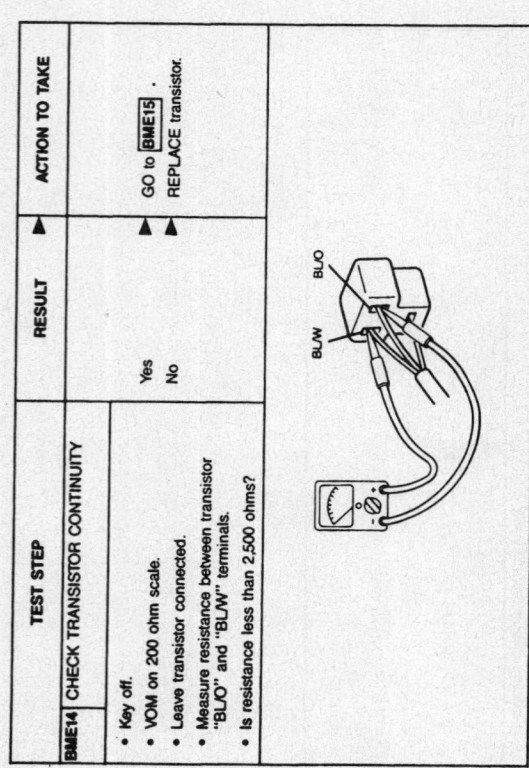

TEST STEP	RESULT ►	ACTION TO TAKE
BME15 CHECK MOTOR TRANSISTOR		
• Disconnect Relay #3. • Disconnect Transistor. • Jump +12V to "BL/W" terminal of Transistor connector. • Does Blower Motor Run?	Yes ► No ►	GO to BME16 . SERVICE "BL/W" wire.

TEST STEP	RESULT ►	ACTION TO TAKE
BME16 CHECK SWITCHING VOLTAGE TO TRANSISTOR		
• Key on. • Blower on "LO." • VOM on 20 volt scale. • Measure voltage at transistor "BL/O" terminal while gradually increasing blower speed. • Does voltage gradually increase with blower speed from 4 volts (±1 volt) (Lo) to 11 volts (±1 volt) (Hi)?	Yes ► No ►	REPLACE transistor. GO to BME17 .

TEST STEP	RESULT ►	ACTION TO TAKE
BME17 CHECK BL/O WIRE		
• Key off. • Disconnect Battery. • Disconnect H.V.A.C. Control Amplifier. • Disconnect Transistor. • Measure resistance.	Yes ►	RECONNECT Battery. RECONNECT Transistor. GO to BME18 .
• Are resistances OK?	No ►	SERVICE wire in question.

From	To	Resistance (OHMS)
H.V.A.C. Control Amplifier BL/O	Battery +	Over 10,000
	Ground	Over 10,000
	Transistor BL/O	0-5

AUTOMATIC TEMPERATURE CONTROL DIAGNOSIS AND TESTING—PROBE

TEST STEP	RESULT ►	ACTION TO TAKE
BME18 CHECK CONTROL AMP GROUND AND POWER		
• Disconnect H.V.A.C. Control Amplifier. • Key on. • Check for 12V at H.V.A.C. Control Amplifier BK/Y. • Check for 0-5 ohms resistance from H.V.A.C. Control Amplifier BK to ground. • Are both ground and power OK?	Yes ► No ►	REPLACE H.V.A.C. Control Amplifier. SERVICE wire in question.

TEST STEP	RESULT ►	ACTION TO TAKE
MODE1 VOLTAGE ACROSS PANEL		
• Disconnect mode motor. • Key on. • VOM 20 volt scale. • Measure voltage between Mode motor "Y/BL" and "R" wires Mode motor "Y/GN" and "R" wires. **Mode** / **Voltage** Panel / 4–7V Others / 0V • Are voltage readings OK?	Yes ► No ►	REPLACE mode servo motor. GO to MODE2 .

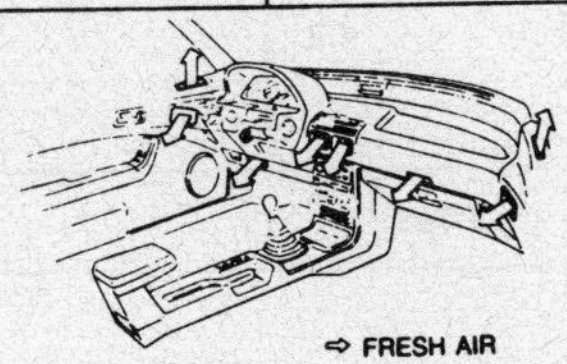
⇨ FRESH AIR

TEST STEP	RESULT ►	ACTION TO TAKE
MODE2 VOLTAGE FOR PANEL		
• Key on. • VOM 20 volt scale. • Measure voltage between HVAC control amplifier Q ("Y/BL" wire) and J ("R" wire) O ("Y/GN" wire) and J ("R" wire) **Mode** / **Voltage** Panel / 4–7V Others / 0V • Are voltage readings OK?	Yes ► No ►	REPAIR wire(s) from HVAC control unit to mode motor. REPLACE HVAC control amplifier.

TEST STEP	RESULT ►	ACTION TO TAKE
MODE3 VOLTAGE ACROSS HILO		
• Disconnect mode motor. • Key on. • VOM 20 volt scale. • Measure voltage between Mode motor "Y/BL" and "BL/W" wires Mode motor "Y/GN" and "BL/W" wires. **Mode** / **Voltage** HiLo / 4–7V Others / 0V • Are voltage readings OK?	Yes ► No ►	REPLACE mode servo motor. GO to MODE4 .

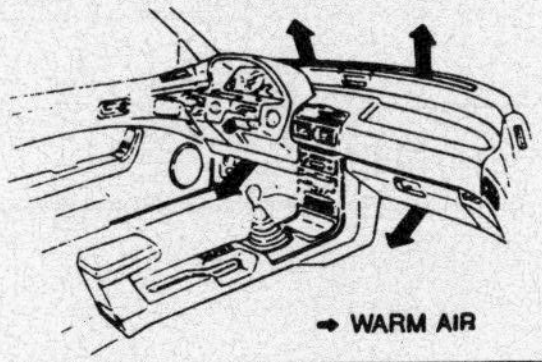
➡ WARM AIR

TEST STEP	RESULT ►	ACTION TO TAKE
MODE4 VOLTAGE FOR HILO		
• Key on. • VOM 20 volt scale. • Measure voltage between HVAC Control amplifier terminals Q ("Y/BL" wire) and H ("BL/W" wire) O ("Y/GN" wire) and H ("BL/W" wire) **Mode** / **Voltage** HiLo 4–7V Others 0V • Are voltage readings OK?	Yes ► No ►	REPAIR wire(s) from HVAC control amplifier to mode motor. REPLACE HVAC control amplifier.

TEST STEP	RESULT ►	ACTION TO TAKE
MODE5 VOLTAGE ACROSS FLOOR		
• Disconnect mode motor. • Key on. • VOM 20 volt scale. • Measure voltage between Mode motor "Y/BL" and "BL" wires Mode motor "Y/GN" and "BL" wires. **Mode** / **Voltage** Floor 4–7V Others 0V • Are voltage readings OK?	Yes ► No ►	REPLACE mode servo motor. GO to **MODE6**.

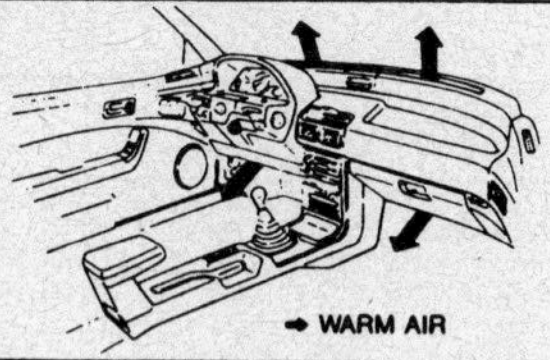
WARM AIR

TEST STEP	RESULT ►	ACTION TO TAKE
MODE6 VOLTAGE FOR FLOOR		
• Key on. • VOM 20 volt scale. • Measure voltage between HVAC Control amplifier terminals Q ("Y/BL" wire) and F ("BL" wire) O ("Y/GN" wire) and F ("BL" wire). **Mode** / **Voltage** Floor 4–7V Others 0V • Are voltage readings OK?	Yes ► No ►	REPAIR wire(s) from HVAC control amplifier to mode monitor. REPLACE HVAC control amplifier.

TEST STEP	RESULT ►	ACTION TO TAKE
MODE7 VOLTAGE ACROSS MIX		
• Disconnect mode motor. • Key on. • VOM 20 volt scale. • Measure voltage between Mode motor "Y/BL" and "BL/BK" wires Mode motor "Y/GN" and "BL/BK" wires. **Mode** / **Voltage** Mix 4–7V Others 0V • Are voltage readings OK?	Yes ► No ►	REPLACE mode servo motor. GO to **MODE8**.

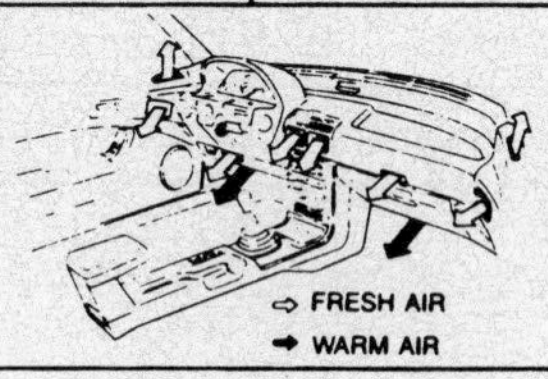
FRESH AIR
WARM AIR

AUTOMATIC TEMPERATURE CONTROL DIAGNOSIS AND TESTING—PROBE

TEST STEP	RESULT ►	ACTION TO TAKE
MODE8 VOLTAGE FOR MIX		
• Key on. • VOM 20 volt scale. • Measure voltage between HVAC control amplifier terminals Q ("Y/BL" wire) and D ("BL/BK" wire) O ("Y/GN" wire) and D ("BL/BK" wire). **Mode** **Voltage** Mix 4–7V Others 0V • Are voltage readings OK?	Yes ► No ►	REPAIR wire(s) from HVAC control amplifier to mode monitor. REPLACE HVAC control amplifier.

TEST STEP	RESULT ►	ACTION TO TAKE
MODE9 VOLTAGE ACROSS DEF		
• Disconnect mode motor. • Key on. • VOM 20 volt scale. • Measure voltage between Mode motor "Y/BL" and "BL/R" wires Mode motor "Y/GN" and "BL/R" wires. **Mode** **Voltage** Def 4–7V Others 0V • Are voltage readings OK?	Yes ► No ►	REPLACE mode servo motor. GO to MODE10 .

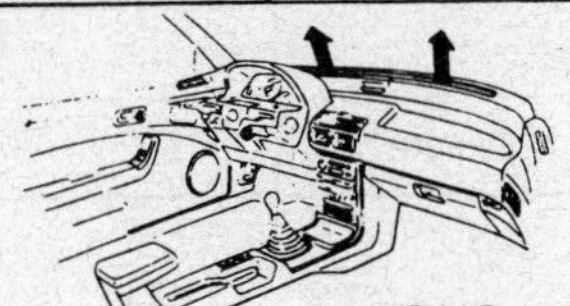
WARM AIR

TEST STEP	RESULT ►	ACTION TO TAKE
MODE10 VOLTAGE FOR DEF		
• Key on. • VOM 20 volt scale. • Measure voltage between Control amplifier terminals. Q ("Y/BL" wire) and D ("BL/R" wire) O ("Y/GN" wire) and D ("BL/R" wire). **Mode** **Voltage** Def 4–7V Others 0V • Are voltage readings OK?	Yes ► No ►	REPAIR wire(s) from control amplifier to mode motor. REPLACE control amplifier.

TEST STEP	RESULT ►	ACTION TO TAKE
MODE11 VOLTAGE ACROSS MOTOR		
• Leave mode motor connected. • Key on. • VOM 20 volt scale. • Measure voltage between mode motor "Y/BK" (+) and "Y/R" (−). • Depress mode buttons in order: Panel, HiLo, Floor, Mix, Def. • Measure voltage between mode motor "Y/R" (+) and "Y/BK" (−). • Depress mode buttons in order: Def, Mix, Floor, HiLo, Panel. • Is voltage above 10 volts each time the mode button is depressed?	Yes ► No ►	REPLACE mode servo motor. GO to MODE12 .
NOTE: Voltage reading 10 volts only when motor operates.		

AUTOMATIC TEMPERATURE CONTROL DIAGNOSIS AND TESTING – PROBE

TEST STEP	RESULT ►	ACTION TO TAKE
MODE12 VOLTAGE FOR MOTOR		
• Key on. • VOM 20 volt scale. • Measure voltage between control amplifier terminals. C ("Y/BK" wire) (+) and A ("Y/R" wire) (–). • Depress mode buttons in order: Panel, HiLo, Floor, Mix, Def. • Measure voltage between control amplifier terminals. A ("Y/R" wire) (+) and C ("Y/BK" wire) (–). • Depress mode buttons in order: Def, Mix, Floor, HiLo, Panel. • Is voltage above 10 volts each time the mode button is depressed?	Yes ► No ►	REPAIR "Y/BK" and/or "Y/R" wire(s). GO to MODE13 .

TEST STEP	RESULT ►	ACTION TO TAKE
MODE13 VOLTAGE ACROSS MODE SWITCH(ES)		
• Disconnect mode motor. • Key on. • VOM 20 volt scale. • Measure voltage between **Mode Motor** / **Mode** / **Voltage** "Y/BL" and "R" / Panel / 4–7V "Y/GN" and "R" / Panel / 4–7V "Y/BL" and "BL/W" / HiLo / 4–7V "Y/GN" and "BL/W" / HiLo / 4–7V "Y/BL" and "BL" / Floor / 4–7V "Y/GN" and "BL" / Floor / 4–7V "Y/BL" and "BL/BK" / Mix / 4–7V "Y/GN" and "BL/BK" / Mix / 4–7V "Y/BL" and "BL/R" / Def / 4–7V "Y/GN" and "BL/R" / Def / 4–7V • Are voltage readings OK?	Yes ► No ►	GO to MODE14 . GO to MODE15 .
NOTE: Voltage is 0 volts when the mode is in other range(s).		

TEST STEP	RESULT ►	ACTION TO TAKE
MODE14 MODE SWITCH(ES) CHECK		
• Disconnect mode motor. • Key off. • VOM 200 ohm scale. • Measure resistance between Mode motor "Y/GN" and "R," "BL/W," "BL," "BL/BK," "BL/R." Mode motor 'Y/BL" and "R," "BL/W," "BL," "BL/BK," "BL/R." • Operate the motor for only one cycle for each measurement by connecting 12 volts to mode motor "Y/BK" wire and ground "Y/R" wire with jumper wire (temporarily). • Is resistance below 5 ohms twice during one cycle?	Yes ► No ►	REPLACE HVAC control amplifier. REPLACE mode servo motor.

TEST STEP	RESULT ►	ACTION TO TAKE
MODE15 VOLTAGE FOR MODE SWITCH(ES)		
• Key on. • VOM 20 volt scale. • Measure voltage between **HVAC Control Unit** / **Mode** / **Voltage** "Y/BL" and "R" / Panel / 4–7V "Y/GN" and "R" / Panel / 4–7V "Y/BL" and "BL/W" / HiLo / 4–7V "Y/GN" and "BL/W" / HiLo / 4–7V "Y/BL" and "BL" / Floor / 4–7V "Y/GN" and "BL" / Floor / 4–7V "Y/BL" and "BL/BK" / Mix / 4–7V "Y/GN" and "BL/BK" / Mix / 4–7V "Y/BL" and "BL/R" / Def / 4–7V "Y/GN" and "BL/R" / Def / 4–7V • Are voltage readings OK?	Yes ► No ►	REPAIR wire(s) in question between control amplifier and mode motor. REPLACE control amplifier.
NOTE: Voltage is 0 volts when the mode is in other range(s).		

AUTOMATIC TEMPERATURE CONTROL DIAGNOSIS AND TESTING—PROBE

TEST STEP	RESULT ►	ACTION TO TAKE
MIX1 VOLTAGE ACROSS MOTOR		
• Do not disconnect motor. • Key on. • VOM 20 volt scale. • Measure voltage between Mix motor "Y/BL" (+) and "Y/W" (−). **Mix Lever** / **Voltage** MAX hot / above 10v Other / 0v Mix motor "Y/W" (+) and "Y/BL" (−) **Mix Lever** / **Voltage** MAX cold / above 10v Other / 0v • Are voltage readings OK?	Yes ► No ►	GO to MIX5. GO to MIX2.

TEST STEP	RESULT ►	ACTION TO TAKE
MIX2 VOLTAGE TO MOTOR FROM HVAC CONTROL AMPLIFIER		
• Key on. • VOM 20 volt scale. • Measure voltage between HVAC control amplifier terminals. E ("Y/BL") (+) and G ("Y/W") (−). **Mix Lever** / **Voltage** MAX hot / above 10v Other / 0v HVAC control amplifier terminals G ("Y/W") (+) and E ("Y/BL") (−) **Mix Lever** / **Voltage** MAX cold / above 10v Other / 0v • Are voltage readings OK?	Yes ► No ►	REPAIR "Y/BL" and/or "Y/W" wire(s) from HVAC control amplifier to motor. GO to MIX3.

TEST STEP	RESULT ►	ACTION TO TAKE
MIX3 POWER TO HVAC CONTROL UNIT		
• Key on. • VOM 20 volt scale. • Measure voltage between HVAC control amplifier terminals R ("BK/Y" wire) and ground. • Is voltage above 10 volts?	Yes ► No ►	GO to MIX4. REPAIR "BK/Y" wire from HVAC control amplifier to ignition switch. NOTE: Check fuses.

TEST STEP	RESULT ►	ACTION TO TAKE
MIX4 GROUND AT HVAC CONTROL AMPLIFIER		
• Key off. • VOM 200 ohm scale. • Measure resistance between HVAC control amplifier terminal 2D ("BK" wire) and ground. • Is resistance below 5 ohms?	Yes ► No ►	REPLACE HVAC control amplifier. REPAIR "BK" wire to ground.

TEST STEP	RESULT ►	ACTION TO TAKE
MIX5 VOLTAGE ACROSS COLD		
• Key on. • VOM 20 volt scale. • Measure voltage between Mix motor "GN/R" wire and Mix motor "GN/BK" wire. **Mix Lever** / **Voltage** MAX hot / 4–7v MAX cold / below 1.5v NOTE: Voltage decreases steadily from hot to cold. • Are voltage readings OK?	Yes ► No ►	GO to MIX6. GO to MIX7.

TEST STEP	RESULT ►	ACTION TO TAKE
MIX6 VOLTAGE FOR COLD		
• Key on. • VOM 20 volt scale. • Measure voltage between HVAC control amplifier terminals K ("GN/R" wire) and L ("GN/BK" wire). **Mix Lever** / **Voltage** MAX hot / 4–7v MAX cold / below 1.5v NOTE: Voltage decreases steadily from hot to cold. • Are voltage readings OK?	Yes ► No ►	REPAIR "GN/R" and/or "GN/BK" wire(s) from control amplifier to mix motor. REPLACE HVAC control amplifier.

TEST STEP	RESULT ►	ACTION TO TAKE
MIX7 VOLTAGE ACROSS HOT		
• Key on. • VOM 20 volt scale. • Measure voltage between mix motor terminals M ("GN/Y" wire) and L ("GN/BK" wire). **Mix Lever** / **Approximate Voltage** MAX hot / below 1.5v MAX cold / 4–7v NOTE: Voltage decreases steadily from cold to hot. • Are voltage readings OK?	Yes ► No ►	REPLACE mix servo motor. GO to **MIX8**.

TEST STEP	RESULT ►	ACTION TO TAKE
MIX8 VOLTAGE FOR HOT		
• Key on. • VOM 20 volt scale. • Measure voltage between HVAC control amplifier terminals M ("GN/Y" wire) and L ("GN/BK" wire). **Mix Lever** / **Approximate Voltage** MAX hot / below 1.5v MAX cold / 4–7v NOTE: Voltage increases steadily from hot to cold. • Are voltage readings OK?	Yes ► No ►	SERVICE "GN/Y" wire from HVAC control amplifier to mix motor. REPLACE control amplifier.

TEST STEP	RESULT ►	ACTION TO TAKE
REC1 REC MOTOR OPERATION		
• Key off. • Disconnect rec motor. • Connect 12 volts to rec motor "BK/Y" and ground "W/GN" wire with jumper wire. • VOM 200 ohm scale. • Measure resistance between **Resistance (ohms)** **Control Unit** / **Rec** / **Fresh** / **During Travel** "GN/BK" & "GN" / Open / Open / 0 ohms "GN/BK" & "GN/R" / Open / 0 ohms / 0 ohms "GN/R" & "GN" / 0 ohms / Open / 0 ohms NOTE: Open = above 10,000 ohms. • Are resistance readings OK?	Yes ► No ►	GO to **REC2**. REPLACE rec servo motor.

AUTOMATIC TEMPERATURE CONTROL DIAGNOSIS AND TESTING—PROBE

TEST STEP	RESULT ►	ACTION TO TAKE
REC2 POWER TO REC MOTOR		
• VOM 20 volt scale. • Measure voltage between rec motor "BK/Y" wire and ground. Key on .... above 10v Key off .... 0v • Are voltage readings OK?	Yes ► No ►	GO to REC3. SERVICE "BK/Y" wire from rec motor to ignition switch.

TEST STEP	RESULT ►	ACTION TO TAKE
REC3 REC SWITCH AT CONTROL AMPLIFIER		
• Disconnect HVAC control amplifier. • Key on. • Connect rec motor "W/GN" wire to ground with jumper wire. • VOM 200 ohm scale. • Measure resistance between Control Unit / Rec / Fresh / During Travel "GN/BL" & "GN" / Open / Open / 0 ohms "GN/BL" & "GN/R" / Open / 0 ohms / 0 ohms "GN/R" & "GN" / 0 ohms / Open / 0 ohms NOTE: Open = above 10,000 ohms. • Are resistance readings OK?	Yes ► No ►	GO to REC4. SERVICE wire(s) in question.

TEST STEP	RESULT ►	ACTION TO TAKE
REC4 REC MOTOR GROUND OPEN CHECK		
• Disconnect rec motor. • Disconnect HVAC control amplifier. • Key off. • VOM 200 ohm scale. • Measure resistance between Rec motor "W/GN" wire and control amplifier "W/GN" wire. • Is resistance below 5 ohms?	Yes ► No ►	GO to REC5. SERVICE open in "W/GN" wire.

TEST STEP	RESULT ►	ACTION TO TAKE
REC5 REC MOTOR SHORT CHECK		
• Disconnect rec motor. • Disconnect HVAC control amplifier. • Disconnect battery. • Key off. • VOM 200 ohm scale. • Measure resistance between Rec motor "W/GN" wire and ground Rec motor "W/GN" wire and battery positive. • Are resistance readings above 10,000 ohms?	Yes ► No ►	REPLACE HVAC control amplifier. SERVICE short in "W/GN" wire.

WIRING SCHEMATICS

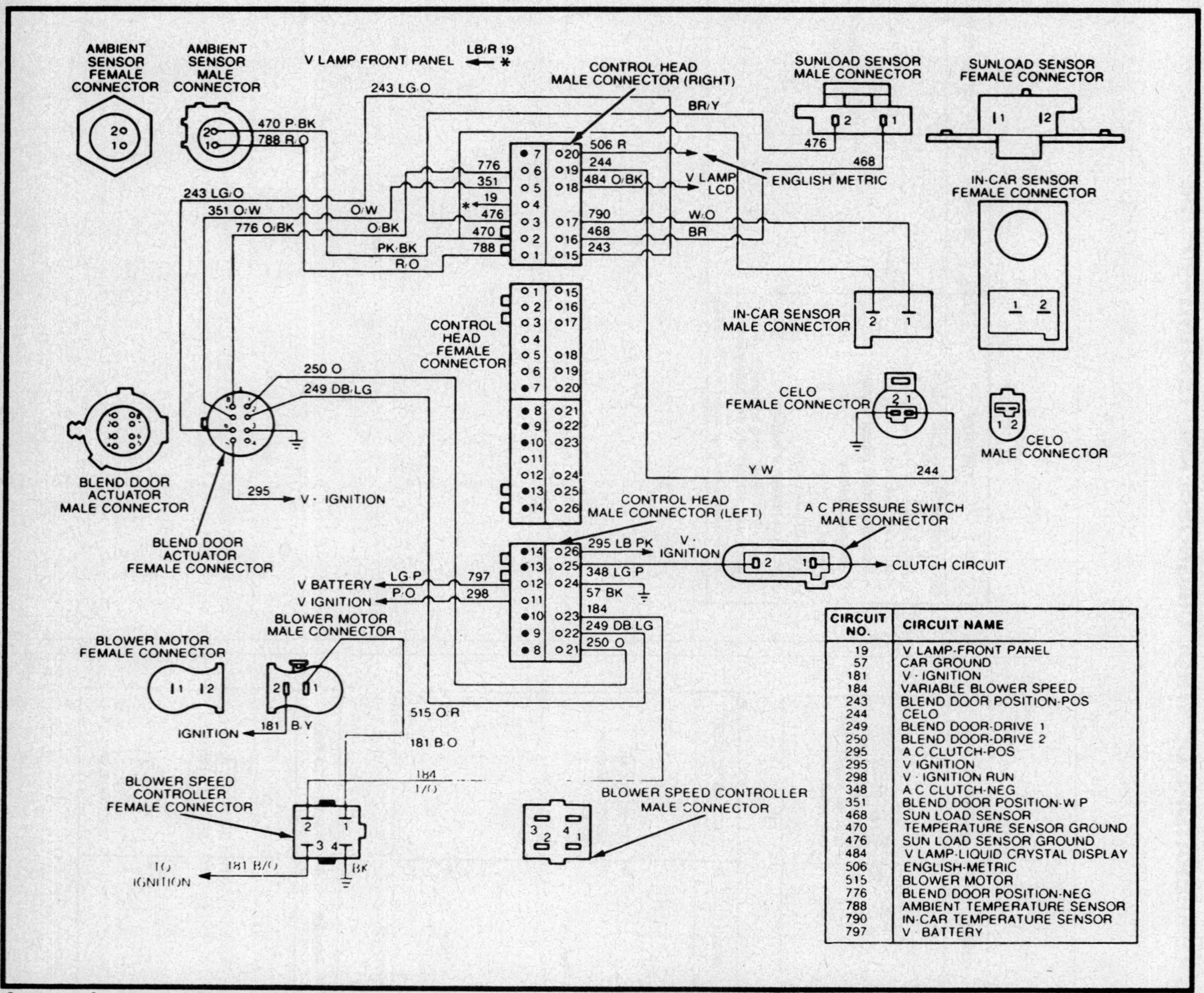
AMBIENT SENSOR FEMALE CONNECTOR
AMBIENT SENSOR MALE CONNECTOR
V LAMP FRONT PANEL
LB/R 19
CONTROL HEAD MALE CONNECTOR (RIGHT)
SUNLOAD SENSOR MALE CONNECTOR
SUNLOAD SENSOR FEMALE CONNECTOR
ENGLISH METRIC
V LAMP LCD
IN-CAR SENSOR FEMALE CONNECTOR
IN-CAR SENSOR MALE CONNECTOR
CONTROL HEAD FEMALE CONNECTOR
CELO FEMALE CONNECTOR
CELO MALE CONNECTOR
BLEND DOOR ACTUATOR MALE CONNECTOR
BLEND DOOR ACTUATOR FEMALE CONNECTOR
V · IGNITION
CONTROL HEAD MALE CONNECTOR (LEFT)
A C PRESSURE SWITCH MALE CONNECTOR
CLUTCH CIRCUIT
V BATTERY
V IGNITION
BLOWER MOTOR MALE CONNECTOR
BLOWER MOTOR FEMALE CONNECTOR
IGNITION
BLOWER SPEED CONTROLLER FEMALE CONNECTOR
BLOWER SPEED CONTROLLER MALE CONNECTOR
TO IGNITION

CIRCUIT NO.	CIRCUIT NAME
19	V LAMP-FRONT PANEL
57	CAR GROUND
181	V · IGNITION
184	VARIABLE BLOWER SPEED
243	BLEND DOOR POSITION-POS
244	CELO
249	BLEND DOOR-DRIVE 1
250	BLEND DOOR-DRIVE 2
295	A C CLUTCH-POS
295	V IGNITION
298	V · IGNITION RUN
348	A C CLUTCH-NEG
351	BLEND DOOR POSITION-W P
468	SUN LOAD SENSOR
470	TEMPERATURE SENSOR GROUND
476	SUN LOAD SENSOR GROUND
484	V LAMP-LIQUID CRYSTAL DISPLAY
506	ENGLISH-METRIC
515	BLOWER MOTOR
776	BLEND DOOR POSITION-NEG
788	AMBIENT TEMPERATURE SENSOR
790	IN-CAR TEMPERATURE SENSOR
797	V · BATTERY

Automatic temperature control system wiring schematic—1989 Taurus, Sable and Continental

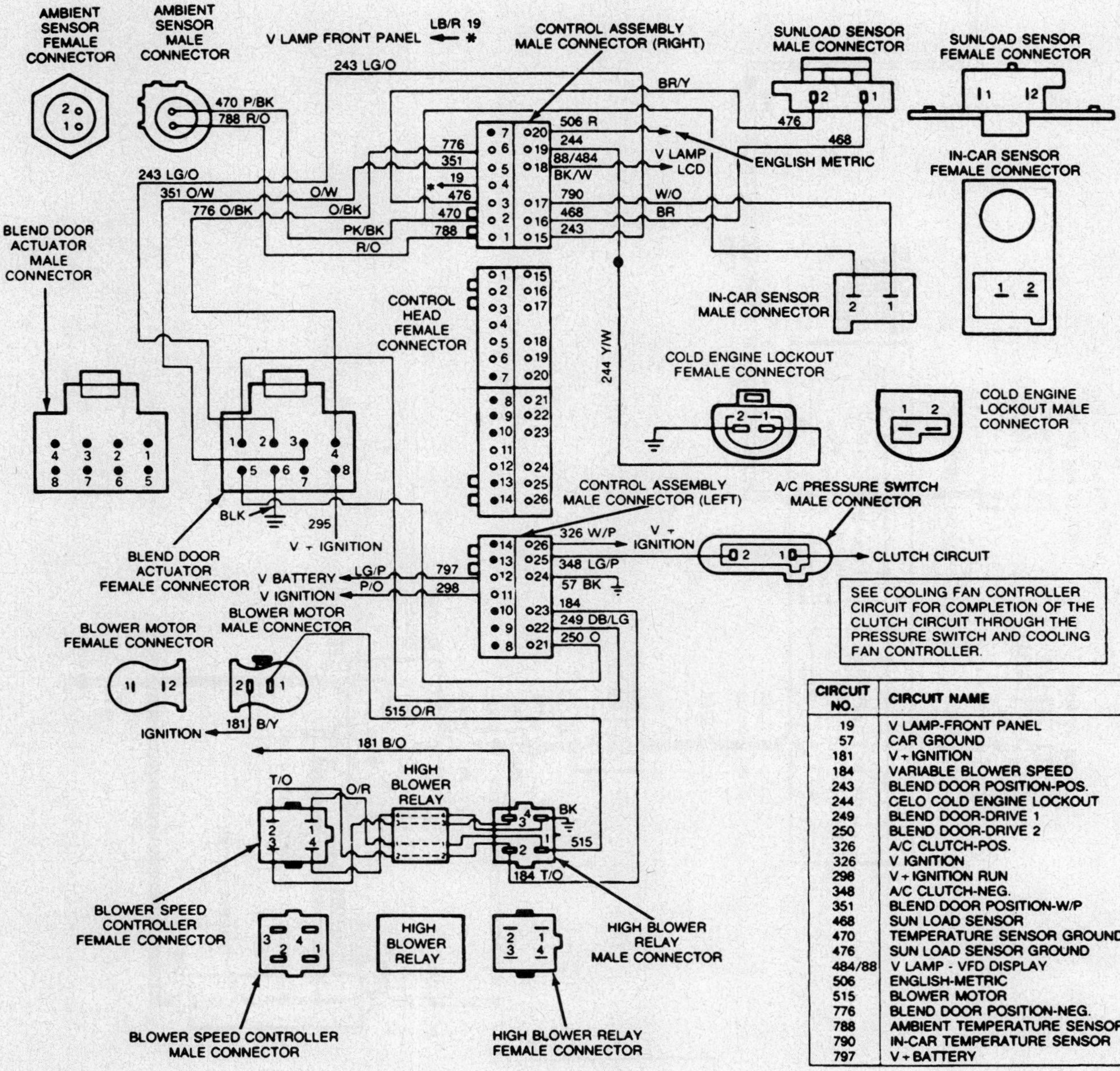
AMBIENT SENSOR FEMALE CONNECTOR
AMBIENT SENSOR MALE CONNECTOR
V LAMP FRONT PANEL
LB/R 19
CONTROL ASSEMBLY MALE CONNECTOR (RIGHT)
SUNLOAD SENSOR MALE CONNECTOR
SUNLOAD SENSOR FEMALE CONNECTOR
243 LG/O
470 P/BK
788 R/O
BR/Y
506 R
V LAMP LCD
ENGLISH METRIC
IN-CAR SENSOR FEMALE CONNECTOR
351 O/W
776 O/BK
O/W
O/BK
PK/BK
R/O
BK/W
W/O
BR
BLEND DOOR ACTUATOR MALE CONNECTOR
CONTROL HEAD FEMALE CONNECTOR
IN-CAR SENSOR MALE CONNECTOR
244 Y/W
COLD ENGINE LOCKOUT FEMALE CONNECTOR
COLD ENGINE LOCKOUT MALE CONNECTOR
BLK
295
V + IGNITION
CONTROL ASSEMBLY MALE CONNECTOR (LEFT)
A/C PRESSURE SWITCH MALE CONNECTOR
326 W/P
CLUTCH CIRCUIT
BLEND DOOR ACTUATOR FEMALE CONNECTOR
V BATTERY
V IGNITION
LG/P
P/O
348 LG/P
57 BK
249 DB/LG
250 O
SEE COOLING FAN CONTROLLER CIRCUIT FOR COMPLETION OF THE CLUTCH CIRCUIT THROUGH THE PRESSURE SWITCH AND COOLING FAN CONTROLLER.
BLOWER MOTOR FEMALE CONNECTOR
BLOWER MOTOR MALE CONNECTOR
515 O/R
IGNITION
181 B/Y
181 B/O
T/O
O/R
HIGH BLOWER RELAY
BK
515
184 T/O
BLOWER SPEED CONTROLLER FEMALE CONNECTOR
HIGH BLOWER RELAY MALE CONNECTOR
BLOWER SPEED CONTROLLER MALE CONNECTOR
HIGH BLOWER RELAY FEMALE CONNECTOR

CIRCUIT NO.	CIRCUIT NAME
19	V LAMP-FRONT PANEL
57	CAR GROUND
181	V+IGNITION
184	VARIABLE BLOWER SPEED
243	BLEND DOOR POSITION-POS.
244	CELO COLD ENGINE LOCKOUT
249	BLEND DOOR-DRIVE 1
250	BLEND DOOR-DRIVE 2
326	A/C CLUTCH-POS.
326	V IGNITION
298	V+IGNITION RUN
348	A/C CLUTCH-NEG.
351	BLEND DOOR POSITION-W/P
468	SUN LOAD SENSOR
470	TEMPERATURE SENSOR GROUND
476	SUN LOAD SENSOR GROUND
484/88	V LAMP - VFD DISPLAY
506	ENGLISH-METRIC
515	BLOWER MOTOR
776	BLEND DOOR POSITION-NEG.
788	AMBIENT TEMPERATURE SENSOR
790	IN-CAR TEMPERATURE SENSOR
797	V+BATTERY

Automatic temperature control system wiring schematic—1990–91 Taurus, Sable and Continental

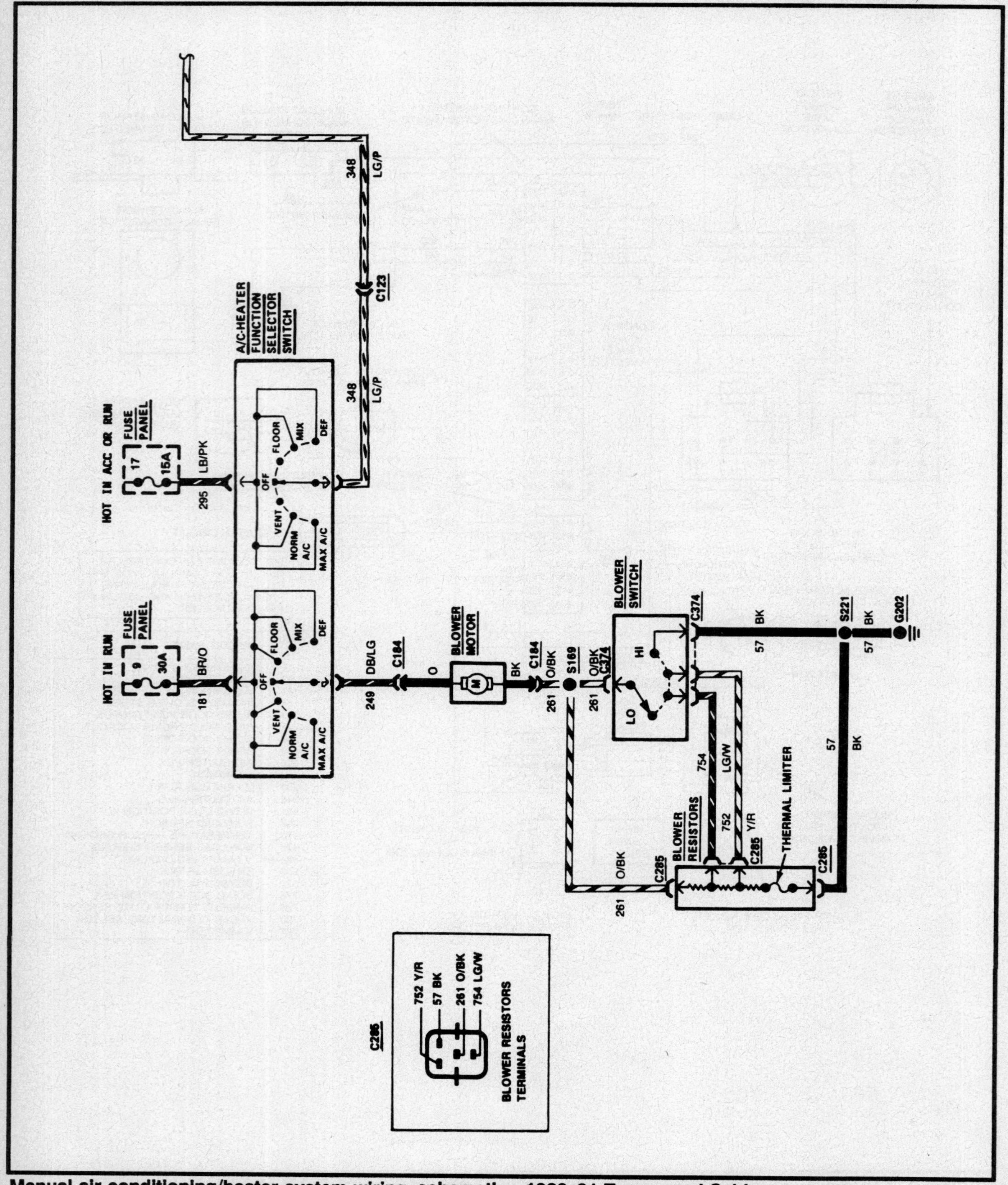
HOT IN RUN
FUSE PANEL
9
30A
181
BR/O
HOT IN ACC OR RUN
FUSE PANEL
17
15A
295
LB/PK
A/C-HEATER FUNCTION SELECTOR SWITCH
OFF
VENT
NORM A/C
MAX A/C
FLOOR
MIX
DEF
348
LG/P
C123
249
DB/LG
C184
O
BLOWER MOTOR
BK
261
O/BK
S169
C374
BLOWER SWITCH
HI
LO
57
BK
S221
G202
754
LG/W
752
Y/R
BLOWER RESISTORS
C285
THERMAL LIMITER
C286
752 Y/R
57 BK
261 O/BK
754 LG/W
BLOWER RESISTORS TERMINALS

Manual air conditioning/heater system wiring schematic—1989–91 Taurus and Sable

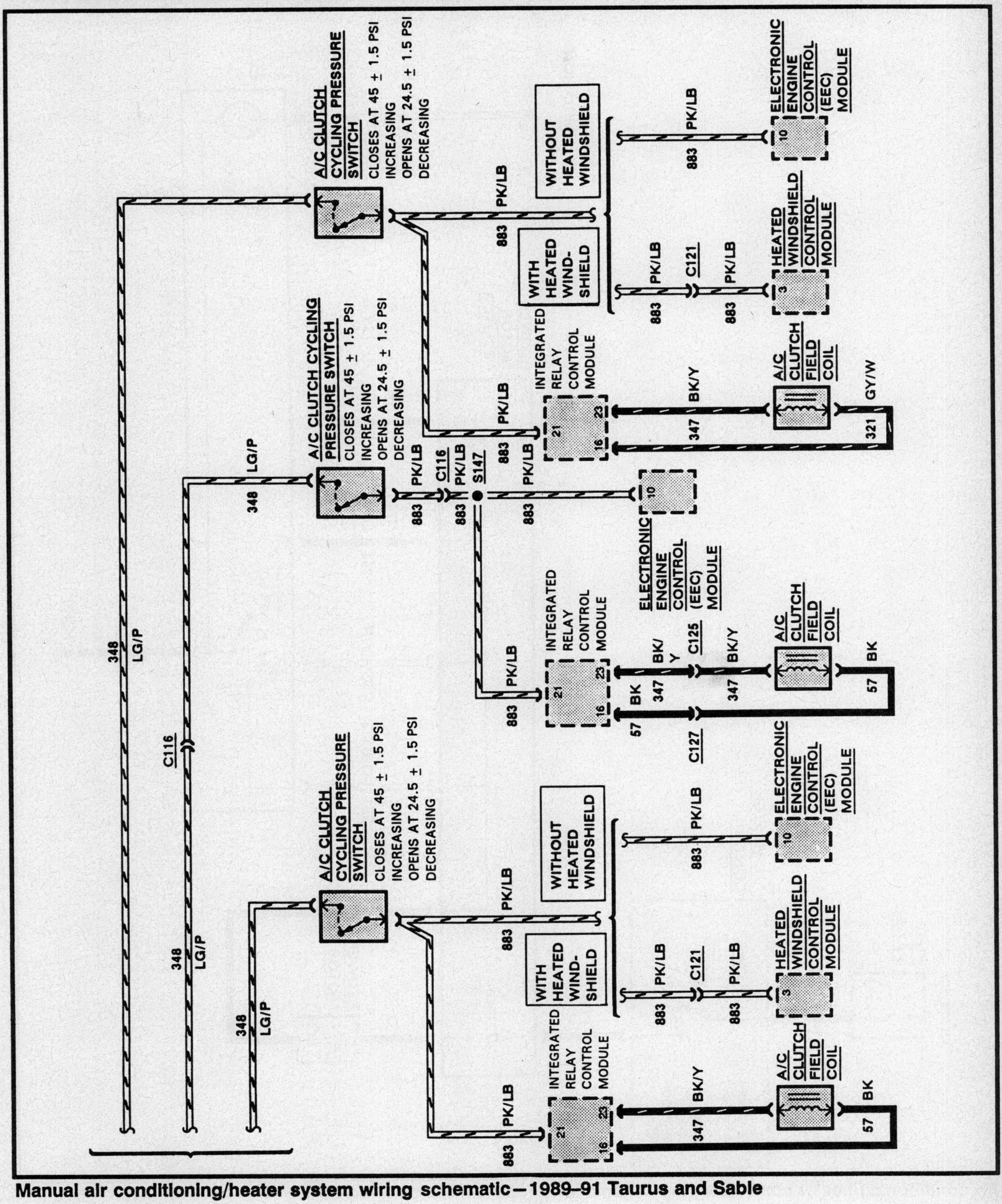
A/C CLUTCH CYCLING PRESSURE SWITCH
CLOSES AT 45 ± 1.5 PSI INCREASING
OPENS AT 24.5 ± 1.5 PSI DECREASING
348
LG/P
C116
883
PK/LB
S147
WITHOUT HEATED WINDSHIELD
WITH HEATED WIND-SHIELD
C121
ELECTRONIC ENGINE CONTROL (EEC) MODULE
HEATED WINDSHIELD CONTROL MODULE
INTEGRATED RELAY CONTROL MODULE
21
23
16
10
3
347
BK/Y
A/C CLUTCH FIELD COIL
321
GY/W
BK/
Y
C125
BK
57
C127
Manual air conditioning/heater system wiring schematic—1989–91 Taurus and Sable

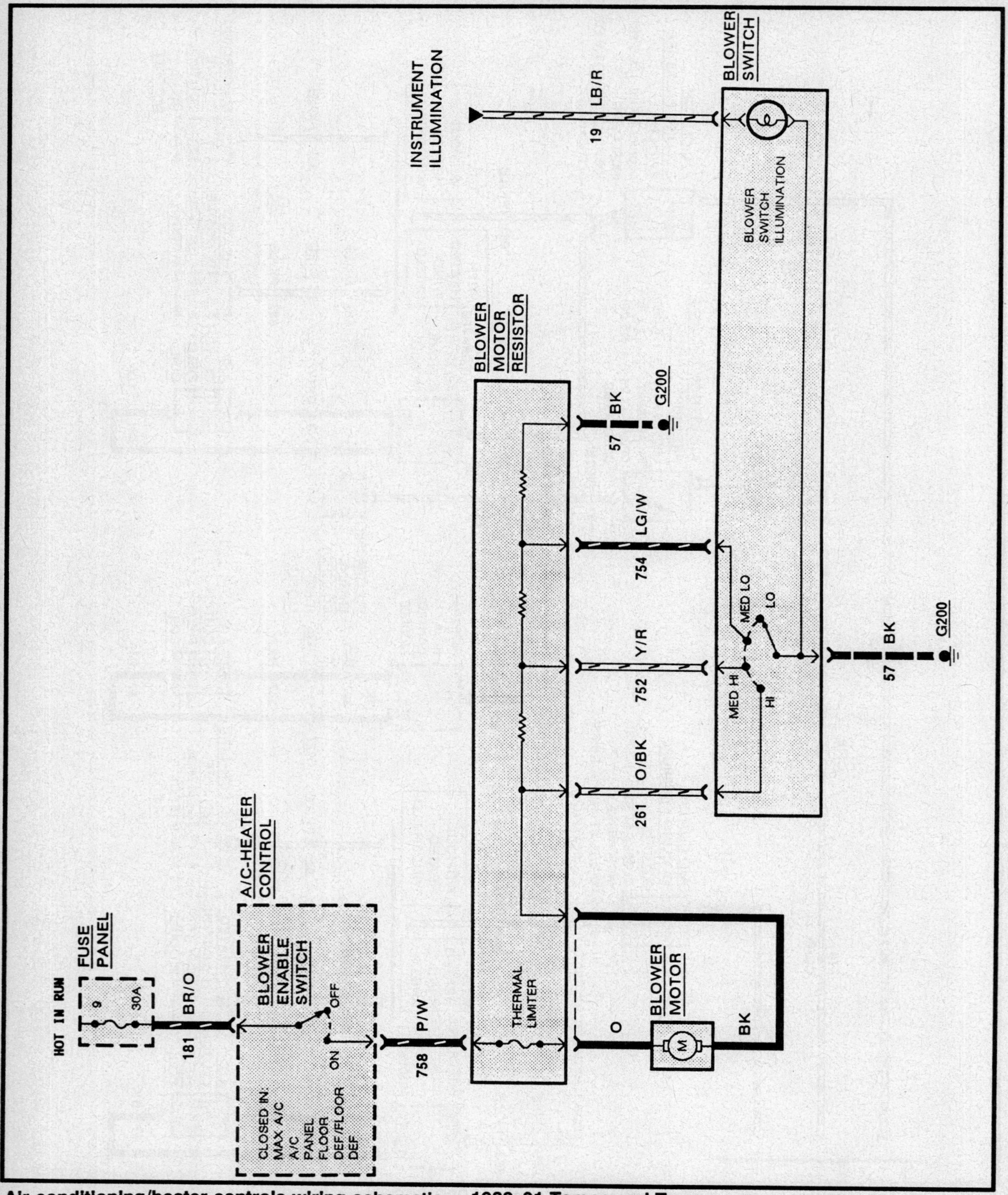
INSTRUMENT ILLUMINATION
BLOWER SWITCH
LB/R
19
BLOWER SWITCH ILLUMINATION
BLOWER MOTOR RESISTOR
BK
57
G200
LG/W
754
MED LO
LO
Y/R
752
MED HI
HI
O/BK
261
A/C-HEATER CONTROL
FUSE PANEL
HOT IN RUN
9
30A
BR/O
181
BLOWER ENABLE SWITCH
OFF
ON
CLOSED IN:
MAX A/C
A/C
PANEL
FLOOR
DEF/FLOOR
DEF
P/W
758
THERMAL LIMITER
O
BLOWER MOTOR
M
BK

Air conditioning/heater controls wiring schematic— 1989–91 Tempo and Topaz

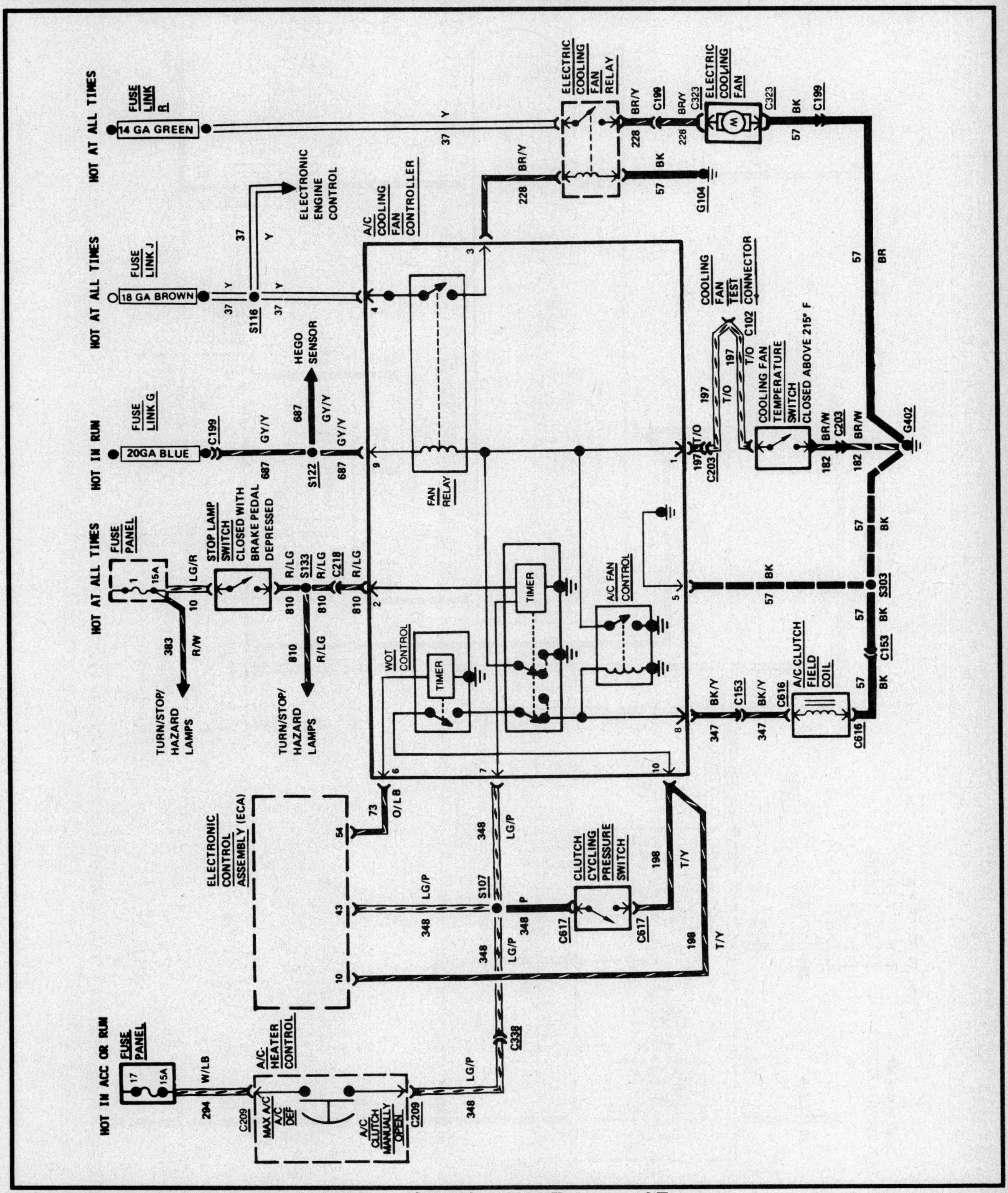
HOT AT ALL TIMES
FUSE LINK R
14 GA GREEN
HOT AT ALL TIMES
FUSE LINK J
18 GA BROWN
HOT IN RUN
FUSE LINK G
20GA BLUE
HOT AT ALL TIMES
FUSE PANEL
STOP LAMP SWITCH CLOSED WITH BRAKE PEDAL DEPRESSED
TURN/STOP/HAZARD LAMPS
ELECTRONIC ENGINE CONTROL
HEGO SENSOR
A/C COOLING FAN CONTROLLER
FAN RELAY
WOT CONTROL
TIMER
A/C FAN CONTROL
ELECTRIC COOLING FAN RELAY
ELECTRIC COOLING FAN
COOLING FAN TEST CONNECTOR
COOLING FAN TEMPERATURE SWITCH CLOSED ABOVE 215° F
A/C CLUTCH FIELD COIL
ELECTRONIC CONTROL ASSEMBLY (ECA)
CLUTCH CYCLING PRESSURE SWITCH
HOT IN ACC OR RUN
A/C-HEATER CONTROL
MAX A/C
A/C
DEF
A/C CLUTCH MANUALLY OPEN

Air conditioning/engine cooling fan wiring schematic – 1989 Tempo and Topaz

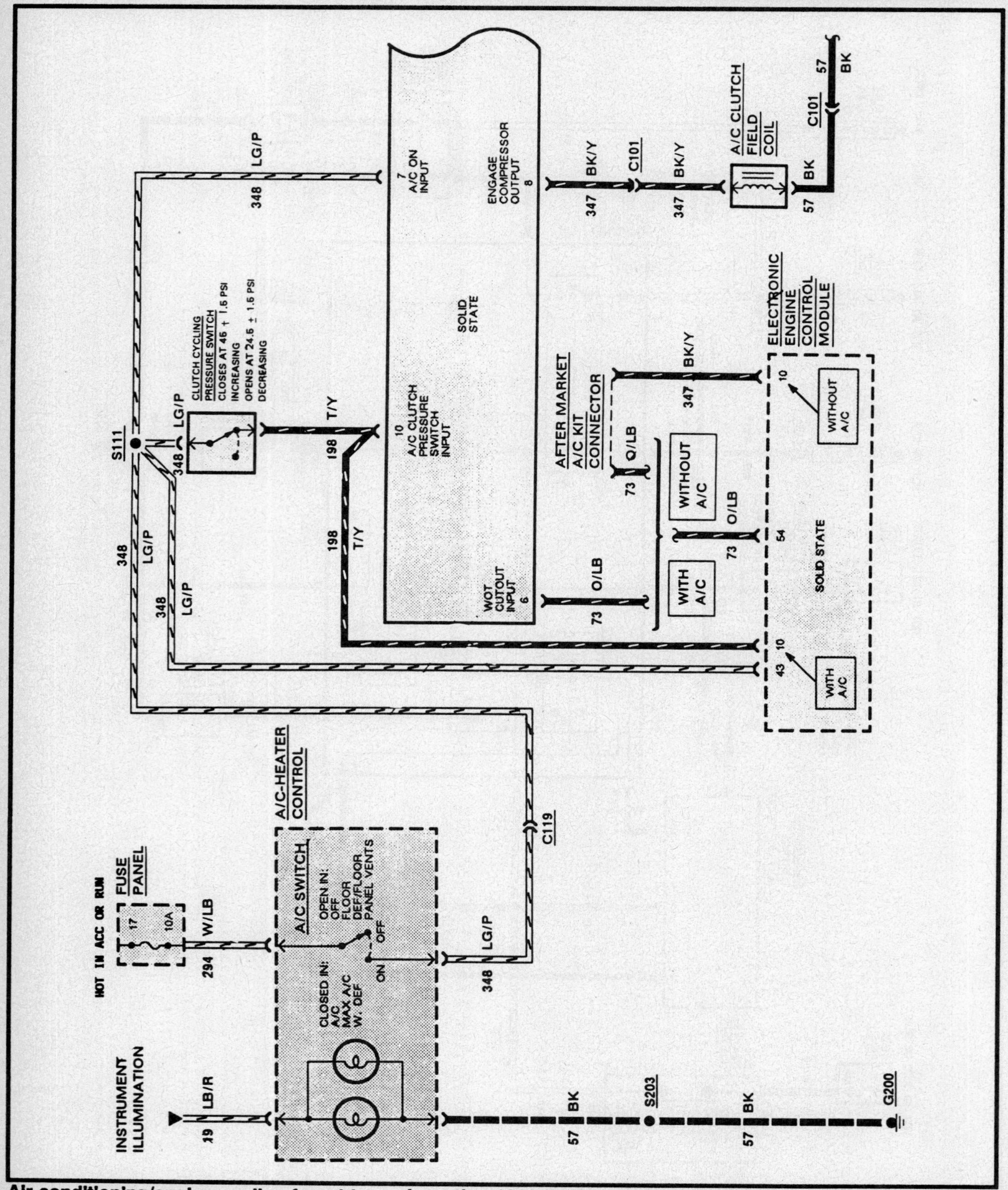
INSTRUMENT ILLUMINATION
HOT IN ACC OR RUN
FUSE PANEL
17
10A
A/C-HEATER CONTROL
A/C SWITCH
OPEN IN: OFF FLOOR DEF/FLOOR PANEL VENTS
CLOSED IN: A/C MAX A/C W. DEF
OFF
ON
19 LB/R
294 W/LB
348 LG/P
C119
57 BK
S203
G200
S111
CLUTCH CYCLING PRESSURE SWITCH
CLOSES AT 46 ± 1.5 PSI INCREASING
OPENS AT 24.5 ± 1.5 PSI DECREASING
198 T/Y
7 A/C ON INPUT
10 A/C CLUTCH PRESSURE SWITCH INPUT
SOLID STATE
ENGAGE COMPRESSOR OUTPUT 8
WOT CUTOUT INPUT 6
347 BK/Y
C101
A/C CLUTCH FIELD COIL
AFTER MARKET A/C KIT CONNECTOR
73 O/LB
WITH A/C
WITHOUT A/C
ELECTRONIC ENGINE CONTROL MODULE
54
43
10

Air conditioning/engine cooling fan wiring schematic—1990–91 Tempo and Topaz

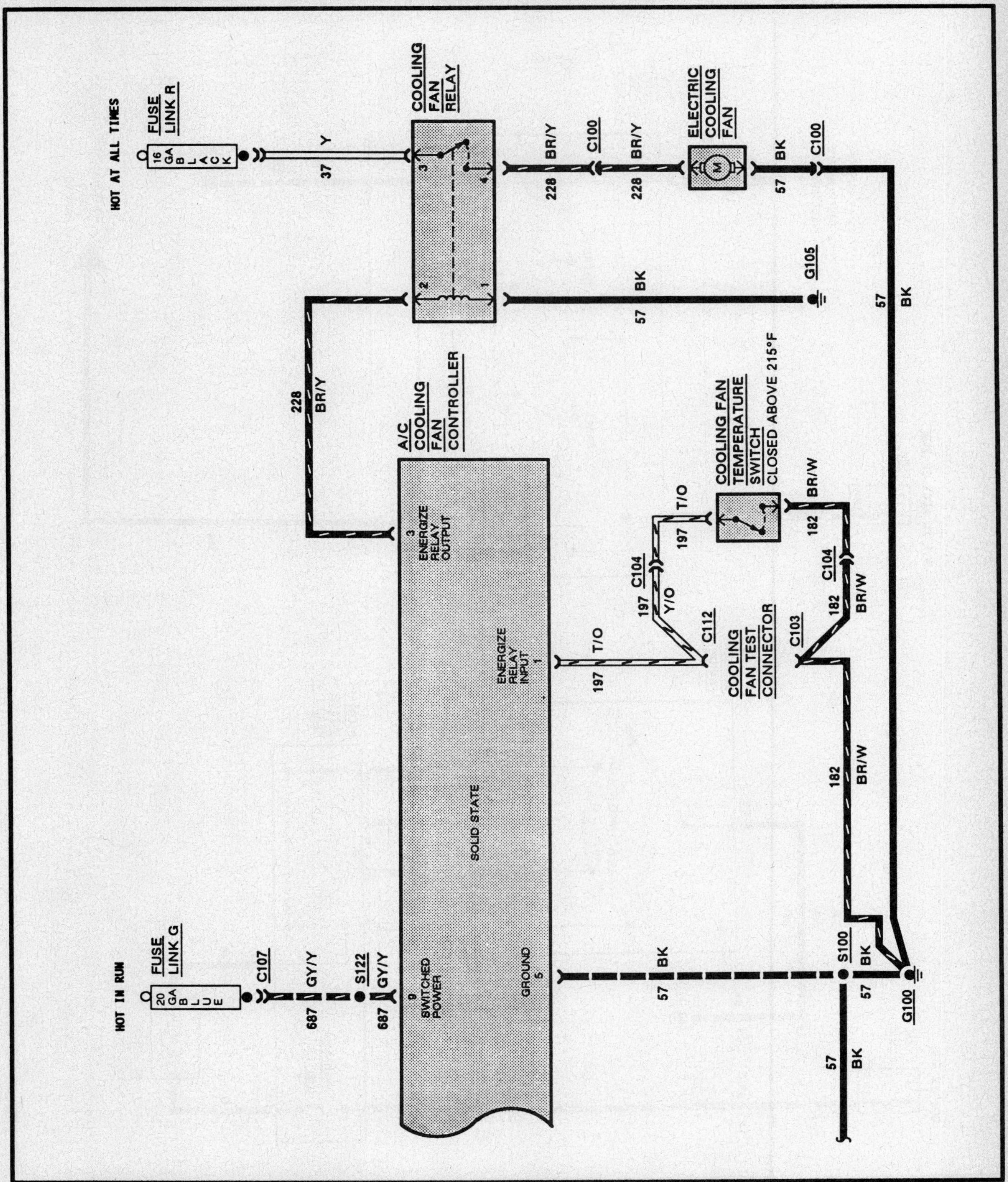
HOT AT ALL TIMES
FUSE LINK R
16 GA BLACK
37
Y
COOLING FAN RELAY
3
4
2
1
228
BR/Y
C100
228
BR/Y
ELECTRIC COOLING FAN
M
57
BK
C100
57
BK
G105
57
BK
228
BR/Y
A/C COOLING FAN CONTROLLER
3 ENERGIZE RELAY OUTPUT
ENERGIZE RELAY INPUT 1
SOLID STATE
GROUND 5
9 SWITCHED POWER
197
T/O
C112
197
Y/O
C104
197
T/O
COOLING FAN TEMPERATURE SWITCH CLOSED ABOVE 215°F
182
BR/W
C104
182
BR/W
C103
COOLING FAN TEST CONNECTOR
182
BR/W
HOT IN RUN
FUSE LINK G
20 GA BLUE
C107
687
GY/Y
S122
687
GY/Y
57
BK
S100
57
BK
G100
57
BK

Air conditioning/engine cooling fan wiring schematic—1990–91 Tempo and Topaz

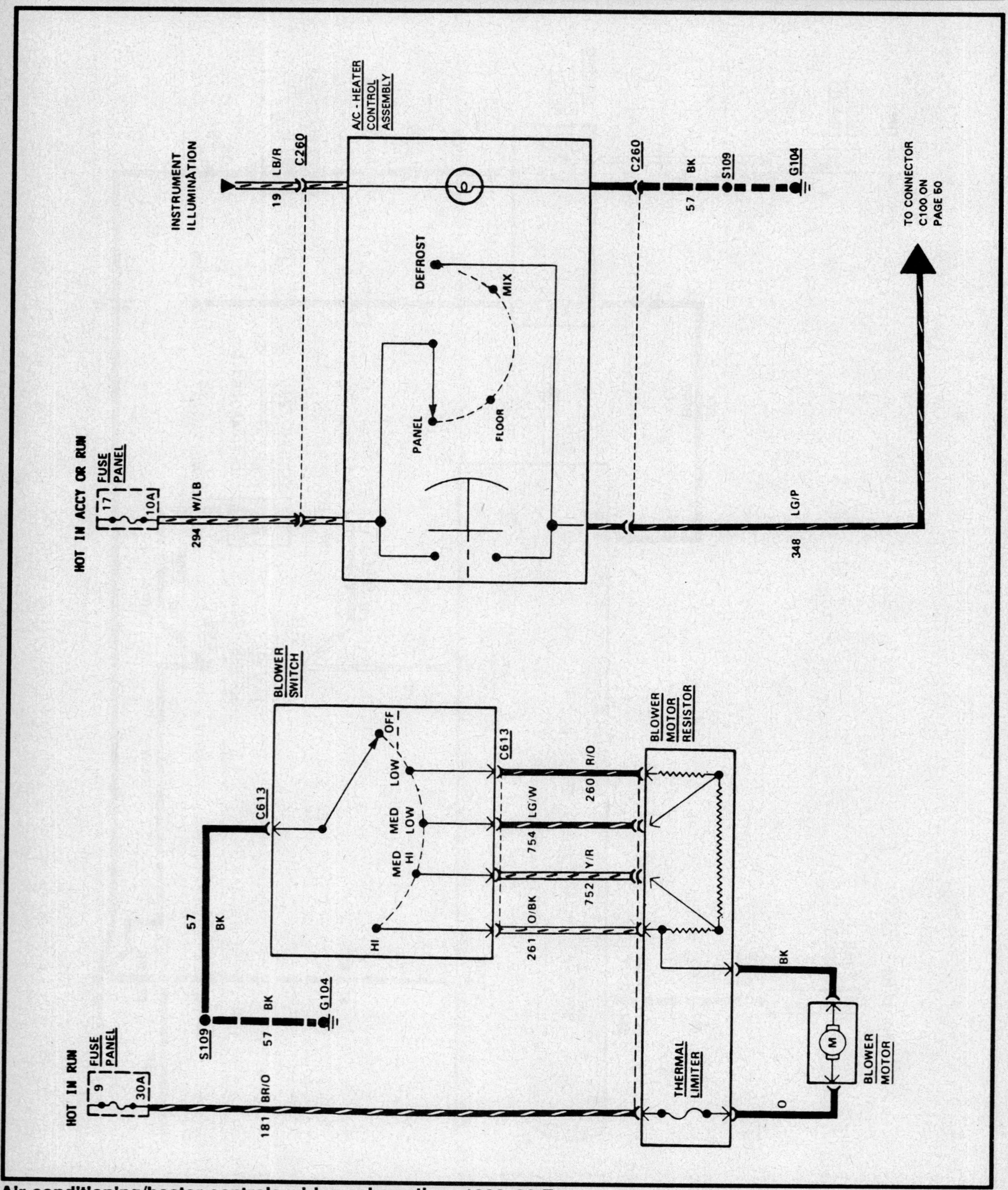
INSTRUMENT ILLUMINATION
19 LB/R
C260
A/C - HEATER CONTROL ASSEMBLY
57 BK
S109
G104
TO CONNECTOR C100 ON PAGE 50
DEFROST
MIX
PANEL
FLOOR
HOT IN ACCY OR RUN
FUSE PANEL
17
10A
294 W/LB
348 LG/P
BLOWER SWITCH
OFF
LOW
MED LOW
MED HI
HI
C613
BLOWER MOTOR RESISTOR
260 R/O
754 LG/W
752 Y/R
261 O/BK
57 BK
HOT IN RUN
9
30A
181 BR/O
THERMAL LIMITER
BK
O
M
BLOWER MOTOR

Air conditioning/heater controls wiring schematic— 1989–90 Escort

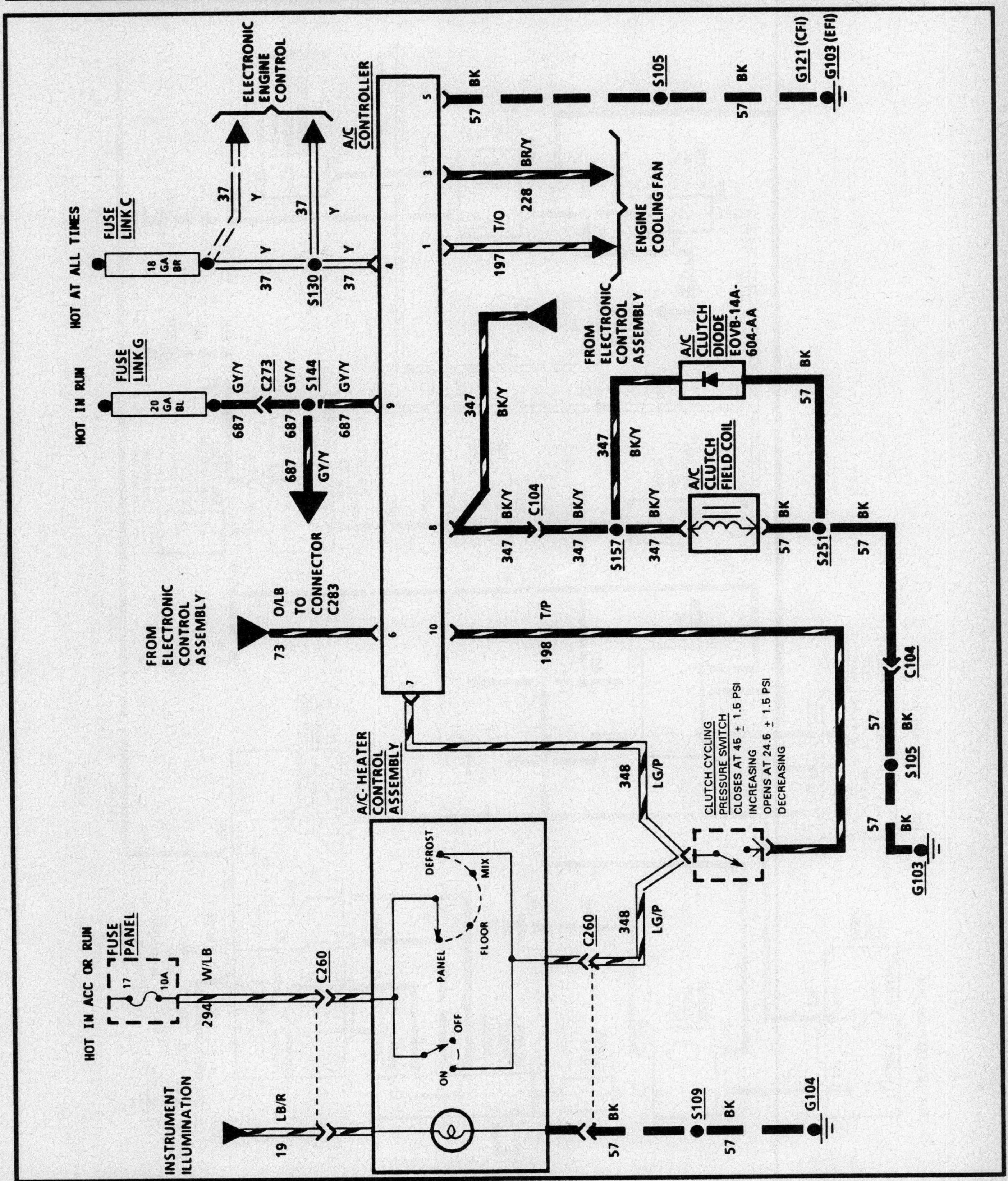
HOT AT ALL TIMES
FUSE LINK C
18 GA BR
HOT IN RUN
FUSE LINK G
20 GA BL
ELECTRONIC ENGINE CONTROL
A/C CONTROLLER
ENGINE COOLING FAN
FROM ELECTRONIC CONTROL ASSEMBLY
TO CONNECTOR C283
A/C CLUTCH DIODE EOVB-14A-604-AA
A/C CLUTCH FIELD COIL
CLUTCH CYCLING PRESSURE SWITCH
CLOSES AT 45 ± 1.5 PSI INCREASING
OPENS AT 24.5 ± 1.5 PSI DECREASING
A/C-HEATER CONTROL ASSEMBLY
HOT IN ACC OR RUN
FUSE PANEL
INSTRUMENT ILLUMINATION
DEFROST
MIX
FLOOR
PANEL
OFF
ON
S105
S130
S144
S157
S251
S109
C273
C104
C260
G121 (CFI)
G103 (EFI)
G103
G104

Air conditioning/engine cooling fan wiring schematic—1989–90 Escort

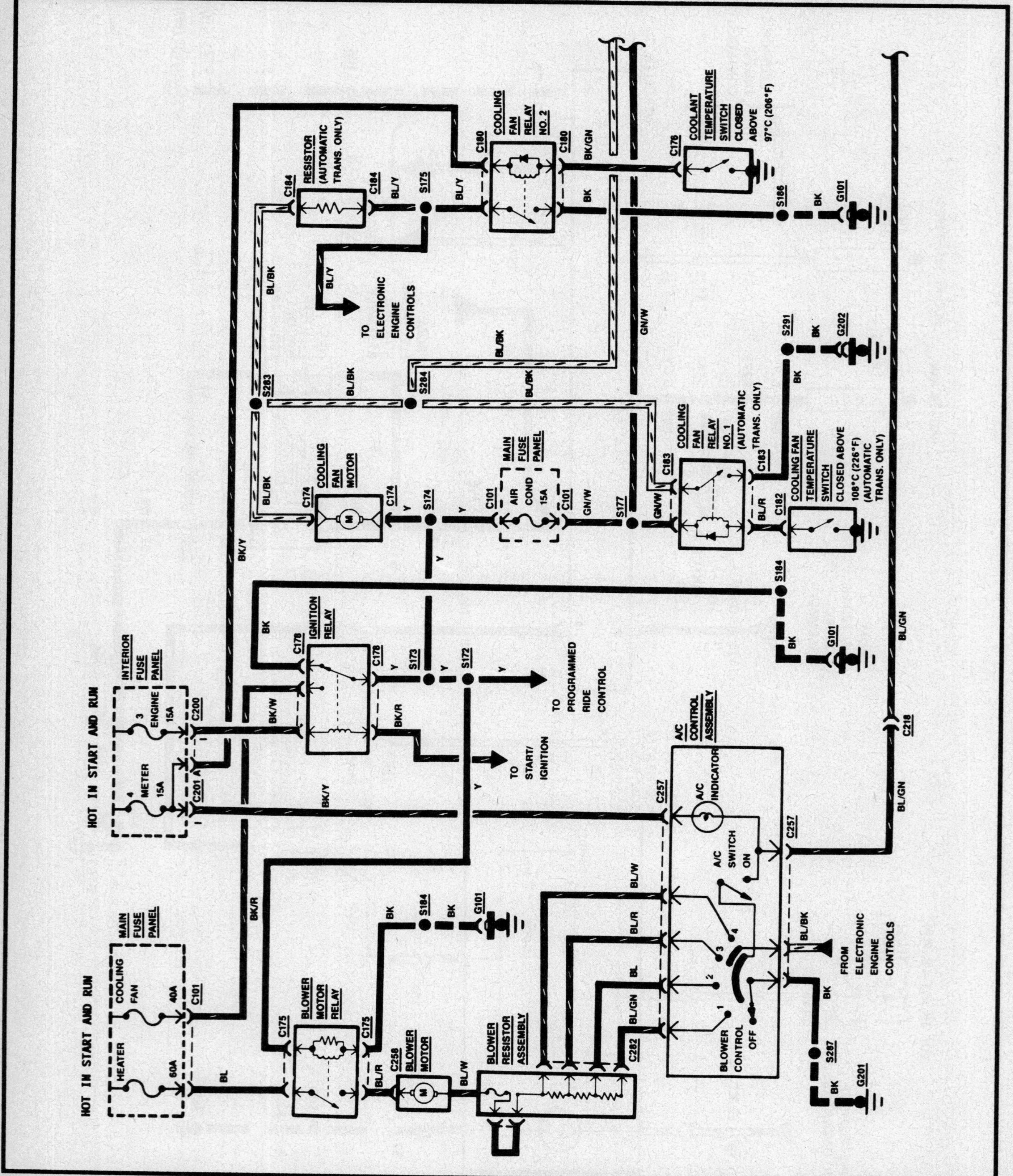
HOT IN START AND RUN
INTERIOR FUSE PANEL
3 ENGINE 15A
4 METER 15A
C200
C201
HOT IN START AND RUN
MAIN FUSE PANEL
COOLING FAN 40A
HEATER 60A
C101
IGNITION RELAY
C178
TO PROGRAMMED RIDE CONTROL
TO START/IGNITION
BLOWER MOTOR RELAY
C175
BLOWER MOTOR
C258
BLOWER RESISTOR ASSEMBLY
C282
A/C CONTROL ASSEMBLY
A/C INDICATOR
A/C SWITCH ON
BLOWER CONTROL OFF
C257
C218
FROM ELECTRONIC ENGINE CONTROLS
S287
G201
S184
G101
COOLING FAN MOTOR
C174
S174
S173
S172
MAIN FUSE PANEL
AIR COND 15A
S177
COOLING FAN RELAY NO. 1 (AUTOMATIC TRANS. ONLY)
C183
C182
COOLING FAN TEMPERATURE SWITCH CLOSED ABOVE 108°C (226°F) (AUTOMATIC TRANS. ONLY)
S291
G202
S283
S284
RESISTOR (AUTOMATIC TRANS. ONLY)
C184
S175
TO ELECTRONIC ENGINE CONTROLS
COOLING FAN RELAY NO. 2
C180
COOLANT TEMPERATURE SWITCH CLOSED ABOVE 97°C (206°F)
C176
S186
BK/Y
BL/BK
BL/Y
GN/W
BK/GN
BL/GN
BK/W
BK/R
BL/R
BL/W
BL
BK
Y

Manual air conditioning/heater/engine cooling fan wiring schematic—1989 Probe

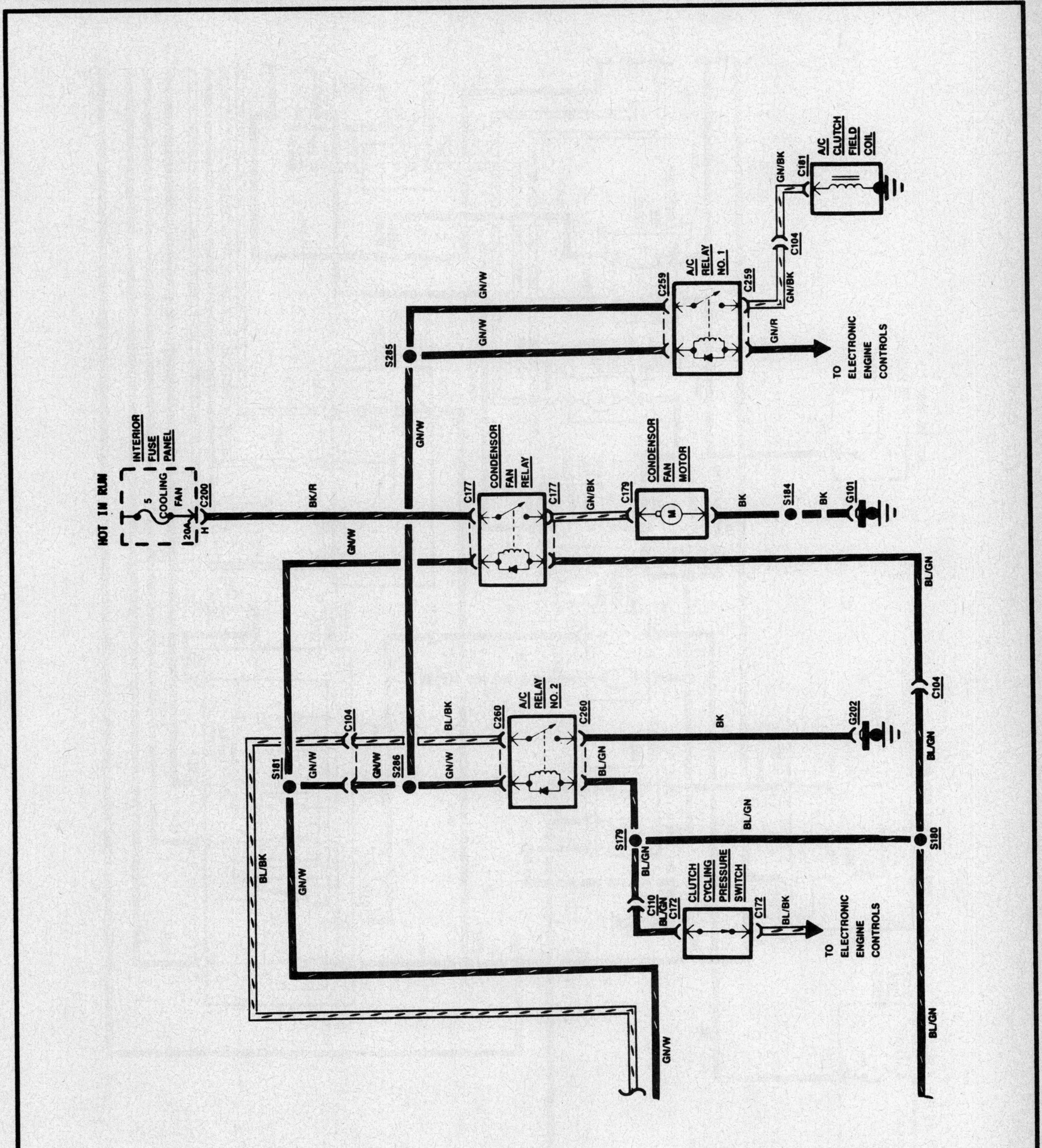
HOT IN RUN
INTERIOR FUSE PANEL
5 COOLING FAN 20A
C200
BK/R
CONDENSOR FAN RELAY
C177
GN/BK
C179
CONDENSOR FAN MOTOR
BK
S184
G101
GN/W
S285
C259
A/C RELAY NO. 1
GN/R
TO ELECTRONIC ENGINE CONTROLS
C104
C181
A/C CLUTCH FIELD COIL
BL/GN
BL/BK
A/C RELAY NO. 2
C260
S181
S286
G202
S179
S180
CLUTCH CYCLING PRESSURE SWITCH
C110
C172

Manual air conditioning/heater/engine cooling fan wiring schematic—1989 Probe

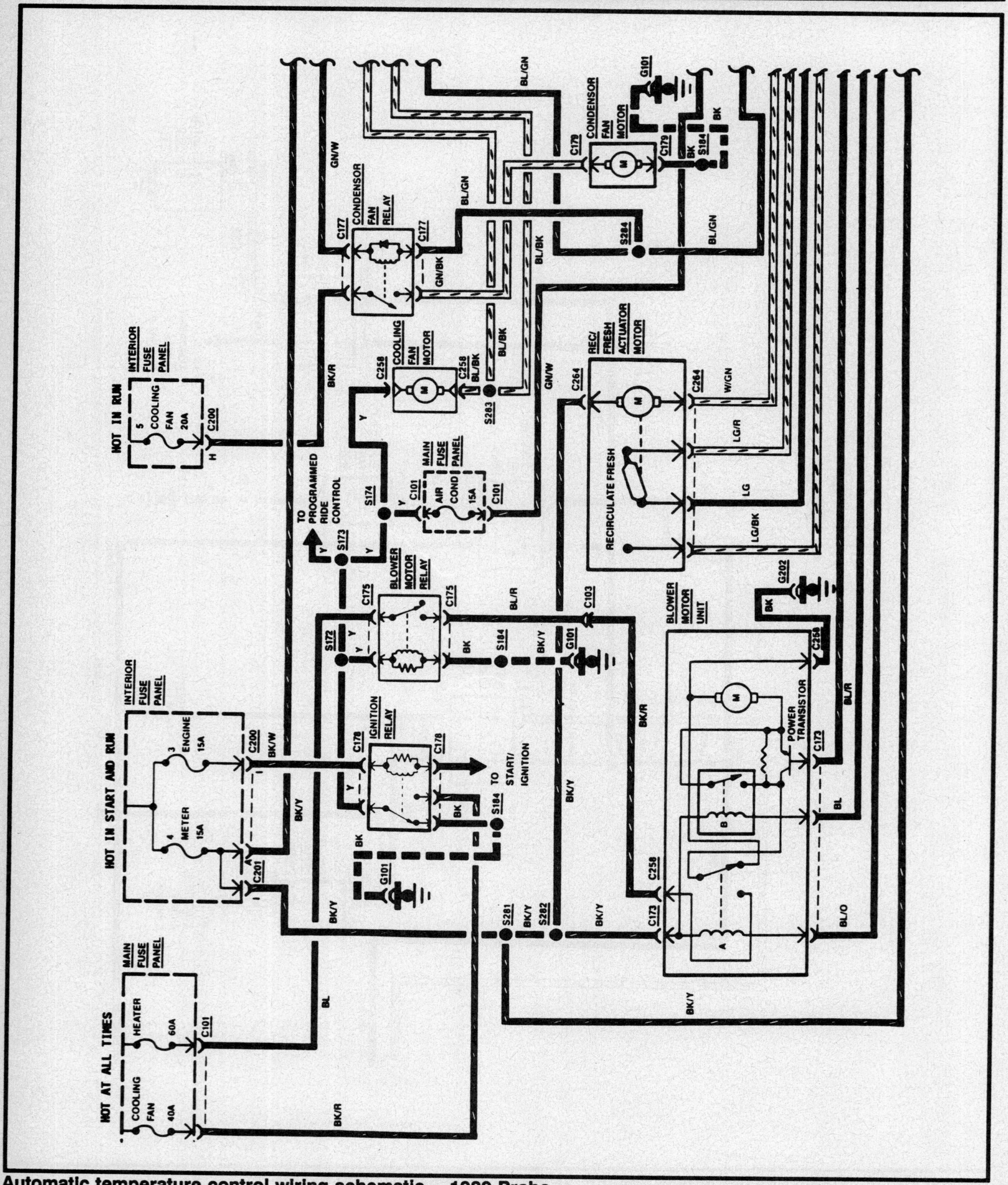
HOT IN RUN
INTERIOR FUSE PANEL
5 COOLING FAN 20A
C200
HOT IN START AND RUN
3 ENGINE 15A
4 METER 15A
C201
HOT AT ALL TIMES
MAIN FUSE PANEL
HEATER 60A
COOLING FAN 40A
C101
TO PROGRAMMED RIDE CONTROL
CONDENSOR FAN RELAY
C177
COOLING FAN MOTOR
C258
MAIN FUSE PANEL
AIR COND 15A
BLOWER MOTOR RELAY
C175
IGNITION RELAY
C178
TO START/ IGNITION
CONDENSOR FAN MOTOR
C179
G101
S184
S284
REC/ FRESH ACTUATOR MOTOR
C264
RECIRCULATE FRESH
C103
G202
BLOWER MOTOR UNIT
POWER TRANSISTOR
C254
C173
S172
S173
S174
S281
S282
S283
BK/R
BK/W
BK/Y
GN/W
GN/BK
BL/GN
BL/BK
BL/R
BL/O
BL
BK
Y
W/GN
LG/R
LG
LG/BK

Automatic temperature control wiring schematic — 1989 Probe

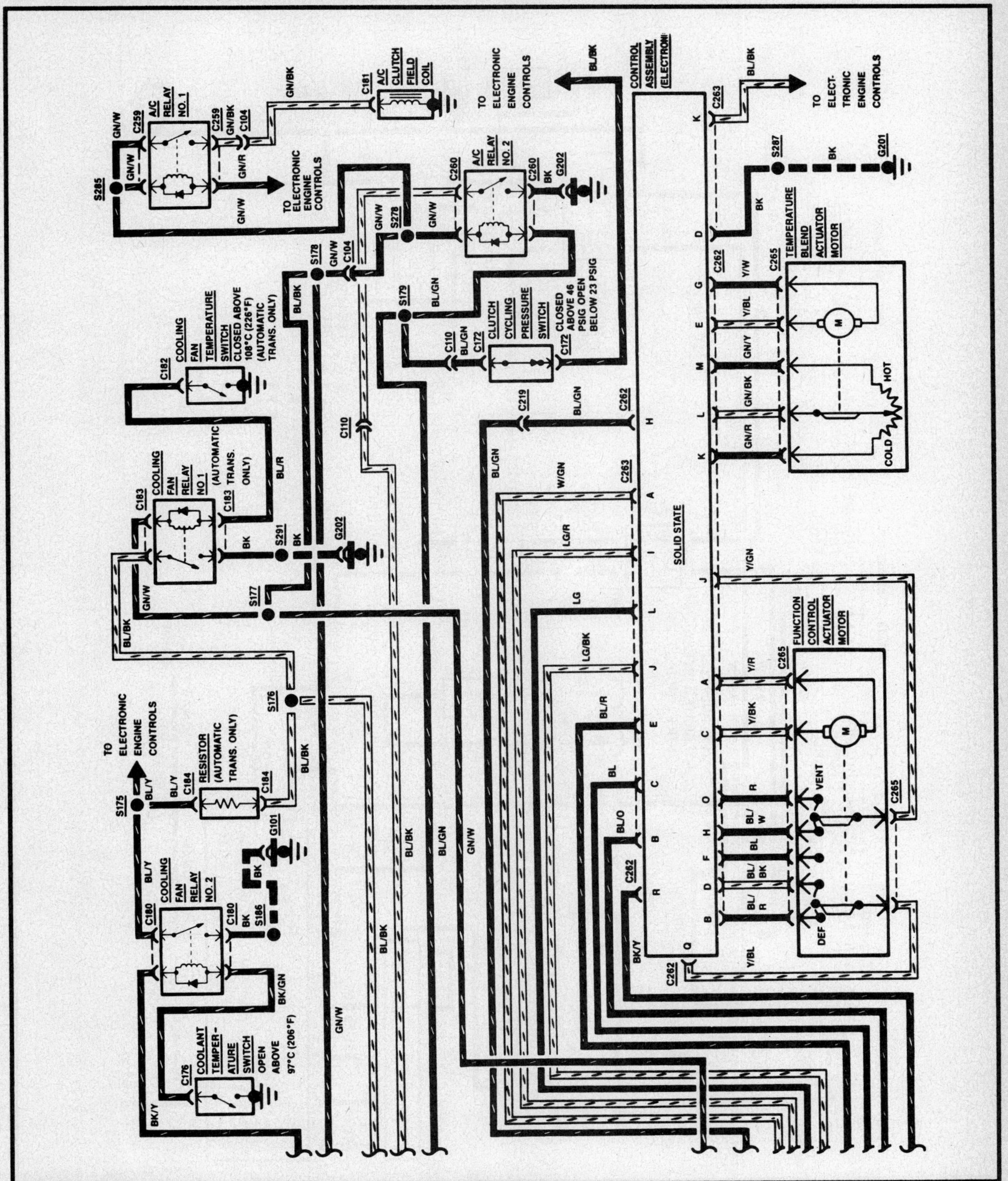
A/C RELAY NO. 1
A/C CLUTCH FIELD COIL
TO ELECTRONIC ENGINE CONTROLS
A/C RELAY NO. 2
CONTROL ASSEMBLY (ELECTRONIC)
TO ELECT-TRONIC ENGINE CONTROLS
COOLING FAN TEMPERATURE SWITCH CLOSED ABOVE 108°C (226°F) (AUTOMATIC TRANS. ONLY)
CLUTCH CYCLING PRESSURE SWITCH
CLOSED ABOVE 46 PSIG OPEN BELOW 23 PSIG
TEMPERATURE BLEND ACTUATOR MOTOR
HOT
COLD
COOLING FAN RELAY NO 1 (AUTOMATIC TRANS. ONLY)
SOLID STATE
FUNCTION CONTROL ACTUATOR MOTOR
VENT
DEF
RESISTOR (AUTOMATIC TRANS. ONLY)
COOLING FAN RELAY NO. 2
COOLANT TEMPER-ATURE SWITCH OPEN ABOVE 97°C (206°F)

Automatic temperature control wiring schematic— 1989 Probe

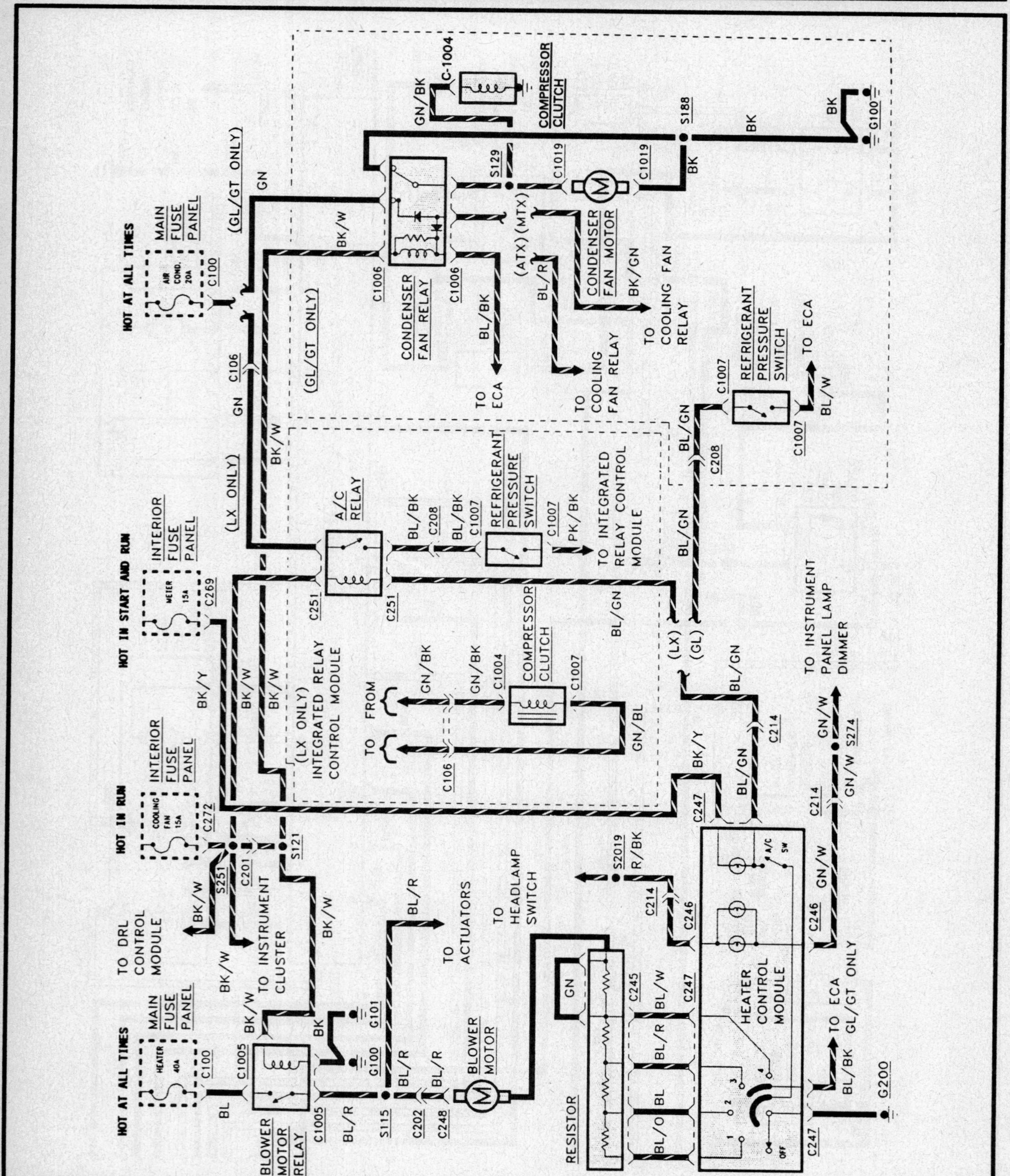
HOT AT ALL TIMES
MAIN FUSE PANEL
HOT IN RUN
INTERIOR FUSE PANEL
HOT IN START AND RUN
HOT AT ALL TIMES
BLOWER MOTOR RELAY
BLOWER MOTOR
TO ACTUATORS
TO HEADLAMP SWITCH
RESISTOR
HEATER CONTROL MODULE
TO ECA GL/GT ONLY
TO INSTRUMENT PANEL LAMP DIMMER
TO DRL CONTROL MODULE
TO INSTRUMENT CLUSTER
(LX ONLY) INTEGRATED RELAY CONTROL MODULE
A/C RELAY
REFRIGERANT PRESSURE SWITCH
TO INTEGRATED RELAY CONTROL MODULE
COMPRESSOR CLUTCH
CONDENSER FAN RELAY
CONDENSER FAN MOTOR
TO COOLING FAN RELAY
TO ECA

Manual air conditioning/heater wiring schematic — 1990–91 Probe

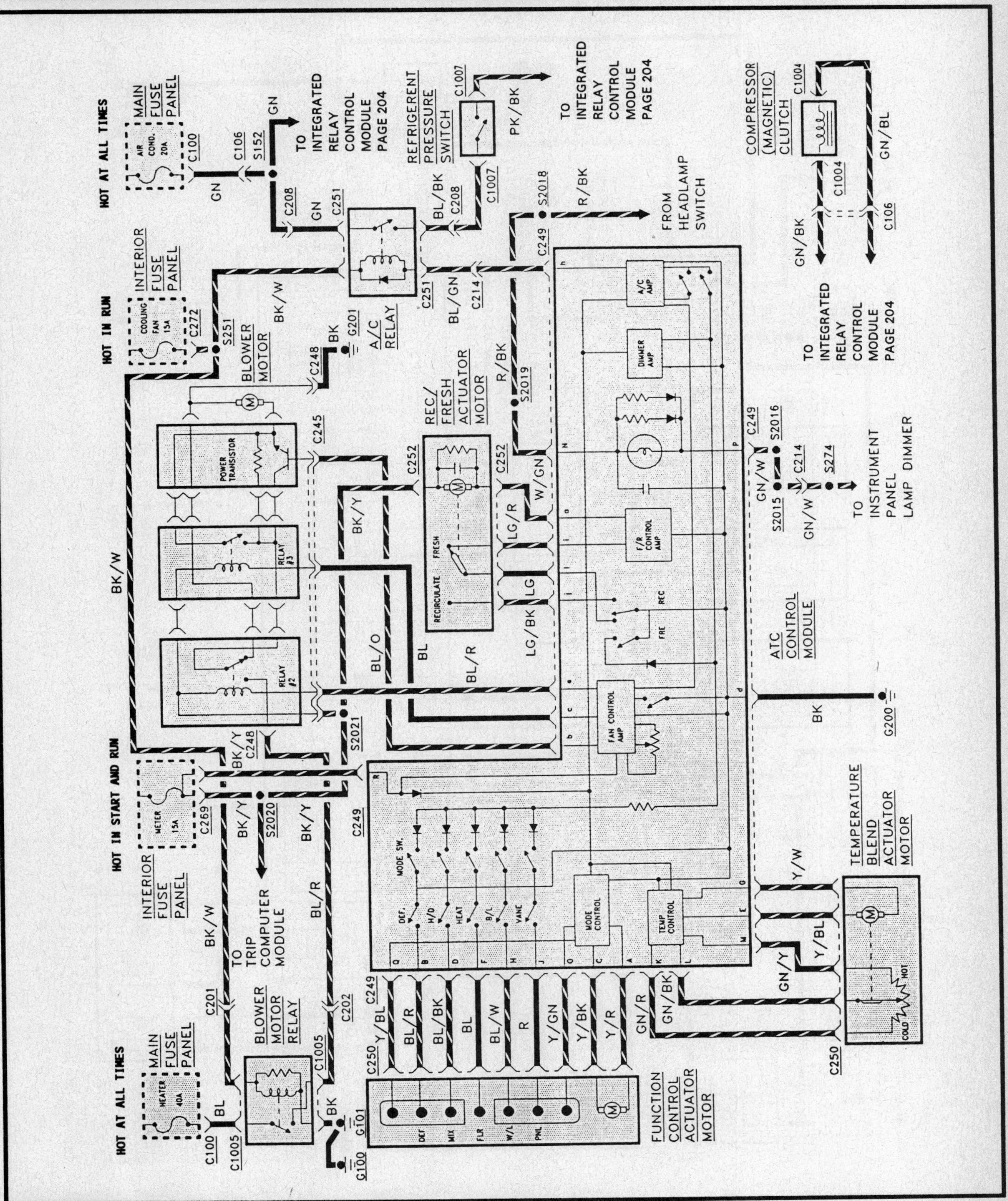
HOT AT ALL TIMES
MAIN FUSE PANEL
HEATER 40A
HOT IN START AND RUN
INTERIOR FUSE PANEL
METER 15A
HOT IN RUN
COOLING FAN 15A
AIR COND. 20A
BLOWER MOTOR RELAY
BLOWER MOTOR
POWER TRANSISTOR
RELAY #3
RELAY #2
A/C RELAY
REFRIGERENT PRESSURE SWITCH
TO INTEGRATED RELAY CONTROL MODULE PAGE 204
COMPRESSOR (MAGNETIC) CLUTCH
FROM HEADLAMP SWITCH
REC/FRESH ACTUATOR MOTOR
ATC CONTROL MODULE
TO INSTRUMENT PANEL LAMP DIMMER
TO TRIP COMPUTER MODULE
FUNCTION CONTROL ACTUATOR MOTOR
TEMPERATURE BLEND ACTUATOR MOTOR

Automatic temperature control wiring schematic — 1990–91 Probe LX

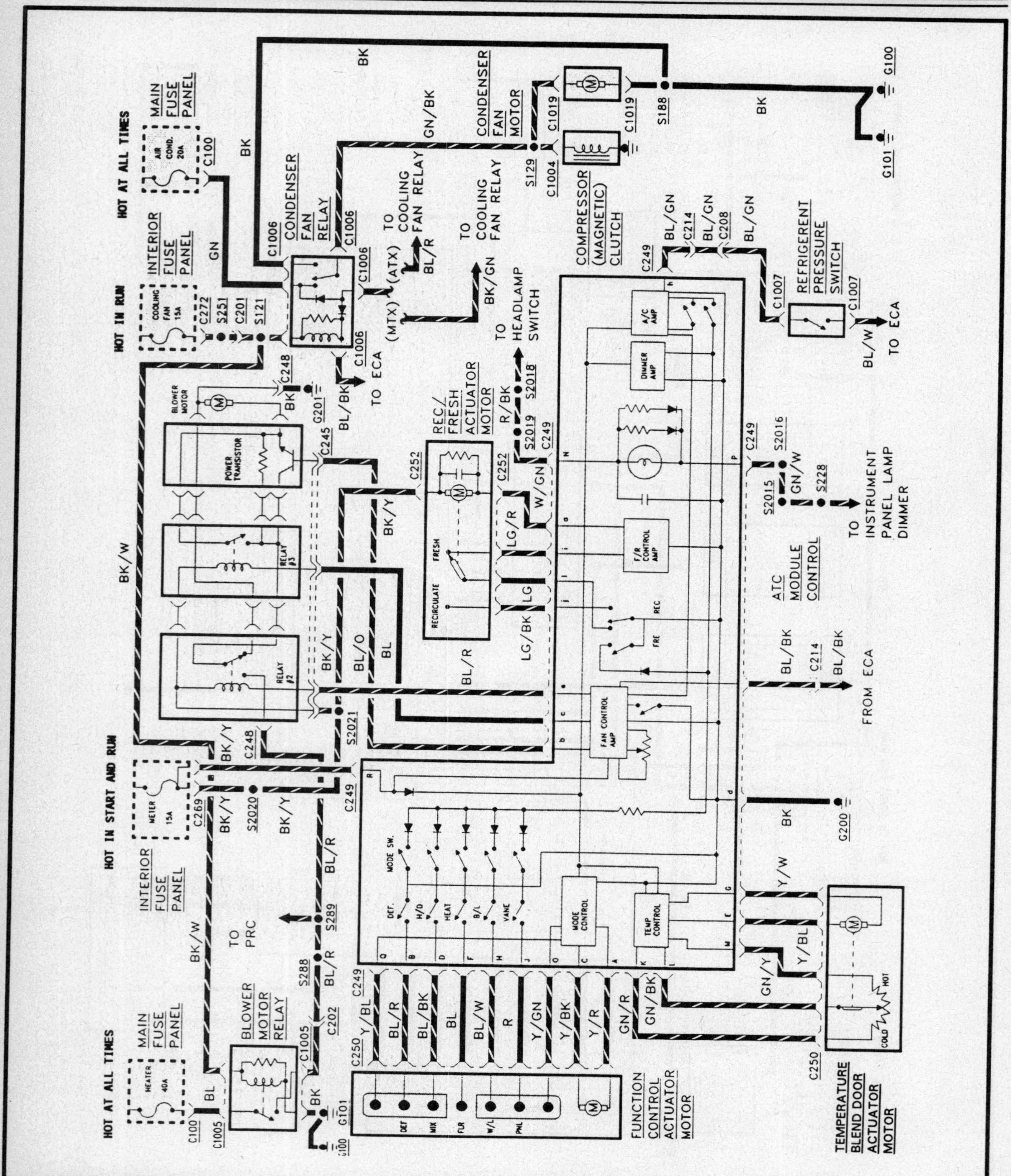
HOT AT ALL TIMES
MAIN FUSE PANEL
AIR COND. 20A
C100
BK
HOT IN RUN
COOLING FAN 15A
INTERIOR FUSE PANEL
C272
S251
C201
S121
GN
C1006
CONDENSER FAN RELAY
TO COOLING FAN RELAY
(ATX)
(MTX)
BL/R
BK/GN
GN/BK
TO COOLING FAN RELAY
CONDENSER FAN MOTOR
C1019
S188
G100
G101
S129
C1004
COMPRESSOR (MAGNETIC CLUTCH)
TO HEADLAMP SWITCH
TO ECA
BL/BK
BLOWER MOTOR
C248
G201
POWER TRANSISTOR
C245
C252
REC/FRESH ACTUATOR MOTOR
R/BK
S2018
S2019
C249
W/GN
FRESH
RECIRCULATE
RELAY #3
RELAY #2
BK/W
BK/Y
BL/O
BL
LG/R
LG
LG/BK
A/C AMP
DIMMER AMP
F/R CONTROL AMP
REC
FRE
FAN CONTROL AMP
BL/GN
C214
C208
C1007
REFRIGERENT PRESSURE SWITCH
BL/W
TO ECA
C249
S2016
S2015
GN/W
S228
TO INSTRUMENT PANEL LAMP DIMMER
ATC MODULE CONTROL
BL/BK
C214
FROM ECA
S2021
HOT IN START AND RUN
METER 15A
C269
S2020
INTERIOR FUSE PANEL
BL/R
TO PRC
S289
S288
MODE SW.
DEF.
H/D
HEAT
B/L
VANE
MODE CONTROL
TEMP CONTROL
BK
G200
Y/W
Y/BL
GN/Y
GN/BK
GN/R
Y/R
Y/BK
Y/GN
R
BL/W
BL/BK
C250
C202
C1005
BLOWER MOTOR RELAY
HOT AT ALL TIMES
MAIN FUSE PANEL
HEATER 40A
C100
C1005
G101
G100
DEF
MIX
FLR
W/L
PNL
FUNCTION CONTROL ACTUATOR MOTOR
HOT
COLD
TEMPERATURE BLEND DOOR ACTUATOR MOTOR

Automatic temperature control wiring schematic – 1990–91 Probe GT

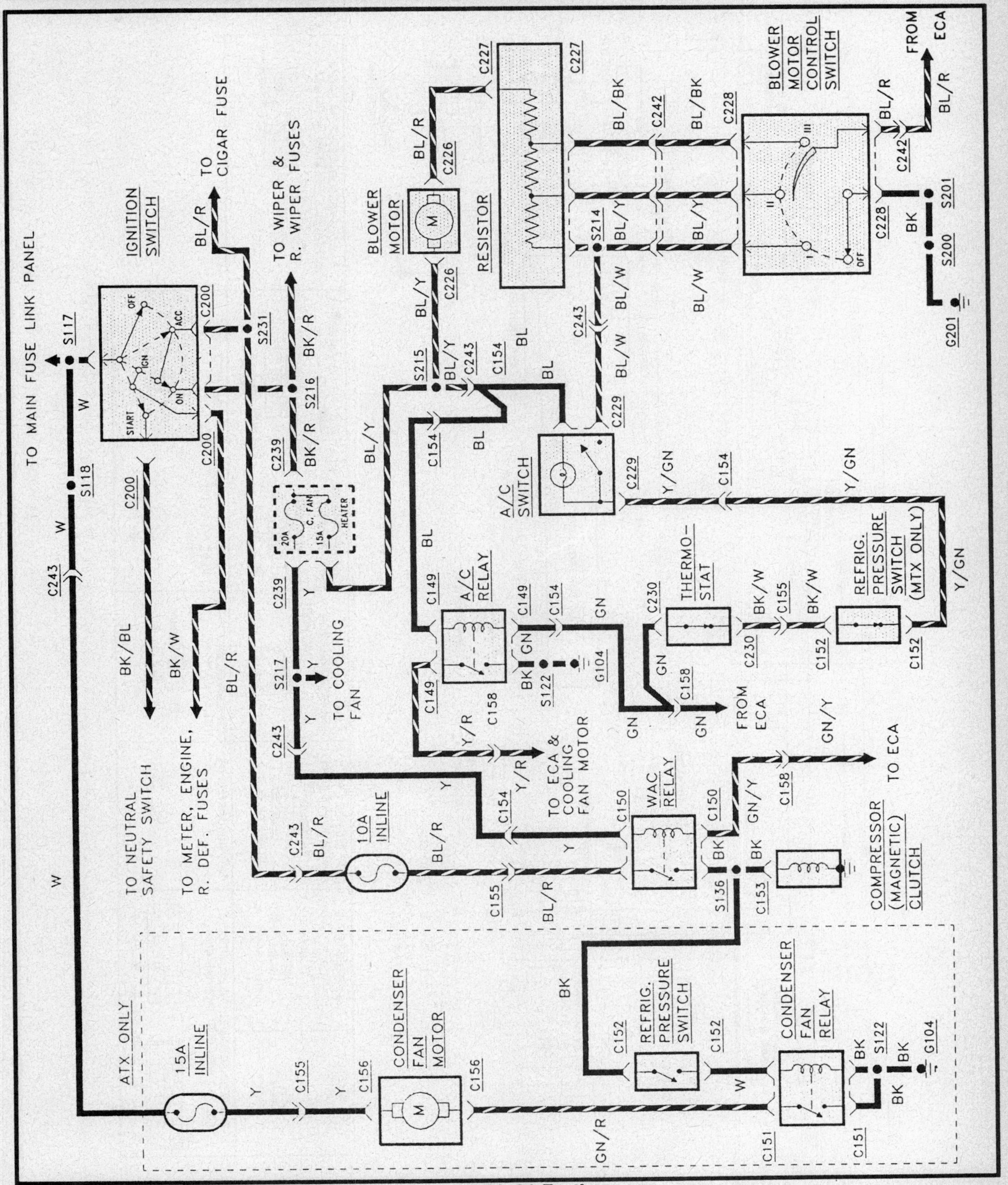
TO MAIN FUSE LINK PANEL
IGNITION SWITCH
TO CIGAR FUSE
TO WIPER & R. WIPER FUSES
BLOWER MOTOR
RESISTOR
BLOWER MOTOR CONTROL SWITCH
FROM ECA
A/C SWITCH
TO NEUTRAL SAFETY SWITCH
TO METER, ENGINE, R. DEF. FUSES
TO COOLING FAN
A/C RELAY
THERMO-STAT
REFRIG. PRESSURE SWITCH (MTX ONLY)
FROM ECA
TO ECA & COOLING FAN MOTOR
10A INLINE
WAC RELAY
TO ECA
COMPRESSOR (MAGNETIC CLUTCH)
ATX ONLY
15A INLINE
CONDENSER FAN MOTOR
REFRIG. PRESSURE SWITCH
CONDENSER FAN RELAY

Air conditioning/heater system wiring schematic – 1990–91 Festiva

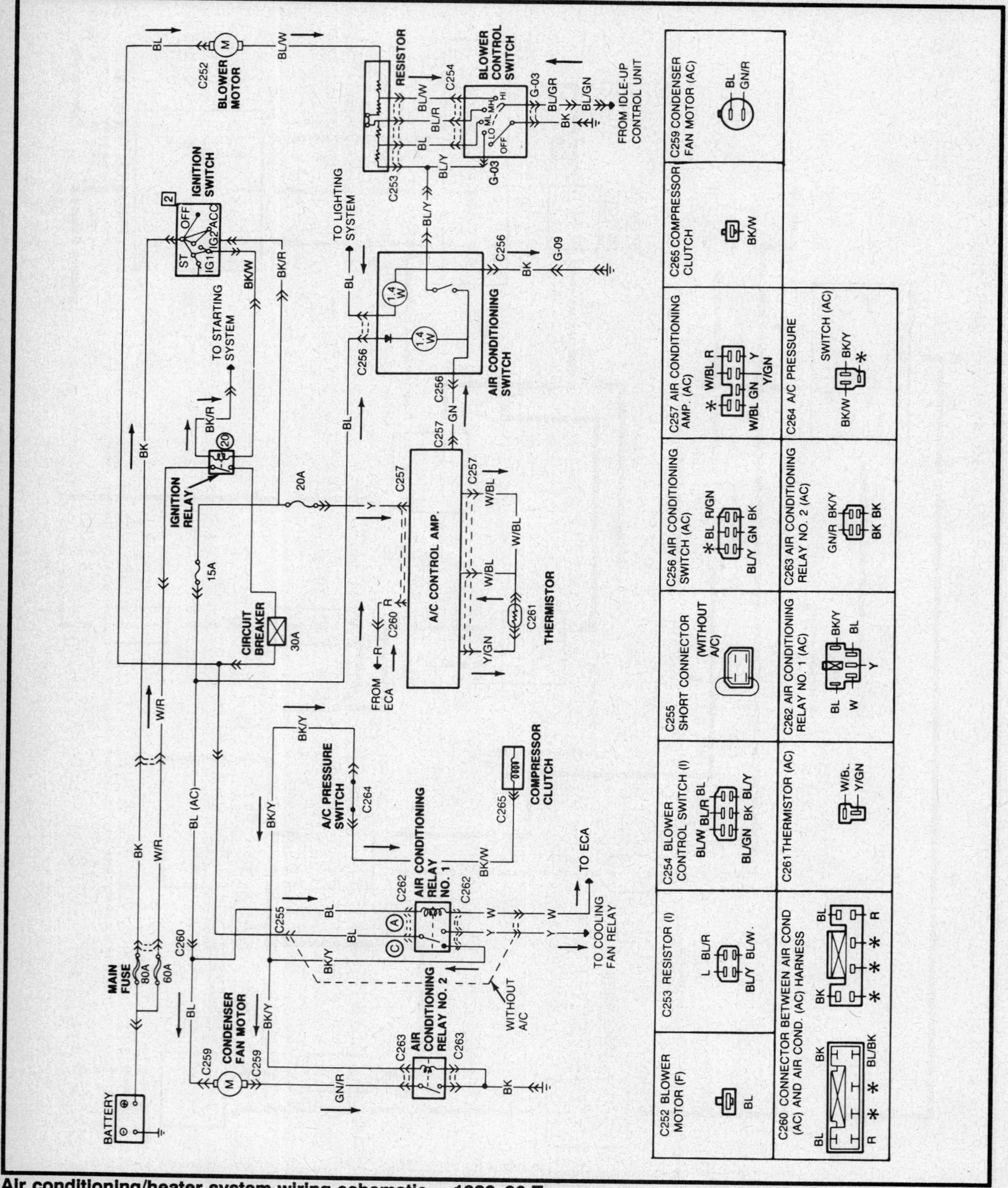
BATTERY
MAIN FUSE
80A
60A
CONDENSER FAN MOTOR
C259
AIR CONDITIONING RELAY NO. 2
C263
AIR CONDITIONING RELAY NO. 1
C262
C255
C260
WITHOUT A/C
TO COOLING FAN RELAY
TO ECA
A/C PRESSURE SWITCH
C264
COMPRESSOR CLUTCH
C265
CIRCUIT BREAKER
30A
15A
20A
IGNITION RELAY
TO STARTING SYSTEM
IGNITION SWITCH
FROM ECA
A/C CONTROL AMP.
C257
C261
THERMISTOR
AIR CONDITIONING SWITCH
C256
TO LIGHTING SYSTEM
G-09
C253
RESISTOR
C254
BLOWER CONTROL SWITCH
G-03
FROM IDLE-UP CONTROL UNIT
BLOWER MOTOR
C252
C252 BLOWER MOTOR (F)
C253 RESISTOR (I)
C254 BLOWER CONTROL SWITCH (I)
C255 SHORT CONNECTOR (WITHOUT A/C)
C256 AIR CONDITIONING SWITCH (AC)
C257 AIR CONDITIONING AMP. (AC)
C265 COMPRESSOR CLUTCH
C259 CONDENSER FAN MOTOR (AC)
C260 CONNECTOR BETWEEN AIR COND (AC) AND AIR COND. (AC) HARNESS
C261 THERMISTOR (AC)
C262 AIR CONDITIONING RELAY NO. 1 (AC)
C263 AIR CONDITIONING RELAY NO. 2 (AC)
C264 A/C PRESSURE SWITCH (AC)

Air conditioning/heater system wiring schematic – 1989–90 Tracer

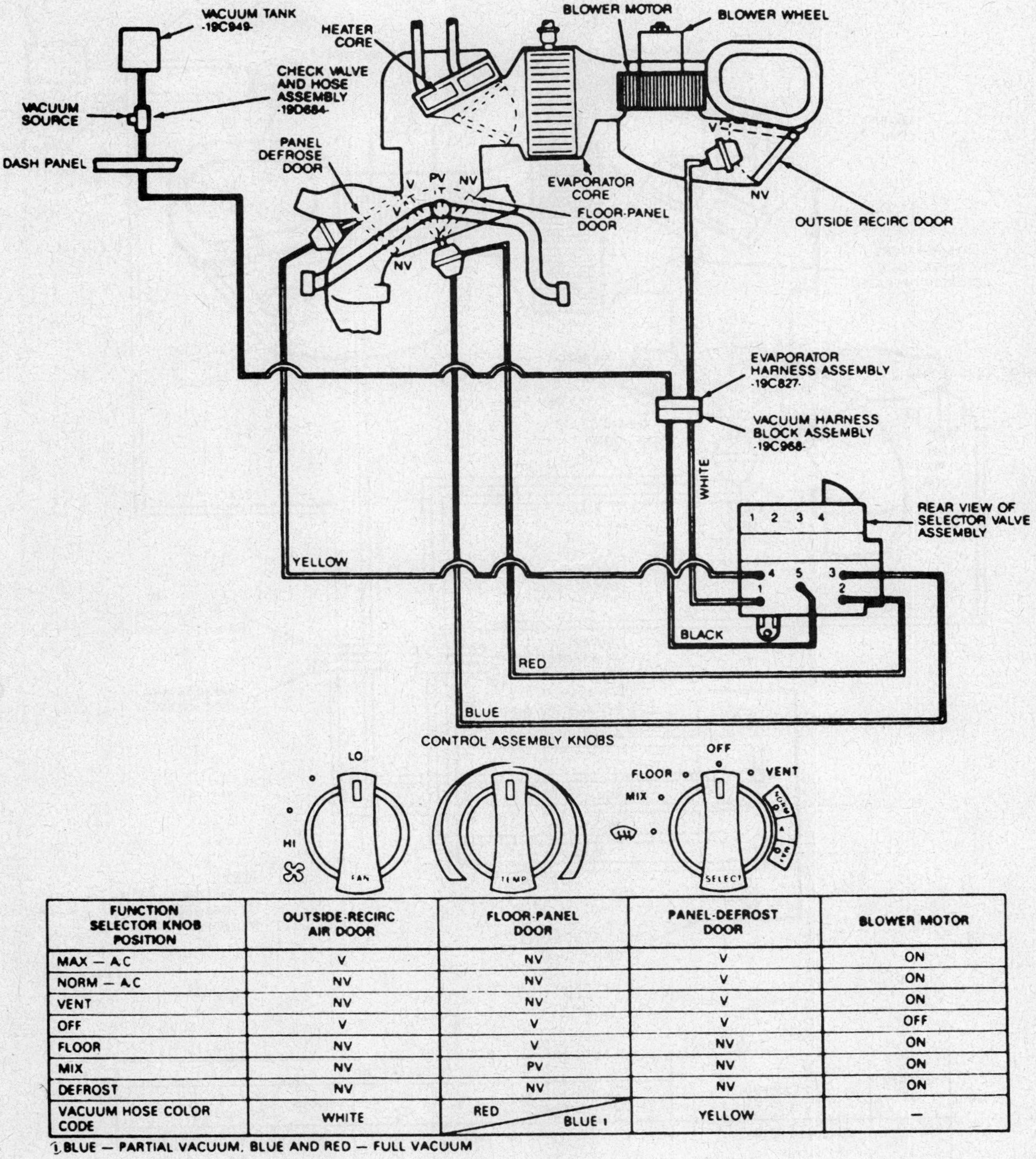
VACUUM TANK
-19C949-
HEATER CORE
CHECK VALVE AND HOSE ASSEMBLY
-19D684-
VACUUM SOURCE
DASH PANEL
PANEL DEFROSE DOOR
V
PV
NV
BLOWER MOTOR
BLOWER WHEEL
EVAPORATOR CORE
FLOOR-PANEL DOOR
OUTSIDE RECIRC DOOR
EVAPORATOR HARNESS ASSEMBLY
-19C827-
VACUUM HARNESS BLOCK ASSEMBLY
-19C968-
WHITE
REAR VIEW OF SELECTOR VALVE ASSEMBLY
1 2 3 4
YELLOW
BLACK
RED
BLUE
CONTROL ASSEMBLY KNOBS
LO
HI
FAN
TEMP
OFF
FLOOR
VENT
MIX
SELECT

FUNCTION SELECTOR KNOB POSITION	OUTSIDE-RECIRC AIR DOOR	FLOOR-PANEL DOOR	PANEL-DEFROST DOOR	BLOWER MOTOR
MAX — A.C	V	NV	V	ON
NORM — A.C	NV	NV	V	ON
VENT	NV	NV	V	ON
OFF	V	V	V	OFF
FLOOR	NV	V	NV	ON
MIX	NV	PV	NV	ON
DEFROST	NV	NV	NV	ON
VACUUM HOSE COLOR CODE	WHITE	RED / BLUE 1	YELLOW	—

1 BLUE — PARTIAL VACUUM. BLUE AND RED — FULL VACUUM

Manual air conditioning vacuum schematic—Taurus and Sable

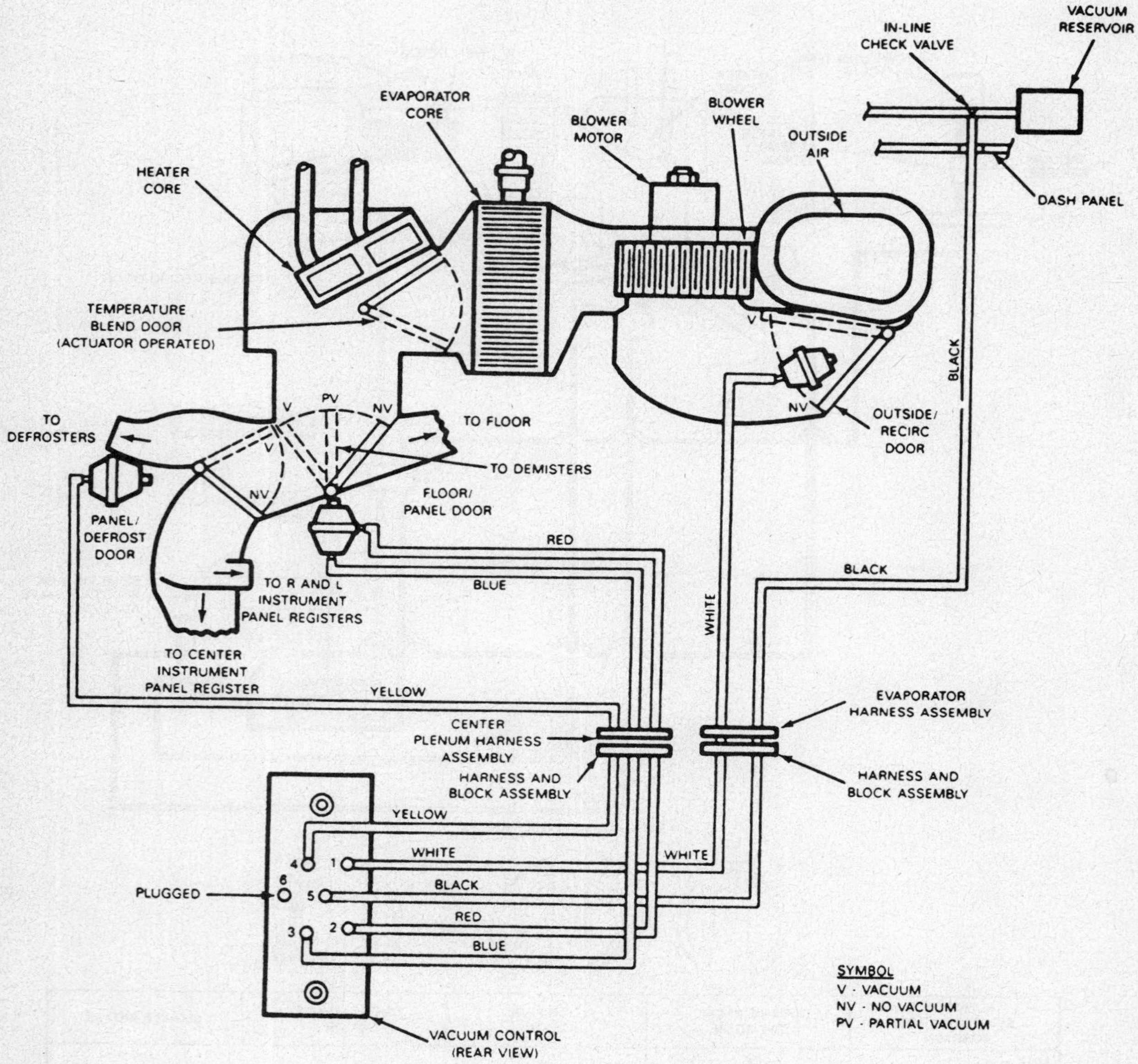
VACUUM RESERVOIR
IN-LINE CHECK VALVE
DASH PANEL
EVAPORATOR CORE
BLOWER MOTOR
BLOWER WHEEL
OUTSIDE AIR
HEATER CORE
TEMPERATURE BLEND DOOR (ACTUATOR OPERATED)
V
PV
NV
TO DEFROSTERS
TO FLOOR
TO DEMISTERS
FLOOR/ PANEL DOOR
OUTSIDE/ RECIRC DOOR
BLACK
PANEL/ DEFROST DOOR
RED
BLUE
TO R AND L INSTRUMENT PANEL REGISTERS
TO CENTER INSTRUMENT PANEL REGISTER
WHITE
YELLOW
CENTER PLENUM HARNESS ASSEMBLY
HARNESS AND BLOCK ASSEMBLY
EVAPORATOR HARNESS ASSEMBLY
HARNESS AND BLOCK ASSEMBLY
PLUGGED
4
1
6
5
3
2
VACUUM CONTROL (REAR VIEW)
SYMBOL
V - VACUUM
NV - NO VACUUM
PV - PARTIAL VACUUM

VACUUM PORT	FUNCTION	SELECTION						
		OFF	MAX A/C (RECIRC)	VENT	PANEL-FLOOR	FLOOR	FLOOR-DEFROST	DEFROST
1	OUTSIDE - RECIRC	V	V	NV	NV	NV	NV	NV
2	FULL FLOOR	NV	NV	NV	NA	V	NA	NV
3	FLOOR - PANEL (PARTIAL)	NV	NA	NV	PV	V	PV	NV
4	PANEL - DEFROST	NV	V	V	V	NV	NV	NV
5	SOURCE	V	V	V	V	V	V	V
6	PLUGGED	-	-	-	-	-	-	-

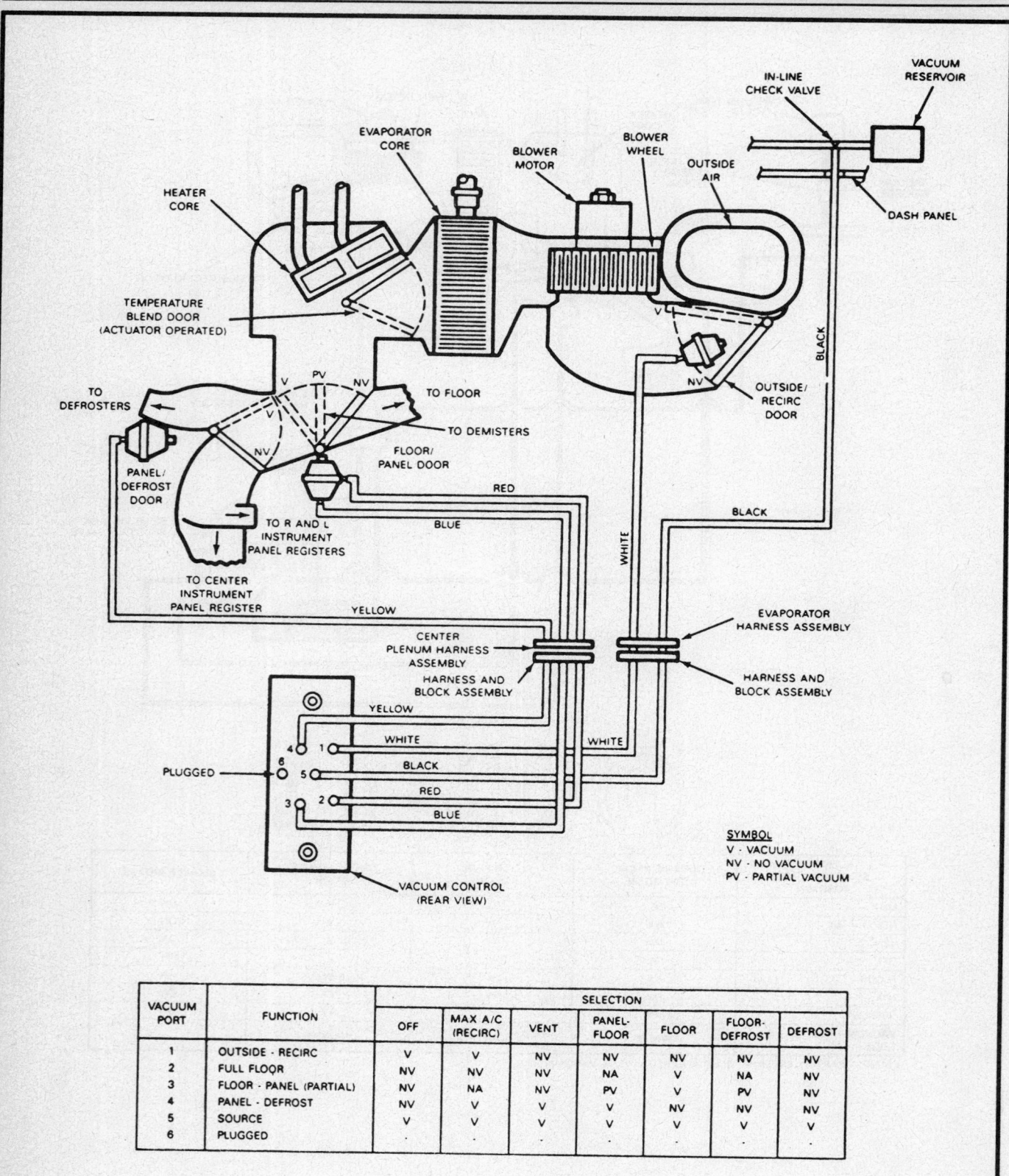

Automatic temperature control vacuum schematic— Taurus, Sable and Continental

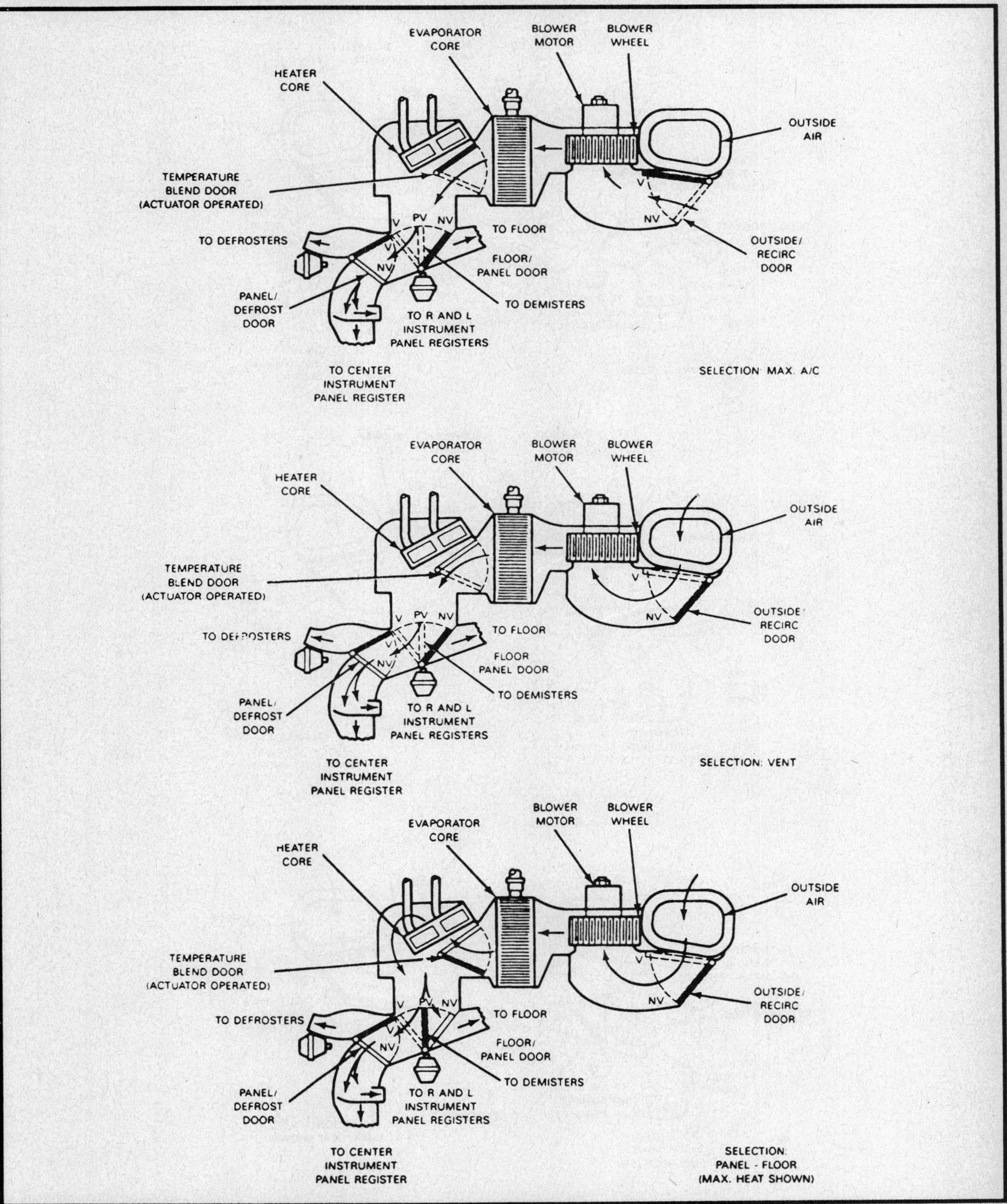
EVAPORATOR CORE
BLOWER MOTOR
BLOWER WHEEL
HEATER CORE
OUTSIDE AIR
TEMPERATURE BLEND DOOR (ACTUATOR OPERATED)
V
PV
NV
TO FLOOR
TO DEFROSTERS
OUTSIDE/ RECIRC DOOR
FLOOR/ PANEL DOOR
PANEL/ DEFROST DOOR
TO DEMISTERS
TO R AND L INSTRUMENT PANEL REGISTERS
TO CENTER INSTRUMENT PANEL REGISTER
SELECTION: MAX. A/C
SELECTION: VENT
SELECTION: PANEL - FLOOR (MAX. HEAT SHOWN)

Automatic temperature control airflow diagram 1 – Taurus, Sable and Continental

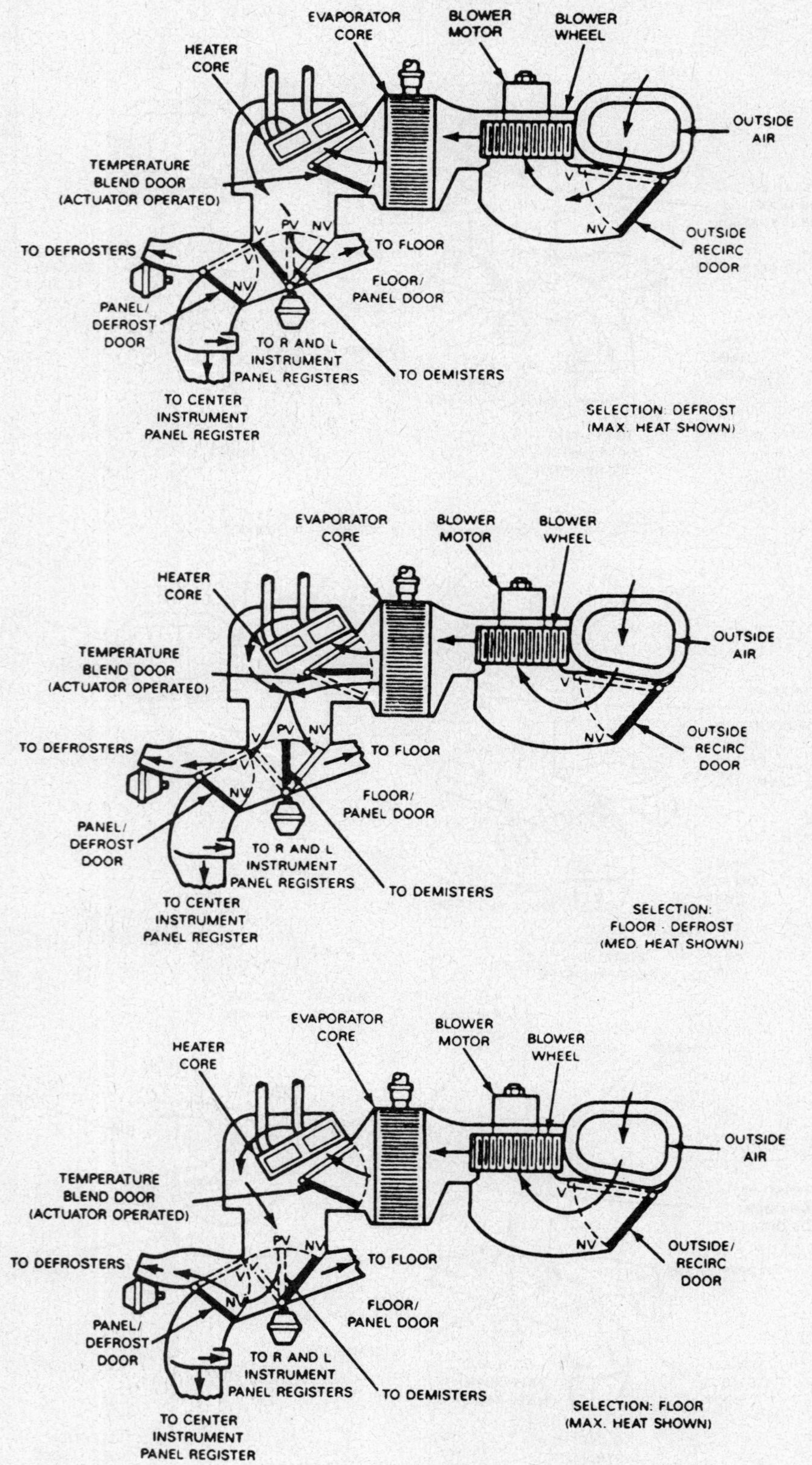
EVAPORATOR CORE
BLOWER MOTOR
BLOWER WHEEL
HEATER CORE
OUTSIDE AIR
TEMPERATURE BLEND DOOR (ACTUATOR OPERATED)
V
PV
NV
TO DEFROSTERS
TO FLOOR
OUTSIDE RECIRC DOOR
FLOOR/ PANEL DOOR
PANEL/ DEFROST DOOR
TO R AND L INSTRUMENT PANEL REGISTERS
TO DEMISTERS
TO CENTER INSTRUMENT PANEL REGISTER
SELECTION: DEFROST (MAX. HEAT SHOWN)
EVAPORATOR CORE
BLOWER MOTOR
BLOWER WHEEL
HEATER CORE
OUTSIDE AIR
TEMPERATURE BLEND DOOR (ACTUATOR OPERATED)
TO DEFROSTERS
TO FLOOR
OUTSIDE RECIRC DOOR
FLOOR/ PANEL DOOR
PANEL/ DEFROST DOOR
TO R AND L INSTRUMENT PANEL REGISTERS
TO DEMISTERS
TO CENTER INSTRUMENT PANEL REGISTER
SELECTION: FLOOR - DEFROST (MED. HEAT SHOWN)
EVAPORATOR CORE
BLOWER MOTOR
BLOWER WHEEL
HEATER CORE
OUTSIDE AIR
TEMPERATURE BLEND DOOR (ACTUATOR OPERATED)
TO DEFROSTERS
TO FLOOR
OUTSIDE/ RECIRC DOOR
FLOOR/ PANEL DOOR
PANEL/ DEFROST DOOR
TO R AND L INSTRUMENT PANEL REGISTERS
TO DEMISTERS
TO CENTER INSTRUMENT PANEL REGISTER
SELECTION: FLOOR (MAX. HEAT SHOWN)

Automatic temperature control airflow diagram 2 – Taurus, Sable and Continental

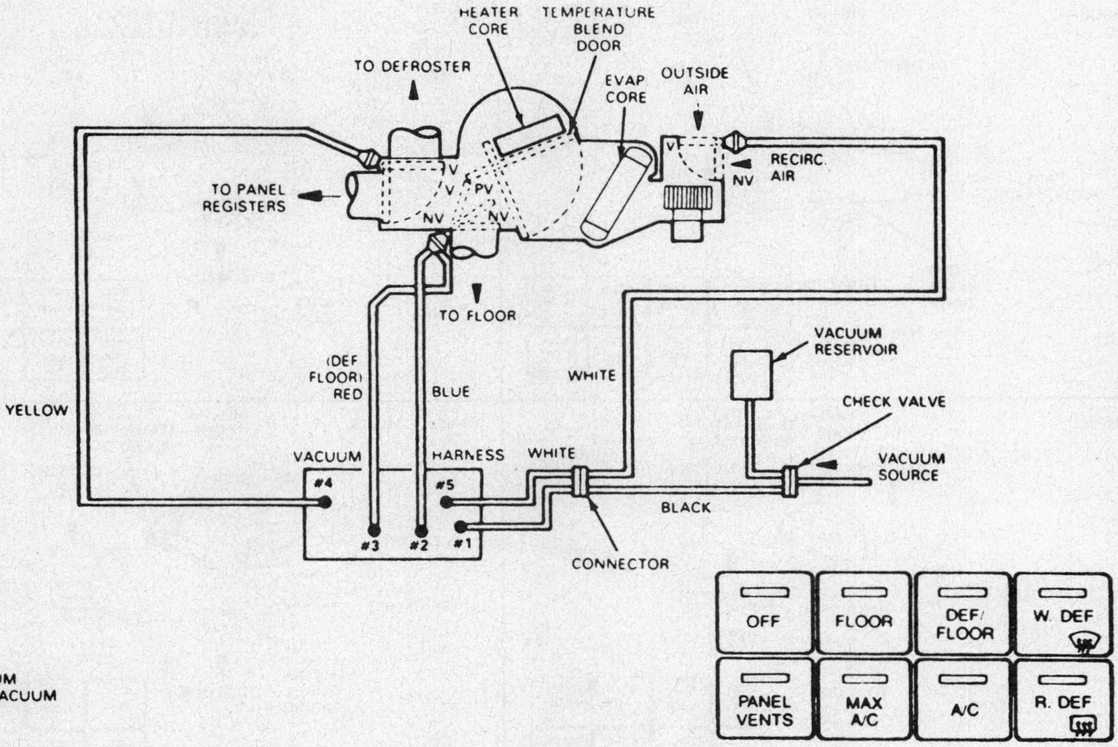
HEATER CORE
TEMPERATURE BLEND DOOR
TO DEFROSTER
EVAP CORE
OUTSIDE AIR
RECIRC. AIR
TO PANEL REGISTERS
V
PV
NV
TO FLOOR
VACUUM RESERVOIR
CHECK VALVE
VACUUM SOURCE
(DEF FLOOR) RED
BLUE
WHITE
YELLOW
VACUUM
HARNESS
BLACK
CONNECTOR
#4
#5
#3
#2
#1
OFF
FLOOR
DEF/ FLOOR
W. DEF
PANEL VENTS
MAX A/C
A/C
R. DEF
V :VACUUM
NV :NO VACUUM
PV :PARTIAL VACUUM

Function (Push-Button Depressed)	Outside-Recirc Door	Floor-Panel Door	Panel-Defrost Door	Blower Motor	A/C Clutch
OFF	V	V	NV	OFF	OFF
FLOOR	NV	V	NV	ON	OFF
DEF/FLOOR	NV	PV	NV	ON	OFF
DEF	NV	NV	NV	ON	ON
PANEL-VENTS	NV	NV	V	ON	OFF
MAX A/C	V	NV	V	ON	ON
A/C	NV	NV	V	ON	ON
VACUUM HOSE COLOR	WHITE	RED / BLUE ①	YELLOW	—	—

①Blue — Partial Vacuum; Blue and Red — Full Vacuum

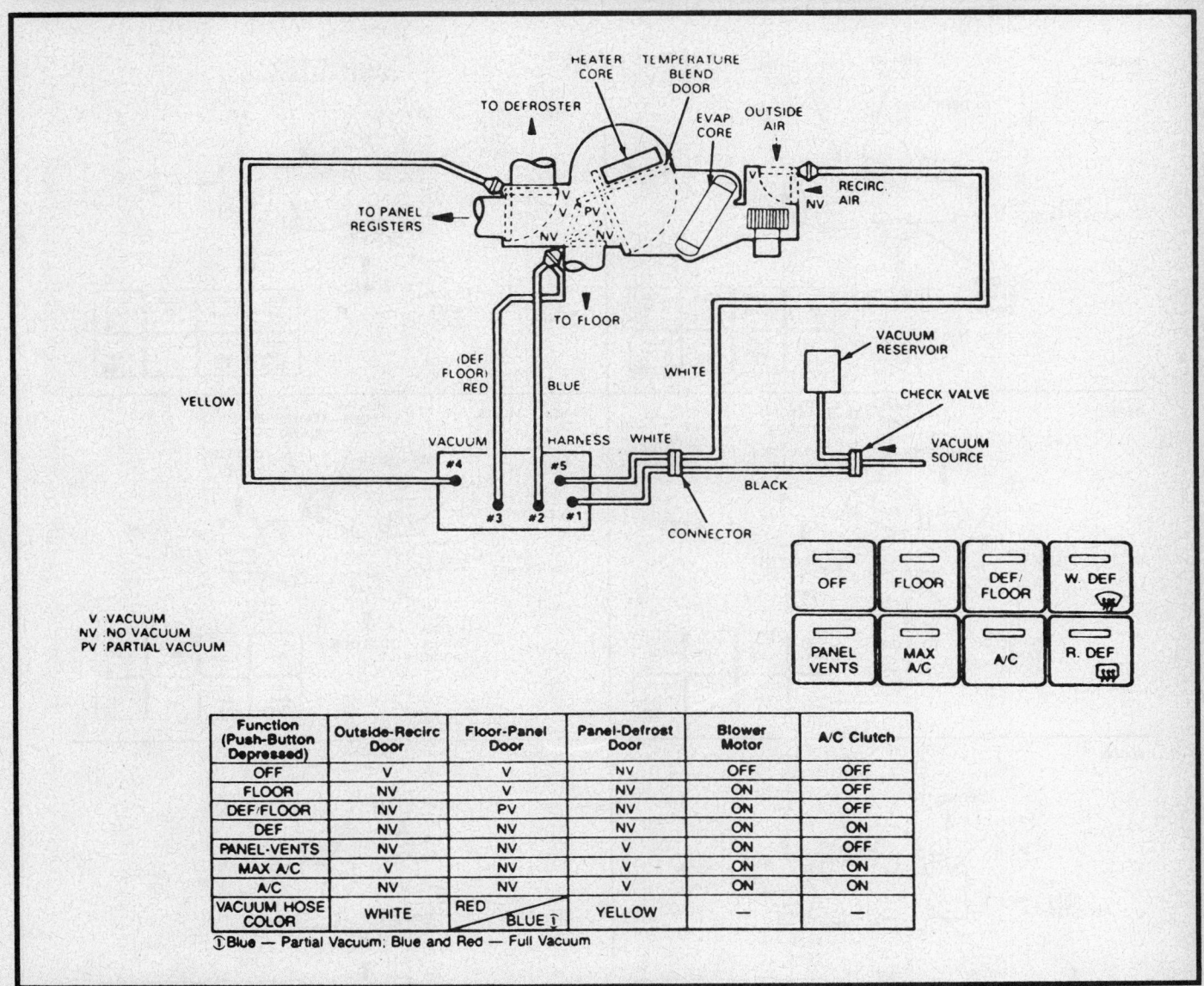

Air conditioning/heater vacuum schematic—Tempo and Topaz

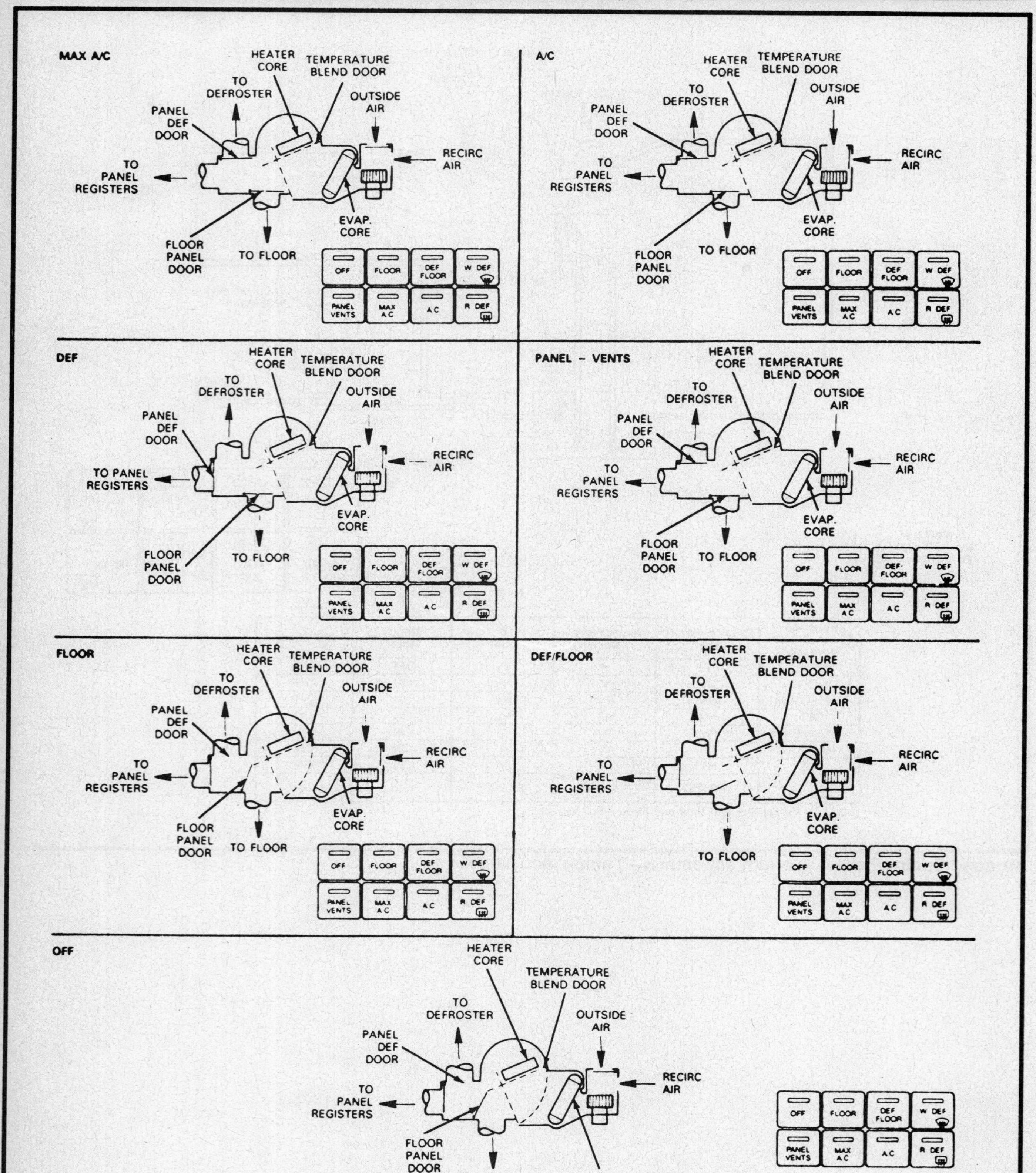
MAX A/C
HEATER CORE
TEMPERATURE BLEND DOOR
TO DEFROSTER
OUTSIDE AIR
PANEL DEF DOOR
RECIRC AIR
TO PANEL REGISTERS
EVAP. CORE
FLOOR PANEL DOOR
TO FLOOR
OFF
FLOOR
DEF FLOOR
W DEF
PANEL VENTS
MAX A C
A C
R DEF
A/C
HEATER CORE
TEMPERATURE BLEND DOOR
TO DEFROSTER
OUTSIDE AIR
PANEL DEF DOOR
RECIRC AIR
TO PANEL REGISTERS
EVAP. CORE
FLOOR PANEL DOOR
TO FLOOR
DEF
HEATER CORE
TEMPERATURE BLEND DOOR
TO DEFROSTER
OUTSIDE AIR
PANEL DEF DOOR
RECIRC AIR
TO PANEL REGISTERS
EVAP. CORE
FLOOR PANEL DOOR
TO FLOOR
PANEL - VENTS
HEATER CORE
TEMPERATURE BLEND DOOR
TO DEFROSTER
OUTSIDE AIR
PANEL DEF DOOR
RECIRC AIR
TO PANEL REGISTERS
EVAP. CORE
FLOOR PANEL DOOR
TO FLOOR
FLOOR
HEATER CORE
TEMPERATURE BLEND DOOR
TO DEFROSTER
OUTSIDE AIR
PANEL DEF DOOR
RECIRC AIR
TO PANEL REGISTERS
EVAP. CORE
FLOOR PANEL DOOR
TO FLOOR
DEF/FLOOR
HEATER CORE
TEMPERATURE BLEND DOOR
TO DEFROSTER
OUTSIDE AIR
RECIRC AIR
TO PANEL REGISTERS
EVAP. CORE
TO FLOOR
OFF
HEATER CORE
TEMPERATURE BLEND DOOR
TO DEFROSTER
OUTSIDE AIR
PANEL DEF DOOR
RECIRC AIR
TO PANEL REGISTERS
FLOOR PANEL DOOR
TO FLOOR
EVAP. CORE

Air conditioning/heater airflow diagram—Tempo and Topaz

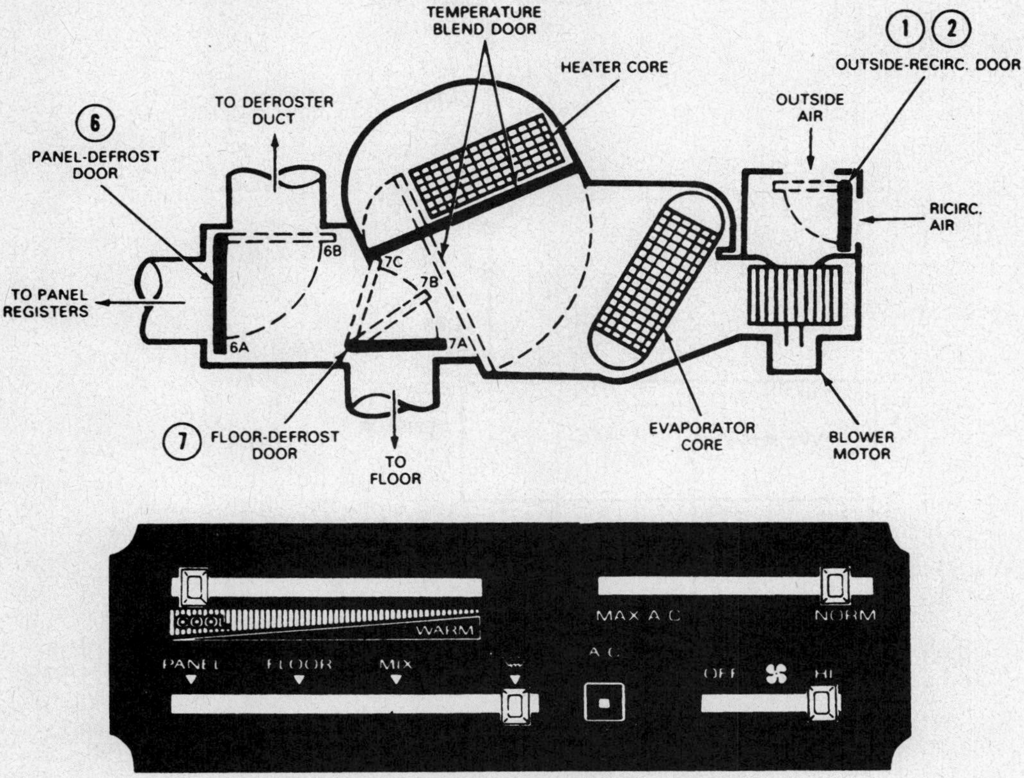
TEMPERATURE BLEND DOOR
HEATER CORE
1 2
OUTSIDE-RECIRC. DOOR
OUTSIDE AIR
RICIRC. AIR
TO DEFROSTER DUCT
6
PANEL-DEFROST DOOR
6B
7C
7B
TO PANEL REGISTERS
6A
7A
7
FLOOR-DEFROST DOOR
TO FLOOR
EVAPORATOR CORE
BLOWER MOTOR
COOL
WARM
MAX A C
NORM
A C
PANEL
FLOOR
MIX
OFF
HI

FUNCTION SELECTOR LEVER/AIR DOOR POSITION CHART

Function Selector Lever Position	Floor-Defrost Door Position	Panel-Defrost Door Position
DEFROST	7A	6A
MIX	7B	6A
FLOOR	7C	6A
PANEL	7A	6B

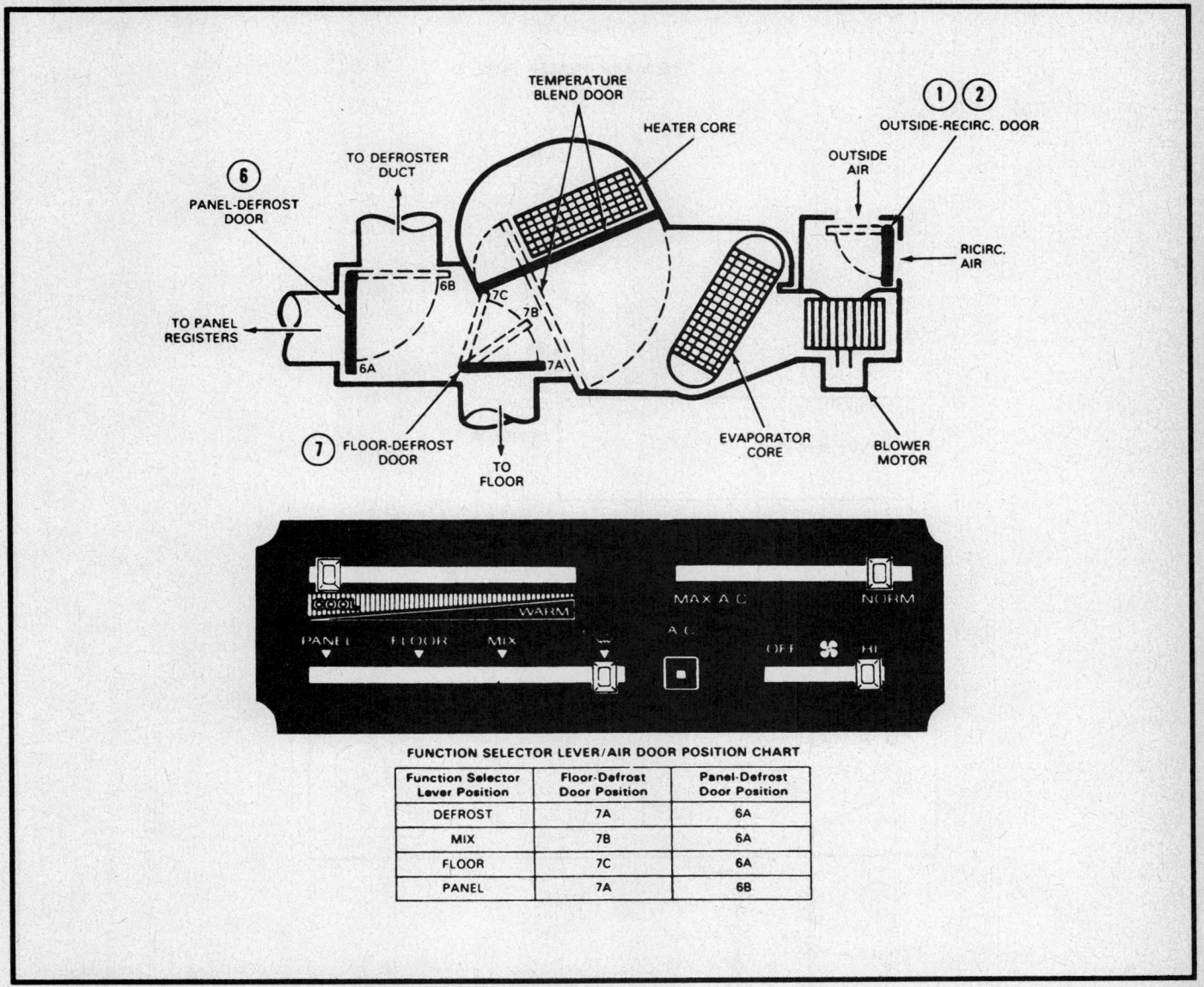

Air conditioning/heater airflow diagram—1989–90 Escort

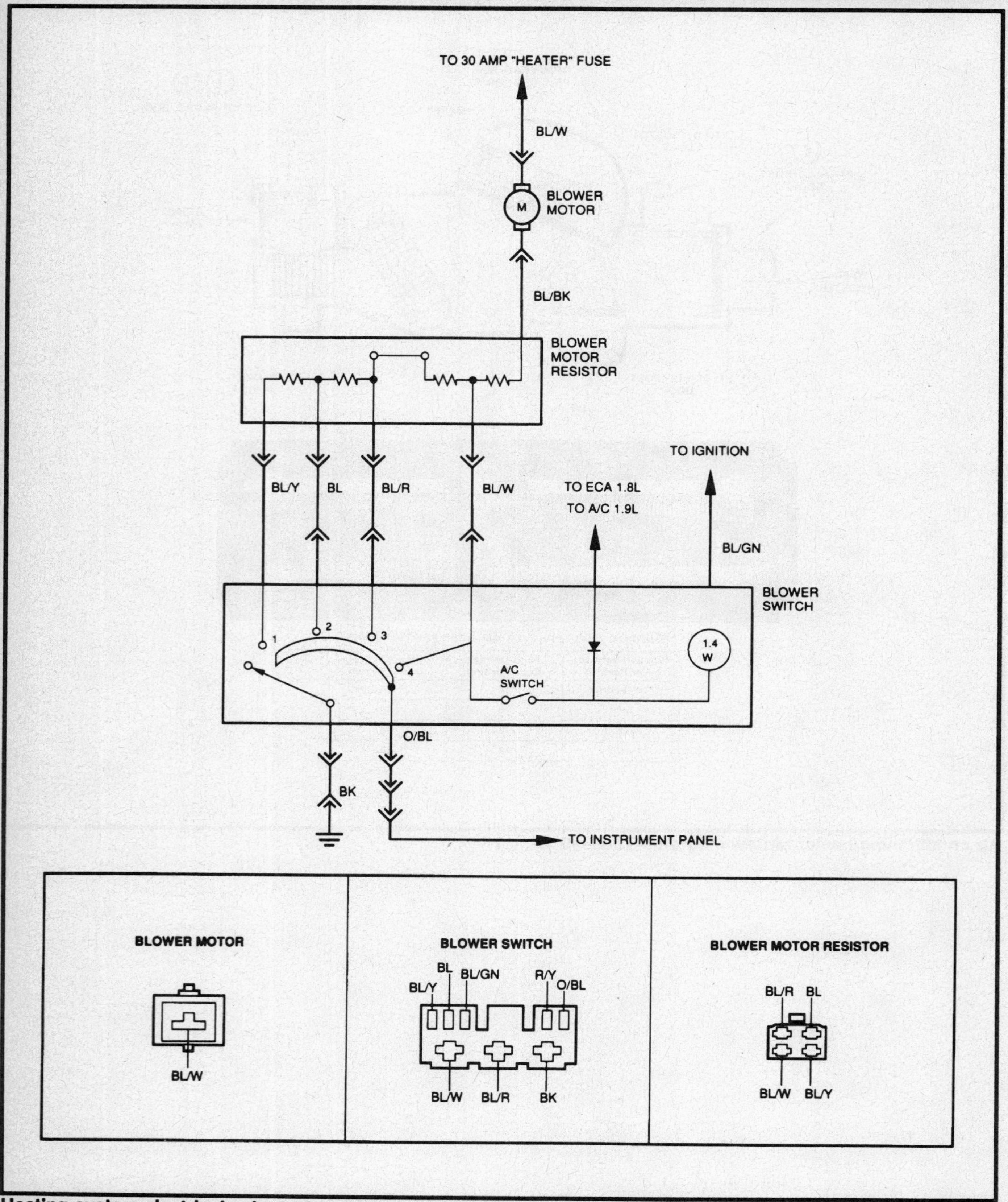
TO 30 AMP "HEATER" FUSE
BL/W
M
BLOWER MOTOR
BL/BK
BLOWER MOTOR RESISTOR
TO IGNITION
BL/Y
BL
BL/R
BL/W
TO ECA 1.8L
TO A/C 1.9L
BL/GN
BLOWER SWITCH
1
2
3
4
1.4 W
A/C SWITCH
O/BL
BK
TO INSTRUMENT PANEL
BLOWER MOTOR
BL/W
BLOWER SWITCH
BL
BL/GN
BL/Y
R/Y
O/BL
BL/W
BL/R
BK
BLOWER MOTOR RESISTOR
BL/R
BL
BL/W
BL/Y

Heating system electrical schematic—1991 Escort and Tracer with 1.8L engine

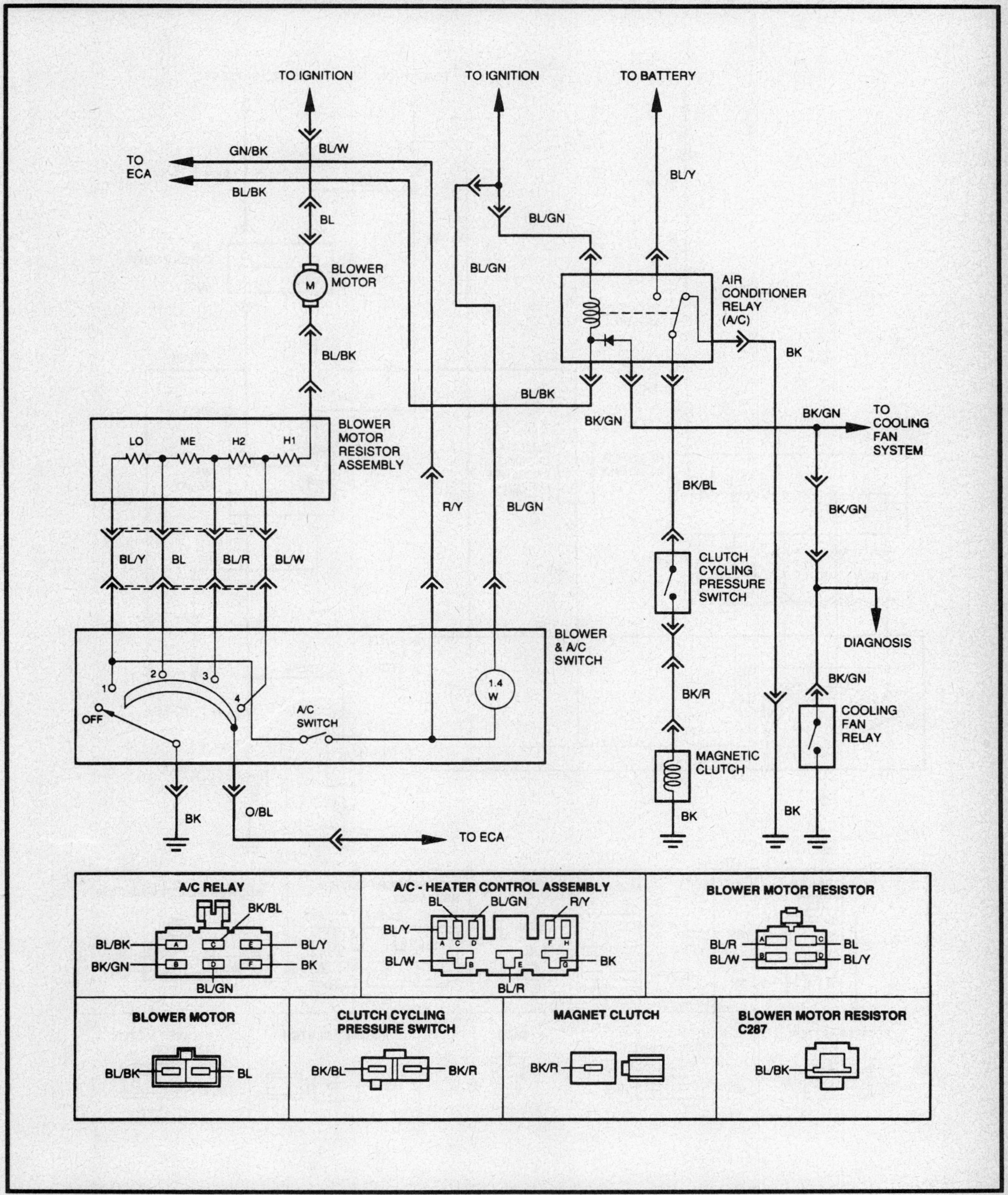
TO IGNITION
TO IGNITION
TO BATTERY
TO ECA
GN/BK
BL/W
BL/BK
BL
BLOWER MOTOR
M
BL/BK
BL/GN
BL/GN
BL/Y
AIR CONDITIONER RELAY (A/C)
BK
BL/BK
BK/GN
BK/GN
TO COOLING FAN SYSTEM
BLOWER MOTOR RESISTOR ASSEMBLY
LO
ME
H2
H1
R/Y
BL/GN
BK/BL
BK/GN
BL/Y
BL
BL/R
BL/W
CLUTCH CYCLING PRESSURE SWITCH
DIAGNOSIS
BLOWER & A/C SWITCH
1.4 W
OFF
A/C SWITCH
BK/R
BK/GN
COOLING FAN RELAY
MAGNETIC CLUTCH
BK
O/BL
TO ECA
BK
BK
A/C RELAY
BK/BL
BL/BK
BK/GN
BL/Y
BK
BL/GN
A/C - HEATER CONTROL ASSEMBLY
BL
BL/GN
R/Y
BL/Y
BL/W
BK
BL/R
BLOWER MOTOR RESISTOR
BL/R
BL/W
BL
BL/Y
BLOWER MOTOR
BL/BK
BL
CLUTCH CYCLING PRESSURE SWITCH
BK/BL
BK/R
MAGNET CLUTCH
BK/R
BLOWER MOTOR RESISTOR C287
BL/BK

Air conditioning system electrical schematic—1991 Escort and Tracer with 1.8L engine

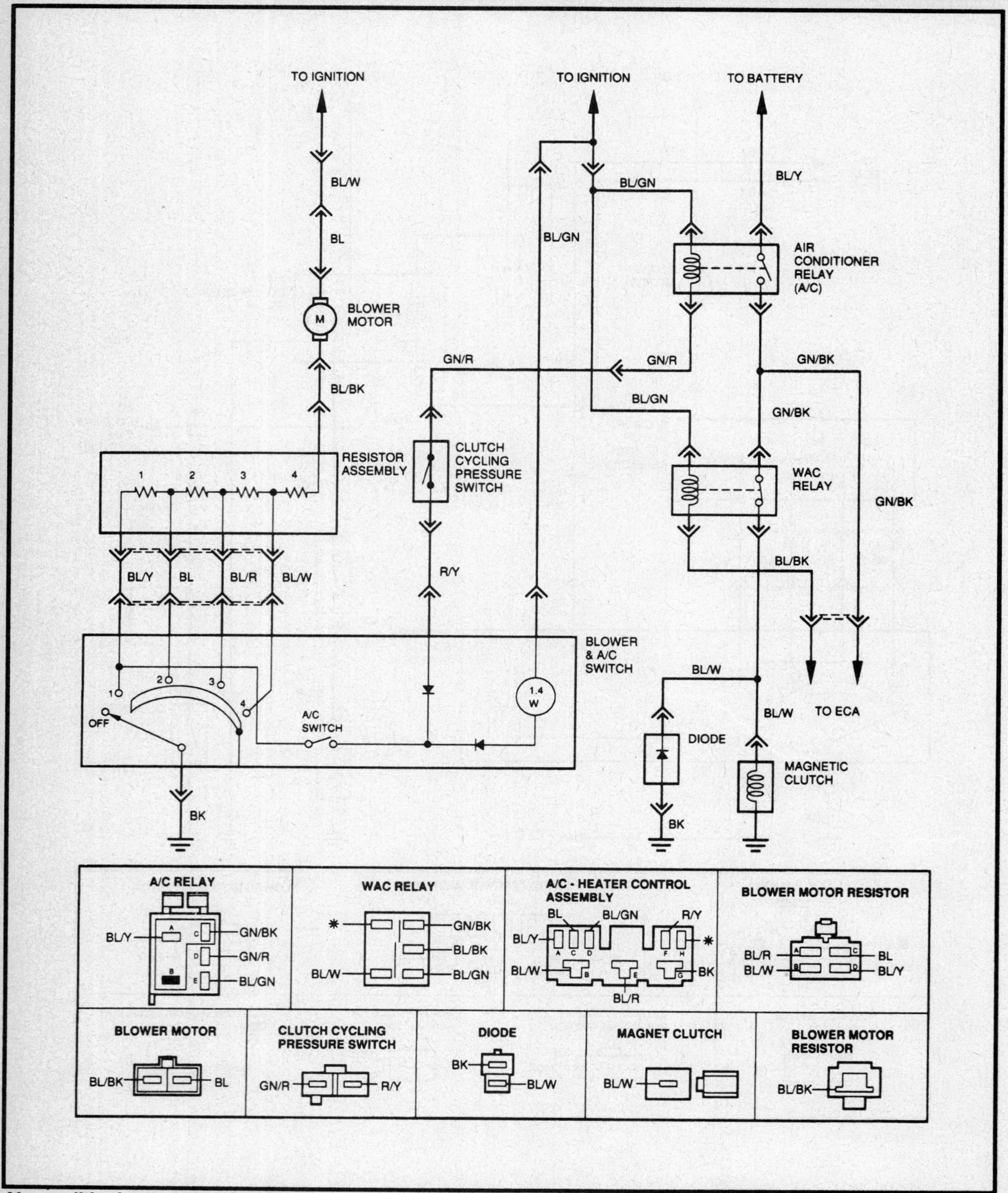
TO IGNITION
TO IGNITION
TO BATTERY
BL/W
BL
BLOWER MOTOR
BL/BK
BL/GN
BL/GN
BL/Y
AIR CONDITIONER RELAY (A/C)
GN/R
GN/R
GN/BK
BL/GN
GN/BK
CLUTCH CYCLING PRESSURE SWITCH
RESISTOR ASSEMBLY
WAC RELAY
GN/BK
R/Y
BL/Y
BL
BL/R
BL/W
BL/BK
BLOWER & A/C SWITCH
OFF
A/C SWITCH
1.4 W
BL/W
BL/W
TO ECA
DIODE
MAGNETIC CLUTCH
BK
BK
A/C RELAY
WAC RELAY
A/C - HEATER CONTROL ASSEMBLY
BLOWER MOTOR RESISTOR
BLOWER MOTOR
CLUTCH CYCLING PRESSURE SWITCH
DIODE
MAGNET CLUTCH
BLOWER MOTOR RESISTOR

Air conditioning system electrical schematic—1991 Escort and Tracer with 1.9L engine

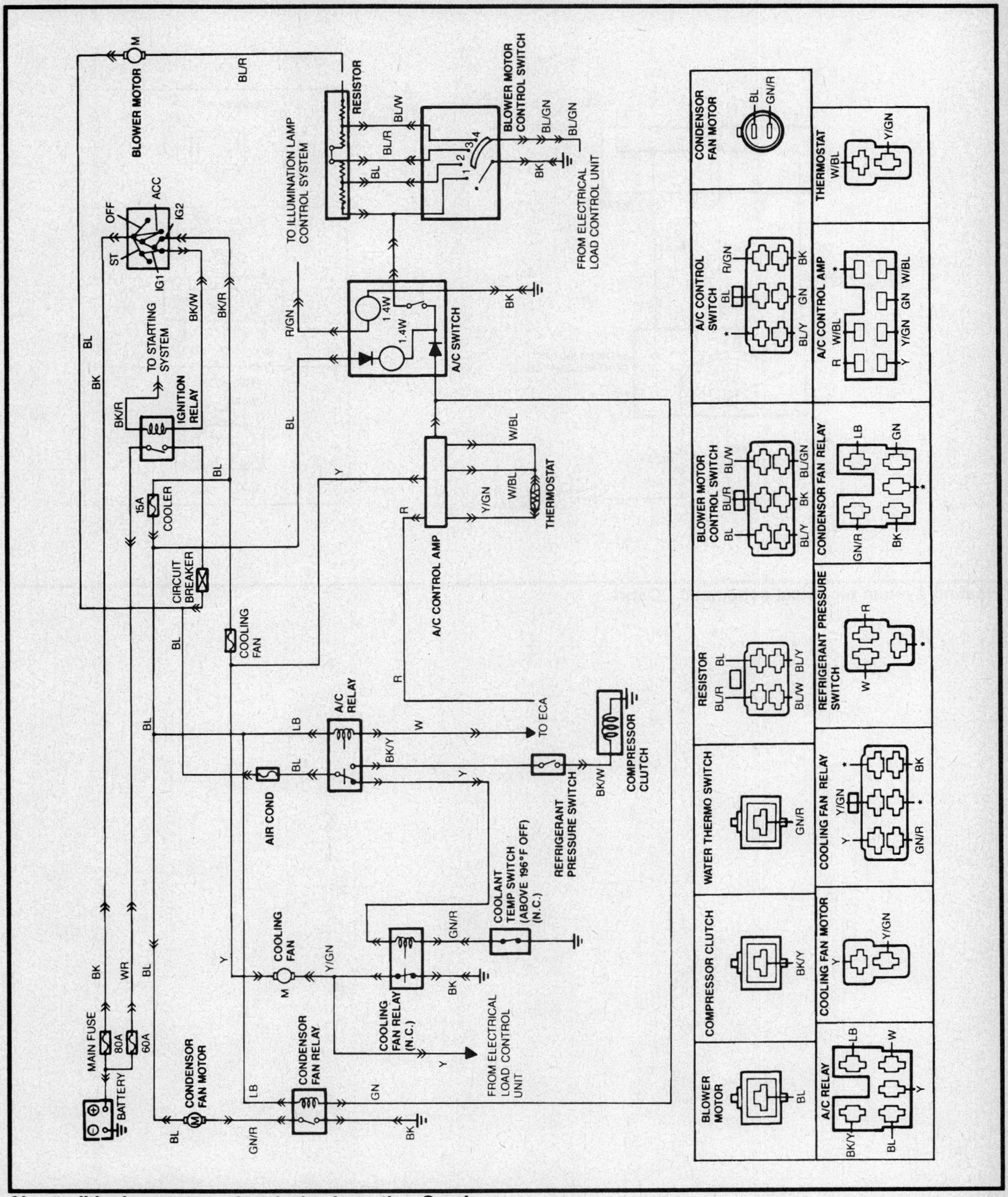
BLOWER MOTOR
M
BL/R
RESISTOR
BLOWER MOTOR CONTROL SWITCH
BL/W
BL/R
BL
BL/GN
BK
FROM ELECTRICAL LOAD CONTROL UNIT
TO ILLUMINATION LAMP CONTROL SYSTEM
OFF
ACC
ST
IG1
IG2
TO STARTING SYSTEM
BK/W
BK/R
R/GN
1.4W
A/C SWITCH
IGNITION RELAY
15A
COOLER
CIRCUIT BREAKER
COOLING FAN
A/C CONTROL AMP
W/BL
Y/GN
THERMOSTAT
R
Y
TO ECA
A/C RELAY
LB
W
BK/Y
AIR COND
COMPRESSOR CLUTCH
REFRIGERANT PRESSURE SWITCH
COOLANT TEMP SWITCH (ABOVE 196°F OFF) (N.C.)
GN/R
COOLING FAN RELAY (N.C.)
FROM ELECTRICAL LOAD CONTROL UNIT
MAIN FUSE
80A
60A
BATTERY
WR
CONDENSOR FAN MOTOR
CONDENSOR FAN RELAY
GN
CONDENSOR FAN MOTOR
A/C CONTROL SWITCH
BLOWER MOTOR CONTROL SWITCH
RESISTOR
WATER THERMO SWITCH
COMPRESSOR CLUTCH
BLOWER MOTOR
THERMOSTAT
A/C CONTROL AMP
CONDENSOR FAN RELAY
REFRIGERANT PRESSURE SWITCH
COOLING FAN RELAY
COOLING FAN MOTOR
A/C RELAY

Air conditioning system electrical schematic—Capri

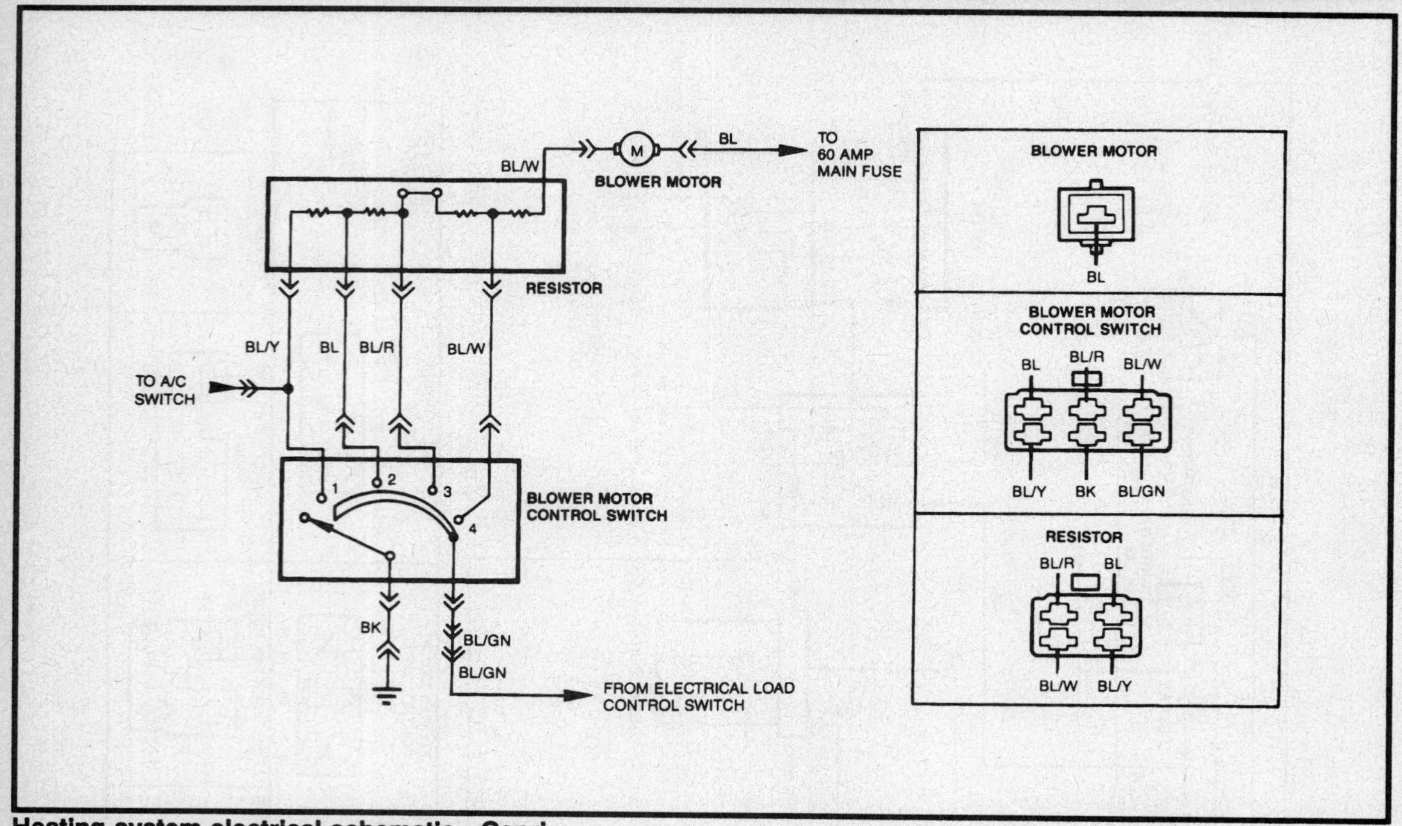
BL/W
BLOWER MOTOR
BL
TO
60 AMP
MAIN FUSE
RESISTOR
BL/Y
BL
BL/R
BL/W
TO A/C
SWITCH
1
2
3
4
BLOWER MOTOR
CONTROL SWITCH
BK
BL/GN
BL/GN
FROM ELECTRICAL LOAD
CONTROL SWITCH
BLOWER MOTOR
BL
BLOWER MOTOR
CONTROL SWITCH
BL
BL/R
BL/W
BL/Y
BK
BL/GN
RESISTOR
BL/R
BL
BL/W
BL/Y

Heating system electrical schematic—Capri

5 FORD/LINCOLN/MERCURY 5

COUGAR • CROWN VICTORIA • GRAND MARQUIS • MARK VII • MUSTANG • THUNDERBIRD • TOWN CAR

SPECIFICATIONS

ENGINE IDENTIFICATION

Year	Model	Engine Displacement cu. in. (liter)	Engine Series Identification (VIN)	No. of Cylinders	Engine Type
1989	Mustang	140 (2.3)	A	4	OHC
	Mustang	302 (5.0) HO	M	8	OHV
	Thunderbird	232 (3.8)	3	6	OHV
	Thunderbird	232 (3.8) SC	R	6	OHV
	Cougar	232 (3.8)	3	6	OHV
	Cougar	232 (3.8) SC	R	6	OHV
	MarK VII	302 (5.0) HO	M	8	OHV
	Crown Victoria	302 (5.0)	F	8	OHV
	Crown Victoria	351 (5.8)	G	8	OHV
	Grand Marquis	302 (5.0)	F	8	OHV
	Grand Marquis	351 (5.8)	G	8	OHV
	Town Car	302 (5.0)	F	8	OHV
1990	Mustang	140 (2.3)	A	4	OHC
	Mustang	302 (5.0) HO	E	8	OHV
	Thunderbird	232 (3.8)	4	6	OHV
	Thunderbird	232 (3.8) SC	R ①	6	OHV
	Cougar	232 (3.8)	4	6	OHV
	Cougar	232 (3.8) SC	R ①	6	OHV
	Mark VII	302 (5.0) HO	E	8	OHV
	Crown Victoria	302 (5.0)	F	8	OHV
	Crown Victoria	351 (5.8)	G	8	OHV
	Grand Marquis	302 (5.0)	F	8	OHV
	Grand Marquis	351 (5.8)	G	8	OHV
	Town Car	302 (5.0)	F	8	OHV
1991	Mustang	140 (2.3)	A	4	OHC
	Mustang	302 (5.0) HO	E	8	OHV
	Thunderbird	232 (3.8)	4	6	OHV
	Thunderbird	232 (3.8) SC	R ①	6	OHV
	Thunderbird	302 (5.0) HO	T	8	OHV
	Cougar	232 (3.8)	4	6	OHV
	Cougar	302 (5.0) HO	T	8	OHV
	Mark VII	302 (5.0) HO	E	8	OHV
	Crown Victoria	302 (5.0)	F	8	OHV
	Crown Victoria	351 (5.8)	G	8	OHV
	Grand Marquis	302 (5.0)	F	8	OHV
	Grand Marquis	351 (5.8)	G	8	OHV
	Town Car	281 (4.6)	W	8	OHC

① Early production could be Code C

REFRIGERANT CAPACITIES

Year	Model	Freon (oz.)	Oil (fl. oz.)	Type
1989	Mustang	38–42	①	②
	Thunderbird	38–42	7	FX-15
	Cougar	38–42	7	FX-15
	Mark VII	38–42	8	10 PA 17
	Crown Victoria	48–52③	8	10 PA 17
	Grand Marquis	48–52③	8	10 PA 17
	Town Car	48–52③	8	10 PA 17
1990	Mustang	38–42	①	④
	Thunderbird	38–42	7	FX-15
	Cougar	38–42	7	FX-15
	Mark VII	38–42	8	10 PA 17
	Crown Victoria	48–52③	8	10 PA 17
	Grand Marquis	48–52③	8	10 PA 17
	Town Car	48–52③	8	10 PA 17
1991	Mustang	38–42	①	④
	Thunderbird	38–42	7	FX-15
	Cougar	38–42	7	FX-15
	Mark VII	38–42	8	10 PA 17
	Crown Victoria	48–52③	7	FX-15
	Grand Marquis	48–52③	7	FX-15
	Town Car	39–41	7	FX-15

① 2.3L Engine—8
5.0L Engine—10
② 2.3L Engine—HR-980
5.0L Engine—6P148
③ 48 oz. is preferred
④ 2.3L Engine—10P15
5.0L Engine—6P148

AIR CONDITIONING BELT TENSION CHART

Year	Model	Engine (L)	Belt Type	Specification ① New	Specification ① Used
1989	Mustang	2.3	V-Ribbed	②	②
	Mustang	5.0	V-Ribbed	②	②
	Thunderbird	3.8	V-Ribbed	②	②
	Cougar	3.8	V-Ribbed	②	②
	Mark VII	5.0	V-Ribbed	②	②
	Crown Victoria	5.0	V-Ribbed	170	140
	Grand Marquis	5.0	V-Ribbed	170	140
	Town Car	5.0	V-Ribbed	170	140
1990	Mustang	2.3	V-Ribbed	②	②
	Mustang	5.0	V-Ribbed	②	②
	Thunderbird	3.8	V-Ribbed	②	②
	Cougar	3.8	V-Ribbed	②	②
	Mark VII	5.0	V-Ribbed	②	②
	Crown Victoria	5.0	V-Ribbed	170	140
	Grand Marquis	5.0	V-Ribbed	170	140
	Town Car	5.0	V-Ribbed	170	140

AIR CONDITIONING BELT TENSION CHART

Year	Model	Engine (L)	Belt Type	Specification ① New	Specification ① Used
1991	Mustang	2.3	V-Ribbed	②	②
	Mustang	5.0	V-Ribbed	②	②
	Thunderbird	3.8	V-Ribbed	②	②
	Thunderbird	5.0	V-Ribbed	②	②
	Cougar	3.8	V-Ribbed	②	②
	Cougar	5.0	V-Ribbed	②	②
	Mark VII	5.0	V-Ribbed	②	②
	Crown Victoria	5.0	V-Ribbed	170	140
	Crown Victoria	5.8	V-Ribbed	170	140
	Grand Marquis	5.0	V-Ribbed	170	140
	Grand Marquis	5.8	V-Ribbed	170	140
	Town Car	4.6	V-Ribbed	②	②

① Lbs. using a belt tension gauge
② Automatic belt tensioner

SYSTEM DESCRIPTION

General Information

The air conditioning system used on Ford rear wheel drive vehicles is the fixed orifice tube-cycling clutch type. The system components consist of the compressor, magnetic clutch, condenser, evaporator, suction accumulator/drier and the necessary connecting refrigerant lines. The fixed orifice tube assembly is the restriction between the high and low pressure liquid refrigerant and meters the flow of liquid refrigerant into the evaporator core. Evaporator temperature is controlled by sensing the pressure within the evaporator with the clutch cycling pressure switch. The pressure switch controls compressor operation as necessary to maintain the evaporator pressure within specified limits.

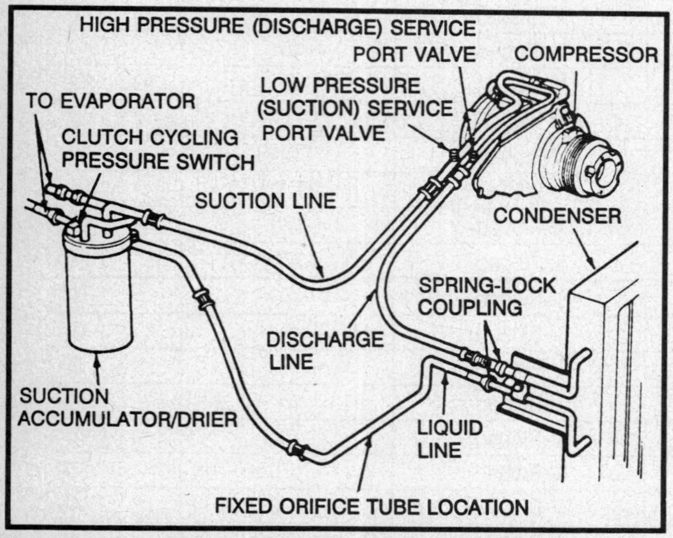
HIGH PRESSURE (DISCHARGE) SERVICE PORT VALVE
COMPRESSOR
LOW PRESSURE (SUCTION) SERVICE PORT VALVE
TO EVAPORATOR
CLUTCH CYCLING PRESSURE SWITCH
SUCTION LINE
CONDENSER
SPRING-LOCK COUPLING
DISCHARGE LINE
SUCTION ACCUMULATOR/DRIER
LIQUID LINE
FIXED ORIFICE TUBE LOCATION

Fixed orifice tube air conditioning system—typical

Service Valve Location

The air conditioning system has a high pressure (discharge) and a low pressure (suction) gauge port valve. These are Schrader valves which provide access to both the high and low pressure sides of the system for service hoses and a manifold gauge set so system pressures can be read. The high pressure gauge port valve is located between the compressor and the condenser, in the high pressure vapor (discharge) hose. The low pressure gauge port valve is located between the suction accumulator/drier and the compressor, in the low pressure vapor (suction) hose.

High side adapter set D81L–19703–A or tool YT–354, 355 or equivalent, is required to connect a manifold gauge set or charging station to the high pressure gauge port valve. Service tee fitting D87P–19703–A, which may be mounted on the clutch cycling pressure switch fitting, is available for use in the low pressure side, to be used in place of the low pressure gauge port valve.

System Discharging

WITHOUT RECOVERY SYSTEM

1. Connect a manifold gauge set as follows:
   a. Turn both manifold gauge set valves all the way to the right, to close the high and low pressure hoses to the center manifold and hose.
   b. Remove the caps from the high and low pressure service gauge port valves.
   c. If the manifold gauge set hoses do not have valve depressing pins in them, install fitting adapters T71P–19703–S and R or equivalent, which have pins, on the low and high pressure hoses.
   d. Connect the high and low pressure hoses or adapters, to the respective high and low pressure service gauge port valves. High side adapter set D81L–19703–A or tool YT–354, 355 or equivalent, is required to connect a manifold gauge set or charging station to the high pressure gauge port valve.

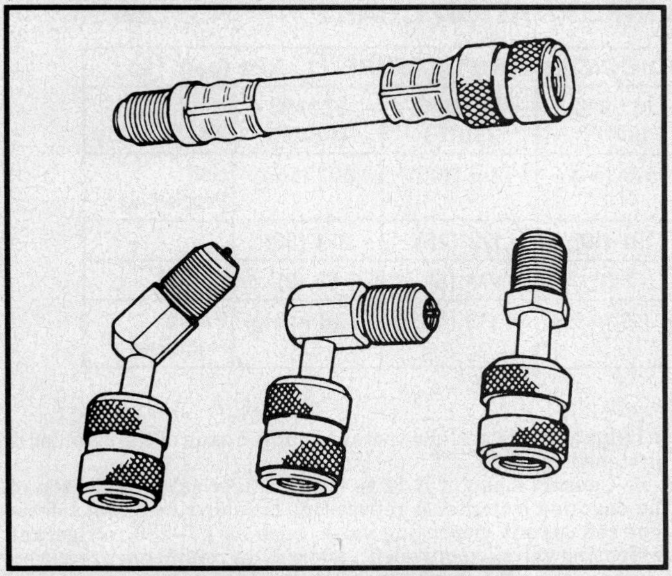

High pressure gauge port valve adapters

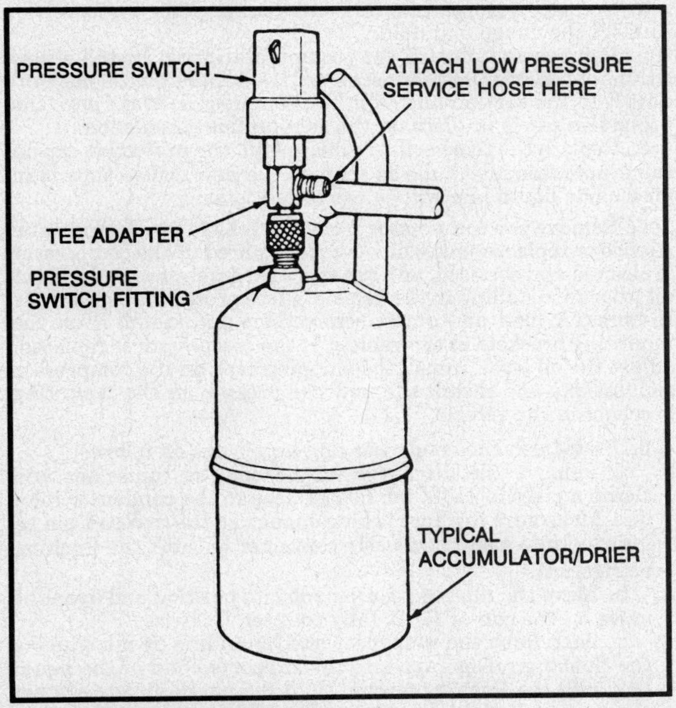
PRESSURE SWITCH
ATTACH LOW PRESSURE SERVICE HOSE HERE
TEE ADAPTER
PRESSURE SWITCH FITTING
TYPICAL ACCUMULATOR/DRIER

Tee adapter tool installation

NOTE: Service tee fitting D87P–19703–A, which may be mounted on the clutch cycling pressure switch fitting, is available for use in the low pressure side, to be used in place of the low pressure gauge port valve.

2. Make sure the center hose connection at the manifold gauge set is tight.
3. Place the open end of the center hose in a garage exhaust outlet.
4. Open the low pressure valve of the manifold gauge set a slight amount and let the refrigerant slowly discharge from the system.
5. When the system is nearly discharged, open the high pressure gauge valve slowly, to avoid refrigerant oil loss. This will allow any refrigerant trapped in the compressor and high pressure discharge line to discharge.
6. As soon as the system is completely discharged, close both the high and low pressure valves to prevent moisture from entering the system.

WITH RECOVERY SYSTEM

The use of refrigerant recovery systems and recycling stations makes possible the recovery and reuse of refrigerant after contaminents and moisture have been removed. If a recovery system or recyling station is used, the following general procedures should be observed, in addition to the operating instructions provided by the equipment manufacturer.

1. Connect the refrigerant recycling station hose(s) to the vehicle air conditioning service ports and the recovery station inlet fitting.

NOTE: Hoses should have shut off devices or check valves within 12 inches of the hose end to minimize the introduction of air into the recycling station and to minimize the amount of refrigerant released when the hose(s) is disconnected.

2. Turn the power to the recycling station **ON** to start the recovery process. Allow the recycling station to pump the refrigerant from the system until the station pressure goes into a vacuum. On some stations the pump will be shut off automatically by a low pressure switch in the electrical system. On other units it may be necessary to manually turn **OFF** the pump.
3. Once the recycling station has evacuated the vehicle air conditioning system, close the station inlet valve, if equipped. Then switch **OFF** the electrical power.
4. Allow the vehicle air conditioning system to remain closed for about 2 minutes. Observe the system vacuum level as shown on the gauge. If the pressure does not rise, disconnect the recycling station hose(s).
5. If the system pressure rises, repeat Steps 2, 3 and 4 until the vacuum level remains stable for 2 minutes.

System Flushing

A refrigerant system can become badly contaminated for a number of reasons:

- The compressor may have failed due to damage or wear.
- The compressor may have been run for some time with a severe leak or an opening in the system.
- The system may have been damaged by a collision and left open for some time.
- The system may not have been cleaned properly after a previous failure.
- The system may have been operated for a time with water or moisture in it.

A badly contaminated system contains water, carbon and other decomposition products. When this condition exists, the system must be flushed with a special flushing agent using equipment designed specially for this purpose.

FLUSHING AGENTS

To be suitable as a flushing agent, a refrigerant must remain in liquid state during the flushing operation in order to wash the inside surfaces of the system components. Refrigerant vapor will not remove contaminent particles. They must be flushed with a liquid.

Some refrigerants are better suited to flushing than others. Neither Refrigerant-12 (R-12) nor Refrigerant-114 (R-114) is suitable for flushing a system because of low vaporization (boil-

REFRIGERANT FLUSHING INFORMATION CHART

Refrigerant	Vaporizes °C(°F) ①	APPROXIMATE CLOSED CONTAINER PRESSURE ① kPa (psi) ②					
		15.57°C (60°F)	21.13°C (70°F)	26.69°C (80°F)	32.25°C (90°F)	37.81°C (100°F)	Adaptability
R-12	−29.80(−21.6)	393 (57)	483 (70)	579 (84)	689 (100)	807 (117)	Self Propelling
F-114	3.56 (38.4)	55.16 (8)	89.63 (13)	131 (19)	172 (25)	221 (32)	
F-11 ③	23.74 (74.7)	27 (8 in Hg)	10 (3 in Hg)	7 (1)	34 (5)	62 (9)	
F-113	47.59 (117.6)	74 (22 in Hg)	64 (19 in Hg)	54 (16 in Hg)	44 (13 in Hg)	27 (8 in Hg)	Pump Required

ing) points: −21.6°F (−29.8°C) for R-12 and 38.4°F (3.5°C) for R-114. Both these refrigerants would be difficult to use and would not do a sufficient job because of the tendency to vaporize rather than remain in a liquid state, especially in high ambient temperatures.

Refrigerant-11 (R-11) and Refrigerant-113 (R-113) are much better suited for use with special flushing equipment. Both have rather high vaporization points: 74.7°F (23.7°C) for R-11 and 117.6°F (47.5°C) for R-113. Both refrigerants also have low closed container pressures. This reduces the danger of an accidental system discharge due to a ruptured hose or fitting. R-113 will do the best job amd is recommended as a flushing refrigerant. Both R-11 and R-113 require a propellant or pump type flushing equipment due to their low closed container pressures. R-12 can be used as a propellant with either flushing refrigerant. R-11 is available in pressurized containers. Although not recommended for regular use, it may become necessary to use R-11 if special flushing equipment is not available. R-11 is more toxic than other refrigerants and should be handled with extra care.

SPECIAL FLUSHING EQUIPMENT

Special refrigerant system flushing equipment is available from a number of air conditioning equipment and usually comes in kit form. A flushing kit, such as model 015–00205 or equivalent, consists of a cylinder for the flushing agent, a nozzle to introduce the flushing agent into the system and a connecting hose.

A second type of equipment, which must be connected into the system, allows for the continuous circulation of the flushing agent through the system. Contaminents are trapped by an external filter/drier. If this equipment is used, follow the manufacturer's instructions and observe all safety precautions.

SYSTEM CLEANING AND FLUSHING

NOTE: Use extreme care and adhere to all safety precautions related to the use of refrigerants when flushing a system.

When it is necessary to flush a refrigerant system, the accumulator/drier must be removed and replaced, because it is impossible to clean. Remove the fixed orifice tube and replace it. If a new tube is not available, carefully wash the contaminated tube in flushing refrigerant or mineral spirits and blow it dry. If the tube does not show signs of damage or deterioration, it may be reused. Install new O-rings.

Any moisture in the evaporator core will be removed during leak testing and system evacuation following the cleaning job. Perorm the cleaning procedure carefully as follows:

1. Check the hose connections at the flushing cylinder outlet and flushing nozzle, to make sure they are secure.
2. Make sure the flushing cylinder is filled with approximately 1 pint of R-113 and the valve assembly on top of the cylinder is tightened securely.
3. Connect a can of R-12 to the Schrader valve at the top of the charging cylinder. A refrigerant hose and a special safety-type refrigerant dispensing valve, such as YT–280 refrigerant dispensing valve or equivalent, and a valve retainer are required for connecting the small can to the cylinder. Make sure all connections are secure.
4. Connect a gauge manifold and discharge the system. Disconnect the gauge manifold.
5. Remove and discard the accumulator/drier. Install a new accumulator/drier and connect it to the evaporator. Do not connect it to the suction line from the compressor. Make sure the protective cap is in place on the suction line connection.
6. Replace the fixed orifice tube. Install the protective cap on the evaporator inlet tube as soon as the new orifice tube is in place. The liquid line will be connected later.
7. Remove the compressor from the vehicle for cleaning and service or replacement, whichever is required. If the compressor is cleaned and serviced, add the specified amount of refrigerant oil prior to installing in the vehicle. Place protective caps on the compressor inlet and outlet connections and install it on the mounting brackets in the vehicle. If the compressor is replaced, adjust the oil level. Install the shipping caps on the compressor connections and install the new compressor on the mounting brackets in the vehicle.
8. Back-flush the condenser and liquid line as follows:
   a. Remove the discharge hose from the condenser and clamp a piece of ½ in. i.d. heater hose to the condenser inlet line. Make sure the hose is long enough so the free end can be inserted into a suitable waste container to catch the flushing refrigerant.
   b. Move the flushing equipment into position and open the valve on the can of R-12, fully counterclockwise.
   c. Back-flush the condenser and liquid line by introducing the flushing refrigerant into the supported end of the liquid line with the flushing nozzle. Hold the nozzle firmly against the open end of the liquid line.
   d. After the liquid line and condenser have been flushed, lay the charging cylinder on it's side so the R-12 will not force more flushing refrigerant into the liquid line. Press the nozzle firmly to the liquid line and admit R-12 to force all flushing refrigerant from the liquid line and condenser.
   e. Remove the heater hose and clamp from the condenser inlet connection.
   f. Stand the flushing cylinder upright and flush the compressor discharge hose. Secure it so the flushing refrigerant goes into the waste container.
   g. Close the dispensing valve of the R-12 can, full clockwise. If there is any flushing refrigerant in the cylinder, it may be left there until the next flushing job. Put the flushing kit and R-12 can in a suitable storage location.

9. Connect all refrigerant lines. All connections should be cleaned and new O-rings should be used. Lubricate new O-rings with clean refrigerant oil.

10. Connect a charging station or manifold gauge set and charge the system with 1 lb. of R-12. Do not evacuate the system until after it has been leak tested.

11. Leak test all connections and components with flame-type leak detector 023–00006, electronic leak detector 055–00014 or 055–00015 or equivalent. If no leaks are found, proceed to Step 12. If leaks are found, service as necessary, check the system and then go to Step 12.

CAUTION

Fumes from flame-type leak detectors are noxious, avoid inhaling them or personal injury may result.

NOTE: Good ventilation is necessary in the area where air conditioning leak testing is to be done. If the surrounding air is contaminated with refrigerant gas, the leak detector will indicate this gas all the time. Odors from other chemicals such as anti-freeze, diesel fuel, disc brake cleaner or other cleaning solvents can cause the same problem. A fan, even in a well ventilated area, is very helpful in removing small traces of air contamination that might affect the leak detector.

12. Evacuate and charge the system with the specified amount of R-12. Operate the system to make sure it is cooling properly.

System Evacuating

1. Connect a manifold gauge set as follows:

a. Turn both manifold gauge set valves all the way to the right, to close the high and low pressure hoses to the center manifold and hose.

b. Remove the caps from the high and low pressure service gauge port valves.

c. If the manifold gauge set hoses do not have valve depressing pins in them, install fitting adapters T71P–19703–S and R or equivalent, which have pins, on the low and high pressure hoses.

d. Connect the high and low pressure hoses or adapters, to the respective high and low pressure service gauge port valves. High side adapter set D81L–19703–A or tool YT–354 or 355 or equivalent is required to connect a manifold gauge set or charging station to the high pressure gauge port valve.

NOTE: Service tee fitting D87P–19703–A, which may be mounted on the clutch cycling pressure switch fitting, is available for use in the low pressure side, to be used in place of the low pressure gauge port valve.

2. Leak test all connections and components with flame-type leak detector 023–00006, electronic leak detector 055–00014 or 055–00015 or equivalent.

CAUTION

Fumes from flame-type leak detectors are noxious, avoid inhaling them or personal injury may result.

NOTE: Good ventilation is necessary in the area where air conditioning leak testing is to be done. If the surrounding air is contaminated with refrigerant gas, the leak detector will indicate this gas all the time. Odors from other chemicals such as anti-freeze, diesel fuel, disc brake cleaner or other cleaning solvents can cause the same problem. A fan, even in a well ventilated area, is very helpful in removing small traces of air contamination that might affect the leak detector.

3. Properly discharge the refrigerant system according the to proper procedure.

4. Make sure both manifold gauge valves are turned all the way to the right. Make sure the center hose connection at the manifold gauge is tight.

5. Connect the manifold gauge set center hose to a vacuum pump.

6. Open the manifold gauge set valves and start the vacuum pump.

7. Evacuate the system with the vacuum pump until the low pressure gauge reads at least 25 in. Hg or as close to 30 in. Hg as possible. Continue to operate the vacuum pump for 15 minutes. If a part of the system has been replaced, continue to operate the vacuum pump for another 20–30 minutes.

8. When evacuation of the system is complete, close the manifold gauge set valves and turn the vacuum pump **OFF**.

9. Observe the low pressure gauge for 5 minutes to ensure that system vacuum is held. If vacuum is held, charge the system. If vacuum is not held for 5 minutes, leak test the system, service the leaks and evacuate the system again.

System Charging

1. Connect a manifold gauge set according to the proper procedure. Properly discharge and evacuate the system.

2. With the manifold gauge set valves closed to the center hose, disconnect the vacuum pump from the manifold gauge set.

3. Connect the center hose of the manifold gauge set to a refrigerant drum or a small can refrigerant dispensing valve tool YT–280, 1034 or equivalent. If a charging station is used, follow the instructions of the manufacturer. If a small can dispensing valve is used, install the small can(s) on the dispensing valve.

NOTE: Use only a safety type dispensing valve.

4. Loosen the center hose at the manifold gauge set and open the refrigerant drum valve or small can dispensing valve. Allow the refrigerant to escape to purge air and moisture from the center hose. Then, tighten the center hose connection at the manifold gauge set.

5. Disconnect the wire harness snap lock connector from the clutch cycling pressure switch and install a jumper wire across the 2 terminals of the connector.

6. Open the manifold gauge set low side valve to allow refrigerant to enter the system. Keep the refrigerant can in an upright position.

CAUTION

Do not open the manifold gauge set high pressure (discharge) gauge valve when charging with a small container. Opening the valve can cause the small refrigerant container to explode, which can result in personal injury.

7. When no more refrigerant is being drawn into the system, start the engine and set the control assembly for MAX cold and HI blower to draw the remaining refrigerant intyo the system. If equipped, press the air conditioning switch. Continue to add refrigerant to the system until the specified weight of R-12 is in the system. Then close the manifold gauge set low pressure valve and the refrigerant supply valve.

8. Remove the jumper wire from the clutch cycling pressure switch snap lock connector. Connect the connector to the pressure switch.

9. Operate the system until pressures stabilize to verify normal operation and system pressures.

10. In high ambient temperatures, it may be necessary to operate a high volume fan positioned to blow air through the radiator and condenser to aid in cooling the engine and prevent excessive refrigerant system pressures.

11. When charging is completed and system operating pressures are normal, disconnect the manifold gauge set from the vehicle. Install the protective caps on the service gauge port valves.

SYSTEM COMPONENTS

Radiator

REMOVAL AND INSTALLATION

1. Disconnect the negative battery cable. Drain the cooling system.
2. Disconnect the upper, lower and overflow hoses at the radiator.
3. On automatic transmission equipped vehicles, disconnect the fluid cooler lines at radiator.
4. Depending on model; remove the 2 top mounting bolts and remove radiator and shroud assembly or remove the shroud mounting bolts and position the shroud aside. If the air conditioner condenser is attached to the radiator, remove the retaining bolts and position the condenser aside. Do not disconnect the refrigerant lines.
5. Remove the radiator attaching bolts or top brackets and lift out the radiator.

To install:

6. If a new radiator is to be installed, transfer the petcock from the old radiator to the new one. If equipped with an automatic transmission, transfer the fluid cooler line fittings from the old radiator.
7. Position the radiator and install, do not tighten the radiator support bolts. If equipped with an automatic transmission, connect the fluid cooler lines. Then tighten the radiator support bolts or shroud and mounting bolts.
8. Connect the radiator hoses. Close the radiator petcock. Fill and bleed the cooling system.
9. Start the engine and bring to operating temperature. Check for leaks.
10. If equpped with an automatic transmission, check the cooler lines for leaks and interference. Check the transmission fluid level.

COOLING SYSTEM BLEEDING

When the entire cooling system is drained, the following procedure should be used to ensure a complete fill.

1. Install the block drain plug, if removed and close the draincock. With the engine off, add anti-freeze to the radiator to a level of 50 percent of the total cooling system capacity. Then add water until it reaches the radiator filler neck seat.

NOTE: On Mustang equipped with the 2.3L engine, disconnect the heater hose at the connection on the thermostat housing. Fill the radiator until coolant is visible at the connection in the thermostat housing or the coolant level in the radiator reaches the radiator filler neck seat. Install the heater hose and tighten the hose clamps.

2. Install the radiator cap to the first notch to keep spillage to a minimum.
3. Start the engine and let it idle until the upper radiator hose is warm. This indicates that the thermostat is open and coolant is flowing through the entire system.
4. Carefully remove the radiator cap and top off the radiator with water. Install the cap on the radiator securely.
5. Fill the coolant recovery reservoir to the FULL COLD mark with anti-freeze, then add water to the FULL HOT mark. This will ensure that a proper mixture is in the reservoir.

Electric Cooling Fan

TESTING

1. Disconnect the electrical connector at the cooling fan motor.
2. Connect a jumper wire between the negative motor lead and ground.
3. Connect another jumper wire between the positive motor lead and the positive terminal of the battery.
4. If the cooling fan motor does not run, it must be replaced.

REMOVAL AND INSTALLATION

Mustang

2.3L ENGINE

1. Disconnect the negative battery cable.
2. Remove the fan wiring harness from the routing clip. Disconnect the wiring harness from the fan motor connector by pulling up on the single lock finger to separate the connectors.
3. Remove the 4 mounting bracket attaching screws and remove the fan assembly from the vehicle.
4. Remove the retaining clip from the end of the motor shaft and remove the fan.

NOTE: A metal burr may be present on the motor after the retaining clip is removed. Deburring of the shaft may be required to remove the fan.

5. Remove the nuts attaching the fan motor to the mounting bracket.
6. Installation is the reverse of the removal procedure. Tighten the fan motor-to-mounting bracket attaching nuts to 48.5–62.0 inch lbs. (5.5–7.0 Nm) and the mounting bracket attaching screws to 70–95 inch lbs. (8.0–10.5 Nm).

Thunderbird and Cougar

3.8L SC ENGINE

1. Disconnect the negative battery cable.
2. Disconnect the fan motor wiring connector at the side of the fan shroud. Remove the male terminal connector retaining clip from the shroud mounting tab.
3. Remove the overflow hose from the fan shroud retaining clip and remove the 2 shroud upper retaining bolts at the radiator support.
4. Lift the cooling fan module past the radiator, disengaging the shroud from the 2 lower retaining clips.
5. Installation is the reverse of the removal procedure. Tighten the shroud retaining bolts to 36 inch lbs. (4 Nm).

Condenser

REMOVAL AND INSTALLATION

Crown Victoria, Grand Marquis and Town Car

NOTE: Whenever the condenser is replaced, it will be necessary to replace the suction accumulator/drier.

1. Disconnect the battery cables and remove the battery.
2. Place a clean container under the radiator draincock and drain the engine coolant. Save the coolant for reuse.
3. Disconnect the upper hose from the radiator.
4. Discharge the refrigerant from the air conditioning system according to the proper procedure.
5. Disconnect the 2 refrigerant lines at the fittings near the radiator on the right side of the vehicle using the spring-lock coupling disconnect procedure. Plug the lines to prevent dirt and excessive moisture from entering.
6. If necessary, remove the 2 retaining screws from the air intake duct and position it away from the radiator/condenser area.

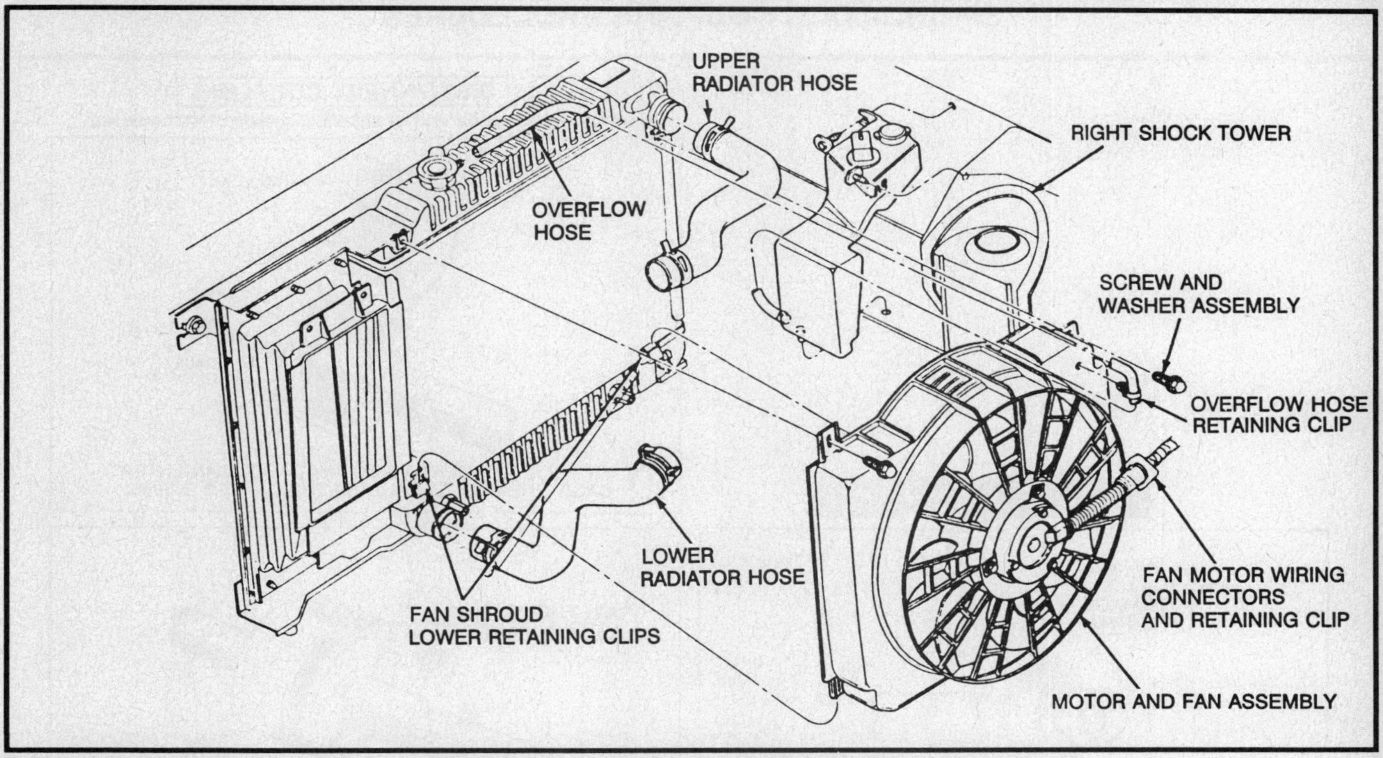
UPPER
RADIATOR HOSE
RIGHT SHOCK TOWER
OVERFLOW
HOSE
SCREW AND
WASHER ASSEMBLY
OVERFLOW HOSE
RETAINING CLIP
LOWER
RADIATOR HOSE
FAN MOTOR WIRING
CONNECTORS
AND RETAINING CLIP
FAN SHROUD
LOWER RETAINING CLIPS
MOTOR AND FAN ASSEMBLY

Cooling fan and motor assembly—Thunderbird and Cougar with 3.8L SC engine

7. Remove the 2 retaining screws from the fan shroud and position it rearward away from the radiator/condenser area.
8. Remove the screw from each of the 2 radiator brackets and tilt the radiator rearward.
9. Remove the 2 retaining screws from the top back side of the condenser assembly and lift the condenser from the vehicle. Remove and retain the 4 corner condenser mounts.

To install:

NOTE: When replacing the condenser in the refrigerant system, 1 oz. (29.5ml) of clean refrigerant oil should be added to the new replacement condenser to maintain the total system oil charge.

10. Attach the 4 corner mounts and position the condenser into the vehicle. Install the 2 condenser retaining screws.
11. Position the radiator and install the radiator brackets and 2 screws.
12. Position the fan shroud and install the 2 retaining screws.
13. If necessary, position the air intake duct and install the 2 retaining screws.
14. Remove the plugs from the 2 refrigerant lines and install new O-rings lubricated with clean refrigerant oil.
15. Connect the condenser inlet tube to the compressor discharge line and the condenser outlet tube to the liquid line using the spring-lock coupling connect procedure.
16. Connect the upper hose to the radiator and fill the cooling system with the previously drained radiator coolant. Replace the radiator cap.
17. Replace the battery and connect the battery cables.
18. Leak test, evacuate and charge the refrigerant system according to the proper procedure. Observe all safety precautions.
19. Check the air conditioning system for proper operation.

Thunderbird, Cougar and Mark VII

NOTE: Whenever the condenser is replaced, it will be necessary to replace the suction accumulator/drier.

1. Disconnect the battery cables and remove the battery.
2. Discharge the refrigerant from the air conditioning system according to the proper procedure.
3. Disconnect the 2 refrigerant lines at the fittings on the right side of the radiator by following the spring-lock coupling disconnect procedure.
4. Remove the 4 bolts attaching the condenser to the radiator support and remove the condenser from the vehicle.

To install:

NOTE: When replacing the condenser in the refrigerant system, 1 oz. (29.5ml) of clean refrigerant oil should be added to the new replacement condenser to maintain the total system oil charge.

5. Position the condenser assembly to the radiator support brackets and install the attaching bolts.
6. Connect the refrigerant lines to the condenser assembly according to the spring-lock coupling connect procedure.
7. Install the battery and connect the battery cables.
8. Leak test, evacuate and charge the refrigerant system according to the proper procedure. Observe all safety precautions.
9. Check the operation of the air conditioning system.

Mustang

NOTE: Whenever the condenser is replaced, it will be necessary to replace the suction accumulator/drier.

1. Disconnect the battery cables and remove the battery and heat shield.

SPRING-LOCK COUPLING PROCEDURES

TO CONNECT COUPLING

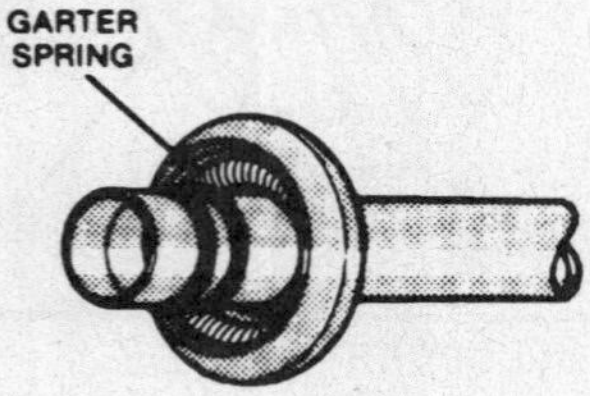
GARTER SPRING

1. CHECK FOR MISSING OR DAMAGED GARTER SPRING — REMOVE DAMAGED SPRING WITH SMALL HOOKED WIRE — INSTALL NEW SPRING IF DAMAGED OR MISSING.

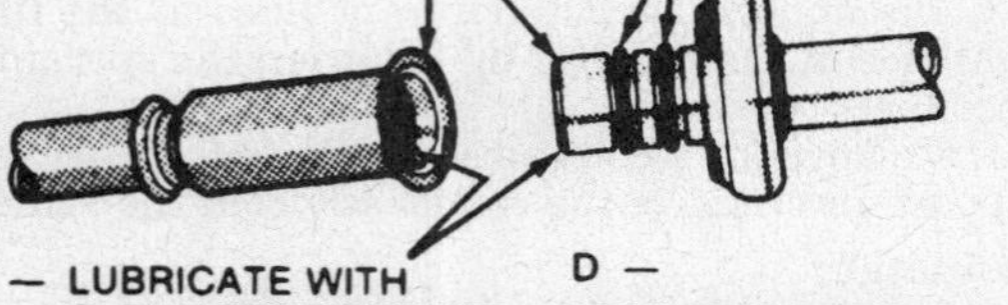
A — CLEAN FITTINGS
B — INSTALL NEW O-RINGS — USE ONLY SPECIFIED O-RINGS
C — LUBRICATE WITH CLEAN REFRIGERANT OIL
D — ASSEMBLE FITTING TOGETHER BY PUSHING WITH A SLIGHT TWISTING MOTION

2.

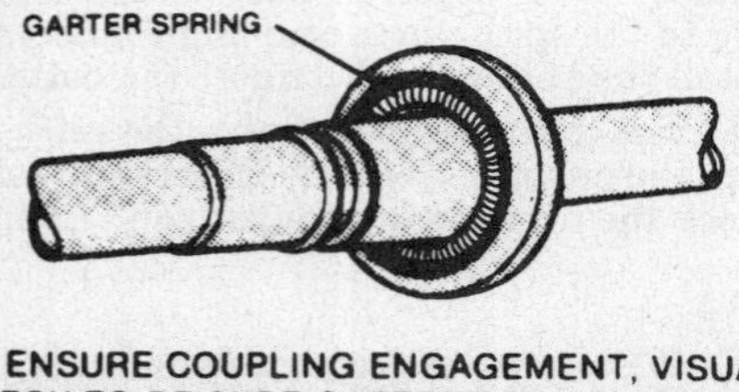
GARTER SPRING

3. TO ENSURE COUPLING ENGAGEMENT, VISUALLY CHECK TO BE SURE GARTER SPRING IS OVER FLARED END OF FEMALE FITTING.

TO DISCONNECT COUPLING

CAUTION — DISCHARGE SYSTEM BEFORE DISCONNECTING COUPLING

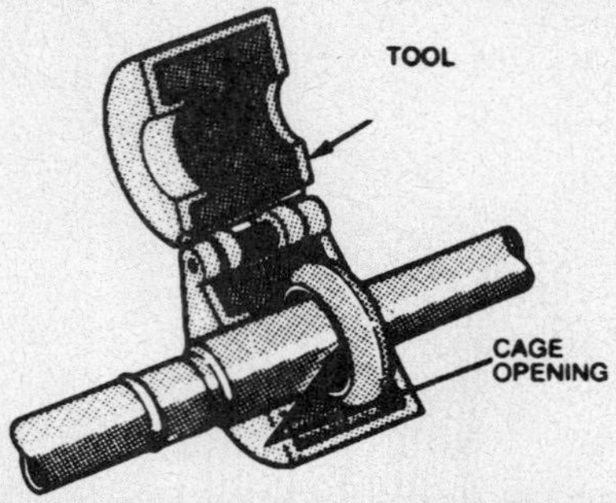
TOOL
CAGE OPENING

(1) FIT TOOL TO COUPLING SO THAT TOOL CAN ENTER CAGE OPENING TO RELEASE THE GARTER SPRING.

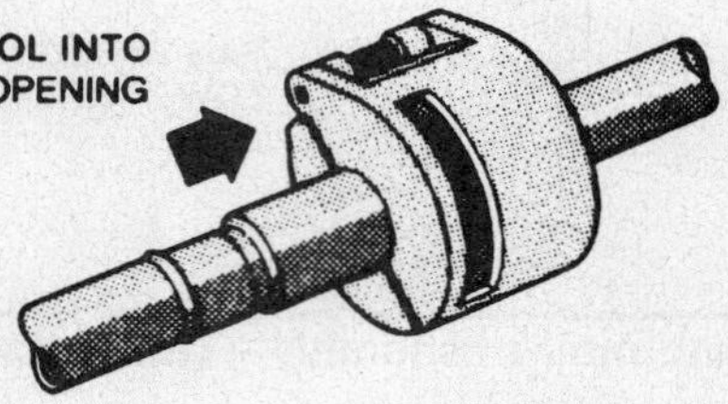
PUSH TOOL INTO CAGE OPENING

(2) PUSH THE TOOL INTO THE CAGE OPENING TO RELEASE THE FEMALE FITTING FROM THE GARTER SPRING.

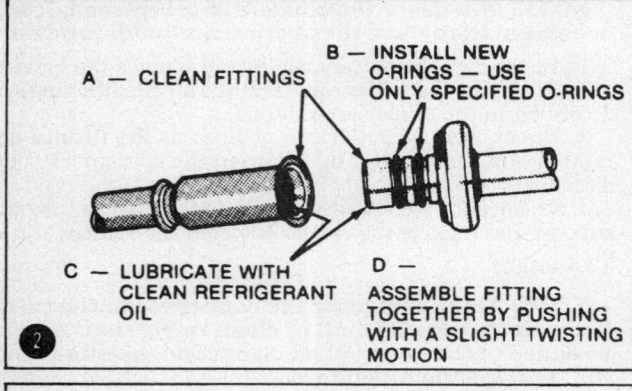

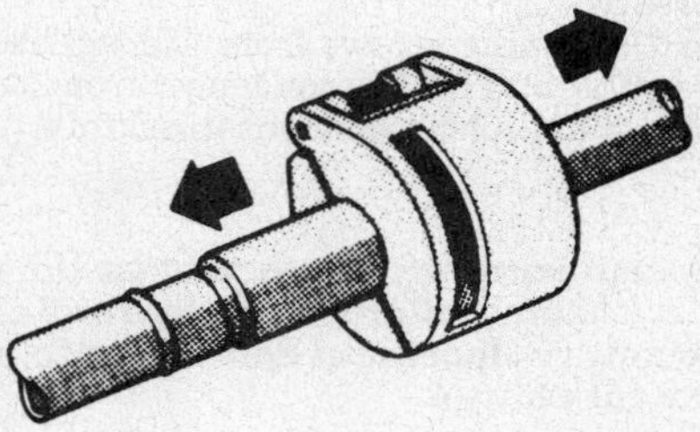

(3) PULL THE COUPLING MALE AND FEMALE FITTINGS APART.

(4) REMOVE THE TOOL FROM THE DISCONNECTED SPRING LOCK COUPLING.

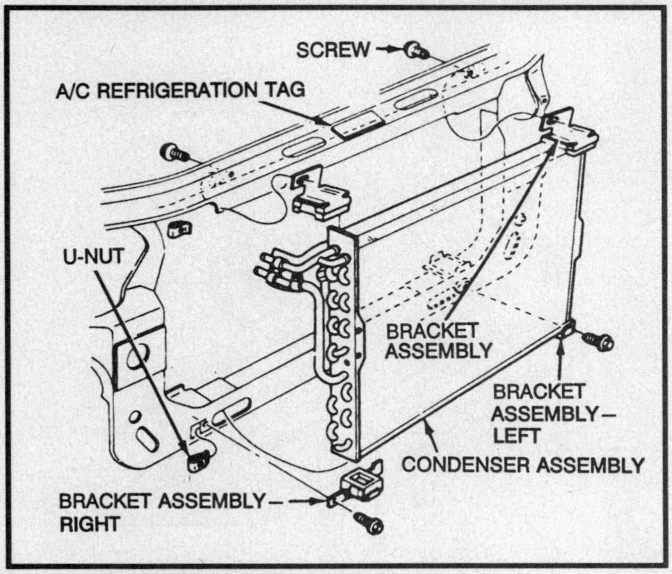
SCREW
A/C REFRIGERATION TAG
U-NUT
BRACKET ASSEMBLY
BRACKET ASSEMBLY—LEFT
CONDENSER ASSEMBLY
BRACKET ASSEMBLY—RIGHT

Condenser Installation—Mark VII

2. Discharge the refrigerant from the air conditioning system according to the proper procedure.
3. Place a clean container under the radiator draincock and drain the coolant from the radiator. Save the coolant for reuse.
4. Disconnect the refrigerant lines at the right side of the radiator according to the spring-lock coupling disconnect procedure.
5. Remove the 2 fan shroud attaching screws. Disengage the fan shroud and position it rearward.
6. Disconnect the upper hose from the radiator, remove the 2 radiator retaining clamps and tilt the radiator rearward.
7. Remove the 2 screws attaching the top of the condenser to the radiator support and lift the condenser from the vehicle. Cap the refrigerant lines to prevent entry of dirt and excessive moisture.

To install:

NOTE: When replacing the condenser in the refrigerant system, 1 oz. (29.5ml) of clean refrigerant oil should be added to the new replacement condenser to maintain the total system oil charge.

8. If the condenser is to be replaced, transfer the rubber isolators from the bottom of the old condenser to the new condenser.
9. Position the condenser assembly to the vehicle making sure the lower isolators are properly seated. Then install the upper 2 condenser attaching screws.
10. Position the radiator to the radiator support and install the 2 retaining clamps.
11. Connect the upper hose to the radiator and fill the radiator with the previously removed coolant.
12. Position the fan shroud to the radiator and install the 2 attaching screws.
13. Connect the refrigerant lines to the condenser according to the spring-lock coupling connect procedure.
14. Install the battery and heat shield, then connect the battery cables.
15. Leak test, evacuate and charge the refrigerant system according to the proper procedure. Observe all safety precautions.
16. Check the operation of the air conditioning system.

Compressor

REMOVAL AND INSTALLATION

Crown Victoria, Grand Marquis and Town Car

NOTE: The suction accumulator/drier and the fixed orifice tube should also be replaced whenever the compressor is replaced.

1. Disconnect the negative battery cable.
2. Discharge the refrigerant from the air conditioning system according to the proper procedure.
3. Loosen the idler pulley to remove the tension from the compressor drive belt. Remove the drive belt from the clutch pulley.
4. Remove the refrigerant lines from the compressor manifolds and disconnect the clutch wires at the wire connector.
5. Remove 1 bolt attaching the top of the compressor to the compressor front bracket.
6. Remove the locknut and stud from the compressor front lower inboard attachment at the front bracket. If the stud does not come out with the locknut, install two 10mm × 1.25 pitch nuts on the stud and remove the stud.
7. Remove 3 compressor lower attaching bolts and remove the compressor.

To install:

NOTE: A new service replacement 10PA17 compressor contains 8 oz. (237ml) of refrigerant oil. Prior to installing the replacement compressor, drain the refrigerant oil from the removed compressor into a calibrated container. Then, drain the refrigerant oil from the new compressor into a clean calibrated container. If the amount of oil drained from the removed compressor was between 3–5 oz. (90–148ml), pour the same amount of clean refrigerant oil into the new compressor. If the amount of oil that was removed from the old compressor is greater than 5 oz. (148ml), pour 5 oz. (148ml) of clean refrigerant oil into the new compressor. If the amount of refrigerant oil that was removed from the old compressor is less than 3 oz. (90ml), pour 3 oz. (90ml) of clean refrigerant oil into the new compressor. This will maintain the total system oil charge within specification.

8. Position the compressor to the mounting brackets and install the 3 lower attaching bolts.
9. Install the stud and locknut at the front lower inboard attachment. A bolt and lock washer may be used in place of the stud and locknut, if desired. The bolt should be 10mm × 1.25 pitch by 2¼ in. long.
10. Install 1 bolt to attach the top of the compressor to the front bracket.
11. Remove the pressure test plate from the compressor. If the compressor is new, remove the shipping cover and install it on the old compressor.
12. Using new O-rings lubricated with clean refrigerant oil, connect the refrigerant hoses to the suction and discharge manifolds. Tighten the suction hose fitting to 21–27 ft. lbs. (28–36Nm) and the discharge hose fitting to 15–20 ft. lbs. (20–27Nm).
13. Connect the clutch wires at the harness connector and attach the connector to the compressor front bracket.
14. Install the belt on the compressor clutch pulley and adjust the belt tension.
15. Leak test, evacuate and charge the system. Observe all safety precautions.
16. Check the operation of the air conditioning system.

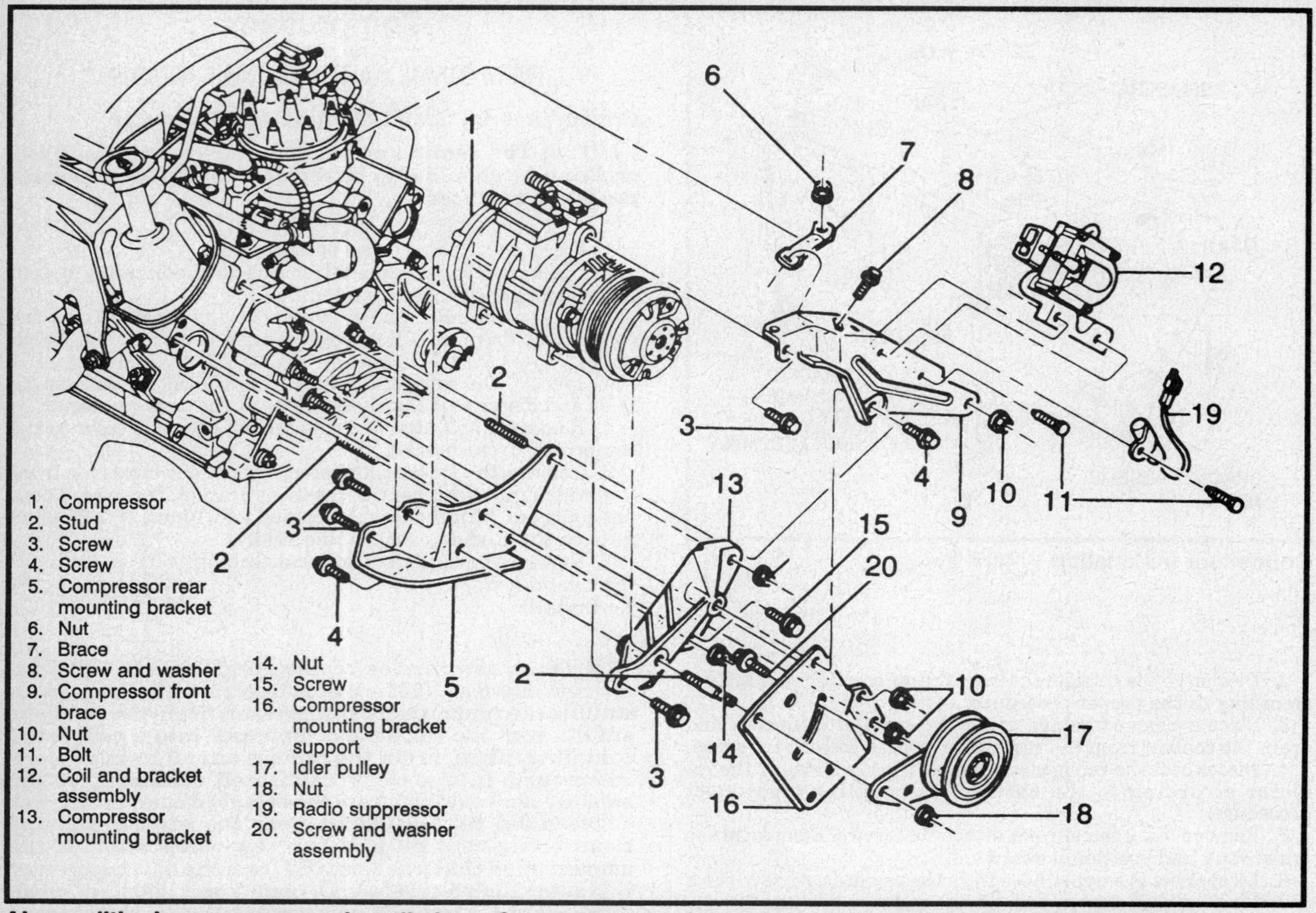
1
2
3
4
5
6
7
8
9
10
11
12
13
14
15
16
17
18
19
20
1. Compressor
2. Stud
3. Screw
4. Screw
5. Compressor rear mounting bracket
6. Nut
7. Brace
8. Screw and washer
9. Compressor front brace
10. Nut
11. Bolt
12. Coil and bracket assembly
13. Compressor mounting bracket
14. Nut
15. Screw
16. Compressor mounting bracket support
17. Idler pulley
18. Nut
19. Radio suppressor
20. Screw and washer assembly

Air conditioning compressor installation—Crown Victoria, Grand Marquis and Town Car with 5.0L engine

Mark VII

NOTE: The suction accumulator/drier and the fixed orifice tube should also be replaced whenever the compressor is replaced.

1. Disconnect the negative battery cable.
2. Discharge the refrigerant from the air conditioning system according to the proper procedure.
3. Disconnect the compressor clutch wires at the field coil connector on the compressor.
4. Disconnect the discharge and suction hoses from the compressor manifolds. Cap the refrigerant lines and compressor manifolds to prevent the entrance of dirt and moisture.
5. Remove the 3 bolts attaching the front of the compressor to the power steering pump support and compressor brace.
6. Remove the 2 bolts mounting the rear compressor brace to the power steering pump support.
7. Remove the compressor and rear compressor brace as a unit.
8. Remove the 2 bolts mounting the rear brace to the compressor. If the compressor is to be replaced, remove the clutch and field coil assembly from the compressor.

To install:

NOTE: A new service replacement 10PA17 compressor contains 8 oz. (237ml) of refrigerant oil. Prior to installing the replacement compressor, drain the refrigerant oil from the removed compressor into a calibrated container. Then, drain the refrigerant oil from the new compressor into a clean calibrated container. If the amount of oil drained from the removed compressor was between 3–5 oz. (90–148ml), pour the same amount of clean refrigerant oil into the new compressor. If the amount of oil that was removed from the old compressor is greater than 5 oz. (148ml), pour 5 oz. (148ml) of clean refrigerant oil into the new compressor. If the amount of refrigerant oil that was removed from the old compressor is less than 3 oz. (90ml), pour 3 oz. (90ml) of clean refrigerant oil into the new compressor. This will maintain the total system oil charge within specification.

9. Mount the compressor rear brace to the compressor.
10. Finger start the bolts attaching the compressor rear brace to the power steering pump support.
11. Tighten the 2 bottom bolts holding the front of the compressor onto the power steering pump support.
12. Tighten the bolt holding the front of the compressor brace to the top front of the compressor.
13. Tighten the 2 started bolts attaching the compressor rear brace to the power steering pump support.
14. Using new O-rings lubricated with clean refrigerant oil, connect the suction and discharge lines to the compressor manifolds.
15. Connect the clutch wires to the field coil connector and install the drive belt.

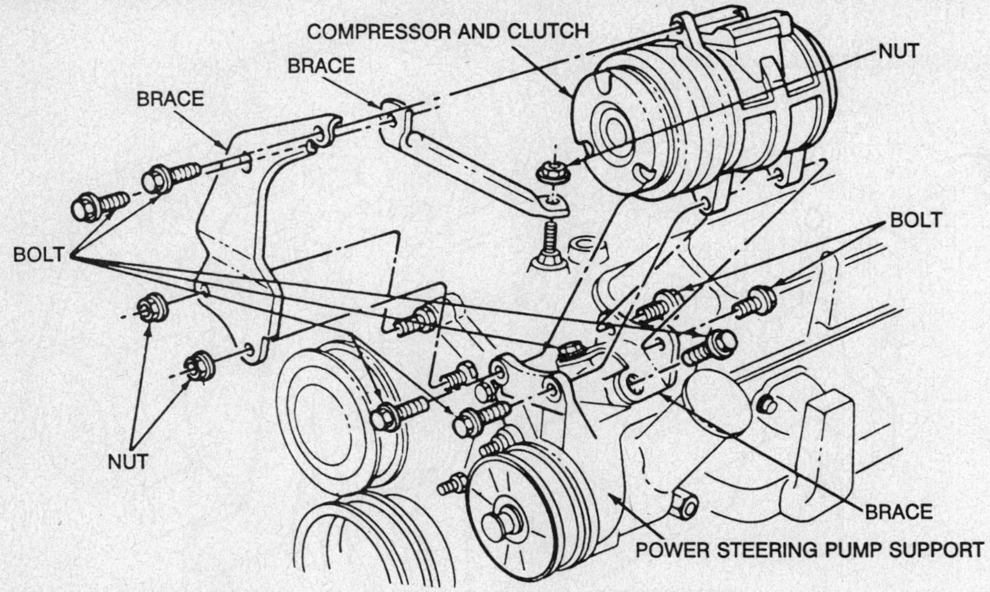
COMPRESSOR AND CLUTCH
BRACE
BRACE
NUT
BOLT
BOLT
NUT
BRACE
POWER STEERING PUMP SUPPORT

Air conditioning compressor installation—Mark VII

16. Leak test, evacuate and charge the air conditioning system. Observe all safety precautions.
17. Check the operation of the air conditioning system.

Thunderbird and Cougar

NOTE: The suction accumulator/drier and the fixed orifice tube should also be replaced whenever the compressor is replaced.

1. Disconnect the negative battery cable.
2. Discharge the refrigerant from the air conditioning system according to the proper procedure.
3. Remove the compressor drive belt and disconnect the compressor clutch wires at the field coil connector on the compressor.
4. Remove the suction and discharge manifold from the compressor. Cap the suction and discharge ports in the manifold and compressor to prevent entry of dirt or moisture.
5. Remove the 4 bolts that secure the compressor to the mounting bracket and remove the compressor.

To install:

NOTE: A new service replacement FX-15 compressor contains 7 oz. (207ml) of refrigerant oil. Prior to installing the replacement compressor, drain the refrigerant oil from the removed compressor into a calibrated container. Then, drain the refrigerant oil from the new compressor into a clean calibrated container. If the amount of oil drained from the removed compressor was between 3–5 oz. (90–148ml), pour the same amount of clean refrigerant oil into the new compressor. If the amount of oil that was removed from the old compressor is greater than 5 oz. (148ml), pour 5 oz. (148ml) of clean refrigerant oil into the new compressor. If the amount of refrigerant oil that was removed from the old compressor is less than 3 oz. (90ml), pour 3 oz. (90ml) of clean refrigerant oil into the new compressor. This will maintain the total system oil charge within specification.

6. Position the compressor on the mounting bracket and install the 4 mounting bolts.
7. Remove the protective caps and install the suction and discharge manifold on the compressor.
8. Connect the clutch wires to the field coil connector and install the compressor drive belt.
9. Leak test, evacuate and charge the air conditioning system. Observe all safety precautions.
10. Check the operation of the air conditioning system.

Mustang

2.3L ENGINE

NOTE: The suction accumulator/drier and the fixed orifice tube should also be replaced whenever the compressor is replaced.

1. Disconnect the negative battery cable.
2. Discharge the refrigerant from the air conditioning system according to the proper procedure.
3. Disconnect the compressor clutch wires at the field coil connector on the compressor.
4. Disconnect the discharge and suction hoses from the compressor manifolds. Cap the refrigerant lines and compressor manifolds to prevent the entrance of dirt and moisture.
5. Remove the screw and washer assembly from the adjusting bracket.
6. Rotate the compressor outboard and remove the drive belts.
7. Remove the compressor mounting bolt attaching the bracket to the compressor lower mounting lug.
8. Remove the compressor and adjusting bracket intact.
9. Remove the clutch field coil and adjusting bracket from the compressor, if the compressor is to be replaced.

To install:

NOTE: A new service replacement HR-980 compressor contains 8 oz. (237ml) of refrigerant oil. Prior to installing the replacement compressor, drain 4 oz. (118ml) of refrigerant oil from the compressor. This will main-

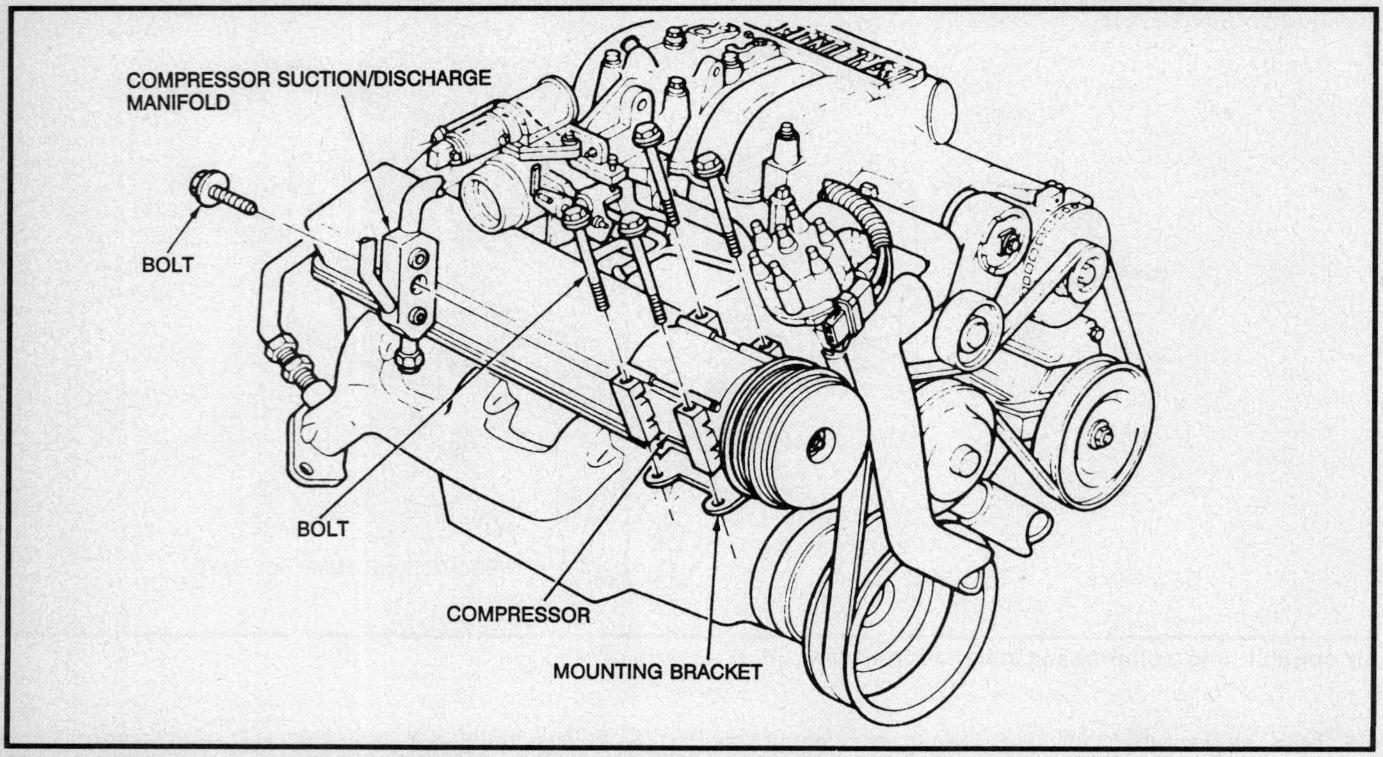
COMPRESSOR SUCTION/DISCHARGE
MANIFOLD
BOLT
BOLT
COMPRESSOR
MOUNTING BRACKET

Air conditioning compressor installation – Thunderbird and Cougar except 3.8L SC engine

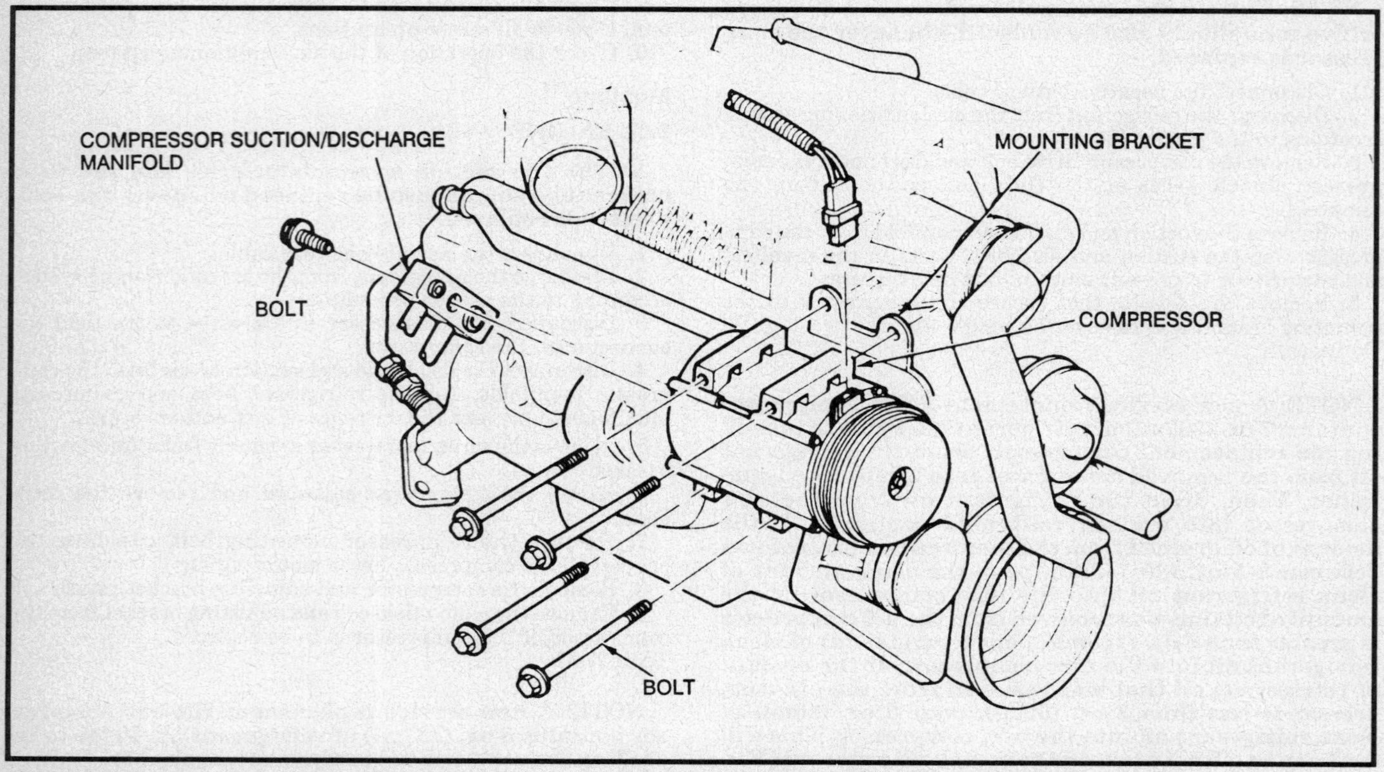
COMPRESSOR SUCTION/DISCHARGE
MANIFOLD
MOUNTING BRACKET
BOLT
COMPRESSOR
BOLT

Air conditioning compressor installation – Thunderbird and Cougar with 3.8L SC engine

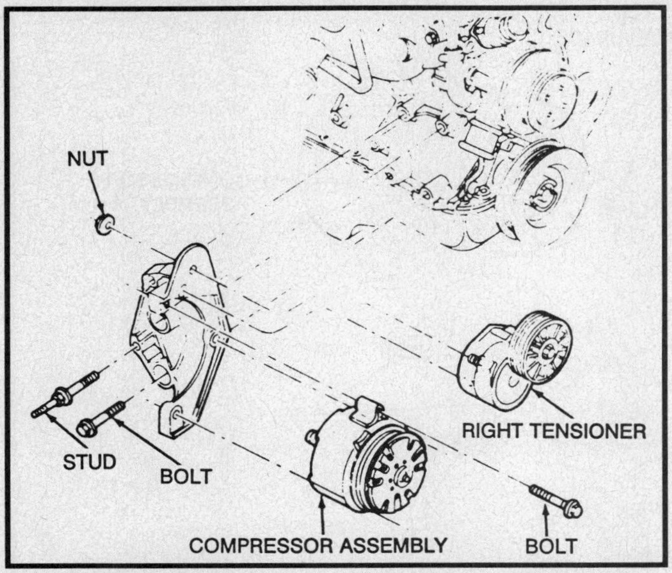
NUT
STUD
BOLT
RIGHT TENSIONER
COMPRESSOR ASSEMBLY
BOLT

Air conditioning compressor installation—Mustang with 2.3L engine

tain the system total oil charge. A new service replacement 10P15C compressor contains 8 oz. (237ml) of refrigerant oil. Prior to installing the replacement compressor, drain the refrigerant oil from the removed compressor into a calibrated container. Then, drain the refrigerant oil from the new compressor into a clean calibrated container. If the amount of oil drained from the removed compressor was between 3–5 oz. (90–148ml), pour the same amount of clean refrigerant oil into the new compressor. If the amount of oil that was removed from the old compressor is greater than 5 oz. (148ml), pour 5 oz. (148ml) of clean refrigerant oil into the new compressor. If the amount of refrigerant oil that was removed from the old compressor is less than 3 oz. (90ml), pour 3 oz. (90ml) of clean refrigerant oil into the new compressor. This will maintain the total system oil charge within specification.

10. Install the clutch field coil and adjusting bracket if it was removed or the compressor was replaced.
11. Install the compressor mounting brackets and drive belt in the reverse order of their removal.
12. Connect the refrigerant lines to the compressor and connect the clutch wires to the field coil connector.
13. Leak test, evacuate and charge the air conditioning system. Observe all safety precautions.
14. Check the operation of the air conditioning system.

5.0L ENGINE

NOTE: The suction accumulator/drier and the fixed orifice tube should also be replaced whenever the compressor is replaced.

1. Disconnect the negative battery cable.
2. Discharge the refrigerant from the air conditioning system according to the proper procedure.
3. Disconnect the compressor clutch wires at the field coil connector on the compressor.
4. Disconnect the discharge and suction hoses from the compressor manifolds. Cap the refrigerant lines and compressor manifolds to prevent the entrance of dirt and moisture.
5. Remove the 2 screws attaching the brace to the rear mounting bracket.
6. Remove the 2 screws attaching the bracket to the compressor lower front mounting lugs.
7. Remove 1 screw attaching the bracket to the compressor upper mounting lug.
8. Remove the compressor/clutch assembly and rear support from the vehicle as a unit.
9. Remove the 2 screws attaching the compressor to the rear support and remove the rear support.
10. If the compressor is to be replaced, remove the clutch and field coil assembly from the compressor.

To install:

NOTE: A new service replacement 6P148 compressor contains 10 oz. (300ml) of refrigerant oil. Prior to installing the replacement compressor, drain the refrigerant oil from the removed compressor into a calibrated container. Then, drain the refrigerant oil from the new compressor into a clean calibrated container. If the amount of oil drained from the removed compressor was between 3–5 oz. (90–148ml), pour the same amount of clean refrigerant oil into the new compressor. If the amount of oil that was removed from the old compressor is greater than 5 oz. (148ml), pour 5 oz. (148ml) of clean refrigerant oil into the new compressor. If the amount of refrigerant oil that was removed from the old compressor is less than 3 oz. (90ml), pour 3 oz. (90ml) of clean refrigerant oil into the new compressor. This will maintain the total system oil charge within specification.

11. Install the compressor and brackets in the reverse order of their removal.
12. Using new O-rings lubricated with clean refrigerant oil, connect the suction and discharge lines to the compressor manifolds. Tighten the suction hose fitting to 21–27 ft. lbs. (28–36Nm) and the discharge hose fitting to 15–20 ft. lbs. (20–27Nm).
13. Connect the clutch wires to the field coil connector and install the drive belt.
14. Leak test, evacuate and charge the air conditioning system. Observe all safety precautions.
15. Check the system for proper operation.

Accumulator/Drier

REMOVAL AND INSTALLATION

Any time a major component of the air conditioning system is replaced, it is necessary to replace the suction accumulator/drier. A major component would be the condenser, compressor, evaporator or a refrigerant hose/line. A fixed orifice tube or O-ring is not considered a major component but the orifice tube should be replaced whenever the compressor is replaced for lack of performance.

The accumulator/drier should also be replaced, if 1 of the following conditions exist:

- The accumulator/drier is perforated.
- The refrigerant system has been opened to the atmosphere for a period of time longer than required to make a minor repair.
- There is evidence of moisture in the system such as internal corrosion of metal refrigerant lines or the refrigerant oil is thick and dark.

NOTE: The compressor oil from vehicles equipped with an FX-15 compressor may have a dark color while maintaining a normal oil viscosity. This is normal for this compressor because carbon from the compressor piston rings may discolor the oil.

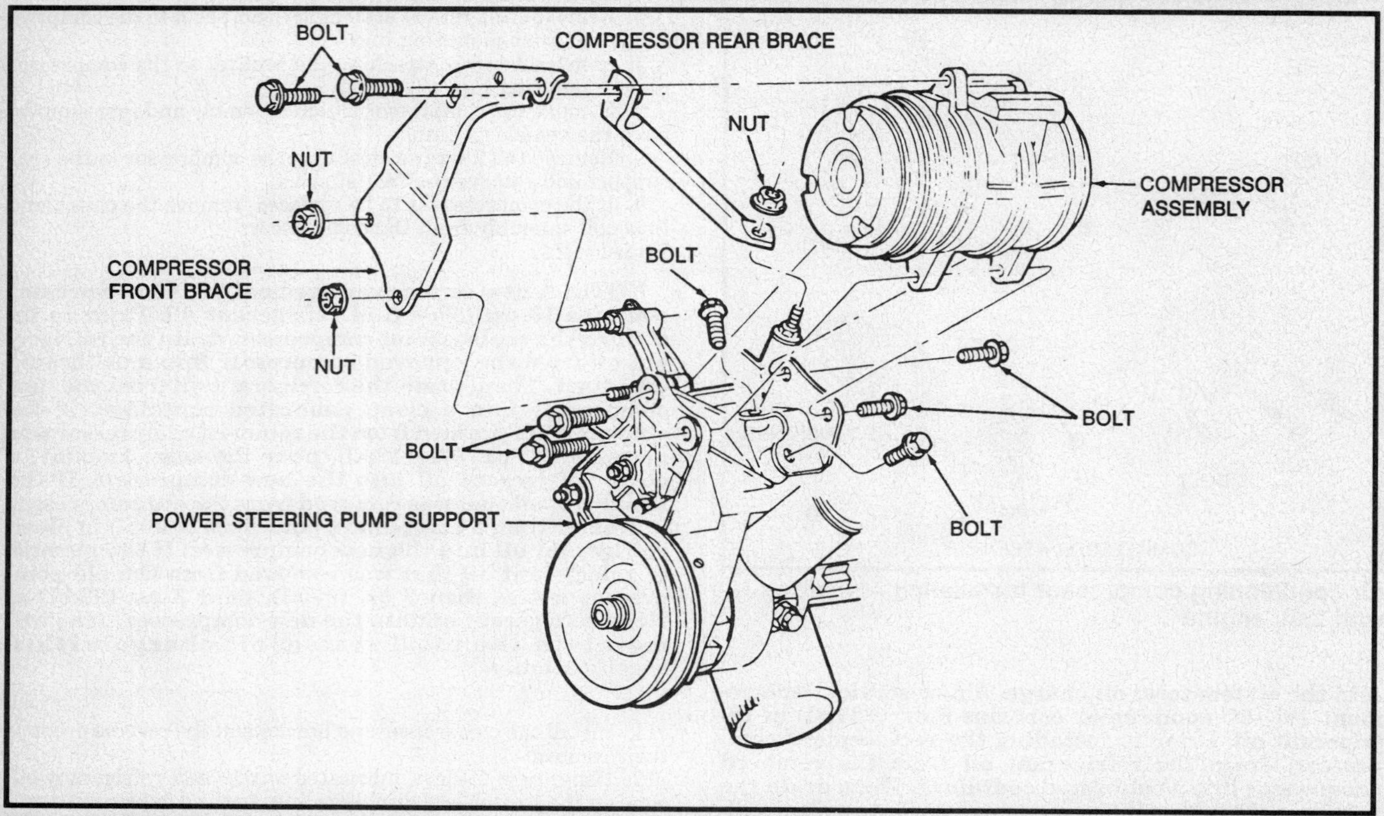
BOLT
COMPRESSOR REAR BRACE
NUT
NUT
COMPRESSOR ASSEMBLY
BOLT
COMPRESSOR FRONT BRACE
NUT
BOLT
BOLT
POWER STEERING PUMP SUPPORT
BOLT

Air conditioning compressor installation – Mustang with 5.0L engine

When replacing the suction accumulator/drier, the following procedure must be used to ensure that the total oil charge in the system is correct after the new accumulator/drier is installed.

1. Drain the oil from the removed accumulator/drier into a suitable measuring container. It may be necessary to drill one or two ½ in. holes in the bottom of the old accumulator/drier to ensure that all the oil has drained out.
2. Add the same amount of clean new refrigerant oil plus 2 oz. to the new accumulator/drier. Use only the proper type of oil for the vehicle being serviced.

Crown Victoria, Grand Marquis and Town Car

1. Disconnect the negative battery cable.
2. Discharge the refrigerant from the air conditioning system according to the proper procedure.
3. Disconnect the electrical connector from the pressure switch and remove the switch by unscrewing it from the accumulator/drier.
4. Disconnect the suction hose from the accumulator/drier according to the spring-lock coupling disconnect procedure.
5. Loosen the fitting connecting the accumulator/drier to the evaporator core. Use 2 wrenches to prevent component damage.
6. Remove the screw attaching the accumulator/drier strap to the mounting bracket.
7. Disconnect the accumulator/drier from the evaporator core. Remove the 2 straps from the accumulator/drier.

To install:

8. Using a new O-ring lubricated with clean refrigerant oil, connect the accumulator/drier to the evaporator core tube. Tighten the connection finger-tight only.
9. Position the strap on the accumulator/drier. Align the strap with the mounting bracket and install the mounting screw. Loosen the connection of the accumulator/drier to the evaporator core, if it is necessary to reposition the accumulator to install the strap attaching screw.
10. Tighten the accumulator/drier to evaporator core fitting using 2 wrenches.
11. Using a new O-ring lubricated with clean refrigerant oil, connect the suction hose to the accumulator/drier using the spring-lock coupling connect procedure.
12. Install a new O-ring lubricated with clean refrigerant oil on the pressure switch nipple of the accumulator/drier. Install the pressure switch and tighten the switch finger-tight only.
13. Connect the electrical connector to the pressure switch.
14. Leak test, evacuate and charge the air conditioning system. Observe all safety precautions.
15. Check the system for proper operation.

Mark VII

1. Disconnect the negative battery cable.
2. Discharge the refrigerant from the air conditioning system according to the proper procedure.
3. Disconnect the suction hose at the compressor. Cap the hose and compressor to prevent the entrance of dirt and moisture.
4. Disconnect the accumulator/drier inlet tube from the evaporator core outlet. Use 2 wrenches to prevent component damage.
5. Disconnect the wire harness connector from the pressure switch on top of the accumulator/drier.
6. Remove the screw holding the accumulator/drier in the accumulator bracket and remove the accumulator/drier.

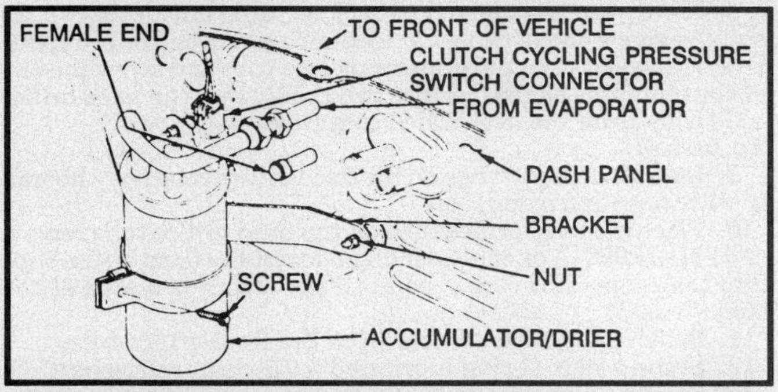
FEMALE END
TO FRONT OF VEHICLE
CLUTCH CYCLING PRESSURE SWITCH CONNECTOR
FROM EVAPORATOR
DASH PANEL
BRACKET
SCREW
NUT
ACCUMULATOR/DRIER

Accumulator/drier installation—Mustang and Mark VII

To install:

7. Position the accumulator/drier to the vehicle and route the suction hose to the compressor.
8. Using a new O-ring lubricated with clean refrigerant oil, connect the accumulator/drier inlet tube to the evaporator core outlet. Tighten the connection using a back-up wrench to prevent component damage.
9. Install the screw in the accumulator/drier bracket.
10. Using a new O-ring lubricated with clean refrigerant oil, connect the suction hose to the compressor.
11. Leak test, evacuate and charge the air conditioning system. Observe all safety precautions.
12. Check the system for proper operation.

Thunderbird and Cougar

1. Disconnect the negative battery cable.
2. Discharge the refrigerant from the air conditioning system according to the proper procedure.
3. On 3.8L SC engine equipped vehicles, disconnect the suction hose at the accumulator/drier. Cap the suction hose to prevent the entrance of dirt and moisture. If equipped with the 3.8L EFI base engine, disconnect the suction hose at the compressor. Cap the suction hose and compressor to prevent the entry of dirt and moisture.
4. Disconnect the accumulator/drier inlet tube from the evaporator core outlet using the spring-lock coupling disconnect procedure.
5. Disconnect the wire harness connector from the pressure switch on top of the accumulator/drier.
6. Remove the screw holding the accumulator/drier in the accumulator bracket and remove the accumulator/drier.

To install:

7. Position the accumulator/drier to the vehicle and route the suction hose to the compressor.
8. Using a new O-ring lubricated with clean refrigerant oil, connect the accumulator/drier inlet tube to the evaporator core outlet using the spring-lock coupling connect procedure.
9. Install the screw in the accumulator/drier bracket.
10. Using a new O-ring lubricated with clean refrigerant oil, connect the suction hose to the accumulator/drier or the compressor, as required.
11. Leak test, evacuate and charge the air conditioning system. Observe all safety precautions.
12. Check the system for proper operation.

Mustang

1. Disconnect the negative battery cable.
2. Discharge the refrigerant from the air conditioning system according to the proper procedure.
3. On 2.3L engine equipped vehicles, remove the speed control servo, if equipped.
4. Disconnect the suction hose at the compressor. Cap the hose and compressor to prevent the entrance of dirt and moisture.

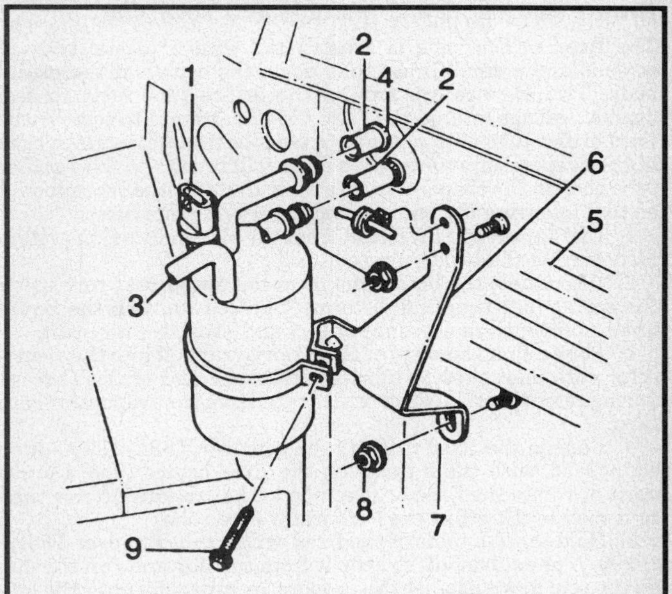
1
2
4
2
6
5
3
8
7
9

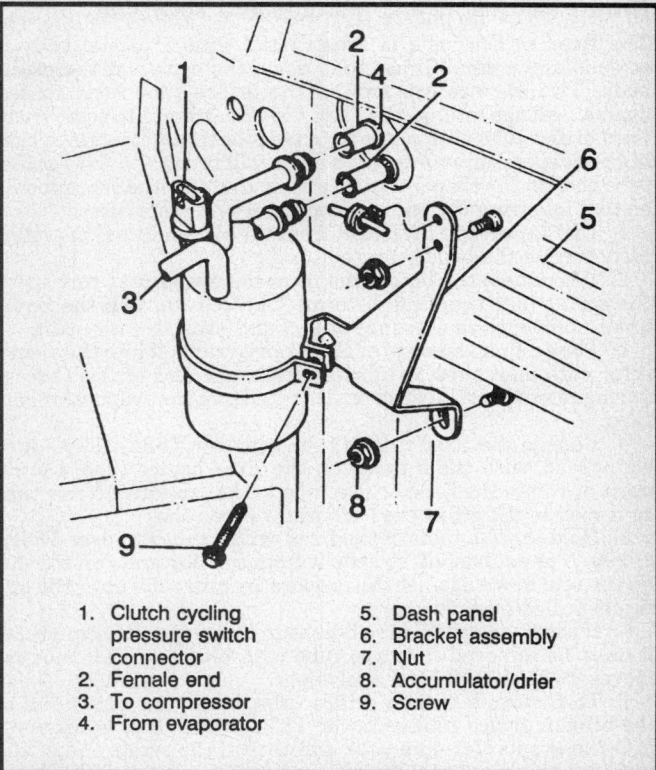

1. Clutch cycling pressure switch connector
2. Female end
3. To compressor
4. From evaporator
5. Dash panel
6. Bracket assembly
7. Nut
8. Accumulator/drier
9. Screw

Accumulator/drier installation—Thunderbird and Cougar

5. Disconnect the accumulator/drier inlet tube from the evaporator core outlet. Use 2 wrenches to prevent component damage.
6. Disconnect the wire harness connector from the pressure switch on top of the accumulator/drier.
7. Remove the screw holding the accumulator/drier in the accumulator bracket and remove the accumulator/drier.

To install:

8. Position the accumulator/drier to the vehicle and route the suction hose to the compressor.
9. Using a new O-ring lubricated with clean refrigerant oil, connect the accumulator/drier inlet tube to the evaporator core outlet. Tighten the connection using a back-up wrench to prevent component damage.
10. Install the screw in the accumulator/drier bracket
11. Using a new O-ring lubricated with clean refrigerant oil, connect the suction hose to the compressor.
12. On 2.3L engine equipped vehicles, install the speed control servo, if equipped.
13. Leak test, evacuate and charge the air conditioning system. Observe all safety precautions.
14. Check the system for proper operation.

Fixed Orifice Tube

REMOVAL AND INSTALLATION

NOTE: The fixed orifice tube should be replaced whenever a compressor is replaced. If high pressure reads extremely high and low pressure (suction) is almost a vacuum, the fixed orifice is plugged and must be replaced.

Crown Victoria, Grand Marquis and Town Car

The fixed orifice tube is constructed with a plastic body, 2 screens and a small brass tube down the center of the orifice body. Two O-rings are around the orifice tube body to seal against leakage around the body. Do not attempt to remove the fixed orifice tube with pliers or to twist or rotate the orifice tube in the evaporator core tube; to do so will break the fixed orifice tube body in the evaporator core tube. Use only the recommended tool following the recommended service procedures.

1. Discharge the refrigerant from the air conditioning system according to the proper procedure.
2. Disconnect the liquid line from the evaporator core using the spring-lock coupling disconnect procedure. Cap the liquid line to prevent the entrance of dirt and excessive moisture.
3. Pour a small amount of clean refrigerant oil into the evaporator core inlet tube to lubricate the tube and orifice O-rings during removal of the fixed orifice tube from the evaporator core tube.
4. Engage the fixed orifice tube remover T83L–19990–A or equivalent, with the 2 tangs on the fixed orifice tube. Do not twist or rotate the fixed orifice tube in the evaporator core tube as it may break off in the evaporator core tube.
5. Hold the T-handle of the fixed orifice tube remover T83L–19990–A or equivalent, to keep it from turning and run the nut on the tool down against the evaporator core tube until the orifice is pulled from the tube.
6. If the fixed orifice tube breaks in the evaporator core tube, it must be removed from the tube with broken orifice tube remover T83L–19990–B or equivalent.
7. To remove a broken orifice tube, insert the screw end of the broken orifice tube remover T83L–19990–B or equivalent, into the evaporator core tube and thread the screw end of the tool into the brass tube in the center of the fixed orifice tube. Pull the fixed orifice tube from the evaporator core tube.
8. If only the brass center tube is removed during Step 7, insert the screw end of broken orifice tube remover T83L–19990–B or equivalent, into the evaporator core tube and screw the end of the tool into the fixed orifice tube body. Pull the fixed orifice tube body from the evaporator core tube.

To install:

9. Lubricate the O-rings on the fixed orifice tube body liberally with clean refrigerant oil.
10. Place the fixed orifice tube on the fixed orifice tube remover T83L–19990–A or equivalent, and insert the fixed orifice tube into the evaporator core tube until the orifice is seated at the stop.
11. Remove the remover tool from the fixed orifice tube.
12. Using a new O-ring lubricated with clean refrigerant oil, connect the liquid line to the evaporator core tube using the spring-lock coupling connect procedure.
13. Leak test, evacuate and charge the system. Observe all safety precautions.
14. Check the system for proper operation.

Mark VII, Thunderbird, Cougar and Mustang

If replacement of the fixed orifice tube is necessary, the liquid line must be replaced or install orifice tube replacement kit E5VY–190695–A or equivalent.

1. Discharge the refrigerant from the air conditioning system according the to proper procedure.
2. Remove the liquid line from the vehicle.
3. Locate the orifice tube by the 3 indented notches or a circular depression in the metal portion of the liquid line.
4. Note the angular position of the ends of the liquid line so it can be reassembled in the correct position.
5. Cut a 2½ in. (63.5mm) section from the tube at the orifice tube location. Do not cut closer than 1 in. (25.4mm) from the start of a bend in the tube.

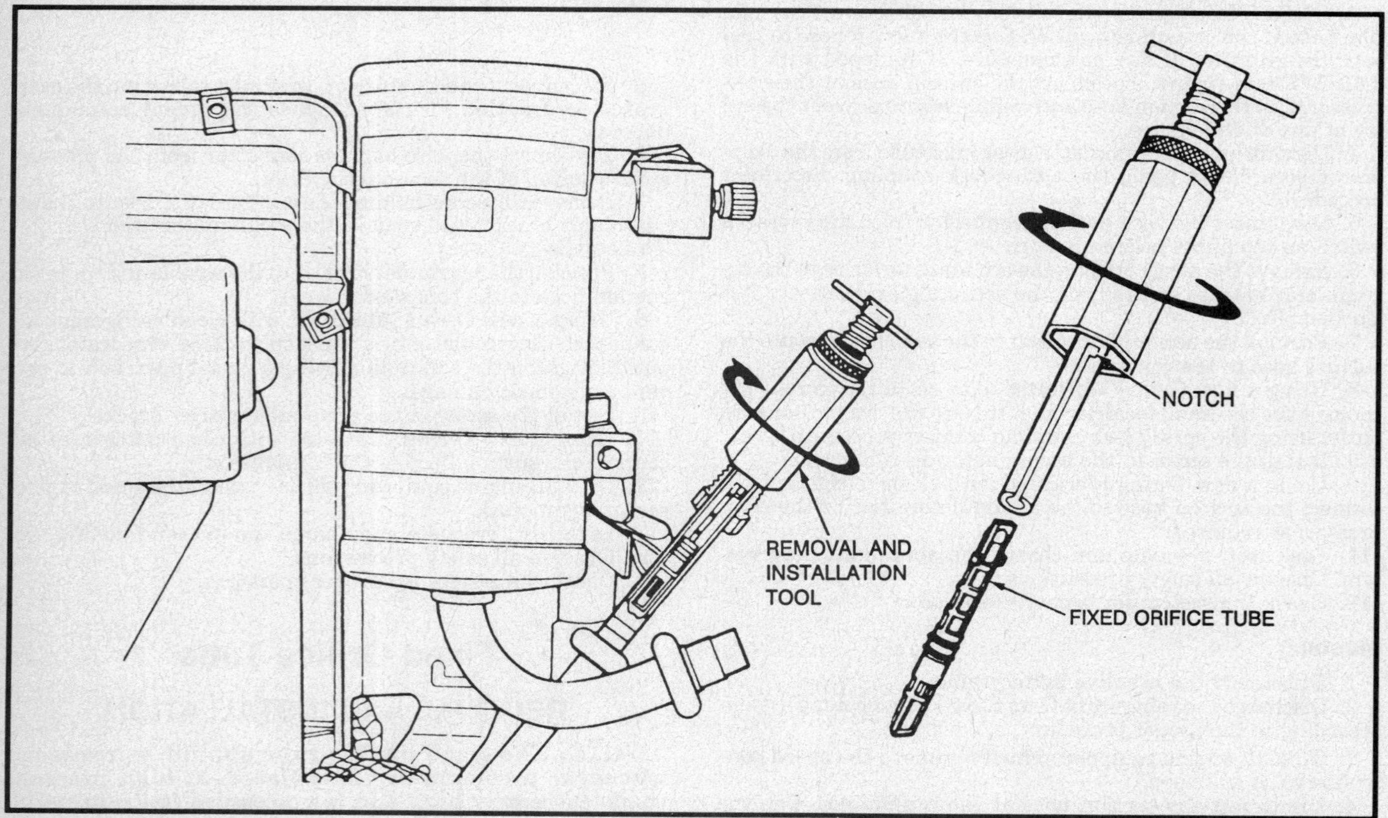
NOTCH
REMOVAL AND
INSTALLATION
TOOL
FIXED ORIFICE TUBE

Fixed orifice tube removal—Crown Victoria, Grand Marquis and Town Car

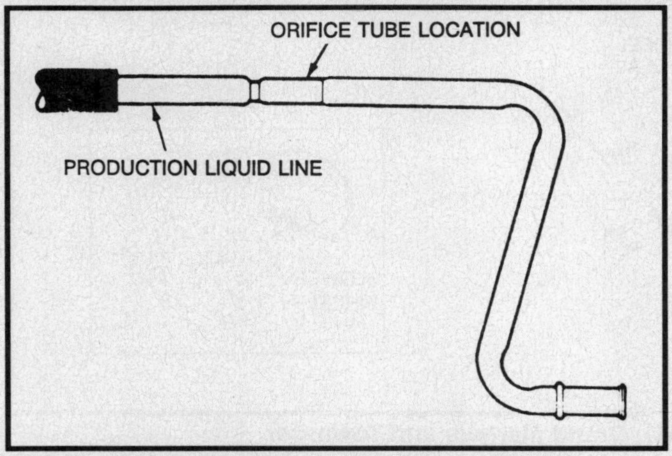
ORIFICE TUBE LOCATION
PRODUCTION LIQUID LINE

Fixed orifice tube location—Mark VII, Thunderbird, Cougar and Mustang

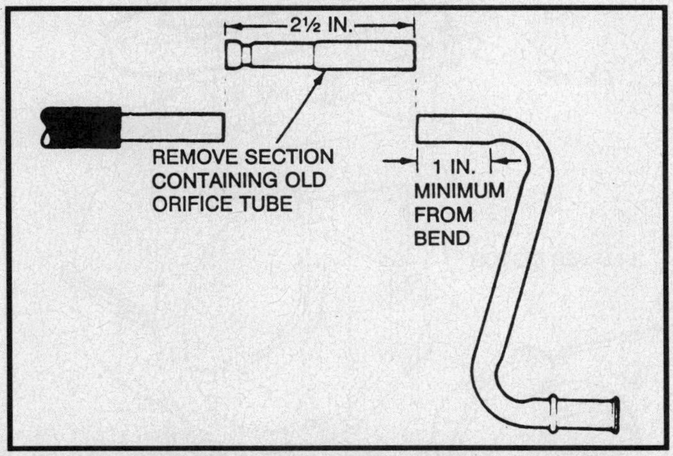
2½ IN.
REMOVE SECTION CONTAINING OLD ORIFICE TUBE
1 IN. MINIMUM FROM BEND

Fixed orifice tube section removed from liquid line—Mark VII, Thunderbird, Cougar and Mustang

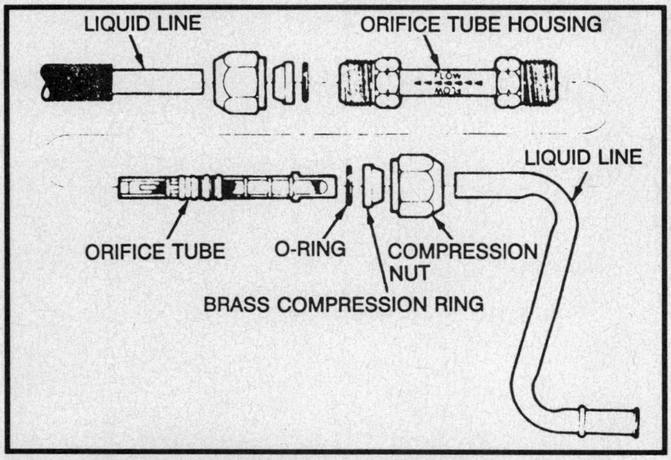
LIQUID LINE
ORIFICE TUBE HOUSING
LIQUID LINE
ORIFICE TUBE
O-RING
COMPRESSION NUT
BRASS COMPRESSION RING

Fixed orifice tube kit disassembled—Mark VII, Thunderbird, Cougar and Mustang

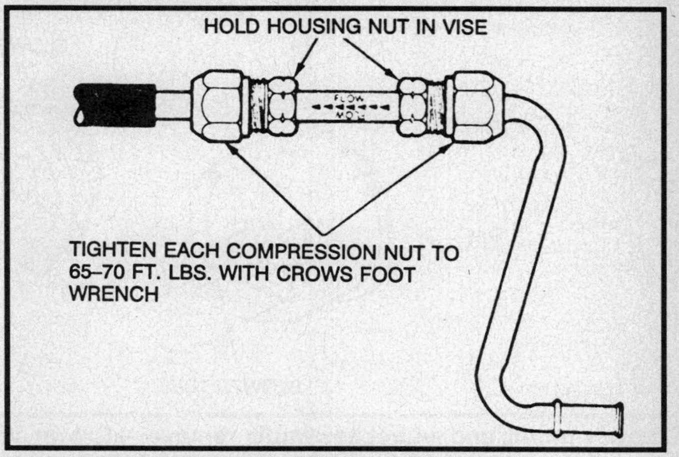
HOLD HOUSING NUT IN VISE
TIGHTEN EACH COMPRESSION NUT TO 65–70 FT. LBS. WITH CROWS FOOT WRENCH

Fixed orifice tube kit installed—Mark VII, Thunderbird, Cougar and Mustang

6. Remove the orifice tube from the housing with pliers. The orifice tube removal tool cannot be used.
7. Flush the 2 pieces of liquid line to remove any contaminants.
8. Lubricate the O-rings with clean refrigerant oil and assemble the orifice tube kit, with the orifice tube installed, to the liquid line. Make sure the flow direction arrow is pointing toward the evaporator end of the liquid line and the taper of each compression ring is toward the compression nut.

NOTE: The inlet tube will be positioned against the orifice tube tabs when correctly assembled.

9. While holding the hex of the tube in a suitable vise, tighten each compression nut to 65–70 ft. lbs. (88–94 Nm) with a crow foot wrench.
10. Install the liquid line on the vehicle using new O-rings lubricated with clean refrigerant oil.
11. Leak test, evacuate and charge the system. Observe all safety precautions.
12. Check the system for proper operation.

Blower Motor

REMOVAL AND INSTALLATION

Crown Victoria, Grand Marquis and Town Car

1. Disconnect the negative battery cable.
2. Disconnect the blower motor lead connector from the wiring harness connector.
3. Remove the blower motor cooling tube from the blower motor.
4. Remove the 4 retaining screws.
5. Turn the motor and wheel assembly slightly to the right so the bottom edge of the mounting plate follows the contour of the wheel well splash panel. Lift up on the blower and remove it from the blower housing.
6. Installation is the reverse of the removal procedure.

Mark VII

1. Disconnect the negative battery cable.
2. Remove the recirculation duct assembly and disconnect the blower electrical connector.
3. Remove the 4 blower motor mounting plate screws and remove the blower motor and wheel assembly from the blower housing.

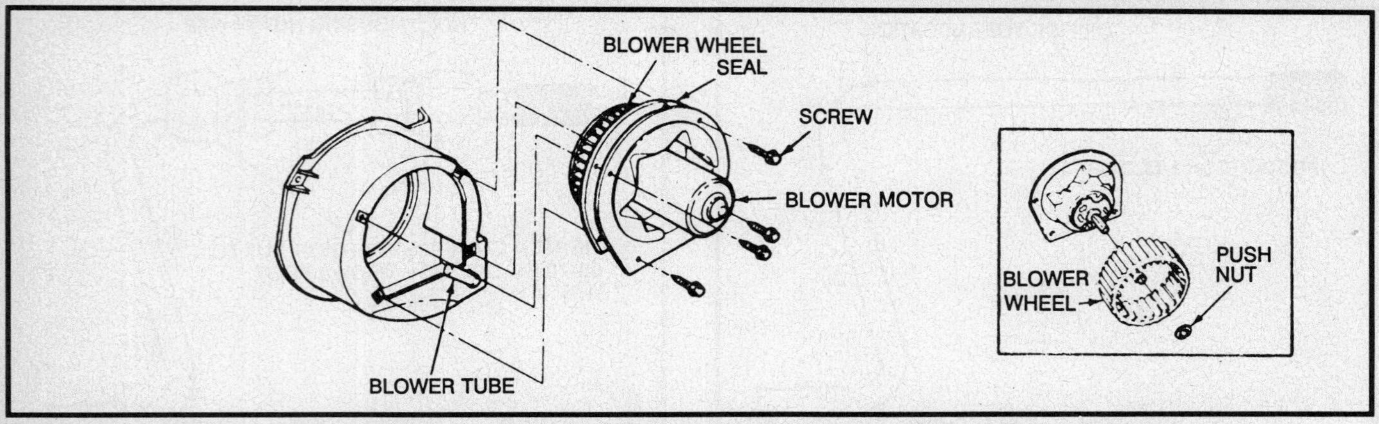
BLOWER WHEEL
SEAL
SCREW
BLOWER MOTOR
BLOWER TUBE
BLOWER
WHEEL
PUSH
NUT

Blower motor and wheel assembly removal – Crown Victoria, Grand Marquis and Town Car.

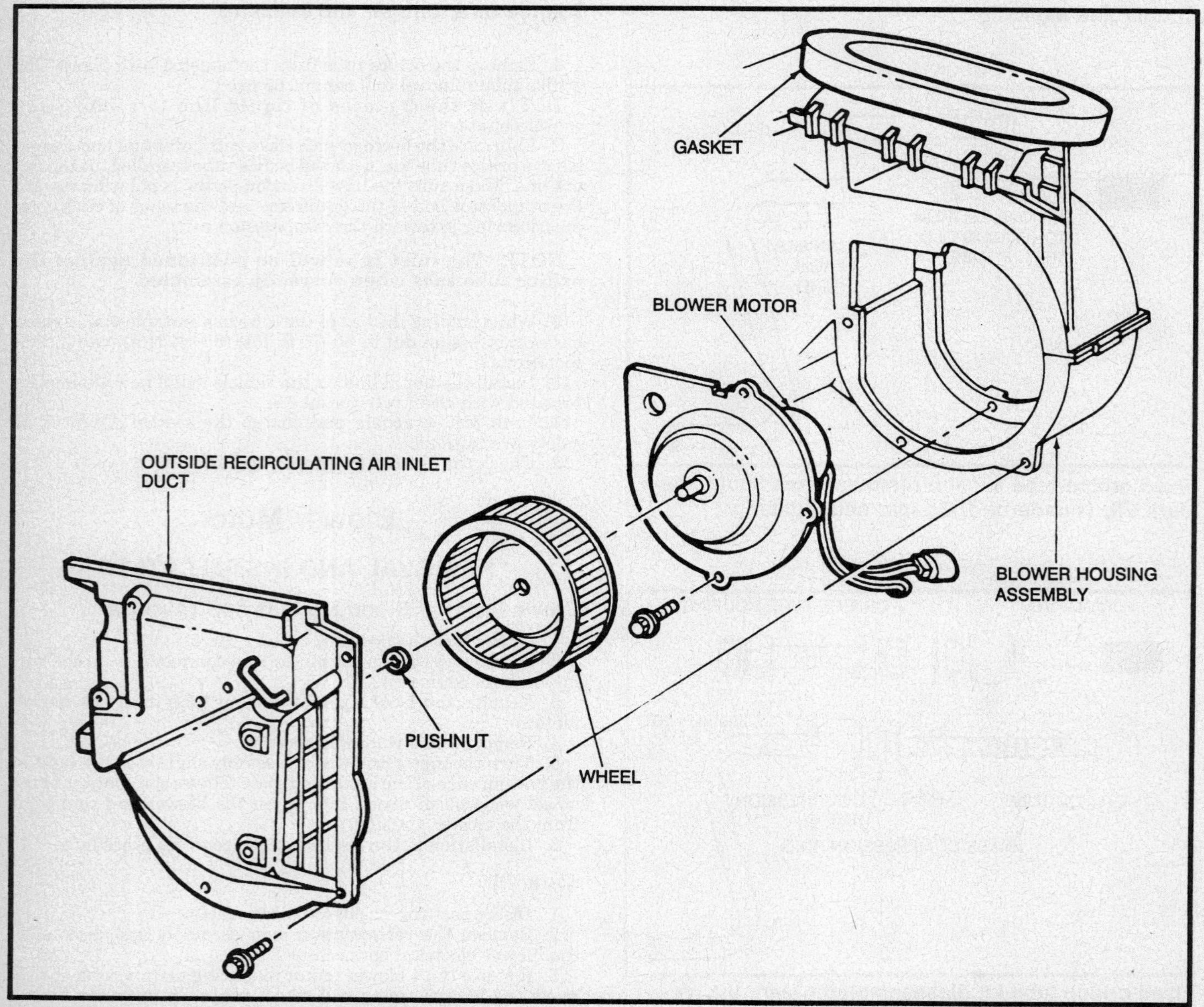
GASKET
BLOWER MOTOR
OUTSIDE RECIRCULATING AIR INLET
DUCT
BLOWER HOUSING
ASSEMBLY
PUSHNUT
WHEEL

Blower motor and wheel assembly disassembled – Mark VII

4. Remove the pushnut from the blower motor shaft and remove the blower wheel from the shaft.
5. Installation is the reverse of the removal procedure.

Thunderbird and Cougar

1. Disconnect the negative battery cable.
2. Remove the glove compartment liner to gain access to the blower motor mounting screws.
3. Remove the 4 blower motor retaining screws and remove the blower motor and wheel assembly from the blower housing.
4. Remove the pushnut from the blower motor shaft and then remove the blower wheel from the motor shaft.
5. Installation is the reverse of the removal procedure.

Mustang

1. Disconnect the negative battery cable. Loosen glove compartment assembly by squeezing the sides together to disengage the retainer tabs.
2. Let the glove compartment and door hang down in front of instrument panel and remove blower motor cooling hose.
3. Disconnect electrical wiring harness. Remove 4 screws attaching motor to housing. Pull motor and wheel out of housing.
4. Installation is the reverse of the removal procedure.

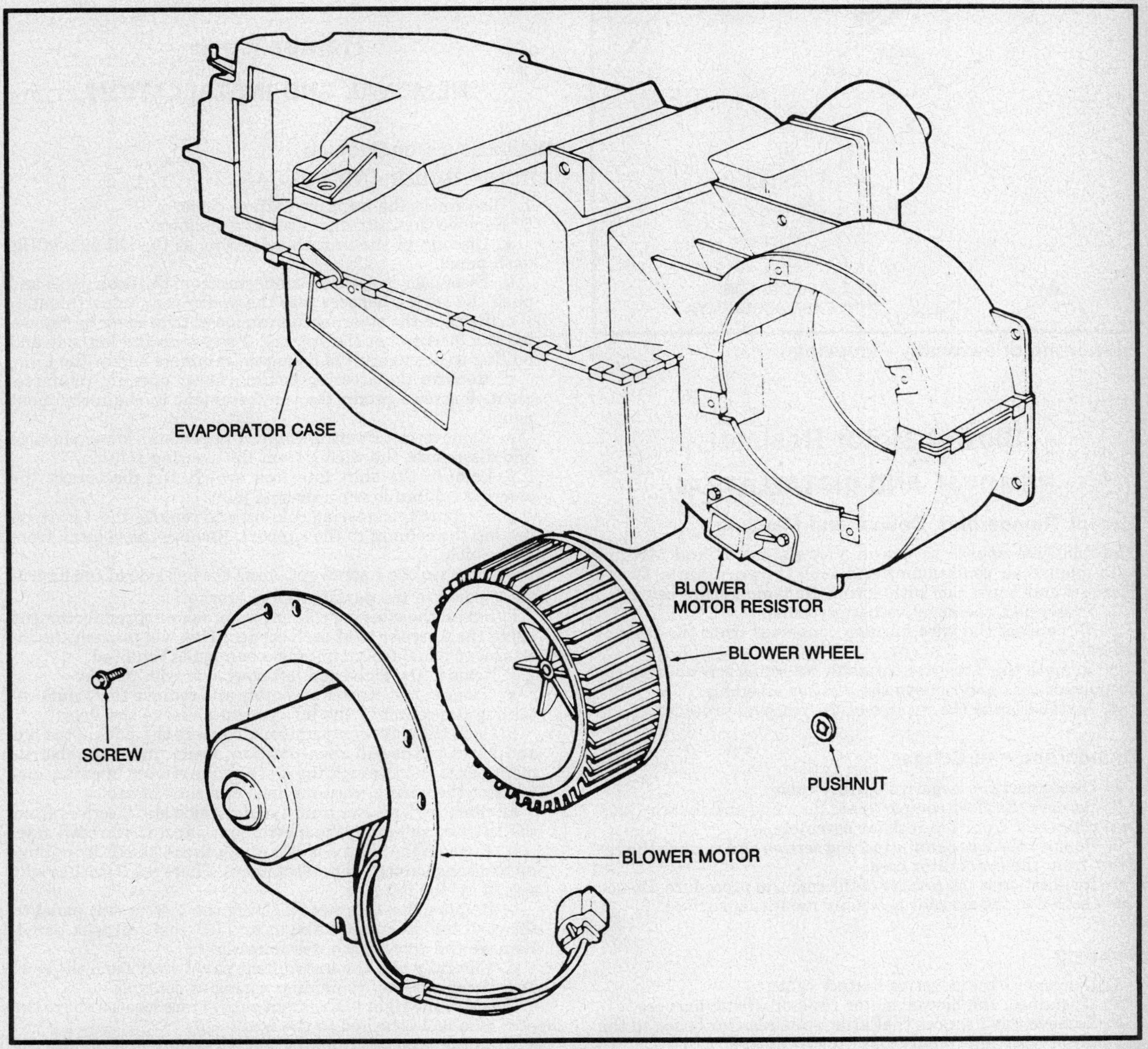
EVAPORATOR CASE
BLOWER
MOTOR RESISTOR
BLOWER WHEEL
SCREW
PUSHNUT
BLOWER MOTOR

Blower motor assembly removal—Thunderbird and Cougar

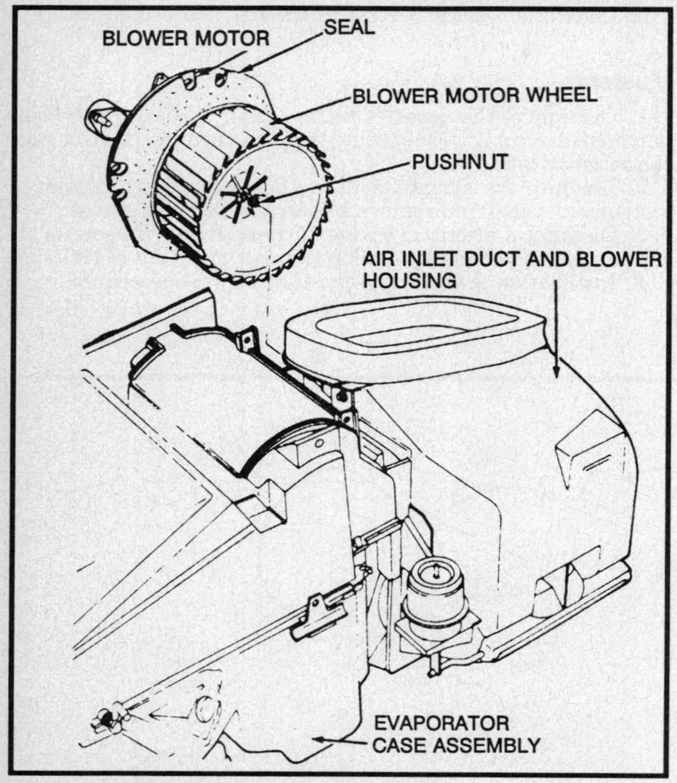
BLOWER MOTOR
SEAL
BLOWER MOTOR WHEEL
PUSHNUT
AIR INLET DUCT AND BLOWER HOUSING
EVAPORATOR CASE ASSEMBLY

Blower motor assembly—Mustang

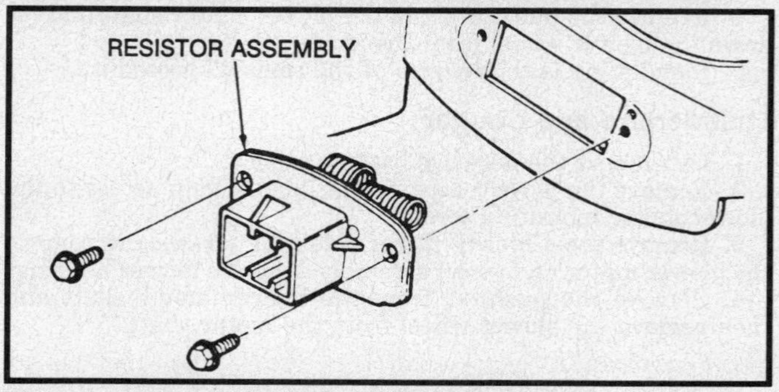
RESISTOR ASSEMBLY

Blower motor resistor installation—typical

Blower Motor Resistor

REMOVAL AND INSTALLATION

Except Thunderbird, Cougar and Mustang

The following applies to Crown Victoria and Grand Marquis with manual air conditioning and 1989 Crown Victoria, Grand Marquis and Town Car with automatic temperature control

1. Disconnect the negative battery cable.
2. Disconnect the wire harness connector from the resistor assembly.
3. Remove the 2 resistor assembly retaining screws from the evaporator case and remove the resistor assembly.
4. Installation is the reverse of the removal procedure.

Thunderbird and Cougar

1. Disconnect the negative battery cable.
2. Remove the glove compartment liner and pull the wire harness connector from the resistor assembly.
3. Remove the 2 resistor attaching screws and remove the resistor from the evaporator case.
4. Installation is the reverse of the removal procedure. Do not apply sealer to the resistor assembly mounting surface.

Mustang

1. Disconnect the negative battery cable.
2. Disconnect the blower motor resistor wiring harness.
3. Remove the 2 screws that attach the resistor board to the evaporator case and remove the resistor assembly.
4. Installation is the reverse of the removal procedure.

Heater Core

REMOVAL AND INSTALLATION

Without Air Conditioning

THUNDERBIRD AND COUGAR

1. Disconnect the negative battery cable.
2. Remove the instrument panel as follows:
   a. Disconnect the underhood wiring at the left side of the dash panel.
   b. Disengage the wiring connector from the dash panel and push the wiring harness into the passenger compartment.
   c. Remove the steering column lower trim cover by removing the 3 screws at the bottom, 1 screw on the left side and pulling to disengage the 5 snap-in retainers across the top.
   d. Remove the steering column lower opening reinforcement. 6 screws retain the reinforcement to the instrument panel.
   e. Remove the steering column upper and lower shrouds and disconnect the wiring from the steering column.
   f. Remove the shift interlock switch and disconnect the steering column lower universal joint.
   g. Support the steering column and remove the 4 nuts retaining the column to the support. Remove the column from the vehicle.
   h. Remove the 1 screw retaining the left side of the instrument panel to the parking brake bracket.
   i. Install the steering column lower opening reinforcement using the 4 screws, 1 at each corner. This will prevent the instrument panel from twisting when being removed.
   j. Remove the right and left cowl side trim panels.
   k. Remove the console assembly and remove the 2 nuts retaining the center of the instrument panel to the floor.
   l. Open the glove compartment, squeeze the sides of the bin and lower to the full open position. From under the instrument panel and through the glove compartment opening, disconnect the wiring, vacuum lines and control cables.
   m. Remove 2 screws from the right side and 2 screws from the left side retaining the instrument panel to the cowl side.
   n. Remove the right and left upper finish panels by pulling up to disengage the snap-in retainers. There are 3 on the right side, 4 on the left side.
   o. Remove the 4 screws retaining the instrument panel to the cowl top. Remove the right and left roof rail trim panel. Remove the door frame weatherstrip.
   p. Carefully pull the instrument panel away from the cowl and disconnect any remaining wiring or controls.
3. Remove the right instrument panel brace located above the heater case and attached to the cowl.
4. Drain the coolant from the cooling system and remove the hoses from the heater core. Plug the hoses and the core.

5. Disconnect the black vacuum supply hose from the in-line vacuum check valve in the engine compartment.
6. Disconnect the blower motor wire harness from the resistor and motor lead.
7. Working under the hood, remove the 3 nuts retaining the heater assembly to the dash panel.
8. In the passenger compartment, remove the screw attaching the heater assembly support bracket to the cowl top panel.
9. Remove the 1 screw retaining the bracket below the heater assembly to the dash panel.
10. Carefully pull the heater assembly away from the dash panel and remove the heater assembly from the vehicle.
11. Remove the 4 heater core access cover attaching screws and remove the access cover.
12. Remove the seal from the heater core tubes and pull the heater core from the case.

To install:

13. Inspect the heater core sealer in the case and replace, if necessary.
14. Install the heater core in the case with the seals on the outside of the case. Install the heater core tube seal on the heater core tubes.
15. Position the heater core access cover and seal on the case and install the 4 attaching screws.
16. Position the heater assembly in the vehicle. Install the screw attaching the heater assembly support bracket to the cowl top panel.
17. Working under the hood, install the 3 nuts retaining the heater assembly to the dash panel.
18. Install 1 screw to retain the bracket below the heater assembly to the dash panel.
19. Connect the blower motor and the harness to the resistor and blower motor lead.
20. Connect the black vacuum supply hose to the vacuum check valve in the engine compartment.
21. Install the right instrument panel brace and install the instrument panel by reversing the removal procedure.
22. Connect the heater hoses to the heater core and fill the cooling system. Check heater operation.

MUSTANG

1. Disconnect the negative battery cable.
2. Remove the floor console and instrument panel as follows:
   a. Remove the 4 screws that attach the console top panel assembly to the console assembly.
   b. Lift the console top panel assembly off the console assembly and disconnect the 2 electrical connectors.
   c. Remove the 2 screws attaching the rear end of the console assembly to the console panel support assembly.
   d. Remove 4 screws attaching the console assembly to the console panel front support.
   e. Remove the 4 screws attaching the console assembly to the instrument panel.
   f. Lift the console assembly off of the transmission tunnel.

NOTE: The console assembly includes a snap-in finish panel which conceals the heater control assembly attaching screws. To gain access to these screws, it is necessary to remove the floor console

   g. Disconnect all underhood wiring connectors from the main wiring harness. Disengage the rubber grommet seal from the dash panel and push the wiring harness and connectors into the passenger compartment.
   h. Remove the 3 bolts attaching the steering column opening cover and reinforcement panel. Remove the cover.

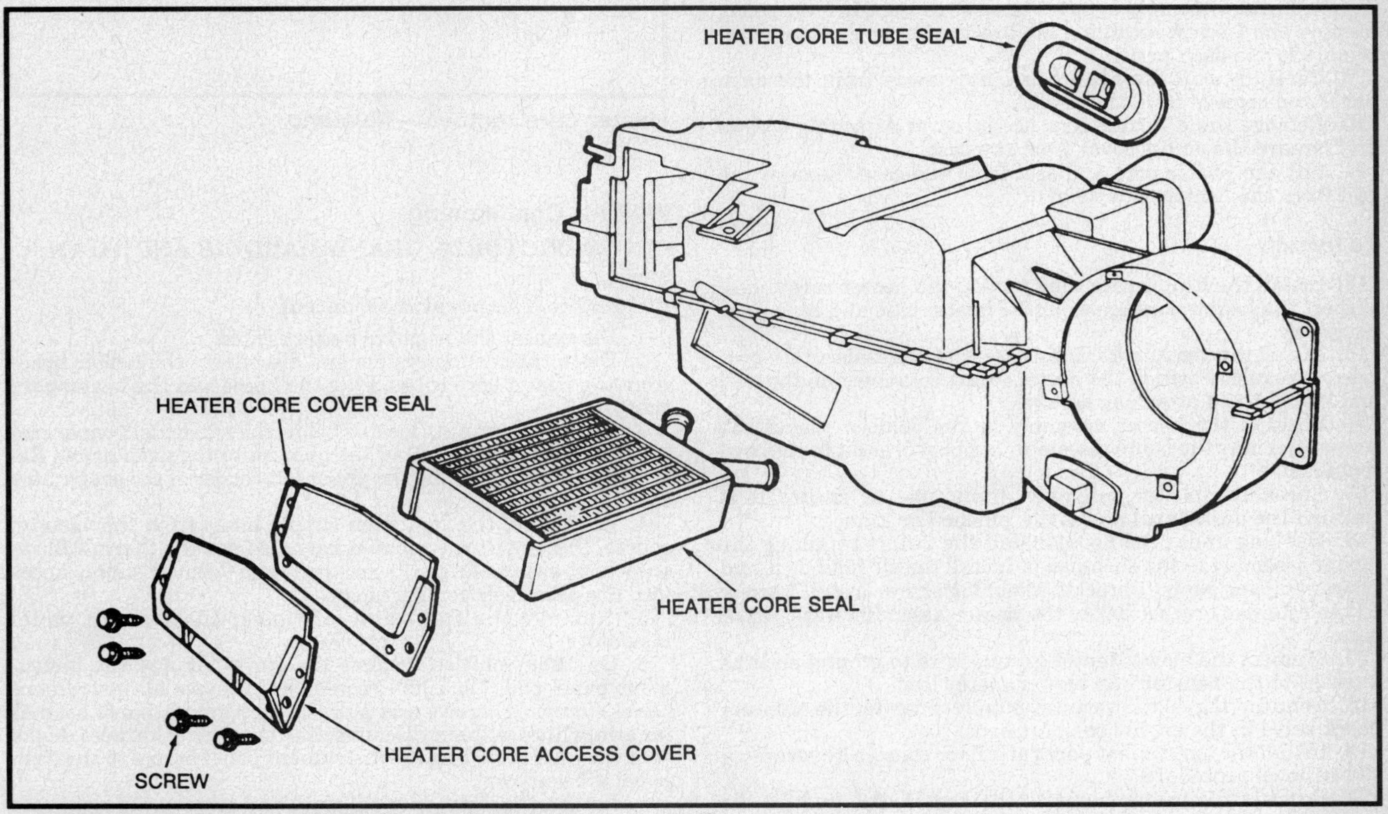
HEATER CORE TUBE SEAL
HEATER CORE COVER SEAL
HEATER CORE SEAL
HEATER CORE ACCESS COVER
SCREW

Heater core removal—Thunderbird and Cougar

i. Remove the steering column opening reinforcement by removing 2 bolts. Remove the 2 bolts retaining the lower steering column opening reinforcement and remove the reinforcement.

j. Remove the 6 steering column retaining nuts. 2 are retaining the hood release mechanism and 4 retain the column to the lower brake pedal support. Lower the steering column to the floor.

k. Remove the steering column upper and lower shrouds and disconnect the wiring from the multi-function switch.

l. Remove the brake pedal support nut and snap out the defroster grille.

m. Remove the screws from the speaker covers. Snap out the speaker covers. Remove the front screws retaining the right and left scuff plates at the cowl trim panel. Remove the right and left side cowl trim panels.

n. Disconnect the wiring at the right and left cowl sides. Remove the cowl side retaining bolts, 1 on each side.

o. Open the glove compartment door and flex the glove compartment bin tabs inward. Drop down the glove compartment door assembly.

p. Remove the 5 cowl top screw attachments. Gently pull the instrument panel away from the cowl. Disconnect the speedometer cable and wire connectors.

3. Drain the coolant from the cooling system and remove the hoses from the heater core. Plug the hoses and the core.

4. Remove the screw attaching the air inlet duct and blower housing assembly support bracket to the cowl top panel.

5. Disconnect the black vacuum supply hose from the in-line vacuum check valve in the engine compartment.

6. Disconnect the blower motor wire harness from the resistor and motor head.

7. Working under the hood, remove the 2 nuts retaining the heater assembly to the dash panel.

8. In the passenger compartment, remove the screw attaching the heater assembly support bracket to the cowl top panel. Remove the 1 screw retaining the bracket below the heater assembly to the dash panel.

9. Carefully pull the heater assembly away from the dash panel and remove from the vehicle.

10. Remove the 4 heater core access cover attaching screws and remove the access cover from the case.

11. Lift the heater core and seal from the case. Remove the seal from the heater core tubes.

To install:

12. Install the heater core tube seal on the heater core tubes. Inspect the heater core sealer in the heater case and replace, if necessary.

13. Install the heater core in the case with the seals on the outside of the case. Position the heater core access cover on the case and install the 4 attaching screws.

14. Position the heater assembly in the vehicle. Install the screw attaching the heater assembly support bracket to the cowl top panel.

15. Check the heater assembly drain tube to ensure it is through the dash panel and is not pinched or kinked.

16. Working under the hood, install the 2 nuts retaining the heater assembly to the dash panel. Install the air inlet duct and blower housing support bracket attaching screw. Install 1 screw to the retainer bracket below the heater assembly to the dash panel.

17. Connect the blower motor ground wire to ground and the harness to the resistor and blower motor lead.

18. Connect the black vacuum supply hose to the vacuum check valve in the engine compartment.

19. Install the instrument panel and floor console by reversing the removal procedure.

20. Connect the heater hoses to the heater core and fill the cooling system. Check the system for proper operation.

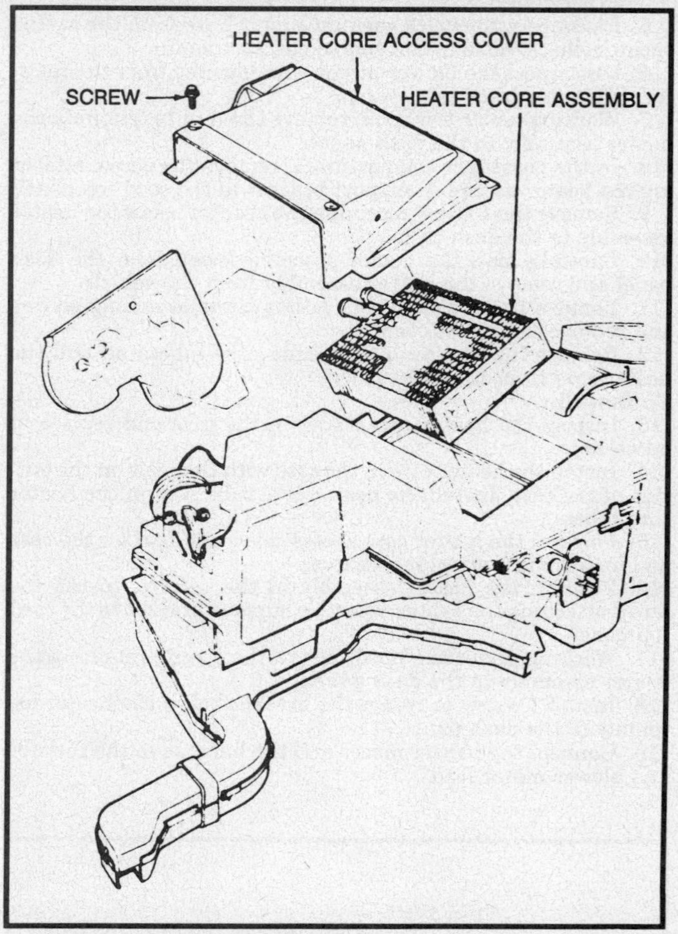
HEATER CORE ACCESS COVER
SCREW
HEATER CORE ASSEMBLY

Heater core removal – Mustang

With Air Conditioning

CROWN VICTORIA, GRAND MARQUIS AND TOWN CAR

Automatic Temperature Control

1. Disconnect the negative battery cable.

2. Drain the cooling system and disconnect the heater hoses from the heater core tubes. Plug the hoses and the heater core tubes.

3. Remove the 3 nuts located below the windshield wiper motor attaching the left end of the plenum to the dash panel. Remove the 1 nut retaining the upper left corner of the evaporator case to the dash panel.

4. Disconnect the 2 vacuum supply hoses from the vacuum source. Disconnect the vacuum harness from the thermal blower lockout switch. Push the grommet and vacuum supply hoses into the passenger compartment.

5. Remove the right and left lower instrument panel insulators.

6. On 1989 vehicles, remove the glove box and the instrument panel pad. On 1990–91 vehicles, remove all instrument panel mounting screws and pull the instrument panel back as far as it will go without disconnecting the wiring harness. Make sure the nuts attaching the instrument panel braces to the dash panel are removed.

7. Loosen the right door sill plate and remove the right side cowl trim panel.

8. On 1989 vehicles, disconnect the temperature control cable from the ATC sensor. Disconnect the vacuum harness line connector from the ATC sensor harness and disconnect the electrical plug from the ATC servo plug. On 1990–91 vehicles, remove the cross body brace and disconnect the wiring harness from the temperature blend door actuator. On all vehicles, disconnect the ATC sensor tube from the evaporator case connector.

9. Disconnect the vacuum jumper harness at the multiple vacuum connector near the floor air distribution duct. Disconnect the white vacuum hose from the outside-recirc door vacuum motor.

10. Remove the left and loosen the right screw attaching the passenger (rear) side of the floor air distribution duct to the plenum. It may be necessary to remove the 2 screws attaching the partial (lower) panel door vacuum motor to the mounting bracket to gain access to the right screw.

11. Remove 1 plastic push fastener retaining the floor air distribution duct to the left end of the plenum and 2 screws on the rear face of the plenum and remove the floor air distribution duct.

12. Remove 2 nuts from the 2 studs along the lower flange of the plenum. Carefully move the plenum rearward to allow the heater core tubes and the stud at the top of the plenum to clear the holes in the dash panel. Remove the plenum from the vehicle by rotating the top of the plenum forward, down and out from under the instrument panel. On 1989 vehicles, carefully pull the lower edge of the instrument panel rearward, as necessary, while rolling the plenum from behind the instrument panel.

13. On 1989 vehicles, remove the ATC servo from the plenum. On all vehicles, remove the 4 retaining screws from the heater core cover and remove the cover from the plenum assembly. Pull the heater core and seal assembly from the plenum assembly.

To install:

14. Carefully install the heater core and seal assembly into the plenum assembly. Visually check to ensure the core seal is properly positioned. Position the heater core cover and install the 4 retaining screws. On 1989 vehicles, install the ATC servo on the plenum.

15. Position the plenum on the rear of the dash panel with the heater core tubes and the stud at the top of the plenum through the holes in the dash panel. Install the 2 nuts removed from the lower flange of the plenum.

16. Install the plastic push fastener retaining the left end of the floor air distribution duct to the left end of the plenum.

17. Install the left screw and tighten the right screw that attach the rear of the floor air distribution duct to the plenum. If necessary, tighten the screws attaching the partial (lower) panel door vacuum motor to the mounting bracket.

18. Connect the white vacuum hose from the outside-recirc door vacuum motor. Connect the vacuum jumper harness at the multiple vacuum connector near the floor air distribution duct.

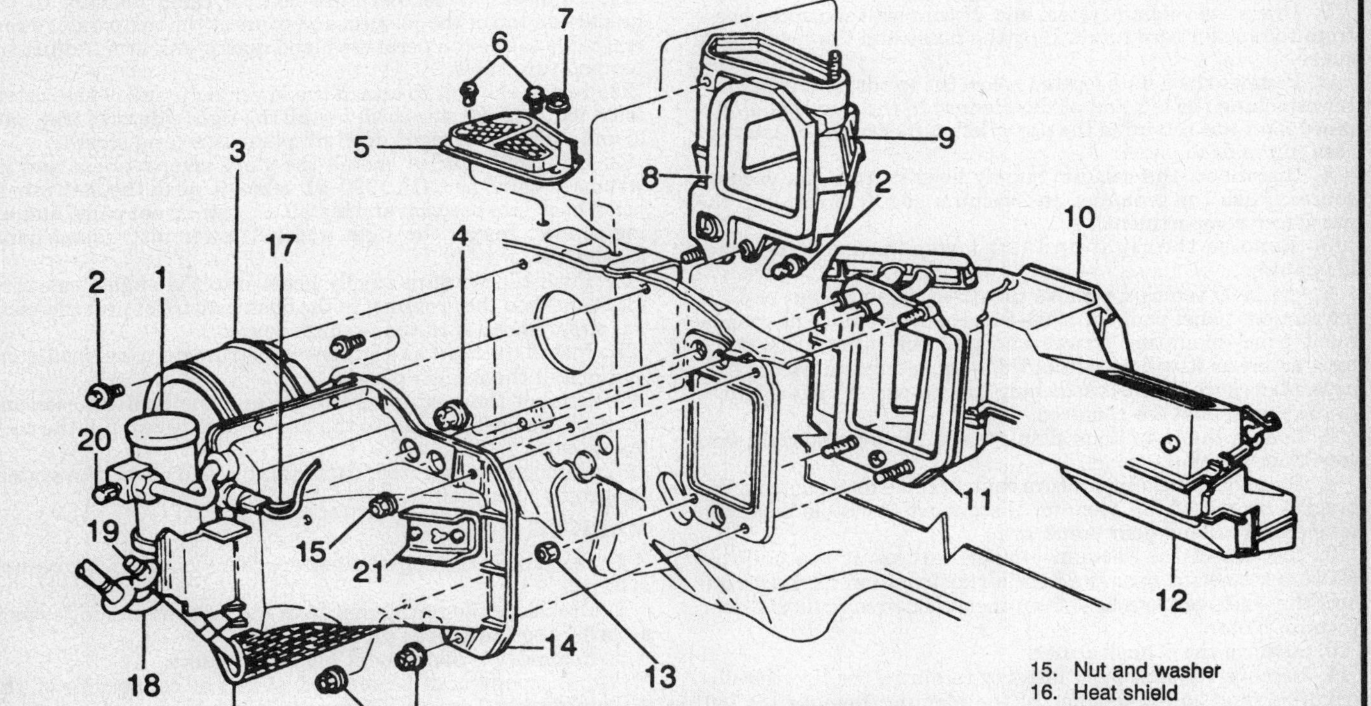
1
2
3
4
5
6
7
8
9
10
11
12
13
14
15
16
17
18
19
20
21

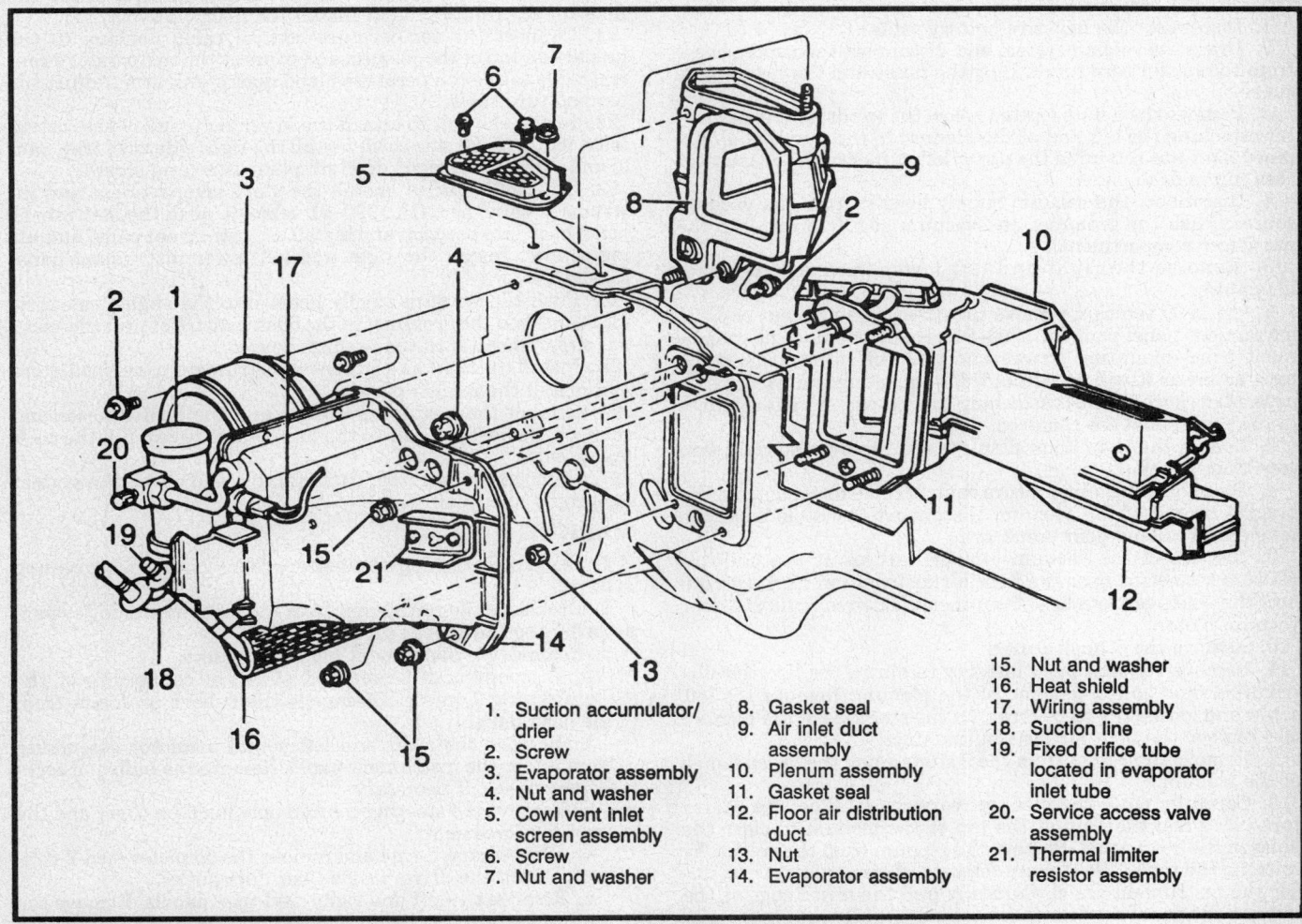

1. Suction accumulator/drier
2. Screw
3. Evaporator assembly
4. Nut and washer
5. Cowl vent inlet screen assembly
6. Screw
7. Nut and washer
8. Gasket seal
9. Air inlet duct assembly
10. Plenum assembly
11. Gasket seal
12. Floor air distribution duct
13. Nut
14. Evaporator assembly
15. Nut and washer
16. Heat shield
17. Wiring assembly
18. Suction line
19. Fixed orifice tube located in evaporator inlet tube
20. Service access valve assembly
21. Thermal limiter resistor assembly

Plenum and evaporator removal—Crown Victoria, Grand Marquis and Town Car

On 1989 vehicles, route and connect the vacuum harness connector at the ATC sensor and connect the electrical plug to the ATC servo plug. Do not block the sensor aspirator exhaust port with the excess vacuum harness.

19. Connect the ATC sensor tube to the evaporator case connector. On 1990–91 vehicles, install the cross body brace and connect the wiring harness to the blend door actuator.

20. Replace the right side cowl trim panel and tighten the screws in the right door sill plate.

21. On 1989 vehicles, install the glove compartment door and instrument panel pad. On 1990–91 vehicles, push the instrument panel back into position and install all instrument panel mounting screws. Install the right and left lower instrument panel insulators.

22. Push the vacuum supply hoses into the engine compartment and seat the grommet in the dash panel. Connect the 2 vacuum supply hoses to the vacuum source and connect the vacuum harness to the thermal blower lockout switch.

23. Install the 1 nut retaining the upper left corner of the evaporator case to the dash panel. Install the 3 nuts located below the windshield wiper motor, that attach the left end of the plenum to the dash panel.

24. Unplug the heater core hoses and tubes and connect the heater hoses to the heater core tubes. Fill the cooling system.

25. Connect the negative battery cable and check the system for proper operation.

Manual Air Conditioning

1. Disconnect the negative battery cable.
2. Drain the cooling system and disconnect the heater hoses from the heater core tubes. Plug the hoses and the heater core tubes.
3. Remove the 3 nuts located below the windshield wiper motor attaching the left end of the plenum to the dash panel. Remove the 1 nut retaining the upper left corner of the evaporator case to the dash panel.
4. Disconnect the vacuum supply hose(s) from the vacuum source. Push the grommet and vacuum supply hoses into the passenger compartment.
5. Remove the right and left lower instrument panel insulators.
6. On 1989 vehicles, remove the glove compartment and the instrument panel pad. On 1990–91 vehicles, remove all instrument panel mounting screws and pull the instrument panel back as far as it will go without disconnecting the wiring harness. Make sure the nuts attaching the instrument panel braces to the dash panel are removed.
7. Loosen the right door sill plate and remove the right side cowl trim panel.
8. Disengage the temperature control cable housing from the bracket on top of the plenum. Disconnect the cable from the temperature blend door crank arm.
9. Disconnect the vacuum jumper harness at the multiple vacuum connector near the floor air distribution duct. Disconnect the white vacuum hose from the outside-recirculating door vacuum motor.
10. Remove the 2 hush panels.
11. Remove 1 plastic push fastener retaining the floor air distribution duct to the left end of the plenum. Remove the left screw and loosen the right screw on the rear face of the plenum and remove the floor air distribution duct.
12. Remove the 2 nuts from the 2 studs along the lower flange of the plenum.
13. Carefully move the plenum rearward to allow the heater core tubes and the stud at the top of the plenum to clear the holes in the dash panel. Remove the plenum from the vehicle by rotating the top of the plenum forward, down and out from under the instrument panel. Carefully pull the lower edge of the instrument panel rearward, as necessary, while rolling the plenum from behind the instrument panel.
14. Remove the 4 retaining screws from the heater core cover and remove the cover from the plenum assembly. Pull the heater core and seal assembly from the plenum assembly.

To install:

15. Carefully install the heater core and seal assembly into the plenum assembly. Visually check to ensure that the core seal is properly positioned. Position the heater core cover and install the 4 retaining screws.
16. Route the vacuum supply hose through the dash panel and seat the grommet in the opening.
17. Position the plenum under the instrument panel with the register duct opening up and the heater core tubes down. Rotate the plenum up behind the instrument panel and position the plenum to the dash panel. Insert the heater core tubes and mounting studs through their respective holes in the dash panel and the evaporator case.
18. Install the 3 nuts on the studs along the lower flange and 1 on the upper flange of the plenum. Install the 3 nuts below the windshield wiper motor to attach the left end of the plenum to the dash panel. Install 1 nut to retain the upper left corner of the evaporator case to the dash panel.
19. Position the floor air distribution duct on the plenum. Install the 2 screws and plastic push fastener. If removed, position the panel door vacuum motor to the mounting bracket and install the 2 attaching screws.
20. Connect the white vacuum hose to the outside-recirculating door vacuum motor. Connect the vacuum jumper harness to the plenum harness at the multiple vacuum connector near the floor air distribution duct. Install the floor duct.
21. Connect the temperature control cable housing to the bracket on top of the plenum and connect the temperature control cable to the temperature blend door crank arm. Adjust the temperature cable.
22. Install the bolt to attach the lower right end of the instrument panel to the side cowl. Install the right side cowl trim panel and tighten the right door sill plate attaching screws.
23. On 1989 vehicles, install the glove compartment and instrument panel pad. On 1990–91 vehicles, push the instrument panel back into position and install all instrument panel mounting screws. Install the right and left lower instrument panel insulators.
24. Push the vacuum supply hoses into the engine compartment and seat the grommet in the dash panel. Connect the vacuum supply hose(s) to the vacuum source.
25. Install the right and left lower instrument panel insulators and install the 2 hush panels.
26. Unplug the heater core tubes and the heater hoses and connect the heater hoses to the heater core tubes. Fill the cooling system.
27. Connect the negative battery cable and check the system for proper operation.

MARK VII

1. Disconnect the negative battery cable and drain the cooling system.
2. Discharge the refrigerant from the air conditioning system according to the proper procedure.
3. Remove the instrument panel as follows:
   a. Disconnect all underhood electrical connectors of the main wiring harness. Disengage the rubber grommet from the dash panel.
   b. Remove the right and left sound insulator assemblies from under the instrument panel. Remove the bulb and socket assemblies, if necessary.
   c. Remove the steering column opening trim cover and the steel reinforcement.
   d. If necessary, locate and remove the demister feed Y-connector from the driver's side floor duct outlet.
   e. Remove the left and right cowl trim panels. Remove the 2 screws attaching the hood release to the cowl panel before removing the left trim panel.

f. Remove the 5 steering column trim shroud screws and remove the shrouds.

g. Disconnect all electrical connector quick couplers from the steering column switches.

h. Remove the 4 nuts attaching the steering column to the support. Lower the column to rest on the seat cushion.

i. Remove the defroster opening grille panel and remove the screws attaching the floor console to the instrument panel and floor. Move the console rearward.

j. Remove the screw(s) attaching the instrument panel to the floor. Remove the screws attaching the instrument panel to the cowls.Remove the bolt or nut attaching the instrument panel to the support bracket.

k. Disconnect the main wiring harness behind the instrument panel, on the right side of the steering column support, at the blower motor and at the left and right cowl panels.

l. Disconnect the radio antenna lead from the radio. Disconnect any vacuum hoses attached to the instrument panel.

m. Remove the right and left A-pillar garnish mouldings.

n. Remove the 3 screws attaching the instrument panel to the dash panel and pull/push the wiring harness and connectors into the passenger compartment. Remove the instrument panel.

4. Remove the evaporator case assembly.

NOTE: Whenever an evaporator case is removed, it will be necessary to replace the suction accumulator/drier.

5. Remove the 5 heater core access cover attaching screws and remove the access cover from the evaporator case.

6. Lift the heater core and seal from the evaporator case. Remove the seal from the heater core tubes.

To install:

7. Install the heater core in the evaporator case.

8. Position the heater core access cover on the evaporator case and install the 5 attaching screws. Install the heater core seal.

9. Install the evaporator case.

10. Install the instrument panel by reversing the removal procedure.

11. Fill the cooling system. Leak test, evacuate and charge the refrigerant system according to the proper procedure. Observe all safety precautions.

12. Connect the negative battery cable and check the system for proper operation.

THUNDERBIRD AND COUGAR

1. Disconnect the negative battery cable and drain the cooling system.

2. Discharge the refrigerant from the air conditioning system according to the proper procedure.

3. Remove the instrument panel as follows:

a. Disconnect the underhood wiring at the left side of the dash panel.

b. Disengage the wiring connector from the dash panel and push the wiring harness into the passenger compartment.

c. Remove the steering column lower trim cover by removing the 3 screws at the bottom, 1 screw on the left side and pulling to disengage the 5 snap-in retainers across the top.

d. Remove the steering column lower opening reinforcement. 6 screws retain the reinforcement to the instrument panel.

e. Remove the steering column upper and lower shrouds and disconnect the wiring from the steering column.

f. Remove the shift interlock switch and disconnect the steering column lower universal joint.

g. Support the steering column and remove the 4 nuts re-

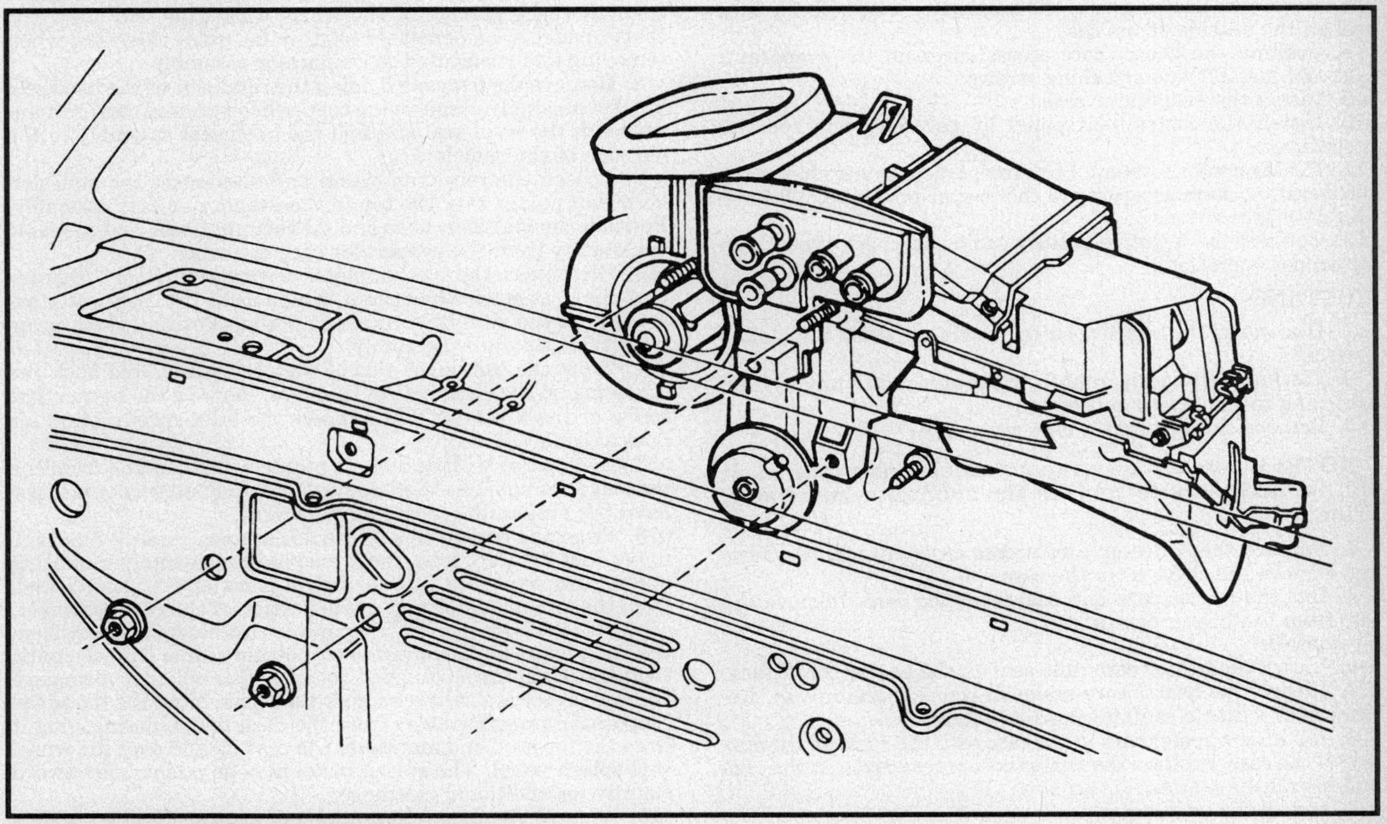

Evaporator assembly installation – Mark VII

taining the column to the support. Remove the column from the vehicle.

h. Remove the 1 screw retaining the left side of the instrument panel to the parking brake bracket.

i. Install the steering column lower opening reinforcement using the 4 screws, 1 at each corner. This will prevent the instrument panel from twisting when being removed.

j. Remove the right and left cowl side trim panels.

k. Remove the console assembly and remove the 2 nuts retaining the center of the instrument panel to the floor.

l. Open the glove compartment, squeeze the sides of the bin and lower to the full open position. From under the instrument panel and through the glove compartment opening, disconnect the wiring, vacuum lines and control cables.

m. Remove 2 screws from the right side and 2 screws from the left side retaining the instrument panel to the cowl side.

n. Remove the right and left upper finish panels by pulling up to disengage the snap-in retainers. There are 3 on the right side, 4 on the left side.

o. Remove the 4 screws retaining the instrument panel to the cowl top. Remove the right and left roof rail trim panel. Remove the door frame weatherstrip.

p. Carefully pull the instrument panel away from the cowl and disconnect any remaining wiring or controls.

4. Remove the evaporator case assembly.

NOTE: Whenever an evaporator case is removed, it will be necessary to replace the suction accumulator/drier.

5. Remove the 4 heater core access cover attaching screws and remove the access cover from the evaporator case.
6. Remove the tube seal from the heater core tubes. Slide the heater core and seals from the evaporator case.

To install:

7. Install the heater core in the evaporator case with the tube seal on the outside of the case.
8. Position the heater core access cover on the evaporator case and install the 4 attaching screws.
9. Install the evaporator case.
10. Install the instrument panel by reversing the removal procedure.
11. Fill the cooling system. Leak test, evacuate and charge the refrigerant system according to the proper procedure. Observe all safety precautions.
12. Connect the negative battery cable and check the system for proper operation.

MUSTANG

1. Disconnect the negative battery cable and drain the cooling system.
2. Discharge the refrigerant from the air conditioning system according to the proper procedure.
3. Remove the evaporator case assembly.

NOTE: Whenever an evaporator case is replaced, it will be necessary to replace the suction accumulator/drier.

4. Remove the 4 heater core access cover attaching screws and remove the cover from the case.
5. Lift the heater core and seal from the case. Remove the seal from the heater core tubes.

To install:

6. Install the heater core tube seal on the heater core tubes.
7. Inspect the heater core sealer in the evaporator case. Replace with suitable caulking cord, if necessary.
8. Install the heater core in the case with the seals on the outside of the case. Position the heater core access cover on the case and install the 4 attaching screws.
9. Install the evaporator case.
10. Fill the cooling system. Leak test, evacuate and charge the refrigerant system according to the proper procedure. Observe all safety precautions.
11. Connect the negative battery cable and check the system for proper operation.

Evaporator

REMOVAL AND INSTALLATION

Crown Victoria, Grand Marquis and Town Car

1. Disconnect the negative battery cable and drain the cooling system. Save the coolant for reuse.
2. Discharge the refrigerant from the air conditioning system according to the proper procedure.

NOTE: Whenever the evaporator case is removed, it will be necessary to replace the suction accumulator/drier.

3. Disconnect the suction hose from the accumulator/drier using the spring-lock coupling disconnect procedure. Plug the openings to prevent dirt and excessive moisture from entering. Position the hose away from the evaporator assembly.
4. Disconnect the connector from the pressure switch on the accumulator/drier.
5. Disconnect the liquid line from the evaporator inlet tube using the spring-lock coupling disconnect procedure and plug the openings. Position the liquid line away from the evaporator assembly.
6. Loosen the heater hose clamps and disconnect the heater hoses from the heater core tubes.
7. Turn the steering wheel to the left to position the right front wheel so the wheel well splash panel support bracket is accessible. Remove the screw and splash panel support bracket from the back portion of the wheel well. This will allow the splash panel to be depressed slightly for extra clearance when removing and replacing the evaporator assembly.
8. Remove the 6 screws holding the right side of the hood seal bracket assembly. Remove the copper hood ground clip from underneath the hood seal and fold the hood seal assembly to the left side of the vehicle.
9. Loosen the retaining clamp and disconnect the emission hose that passes over the top of the evaporator case assembly. Position the emission hose and all vacuum hoses and movable wires away from the evaporator case assembly.
10. Disconnect the blower motor wiring connectors. Disconnect the 2 large wire harnesses, which cross the evaporator assembly, at the various connecting points. Position them away from the evaporator assembly.
11. From the passenger side of the dash panel, fold back the carpeting on the right side of the floor. Remove the bottom left screw of the 2 screws that support the inlet recirculation air duct assembly.
12. If equipped with automatic temperature control, from the passenger compartment, disconnect the ambient sensor air tube from the evaporator sensor air tube port.
13. From the engine side of the dash panel, remove 3 nuts, 1 upper and 2 lower, from the 3 evaporator assembly mounting studs. Also remove 2 screws, 1 drill-point and 1 sheet metal, from the blower motor and wheel portion of the case assembly.
14. Pull the bottom of the evaporator case assembly away from the dash panel to disengage the 2 bottom studs. On automatic temperature control equipped vehicles, this will also disengage the evaporator ambient sensor air tube port. Move the top of the evaporator assembly away from the dash panel, disengaging it from the top stud and maneuver the case up and over the wheel well splash panel. The splash panel may be pushed downward slightly for additional clearance.
15. Remove the dash panel seal and remove the heat shield from the bottom of the evaporator case.

16. Remove the 6 screws attaching the 2 halves of the evaporator case together. Separate the 2 halves of the evaporator case and remove the evaporator core and suction accumulator/drier assembly.

17. Disconnect the suction accumulator/drier inlet from the evaporator core outlet tube. Remove the retaining screw from the accumulator/drier and evaporator core mounting brackets and remove the accumulator/drier from the evaporator core.

To install:

NOTE: When replacing the evaporator, 3 fluid oz. (90ml) of clean refrigerant oil should be added to the new evaporator to maintain the total system oil charge.

18. Attach the suction accumulator/drier to the evaporator core mounting bracket with the retaining screw. Install a new O-ring lubricated with clean refrigerant oil and connect the accumulator/drier inlet connection to the outlet tube of the evaporator core. Tighten using a backup wrench to prevent component damage.

19. Position the evaporator core assembly to the right half of the evaporator case. Apply caulking cord or similar sealer to the case flange and around the evaporator core tubes.

20. Position the evaporator case left half and dash panel gasket to the case right half. Install the support strap on the evaporator inlet tube. Install the 7 screws to attach the 2 halves of the case together. The center screw on the front of the case also attaches the support strap.

21. Install the dash panel seal. Install a new heat shield on the bottom of the evaporator case assembly with staples.

22. Position the evaporator assembly near the dash panel by maneuvering it down past the wheel splash panel. If necessary, push the splash panel downward slightly for extra clearance.

23. On automatic temperature control equipped vehicles, engage the sensor air tube port into the dash panel port opening.

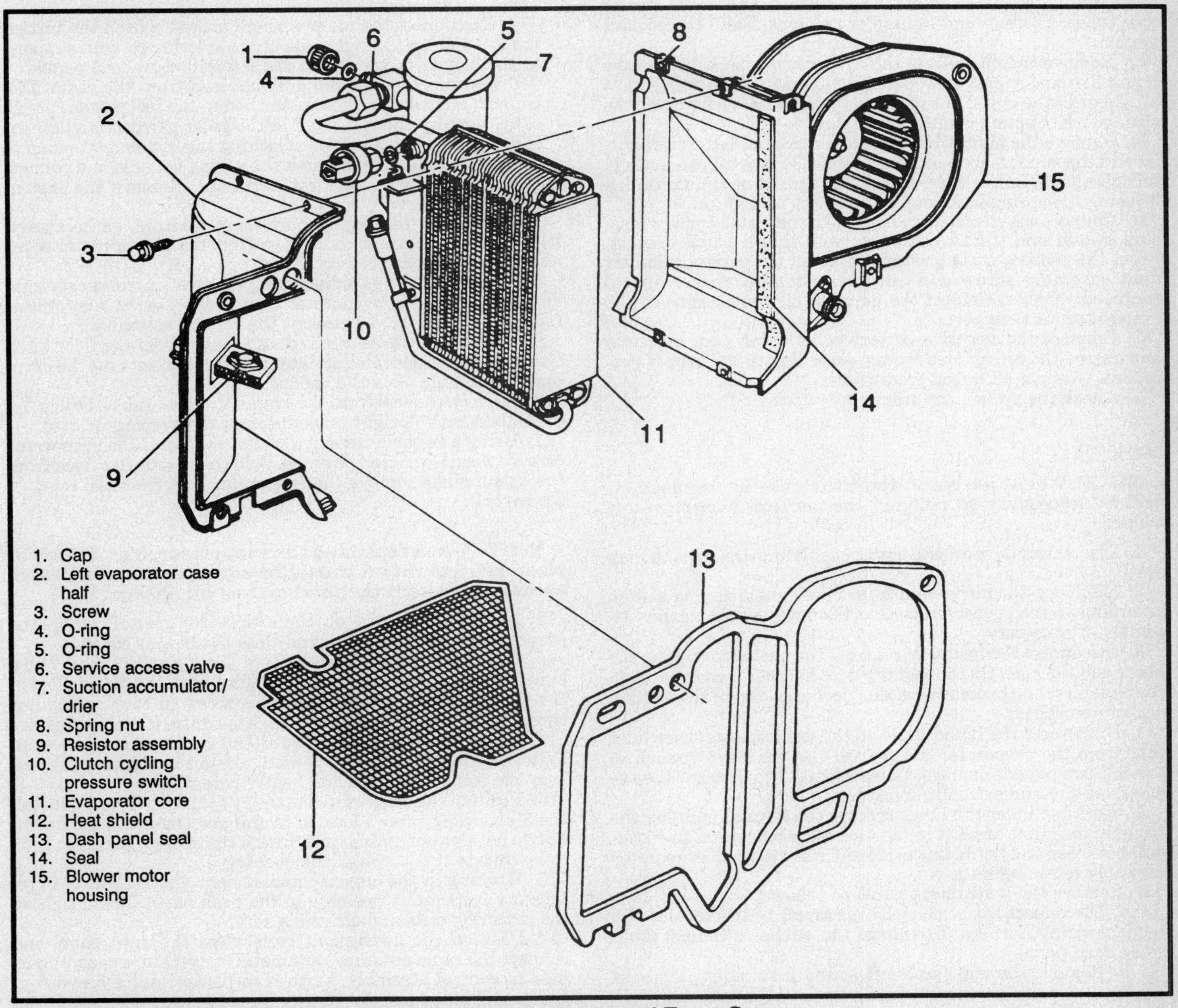
1
2
3
4
5
6
7
8
9
10
11
12
13
14
15
1. Cap
2. Left evaporator case half
3. Screw
4. O-ring
5. O-ring
6. Service access valve
7. Suction accumulator/drier
8. Spring nut
9. Resistor assembly
10. Clutch cycling pressure switch
11. Evaporator core
12. Heat shield
13. Dash panel seal
14. Seal
15. Blower motor housing

Evaporator core removal—Crown Victoria, Grand Marquis and Town Car

On all vehicles, engage the 2 bottom studs into the evaporator assembly stud holes. Move the top of the evaporator assembly toward the dash panel while engaging the top dash panel stud into the evaporator assembly stud hole. Replace, but do not tighten, the 3 stud nuts.

24. Replace the 2 screws, being careful to return the drill point screw to the correct hole which is located on top of the case and to the right of the blower motor and wheel assembly. Tighten the 3 stud nuts that were previously installed.

25. Position the 2 large wire harnesses across the evaporator case assembly and connect the various connectors. Connect the blower motor electrical connectors.

26. Place the emission hose clamp on the hose, tighten the clamp and position it over the evaporator case assembly along with the vacuum hoses and wires previously removed.

27. Unfold the hood seal bracket assembly and insert the copper hood ground clip under the hood seal. Install the 6 screws which secure the right side of the hood seal bracket assembly.

28. Place the heater core hose clamps onto the heater hoses and carefully connect the hoses to the inlet and outlet heater core tubes. Position and tighten the clamps. Refill the coolant system.

29. Remove the plugs from the evaporator inlet tube and the liquid line and install new O-rings dipped in clean refrigerant oil. Connect the liquid line to the evaporator inlet tube using the spring-lock coupling connect procedure.

30. Remove the plugs from the suction accumulator/drier outlet and the suction hose and install new O-rings dipped in clean refrigerant oil. Connect the suction hose to the accumulator/drier using the spring-lock coupling connect procedure.

31. Connect the electrical connector to the clutch cycling pressure switch and install the wheel well splash panel bracket. From the passenger compartment, install the recirculation air duct assembly screw. On automatic temperature control equipped vehicles, connect the ambient air sensor tube to the evaporator air tube port.

32. Connect the negative battery cable. Leak test, evacuate and charge the refrigerant system according to the proper procedure. Observe all safety precautions.

33. Check the system for proper operation.

Mark VII

NOTE: Whenever an evaporator case is replaced, it will be necessary to replace the suction accumulator/drier.

1. Disconnect the negative battery cable and drain the cooling system.

2. Discharge the refrigerant from the air conditioning system according to the proper procedure. Remove the air cleaner assembly, if necessary.

3. Disconnect the heater hoses from the heater core. Plug the hoses and the core. Disconnect the wire harness connector from the clutch cycling pressure switch, located on top of the suction accumulator/drier.

4. Disconnect the liquid line and the accumulator/drier inlet tube from the evaporator core tubes. Use a backup wrench to prevent component damage. Cap all fittings to prevent the entrance of dirt and excessive moisture.

5. Working under the hood, remove the 2 nuts retaining the accumulator/drier bracket to the dash panel. Position the accumulator/drier and liquid line aside and remove the 2 evaporator assembly retaining nuts.

6. Remove the instrument panel as follows:

a. Disconnect all underhood electrical connectors of the main wiring harness. Disengage the rubber grommet from the dash panel.

b. Remove the right and left sound insulator assemblies from under the instrument panel. Remove the bulb and socket assemblies, if necessary.

c. Remove the steering column opening trim cover and the steel reinforcement.

d. If necessary, locate and remove the demister feed Y-connector from the driver's side floor duct outlet.

e. Remove the left and right cowl trim panels. Remove the 2 screws attaching the hood release to the cowl panel before removing the left trim panel.

f. Remove the 5 steering column trim shroud screws and remove the shrouds.

g. Disconnect all electrical connector quick couplers from the steering column switches.

h. Remove the 4 nuts attaching the steering column to the support. Lower the column to rest on the seat cushion.

i. Remove the defroster opening grille panel and remove the screws attaching the floor console to the instrument panel and floor. Move the console rearward.

j. Remove the screw(s) attaching the instrument panel to the floor. Remove the screws attaching the instrument panel to the cowls. Remove the bolt or nut attaching the instrument panel to the support bracket.

k. Disconnect the main wiring harness behind the instrument panel, on the right side of the steering column support, at the blower motor and at the left and right cowl panels.

l. Disconnect the radio antenna lead from the radio. Disconnect any vacuum hoses attached to the instrument panel.

m. Remove the right and left A-pillar garnish mouldings.

n. Remove the 3 screws attaching the instrument panel to the dash panel and pull/push the wiring harness and connectors into the passenger compartment. Remove the instrument panel.

7. Disconnect the wiring harness connectors, as necessary. Disconnect the harness connectors from the blower motor wires and blower motor speed controller.

8. Disconnect the automatic temperature control sensor hose and elbow from the evaporator case. Disconnect the automatic temperature control harness at the control assembly.

9. Disconnect the rear seat duct adapter from the floor duct. Remove the 3 evaporator attaching screws and remove the evaporator assembly from the vehicle.

10. Remove the seal from the evaporator core tubes. Drill a $^3/_{16}$ in. hole in both upright tabs on top of the evaporator case.

11. Using a suitable cutting tool, cut the top of the evaporator case between the raised outlines. Fold the cutout flap back from the opening and remove the evaporator core from the case.

To install:

NOTE: When replacing the evaporator, 3 oz. (90ml) of clean refrigerant oil should be added to the new evaporator to maintain the total system oil charge.

12. Install a new seal on the evaporator core. Position the evaporator core in the case and close the cutout cover.

13. Install a spring nut on each of the 2 upright tabs. Make sure the hole in the spring nut is aligned with the hole drilled in the tab flange. Install and tighten a screw in each spring nut through the hole in the tab or flange to secure the cutout cover.

14. Install caulking cord or equivalent sealer, to seal the evaporator case against air leakage along the cut line. Install the seal over the evaporator core and heater core tubes.

15. Position the evaporator assembly to the dash panel. Install the 3 attaching screws located in the passenger compartment, but do not tighten at this time. Check the evaporator drain tube to be certain it is through the opening.

16. Working in the engine compartment, install 2 nuts to retain the evaporator assembly to the dash panel. Then, tighten the retaining nuts and attaching screws.

17. Position the instrument panel near the dash panel and connect the radio antenna, automatic temperature control harness to control assembly, harness to blower motor speed controller and blower motor wires. Also attach any additional wire harness connectors disconnected during removal.

18. Move the instrument panel into position and install the attaching screws. Connect the automatic temperature control sensor hose and elbow assembly.

NOTE: Make sure the air conditioning plenum (attached to the instrument panel) is correctly aligned and sealed at the evaporator outlet opening. Air leakage to the floor area will result if the plenum is not sealed at the evaporator case outlet.

19. Install the nut retaining the instrument panel to the brake pedal and steering column support. Position the steering column to the brake pedal and steering column support and install the retaining nuts.
20. Install the steering column opening reinforcement and shroud. Install the screws to attach the lower center of the instrument panel to the floor brace.
21. Install the defroster opening grille and the right and left side cowl trim panels. Install the right and left instrument panel sound insulators.
22. Install the rear seat duct adapter and the console assembly. Install the instrument panel right hand finish panel and the steering column opening cover.
23. Position the accumulator/drier mounting bracket over the studs on the dash panel and loosely install the 2 nuts.
24. Connect the accumulator/drier inlet tube to the evaporator core outlet tube using a new O-ring lubricated with clean refrigerant oil. Do not tighten the connection.
25. Connect the liquid line to the evaporator core inlet tube using a new O-ring lubricated with clean refrigerant oil. Do not tighten the connection.
26. Tighten the 2 nuts retaining the accumulator/drier to the dash panel. Tighten the 2 refrigerant line connections at the evaporator core. Use a backup wrench to prevent component damage.

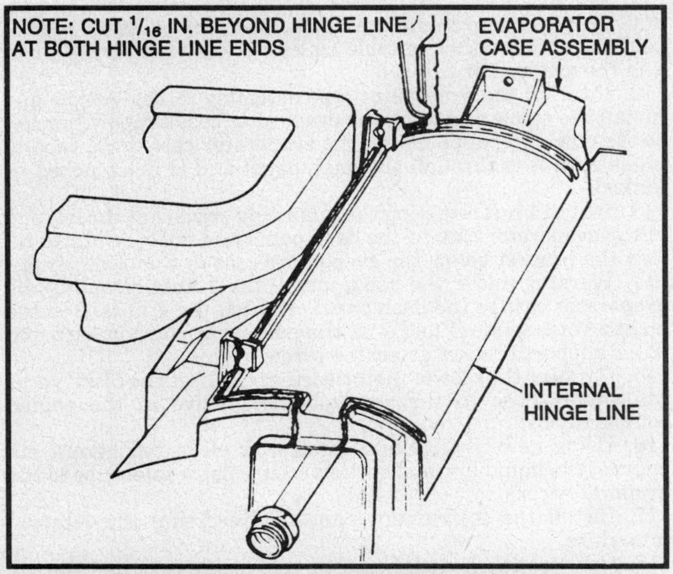
NOTE: CUT 1/16 IN. BEYOND HINGE LINE
AT BOTH HINGE LINE ENDS
EVAPORATOR
CASE ASSEMBLY
INTERNAL
HINGE LINE

Evaporator case cutting—Mark VII and Mustang

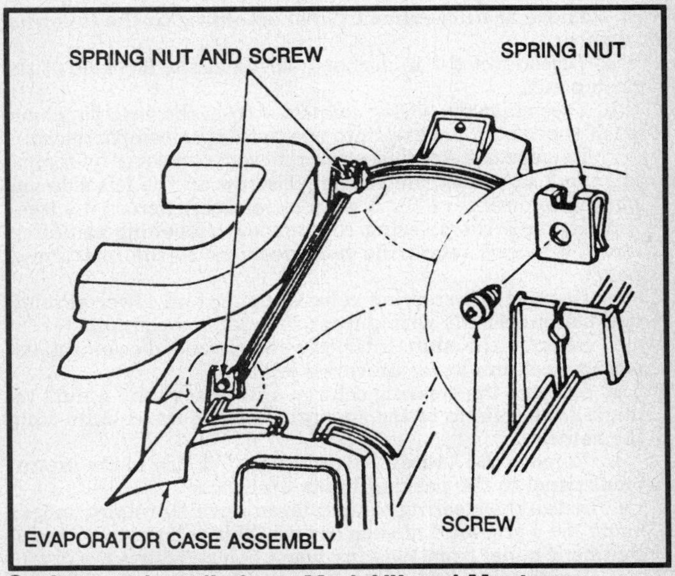
SPRING NUT AND SCREW
SPRING NUT
EVAPORATOR CASE ASSEMBLY
SCREW

Spring nut installation—Mark VII and Mustang

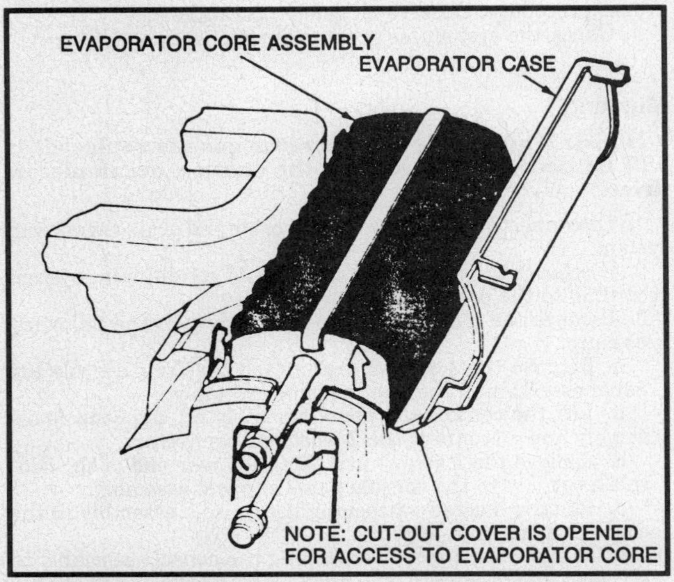
EVAPORATOR CORE ASSEMBLY
EVAPORATOR CASE
NOTE: CUT-OUT COVER IS OPENED
FOR ACCESS TO EVAPORATOR CORE

Evaporator core removal—Mark VII and Mustang

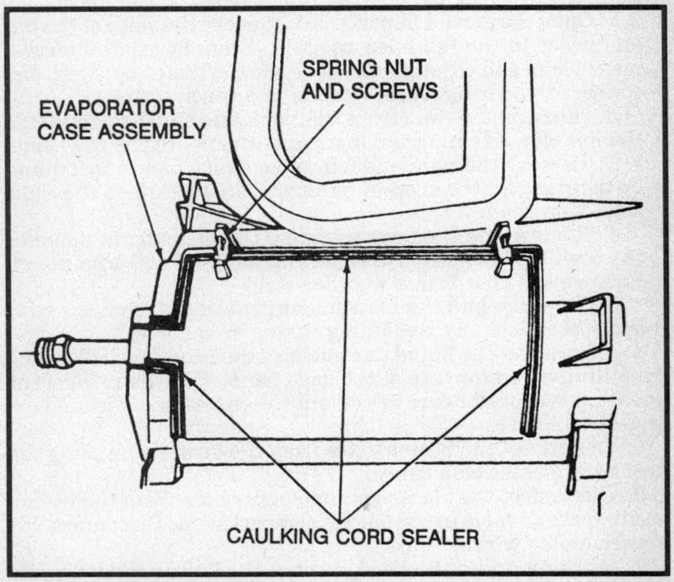
SPRING NUT
AND SCREWS
EVAPORATOR
CASE ASSEMBLY
CAULKING CORD SEALER

Caulking cord installation—Mark VII and Mustang

27. Connect the harness connector to the clutch cycling pressure switch. Connect the heater hoses to the heater core and fill the cooling system.
28. Connect the negative battery cable. Leak test, evacuate and charge the refrigerant system according to the proper procedure. Observe all safety precautions.
29. Check the automatic temperature control system and all instrument panel functions for proper operation.

Thunderbird and Cougar

NOTE: Whenever an evaporator case is removed, it will be necessary to replace the suction accumulator/drier.

1. Disconnect the negative battery cable and drain the cooling system.
2. Discharge the refrigerant from the air conditioning system according to the proper procedure.
3. Remove the instrument panel according to the following procedure:
   a. Disconnect the underhood wiring at the left side of the dash panel.
   b. Disengage the wiring connector from the dash panel and push the wiring harness into the passenger compartment.
   c. Remove the steering column lower trim cover by removing the 3 screws at the bottom, 1 screw on the left side and pulling to disengage the 5 snap-in retainers across the top.
   d. Remove the steering column lower opening reinforcement. 6 screws retain the reinforcement to the instrument panel.
   e. Remove the steering column upper and lower shrouds and disconnect the wiring from the steering column.
   f. Remove the shift interlock switch and disconnect the steering column lower universal joint.
   g. Support the steering column and remove the 4 nuts retaining the column to the support. Remove the column from the vehicle.
   h. Remove the 1 screw retaining the left side of the instrument panel to the parking brake bracket.
   i. Install the steering column lower opening reinforcement using the 4 screws, 1 at each corner. This will prevent the instrument panel from twisting when being removed.
   j. Remove the right and left cowl side trim panels.
   k. Remove the console assembly and remove the 2 nuts retaining the center of the instrument panel to the floor.
   l. Open the glove compartment, squeeze the sides of the bin and lower to the full open position. From under the instrument panel and through the glove compartment opening, disconnect the wiring, vacuum lines and control cables.
   m. Remove 2 screws from the right side and 2 screws from the left side retaining the instrument panel to the cowl side.
   n. Remove the right and left upper finish panels by pulling up to disengage the snap-in retainers. There are 3 on the right side, 4 on the left side.
   o. Remove the 4 screws retaining the instrument panel to the cowl top. Remove the right and left roof rail trim panel. Remove the door frame weather-strip.
   p. Carefully pull the instrument panel away from the cowl and disconnect any remaining wiring or controls.
4. Disconnect the liquid line and accumulator/drier inlet tube from the evaporator core at the dash panel. Cap the refrigerant lines and evaporator core to prevent the entrance of dirt and excessive moisture.
5. Disconnect the heater hoses from the heater core. Plug the hoses and heater core tubes.
6. Disconnect the black vacuum supply hose from the in-line vacuum check valve in the engine compartment. Disconnect the blower motor wiring.
7. Working under the hood, remove the 2 nuts retaining the evaporator case to the dash panel. In the passenger compartment, remove the screw attaching the evaporator case support bracket to the cowl top panel.
8. Remove 1 nut retaining the bracket below the evaporator case to the dash panel. Carefully pull the evaporator case away from the dash panel and remove the evaporator case assembly from the vehicle.
9. Using a suitable cutting tool, cut the top of the evaporator case to gain access to the evaporator core. Remove the old evaporator core from the case.

To install:

NOTE: When replacing the evaporator, 3 fluid oz. (90ml) of clean refrigerant oil should be added to the new evaporator to maintain the total system oil charge.

10. Make sure all burrs are removed from the sawed edges of the evaporator case. Hold the cover against the case firmly and drill five $^3/_{16}$ in. diameter holes for the attaching screws.
11. Install the new evaporator in the evaporator case and install the service cover and the 5 attaching screws. Run a bead of caulking cord or other suitable sealer, between the service cover and the evaporator case.
12. Position the evaporator case assembly in the vehicle and install the screw attaching the evaporator case support bracket to the cowl top panel. Check the evaporator case drain tube to make sure it is through the dash panel and is not pinched or kinked.
13. Install 1 nut retaining the mounting bracket at the left end of the evaporator case to the dash panel and another nut to retain the bracket below the evaporator case to the dash panel.
14. Working under the hood, install the 2 nuts retaining the evaporator case to the dash panel. Tighten the 4 nuts, 2 in the engine compartment and 2 in the passenger comparment and the 1 support bracket attaching screw.
15. Connect the blower motor wiring. Connect the black vacuum supply hose to the vacuum check valve in the engine compartment.
16. Using new O-rings lubricated with clean refrigerant oil, connect the liquid line and suction accumulator inlet tube to the evaporator core.
17. Install the instrument panel by reversing the removal procedure.
18. Connect the heater hoses to the heater core and fill the cooling system.
19. Leak test, evacuate and charge the system according to the proper procedure. Observe all safety precautions.
20. Check the system for proper operation.

Mustang

NOTE: Whenever an evaporator core is replaced, it will be necessary to replace the suction accumulator/drier.

1. Disconnect the negative battery cable and drain the cooling system.
2. Discharge the refrigerant from the air conditioning system according to the proper procedure.
3. Remove the instrument panel according to the following procedure:
   a. Remove the 4 screws that attach the floor console top panel assembly to the floor console assembly.
   b. Lift the console top panel assembly off the console assembly and disconnect the 2 electrical connectors.
   c. Remove the 2 screws attaching the rear end of the console assembly to the console panel support assembly.
   d. Remove 4 screws attaching the console assembly to the console panel front support.
   e. Remove the 4 screws attaching the console assembly to the instrument panel.
   f. Lift the console assembly off of the transmission tunnel.

NOTE: The console assembly includes a snap-in finish panel which conceals the heater and air conditioning control assembly attaching screws. To gain access to these screws, it is necessary to remove the floor console.

g. Disconnect all underhood wiring connectors from the main wiring harness. Disengage the rubber grommet seal from the dash panel and push the wiring harness and connectors into the passenger compartment.

h. Remove the 3 bolts attaching the steering column opening cover and reinforcement panel. Remove the cover.

i. Remove the steering column opening reinforcement by removing 2 bolts. Remove the 2 bolts retaining the lower steering column opening reinforcement and remove the reinforcement.

j. Remove the 6 steering column retaining nuts. 2 are retaining the hood release mechanism and 4 retain the column to the lower brake pedal support. Lower the steering column to the floor.

k. Remove the steering column upper and lower shrouds and disconnect the wiring from the multi-function switch.

l. Remove the brake pedal support nut and snap out the defroster grille.

m. Remove the screws from the speaker covers. Snap out the speaker covers. Remove the front screws retaining the right and left scuff plates at the cowl trim panel. Remove the right and left side cowl trim panels.

n. Disconnect the wiring at the right and left cowl sides. Remove the cowl side retaining bolts, 1 on each side.

o. Open the glove compartment door and flex the glove compartment bin tabs inward. Drop down the glove compartment door assembly.

p. Remove the 5 cowl top screw attachments. Gently pull the instrument panel away from the cowl. Disconnect the speedometer cable and wire connectors.

4. Disconnect the liquid line and the accumulator/drier inlet tube from the evaporator core at the dash panel. Cap the refrigerant lines and evaporator core tube to prevent the entrance of dirt and excessive moisture.
5. Disconnect the heater hoses from the heater core tubes and plug the hoses and tubes.
6. Remove the screw attaching the air inlet duct and blower housing assembly support brace to the cowl top panel.
7. Disconnect the black vacuum supply hose from the in-line vacuum check valve in the engine compartment. Disconnect the blower motor wires from the wire harness and disconnect the wire harness from the blower motor resistor.
8. Working under the hood, remove the 2 nuts retaining the evaporator case to the dash panel. Inside the passenger compartment, remove the 2 screws attaching the evaporator case support brackets to the cowl top panel.
9. Remove the 1 screw retaining the bracket below the evaporator case to the dash panel. Carefully pull the evaporator case away from the dash panel and remove the evaporator case assembly from the vehicle.
10. Remove the 4 screws retaining the air inlet duct to the evaporator case and remove the duct. Remove the foam seal from the evaporator core tubes.
11. Drill a $^{3}/_{16}$ in. hole in both upright tabs on top of the evaporator case. Using a suitable cutting tool, cut the top of the evaporator case between the raised outlines.
12. Remove the 2 screws retaining the blower motor resistor to the evaporator case and remove the resistor. Fold the cutout flap from the opening and lift the evaporator core from the case.

To install:

NOTE: When replacing the evaporator, 3 oz. (90ml) of clean refrigerant oil should be added to the new evaporator to maintain the total system oil charge.

13. Transfer 2 foam core seals to the new evaporator core. Position the evaporator core in the case and close the cutout cover.
14. Install a spring nut on each of the 2 upright tabs. Make sure the hole in the spring nut is aligned with the hole drilled in the tab. Install and tighten a screw in each spring nut through the hole in the tab to secure the cutout cover in the closed position.
15. Install caulking cord or other suitable sealer, to seal the evaporator case against leakage along the cut line. Using new caulking cord, assemble the air inlet duct to the evaporator case.
16. Install the blower motor resistor and the foam seal over the evaporator core and heater core tubes.
17. Position the evaporator case assembly in the vehicle. Install the screws attaching the evaporator case support brackets to the cowl top panel. Check the evaporator case drain tube to ensure it is through the dash panel and is not pinched or kinked.
18. Install 1 screw retaining the bracket below the evaporator case to the dash panel. Working under the hood, install the 2 nuts retaining the evaporator case to the dash panel. Tighten the 4 nuts and 2 screws in the engine compartment. Tighten the 2 screws in the passenger compartment and the 2 support bracket attaching screws.
19. Connect the blower motor wire harness to the resistor and blower motor. Connect the black vacuum supply hose to the vacuum check valve in the engine compartment.
20. Using new O-rings lubricated with clean refrigerant oil, connect the liquid line and suction accumulator inlet to the evaporator core tubes. Tighten each connection using a backup wrench to prevent component damage.
21. Install the instrument panel by reversing the removal procedure.
22. Connect the heater hoses to the heater core and fill the cooling system.
23. Connect the negative battery cable. Leak test, evacuate and charge the refrigerant system according to the proper procedure. Observe all safety precautions.
24. Check the system for proper operation.

Refrigerant Lines

REMOVAL AND INSTALLATION

NOTE: Whenever a refrigerant line is replaced, it will be necessary to replace the suction accumulator/drier.

1. Disconnect the negative battery cable. Discharge the refrigerant from the air conditioning system.
2. Disconnect the refrigerant line using a wrench on each side of the fitting or the spring-lock coupling disconnect procedure, whichever is necessary. Remove the refrigerant line.
3. Route the new refrigerant line with the protective caps installed.
4. Connect the refrigerant line into the system using new O-rings lubricated with clean refrigerant oil. Tighten the connection using 2 wrenches or the spring-lock coupling connect procedure, whichever is necessary.
5. Connect the negative battery cable. Leak test, evacuate and charge the refrigerant system according to the proper procedure. Observe all safety precautions.

Manual Control Head

REMOVAL AND INSTALLATION

Crown Victoria and Grand Marquis

1989

1. Disconnect the negative battery cable.
2. Pull the knobs from the radio control shafts. Open the ash tray and remove the 2 screws attaching the center finish panel to the instrument panel at the ash tray opening.
3. Pull the lower edge of the center finish panel away from

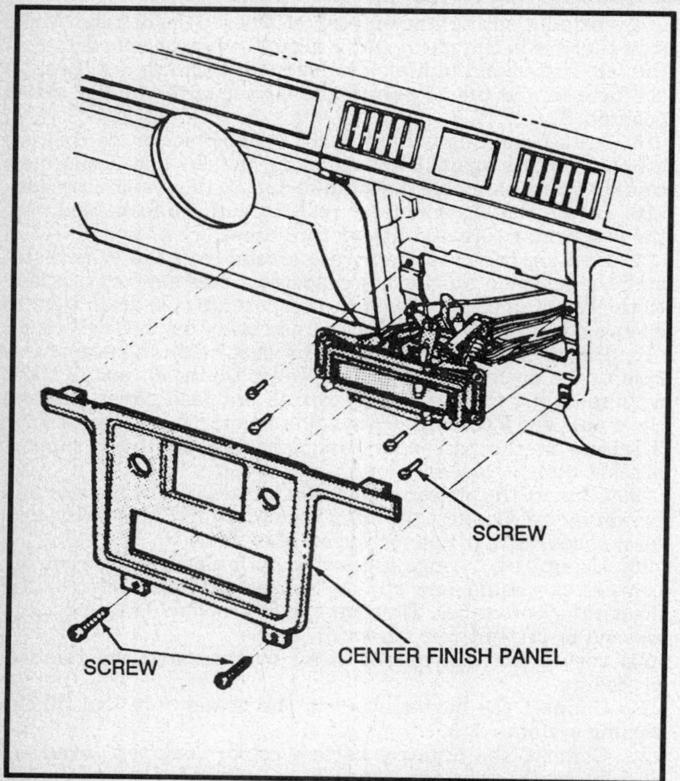
SCREW
SCREW
CENTER FINISH PANEL

Manual control assembly removal—1989 Crown Victoria and Grand Marquis

the instrument panel and disengage the upper tabs of the finish panel from the instrument panel.

4. Remove the 4 screws attaching the control assembly to the instrument panel. Pull the control assembly from the instrument panel opening and disconnect the wire connectors from the control assembly. Disconnect the vacuum harness and temperature control cable from the control assembly.

To install:

5. Connect the temperature cable, wire connectors and the vacuum harness to the control assembly.

NOTE: Push on the vacuum harness retaining nut. Do not attempt to screw onto the post.

6. Position the control assembly to the instrument panel and install the 4 attaching screws. Position the center finish panel to the instrument panel and install the 2 attaching screws.

7. Install the knobs on the radio control shafts. Connect the negative battery cable and check the system for proper operation.

1990–91

1. Disconnect the negative battery cable.
2. Remove the left and right instrument panel moulding assemblies. Remove the cluster finish panel screws that were under the mouldings and also the 6 screws along the top surface of the cluster finish panel.
3. Pull off the knob from the headlight auto dim switch. Remove the headlight switch shaft as follows:
   a. Locate the headlight switch assembly body under the instrument panel.
   b. Push the spring loaded shaft release button located on the side of the switch body and simultaneously pull out the headlight switch shaft.
4. Remove the steering column close out bolster panel by removing the 2 screws on the left side, 1 screw on the right side and 3 screws from the bottom.
5. Remove the 2 screws retaining the steering column close out bolster panel bracket and remove the bracket.
6. Lower the steering column and remove the shift position indicator and cable assembly as follows:
   a. Place the shift lever in 1 position.
   b. Remove the shift position indicator cable from the steering column arm.
   c. Remove the bolt from the steering column shift position indicator bracket
7. Remove the 4 nuts holding the steering column and let the steering column rest on the front seat.
8. Remove the cluster finish panel.

NOTE: Remove the electrical connectors from the accessory push button switches.

9. Remove the center finish panel as follows:
   a. The center finish panel is retained by 2 screws on the top and 2 snap-in tabs on the bottom.
   b. Remove the 2 top screws and gently rock the top back while unsnapping the bottom from the instrument panel.
   c. Remove the electrical connector from the clock.
10. Remove the 4 screws from the air conditioning control assembly and pull the control out of the instrument panel. Remove the 2 electrical connectors, the temperature cable and the vacuum connector from the control assembly.

To install:

11. Connect the temperature cable, 2 electrical connectors and the vacuum connector to the control assembly. Position the control assembly in the instrument panel and attach with the 4 screws.
12. Install the electrical connector to the clock on the center finish panel. Install the center finish panel by snapping in the bottom and using the 2 screws on the top.
13. Position the cluster finish panel. Raise the steering column and install the 4 nuts to the steering column bracket.
14. Install the bolt to the steering column shift position indicator bracket and install the shift position indicator cable to the steering column arm.
15. Position the steering column close out bolster panel bracket and install with the 2 screws. Install the steering column close out bolster panel.
16. Install the cluster finish panel screws and snap in the headlight switch knob/shaft assembly. Install the headlight auto dim knob.

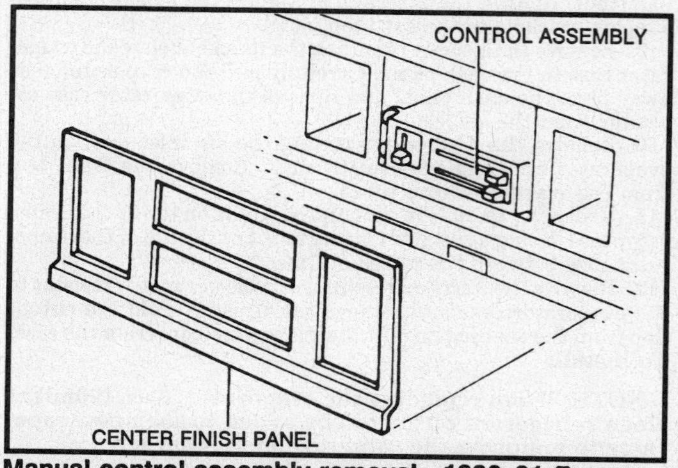
CONTROL ASSEMBLY
CENTER FINISH PANEL

Manual control assembly removal—1990–91 Crown Victoria and Grand Marquis

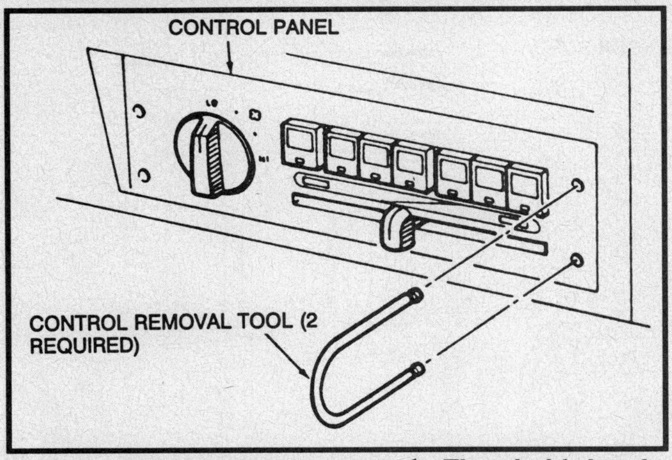
CONTROL PANEL
CONTROL REMOVAL TOOL (2 REQUIRED)

Manual control assembly removal—Thunderbird and Cougar

17. Position the left and right instrument panel moulding assemblies and install by snapping into place.
18. Connect the negative battery cable and check the system for proper operation.

Thunderbird and Cougar

1. Disconnect the negative battery cable.
2. Insert removal tool T87P–19061–A or equivalent, in the retaining clip access holes. Apply a side load away from the control to disengage the clips.
3. Pull the control assembly from the instrument panel opening and disconnect the wire connectors from the control assembly. Disconnect the vacuum harness and the temperature control cable from the control assembly.

To install:

4. Connect the temperature cable, wire connectors and vacuum harness to the control assembly.

NOTE: Push on the vacuum harness retaining nuts. Do not attempt to screw on to post.

5. Position the control assembly in the instrument panel opening. Engage it in the track in the instrument panel and push it in until it latches firmly in place.
6. Connect the negative battery cable and check the system for proper operation.

Mustang

1. Disconnect the negative battery cable.
2. Remove the snap-in trim moulding in the floor console to expose the 4 control assembly attaching screws. Remove the 4 screws attaching the control assembly to the instrument panel.
3. Roll the control out of the opening in the console. Disconnect the fan switch connectors and temperature control cable. Disconnect the vacuum hose connector and electrical connector from the back of the function selector knob. Disconnect the connector for the control assembly illumination bulbs.
4. Remove the control assembly.

To install:

5. Connect the temperature cable to the geared arm on the temperature control.
6. Install the electrical connector at the following locations: blower switch, control assembly illumination bulbs and function selector switch.
7. Install the vacuum harness connector for the function selector knob.
8. Roll the control assembly into position against the instrument panel and install the 4 attaching screws.
9. Snap the console trim moulding into position, connect the negative battery cable and check the system for proper operation.

Manual Control Cables

ADJUSTMENT

1989 Crown Victoria, Grand Marquis and Town Car with Automatic Temperature Control

1. Remove the instrument panel pad.
2. Move the temperature selector lever to the **75°F** position.
3. The control arm of the Automatic Temperature Control

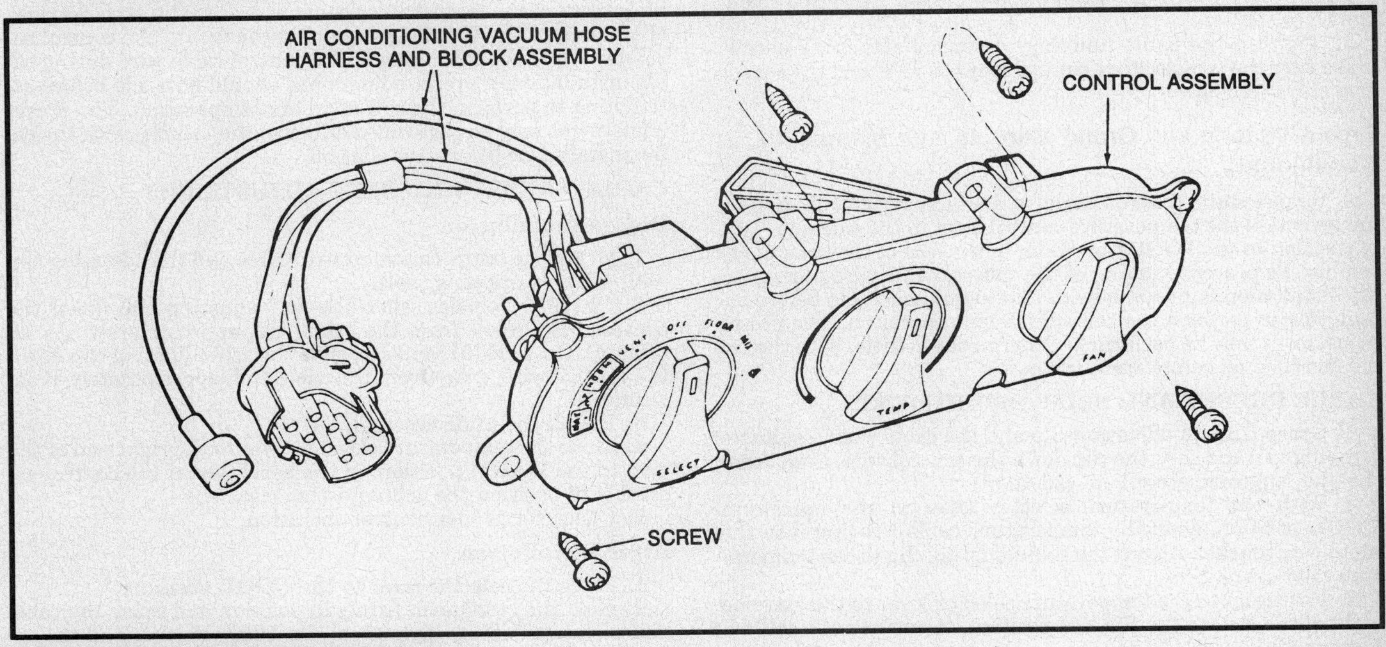
AIR CONDITIONING VACUUM HOSE HARNESS AND BLOCK ASSEMBLY
CONTROL ASSEMBLY
SCREW
SELECT
TEMP
FAN

Manual control assembly—Mustang

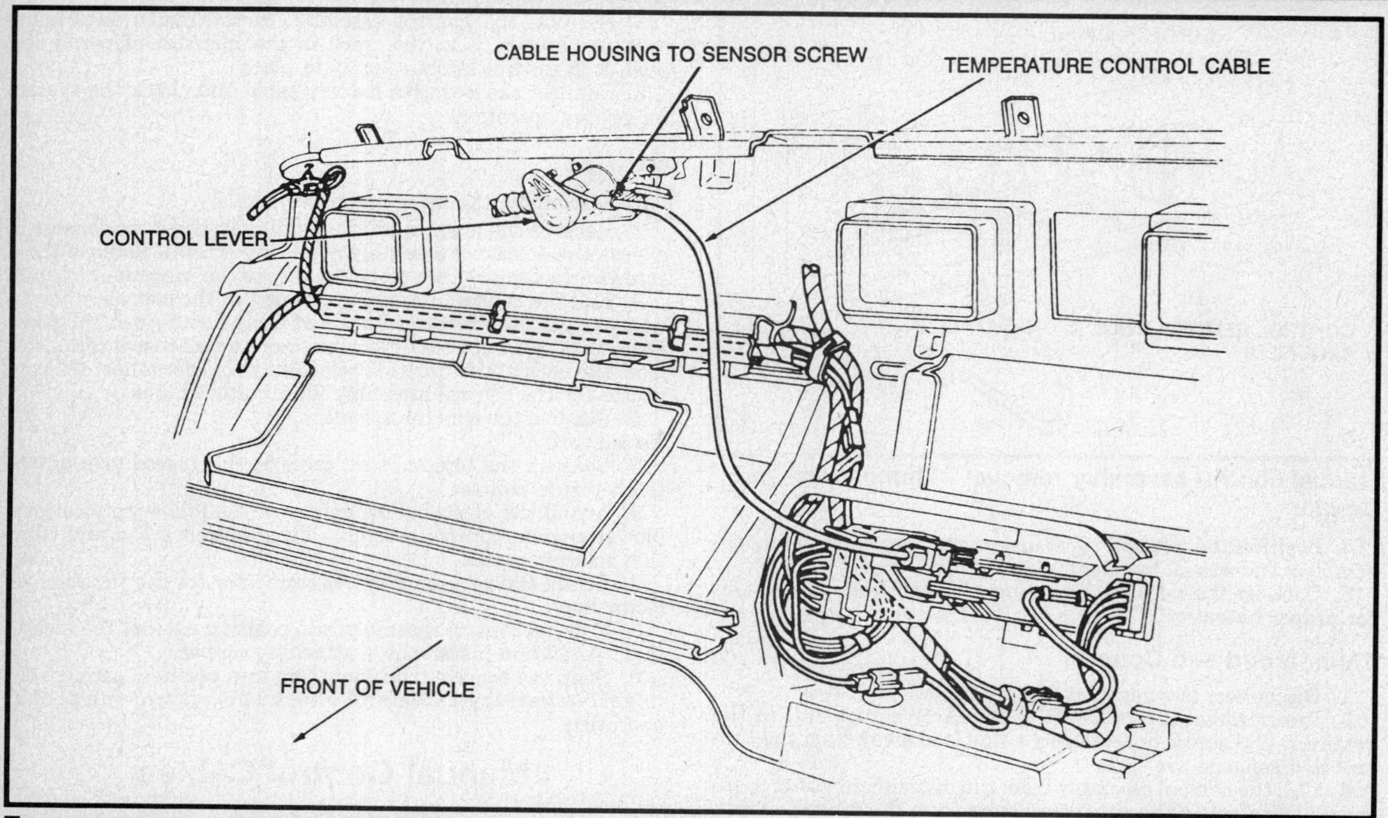
CABLE HOUSING TO SENSOR SCREW
TEMPERATURE CONTROL CABLE
CONTROL LEVER
FRONT OF VEHICLE

Temperature control cable adjustment and sensor calibration—1989 Crown Victoria, Grand Marquis and Town Car with Automatic Temperature Control

(ATC) sensor should be aligned with the arrow on the sensor body.

4. If it is not, loosen the cable housing-to-sensor attaching screw and align the sensor control arm with the arrow while maintaining the 75°F position of the temperature selector control lever.

5. Tighten the cable housing-to-sensor attaching screw. Make sure the temperature control stays at 75°F and the sensor arm stays locked.

Crown Victoria and Grand Marquis with Manual Air Conditioning

The temperature control cable is self-adjusting with a firm movement of the temperature control lever to the extreme right of the slot, to the **WARM** position, in the face of the control assembly. To prevent kinking of the control cable wire during cable installation, a preset adjustment should be made before attempting to perform the self-adjustment operation. The preset adjustment may be performed either in the vehicle, with the cable installed or before installation.

CABLE PRESET AND SELF-ADJUSTMENT

1. Grasp the self-adjusting clip and the cable with a suitable gripping tool and slide the clip down the control wire, away from the end, approximately 1 in. (25.4mm).

2. With the temperature selector lever in the maximum **COOL** position, snap the temperature cable housing into the mounting bracket. Attach the self-adjusting clip to the temperature door crank arm.

3. Firmly move the temperature selector lever to the extreme right of the slot, to the **WARM** position, to position the self-adjusting clip.

4. Check for proper control operation.

Thunderbird and Cougar

The temperature control cable is self-adjusting with a firm movement of the temperature control lever to the extreme right of the slot, to the **WARM** position, in the face of the control assembly. To prevent kinking of the control cable wire during cable installation, a preset adjustment should be made before attempting to perform the self-adjustment operation. The preset adjustment may be performed either in the vehicle, with the cable installed or before installation.

CABLE PRESET AND SELF-ADJUSTMENT

Before Installation

1. Grasp the temperature control cable and the adjusting clip with suitable gripping tools.

2. On 1989 vehicles, slide the self-adjusting clip down the control wire, away from the cable end, approximately 1½ in. (38mm). On 1990–91 vehicles, slide the self-adjusting clip down the control wire, away from the cable end, approximately ¾ in. (18mm).

3. Install the cable assembly.

4. Move the temperature selector lever to the right end of the slot, to the **WARM** position, in the bezel face of the control assembly to position the self-adjusting clip.

5. Check for proper control operation.

After Installation

1. Move the selector lever to the **COOL** position.

2. Hold the crank arm firmly in position and grasp the cable end with a suitable gripping tool. On 1989 vehicles, pull the cable wire through the self-adjusting clip until there is a space of

approximately 1½ in. (38mm) between the clip and the cable end. On 1990–91 vehicles, pull the cable wire through the self-adjusting clip until there is a space of approximately ¾ in. (18mm) between the clip and the cable end.

3. Move the selector lever to the right of the slot to position the self-adjusting clip.
4. Check for proper control operation.

Mustang

The temperature control cable is self-adjusting with the movement of the temperature selector knob to it's fully clockwise position in the red band on the face of the control assembly. To prevent kinking of the control wire, a preset adjustment should be made before attempting to perform the self-adjustment operation. The preset adjustment may be performed either with the cable installed in the vehicle or before cable installation.

CABLE PRESET AND SELF-ADJUSTMENT

Before Installation

1. Insert the end of a suitable tool in the end loop of the temperature control cable, at the temperature door crank arm end.
2. Slide the self-adjusting clip down the control wire, away from the end loop, approximately 1 in. (25mm).
3. Install the cable assembly.
4. Turn the temperature control knob fully clockwise to position the self-adjusting clip.
5. Check for proper control operation.

After Installation

1. Turn the temperature selector knob to the **COOL** position.
2. Hold the temperature door crank arm firmly in position, insert a suitable tool into the wire end loop and pull the cable wire through the self-adjusting clip until there is a space of approximately 1 in. (25mm) between the clip and the wire end loop.
3. Turn the temperature control knob fully clockwise to position the self-adjusting clip.
4. Check for proper control operation.

REMOVAL AND INSTALLATION

1989 Crown Victoria, Grand Marquis and Town Car with Automatic Temperature Control

1. Disconnect the negative battery cable.
2. Remove the instrument panel pad as follows:
   a. Remove the 2 screws attaching the instrument panel pad to the instrument panel at each defroster opening. Use extreme care not to drop the screws into the defroster openings.
   b. Remove 1 screw attaching each outboard end of the pad to the instrument panel.
   c. On Crown Victoria, remove 1 pad attaching the screw near the upper right corner of the glove compartment door.
   d. Remove the 5 screws attaching the lower edge of the pad to the instrument panel. Pull the instrument panel pad rearward and remove it from the vehicle.
3. Remove the 1 screw attaching the cable to the Automatic Temperature Control (ATC) sensor and remove the cable from the sensor.
4. If equipped with a mechanically controlled radio, pull the knobs from the radio control shafts.
5. Open the ash tray and remove the 2 screws attaching the center finish panel to the instrument panel at the ash tray opening.
6. Pull the lower edge of the center finish panel away from the instrument panel and disengage the upper tabs of the finish panel from the instrument panel.
7. Remove the 4 screws attaching the control assembly to the instrument panel and pull the control out of the opening.

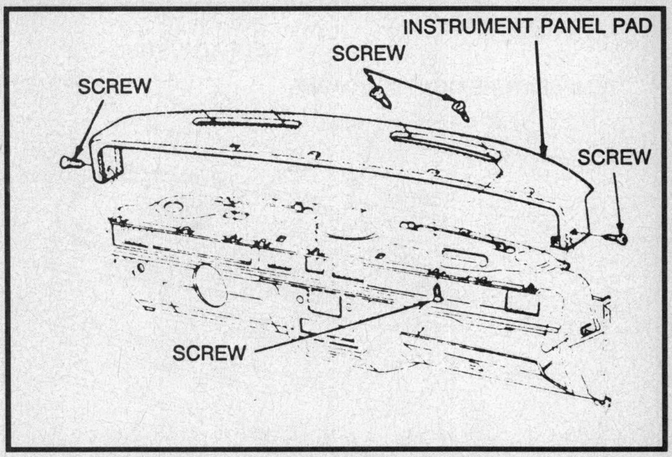
INSTRUMENT PANEL PAD
SCREW
SCREW
SCREW
SCREW

Instrument panel pad removal—1989 Crown Victoria, Grand Marquis and Town Car

8. Remove the pushnut retaining the cable end loop on the temperature lever arm. Disconnect the cable housing from the control assembly.
9. Note the cable routing and remove the cable from the vehicle.

To install:

10. Route the cable behind the instrument panel and connect the cable to the sensor. Loosely assemble, but do not tighten the attaching screw at this time.
11. Connect the other end of the control cable to the temperature lever arm of the control assembly. Snap the cable housing into place at the control assembly.
12. Install a new pushnut to retain the cable end loop on the temperature lever arm.
13. Position the control assembly to the instrument panel and install the 4 attaching screws.
14. Position the center finish panel to the instrument panel and install the 2 attaching screws.
15. Install the knobs on the radio shafts, if equipped.
16. Adjust the temperature control cable. Install the instrument panel pad by reversing the removal procedure.
17. Connect the negative battery cable and check the system for proper operation.

Crown Victoria and Grand Marquis with Manual Air Conditioning

1989

1. Disconnect the negative battery cable.
2. Remove the glove compartment door stops and allow the door to hang by the hinge. Pull the knobs from the radio control shafts.
3. Open the ash tray and remove the 2 screws attaching the center finish panel to the instrument panel at the ash tray opening.
4. Pull the lower edge of the center finish panel away from the instrument panel and disengage the upper tabs of the finish panel from the instrument panel.
5. Remove the 4 screws attaching the control assembly to the instrument panel and pull the control from the opening.
6. Remove the pushnut retaining the cable end loop on the temperature lever arm. Disconnect the cable housing from the control assembly.
7. Through the glove compartment opening, disconnect the temperature cable from the plenum temperature blend door crank arm and cable mounting bracket. Note the cable routing and remove the cable from the vehicle.

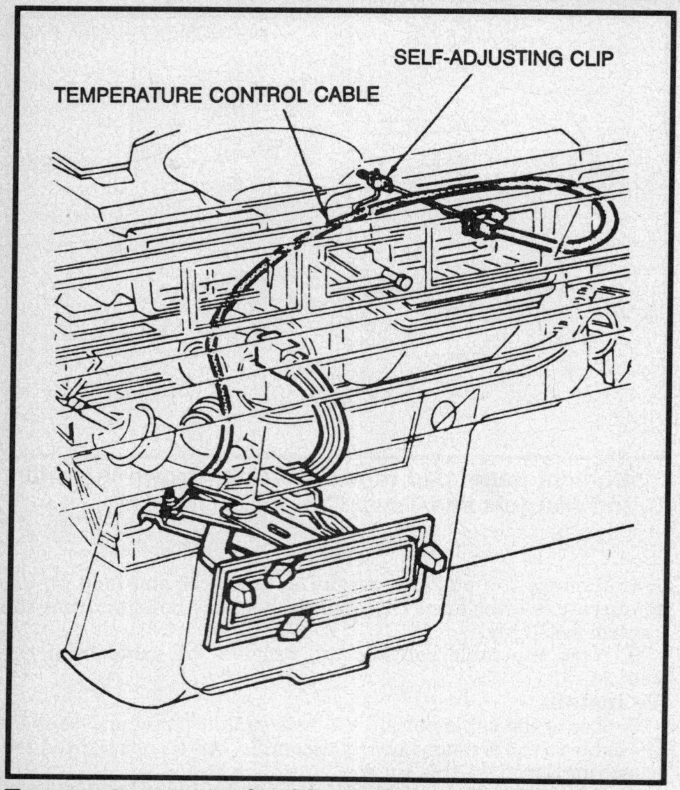
SELF-ADJUSTING CLIP
TEMPERATURE CONTROL CABLE

Temperature control cable routing—1989 Crown Victoria and Grand Marquis

To install:

8. Check to make sure the self-adjusting clip is at least 1 in. (25.4mm) from the end loop of the control cable.
9. Route the cable behind the instrument panel and connect the control cable to the mounting bracket on the plenum. Install the self-adjusting clip on the temperature blend door crank arm.
10. Connect the other end of the control cable to the temperature lever arm on the control assembly. Snap the cable housing into place at the control assembly and install a new pushnut to retain the cable end loop on the temperature lever arm.
11. Position the control assembly to the instrument panel and install the 4 attaching screws.
12. Position the center finish panel to the instrument panel and install the 2 attaching screws. Install the knobs on the radio control shafts.
13. Force the temperature lever to the extreme right end of the slot, to the **WARM** position, to position the self-adjusting clip on the control cable. Check the temperature selector lever for proper operation.
14. Install the glove compartment door stop and connect the negative battery cable.
15. Check the system for proper operation.

1990–91

1. Disconnect the negative battery cable.
2. Press the glove compartment door stops inward and allow the door to hang by the hinge.
3. Remove the control assembly from the instrument panel. Disconnect the cable housing from the control assembly and disengage the cable from the temperature control lever.
4. Through the glove compartment opening, disconnect the temperature cable from the plenum temperature blend door crank arm and cable mounting bracket. Note the cable routing and remove the cable from the vehicle.

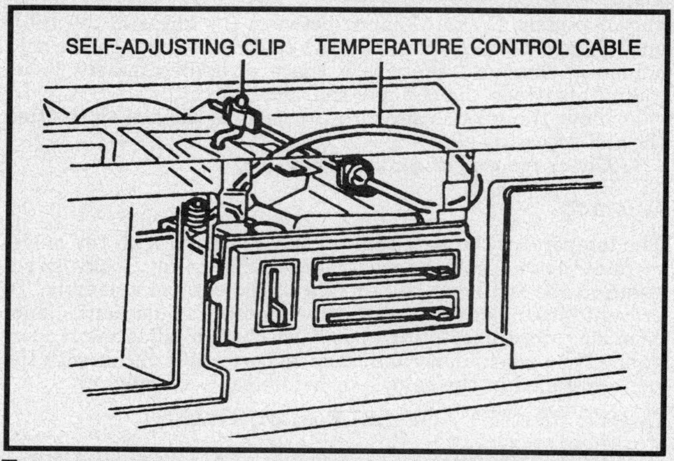
SELF-ADJUSTING CLIP
TEMPERATURE CONTROL CABLE

Temperature control cable routing—1990–91 Crown Victoria and Grand Marquis

To install:

5. Check to make sure the self-adjusting clip is at least 1 in. (25.4mm) from the end loop of the control cable.
6. Route the cable behind the instrument panel and connect the control cable to the mounting bracket on the plenum. Install the self-adjusting clip on the temperature blend door crank arm.
7. Connect the other end of the control cable to the temperature lever arm on the control assembly. Snap the cable housing into place at the control assembly.
8. Install the control assembly in the instrument panel and return the glove compartment door to the normal position.
9. Connect the negative battery cable and check the system for proper operation.

Thunderbird and Cougar

1. Disconnect the negative battery cable.
2. Remove the control assembly and disconnect the cable housing from the control assembly.
3. Disconnect the temperature cable from the plenum temperature blend door crank arm and the cable mounting bracket. Note the cable routing and remove the cable from the vehicle.

To install:

4. On 1989 vehicles, check to ensure the self-adjusting clip is at least 1½ in. (38mm) from the end loop of the control cable. On 1990–91 vehicles, check to ensure the self-adjusting clip is at least ¾ in. (18mm) from the end loop of the control cable.
5. Route the cable behind the instrument panel and connect the control cable to the mounting bracket on the plenum. Install the self-adjusting clip on the temperature blend door crank arm.
6. Connect the cable to the temperature control lever and snap the cable housing into place at the control assembly. Install the control assembly.
7. Move the temperature lever firmly to the extreme right end of the slot, to the **WARM** position, to position the self-adjusting clip on the control cable. Check the temperature selector lever for proper operation.
8. Connect the negative battery cable and check the system for proper operation.

Mustang

1. Disconnect the negative battery cable.
2. Remove the control assembly from the instrument panel.
3. Disengage the temperature control cable from the cable actuator on the control assembly. Disconnect the temperature cable from the plenum temperature blend door crank arm and cable mounting bracket.
4. Note the cable routing and remove the cable from the vehicle.

To install:

5. Check to ensure the self-adjusting clip is at least 1 in. (25.4mm) from the end loop of the control cable.
6. Route the cable behind the instrument panel and connect the control cable to the mounting bracket on the plenum. Install the self-adjusting clip on the temperature blend door crank arm.
7. Engage the cable end with the cable actuator on the control assembly. Install the control assembly in the instrument panel.
8. Turn the temperature control knob all the way to the right, to the **WARM** position, to position the self-adjusting clip on the control cable. Check the temperature control knob for proper operation.
9. Connect the negative battery cable and check the system for proper operation.

Electronic Control Head

REMOVAL AND INSTALLATION

Crown Victoria, Grand Marquis and Town Car

1989

1. Disconnect the negative battery cable.
2. If equipped with a mechanically controlled radio, pull the knobs from the radio control shafts.
3. Open the ash tray and remove the 2 screws attaching the center finish panel to the instrument panel at the ash tray opening.
4. Pull the lower edge of the center finish panel away from the instrument panel and disengage the upper tabs of the finish panel from the instrument panel.
5. Remove the 4 screws attaching the control assembly to the instrument panel and pull the control assembly from the instrument panel opening.
6. Disconnect the wire connectors, vacuum harness and temperature control cable from the control assembly.

To install:

7. Connect the temperature cable to the control assembly. Use a new pushnut to retain the cable end loop to the control arm.
8. Connect the wire connectors and the vacuum harness to the control assembly.

NOTE: Push on the vacuum harness retaining nut. Do not attempt to screw onto post.

9. Position the control assembly to the instrument panel opening and install the 4 screws. Position the center finish panel to the instrument panel and install the 2 attaching screws.
10. Install the knobs on the radio control shafts, if equipped.
11. Connect the negative battery cable and check the system for proper operation.

1990–91

1. Disconnect the negative battery cable.
2. Remove the left and right instrument panel moulding assemblies. Remove the cluster finish panel screws that were under the mouldings and also the 6 screws along the top surface of the cluster finish panel.
3. Pull off the knob from the headlight auto dim switch. Remove the headlight switch shaft as follows:
   a. Locate the headlight switch assembly body under the instrument panel.
   b. Push the spring loaded shaft release button located on the side of the switch body and simultaneously pull out the headlight switch shaft.
4. Remove the steering column close out bolster panel by removing the 2 screws on the left side, 1 screw on the right side and 3 screws from the bottom.
5. Remove the 2 screws retaining the steering column close out bolster panel bracket and remove the bracket.

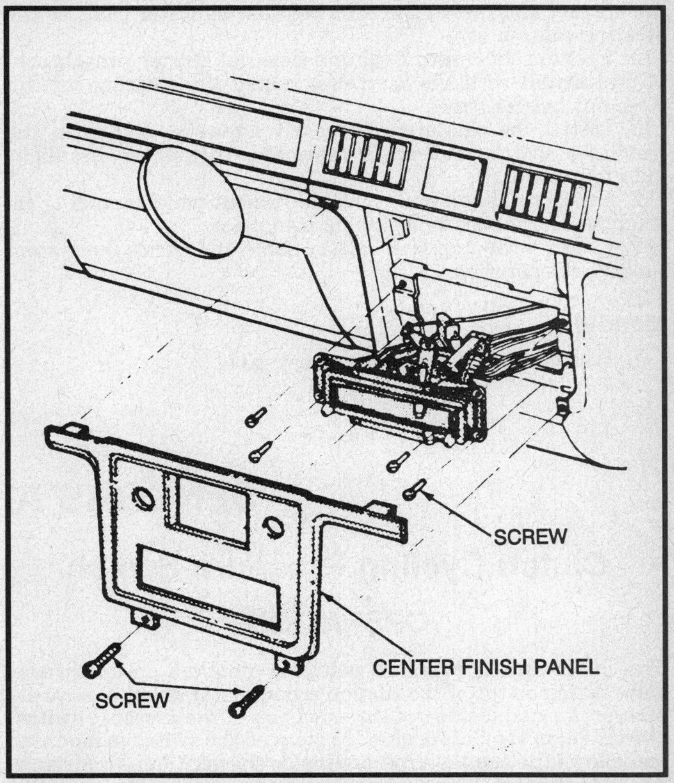
SCREW
CENTER FINISH PANEL
SCREW

Control assembly removal—1989 Crown Victoria and Grand Marquis

6. Lower the steering column and remove the shift position indicator and cable assembly as follows:
   a. Place the shift lever in **1** position.
   b. Remove the shift position indicator cable from the steering column arm.
   c. Remove the bolt from the steering column shift position indicator bracket
7. Remove the 4 nuts holding the steering column and let the steering column rest on the front seat.
8. Remove the cluster finish panel.

NOTE: Remove the electrical connectors from the accessory push button switches.

9. Remove the center finish panel as follows:
   a. The center finish panel is retained by 2 screws on the top and 2 snap-in tabs on the bottom.
   b. Remove the 2 top screws and gently rock the top back while unsnapping the bottom from the instrument panel.
   c. Remove the electrical connector from the clock.
10. Remove the 4 screws from the air conditioning control assembly and pull the control out of the instrument panel. Remove the electrical connectors and the vacuum connector from the control assembly.

To install:

11. Connect the electrical connectors and the vacuum connector to the control assembly. Position the control assembly in the instrument panel and attach with the 4 screws.
12. Install the electrical connector to the clock on the center finish panel. Install the center finish panel by snapping in the bottom and using the 2 screws on the top.
13. Position the cluster finish panel. Raise the steering column and install the 4 nuts to the steering column bracket.
14. Install the bolt to the steering column shift position indica-

tor bracket and install the shift position indicator cable to the steering column arm.

15. Position the steering column close out bolster panel bracket and install with the 2 screws. Install the steering column close out bolster panel.

16. Install the cluster finish panel screws and snap in the headlight switch knob/shaft assembly. Install the headlight auto dim knob.

17. Position the left and right instrument panel moulding assemblies and install by snapping into place.

18. Connect the negative battery cable and check the system for proper operation.

Mark VII

1. Disconnect the negative battery cable.

2. Remove the instrument panel center finish panel right insert; it is a snap fit.

3. Remove the 4 screws attaching the control assembly to the instrument panel.

4. Slide the control assembly out from the instrument panel opening and disconnect the 2 harness connectors from the control assembly by disengaging the latches on the bottom of the control.

To install:

5. Connect the 2 harness connectors to the control assembly.

6. Position the control assembly to the instrument panel opening and install the 4 attaching screws.

7. Position the instrument panel center finish panel on the instrument panel and snap in.

8. Connect the negative battery cable and check the system for proper operation.

SENSORS AND SWITCHES

Clutch Cycling Pressure Switch

OPERATION

The clutch cycling pressure switch is mounted on a Schrader valve fitting on top of the suction accumulator/drier. A valve depressor, located inside the threaded end of the pressure switch, presses in on the Schrader valve stem as the switch is mounted and allows the suction pressure inside the accumulator/drier to act on the switch. The electrical switch contacts will open when the suction pressure drops to 23–26 psi. and close when the suction pressure rises to approximately 45 psi. or above. Ambient temperatures below approximately 45°F (9°C) will also open the clutch cycling pressure switch contacts because of the pressure/temperature relationship of the refrigerant in the system. The electrical switch contacts control the electrical circuit to the compressor magnetic clutch coil. When the switch contacts are closed, the magnetic clutch coil is energized and the air conditioning clutch is engaged to drive the compressor. When the switch contacts are open, the compressor magnetic clutch coil is de-energized, the air conditioning clutch is disengaged and the compressor does not operate. The clutch cycling pressure switch, when functioning properly, will control the evaporator core pressure at a point where the plate/fin surface temperature will be maintained slightly above freezing which prevents evaporator icing and the blockage of airflow.

REMOVAL AND INSTALLATION

1. Disconnect the negative battery cable.

2. Disconnect the wire harness connector from the pressure switch.

3. Unscrew the pressure switch from the top of the suction accumulator/drier.

To install:

4. Lubricate the O-ring on the accumulator nipple with clean refrigerant oil.

5. Screw the pressure switch on the accumulator nipple. Hand tighten only.

6. Connect the wire connector to the pressure switch.

7. Check the pressure switch installation for refrigerant leaks. Connect the negative battery cable and check the system for proper operation.

Thermal Blower Lock Out Switch (TBL)

OPERATION

The TBL is used on Crown Victoria, Grand Marquis and Town Car with automatic temperature control. It is a combination vacuum valve and a single-pole single-throw switch powered by a thermal element. The TBL is located in the heater supply hose in the engine compartment with the thermal element of the switch in contact with the engine coolant. In the FLOOR function lever position and with a cold engine, the blower is locked out and the outside-recirc door is in the RECIRC position.

When the engine coolant warms up to approximately 120°F (49°C), the electrical switch contacts close permitting the blower to operate and the outside-recirc door to move to the outside position.

REMOVAL AND INSTALLATION

1. Disconnect the negative battery cable and drain the cooling system.

2. Disconnect the electrical and vacuum connectors from the TBL.

3. Loosen the hose clamps at the TBL and remove the TBL from the hose.

To install:

4. Slide the new hose clamps over the ends of the hoses. Apply soapy water to the ends of the hoses.

5. Insert the TBL in the hose ends and tighten the clamps to 16–22 inch lbs. (1.80–2.48 Nm).

6. Connect the electrical and vacuum connectors to the TBL. Fill the cooling system.

7. Connect the negative battery cable and check the air conditioning system for proper operation.

Coolant Temperature Switch

OPERATION

During cool or cold weather, the engine coolant temperature switch on Mark VII vehicles controls a cold engine lock out function when the automatic temperature control system is set for automatic operation. During lock out, the fan will not operate until engine coolant temperature reaches the point where the

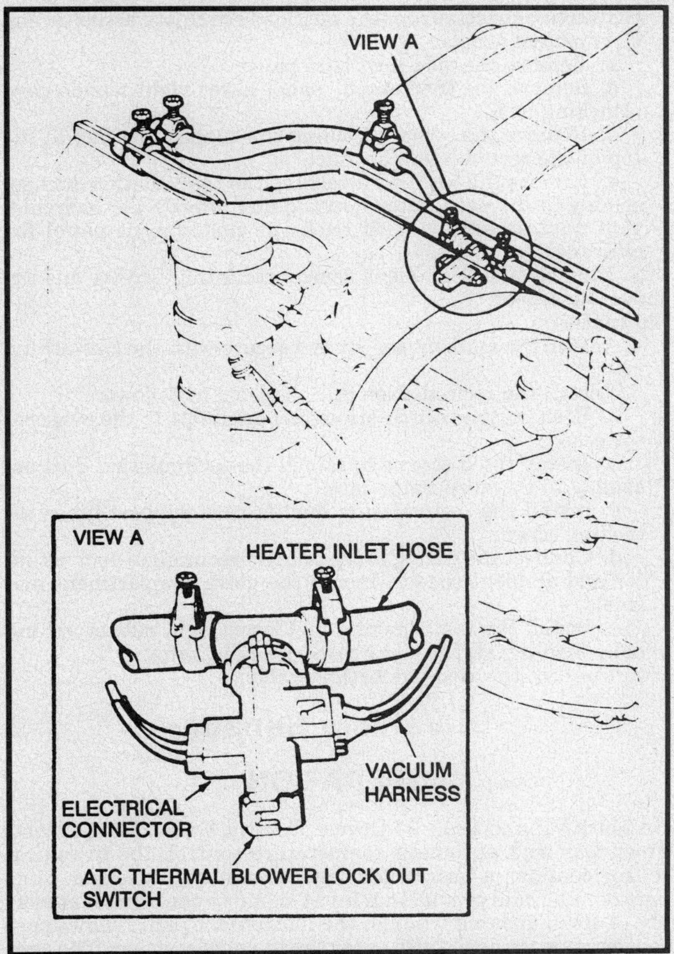
VIEW A
VIEW A
HEATER INLET HOSE
VACUUM HARNESS
ELECTRICAL CONNECTOR
ATC THERMAL BLOWER LOCK OUT SWITCH

Thermal blower lock out switch—Crown Victoria, Grand Marquis and Town Car with automatic temperature control

temperature of the air being discharged from the floor outlets rises to a minimum of 100°F (68°C).

REMOVAL AND INSTALLATION

MARK VII

1. Disconnect the negative battery cable and drain the cooling system.
2. Disconnect the electrical connector from the coolant temperature switch and remove the switch from the heater inlet hose fitting.

To install:

3. Install the coolant temperature switch and tighten to 8–18 ft. lbs. (11–24 Nm).
4. Connect the electrical connector and fill the cooling system.
5. Start the engine and check for coolant leaks. Add coolant as necessary.

Blower Speed Controller (BSC)

OPERATION

The blower speed controller is used on Mark VII and 1990–91 Crown Victoria, Grand Marquis and Town Car with automatic temperature control. The BSC is located in the evaporator case. It's function is to convert low current signals from the electronic control assembly to a high current, variable ground feed to the blower motor. Blower motor speed is infinitely variable and is controlled by the electronic control assembly software. A delay function provides a gradual increase or decrease in blower motor speed under all conditions.

NOTE: The system should not be operated with the blower motor disconnected. Damage may occur to the BSC if cooling air is not provided by the blower motor.

REMOVAL AND INSTALLATION

Crown Victoria, Grand Marquis and Town Car

1. Disconnect the negative battery cable.
2. Disconnect the wire harness connector from the blower speed controller.
3. Remove the 2 retaining screws securing the blower speed controller to the evaporator case and remove the blower speed controller.
4. Installation is the reverse of the removal procedure.

Mark VII

1. Disconnect the negative battery cable.
2. Disengage the glove compartment door stops and allow the door to hang by the hinge.
3. Remove the screw attaching the lower right end of the instrument panel to the side cowl panel.
4. Loosen the floor console and move it rearward. Remove the control assembly and remove the screws attaching the instrument panel to the floorpan.
5. Working through the glove compartment opening, disconnect the snap-lock wire connector from the blower speed controller.
6. Remove the 3 screws attaching the blower speed controller to the evaporator case and remove the blower speed controller.

CAUTION

Do not touch the fins of the controller if it has been operated recently. They will be hot and a burn could result.

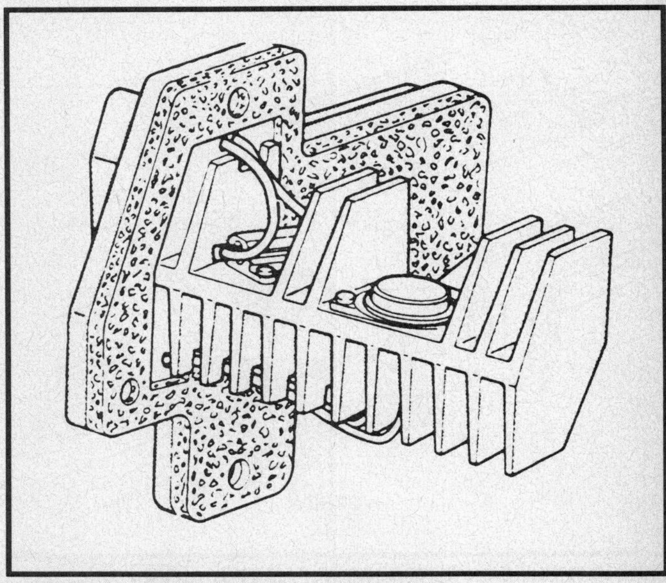

Blower speed controller—Mark VII

To install:

7. Position the blower speed controller to the evaporator case and install the 3 attaching screws. Connect the wire connector to the blower speed controller.
8. Install the screws to attach the instrument panel to the floorpan. Install the control assembly.
9. Move the floor console forward to the instrument panel and secure in place.
10. Install the screw to attach the lower right end of the instrument panel to the side cowl. Close the glove compartment door.
11. Connect the negative battery cable and check the system for proper operation.

Ambient Sensor

OPERATION

The ambient temperature sensor is used on Mark VII and 1990–91 Crown Victoria, Grand Marquis and Town Car with automatic temperature control. The sensor contains a thermister which measures the temperature of the outside air and provides an input signal to the control assembly. On 1990–91 Crown Victoria, Grand Marquis and Town Car, the sensor is located in front of the condenser on the hood latch support brace. On Mark VII, the sensor is located in the outside air intake duct of the evaporator case.

REMOVAL AND INSTALLATION

Crown Victoria, Grand Marquis and Town Car

1. Disconnect the negative battery cable.
2. Disconnect the electrical connector from the ambient sensor.
3. Remove the mounting screw and remove the ambient sensor and bracket assembly.
4. Installation is the reverse of the removal procedure.

Mark VII

1. Disconnect the negative battery cable.
2. Remove the recirculation duct housing as follows:
   a. Remove the glove compartment and shield. Disconnect the wire connector from the outside-recirculate actuator and the ambient sensor.
   b. Remove the side cowl trim panel.
   c. Remove the instrument panel lower right-to-side cowl attaching bolt.
   d. Remove the screw attaching the support bracket to the top of the recirculation air duct.
   e. Remove the 5 screws attaching the recirculation duct assembly to the evaporator housing and remove the recirculation duct assembly. Pull back the instrument panel for clearance.
3. Remove the 2 ambient sensor mounting screws and remove the sensor.

To install:

4. Install the ambient sensor and secure with the 2 attaching screws.
5. Install the recirculation duct housing as follows:
   a. Position the recirculation duct assembly to the evaporator case.
   b. Install the 5 screws to attach the recirculation duct assembly to the evaporator case.
   c. Install the recirculation duct-to-cowl support brace attaching screw.
   d. Connect the wiring to the outside-recirculate door actuator and ambient sensor. Install the glove compartment and shield.
   e. Install the instrument panel lower right side attaching bolt, then install the right cowl side trim panel.
6. Connect the negative battery cable.

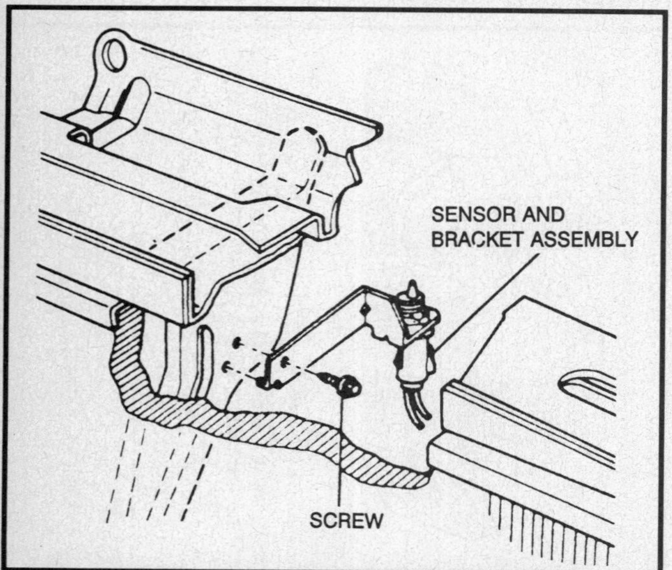
SENSOR AND
BRACKET ASSEMBLY
SCREW

Ambient temperature sensor removal—1990–91 Crown Victoria, Grand Marquis and Town Car

In-Vehicle Sensor

OPERATION

On Mark VII and 1990–91 Crown Victoria, Grand Marquis and Town Car with automatic temperature control, the in-vehicle sensor contains a thermistor that senses the passenger compartment air and provides an input signal to the control assembly. A small opening through the instrument panel allows passenger compartment air to enter the in-vehicle sensor. The sensor is located behind the instrument panel directly above the control assembly and clock on 1990–91 Crown Victoria, Grand Marquis and Town Car. On 1989 Mark VII, the sensor is located behind the warning light module in the upper right corner of the instrument cluster. On 1990–91 Mark VII, the sensor is located behind the right lower instrument panel finish panel.

On 1989 Crown Victoria, Grand Marquis and Town Car with automatic temperature control, the in-vehicle sensor contains a bimetallic sensor that senses the passenger compartment air temperatures. The bimetallic sensor controls a vacuum modulator and higher temperatures cause higher vacuum gauge readings. A bias to the vacuum output level is accomplished by means of a control arm attached by a cable assembly to the temperature control lever. The modulated vacuum ouput is the result of the effects of the control bias and the temperature of the air across the bimetallic sensor. The sensor is located behind the instrument panel above the glove compartment. A small opening in the instrument panel allows passenger compartment air to enter the sensor.

REMOVAL AND INSTALLATION

Crown Victoria, Grand Marquis and Town Car

1989

1. Disconnect the negative battery cable.
2. Remove the instrument panel pad as follows:
   a. Remove the 2 screws attaching the instrument panel pad to the instrument panel at each defroster opening. Use extreme care not to drop the screws into the defroster openings.

b. Remove 1 screw attaching each outboard end of the pad to the instrument panel.

c. On Crown Victoria, remove 1 pad attaching the screw near the upper right corner of the glove compartment door.

d. Remove the 5 screws attaching the lower edge of the pad to the instrument panel. Pull the instrument panel pad rearward and remove it from the vehicle.

3. Remove the 2 mounting screws from the sensor assembly and remove the control cable housing-to-sensor attaching screw.

4. Disconnect the cable end loop from the lever arm. Remove the cable from the sensor assembly.

NOTE: Secure the control cable with tape or wire to prevent it from falling from sight behind the instrument panel.

5. Disconnect the sensor vacuum harness from the servo vacuum harness.

6. Remove the ambient air hose from the end of the sensor assembly by rotating the sensor assembly in a clockwise direction. Remove the sensor assembly.

To install:

7. Connect the ambient air hose to the sensor by turning it couterclockwise.

8. Route and connect the vacuum harness connector to the jumper line connector. Make sure the locking tab is snapped onto the jumper line connector.

9. Position the sensor assembly to the screw mounting bosses and install the 2 mounting screws.

NOTE: Use a mirror to help align the sensor screw holes to the mounting bosses. If necessary, position a suitable light on the windshield for additional light. A small amount of body caulk in the end of the ratchet socket will help prevent the screws from falling from the socket.

10. Remove the tape or wire securing the cable and connect the control cable to the lever arm. Loosely install the attaching screw and adjust the cable.

11. Do not block the sensor aspirator exhaust port with the excess vacuum harness.

12. Install the instrument panel pad by reversing the removal procedure.

13. Connect the negative battery cable and check the air conditioning system for proper operation.

1990–91

1. Disconnect the negative battery cable.

2. Remove the left and right instrument panel moulding assemblies. Remove the cluster finish panel screws that were under the mouldings and also the 6 screws along the top surface of the cluster finish panel.

3. Pull off the knob from the headlight auto dim switch. Remove the headlight switch shaft as follows:

a. Locate the headlight switch assembly body under the instrument panel.

b. Push the spring loaded shaft release button located on the side of the switch body and simultaneously pull out the headlight switch shaft.

4. Remove the steering column close out bolster panel by removing the 2 screws on the left side, 1 screw on the right side and 3 screws from the bottom.

5. Remove the 2 screws retaining the steering column close out bolster panel bracket and remove the bracket.

6. Lower the steering column and remove the shift position indicator and cable assembly as follows:

a. Place the shift lever in **1** position.

b. Remove the shift position indicator cable from the steering column arm.

c. Remove the bolt from the steering column shift position indicator bracket

7. Remove the 4 nuts holding the steering column and let the steering column rest on the front seat.

8. Remove the cluster finish panel.

NOTE: Remove the electrical connectors from the accessory push button switches.

9. Remove the center finish panel as follows:

a. The center finish panel is retained by 2 screws on the top and 2 snap-in tabs on the bottom.

b. Remove the 2 top screws and gently rock the top back while unsnapping the bottom from the instrument panel.

c. Remove the electrical connector from the clock.

10. Grasp the handle on the front of the sensor assembly, remove the 2 screws and rotate the sensor down and out of the instrument panel.

11. Disconnect the electrical lead and the air hose from the sensor.

To install:

12. Connect the electrical lead and the air hose to the sensor.

13. Using the handle on the front of the sensor, position the

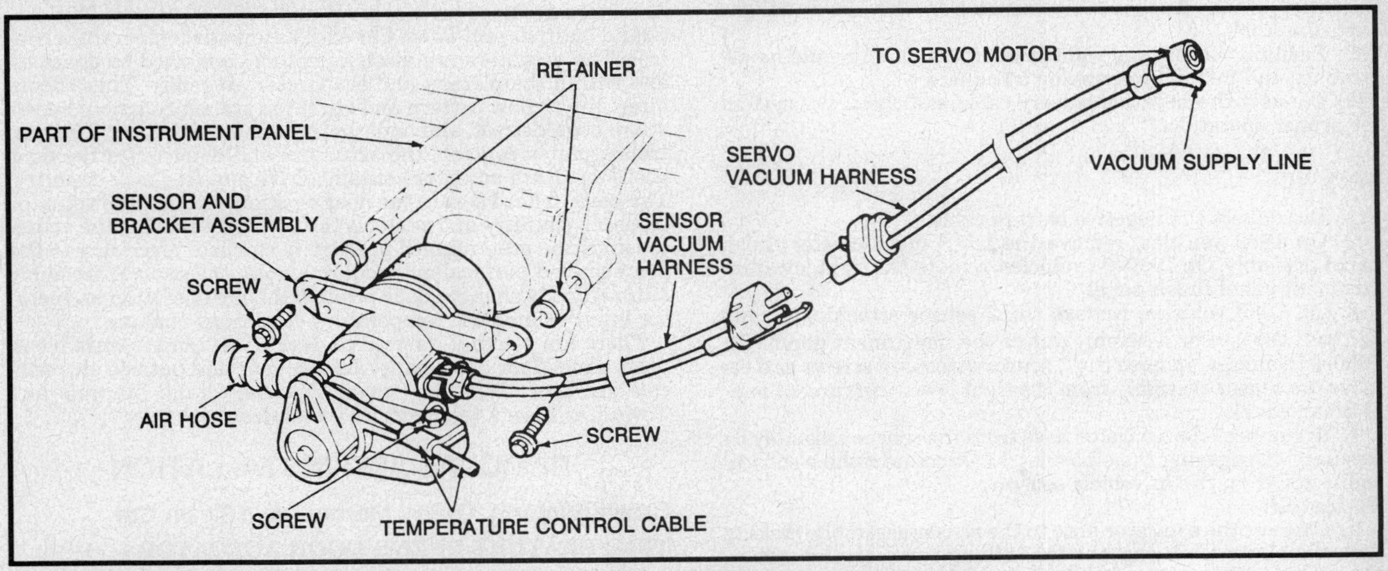
RETAINER
TO SERVO MOTOR
PART OF INSTRUMENT PANEL
SERVO VACUUM HARNESS
VACUUM SUPPLY LINE
SENSOR AND BRACKET ASSEMBLY
SENSOR VACUUM HARNESS
SCREW
AIR HOSE
SCREW
SCREW
TEMPERATURE CONTROL CABLE

In-vehicle sensor removal—1989 Crown Victoria, Grand Marquis and Town Car

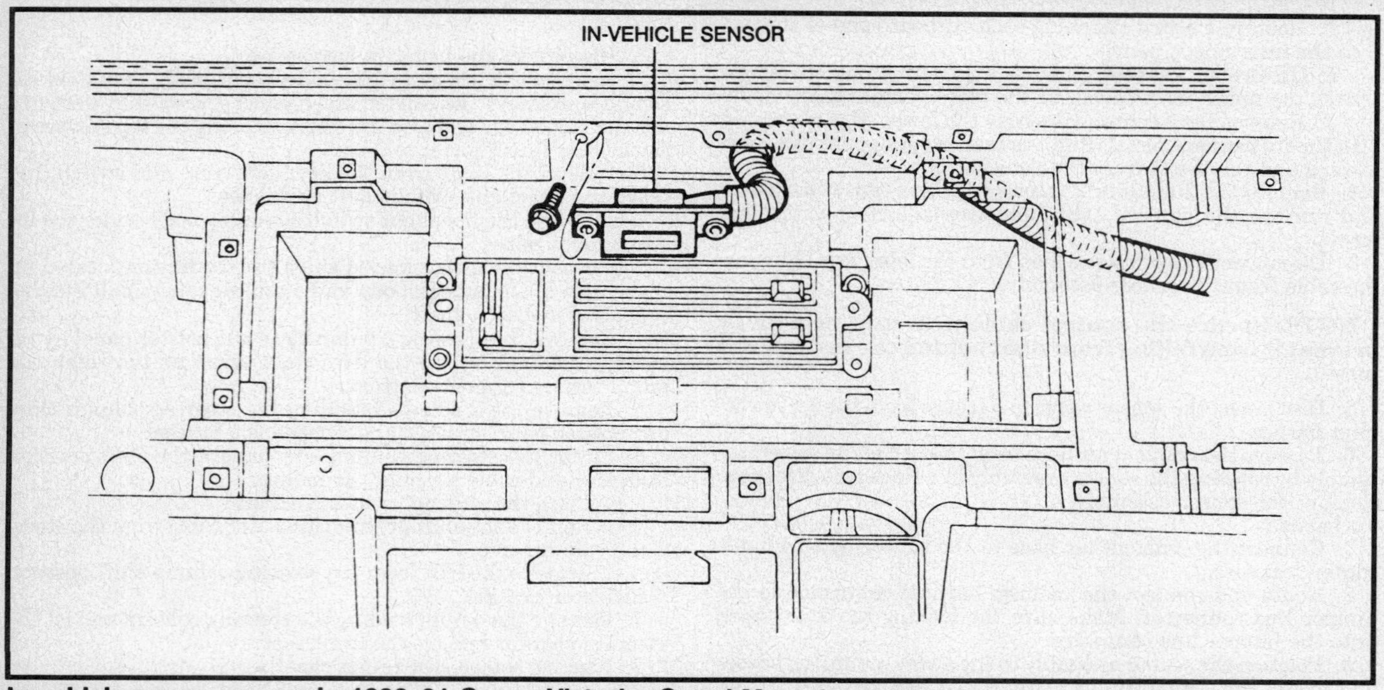
IN-VEHICLE SENSOR

In-vehicle sensor removal—1990–91 Crown Victoria, Grand Marquis and Town Car

sensor on the instrument panel and install the 2 attaching screws.

14. Install the electrical connector to the clock on the center finish panel. Install the center finish panel by snapping in the bottom and using the 2 screws on the top.
15. Position the cluster finish panel. Raise the steering column and install the 4 nuts to the steering column bracket.
16. Install the bolt to the steering column shift position indicator bracket and install the shift position indicator cable to the steering column arm.
17. Position the steering column close out bolster panel bracket and install with the 2 screws. Install the steering column close out bolster panel.
18. Install the cluster finish panel screws and snap in the headlight switch knob/shaft assembly. Install the headlight auto dim knob.
19. Position the left and right instrument panel moulding assemblies and install by snapping into place.
20. Connect the negative battery cable and check the system for proper operation.

Mark VII

1. Disconnect the negative battery cable.
2. On 1989 vehicles, remove the instrument cluster finish panel assembly. On 1990–91 vehicles, remove the right lower instrument panel finish panel.
3. On 1989 vehicles, remove the 2 sensor attaching screws and pull the sensor assembly out of the instrument panel. On 1990–91 vehicles, remove the 2 sensor attaching screws and remove the sensor assembly from the right lower instrument panel finish panel.
4. Disconnect the aspirator hose from the sensor assembly by carefully disengaging the elbow latch. Disconnect the electrical connector from the in-vehicle sensor.

To install:

5. Connect the aspirator hose to the sensor assembly, making sure the elbow latch engages the locking ramp on the sensor. Connect the electrical connector.
6. Position the sensor assembly and install the 2 attaching screws.
7. On 1989 vehicles, install the instrument cluster finish panel. On 1990–91 vehicles, install the right lower instrument panel finish panel.
8. Connect the negative battery cable and check the system for proper operation.

Automatic Temperature Control Actuators

OPERATION

Actuators are used on Mark VII and 1990–91 Crown Victoria, Grand Marquis and Town Car with automatic temperature control. The actuators are electric motors connected to doors on and within the plenum and evaporator assembly. These doors direct the airflow pattern and enact the system functional operation: heat, defrost, air conditioning, temperature, etc. The control assembly controls the actuators and determines the door positions. Each actuator contains drive and feedback circuitry. The control head senses the door position through the actuator feedback circuitry and controls the door by powering the actuator until the programmed position is reached. According to the programmed performance requirements, the control assembly automatically changes door position during operation as operator input or ambient temperature conditions change.

There are 4 actuators used on Mark VII: temperature blend door, panel/floor door, panel/defrost door and outside air/recirculation door. 1990–91 Crown Victoria, Grand Marquis and Town Car have a temperature blend door actuator.

REMOVAL AND INSTALLATION

Crown Victoria, Grand Marquis and Town Car

TEMPERATURE BLEND DOOR ACTUATOR

1. Disconnect the negative battery cable.

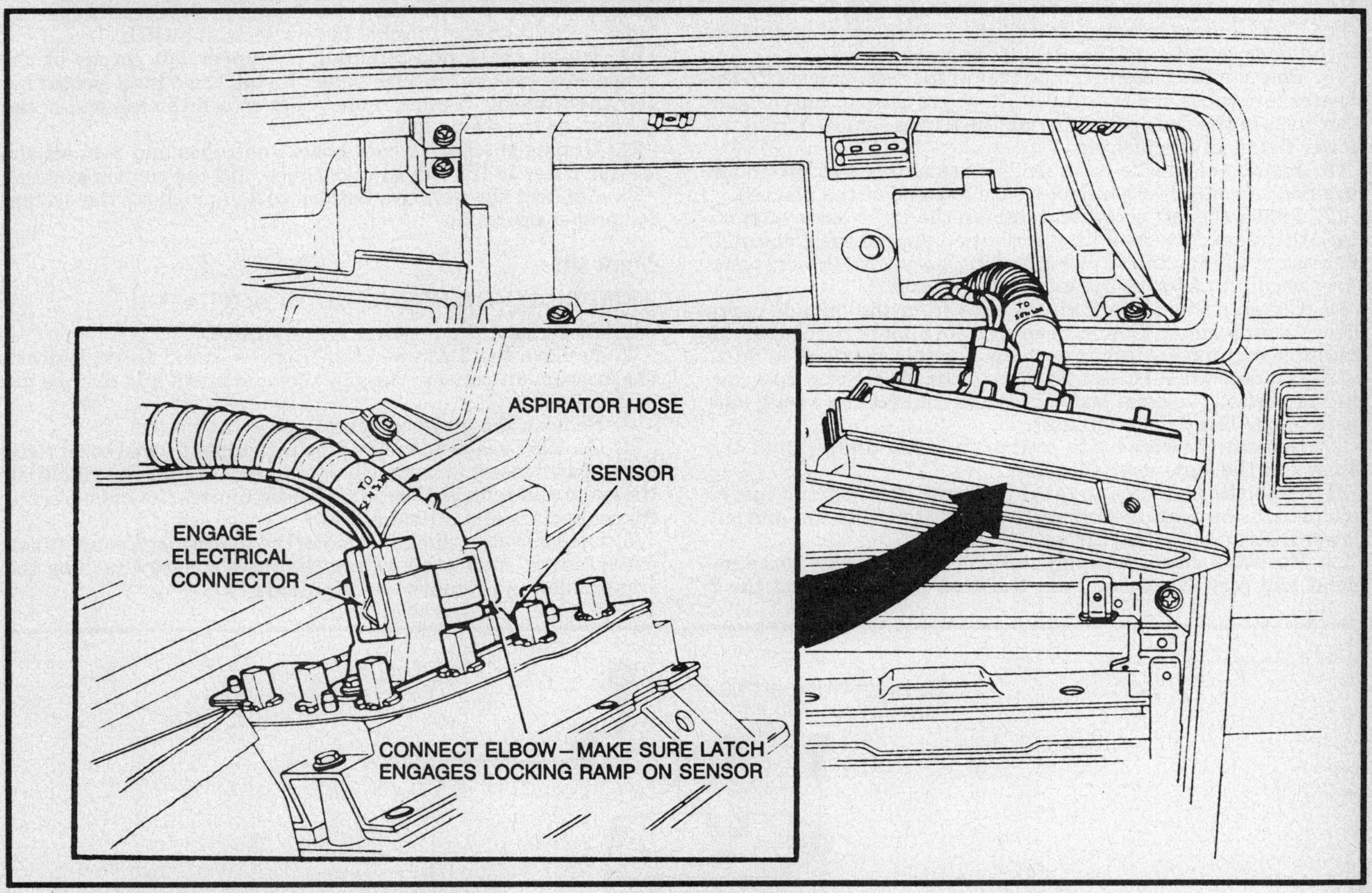
ASPIRATOR HOSE
SENSOR
ENGAGE ELECTRICAL CONNECTOR
CONNECT ELBOW—MAKE SURE LATCH ENGAGES LOCKING RAMP ON SENSOR

In-vehicle sensor removal—1989 Mark VII

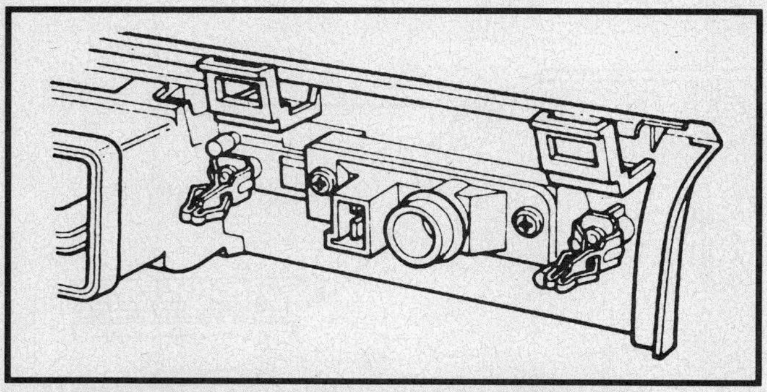

In-vehicle sensor removal—1990–91 Mark VII

2. Drain the cooling system and disconnect the heater hoses from the heater core tubes. Plug the hoses and the heater core tubes.
3. Remove the 3 nuts located below the windshield wiper motor attaching the left end of the plenum to the dash panel. Remove the 1 nut retaining the upper left corner of the evaporator case to the dash panel.
4. Disconnect the 2 vacuum supply hoses from the vacuum source. Disconnect the vacuum harness from the thermal blower lockout switch. Push the grommet and vacuum supply hoses into the passenger compartment.
5. Remove the right and left lower instrument panel insulators.
6. Remove all instrument panel mounting screws and pull the instrument panel back as far as it will go without disconnecting the wiring harness. Make sure the nuts attaching the instrument panel braces to the dash panel are removed.
7. Loosen the right door sill plate and remove the right side cowl trim panel.
8. Remove the cross body brace and disconnect the wiring harness from the temperature blend door actuator. Disconnect the ATC sensor tube from the evaporator case connector.
9. Disconnect the vacuum jumper harness at the multiple vacuum connector near the floor air distribution duct. Disconnect the white vacuum hose from the outside-recirc door vacuum motor.
10. Remove the left and loosen the right screw attaching the passenger (rear) side of the floor air distribution duct to the plenum. It may be necessary to remove the 2 screws attaching the partial (lower) panel door vacuum motor to the mounting bracket to gain access to the right screw.
11. Remove 1 plastic push fastener retaining the floor air distribution duct to the left end of the plenum and 2 screws on the rear face of the plenum and remove the floor air distribution duct.
12. Remove 2 nuts from the 2 studs along the lower flange of the plenum. Carefully move the plenum rearward to allow the heater core tubes and the stud at the top of the plenum to clear the holes in the dash panel.
13. Remove the 4 screws and remove the blend door actuator from the plenum.

To install:

14. Position the blend door actuator on the plenum assembly.

Be sure the actuator cam is properly engaged with the temperature blend door crank arm. Install the 4 screws that secure the blend door actuator to the plenum assembly.

15. Position the plenum on the rear of the dash panel with the heater core tubes and the stud at the top of the plenum through the holes in the dash panel. Install the 2 nuts removed from the lower flange of the plenum.

16. Install the plastic push fastener retaining the left end of the floor air distribution duct to the left end of the plenum.

17. Install the left screw and tighten the right screw that attach the rear of the floor air distribution duct to the plenum. If necessary, tighten the screws attaching the partial (lower) panel door vacuum motor to the mounting bracket.

18. Connect the white vacuum hose from the outside-recirc door vacuum motor. Connect the vacuum jumper harness at the multiple vacuum connector near the floor air distribution duct.

19. Connect the ATC sensor tube to the evaporator case connector. Install the cross body brace and connect the wiring harness to the blend door actuator.

20. Replace the right side cowl trim panel and tighten the screws in the right door sill plate.

21. Push the instrument panel back into position and install all instrument panel mounting screws. Install the right and left lower instrument panel insulators.

22. Push the vacuum supply hoses into the engine compartment and seat the grommet in the dash panel. Connect the 2 vacuum supply hoses to the vacuum source and connect the vacuum harness to the thermal blower lockout switch.

23. Install the 1 nut retaining the upper left corner of the evaporator case to the dash panel. Install the 3 nuts located below the windshield wiper motor, that attach the left end of the plenum to the dash panel.

24. Unplug the heater core hoses and tubes and connect the heater hoses to the heater core tubes. Fill the cooling system.

25. Connect the negative battery cable and check the system for proper operation.

Mark VII

TEMPERATURE BLEND DOOR ACTUATOR

1. Disconnect the negative battery cable.
2. Remove the 2 screws attaching the sound shield beneath the instrument panel at the glove compartment and remove the sound shield.
3. Remove the glove compartment.
4. On 1989 vehicles, remove the instrument panel bezel right finish panel insert (snap in clips), remove the 4 screws retaining the radio and remove the radio and disconnect the radio electrical connectors and antenna lead.
5. On 1990–91 vehicles, remove the instrument panel finish panel center (snap in clips), remove the 4 screws attaching the trip-minder and remove the tripminder.

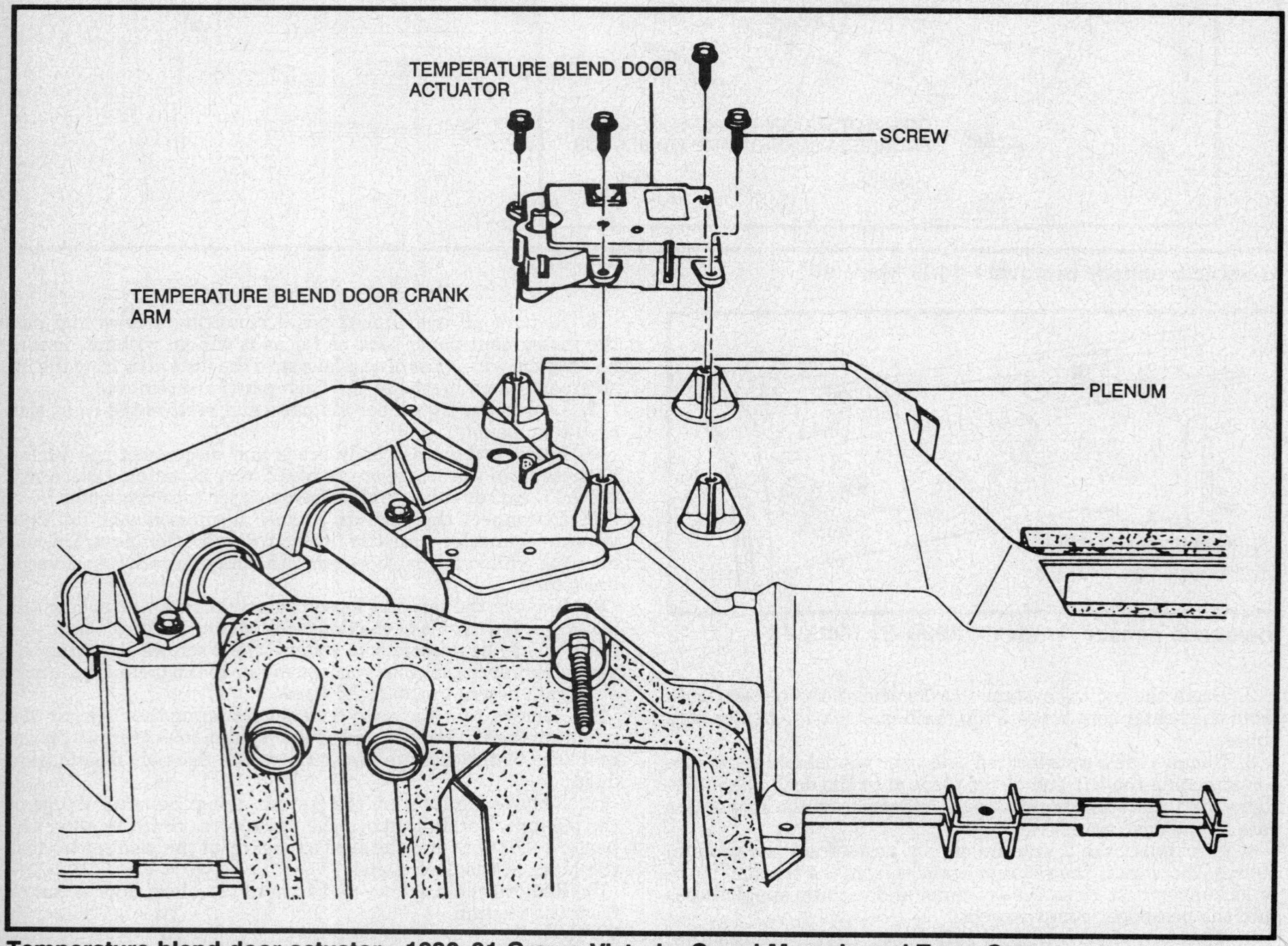
TEMPERATURE BLEND DOOR ACTUATOR
SCREW
TEMPERATURE BLEND DOOR CRANK ARM
PLENUM

Temperature blend door actuator—1990–91 Crown Victoria, Grand Marquis and Town Car

6. Disconnect the electrical connector from the actuator. Remove the pushnut from the actuator arm and disconnect the link from the arm.

7. Remove the 3 screws attaching the actuator and remove the actuator.

To install:

8. Connect the negative battery cable.

9. Mount the actuator, keeping the screws loose. Connect the link from the actuator to the blend door crank arm and install the pushnut.

10. Connect the electrical connector and turn the ignition to the **RUN** position. Perform the calibration procedure as follows:

NOTE: Perform the calibration with the ambient temperature at 50–90°F (10–33°C) and with the engine at idle and at normal operating temperature.

a. Make sure the 3 screws that attach the actuator to the evaporator case are loose.

b. Set the control at **90**.

c. Push the **OFF/AUTO** and **DEFROST** buttons simultaneously. The control should display 88.

d. Push the **WARM** button. The control should display 90.

e. Push the **COOL** button so 85 is displayed. make sure the control is in AUTO. The OFF/AUTO indicator should be lit.

f. Measure the discharge air temperature at the driver's floor duct. There are 3 openings in the duct. Measure the temperature in the long thin slot, closest to the dash panel.

g. Slide the actuator until the temperature is 121–129°F (50–54°C). Allow at least 5 minutes for the temperature to stabilize.

h. Tighten the actuator screws and recheck the temperature.

NOTE: The setting can change when the screws are tightened. Recheck after the screws are tightened.

11. With the control assembly in AUTO, set the temperature to 60°F (15°C). The blend door should move to the full air conditioning position.

12. Change the temperature to 90°F (32°C). The blend door should move to full heat.

13. Turn the ignition to the **OFF** position. Securely attach the actuator cover with the 3 screws.

14. On 1989 vehicles, connect the radio electrical connectors and antenna lead. Install the radio and the instrument panel bezel right finish panel insert.

15. On 1990–91 vehicles, install the trip-minder and the instrument panel finish panel center.

16. Attach the glove compartment and sound shield beneath the instrument panel.

PANEL/FLOOR DOOR ACTUATOR

1. Disconnect the negative battery cable.

2. Loosen the instrument panel and pull it back from the cowl.

3. Loosen the evaporator assembly from the dash panel and pull it back to expose the actuator on the driver's side end of the assembly.

4. Remove the actuator cover by removing the 2 screws and 1 pushnut.

5. Disconnect the electrical connector and remove the nut and link from the actuator arm.

6. Note the position of the actuator screws in the slots so the new actuator can be installed in the same approximate position. Remove the 3 screws and remove the actuator.

To install:

7. Make sure the panel/floor door is not obstructed by moving the crank arm through it's full range of travel.

8. Attach the actuator loosely to the evaporator assembly. Attach the link to the actuator arm with the nut. Adjust the actuator so the position is the same as the original actuator and tighten the 3 screws.

9. Attach the electrical connector and connect the negative battery cable.

10. Turn the ignition switch to the **RUN** position.

11. Depress the **FLOOR** button on the control assembly. The panel/floor door should move to the FLOOR position. Make sure the link to the crank arm has a minimum 0.03 in. (0.76mm) compression.

12. Depress the **PANEL** button on the control assembly. The function door should move to the PANEL position. Make sure the link has a minimum 0.03 in. (0.76mm) compression.

13. Repeat Steps 11 and 12 several times to ensure correct actuator operation.

14. If the link does not have 0.03 in. (0.76mm) minimum compression at each end of it's travel, readjust the actuator.

15. Disconnect the negative battery cable.

16. Attach the actuator cover and secure the evaporator assembly to the dash panel. Attach the instrument panel and associated components.

17. Connect the negative battery cable.

PANEL/DEFROST DOOR ACTUATOR

1. Disconnect the negative battery cable.

2. Loosen the instrument panel and pull it back from the cowl to expose the air conditioning plenum chamber assembly attached to the instrument panel.

3. Disconnect the electrical connector from the electric actuator attached to the air conditioning plenum chamber assembly.

4. Remove the black PVC sound cover from the top of the actuator.

5. Remove the nut from the pin on the actuator arm and disconnect the link.

6. Remove the actuator from the air conditioning plenum chamber assembly duct by removing the 3 screws.

To install:

NOTE: Be sure to install the correct actuator. It should have a silver arm.

7. Install a new tie strap and securely fasten both halves of the actuator sound cover.

8. Attach the actuator to the air conditioning plenum chamber assembly. To ensure that the panel/defrost door is not obstructed, move the crank arm through it's full travel.

9. Attach the link from the panel/defrost door crank arm to the actuator arm and secure with a pushnut.

10. Attach the electrical connector to the actuator and connect the negative battery cable.

11. Turn the ignition switch to the **RUN** position.

12. Depress the **DEF** button on the control panel. The actuator should position the panel/defrost door in the DEFROST position.

13. Depress the **OFF** button on the control panel. The actuator should position the door in the PANEL position.

14. Repeat Steps 12 and 13 several times to ensure correct actuator operation.

15. Disconnect the negative battery cable.

16. Securely fasten the top half of the sound cover to the actuator with a new tie strap.

17. Reattach the instrument panel and associated components. Connect the negative battery cable.

OUTSIDE AIR/RECIRCULATION DOOR ACTUATOR

1. Disconnect the negative battery cable.

2. Remove the recirculation duct housing as follows:

a. Remove the glove compartment and shield. Disconnect the wire connector from the outside-recirculation actuator and the ambient sensor.

b. Remove the side cowl trim panel.

c. Remove the instrument panel lower right-to-side cowl attaching bolt.

d. Remove the screw attaching the support bracket to the top of the recirculation air duct.

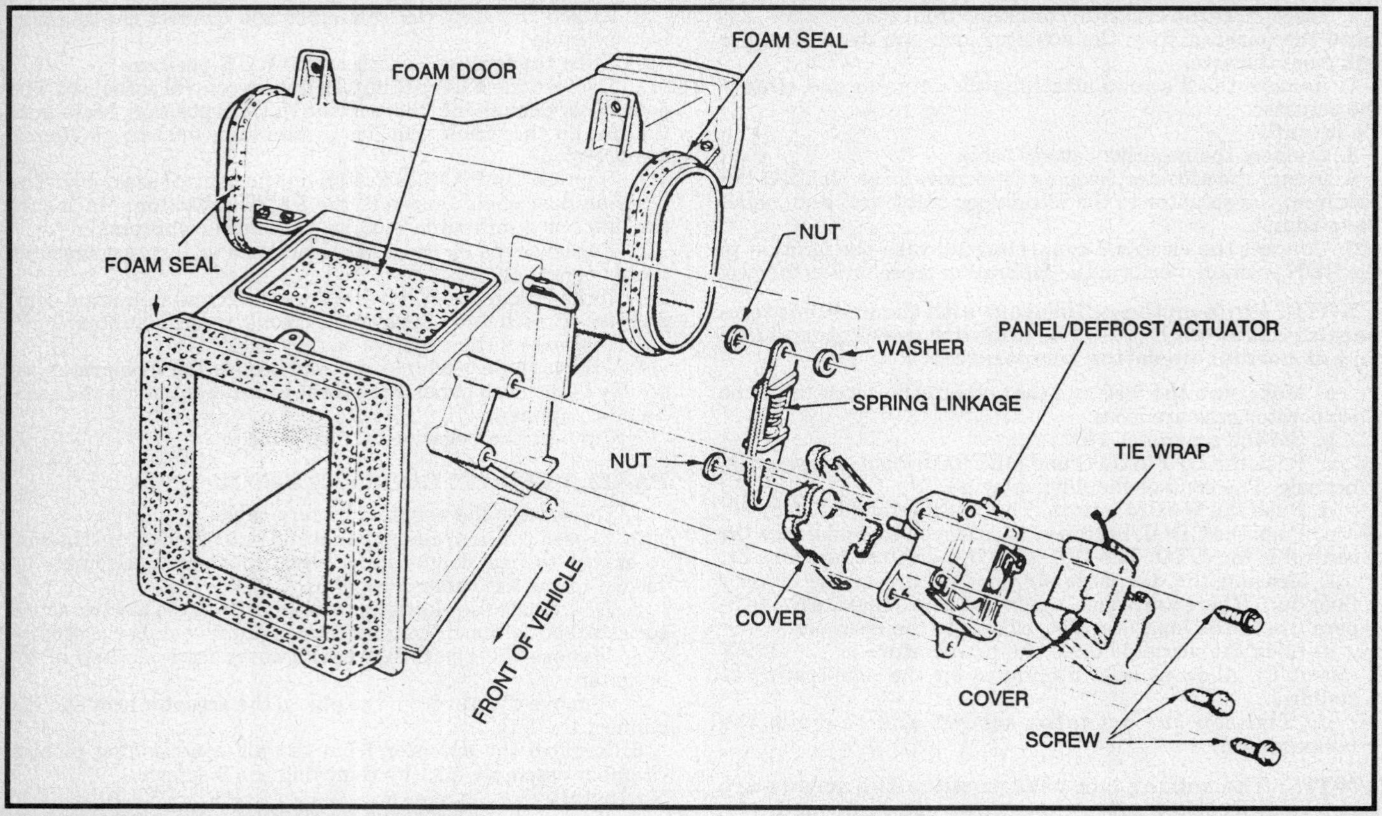
FOAM SEAL
FOAM DOOR
FOAM SEAL
NUT
PANEL/DEFROST ACTUATOR
WASHER
SPRING LINKAGE
NUT
TIE WRAP
FRONT OF VEHICLE
COVER
COVER
SCREW

Panel/defrost door actuator—Mark VII

e. Remove the 5 screws attaching the recirculation duct assembly to the evaporator housing and remove the recirculation duct assembly. Pull back the instrument panel for clearance.

3. Remove the pushnut from the pin on the actuator arm and disconnect the link.
4. Remove the actuator from the recirculation duct by removing the 3 attaching screws.

To install:

NOTE: Be sure to install the correct actuator. It should have a black arm.

5. Attach the actuator to the blower housing. Make sure the outside/recirculation door is not obstructed by moving the crank arm through it's travel.
6. Attach the link from the outside/recirculation door crank arm on the blower housing to the output arm pin on the actuator and secure with a pushnut.
7. Install the recirculation duct by reversing the removal procedure.
8. Connect the negative battery cable and turn the ignition switch to the **RUN** position.
9. Depress the **FLOOR** button on the control panel. The actuator should position the outside/recirculation door in the outside air/recirculate position.
10. Depress the **OFF** button on the control panel. The door should move to the recirculate position.
11. Install the glove compartment and sound shield beneath the instrument panel at the glove compartment.

Servo Motor Assembly

OPERATION

The servo motor assembly is a large calibrated vacuum motor and vacuum diverter valve used on 1989 Crown Victoria, Grand Marquis and Town Car with automatic temperature control. It is located behind the lower edge of the glove compartment on the mounting bracket attached to the plenum assembly. The calibrated vacuum motor provides specific temperature blend door positions for given vacuum levels. The attached vacuum diverter valve controls recirculating or outside air operation.

REMOVAL AND INSTALLATION

1989 Crown Victoria, Grand Marquis and Town Car

1. Disconnect the negative battery cable.
2. Disconnect the glove compartment door stop and let the door hang by the hinges.
3. Remove the vacuum hose from the servo motor and unplug the electrical harness connectors.
4. Remove the 2 screws from the servo motor assembly mounting bracket and position the servo for access to the vacuum diverter valve.
5. Remove the retaining pushnut and vacuum connector clip, unplug the multiple vacuum connector from the vacuum diverter valve.
6. Remove the pushnut that retains the servo motor overtravel spring and arm link to the blend door crank arm. Remove the servo assembly from the vehicle.
7. Installation is the reverse of the removal procedure.

Vacuum Motors

OPERATION

Vacuum motors are used on all vehicles except Mark VII. The vacuum motors operate the doors which in turn direct the air-

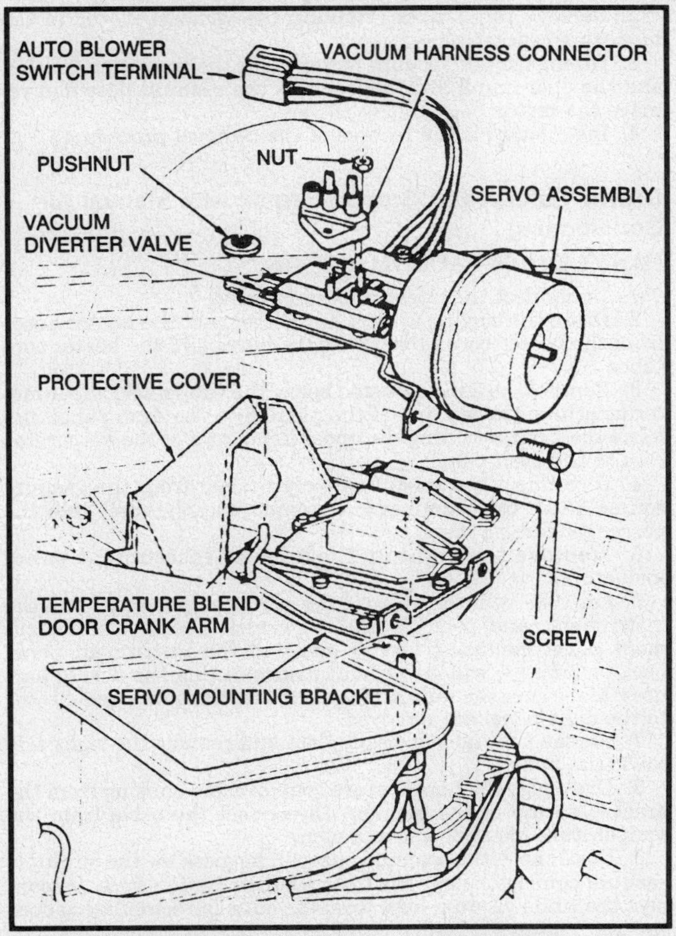
AUTO BLOWER SWITCH TERMINAL
VACUUM HARNESS CONNECTOR
PUSHNUT
NUT
SERVO ASSEMBLY
VACUUM DIVERTER VALVE
PROTECTIVE COVER
TEMPERATURE BLEND DOOR CRANK ARM
SCREW
SERVO MOUNTING BRACKET

Servo motor assembly removal—1989 Crown Victoria, Grand Marquis and Town Car

flow through the system. A vacuum selector valve, controlled by the function control lever, distributes the vacuum to the various door vacuum motors.

REMOVAL AND INSTALLATION

Crown Victoria, Grand Marquis and Town Car with Automatic Temperature Control

PANEL DOOR VACUUM MOTOR

1. Disconnect the negative battery cable.
2. Drain the cooling system and disconnect the heater hoses from the heater core tubes. Plug the hoses and the heater core tubes.
3. Remove the 3 nuts located below the windshield wiper motor attaching the left end of the plenum to the dash panel. Remove the 1 nut retaining the upper left corner of the evaporator case to the dash panel.
4. Disconnect the 2 vacuum supply hoses from the vacuum source. Disconnect the vacuum harness from the thermal blower lockout switch. Push the grommet and vacuum supply hoses into the passenger compartment.
5. Remove the right and left lower instrument panel insulators.
6. On 1989 vehicles, remove the glove box and the instrument panel pad. On 1990–91 vehicles, remove all instrument panel mounting screws and pull the instrument panel back as far as it will go without disconnecting the wiring harness. Make sure the nuts attaching the instrument panel braces to the dash panel are removed.
7. Loosen the right door sill plate and remove the right side cowl trim panel.
8. On 1989 vehicles, disconnect the temperature control cable from the ATC sensor. Disconnect the vacuum harness line connector from the ATC sensor harness and disconnect the electrical plug from the ATC servo plug. On 1990–91 vehicles, remove the cross body brace and disconnect the wiring harness from the temperature blend door actuator. On all vehicles, disconnect the ATC sensor tube from the evaporator case connector.
9. Disconnect the vacuum jumper harness at the multiple vacuum connector near the floor air distribution duct. Disconnect the white vacuum hose from the outside-recirc door vacuum motor.
10. Remove the left and loosen the right screw attaching the passenger (rear) side of the floor air distribution duct to the plenum. It may be necessary to remove the 2 screws attaching the partial (lower) panel door vacuum motor to the mounting bracket to gain access to the right screw.
11. Remove 1 plastic push fastener retaining the floor air distribution duct to the left end of the plenum and 2 screws on the rear face of the plenum and remove the floor air distribution duct.
12. Remove 2 nuts from the 2 studs along the lower flange of the plenum. Carefully move the plenum rearward to allow the heater core tubes and the stud at the top of the plenum to clear the holes in the dash panel. Remove the plenum from the vehicle by rotating the top of the plenum forward, down and out from under the instrument panel. On 1989 vehicles, carefully pull the lower edge of the instrument panel rearward, as necessary, while rolling the plenum from behind the instrument panel.
13. Reach through the defroster nozzle opening and remove the sleeve nut attaching the vacuum motor arm to the door.
14. Remove the 2 screws attaching the vacuum motor to the mounting bracket. Disengage the vacuum motor from the plenum and disconnect the vacuum hose from the vacuum motor.

To install:

15. Position the vacuum motor to the mounting bracket and the door bracket. Install the 2 screws to attach the motor to the mounting bracket.
16. Connect the vacuum motor arm to the panel door with a new sleeve nut. Connect the vacuum hose to the vacuum motor. The blue hose connects to the upper vacuum motor and the orange hose connects to the lower vacuum motor.
17 Position the plenum on the rear of the dash panel with the heater core tubes and the stud at the top of the plenum through the holes in the dash panel. Install the 2 nuts removed from the lower flange of the plenum.
18. Install the plastic push fastener retaining the left end of the floor air distribution duct to the left end of the plenum.
19. Install the left screw and tighten the right screw that attach the rear of the floor air distribution duct to the plenum. If necessary, tighten the screws attaching the partial (lower) panel door vacuum motor to the mounting bracket.
20. Connect the white vacuum hose from the outside-recirc door vacuum motor. Connect the vacuum jumper harness at the multiple vacuum connector near the floor air distribution duct. On 1989 vehicles, route and connect the vacuum harness connector at the ATC sensor and connect the electrical plug to the ATC servo plug. Do not block the sensor aspirator exhaust port with the excess vacuum harness.
21. Connect the ATC sensor tube to the evaporator case connector. On 1990–91 vehicles, install the cross body brace and connect the wiring harness to the blend door actuator.
22. Replace the right side cowl trim panel and tighten the screws in the right door sill plate.

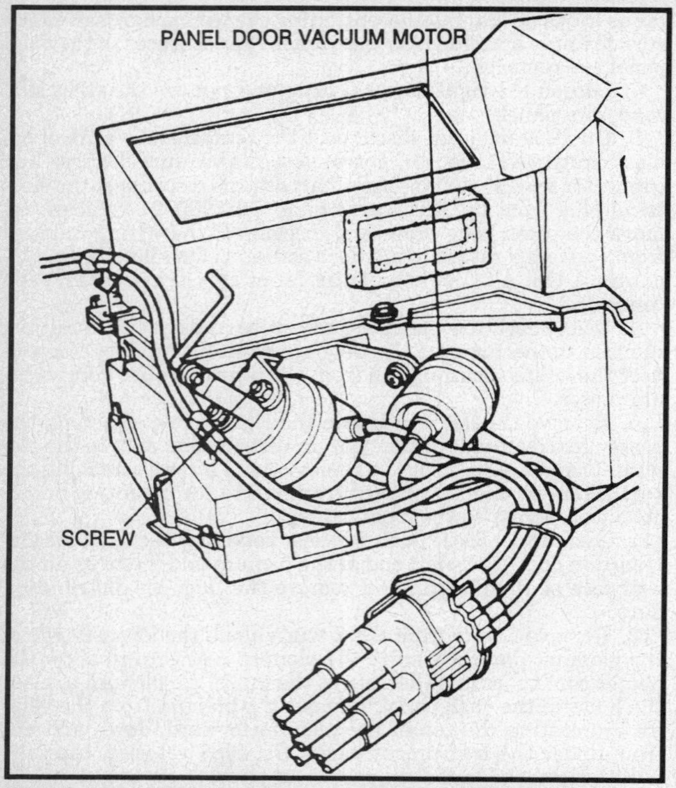
PANEL DOOR VACUUM MOTOR
SCREW

Panel door vacuum motor removal—1990–91 Crown Victoria, Grand Marquis and Town Car with automatic temperature control

23. On 1989 vehicles, install the glove compartment door and instrument panel pad. On 1990–91 vehicles, push the instrument panel back into position and install all instrument panel mounting screws. Install the right and left lower instrument panel insulators.
24. Push the vacuum supply hoses into the engine compartment and seat the grommet in the dash panel. Connect the 2 vacuum supply hoses to the vacuum source and connect the vacuum harness to the thermal blower lockout switch.
25. Install the 1 nut retaining the upper left corner of the evaporator case to the dash panel. Install the 3 nuts located below the windshield wiper motor, that attach the left end of the plenum to the dash panel.
26. Unplug the heater core hoses and tubes and connect the heater hoses to the heater core tubes. Fill the cooling system.
27. Connect the negative battery cable and check the system for proper operation.

FLOOR/DEFROST DOOR VACUUM MOTOR

1. Remove the floor air distribution duct assembly.
2. Remove the pushnut retaining the vacuum motor arm to the floor/defrost door crank arm. Remove the 2 nuts retaining the vacuum motor to the motor bracket.
3. Disengage the motor from the mounting bracket and the motor arm from the door crank arm. Remove the motor from the plenum and disconnect the vacuum hoses from the motor.
4. Installation is the reverse of the removal procedure.

OUTSIDE/RECIRCULATING DOOR VACUUM MOTOR

1. Remove the spring nut retaining the outside/recirculating door vacuum motor arm to the outside/recirculating door crank arm.
2. Remove the 2 nuts retaining the vacuum motor to the mounting bracket.
3. Disengage the vacuum motor from the mounting bracket and the door crank arm. Disconnect the vacuum hose and remove the motor.
4. Installation is the reverse of the removal procedure.

Crown Victoria and Grand Marquis with Manual Air Conditioning

PANEL DOOR VACUUM MOTOR

1. Disconnect the negative battery cable.
2. Drain the cooling system and disconnect the heater hoses from the heater core tubes. Plug the hoses and the heater core tubes.
3. Remove the 3 nuts located below the windshield wiper motor attaching the left end of the plenum to the dash panel. Remove the 1 nut retaining the upper left corner of the evaporator case to the dash panel.
4. Disconnect the vacuum supply hose(s) from the vacuum source. Push the grommet and vacuum supply hoses into the passenger compartment.
5. Remove the right and left lower instrument panel insulators.
6. On 1989 vehicles, remove the glove compartment and the instrument panel pad. On 1990–91 vehicles, remove all instrument panel mounting screws and pull the instrument panel back as far as it will go without disconnecting the wiring harness. Make sure the nuts attaching the instrument panel braces to the dash panel are removed.
7. Loosen the right door sill plate and remove the right side cowl trim panel.
8. Disengage the temperature control cable housing from the bracket on top of the plenum. Disconnect the cable from the temperature blend door crank arm.
9. Disconnect the vacuum jumper harness at the multiple vacuum connector near the floor air distribution duct. Disconnect the white vacuum hose from the outside-recirculating door vacuum motor.
10. Remove the 2 hush panels.
11. Remove 1 plastic push fastener retaining the floor air distribution duct to the left end of the plenum. Remove the left screw and loosen the right screw on the rear face of the plenum and remove the floor air distribution duct.
12. Remove the 2 nuts from the 2 studs along the lower flange of the plenum.
13. Carefully move the plenum rearward to allow the heater core tubes and the stud at the top of the plenum to clear the holes in the dash panel. Remove the plenum from the vehicle by rotating the top of the plenum forward, down and out from under the instrument panel. Carefully pull the lower edge of the instrument panel rearward, as necessary, while rolling the plenum from behind the instrument panel.
14. Reach through the defroster nozzle opening and remove the sleeve nut attaching the vacuum motor arm to the door.
15. Remove the 2 screws attaching the vacuum motor to the mounting bracket. Disengage the vacuum motor from the plenum and disconnect the vacuum hose from the vacuum motor.

To install:

16. Position the vacuum motor to the mounting bracket and the door bracket. Install 2 screws to attach the motor to the mounting bracket.
17. Connect the vacuum motor arm to the panel door with a new sleeve nut. Connect the vacuum hose to the vacuum motor.
18. Position the plenum under the instrument panel with the register duct opening up and the heater core tubes down. Rotate the plenum up behind the instrument panel and position the plenum to the dash panel. Insert the heater core tubes and mounting studs through their respective holes in the dash panel and the evaporator case.

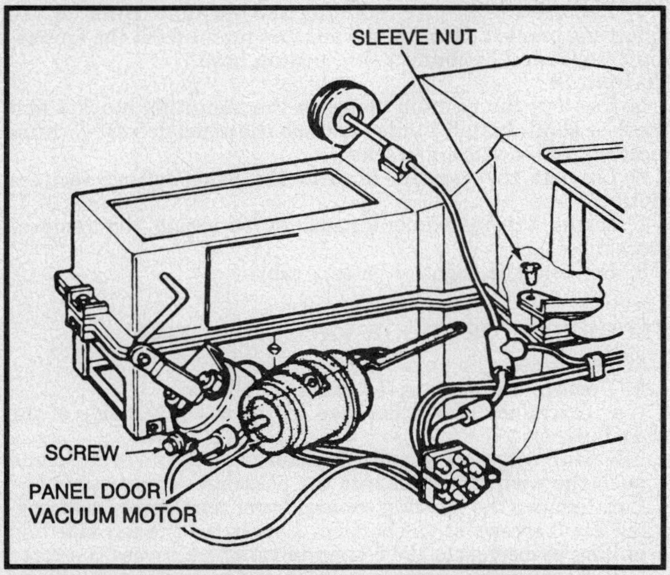
SLEEVE NUT
SCREW
PANEL DOOR
VACUUM MOTOR

Panel door vacuum motor removal—1989 Crown Victoria and Grand Marquis with manual air conditioning

19. Install the 3 nuts on the studs along the lower flange and 1 on the upper flange of the plenum. Install the 3 nuts below the windshield wiper motor to attach the left end of the plenum to the dash panel. Install 1 nut to retain the upper left corner of the evaporator case to the dash panel.
20. Position the floor air distribution duct on the plenum. Install the 2 screws and plastic push fastener. If removed, position the panel door vacuum motor to the mounting bracket and install the 2 attaching screws.
21. Connect the white vacuum hose to the outside-recirculating door vacuum motor. Connect the vacuum jumper harness to the plenum harness at the multiple vacuum connector near the floor air distribution duct. Install the floor duct.
22. Connect the temperature control cable housing to the bracket on top of the plenum and connect the temperature control cable to the temperature blend door crank arm. Adjust the temperature cable.
23. Install the bolt to attach the lower right end of the instrument panel to the side cowl. Install the right side cowl trim panel and tighten the right door sill plate attaching screws.
24. On 1989 vehicles, install the glove compartment and instrument panel pad. On 1990–91 vehicles, push the instrument panel back into position and install all instrument panel mounting screws. Install the right and left lower instrument panel insulators.
25. Push the vacuum supply hoses into the engine compartment and seat the grommet in the dash panel. Connect the vacuum supply hose(s) to the vacuum source.
26. Install the right and left lower instrument panel insulators and install the 2 hush panels.
27. Unplug the heater core tubes and the heater hoses and connect the heater hoses to the heater core tubes. Fill the cooling system.
28. Connect the negative battery cable and check the system for proper operation.

FLOOR/DEFROST DOOR VACUUM MOTOR

1. Remove the floor air distribution duct assembly.
2. Remove the pushnut retaining the vacuum motor arm to the floor/defrost door crank arm. Remove the 2 nuts retaining the vacuum motor to the motor bracket.
3. Disengage the motor from the mounting bracket and the motor arm from the door crank arm. Remove the motor from the plenum and disconnect the vacuum hoses from the motor.
4. Installation is the reverse of the removal procedure.

OUTSIDE/RECIRCULATING DOOR VACUUM MOTOR

1. Remove the spring nut retaining the outside/recirculating air door vacuum motor arm to the door crank arm.
2. Disengage the vacuum motor arm and washer and the assist spring and second washer from the crank arm. Disconnect the white vacuum hose connector from the vacuum motor.
3. Remove the 2 nuts retaining the vacuum motor and the assist spring bracket to the air inlet duct mounting bracket. Remove the vacuum motor and the assist spring mounting bracket.
4. Installation is the reverse of the removal procedure.

Thunderbird and Cougar

PANEL/DEFROST DOOR VACUUM MOTOR

1. Disconnect the negative battery cable.
2. Remove the instrument panel as follows:
   a. Disconnect the underhood wiring at the left side of the dash panel.
   b. Disengage the wiring connector from the dash panel and push the wiring harness into the passenger compartment.
   c. Remove the steering column lower trim cover by removing the 3 screws at the bottom, 1 screw on the left side and pulling to disengage the 5 snap-in retainers across the top.
   d. Remove the steering column lower opening reinforcement. 6 screws retain the reinforcement to the instrument panel.
   e. Remove the steering column upper and lower shrouds and disconnect the wiring from the steering column.

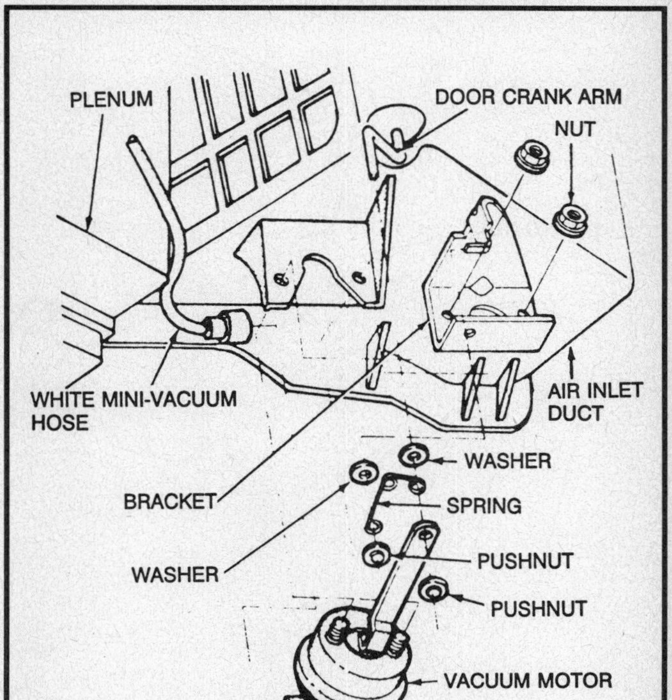
PLENUM
DOOR CRANK ARM
NUT
WHITE MINI-VACUUM HOSE
AIR INLET DUCT
WASHER
BRACKET
SPRING
WASHER
PUSHNUT
PUSHNUT
VACUUM MOTOR

Outside/recirculating air door vacuum motor removal—1989 Crown Victoria and Grand Marquis with manual air conditioning

f. Remove the shift interlock switch and disconnect the steering column lower universal joint.

g. Support the steering column and remove the 4 nuts retaining the column to the support. Remove the column from the vehicle.

h. Remove the 1 screw retaining the left side of the instrument panel to the parking brake bracket.

i. Install the steering column lower opening reinforcement using the 4 screws, 1 at each corner. This will prevent the instrument panel from twisting when being removed.

j. Remove the right and left cowl side trim panels.

k. Remove the console assembly and remove the 2 nuts retaining the center of the instrument panel to the floor.

l. Open the glove compartment, squeeze the sides of the bin and lower to the full open position. From under the instrument panel and through the glove compartment opening, disconnect the wiring, vacuum lines and control cables.

m. Remove 2 screws from the right side and 2 screws from the left side retaining the instrument panel to the cowl side.

n. Remove the right and left upper finish panels by pulling up to disengage the snap-in retainers. There are 3 on the right side, 4 on the left side.

o. Remove the 4 screws retaining the instrument panel to the cowl top. Remove the right and left roof rail trim panel. Remove the door frame weatherstrip.

p. Carefully pull the instrument panel away from the cowl and disconnect any remaining wiring or controls.

3. Remove the spring nut retaining the panel/defrost door vacuum motor arm to the door shaft.

4. Remove the 2 nuts retaining the vacuum motor to the mounting bracket. Remove the vacuum motor from the mounting bracket and disconnect the vacuum hose.

To install:

5. Position the vacuum motor to the mounting bracket and the door shaft. Install 2 nuts to attach the panel/defrost vacuum motor to the mounting bracket.

6. Connect the vacuum hose to the panel/defrost vacuum motor.

7. Install the instrument panel by reversing the removal procedure.

8. Connect the negative battery cable.

FLOOR/DEFROST DOOR VACUUM MOTOR

1. Disconnect the negative battery cable.

2. Remove the instrument panel as follows:

a. Disconnect the underhood wiring at the left side of the dash panel.

b. Disengage the wiring connector from the dash panel and push the wiring harness into the passenger compartment.

c. Remove the steering column lower trim cover by removing the 3 screws at the bottom, 1 screw on the left side and pulling to disengage the 5 snap-in retainers across the top.

d. Remove the steering column lower opening reinforcement. Six screws retain the reinforcement to the instrument panel.

e. Remove the steering column upper and lower shrouds and disconnect the wiring from the steering column.

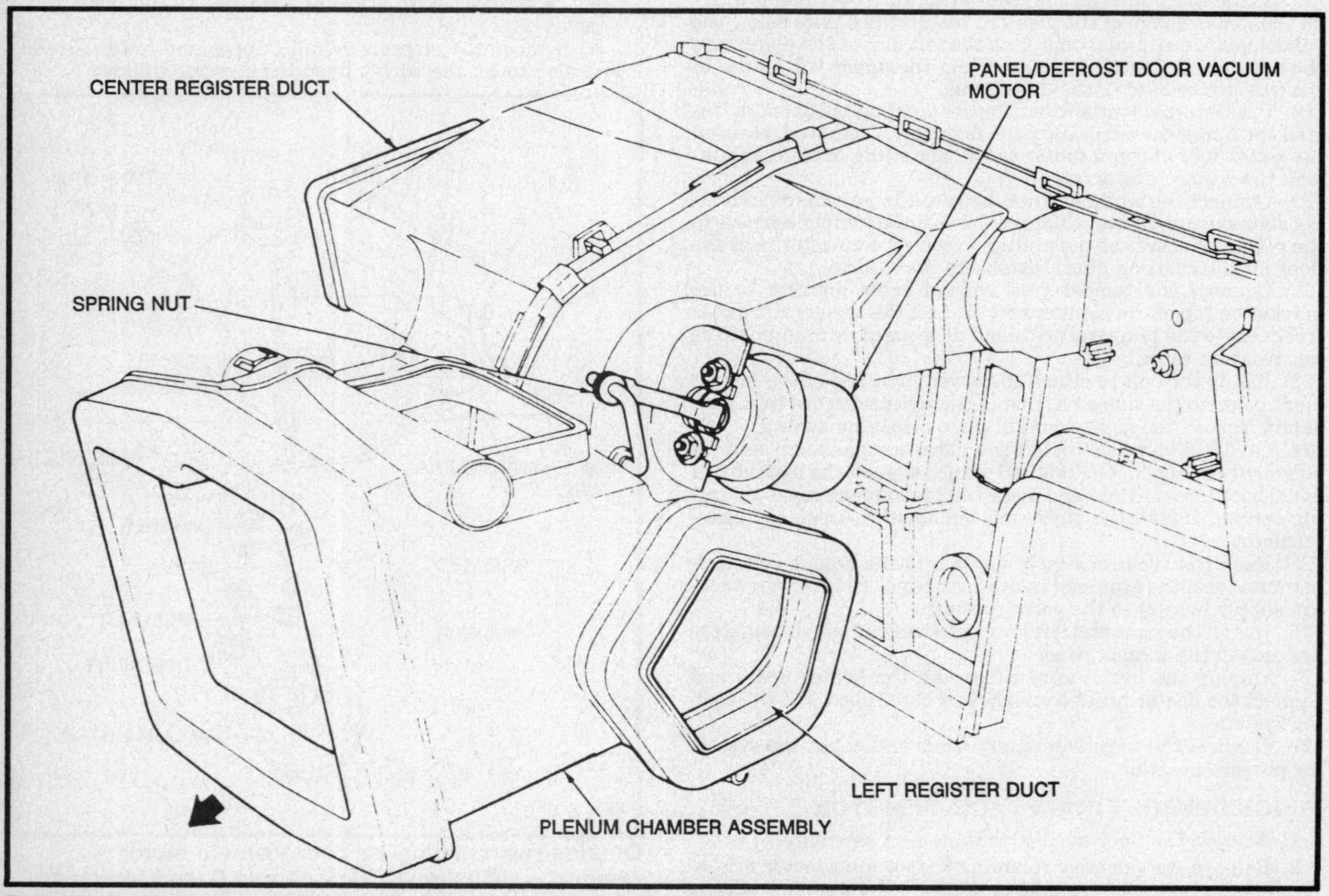
CENTER REGISTER DUCT
PANEL/DEFROST DOOR VACUUM MOTOR
SPRING NUT
LEFT REGISTER DUCT
PLENUM CHAMBER ASSEMBLY

Panel/defrost door vacuum motor—Thunderbird and Cougar

f. Remove the shift interlock switch and disconnect the steering column lower universal joint.

g. Support the steering column and remove the 4 nuts retaining the column to the support. Remove the column from the vehicle.

h. Remove the 1 screw retaining the left side of the instrument panel to the parking brake bracket.

i. Install the steering column lower opening reinforcement using the 4 screws, 1 at each corner. This will prevent the instrument panel from twisting when being removed.

j. Remove the right and left cowl side trim panels.

k. Remove the console assembly and remove the 2 nuts retaining the center of the instrument panel to the floor.

l. Open the glove compartment, squeeze the sides of the bin and lower to the full open position. From under the instrument panel and through the glove compartment opening, disconnect the wiring, vacuum lines and control cables.

m. Remove 2 screws from the right side and 2 screws from the left side retaining the instrument panel to the cowl side.

n. Remove the right and left upper finish panels by pulling up to disengage the snap-in retainers. There are 3 on the right side, 4 on the left side.

o. Remove the 4 screws retaining the instrument panel to the cowl top. Remove the right and left roof rail trim panel. Remove the door frame weatherstrip.

p. Carefully pull the instrument panel away from the cowl and disconnect any remaining wiring or controls.

3. Remove the 2 nuts retaining the vacuum motor to the mounting bracket.

4. Disconnect the vacuum hoses from the vacuum motor and disengage the motor arm from the floor/defrost door crank arm. Remove the vacuum motor.

To install:

5. Engage the motor arm to the floor/defrost door crank arm. Position the vacuum motor on the mounting bracket and install the 2 retaining nuts.

6. Connect the vacuum hoses.

7. Install the instrument panel by reversing the removal procedure.

8. Connect the negative battery cable.

OUTSIDE/RECIRCULATING DOOR VACUUM MOTOR

1. Working between the outside/recirculating air inlet duct and the dash panel, remove the 2 screws retaining the vacuum motor to the mounting bracket.

2. Disconnect the vacuum hose from the vacuum motor.

3. Disengage the vacuum motor arm from the outside/recirculating air door operating link and remove the vacuum motor.

4. Installation is the reverse of the removal procedure.

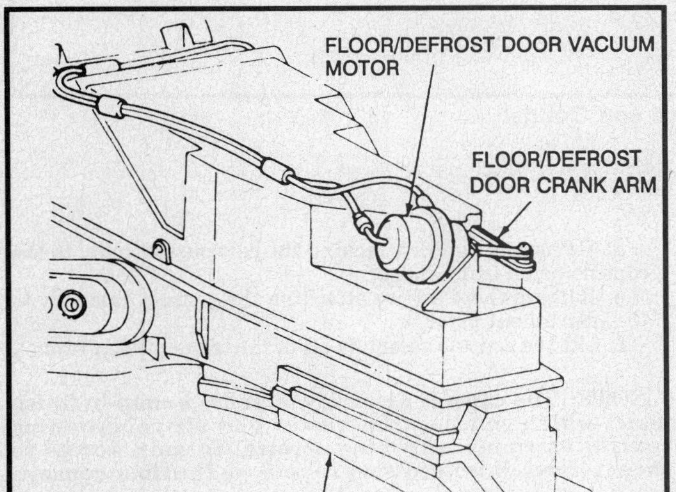
FLOOR/DEFROST DOOR VACUUM MOTOR
FLOOR/DEFROST DOOR CRANK ARM
FLOOR AIR DISTRIBUTION DUCT

Floor/defrost door vacuum motor—Thunderbird and Cougar

Mustang

PANEL/DEFROST DOOR VACUUM MOTOR

1. Disconnect the negative battery cable.

2. Remove the instrument panel according to the following procedure:

a. Remove the 4 screws that attach the floor console top panel assembly to the floor console assembly.

b. Lift the console top panel assembly off the console assembly and disconnect the 2 electrical connectors.

c. Remove the 2 screws attaching the rear end of the console assembly to the console panel support assembly.

d. Remove 4 screws attaching the console assembly to the console panel front support.

e. Remove the 4 screws attaching the console assembly to the instrument panel.

f. Lift the console assembly off of the transmission tunnel.

NOTE: The console assembly includes a snap-in finish panel which conceals the heater and air conditioning control assembly attaching screws. To gain access to these screws, it is necessary to remove the floor console.

g. Disconnect all underhood wiring connectors from the main wiring harness. Disengage the rubber grommet seal from the dash panel and push the wiring harness and connectors into the passenger compartment.

h. Remove the 3 bolts attaching the steering column opening cover and reinforcement panel. Remove the cover.

i. Remove the steering column opening reinforcement by removing 2 bolts. Remove the 2 bolts retaining the lower steering column opening reinforcement and remove the reinforcement.

j. Remove the 6 steering column retaining nuts; 2 retain the hood release mechanism and 4 retain the column to the lower brake pedal support. Lower the steering column to the floor.

k. Remove the steering column upper and lower shrouds and disconnect the wiring from the multi-function switch.

l. Remove the brake pedal support nut and snap out the defroster grille.

m. Remove the screws from the speaker covers. Snap out the speaker covers. Remove the front screws retaining the right and left scuff plates at the cowl trim panel. Remove the right and left side cowl trim panels.

n. Disconnect the wiring at the right and left cowl sides. Remove the cowl side retaining bolts, 1 on each side.

o. Open the glove compartment door and flex the glove compartment bin tabs inward. Drop down the glove compartment door assembly.

p. Remove the 5 cowl top screw attachments. Gently pull the instrument panel away from the cowl. Disconnect the speedometer cable and wire connectors.

3. Remove the spring nut retaining the panel/defrost door vacuum motor arm to the door shaft.

4. Remove the 2 nuts retaining the vacuum motor to the mounting bracket. Remove the vacuum motor from the mounting bracket and disconnect the vacuum hose.

To install:

5. Position the vacuum motor to the mounting bracket and door shaft. Install 2 nuts to attach the panel/defrost vacuum motor to the mounting bracket.

6. Connect the vacuum hose to the panel/defrost vacuum motor.

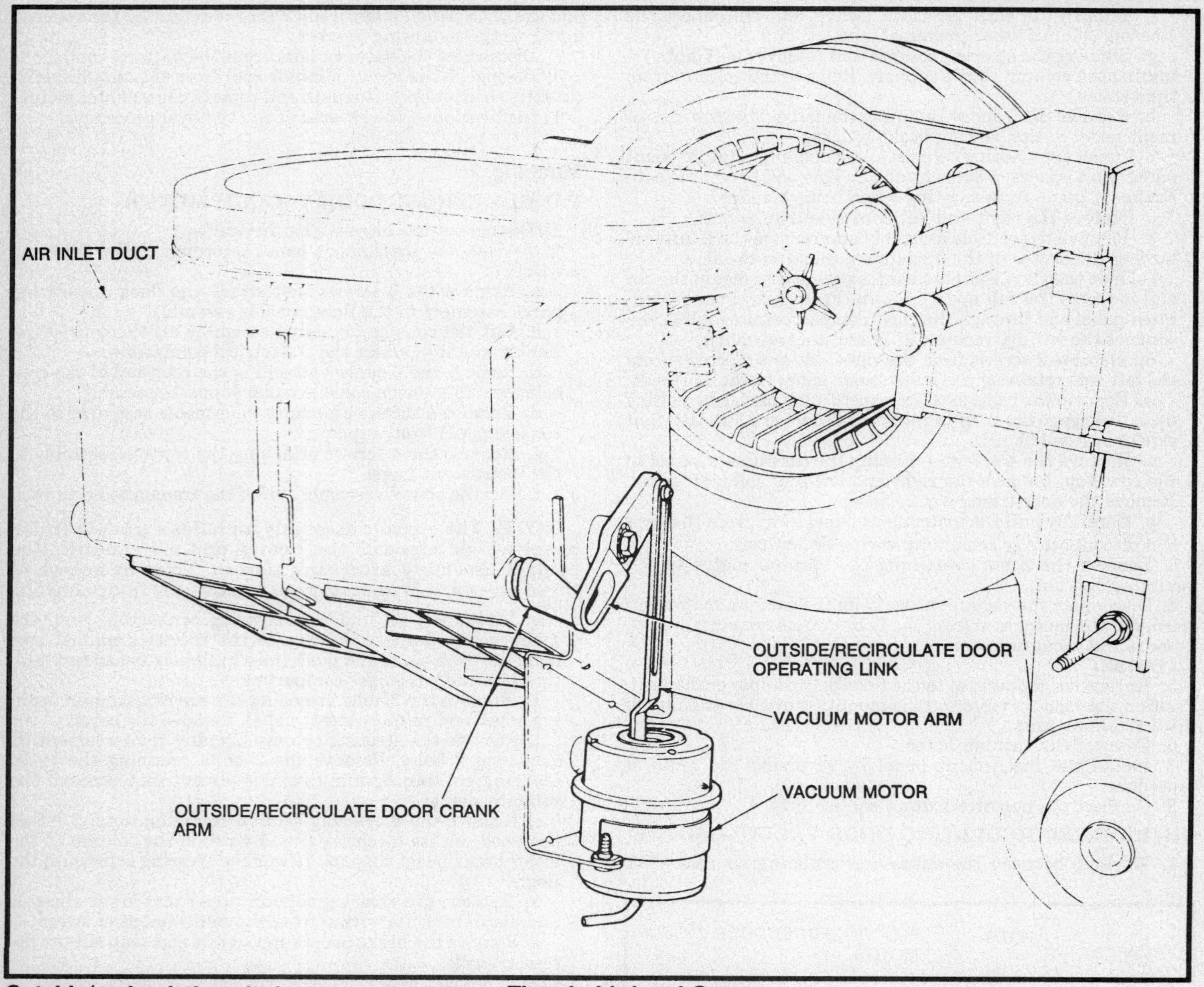
AIR INLET DUCT
OUTSIDE/RECIRCULATE DOOR OPERATING LINK
VACUUM MOTOR ARM
VACUUM MOTOR
OUTSIDE/RECIRCULATE DOOR CRANK ARM

Outside/recirculating air door vacuum motor– Thunderbird and Cougar

7. Install the instrument panel by reversing the removal procedure.
8. Connect the negative battery cable.

FLOOR/DEFROST DOOR VACUUM MOTOR

1. Disconnect the negative battery cable and drain the cooling system.
2. Discharge the refrigerant from the air conditioning system according the to proper procedure.
3. Remove the instrument panel according to the following procedure:
   a. Remove the 4 screws that attach the floor console top panel assembly to the floor console assembly.
   b. Lift the console top panel assembly off the console assembly and disconnect the 2 electrical connectors.
   c. Remove the 2 screws attaching the rear end of the console assembly to the console panel support assembly.
   d. Remove 4 screws attaching the console assembly to the console panel front support.
   e. Remove the 4 screws attaching the console assembly to the instrument panel.
   f. Lift the console assembly off of the transmission tunnel.

NOTE: The console assembly includes a snap-in finish panel which conceals the heater and air conditioning control assembly attaching screws. To gain access to these screws, it is necessary to remove the floor console.

   g. Disconnect all underhood wiring connectors from the main wiring harness. Disengage the rubber grommet seal from the dash panel and push the wiring harness and connectors into the passenger compartment.
   h. Remove the 3 bolts attaching the steering column open-

ing cover and reinforcement panel. Remove the cover.

i. Remove the steering column opening reinforcement by removing 2 bolts. Remove the 2 bolts retaining the lower steering column opening reinforcement and remove the reinforcement.

j. Remove the 6 steering column retaining nuts; 2 retain the hood release mechanism and 4 retain the column to the lower brake pedal support. Lower the steering column to the floor.

k. Remove the steering column upper and lower shrouds and disconnect the wiring from the multi-function switch.

l. Remove the brake pedal support nut and snap out the defroster grille.

m. Remove the screws from the speaker covers. Snap out the speaker covers. Remove the front screws retaining the right and left scuff plates at the cowl trim panel. Remove the right and left side cowl trim panels.

n. Disconnect the wiring at the right and left cowl sides. Remove the cowl side retaining bolts, 1 on each side.

o. Open the glove compartment door and flex the glove compartment bin tabs inward. Drop down the glove compartment door assembly.

p. Remove the 5 cowl top screw attachments. Gently pull the instrument panel away from the cowl. Disconnect the speedometer cable and wire connectors.

4. Disconnect the liquid line and the accumulator/drier inlet tube from the evaporator core at the dash panel. Cap the refrigerant lines and evaporator core tube to prevent the entrance of dirt and excessive moisture.

5. Disconnect the heater hoses from the heater core tubes and plug the hoses and tubes.

6. Remove the screw attaching the air inlet duct and blower housing assembly support brace to the cowl top panel.

7. Disconnect the black vacuum supply hose from the in-line vacuum check valve in the engine compartment. Disconnect the blower motor wires from the wire harness and disconnect the wire harness from the blower motor resistor.

8. Working under the hood, remove the 2 nuts retaining the evaporator case to the dash panel. Inside the passenger compartment, remove the 2 screws attaching the evaporator case support brackets to the cowl top panel.

9. Remove the 1 screw retaining the bracket below the evaporator case to the dash panel. Carefully pull the evaporator case away from the dash panel and remove the evaporator case assembly from the vehicle.

10. Remove the 2 nuts that attach the vacuum motor to the case and disconnect the vacuum hose from the motor.

11. Remove the spring nut that attaches the motor crank arm to the shaft and remove the motor.

To install:

12. Position the motor and install the spring nut that attaches the motor crank arm to the shaft.

13. Connect the vacuum hose to the motor and install the 2 nuts that attach the vacuum motor to the case.

14. Position the evaporator case assembly in the vehicle. Install the screws attaching the evaporator case support brackets to the cowl top panel. Check the evaporator case drain tube to ensure it is through the dash panel and is not pinched or kinked.

15. Install 1 screw retaining the bracket below the evaporator case to the dash panel. Working under the hood, install the 2 nuts retaining the evaporator case to the dash panel. Tighten the 4 nuts and 2 screws in the engine compartment. Tighten the 2 screws in the passenger compartment and the 2 support bracket attaching screws.

16. Connect the blower motor wire harness to the resistor and blower motor. Connect the black vacuum supply hose to the vacuum check valve in the engine compartment.

17. Using new O-rings lubricated with clean refrigerant oil, connect the liquid line and suction accumulator inlet to the evaporator core tubes. Tighten each connection using a backup wrench to prevent component damage.

18. Install the instrument panel by reversing the removal procedure.

19. Connect the heater hoses to the heater core and fill the cooling system.

20. Connect the negative battery cable. Leak test, evacuate and charge the refrigerant system according to the proper procedure. Observe all safety precautions.

21. Check the system for proper operation.

OUTSIDE/RECIRCULATING DOOR VACUUM MOTOR

1. Remove the glove compartment. Disconnect the vacuum hose from the vacuum motor.
2. Remove the motor arm retainer from the outside/recirculating door shaft.
3. Remove the 2 nuts retaining the vacuum motor to the mounting bracket and remove the motor.
4. Installation is the reverse of the removal procedure.

HEATING SYSTEM DIAGNOSIS AND TESTING

CONDITION	POSSIBLE SOURCE	ACTION
• Insufficient, Erratic, or No Heat or Defrost	• Low radiator coolant due to: • Coolant leaks.	• Check radiator cap pressure. Replace if below minimum pressure. • Fill to level. Pressure test for engine cooling system and heater system leaks. Service as required.
	• Engine overheating.	• Remove bugs, leaves, etc. from radiator or condenser fins. • Check for: Loose fan belt Sticking thermostat Incorrect ignition timing Water pump impeller damage Restricted cooling system • Service as required.
	• Loose fan belt.	• Replace if cracked or worn and/or adjust belt tension.
	• Thermostat.	• Check coolant temperature at radiator filler neck. If under 170°F, check thermostat.
	• Plugged or partially plugged heater core.	• Clean and backflush engine cooling system and heater core.
	• Loose or improperly adjusted control cables.	• Adjust to specification.
	• Vacuum hoses crossed, collapsed, or kinked (if applicable).	• Check to see if door vacuum motors respond properly to movements of the Function Selector Lever and the Temperature Control Lever. Visually check vacuum hoses, and service as required.
	• Air flow control doors sticking or binding.	• Check to see if door vacuum motors or cable operated blend door respond properly to movements of Function and Temperature Control Levers. If hesitation in movement is noticed, disconnect vacuum motor arm from door crank arm, and move crank arm by hand. Service sticking or binding door as required.
	• Vacuum motor or hose leaks (if applicable).	• Disconnect multiple vacuum connector from back of Control Assembly, and check each connector opening with hand operated vacuum pump. If one line leaks vacuum, test motor by itself before replacing. (Be careful of vacuum hoses that operate two motors at same time.) Service vacuum hose(s), or replace vacuum motor as required.

CONDITION	POSSIBLE SOURCE	ACTION
• Air flow changes direction when vehicle is accelerated	• Vacuum system leak (if applicable).	• Check vacuum system with hand vacuum pump from control head connector. Service tubing, or replace damaged components as required.
• Insufficient, erratic, or no heat or defrost	• Kinked, clogged, collapsed, soft, swollen, or decomposed engine cooling system or heater system hoses.	• Replace damaged hoses and back-flush engine cooling system. Then back-flush heater system, until all particles have been removed.
	• Blocked air inlet.	• Check cowl air inlet for leaves, foreign material, etc. Remove as required.

HEATING SYSTEM DIAGNOSIS AND TESTING

CONDITION	POSSIBLE SOURCE	RESOLUTION
• Air Comes Out of Defroster Outlet in Any Function Selector Lever Position	• Vacuum system (indicates a very bad leak).	• Listen for vacuum system leak. Look for disconnected vacuum hose connector. Use hand-operated vacuum pump, and check vacuum motors for diaphragm leak. Also check for leaking vacuum selector valve on control assembly, check valve, and leaking vacuum reservoir tank. Service hoses, or replace components as required.
• Cowl Ventilation System Leaks Air When in OFF Position	• Recirc door not properly sealing in recirc position.	• Check operation of recirc door for proper seal, kinked, or binding door. Service as required.
• Blower Does Not Operate Properly	• Blower motor.	• Run a #10 gauge jumper wire directly from the (grounded) negative battery terminal to the negative lead (black wire) of the blower motor. If the motor runs, the problem must be external to the motor. If the motor will not run, check the ground connection for good electrical contact. If this connection is good, the motor is inoperative and should be replaced.
	• Blower resistor.	• Check continuity of resistors for opens or check thermal limiter for continuity, if so equipped. (A blown thermal limiter will allow motor operation on Hi blower only). Service or replace as required.
	• Blower wire harness.	• Check for proper installation of harness connector terminal connectors. • Check wire-to-terminal continuity. • Check continuity of wires in harness for shorts (a short to ground will cause motor to operate with no control over the motor), opens, abrasion, etc. • Service as required.
	• Blower switch(es).	• Check blower switch(es) for proper contact. Replace switch(es) as required.
	• Vacuum selector valve.	• Check vacuum selector valve for proper contacts. Replace if required.

SPECIAL SERVICE TOOLS

ROTUNDA EQUIPMENT

Model	Description
021-00012	Pressure Tester
007-00001	Digital Volt/Ohm Meter

AIR CONDITIONING SYSTEM DIAGNOSIS AND TESTING
INSUFFICIENT OR NO COOLING

TEST STEP	RESULT ▶	ACTION TO TAKE
A1 VERIFY THE CONDITION		
• Check system operation. Verify the charge in the system.	System cooling properly ▶	INSTRUCT vehicle owner on proper use of the system.
	System not cooling properly ▶	GO to **A2**.
A2 CHECK COOLING FAN		
• Does vehicle have an electro-drive cooling fan?	Yes ▶	GO to **A3**.
	No ▶	GO to **A5**.
A3 CHECK A/C COMPRESSOR CLUTCH		
• Does the A/C compressor clutch engage?	Yes ▶	GO to **A4**.
	No ▶	REFER to clutch circuit diagnosis
A4 CHECK OPERATION OF COOLING FAN		
• Check to ensure electro-drive cooling fan runs when the A/C compressor clutch is engaged.	Yes ▶	GO to **A5**.
	No ▶	Check cooling fan
A5 COMPONENT CHECK		
Underhood check of the following: • Loose, missing or damaged compressor drive belt. • Loose or disconnected A/C clutch or clutch cycling pressure switch wires/connectors. • Disconnected resistor assembly. • Loose vacuum lines or misadjusted control cables. Inside vehicle check for: • Blown fuse/proper blower motor operation. • Vacuum motors/temperature door movement — full travel. • Control electrical and vacuum connections.	OK but still not cooling ▶ Not OK ▶	GO to **A7**. SERVICE and GO to **A6**.
A6 CHECK SYSTEM		
• Check system operation.	OK ▶	Condition Corrected. GO to **A1**.
	Not OK ▶	GO to **A7**.

AIR CONDITIONING SYSTEM DIAGNOSIS AND TESTING—INSUFFICIENT OR NO COOLING

TEST STEP	RESULT ▶	ACTION TO TAKE
A7 CHECK COMPRESSOR CLUTCH		
• Use refrigerant system pressure/clutch cycle rate and timing evaluation charts. After preparing vehicle as follows: 1. Hook up manifold gauge set. 2. Set function control at max. A/C 3. Set blower switch on high. 4. Set temperature lever full cold. 5. Close doors and windows. 6. Use a thermometer to check temperature at center discharge register, record outside temperature. 7. Run engine at approximately 1500 rpm with compressor clutch engaged. 8. Stabilize with above conditions for 10-15 minutes. • Check compressor clutch off/on time with watch. Refer to charts for normal clutch cycle timing rates.	Compressor cycles very rapidly (1 second on) (1 second off) ▶	GO to **A8**.
	Compressor runs continuously (normal operation in ambient temperature above 27°C (80°F) depending on humidity conditions) ▶	GO to **A9**.
	Compressor cycles slow ▶	GO to **A8**.
A8 CHECK CLUTCH CYCLING PRESSURE SWITCH		
• Bypass clutch cycling pressure switch with jumper wire. Compressor on continuously. • Hand feel evaporator inlet and outlet tubes.	Outlet tube same temperature approximately −2°C - 4°C (28°F - 40°F) or slightly colder than inlet tube (after fixed orifice) ▶	REPLACE clutch cycling pressure switch. Do not discharge system. Switch fitting has Schrader Valve. GO to **A9**.
	Inlet tube warm or (after fixed orifice) colder than outlet tube ▶	GO to **A10**.
A9 CHECK SYSTEM PRESSURES		
• Compare readings with normal system pressure ranges.	Clutch cycles within limits, system pressure within limits ▶	System OK. GO to **A1**.
	Compressor runs continuously (normal operation in ambient temperature above 27°C (80°F) depending on humidity conditions) ▶	GO to **A11**.
	Compressor cycles high or low ON above 259 kPa (52 psi) OFF below 144 kPa (20 psi) ▶	REPLACE clutch cycling pressure switch. Do not discharge system. Switch fitting has Schrader valve. CHECK system. OK — GO to **A1**. NOT OK — REINSTALL original switch. GO to **A10**.

TEST STEP	RESULT ▶	ACTION TO TAKE
A10 CHECK SYSTEM		
• Leak check system.	Leak found ▶	SERVICE, discharge, evacuate and charge system. System OK, GO to **A1**.
	No leak found ▶	Low refrigerant charge or moisture in system. Discharge, evacuate and charge system. System OK.
A11 CHECK CLUTCH CYCLING		
• Disconnect blower motor wire and check for clutch cycling off at 144 kPa (20 psi) (suction pressure).	Clutch cycles OFF at 144-179 kPa (20-26 psi) ▶	CONNECT blower motor wire. System OK, GO to **A1**.
	Pressure falls below 144 kPa (20 psi) ▶	REPLACE clutch cycling pressure switch. Do not discharge system. Switch fitting has Schrader valve. System OK, GO to **A1**.

COMPRESSOR CLUTCH CIRCUIT DIAGNOSIS AND TESTING—ALL 1989 VEHICLES, 1990–91 THUNDERBIRD AND COUGAR WITH 3.8L SC ENGINE AND 1990–91 MUSTANG

TEST STEP	RESULT	▶	ACTION TO TAKE
B1 CHECK SYSTEM OPERATION			
• Turn blower switch On. • Depress A/C push-button. • Turn ignition switch to Run position. • Compressor clutch should engage and engine cooling fan should operate.	Clutch and fan operate	▶	System OK.
	Clutch and fan do not operate	▶	GO to **B2**.
	Only clutch operates	▶	Check cooling fan
	Only fan operates	▶	GO to **B5**.
B2 CHECK FOR VOLTAGE			
• Check for voltage at circuit 348 (LG/P) wire at the clutch cycling pressure switch connector.	Voltage present	▶	GO to **B3**.
	No voltage	▶	GO to **B8**.
B3 BY-PASS PRESSURE SWITCH			
• Disconnect connector at clutch cycling pressure switch. • Jumper connector pins. • Clutch should engage.	OK	▶	GO to **B4**.
	NOT OK	▶	GO to **B5**.
B4 CHECK SYSTEM PRESSURE			
• Connect manifold gauge set and check system pressure.	Pressure above 55 psi.	▶	REPLACE clutch cycling pressure switch. GO to **A1**.
	Pressure below 55 psi (ambient temperature above 50°F)	▶	CHECK refrigerant system for leaks. SERVICE and CHARGE system as necessary. GO to **A1**.
B5 CHECK VOLTAGE AT CLUTCH			
• Check for voltage at clutch field coil.	Voltage present	▶	GO to **B7**.
	No voltage	▶	GO to **B6**.
B6 CHECK VOLTAGE AT CONTROLLER			
• Check for voltage at cooling fan controller	Voltage present	▶	CHECK for open in circuit 347 (BK Y). SERVICE as necessary. GO to **A1**.
	No voltage	▶	GO to **B8**.

COMPRESSOR CLUTCH CIRCUIT DIAGNOSIS AND TESTING—1990–91 CROWN VICTORIA, GRAND MARQUIS, TOWN CAR, MARK VII AND 3.8L BASE ENGINE EQUIPPED THUNDERBIRD AND COUGAR

TEST STEP	RESULT	▶	ACTION TO TAKE
B1 CHECK SYSTEM OPERATION			
• Turn blower switch On. • Turn A/C On. • Turn ignition switch to Run position. • Compressor clutch should engage.	Clutch operates	▶	System OK.
	Clutch does not operate	▶	GO to **B2**.
B2 CHECK FOR VOLTAGE			
• Check for voltage at circuit 348 (LG/P) wire at the clutch cycling pressure switch connector.	Voltage present	▶	GO to **B3**.
	No voltage	▶	GO to **B8**.
B3 BY-PASS PRESSURE SWITCH			
• Disconnect connector at clutch cycling pressure switch. • Jumper connector pins. • Clutch should engage.	OK	▶	GO to **B4**.
	NOT OK	▶	GO to **B5**.
B4 CHECK SYSTEM PRESSURE			
• Connect manifold gauge set and check system pressure.	Pressure above 55 psi	▶	REPLACE clutch cycling pressure switch. GO to **A1**.
	Pressure below 55 psi (ambient temperature above 50°F)	▶	CHECK refrigerant system for leaks. SERVICE and CHARGE system as necessary. GO to **A1**.
B5 CHECK VOLTAGE AT CLUTCH			
• Check for voltage at clutch field coil.	Voltage present	▶	GO to **B6**.
	No voltage	▶	GO to **B7**.

COMPRESSOR CLUTCH CIRCUIT DIAGNOSIS AND TESTING – 1989 MARK VII, THUNDERBIRD, COUGAR AND MUSTANG AND 1990–91 THUNDERBIRD AND COUGAR WITH 3.8L SC ENGINE

	TEST STEP	RESULT ▶	ACTION TO TAKE
B7	CHECK VOLTAGE		
	• Check for voltage at pin 16 of cooling fan controller.	Voltage present ▶	GO to **B9**.
		No voltage ▶	REPLACE clutch field coil. GO to **B1**.
B8	CHECK FUSE		
	• Check Fuse 17 in fuse panel for continuity.	(OK) ▶	GO to **B9**.
		(NOT OK) ▶	CHECK for short. SERVICE as necessary. REPLACE fuse. GO to **B1**.
B9	CHECK A/C CONTROLS		
	• Move Function selector lever to DEFROST postion. • Check for voltage at circuit 348 (LG/P) wire at the clutch cycling pressure switch connector.	Voltage present ▶	GO to **B11**.
		No voltage ▶	GO to **B10**.
B10	CHECK CIRCUIT 296		
	• Remove connector from A/C push-button switch. • Check for voltage at circuit 296 (W/LB).	Voltage present ▶	GO to **B11**.
		No voltage ▶	CHECK for open in Circuit 296. SERVICE as necessary. GO to **B1**.
B11	CHECK A/C CONTROLS		
	• Check A/C push button switch and Function switch for continuity. **NOTE: A/C push-button switch must be depressed. Function switch must be in DEFROST position.**	No continuity through function switch ▶	REPLACE Function switch. GO to **B1**.
		Continuity through function switch ▶	CHECK for open in circuit 348 (LG/P) between control assembly and clutch cycling pressure switch. SERVICE as necessary. GO to **B1**.

COMPRESSOR CLUTCH CIRCUIT DIAGNOSIS AND TESTING – 1989 CROWN VICTORIA, GRAND MARQUIS AND TOWN CAR

	TEST STEP	RESULT ▶	ACTION TO TAKE
B7	CHECK VOLTAGE		
	• Check for voltage at Pin 16 of cooling fan controller.	Voltage present ▶	GO to **B9**.
		No voltage ▶	REPLACE clutch field coil. GO to **B1**.
B8	CHECK FUSE		
	• Check fuse 17 in fuse panel for continuity.	(OK) ▶	GO to **B9**.
		(NOT OK) ▶	CHECK for short. SERVICE as necessary. REPLACE fuse. GO to **B1**.
B9	CHECK A/C CONTROLS		
	• Move function selector lever to DEFROST postion. • Check for voltage at Circuit 348 (LG/P) Wire at the clutch cycling pressure switch connector.	Voltage present ▶	GO to **B11**.
		No voltage ▶	GO to **B10**.
B10	CHECK CIRCUIT 296		
	• Check for voltage at Circuit 296 (W/P).	Voltage present ▶	GO to **B11**.
		No voltage ▶	CHECK for open in Circuit 296. SERVICE as necessary. GO to **B1**.
B11	CHECK WOT CUTOUT RELAY		
	• Check A/C push button switch and Function switch for continuity. **NOTE: A/C push-button switch must be depressed. Function switch must be in DEFROST position.** • Check that WOT cutout relay contacts are closed.	Contacts closed ▶	GO to **B1**.
		Contacts open ▶	REPLACE or SERVICE relay or circuit as necessary. GO to **B1**.

COMPRESSOR CLUTCH CIRCUIT DIAGNOSIS AND TESTING—1990–91 MUSTANG

TEST STEP	RESULT ▶	ACTION TO TAKE
B7 CHECK VOLTAGE		
• Check Circuit 60 (BK/LG) at the clutch field coil for continuity to ground.	No continuity ▶	SERVICE open in Circuit 60 to ground.
	Continuity ▶	REPLACE clutch field coil. GO to **B1**.
B8 CHECK FUSE		
• Check Fuse 17 in fuse panel for continuity.	OK ▶	GO to **B9**.
	Not OK ▶	CHECK for short. SERVICE as necessary. REPLACE fuse. GO to **B1**.
B9 CHECK A/C CONTROLS		
• Move Function selector lever to DEFROST postion. • Check for voltage at circuit 348 (LG/P) wire at the clutch cycling pressure switch connector.	Voltage present ▶	GO to **B11**.
	No voltage ▶	GO to **B10**.
B10 CHECK CIRCUIT 296		
• Remove connector from A/C push-button switch. • Check for voltage at circuit 296 (W/LB).	Voltage present ▶	GO to **B11**.
	No voltage ▶	CHECK for open in Circuit 296. SERVICE as necessary. GO to **B1**.
B11 CHECK A/C CONTROLS		
• Check A/C push button switch and Function switch for continuity. **NOTE: A/C push-button switch must be depressed. Function switch must be in DEFROST position.**	No continuity through function switch ▶	REPLACE Function switch. GO to **B1**.
	Continuity through function switch ▶	CHECK for open in circuit 348 (LG/P) between control assembly and clutch cycling pressure switch. SERVICE as necessary. GO to **B1**.

COMPRESSOR CLUTCH CIRCUIT DIAGNOSIS AND TESTING—1990–91 MARK VII AND 3.8L BASE ENGINE EQUIPPED THUNDERBIRD AND COUGAR

TEST STEP	RESULT ▶	ACTION TO TAKE
B6 CHECK FUSE		
• Check Fuse 17 in fuse panel for continuity.	OK ▶	GO to **B7**.
	Not OK ▶	CHECK for short. SERVICE as necessary. REPLACE fuse. GO to **B1**.
B7 CHECK A/C CONTROLS		
• Move Function selector lever to DEFROST position. • Check for voltage at circuit 348 (LG/P) wire at the clutch cycling pressure switch connector.	Voltage present ▶	GO to **B9**.
	No voltage ▶	GO to **B8**.
B8 CHECK CIRCUIT 296		
• Remove connector from A/C switch. • Check for voltage at circuit 296 (W/LB).	Voltage present ▶	GO to **B9**.
	No voltage ▶	CHECK for open in Circuit 296. SERVICE as necessary. GO to **B1**.
B9 CHECK A/C CONTROLS		
• Check A/C switch for continuity.	No continuity through switch ▶	REPLACE switch. GO to **B1**.
	Continuity through switch ▶	CHECK for open in circuit 348 (LG/P) between control assembly and clutch cycling pressure switch. SERVICE as necessary. GO to **B1**.

COMPRESSOR CLUTCH CIRCUIT DIAGNOSIS AND TESTING—1990–91 CROWN VICTORIA, GRAND MARQUIS AND TOWN CAR

	TEST STEP	RESULT ▶	ACTION TO TAKE
B6	CHECK FUSE		
	• Check fuse 17 in fuse panel for continuity.	(OK) ▶	GO to **B7**.
		(OK crossed out) ▶	CHECK for short. SERVICE as necessary. REPLACE fuse. GO to **B1**.
B7	CHECK A/C CONTROLS		
	• Move function selector lever to DEFROST position. • Check for voltage at Circuit 348 (LG/P) wire at the clutch cycling pressure switch connector.	Voltage present ▶	GO to **B9**.
		No voltage ▶	GO to **B8**.
B8	CHECK CIRCUIT 296		
	• Check for voltage at Circuit 296 (W/P).	Voltage present ▶	GO to **B9**.
		No voltage ▶	CHECK for open in Circuit 296. SERVICE as necessary. GO to **B1**.
B9	CHECK WOT CUTOUT RELAY		
	• Check A/C switch for continuity. **NOTE: A/C must be ON.**	Contacts closed ▶	GO to **B1**.
	• Check that WOT cutout relay contacts are closed.	Contacts open ▶	REPLACE or SERVICE relay or circuit as necessary. GO to **B1**.

NORMAL REFRIGERANT SYSTEM PRESSURE/TEMPERATURE RELATIONSHIPS—EXCEPT CROWN VICTORIA, GRAND MARQUIS AND TOWN CAR

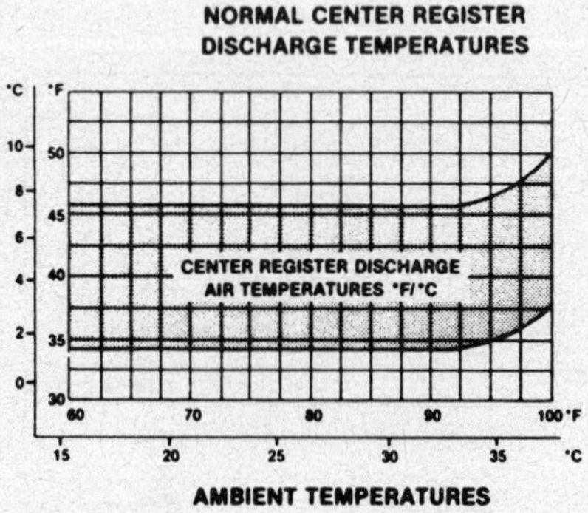
NORMAL CENTER REGISTER DISCHARGE TEMPERATURES
CENTER REGISTER DISCHARGE AIR TEMPERATURES °F/°C
AMBIENT TEMPERATURES

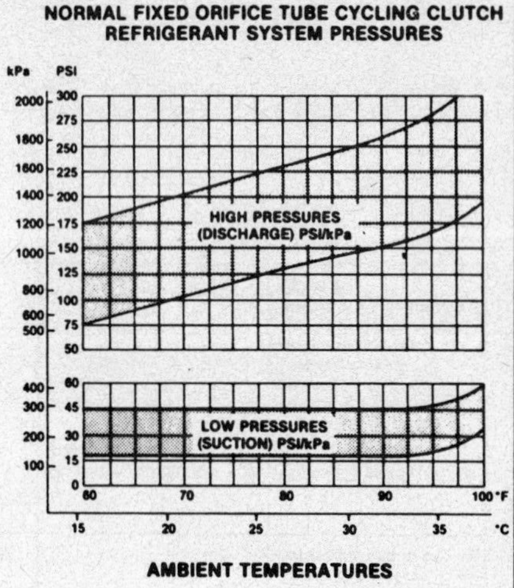
NORMAL FIXED ORIFICE TUBE CYCLING CLUTCH REFRIGERANT SYSTEM PRESSURES
HIGH PRESSURES (DISCHARGE) PSI/kPa
LOW PRESSURES (SUCTION) PSI/kPa
AMBIENT TEMPERATURES

NORMAL REFRIGERANT SYSTEM PRESSURE/TEMPERATURE RELATIONSHIPS—CROWN VICTORIA, GRAND MARQUIS AND TOWN CAR

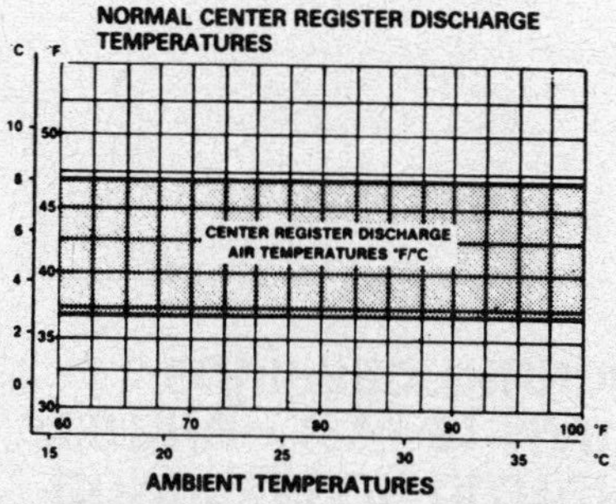
NORMAL CENTER REGISTER DISCHARGE TEMPERATURES
CENTER REGISTER DISCHARGE AIR TEMPERATURES °F/°C
AMBIENT TEMPERATURES

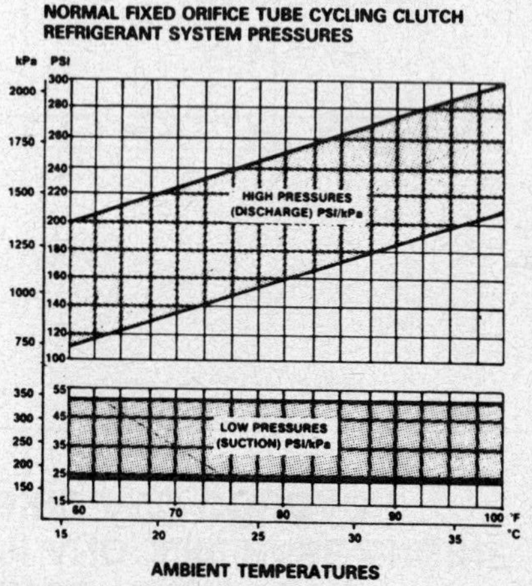
NORMAL FIXED ORIFICE TUBE CYCLING CLUTCH REFRIGERANT SYSTEM PRESSURES
HIGH PRESSURES (DISCHARGE) PSI/kPa
LOW PRESSURES (SUCTION) PSI/kPa
AMBIENT TEMPERATURES

NORMAL CLUTCH CYCLE RATES AND TIMES EXCEPT CROWN VICTORIA, GRAND MARQUIS AND TOWN CAR

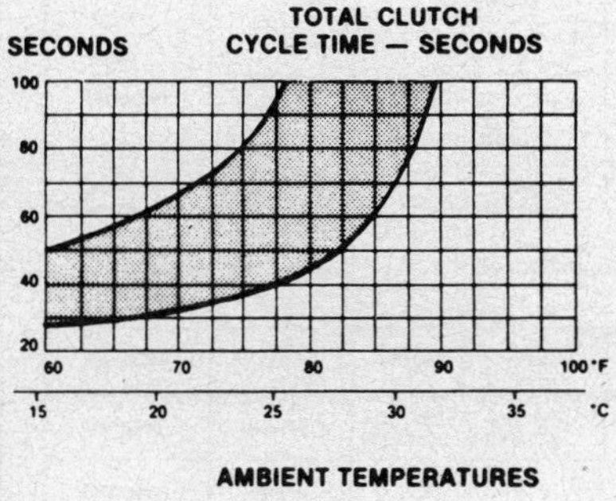
SECONDS
TOTAL CLUTCH CYCLE TIME — SECONDS
100
80
60
40
20
60
70
80
90
100 °F
15
20
25
30
35
°C
AMBIENT TEMPERATURES

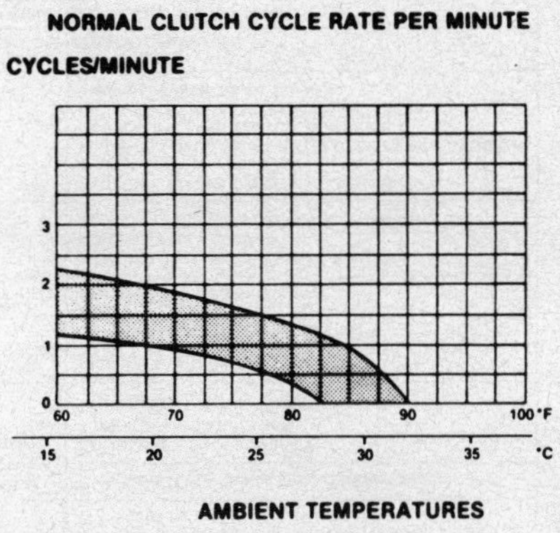
NORMAL CLUTCH CYCLE RATE PER MINUTE
CYCLES/MINUTE
3
2
1
0
60
70
80
90
100 °F
15
20
25
30
35
°C
AMBIENT TEMPERATURES

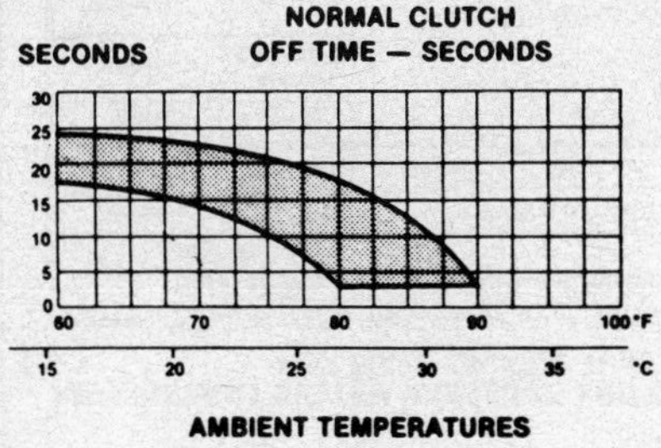
SECONDS
NORMAL CLUTCH OFF TIME — SECONDS
30
25
20
15
10
5
0
60
70
80
90
100 °F
15
20
25
30
35
°C
AMBIENT TEMPERATURES

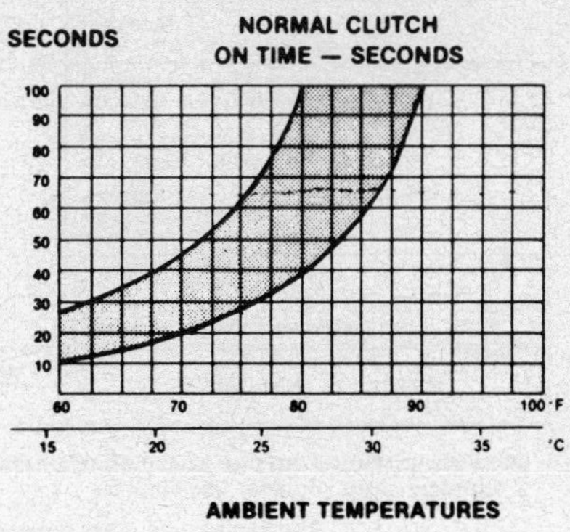
SECONDS
NORMAL CLUTCH ON TIME — SECONDS
100
90
80
70
60
50
40
30
20
10
60
70
80
90
100 °F
15
20
25
30
35
°C
AMBIENT TEMPERATURES

NORMAL CLUTCH CYCLE RATES AND TIMES CROWN VICTORIA, GRAND MARQUIS AND TOWN CAR

IMPORTANT — TEST REQUIREMENTS

The following test conditions must be established to obtain accurate clutch cycle rate and cycle time readings:

- Run engine at 1500 rpm for 10 minutes.
- Operate A/C system on max A/C (recirculating air).
- Run blower at max speed.
- Stabilize in car temperature @ 70°F to 80°F (21°C to 22°C).

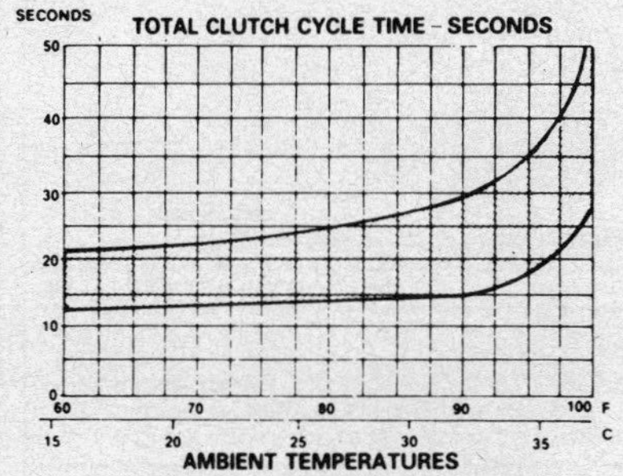
SECONDS
TOTAL CLUTCH CYCLE TIME - SECONDS
50
40
30
20
10
0
60
70
80
90
100 F
15
20
25
30
35
C
AMBIENT TEMPERATURES

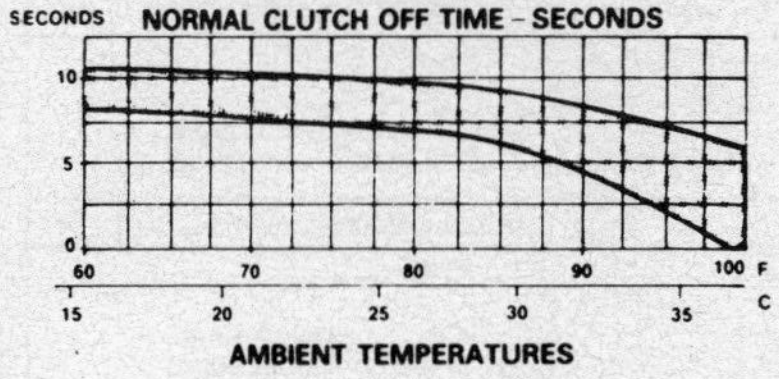
SECONDS
NORMAL CLUTCH OFF TIME - SECONDS
10
5
0
60
70
80
90
100 F
15
20
25
30
35
C
AMBIENT TEMPERATURES

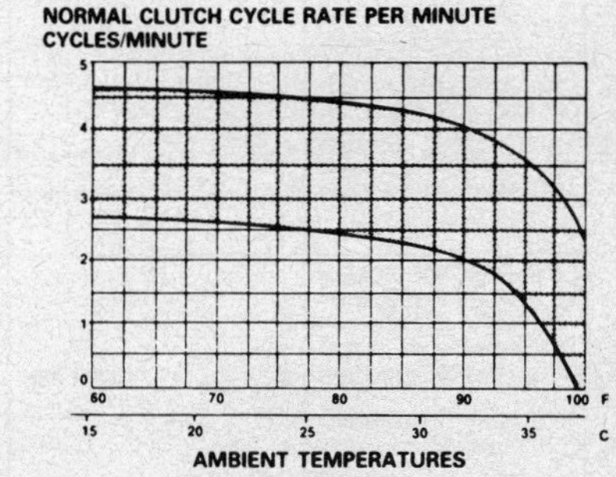
NORMAL CLUTCH CYCLE RATE PER MINUTE
CYCLES/MINUTE
5
4
3
2
1
0
60
70
80
90
100 F
15
20
25
30
35
C
AMBIENT TEMPERATURES

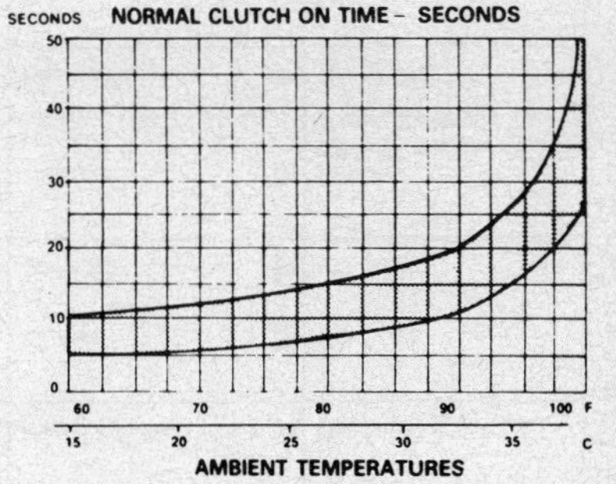
SECONDS
NORMAL CLUTCH ON TIME - SECONDS
50
40
30
20
10
0
60
70
80
90
100 F
15
20
25
30
35
C
AMBIENT TEMPERATURES

REFRIGERANT SYSTEM AND CLUTCH CYCLE RATE AND TIMING EVALUATION

REFRIGERANT SYSTEM PRESSURE AND CLUTCH CYCLE TIMING EVALUATION CHART FOR FIXED ORIFICE TUBE CYCLING CLUTCH SYSTEMS

NOTE: System test requirements must be met to obtain accurate test readings for evaluation. Refer to the normal refrigerant system pressure/temperature and the normal clutch cycle rate and times charts.

HIGH (DISCHARGE) PRESSURE	LOW (SUCTION) PRESSURE	CLUTCH CYCLE TIME			COMPONENT — CAUSES
		RATE	ON	OFF	
HIGH	HIGH	CONTINUOUS RUN			CONDENSER — Inadequate Airflow
HIGH	NORMAL TO HIGH				ENGINE OVERHEATING
NORMAL TO HIGH	NORMAL				REFRIGERANT OVERCHARGE (a) AIR IN REFRIGERANT HUMIDITY OR AMBIENT TEMP VERY HIGH (b)
NORMAL	HIGH				FIXED ORIFICE TUBE — Missing O Rings Leaking/Missing
NORMAL	NORMAL	SLOW OR NO CYCLE	LONG OR CONTINUOUS	NORMAL OR NO CYCLE	MOISTURE IN REFRIGERANT SYSTEM EXCESSIVE REFRIGERANT OIL
NORMAL	LOW	SLOW	LONG	LONG	CLUTCH CYCLING SWITCH — Low Cut-Out
NORMAL TO LOW	HIGH	CONTINUOUS RUN			Compressor — Low Performance
NORMAL TO LOW	NORMAL TO HIGH				A/C SUCTION LINE — Partially Restricted or Plugged (c)
NORMAL TO LOW	NORMAL	FAST	SHORT	NORMAL	EVAPORATOR - Low or Restricted Airflow
			SHORT TO VERY SHORT	NORMAL TO LONG	CONDENSER, FIXED ORIFICE TUBE, OR A/C LIQUID LINE — Partially Restricted or Plugged
			SHORT TO VERY SHORT	SHORT TO VERY SHORT	LOW REFRIGERANT CHARGE
			SHORT TO VERY SHORT	LONG	EVAPORATOR CORE — Partially Restricted or Plugged
NORMAL TO LOW	LOW	CONTINUOUS RUN			A/C SUCTION LINE — Partially Restricted or Plugged (d) CLUTCH CYCLING SWITCH — Sticking Closed
ERRATIC OPERATION OR COMPRESSOR NOT RUNNING		—	—	—	CLUTCH CYCLING SWITCH — Dirty Contacts or Sticking Open POOR CONNECTION AT A/C CLUTCH CONNECTOR OR CLUTCH CYCLING SWITCH CONNECTOR A/C ELECTRICAL CIRCUIT ERRATIC — See A/C Electrical Circuit Wiring Diagram

ADDITIONAL POSSIBLE CAUSE COMPONENTS ASSOCIATED WITH INADEQUATE COMPRESSOR OPERATION

- COMPRESSOR DRIVE BELT — Loose • COMPRESSOR CLUTCH — Slipping
- CLUTCH COIL Open — Shorted, or Loose Mounting
- CONTROL ASSEMBLY SWITCH — Dirty Contacts or Sticking Open
- CLUTCH WIRING CIRCUIT — High Resistance, Open or Blown Fuse
- COMPRESSOR OPERATION INTERRUPTED BY ENGINE COMPUTER

ADDITIONAL POSSIBLE CAUSE COMPONENTS ASSOCIATED WITH A DAMAGED COMPRESSOR

- CLUTCH CYCLING SWITCH - Sticking Closed or Compressor Clutch Seized
- SUCTION ACCUMULATOR DRIER — Refrigerant Oil Bleed Hole Plugged
- REFRIGERANT LEAKS

(a) Compressor may make noise on initial run. This is slugging condition caused by excessive liquid refrigerant
(b) Compressor clutch may not cycle in ambient temperatures above 80°F depending on humidity conditions
(c) Low pressure reading will be **normal to high** if pressure is taken at accumulator and if restriction is downstream of service access valve
(d) Low pressure reading will be **low** if pressure is taken near the compressor and restriction is upstream of service access valve

MANUAL AIR CONDITIONING AND HEATER SYSTEM VACUUM LEAK DIAGNOSIS

	TEST STEP	RESULT ▶	ACTION TO TAKE
A0	CHECK CONNECTORS		
	• Check in-line and control assembly multiple connectors for proper installation. • Listen for hiss.	Hiss stops ▶	RECHECK system for proper operation.
		Hiss continues ▶	GO to **A1**.
A1	DETERMINE LEAKING VALVE		
	• Move function lever to determine what Selector Valve positions are leaking.	All leak ▶	GO to **A2**.
		Some leak but not all ▶	GO to **A4**.
A2	CHECK SOURCE TUBE		
	• Check vacuum source tube (black) from reservoir to control assembly for cut or disconnection. • Listen for hiss.	Hiss stops ▶	SERVICE tube. RECHECK system for proper operation.
		Hiss continues ▶	GO to **A3**.
A3	PINCH OFF SOURCE TUBE		
	• Pinch off source tube (black) at control assembly. • Listen for hiss.	Hiss stops ▶	REPLACE selector valve. RECHECK system for proper operation.
		Hiss continues ▶	RECHECK source tube (black), connections, reservoir and check valve. SERVICE or REPLACE as required.
A4	DETERMINE LEAKING TUBE(S)		
	• Determine what color tube(s) are used in leaking function selector valve position(s). (Refer to air flow schematic and vacuum control chart.) • Pinch off suspect tube(s), one at a time, near each respective vacuum motor. • Listen for hiss.	Hiss stops ▶	CHECK tube connection to vacuum motor and SERVICE and/or RECONNECT if loose or split. RECHECK for hiss. If hiss still continues, REPLACE vacuum motor.* RECHECK system for proper operation.
		Hiss continues ▶	GO to **A5**.
A5	PINCH OFF SUSPECT TUBE(S)		
	• Pinch off suspect tube(s), one at a time, near control assembly and/or in-line connector. • Listen for hiss.	Hiss stops ▶	CHECK tube for cut or damage. SERVICE if required. RECHECK system for proper operation.
		Hiss continues ▶	REPLACE function vacuum selector valve.

*Never manually operate any vacuum motor or vacuum motor controlled door — this may cause internal damage to the vacuum motor diaphragm.

MANUAL HEATING AND AIR CONDITIONING DIAGNOSIS AND TESTING

Condition	Diagnosis and Resolution
Low radiator coolant due to: • Coolant leaks • Engine overheating	Check radiator cap pressure. Replace if below minimum pressure. Fill to level. Pressure test for engine cooling system and heat system leaks. Service as required.
	Remove bugs, leaves, etc. from radiator or condenser fins. Check for: Loose fan belt Sticking thermostat Incorrect ignition timing Water pump impeller damage Restricted cooling system Service as required.
Loose fan belt	Replace if cracked or worn and/or adjust belt tension.
Thermostat	Check thermostat.
Plugged or partially plugged heater core	Clean and backflush engine cooling system and heater core separately.
Loose or improperly adjusted control cable	Reconnect and/or adjust to specifications.
Vacuum hoses crossed or kinked	Check to see if door vacuum motors respond properly to movements of the Function Selector Lever. Visually check vacuum hoses, and service as required.
Air flow control doors sticking or binding	Check to see if doors and vacuum motors respond properly to movements of Function Selector Lever. If hesitation in movement is noticed, disconnect vacuum motor arm or cable from door crank arm, and move crank arm by hand. Service sticking or binding door as required.
Vacuum motor diaphragm or hose leaks	Disconnect multiple vacuum connector from Control Assembly selector valve and check each connector opening with hand operated vacuum pump. If one line leaks vacuum, test motor by itself before replacing. Service vacuum hose(s), or replace vacuum motor as required. Refer to the appropriate system vacuum leak tests.

INSUFFICIENT, ERRATIC, OR NO HEAT OR DEFROST

Condition	Action
Kinked, clogged, collapsed, soft, swollen, or decomposed engine cooling or heater system hoses.	Replace damaged hoses and backflush engine cooling system, then backflush heater core separately, until all particles have been removed.
Blocked air inlet.	Check cowl air inlet for leaves, foreign material, etc. Remove as required.

TOO MUCH HEAT

Condition	Action
Loose or improperly adjusted control cable.	Reconnect and/or adjust as specified for applicable system.
ATC sensor improperly adjusted.	Readjust as required.

AIR FLOW CHANGES DIRECTION WHEN VEHICLE IS ACCELERATED

Condition	Action
Vacuum system leak.	Check vacuum system (including check valve) with hand vacuum pump from control vacuum selector connector. Service tubing, or replace damaged components as required.

AIR COMES OUT OF DEFROSTER OUTLET IN ANY FUNCTION SELECTOR LEVER POSITION

Condition	Resolution
Vacuum system (this indicates a very bad leak, and is usually easy to locate).	Listen for vacuum system leak. Look for disconnected vacuum hose connector. Use hand-operated vacuum pump, and check vacuum motors for diaphragm leak. Also check for leaking check valve, and leaking vacuum reservoir tank. Service hoses, or replace components as required. Refer to appropriate system vacuum leak tests.

BLOWER DOES NOT OPERATE

Condition	Resolution
Check fuse	Check fuse 9 for continuity. If OK, check blower motor. If not OK, replace fuse.
Blower motor	Run a 10 gauge or larger jumper wire directly from the positive battery terminal to the positive lead (orange/black wire) of the blower motor, also run a 10 gauge wire from frame ground to the negative lead (black) of the blower motor. If the motor runs, check the electrical circuits for continuity.
Blower resistor	Check continuity of resistors and thermal limiter for an open circuit (self-powered test light). Or check thermal limiter for continuity, if so equipped. (A blown thermal limiter will allow motor operation on Hi-blower only.) Service or replace as required.
Blower wire harness	Check for proper installation of wire harness terminal connectors. Check wire-to-terminal continuity. Check continuity of wires in harness for open circuits, etc. Service as required.
Blower switch(s)	Check blower switch for proper contact. Replace switch if required.
Selector valve switch	Check selector valve electrical switch for proper contact. Replace if required.

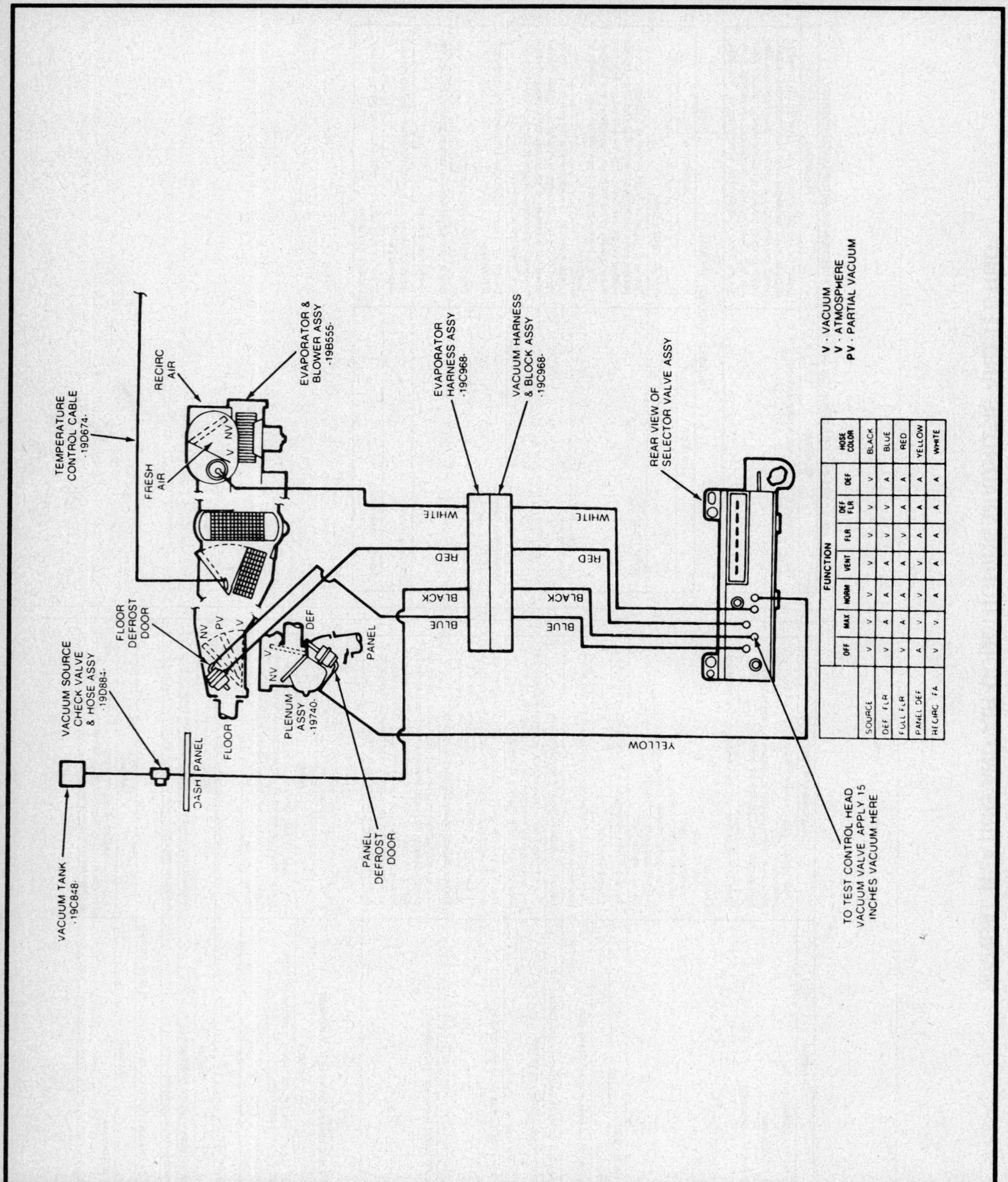
TEMPERATURE CONTROL CABLE -19D674-
RECIRC AIR
EVAPORATOR & BLOWER ASSY -19B555-
FRESH AIR
EVAPORATOR HARNESS ASSY -19C968-
VACUUM HARNESS & BLOCK ASSY -19C968-
REAR VIEW OF SELECTOR VALVE ASSY
V · VACUUM
V · ATMOSPHERE
PV · PARTIAL VACUUM
WHITE
RED
BLACK
BLUE
YELLOW
FLOOR DEFROST DOOR
VACUUM SOURCE CHECK VALVE & HOSE ASSY -19D884-
DEF
PANEL
PLENUM ASSY -19740-
FLOOR
DASH PANEL
VACUUM TANK -19C848-
PANEL DEFROST DOOR
TO TEST CONTROL HEAD VACUUM VALVE APPLY 15 INCHES VACUUM HERE

	FUNCTION							HOSE COLOR
	OFF	MAX	NORM	VENT	FLR	DEF FLR	DEF	
SOURCE	V	V	V	V	V	V	V	BLACK
DEF FLR	V	A	A	A	V	V	A	BLUE
FULL FLR	V	A	A	A	V	A	A	RED
PANEL DEF	A	V	V	V	A	A	A	YELLOW
RECIRC FA	V	V	A	A	A	A	A	WHITE

Vacuum schematic and selector test—Thunderbird and Cougar

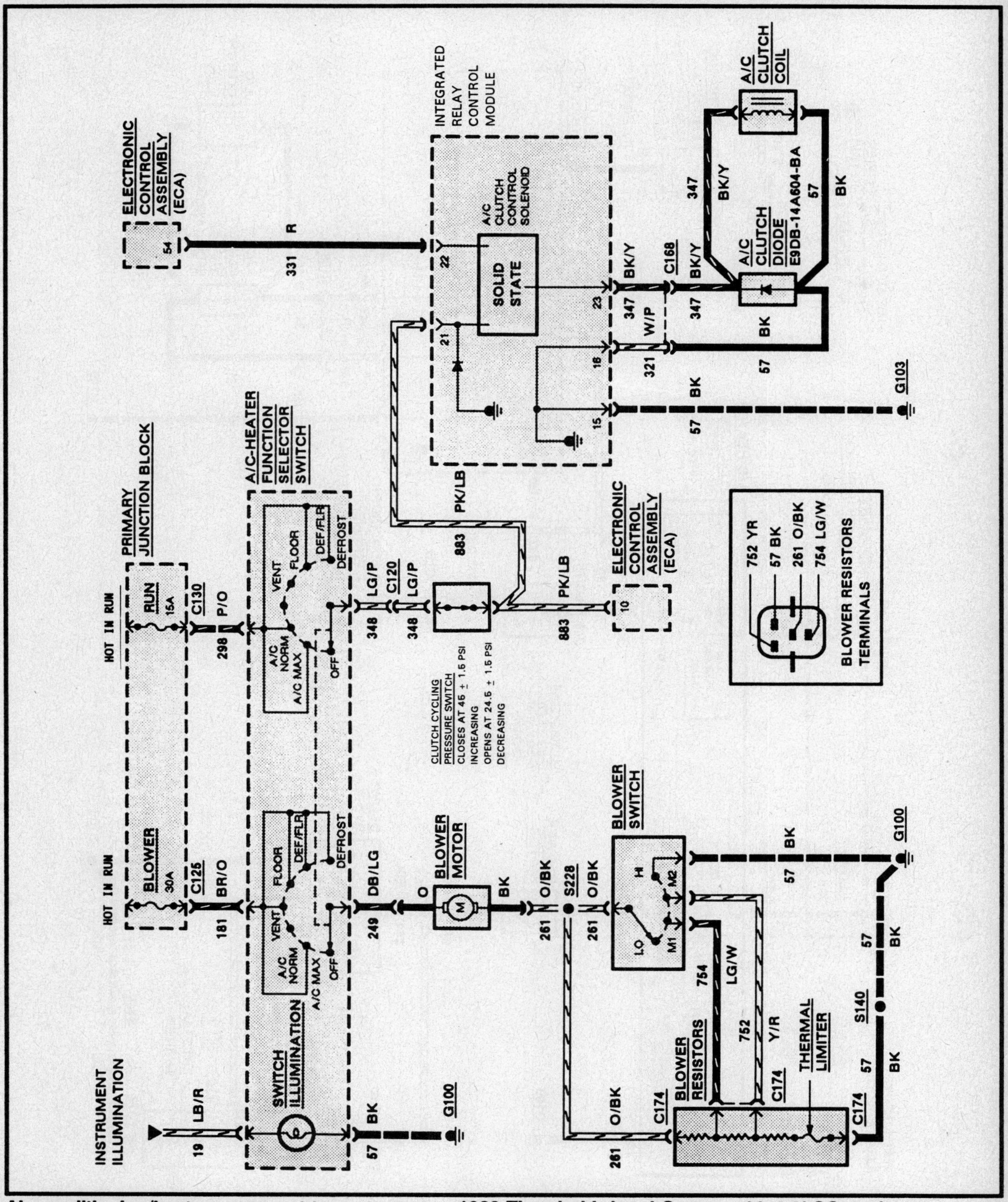
ELECTRONIC CONTROL ASSEMBLY (ECA)
INTEGRATED RELAY CONTROL MODULE
A/C CLUTCH CONTROL SOLENOID
SOLID STATE
A/C CLUTCH COIL
A/C CLUTCH DIODE E9DB-14A604-BA
PRIMARY JUNCTION BLOCK
HOT IN RUN
RUN 15A
BLOWER 30A
A/C-HEATER FUNCTION SELECTOR SWITCH
A/C NORM
A/C MAX
VENT
FLOOR
DEF/FLR
DEFROST
OFF
CLUTCH CYCLING PRESSURE SWITCH
CLOSES AT 45 ± 1.5 PSI INCREASING
OPENS AT 24.5 ± 1.5 PSI DECREASING
BLOWER MOTOR
BLOWER SWITCH
BLOWER RESISTORS
THERMAL LIMITER
INSTRUMENT ILLUMINATION
SWITCH ILLUMINATION
752 YR
57 BK
261 O/BK
754 LG/W
BLOWER RESISTORS TERMINALS
G100
G103
S140
S228
C125
C130
C120
C168
C174

Air conditioning/heater system wiring schematic – 1989 Thunderbird and Cougar with 3.8l SC engine

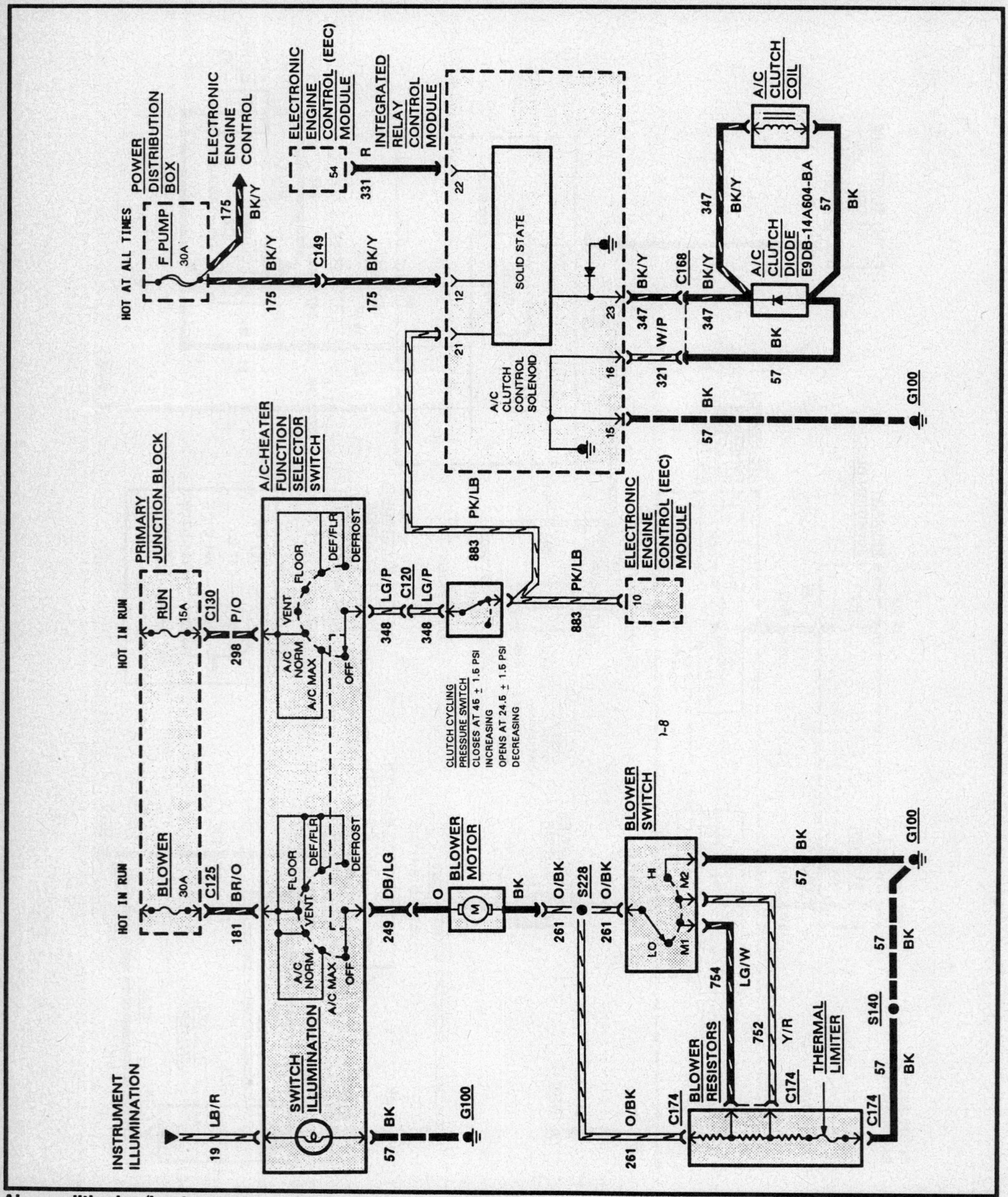
HOT AT ALL TIMES
F PUMP 30A
POWER DISTRIBUTION BOX
ELECTRONIC ENGINE CONTROL
175 BK/Y
C149
ELECTRONIC ENGINE CONTROL (EEC) MODULE
54
331 R
INTEGRATED RELAY CONTROL MODULE
SOLID STATE
A/C CLUTCH CONTROL SOLENOID
22
12
21
23
16
15
347 BK/Y
C168
347 W/P
321
A/C CLUTCH DIODE E9DB-14A604-BA
A/C CLUTCH COIL
57 BK
G100
HOT IN RUN
RUN 15A
PRIMARY JUNCTION BLOCK
C130
298 P/O
A/C-HEATER FUNCTION SELECTOR SWITCH
A/C NORM
A/C MAX
OFF
VENT
FLOOR
DEF/FLR
DEFROST
348 LG/P
C120
883 PK/LB
10
CLUTCH CYCLING PRESSURE SWITCH
CLOSES AT 45 ± 1.5 PSI INCREASING
OPENS AT 24.5 ± 1.5 PSI DECREASING
BLOWER 30A
C125
181 BR/O
INSTRUMENT ILLUMINATION
19 LB/R
SWITCH ILLUMINATION
249 DB/LG
BLOWER MOTOR
O
BK
261 O/BK
S228
BLOWER SWITCH
LO
M1
M2
HI
754 LG/W
752 Y/R
BLOWER RESISTORS
C174
THERMAL LIMITER
S140

Air conditioning/heater system wiring schematic — 1990–91 Thunderbird and Cougar with 3.8l SC engine

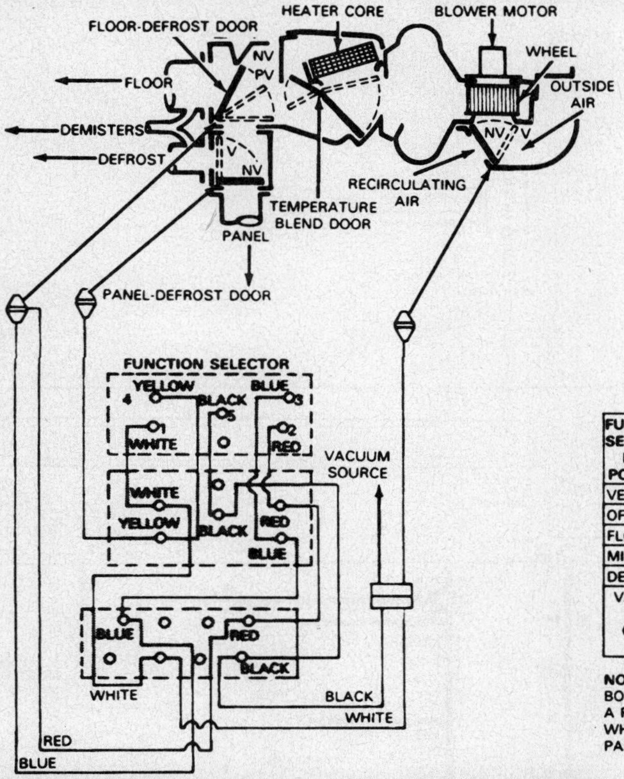
FLOOR-DEFROST DOOR
HEATER CORE
BLOWER MOTOR
WHEEL
OUTSIDE AIR
FLOOR
DEMISTERS
DEFROST
NV
PV
V
RECIRCULATING AIR
TEMPERATURE BLEND DOOR
PANEL
PANEL-DEFROST DOOR
FUNCTION SELECTOR
YELLOW
BLUE
BLACK
WHITE
RED
VACUUM SOURCE

NOTE: DOOR POSITIONS SHOWN REFLECT A FUNCTION SELECTOR KNOB SETTING IN THE OFF POSITION

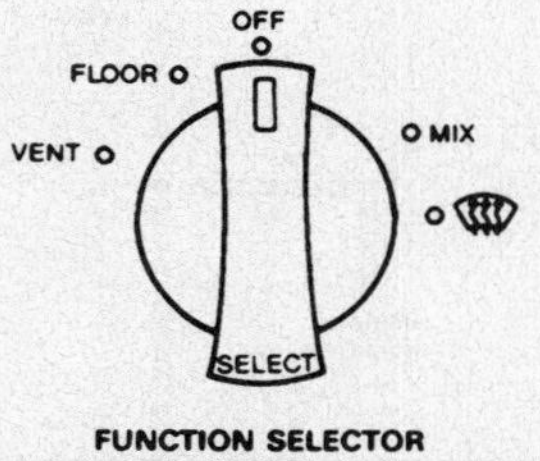
OFF
FLOOR
MIX
VENT
SELECT

FUNCTION SELECTOR KNOB

FUNCTION SELECTOR KNOB POSITION	OUTSIDE RECIRC AIR DOOR	FLOOR-DEFROST DOOR	PANEL-DEFROST DOOR	BLOWER MOTOR
VENT	NV	NV	V	ON
OFF	V	V	V	OFF
FLOOR	NV	V	NV	ON
MIX	NV	PV	NV	ON
DEFROST	NV	NV	NV	ON
VACUUM HOSE COLOR CODE	WHITE	RED / BLUE	YELLOW	–

NOTE: WHEN VACUUM IS APPLIED TO BOTH FLOOR-DEFROST VACUUM LINES (RED/BLUE), A FULL VACUUM CONDITION EXISTS. WHEN APPLIED TO BLUE LINE ONLY, PARTIAL VACUUM EXISTS.

Heater system vacuum schematic and selector test— Mustang

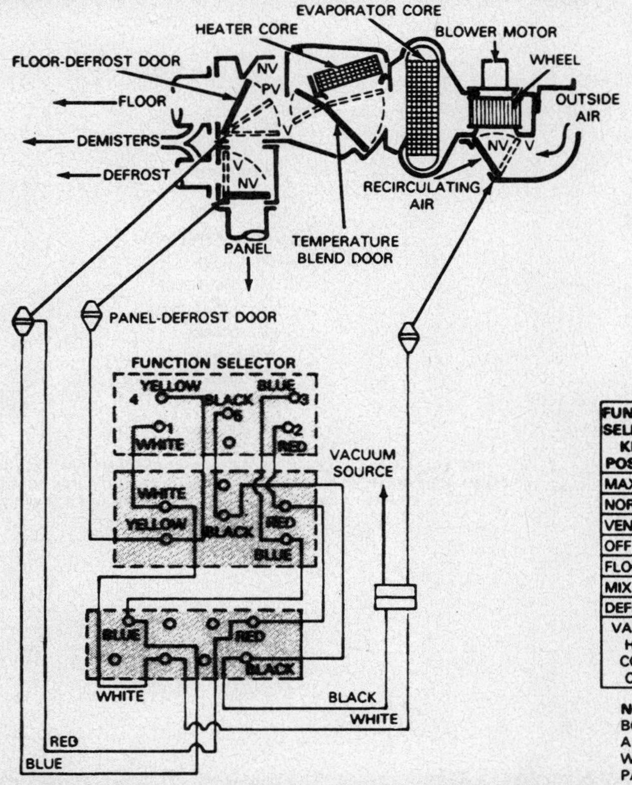
EVAPORATOR CORE
HEATER CORE
BLOWER MOTOR
FLOOR-DEFROST DOOR
WHEEL
OUTSIDE AIR
FLOOR
DEMISTERS
DEFROST
NV
PV
V
RECIRCULATING AIR
PANEL
TEMPERATURE BLEND DOOR
PANEL-DEFROST DOOR
FUNCTION SELECTOR
YELLOW
BLUE
BLACK
WHITE
RED
VACUUM SOURCE

NOTE: DOOR POSITIONS SHOWN REFLECT A FUNCTION SELECTOR KNOB SETTING IN THE MAX A/C POSITION

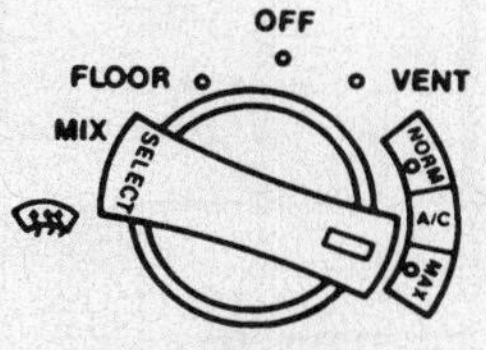
OFF
FLOOR
VENT
MIX
SELECT
NORM
A/C
MAX

FUNCTION SELECTOR KNOB

FUNCTION SELECTOR KNOB POSITION	OUTSIDE RECIRC AIR DOOR	FLOOR-DEFROST DOOR	PANEL-DEFROST DOOR	BLOWER MOTOR
MAX A/C	V	NV	V	ON
NORM A/C	NV	NV	V	ON
VENT	NV	NV	V	ON
OFF	V	V	V	OFF
FLOOR	NV	V	NV	ON
MIX	NV	PV	NV	ON
DEFROST	NV	NV	NV	ON
VACUUM HOSE COLOR CODE	WHITE	RED / BLUE	YELLOW	–

NOTE: WHEN VACUUM IS APPLIED TO BOTH FLOOR-DEFROST VACUUM LINES (RED/BLUE) A FULL VACUUM CONDITION EXISTS. WHEN APPLIED TO BLUE LINE ONLY, PARTIAL VACUUM EXISTS.

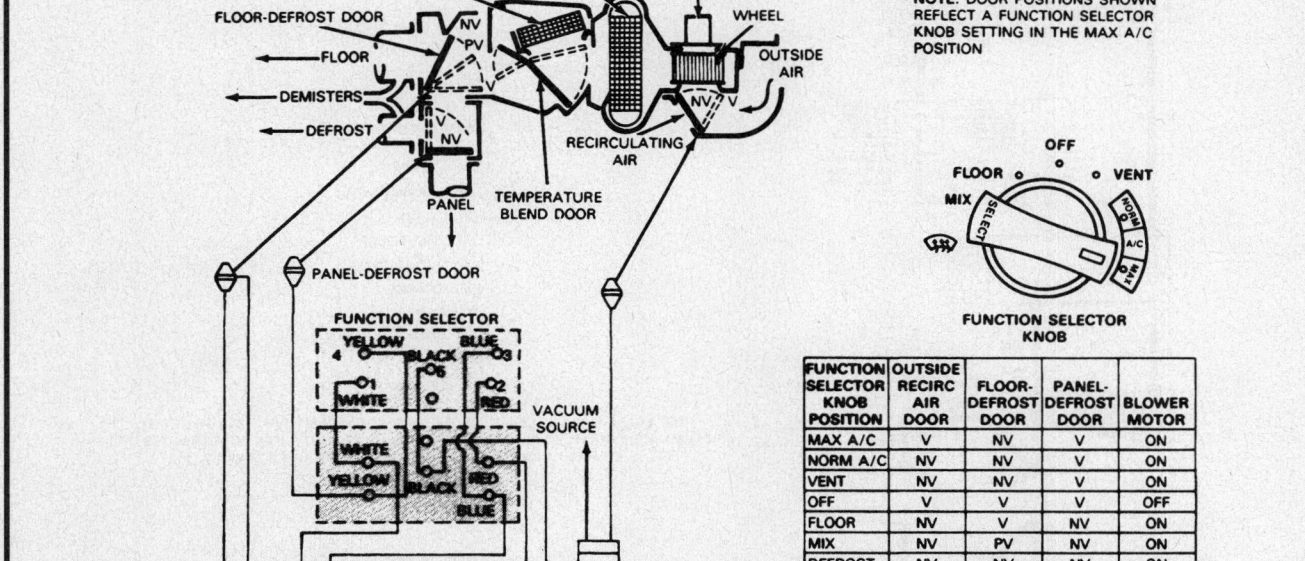

Air conditioning/heater system vacuum schematic and selector test—Mustang

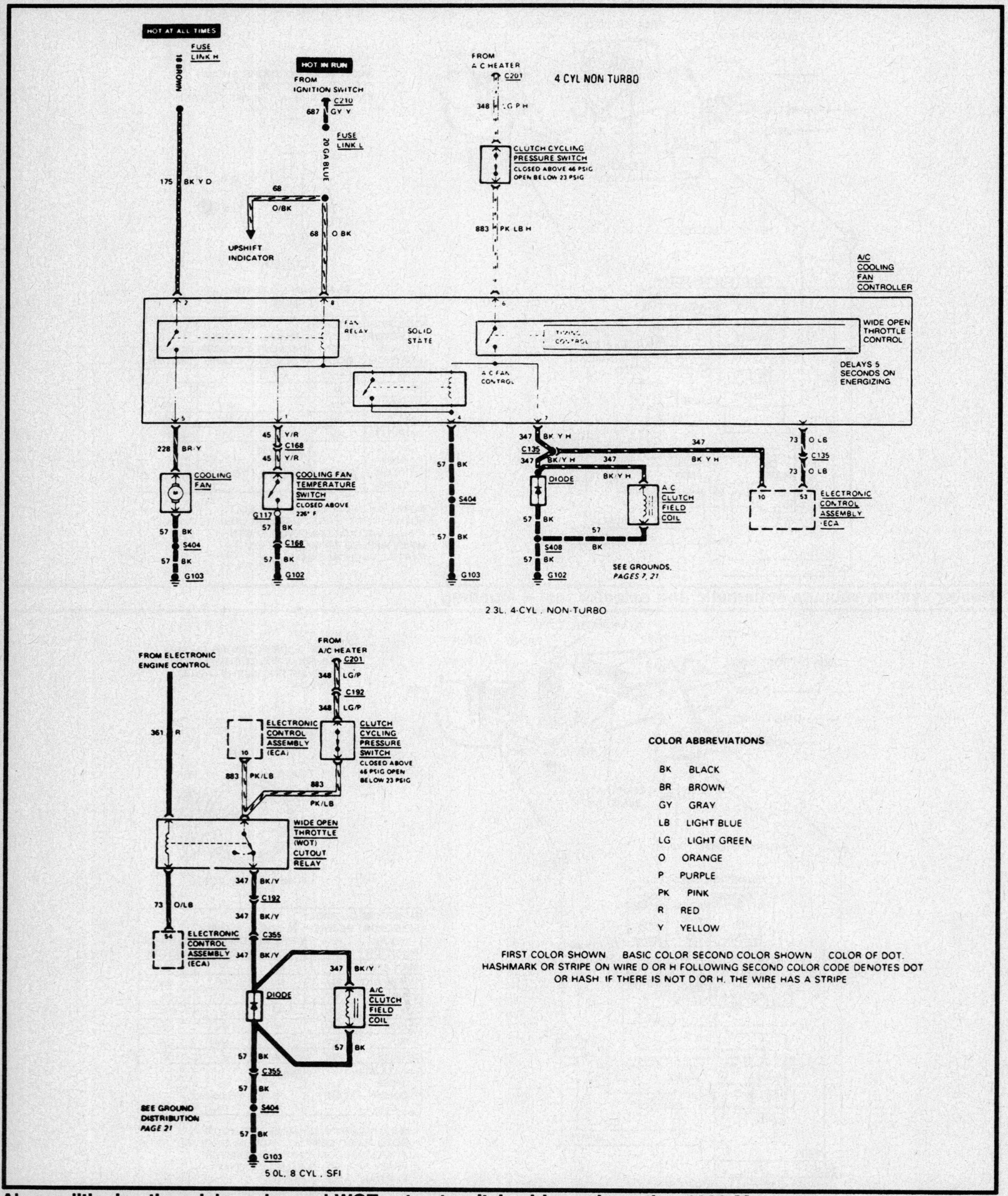
HOT AT ALL TIMES
FUSE LINK H
18 BROWN
175 BK Y D
HOT IN RUN
FROM IGNITION SWITCH
C210
687 GY Y
20 GA BLUE
FUSE LINK L
68
O/BK
68 O BK
UPSHIFT INDICATOR
FROM A C HEATER
C201
4 CYL NON TURBO
348 LG P H
CLUTCH CYCLING PRESSURE SWITCH
CLOSED ABOVE 46 PSIG
OPEN BELOW 23 PSIG
883 PK LB H
A/C COOLING FAN CONTROLLER
FAN RELAY
SOLID STATE
WIDE OPEN THROTTLE CONTROL
A C FAN CONTROL
DELAYS 5 SECONDS ON ENERGIZING
228 BR Y
COOLING FAN
45 Y/R
C168
45 Y/R
COOLING FAN TEMPERATURE SWITCH
CLOSED ABOVE 226° F
G117
57 BK
S404
G103
C168
G102
347 BK Y H
C135
347 BK/Y H
DIODE
A C CLUTCH FIELD COIL
347 BK Y H
73 O LB
C135
73 O LB
ELECTRONIC CONTROL ASSEMBLY ECA
S408
SEE GROUNDS, PAGES 7, 21
2 3L, 4-CYL, NON-TURBO
FROM ELECTRONIC ENGINE CONTROL
361 R
FROM A/C HEATER
C201
348 LG/P
C192
348 LG/P
ELECTRONIC CONTROL ASSEMBLY (ECA)
CLUTCH CYCLING PRESSURE SWITCH
CLOSED ABOVE 46 PSIG OPEN BELOW 23 PSIG
883 PK/LB
883
PK/LB
WIDE OPEN THROTTLE (WOT) CUTOUT RELAY
347 BK/Y
C192
347 BK/Y
73 O/LB
ELECTRONIC CONTROL ASSEMBLY (ECA)
C355
347 BK/Y
DIODE
A/C CLUTCH FIELD COIL
57 BK
C355
S404
G103
SEE GROUND DISTRIBUTION PAGE 21
5 0L, 8 CYL, SFI
COLOR ABBREVIATIONS
BK BLACK
BR BROWN
GY GRAY
LB LIGHT BLUE
LG LIGHT GREEN
O ORANGE
P PURPLE
PK PINK
R RED
Y YELLOW
FIRST COLOR SHOWN BASIC COLOR SECOND COLOR SHOWN COLOR OF DOT.
HASHMARK OR STRIPE ON WIRE D OR H FOLLOWING SECOND COLOR CODE DENOTES DOT
OR HASH IF THERE IS NOT D OR H, THE WIRE HAS A STRIPE

Air conditioning time delay relay and WOT cut-out switch wiring schematic—1989 Mustang

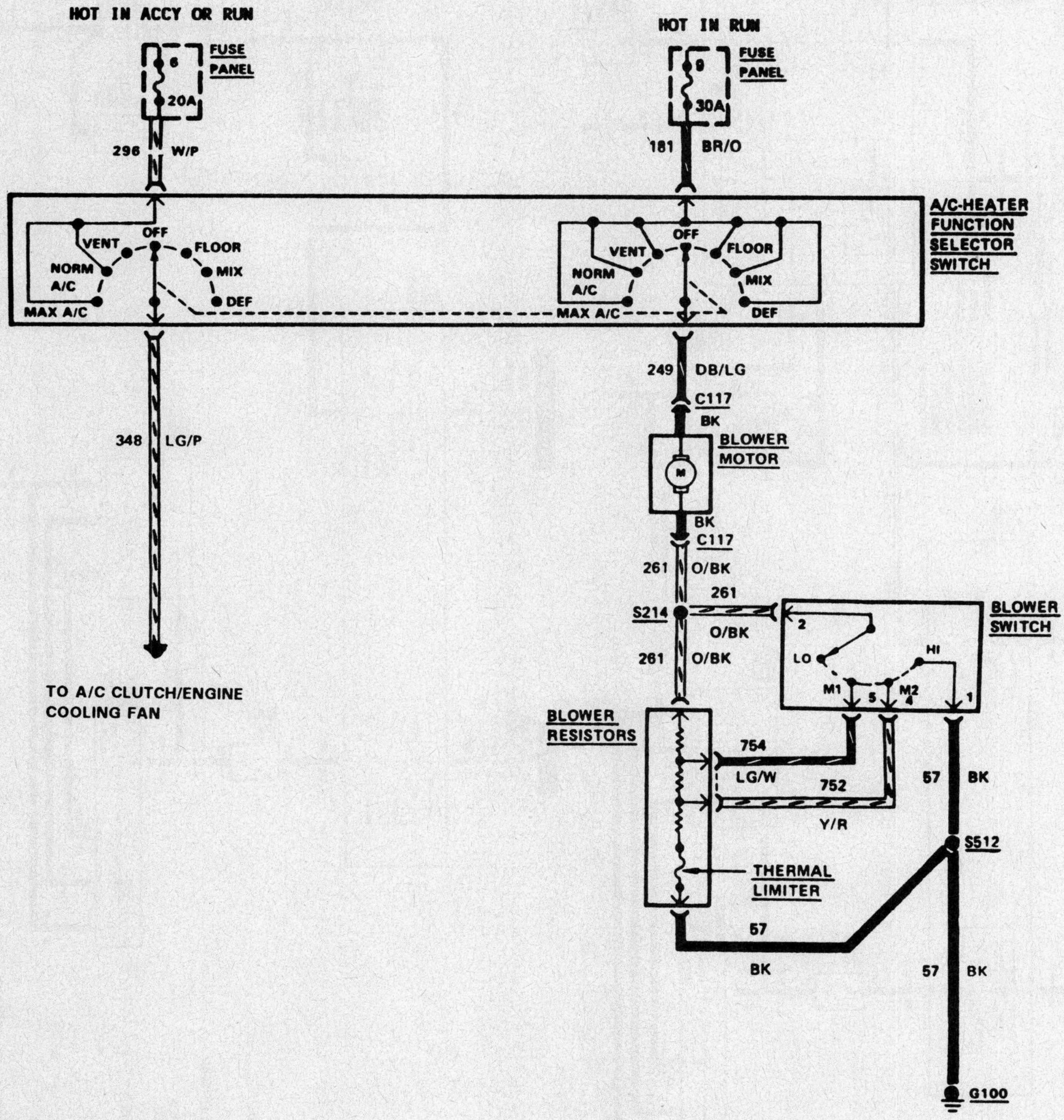
HOT IN ACCY OR RUN
FUSE PANEL
6
20A
296
W/P
HOT IN RUN
FUSE PANEL
9
30A
181
BR/O
A/C-HEATER FUNCTION SELECTOR SWITCH
VENT
OFF
FLOOR
NORM A/C
MIX
DEF
MAX A/C
348
LG/P
TO A/C CLUTCH/ENGINE COOLING FAN
249
DB/LG
C117
BK
BLOWER MOTOR
M
261
O/BK
S214
BLOWER SWITCH
2
LO
HI
M1
5
M2
4
1
BLOWER RESISTORS
754
LG/W
752
Y/R
57
BK
S512
THERMAL LIMITER
G100

Air conditioning/heater system wiring schematic—1989 Mustang

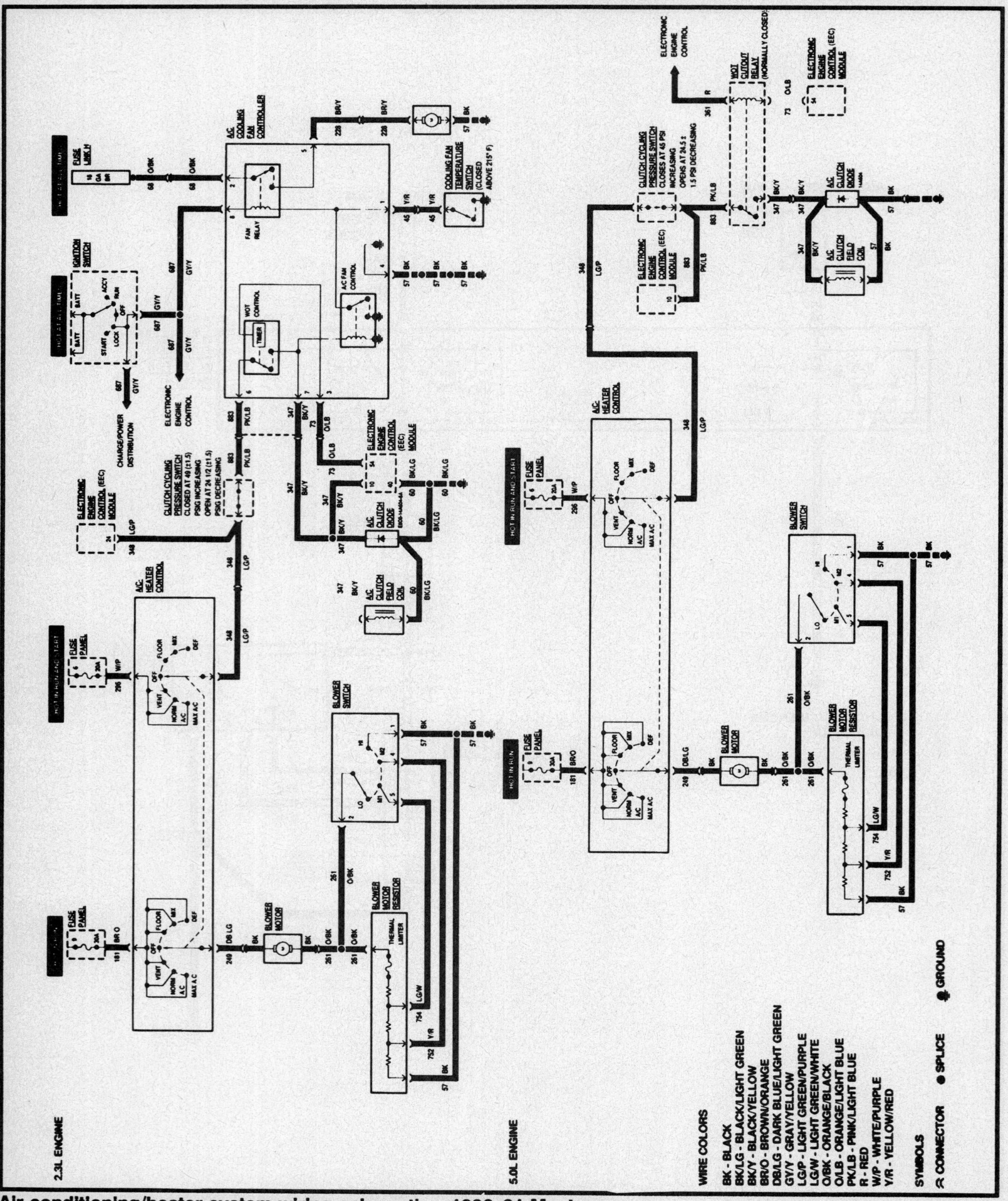
2.3L ENGINE
5.0L ENGINE
HOT AT ALL TIMES
FUSE LINK H
IGNITION SWITCH
CHARGE/POWER DISTRIBUTION
ELECTRONIC ENGINE CONTROL
A/C COOLING FAN CONTROLLER
FAN RELAY
WOT CONTROL
TIMER
A/C FAN CONTROL
COOLING FAN TEMPERATURE SWITCH (CLOSED ABOVE 215° F)
ELECTRONIC ENGINE CONTROL (EEC) MODULE
CLUTCH CYCLING PRESSURE SWITCH
CLOSED AT 40 (±1.5) PSIG INCREASING
OPEN AT 24 1/2 (±1.5) PSIG DECREASING
A/C CLUTCH DIODE
A/C CLUTCH FIELD COIL
A/C HEATER CONTROL
HOT IN RUN AND START
HOT IN RUN
FUSE PANEL
BLOWER SWITCH
BLOWER MOTOR
BLOWER MOTOR RESISTOR
THERMAL LIMITER
CLUTCH CYCLING PRESSURE SWITCH
CLOSES AT 45 PSI INCREASING
OPENS AT 24.5 ± 1.5 PSI DECREASING
WOT CUTOUT RELAY (NORMALLY CLOSED)
WIRE COLORS
BK - BLACK
BK/LG - BLACK/LIGHT GREEN
BK/Y - BLACK/YELLOW
BR/O - BROWN/ORANGE
DB/LG - DARK BLUE/LIGHT GREEN
GY/Y - GRAY/YELLOW
LG/P - LIGHT GREEN/PURPLE
LG/W - LIGHT GREEN/WHITE
O/BK - ORANGE/BLACK
O/LB - ORANGE/LIGHT BLUE
PK/LB - PINK/LIGHT BLUE
R - RED
W/P - WHITE/PURPLE
Y/R - YELLOW/RED
SYMBOLS
CONNECTOR
SPLICE
GROUND

Air conditioning/heater system wiring schematic – 1990–91 Mustang

SYSTEM DIAGNOSIS

Automatic Temperature Control Systems

Crown Victoria, Grand Marquis and Town Car

DIAGNOSIS AND TESTING

Due to the interactions of all heating, ventilation and air conditioning functions in an automatic temperature control system, it is essential that the entire climate control system be checked to fully analyze the proper failure condition(s) and isolate the inoperative component(s). After a preliminary check to verify the complaint, a check of the supporting systems should be performed:

- Heat to heater core
- Refrigerant to evaporator core
- Air distribution for proper location and quantity

The following is divided into 2 parts. The first part contains a general checkout procedure to be used when the fault is not fully defined or more than 1 problem exists. The second part contains a detailed checkout procedure to isolate the fault to a component.

SYSTEM CHECK

The engine must be warm and above 1200 rpm. The vehicle interior must be 70°–80°F (21°–27°C).

1. Check the air distribution for proper operation in each function. If the fault is found, it must be corrected before proceeding to the detailed checkout procedure.
2. Set the function selector to the **VENT** position. Check the blower operation in low and high. If okay, move the selector to **AUTO**. If the blower does not operate properly in all positions, correct the inoperative component and proceed. Follow the diagnosis procedure in the auto blower diagnostic chart.
3. Cycle the temperature lever from 65°–85°F and observe the blower speed change and discharge temperature change. The automatic temperature control performance chart indicates the relationship of these functions.
4. Move the temperature lever back to 65°F and observe the blower and temperature outputs.
5. With the temperature lever still at 65°F, move the function lever to **NORM A/C**.The fresh air/recirculating door should open and the air conditioning compressor clutch should engage to produce colder discharge temperatures.
6. Move the temperature lever to 72°–75°F. The blower speed should reduce to low or medium low and the discharge temperature rise to a more moderate level.

COMPONENT CHECK

Automatic temperature control malfunctions can be divided into 3 groups.

- Improper discharge temperature control
- Improper blower speed control
- Improper system inlet control

The most common cause of failures in the system are vacuum leaks and aspirator hose connections. Cable adjustment is also a problem on 1989 vehicles. The following is a detailed checkout procedure to fully analyze the automatic temperature control system and isolate the inoperative component.

A vacuum gauge, voltmeter and continuity tester are required to perform the tests. The engine must be warm, run for at least 10 minutes, above 1200 rpm and the vehicle interior temperature must be 70°–80°F (21°–27°C).

Insufficient or No Heat—1989 Vehicles

Observe the servo vacuum with the temperature lever at 85°F. If 3 in. Hg. or lower, check for hot heater hoses to and from the heater core and that the servo positions the blend door in the full heat position. If over 3 in. Hg., disconnect the line from the servo and note the discharge temperature. If heat is available, check the sensor cable adjustment. If okay, replace the sensor. If no heat is available, correct the fault in the cooling system.

Insufficient or No Cooling—1989 Vehicles

Observe the servo vacuum with the temperature lever at 65°F. If over 12 in. Hg. and there is no cooling, check the refrigerant circuit and recirc door circuit. If under 12 in. Hg., check the sensor cable adjustment. If okay, ensure vacuum is available at the sensor. If okay, replace the sensor.

Discharge Temperature Rises on Acceleration—1989 Vehicles

Observe the servo vacuum under load. If it drops, an inoperative check valve or a vacuum leak exists. A severe leak will result in an air distribution shift to DEFROST.

AUTOMATIC TEMPERATURE CONTROL PERFORMANCE CHECK AT 70°–80°F INTERIOR TEMPERATURE—1990–91 CROWN VICTORIA, GRAND MARQUIS AND TOWN CAR

Temperature Lever Position	Discharge Temperature	Auto Blower Speeds
65	Cool	Hi Med Hi Med Lo Lo Med Lo Med Hi
85	Warm	Hi

AUTOMATIC TEMPERATURE CONTROL PERFORMANCE CHECK AT 70°–80°F INTERIOR TEMPERATURE—1989 CROWN VICTORIA, GRAND MARQUIS AND TOWN CAR

Temperature Lever Position	Servo Vacuum①	Discharge Temperature	Auto Blower Speeds
65	High (12 in. hg. min.)	Cool	Hi Med Hi Med Lo Lo Med Lo Med Hi
85	Low (0-3 in. hg.)	Warm	Hi

①Vacuum level changes approximately .3 in. hg. per degree Fahrenheit interior change.

AUTO BLOWER DIAGNOSIS—1989 CROWN VICTORIA, GRAND MARQUIS AND TOWN CAR

CONDITION	POSSIBLE SOURCE	ACTION
• No blower any speed, any function.	• Blower leads disconnected at blower motor. • 30 amp fuse in blower circuit open. • Motor inoperative. • Connector at control head open.	• Connect blower leads. • Replace fuse. • Replace blower motor. • Service open at control head.
• No blower in FLOOR Position. **NOTE: Engine coolant Temperature must be above 43°C (110°F).**	• Open in TBL circuit at: a. Control Head b. Upper right side of I/P c. At TBL switch under hood • Low coolant level (not activating switch). • Inoperative or missing TBL.	• Service open as necessary. (Two wires in circuit Dark Blue and Orange). • Service coolant level as necessary. • Replace TBL.
• Blower does not shut off in OFF position.	• Selector switch in control head inoperative. • Short in 14401 harness.	• Replace selector switch. • Service short as necesary.
• Blower on at all times in FLOOR position (no cold engine lockout). **NOTE: Engine coolant temperature must be below 43°C (110°F) for cold engine lockout operation.**	• Inoperative TBL. • Short in TBL circuit wiring (dark blue and orange).	• Replace TBL. • Service short in wiring.
• Low blower speed only, no intermediate or high speeds.	• Connector at blower switch open at control head (grey). • Connector at ash tray open at blower switch jumper (green).	• Service open at connector. • Service open at connector.
• Low blower only in AUTO., manual speeds OK.	• ATC servo connector open. • ATC servo inoperative. • ATC sensor inoperative.	• Service open connector. • Replace servo. • Replace sensor.
• High blower only, no low or intermediate speeds. AUTO high OK, no other speeds in AUTO. **NOTE: High blower grounds directly to buss bar. Does not need resistor connector.**	• Blower resistor connector open. • Connector for resistor jumper open (under hood). • Resistor inoperative (open thermal blower limiter). • Ground wire not connected under hood.	• Service connector as necessary. • Service open in connector. • Replace resistor. • Secure ground wire as necessary.
• AUTO high run in low speed, all other AUTO and manual speeds OK.	• Ground wire on ATC jumper harness not connected to buss bar.	• Secure ground wire to buss bar. (AUTO high grounds from servo switch through ATC jumper harness.)
• Manual high runs in low, all other speeds OK.	• Ground wire from 14401 harness not connected to buss bar.	• Secure ground wire to buss bar.
• Low and high speeds OK, no intermediate speeds.	• Connectors in right cowl panel open or misconnected.	• Service connectors in right cowl panel as necessary.
• Does not change speed in AUTO, manual speeds OK (move temperature lever to extreme positions). **NOTE: Auto blower speed changes are determined by ATC servo position. High blower at each extreme (heat — no vacuum, cool-high vacuum), lower in center position.**	• Servo moving (temperature changing). • Servo not moving a. Vacuum circuit from sensor. b. Door jammed in plenum. c. Inoperative servo.	• Low speed only replace servo. • Service as follows: a. Service vacuum circuit from sensor. b. Free up door in plenum c. Replace servo.

AUTO BLOWER DIAGNOSIS—1990–91 CROWN VICTORIA, GRAND MARQUIS AND TOWN CAR

CONDITION	POSSIBLE SOURCE	ACTION
• No Blower Any Speed, Any Function	• Blower leads disconnected at blower motor. • 30 amp fuse in blower circuit open. • Motor inoperative. • Connector at control head open.	• Connect blower leads. • Replace fuse. • Replace blower motor. • Service open at control head.
• No Blower in FLOOR Position **NOTE: Engine coolant temperature must be above 43°C (110°F).**	• Open in TBL circuit at: a. Control Head b. Upper right side of I/P c. At TBL switch under hood • Low coolant level (not activating switch). • Inoperative or missing TBL.	• Service open as necessary. (Two wires in circuit Dark Blue and Orange). • Service coolant level as necessary. • Replace TBL.
• Blower Does Not Shut Off in OFF Position.	• Selector switch in control head inoperative. • Short in 14401 harness.	• Replace selector switch. • Service short as necesary.
• Blower On At All Times in FLOOR Position (No Cold Engine Lockout) **NOTE: Engine coolant temperature must be below 43°C (110°F) for cold engine lockout operation.**	• Inoperative TBL. • Short in TBL circuit wiring (dark blue and orange).	• Replace TBL. • Service short in wiring.
• Low Blower Speed Only, No Intermediate or High Speeds	• Connector at blower switch open at control head (gray). • Connector at ash receptacle open at blower switch jumper (green).	• Service open at connector. • Service open at connector.
• Low Blower Only in AUTO, Manual Speeds OK	• ATC servo connector open. • ATC servo inoperative. • ATC sensor inoperative.	• Service open connector. • Replace servo. • Replace sensor.
• High Blower Only, No Low or Intermediate Speeds. AUTO High OK, No Other Speeds in AUTO **NOTE: High blower grounds directly to buss bar. Does not need resistor connector.**	• Ground wire not connected under hood.	• Secure ground wire as necessary.
• AUTO High Run in Low Speed, All Other AUTO and Manual Speeds OK	• Ground wire on ATC jumper harness not connected to buss bar.	• Secure ground wire to buss bar. (AUTO high grounds from servo switch through ATC jumper harness.)
• Manual High Runs in Low, All Other Speeds OK	• Ground wire from 14401 harness not connected to buss bar.	• Secure ground wire to buss bar.
• Low and High Speeds OK, No Intermediate Speeds	• Connectors in right cowl panel open or misconnected.	• Service connectors in right cowl panel as necessary.

HISSING AUTOMATIC TEMPERATURE CONTROL VACUUM SYSTEM OR CONTROL ASSEMBLY SELECTOR VALVE—CROWN VICTORIA, GRAND MARQUIS AND TOWN CAR

TEST STEP	RESULT	ACTION TO TAKE
A0 CHECK CONNECTORS		
• Check in-line and control assembly multiple connectors for proper installation	Hiss stops ▶	RECHECK system for proper operation.
• Listen for hiss.	Hiss continues ▶	GO to **A1**.
A1 DETERMINE LEAKING VALVE POSITION(S)		
• Move function lever to determine what selector valve position(s) are leaking.	All leak ▶	REFER to "All Function Selector Valve Positions Leak" diagnostic chart.
	Some leak but not all ▶	GO to **A2**.
A2 DETERMINE LEAKING TUBE(S) COLOR		
• Determine what color tube(s) are used in leaking function selector valve positions (Refer to Air Flow Schematic and Vacuum Control Chart). • Pinch off suspect tube(s), one at a time, near each respective vacuum motor.	Hiss stops ▶	CHECK tube connection to vacuum motor and REPAIR and/or RE-CONNECT if loose or split. If hiss still continues, REPLACE vacuum motor.*
• Listen for hiss.	Hiss continues ▶	GO to **A3**.
A3 PINCH OFF SUSPECT TUBE(S)		
• Pinch off suspect tube(s), one at a time, near control assembly and/or in-line connector.	Hiss stops ▶	CHECK tube for cut or damage. REPAIR if required.
• Listen for hiss.	Hiss continues ▶	REPLACE function vacuum selector valve.

*Never manually operate any vacuum motor or vacuum motor controlled door — this may cause internal damage to the vacuum motor diaphragm.

ALL FUNCTION SELECTOR VALVE POSITIONS LEAK 1989 CROWN VICTORIA, GRAND MARQUIS AND TOWN CAR

TEST STEP	RESULT	ACTION TO TAKE
B0 MOVE TEMPERATURE CONTROL LEVER		
• Move temperature control lever from 65° to 85°.	Hiss stops at some settings ▶	REFER to "Some Temperature Control Lever Positions Leak" diagnostic chart.
	Hiss continues ▶	GO to **B1**.
B1 CHECK VACUUM SOURCE TUBE		
• Check vacuum source tube (black) from reservoir to control assembly for cut or disconnection. Also check at diverter valve, TBL Switch and sensor.	Hiss stops ▶	SERVICE tube.
	Hiss continues ▶	GO to **B2**.
B2 PINCH OFF SOURCE TUBE		
• Pinch off source tube (black) at control assembly.	Hiss stops ▶	REPLACE selector valve.
	Hiss continues ▶	GO to **B3**.
B3 PINCH OFF SOURCE TUBE		
• Pinch off source tube (black) at diverter valve.	Hiss stops ▶	REPLACE servo assembly.
	Hiss continues ▶	GO to **B4**.
B4 PINCH OFF SOURCE TUBE		
• Pinch off source tube (black) at TBL Switch.	Hiss stops ▶	REPLACE TBL Switch.
	Hiss continues ▶	GO to **B5**.
B5 PINCH OFF SOURCE TUBE		
• Pinch off source tube (black) at ATC Sensor.	Hiss stops ▶	GO to **B6**.
	Hiss continues ▶	RECHECK source tubes (black), connections, reservoir and check valve.
B6 PINCH OFF TAN TUBE		
• Pinch off tan tube at ATC Sensor.	Hiss stops ▶	GO to **B7**.
	Hiss continues ▶	REPLACE ATC Sensor.
B7 PINCH OFF TAN TUBE		
• Pinch off tan tube at servo motor.	Hiss stops ▶	REPLACE servo motor.
	Hiss continues ▶	SERVICE tube.

ALL FUNCTION SELECTOR VALVE POSITIONS LEAK 1990–91 CROWN VICTORIA, GRAND MARQUIS AND TOWN CAR

TEST STEP	RESULT ▶	ACTION TO TAKE
B0 MOVE TEMPERATURE CONTROL LEVER		
• Move temperature control lever from 65° to 85°.	Hiss stops at some settings ▶	REFER to "Some Temperature Control Lever Positions Leak" diagnostic chart.
	Hiss continues ▶	GO to **B1**.
B1 CHECK VACUUM SOURCE TUBE		
• Check vacuum source tube (black) from reservoir to control assembly for cut or disconnection.	Hiss stops ▶	SERVICE tube.
	Hiss continues ▶	GO to **B2**.
B2 PINCH OFF SOURCE TUBE		
• Pinch off source tube (black) at control assembly.	Hiss stops ▶	REPLACE selector valve.
	Hiss continues ▶	GO to **B3**.
B3 PINCH OFF SOURCE TUBE		
• Pinch off source tube (black) at TBL Switch.	Hiss stops ▶	REPLACE TBL Switch.
	Hiss continues ▶	GO to **B4**.
B4 PINCH OFF SOURCE TUBE		
• Pinch off source tube (black) at ATC Sensor.	Hiss stops ▶	SERVICE tube.
	Hiss continues ▶	RECHECK source tubes (black), connections, reservoir and check valve.

SOME TEMPERATURE CONTROL LEVER POSITIONS LEAK—1989 CROWN VICTORIA, GRAND MARQUIS AND TOWN CAR

TEST STEP	RESULT ▶	ACTION TO TAKE
C0 PINCH OFF SOURCE TUBE		
• Pinch off source tube (black) at diverter valve.	Hiss stops ▶	GO to **C1**.
	Hiss continues	GO to **C3**.
C1 PINCH OFF PURPLE TUBE		
• Pinch off purple tube at diverter valve.	Hiss stops ▶	GO to **C2**.
	Hiss continues	REPLACE servo assembly.
C2 PINCH OFF PURPLE TUBE		
• Pinch off purple tube at control assembly.	Hiss stops ▶	REPLACE selector valve.
	Hiss continues	SERVICE tube.
C3 PINCH OFF SOURCE TUBE		
• Pinch off source tube (black) at ATC Sensor.	Hiss stops ▶	GO to **C4**.
	Hiss continues	RECHECK source tubes (black), connections, reservoir and check valve.
C4 PINCH OFF TAN TUBE		
• Pinch off tan tube at ATC Sensor.	Hiss stops ▶	GO to **C5**.
	Hiss continues	REPLACE ATC Sensor.
C5 PINCH OFF TAN TUBE		
• Pinch off tan tube at servo motor.	Hiss stops ▶	REPLACE servo motor
	Hiss continues	SERVICE tube.

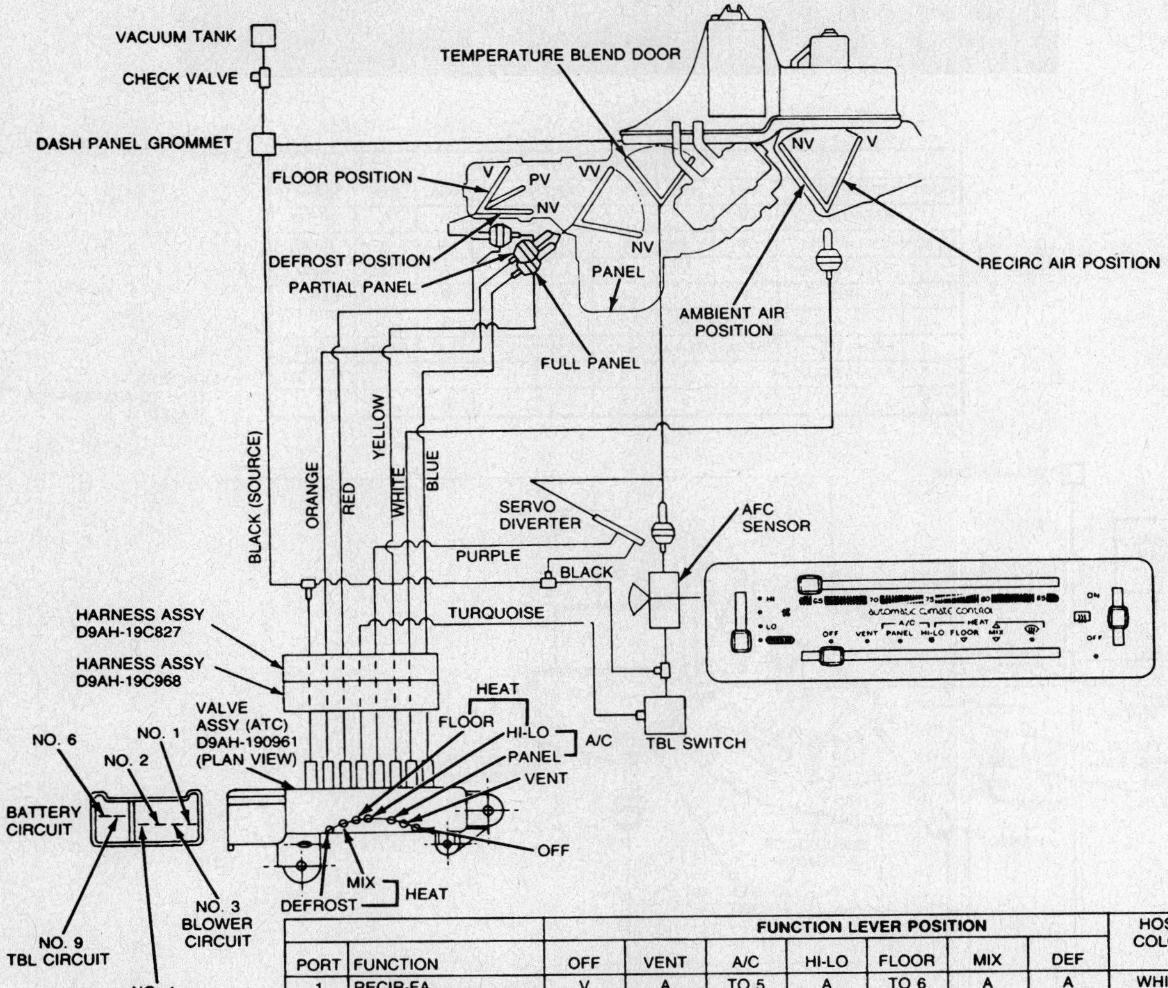
VACUUM TANK
CHECK VALVE
DASH PANEL GROMMET
TEMPERATURE BLEND DOOR
FLOOR POSITION
V
PV
VV
NV
NV
V
NV
DEFROST POSITION
PARTIAL PANEL
PANEL
RECIRC AIR POSITION
AMBIENT AIR POSITION
FULL PANEL
BLACK (SOURCE)
ORANGE
RED
YELLOW
WHITE
BLUE
SERVO DIVERTER
AFC SENSOR
PURPLE
BLACK
TURQUOISE
HARNESS ASSY D9AH-19C827
HARNESS ASSY D9AH-19C968
HEAT
VALVE ASSY (ATC) D9AH-190961 (PLAN VIEW)
FLOOR
HI-LO
A/C
PANEL
VENT
TBL SWITCH
NO. 6
NO. 1
NO. 2
BATTERY CIRCUIT
OFF
MIX
HEAT
DEFROST
NO. 3 BLOWER CIRCUIT
NO. 9 TBL CIRCUIT
NO. 4 CLUTCH CIRCUIT

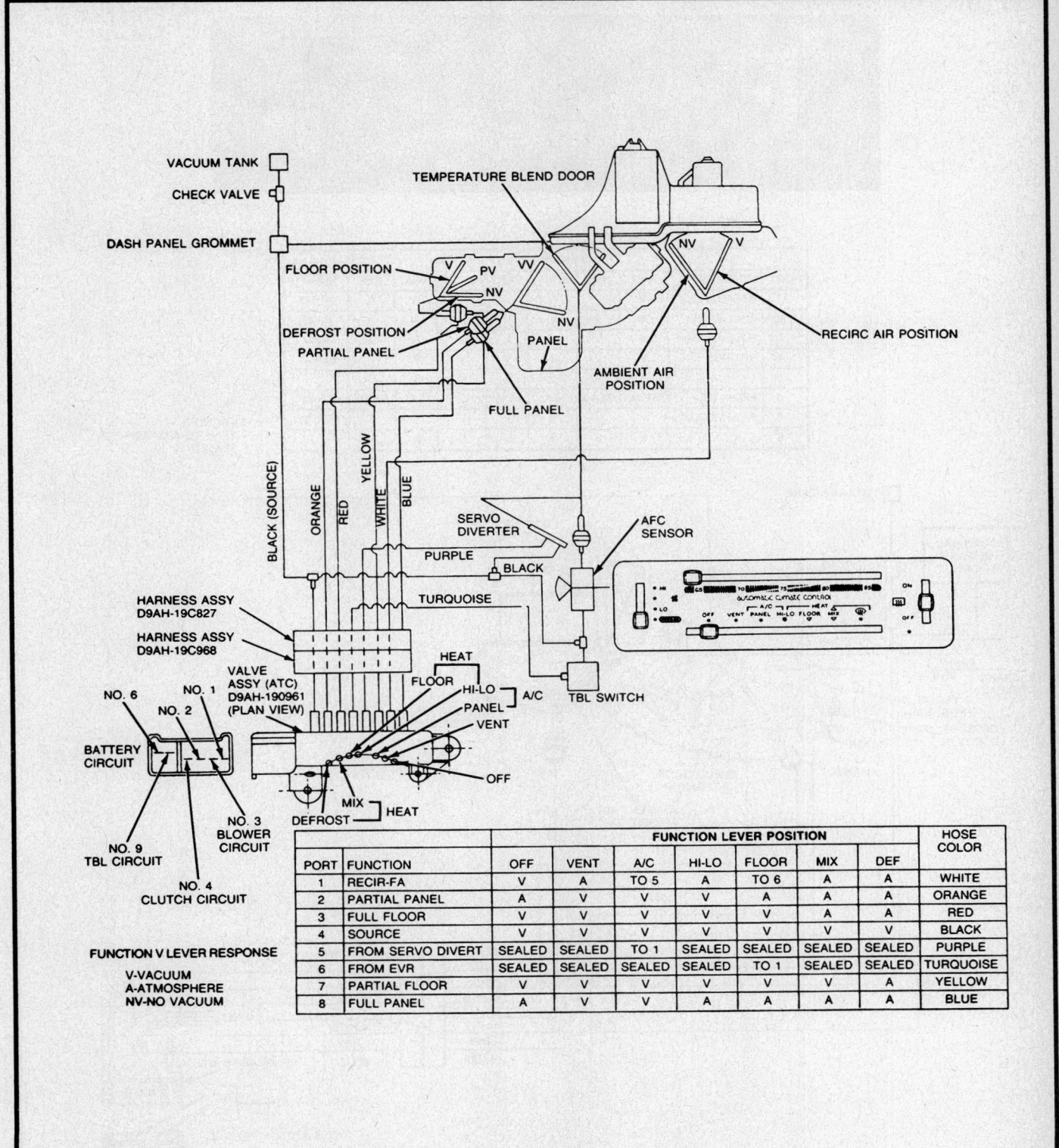

		FUNCTION LEVER POSITION							HOSE COLOR
PORT	FUNCTION	OFF	VENT	A/C	HI-LO	FLOOR	MIX	DEF	
1	RECIR-FA	V	A	TO 5	A	TO 6	A	A	WHITE
2	PARTIAL PANEL	A	V	V	V	A	A	A	ORANGE
3	FULL FLOOR	V	V	V	V	V	A	A	RED
4	SOURCE	V	V	V	V	V	V	V	BLACK
5	FROM SERVO DIVERT	SEALED	SEALED	TO 1	SEALED	SEALED	SEALED	SEALED	PURPLE
6	FROM EVR	SEALED	SEALED	SEALED	SEALED	TO 1	SEALED	SEALED	TURQUOISE
7	PARTIAL FLOOR	V	V	V	V	V	V	A	YELLOW
8	FULL PANEL	A	V	V	A	A	A	A	BLUE

FUNCTION V LEVER RESPONSE
V-VACUUM
A-ATMOSPHERE
NV-NO VACUUM

Automatic temperature control system airflow and vacuum control chart—1989 Crown Victoria, Grand Marquis and Town Car

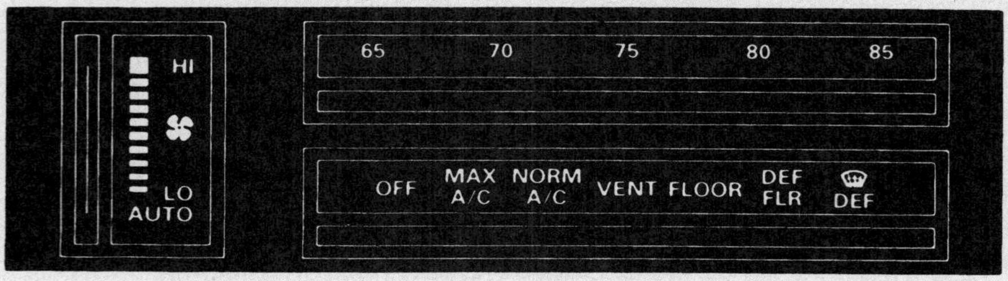
HI
LO
AUTO
65
70
75
80
85
OFF
MAX A/C
NORM A/C
VENT
FLOOR
DEF FLR
DEF

PORT	FUNCTION	MODE LEVER POSITION OFF	MAX	NORM	VENT	FLOOR	MIX	DEF	HOSE COLOR
1	RECIRC-F/A	V	V	A	A	A	A	A	WHITE
2	FULL PANEL	A	V	V	V	A	A	A	BLUE
3	FULL FLOOR	V	V	V	V	V	A	A	RED
4	SOURCE	V	V	V	V	V	V	V	BLACK
5		S	S	S	S	S	S	S	
6	FROM TBL	SEAL	SEAL	SEAL	SEAL	TO 1	SEAL	SEAL	GRAY
7	PART FLOOR	V	V	V	V	V	V	A	YELLOW
8		S	S	S	S	S	S	S	

V = VACUUM
A = VENT TO ATMOSPHERE
S = SEALED

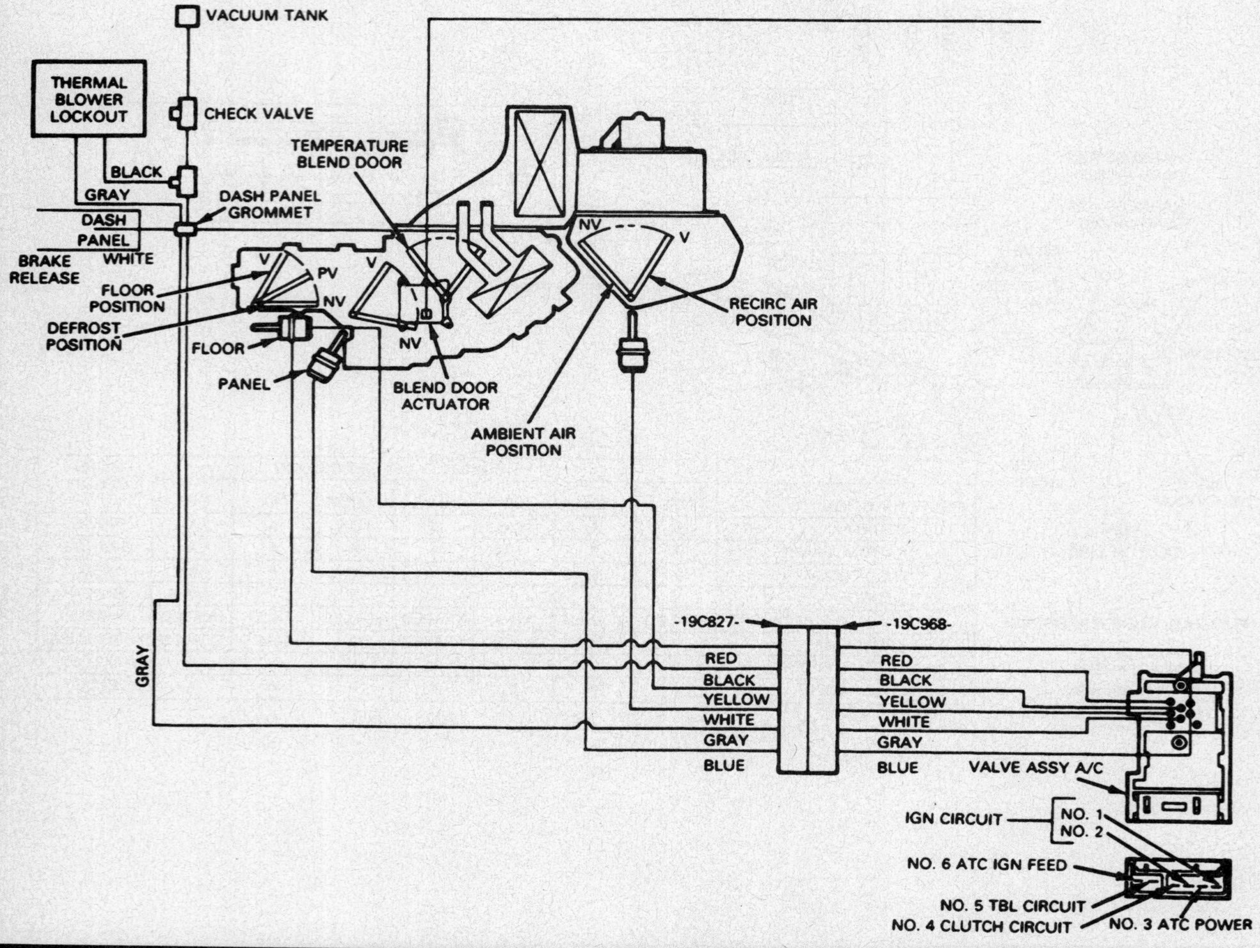
VACUUM TANK
THERMAL BLOWER LOCKOUT
CHECK VALVE
BLACK
GRAY
DASH PANEL
DASH PANEL GROMMET
TEMPERATURE BLEND DOOR
BRAKE RELEASE
WHITE
FLOOR POSITION
DEFROST POSITION
FLOOR
PANEL
V
PV
NV
BLEND DOOR ACTUATOR
AMBIENT AIR POSITION
RECIRC AIR POSITION
-19C827-
-19C968-
RED
BLACK
YELLOW
WHITE
GRAY
BLUE
VALVE ASSY A/C
IGN CIRCUIT
NO. 1
NO. 2
NO. 6 ATC IGN FEED
NO. 5 TBL CIRCUIT
NO. 4 CLUTCH CIRCUIT
NO. 3 ATC POWER

Automatic temperature control system airflow and vacuum control chart—1990–91 Crown Victoria, Grand Marquis and Town Car

SWITCH SCHEMATIC	TERMINAL CONNECTIONS						
	OFF	A/C		VENT	HEAT		DEFROST
		MAX	NORM		FLR	MIX	
5, 6	5-6	5-6	5-6	5-6	NONE	5-6	5-6
CURRENT							
1, 3; 2, 4	NONE	1-3 2-4	1-3 2-4	1-3	1-3	1-3 2-4	1-3 2-4
CURRENT/AMPS							

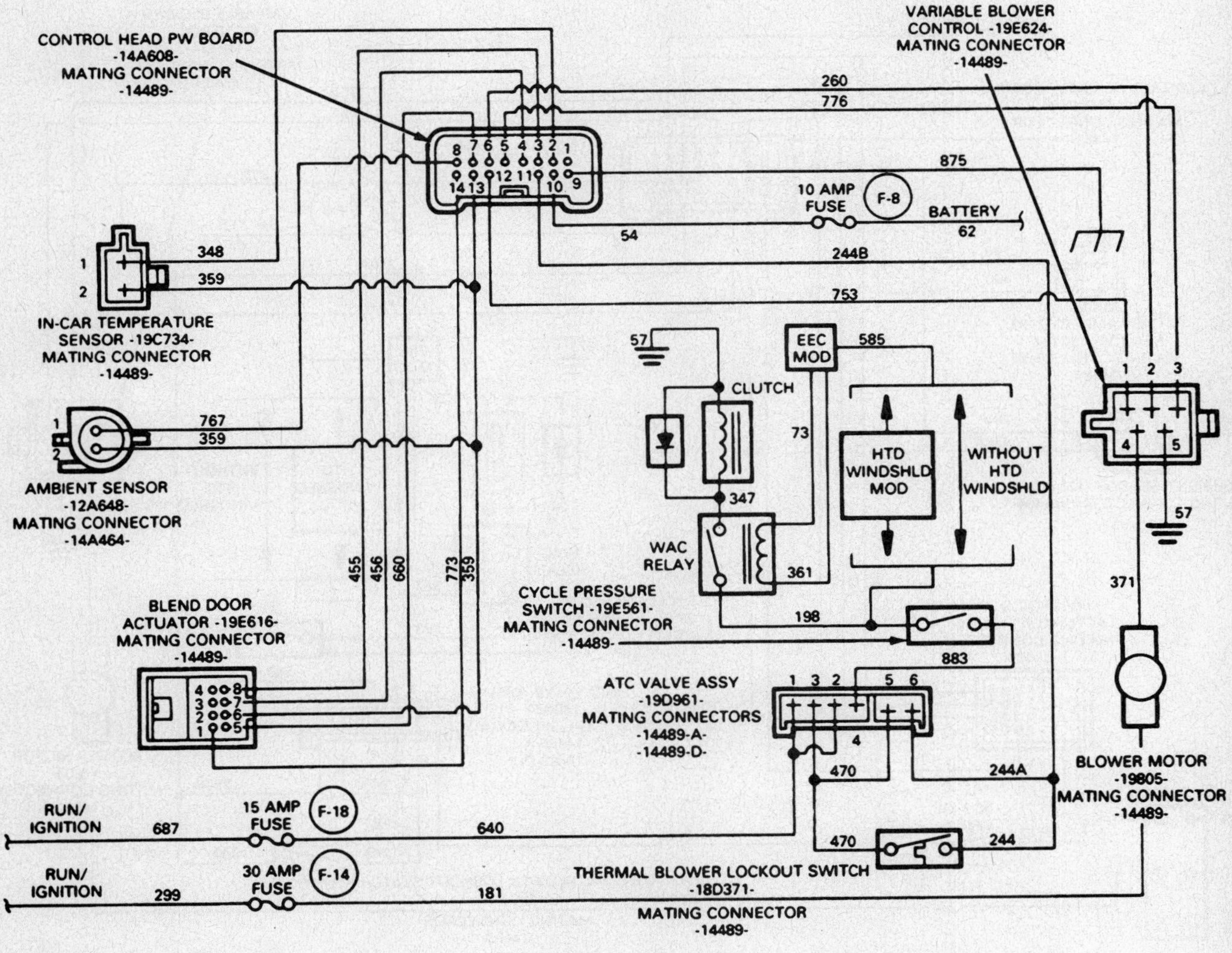
CONTROL HEAD PW BOARD
-14A608-
MATING CONNECTOR
-14489-
VARIABLE BLOWER
CONTROL -19E624-
MATING CONNECTOR
-14489-
260
776
875
10 AMP FUSE
F-8
BATTERY
62
54
244B
753
348
359
IN-CAR TEMPERATURE
SENSOR -19C734-
MATING CONNECTOR
-14489-
57
EEC MOD
585
CLUTCH
73
HTD WINDSHLD MOD
WITHOUT HTD WINDSHLD
767
359
AMBIENT SENSOR
-12A648-
MATING CONNECTOR
-14A464-
347
WAC RELAY
361
371
455
456
660
773
359
BLEND DOOR
ACTUATOR -19E616-
MATING CONNECTOR
-14489-
CYCLE PRESSURE
SWITCH -19E561-
MATING CONNECTOR
-14489-
198
883
ATC VALVE ASSY
-19D961-
MATING CONNECTORS
-14489-A-
-14489-D-
470
244A
BLOWER MOTOR
-19805-
MATING CONNECTOR
-14489-
RUN/ IGNITION
687
15 AMP FUSE
F-18
640
470
244
RUN/ IGNITION
299
30 AMP FUSE
F-14
181
THERMAL BLOWER LOCKOUT SWITCH
-18D371-
MATING CONNECTOR
-14489-

Automatic temperature control system wiring schematic and continuity test—1990–91 Town Car

SWITCH SCHEMATIC	TERMINAL CONNECTIONS						
	OFF	A/C		VENT	HEAT		DEFROST
		MAX	NORM		FLR	MIX	
5, 6	5-6	5-6	5-6	5-6	NONE	5-6	5-6
CURRENT							
1, 2, 3, 4	NONE	1-3 2-4	1-3 2-4	1-3	1-3	1-3 2-4	1-3 2-4
CURRENT/AMPS							

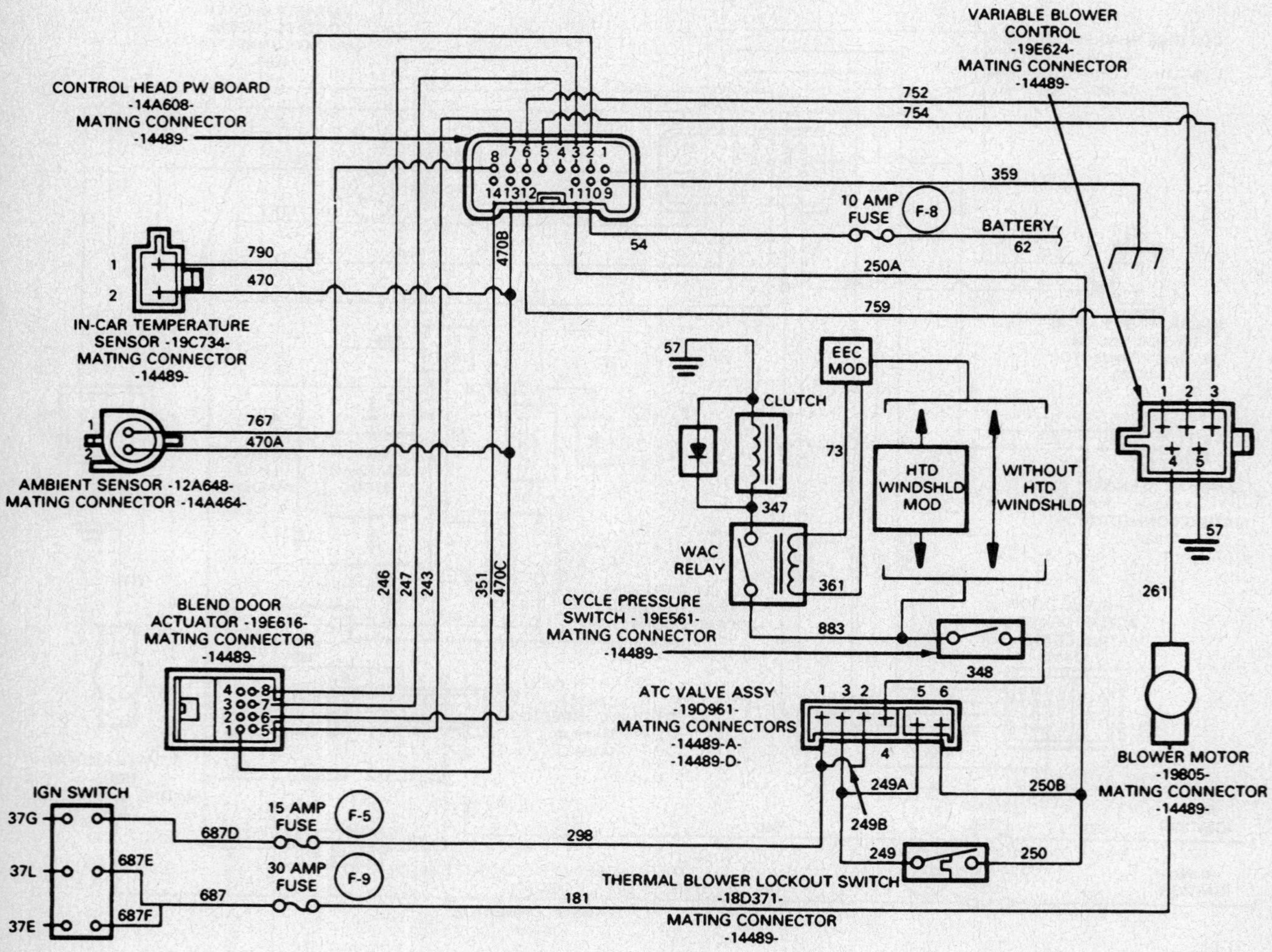
VARIABLE BLOWER CONTROL -19E624- MATING CONNECTOR -14489-
CONTROL HEAD PW BOARD -14A608- MATING CONNECTOR -14489-
752
754
359
10 AMP FUSE
F-8
BATTERY
62
54
250A
759
790
470
IN-CAR TEMPERATURE SENSOR -19C734- MATING CONNECTOR -14489-
470B
57
EEC MOD
CLUTCH
73
HTD WINDSHLD MOD
WITHOUT HTD WINDSHLD
347
WAC RELAY
361
767
470A
AMBIENT SENSOR -12A648- MATING CONNECTOR -14A464-
246
247
243
351
470C
BLEND DOOR ACTUATOR -19E616- MATING CONNECTOR -14489-
CYCLE PRESSURE SWITCH - 19E561- MATING CONNECTOR -14489-
883
348
ATC VALVE ASSY -19D961- MATING CONNECTORS -14489-A- -14489-D-
249A
250B
249B
249
250
261
BLOWER MOTOR -19805- MATING CONNECTOR -14489-
IGN SWITCH
37G
37L
37E
687D
687E
687F
687
15 AMP FUSE
F-5
30 AMP FUSE
F-9
298
181
THERMAL BLOWER LOCKOUT SWITCH -18D371- MATING CONNECTOR -14489-

Automatic temperature control system wiring schematic and continuity test—1990–91 Crown Victoria and Grand Marquis

BLOWER SPEED CONTROLLER FUNCTIONAL TEST 1, SYMPTOM—BLOWER WILL NOT RUN—1990–91 CROWN VICTORIA, GRAND MARQUIS AND TOWN CAR

Test Condition:
Start engine, set control to MAX A/C, set blower switch to any blower speed. If blower does not turn on:

TEST STEP		RESULT	▶ ACTION TO TAKE
B1	VOLTAGE CHECK		
	• Disconnect blower speed controller (BSC) connector. Turn ignition to ON position and measure voltage between pin 4 and pin 5.	0 volts ▶	CHECK fuse
		More than 10 volts ▶	GO to **B2.**
B2	VOLTAGE CHECK		
	• Measure voltage between pin 2 and pin 5 of BSC.	Less than 9 volts ▶	CHECK wiring
		More than 10 volts ▶	REPLACE BSC.

BLOWER SPEED CONTROLLER FUNCTIONAL TEST 3, SYMPTOM—NO MEDIUM OR LOW BLOWER SPEEDS 1990–91 CROWN VICTORIA, GRAND MARQUIS AND TOWN CAR

Test Condition:
Start engine, set control to MAX A/C, set blower switch to MED or LOW. If there is no blower operation:

TEST STEP		RESULT	▶ ACTION TO TAKE
D1	VOLTAGE CHECK		
	• Disconnect blower speed controller (BSC) connector. Turn ignition to ON position and measure voltage between pin 2 and pin 5.	More than 10 volts ▶	REPLACE BSC.
		Less than 9 volts ▶	CHECK wiring

BLOWER SPEED CONTROLLER FUNCTIONAL TEST 2, SYMPTOM—HIGH BLOWER ALWAYS ON IN ALL SWITCH POSITIONS—1990–91 CROWN VICTORIA, GRAND MARQUIS AND TOWN CAR

Test Condition:
Start engine, set control to MAX A/C, set blower switch to MED. If blower remains in high speed:

TEST STEP		RESULT	▶ ACTION TO TAKE
C1	CHECK BLOWER SWITCH		
	• Disconnect blower speed controller (BSC) connector. Turn ignition to ON position and measure voltage between pin 3 and pin 5 of BSC while changing blower speeds.	More than 10 volts (for all blower speeds) ▶	CHECK wiring
		0 volts (for low speeds) ▶	GO to **C2.**
C2	CHECK BLOWER SWITCH		
	• Disconnect pin 2 from connector. Reconnect plug. Set control to low blower.	If blower is off (at low speed) (0 voltage at blower) ▶	CHECK wiring
		Blower is on at high speed. ▶	REPLACE BSC.

BLOWER SPEED CONTROLLER FUNCTIONAL TEST 4, SYMPTOM—NO HIGH BLOWER SPEED—1990–91 CROWN VICTORIA, GRAND MARQUIS AND TOWN CAR

Test Condition:
Start engine, set control to MAX A/C, set blower switch to LOW or MED (blower turns), then switch blower to high speed. If blower does not go to full high speed:

TEST STEP		RESULT	▶ ACTION TO TAKE
E1	VOLTAGE CHECK		
	• Disconnect blower speed controller (BSC) connector. Turn ignition to ON position and measure voltage between pin 3 and pin 5.	0 volts (on HI speed) ▶	CHECK wiring
		More than 10 volts (on HI speed) ▶	REPLACE BSC.

AUTOMATIC TEMPERATURE CONTROL QUICK TEST—1990–91 CROWN VICTORIA, GRAND MARQUIS AND TOWN CAR

Test Condition:

The following is a "quick guide" and assumes that interior temperature is 70-80°F. It also assumes that there is a reasonable chance that A/C refrigerant system (compressor, etc.) is functioning.

	TEST STEP	RESULT	ACTION TO TAKE
1	• Operate System	• No blower operation	• Verify that blower motor leads are connected at blower motor. • Verify that four fuses are good (two in underhood power distribution box and two under dash). • Verify that blower motor works. • Verify power wiring continuity between fuse panel and ATC control assembly. • If fuses are good, blower motor is functional and there is continuity between fuse panel and ATC control assembly. Replace electro-vacuum switch on control assembly.
		• Mode selections incorrect or erratic	• Check for pinched or poorly connected vacuum lines. • Replace electro-vacuum switch on control assembly.
		• No blower operation in AUTO, or from LO to HI	• Make sure that blower motor and VBC have a good electrical connection. • Check 30 amp fuse (underhood power distribution box and under dash). • If above are good, suspect either a wiring short or a damaged ATC control module.

	TEST STEP	RESULT	ACTION TO TAKE
2	• Operate System • Select Different Blower Speeds	• Blower stays at maximum speed in all settings	• Refer to variable blower speed control functional test. • Verify wiring continuity between VBC and the ATC control module. • If above checks OK, replace the ATC control module.
		• With blower switch in AUTO, discharge temperature will not change with change in temperature lever position. Blower speed does change with temperature lever change	• Verify that blend door actuator electrical connection is good and that wiring continuity exists between blend door actuator and ATC control module. • Refer to blend door actuator functional test.
		• With blower switch in AUTO, discharge temperature remains at full heat no matter what position temperature lever is in. Blower at maximum speed	• Verify that aspirator hose is connected at dash panel and to in-car temperature sensor. • Verify that in-car temperature sensor electrical connection is connected and that electrical continuity exists between sensor and ATC control module. • Verify ambient temperature sensor electrical connection is connected and that electrical continuity exists between sensor and ATC control module.
		• With blower switch in AUTO, blower speed does not change when temperature lever is slowly moved from 65°F to 85°F. Discharge temperature does change	• Verify that in-car temperature sensor electrical connection is good and that wiring continuity exists between sensor and ATC control module.

AUTOMATIC TEMPERATURE CONTROL QUICK TEST 1990–91 CROWN VICTORIA, GRAND MARQUIS AND TOWN CAR

	TEST STEP	RESULT	ACTION TO TAKE
3	• Operate System. Set temperature selector lever between 72°F and 78°F NOTE: With ambient temperature approximately 24°C (75°F) blower speed should be lower when temperature lever is set between 72°F and 78°F and higher when not in this range.	• Blower speed oscillates rapidly or constantly changes	• Verify that ambient temperature sensor electrical connection is good and that wiring continuity exists between sensor and ATC control module. • Refer to variable blower controller functional test.
4	• Change Blower Speed Setting	• Blower speed does not change • System operates correctly, but does not "seem" to reach maximum heat or cool	• Refer to variable blower controller functional test. • If above checks OK, replace the ATC control module. • Check for loose or intermittent wire connection to ATC control module pin 11 (circuit 244, Y/W) or pin 10 (circuit 54, LG/Y). • Disconnect vehicle battery for 2 minutes and allow system to re-calibrate.
5	• Set Select Lever To Floor NOTE: Engine coolant temperature must be above 43°C (110°F).	• No blower in floor position	• Refer to thermal blower lockout switch functional test. • Verify that circuits 244 (Y/W) and 470 (PK/BK) going to Thermal Blower Lockout have a good connection. • Check for low coolant level.
6	• Set Select Lever To Floor NOTE: Engine coolant temperature must be above 43°C (110°F).	• Blower on at all times (no cold engine lockout)	• Refer to thermal blower lockout switch functional test.
7	• Set Blower Switch To OFF	• Blower does not stop running	• Check for short in 14401 harness. • Replace electro-vacuum selector valve.
8	• Operate System	• Alternates between long periods of heat and long periods of cool	• Verify that aspirator hose is connected at dash panel and to in-car sensor. • Check aspirator tube for blockages.

BLEND DOOR ACTUATOR FUNCTIONAL TEST 1990–91 CROWN VICTORIA, GRAND MARQUIS AND TOWN CAR

TEST STEP	RESULT	ACTION TO TAKE
A1 CHECK BLEND DOOR ACTUATOR		
• Disconnect electrical connector from rear of ATC control module and drive actuator in both directions using any 9-12 volt battery. • The following pins can be jumped to use vehicle battery. The ignition switch must be in RUN position: a) Pin 4 (456, W/LG) (+), to Pin 3 (455, GY/R) (-). This drives actuator CW — maximum cooling. b) Pin 4 (456, W/LG) (-), to Pin 3 (455, GY/R) (+). This drives actuator CCW — maximum heating.	Actuator drives both directions. ▶ Actuator does not drive in both directions. ▶	GO to **A2**. REPLACE blend door actuator.
A2 MEASURE ACTUATOR RESISTANCE		
• Using technique outlined in Step b (above), set actuator to full CCW travel (power 15-20 seconds). • Using any digital or dial type volt-ohmmeter, measure resistance at ATC control module connector as follows: a) Pin 7 (660, Y/LG) to pin 13 (359, BK/W) — 4,500-6,000 ohms b) Pin 14 (773, DG/O) to pin 13 (359, BK/W) — 3,500-6,000 ohms c) Pin 14 (773, DG/O) to pin 7 (660, Y/LG) — 250-1,500 ohms.	All resistance OK ▶ Any resistance not OK ▶	GO to **A3**. REPLACE blend door actuator.
A3 CHECK VEHICLE WIRING		
• Check vehicle wiring harness and connector continuity as shown below. Disconnect connectors from both ATC control module and blend door actuator. Use any digital or dial type volt-ohmmeter: **ATC MODULE CONNECTOR** — **ACTUATOR CONNECTOR** Pin 4 (456, W/LG) to — Pin 7 Pin 3 (455, GY/R) to — Pin 8 Pin 7 (660, Y/LG) to — Pin 5 Pin 13 (359, BK/W) to — Pin 6 Pin 14 (773, DG/O) to — Pin 1	Continuity bad ▶ Continuity good ▶	SERVICE/REPLACE wiring harness. REPLACE ATC control module.

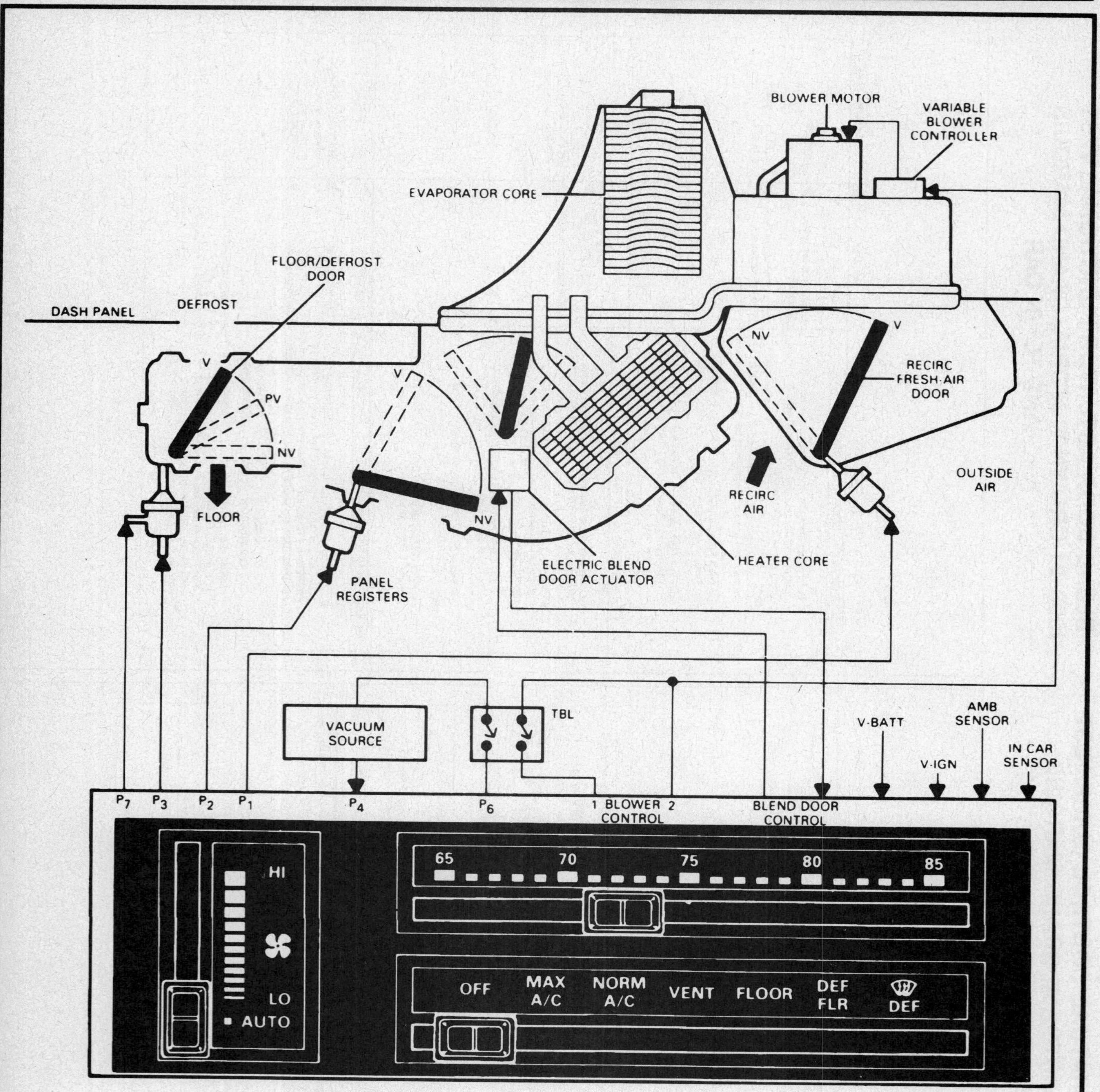
BLOWER MOTOR
VARIABLE BLOWER CONTROLLER
EVAPORATOR CORE
FLOOR/DEFROST DOOR
DASH PANEL
DEFROST
V
PV
NV
FLOOR
V
NV
PANEL REGISTERS
ELECTRIC BLEND DOOR ACTUATOR
HEATER CORE
RECIRC AIR
NV
V
RECIRC FRESH-AIR DOOR
OUTSIDE AIR
VACUUM SOURCE
TBL
V-BATT
AMB SENSOR
V-IGN
IN CAR SENSOR
P7 P3 P2 P1 P4 P6
1 BLOWER 2 CONTROL
BLEND DOOR CONTROL
HI
LO
AUTO
65 70 75 80 85
OFF
MAX A/C
NORM A/C
VENT
FLOOR
DEF FLR
DEF

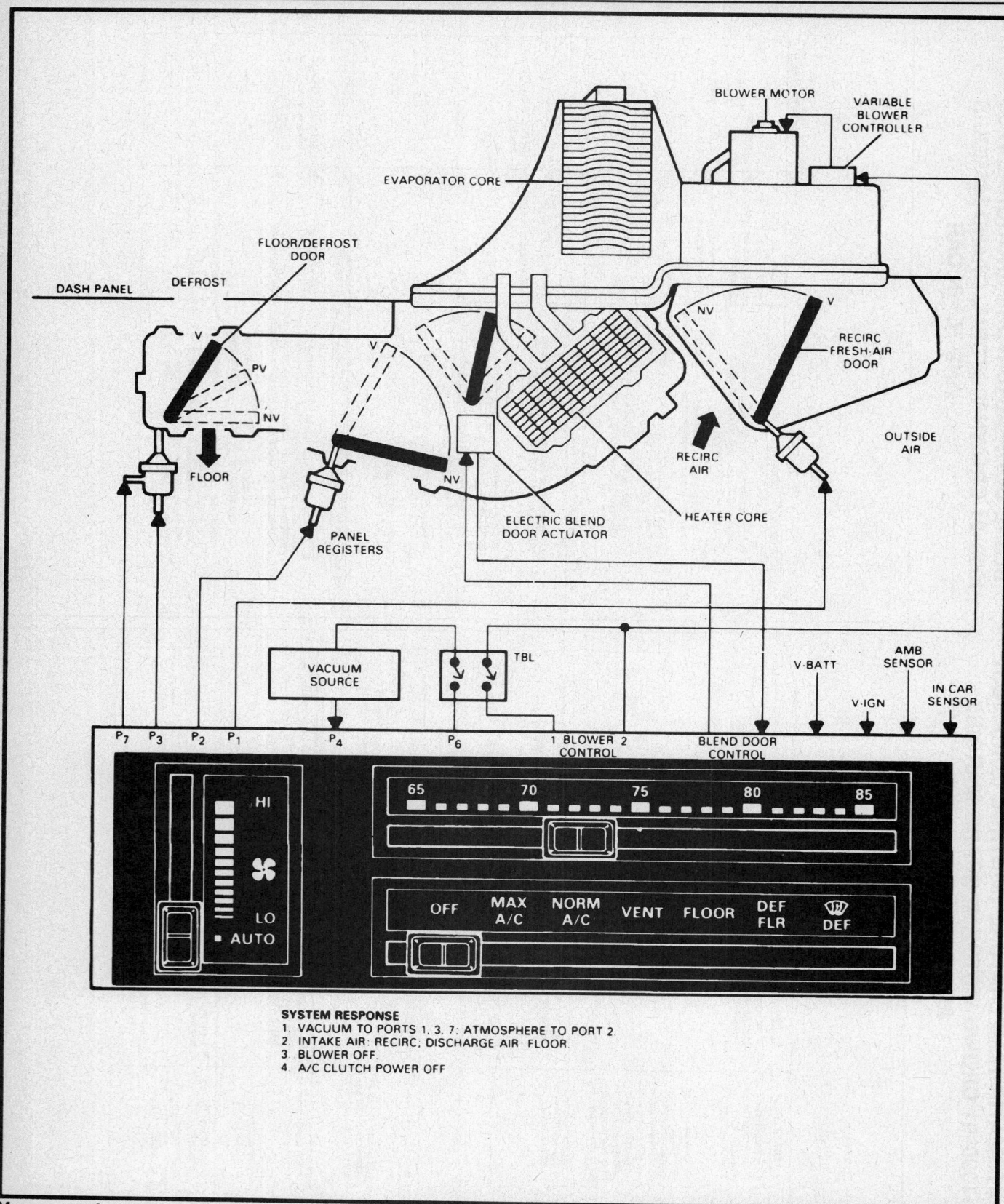

SYSTEM RESPONSE

1. VACUUM TO PORTS 1, 3, 7: ATMOSPHERE TO PORT 2.
2. INTAKE AIR: RECIRC; DISCHARGE AIR FLOOR.
3. BLOWER OFF.
4. A/C CLUTCH POWER OFF

Vacuum schematic—system function: off—1991 Crown Victoria, Grand Marquis and Town Car

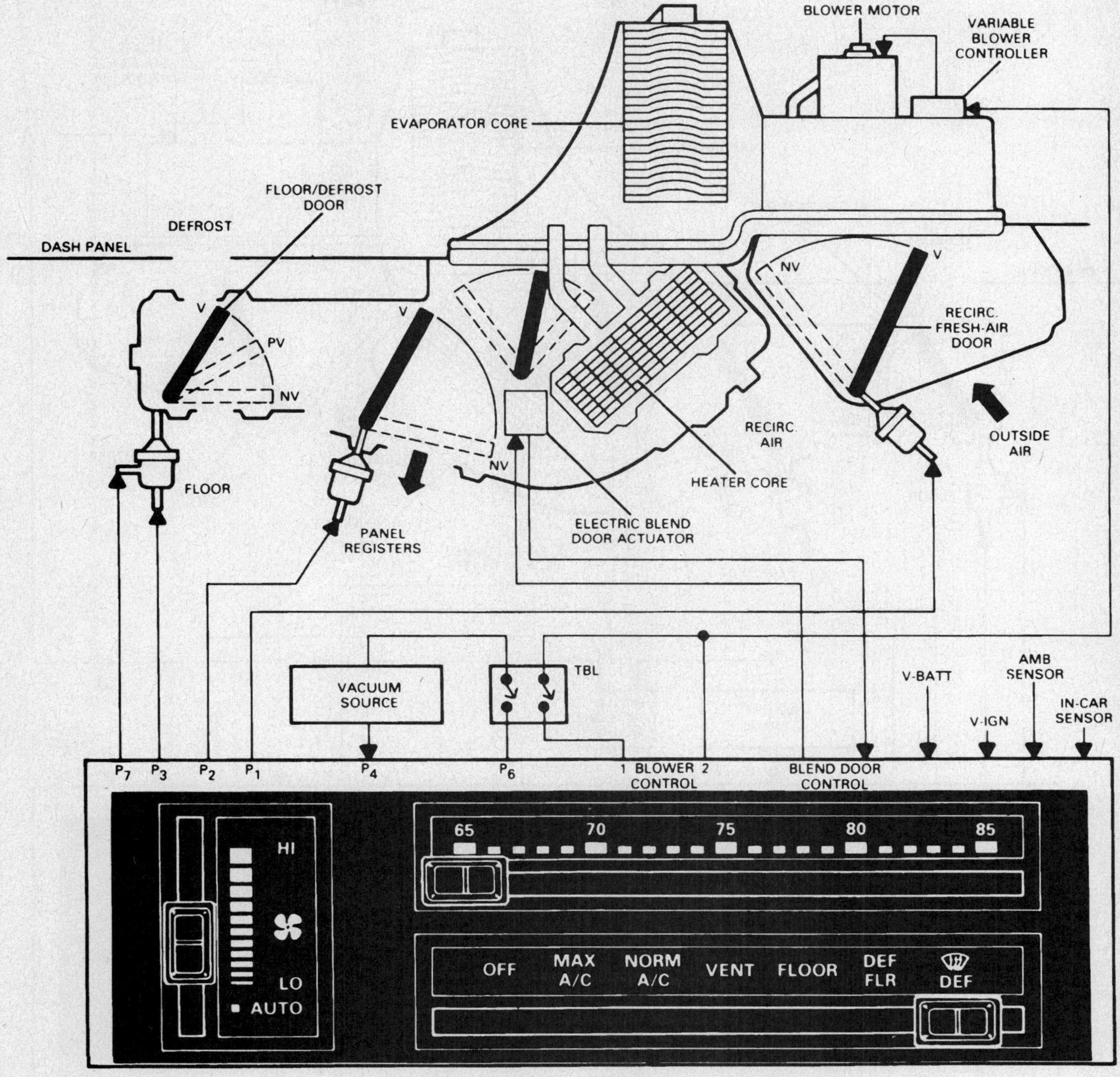
BLOWER MOTOR
VARIABLE BLOWER CONTROLLER
EVAPORATOR CORE
FLOOR/DEFROST DOOR
DEFROST
DASH PANEL
V
PV
NV
V
NV
RECIRC. FRESH-AIR DOOR
RECIRC. AIR
OUTSIDE AIR
HEATER CORE
FLOOR
PANEL REGISTERS
ELECTRIC BLEND DOOR ACTUATOR
VACUUM SOURCE
TBL
V-BATT
AMB SENSOR
V-IGN
IN-CAR SENSOR
P7 P3 P2 P1 P4 P6
1 BLOWER 2 CONTROL
BLEND DOOR CONTROL
65 70 75 80 85
HI
LO
AUTO
OFF
MAX A/C
NORM A/C
VENT
FLOOR
DEF FLR
DEF

SYSTEM RESPONSE
1. MODE DOORS WILL RESPOND TO CUSTOMER SELECTION.
2. BLEND DOOR GOES TO:
   A. FULL HEAT POSITION IF 85° IS SELECTED.
   B. FULL COOL POSITION IF 65° IS SELECTED.
3. BLOWER SPEED GOES TO:
   A. MAXIMUM IF AUTO IS SELECTED.
   B. FROM LOW TO HIGH BASED ON CUSTOMER SELECTION.
4. A/C CLUTCH POWER ON IN ALL MODES EXCEPT FLOOR & VENT.

Vacuum schematic – system function: any mode, auto or manual blower, temperature lever at 65° or 75°F – 1991 Crown Victoria, Grand Marquis and Town Car

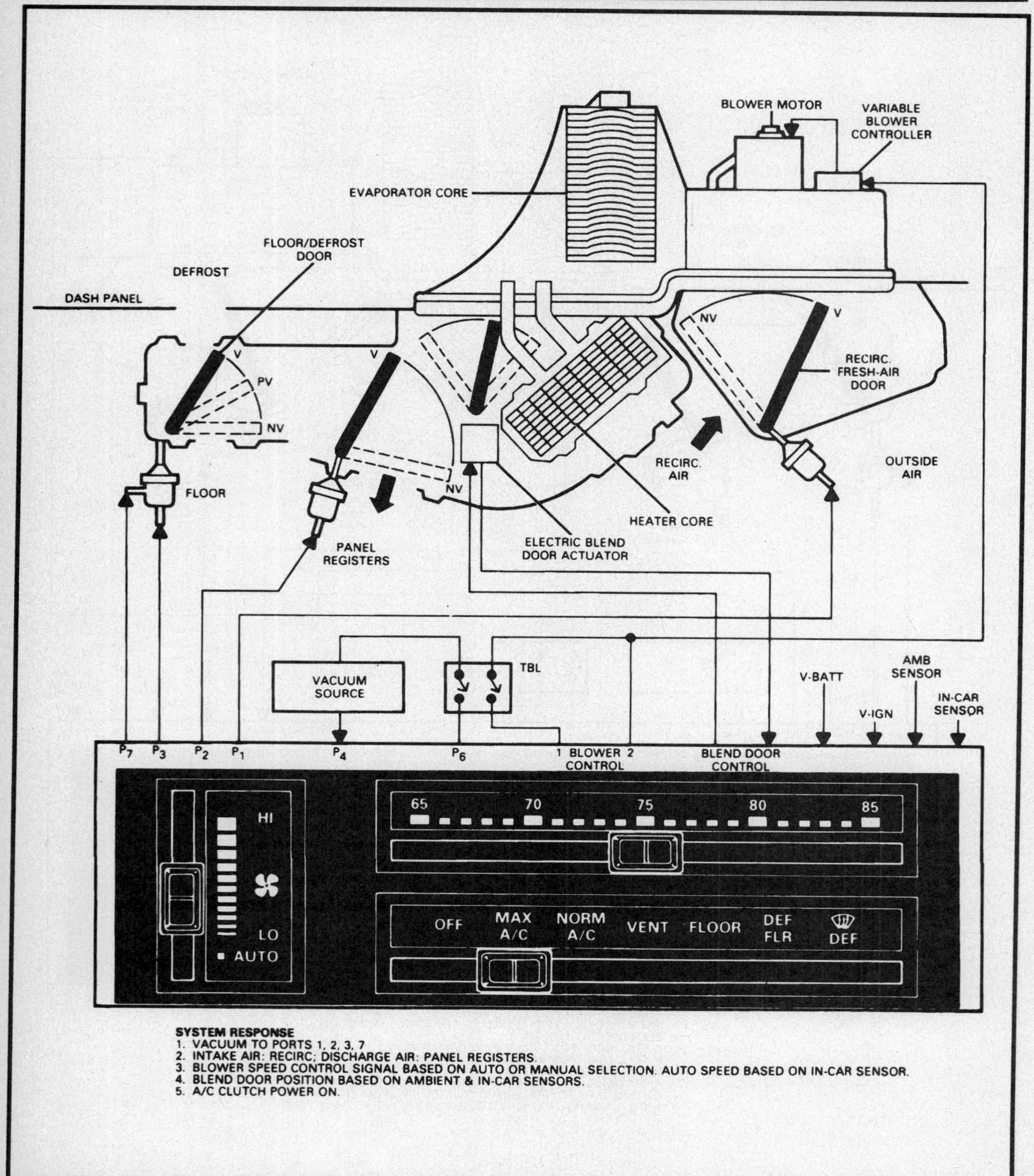
BLOWER MOTOR
VARIABLE BLOWER CONTROLLER
EVAPORATOR CORE
FLOOR/DEFROST DOOR
DEFROST
DASH PANEL
V
PV
NV
FLOOR
PANEL REGISTERS
RECIRC. FRESH-AIR DOOR
RECIRC. AIR
OUTSIDE AIR
HEATER CORE
ELECTRIC BLEND DOOR ACTUATOR
VACUUM SOURCE
TBL
V-BATT
AMB SENSOR
V-IGN
IN-CAR SENSOR
P7
P3
P2
P1
P4
P6
1 BLOWER 2 CONTROL
BLEND DOOR CONTROL
65
70
75
80
85
HI
LO
AUTO
OFF
MAX A/C
NORM A/C
VENT
FLOOR
DEF FLR
DEF
SYSTEM RESPONSE
1. VACUUM TO PORTS 1, 2, 3, 7
2. INTAKE AIR: RECIRC; DISCHARGE AIR: PANEL REGISTERS.
3. BLOWER SPEED CONTROL SIGNAL BASED ON AUTO OR MANUAL SELECTION. AUTO SPEED BASED ON IN-CAR SENSOR.
4. BLEND DOOR POSITION BASED ON AMBIENT & IN-CAR SENSORS.
5. A/C CLUTCH POWER ON.

Vacuum schematic—system function: MAX A/C, auto or manual blower—1991 Crown Victoria, Grand Marquis and Town Car

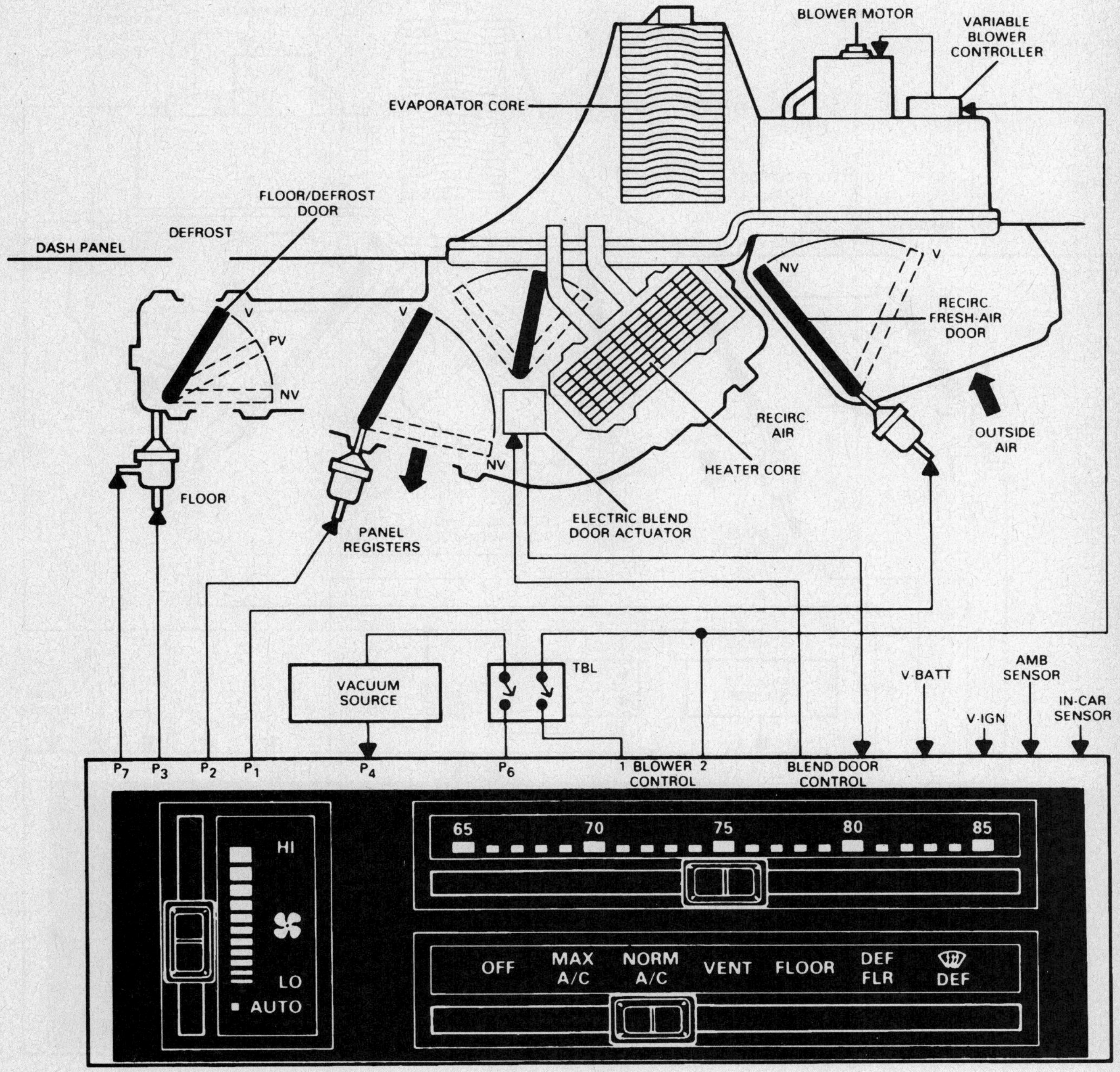
BLOWER MOTOR
VARIABLE BLOWER CONTROLLER
EVAPORATOR CORE
FLOOR/DEFROST DOOR
DEFROST
DASH PANEL
V
PV
NV
V
NV
RECIRC. FRESH-AIR DOOR
RECIRC. AIR
OUTSIDE AIR
HEATER CORE
FLOOR
ELECTRIC BLEND DOOR ACTUATOR
PANEL REGISTERS
TBL
VACUUM SOURCE
V-BATT
AMB SENSOR
V-IGN
IN-CAR SENSOR
P7 P3 P2 P1 P4 P6
1 BLOWER 2 CONTROL
BLEND DOOR CONTROL
HI
LO
AUTO
65 70 75 80 85
OFF
MAX A/C
NORM A/C
VENT
FLOOR
DEF FLR
DEF

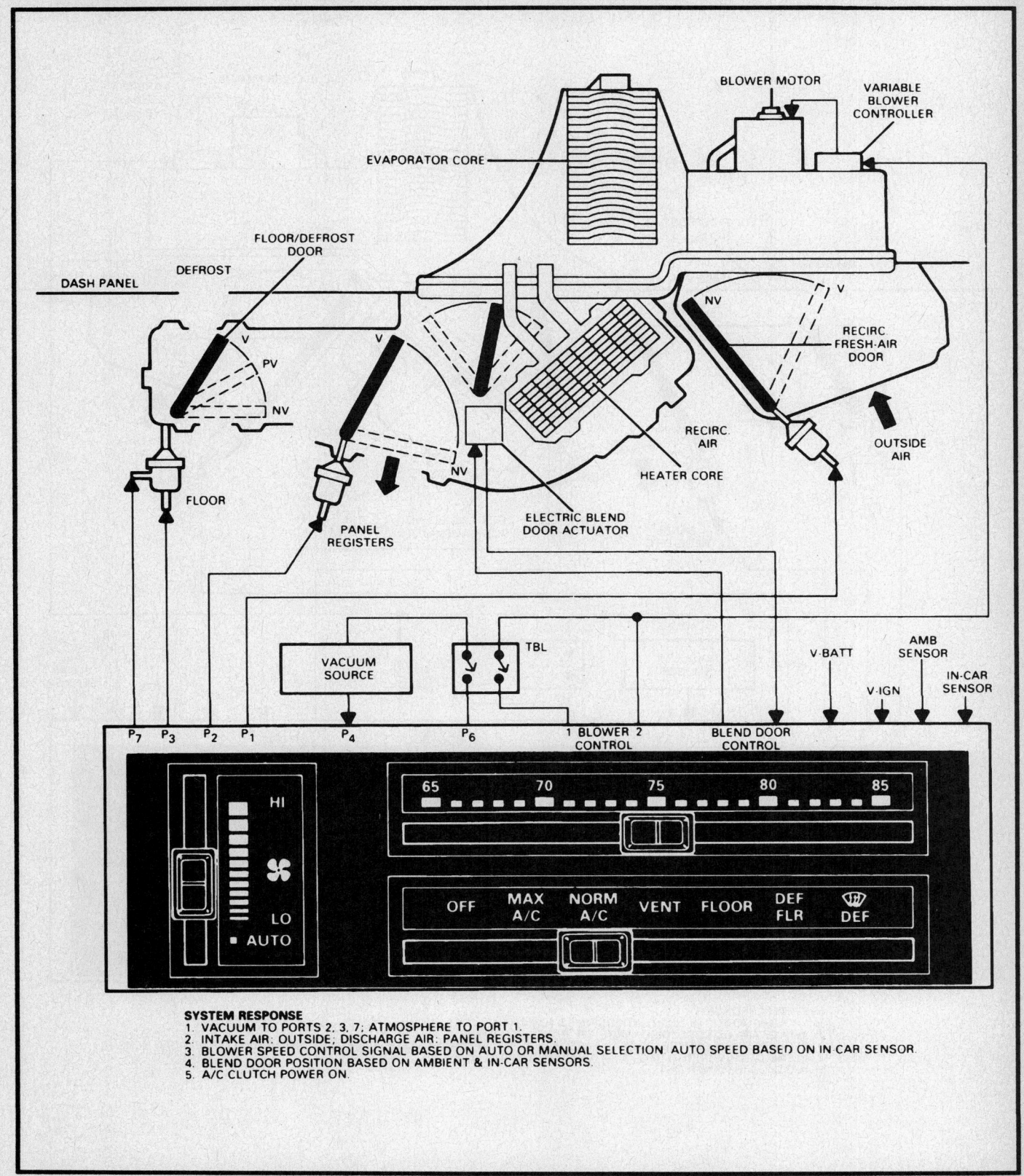

SYSTEM RESPONSE
1. VACUUM TO PORTS 2, 3, 7; ATMOSPHERE TO PORT 1.
2. INTAKE AIR: OUTSIDE; DISCHARGE AIR: PANEL REGISTERS.
3. BLOWER SPEED CONTROL SIGNAL BASED ON AUTO OR MANUAL SELECTION. AUTO SPEED BASED ON IN CAR SENSOR.
4. BLEND DOOR POSITION BASED ON AMBIENT & IN-CAR SENSORS.
5. A/C CLUTCH POWER ON.

Vacuum schematic—system function: NORM A/C, auto or manual blower—1991 Crown Victoria, Grand Marquis and Town Car

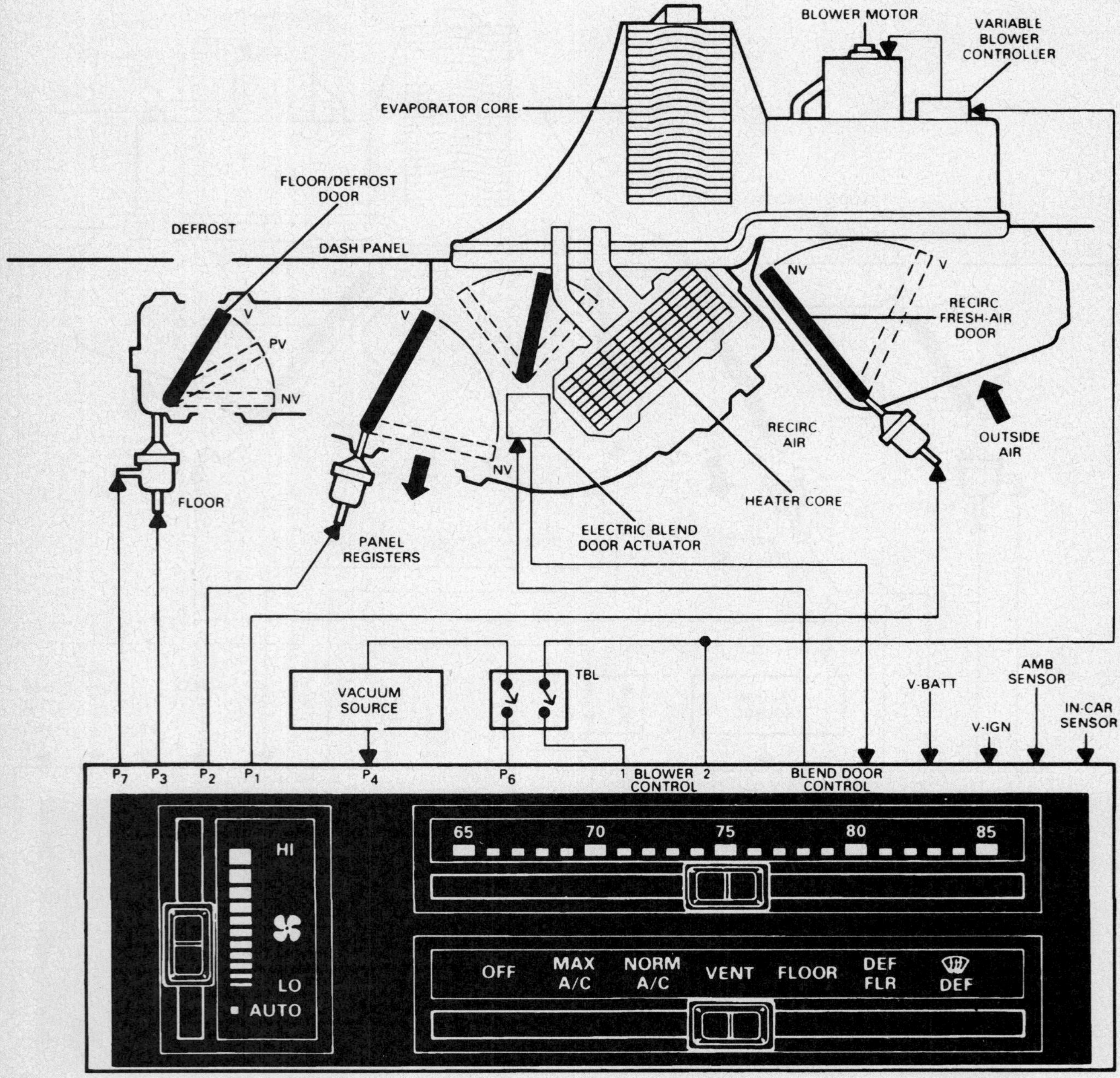
BLOWER MOTOR
VARIABLE BLOWER CONTROLLER
EVAPORATOR CORE
FLOOR/DEFROST DOOR
DEFROST
DASH PANEL
V
PV
NV
V
NV
NV
V
RECIRC FRESH-AIR DOOR
RECIRC AIR
OUTSIDE AIR
FLOOR
PANEL REGISTERS
ELECTRIC BLEND DOOR ACTUATOR
HEATER CORE
VACUUM SOURCE
TBL
V-BATT
V-IGN
AMB SENSOR
IN-CAR SENSOR
P7 P3 P2 P1 P4 P6
1 BLOWER 2 CONTROL
BLEND DOOR CONTROL
HI
LO
AUTO
65 70 75 80 85
OFF
MAX A/C
NORM A/C
VENT
FLOOR
DEF FLR
DEF

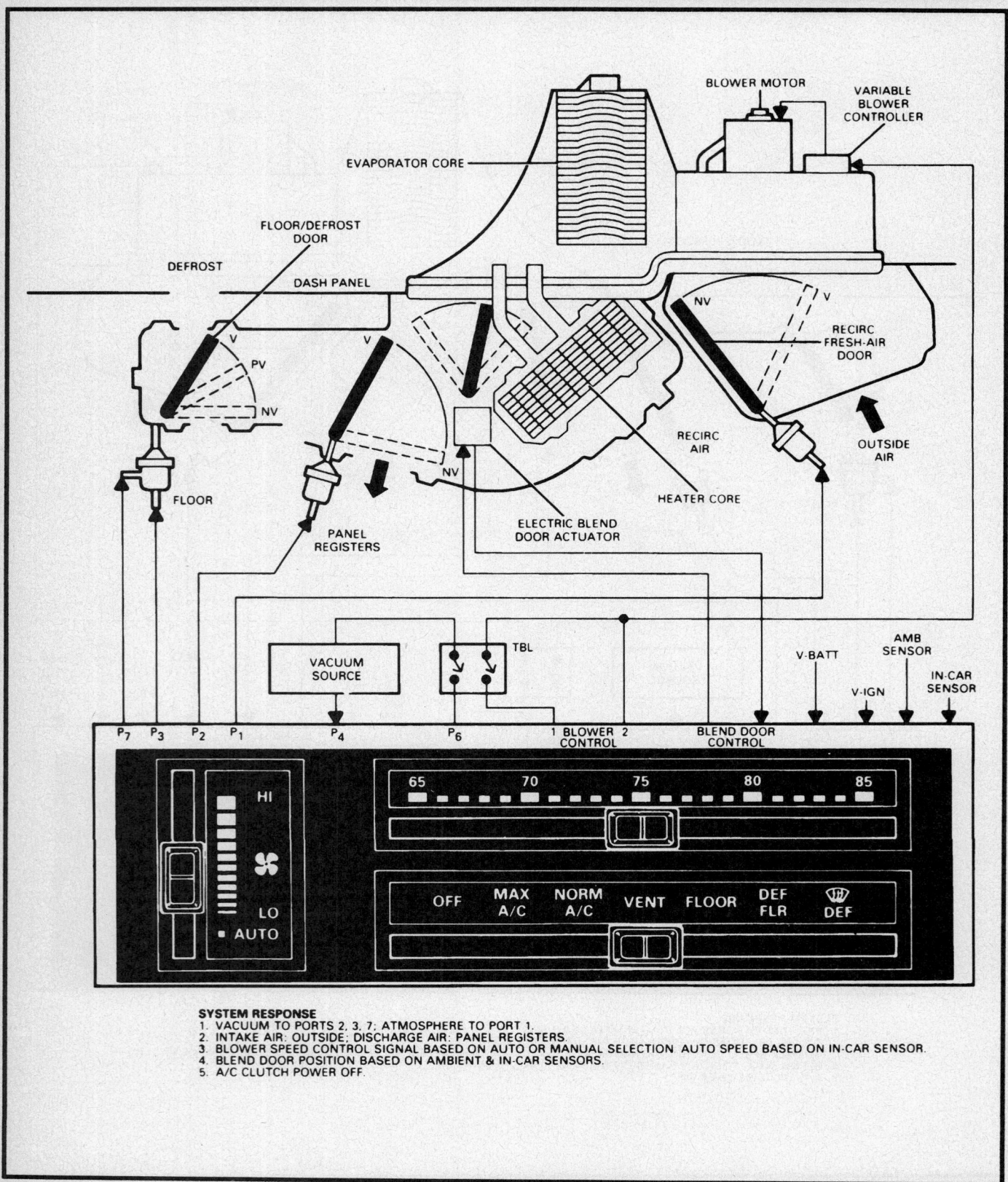

SYSTEM RESPONSE

1. VACUUM TO PORTS 2, 3, 7; ATMOSPHERE TO PORT 1.
2. INTAKE AIR: OUTSIDE; DISCHARGE AIR: PANEL REGISTERS.
3. BLOWER SPEED CONTROL SIGNAL BASED ON AUTO OR MANUAL SELECTION. AUTO SPEED BASED ON IN-CAR SENSOR.
4. BLEND DOOR POSITION BASED ON AMBIENT & IN-CAR SENSORS.
5. A/C CLUTCH POWER OFF.

Vacuum schematic—system function: VENT, auto or manual blower—1991 Crown Victoria, Grand Marquis and Town Car

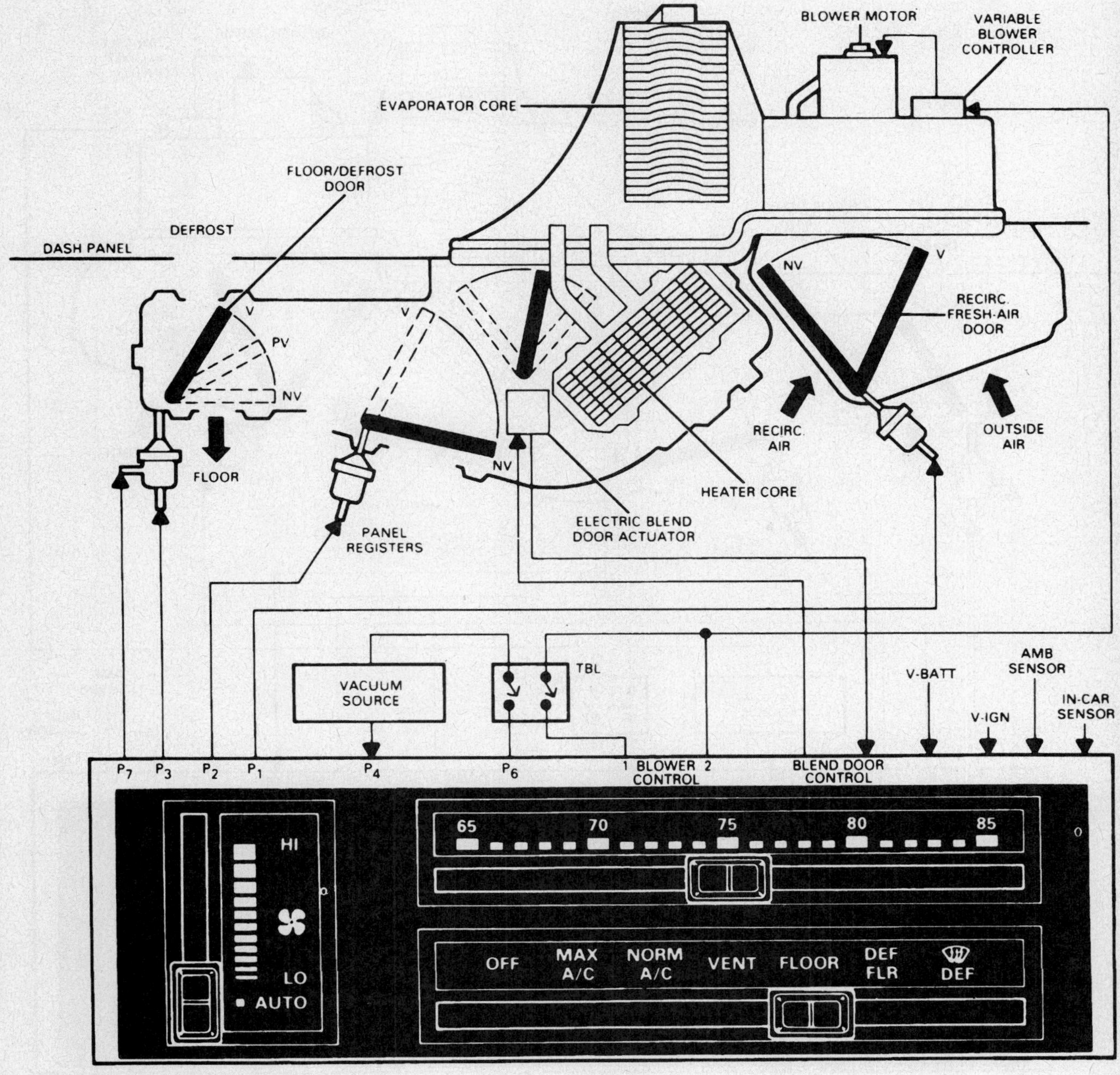
BLOWER MOTOR
VARIABLE BLOWER CONTROLLER
EVAPORATOR CORE
FLOOR/DEFROST DOOR
DEFROST
DASH PANEL
V
PV
NV
FLOOR
V
NV
PANEL REGISTERS
ELECTRIC BLEND DOOR ACTUATOR
HEATER CORE
RECIRC. AIR
NV
V
RECIRC. FRESH-AIR DOOR
OUTSIDE AIR
VACUUM SOURCE
TBL
V-BATT
AMB SENSOR
V-IGN
IN-CAR SENSOR
P7 P3 P2 P1 P4 P6
1 BLOWER 2 CONTROL
BLEND DOOR CONTROL
65 70 75 80 85
HI
LO
AUTO
OFF
MAX A/C
NORM A/C
VENT
FLOOR
DEF FLR
DEF

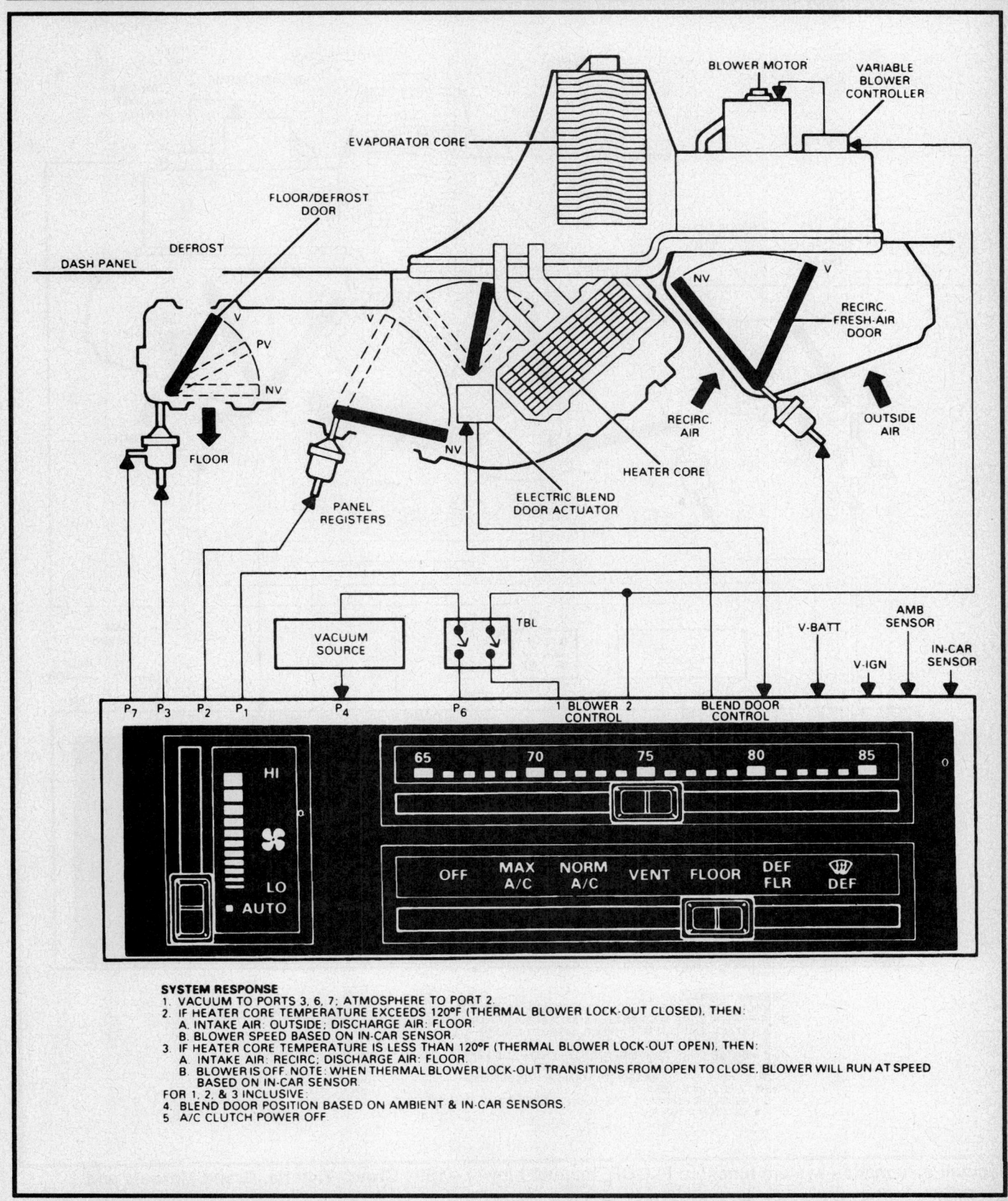

SYSTEM RESPONSE
1. VACUUM TO PORTS 3, 6, 7; ATMOSPHERE TO PORT 2.
2. IF HEATER CORE TEMPERATURE EXCEEDS 120°F (THERMAL BLOWER LOCK-OUT CLOSED), THEN:
   A. INTAKE AIR: OUTSIDE; DISCHARGE AIR: FLOOR.
   B. BLOWER SPEED BASED ON IN-CAR SENSOR.
3. IF HEATER CORE TEMPERATURE IS LESS THAN 120°F (THERMAL BLOWER LOCK-OUT OPEN), THEN:
   A. INTAKE AIR: RECIRC; DISCHARGE AIR: FLOOR.
   B. BLOWER IS OFF. NOTE: WHEN THERMAL BLOWER LOCK-OUT TRANSITIONS FROM OPEN TO CLOSE, BLOWER WILL RUN AT SPEED BASED ON IN-CAR SENSOR.

FOR 1, 2, & 3 INCLUSIVE:

4. BLEND DOOR POSITION BASED ON AMBIENT & IN-CAR SENSORS.
5. A/C CLUTCH POWER OFF.

Vacuum schematic—system function: FLOOR, auto blower—1991 Crown Victoria, Grand Marquis and Town Car

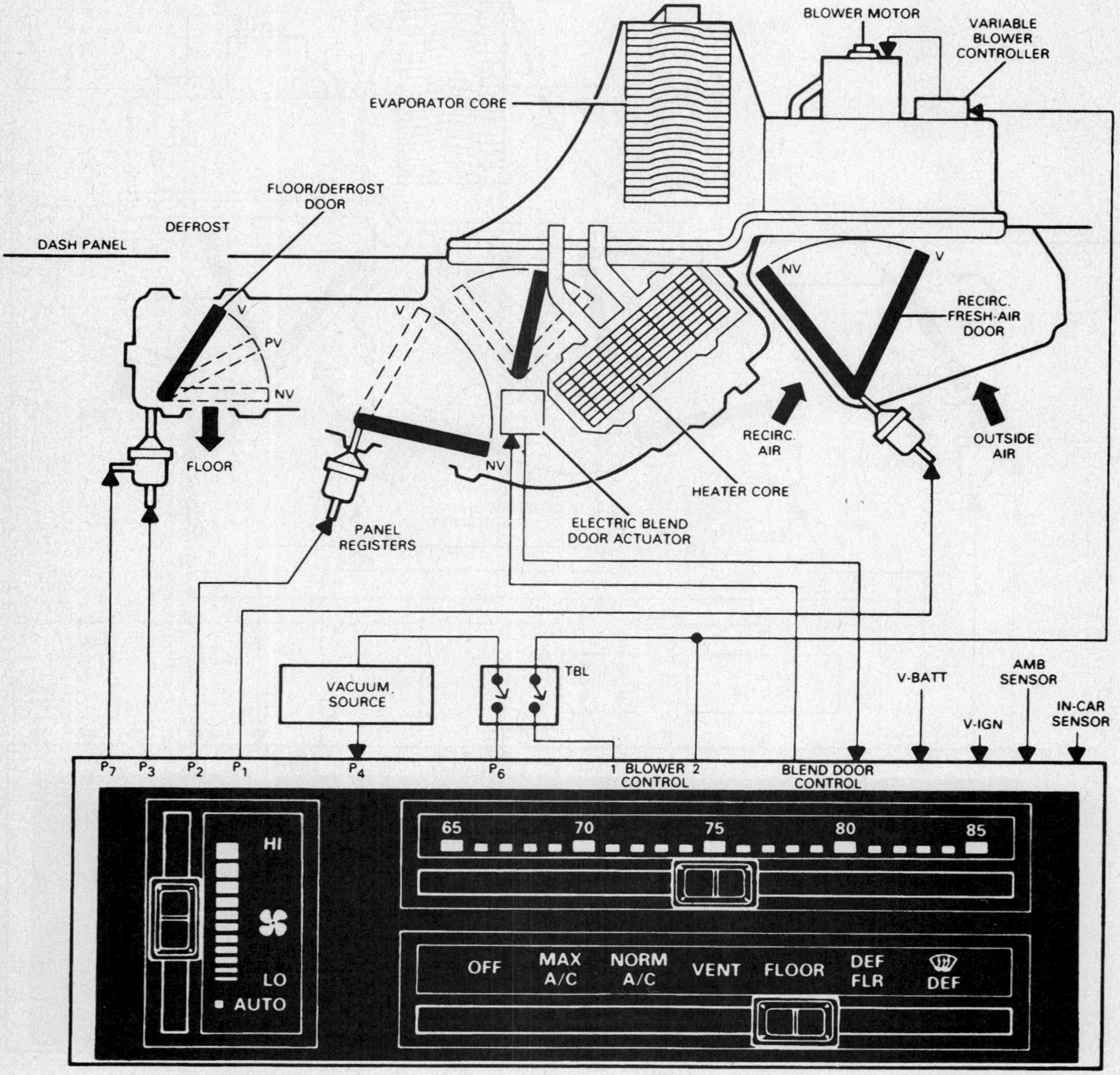
BLOWER MOTOR
VARIABLE BLOWER CONTROLLER
EVAPORATOR CORE
FLOOR/DEFROST DOOR
DEFROST
DASH PANEL
V
PV
NV
FLOOR
V
NV
PANEL REGISTERS
NV
V
RECIRC. FRESH-AIR DOOR
RECIRC. AIR
OUTSIDE AIR
HEATER CORE
ELECTRIC BLEND DOOR ACTUATOR
VACUUM SOURCE
TBL
V-BATT
AMB SENSOR
V-IGN
IN-CAR SENSOR
P7 P3 P2 P1 P4 P6
1 BLOWER 2 CONTROL
BLEND DOOR CONTROL
65 70 75 80 85
HI
LO
AUTO
OFF
MAX A/C
NORM A/C
VENT
FLOOR
DEF FLR
DEF

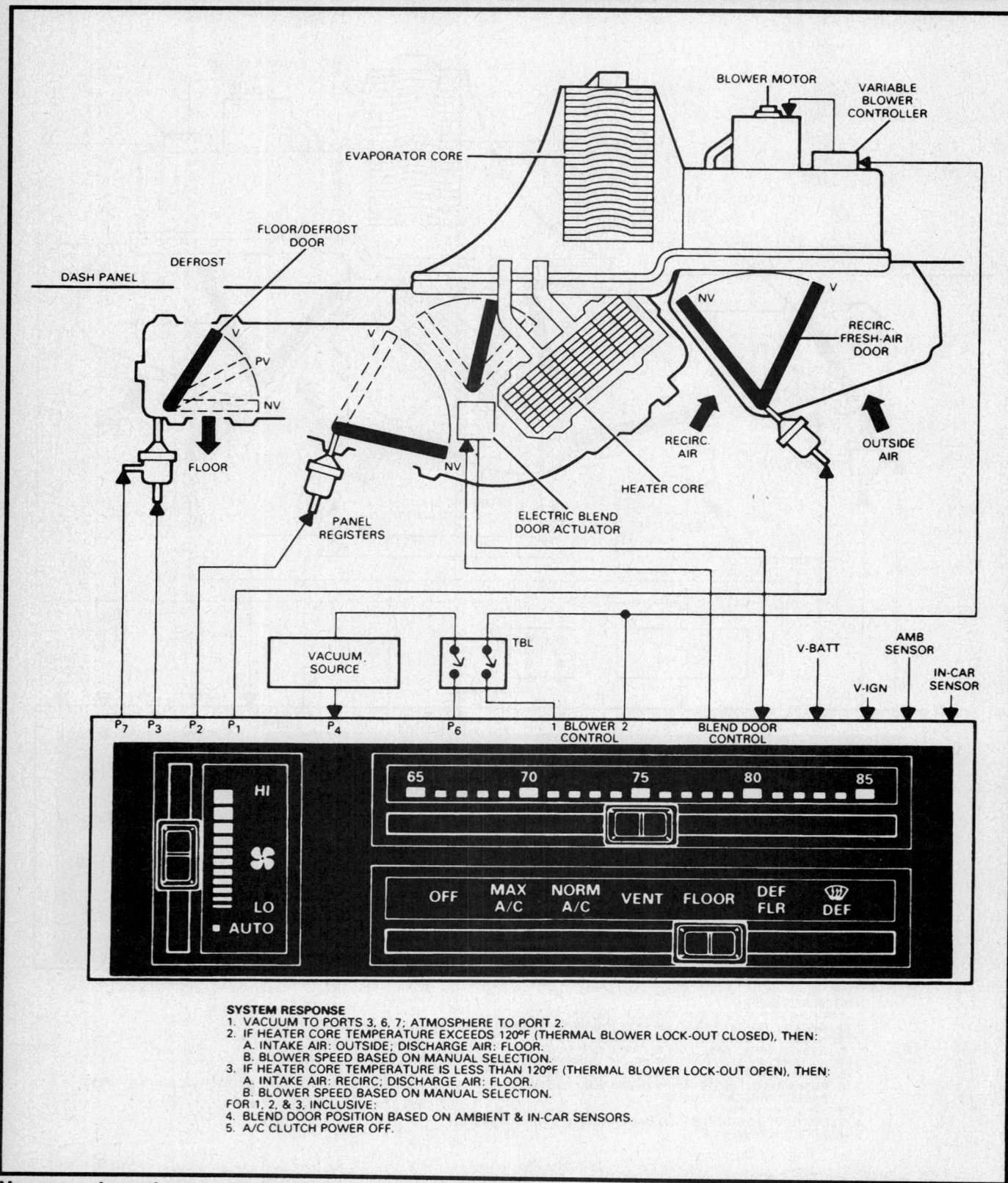

SYSTEM RESPONSE

1. VACUUM TO PORTS 3, 6, 7; ATMOSPHERE TO PORT 2.
2. IF HEATER CORE TEMPERATURE EXCEEDS 120°F (THERMAL BLOWER LOCK-OUT CLOSED), THEN:
   A. INTAKE AIR: OUTSIDE; DISCHARGE AIR: FLOOR.
   B. BLOWER SPEED BASED ON MANUAL SELECTION.
3. IF HEATER CORE TEMPERATURE IS LESS THAN 120°F (THERMAL BLOWER LOCK-OUT OPEN), THEN:
   A. INTAKE AIR: RECIRC; DISCHARGE AIR: FLOOR.
   B. BLOWER SPEED BASED ON MANUAL SELECTION.

FOR 1, 2, & 3, INCLUSIVE:

4. BLEND DOOR POSITION BASED ON AMBIENT & IN-CAR SENSORS.
5. A/C CLUTCH POWER OFF.

Vacuum schematic—system function: FLOOR, manual blower—1991 Crown Victoria, Grand Marquis and Town Car

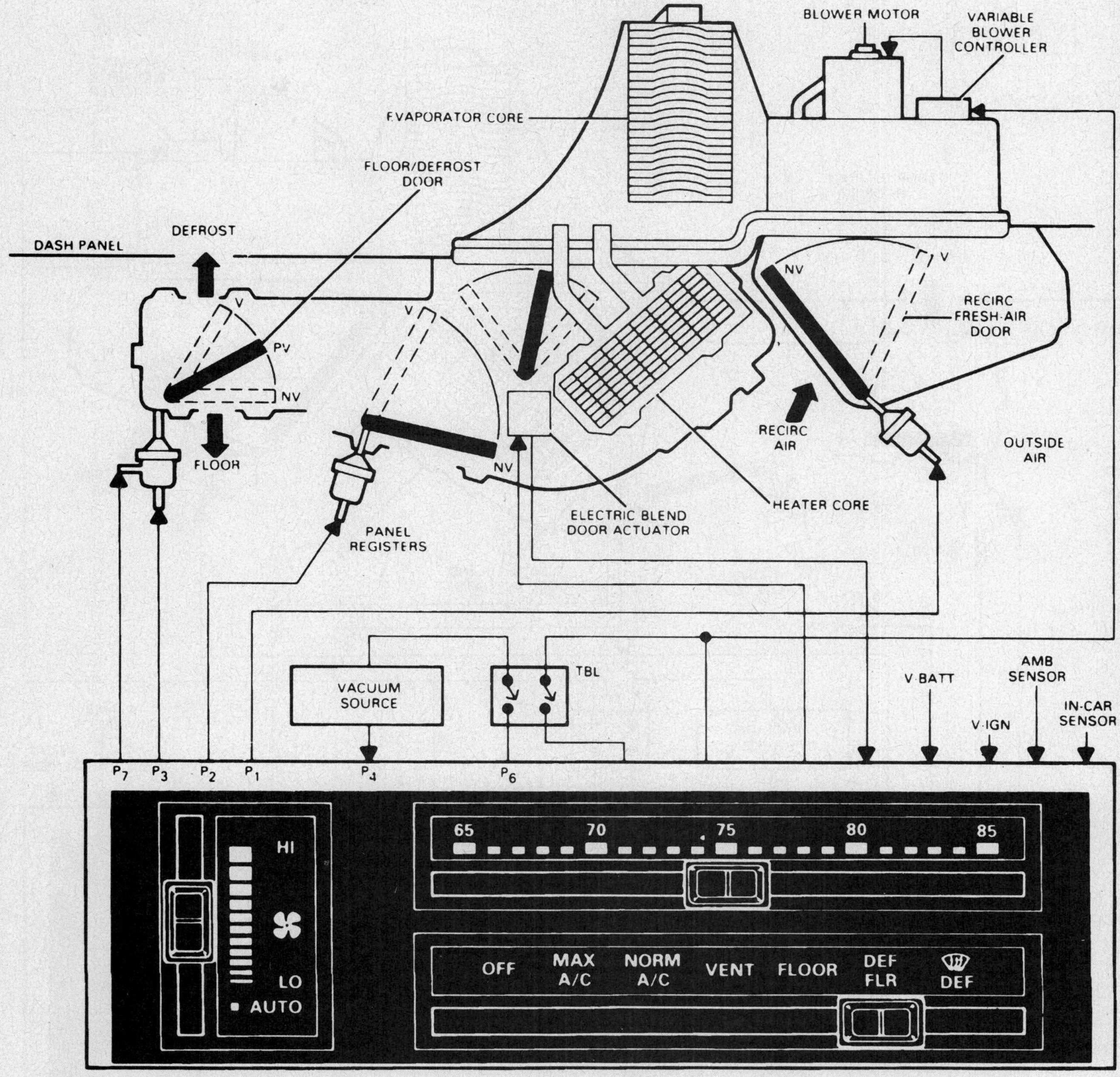
BLOWER MOTOR
VARIABLE BLOWER CONTROLLER
EVAPORATOR CORE
FLOOR/DEFROST DOOR
DEFROST
DASH PANEL
V
PV
NV
FLOOR
V
NV
RECIRC FRESH-AIR DOOR
RECIRC AIR
OUTSIDE AIR
ELECTRIC BLEND DOOR ACTUATOR
HEATER CORE
PANEL REGISTERS
VACUUM SOURCE
TBL
V-BATT
AMB SENSOR
V-IGN
IN-CAR SENSOR
P7 P3 P2 P1 P4 P6
HI
LO
AUTO
65 70 75 80 85
OFF
MAX A/C
NORM A/C
VENT
FLOOR
DEF FLR
DEF

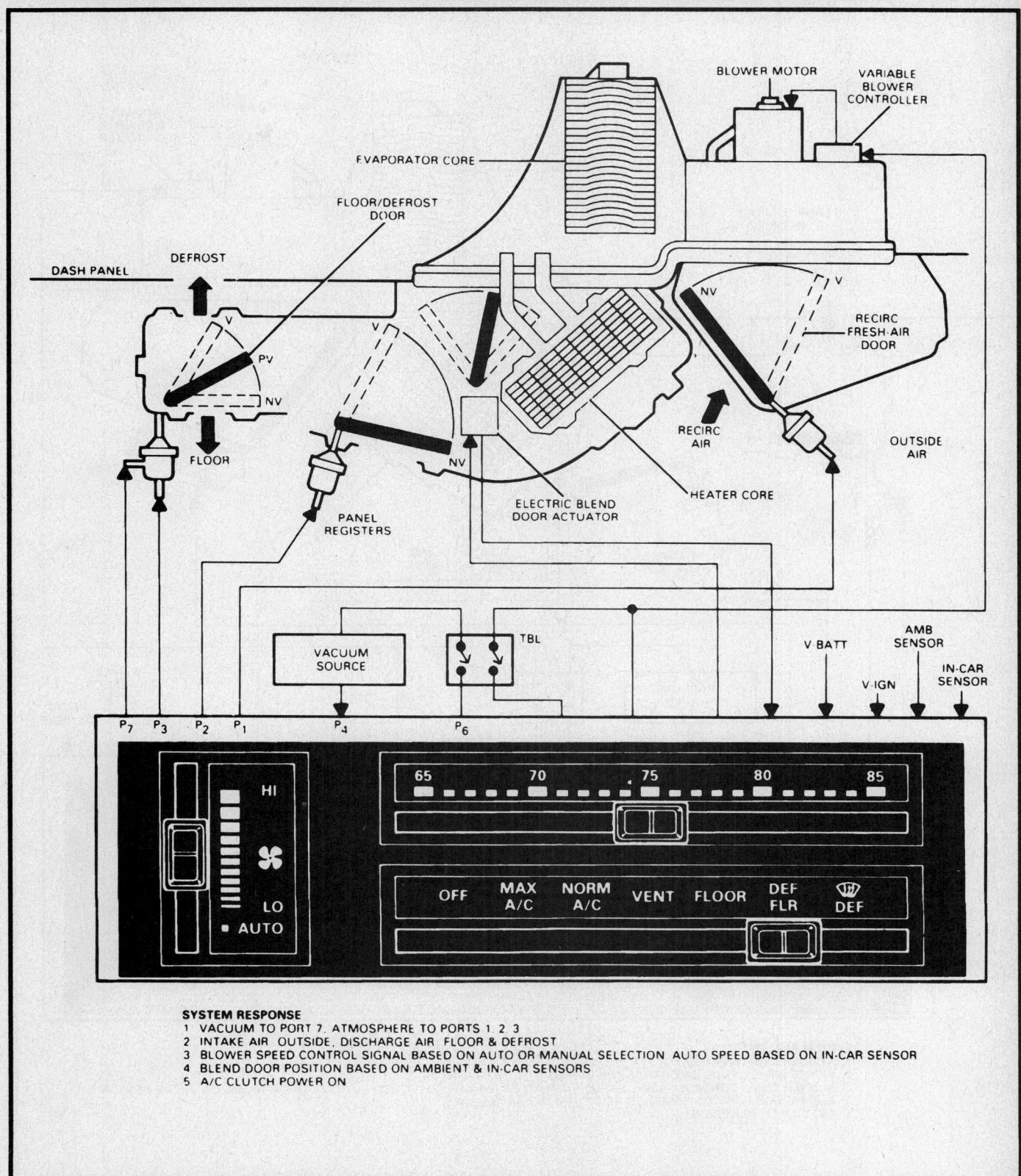

SYSTEM RESPONSE
1. VACUUM TO PORT 7. ATMOSPHERE TO PORTS 1, 2, 3
2. INTAKE AIR: OUTSIDE, DISCHARGE AIR: FLOOR & DEFROST
3. BLOWER SPEED CONTROL SIGNAL BASED ON AUTO OR MANUAL SELECTION. AUTO SPEED BASED ON IN-CAR SENSOR
4. BLEND DOOR POSITION BASED ON AMBIENT & IN-CAR SENSORS
5. A/C CLUTCH POWER ON

Vacuum schematic—system function: DEF/FLR, auto or manual blower—1991 Crown Victoria, Grand Marquis and Town Car

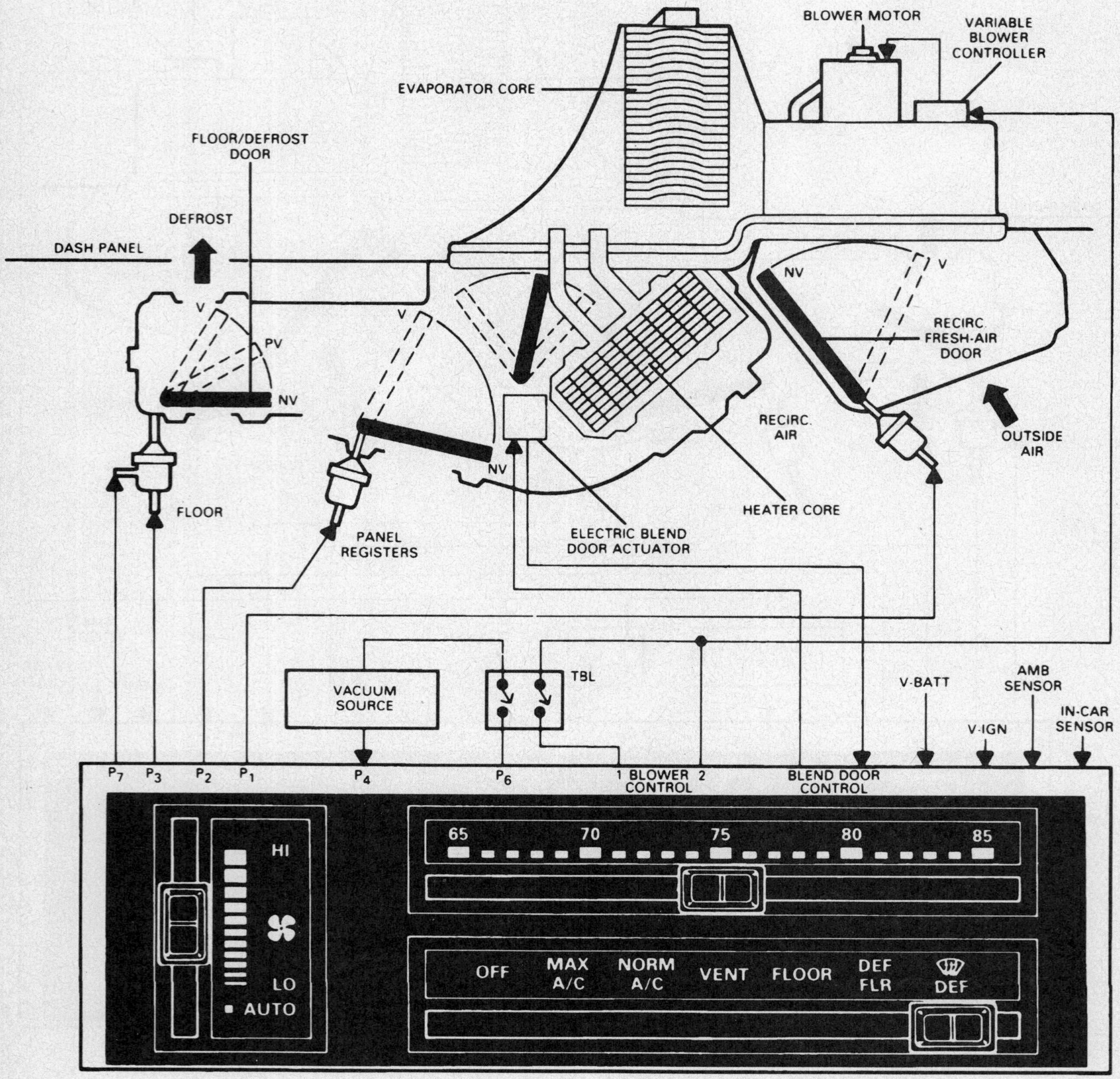
BLOWER MOTOR
VARIABLE BLOWER CONTROLLER
EVAPORATOR CORE
FLOOR/DEFROST DOOR
DEFROST
DASH PANEL
V
PV
NV
V
NV
NV
V
RECIRC. FRESH-AIR DOOR
RECIRC. AIR
OUTSIDE AIR
HEATER CORE
FLOOR
PANEL REGISTERS
ELECTRIC BLEND DOOR ACTUATOR
VACUUM SOURCE
TBL
V-BATT
AMB SENSOR
V-IGN
IN-CAR SENSOR
P7
P3
P2
P1
P4
P6
1 BLOWER 2
CONTROL
BLEND DOOR CONTROL
HI
LO
AUTO
65
70
75
80
85
OFF
MAX A/C
NORM A/C
VENT
FLOOR
DEF FLR
DEF

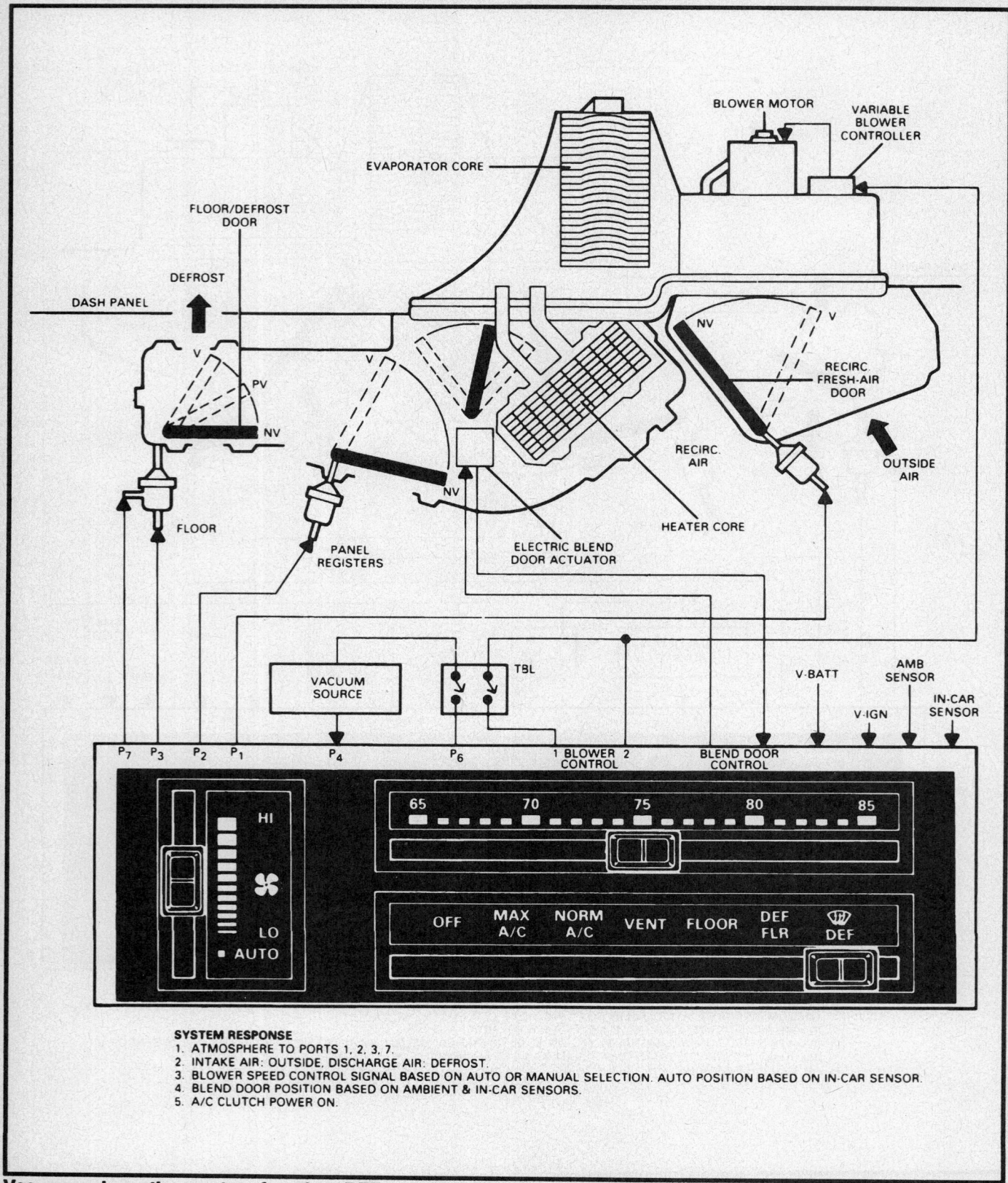

SYSTEM RESPONSE

1. ATMOSPHERE TO PORTS 1, 2, 3, 7.
2. INTAKE AIR: OUTSIDE, DISCHARGE AIR: DEFROST.
3. BLOWER SPEED CONTROL SIGNAL BASED ON AUTO OR MANUAL SELECTION. AUTO POSITION BASED ON IN-CAR SENSOR.
4. BLEND DOOR POSITION BASED ON AMBIENT & IN-CAR SENSORS.
5. A/C CLUTCH POWER ON.

Vacuum schematic—system function: DEF, auto or manual blower—1991 Crown Victoria, Grand Marquis and Town Car

Long Periods of Heat, Then Long Periods of Cool or Long Periods of Cool, Then Long Periods of Heat

Aspirator hose blocked or disconnected. The sensor is not sampling interior air.

Thermal Blower Lock Out Switch

The 3 failures associated with the thermal blower lock out switch are:

- Short across the 2 terminals of the harness connector
- Vacuum leak
- Coolant leaks

Check all function selector valve positions for vacuum leaks. Electrical functions can be checked as follows:

Blower Inoperative in FLOOR Position

Engine temperature must be over 110°F (43°C). Unplug the electrical connector from the thermal blower lock out switch. Short across the 2 terminals of the harness connector. If the blower comes on, replace the thermal blower lock out switch. If the blower does not come on, there is an open between the selector switch and the thermal blower lock out switch.

Blower On at All Times In FLOOR Position

If the blower is on with the engine coolant under 110°F (43°C), disconnect the harness connector from the thermal blower lock out switch. If the blower turns off, replace the thermal blower lock out switch. If the blower continues to run, there is a short in the circuit between the selector switch and the thermal blower lock out switch.

Mark VII

DIAGNOSIS AND TESTING

The control head will detect some system faults occurring during normal operation and has the capability to test for other faults during the Self-Test. If an actuator fault is detected by the control assembly during normal operation, the Vacuum Fluorescent Display (VFD) or function LED will blink.

To display the error codes for the fault detected, initiate the Self-Test by pushing the **OFF/AUTO** and **DEFROST** simultaneously and then **A/C** within 2 seconds.

Error codes for any faults found during the Self-Test will appear along with error codes for any faults found during normal operation. The Self-Test can be initiated at any time with the resulting error codes being displayed. Normal operation of the system stops when the Self-Test is activated. To exit the Self-Test and restart the system, push the **COOL** button.

NOTE: The in-vehicle temperature should be greater than 50°F (10°C) for all error codes shown to be valid.

If error codes appear during the Self-Test, check the error code key and perform the pinpoint tests indicated. If a malfunction exists, but no error code appears during the Self-Test, check pinpoint tests H through P.

AUTOMATIC TEMPERATURE CONTROL FUNCTIONAL TEST

1. Turn the ignition **OFF**, then **ON**, to reset the system.
2. Make sure the engine is warm. The coolant temperature should be at least 120°F (49°C).
3. Set the control assembly to **AUTO: 90°F**.
   a. Wait 40 seconds, minimum.
   b. Verify that the system goes to high blower and that warm air is being discharged from the floor.
   c. Verify that the recirc door is in the OUTSIDE AIR position.
   d. Verify that warm air is bleeding out of the defroster nozzle.
   e. Enter the Self-Test.
   f. Record all faults and error codes displayed.
   g. Exit the Self-Test.
   h. Diagnose the system according to the error code key if any error codes are displayed. If any error codes were displayed during the AUTO: 90°F test, turn the vehicle ignition **OFF**, then **ON**, to reset the system.
4. Set the control assembly to **AUTO: 60°F**.
   a. Verify that the system goes to low blower, then back to high blower as the temperature setting changes.
   b. Wait 40 seconds, minimum.
   c. Verify that cool air is being discharged from the panel.
   d. Verify that the recirc door is in the RECIRC position.
   e. Enter the Self-Test.
   f. Record all faults and error codes displayed.
   g. Exit the Self-Test.
   h. Diagnose the system according to the error code key if any error codes are displayed.
5. Repeat Step 3.
6. Check pinpoint tests H through P for diagnosis if any other faults still exist.

NOTE: When diagnosing a vehicle that is idling, it is likely that the system will discharge cool air from the panel, even at an 85°F set point. This is because engine heat will cause the ambient sensor to be very warm. Drive the vehicle for final checkout.

ERROR CODE KEY—MARK VII

ERROR CODE	CONDITION	DIAGNOSTIC/SERVICE PROCEDURE
01	Blend actuator out of position ▶	Pinpoint Test A
02	Panel/Floor actuator out of position ▶	Pinpoint Test B
03	Pan/Def actuator out of position ▶	Pinpoint Test C
04	OA/Recirc actuator out of position ▶	Pinpoint Test D
05	Blend actuator over current ▶	Pinpoint Test A
06	Panel/Floor actuator over current ▶	Pinpoint Test B
07	Pan/Def actuator over current ▶	Pinpoint Test C
08	OA/Recirc actuator over current ▶	Pinpoint Test D
09	No faults found in Self-Test. Go to Pinpoint Tests H through P. ▶	—
10	If it appears with any other code, ignore it. If it appears alone, it is the same as 88. ▶	—
11	Clutch signal low	Pinpoint Test E
12	Sensor string open*	Pinpoint Test F
13	Sensor string shorted	Pinpoint Test F
14	Control assembly inoperative	Replace control assembly
15	Blower signal shorted to B+	Pinpoint Test G
88	No faults found in Self-Test. Go to Pinpoint Tests H through P.	—

***If vehicle interior is very cold this error code (12) may appear in Self-Test.**

PINPOINT TEST INDEX—MARK VII

PINPOINT TEST	TITLE
A	Blend Door Actuator Diagnosis
B	Panel/Floor Door Actuator Diagnosis
C	Panel/Defrost Door Actuator Diagnosis
D	Outside Air/Recirc Door Actuator Diagnosis
E	Clutch Signal Low
F	Sensor Diagnosis
G	Blower Always Off
H	Diagnosis When Self-Test Indicates No Errors Found
J	No Clutch Operation
K	No Blower
L	High Blower Only
M	Fixed Blower Speed
P	Clutch Does Not Disengage When In OFF

PINPOINT TEST A: BLEND DOOR ACTUATOR DIAGNOSIS—MARK VII

	TEST STEP	RESULT ▶	ACTION TO TAKE
A1	ANALYZE ERROR CODES		
	• Refer to error code key. • Check error codes recorded during Self-Test.	5 displayed ▶ 1 displayed but not 5 ▶	GO to **A2**. GO to **A7**.
A2	ISOLATE CONNECTOR		
	• Disconnect Connector J-1 (passenger side) from control assembly. • Turn ignition to OFF, then to RUN to restart system. • Enter Self-Test.	5 displayed ▶ 5 not displayed ▶	GO to **A3**. GO to **A4**.
A3	TEST CONTROL ASSEMBLY		
	• Replace control assembly and test according to EATC Self-Test.	OK ▶ NOT OK ▶	Blend door actuator OK. GO to **A1**.
A4	ISOLATE WIRING HARNESS/ACTUATOR		
	• Reconnect wiring harness to control assembly and disconnect wiring harness from actuator. • Turn ignition to OFF, then to RUN to restart system. • Enter Self-Test.	5 displayed ▶ 5 not displayed ▶	GO to **A5**. GO to **A6**.
A5	TEST WIRING HARNESS		
	• Service/Replace wiring harness, connect and test according to EATC Self-Test.	OK ▶ NOT OK ▶	Blend door actuator OK. GO to **A1**.
A6	TEST ACTUATOR		
	• Replace actuator and test according to EATC Self-Test.	OK ▶ NOT OK ▶	Blend door actuator OK. GO to **A1**.
A7	CHECK ACTUATOR		
	• Disconnect both connectors from control assembly and drive actuator in both directions with a 9-12V battery. (One second maximum in either direction.) The following Pins can be jumped to connect the actuator to the battery. Make certain ignition is in RUN. J-1 (Passenger Side) — J-2 (Driver's Side) Trial 1: Pin 7 to Pin 8 Pin 8 to Pin 4 Trial 2: Pin 7 to Pin 4 Pin 8 to Pin 8 **CAUTION: Any other combination could cause severe damage to other components of the electrical or air conditioning systems.**	Actuator drives ▶ Actuator does not drive ▶	GO to **A8**. GO to **A9**.

PINPOINT TEST A: BLEND DOOR ACTUATOR DIAGNOSIS—MARK VII

	TEST STEP	RESULT ▶	ACTION TO TAKE
A8	TEST CONTROL ASSEMBLY		
	• Reconnect control assembly and test according to EATC Self-Test.	OK ▶ NOT OK ▶	Blend door actuator OK. GO to **A10**.
A9	TEST CONTINUITY		
	• Check wiring harness and connector continuity. Make certain that all connectors are connected. Check for damaged or pushed out terminals.	OK ▶ NOT OK ▶	GO to **A6**. GO to **A5**.
A10	TEST RESISTANCES		
	• Measure resistance using Rotunda DVOM 007-00001 or equivalent, as shown below at the control assembly connector J-1 (passenger side). Pin 4-5 500-600 ohms Pin 4-2 40-550 ohms Pin 5-2 200-600 ohms	OK ▶ NOT OK ▶	GO to **A3**. GO to **A9**.

PINPOINT TEST B: PANEL/FLOOR DOOR ACTUATOR DIAGNOSIS—MARK VII

TEST STEP	RESULT ▶	ACTION TO TAKE
B1 ANALYZE ERROR CODES		
• Refer to error code key. • Check error codes recorded during Self-Test.	6 displayed ▶	GO to **B2**.
	2 displayed but not 6 ▶	GO to **B7**.
B2 ISOLATE CONNECTOR		
• Disconnect connector J-1 (passenger side) from control assembly.	6 displayed ▶	GO to **B3**.
• Turn ignition to OFF, then to RUN to restart system. • Enter Self-Test.	6 not displayed ▶	GO to **B4**.
B3 TEST CONTROL ASSEMBLY		
• Replace control assembly and test according to EATC Self-Test.	(OK) ▶	Panel/Floor door actuator OK.
	(NOT OK) ▶	GO to **B1**.
B4 ISOLATE WIRING HARNESS/ACTUATOR		
• Reconnect wiring harness to control assembly and disconnect wiring harness from actuator.	6 displayed ▶	GO to **B5**.
• Turn ignition to OFF, then RUN to restart system. • Enter Self-Test.	6 not displayed ▶	GO to **B6**.
B5 TEST WIRING HARNESS		
• Service/replace wiring harness, connect and test according to EATC Self-Test.	(OK) ▶	Panel/Floor door actuator OK.
	(NOT OK) ▶	GO to **B1**.
B6 TEST ACTUATOR		
• Replace actuator and test according to EATC Self-Test.	(OK) ▶	Panel/Floor door actuator OK.
	(NOT OK) ▶	GO to **B1**.

TEST STEP	RESULT ▶	ACTION TO TAKE
B7 CHECK ACTUATOR		
• Disconnect both connectors from control assembly and drive actuator in both directions with a 9-12V battery (one second maximum in either direction). The following Pins can be jumped to connect the actuator to the battery. Make certain ignition is in RUN.	Actuator drives ▶	GO to **B8**.
	Actuator does not drive ▶	GO to **B9**.
J-1 (Passenger Side) — J-2 (Driver's Side) Trial 1: Pin 6 to Pin 8 Pin 9 to Pin 4 Trial 2: Pin 6 to Pin 4 Pin 9 to Pin 8 **CAUTION: Any other combination could cause severe damage to other components of the electrical or air conditioning systems.**		
B8 TEST CONTROL ASSEMBLY		
• Reconnect control assembly and test according to EATC Self-Test.	(OK) ▶	Floor/Panel door actuator OK.
	(NOT OK) ▶	GO to **B10**.
B9 TEST CONTINUITY		
• Check wiring harness and connector continuity Make certain that the connectors are connected.	(OK) ▶	GO to **B6**.
	(NOT OK) ▶	GO to **B5**.
B10 TEST RESISTANCES		
• Measure resistance as shown below at the control assembly connector J-1 (passenger side) with the connector disconnected.	(OK) ▶	GO to **B3**.
Pin 4-5 500-600 ohms Pin 13-4 75-550 ohms Pin 13-5 200-600 ohms	(NOT OK) ▶	GO to **B9**.

PINPOINT TEST C: PANEL/DEFROST DOOR ACTUATOR DIAGNOSIS

TEST STEP	RESULT	ACTION TO TAKE
C1 ANALYZE ERROR CODES		
• Check error codes recorded during Self-Test. Refer to error code key.	7 displayed	GO to **C2**.
	3 displayed, 7 not displayed, door does not drive	GO to **C7**.
	3 displayed, 7 not displayed, door drives continuously	GO to **C9**.
C2 ISOLATE CONNECTOR		
• Disconnect Pin 9 from connector J-2 (drivers side) from control assembly. • Leave connector on. • Turn ignition to OFF, then ON to restart system. • Enter Self-Test.	7 not displayed	GO to **C4**.
	7 displayed	GO to **C3**.
C3 TEST CONTROL ASSEMBLY		
• Replace control assembly and test according to EATC Self-Test.	OK	Panel/Defrost door actuator OK.
	~~OK~~	GO to **C1**.
C4 ISOLATE WIRING HARNESS/ACTUATOR		
• Reconnect wiring harness to control assembly and disconnect wiring harness from actuator. • Turn ignition to OFF, then to RUN to restart the system. • Enter Self-Test.	7 not displayed	GO to **C6**.
	7 displayed	GO to **C5**.
C5 TEST WIRING HARNESS		
• Service/replace wiring harness and test according to EATC Self-Test.	OK	Panel/Defrost door actuator OK.
	~~OK~~	GO to **C1**.
C6 TEST ACTUATOR		
• Replace actuator and test according to EATC Self-Test.	OK	Panel/Defrost door actuator OK.
	~~OK~~	GO to **C1**.

TEST STEP	RESULT	ACTION TO TAKE
C7 CHECK ACTUATOR		
• Set the control to HI AUTO. • Disconnect connector J-2 (driver's side) from control assembly. The blower should still be operating. • Jump the following J-2 pins to connect the battery to the actuator. Pin 8 to Pin 9 Pin 4 to Pin 10 **CAUTION: Any other combination could cause severe damage to other components of the electrical or air conditioning systems.**	Actuator drives freely. (Goes from Panel to Defrost or from Defrost to Panel in less than 10 seconds).	GO to **C8**.
	Actuator drives but is restricted. (Does not go from Panel to Defrost or from Defrost to Panel in less than 10 seconds).	GO to **C10**.
C8 TEST CONTROL ASSEMBLY		
• Reconnect control assembly and test according to EATC Self-Test.	OK	Panel/Defrost door actuator OK.
	~~OK~~	GO to **C3**.
C9 TEST CONTINUITY		
• Circuit 776 (O/BK) from the Panel/Defrost actuator to Pin 3 of connector J-2 could be open or disconnected. Make certain that the connector is connected.	OK	GO to **C13**.
	~~OK~~	SERVICE and RETEST.
C10 CHECK ACTUATOR CLEARANCE		
• Actuator may be tangled in wiring harness or internally restricted.	Externally restricted	CLEAR and RETEST.
	Internally restricted	REPLACE actuator and RETEST.
C11 CHECK CONTINUITY		
• Check continuity between Pins 10 and 9 on connector J-2.	Open	GO to **C12**.
	Less than 100 ohms	GO to **C6**.
C12 CHECK ACTUATOR CONNECTION		
• Check to make sure actuator is connected.	OK	GO to **C6**.
	~~OK~~	CONNECT and RETEST.
C13 CHANGE ACTUATOR		
• Change actuator and test.	OK	Panel/Defrost door actuator OK.
	~~OK~~	GO to **C3**.

PINPOINT TEST D: OUTSIDE AIR/RECIRCULATING DOOR ACTUATOR DIAGNOSIS—MARK VII

TEST STEP	RESULT ▶	ACTION TO TAKE
D1 ANALYZE ERROR CODES		
• Check error codes recorded during Self-Test. Refer to error code key.	8 displayed ▶	GO to **D2**.
	4 displayed, 8 not displayed, door does not drive ▶	GO to **D7**.
	4 displayed, 8 not displayed, and door drives continuously ▶	GO to **D9**.
D2 ISOLATE CONNECTOR		
• Disconnect connector J-1 (passenger side) from control assembly. • Turn ignition to OFF, then ON to restart system. • Enter Self-Test.	8 not displayed ▶	GO to **D4**.
	8 displayed ▶	GO to **D3**.
D3 TEST CONTROL ASSEMBLY		
• Replace control assembly and test according to EATC Self-Test.	OK ▶	Outside Air/Recirc door actuator OK.
	NOT OK ▶	GO to **D1**.
D4 ISOLATE WIRING HARNESS/ACTUATOR		
• Reconnect wiring harness to control assembly and disconnect wiring harness from actuator. • Turn ignition to OFF, then to RUN to restart the system. • Enter Self-Test.	8 not displayed ▶	GO to **D6**.
	8 displayed ▶	GO to **D5**.
D5 TEST WIRING HARNESS		
• Service/replace wiring harness and test according to EATC Self-Test.	OK ▶	Outside Air/Recirc door actuator OK.
	NOT OK ▶	GO to **D1**.
D6 TEST ACTUATOR		
• Replace actuator and test according to EATC Self-Test.	OK ▶	Outside Air/Recirc door actuator OK.
	NOT OK ▶	GO to **D1**.
D7 CHECK ACTUATOR		
• Disconnect both connectors from control assembly and drive actuator with a 9-12V battery (positive to Pin 1, negative to Pin 3 of connector J-1). • The following Pins may be jumped to connect the battery to the actuator: J-1 — J-2 Pin 1 to Pin 8 Pin 3 to Pin 4 **CAUTION: Any other combination could cause severe damage to other components of the electrical or air conditioning systems.**	Actuator drives freely (Goes from fresh to recirc or vice versa in under 10 seconds) ▶	GO to **D8**.
	Actuator does not drive ▶	GO to **D11**.
	Actuator drives but is restricted (Does not go from fresh to recirc or vice versa in under 10 seconds) ▶	GO to **D10**.
D8 TEST CONTROL ASSEMBLY		
• Reconnect control assembly and test according to EATC Self-Test.	OK ▶	Outside Air/Recirc door actuator OK.
	NOT OK ▶	GO to **D3**.
D9 TEST CONTINUITY		
• Circuit 248 (Y/LB) connecting Pin 12 of control assembly connector J-1 to Outside Air/Recirc door actuator could be open or disconnected. Make certain that the connector is connected.	OK ▶	GO to **D6**.
	NOT OK ▶	SERVICE and RETEST.
D10 CHECK ACTUATOR CLEARANCE		
• Actuator may be internally or externally restricted.	Externally restricted ▶	CLEAR and RETEST.
	Internally restricted ▶	REPLACE actuator and RETEST.
D11 CHECK CONTINUITY		
• Check continuity between Pins 1 and 3 on connector J-1.	Open ▶	GO to **D12**.
	Less than 100 Ohms ▶	GO to **D6**.
D12 CHECK ACTUATOR CONNECTION		
• Check to make sure actuator is connected.	OK ▶	GO to **D6**.
	NOT OK ▶	CONNECT and RETEST.
D13 CHANGE ACTUATOR		
• Change actuator and test.	OK ▶	Outside Air/Recirc door actuator OK.
	NOT OK ▶	GO to **D3**.

(1) **Disregard any other error codes displayed at this time.**

PINPOINT TEST E: CLUTCH SIGNAL LOW—MARK VII

TEST STEP		RESULT ▶	ACTION TO TAKE
E1	MEASURE VOLTAGE		
	• Measure voltage using Rotunda DVOM 007-00001 or equivalent, on Circuit 321 GY/W while control assembly is operating and set on AUTO (Pin 2 on blower speed controller connector).	5 to 7V ▶	REPLACE control assembly.
		Less than 5V ▶	REPLACE blower speed controller.

PINPOINT TEST F: SENSOR DIAGNOSIS—MARK VII

TEST STEP		RESULT ▶	ACTION TO TAKE
F1	MEASURE RESISTANCE		
	• Remove control assembly connectors. • Measure resistance between Pin 10 and Pin 14 of connector J1 (passenger side). The resistance should be as shown.	Resistance not to specification ▶	CHECK for short in wiring. If OK, REPLACE ambient sensor.
		Resistance is to specification ▶	GO to **F2**.

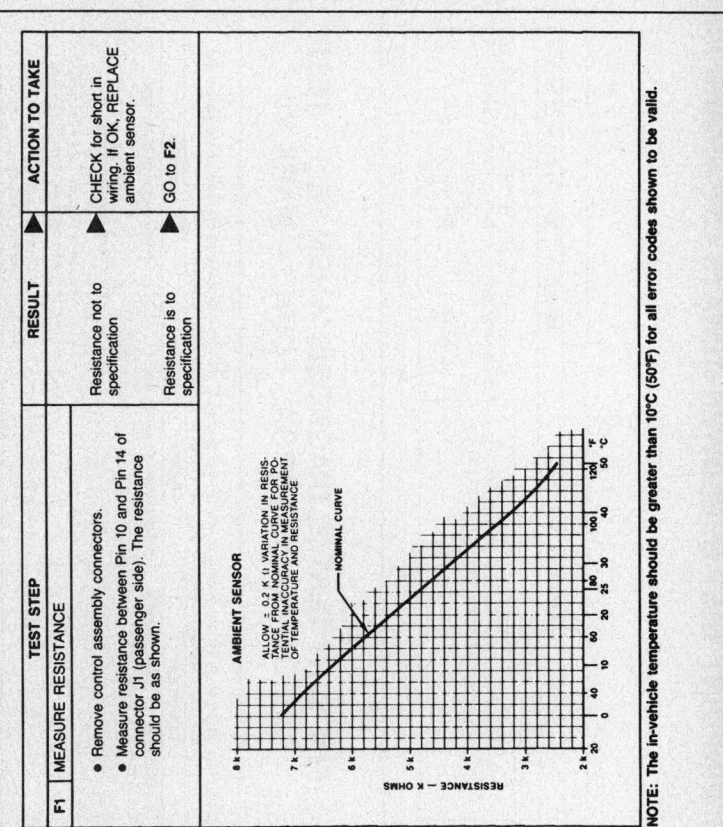

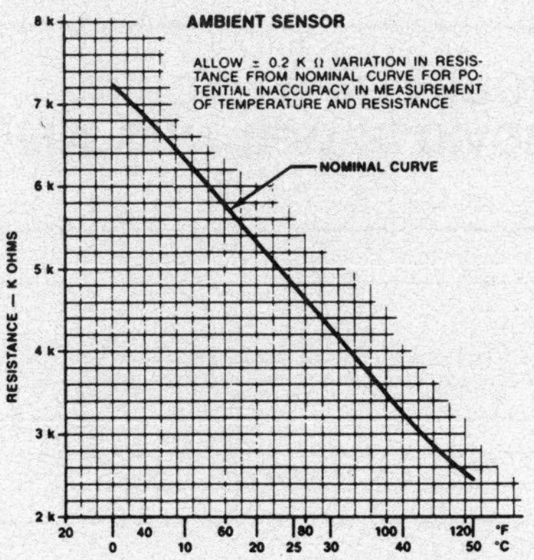
AMBIENT SENSOR
ALLOW ± 0.2 K Ω VARIATION IN RESISTANCE FROM NOMINAL CURVE FOR POTENTIAL INACCURACY IN MEASUREMENT OF TEMPERATURE AND RESISTANCE
NOMINAL CURVE
RESISTANCE — K OHMS
8 k
7 k
6 k
5 k
4 k
3 k
2 k
20 40 60 80 100 120 °F
0 10 20 25 30 40 50 °C

NOTE: The in-vehicle temperature should be greater than 10°C (50°F) for all error codes shown to be valid.

PINPOINT TEST F: SENSOR DIAGNOSIS—MARK VII

TEST STEP		RESULT ▶	ACTION TO TAKE
F2	MEASURE RESISTANCE		
	• Measure the resistance between Pin 2 and Pin 7 of connector J-2 (drivers side). The resistance should be as shown.	Resistance not to specification ▶	CHECK wiring. If OK, REPLACE in-vehicle sensor.
		Resistance is to specification ▶	Sensor OK. REPLACE control assembly.

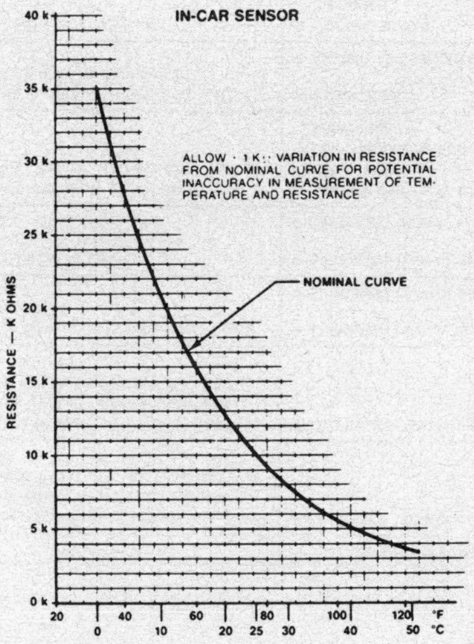
IN-CAR SENSOR
ALLOW ± 1 K Ω VARIATION IN RESISTANCE FROM NOMINAL CURVE FOR POTENTIAL INACCURACY IN MEASUREMENT OF TEMPERATURE AND RESISTANCE
NOMINAL CURVE
RESISTANCE — K OHMS
40 k
35 k
30 k
25 k
20 k
15 k
10 k
5 k
0 k
20 40 60 80 100 120 °F
0 10 20 25 30 40 50 °C

NOTE: The in-vehicle temperature should be greater than 10°C (50°F) for all error codes shown to be valid.

PINPOINT TEST G: BLOWER ALWAYS OFF—MARK VII

TEST STEP		RESULT	ACTION TO TAKE
G1	MEASURE VOLTAGE		
	• Measure voltage between Pin 1 (Circuit 184 T/O) on the blower controller and Pin 5 (Circuit 57 BK) with the control assembly in HI AUTO.	Greater than 10V ▶	REPLACE control assembly.
		Less than 10V ▶	REPLACE blower controller.

PINPOINT TEST H: DIAGNOSIS WHEN SELF—TEST INDICATES NO ERRORS FOUND—MARK VII

NOTE: This diagnosis is for the electronic part of the system. If there is a problem in the mechanical part of the system, diagnostic techniques should be located in the appropriate manual.

CONDITION	POSSIBLE SOURCE	ACTION
Cool Discharge Air When System is Set to AUTO/32°C (AUTO/90°F)	• Blend door not in max heat.	• Check position of blend door. • Check link attachment • Go to Pinpoint Test A (assume 1 was displayed during Self-Test).
	• Heater system malfunction.	• Diagnose according to appropriate service manual.
Warm Discharge Air When System is Set to AUTO/15°C (AUTO/60°F)	• Clutch circuit malfunction.	• Test clutch circuit. Go to Pinpoint Test J.
	• Blend door not in max A/C position (counterclockwise).	• Check position of blend door. • Check link attachment. • Go to Pinpoint Test A (assume 1 was displayed on Self-Test).
	• Outside Air/Recirc door not in recirc.	• Test Outside Air/Recirc door. Go to Pinpoint Test D (assume 4 was displayed during Self-Test).
Air Out Wrong Registers	• Panel/Floor door out of position.	• Go to Pinpoint Test B, assume 2 was displayed. • Check link attachment.
	• Panel/Defrost door out of position.	• Go to Pinpoint Test C, assume 3 was displayed. • Check link attachment.
No Blower	• Damaged CELO switch/wiring. • Damaged blower controller. • Damaged control assembly. • Damaged blower motor. • Damaged wiring.	• Go to Pinpoint Test K.
High Blower Only	• Damaged control. • Damaged blower controller. • Damaged wiring.	• Go to Pinpoint Test L.

PINPOINT TEST H: DIAGNOSIS WHEN SELF—TEST INDICATES NO ERRORS FOUND—MARK VII

CONDITION	POSSIBLE SOURCE	ACTION
No Low Blower in LO Mode but Goes to Low When Temperature Setting Changes From 15°C to 32°C (60°F to 90°F)	• Damaged control assembly.	• Replace control assembly.
No High Blower in HI AUTO but Goes to High When Temperature Setting Changes From 15°C to 32°C (60°F to 90°F)	• Damaged control assembly.	• Replace control assembly.
Blower Speed Does Not Vary, Fixed Between OFF and HI	• Damaged blower controller. • Damaged control assembly.	• GO to Pinpoint Test M.
Clutch is On in OFF.	• Damaged control assembly. • Damaged blower speed controller.	• GO to Pinpoint Test P.
Control Assembly Digits and LED's Do Not Light Up. Blower On	• Control assembly ignition Circuit 296 W/P not connected to the control assembly.	• Service wiring.
Control Assembly Digits and LED's Do Not Light Up. Blower Off	• Fuse open. • Ignition Circuit 296 W/P open.	• Replace fuse. • Check Circuit 296 W/P.
One LED Does Not Light	• Control assembly worn or damaged.	• Replace control assembly.
Cold Air is Delivered During Heating When Engine is Cold	• Damaged wiring.	• Place system at AUTO/32°C (AUTO/90°F) with ignition in OFF, ground Circuit 244 Y/W at engine temperature switch. If blower is on, check wiring. If OK, replace control assembly.
	• Damaged engine temperature switch.	• Replace engine temperature switch.
Temperature Set Point Does Not Repeat After Turning Ignition Off	• Damaged control assembly.	• Check fuse/wiring. Replace control assembly.
Interior Temperature Too Warm or Too Cool	• Control assembly not within calibration limits. • Customer does not feel interior temperature is correct.	• Adjust control assembly calibration.
VFD Does Not Dim Properly	• Inoperative/not connected wiring.	• Check wiring (Circuits 14 and 19).

PINPOINT TEST H: DIAGNOSIS WHEN SELF—TEST INDICATES NO ERRORS FOUND— MARK VII

CONDITION	• POSSIBLE SOURCE	• ACTION
Control Assembly Temperature Display Does Not Switch From Farenheit to Centigrade When E/M Trip Computer Button is Pushed	• Damaged wiring, trip computer, or control assembly.	• **CAUTION: Accidental shorting of the wrong pin could destroy the control assembly.** • Short Pin 14 of connector J-2 (Circuit 506 R) to ground. Turn ignition switch to ON. If the display does not switch from F to C, Circuit 506R is shorted at the control assembly and the control assembly is defective.
System Does Not Control Temperature	• Sensor hose not connected to aspirator.	• Inspect and service.
	• Aspirator not secured to evaporator case.	• Inspect and service.
	• Sensor seals missing or not installed properly.	• Inspect and service.
	• Aspirator or sensor hose blocked with foreign material.	• Inspect and service.
	• Damaged aspirator hose.	• Inspect and service.
Outside Air/Recirc or Panel Defrost Door Runs Continuously	• Feedback circuit open.	• Check connectors.
		• Check wiring harness.
		• Check actuator.

PINPOINT TEST J: NO CLUTCH OPERATION—MARK VII

TEST STEP		RESULT	▶	ACTION TO TAKE
J1	CHECK CLUTCH ENGAGEMENT			
	• Jump Circuit 575 Y/BK (Pin 6) to Circuit 348 LG/P (Pin 4) on blower controller. Leave jumper on until it is determined that no short exists.	Clutch engages and does not blow fuse while operating	▶	GO to J3.
		Clutch does not engage	▶	GO to J2.
		20A fuse blows immediately or after driving/ operation	▶	Clutch is shorted. CHECK diode in wiring harness across clutch. SERVICE short, then test to see if the control assembly will turn the clutch off and on. If not, REPLACE blower controller.
J2	MEASURE VOLTAGE			
	• Measure voltage at blower speed controller connector Circuit 575 BK (Pin 6).	Zero volts	▶	CHECK battery circuit.
		Greater than 10V	▶	DIAGNOSE damaged clutch.
J3	MEASURE VOLTAGE			
	• Set control assembly to AUTO. • Measure voltage between Circuit 321 GY/W (Pin 2) and ground.	5 to 7V	▶	REPLACE blower controller.
		Greater than 7V	▶	GO to J4.
J4	CHECK CONTINUITY			
	• Check continuity of Circuit 321 GY/W	OK	▶	REPLACE control assembly.
		NOT OK	▶	SERVICE and test according to EATC SELF-TEST.

NOTE: Repeated failure of blower speed controllers indicates that there is a short circuit in Circuit 348 LG/P in the engine compartment or a reversed or leaky clutch diode.

PINPOINT TEST K: NO BLOWER—MARK VII

	TEST STEP	RESULT	▶	ACTION TO TAKE
K1	TEST BLOWER			
	• Set control assembly to AUTO/15°C (AUTO/60°F) with engine running.	High blower	▶	GO to K2.
		No blower	▶	GO to K4.
K2	TEST BLOWER			
	• Set control assembly to AUTO/32°C (AUTO/90°F) with engine running warm. • Disconnect cold engine lock-out switch in engine compartment.	High blower	▶	REPLACE CELO switch.
		No blower	▶	GO to K3.
K3	MEASURE RESISTANCE			
	• Disconnect control assembly connector J-2 (drivers side) while leaving the Cold Engine Lock-Out Switch (CELO) switch disconnected. • Measure the resistance between Pin 6 on J-2 and ground.	Open	▶	REPLACE control assembly.
		Short	▶	SERVICE wiring harness.
K4	CHECK BLOWER FUSE			
	• Check fuse, replace if blown, test blower operation.	OK	▶	Blower OK.
		NOT OK	▶	GO to K5.
K5	CHECK BLOWER MOTOR			
	• Ground Circuit 515 O/R on the blower connector.	High blower	▶	GO to K6.
		No blower	▶	REPLACE blower motor on B+ line to blower.
K6	CHECK BLOWER SPEED CONTROLLER			
	• Ground Circuit 184 T/O (Pin 1) at the blower motor speed controller connector.	High blower	▶	GO to K7.
		No blower	▶	REPLACE blower speed controller.
K7	CHECK CONTROL ASSEMBLY			
	• Ground Circuit 184 T/O (Pin 5) at J-2 of the control assembly.	High blower	▶	REPLACE control assembly.
		No blower	▶	SERVICE wiring harness.

PINPOINT TEST L: HIGH BLOWER ONLY—MARK VII

	TEST STEP	RESULT	▶	ACTION TO TAKE
L1	TEST CONTROLLER			
	• Disconnect connector J-2 (driver's side) from control assembly. • Short Pins 8 and 5.	Blower turns off	▶	REPLACE control assembly.
		Blower stays in HIGH	▶	REPLACE blower controller.

PINPOINT TEST M: FIXED BLOWER SPEED—MARK VII

	TEST STEP	RESULT	▶	ACTION TO TAKE
M1	TEST CONTROLLER			
	• Disconnect connector J-2 (driver's side) from control assembly. • Jump Pins 5 and 4	Goes to high blower	▶	REPLACE control assembly.
		Stays the same	▶	REPLACE blower speed controller.

PINPOINT TEST P: CLUTCH DOES NOT DISENGAGE WHEN IN OFF OR ECON—MARK VII

	TEST STEP	RESULT	▶	ACTION TO TAKE
P1	TEST CLUTCH			
	• Disconnect connector J-2 (driver's side) from control assembly.	Clutch disengages	▶	REPLACE control assembly.
		Clutch stays on	▶	REPLACE blower controller.

ACTUATOR INFORMATION AND IDENTIFICATION MARK VII

	Actuator			
	Temp. Blend Door	Floor/Panel Mode Door	Outside Air/ Recirculation Door	Panel/ Defrost Door
Type	Continuous	Continuous	Two Position	Two Position
Rotation (Arm Side)	CW/CCW	CW/CCW	CCW	CCW
Operating Range	180°	180°	360°	360°
Sound Shields	No	No	Yes	Yes
Arm Color	Silver	Silver	Black	Silver
Arm Ship Position	A	A	Pos. 2	Pos. 2
Mounting Location	B	C	D	E

Function	Max. Heat	Max. A/C	Air to Floor	Air to Plenum	Outside Air	Recirc.	Defrost	Panel
Arm Position	1	2	1	2	1	2	1	2
Resistance	—	—	—	—	0K Ohms	6.8K Ohms	0K Ohms	6.8K Ohms
Feedback Ratio	.087	.686	.087	.686	—	—	—	—
Between Terminals	F	F	F	F	G	G	G	G

A. Feedback Ratio (FBR) — .34-.36 with a clockwise torque applied to actuator arm from arm side
B. Front Center of Evaporator Assembly directly behind radio
C. Top Left Corner (Driver's Side) of Evaporator Assembly
D. Attached to Panel/Defrost Plenum which is mounted to underside of Instrument Panel
E. Right Front of Evaporator Assembly directly behind Glove Box Opening
F. The Feedback Ratio (FBR) equals the ratio of resistance across terminals F&D divided by the resistance across terminals C&D
G. The resistance is measured between the B+ and Feedback terminals

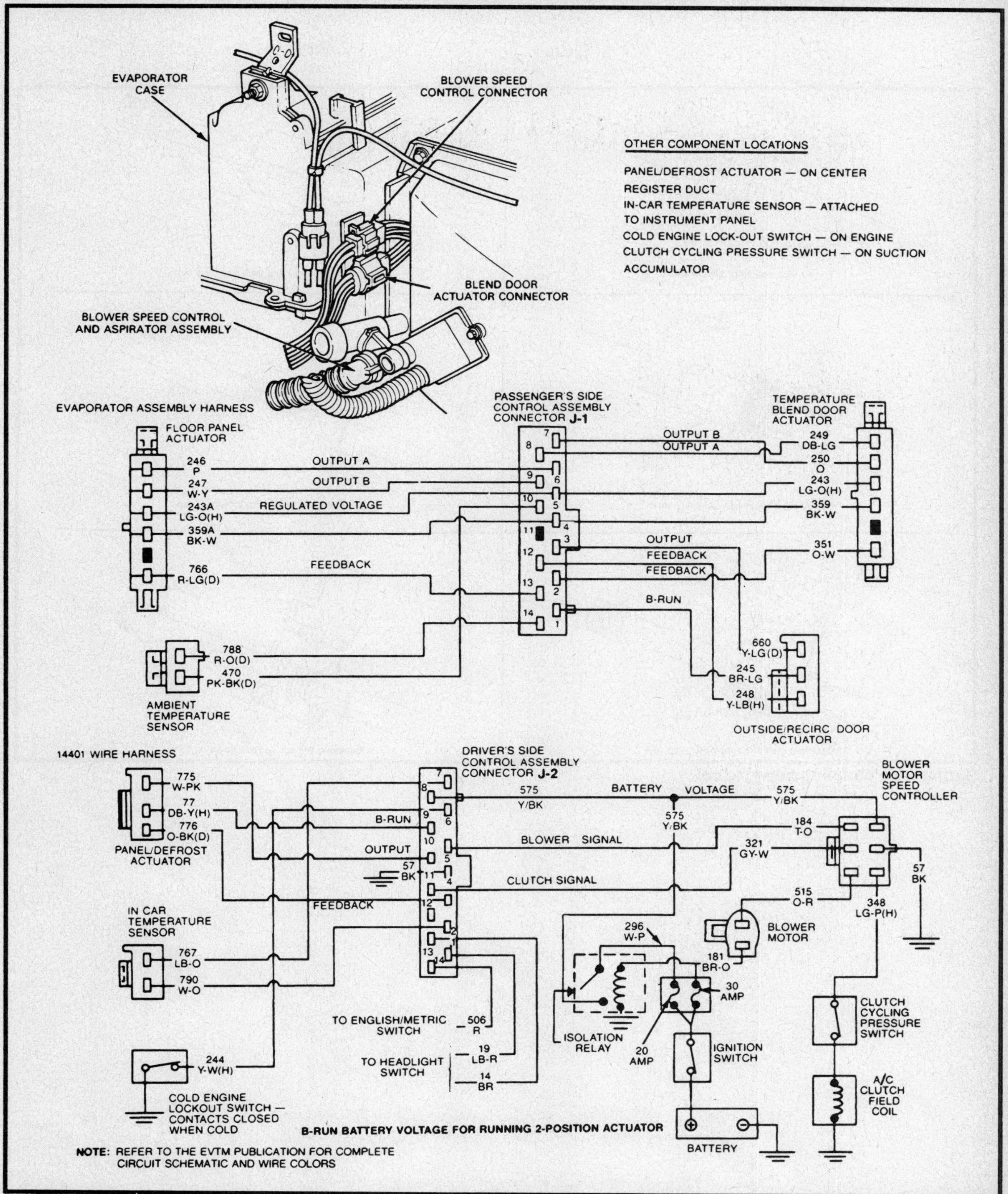
EVAPORATOR CASE
BLOWER SPEED CONTROL CONNECTOR
OTHER COMPONENT LOCATIONS
PANEL/DEFROST ACTUATOR — ON CENTER REGISTER DUCT
IN-CAR TEMPERATURE SENSOR — ATTACHED TO INSTRUMENT PANEL
COLD ENGINE LOCK-OUT SWITCH — ON ENGINE
CLUTCH CYCLING PRESSURE SWITCH — ON SUCTION ACCUMULATOR
BLEND DOOR ACTUATOR CONNECTOR
BLOWER SPEED CONTROL AND ASPIRATOR ASSEMBLY
EVAPORATOR ASSEMBLY HARNESS
FLOOR PANEL ACTUATOR
246 P
247 W-Y
243A LG-O(H)
359A BK-W
766 R-LG(D)
OUTPUT A
OUTPUT B
REGULATED VOLTAGE
FEEDBACK
PASSENGER'S SIDE CONTROL ASSEMBLY CONNECTOR J-1
OUTPUT B
OUTPUT A
OUTPUT
FEEDBACK
FEEDBACK
B-RUN
TEMPERATURE BLEND DOOR ACTUATOR
249 DB-LG
250 O
243 LG-O(H)
359 BK-W
351 O-W
788 R-O(D)
470 PK-BK(D)
AMBIENT TEMPERATURE SENSOR
660 Y-LG(D)
245 BR-LG
248 Y-LB(H)
OUTSIDE/RECIRC DOOR ACTUATOR
14401 WIRE HARNESS
775 W-PK
77 DB-Y(H)
776 O-BK(D)
PANEL/DEFROST ACTUATOR
DRIVER'S SIDE CONTROL ASSEMBLY CONNECTOR J-2
575 Y/BK
BATTERY VOLTAGE
575 Y/BK
575 Y/BK
BLOWER MOTOR SPEED CONTROLLER
B-RUN
OUTPUT
57 BK
BLOWER SIGNAL
184 T-O
321 GY-W
CLUTCH SIGNAL
57 BK
FEEDBACK
515 O-R
348 LG-P(H)
IN CAR TEMPERATURE SENSOR
767 LB-O
790 W-O
296 W-P
BLOWER MOTOR
181 BR-O
30 AMP
ISOLATION RELAY
20 AMP
IGNITION SWITCH
CLUTCH CYCLING PRESSURE SWITCH
TO ENGLISH/METRIC SWITCH
506 R
TO HEADLIGHT SWITCH
19 LB-R
14 BR
244 Y-W(H)
COLD ENGINE LOCKOUT SWITCH — CONTACTS CLOSED WHEN COLD
A/C CLUTCH FIELD COIL
B-RUN BATTERY VOLTAGE FOR RUNNING 2-POSITION ACTUATOR
BATTERY
NOTE: REFER TO THE EVTM PUBLICATION FOR COMPLETE CIRCUIT SCHEMATIC AND WIRE COLORS

Automatic temperature control wiring schematic— Mark VII

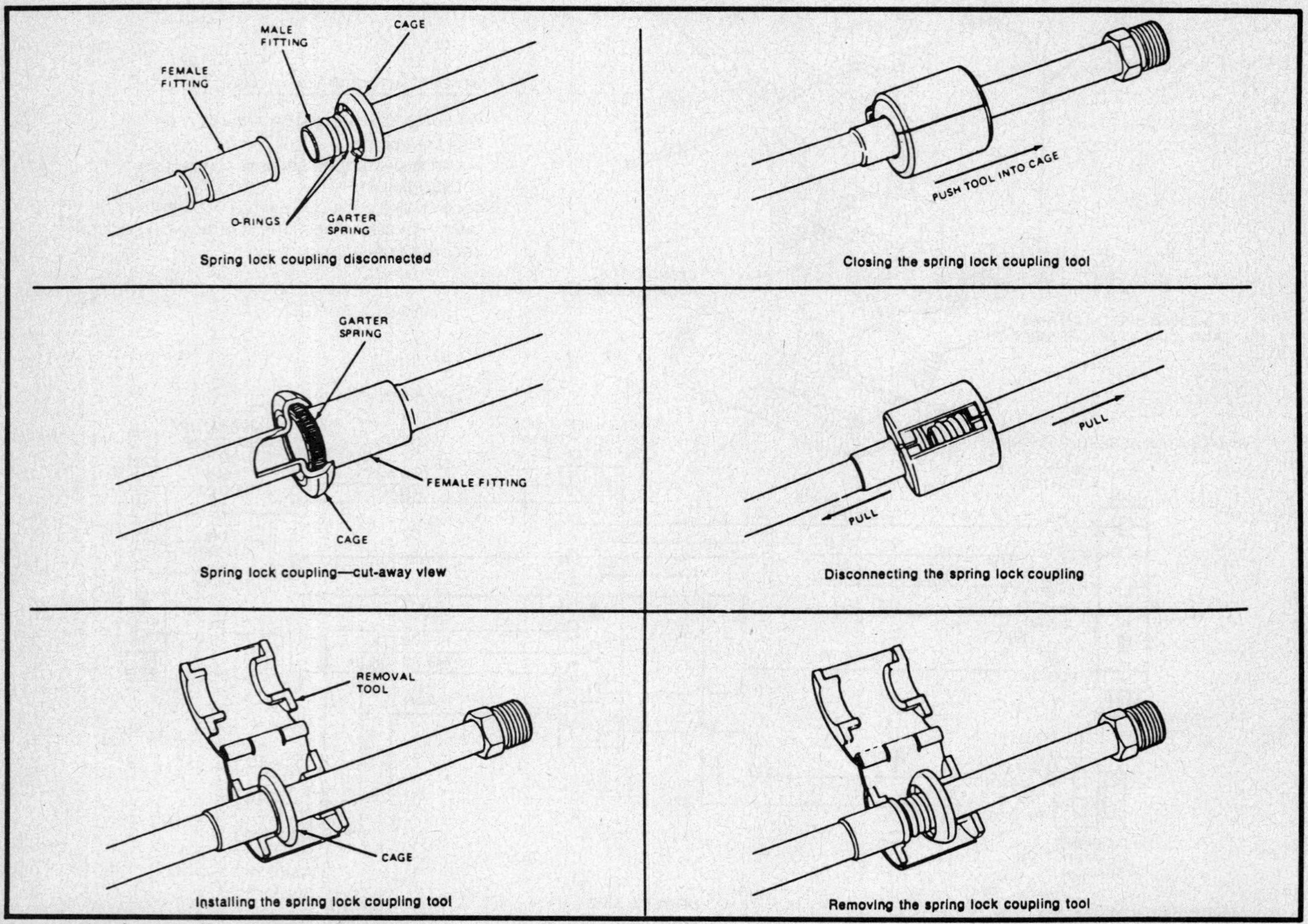
MALE FITTING
CAGE
FEMALE FITTING
O-RINGS
GARTER SPRING
Spring lock coupling disconnected
PUSH TOOL INTO CAGE
Closing the spring lock coupling tool
GARTER SPRING
FEMALE FITTING
CAGE
Spring lock coupling—cut-away view
PULL
PULL
Disconnecting the spring lock coupling
REMOVAL TOOL
CAGE
Installing the spring lock coupling tool
Removing the spring lock coupling tool

Spring lock coupling service tool

6 GENERAL MOTORS CORPORATION 6

FRONT WHEEL DRIVE VEHICLES

SPECIFICATIONS

VEHICLE IDENTIFICATION CHART

It is important for servicing and ordering parts to be certain of the vehicle and engine identification. The VIN (vehicle identification number) is a 17 digit number visible through the windshield on the driver's side of the dash and contains the vehicle and engine identification codes. The tenth digit indicates model year and the eighth digit indicates engine code. It can be interpreted as follows:

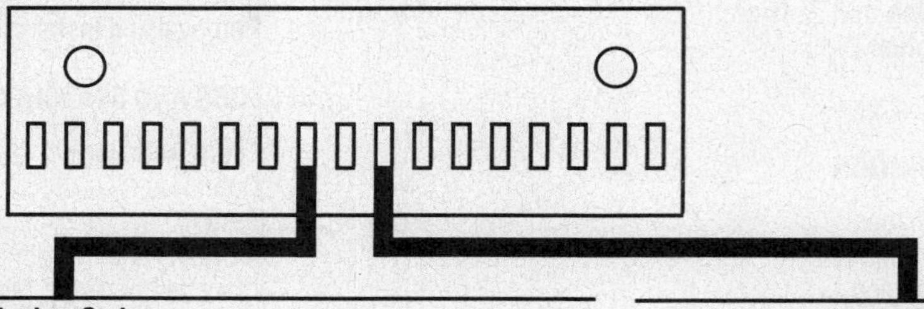

Engine Code

Code	Cu. In.	Liters	Cyl.	Fuel Sys.	Eng. Mfg.
6	98	1.6	4	TBI	—
K	121	2.0	4	TBI	Brazil
M	121	2.0	4	MFI	①
1	121	2.0	4	TBI	Chevrolet
G	134	2.2	4	TBI	Chevrolet
A	138	2.3	4	MFI	Oldsmobile
D	138	2.3	4	MFI	Oldsmobile
R	151	2.5	4	TBI	Pontiac
V	151	2.5	4	TBI	Pontiac
W	173	2.8	6	MFI	Chevrolet
T	192	3.1	6	MFI	Chevrolet
N	204	3.3	6	SFI	Buick
3	231	3.8	6	SFI	Buick
C	231	3.8	6	SFI	Buick
5	273	4.3	8	SFI	Cadillac
3	273	4.3	8	SFI	Cadillac
B	300	4.9	8	SFI	Cadillac

① Chevrolet-Pontiac-GM of Canada

Model Year

Code	Year
K	1989
L	1990
M	1991

REFRIGERANT CAPACITIES

Year	Model	Freon (oz.)	Oil (fl. oz.)	Type
1989	A Body	44.0	8	①
	C Body	46.0	8	HR-6
	H Body	38.5	8	HR-6
	E and K Body	38.0	8	HR-6
	V Body	36.0	8	HR-6
	J Body	36.0	8	V-5
	L Body	36.0	8	V-5
	N Body	36.0	8	V-5
	T Body	35.0	8	V-5
	W Body	44.0②	8	HR-6

REFRIGERANT CAPACITIES

Year	Model	Freon (oz.)	Oil (fl. oz.)	Type
1990	A Body	44.0	8	①
	C Body	46.0	8	HR-6
	H Body	38.5	8	HR-6
	E and K Body	38.0	8	HR-6
	V Body	36.0	8	HR-6
	J Body	36.0	8	V-5
	L Body	36.0	8	V-5
	N Body	36.0	8	V-5
	T Body	35.0	8	V-5
	W Body	44.0②	8	HR-6
1991	A Body	44.0	8	①
	C Body	46.0	8	HR-6
	H Body	38.5	8	HR-6
	E and K Body	38.0	8	HR-6
	V Body	36.0	8	HR-6
	J Body	36.0	8	V-5
	L Body	36.0	8	V-5
	N Body	36.0	8	V-5
	T Body	35.0	8	V-5
	W Body	44.0②	8	HR-6

① HR-6 and V-5 compressors
② Freon capacity 36.0 oz. with V-5 compressor

AIR CONDITIONING BELT TENSION CHART

Year	Engine VIN	Engine (L)	Belt Type	New	Used
1989	6	1.6	V-Belt	155	80
	K	2.0	V-Belt	155	80
	M	2.0	Serpentine	①	①
	1	2.0	Serpentine	①	①
	R	2.5	Serpentine	①	①
	U	2.5	Serpentine	①	①
	W	2.8	Serpentine	①	①
	T	3.1	Serpentine	①	①
	N	3.3	Serpentine	①	①
	C	3.8	Serpentine	①	①
	5	4.3	Serpentine	①	①
1990	6	1.6	V-Belt	155	80
	K	2.0	V-Belt	155	80
	M	2.0	Serpentine	①	①
	1	2.0	Serpentine	①	①
	G	2.2	Serpentine	①	①
	A	2.3	Serpentine	①	①
	D	2.3	Serpentine	①	①

AIR CONDITIONING BELT TENSION CHART

Year	Engine VIN	Engine (L)	Belt Type	New	Used
1990	R	2.5	Serpentine	①	①
	U	2.5	Serpentine	①	①
	W	2.8	Serpentine	①	①
	T	3.1	Serpentine	①	①
	N	3.3	Serpentine	①	①
	C	3.8	Serpentine	①	①
	3	4.3	Serpentine	①	①
1991	6	1.6	V-Belt	155	80
	1	2.0	Serpentine	①	①
	G	2.2	Serpentine	①	①
	A	2.3	Serpentine	①	①
	D	2.3	Serpentine	①	①
	R	2.5	Serpentine	①	①
	U	2.5	Serpentine	①	①
	T	3.1	Serpentine	①	①
	N	3.3	Serpentine	①	①
	C	3.8	Serpentine	①	①
	3	4.3	Serpentine	①	①
	B	4.9	Serpentine	①	①

① Automatic dynamic tensioner

BODY DESIGNATION DATA

Year	Manufacturer	Model	Body Designation
1989	Buick	Century	A
	Chevrolet	Celebrity	A
	Oldsmobile	Cutlass Ciera, Cruiser	A
	Pontiac	6000	A
	Buick	Electra, Park Avenue	C
	Cadillac	DeVille, Fleetwood	C
	Oldsmobile	Ninety Eight, Regency	C
	Buick	Reatta	E
	Buick	LeSabre	H
	Oldsmobile	Delta 88, Royale	H
	Pontiac	Bonneville	H
	Buick	Skyhawk	J
	Chevrolet	Cavalier	J
	Pontiac	Sunbird	J
	Cadillac	Seville	K
	Chevrolet	Beretta, Corsica	L
	Buick	Somerset, Skylark	N
	Oldsmobile	Cutlass Calais	N

BODY DESIGNATION DATA

Year	Manufacturer	Model	Body Designation
1989	Pontiac	Grand AM	N
	Pontiac	LeMans	T
	Cadillac	Allante	V
	Buick	Regal	W
	Chevrolet	Lumina	W
	Oldsmobile	Cutlass Supreme	W
	Pontiac	Grand Prix	W
1990	Buick	Century	A
	Chevrolet	Celebrity	A
	Oldsmobile	Cutlass Ciera, Cruiser	A
	Pontiac	6000	A
	Buick	Electra, Park Avenue	C
	Cadillac	DeVille, Fleetwood	C
	Oldsmobile	Ninety Eight, Regency	C
	Buick	Reatta	E
	Buick	LeSabre	H
	Oldsmobile	Delta 88, Royale	H
	Pontiac	Bonneville	H
	Chevrolet	Cavalier	J
	Pontiac	Sunbird	J
	Cadillac	Seville	K
	Chevrolet	Beretta, Corsica	L
	Buick	Somerset, Skylark	N
	Oldsmobile	Cutlass Calais	N
	Pontiac	Grand AM	N
	Pontiac	LeMans	T
	Cadillac	Allante	V
	Buick	Regal	W
	Chevrolet	Lumina	W
	Oldsmobile	Cutlass Supreme	W
	Pontiac	Grand Prix	W
1991	Buick	Century	A
	Oldsmobile	Cutlass Ciera, Cruiser	A
	Pontiac	6000	A
	Buick	Electra, Park Avenue, Park Avenue Ultra	C
	Cadillac	DeVille, Fleetwood	C
	Oldsmobile	Ninety Eight, Regency	C
	Buick	Reatta	E
	Buick	LeSabre	H
	Oldsmobile	Delta 88, Royale	H
	Pontiac	Bonneville	H
	Chevrolet	Cavalier	J
	Pontiac	Sunbird	J
	Cadillac	Seville	K
	Chevrolet	Beretta, Corsica	L

BODY DESIGNATION DATA

Year	Manufacturer	Model	Body Designation
1991	Buick	Somerset, Skylark	N
	Oldsmobile	Cutlass Calais	N
	Pontiac	Grand AM	N
	Pontiac	LeMans	T
	Cadillac	Allante	V
	Buick	Regal	W
	Chevrolet	Lumina	W
	Oldsmobile	Cutlass Supreme	W
	Pontiac	Grand Prix	W

SYSTEM DESCRIPTION

General Information

The heater and air conditioning systems are controlled manually or electronically. The systems differ mainly in the way air temperature and the routing of air flow are controlled. The manual system controls air temperature through a cable-actuated lever and air flow through a vacuum switching valve and vacuum actuators. With Electronic Climate Control (ECC) systems, both temperature and air flow are controlled by the BCM through the Climate Control Panel (CCP).

The heating system provides heating, ventilation and defrosting for the windshield and side windows. The heater core is a heat exchanger supplied with coolant from the engine cooling system. Temperature is controlled by the temperature valve which moves an air door that directs air flow through the heater core for more heat or bypasses the heater core for less heat.

Vacuum actutors control the mode doors which direct air flow to the outlet ducts. The mode selector on the control panel directs engine vacuum to the actuators. The position of the mode doors determines whether air flows from the floor, panel, defrost or panel and defrost ducts (bi-level mode).

There are 2 types of compressors used on front-wheel drive car air conditioning sytems. The HR-6 compressor, used on Cycling Clutch Orifice Tube (CCOT) systems, is a 6 cylinder axial compressor consisting of 3 double-ended pistons actuated by a swash plate shaft assembly. The compressor cycles on and off according to system demands. The compressor driveshaft is driven by the serpentine belt when the electro-magnetic clutch is engaged.

The V-5 compressor, used on Variable Displacement Orifice Tube (VDOT) systems, is designed to meet the demands of the air conditioning system without cycling. The compressor employs a variable angle wobble plate controlling the displacement of 5 axially oriented cylinders. Displacement is controlled by a bellows actuated control valve located in the rear head of the compressor. The electro-magnetic compressor clutch connects the compressor shaft to the serpentine drive belt when the coil is energized.

Service Valve Locations

The high-side service valve is normally located in the refrigerant line near the discharge fitting of the compressor.

The low-side service valve is normally located on the accumulator or in the condenser-to-evaporator refrigerant line.

System Discharging

R-12 refrigerant is a chloroflourocarbon which, when released into the atmosphere, can contribute to the depletion on the ozone layer in the upper atmosphere. Ozone filters out harmful radiation from the sun. In order to protect the ozone layer, an approved R-12 Recovery/Recycling machine that meets SAE standards should be employed when discharging the system. Follow the operating instructions provided with the approved equipment exactly to properly discharge the system.

System Evacuating

If the air conditioning system has been opened to the atmosphere, it should be air and moisture free before being recharged with refrigerant. Moisture and air mixed with refrigerant will

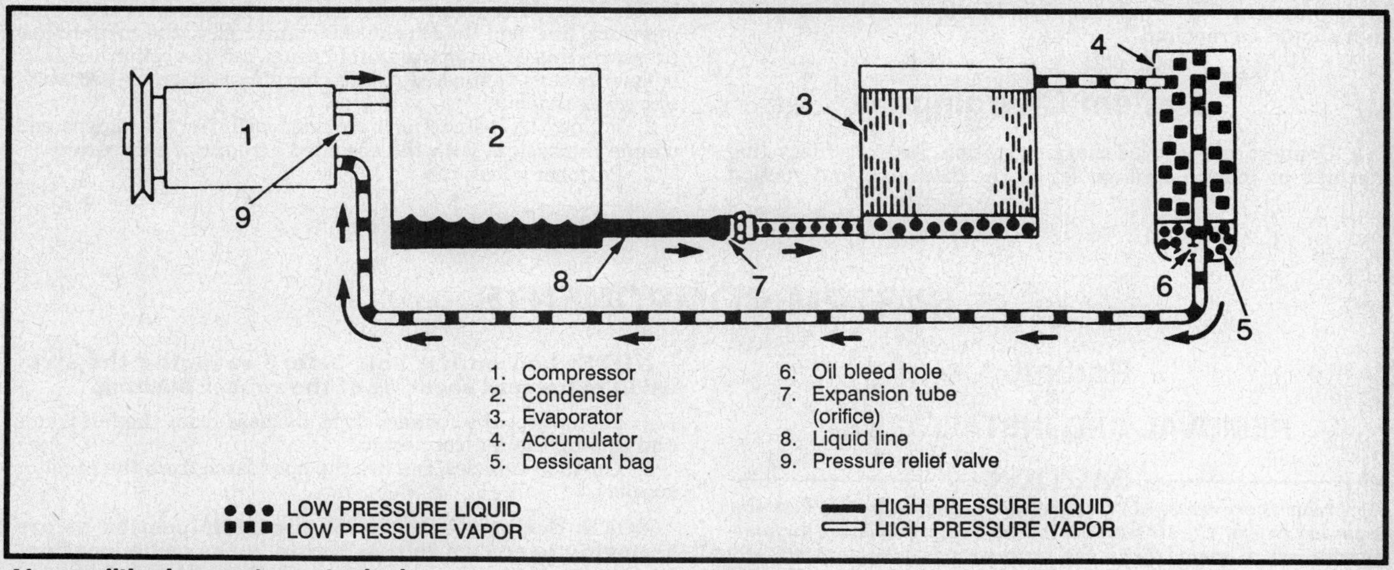
1
2
3
4
5
6
7
8
9
1. Compressor
2. Condenser
3. Evaporator
4. Accumulator
5. Dessicant bag
6. Oil bleed hole
7. Expansion tube (orifice)
8. Liquid line
9. Pressure relief valve
LOW PRESSURE LIQUID
LOW PRESSURE VAPOR
HIGH PRESSURE LIQUID
HIGH PRESSURE VAPOR

Air conditioning system—typical

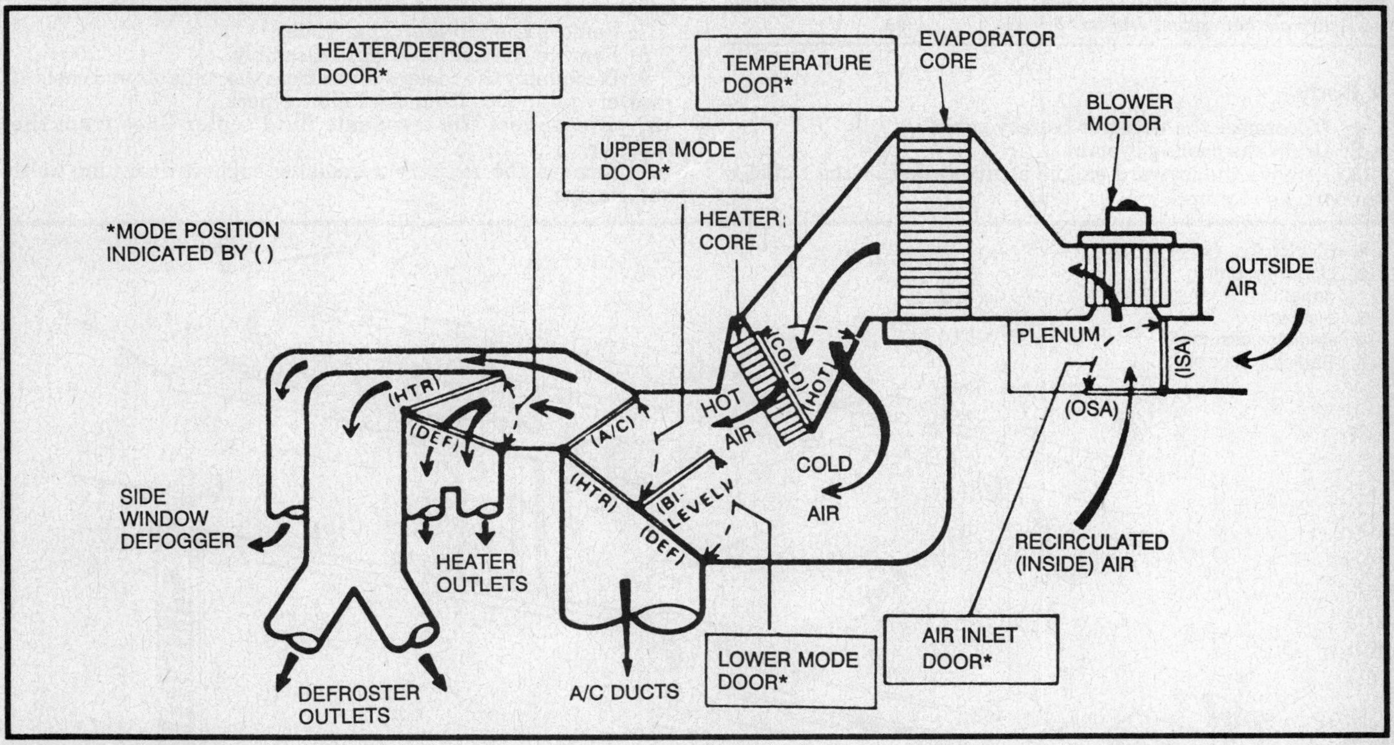
HEATER/DEFROSTER DOOR*
TEMPERATURE DOOR*
EVAPORATOR CORE
BLOWER MOTOR
UPPER MODE DOOR*
*MODE POSITION INDICATED BY ( )
HEATER CORE
OUTSIDE AIR
PLENUM
(ISA)
(OSA)
(HTR)
(DEF)
(A/C)
(COLD)
(HOT)
HOT AIR
COLD AIR
(HTR)
(BI-LEVEL)
(DEF)
SIDE WINDOW DEFOGGER
HEATER OUTLETS
RECIRCULATED (INSIDE) AIR
AIR INLET DOOR*
LOWER MODE DOOR*
DEFROSTER OUTLETS
A/C DUCTS

Air flow—typical

raise the compressor head pressure, possibly damage the system's components and will reduce the performance of the system. In addition, air and moisture in the system can lead to internal corrosion of the system components. Moisture will boil at normal room temperature when exposed to a vacuum. To evacuate, or rid the system of air and moisture:

1. Leak test the system and repair any leaks found.
2. Connect an approved charging station, Recovery/Recycling machine or manifold gauge set and vacuum pump to the discharge and suction ports. The red hose is normally connected to the discharge (high pressure) line. The blue hose is connected to the suction (low pressure) line. If using a manifold gauge set, the center (usually yellow) hose is connected to the charging station or Recovery/Recycling machine.
3. Open the discharge and suction ports and start the vacuum pump. If the pump is not able to pull at least 26 in. Hg of vacuum there is a leak that must be repaired before evacuation can occur.
4. Once the system has reached at least 26 in. Hg of vacuum, allow the system to evacuate for at least 10 minutes. The longer the system is evacuated, the more moisture will be removed.
5. Close all valves and turn the pump off. If the system loses

more than 2 in. Hg of vacuum after 15 minutes, there is a leak that should be repaired.

System Charging

1. Connect an approved charging station, Recovery/Recycling machine or manifold gauge set to the discharge and suction ports. The red hose is normally connected to the discharge (high pressure) line, and the blue hose is connected to the suction (low pressure) line. If using a manifold gauge set, the center (usually yellow) hose is connected to the charging station or Recovery/Recycling machine.
2. Follow the instructions provided with the equipment and charge the system with the specified amount of refrigerant.
3. Perform a leak test.

SYSTEM COMPONENTS

Radiator

REMOVAL AND INSTALLATION

CAUTION

Some vehicles are equipped with the Supplemental Inflatable Restraint or air bag system. The air bag system must be disabled before performing service on or around the air bag, instrument panel components, wiring and sensors. Failure to follow safety and disabling procedures could result in accidental air bag deployment, possible personal injury and unnecessary air bag system repairs.

A Body

1. Disconnect the negative battery cable.
2. Drain the cooling system.
3. Remove the forward engine strut bracket at the radiator support, as required.

NOTE: Loosen the bolt before swinging the strut aside to prevent shearing of the rubber bushing.

4. Disconnect the forward light harness from the fan frame and unplug the fan connector.
5. On 1989 vehicles, remove the hood latch from the radiator support.

NOTE: Scribe a line around the latch location before removing to ensure reinstallation in the same location.

6. If equipped with 2.5L engine, remove the air intake resonator mounting nut and remove the resonator.
7. Remove the fan attaching bolts.
8. Remove the fan and frame assembly.
9. Disconnect the coolant hoses from the radiator and coolant recovery tank hose from the radiator neck.
10. Disconnect the transaxle fluid cooler lines from the radiator.
11. Remove the radiator-to-radiator support attaching bolts and clamps.

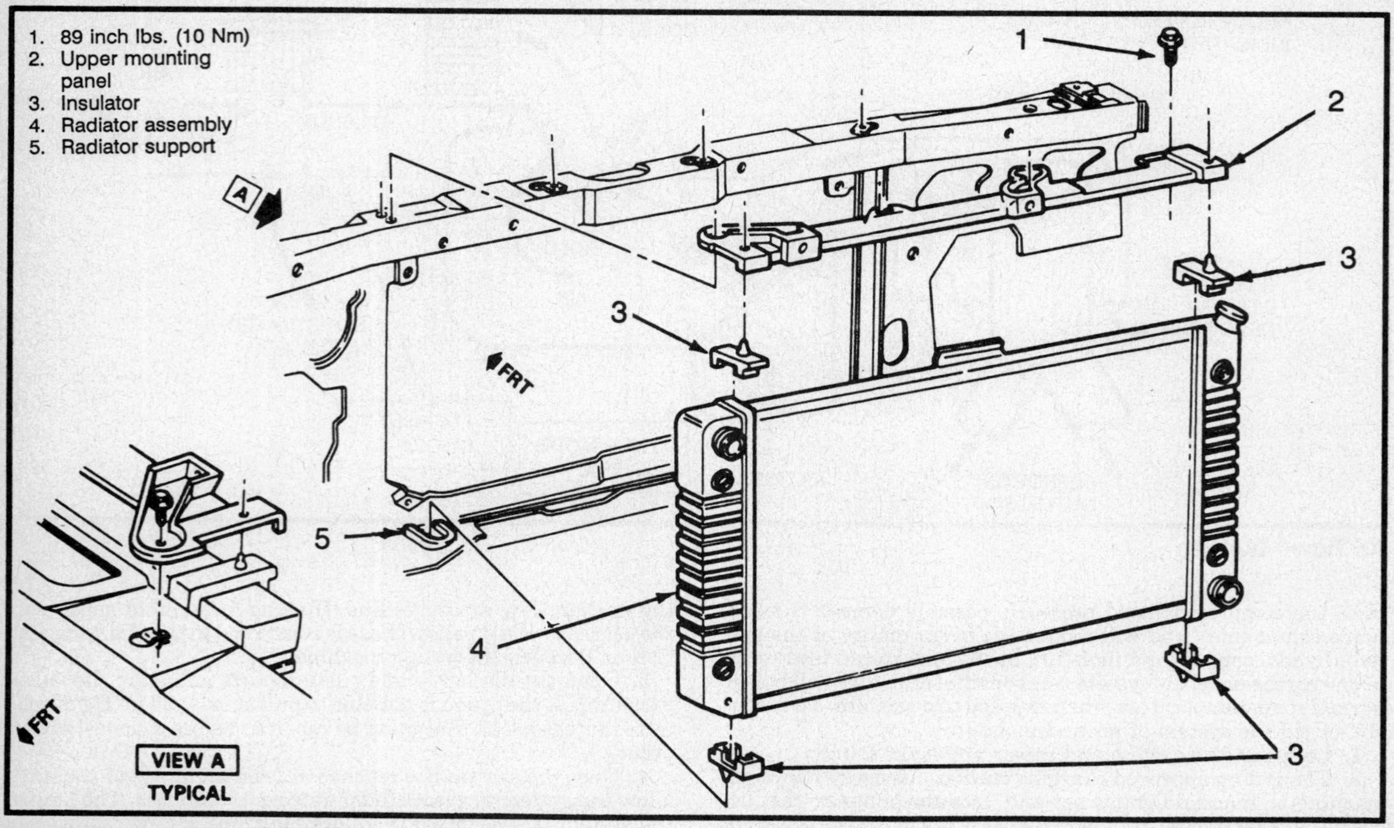
1. 89 inch lbs. (10 Nm)
2. Upper mounting panel
3. Insulator
4. Radiator assembly
5. Radiator support
1
2
3
3
3
4
5
A
FRT
FRT
VIEW A
TYPICAL

Radiator mounting—A body

12. Remove the radiator.

To install:

13. Position the radiator in the vehicle.
14. Install the radiator attaching bolts. Tighten to 89 inch lbs. (10 Nm).
15. Connect the transaxle fluid cooler lines to the radiator.
16. Connect the coolant hoses to the radiator.
17. On 1989 models, install the hood latch observing scribe marks made during removal.
18. Connect the coolant recovery hose to the radiator neck.
19. Install the fan frame and assembly. Tighten to 89 inch lbs. (10 Nm).
20. Connect the fan connector.
21. If equipped with 2.5L engine, install the air intake resonator and mounting nut.
22. Connect the forward engine strut and bracket, if removed. Tighten the attaching bolts to 17 ft. lbs. (23 Nm).
23. Connect negative battery cable.
24. Fill cooling system and check for leaks. Start engine and allow engine to come to normal operating temperature. Recheck for coolant leaks. Allow engine to warm up sufficiently to confirm operation of cooling fan.

C and H Body

1. Disconnect the negative battery cable. Drain the cooling system into a clean container for reuse.
2. If equipped, disable the Supplemental Inflatable Restraint (SIR) system by performing the following:
   a. Remove the SIR fuse from the fuse panel.
   b. Remove the left side sound insulator.
   c. Remove the Connector Positive Assurance (CPA) from the yellow 2-way SIR harness connector at the base of the steering column and separate the connector.
3. Remove the upper fan mounting bolts. On Deville and Fleetwood, remove the left and right cooling fans.
4. Remove the upper air cleaner duct and/or silencer, as required.
5. Remove the upper radiator panel.
6. Disconnect the coolant hoses from the radiator and coolant recovery tank hose from the radiator neck.
7. Disconnect the cooling fan connector.
8. Disconnect the transaxle oil cooler lines from the radiator side tank.
9. Remove the radiator from the vehicle.

To install:

10. Position radiator in the vehicle, locating the bottom of the radiator in the lower mounting pads.
11. Connect the radiator to the radiator support attaching clamp and bolts Tighten to 88 inch lbs. (10 Nm).
12. Connect the transaxle oil cooler lines. Tighten nuts to 20 ft. lbs. (27 Nm).
13. Install the upper radiator panel.
14. Install the upper air cleaner duct and/or silencer, if removed.
15. Connect the coolant recovery hose to the radiator neck.
16. Install the fan assembly and the fan attaching bolts. Tighten to 84 inch lbs. (10 Nm). On Deville and Fleetwood, install the left and right cooling fans.
17. Connect the cooling fan electrical connector(s).
18. If equipped, enable the Supplemental Inflatable Restraint (SIR) system by performing the following:
   a. Connect the yellow 2-way SIR connector and insert the Connect Positive Assurance (CPA) at the base of the steering column.
   b. Install the left side sound insulator.
   c. Install the SIR fuse in the fuse panel.
19. Connect the negative battery cable.
20. Fill cooling system and check for leaks. Start engine and allow engine to come to normal operating temperature. Recheck for coolant leaks. Allow engine to warm up sufficiently to confirm operation of cooling fan.

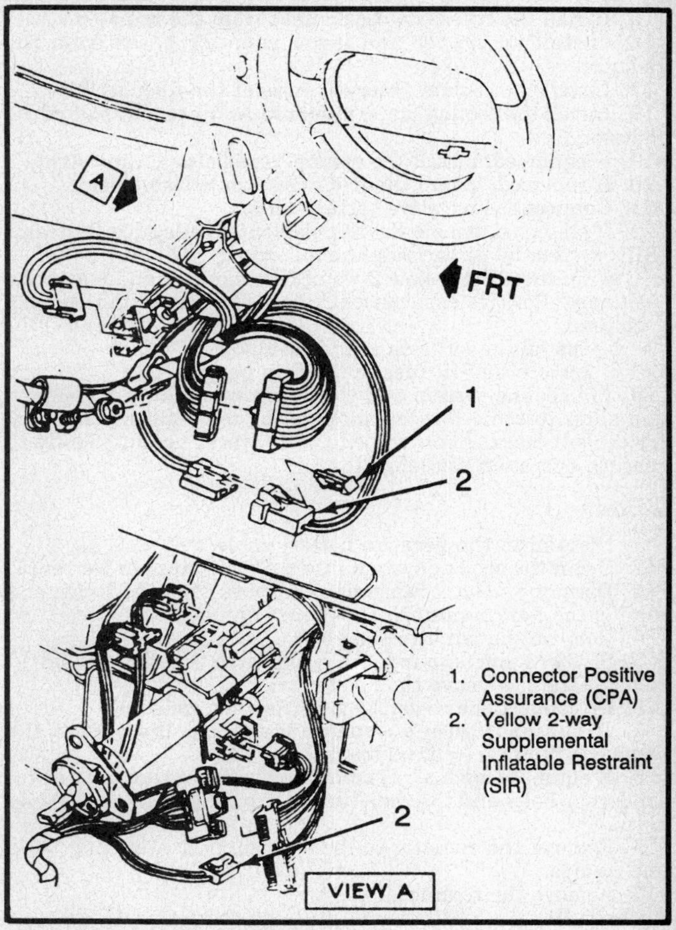
A
FRT
1
2
1. Connector Positive Assurance (CPA)
2. Yellow 2-way Supplemental Inflatable Restraint (SIR)
2
VIEW A

Two-way sir harness connector

E, K AND V BODY

1. Disconnect the negative battery cable. Drain the cooling system into a clean container for reuse.
2. If equipped, disable the Supplemental Inflatable Restraint (SIR) system by performing the following:
   a. Remove the SIR fuse from the fuse panel.
   b. Remove the left side sound insulator.
   c. Remove the Connector Positive Assurance (CPA) from the yellow 2-way SIR harness connector at the base of the steering column and separate the connector.
3. Remove the radiator support cover.
4. Remove the front radiator splash shield, as required.
5. If equipped, remove the engine-to-radiator torque strut.
6. Remove the cooling fan(s) mounted on the engine side of the radiator.
7. Remove the coolant reservoir hose at the filler neck.
8. Remove the upper and lower radiator hoses from the radiator.
9. Remove the transaxle cooler lines from the radiator.
10. If equipped, remove the engine oil cooler lines from the left side radiator end tank.
11. Remove the radiator from the vehicle.

To install:

12. Position the radiator in the vehicle. Ensure that the radiator is properly seated in the rubber mounts.
13. Install the radiator support cover.
14. If equipped, install the engine oil cooler lines to the radiator.

15. Install the transaxle cooler lines from the radiator.
16. Install the upper and lower radiator hoses from the radiator.
17. Install the coolant reservoir hose at the filler neck.
18. Install the cooling fan(s) mounted on the engine side of the radiator.
19. If equipped, install the engine-to-radiator torque strut.
20. If removed, install the front radiator splash shield.
21. Connect the negative battery cable.
22. If equipped, enable the Supplemental Inflatable Restraint (SIR) system by performing the following:
   a. Connect the yellow 2-way SIR connector and insert the Connect Positive Assurance (CPA) at the base of the steering column.
   b. Install the left side sound insulator.
   c. Install the SIR fuse in the fuse panel.
23. Fill cooling system and check for leaks. Start the engine and allow to come to normal operating temperature. Recheck for coolant leaks. Allow the engine to warm up sufficiently to confirm operation of cooling fan.

J Body

1. Disconnect the negative battery cable.
2. Drain the cooling system into a clean container for reuse.
3. Disconnect the forward light harness from the frame and unplug the fan connector.
4. Remove the fan attaching bolts.
5. Scribe a line around the hood latch location to aid in reinstallation. Remove the hood latch.
6. Disconnect the coolant hoses from the radiator.
7. If equipped with automatic transaxle, disconnect the transaxle fluid cooler lines from the radiator.
8. If equipped with air conditioning, remove the radiator-to-condenser bolts and the radiator tank to refrigerant line clamp bolt.
9. Remove the radiator-to-radiator support attaching bolts and clamps.
10. Remove the radiator.

To install:

11. Position the radiator in the vehicle.
12. Install the radiator-to-radiator support attaching bolts and clamps.
13. If equipped with automatic transaxle, connect the transaxle fluid cooler lines from the radiator.
14. If equipped with air conditioning, install the radiator-to-condenser bolts and the radiator tank to refrigerant line clamp bolt.
15. Connect the coolant hoses to the radiator.
16. Install the hood latch. Observe the scribe mark made during removal.
17. Install the cooling fan attaching bolts.
18. Connect the forward light harness to the frame and connect the fan connector.
19. Connect the negative battery cable.
20. Fill cooling system and check for leaks. Start the engine and allow to come to normal operating temperature. Recheck for coolant leaks. Allow the engine to warm up sufficiently to confirm operation of cooling fan.

L Body

1. Disconnect the negative battery cable. Drain the cooling system into a clean container for reuse.
2. If equipped, disable the Supplemental Inflatable Restraint (SIR) system by performing the following:
   a. Remove the SIR fuse from the fuse panel.
   b. Remove the left side sound insulator.
   c. Remove the Connector Positive Assurance (CPA) from the yellow 2-way SIR harness connector at the base of the steering column and separate the connector.
3. Remove the air cleaner duct work and air cleaner, as required.
4. Remove the electric cooling fan assembly.
5. Remove the coolant recovery reservoir hose from the filler neck.
6. If equipped with an automatic transaxle, disconnect the transaxle fluid cooler lines from the radiator. Cap the lines to prevent the loss of transaxle fluid.
7. Remove the upper radiator hoses.
8. Remove the left and right radiator air baffles, as required.
9. If equipped with Supplemental Inflatable Restraint (SIR), remove the forward discriminating sensor and set aside.
10. On GTZ models, remove the upper radiator air baffle.
11. Remove the upper radiator support and mount bolts.
12. Remove the upper condenser-to-radiator bolts.
13. Raise and safely support the vehicle.
14. Remove the lower radiator hose.
15. Remove the lower condenser-to-radiator bolts.
16. Lower the vehicle.
17. Remove the radiator.

To install:

18. Install the radiator.
19. Raise and safely support the vehicle.
20. Install the lower condenser-to-radiator bolts.
21. Install the lower radiator hose.
22. Lower the vehicle.
23. Install the upper condenser-to-radiator bolts.
24. Install the upper radiator support and mount bolts.
25. On GTZ models, install the upper radiator air baffle.
26. If equipped with Supplemental Inflatable Restraint (SIR), install the forward discriminating sensor.

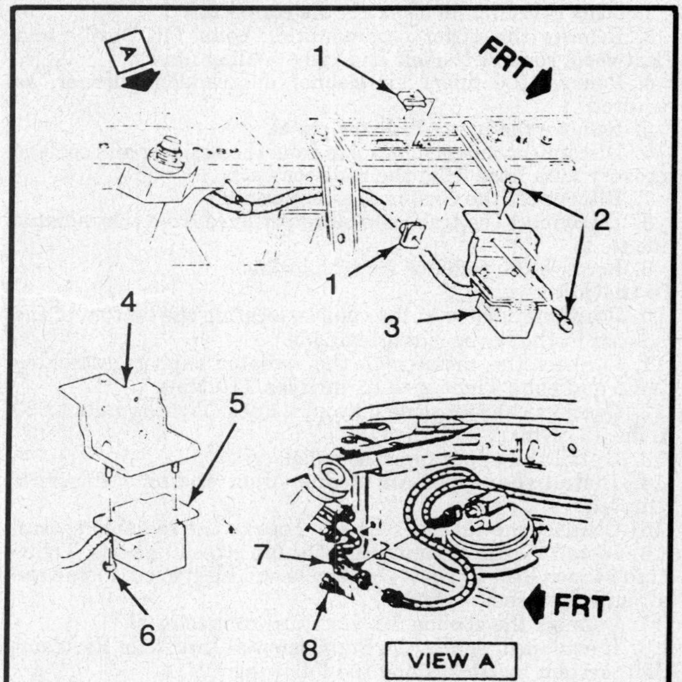
A
FRT
1
2
1
3
4
5
7
6
8
FRT
VIEW A

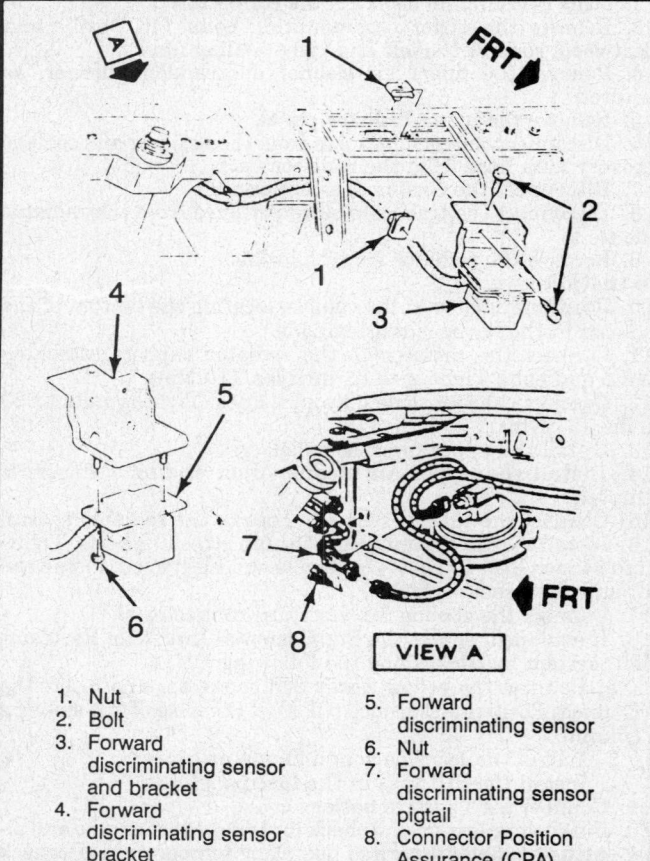

1. Nut
2. Bolt
3. Forward discriminating sensor and bracket
4. Forward discriminating sensor bracket
5. Forward discriminating sensor
6. Nut
7. Forward discriminating sensor pigtail
8. Connector Position Assurance (CPA)

Forward discriminating sensor installation – L body

27. If removed, install the left and right radiator air baffles.
28. Install the upper and lower radiator hoses.
29. If equipped with an automatic transaxle, connect the transaxle fluid cooler lines to the radiator.
30. Install the coolant recovery reservoir hose to the filler neck.
31. Install the electric cooling fan assembly.
32. If removed, install the air cleaner duct work and air cleaner.
33. Connect the negative battery cable.
34. If equipped, enable the Supplemental Inflatable Restraint (SIR) system by performing the following:
   a. Connect the yellow 2-way SIR connector and insert the Connect Positive Assurance (CPA) at the base of the steering column.
   b. Install the left side sound insulator.
   c. Install the SIR fuse in the fuse panel.
35. Fill cooling system and check for leaks. Start the engine and allow to come to normal operating temperature. Recheck for coolant leaks. Allow the engine to warm up sufficiently to confirm operation of cooling fan.

N Body

1. Disconnect the negative battery cable.
2. Drain the cooling system into a clean container for reuse.
3. Remove the forward light harness from the frame and unplug the fan connector.
4. Remove the cooling fan attaching bolts and remove the cooling fan.
5. Remove the hood latch from the radiator support. Scribe a line around the hood latch location before removing to aid reinstallation.
6. Disconnect the coolant hoses from the radiator.
7. Disconnect the transaxle fluid cooler lines from the radiator. Cap the lines to prevent the loss of transaxle fluid.
8. If equipped with air conditioning, remove the radiator-to-condenser bolts and the radiator tank-to-refrigerant line clamp bolt.
9. Remove the radiator-to-radiator support attaching bolts and clamps.
10. Remove the radiator.

To install:

11. Position the radiator in the vehicle. Ensure that the radiator is seated on the lower mounting pads.
12. Install the radiator-to-radiator support attaching clamp and bolts.
13. If equipped with air conditioning, install the radiator-to-condenser bolts and the condenser-to-refrigerant line clamp bolt.
14. Connect the transaxle fluid cooler line bolts.
15. Connect the coolant hoses to the radiator.
16. Install the hood latch using scribe mark made during removal.
17. Install the cooling fan. Ensure that the bottom leg of the frame fits into the rubber grommet at the lower radiator support.
18. Connect the fan connector.
19. If equipped, ensure that the engine ground strap is connected to the strut brace.
20. Attach the forward light harness to the fan frame.
21. Connect the negative battery cable.
22. Fill cooling system and check for leaks. Start the engine and allow to come to normal operating temperature. Recheck for coolant leaks. Allow the engine to warm up sufficiently to confirm operation of cooling fan.

T Body

1. Disconnect the negative battery cable.
2. Drain the engine coolant into a clean container for reuse.
3. Disconnect the upper and lower radiator hoses.
4. Disconnect the coolant reservoir hose.
5. Disconnect the cooling fan motor connector, oxygen sensor and temperature sensor.
6. Remove the radiator-to-radiator support bolts.
7. Remove the radiator.
8. Remove the radiator fan shroud with motor from the radiator assembly.

To install:

9. Install the fan motor and shroud to the radiator assembly.
10. Install the radiator and attaching bolts.
11. Connect the temperature sensor, oxygen sensor and fan motor connectors.
12. Connect the coolant reservoir hose.
13. Connect the lower radiator hose.
14. Fill the cooling system. Bleed air through the upper hose connection.
15. Connect the upper radiator hose.
16. Start the engine and allow to come to normal operating temperature. Recheck for coolant leaks. Allow the engine to warm up sufficiently to confirm operation of cooling fan.

W Body

1. Disconnect the negative battery cable.
2. Drain the cooling system into a clean container for reuse.
3. Remove the coolant recovery reservoir.
4. Remove the air cleaner assembly.
5. Remove the engine strut brace bolts from the upper tie bar and rotate the strut(s) and brace(s) rearward. To prevent shearing of the rubber bushing(s), loosen the bolt(s) on the engine strut(s) before swinging the strut(s).
6. Remove the air intake resonator mounting nut.
7. Remove the upper radiator mounting panel bolts and clamps.
8. Disconnect the cooling fan electrical connector(s).
9. Remove the upper radiator mounting panel with the cooling fan(s) attached.
10. Disconnect the upper and lower hoses at the radiator.
11. If equipped, disconnect the low coolant sensor electrical connector and remove the sensor.
12. If equipped with an automatic transaxle, disconnect the transaxle fluid cooler lines from the radiator. Cap the lines to prevent the loss of transaxle fluid.
13. Remove the radiator from the vehicle.

To install:

14. Install the radiator in the vehicle. Ensure that the radiator is seated in lower insulator pads.
15. If equipped, connect the transaxle fluid cooler lines.
16. Install the low coolant sensor in the radiator. Connect the sensor electrical connector.
17. Connect the upper and lower radiator hoses.
18. Install the upper radiator mounting panel with the cooling fan(s) attached.
19. Connect the cooling fan electrical connector(s).
20. Install the upper radiator mounting panel bolts and clamps.
21. Install the coolant reservoir.
22. Swing the engine strut(s) into the proper position.
23. Install the air cleaner assembly.
24. Connect the negative battery cable.
25. Fill cooling system and check for leaks. Start the engine and allow to come to normal operating temperature. Recheck for coolant leaks. Allow the engine to warm up sufficiently to confirm operation of cooling fan.

COOLING SYSTEM BLEEDING

Except T Body

1. Fill the cooling system with the proper ratio of coolant and water.

2. If equipped with the 3.1L engine, open the the air bleed vent on the bypass pipe 2–3 turns.
3. Set the heater controls to heat and the temperature controls to the warmest setting.
4. Start the engine and add coolant as necessary to keep the radiator level just below the filler neck.
5. If equipped with the 3.1L engine, observe the air bleed vent. Close the vent when coolant begins to come out of the vent.
6. Allow the engine to come to normal operating temperature; indicated by the upper radiator hose becoming hot.
7. The air coming out of the heater should be getting hot.
8. Check the coolant level in the radiator and coolant reservoir. Install the radiator cap, turning it until the arrows align with the overflow tube.

T Body

1. Disconnect the negative battery cable.
2. Drain the engine coolant into a clean container for reuse.
3. Remove the hose from the reservoir tank.
4. Disconnect the upper and lower radiator hoses.
5. Disconnect the fan motor, oxygen sensor and temperature sensor connectors.
6. Remove the bolts from the radiator support.
7. Remove the radiator from the vehicle.

NOTE: The radiator will be approximately ½ of coolant.

To install:

8. Place the radiator in the vehicle.
9. Connect the fan motor with the fan shroud to the radiator.
10. Install the radiator attaching bolts.
11. Connect the fan motor, oxygen sensor and temperature sensor connectors.
12. Connect the radiator hoses.
13. Connect the reservoir tank hose to the radiator.
14. Connect the upper and lower radiator hoses.
15. Connect the negative battery cable.
16. Fill cooling system and check for leaks. Start the engine and allow to come to normal operating temperature. Recheck for coolant leaks. Allow the engine to warm up sufficiently to confirm operation of cooling fan.

Cooling Fan

TESTING

1. Check fuse or circuit breaker for power to cooling fan motor.
2. Remove connector(s) at cooling fan motor(s). Connect jumper wire and apply battery voltage to the positive terminal of the cooling fan motor.
3. Using an ohmmeter, check for continuity in cooling fan motor.

NOTE: Remove the cooling fan connector at the fan motor before performing continuity checks. Perform continuity check of the motor windings only. The cooling fan control circuit is connected electrically to the ECM through the cooling fan relay center. Ohmmeter battery voltage must not be applied to the ECM.

4. Ensure proper continuity of cooling fan motor ground circuit at chassis ground connector.

REMOVAL AND INSTALLATION

A Body

1. Disconnect the negative battery cable.
2. Remove the air cleaner, as required.
3. Remove the engine strut brace bolts from the upper tie bar and rotate the strut(s) and braces(s) rearward, as required, for access to the fan assembly

NOTE: To prevent shearing of the rubber bushing(s), loosen the bolt(s) on the engine strut(s) before rotating.

4. Disconnect the wiring harness from the fan motor(s) and fan frame(s).
5. Remove the fan frame attaching bolts.
6. Remove the fan frame assembly from the vehicle.

To install:

7. Position the fan frame assembly in the vehicle and install the attaching bolts.
8. Connect the wiring harness to the fan motor(s).
9. If removed, rotate the strut bar(s) into position and install the strut bar brace attaching bolts.
10. If removed, install the air cleaner.
11. Connect negative battery cable.

C and H Body

EXCEPT DEVILLE AND FLEETWOOD

1. Disconnect the negative battery cable.
2. Disconnect the wiring harness from the motor and the fan frame.
3. Remove the fan guard and hose support, as required.
4. Remove the fan assembly from the radiator support.

To install:

5. Install the fan assembly to the radiator support.
6. Connect the wiring harness.
7. Connect the negative battery cable.

DEVILLE AND FLEETWOOD

1. Disconnect the negative battery cable.
2. Raise and safely support the vehicle.
3. Disconnect the electrical connector(s) from the fan assembly.
4. Remove the screws attaching the fan(s) to the lower radiator cradle.
5. Lower the vehicle.
6. If removing the right side fan, disconnect the air conditioning accumulator from the bracket and set aside.
7. Remove the air cleaner intake duct.
8. Remove the screws attaching the fan(s) to the upper radiator mounting panel.
9. Remove the upper radiator mounting panel.
10. Remove the cooling fan(s) from the vehicle.

To install:

11. Position the cooling fan(s) in the vehicle.

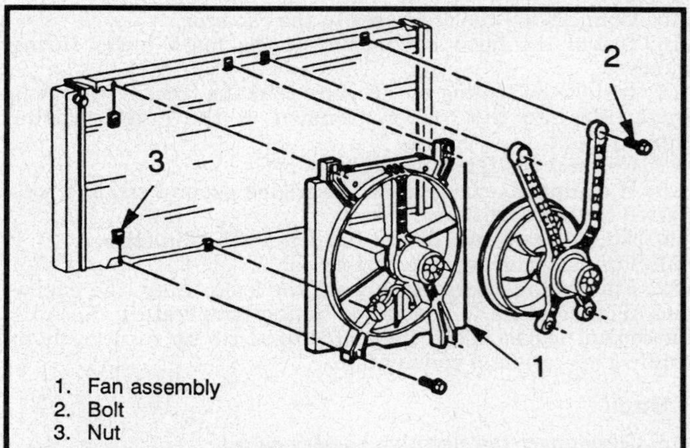
2
3
1
1. Fan assembly
2. Bolt
3. Nut

Cooling fan mounting—C and H body

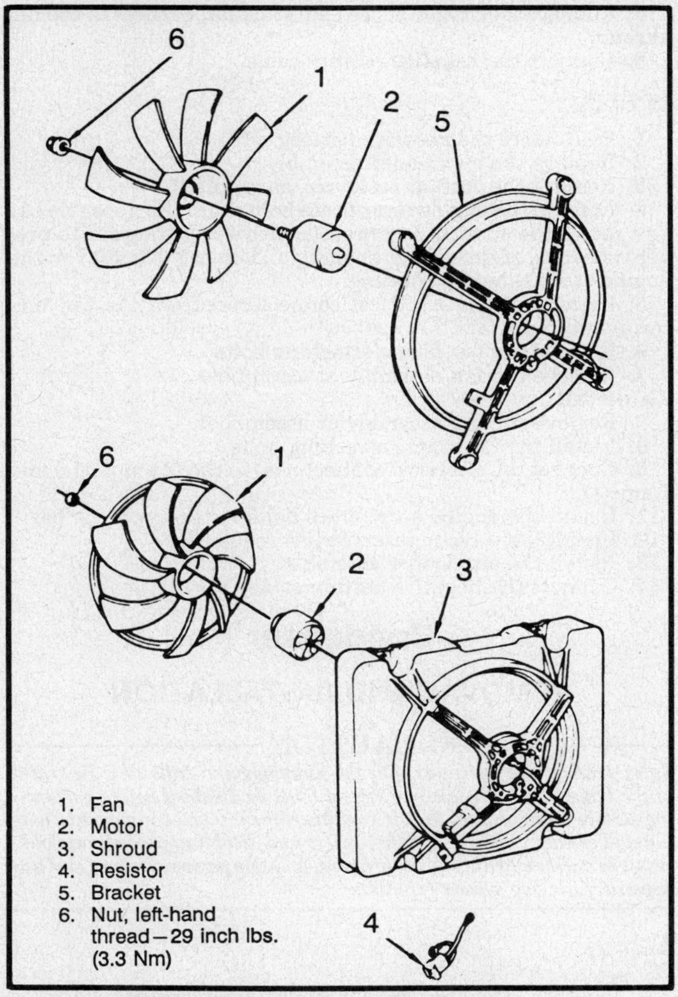
6
1
2
5
6
1
2
3
4
1. Fan
2. Motor
3. Shroud
4. Resistor
5. Bracket
6. Nut, left-hand thread—29 inch lbs. (3.3 Nm)

Electric cooling fan—disassembled

12. Install the upper radiator mounting panel.
13. Install the upper fan mounting screws. Do not tighten at this time.
14. Raise and safely support the vehicle.
15. Connect the cooling fan electrical connector(s).
16. Install the lower fan mounting screws.
17. Lower the vehicle.
18. Install the upper fan mounting screws.
19. If the right side fan was removed, install the air conditioning accumulator in its bracket.
20. Install the air cleaner intake duct.
21. Connect the negative battery cable.

E, K and V Body

FRONT COOLING FAN

1. Disconnect the negative battery cable.
2. Disconnect the cooling fan electrical connector.
3. Remove the front finish panel, grille or cowl, as required.
4. If equipped, remove the radiator support to gain access to the cooling fan.
5. Remove the cooling fan attaching screws.
6. Remove the cooling fan.

To install:

7. Install the cooling fan in the vehicle.
8. If removed, install the radiator support.
9. Install the front finish panel, grille or cowl, as required.
10. Connect the fan electrical connector.
11. Connect the negative battery cable.

LEFT AND RIGHT SIDE COOLING FAN

1. Disconnect the negative battery cable.
2. Disconnect the cooling fan electrical connector.
3. Remove the upper engine-to-radiator torque strut, as required.
4. Remove the cooling fan attaching bolts.
5. Remove the cooling fan.

To install:

6. Install the cooling fan.
7. If removed, install the upper engine-to-radiator torque strut.
8. Connect the cooling fan electrical connector.
9. Connect the negative battery cable.

J Body

EXCEPT 2.8L AND 3.1L ENGINES

1. Disconnect the negative battery cable.
2. Remove the air cleaner duct.
3. Disconnect the wiring harness from the motor and fan frame.
4. Remove the fan assembly from the radiator support.

To install:

5. Install the fan assembly to the radiator support.
6. Connect the wiring harness from the motor and fan frame.
7. Install the air cleaner duct.
8. Connect the negative battery cable.

2.8L AND 3.1L ENGINES

1. Disconnect the negative battery cable.
2. Remove the air cleaner duct and air cleaner.
3. Drain the engine coolant into a clean container to a level below the radiator inlet (upper) hose.
4. Disconnect the radiator inlet (upper) hose and position aside.
5. If equipped with automatic transaxle, disconnect the transaxle fluid cooler lines at the radiator and position aside.
6. Disconnect the wiring harness connector at the coolant fan.
7. Remove the fan assembly from the radiator support.

To install:

8. Install the fan assembly from the radiator support.
9. Connect the wiring harness connector at the coolant fan.
10. If equipped with automatic transaxle, connect the transaxle fluid cooler lines at the radiator and position aside.
11. Connect the radiator inlet (upper) hose.
12. Remove the air cleaner duct and air cleaner.
13. Connect the negative battery cable.
14. Fill cooling system and check for leaks. Start the engine and allow to come to normal operating temperature. Recheck for coolant leaks. Allow the engine to warm up sufficiently to confirm operation of cooling fan.

L Body

1. Disconnect the negative battery cable.
2. Remove the air cleaner intake duct and air cleaner housing, as required.
3. Disconnect the coolant fan electrical connector.
4. Remove the fan frame attaching bolts.
5. Remove the fan assembly.

To install:

6. Install the fan assembly.
7. Install the fan frame attaching bolts.
8. Connect the coolant fan electrical connector.
9. If removed, install the air cleaner intake duct and air cleaner housing.

10. Connect the negative battery cable.

N Body

EXCEPT 2.3L ENGINE

1. Disconnect the negative battery cable.
2. Disconnect the wiring harness from the motor and fan frame.
3. Fan guard and hose support, as required.
4. Remove the fan assembly from the radiator support.

To install:

5. Install the fan assembly on the radiator support.
6. If removed, install the fan guard and hose support.
7. Connect the wiring harness to the motor and fan frame.
8. Connect the negative battery cable.

2.3L ENGINE

1. Disconnect the negative battery cable.
2. Remove the air cleaner-to-throttle body duct.
3. Disconnect the electrical connectors from the Throttle Position Sensor (TPS), Idle Air Control (IAC) and the Manifold Absolute Pressure (MPS) sensor. Position aside.
4. Disconnect the vacuum harness assembly from the throttle body and position aside.
5. Disconnect the MAP sensor vacuum hose from the intake manifold.
6. Remove the cooling fan shroud retaining bolts and remove the shroud including the MAP sensor.
7. Remove the cooling fan to upper radiator support bolt, remaining upper radiator support bolt and upper radiator support.
8. Disconnect the electrical connector from the cooling fan.
9. Lift the fan assembly out of the 2 lower insulators. Rotate the bracket so the 2 lower bracket legs point upward. Move the fan assembly toward the left side until the fan blade overlaps the radiator tank to core seam by approximately 1 inch (25mm). Remove the fan assembly.

NOTE: Due to the narrow clearance, special care must be taken not to damage the lock tang on the TPS with the fan bracket when removing and installing the fan assembly.

To install:

10. Rotate the fan assembly so the 2 lower legs face upward. Install the fan assembly down between the throttle body and the radiator while overlapping the radiator tank to core seam with the fan blade approximately 1 inch (25mm).
11. Rotate the fan bracket and insert the 2 lower legs into the insulators.
12. Connect the cooling fan electrical connector.
13. Install the upper radiator support.
14. Install the cooling fan shroud.
15. Install the cooling fan-to-upper radiator support mounting bolt.
16. Connect the MAP sensor vacuum hose to the intake manifold.
17. Connect the TPS, IAC and MAP sensor connectors.
18. Install the vacuum harness assembly to the throttle body.
19. Install the air cleaner to the throttle body.
20. Connect the negative battery cable.

T Body

1. Disconnect the negative battery cable.
2. Disconnect the cooling fan electrical connector.
3. Disconnect the oxygen sensor plug from the fan shroud.
4. Disconnect the fan shroud-to-radiator support attaching bolts.
5. Remove the fan motor and shroud assembly.

To install:

6. Install the fan motor and shroud assembly.
7. Install the fan shroud-to-radiator support attaching bolts.
8. Connect the oxygen sensor plug and fan harness to the fan shroud.
9. Connect the negative battery cable.

W Body

1. Disconnect the negative battery cable.
2. Remove the air cleaner assembly.
3. Remove the coolant reservoir, as required.
4. Remove the engine strut brace bolts from the upper tie bar and rotate the strut(s) and brace(s) rearward. In order to prevent shearing of the rubber bushing(s), loosen the bolt(s) on the engine strut(s) before rotating.
5. Disconnect the electrical connector(s) from the fan motor(s) and frame(s).
6. Remove the fan frame attaching bolts.
7. Remove the fan assembly or assemblies.

To install:

8. Remove the fan assembly or assemblies.
9. Install the fan frame attaching bolts.
10. Connect the electrical connector(s) to the fan motor(s) and frame(s).
11. Install the engine strut brace bolts to the upper tie bar.
12. Install the coolant reservoir, as required.
13. Install the air cleaner assembly.
14. Connect the negative battery cable.

Condenser

REMOVAL AND INSTALLATION

CAUTION

Some vehicles are equipped with the Supplemental Inflatable Restraint or air bag system. The air bag system must be disabled before performing service on or around the air bag, instrument panel components, wiring and sensors. Failure to follow safety and disabling procedures could result in accidental air bag deployment, possible personal injury and unnecessary air bag system repairs.

A Body

1. Properly discharge the air conditioning system.
2. Disconnect the high-pressure and liquid lines at the condenser fittings. Discard the O-rings.

NOTE: Use a backup wrench on the condenser fittings when removing the high-pressure and liquid lines. Cap both refrigerant lines when opening the system to prevent the entry of dirt and moisture and the loss of refrigerant lubricant.

3. Remove the condenser attaching bolts from the center support.
4. Remove the engine strut bracket and upper radiator support. Lean radiator back.
5. Remove the condenser.

To install:

6. Position the condenser in the vehicle.

NOTE: If replacing the condenser or if the original condenser was flushed during service, add 1 fluid oz. (30ml) of refrigerant lubricant to the system.

7. Install the upper radiator support and engine strut bracket.
8. Install the condenser attaching bolts.
9. Replace the condenser fitting O-rings. Lubricate the O-rings with refrigerant oil.
10. Connect the condenser high-pressure and liquid lines.

NOTE: Use a backup wrench on the condenser fittings when tightening lines.

11. Evacuate, charge and leak test the system.

C and H Body

1. Disconnect the negative battery cable. Remove battery hold-down and battery, as required.
2. If equipped, disable the Supplemental Inflatable Restraint (SIR) system by performing the following:
   a. Remove the SIR fuse from the fuse panel.
   b. Remove the left side sound insulator.
   c. Remove the Connector Positive Assurance (CPA) from the yellow 2-way SIR harness connector at the base of the steering column and separate the connector.
3. Properly discharge the air conditioning system.
4. Disconnect the cooling fans and remove, as required. If equipped, disconnect the auxiliary transaxle cooler lines.
5. Remove the upper radiator support.
6. Remove the coolant overflow tube from the radiator.
7. Disconnect the refrigerant lines at the condenser. Discard the O-rings.

NOTE: Use a backup wrench on the condenser fittings when removing the high-pressure and liquid lines. Cap both refrigerant lines when opening the system to prevent the entry of dirt and moisture and the loss of refrigerant lubricant.

8. Remove the condenser support bolts.
9. Remove the condenser from the vehicle.

To install:

NOTE: If replacing the condenser or if the original condenser was flushed during service, add 1 fluid oz. (30ml) of refrigerant lubricant to the system.

10. Position the condenser in the vehicle.
11. Install the condenser support bolts.
12. If equipped, connect the auxiliary transaxle cooler lines.
13. Install the upper radiator support.
14. Connect the condenser refrigerant lines.

NOTE: Use a backup wrench on the condenser fittings when tightening lines.

15. Connect the coolant overflow tube to the radiator.
16. If removed, install the cooling fans and connect the electrical connectors.
17. Install the battery and connect the negative battery cable.
18. If equipped, enable the Supplemental Inflatable Restraint (SIR) system by performing the following:
   a. Connect the yellow 2-way SIR connector and insert the Connect Positive Assurance (CPA) at the base of the steering column.
   b. Install the left side sound insulator.
   c. Install the SIR fuse in the fuse panel.
19. Evacuate, recharge and leak test the air conditioning system.

E, K and V Body

EXCEPT ELDORADO AND SEVILLE

1. Disconnect the negative battery cable. Drain the cooling system into a clean container for reuse.
2. If equipped, disable the Supplemental Inflatable Restraint (SIR) system by performing the following:
   a. Remove the SIR fuse from the fuse panel.
   b. Remove the left side sound insulator.
   c. Remove the Connector Positive Assurance (CPA) from the yellow 2-way SIR harness connector at the base of the steering column and separate the connector.
3. Properly discharge the air conditioning system.
4. Remove the upper engine-to-radiator torque strut, as required.
5. Remove the cooling fan(s) located on the engine side of the radiator.
6. Remove the radiator.
7. Disconnect the refrigerant lines at the condenser fittings. Discard the O-rings.

NOTE: Use a backup wrench on the condenser fittings when tightening lines. Cap the refrigerant lines when opening the system to prevent the entry of dirt and moisture and the loss of refrigerant lubricant.

8. Remove the refrigerant hose bracket, as required.
9. Remove the condenser attaching bolts.
10. Remove the condenser.

To install:

NOTE: If replacing the condenser or if the original condenser was flushed during service, add 1 fluid oz. (30ml) of refrigerant lubricant to the system.

11. Install the condenser in the vehicle. Ensure that the condenser is properly positioned in the mounting insulator.
12. Install the condenser attaching bolts.
13. Install new O-rings on the condenser refrigerant line fittings. Lubricate with refrigerant oil.
14. Connect the refrigerant lines at the condenser fittings. Use a backup wrench on the condenser fittings.
15. If removed, install the refrigerant hose bracket.
16. Install the radiator.
17. Install the cooling fan(s).
18. If removed, install the upper engine-to-radiator torque strut.
19. Connect the negative battery cable.
20. If equipped, enable the Supplemental Inflatable Restraint (SIR) system by performing the following:
   a. Connect the yellow 2-way SIR connector and insert the Connect Positive Assurance (CPA) at the base of the steering column.
   b. Install the left side sound insulator.
   c. Install the SIR fuse in the fuse panel.
21. Evacuate, recharge and leak test the air conditioning system.
22. Fill cooling system and check for leaks. Start the engine and allow to come to normal operating temperature. Recheck for coolant leaks. Allow the engine to warm up sufficiently to confirm operation of cooling fans.

ELDORADO AND SEVILLE

1. Disconnect the negative battery cable. Properly discharge the air conditioning system.
2. If equipped, disable the Supplemental Inflatable Restraint (SIR) system by performing the following:
   a. Remove the SIR fuse from the fuse panel.
   b. Remove the left side insulator.
   c. Remove the Connector Positive Assurance (CPA) from the yellow 2-way SIR harness connector at the base of the steering column and separate the connector.
3. Remove the engine support bracket from the radiator top support bracket.
4. Remove the radiator top support bracket.
5. Remove the cooling fan(s) on the engine side of the radiator.
6. Disconnect the refrigerant lines at the condenser fittings. Discard the O-rings.

NOTE: Use a backup wrench on the condenser fittings. Cap the refrigerant lines when opening the system to prevent the entry of dirt and moisture and the loss of refrigerant lubricant.

7. Remove the condenser support screws and remove the condenser.

To install:

NOTE: If replacing the condenser or if the original condenser was flushed during service, add 1 fluid oz. (30ml) of refrigerant lubricant to the system.

8. Install the condenser in the vehicle. Ensure that the condenser is properly seated in the insulators.
9. Install new O-rings on the condenser fittings. Lubricate with refrigerant oil.
10. Connect the refrigerant lines to the condenser.

NOTE: Use a backup wrench on the condenser fittings when tightening lines.

11. Install the cooling fan(s).
12. Install the radiator top support bracket.
13. Install the engine support bracket to the radiator top support bracket.
14. Evacuate, recharge and leak test the air conditioning system.
15. Connect the negative battery cable.
16. If equipped, enable the Supplemental Inflatable Restraint (SIR) system by performing the following:
    a. Connect the yellow 2-way SIR connector and insert the Connect Positive Assurance (CPA) at the base of the steering column.
    b. Install the left side sound insulator.
    c. Install the SIR fuse in the fuse panel.

J Body

FIRENZA, SKYHAWK AND 1989 CAVALIER

1. Disconnect the negative battery cable.
2. Properly discharge the air conditioning system.
3. Drain the cooling system into a clean container for reuse.
4. Remove the air cleaner inlet and air cleaner assembly.
5. Remove the battery.
6. Remove the fan assembly.
7. Remove the upper and lower radiator hoses.
8. Disconnect the transaxle fluid lines from the radiator. Cap the lines to prevent fluid loss.
9. Disconnect the radiator coolant recovery hose clamp and hose.
10. Remove the right side radiator/condenser baffle.
11. Remove the hood latch.
12. Disconnect the low coolant sensor. Remove the radiator bracket and the radiator.
13. Disconnect the refrigerant lines at the condenser. Discard the O-rings.

NOTE: Use a backup wrench on the condenser fittings when removing the high-pressure and liquid lines. Cap both refrigerant lines when opening the system to prevent the entry of dirt and moisture and the loss of refrigerant lubricant.

14. Remove the condenser brackets and remove the condenser.

To install:

NOTE: If replacing the condenser or if the original condenser was flushed during service, add 1 fluid oz. (30ml) of refrigerant lubricant to the system.

15. Install the condenser in the vehicle and install the condenser brackets.
16. Install new O-rings on the condenser refrigerant line fittings. Lubricate with refrigerant oil.

NOTE: Use a backup wrench on the condenser fittings when tightening lines.

17. Install the radiator and brackets. Connect the low coolant sensor.
18. Install the hood latch.
19. Install the right side radiator/condenser baffle.
20. Connect the radiator coolant recovery hose and clamp.
21. Connect the transaxle fluid cooler lines to the transaxle.
22. Connect the upper and lower radiator hoses.
23. Install the fan assembly.
24. Install the battery.
25. Install the air cleaner inlet and air cleaner assembly.
26. Evacuate, recharge and leak test the air conditioning system.
27. Connect the negative battery cable.
28. Fill cooling system and check for leaks. Start the engine and allow to come to normal operating temperature. Recheck for coolant leaks. Allow the engine to warm up sufficiently to confirm operation of cooling fan.

1990–91 CAVALIER

1. Disconnect the negative battery cable.
2. Properly discharge the air conditioning system.
3. Remove the right and left headlight trim.
4. Remove the center grille assembly.
5. Remove the right and left headlight housings.
6. Remove the hood bracket and latch assembly.
7. Disconnect the refrigerant lines from the condenser. Discard the O-rings.

NOTE: Use a backup wrench on the condenser fittings when removing the high-pressure and liquid lines. Cap both refrigerant lines when opening the system to prevent the entry of dirt and moisture and the loss of refrigerant lubricant.

8. Remove the condenser air deflector shield.
9. Remove the condenser mounting brackets and the condenser.

To install:

NOTE: If replacing the condenser or if the original condenser was flushed during service, add 1 fluid oz. (30ml) of refrigerant lubricant to the system.

10. Install the condenser in the vehicle and install the brackets.
11. Install the condenser air deflector shield.
12. Install new O-rings on the refrigerant line fittings. Lubricate with refrigerant oil.
13. Connect the refrigerant lines to the condenser.

NOTE: Use a backup wrench on the condenser fittings when tightening lines.

14. Install the hood latch and bracket assembly.
15. Install the left and right side headlight housings.
16. Install the center grille assembly.
17. Install the headlight trim.
18. Connect the negative battery cable.
19. Evacuate, recharge and leak test the air conditioning system.

SUNBIRD

1. Disconnect the negative battery cable.
2. Properly discharge the air conditioning system.
3. Remove hood latch assembly and cable from latch.
4. On Sunbird GT and SE, perform the following:
    a. Remove the header filler panels and brackets.
    b. Manually open the headlight doors by turning the headlight door actuator knob.
    c. Remove the 4 retaining bolts from the headlight door actuators and pull the actuator assemblies forward as far as possible.
5. On Sunbird LE, remove the front end panel center brace.
6. Disconnect the refrigerant lines at the condenser. Discard the O-rings.

NOTE: Use a backup wrench on the condenser fittings when removing the high-pressure and liquid lines. Cap both refrigerant lines when opening the system to prevent the entry of dirt and moisture and the loss of refrigerant lubricant.

7. Remove the condenser upper mounting brackets.
8. Remove the condenser.

To install:

NOTE: If replacing the condenser or if the original condenser was flushed during service, add 1 fluid oz. (30ml) of refrigerant lubricant to the system.

9. Install the condenser in the vehicle.
10. Install the condenser upper mounting brackets.
11. Replace the O-rings on the condenser refrigerant lines. Lubricate with refrigerant oil.
12. Connect the high pressure and liquid lines at the condenser.

NOTE: Use a backup wrench on the condenser fittings when tightening lines.

13. On Sunbird GT and SE, perform the following:
    a. Install the headlight door actuator assemblies and retaining bolts to the headlight mounting panel.
    b. Manually close the headlight doors by turning the headlight door actuator knob.
    c. Install the header filler panels and brackets.
14. On Sunbird LE, install the front end panel center brace.
15. Install the cable to latch and hood latch assembly.
16. Evacuate, recharge and leak test the air conditioning system.
17. Connect the negative battery cable.

L Body

1. Disconnect the negative battery cable.
2. If equipped, disable the Supplemental Inflatable Restraint (SIR) system by performing the following:
    a. Remove the SIR fuse from the fuse panel.
    b. Remove the left side sound insulator.
    c. Remove the Connector Positive Assurance (CPA) from the yellow 2-way SIR harness connector at the base of the steering column and separate the connector.
3. Properly discharge the air conditioning system.
4. Remove the radiator upper baffle, as required.
5. Remove the air cleaner assembly.
6. Remove the engine cooling fan.
7. If equipped with SIR, remove the forward discriminating sensor and set aside.

NOTE: Use a backup wrench on the condenser fittings when removing the high-pressure and liquid lines. Cap the refrigerant lines when opening the system to prevent the entry of dirt and moisture and the loss of refrigerant lubricant.

8. Disconnect the evaporator tube from the condenser. Discard the O-ring.
9. Disconnect the compressor-to-condenser hose from the condenser inlet. Discard the O-ring.
10. Remove the screws attaching the condenser to the radiator.
11. Remove the bolts and radiator upper mounting brackets.
12. Remove the condenser from the vehicle by tipping the radiator toward the engine.

To install:

NOTE: If replacing the condenser or if the original condenser was flushed during service, add 1 fluid oz. (30ml) of refrigerant lubricant to the system.

13. Install the condenser into position by tipping the radiator toward the engine.
14. Install the radiator upper mounting brackets and bolts.
15. Install the screws attaching the condenser to the radiator.
16. Install new O-rings on the condenser refrigerant line fittings. Lubricate with refrigerant oil.
17. Connect the refrigerant line to the condenser inlet.
18. Connect the evaporator tube-to-condenser outlet.

NOTE: Use a backup wrench on the condenser fittings when tightening lines.

19. Install the forward discriminating sensor.
20. Install the engine cooling fan.
21. Install the air cleaner assembly.
22. If removed, install the upper radiator air baffle.
23. If equipped, enable the Supplemental Inflatable Restraint (SIR) system by performing the following:
    a. Connect the yellow 2-way SIR connector and insert the Connect Positive Assurance (CPA) at the base of the steering column.
    b. Install the left side sound insulator.
    c. Install the SIR fuse in the fuse panel.
24. Evacuate, recharge and leak test the air conditioning system.
25. Connect the negative battery cable.
26. Fill cooling system and check for leaks. Start the engine and allow to come to normal operating temperature. Recheck for coolant leaks. Allow the engine to warm up sufficiently to confirm operation of cooling fan.

N Body

1. Disconnect the negative battery cable.
2. Properly discharge the air conditioning system.
3. Remove the grille and moulding.
4. Remove the headlights.
5. Remove the headlight mounting panel/front end panel and mounting brackets.
6. Remove the hood latch assembly. Scribe a mark on the radiator support for use during reinstallation.
7. Remove the condenser retainers and splash shields.
8. Disconnect the lines at the condenser. Discard the O-rings.

NOTE: Use a backup wrench on the condenser fittings when removing the high-pressure and liquid lines. Cap the refrigerant lines when opening the system to prevent the entry of dirt and moisture and the loss of refrigerant lubricant.

9. Carefully remove the condenser from the vehicle.
10. Transfer the splash shields, as required.

To install:

NOTE: If replacing the condenser or if the original condenser was flushed during service, add 1 fluid oz. (30ml) of refrigerant lubricant to the system.

11. Install the condenser in the vehicle.
12. Install the condenser retainers and splash shield.
13. Install new O-rings on the condenser refrigerant line fittings. Lubricate with refrigerant oil.
14. Connect the refrigerant lines at the condenser.

NOTE: Use a backup wrench on the condenser fittings when tightening lines.

15. Install the headlight mounting panel/front end panel and mounting brackets.
16. Install the hood latch assembly.
17. Install the headlight assemblies.
18. Install the grille and moulding to the headlight mounting panel/front end panel.

19. Evacuate, recharge and leak test the air conditioning system.
20. Connect the negative battery cable.

T Body

1. Disconnect the negative battery cable.
2. Properly discharge the air conditioning system.
3. Drain the engine coolant into a clean container for reuse.
4. Disconnect the lower coolant hose at the radiator.
5. Disconnect the upper coolant hose at the engine block.
6. If equipped, move the power steering reservoir toward the dash.
7. Remove the radiator.
8. Disconnect the coolant fan wire harness.
9. Disconnect the lower pressure cut-off switch connector.
10. Disconnect the condenser-to-evaporator line at the orifice tube.
11. Disconnect the compressor-to-accumulator hose at the accumulator.
12. Disconnect the condenser-to-compressor hose at the accumulator.

NOTE: Use a backup wrench on the condenser fittings when removing the high-pressure and liquid lines. Discard the O-rings. Cap the refrigerant lines when opening the system to prevent the entry of dirt and moisture and the loss of refrigerant lubricant.

13. Remove the tube from the retaining clamp.
14. Remove the condenser attaching screws.
15. Remove the condenser.
16. Remove the condenser-to-orifice tube at the condenser.

To install:

NOTE: If replacing the condenser or if the original condenser was flushed during service, add 1 fluid oz. (30ml) of refrigerant lubricant to the system.

17. Install the condenser-to-orifice tube at the condenser.
18. install the condenser.
19. Install the attaching screws.
20. Install the tube to the retaining clamp.
21. Install the new O-rings to the refrigerant lines. Lubricate with refrigerant oil.
22. Connect the condenser-to-compressor hose at the condenser.

NOTE: Use a backup wrench on the condenser fittings when tightening lines.

23. Connect the compressor-to-accumulator hose at the accumulator.
24. Connect the condenser-to-evaporator line at the orifice tube.
25. Connect the lower pressure cut-off switch connector.
26. Connect the coolant fan wire harness.
27. Install the radiator.
28. If equipped, reposition the power steering reservoir.
29. Connect the upper coolant hose at the engine block.
30. Connect the lower coolant hose at the radiator.
31. Evacuate, recharge and leak test the air conditioning system.
32. Connect the negative battery cable.
33. Fill cooling system and check for leaks. Start the engine and allow to come to normal operating temperature. Recheck for coolant leaks. Allow the engine to warm up sufficiently to confirm operation of cooling fan.

W Body

1. Disconnect the negative battery cable.
2. Air cleaner assembly and duct.
3. Properly discharge the air conditioning system.
4. Remove the coolant recovery reservoir, as required.
5. Remove the engine strut brace bolts from the upper tie bar and rotate the strut(s) and brace(s) rearward. In order to prevent shearing of the rubber bushing(s), loosen the bolt(s) on the engine strut(s) before swinging the strut(s).
6. Remove the air intake resonator mounting nut, as required.
7. Disconnect the condenser refrigerant lines. Discard the O-rings.

NOTE: Use a backup wrench on the condenser fittings when removing the high-pressure and liquid lines. Cap the refrigerant lines when opening the system to prevent the entry of dirt and moisture and the loss of refrigerant lubricant.

8. Remove the upper radiator mounting panel bolts and clamps.
9. Disconnect the electrical connector from fan(s).
10. Remove the upper radiator mounting panel with the cooling fan(s) attached.
11. Tilt the radiator rearward.
12. Remove the condenser.

To install:

13. Install the condenser.
14. Install the upper radiator mounting panel with the fan(s) attached.
15. Connect the cooling fan(s) electrical connector(s).
16. Install the upper radiator mounting panel bolts and clamps.
17. Install new O-rings to the condenser refrigerant lines. Lubricate with refrigerant oil.
18. Connect the condenser refrigerant lines.

NOTE: Use a backup wrench on the condenser fittings when tightening lines.

19. If removed, install the air intake resonator mounting nut.
20. If removed, install the coolant recovery reservoir.
21. Swing the engine strut(s) into position.
22. Install the air cleaner assembly and duct.
23. Evacuate, recharge and leak test the air conditioning system.
24. Connect the negative battery cable.

Compressor

REMOVAL AND INSTALLATION

A Body

1. Disconnect the negative battery cable.
2. Disconnect the electrical connectors from the compressor.
3. Properly discharge the air conditioning system.
4. Remove the coupled hose assembly from the rear of the compressor. Discard the O-rings.

NOTE: Cap the refrigerant lines when opening the system to prevent the entry of dirt and moisture and the loss of refrigerant lubricant.

5. Release the drive belt tension and remove the belt from the compressor.
6. Remove the compressor attaching bolts.
7. Remove the compressor.
8. Drain and measure the refrigerant oil from the compressor. Discard the old oil.

To install:

9. If the compressor is to be replaced, drain the oil from the new compressor and discard. Add new refrigerant oil equivalent to the amount that was drained from the compressor upon removal.
10. Position the compressor in the vehicle.

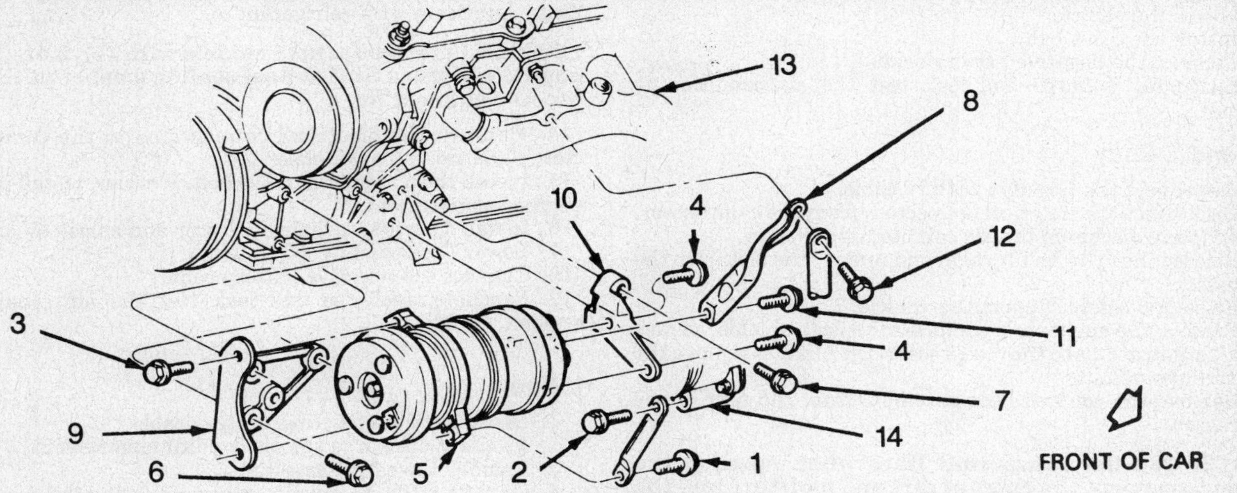
13
8
10
4
12
3
11
4
7
9
14
6
5
2
1
FRONT OF CAR

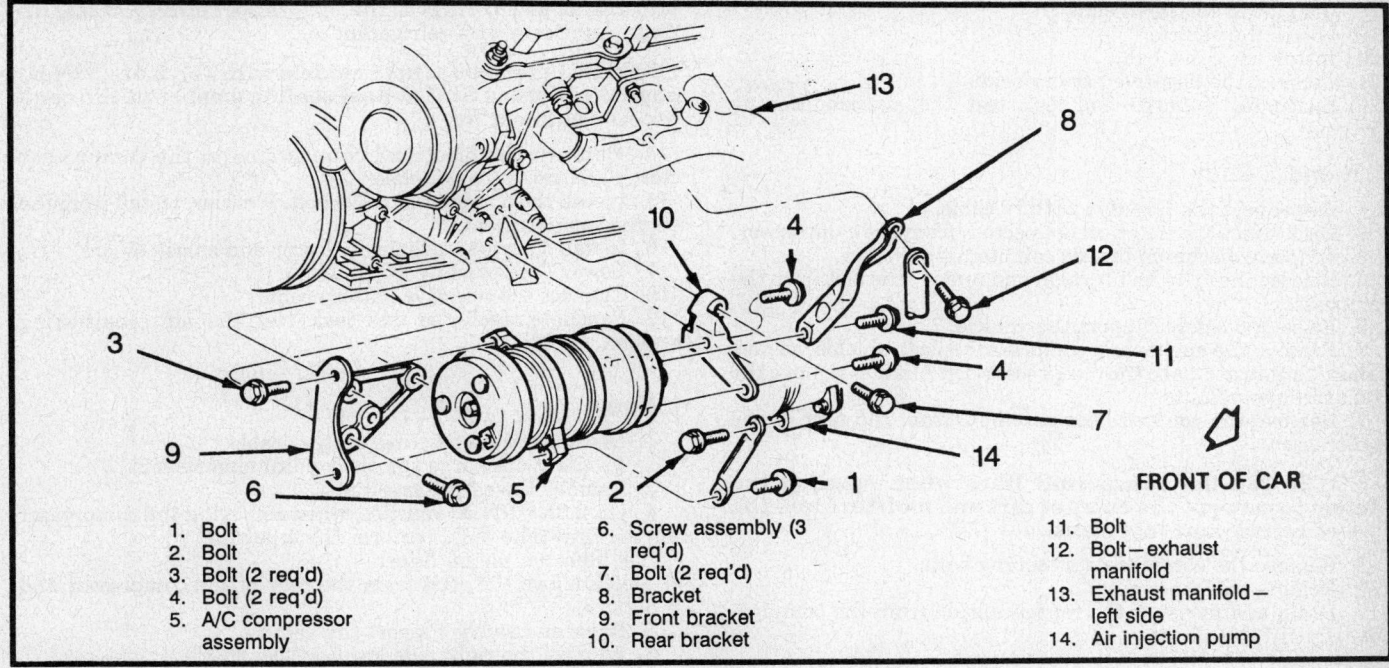

1. Bolt
2. Bolt
3. Bolt (2 req'd)
4. Bolt (2 req'd)
5. A/C compressor assembly
6. Screw assembly (3 req'd)
7. Bolt (2 req'd)
8. Bracket
9. Front bracket
10. Rear bracket
11. Bolt
12. Bolt—exhaust manifold
13. Exhaust manifold—left side
14. Air injection pump

HR-6 compressor mounting

11. Install the compressor attaching bolts.
12. Install new O-rings to the coupled hose assembly. Lubricate the O-rings with refrigerant oil.
13. Install the coupled hose assembly to the back of the compressor.
14. Install the drive belt.
15. Connect the electrical connectors to the compressor.
16. Evacuate, recharge and leak test the system.
17. Connect negative battery cable.

C and H Body

EXCEPT DEVILLE AND FLEETWOOD

1. Disconnect the negative battery cable.
2. Properly discharge the air conditioning system.
3. Release the belt tension and remove the drive belt.
4. Disconnect the compressor electrical connector(s).
5. Remove the compressor pivot bolts.
6. Raise and safely support the vehicle.
7. Remove the splash shield(s) as required.
8. Remove the compressor adjusting bolts.
9. Remove the coupled hose assembly from the rear of the compressor. Discard the O-rings.

NOTE: Cap the refrigerant lines when opening the system to prevent the entry of dirt and moisture and the loss of refrigerant lubricant.

10. Remove the compressor from the vehicle.
11. Drain and measure the refrigerant oil from the compressor. Discard the old oil.

To install:

12. If the compressor is to be replaced, drain the oil from the new compressor and discard. Add new refrigerant oil equivalent to the amount that was drained from the compressor upon removal.
13. Position the compressor in the vehicle and install the mounting bolts.
14. Install new O-rings on the coupled hose assembly. Lubricate the O-rings with refrigerant oil.
15. Install the splash shield(s).
16. Lower the vehicle.
17. Install the compressor pivot bolts.
18. Connect the compressor electrical connector(s).
19. Connect the negative battery cable.
20. Evacuate, recharge and leak test the air conditioning system.

DEVILLE AND FLEETWOOD

1. Disconnect the negative battery cable.
2. Properly discharge the air conditioning system.
3. Release the drive belt tension and remove the drive belt.
4. Raise and safely support the vehicle.
5. Remove the splash shield(s), as required to gain access to the compressor.
6. Disconnect the electrical connectors.
7. Remove the coupled hose assembly. Discard the O-rings.

NOTE: Cap the refrigerant lines when opening the system to prevent the entry of dirt and moisture and the loss of refrigerant lubricant.

8. Loosen the AIR pump-to-compressor brace bolt 1 turn.
9. Remove the compressor mounting bolts and the compressor.
10. Remove the compressor port O-rings.
11. Drain and measure the refrigerant oil from the compressor. Discard the old oil.

To install:

12. If the compressor is to be replaced, drain the oil from the new compressor and discard. Add new refrigerant oil equivalent to the amount that was drained from the compressor upon removal.
13. Position the compressor in the vehicle and install the mounting bolts.
14. Tighten the AIR pump-to-compressor brace bolt.
15. Install new O-rings on the coupled hose assembly. Lubricate the O-rings with refrigerant oil.
16. Install the coupled hose assembly to the compressor.
17. Connect the electrical connector(s).

18. Install the splash shield(s).
19. Lower the vehicle.
20. Install the drive belt.
21. Connect the negative battery cable.
22. Evacuate, recharge and leak test the air conditioning system.

E, K and V Body

1. Disconnect the negative battery cable.
2. Disconnect the electrical connectors from the compressor.
3. Properly discharge the air conditioning system.
4. Release the drive belt tension and remove the belt from the compressor.
5. Raise and safely support the vehicle.
6. Remove the engine and compressor splash shields, as necessary, to gain access to the compressor. On Allante, remove the front bumper valance.
7. Remove the coupled hose assembly from the rear of the compressor.

NOTE: Cap the refrigerant lines when opening the system to prevent the entry of dirt and moisture and the loss of refrigerant lubricant.

8. Remove the compressor attaching bolts.
9. Remove the compressor.
10. Drain and measure the refrigerant oil from the compressor. Discard the old oil.

To install:

11. If the compressor is to be replaced, drain the oil from the new compressor and discard. Add new refrigerant oil equivalent to the amount that was drained from the compressor upon removal.
12. Position the compressor in the vehicle.
13. Install the compressor attaching bolts.
14. Install new O-rings to the coupled hose assembly. Lubricate the O-rings with refrigerant oil.
15. Install the coupled hose assembly to the back of the compressor.
16. Install the engine and compressor splash shields. On Allante, install the front bumper valance.
17. Lower the vehicle.
18. Install the drive belt.
19. Connect the electrical connectors to the compressor.
20. Evacuate, recharge and leak test the system.
21. Connect negative battery cable.

J Body

1. Disconnect the negative battery cable.
2. Properly discharge the air conditioning system.
3. Remove the compressor drive belt.
4. Raise and safely support the vehicle.
5. Remove the right side air deflector and splash shield.
6. Disconnect the electrical connections at the compressor switches.
7. Remove the compressor/condenser hose assembly at the rear of the compressor and discard the O-rings.

NOTE: Cap the refrigerant lines when opening the system to prevent the entry of dirt and moisture and the loss of refrigerant lubricant.

8. Remove the compressor attaching bolts.
9. Remove the compressor.
10. Drain and measure the refrigerant oil from the compressor. Discard the old oil.

To install:

11. If the compressor is to be replaced, drain the oil from the new compressor and discard. Add new refrigerant oil equivalent to the amount drained from the old compressor.
12. Install the compressor in the vehicle.
13. Install new O-rings to the compressor refrigerant line fittings. Lubricate with refrigerant oil.

NOTE: Late 1990 – 1991 models with the 2.0L (VIN K) engine will use a Stat-O-Seal sealing washer at the compressor connection.

14. Connect the electrical connections to the compressor clutch and pressure switches.
15. Install the compressor drive belt. If easier, install from the engine compartment.
16. Install the right side air deflector and splash shield.
17. Lower the vehicle.
18. Connect the negative battery cable.
19. Evacuate, recharge and leak test the air conditioning system.

L Body

1. Disconnect the negative battery cable.
2. Properly discharge the air conditioning system.
3. Remove the serpentine belt.
4. On 2.3L (VIN A) vehicles, when removing the compressor for the first time only, perform the following:
   a. Remove the oil filter.
   b. Remove the stud from the rear of the compressor and discard.
5. Raise and safely support the vehicle.
6. Remove the right side lower splash shield.
7. Disconnect the compressor electrical connector.
8. Remove the bolt attaching the compressor refrigerant line assembly and disconnect the refrigerant line. Discard the O-rings.

NOTE: Cap the refrigerant lines when opening the system to prevent the entry of dirt and moisture and the loss of refrigerant lubricant.

9. Remove the compressor mounting bolts.
10. Remove the compressor.
11. Drain and measure the refrigerant oil from the compressor. Discard the old oil.

To install:

12. If the compressor is to be replaced, drain the oil from the new compressor and discard. Add new refrigerant oil equivalent to the amount drained from the old compressor.
13. Install the compressor in the vehicle.
14. Install the compressor mounting bolts.
15. Install new O-rings to the compressor refrigerant line fittings. Lubricate with refrigerant oil.
16. Install the bolt attaching the compressor refrigerant line assembly.
17. Connect the compressor electrical connector.
18. Install the right side lower splash shield.
19. Lower the vehicle.
20. Install the serpentine belt.
21. Evacuate, recharge and leak test the air conditioning system.
22. Connect the negative battery cable.

N Body

1. Disconnect the negative battery cable.
2. Properly discharge the air conditioning system.
3. If equipped with the 2.3L engine, when removing the compressor for the first time only, perform the following:
   a. Remove the oil filter.
   b. Using a 7mm socket, remove the stud in the back of the compressor.
   c. Discard the stud.
   d. Install the oil filter.
4. If equipped with the 2.0L or 3.3L engine, remove the serpentine belt.

5. If equipped with the 3.3L engine, install a suitable engine support fixture.
6. Raise and safely support the vehicle.
7. Remove the right side splash shield.
8. If equipped with the 3.3L engine, remove the lower support bracket. Lower the vehicle.
9. If equipped with the 2.3L or 2.5L engine, remove the serpentine belt.
10. Disconnect the compressor electrical connector.
11. Remove the refrigerant line assembly from the back of the compressor. Discard the O-rings.

NOTE: Cap the refrigerant lines when opening the system to prevent the entry of dirt and moisture and the loss of refrigerant lubricant.

12. Remove the compressor attaching bolts.
13. Remove the compressor.
14. Drain and measure the refrigerant oil from the compressor. Discard the old oil.

To install:

15. If the compressor is to be replaced, drain the oil from the new compressor and discard. Add new refrigerant oil equivalent to the amount drained from the old compressor.
16. Install the compressor and attaching bolts.
17. Install new O-rings to the compressor refrigerant lines. Lubricate with refrigerant oil.
18. Install the refrigerant line assembly to the back of the compressor.
19. Connect the compressor electrical connector.
20. If equipped with the 2.3L or 2.5L engine, install the serpentine belt.
21. If equipped with the 3.3L engine, raise and safely support the vehicle. Install the lower support bracket.
22. Install the right side splash shield.
23. Lower the vehicle.
24. If equipped with the 3.3L engine, remove the engine support fixture.
25. If equipped with the 2.0L or 3.3L engine, install the serpentine belt.
26. Evacuate, recharge and leak test the air conditioning system.
27. Connect the negative battery cable.

T Body

1. Disconnect the negative battery cable.
2. Properly discharge the air conditioning system.
3. Raise and safely support the vehicle.
4. Disconnect the compressor electrical connector.
5. If equipped with the 1.6L engine, remove the heat shield nuts, strut bolt, heat shield and strut.
6. If equipped with the 2.0L engine, remove the compressor cover plate.
7. Disconnect the compressor block fitting. Discard the O-rings.

NOTE: Cap the refrigerant lines when opening the system to prevent the entry of dirt and moisture and the loss of refrigerant lubricant.

8. Relieve the drive belt tension.
9. Remove the drive belt.
10. Remove the compressor mounting bolts.
11. Remove the compressor from the vehicle.
12. Drain and measure the refrigerant oil from the compressor. Discard the old oil.

To install:

13. If the compressor is to be replaced, drain the oil from the new compressor and discard. Add new refrigerant oil equivalent to the amount drained from the old compressor.
14. Install the compressor and mounting bolts.
15. Install the drive belt.
16. Adjust the drive belt tension.
17. Connect the compressor block fitting. Discard the O-rings.
18. If equipped with the 2.0L engine, install the compressor cover plate.
19. If equipped with the 1.6L engine, install the heat shield nuts, strut bolt, heat shield and strut.
20. Connect the compressor electrical connector.
21. Evacuate, recharge and leak test the air conditioning system.
22. Connect the negative battery cable.

W Body

2.5L AND 3.1L ENGINES

1. Disconnect the negative battery cable.
2. Properly discharge the air conditioning system.
3. Remove the serpentine belt.
4. Remove the coolant recovery reservoir.
5. Disconnect the refrigerant hose assembly from the compressor. Discard the O-rings.

NOTE: Cap the refrigerant lines when opening the system to prevent the entry of dirt and moisture and the loss of refrigerant lubricant.

6. Disconnect the compressor clutch electrical connector.
7. Remove the compressor mounting bolts.
8. Remove the compressor.
9. Drain and measure the refrigerant oil from the compressor. Discard the old oil.

To install:

10. If the compressor is to be replaced, drain the oil from the new compressor and discard. Add new refrigerant oil equivalent to the amount drained from the old compressor.
11. Install the compressor and attaching bolts.
12. Install the compressor in the vehicle.
13. Install the compressor mounting bolts.
14. Connect the compressor clutch electrical connector.
15. Install new O-rings on the compressor refrigerant line fittings. Lubricate with refrigerant oil.
16. Connect the compressor refrigerant lines.
17. Install the coolant recovery reservoir.
18. Install the serpentine belt.
19. Evacuate, recharge and leak test the air conditioning system.
20. Connect the negative battery cable.

3.4L ENGINE

1. Disconnect the negative battery cable.
2. Remove the air cleaner assembly.
3. Properly discharge the air conditioning system.
4. Remove the coolant recovery reservoir.
5. Remove the serpentine belt.
6. Remove the engine torque strut.
7. Remove the engine torque strut bracket at the frame.
8. If equipped with manual transaxle, remove the engine torque strut bracket pencil brace.
9. Remove the right and left side cooling fan retaining bolts.
10. Remove the upper radiator mounting panel bolts and the panel.
11. Disconnect the cooling fan connectors.
12. Disconnect the refrigerant line manifold from the compressor. Discard the O-rings.

NOTE: Cap the refrigerant lines when opening the system to prevent the entry of dirt and moisture and the loss of refrigerant lubricant.

13. Disconnect the compressor electrical connector.
14. Remove the compressor retaining bolts.
15. Remove the compressor from the vehicle.
16. Drain and measure the refrigerant oil from the compressor. Discard the old oil.

To install:

17. If the compressor is to be replaced, drain the oil from the new compressor and discard. Add new refrigerant oil equivalent to the amount drained from the old compressor.
18. Install the compressor and attaching bolts.
19. Install the compressor in the vehicle.
20. Install the compressor retaining bolts.
21. Connect the compressor electrical connector.
22. Install new O-rings on the compressor refrigerant lines. Lubricate with refrigerant oil.
23. Connect the compressor manifold.
24. Connect the cooling fan connectors.
25. Install the upper radiator mounting panel bolts and the panel.
26. Install the right and left side cooling fan retaining bolts.
27. If equipped with manual transaxle, install the engine torque strut bracket pencil brace.
28. Install the engine torque strut bracket at the frame.
29. Install the engine torque strut.
30. Install the serpentine belt.
31. Install the coolant recovery reservoir.
32. Evacuate, recharge and leak test the air conditioning system.
33. Install the air cleaner assembly.
34. Connect the negative battery cable.

Accumulator

REMOVAL AND INSTALLATION

1. Disconnect the negative battery cable.
2. Properly discharge the air conditioning system.
3. Disconnect the low-pressure lines at the inlet and outlet fittings on the accumulator.

NOTE: Cap the refrigerant lines when opening the system to prevent the entry of dirt and moisture and the loss of refrigerant lubricant.

4. Disconnect the pressure cycling switch connection and remove the switch, as required.
5. Loosen the lower strap bolt and spread the strap. Turn the accumulator and remove.
6. Drain and measure the oil in the accumulator. Discard the old oil.

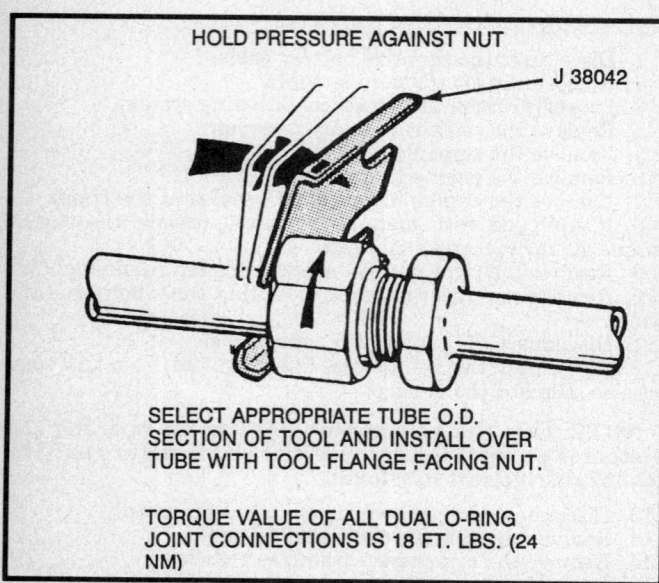

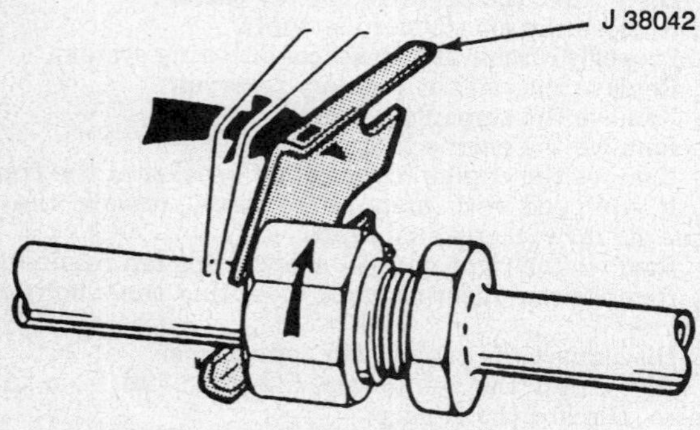
HOLD PRESSURE AGAINST NUT
J 38042
SELECT APPROPRIATE TUBE O.D. SECTION OF TOOL AND INSTALL OVER TUBE WITH TOOL FLANGE FACING NUT.
TORQUE VALUE OF ALL DUAL O-RING JOINT CONNECTIONS IS 18 FT. LBS. (24 NM)

Dual o-ring joint and tool

To install:

7. Add new oil equivalent to the amount drained from the old accumulator. Add an additional 2–3 oz. (60–90ml) of oil to compensate for the oil retained by the accumulator dessicant.
8. Position the accumulator in the securing bracket and tighten the clamp bolt.
9. Install new O-rings at the inlet and outlet connections on the accumulator. Lubricate the O-rings with refrigerant oil.
10. Connect the low-pressure inlet and outlet lines.
11. Evacuate, charge and leak test the system.
12. Connect the negative battery cable.

Fixed Orifice Tube

REMOVAL AND INSTALLATION

1. Properly discharge the air conditioning system.
2. Loosen the fitting at the liquid line outlet on the condenser or evaporator inlet pipe and disconnect. Discard the O-ring.

NOTE: Use a backup wrench on the condenser outlet fitting when loosening the lines.

3. On 1990-91 vehicles equipped with the 2.0L (VIN K) engine, remove the expansion tube by performing the following:
   a. Loosen the nut and separate the front evaporator tube from the rear evaporator tube near the compressor to gain access to the expansion tube.
   b. Carefully remove the tube with needle-nose pliers or special tool J-26549D.
   c. Inspect the tube for contamination or metal cuttings.
4. Carefully, remove the fixed orifice tube from the tube fitting in the evaporator inlet line.
5. In the event that the restricted or plugged orifice tube is difficult to remove, perform the following:
   a. Remove as much of the impacted residue as possible.
   b. Using a hair dryer, epoxy drier or equivalent, carefully apply heat approximately ¼ in. from the dimples on the inlet pipe. Do not overheat the pipe.

NOTE: If the system has a pressure switch near the orifice tube, it should be removed prior to heating the pipe to avoid damage to the switch.

   c. While applying heat, use special tool J 26549-C or equivalent to grip the orifice tube. Use a turning motion along with a push-pull motion to loosen the impacted orifice tube and remove it.
6. Swab the inside of the evaporator inlet pipe with R-11 to remove any remaining residue.
7. Add 1 oz. of 525 viscosity refrigerant oil to the system.

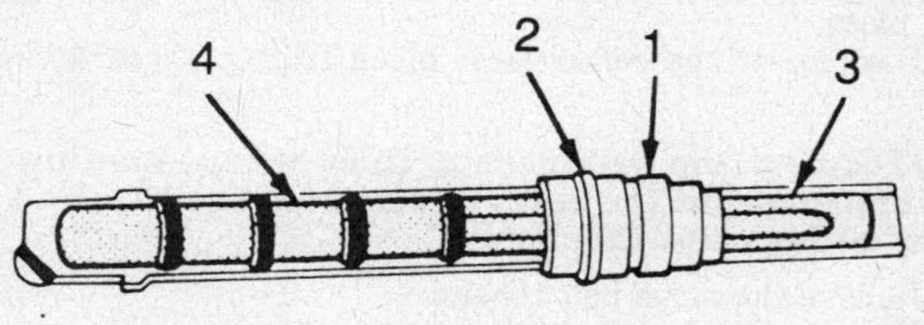
4
2
1
3

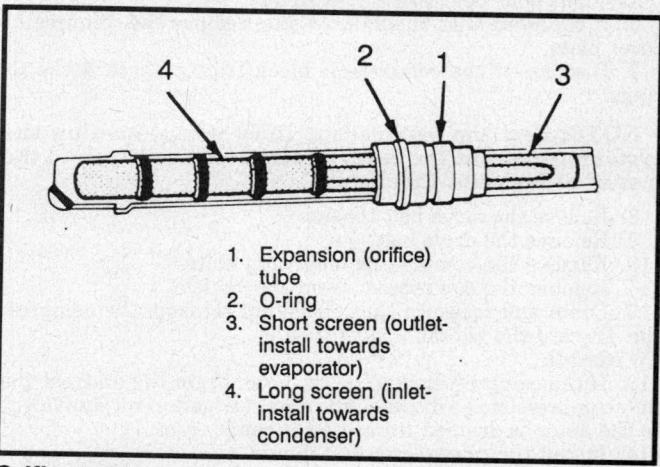

1. Expansion (orifice) tube
2. O-ring
3. Short screen (outlet-install towards evaporator)
4. Long screen (inlet-install towards condenser)

Orifice tube

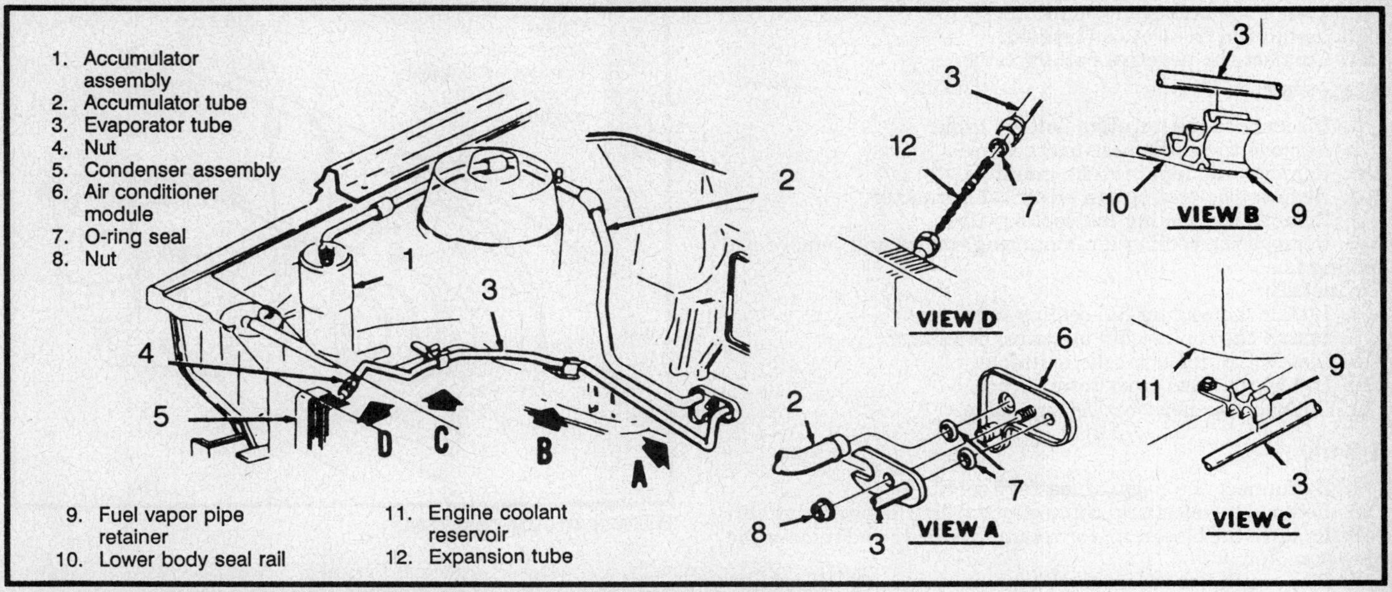
1. Accumulator assembly
2. Accumulator tube
3. Evaporator tube
4. Nut
5. Condenser assembly
6. Air conditioner module
7. O-ring seal
8. Nut
9. Fuel vapor pipe retainer
10. Lower body seal rail
11. Engine coolant reservoir
12. Expansion tube
VIEW A
VIEW B
VIEW C
VIEW D

Evaporator and accumulator tube installation—2.0L engine (VIN K)

8. Lubricate the new O-ring and orifice tube with refrigerant oil and insert into the inlet pipe.

NOTE: Ensure that the new orifice tube is inserted in the inlet tube with the smaller screen end first.

9. Connect the evaporator inlet pipe with the condenser outlet fitting.

NOTE: Use a backup wrench on the condenser outlet fitting when tightening the lines.

10. Evacuate, recharge and leak test the system.

Blower Motor

REMOVAL AND INSTALLATION

A, C, H, L and T Body

EXCEPT 1991 CENTURY AND CUTLASS CIERA AND CRUISER

1. Disconnect the negative battery cable.
2. Disconnect the electrical connections at the blower motor.
3. Remove the bolts attaching the blower motor to the evaporator case.
4. Remove the blower motor.

NOTE: If equipped with 2.8L or 3.1L engines, it may be necessary to rotate the alternator away in order to completely remove the blower motor.

To install:

5. Position the blower motor in the evaporator case and install the attaching bolts.
6. Connect the electrical connectors at the blower motor.
7. Connect the negative battery cable.

1991 CENTURY AND CUTLASS CIERA AND CRUISER

1. Disconnect the negative battery cable.
2. Remove the wiper arms.
3. Remove the cowl panel.
4. Disconnect the blower motor electrical connector and vent tube.
5. Remove the blower motor attaching screws.
6. Remove the fan retaining nut from the blower motor shaft through the plenum opening.
7. Remove the fan from the blower motor while removing the blower motor from the vehicle.

To install:

8. Holding the fan through the plenum opening, position the blower motor in the evaporator housing while installing the fan to the blower motor.
9. Install the fan retaining nut to the blower motor shaft through the plenum opening.
10. Install the blower motor attaching screws.
11. Connect the electrical connector and vent tube.
12. Install the cowl panel.
13. Install the wiper arms.
14. Connect the negative battery cable.

E, K and V Body

EXCEPT ALLANTE

1. Disconnect the negative battery cable.
2. Remove the front of cowl shield.
3. Remove the bulkhead connector.
4. Remove the ESC module and bracket, as required.
5. Remove the power steering pump bracket and support, as required.
6. Remove the coil electrical connectors.
7. Remove the coil and bracket assembly and position aside.
8. Remove the blower motor cooling tube.
9. Disconnect the blower motor electrical connector.
10. Remove the blower motor mounting screws.
11. Remove the blower motor fan from the blower motor.
12. Remove the blower motor.

To install:

13. Install the blower motor.
14. Install the blower motor fan from the blower motor.
15. Install the blower motor mounting screws.
16. Connect the blower motor electrical connector.
17. Install the blower motor cooling tube.
18. Install the coil and bracket assembly.
19. Install the coil electrical connectors.
20. If removed, install the power steering pump bracket and support.
21. If removed, install the ESC module and bracket.

22. Install the bulkhead connector.
23. Install the front of cowl shield.
24. Connect the negative battery cable.

ALLANTE

1. Disconnect the negative battery cable.
2. Remove the cowl cross-tower brace.
3. Remove the upper intake manifold.
4. Remove the cooling fan electrical connector.
5. Remove the cooling fan cooling tube.
6. Remove the cooling fan mounting screws and remove the cooling fan.

To install:

7. Install the cooling fan cooling tube.
8. Install the cooling fan electrical connector.
9. Install the upper intake manifold.
10. Install the cowl cross-tower brace.
11. Connect the negative battery cable.

J Body

1. Disconnect the negative battery cable.
2. Remove the electrical connections from the blower motor.
3. Remove the blower motor retaining screws and remove the blower motor.
4. Remove the nut from the blower motor shaft, while holding the blower motor cage.
5. Remove the cage from the blower motor shaft.

To install:

6. Install the cage to the blower motor shaft.
7. Install the nut to the blower motor shaft, while holding the cage.
8. Install the blower motor and retaining screw.
9. Connect the blower motor electrical connections at the blower motor.
10. Connect the negative battery cable.

N Body

1. Disconnect the negative battery cable.
2. If equipped with the 2.5L or 3.3L engine, remove the power steering high pressure hose from the pump.
3. Remove the electrical connector from the blower motor.
4. Remove the blower motor cooling tube.
5. Remove the blower motor retaining screws and the blower motor.

To install:

6. Install the blower motor and retaining screws.
7. Install the blower motor cooling tube.
8. Connect the electrical connector.
9. If equipped with the 2.5L or 3.3L engine, install the power steering high pressure hose to the pump.
10. Connect the negative battery cable.

W Body

1. Disconnect the negative battery cable.
2. Remove the right side sound insulator.
3. Remove the convenience center rear screws. Loosen the front screw and slide the convenience center out.
4. Grasp the carpet at the top side of the cowl and pull forward.
5. Disconnect the blower motor electrical connection.
6. Disconnect the harness from the clip.
7. Remove the blower motor mounting screws.
8. Remove the blower motor.

To install:

9. Install the blower motor.
10. Connect the harness clip.
11. Connect the blower motor electrical connector.
12. Replace the carpet at the cowl.
13. Place the convenience center into position. Install the front and rear screws.

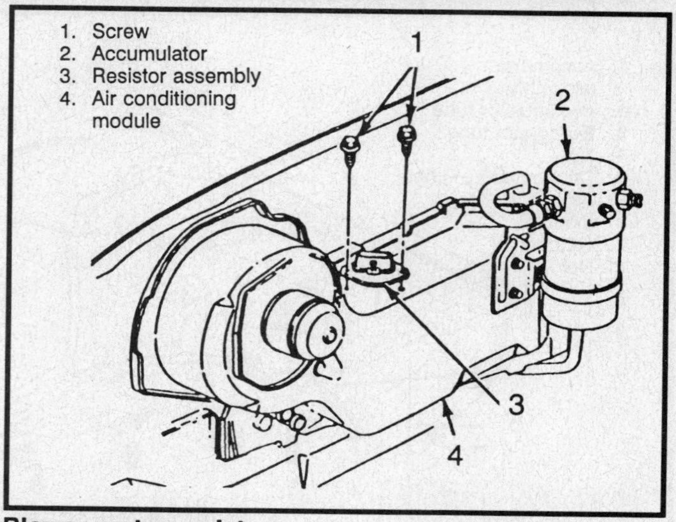
1. Screw
2. Accumulator
3. Resistor assembly
4. Air conditioning module
1
2
3
4

Blower motor resistor

14. Install the right side lower insulator panel.
15. Connect the negative battery cable.

Blower Motor Resistor/Power Module

REMOVAL AND INSTALLATION

1. Disconnect the negative battery cable.
2. Disconnect the electrical connector at the resistor.
3. Remove the resistor attaching screws.
4. Remove the resistor from the evaporator case.

To install:

5. Position the resistor in the evaporator case. Install the attaching screws.
6. Connect the electrical connector.
7. Connect the negative battery cable.

Heater Core

REMOVAL AND INSTALLATION

CAUTION

Some vehicles are equipped with the Supplemental Inflatable Restraint or air bag system. The air bag system must be disabled before performing service on or around the air bag, instrument panel components, wiring and sensors. Failure to follow safety and disabling procedures could result in accidental air bag deployment, possible personal injury and unnecessary air bag system repairs.

A Body

1. Disconnect the negative battery cable.
2. Drain the cooling system.
3. Disconnect the heater hoses from the heater core inlet and outlet connections in the engine compartment.
4. Blow residual coolant from the heater core using shop air.
5. Working inside the vehicle, remove the lower instrument panel sound insulator panel.
6. Remove the heater floor outlet duct screws or clips and remove the duct.
7. Remove the heater core cover by removing the attaching screws and clips.
8. Remove the heater core cover.
9. Remove the heater core retaining straps and remove the heater core.

To install:

10. Position the heater core in the housing and install the retaining straps.
11. Position the heater core cover on the housing and install the attaching screws and clips.
12. Install the floor outlet duct and attaching screws or clips.
13. Install the lower instrument panel sound insulator panel.
14. Working in the engine compartment, connect the heater core inlet and outlet hoses.
15. Fill the cooling system.
16. Start the engine and check for coolant leaks. Allow the engine to warm up sufficiently to confirm the proper operation of the heater. Recheck for leaks. Top-up coolant.

C and H Body

EXCEPT DEVILLE AND FLEETWOOD

1. Disconnect the negative battery cable. Drain the cooling system into a clean container for reuse.
2. If equipped, disable the Supplemental Inflatable Restraint (SIR) system by performing the following:
   a. Remove the SIR fuse from the fuse panel.
   b. Remove the left side sound insulator.
   c. Remove the Connector Positive Assurance (CPA) from the yellow 2-way SIR harness connector at the base of the steering column and separate the connector.
3. Remove the splash shield(s), as required, to gain access to the heater hoses.
4. Disconnect the heater hoses from the heater core.
5. Working inside the vehicle, remove the right side sound insulator.
6. Remove the center and lower instrument panel trim plates.
7. If equipped with Electronic Climate Control (ECC), perform the following:
   a. Disconnect the wire and hoses from the programmer.
   b. Remove the programmer linkage cover and linkage.
   c. Remove the programmer attaching bolts and remove the programmer.
8. Remove the heater core cover.
9. Remove the heater core.

To install:

10. Install the heater core in the vehicle.
11. Install the heater core cover.
12. If equipped with Electronic Climate Control (ECC) perform the following:
    a. Install the programmer attaching bolts and remove the programmer.
    b. Install the programmer linkage cover and linkage.
    c. Connect the wire and hoses from the programmer.
13. Install the lower and center trim plates.
14. Install the right sound insulator.
15. Working inside the engine compartment, connect the heater hoses to the heater core.
16. Install the splash shield(s).
17. Connect the negative battery cable.
18. If equipped, enable the Supplemental Inflatable Restraint (SIR) system by performing the following:
    a. Connect the yellow 2-way SIR connector and insert the Connect Positive Assurance (CPA) at the base of the steering column.
    b. Install the left side sound insulator.
    c. Install the SIR fuse in the fuse panel.
19. Fill cooling system and check for leaks. Start the engine and allow to come to normal operating temperature. Recheck for coolant leaks. Allow the engine to warm up sufficiently to confirm operation of cooling fan.

DEVILLE AND FLEETWOOD

1. Disconnect the negative battery cable. Remove the junction block cover nut and cover.
2. If equipped, disable the Supplemental Inflatable Restraint (SIR) system by performing the following:
   a. Remove the SIR fuse from the fuse panel.
   b. Remove the left side sound insulator.
   c. Remove the Connector Positive Assurance (CPA) from the yellow 2-way SIR harness connector at the base of the steering column and separate the connector.
3. Drain the cooling system into a clean container for reuse.
4. Remove the heater core inlet and outlet coolant hoses.
5. Working inside the vehicle, remove the glove box and sound insulators.
6. Remove the screw attaching the BCM bracket to the air conditioning module case.
7. Remove the programmer air mix valve link and shield.
8. Disconnect the programmer wiring and vacuum harness connectors.
9. Remove the module assembly heater core cover.
10. Remove the heater core retaining screws.
11. Remove the heater core.

To install:

12. Position the heater core in the vehicle. Install the retaining screws.
13. Install the module assembly heater core cover.
14. Connect the programmer wiring and vacuum harness connectors.
15. Adjust the air mix valve by performing the following:
    a. Set the temperature on the Climate Control Panel (CCP) for 90°F (32°C). Allow 1–2 minutes for the programmer to travel to the maximum heat position.
    b. Snap the threaded rod from the plastic retainer on the programmer output arm.
    c. Check the air mix valve for free travel. Push the valve to the maximum air conditioning position and check for binding.
    d. Pre-load the air mix valve in the maximum heat position by pulling the threaded rod to ensure the valve is sealing. The programmer output arm should be in the maximum heat position.
    e. Snap the threaded rod into the plastic retainer on the programmer arm and the air mix valve travel to the maximum air conditioning position.
    f. Set the temperature on the CCP for 60°F (16°C). Verify the programmer arm and air mix valve travel to the maximum air condition position.
16. Install the programmer air mix valve link and shield.
17. Install the screw attaching the BCM bracket to the air conditioning module case.
18. Install the glove box and sound insulators.
19. Working in the engine compartment, connect the heater core inlet and outlet hoses.
20. Install the junction block cover nut and cover.
21. Connect the negative battery cable.
22. If equipped, enable the Supplemental Inflatable Restraint (SIR) system by performing the following:
    a. Connect the yellow 2-way SIR connector and insert the Connect Positive Assurance (CPA) at the base of the steering column.
    b. Install the left side sound insulator.
    c. Install the SIR fuse in the fuse panel.
23. Fill cooling system and check for leaks. Start the engine and allow to come to normal operating temperature. Recheck for coolant leaks.

E, K and V Body

1. Disconnect the negative battery cable. Drain the cooling system into a clean container for reuse.
2. If equipped, disable the Supplemental Inflatable Restraint (SIR) system by performing the following:
   a. Remove the SIR fuse from the fuse panel.
   b. Remove the left side sound insulator.

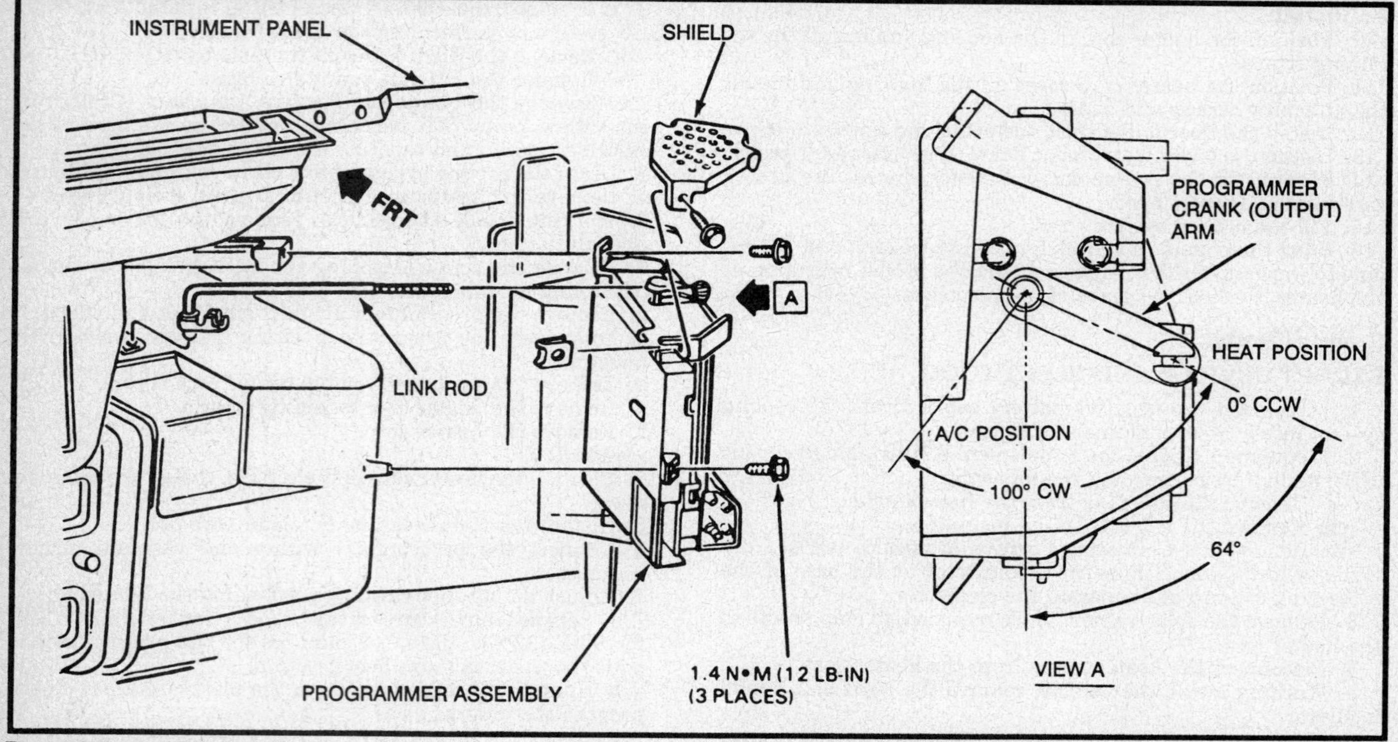
INSTRUMENT PANEL
SHIELD
FRT
A
LINK ROD
PROGRAMMER CRANK (OUTPUT) ARM
HEAT POSITION
0° CCW
A/C POSITION
100° CW
64°
1.4 N•M (12 LB-IN)
(3 PLACES)
PROGRAMMER ASSEMBLY
VIEW A

Programmer linkage

c. Remove the Connector Positive Assurance (CPA) from the yellow 2-way SIR harness connector at the base of the steering column and separate the connector.

3. Remove the console, instrument panel and right side sound insulator panel, as required.
4. Remove the programmer and electrical connectors.
5. Remove the BCM electrical connectors. Remove the BCM and mounting bracket.
6. Remove the PCM (ECM) electrical connectors. Remove the PCM (ECM) and mounting bracket.
7. Remove the heater core housing.
8. Disconnect the inlet and outlet hoses from the heater core.
9. Remove the heater core retaining screws.
10. Remove the heater core from the vehicle.

To install:

11. Install the heater core in the vehicle.
12. Connect the inlet and outlet hoses from the heater core.
13. Install the retaining screws.
14. Install the PCM (ECM) and mounting bracket. Install the PCM (ECM) electrical connectors.
15. Install the BCM and mounting bracket. Install the BCM electrical connectors.
16. Install the programmer and electrical connectors.
17. Install the console, instrument panel and right side sound insulator panel.
18. Connect the negative battery cable.
19. If equipped, enable the Supplemental Inflatable Restraint (SIR) system by performing the following:
    a. Connect the yellow 2-way SIR connector and insert the Connect Positive Assurance (CPA) at the base of the steering column.
    b. Install the left side sound insulator.
    c. Install the SIR fuse in the fuse panel.
20. Fill cooling system and check for leaks. Start the engine and allow to come to normal operating temperature. Recheck for coolant leaks. Allow the engine to warm up sufficiently to confirm operation of cooling fan.

J Body

1. Disconnect the negative battery cable.
2. Drain the cooling system into a clean container for reuse.
3. Raise and safely support the vehicle.
4. If equipped, remove the rear lateral transaxle strut mount.
5. Remove the drain tube from the heater case.
6. Disconnect the heater hoses from the heater core.
7. Lower the vehicle.
8. Remove the right and left side sound insulators, the steering column trim cover and the heater outlet duct.
9. Carefully remove the heater core cover, pulling it straight to the rear to avoid breaking the drain tube.
10. Loosen the heater core clamps and remove the heater core.

To install:

11. Install the heater core.
12. Install the heater core cover.
13. Install the heater outlet duct, steering column trim cover and the right and left side sound insulators.
14. Raise and safely support the vehicle.
15. Connect the heater hoses to the heater core.
16. Connect the drain tube to the heater case.
17. If removed, install the lateral transaxle strut (mount).
18. Lower the vehicle.
19. Connect the negative battery cable.
20. Fill cooling system and check for leaks. Start the engine and allow to come to normal operating temperature. Recheck for coolant leaks. Allow the engine to warm up sufficiently to confirm operation of cooling fan.

L Body

1989–90

1. Drain the cooling system into a clean container for reuse.
2. Disconnect the heater core inlet and outlet hoses at the heater core.
3. Remove the heater outlet deflector.

4. Remove the heater core cover.
5. Remove the heater core and retaining straps.

To install:

6. Install the heater core and retaining straps.
7. Install the heater core cover.
8. Install the heater outlet deflector.
9. Connect the inlet and outlet hoses at the heater core.
10. Fill cooling system and check for leaks. Start the engine and allow to come to normal operating temperature. Recheck for coolant leaks. Allow the engine to warm up sufficiently to confirm operation of cooling fan.

1991

1. Disconnect the negative battery cable.
2. If equipped, disable the Supplemental Inflatable Restraint (SIR) system by performing the following:
   a. Remove the SIR fuse from the fuse panel.
   b. Remove the left side sound insulator.
   c. Remove the Connector Positive Assurance (CPA) from the yellow 2-way SIR harness connector at the base of the steering column and separate the connector.
3. Remove the instrument panel.
4. Remove the screws and the floor outlet, turning clockwise and to the right to release from the rear floor air outlet.
5. Drain the cooling system into a clean container for reuse.
6. Raise and safely support the vehicle.
7. Disconnect the heater hoses from the heater core.
8. Remove the drain tube elbow from the heater core cover.
9. Lower the vehicle.
10. Remove the heater core screw, clamps and the heater core from the vehicle.

To install:

11. Install the heater core screw, clamps and the heater core from the vehicle.
12. Raise and safely support the vehicle.
13. Install the drain tube elbow from the heater core cover.
14. Connect the heater hoses from the heater core.
15. Lower the vehicle.
16. Install the screws and the floor outlet to the rear floor air outlet.
17. Install the instrument panel.
18. If equipped, enable the SIR system.
19. Connect the negative battery cable.
20. If equipped, enable the Supplemental Inflatable Restraint (SIR) system by performing the following:
   a. Connect the yellow 2-way SIR connector and insert the Connect Positive Assurance (CPA) at the base of the steering column.
   b. Install the left side sound insulator.
   c. Install the SIR fuse in the fuse panel.
21. Fill cooling system and check for leaks. Start the engine and allow to come to normal operating temperature. Recheck for coolant leaks. Allow the engine to warm up sufficiently to confirm operation of cooling fan.

N Body

1. Disconnect the negative battery cable.
2. Drain the cooling system into a clean container for reuse.
3. Raise and safely support the vehicle.
4. Disconnect the heater hoses at the heater core.
5. Remove the drain tube.
6. Lower the vehicle.
7. Remove the right and left sound insulator.
8. Remove the floor air outlet duct and hoses.
9. Remove the heater core cover.
10. Remove the heater core.

To install:

11. Install the heater core.
12. Install the heater core cover.
13. Install the floor air outlet duct and hoses to the duct.
14. Install the right and left sound insulators.
15. Raise and safely support the vehicle.
16. Install the drain tube.
17. Connect the heater hose to the heater core.
18. Lower the vehicle.
19. Connect the negative battery cable.
20. Fill cooling system and check for leaks. Start the engine and allow to come to normal operating temperature. Recheck for coolant leaks. Allow the engine to warm up sufficiently to confirm operation of cooling fan.

T Body

1. Disconnect the negative battery cable.
2. Drain the engine coolant into a clean container for reuse.
3. Disconnect the heater hoses at the heater core.
4. Remove the evaporator drain hose at the heater case.
5. If equipped with a manual transaxle, remove the gear shift boot.
6. Remove the package shelf.
7. Remove the front floor console shift plate and front center console.
8. Remove the 2 glove box straps.
9. Remove the hush panel.
10. Remove the 2 retainers, bend the tab and remove outer heater case cover.
11. Remove the heater case cover clips and screws. Remove the heater case cover.
12. Remove the 3 heater core clamps. Remove the heater core.

To install:

13. Install the heater core.
14. Install the heater core cover.
15. Install the heater case cover.
16. Install the hush panel.
17. Install the glove box.
18. Install the front center console and shift plate.
19. Install the package shelf.
20. If equipped with a manual transaxle, install the gear shift boot.
21. Connect the heater core hoses at the dash panel.
22. Connect the negative battery cable.
23. Fill cooling system and check for leaks. Start the engine and allow to come to normal operating temperature. Recheck for coolant leaks. Allow the engine to warm up sufficiently to confirm operation of cooling fan.

W Body

1. Disconnect the negative battery cable.
2. Drain the engine coolant into a clean container for reuse.
3. Remove the upper weatherstrip from the body.
4. Remove the upper secondary cowl.
5. Remove the lower secondary cowl upper nut.
6. Disconnect the heater hoses from the heater core.
7. Working inside the vehicle, remove the right and left side instrument panel sound insulators.
8. Remove the rear seat heater duct adapter.
9. Remove the lower heater duct.
10. Remove the heater core cover screws.
11. Remove the heater core cover.
12. Remove the heater core from the vehicle.

To install:

13. Install the heater core in the vehicle.
14. Install the heater core cover.
15. Install the heater core cover screws.
16. Install the lower heater duct.
17. Install the rear seat heater duct adapter.
18. Install the right and left side instrument panel sound insulators.
19. Working inside the engine compartment, connect the heater hoses to the heater core.
20. Install the lower secondary cowl upper nut.

21. Install the upper secondary cowl.
22. Install the upper weatherstrip from the body.
23. Connect the negative battery cable.
24. Fill cooling system and check for leaks. Start the engine and allow to come to normal operating temperature. Recheck for coolant leaks. Allow the engine to warm up sufficiently to confirm operation of cooling fan.

Evaporator

REMOVAL AND INSTALLATION

CAUTION

Some vehicles are equipped with the Supplemental Inflatable Restraint or air bag system. The air bag system must be disabled before performing service on or around the air bag, instrument panel components, wiring and sensors. Failure to follow safety and disabling procedures could result in accidental air bag deployment, possible personal injury and unnecessary air bag system repairs.

A Body

1. Disconnect the negative battery cable.
2. Remove the air cleaner.
3. Properly discharge the air conditioning system.
4. Disconnect the module electrical connectors, disconnect the harness straps and move the harness aside.
5. Remove the heater hose routing bracket from the back of the cover.
6. Disconnect the liquid line at the evaporator inlet and low pressure line at the evaporator outlet.

NOTE: Cap the refrigerant lines when opening the system to prevent the entry of dirt and moisture and the loss of refrigerant lubricant.

7. Remove the blower motor resistor from the top of the cover.
8. Disconnect the blower motor electrical connector.
9. If equipped with the 2.8L engine, remove the alternator bracket bolts, alternator rear brace bolt, alternator pivot bolt and move the alternator away from the module.
10. Remove the evaporator core.

To install:

NOTE: If replacing the evaporator or if the original evaporator was flushed during service, add 2–3 fluid oz. (60–90ml) of refrigerant lubricant to the system.

11. Clean the old gasket material from the cowl.
12. Install the evaporator core in the module.
13. Apply permagum sealer to the case and install the cover using a new gasket.
14. Install the cover attaching screws.
15. If equipped with the 2.8L engine, position the alternator and install the pivot bolts, rear brace bolt and alternator bracket bolts.
16. Connect the blower motor electrical connector.
17. Install the resistor to the top of the cover.
18. Install new O-rings to the liquid and low pressure lines. Lubricate O-rings with refrigerant oil.
19. Connect the liquid line at the evaporator inlet and low pressure line at the evaporator outlet.
20. Install the heater hose routing bracket to the cover.
21. Route the cowl harness in the straps and connect the module electrical connectors.
22. Evacuate, recharge and leak test the system.
23. Connect the negative battery cable.

C and H Body

EXCEPT DEVILLE AND FLEETWOOD

1. Disconnect the negative battery cable. Drain the cooling system into a clean container for reuse.
2. If equipped, disable the Supplemental Inflatable Restraint (SIR) system by performing the following:
   a. Remove the SIR fuse from the fuse panel.
   b. Remove the left side sound insulator.
   c. Remove the Connector Positive Assurance (CPA) from the yellow 2-way SIR harness connector at the base of the steering column and separate the connector.
3. Remove the engine compartment sight shield. Properly discharge the air conditioning system.
4. Disconnect the evaporator and blower module electrical connectors. Remove th relay bracket assembly and set aside.
5. Disconnect the electrical connector from the pressure cycling switch.
6. Disconnect the refrigerant lines from the accumulator.
7. Remove the accumulator from the bracket and install the sealing caps.
8. Disconnect the condenser-to-evaporator tube. Use a backup wrench on the evaporator fitting.

NOTE: Cap the refrigerant lines when opening the system to prevent the entry of dirt and moisture and the loss of refrigerant lubricant.

9. Remove the power steering pump from its mounting position and set aside.
10. Remove the vacuum tank.
11. Disconnect the blower motor electrical connection and cooling tube. Remove the blower motor from the module.
12. Remove the exhaust manifold heat shield.
13. Disconnect the heater hoses from the heater core.
14. Disconnect the blower motor resistor electrical connector. Remove the blower motor resistor from the module.
15. Disconnect the evaporator outlet line and support bracket. Use a backup wrench on the evaporator fitting.
16. Working inside the vehicle, remove the right side sound insulator.
17. Remove the floor air outlet duct.
18. Remove the evaporator and blower module bolts from under the instrument panel (behind the carpet.)
19. Raise and safely support the vehicle.
20. Remove the lower the evaporator and blower module bolts.
21. Cut the rubber blower barrier along the guide line (molded into the barrier).
22. Lower the vehicle.
23. Remove the upper evaporator and blower module bolts.
24. Finish cutting the rubber barrier along the guide lines (molded into the barrier).
25. Remove the evaporator from the module.

To install:

NOTE: If replacing the evaporator or if the original evaporator was flushed during service, add 2–3 fluid oz. (60–90ml) of refrigerant lubricant to the system.

26. Install the evaporator in the module.
27. Using strip-caulk, thoroughly seal the seam where the barrier had been cut.
28. Install the upper evaporator and blower module bolts.
29. Raise and safely support the vehicle.
30. Install the lower evaporator and blower module bolts.
31. Lower the vehicle.
32. Install the evaporator and blower module bolts (behind the carpet) under the instrument panel.
33. Install the floor air outlet duct.
34. Install the right side sound insulator.
35. Install the evaporator outlet line and support bracket. Use a backup wrench on the evaporator fitting. Install new O-rings. Lubricate with refrigerant oil.

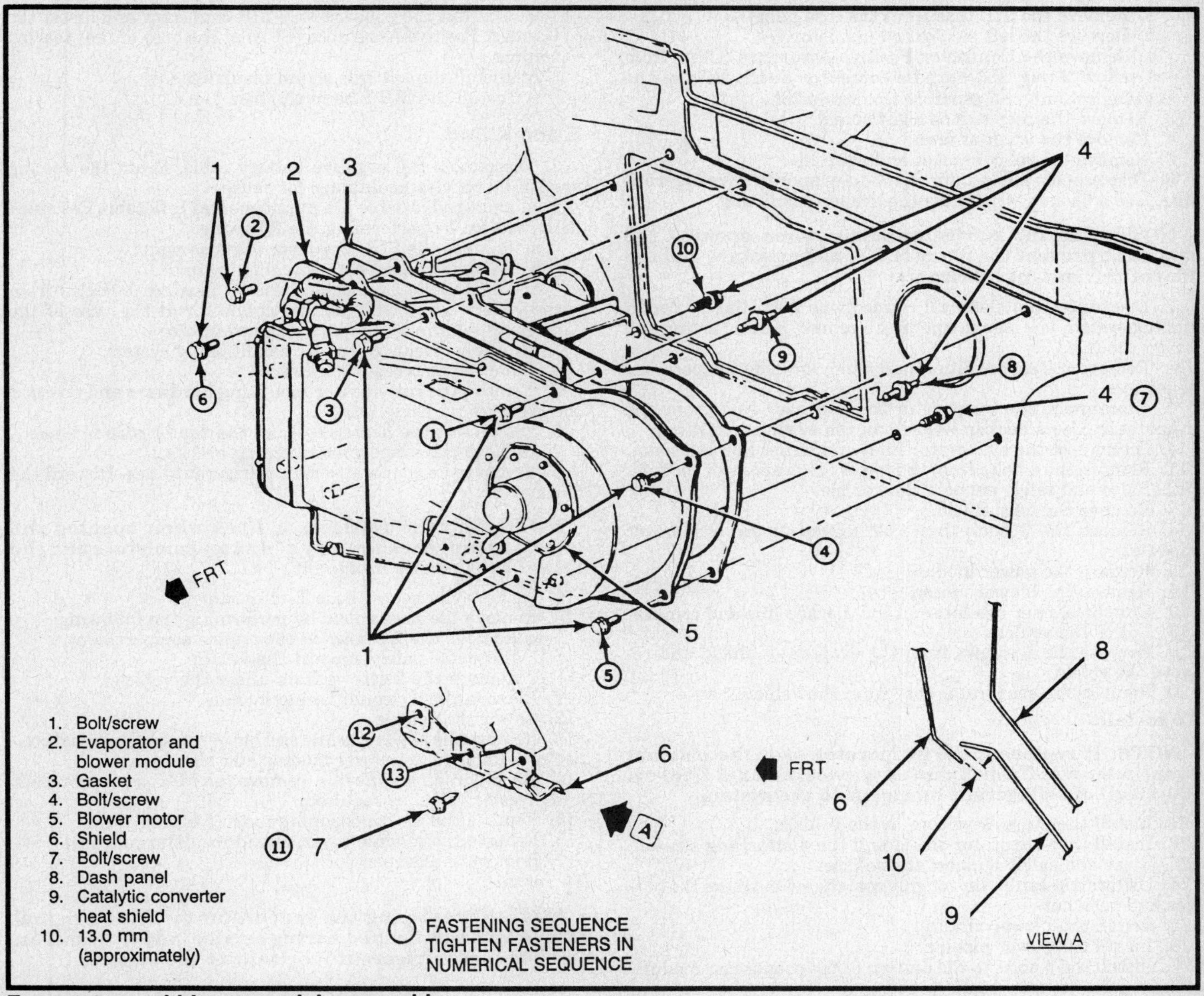
FRT
FRT
A
1. Bolt/screw
2. Evaporator and blower module
3. Gasket
4. Bolt/screw
5. Blower motor
6. Shield
7. Bolt/screw
8. Dash panel
9. Catalytic converter heat shield
10. 13.0 mm (approximately)
FASTENING SEQUENCE
TIGHTEN FASTENERS IN NUMERICAL SEQUENCE
VIEW A

Evaporator and blower module assembly

36. Install the blower motor resistor. Connect electrical connnector.
37. Connect the heater hoses to the heater core.
38. Install the exhaust manifold heat shield.
39. Install the blower motor. Connect the electrical connector and cooling tube.
40. Install the vacuum tank.
41. Install the power steering pump.
42. Connect the evaporator refrigerant lines using new O-rings. Lubricate with refrigerant oil. Use a backup wrench on the evaporator fitting.
43. Remove accumulator sealing caps. Install the accumulator and bracket using new O-rings. Lubricate with refrigerant oil.
44. Connect electrical connector to the pressure cycling switch.
45. Connect the evaporator and blower module electrical connectors. Install the relay bracket.
46. Install the engine compartment rear sight shield.
47. Connect the negative battery cable.
48. Evacuate, recharge and leak test the air conditioning system.
49. If equipped, enable the Supplemental Inflatable Restraint (SIR) system by performing the following:
   a. Connect the yellow 2-way SIR connector and insert the Connect Positive Assurance (CPA) at the base of the steering column.
   b. Install the left side sound insulator.
   c. Install the SIR fuse in the fuse panel.
50. Fill cooling system and check for leaks. Start the engine and allow to come to normal operating temperature. Recheck for coolant leaks. Allow the engine to warm up sufficiently to confirm operation of cooling fan.

DEVILLE AND FLEETWOOD

1. Disconnect the negative battery cable. Properly discharge the air conditioning system.
2. If equipped, disable the Supplemental Inflatable Restraint (SIR) system by performing the following:

a. Remove the SIR fuse from the fuse panel.
b. Remove the left side sound insulator.
c. Remove the Connector Positive Assurance (CPA) from the yellow 2-way SIR harness connector at the base of the steering column and separate the connector.

3. Remove the rear engine sight shield.
4. Remove the vacuum tank.
5. Remove the relay bracket and set aside.
6. Disconnect the accumulator-to-evaporator refrigerant line. Use a backup wrench on the evaporator fitting.

NOTE: Cap the refrigerant lines when opening the system to prevent the entry of dirt and moisture and the loss of refrigerant lubricant.

7. Disconnect the electrical connections from the air conditioning system low side temperature sensor, blower motor and power module.
8. Remove the air conditioning system low side temperature sensor.
9. Disconnect the evaporator-to-condenser line from the evaporator. Use a backup wrench on the evaporator fitting.
10. Disconnect the evaporator inlet and outlet line brackets.
11. Remove the 4 bolts from the top of the evaporator module.
12. Raise and safely support the vehicle.
13. Remove the heat shield.
14. Remove the 3 bolts from the bottom of the evaporator module.
15. Remove the power module.
16. Remove the blower motor.
17. Cut the barrier insulator on the marked line and remove.
18. Lower the vehicle.
19. Remove the 4 screws from the evaporator shield and remove the shield.
20. Remove the evaporator core from the vehicle.

To install:

NOTE: If replacing the evaporator or if the original evaporator was flushed during service, add 2–3 fluid oz. (60–90ml) of refrigerant lubricant to the system.

21. Install the evaporator core in the vehicle.
22. Install the evaporator shield and the 4 attaching screws.
23. Raise and safely support the vehicle.
24. Using strip-caulk, thoroughly seal the seam where the barrier had been cut.
25. Install the blower motor.
26. Install the power module.
27. Install the 3 bolts to the bottom of the evaporator module.
28. Install the heat shield.
29. Lower the vehicle.
30. Install the 4 bolts to the top of the evaporator module.
31. Connect the evaporator-to-condenser line from the evaporator. Use a backup wrench on the evaporator fitting. Use new O-rings. Lubricate with refrigerant oil.
32. Connect the evaporator inlet and outlet line brackets.
33. Install the air conditioning system low side temperature sensor.
34. Connect the electrical connections from the air conditioning system low side temperature sensor, blower motor and power module.
35. Connect the accumulator-to-evaporator refrigerant line. Use a backup wrench on the evaporator fitting. Use new O-rings. Lubricate with refrigerant oil.
36. Install the relay bracket and set aside.
37. Install the vacuum tank.
38. Install the rear engine sight shield.
39. Evacuate, recharge and leak test the air conditioning system.
40. Connect the negative battery cable.
41. If equipped, enable the Supplemental Inflatable Restraint (SIR) system by performing the following:
    a. Connect the yellow 2-way SIR connector and insert the Connect Positive Assurance (CPA) at the base of the steering column.
    b. Install the left side sound insulator.
    c. Install the SIR fuse in the fuse panel.

E and K Body

1. Disconnect the negative battery cable. Drain the cooling system into a clean container for reuse.
2. If equipped, disable the Supplemental Inflatable Restraint (SIR) system by performing the following:
    a. Remove the SIR fuse from the fuse panel.
    b. Remove the left side sound insulator.
    c. Remove the Connector Positive Assurance (CPA) from the yellow 2-way SIR harness connector at the base of the steering column and separate the connector.
3. Properly discharge the air conditioning system.
4. Remove the cross-tower brace.
5. Remove the relay center mounting hardware and position the relay center aside.
6. Disconnect the heater hoses at the heater core fittings.
7. Remove the evaporator retaining bracket.
8. Remove the evaporator core refrigerant lines. Discard the O-rings.

NOTE: Cap the refrigerant lines when opening the system to prevent the entry of dirt and moisture and the loss of refrigerant lubricant.

9. Remove the heater hose T-connector.
10. Remove the heat shield by performing the following:
    a. Remove the 2 screws in the engine compartment.
    b. Raise and safely support the vehicle.
    c. Remove the 2 screws from under the vehicle.
11. Remove the air conditioning module.
12. Lower the vehicle.
13. Remove the power module and blower motor electrical connectors. Remove the power module and blower motor.
14. On Eldorado and Seville, remove the MAP sensor bracket and diverter valve, as required.
15. Remove the air conditioning module cover screws.
16. Remove the module cover, sound insulator and seal.
17. Remove the evaporator.

To install:

NOTE: If replacing the evaporator or if the original evaporator was flushed during service, add 2–3 fluid oz. (60–90ml) of refrigerant lubricant to the system.

18. Install the evaporator in the case.
19. Install the module cover, retaining screws, sound insulator and seal.
20. Install the power module and blower motor. Connect the power module and blower motor electrical connectors.
21. On Eldorado and Seville, install the MAP sensor bracket and diverter valve, as required.
22. Raise the vehicle.
23. Install the air conditioning module.
24. Install the heat shield by performing the following:
    a. Install the 2 screws from under the vehicle.
    b. Lower the vehicle.
    c. Install the 2 screws in the engine compartment.
25. Install the heater hose T-connector.
26. Install new O-rings on the evaporator core refrigerant lines. Lubricate with refrigerant oil. Connect the evaporator core refrigerant lines.
27. Install the evaporator retaining bracket.
28. Connect the heater hoses at the heater core fittings.
29. Install the relay center mounting hardware.
30. Install the cross-tower brace.
31. Evacuate, recharge and leak test the air conditioning system.

32. Connect the negative battery cable.
33. If equipped, enable the Supplemental Inflatable Restraint (SIR) system by performing the following:
   a. Connect the yellow 2-way SIR connector and insert the Connect Positive Assurance (CPA) at the base of the steering column.
   b. Install the left side sound insulator.
   c. Install the SIR fuse in the fuse panel.
34. Fill cooling system and check for leaks. Start the engine and allow to come to normal operating temperature. Recheck for coolant leaks. Allow the engine to warm up sufficiently to confirm operation of cooling fan.

V Body

1. Disconnect the negative battery cable. Properly discharge the air conditioning system.
2. If equipped, disable the Supplemental Inflatable Restraint (SIR) system by performing the following:
   a. Remove the SIR fuse from the fuse panel.
   b. Remove the left side sound insulator.
   c. Remove the Connector Positive Assurance (CPA) from the yellow 2-way SIR harness connector at the base of the steering column and separate the connector.
3. Remove the cross-tower brace.
4. Remove the upper intake manifold.
5. Remove the power module.
6. Remove the evaporator line block fitting bolt. Detach the inlet and outlet lines from the evaporator. Discard the O-rings.

NOTE: Cap the refrigerant lines when opening the system to prevent the entry of dirt and moisture and the loss of refrigerant lubricant.

7. Disconnect the wire harness tie strap near the evaporator line fitting.
8. Remove the blower motor.
9. Remove the heat shield.
10. Remove the 6 large evaporator module noise barrier cover screws.
11. Remove the 5 small module noise barrier cover screws.
12. Remove the 3 small barrier clips.
13. Remove the plastic barrier cover and seal gasket.
14. Remove the evaporator core retaining screw and evaporator from the vehicle.

To install:

NOTE: If replacing the evaporator or if the original evaporator was flushed during service, add 2–3 fluid oz. (60–90ml) of refrigerant lubricant to the system.

15. Install the evaporator core retaining screw and evaporator from the vehicle.
16. Install the plastic barrier cover and seal gasket.
17. Install the 3 small barrier clips.
18. Install the 5 small module noise barrier cover screws.
19. Install the 6 large evaporator module noise barrier cover screws.
20. Install the heat shield.
21. Install the blower motor.
22. Connect the wire harness tie strap near the evaporator line fitting.
23. Install new O-rings on the evaporator refrigerant lines. Lubricate with refrigerant oil. Connect the evaporator refrigerant lines to the evaporator. Install the evaporator line block fitting bolt.
24. Install the power module.
25. Install the upper intake manifold.
26. Install the cross-tower brace.
27. Connect the negative battery cable.
28. If equipped, enable the Supplemental Inflatable Restraint (SIR) system by performing the following:
   a. Connect the yellow 2-way SIR connector and insert the Connect Positive Assurance (CPA) at the base of the steering column.
   b. Install the left side sound insulator.
   c. Install the SIR fuse in the fuse panel.
29. Fill cooling system and check for leaks. Start the engine and allow to come to normal operating temperature. Recheck for coolant leaks. Allow the engine to warm up sufficiently to confirm operation of cooling fan.

J Body

1. Disconnect the negative battery cable.
2. Properly discharge the air conditioning system.
3. Drain the cooling system into a clean container for reuse.
4. Raise and safely support the vehicle.
5. If equipped, remove the rear lateral transaxle strut (mount).
6. Disconnect the heater hoses and evaporator lines at the heater core and the evaporator core. Discard the evaporator O-rings.

NOTE: Cap the refrigerant lines when opening the system to prevent the entry of dirt and moisture and the loss of refrigerant lubricant.

7. Remove the drain tube.
8. Lower the vehicle.
9. Remove the right and left side sound insulators, the steering column trim cover, the heater outlet and the instrument panel compartment.
10. Remove the heater cover, pulling it straight to the rear in order to avoid breaking the drain tube.
11. Remove the heater core clamps and the heater core.
12. Remove the screws holding the defroster vacuum actuator to the module case.
13. Remove the evaporator cover and the evaporator core.

To install:

NOTE: If replacing the evaporator or if the original evaporator was flushed during service, add 2–3 fluid oz. (60–90ml) of refrigerant lubricant to the system.

14. Install the evaporator core and cover.
15. Install the screws holding the defroster vacuum actuator to the module case.
16. Install the heater core and clamps.
17. Install the heater core cover.
18. Install the instrument panel compartment, heater outlet duct, steering column trim cover and the right and left side sound insulator panels.
19. Raise and safely support the vehicle.
20. Connect the drain tube.
21. Connect the heater hoses and the evaporator lines. Install new O-rings on the evaporator refrigerant line fittings. Lubricate with refrigerant oil.
22. If removed, install the rear lateral transaxle strut (mount).
23. Evacuate, recharge and leak test the air conditioning system.
24. Connect the negative battery cable.
25. Fill cooling system and check for leaks. Start the engine and allow to come to normal operating temperature. Recheck for coolant leaks. Allow the engine to warm up sufficiently to confirm operation of cooling fan.

L Body

1. Disconnect the negative battery cable.
2. If equipped, disable the Supplemental Inflatable Restraint (SIR) system by performing the following:
   a. Remove the SIR fuse from the fuse panel.
   b. Remove the left side sound insulator.
   c. Remove the Connector Positive Assurance (CPA) from the yellow 2-way SIR harness connector at the base of the steering column and separate the connector.

3. Properly discharge the air conditioning system.
4. Remove the instrument panel assembly.
5. Remove the screws and the floor outlet, turning clockwise and to the right to release from the rear floor air outlet.
6. Raise and safely support the vehicle.
7. Remove the bolt from the mating block at the air conditioning module and disconnect the refrigerant lines from the module. Discard the O-rings.

NOTE: Cap the refrigerant lines when opening the system to prevent the entry of dirt and moisture and the loss of refrigerant lubricant.

8. If equipped with the 2.3L engine, remove the bolt from the tube retaining clamp.
9. Remove the drain tube elbow from the heater core cover.
10. Lower the vehicle.
11. Remove the screws and heater core cover.
12. Remove the heater core clamp screws and clamps and gently lower the heater core.
13. Remove the screws and evaporator cover.
14. Remove the screw from the evaporator securing clamp.
15. Remove the evaporator from the vehicle.

To install:

NOTE: If replacing the evaporator or if the original evaporator was flushed during service, add 3 fluid oz. (90ml) of refrigerant lubricant to the system.

16. Position the evaporator in the vehicle.
17. Install the evaporator securing clamp and screw.
18. Install the evaporator cover and screws.
19. Install the clamps and screws after positioning the heater core.
20. Install the heater core cover and screws.
21. Raise and safely support the vehicle.
22. Install the drain tube elbow to heater core cover.
23. Install new O-rings to the evaporator mating block fittings. Lubricate with refrigerant oil.
24. Install the bolt through the mating block at the air conditioner module.
25. Install the tube retaining clamp bolt.
26. If equipped with the 2.3L engine, install the bolt from the tube retaining clamp.
27. Install the bolt from the mating block at the air conditioning module and disconnect the refrigerant lines from the module. Discard the O-rings.
28. Lower the vehicle.
29. Install the screws and the floor outlet to the rear floor air outlet.
30. Install the instrument panel assembly.
31. Evacuate, recharge and leak test the air conditioning system.
32. If equipped, enable the Supplemental Inflatable Restraint (SIR) system by performing the following:
   a. Connect the yellow 2-way SIR connector and insert the Connect Positive Assurance (CPA) at the base of the steering column.
   b. Install the left side sound insulator.
   c. Install the SIR fuse in the fuse panel.
33. Connect the negative battery cable.

N Body

1. Disconnect the negative battery cable.
2. Drain the cooling system into a clean container for reuse.
3. Properly discharge the air conditioning system.
4. Raise and safely support the vehicle.
5. Disconnect the heater hoses at the heater core.
6. Remove the drain tube.
7. Disconnect the block fitting at the evaporator and discard the O-rings.

NOTE: Cap the refrigerant lines when opening the system to prevent the entry of dirt and moisture and the loss of refrigerant lubricant.

8. Lower the vehicle.
9. Remove the right and left sound insulators.
10. Remove the floor air outlet duct and hoses from the duct.
11. Remove the heater core cover.
12. Remove the heater core.
13. Remove the evaporator core cover.
14. Remove the evaporator core.

To install:

NOTE: If replacing the evaporator or if the original evaporator was flushed during service, add 3 fluid oz. (90ml) of refrigerant lubricant to the system.

15. Install the evaporator core.
16. Install the evaporator core cover.
17. Install the heater core.
18. Install the heater core cover.
19. Install the floor air outlet duct and hoses.
20. Install the right and left sound insulators.
21. Raise and safely support the vehicle.
22. Install new O-rings on the evaporator refrigerant lines. Lubricate with refrigerant oil.
23. Connect the block fitting to the evaporator.
24. Install the drain tube.
25. Connect the heater hoses to the heater core.
26. Lower the vehicle.
27. Evacuate, recharge and leak test the air conditioning system.
28. Connect the negative battery cable.
29. Fill cooling system and check for leaks. Start the engine and allow to come to normal operating temperature. Recheck for coolant leaks. Allow the engine to warm up sufficiently to confirm operation of cooling fan.

T Body

1. Disconnect the negative battery cable.
2. Properly discharge the air conditioning system.
3. Drain the engine coolant into a clean container for reuse.
4. Remove the heater core.
5. Disconnect the accumulator-to-evaporator pipe and the orifice tube to the evaporator at the dash panel.
6. Remove the evaporator cover screws and evaporator cover.
7. Remove the evaporator refrigerant lines. Discard the O-rings.

NOTE: Cap the refrigerant lines when opening the system to prevent the entry of dirt and moisture and the loss of refrigerant lubricant.

8. Remove the evaporator brackets.
9. Remove the evaporator.

To install:

NOTE: If replacing the evaporator or if the original evaporator was flushed during service, add 2–3 fluid oz. (60–90ml) of refrigerant lubricant to the system.

10. Install the evaporator core.
11. Install the pipe clamps.
12. Install the evaporator bracket and screws.
13. Install the evaporator cover.
14. Connect the accumulator-to-evaporator pipe and orifice tube to the evaporator at the dash panel.
15. Install the heater core.
16. Evacuate, recharge and leak test the air conditioning system.
17. Connect the negative battery cable.
18. Fill cooling system and check for leaks. Start the engine

and allow to come to normal operating temperature. Recheck for coolant leaks. Allow the engine to warm up sufficiently to confirm operation of cooling fan.

W Body

1. Disconnect the negative battery cable.
2. Properly discharge the air conditioning system.
3. Drain the engine coolant into a clean container for reuse.
4. Remove the heater core.
5. Disconnect the evaporator core block connection at the cowl. Discard the O-rings.

NOTE: Cap the refrigerant lines when opening the system to prevent the entry of dirt and moisture and the loss of refrigerant lubricant.

6. Remove the evaporator core.

To install:

NOTE: If replacing the evaporator or if the original evaporator was flushed during service, add 3 fluid oz. (90ml) of refrigerant lubricant to the system.

7. Install the evaporator core.
8. Install new O-rings to the evaporator refrigerant line connections. Lubricate with refrigerant oil.
9. Connect the evaporator core block connection at the cowl.
10. Install the heater core.
11. Evacuate, recharge and leak test the air conditioning system.
12. Connect the negative battery cable.
13. Fill cooling system and check for leaks. Start the engine and allow to come to normal operating temperature. Recheck for coolant leaks. Allow the engine to warm up sufficiently to confirm operation of cooling fan.

Refrigerant Lines

REMOVAL AND INSTALLATION

1. Disconnect the negative battery cable.
2. Properly discharge the air conditioning system.
3. Disconnect the refrigerant line connectors, using a backup wrench as required.
4. Remove refrigerant line support or routing brackets, as required.
5. Remove refrigerant line.

To install:

6. Position new refrigerant line in place, leaving protective caps installed until ready to connect.
7. Install new O-rings on refrigerant line connector fittings. Lubricate with refrigerant oil.
8. Connect refrigerant line, using a backup wrench, as required.
9. Install refrigerant line support or routing brackets, as required.
10. Evacuate, recharge and leak test the system.
11. Connect the negative battery cable.

Manual Control Head

REMOVAL AND INSTALLATION

A and N Body

1. Disconnect the negative battery cable.
2. Remove the hush panel, as required.
3. Remove the instrument panel trim plate.
4. Remove the control head attaching screws and pull the control head out.
5. Disconnect the electrical and vacuum connectors at the back of the control head. Disconnect the temperature control cable.
6. Remove the control head.

To install:

7. Position control head near the mounting location. Connect the electrical and vacuum connectors and cables to the back of the control head. Connect the temperature control.
8. Install the control head and attaching screws.
9. Install the instrument panel trim plate.
10. Install the hush panel, if removed.
11. Connect the negative battery cable.

J Body

1. Disconnect the negative battery cable.
2. Remove the steering column opening filler, as required.
3. Remove the cigar lighter and control assembly trim plate.
4. Remove the screws attaching the air conditioning control assembly and pull rearward.
5. Disconnect the electrical and vacuum connectors and temperature control cable from the air conditioning control assembly.
6. Remove the control assembly.

To install:

7. Connect the electrical and vacuum connections and the temperature control cable to the control assembly.
8. Install the screws attaching the control assembly to the instrument panel.
9. Install the cigar lighter and control assembly trim plate.
10. Install the steering column opening filler.
11. Connect the negative battery cable.

L Body

1989–90

1. Disconnect the negative battery cable.
2. Remove the left side hush panel.
3. On Beretta, remove the 2 screws from the bottom of the trim panel.
4. Pull the bottom of the trim panel out to release the tabs at the top.
5. Remove the trim panel.
6. Remove the 2 screws at the top of the assembly.
7. Remove the 2 screws from the front underside of the assembly.
8. Pull the assembly away from the carrier.
9. If equipped with air conditioning, disconnect the electrical and vacuum harness from the back of the heater and air conditioner control assembly.
10. Without air conditioning, remove the 2 cables from the control module.
11. Disconnect the antenna connector.
12. Disconnect the electrical connectors.
13. Remove the accessory center assembly.

To install:

14. Position the accessory center near its mounting position.
15. Connect the electrical connectors.
16. Connect the antenna connector.
17. Without air conditioning, install the 2 cables to the control module.
18. If equipped with air conditioning, connect the electrical and vacuum harness to the back of the heater and air conditioner control assembly.
19. Install the 2 screws at the top of the assembly.
20. Install the 2 screws to the front underside of the assembly.
21. Install the trim panel.
22. Push the bottom of the trim panel into place.
23. On Beretta, install the 2 screws to the bottom of the trim panel.
24. Install the left side hush panel.
25. Connect the negative battery cable.

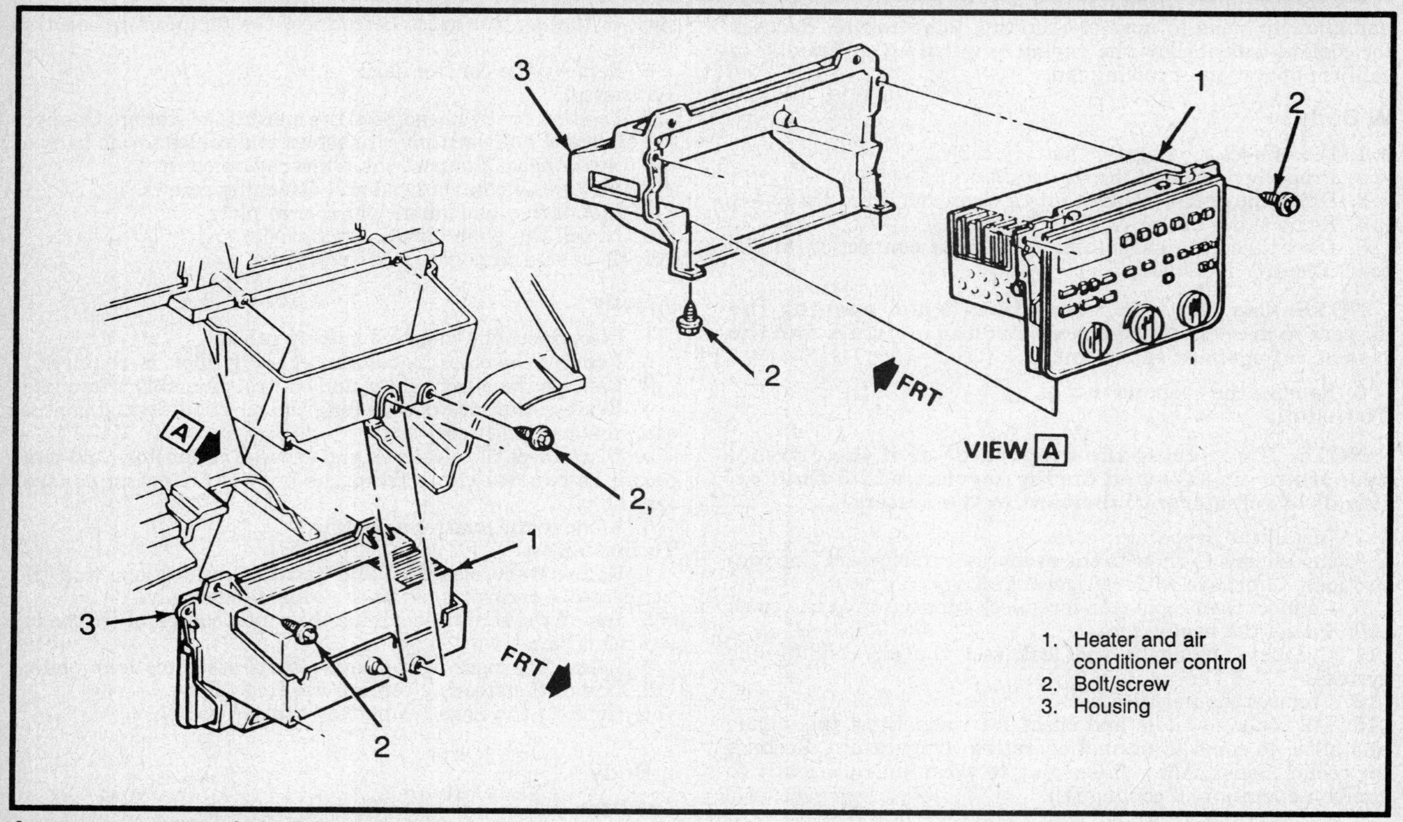
3
1
2
2
FRT
VIEW A
A
2,
1
3
FRT
2
1. Heater and air conditioner control
2. Bolt/screw
3. Housing

Accessory center housing—L body

1991

1. Disconnect the negative battery cable.
2. Remove the trim bezel.
3. Remove the screws to the control panel.
4. Disconnect the electrical and vacuum connectors.
5. Remove the control panel.

To install:

6. Position the control panel near its mounting location.
7. Connect the electrical and vacuum connectors.
8. Install the attaching screws.
9. Install the trim bezel.
10. Connect the negative battery cable.

T Body

1. Disconnect the negative battery cable.
2. If equipped with a manual transaxle, remove the gear shift lever boot.
3. Remove the package shelf.
4. Remove the front floor console shift plate and the front center console.
5. Remove the 2 retainer, bend the tab and remove the cover.
6. Remove the temperature control cable from the actuating lever and the air distributor.
7. Remove the screw underneath the control unit.
8. Disconnect the electrical and vacuum connectors and the control cable.

To install:

9. Install the electrical and vacuum connectors.
10. Attach the control unit with the screw underneath.
11. Connect the temperature control cable to the actuating lever and air distributor.
12. Install the outer heater case cover with the 2 retainers and bend the tab into position.
13. Install the front floor console shift plate and the front center console.
14. Install the package shelf.
15. If equipped with a manual transaxle, install the gear shift lever boot.
16. Connect the negative battery cable.

W Body

1. Disconnect the negative battery cable.
2. Remove the instrument panel trim plate.
3. Loosen the control assembly attaching screws. Pull assembly out.
4. Disconnect cables and electrical connectors, as required.
5. Remove control assembly.

To install:

6. Connect electrical connectors and cables, as required.
7. Install control assembly attaching screws.
8. Install the instrument panel trim plate.
9. Connect the negative battery cable.

Manual Control Cables

ADJUSTMENT

A and J Body

1. Attach the cable to the control assembly.
2. Place the control lever in the **OFF** position.
3. Place the opposite loop of cable on the lever or actuator post.
4. Push the sheath toward the lever until the lever or actua-

tor seats and the lash is out of the cable and control.

5. Tighten the screw to secure the cable.

REMOVAL AND INSTALLATION

A and T Body

1. Disconnect the negative battery cable.
2. Remove control head.
3. Disconnect the cable at the control head and lever or actuator ends by removing the push-on nuts.
4. Remove the control cable.

To install:

5. Position the control cable and connect at the lever or actuator and control assembly. Install the push-on nuts.
6. Install the control head.
7. Connect the negative battery cable.

J Body

1. Disconnect the negative battery cable.
2. Remove the right side sound insulator, instrument panel compartment and lower right side of the heater outlet duct.
3. Disconnect the temperature cable at the temperature valve.
4. Steering column trim cover.
5. Remove the right side trim cover.
6. Remove the screws attaching the heater and air conditioner control to the instrument panel.
7. Disconnect the temperature cable from the air conditioner control assembly.

To install:

8. Connect the cable to the air conditioner control assembly.
9. Install the screws attaching the heater and the air conditioner control to the instrument panel.
10. Install the right side trim cover.
11. Install the steering column trim cover.
12. Install the temperature cable at the temperature valve.
13. Install the lower right side of the heater outlet duct, instrument panel compartment and the right side sound insulator.
14. Connect the negative battery cable.

N and W Body

1. Disconnect the negative battery cable.
2. Remove the screws securing the cluster trim plate to the instrument panel.
3. Tilt the top of the cluster trim plate downward releasing the clips that mount the bottom of the trim plate to the dash. Remove the trim plate.
4. Remove the screws attaching the accessory trim center plate to the dash.
5. Tilt the top of accessory trim plate downward releasing the clips that mount the bottom of the plate to the instrument panel. Remove the plate.
6. Remove the screws attaching the control assembly to the dash.
7. Remove the control assembly from the dash.
8. Disconnect the control assembly electrical connectors.
9. Remove the control assembly.

To install:

10. Install the control assembly.
11. Connect the control assembly electrical connectors.
12. Install the control assembly attaching screws.
13. Push the mounting clips into place and roll the top of the accessory trim plate upward into position.
14. Install the screws attaching the accessory trim plate to the dash.
15. Push the mounting clips into place and roll the top of the cluster trim plate upward into position.

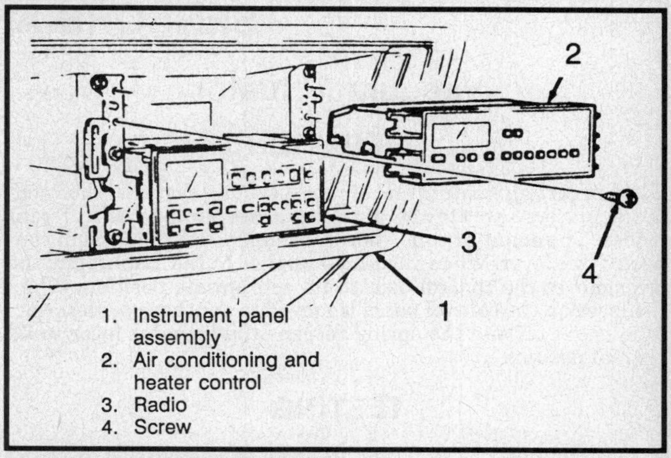
2
3
4
1
1. Instrument panel assembly
2. Air conditioning and heater control
3. Radio
4. Screw

Electronic comfort controls

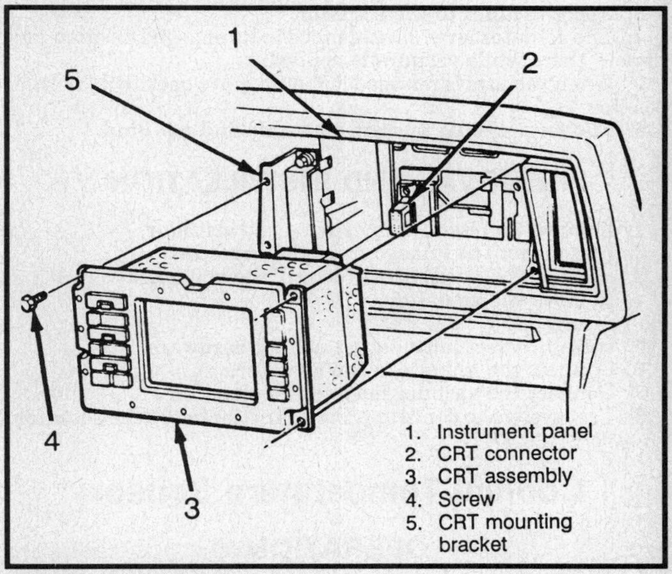
1
2
5
4
3
1. Instrument panel
2. CRT connector
3. CRT assembly
4. Screw
5. CRT mounting bracket

CRT control panel

16. Install the screws attaching the cluster trim plate to the instrument panel.
17. Connect the negative battery cable.

Electronic Climate Control Panel

REMOVAL AND INSTALLATION

C, H, E, K and V Body

1. Disconnect the negative battery cable.
2. Remove the instrument panel trim plate(s) to gain access to the electronic control panel.
3. Remove the control panel attaching screws.
4. Pull the control panel out far enough to disconnect the electrical connector. Remove control panel

To install:

5. Connect control panel electrical connector.
6. Install control panel attaching screws.
7. Install the instrument panel trim plate(s).
8. Connect the negative battery cable.

SENSORS AND SWITCHES

Vacuum Actuator

OPERATION

Used on certain heating and air conditioning systems, the vacuum actuators operate the air doors determining the different modes. The actuator consists of a spring loaded diaphragm connected to a lever. When vacuum is applied to the diaphragm, the lever moves the control door to its appropriate position. When the lever on the control panel is moved to another position, vacuum is cut off and the spring returns the actuator lever to its normal position.

TESTING

1. Disconnect the vacuum line from the actuator.
2. Attach a hand-held vacuum pump to the actuator.
3. Apply vacuum to the actuator.
4. The actuator lever should move to its engaged position and remain there while vacuum is applied.
5. When vacuum is released it should move back to its normal position.
6. The lever should operate smoothly and not bind.

REMOVAL AND INSTALLATION

1. Remove the vacuum lines from the actuator.
2. Disconnect the linkage from the actuator.
3. Remove the hardware attaching the actuator.
4. Remove the actuator.

To install:

5. Install the actuator and attaching hardware.
6. Connect the linkage to the actuator.
7. Connect the vacuum lines to the actuator.
8. Test system to confirm proper functioning of the actuator.

Coolant Temperature Sensor

OPERATION

The coolant temperature sensor provides an engine temperature signal to the ECM. The ECM controls operation of the cooling fans and, in cases of high engine temperature, deengergizes the compressor clutch. On 2.5L engines, the coolant temperature sensor is located on the top left side front of the engine below the coolant outlet. On 2.8L engines, the coolant temperature sensor is located on the left side side of the engine, below the throttle body. On 3.3L engines, the coolant temperature is located on the top right side side of the engine below the alternator. On VIN 3.1L engines, the coolant temperature sensor is located on the top left side side of the engine.

REMOVAL AND INSTALLATION

1. Disconnect the negative battery cable.
2. Drain the cooling system into a clean container for reuse.
3. Disconnect the electrical connector from the coolant temperature sensor.
4. Remove the coolant temperature sensor.

To install:

5. Install the coolant temperature sensor.
6. Connect the electrical connector.
7. Fill the cooling system.
8. Connect the negative battery cable.
9. Start the engine and check for leaks.

High-Side Temperature Sensor

OPERATION

The high-side temperature sensor is located in the high pressure refrigerant line between the condenser and the orifice tube. The BCM monitors refrigerant temperature and determines the pressure based on the pressure-temperature relationship.

REMOVAL AND INSTALLATION

1. Disconnect the negative battery cable.
2. Properly discharge the air conditioning system.
3. Disconnect the electrical connector from the sensor.
4. Unscrew and remove the sensor. Discard the O-ring.

To install:

5. Install a new O-ring. Lubricate with refrigerant oil. Install the sensor.
6. Connect electrical connector to the sensor.
7. Connect the negative battery cable.
8. Evacuate, recharge and leak test the air conditioning system.

Low-Side Temperature Sensor

OPERATION

The low-side temperature sensor is in the low pressure refrigerant line between the orifice tube and the evaporator. The BCM monitors low-side pressure to determine the maintain system pressure based on the pressure-temperature relationship.

REMOVAL AND INSTALLATION

1. Disconnect the negative battery cable.
2. Properly discharge the air conditioning system.
3. Disconnect the electrical connector from the sensor.
4. Unscrew and remove the sensor. Discard the O-ring.

To install:

5. Install a new O-ring. Lubricate with refrigerant oil. Install the sensor.
6. Connect electrical connector to the sensor.
7. Connect the negative battery cable.
8. Evacuate, recharge and leak test the air conditioning system.

In-Vehicle Temperature Sensor

OPERATION

Located behind the "Cadillac" emblem on the upper trim pad, the in-vehicle temperature sensor monitors the temperature inside the passenger compartment. To provide accurate temperature readings, a small amount of air is drawn into the sensor housing, through the aspirator, passing over the thermistor.

REMOVAL AND INSTALLATION

1. Disconnect the negative battery cable.
2. Remove the instrument panel upper trim pad.
3. Remove the screws and the sensor.

To install:

4. Install the new sensor.
5. Install the instrument panel upper trim pad.
6. Connect the negative battery cable.

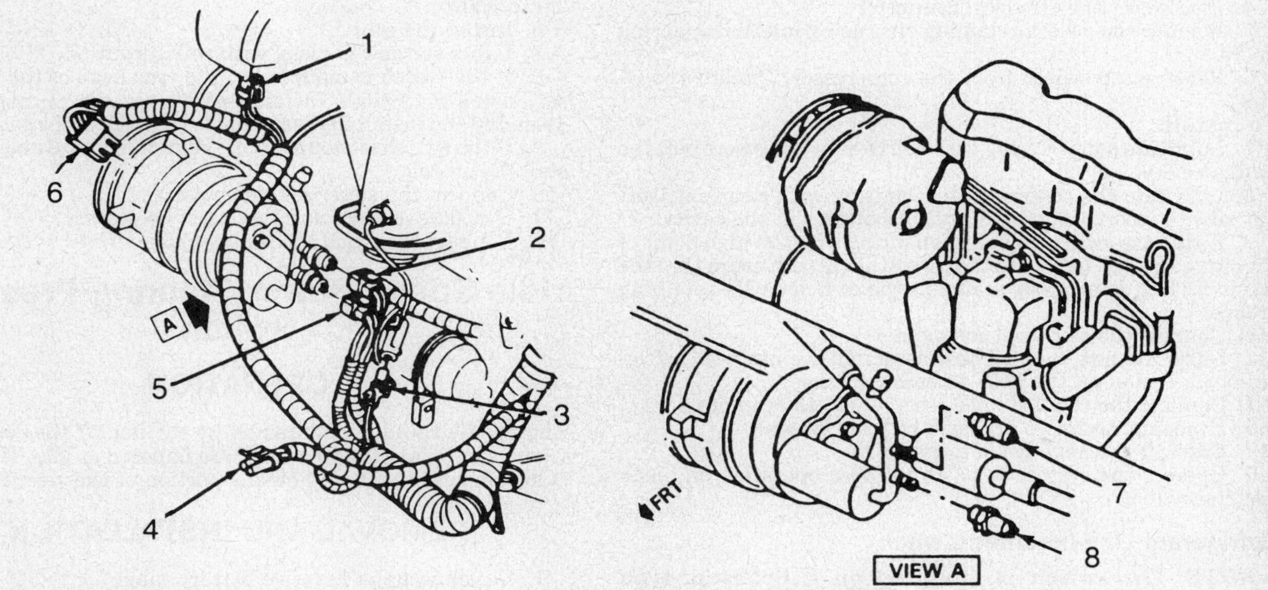
1
2
3
4
5
6
A
FRT
7
8
VIEW A
1 ALTERNATOR CONNECTOR
2 A/C LOW PRESSURE SWITCH CONNECTOR
3 O2 SENSOR CONNECTOR
4 ELECTRIC COOLING FAN CONNECTOR
5 A/C HIGH PRESSURE SWITCH CONNECTOR
6 A/C COMPRESSOR CLUTCH CONNECTOR
7 LOW PRESSURE SWITCH 4.8 N·m (42 LB. IN.)
8 HIGH PRESSURE SWITCH 4.8 N·m (42 LB. IN.)

Compressor high and low pressure switch location— 2.5L engine (VIN R)

Outside Temperature Sensor

OPERATION

The outside temperature sensor is located behind the radiator grille and provides an input to the BCM for display upon request on the Climate Control Panel (CCP).

REMOVAL AND INSTALLATION

1. Disconnect the negative battery cable.
2. Remove the grille.
3. Disconnect the electrical connector from the sensor.
4. Remove the attaching screw and the sensor.

To install:

5. Install the sensor and attaching screw.
6. Connect the electrical connector to the sensor.
7. Connect the negative battery cable.

High-Pressure Compressor Cut-Off Switch

OPERATION

The function of the switch is to protect the engine from overheating in the event of excessively high compressor head pressure and to deenergize the compressor clutch before the high pressure relief valve discharge pressure is reached. The switch is mounted on the back of the compressor or on the refrigerant hose assembly near the back of the compressor. Servicing a switch mounted on the back of the compressor requires that the system be discharged. Switches mounted on the coupled hose

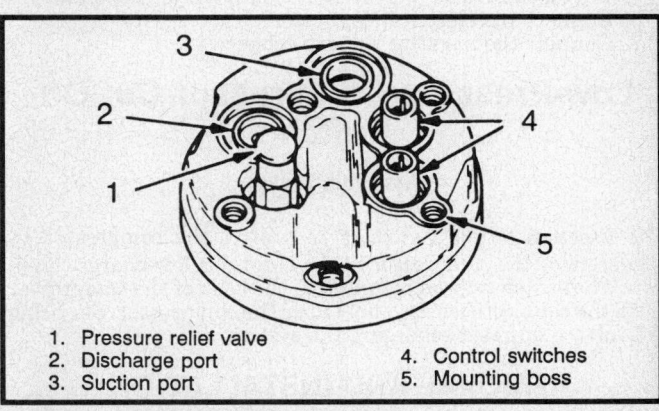

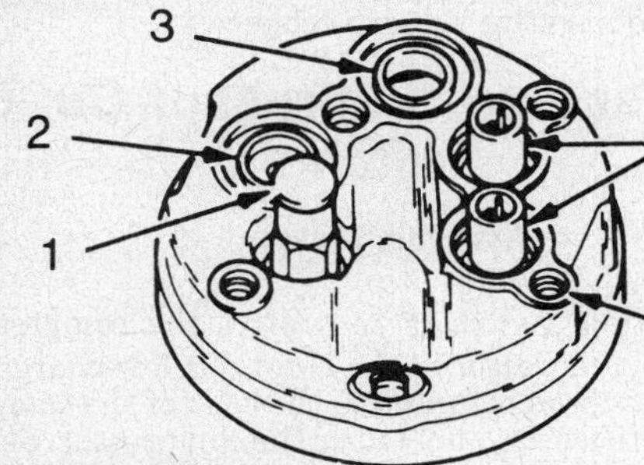
1
2
3
4
5
1. Pressure relief valve
2. Discharge port
3. Suction port
4. Control switches
5. Mounting boss

Compressor high and low pressure switch location— 2.8L engine (VIN W)

assembly are mounted on Schrader-type valves and do not require discharging the system to be serviced.

REMOVAL AND INSTALLATION

Compressor-Mounted Switch

NOTE: The system must be discharged in order to service the high pressure relief switch mounted to the back of the compressor.

1. Disconnect the negative battery cable.
2. Properly discharge the air conditioning system.

3. Remove the coupled hose assembly at the rear of the compressor.
4. Disconnect the electrical connector.
5. Remove the switch retaining ring using internal snapring pliers.
6. Remove the switch from the compressor. Discard the O-ring.

To install:

7. Lubricate a new O-ring with refrigerant oil. Insert into the switch cavity.
8. Lubricate the control switch housing with clean refrigerant oil and insert the switch until it bottoms in the cavity.
9. Install the switch retaining snapring with the high point of the curved sides adjacent to the switch housing. Ensure that the retaining ring is properly seated in the switch cavity retaining groove.
10. Connect the electrical connector.
11. Lubricate new coupled hose assembly O-rings with refrigerant oil. Install on the hose assembly fittings.
12. Connect the coupled hose assembly to the compressor.
13. Evacuate, recharge and leak test the system.
14. Connect the negative battery cable.
15. Operate the system to ensure proper operation and leak test the switch.

Refrigerant Line-Mounted Switch

NOTE: The switch is mounted on a Schrader-type valve and does not require that the system be discharged.

1. Disconnect the negative battery cable.
2. Disconnect the electrical connector.
3. Remove the switch from the coupled hose assembly. Discard the O-ring.

To install:

4. Lubricate a new O-ring with refrigerant oil.
5. Install the O-ring on the switch and install the switch.
6. Connect the electrical connector.
7. Connect the negative battery cable.

Low-Pressure Compressor Cut-Off Switch

OPERATION

The function of the switch is to protect the compressor by deenergizing the compressor in the event of a low-charge condition. The switch may be mounted at the back of the compressor or on the coupled hose assembly near the compressor. Servicing the valve requires discharging the system.

REMOVAL AND INSTALLATION

1. Disconnect the negative battery cable.
2. Properly discharge the air conditioning system.
3. Disconnect the electrical connector(s).
4. If the switch is mounted to the rear head of the compressor, remove the coupled hose assembly to gain access to the switch. Remove the switch.
5. If the switch is mounted to the coupled hose assembly, remove the switch from its mounting position.

To install:

6. Install the switch.
7. Lubricate new O-rings with refrigerant oil.
8. If the switch is mounted to the rear head of the compressor, install the switch. Install new O-rings on the coupled hose assembly and install the assembly to the back of the compressor.
9. If the switch is mounted on the coupled hose assembly, install the switch.
10. Connect the electrical connector(s).
11. Evacuate, charge and leak test the system.
12. Connect the negative battery cable.

Idle Speed Power Steering Pressure Switch

OPERATION

Engine idle speed is maintained by cutting off the compressor when high power steering loads are imposed at idle. The switch is located on the pinion housing portion of the steering rack.

REMOVAL AND INSTALLATION

1. Disconnect the negative battery cable.
2. Disconnect the electrical connector.
3. Remove the switch.

To install:

4. Install the switch.
5. Connect the electrical connector.
6. Connect the negative battery cable.
7. Allow the engine to come to normal operating temperature and confirm the proper operation of the switch.

Pressure Cycling Switch

OPERATION

The pressure cycling switch controls the refrigeration cycle by sensing low-side pressure as an indicator of evaporator temperature. The pressure cycling switch is the freeze-protection device in the system and senses refrigerant pressure on the suction side.

REMOVAL AND INSTALLATION

NOTE: The switch is mounted on a Schrader valve on the accumulator. The system need not be discharged to remove the pressure cycling switch.

1. Disconnect the negative battery cable.
2. Disconnect the electrical connector.
3. Remove the switch and O-ring seal. Discard the O-ring.

To install:

4. Install a new O-ring. Lubricate with refrigerant oil.
5. Install the switch to the accumulator.
6. Connect the electrical connector.
7. Connect the negative battery cable.

CCOT SYSTEM DIAGNOSTIC PROCEDURE

C.C.O.T. SYSTEM AIR CONDITIONING DIAGNOSIS INSUFFICIENT COOLING "CHART A"

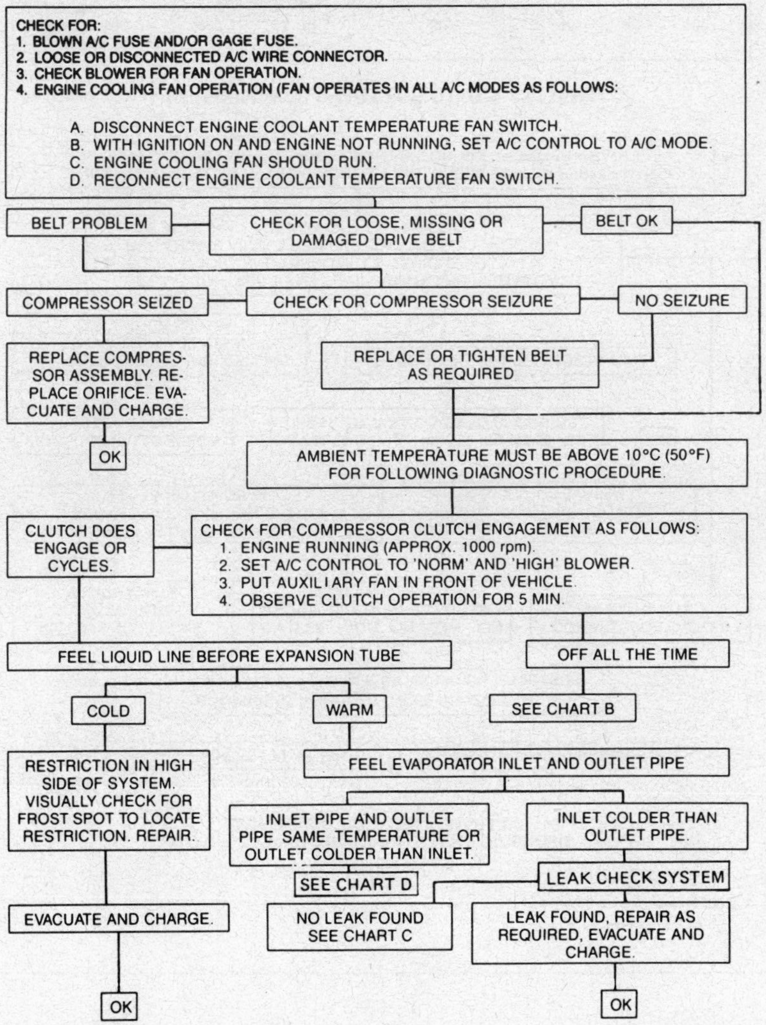
CHECK FOR:
1. BLOWN A/C FUSE AND/OR GAGE FUSE.
2. LOOSE OR DISCONNECTED A/C WIRE CONNECTOR.
3. CHECK BLOWER FOR FAN OPERATION.
4. ENGINE COOLING FAN OPERATION (FAN OPERATES IN ALL A/C MODES AS FOLLOWS:
A. DISCONNECT ENGINE COOLANT TEMPERATURE FAN SWITCH.
B. WITH IGNITION ON AND ENGINE NOT RUNNING, SET A/C CONTROL TO A/C MODE.
C. ENGINE COOLING FAN SHOULD RUN.
D. RECONNECT ENGINE COOLANT TEMPERATURE FAN SWITCH.
BELT PROBLEM
CHECK FOR LOOSE, MISSING OR DAMAGED DRIVE BELT
BELT OK
COMPRESSOR SEIZED
CHECK FOR COMPRESSOR SEIZURE
NO SEIZURE
REPLACE COMPRESSOR ASSEMBLY. REPLACE ORIFICE. EVACUATE AND CHARGE.
REPLACE OR TIGHTEN BELT AS REQUIRED
OK
AMBIENT TEMPERATURE MUST BE ABOVE 10°C (50°F) FOR FOLLOWING DIAGNOSTIC PROCEDURE.
CLUTCH DOES ENGAGE OR CYCLES.
CHECK FOR COMPRESSOR CLUTCH ENGAGEMENT AS FOLLOWS:
1. ENGINE RUNNING (APPROX. 1000 rpm).
2. SET A/C CONTROL TO 'NORM' AND 'HIGH' BLOWER.
3. PUT AUXILIARY FAN IN FRONT OF VEHICLE.
4. OBSERVE CLUTCH OPERATION FOR 5 MIN.
FEEL LIQUID LINE BEFORE EXPANSION TUBE
OFF ALL THE TIME
COLD
WARM
SEE CHART B
RESTRICTION IN HIGH SIDE OF SYSTEM. VISUALLY CHECK FOR FROST SPOT TO LOCATE RESTRICTION. REPAIR.
FEEL EVAPORATOR INLET AND OUTLET PIPE
INLET PIPE AND OUTLET PIPE SAME TEMPERATURE OR OUTLET COLDER THAN INLET.
INLET COLDER THAN OUTLET PIPE.
SEE CHART D
LEAK CHECK SYSTEM
EVACUATE AND CHARGE.
NO LEAK FOUND SEE CHART C
LEAK FOUND, REPAIR AS REQUIRED, EVACUATE AND CHARGE.
OK
OK

C.C.O.T SYSTEM AIR CONDITIONING DIAGNOSIS INSUFFICIENT COOLING "CHART B"

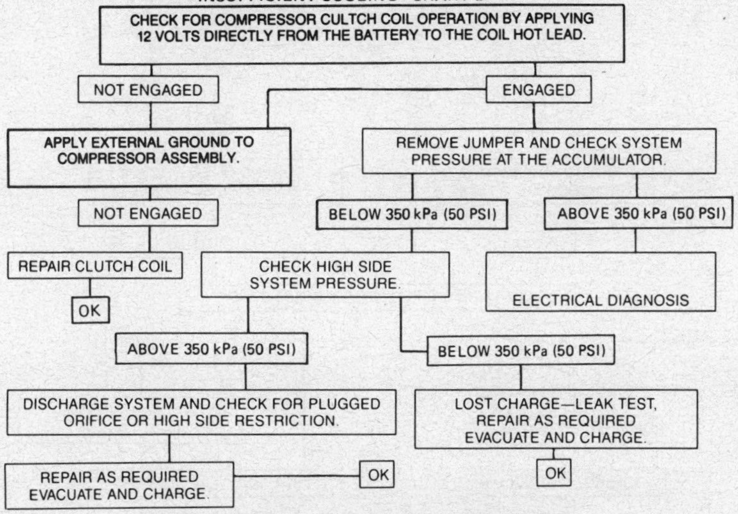
CHECK FOR COMPRESSOR CULTCH COIL OPERATION BY APPLYING 12 VOLTS DIRECTLY FROM THE BATTERY TO THE COIL HOT LEAD.
NOT ENGAGED
ENGAGED
APPLY EXTERNAL GROUND TO COMPRESSOR ASSEMBLY.
REMOVE JUMPER AND CHECK SYSTEM PRESSURE AT THE ACCUMULATOR.
NOT ENGAGED
BELOW 350 kPa (50 PSI)
ABOVE 350 kPa (50 PSI)
REPAIR CLUTCH COIL
CHECK HIGH SIDE SYSTEM PRESSURE.
ELECTRICAL DIAGNOSIS
OK
ABOVE 350 kPa (50 PSI)
BELOW 350 kPa (50 PSI)
DISCHARGE SYSTEM AND CHECK FOR PLUGGED ORIFICE OR HIGH SIDE RESTRICTION.
LOST CHARGE—LEAK TEST, REPAIR AS REQUIRED EVACUATE AND CHARGE.
REPAIR AS REQUIRED EVACUATE AND CHARGE.
OK
OK

C.C.O.T. SYSTEM AIR CONDITIONING DIAGNOSIS INSUFFICIENT COOLING "CHART C"

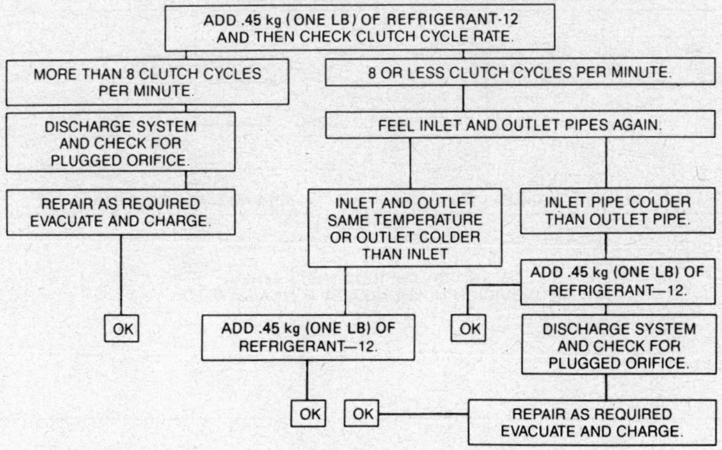
ADD .45 kg (ONE LB) OF REFRIGERANT-12 AND THEN CHECK CLUTCH CYCLE RATE.
MORE THAN 8 CLUTCH CYCLES PER MINUTE.
8 OR LESS CLUTCH CYCLES PER MINUTE.
DISCHARGE SYSTEM AND CHECK FOR PLUGGED ORIFICE.
FEEL INLET AND OUTLET PIPES AGAIN.
REPAIR AS REQUIRED EVACUATE AND CHARGE.
INLET AND OUTLET SAME TEMPERATURE OR OUTLET COLDER THAN INLET
INLET PIPE COLDER THAN OUTLET PIPE.
ADD .45 kg (ONE LB) OF REFRIGERANT—12.
OK
ADD .45 kg (ONE LB) OF REFRIGERANT—12.
OK
DISCHARGE SYSTEM AND CHECK FOR PLUGGED ORIFICE.
OK
OK
REPAIR AS REQUIRED EVACUATE AND CHARGE.

CCOT SYSTEM DIAGNOSTIC PROCEDURE (CONT.)

**C.C.O.T. SYSTEM AIR CONDITIONING DIAGNOSIS
INSUFFICIENT COOLING " CHART D"**

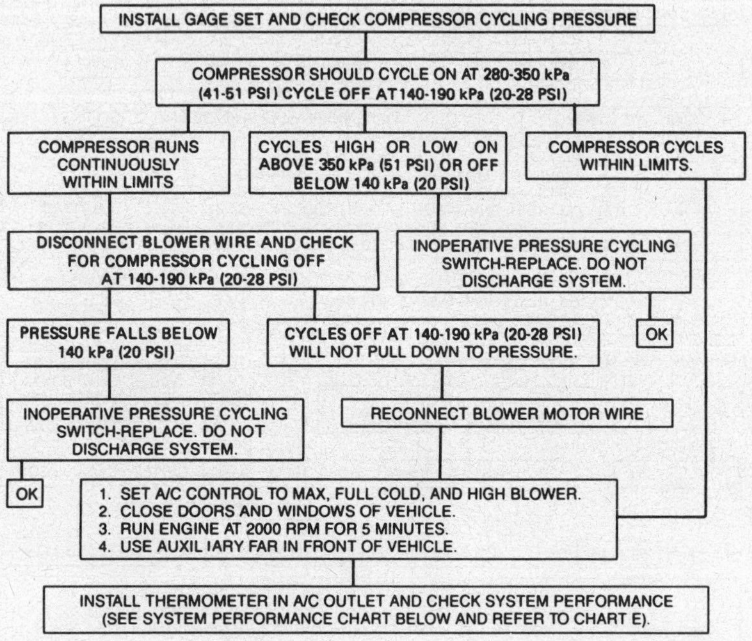
INSTALL GAGE SET AND CHECK COMPRESSOR CYCLING PRESSURE
COMPRESSOR SHOULD CYCLE ON AT 280-350 kPa (41-51 PSI) CYCLE OFF AT 140-190 kPa (20-28 PSI)
COMPRESSOR RUNS CONTINUOUSLY WITHIN LIMITS
CYCLES HIGH OR LOW ON ABOVE 350 kPa (51 PSI) OR OFF BELOW 140 kPa (20 PSI)
COMPRESSOR CYCLES WITHIN LIMITS.
DISCONNECT BLOWER WIRE AND CHECK FOR COMPRESSOR CYCLING OFF AT 140-190 kPa (20-28 PSI)
INOPERATIVE PRESSURE CYCLING SWITCH-REPLACE. DO NOT DISCHARGE SYSTEM.
OK
PRESSURE FALLS BELOW 140 kPa (20 PSI)
CYCLES OFF AT 140-190 kPa (20-28 PSI) WILL NOT PULL DOWN TO PRESSURE.
INOPERATIVE PRESSURE CYCLING SWITCH-REPLACE. DO NOT DISCHARGE SYSTEM.
RECONNECT BLOWER MOTOR WIRE
OK
1. SET A/C CONTROL TO MAX, FULL COLD, AND HIGH BLOWER.
2. CLOSE DOORS AND WINDOWS OF VEHICLE.
3. RUN ENGINE AT 2000 RPM FOR 5 MINUTES.
4. USE AUXIL IARY FAR IN FRONT OF VEHICLE.
INSTALL THERMOMETER IN A/C OUTLET AND CHECK SYSTEM PERFORMANCE (SEE SYSTEM PERFORMANCE CHART BELOW AND REFER TO CHART E).

PERFORMANCE CHART FOR C.C.O.T. SYSTEMS

TEMPERATURE OF AIR ENTERING CONDENSER	°F (°C)	70 (21)	80 (27)	90 (32)	100 (38)
COMPRESSOR OUT PRESSURE	PSI (KPA)	135-170 (950-1200)	165-200 (1150-1400)	200-245 (1400-1700)	245-300 (1700-2050)
ACCUMULATOR PRESSURE	PSI (KPA)	22-28 (150-193)	22-29 (150-200)	26-35 (180-240)	30-40 (205-275)
AVERAGE A/C AIR DISCHARGE	°F (°C)	36-43 (2.2-6.0)	36-43 (2.2-6.0)	36-43 (2.2-6.0)	42-48 (5.5-9.0)

**C.C.O.T. SYSTEM AIR CONDITIONING DIAGNOSIS
INSUFFICIENT COOLING "CHART E"**

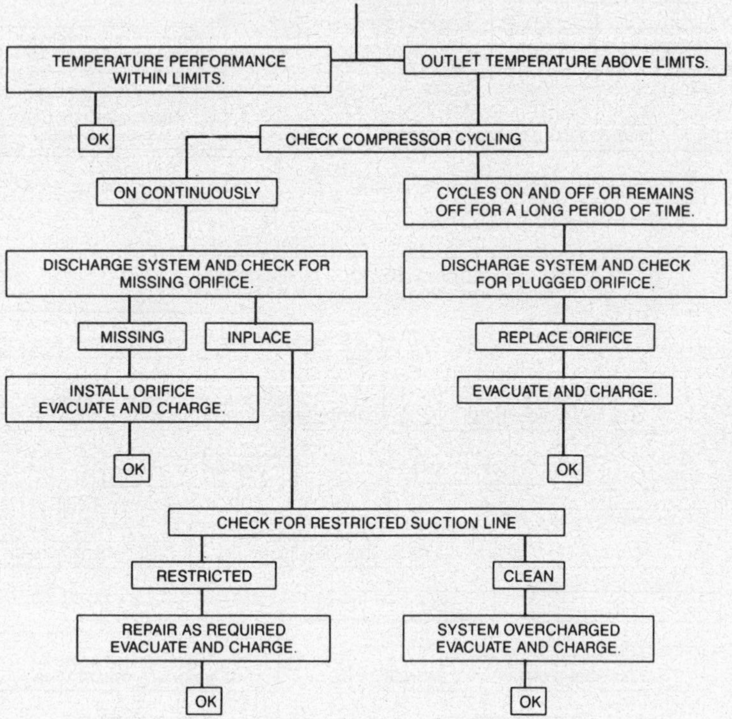
TEMPERATURE PERFORMANCE WITHIN LIMITS.
OUTLET TEMPERATURE ABOVE LIMITS.
OK
CHECK COMPRESSOR CYCLING
ON CONTINUOUSLY
CYCLES ON AND OFF OR REMAINS OFF FOR A LONG PERIOD OF TIME.
DISCHARGE SYSTEM AND CHECK FOR MISSING ORIFICE.
DISCHARGE SYSTEM AND CHECK FOR PLUGGED ORIFICE.
MISSING
INPLACE
REPLACE ORIFICE
INSTALL ORIFICE EVACUATE AND CHARGE.
EVACUATE AND CHARGE.
OK
OK
CHECK FOR RESTRICTED SUCTION LINE
RESTRICTED
CLEAN
REPAIR AS REQUIRED EVACUATE AND CHARGE.
SYSTEM OVERCHARGED EVACUATE AND CHARGE.
OK
OK

VDOT SYSTEM DIAGNOSTIC PROCEDURE – 1989–90

V–5 SYSTEM AIR CONDITIONING DIAGNOSIS INSUFFICIENT COOLING "CHART A"

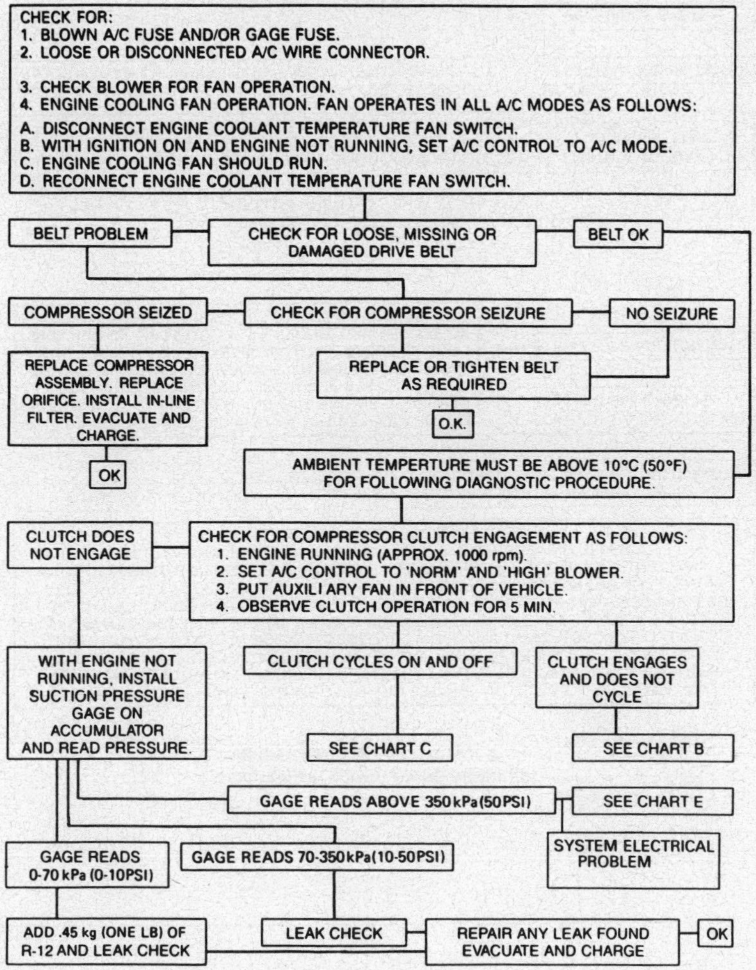
CHECK FOR:
1. BLOWN A/C FUSE AND/OR GAGE FUSE.
2. LOOSE OR DISCONNECTED A/C WIRE CONNECTOR.
3. CHECK BLOWER FOR FAN OPERATION.
4. ENGINE COOLING FAN OPERATION. FAN OPERATES IN ALL A/C MODES AS FOLLOWS:
A. DISCONNECT ENGINE COOLANT TEMPERATURE FAN SWITCH.
B. WITH IGNITION ON AND ENGINE NOT RUNNING, SET A/C CONTROL TO A/C MODE.
C. ENGINE COOLING FAN SHOULD RUN.
D. RECONNECT ENGINE COOLANT TEMPERATURE FAN SWITCH.
BELT PROBLEM
CHECK FOR LOOSE, MISSING OR DAMAGED DRIVE BELT
BELT OK
COMPRESSOR SEIZED
CHECK FOR COMPRESSOR SEIZURE
NO SEIZURE
REPLACE COMPRESSOR ASSEMBLY. REPLACE ORIFICE. INSTALL IN-LINE FILTER. EVACUATE AND CHARGE.
REPLACE OR TIGHTEN BELT AS REQUIRED
O.K.
OK
AMBIENT TEMPERTURE MUST BE ABOVE 10°C (50°F) FOR FOLLOWING DIAGNOSTIC PROCEDURE.
CLUTCH DOES NOT ENGAGE
CHECK FOR COMPRESSOR CLUTCH ENGAGEMENT AS FOLLOWS:
1. ENGINE RUNNING (APPROX. 1000 rpm).
2. SET A/C CONTROL TO 'NORM' AND 'HIGH' BLOWER.
3. PUT AUXILIARY FAN IN FRONT OF VEHICLE.
4. OBSERVE CLUTCH OPERATION FOR 5 MIN.
WITH ENGINE NOT RUNNING, INSTALL SUCTION PRESSURE GAGE ON ACCUMULATOR AND READ PRESSURE.
CLUTCH CYCLES ON AND OFF
CLUTCH ENGAGES AND DOES NOT CYCLE
SEE CHART C
SEE CHART B
GAGE READS ABOVE 350 kPa (50 PSI)
SEE CHART E
SYSTEM ELECTRICAL PROBLEM
GAGE READS 0-70 kPa (0-10PSI)
GAGE READS 70-350 kPa (10-50 PSI)
ADD .45 kg (ONE LB) OF R-12 AND LEAK CHECK
LEAK CHECK
REPAIR ANY LEAK FOUND EVACUATE AND CHARGE
OK

V–5 SYSTEM AIR CONDITIONING DIAGNOSIS INSUFFICIENT COOLING "CHART B"

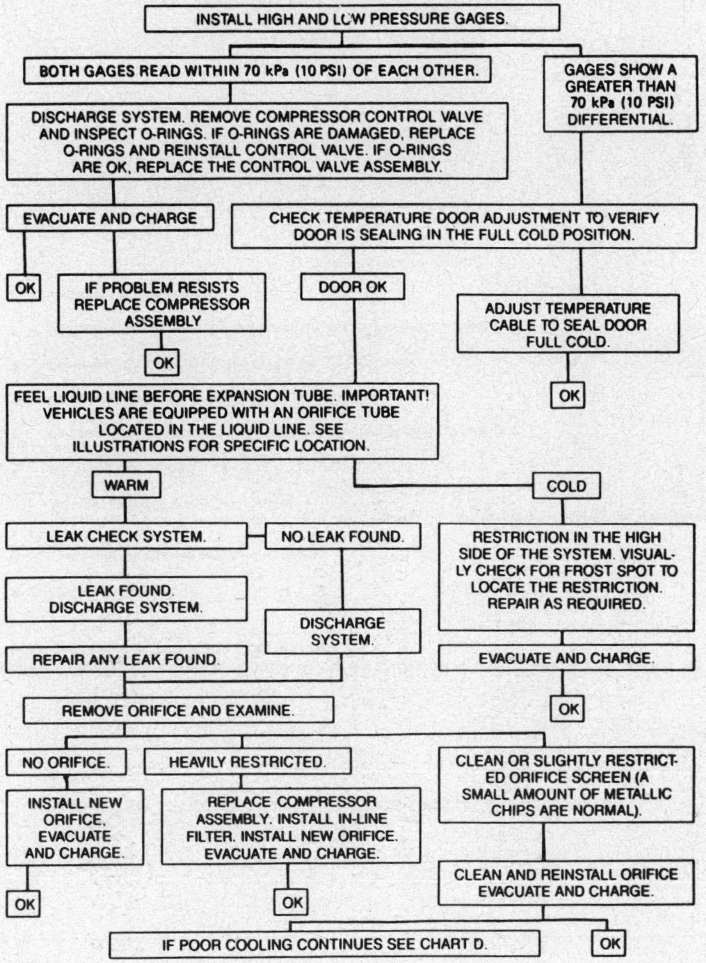
INSTALL HIGH AND LOW PRESSURE GAGES.
BOTH GAGES READ WITHIN 70 kPa (10 PSI) OF EACH OTHER.
GAGES SHOW A GREATER THAN 70 kPa (10 PSI) DIFFERENTIAL.
DISCHARGE SYSTEM. REMOVE COMPRESSOR CONTROL VALVE AND INSPECT O-RINGS. IF O-RINGS ARE DAMAGED, REPLACE O-RINGS AND REINSTALL CONTROL VALVE. IF O-RINGS ARE OK, REPLACE THE CONTROL VALVE ASSEMBLY.
EVACUATE AND CHARGE
CHECK TEMPERATURE DOOR ADJUSTMENT TO VERIFY DOOR IS SEALING IN THE FULL COLD POSITION.
OK
IF PROBLEM RESISTS REPLACE COMPRESSOR ASSEMBLY
DOOR OK
ADJUST TEMPERATURE CABLE TO SEAL DOOR FULL COLD.
OK
OK
FEEL LIQUID LINE BEFORE EXPANSION TUBE. IMPORTANT! VEHICLES ARE EQUIPPED WITH AN ORIFICE TUBE LOCATED IN THE LIQUID LINE. SEE ILLUSTRATIONS FOR SPECIFIC LOCATION.
WARM
COLD
LEAK CHECK SYSTEM.
NO LEAK FOUND.
RESTRICTION IN THE HIGH SIDE OF THE SYSTEM. VISUALLY CHECK FOR FROST SPOT TO LOCATE THE RESTRICTION. REPAIR AS REQUIRED.
LEAK FOUND. DISCHARGE SYSTEM.
DISCHARGE SYSTEM.
REPAIR ANY LEAK FOUND.
EVACUATE AND CHARGE.
OK
REMOVE ORIFICE AND EXAMINE.
NO ORIFICE.
HEAVILY RESTRICTED.
CLEAN OR SLIGHTLY RESTRICTED ORIFICE SCREEN (A SMALL AMOUNT OF METALLIC CHIPS ARE NORMAL).
INSTALL NEW ORIFICE, EVACUATE AND CHARGE.
REPLACE COMPRESSOR ASSEMBLY. INSTALL IN-LINE FILTER. INSTALL NEW ORIFICE. EVACUATE AND CHARGE.
CLEAN AND REINSTALL ORIFICE EVACUATE AND CHARGE.
OK
OK
IF POOR COOLING CONTINUES SEE CHART D.
OK

VDOT SYSTEM DIAGNOSTIC PROCEDURE 1989–90 (CONT.)

V-5 SYSTEM AIR CONDITIONING DIAGNOSIS INSUFFICIENT COOLING "CHART C"

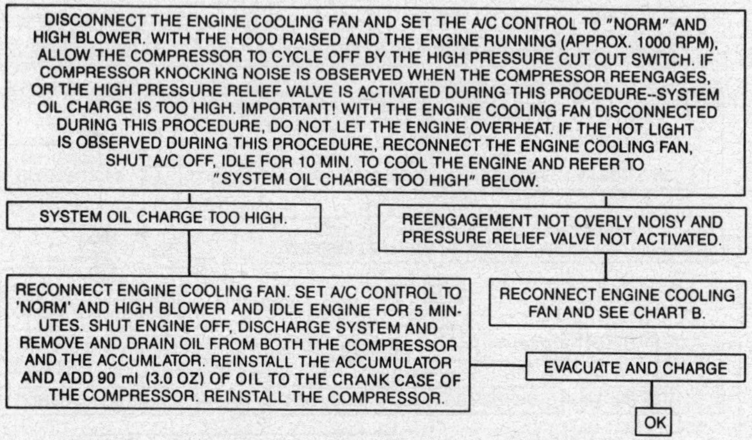
DISCONNECT THE ENGINE COOLING FAN AND SET THE A/C CONTROL TO "NORM" AND HIGH BLOWER. WITH THE HOOD RAISED AND THE ENGINE RUNNING (APPROX. 1000 RPM), ALLOW THE COMPRESSOR TO CYCLE OFF BY THE HIGH PRESSURE CUT OUT SWITCH. IF COMPRESSOR KNOCKING NOISE IS OBSERVED WHEN THE COMPRESSOR REENGAGES, OR THE HIGH PRESSURE RELIEF VALVE IS ACTIVATED DURING THIS PROCEDURE--SYSTEM OIL CHARGE IS TOO HIGH. IMPORTANT! WITH THE ENGINE COOLING FAN DISCONNECTED DURING THIS PROCEDURE, DO NOT LET THE ENGINE OVERHEAT. IF THE HOT LIGHT IS OBSERVED DURING THIS PROCEDURE, RECONNECT THE ENGINE COOLING FAN, SHUT A/C OFF, IDLE FOR 10 MIN. TO COOL THE ENGINE AND REFER TO "SYSTEM OIL CHARGE TOO HIGH" BELOW.
SYSTEM OIL CHARGE TOO HIGH.
REENGAGEMENT NOT OVERLY NOISY AND PRESSURE RELIEF VALVE NOT ACTIVATED.
RECONNECT ENGINE COOLING FAN. SET A/C CONTROL TO 'NORM' AND HIGH BLOWER AND IDLE ENGINE FOR 5 MINUTES. SHUT ENGINE OFF, DISCHARGE SYSTEM AND REMOVE AND DRAIN OIL FROM BOTH THE COMPRESSOR AND THE ACCUMLATOR. REINSTALL THE ACCUMULATOR AND ADD 90 ml (3.0 OZ) OF OIL TO THE CRANK CASE OF THE COMPRESSOR. REINSTALL THE COMPRESSOR.
RECONNECT ENGINE COOLING FAN AND SEE CHART B.
EVACUATE AND CHARGE
OK

V–5 SYSTEM AIR CONDITIONING DIAGNOSIS INSUFFICIENT COOLING "CHART D"

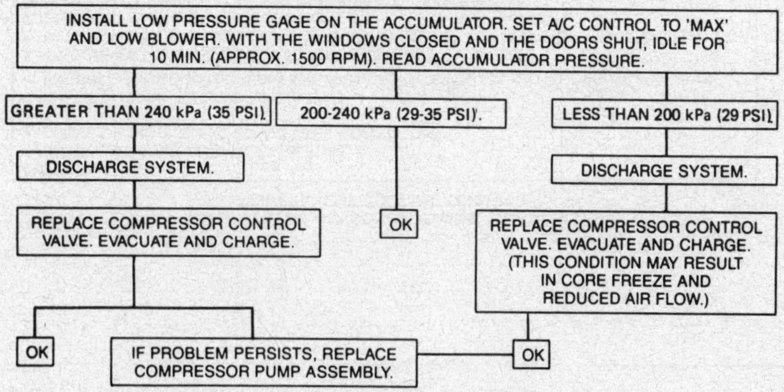
INSTALL LOW PRESSURE GAGE ON THE ACCUMULATOR. SET A/C CONTROL TO 'MAX' AND LOW BLOWER. WITH THE WINDOWS CLOSED AND THE DOORS SHUT, IDLE FOR 10 MIN. (APPROX. 1500 RPM). READ ACCUMULATOR PRESSURE.
GREATER THAN 240 kPa (35 PSI)
200-240 kPa (29-35 PSI)
LESS THAN 200 kPa (29 PSI)
DISCHARGE SYSTEM.
DISCHARGE SYSTEM.
REPLACE COMPRESSOR CONTROL VALVE. EVACUATE AND CHARGE.
OK
REPLACE COMPRESSOR CONTROL VALVE. EVACUATE AND CHARGE. (THIS CONDITION MAY RESULT IN CORE FREEZE AND REDUCED AIR FLOW.)
OK
IF PROBLEM PERSISTS, REPLACE COMPRESSOR PUMP ASSEMBLY.
OK

VDOT SYSTEM DIAGNOSTIC PROCEDURE—1991

V-5 SYSTEM AIR CONDITIONING DIAGNOSIS INSUFFICIENT COOLING

STEP 1 – Preliminary Checks

Repair the following as necessary. If outlet air temperature with A/C on is normal after making the following repairs, the system is operating normally.

- A/C fuse
- Clutch coil or rear head switch connections
- Temperature valve. Move temperature valve lever rapidly from cold to hot. Listen for temperature valve hitting at each end. Adjust as necessary.
- A/C blower operation.
- Compressor belt. Check condition and tension of belt. Replace as necessary.
- Engine cooling fan operation. Refer to service manual for diagnosis.
- Condensor. Check for restricted airflow through condensor.
- Compressor clutch operation and condition (overheated or discolored)
- Clutch driver (freewheeling)

VDOT SYSTEM DIAGNOSTIC PROCEDURE – 1991 (CONT.)

V-5 SYSTEM AIR CONDITIONING DIAGNOSIS INSUFFICIENT COOLING

STEP 2 – Checking Refrigerant Charge

NOTE: Ambient temperature should be above 16°C (60°F) and engine at normal operating temperature.

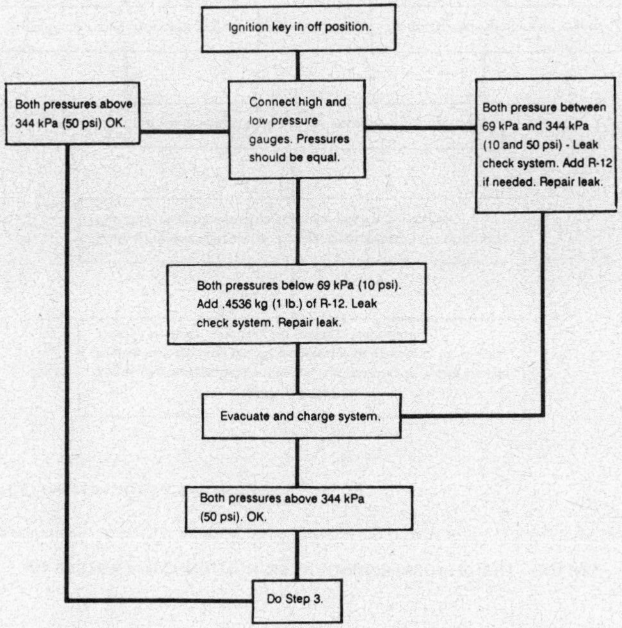
Ignition key in off position.
Connect high and low pressure gauges. Pressures should be equal.
Both pressures above 344 kPa (50 psi) OK.
Both pressure between 69 kPa and 344 kPa (10 and 50 psi) - Leak check system. Add R-12 if needed. Repair leak.
Both pressures below 69 kPa (10 psi). Add .4536 kg (1 lb.) of R-12. Leak check system. Repair leak.
Evacuate and charge system.
Both pressures above 344 kPa (50 psi). OK.
Do Step 3.

V-5 SYSTEM AIR CONDITIONING DIAGNOSIS INSUFFICIENT COOLING

STEP 3 – Checking Compressor Clutch Engagement

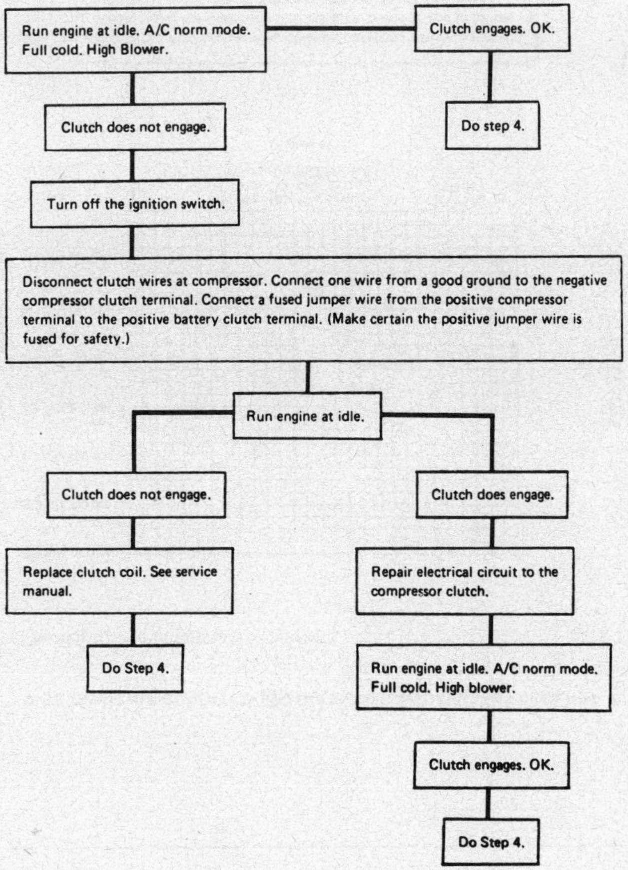
Run engine at idle. A/C norm mode. Full cold. High Blower.
Clutch engages. OK.
Do step 4.
Clutch does not engage.
Turn off the ignition switch.
Disconnect clutch wires at compressor. Connect one wire from a good ground to the negative compressor clutch terminal. Connect a fused jumper wire from the positive compressor terminal to the positive battery clutch terminal. (Make certain the positive jumper wire is fused for safety.)
Run engine at idle.
Clutch does not engage.
Replace clutch coil. See service manual.
Do Step 4.
Clutch does engage.
Repair electrical circuit to the compressor clutch.
Run engine at idle. A/C norm mode. Full cold. High blower.
Clutch engages. OK.
Do Step 4.

V-5 SYSTEM AIR CONDITIONING DIAGNOSIS INSUFFICIENT COOLING

STEP 4 – Checking System Performance

IMPORTANT
Follow this test procedure exactly. It is designed to create enough cooling load to cause the V5 compressor to operate at full stroke. This is absolutely necessary for accurate test results.

Close all vehicle windows and doors. Open hood. A/C norm mode. Full cold. High blower. Run engine at idle for 5 minutes.

Feed liquid line on both sides of expansion (orifice) tube.

- Same temperature. Discharge system.
  - Expansion tube missing.
  - Install expansion tube.
  - Evacuate and charge system.
  - Note outlet temperature. If outlet temperature is not within specifications, follow Step 4 again.
- Noticeable temperature difference.
  - Record low and high side pressures after A/C system has been operating for 5 minutes or more. On engines with cooling fans that cycle, take pressure readings with engine cooling fan on.
  - Locate the intersection of the low and high side pressures on the Diagnostic Chart

V-5 SYSTEM AIR CONDITIONING DIAGNOSIS INSUFFICIENT COOLING

STEP 4 – Checking System Performance (Continued)

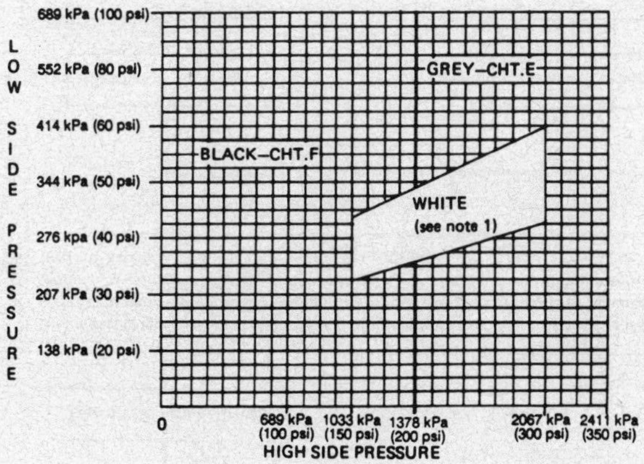
LOW SIDE PRESSURE
689 kPa (100 psi)
552 kPa (80 psi)
414 kPa (60 psi)
344 kPa (50 psi)
276 kpa (40 psi)
207 kPa (30 psi)
138 kPa (20 psi)
0
GREY–CHT.E
BLACK–CHT.F
WHITE
(see note 1)
689 kPa (100 psi)
1033 kPa (150 psi)
1378 kPa (200 psi)
2067 kPa (300 psi)
2411 kPa (350 psi)
HIGH SIDE PRESSURE

(Figure 1)

Humidity and temperature variables can create borderline diagnostic conditions. If the Diagnostic Chart (Figure 1) directs you to follow procedures in one step, but those procedures do not lead you to correct the problem, follow the procedures for the other step.

- Low and high side pressures intersect in the black area of the chart. Do Step 5.
- Low and high side pressures intersect in the white area of the chart. No trouble found. All components of the A/C system are functioning properly.
- Low and high side pressures intersect in the gray area of the chart. Do Step. 6.

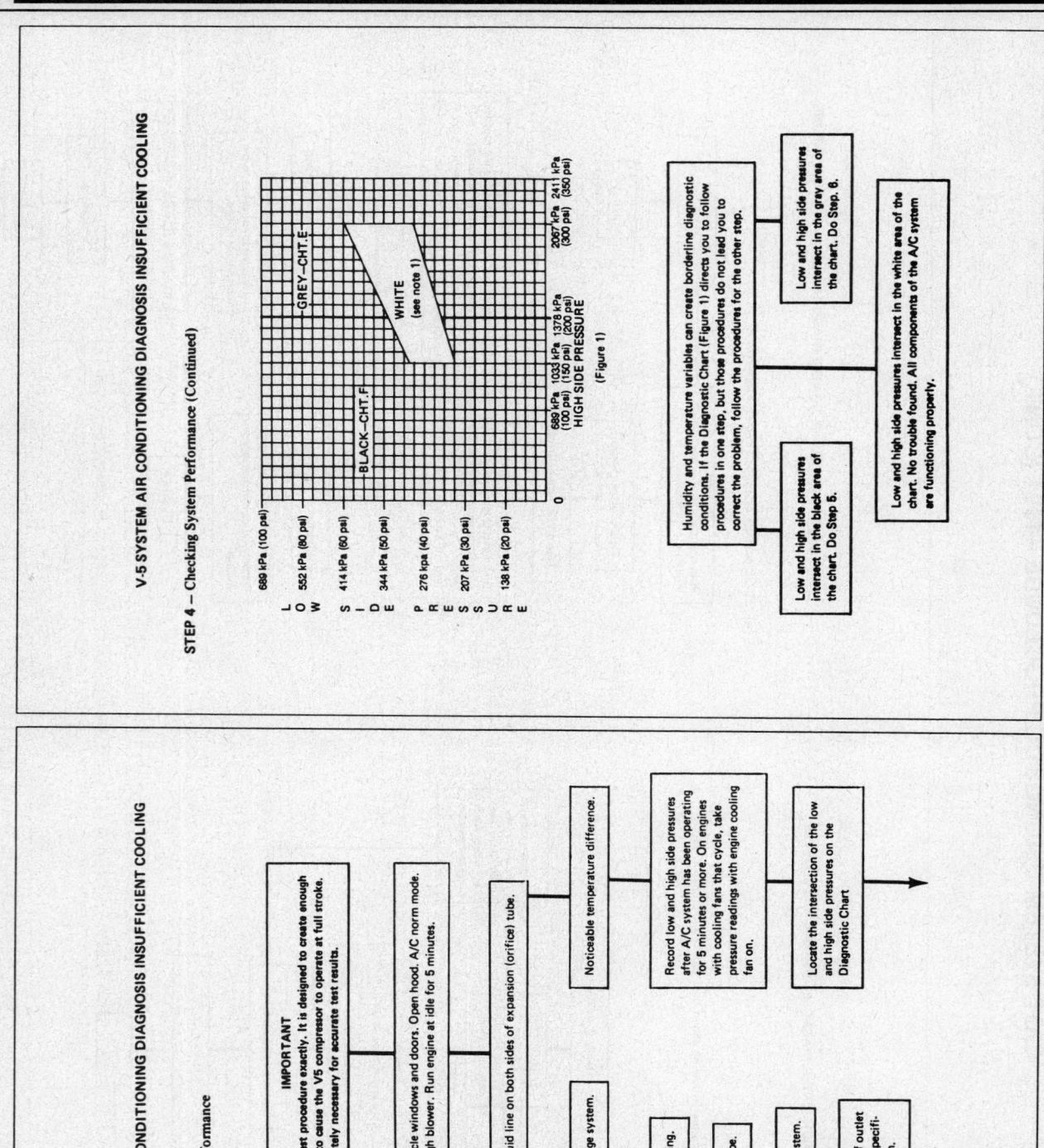

VDOT SYSTEM DIAGNOSTIC PROCEDURE – 1991 (CONT.)

V-5 SYSTEM AIR CONDITIONING DIAGNOSIS INSUFFICIENT COOLING

STEP 5 – Black Zone Performance Checks

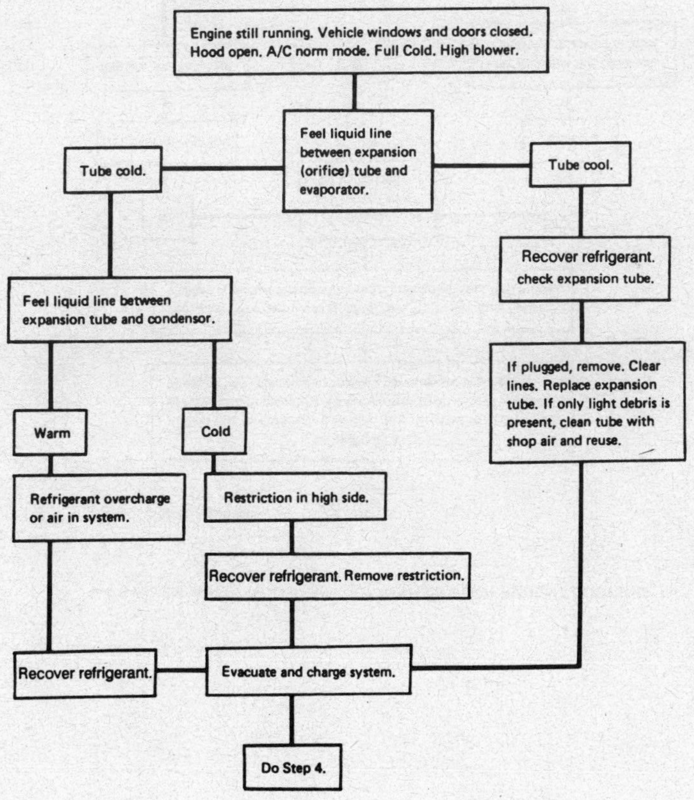
Engine still running. Vehicle windows and doors closed. Hood open. A/C norm mode. Full Cold. High blower.
Feel liquid line between expansion (orifice) tube and evaporator.
Tube cold.
Tube cool.
Feel liquid line between expansion tube and condensor.
Warm
Cold
Refrigerant overcharge or air in system.
Restriction in high side.
Recover refrigerant. Remove restriction.
Recover refrigerant.
Evacuate and charge system.
Do Step 4.
Recover refrigerant. check expansion tube.
If plugged, remove. Clear lines. Replace expansion tube. If only light debris is present, clean tube with shop air and reuse.

V-5 SYSTEM AIR CONDITIONING DIAGNOSIS INSUFFICIENT COOLING

STEP 6 – Grey Zone Performance Checks

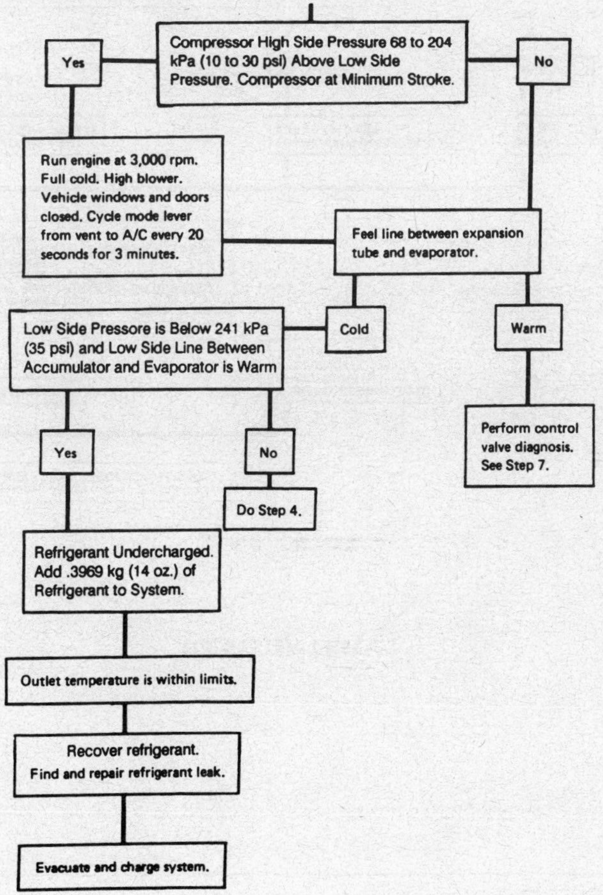
Compressor High Side Pressure 68 to 204 kPa (10 to 30 psi) Above Low Side Pressure. Compressor at Minimum Stroke.
Yes
No
Run engine at 3,000 rpm. Full cold. High blower. Vehicle windows and doors closed. Cycle mode lever from vent to A/C every 20 seconds for 3 minutes.
Feel line between expansion tube and evaporator.
Cold
Warm
Low Side Pressore is Below 241 kPa (35 psi) and Low Side Line Between Accumulator and Evaporator is Warm
Perform control valve diagnosis. See Step 7.
Yes
No
Do Step 4.
Refrigerant Undercharged. Add .3969 kg (14 oz.) of Refrigerant to System.
Outlet temperature is within limits.
Recover refrigerant. Find and repair refrigerant leak.
Evacuate and charge system.

VDOT SYSTEM DIAGNOSTIC PROCEDURE 1991 (CONT.)

V-5 SYSTEM AIR CONDITIONING DIAGNOSIS INSUFFICIENT COOLING

STEP 7 – Control Valve Diagnosis

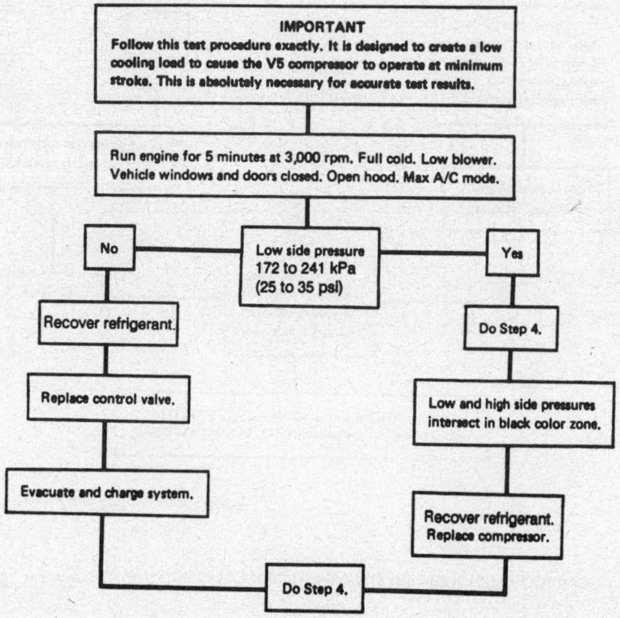
IMPORTANT
Follow this test procedure exactly. It is designed to create a low cooling load to cause the V5 compressor to operate at minimum stroke. This is absolutely necessary for accurate test results.
Run engine for 5 minutes at 3,000 rpm. Full cold. Low blower. Vehicle windows and doors closed. Open hood. Max A/C mode.
Low side pressure 172 to 241 kPa (25 to 35 psi)
No
Yes
Recover refrigerant.
Replace control valve.
Evacuate and charge system.
Do Step 4.
Low and high side pressures intersect in black color zone.
Recover refrigerant. Replace compressor.
Do Step 4.

ECC SYSTEM CHECK

ECC SYSTEM CHECK

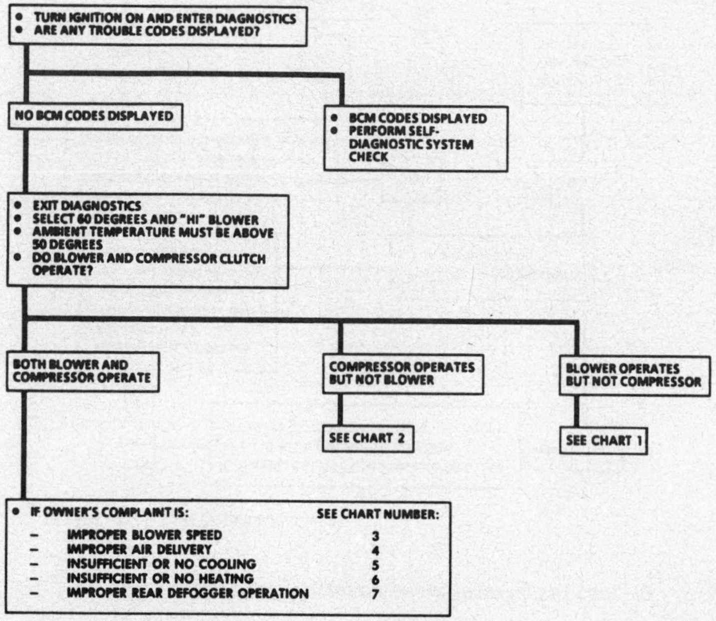
• TURN IGNITION ON AND ENTER DIAGNOSTICS
• ARE ANY TROUBLE CODES DISPLAYED?
NO BCM CODES DISPLAYED
• BCM CODES DISPLAYED
• PERFORM SELF-DIAGNOSTIC SYSTEM CHECK
• EXIT DIAGNOSTICS
• SELECT 60 DEGREES AND "HI" BLOWER
• AMBIENT TEMPERATURE MUST BE ABOVE 50 DEGREES
• DO BLOWER AND COMPRESSOR CLUTCH OPERATE?
BOTH BLOWER AND COMPRESSOR OPERATE
COMPRESSOR OPERATES BUT NOT BLOWER
BLOWER OPERATES BUT NOT COMPRESSOR
SEE CHART 2
SEE CHART 1
• IF OWNER'S COMPLAINT IS: SEE CHART NUMBER:
– IMPROPER BLOWER SPEED 3
– IMPROPER AIR DELIVERY 4
– INSUFFICIENT OR NO COOLING 5
– INSUFFICIENT OR NO HEATING 6
– IMPROPER REAR DEFOGGER OPERATION 7

EEC SYSTEM DIAGNOSIS—DEVILLE AND FLEETWOOD

CHART #1

NO COMPRESSOR OPERATION

- CHECK AND REPAIR ALL ECM & BCM TROUBLE CODES
- OUTSIDE TEMPERATURE MUST BE ABOVE 50°F

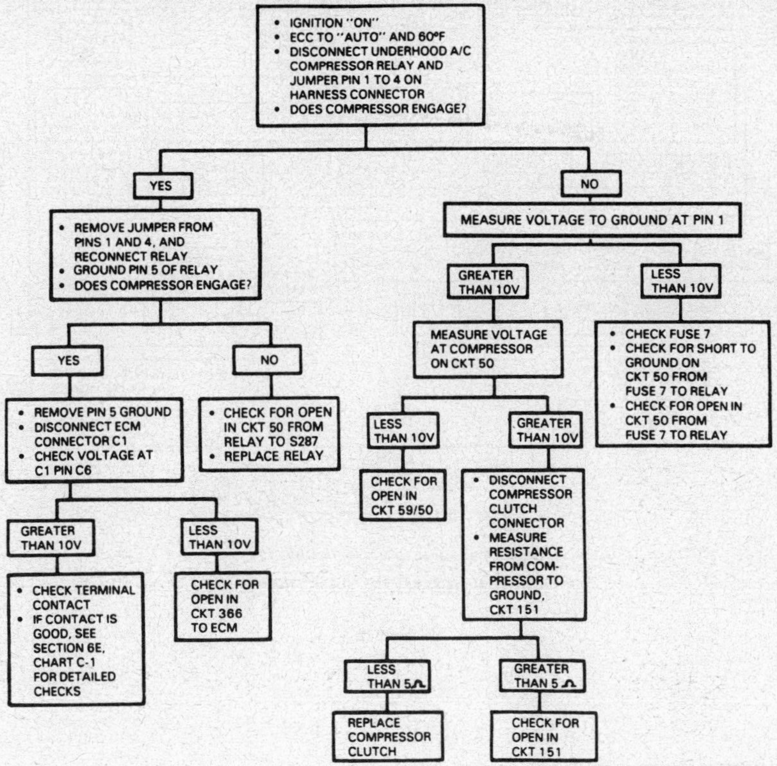
• IGNITION "ON"
• ECC TO "AUTO" AND 60°F
• DISCONNECT UNDERHOOD A/C COMPRESSOR RELAY AND JUMPER PIN 1 TO 4 ON HARNESS CONNECTOR
• DOES COMPRESSOR ENGAGE?
YES
NO
• REMOVE JUMPER FROM PINS 1 AND 4, AND RECONNECT RELAY
• GROUND PIN 5 OF RELAY
• DOES COMPRESSOR ENGAGE?
YES
NO
• REMOVE PIN 5 GROUND
• DISCONNECT ECM CONNECTOR C1
• CHECK VOLTAGE AT C1 PIN C6
• CHECK FOR OPEN IN CKT 50 FROM RELAY TO S287
• REPLACE RELAY
GREATER THAN 10V
LESS THAN 10V
• CHECK TERMINAL CONTACT
• IF CONTACT IS GOOD, SEE SECTION 6E, CHART C-1 FOR DETAILED CHECKS
CHECK FOR OPEN IN CKT 366 TO ECM
MEASURE VOLTAGE TO GROUND AT PIN 1
GREATER THAN 10V
LESS THAN 10V
MEASURE VOLTAGE AT COMPRESSOR ON CKT 50
• CHECK FUSE 7
• CHECK FOR SHORT TO GROUND ON CKT 50 FROM FUSE 7 TO RELAY
• CHECK FOR OPEN IN CKT 50 FROM FUSE 7 TO RELAY
LESS THAN 10V
GREATER THAN 10V
CHECK FOR OPEN IN CKT 59/50
• DISCONNECT COMPRESSOR CLUTCH CONNECTOR
• MEASURE RESISTANCE FROM COMPRESSOR TO GROUND, CKT 151
LESS THAN 5Ω
GREATER THAN 5Ω
REPLACE COMPRESSOR CLUTCH
CHECK FOR OPEN IN CKT 151

CHART #2

NO BLOWER OPERATION

- ECC SYSTEM CHECK MUST BE PERFORMED FIRST

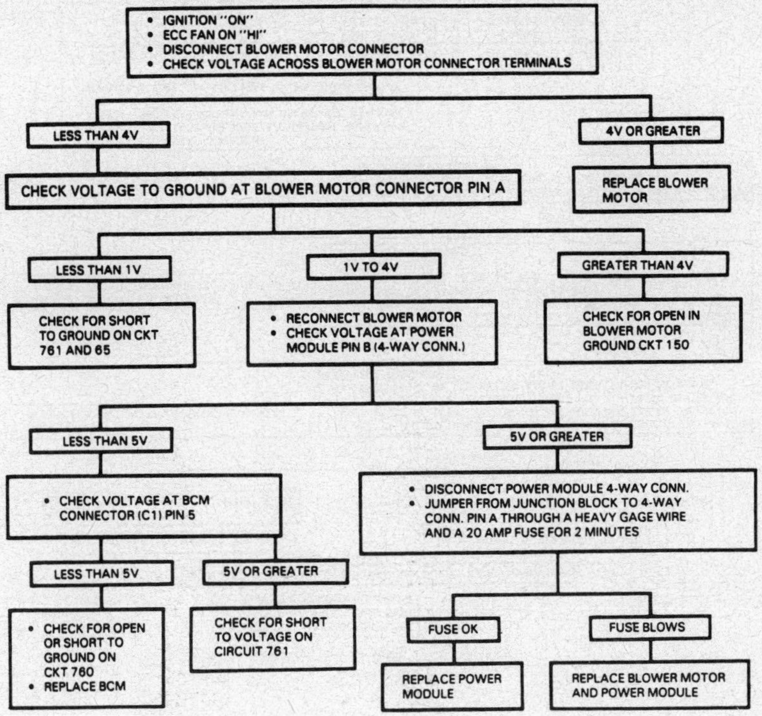
• IGNITION "ON"
• ECC FAN ON "HI"
• DISCONNECT BLOWER MOTOR CONNECTOR
• CHECK VOLTAGE ACROSS BLOWER MOTOR CONNECTOR TERMINALS
LESS THAN 4V
4V OR GREATER
CHECK VOLTAGE TO GROUND AT BLOWER MOTOR CONNECTOR PIN A
REPLACE BLOWER MOTOR
LESS THAN 1V
1V TO 4V
GREATER THAN 4V
CHECK FOR SHORT TO GROUND ON CKT 761 AND 65
• RECONNECT BLOWER MOTOR
• CHECK VOLTAGE AT POWER MODULE PIN B (4-WAY CONN.)
CHECK FOR OPEN IN BLOWER MOTOR GROUND CKT 150
LESS THAN 5V
5V OR GREATER
• CHECK VOLTAGE AT BCM CONNECTOR (C1) PIN 5
• DISCONNECT POWER MODULE 4-WAY CONN.
• JUMPER FROM JUNCTION BLOCK TO 4-WAY CONN. PIN A THROUGH A HEAVY GAGE WIRE AND A 20 AMP FUSE FOR 2 MINUTES
LESS THAN 5V
5V OR GREATER
• CHECK FOR OPEN OR SHORT TO GROUND ON CKT 760
• REPLACE BCM
CHECK FOR SHORT TO VOLTAGE ON CIRCUIT 761
FUSE OK
FUSE BLOWS
REPLACE POWER MODULE
REPLACE BLOWER MOTOR AND POWER MODULE

CHART #3

IMPROPER BLOWER SPEED

- ECC SYSTEM CHECK MUST BE PERFORMED FIRST

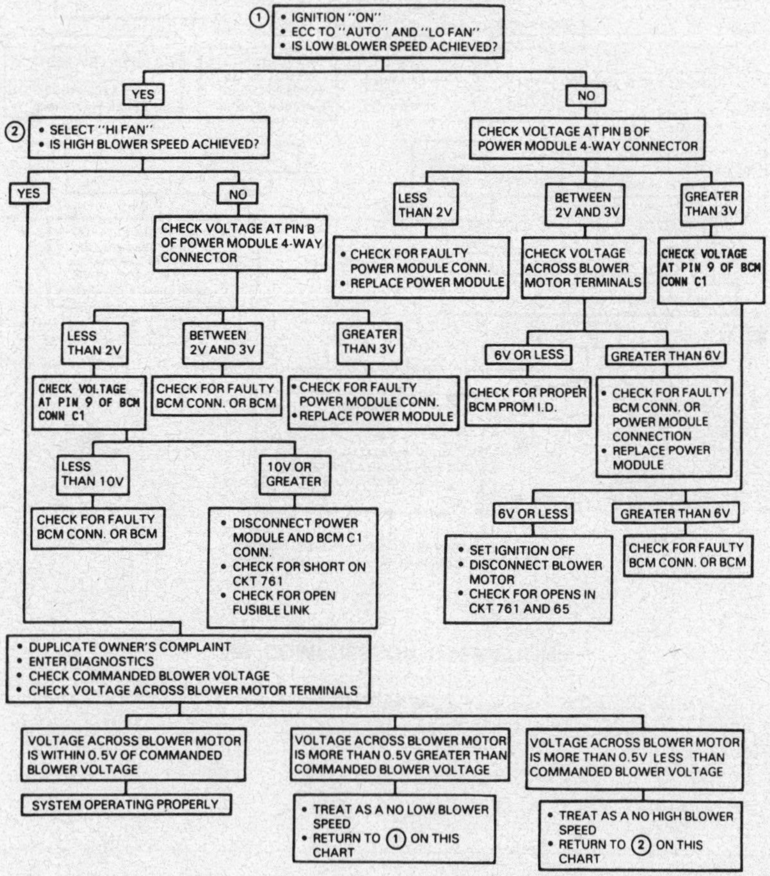
① • IGNITION "ON" • ECC TO "AUTO" AND "LO FAN" • IS LOW BLOWER SPEED ACHIEVED?
YES
NO
② • SELECT "HI FAN" • IS HIGH BLOWER SPEED ACHIEVED?
CHECK VOLTAGE AT PIN B OF POWER MODULE 4-WAY CONNECTOR
YES
NO
CHECK VOLTAGE AT PIN B OF POWER MODULE 4-WAY CONNECTOR
LESS THAN 2V
BETWEEN 2V AND 3V
GREATER THAN 3V
• CHECK FOR FAULTY POWER MODULE CONN. • REPLACE POWER MODULE
CHECK VOLTAGE ACROSS BLOWER MOTOR TERMINALS
CHECK VOLTAGE AT PIN 9 OF BCM CONN C1
LESS THAN 2V
BETWEEN 2V AND 3V
GREATER THAN 3V
CHECK VOLTAGE AT PIN 9 OF BCM CONN C1
CHECK FOR FAULTY BCM CONN. OR BCM
• CHECK FOR FAULTY POWER MODULE CONN. • REPLACE POWER MODULE
6V OR LESS
GREATER THAN 6V
CHECK FOR PROPER BCM PROM I.D.
• CHECK FOR FAULTY BCM CONN. OR POWER MODULE CONNECTION • REPLACE POWER MODULE
LESS THAN 10V
10V OR GREATER
CHECK FOR FAULTY BCM CONN. OR BCM
• DISCONNECT POWER MODULE AND BCM C1 CONN. • CHECK FOR SHORT ON CKT 761 • CHECK FOR OPEN FUSIBLE LINK
6V OR LESS
GREATER THAN 6V
• SET IGNITION OFF • DISCONNECT BLOWER MOTOR • CHECK FOR OPENS IN CKT 761 AND 65
CHECK FOR FAULTY BCM CONN. OR BCM
• DUPLICATE OWNER'S COMPLAINT • ENTER DIAGNOSTICS • CHECK COMMANDED BLOWER VOLTAGE • CHECK VOLTAGE ACROSS BLOWER MOTOR TERMINALS
VOLTAGE ACROSS BLOWER MOTOR IS WITHIN 0.5V OF COMMANDED BLOWER VOLTAGE
VOLTAGE ACROSS BLOWER MOTOR IS MORE THAN 0.5V GREATER THAN COMMANDED BLOWER VOLTAGE
VOLTAGE ACROSS BLOWER MOTOR IS MORE THAN 0.5V LESS THAN COMMANDED BLOWER VOLTAGE
SYSTEM OPERATING PROPERLY
• TREAT AS A NO LOW BLOWER SPEED • RETURN TO ① ON THIS CHART
• TREAT AS A NO HIGH BLOWER SPEED • RETURN TO ② ON THIS CHART

CHART #4

IMPROPER AIR DELIVERY

- ECC SYSTEM CHECK MUST BE PERFORMED FIRST
- PROGRAMMER MUST BE MOUNTED IN ITS NORMAL ORIENTATION FOR ALL TESTS

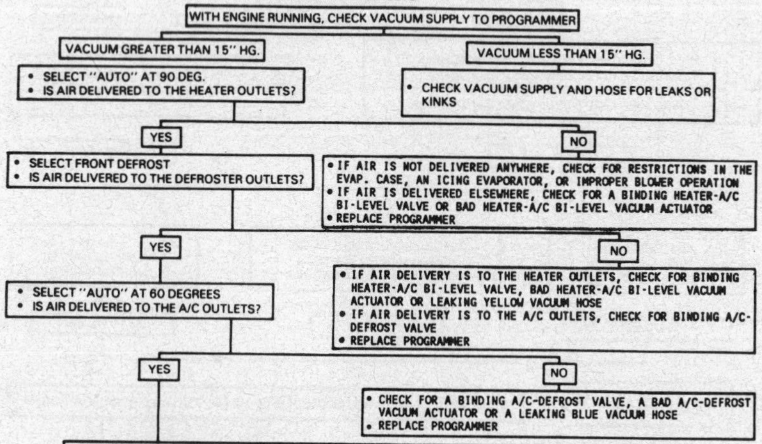
WITH ENGINE RUNNING, CHECK VACUUM SUPPLY TO PROGRAMMER
VACUUM GREATER THAN 15" HG.
VACUUM LESS THAN 15" HG.
• SELECT "AUTO" AT 90 DEG. • IS AIR DELIVERED TO THE HEATER OUTLETS?
• CHECK VACUUM SUPPLY AND HOSE FOR LEAKS OR KINKS
YES
NO
• SELECT FRONT DEFROST • IS AIR DELIVERED TO THE DEFROSTER OUTLETS?
• IF AIR IS NOT DELIVERED ANYWHERE, CHECK FOR RESTRICTIONS IN THE EVAP. CASE, AN ICING EVAPORATOR, OR IMPROPER BLOWER OPERATION • IF AIR IS DELIVERED ELSEWHERE, CHECK FOR A BINDING HEATER-A/C BI-LEVEL VALVE OR BAD HEATER-A/C BI-LEVEL VACUUM ACTUATOR • REPLACE PROGRAMMER
YES
NO
• SELECT "AUTO" AT 60 DEGREES • IS AIR DELIVERED TO THE A/C OUTLETS?
• IF AIR DELIVERY IS TO THE HEATER OUTLETS, CHECK FOR BINDING HEATER-A/C BI-LEVEL VALVE, BAD HEATER-A/C BI-LEVEL VACUUM ACTUATOR OR LEAKING YELLOW VACUUM HOSE • IF AIR DELIVERY IS TO THE A/C OUTLETS, CHECK FOR BINDING A/C-DEFROST VALVE • REPLACE PROGRAMMER
YES
NO
• CHECK FOR A BINDING A/C-DEFROST VALVE, A BAD A/C-DEFROST VACUUM ACTUATOR OR A LEAKING BLUE VACUUM HOSE • REPLACE PROGRAMMER

- DUPLICATE OWNER'S COMPLAINT
- ENTER DIAGNOSTICS AND NOTE A/C-DEFROST MODE VALVE STATUS ("LO FAN" SYMBOL) AND HEATER-A/C BI-LEVEL MODE VALVE STATUS ("HI FAN" SYMBOL)
- COMPARE ACTUAL AIR DELIVERY TO THE TABLE BELOW:

IF STATUS LIGHT IS:

A/C-DEFROST VALVE (LO FAN)	HEATER-A/C BI-LEVEL VALVE (HI FAN)	AIR SHOULD BE DIRECTED TO: (COMMAND AIR DELIVERY)
OFF	ON	HEATER DUCTS
OFF	OFF	DEFROSTER DUCTS
ON	OFF	A/C DUCTS

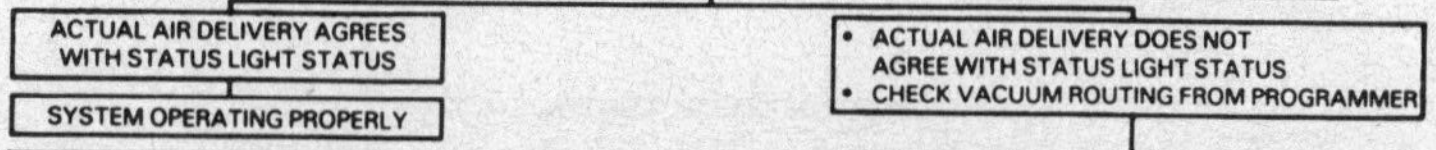
ACTUAL AIR DELIVERY AGREES WITH STATUS LIGHT STATUS
SYSTEM OPERATING PROPERLY
• ACTUAL AIR DELIVERY DOES NOT AGREE WITH STATUS LIGHT STATUS • CHECK VACUUM ROUTING FROM PROGRAMMER

COMPARE COMMANDED VS. ACTUAL AIR DELIVERY AND PERFORM THE INDICATED CHECKS:

	ACTUAL AIR DELIVERY		
COMMANDED AIR DELIVERY	HEATER DUCTS	DEFROSTER DUCTS	A/C DUCTS
HEATER DUCTS	SYSTEM OK	• CHECK FOR BINDING HEATER-A/C BI-LEVEL VALVE • REPLACE PROGRAMMER	REPLACE PROGRAMMER
DEFROSTER DUCTS	• CHECK FOR BINDING HEATER-A/C BI-LEVEL VALVE • CHECK FOR LEAK IN HEATER-A/C BI-LEVEL VALVE VAC HOSE • REPLACE PROGRAMMER	SYSTEM OK	• CHECK FOR BINDING A/C-DEF VALVE REPLACE PROGRAMMER
A/C DUCTS	• CHECK PROGRAMMER VACUUM SUPPLY CHECK FOR LEAKS IN THE BLUE VAC. HOSE AND YELLOW VAC. HOSE • REPLACE PROGRAMMER	• CHECK FOR BINDING A/C-DEF VALVE • CHECK FOR LEAK IN A/C-DEF VALVE VAC. HOSE • REPLACE PROGRAMMER	SYSTEM OK

EEC SYSTEM DIAGNOSIS—DEVILLE AND FLEETWOOD (CONT.)

CHART #5
INSUFFICIENT OR NO COOLING

- ECC SYSTEM CHECK MUST BE PERFORMED

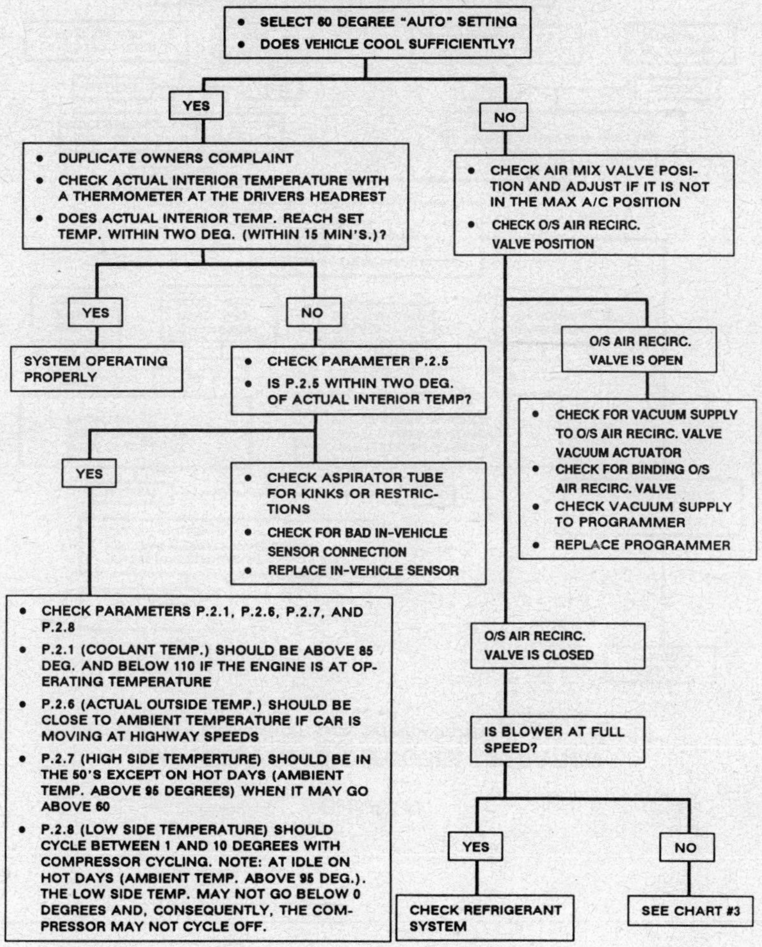
SELECT 60 DEGREE "AUTO" SETTING
DOES VEHICLE COOL SUFFICIENTLY?
YES
NO
DUPLICATE OWNERS COMPLAINT
CHECK ACTUAL INTERIOR TEMPERATURE WITH A THERMOMETER AT THE DRIVERS HEADREST
DOES ACTUAL INTERIOR TEMP. REACH SET TEMP. WITHIN TWO DEG. (WITHIN 15 MIN'S.)?
CHECK AIR MIX VALVE POSITION AND ADJUST IF IT IS NOT IN THE MAX A/C POSITION
CHECK O/S AIR RECIRC. VALVE POSITION
YES
NO
SYSTEM OPERATING PROPERLY
CHECK PARAMETER P.2.5
IS P.2.5 WITHIN TWO DEG. OF ACTUAL INTERIOR TEMP?
O/S AIR RECIRC. VALVE IS OPEN
CHECK FOR VACUUM SUPPLY TO O/S AIR RECIRC. VALVE VACUUM ACTUATOR
CHECK FOR BINDING O/S AIR RECIRC. VALVE
CHECK VACUUM SUPPLY TO PROGRAMMER
REPLACE PROGRAMMER
YES
CHECK ASPIRATOR TUBE FOR KINKS OR RESTRICTIONS
CHECK FOR BAD IN-VEHICLE SENSOR CONNECTION
REPLACE IN-VEHICLE SENSOR
CHECK PARAMETERS P.2.1, P.2.6, P.2.7, AND P.2.8
P.2.1 (COOLANT TEMP.) SHOULD BE ABOVE 85 DEG. AND BELOW 110 IF THE ENGINE IS AT OPERATING TEMPERATURE
P.2.6 (ACTUAL OUTSIDE TEMP.) SHOULD BE CLOSE TO AMBIENT TEMPERATURE IF CAR IS MOVING AT HIGHWAY SPEEDS
P.2.7 (HIGH SIDE TEMPERTURE) SHOULD BE IN THE 50'S EXCEPT ON HOT DAYS (AMBIENT TEMP. ABOVE 95 DEGREES) WHEN IT MAY GO ABOVE 60
P.2.8 (LOW SIDE TEMPERATURE) SHOULD CYCLE BETWEEN 1 AND 10 DEGREES WITH COMPRESSOR CYCLING. NOTE: AT IDLE ON HOT DAYS (AMBIENT TEMP. ABOVE 95 DEG.). THE LOW SIDE TEMP. MAY NOT GO BELOW 0 DEGREES AND, CONSEQUENTLY, THE COMPRESSOR MAY NOT CYCLE OFF.
O/S AIR RECIRC. VALVE IS CLOSED
IS BLOWER AT FULL SPEED?
YES
NO
CHECK REFRIGERANT SYSTEM
SEE CHART #3

CHART #6
INSUFFICIENT OR NO HEATING

- ECC SYSTEM CHECK MUST BE PERFORMED FIRST

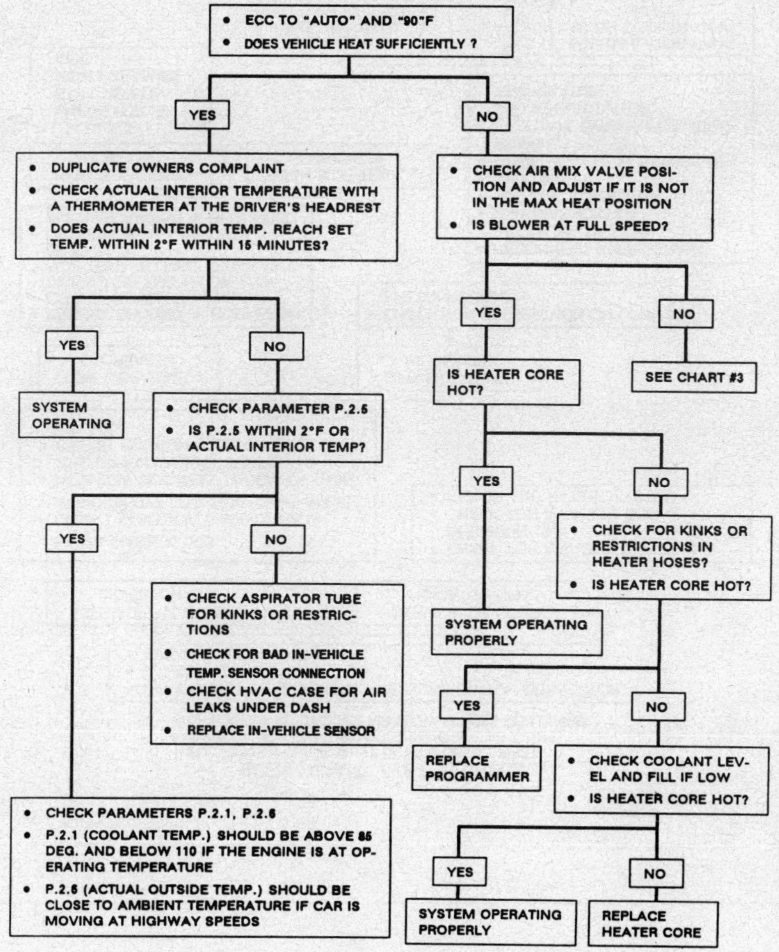
ECC TO "AUTO" AND "90"F
DOES VEHICLE HEAT SUFFICIENTLY ?
YES
NO
DUPLICATE OWNERS COMPLAINT
CHECK ACTUAL INTERIOR TEMPERATURE WITH A THERMOMETER AT THE DRIVER'S HEADREST
DOES ACTUAL INTERIOR TEMP. REACH SET TEMP. WITHIN 2°F WITHIN 15 MINUTES?
CHECK AIR MIX VALVE POSITION AND ADJUST IF IT IS NOT IN THE MAX HEAT POSITION
IS BLOWER AT FULL SPEED?
YES
NO
SYSTEM OPERATING
CHECK PARAMETER P.2.5
IS P.2.5 WITHIN 2°F OR ACTUAL INTERIOR TEMP?
YES
NO
IS HEATER CORE HOT?
SEE CHART #3
YES
NO
CHECK ASPIRATOR TUBE FOR KINKS OR RESTRICTIONS
CHECK FOR BAD IN-VEHICLE TEMP. SENSOR CONNECTION
CHECK HVAC CASE FOR AIR LEAKS UNDER DASH
REPLACE IN-VEHICLE SENSOR
CHECK FOR KINKS OR RESTRICTIONS IN HEATER HOSES?
IS HEATER CORE HOT?
SYSTEM OPERATING PROPERLY
YES
NO
REPLACE PROGRAMMER
CHECK COOLANT LEVEL AND FILL IF LOW
IS HEATER CORE HOT?
CHECK PARAMETERS P.2.1, P.2.6
P.2.1 (COOLANT TEMP.) SHOULD BE ABOVE 85 DEG. AND BELOW 110 IF THE ENGINE IS AT OPERATING TEMPERATURE
P.2.6 (ACTUAL OUTSIDE TEMP.) SHOULD BE CLOSE TO AMBIENT TEMPERATURE IF CAR IS MOVING AT HIGHWAY SPEEDS
YES
NO
SYSTEM OPERATING PROPERLY
REPLACE HEATER CORE

EEC SYSTEM DIAGNOSIS—DEVILLE AND FLEETWOOD (CONT.)

CHART #7

IMPROPER REAR DEFOGGER OPERATION

- ECC SYSTEM CHECK MUST BE PERFORMED FIRST

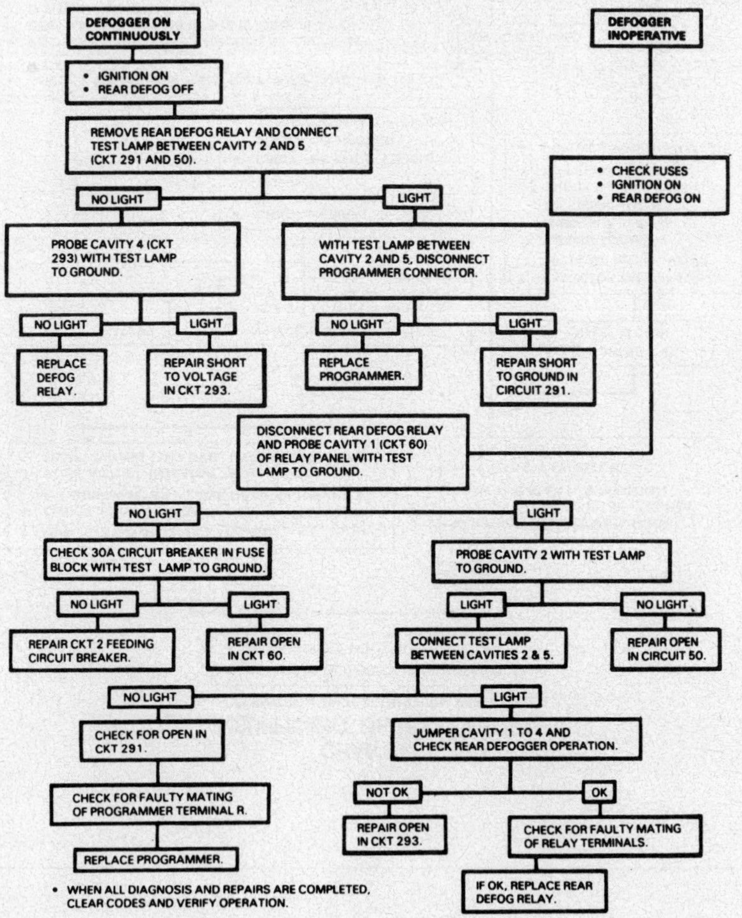
DEFOGGER ON CONTINUOUSLY
• IGNITION ON
• REAR DEFOG OFF
REMOVE REAR DEFOG RELAY AND CONNECT TEST LAMP BETWEEN CAVITY 2 AND 5 (CKT 291 AND 50).
NO LIGHT
LIGHT
PROBE CAVITY 4 (CKT 293) WITH TEST LAMP TO GROUND.
WITH TEST LAMP BETWEEN CAVITY 2 AND 5, DISCONNECT PROGRAMMER CONNECTOR.
NO LIGHT
LIGHT
REPLACE DEFOG RELAY.
REPAIR SHORT TO VOLTAGE IN CKT 293.
NO LIGHT
LIGHT
REPLACE PROGRAMMER.
REPAIR SHORT TO GROUND IN CIRCUIT 291.
DEFOGGER INOPERATIVE
• CHECK FUSES
• IGNITION ON
• REAR DEFOG ON
DISCONNECT REAR DEFOG RELAY AND PROBE CAVITY 1 (CKT 60) OF RELAY PANEL WITH TEST LAMP TO GROUND.
NO LIGHT
LIGHT
CHECK 30A CIRCUIT BREAKER IN FUSE BLOCK WITH TEST LAMP TO GROUND.
NO LIGHT
LIGHT
REPAIR CKT 2 FEEDING CIRCUIT BREAKER.
REPAIR OPEN IN CKT 60.
PROBE CAVITY 2 WITH TEST LAMP TO GROUND.
LIGHT
NO LIGHT
REPAIR OPEN IN CIRCUIT 50.
CONNECT TEST LAMP BETWEEN CAVITIES 2 & 5.
NO LIGHT
LIGHT
CHECK FOR OPEN IN CKT 291.
CHECK FOR FAULTY MATING OF PROGRAMMER TERMINAL R.
REPLACE PROGRAMMER.
JUMPER CAVITY 1 TO 4 AND CHECK REAR DEFOGGER OPERATION.
NOT OK
OK
REPAIR OPEN IN CKT 293.
CHECK FOR FAULTY MATING OF RELAY TERMINALS.
IF OK, REPLACE REAR DEFOG RELAY.

- WHEN ALL DIAGNOSIS AND REPAIRS ARE COMPLETED, CLEAR CODES AND VERIFY OPERATION.

REFRIGERANT SYSTEM CHECK

- ECC SYSTEM CHECK MUST BE PERFORMED FIRST
- AMBIENT TEMPERATURE MUST BE ABOVE 10°C (50°F)
- CHECK FOR RESTRICTED AIR FLOW ACROSS CONDENSER

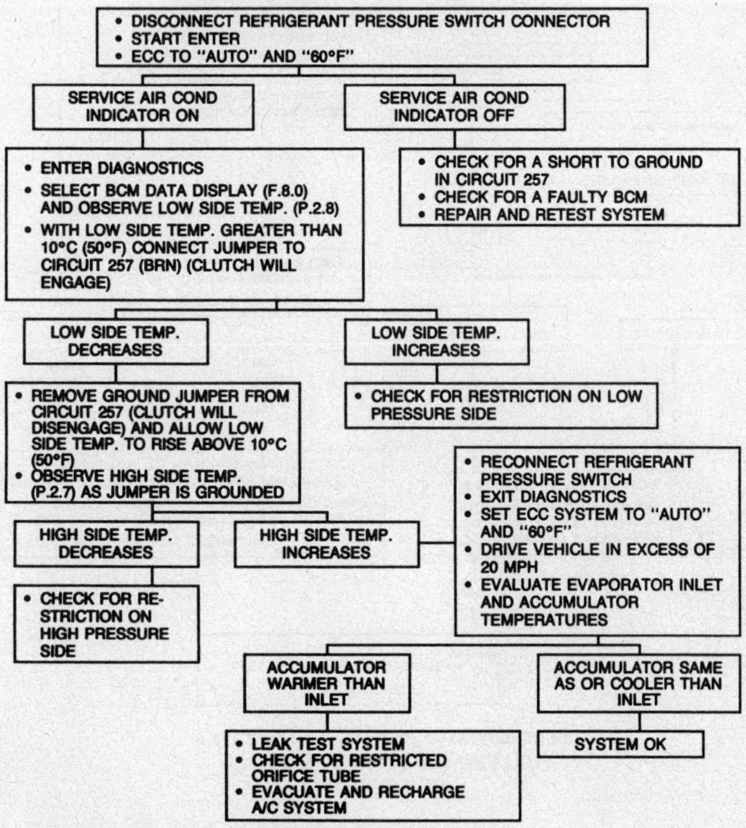
• DISCONNECT REFRIGERANT PRESSURE SWITCH CONNECTOR
• START ENTER
• ECC TO "AUTO" AND "60°F"
SERVICE AIR COND INDICATOR ON
SERVICE AIR COND INDICATOR OFF
• ENTER DIAGNOSTICS
• SELECT BCM DATA DISPLAY (F.8.0) AND OBSERVE LOW SIDE TEMP. (P.2.8)
• WITH LOW SIDE TEMP. GREATER THAN 10°C (50°F) CONNECT JUMPER TO CIRCUIT 257 (BRN) (CLUTCH WILL ENGAGE)
• CHECK FOR A SHORT TO GROUND IN CIRCUIT 257
• CHECK FOR A FAULTY BCM
• REPAIR AND RETEST SYSTEM
LOW SIDE TEMP. DECREASES
LOW SIDE TEMP. INCREASES
• REMOVE GROUND JUMPER FROM CIRCUIT 257 (CLUTCH WILL DISENGAGE) AND ALLOW LOW SIDE TEMP. TO RISE ABOVE 10°C (50°F)
• OBSERVE HIGH SIDE TEMP. (P.2.7) AS JUMPER IS GROUNDED
• CHECK FOR RESTRICTION ON LOW PRESSURE SIDE
HIGH SIDE TEMP. DECREASES
HIGH SIDE TEMP. INCREASES
• CHECK FOR RE-STRICTION ON HIGH PRESSURE SIDE
• RECONNECT REFRIGERANT PRESSURE SWITCH
• EXIT DIAGNOSTICS
• SET ECC SYSTEM TO "AUTO" AND "60°F"
• DRIVE VEHICLE IN EXCESS OF 20 MPH
• EVALUATE EVAPORATOR INLET AND ACCUMULATOR TEMPERATURES
ACCUMULATOR WARMER THAN INLET
ACCUMULATOR SAME AS OR COOLER THAN INLET
• LEAK TEST SYSTEM
• CHECK FOR RESTRICTED ORIFICE TUBE
• EVACUATE AND RECHARGE A/C SYSTEM
SYSTEM OK

- BELOW 20 MPH EXTENDED COMPRESSOR AT IDLE IS POSSIBLE
- WHEN ALL DIAGNOSIS AND REPAIRS ARE COMPLETED, CLEAR CODES AND VERIFY OPERATION

SYSTEM RESPONSE CHART

AIR DELIVERY MODE (SELECT BCM DATA BD24 TO SEE MODE NO.)		"AUTO" SELECTED	"AUTO" OF "ECON" SELECTED			"OFF" SELECTED	ANY SETTING EXCEPT "DEF" OR "OFF" SELECTED		"DEF" SELECTED	ANY SETTING EXCEPT "DEF OR OFF" SELECTED
		#0 MAX A/C	#1 A/C	#2 INTER-MEDIATE	#3 HEATER	#4 OFF	#5 NORMAL PURGE	#6 COLD PURGE	#7 FRONT DEFROST	#8* A/C PURGE
NORM FAN (SELECTED BCM DATA BD20 TO SEE COMMANDED BLOWER SPEED)		VARIABLE SPEED BASED ON PROGRAM NUMBER				OFF	OFF THEN LO	OFF	VARIABLE SPEED BASED ON PROGRAM NUMBER	MEDIUM
AIR INLET VALVE	ORANGE HOSE	VACUUM	VENT							
	VALVE POSITION	INSIDE AIR	OUTSIDE AIR							
UP-DOWN VALVE	POSITION THE CCDIC UP - DOWN LEVER IN THE "NORMAL" POSITION									
	VALVE POSITION	AIR DIRECTED UP			AIR DIRECTED TO FLOOR			AIR DIRECTED UP		AIR DIRECTED TO FLOOR
A/C-DEF VALVE	BLUE HOSE	VACUUM		VENT			VACUUM	VENT		
	VALVE POSITION	AIR DIRECTED OUT A/C VENTS		AIR DIRECTED OUT DEFROSTER OUTLETS			AIR DIRECTED OUT A/C VENTS	AIR DIRECTED OUT DEFROSTER OUTLETS		AIR DIRECTED OUT HEATER VENT
COMPRESSOR		ENABLED EXCEPT IN "OFF" AND "ECON" SETTINGS								

*A/C Purge, mode number 8 was a feature added to Allantes built after April 1989.

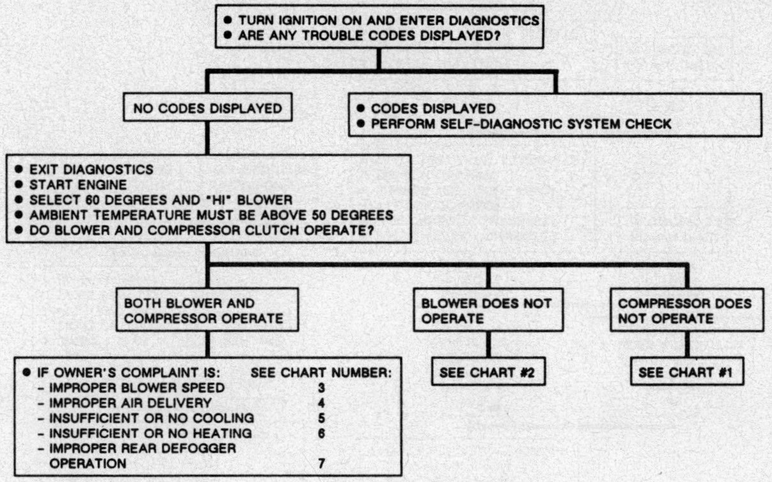

● TURN IGNITION ON AND ENTER DIAGNOSTICS
● ARE ANY TROUBLE CODES DISPLAYED?
NO CODES DISPLAYED
● CODES DISPLAYED
● PERFORM SELF-DIAGNOSTIC SYSTEM CHECK
● EXIT DIAGNOSTICS
● START ENGINE
● SELECT 60 DEGREES AND "HI" BLOWER
● AMBIENT TEMPERATURE MUST BE ABOVE 50 DEGREES
● DO BLOWER AND COMPRESSOR CLUTCH OPERATE?
BOTH BLOWER AND COMPRESSOR OPERATE
BLOWER DOES NOT OPERATE
COMPRESSOR DOES NOT OPERATE
● IF OWNER'S COMPLAINT IS: SEE CHART NUMBER:
- IMPROPER BLOWER SPEED 3
- IMPROPER AIR DELIVERY 4
- INSUFFICIENT OR NO COOLING 5
- INSUFFICIENT OR NO HEATING 6
- IMPROPER REAR DEFOGGER OPERATION 7
SEE CHART #2
SEE CHART #1

COMPRESSOR ELECTRICAL SYSTEM
E, K AND V BODY CADILLAC

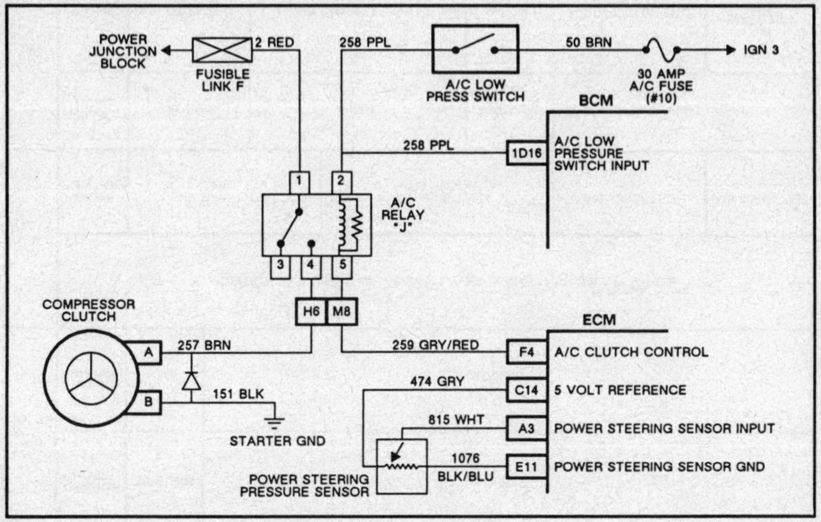
POWER JUNCTION BLOCK
FUSIBLE LINK F
2 RED
258 PPL
A/C LOW PRESS SWITCH
50 BRN
30 AMP A/C FUSE (#10)
IGN 3
BCM
258 PPL
1D16
A/C LOW PRESSURE SWITCH INPUT
A/C RELAY "J"
1
2
3
4
5
H6
M8
COMPRESSOR CLUTCH
A
B
257 BRN
151 BLK
STARTER GND
ECM
259 GRY/RED
F4
A/C CLUTCH CONTROL
474 GRY
C14
5 VOLT REFERENCE
815 WHT
A3
POWER STEERING SENSOR INPUT
1076 BLK/BLU
E11
POWER STEERING SENSOR GND
POWER STEERING PRESSURE SENSOR

EEC SYSTEM DIAGNOSIS
E, K AND V BODY CADILLAC (CONT.)

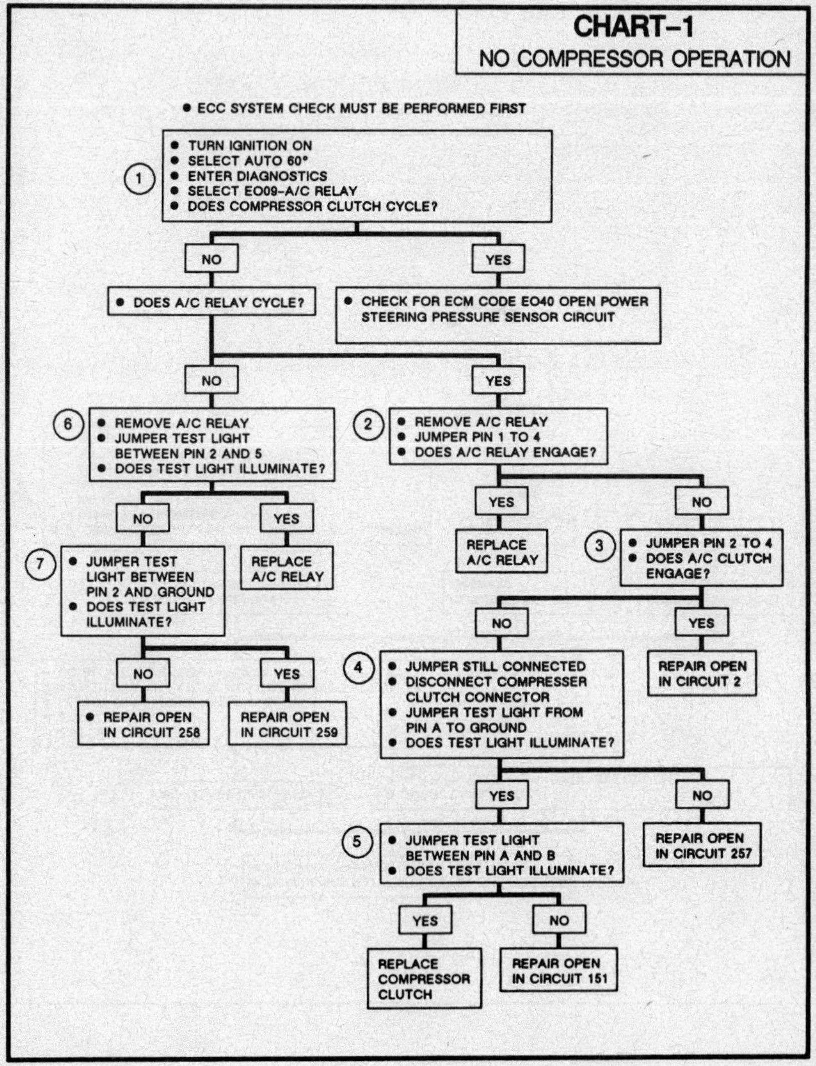
CHART–1
NO COMPRESSOR OPERATION
• ECC SYSTEM CHECK MUST BE PERFORMED FIRST
1
• TURN IGNITION ON
• SELECT AUTO 60°
• ENTER DIAGNOSTICS
• SELECT EO09–A/C RELAY
• DOES COMPRESSOR CLUTCH CYCLE?
NO
YES
• DOES A/C RELAY CYCLE?
• CHECK FOR ECM CODE EO40 OPEN POWER STEERING PRESSURE SENSOR CIRCUIT
NO
YES
6
• REMOVE A/C RELAY
• JUMPER TEST LIGHT BETWEEN PIN 2 AND 5
• DOES TEST LIGHT ILLUMINATE?
2
• REMOVE A/C RELAY
• JUMPER PIN 1 TO 4
• DOES A/C RELAY ENGAGE?
NO
YES
7
• JUMPER TEST LIGHT BETWEEN PIN 2 AND GROUND
• DOES TEST LIGHT ILLUMINATE?
REPLACE A/C RELAY
YES
NO
REPLACE A/C RELAY
3
• JUMPER PIN 2 TO 4
• DOES A/C CLUTCH ENGAGE?
NO
YES
• REPAIR OPEN IN CIRCUIT 258
• REPAIR OPEN IN CIRCUIT 259
NO
YES
4
• JUMPER STILL CONNECTED
• DISCONNECT COMPRESSER CLUTCH CONNECTOR
• JUMPER TEST LIGHT FROM PIN A TO GROUND
• DOES TEST LIGHT ILLUMINATE?
REPAIR OPEN IN CIRCUIT 2
YES
NO
5
• JUMPER TEST LIGHT BETWEEN PIN A AND B
• DOES TEST LIGHT ILLUMINATE?
REPAIR OPEN IN CIRCUIT 257
YES
NO
REPLACE COMPRESSOR CLUTCH
REPAIR OPEN IN CIRCUIT 151

BLOWER MOTOR ELECTRICAL CIRCUIT E, K AND V BODY CADILLAC

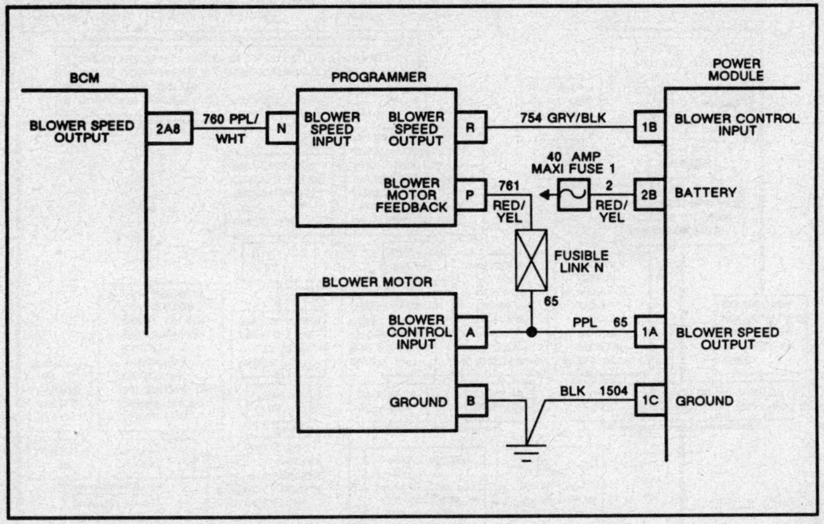
BCM
BLOWER SPEED OUTPUT
2A8
760 PPL/ WHT
PROGRAMMER
N
BLOWER SPEED INPUT
BLOWER SPEED OUTPUT
R
754 GRY/BLK
BLOWER MOTOR FEEDBACK
P
761 RED/ YEL
40 AMP MAXI FUSE 1
2 RED/ YEL
FUSIBLE LINK N
65
BLOWER MOTOR
BLOWER CONTROL INPUT
A
PPL 65
GROUND
B
BLK 1504
POWER MODULE
1B
BLOWER CONTROL INPUT
2B
BATTERY
1A
BLOWER SPEED OUTPUT
1C
GROUND

EEC SYSTEM DIAGNOSIS E, K AND V BODY CADILLAC (CONT.)

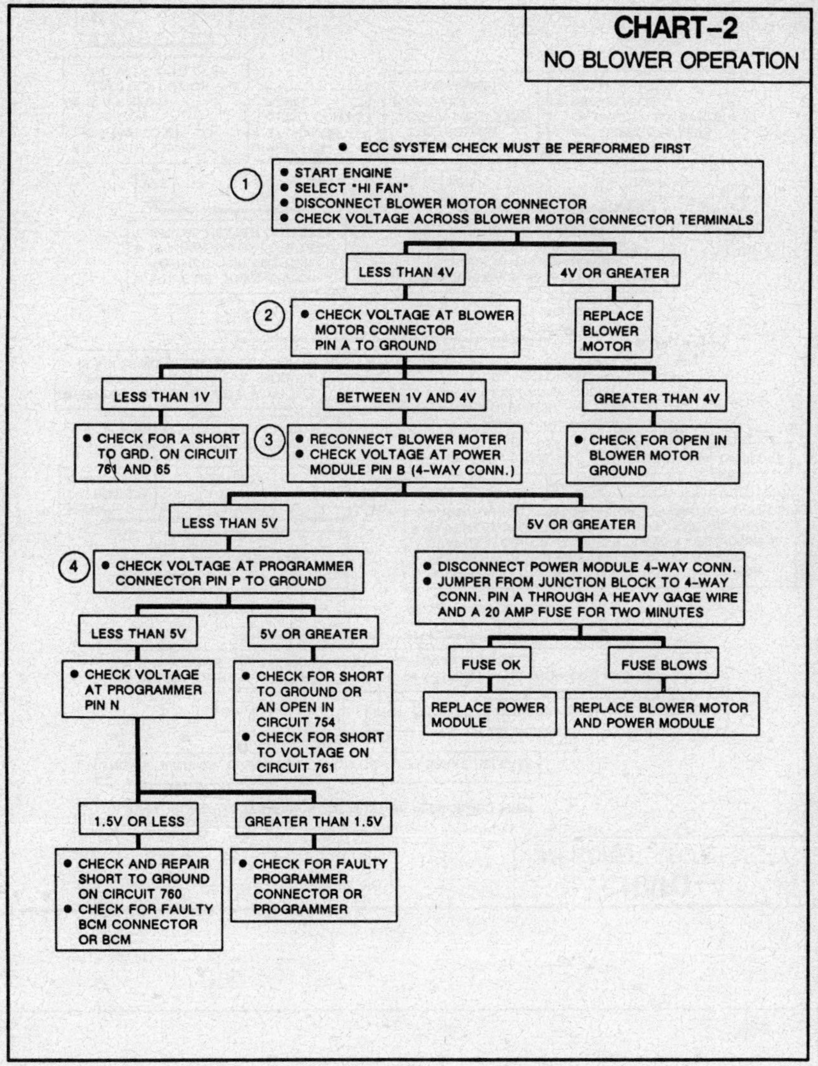
CHART–2
NO BLOWER OPERATION
● ECC SYSTEM CHECK MUST BE PERFORMED FIRST
1
● START ENGINE
● SELECT "HI FAN"
● DISCONNECT BLOWER MOTOR CONNECTOR
● CHECK VOLTAGE ACROSS BLOWER MOTOR CONNECTOR TERMINALS
LESS THAN 4V
4V OR GREATER
2
● CHECK VOLTAGE AT BLOWER MOTOR CONNECTOR PIN A TO GROUND
REPLACE BLOWER MOTOR
LESS THAN 1V
BETWEEN 1V AND 4V
GREATER THAN 4V
● CHECK FOR A SHORT TO GRD. ON CIRCUIT 761 AND 65
3
● RECONNECT BLOWER MOTER
● CHECK VOLTAGE AT POWER MODULE PIN B (4-WAY CONN.)
● CHECK FOR OPEN IN BLOWER MOTOR GROUND
LESS THAN 5V
5V OR GREATER
4
● CHECK VOLTAGE AT PROGRAMMER CONNECTOR PIN P TO GROUND
● DISCONNECT POWER MODULE 4-WAY CONN.
● JUMPER FROM JUNCTION BLOCK TO 4-WAY CONN. PIN A THROUGH A HEAVY GAGE WIRE AND A 20 AMP FUSE FOR TWO MINUTES
LESS THAN 5V
5V OR GREATER
FUSE OK
FUSE BLOWS
● CHECK VOLTAGE AT PROGRAMMER PIN N
● CHECK FOR SHORT TO GROUND OR AN OPEN IN CIRCUIT 754
● CHECK FOR SHORT TO VOLTAGE ON CIRCUIT 761
REPLACE POWER MODULE
REPLACE BLOWER MOTOR AND POWER MODULE
1.5V OR LESS
GREATER THAN 1.5V
● CHECK AND REPAIR SHORT TO GROUND ON CIRCUIT 760
● CHECK FOR FAULTY BCM CONNECTOR OR BCM
● CHECK FOR FAULTY PROGRAMMER CONNECTOR OR PROGRAMMER

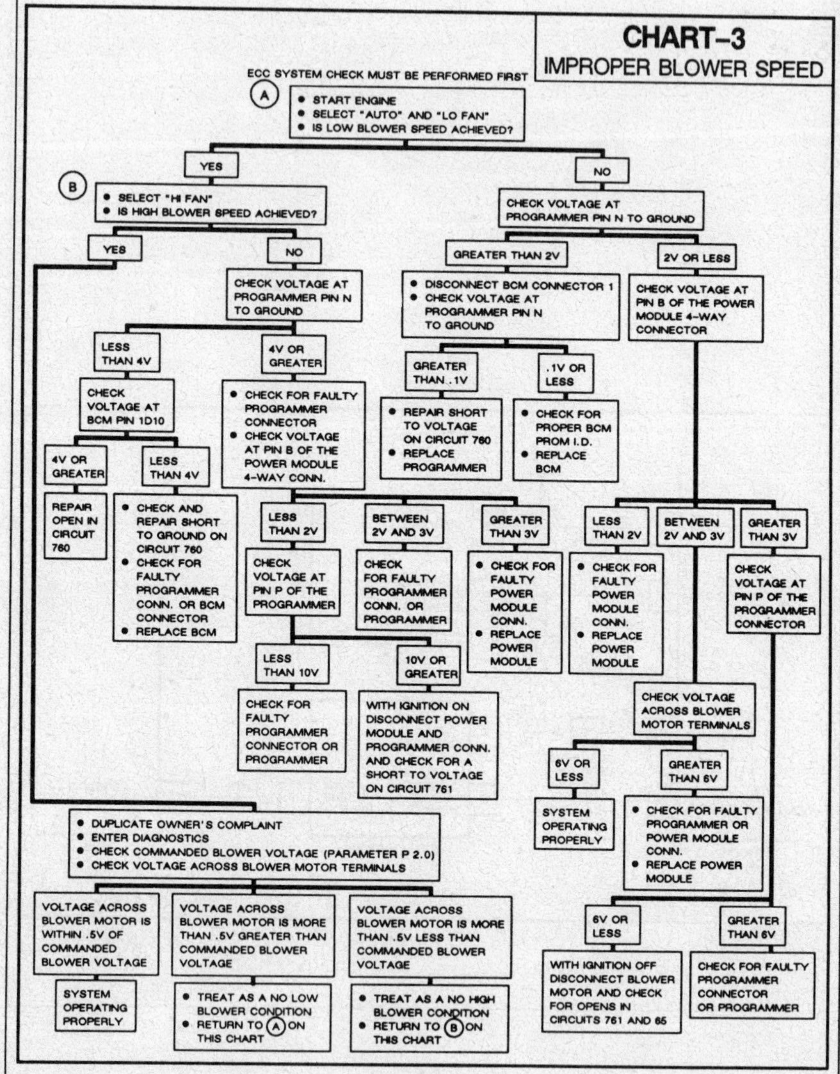
CHART–3
IMPROPER BLOWER SPEED
ECC SYSTEM CHECK MUST BE PERFORMED FIRST
A
• START ENGINE
• SELECT "AUTO" AND "LO FAN"
• IS LOW BLOWER SPEED ACHIEVED?
YES
NO
B
• SELECT "HI FAN"
• IS HIGH BLOWER SPEED ACHIEVED?
YES
NO
CHECK VOLTAGE AT PROGRAMMER PIN N TO GROUND
LESS THAN 4V
4V OR GREATER
CHECK VOLTAGE AT BCM PIN 1D10
4V OR GREATER
LESS THAN 4V
REPAIR OPEN IN CIRCUIT 760
• CHECK AND REPAIR SHORT TO GROUND ON CIRCUIT 760
• CHECK FOR FAULTY PROGRAMMER CONN. OR BCM CONNECTOR
• REPLACE BCM
• CHECK FOR FAULTY PROGRAMMER CONNECTOR
• CHECK VOLTAGE AT PIN B OF THE POWER MODULE 4-WAY CONN.
LESS THAN 2V
BETWEEN 2V AND 3V
GREATER THAN 3V
CHECK VOLTAGE AT PIN P OF THE PROGRAMMER
CHECK FOR FAULTY PROGRAMMER CONN. OR PROGRAMMER
• CHECK FOR FAULTY POWER MODULE CONN.
• REPLACE POWER MODULE
LESS THAN 10V
10V OR GREATER
CHECK FOR FAULTY PROGRAMMER CONNECTOR OR PROGRAMMER
WITH IGNITION ON DISCONNECT POWER MODULE AND PROGRAMMER CONN. AND CHECK FOR A SHORT TO VOLTAGE ON CIRCUIT 761
CHECK VOLTAGE AT PROGRAMMER PIN N TO GROUND
GREATER THAN 2V
2V OR LESS
• DISCONNECT BCM CONNECTOR 1
• CHECK VOLTAGE AT PROGRAMMER PIN N TO GROUND
GREATER THAN .1V
.1V OR LESS
• REPAIR SHORT TO VOLTAGE ON CIRCUIT 760
• REPLACE PROGRAMMER
• CHECK FOR PROPER BCM PROM I.D.
• REPLACE BCM
CHECK VOLTAGE AT PIN B OF THE POWER MODULE 4-WAY CONNECTOR
LESS THAN 2V
BETWEEN 2V AND 3V
GREATER THAN 3V
• CHECK FOR FAULTY POWER MODULE CONN.
• REPLACE POWER MODULE
CHECK VOLTAGE AT PIN P OF THE PROGRAMMER CONNECTOR
CHECK VOLTAGE ACROSS BLOWER MOTOR TERMINALS
6V OR LESS
GREATER THAN 6V
SYSTEM OPERATING PROPERLY
• CHECK FOR FAULTY PROGRAMMER OR POWER MODULE CONN.
• REPLACE POWER MODULE
6V OR LESS
GREATER THAN 6V
WITH IGNITION OFF DISCONNECT BLOWER MOTOR AND CHECK FOR OPENS IN CIRCUITS 761 AND 65
CHECK FOR FAULTY PROGRAMMER CONNECTOR OR PROGRAMMER
• DUPLICATE OWNER'S COMPLAINT
• ENTER DIAGNOSTICS
• CHECK COMMANDED BLOWER VOLTAGE (PARAMETER P 2.0)
• CHECK VOLTAGE ACROSS BLOWER MOTOR TERMINALS
VOLTAGE ACROSS BLOWER MOTOR IS WITHIN .5V OF COMMANDED BLOWER VOLTAGE
SYSTEM OPERATING PROPERLY
VOLTAGE ACROSS BLOWER MOTOR IS MORE THAN .5V GREATER THAN COMMANDED BLOWER VOLTAGE
• TREAT AS A NO LOW BLOWER CONDITION
• RETURN TO A ON THIS CHART
VOLTAGE ACROSS BLOWER MOTOR IS MORE THAN .5V LESS THAN COMMANDED BLOWER VOLTAGE
• TREAT AS A NO HIGH BLOWER CONDITION
• RETURN TO B ON THIS CHART

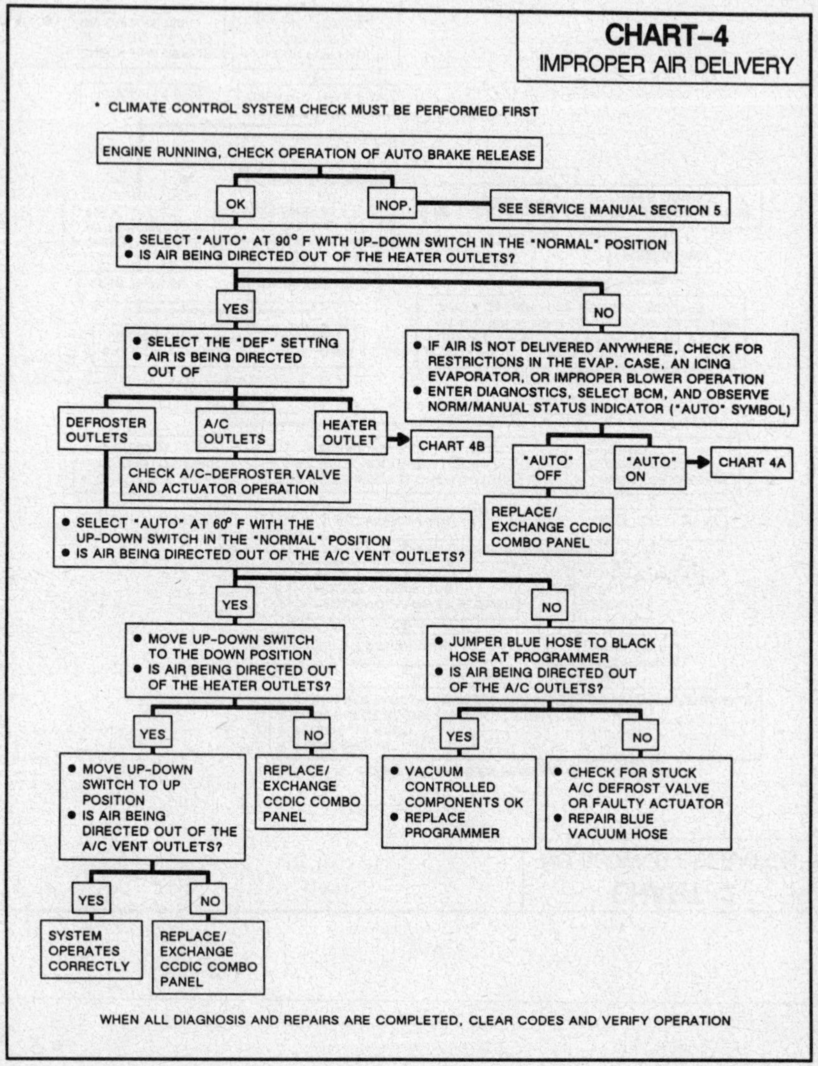
CHART–4
IMPROPER AIR DELIVERY
• CLIMATE CONTROL SYSTEM CHECK MUST BE PERFORMED FIRST
ENGINE RUNNING, CHECK OPERATION OF AUTO BRAKE RELEASE
OK
INOP.
SEE SERVICE MANUAL SECTION 5
• SELECT "AUTO" AT 90° F WITH UP-DOWN SWITCH IN THE "NORMAL" POSITION
• IS AIR BEING DIRECTED OUT OF THE HEATER OUTLETS?
YES
NO
• SELECT THE "DEF" SETTING
• AIR IS BEING DIRECTED OUT OF
DEFROSTER OUTLETS
A/C OUTLETS
HEATER OUTLET
CHART 4B
CHECK A/C-DEFROSTER VALVE AND ACTUATOR OPERATION
• IF AIR IS NOT DELIVERED ANYWHERE, CHECK FOR RESTRICTIONS IN THE EVAP. CASE, AN ICING EVAPORATOR, OR IMPROPER BLOWER OPERATION
• ENTER DIAGNOSTICS, SELECT BCM, AND OBSERVE NORM/MANUAL STATUS INDICATOR ("AUTO" SYMBOL)
"AUTO" OFF
"AUTO" ON
CHART 4A
REPLACE/ EXCHANGE CCDIC COMBO PANEL
• SELECT "AUTO" AT 60° F WITH THE UP-DOWN SWITCH IN THE "NORMAL" POSITION
• IS AIR BEING DIRECTED OUT OF THE A/C VENT OUTLETS?
YES
NO
• MOVE UP-DOWN SWITCH TO THE DOWN POSITION
• IS AIR BEING DIRECTED OUT OF THE HEATER OUTLETS?
YES
NO
• MOVE UP-DOWN SWITCH TO UP POSITION
• IS AIR BEING DIRECTED OUT OF THE A/C VENT OUTLETS?
YES
NO
SYSTEM OPERATES CORRECTLY
REPLACE/ EXCHANGE CCDIC COMBO PANEL
REPLACE/ EXCHANGE CCDIC COMBO PANEL
• JUMPER BLUE HOSE TO BLACK HOSE AT PROGRAMMER
• IS AIR BEING DIRECTED OUT OF THE A/C OUTLETS?
YES
NO
• VACUUM CONTROLLED COMPONENTS OK
• REPLACE PROGRAMMER
• CHECK FOR STUCK A/C DEFROST VALVE OR FAULTY ACTUATOR
• REPAIR BLUE VACUUM HOSE
WHEN ALL DIAGNOSIS AND REPAIRS ARE COMPLETED, CLEAR CODES AND VERIFY OPERATION

EEC SYSTEM DIAGNOSIS
E, K AND V BODY CADILLAC (CONT.)

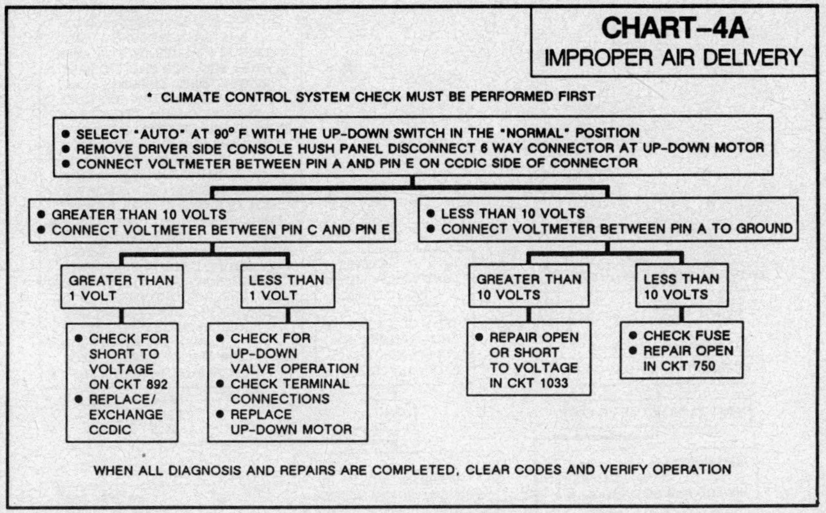
CHART–4A
IMPROPER AIR DELIVERY
• CLIMATE CONTROL SYSTEM CHECK MUST BE PERFORMED FIRST
● SELECT "AUTO" AT 90° F WITH THE UP-DOWN SWITCH IN THE "NORMAL" POSITION
● REMOVE DRIVER SIDE CONSOLE HUSH PANEL DISCONNECT 6 WAY CONNECTOR AT UP-DOWN MOTOR
● CONNECT VOLTMETER BETWEEN PIN A AND PIN E ON CCDIC SIDE OF CONNECTOR
● GREATER THAN 10 VOLTS
● CONNECT VOLTMETER BETWEEN PIN C AND PIN E
● LESS THAN 10 VOLTS
● CONNECT VOLTMETER BETWEEN PIN A TO GROUND
GREATER THAN 1 VOLT
LESS THAN 1 VOLT
GREATER THAN 10 VOLTS
LESS THAN 10 VOLTS
● CHECK FOR SHORT TO VOLTAGE ON CKT 892
● REPLACE/ EXCHANGE CCDIC
● CHECK FOR UP-DOWN VALVE OPERATION
● CHECK TERMINAL CONNECTIONS
● REPLACE UP-DOWN MOTOR
● REPAIR OPEN OR SHORT TO VOLTAGE IN CKT 1033
● CHECK FUSE
● REPAIR OPEN IN CKT 750
WHEN ALL DIAGNOSIS AND REPAIRS ARE COMPLETED, CLEAR CODES AND VERIFY OPERATION

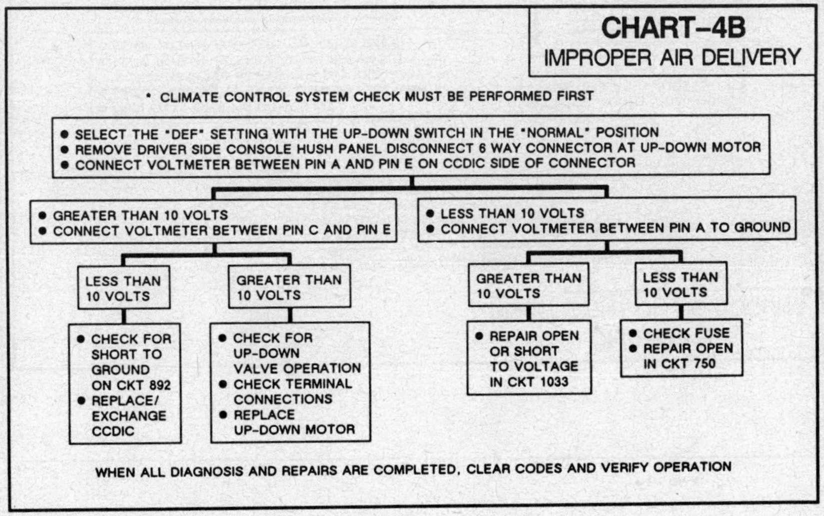
CHART–4B
IMPROPER AIR DELIVERY
• CLIMATE CONTROL SYSTEM CHECK MUST BE PERFORMED FIRST
● SELECT THE "DEF" SETTING WITH THE UP-DOWN SWITCH IN THE "NORMAL" POSITION
● REMOVE DRIVER SIDE CONSOLE HUSH PANEL DISCONNECT 6 WAY CONNECTOR AT UP-DOWN MOTOR
● CONNECT VOLTMETER BETWEEN PIN A AND PIN E ON CCDIC SIDE OF CONNECTOR
● GREATER THAN 10 VOLTS
● CONNECT VOLTMETER BETWEEN PIN C AND PIN E
● LESS THAN 10 VOLTS
● CONNECT VOLTMETER BETWEEN PIN A TO GROUND
LESS THAN 10 VOLTS
GREATER THAN 10 VOLTS
GREATER THAN 10 VOLTS
LESS THAN 10 VOLTS
● CHECK FOR SHORT TO GROUND ON CKT 892
● REPLACE/ EXCHANGE CCDIC
● CHECK FOR UP-DOWN VALVE OPERATION
● CHECK TERMINAL CONNECTIONS
● REPLACE UP-DOWN MOTOR
● REPAIR OPEN OR SHORT TO VOLTAGE IN CKT 1033
● CHECK FUSE
● REPAIR OPEN IN CKT 750
WHEN ALL DIAGNOSIS AND REPAIRS ARE COMPLETED, CLEAR CODES AND VERIFY OPERATION

ELECTRONIC CLIMATE CONTROL CIRCUIT
E, K AND V BODY CADILLAC

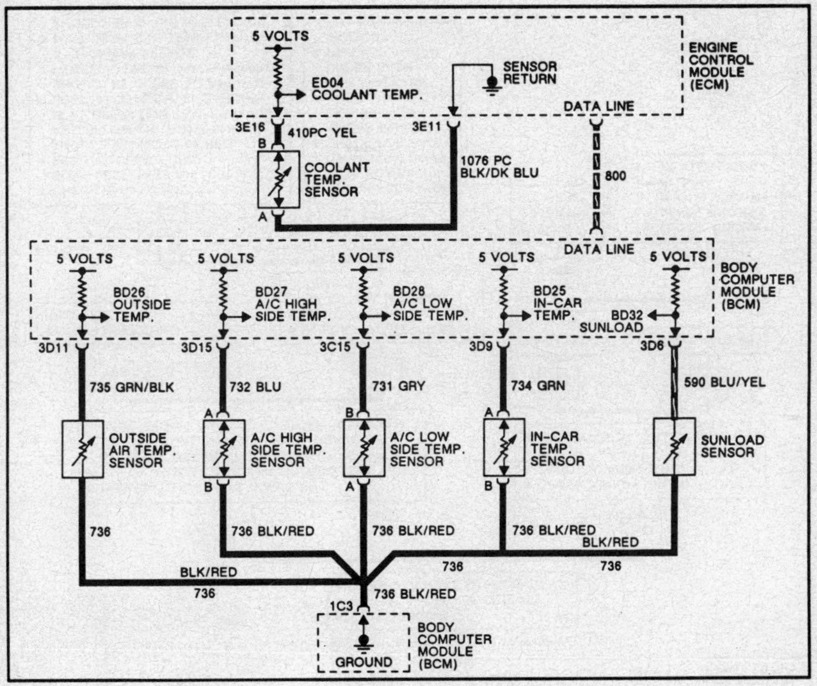
5 VOLTS
ED04 COOLANT TEMP.
SENSOR RETURN
ENGINE CONTROL MODULE (ECM)
DATA LINE
3E16
410PC YEL
3E11
COOLANT TEMP. SENSOR
1076 PC BLK/DK BLU
800
DATA LINE
BODY COMPUTER MODULE (BCM)
BD26 OUTSIDE TEMP.
BD27 A/C HIGH SIDE TEMP.
BD28 A/C LOW SIDE TEMP.
BD25 IN-CAR TEMP.
BD32 SUNLOAD
3D11
3D15
3C15
3D9
3D6
735 GRN/BLK
732 BLU
731 GRY
734 GRN
590 BLU/YEL
OUTSIDE AIR TEMP. SENSOR
A/C HIGH SIDE TEMP. SENSOR
A/C LOW SIDE TEMP. SENSOR
IN-CAR TEMP. SENSOR
SUNLOAD SENSOR
736
736 BLK/RED
BLK/RED
1C3
GROUND
BODY COMPUTER MODULE (BCM)

EEC SYSTEM DIAGNOSIS—E, K AND V BODY CADILLAC (CONT.)

CHART–5
INSUFFICIENT OR NO COOLING

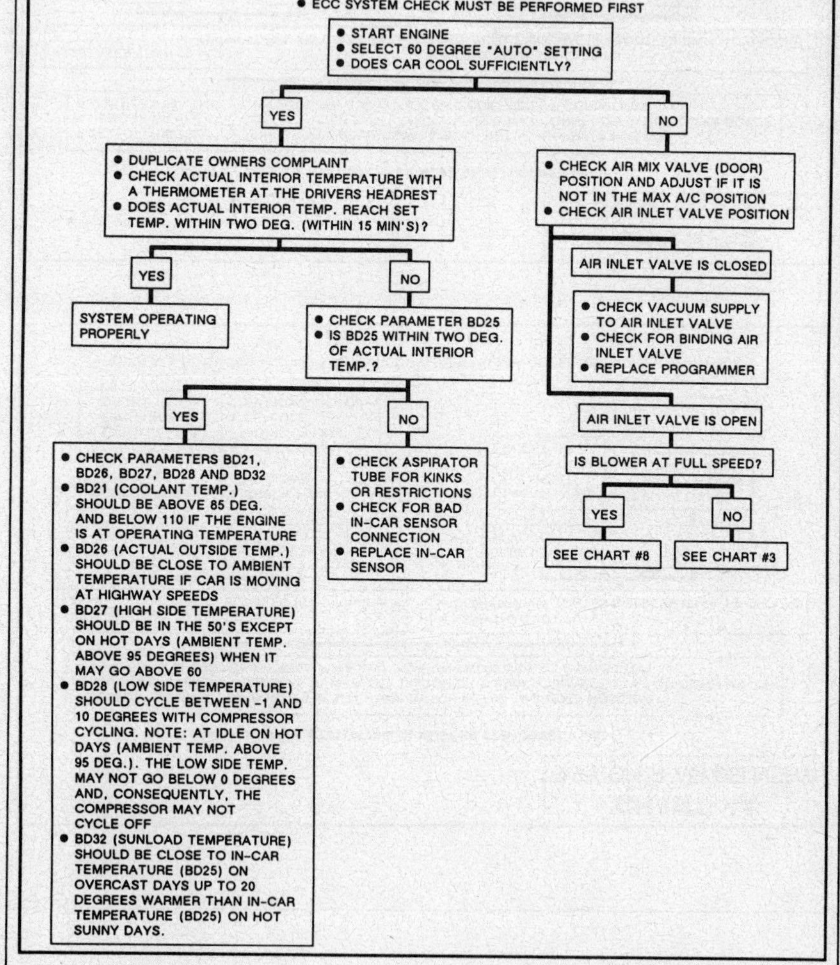
• ECC SYSTEM CHECK MUST BE PERFORMED FIRST
• START ENGINE
• SELECT 60 DEGREE "AUTO" SETTING
• DOES CAR COOL SUFFICIENTLY?
YES
NO
• DUPLICATE OWNERS COMPLAINT
• CHECK ACTUAL INTERIOR TEMPERATURE WITH A THERMOMETER AT THE DRIVERS HEADREST
• DOES ACTUAL INTERIOR TEMP. REACH SET TEMP. WITHIN TWO DEG. (WITHIN 15 MIN'S)?
YES
SYSTEM OPERATING PROPERLY
NO
• CHECK PARAMETER BD25
• IS BD25 WITHIN TWO DEG. OF ACTUAL INTERIOR TEMP.?
YES
• CHECK PARAMETERS BD21, BD26, BD27, BD28 AND BD32
• BD21 (COOLANT TEMP.) SHOULD BE ABOVE 85 DEG. AND BELOW 110 IF THE ENGINE IS AT OPERATING TEMPERATURE
• BD26 (ACTUAL OUTSIDE TEMP.) SHOULD BE CLOSE TO AMBIENT TEMPERATURE IF CAR IS MOVING AT HIGHWAY SPEEDS
• BD27 (HIGH SIDE TEMPERATURE) SHOULD BE IN THE 50'S EXCEPT ON HOT DAYS (AMBIENT TEMP. ABOVE 95 DEGREES) WHEN IT MAY GO ABOVE 60
• BD28 (LOW SIDE TEMPERATURE) SHOULD CYCLE BETWEEN -1 AND 10 DEGREES WITH COMPRESSOR CYCLING. NOTE: AT IDLE ON HOT DAYS (AMBIENT TEMP. ABOVE 95 DEG.). THE LOW SIDE TEMP. MAY NOT GO BELOW 0 DEGREES AND, CONSEQUENTLY, THE COMPRESSOR MAY NOT CYCLE OFF
• BD32 (SUNLOAD TEMPERATURE) SHOULD BE CLOSE TO IN-CAR TEMPERATURE (BD25) ON OVERCAST DAYS UP TO 20 DEGREES WARMER THAN IN-CAR TEMPERATURE (BD25) ON HOT SUNNY DAYS.
NO
• CHECK ASPIRATOR TUBE FOR KINKS OR RESTRICTIONS
• CHECK FOR BAD IN-CAR SENSOR CONNECTION
• REPLACE IN-CAR SENSOR
• CHECK AIR MIX VALVE (DOOR) POSITION AND ADJUST IF IT IS NOT IN THE MAX A/C POSITION
• CHECK AIR INLET VALVE POSITION
AIR INLET VALVE IS CLOSED
• CHECK VACUUM SUPPLY TO AIR INLET VALVE
• CHECK FOR BINDING AIR INLET VALVE
• REPLACE PROGRAMMER
AIR INLET VALVE IS OPEN
IS BLOWER AT FULL SPEED?
YES
SEE CHART #8
NO
SEE CHART #3

CHART–6
INSUFFICIENT OR NO HEATING

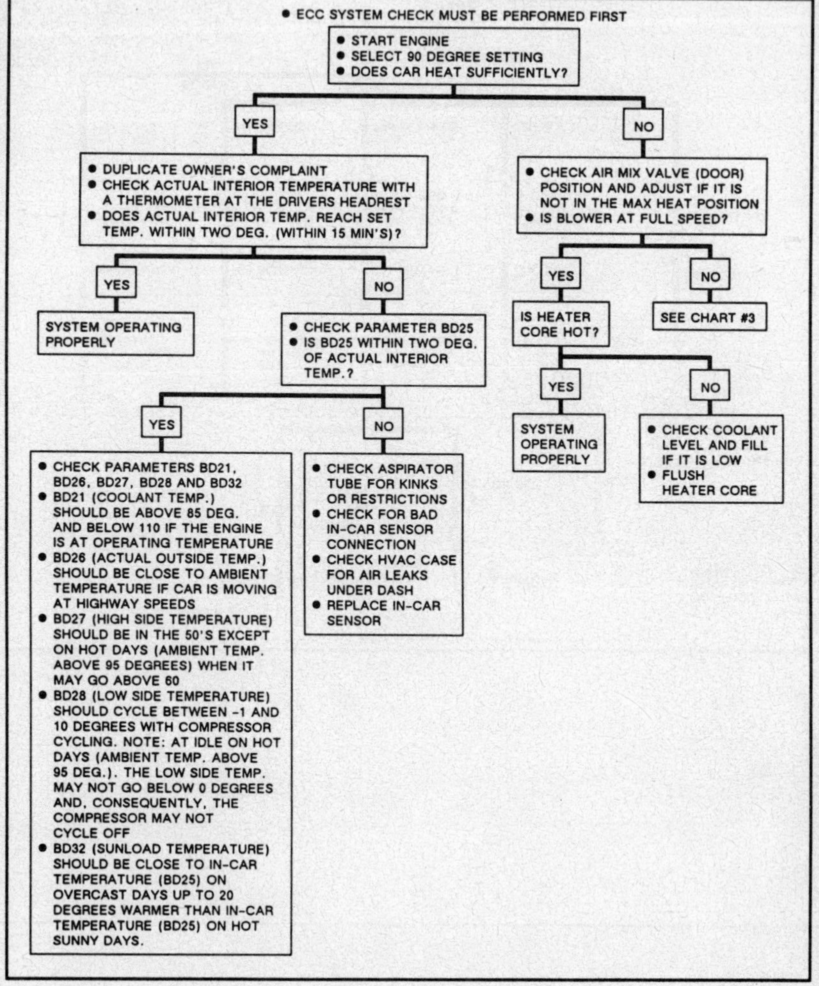
• ECC SYSTEM CHECK MUST BE PERFORMED FIRST
• START ENGINE
• SELECT 90 DEGREE SETTING
• DOES CAR HEAT SUFFICIENTLY?
YES
NO
• DUPLICATE OWNER'S COMPLAINT
• CHECK ACTUAL INTERIOR TEMPERATURE WITH A THERMOMETER AT THE DRIVERS HEADREST
• DOES ACTUAL INTERIOR TEMP. REACH SET TEMP. WITHIN TWO DEG. (WITHIN 15 MIN'S)?
YES
SYSTEM OPERATING PROPERLY
NO
• CHECK PARAMETER BD25
• IS BD25 WITHIN TWO DEG. OF ACTUAL INTERIOR TEMP.?
YES
• CHECK PARAMETERS BD21, BD26, BD27, BD28 AND BD32
• BD21 (COOLANT TEMP.) SHOULD BE ABOVE 85 DEG. AND BELOW 110 IF THE ENGINE IS AT OPERATING TEMPERATURE
• BD26 (ACTUAL OUTSIDE TEMP.) SHOULD BE CLOSE TO AMBIENT TEMPERATURE IF CAR IS MOVING AT HIGHWAY SPEEDS
• BD27 (HIGH SIDE TEMPERATURE) SHOULD BE IN THE 50'S EXCEPT ON HOT DAYS (AMBIENT TEMP. ABOVE 95 DEGREES) WHEN IT MAY GO ABOVE 60
• BD28 (LOW SIDE TEMPERATURE) SHOULD CYCLE BETWEEN -1 AND 10 DEGREES WITH COMPRESSOR CYCLING. NOTE: AT IDLE ON HOT DAYS (AMBIENT TEMP. ABOVE 95 DEG.). THE LOW SIDE TEMP. MAY NOT GO BELOW 0 DEGREES AND, CONSEQUENTLY, THE COMPRESSOR MAY NOT CYCLE OFF
• BD32 (SUNLOAD TEMPERATURE) SHOULD BE CLOSE TO IN-CAR TEMPERATURE (BD25) ON OVERCAST DAYS UP TO 20 DEGREES WARMER THAN IN-CAR TEMPERATURE (BD25) ON HOT SUNNY DAYS.
NO
• CHECK ASPIRATOR TUBE FOR KINKS OR RESTRICTIONS
• CHECK FOR BAD IN-CAR SENSOR CONNECTION
• CHECK HVAC CASE FOR AIR LEAKS UNDER DASH
• REPLACE IN-CAR SENSOR
• CHECK AIR MIX VALVE (DOOR) POSITION AND ADJUST IF IT IS NOT IN THE MAX HEAT POSITION
• IS BLOWER AT FULL SPEED?
YES
IS HEATER CORE HOT?
YES
SYSTEM OPERATING PROPERLY
NO
• CHECK COOLANT LEVEL AND FILL IF IT IS LOW
• FLUSH HEATER CORE
NO
SEE CHART #3

REAR DEFOGGER ELECTRICAL CIRCUIT
E, K AND V BODY CADILLAC

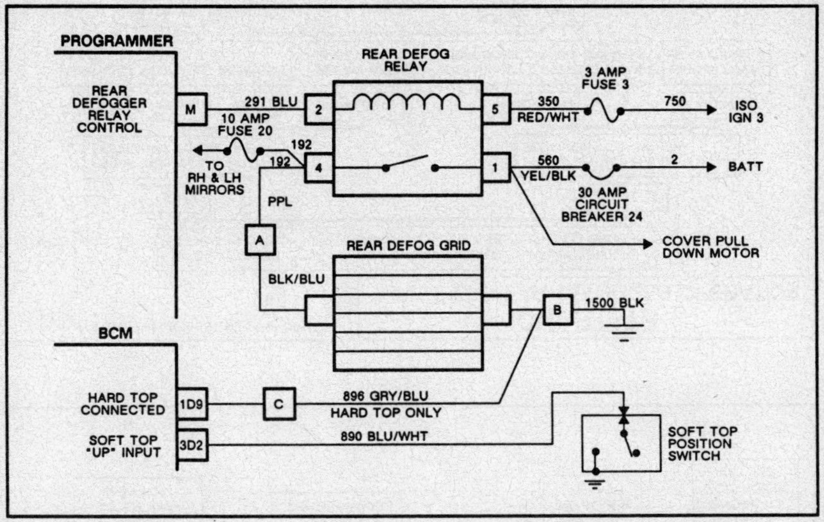
PROGRAMMER
REAR DEFOGGER RELAY CONTROL
M
291 BLU
10 AMP FUSE 20
192
192
TO RH & LH MIRRORS
REAR DEFOG RELAY
2
4
5
1
350 RED/WHT
3 AMP FUSE 3
750
ISO IGN 3
560 YEL/BLK
30 AMP CIRCUIT BREAKER 24
2
BATT
COVER PULL DOWN MOTOR
PPL
A
REAR DEFOG GRID
BLK/BLU
B
1500 BLK
BCM
HARD TOP CONNECTED
1D9
C
896 GRY/BLU
HARD TOP ONLY
SOFT TOP "UP" INPUT
3D2
890 BLU/WHT
SOFT TOP POSITION SWITCH

EEC SYSTEM DIAGNOSIS
E, K AND V BODY CADILLAC (CONT.)

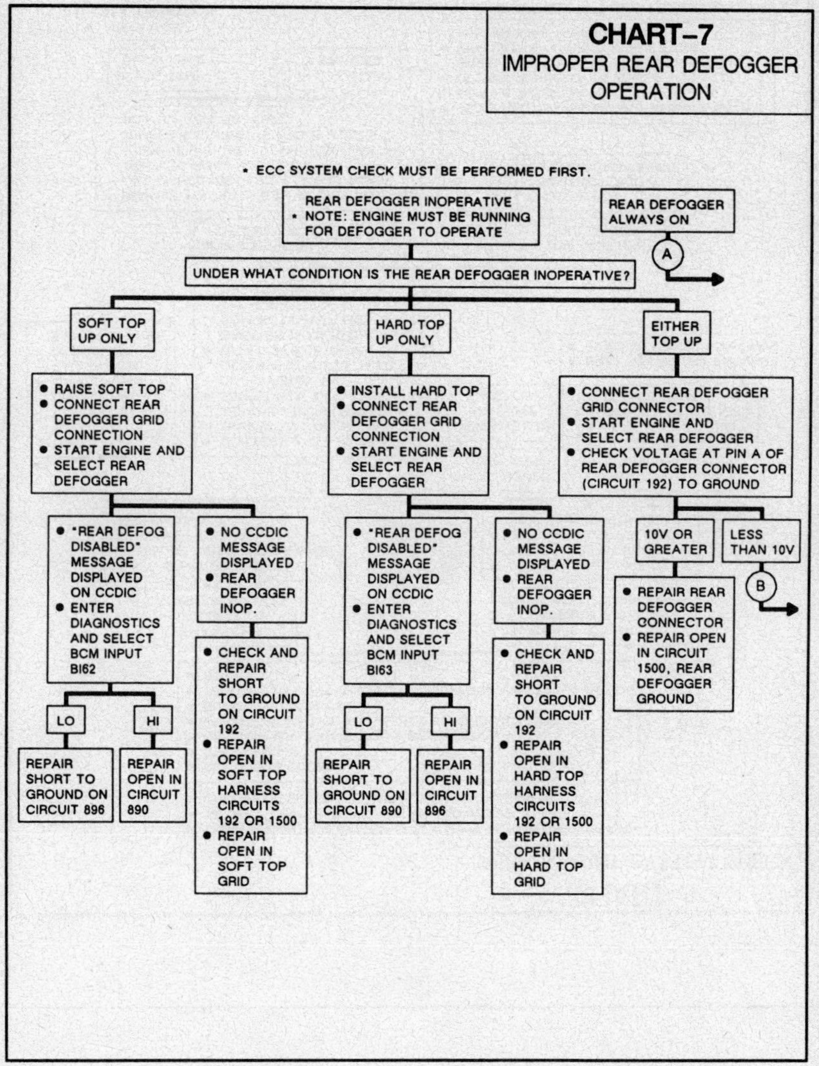
CHART–7
IMPROPER REAR DEFOGGER OPERATION
• ECC SYSTEM CHECK MUST BE PERFORMED FIRST.
REAR DEFOGGER INOPERATIVE
• NOTE: ENGINE MUST BE RUNNING FOR DEFOGGER TO OPERATE
REAR DEFOGGER ALWAYS ON
A
UNDER WHAT CONDITION IS THE REAR DEFOGGER INOPERATIVE?
SOFT TOP UP ONLY
HARD TOP UP ONLY
EITHER TOP UP
• RAISE SOFT TOP
• CONNECT REAR DEFOGGER GRID CONNECTION
• START ENGINE AND SELECT REAR DEFOGGER
• INSTALL HARD TOP
• CONNECT REAR DEFOGGER GRID CONNECTION
• START ENGINE AND SELECT REAR DEFOGGER
• CONNECT REAR DEFOGGER GRID CONNECTOR
• START ENGINE AND SELECT REAR DEFOGGER
• CHECK VOLTAGE AT PIN A OF REAR DEFOGGER CONNECTOR (CIRCUIT 192) TO GROUND
• "REAR DEFOG DISABLED" MESSAGE DISPLAYED ON CCDIC
• ENTER DIAGNOSTICS AND SELECT BCM INPUT BI62
• NO CCDIC MESSAGE DISPLAYED
• REAR DEFOGGER INOP.
• "REAR DEFOG DISABLED" MESSAGE DISPLAYED ON CCDIC
• ENTER DIAGNOSTICS AND SELECT BCM INPUT BI63
• NO CCDIC MESSAGE DISPLAYED
• REAR DEFOGGER INOP.
10V OR GREATER
LESS THAN 10V
B
• REPAIR REAR DEFOGGER CONNECTOR
• REPAIR OPEN IN CIRCUIT 1500, REAR DEFOGGER GROUND
LO
HI
REPAIR SHORT TO GROUND ON CIRCUIT 896
REPAIR OPEN IN CIRCUIT 890
• CHECK AND REPAIR SHORT TO GROUND ON CIRCUIT 192
• REPAIR OPEN IN SOFT TOP HARNESS CIRCUITS 192 OR 1500
• REPAIR OPEN IN SOFT TOP GRID
LO
HI
REPAIR SHORT TO GROUND ON CIRCUIT 890
REPAIR OPEN IN CIRCUIT 896
• CHECK AND REPAIR SHORT TO GROUND ON CIRCUIT 192
• REPAIR OPEN IN HARD TOP HARNESS CIRCUITS 192 OR 1500
• REPAIR OPEN IN HARD TOP GRID

EEC SYSTEM DIAGNOSIS—E, K AND V BODY CADILLAC (CONT.)

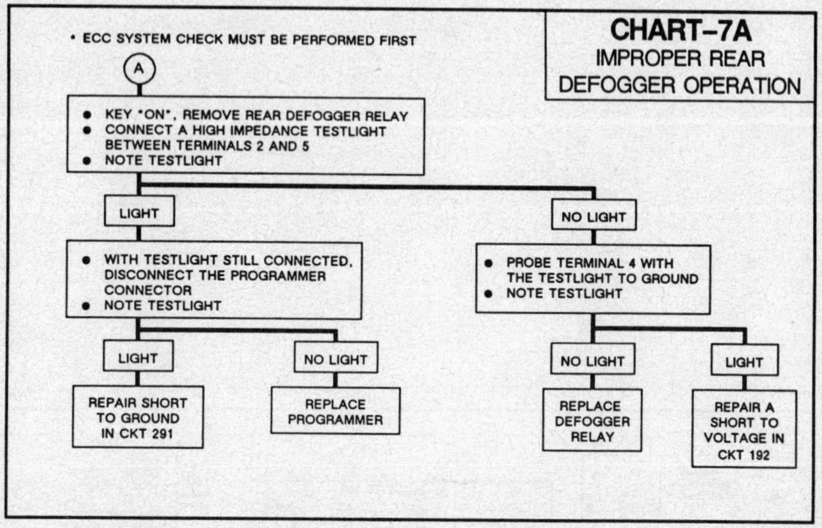
CHART–7A
IMPROPER REAR DEFOGGER OPERATION
* ECC SYSTEM CHECK MUST BE PERFORMED FIRST
A
● KEY "ON", REMOVE REAR DEFOGGER RELAY ● CONNECT A HIGH IMPEDANCE TESTLIGHT BETWEEN TERMINALS 2 AND 5 ● NOTE TESTLIGHT
LIGHT
● WITH TESTLIGHT STILL CONNECTED, DISCONNECT THE PROGRAMMER CONNECTOR ● NOTE TESTLIGHT
LIGHT
REPAIR SHORT TO GROUND IN CKT 291
NO LIGHT
REPLACE PROGRAMMER
NO LIGHT
● PROBE TERMINAL 4 WITH THE TESTLIGHT TO GROUND ● NOTE TESTLIGHT
NO LIGHT
REPLACE DEFOGGER RELAY
LIGHT
REPAIR A SHORT TO VOLTAGE IN CKT 192

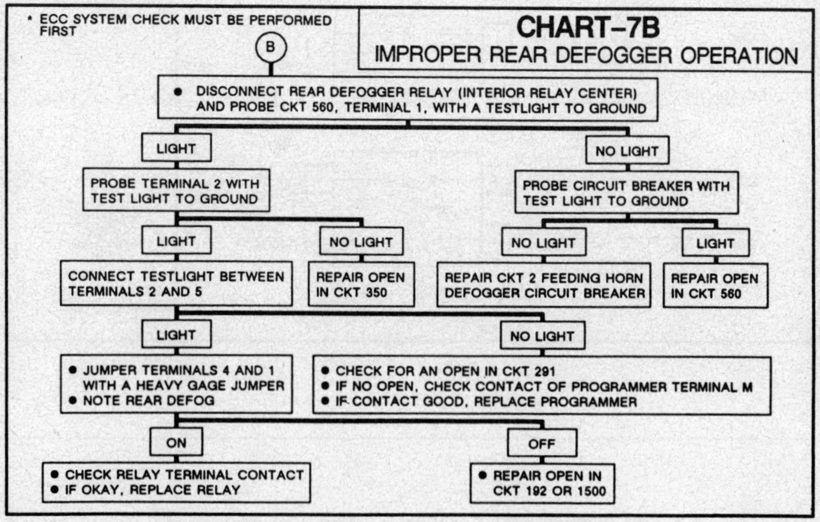
CHART–7B
IMPROPER REAR DEFOGGER OPERATION
* ECC SYSTEM CHECK MUST BE PERFORMED FIRST
B
● DISCONNECT REAR DEFOGGER RELAY (INTERIOR RELAY CENTER) AND PROBE CKT 560, TERMINAL 1, WITH A TESTLIGHT TO GROUND
LIGHT
PROBE TERMINAL 2 WITH TEST LIGHT TO GROUND
LIGHT
CONNECT TESTLIGHT BETWEEN TERMINALS 2 AND 5
NO LIGHT
REPAIR OPEN IN CKT 350
LIGHT
● JUMPER TERMINALS 4 AND 1 WITH A HEAVY GAGE JUMPER ● NOTE REAR DEFOG
ON
● CHECK RELAY TERMINAL CONTACT ● IF OKAY, REPLACE RELAY
OFF
● REPAIR OPEN IN CKT 192 OR 1500
NO LIGHT
● CHECK FOR AN OPEN IN CKT 291 ● IF NO OPEN, CHECK CONTACT OF PROGRAMMER TERMINAL M ● IF CONTACT GOOD, REPLACE PROGRAMMER
NO LIGHT
PROBE CIRCUIT BREAKER WITH TEST LIGHT TO GROUND
NO LIGHT
REPAIR CKT 2 FEEDING HORN DEFOGGER CIRCUIT BREAKER
LIGHT
REPAIR OPEN IN CKT 560

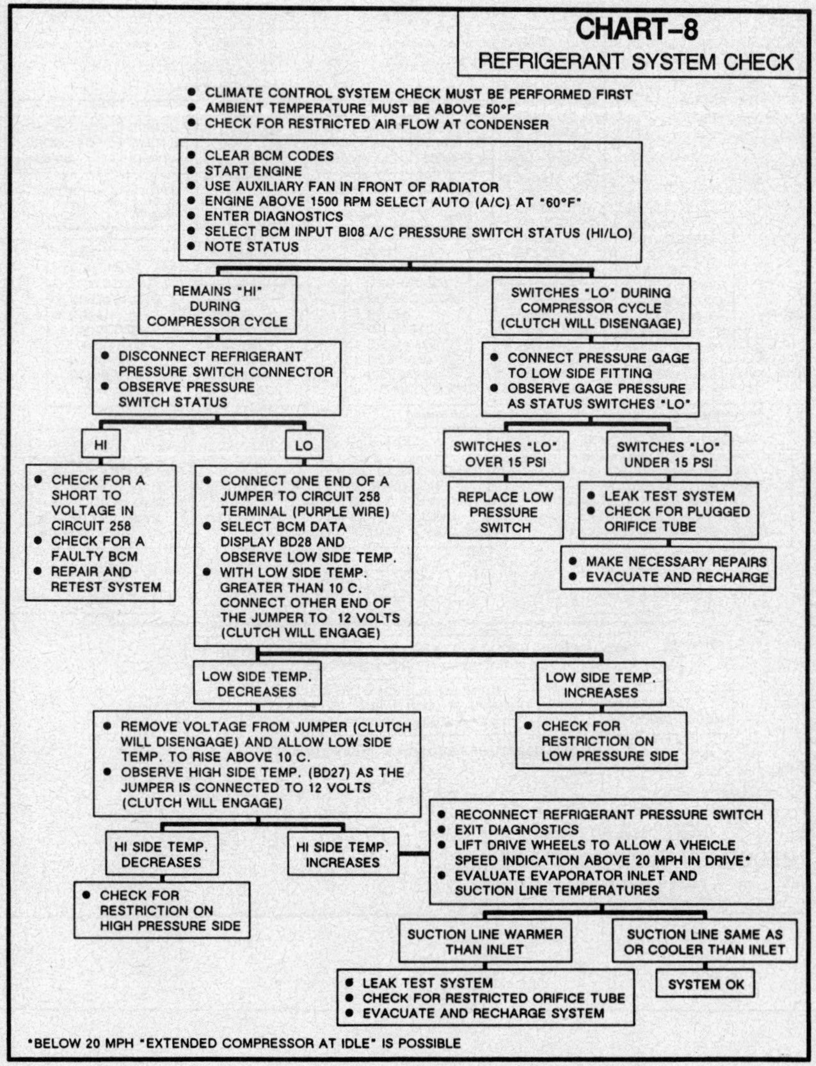
CHART–8
REFRIGERANT SYSTEM CHECK
● CLIMATE CONTROL SYSTEM CHECK MUST BE PERFORMED FIRST ● AMBIENT TEMPERATURE MUST BE ABOVE 50°F ● CHECK FOR RESTRICTED AIR FLOW AT CONDENSER
● CLEAR BCM CODES ● START ENGINE ● USE AUXILIARY FAN IN FRONT OF RADIATOR ● ENGINE ABOVE 1500 RPM SELECT AUTO (A/C) AT "60°F" ● ENTER DIAGNOSTICS ● SELECT BCM INPUT BI08 A/C PRESSURE SWITCH STATUS (HI/LO) ● NOTE STATUS
REMAINS "HI" DURING COMPRESSOR CYCLE
● DISCONNECT REFRIGERANT PRESSURE SWITCH CONNECTOR ● OBSERVE PRESSURE SWITCH STATUS
HI
● CHECK FOR A SHORT TO VOLTAGE IN CIRCUIT 258 ● CHECK FOR A FAULTY BCM ● REPAIR AND RETEST SYSTEM
LO
● CONNECT ONE END OF A JUMPER TO CIRCUIT 258 TERMINAL (PURPLE WIRE) ● SELECT BCM DATA DISPLAY BD28 AND OBSERVE LOW SIDE TEMP. ● WITH LOW SIDE TEMP. GREATER THAN 10 C. CONNECT OTHER END OF THE JUMPER TO 12 VOLTS (CLUTCH WILL ENGAGE)
LOW SIDE TEMP. DECREASES
● REMOVE VOLTAGE FROM JUMPER (CLUTCH WILL DISENGAGE) AND ALLOW LOW SIDE TEMP. TO RISE ABOVE 10 C. ● OBSERVE HIGH SIDE TEMP. (BD27) AS THE JUMPER IS CONNECTED TO 12 VOLTS (CLUTCH WILL ENGAGE)
HI SIDE TEMP. DECREASES
● CHECK FOR RESTRICTION ON HIGH PRESSURE SIDE
HI SIDE TEMP. INCREASES
● RECONNECT REFRIGERANT PRESSURE SWITCH ● EXIT DIAGNOSTICS ● LIFT DRIVE WHEELS TO ALLOW A VHEICLE SPEED INDICATION ABOVE 20 MPH IN DRIVE* ● EVALUATE EVAPORATOR INLET AND SUCTION LINE TEMPERATURES
SUCTION LINE WARMER THAN INLET
● LEAK TEST SYSTEM ● CHECK FOR RESTRICTED ORIFICE TUBE ● EVACUATE AND RECHARGE SYSTEM
SUCTION LINE SAME AS OR COOLER THAN INLET
SYSTEM OK
LOW SIDE TEMP. INCREASES
● CHECK FOR RESTRICTION ON LOW PRESSURE SIDE
SWITCHES "LO" DURING COMPRESSOR CYCLE (CLUTCH WILL DISENGAGE)
● CONNECT PRESSURE GAGE TO LOW SIDE FITTING ● OBSERVE GAGE PRESSURE AS STATUS SWITCHES "LO"
SWITCHES "LO" OVER 15 PSI
REPLACE LOW PRESSURE SWITCH
SWITCHES "LO" UNDER 15 PSI
● LEAK TEST SYSTEM ● CHECK FOR PLUGGED ORIFICE TUBE
● MAKE NECESSARY REPAIRS ● EVACUATE AND RECHARGE
*BELOW 20 MPH "EXTENDED COMPRESSOR AT IDLE" IS POSSIBLE

EEC SYSTEM DIAGNOSIS
E BODY, EXCEPT ELDORADO

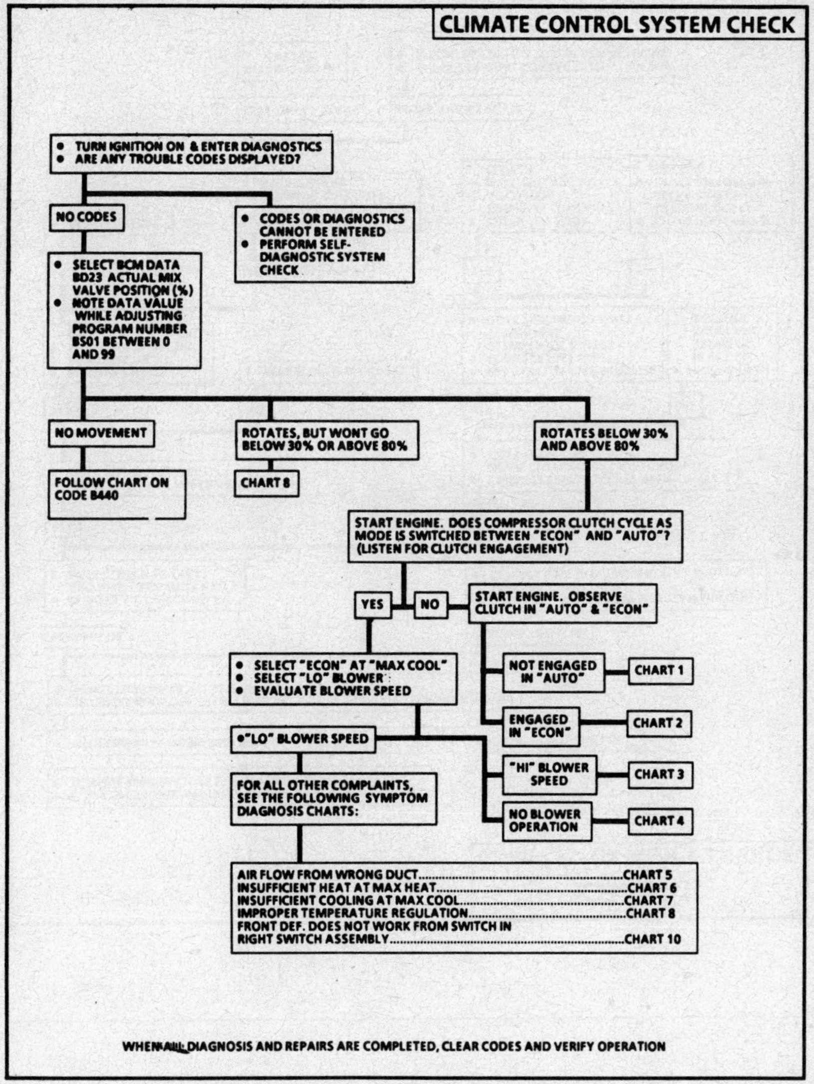
CLIMATE CONTROL SYSTEM CHECK
• TURN IGNITION ON & ENTER DIAGNOSTICS
• ARE ANY TROUBLE CODES DISPLAYED?
NO CODES
• CODES OR DIAGNOSTICS CANNOT BE ENTERED
• PERFORM SELF-DIAGNOSTIC SYSTEM CHECK
• SELECT BCM DATA BD23 ACTUAL MIX VALVE POSITION (%)
• NOTE DATA VALUE WHILE ADJUSTING PROGRAM NUMBER BS01 BETWEEN 0 AND 99
NO MOVEMENT
ROTATES, BUT WONT GO BELOW 30% OR ABOVE 80%
ROTATES BELOW 30% AND ABOVE 80%
FOLLOW CHART ON CODE B440
CHART 8
START ENGINE. DOES COMPRESSOR CLUTCH CYCLE AS MODE IS SWITCHED BETWEEN "ECON" AND "AUTO"? (LISTEN FOR CLUTCH ENGAGEMENT)
YES
NO
START ENGINE. OBSERVE CLUTCH IN "AUTO" & "ECON"
• SELECT "ECON" AT "MAX COOL"
• SELECT "LO" BLOWER
• EVALUATE BLOWER SPEED
NOT ENGAGED IN "AUTO"
CHART 1
ENGAGED IN "ECON"
CHART 2
•"LO" BLOWER SPEED
"HI" BLOWER SPEED
CHART 3
NO BLOWER OPERATION
CHART 4
FOR ALL OTHER COMPLAINTS, SEE THE FOLLOWING SYMPTOM DIAGNOSIS CHARTS:
AIR FLOW FROM WRONG DUCT....CHART 5
INSUFFICIENT HEAT AT MAX HEAT....CHART 6
INSUFFICIENT COOLING AT MAX COOL....CHART 7
IMPROPER TEMPERATURE REGULATION....CHART 8
FRONT DEF. DOES NOT WORK FROM SWITCH IN RIGHT SWITCH ASSEMBLY....CHART 10
WHEN ALL DIAGNOSIS AND REPAIRS ARE COMPLETED, CLEAR CODES AND VERIFY OPERATION

COMPRESSOR ELECTRICAL SYSTEM
E BODY (EXCEPT ELDORADO)

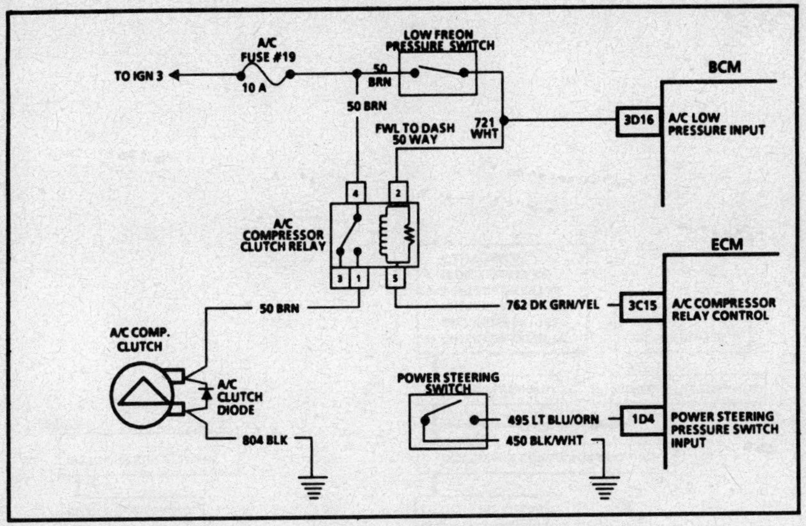
TO IGN 3
A/C FUSE #19
10 A
LOW FREON PRESSURE SWITCH
50 BRN
50 BRN
FWL TO DASH 50 WAY
721 WHT
BCM
3D16
A/C LOW PRESSURE INPUT
A/C COMPRESSOR CLUTCH RELAY
4
2
3
1
5
ECM
50 BRN
762 DK GRN/YEL
3C15
A/C COMPRESSOR RELAY CONTROL
A/C COMP. CLUTCH
A/C CLUTCH DIODE
804 BLK
POWER STEERING SWITCH
495 LT BLU/ORN
450 BLK/WHT
1D4
POWER STEERING PRESSURE SWITCH INPUT

EEC SYSTEM DIAGNOSIS – E BODY, EXCEPT ELDORADO (CONT.)

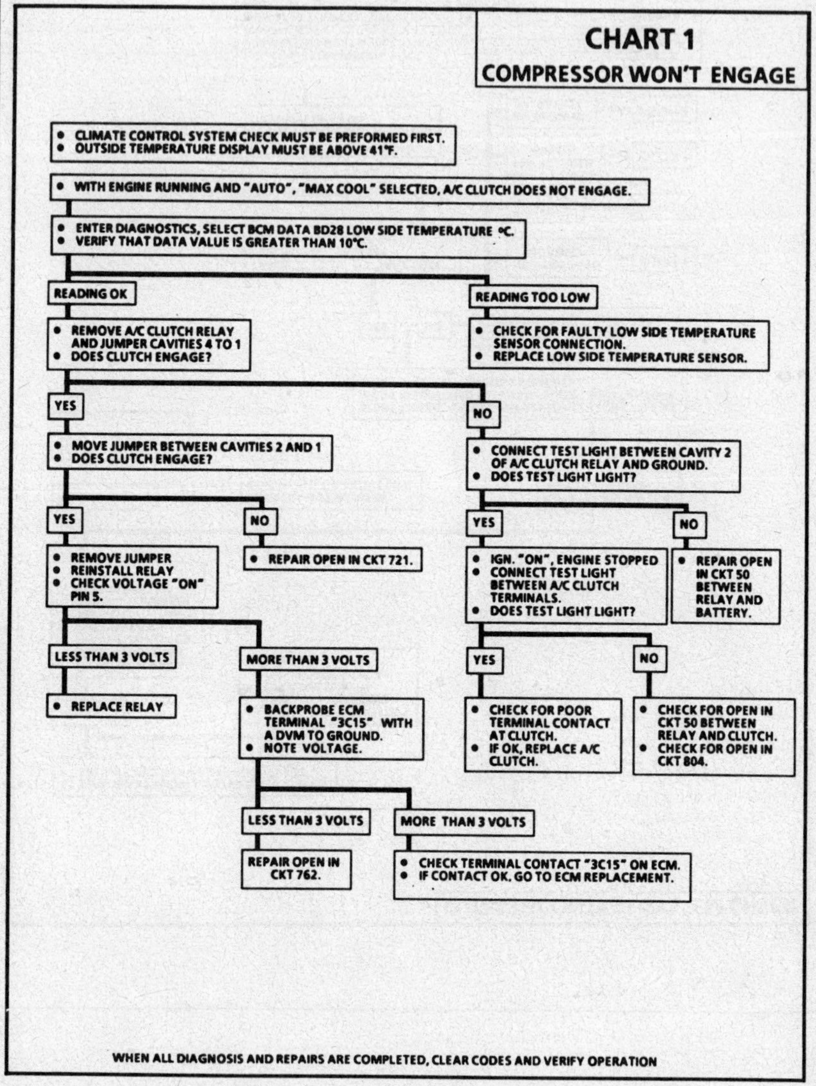
CHART 1
COMPRESSOR WON'T ENGAGE
• CLIMATE CONTROL SYSTEM CHECK MUST BE PREFORMED FIRST.
• OUTSIDE TEMPERATURE DISPLAY MUST BE ABOVE 41°F.
• WITH ENGINE RUNNING AND "AUTO", "MAX COOL" SELECTED, A/C CLUTCH DOES NOT ENGAGE.
• ENTER DIAGNOSTICS, SELECT BCM DATA BD28 LOW SIDE TEMPERATURE °C.
• VERIFY THAT DATA VALUE IS GREATER THAN 10°C.
READING OK
READING TOO LOW
• REMOVE A/C CLUTCH RELAY AND JUMPER CAVITIES 4 TO 1
• DOES CLUTCH ENGAGE?
• CHECK FOR FAULTY LOW SIDE TEMPERATURE SENSOR CONNECTION.
• REPLACE LOW SIDE TEMPERATURE SENSOR.
YES
NO
• MOVE JUMPER BETWEEN CAVITIES 2 AND 1
• DOES CLUTCH ENGAGE?
• CONNECT TEST LIGHT BETWEEN CAVITY 2 OF A/C CLUTCH RELAY AND GROUND.
• DOES TEST LIGHT LIGHT?
YES
NO
YES
NO
• REMOVE JUMPER
• REINSTALL RELAY
• CHECK VOLTAGE "ON" PIN 5.
• REPAIR OPEN IN CKT 721.
• IGN. "ON", ENGINE STOPPED
• CONNECT TEST LIGHT BETWEEN A/C CLUTCH TERMINALS.
• DOES TEST LIGHT LIGHT?
• REPAIR OPEN IN CKT 50 BETWEEN RELAY AND BATTERY.
LESS THAN 3 VOLTS
MORE THAN 3 VOLTS
YES
NO
• REPLACE RELAY
• BACKPROBE ECM TERMINAL "3C15" WITH A DVM TO GROUND.
• NOTE VOLTAGE.
• CHECK FOR POOR TERMINAL CONTACT AT CLUTCH.
• IF OK, REPLACE A/C CLUTCH.
• CHECK FOR OPEN IN CKT 50 BETWEEN RELAY AND CLUTCH.
• CHECK FOR OPEN IN CKT 804.
LESS THAN 3 VOLTS
MORE THAN 3 VOLTS
REPAIR OPEN IN CKT 762.
• CHECK TERMINAL CONTACT "3C15" ON ECM.
• IF CONTACT OK. GO TO ECM REPLACEMENT.
WHEN ALL DIAGNOSIS AND REPAIRS ARE COMPLETED, CLEAR CODES AND VERIFY OPERATION

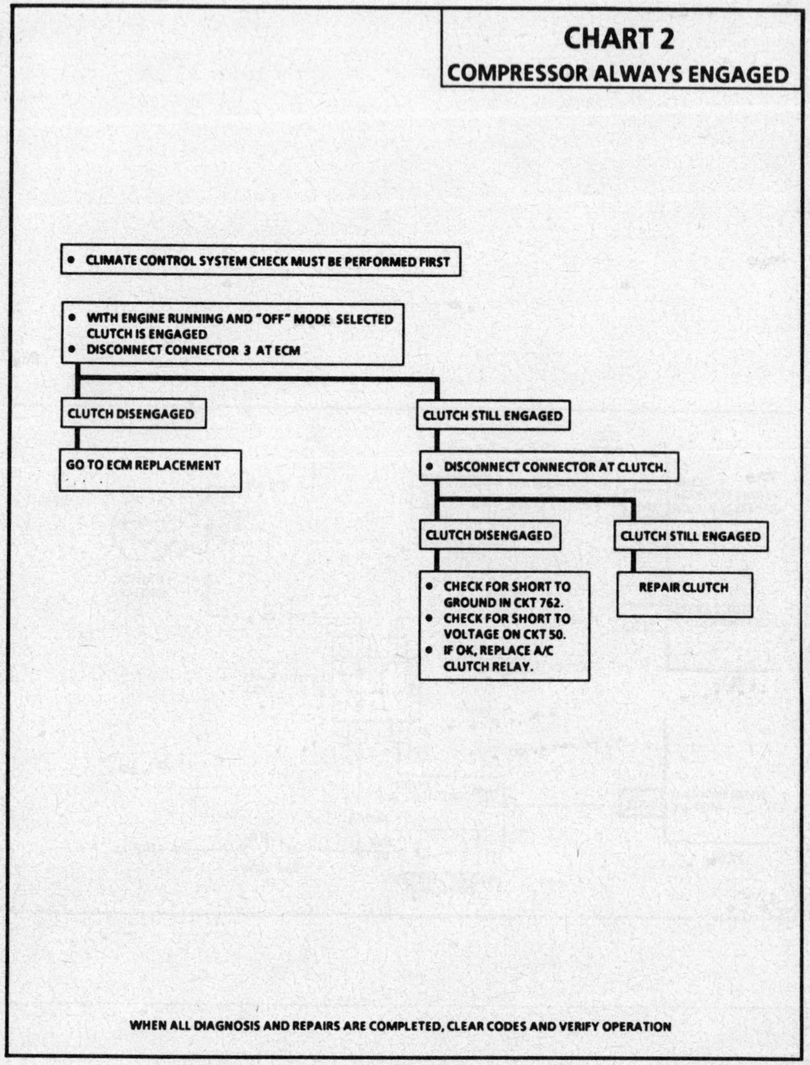
CHART 2
COMPRESSOR ALWAYS ENGAGED
• CLIMATE CONTROL SYSTEM CHECK MUST BE PERFORMED FIRST
• WITH ENGINE RUNNING AND "OFF" MODE SELECTED CLUTCH IS ENGAGED
• DISCONNECT CONNECTOR 3 AT ECM
CLUTCH DISENGAGED
CLUTCH STILL ENGAGED
GO TO ECM REPLACEMENT
• DISCONNECT CONNECTOR AT CLUTCH.
CLUTCH DISENGAGED
CLUTCH STILL ENGAGED
• CHECK FOR SHORT TO GROUND IN CKT 762.
• CHECK FOR SHORT TO VOLTAGE ON CKT 50.
• IF OK, REPLACE A/C CLUTCH RELAY.
REPAIR CLUTCH
WHEN ALL DIAGNOSIS AND REPAIRS ARE COMPLETED, CLEAR CODES AND VERIFY OPERATION

BLOWER CONTROL CIRCUIT
E BODY (EXCEPT ELDORADO)

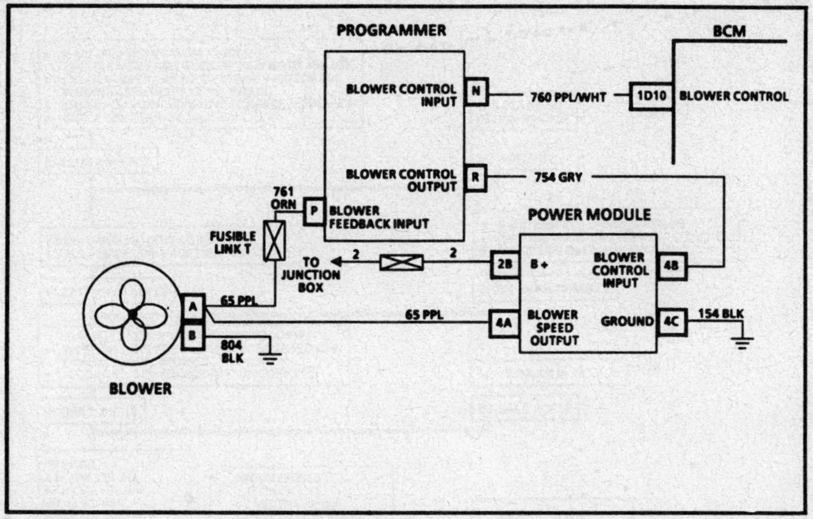
PROGRAMMER
BCM
BLOWER CONTROL INPUT
N
760 PPL/WHT
1D10
BLOWER CONTROL
BLOWER CONTROL OUTPUT
R
754 GRY
761 ORN
P
BLOWER FEEDBACK INPUT
POWER MODULE
FUSIBLE LINK T
TO JUNCTION BOX
2
2
2B
B+
BLOWER CONTROL INPUT
4B
A
65 PPL
65 PPL
4A
BLOWER SPEED OUTPUT
GROUND
4C
154 BLK
B
804 BLK
BLOWER

EEC SYSTEM DIAGNOSIS
E BODY, EXCEPT ELDORADO (CONT.)

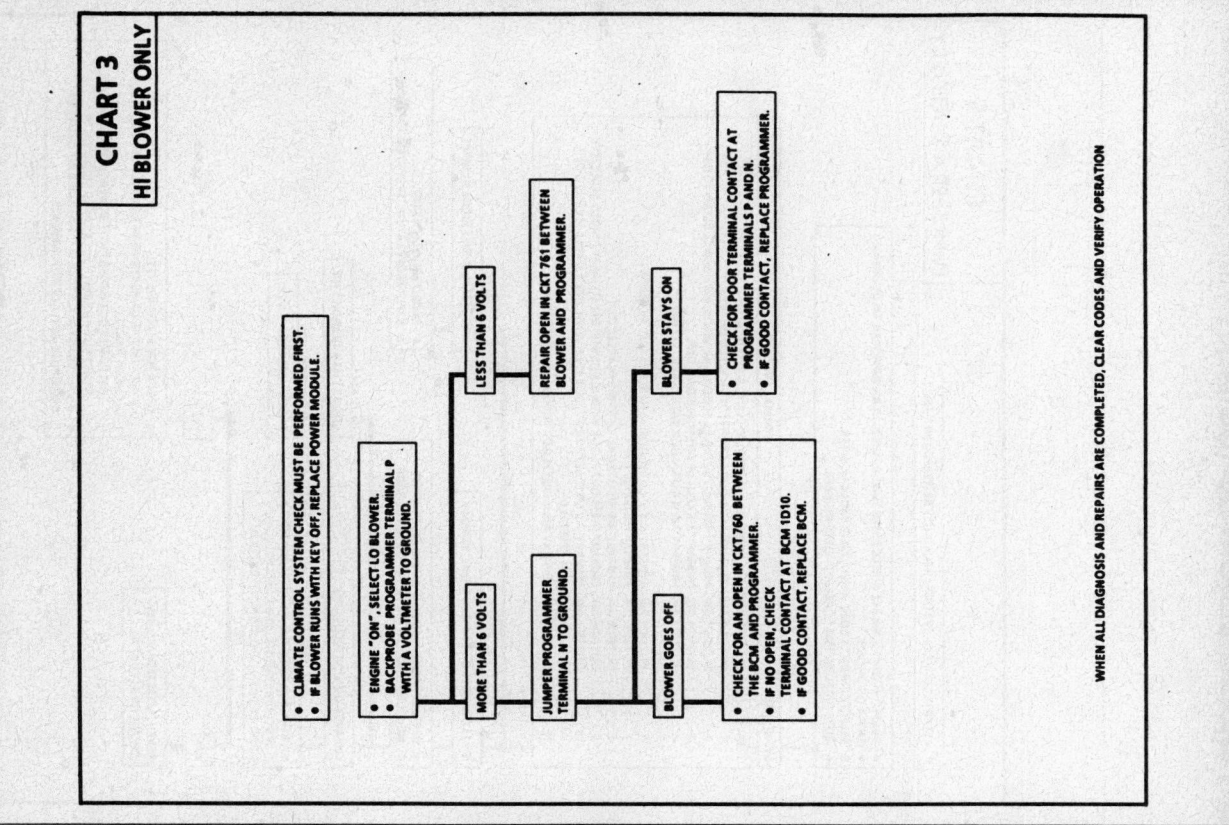

CHART 3
HI BLOWER ONLY

- CLIMATE CONTROL SYSTEM CHECK MUST BE PERFORMED FIRST.
- IF BLOWER RUNS WITH KEY OFF, REPLACE POWER MODULE.

- ENGINE "ON", SELECT LO BLOWER.
- BACKPROBE PROGRAMMER TERMINAL P WITH A VOLTMETER TO GROUND.

MORE THAN 6 VOLTS

JUMPER PROGRAMMER TERMINAL N TO GROUND.

BLOWER GOES OFF

- CHECK FOR AN OPEN IN CKT 760 BETWEEN THE BCM AND PROGRAMMER.
- IF NO OPEN, CHECK TERMINAL CONTACT AT BCM 1D10.
- IF GOOD CONTACT, REPLACE BCM.

BLOWER STAYS ON

- CHECK FOR POOR TERMINAL CONTACT AT PROGRAMMER TERMINALS P AND N.
- IF GOOD CONTACT, REPLACE PROGRAMMER.

LESS THAN 6 VOLTS

REPAIR OPEN IN CKT 761 BETWEEN BLOWER AND PROGRAMMER.

WHEN ALL DIAGNOSIS AND REPAIRS ARE COMPLETED, CLEAR CODES AND VERIFY OPERATION

EEC SYSTEM DIAGNOSIS – E BODY, EXCEPT ELDORADO (CONT.)

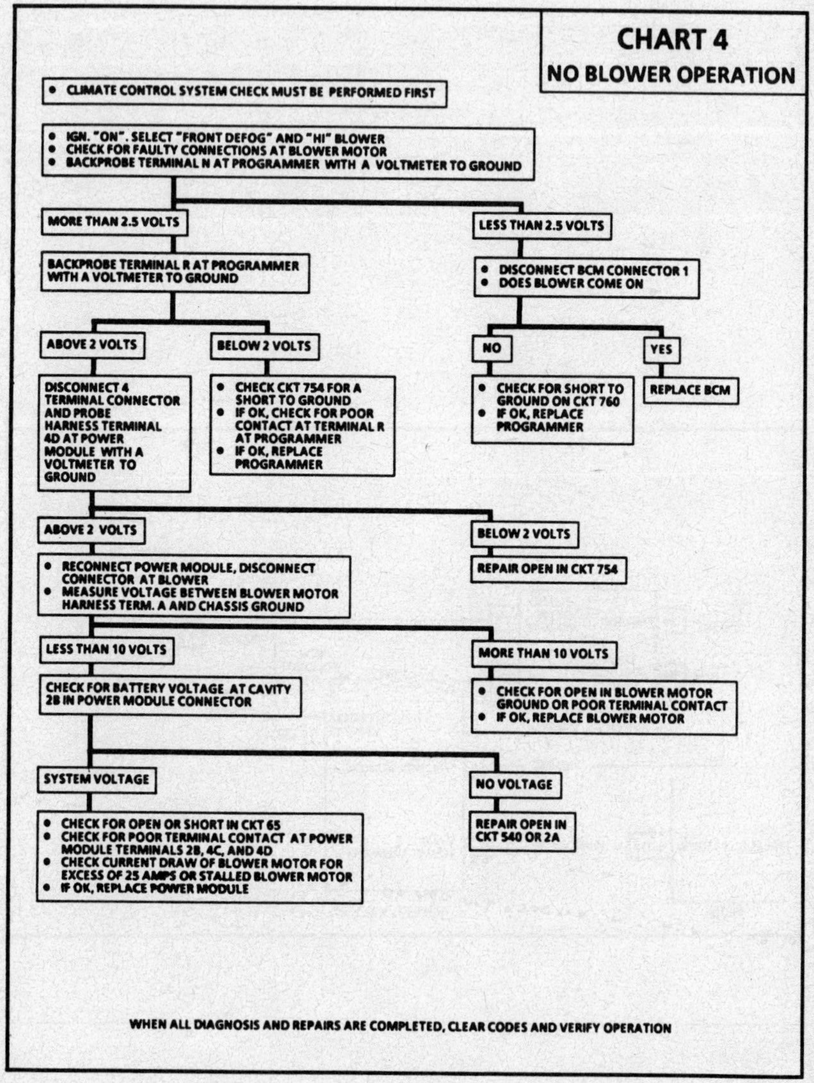
CHART 4
NO BLOWER OPERATION
• CLIMATE CONTROL SYSTEM CHECK MUST BE PERFORMED FIRST
• IGN. "ON". SELECT "FRONT DEFOG" AND "HI" BLOWER
• CHECK FOR FAULTY CONNECTIONS AT BLOWER MOTOR
• BACKPROBE TERMINAL N AT PROGRAMMER WITH A VOLTMETER TO GROUND
MORE THAN 2.5 VOLTS
LESS THAN 2.5 VOLTS
BACKPROBE TERMINAL R AT PROGRAMMER WITH A VOLTMETER TO GROUND
• DISCONNECT BCM CONNECTOR 1
• DOES BLOWER COME ON
ABOVE 2 VOLTS
BELOW 2 VOLTS
NO
YES
DISCONNECT 4 TERMINAL CONNECTOR AND PROBE HARNESS TERMINAL 4D AT POWER MODULE WITH A VOLTMETER TO GROUND
• CHECK CKT 754 FOR A SHORT TO GROUND
• IF OK, CHECK FOR POOR CONTACT AT TERMINAL R AT PROGRAMMER
• IF OK, REPLACE PROGRAMMER
• CHECK FOR SHORT TO GROUND ON CKT 760
• IF OK, REPLACE PROGRAMMER
REPLACE BCM
ABOVE 2 VOLTS
BELOW 2 VOLTS
• RECONNECT POWER MODULE, DISCONNECT CONNECTOR AT BLOWER
• MEASURE VOLTAGE BETWEEN BLOWER MOTOR HARNESS TERM. A AND CHASSIS GROUND
REPAIR OPEN IN CKT 754
LESS THAN 10 VOLTS
MORE THAN 10 VOLTS
CHECK FOR BATTERY VOLTAGE AT CAVITY 2B IN POWER MODULE CONNECTOR
• CHECK FOR OPEN IN BLOWER MOTOR GROUND OR POOR TERMINAL CONTACT
• IF OK, REPLACE BLOWER MOTOR
SYSTEM VOLTAGE
NO VOLTAGE
• CHECK FOR OPEN OR SHORT IN CKT 65
• CHECK FOR POOR TERMINAL CONTACT AT POWER MODULE TERMINALS 2B, 4C, AND 4D
• CHECK CURRENT DRAW OF BLOWER MOTOR FOR EXCESS OF 25 AMPS OR STALLED BLOWER MOTOR
• IF OK, REPLACE POWER MODULE
REPAIR OPEN IN CKT 540 OR 2A
WHEN ALL DIAGNOSIS AND REPAIRS ARE COMPLETED, CLEAR CODES AND VERIFY OPERATION

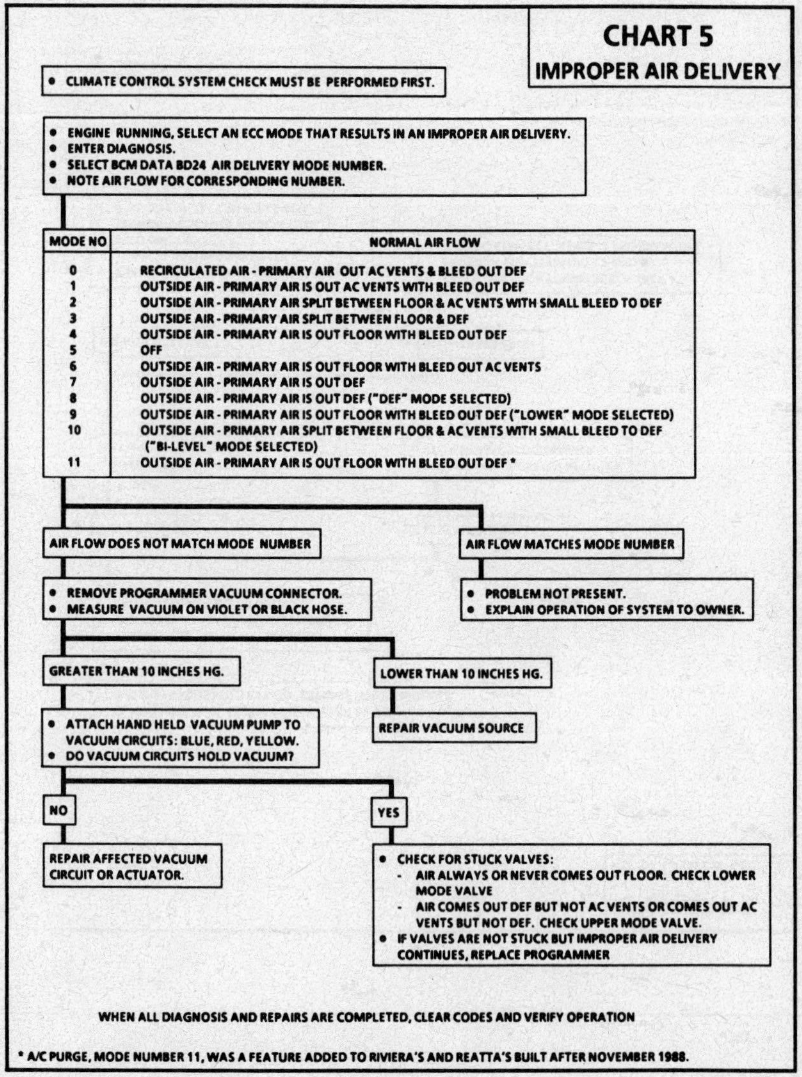
CHART 5
IMPROPER AIR DELIVERY
• CLIMATE CONTROL SYSTEM CHECK MUST BE PERFORMED FIRST.
• ENGINE RUNNING, SELECT AN ECC MODE THAT RESULTS IN AN IMPROPER AIR DELIVERY.
• ENTER DIAGNOSIS.
• SELECT BCM DATA BD24 AIR DELIVERY MODE NUMBER.
• NOTE AIR FLOW FOR CORRESPONDING NUMBER.
MODE NO
NORMAL AIR FLOW
0 RECIRCULATED AIR - PRIMARY AIR OUT AC VENTS & BLEED OUT DEF
1 OUTSIDE AIR - PRIMARY AIR IS OUT AC VENTS WITH BLEED OUT DEF
2 OUTSIDE AIR - PRIMARY AIR SPLIT BETWEEN FLOOR & AC VENTS WITH SMALL BLEED TO DEF
3 OUTSIDE AIR - PRIMARY AIR SPLIT BETWEEN FLOOR & DEF
4 OUTSIDE AIR - PRIMARY AIR IS OUT FLOOR WITH BLEED OUT DEF
5 OFF
6 OUTSIDE AIR - PRIMARY AIR IS OUT FLOOR WITH BLEED OUT AC VENTS
7 OUTSIDE AIR - PRIMARY AIR IS OUT DEF
8 OUTSIDE AIR - PRIMARY AIR IS OUT DEF ("DEF" MODE SELECTED)
9 OUTSIDE AIR - PRIMARY AIR IS OUT FLOOR WITH BLEED OUT DEF ("LOWER" MODE SELECTED)
10 OUTSIDE AIR - PRIMARY AIR SPLIT BETWEEN FLOOR & AC VENTS WITH SMALL BLEED TO DEF ("BI-LEVEL" MODE SELECTED)
11 OUTSIDE AIR - PRIMARY AIR IS OUT FLOOR WITH BLEED OUT DEF *
AIR FLOW DOES NOT MATCH MODE NUMBER
AIR FLOW MATCHES MODE NUMBER
• REMOVE PROGRAMMER VACUUM CONNECTOR.
• MEASURE VACUUM ON VIOLET OR BLACK HOSE.
• PROBLEM NOT PRESENT.
• EXPLAIN OPERATION OF SYSTEM TO OWNER.
GREATER THAN 10 INCHES HG.
LOWER THAN 10 INCHES HG.
• ATTACH HAND HELD VACUUM PUMP TO VACUUM CIRCUITS: BLUE, RED, YELLOW.
• DO VACUUM CIRCUITS HOLD VACUUM?
REPAIR VACUUM SOURCE
NO
YES
REPAIR AFFECTED VACUUM CIRCUIT OR ACTUATOR.
• CHECK FOR STUCK VALVES:
- AIR ALWAYS OR NEVER COMES OUT FLOOR. CHECK LOWER MODE VALVE
- AIR COMES OUT DEF BUT NOT AC VENTS OR COMES OUT AC VENTS BUT NOT DEF. CHECK UPPER MODE VALVE.
• IF VALVES ARE NOT STUCK BUT IMPROPER AIR DELIVERY CONTINUES, REPLACE PROGRAMMER
WHEN ALL DIAGNOSIS AND REPAIRS ARE COMPLETED, CLEAR CODES AND VERIFY OPERATION
* A/C PURGE, MODE NUMBER 11, WAS A FEATURE ADDED TO RIVIERA'S AND REATTA'S BUILT AFTER NOVEMBER 1988.

AIR MIX VALVE ADJUSTMENT
E BODY (EXCEPT ELDORADO)

AIR MIX VALVE ADJUSTMENT PROCEDURE

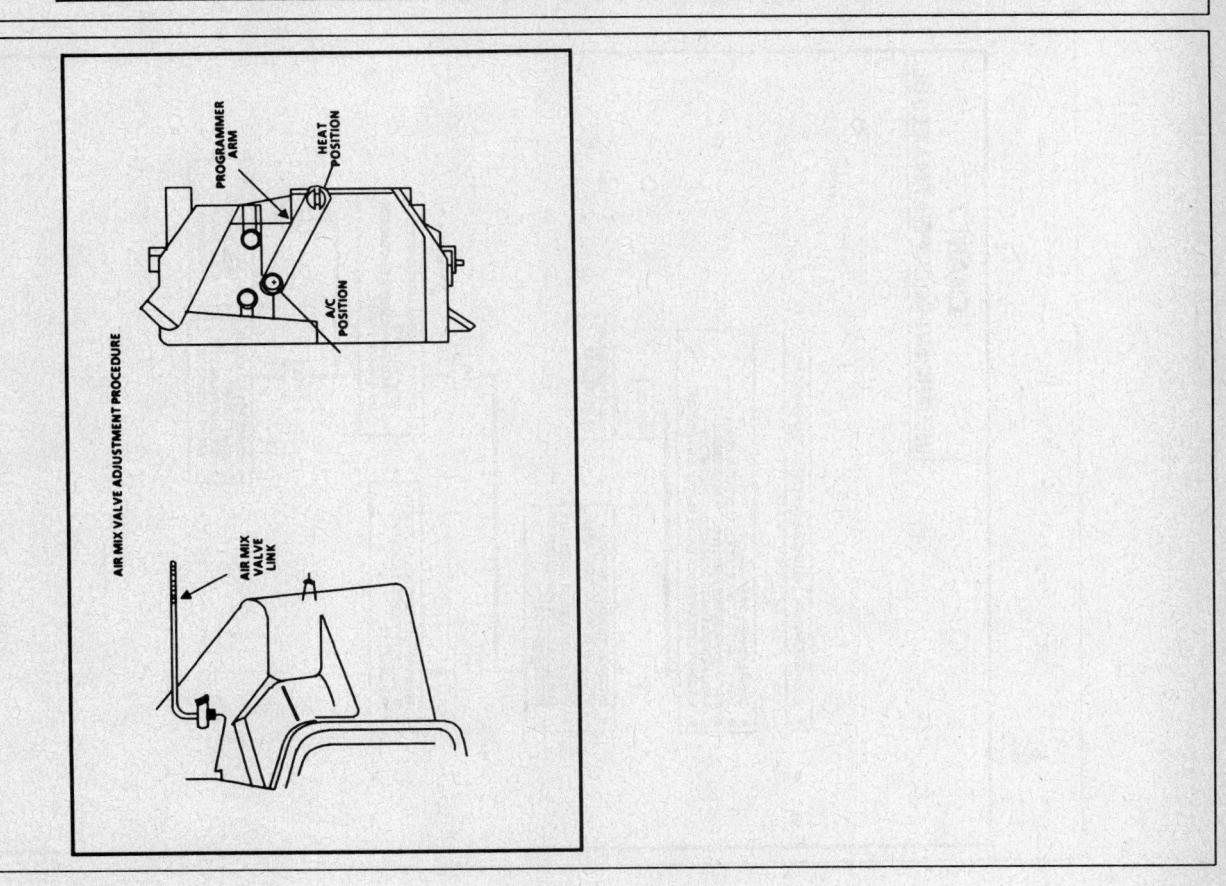

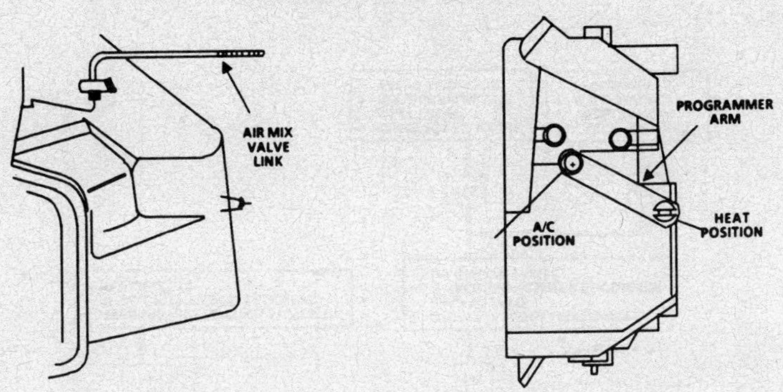
AIR MIX
VALVE
LINK
PROGRAMMER
ARM
A/C
POSITION
HEAT
POSITION

EEC SYSTEM DIAGNOSIS
E BODY, EXCEPT ELDORADO (CONT.)

CHART 6
INSUFFICIENT HEAT AT MAX HEAT

- CLIMATE CONTROL SYSTEM CHECK MUST BE PERFORMED FIRST.

- ENGINE RUNNING AND WARM. SELECT "AUTO" AND 90°F.
- VISUALLY CHECK AIR MIX VALVE.
- IS VALVE IN MAX HEAT POSITION ?

YES:
- TEMPERATURE CONTROL SYSTEM OK.
- IF INSUFFICIENT HEAT, CONDITION CONTINUES, CHECK COOLING SYSTEM

NO:
ADJUST OR REPAIR AS NECESSARY.

WHEN ALL DIAGNOSIS AND REPAIRS ARE COMPLETED, CLEAR CODES AND VERIFY OPERATION

EEC SYSTEM DIAGNOSIS—E BODY, EXCEPT ELDORADO (CONT.)

CHART 7
INSUFFICIENT COOLING AT MAX COOL

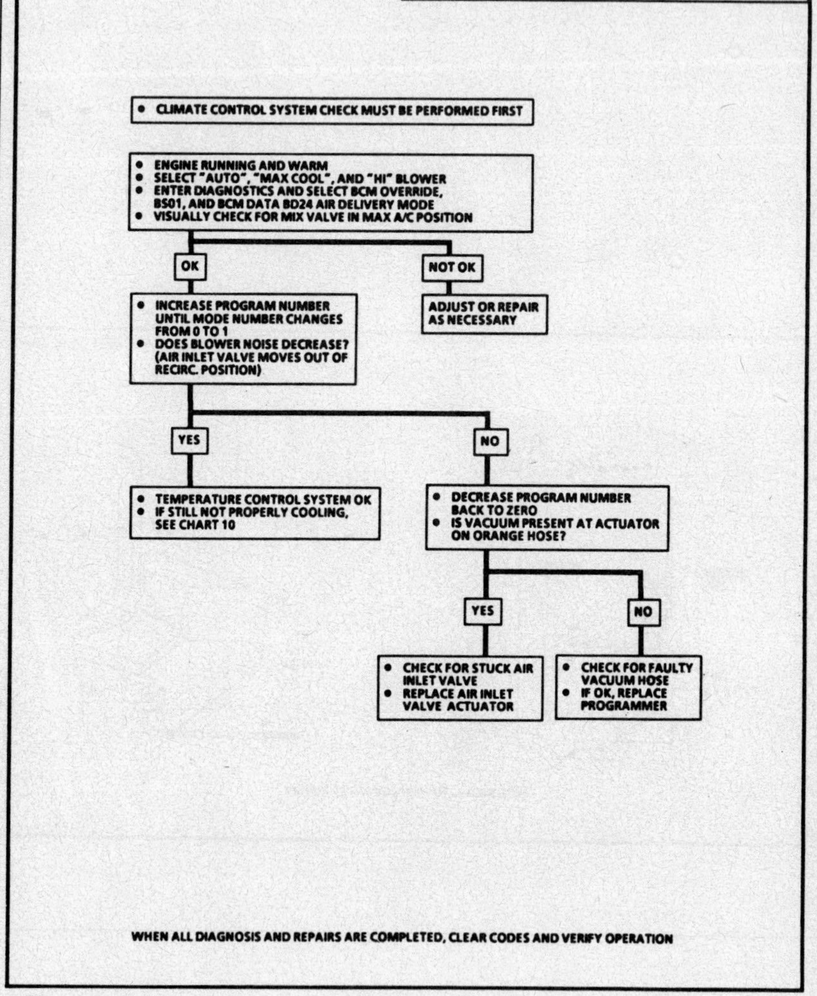
• CLIMATE CONTROL SYSTEM CHECK MUST BE PERFORMED FIRST
• ENGINE RUNNING AND WARM • SELECT "AUTO", "MAX COOL", AND "HI" BLOWER • ENTER DIAGNOSTICS AND SELECT BCM OVERRIDE, BS01, AND BCM DATA BD24 AIR DELIVERY MODE • VISUALLY CHECK FOR MIX VALVE IN MAX A/C POSITION
OK
NOT OK
ADJUST OR REPAIR AS NECESSARY
• INCREASE PROGRAM NUMBER UNTIL MODE NUMBER CHANGES FROM 0 TO 1 • DOES BLOWER NOISE DECREASE? (AIR INLET VALVE MOVES OUT OF RECIRC. POSITION)
YES
NO
• TEMPERATURE CONTROL SYSTEM OK • IF STILL NOT PROPERLY COOLING, SEE CHART 10
• DECREASE PROGRAM NUMBER BACK TO ZERO • IS VACUUM PRESENT AT ACTUATOR ON ORANGE HOSE?
YES
NO
• CHECK FOR STUCK AIR INLET VALVE • REPLACE AIR INLET VALVE ACTUATOR
• CHECK FOR FAULTY VACUUM HOSE • IF OK, REPLACE PROGRAMMER
WHEN ALL DIAGNOSIS AND REPAIRS ARE COMPLETED, CLEAR CODES AND VERIFY OPERATION

CHART 8
IMPROPER TEMPERATURE REGULATION

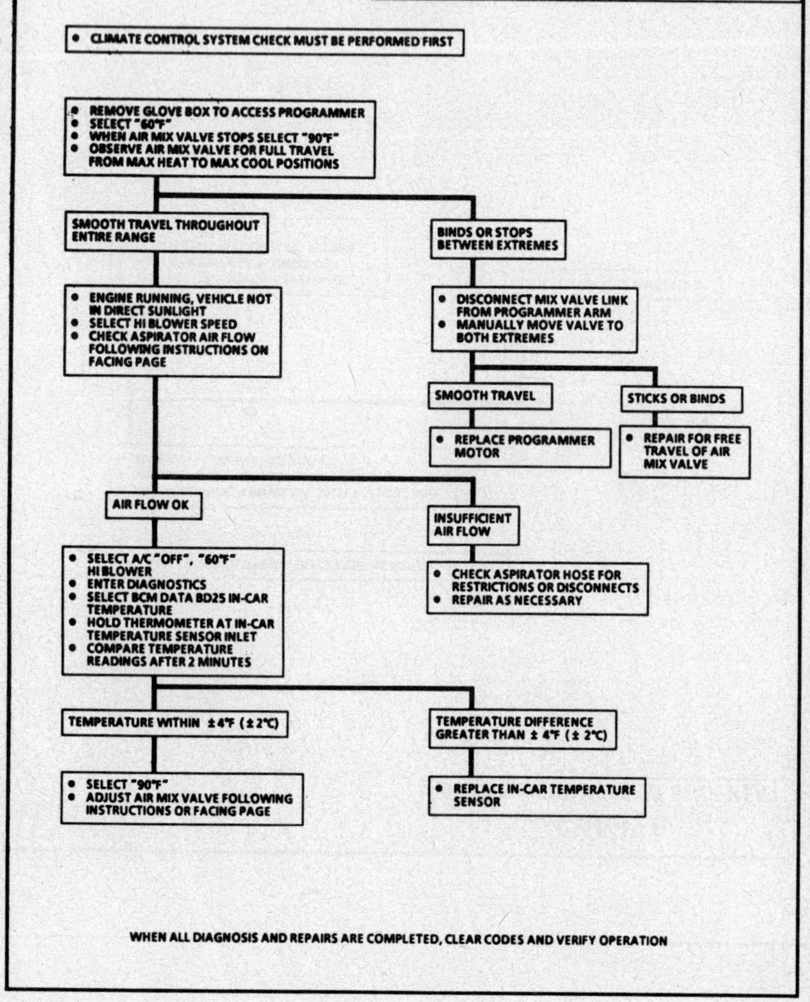
• CLIMATE CONTROL SYSTEM CHECK MUST BE PERFORMED FIRST
• REMOVE GLOVE BOX TO ACCESS PROGRAMMER • SELECT "60°F" • WHEN AIR MIX VALVE STOPS SELECT "90°F" • OBSERVE AIR MIX VALVE FOR FULL TRAVEL FROM MAX HEAT TO MAX COOL POSITIONS
SMOOTH TRAVEL THROUGHOUT ENTIRE RANGE
BINDS OR STOPS BETWEEN EXTREMES
• ENGINE RUNNING, VEHICLE NOT IN DIRECT SUNLIGHT • SELECT HI BLOWER SPEED • CHECK ASPIRATOR AIR FLOW FOLLOWING INSTRUCTIONS ON FACING PAGE
• DISCONNECT MIX VALVE LINK FROM PROGRAMMER ARM • MANUALLY MOVE VALVE TO BOTH EXTREMES
SMOOTH TRAVEL
STICKS OR BINDS
• REPLACE PROGRAMMER MOTOR
• REPAIR FOR FREE TRAVEL OF AIR MIX VALVE
AIR FLOW OK
INSUFFICIENT AIR FLOW
• SELECT A/C "OFF", "60°F" HI BLOWER • ENTER DIAGNOSTICS • SELECT BCM DATA BD25 IN-CAR TEMPERATURE • HOLD THERMOMETER AT IN-CAR TEMPERATURE SENSOR INLET • COMPARE TEMPERATURE READINGS AFTER 2 MINUTES
• CHECK ASPIRATOR HOSE FOR RESTRICTIONS OR DISCONNECTS • REPAIR AS NECESSARY
TEMPERATURE WITHIN ±4°F (±2°C)
TEMPERATURE DIFFERENCE GREATER THAN ± 4°F (± 2°C)
• SELECT "90°F" • ADJUST AIR MIX VALVE FOLLOWING INSTRUCTIONS OR FACING PAGE
• REPLACE IN-CAR TEMPERATURE SENSOR
WHEN ALL DIAGNOSIS AND REPAIRS ARE COMPLETED, CLEAR CODES AND VERIFY OPERATION

EEC SYSTEM DIAGNOSIS
E BODY, EXCEPT ELDORADO (CONT.)

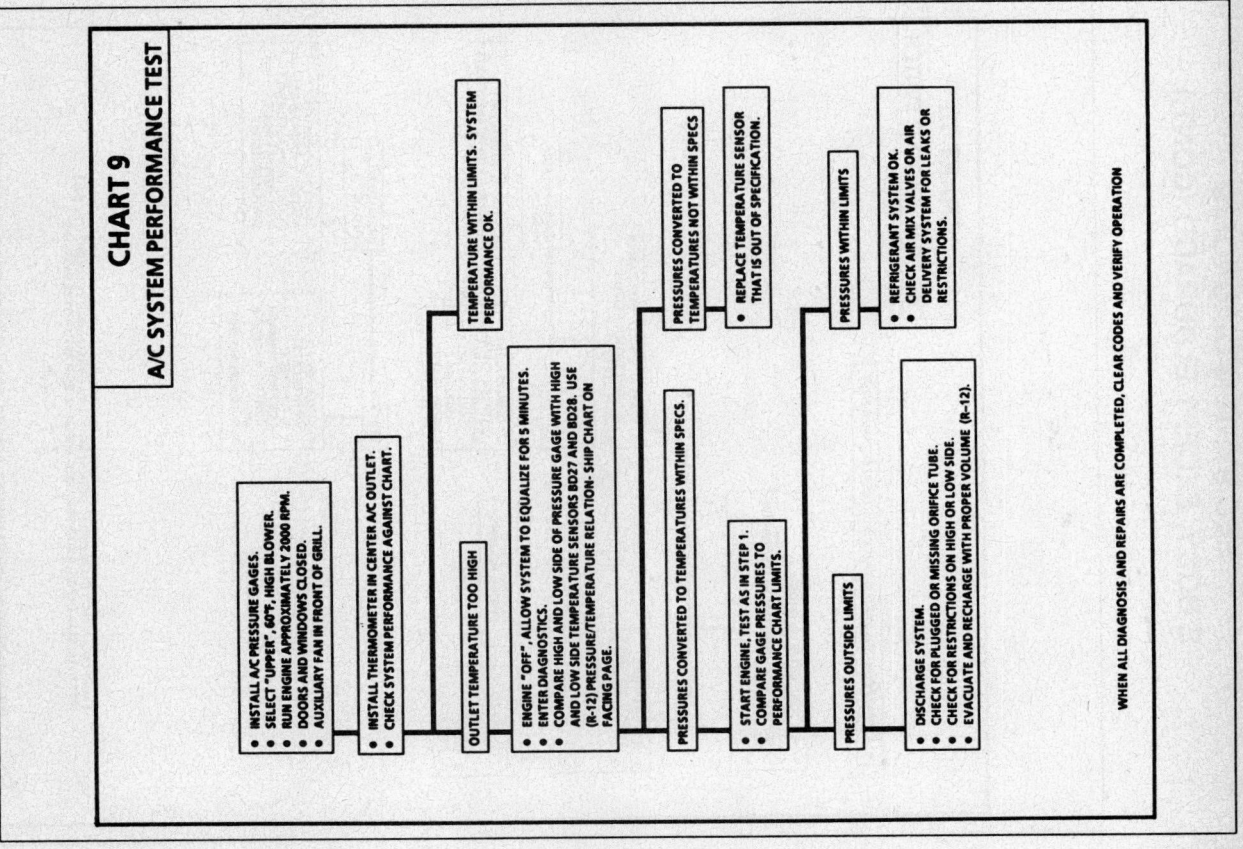

CHART 9
A/C SYSTEM PERFORMANCE TEST

- INSTALL A/C PRESSURE GAGES.
- SELECT "UPPER", 60°F, HIGH BLOWER.
- RUN ENGINE APPROXIMATELY 2000 RPM.
- DOORS AND WINDOWS CLOSED.
- AUXILIARY FAN IN FRONT OF GRILL.

- INSTALL THERMOMETER IN CENTER A/C OUTLET.
- CHECK SYSTEM PERFORMANCE AGAINST CHART.

OUTLET TEMPERATURE TOO HIGH

- ENGINE "OFF", ALLOW SYSTEM TO EQUALIZE FOR 5 MINUTES.
- ENTER DIAGNOSTICS.
- COMPARE HIGH AND LOW SIDE OF PRESSURE GAGE WITH HIGH AND LOW SIDE TEMPERATURE SENSORS BD27 AND BD28. USE (R-12) PRESSURE/TEMPERATURE RELATION- SHIP CHART ON FACING PAGE.

TEMPERATURE WITHIN LIMITS. SYSTEM PERFORMANCE OK.

PRESSURES CONVERTED TO TEMPERATURES WITHIN SPECS.

- START ENGINE, TEST AS IN STEP 1.
- COMPARE GAGE PRESSURES TO PERFORMANCE CHART LIMITS.

PRESSURES CONVERTED TO TEMPERATURES NOT WITHIN SPECS

- REPLACE TEMPERATURE SENSOR THAT IS OUT OF SPECIFICATION.

PRESSURES OUTSIDE LIMITS

- DISCHARGE SYSTEM.
- CHECK FOR PLUGGED OR MISSING ORIFICE TUBE.
- CHECK FOR RESTRICTIONS ON HIGH OR LOW SIDE.
- EVACUATE AND RECHARGE WITH PROPER VOLUME (R-12).

PRESSURES WITHIN LIMITS

- REFRIGERANT SYSTEM OK.
- CHECK AIR MIX VALVES OR AIR DELIVERY SYSTEM FOR LEAKS OR RESTRICTIONS.

WHEN ALL DIAGNOSIS AND REPAIRS ARE COMPLETED, CLEAR CODES AND VERIFY OPERATION

DEFROST SWITCH CIRCUIT
E BODY (EXCEPT ELDORADO)

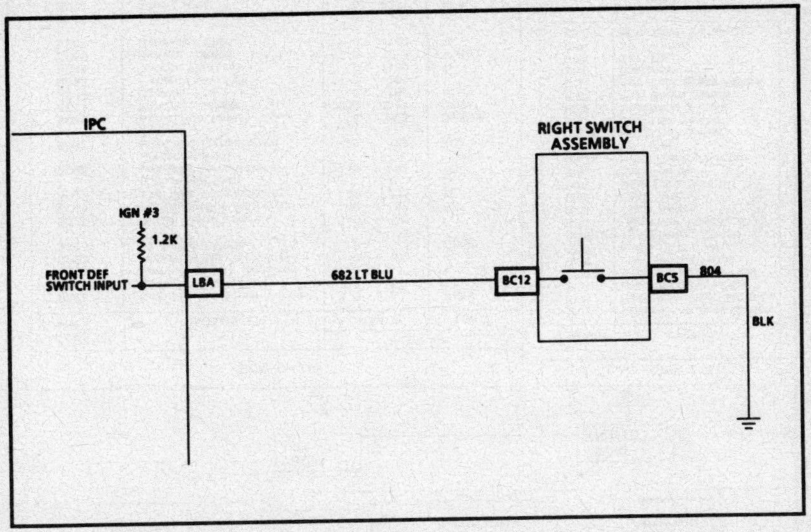
IPC
IGN #3
1.2K
FRONT DEF SWITCH INPUT
LBA
682 LT BLU
BC12
RIGHT SWITCH ASSEMBLY
BC5
804
BLK

EEC SYSTEM DIAGNOSIS
E BODY, EXCEPT ELDORADO (CONT.)

CHART 10
NO "DEF" FROM IP SWITCH

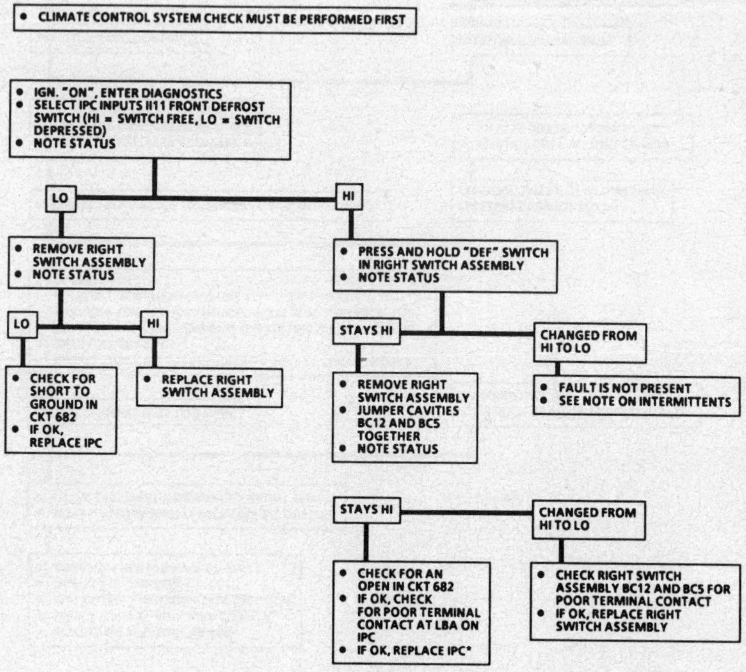
• CLIMATE CONTROL SYSTEM CHECK MUST BE PERFORMED FIRST
• IGN. "ON", ENTER DIAGNOSTICS
• SELECT IPC INPUTS II11 FRONT DEFROST SWITCH (HI = SWITCH FREE, LO = SWITCH DEPRESSED)
• NOTE STATUS
LO
HI
• REMOVE RIGHT SWITCH ASSEMBLY
• NOTE STATUS
LO
HI
• CHECK FOR SHORT TO GROUND IN CKT 682
• IF OK, REPLACE IPC
• REPLACE RIGHT SWITCH ASSEMBLY
• PRESS AND HOLD "DEF" SWITCH IN RIGHT SWITCH ASSEMBLY
• NOTE STATUS
STAYS HI
CHANGED FROM HI TO LO
• REMOVE RIGHT SWITCH ASSEMBLY
• JUMPER CAVITIES BC12 AND BC5 TOGETHER
• NOTE STATUS
• FAULT IS NOT PRESENT
• SEE NOTE ON INTERMITTENTS
STAYS HI
CHANGED FROM HI TO LO
• CHECK FOR AN OPEN IN CKT 682
• IF OK, CHECK FOR POOR TERMINAL CONTACT AT LBA ON IPC
• IF OK, REPLACE IPC*
• CHECK RIGHT SWITCH ASSEMBLY BC12 AND BC5 FOR POOR TERMINAL CONTACT
• IF OK, REPLACE RIGHT SWITCH ASSEMBLY

* FAULT COULD ALSO BE CAUSED BY OPEN IN RIGHT SWITCH ASSEMBLIES GROUND. (Ckt. 804) HOWEVER, REAR DEFOG. AND WINDSHIELD WIPERS WOULD ALSO NOT BE WORKING

WHEN ALL DIAGNOSIS AND REPAIRS ARE COMPLETED, CLEAR CODES AND VERIFY OPERATION

BCM ACCESS—EEC SYSTEMS WITH CONTROL HEAD DISPLAY

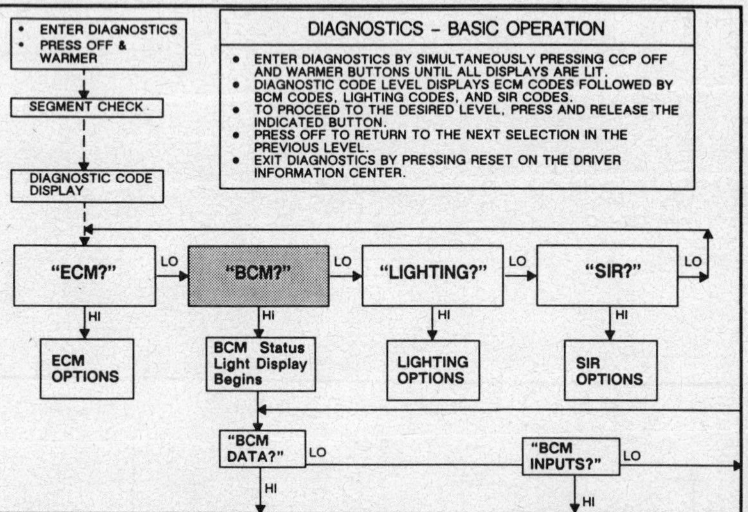
• ENTER DIAGNOSTICS
• PRESS OFF & WARMER
SEGMENT CHECK
DIAGNOSTIC CODE DISPLAY
"ECM?"
LO
"BCM?"
LO
"LIGHTING?"
LO
"SIR?"
LO
HI
ECM OPTIONS
BCM Status Light Display Begins
LIGHTING OPTIONS
SIR OPTIONS
"BCM DATA?"
LO
"BCM INPUTS?"
LO
HI

DIAGNOSTICS – BASIC OPERATION

- ENTER DIAGNOSTICS BY SIMULTANEOUSLY PRESSING CCP OFF AND WARMER BUTTONS UNTIL ALL DISPLAYS ARE LIT.
- DIAGNOSTIC CODE LEVEL DISPLAYS ECM CODES FOLLOWED BY BCM CODES, LIGHTING CODES, AND SIR CODES.
- TO PROCEED TO THE DESIRED LEVEL, PRESS AND RELEASE THE INDICATED BUTTON.
- PRESS OFF TO RETURN TO THE NEXT SELECTION IN THE PREVIOUS LEVEL.
- EXIT DIAGNOSTICS BY PRESSING RESET ON THE DRIVER INFORMATION CENTER.

BCM DATA

PARAMETER NUMBER	PARAMETER	DISPLAY RANGE	DISPLAY UNITS
BD20	Commanded Blower Voltage	-2.9 - 18.0	Volts
BD21	Coolant Temperature	-40 - 151	°C
BD22	Commanded Air Mix Door	0 - 100	%
BD23	Actual Air Mix Door Position	0 - 100	%
BD24	Air Delivery Mode	0 - 7	Code
BD25	In-Car Temperature	-40 - 102	°C
BD26	Actual Outside Air Temp	-40 - 93	°C
BD27	High Side Temperature - (Condenser Out)	-40 - 215	°C
BD28	Low Side Temperature - (Evaporator In)	-40 - 93	°C
BD32	Sun Load Temperature	-40 - 102	°C
BD40	Actual Fuel Level	0 - 25.5	Gallons
BD41	PRND321 Sensor	0000 - 1111	Code
BD42	Dimming Pot	0 - 100	%
BD43	Twilight Delay Pot	0 - 100	%
BD44	Twilight Photocell	0 - 100	%
BD50	Battery Voltage	0 - 16.3	Volts
BD51	Generator Field	0 - 100	%
BD60	Car Speed	0 - 159	MPH
BD61	Engine RPM	0 - 6375	RPM
BD71	Oil Pressure	0 - 85.0	PSI
BD98	Ignition Cycle Counter	0 - 99	Key Cycles
BD99	BCM PROM ID	0 - 9999	Code ●

● *PROM ID Code Number Identifies An Individual Calibration And Is Periodically Updated; Refer To Latest Service Publication For Correct ID Number.*

BCM INPUTS ▼

INPUT NUMBER	INPUT
BI03	Driver Door Jamb Switch
BI04	Passenger Door Jamb Sw
BI08	Low Refrig Press Sw
BI09	Washer Fluid Level Sw
BI10	Low Coolant Level
BI21	Brake Fluid Level
BI30	Time/Temp. Switch
BI51	Generator Feedback
BI55	Trunk Switch
BI60	Theft Alarm
BI61	Door Lock Switch
BI62	Soft Top Up
BI63	Hard Top Connected
BI64	Oil Level
BI90	Right Turn Switch
BI91	Left Turn Switch
BI92	Headlamp Switch
BI93	High Beam Switch
BI94	Anti-Lock Brake Failure
BI95	Brake Switch
BI96	SDD Fault
BI97	TCS Active
BI98	Mini-Spare Installed

KEY

To Select Another Test Within A Particular Test Type Press:
Hi - To Increment
Lo - To Decrement

▼ *"HI" = High Signal Voltage*
▼ *"LO" = Low Signal Voltage*
▼ *"O" = Input Same Since Displayed*
▼ *"X" = Input Changed Since Displayed*

BCM ACCESS—EEC SYSTEMS WITH CONTROL HEAD DISPLAY

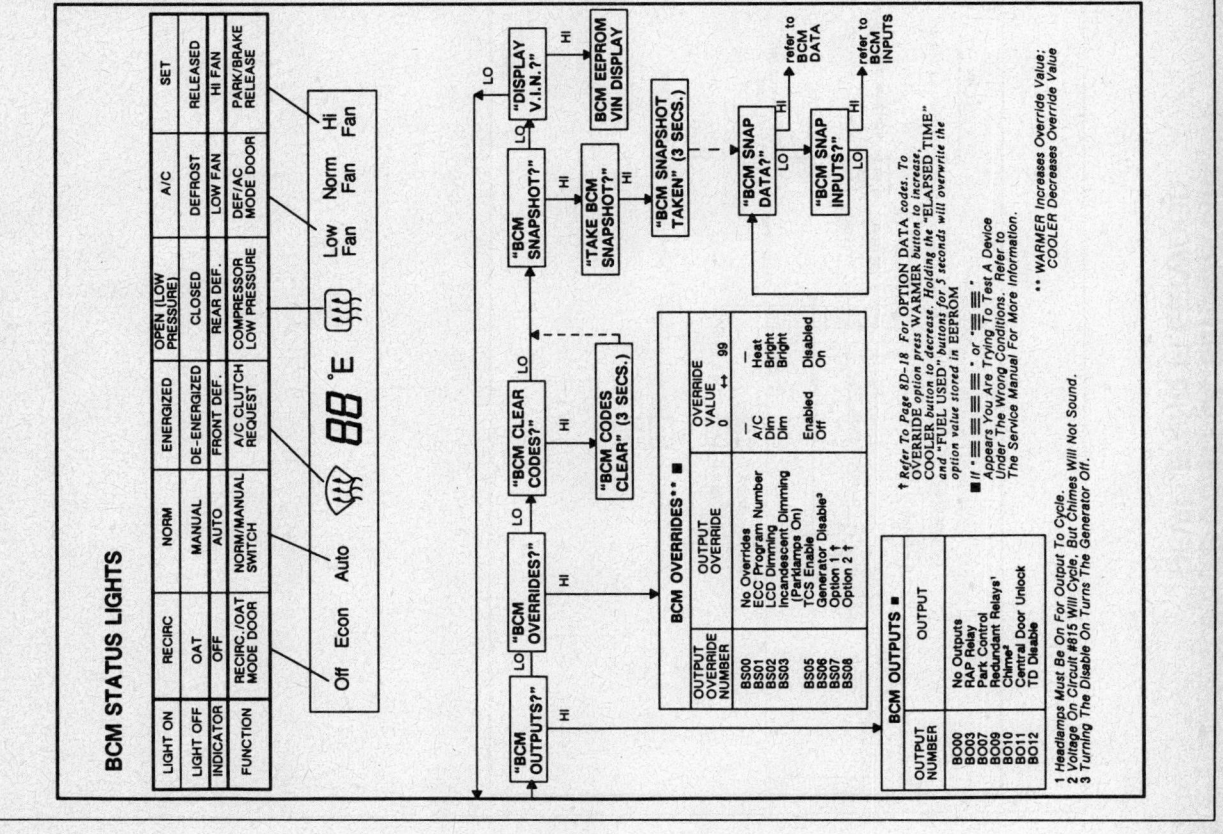

BCM STATUS LIGHTS

LIGHT ON	RECIRC	NORM	ENERGIZED	OPEN (LOW PRESSURE)	A/C	SET
LIGHT OFF	OAT	MANUAL	DE-ENERGIZED	CLOSED	DEFROST	RELEASED
INDICATOR	OFF	AUTO	FRONT DEF.	REAR DEF.	LOW FAN	HI FAN
FUNCTION	RECIRC./OAT MODE DOOR	NORM/MANUAL SWITCH	A/C CLUTCH REQUEST	COMPRESSOR LOW PRESSURE	DEF/AC MODE DOOR	PARK/BRAKE RELEASE

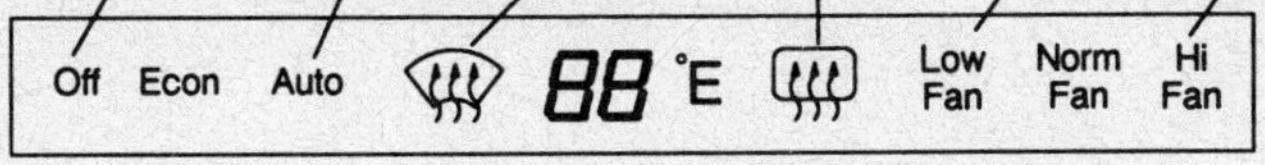
Off
Econ
Auto
88 °E
Low Fan
Norm Fan
Hi Fan

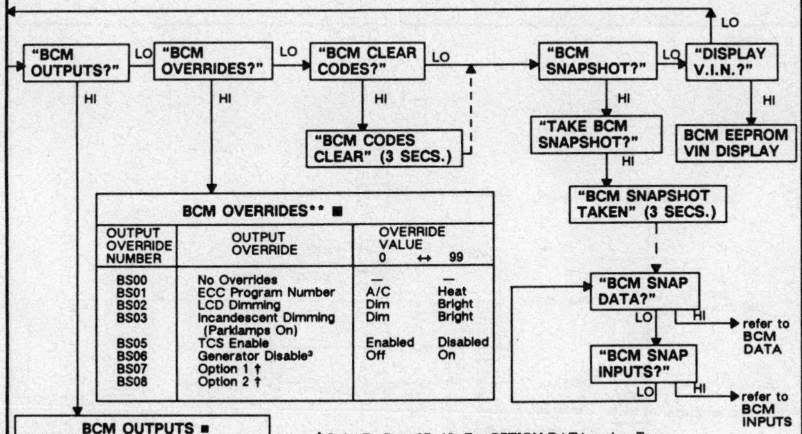
"BCM OUTPUTS?"
LO
"BCM OVERRIDES?"
LO
"BCM CLEAR CODES?"
LO
"BCM SNAPSHOT?"
LO
"DISPLAY V.I.N.?"
LO
HI
"BCM CODES CLEAR" (3 SECS.)
"TAKE BCM SNAPSHOT?"
"BCM SNAPSHOT TAKEN" (3 SECS.)
BCM EEPROM VIN DISPLAY
"BCM SNAP DATA?"
"BCM SNAP INPUTS?"
refer to BCM DATA
refer to BCM INPUTS

BCM OVERRIDES ■**

OUTPUT OVERRIDE NUMBER	OUTPUT OVERRIDE	OVERRIDE VALUE 0	↔ 99
BS00	No Overrides	—	—
BS01	ECC Program Number	A/C	Heat
BS02	LCD Dimming	Dim	Bright
BS03	Incandescent Dimming (Parklamps On)	Dim	Bright
BS05	TCS Enable	Enabled	Disabled
BS06	Generator Disable[3]	Off	On
BS07	Option 1 †		
BS08	Option 2 †		

BCM OUTPUTS ■

OUTPUT NUMBER	OUTPUT
BO00	No Outputs
BO03	RAP Relay
BO07	Park Control
BO09	Redundant Relays[1]
BO10	Chime[2]
BO11	Central Door Unlock
BO12	TD Disable

† *Refer To Page 8D-18 For OPTION DATA codes. To OVERRIDE option press WARMER button to increase, COOLER button to decrease. Holding the "ELAPSED TIME" and "FUEL USED" buttons for 5 seconds will overwrite the option value stored in EEPROM*

■ *If "☰☰☰☰" or "☰☰" Appears You Are Trying To Test A Device Under The Wrong Conditions. Refer to The Service Manual For More Information.*

** *WARMER Increases Override Value; COOLER Decreases Override Value*

1 *Headlamps Must Be On For Output To Cycle.*
2 *Voltage On Circuit #815 Will Cycle, But Chimes Will Not Sound.*
3 *Turning The Disable On Turns The Generator Off.*

BCM DIAGNOSTIC CHARTS FLEETWOOD AND DEVILLE

CODE F10
OUTSIDE AIR TEMPERATURE SENSOR CIRCUIT PROBLEM

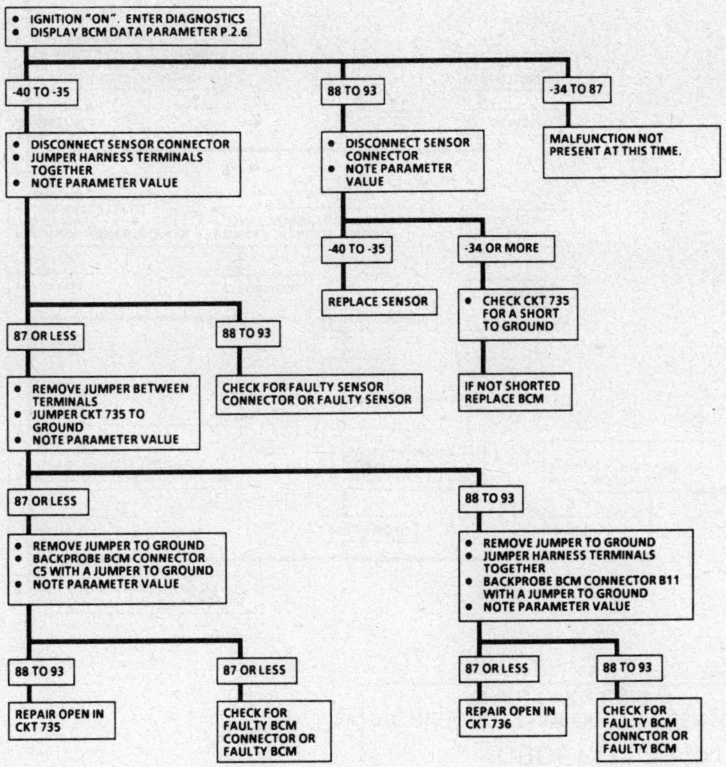
• IGNITION "ON". ENTER DIAGNOSTICS
• DISPLAY BCM DATA PARAMETER P.2.6
-40 TO -35
88 TO 93
-34 TO 87
• DISCONNECT SENSOR CONNECTOR
• JUMPER HARNESS TERMINALS TOGETHER
• NOTE PARAMETER VALUE
• DISCONNECT SENSOR CONNECTOR
• NOTE PARAMETER VALUE
MALFUNCTION NOT PRESENT AT THIS TIME.
-40 TO -35
-34 OR MORE
REPLACE SENSOR
• CHECK CKT 735 FOR A SHORT TO GROUND
IF NOT SHORTED REPLACE BCM
87 OR LESS
88 TO 93
CHECK FOR FAULTY SENSOR CONNECTOR OR FAULTY SENSOR
• REMOVE JUMPER BETWEEN TERMINALS
• JUMPER CKT 735 TO GROUND
• NOTE PARAMETER VALUE
87 OR LESS
88 TO 93
• REMOVE JUMPER TO GROUND
• BACKPROBE BCM CONNECTOR C5 WITH A JUMPER TO GROUND
• NOTE PARAMETER VALUE
• REMOVE JUMPER TO GROUND
• JUMPER HARNESS TERMINALS TOGETHER
• BACKPROBE BCM CONNECTOR B11 WITH A JUMPER TO GROUND
• NOTE PARAMETER VALUE
88 TO 93
87 OR LESS
87 OR LESS
88 TO 93
REPAIR OPEN IN CKT 735
CHECK FOR FAULTY BCM CONNECTOR OR FAULTY BCM
REPAIR OPEN IN CKT 736
CHECK FOR FAULTY BCM CONNCTOR OR FAULTY BCM

CLIMATE CONTROL SENSOR CIRCUIT DEVILLE AND FLEETWOOD

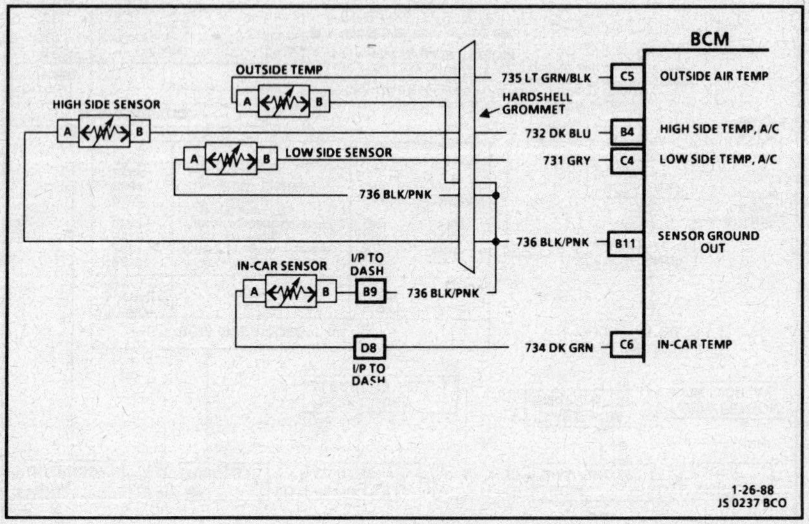
BCM
OUTSIDE TEMP
HIGH SIDE SENSOR
LOW SIDE SENSOR
IN-CAR SENSOR
A
B
HARDSHELL GROMMET
735 LT GRN/BLK
732 DK BLU
731 GRY
736 BLK/PNK
734 DK GRN
C5
B4
C4
B11
C6
B9
D8
I/P TO DASH
OUTSIDE AIR TEMP
HIGH SIDE TEMP, A/C
LOW SIDE TEMP, A/C
SENSOR GROUND OUT
IN-CAR TEMP
1-26-88
JS 0237 BCO

BCM DIAGNOSTIC CHARTS FLEETWOOD AND DEVILLE (CONT.)

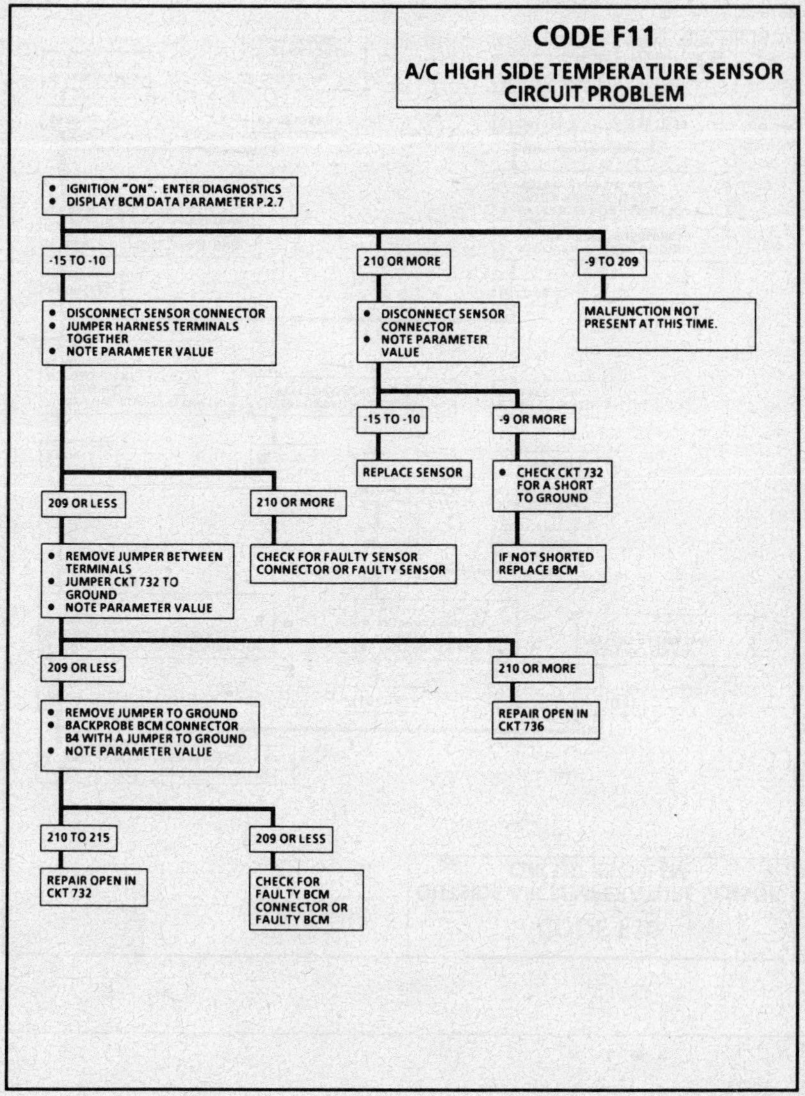
CODE F11
A/C HIGH SIDE TEMPERATURE SENSOR CIRCUIT PROBLEM
• IGNITION "ON". ENTER DIAGNOSTICS
• DISPLAY BCM DATA PARAMETER P.2.7
-15 TO -10
210 OR MORE
-9 TO 209
• DISCONNECT SENSOR CONNECTOR
• JUMPER HARNESS TERMINALS TOGETHER
• NOTE PARAMETER VALUE
• DISCONNECT SENSOR CONNECTOR
• NOTE PARAMETER VALUE
MALFUNCTION NOT PRESENT AT THIS TIME.
-15 TO -10
-9 OR MORE
REPLACE SENSOR
• CHECK CKT 732 FOR A SHORT TO GROUND
IF NOT SHORTED REPLACE BCM
209 OR LESS
210 OR MORE
• REMOVE JUMPER BETWEEN TERMINALS
• JUMPER CKT 732 TO GROUND
• NOTE PARAMETER VALUE
CHECK FOR FAULTY SENSOR CONNECTOR OR FAULTY SENSOR
209 OR LESS
210 OR MORE
• REMOVE JUMPER TO GROUND
• BACKPROBE BCM CONNECTOR B4 WITH A JUMPER TO GROUND
• NOTE PARAMETER VALUE
REPAIR OPEN IN CKT 736
210 TO 215
209 OR LESS
REPAIR OPEN IN CKT 732
CHECK FOR FAULTY BCM CONNECTOR OR FAULTY BCM

BCM DIAGNOSTIC CHARTS – FLEETWOOD AND DEVILLE (CONT.)

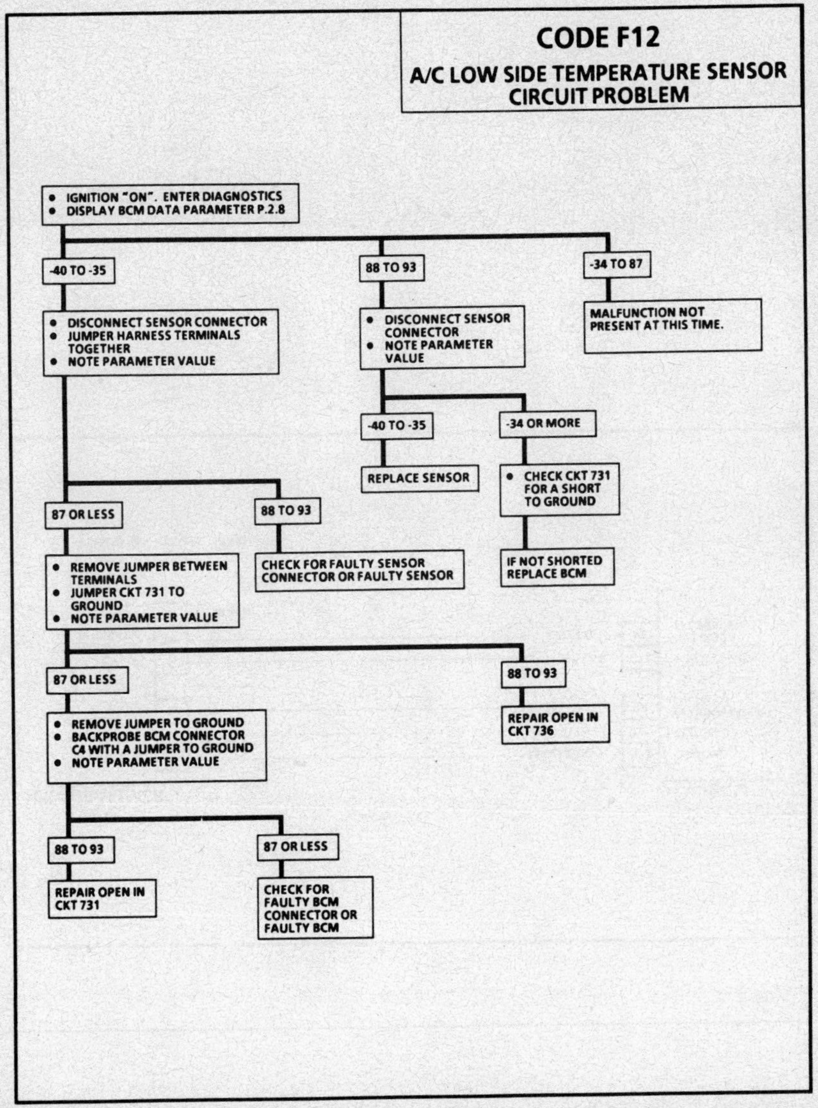
CODE F12
A/C LOW SIDE TEMPERATURE SENSOR CIRCUIT PROBLEM
• IGNITION "ON". ENTER DIAGNOSTICS • DISPLAY BCM DATA PARAMETER P.2.8
-40 TO -35
88 TO 93
-34 TO 87
MALFUNCTION NOT PRESENT AT THIS TIME.
• DISCONNECT SENSOR CONNECTOR • JUMPER HARNESS TERMINALS TOGETHER • NOTE PARAMETER VALUE
• DISCONNECT SENSOR CONNECTOR • NOTE PARAMETER VALUE
-40 TO -35
-34 OR MORE
REPLACE SENSOR
• CHECK CKT 731 FOR A SHORT TO GROUND
IF NOT SHORTED REPLACE BCM
87 OR LESS
88 TO 93
CHECK FOR FAULTY SENSOR CONNECTOR OR FAULTY SENSOR
• REMOVE JUMPER BETWEEN TERMINALS • JUMPER CKT 731 TO GROUND • NOTE PARAMETER VALUE
87 OR LESS
88 TO 93
REPAIR OPEN IN CKT 736
• REMOVE JUMPER TO GROUND • BACKPROBE BCM CONNECTOR C4 WITH A JUMPER TO GROUND • NOTE PARAMETER VALUE
88 TO 93
87 OR LESS
REPAIR OPEN IN CKT 731
CHECK FOR FAULTY BCM CONNECTOR OR FAULTY BCM

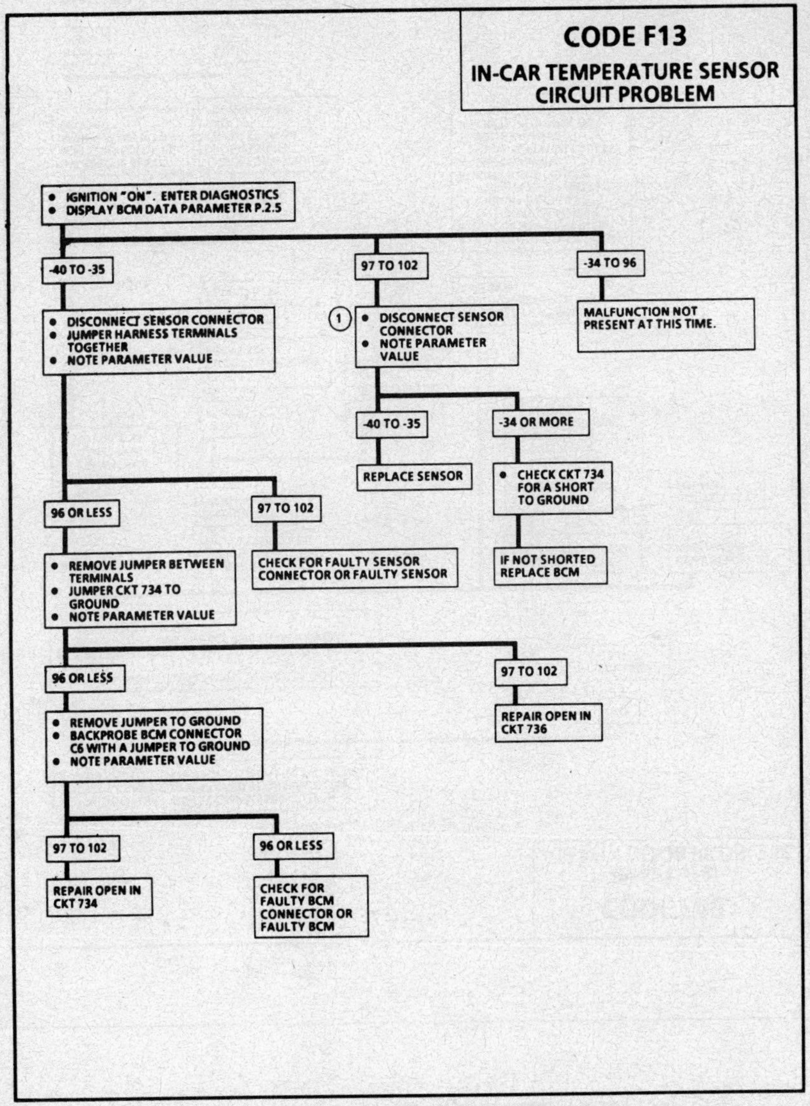
CODE F13
IN-CAR TEMPERATURE SENSOR CIRCUIT PROBLEM
• IGNITION "ON". ENTER DIAGNOSTICS • DISPLAY BCM DATA PARAMETER P.2.5
-40 TO -35
97 TO 102
-34 TO 96
MALFUNCTION NOT PRESENT AT THIS TIME.
• DISCONNECT SENSOR CONNECTOR • JUMPER HARNESS TERMINALS TOGETHER • NOTE PARAMETER VALUE
1
• DISCONNECT SENSOR CONNECTOR • NOTE PARAMETER VALUE
-40 TO -35
-34 OR MORE
REPLACE SENSOR
• CHECK CKT 734 FOR A SHORT TO GROUND
IF NOT SHORTED REPLACE BCM
96 OR LESS
97 TO 102
CHECK FOR FAULTY SENSOR CONNECTOR OR FAULTY SENSOR
• REMOVE JUMPER BETWEEN TERMINALS • JUMPER CKT 734 TO GROUND • NOTE PARAMETER VALUE
96 OR LESS
97 TO 102
REPAIR OPEN IN CKT 736
• REMOVE JUMPER TO GROUND • BACKPROBE BCM CONNECTOR C6 WITH A JUMPER TO GROUND • NOTE PARAMETER VALUE
97 TO 102
96 OR LESS
REPAIR OPEN IN CKT 734
CHECK FOR FAULTY BCM CONNECTOR OR FAULTY BCM

PROGRAMMER ELECTRICAL CIRCUIT DEVILLE AND FLEETWOOD

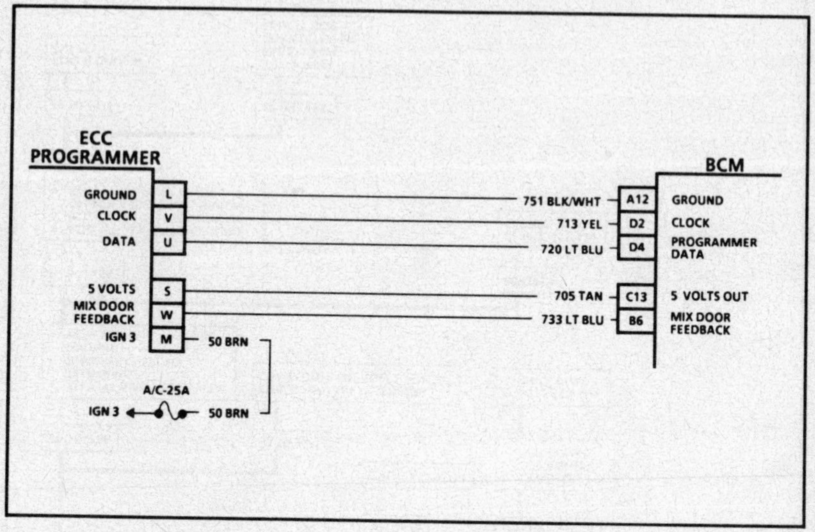
ECC PROGRAMMER
GROUND L
CLOCK V
DATA U
5 VOLTS S
MIX DOOR FEEDBACK W
IGN 3 M
751 BLK/WHT
713 YEL
720 LT BLU
705 TAN
733 LT BLU
50 BRN
A/C-25A
IGN 3
50 BRN
BCM
A12 GROUND
D2 CLOCK
D4 PROGRAMMER DATA
C13 5 VOLTS OUT
B6 MIX DOOR FEEDBACK

BCM DIAGNOSTIC CHARTS FLEETWOOD AND DEVILLE (CONT.)

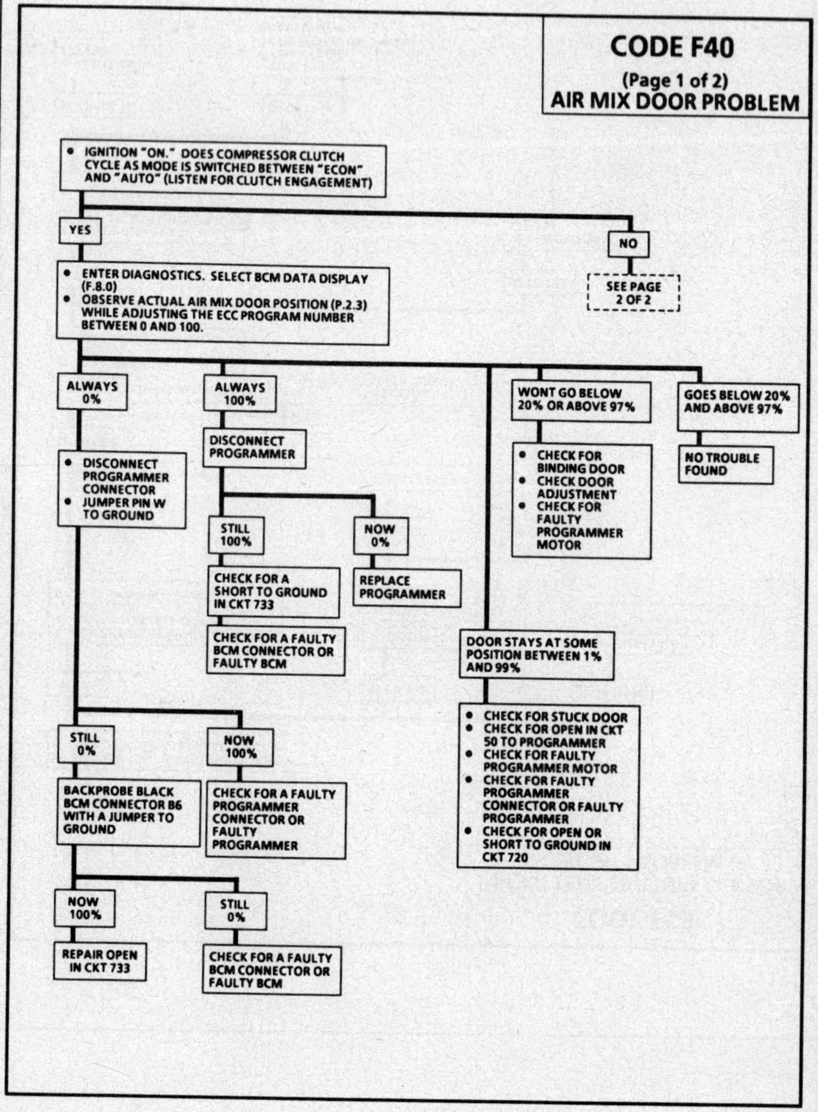
CODE F40
(Page 1 of 2)
AIR MIX DOOR PROBLEM
• IGNITION "ON." DOES COMPRESSOR CLUTCH CYCLE AS MODE IS SWITCHED BETWEEN "ECON" AND "AUTO" (LISTEN FOR CLUTCH ENGAGEMENT)
YES
NO
SEE PAGE 2 OF 2
• ENTER DIAGNOSTICS. SELECT BCM DATA DISPLAY (F.8.0)
• OBSERVE ACTUAL AIR MIX DOOR POSITION (P.2.3) WHILE ADJUSTING THE ECC PROGRAM NUMBER BETWEEN 0 AND 100.
ALWAYS 0%
ALWAYS 100%
WONT GO BELOW 20% OR ABOVE 97%
GOES BELOW 20% AND ABOVE 97%
• DISCONNECT PROGRAMMER CONNECTOR
• JUMPER PIN W TO GROUND
DISCONNECT PROGRAMMER
• CHECK FOR BINDING DOOR
• CHECK DOOR ADJUSTMENT
• CHECK FOR FAULTY PROGRAMMER MOTOR
NO TROUBLE FOUND
STILL 100%
NOW 0%
CHECK FOR A SHORT TO GROUND IN CKT 733
REPLACE PROGRAMMER
CHECK FOR A FAULTY BCM CONNECTOR OR FAULTY BCM
DOOR STAYS AT SOME POSITION BETWEEN 1% AND 99%
• CHECK FOR STUCK DOOR
• CHECK FOR OPEN IN CKT 50 TO PROGRAMMER
• CHECK FOR FAULTY PROGRAMMER MOTOR
• CHECK FOR FAULTY PROGRAMMER CONNECTOR OR FAULTY PROGRAMMER
• CHECK FOR OPEN OR SHORT TO GROUND IN CKT 720
STILL 0%
NOW 100%
BACKPROBE BLACK BCM CONNECTOR B6 WITH A JUMPER TO GROUND
CHECK FOR A FAULTY PROGRAMMER CONNECTOR OR FAULTY PROGRAMMER
NOW 100%
STILL 0%
REPAIR OPEN IN CKT 733
CHECK FOR A FAULTY BCM CONNECTOR OR FAULTY BCM

CODE F40
(Page 2 of 2)
AIR MIX DOOR PROBLEM

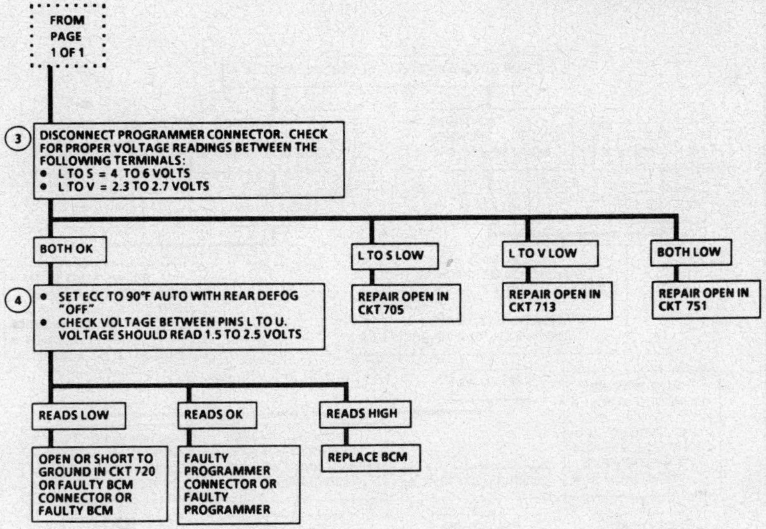
FROM PAGE 1 OF 1
3
DISCONNECT PROGRAMMER CONNECTOR. CHECK FOR PROPER VOLTAGE READINGS BETWEEN THE FOLLOWING TERMINALS:
• L TO S = 4 TO 6 VOLTS
• L TO V = 2.3 TO 2.7 VOLTS
BOTH OK
L TO S LOW
L TO V LOW
BOTH LOW
REPAIR OPEN IN CKT 705
REPAIR OPEN IN CKT 713
REPAIR OPEN IN CKT 751
4
• SET ECC TO 90°F AUTO WITH REAR DEFOG "OFF"
• CHECK VOLTAGE BETWEEN PINS L TO U. VOLTAGE SHOULD READ 1.5 TO 2.5 VOLTS
READS LOW
READS OK
READS HIGH
OPEN OR SHORT TO GROUND IN CKT 720 OR FAULTY BCM CONNECTOR OR FAULTY BCM
FAULTY PROGRAMMER CONNECTOR OR FAULTY PROGRAMMER
REPLACE BCM

LOW PRESSURE ELECTRICAL CIRCUIT DEVILLE AND FLEETWOOD

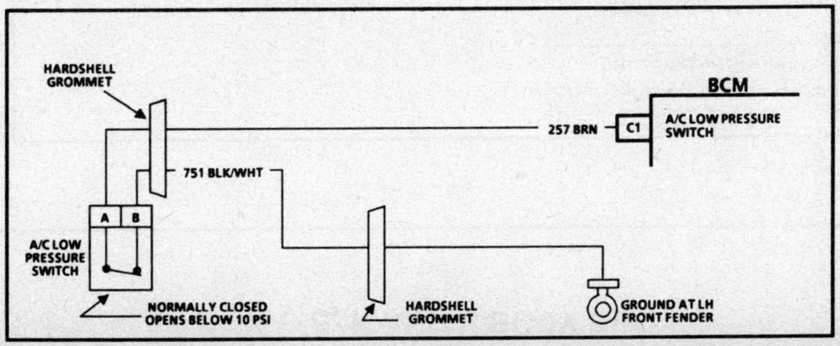
HARDSHELL GROMMET
BCM
257 BRN
C1
A/C LOW PRESSURE SWITCH
751 BLK/WHT
A
B
A/C LOW PRESSURE SWITCH
NORMALLY CLOSED OPENS BELOW 10 PSI
HARDSHELL GROMMET
GROUND AT LH FRONT FENDER

CODES F46, F47, AND/OR F48
REFRIGERANT SYSTEM PROBLEM

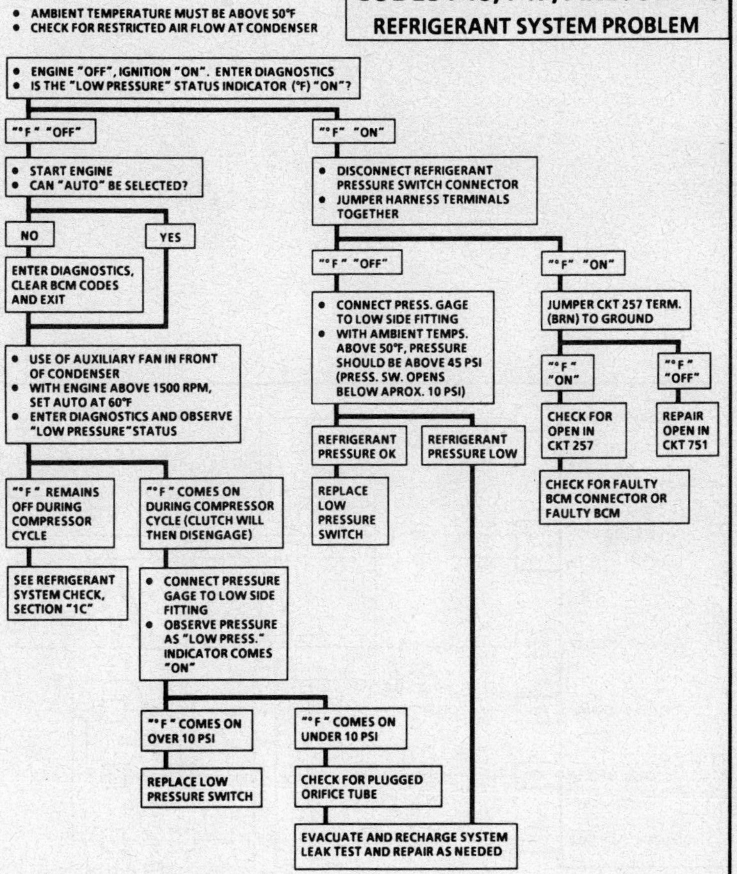
• AMBIENT TEMPERATURE MUST BE ABOVE 50°F
• CHECK FOR RESTRICTED AIR FLOW AT CONDENSER
• ENGINE "OFF", IGNITION "ON". ENTER DIAGNOSTICS
• IS THE "LOW PRESSURE" STATUS INDICATOR (°F) "ON"?
"°F" "OFF"
"°F" "ON"
• START ENGINE
• CAN "AUTO" BE SELECTED?
NO
YES
ENTER DIAGNOSTICS, CLEAR BCM CODES AND EXIT
• USE OF AUXILIARY FAN IN FRONT OF CONDENSER
• WITH ENGINE ABOVE 1500 RPM, SET AUTO AT 60°F
• ENTER DIAGNOSTICS AND OBSERVE "LOW PRESSURE" STATUS
"°F" REMAINS OFF DURING COMPRESSOR CYCLE
"°F" COMES ON DURING COMPRESSOR CYCLE (CLUTCH WILL THEN DISENGAGE)
SEE REFRIGERANT SYSTEM CHECK, SECTION "1C"
• CONNECT PRESSURE GAGE TO LOW SIDE FITTING
• OBSERVE PRESSURE AS "LOW PRESS." INDICATOR COMES "ON"
"°F" COMES ON OVER 10 PSI
"°F" COMES ON UNDER 10 PSI
REPLACE LOW PRESSURE SWITCH
CHECK FOR PLUGGED ORIFICE TUBE
EVACUATE AND RECHARGE SYSTEM LEAK TEST AND REPAIR AS NEEDED
• DISCONNECT REFRIGERANT PRESSURE SWITCH CONNECTOR
• JUMPER HARNESS TERMINALS TOGETHER
"°F" "OFF"
"°F" "ON"
• CONNECT PRESS. GAGE TO LOW SIDE FITTING
• WITH AMBIENT TEMPS. ABOVE 50°F, PRESSURE SHOULD BE ABOVE 45 PSI (PRESS. SW. OPENS BELOW APROX. 10 PSI)
REFRIGERANT PRESSURE OK
REFRIGERANT PRESSURE LOW
REPLACE LOW PRESSURE SWITCH
JUMPER CKT 257 TERM. (BRN) TO GROUND
"°F" "ON"
"°F" "OFF"
CHECK FOR OPEN IN CKT 257
REPAIR OPEN IN CKT 751
CHECK FOR FAULTY BCM CONNECTOR OR FAULTY BCM

WHEN ALL DIAGNOSES AND REPAIRS ARE COMPLETED, CLEAR CODES AND CONFIRM "CLOSED LOOP" OPERATION AND NO "SERVICE ENGINE SOON" LIGHT.

BCM DIAGNOSTIC CHARTS E, K AND V BODY BODY

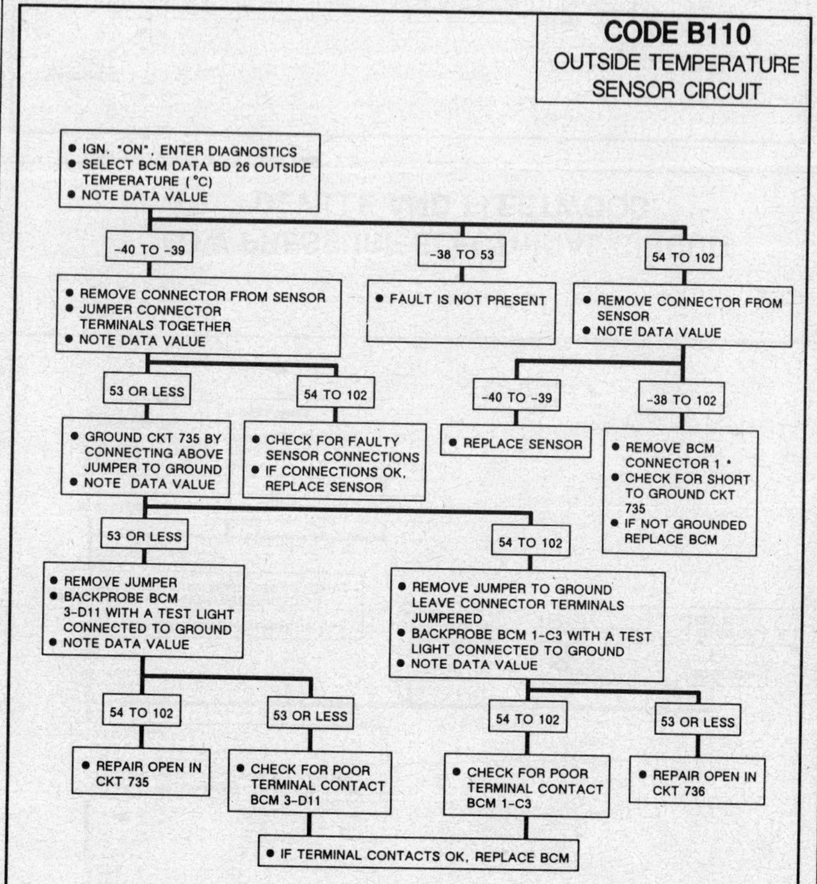
CODE B110
OUTSIDE TEMPERATURE SENSOR CIRCUIT
• IGN. "ON", ENTER DIAGNOSTICS • SELECT BCM DATA BD 26 OUTSIDE TEMPERATURE (°C) • NOTE DATA VALUE
-40 TO -39
-38 TO 53
54 TO 102
• REMOVE CONNECTOR FROM SENSOR • JUMPER CONNECTOR TERMINALS TOGETHER • NOTE DATA VALUE
• FAULT IS NOT PRESENT
• REMOVE CONNECTOR FROM SENSOR • NOTE DATA VALUE
53 OR LESS
54 TO 102
-40 TO -39
-38 TO 102
• GROUND CKT 735 BY CONNECTING ABOVE JUMPER TO GROUND • NOTE DATA VALUE
• CHECK FOR FAULTY SENSOR CONNECTIONS • IF CONNECTIONS OK, REPLACE SENSOR
• REPLACE SENSOR
• REMOVE BCM CONNECTOR 1 * • CHECK FOR SHORT TO GROUND CKT 735 • IF NOT GROUNDED REPLACE BCM
53 OR LESS
54 TO 102
• REMOVE JUMPER • BACKPROBE BCM 3-D11 WITH A TEST LIGHT CONNECTED TO GROUND • NOTE DATA VALUE
• REMOVE JUMPER TO GROUND LEAVE CONNECTOR TERMINALS JUMPERED • BACKPROBE BCM 1-C3 WITH A TEST LIGHT CONNECTED TO GROUND • NOTE DATA VALUE
54 TO 102
53 OR LESS
54 TO 102
53 OR LESS
• REPAIR OPEN IN CKT 735
• CHECK FOR POOR TERMINAL CONTACT BCM 3-D11
• CHECK FOR POOR TERMINAL CONTACT BCM 1-C3
• REPAIR OPEN IN CKT 736
• IF TERMINAL CONTACTS OK, REPLACE BCM

* WHEN THE REPAIR IS COMPLETE, MOMENTARILY DISCONNECT THE OUTSIDE TEMPERATURE SENSOR CONNECTOR WITH THE KEY "ON" TO RESET OUTSIDE TEMPERATURE AND ALLOW A/C OPERATION.

WHEN ALL DIAGNOSIS AND REPAIRS ARE COMPLETED, CLEAR CODES AND VERIFY PROPER OPERATION

TEMPERATURE SENSOR CIRCUITS E, K AND V BODY CADILLAC

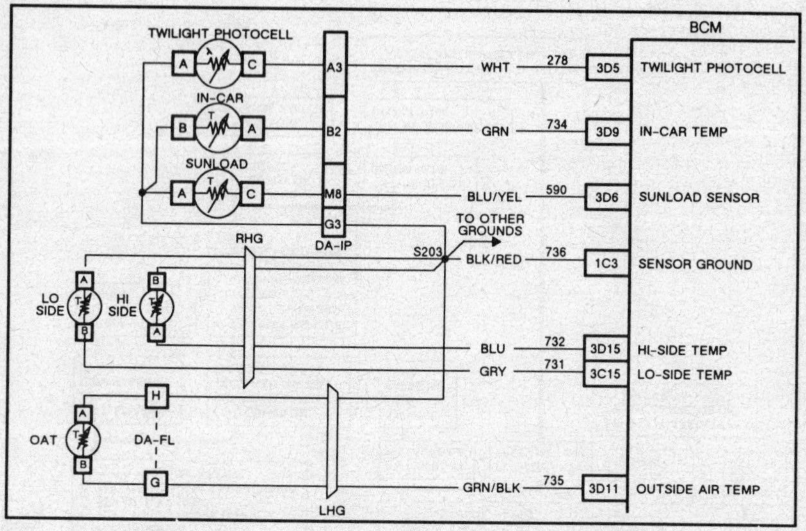
BCM
TWILIGHT PHOTOCELL
IN-CAR
SUNLOAD
A3
B2
M8
G3
DA-IP
WHT
278
3D5
TWILIGHT PHOTOCELL
GRN
734
3D9
IN-CAR TEMP
BLU/YEL
590
3D6
SUNLOAD SENSOR
TO OTHER GROUNDS
S203
BLK/RED
736
1C3
SENSOR GROUND
RHG
LO SIDE
HI SIDE
BLU
732
3D15
HI-SIDE TEMP
GRY
731
3C15
LO-SIDE TEMP
OAT
DA-FL
LHG
GRN/BLK
735
3D11
OUTSIDE AIR TEMP

BCM DIAGNOSTIC CHARTS—E, K AND V BODY (CONT.)

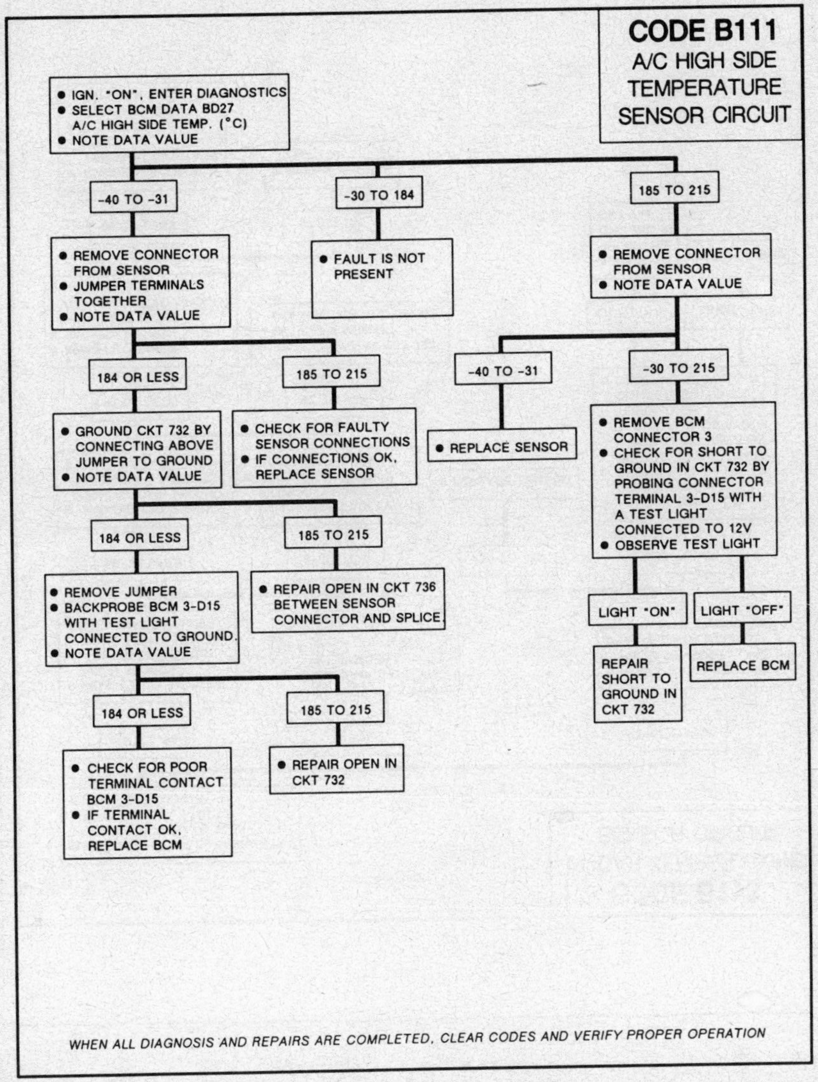
CODE B111
A/C HIGH SIDE TEMPERATURE SENSOR CIRCUIT
● IGN. "ON", ENTER DIAGNOSTICS
● SELECT BCM DATA BD27 A/C HIGH SIDE TEMP. (°C)
● NOTE DATA VALUE
-40 TO -31
-30 TO 184
185 TO 215
● REMOVE CONNECTOR FROM SENSOR
● JUMPER TERMINALS TOGETHER
● NOTE DATA VALUE
● FAULT IS NOT PRESENT
● REMOVE CONNECTOR FROM SENSOR
● NOTE DATA VALUE
184 OR LESS
185 TO 215
-40 TO -31
-30 TO 215
● GROUND CKT 732 BY CONNECTING ABOVE JUMPER TO GROUND
● NOTE DATA VALUE
● CHECK FOR FAULTY SENSOR CONNECTIONS
● IF CONNECTIONS OK, REPLACE SENSOR
● REPLACE SENSOR
● REMOVE BCM CONNECTOR 3
● CHECK FOR SHORT TO GROUND IN CKT 732 BY PROBING CONNECTOR TERMINAL 3-D15 WITH A TEST LIGHT CONNECTED TO 12V
● OBSERVE TEST LIGHT
184 OR LESS
185 TO 215
● REMOVE JUMPER
● BACKPROBE BCM 3-D15 WITH TEST LIGHT CONNECTED TO GROUND.
● NOTE DATA VALUE
● REPAIR OPEN IN CKT 736 BETWEEN SENSOR CONNECTOR AND SPLICE
LIGHT "ON"
LIGHT "OFF"
REPAIR SHORT TO GROUND IN CKT 732
REPLACE BCM
184 OR LESS
185 TO 215
● CHECK FOR POOR TERMINAL CONTACT BCM 3-D15
● IF TERMINAL CONTACT OK, REPLACE BCM
● REPAIR OPEN IN CKT 732
WHEN ALL DIAGNOSIS AND REPAIRS ARE COMPLETED, CLEAR CODES AND VERIFY PROPER OPERATION

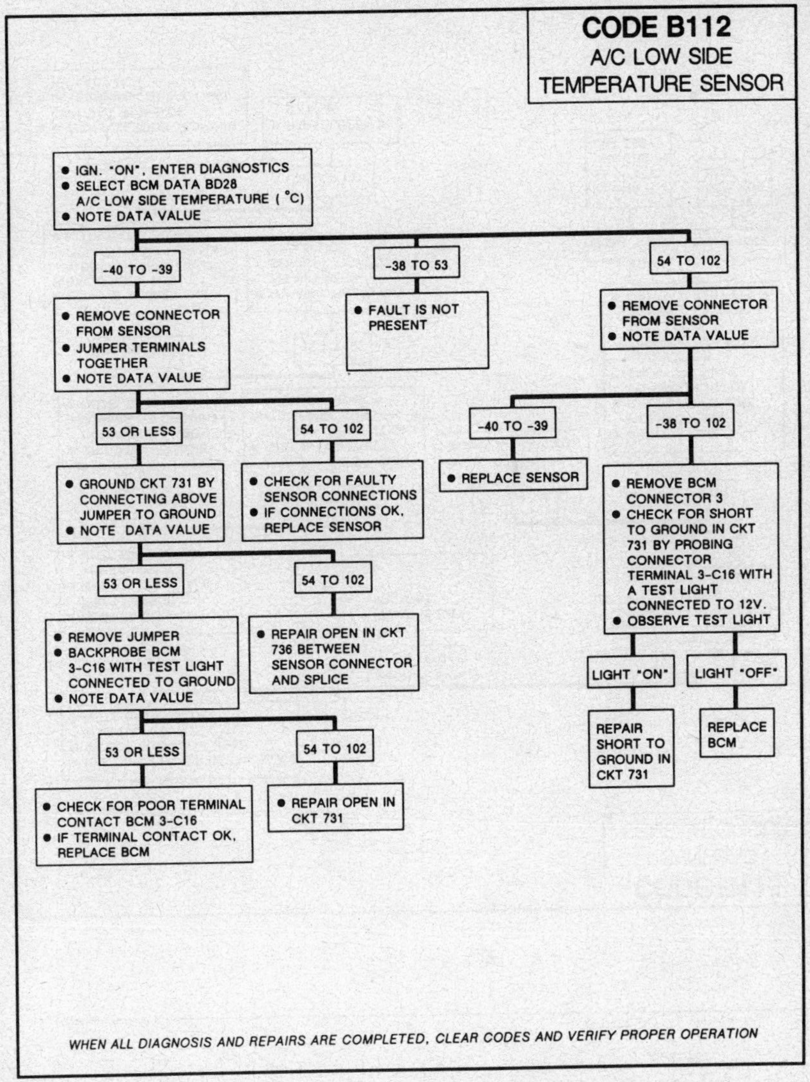
CODE B112
A/C LOW SIDE TEMPERATURE SENSOR
● IGN. "ON", ENTER DIAGNOSTICS
● SELECT BCM DATA BD28 A/C LOW SIDE TEMPERATURE (°C)
● NOTE DATA VALUE
-40 TO -39
-38 TO 53
54 TO 102
● REMOVE CONNECTOR FROM SENSOR
● JUMPER TERMINALS TOGETHER
● NOTE DATA VALUE
● FAULT IS NOT PRESENT
● REMOVE CONNECTOR FROM SENSOR
● NOTE DATA VALUE
53 OR LESS
54 TO 102
-40 TO -39
-38 TO 102
● GROUND CKT 731 BY CONNECTING ABOVE JUMPER TO GROUND
● NOTE DATA VALUE
● CHECK FOR FAULTY SENSOR CONNECTIONS
● IF CONNECTIONS OK, REPLACE SENSOR
● REPLACE SENSOR
● REMOVE BCM CONNECTOR 3
● CHECK FOR SHORT TO GROUND IN CKT 731 BY PROBING CONNECTOR TERMINAL 3-C16 WITH A TEST LIGHT CONNECTED TO 12V.
● OBSERVE TEST LIGHT
53 OR LESS
54 TO 102
● REMOVE JUMPER
● BACKPROBE BCM 3-C16 WITH TEST LIGHT CONNECTED TO GROUND
● NOTE DATA VALUE
● REPAIR OPEN IN CKT 736 BETWEEN SENSOR CONNECTOR AND SPLICE
LIGHT "ON"
LIGHT "OFF"
REPAIR SHORT TO GROUND IN CKT 731
REPLACE BCM
53 OR LESS
54 TO 102
● CHECK FOR POOR TERMINAL CONTACT BCM 3-C16
● IF TERMINAL CONTACT OK, REPLACE BCM
● REPAIR OPEN IN CKT 731
WHEN ALL DIAGNOSIS AND REPAIRS ARE COMPLETED, CLEAR CODES AND VERIFY PROPER OPERATION

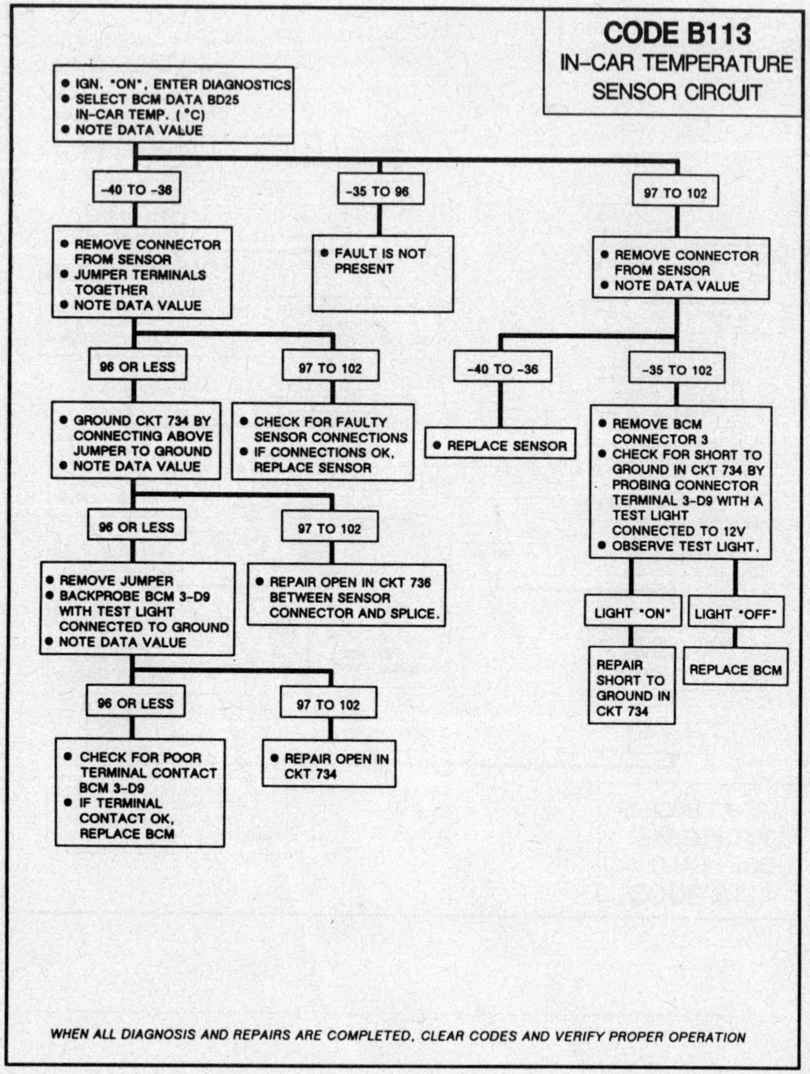
CODE B113
IN-CAR TEMPERATURE
SENSOR CIRCUIT
● IGN. "ON", ENTER DIAGNOSTICS ● SELECT BCM DATA BD25 IN-CAR TEMP. (°C) ● NOTE DATA VALUE
-40 TO -36
-35 TO 96
97 TO 102
● REMOVE CONNECTOR FROM SENSOR ● JUMPER TERMINALS TOGETHER ● NOTE DATA VALUE
● FAULT IS NOT PRESENT
● REMOVE CONNECTOR FROM SENSOR ● NOTE DATA VALUE
96 OR LESS
97 TO 102
-40 TO -36
-35 TO 102
● GROUND CKT 734 BY CONNECTING ABOVE JUMPER TO GROUND ● NOTE DATA VALUE
● CHECK FOR FAULTY SENSOR CONNECTIONS ● IF CONNECTIONS OK, REPLACE SENSOR
● REPLACE SENSOR
● REMOVE BCM CONNECTOR 3 ● CHECK FOR SHORT TO GROUND IN CKT 734 BY PROBING CONNECTOR TERMINAL 3-D9 WITH A TEST LIGHT CONNECTED TO 12V ● OBSERVE TEST LIGHT.
96 OR LESS
97 TO 102
● REMOVE JUMPER ● BACKPROBE BCM 3-D9 WITH TEST LIGHT CONNECTED TO GROUND ● NOTE DATA VALUE
● REPAIR OPEN IN CKT 736 BETWEEN SENSOR CONNECTOR AND SPLICE.
LIGHT "ON"
LIGHT "OFF"
REPAIR SHORT TO GROUND IN CKT 734
REPLACE BCM
96 OR LESS
97 TO 102
● CHECK FOR POOR TERMINAL CONTACT BCM 3-D9 ● IF TERMINAL CONTACT OK, REPLACE BCM
● REPAIR OPEN IN CKT 734
WHEN ALL DIAGNOSIS AND REPAIRS ARE COMPLETED, CLEAR CODES AND VERIFY PROPER OPERATION

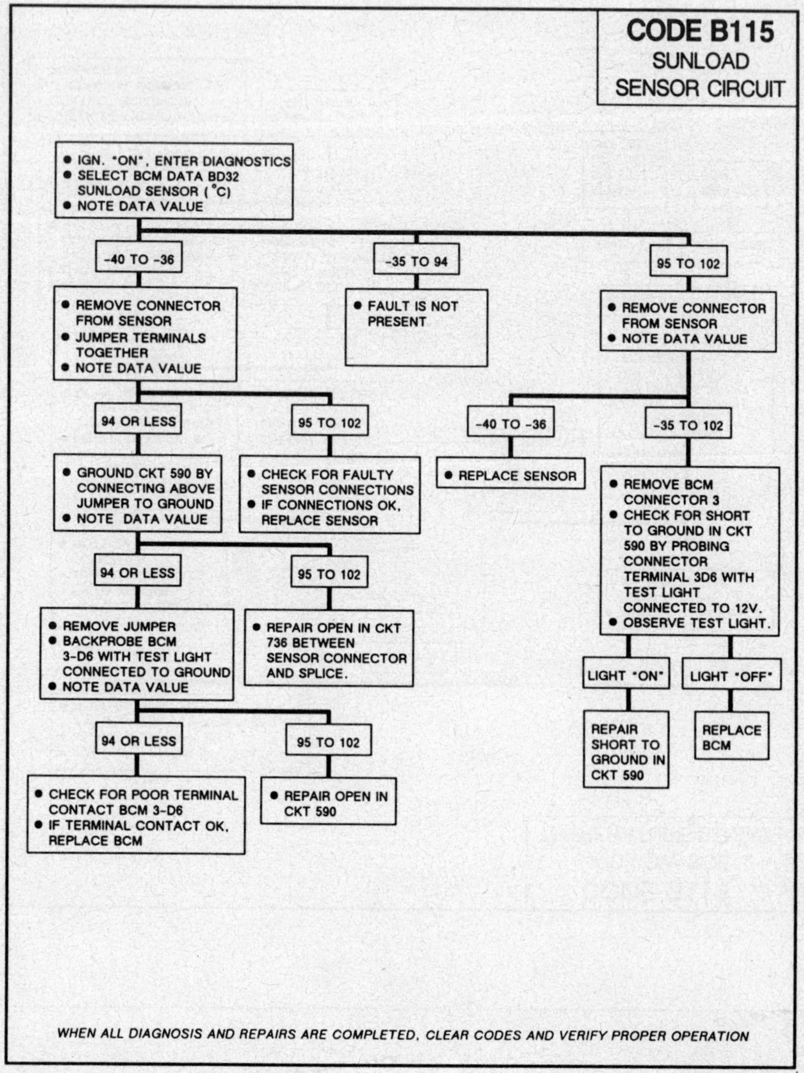
CODE B115
SUNLOAD
SENSOR CIRCUIT
● IGN. "ON", ENTER DIAGNOSTICS ● SELECT BCM DATA BD32 SUNLOAD SENSOR (°C) ● NOTE DATA VALUE
-40 TO -36
-35 TO 94
95 TO 102
● REMOVE CONNECTOR FROM SENSOR ● JUMPER TERMINALS TOGETHER ● NOTE DATA VALUE
● FAULT IS NOT PRESENT
● REMOVE CONNECTOR FROM SENSOR ● NOTE DATA VALUE
94 OR LESS
95 TO 102
-40 TO -36
-35 TO 102
● GROUND CKT 590 BY CONNECTING ABOVE JUMPER TO GROUND ● NOTE DATA VALUE
● CHECK FOR FAULTY SENSOR CONNECTIONS ● IF CONNECTIONS OK, REPLACE SENSOR
● REPLACE SENSOR
● REMOVE BCM CONNECTOR 3 ● CHECK FOR SHORT TO GROUND IN CKT 590 BY PROBING CONNECTOR TERMINAL 3D6 WITH TEST LIGHT CONNECTED TO 12V. ● OBSERVE TEST LIGHT.
94 OR LESS
95 TO 102
● REMOVE JUMPER ● BACKPROBE BCM 3-D6 WITH TEST LIGHT CONNECTED TO GROUND ● NOTE DATA VALUE
● REPAIR OPEN IN CKT 736 BETWEEN SENSOR CONNECTOR AND SPLICE.
LIGHT "ON"
LIGHT "OFF"
REPAIR SHORT TO GROUND IN CKT 590
REPLACE BCM
94 OR LESS
95 TO 102
● CHECK FOR POOR TERMINAL CONTACT BCM 3-D6 ● IF TERMINAL CONTACT OK, REPLACE BCM
● REPAIR OPEN IN CKT 590
WHEN ALL DIAGNOSIS AND REPAIRS ARE COMPLETED, CLEAR CODES AND VERIFY PROPER OPERATION

DATA CIRCUIT SCHEMATIC
E, K AND V BODY CADILLAC

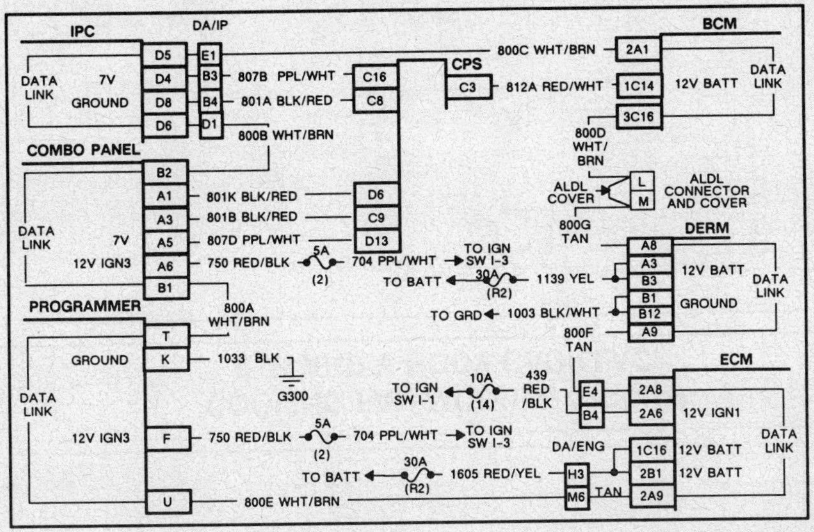
IPC
DA/IP
BCM
DATA LINK
7V
GROUND
D5 D4 D8 D6
E1 B3 B4 D1
807B PPL/WHT
801A BLK/RED
800B WHT/BRN
C16 C8
CPS
C3
800C WHT/BRN
812A RED/WHT
2A1 1C14 3C16
12V BATT
800D WHT/BRN
ALDL COVER
L M
ALDL CONNECTOR AND COVER
COMBO PANEL
B2 A1 A3 A5 A6 B1
801K BLK/RED
801B BLK/RED
807D PPL/WHT
750 RED/BLK
12V IGN3
D6 C9 D13
5A (2)
704 PPL/WHT
TO IGN SW I-3
TO BATT
30A (R2)
1139 YEL
TO GRD
1003 BLK/WHT
800G TAN
DERM
A8 A3 B3 B1 B12 A9
GROUND
800F TAN
PROGRAMMER
800A WHT/BRN
T K F U
1033 BLK
G300
TO IGN SW I-1
10A (14)
439 RED /BLK
E4 B4
ECM
2A8 2A6 1C16 2B1 2A9
12V IGN1
DA/ENG
H3 M6
TAN
1605 RED/YEL
800E WHT/BRN

BCM DIAGNOSTIC CHARTS—E, K AND V BODY (CONT.)

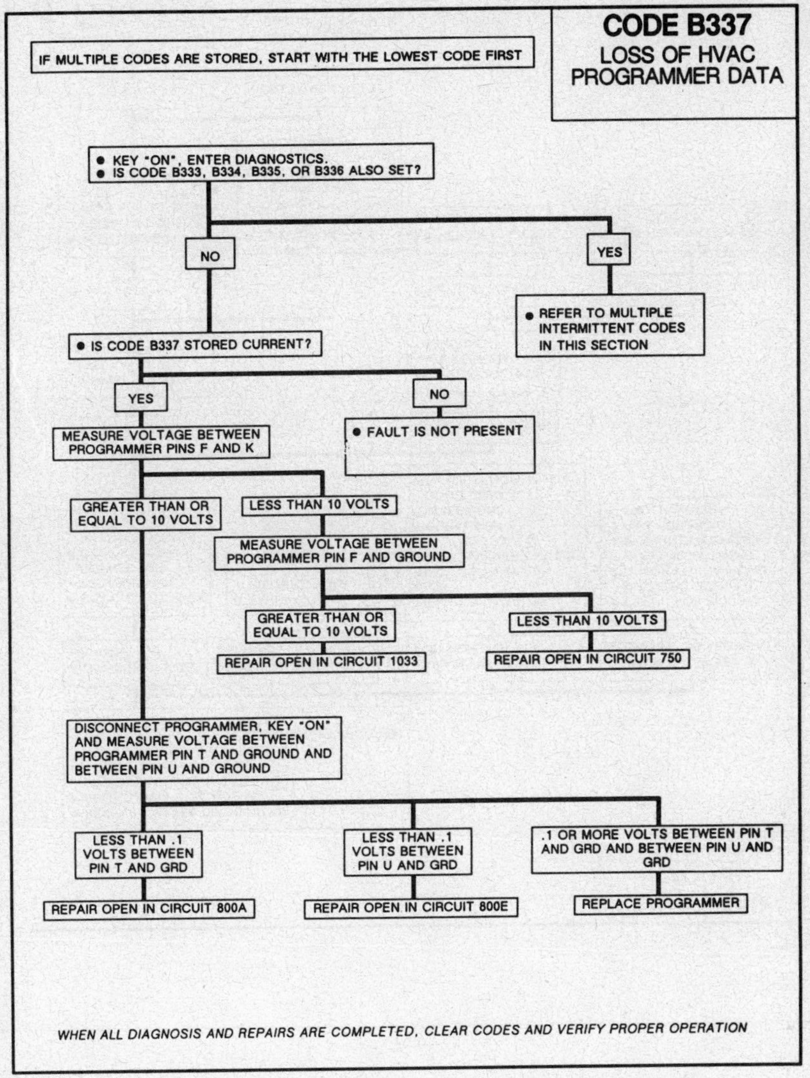
CODE B337
LOSS OF HVAC PROGRAMMER DATA
IF MULTIPLE CODES ARE STORED, START WITH THE LOWEST CODE FIRST
• KEY "ON", ENTER DIAGNOSTICS.
• IS CODE B333, B334, B335, OR B336 ALSO SET?
NO
YES
• REFER TO MULTIPLE INTERMITTENT CODES IN THIS SECTION
• IS CODE B337 STORED CURRENT?
YES
NO
• FAULT IS NOT PRESENT
MEASURE VOLTAGE BETWEEN PROGRAMMER PINS F AND K
GREATER THAN OR EQUAL TO 10 VOLTS
LESS THAN 10 VOLTS
MEASURE VOLTAGE BETWEEN PROGRAMMER PIN F AND GROUND
GREATER THAN OR EQUAL TO 10 VOLTS
LESS THAN 10 VOLTS
REPAIR OPEN IN CIRCUIT 1033
REPAIR OPEN IN CIRCUIT 750
DISCONNECT PROGRAMMER, KEY "ON" AND MEASURE VOLTAGE BETWEEN PROGRAMMER PIN T AND GROUND AND BETWEEN PIN U AND GROUND
LESS THAN .1 VOLTS BETWEEN PIN T AND GRD
LESS THAN .1 VOLTS BETWEEN PIN U AND GRD
.1 OR MORE VOLTS BETWEEN PIN T AND GRD AND BETWEEN PIN U AND GRD
REPAIR OPEN IN CIRCUIT 800A
REPAIR OPEN IN CIRCUIT 800E
REPLACE PROGRAMMER
WHEN ALL DIAGNOSIS AND REPAIRS ARE COMPLETED, CLEAR CODES AND VERIFY PROPER OPERATION

AIR MIX DOOR VALVE CIRCUIT
E, K AND V BODY CADILLAC

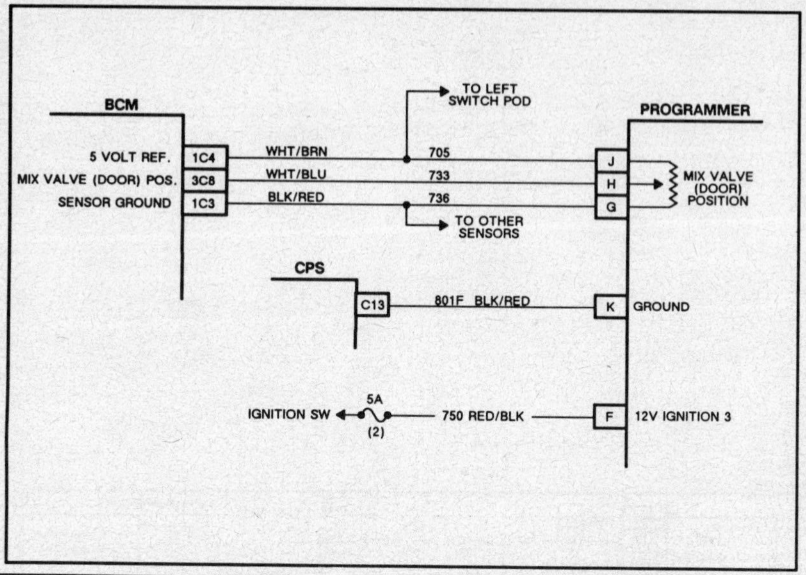
BCM
5 VOLT REF.
MIX VALVE (DOOR) POS.
SENSOR GROUND
1C4
3C8
1C3
WHT/BRN
WHT/BLU
BLK/RED
705
733
736
TO LEFT SWITCH POD
TO OTHER SENSORS
PROGRAMMER
J
H
G
MIX VALVE (DOOR) POSITION
CPS
C13
801F BLK/RED
K
GROUND
IGNITION SW
5A
(2)
750 RED/BLK
F
12V IGNITION 3

COOLING FAN MODULE CIRCUIT
E, K AND V BODY CADILLAC

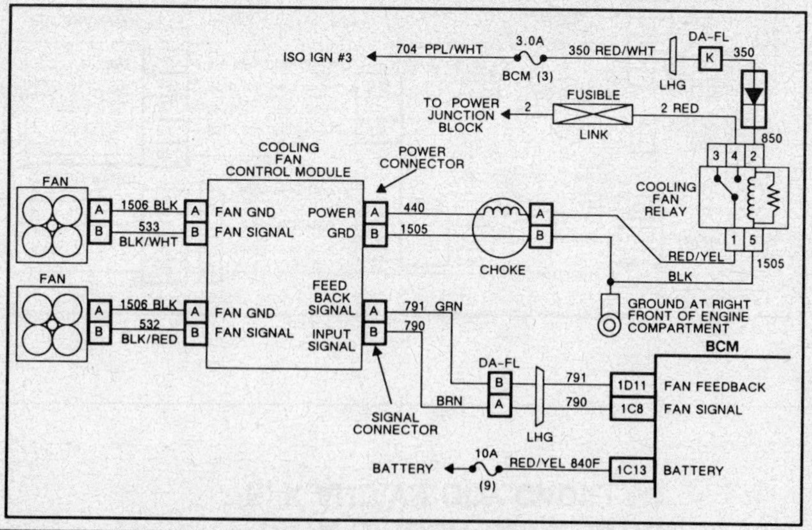
ISO IGN #3
704 PPL/WHT
3.0A
BCM (3)
350 RED/WHT
LHG
DA-FL
K
350
TO POWER JUNCTION BLOCK
2
FUSIBLE LINK
2 RED
850
COOLING FAN CONTROL MODULE
POWER CONNECTOR
COOLING FAN RELAY
FAN
1506 BLK
533
BLK/WHT
FAN GND
FAN SIGNAL
POWER
GRD
440
1505
CHOKE
RED/YEL
BLK
1505
FAN
1506 BLK
532
BLK/RED
FEED BACK SIGNAL
INPUT SIGNAL
791 GRN
790
GROUND AT RIGHT FRONT OF ENGINE COMPARTMENT
BCM
DA-FL
BRN
LHG
791
790
1D11
1C8
FAN FEEDBACK
FAN SIGNAL
SIGNAL CONNECTOR
BATTERY
10A
(9)
RED/YEL 840F
1C13
BATTERY

BCM DIAGNOSTIC CHARTS—E, K AND V BODY (CONT.)

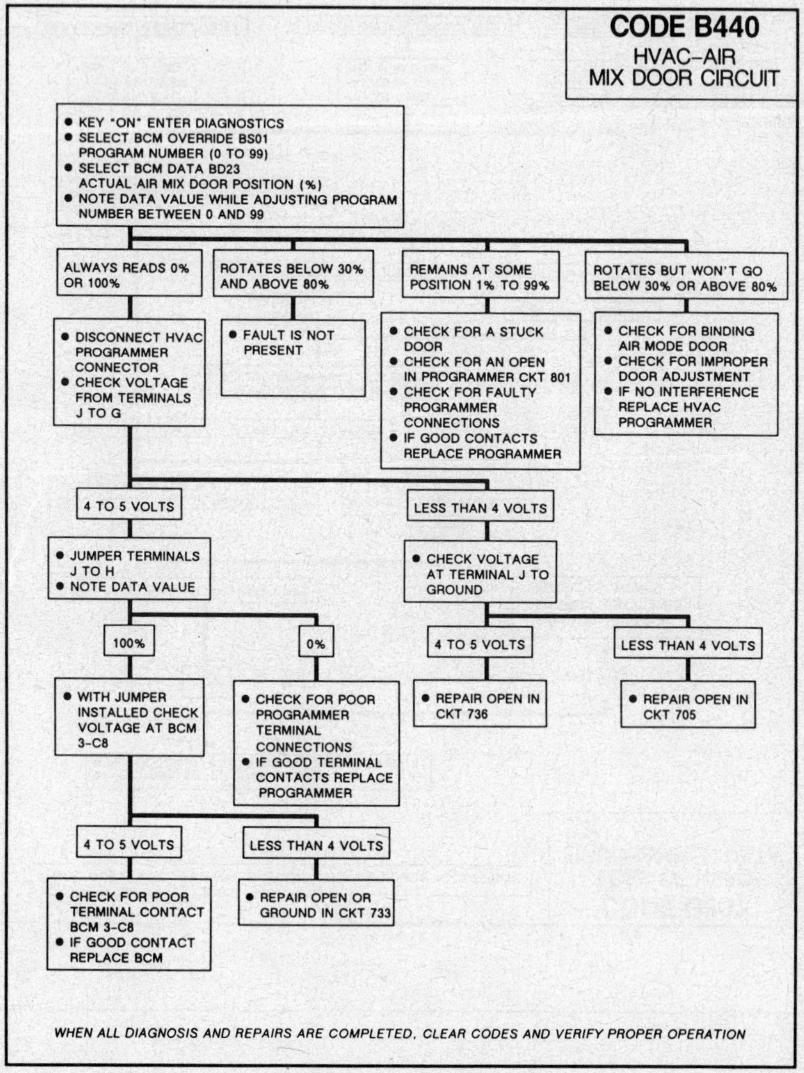
CODE B440
HVAC–AIR MIX DOOR CIRCUIT
• KEY "ON" ENTER DIAGNOSTICS
• SELECT BCM OVERRIDE BS01 PROGRAM NUMBER (0 TO 99)
• SELECT BCM DATA BD23 ACTUAL AIR MIX DOOR POSITION (%)
• NOTE DATA VALUE WHILE ADJUSTING PROGRAM NUMBER BETWEEN 0 AND 99
ALWAYS READS 0% OR 100%
ROTATES BELOW 30% AND ABOVE 80%
REMAINS AT SOME POSITION 1% TO 99%
ROTATES BUT WON'T GO BELOW 30% OR ABOVE 80%
• DISCONNECT HVAC PROGRAMMER CONNECTOR
• CHECK VOLTAGE FROM TERMINALS J TO G
• FAULT IS NOT PRESENT
• CHECK FOR A STUCK DOOR
• CHECK FOR AN OPEN IN PROGRAMMER CKT 801
• CHECK FOR FAULTY PROGRAMMER CONNECTIONS
• IF GOOD CONTACTS REPLACE PROGRAMMER
• CHECK FOR BINDING AIR MODE DOOR
• CHECK FOR IMPROPER DOOR ADJUSTMENT
• IF NO INTERFERENCE REPLACE HVAC PROGRAMMER
4 TO 5 VOLTS
LESS THAN 4 VOLTS
• JUMPER TERMINALS J TO H
• NOTE DATA VALUE
• CHECK VOLTAGE AT TERMINAL J TO GROUND
100%
0%
4 TO 5 VOLTS
LESS THAN 4 VOLTS
• WITH JUMPER INSTALLED CHECK VOLTAGE AT BCM 3-C8
• CHECK FOR POOR PROGRAMMER TERMINAL CONNECTIONS
• IF GOOD TERMINAL CONTACTS REPLACE PROGRAMMER
• REPAIR OPEN IN CKT 736
• REPAIR OPEN IN CKT 705
4 TO 5 VOLTS
LESS THAN 4 VOLTS
• CHECK FOR POOR TERMINAL CONTACT BCM 3-C8
• IF GOOD CONTACT REPLACE BCM
• REPAIR OPEN OR GROUND IN CKT 733
WHEN ALL DIAGNOSIS AND REPAIRS ARE COMPLETED, CLEAR CODES AND VERIFY PROPER OPERATION

BCM DIAGNOSTIC CHARTS—E, K AND V BODY (CONT.)

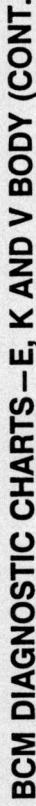

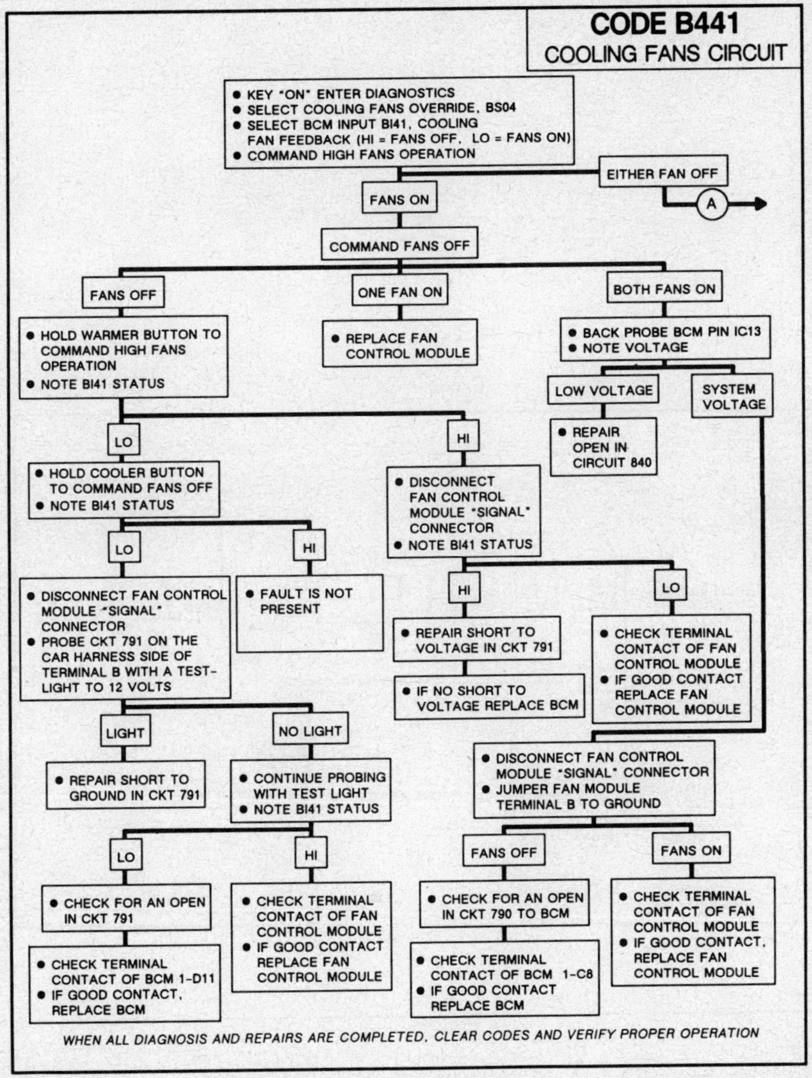
CODE B441
COOLING FANS CIRCUIT
• KEY "ON" ENTER DIAGNOSTICS
• SELECT COOLING FANS OVERRIDE, BS04
• SELECT BCM INPUT BI41, COOLING FAN FEEDBACK (HI = FANS OFF, LO = FANS ON)
• COMMAND HIGH FANS OPERATION
EITHER FAN OFF
A
FANS ON
COMMAND FANS OFF
FANS OFF
ONE FAN ON
BOTH FANS ON
• HOLD WARMER BUTTON TO COMMAND HIGH FANS OPERATION
• NOTE BI41 STATUS
• REPLACE FAN CONTROL MODULE
• BACK PROBE BCM PIN IC13
• NOTE VOLTAGE
LOW VOLTAGE
SYSTEM VOLTAGE
• REPAIR OPEN IN CIRCUIT 840
LO
HI
• HOLD COOLER BUTTON TO COMMAND FANS OFF
• NOTE BI41 STATUS
• DISCONNECT FAN CONTROL MODULE "SIGNAL" CONNECTOR
• NOTE BI41 STATUS
LO
HI
• DISCONNECT FAN CONTROL MODULE "SIGNAL" CONNECTOR
• PROBE CKT 791 ON THE CAR HARNESS SIDE OF TERMINAL B WITH A TEST-LIGHT TO 12 VOLTS
• FAULT IS NOT PRESENT
HI
LO
• REPAIR SHORT TO VOLTAGE IN CKT 791
• IF NO SHORT TO VOLTAGE REPLACE BCM
• CHECK TERMINAL CONTACT OF FAN CONTROL MODULE
• IF GOOD CONTACT REPLACE FAN CONTROL MODULE
LIGHT
NO LIGHT
• REPAIR SHORT TO GROUND IN CKT 791
• CONTINUE PROBING WITH TEST LIGHT
• NOTE BI41 STATUS
• DISCONNECT FAN CONTROL MODULE "SIGNAL" CONNECTOR
• JUMPER FAN MODULE TERMINAL B TO GROUND
LO
HI
FANS OFF
FANS ON
• CHECK FOR AN OPEN IN CKT 791
• CHECK TERMINAL CONTACT OF BCM 1-D11
• IF GOOD CONTACT, REPLACE BCM
• CHECK TERMINAL CONTACT OF FAN CONTROL MODULE
• IF GOOD CONTACT REPLACE FAN CONTROL MODULE
• CHECK FOR AN OPEN IN CKT 790 TO BCM
• CHECK TERMINAL CONTACT OF BCM 1-C8
• IF GOOD CONTACT REPLACE BCM
• CHECK TERMINAL CONTACT OF FAN CONTROL MODULE
• IF GOOD CONTACT, REPLACE FAN CONTROL MODULE
WHEN ALL DIAGNOSIS AND REPAIRS ARE COMPLETED, CLEAR CODES AND VERIFY PROPER OPERATION

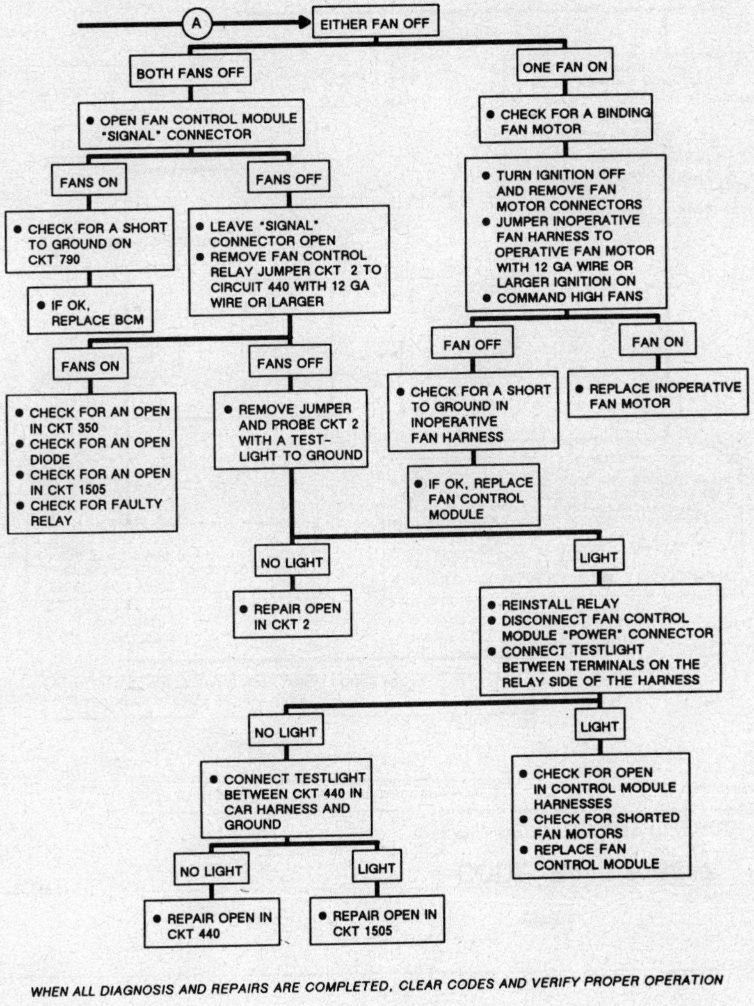
A
EITHER FAN OFF
BOTH FANS OFF
ONE FAN ON
• OPEN FAN CONTROL MODULE "SIGNAL" CONNECTOR
• CHECK FOR A BINDING FAN MOTOR
FANS ON
FANS OFF
• CHECK FOR A SHORT TO GROUND ON CKT 790
• IF OK, REPLACE BCM
• LEAVE "SIGNAL" CONNECTOR OPEN
• REMOVE FAN CONTROL RELAY JUMPER CKT 2 TO CIRCUIT 440 WITH 12 GA WIRE OR LARGER
• TURN IGNITION OFF AND REMOVE FAN MOTOR CONNECTORS
• JUMPER INOPERATIVE FAN HARNESS TO OPERATIVE FAN MOTOR WITH 12 GA WIRE OR LARGER IGNITION ON
• COMMAND HIGH FANS
FAN OFF
FAN ON
• CHECK FOR A SHORT TO GROUND IN INOPERATIVE FAN HARNESS
• IF OK, REPLACE FAN CONTROL MODULE
• REPLACE INOPERATIVE FAN MOTOR
FANS ON
FANS OFF
• CHECK FOR AN OPEN IN CKT 350
• CHECK FOR AN OPEN DIODE
• CHECK FOR AN OPEN IN CKT 1505
• CHECK FOR FAULTY RELAY
• REMOVE JUMPER AND PROBE CKT 2 WITH A TEST-LIGHT TO GROUND
NO LIGHT
LIGHT
• REPAIR OPEN IN CKT 2
• REINSTALL RELAY
• DISCONNECT FAN CONTROL MODULE "POWER" CONNECTOR
• CONNECT TESTLIGHT BETWEEN TERMINALS ON THE RELAY SIDE OF THE HARNESS
NO LIGHT
LIGHT
• CONNECT TESTLIGHT BETWEEN CKT 440 IN CAR HARNESS AND GROUND
• CHECK FOR OPEN IN CONTROL MODULE HARNESSES
• CHECK FOR SHORTED FAN MOTORS
• REPLACE FAN CONTROL MODULE
NO LIGHT
LIGHT
• REPAIR OPEN IN CKT 440
• REPAIR OPEN IN CKT 1505
WHEN ALL DIAGNOSIS AND REPAIRS ARE COMPLETED, CLEAR CODES AND VERIFY PROPER OPERATION

LOW REFRIGERANT PRESSURE SWITCH CIRCUIT
E, K AND V BODY CADILLAC

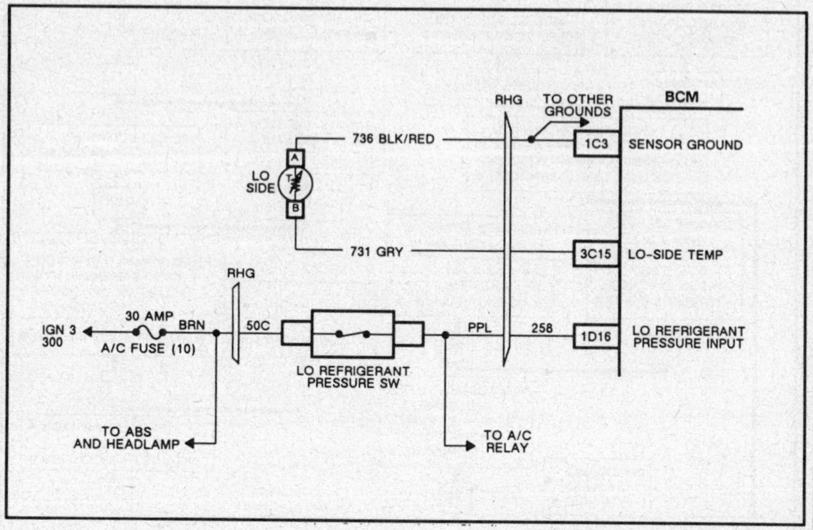
RHG
TO OTHER GROUNDS
BCM
736 BLK/RED
1C3
SENSOR GROUND
LO SIDE
A
B
731 GRY
3C15
LO-SIDE TEMP
RHG
IGN 3
300
30 AMP
A/C FUSE (10)
BRN
50C
LO REFRIGERANT PRESSURE SW
PPL
258
1D16
LO REFRIGERANT PRESSURE INPUT
TO ABS AND HEADLAMP
TO A/C RELAY

BCM DIAGNOSTIC CHARTS – E, K AND V BODY (CONT.)

CODE B446 & B447
LOW REFRIGERANT CHARGE

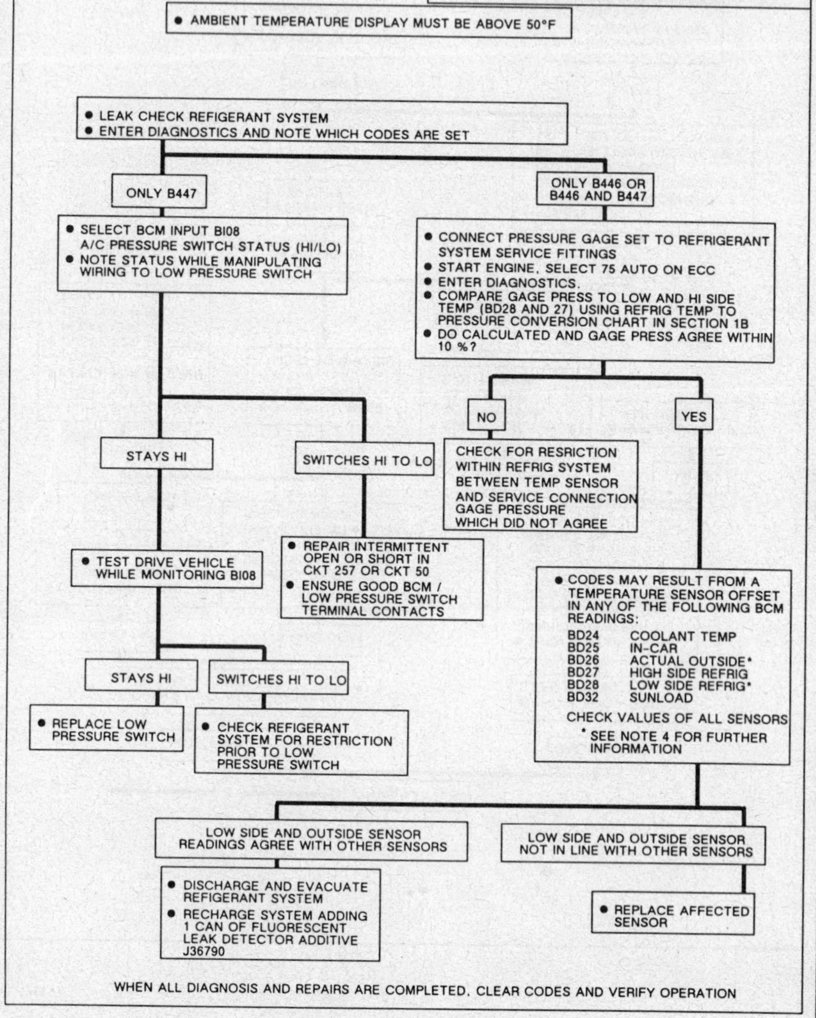
• AMBIENT TEMPERATURE DISPLAY MUST BE ABOVE 50°F
• LEAK CHECK REFIGERANT SYSTEM
• ENTER DIAGNOSTICS AND NOTE WHICH CODES ARE SET
ONLY B447
ONLY B446 OR B446 AND B447
• SELECT BCM INPUT BI08 A/C PRESSURE SWITCH STATUS (HI/LO)
• NOTE STATUS WHILE MANIPULATING WIRING TO LOW PRESSURE SWITCH
• CONNECT PRESSURE GAGE SET TO REFRIGERANT SYSTEM SERVICE FITTINGS
• START ENGINE. SELECT 75 AUTO ON ECC
• ENTER DIAGNOSTICS.
• COMPARE GAGE PRESS TO LOW AND HI SIDE TEMP (BD28 AND 27) USING REFRIG TEMP TO PRESSURE CONVERSION CHART IN SECTION 1B
• DO CALCULATED AND GAGE PRESS AGREE WITHIN 10 %?
NO
YES
STAYS HI
SWITCHES HI TO LO
CHECK FOR RESRICTION WITHIN REFRIG SYSTEM BETWEEN TEMP SENSOR AND SERVICE CONNECTION GAGE PRESSURE WHICH DID NOT AGREE
• TEST DRIVE VEHICLE WHILE MONITORING BI08
• REPAIR INTERMITTENT OPEN OR SHORT IN CKT 257 OR CKT 50
• ENSURE GOOD BCM / LOW PRESSURE SWITCH TERMINAL CONTACTS
• CODES MAY RESULT FROM A TEMPERATURE SENSOR OFFSET IN ANY OF THE FOLLOWING BCM READINGS:
BD24 COOLANT TEMP
BD25 IN-CAR
BD26 ACTUAL OUTSIDE*
BD27 HIGH SIDE REFRIG
BD28 LOW SIDE REFRIG*
BD32 SUNLOAD
CHECK VALUES OF ALL SENSORS
* SEE NOTE 4 FOR FURTHER INFORMATION
STAYS HI
SWITCHES HI TO LO
• REPLACE LOW PRESSURE SWITCH
• CHECK REFIGERANT SYSTEM FOR RESTRICTION PRIOR TO LOW PRESSURE SWITCH
LOW SIDE AND OUTSIDE SENSOR READINGS AGREE WITH OTHER SENSORS
LOW SIDE AND OUTSIDE SENSOR NOT IN LINE WITH OTHER SENSORS
• DISCHARGE AND EVACUATE REFRIGERANT SYSTEM
• RECHARGE SYSTEM ADDING 1 CAN OF FLUORESCENT LEAK DETECTOR ADDITIVE J36790
• REPLACE AFFECTED SENSOR
WHEN ALL DIAGNOSIS AND REPAIRS ARE COMPLETED, CLEAR CODES AND VERIFY OPERATION

BCM DIAGNOSTIC CHARTS – E, K AND V BODY (CONT.)

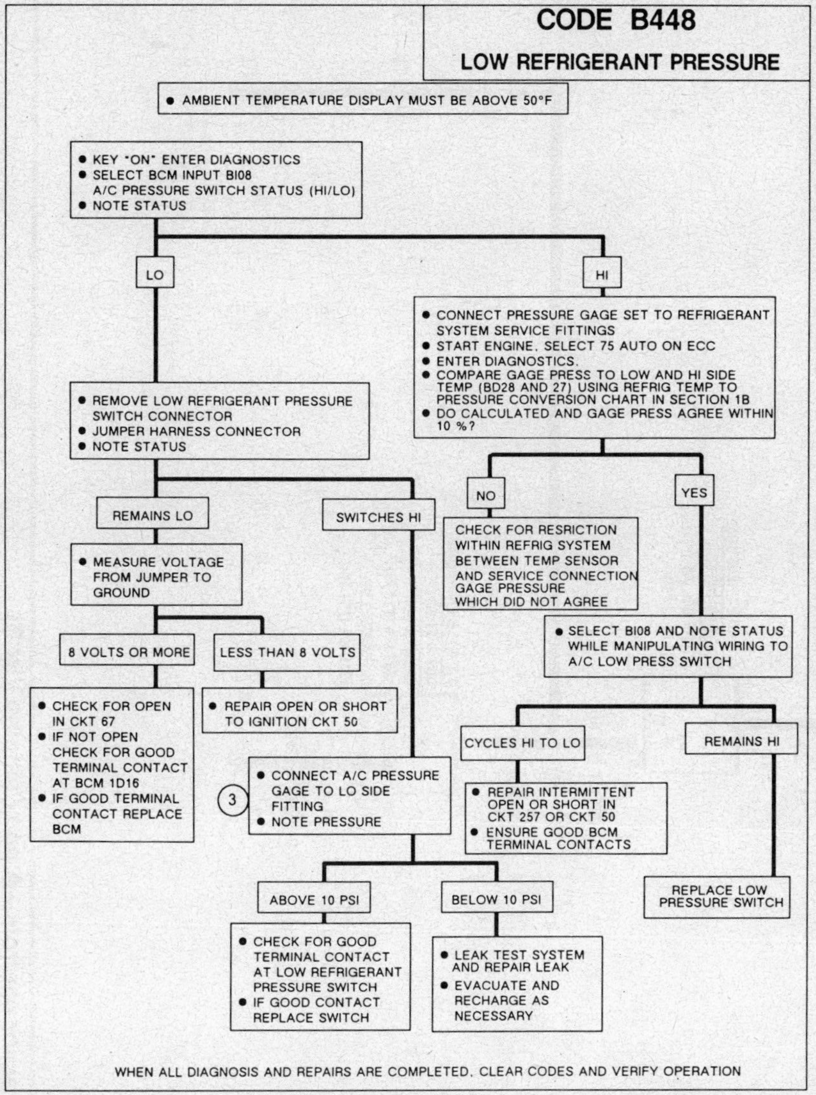
CODE B448
LOW REFRIGERANT PRESSURE
● AMBIENT TEMPERATURE DISPLAY MUST BE ABOVE 50°F
● KEY "ON" ENTER DIAGNOSTICS
● SELECT BCM INPUT BI08
A/C PRESSURE SWITCH STATUS (HI/LO)
● NOTE STATUS
LO
HI
● CONNECT PRESSURE GAGE SET TO REFRIGERANT SYSTEM SERVICE FITTINGS
● START ENGINE, SELECT 75 AUTO ON ECC
● ENTER DIAGNOSTICS.
● COMPARE GAGE PRESS TO LOW AND HI SIDE TEMP (BD28 AND 27) USING REFRIG TEMP TO PRESSURE CONVERSION CHART IN SECTION 1B
● DO CALCULATED AND GAGE PRESS AGREE WITHIN 10 %?
● REMOVE LOW REFRIGERANT PRESSURE SWITCH CONNECTOR
● JUMPER HARNESS CONNECTOR
● NOTE STATUS
NO
YES
CHECK FOR RESRICTION WITHIN REFRIG SYSTEM BETWEEN TEMP SENSOR AND SERVICE CONNECTION GAGE PRESSURE WHICH DID NOT AGREE
REMAINS LO
SWITCHES HI
● MEASURE VOLTAGE FROM JUMPER TO GROUND
● SELECT BI08 AND NOTE STATUS WHILE MANIPULATING WIRING TO A/C LOW PRESS SWITCH
8 VOLTS OR MORE
LESS THAN 8 VOLTS
● CHECK FOR OPEN IN CKT 67
● IF NOT OPEN CHECK FOR GOOD TERMINAL CONTACT AT BCM 1D16
● IF GOOD TERMINAL CONTACT REPLACE BCM
● REPAIR OPEN OR SHORT TO IGNITION CKT 50
CYCLES HI TO LO
REMAINS HI
3
● CONNECT A/C PRESSURE GAGE TO LO SIDE FITTING
● NOTE PRESSURE
● REPAIR INTERMITTENT OPEN OR SHORT IN CKT 257 OR CKT 50
● ENSURE GOOD BCM TERMINAL CONTACTS
ABOVE 10 PSI
BELOW 10 PSI
REPLACE LOW PRESSURE SWITCH
● CHECK FOR GOOD TERMINAL CONTACT AT LOW REFRIGERANT PRESSURE SWITCH
● IF GOOD CONTACT REPLACE SWITCH
● LEAK TEST SYSTEM AND REPAIR LEAK
● EVACUATE AND RECHARGE AS NECESSARY
WHEN ALL DIAGNOSIS AND REPAIRS ARE COMPLETED, CLEAR CODES AND VERIFY OPERATION

HIGH SIDE AND COOLANT TEMPERATURE SENSOR CIRCUITS E, K AND V BODY CADILLAC

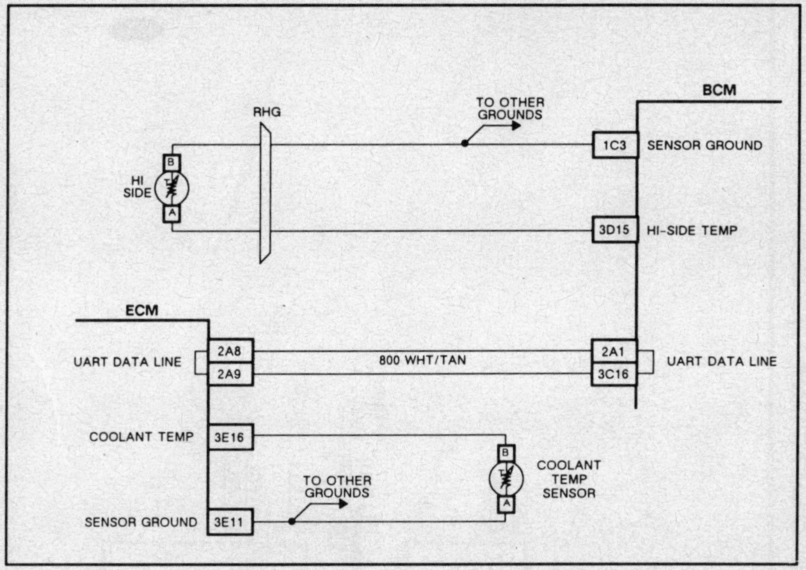
BCM
RHG
TO OTHER GROUNDS
1C3
SENSOR GROUND
HI SIDE
B
A
3D15
HI-SIDE TEMP
ECM
UART DATA LINE
2A8
2A9
800 WHT/TAN
2A1
3C16
UART DATA LINE
COOLANT TEMP
3E16
COOLANT TEMP SENSOR
TO OTHER GROUNDS
SENSOR GROUND
3E11

WIRING SCHEMATICS

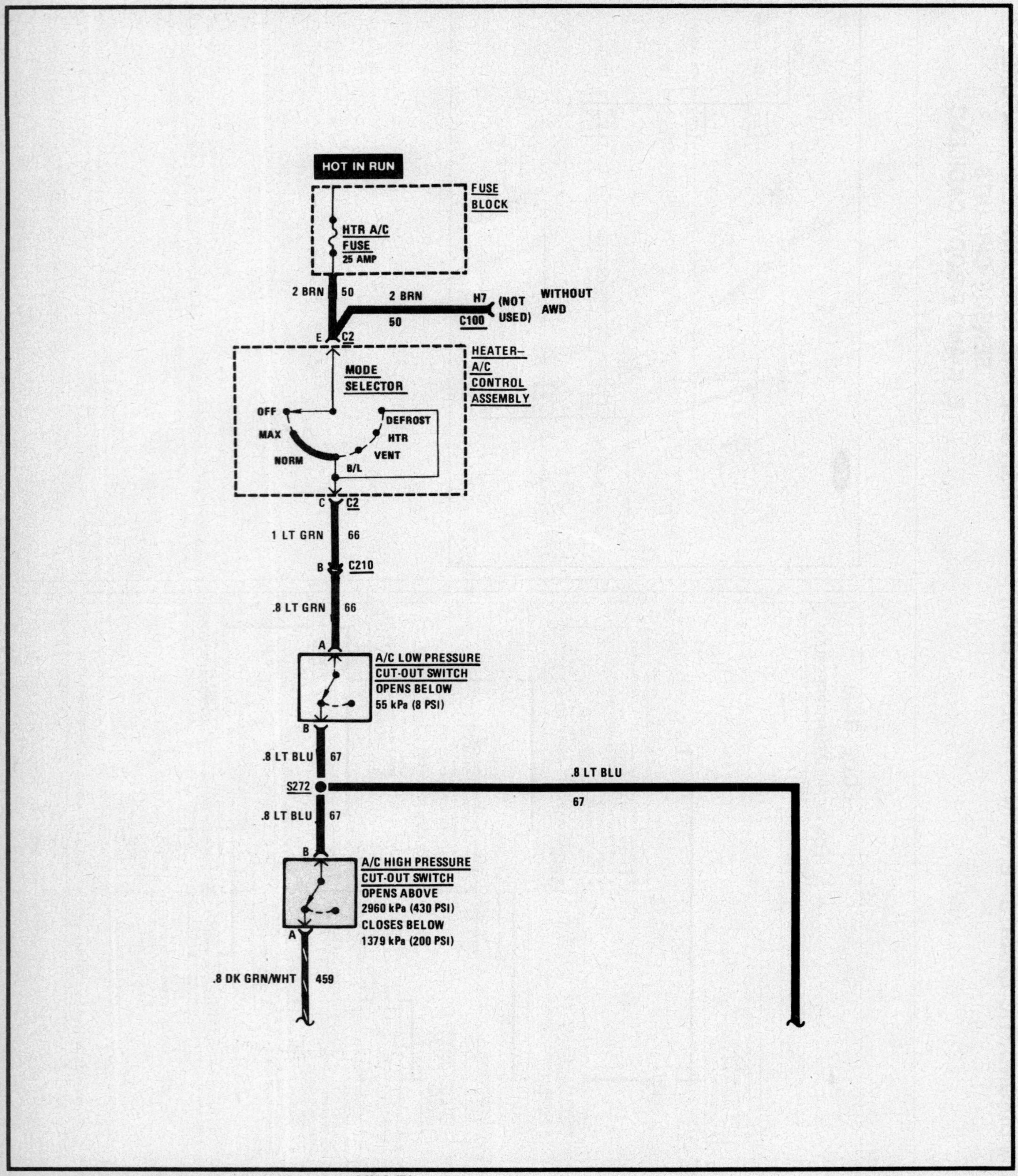
HOT IN RUN
FUSE BLOCK
HTR A/C FUSE
25 AMP
2 BRN
50
2 BRN
H7
(NOT USED)
WITHOUT AWD
50
C100
E
C2
HEATER-A/C CONTROL ASSEMBLY
MODE SELECTOR
OFF
DEFROST
MAX
HTR
VENT
NORM
B/L
C
C2
1 LT GRN
66
B
C210
.8 LT GRN
66
A
A/C LOW PRESSURE CUT-OUT SWITCH
OPENS BELOW
55 kPa (8 PSI)
B
.8 LT BLU
67
S272
.8 LT BLU
67
.8 LT BLU
67
B
A/C HIGH PRESSURE CUT-OUT SWITCH
OPENS ABOVE
2960 kPa (430 PSI)
CLOSES BELOW
1379 kPa (200 PSI)
A
.8 DK GRN/WHT
459

Compressor controls—A body (engine VIN R)

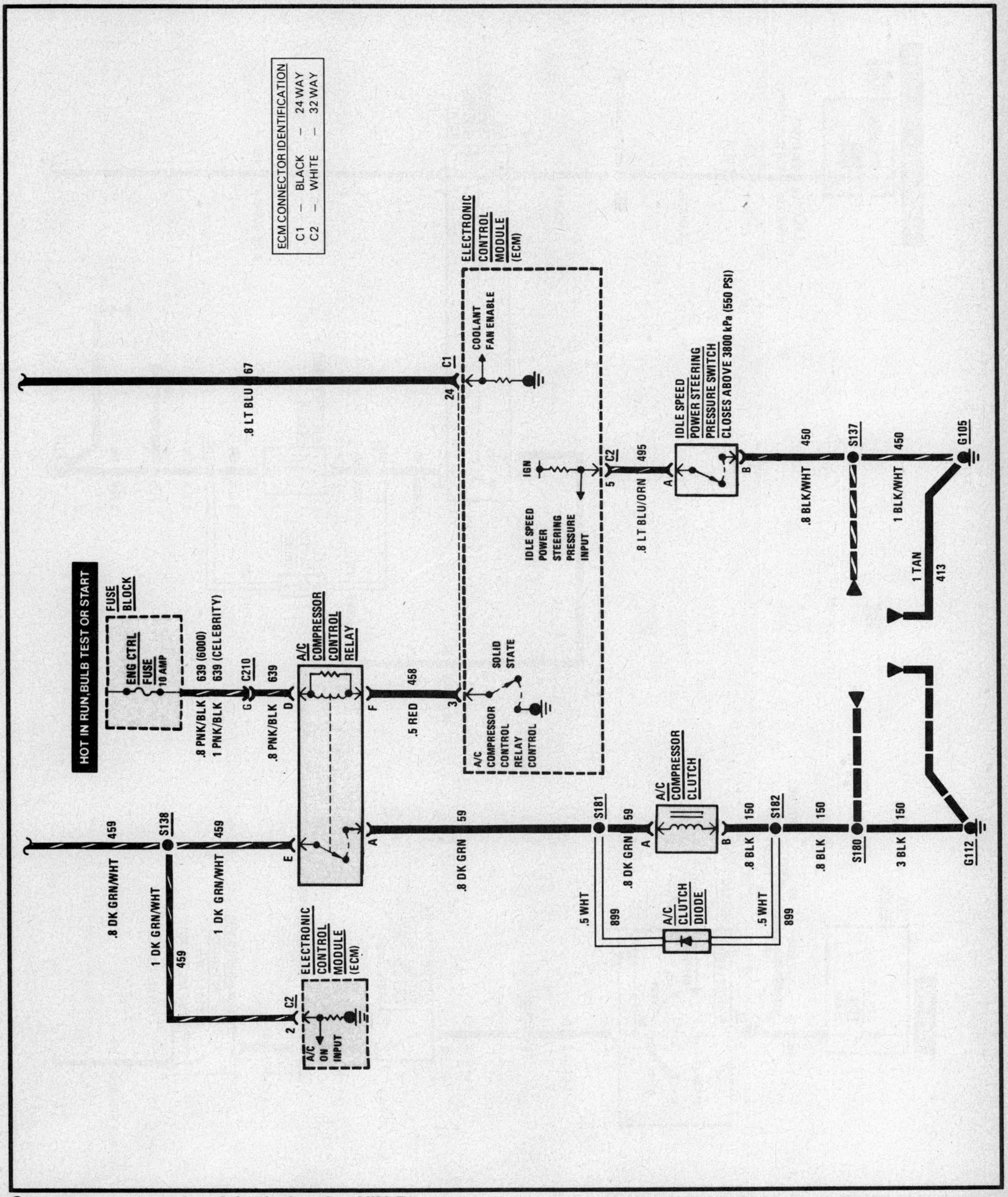
ECM CONNECTOR IDENTIFICATION
C1 – BLACK – 24 WAY
C2 – WHITE – 32 WAY
HOT IN RUN, BULB TEST OR START
FUSE BLOCK
ENG CTRL FUSE 10 AMP
639 (6000)
639 (CELEBRITY)
.8 PNK/BLK
1 PNK/BLK
C210
639
.8 PNK/BLK
A/C COMPRESSOR CONTROL RELAY
458
.5 RED
ELECTRONIC CONTROL MODULE (ECM)
A/C COMPRESSOR CONTROL RELAY CONTROL
SOLID STATE
COOLANT FAN ENABLE
.8 LT BLU
67
IDLE SPEED POWER STEERING PRESSURE INPUT
IGN
495
.8 LT BLU/ORN
IDLE SPEED POWER STEERING PRESSURE SWITCH CLOSES ABOVE 3800 kPa (550 PSI)
450
.8 BLK/WHT
S137
1 BLK/WHT
G105
1 TAN
413
459
.8 DK GRN/WHT
S138
1 DK GRN/WHT
59
.8 DK GRN
S181
A/C COMPRESSOR CLUTCH
150
.8 BLK
S182
S180
3 BLK
G112
.5 WHT
899
A/C CLUTCH DIODE
A/C ON INPUT

Compressor controls—A body (engine VIN R)

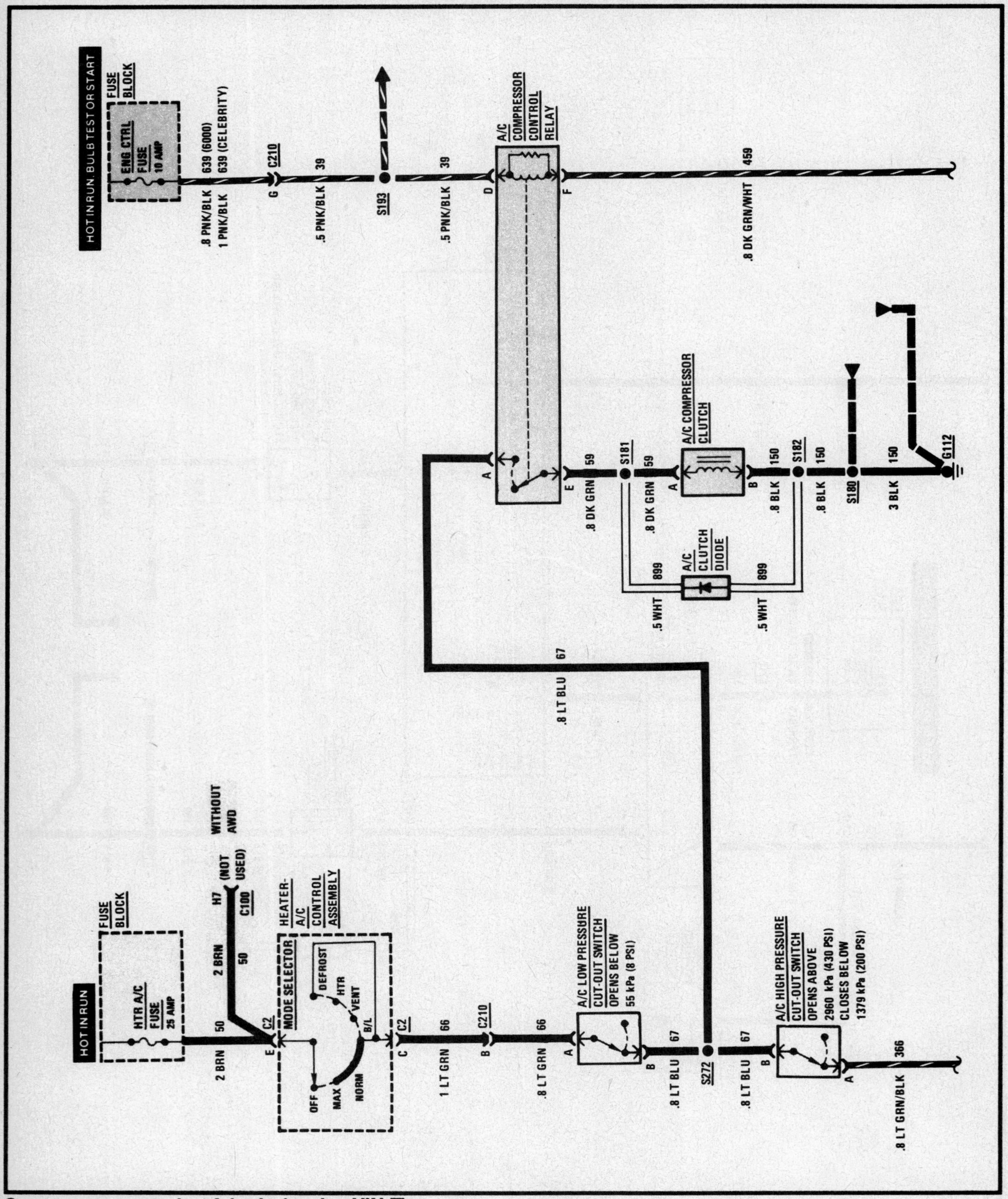
HOT IN RUN, BULB TEST OR START
FUSE BLOCK
ENG CTRL FUSE 10 AMP
639 (6000)
639 (CELEBRITY)
.8 PNK/BLK
1 PNK/BLK
C210
G
39
.5 PNK/BLK
S193
39
.5 PNK/BLK
D
A/C COMPRESSOR CONTROL RELAY
F
459
.8 DK GRN/WHT
A
E
59
.8 DK GRN
S181
59
.8 DK GRN
A/C COMPRESSOR CLUTCH
B
150
.8 BLK
S182
150
.8 BLK
S180
150
3 BLK
G112
A/C CLUTCH DIODE
899
.5 WHT
899
.5 WHT
67
.8 LT BLU
HOT IN RUN
FUSE BLOCK
HTR A/C FUSE 25 AMP
50
2 BRN
C2
E
H7
(NOT USED)
WITHOUT AWD
C100
2 BRN
50
HEATER-A/C CONTROL ASSEMBLY
MODE SELECTOR
DEFROST
HTR
VENT
B/L
OFF
MAX
NORM
C2
C
66
1 LT GRN
C210
B
66
.8 LT GRN
A/C LOW PRESSURE CUT-OUT SWITCH
OPENS BELOW 55 kPa (8 PSI)
A
B
67
.8 LT BLU
S272
67
.8 LT BLU
A/C HIGH PRESSURE CUT-OUT SWITCH
OPENS ABOVE 2960 kPa (430 PSI)
CLOSES BELOW 1379 kPa (200 PSI)
B
A
366
.8 LT GRN/BLK

Compressor controls—A body (engine VIN T)

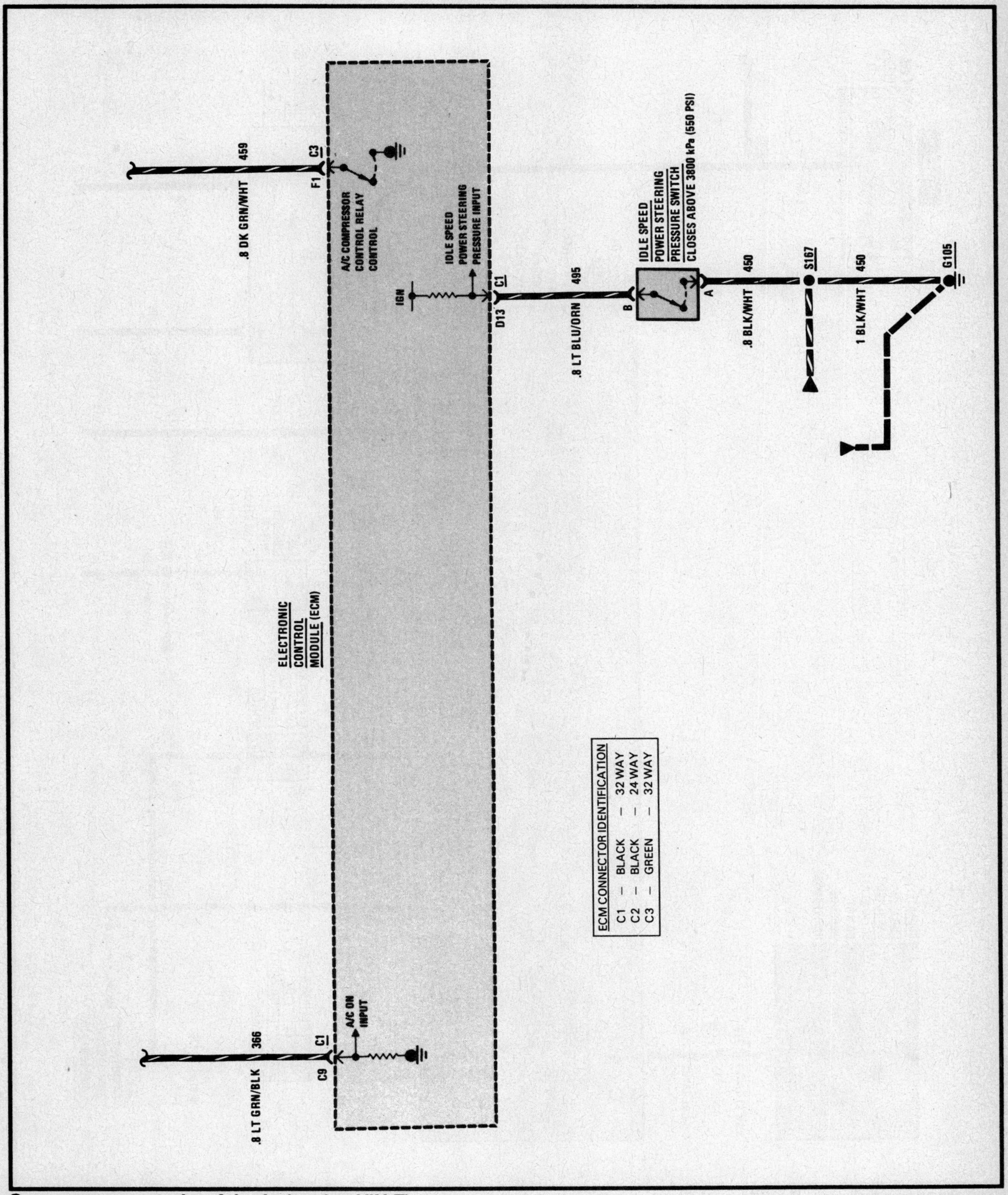
.8 DK GRN/WHT
459
C3
F1
A/C COMPRESSOR CONTROL RELAY CONTROL
IDLE SPEED POWER STEERING PRESSURE INPUT
IGN
C1
D13
495
.8 LT BLU/ORN
B
A
IDLE SPEED POWER STEERING PRESSURE SWITCH CLOSES ABOVE 3800 kPa (550 PSI)
450
.8 BLK/WHT
S167
450
1 BLK/WHT
G105
ELECTRONIC CONTROL MODULE (ECM)
ECM CONNECTOR IDENTIFICATION
C1 – BLACK – 32 WAY
C2 – BLACK – 24 WAY
C3 – GREEN – 32 WAY
A/C ON INPUT
C1
C9
366
.8 LT GRN/BLK

Compressor controls—A body (engine VIN T)

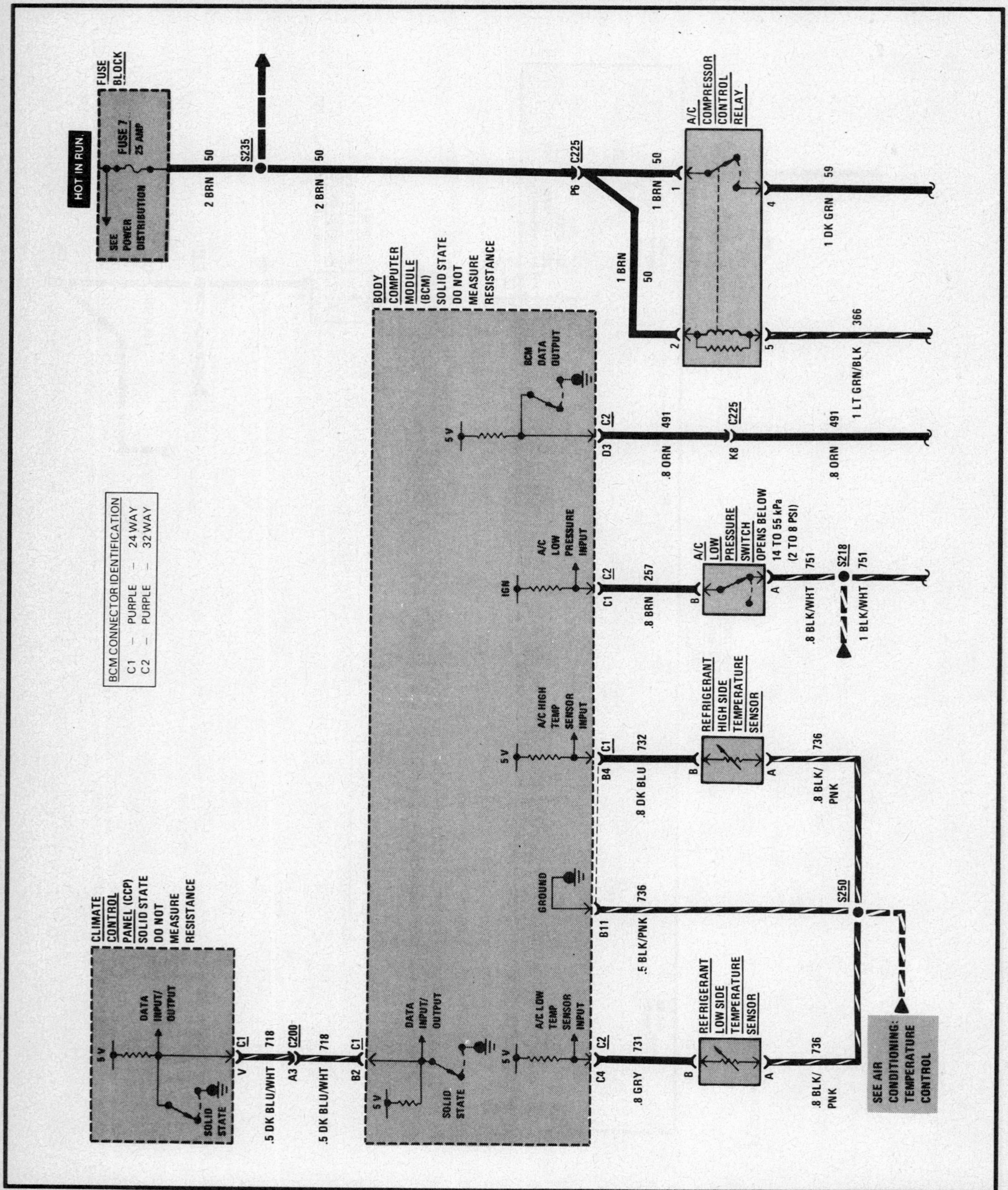
HOT IN RUN.
FUSE BLOCK
FUSE 7 25 AMP
SEE POWER DISTRIBUTION
S235
C225
A/C COMPRESSOR CONTROL RELAY
2 BRN
50
1 BRN
1 DK GRN
59
366
1 LT GRN/BLK
BODY COMPUTER MODULE (BCM) SOLID STATE DO NOT MEASURE RESISTANCE
BCM DATA OUTPUT
491
.8 ORN
BCM CONNECTOR IDENTIFICATION
C1 – PURPLE – 24 WAY
C2 – PURPLE – 32 WAY
A/C LOW PRESSURE INPUT
IGN
257
.8 BRN
A/C LOW PRESSURE SWITCH OPENS BELOW 14 TO 55 kPa (2 TO 8 PSI)
751
.8 BLK/WHT
S218
1 BLK/WHT
A/C HIGH TEMP SENSOR INPUT
732
.8 DK BLU
REFRIGERANT HIGH SIDE TEMPERATURE SENSOR
736
.8 BLK/PNK
GROUND
.5 BLK/PNK
S250
CLIMATE CONTROL PANEL (CCP) SOLID STATE DO NOT MEASURE RESISTANCE
DATA INPUT/OUTPUT
SOLID STATE
718
C200
.5 DK BLU/WHT
A/C LOW TEMP SENSOR INPUT
731
.8 GRY
REFRIGERANT LOW SIDE TEMPERATURE SENSOR
SEE AIR CONDITIONING: TEMPERATURE CONTROL
5 V

Compressor controls – DeVille and Fleetwood

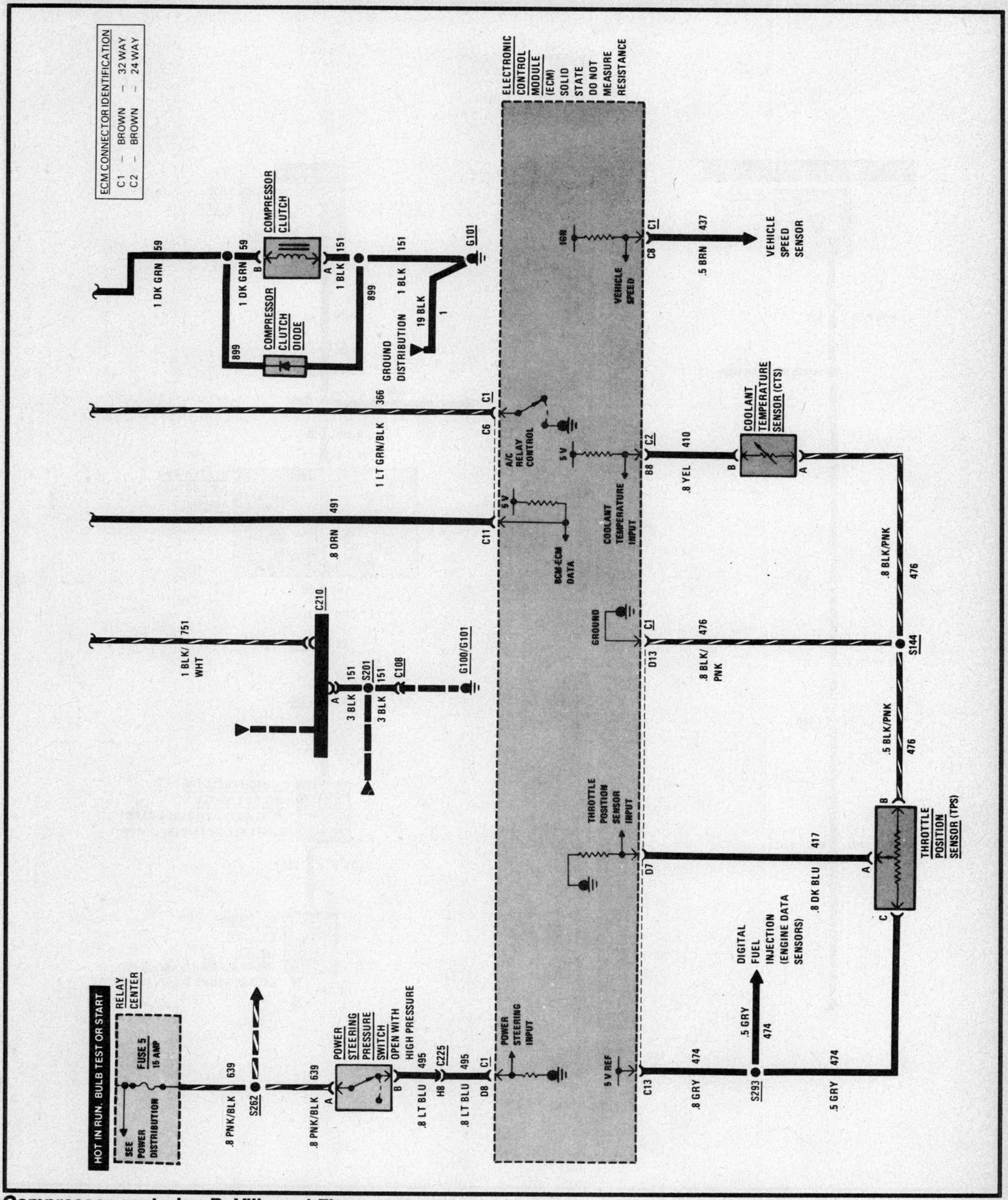
ECM CONNECTOR IDENTIFICATION
C1 – BROWN – 32 WAY
C2 – BROWN – 24 WAY
COMPRESSOR CLUTCH
COMPRESSOR CLUTCH DIODE
GROUND DISTRIBUTION
G101
ELECTRONIC CONTROL MODULE (ECM) SOLID STATE DO NOT MEASURE RESISTANCE
VEHICLE SPEED SENSOR
COOLANT TEMPERATURE SENSOR (CTS)
A/C RELAY CONTROL
COOLANT TEMPERATURE INPUT
BCM-ECM DATA
VEHICLE SPEED
GROUND
THROTTLE POSITION SENSOR INPUT
THROTTLE POSITION SENSOR (TPS)
DIGITAL FUEL INJECTION (ENGINE DATA SENSORS)
POWER STEERING INPUT
5 V REF
POWER STEERING PRESSURE SWITCH OPEN WITH HIGH PRESSURE
HOT IN RUN, BULB TEST OR START
RELAY CENTER
FUSE 5 15 AMP
SEE POWER DISTRIBUTION
S262
S293
S144
S201
C108
C210
C225
G100/G101

Compressor controls—DeVille and Fleetwood

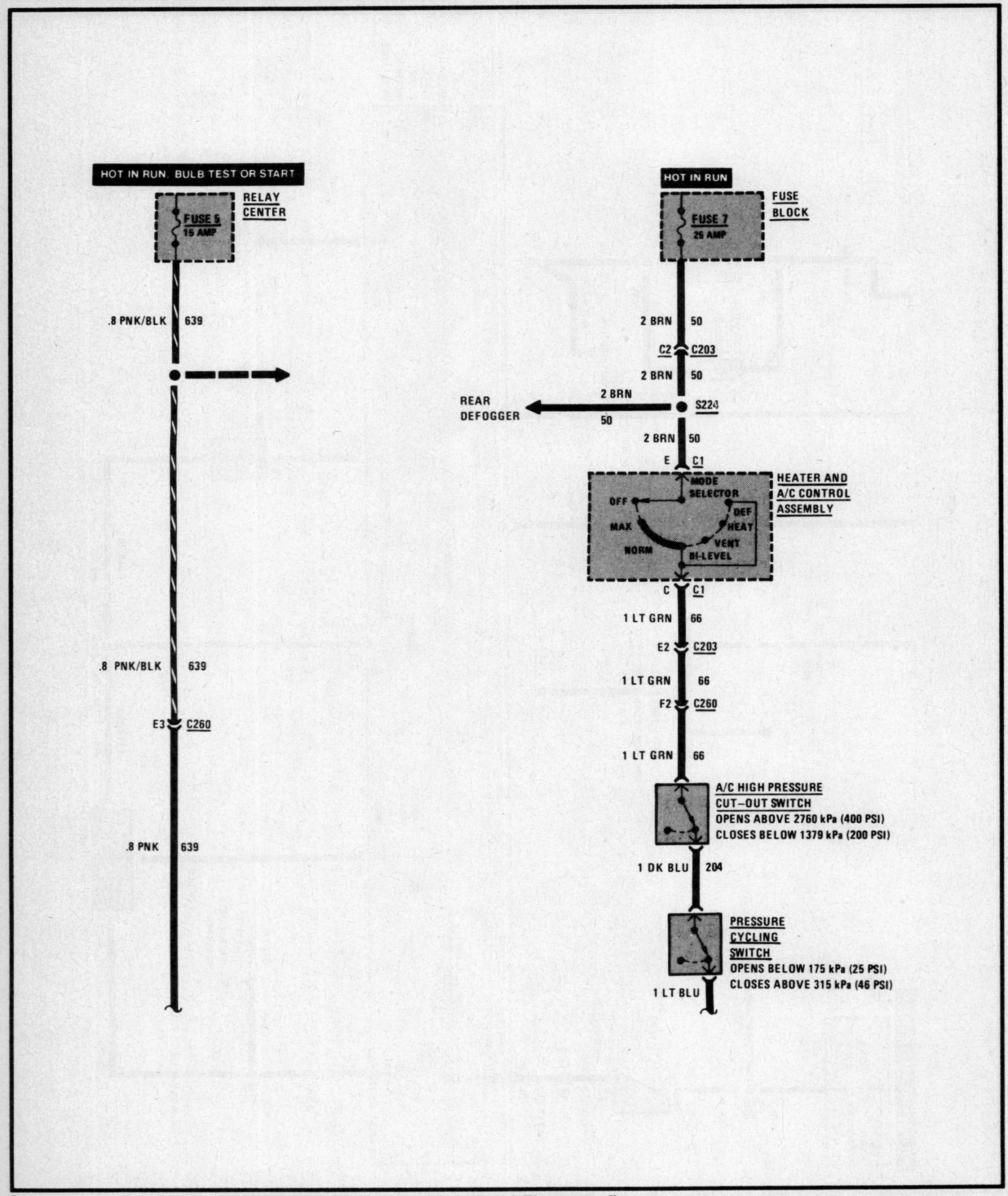
HOT IN RUN, BULB TEST OR START
RELAY CENTER
FUSE 5 15 AMP
.8 PNK/BLK 639
.8 PNK/BLK 639
E3 C260
.8 PNK 639
HOT IN RUN
FUSE BLOCK
FUSE 7 25 AMP
2 BRN 50
C2 C203
2 BRN 50
REAR DEFOGGER
2 BRN
50
S224
2 BRN 50
E C1
MODE SELECTOR
HEATER AND A/C CONTROL ASSEMBLY
OFF
DEF
MAX
HEAT
VENT
NORM
BI-LEVEL
C C1
1 LT GRN 66
E2 C203
1 LT GRN 66
F2 C260
1 LT GRN 66
A/C HIGH PRESSURE CUT-OUT SWITCH
OPENS ABOVE 2760 kPa (400 PSI)
CLOSES BELOW 1379 kPa (200 PSI)
1 DK BLU 204
PRESSURE CYCLING SWITCH
OPENS BELOW 175 kPa (25 PSI)
CLOSES ABOVE 315 kPa (46 PSI)
1 LT BLU

Compressor controls – C and H body (except DeVille and Fleetwood)

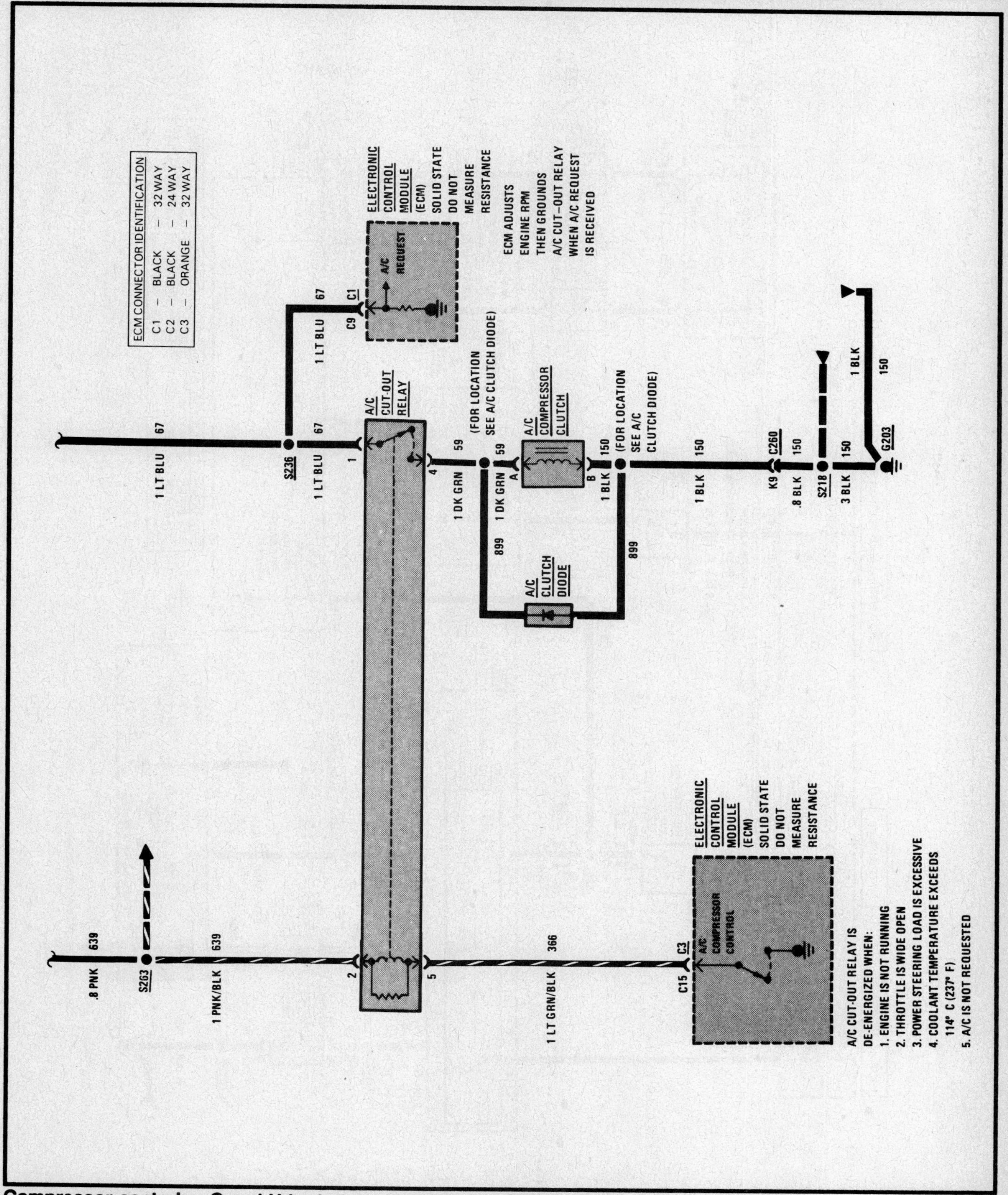
ECM CONNECTOR IDENTIFICATION
C1 – BLACK – 32 WAY
C2 – BLACK – 24 WAY
C3 – ORANGE – 32 WAY
ELECTRONIC CONTROL MODULE (ECM) SOLID STATE DO NOT MEASURE RESISTANCE
A/C REQUEST
ECM ADJUSTS ENGINE RPM THEN GROUNDS A/C CUT-OUT RELAY WHEN A/C REQUEST IS RECEIVED
C1
C9
67
1 LT BLU
A/C CUT-OUT RELAY
S236
1
2
4
5
59
1 DK GRN
(FOR LOCATION SEE A/C CLUTCH DIODE)
A/C COMPRESSOR CLUTCH
A
B
150
(FOR LOCATION SEE A/C CLUTCH DIODE)
899
A/C CLUTCH DIODE
1 BLK
C260
K9
.8 BLK
S218
3 BLK
G203
.8 PNK
639
S263
1 PNK/BLK
366
1 LT GRN/BLK
C3
C15
A/C COMPRESSOR CONTROL
A/C CUT-OUT RELAY IS DE-ENERGIZED WHEN:
1. ENGINE IS NOT RUNNING
2. THROTTLE IS WIDE OPEN
3. POWER STEERING LOAD IS EXCESSIVE
4. COOLANT TEMPERATURE EXCEEDS 114° C (237° F)
5. A/C IS NOT REQUESTED

Compressor controls – C and H body (except DeVille and Fleetwood)

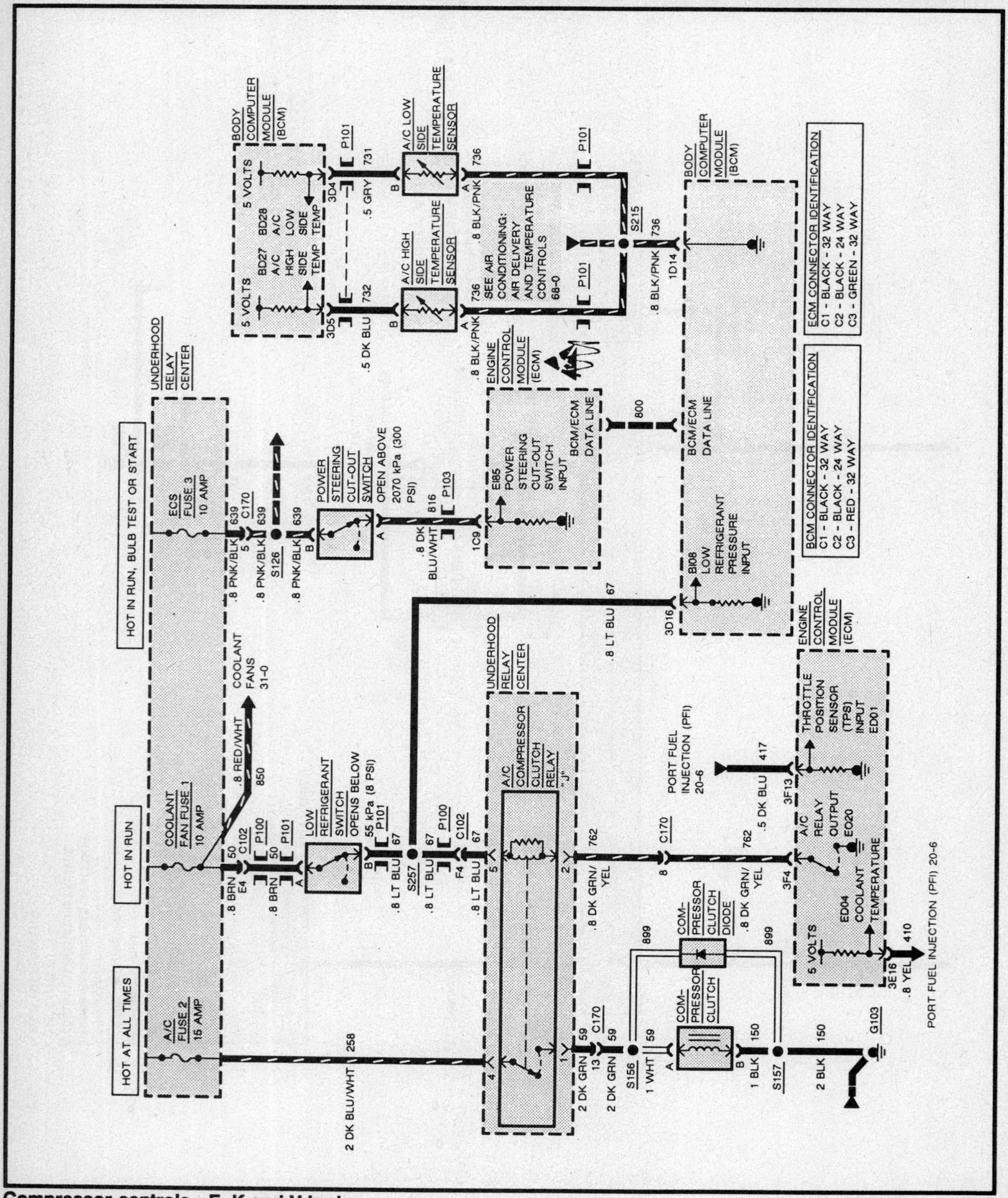
HOT AT ALL TIMES
HOT IN RUN
HOT IN RUN, BULB TEST OR START
UNDERHOOD RELAY CENTER
A/C FUSE 2 15 AMP
COOLANT FAN FUSE 1 10 AMP
ECS FUSE 3 10 AMP
COOLANT FANS 31-0
LOW REFRIGERANT SWITCH OPENS BELOW 55 kPa (8 PSI)
POWER STEERING CUT-OUT SWITCH OPEN ABOVE 2070 kPa (300 PSI)
BODY COMPUTER MODULE (BCM)
A/C HIGH SIDE TEMPERATURE SENSOR
A/C LOW SIDE TEMPERATURE SENSOR
SEE AIR CONDITIONING: AIR DELIVERY AND TEMPERATURE CONTROLS 68-0
ENGINE CONTROL MODULE (ECM)
E185 POWER STEERING CUT-OUT SWITCH INPUT
BCM/ECM DATA LINE
B108 LOW REFRIGERANT PRESSURE INPUT
A/C COMPRESSOR CLUTCH RELAY "J"
COMPRESSOR CLUTCH DIODE
COMPRESSOR CLUTCH
PORT FUEL INJECTION (PFI) 20-6
THROTTLE POSITION SENSOR (TPS) INPUT ED01
A/C RELAY OUTPUT EO20
ED04 COOLANT TEMPERATURE
PORT FUEL INJECTION (PFI) 20-6
BCM CONNECTOR IDENTIFICATION
C1 - BLACK - 32 WAY
C2 - BLACK - 24 WAY
C3 - RED - 32 WAY
ECM CONNECTOR IDENTIFICATION
C1 - BLACK - 32 WAY
C2 - BLACK - 24 WAY
C3 - GREEN - 32 WAY

Compressor controls – E, K and V body

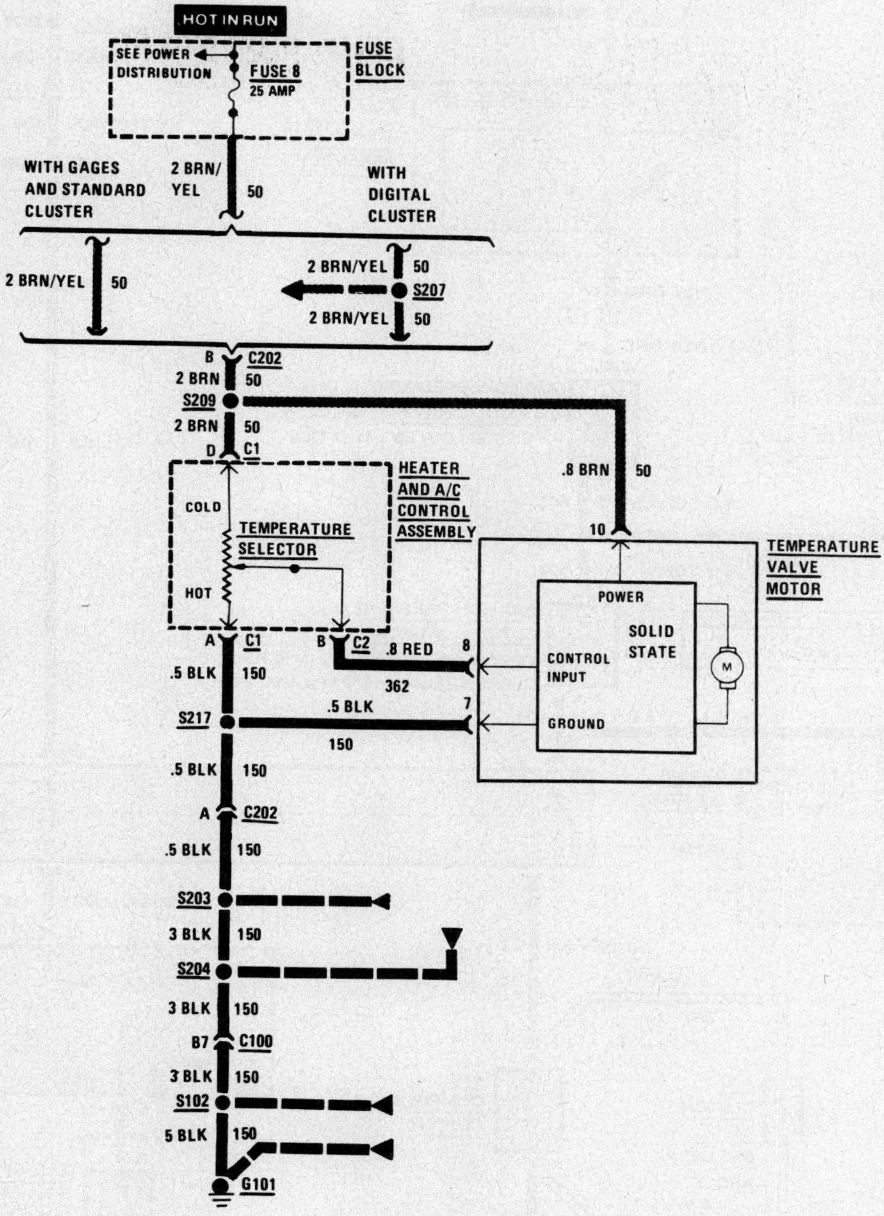
HOT IN RUN
SEE POWER DISTRIBUTION
FUSE 8
25 AMP
FUSE BLOCK
WITH GAGES AND STANDARD CLUSTER
2 BRN/YEL
50
WITH DIGITAL CLUSTER
2 BRN/YEL
50
2 BRN/YEL
50
S207
2 BRN/YEL
50
B
C202
2 BRN
50
S209
2 BRN
50
D
C1
HEATER AND A/C CONTROL ASSEMBLY
COLD
TEMPERATURE SELECTOR
HOT
.8 BRN
50
10
TEMPERATURE VALVE MOTOR
POWER
SOLID STATE
CONTROL INPUT
GROUND
M
A
C1
B
C2
.8 RED
8
362
.5 BLK
150
S217
.5 BLK
7
150
.5 BLK
150
A
C202
.5 BLK
150
S203
3 BLK
150
S204
3 BLK
150
B7
C100
3 BLK
150
S102
5 BLK
150
G101

Compressor controls—L and J body

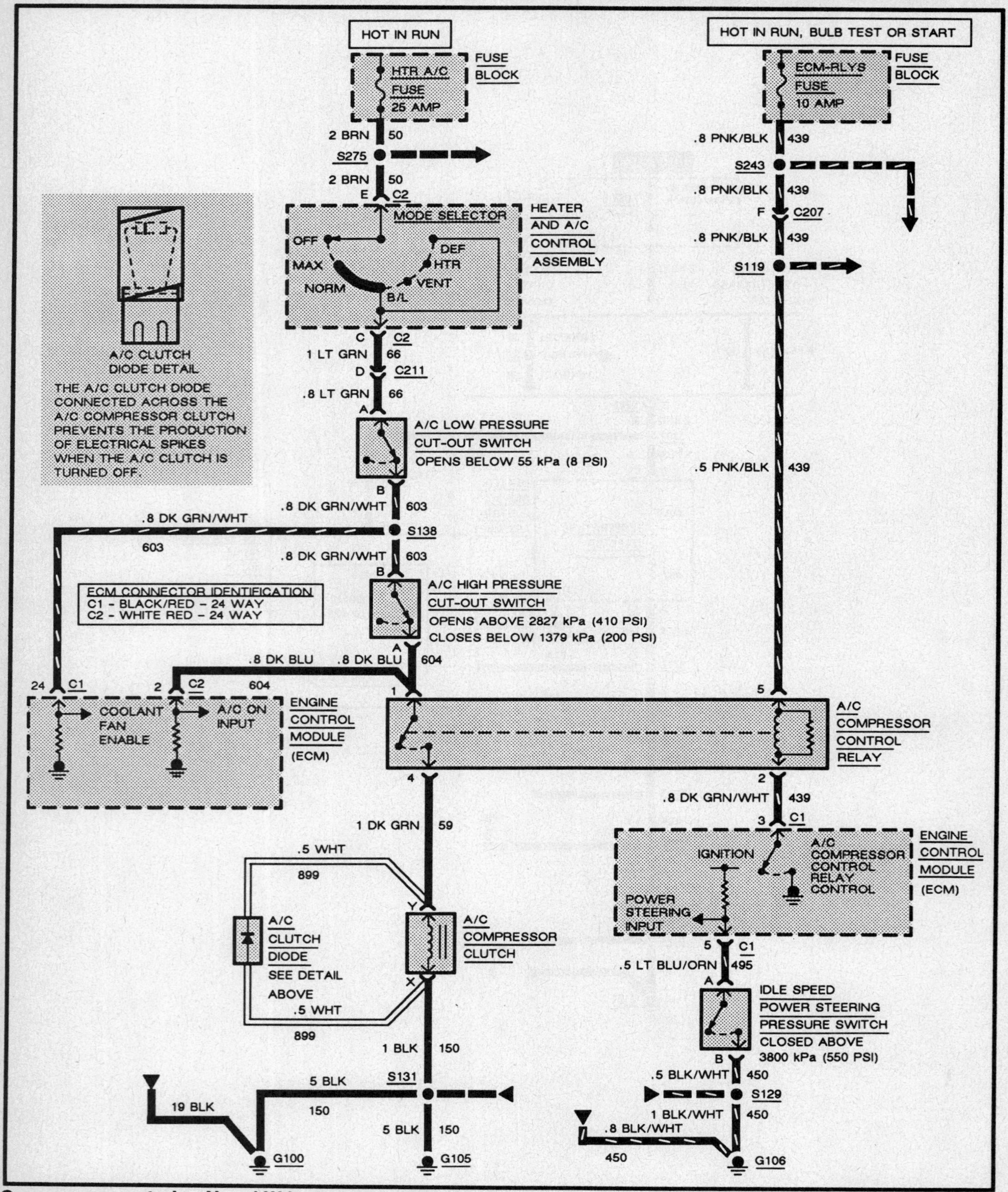
HOT IN RUN
HTR A/C FUSE 25 AMP
FUSE BLOCK
HOT IN RUN, BULB TEST OR START
ECM-RLYS FUSE 10 AMP
FUSE BLOCK
2 BRN 50
S275
2 BRN 50
E C2
MODE SELECTOR
OFF
MAX
NORM
DEF
HTR
VENT
B/L
HEATER AND A/C CONTROL ASSEMBLY
C C2
1 LT GRN 66
D C211
.8 LT GRN 66
A
A/C LOW PRESSURE CUT-OUT SWITCH
OPENS BELOW 55 kPa (8 PSI)
B
.8 DK GRN/WHT 603
.8 DK GRN/WHT
603
S138
.8 DK GRN/WHT 603
B
A/C HIGH PRESSURE CUT-OUT SWITCH
OPENS ABOVE 2827 kPa (410 PSI)
CLOSES BELOW 1379 kPa (200 PSI)
A
A/C CLUTCH DIODE DETAIL
THE A/C CLUTCH DIODE CONNECTED ACROSS THE A/C COMPRESSOR CLUTCH PREVENTS THE PRODUCTION OF ELECTRICAL SPIKES WHEN THE A/C CLUTCH IS TURNED OFF.
ECM CONNECTOR IDENTIFICATION
C1 - BLACK/RED - 24 WAY
C2 - WHITE RED - 24 WAY
.8 DK BLU
.8 DK BLU 604
24 C1
2 C2
604
COOLANT FAN ENABLE
A/C ON INPUT
ENGINE CONTROL MODULE (ECM)
1
5
A/C COMPRESSOR CONTROL RELAY
4
2
.8 PNK/BLK 439
S243
.8 PNK/BLK 439
F C207
.8 PNK/BLK 439
S119
.5 PNK/BLK 439
.8 DK GRN/WHT 439
3 C1
IGNITION
A/C COMPRESSOR CONTROL RELAY CONTROL
POWER STEERING INPUT
ENGINE CONTROL MODULE (ECM)
5 C1
.5 LT BLU/ORN 495
A
IDLE SPEED POWER STEERING PRESSURE SWITCH
CLOSED ABOVE 3800 kPa (550 PSI)
B
.5 BLK/WHT 450
S129
1 BLK/WHT 450
.8 BLK/WHT
450
G106
1 DK GRN 59
.5 WHT
899
Y
A/C CLUTCH DIODE
SEE DETAIL ABOVE
A/C COMPRESSOR CLUTCH
X
.5 WHT
899
1 BLK 150
5 BLK
S131
150
19 BLK
5 BLK 150
G100
G105

Compressor controls – N and W body (engine VIN U)

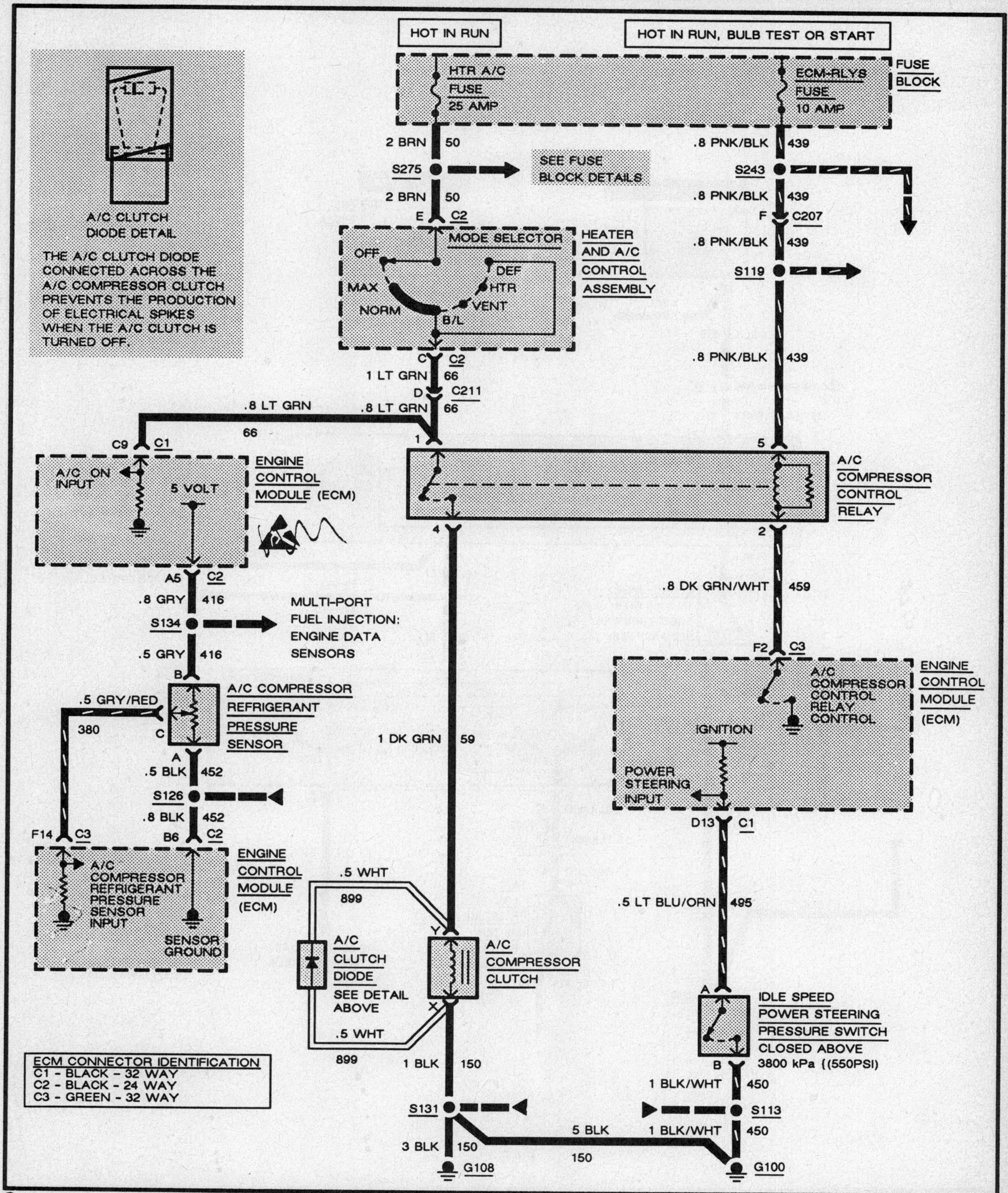
HOT IN RUN
HOT IN RUN, BULB TEST OR START
HTR A/C FUSE 25 AMP
ECM-RLYS FUSE 10 AMP
FUSE BLOCK
2 BRN 50
.8 PNK/BLK 439
S275
SEE FUSE BLOCK DETAILS
S243
2 BRN 50
.8 PNK/BLK 439
E C2
F C207
MODE SELECTOR
HEATER AND A/C CONTROL ASSEMBLY
OFF
DEF
MAX
HTR
NORM
VENT
B/L
.8 PNK/BLK 439
S119
C C2
1 LT GRN 66
D C211
.8 LT GRN
.8 LT GRN 66
66
.8 PNK/BLK 439
C9 C1
1
5
A/C ON INPUT
5 VOLT
ENGINE CONTROL MODULE (ECM)
A/C COMPRESSOR CONTROL RELAY
4
2
A5 C2
.8 GRY 416
S134
MULTI-PORT FUEL INJECTION: ENGINE DATA SENSORS
.5 GRY 416
.8 DK GRN/WHT 459
F2 C3
B
A/C COMPRESSOR REFRIGERANT PRESSURE SENSOR
.5 GRY/RED
380
C
A/C COMPRESSOR CONTROL RELAY CONTROL
ENGINE CONTROL MODULE (ECM)
IGNITION
1 DK GRN 59
A
.5 BLK 452
S126
.8 BLK 452
POWER STEERING INPUT
D13 C1
F14 C3
B6 C2
A/C COMPRESSOR REFRIGERANT PRESSURE SENSOR INPUT
SENSOR GROUND
ENGINE CONTROL MODULE (ECM)
.5 WHT
899
.5 LT BLU/ORN 495
Y
A/C CLUTCH DIODE
SEE DETAIL ABOVE
A/C COMPRESSOR CLUTCH
X
.5 WHT
899
A
IDLE SPEED POWER STEERING PRESSURE SWITCH
CLOSED ABOVE 3800 kPa ((550PSI)
B
ECM CONNECTOR IDENTIFICATION
C1 - BLACK - 32 WAY
C2 - BLACK - 24 WAY
C3 - GREEN - 32 WAY
1 BLK 150
1 BLK/WHT 450
S131
S113
5 BLK
1 BLK/WHT 450
3 BLK 150
150
G108
G100
A/C CLUTCH DIODE DETAIL
THE A/C CLUTCH DIODE CONNECTED ACROSS THE A/C COMPRESSOR CLUTCH PREVENTS THE PRODUCTION OF ELECTRICAL SPIKES WHEN THE A/C CLUTCH IS TURNED OFF.

Compressor controls—N and W body (engine VIN D and A)

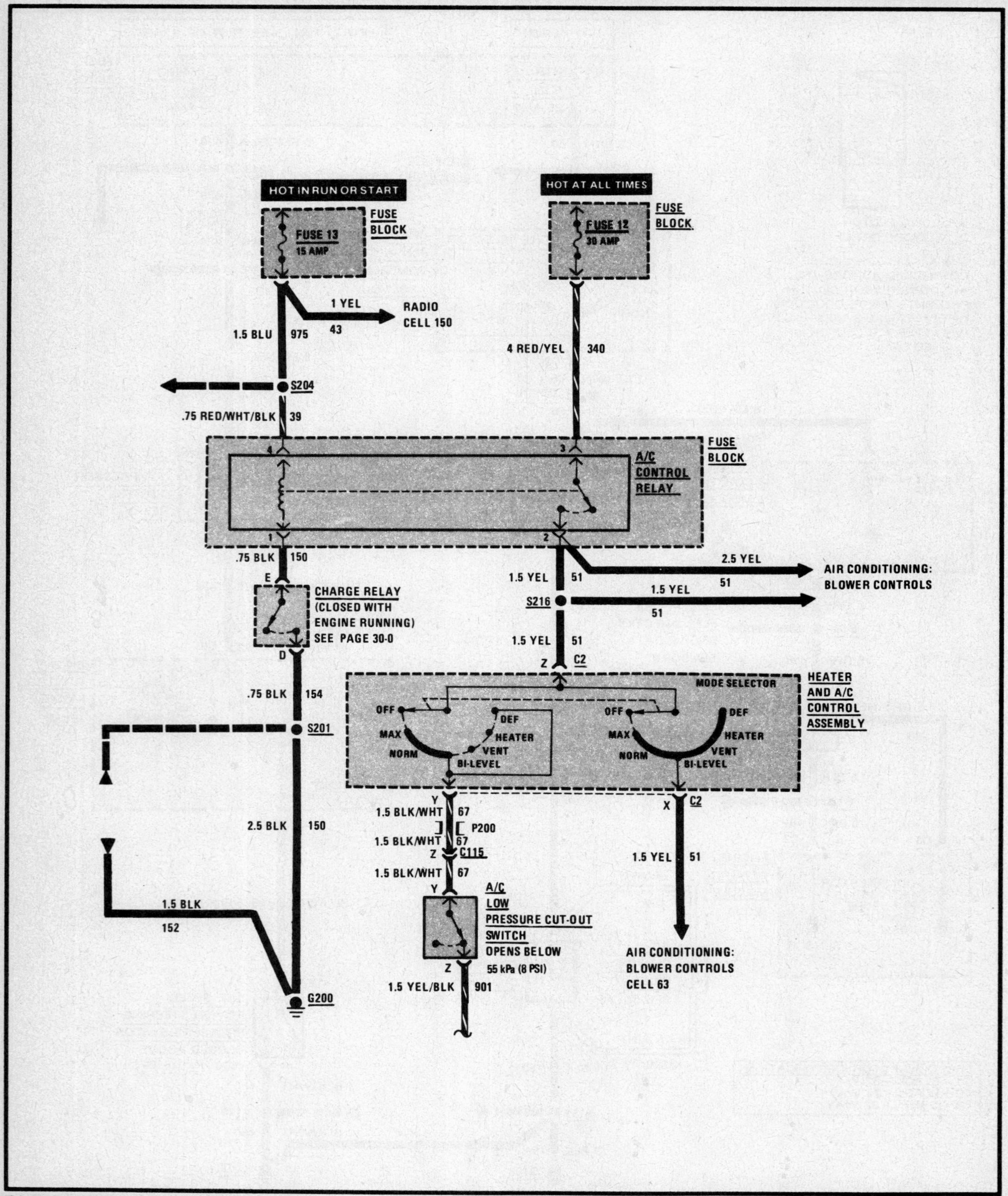
HOT IN RUN OR START
FUSE 13
15 AMP
FUSE BLOCK
HOT AT ALL TIMES
FUSE 12
30 AMP
FUSE BLOCK
1 YEL
43
RADIO
CELL 150
1.5 BLU
975
4 RED/YEL
340
S204
.75 RED/WHT/BLK
39
FUSE BLOCK
A/C CONTROL RELAY
.75 BLK
150
2.5 YEL
51
AIR CONDITIONING:
BLOWER CONTROLS
1.5 YEL
51
S216
1.5 YEL
51
CHARGE RELAY
(CLOSED WITH
ENGINE RUNNING)
SEE PAGE 30-0
1.5 YEL
51
C2
.75 BLK
154
S201
MODE SELECTOR
OFF
DEF
MAX
HEATER
NORM
VENT
BI-LEVEL
HEATER AND A/C CONTROL ASSEMBLY
1.5 BLK/WHT
67
P200
C115
2.5 BLK
150
1.5 YEL
51
A/C LOW PRESSURE CUT-OUT SWITCH
OPENS BELOW
55 kPa (8 PSI)
1.5 BLK
152
1.5 YEL/BLK
901
AIR CONDITIONING:
BLOWER CONTROLS
CELL 63
G200

Compressor controls—T body

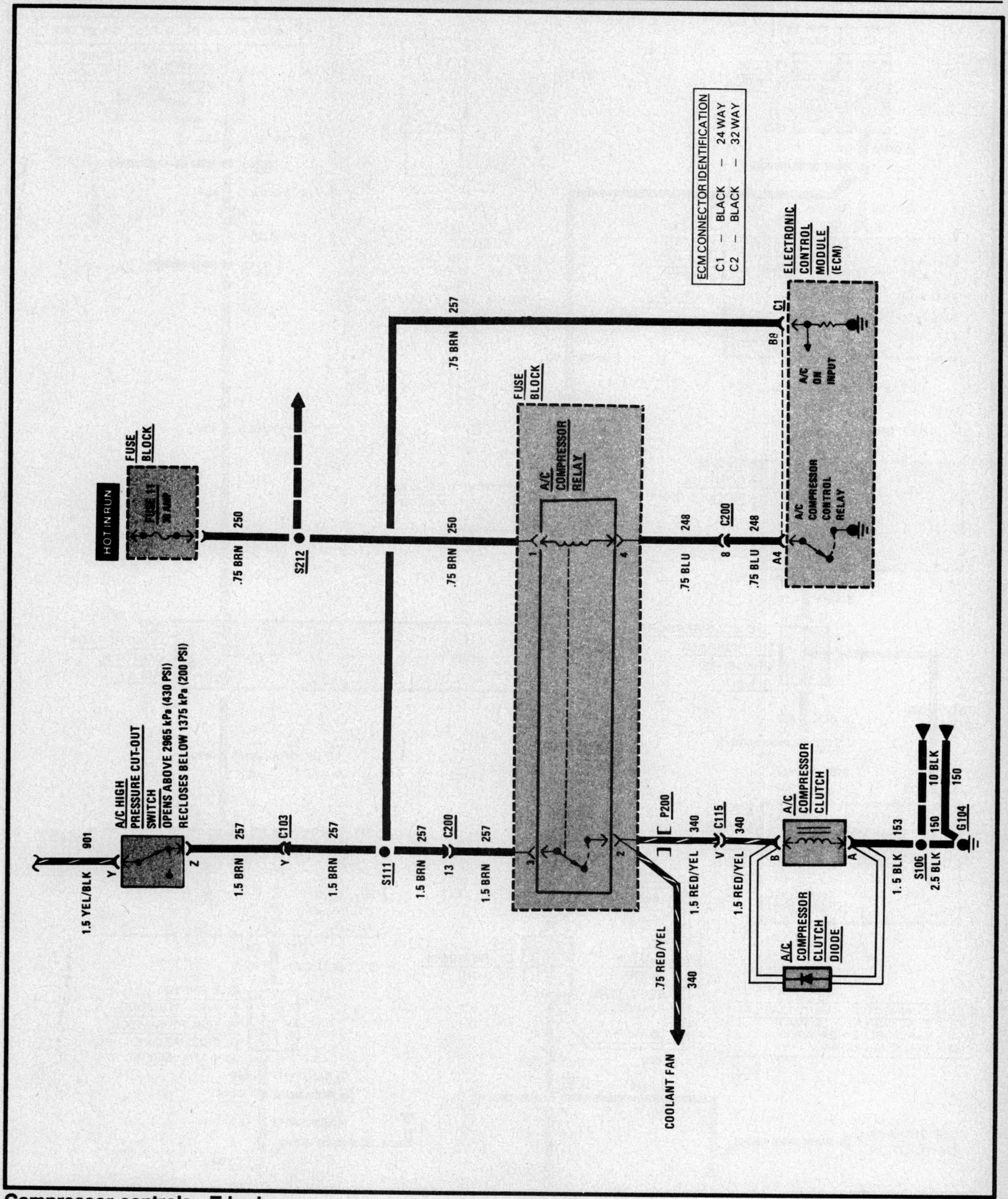
ECM CONNECTOR IDENTIFICATION
C1 – BLACK – 24 WAY
C2 – BLACK – 32 WAY
ELECTRONIC CONTROL MODULE (ECM)
C1
B8
A/C ON INPUT
A/C COMPRESSOR CONTROL RELAY
A4
HOT IN RUN
FUSE BLOCK
FUSE 11 20 AMP
.75 BRN 250
S212
.75 BRN 257
FUSE BLOCK
A/C COMPRESSOR RELAY
.75 BRN 250
.75 BLU 248
C200
8
.75 BLU 248
A/C HIGH PRESSURE CUT-OUT SWITCH
OPENS ABOVE 2965 kPa (430 PSI)
RECLOSES BELOW 1375 kPa (200 PSI)
1.5 YEL/BLK 901
1.5 BRN 257
C103
1.5 BRN 257
S111
1.5 BRN 257
C200
13
1.5 BRN 257
P200
1.5 RED/YEL 340
C115
1.5 RED/YEL 340
A/C COMPRESSOR CLUTCH
A/C COMPRESSOR CLUTCH DIODE
1.5 BLK 153
S106
2.5 BLK 150
10 BLK 150
G104
.75 RED/YEL 340
COOLANT FAN

Compressor controls—T body

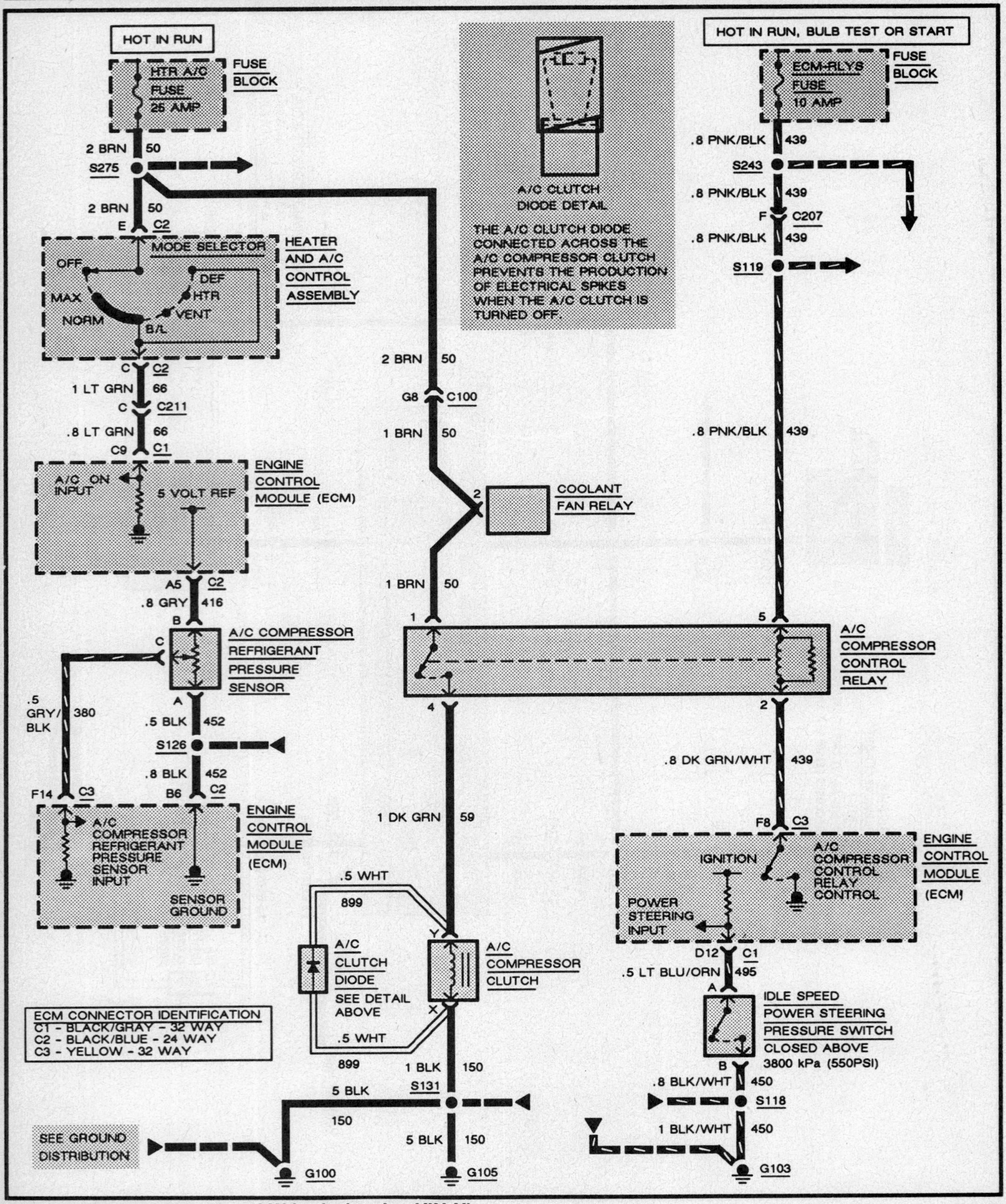
HOT IN RUN
HTR A/C FUSE 25 AMP
FUSE BLOCK
2 BRN 50
S275
2 BRN 50
E C2
MODE SELECTOR
HEATER AND A/C CONTROL ASSEMBLY
OFF
DEF
HTR
MAX
VENT
NORM
B/L
C C2
1 LT GRN 66
C C211
.8 LT GRN 66
C9 C1
ENGINE CONTROL MODULE (ECM)
A/C ON INPUT
5 VOLT REF
A5 C2
.8 GRY 416
B
A/C COMPRESSOR REFRIGERANT PRESSURE SENSOR
C
A
.5 GRY/BLK 380
.5 BLK 452
S126
.8 BLK 452
F14 C3
B6 C2
ENGINE CONTROL MODULE (ECM)
A/C COMPRESSOR REFRIGERANT PRESSURE SENSOR INPUT
SENSOR GROUND
ECM CONNECTOR IDENTIFICATION
C1 - BLACK/GRAY - 32 WAY
C2 - BLACK/BLUE - 24 WAY
C3 - YELLOW - 32 WAY
SEE GROUND DISTRIBUTION
G100
A/C CLUTCH DIODE DETAIL
THE A/C CLUTCH DIODE CONNECTED ACROSS THE A/C COMPRESSOR CLUTCH PREVENTS THE PRODUCTION OF ELECTRICAL SPIKES WHEN THE A/C CLUTCH IS TURNED OFF.
2 BRN 50
G8 C100
1 BRN 50
2
COOLANT FAN RELAY
1 BRN 50
1
4
1 DK GRN 59
.5 WHT
899
Y
A/C CLUTCH DIODE
SEE DETAIL ABOVE
A/C COMPRESSOR CLUTCH
X
.5 WHT
899
1 BLK 150
S131
5 BLK
150
5 BLK 150
G105
HOT IN RUN, BULB TEST OR START
ECM-RLYS FUSE 10 AMP
FUSE BLOCK
.8 PNK/BLK 439
S243
.8 PNK/BLK 439
F C207
.8 PNK/BLK 439
S119
.8 PNK/BLK 439
5
A/C COMPRESSOR CONTROL RELAY
2
.8 DK GRN/WHT 439
F8 C3
ENGINE CONTROL MODULE (ECM)
IGNITION
A/C COMPRESSOR CONTROL RELAY CONTROL
POWER STEERING INPUT
D12 C1
.5 LT BLU/ORN 495
A
IDLE SPEED POWER STEERING PRESSURE SWITCH
CLOSED ABOVE 3800 kPa (550PSI)
B
.8 BLK/WHT 450
S118
1 BLK/WHT 450
G103

Compressor controls—N and W body (engine VIN N)

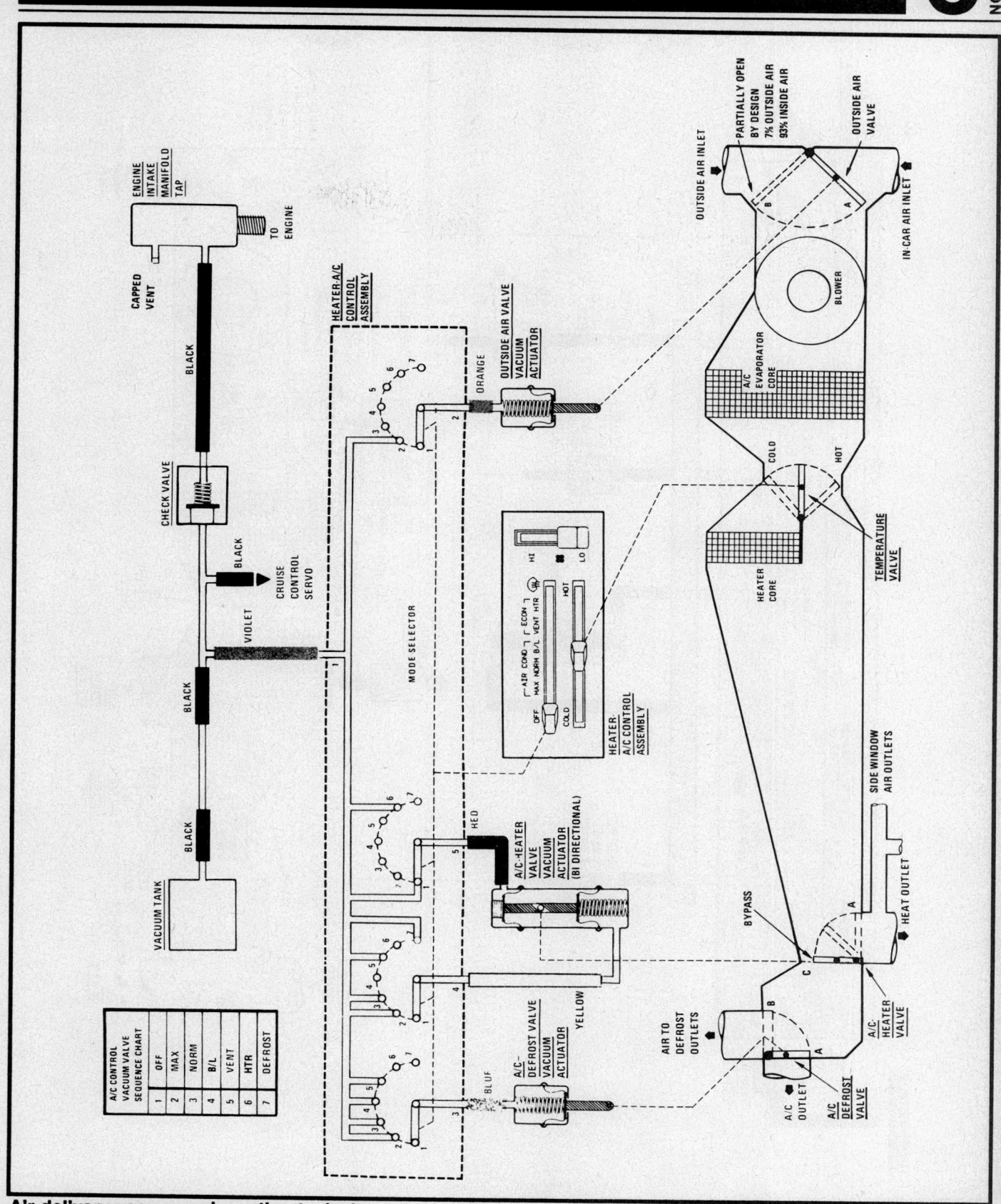

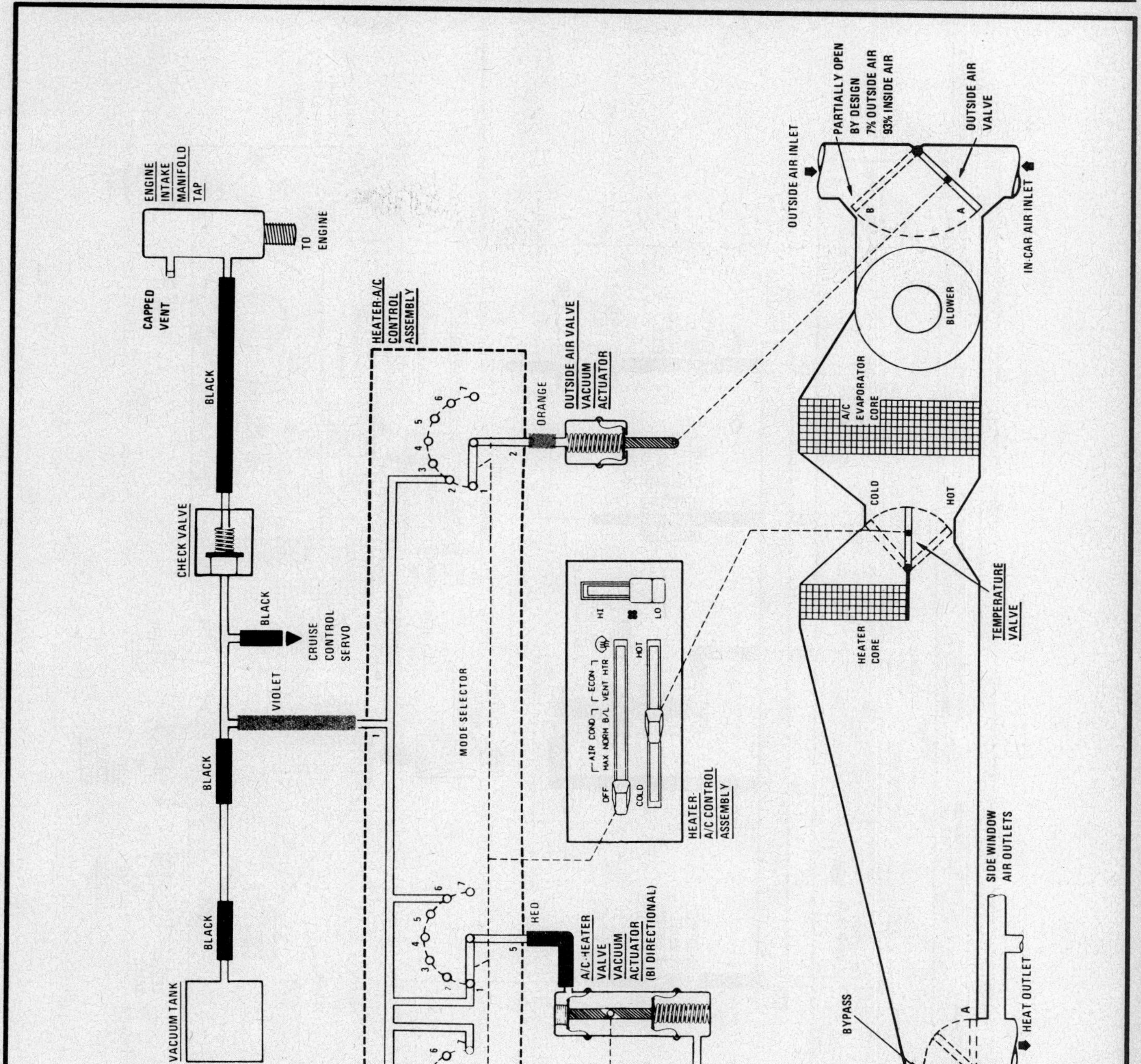
ENGINE INTAKE MANIFOLD TAP
TO ENGINE
CAPPED VENT
BLACK
CHECK VALVE
BLACK
CRUISE CONTROL SERVO
VIOLET
BLACK
BLACK
VACUUM TANK
HEATER-A/C CONTROL ASSEMBLY
MODE SELECTOR
ORANGE
OUTSIDE AIR VALVE VACUUM ACTUATOR
RED
A/C-HEATER VALVE VACUUM ACTUATOR (BI DIRECTIONAL)
YELLOW
BLUE
A/C-DEFROST VALVE VACUUM ACTUATOR
A/C CONTROL VACUUM VALVE SEQUENCE CHART
1 OFF
2 MAX
3 NORM
4 B/L
5 VENT
6 HTR
7 DEFROST
AIR COND
ECON
OFF MAX NORM B/L VENT HTR
COLD
HOT
HI
LO
HEATER-A/C CONTROL ASSEMBLY
PARTIALLY OPEN BY DESIGN 7% OUTSIDE AIR 93% INSIDE AIR
OUTSIDE AIR VALVE
OUTSIDE AIR INLET
IN-CAR AIR INLET
BLOWER
A/C EVAPORATOR CORE
COLD
HOT
TEMPERATURE VALVE
HEATER CORE
SIDE WINDOW AIR OUTLETS
HEAT OUTLET
BYPASS
A/C-HEATER VALVE
AIR TO DEFROST OUTLETS
A/C OUTLET
A/C DEFROST VALVE

Air delivery vacuum schematic—typical

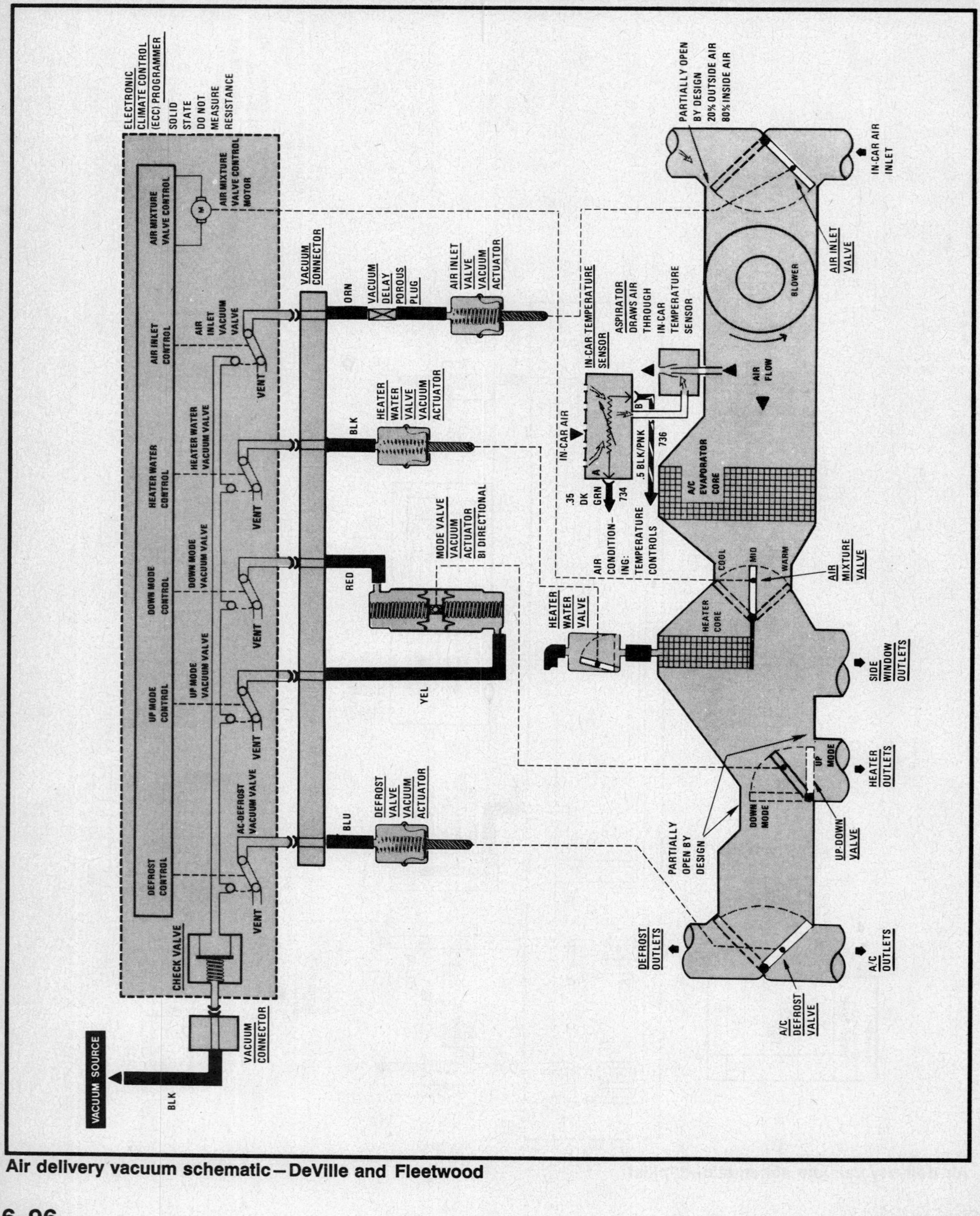
ELECTRONIC CLIMATE CONTROL (ECC) PROGRAMMER
SOLID STATE DO NOT MEASURE RESISTANCE
AIR MIXTURE VALVE CONTROL
M
AIR MIXTURE VALVE CONTROL MOTOR
AIR INLET CONTROL
AIR INLET VACUUM VALVE
HEATER WATER CONTROL
HEATER WATER VACUUM VALVE
DOWN MODE CONTROL
DOWN MODE VACUUM VALVE
UP MODE CONTROL
UP MODE VACUUM VALVE
DEFROST CONTROL
AC-DEFROST VACUUM VALVE
VENT
CHECK VALVE
VACUUM CONNECTOR
VACUUM SOURCE
BLK
ORN
VACUUM DELAY POROUS PLUG
AIR INLET VALVE VACUUM ACTUATOR
HEATER WATER VALVE VACUUM ACTUATOR
MODE VALVE VACUUM ACTUATOR BI DIRECTIONAL
RED
YEL
BLU
DEFROST VALVE VACUUM ACTUATOR
IN-CAR TEMPERATURE SENSOR
ASPIRATOR DRAWS AIR THROUGH IN-CAR TEMPERATURE SENSOR
IN-CAR AIR
A
B
.35 DK GRN
734
.5 BLK/PNK
736
AIR CONDITIONING: TEMPERATURE CONTROLS
PARTIALLY OPEN BY DESIGN 20% OUTSIDE AIR 80% INSIDE AIR
IN-CAR AIR INLET
AIR INLET VALVE
BLOWER
AIR FLOW
A/C EVAPORATOR CORE
COOL
MID
WARM
AIR MIXTURE VALVE
HEATER WATER VALVE
HEATER CORE
SIDE WINDOW OUTLETS
UP MODE
DOWN MODE
HEATER OUTLETS
UP-DOWN VALVE
PARTIALLY OPEN BY DESIGN
DEFROST OUTLETS
A/C OUTLETS
A/C DEFROST VALVE

Air delivery vacuum schematic—DeVille and Fleetwood

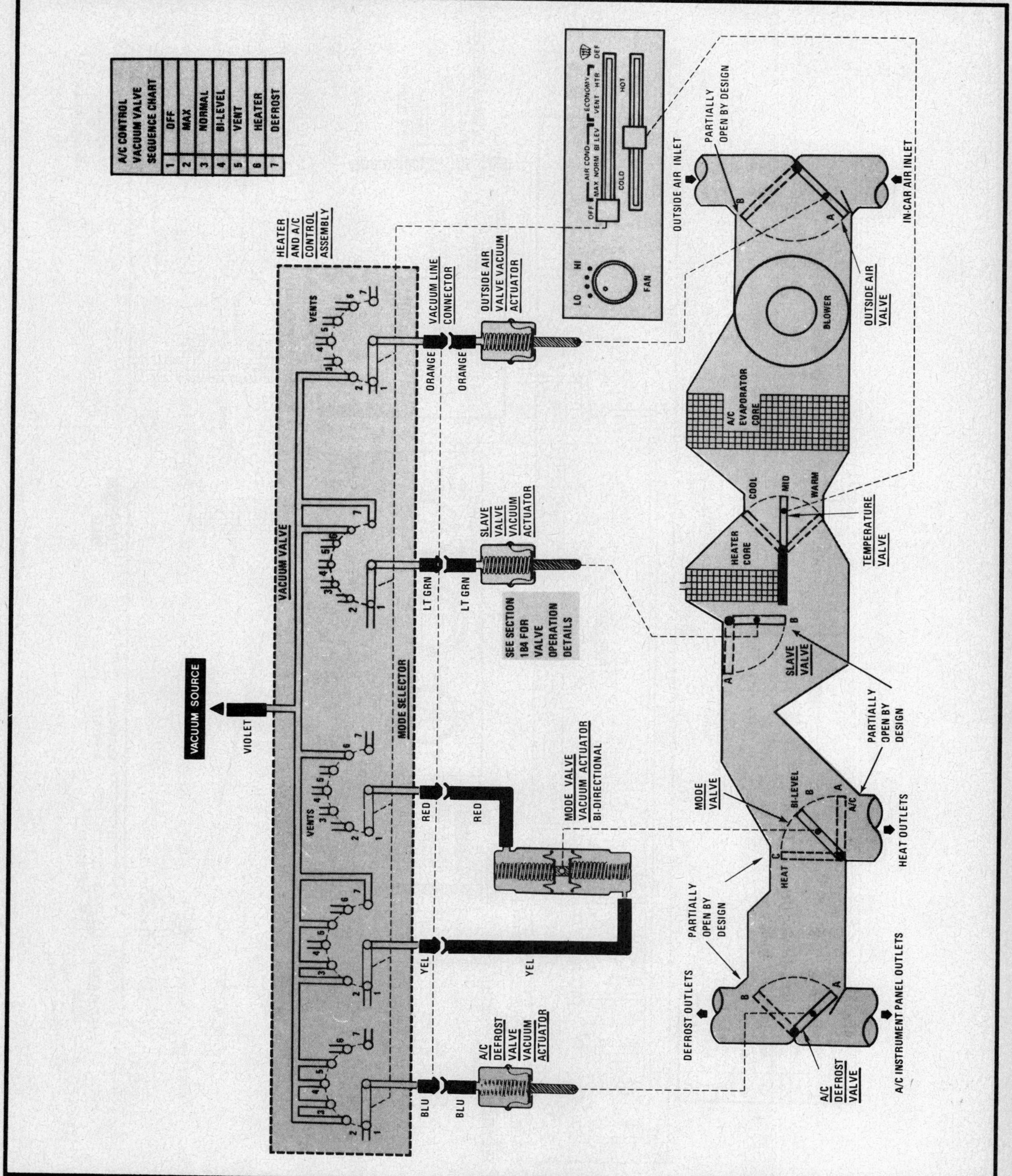
A/C CONTROL VACUUM VALVE SEQUENCE CHART
1 OFF
2 MAX
3 NORMAL
4 BI-LEVEL
5 VENT
6 HEATER
7 DEFROST
HEATER AND A/C CONTROL ASSEMBLY
VACUUM SOURCE
VIOLET
VACUUM VALVE
MODE SELECTOR
VENTS
VACUUM LINE CONNECTOR
ORANGE
OUTSIDE AIR VALVE VACUUM ACTUATOR
LT GRN
SLAVE VALVE VACUUM ACTUATOR
SEE SECTION 1B4 FOR VALVE OPERATION DETAILS
RED
MODE VALVE VACUUM ACTUATOR BI-DIRECTIONAL
YEL
BLU
A/C DEFROST VALVE VACUUM ACTUATOR
OFF
AIR COND
MAX
NORM
BI LEV
VENT
ECONOMY
HTR
DEF
COLD
HOT
LO
HI
FAN
OUTSIDE AIR INLET
PARTIALLY OPEN BY DESIGN
IN-CAR AIR INLET
OUTSIDE AIR VALVE
BLOWER
A/C EVAPORATOR CORE
COOL
MID
WARM
TEMPERATURE VALVE
HEATER CORE
SLAVE VALVE
PARTIALLY OPEN BY DESIGN
MODE VALVE
BI-LEVEL
A/C
HEAT
HEAT OUTLETS
PARTIALLY OPEN BY DESIGN
DEFROST OUTLETS
A/C INSTRUMENT PANEL OUTLETS
A/C DEFROST VALVE

Air delivery vacuum schematic—C and H body (except Cadillac)

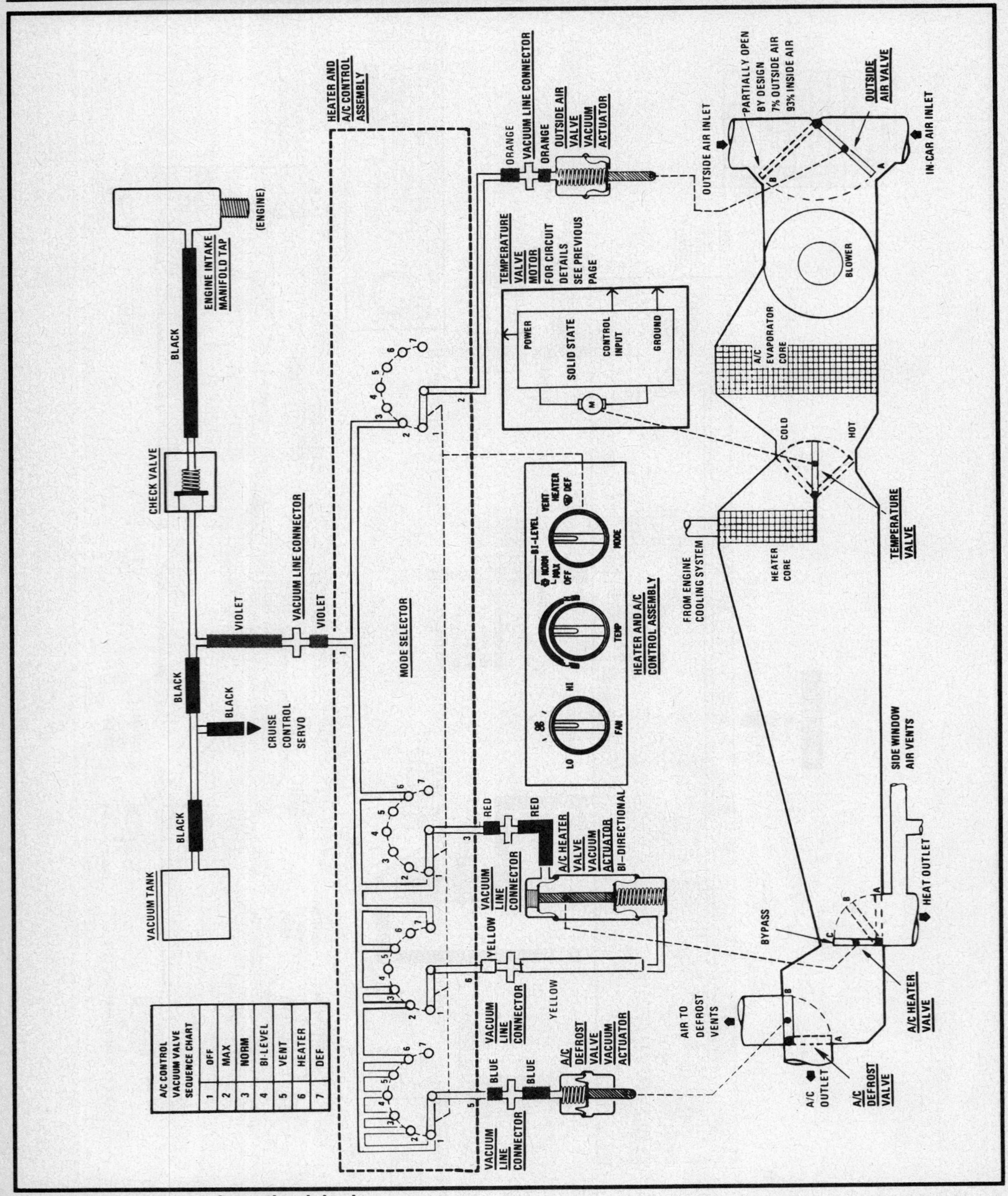
HEATER AND A/C CONTROL ASSEMBLY
VACUUM LINE CONNECTOR
ORANGE
OUTSIDE AIR VALVE VACUUM ACTUATOR
PARTIALLY OPEN BY DESIGN 7% OUTSIDE AIR 93% INSIDE AIR
OUTSIDE AIR VALVE
OUTSIDE AIR INLET
IN-CAR AIR INLET
(ENGINE)
ENGINE INTAKE MANIFOLD TAP
BLACK
TEMPERATURE VALVE MOTOR FOR CIRCUIT DETAILS SEE PREVIOUS PAGE
POWER
SOLID STATE
CONTROL INPUT
GROUND
BLOWER
A/C EVAPORATOR CORE
COLD
HOT
CHECK VALVE
TEMPERATURE VALVE
VACUUM LINE CONNECTOR
VIOLET
MODE SELECTOR
BI-LEVEL
NORM
MAX
OFF
VENT
HEATER
DEF
MODE
TEMP
HEATER AND A/C CONTROL ASSEMBLY
FROM ENGINE COOLING SYSTEM
HEATER CORE
CRUISE CONTROL SERVO
LO
HI
FAN
SIDE WINDOW AIR VENTS
RED
A/C HEATER VALVE VACUUM ACTUATOR
BI-DIRECTIONAL
VACUUM TANK
VACUUM LINE CONNECTOR
HEAT OUTLET
YELLOW
BYPASS
A/C HEATER VALVE
A/C CONTROL VACUUM VALVE SEQUENCE CHART
1 OFF
2 MAX
3 NORM
4 BI-LEVEL
5 VENT
6 HEATER
7 DEF
AIR TO DEFROST VENTS
BLUE
A/C DEFROST VALVE VACUUM ACTUATOR
A/C OUTLET
A/C DEFROST VALVE

Air delivery vacuum schematic—L body

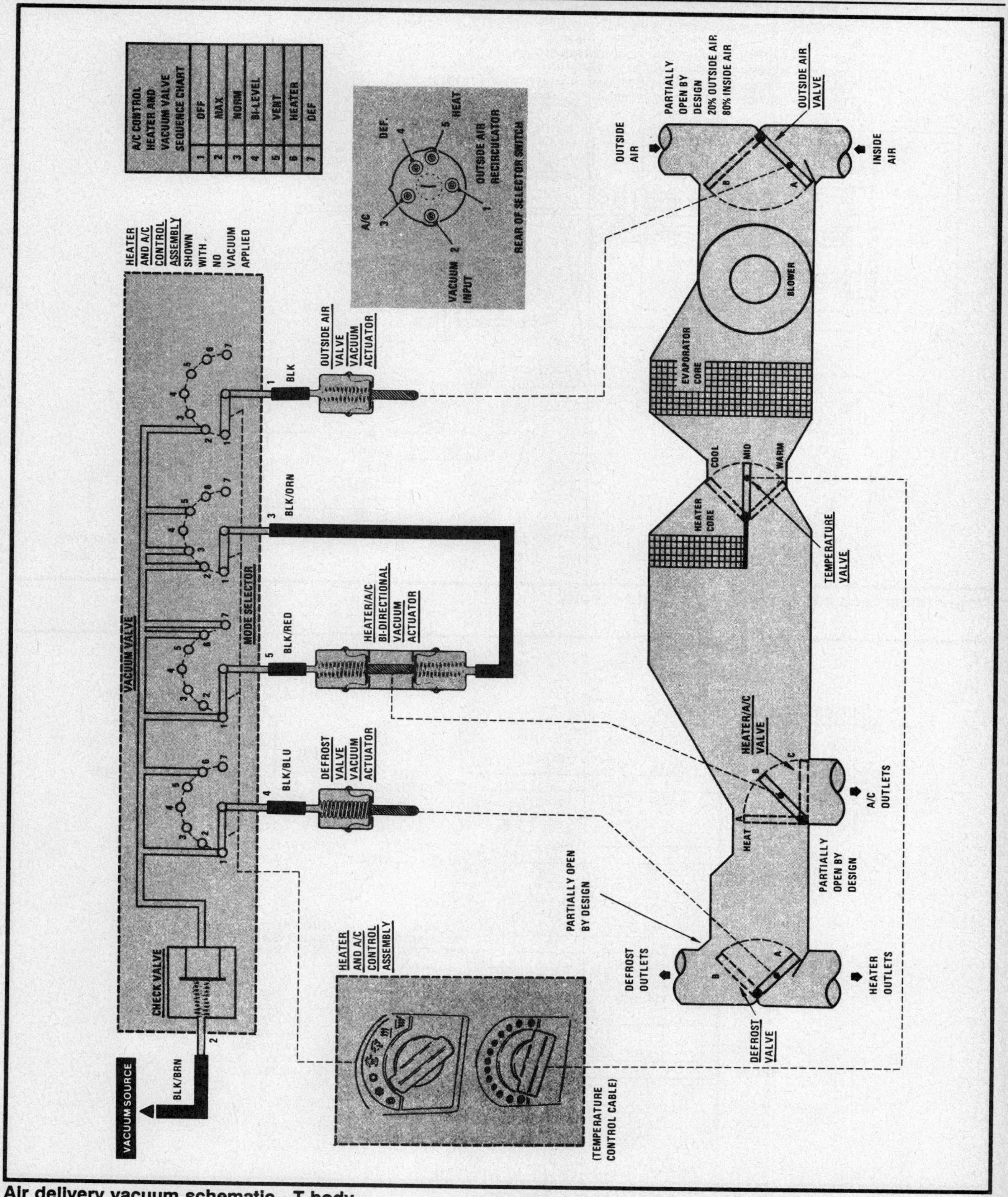

A/C CONTROL HEATER AND VACUUM VALVE SEQUENCE CHART
1 OFF
2 MAX
3 NORM
4 BI-LEVEL
5 VENT
6 HEATER
7 DEF
HEATER AND A/C CONTROL ASSEMBLY SHOWN WITH NO VACUUM APPLIED
A/C
DEF.
HEAT
VACUUM INPUT
OUTSIDE AIR RECIRCULATOR
REAR OF SELECTOR SWITCH
OUTSIDE AIR
PARTIALLY OPEN BY DESIGN 20% OUTSIDE AIR 80% INSIDE AIR
OUTSIDE AIR VALVE
INSIDE AIR
BLOWER
EVAPORATOR CORE
OUTSIDE AIR VALVE VACUUM ACTUATOR
BLK
BLK/ORN
BLK/RED
BLK/BLU
BLK/BRN
VACUUM VALVE
MODE SELECTOR
HEATER/A/C BI-DIRECTIONAL VACUUM ACTUATOR
DEFROST VALVE VACUUM ACTUATOR
COOL
MID
WARM
HEATER CORE
TEMPERATURE VALVE
HEATER/A/C VALVE
A/C OUTLETS
HEAT
PARTIALLY OPEN BY DESIGN
PARTIALLY OPEN BY DESIGN
CHECK VALVE
VACUUM SOURCE
HEATER AND A/C CONTROL ASSEMBLY
DEFROST OUTLETS
HEATER OUTLETS
DEFROST VALVE
(TEMPERATURE CONTROL CABLE)

Air delivery vacuum schematic—T body

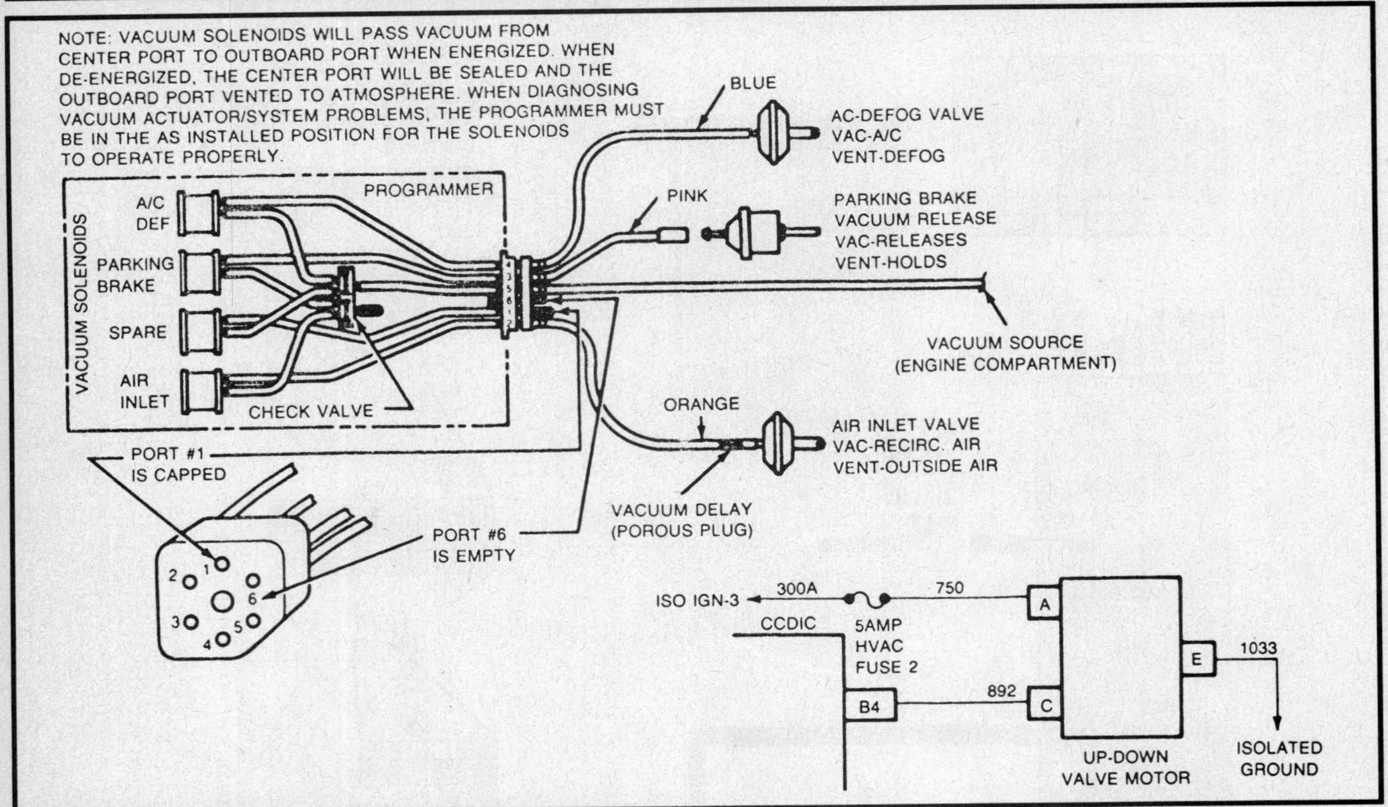
NOTE: VACUUM SOLENOIDS WILL PASS VACUUM FROM CENTER PORT TO OUTBOARD PORT WHEN ENERGIZED. WHEN DE-ENERGIZED, THE CENTER PORT WILL BE SEALED AND THE OUTBOARD PORT VENTED TO ATMOSPHERE. WHEN DIAGNOSING VACUUM ACTUATOR/SYSTEM PROBLEMS, THE PROGRAMMER MUST BE IN THE AS INSTALLED POSITION FOR THE SOLENOIDS TO OPERATE PROPERLY.
BLUE
AC-DEFOG VALVE
VAC-A/C
VENT-DEFOG
PROGRAMMER
A/C
DEF
VACUUM SOLENOIDS
PARKING
BRAKE
SPARE
AIR
INLET
CHECK VALVE
PINK
PARKING BRAKE
VACUUM RELEASE
VAC-RELEASES
VENT-HOLDS
VACUUM SOURCE
(ENGINE COMPARTMENT)
ORANGE
AIR INLET VALVE
VAC-RECIRC. AIR
VENT-OUTSIDE AIR
VACUUM DELAY
(POROUS PLUG)
PORT #1
IS CAPPED
PORT #6
IS EMPTY
ISO IGN-3
300A
750
CCDIC
5AMP
HVAC
FUSE 2
B4
892
A
C
E
1033
UP-DOWN
VALVE MOTOR
ISOLATED
GROUND

Programmer vacuum connector—E, K and V body

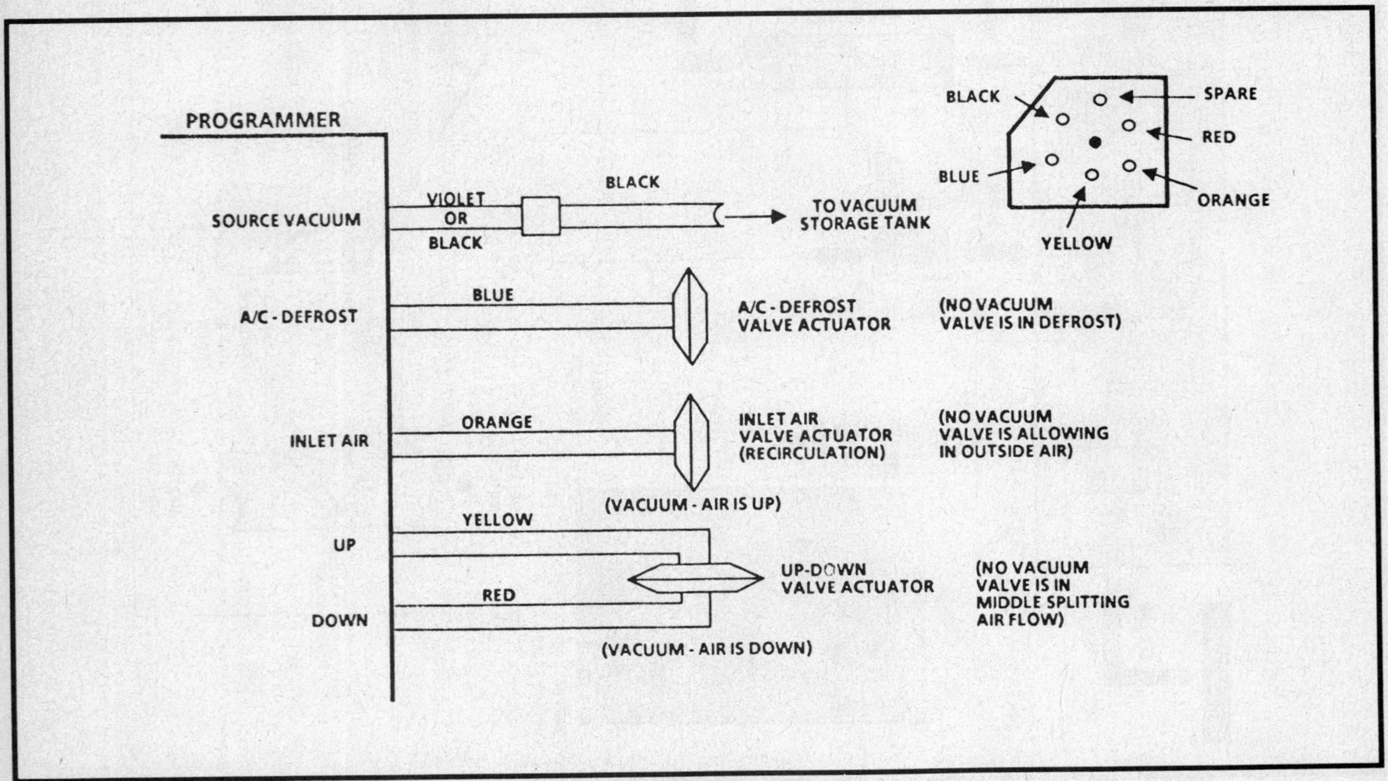
PROGRAMMER
SOURCE VACUUM
VIOLET
OR
BLACK
BLACK
TO VACUUM
STORAGE TANK
A/C - DEFROST
BLUE
A/C - DEFROST
VALVE ACTUATOR
(NO VACUUM
VALVE IS IN DEFROST)
INLET AIR
ORANGE
INLET AIR
VALVE ACTUATOR
(RECIRCULATION)
(NO VACUUM
VALVE IS ALLOWING
IN OUTSIDE AIR)
(VACUUM - AIR IS UP)
UP
YELLOW
DOWN
RED
UP-DOWN
VALVE ACTUATOR
(NO VACUUM
VALVE IS IN
MIDDLE SPLITTING
AIR FLOW)
(VACUUM - AIR IS DOWN)
BLACK
SPARE
RED
BLUE
ORANGE
YELLOW

Programmer vacuum connector—E body (except Eldorado)

7 GENERAL MOTORS CORPORATION 7

CADILLAC BROUGHAM • CAMARO • CAPRICE • CAPRICE WAGON • CORVETTE
CUSTOM CRUISER • ESTATE WAGON • FIREBIRD • ROADMASTER • SAFARI

SPECIFICATIONS

VEHICLE IDENTIFICATION CHART

It is important for servicing and ordering parts to be certain of the vehicle and engine identification. The VIN (vehicle identification number) is a 17 digit number visible through the windshield on the driver's side of the dash and contains the vehicle and engine identification codes. The tenth digit indicates model year and the eighth digit indicates engine code. It can be interpreted as follows:

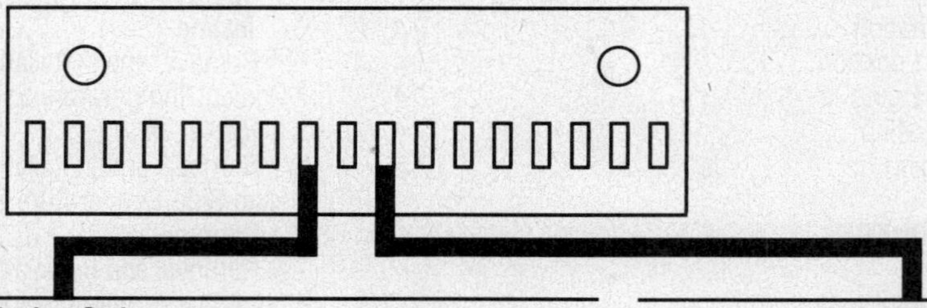

Engine Code

Code	Cu. In.	Liters	Cyl.	Fuel Sys.	Eng. Mfg.
S	173	2.8	V6	PFI	CPC
T	191	3.1	V6	PFI	CPC
2	262	4.3	V6	TBI	CPC
Z	262	4.3	V6	TBI	CPC
E	305	5.0	V8	TBI	BOC
F	305	5.0	V8	PFI	CPC
Y	307	5.0	V8	4bbl	BOC
7	350	5.7	V8	TBI	CPC
8	350	5.7	V8	PFI	CPC
J	350	5.7	V8	PFI	Chevrolet

Model Year

Code	Year
K	1989
L	1990
M	1991

REFRIGERANT CAPACITIES

Year	Model	Freon (oz.)	Oil (fl. oz.)	Type ①
1989	Caprice	56.0	6	R-4
	Estate Wagon	56.0	6	R-4
	Custom Cruiser	56.0	6	R-4
	Safari	56.0	6	R-4
	Cadillac Brougham	53.3	6	R-4
	Camaro	36.0	6	R-4
	Firebird	36.0	6	R-4
	Corvette	36.0	—	10PA17/10PA20
1990	Caprice	56.0	6	R-4
	Estate Wagon	56.0	6	R-4
	Custom Cruiser	56.0	6	R-4
	Cadillac Brougham	53.3	6	R-4
	Camaro	36.0	6	R-4
	Firebird	36.0	6	R-4
	Corvette	36.0	—	10PA17/10PA20

REFRIGERANT CAPACITIES

Year	Model	Freon (oz.)	Oil (fl. oz.)	Type ①
1991	Caprice	49.5	6	R-4
	Estate Wagon	49.5	6	R-4
	Custom Cruiser	49.5	6	R-4
	Roadmaster	49.5	6	R-4
	Cadillac Brougham	53.3	6	R-4
	Camaro	36	6	R-4
	Firebird	36	6	R-4
	Corvette	36	—	10PA17/10PA20

① Compressor

AIR CONDITIONING BELT TENSION CHART

Year	Model	Engine (L)	Belt Type	New	Used
1989	Caprice	All Engines	V-Belt ②	③	④
	Estate Wagon	All Engines	V-Belt ②	③	④
	Custom Cruiser	All Engines	V-Belt ②	③	④
	Safari	All Engines	V-Belt ②	③	④
	Cadillac Brougham	5.0L	V-Belt	169	112
	Cadillac Brougham	5.7L	Serpentine	②	②
	Camaro	All Engines	V-Belt ②	③	④
	Firebird	All Engines	V-Belt ②	③	④
	Corvette	All Engines	Serpentine	⑤	②
1990	Caprice	All Engines	V-Belt ②	③	④
	Estate Wagon	All Engines	V-Belt ②	③	④
	Custom Cruiser	All Engines	V-Belt ②	③	④
	Cadillac Brougham	5.0L	V-Belt	169	112
	Cadillac Brougham	5.7L	Serpentine	②	②
	Camaro	All Engines	V-Belt ②	③	④
	Firebird	All Engines	Serpentine	②	②
	Corvette	All Engines	Serpentine	②	②
1991	Caprice	All Engines	Serpentine	②	②
	Estate Wagon	All Engines	Serpentine	②	②
	Custom Cruiser	All Engines	Serpentine	②	②
	Roadmaster	All Engines	Serpentine	②	②
	Cadillac Brougham	All Engines	Serpentine	②	②
	Camaro	All Engines	Serpentine	②	②
	Firebird	All Engines	Serpentine	②	②
	Corvette	All Engines	Serpentine	②	②

① Lbs.
② If equipped with serpentine belt—no adjustment necessary
③ New belts
5/16" wide—80 lbs.
3/8" & 13/32" wide—140 lbs.
7/16" wide—165 lbs.
④ Used belts
5/16" wide—50 lbs.
3/8" & 13/32" wide—740 lbs.
7/16" wide—90 lbs.

SYSTEM DESCRIPTION

General Information

The heater and air conditioning systems are controlled manually or electronically. The systems differ mainly in the way air temperature and the routing of air flow are controlled. The manual system controls air temperature through a cable-actuated lever and air flow through a vacuum switching valve and vacuum actuators. With Electronic Climate Control (ECC) systems, both temperature and air flow are controlled by the BCM through the Climate Control Panel (CCP).

The heating system provides heating, ventilation and defrosting for the windshield and side windows. The heater core is a heat exchanger supplied with coolant from the engine cooling system. Temperature is controlled by the temperature valve which moves an air door that directs air flow through the heater core for more heat or bypasses the heater core for less heat.

Vacuum actuators control the mode doors which direct air flow to the outlet ducts. The mode selector on the control panel directs engine vacuum to the actuators. The position of the mode doors determines whether air flows from the floor, panel, defrost or panel and defrost ducts (bi-level mode).

The refrigeration system used is designated the Cycling Clutch Orifice Tube (CCOT). In this type of system, the compressor cycles on and off to maintain proper cooling and to prevent evaporator freeze-up. The orifice tube provides a restriction in the high-pressure refrigerant line which meters the flow of refrigerant into the evaporator as a low-pressure liquid.

There are 2 types of compressors used on air conditioning systems. The R-4 compressor, used on Caprice, Estate Wagon, Custom Cruiser, Safari, Roadmaster, Cadillac Brougham, Camaro and Firebird vehicles, is a light weight fixed displacement refrigerant pump with 4 cylinders arranged radially, extending straight out from the center of the compressor. The compressor driveshaft is driven by the V-belt or serpentine belt when the electro-magnetic clutch is engaged.

The 10PA17 and 10PA20 compressors, used on Corvette, are conventional swash plate compressors with 5 double-ended pistons. The 10PA20 compressor is used on vehicles equipped with the L98 engine and the 10PA 17 compressor is used on vehicles equipped with the LT5 engine. The compressor driveshaft is driven by the serpentine belt when the electro-magnetic clutch is engaged.

Service Valve Locations

The high-side fitting is normally located in the refrigerant line near the compressor.

The low-side fitting is normally located on the accumulator or in the condenser-to-evaporator refrigerant line.

System Discharging

R-12 refrigerant is a chlorofluorocarbon which, when released into the atmosphere, can contribute to the depletion on the ozone layer in the upper atmosphere. Ozone filters out harmful radiation from the sun. In order to protect the ozone layer, an approved R-12 Recovery/Recycling machine that meets SAE standard J1991 should be employed when discharging the system. Follow the operating instructions provided with the approved equipment exactly to properly discharge the system.

System Evacuating

If the air conditioning system has been opened to the atmosphere, it should be air and moisture free before being recharged with refrigerant. Moisture and air mixed with refrigerant will raise the compressor head pressure, resulting in possible damage to the system's components. In addition, air and moisture in the system can lead to internal corrosion of the system components. Moisture will boil at normal room temperature when exposed to a vacuum. To evacuate the system:

1. Leak test the system and repair any leaks found.
2. Connect an approved charging station, Recovery/Recycling machine or manifold gauge set and vacuum pump to the discharge and suction ports. The red hose is normally connected to the discharge (high pressure) line. The blue hose is connected to the suction (low pressure) line. If using a manifold gauge set, the center (usually yellow) hose is connected to the charging station or Recovery/Recycling machine.
3. Open the discharge and suction ports and start the vacuum pump. If the pump is not able to pull at least 26 in. Hg of vacuum there is a leak that must be repaired before evacuation can occur.
4. Once the system has reached at least 26 in. Hg of vacuum, allow the system to evacuate for at least 10 minutes. The longer the system is evacuated, the more moisture will be removed.
5. Close all valves and turn the pump off. If the system loses more than 2 in. Hg of vacuum after 15 minutes, there is a leak that should be repaired.

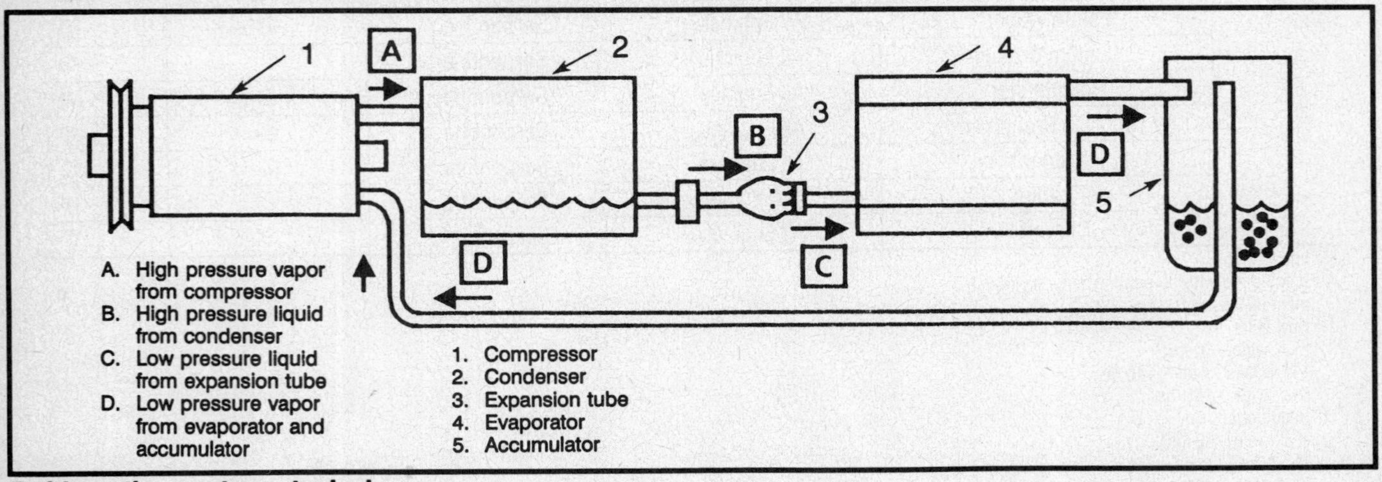
1
2
3
4
5
A
B
C
D
D
D
A. High pressure vapor from compressor
B. High pressure liquid from condenser
C. Low pressure liquid from expansion tube
D. Low pressure vapor from evaporator and accumulator
1. Compressor
2. Condenser
3. Expansion tube
4. Evaporator
5. Accumulator

Refrigeration system—typical

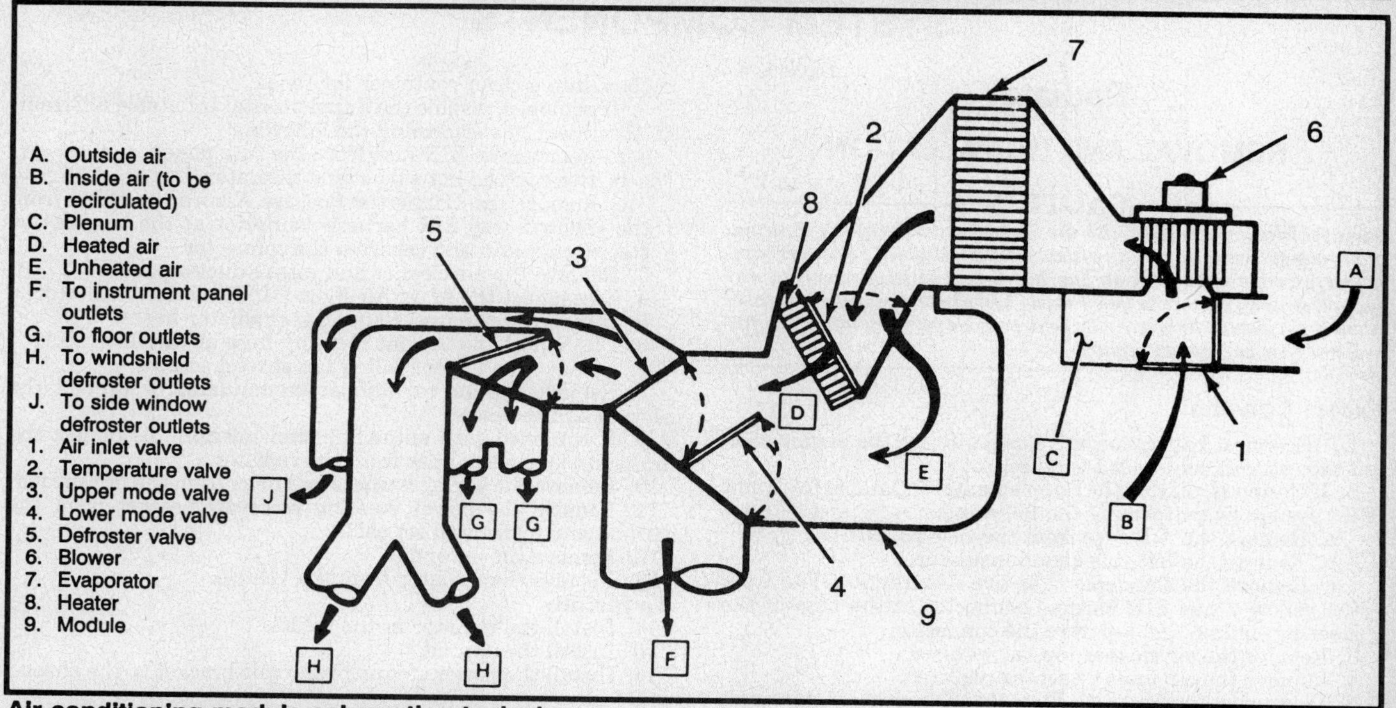
A. Outside air
B. Inside air (to be recirculated)
C. Plenum
D. Heated air
E. Unheated air
F. To instrument panel outlets
G. To floor outlets
H. To windshield defroster outlets
J. To side window defroster outlets
1. Air inlet valve
2. Temperature valve
3. Upper mode valve
4. Lower mode valve
5. Defroster valve
6. Blower
7. Evaporator
8. Heater
9. Module

Air conditioning module schematic—typical

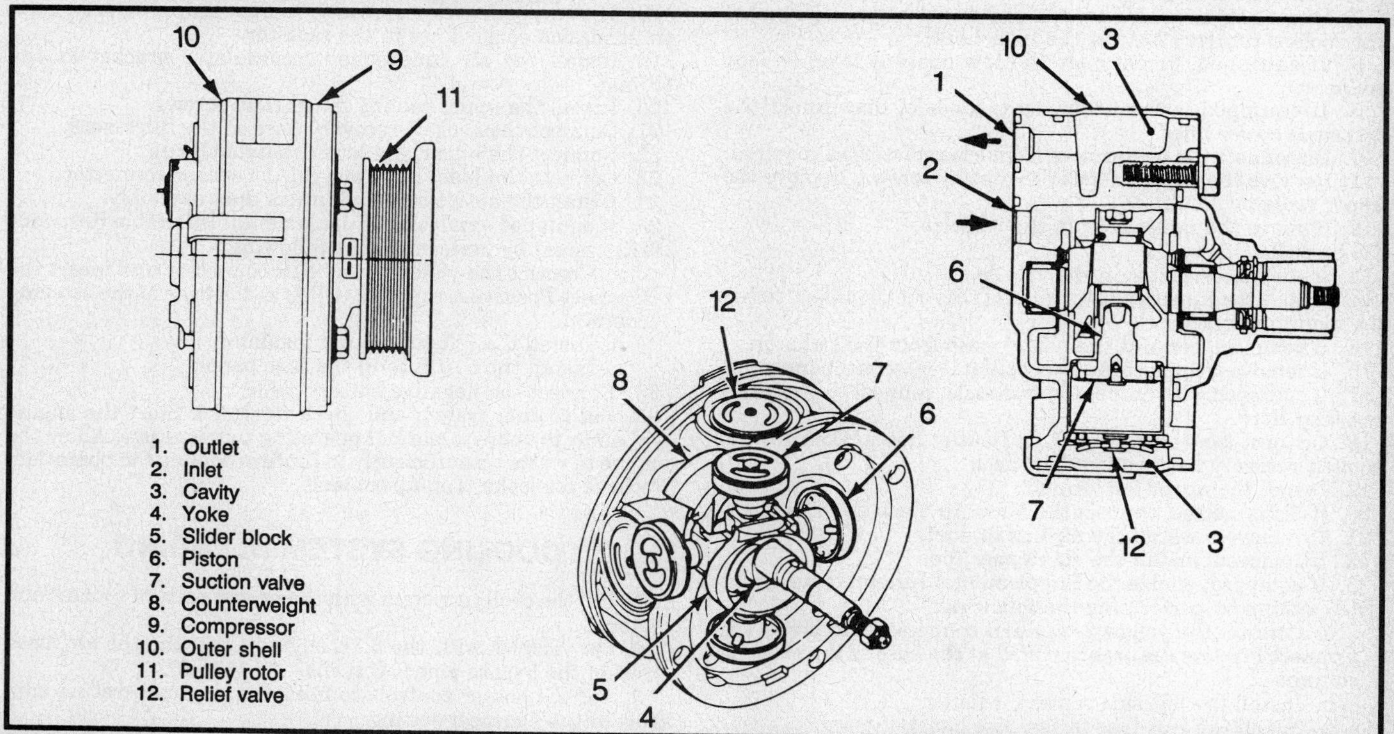
1. Outlet
2. Inlet
3. Cavity
4. Yoke
5. Slider block
6. Piston
7. Suction valve
8. Counterweight
9. Compressor
10. Outer shell
11. Pulley rotor
12. Relief valve

R-4 compressor components

System Charging

1. Connect an approved charging station, Recovery/Recycling machine or manifold gauge set to the discharge and suction ports. The red hose is normally connected to the discharge (high pressure) line and the blue hose is connected to the suction (low pressure) line. If using a manifold gauge set, the center (usually yellow) hose is connected to the charging station or Recovery/Recycling machine.
2. Follow the instructions provided with the equipment and charge the system with the specified amount of refrigerant.
3. Perform a leak test.

SYSTEM COMPONENTS

Radiator

REMOVAL AND INSTALLATION

CAUTION

Some vehicles are equipped with the Supplemental Inflatable Restraint or air bag system. The air bag system must be disabled before performing service on or around the air bag, instrument panel components, wiring and sensors. Failure to follow safety and disabling procedures could result in accidental air bag deployment, possible personal injury and unnecessary air bag system repairs.

Except Corvette

1. Disconnect battery negative cable. Drain the engine coolant into a clean container for reuse.
2. If equipped, disable the Supplemental Inflatable Restraint (SIR) system by performing the following:
   a. Remove the SIR fuse from the fuse panel.
   b. Remove the left side sound insulator.
   c. Remove the Connector Positive Assurance (CPA) from the yellow 2-way SIR harness connector at the base of the steering column and separate the connector.
3. Remove the air cleaner top, as required.
4. Remove the air intake duct, as required.
5. Disconnect the Mass Air Flow (MAF) sensor, as required.
6. Remove the upper fan shroud.
7. Disconnect the radiator inlet and outlet hoses. Disconnect the coolant recovery hose at the filler heck.
8. If equipped, disconnect the low coolant level sensor connector.
9. If equipped with automatic transaxle, disconnect the transaxle cooler lines.
10. Disconnect the heater hose from the radiator, as required.
11. Remove the upper radiator mounting screws. Remove the upper radiator mount.
12. Remove the radiator from the vehicle.

To install:

13. Install the radiator in the vehicle.
14. Install the upper radiator mount. Install the upper radiator mounting screws.
15. If removed, connect the heater hose from the radiator.
16. If removed, connect the low coolant level sensor connector.
17. If equipped with automatic transaxle, connect the transaxle cooler lines.
18. Connect the radiator inlet and outlet hoses. Connect the coolant recovery hose at the filler heck.
19. Install the upper fan shroud.
20. If disconnected, connect the Mass Air Flow (MAF) sensor.
21. If removed, install the air intake duct.
22. If removed, install the air cleaner top.
23. If equipped, enable the Supplemental Inflatable Restraint (SIR) system by performing the following:
   a. Connect the yellow 2-way SIR connector and insert the Connect Positive Assurance (CPA) at the base of the steering column.
   b. Install the left side sound insulator.
   c. Install the SIR fuse in the fuse panel.
24. Connect the negative battery cable.
25. Fill cooling system and check for leaks. Start the engine and allow to come to normal operating temperature. Allow the engine to warm up sufficiently to confirm cooling fan operation. Recheck for leaks. Top-up coolant.

Corvette

1. Disconnect the negative battery cable. Drain the engine coolant into a clean container for reuse.
2. If equipped, disable the Supplemental Inflatable Restraint (SIR) system by performing the following:
   a. Remove the SIR fuse from the fuse panel.
   b. Remove the left side sound insulator.
   c. Remove the Connector Positive Assurance (CPA) from the yellow 2-way SIR harness connector at the base of the steering column and separate the connector.
3. Remove the air cleaner and intake duct assembly.
4. Disconnect the Mass Air Flow (MAF) sensor connector.
5. Disconnect the upper and lower radiator hoses.
6. Disconnect the coolant recovery hose at the filler neck.
7. Remove the upper cooling fan shroud screws.
8. Remove the air conditioner accumulator bracket at the shroud and set aside.
9. If equipped with automatic transmission, disconnect the transmission cooler lines from the radiator.
10. Remove the wiring harness and relay from the fan shroud.
11. Remove the power steering reservoir bracket from the shroud and frame and set aside.
12. Remove the shroud.
13. Remove the radiator from the vehicle.

To install:

14. Install the radiator in the vehicle.
15. Install the shroud.
16. Install the power steering reservoir bracket to the shroud and frame.
17. Install the wiring harness and relay to the fan shroud.
18. If equipped with automatic transmission, connect the transmission cooler lines to the radiator.
19. Install the air conditioner accumulator bracket at the shroud.
20. Install the upper cooling fan shroud screws.
21. Connect the coolant recovery hose at the filler neck.
22. Connect the upper and lower radiator hoses.
23. Connect the Mass Air Flow (MAF) sensor connector.
24. Install the air cleaner and intake duct assembly.
25. If equipped, enable the Supplemental Inflatable Restraint (SIR) system by performing the following:
   a. Connect the yellow 2-way SIR connector and insert the Connect Positive Assurance (CPA) at the base of the steering column.
   b. Install the left side sound insulator.
   c. Install the SIR fuse in the fuse panel.
26. Connect the negative battery cable.
27. Fill cooling system and check for leaks. Start the engine and allow to come to normal operating temperature. Allow the engine to warm up sufficiently to confirm cooling fan operation. Recheck for leaks. Top-up coolant.

COOLING SYSTEM BLEEDING

1. Fill the cooling system with the proper ratio of coolant and water.
2. On vehicles with the 3.1L engine, open the the air bleed vent on the bypass pipe 2–3 turns.
3. Set the heater controls to heat and the temperature controls to the warmest setting.
4. Start the engine and add coolant as necessary to keep the radiator level just below the filler neck.
5. On vehicles with the 3.1L engine, observe the air bleed vent. Close the vent when coolant begins to come out of the vent.
6. Allow the engine to come to normal operating temperature; indicated by the upper radiator hose becoming hot.
7. The air coming out of the heater should be getting hot.
8. Check the coolant level in the radiator and coolant reser-

voir. Install the radiator cap, turning it until the arrows align with the overflow tube.

Cooling Fan

TESTING

1. Check fuse or circuit breaker for power to cooling fan motor.
2. Remove connector(s) at cooling fan motor(s). Connect jumper wire and apply
battery voltage to the positive terminal of the cooling fan motor.
3. Using an ohmmeter, check for continuity in cooling fan motor.

NOTE: Remove the cooling fan connector at the fan motor before performing continuity checks. Perform continuity check of the motor windings only. The cooling fan control circuit is connected electrically to the ECM through the cooling fan relay. Ohmmeter battery voltage must not be applied to the ECM.

4. Ensure proper continuity of cooling fan motor ground circuit at chassis ground connector.

REMOVAL AND INSTALLATION

CAUTION

Some vehicles are equipped with the Supplemental Inflatable Restraint or air bag system. The air bag system must be disabled before performing service on or around the air bag, instrument panel components, wiring and sensors. Failure to follow safety and disabling procedures could result in accidental air bag deployment, possible personal injury and unnecessary air bag system repairs.

Camaro and Firebird

1. Disconnect the negative battery cable. If equipped, remove the air cleaner top.
2. If equipped, disable the Supplemental Inflatable Restraint (SIR) system by performing the following:
   a. Remove the SIR fuse from the fuse panel.
   b. Remove the left side sound insulator.
   c. Remove the Connector Positive Assurance (CPA) from the yellow 2-way SIR harness connector at the base of the steering column and separate the connector.
3. Disconnect the wiring harness.
4. Remove the cooling fan-to-radiator support bolts.
5. Remove the cooling fan bracket.
6. Remove the cooling fan assembly.

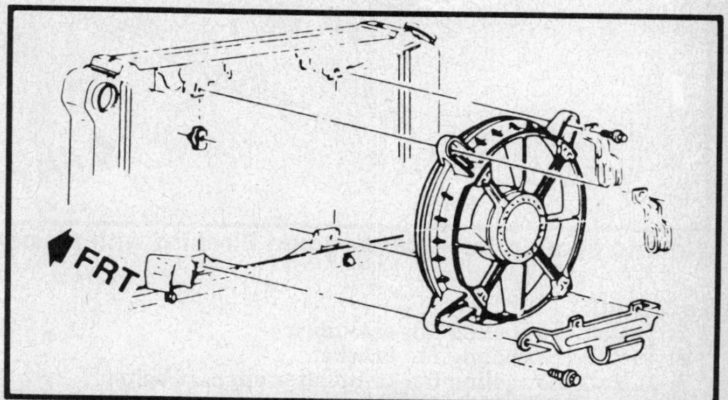
FRT

Electric cooling fan—Camaro and Firebird without air conditioning

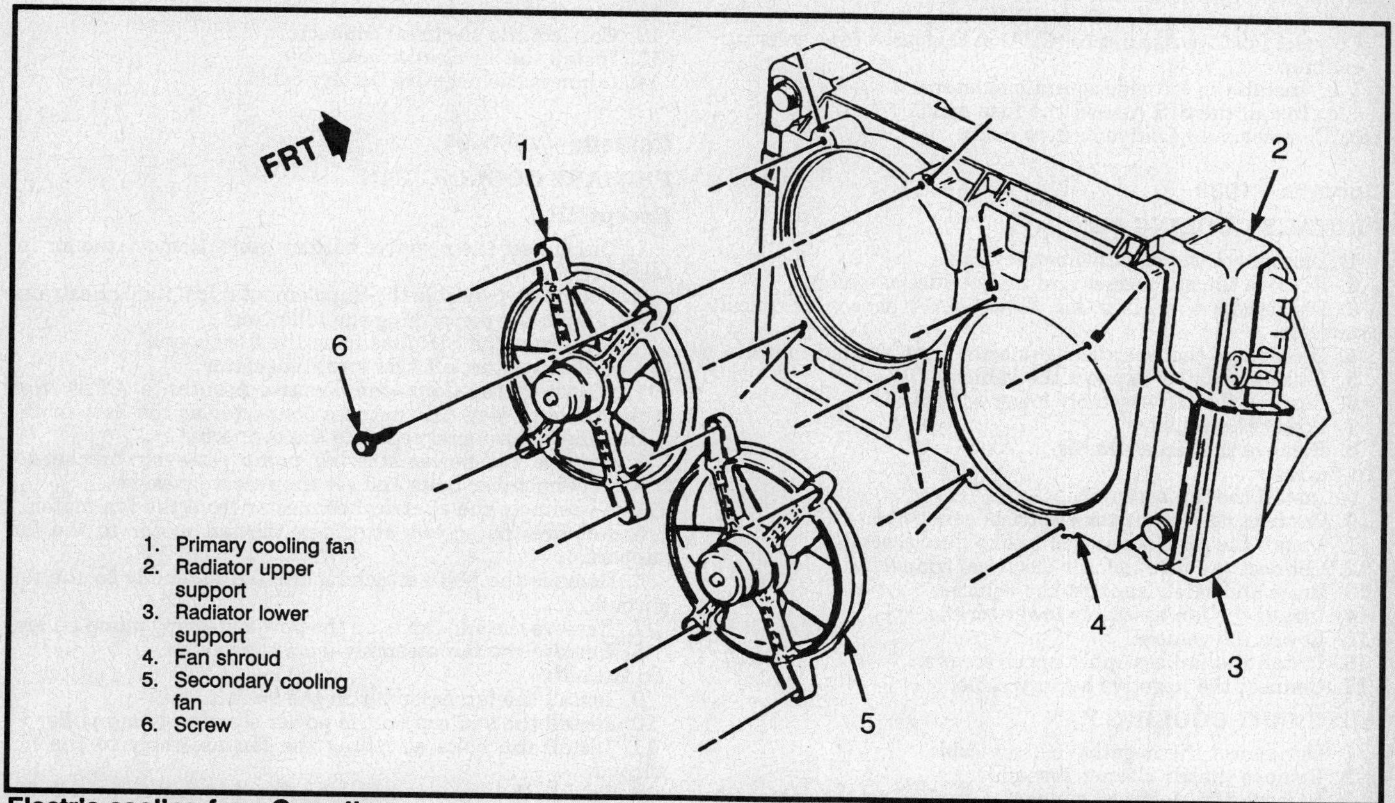
FRT
1
2
3
4
5
6
1. Primary cooling fan
2. Radiator upper support
3. Radiator lower support
4. Fan shroud
5. Secondary cooling fan
6. Screw

Electric cooling fan—Corvette

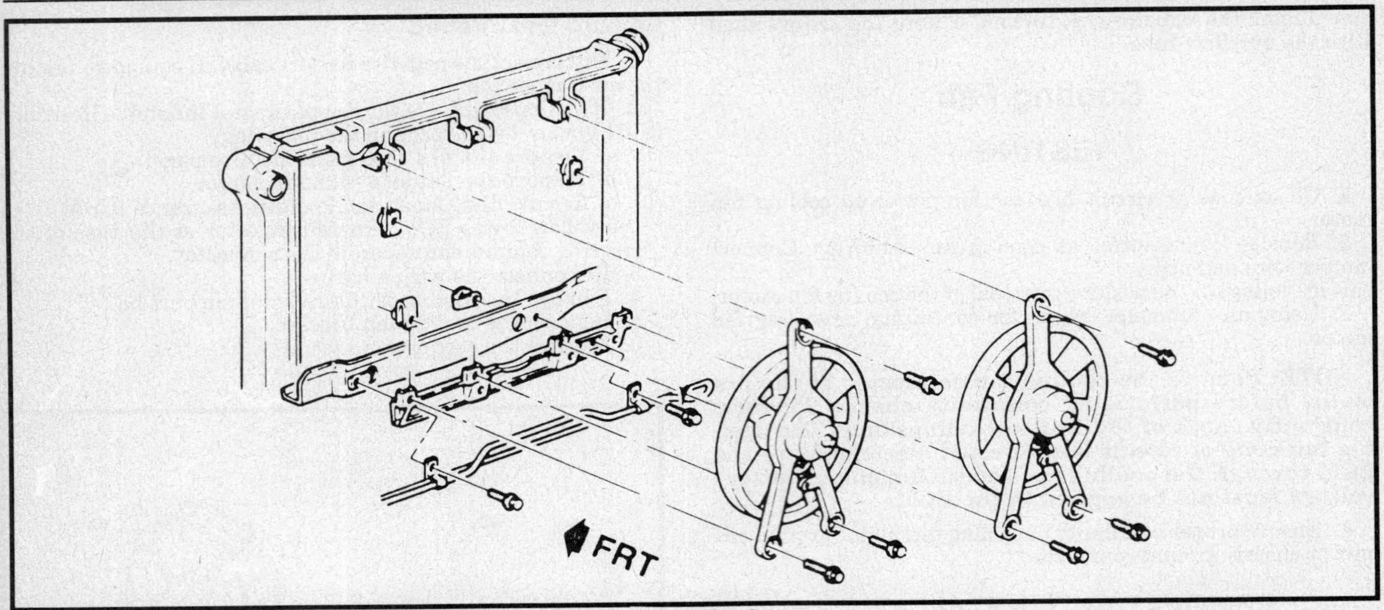
FRT

Electric cooling fan—Camaro and Firebird with air conditioning

To install:

7. Install the cooling fan assembly.
8. Install the cooling fan bracket.
9. Install the cooling fan-to-radiator support bolts.
10. Connect the wiring harness.
11. If equipped, install the air cleaner top.
12. If equipped, enable the Supplemental Inflatable Restraint (SIR) system by performing the following:
    a. Connect the yellow 2-way SIR connector and insert the Connect Positive Assurance (CPA) at the base of the steering column.
    b. Install the left side sound insulator.
    c. Install the SIR fuse in the fuse panel.
13. Connect the negative battery cable.

Corvette—1989

PRIMARY COOLING FAN

1. Disconnect the negative battery cable.
2. Remove the air cleaner and intake duct assembly.
3. Disconnect the Mass Air Flow (MAF) sensor electrical connector.
4. Disconnect the electrical connector from the fan motor.
5. Raise and safely support the vehicle.
6. Remove the fan assembly lower screws.
7. Lower the vehicle.
8. Remove the fan assembly.

To install:

9. Install the fan assembly.
10. Connect the fan motor electrical connector.
11. Install the air cleaner and intake duct assembly.
12. Connect the MAF sensor electrical connector.
13. Raise and safely support the vehicle.
14. Install the fan assembly lower screws.
15. Lower the vehicle.
16. Install the fan assembly upper screws.
17. Connect the negative battery cable.

AUXILIARY COOLING FAN

1. Disconnect the negative battery cable.
2. Remove the air cleaner assembly.
3. Remove the electrical connector by feeding the grommet and harness through the baffle.
4. Remove the upper fan screws.
5. Raise and safely support the vehicle.
6. Remove the lower fan screw.
7. Remove the fan assembly.

To install:

8. Install the fan assembly and lower screw.
9. Feed the harness and grommet through the baffle.
10. Lower the vehicle.
11. Install the upper fan screws.
12. Connect the electrical connector.
13. Install the air cleaner assembly.
14. Connect the negative battery cable.

Corvette—1990–91

PRIMARY COOLING FAN

Except ZR-1

1. Disconnect the negative battery cable. Remove the air intake duct.
2. If equipped, disable the Supplemental Inflatable Restraint (SIR) system by performing the following:
    a. Remove the SIR fuse from the fuse panel.
    b. Remove the left side sound insulator.
    c. Remove the Connector Positive Assurance (CPA) from the yellow 2-way SIR harness connector at the base of the steering column and separate the connector.
3. Remove the power steering pump reservoir bracket-to-front crossmember bolts and set the reservoir aside.
4. Disconnect the electrical connector from the fan motor.
5. Remove the screws attaching the fan motor to the fan support.
6. Remove the bolts attaching the fan assembly to the fan shroud.
7. Remove the end cap from the power steering pump pulley.
8. Remove the fan assembly from the vehicle.

To install:

9. Install the fan assembly in the vehicle.
10. Install the end cap on the power steering pump pulley.
11. Install the bolts attaching the fan assembly to the fan shroud.
12. Install the screws attaching the fan motor to the fan support.

13. Connect the electrical connector from the fan motor.
14. Install the power steering pump reservoir bracket-to-front crossmember bolts and set the reservoir aside.
15. If equipped, enable the Supplemental Inflatable Restraint (SIR) system by performing the following:
    a. Connect the yellow 2-way SIR connector and insert the Connect Positive Assurance (CPA) at the base of the steering column.
    b. Install the left side sound insulator.
    c. Install the SIR fuse in the fuse panel.
16. Connect the negative battery cable.
17. Install the air intake duct.

ZR-1

1. Disconnect the negative battery cable. Drain the engine coolant into a clean container for reuse.
2. If equipped, disable the Supplemental Inflatable Restraint (SIR) system by performing the following:
    a. Remove the SIR fuse from the fuse panel.
    b. Remove the left side sound insulator.
    c. Remove the Connector Positive Assurance (CPA) from the yellow 2-way SIR harness connector at the base of the steering column and separate the connector.
3. Remove the air intake duct.
4. Disconnect the coolant hoses from the radiator.
5. Remove the hose and inlet pipe assembly from the vehicle.
6. Disconnect the cooling fan electrical connector.
7. Remove the screws attaching the fan motor to the motor support.
8. Remove the bolt attaching the air conditioner discharge line clamp to the crossmember.
9. Remove the bolts attaching the fan assembly to the fan shroud.
10. Remove the bolts attaching the fan assembly to the fan shroud.
11. Remove the end cap from the power steering pump pulley.
12. Remove the fan assembly from the vehicle.

To install:

13. Install the fan assembly in the vehicle.
14. Install the end cap to the power steering pump pulley.
15. Install the bolts attaching the fan assembly to the fan shroud.
16. Install the bolt attaching the air conditioner discharge line clamp to the crossmember.
17. Install the screws attaching the fan motor to the motor support.
18. Connect the cooling fan electrical connector.
19. Install the hose and inlet pipe assembly to the vehicle.
20. Connect the coolant hoses to the radiator.
21. Install the air intake duct.
22. If equipped, enable the Supplemental Inflatable Restraint (SIR) system by performing the following:
    a. Connect the yellow 2-way SIR connector and insert the Connect Positive Assurance (CPA) at the base of the steering column.
    b. Install the left side sound insulator.
    c. Install the SIR fuse in the fuse panel.
23. Connect the negative battery cable.
24. Fill cooling system and check for leaks. Start the engine and allow to come to normal operating temperature. Allow the engine to warm up sufficiently to confirm cooling fan operation. Recheck for leaks. Top-up coolant.

AUXILIARY COOLING FAN

Except ZR-1

1. Disconnect the negative battery cable. Remove the upper right bolt attaching the fan assembly to the shroud.
2. If equipped, disable the Supplemental Inflatable Restraint (SIR) system by performing the following:
    a. Remove the SIR fuse from the fuse panel.
    b. Remove the left side sound insulator.
    c. Remove the Connector Positive Assurance (CPA) from the yellow 2-way SIR harness connector at the base of the steering column and separate the connector.
3. Raise and safely support the vehicle.
4. Disconnect the electrical connector from the fan motor.
5. Remove the bolts attaching the fan assembly to the fan shroud.
6. Remove the fan assembly from the vehicle.

To install:

7. Install the fan assembly in the vehicle.
8. Install the bolts attaching the fan assembly to the fan shroud.
9. Connect the electrical connector to the fan motor.
10. Lower the vehicle.
11. Install the upper right bolt attaching the fan assembly to the shroud.
12. If equipped, enable the Supplemental Inflatable Restraint (SIR) system by performing the following:
    a. Connect the yellow 2-way SIR connector and insert the Connect Positive Assurance (CPA) at the base of the steering column.
    b. Install the left side sound insulator.
    c. Install the SIR fuse in the fuse panel.
13. Connect the negative battery cable.

ZR-1

1. Disconnect the negative battery cable. Remove the upper right attaching fan assembly to the shroud.
2. If equipped, disable the Supplemental Inflatable Restraint (SIR) system by performing the following:
    a. Remove the SIR fuse from the fuse panel.
    b. Remove the left side sound insulator.
    c. Remove the Connector Positive Assurance (CPA) from the yellow 2-way SIR harness connector at the base of the steering column and separate the connector.
3. Raise and safely support the vehicle.
4. Disconnect the electrical connector from the fan motor.
5. Remove the bolts attaching the fan assembly to the fan shroud.
6. Remove the fan assembly.

To install:

7. Install the fan assembly.
8. Remove the bolts attaching the fan assembly to the fan shroud.
9. Disconnect the electrical connector from the fan motor.
10. Lower the vehicle.
11. Remove the upper right attaching fan assembly to the shroud.
12. If equipped, enable the Supplemental Inflatable Restraint (SIR) system by performing the following:
    a. Connect the yellow 2-way SIR connector and insert the Connect Positive Assurance (CPA) at the base of the steering column.
    b. Install the left side sound insulator.
    c. Install the SIR fuse in the fuse panel.
13. Connect the negative battery cable.

Condenser

REMOVAL AND INSTALLATION

CAUTION

Some vehicles are equipped with the Supplemental Inflatable Restraint or air bag system. The air bag system must be disabled before performing service on or around the air bag, instrument panel components, wiring and sensors. Failure to follow safety and disabling procedures could result in accidental air bag deployment, possible personal injury and unnecessary air bag system repairs.

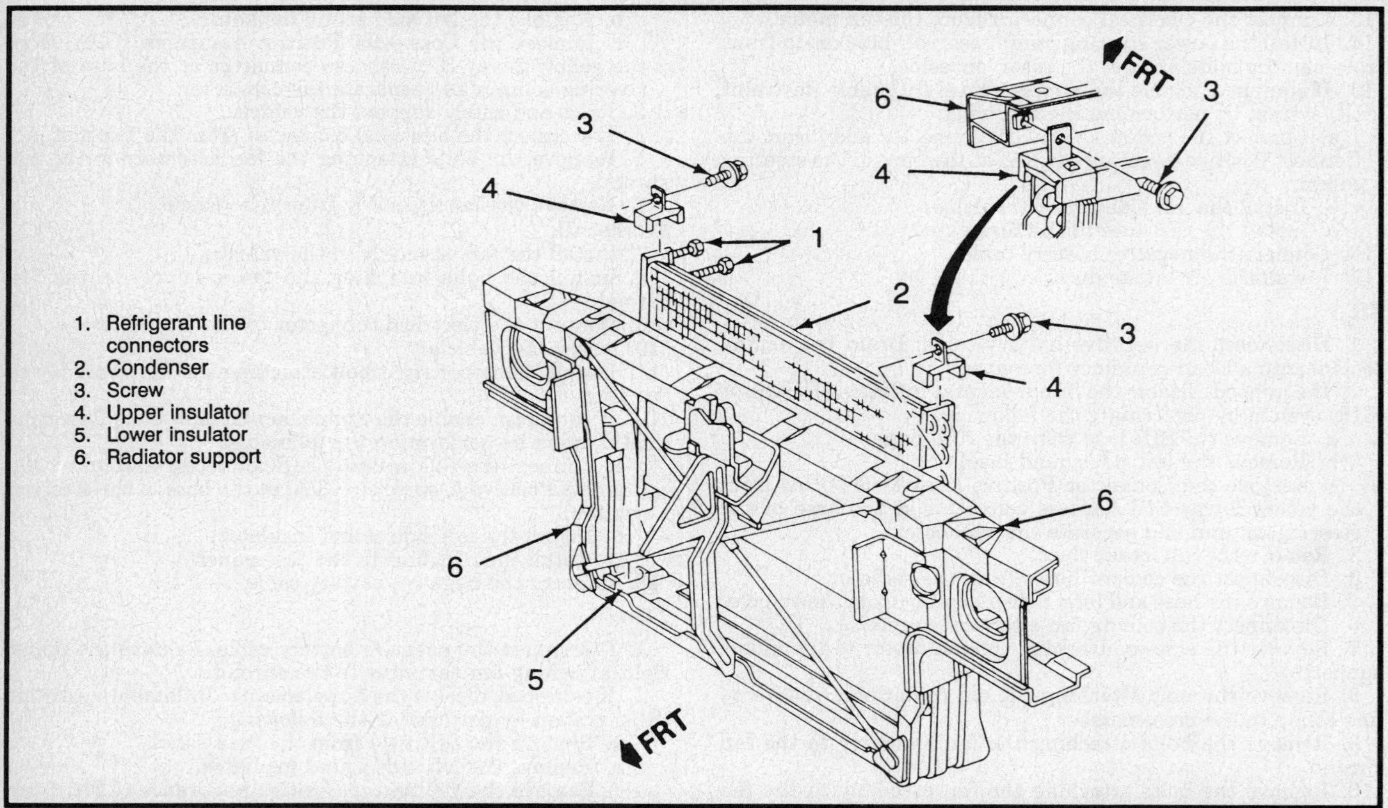
FRT
6
3
4
3
4
1
2
3
4
6
6
5
FRT
1. Refrigerant line connectors
2. Condenser
3. Screw
4. Upper insulator
5. Lower insulator
6. Radiator support

Condenser removed—Caprice and Caprice Wagon, Custom Cruiser, Estate Wagon, Safari and Roadmaster

Cadillac Brougham, Caprice, Custom Cruiser, Estate Wagon, Safari and Roadmaster

1. Disconnect the negative battery cable.
2. Properly discharge the air conditioning system. Drain the engine coolant into a clean container for reuse.
3. If equipped, disable the Supplemental Inflatable Restraint (SIR) system by performing the following:
   a. Remove the SIR fuse from the fuse panel.
   b. Remove the left side sound insulator.
   c. Remove the Connector Positive Assurance (CPA) from the yellow 2-way SIR harness connector at the base of the steering column and separate the connector.
4. Remove the radiator.
5. Disconnect the refrigerant lines at the condenser. Discard the O-rings.

NOTE: Use a backup wrench on the condenser fittings when removing the high-pressure and liquid lines. Cap the refrigerant lines when opening the system to prevent the entry of dirt and moisture and the loss of refrigerant lubricant.

6. Remove the top condenser insulator retainer screws and the insulators.
7. Remove the condenser from the vehicle by tilting to the rear and lifting gently out of the lower condenser insulators.

To install:

NOTE: If replacing the condenser or if the original condenser was flushed during service, add 1 fluid oz. (30ml) of refrigerant lubricant to the system.

8. Install the condenser in the vehicle. Ensure that the condenser is seated properly in the lower insulators.
9. Install the upper condenser insulators and retainers.
10. Replace the condenser fitting O-rings. Lubricate the O-rings with refrigerant oil.
11. Install the condenser refrigerant lines.

NOTE: Use a backup wrench on the condenser fittings when tightening lines.

12. Install the radiator.
13. Evacuate, recharge and leak test the air conditioning system.
14. If equipped, enable the Supplemental Inflatable Restraint (SIR) system by performing the following:
   a. Connect the yellow 2-way SIR connector and insert the Connect Positive Assurance (CPA) at the base of the steering column.
   b. Install the left side sound insulator.
   c. Install the SIR fuse in the fuse panel.
15. Connect the negative battery cable.
16. Fill cooling system and check for leaks. Start the engine and allow to come to normal operating temperature. Allow the engine to warm up sufficiently to confirm cooling fan operation. Recheck for leaks. Top-up coolant.

Camaro and Firebird

1. Disconnect the negative battery cable. Properly discharge the air conditioning system.
2. If equipped, disable the Supplemental Inflatable Restraint (SIR) system by performing the following:
   a. Remove the SIR fuse from the fuse panel.
   b. Remove the left side sound insulator.
   c. Remove the Connector Positive Assurance (CPA) from the yellow 2-way SIR harness connector at the base of the steering column and separate the connector.
3. Remove the air cleaner and/or the air intake duct work, as required.

4. Remove the radiator shroud retaining screws. Disconnect the cooling fan electrical connections and remove the shroud.
5. Disconnect the refrigerant lines at the condenser. Discard the O-rings.

NOTE: Use a backup wrench on the condenser fittings when removing the high-pressure and liquid lines. Cap the refrigerant lines when opening the system to prevent the entry of dirt and moisture and the loss of refrigerant lubricant.

6. Remove the top condenser insulator retainer screws and the insulators.
7. Remove the condenser from the vehicle by tilting to the rear and lifting gently out of the lower condenser insulators.

To install:

NOTE: If replacing the condenser or if the original condenser was flushed during service, add 1 fluid oz. (30ml) of refrigerant lubricant to the system.

8. Install the condenser in the vehicle. Ensure that the condenser is seated properly in the lower insulators.
9. Install the upper condenser insulators and retainers.
10. Replace the condenser fitting O-rings. Lubricate the O-rings with refrigerant oil.
11. Install the condenser refrigerant lines.

NOTE: Use a backup wrench on the condenser fittings when tightening lines.

12. Connect the cooling fan electrical connections and install the shroud. Install the radiator shroud retaining screws.
13. If removed, install the air cleaner and/or the air intake duct work.
14. Evacuate, recharge and leak test the air conditioning system.
15. If equipped, enable the Supplemental Inflatable Restraint (SIR) system by performing the following:
    a. Connect the yellow 2-way SIR connector and insert the Connect Positive Assurance (CPA) at the base of the steering column.
    b. Install the left side sound insulator.
    c. Install the SIR fuse in the fuse panel.
16. Connect the negative battery cable.

Corvette – 1989

1. Disconnect the negative battery cable.
2. Remove the radiator cap.
3. Remove the air cleaner assembly.
4. Remove the accumulator attaching screw and reposition the accumulator away from the condenser.
5. Remove the accumulator bracket.
6. Remove the upper fan retaining screws and reposition the fan.
7. Disconnect the cooling fan relay electrical connector.
8. Remove the upper fan support shroud.
9. Disconnect the accumulator and compressor refrigerant lines from the condenser. Discard the O-rings.

NOTE: Use a backup wrench on the condenser fittings when removing the high-pressure and liquid lines. Cap the refrigerant lines when opening the system to prevent the entry of dirt and moisture and the loss of refrigerant lubricant.

10. Remove the condenser.

To install:

11. Install the condenser.
12. Replace the condenser fitting O-rings. Lubricate the O-rings with refrigerant oil.
13. Connect the refrigerant lines to the condenser.

NOTE: Use a backup wrench on the condenser fittings when tightening lines.

14. Install the upper fan support shroud.
15. Connect the cooling fan electrical connector.
16. Install the upper fan retaining screws.
17. Install the accumulator bracket.
18. Install the accumulator.
19. Install the air cleaner assembly.
20. Install the radiator cap.
21. Connect the negative battery cable.

Corvette – 1990–91

EXCEPT ZR-1

1. Disconnect the negative battery cable. Properly discharge the air conditioning system.
2. If equipped, disable the Supplemental Inflatable Restraint (SIR) system by performing the following:
    a. Remove the SIR fuse from the fuse panel.
    b. Remove the left side sound insulator.
    c. Remove the Connector Positive Assurance (CPA) from the yellow 2-way SIR harness connector at the base of the steering column and separate the connector.
3. Remove the cooling fans, as required, to provide room to tilt the radiator back when removing the condenser.
4. Remove the upper radiator support.
5. Disconnect the accumulator and compressor refrigerant lines from the condenser. Discard the O-rings.

NOTE: Use a backup wrench on the condenser fittings when removing the high-pressure and liquid lines. Cap the refrigerant lines when opening the system to prevent the entry of dirt and moisture and the loss of refrigerant lubricant.

6. Remove the condenser.

To install:

7. Install the condenser.
8. Replace the condenser fitting O-rings. Lubricate the O-rings with refrigerant oil.
9. Connect the refrigerant lines to the condenser.

NOTE: Use a backup wrench on the condenser fittings when tightening lines.

10. Install the upper radiator support.
11. If removed, install the cooling fans.
12. Evacuate, recharge and leak test the air conditioning system.
13. If equipped, enable the Supplemental Inflatable Restraint (SIR) system by performing the following:
    a. Connect the yellow 2-way SIR connector and insert the Connect Positive Assurance (CPA) at the base of the steering column.
    b. Install the left side sound insulator.
    c. Install the SIR fuse in the fuse panel.
14. Connect the negative battery cable.

ZR-1

1. Disconnect the negative battery cable. Properly discharge the air conditioning system.
2. If equipped, disable the Supplemental Inflatable Restraint (SIR) system by performing the following:
    a. Remove the SIR fuse from the fuse panel.
    b. Remove the left side sound insulator.
    c. Remove the Connector Positive Assurance (CPA) from the yellow 2-way SIR harness connector at the base of the steering column and separate the connector.
3. Remove the upper radiator support.
4. Disconnect the accumulator and compressor refrigerant lines from the condenser. Discard the O-rings.

NOTE: Use a backup wrench on the condenser fittings when removing the high-pressure and liquid lines. Cap the refrigerant lines when opening the system to prevent the entry of dirt and moisture and the loss of refrigerant lubricant.

5. Remove the condenser and oil cooler assembly from the vehicle.
6. Remove the screws attaching the oil cooler to the condenser.
7. Remove the screws attaching the condenser bracket to the condenser.

To install:

8. Install the screws attaching the condenser bracket to the condenser.
9. Install the screws attaching the oil cooler to the condenser.
10. Install the condenser and oil cooler assembly in the vehicle.
11. Replace the condenser fitting O-rings. Lubricate the O-rings with refrigerant oil.
12. Connect the refrigerant lines to the condenser.

NOTE: Use a backup wrench on the condenser fittings when tightening lines.

13. Install the upper radiator support.
14. Evacuate, recharge and leak test the air conditioning system.
15. If equipped, enable the Supplemental Inflatable Restraint (SIR) system by performing the following:
    a. Connect the yellow 2-way SIR connector and insert the Connect Positive Assurance (CPA) at the base of the steering column.
    b. Install the left side sound insulator.
    c. Install the SIR fuse in the fuse panel.
16. Connect the negative battery cable.

Compressor

REMOVAL AND INSTALLATION

Caprice, Custom Cruiser, Estate Wagon, Safari and Roadmaster

1. Disconnect the negative battery cable.
2. Properly discharge the air conditioning system.
3. Remove the serpentine belt.
4. Disconnect the compressor electrical connectors.
5. Remove the screw and lock washer from the refrigerant line connector block at the rear of the compressor.
6. Disconnect the refrigerant line connector block and remove the O-rings.

NOTE: On 1990–91 vehicles, oval cross-section O-rings have been installed to provide more effective sealing of the refrigerant line connections at the rear of the compressor. New oval cross-section O-rings should be used when installing the refrigerant hose connector block to the compressor. Discard the old O-rings.

NOTE: Cap the refrigerant lines when opening the system to prevent the entry of dirt and moisture and the loss of refrigerant lubricant.

7. Remove the compressor brace nuts from the braces at the rear of the compressor.
8. Remove the compressor mounting bolts.
9. Remove the compressor.
10. Drain and measure the refrigerant oil from the compressor. Discard the old oil.

To install:

11. If the compressor is to be replaced, drain the oil from the new compressor and discard. Add new refrigerant oil equivalent to the amount that was drained from the old compressor upon removal.
12. Position the compressor in the vehicle.
13. Install the compressor mounting bolts.
14. Install the compressor braces and attaching nuts to the rear of the compressor.
15. Replace the compressor fitting O-rings with the same type as were originally installed. Lubricate the O-rings with refrigerant oil.
16. Connect the compressor electrical connectors.
17. Install the serpentine belt.
18. Evacuate, recharge and leak test the air conditioning system.
19. Connect the negative battery cable.

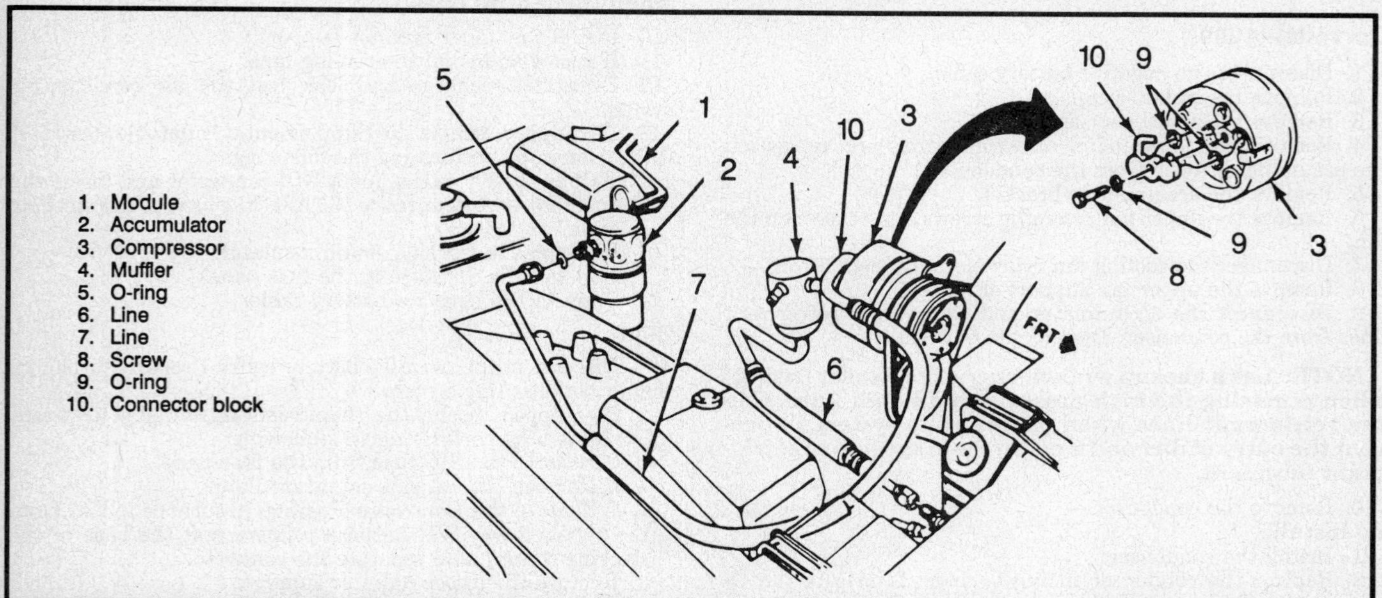
1. Module
2. Accumulator
3. Compressor
4. Muffler
5. O-ring
6. Line
7. Line
8. Screw
9. O-ring
10. Connector block
5
1
2
4
10
3
10
9
9
3
8
7
6
FRT

Compressor and refrigerant hose installation—typical

Cadillac Brougham

5.0L ENGINE

1. Disconnect the negative battery cable.
2. Properly discharge the air conditioning system.
3. Disconnect the compressor electrical connectors.
4. Loosen the pivot bolt and 2 adjusting bolts.
5. Remove the bolt securing the refrigerant line coupling to the rear of the compressor. Discard the O-rings.
6. Remove the compressor drive belt.
7. Remove the 2 through bolts and remove the compressor from the vehicle.
8. Drain and measure the refrigerant oil from the compressor. Discard the old oil.

To install:

9. If the compressor is to be replaced, drain the oil from the new compressor and discard. Add new refrigerant oil equivalent to the amount that was drained from the old compressor upon removal.
10. Position the compressor in the vehicle.
11. Install the compressor through bolts.
12. Install the compressor drive belt. Check and adjust drive belt tension.
13. Replace the compressor fitting O-rings. Lubricate the O-rings with refrigerant oil.
14. Connect the refrigerant line coupling at the rear of the compressor.
15. Connect the compressor electrical connectors.
16. Evacuate, recharge and leak test the air conditioning system.
17. Connect the negative battery cable.

5.7L ENGINE

1. Disconnect the negative battery cable.
2. Properly discharge the air conditioning system.
3. Remove the serpentine belt.
4. Disconnect the refrigerant line fitting bolt and separate the coupling. Discard the O-rings.
5. Disconnect the compressor electrical connectors.
6. Remove the 2 nuts and 3 bolts from the rear of the compressor.
7. Remove the compressor from the vehicle.
8. Drain and measure the refrigerant oil from the compressor. Discard the old oil.

To install:

9. If the compressor is to be replaced, drain the oil from the new compressor and discard. Add new refrigerant oil equivalent to the amount that was drained from the old compressor upon removal.
10. Position the compressor in the vehicle.
11. Install the 3 bolts and 2 nuts at the rear of the compressor.
12. Connect the compressor electrical connectors.
13. Replace the compressor fitting O-rings. Lubricate the O-rings with refrigerant oil.
14. Connect the refrigerant line coupling at the rear of the compressor.
15. Install the serpentine belt.
16. Evacuate, recharge and leak test the air conditioning system.
17. Connect the negative battery cable.

Camaro and Firebird

1. Disconnect the negative battery cable.
2. Properly discharge the air conditioning system.
3. Remove the serpentine belt.
4. Disconnect the compressor electrical connectors.
5. Disconnect the refrigerant line coupler at the rear of the compressor.

NOTE: Cap the refrigerant lines when opening the system to prevent the entry of dirt and moisture and the loss of refrigerant lubricant.

6. Remove the O-rings.

NOTE: On 1990–91 vehicles, oval cross-section O-rings have been installed to provide more effective sealing of the refrigerant line connections at the rear of the compressor. New oval cross-section O-rings should be used when installing the refrigerant hose connector block to the compressor. Discard the old O-rings.

7. Remove the compressor brace nuts and remove the brace.
8. Remove the compressor mounting bolts and nut. Remove the compressor.
9. Remove the fuel feed shield and attaching screws.
10. Drain and measure the refrigerant oil from the compressor. Discard the old oil.

To install:

11. If the compressor is to be replaced, drain the oil from the new compressor and discard. Add new refrigerant oil equivalent to the amount that was drained from the old compressor upon removal.
12. Install the fuel feed shield and attaching screws.
13. Position the compressor in the vehicle.
14. Install the compressor mounting bolts and nut.
15. Install the compressor brace and brace attaching nuts.
16. Replace the compressor refrigerant line coupler O-rings with the same type as were originally installed. Lubricate the O-rings with refrigerant oil.
17. Install the refrigerant line coupler to the rear of the compressor.
18. Connect the compressor electrical connectors.
19. Install the serpentine belt.
20. Evacuate, recharge and leak test the air conditioning system.
21. Connect the negative battery cable.

Corvette

Except ZR-1

1. Disconnect the negative battery cable.
2. Properly discharge the air conditioning system.
3. Remove the serpentine belt.
4. Disconnect the compressor electrical connector.
5. Disconnect the refrigerant line coupler from the compressor. Discard the O-ring.
6. Remove the compressor mounting bolts.
7. Remove the compressor from the vehicle.
8. Drain and measure the refrigerant oil from the compressor. Discard the old oil.

To install:

9. If the compressor is to be replaced, drain the oil from the new compressor and discard. Add new refrigerant oil equivalent to the amount that was drained from the old compressor upon removal.
10. Install the fuel feed shield and attaching screws.
11. Position the compressor in the vehicle.
12. Install the compressor mounting bolts.
13. Replace the condenser fitting O-rings. Lubricate the O-rings with refrigerant oil.
14. Connect the refrigerant line coupler at the rear of the compressor.
15. Connect the compressor electrical connectors.
16. Install the serpentine belt.
17. Evacuate, recharge and leak test the air conditioning system.
18. Connect the negative battery cable.

ZR-1

1. Disconnect the negative battery cable.

2. Properly discharge the air conditioning system.
3. Remove the throttle body by performing the following:
   a. Drain the engine coolant into a clean container for reuse.
   b. Remove the air intake duct.
   c. Disconnect the Manifold Air Temperature (MAT) sensor, Throttle Position Switch (TPS) and Idle Air Control (IAC) valve electrical connectors.
   d. Remove the ventilation breather hose from the left and right side of the throttle body extension.
   e. Remove the cable shield clamps from the throttle body and set the cable aside. Remove the throttle and cruise control cable clamps from the throttle body and set the cables aside.
   f. Remove the throttle body extension front the throttle body.
   g. Disconnect the vacuum hose from the bottom of the extension.
   h. Remove the throttle body from the plenum.
4. Remove the serpentine belt.
5. Disconnect the engine oil temperature sensor.
6. Remove the alternator by performing the following:
   a. Remove the water pump pulley.
   b. Remove the alternator support bracket.
   c. Remove the alternator lower mounting bolt.
   d. Disconnect the alternator electrical connectors.
   e. Remove the alternator from the vehicle.
7. Disconnect the refrigerant line coupler from the rear of the compressor. Discard the O-rings.
8. Disconnect the compressor electrical connectors.
9. Remove the compressor from the vehicle.
10. Drain and measure the refrigerant oil from the compressor. Discard the old oil.

To install:

11. If the compressor is to be replaced, drain the oil from the new compressor and discard. Add new refrigerant oil equivalent to the amount that was drained from the old compressor upon removal.
12. Install the compressor.
13. Connect the compressor electrical connectors.
14. Replace the compressor refrigerant line coupler O-rings. Lubricate the O-rings with refrigerant oil.
15. Connect the refrigerant line coupler to the rear of the compressor.
16. Install the alternator by performing the following:
   a. Position the alternator in the vehicle.
   b. Install the upper mounting bolts.
   c. Connect the alternator electrical connectors.
   d. Install the alternator lower mounting bolt.
   e. Install the alternator support bracket.
   f. Install the water pump pulley.
17. Connect the engine oil temperature sensor.
18. Install the serpentine belt.
19. Install the throttle body by performing the following:
   a. Ensure that all gasket surfaces are thoroughly clean and free of gasket material.
   b. Install the throttle body to the plenum.
   c. Connect the vacuum hose to the bottom of the extension.
   d. Install the throttle body extension to the throttle body.
   e. Install the cable shield clamps to the throttle body and set the cable aside. Install the throttle and cruise control cable clamps to the throttle body and set the cables aside.
   f. Install the ventilation breather hose to the left and right side of the throttle body extension.
   g. Connect the Manifold Air Temperature (MAT) sensor, Throttle Position Switch (TPS) and Idle Air Control (IAC) valve electrical connectors.
   h. Install the air intake duct.
20. Evacuate, recharge and leak test the air conditioning system.
21. Connect the negative battery cable.
22. Fill cooling system and check for leaks. Start the engine and allow to come to normal operating temperature. Allow the engine to warm up sufficiently to confirm cooling fan operation. Recheck for leaks. Top-up coolant.

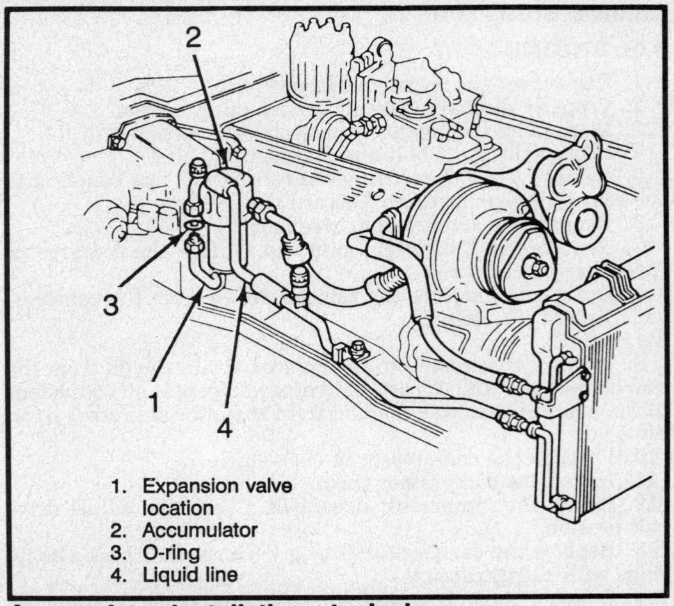
2
3
1
4
1. Expansion valve location
2. Accumulator
3. O-ring
4. Liquid line

Accumulator installation—typical

Accumulator

REMOVAL AND INSTALLATION

1. Disconnect the negative battery cable.
2. Properly discharge the air conditioning system.
3. Disconnect the low-pressure lines at the inlet and outlet fittings on the accumulator.

NOTE: Cap the refrigerant lines when opening the system to prevent the entry of dirt and moisture and the loss of refrigerant lubricant.

4. Disconnect the pressure cycling switch connection and remove the switch, as required.
5. Loosen the lower strap bolt and spread the strap. Turn the accumulator and remove.
6. Drain and measure the oil in the accumulator. Discard the old oil.

To install:

7. Add new oil equivalent to the amount drained from the old accumulator. Add an additional 2–3 oz. (60–90ml) of oil to compensate for the oil retained by the accumulator dessicant.
8. Position the accumulator in the securing bracket and tighten the clamp bolt.
9. Install new O-rings at the inlet and outlet connections on the accumulator. Lubricate the O-rings with refrigerant oil.
10. Connect the low-pressure inlet and outlet lines.
11. Evacuate, charge and leak test the system.
12. Connect the negative battery cable.

Fixed Orifice Tube

REMOVAL AND INSTALLATION

1. Properly discharge the air conditioning system.
2. Loosen the fitting at the liquid line outlet on the condenser or evaporator inlet pipe and disconnect. Discard the O-ring.

NOTE: Use a backup wrench on the condenser outlet fitting when loosening the lines.

3. Carefully, remove the fixed orifice tube from the tube fitting in the evaporator inlet line.
4. In the event that the restricted or plugged orifice tube is difficult to remove, perform the following:
   a. Remove as much of the impacted residue as possible.
   b. Using a hair dryer, epoxy drier or equivalent, carefully apply heat approximately ¼ in. from the dimples on the inlet pipe. Do not overheat the pipe.

NOTE: If the system has a pressure switch near the orifice tube, it should be removed prior to heating the pipe to avoid damage to the switch.

   c. While applying heat, use special tool J 26549-C or equivalent to grip the orifice tube. Use a turning motion along with a push-pull motion to loosen the impacted orifice tube and remove it.
5. Swab the inside of the evaporator inlet pipe with solvent to remove any remaining residue.
6. Add 1 oz. of 525 viscosity refrigerant oil to the system.
7. Lubricate the new O-ring and orifice tube with refrigerant oil and insert into the inlet pipe.

NOTE: Ensure that the new orifice tube is inserted in the inlet tube with the smaller screen end first.

8. Connect the evaporator inlet pipe with the condenser outlet fitting.

NOTE: Use a backup wrench on the condenser outlet fitting when tightening the lines.

9. Evacuate, recharge and leak test the system.

Blower Motor

REMOVAL AND INSTALLATION

1989–90 Caprice, Custom Cruiser, Estate Wagon and Safari

1. Disconnect the negative battery cable.
2. Disconnect the blower motor electrical connectors.
3. Remove the blower motor cooling tube.
4. Remove the blower motor retaining screws.
5. Lift the blower motor and fan assembly straight up and out of the upper case of the air conditioning module.
6. Remove the sealer from the blower motor mounting flange and the mating surface of the upper case.

To install:

7. Apply fresh sealer to the blower motor mounting flange.
8. Install the blower motor and fan assembly. Install the retaining screws.
9. Install the cooling tube.
10. Connect the blower motor electrical connectors.
11. Connect the negative battery cable.
12. Test the operation of the blower motor to ensure that it functions on all speeds.

1991 Caprice, Custom Cruiser and Roadmaster

1. Disconnect the negative battery cable.
2. Remove the right side instrument panel sound insulator.
3. Disconnect the blower motor electrical connector.
4. Remove the right side hing pillar trim finish panel by pulling away from the front body hinge pillar.
5. Remove the screw from the secondary ECM bracket. Swing the ECM module aside to provide clearance for the removal and installation of the blower motor and fan.
6. Remove 2 of the mounting screws allowing the third,

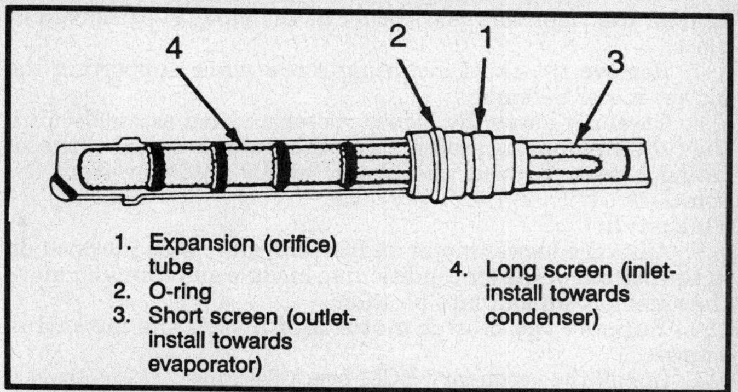
4
2
1
3
1. Expansion (orifice) tube
2. O-ring
3. Short screen (outlet-install towards evaporator)
4. Long screen (inlet-install towards condenser)

Expansion (orifice) tube

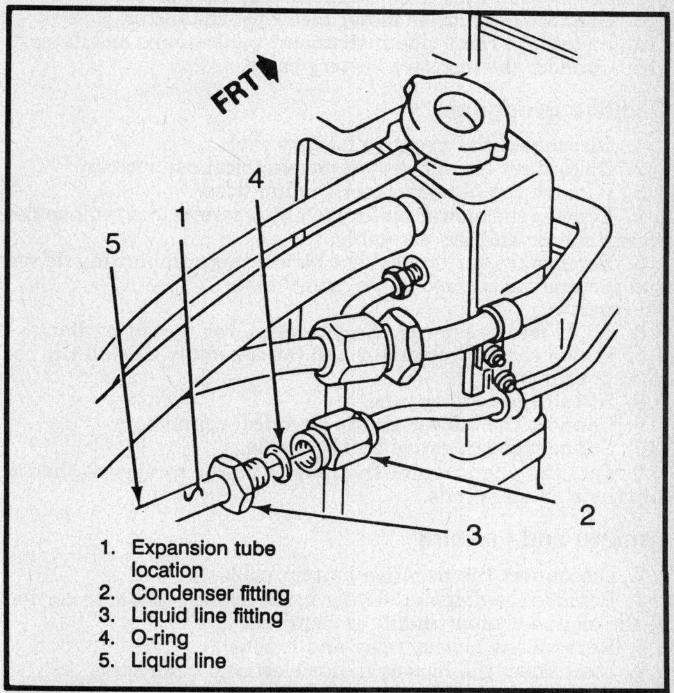
FRT
4
1
5
2
3
1. Expansion tube location
2. Condenser fitting
3. Liquid line fitting
4. O-ring
5. Liquid line

Expansion tube location—1991 Caprice, Custom Cruiser and Roadmaster

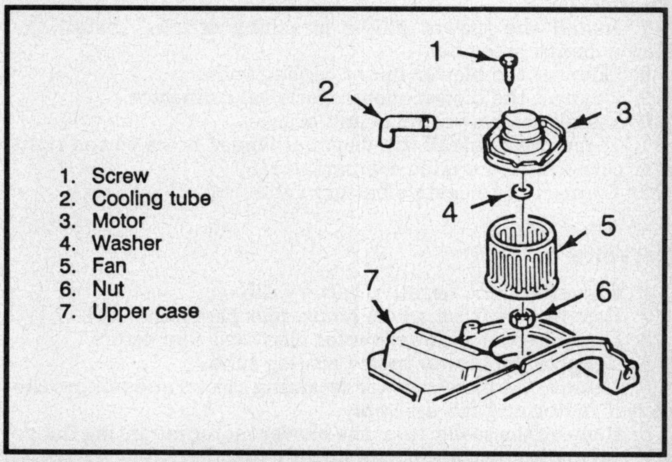
1
2
3
4
5
6
7
1. Screw
2. Cooling tube
3. Motor
4. Washer
5. Fan
6. Nut
7. Upper case

Blower motor and fan assembly—1989–90 Caprice, Custom Cruiser, Estate Wagon and Safari

nearest the right side rear corner of the module, to remain in place.

7. Remove the third mounting screw while supporting the blower motor assembly.

8. Carefully lower the blower motor and fan assembly until the rubber mounting grommets on the motor are clear of the locating bosses. Remove the blower motor assembly from the vehicle.

To install:

9. Align the blower motor and fan assembly with the opening in the bottom of the air conditioning module and carefully move the assembly up and into position.

10. Support the blower motor and install the mounting screws.

11. Install the secondary ECM bracket screw.

12. Install the right side hinge pillar trim finish panel by pressing into position until the retainers snap into place.

13. Connect the blower motor electrical connector.

14. Install the right side instrument panel sound insulator.

15. Connect the negative battery cable.

Cadillac Brougham

1. Disconnect the negative battery cable.
2. Disconnect the blower motor electrical connectors.
3. Remove the blower motor cooling tube.
4. Remove the blower motor retaining screws and remove the blower motor and fan assembly.
5. Remove the sealer from the blower motor mounting flange and the mating surface of the upper case.

To install:

6. Apply fresh sealer to the blower motor mounting flange.
7. Install the blower motor and fan assembly. Install the retaining screws.
8. Install the cooling tube.
9. Connect the blower motor electrical connectors.
10. Connect the negative battery cable.
11. Test the operation of the blower motor to ensure that it functions on all speeds.

Camaro and Firebird

1. Disconnect the negative battery cable.
2. Remove the diagonal fender brace at the right rear corner of the engine compartment, as required.
3. Remove the blower relay and bracket.
4. Disconnect the blower motor electrical connector.
5. Disconnect the blower motor cooling tube.
6. Remove the blower motor attaching screws. Remove the blower motor assembly.

To install:

7. Install the blower motor attaching screws. Install the blower motor assembly.
8. Connect the blower motor cooling tube.
9. Connect the blower motor electrical connector.
10. Install the blower relay and bracket.
11. If removed, install the diagonal fender brace to the right rear corner of the engine compartment.
12. Connect the negative battery cable.

Corvette

1. Disconnect the negative battery cable.
2. Remove the front wheel house rear panel and seal.
3. Disconnect the blower motor electrical connectors.
4. Remove the blower motor cooling tube.
5. Remove the blower motor retaining screws and remove the blower motor and fan assembly.
6. Remove the sealer from the blower motor mounting flange and the mating surface of the upper case.

To install:

7. Apply fresh sealer to the blower motor mounting flange.

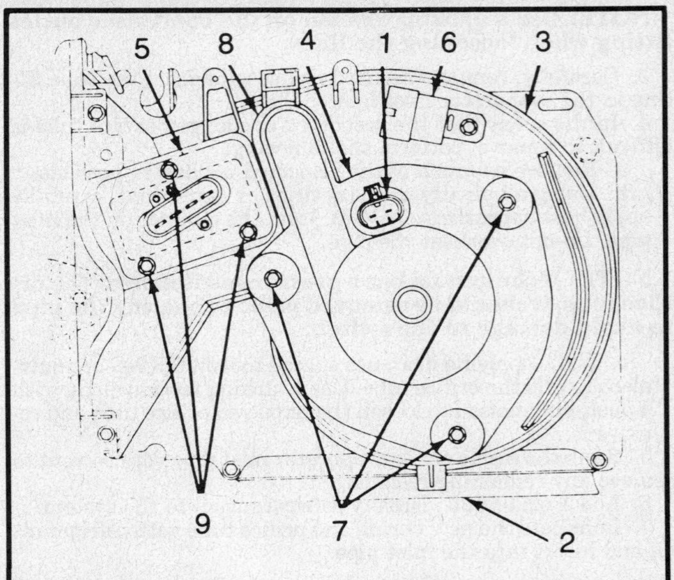
5
8
4
1
6
3
9
7
2

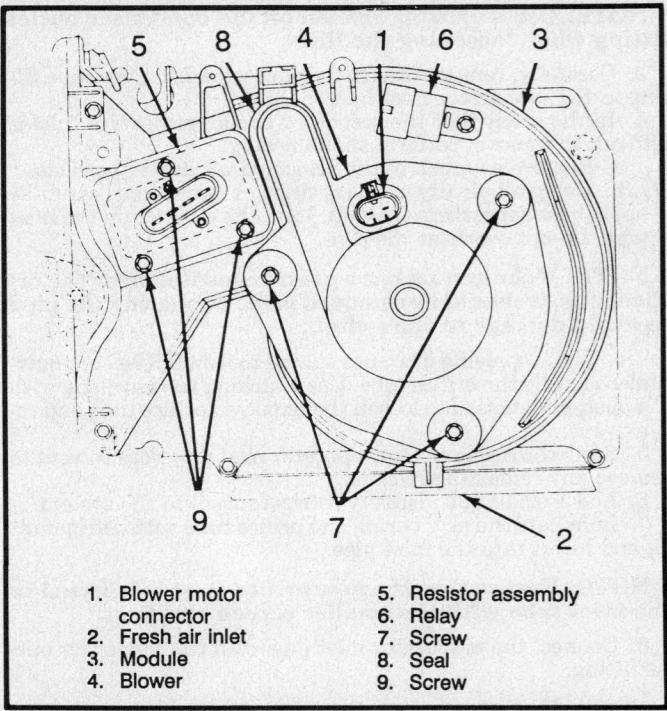

1. Blower motor connector
2. Fresh air inlet
3. Module
4. Blower
5. Resistor assembly
6. Relay
7. Screw
8. Seal
9. Screw

Blower motor housing from below—1991 Caprice, Custom Cruiser and Roadmaster

8. Install the blower motor and fan assembly. Install the retaining screws.
9. Install the cooling tube.
10. Connect the blower motor electrical connectors.
11. Install the front wheel house rear panel and seal.
12. Connect the negative battery cable.
13. Test the operation of the blower motor to ensure that it functions on all speeds.

Blower Motor Resistor/Power Module

REMOVAL AND INSTALLATION

1. Disconnect the negative battery cable.
2. Disconnect the electrical connector at the resistor.
3. Remove the resistor attaching screws.
4. Remove the resistor from the evaporator case.

To install:

5. Position the resistor in the evaporator case. Install the attaching screws.
6. Connect the electrical connector.
7. Connect the negative battery cable.

Heater Core

REMOVAL AND INSTALLATION

1989–90 Caprice, Custom Cruiser, Estate Wagon and Safari

1. Disconnect the negative battery cable.
2. Drain the engine coolant into a clean container for reuse.
3. Disconnect the heater hoses at the inlet and outlet pipes.
4. Remove the air conditioning module upper case by performing the following:
   a. Remove the blower motor assembly, as required.

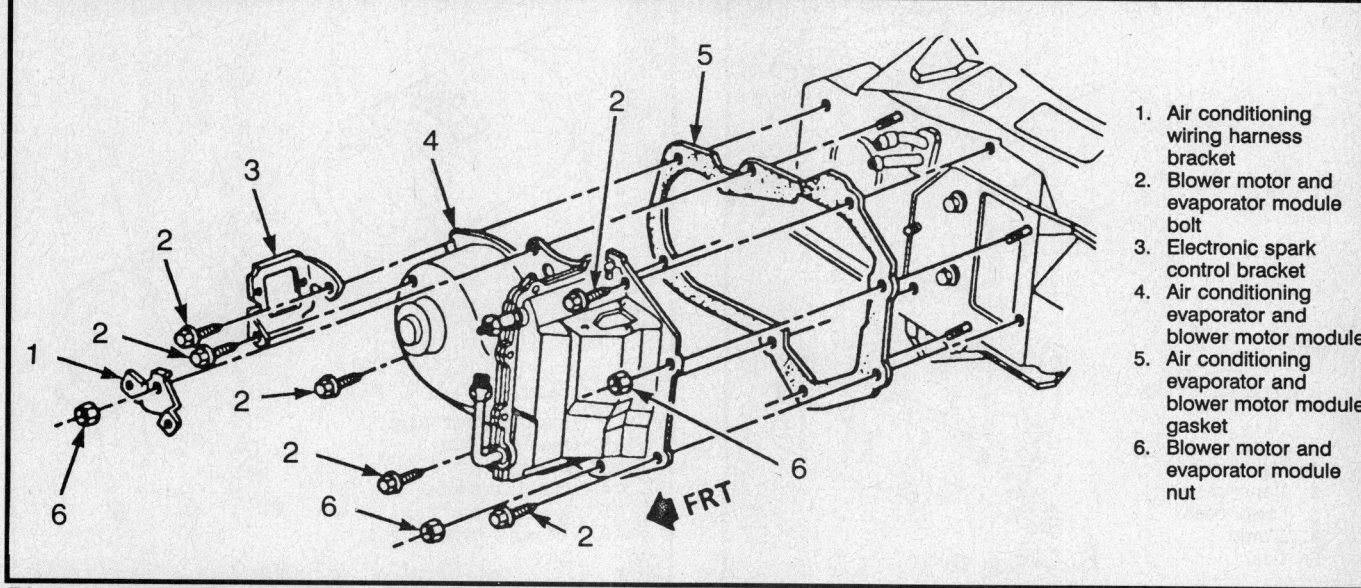

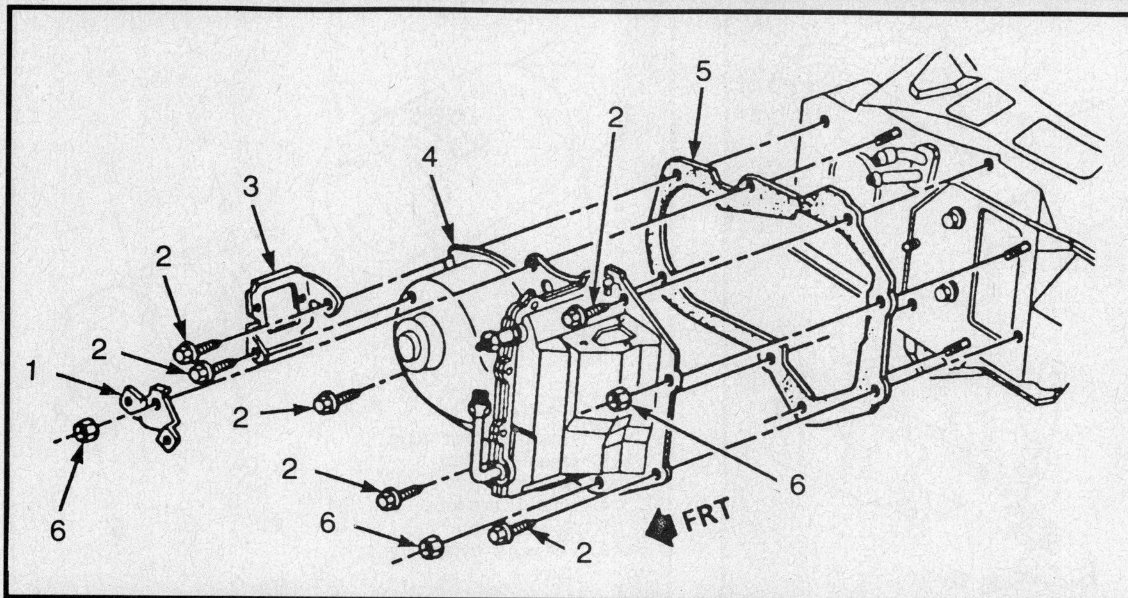
1. Air conditioning wiring harness bracket
2. Blower motor and evaporator module bolt
3. Electronic spark control bracket
4. Air conditioning evaporator and blower motor module
5. Air conditioning evaporator and blower motor module gasket
6. Blower motor and evaporator module nut
FRT

Blower motor and evaporator module installation— Corvette

b. Remove the hood cowl seal by pulling the seal up and off the air conditioning module flange above the air inlet screen.
c. Remove both halves of the air inlet screen.
d. Remove the right side windshield wiper arm.
e. Remove the air conditioning module ground strap from the dash panel.
f. Disconnect the electrical connectors.
g. Remove the air conditioning module flange mounting screws. Remove the air conditioning module upper case.
5. Remove the heater core mounting clamp.
6. Remove the heater core and the heater core pipes seal.

To install:

7. Install the heater core by fitting the base of the heater core into the mounting clip at the bottom of the air conditioning module lower case.
8. Install the core pipes seal.
9. Install the air conditioning module upper case by performing the following:
a. Install the air conditioning module upper case. Install the air conditioning module flange mounting screws.
b. Connect the electrical connectors.
c. Install the air conditioning module ground strap to the dash panel.
d. Install the right side windshield wiper arm.
e. Install both halves of the air inlet screen.
f. Install the hood cowl seal.
g. If removed, install the blower motor assembly.
10. Connect the heater hoses to the inlet and outlet pipes on the heater core.
11. Connect the negative battery cable.
12. Fill cooling system and check for leaks. Start the engine and allow to come to normal operating temperature. Allow the engine to warm up sufficiently to confirm cooling fan operation. Recheck for leaks. Top-up coolant.

1991 Caprice, Custom Cruiser and Roadmaster

1. Disconnect the negative battery cable.
2. Drain the engine coolant into a clean container for reuse.
3. Remove the screw holding the hot water bypass valve to the cowl panel.
4. Release the heater inlet and outlet pipe quick-disconnect fitting by squeezing both release tabs at the base of the heater core tube and pulling on the pipe to disengage the fitting.
5. Remove the air conditioning module lower case by performing the following:
a. Remove the right side instrument panel sound insulator.
b. Remove the lower instrument panel reinforcement.
c. Disconnect the 2 vacuum harness connectors at the lower evaporator case and remove from the case. Position the vacuum harnesses aside.
d. Remove the right side hinge pillar trim finish panel by pulling away from the front body hinge pillar.

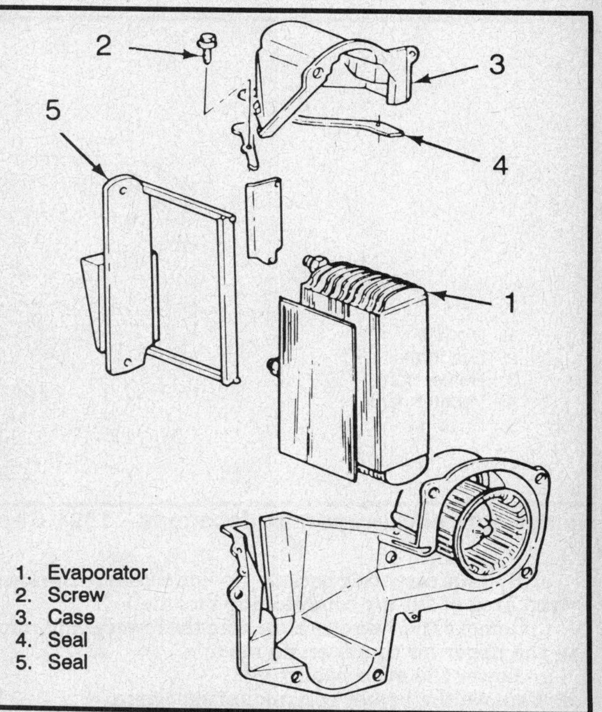
1. Evaporator
2. Screw
3. Case
4. Seal
5. Seal

Evaporator housing—Camaro and Firebird

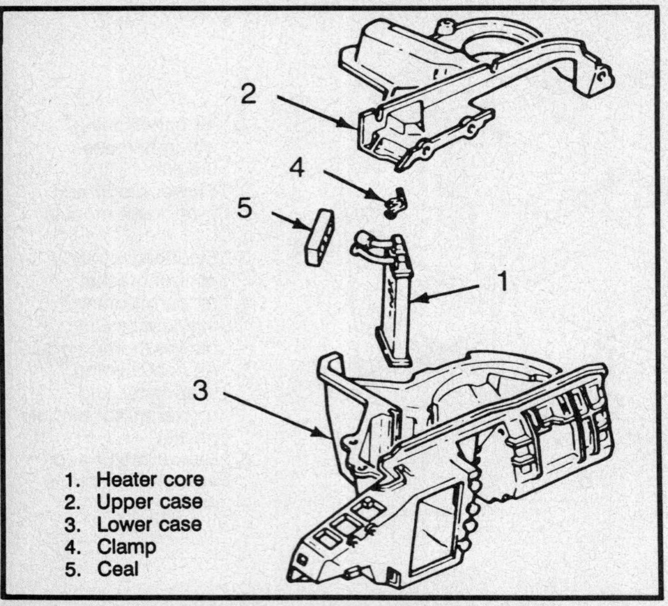
2
4
5
1
3
1. Heater core
2. Upper case
3. Lower case
4. Clamp
5. Ceal

Heater core installation—1989–90 Caprice, Custom Cruiser, Estate Wagon and Safari

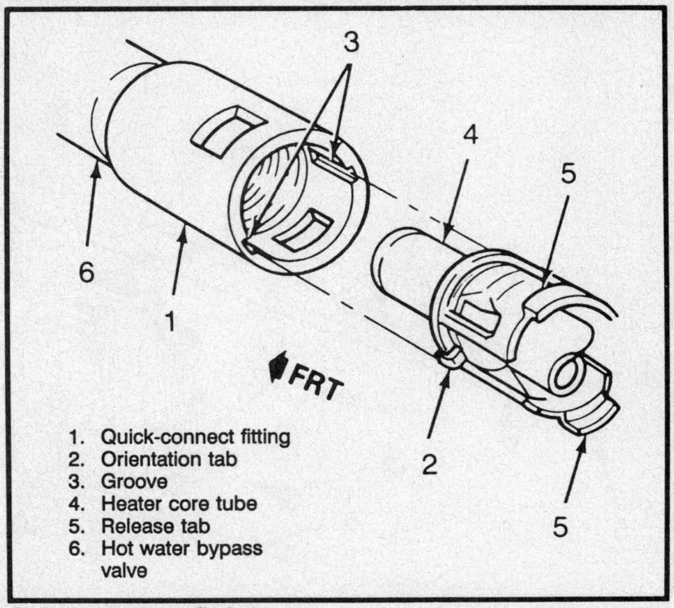
3
4
5
6
1
FRT
2
5
1. Quick-connect fitting
2. Orientation tab
3. Groove
4. Heater core tube
5. Release tab
6. Hot water bypass valve

Quick-connect fitting

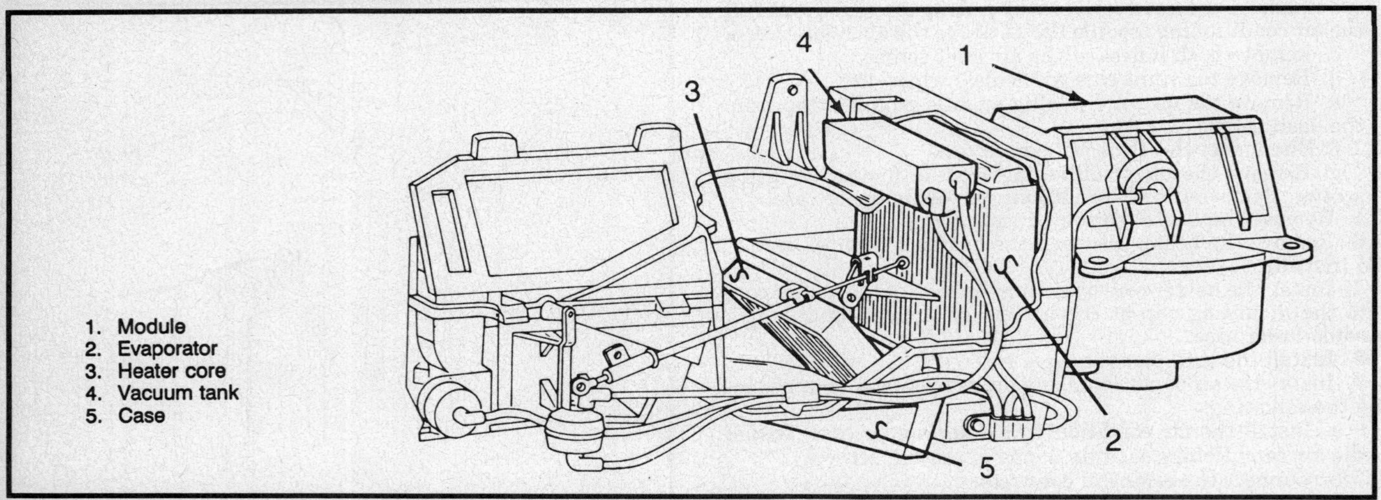
4
1
3
2
5
1. Module
2. Evaporator
3. Heater core
4. Vacuum tank
5. Case

Heater core and evaporator locations—1991 Caprice, Custom Cruiser and Roadmaster

e. Roll the carpeting back to provide access to the lower forward area of the air conditioning module.

f. Remove the 7 screws attaching the lower evaporator case to the upper air conditioning module.

g. Lower the evaporator case.

6. Remove the heater core mounting clamp.

7. Remove the heater core and the heater core pipes seal.

To install:

8. Install the heater core by fitting the base of the heater core into the mounting clip at the bottom of the air conditioning module lower case.

9. Install the core pipes seal.

10. Install the air conditioning module lower case by performing the following:

a. Place the evaporator case into position.

b. Install the 7 screws attaching the lower evaporator case to the upper air conditioing module.

c. Fit the carpeting back in place under the air conditioning module and against the cowl panel.

d. Install the right side hinge pillar trim finish panel.

e. Connect the 2 vacuum harness connectors to the lower evaporator case. Ensure that the vacuum lines are routed properly.

f. Install the lower instrument panel reinforcement.

g. Install the right side instrument panel sound insulator.

11. Connect the heater core inlet and outlet pipe quick-connect fittings.

NOTE: Ensure that the quick-connect orientation tabs are properly aligned before connecting the fittings. Do not rely on an audible click alone to verify proper connection. Test for proper engagement by pushing the fittings together and then pulling back.

12. Connect the negative battery cable.

13. Fill cooling system and check for leaks. Start the engine and allow to come to normal operating temperature. Allow the engine to warm up sufficiently to confirm cooling fan operation. Recheck for leaks. Top-up coolant.

Cadillac Brougham

1. Disconnect the negative battery cable.
2. Drain the engine coolant into a clean container for reuse.
3. Disconnect the blower motor, compressor cycling switch, power module and radio lead-in electrical connectors. Position the wiring harness aside.
4. Remove the compressor cycling switch, as required.
5. Remove the right side windshield washer nozzle.
6. Remove the right side secondary air inlet screen from the plenum.
7. Partially remove the rubber moulding above the plenum. Remove 1 screw on the right side.
8. Remove the remaining screws and remove the primary inlet screen.
9. Remove the blower motor.
10. Remove the air conditioning module cover.
11. Disconnect the heater hoses.
12. Remove the screw and retainer holding the heater core to the frame top.
13. Remove the heater core by performing the following:
   a. Set the temperature valve to the **MAX** heat position.
   b. Reach through the temperature housing and push the lower forward corner of the heater core away from the housing.
   c. Rotate the core until it is parallel to the housing. This will cause the heater core to snap out of the lower clamp.
   d. Remove the heater core.

To install:

14. Remove the old sealer and clean all sealing surfaces. Install new sealer.
15. Position the heater core in the vehicle. Push down firmly to seat the heater core in the bottom clip.
16. Fasten the heater core to the frame top with 1 screw and retainer.
17. Connect the heater hose to the heater core inlet and outlet fittings.
18. Install the air conditioner module cover.
19. Install the blower motor.
20. Install the primary and secondary screens and rubber moulding.
21. Install the right side windshield washer nozzle.
22. If removed, install the pressure cycling switch.
23. Connect the blower motor, compressor cycling switch, power module and radio lead-in electrical connectors. Reposition the wiring harness.
24. Connect the negative battery cable.
25. Fill cooling system and check for leaks. Start the engine and allow to come to normal operating temperature. Allow the engine to warm up sufficiently to confirm cooling fan operation. Recheck for leaks. Top-up coolant.

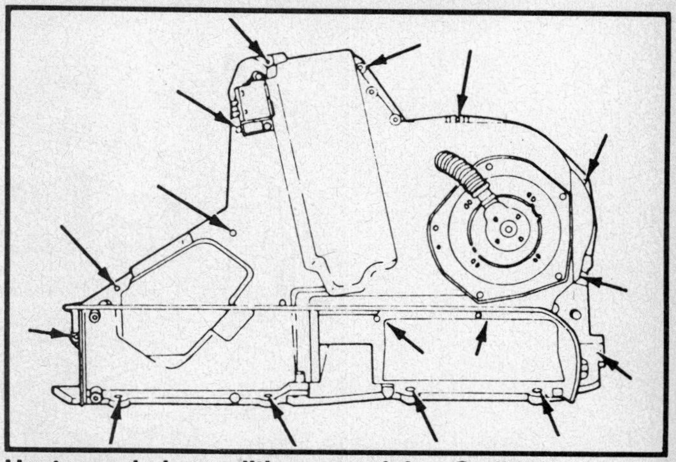

Heater and air conditioner module—Cadillac Brougham

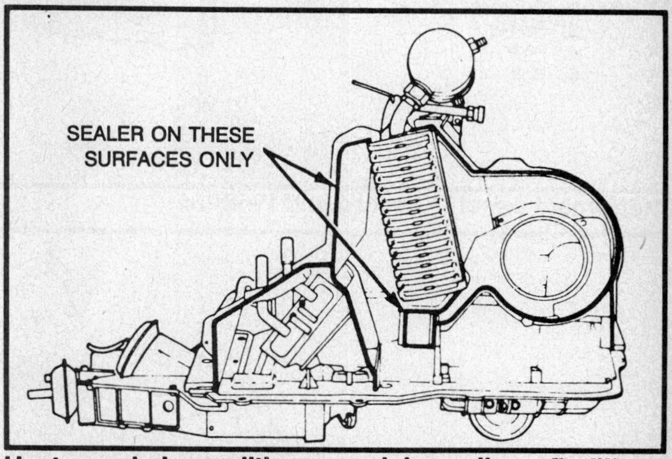
SEALER ON THESE SURFACES ONLY

Heater and air conditioner module sealing—Cadillac Brougham

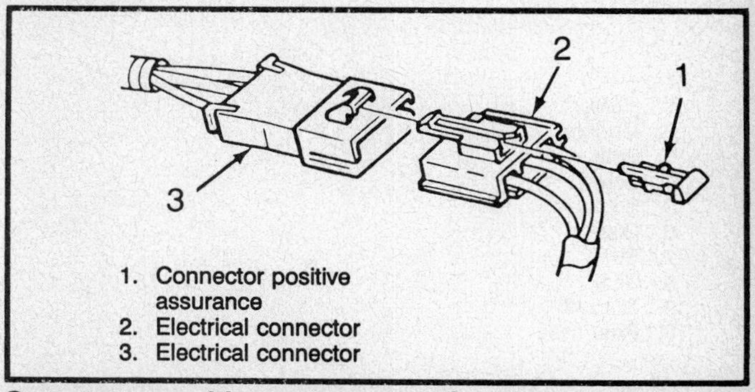
2
1
3
1. Connector positive assurance
2. Electrical connector
3. Electrical connector

Connector positive assurance—Supplement Inflatable Restraint (SIR) system

Camaro and Firebird

CAUTION

Some vehicles are equipped with the Supplemental Inflatable Restraint or air bag system. The air bag system must be disabled before performing service on or around the air bag, instrument panel components, wiring and sensors. Failure to follow safety and disabling procedures could result in accidental air bag deployment, possible personal injury and unnecessary air bag system repairs.

1. Disconnect the negative battery cable.
2. If equipped, disable the Supplemental Inflatable Restraint (SIR) system by performing the following:
   a. Remove the SIR fuse from the fuse panel.
   b. Remove the left side sound insulator.
   c. Remove the Connector Positive Assurance (CPA) from the yellow 2-way SIR harness connector at the base of the steering column and separate the connector.
3. Drain the engine coolant into a clean container for reuse.
4. Disconnect the heater hoses from the heater core inlet and outlet fittings on the firewall.
5. Remove the console by performing the following:
   a. Remove the console trim plates.
   b. Remove the heater and air conditioning control assembly.
   c. Remove the radio.
   d. Remove the shifter handle and retainer, as required.
   e. Remove the parking brake handle grip.

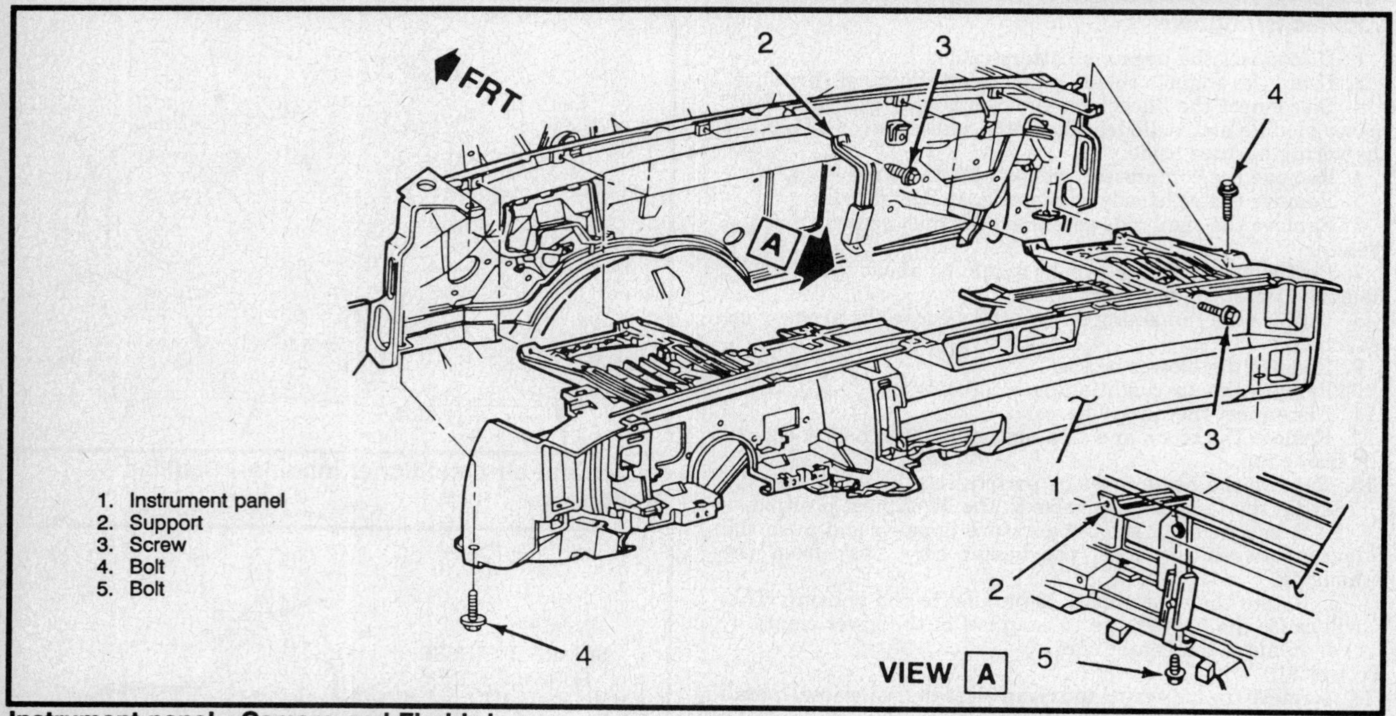
FRT
A
VIEW A
1. Instrument panel
2. Support
3. Screw
4. Bolt
5. Bolt

Instrument panel—Camaro and Firebird

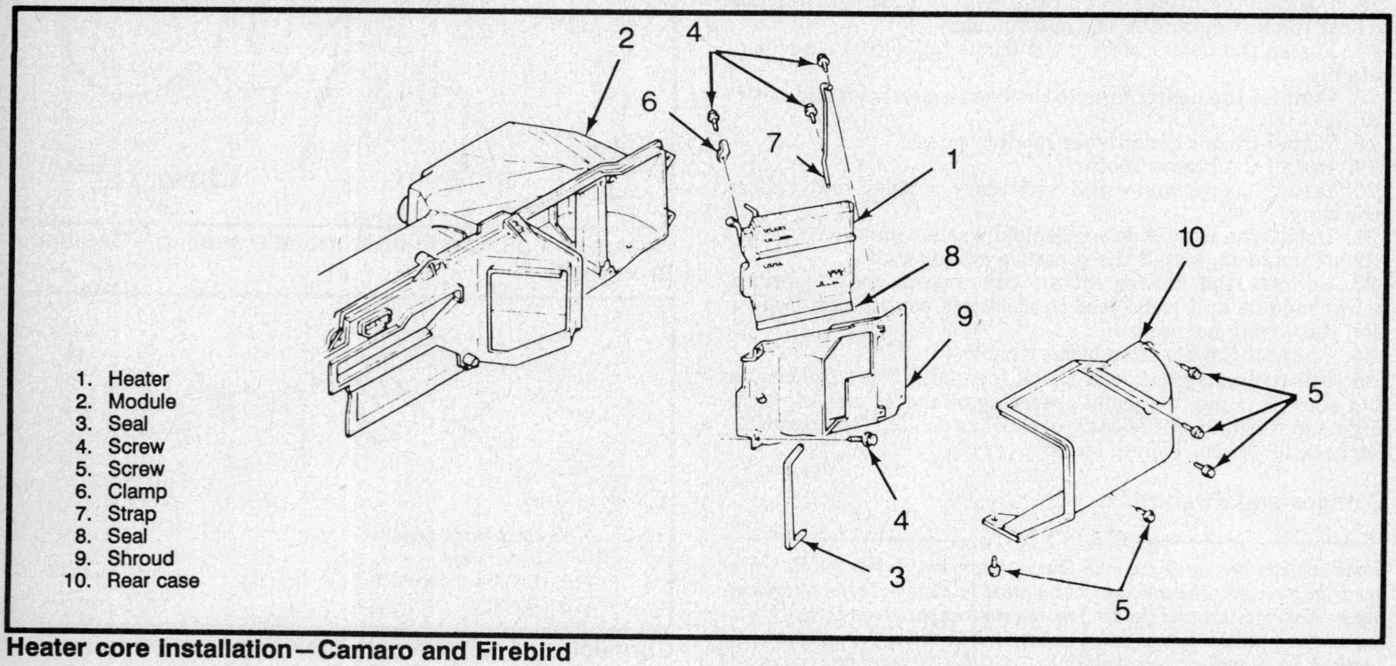
1. Heater
2. Module
3. Seal
4. Screw
5. Screw
6. Clamp
7. Strap
8. Seal
9. Shroud
10. Rear case

Heater core installation—Camaro and Firebird

f. Remove the console-mounted switches and disconnect the electrical connectors.
g. Remove the upper floor console.
h. Remove the lower floor console.

6. Remove the instrument panel by performing the following:
a. Remove the instrument panel pad.
b. Remove the instrument panel sound insulators.
c. Remove the knee bolster.
d. Remove the instrument panel cluster.
e. Remove the steering column retaining nuts. Lower the steering column.
f. Remove the upper and lower instrument panel-to-cowl screws.
g. Disconnect the instrument panel electrical harness at the cowl connector and under dash panel.
h. Remove the instrument panel.

7. Remove the screws from the top, bottom and right side flanges of the rear case.
8. Remove the rear case from the air conditioning module.
9. Remove the core shroud screws.

10. Remove the core shroud, heater core and heater mounting strap as an assembly.
11. Remove the heater core mounting strap.
12. Remove the heater core from the core shroud.
13. Remove the shroud seal from the shroud.

To install:

14. Install the heater core and heater mounting strap to the core shroud.
15. Install the shroud seal to the shroud.
16. Install the heater core heater mounting strap and core shroud as an assembly to the interior of the air conditioning module. Guide both heater core tubes into position into the holes in the dash panel.
17. Install the core shroud screws.
18. Replace the original rear case flange sealer with fresh sealer.
19. Install the rear case to the air conditioning module.
20. Install the rear case flange mounting screws.
21. Install the instrument panel by performing the following:
    a. Install the instrument panel.
    b. Connect the instrument panel electrical harness at the cowl connector and under dash panel.
    c. Install the upper and lower instrument panel-to-cowl screws.
    d. Raise the steering column. Install the steering column retaining nuts.
    e. Install the instrument panel cluster.
    f. Install the knee bolster.
    g. Install the instrument panel sound insulators.
    h. Install the instrument panel pad.
22. Install the console by performing the following:
    a. Install the lower floor console.
    b. Install the upper floor console.
    c. Install the console-mounted switches and disconnect the electrical connectors.
    d. Install the parking brake handle grip.
    e. If removed, install the shifter handle and retainer.
    f. Install the radio.
    g. Install the heater and air conditioning control assembly.
    h. Install the console trim plates.
23. Connect the heater hoses to the heater core inlet and outlet fittings.
24. If equipped, enable the Supplemental Inflatable Restraint (SIR) system by performing the following:
    a. Connect the yellow 2-way SIR connector and insert the Connect Positive Assurance (CPA) at the base of the steering column.
    b. Install the left side sound insulator.
    c. Install the SIR fuse in the fuse panel.
25. Connect the negative battery cable.
26. Fill cooling system and check for leaks. Start the engine and allow to come to normal operating temperature. Allow the engine to warm up sufficiently to confirm cooling fan operation. Recheck for leaks. Top-up coolant.

Corvette

CAUTION

Some vehicles are equipped with the Supplemental Inflatable Restraint or air bag system. The air bag system must be disabled before performing service on or around the air bag, instrument panel components, wiring and sensors. Failure to follow safety and disabling procedures could result in accidental air bag deployment, possible personal injury and unnecessary air bag system repairs.

1. Disconnect the negative battery cable.
2. If equipped, disable the Supplemental Inflatable Restraint (SIR) system by performing the following:
    a. Remove the SIR fuse from the fuse panel.
    b. Remove the left side sound insulator.
    c. Remove the Connector Positive Assurance (CPA) from the yellow 2-way SIR harness connector at the base of the steering column and separate the connector.
3. Drain the engine coolant into a clean container for reuse.
4. Remove the upper instrument panel trim pad.
5. Disconnect the in-vehicle temperature sensor aspirator hose.
6. Disconnect the in-vehicle temperature sensor connector.
7. Remove the right side knee bolster brace.
8. Remove the floor heat deflector.
9. Remove the relays from the multi-use relay bracket.
10. Loosen the nuts retaining the wiring harness retainer to the radio receiver. Slide the wiring harness retainer from the radio receiver.
11. Remove the harnesses from the wiring harness retainer. Remove the wiring harness retainer.
12. Remove the carrier nuts from the right side pillar.
13. Remove the multi-use bracket.
14. Remove the passenger knee bolster brace attachments.
15. Remove the side window defroster duct rose bud clip and duct hose from the knee bolster brace.
16. Pull the carrier back and remove the passenger knee bolster brace.
17. Disconnect the electrical connections from the radio receiver.
18. Disconnect the cruise control module electrical connector.
19. Remove the side window defroster duct from the rear of the heater case.
20. Remove the fuse block from the carrier.
21. Disconnect the vacuum hose from the actuator.
22. Remove the vacuum line retainer tape on the heater.
23. Remove the wiring harness from the retainer clip on the bottom of rear heater case.
24. Remove the side window defroster duct extension from the heater case.
25. Remove the rear heater case half.
26. Remove the high fill reservoir.
27. Disconnect the heater hoses from the heater core.
28. Remove the heater core from the case.

To install:

29. Install the heater core in the case.
30. Connect the heater hoses to the heater core.
31. Install the high fill reservoir.
32. Install the rear heater case half.
33. Install the side window defroster duct extension to the defroster duct.
34. Connect the harnesses to the retainer clip on the bottom of the rear heater case.
35. Install the vacuum line and tape onto the retainer.
36. Connect the vacuum hose to the actuator.
37. Install the fuse block to the carrier.
38. Install the side window defroster duct to the rear of the heater case.
39. Connect the radio receiver and cruise control module electrical connectors.
40. Install the multi-use relay bracket and knee bolster brace.
41. Install the side window defroster duct hose and rose bud clip to the knee bolster brace.
42. Install the carrier-to-pillar attachments.
43. Install the wiring harness to the harness retainer. Connect the wiring harness retainer to the radio receiver.
44. Install the relays to the multi-use relay bracket.
45. Install the floor heat deflector.
46. Install the right side knee bolster brace.
47. Connect the in-vehicle temperature sensor connectors.
48. Connect the in-vehicle temperature sensor aspirator hose.
49. Install the instrument panel upper trim pad.
50. If equipped, enable the Supplemental Inflatable Restraint (SIR) system by performing the following:
    a. Connect the yellow 2-way SIR connector and insert the

Connect Positive Assurance (CPA) at the base of the steering column.

b. Install the left side sound insulator.

c. Install the SIR fuse in the fuse panel.

51. Connect the negative battery cable.

52. Fill cooling system and check for leaks. Start the engine and allow to come to normal operating temperature. Allow the engine to warm up sufficiently to confirm cooling fan operation. Recheck for leaks. Top-up coolant.

Evaporator

REMOVAL AND INSTALLATION

1989–90 Caprice, Custom Cruiser, Estate Wagon and Safari

1. Disconnect the negative battery cable.
2. Properly discharge the air conditioning system.
3. Disconnect the refrigerant lines at the evaporator inlet and outlet fittings. Discard the O-rings.

NOTE: Cap the refrigerant lines when opening the system to prevent the entry of dirt and moisture and the loss of refrigerant lubricant.

4. Remove the expansion tube, as required.
5. Remove the air conditioning module upper case.
6. Remove the evaporator clamp.
7. Remove the evaporator and seals pulling straight up and out of the air conditioning module lower case.

To install:

8. Ensure that seals are properly positioned on the air conditioning module mounting flanges.
9. Install the evaporator clamp.
10. Install the air conditioning module upper case.
11. If removed, install the expansion tube.
12. Add 3 oz. (90ml) of refrigerant oil to the system.
13. Replace the evaporator fitting O-rings. Lubricate the O-rings with refrigerant oil.
14. Connect the refrigerant lines to the evaporator inlet and outlet fittings.
15. Evacuate, recharge and leak test the air conditioning system.
16. Connect the negative battery cable.

1991 Caprice, Custom Cruiser and Roadmaster

1. Disconnect the negative battery cable.
2. Properly discharge the air conditioning system.
3. Disconnect the refrigerant lines at the evaporator inlet and outlet fittings. Discard the O-rings.

NOTE: Cap the refrigerant lines when opening the system to prevent the entry of dirt and moisture and the loss of refrigerant lubricant.

4. Remove the air conditioning module lower case.
5. Remove the evaporator mounting bracket.
6. Remove the evaporator by sliding rearward and down.

To install:

7. Ensure that seals are properly positioned on the air conditioning module mounting flanges.
8. Install the evaporator mounting bracket.
9. Install the air conditioning module upper case.
10. Add 3 oz. (90ml) of refrigerant oil to the system.
11. Replace the evaporator fitting O-rings. Lubricate the O-rings with refrigerant oil.
12. Connect the refrigerant lines to the evaporator inlet and outlet fittings.
13. Evacuate, recharge and leak test the air conditioning system.
14. Connect the negative battery cable.

Cadillac Brougham

1. Disconnect the negative battery cable.
2. Properly discharge the air conditioning system.
3. Disconnect the blower motor, compressor cycling switch, power module and radio lead-in electrical connectors. Position the wiring harness aside.
4. Remove the compressor cycling switch, as required.
5. Remove the right side windshield washer nozzle.
6. Remove the right side secondary air inlet screen from the plenum.
7. Partially remove the rubber moulding above the plenum. Remove 1 screw on the right side.
8. Remove the remaining screws and remove the primary inlet screen.
9. Remove the blower motor.
10. Disconnect the evaporator-to-accumulator connection at the top of the accumulator. Discard the O-rings.

NOTE: Cap the refrigerant lines when opening the system to prevent the entry of dirt and moisture and the loss of refrigerant lubricant.

11. Partially remove the accumulator bracket.
12. Remove the top of the evaporator case.
13. Disconnect the condenser-to-evaporator line. Discard the O-ring.

NOTE: Cap the refrigerant lines when opening the system to prevent the entry of dirt and moisture and the loss of refrigerant lubricant.

14. Remove the evaporator core by lifting straight up and out of the air conditioning module.

To install:

15. Install the evaporator core in the vehicle.
16. Replace the evaporator fitting O-rings. Lubricate the O-rings with refrigerant oil.
17. Connect the condenser-to-evaporator refrigerant lines.
18. Connect the evaporator-to-accumulator connection at the top of the accumulator.
19. Install the accumulator bracket and evaporator case cover.
20. Install the blower motor.
21. Install the primary and secondary screens and rubber moulding.
22. Install the right side windshield washer nozzle.
23. If removed, install the pressure cycling switch.
24. Connect the blower motor, compressor cycling switch, power module and radio lead-in electrical connectors. Reposition the wiring harness.
25. Connect the negative battery cable.
26. Evacuate, recharge and leak test the air conditioning system.

Camaro and Firebird

1. Disconnect the negative battery cable.
2. Properly discharge the air conditioning system.
3. Remove the accumulator. Discard the O-rings.

NOTE: Cap the refrigerant lines when opening the system to prevent the entry of dirt and moisture and the loss of refrigerant lubricant.

4. Disconnect the blower motor resistor electrical connector. Remove the blower motor resistor.
5. Remove the blower relay and bracket.
6. Remove the upper evaporator case and seal.
7. Disconnect the refrigerant line from the lower fitting of the evaporator.

NOTE: Cap the refrigerant lines when opening the system to prevent the entry of dirt and moisture and the loss of refrigerant lubricant.

8. Remove the evaporator and seal.
9. Remove the expansion tube and O-ring from the lower fitting of the evaporator, as required.

To install:

10. Install the evaporator and seal.
11. Replace the O-rings. Lubricate with refrigerant oil.
12. If removed, install the expansion tube.
13. Connect the refrigerant line to the lower fitting of the evaporator.
14. Install the upper evaporator seal and case.
15. Install the blower relay and bracket assembly.
16. Install the blower motor resistor assembly. Connect the electrical connector.
17. Install the accumulator.
18. Evacuate, recharge and leak test the air conditioning system.
19. Connect the negative battery cable.

Corvette

1. Disconnect the negative battery cable.
2. Properly discharge the air conditioning system.
3. Drain the engine coolant into a clean container for reuse.
4. Remove the front wheel house rear panel and seal.
5. Disconnect the blower motor electrical connectors.
6. Disconnect the evaporator outlet hose.

NOTE: Cap the refrigerant lines when opening the system to prevent the entry of dirt and moisture and the loss of refrigerant lubricant.

7. Remove the pressure cycling switch.
8. Disconnect the heater hoses.
9. Disconnect the evaporator inlet line and remove the expansion tube.
10. Remove the vapor pipe bracket from the evaporator case.
11. Remove the right side rear bolt from the upper front fender.
12. Remove the bulkhead bolts and nuts securing the evaporator and blower assembly to the bulkhead.
13. Remove the evaporator case from the vehicle.
14. Split the evaporator case and remove the evaporator core.

To install:

15. Add 3 oz. (90ml) of refrigerant oil to the system.
16. Position the evaporator core seal between the evaporator case halves.
17. Install the evaporator core in the evaporator case.
18. Install the evaporator case in the vehicle.
19. Install the rear right side bolt to the upper front fender.
20. Install the vapor pipe bracket to the evaporator case.
21. Replace the evaporator fitting O-rings. Lubricate the O-rings with refrigerant oil.
22. Install the orifice tube into the evaporator inlet line. Connect the line.
23. Connect the heater hoses.
24. Install the pressure cycling switch.
25. Connect the blower motor electrical connectors.
26. Install the front panel and seal at the wheel house.
27. Evacuate, recharge and leak test the air conditioning system.
28. Connect the negative battery cable.
29. Fill cooling system and check for leaks. Start the engine and allow to come to normal operating temperature. Allow the engine to warm up sufficiently to confirm cooling fan operation. Recheck for leaks. Top-up coolant.

Refrigerant Lines

REMOVAL AND INSTALLATION

1. Disconnect the negative battery cable.
2. Properly discharge the air conditioning system.
3. Disconnect the refrigerant line connectors, using a backup wrench as required.
4. Remove refrigerant line support or routing brackets, as required.
5. Remove refrigerant line.

To install:

6. Position new refrigerant line in place, leaving protective caps installed until ready to connect.
7. Install new O-rings on refrigerant line connector fittings. Lubricate with refrigerant oil.
8. Connect refrigerant line, using a backup wrench, as required.
9. Install refrigerant line support or routing brackets, as required.
10. Evacuate, recharge and leak test the system.
11. Connect the negative battery cable.

Manual Control Head

REMOVAL AND INSTALLATION

Caprice, Custom Cruiser, Estate Wagon, Safari and Roadmaster

1. Disconnect the negative battery cable.
2. On 1991 Caprice and Roadmaster, remove the steering column opening filler. Loosen the steering column mounting nuts.
3. Remove the trim plates, as required to gain access to the control panel attaching screws.
4. Remove the control assembly attaching screws.
3. Pull the control assembly out of the instrument panel fan enough to disconnect the control cable assembly ends, electrical and vacuum harness connectors.
5. Disconnect the control cables by performing the following:
   a. Remove the push nut retainer from the pin for the temperature control cable.
   b. Pull the control cable sheath retainer clips from the control assembly and tilt the control assembly to slip the cable ends off the pins of the mode lever.
6. Remove the heater blower switch knob and spring clip and remove the blower switch, as required.
7. Remove the control assembly.

To install:

8. If removed, hold the blower switch in position and install the spring clip. Install the blower switch knob.
9. Place the control assembly in position. Connect the control cables by slipping the end loops over the pins of the mode lever. If equipped, press the retainer clips into the slots in the control assembly.
10. If equipped, connect the control cable and push nut retainer. Press the cable sheath retainer clip into the slot in the control assembly.
11. Connect the vacuum harness and electrical connectors.
12. Install the control assembly and attaching screws.
13. Install the instrument panel trim plate.
14. On 1991 Caprice and Roadmaster, tighten the steering column mounting nuts. Install the steering column opening filler.
13. Connect the negative battery cable.

Camaro and Firebird

1. Disconnect the negative battery cable.
2. Remove the radio and air conditioning control console trim plate.
3. Remove the control assembly retaining screws.
4. Pull the control assembly out far enough to reach the vacuum, electrical and temperature control cable connections.
5. Disconnect the blower switch connnector.
6. Disconnect the rotary selector switch connector.
7. Disconnect the control assembly dial lamp wire connector.

8. Disconnect the vacuum harness.
9. Pull the temperature selector control cable from the control assembly. Slip the temperature control cable loop off the lever.
10. Remove the control assembly.

To install:

11. Place the control assembly in position.
12. Slip the temperature control cable loop into position on the lever arm. Press the temperature control clip into the slot in the control assembly.
13. Connect the vacuum selector valve harness connector.
14. Connect the control assembly dial lamp wire connector cable clip to the instrument panel harness.
15. Connect the rotary selector switch connector.
16. Connect the blower switch connnector.
17. Install the control assembly.
18. Install the radio and air conditioning control console trim plate.
19. Connect the negative battery cable.

Corvette

1. Disconnect the negative battery cable.
2. Remove the instrument panel trim plate.
3. Remove the heater and control panel attaching screws.
4. Slide control panel out far enough to disconnect the control cables, and electrical and vacuum connectors.
5. Remove control panel.

To install:

6. Place the control panel in position.
7. Connect the control cables, and electrical and vacuum connectors.
8. Install the heater and control panel attaching screws.
9. Install the instrument panel trim plate.
10. Connect the negative battery cable.

Manual Control Cables

ADJUSTMENT

Except 1989-90 Caprice, Custom Cruiser, Estate Wagon and Safari

The control cables have a self-adjusting sliding clip at the air valve end. To adjust the cable, move the control lever back and forth briskly from one extreme of travel to the other. If the clip requires adjustment, added effort will be required to move the lever through the final part of its travel. When the control cable adjustment is correct, the valve will be heard hitting the stop at both extremes of lever travel.

1989-90 Caprice, Custom Cruiser, Estate Wagon and Safari

1. Disconnect the negative battery cable.
2. Remove the instrument panel compartment.
3. Move the temperature control lever to the full **HOT** position.

NOTE: The temperature control lever must be in contact with the right end of the lower slot in the control assembly dial before beginning the adjustment.

4. Rotate the turnbuckle in the temperature control cable until the temperature control lever moves to the left approximately 0.17 in. (4.2mm) from the end of the slot.
5. Move the temperature control lever to the full **COLD** position and then back to the full **HOT** position. Repeat the adjustment procedure, if the lever does not spring back approximately 0.17 in (4.2mm) from the end of the lower slot in the control assembly dial when it is released in the full **HOT** position.

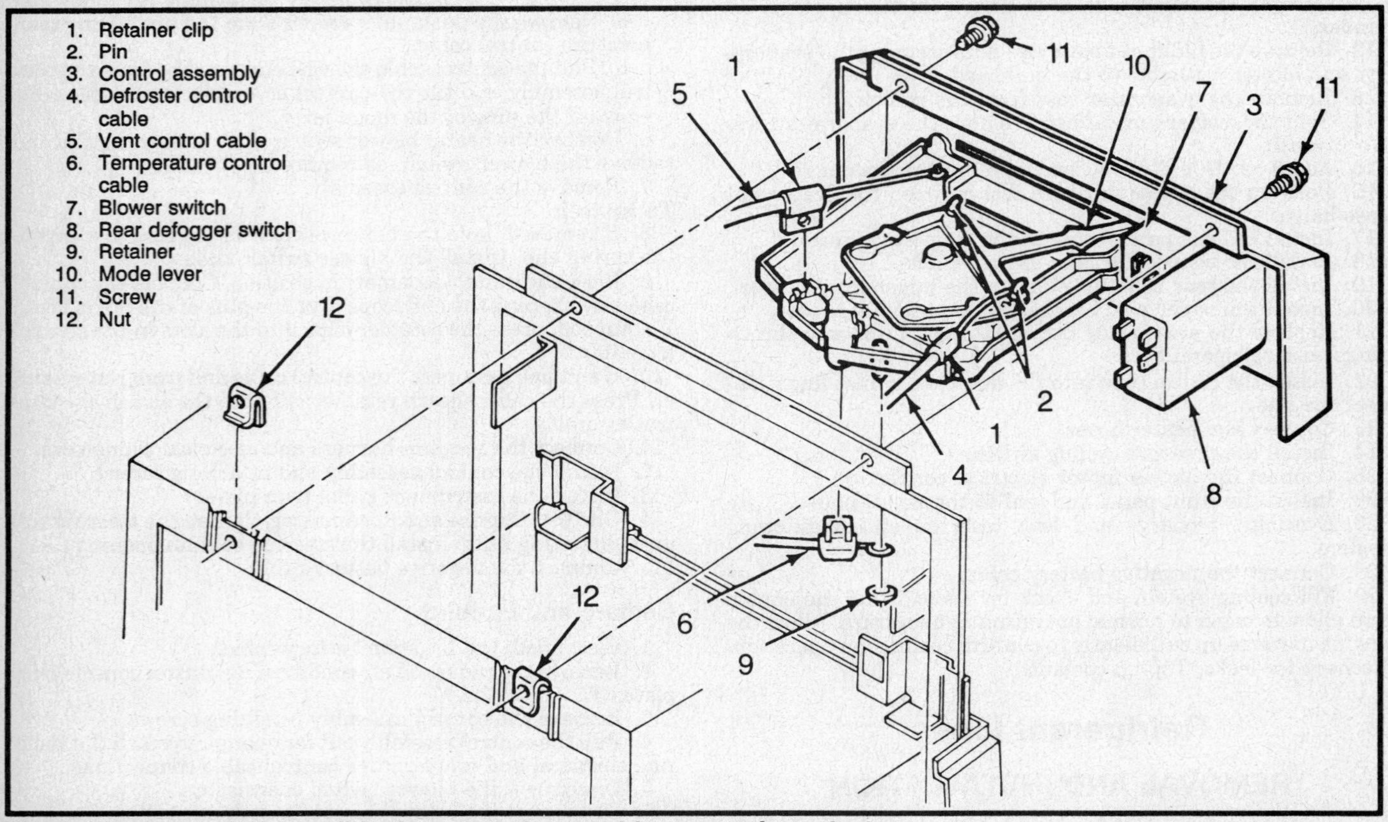
1. Retainer clip
2. Pin
3. Control assembly
4. Defroster control cable
5. Vent control cable
6. Temperature control cable
7. Blower switch
8. Rear defogger switch
9. Retainer
10. Mode lever
11. Screw
12. Nut
1
2
3
4
5
6
7
8
9
10
11
12

Manual heater and air conditioning control assembly removal—typical

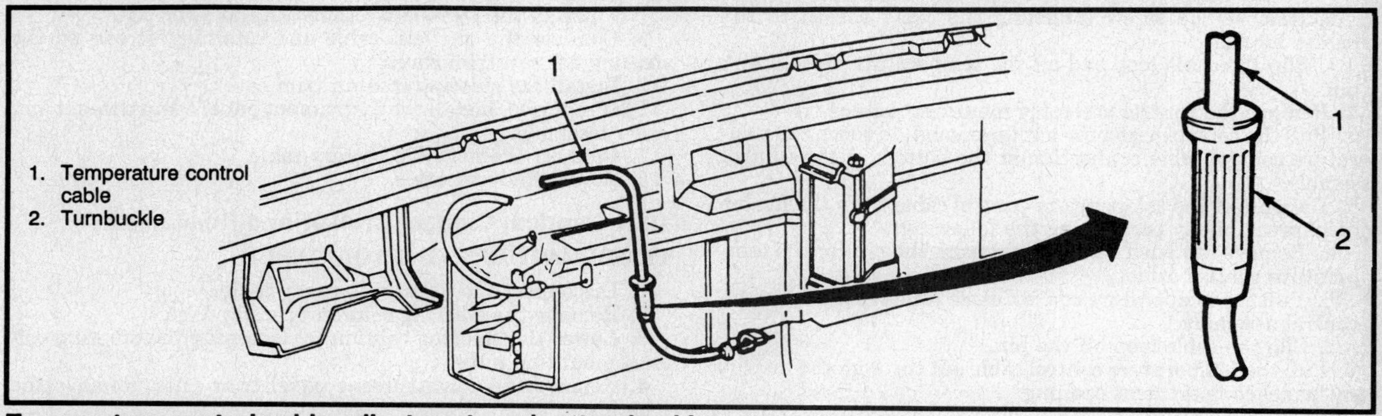
1
2
1. Temperature control cable
2. Turnbuckle
Temperature control cable adjustment—using turnbuckle

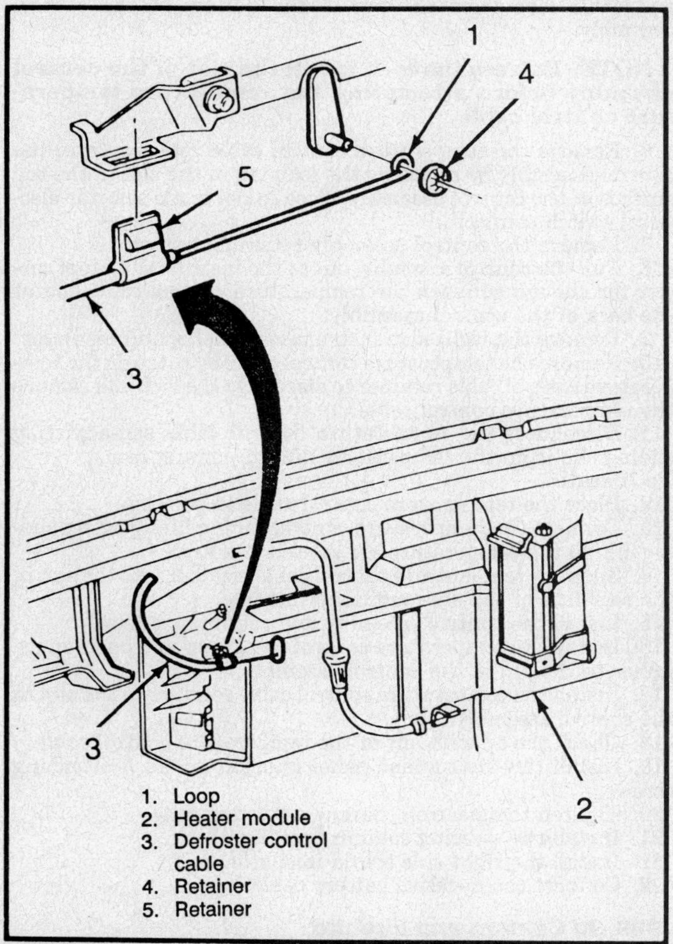
1
4
5
3
3
2
1. Loop
2. Heater module
3. Defroster control cable
4. Retainer
5. Retainer
Defroster control cable removal—typical

REMOVAL AND INSTALLATION

1989–90 Caprice, Custom Cruiser, Estate Wagon and Safari

DEFROSTER AND VENT CONTROL CABLE

1. Disconnect the negative battery cable.
2. Remove the instrument panel compartment.
3. Disconnect the defroster control cable, as required, by performing the following:
   a. Remove the push nut retainer from the end of the defroster valve lever pin.
   b. Snap the defroster cable retainer out of the bracket on the heater module.
   c. Slip the cable end loop off the lever pin.
4. Disconnect the vent control cable from the heater module, as required, by performing the following:
   a. Remove the push nut retainer from the end of the vent valve lever pin.
   b. Remove the retaining screw and vent control cable from the heater module.
   c. Slip the cable end loop off the lever pin.
5. Remove the control assembly retaining screws.
6. Pull the control assembly out of the instrument panel far enough to reach the 2 control cable ends at the top of the control assembly.
7. Pull the defroster and/or vent control cable retainer(s) from the control assembly and tilt the control assembly to slip the cable loop(s) off the pin(s) of the mode lever.
8. Remove the defroster and/or vent control cable.

To install:

9. Guide the defroster and/or vent cable(s) into position, ensuring that there are no kinks in the cable(s).
10. Slip the cable end loop(s) over the pin(s) of the mode lever.
11. Press the cable retainer(s) into the slot(s) in the control assembly.
12. Install the control assembly.
13. Connect the defroster control cable to the heater module, as required, by performing the following:
    a. Slip the defroster control cable end loop over the pin on the defroster valve lever and install the push nut retainer.
    b. Snap the defroster control cable retainer into the slot in the mounting bracket on the heater module.
14. Connect the vent control cable to the heater module, as required, by performing the following:
    a. Slip the vent control cable end loop over the pin on the vent valve lever and install the push nut retainer.
    b. Install the screw holding the vent control cable retainer to the heater module.
15. Install the instrument panel compartment.
16. Connect the negative battery cable.
17. Adjust the vent control cable.

TEMPERATURE CONTROL CABLE

1. Disconnect the negative battery cable.
2. Remove the instrument panel compartment.
3. Disconnect the temperature control cable from the valve crank by performing the following:
   a. Remove the retainer from the temperature valve crank pin.

b. Remove the screw attaching the cable sheath to the heater module.

c. Slip the cable loop end off the temperature valve crank pin.

4. Remove the control assembly mounting screws.

5. Pull the control assembly out far enough to reach the temperature control cable connection at the bottom of the control assembly.

6. Disconnect the temperature control cable from the heater control assembly by performing the following:

a. Remove the push nut retainer from the pin for the temperature control cable.

b. Pull the temperature control cable retainer clip from the control assembly.

c. Slip the cable loop off the pin.

7. Pull the temperature control cable out through the instrument panel compartment opening.

To install:

8. Guide the temperature control cable into position, ensuring that there are no kinks in the cable.

9. Connect the temperature control cable to the control assembly by performing the following:

a. Slip the cable loop onto the temperature control lever pin.

b. Install the push nut retainer.

c. Press the temperature control cable retainer clip into the slot in the control assembly.

10. Install the heater control assembly attaching screws.

11. Slip the temperature control cable loop end onto the temperature valve lever and install the retainer.

12. Install the cable retaining screw.

13. Install the instrument panel compartment.

14. Connect the negative battery cable.

15. Adjust the temperature control cable.

VENT CABLES

1. Disconnect the negative battery cable.

2. Lower the steering column trim cover enough to gain access to the air vent cable attaching screws in the cover.

3. Remove the air vent cable attaching screws for the cable(s) to be replaced.

4. If the center and/or right air vent cable is to be removed, remove the instrument panel compartment and valve assembly.

5. Disconnect the left, center and/or right air vent cable at the heater module by performing the following:

a. Remove the push nut retainer from the lever pin.

b. Remove the screw holding the cable retainer to the heater module or pop the cable retainer out of the slot in the bottom of the heater module. Slip the cable end loop off the lever pin.

6. Remove the cable(s).

NOTE: Note the routing of the cable(s) before removal as a reference for installation.

To install:

7. Place the cable(s) in position, ensuring that there are no kinks.

NOTE: Route the right air vent cable between the instrument panel reinforcement and the instrument panel near the bottom center of the instrument panel compartment opening.

8. Connect the vent cable(s) to the heater module by performing the following:

a. Hold the center cable end loop on the lever pin while snapping the cable retainer into the slot in the bottom of the heater module case.

b. Slip the left or right cable end loop onto the lever pin and install the screw holding the cable retainer to the heater module.

c. Install the push nut retainer to the lever pin.

9. Connect the air vent cable and retaining screws to the steering column trim cover.

10. Install the steering column trim cover.

11. If removed, install the instrument panel compartment and valve assembly.

12. Connect the negative battery cable.

13. Adjust the vent cable.

1991 Caprice, Custom Cruiser and Roadmaster

TEMPERATURE CONTROL CABLE

1. Disconnect the negative battery cable.

2. Remove the steering column opening filler.

3. Lower the steering column by loosening the steering column mounting nuts.

4. Remove the 8 instrument panel trim nuts. Remove the trim plate.

5. Remove the temperature control cable push-on retainer and cable loop from the pin at the bottom of the control assembly.

NOTE: Release the lock tab in the slot of the control assembly before attempting the remove the temperature control cable.

6. Remove the temperature control cable retainer from the control assembly by releasing the lock tab in the slot in the top surface of the control assembly, close to the mode selector electrical switch connector.

7. Remove the control assembly retaining screws.

8. Pull the control assembly out of the instrument panel carrier far enough to reach the temperature control cable end at the back of the control assembly.

9. Remove the right side instrument panel sound insulator.

10. Remove the temperature control cable by rotating the temperature control cable retainer to disengage the lock and remove the temperature control cable.

11. Disconnect the temperature control cable self-adjusting sliding clip from the temperature air valve crank arm.

To install:

12. Place the temperature control cable in position.

13. Connect the temperature control cable self-adjusting sliding clip to the temperature air valve crank arm.

14. Snap the temperature control cable retainer into the slot in the rear face of the air conditioner module.

15. Install the control assembly and retaining screws.

16. Install the temperature control cable loop and push-on retainer to the pin at the control assembly.

17. Install the temperature control cable retainer to the slot in the control assembly.

18. Check the adjustment of the temperature control cable.

19. Install the instrument panel trim plate and 8 attaching screws.

20. Tighten the steering column mounting nuts.

21. Install the steering column opening filler.

21. Install the right side sound insulator.

22. Connect the negative battery cable.

1989–90 Camaro and Firebird

DEFROSTER CONTROL CABLE

1. Disconnect the negative battery cable.

2. Remove the left side sound insulator.

3. Disconnect the defroster control cable by performing the following:

a. Remove the push nut retainer holding the cable self-adjusting clip to the defroster valve lever pin.

b. Disengage the cable clamp from the slot in the bracket on the heater module.

4. Remove the radio and heater control trim plate.

5. Remove the control assembly mounting screws. Pull the

control assembly out far enough to reach the defroster control cable connection.

6. Pull the defroster control cable clip from the control assembly.
7. Tilt the control assembly to slip the defroster control cable end loop off the pin of the mode lever.
8. Remove the defroster control cable.

To install:

9. Install the defroster control cable.
10. Tilt the control assembly and slip the defroster control cable end loop onto the pin of the mode lever.
11. Press the defroster control cable clip into the slot in the control assembly.
12. Install the control assembly.
13. Install the radio and heater control trim plate.
14. Connect the defroster control cable at the heater module by performing the following:
    a. Fit the cable self-adjusting clip onto the defroster valve lever pin.
    b. Snap the cable clamp into the slot in the bracket on the heater module.
    c. Install the push nut retainer to the defroster valve lever pin.
15. Install the left side sound insulator.
16. Connect the negative battery cable.
17. Adjust the defroster control cable.

VENT CONTROL CABLE

1. Disconnect the negative battery cable.
2. Remove the right side sound insulator.
3. Disconnect the vent control cable by performing the following:
    a. Remove the push nut retainer holding the cable self-adjusting clip to the vent valve lever pin.
    b. Disengage the cable clamp from the slot in the bracket on the heater module.
4. Remove the radio and heater control trim plate.
5. Remove the control assembly mounting screws. Pull the control assembly out far enough to reach the vent control cable connection.
6. Pull the vent control cable clip from the control assembly.
7. Tilt the control assembly to slip the vent control cable end loop off the pin of the mode lever.
8. Remove the vent control cable.

To install:

9. Install the vent control cable.
10. Tilt the control assembly and slip the vent control cable end loop onto the pin of the mode lever.
11. Press the vent control cable clip into the slot in the control assembly.
12. Install the control assembly.
13. Install the radio and heater control trim plate.
14. Connect the vent control cable at the heater module by performing the following:
    a. Fit the cable self-adjusting clip onto the vent valve lever pin.
    b. Snap the cable clamp into the slot in the bracket on the heater module.
    c. Install the push nut retainer to the vent valve lever pin.
15. Install the right side sound insulator.
16. Connect the negative battery cable.
17. Adjust the vent control cable.

LEFT AND RIGHT VENT CABLE

1. Disconnect the negative battery cable.
2. Remove the left and right side sound insulators.

NOTE: If servicing the left air vent cable, remove only the left side sound insulator.

3. Remove the screws attaching the cable(s) to the steering column cover.
4. Disconnect the air vent cables by performing the following:
    a. Disengage the cable clamp(s) at the vent duct(s).
    b. Disengage the Z-shaped cable end(s) from the vent valve lever(s).
    c. Remove the air vent cable(s), noting the cable position for reference during installation.

To install:

5. Place the cable(s) into position under the instrument panel.
6. Connect the air vent cable(s) by performing the following:
    a. Engage the Z-shaped cable end(s) to the vent valve lever(s).
    b. Snap the cable clamp(s) into the slot of the bracket formed on the vent duct(s).
7. Install the air vent cable bracket(s) and screws at the steering colum cover.
8. Install the sound insulator(s).
9. Connect the negative battery cable.
10. Adjust the vent cable(s).

Camaro and Firebird

TEMPERATURE CONTROL CABLE

1. Disconnect the negative battery cable.
2. Remove the right side sound insulator.
3. Remove the cable cover.
4. Disconnect the temperature control cable by performing the following:
    a. Remove the push nut retainer holding the cable self-adjusting clip to the temperature valve lever pin.
    b. Disengage the cable clamp from the slot in the bracket on the heater module.
5. Remove the radio and heater control trim plate.
6. Remove the control assembly mounting screws. Pull the control assembly out far enough to reach the temperature control cable connection.
7. Pull the temperature control cable clip from the control assembly.
8. Tilt the control assembly to slip the temperature control cable end loop off the pin of the mode lever.
9. Remove the temperature control cable.

To install:

10. Install the temperature control cable.
11. Tilt the control assembly and slip the temperature control cable end loop onto the pin of the mode lever.
12. Press the temperature control cable clip into the slot in the control assembly.
13. Install the control assembly.
14. Install the radio and heater control trim plate.
15. Connect the temperature control cable at the heater module by performing the following:
    a. Fit the cable self-adjusting clip onto the temperature valve lever pin.
    b. Snap the cable clamp into the slot in the bracket on the heater module.
    c. Install the push nut retainer to the temperature valve lever pin.
16. Install the cable cover.
17. Install the right side sound insulator.
18. Connect the negative battery cable.
19. Adjust the temperature control cable.

Corvette

TEMPERATURE CONTROL CABLE

1. Disconnect the negative battery cable.
2. Remove the heater and air conditioner control panel.
3. Remove the radio.
4. Remove the right side sound insulator.
5. Remove the screws and retaining clips securing the cable.
6. Remove the temperature control cable.

To install:

7. Route the temperature control cable to the heater and air conditioner control assembly.
8. Install the retaining clips and screws.
9. Install the right side sound insulator.
10. Install the radio.
11. Install the heater and air conditioner control assembly.
12. Connect the negative battery cable.
13. Adjust the temperature control cable.

Electronic Control Head

REMOVAL AND INSTALLATION

Custom Cruiser and Roadmaster

1. Disconnect the negative battery cable.
2. Remove the steering column opening filler.
3. Loosen the steering column mounting nuts.
4. Remove the 8 instrument panel trim plate screws. Remove the trim plate by pulling straight away from the instrument panel carrier snapping the 7 trim plate integral retaining clips out of the slots in the instrument panel carrier.
5. Pull the control assembly out of the instrument panel carrier fan enough to reach the electrical connectors. Disconnect the connectors.
6. Remove the control assembly.

To install:

7. Install the control assembly.
8. Connect the electrical connectors.
9. Install the control assembly and retaining screws.
10. Position the instrument panel trim plate to the instrument panel carrier. Press forward along the lower edge of the trim plate to snap the 7 trim plate integral retaining clips into the slots in the instrument panel carrier.
11. Install the 8 instrument panel trim plate screws.
12. Tighten the steering column mounting nuts.
13. Install the steering column opening filler.
14. Connect the negative battery cable.

Cadillac Brougham

1. Disconnect the negative battery cable.
2. Remove the center instrument panel trim plate.
3. Remove the Electronic Climate Control (ECC) head from the panel.
4. Disconnect the electrical connector from the control head and remove the control head from the vehicle.

To install:

5. Connect the electrical connector to the control head and install the control head in the vehicle.
6. Install the center instrument panel trim plate.
7. Connect the negative battery cable.

Corvette

1. Disconnect the negative battery cable.
2. Remove the instrument panel trim plate.
3. Remove the instrument panel upper trim pad assembly.
4. Remove the control head screws.
5. Remove the control enough to disconnect the electrical connector.

To install:

6. Connect the electrical connector to the back of the control head.
7. Install the control head screws.
8. Install the instrument panel upper trim pad assembly.
9. Install the instrument panel trim plate.
10. Connect the negative battery cable.

SENSORS AND SWITCHES

Vacuum Actuator

OPERATION

Used on certain heating and air conditioning systems, the vacuum actuators operate the air doors determining the different modes. The actuator consists of a spring loaded diaphragm connected to a lever. When vacuum is applied to the diaphragm, the lever moves the control door to its appropriate position. When the lever on the control panel is moved to another position, vacuum is cut off and the spring returns the actuator lever to its normal position.

TESTING

1. Disconnect the vacuum line from the actuator.
2. Attach a hand-held vacuum pump to the actuator.
3. Apply vacuum to the actuator.
4. The actuator lever should move to its engaged position and remain there while vacuum is applied.
5. When vacuum is released it should move back to its normal position.
6. The lever should operate smoothly and not bind.

REMOVAL AND INSTALLATION

1. Remove the vacuum lines from the actuator.
2. Disconnect the linkage from the actuator.
3. Remove the hardware attaching the actuator.
4. Remove the actuator.

To install:

5. Install the actuator and attaching hardware.
6. Connect the linkage to the actuator.
7. Connect the vacuum lines to the actuator.
8. Test system to confirm proper functioning of the actuator.

Coolant Temperature Sensor

OPERATION

The coolant temperature sensor provides an engine temperature signal to the ECM. The ECM controls operation of the cooling fans and, in cases of high engine temperature, deenergizes the compressor clutch. On 2.8L and 3.1L V6 engines, the coolant temperature sensor is located on the top front of the engine below the intake plenum. On 4.3L V6 engines, the coolant temperature sensor is located on the front of the engine, near the coolant outlet. On 5.0L V8 (VIN Y) engines, the coolant temperature is located on the top left side of the engine. On 5.0L (VIN E) engines, the coolant temperature sensor is located on the top left side of the engine or near the thermostat housing. On 5.0L (VIN F) and 5.7L (VIN 8) engines, the coolant temperature sensor is located on the left front of the engine. On 5.7L (VIN 7) engines, the coolant temperature sensor is located on the left side of the engine, at the front of the intake manifold. On 5.7L (VIN J) engines, the coolant temperature sensor is located under the plenum, next to No. 1 cylinder injector.

REMOVAL AND INSTALLATION

1. Disconnect the negative battery cable.
2. Drain the cooling system into a clean container for reuse.
3. Disconnect the electrical connector from the coolant temperature sensor.
4. Remove the coolant temperature sensor.

To install:

5. Install the coolant temperature sensor.
6. Connect the electrical connector.
7. Fill the cooling system.
8. Connect the negative battery cable.
9. Start the engine and check for leaks.

High-Side Temperature Sensor

OPERATION

The high-side temperature sensor is located in the high pressure refrigerant line between the condenser and the orifice tube. The BCM monitors refrigerant temperature and determines the pressure based on the pressure-temperature relationship.

REMOVAL AND INSTALLATION

1. Disconnect the negative battery cable.
2. Properly discharge the air conditioning system.
3. Disconnect the electrical connector from the sensor.
4. Unscrew and remove the sensor. Discard the O-ring.

To install:

5. Install a new O-ring. Lubricate with refrigerant oil. Install the sensor.
6. Connect electrical connector to the sensor.
7. Connect the negative battery cable.
8. Evacuate, recharge and leak test the air conditioning system.

Low-Side Temperature Sensor

OPERATION

The low-side temperature sensor is in the low pressure refrigerant line between the orifice tube and the evaporator. The BCM monitors low-side pressure to determine the maintain system pressure based on the pressure-temperature relationship.

REMOVAL AND INSTALLATION

1. Disconnect the negative battery cable.
2. Properly discharge the air conditioning system.
3. Disconnect the electrical connector from the sensor.
4. Unscrew and remove the sensor. Discard the O-ring.

To install:

5. Install a new O-ring. Lubricate with refrigerant oil. Install the sensor.
6. Connect electrical connector to the sensor.
7. Connect the negative battery cable.
8. Evacuate, recharge and leak test the air conditioning system.

In-Vehicle Temperature Sensor

OPERATION

On Roadmaster, the in-vehicle temperature sensor is located at the top of the instrument panel carrier, to the right of the radio; on the far right side of the instrument panel on Cadillac Brougham and in the bow assembly-roof center on Corvette coupes and in the stowage lid on convertibles.

The in-vehicle temperature sensor monitors the temperature inside the passenger compartment. To provide accurate temperature readings, a small amount of air is drawn into the sensor housing, through the aspirator, passing over the thermistor.

REMOVAL AND INSTALLATION

1. Disconnect the negative battery cable.
2. Remove the necessary instrument panel trim pieces.
3. Remove the screws and the sensor.

To install:

4. Install the new sensor.
5. Install the instrument panel trim pieces.
6. Connect the negative battery cable.

Outside Temperature Sensor

OPERATION

The outside temperature sensor is located behind the radiator grille and provides an input to the BCM for display upon request on the Climate Control Panel (CCP).

REMOVAL AND INSTALLATION

1. Disconnect the negative battery cable.
2. Remove the grille, as required.
3. Disconnect the electrical connector from the sensor.
4. Remove the attaching screw and the sensor.

To install:

5. Install the sensor and attaching screw.
6. Connect the electrical connector to the sensor.
7. Connect the negative battery cable.

High-Pressure Compressor Cut-Off Switch

OPERATION

The function of the switch is to protect the engine from overheating in the event of excessively high compressor head pressure and to deenergize the compressor clutch before the high pressure relief valve discharge pressure is reached. The switch is mounted on the back of the compressor or on the refrigerant hose assembly near the back of the compressor. Servicing a switch mounted on the back of the compressor requires that the system be discharged. Switches mounted on the coupled hose assembly are mounted on Schrader-type valves and do not require discharging the system to be serviced.

REMOVAL AND INSTALLATION

Compressor-Mounted Switch

NOTE: The system must be discharged in order to service the high pressure relief switch mounted to the back of the compressor.

1. Disconnect the negative battery cable.
2. Properly discharge the air conditioning system.
3. Remove the coupled hose assembly at the rear of the compressor.
4. Disconnect the electrical connector.
5. Remove the switch retaining ring using internal snapring pliers.
6. Remove the switch from the compressor. Discard the O-ring.

To install:

7. Lubricate a new O-ring with refrigerant oil. Insert into the switch cavity.
8. Lubricate the control switch housing with clean refrigerant oil and insert the switch until it bottoms in the cavity.
9. Install the switch retaining snapring with the high point of the curved sides adjacent to the switch housing. Ensure that the retaining ring is properly seated in the switch cavity retaining groove.
10. Connect the electrical connector.
11. Lubricate new coupled hose assembly O-rings with refrigerant oil. Install on the hose assembly fittings.
12. Connect the coupled hose assembly to the compressor.
13. Evacuate, recharge and leak test the system.
14. Connect the negative battery cable.
15. Operate the system to ensure proper operation and leak test the switch.

Refrigerant Line-Mounted Switch

NOTE: The switch is mounted on a Schrader-type valve and does not require that the system be discharged.

1. Disconnect the negative battery cable.
2. Disconnect the electrical connector.
3. Remove the switch from the coupled hose assembly. Discard the O-ring.

To install:

4. Lubricate a new O-ring with refrigerant oil.
5. Install the O-ring on the switch and install the switch.
6. Connect the electrical connector.
7. Connect the negative battery cable.

Low-Pressure Compressor Cut-Off Switch

OPERATION

The function of the switch is to protect the compressor by deenergizing the compressor in the event of a low-charge condition. The switch may be mounted at the back of the compressor or on the coupled hose assembly near the compressor. Servicing the valve requires discharging the system.

REMOVAL AND INSTALLATION

1. Disconnect the negative battery cable.
2. Properly discharge the air conditioning system.
3. Disconnect the electrical connector(s).
4. If the switch is mounted to the rear head of the compressor, remove the coupled hose assembly to gain access to the switch. Remove the switch.
5. If the switch is mounted to the coupled hose assembly, remove the switch from its mounting position.

To install:

6. Install the switch.
7. Lubricate new O-rings with refrigerant oil.
8. If the switch is mounted to the rear head of the compressor, install the switch. Install new O-rings on the coupled hose assembly and install the assembly to the back of the compressor.
9. If the switch is mounted on the coupled hose assembly, install the switch.
10. Connect the electrical connector(s).
11. Evacuate, charge and leak test the system.
12. Connect the negative battery cable.

Idle Speed Power Steering Pressure Switch

OPERATION

Engine idle speed is maintained by cutting off the compressor when high power steering loads are imposed at idle. The switch is located on the pinion housing portion of the steering rack.

REMOVAL AND INSTALLATION

1. Disconnect the negative battery cable.
2. Disconnect the electrical connector.
3. Remove the switch.

To install:

4. Install the switch.
5. Connect the electrical connector.
6. Connect the negative battery cable.
7. Allow the engine to come to normal operating temperature and confirm the proper operation of the switch.

Pressure Cycling Switch

OPERATION

The pressure cycling switch controls the refrigeration cycle by sensing low-side pressure as an indicator of evaporator temperature. The pressure cycling switch is the freeze-protection device in the system and senses refrigerant pressure on the suction side.

REMOVAL AND INSTALLATION

NOTE: The switch is mounted on a Schrader valve on the accumulator. The system need not be discharged to remove the pressure cycling switch.

1. Disconnect the negative battery cable.
2. Disconnect the electrical connector.
3. Remove the switch and O-ring seal. Discard the O-ring.

To install:

4. Install a new O-ring. Lubricate with refrigerant oil.
5. Install the switch to the accumulator.
6. Connect the electrical connector.
7. Connect the negative battery cable.

SYSTEM DIAGNOSIS

Entering Diagnostic Mode

CORVETTE

To enter the diagnostic mode, push and hold the fan up and fan down arrows at the same time for approximately 5 seconds. The LCD will show "00." Push the auto fan button and the LCD will show any fault codes stored in the memory.

Entering Diagnostic Mode

CUSTOM CRUISER AND ROADMASTER

To enter the diagnostic mode, press the **EXT TEMP** switch followed by the **OFF** switch. Within approximately 5 seconds, the LCD will display any fault codes stored in the memory.

HEATING SYSTEM DIAGNOSIS

INSUFFICIENT HEATING OR DEFROSTING

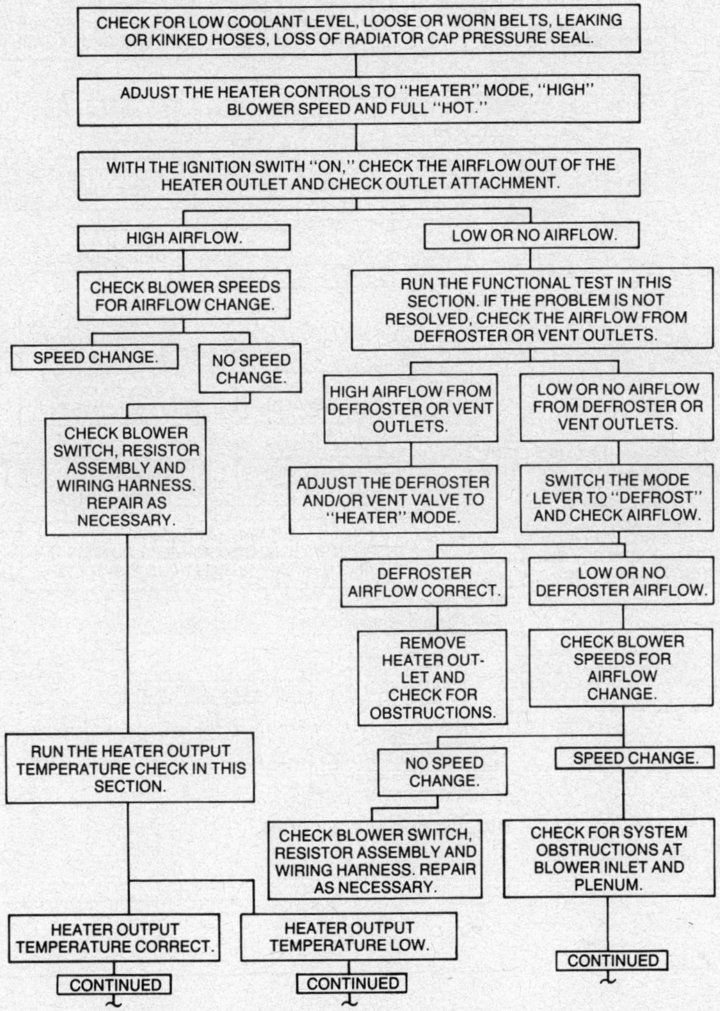
CHECK FOR LOW COOLANT LEVEL, LOOSE OR WORN BELTS, LEAKING OR KINKED HOSES, LOSS OF RADIATOR CAP PRESSURE SEAL.
ADJUST THE HEATER CONTROLS TO "HEATER" MODE, "HIGH" BLOWER SPEED AND FULL "HOT."
WITH THE IGNITION SWITH "ON," CHECK THE AIRFLOW OUT OF THE HEATER OUTLET AND CHECK OUTLET ATTACHMENT.
HIGH AIRFLOW.
LOW OR NO AIRFLOW.
CHECK BLOWER SPEEDS FOR AIRFLOW CHANGE.
RUN THE FUNCTIONAL TEST IN THIS SECTION. IF THE PROBLEM IS NOT RESOLVED, CHECK THE AIRFLOW FROM DEFROSTER OR VENT OUTLETS.
SPEED CHANGE.
NO SPEED CHANGE.
HIGH AIRFLOW FROM DEFROSTER OR VENT OUTLETS.
LOW OR NO AIRFLOW FROM DEFROSTER OR VENT OUTLETS.
CHECK BLOWER SWITCH, RESISTOR ASSEMBLY AND WIRING HARNESS. REPAIR AS NECESSARY.
ADJUST THE DEFROSTER AND/OR VENT VALVE TO "HEATER" MODE.
SWITCH THE MODE LEVER TO "DEFROST" AND CHECK AIRFLOW.
DEFROSTER AIRFLOW CORRECT.
LOW OR NO DEFROSTER AIRFLOW.
REMOVE HEATER OUTLET AND CHECK FOR OBSTRUCTIONS.
CHECK BLOWER SPEEDS FOR AIRFLOW CHANGE.
RUN THE HEATER OUTPUT TEMPERATURE CHECK IN THIS SECTION.
NO SPEED CHANGE.
SPEED CHANGE.
CHECK BLOWER SWITCH, RESISTOR ASSEMBLY AND WIRING HARNESS. REPAIR AS NECESSARY.
CHECK FOR SYSTEM OBSTRUCTIONS AT BLOWER INLET AND PLENUM.
HEATER OUTPUT TEMPERATURE CORRECT.
HEATER OUTPUT TEMPERATURE LOW.
CONTINUED
CONTINUED
CONTINUED

INSUFFICIENT HEATING OR DEFROSTING (Continued)

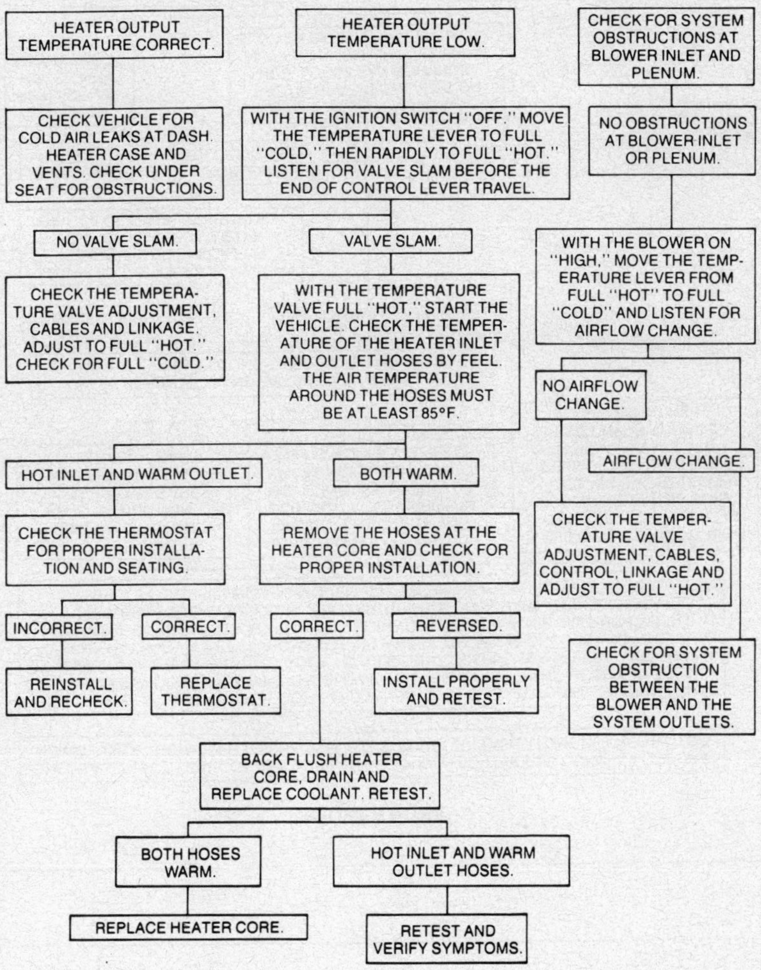
HEATER OUTPUT TEMPERATURE CORRECT.
HEATER OUTPUT TEMPERATURE LOW.
CHECK FOR SYSTEM OBSTRUCTIONS AT BLOWER INLET AND PLENUM.
CHECK VEHICLE FOR COLD AIR LEAKS AT DASH. HEATER CASE AND VENTS. CHECK UNDER SEAT FOR OBSTRUCTIONS.
WITH THE IGNITION SWITCH "OFF." MOVE THE TEMPERATURE LEVER TO FULL "COLD," THEN RAPIDLY TO FULL "HOT." LISTEN FOR VALVE SLAM BEFORE THE END OF CONTROL LEVER TRAVEL.
NO OBSTRUCTIONS AT BLOWER INLET OR PLENUM.
NO VALVE SLAM.
VALVE SLAM.
WITH THE BLOWER ON "HIGH," MOVE THE TEMPERATURE LEVER FROM FULL "HOT" TO FULL "COLD" AND LISTEN FOR AIRFLOW CHANGE.
CHECK THE TEMPERATURE VALVE ADJUSTMENT, CABLES AND LINKAGE. ADJUST TO FULL "HOT." CHECK FOR FULL "COLD."
WITH THE TEMPERATURE VALVE FULL "HOT," START THE VEHICLE. CHECK THE TEMPERATURE OF THE HEATER INLET AND OUTLET HOSES BY FEEL. THE AIR TEMPERATURE AROUND THE HOSES MUST BE AT LEAST 85°F.
NO AIRFLOW CHANGE.
AIRFLOW CHANGE.
HOT INLET AND WARM OUTLET.
BOTH WARM.
CHECK THE TEMPERATURE VALVE ADJUSTMENT, CABLES, CONTROL, LINKAGE AND ADJUST TO FULL "HOT."
CHECK THE THERMOSTAT FOR PROPER INSTALLATION AND SEATING.
REMOVE THE HOSES AT THE HEATER CORE AND CHECK FOR PROPER INSTALLATION.
INCORRECT.
CORRECT.
CORRECT.
REVERSED.
CHECK FOR SYSTEM OBSTRUCTION BETWEEN THE BLOWER AND THE SYSTEM OUTLETS.
REINSTALL AND RECHECK.
REPLACE THERMOSTAT.
INSTALL PROPERLY AND RETEST.
BACK FLUSH HEATER CORE, DRAIN AND REPLACE COOLANT. RETEST.
BOTH HOSES WARM.
HOT INLET AND WARM OUTLET HOSES.
REPLACE HEATER CORE.
RETEST AND VERIFY SYMPTOMS.

HEATING SYSTEM DIAGNOSIS

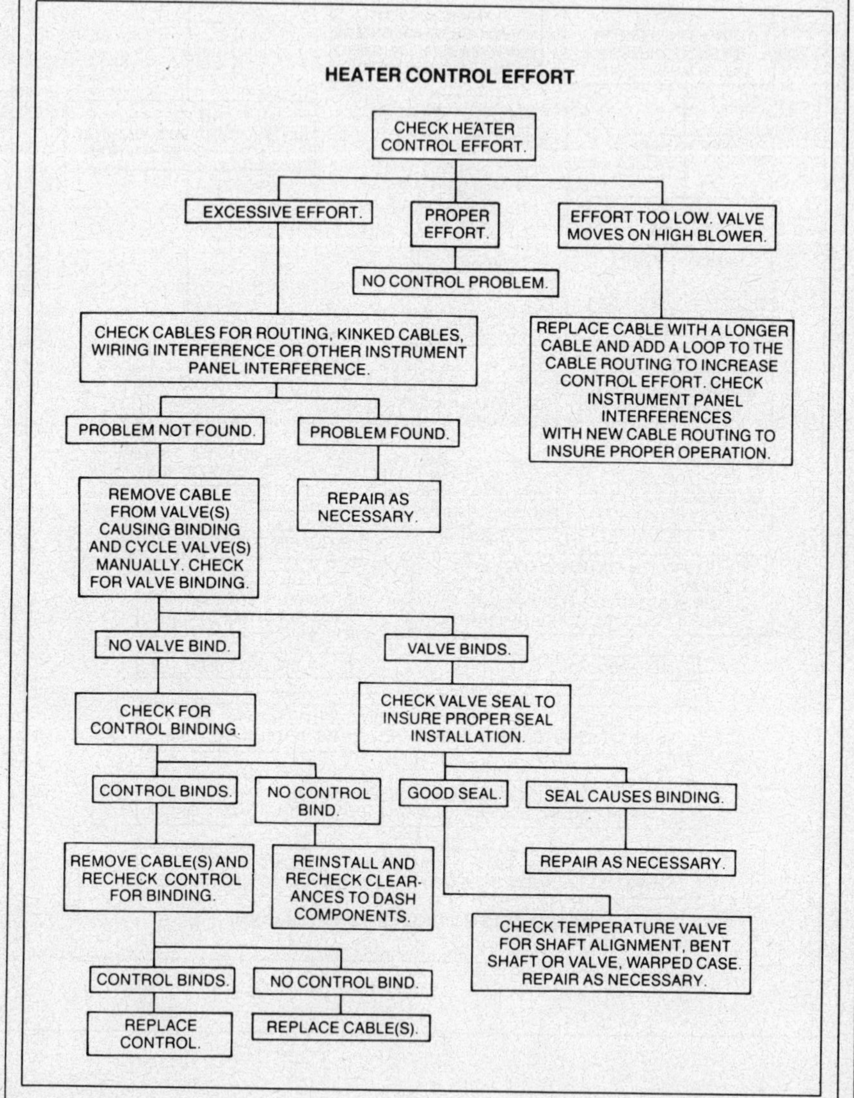
HEATER CONTROL EFFORT
CHECK HEATER CONTROL EFFORT.
EXCESSIVE EFFORT.
PROPER EFFORT.
EFFORT TOO LOW. VALVE MOVES ON HIGH BLOWER.
NO CONTROL PROBLEM.
CHECK CABLES FOR ROUTING, KINKED CABLES, WIRING INTERFERENCE OR OTHER INSTRUMENT PANEL INTERFERENCE.
REPLACE CABLE WITH A LONGER CABLE AND ADD A LOOP TO THE CABLE ROUTING TO INCREASE CONTROL EFFORT. CHECK INSTRUMENT PANEL INTERFERENCES WITH NEW CABLE ROUTING TO INSURE PROPER OPERATION.
PROBLEM NOT FOUND.
PROBLEM FOUND.
REMOVE CABLE FROM VALVE(S) CAUSING BINDING AND CYCLE VALVE(S) MANUALLY. CHECK FOR VALVE BINDING.
REPAIR AS NECESSARY.
NO VALVE BIND.
VALVE BINDS.
CHECK FOR CONTROL BINDING.
CHECK VALVE SEAL TO INSURE PROPER SEAL INSTALLATION.
CONTROL BINDS.
NO CONTROL BIND.
GOOD SEAL.
SEAL CAUSES BINDING.
REMOVE CABLE(S) AND RECHECK CONTROL FOR BINDING.
REINSTALL AND RECHECK CLEARANCES TO DASH COMPONENTS.
REPAIR AS NECESSARY.
CHECK TEMPERATURE VALVE FOR SHAFT ALIGNMENT, BENT SHAFT OR VALVE, WARPED CASE. REPAIR AS NECESSARY.
CONTROL BINDS.
NO CONTROL BIND.
REPLACE CONTROL.
REPLACE CABLE(S).

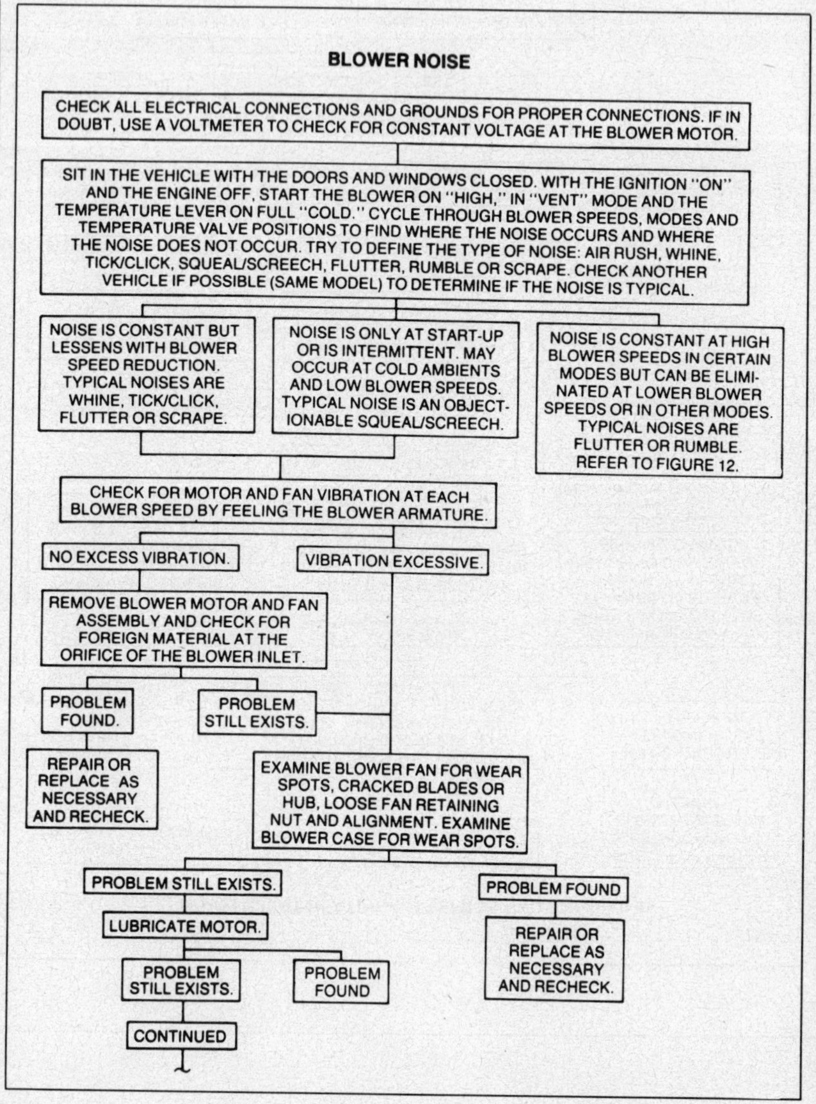
BLOWER NOISE
CHECK ALL ELECTRICAL CONNECTIONS AND GROUNDS FOR PROPER CONNECTIONS. IF IN DOUBT, USE A VOLTMETER TO CHECK FOR CONSTANT VOLTAGE AT THE BLOWER MOTOR.
SIT IN THE VEHICLE WITH THE DOORS AND WINDOWS CLOSED. WITH THE IGNITION "ON" AND THE ENGINE OFF, START THE BLOWER ON "HIGH," IN "VENT" MODE AND THE TEMPERATURE LEVER ON FULL "COLD." CYCLE THROUGH BLOWER SPEEDS, MODES AND TEMPERATURE VALVE POSITIONS TO FIND WHERE THE NOISE OCCURS AND WHERE THE NOISE DOES NOT OCCUR. TRY TO DEFINE THE TYPE OF NOISE: AIR RUSH, WHINE, TICK/CLICK, SQUEAL/SCREECH, FLUTTER, RUMBLE OR SCRAPE. CHECK ANOTHER VEHICLE IF POSSIBLE (SAME MODEL) TO DETERMINE IF THE NOISE IS TYPICAL.
NOISE IS CONSTANT BUT LESSENS WITH BLOWER SPEED REDUCTION. TYPICAL NOISES ARE WHINE, TICK/CLICK, FLUTTER OR SCRAPE.
NOISE IS ONLY AT START-UP OR IS INTERMITTENT. MAY OCCUR AT COLD AMBIENTS AND LOW BLOWER SPEEDS. TYPICAL NOISE IS AN OBJECTIONABLE SQUEAL/SCREECH.
NOISE IS CONSTANT AT HIGH BLOWER SPEEDS IN CERTAIN MODES BUT CAN BE ELIMINATED AT LOWER BLOWER SPEEDS OR IN OTHER MODES. TYPICAL NOISES ARE FLUTTER OR RUMBLE. REFER TO FIGURE 12.
CHECK FOR MOTOR AND FAN VIBRATION AT EACH BLOWER SPEED BY FEELING THE BLOWER ARMATURE.
NO EXCESS VIBRATION.
VIBRATION EXCESSIVE.
REMOVE BLOWER MOTOR AND FAN ASSEMBLY AND CHECK FOR FOREIGN MATERIAL AT THE ORIFICE OF THE BLOWER INLET.
PROBLEM FOUND.
PROBLEM STILL EXISTS.
REPAIR OR REPLACE AS NECESSARY AND RECHECK.
EXAMINE BLOWER FAN FOR WEAR SPOTS, CRACKED BLADES OR HUB, LOOSE FAN RETAINING NUT AND ALIGNMENT. EXAMINE BLOWER CASE FOR WEAR SPOTS.
PROBLEM STILL EXISTS.
PROBLEM FOUND
LUBRICATE MOTOR.
REPAIR OR REPLACE AS NECESSARY AND RECHECK.
PROBLEM STILL EXISTS.
PROBLEM FOUND
CONTINUED

HEATING SYSTEM DIAGNOSIS

BLOWER NOISE (Continued)

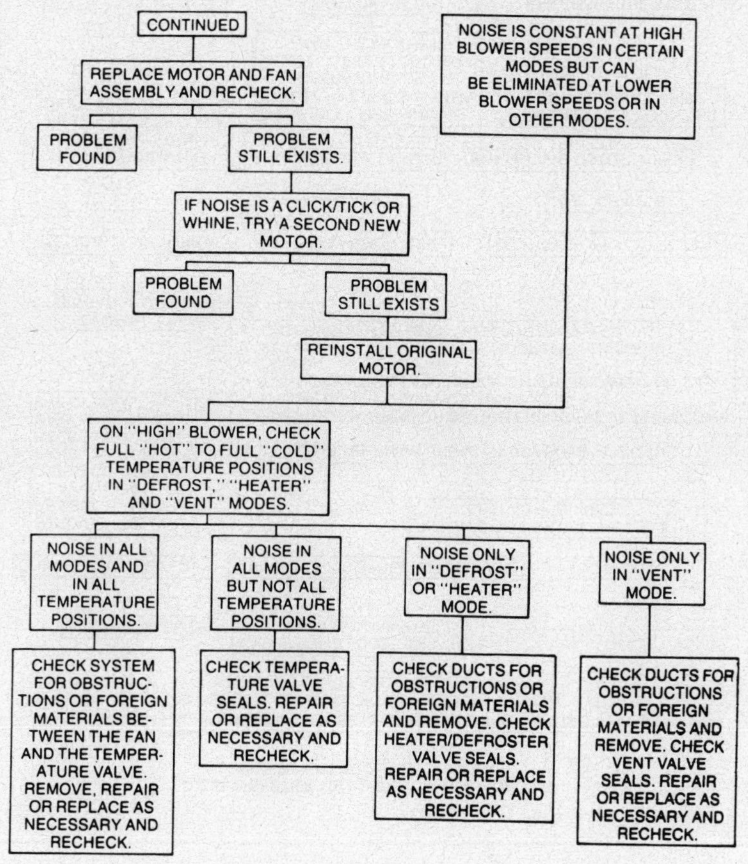
CONTINUED
REPLACE MOTOR AND FAN ASSEMBLY AND RECHECK.
PROBLEM FOUND
PROBLEM STILL EXISTS.
IF NOISE IS A CLICK/TICK OR WHINE, TRY A SECOND NEW MOTOR.
PROBLEM FOUND
PROBLEM STILL EXISTS
REINSTALL ORIGINAL MOTOR.
NOISE IS CONSTANT AT HIGH BLOWER SPEEDS IN CERTAIN MODES BUT CAN BE ELIMINATED AT LOWER BLOWER SPEEDS OR IN OTHER MODES.
ON "HIGH" BLOWER, CHECK FULL "HOT" TO FULL "COLD" TEMPERATURE POSITIONS IN "DEFROST," "HEATER" AND "VENT" MODES.
NOISE IN ALL MODES AND IN ALL TEMPERATURE POSITIONS.
CHECK SYSTEM FOR OBSTRUCTIONS OR FOREIGN MATERIALS BETWEEN THE FAN AND THE TEMPERATURE VALVE. REMOVE, REPAIR OR REPLACE AS NECESSARY AND RECHECK.
NOISE IN ALL MODES BUT NOT ALL TEMPERATURE POSITIONS.
CHECK TEMPERATURE VALVE SEALS. REPAIR OR REPLACE AS NECESSARY AND RECHECK.
NOISE ONLY IN "DEFROST" OR "HEATER" MODE.
CHECK DUCTS FOR OBSTRUCTIONS OR FOREIGN MATERIALS AND REMOVE. CHECK HEATER/DEFROSTER VALVE SEALS. REPAIR OR REPLACE AS NECESSARY AND RECHECK.
NOISE ONLY IN "VENT" MODE.
CHECK DUCTS FOR OBSTRUCTIONS OR FOREIGN MATERIALS AND REMOVE. CHECK VENT VALVE SEALS. REPAIR OR REPLACE AS NECESSARY AND RECHECK.

EXCESSIVE HEAT

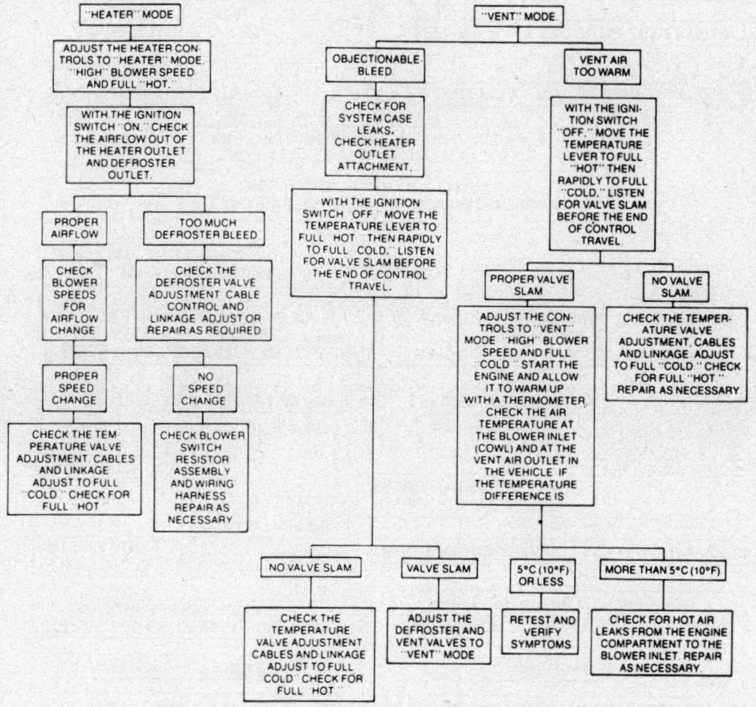
"HEATER" MODE
ADJUST THE HEATER CONTROLS TO "HEATER" MODE, "HIGH" BLOWER SPEED AND FULL "HOT."
WITH THE IGNITION SWITCH "ON," CHECK THE AIRFLOW OUT OF THE HEATER OUTLET AND DEFROSTER OUTLET.
PROPER AIRFLOW
CHECK BLOWER SPEEDS FOR AIRFLOW CHANGE
TOO MUCH DEFROSTER BLEED
CHECK THE DEFROSTER VALVE ADJUSTMENT CABLE CONTROL AND LINKAGE ADJUST OR REPAIR AS REQUIRED
PROPER SPEED CHANGE
CHECK THE TEMPERATURE VALVE ADJUSTMENT CABLES AND LINKAGE ADJUST TO FULL "COLD." CHECK FOR FULL "HOT."
NO SPEED CHANGE
CHECK BLOWER SWITCH RESISTOR ASSEMBLY AND WIRING HARNESS REPAIR AS NECESSARY
"VENT" MODE
OBJECTIONABLE BLEED
CHECK FOR SYSTEM CASE LEAKS. CHECK HEATER OUTLET ATTACHMENT.
WITH THE IGNITION SWITCH "OFF," MOVE THE TEMPERATURE LEVER TO FULL "HOT," THEN RAPIDLY TO FULL "COLD," LISTEN FOR VALVE SLAM BEFORE THE END OF CONTROL TRAVEL.
NO VALVE SLAM
CHECK THE TEMPERATURE VALVE ADJUSTMENT CABLES AND LINKAGE ADJUST TO FULL "COLD." CHECK FOR FULL "HOT."
VALVE SLAM
ADJUST THE DEFROSTER AND VENT VALVES TO "VENT" MODE
VENT AIR TOO WARM
WITH THE IGNITION SWITCH "OFF," MOVE THE TEMPERATURE LEVER TO FULL "HOT" THEN RAPIDLY TO FULL "COLD," LISTEN FOR VALVE SLAM BEFORE THE END OF CONTROL TRAVEL.
PROPER VALVE SLAM
ADJUST THE CONTROLS TO "VENT" MODE "HIGH" BLOWER SPEED AND FULL "COLD." START THE ENGINE AND ALLOW IT TO WARM UP WITH A THERMOMETER, CHECK THE AIR TEMPERATURE AT THE BLOWER INLET (COWL) AND AT THE VENT AIR OUTLET IN THE VEHICLE. IF THE TEMPERATURE DIFFERENCE IS
5°C (10°F) OR LESS
RETEST AND VERIFY SYMPTOMS
MORE THAN 5°C (10°F)
CHECK FOR HOT AIR LEAKS FROM THE ENGINE COMPARTMENT TO THE BLOWER INLET. REPAIR AS NECESSARY.
NO VALVE SLAM.
CHECK THE TEMPERATURE VALVE ADJUSTMENT, CABLES AND LINKAGE. ADJUST TO FULL "COLD." CHECK FOR FULL "HOT." REPAIR AS NECESSARY.

C.C.O.T. SYSTEM AIR CONDITIONING DIAGNOSIS INSUFFICIENT COOLING "CHART A"

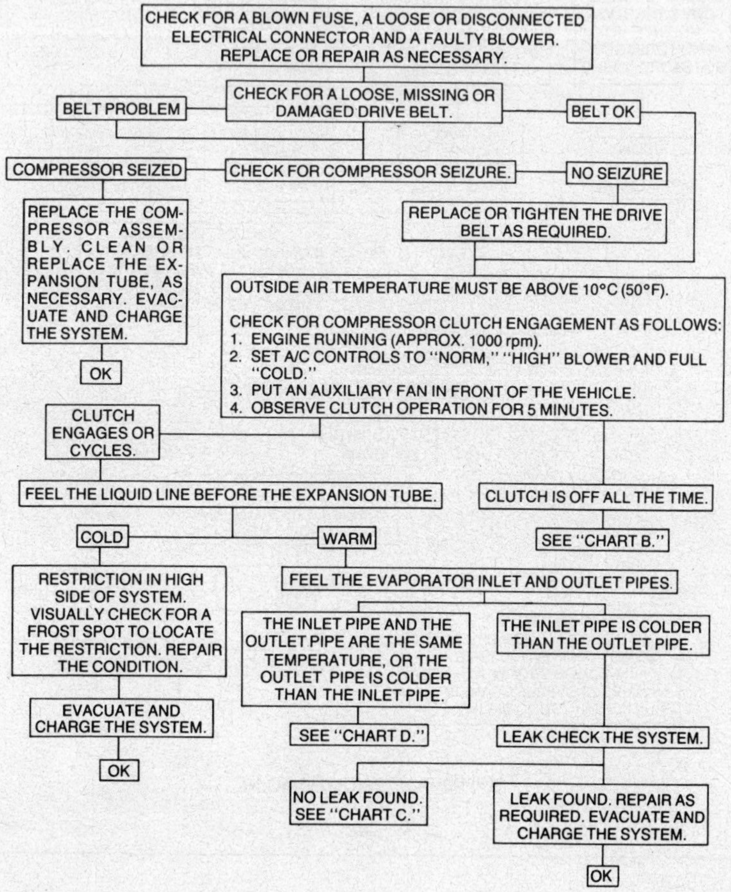
CHECK FOR A BLOWN FUSE, A LOOSE OR DISCONNECTED ELECTRICAL CONNECTOR AND A FAULTY BLOWER. REPLACE OR REPAIR AS NECESSARY.
CHECK FOR A LOOSE, MISSING OR DAMAGED DRIVE BELT.
BELT PROBLEM
BELT OK
CHECK FOR COMPRESSOR SEIZURE.
COMPRESSOR SEIZED
NO SEIZURE
REPLACE THE COMPRESSOR ASSEMBLY. CLEAN OR REPLACE THE EXPANSION TUBE, AS NECESSARY. EVACUATE AND CHARGE THE SYSTEM.
OK
REPLACE OR TIGHTEN THE DRIVE BELT AS REQUIRED.
OUTSIDE AIR TEMPERATURE MUST BE ABOVE 10°C (50°F).
CHECK FOR COMPRESSOR CLUTCH ENGAGEMENT AS FOLLOWS:
1. ENGINE RUNNING (APPROX. 1000 rpm).
2. SET A/C CONTROLS TO "NORM," "HIGH" BLOWER AND FULL "COLD."
3. PUT AN AUXILIARY FAN IN FRONT OF THE VEHICLE.
4. OBSERVE CLUTCH OPERATION FOR 5 MINUTES.
CLUTCH ENGAGES OR CYCLES.
CLUTCH IS OFF ALL THE TIME.
SEE "CHART B."
FEEL THE LIQUID LINE BEFORE THE EXPANSION TUBE.
COLD
WARM
RESTRICTION IN HIGH SIDE OF SYSTEM. VISUALLY CHECK FOR A FROST SPOT TO LOCATE THE RESTRICTION. REPAIR THE CONDITION.
EVACUATE AND CHARGE THE SYSTEM.
OK
FEEL THE EVAPORATOR INLET AND OUTLET PIPES.
THE INLET PIPE AND THE OUTLET PIPE ARE THE SAME TEMPERATURE, OR THE OUTLET PIPE IS COLDER THAN THE INLET PIPE.
SEE "CHART D."
THE INLET PIPE IS COLDER THAN THE OUTLET PIPE.
LEAK CHECK THE SYSTEM.
NO LEAK FOUND. SEE "CHART C."
LEAK FOUND. REPAIR AS REQUIRED. EVACUATE AND CHARGE THE SYSTEM.
OK

C.C.O.T. SYSTEM AIR CONDITIONING DIAGNOSIS INSUFFICIENT COOLING "CHART B"

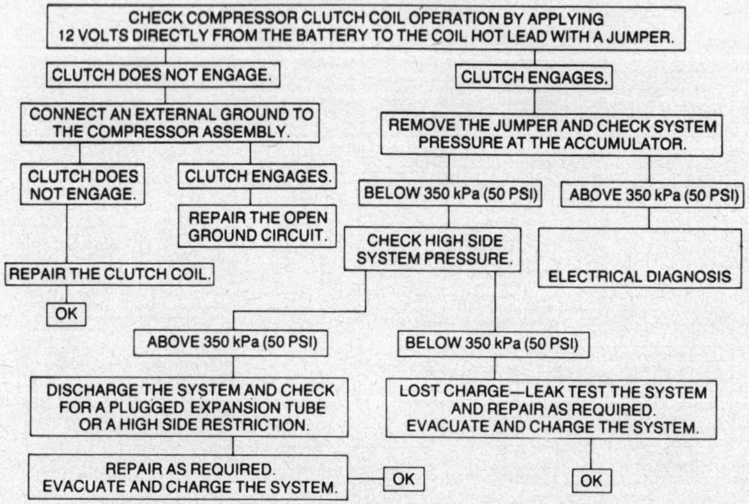
CHECK COMPRESSOR CLUTCH COIL OPERATION BY APPLYING 12 VOLTS DIRECTLY FROM THE BATTERY TO THE COIL HOT LEAD WITH A JUMPER.
CLUTCH DOES NOT ENGAGE.
CLUTCH ENGAGES.
CONNECT AN EXTERNAL GROUND TO THE COMPRESSOR ASSEMBLY.
CLUTCH DOES NOT ENGAGE.
CLUTCH ENGAGES.
REPAIR THE OPEN GROUND CIRCUIT.
REPAIR THE CLUTCH COIL.
OK
REMOVE THE JUMPER AND CHECK SYSTEM PRESSURE AT THE ACCUMULATOR.
BELOW 350 kPa (50 PSI)
ABOVE 350 kPa (50 PSI)
CHECK HIGH SIDE SYSTEM PRESSURE.
ELECTRICAL DIAGNOSIS
ABOVE 350 kPa (50 PSI)
BELOW 350 kPa (50 PSI)
DISCHARGE THE SYSTEM AND CHECK FOR A PLUGGED EXPANSION TUBE OR A HIGH SIDE RESTRICTION.
REPAIR AS REQUIRED. EVACUATE AND CHARGE THE SYSTEM.
OK
LOST CHARGE—LEAK TEST THE SYSTEM AND REPAIR AS REQUIRED. EVACUATE AND CHARGE THE SYSTEM.
OK

C.C.O.T. SYSTEM AIR CONDITIONING DIAGNOSIS INSUFFICIENT COOLING "CHART C"

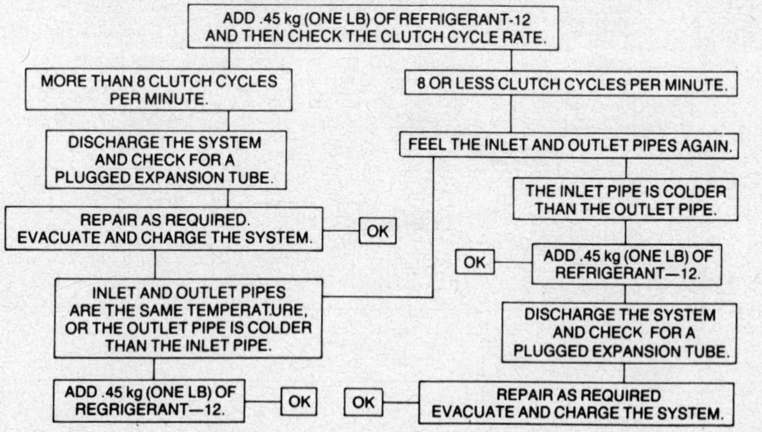
ADD .45 kg (ONE LB) OF REFRIGERANT-12 AND THEN CHECK THE CLUTCH CYCLE RATE.
MORE THAN 8 CLUTCH CYCLES PER MINUTE.
8 OR LESS CLUTCH CYCLES PER MINUTE.
DISCHARGE THE SYSTEM AND CHECK FOR A PLUGGED EXPANSION TUBE.
REPAIR AS REQUIRED. EVACUATE AND CHARGE THE SYSTEM.
OK
FEEL THE INLET AND OUTLET PIPES AGAIN.
THE INLET PIPE IS COLDER THAN THE OUTLET PIPE.
ADD .45 kg (ONE LB) OF REFRIGERANT—12.
OK
DISCHARGE THE SYSTEM AND CHECK FOR A PLUGGED EXPANSION TUBE.
INLET AND OUTLET PIPES ARE THE SAME TEMPERATURE, OR THE OUTLET PIPE IS COLDER THAN THE INLET PIPE.
ADD .45 kg (ONE LB) OF REGRIGERANT—12.
OK
OK
REPAIR AS REQUIRED EVACUATE AND CHARGE THE SYSTEM.

AIR CONDITIONING SYSTEM DIAGNOSIS

**C.C.O.T. SYSTEM AIR CONDITIONING DIAGNOSIS
INSUFFICIENT COOLING "CHART D"**

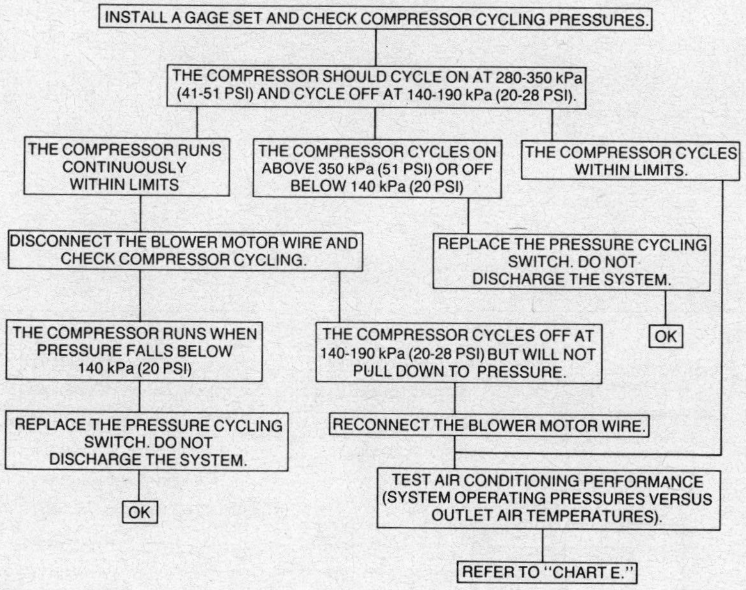
INSTALL A GAGE SET AND CHECK COMPRESSOR CYCLING PRESSURES.
THE COMPRESSOR SHOULD CYCLE ON AT 280-350 kPa (41-51 PSI) AND CYCLE OFF AT 140-190 kPa (20-28 PSI).
THE COMPRESSOR RUNS CONTINUOUSLY WITHIN LIMITS
THE COMPRESSOR CYCLES ON ABOVE 350 kPa (51 PSI) OR OFF BELOW 140 kPa (20 PSI)
THE COMPRESSOR CYCLES WITHIN LIMITS.
DISCONNECT THE BLOWER MOTOR WIRE AND CHECK COMPRESSOR CYCLING.
REPLACE THE PRESSURE CYCLING SWITCH. DO NOT DISCHARGE THE SYSTEM.
OK
THE COMPRESSOR RUNS WHEN PRESSURE FALLS BELOW 140 kPa (20 PSI)
THE COMPRESSOR CYCLES OFF AT 140-190 kPa (20-28 PSI) BUT WILL NOT PULL DOWN TO PRESSURE.
REPLACE THE PRESSURE CYCLING SWITCH. DO NOT DISCHARGE THE SYSTEM.
RECONNECT THE BLOWER MOTOR WIRE.
OK
TEST AIR CONDITIONING PERFORMANCE (SYSTEM OPERATING PRESSURES VERSUS OUTLET AIR TEMPERATURES).
REFER TO "CHART E."

**C.C.O.T. SYSTEM AIR CONDITIONING DIAGNOSIS
INSUFFICIENT COOLING "CHART E"**

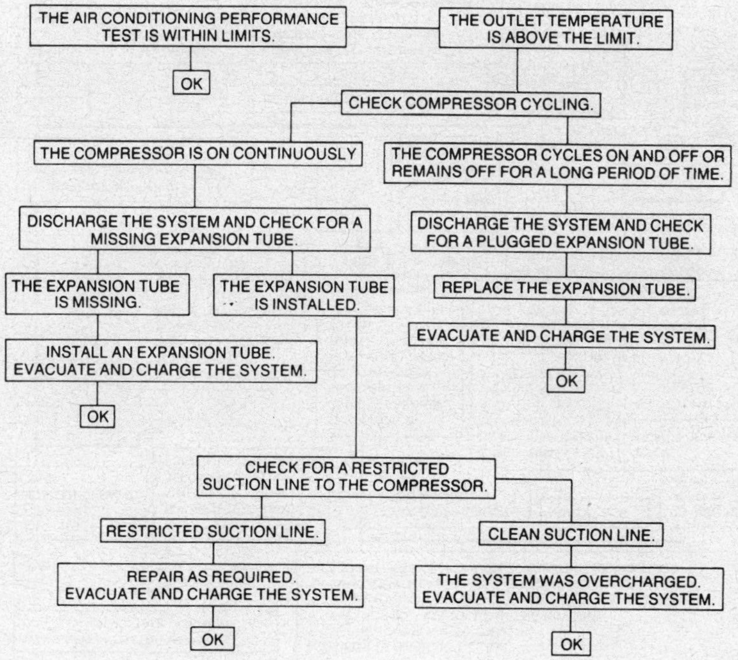
THE AIR CONDITIONING PERFORMANCE TEST IS WITHIN LIMITS.
THE OUTLET TEMPERATURE IS ABOVE THE LIMIT.
OK
CHECK COMPRESSOR CYCLING.
THE COMPRESSOR IS ON CONTINUOUSLY
THE COMPRESSOR CYCLES ON AND OFF OR REMAINS OFF FOR A LONG PERIOD OF TIME.
DISCHARGE THE SYSTEM AND CHECK FOR A MISSING EXPANSION TUBE.
DISCHARGE THE SYSTEM AND CHECK FOR A PLUGGED EXPANSION TUBE.
THE EXPANSION TUBE IS MISSING.
THE EXPANSION TUBE IS INSTALLED.
REPLACE THE EXPANSION TUBE.
INSTALL AN EXPANSION TUBE. EVACUATE AND CHARGE THE SYSTEM.
EVACUATE AND CHARGE THE SYSTEM.
OK
OK
CHECK FOR A RESTRICTED SUCTION LINE TO THE COMPRESSOR.
RESTRICTED SUCTION LINE.
CLEAN SUCTION LINE.
REPAIR AS REQUIRED. EVACUATE AND CHARGE THE SYSTEM.
THE SYSTEM WAS OVERCHARGED. EVACUATE AND CHARGE THE SYSTEM.
OK
OK

ECC SYSTEM DIAGNOSIS—CUSTOM CRUISER AND ROADMASTER

A	50 BRN WIRE FROM NO. 6 FUSE (20A) — HOT IN RUN
B	640 ORN WIRE FROM NO. 4 FUSE (10A) — ALWAYS HOT
C	198 LT GRN/BLK
D	198 LT GRN/BLK TO SENSORS
E	1218 BRN/WHT
F	1217 LT BLU
G	1236 WHT/BLK
H	1199 DK BLU
J	TEMPERATURE AIR VALVE POSITION INPUT
K	5 VOLT REFERENCE VOLTAGE
L	B TERMINAL (IGNITION VOLTAGE)
M	C1 TERMINAL (BATTERY VOLTAGE)
N	C9 TERMINAL (ANALOG GROUND)
P	C6 TERMINAL (FEEDBACK)
Q	C12 TERMINAL (REFERENCE VOLTAGE)
R	G TERMINAL (MOTOR DRIVE –)
S	F TERMINAL (MOTOR DRIVE +)
T	C8 TERMINAL (GROUND)
U	C5 TERMINAL (REFERENCE VOLTAGE)
V	C10 TERMINAL (MOTOR DRIVE)
W	C9 TERMINAL (MOTOR DRIVE)
15	MICROPROCESSOR
16	TEMPERATURE AIR VALVE ACTUATOR

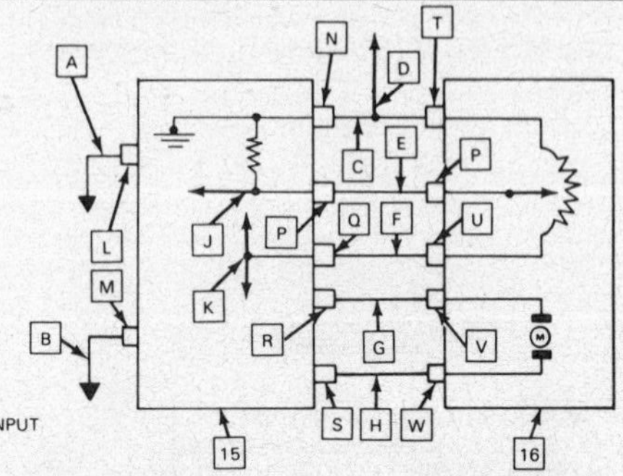
A
B
C
D
E
F
G
H
J
K
L
M
N
P
Q
R
S
T
U
V
W
15
16

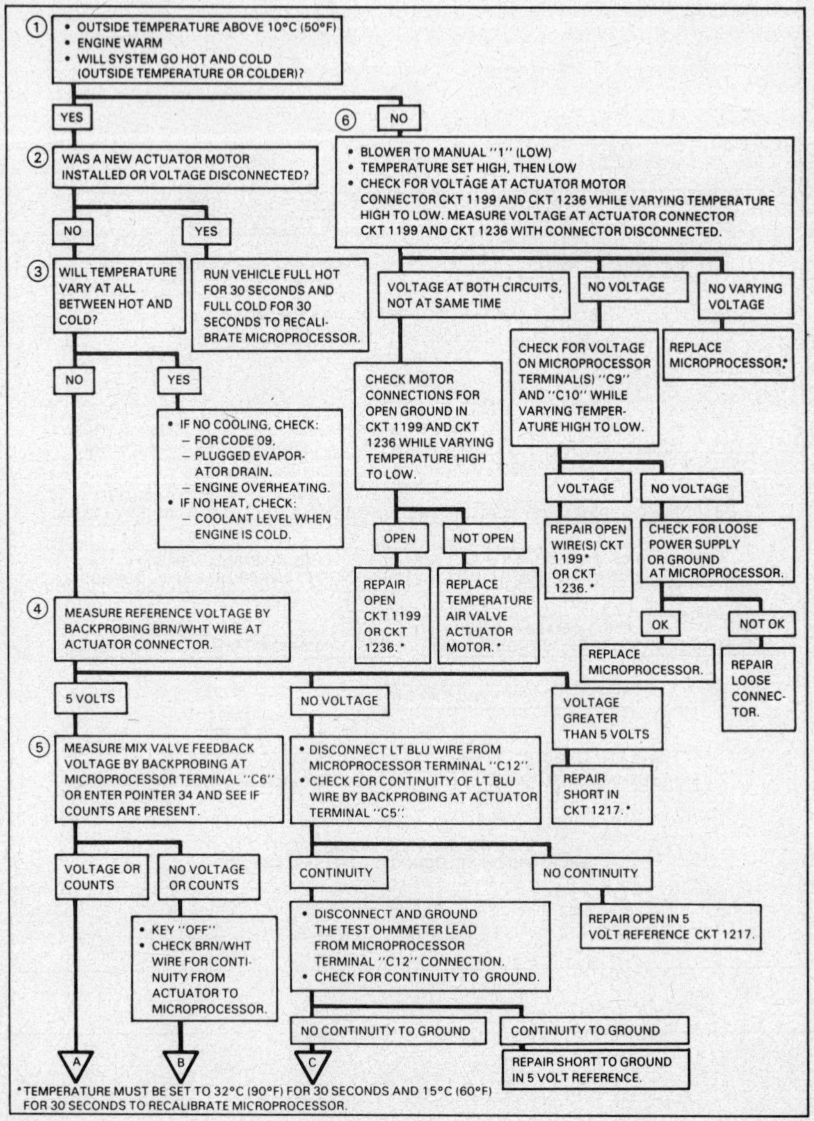
1
• OUTSIDE TEMPERATURE ABOVE 10°C (50°F)
• ENGINE WARM
• WILL SYSTEM GO HOT AND COLD (OUTSIDE TEMPERATURE OR COLDER)?
YES
NO
2
WAS A NEW ACTUATOR MOTOR INSTALLED OR VOLTAGE DISCONNECTED?
NO
YES
RUN VEHICLE FULL HOT FOR 30 SECONDS AND FULL COLD FOR 30 SECONDS TO RECALIBRATE MICROPROCESSOR.
3
WILL TEMPERATURE VARY AT ALL BETWEEN HOT AND COLD?
NO
YES
• IF NO COOLING, CHECK:
– FOR CODE 09.
– PLUGGED EVAPORATOR DRAIN.
– ENGINE OVERHEATING.
• IF NO HEAT, CHECK:
– COOLANT LEVEL WHEN ENGINE IS COLD.
4
MEASURE REFERENCE VOLTAGE BY BACKPROBING BRN/WHT WIRE AT ACTUATOR CONNECTOR.
5 VOLTS
NO VOLTAGE
VOLTAGE GREATER THAN 5 VOLTS
REPAIR SHORT IN CKT 1217.*
5
MEASURE MIX VALVE FEEDBACK VOLTAGE BY BACKPROBING AT MICROPROCESSOR TERMINAL "C6" OR ENTER POINTER 34 AND SEE IF COUNTS ARE PRESENT.
VOLTAGE OR COUNTS
NO VOLTAGE OR COUNTS
• KEY "OFF"
• CHECK BRN/WHT WIRE FOR CONTINUITY FROM ACTUATOR TO MICROPROCESSOR.
• DISCONNECT LT BLU WIRE FROM MICROPROCESSOR TERMINAL "C12".
• CHECK FOR CONTINUITY OF LT BLU WIRE BY BACKPROBING AT ACTUATOR TERMINAL "C5".
CONTINUITY
NO CONTINUITY
REPAIR OPEN IN 5 VOLT REFERENCE CKT 1217.
• DISCONNECT AND GROUND THE TEST OHMMETER LEAD FROM MICROPROCESSOR TERMINAL "C12" CONNECTION.
• CHECK FOR CONTINUITY TO GROUND.
NO CONTINUITY TO GROUND
CONTINUITY TO GROUND
REPAIR SHORT TO GROUND IN 5 VOLT REFERENCE.
A
B
C
6
• BLOWER TO MANUAL "1" (LOW)
• TEMPERATURE SET HIGH, THEN LOW
• CHECK FOR VOLTAGE AT ACTUATOR MOTOR CONNECTOR CKT 1199 AND CKT 1236 WHILE VARYING TEMPERATURE HIGH TO LOW. MEASURE VOLTAGE AT ACTUATOR CONNECTOR CKT 1199 AND CKT 1236 WITH CONNECTOR DISCONNECTED.
VOLTAGE AT BOTH CIRCUITS, NOT AT SAME TIME
NO VOLTAGE
NO VARYING VOLTAGE
REPLACE MICROPROCESSOR.*
CHECK MOTOR CONNECTIONS FOR OPEN GROUND IN CKT 1199 AND CKT 1236 WHILE VARYING TEMPERATURE HIGH TO LOW.
OPEN
NOT OPEN
REPAIR OPEN CKT 1199 OR CKT 1236.*
REPLACE TEMPERATURE AIR VALVE ACTUATOR MOTOR.*
CHECK FOR VOLTAGE ON MICROPROCESSOR TERMINAL(S) "C9" AND "C10" WHILE VARYING TEMPERATURE HIGH TO LOW.
VOLTAGE
NO VOLTAGE
REPAIR OPEN WIRE(S) CKT 1199* OR CKT 1236.*
CHECK FOR LOOSE POWER SUPPLY OR GROUND AT MICROPROCESSOR.
OK
NOT OK
REPLACE MICROPROCESSOR.
REPAIR LOOSE CONNECTOR.
*TEMPERATURE MUST BE SET TO 32°C (90°F) FOR 30 SECONDS AND 15°C (60°F) FOR 30 SECONDS TO RECALIBRATE MICROPROCESSOR.

EEC SYSTEM DIAGNOSIS—CUSTOM CRUISER AND ROADMASTER (CONT'D)

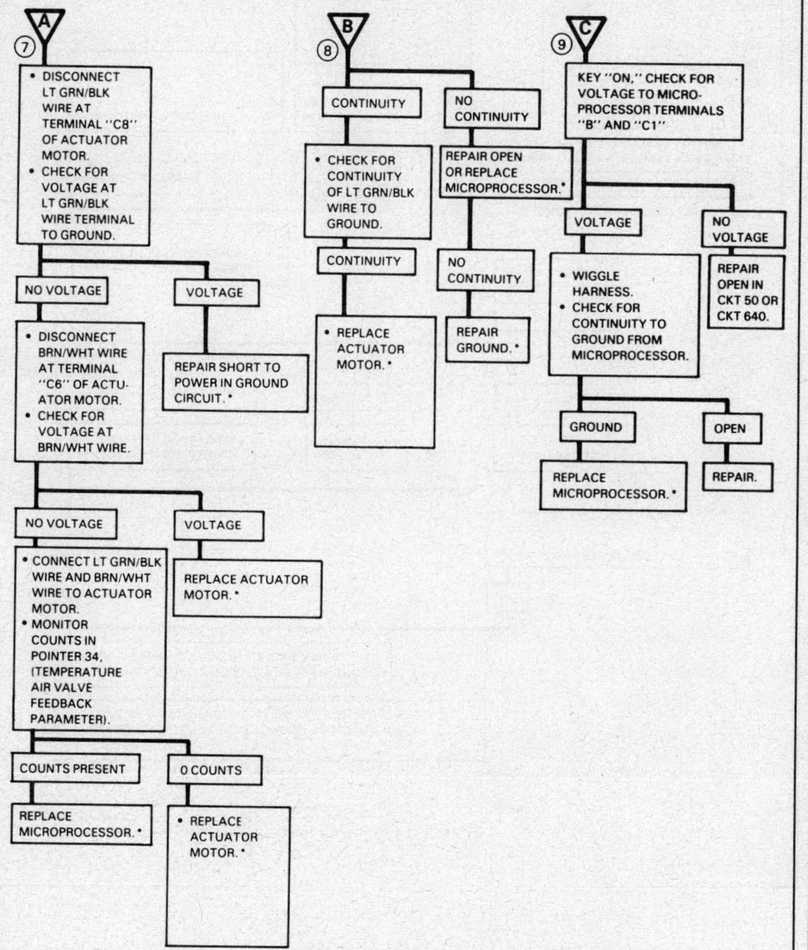
A
7
• DISCONNECT LT GRN/BLK WIRE AT TERMINAL "C8" OF ACTUATOR MOTOR.
• CHECK FOR VOLTAGE AT LT GRN/BLK WIRE TERMINAL TO GROUND.
NO VOLTAGE
VOLTAGE
REPAIR SHORT TO POWER IN GROUND CIRCUIT.*
• DISCONNECT BRN/WHT WIRE AT TERMINAL "C6" OF ACTUATOR MOTOR.
• CHECK FOR VOLTAGE AT BRN/WHT WIRE.
NO VOLTAGE
VOLTAGE
REPLACE ACTUATOR MOTOR.*
• CONNECT LT GRN/BLK WIRE AND BRN/WHT WIRE TO ACTUATOR MOTOR.
• MONITOR COUNTS IN POINTER 34, (TEMPERATURE AIR VALVE FEEDBACK PARAMETER).
COUNTS PRESENT
0 COUNTS
REPLACE MICROPROCESSOR.*
• REPLACE ACTUATOR MOTOR.*
B
8
CONTINUITY
NO CONTINUITY
• CHECK FOR CONTINUITY OF LT GRN/BLK WIRE TO GROUND.
REPAIR OPEN OR REPLACE MICROPROCESSOR.*
CONTINUITY
NO CONTINUITY
• REPLACE ACTUATOR MOTOR.*
REPAIR GROUND.*
C
9
KEY "ON," CHECK FOR VOLTAGE TO MICRO-PROCESSOR TERMINALS "B" AND "C1"
VOLTAGE
NO VOLTAGE
REPAIR OPEN IN CKT 50 OR CKT 640.
• WIGGLE HARNESS.
• CHECK FOR CONTINUITY TO GROUND FROM MICROPROCESSOR.
GROUND
OPEN
REPLACE MICROPROCESSOR.*
REPAIR.

*TEMPERATURE MUST BE SET TO 32°C (90°F) FOR 30 SECONDS AND 15°C (60°F) FOR 30 SECONDS TO RECALIBRATE MICROPROCESSOR.

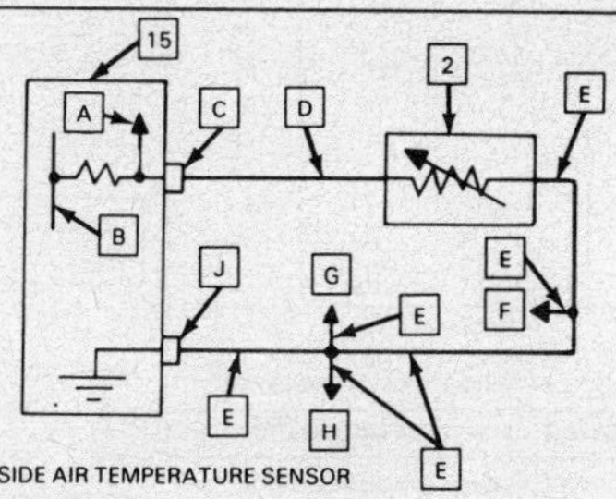
15
A
B
C
D
2
E
J
G
E
F
E
H
E

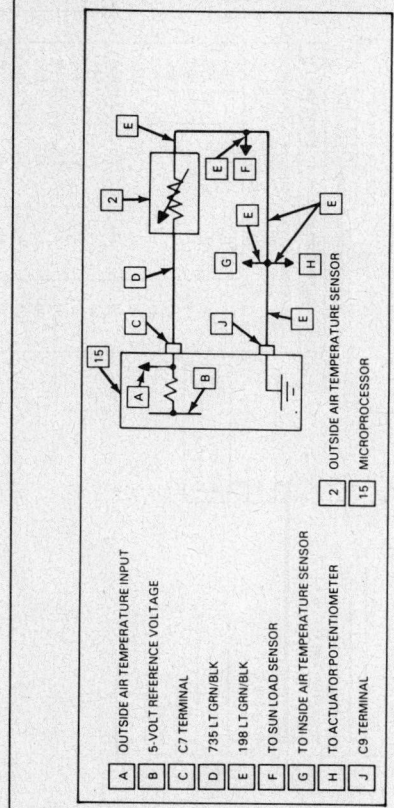

A	OUTSIDE AIR TEMPERATURE INPUT
B	5-VOLT REFERENCE VOLTAGE
C	C7 TERMINAL
D	735 LT GRN/BLK
E	198 LT GRN/BLK
F	TO SUN LOAD SENSOR
G	TO INSIDE AIR TEMPERATURE SENSOR
H	TO ACTUATOR POTENTIOMETER
J	C9 TERMINAL
2	OUTSIDE AIR TEMPERATURE SENSOR
15	MICROPROCESSOR

ECC SYSTEM DIAGNOSIS—CUSTOM CRUISER AND ROADMASTER (CONT'D)

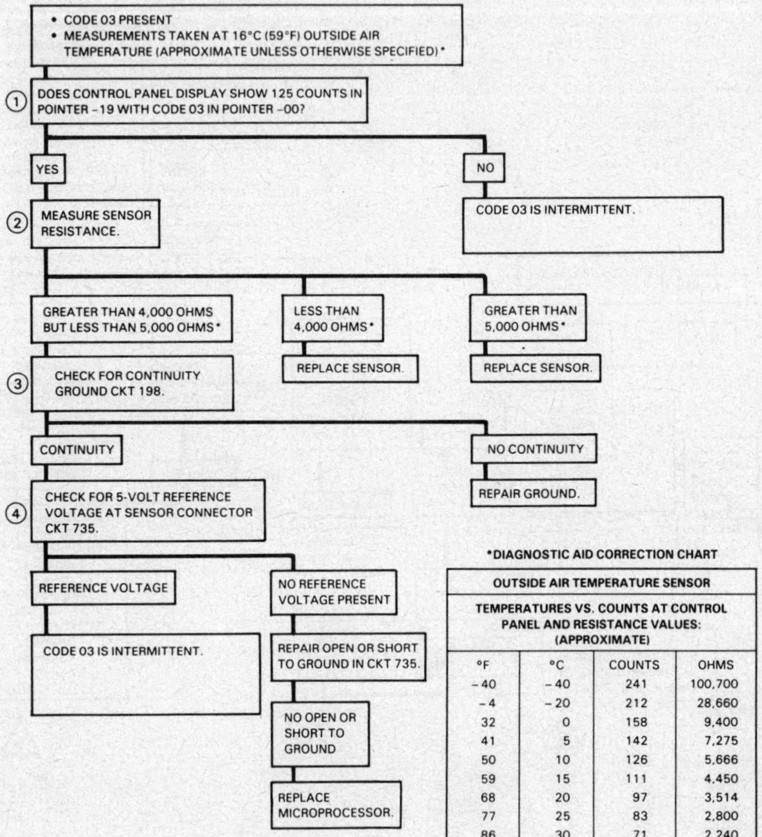
• CODE 03 PRESENT
• MEASUREMENTS TAKEN AT 16°C (59°F) OUTSIDE AIR TEMPERATURE (APPROXIMATE UNLESS OTHERWISE SPECIFIED)*
1 DOES CONTROL PANEL DISPLAY SHOW 125 COUNTS IN POINTER –19 WITH CODE 03 IN POINTER –00?
YES
NO
CODE 03 IS INTERMITTENT.
2 MEASURE SENSOR RESISTANCE.
GREATER THAN 4,000 OHMS BUT LESS THAN 5,000 OHMS*
LESS THAN 4,000 OHMS*
GREATER THAN 5,000 OHMS*
REPLACE SENSOR.
REPLACE SENSOR.
3 CHECK FOR CONTINUITY GROUND CKT 198.
CONTINUITY
NO CONTINUITY
REPAIR GROUND.
4 CHECK FOR 5-VOLT REFERENCE VOLTAGE AT SENSOR CONNECTOR CKT 735.
REFERENCE VOLTAGE
NO REFERENCE VOLTAGE PRESENT
CODE 03 IS INTERMITTENT.
REPAIR OPEN OR SHORT TO GROUND IN CKT 735.
NO OPEN OR SHORT TO GROUND
REPLACE MICROPROCESSOR.

*DIAGNOSTIC AID CORRECTION CHART

OUTSIDE AIR TEMPERATURE SENSOR

TEMPERATURES VS. COUNTS AT CONTROL PANEL AND RESISTANCE VALUES: (APPROXIMATE)

°F	°C	COUNTS	OHMS
–40	–40	241	100,700
–4	–20	212	28,660
32	0	158	9,400
41	5	142	7,275
50	10	126	5,666
59	15	111	4,450
68	20	97	3,514
77	25	83	2,800
86	30	71	2,240
95	35	61	1,800
104	40	52	1,460
113	45	44	1,190
131	55	31	800
167	75	16	390

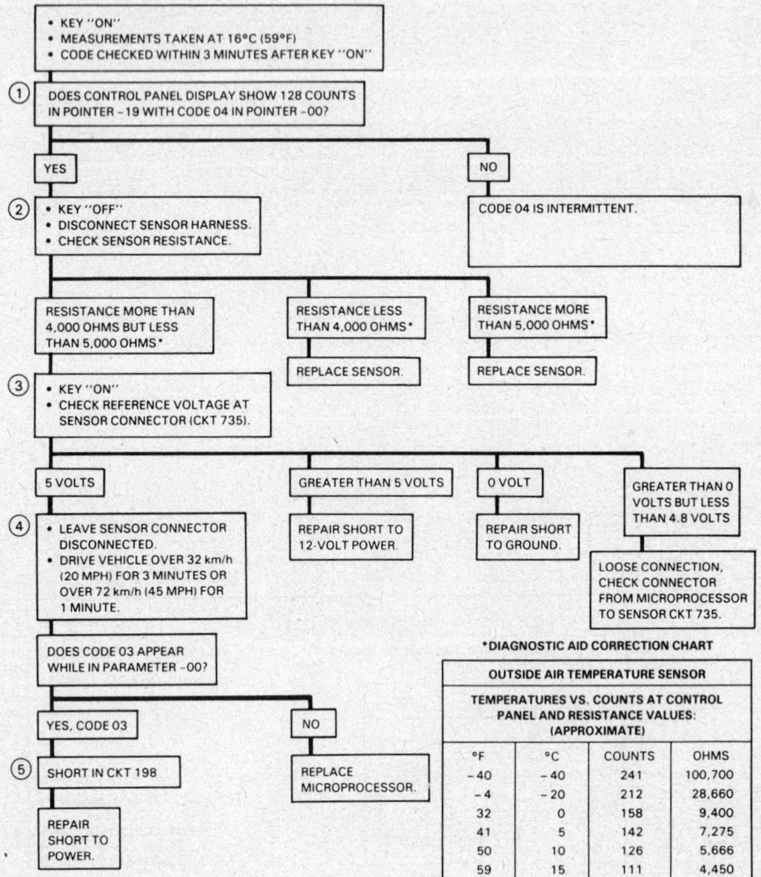
• KEY "ON"
• MEASUREMENTS TAKEN AT 16°C (59°F)
• CODE CHECKED WITHIN 3 MINUTES AFTER KEY "ON"
1 DOES CONTROL PANEL DISPLAY SHOW 128 COUNTS IN POINTER –19 WITH CODE 04 IN POINTER –00?
YES
NO
CODE 04 IS INTERMITTENT.
2 • KEY "OFF" • DISCONNECT SENSOR HARNESS. • CHECK SENSOR RESISTANCE.
RESISTANCE MORE THAN 4,000 OHMS BUT LESS THAN 5,000 OHMS*
RESISTANCE LESS THAN 4,000 OHMS*
RESISTANCE MORE THAN 5,000 OHMS*
REPLACE SENSOR.
REPLACE SENSOR.
3 • KEY "ON" • CHECK REFERENCE VOLTAGE AT SENSOR CONNECTOR (CKT 735).
5 VOLTS
GREATER THAN 5 VOLTS
0 VOLT
GREATER THAN 0 VOLTS BUT LESS THAN 4.8 VOLTS
4 • LEAVE SENSOR CONNECTOR DISCONNECTED. • DRIVE VEHICLE OVER 32 km/h (20 MPH) FOR 3 MINUTES OR OVER 72 km/h (45 MPH) FOR 1 MINUTE.
REPAIR SHORT TO 12-VOLT POWER.
REPAIR SHORT TO GROUND.
LOOSE CONNECTION, CHECK CONNECTOR FROM MICROPROCESSOR TO SENSOR CKT 735.
DOES CODE 03 APPEAR WHILE IN PARAMETER –00?
YES, CODE 03
NO
5 SHORT IN CKT 198
REPLACE MICROPROCESSOR.
REPAIR SHORT TO POWER.

*DIAGNOSTIC AID CORRECTION CHART

OUTSIDE AIR TEMPERATURE SENSOR

TEMPERATURES VS. COUNTS AT CONTROL PANEL AND RESISTANCE VALUES: (APPROXIMATE)

°F	°C	COUNTS	OHMS
–40	–40	241	100,700
–4	–20	212	28,660
32	0	158	9,400
41	5	142	7,275
50	10	126	5,666
59	15	111	4,450
68	20	97	3,514
77	25	83	2,800
86	30	71	2,240
95	35	61	1,800
104	40	52	1,460
113	45	44	1,190
131	55	31	800
167	75	16	390

ECC SYSTEM DIAGNOSIS—CUSTOM CRUISER AND ROADMASTER (CONT'D)

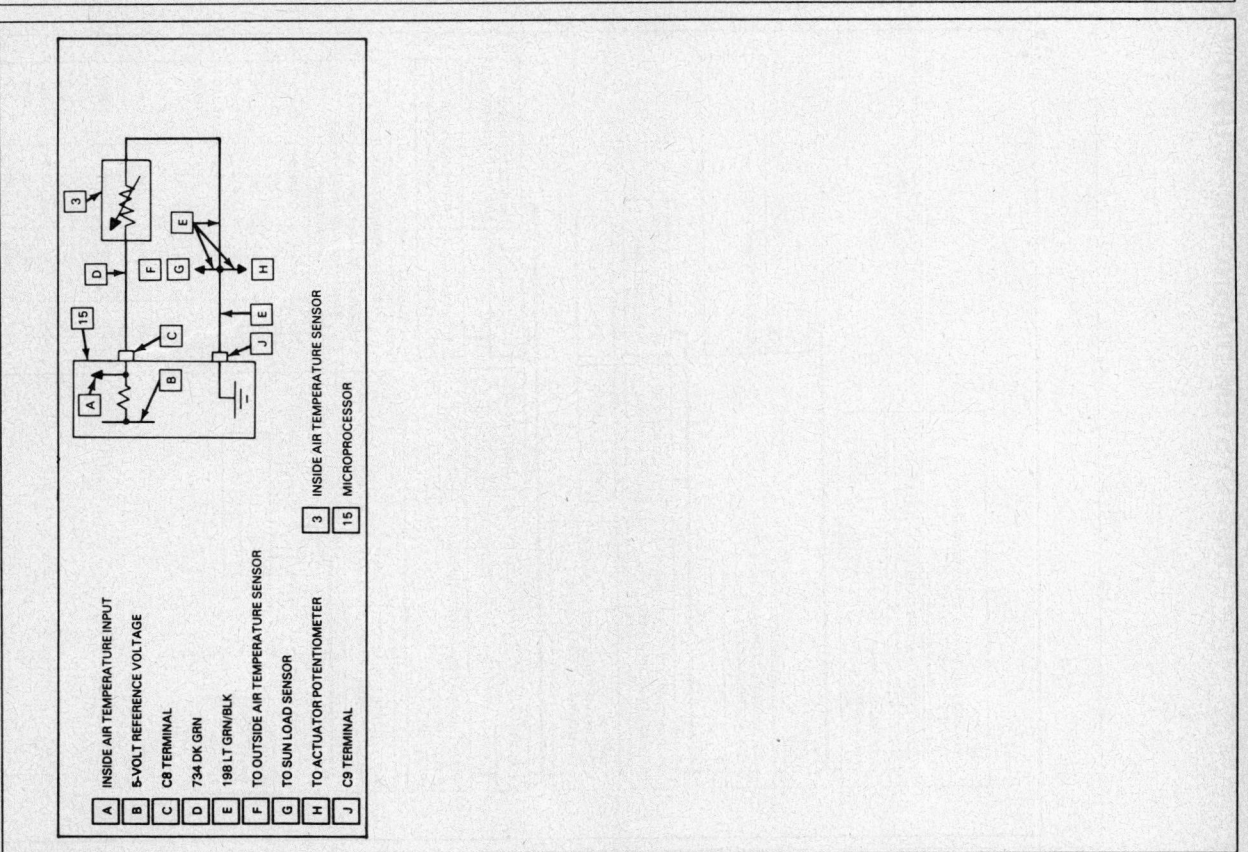

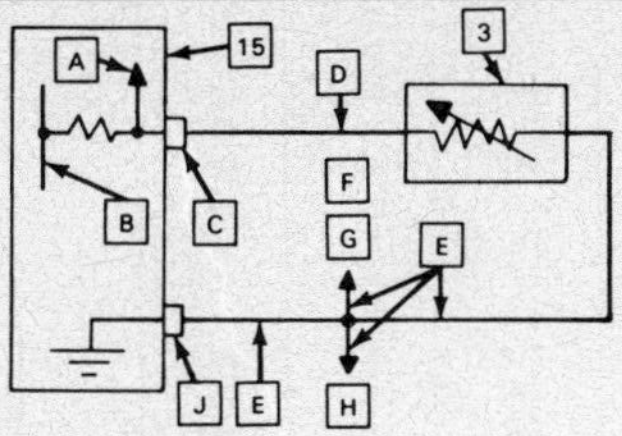
A
B
C
D
E
F
G
H
J
3
15

- A INSIDE AIR TEMPERATURE INPUT
- B 5-VOLT REFERENCE VOLTAGE
- C C8 TERMINAL
- D 734 DK GRN
- E 198 LT GRN/BLK
- F TO OUTSIDE AIR TEMPERATURE SENSOR
- G TO SUN LOAD SENSOR
- H TO ACTUATOR POTENTIOMETER
- J C9 TERMINAL
- 3 INSIDE AIR TEMPERATURE SENSOR
- 15 MICROPROCESSOR

- CODE 05 PRESENT
- MEASUREMENTS TAKEN AT APPROXIMATELY 15°C (59°F) INSIDE THE VEHICLE (UNLESS OTHERWISE SPECIFIED)*

(1) DOES CONTROL PANEL DISPLAY SHOW 128 COUNTS IN POINTER –02 WITH CODE 05 IN POINTER –00?

- NO: CODE 05 IS INTERMITTENT.
- YES:

(2)
- DISCONNECT SENSOR CONNECTOR.
- MEASURE SENSOR RESISTANCE.

- LESS THAN 4,000 OHMS*: REPLACE SENSOR.
- GREATER THAN 5,000 OHMS*: REPLACE SENSOR.
- GREATER THAN 4,000 OHMS BUT LESS THAN 5,000 OHMS*:

(3) CHECK FOR CONTINUITY AT SENSOR CONNECTOR TO GROUND, CKT 198.

- NO CONTINUITY: REPAIR GROUND.
- CONTINUITY:

(4) CHECK FOR 5-VOLT REFERENCE VOLTAGE AT SENSOR CONNECTOR, CKT 734.

- NO REFERENCE VOLTAGE: REPAIR OPEN IN CKT 734 OR IF NOT OPEN, REPLACE MICROPROCESSOR.
- REFERENCE VOLTAGE: CHECK FOR SHORT TO 5-VOLT REFERENCE VOLTAGE BY MEASURING VOLTAGE WITH REFERENCE CKT 734 DISCONNECTED AT MICROPROCESSOR TERMINAL "C8"
  - NO VOLTAGE: CODE 05 IS INTERMITTENT.
  - VOLTAGE: REPAIR SHORT TO POWER IN REFERENCE CKT 734 WIRE.

*DIAGNOSTIC AID CORRECTION CHART

INSIDE AIR TEMPERATURE SENSOR

TEMPERATURES VS. COUNTS AT CONTROL PANEL AND RESISTANCE VALUES: (APPROXIMATE)

°F	°C	COUNTS	OHMS
–40	–40	248	100,700
–22	–30	242	52,670
–04	–20	232	28,660
14	–10	217	16,160
32	0	197	9,400
41	5	184	7,275
50	10	171	5,670
59	15	156	4,450
68	20	142	3,515
77	25	127	2,800
86	30	113	2,235
95	35	100	1,800
104	40	87	1,460
122	50	66	973
140	60	49	667
158	70	36	467
176	80	27	332
185	85	23	282

ECC SYSTEM DIAGNOSIS—CUSTOM CRUISER AND ROADMASTER (CONT'D)

- KEY "ON"
- MEASUREMENTS TAKEN AT APPROXIMATELY 15°C (59°F) INSIDE THE VEHICLE (UNLESS OTHERWISE SPECIFIED)*
- CODES CHECKED WITHIN 3 MINUTES AFTER KEY "ON"

(1) DOES CONTROL PANEL DISPLAY SHOW 125 COUNTS IN PARAMETER -02 WITH CODE 06 IN PARAMETER -00?

- YES
- NO → CODE 06 IS INTERMITTENT.

(2)
- DISCONNECT SENSOR HARNESS.
- CHECK SENSOR RESISTANCE.

- RESISTANCE GREATER THAN 4,000 OHMS BUT LESS THAN 5,000 OHMS*
- RESISTANCE LESS THAN 4,000 OHMS* → REPLACE SENSOR.
- RESISTANCE GREATER THAN 5,000 OHMS* → REPLACE SENSOR.

(3)
- KEY "ON"
- CHECK 5-VOLT REFERENCE VOLTAGE AT SENSOR CONNECTOR, CKT 734.

- 5 VOLTS
- GREATER THAN 5 VOLTS → REPAIR SHORT.
- 0 VOLTS → REPAIR SHORT TO GROUND.
- GREATER THAN 0 VOLTS BUT LESS THAN 4.8 VOLTS → CHECK CONNECTOR "C8" FOR PROPER CONTACT.

(4)
- LEAVE SENSOR CONNECTOR DISCONNECTED.
- KEY "OFF"
- KEY "ON"

DOES CODE 05 APPEAR WHILE IN PARAMETER -00?

- YES → REPAIR SHORT TO GROUND IN CKT 198.
- NO → REPLACE MICROPROCESSOR.

*DIAGNOSTIC AID CORRECTION CHART

INSIDE AIR TEMPERATURE SENSOR

TEMPERATURES VS. COUNTS AT CONTROL PANEL AND RESISTANCE VALUES: (APPROXIMATE)

°F	°C	COUNTS	OHMS
–40	–40	248	100,700
–22	–30	242	52,670
–04	–20	232	28,660
14	–10	217	16,160
32	0	197	9,400
41	5	184	7,275
50	10	171	5,670
59	15	156	4,450
68	20	142	3,515
77	25	127	2,800
86	30	113	2,235
95	35	100	1,800
104	40	87	1,460
122	50	66	973
140	60	49	667
158	70	36	467
176	80	27	332
185	85	23	282

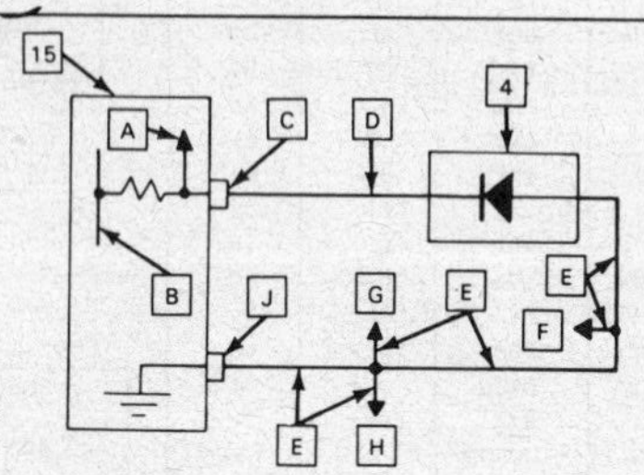
15
A
B
C
D
4
E
F
G
E
J
E
H

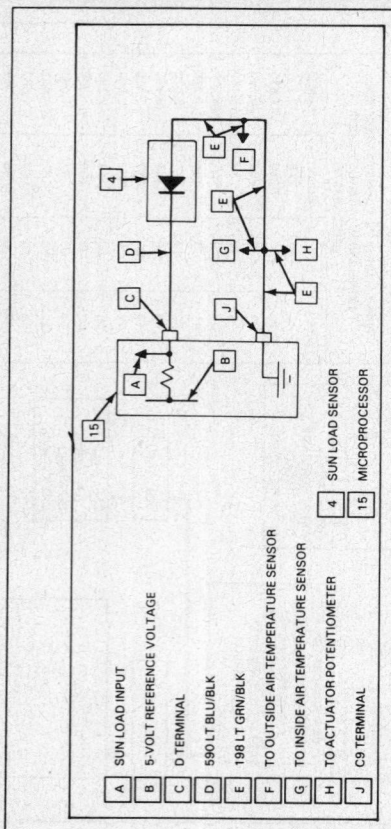

- A SUN LOAD INPUT
- B 5-VOLT REFERENCE VOLTAGE
- C D TERMINAL
- D 590 LT BLU/BLK
- E 198 LT GRN/BLK
- F TO OUTSIDE AIR TEMPERATURE SENSOR
- G TO INSIDE AIR TEMPERATURE SENSOR
- H TO ACTUATOR POTENTIOMETER
- J C9 TERMINAL
- 4 SUN LOAD SENSOR
- 15 MICROPROCESSOR

ECC SYSTEM DIAGNOSIS—CUSTOM CRUISER AND ROADMASTER (CONT'D)

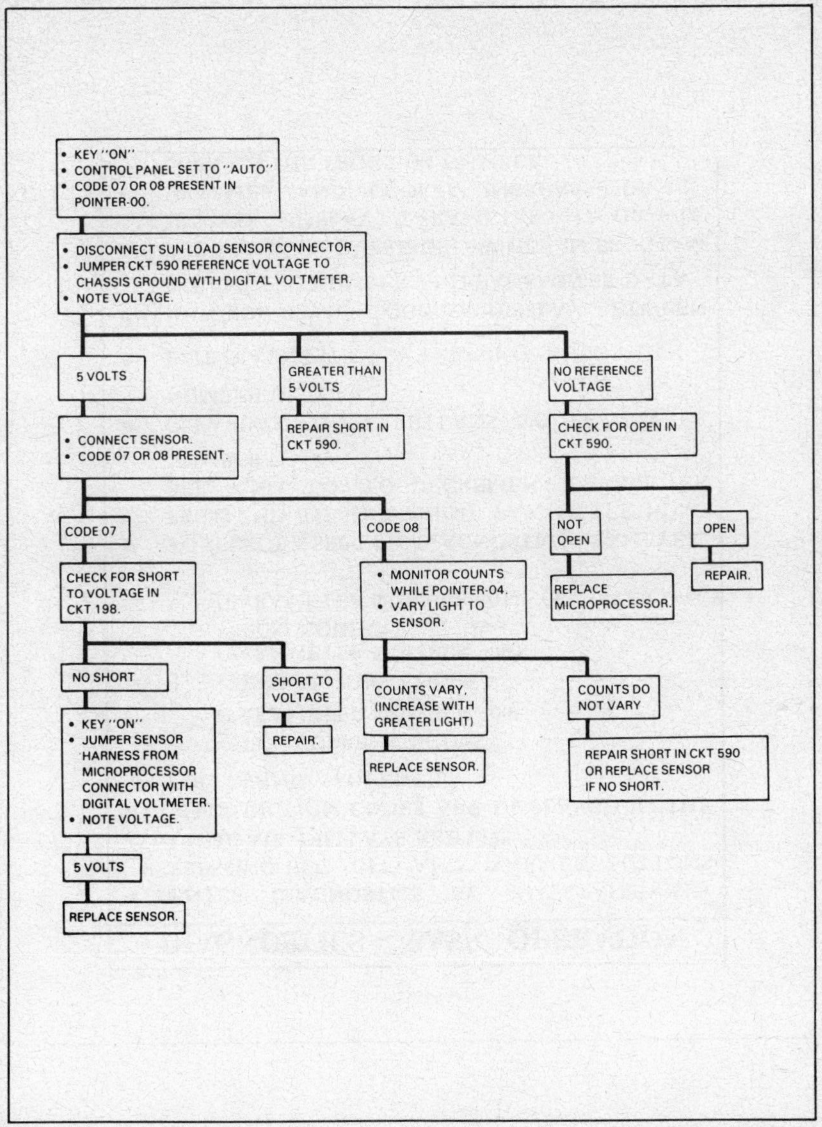
• KEY "ON"
• CONTROL PANEL SET TO "AUTO"
• CODE 07 OR 08 PRESENT IN POINTER-00.
• DISCONNECT SUN LOAD SENSOR CONNECTOR.
• JUMPER CKT 590 REFERENCE VOLTAGE TO CHASSIS GROUND WITH DIGITAL VOLTMETER.
• NOTE VOLTAGE.
5 VOLTS
GREATER THAN 5 VOLTS
NO REFERENCE VOLTAGE
• CONNECT SENSOR.
• CODE 07 OR 08 PRESENT.
REPAIR SHORT IN CKT 590.
CHECK FOR OPEN IN CKT 590.
NOT OPEN
OPEN
REPLACE MICROPROCESSOR.
REPAIR.
CODE 07
CODE 08
CHECK FOR SHORT TO VOLTAGE IN CKT 198.
• MONITOR COUNTS WHILE POINTER-04.
• VARY LIGHT TO SENSOR.
NO SHORT
SHORT TO VOLTAGE
REPAIR.
COUNTS VARY, (INCREASE WITH GREATER LIGHT)
COUNTS DO NOT VARY
REPLACE SENSOR.
REPAIR SHORT IN CKT 590 OR REPLACE SENSOR IF NO SHORT.
• KEY "ON"
• JUMPER SENSOR HARNESS FROM MICROPROCESSOR CONNECTOR WITH DIGITAL VOLTMETER.
• NOTE VOLTAGE.
5 VOLTS
REPLACE SENSOR.

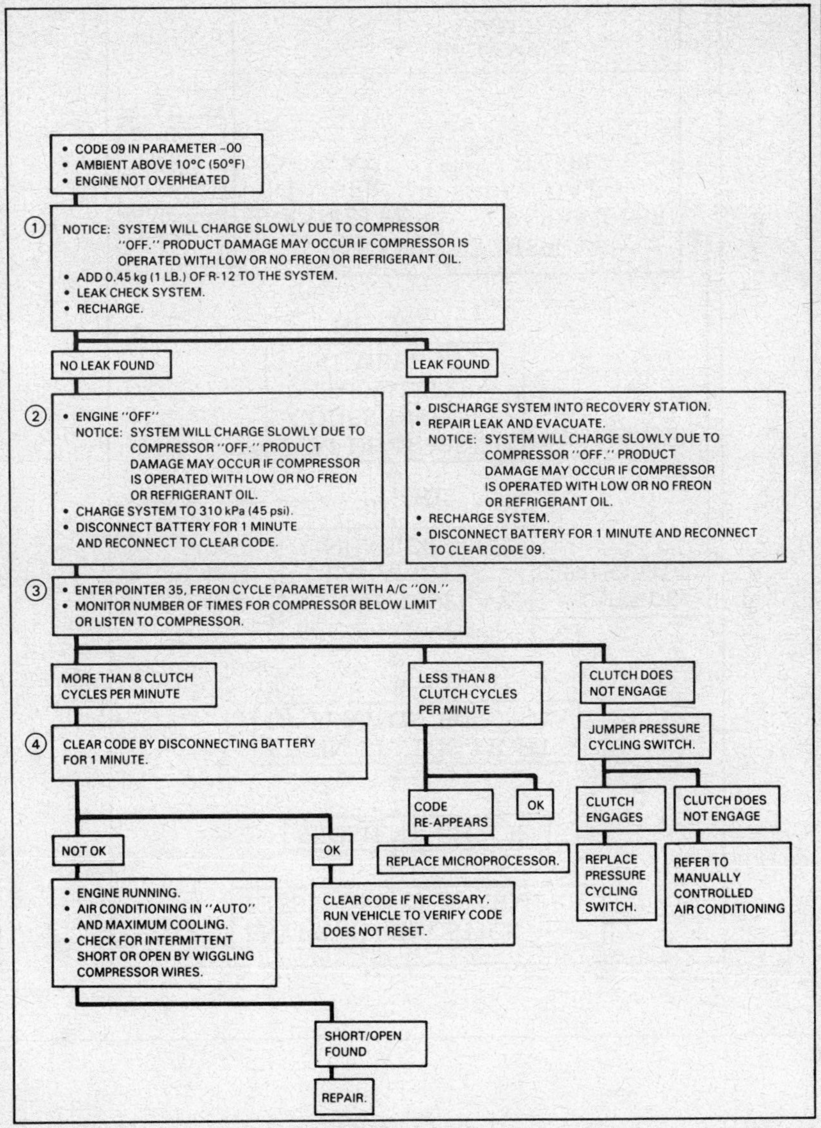
• CODE 09 IN PARAMETER -00
• AMBIENT ABOVE 10°C (50°F)
• ENGINE NOT OVERHEATED
1
NOTICE: SYSTEM WILL CHARGE SLOWLY DUE TO COMPRESSOR "OFF." PRODUCT DAMAGE MAY OCCUR IF COMPRESSOR IS OPERATED WITH LOW OR NO FREON OR REFRIGERANT OIL.
• ADD 0.45 kg (1 LB.) OF R-12 TO THE SYSTEM.
• LEAK CHECK SYSTEM.
• RECHARGE.
NO LEAK FOUND
LEAK FOUND
2
• ENGINE "OFF"
NOTICE: SYSTEM WILL CHARGE SLOWLY DUE TO COMPRESSOR "OFF." PRODUCT DAMAGE MAY OCCUR IF COMPRESSOR IS OPERATED WITH LOW OR NO FREON OR REFRIGERANT OIL.
• CHARGE SYSTEM TO 310 kPa (45 psi).
• DISCONNECT BATTERY FOR 1 MINUTE AND RECONNECT TO CLEAR CODE.
• DISCHARGE SYSTEM INTO RECOVERY STATION.
• REPAIR LEAK AND EVACUATE.
NOTICE: SYSTEM WILL CHARGE SLOWLY DUE TO COMPRESSOR "OFF." PRODUCT DAMAGE MAY OCCUR IF COMPRESSOR IS OPERATED WITH LOW OR NO FREON OR REFRIGERANT OIL.
• RECHARGE SYSTEM.
• DISCONNECT BATTERY FOR 1 MINUTE AND RECONNECT TO CLEAR CODE 09.
3
• ENTER POINTER 35, FREON CYCLE PARAMETER WITH A/C "ON."
• MONITOR NUMBER OF TIMES FOR COMPRESSOR BELOW LIMIT OR LISTEN TO COMPRESSOR.
MORE THAN 8 CLUTCH CYCLES PER MINUTE
LESS THAN 8 CLUTCH CYCLES PER MINUTE
CLUTCH DOES NOT ENGAGE
4
CLEAR CODE BY DISCONNECTING BATTERY FOR 1 MINUTE.
JUMPER PRESSURE CYCLING SWITCH.
CODE RE-APPEARS
OK
CLUTCH ENGAGES
CLUTCH DOES NOT ENGAGE
NOT OK
OK
REPLACE MICROPROCESSOR.
REPLACE PRESSURE CYCLING SWITCH.
REFER TO MANUALLY CONTROLLED AIR CONDITIONING
• ENGINE RUNNING.
• AIR CONDITIONING IN "AUTO" AND MAXIMUM COOLING.
• CHECK FOR INTERMITTENT SHORT OR OPEN BY WIGGLING COMPRESSOR WIRES.
CLEAR CODE IF NECESSARY. RUN VEHICLE TO VERIFY CODE DOES NOT RESET.
SHORT/OPEN FOUND
REPAIR.

DIAGNOSTICS – BASIC OPERATION

- ENTER DIAGNOSTICS BY SIMULTANEOUSLY PRESSING ECC 'OFF' AND 'WARMER' BUTTONS UNTIL ALL DISPLAYS ARE LIT.
- MALFUNCTION CODES ARE DISPLAYED IN THE FOLLOWING SEQUENCE:
  - . . – ECC CURRENT CODES (PARAMETER NUMBER –00)
  - 1. . – ECC HISTORY CODES (PARAMETER NUMBER –00)
  - . . – ECM CODES (PARAMETER NUMBER –01)* (5.7 LITER ONLY
- TO SELECT A SPECIFIC DIAGNOSTIC PARAMETER, PRESS 'HI' TO INCREMENT PARAMETER NUMBER, AND 'LO' TO DECREMENT PARAMETER NUMBER.
- CLEARING CODES RETURNS TO PARAMETER NUMBER DISPLAY.
- EXIT DIAGNOSTICS BY PRESSING 'AUTO'.
- 'OUTSIDE TEMP' TOGGLES DISPLAY BETWEEN PARAMETER NUMBER AND PARAMETER DATA.
- ECC PROGRAM OVERRIDE: WHILE IN PROGRAM NUMBER DISPLAY, PARAMETER –11 OR –02, 'WARMER' AND 'COOLER' INCREASES OR DECREASES THE PROGRAM NUMBER.

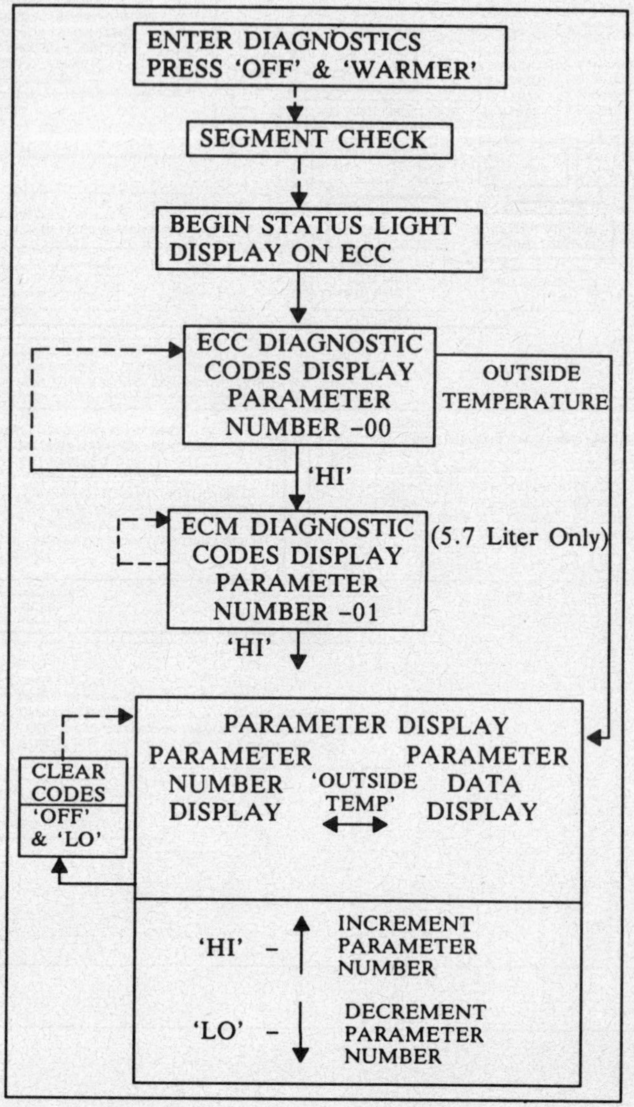
ENTER DIAGNOSTICS
PRESS 'OFF' & 'WARMER'
SEGMENT CHECK
BEGIN STATUS LIGHT DISPLAY ON ECC
ECC DIAGNOSTIC CODES DISPLAY PARAMETER NUMBER –00
OUTSIDE TEMPERATURE
'HI'
ECM DIAGNOSTIC CODES DISPLAY PARAMETER NUMBER –01
(5.7 Liter Only)
'HI'
PARAMETER DISPLAY
PARAMETER NUMBER DISPLAY
'OUTSIDE TEMP'
PARAMETER DATA DISPLAY
CLEAR CODES
'OFF' & 'LO'
'HI' – INCREMENT PARAMETER NUMBER
'LO' – DECREMENT PARAMETER NUMBER

ECC SYSTEM DIAGNOSIS—CADILLAC BROUGHAM (CONT'D)

PARAMETER NUMBER – 00

ECC DIAGNOSTIC CODES

CODE	DESCRIPTION
00	NO ECC SYSTEM FAULTS
10	OUTSIDE AIR TEMPERATURE SENSOR CIRCUIT PROBLEM
12	EVAPORATOR INLET SENSOR CIRCUIT PROBLEM
13	IN-CAR TEMPERATURE SENSOR CIRCUIT PROBLEM
19	BLOWER MOTOR PROBLEM
32	ECM-ECC DATA PROBLEM *
40	AIR MIX VALVE PROBLEM
48	VERY LOW A/C REFRIGERANT PRESSURE CONDITION (COMP. OFF) *
49	HIGH ENGINE TEMPERATURE (COMP. OFF) *
55	SHORTED COOLANT TEMPERATURE SENSOR **

* 5.7 LITER ONLY
** 5.0 LITER ONLY

PARAMETER NUMBER – 01

ECM DIAGNOSTIC CODES *

CODE	DESCRIPTION
00	NO ECM FAULTS
12	NO ENGINE RPM REFERENCE PULSES
13	OXYGEN SENSOR CIRCUIT FAULT
14	SHORTED COOLANT SENSOR CIRCUIT
15	OPEN COOLANT SENSOR CIRCUIT
21	OPEN THROTTLE POSITION SENSOR CIRCUIT
22	SHORTED THROTTLE POSITION SENSOR CIRCUIT
23	OPEN MAT SENSOR CIRCUIT
24	VEHICLE SPEED SENSOR CIRCUIT PROBLEM
25	SHORTED MAT SENSOR CIRCUIT
32	EGR SYSTEM FAULT
33	OPEN MAP SENSOR CIRCUIT
34	SHORTED MAP SENSOR CIRCUIT
42	EST/BYPASS CIRCUIT PROBLEM
43	ESC FAILURE
44	LEAN OXYGEN SIGNAL
45	RICH OXYGEN SIGNAL
51	PROM ERROR
52	BACKUP FUEL CAL-PAK MISSING
53	VATS CIRCUIT MALFUNCTION
54	FUEL PUMP RELAY FAILURE
55	A/D CONVERTER ERROR

* 5.7 LITER ONLY

STATUS LIGHTS

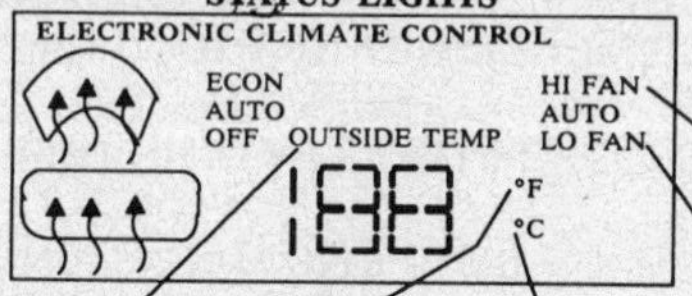
ELECTRONIC CLIMATE CONTROL
ECON
AUTO
OFF
OUTSIDE TEMP
HI FAN
AUTO
LO FAN
°F
°C

ECC STATUS LIGHT DISPLAY	FUNCTION	A/C CLUTCH COMMAND	COMPRESSOR LOW PRESSURE SWITCH INPUT	HEATER WATER VALVE OUTPUT	A/C-HTR MODE VALVE OUTPUT	DEF-HTR MODE VALVE OUTPUT
	INDICATOR	OUTSIDE TEMP	°F	°C	LO FAN	HI FAN
	LIGHT ON	ENABLES	OPEN (LOW PRESSURE)	OPEN	A/C	DEF/A/C
	LIGHT OFF	DISABLED	CLOSED	CLOSED (MAX A/C	HEATER/ DEFROST	HEATER

PARAMETERS

NUMBER	DESCRIPTION	RANGE	UNITS
-00	ECC SYSTEM FAULTS †		CODE
-01	ECM FAULTS * ††		CODE
-02	PROGRAM NUMBER (IN COUNTS) **	0 - 255‡	COUNTS
-10	IGNITION VOLTAGE	9.0 - 16.0	VOLTS
-11	PROGRAM NUMBER (IN PERCENT) **	0 - 100	%
-12	VEHICLE SPEED	0 - 199	MPH
-19	ACTUAL BLOWER VOLTAGE	-3.3 - 18.0	VOLTS
-20	COMMANDED BLOWER VOLTAGE	-3.3 - 18.0	VOLTS
-21	ENGINE COOLANT TEMPERATURE	-22 - 161	°C
-22	COMMANDED MIX VALVE POSITION	0 - 255‡	COUNTS
-23	ACTUAL MIX VALVE POSITION	0 - 255‡	COUNTS
-24	AIR DELIVERY MODE	0 - 6	CODE⊕
-25	IN-CAR TEMPERATURE	-40 - 102	°C
-26	OUTSIDE AIR TEMPERATURE	-40 - 93	°C
-28	EVAPORATOR INLET TEMPERATURE	-40 - 93	°C
-29	5.0 LITER VS. 5.7 LITER ENGINE (00 - 5.0 L, 01 - 5.7 L)	00 - 01	CODE
-30	IGNITION CYCLE COUNTER	0 - 99	COUNTS
-31	HVAC CALIBRATION I.D.	0 - 999	CODE❑

❑ PROM ID CODE NUMBER IDENTIFIES AN INDIVIDUAL CALIBRATION AND IS PERIODICALLY UPDATED: REFER TO LATEST SERVICE PUBLICATION FOR CORRECT ID NUMBER

* 5.7 LITER ENGINE ONLY

** 'WARMER' INCREASES PROGRAM NUMBER: 'COOLER' DECREASES PROGRAM NUMBER

‡ FOR PARAMETER VALUES GREATER THAN 199; THE LEADING 2 IS DISPLAYED AS 7 (I.E. 255 = 755)

AIR DELIVERY MODE

CODE NO.	MODE
0	MAX A/C
1	A/C
2	HEATER/DEFROST
3	HEATER
4	DEFROST
5	DELAY
6	OFF

ECC SYSTEM DIAGNOSIS—CADILLAC BROUGHAM (CONT'D)

ECC SYSTEM CHECK

- IF YOU HAVE NOT REVIEWED THE BASIC INFORMATION ON THE COMPUTER SELF-DIAGNOSTICS SEE CONTENTS UNDER "SELF DIAGNOSTIC FEATURES" IN THIS SECTION.

(1)
- IGNITION 'ON'
- DOES CCP DISPLAY AND RESPOND TO KEYBOARD PUSHBUTTONS?

YES — go to step 2 | NO — SEE CHART A

(2)
- ENTER DIAGNOSTICS
- ARE ANY TROUBLE CODES DISPLAYED?

NO — go to step 3 | YES — SEE CORRESPONDING CHART

(3)
- EXIT DIAGNOSTICS
- SELECT 'LO' TEMP.
- AMBIENT TEMPERATURE MUST BE ABOVE 50°F
- DOES COMPRESSOR OPERATE?

YES — see complaint list below | NO — SEE CHART B FOR 5.0 LITER ENGINE; SEE CHART B, FOR 5.7 LITER ENGINE

- IF OWNER'S COMPLAINT IS:

IF OWNER'S COMPLAINT IS:	SEE CHART NUMBER:
– IMPROPER AIR DELIVERY	C
– INSUFFICIENT OR NO COOLING	D
– INSUFFICIENT OR NO HEATING	E
– IMPROPER REAR DEFOGGER OPERATION	F
– IMPROPER BLOWER SPEED	19

WHEN ALL DIAGNOSIS AND REPAIRS ARE COMPLETED, CLEAR CODES AND VERIFY OPERATION

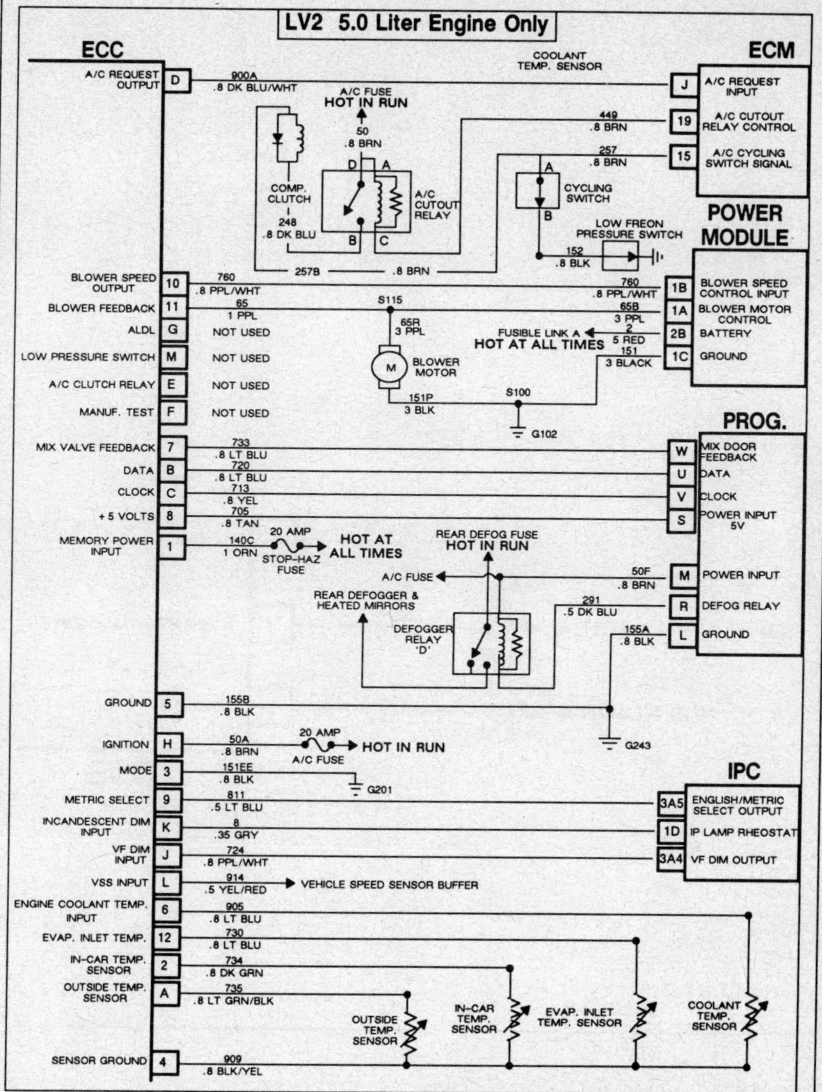
LV2 5.0 Liter Engine Only
ECC
ECM
POWER MODULE
PROG.
IPC
A/C REQUEST OUTPUT
BLOWER SPEED OUTPUT
BLOWER FEEDBACK
ALDL
LOW PRESSURE SWITCH
A/C CLUTCH RELAY
MANUF. TEST
MIX VALVE FEEDBACK
DATA
CLOCK
+5 VOLTS
MEMORY POWER INPUT
GROUND
IGNITION
MODE
METRIC SELECT
INCANDESCENT DIM INPUT
VF DIM INPUT
VSS INPUT
ENGINE COOLANT TEMP. INPUT
EVAP. INLET TEMP.
IN-CAR TEMP. SENSOR
OUTSIDE TEMP. SENSOR
SENSOR GROUND
NOT USED
A/C REQUEST INPUT
A/C CUTOUT RELAY CONTROL
A/C CYCLING SWITCH SIGNAL
BLOWER SPEED CONTROL INPUT
BLOWER MOTOR CONTROL
BATTERY
MIX DOOR FEEDBACK
POWER INPUT 5V
POWER INPUT
DEFOG RELAY
ENGLISH/METRIC SELECT OUTPUT
IP LAMP RHEOSTAT
VF DIM OUTPUT
COOLANT TEMP. SENSOR
A/C FUSE HOT IN RUN
COMP. CLUTCH
A/C CUTOUT RELAY
CYCLING SWITCH
LOW FREON PRESSURE SWITCH
BLOWER MOTOR
FUSIBLE LINK A
HOT AT ALL TIMES
20 AMP STOP-HAZ FUSE
REAR DEFOG FUSE HOT IN RUN
A/C FUSE
REAR DEFOGGER & HEATED MIRRORS
DEFOGGER RELAY 'D'
20 AMP A/C FUSE
HOT IN RUN
VEHICLE SPEED SENSOR BUFFER
OUTSIDE TEMP. SENSOR
IN-CAR TEMP. SENSOR
EVAP. INLET TEMP. SENSOR
S115
S100
G102
G243
G201
900A .8 DK BLU/WHT
449 .8 BRN
257 .8 BRN
248 .8 DK BLU
257B
152 .8 BLK
760 .8 PPL/WHT
65 1 PPL
65B 3 PPL
65R 3 PPL
2 5 RED
151 3 BLACK
151P 3 BLK
733 .8 LT BLU
720 .8 LT BLU
713 .8 YEL
705 .8 TAN
140C 1 ORN
50F .8 BRN
291 .5 DK BLU
155A .8 BLK
155B .8 BLK
50A .8 BRN
151EE .8 BLK
811 .5 LT BLU
8 .35 GRY
724 .8 PPL/WHT
914 .5 YEL/RED
905 .8 LT BLU
730 .8 LT BLU
734 .8 DK GRN
735 .8 LT GRN/BLK
909 .8 BLK/YEL

ECC SYSTEM DIAGNOSIS—CADILLAC BROUGHAM (CONT'D)

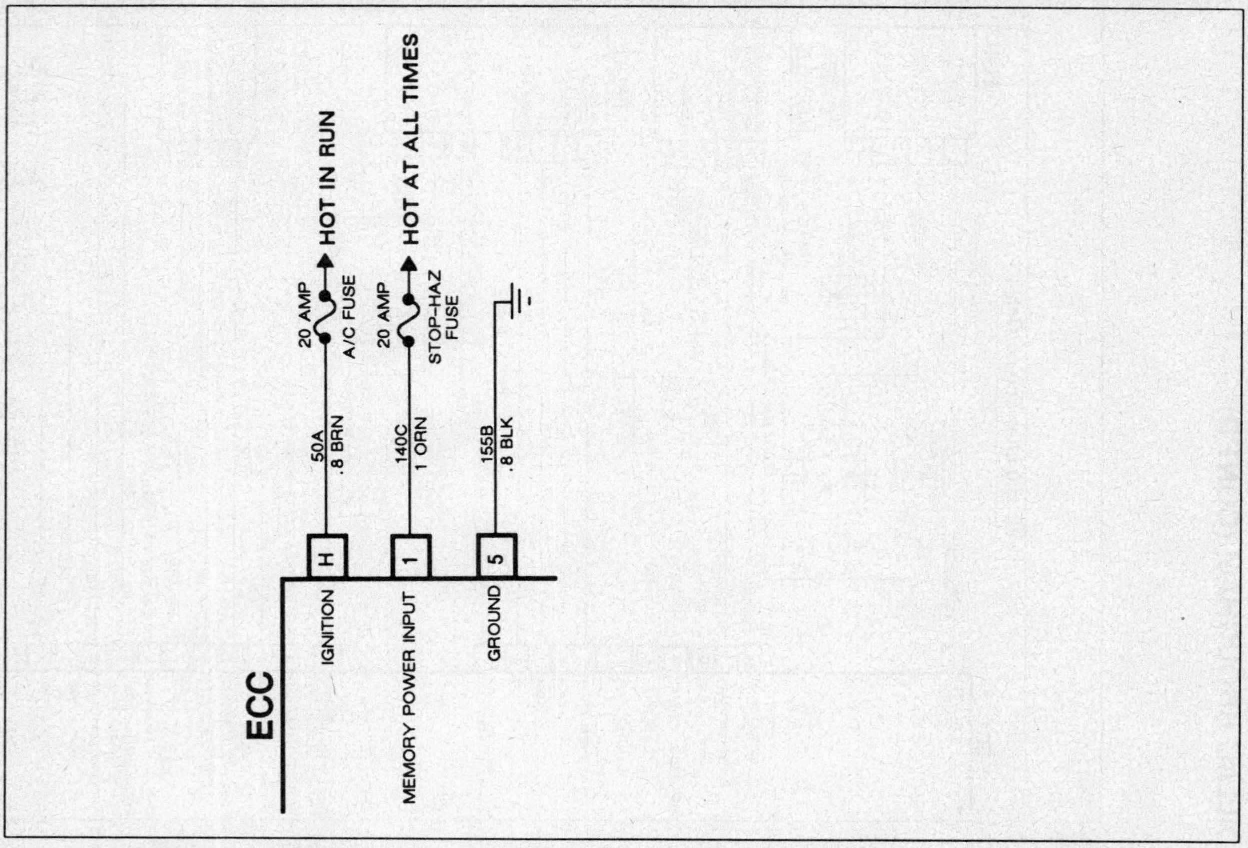
ECC
IGNITION
MEMORY POWER INPUT
GROUND
H
1
5
50A
.8 BRN
140C
1 ORN
155B
.8 BLK
20 AMP
A/C FUSE
HOT IN RUN
20 AMP
STOP-HAZ FUSE
HOT AT ALL TIMES

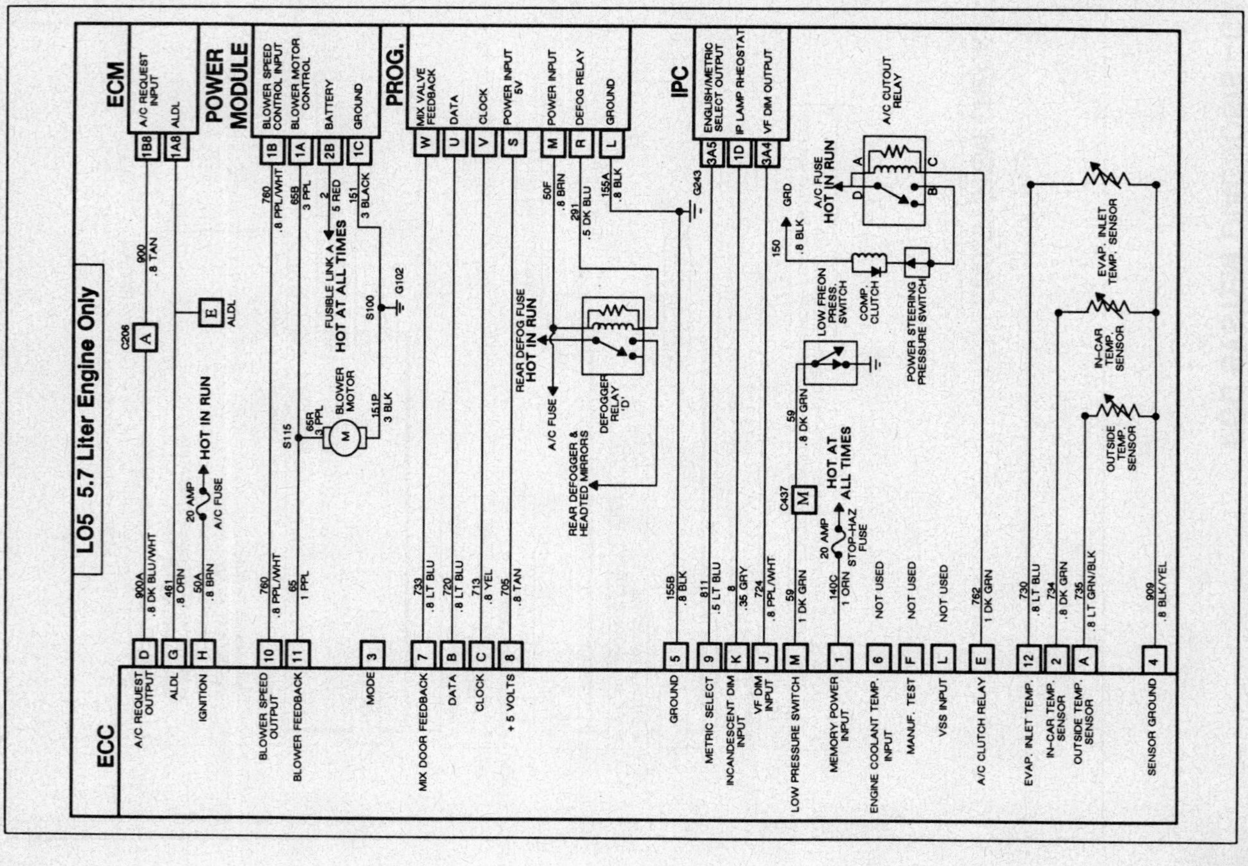
LO5 5.7 Liter Engine Only
ECC
A/C REQUEST OUTPUT
ALDL
IGNITION
BLOWER SPEED OUTPUT
BLOWER FEEDBACK
MODE
MIX DOOR FEEDBACK
DATA
CLOCK
+5 VOLTS
GROUND
METRIC SELECT
INCANDESCENT DIM INPUT
VF DIM INPUT
LOW PRESSURE SWITCH
MEMORY POWER INPUT
ENGINE COOLANT TEMP. INPUT
MANUF. TEST
VSS INPUT
A/C CLUTCH RELAY
EVAP. INLET TEMP.
IN-CAR TEMP. SENSOR
OUTSIDE TEMP. SENSOR
SENSOR GROUND
ECM
A/C REQUEST INPUT
POWER MODULE
BLOWER SPEED CONTROL INPUT
BLOWER MOTOR CONTROL
BATTERY
PROG.
MIX VALVE FEEDBACK
POWER INPUT 5V
POWER INPUT
DEFOG RELAY
IPC
ENGLISH/METRIC SELECT OUTPUT
IP LAMP RHEOSTAT
VF DIM OUTPUT
A/C CUTOUT RELAY
BLOWER MOTOR
FUSIBLE LINK A
HOT AT ALL TIMES
HOT IN RUN
A/C FUSE
20 AMP
STOP-HAZ FUSE
REAR DEFOG FUSE
DEFOGGER RELAY 'D'
REAR DEFOGGER & HEADED MIRRORS
LOW FREON PRESS. SWITCH
COMP. CLUTCH
POWER STEERING PRESSURE SWITCH
EVAP. INLET TEMP. SENSOR
IN-CAR TEMP. SENSOR
OUTSIDE TEMP. SENSOR
NOT USED

ECC SYSTEM DIAGNOSIS—CADILLAC BROUGHAM (CONT'D)

CHART A
NO DISPLAY ON CCP

- TURN IGNITION "ON". TURN HEADLAMPS "OFF"

(1) CHECK FOR BLOWN A/C OR STOP-HAZ FUSE

- FUSES OK → (2)
- A/C FUSE BLOWN
  - REPAIR SHORT IN CKT 50
  - REPLACE A/C FUSE
- STOP-HAZ FUSE BLOWN
  - REPAIR SHORT IN CKT 140C
  - REPLACE STOP-HAZ FUSE

(2)
- MEASURE VOLTAGE FROM ECC CONN. PIN H TO EXTERNAL GROUND
- GREATER THAN 10 VOLTS?

- YES → (3)
- NO → REPAIR OPEN IN CKT 50

(3)
- MEASURE VOLTAGE FROM ECC CONN. PIN 1 TO EXTERNAL GROUND
- GREATER THAN 10 VOLTS?

- YES → (4)
- NO → REPAIR OPEN IN CKT 140C

(4)
- MEASURE VOLTAGE BETWEEN ECC CONN. PIN 1 AND 5
- GREATER THAN 10 VOLTS?

- YES → (5)
- NO → REPAIR OPEN IN CKT 155

(5) CHECK FOR FAULTY ECC CONNECTOR OR FAULTY ECC HEAD

WHEN ALL DIAGNOSIS AND REPAIRS ARE COMPLETED, CLEAR CODES AND VERIFY OPERATION

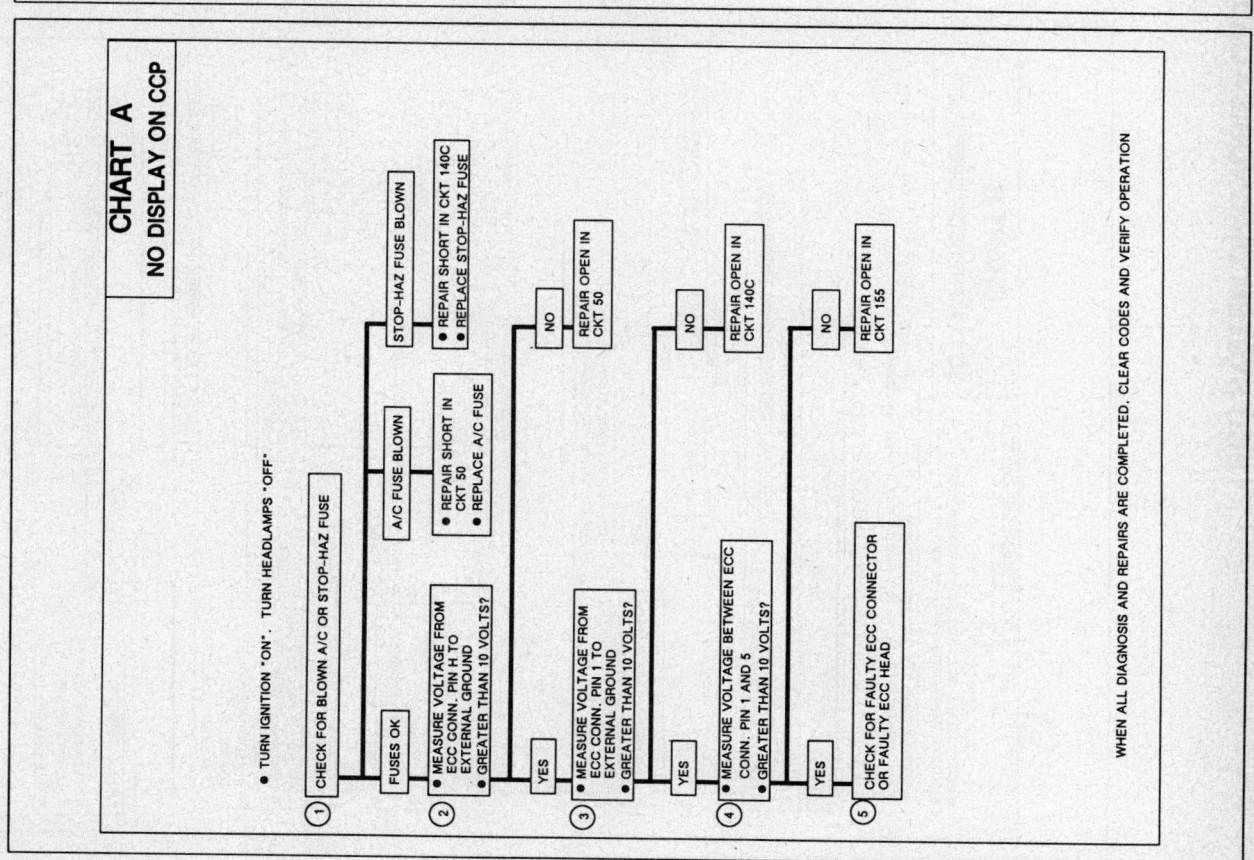

LV2 5.0 LITER ENGINE ONLY

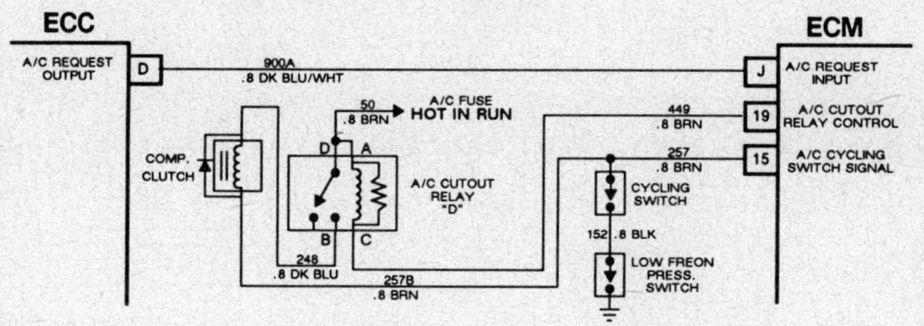
ECC
A/C REQUEST OUTPUT
D
900A
.8 DK BLU/WHT
50
.8 BRN
A/C FUSE
HOT IN RUN
COMP. CLUTCH
A/C CUTOUT RELAY "D"
248
.8 DK BLU
257B
.8 BRN
449
.8 BRN
257
.8 BRN
CYCLING SWITCH
152 .8 BLK
LOW FREON PRESS. SWITCH
ECM
J
A/C REQUEST INPUT
19
A/C CUTOUT RELAY CONTROL
15
A/C CYCLING SWITCH SIGNAL

ECC SYSTEM DIAGNOSIS—CADILLAC BROUGHAM (CONT'D)

CHART B
NO COMPRESSOR OPERATION

LV2 5.0 LITER ENGINE ONLY

- ECC SYSTEM CHECK MUST BE PERFORMED FIRST
- OUTSIDE TEMPERATURE MUST BE ABOVE 43°F

- TURN IGNITION "ON" AND START ENGINE
- ENGINE WARM AND IDLING, SET ECC TO "AUTO" AND "60" TEMP.
- ENTER DIAGNOSTICS
- DOES A/C CLUTCH STATUS LIGHT (OUTSIDE TEMP.) REMAIN ON?

NO:
- CHECK PARAMETER -26
- DOES IT AGREE WITH AMBIENT TEMPERATURE?
  - **YES:** REPLACE ECC HEAD
  - **NO:** ALLOW SEVERAL MINUTES FOR OAT READING TO ADJUST, REPLACE OAT SENSOR IF STILL DOENS'T AGREE WITH AMBIENT TEMPERATURE.

YES:
- DISCONNECT UNDERHOOD A/C RELAY
- JUMPER PIN D TO B
- DOES COMPRESSOR ENGAGE?

YES:
- REMOVE JUMPER
- MEASURE VOLTAGE AT PIN A
- GREATER THAN 10 VOLTS?
  - **NO:** REPAIR OPEN IN CKT 50 BETWEEEN PIN A AND D OF A/C CUTOUT RELAY
  - **YES:**
    - RECONNECT A/C RELAY
    - GROUND PIN C
    - DOES COMP. ENGAGE?
      - **NO:** REPLACE A/C RELAY
      - **YES:**
        - UNGROUND PIN C
        - DISCONNECT ECM CONNECTOR
        - MEASURE VOLTAGE AT ECM PIN 19
        - LESS THAN 0.5 VOLTS?
          - **YES:** REPAIR OPEN IN CKT 449
          - **NO:**
            - CHECK TERMINAL CONTACT
            - CHECK FOR A FAULTY A/C CYCLING SWITCH
            - REPLACE ECM

NO:
- MEASURE VOLTAGE AT PIN D
- GREATER THAN 10 VOLTS?
  - **NO:**
    - RECONNECT A/C RELAY
    - CHECK FOR A BLOWN A/C FUSE
    - CHECK FOR AN OPEN IN CKT 50
  - **YES:**
    - MEASURE VOLTAGE AT COMPRESSOR ON CKT 248
    - GREATER THAN 10 VOLTS?
      - **NO:** REPAIR OPEN IN CKT 248
      - **YES:**
        - DISCONNECT CYCLING SWITCH
        - MEASURE VOLTAGE AT COMPRESSOR CKT 257B
        - GREATER THAN 10 VOLTS?
          - **NO:** REPLACE COMP. CLUTCH COIL
          - **YES:**
            - JUMPER CYCLING SWITCH CONNECTOR
            - GREATER THAN 10 VOLTS?
              - **NO:** REPLACE CYCLING SWITCH
              - **YES:**
                - DISCONNECT LOW PRESSURE SWITCH
                - JUMPER SWITCH CONNECTOR
                - GREATER THAN 10 VOLTS?
                  - **YES:** OPEN IN CKT 152 OR CKT 257
                  - **NO:** REFRIGERANT CHECK

LO5 5.7 Liter Engine Only

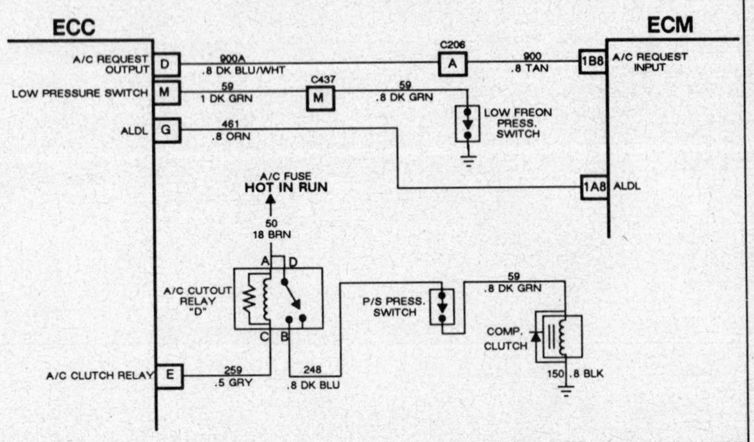
ECC
ECM
A/C REQUEST OUTPUT
D
900A
.8 DK BLU/WHT
C206
A
900
.8 TAN
1B8
A/C REQUEST INPUT
LOW PRESSURE SWITCH
M
59
1 DK GRN
C437
M
59
.8 DK GRN
LOW FREON PRESS. SWITCH
ALDL
G
461
.8 ORN
1A8
ALDL
A/C FUSE
HOT IN RUN
50
18 BRN
A/C CUTOUT RELAY "D"
A
D
C
B
P/S PRESS. SWITCH
59
.8 DK GRN
COMP. CLUTCH
A/C CLUTCH RELAY
E
259
.5 GRY
248
.8 DK BLU
150
.8 BLK

ECC SYSTEM DIAGNOSIS—CADILLAC BROUGHAM (CONT'D)

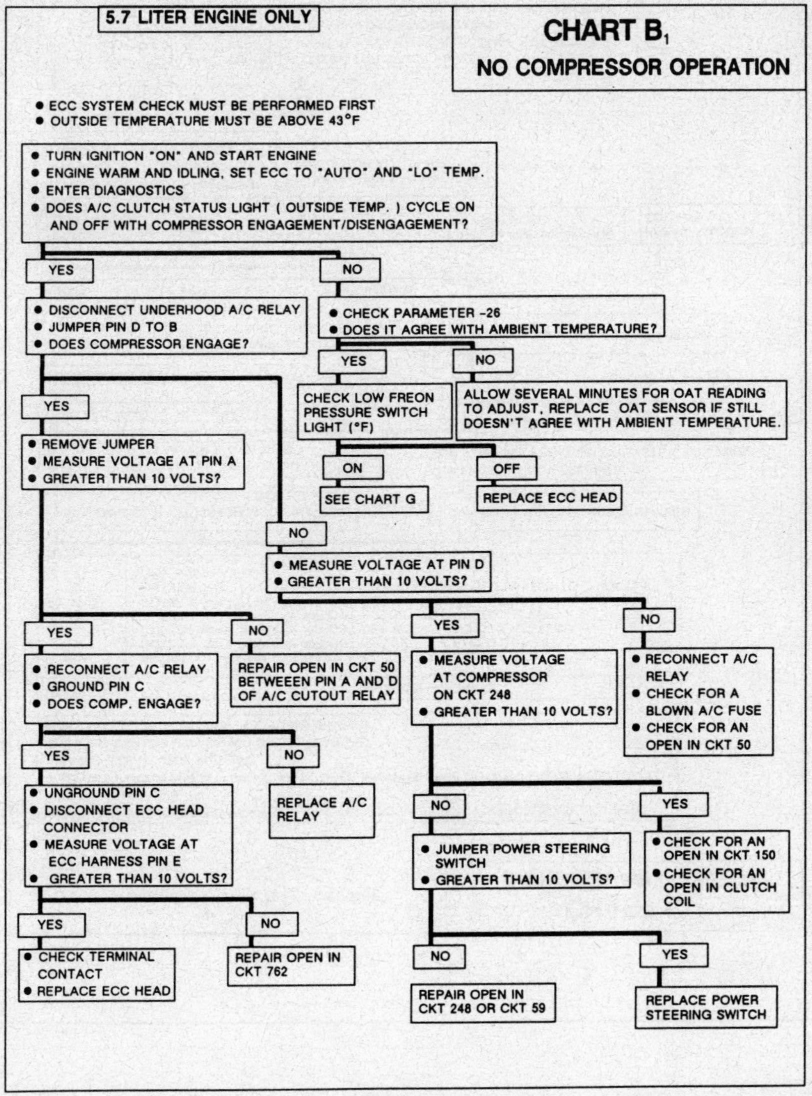
5.7 LITER ENGINE ONLY
CHART B1
NO COMPRESSOR OPERATION
• ECC SYSTEM CHECK MUST BE PERFORMED FIRST
• OUTSIDE TEMPERATURE MUST BE ABOVE 43°F
• TURN IGNITION "ON" AND START ENGINE
• ENGINE WARM AND IDLING, SET ECC TO "AUTO" AND "LO" TEMP.
• ENTER DIAGNOSTICS
• DOES A/C CLUTCH STATUS LIGHT (OUTSIDE TEMP.) CYCLE ON AND OFF WITH COMPRESSOR ENGAGEMENT/DISENGAGEMENT?
YES
NO
• DISCONNECT UNDERHOOD A/C RELAY
• JUMPER PIN D TO B
• DOES COMPRESSOR ENGAGE?
• CHECK PARAMETER -26
• DOES IT AGREE WITH AMBIENT TEMPERATURE?
YES
NO
CHECK LOW FREON PRESSURE SWITCH LIGHT (°F)
ALLOW SEVERAL MINUTES FOR OAT READING TO ADJUST, REPLACE OAT SENSOR IF STILL DOESN'T AGREE WITH AMBIENT TEMPERATURE.
ON
OFF
SEE CHART G
REPLACE ECC HEAD
YES
• REMOVE JUMPER
• MEASURE VOLTAGE AT PIN A
• GREATER THAN 10 VOLTS?
NO
• MEASURE VOLTAGE AT PIN D
• GREATER THAN 10 VOLTS?
YES
NO
• RECONNECT A/C RELAY
• GROUND PIN C
• DOES COMP. ENGAGE?
REPAIR OPEN IN CKT 50 BETWEEEN PIN A AND D OF A/C CUTOUT RELAY
YES
NO
• MEASURE VOLTAGE AT COMPRESSOR ON CKT 248
• GREATER THAN 10 VOLTS?
• RECONNECT A/C RELAY
• CHECK FOR A BLOWN A/C FUSE
• CHECK FOR AN OPEN IN CKT 50
YES
NO
• UNGROUND PIN C
• DISCONNECT ECC HEAD CONNECTOR
• MEASURE VOLTAGE AT ECC HARNESS PIN E
• GREATER THAN 10 VOLTS?
REPLACE A/C RELAY
NO
YES
• JUMPER POWER STEERING SWITCH
• GREATER THAN 10 VOLTS?
• CHECK FOR AN OPEN IN CKT 150
• CHECK FOR AN OPEN IN CLUTCH COIL
YES
NO
• CHECK TERMINAL CONTACT
• REPLACE ECC HEAD
REPAIR OPEN IN CKT 762
NO
YES
REPAIR OPEN IN CKT 248 OR CKT 59
REPLACE POWER STEERING SWITCH

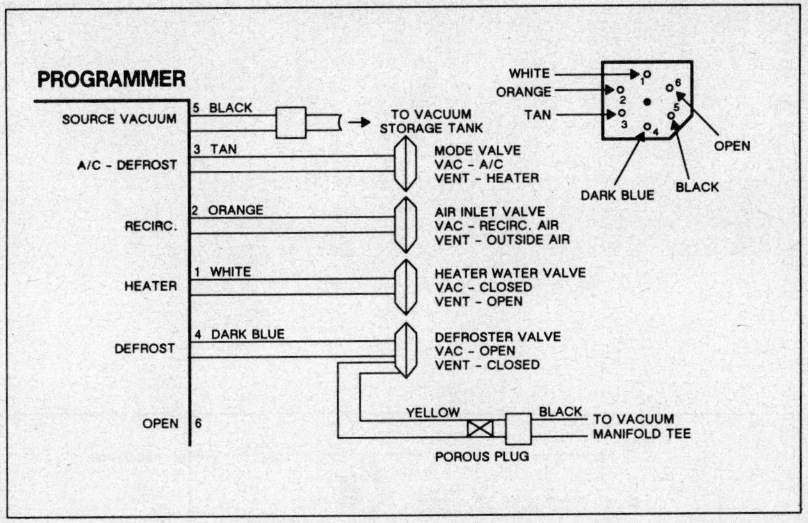
PROGRAMMER
SOURCE VACUUM
5 BLACK
TO VACUUM STORAGE TANK
A/C - DEFROST
3 TAN
MODE VALVE
VAC - A/C
VENT - HEATER
RECIRC.
2 ORANGE
AIR INLET VALVE
VAC - RECIRC. AIR
VENT - OUTSIDE AIR
HEATER
1 WHITE
HEATER WATER VALVE
VAC - CLOSED
VENT - OPEN
DEFROST
4 DARK BLUE
DEFROSTER VALVE
VAC - OPEN
VENT - CLOSED
OPEN
6
YELLOW
BLACK
TO VACUUM MANIFOLD TEE
POROUS PLUG
WHITE
ORANGE
TAN
OPEN
DARK BLUE
BLACK

CHART C
IMPROPER AIR DELIVERY

- ECC SYSTEM CHECK MUST BE PERFORMED FIRST

(1)
- ENGINE RUNNING, SELECT AN ECC MODE THAT RESULTS IN AN IMPROPER AIR DELIVERY
- ENTER DIAGNOSIS
- SELECT PARAMETER -11, PROGRAM NUMBER AND PUSH THE COOLER/WARMER BUTTON TO INITIATE OVER-RIDE FEATURE
- SELECT PARAMETER -24, AIR DELIVERY MODE
- NOTE AIRFLOW FOR CORRESPONDING NUMBER

MODE NO.	NORMAL AIR FLOW
0	RECIRCULATED AIR - PRIMARY AIR OUT A/C VENTS & BLEED OUT DEF
1	OUTSIDE AIR - PRIMARY AIR OUT A/C VENTS & BLEED OUT DEF
2	OUTSIDE AIR - PRIMARY AIR OUT DEF WITH BLEED OUT HEATER
3	OUTSIDE AIR - PRIMARY AIR OUT FLOOR WITH BLEED OUT DEF
4	OUTSIDE AIR - PRIMARY AIR OUT DEF WITH BLEED OUT HEATER
5	OUTSIDE AIR - PRIMARY AIR DEF WITH BLOWER SPEED LIMITED TO 7 VOLTS
6	OFF - NO AIR FLOW

AIR FLOW DOES NOT MATCH MODE NUMBER

(2)
- REMOVE PROGRAMMER VACUUM CONNECTOR
- MEASURE VACUUM ON BLACK HOSE

GREATER THAN 10 INCHES HG.

TURN ENGINE OFF

(3)
- ATTACH HAND HELD VACUUM PUMP TO VACUUM CIRCUITS: TAN, WHITE, DARK BLUE, ORANGE.
- DO VACUUM CIRCUITS HOLD VACUUM?

(NOTE: DARK BLUE HOSE WILL SLOWLY LEAK VACUUM)

YES

TURN IGNITION OFF

- CHECK VOLTAGE BETWEEN PIN 'M' AND 'L' OF PROGRAMMER
- GREATER THAN 10 VOLTS?

NO

REPAIR OPEN CKT 50 F BETWEEN SPLICE 433 AND PIN 'M'

YES

- CHECK FOR STUCK VALVES:
  - AIR ALWAYS OR NEVER COMES OUT FLOOR: CHECK LOWER MODE VALVE
  - AIR COMES OUT DEF BUT NOT A/C VENTS OR COMES OUT A/C VENTS BUT NOT DEF: CHECK UPPER MODE VALVE
- IF VALVES ARE NOT STUCK BUT IMPROPER AIR DELIVERY CONTINUES, REPLACE PROGRAMMER

NO

REPAIR AFFECTED VACUUM CIRCUIT OR ACTUATOR

LOWER THAN 10 INCHES HG.

DOES PARKING BRAKE RELEASE OK?

YES

REPAIR KINK IN VACUUM SUPPLY HOSE

NO

REPAIR VACUUM SOURCE

AIR FLOW MATCHES MODE NUMBER

- PROBLEM NOT PRESENT
- EXPLAIN OPERATION OF SYSTEM TO OWNER

WHEN ALL DIAGNOSIS AND REPAIRS ARE COMPLETED, CLEAR CODES AND VERIFY OPERATION

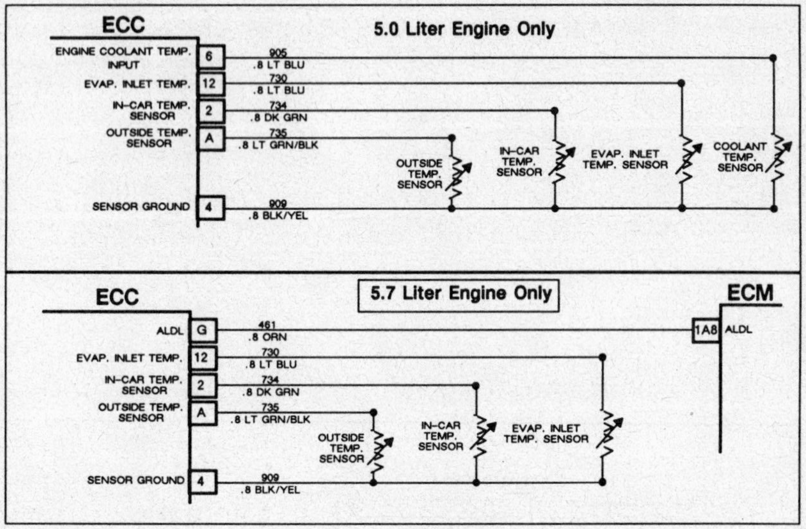
ECC
5.0 Liter Engine Only
ENGINE COOLANT TEMP. INPUT
6
905
.8 LT BLU
EVAP. INLET TEMP.
12
730
.8 LT BLU
IN-CAR TEMP. SENSOR
2
734
.8 DK GRN
OUTSIDE TEMP. SENSOR
A
735
.8 LT GRN/BLK
SENSOR GROUND
4
909
.8 BLK/YEL
OUTSIDE TEMP. SENSOR
IN-CAR TEMP. SENSOR
EVAP. INLET TEMP. SENSOR
COOLANT TEMP. SENSOR
ECC
5.7 Liter Engine Only
ECM
ALDL
G
461
.8 ORN
1A8
ALDL
EVAP. INLET TEMP.
12
730
.8 LT BLU
IN-CAR TEMP. SENSOR
2
734
.8 DK GRN
OUTSIDE TEMP. SENSOR
A
735
.8 LT GRN/BLK
SENSOR GROUND
4
909
.8 BLK/YEL
OUTSIDE TEMP. SENSOR
IN-CAR TEMP. SENSOR
EVAP. INLET TEMP. SENSOR

ECC SYSTEM DIAGNOSIS—CADILLAC BROUGHAM (CONT'D)

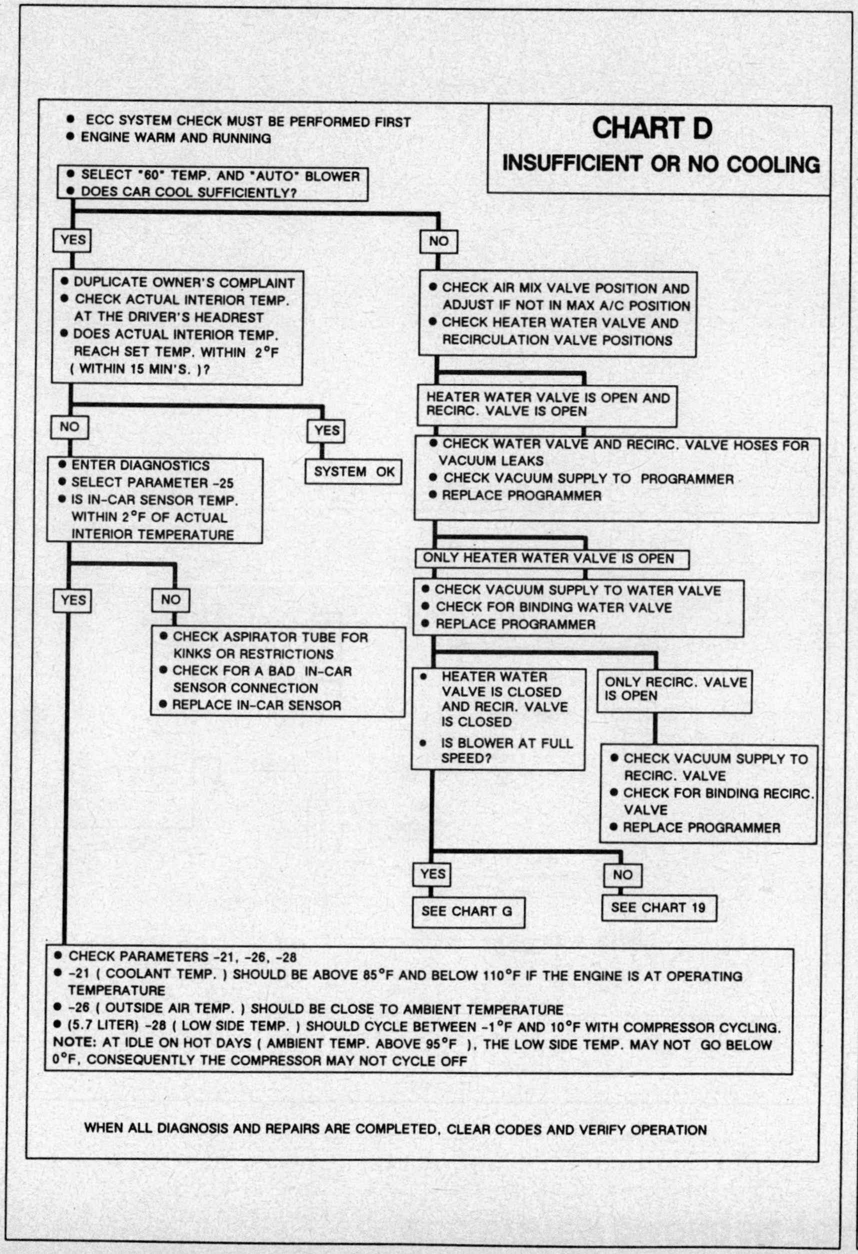
CHART D
INSUFFICIENT OR NO COOLING
• ECC SYSTEM CHECK MUST BE PERFORMED FIRST
• ENGINE WARM AND RUNNING
• SELECT "60" TEMP. AND "AUTO" BLOWER
• DOES CAR COOL SUFFICIENTLY?
YES
NO
• DUPLICATE OWNER'S COMPLAINT
• CHECK ACTUAL INTERIOR TEMP. AT THE DRIVER'S HEADREST
• DOES ACTUAL INTERIOR TEMP. REACH SET TEMP. WITHIN 2°F (WITHIN 15 MIN'S.)?
• CHECK AIR MIX VALVE POSITION AND ADJUST IF NOT IN MAX A/C POSITION
• CHECK HEATER WATER VALVE AND RECIRCULATION VALVE POSITIONS
HEATER WATER VALVE IS OPEN AND RECIRC. VALVE IS OPEN
• CHECK WATER VALVE AND RECIRC. VALVE HOSES FOR VACUUM LEAKS
• CHECK VACUUM SUPPLY TO PROGRAMMER
• REPLACE PROGRAMMER
NO
YES
SYSTEM OK
• ENTER DIAGNOSTICS
• SELECT PARAMETER -25
• IS IN-CAR SENSOR TEMP. WITHIN 2°F OF ACTUAL INTERIOR TEMPERATURE
ONLY HEATER WATER VALVE IS OPEN
• CHECK VACUUM SUPPLY TO WATER VALVE
• CHECK FOR BINDING WATER VALVE
• REPLACE PROGRAMMER
YES
NO
• CHECK ASPIRATOR TUBE FOR KINKS OR RESTRICTIONS
• CHECK FOR A BAD IN-CAR SENSOR CONNECTION
• REPLACE IN-CAR SENSOR
• HEATER WATER VALVE IS CLOSED AND RECIR. VALVE IS CLOSED
• IS BLOWER AT FULL SPEED?
ONLY RECIRC. VALVE IS OPEN
• CHECK VACUUM SUPPLY TO RECIRC. VALVE
• CHECK FOR BINDING RECIRC. VALVE
• REPLACE PROGRAMMER
YES
NO
SEE CHART G
SEE CHART 19
• CHECK PARAMETERS -21, -26, -28
• -21 (COOLANT TEMP.) SHOULD BE ABOVE 85°F AND BELOW 110°F IF THE ENGINE IS AT OPERATING TEMPERATURE
• -26 (OUTSIDE AIR TEMP.) SHOULD BE CLOSE TO AMBIENT TEMPERATURE
• (5.7 LITER) -28 (LOW SIDE TEMP.) SHOULD CYCLE BETWEEN -1°F AND 10°F WITH COMPRESSOR CYCLING.
NOTE: AT IDLE ON HOT DAYS (AMBIENT TEMP. ABOVE 95°F), THE LOW SIDE TEMP. MAY NOT GO BELOW 0°F, CONSEQUENTLY THE COMPRESSOR MAY NOT CYCLE OFF
WHEN ALL DIAGNOSIS AND REPAIRS ARE COMPLETED, CLEAR CODES AND VERIFY OPERATION

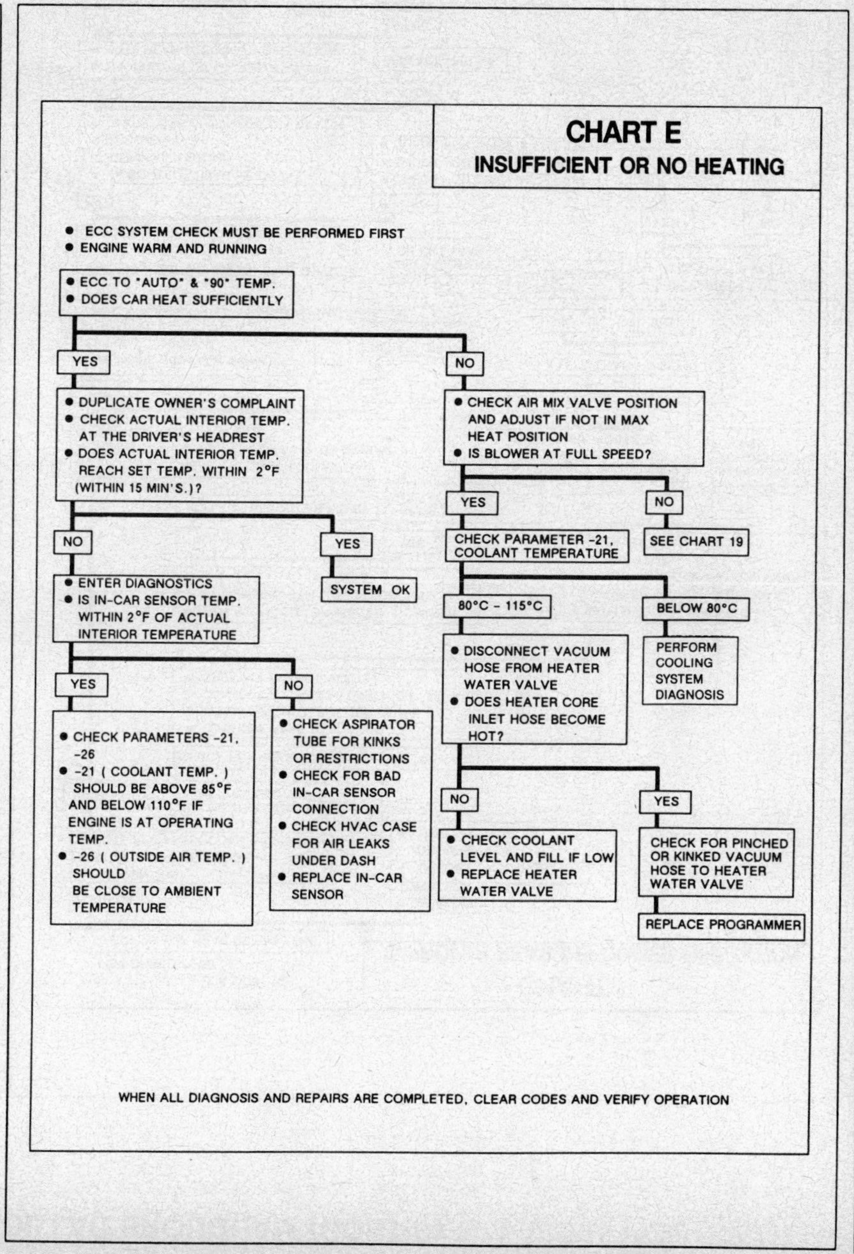
CHART E
INSUFFICIENT OR NO HEATING
• ECC SYSTEM CHECK MUST BE PERFORMED FIRST
• ENGINE WARM AND RUNNING
• ECC TO "AUTO" & "90" TEMP.
• DOES CAR HEAT SUFFICIENTLY
YES
NO
• DUPLICATE OWNER'S COMPLAINT
• CHECK ACTUAL INTERIOR TEMP. AT THE DRIVER'S HEADREST
• DOES ACTUAL INTERIOR TEMP. REACH SET TEMP. WITHIN 2°F (WITHIN 15 MIN'S.)?
• CHECK AIR MIX VALVE POSITION AND ADJUST IF NOT IN MAX HEAT POSITION
• IS BLOWER AT FULL SPEED?
YES
NO
CHECK PARAMETER -21, COOLANT TEMPERATURE
SEE CHART 19
NO
YES
SYSTEM OK
• ENTER DIAGNOSTICS
• IS IN-CAR SENSOR TEMP. WITHIN 2°F OF ACTUAL INTERIOR TEMPERATURE
80°C - 115°C
BELOW 80°C
• DISCONNECT VACUUM HOSE FROM HEATER WATER VALVE
• DOES HEATER CORE INLET HOSE BECOME HOT?
PERFORM COOLING SYSTEM DIAGNOSIS
YES
NO
• CHECK PARAMETERS -21, -26
• -21 (COOLANT TEMP.) SHOULD BE ABOVE 85°F AND BELOW 110°F IF ENGINE IS AT OPERATING TEMP.
• -26 (OUTSIDE AIR TEMP.) SHOULD BE CLOSE TO AMBIENT TEMPERATURE
• CHECK ASPIRATOR TUBE FOR KINKS OR RESTRICTIONS
• CHECK FOR BAD IN-CAR SENSOR CONNECTION
• CHECK HVAC CASE FOR AIR LEAKS UNDER DASH
• REPLACE IN-CAR SENSOR
NO
YES
• CHECK COOLANT LEVEL AND FILL IF LOW
• REPLACE HEATER WATER VALVE
CHECK FOR PINCHED OR KINKED VACUUM HOSE TO HEATER WATER VALVE
REPLACE PROGRAMMER
WHEN ALL DIAGNOSIS AND REPAIRS ARE COMPLETED, CLEAR CODES AND VERIFY OPERATION

ECC SYSTEM DIAGNOSIS—CADILLAC BROUGHAM (CONT'D)

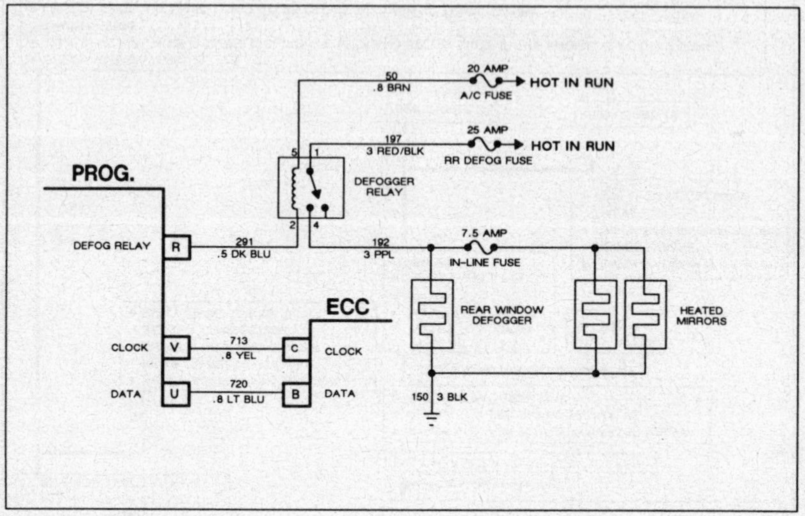
PROG.
DEFOG RELAY
R
CLOCK
V
DATA
U
291
.5 DK BLU
713
.8 YEL
720
.8 LT BLU
ECC
C
CLOCK
B
DATA
DEFOGGER RELAY
5
1
2
4
50
.8 BRN
20 AMP
A/C FUSE
HOT IN RUN
197
3 RED/BLK
25 AMP
RR DEFOG FUSE
HOT IN RUN
192
3 PPL
7.5 AMP
IN-LINE FUSE
REAR WINDOW DEFOGGER
HEATED MIRRORS
150
3 BLK

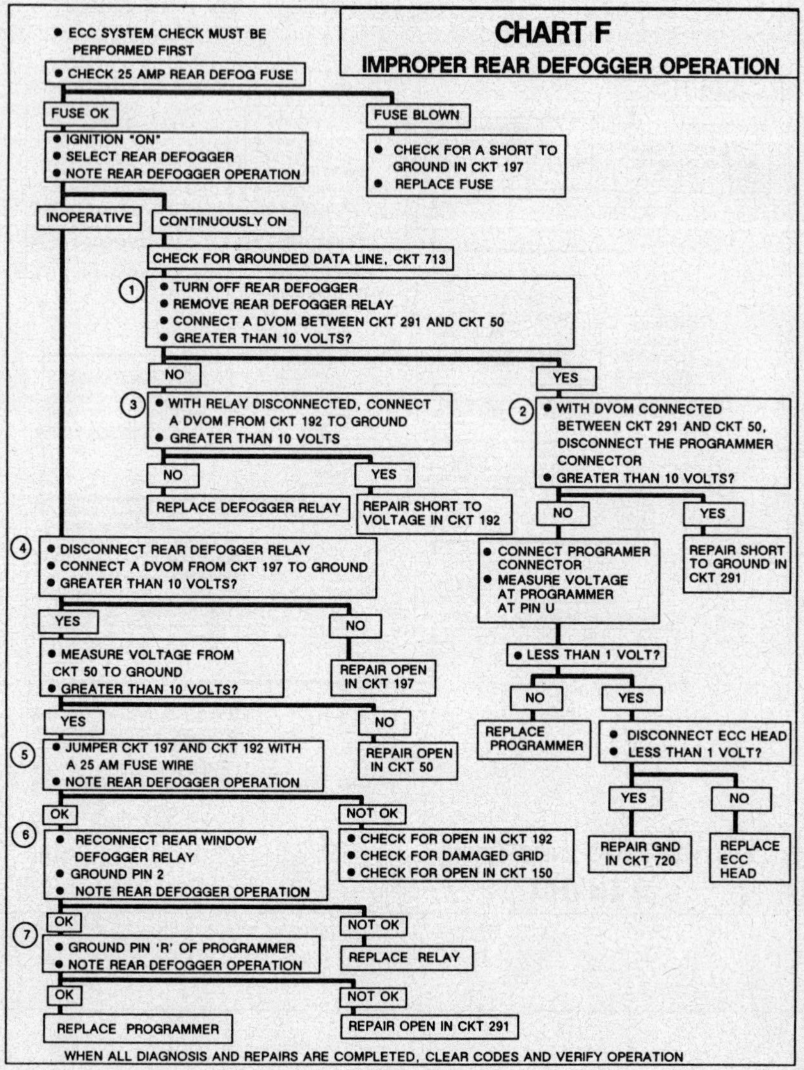
CHART F
IMPROPER REAR DEFOGGER OPERATION
• ECC SYSTEM CHECK MUST BE PERFORMED FIRST
• CHECK 25 AMP REAR DEFOG FUSE
FUSE OK
FUSE BLOWN
• IGNITION "ON"
• SELECT REAR DEFOGGER
• NOTE REAR DEFOGGER OPERATION
• CHECK FOR A SHORT TO GROUND IN CKT 197
• REPLACE FUSE
INOPERATIVE
CONTINUOUSLY ON
CHECK FOR GROUNDED DATA LINE, CKT 713
1
• TURN OFF REAR DEFOGGER
• REMOVE REAR DEFOGGER RELAY
• CONNECT A DVOM BETWEEN CKT 291 AND CKT 50
• GREATER THAN 10 VOLTS?
NO
YES
3
• WITH RELAY DISCONNECTED, CONNECT A DVOM FROM CKT 192 TO GROUND
• GREATER THAN 10 VOLTS
NO
YES
REPLACE DEFOGGER RELAY
REPAIR SHORT TO VOLTAGE IN CKT 192
2
• WITH DVOM CONNECTED BETWEEN CKT 291 AND CKT 50, DISCONNECT THE PROGRAMMER CONNECTOR
• GREATER THAN 10 VOLTS?
NO
YES
REPAIR SHORT TO GROUND IN CKT 291
• CONNECT PROGRAMER CONNECTOR
• MEASURE VOLTAGE AT PROGRAMMER AT PIN U
• LESS THAN 1 VOLT?
NO
YES
REPLACE PROGRAMMER
• DISCONNECT ECC HEAD
• LESS THAN 1 VOLT?
YES
NO
REPAIR GND IN CKT 720
REPLACE ECC HEAD
4
• DISCONNECT REAR DEFOGGER RELAY
• CONNECT A DVOM FROM CKT 197 TO GROUND
• GREATER THAN 10 VOLTS?
YES
NO
REPAIR OPEN IN CKT 197
• MEASURE VOLTAGE FROM CKT 50 TO GROUND
• GREATER THAN 10 VOLTS?
YES
NO
REPAIR OPEN IN CKT 50
5
• JUMPER CKT 197 AND CKT 192 WITH A 25 AM FUSE WIRE
• NOTE REAR DEFOGGER OPERATION
OK
NOT OK
• CHECK FOR OPEN IN CKT 192
• CHECK FOR DAMAGED GRID
• CHECK FOR OPEN IN CKT 150
6
• RECONNECT REAR WINDOW DEFOGGER RELAY
• GROUND PIN 2
• NOTE REAR DEFOGGER OPERATION
OK
NOT OK
REPLACE RELAY
7
• GROUND PIN 'R' OF PROGRAMMER
• NOTE REAR DEFOGGER OPERATION
OK
NOT OK
REPLACE PROGRAMMER
REPAIR OPEN IN CKT 291
WHEN ALL DIAGNOSIS AND REPAIRS ARE COMPLETED, CLEAR CODES AND VERIFY OPERATION

ECC SYSTEM DIAGNOSIS—CADILLAC BROUGHAM (CONT'D)

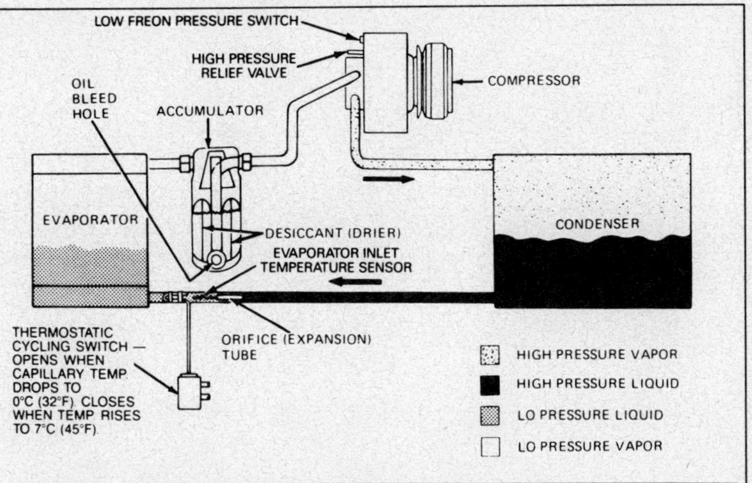
LOW FREON PRESSURE SWITCH
HIGH PRESSURE RELIEF VALVE
COMPRESSOR
OIL BLEED HOLE
ACCUMULATOR
EVAPORATOR
CONDENSER
DESICCANT (DRIER)
EVAPORATOR INLET TEMPERATURE SENSOR
THERMOSTATIC CYCLING SWITCH — OPENS WHEN CAPILLARY TEMP. DROPS TO 0°C (32°F). CLOSES WHEN TEMP. RISES TO 7°C (45°F).
ORIFICE (EXPANSION) TUBE
HIGH PRESSURE VAPOR
HIGH PRESSURE LIQUID
LO PRESSURE LIQUID
LO PRESSURE VAPOR

REFRIGERANT 12 CAPACITY — 3.30 LBS.

COMPONENT REPLACED	COMPRESSOR	EVAPORATOR	CONDENSOR	ACCUMULATOR
OIL DISTRIBUTION	DRAIN OIL, MEASURE, AND REPLACE WITH SAME AMOUNT OF NEW OIL	ADD 90 ML (3 FL. OZ.)	ADD 30 ML (1 FL. OZ.)	ADD 105 ML (3.5 FL. OZ.)

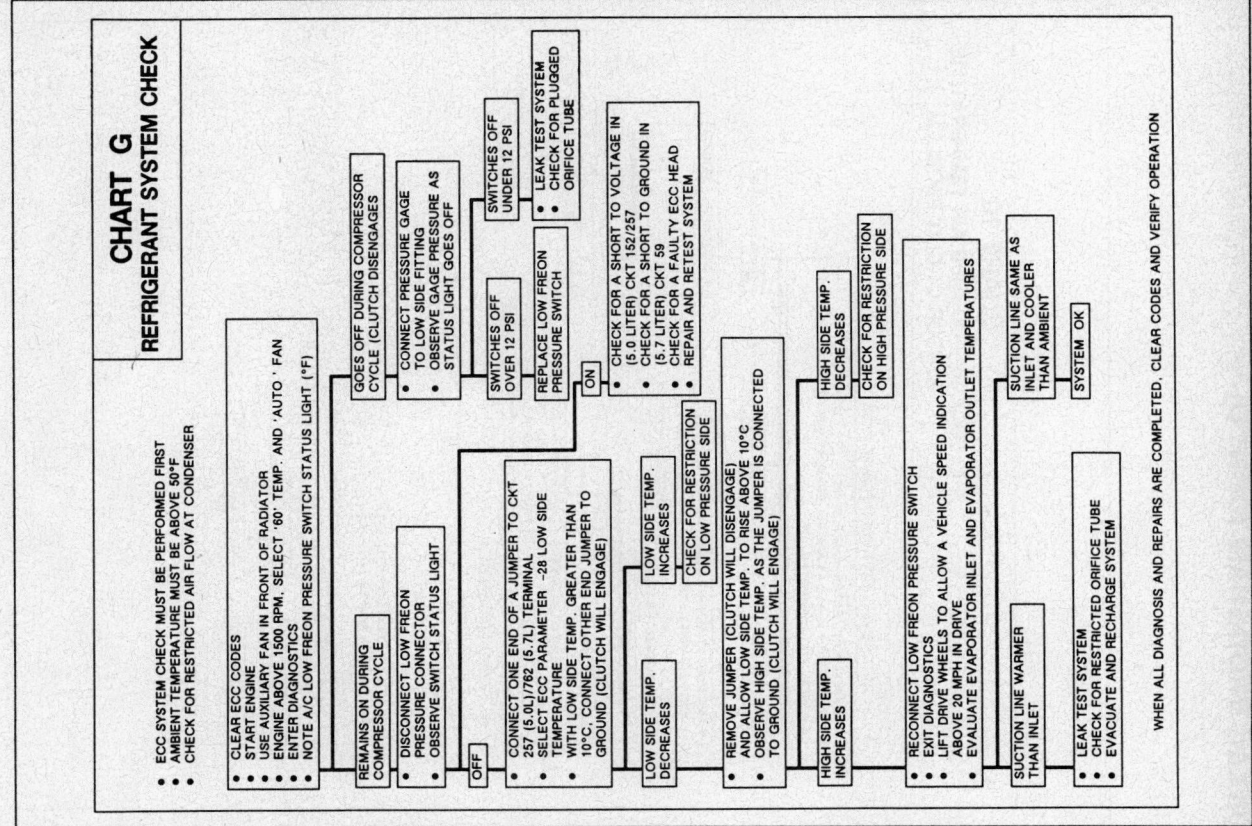

CHART G
REFRIGERANT SYSTEM CHECK

- ECC SYSTEM CHECK MUST BE PERFORMED FIRST
- AMBIENT TEMPERATURE MUST BE ABOVE 50°F
- CHECK FOR RESTRICTED AIR FLOW AT CONDENSER

- CLEAR ECC CODES
- START ENGINE
- USE AUXILIARY FAN IN FRONT OF RADIATOR
- ENGINE ABOVE 1500 RPM, SELECT '60' TEMP. AND 'AUTO ' FAN
- ENTER DIAGNOSTICS
- NOTE A/C LOW FREON PRESSURE SWITCH STATUS LIGHT (°F)

REMAINS ON DURING COMPRESSOR CYCLE

- DISCONNECT LOW FREON PRESSURE CONNECTOR
- OBSERVE SWITCH STATUS LIGHT

OFF

- CONNECT ONE END OF A JUMPER TO CKT 257 (5.0L)/762 (5.7L) TERMINAL
- SELECT ECC PARAMETER -28 LOW SIDE TEMPERATURE
- WITH LOW SIDE TEMP. GREATER THAN 10°C, CONNECT OTHER END JUMPER TO GROUND (CLUTCH WILL ENGAGE)

LOW SIDE TEMP. DECREASES

LOW SIDE TEMP. INCREASES

CHECK FOR RESTRICTION ON LOW PRESSURE SIDE

ON

- CHECK FOR A SHORT TO VOLTAGE IN (5.0 LITER) CKT 152/257
- CHECK FOR A SHORT TO GROUND IN (5.7 LITER) CKT 59
- CHECK FOR A FAULTY ECC HEAD
- REPAIR AND RETEST SYSTEM

GOES OFF DURING COMPRESSOR CYCLE (CLUTCH DISENGAGES

- CONNECT PRESSURE GAGE TO LOW SIDE FITTING
- OBSERVE GAGE PRESSURE AS STATUS LIGHT GOES OFF

SWITCHES OFF OVER 12 PSI

REPLACE LOW FREON PRESSURE SWITCH

SWITCHES OFF UNDER 12 PSI

- LEAK TEST SYSTEM
- CHECK FOR PLUGGED ORIFICE TUBE

- REMOVE JUMPER (CLUTCH WILL DISENGAGE) AND ALLOW LOW SIDE TEMP. TO RISE ABOVE 10°C
- OBSERVE HIGH SIDE TEMP. AS THE JUMPER IS CONNECTED TO GROUND (CLUTCH WILL ENGAGE)

HIGH SIDE TEMP. INCREASES

HIGH SIDE TEMP. DECREASES

CHECK FOR RESTRICTION ON HIGH PRESSURE SIDE

- RECONNECT LOW FREON PRESSURE SWITCH
- EXIT DIAGNOSTICS
- LIFT DRIVE WHEELS TO ALLOW A VEHICLE SPEED INDICATION ABOVE 20 MPH IN DRIVE
- EVALUATE EVAPORATOR INLET AND EVAPORATOR OUTLET TEMPERATURES

SUCTION LINE WARMER THAN INLET

- LEAK TEST SYSTEM
- CHECK FOR RESTRICTED ORIFICE TUBE
- EVACUATE AND RECHARGE SYSTEM

SUCTION LINE SAME AS INLET AND COOLER THAN AMBIENT

SYSTEM OK

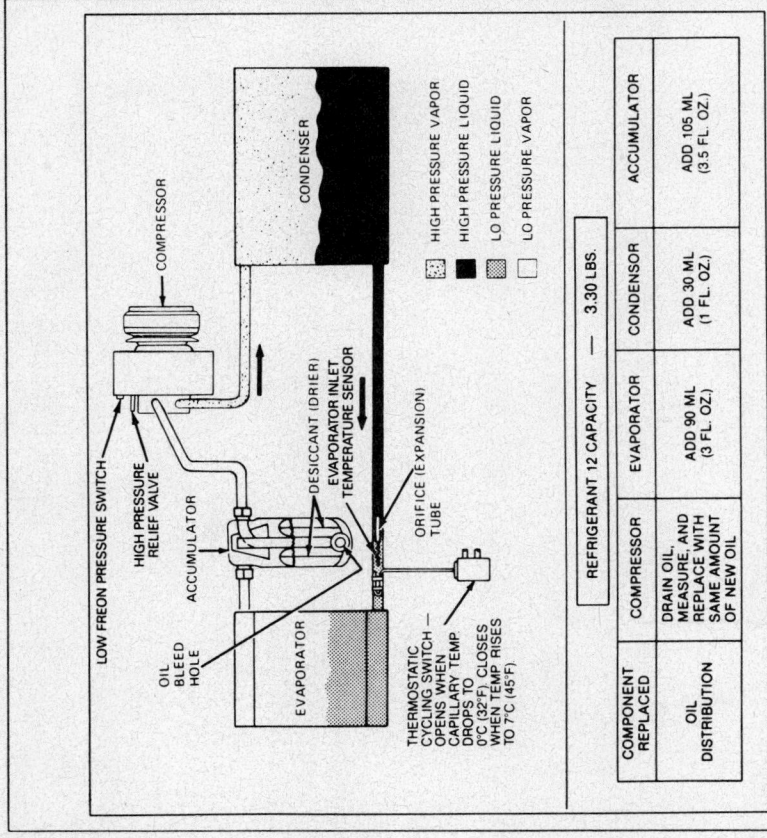

WHEN ALL DIAGNOSIS AND REPAIRS ARE COMPLETED, CLEAR CODES AND VERIFY OPERATION

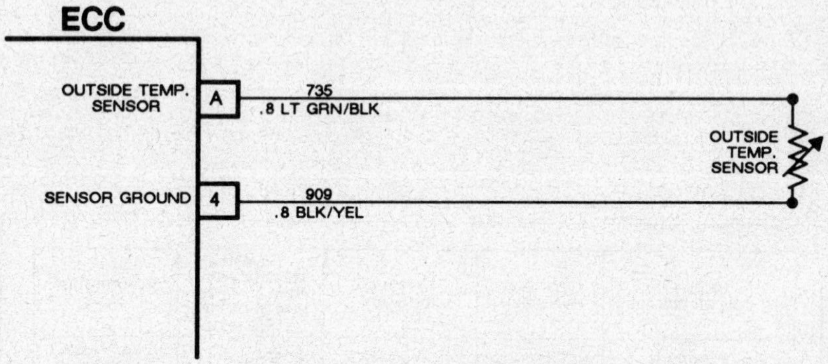
ECC
OUTSIDE TEMP. SENSOR
A
735
.8 LT GRN/BLK
SENSOR GROUND
4
909
.8 BLK/YEL
OUTSIDE TEMP. SENSOR

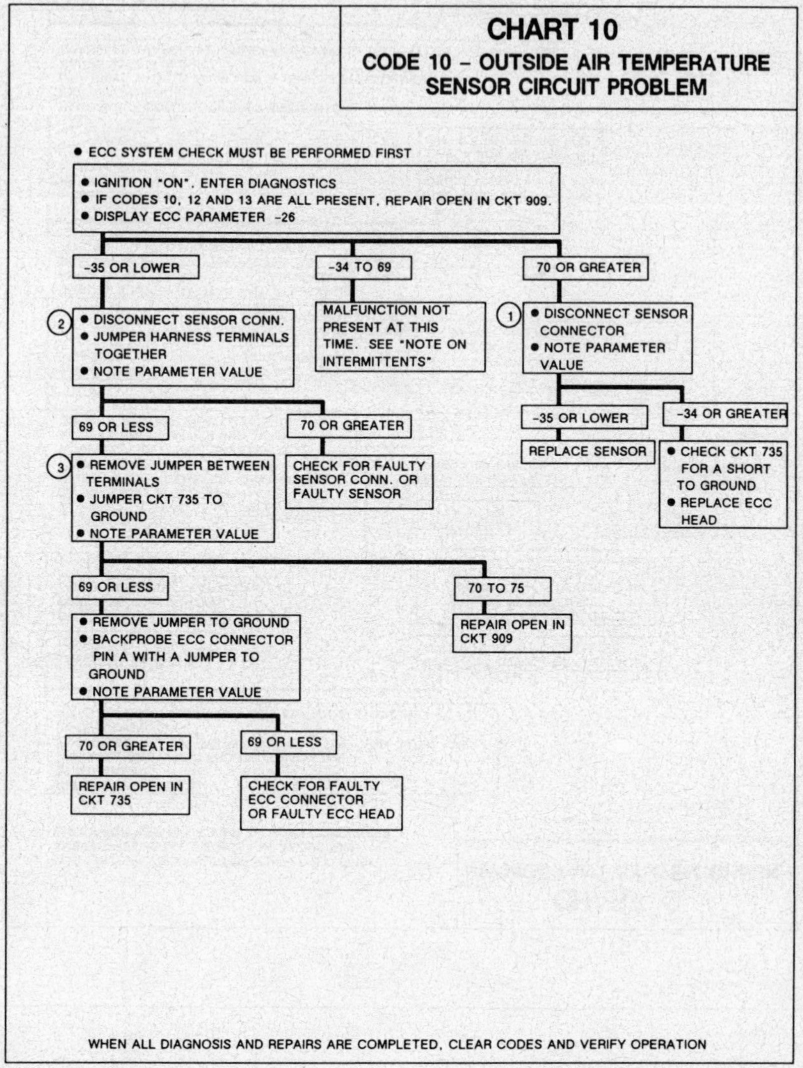
CHART 10
CODE 10 – OUTSIDE AIR TEMPERATURE SENSOR CIRCUIT PROBLEM
• ECC SYSTEM CHECK MUST BE PERFORMED FIRST
• IGNITION "ON". ENTER DIAGNOSTICS
• IF CODES 10, 12 AND 13 ARE ALL PRESENT, REPAIR OPEN IN CKT 909.
• DISPLAY ECC PARAMETER -26
-35 OR LOWER
-34 TO 69
70 OR GREATER
2
• DISCONNECT SENSOR CONN.
• JUMPER HARNESS TERMINALS TOGETHER
• NOTE PARAMETER VALUE
MALFUNCTION NOT PRESENT AT THIS TIME. SEE "NOTE ON INTERMITTENTS"
1
• DISCONNECT SENSOR CONNECTOR
• NOTE PARAMETER VALUE
69 OR LESS
70 OR GREATER
-35 OR LOWER
-34 OR GREATER
REPLACE SENSOR
• CHECK CKT 735 FOR A SHORT TO GROUND
• REPLACE ECC HEAD
3
• REMOVE JUMPER BETWEEN TERMINALS
• JUMPER CKT 735 TO GROUND
• NOTE PARAMETER VALUE
CHECK FOR FAULTY SENSOR CONN. OR FAULTY SENSOR
69 OR LESS
70 TO 75
• REMOVE JUMPER TO GROUND
• BACKPROBE ECC CONNECTOR PIN A WITH A JUMPER TO GROUND
• NOTE PARAMETER VALUE
REPAIR OPEN IN CKT 909
70 OR GREATER
69 OR LESS
REPAIR OPEN IN CKT 735
CHECK FOR FAULTY ECC CONNECTOR OR FAULTY ECC HEAD
WHEN ALL DIAGNOSIS AND REPAIRS ARE COMPLETED, CLEAR CODES AND VERIFY OPERATION

ECC SYSTEM DIAGNOSIS—CADILLAC BROUGHAM (CONT'D)

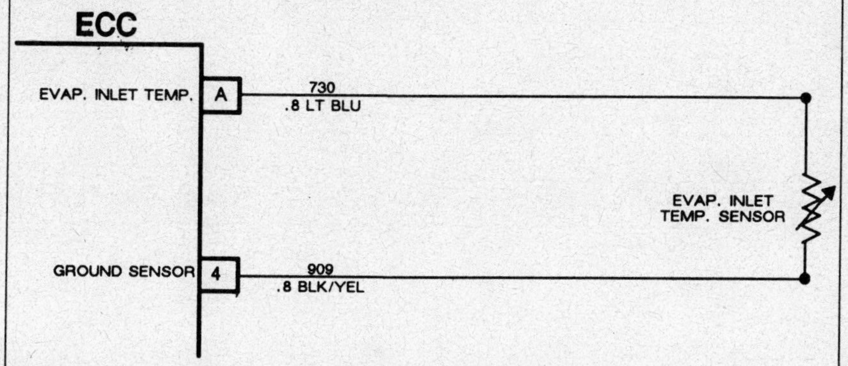
ECC
EVAP. INLET TEMP.
A
730
.8 LT BLU
GROUND SENSOR
4
909
.8 BLK/YEL
EVAP. INLET
TEMP. SENSOR

CHART 12

CODE 12 – EVAPORATOR INLET TEMPERATURE SENSOR CIRCUIT PROBLEM

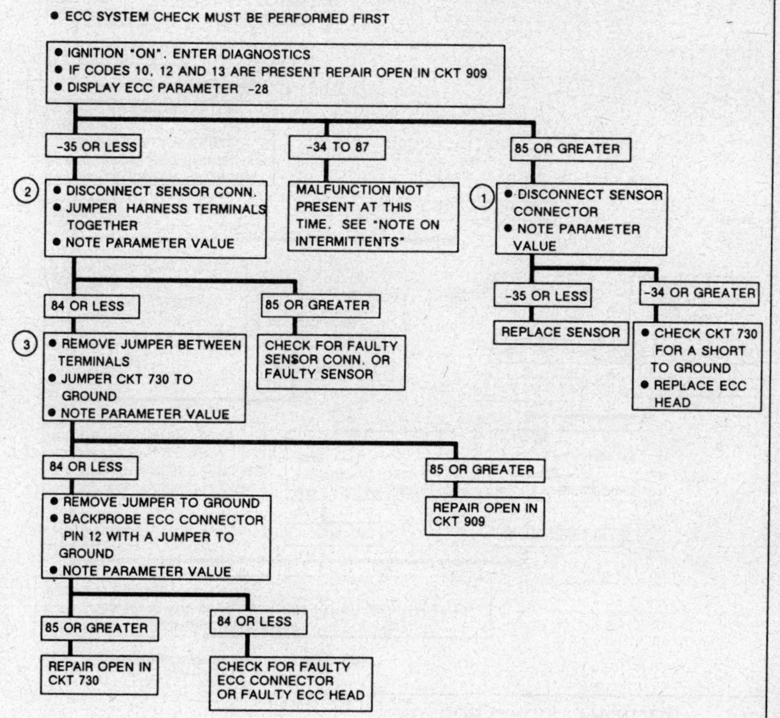
• ECC SYSTEM CHECK MUST BE PERFORMED FIRST
• IGNITION "ON". ENTER DIAGNOSTICS
• IF CODES 10, 12 AND 13 ARE PRESENT REPAIR OPEN IN CKT 909
• DISPLAY ECC PARAMETER -28
-35 OR LESS
-34 TO 87
85 OR GREATER
2
• DISCONNECT SENSOR CONN.
• JUMPER HARNESS TERMINALS TOGETHER
• NOTE PARAMETER VALUE
MALFUNCTION NOT PRESENT AT THIS TIME. SEE "NOTE ON INTERMITTENTS"
1
• DISCONNECT SENSOR CONNECTOR
• NOTE PARAMETER VALUE
84 OR LESS
85 OR GREATER
-35 OR LESS
-34 OR GREATER
REPLACE SENSOR
• CHECK CKT 730 FOR A SHORT TO GROUND
• REPLACE ECC HEAD
3
• REMOVE JUMPER BETWEEN TERMINALS
• JUMPER CKT 730 TO GROUND
• NOTE PARAMETER VALUE
CHECK FOR FAULTY SENSOR CONN. OR FAULTY SENSOR
84 OR LESS
85 OR GREATER
• REMOVE JUMPER TO GROUND
• BACKPROBE ECC CONNECTOR PIN 12 WITH A JUMPER TO GROUND
• NOTE PARAMETER VALUE
REPAIR OPEN IN CKT 909
85 OR GREATER
84 OR LESS
REPAIR OPEN IN CKT 730
CHECK FOR FAULTY ECC CONNECTOR OR FAULTY ECC HEAD

WHEN ALL DIAGNOSIS AND REPAIRS ARE COMPLETED, CLEAR CODES AND VERIFY OPERATION

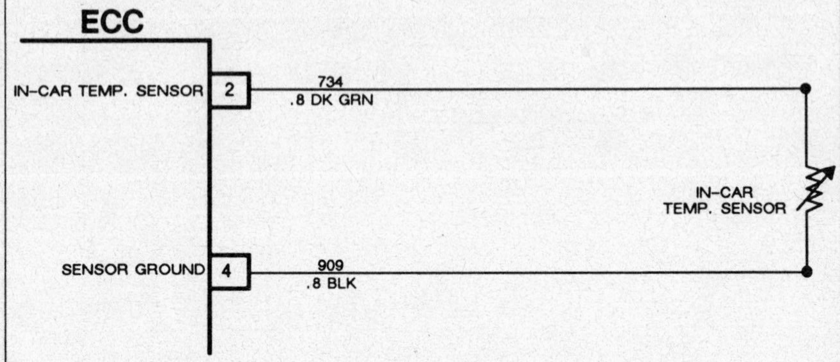
ECC
IN-CAR TEMP. SENSOR
2
734
.8 DK GRN
SENSOR GROUND
4
909
.8 BLK
IN-CAR
TEMP. SENSOR

CHART 13

CODE 13 – IN-CAR TEMPERATURE SENSOR CIRCUIT PROBLEM

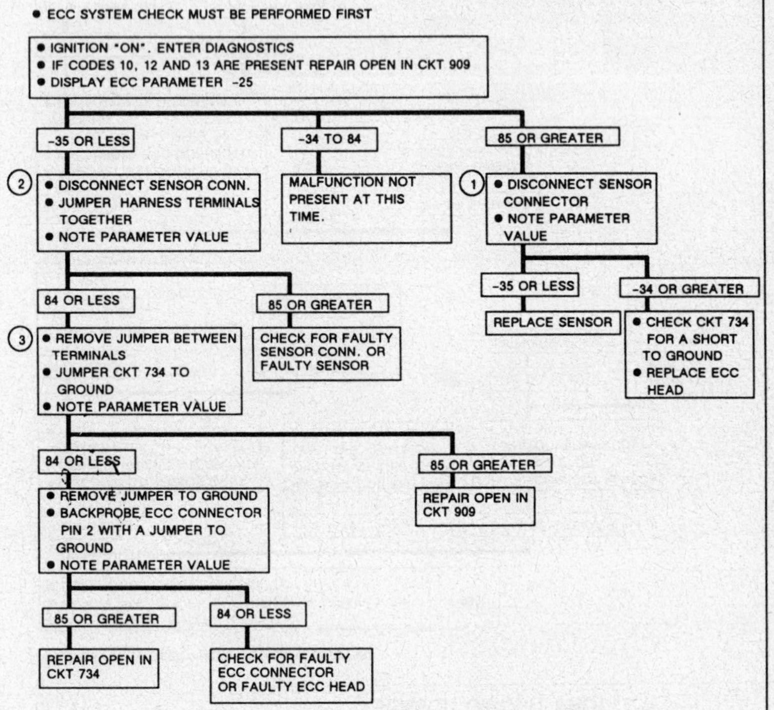
• ECC SYSTEM CHECK MUST BE PERFORMED FIRST
• IGNITION "ON". ENTER DIAGNOSTICS
• IF CODES 10, 12 AND 13 ARE PRESENT REPAIR OPEN IN CKT 909
• DISPLAY ECC PARAMETER -25
-35 OR LESS
-34 TO 84
85 OR GREATER
2
• DISCONNECT SENSOR CONN.
• JUMPER HARNESS TERMINALS TOGETHER
• NOTE PARAMETER VALUE
MALFUNCTION NOT PRESENT AT THIS TIME.
1
• DISCONNECT SENSOR CONNECTOR
• NOTE PARAMETER VALUE
-35 OR LESS
-34 OR GREATER
REPLACE SENSOR
• CHECK CKT 734 FOR A SHORT TO GROUND
• REPLACE ECC HEAD
84 OR LESS
85 OR GREATER
3
• REMOVE JUMPER BETWEEN TERMINALS
• JUMPER CKT 734 TO GROUND
• NOTE PARAMETER VALUE
CHECK FOR FAULTY SENSOR CONN. OR FAULTY SENSOR
84 OR LESS
85 OR GREATER
• REMOVE JUMPER TO GROUND
• BACKPROBE ECC CONNECTOR PIN 2 WITH A JUMPER TO GROUND
• NOTE PARAMETER VALUE
REPAIR OPEN IN CKT 909
85 OR GREATER
84 OR LESS
REPAIR OPEN IN CKT 734
CHECK FOR FAULTY ECC CONNECTOR OR FAULTY ECC HEAD

WHEN ALL DIAGNOSIS AND REPAIRS ARE COMPLETED, CLEAR CODES AND VERIFY OPERATION

ECC SYSTEM DIAGNOSIS—CADILLAC BROUGHAM (CONT'D)

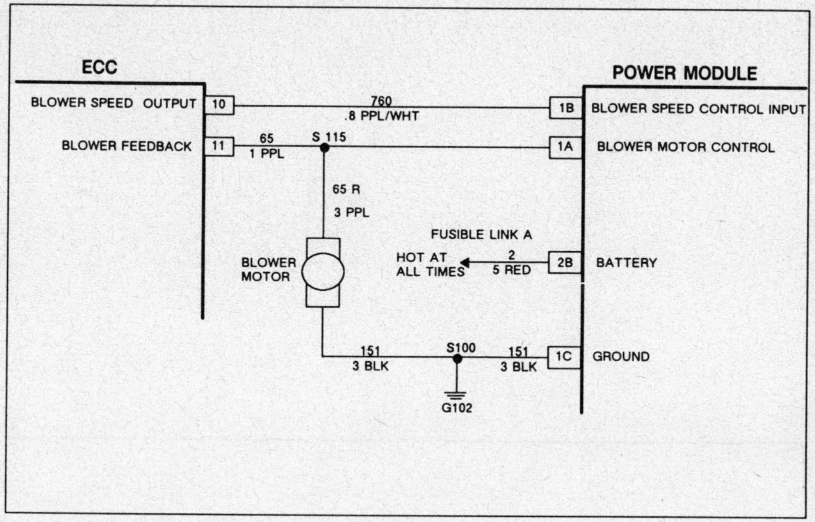
ECC
BLOWER SPEED OUTPUT
BLOWER FEEDBACK
10
11
760
.8 PPL/WHT
65
1 PPL
S 115
65 R
3 PPL
BLOWER MOTOR
FUSIBLE LINK A
HOT AT ALL TIMES
2
5 RED
151
3 BLK
S100
G102
POWER MODULE
1B
BLOWER SPEED CONTROL INPUT
1A
BLOWER MOTOR CONTROL
2B
BATTERY
1C
GROUND

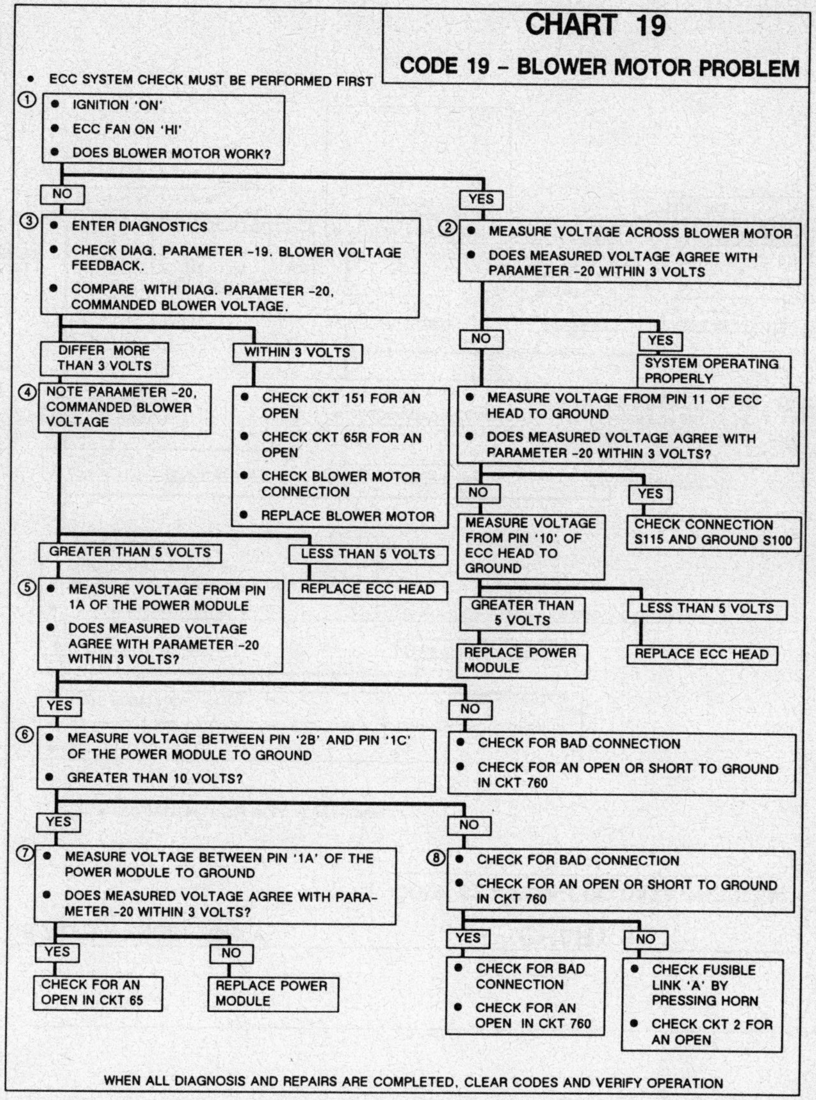
CHART 19
CODE 19 – BLOWER MOTOR PROBLEM
• ECC SYSTEM CHECK MUST BE PERFORMED FIRST
① • IGNITION 'ON' • ECC FAN ON 'HI' • DOES BLOWER MOTOR WORK?
NO
YES
③ • ENTER DIAGNOSTICS • CHECK DIAG. PARAMETER -19. BLOWER VOLTAGE FEEDBACK. • COMPARE WITH DIAG. PARAMETER -20, COMMANDED BLOWER VOLTAGE.
② • MEASURE VOLTAGE ACROSS BLOWER MOTOR • DOES MEASURED VOLTAGE AGREE WITH PARAMETER -20 WITHIN 3 VOLTS
DIFFER MORE THAN 3 VOLTS
WITHIN 3 VOLTS
NO
YES
SYSTEM OPERATING PROPERLY
④ NOTE PARAMETER -20, COMMANDED BLOWER VOLTAGE
• CHECK CKT 151 FOR AN OPEN • CHECK CKT 65R FOR AN OPEN • CHECK BLOWER MOTOR CONNECTION • REPLACE BLOWER MOTOR
• MEASURE VOLTAGE FROM PIN 11 OF ECC HEAD TO GROUND • DOES MEASURED VOLTAGE AGREE WITH PARAMETER -20 WITHIN 3 VOLTS?
NO
YES
MEASURE VOLTAGE FROM PIN '10' OF ECC HEAD TO GROUND
CHECK CONNECTION S115 AND GROUND S100
GREATER THAN 5 VOLTS
LESS THAN 5 VOLTS
REPLACE ECC HEAD
⑤ • MEASURE VOLTAGE FROM PIN 1A OF THE POWER MODULE • DOES MEASURED VOLTAGE AGREE WITH PARAMETER -20 WITHIN 3 VOLTS?
GREATER THAN 5 VOLTS
LESS THAN 5 VOLTS
REPLACE POWER MODULE
REPLACE ECC HEAD
YES
NO
⑥ • MEASURE VOLTAGE BETWEEN PIN '2B' AND PIN '1C' OF THE POWER MODULE TO GROUND • GREATER THAN 10 VOLTS?
• CHECK FOR BAD CONNECTION • CHECK FOR AN OPEN OR SHORT TO GROUND IN CKT 760
YES
NO
⑦ • MEASURE VOLTAGE BETWEEN PIN '1A' OF THE POWER MODULE TO GROUND • DOES MEASURED VOLTAGE AGREE WITH PARA-METER -20 WITHIN 3 VOLTS?
⑧ • CHECK FOR BAD CONNECTION • CHECK FOR AN OPEN OR SHORT TO GROUND IN CKT 760
YES
NO
CHECK FOR AN OPEN IN CKT 65
REPLACE POWER MODULE
YES
NO
• CHECK FOR BAD CONNECTION • CHECK FOR AN OPEN IN CKT 760
• CHECK FUSIBLE LINK 'A' BY PRESSING HORN • CHECK CKT 2 FOR AN OPEN
WHEN ALL DIAGNOSIS AND REPAIRS ARE COMPLETED, CLEAR CODES AND VERIFY OPERATION

ECC SYSTEM DIAGNOSIS—CADILLAC BROUGHAM (CONT'D)

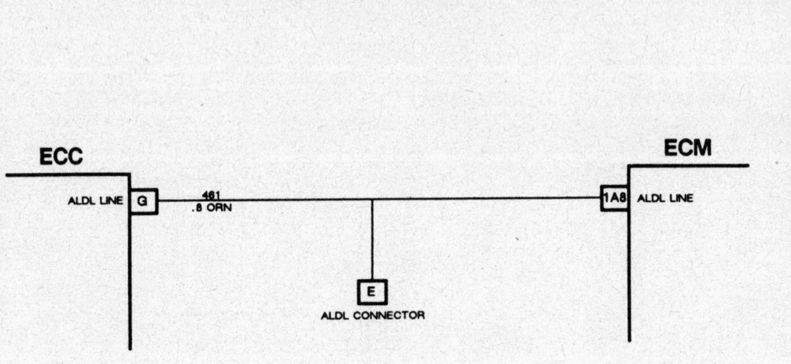
5.7 Liter Engine Only
ECC
ALDL LINE
G
461
.8 ORN
1A8
ALDL LINE
ECM
E
ALDL CONNECTOR

5.7 LITER ENGINE ONLY

CHART 32

CODE 32 – ECM–ECC DATA PROBLEM

• ECC SYSTEM CHECK MUST BE PERFORMED FIRST

(1)
- KEY OFF
- MEASURE RESISTANCE FROM PIN E OF THE ALDL CONNECTOR TO GROUND
- NOTE RESISTANCE

LESS THAN 500 OHMS → CHECK FOR A SHORT TO GROUND ON CKT 461

GREATER THAN 500 OHMS →

(2)
- KEY ON, ENGINE NOT RUNNING
- MEASURE VOLTAGE AT PIN E OF ALDL CONNECTOR TO GROUND
- NOTE VOLTAGE

VOLTAGE FLUCTUATION BETWEEN .5 AND 5 VOLTS → WILL COMPRESSOR CLUTCH ENGAGE?
- NO → CHECK FOR OPEN BETWEEN ALDL AND ECC HEAD IN CKT 461 → REPLACE ECC HEAD
- YES → FAULT NOT PRESENT AT THIS TIME.

FIXED VOLTAGE OVER .5V →
- DISCONNECT ECC HEAD
- NOTE VOLTAGE

  - FIXED VOLTAGE OVER .5V → • CHECK FOR SHORT TO VOLTAGE ON CIRCUIT 461
  - VOLTAGE FLUCTUATION BETWEEN .5 AND 5 VOLTS → REPLACE EGC
  - FIXED BETWEEN 0 AND .5 → OPEN BETWEEN ALDL AND ECM IN CKT 461

FIXED BETWEEN 0 AND .5 VOLTS → CHECK FOR SHORT TO GROUND OR CKT 461

WHEN ALL DIAGNOSIS AND REPAIRS ARE COMPLETED, CLEAR CODES AND VERIFY OPERATION

ECC SYSTEM DIAGNOSIS—CADILLAC BROUGHAM (CONT'D)

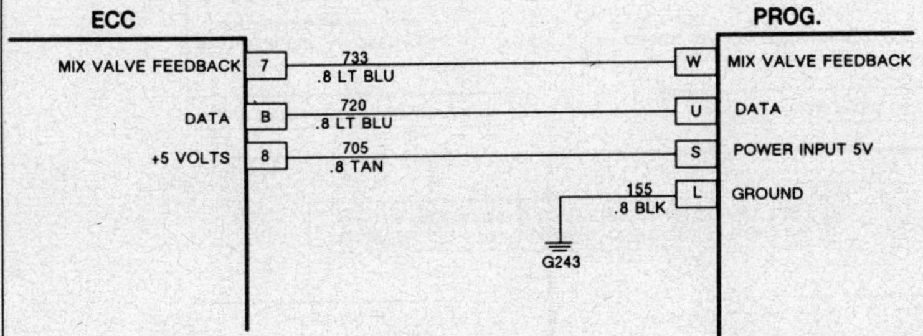
ECC
MIX VALVE FEEDBACK
DATA
+5 VOLTS
7
B
8
733
.8 LT BLU
720
.8 LT BLU
705
.8 TAN
155
.8 BLK
G243
PROG.
W
U
S
L
MIX VALVE FEEDBACK
DATA
POWER INPUT 5V
GROUND

CHART 40

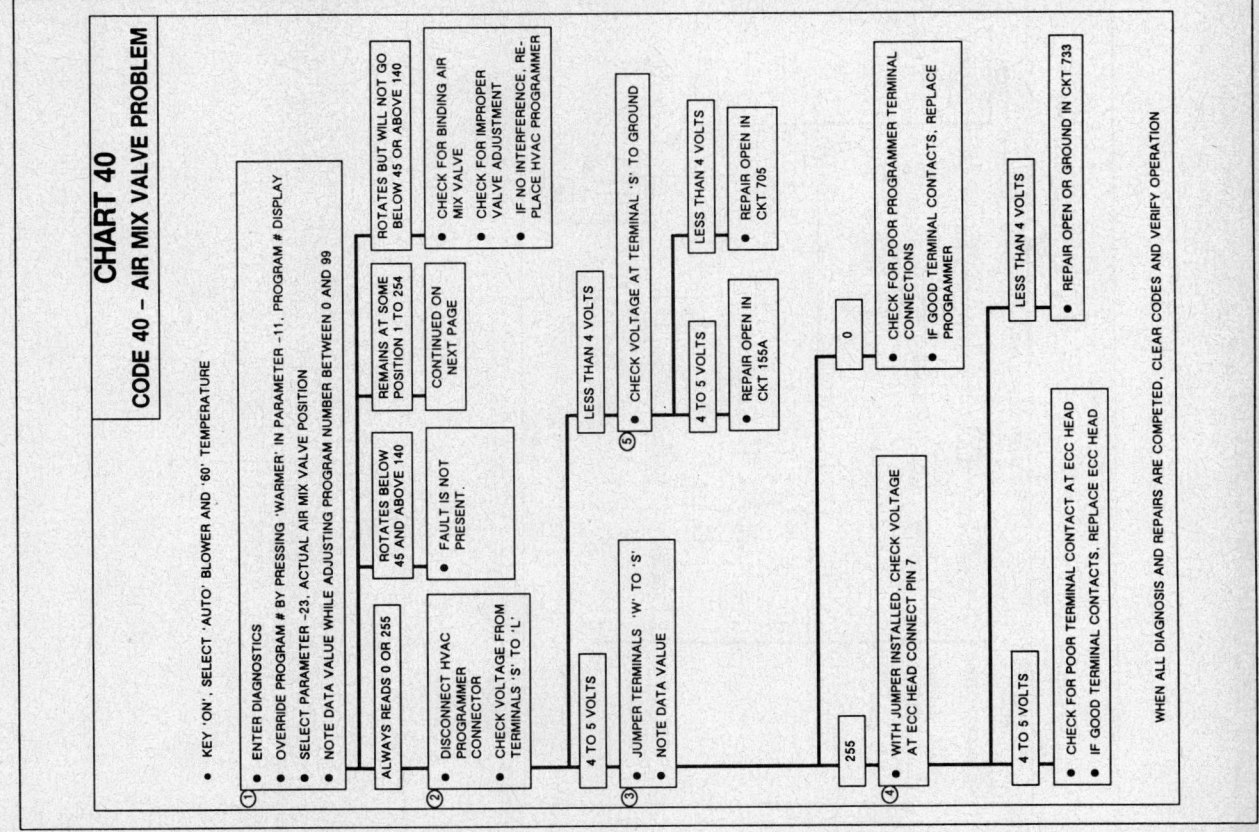

CODE 40 – AIR MIX VALVE PROBLEM

- KEY 'ON', SELECT 'AUTO' BLOWER AND '60' TEMPERATURE

(1)
- ENTER DIAGNOSTICS
- OVERRIDE PROGRAM # BY PRESSING 'WARMER' IN PARAMETER -11, PROGRAM # DISPLAY
- SELECT PARAMETER -23, ACTUAL AIR MIX VALVE POSITION
- NOTE DATA VALUE WHILE ADJUSTING PROGRAM NUMBER BETWEEN 0 AND 99

ALWAYS READS 0 OR 255

(2)
- DISCONNECT HVAC PROGRAMMER CONNECTOR
- CHECK VOLTAGE FROM TERMINALS 'S' TO 'L'

ROTATES BELOW 45 AND ABOVE 140

- FAULT IS NOT PRESENT.

REMAINS AT SOME POSITION 1 TO 254

CONTINUED ON NEXT PAGE

ROTATES BUT WILL NOT GO BELOW 45 OR ABOVE 140

- CHECK FOR BINDING AIR MIX VALVE
- CHECK FOR IMPROPER VALVE ADJUSTMENT
- IF NO INTERFERENCE, REPLACE HVAC PROGRAMMER

4 TO 5 VOLTS

(3)
- JUMPER TERMINALS 'W' TO 'S'
- NOTE DATA VALUE

LESS THAN 4 VOLTS

(5)
- CHECK VOLTAGE AT TERMINAL 'S' TO GROUND

4 TO 5 VOLTS

- REPAIR OPEN IN CKT 155A

LESS THAN 4 VOLTS

- REPAIR OPEN IN CKT 705

255

(4)
- WITH JUMPER INSTALLED, CHECK VOLTAGE AT ECC HEAD CONNECT PIN 7

0

- CHECK FOR POOR PROGRAMMER TERMINAL CONNECTIONS
- IF GOOD TERMINAL CONTACTS, REPLACE PROGRAMMER

4 TO 5 VOLTS

- CHECK FOR POOR TERMINAL CONTACT AT ECC HEAD
- IF GOOD TERMINAL CONTACTS, REPLACE ECC HEAD

LESS THAN 4 VOLTS

- REPAIR OPEN OR GROUND IN CKT 733

WHEN ALL DIAGNOSIS AND REPAIRS ARE COMPETED, CLEAR CODES AND VERIFY OPERATION

ECC SYSTEM DIAGNOSIS – CADILLAC BROUGHAM (CONT'D)

CHART 40
CODE 40 – AIR MIX VALVE PROBLEM (CONTINUED)

CONTINUED FROM PAGE 43 CODE 40 – AIR MIX VALVE PROBLEM

- ENTER ECC PARAMETER -22, COMMANDED AIR MIX VALVE POSITION NOTE DATA VALUE WHILE ADJUSTING PROGRAM NUMBER BETWEEN 0 AND 99

WILL RANGE FROM 0–255

- CHECK FOR A STUCK VALVE
- CHECK FOR AN OPEN IN PROGRAMMER CIRCIUT 155A
- CHECK PROGRAM POWER VOLTAGES
- CHECK PROGRAMMER CONNECTORS
- IF NO TROUBLE FOUND, REPLACE PROGRAMMER

REMAINS AT SOME VALUE FROM 0–255

- CHECK VOLTAGE AT PIN 'U' OF PROGRAMMER

THIS SHOULD BE A SERIAL DATA VOLTAGE FLUCTUATING FROM 1–5V

< .1

REPAIR SHORT TO GROUND IN CKT 720

A CONSTANT, NON-FLUCTUATING VOLTAGE BETWEEN 1 AND 4.9 VOLTS

DISCONNECT THE PROGRAMMER. CONTIUNE TO MONITOR THE VOLTAGE AT PIN U OF THE PROGRAM CONNECTOR

FLUCTUATES FROM 1 TO 4.9 VOLTS

- CHECK FOR AN OPEN IN PROGRAMMER CKT 155A
- CHECK PROGRAM POWER VOLTAGE
- CHECK FOR FAULTY PROGRAMMER CONNECTIONS
- IF GOOD CONTACS, REPLACE PROGRAMMER

CONSTANT, NON-FLUCTUATING

- CHECK CKT 720 FOR A SHORT TO VOLTAGE
- CHECK FOR PROPER ECC HEAD CONNECTION
- CHECK POWER AND GROUND VOLTAGES AT THE ECC HEAD PINS I, H, AND 5
- IF OK, REPLACE ECC HEAD

> 4.9

REPAIR SHORT TO VOLTAGE OR OPEN IN CKT 720

WHEN ALL DIAGNOSIS AND REPAIRS ARE COMPETED, CLEAR CODES AND VERIFY OPERATION

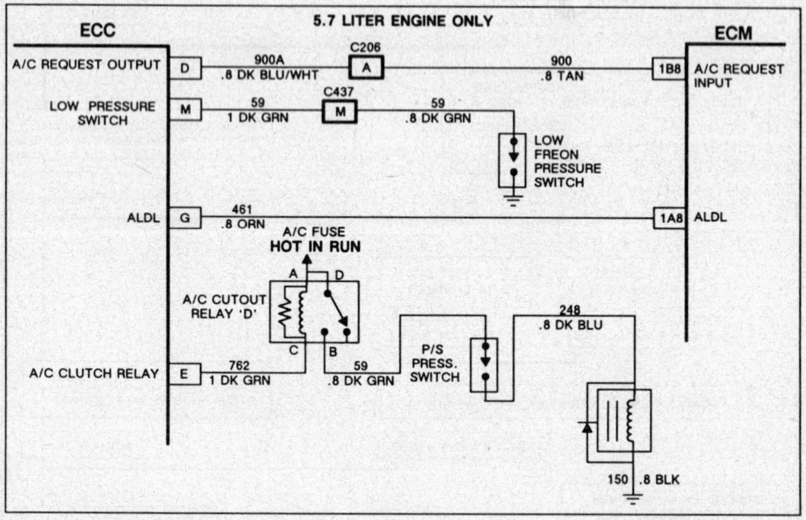
5.7 LITER ENGINE ONLY
ECC
ECM
A/C REQUEST OUTPUT
D
900A
.8 DK BLU/WHT
C206
A
900
.8 TAN
1B8
A/C REQUEST INPUT
LOW PRESSURE SWITCH
M
59
1 DK GRN
C437
M
59
.8 DK GRN
LOW FREON PRESSURE SWITCH
ALDL
G
461
.8 ORN
1A8
ALDL
A/C FUSE
HOT IN RUN
A
D
A/C CUTOUT RELAY 'D'
C
B
248
.8 DK BLU
A/C CLUTCH RELAY
E
762
1 DK GRN
59
.8 DK GRN
P/S PRESS. SWITCH
150
.8 BLK

ECC SYSTEM DIAGNOSIS—CADILLAC BROUGHAM (CONT'D)

CHART 48/49
CODES 48, 49 – COMPRESSOR OFF

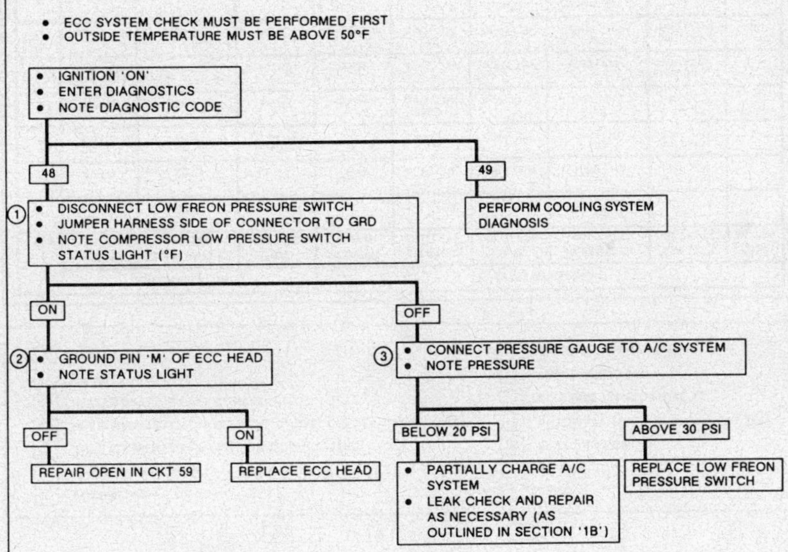
• ECC SYSTEM CHECK MUST BE PERFORMED FIRST
• OUTSIDE TEMPERATURE MUST BE ABOVE 50°F
• IGNITION 'ON'
• ENTER DIAGNOSTICS
• NOTE DIAGNOSTIC CODE
48
49
PERFORM COOLING SYSTEM DIAGNOSIS
1
• DISCONNECT LOW FREON PRESSURE SWITCH
• JUMPER HARNESS SIDE OF CONNECTOR TO GRD
• NOTE COMPRESSOR LOW PRESSURE SWITCH STATUS LIGHT (°F)
ON
OFF
2
• GROUND PIN 'M' OF ECC HEAD
• NOTE STATUS LIGHT
3
• CONNECT PRESSURE GAUGE TO A/C SYSTEM
• NOTE PRESSURE
OFF
ON
REPAIR OPEN IN CKT 59
REPLACE ECC HEAD
BELOW 20 PSI
ABOVE 30 PSI
• PARTIALLY CHARGE A/C SYSTEM
• LEAK CHECK AND REPAIR AS NECESSARY (AS OUTLINED IN SECTION '1B')
REPLACE LOW FREON PRESSURE SWITCH

WHEN ALL DIAGNOSIS AND REPAIRS ARE COMPLETED, CLEAR CODES AND VERIFY OPERATION

5.0 Liter Engine Only

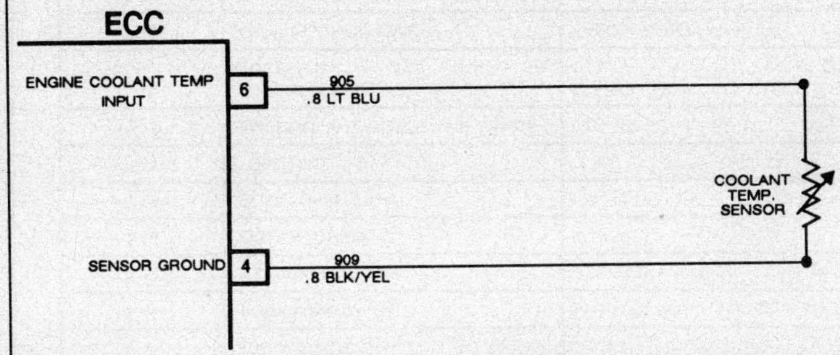
ECC
ENGINE COOLANT TEMP INPUT
6
905
.8 LT BLU
SENSOR GROUND
4
909
.8 BLK/YEL
COOLANT TEMP. SENSOR

CHART 55
CODE 55 – SHORTED COOLANT TEMPERATURE SENSOR

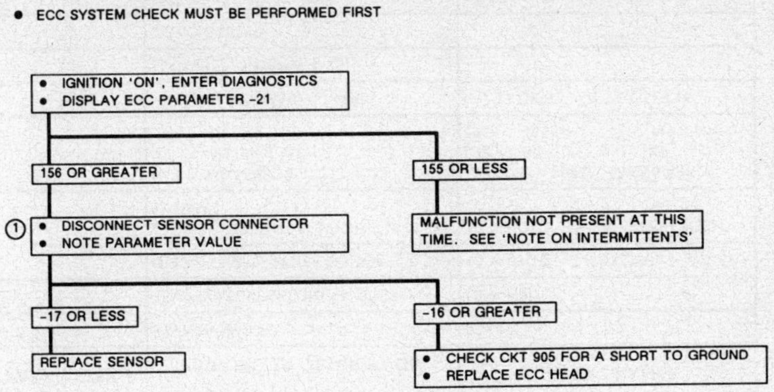
• ECC SYSTEM CHECK MUST BE PERFORMED FIRST
• IGNITION 'ON', ENTER DIAGNOSTICS
• DISPLAY ECC PARAMETER -21
156 OR GREATER
155 OR LESS
MALFUNCTION NOT PRESENT AT THIS TIME. SEE 'NOTE ON INTERMITTENTS'
1
• DISCONNECT SENSOR CONNECTOR
• NOTE PARAMETER VALUE
-17 OR LESS
-16 OR GREATER
REPLACE SENSOR
• CHECK CKT 905 FOR A SHORT TO GROUND
• REPLACE ECC HEAD

WHEN ALL DIAGNOSIS AND REPAIRS ARE COMPLETED, CLEAR CODES AND VERIFY OPERATION

ECC SYSTEM DIAGNOSIS—CORVETTE

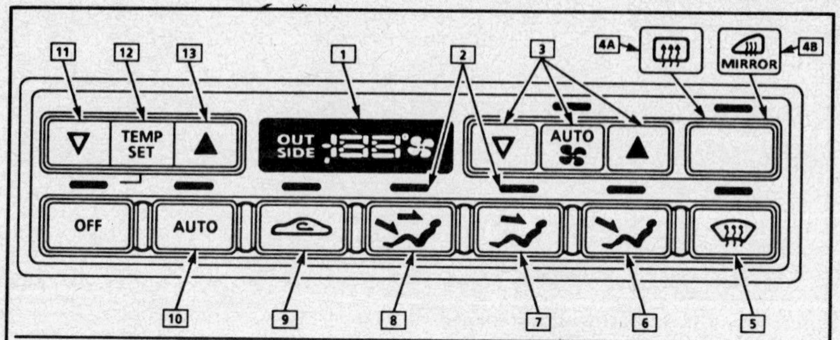
11
12
13
1
2
3
4A
4B
MIRROR
TEMP SET
OUT SIDE
AUTO
OFF
AUTO
10
9
8
7
6
5

1 LCD DISPLAY
2 LED MODE INDICATORS
3 AUTO BLOWER/FAN UP/FAN DOWN/DIAGNOSTICS
4A HEATED MIRRORS/REAR DEFROST - COUPES CONVERTIBLE HARDTOP
4B HEATED MIRRORS/ONLY CONVERTIBLE
5 DEFROST/DEFOGGER
6 HEATER
7 VENT
8 BI-LEVEL
9 RECIRCULATION
10 AUTOMATIC (FROM TEMPERATURE SET)
11 DECREASE TEMPERATURE
12 TEMPERATURE SET
13 INCREASE TEMPERATURE

	CONTROL SETTINGS			SYSTEM RESPONSE					
STEP	MODE CONTROL	TEMPERATURE SETTING	FAN SETTING	BLOWER SPEED	HEATER OUTLETS	A/C OUTLETS	DEFROSTER OUTLETS	S.W.D.** OUTLETS	*SEE NOTES
1	OFF	60°F	MANUAL 1	OFF	NO AIRFLOW	NO AIRFLOW	NO AIRFLOW	NO AIRFLOW	
2	AUTO	60°F	MANUAL 1	LOW	NO AIRFLOW	AIRFLOW	NO AIRFLOW	MINIMAL AIRFLOW	
3	AUTO	60°F	MAN 1 TO AUTO	LOW TO HIGH	NO AIRFLOW	AIRFLOW	NO AIRFLOW	MINIMAL AIRFLOW	A
4	RECIRC	60°F	AUTO	HIGH	NO AIRFLOW	AIRFLOW	NO AIRFLOW	MINIMAL AIRFLOW	
5	BI-LEVEL	60°F	AUTO	HIGH	AIRFLOW	AIRFLOW	AIRFLOW	MINIMAL AIRFLOW	
6	VENT	60°F	AUTO	HIGH	NO AIRFLOW	AIRFLOW	NO AIRFLOW	MINIMAL AIRFLOW	B
7	HTR	90°F	AUTO	HIGH	AIRFLOW	NO AIRFLOW	MINIMAL AIRFLOW	AIRFLOW	C
8	DEF	90°F	AUTO	HIGH	MINIMAL AIRFLOW	NO AIRFLOW	AIRFLOW	AIRFLOW	C

** ONLY A SMALL QUANTITY OF AIR WILL BE DISCHARGED AT THESE

COOLING FUNCTIONAL TEST

1. DOOR OR WIDOWS CLOSED
2. TEMPERATURE INDICATORS AT CONDENSER INLET AND RH UPPER COOLING OUTLET
3. CLOSE LH SIDE, CENTER AND LOWER RH COOLING OUTLETS
4. START ENGINE AND RUN AT 2000 RPM
5. SET TEMPERATURE TO 60°F (MAX COOL) BY PRESSING COOL BUTTON
6. AFTER ONE MINUTE THE AIR TEMPERATURE DROP AT THE RH UPPER COOLING OUTLET SHOULD BE AS FOLLOWS.

CONDENSER INLET TEMPERATURE (F°)	70	80	90-100
CENTER OUTLET TEMPERATURE DROP (F° MINIMUM)	20	25	30

*NOTES

A. NOTICEABLE BLOWER SPEED INCREASE MUST OCCUR FROM MANUAL (1) TO AUTO
B. LISTEN FOR REDUCTION OF AIR NOISE DUE TO RECIRCULATION DOOR CLOSING.
C. CHECK FOR SMALL AMOUNT OF AIR FLOW AT S.W.D. OUTLETS.

PARAMETER #	PARAMETER DESCRIPTION	DISPLAY RANGE
0	SYSTEM FAULTS	00 - 10
1	TEMPERATURE SETTING IN DEGREES	60°F - 90°F
2	IN-CAR TEMPERATURE SENSOR	10 = (HOT) - 130 (230) = (COLD)
3	OUTSIDE AMBIENT TEMPERATURE SENSOR	10 = (HOT) - 130 (230) = (COLD)
4	SUN LOAD SENSOR	MAX LIGHT / MAX DARK L98 38 / 183 LT5 115 / - 110 (210)
* 5	IGNITION SYSTEM VOLTAGE	0 = 9 VOLTS -155 (255) = 16
* 6	ENGINE SPEED (RPM ÷ 25)	
* 7	VEHICLE SPEED	
9	SYSTEM MODE (00 = OFF 01 = RECIRCULATION, 02 = A/C 03 = BI-LEVEL, 04 = HEATER 06 = DEFROST, 07 = VENT 10 = MANUAL RECIRCULATION)	AUTO MODE WILL DISPLAY 01-04 DEPENDING ON SET TEMPERATURE.
* 10	BLOWER PWM (PULSE WIDTH MODULATION)	0 = 0 VOLTS 128 = 14 VOLTS
* 11	PROGRAM NUMBER	00 = (COLD) - 155 (255) = (HOT)
* 12	MIX NUMBER	-155 (255) = (COLD) 00 = (HOT)
* 16	COOLANT TEMP.	°C
* 17	SOLAR CORRECTION	114 - MAX LIGHT 128 MAX DARK
* 30	STORED FULL HOT VALUE	0 - 50
* 31	TEMPERATURE DOOR TRAVEL RANGE	100 - 200
34	TEMPERATURE DOOR POSITION REQUESTED	00 = FULL HOT -153 (253) = FULL COLD
* 35	COMPRESSOR ON TIME	.1 SECOND INCREMENTS
* 36	NUMBER OF TIMES BELOW CRITICAL TIME	
* 37	SOFTWARE VERSION NUMBER	

* - NOT USED FOR SYSTEM DIAGNOSIS

NOTE: A MINUS (-) SIGN TO THE LEFT OF THE PARAMETER DISPLAY RANGE FIGURE WILL INDICATE AN ADDITIONAL 100 TO THE DISPLAY

EXAMPLE: - 130 = 230

ECC SYSTEM DIAGNOSIS—CORVETTE (CONT'D)

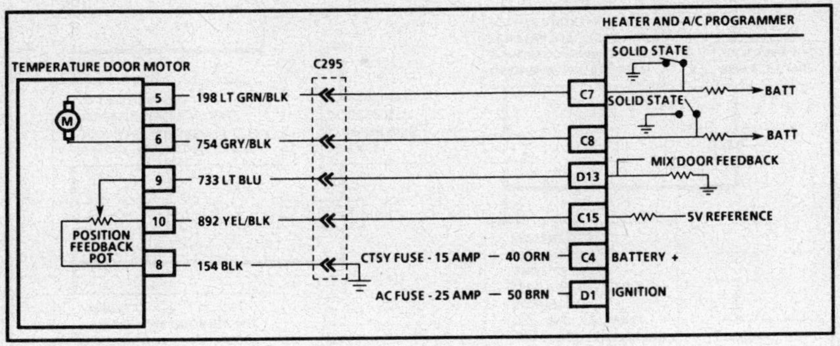
TEMPERATURE DOOR MOTOR
M
POSITION FEEDBACK POT
5
6
9
10
8
198 LT GRN/BLK
754 GRY/BLK
733 LT BLU
892 YEL/BLK
154 BLK
C295
CTSY FUSE - 15 AMP — 40 ORN
AC FUSE - 25 AMP — 50 BRN
HEATER AND A/C PROGRAMMER
C7
C8
D13
C15
C4
D1
SOLID STATE
SOLID STATE
BATT
BATT
MIX DOOR FEEDBACK
5V REFERENCE
BATTERY +
IGNITION

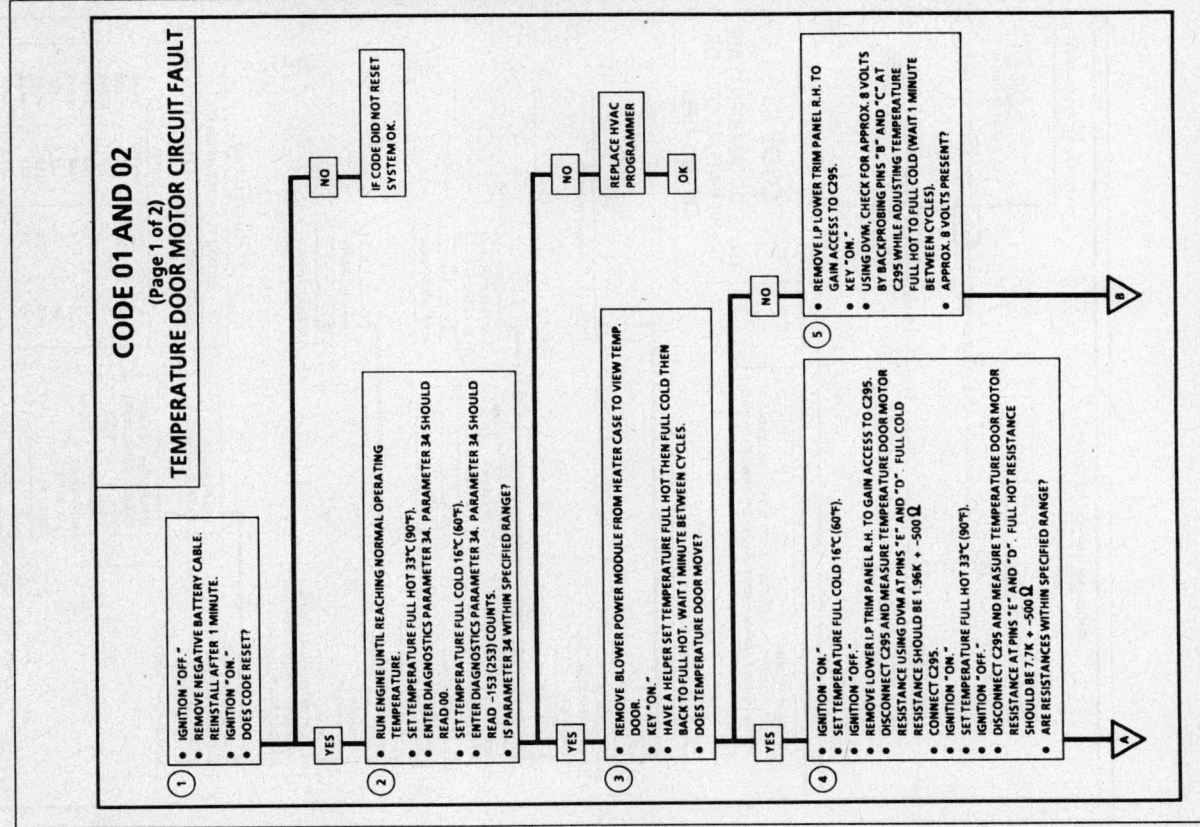

CODE 01 AND 02
(Page 1 of 2)
TEMPERATURE DOOR MOTOR CIRCUIT FAULT

(1)
- IGNITION "OFF."
- REMOVE NEGATIVE BATTERY CABLE. REINSTALL AFTER 1 MINUTE.
- IGNITION "ON."
- DOES CODE RESET?

NO → IF CODE DID NOT RESET SYSTEM OK.

YES ↓

(2)
- RUN ENGINE UNTIL REACHING NORMAL OPERATING TEMPERATURE.
- SET TEMPERATURE FULL HOT 33°C (90°F).
- ENTER DIAGNOSTICS PARAMETER 34. PARAMETER 34 SHOULD READ 00.
- SET TEMPERATURE FULL COLD 16°C (60°F).
- ENTER DIAGNOSTICS PARAMETER 34. PARAMETER 34 SHOULD READ −153 (253) COUNTS.
- IS PARAMETER 34 WITHIN SPECIFIED RANGE?

NO → REPLACE HVAC PROGRAMMER → OK

YES ↓

(3)
- REMOVE BLOWER POWER MODULE FROM HEATER CASE TO VIEW TEMP. DOOR.
- KEY "ON."
- HAVE A HELPER SET TEMPERATURE FULL HOT THEN FULL COLD THEN BACK TO FULL HOT. WAIT 1 MINUTE BETWEEN CYCLES.
- DOES TEMPERATURE DOOR MOVE?

YES ↓

(4)
- IGNITION "ON."
- SET TEMPERATURE FULL COLD 16°C (60°F).
- IGNITION "OFF."
- REMOVE LOWER I.P TRIM PANEL R.H. TO GAIN ACCESS TO C295.
- DISCONNECT C295 AND MEASURE TEMPERATURE DOOR MOTOR RESISTANCE USING DVM AT PINS "E" AND "D". FULL COLD RESISTANCE SHOULD BE 1.96K + −500 Ω
- CONNECT C295.
- IGNITION "ON."
- SET TEMPERATURE FULL HOT 33°C (90°F).
- IGNITION "OFF."
- DISCONNECT C295 AND MEASURE TEMPERATURE DOOR MOTOR RESISTANCE AT PINS "E" AND "D". FULL HOT RESISTANCE SHOULD BE 7.7K + −500 Ω
- ARE RESISTANCES WITHIN SPECIFIED RANGE?

→ A

NO ↓

(5)
- REMOVE I.P LOWER TRIM PANEL R.H. TO GAIN ACCESS TO C295.
- KEY "ON."
- USING DVM, CHECK FOR APPROX. 8 VOLTS BY BACKPROBING PINS "B" AND "C" AT C295 WHILE ADJUSTING TEMPERATURE FULL HOT TO FULL COLD (WAIT 1 MINUTE BETWEEN CYCLES).
- APPROX. 8 VOLTS PRESENT?

→ B

ECC SYSTEM DIAGNOSIS—CORVETTE (CONT'D)

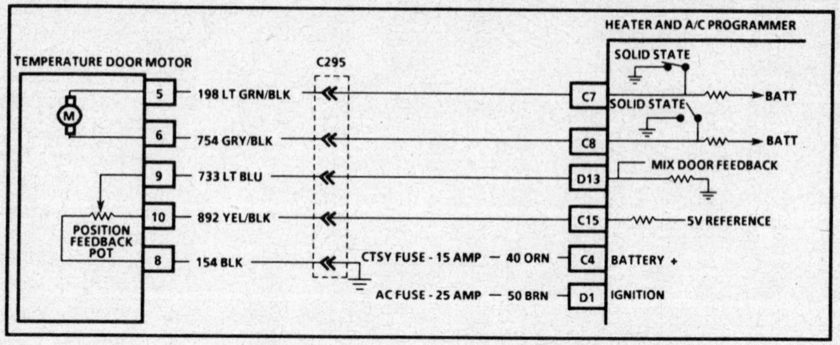
TEMPERATURE DOOR MOTOR
C295
HEATER AND A/C PROGRAMMER
M
5
198 LT GRN/BLK
C7
SOLID STATE
BATT
6
754 GRY/BLK
C8
SOLID STATE
BATT
9
733 LT BLU
D13
MIX DOOR FEEDBACK
POSITION FEEDBACK POT
10
892 YEL/BLK
C15
5V REFERENCE
8
154 BLK
CTSY FUSE - 15 AMP — 40 ORN
C4
BATTERY +
AC FUSE - 25 AMP — 50 BRN
D1
IGNITION

CODE 01 AND 02

(Page 2 of 2)

TEMPERATURE DOOR MOTOR CIRCUIT FAULT

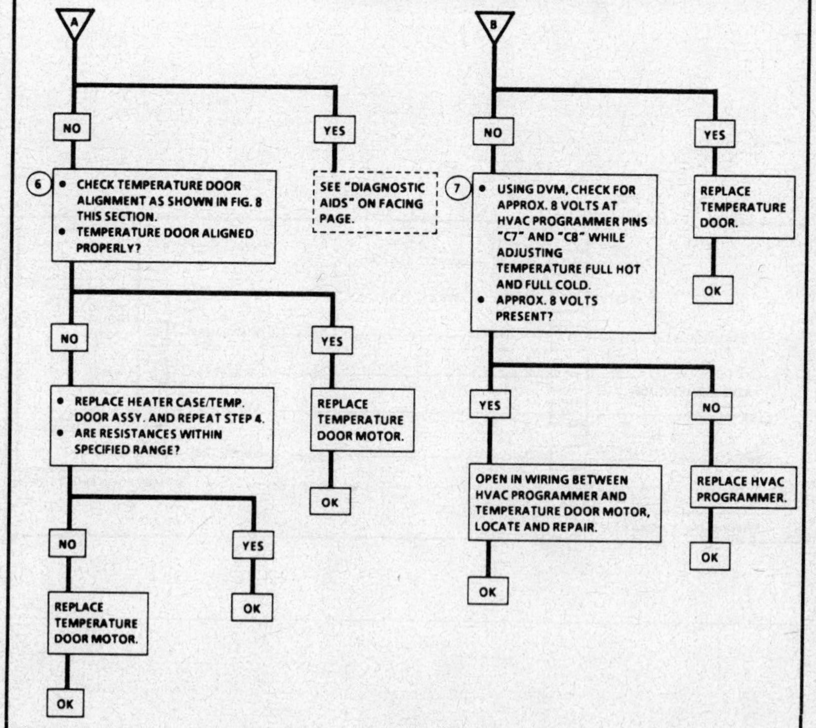
A
NO
YES
6
• CHECK TEMPERATURE DOOR ALIGNMENT AS SHOWN IN FIG. 8 THIS SECTION.
• TEMPERATURE DOOR ALIGNED PROPERLY?
SEE "DIAGNOSTIC AIDS" ON FACING PAGE.
NO
YES
• REPLACE HEATER CASE/TEMP. DOOR ASSY. AND REPEAT STEP 4.
• ARE RESISTANCES WITHIN SPECIFIED RANGE?
REPLACE TEMPERATURE DOOR MOTOR.
OK
NO
YES
REPLACE TEMPERATURE DOOR MOTOR.
OK
OK
B
NO
YES
7
• USING DVM, CHECK FOR APPROX. 8 VOLTS AT HVAC PROGRAMMER PINS "C7" AND "C8" WHILE ADJUSTING TEMPERATURE FULL HOT AND FULL COLD.
• APPROX. 8 VOLTS PRESENT?
REPLACE TEMPERATURE DOOR.
OK
YES
NO
OPEN IN WIRING BETWEEN HVAC PROGRAMMER AND TEMPERATURE DOOR MOTOR, LOCATE AND REPAIR.
OK
REPLACE HVAC PROGRAMMER.
OK

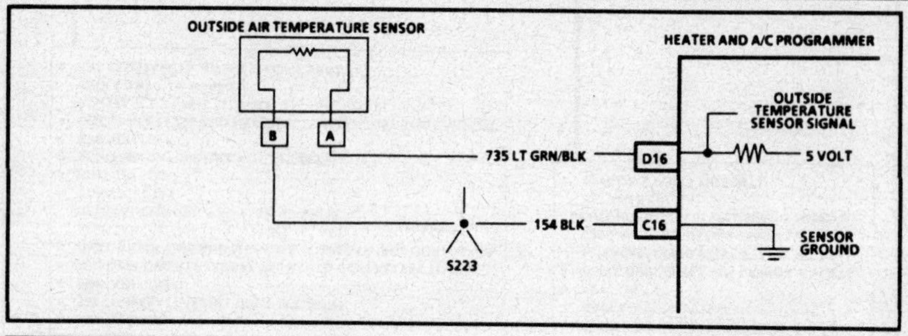
OUTSIDE AIR TEMPERATURE SENSOR
HEATER AND A/C PROGRAMMER
B
A
735 LT GRN/BLK
D16
OUTSIDE TEMPERATURE SENSOR SIGNAL
5 VOLT
154 BLK
C16
SENSOR GROUND
S223

CODE 03

OUTSIDE (AMBIENT) AIR TEMPERATURE SENSOR CIRCUIT OPEN

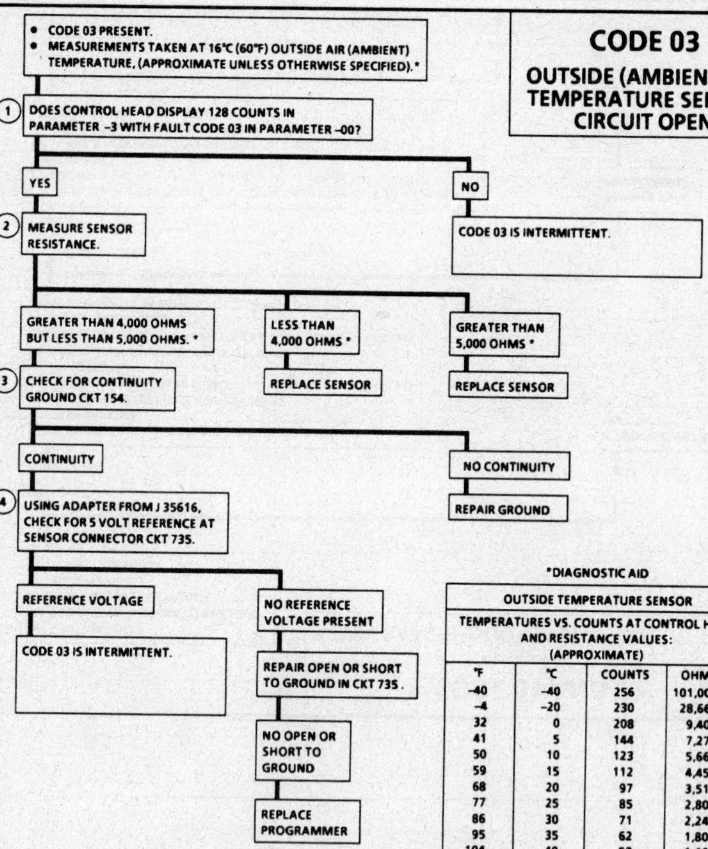
• CODE 03 PRESENT.
• MEASUREMENTS TAKEN AT 16°C (60°F) OUTSIDE AIR (AMBIENT) TEMPERATURE, (APPROXIMATE UNLESS OTHERWISE SPECIFIED).*
1
DOES CONTROL HEAD DISPLAY 128 COUNTS IN PARAMETER –3 WITH FAULT CODE 03 IN PARAMETER –00?
YES
NO
CODE 03 IS INTERMITTENT.
2
MEASURE SENSOR RESISTANCE.
GREATER THAN 4,000 OHMS BUT LESS THAN 5,000 OHMS. *
LESS THAN 4,000 OHMS *
REPLACE SENSOR
GREATER THAN 5,000 OHMS *
REPLACE SENSOR
3
CHECK FOR CONTINUITY GROUND CKT 154.
CONTINUITY
NO CONTINUITY
REPAIR GROUND
4
USING ADAPTER FROM J 35616, CHECK FOR 5 VOLT REFERENCE AT SENSOR CONNECTOR CKT 735.
REFERENCE VOLTAGE
CODE 03 IS INTERMITTENT.
NO REFERENCE VOLTAGE PRESENT
REPAIR OPEN OR SHORT TO GROUND IN CKT 735.
NO OPEN OR SHORT TO GROUND
REPLACE PROGRAMMER

*DIAGNOSTIC AID

OUTSIDE TEMPERATURE SENSOR

TEMPERATURES VS. COUNTS AT CONTROL HEAD AND RESISTANCE VALUES: (APPROXIMATE)

°F	°C	COUNTS	OHMS
–40	–40	256	101,000
–4	–20	230	28,660
32	0	208	9,400
41	5	144	7,275
50	10	123	5,666
59	15	112	4,450
68	20	97	3,514
77	25	85	2,800
86	30	71	2,240
95	35	62	1,800
104	40	53	1,460
113	45	44	1,190
131		32	N.A.
170		0-16	N.A.

ECC SYSTEM DIAGNOSIS—CORVETTE (CONT'D)

CODE 04
OUTSIDE AIR TEMPERATURE SENSOR CIRCUIT SHORT

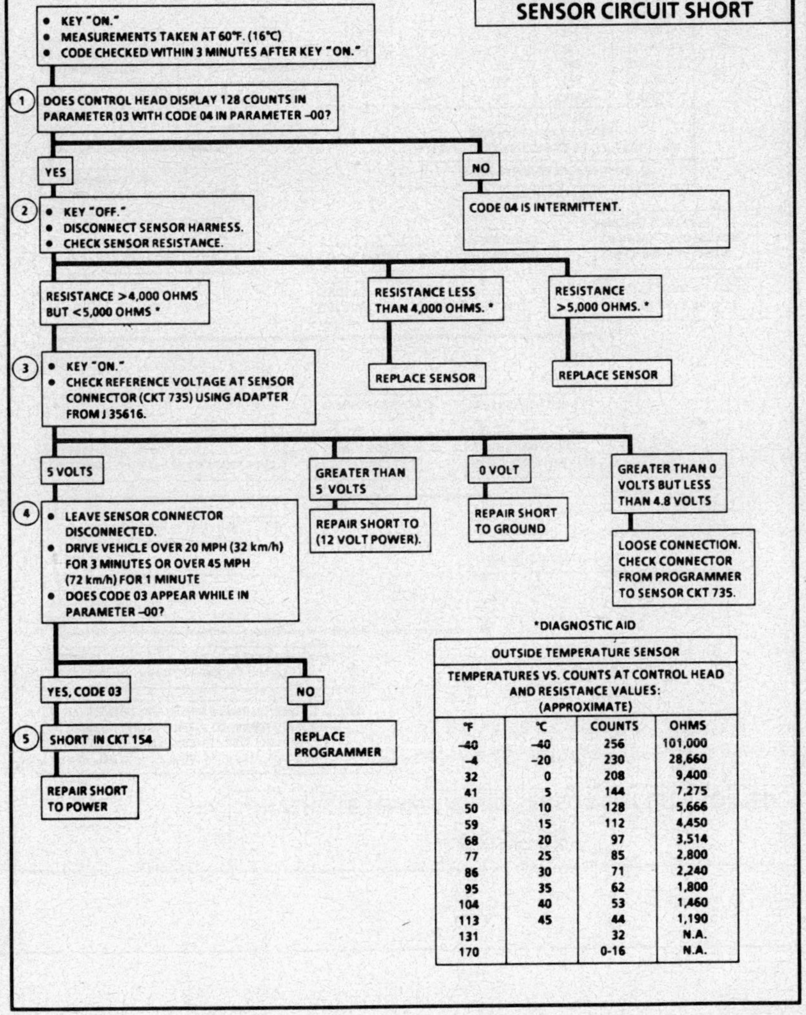
• KEY "ON."
• MEASUREMENTS TAKEN AT 60°F. (16°C)
• CODE CHECKED WITHIN 3 MINUTES AFTER KEY "ON."
1 DOES CONTROL HEAD DISPLAY 128 COUNTS IN PARAMETER 03 WITH CODE 04 IN PARAMETER –00?
YES
NO
CODE 04 IS INTERMITTENT.
2 • KEY "OFF." • DISCONNECT SENSOR HARNESS. • CHECK SENSOR RESISTANCE.
RESISTANCE >4,000 OHMS BUT <5,000 OHMS *
RESISTANCE LESS THAN 4,000 OHMS. *
RESISTANCE >5,000 OHMS. *
REPLACE SENSOR
REPLACE SENSOR
3 • KEY "ON." • CHECK REFERENCE VOLTAGE AT SENSOR CONNECTOR (CKT 735) USING ADAPTER FROM J 35616.
5 VOLTS
GREATER THAN 5 VOLTS
0 VOLT
GREATER THAN 0 VOLTS BUT LESS THAN 4.8 VOLTS
REPAIR SHORT TO (12 VOLT POWER).
REPAIR SHORT TO GROUND
LOOSE CONNECTION. CHECK CONNECTOR FROM PROGRAMMER TO SENSOR CKT 735.
4 • LEAVE SENSOR CONNECTOR DISCONNECTED. • DRIVE VEHICLE OVER 20 MPH (32 km/h) FOR 3 MINUTES OR OVER 45 MPH (72 km/h) FOR 1 MINUTE • DOES CODE 03 APPEAR WHILE IN PARAMETER –00?
YES, CODE 03
NO
REPLACE PROGRAMMER
5 SHORT IN CKT 154
REPAIR SHORT TO POWER

*DIAGNOSTIC AID

OUTSIDE TEMPERATURE SENSOR

TEMPERATURES VS. COUNTS AT CONTROL HEAD AND RESISTANCE VALUES: (APPROXIMATE)

°F	°C	COUNTS	OHMS
–40	–40	256	101,000
–4	–20	230	28,660
32	0	208	9,400
41	5	144	7,275
50	10	128	5,666
59	15	112	4,450
68	20	97	3,514
77	25	85	2,800
86	30	71	2,240
95	35	62	1,800
104	40	53	1,460
113	45	44	1,190
131		32	N.A.
170		0-16	N.A.

CODE 05
IN-VEHICLE TEMPERATURE SENSOR CIRCUIT OPEN

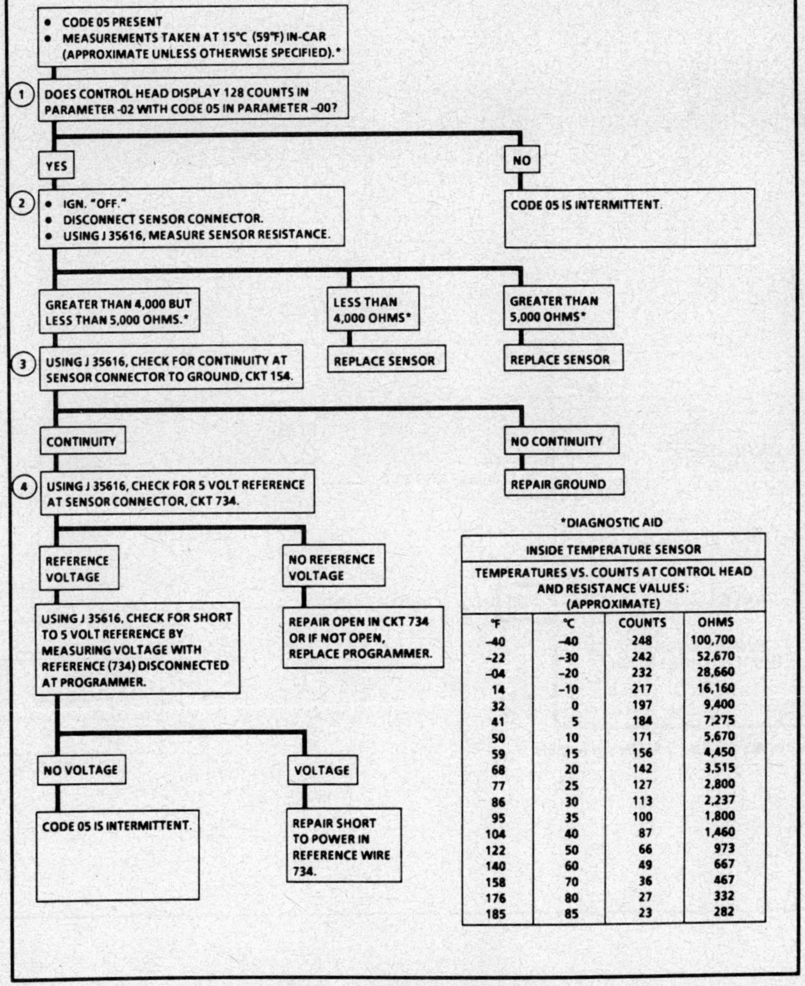
• CODE 05 PRESENT
• MEASUREMENTS TAKEN AT 15°C (59°F) IN-CAR (APPROXIMATE UNLESS OTHERWISE SPECIFIED).*
1 DOES CONTROL HEAD DISPLAY 128 COUNTS IN PARAMETER -02 WITH CODE 05 IN PARAMETER –00?
YES
NO
CODE 05 IS INTERMITTENT.
2 • IGN. "OFF." • DISCONNECT SENSOR CONNECTOR. • USING J 35616, MEASURE SENSOR RESISTANCE.
GREATER THAN 4,000 BUT LESS THAN 5,000 OHMS.*
LESS THAN 4,000 OHMS*
GREATER THAN 5,000 OHMS*
REPLACE SENSOR
REPLACE SENSOR
3 USING J 35616, CHECK FOR CONTINUITY AT SENSOR CONNECTOR TO GROUND, CKT 154.
CONTINUITY
NO CONTINUITY
REPAIR GROUND
4 USING J 35616, CHECK FOR 5 VOLT REFERENCE AT SENSOR CONNECTOR, CKT 734.
REFERENCE VOLTAGE
NO REFERENCE VOLTAGE
USING J 35616, CHECK FOR SHORT TO 5 VOLT REFERENCE BY MEASURING VOLTAGE WITH REFERENCE (734) DISCONNECTED AT PROGRAMMER.
REPAIR OPEN IN CKT 734 OR IF NOT OPEN, REPLACE PROGRAMMER.
NO VOLTAGE
VOLTAGE
CODE 05 IS INTERMITTENT.
REPAIR SHORT TO POWER IN REFERENCE WIRE 734.

*DIAGNOSTIC AID

INSIDE TEMPERATURE SENSOR

TEMPERATURES VS. COUNTS AT CONTROL HEAD AND RESISTANCE VALUES: (APPROXIMATE)

°F	°C	COUNTS	OHMS
–40	–40	248	100,700
–22	–30	242	52,670
–04	–20	232	28,660
14	–10	217	16,160
32	0	197	9,400
41	5	184	7,275
50	10	171	5,670
59	15	156	4,450
68	20	142	3,515
77	25	127	2,800
86	30	113	2,237
95	35	100	1,800
104	40	87	1,460
122	50	66	973
140	60	49	667
158	70	36	467
176	80	27	332
185	85	23	282

CODE 06

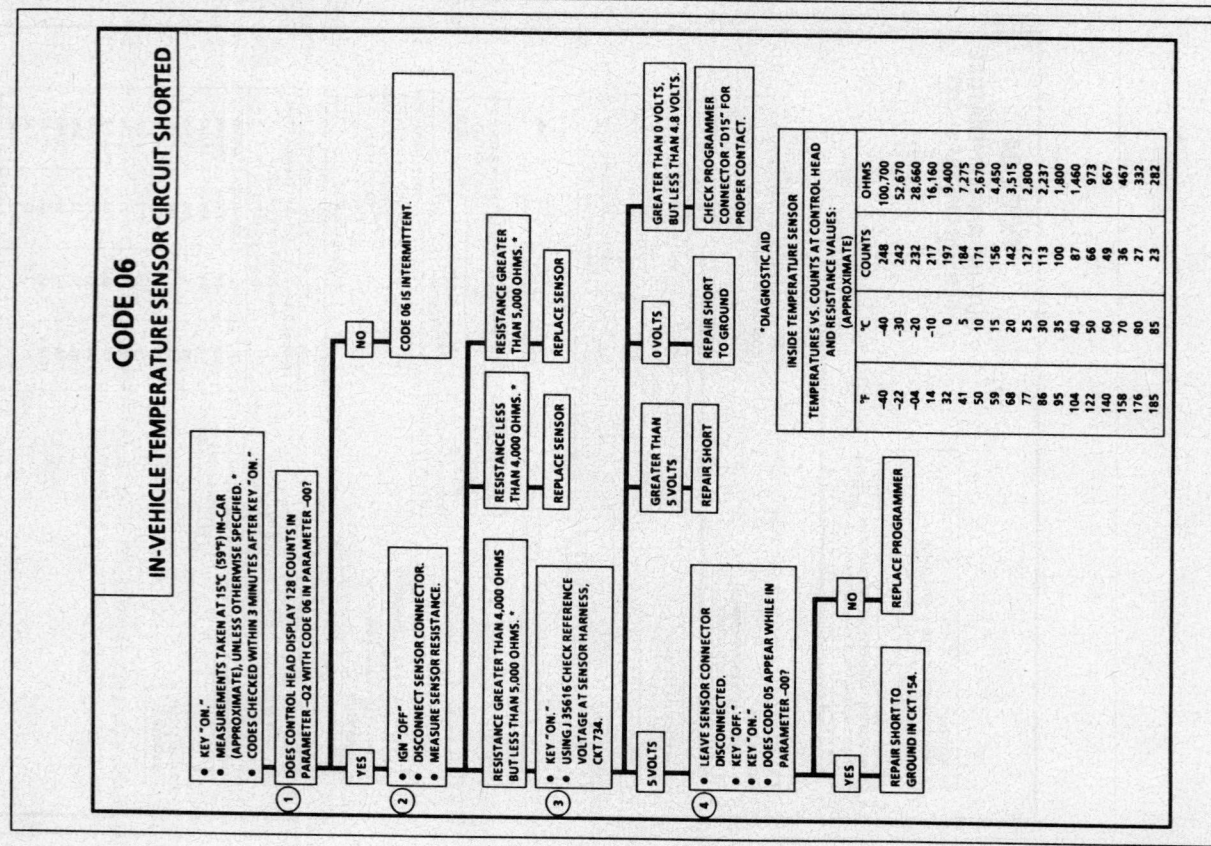

IN-VEHICLE TEMPERATURE SENSOR CIRCUIT SHORTED

- KEY "ON."
- MEASUREMENTS TAKEN AT 15°C (59°F) IN-CAR (APPROXIMATE), UNLESS OTHERWISE SPECIFIED. *
- CODES CHECKED WITHIN 3 MINUTES AFTER KEY "ON."

1 DOES CONTROL HEAD DISPLAY 128 COUNTS IN PARAMETER –02 WITH CODE 06 IN PARAMETER –00?

- YES → 2
- NO → CODE 06 IS INTERMITTENT.

2
- IGN "OFF"
- DISCONNECT SENSOR CONNECTOR.
- MEASURE SENSOR RESISTANCE.

- RESISTANCE GREATER THAN 4,000 OHMS BUT LESS THAN 5,000 OHMS. * → 3
- RESISTANCE LESS THAN 4,000 OHMS. * → REPLACE SENSOR
- RESISTANCE GREATER THAN 5,000 OHMS. * → REPLACE SENSOR

3
- KEY "ON."
- USING J 35616 CHECK REFERENCE VOLTAGE AT SENSOR HARNESS, CKT 734.

- 5 VOLTS → 4
- GREATER THAN 5 VOLTS → REPAIR SHORT
- 0 VOLTS → REPAIR SHORT TO GROUND
- GREATER THAN 0 VOLTS, BUT LESS THAN 4.8 VOLTS. → CHECK PROGRAMMER CONNECTOR "D15" FOR PROPER CONTACT.

4
- LEAVE SENSOR CONNECTOR DISCONNECTED.
- KEY "OFF."
- KEY "ON."
- DOES CODE 05 APPEAR WHILE IN PARAMETER –00?

- YES → REPAIR SHORT TO GROUND IN CKT 154.
- NO → REPLACE PROGRAMMER

*DIAGNOSTIC AID

INSIDE TEMPERATURE SENSOR

TEMPERATURES VS. COUNTS AT CONTROL HEAD AND RESISTANCE VALUES: (APPROXIMATE)

°F	°C	COUNTS	OHMS
–40	–40	248	100,700
–22	–30	242	52,670
–04	–20	232	28,660
14	–10	217	16,160
32	0	197	9,400
41	5	184	7,275
50	10	171	5,670
59	15	156	4,450
68	20	142	3,515
77	25	127	2,800
86	30	113	2,237
95	35	100	1,800
104	40	87	1,460
122	50	66	973
140	60	49	667
158	70	36	467
176	80	27	332
185	85	23	282

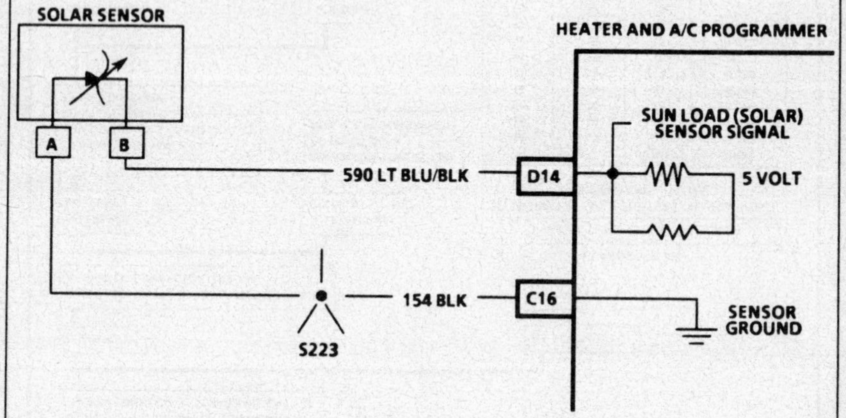
SOLAR SENSOR
A
B
HEATER AND A/C PROGRAMMER
SUN LOAD (SOLAR) SENSOR SIGNAL
5 VOLT
590 LT BLU/BLK
D14
154 BLK
C16
S223
SENSOR GROUND

ECC SYSTEM DIAGNOSIS—CORVETTE (CONT'D)

CODE 07 AND 08
SOLAR SENSOR (SUN LOAD) CIRCUIT OPEN OR SHORTED

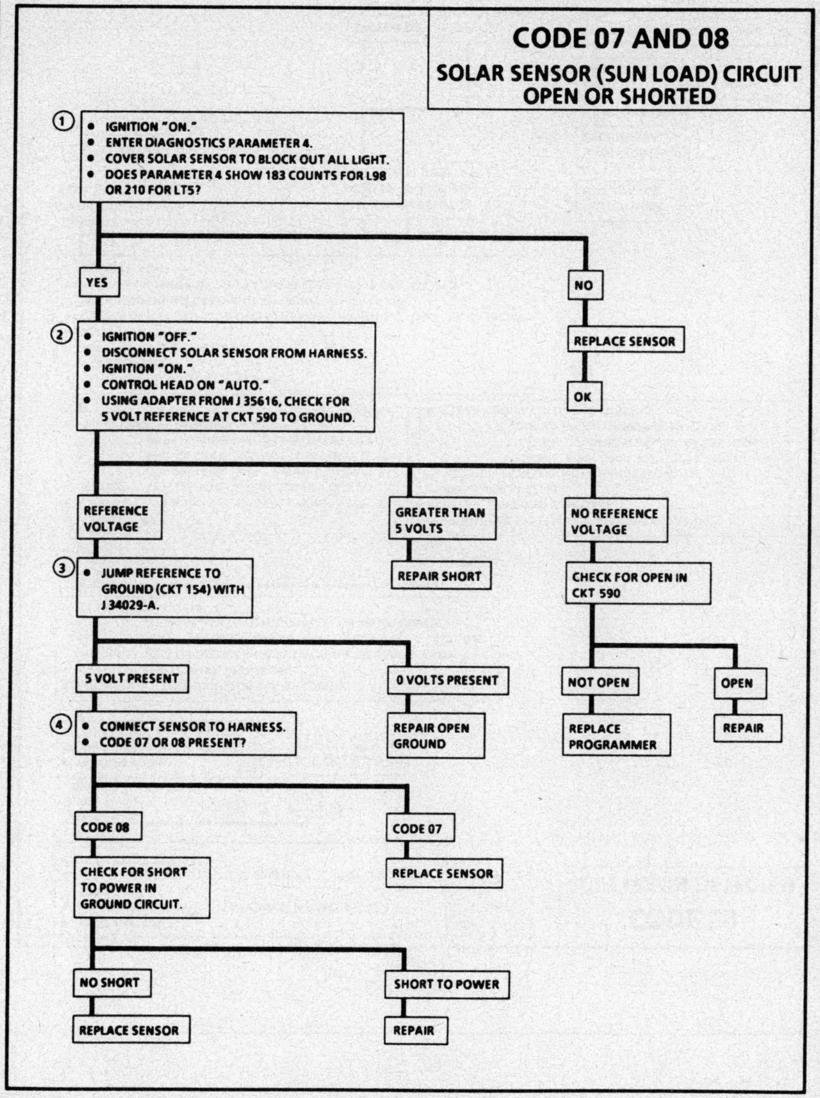
1
IGNITION "ON."
ENTER DIAGNOSTICS PARAMETER 4.
COVER SOLAR SENSOR TO BLOCK OUT ALL LIGHT.
DOES PARAMETER 4 SHOW 183 COUNTS FOR L98 OR 210 FOR LT5?
YES
NO
REPLACE SENSOR
OK
2
IGNITION "OFF."
DISCONNECT SOLAR SENSOR FROM HARNESS.
IGNITION "ON."
CONTROL HEAD ON "AUTO."
USING ADAPTER FROM J 35616, CHECK FOR 5 VOLT REFERENCE AT CKT 590 TO GROUND.
REFERENCE VOLTAGE
GREATER THAN 5 VOLTS
REPAIR SHORT
NO REFERENCE VOLTAGE
CHECK FOR OPEN IN CKT 590
NOT OPEN
REPLACE PROGRAMMER
OPEN
REPAIR
3
JUMP REFERENCE TO GROUND (CKT 154) WITH J 34029-A.
5 VOLT PRESENT
0 VOLTS PRESENT
REPAIR OPEN GROUND
4
CONNECT SENSOR TO HARNESS.
CODE 07 OR 08 PRESENT?
CODE 08
CHECK FOR SHORT TO POWER IN GROUND CIRCUIT.
NO SHORT
REPLACE SENSOR
SHORT TO POWER
REPAIR
CODE 07
REPLACE SENSOR

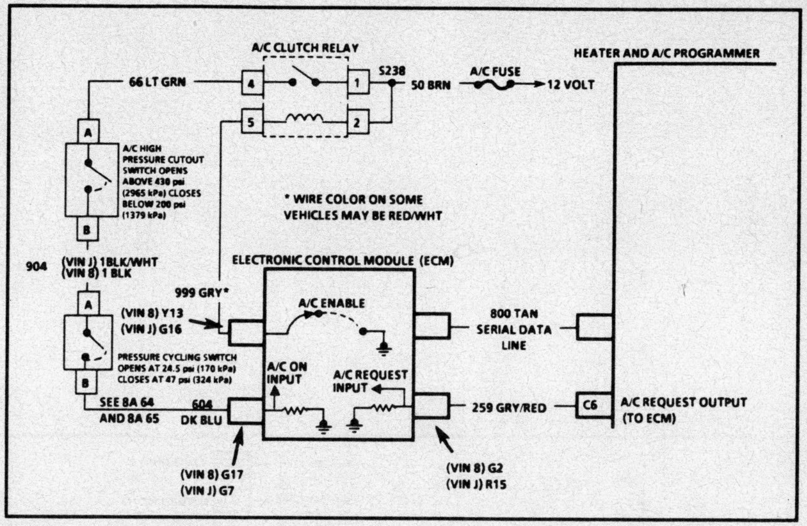
A/C CLUTCH RELAY
66 LT GRN
S238
50 BRN
A/C FUSE
12 VOLT
HEATER AND A/C PROGRAMMER
A/C HIGH PRESSURE CUTOUT SWITCH OPENS ABOVE 430 psi (2965 kPa) CLOSES BELOW 200 psi (1379 kPa)
* WIRE COLOR ON SOME VEHICLES MAY BE RED/WHT
904
(VIN J) 1BLK/WHT
(VIN 8) 1 BLK
ELECTRONIC CONTROL MODULE (ECM)
999 GRY*
(VIN 8) Y13
(VIN J) G16
A/C ENABLE
800 TAN
SERIAL DATA LINE
PRESSURE CYCLING SWITCH OPENS AT 24.5 psi (170 kPa) CLOSES AT 47 psi (324 kPa)
A/C ON INPUT
A/C REQUEST INPUT
SEE 8A 64 AND 8A 65
604
DK BLU
259 GRY/RED
C6
A/C REQUEST OUTPUT (TO ECM)
(VIN 8) G17
(VIN J) G7
(VIN 8) G2
(VIN J) R15

ECC SYSTEM DIAGNOSIS—CORVETTE (CONT'D)

CODE 09
LOW FREON DETECTED

1.
- IGNITION "OFF."
- REMOVE NEGATIVE BATTERY CABLE. INSTALL AFTER 1 MINUTE.
- RUN ENGINE 5 MINUTES, 1000 RPM WITH AC IN RECIRC MODE.
- DOES CODE 09 RESET?

YES
- START ENGINE.
- AMBIENT ABOVE 10ºC (50ºF).
- ENGINE NOT OVERHEATED.

NO
IF CODE 09 DID NOT RESET SYSTEM OK

2. REFER TO HVAC, SECTION 1C FOR THE FOLLOWING:
- ADD 1 LB. OF R-12 USING J 23575-01.
  NOTICE: SYSTEM WILL CHARGE SLOWLY DUE TO COMPRESSOR "OFF." PRODUCT DAMAGE MAY OCCUR IF COMPRESSOR IS OPERATED WITH LOW/NO FREON OR REFRIGERANT OIL.
- LEAK CHECK SYSTEM.

NO LEAK FOUND

3.
- ENGINE "OFF."
- CHARGE SYSTEM TO 45 psi (310 kPa) USING J 23575-01.
  NOTICE: SYSTEM WILL CHARGE SLOWLY DUE TO COMPRESSOR "OFF." PRODUCT DAMAGE MAY OCCUR IF COMPRESSOR IS OPERATED WITH LOW/NO FREON OR REFRIGERANT OIL.
- CLEAR CODE AS OUTLINED IN STEP 1.

LEAK FOUND
- DISCHARGE SYSTEM INTO RECOVERY STATION.
- REPAIR LEAK AND EVACUATE.
- RECHARGE SYSTEM.
  NOTICE: SYSTEM WILL CHARGE SLOWLY DUE TO COMPRESSOR "OFF." PRODUCT DAMAGE MAY OCCUR IF COMPRESSOR IS OPERATED WITH LOW/NO FREON OR REFRIGERANT OIL.
- CLEAR CODE AS OUTLINED IN STEP 1.

4.
- CLEAR CODE AS OUTLINED IN STEP 1.
- START ENGINE.
- AMBIENT ABOVE 10ºC (50ºF).
- A/C IN AUTO MODE.
- ENTER POINTER 35, FREON CYCLE PARAMETER WITH A/C "ON" OR USE TECH 1 WITH 1990 ENGINE CARTRIDGE TO MONITOR A/C CLUTCH.
- MONITOR NUMBER OF TIMES COMPRESSOR CYCLES OR LISTEN TO COMPRESSOR.

MORE THAN 8 CLUTCH CYCLES PER MINUTE.

5.
- CLEAR CODE AS OUTLINED IN STEP 1
- PERFORM COOLING SYSTEM DIAGNOSIS

LESS THAN 8 CLUTCH CYCLES PER MINUTE. DOES CODE 09 RESET?
- NO: SYSTEM OK
- YES: REPLACE PROGRAMMER

CLUTCH DOES NOT ENGAGE.
JUMPER PRESSURE CYCLING SWITCH.
- CLUTCH ENGAGES: REPLACE PRESSURE CYCLING SWITCH.
- CLUTCH DOES NOT ENGAGE: REFER TO HVAC, SECTION 1C, INSUFFICIENT COOLING CHART B FOR FURTHER CIRCUIT DIAGNOSIS.

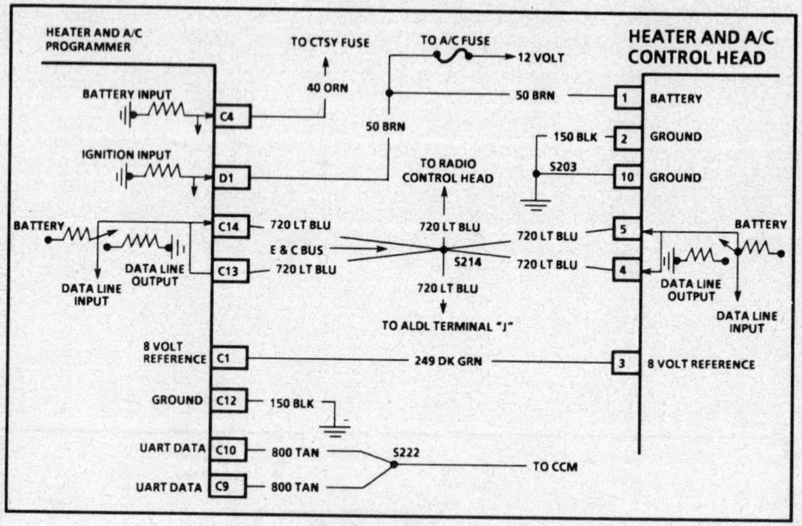
HEATER AND A/C PROGRAMMER
HEATER AND A/C CONTROL HEAD
TO CTSY FUSE
40 ORN
TO A/C FUSE
12 VOLT
50 BRN
50 BRN
BATTERY INPUT
C4
IGNITION INPUT
D1
TO RADIO CONTROL HEAD
150 BLK
S203
1 BATTERY
2 GROUND
10 GROUND
BATTERY
C14
720 LT BLU
E & C BUS
C13
720 LT BLU
DATA LINE OUTPUT
DATA LINE INPUT
720 LT BLU
S214
720 LT BLU
TO ALDL TERMINAL "J"
720 LT BLU
720 LT BLU
5
4
BATTERY
DATA LINE OUTPUT
DATA LINE INPUT
8 VOLT REFERENCE
C1
249 DK GRN
3 8 VOLT REFERENCE
GROUND
C12
150 BLK
UART DATA
C10
800 TAN
S222
TO CCM
UART DATA
C9
800 TAN

WIRING SCHEMATICS

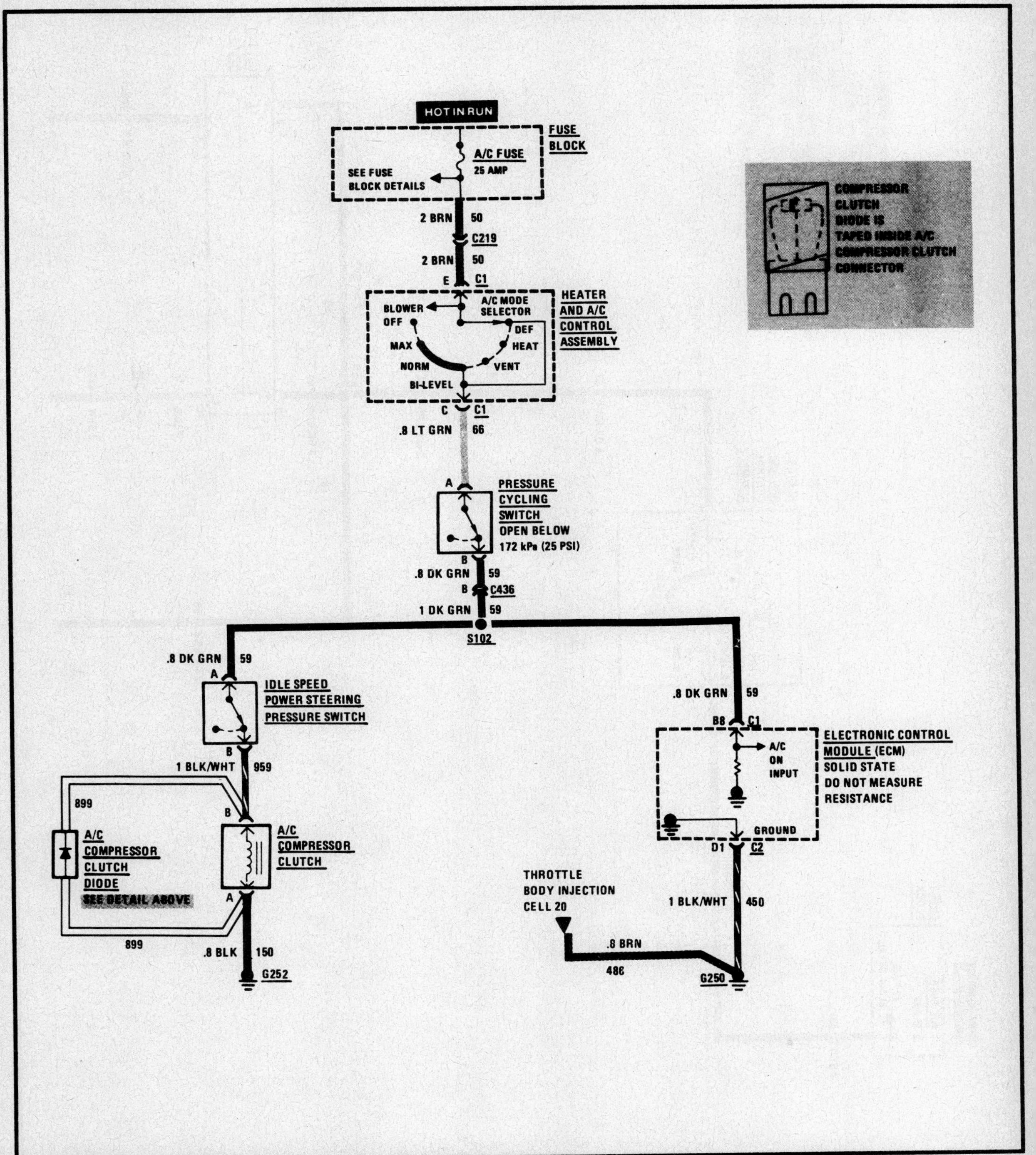
HOT IN RUN
FUSE BLOCK
A/C FUSE
25 AMP
SEE FUSE BLOCK DETAILS
2 BRN
50
C219
2 BRN
50
E
C1
HEATER AND A/C CONTROL ASSEMBLY
BLOWER OFF
A/C MODE SELECTOR
DEF
HEAT
MAX
NORM
VENT
BI-LEVEL
C
C1
.8 LT GRN
66
A
PRESSURE CYCLING SWITCH
OPEN BELOW 172 kPa (25 PSI)
B
.8 DK GRN
59
B
C436
1 DK GRN
59
S102
.8 DK GRN
59
A
IDLE SPEED POWER STEERING PRESSURE SWITCH
B
1 BLK/WHT
959
899
B
A/C COMPRESSOR CLUTCH DIODE
SEE DETAIL ABOVE
A/C COMPRESSOR CLUTCH
A
899
.8 BLK
150
G252
.8 DK GRN
59
B8
C1
ELECTRONIC CONTROL MODULE (ECM)
SOLID STATE
DO NOT MEASURE RESISTANCE
A/C ON INPUT
GROUND
D1
C2
THROTTLE BODY INJECTION CELL 20
1 BLK/WHT
450
.8 BRN
486
G250
COMPRESSOR CLUTCH DIODE IS TAPED INSIDE A/C COMPRESSOR CLUTCH CONNECTOR

Compressor controls schematic—Caprice, Estate Wagon, Custom Cruiser, Safari and Roadmaster

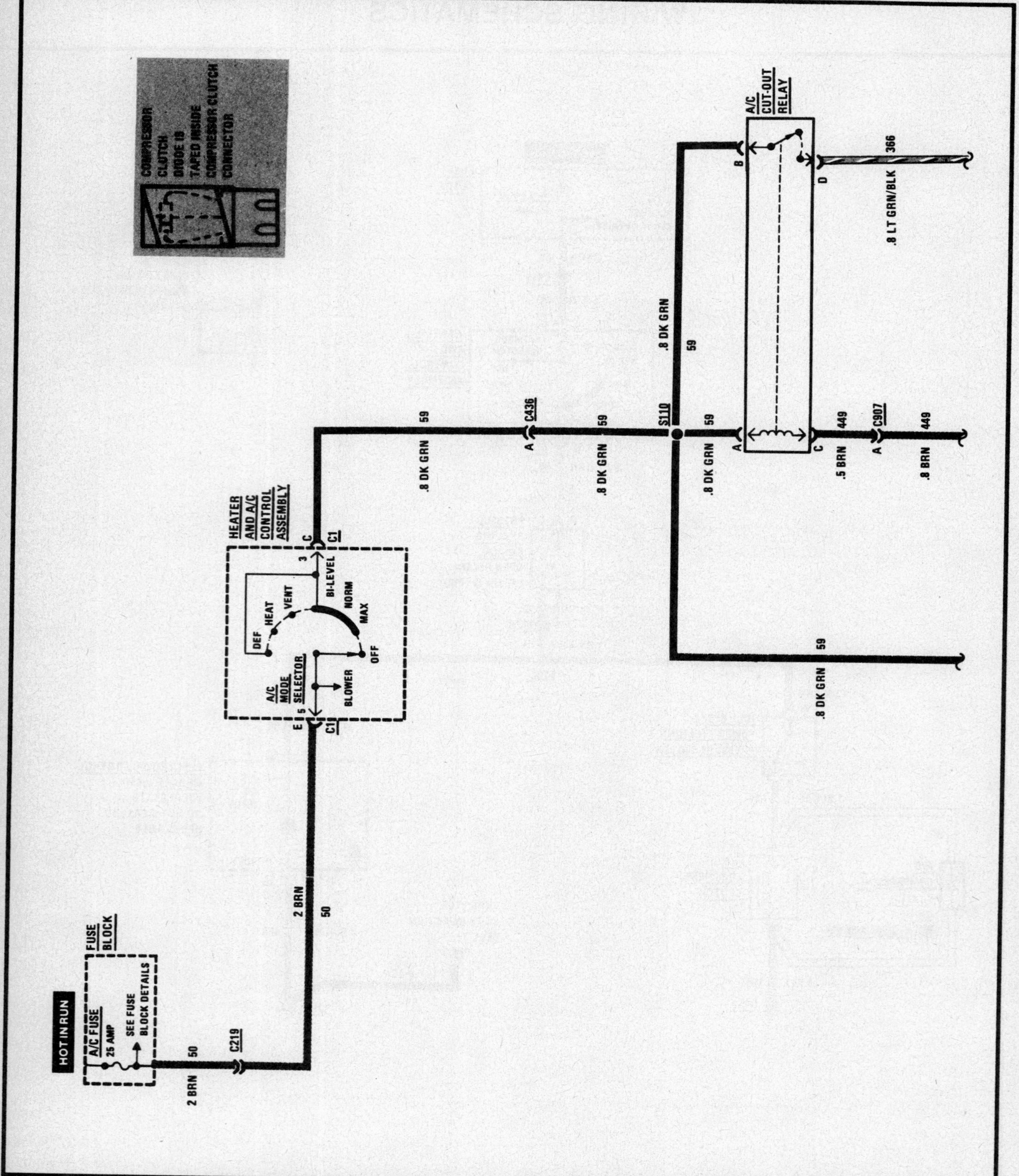
COMPRESSOR CLUTCH DIODE IS TAPED INSIDE COMPRESSOR CLUTCH CONNECTOR
A/C CUT-OUT RELAY
B
D
366
.8 LT GRN/BLK
.8 DK GRN
59
C436
A
S110
C
449
C907
.5 BRN
.8 BRN
HEATER AND A/C CONTROL ASSEMBLY
C1
3
BI-LEVEL
NORM
MAX
VENT
HEAT
DEF
OFF
BLOWER
A/C MODE SELECTOR
E
5
2 BRN
50
FUSE BLOCK
HOT IN RUN
A/C FUSE
25 AMP
SEE FUSE BLOCK DETAILS
C219

Compressor controls schematic—Caprice, Estate Wagon, Custom Cruiser, Safari and Roadmaster

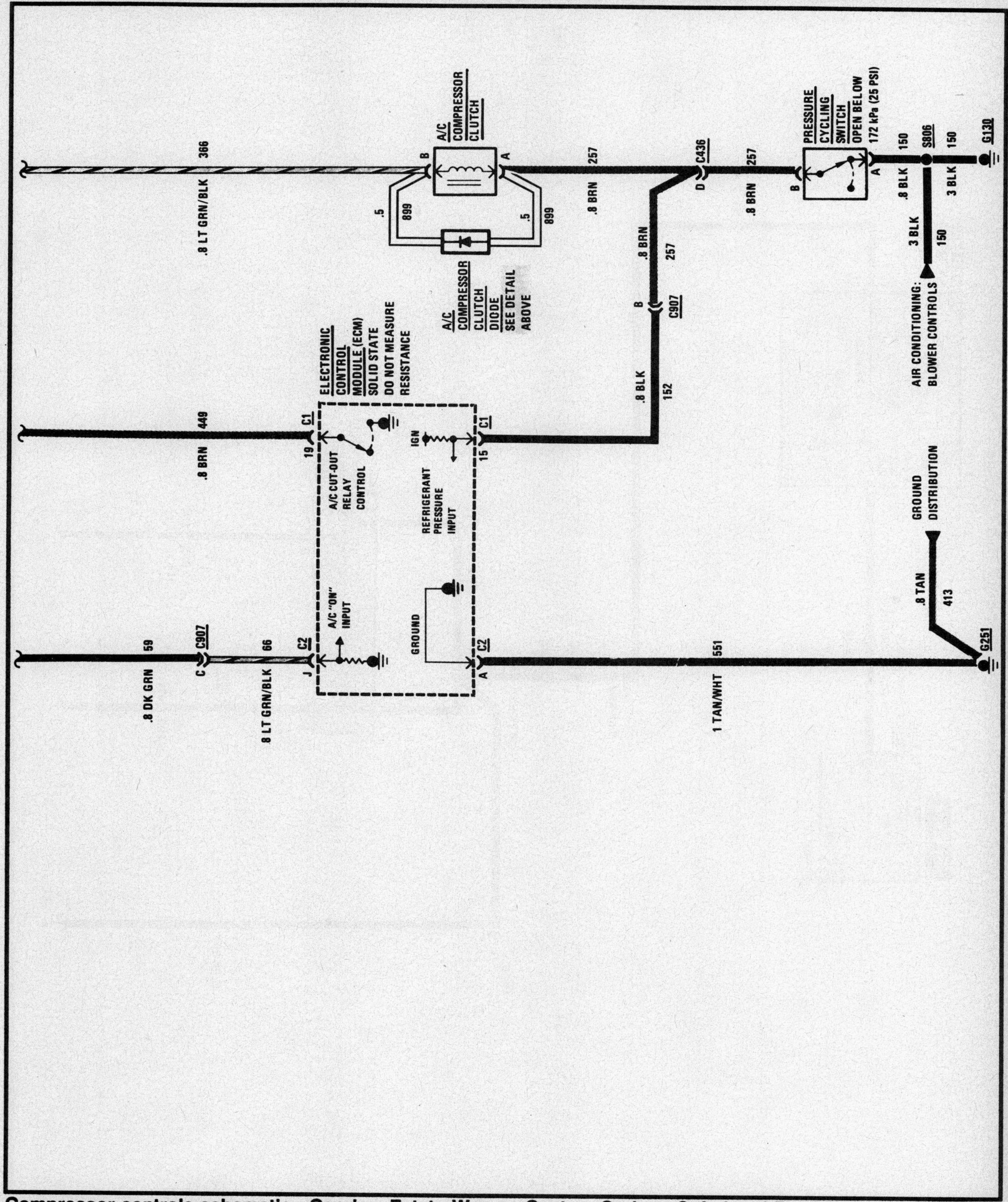
A/C COMPRESSOR CLUTCH
PRESSURE CYCLING SWITCH OPEN BELOW 172 kPa (25 PSI)
A/C COMPRESSOR CLUTCH DIODE SEE DETAIL ABOVE
ELECTRONIC CONTROL MODULE (ECM) SOLID STATE DO NOT MEASURE RESISTANCE
A/C CUT-OUT RELAY CONTROL
REFRIGERANT PRESSURE INPUT
IGN
GROUND
A/C "ON" INPUT
AIR CONDITIONING: BLOWER CONTROLS
GROUND DISTRIBUTION
.8 LT GRN/BLK 366
.8 BRN 449
.8 DK GRN 59
C907
.8 LT GRN/BLK 66
C1
C2
.8 BRN 257
C436
.8 BLK 152
.8 BLK 150
3 BLK 150
S806
G130
G251
.8 TAN 413
1 TAN/WHT 551
.5 899

Compressor controls schematic—Caprice, Estate Wagon, Custom Cruiser, Safari and Roadmaster

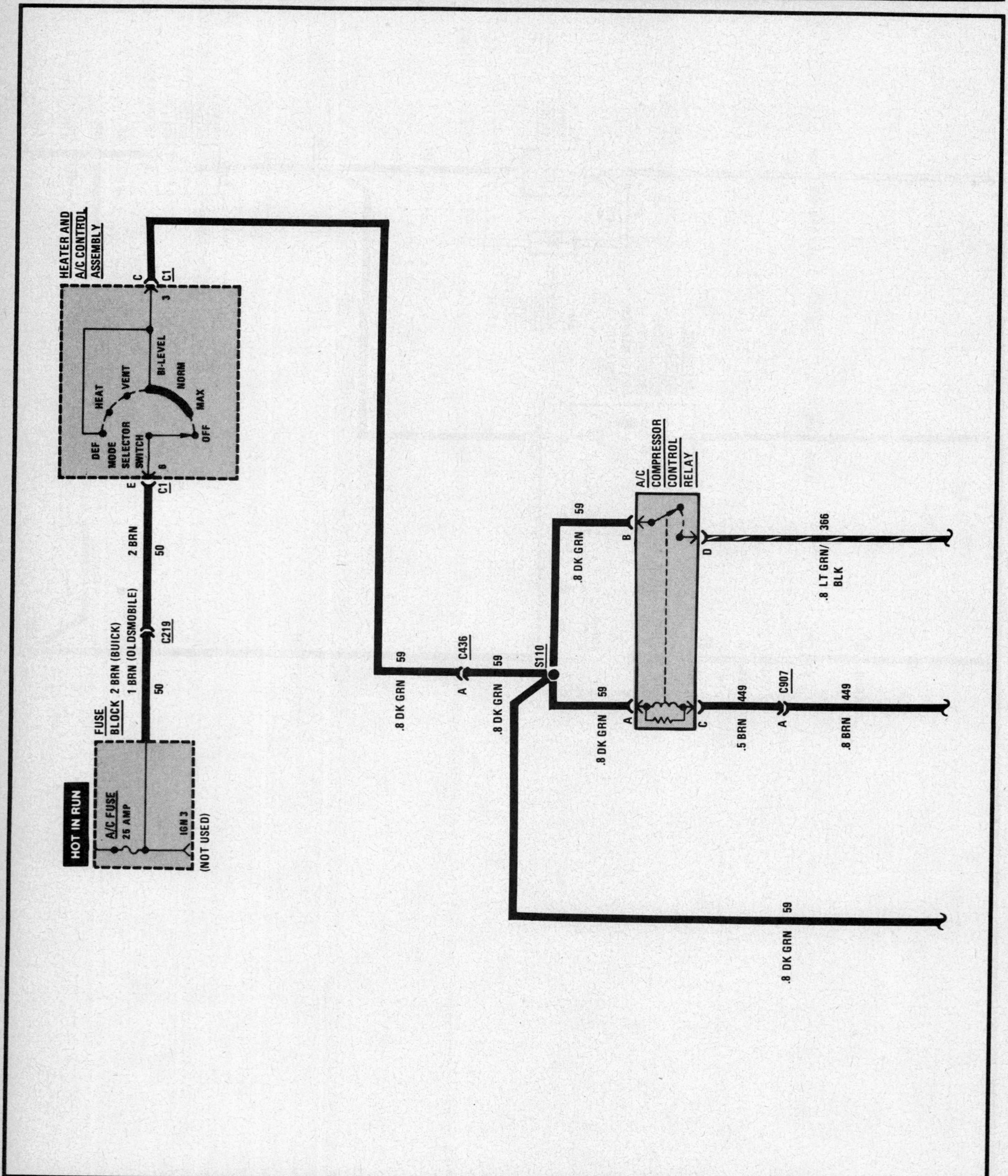
HEATER AND
A/C CONTROL
ASSEMBLY
C
C1
3
DEF
HEAT
VENT
BI-LEVEL
NORM
MAX
OFF
MODE
SELECTOR
SWITCH
6
E
C1
2 BRN
50
FUSE
BLOCK
2 BRN (BUICK)
1 BRN (OLDSMOBILE)
C219
50
HOT IN RUN
A/C FUSE
25 AMP
IGN 3
(NOT USED)
.8 DK GRN
59
C436
A
59
.8 DK GRN
S110
A/C
COMPRESSOR
CONTROL
RELAY
59
.8 DK GRN
B
D
366
.8 LT GRN/
BLK
59
A
.8 DK GRN
C
449
.5 BRN
C907
A
449
.8 BRN
59
.8 DK GRN

Compressor controls schematic—Caprice, Estate Wagon, Custom Cruiser, Safari and Roadmaster

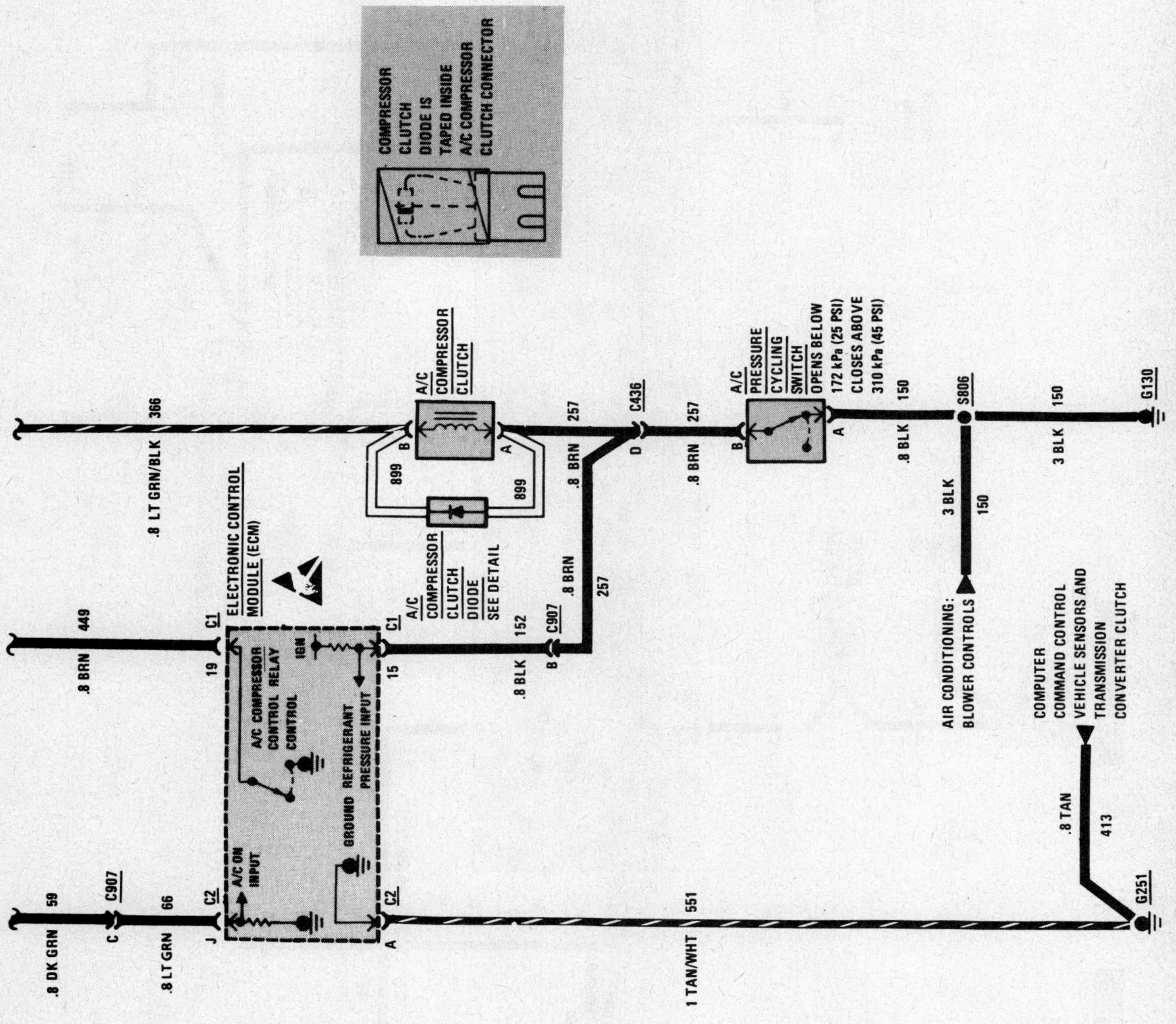
COMPRESSOR CLUTCH DIODE IS TAPED INSIDE A/C COMPRESSOR CLUTCH CONNECTOR
A/C COMPRESSOR CLUTCH
A/C PRESSURE CYCLING SWITCH
OPENS BELOW 172 kPa (25 PSI)
CLOSES ABOVE 310 kPa (45 PSI)
.8 LT GRN/BLK 366
257
C436
.8 BRN
.8 BRN 257
899
B
A
D
S806
G130
.8 BLK 150
3 BLK 150
A/C COMPRESSOR CLUTCH DIODE SEE DETAIL
ELECTRONIC CONTROL MODULE (ECM)
.8 BRN 449
C1
19
A/C COMPRESSOR CONTROL RELAY CONTROL
IGN
REFRIGERANT PRESSURE INPUT
GROUND
A/C ON INPUT
15
.8 BLK 152
C907
AIR CONDITIONING: BLOWER CONTROLS
COMPUTER COMMAND CONTROL VEHICLE SENSORS AND TRANSMISSION CONVERTER CLUTCH
.8 TAN 413
G251
.8 DK GRN 59
C
.8 LT GRN 66
J
C2
1 TAN/WHT 551

Compressor controls schematic—Caprice, Estate Wagon, Custom Cruiser, Safari and Roadmaster

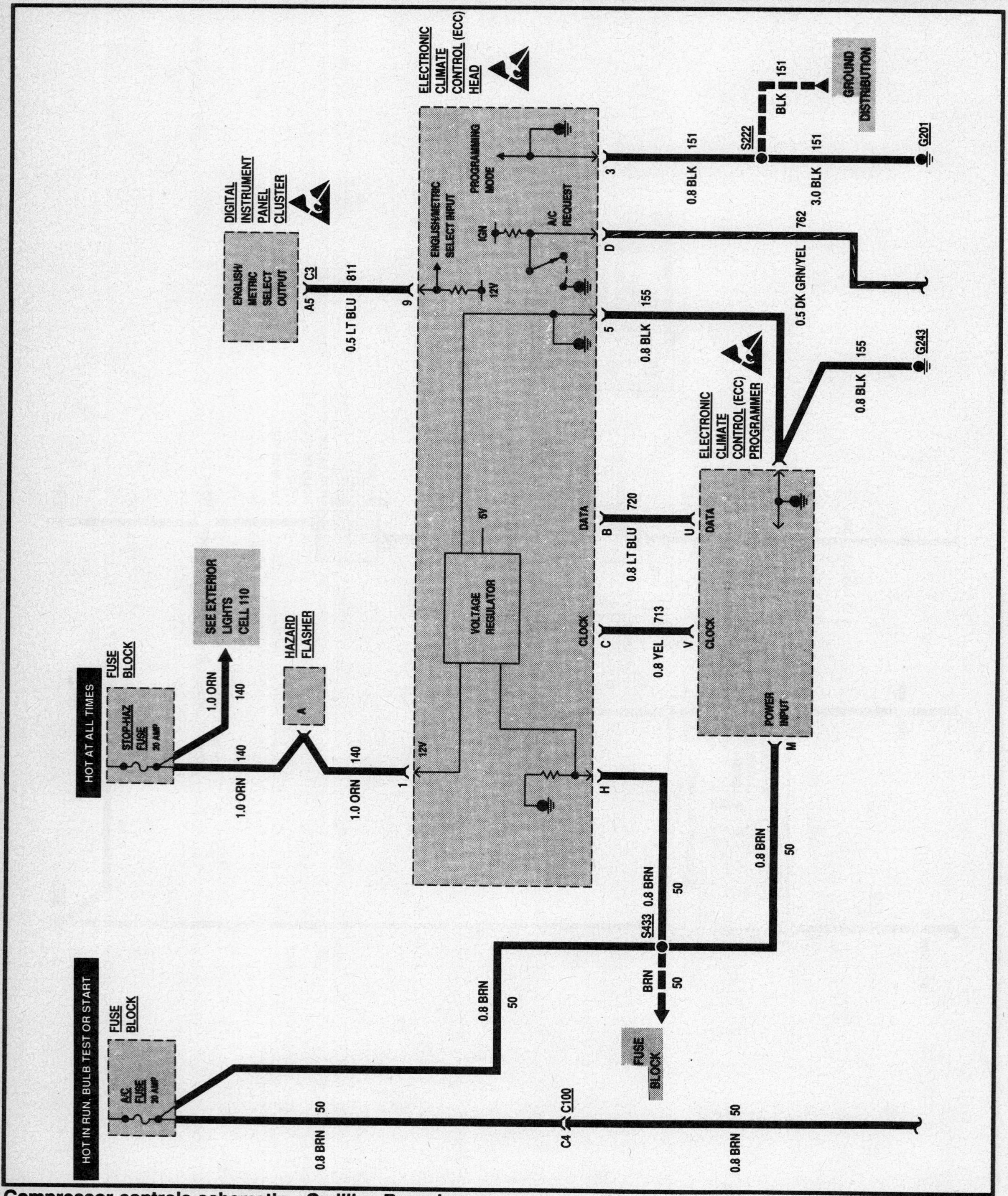
ELECTRONIC CLIMATE CONTROL (ECC) HEAD
GROUND DISTRIBUTION
DIGITAL INSTRUMENT PANEL CLUSTER
ENGLISH/ METRIC SELECT OUTPUT
PROGRAMMING MODE
ENGLISH/METRIC SELECT INPUT
IGN
A/C REQUEST
12V
5V
VOLTAGE REGULATOR
DATA
CLOCK
ELECTRONIC CLIMATE CONTROL (ECC) PROGRAMMER
POWER INPUT
HOT AT ALL TIMES
FUSE BLOCK
STOP-HAZ FUSE 20 AMP
SEE EXTERIOR LIGHTS CELL 110
HAZARD FLASHER
HOT IN RUN, BULB TEST OR START
A/C FUSE 20 AMP
0.8 BLK 151
3.0 BLK 151
S222
G201
BLK 151
0.5 DK GRN/YEL 762
0.8 BLK 155
G243
0.5 LT BLU 811
C3
A5
0.8 LT BLU 720
0.8 YEL 713
1.0 ORN 140
0.8 BRN 50
S433
BRN 50
FUSE BLOCK
C100
C4

Compressor controls schematic—Cadillac Brougham

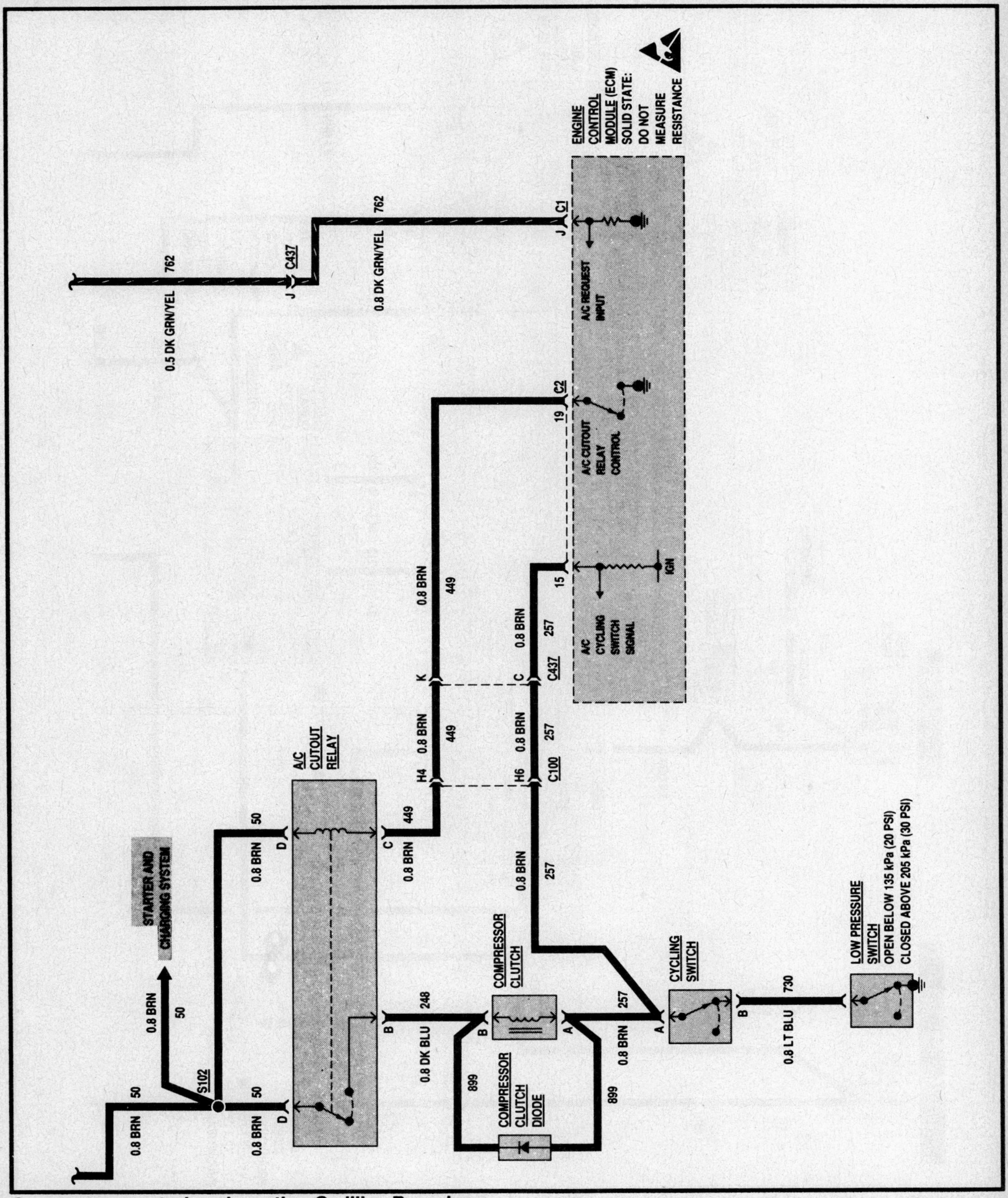
ENGINE CONTROL MODULE (ECM) SOLID STATE: DO NOT MEASURE RESISTANCE
762
0.5 DK GRN/YEL
J
C437
0.8 DK GRN/YEL
J
C1
A/C REQUEST INPUT
C2
19
A/C CUTOUT RELAY CONTROL
0.8 BRN
449
15
IGN
A/C CYCLING SWITCH SIGNAL
0.8 BRN
257
K
C
C437
H4
H6
C100
A/C CUTOUT RELAY
STARTER AND CHARGING SYSTEM
50
0.8 BRN
D
C
S102
B
248
0.8 DK BLU
COMPRESSOR CLUTCH
A
899
COMPRESSOR CLUTCH DIODE
CYCLING SWITCH
730
0.8 LT BLU
LOW PRESSURE SWITCH
OPEN BELOW 135 kPa (20 PSI)
CLOSED ABOVE 205 kPa (30 PSI)

Compressor controls schematic—Cadillac Brougham

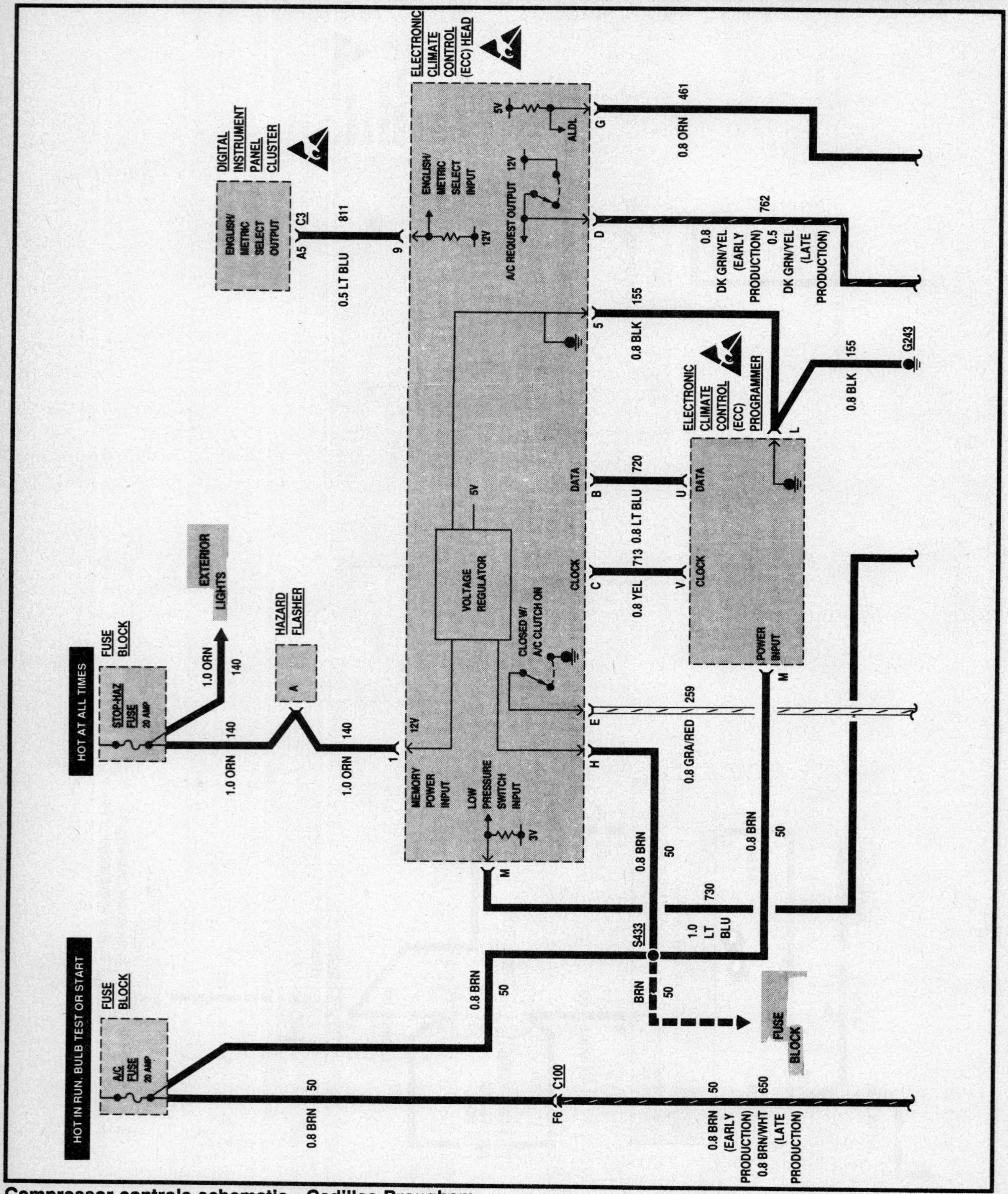
ELECTRONIC CLIMATE CONTROL (ECC) HEAD
DIGITAL INSTRUMENT PANEL CLUSTER
ENGLISH/ METRIC SELECT OUTPUT
ENGLISH/ METRIC SELECT INPUT
A/C REQUEST OUTPUT
ALDL
VOLTAGE REGULATOR
CLOSED W/ A/C CLUTCH ON
MEMORY POWER INPUT
LOW PRESSURE SWITCH INPUT
DATA
CLOCK
ELECTRONIC CLIMATE CONTROL (ECC) PROGRAMMER
POWER INPUT
HOT AT ALL TIMES
FUSE BLOCK
STOP-HAZ FUSE 20 AMP
HAZARD FLASHER
EXTERIOR LIGHTS
HOT IN RUN, BULB TEST OR START
A/C FUSE 20 AMP
0.5 LT BLU 811
0.8 ORN 461
0.8 DK GRN/YEL (EARLY PRODUCTION) 0.5 DK GRN/YEL (LATE PRODUCTION) 762
0.8 BLK 155
G243
0.8 LT BLU 720
0.8 YEL 713
0.8 GRA/RED 259
1.0 ORN 140
0.8 BRN 50
1.0 LT BLU 730
S433
C100
F6
0.8 BRN (EARLY PRODUCTION) 0.8 BRN/WHT (LATE PRODUCTION) 650

Compressor controls schematic – Cadillac Brougham

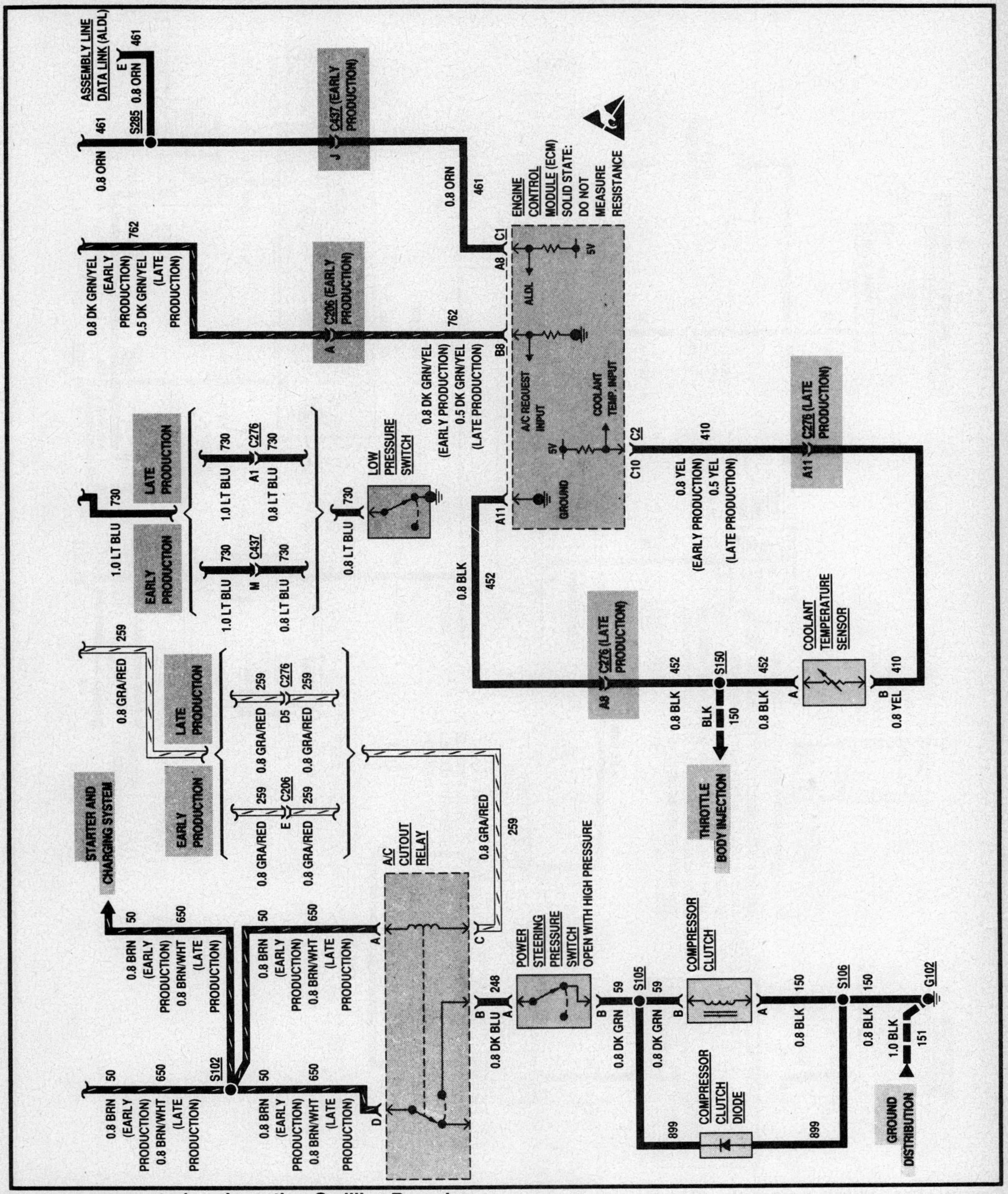
ASSEMBLY LINE DATA LINK (ALDL)
C437 (EARLY PRODUCTION)
ENGINE CONTROL MODULE (ECM) SOLID STATE: DO NOT MEASURE RESISTANCE
ALDL
A/C REQUEST INPUT
COOLANT TEMP. INPUT
GROUND
C206 (EARLY PRODUCTION)
EARLY PRODUCTION
LATE PRODUCTION
LOW PRESSURE SWITCH
C276 (LATE PRODUCTION)
COOLANT TEMPERATURE SENSOR
THROTTLE BODY INJECTION
STARTER AND CHARGING SYSTEM
A/C CUTOUT RELAY
POWER STEERING PRESSURE SWITCH OPEN WITH HIGH PRESSURE
COMPRESSOR CLUTCH
COMPRESSOR CLUTCH DIODE
GROUND DISTRIBUTION
0.8 ORN
0.8 DK GRN/YEL (EARLY PRODUCTION) 0.5 DK GRN/YEL (LATE PRODUCTION)
1.0 LT BLU
0.8 LT BLU
0.8 GRA/RED
0.8 BRN (EARLY PRODUCTION) 0.8 BRN/WHT (LATE PRODUCTION)
0.8 BLK
0.8 YEL (EARLY PRODUCTION) 0.5 YEL (LATE PRODUCTION)
0.8 DK BLU
0.8 DK GRN
1.0 BLK
S265
S102
S150
S105
S106
G102

Compressor controls schematic – Cadillac Brougham

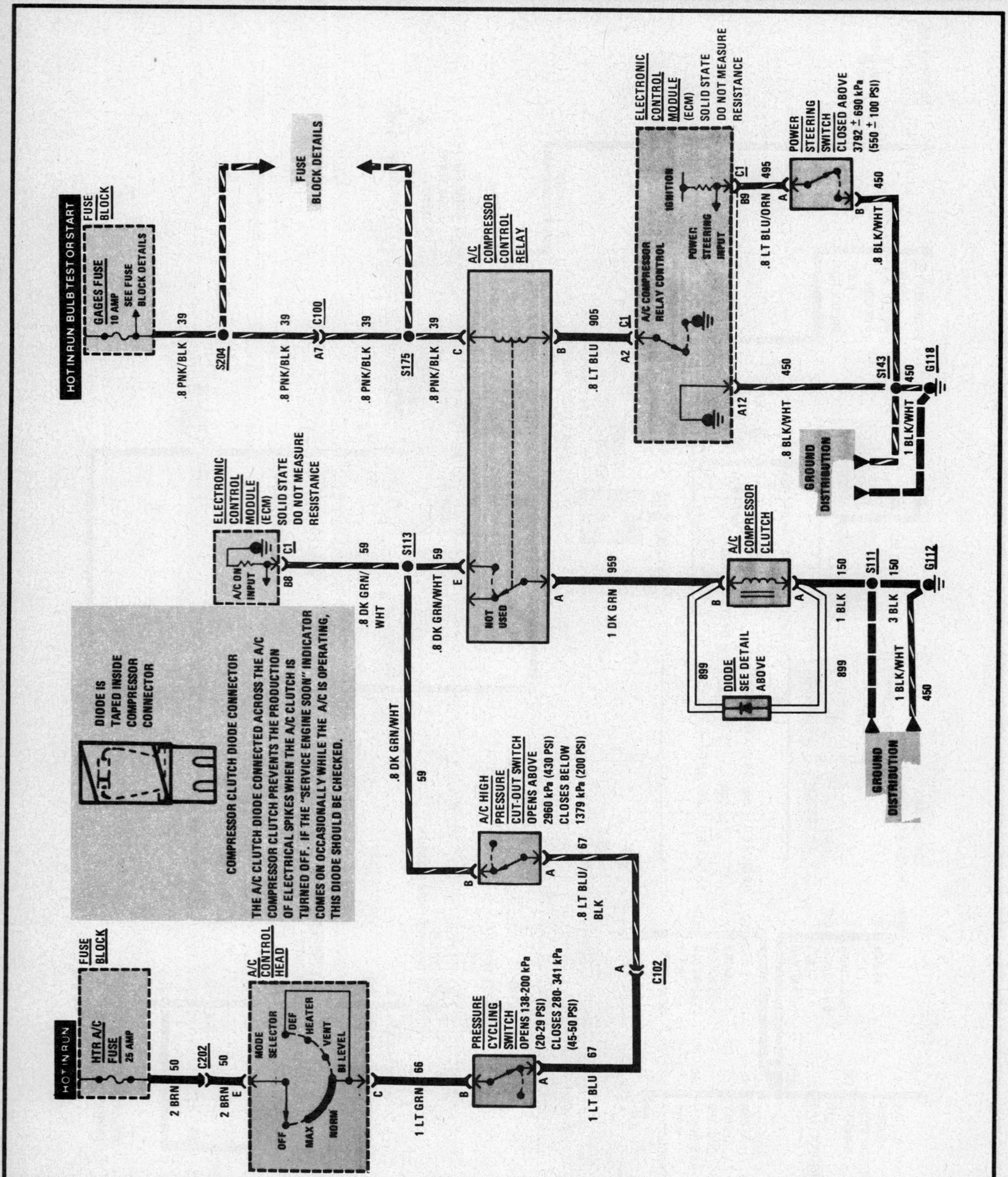
HOT IN RUN BULB TEST OR START
FUSE BLOCK
GAGES FUSE
10 AMP
SEE FUSE BLOCK DETAILS
FUSE BLOCK DETAILS
.8 PNK/BLK
39
S204
C100
A7
S175
C
A/C COMPRESSOR CONTROL RELAY
905
B
.8 LT BLU
C1
A2
ELECTRONIC CONTROL MODULE (ECM)
SOLID STATE
DO NOT MEASURE RESISTANCE
A/C COMPRESSOR RELAY CONTROL
POWER STEERING INPUT
IGNITION
B9
495
.8 LT BLU/ORN
POWER STEERING SWITCH
CLOSED ABOVE
3792 ± 690 kPa
(550 ± 100 PSI)
450
.8 BLK/WHT
A12
S143
G118
1 BLK/WHT
GROUND DISTRIBUTION
A/C ON INPUT
B8
59
S113
.8 DK GRN/WHT
E
NOT USED
A
959
1 DK GRN
A/C COMPRESSOR CLUTCH
150
S111
G112
1 BLK
3 BLK
899
DIODE
SEE DETAIL ABOVE
1 BLK/WHT
DIODE IS TAPED INSIDE COMPRESSOR CONNECTOR
COMPRESSOR CLUTCH DIODE CONNECTOR
THE A/C CLUTCH DIODE CONNECTED ACROSS THE A/C COMPRESSOR CLUTCH PREVENTS THE PRODUCTION OF ELECTRICAL SPIKES WHEN THE A/C CLUTCH IS TURNED OFF. IF THE "SERVICE ENGINE SOON" INDICATOR COMES ON OCCASIONALLY WHILE THE A/C IS OPERATING, THIS DIODE SHOULD BE CHECKED.
A/C HIGH PRESSURE CUT-OUT SWITCH
OPENS ABOVE
2960 kPa (430 PSI)
CLOSES BELOW
1379 kPa (200 PSI)
67
.8 LT BLU/BLK
C102
HOT IN RUN
HTR A/C FUSE
25 AMP
50
C202
2 BRN
A/C CONTROL HEAD
MODE SELECTOR
DEF
HEATER
VENT
BI LEVEL
NORM
MAX
OFF
66
1 LT GRN
PRESSURE CYCLING SWITCH
OPENS 138-200 kPa
(20-29 PSI)
CLOSES 280- 341 kPa
(45-50 PSI)
1 LT BLU

Compressor controls schematic—Camaro and Firebird

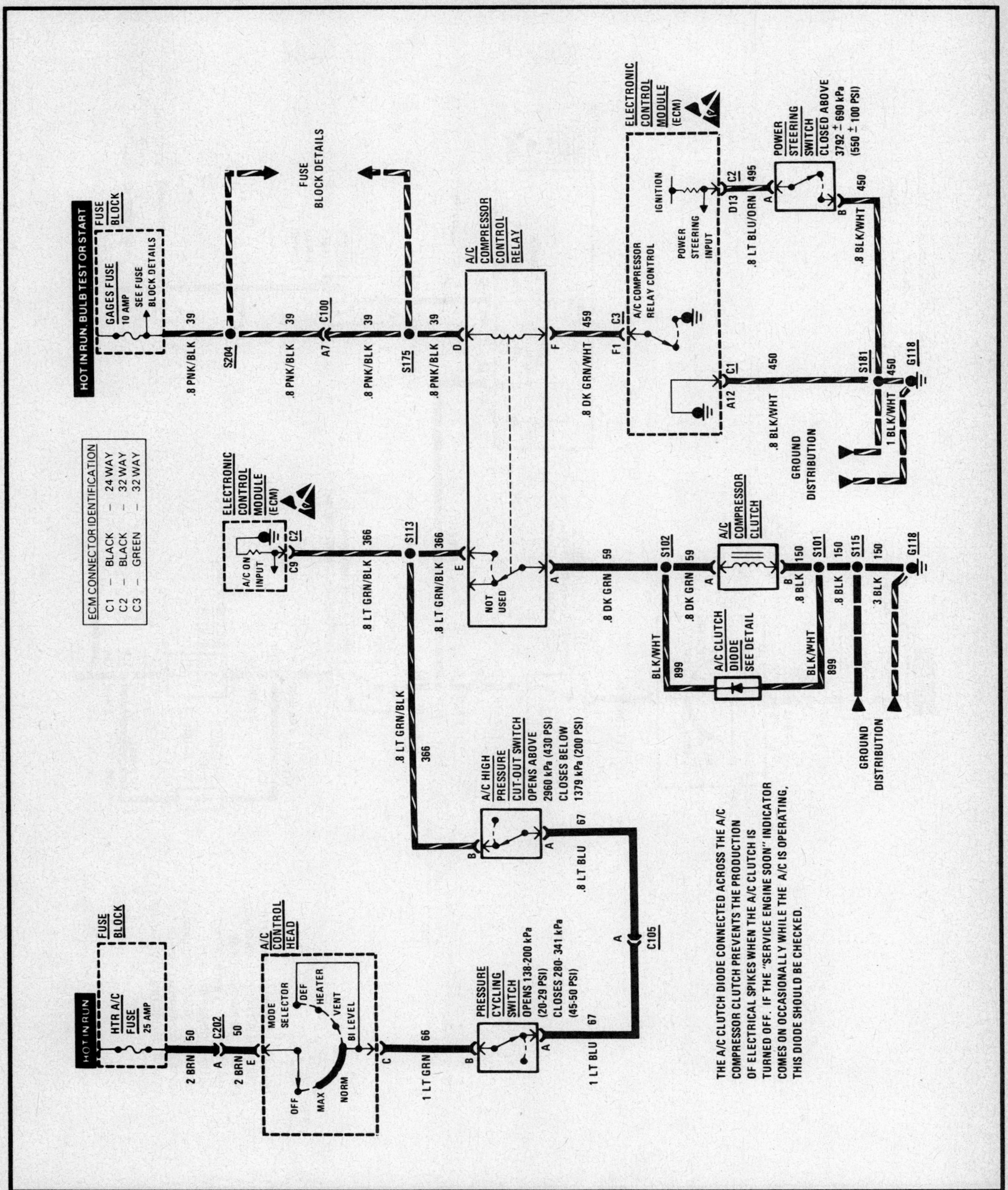
HOT IN RUN, BULB TEST OR START
FUSE BLOCK
GAGES FUSE 10 AMP
SEE FUSE BLOCK DETAILS
FUSE BLOCK DETAILS
ECM CONNECTOR IDENTIFICATION
C1 – BLACK – 24 WAY
C2 – BLACK – 32 WAY
C3 – GREEN – 32 WAY
ELECTRONIC CONTROL MODULE (ECM)
A/C ON INPUT
A/C COMPRESSOR CONTROL RELAY
NOT USED
A/C COMPRESSOR RELAY CONTROL
POWER STEERING INPUT
IGNITION
POWER STEERING SWITCH CLOSED ABOVE 3792 ± 690 kPa (550 ± 100 PSI)
A/C COMPRESSOR CLUTCH
A/C CLUTCH DIODE SEE DETAIL
GROUND DISTRIBUTION
HOT IN RUN
HTR A/C FUSE 25 AMP
A/C CONTROL HEAD
MODE SELECTOR
OFF
MAX
NORM
DEF
HEATER
VENT
BI LEVEL
PRESSURE CYCLING SWITCH OPENS 138-200 kPa (20-29 PSI) CLOSES 280- 341 kPa (45-50 PSI)
A/C HIGH PRESSURE CUT-OUT SWITCH OPENS ABOVE 2960 kPa (430 PSI) CLOSES BELOW 1379 kPa (200 PSI)
THE A/C CLUTCH DIODE CONNECTED ACROSS THE A/C COMPRESSOR CLUTCH PREVENTS THE PRODUCTION OF ELECTRICAL SPIKES WHEN THE A/C CLUTCH IS TURNED OFF. IF THE "SERVICE ENGINE SOON" INDICATOR COMES ON OCCASIONALLY WHILE THE A/C IS OPERATING, THIS DIODE SHOULD BE CHECKED.

Compressor controls schematic—Camaro and Firebird

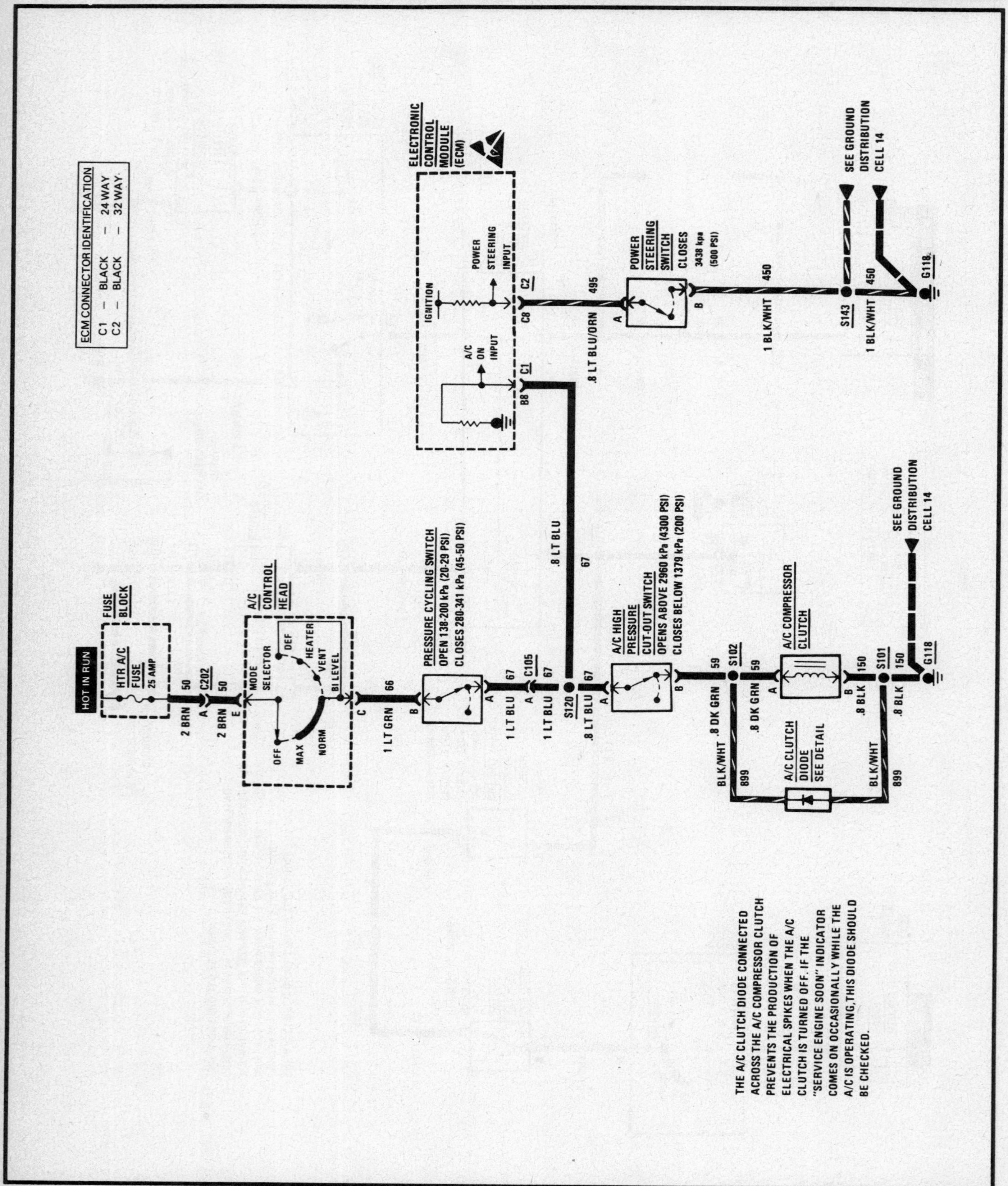
ECM CONNECTOR IDENTIFICATION
C1 – BLACK – 24 WAY
C2 – BLACK – 32 WAY
ELECTRONIC CONTROL MODULE (ECM)
IGNITION
POWER STEERING INPUT
A/C ON INPUT
HOT IN RUN
FUSE BLOCK
HTR A/C FUSE 25 AMP
C202
2 BRN
50
A/C CONTROL HEAD
MODE SELECTOR
DEF
HEATER
VENT
BI LEVEL
OFF
MAX
NORM
1 LT GRN
66
PRESSURE CYCLING SWITCH
OPEN 138-200 kPa (20-29 PSI)
CLOSES 280-341 kPa (45-50 PSI)
1 LT BLU
67
C105
S120
.8 LT BLU
A/C HIGH PRESSURE CUT-OUT SWITCH
OPENS ABOVE 2960 kPa (4300 PSI)
CLOSES BELOW 1379 kPa (200 PSI)
.8 LT BLU/ORN
495
POWER STEERING SWITCH
CLOSES 3438 kpa (500 PSI)
1 BLK/WHT
450
S143
G118
SEE GROUND DISTRIBUTION CELL 14
.8 DK GRN
59
S102
A/C COMPRESSOR CLUTCH
.8 BLK
150
S101
BLK/WHT
899
A/C CLUTCH DIODE SEE DETAIL
THE A/C CLUTCH DIODE CONNECTED ACROSS THE A/C COMPRESSOR CLUTCH PREVENTS THE PRODUCTION OF ELECTRICAL SPIKES WHEN THE A/C CLUTCH IS TURNED OFF. IF THE "SERVICE ENGINE SOON" INDICATOR COMES ON OCCASIONALLY WHILE THE A/C IS OPERATING, THIS DIODE SHOULD BE CHECKED.

Compressor controls schematic—Camaro and Firebird

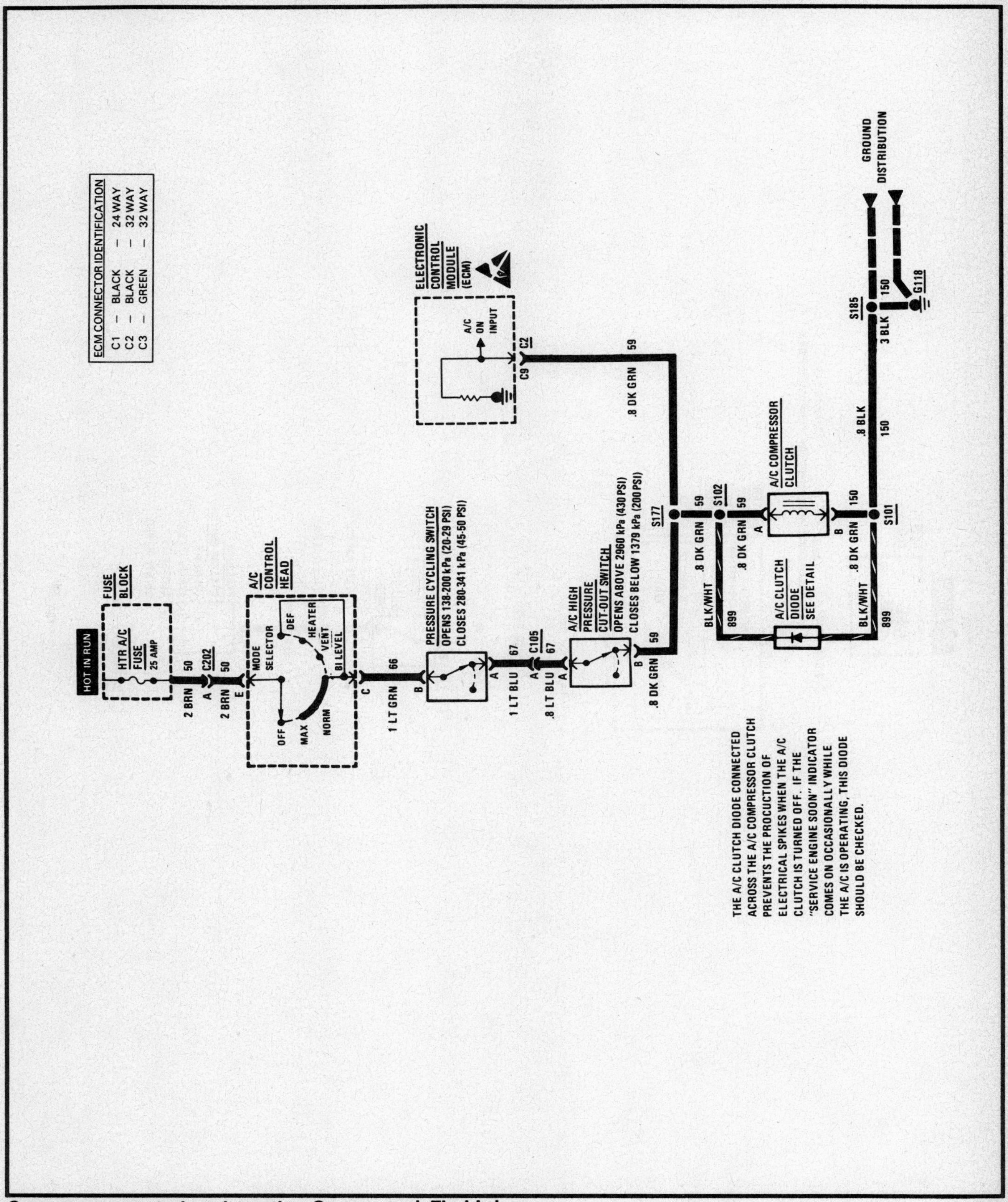

ECM CONNECTOR IDENTIFICATION
C1 – BLACK – 24 WAY
C2 – BLACK – 32 WAY
C3 – GREEN – 32 WAY
ELECTRONIC CONTROL MODULE (ECM)
A/C ON INPUT
C2
C9
59
.8 DK GRN
GROUND DISTRIBUTION
S185
3 BLK
150
G118
.8 BLK
A/C COMPRESSOR CLUTCH
S177
S102
S101
HOT IN RUN
FUSE BLOCK
HTR A/C FUSE 25 AMP
50
C202
A
2 BRN
E
A/C CONTROL HEAD
MODE SELECTOR
DEF
HEATER
VENT
BI LEVEL
OFF
MAX
NORM
C
66
1 LT GRN
B
PRESSURE CYCLING SWITCH
OPENS 138-200 kPa (20-29 PSI)
CLOSES 280-341 kPa (45-50 PSI)
67
C105
1 LT BLU
.8 LT BLU
A/C HIGH PRESSURE CUT-OUT SWITCH
OPENS ABOVE 2960 kPa (430 PSI)
CLOSES BELOW 1379 kPa (200 PSI)
BLK/WHT
899
A/C CLUTCH DIODE SEE DETAIL
.8 DK GRN
THE A/C CLUTCH DIODE CONNECTED ACROSS THE A/C COMPRESSOR CLUTCH PREVENTS THE PROCUCTION OF ELECTRICAL SPIKES WHEN THE A/C CLUTCH IS TURNED OFF. IF THE "SERVICE ENGINE SOON" INDICATOR COMES ON OCCASIONALLY WHILE THE A/C IS OPERATING, THIS DIODE SHOULD BE CHECKED.

Compressor controls schematic—Camaro and Firebird

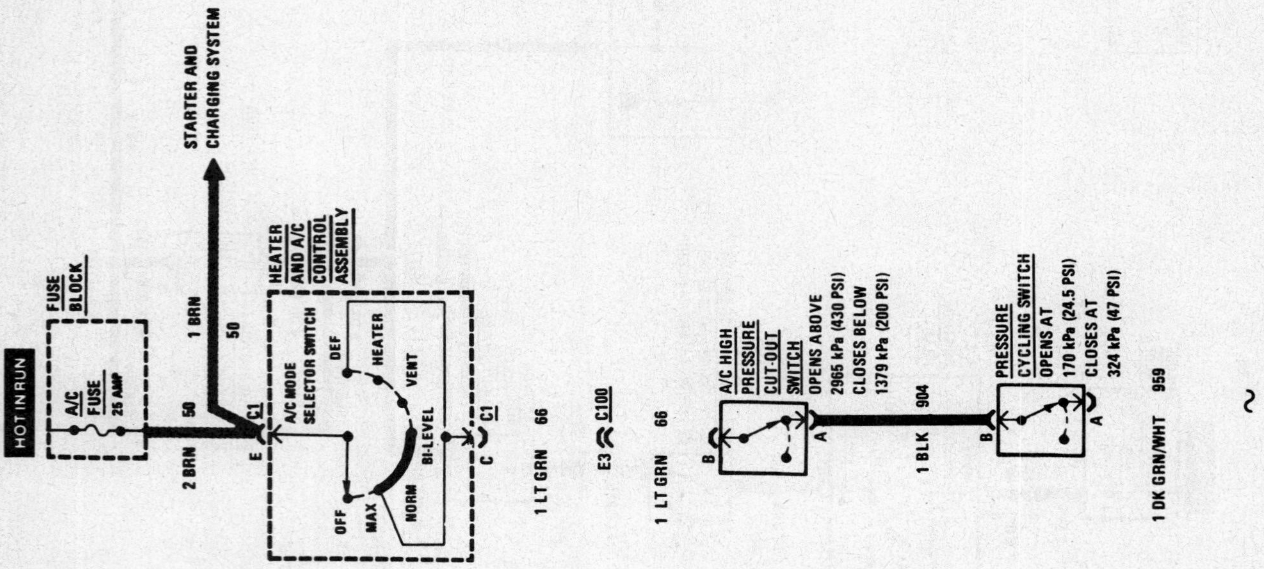
HOT IN RUN
FUSE BLOCK
A/C FUSE 25 AMP
2 BRN 50
1 BRN 50
STARTER AND CHARGING SYSTEM
HEATER AND A/C CONTROL ASSEMBLY
E C1
A/C MODE SELECTOR SWITCH
OFF
MAX
NORM
BI-LEVEL
VENT
HEATER
DEF
C C1
1 LT GRN 66
E3 C100
1 LT GRN 66
B
A
A/C HIGH PRESSURE CUT-OUT SWITCH
OPENS ABOVE 2965 kPa (430 PSI)
CLOSES BELOW 1379 kPa (200 PSI)
1 BLK 904
B
A
PRESSURE CYCLING SWITCH
OPENS AT 170 kPa (24.5 PSI)
CLOSES AT 324 kPa (47 PSI)
1 DK GRN/WHT 959

Compressor controls schematic—Corvette

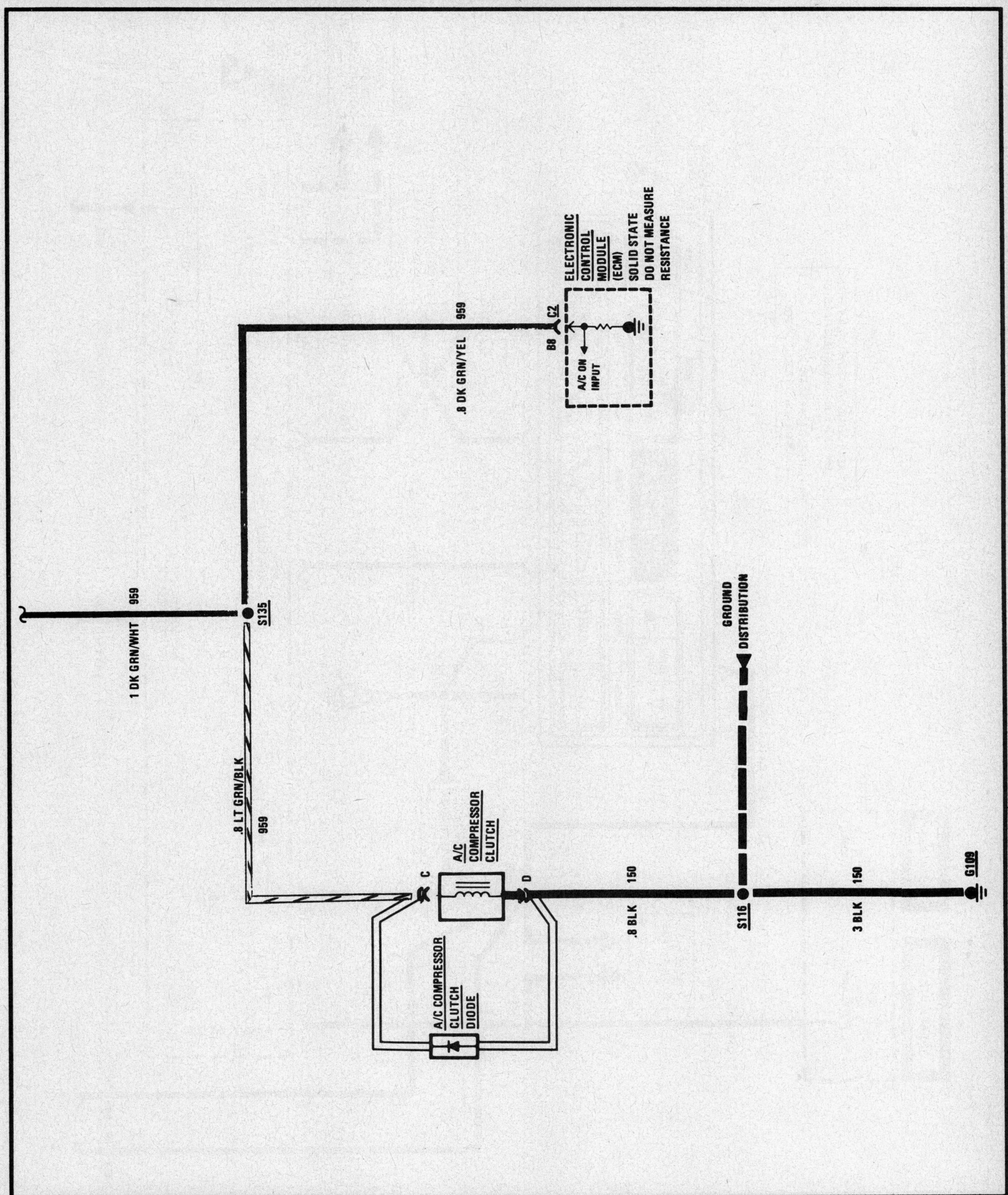
ELECTRONIC CONTROL MODULE (ECM)
SOLID STATE DO NOT MEASURE RESISTANCE
A/C ON INPUT
C2
B8
959
.8 DK GRN/YEL
1 DK GRN/WHT
959
S135
.8 LT GRN/BLK
959
A/C COMPRESSOR CLUTCH
C
D
A/C COMPRESSOR CLUTCH DIODE
150
.8 BLK
S116
GROUND DISTRIBUTION
150
3 BLK
G109

Compressor controls schematic—Corvette

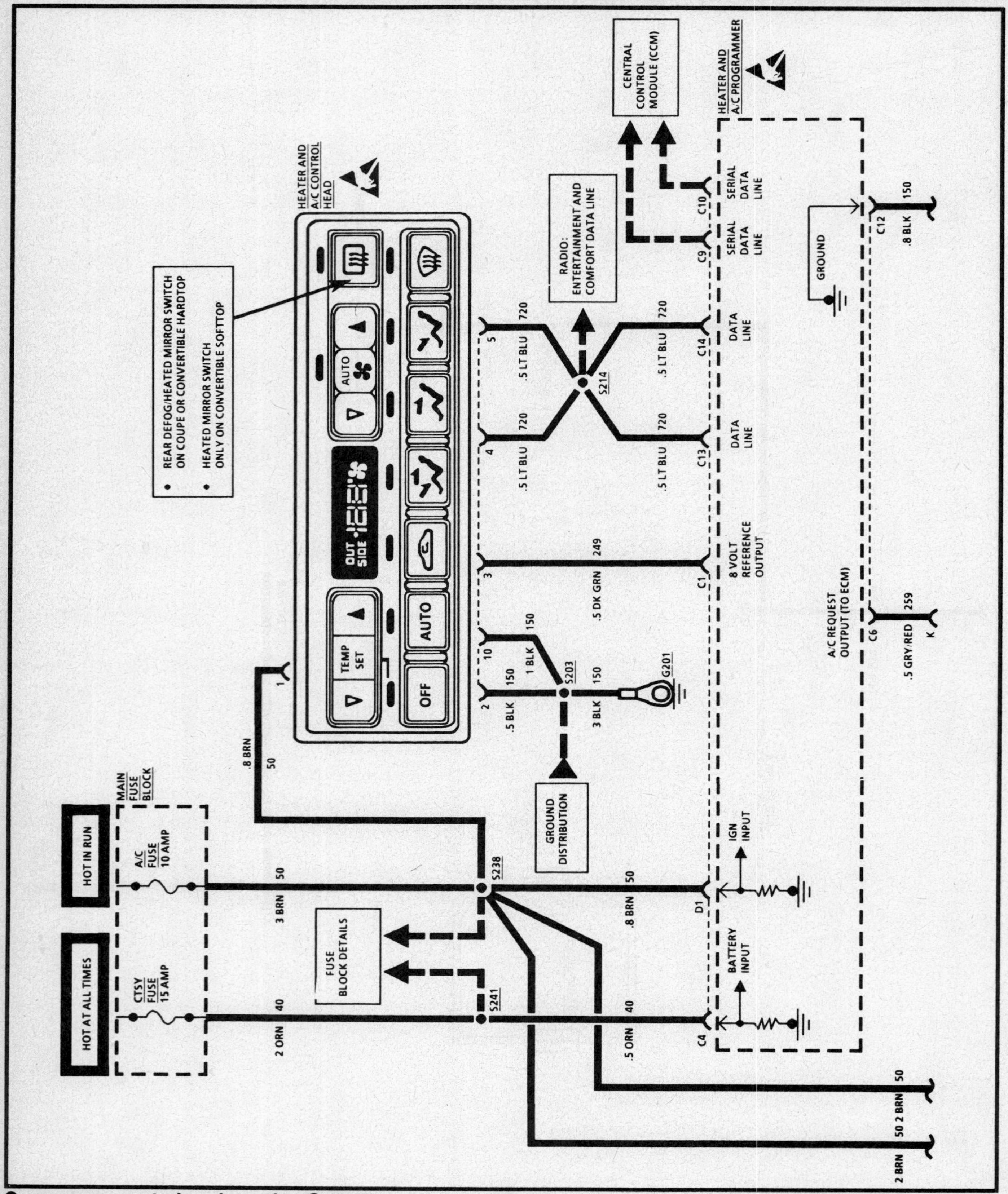
HOT IN RUN
HOT AT ALL TIMES
MAIN FUSE BLOCK
A/C FUSE 10 AMP
CTSY FUSE 15 AMP
3 BRN 50
2 ORN 40
.8 BRN 50
S238
S241
FUSE BLOCK DETAILS
GROUND DISTRIBUTION
.8 BRN 50
.5 ORN 40
D1
C4
IGN INPUT
BATTERY INPUT
2 BRN 50 2 BRN 50
REAR DEFOG/HEATED MIRROR SWITCH ON COUPE OR CONVERTIBLE HARDTOP
HEATED MIRROR SWITCH ONLY ON CONVERTIBLE SOFTTOP
HEATER AND A/C CONTROL HEAD
TEMP SET
OFF
AUTO
OUT SIDE
1
2
10
3
4
5
.5 BLK 150
1 BLK 150
S203
3 BLK 150
G201
.5 DK GRN 249
.5 LT BLU 720
S214
RADIO: ENTERTAINMENT AND COMFORT DATA LINE
CENTRAL CONTROL MODULE (CCM)
HEATER AND A/C PROGRAMMER
C1
C13
C14
C9
C10
8 VOLT REFERENCE OUTPUT
DATA LINE
SERIAL DATA LINE
GROUND
C12
.8 BLK 150
C6
.5 GRY/RED 259
K
A/C REQUEST OUTPUT (TO ECM)

Compressor controls schematic—Corvette

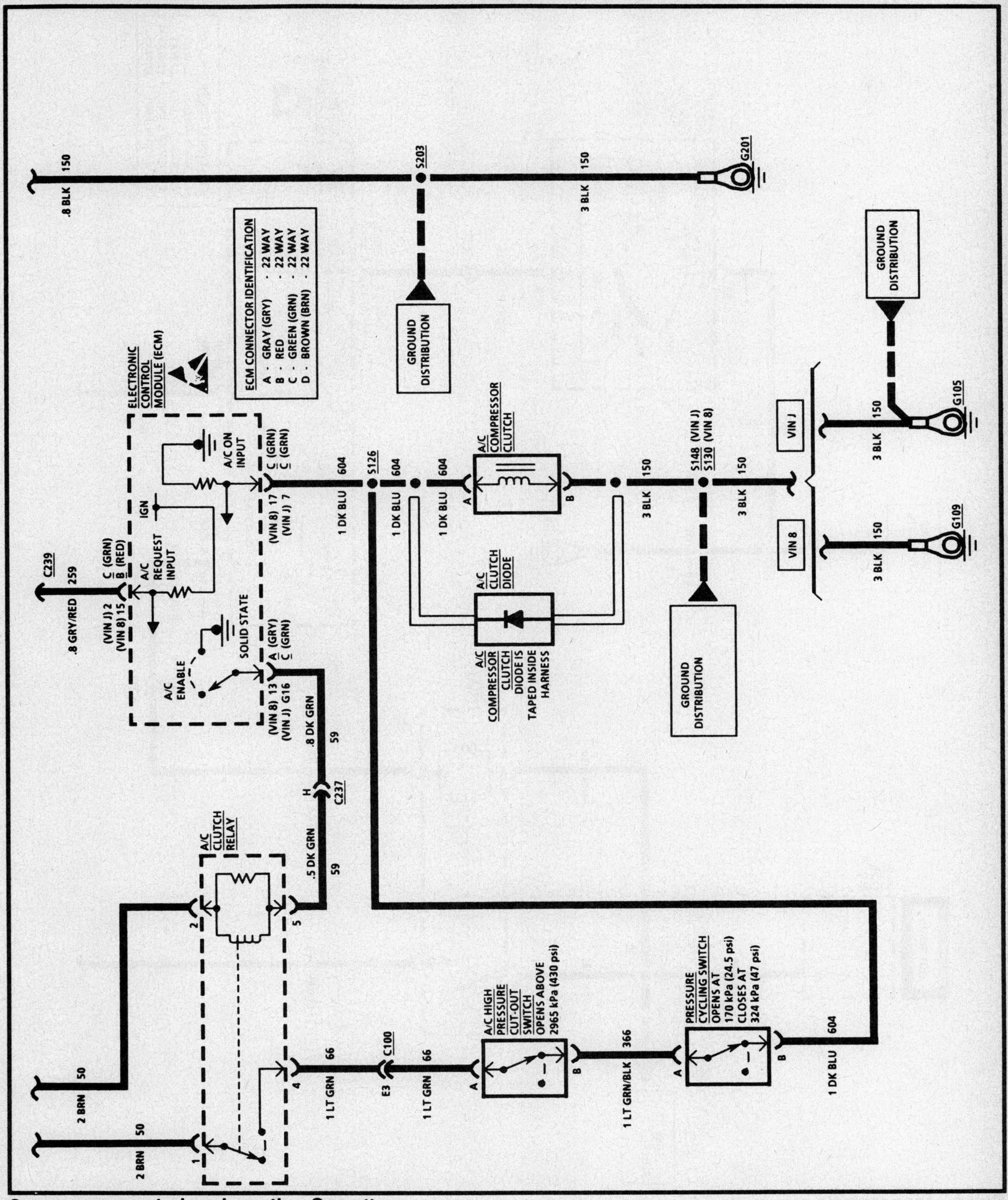
.8 BLK 150
S203
3 BLK 150
G201
ECM CONNECTOR IDENTIFICATION
A - GRAY (GRY) - 22 WAY
B - RED - 22 WAY
C - GREEN (GRN) - 22 WAY
D - BROWN (BRN) - 22 WAY
GROUND DISTRIBUTION
ELECTRONIC CONTROL MODULE (ECM)
A/C ON INPUT
IGN
A/C REQUEST INPUT
C (GRN)
B (RED)
C239
259
.8 GRY/RED
(VIN J) 2
(VIN 8) 15
SOLID STATE
A/C ENABLE
A (GRY)
C (GRN)
(VIN 8) 13
(VIN J) G16
(VIN 8) 17
(VIN J) 7
.8 DK GRN
59
604
1 DK BLU
S126
A/C COMPRESSOR CLUTCH
A/C CLUTCH DIODE
A/C COMPRESSOR CLUTCH DIODE IS TAPED INSIDE HARNESS
S148 (VIN J)
S130 (VIN 8)
3 BLK 150
VIN J
VIN 8
G105
G109
H
C237
A/C CLUTCH RELAY
.5 DK GRN
2 BRN 50
66
1 LT GRN
C100
E3
A/C HIGH PRESSURE CUT-OUT SWITCH OPENS ABOVE 2965 kPa (430 psi)
366
1 LT GRN/BLK
PRESSURE CYCLING SWITCH OPENS AT 170 kPa (24.5 psi) CLOSES AT 324 kPa (47 psi)

Compressor controls schematic—Corvette

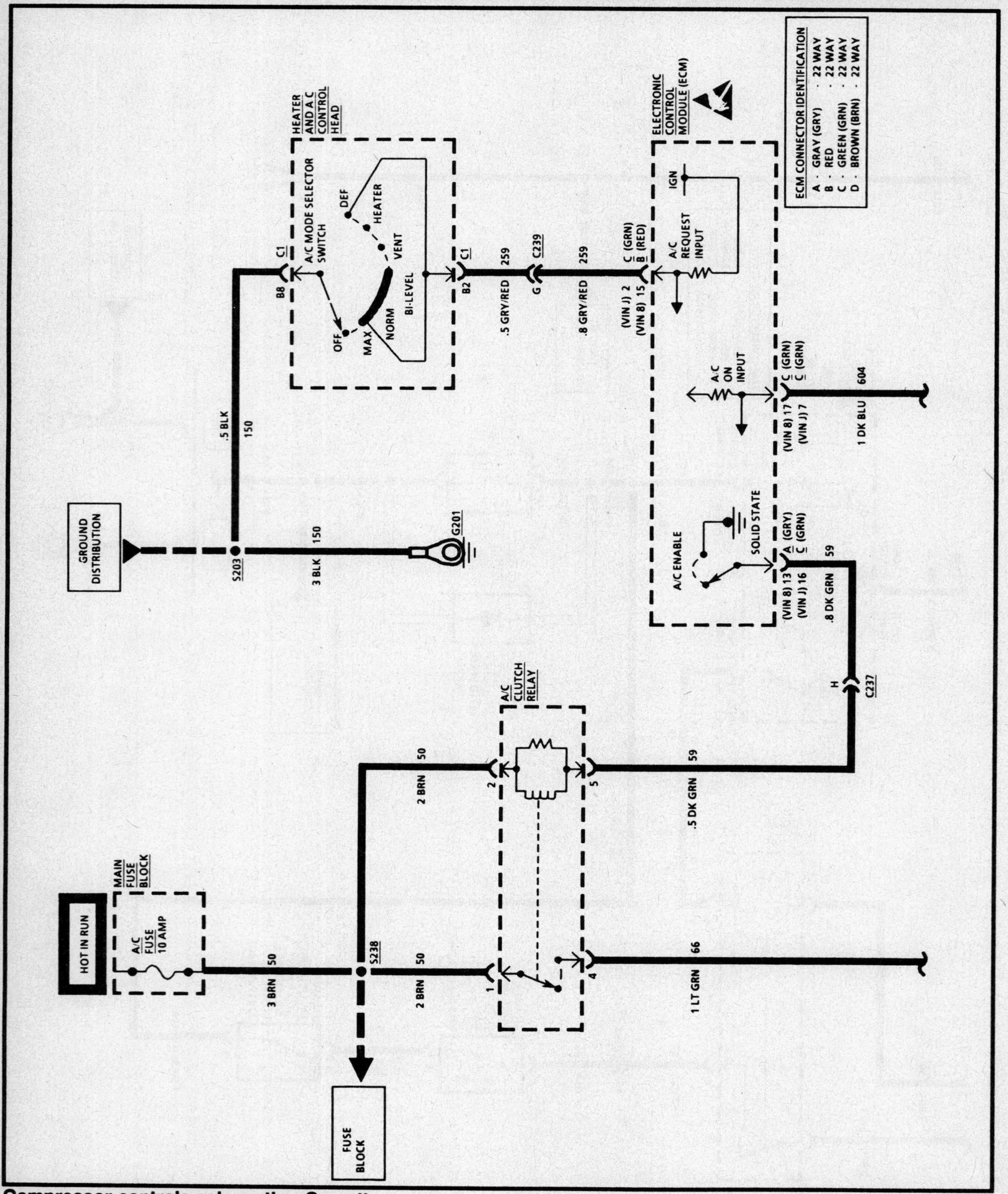
HEATER AND A/C CONTROL HEAD
A/C MODE SELECTOR SWITCH
DEF
HEATER
VENT
BI-LEVEL
NORM
MAX
OFF
C1
B8
B2
259
.5 GRY/RED
C239
G
.8 GRY/RED
C (GRN)
B (RED)
(VIN J) 2
(VIN 8) 15
ELECTRONIC CONTROL MODULE (ECM)
IGN
A/C REQUEST INPUT
A/C ON INPUT
(VIN 8) 17 C (GRN)
(VIN J) 7 C (GRN)
604
1 DK BLU
A/C ENABLE
SOLID STATE
(VIN 8) 13 A (GRY)
(VIN J) 16 C (GRN)
59
.8 DK GRN
H
C237
ECM CONNECTOR IDENTIFICATION
A : GRAY (GRY) : 22 WAY
B : RED : 22 WAY
C : GREEN (GRN) : 22 WAY
D : BROWN (BRN) : 22 WAY
GROUND DISTRIBUTION
S203
.5 BLK
150
3 BLK
150
G201
A/C CLUTCH RELAY
2 BRN
50
2
5
59
.5 DK GRN
MAIN FUSE BLOCK
HOT IN RUN
A/C FUSE 10 AMP
3 BRN
50
S238
2 BRN
50
1
4
66
1 LT GRN
FUSE BLOCK

Compressor controls schematic—Corvette

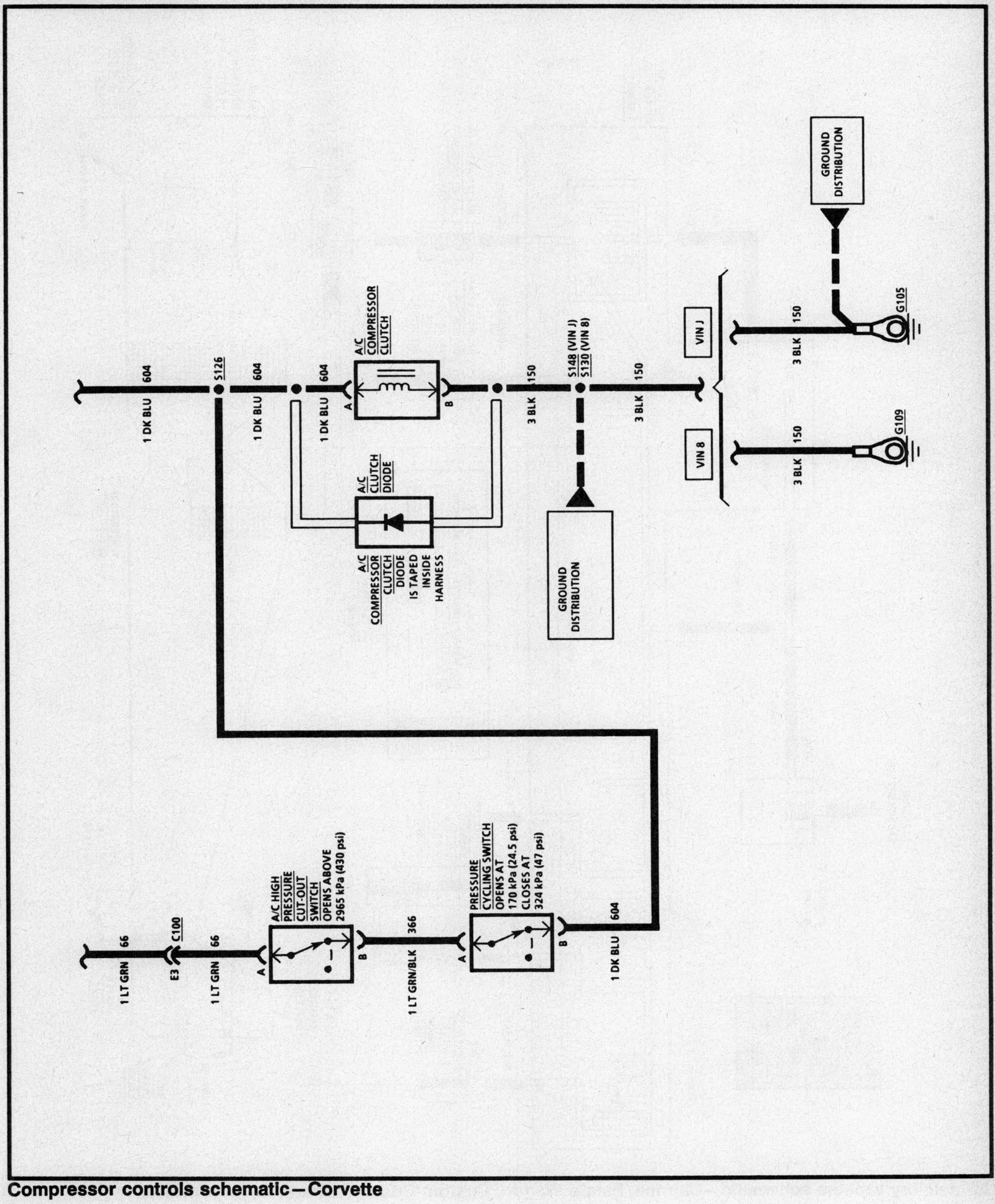
GROUND DISTRIBUTION
G105
150
3 BLK
VIN J
VIN 8
G109
150
3 BLK
A/C COMPRESSOR CLUTCH
604
1 DK BLU
S126
604
1 DK BLU
604
1 DK BLU
A
B
150
3 BLK
S148 (VIN J)
S130 (VIN 8)
150
3 BLK
A/C CLUTCH DIODE
A/C COMPRESSOR CLUTCH DIODE IS TAPED INSIDE HARNESS
GROUND DISTRIBUTION
A/C HIGH PRESSURE CUT-OUT SWITCH OPENS ABOVE 2965 kPa (430 psi)
PRESSURE CYCLING SWITCH OPENS AT 170 kPa (24.5 psi) CLOSES AT 324 kPa (47 psi)
66
1 LT GRN
C100
E3
66
1 LT GRN
A
B
366
1 LT GRN/BLK
A
B
604
1 DK BLU

Compressor controls schematic—Corvette

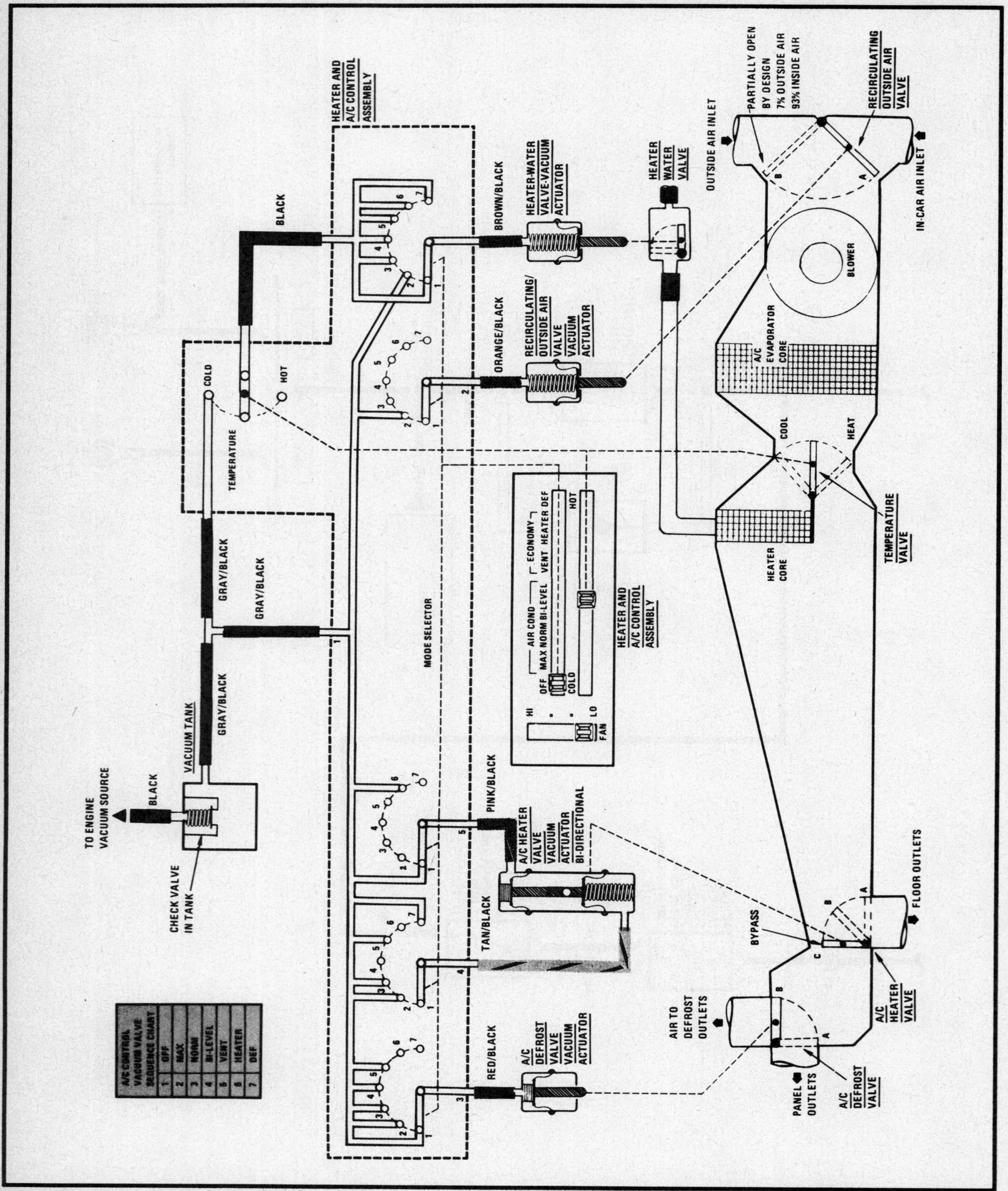
HEATER AND A/C CONTROL ASSEMBLY
BLACK
BROWN/BLACK
HEATER-WATER VALVE-VACUUM ACTUATOR
HEATER WATER VALVE
OUTSIDE AIR INLET
PARTIALLY OPEN BY DESIGN 7% OUTSIDE AIR 93% INSIDE AIR
RECIRCULATING OUTSIDE AIR VALVE
IN-CAR AIR INLET
BLOWER
A/C EVAPORATOR CORE
ORANGE/BLACK
RECIRCULATING/ OUTSIDE AIR VALVE VACUUM ACTUATOR
COLD
HOT
TEMPERATURE
COOL
HEAT
TEMPERATURE VALVE
HEATER CORE
GRAY/BLACK
MODE SELECTOR
AIR COND
MAX NORM BI-LEVEL
VENT HEATER DEF
ECONOMY
OFF
FAN
HI
LO
VACUUM TANK
TO ENGINE VACUUM SOURCE
CHECK VALVE IN TANK
PINK/BLACK
A/C HEATER VALVE VACUUM ACTUATOR BI-DIRECTIONAL
TAN/BLACK
FLOOR OUTLETS
BYPASS
A/C HEATER VALVE
AIR TO DEFROST OUTLETS
RED/BLACK
A/C DEFROST VALVE VACUUM ACTUATOR
PANEL OUTLETS
A/C DEFROST VALVE
A/C CONTROL VACUUM VALVE SEQUENCE CHART
1 OFF
2 MAX
3 NORM
4 BI-LEVEL
5 VENT
6 HEATER
7 DEF

Air delivery vacuum schematic—Caprice, Estate Wagon, Custom Cruiser, Safari and Roadmaster

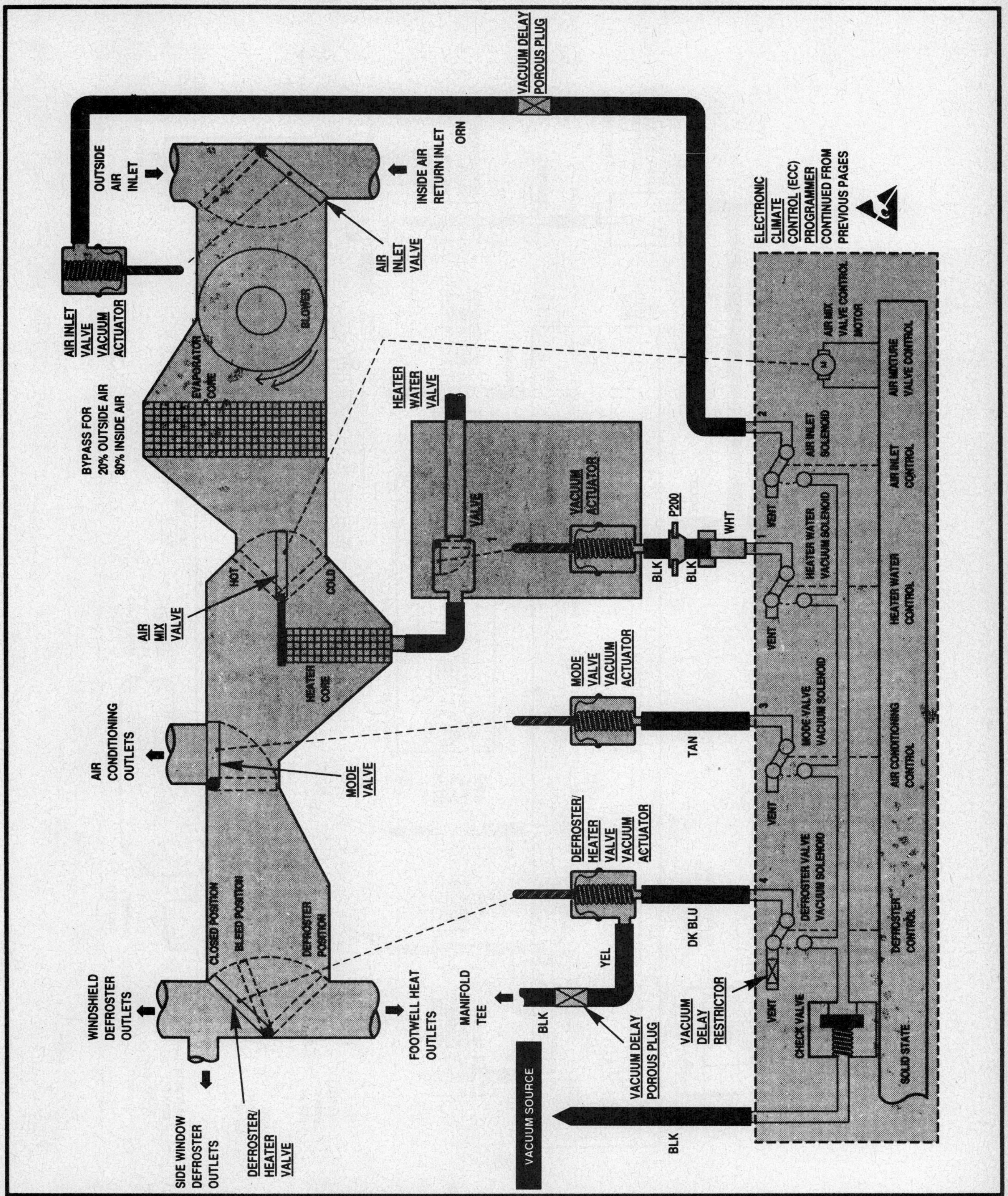
VACUUM DELAY POROUS PLUG
OUTSIDE AIR INLET
INSIDE AIR RETURN INLET
ORN
AIR INLET VALVE
AIR INLET VALVE VACUUM ACTUATOR
BLOWER
EVAPORATOR CORE
BYPASS FOR 20% OUTSIDE AIR 80% INSIDE AIR
ELECTRONIC CLIMATE CONTROL (ECC) PROGRAMMER CONTINUED FROM PREVIOUS PAGES
AIR MIX VALVE CONTROL MOTOR
AIR MIXTURE VALVE CONTROL
HEATER WATER VALVE
VALVE
VACUUM ACTUATOR
P200
WHT
BLK
BLK
AIR INLET SOLENOID
AIR INLET CONTROL
VENT
HEATER WATER VACUUM SOLENOID
HEATER WATER CONTROL
HOT
COLD
AIR MIX VALVE
HEATER CORE
MODE VALVE VACUUM ACTUATOR
TAN
MODE VALVE VACUUM SOLENOID
AIR CONDITIONING CONTROL
AIR CONDITIONING OUTLETS
MODE VALVE
DEFROSTER/ HEATER VALVE VACUUM ACTUATOR
DK BLU
DEFROSTER VALVE VACUUM SOLENOID
DEFROSTER CONTROL
CLOSED POSITION
BLEED POSITION
DEFROSTER POSITION
YEL
WINDSHIELD DEFROSTER OUTLETS
FOOTWELL HEAT OUTLETS
MANIFOLD TEE
BLK
VACUUM DELAY POROUS PLUG
VACUUM DELAY RESTRICTOR
CHECK VALVE
SOLID STATE
VACUUM SOURCE
BLK
SIDE WINDOW DEFROSTER OUTLETS
DEFROSTER/ HEATER VALVE

Air delivery vacuum schematic– Cadillac Brougham

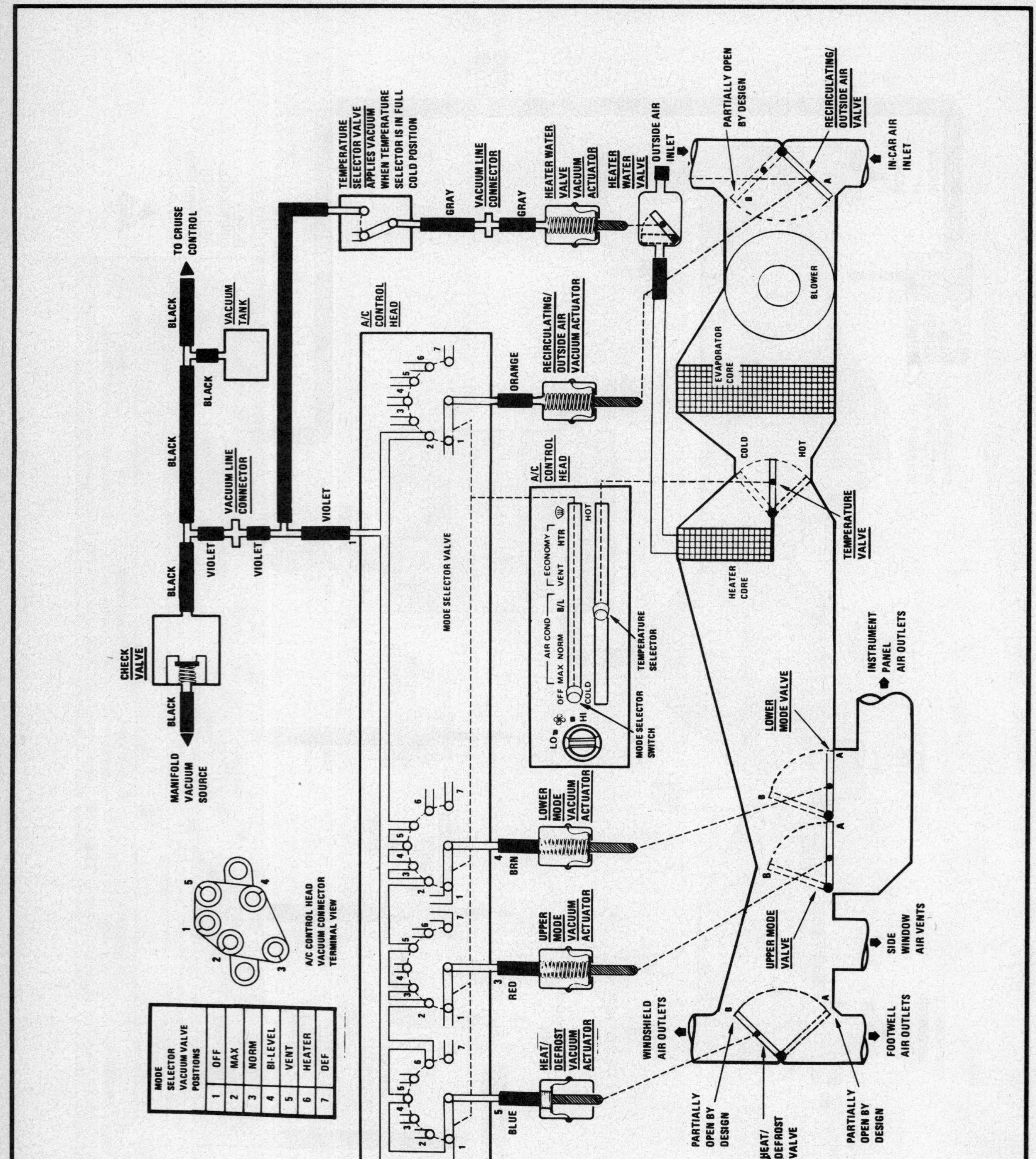
TO CRUISE CONTROL
BLACK
VACUUM TANK
VACUUM LINE CONNECTOR
VIOLET
CHECK VALVE
MANIFOLD VACUUM SOURCE
TEMPERATURE SELECTOR VALVE APPLIES VACUUM WHEN TEMPERATURE SELECTOR IS IN FULL COLD POSITION
GRAY
HEATER WATER VALVE VACUUM ACTUATOR
HEATER WATER VALVE
OUTSIDE AIR INLET
PARTIALLY OPEN BY DESIGN
RECIRCULATING/ OUTSIDE AIR VALVE
IN-CAR AIR INLET
BLOWER
EVAPORATOR CORE
A/C CONTROL HEAD
ORANGE
RECIRCULATING/ OUTSIDE AIR VACUUM ACTUATOR
COLD
HOT
TEMPERATURE VALVE
HEATER CORE
MODE SELECTOR VALVE
OFF MAX NORM AIR COND B/L VENT ECONOMY HTR
TEMPERATURE SELECTOR
MODE SELECTOR SWITCH
LO HI
INSTRUMENT PANEL AIR OUTLETS
LOWER MODE VALVE
LOWER MODE VACUUM ACTUATOR
BRN
UPPER MODE VACUUM ACTUATOR
RED
UPPER MODE VALVE
SIDE WINDOW AIR VENTS
HEAT/ DEFROST VACUUM ACTUATOR
BLUE
WINDSHIELD AIR OUTLETS
FOOTWELL AIR OUTLETS
PARTIALLY OPEN BY DESIGN
HEAT/ DEFROST VALVE
A/C CONTROL HEAD VACUUM CONNECTOR TERMINAL VIEW
MODE SELECTOR VACUUM VALVE POSITIONS
1 OFF
2 MAX
3 NORM
4 BI-LEVEL
5 VENT
6 HEATER
7 DEF

Air delivery vacuum schematic—Camaro and Firebird

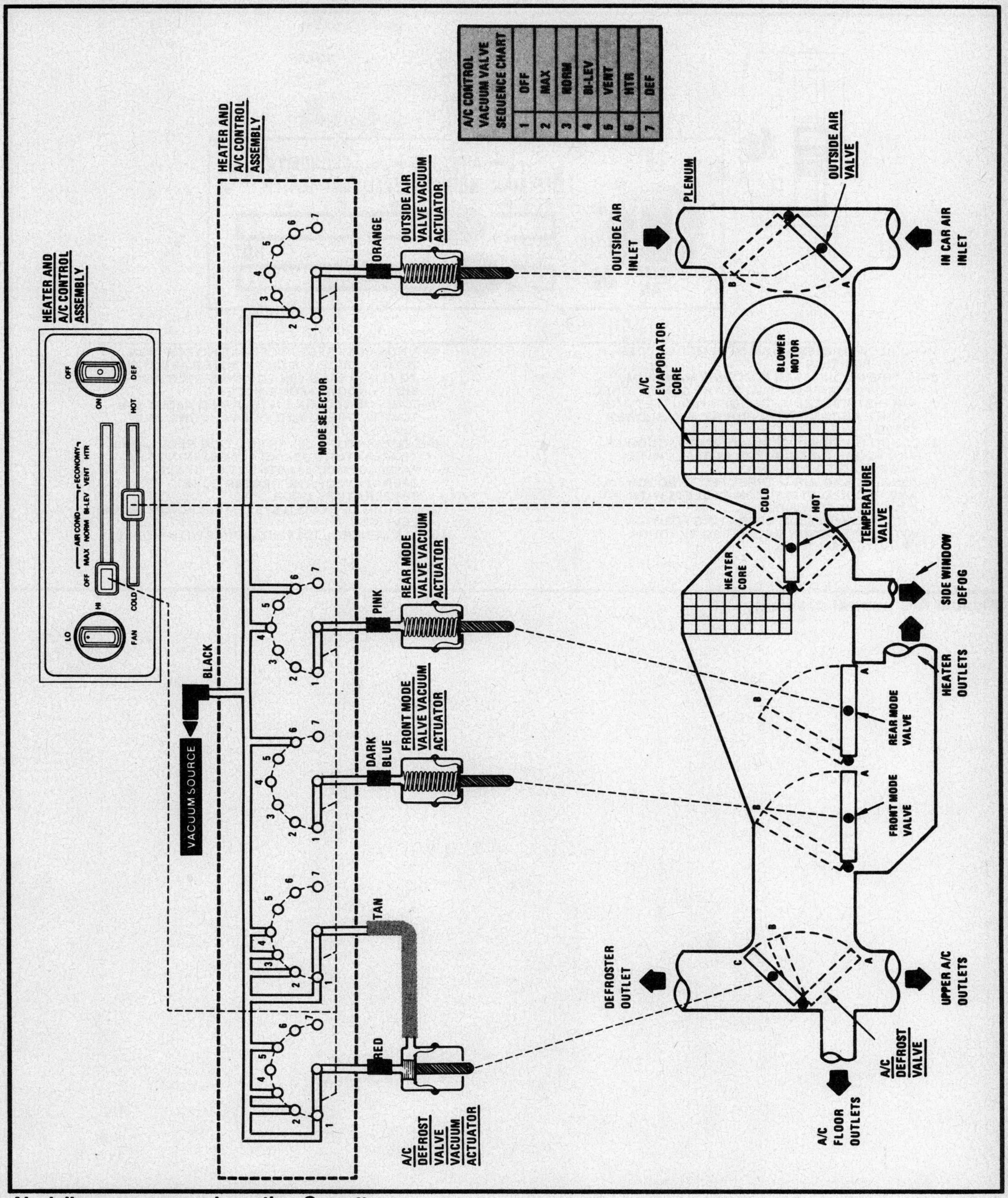
HEATER AND A/C CONTROL ASSEMBLY
LO
HI
FAN
OFF
AIR COND
ECONOMY
MAX
NORM
BI-LEV
VENT
HTR
COLD
HOT
ON
DEF
VACUUM SOURCE
BLACK
HEATER AND A/C CONTROL ASSEMBLY
MODE SELECTOR
ORANGE
PINK
DARK BLUE
TAN
RED
OUTSIDE AIR VALVE VACUUM ACTUATOR
REAR MODE VALVE VACUUM ACTUATOR
FRONT MODE VALVE VACUUM ACTUATOR
A/C DEFROST VALVE VACUUM ACTUATOR
A/C CONTROL VACUUM VALVE SEQUENCE CHART
1 OFF
2 MAX
3 NORM
4 BI-LEV
5 VENT
6 HTR
7 DEF
OUTSIDE AIR INLET
PLENUM
OUTSIDE AIR VALVE
IN CAR AIR INLET
BLOWER MOTOR
A/C EVAPORATOR CORE
COLD
HOT
TEMPERATURE VALVE
HEATER CORE
SIDE WINDOW DEFOG
HEATER OUTLETS
REAR MODE VALVE
FRONT MODE VALVE
DEFROSTER OUTLET
UPPER A/C OUTLETS
A/C DEFROST VALVE
A/C FLOOR OUTLETS

Air delivery vacuum schematic—Corvette

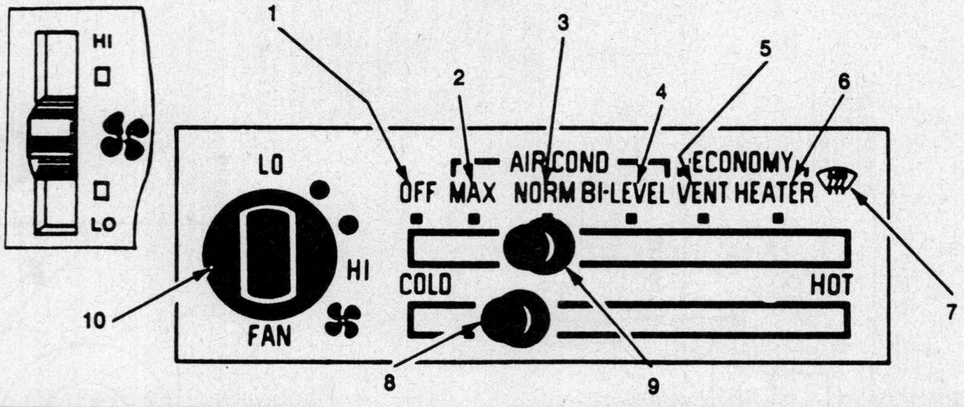
HI
LO
LO
HI
FAN
OFF
MAX
AIR COND
NORM
BI-LEVEL
ECONOMY
VENT
HEATER
COLD
HOT
1
2
3
4
5
6
7
8
9
10

1—NO BLOWER OPERATION WITH MODE LEVER IN "OFF" POSITION
2—IN THIS MODE LEVER POSITION, MAXIMUM COOLING IF OFFERED WITH THE CONDITIONED AIR DISTRIBUTED THROUGH I.P. OUTLET AND SLIGHT AMOUNT TO FLOOR AT ANY BLOWER SPEED
3—CONDITIONED AIR IS DIRECTED THROUGH I.P. AND FLOOR DISTRIBUTOR OUTLETS WITH SOME ALSO TO WINDSHIELD
4—CONDITIONED AIR IS DIRECTED THROUGH I.P. AND FLOOR DISTRIBUTOR OUTLETS WITH SOME ALSO TO WINDSHIELD
5—A NON-COMPRESSOR OPERATING POSITION, WITH OUTSIDE AIR DELIVERED THROUGH I.P. OUTLETS
6—A NON-COMPRESSOR OPERATING POSITION WITH OUTSIDE AIR DISTRIBUTED ABOUT 80% TO FLOOR (AND 20% TO WINDSHIELD AND SIDE WINDOWS - SOME MODELS)
7—CONDITIONED AIR DISTRIBUTED ABOUT 80% TO WINDSHIELD AND SIDE WINDOWS, AND 20% TO FLOOR
8—TEMPERATURE LEVER POSITION REGULATES TEMPERATURE OF THE AIR ENTERING THE PASSENGER COMPARTMENT BY CABLE OPERATION OF THE HEATER CORE TEMPERATURE DOOR
9—VACUUM OPERATED SYSTEM SELECTOR (MODE) LEVER
10—FAN CONTROL (DESIGN VARIES WITH MODEL)

Manual A/C control assembly

8 CHRYSLER CORPORATION 8

CARAVAN • DAKOTA • PICK-UP • RAMCHARGER • TOWN & COUNTRY • VAN • VOYAGER

SPECIFICATIONS

SYSTEM DESCRIPTION

SYSTEM COMPONENTS

SENSORS AND SWITCHES

REAR AUXILIARY SYSTEM

SYSTEM DIAGNOSIS

SPECIFICATIONS

ENGINE IDENTIFICATION

Year	Model	Engine Displacement cu. in. (liter)	Engine Series Identification (VIN)	No. of Cylinders	Engine Type
1989	Caravan	153 (2.5)	K	4	OHC
	Caravan	153 (2.5)	J	4	OHC
	Caravan	181 (3.0)	3	6	OHC
	Voyager	153 (2.5)	K	4	OHC
	Voyager	153 (2.5)	J	4	OHC
	Voyager	181 (3.0)	3	6	OHC
	Dakota	153 (2.5)	K	4	OHC
	Dakota	239 (3.9)	X	6	OHV
	B100 Van	239 (3.9)	X	6	OHV
	B100 Van	318 (5.2)	Y	8	OHV
	B150 Van	239 (3.9)	W	8	OHV
	B150 Van	318 (5.2)	Y	8	OHV
	B250 Van	239 (3.9)	X	6	OHV
	B250 Van	318 (5.2)	Y	8	OHV
	B250 Van	360 (5.9)	Z	8	OHV
	B350 Van	318 (5.2)	Y	8	OHV
	B350 Van	360 (5.9)	Z	8	OHV
	D100 Pick-Up	239 (3.9)	X	6	OHV
	D100 Pick-Up	318 (5.2)	Y	8	OHV
	D100 Pick-Up	360 (5.9)	Z	8	OHV
	W100 Pick-Up	318 (5.2)	Y	8	OHV
	W100 Pick-Up	360 (5.9)	Z	8	OHV
	D150 Pick-Up	239 (3.9)	X	6	OHV
	D150 Pick-Up	318 (5.2)	Y	8	OHV
	D150 Pick-Up	360 (5.9)	Z	8	OHV
	W150 Pick-Up	239 (3.9)	X	6	OHV
	W150 Pick-Up	318 (5.2)	Y	8	OHV
	W150 Pick-Up	360 (5.9)	Z	8	OHV
	AD150 Ramcharger	318 (5.2)	Y	8	OHV
	AD150 Ramcharger	360 (5.9)	Z	8	OHV
	AW150 Ramcharger	318 (5.2)	Y	8	OHV
	AW150 Ramcharger	360 (5.9)	Z	8	OHV
	D250 Pick-Up	239 (3.9)	X	6	OHV
	D250 Pick-Up	318 (5.2)	Y	8	OHV
	D250 Pick-Up	360 (5.9)	Z	8	OHV
	D250 Pick-Up	360 (5.9)	8	6	OHV Turbo diesel
	W250 Pick-Up	318 (5.2)	Y	8	OHV
	W250 Pick-Up	360 (5.9)	Z	8	OHV
	W250 Pick-Up	360 (5.9)	8	6	OHV Turbo diesel
	D350 Pick-Up	360 (5.9)	Z	8	OHV
	D350 Pick-Up	360 (5.9)	8	6	OHV Turbo diesel
	W350 Pick-Up	360 (5.9)	Z	8	OHV
	W350 Pick-Up	360 (5.9)	8	6	OHV Turbo diesel

ENGINE IDENTIFICATION

Year	Model	Engine Displacement cu. in. (liter)	Engine Series Identification (VIN)	No. of Cylinders	Engine Type
1990	Caravan	153 (2.5)	K	4	OHC
	Caravan	153 (2.5)	J	4	OHC
	Caravan	181 (3.0)	3	6	OHC
	Caravan	201 (3.3)	R	6	OHV
	Voyager	153 (2.5)	K	4	OHC
	Voyager	153 (2.5)	J	4	OHC
	Voyager	181 (3.0)	3	6	OHC
	Voyager	201 (3.3)	R	6	OHV
	Town & Country	201 (3.3)	R	6	OHV
	Dakota	153 (2.5)	K	4	OHC
	Dakota	239 (3.9)	X	6	OHV
	B150 Van	239 (3.9)	X	6	OHV
	B150 Van	318 (5.2)	Y	8	OHV
	B250 Van	239 (3.9)	X	6	OHV
	B250 Van	318 (5.2)	Y	8	OHV
	B250 Van	360 (5.9)	Z	8	OHV
	B250 Van	360 (5.9)	5	8	OHV
	B350 Van	318 (5.2)	Y	8	OHV
	B350 Van	360 (5.9)	Z	8	OHV
	B350 Van	360 (5.9)	5	8	OHV
	D150 Pick-Up	239 (3.9)	X	6	OHV
	D150 Pick-Up	318 (5.2)	Y	8	OHV
	D150 Pick-Up	360 (5.9)	Z	8	OHV
	W150 Pick-Up	239 (3.9)	X	6	OHV
	W150 Pick-Up	318 (5.2)	Y	8	OHV
	W150 Pick-Up	360 (5.9)	Z	8	OHV
	AD150 Ramcharger	318 (5.2)	Y	8	OHV
	AD150 Ramcharger	360 (5.9)	Z	8	OHV
	AW150 Ramcharger	318 (5.2)	Y	8	OHV
	AW150 Ramcharger	360 (5.9)	Z	8	OHV
	D250 Pick-Up	239 (3.9)	X	6	OHV
	D250 Pick-Up	318 (5.2)	Y	8	OHV
	D250 Pick-Up	360 (5.9)	Z	8	OHV
	D250 Pick-Up	360 (5.9)	5	8	OHV
	D250 Pick-Up	360 (5.9)	8	6	OHV Turbo diesel
	W250 Pick-Up	318 (5.2)	Y	8	OHV
	W250 Pick-Up	360 (5.9)	Z	8	OHV
	W250 Pick-Up	360 (5.9)	5	8	OHV
	W250 Pick-Up	360 (5.9)	8	6	OHV Turbo diesel
	D350 Pick-Up	360 (5.9)	Z	8	OHV
	D350 Pick-Up	360 (5.9)	5	8	OHV
	D350 Pick-Up	360 (5.9)	8	6	OHV Turbo diesel
	W350 Pick-Up	360 (5.9)	Z	8	OHV
	W350 Pick-Up	360 (5.9)	5	8	OHV
	W350 Pick-Up	360 (5.9)	8	6	OHV Turbo diesel

ENGINE IDENTIFICATION

Year	Model	Engine Displacement cu. in. (liter)	Engine Series Identification (VIN)	No. of Cylinders	Engine Type
1991	Caravan	153 (2.5)	K	4	OHC
	Caravan	181 (3.0)	3	6	OHC
	Caravan	201 (3.3)	R	6	OHV
	Voyager	153 (2.5)	K	4	OHC
	Voyager	181 (3.0)	3	6	OHC
	Voyager	201 (3.3)	R	6	OHV
	Town & Country	201 (3.3)	R	6	OHV
	Dakota	153 (2.5)	K	4	OHC
	Dakota	239 (3.9)	X	6	OHV
	Dakota	318 (5.2)	Y	8	OHV
	B150 Van	239 (3.9)	X	6	OHV
	B150 Van	318 (5.2)	Y	8	OHV
	B250 Van	239 (3.9)	X	6	OHV
	B250 Van	318 (5.2)	Y	8	OHV
	B250 Van	360 (5.9)	Z	8	OHV
	B250 Van	360 (5.9)	5	8	OHV
	B350 Van	318 (5.2)	Y	8	OHV
	B350 Van	360 (5.9)	Z	8	OHV
	B350 Van	360 (5.9)	5	8	OHV
	D150 Pick-Up	239 (3.9)	X	6	OHV
	D150 Pick-Up	318 (5.2)	Y	8	OHV
	D150 Pick-Up	360 (5.9)	Z	8	OHV
	W150 Pick-Up	239 (3.9)	X	6	OHV
	W150 Pick-Up	318 (5.2)	Y	8	OHV
	W150 Pick-Up	360 (5.9)	Z	8	OHV
	AD150 Ramcharger	318 (5.2)	Y	8	OHV
	AD150 Ramcharger	360 (5.9)	Z	8	OHV
	AW150 Ramcharger	318 (5.2)	Y	8	OHV
	AW150 Ramcharger	360 (5.9)	Z	8	OHV
	D250 Pick-Up	239 (3.9)	X	6	OHV
	D250 Pick-Up	318 (5.2)	Y	8	OHV
	D250 Pick-Up	360 (5.9)	Z	8	OHV
	D250 Pick-Up	360 (5.9)	5	8	OHV
	D250 Pick-Up	360 (5.9)	8	6	OHV Turbo diesel
	W250 Pick-Up	318 (5.2)	Y	8	OHV
	W250 Pick-Up	360 (5.9)	Z	8	OHV
	W250 Pick-Up	360 (5.9)	5	8	OHV
	W250 Pick-Up	360 (5.9)	8	6	OHV Turbo diesel
	D350 Pick-Up	360 (5.9)	Z	8	OHV
	D350 Pick-Up	360 (5.9)	5	8	OHV
	D350 Pick-Up	360 (5.9)	8	6	OHV Turbo diesel
	W350 Pick-Up	360 (5.9)	Z	8	OHV
	W350 Pick-Up	360 (5.9)	5	8	OHV
	W350 Pick-Up	360 (5.9)	8	6	OHV Turbo diesel

REFRIGERANT CAPACITIES

Year	Model	Freon (oz.)	Oil (fl. oz.) ①	Type
1989	Caravan	38 ②	11.25	Fixed Displacement
	Caravan	38 ②	12.75	Variable Displacement
	Voyager	38 ②	11.25	Fixed Displacement
	Voyager	38 ②	12.75	Variable Displacement
	Pick-Up	44	11.75	Fixed Displacement
	Ramcharger	44	11.75	Fixed Displacement
	Vans	49 ③	11.25	Fixed Displacement
1990	Caravan	32 ④	11.25	Fixed Displacement
	Caravan	32 ④	12.75	Variable Displacement
	Voyager	32 ④	11.25	Fixed Displacement
	Voyager	32 ④	12.75	Variable Displacement
	Town & Country	32 ④	12.75	Variable Displacement
	Pick-Up	44	11.25	Fixed Displacement
	Ramcharger	44	11.25	Fixed Displacement
	Vans	49 ③	11.25	Fixed Displacement
1991	Caravan	32 ④	11.25	Fixed Displacement
	Caravan	32 ④	12.75	Variable Displacement
	Voyager	32 ④	11.25	Fixed Displacement
	Voyager	32 ④	12.75	Variable Displacement
	Town & Country	32 ④	12.75	Variable Displacement
	Pick-Up	40	11.25	Fixed Displacement
	Ramcharger	40	11.25	Fixed Displacement
	Vans	45 ③	13.75	Fixed Displacement

① Total system capacity—Add 2 oz. with rear air conditioning.
② With rear air conditioning—44 oz.
③ With rear air conditioning—65 oz.
④ With rear air conditioning—43 oz.

AIR CONDITIONING BELT TENSION CHART

Year	Model	Engine (L)	Belt Type	Specification ① New	Used
1989	All	2.5	V	5/16	7/16
	All	3.0	V	5/16	5/16
	All	3.3	Serpentine	②	②
	All	3.9	Dual V	1/4	5/16
	All	5.2	Dual V	1/4	5/16
	All	5.9	Dual V	1/4	5/16
1990	All	2.5	V	5/16	7/16
	All	3.0	V	5/16	7/16
	All	3.3	Serpentine	②	②
	All	3.9	Dual V	1/4	5/16
	All	5.2	Dual V	1/4	5/16
	All	5.9	Dual V	1/4	5/16

AIR CONDITIONING BELT TENSION CHART

Year	Model	Engine (L)	Belt Type	Specification ① New	Specification ① Used
1991	All	2.5	V	5/16	7/16
	All	3.0	V	5/16	7/16
	All	3.3	Serpentine	②	②
	All	3.9	Dual V	1/4	5/16
	All ③	5.2	Dual V	1/4	5/16
	Dakota	5.2	Serpentine	②	②
	All	5.9	Dual V	1/4	5/16

① Inches of deflection at the midpoint of the belt using 10 lbs. force
② Automatic dynamic tensioner
③ Except Dakota

SYSTEM DESCRIPTION

General Information

The air flow system pulls outside air through the cowl opening at the base of the windshield and into the plenum chamber above the heater/air conditioning housing. On air conditioned vehicles, the air passes through the evaporator, then is either directed through or around the heater core by adjusting the blend air door with the TEMP control on the control panel. The air flow can be directed from the panel, panel and floor (bi-level) or floor and defrost outlets. The velocity of the flow can be controlled with the blower speed switch on the control panel.

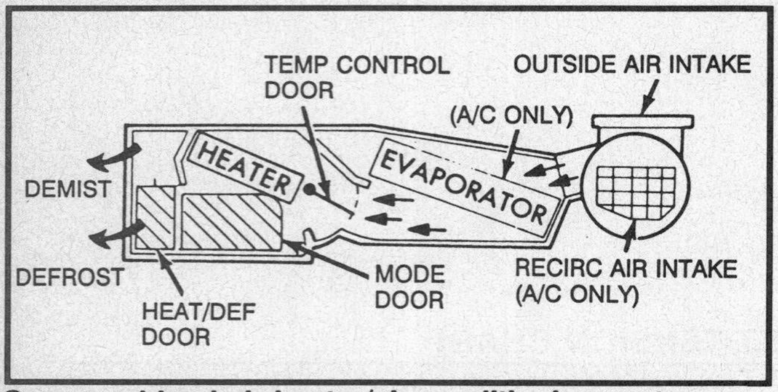
TEMP CONTROL DOOR
OUTSIDE AIR INTAKE
(A/C ONLY)
HEATER
EVAPORATOR
DEMIST
DEFROST
HEAT/DEF DOOR
MODE DOOR
RECIRC AIR INTAKE (A/C ONLY)

Common blend air heater/air conditioning system—Caravan, Voyager and Town & Country

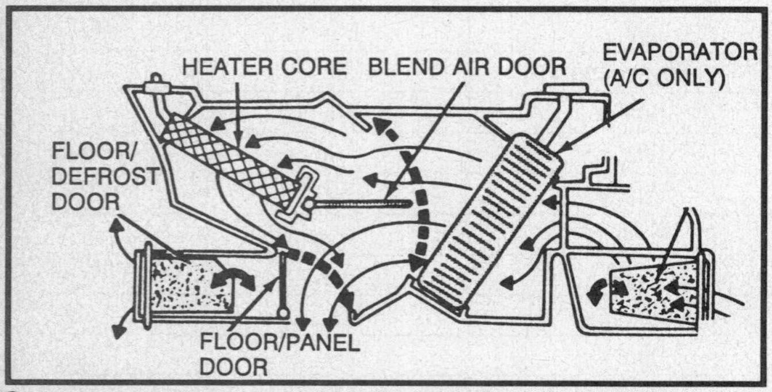
HEATER CORE
BLEND AIR DOOR
EVAPORATOR (A/C ONLY)
FLOOR/ DEFROST DOOR
FLOOR/PANEL DOOR

Common blend air heater/air conditioning system—Pick-Ups and Ramcharger

On air conditioned vehicles, the intake of outside air can be shut off by moving the TEMP control knob to the RECIRC position or depressing the MAX A/C button, which closes the recirculation door and recirculates existing air inside the passenger compartment. Depressing the DEFROST or A/C button may engage the compressor and remove heat and humidity from the air before it is directed through or around the heater core. Forced ventilation is directed from the instrument panel and/or floor outlets when the selector on the control panel is on the panel or bi-level position. The temperature of the forced vent air can be regulated with the TEMP control knob.

On Caravan, Voyager, Town & Country and Dakota, the side window demisters receive air from the heater/air conditioning housing and direct the flow to the front windows. The outlets are located on the top outer corners of the instrument panel. The side demisters operate when the mode control selector is in the FLOOR or DEFROST setting.

Service Valve Location

2.5L, 3.9L, 5.2L and 5.9L Engines

The discharge (high pressure) service port is located on the discharge line near the compressor. The suction (low pressure) service port is located on the compressor.

3.0L and 3.3L Engines

The discharge (high pressure) service port is located on the discharge line. The suction (low pressure) service port is located on the suction line between the compressor and the expansion valve.

System Discharging

R-12 refrigerant is a chloroflourocarbon which, when mishandled, can contribute to the depletion on the ozone layer in the upper atmosphere. Ozone filters out harmful radiation from the sun. In order to protect the ozone layer, an approved R-12 Recovery/Recycling machine that meets SAE standard J1991 should be employed when discharging the system. Follow the operating instructions provided with the approved equipment exactly to properly discharge the system.

System Evacuating

If the air conditioning system has been opened to the atmosphere, it should be air and moisture free before being recharged with refrigerant. Moisture and air mixed with refrigerant will raise the compressor head pressure, possibly damage the system's components and will reduce the performance of the system. Moisture will boil at normal room temperature when exposed to a vacuum. To evacuate or rid the system of air and moisture:

1. Leak test the system and repair any leaks found.
2. Connect an approved charging station, Recovery/Recycling machine or manifold gauge set and vacuum pump to the discharge and suction ports. The red hose is normally connected to the discharge (high pressure) line and the blue hose is connected to the suction (low pressure) line.
3. Open the discharge and suction ports and start the vacuum pump. If the pump is not able to pull at least 26 in. Hg vacuum, there is a leak that must be repaired before evacuation can occur.
4. Once the system has reached at least 26 in. Hg vacuum, allow the system to evacuate for at least 15 minutes. The longer the system is evacuated, the more contaminants will be removed.
5. Close all valves and turn the pump off. If the system loses more than 2 in. Hg vacuum after 15 minutes, there is a leak that should be repaired.

System Charging

1. Connect an approved charging station, Recovery/Recycling machine or manifold gauge set to the discharge and suction ports. The red hose is normally connected to the discharge (high pressure) line and the blue hose is connected to the suction (low pressure) line.
2. Follow the instructions provided with the equipment and charge the system with the specified amount of refrigerant.
3. Perform a leak test.

SYSTEM COMPONENTS

Radiator

REMOVAL AND INSTALLATION

1. Disconnect the negative battery cable.
2. Drain the coolant.
3. Remove the upper hose and coolant reserve tank hose from the radiator.
4. If equipped with an electric cooling fan, remove the fan assembly.
5. If equipped with a belt-driven fan, remove the shroud from the radiator and position it over the fan and away from the radiator.
6. Raise the vehicle and support safely. Remove the lower hose from the radiator.
7. Disconnect the automatic transaxle cooler hoses, if equipped, and plug them. Lower the vehicle.
8. Remove the mounting brackets and screws and carefully lift the radiator from the engine compartment.

To install:

9. Lower the radiator into position.
10. Install the mounting brackets or screws.
11. Raise the vehicle and support safely. Connect the automatic transaxle cooler lines, if equipped.
12. Connect the lower hose and lower the vehicle.
13. Install the electric cooling fan or shroud.
14. Connect the upper hose and coolant reserve tank hose.
15. Fill the system with coolant and bleed, if necessary.
16. Connect the negative battery cable, run the vehicle until the thermostat opens, fill the radiator completely and check the automatic transaxle fluid level, if equipped.
17. Once the vehicle has cooled, recheck the coolant level.

COOLING SYSTEM BLEEDING

The 3.0L, 3.9L, 5.2L and both 5.9L engines are self-bleeding and require no system bleeding when refilling the cooling system.

2.5L and 3.3L Engines

1. On 2.5L engine, remove the plug on the top of the thermostat houisng.
2. On 3.3L engine, remove the engine temperature sending unit, the single-terminal switch located on the cylinder head to the right of the thermostat housing.
3. To vent air from the system, fill the radiator until coolant comes out the hole vacated by the plug or switch.
4. Install the plug or switch and continue to fill the radiator.

Electric Cooling Fan

CAUTION

Make sure the key is in the OFF position when checking the electric cooling fan. If not, the fan could turn ON at any time, causing serious personal injury.

TESTING

1. Unplug the fan connector.
2. Using a jumper wire, connect the female terminal of the fan connector to the negative battery terminal.
3. The fan should turn on when the male terminal is connected to the positive battery terminal.
4. If not, the fan is defective and should be replaced.

REMOVAL AND INSTALLATION

1. Disconnect the negative battery cable.
2. Unplug the connector.
3. Remove the mounting screws.
4. Remove the fan assembly from the vehicle.
5. The installation is the reverse of the removal procedure.
6. Connect the negative battery cable and check the fan for proper operation.

Condenser

REMOVAL AND INSTALLATION

Caravan, Voyager and Town & Country

1. Disconnect the negative battery cable.
2. Properly discharge the air conditioning system.

3. Remove the headlight bezels in order to gain access to the grille. Remove the grille assembly. A hidden screw fastens the grille to the center vertical support.
4. Remove the refrigerant lines attaching nut and separate the lines from the condenser sealing plate. Discard the gasket.
5. Cover the exposed ends of the lines to minimize contamination.
6. Remove the bolts that attach the condenser to the radiator support.
7. Remove the condenser from the vehicle.

To install:

8. Position the condenser and install the bolts.
9. Coat the new gasket with wax-free refrigerant oil and install. Connect the lines to the condenser sealing plate and tighten the nut.
10. Install the grille assembly.
11. Evacuate and recharge the air conditioning system. Add 1 oz. of refrigerant oil during the recharge.
12. Connect the negative battery cable and check the entire climate control system for proper operation and leaks.

Pick-Up, Ramcharger and Van

1. Disconnect the negative battery cable.
2. Properly discharge the air conditioning system.
3. Remove the radiator assembly.
4. Remove the refrigerant lines attaching nut and separate the lines from the condenser sealing plate. Discard the gasket.
5. Cover the exposed ends of the lines to minimize contamination.
6. Remove the bolts that attach the condenser to the radiator support.
7. Lift the condenser and remove from the vehicle.

To install:

8. Position the condenser and install the bolts.
9. Coat the new gasket with wax-free refrigerant oil and install. Connect the lines to the condenser sealing plate and tighten the nut.
10. Install the radiator and fill with coolant.
11. Evacuate and recharge the air conditioning system. Add 1 oz. of refrigerant oil during the recharge.
12. Connect the negative battery cable and check the entire climate control system for proper operation and leaks.

Compressor

REMOVAL AND INSTALLATION

1. Disconnect the negative battery cable.
2. Properly discharge the air conditioning system.
3. Remove the compressor drive belt(s). Disconnect the compressor lead.
4. Raise and safely support the vehicle, if necessary. Remove the refrigerant lines from the compressor and discard the gaskets. Cover the exposed ends of the lines to minimize contamination.
5. Remove the compressor mounting nuts and bolts.
6. Lift the compressor off of its mounting studs and remove from the engine compartment.

To install:

7. Install the compressor and tighten all mounting nuts and bolts.
8. Coat the new gaskets with wax-free refrigerant oil and install. Connect the refrigerant lines to the compressor and tighten the bolts.
9. Install the drive belt(s) and adjust to specification. Connect the electrical lead.
10. Evacuate and recharge the air conditioning system.
11. Connect the negative battery cable and check the entire climate control system for proper operation and leaks.

Receiver/Drier

REMOVAL AND INSTALLATION

1. Disconnect the negative battery cable.
2. Properly discharge the air conditioning system.
3. Remove the nuts that fasten the refrigerant lines to sides of the receiver/drier assembly.
4. Remove the refrigerant lines from the receiver/drier and discard the gaskets. Cover the exposed ends of the lines to minimize contamination.
5. Remove the mounting strap bolts and remove the receiver/drier from the engine compartment.

To install:

6. Transfer the mounting strap to the new receiver/drier.
7. Coat the new gaskets with wax-free refrigerant oil and install. Connect the refrigerant lines to the receiver/drier and tighten the nuts.
8. Evacuate and recharge the air conditioning system. Add 1 oz. of refrigerant oil during the recharge. Check for leaks.

Expansion Valve (H-Valve)

TESTING

1. Connect a manifold gauge set or charging station to the air conditioning system. Verify adequate refrigerant level.
2. Disconnect and plug the vacuum hose at the water control valve.
3. Disconnect the low pressure or differential pressure cut off switch connector and jump the wires inside the boot.
4. Close all doors, windows and vents to the passenger compartment.
5. Set controls to **MAX A/C**, full heat and high blower speed.
6. Start the engine and hold the idle speed at 1000 rpm. After the engine has reached normal operating temperature, allow the passenger compartment to heat up to create the need for maximum refrigerant flow into the evaporator.
7. The discharge (high pressure) gauge should read 140–240 psi and suction (low pressure) gauge should read 20–30 psi, providing the refrigerant charge is sufficient.
8. If the suction side is within specifications, freeze the expansion valve control head using a very cold substance (liquid CO_2 or dry ice) for 30 seconds:
   a. If equipped with a silver H-valve used with fixed displacement compressor, the suction side pressure should drop to 15 in. Hg vacuum. If not, the expansion valve is stuck open and should be replaced.
   b. If equipped with a black H-valve used with variable displacement compressor, the discharge pressure should drop about 15 percent. If not, the expansion valve is stuck open and should be replaced.
9. Allow the expansion valve to thaw. As it thaws, the pressures should stabilize to the values in Step 7. If not, replace the expansion valve.
10. Once the test is complete, put the vacuum line and connector back in the original locations, and perform the overall performance test.

REMOVAL AND INSTALLATION

1. Disconnect the negative battery cable.
2. Properly discharge the air conditioning system.
3. Disconnect the low or differential pressure cut off switch.
4. Remove the attaching bolt at the center of the refrigerant plumbing sealing plate.
5. Pull the refrigerant lines assembly away from the expansion valve. Cover the exposed ends of the lines to minimize contamination.

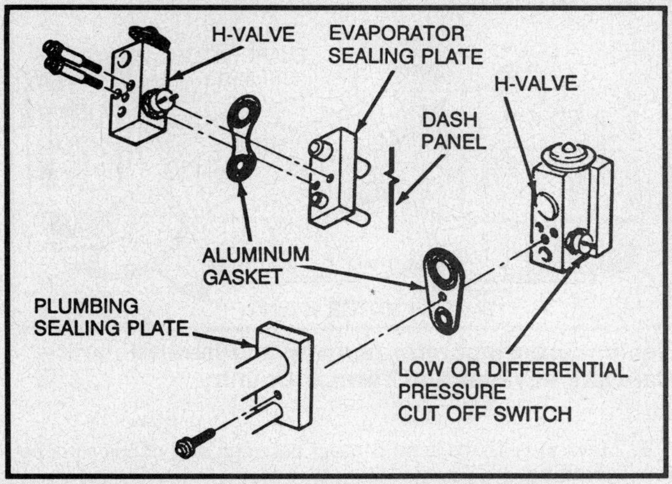
H-VALVE
EVAPORATOR SEALING PLATE
H-VALVE
DASH PANEL
ALUMINUM GASKET
PLUMBING SEALING PLATE
LOW OR DIFFERENTIAL PRESSURE CUT OFF SWITCH

Exploded view of the expansion valve (H-valve)

6. Remove the 2 Torx® screws that mount the expansion valve to the evaporator sealing plate.
7. Remove the valve and discard the gaskets.

To install:

8. Transfer the low pressure cutoff switch to the new valve, if necessary.
9. Coat the new "figure-8" gasket with wax-free refrigerant oil and install to the evaporator sealing plate.
10. Install the expansion valve and torque the Torx® screws to 100 inch lbs.
11. Lubricate the remaining gasket and install with the refrigerant plumbing to the expansion valve. Torque the attaching bolt to 200 inch lbs.
12. Connect the low or differential pressure cut off switch connector.
13. Evacuate and recharge the air conditioning system.
14. Connect the negative battery cable and check the entire climate control system for proper operation and leaks.

Blower Motor

REMOVAL AND INSTALLATION

Caravan, Voyager and Town & Country

1989–90

1. Disconnect the negative battery cable.
2. Disconnect the blower motor lead under the right side of the instrument panel.
3. Remove 5 attaching screws securing the blower to the heater/air conditioning housing.
4. Lower the blower from its cavity and remove it from the vehicle.
5. Remove the fan from the blower.
6. The installation is the reverse of the removal procedure.
7. Connect the negative battery cable and check the blower motor for proper operation.

1991

1. Disconnect the negative battery cable.
2. Remove the steering column cover and left and right side underpanel silencers.
3. Remove the center bezel by unclipping it from the instrument panel.
4. Remove the accessory switch carrier and the heater/air conditioning control head.
5. Remove storage bin and lower right instrument panel.
6. Disconnect the blower motor lead under the right side of the instrument panel.
7. Remove the attaching screws, remove the blower from its cavity and remove it from the vehicle.
8. The installation is the reverse of the removal procedure.
9. Connect the negative battery cable and check the blower motor for proper operation.

Dakota

1. Disconnect the negative battery cable.
2. Remove the steering column cover, intermittent wiper control and the lower instrument panel module retaining screw to the right of the steering column.
3. Remove the center distribution duct retaining screws and panel support screw at the bottom of the module.
4. Remove the courtesy light at the lower right corner of the module and the screw near the ash receiver.
5. Open the glovebox and remove the screws along the top edge.
6. Move the instrument panel out and down far enough to unclip the wiring harness and antenna cable. If equipped with monaural radio, disconnect the speaker wire. Disconnect the glovebox light wire and remove the instrument panel from the vehicle.
7. If equipped with air conditioning, disconnect the 2 vacuum lines from the recirculating air door actuator and disconnect the blower lead wires.
8. Remove 2 screws at the top of the blower housing, 5 screws from around the housing and remove the blower housing from the unit.
9. Remove 3 screw attaching the blower to the unit and remove the blower from the vehicle.
10. Remove the fan from the blower motor.

To install:

11. Install the fan to the blower motor and secure the clip.
12. Install the blower to the unit and install the blower housing.
13. Connect the 2 vacuum lines from the recirculating air door actuator, if equipped, and connect the blower lead wires.
14. Hold the module in position and clip the wiring harness and antenna cable in place. Connect the monaural radio speaker wire, if equipped. Connect the glovebox light wire.
15. Install the retaining screws along the top of the inside of the glovebox.
16. Install the courtesy light at the lower right corner of the module and the screw near the ash receiver.
17. Install the panel support screw at the bottom of the module and the center distribution duct retaining screws.
18. Install the lower instrument panel module retaining screw to the right of the steering column, intermittent wiper control and the steering column cover.
19. Connect the negative battery cable and check the blower motor for proper operation.

Van

WITHOUT AIR CONDITIONING

1. Disconnect the negative battery cable.
2. Remove the air intake duct and top half of the fan shroud, if necessary. Disconnect the blower connector.
3. Remove the 7 screws that fasten the back plate to the heater housing.
4. Remove the blower motor from the vehicle.
5. Remove the spring clip fastening the blower wheel to the blower shaft and pull off the wheel.
6. Remove the vent tube.
7. Remove the nuts fastening the blower motor to the back plate and remove the motor.

To install:

8. Check the seal for breaks and adhesion, repair as necessary.

9. Install the blower motor to the back plate.
10. Install the vent tube.
11. Install the blower wheel to the shaft and secure the spring clip.
12. Install the assembly to the heater housing and install the 7 screws.
13. Connect the conector.
14. Install the fan shroud and air duct, if they were removed.
15. Connect the negative battery cable and check the blower motor for proper operation.

WITH AIR CONDITIONING

1. Disconnect the negative battery cable.
2. Remove the air intake duct and top half of the fan shroud.
3. Disconnect the blower connector.
4. Remove the blower motor cooling tube.
5. Remove the retaining nuts and washers from the studs holding the blower.
6. Pull the air conditioning lines inboard and upward while removing the blower assembly from the vehicle. Remove the spring clip fastening the blower wheel to the blower shaft and pull off the wheel.

To install:

7. Install the blower wheel to the shaft and install the spring clip. Inspect the blower mounting plate seal and repair, as necessary. Apply rubber adhesive to the seal to aid in assembly.
8. Install the blower into the housing and install the washers and nuts.
9. Install the cooling tube.
10. Connect the connector.
11. Install the fan shroud and air intake duct.
12. Connect the negative battery cable and check the blower motor for proper operation.

Pick-Up and Ramcharger

1. Disconnect the negative battery cable.
2. Disconnect the blower connector.
3. Remove the blower motor cooling tube.
4. Remove the screws or retaining nuts retaining the blower plate to the housing.
5. Remove the assembly from the housing.
6. Remove the spring clip fastening the blower wheel to the blower shaft and pull off the wheel. Remove the blower from the plate.

To install:

7. Inspect the blower mounting plate seal and repair, as necessary.
8. Install the blower to the plate. Install the blower wheel to the shaft and install the spring clip.
9. Install the blower into the housing and install the screws or washers and nuts.
10. Install the cooling tube.
11. Connect the connector.
12. Connect the negative battery cable and check the blower motor for proper operation.

Blower Motor Resistor

REMOVAL AND INSTALLATION

The resistor block is located at the left rear corner of the engine compartment on Caravan, Voyager and Town & Country and behind the glovebox on Pick-up, Ramcharger and Van.

1. Disconnect the negative battery cable.
2. Remove the glovebox, if necessary. Locate the resistor block and disconnect the wire harness.
3. Remove the attaching screws and remove the resistor from the housing.

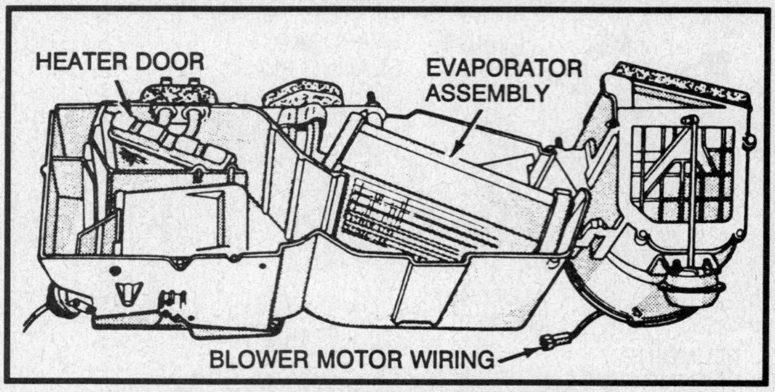
HEATER DOOR
EVAPORATOR ASSEMBLY
BLOWER MOTOR WIRING

Heater core/evaporator housing and internal parts—Caravan, Voyager and Town & Country

4. Make sure there is no contact between any of the coils before installing.
5. The installation is the reverse of the removal procedure. Make sure the foam seal is in good condition.
6. Connect the negative battery cable and check the blower system for proper operation.

Heater Core and Evaporator

REMOVAL AND INSTALLATION

Caravan, Voyager and Town & Country

1989–90

1. Disconnect the negative battery cable. Properly discharge the air conditioning system, if equipped. Drain the cooling system.
2. Remove the lower steering column cover.
3. Remove the lower reinforcement under the steering column, right side cowl and sill trim. Remove the bolt holding the right side instrument panel to the right cowl.
4. Loosen the 2 brackets supporting the lower edge of the heater housing. Remove the instrument panel trim covering and reinforcement. Remove the retaining screws from the right side to the steering column.
5. Disconnect the vacuum lines at the brake booster and water valve.
6. Clamp off the heater hoses near the heater core and remove the hoses from the core tubes. Plug the hose ends and the core tubes to prevent spillage of coolant.
7. If equipped with air conditioning, remove the H-valve and condensation tube.
8. Disconnect the blower motor wiring, resistor wiring and the temperature control cable. Disconnect the vacuum harness at the connection at the top of the unit.
9. Remove the retaining nuts from the package mounting studs at the firewall. Disconnect the hanger strap from the package and rotate it aside.
10. Pull the right side of the instrument panel out as far as possible. Fold the carpeting and insulation back to provide a little more working room and to prevent spillage from staining the carpeting.
11. Remove the entire housing assembly from the dash panel and remove it from the vehicle.
12. To disassemble the housing assembly, remove the vacuum diaphragm and retaining screws from the cover and remove the cover.
13. Remove the retaining screw from the heater core and/or evaporator and remove from the housing assembly.

To install:

14. Remove the temperature control door from the unit and clean the unit out with solvent. Lubricate the lower pivot rod

and its well and install. Wrap the heater core and/or evaporator with foam tape and place in position. Secure with the screws.

15. Assemble the unit, making sure all vacuum tubes are properly routed.
16. Install the assembly to the vehicle and connect the vacuum harness. Install the nuts to the firewall and install the condensation tube. Fold the carpeting back into position.
17. Connect the hanger strap from the package and rotate it aside. Install the 2 brackets supporting the lower edge of the heater housing. Connect the blower motor wiring, resistor wiring and the temperature control cable.
18. Install the retaining screws from the right side to the steering column. Install the instrument panel trim covering and reinforcement.
19. Install the bolt holding the right side instrument panel to the right cowl. Install the lower reinforcement under the steering column, right side cowl and sill trim.
20. Connect the vacuum lines at the brake booster and water valve.
21. Connect the heater hoses to the core tubes.
22. Using new gaskets, install the H-valve and connect the refrigerant lines. Install the condensation tube.
23. Evacuate and recharge the air conditioning system, if equipped. Add 2 oz. of refrigerant oil during the recharge. Fill the cooling system.
24. Connect the negative battery cable and check the entire climate control system for proper operation and leaks.
25. Connect the negative battery cable and check the entire climate control system for proper operation and leakage.

1991

1. Disconnect the negative battery cable. Properly discharge the air conditioning system, if equipped. Drain the cooling system.
2. Remove the steering column cover and left and right side underpanel silencers.
3. Remove the center bezel by unclipping it from the instrument panel.
4. Remove the accessory switch carrier and the heater/air conditioning control head.
5. Remove storage bin and lower right instrument panel.
6. Disconnect the blower motor lead under the right side of the instrument panel.
7. Remove the right side 40-way connector wiring bracket.
8. Remove the lower right reinforcement, body computer bracket and mid-to-lower reinforcement as an assembly.
9. Disconnect the vacuum lines at the brake booster and water valve.
10. Clamp off the heater hoses near the heater core and remove the hoses from the core tubes. Plug the hose ends and the core tubes to prevent spillage of coolant.
11. If equipped with air conditioning, remove the H-valve and condensation tube.
12. Disconnect the the temperature control cable and vacuum harness at the connection at the top of the unit.
13. Remove the retaining nuts from the package mounting studs at the firewall. Disconnect the hanger strap from the package and rotate it aside.
14. Fold the carpeting and insulation back to provide a little more working room and to prevent spillage from staining the carpeting.
15. Remove the entire housing assembly from the dash panel and remove it from the vehicle.
16. To disassemble the housing assembly, remove the vacuum diaphragm and retaining screws from the cover, then remove the cover.
17. Remove the retaining screw from the heater core and/or evaporator and remove from the housing assembly.

To install:

18. Remove the temperature control door from the unit and clean the unit out with solvent. Lubricate the lower pivot rod and its well and install. Wrap the heater core and/or evaporator with foam tape and place in position. Secure with the screws.
19. Assemble the unit, making sure all vacuum tubes are properly routed.
20. Install the assembly to the vehicle and connect the vacuum harness. Install the nuts to the firewall and install the condensation tube. Fold the carpeting back into position.
22. Connect the hanger strap from the package and rotate it aside. Connect the blower motor wiring and temperature control cable.
23. Install the lower right reinforcement, body computer bracket and mid-to-lower reinforcement as an assembly.
24. Install the right side 40-way connector wiring bracket.
25. Install the lower right instrument panel and storage bin.
26. Install the heater/air conditioning control head and accessory switch carrier.
27. Install the center bezel to the instrument panel.
28. Install the underpanel silencers and steering column cover.
29. Install the vacuum lines at the brake booster and water valve.
30. Connect the heater hoses to the core tubes.
31. Using new gaskets, install the H-valve and connect the refrigerant lines. Install the condensation tube.
32. Evacuate and recharge the air conditioning system, if equipped. Add 2 oz. of refrigerant oil during the recharge. Fill the cooling system.
33. Connect the negative battery cable and check the entire climate control system for proper operation and leaks.
34. Connect the negative battery cable and check the entire climate control system for proper operation and leakage.

Dakota

1. Disconnect the negative battery cable. Properly discharge the air conditioning system, if equipped. Drain the coolant.
2. Remove the steering column cover, intermittent wiper control and the lower instrument panel module retaining screw to the right of the steering column.
3. Remove the center distribution duct retaining screws and panel support screw at the bottom of the module.
4. Remove the courtesy light at the lower right corner of the module and the screw near the ash tray.
5. Open the glovebox and remove the screws along the top edge.
6. Move the module out and down far enough to unclip the wiring harness and antenna cable. If equipped with a monaural radio, disconnect the speaker wire. Disconnect the glovebox light wire and remove the module from the vehicle.
7. Remove the center air distribution duct.
8. Remove the antenna wire from retaining clip at the right end of the heater unit.
9. Disconnect the blower motor connector and remove the thermal insulator retainer from the heater unit.

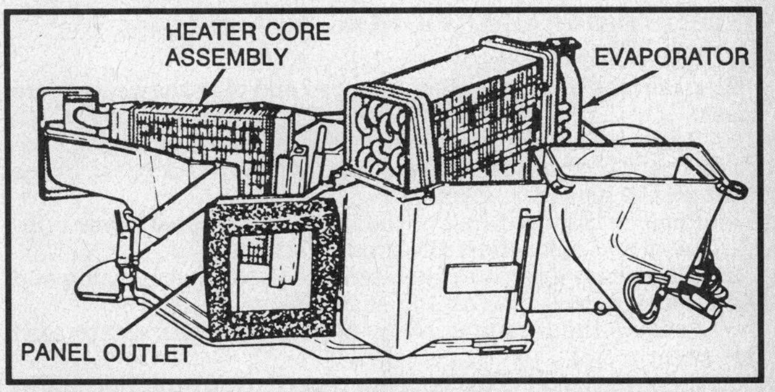
HEATER CORE ASSEMBLY
EVAPORATOR
PANEL OUTLET

Heater core/evaporator housing and internal parts—Pick-Ups and Ramcharger

10. Disconnect the demister hoses from the adaptor at the top of the heater/air conditioning unit.
11. Disconnect the vacuum harness connector from the air conditioning control hose and vacuum feed line from the check valve.
12. Disconnect the temperature control cable flag retainer from the heater unit and remove the adjusting clip from the blend air door crank.
13. Disconnect the heater hoses from the core tubes and plug them.
14. Remove the condensation drain tube, if equipped.
15. Remove 4 heater/air conditioning housing attaching nuts from the rear engine compartment dash panel.
16. Remove the housing support attaching screw and rotate the brace aside.
17. Remove the heater/air conditioning housing from the vehicle.
18. To disassemble the housing assembly, vacuum diaphragm and retaining screws from the cover and remove the cover.
19. Remove the retaining screw from the heater core and/or evaporator and remove from the housing assembly.

To install:

20. Remove the temperature control door from the unit and clean the unit out with solvent. Lubricate the lower pivot rod and its well and install. Wrap the heater core and/or evaporator with foam tape and place in position. Secure with the screw.
21. Assemble the unit, making sure all vacuum tubing is properly routed.
22. Install the assembly to the vehicle and connect the vacuum harness. Install the nuts to the firewall and install the condensation tube. Install the support brace to the housing.
23. Connect the demister hoses to the adaptor at the top of the heater unit.
24. Connect the blower motor connector and install the thermal insulator retainer to the heater unit.
25. Connect the vacuum harness connector to the air conditioning control hose and vacuum feed line to the check valve.
26. Connect the temperature control cable flag retainer to the heater unit and install the adjusting clip from the blend air door crank.
27. Install the center air distribution duct.
28. Install the antenna wire from retaining clip at the right end of the heater unit.
29. Install the instrument panel module and all related parts.
30. Connect the heater hoses to the core tubes.
31. Using new gaskets, install the H-valve and connect the refrigerant lines.
32. Evacuate and recharge the air conditioning system. If the evaporator was replaced, add 2 oz. of refrigerant oil during the recharge. Fill the cooling system.
33. Connect the negative battery cable and check the entire climate control system for proper operation and leaks.

Pick-Up and Ramcharger

WITHOUT AIR CONDITIONING

1. Disconnect the negative battery cable.
2. Drain the cooling system. Remove and plug the heater core hoses.
3. Remove the right side cowl trim panel, if equipped. Remove the glovebox assembly. Remove the structural brace through the glovebox opening.
4. Remove the right half of the instrument panel lower reinforcement and disconnect the ground strap.
5. Disconnect the control cables from the heater housing and the blower motor wires on the engine side.
6. Remove the retaining screw between the package to cowl side sheet metal.
7. Remove the 6 heater housing retaining nuts on the engine side of the heater assembly and remove the heater housing assembly.
8. Remove the heater housing cover retaining screws and the mode door crank. Separate the cover from the housing.
9. Carefully lift the heater core from the heater housing.

To install:

10. Clean the inside of the housing. Install the heater core into the housing.
11. Install the housing cover. Inspect the dash panel seal for damage and repair, as required.
12. Install the assembly to the dash panel and install the retaining nuts.
13. Install the cowl side retaining screws.
14. Connect the blower motor connector.
15. Connect the control cables.
16. Install the right lower instrument panel reinforcement, structural brace, glovebox and cowl side trim panel, if equipped.
17. Connect the heater hoses.
18. Refill the radiator.
19. Connect the negative battery cable, run the vehicle until the thermostat opens, fill the radiator completely and check the operation of the heater.
20. Once the vehicle has cooled, recheck the coolant level.

WITH AIR CONDITIONING

1. Disconnect the negative battery cable. Properly discharge the air conditioning system. Drain the cooling system. Disconnect and plug the heater hoses and the refrigerant lines.
2. Remove the condensation tube from the housing.
3. Move the transfer case and gear shift levers away from the instrument panel, if equipped.
4. Remove the right side cowl trim panel, if equipped. Remove the glovebox and swing it out from the bottom.
5. Remove the structural brace from the through hole in the glovebox opening. Remove the ash tray.
6. Remove the right lower half of the dash reinforcement by removing the retaining screws holding it to the instrument panel and to the cowl side trim panel.
7. Disconnect the radio ground strap, if equipped. Remove the center and floor air distribution ducts.
8. Disconnect the temperature control cable from the assembly and tape it aside.
9. Disconnect the vacuum lines from the extension on the control unit and unclip the vacuum lines from the defroster duct.
10. Remove the wiring connector from the resistor block. Remove the blower motor electrical connector from the engine side of the assembly.
11. Disconnect the vacuum lines on the engine side and make sure the grommet is free from the dash panel.
12. Remove the retaining nuts on the engine side. Remove the screw that retains the assembly to the cowl side of the sheetmetal.
13. Remove the assembly from the vehicle.
14. Remove the vacuum actuators, door crank levers, evaporator case cover retaining nuts and screws and the heater core retaining screws. Lift the cover off of the assembly and remove the heater core from its mounting.

To install:

15. Clean the inside of the housing. Install the heater core into the housing.
16. Install the housing cover, retaining screws and nuts, levers and actuators.
17. Inspect the dash panel seals for damage and repair, as required.
18. Feed the vacuum lines through the hole in the dash panel, install the assembly to the dash panel and install all retaining nuts and screws.
19. Connect the resistor block and blower motor.
20. Connect the vacuum lines to the extension on the control unit and clip the vacuum lines to the defroster duct.
21. Connect the temperature control cable to the assembly.

22. Connect the radio ground strap, if equipped. Install the center and floor air distribution ducts.
23. Install the dash reinforcement, structural brace, glovebox and right side cowl trim panel, if equipped. Install the ash tray.
24. Install the condensation tube.
25. Connect the heater hoses and vacuum lines.
26. Install a new gasket and connect the refrigerant lines.
27. Evacuate and recharge the air conditioning system. Refill the radiator.
28. Connect the negative battery cable and check the entire climate control system for proper operation and leaks.

Van

WITHOUT AIR CONDITIONING

1. Disconnect the negative battery cable.
2. Drain the cooling system. Disconnect and plug the heater hoses.
3. Disconnect the temperature control cable from the heater core cover and the blend door crank. Disconnect the vent cable.
4. Disconnect the blower motor connector.
5. Remove the screws retaining the heater assembly to the side cowl and the nuts fastening the heater assembly to the dash panel.
6. Remove the heater unit from the vehicle.
7. Remove the back plate and remove the screws holding the heater core cover to the heater housing. Lift the cover from the housing.
8. Remove the retaining screws from the heater core and remove the core from the heater housing.

To install:

9. Clean out the inside of the housing. Place the heater core into the housing and fasten.
10. Position the blend air door and right vent door in the housing and fasten the heater core cover to the housing.
11. Check the dash panel and side cowl seals for breaks and lack of adhesion. Repair as required.
12. Install the heater assembly to the vehicle.
13. Connect the blower connector.
14. Connect the cables.
15. Connect the heater hoses.
16. Refill the radiator.
17. Connect the negative battery cable, run the vehicle until

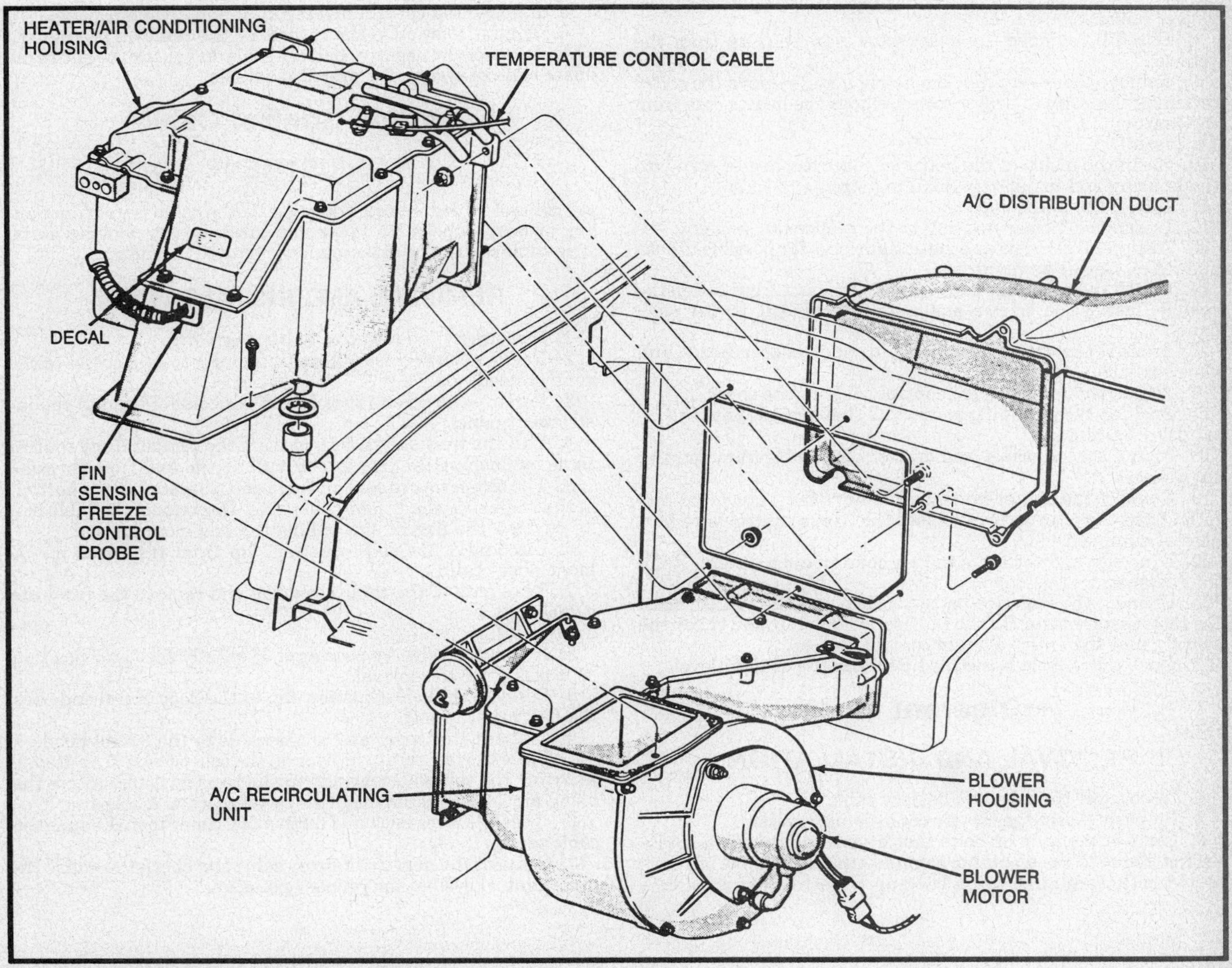
HEATER/AIR CONDITIONING HOUSING
TEMPERATURE CONTROL CABLE
A/C DISTRIBUTION DUCT
DECAL
FIN SENSING FREEZE CONTROL PROBE
A/C RECIRCULATING UNIT
BLOWER HOUSING
BLOWER MOTOR

Heater core/evaporator housing and blower housing—Van

the thermostat opens, fill the radiator completely and check the operation of the heater.

18. Once the vehicle has cooled, recheck the coolant level.

WITH AIR CONDITIONING

1. Disconnect the negative battery cable. Properly discharge the air conditioning system completely.
2. Disconnect the freeze control connector from the wire harness at the H-valve, if equipped.
3. Drain the cooling system. Place a layer of non-conductive waterproof material over the alternator to prevent coolant from spilling on it when disconnecting the heater hoses. Disconnect and cap the heater hoses.
4. Slowly disconnect the refrigerant plumbing from the H-valve. Remove the 2 screws from the filter drier bracket and swing the plumbing aside towards the center of the vehicle.
5. Remove the temperature control cable from the cover.
6. Working from inside the vehicle, remove the glovebox, spot cooler bezel and the appearance shield. Working through the glovebox opening and under the instrument panel, remove the screws and nuts attaching the evaporator core housing to the dash panel.
7. Remove the 2 screws from the flange connection to the blower housing. Separate the evaporator core housing from the blower housing.
8. Carefully remove the evaporator core housing from the vehicle.
9. Remove the cover from the housing and remove the screw retaining the strap to heater core. Remove the heater core from the housing.

To install:

10. Clean the inside of the housing. Place the heater core into the housing and install the retaining strap and screw.
11. Install the housing cover.
12. Install the blower housing to the evaporator housing.
13. Inspect all air seals and mating surfaces for possible breaks and leaks. Repair as required.
14. Install the assembly to the dash panel and from inside the vehicle, install the screws and nuts attaching it to the dash panel.
15. Install the appearance shield, spot cooler bezel and glovebox.
16. Attach the temperature control cable to the cover.
17. Position the plumbing and install the 2 screws onto the filter drier bracket.
18. Install a new gasket and connect the refrigerant lines to the H-valve.
19. Connect the heater hoses and remove the waterproof material from the alternator. Connect the freeze control wire harness, if equipped.
20. Evacuate and recharge the air conditioning system. Refill the radiator.
21. Connect the negative battery cable, run the vehicle until the thermostat opens, fill the radiator completely and check the operation of the entire climate control system.
22. Once the vehicle has cooled, recheck the coolant level.

Refrigerant Lines

REMOVAL AND INSTALLATION

1. Disconnect the negative battery cable.
2. Properly discharge the air conditioning system.
3. Remove the nuts or bolts that attach the refrigerant line sealing plates to the adjoining components. If the lines are connected with flare nuts, use a back-up wrench when disassembling. Cover the exposed ends of the lines to minimize contamination.
4. Remove the lines and discard the gaskets or O-rings.

To install:

5. Coat the new gaskets or O-rings with wax-free refrigerant oil and install. Connect the refrigerant lines to the adjoining components and tighten the nuts or bolts.
6. Evacuate and recharge the air conditioning system.
7. Connect the negative battery cable and check the entire climate control system for proper operation and leaks.

Manual Control Head

REMOVAL AND INSTALLATION

1. Disconnect the negative battery cable.
2. Remove the necessary bezel(s) in order to gain access to the control head.
3. Remove the screws that fasten the control head to the instrument panel.
4. Pull the unit out and unplug the electrical and vacuum connectors. Disconnect the temperature control cable by pushing the flag in and pulling the end from its seat.
5. Remove the control head from the instrument panel.
6. The installation is the reverse of the removal procedure.
7. Connect the negative battery cable and check the entire climate control system for proper operation.

Manual Control Cable

ADJUSTMENT

All control cables are self-adjusting. If the cable is not functioning properly, check for kinks and lubricate dry moving parts. The cable cannot be disassembled; replace if faulty.

REMOVAL AND INSTALLATION

1. Disconnect the negative battery cable.
2. Remove the necessary bezel(s) in order to gain access to the control head.
3. Remove the screws that fasten the control head to the instrument panel.
4. Pull the unit out and disconnect the temperature control cable by pushing the flag in and pulling the end from its seat.
5. The temperature control cable end is located at the bottom of the heater/air conditioning housing. Disconnect the cable end by pushing the flag in and pulling the end from its seat.
6. Disconnect the self-adjusting clip from the blend air or mode door crank.
7. Take note of the cable's routing and remove the from the vehicle.

To install:

8. Install the cable by routing it in exactly the same position as it was prior to removal.
9. Connect the self-adjusting clip to the door crank and click the flag into the seat.
10. Connect the upper end of the cable to the contol head.
11. Place the temperature lever on the coolest side of its travel. Allowing the self-adjusting clip to slide on the cable, rotate the blend air door counterclockwise by hand until it stops.
12. Cycle the lever back and forth a few times to make sure the cable moves freely.
13. Connect the negative battery cable and check the entire climate control system for proper operation.

SENSORS AND SWITCHES

Electronic Cycling Clutch Switch

OPERATION

The following vehicles are equipped with an Electronic Cycling Clutch Switch (ECCS):

- Caravan and Voyager with 2.5L engine
- 1989 Van with rear air conditioning
- 1991 Pick-Up and Ramcharger

The ECCS is located on the refrigerant plumbing near the H-valve. The ECCS prevents evaporator freeze-up by signaling the engine controller (SMEC or SBEC) to cycle the compressor clutch coil by monitoring the temperature of the suction line. The ECCS uses a thermistor probe in a capillary tube, inserted into a well on the suction line. The well must be filled with special conductive grease to prevent corrosion and allow thermal transfer to the probe. The switch is a sealed unit that should be replaced if found to be defective.

TESTING

The compressor clutch coil should cycle 2–3 times per minute at ambient temperatures of 68–90°F (20–32°C). At temperatures above 90°F (32°C), the coil may not cycle at all.

1. Test the switch in an area with ambient temperature of at least 70°F (21°C).
2. Disconnect the switch connector. Supply 12 volts to pin 2, and ground pin 4 of the ECCS connector.
3. Check for continuity between pins 1 and 3.
4. If coninuity is not detected, the switch is faulty and should be replaced.
5. If there is continuity, inspect the rest of the system for an open circuit.

REMOVAL AND INSTALLATION

1. Disconnect the negative battery cable.
2. Disconnect the ECCS connector.
3. Remove the plastic wire tie holding the bulb against the suction line.
4. Remove the mounting screw on the refrigerant line manifold plate at the H-valve.
5. Separate the switch from the refrigerant manifold and pull the capillary tube out of the capillary tube well on the suction line.

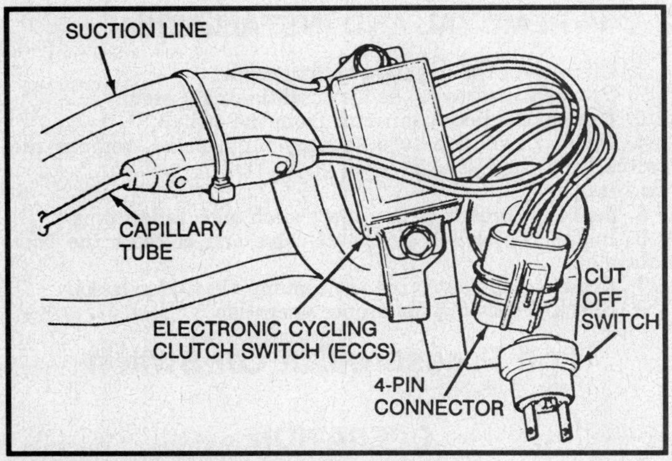
SUCTION LINE
CAPILLARY TUBE
ELECTRONIC CYCLING CLUTCH SWITCH (ECCS)
4-PIN CONNECTOR
CUT OFF SWITCH

Typical electronic cycling clutch switch

NOTE: The capillary tube well is filled with special temperature conductive grease. If reusing the switch, try to save all the grease. If replacing the switch, new grease will be supplied in the replacement switch package.

To install:

6. Fill the well with the special grease and insert the capillary tube.
7. Mount the switch to the refrigerant manifold.
8. Tie the bulb with a new wire tie.
9. Connect the ECCS connector.
10. Connect the negative battery cable and check the entire climate control system for proper operation.

Damped Pressure Cycling Switch

OPERATION

The following vehicles are equipped with a damped pressure switch:

- 1989 Van without rear air conditioning
- 1989–90 Pick-Up and Ramcharger

The damped pressure cycling switch is mounted on a shrader valve on the suction line near the H-valve. It is wired in series with the compressor clutch coil and is an on/off switch that controls the compressor depending on the pressure it is sensing in the suction line. The switch is a sealed unit that should be replaced if found to be defective.

TESTING

The compressor clutch coil should cycle 2–3 times per minute at ambient temperatures of 68–90°F (20–32°C). At temperatures above 90°F (32°C), the coil may not cycle at all.

1. Disconnect the wires from the switch.
2. Check for switch continuity. The switch should be closed at temperatures above 45°F (7°C).
3. If the contacts are closed, reconnect the switch, set the temperature control lever to its coolest position, turn the blower on low speed and operate the engine at 1000 rpm for 5 minutes to allow the air conditioning system to stabilize.
4. If the damped pressure switch is good and the clutch does not engage properly, inspect the rest of the system for an open circuit.

REMOVAL AND INSTALLATION

1. Disconnect the negative battery cable.
2. Disconnect the connector from the switch.
3. The switch is mounted on a shrader valve and will vent a small amount of refrigerant when removed. Rotate the switch counterclockwise quickly to remove.

To install:

4. Replace the O-ring and lubricate with refrigerant oil.
5. Install the switch to the schrader valve.
6. Connect the connector.
7. Connect the negative battery cable and check the entire climate control system for proper operation and leaks.

Fin Sensing Cycling Clutch Switch

OPERATION

The following vehicles are equipped with a fin sensing cycling clutch switch:

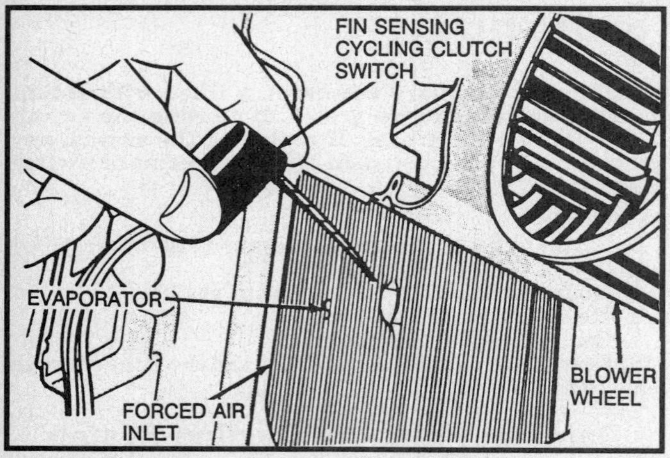
FIN SENSING
CYCLING CLUTCH
SWITCH
EVAPORATOR
BLOWER
WHEEL
FORCED AIR
INLET

Installing the fin-sensing cycling clutch switch

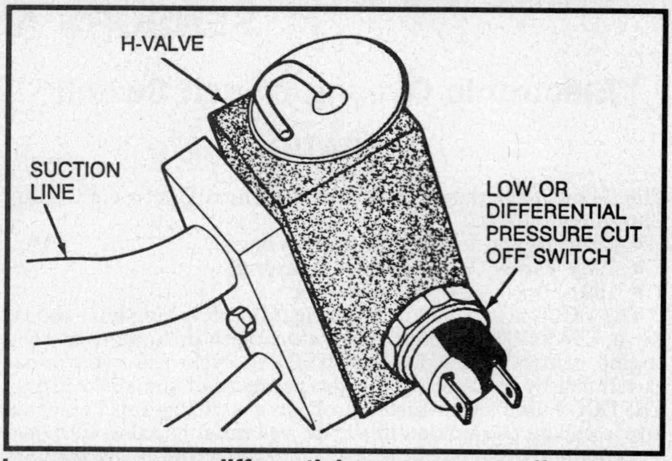
H-VALVE
SUCTION
LINE
LOW OR
DIFFERENTIAL
PRESSURE CUT
OFF SWITCH

Low pressure or differential pressure cut off switch location

- 1989–91 Dakota
- 1990–91 Van

The Fin Sensing Cycling Clutch Switch (FSSC) is located in the heater/air conditioning housing near the blower motor and is inserted into the evaporator fins. The FCCS prevents evaporator freeze-up by cycling the compressor clutch coil off when the evaporator temperature drops below freezing point. The coil will be cycled back on when the temperature rises above the freeze point. The FCCS uses a thermistor probe in a capillary tube inserted between the evaporator fins. The switch is a sealed unit that should be replaced if found to be defective.

TESTING

The compressor clutch coil should cycle 2–3 times per minute at ambient temperatures of 68–90°F (20–32°C). At temperatures above 90°F (32°C), the coil may not cycle at all.

1. Test the switch in an area with ambient temperature of at least 70°F (21°C).
2. Disconnect the switch connector, located behind the glovebox. Use a suitable jumper wire to jump between the outer wires of the harness connector.
3. If the compressor clutch engages, check for continuity between pins 1 and 3 of the FSSC connector. If there is no continuity, replace the switch.
4. If the compressor clutch did not engage, inspect the rest of the system for an open circuit.

REMOVAL AND INSTALLATION

1. Disconnect the negative battery cable.
2. On Dakota, remove the blower housing. On Vans, remove the heater/air conditioning housing and disassemble.
3. Disconnect the connector, push the wire grommet through the housing and feed the connector through the unit housing.
4. Remove the switch from the evaporator.
5. The installation is the reverse of the removal procedure.
6. Evacuate and recharge the air conditioning system, if it was discharged.
7. Connect the negative battery cable and check the entire climate control system for proper operation and leaks.

Low Pressure Cut Off and Differential Pressure Cut Off Switches

OPERATION

The low pressure cut off switch monitors the refrigerant gas pressure on the suction side of the system and is only used with fixed displacement compressors. The Differential pressure cut off switch monitors the liquid refrigerant pressure on the liquid side of the system and is only used with variable displacement compressors. The switches operate similarly in that they turn off voltage to the compressor clutch coil when the monitored pressure drops to levels that could damage the compressor. The switches are sealed units that must be replaced, if faulty.

TESTING

1. Start the engine and allow to idle. Turn the air conditioner **ON**.
2. Disconnect the switch connector and use a jumper wire to jump between terminals inside the connector boot.
3. If the compressor clutch does not engage, inspect the system for an open circuit.
4. If the clutch engages, connect an air conditioning manifold gauge to the system.
5. Read the low pressure gauge. The low pressure cut off switch should complete the circuit at pressures of at least 14 psi. The differential pressure switch will complete the circuit at pressure of at least 41 psi. Check the system for leaks if the pressures are too low.
6. If the pressures are nominal and the system works when the terminals are jumped, the cut off switch is faulty and should be replaced.

REMOVAL AND INSTALLATION

1. Disconnect the negative battery cable.
2. Properly discharge the air conditioning system.
3. Unplug the boot connector from the switch.
4. Using an oil pressure sending unit socket, remove the switch from the H-valve.

To install:

5. Seal the threads of the new switch with teflon tape.
6. Install the switch to the H-valve and connect the boot connector.
7. Evacuate and recharge the system. Check for leaks.
8. Check the switch for proper operation.

High Pressure Cut Off Switch

OPERATION

The high pressure cut off switch used in vehicles equipped with

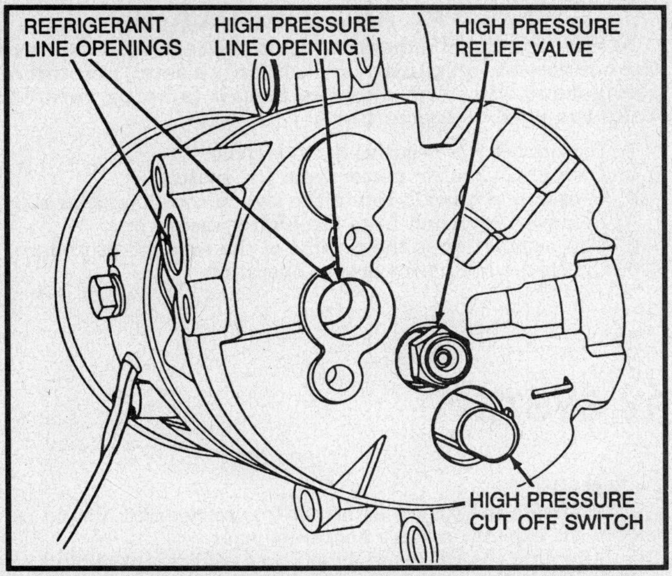
REFRIGERANT
LINE OPENINGS
HIGH PRESSURE
LINE OPENING
HIGH PRESSURE
RELIEF VALVE
HIGH PRESSURE
CUT OFF SWITCH

Rear view of the variable displacement compressor

a variable displacement compressor and is located on or near the high pressure relief valve. The function of the switch is to disengage the compressor clutch by monitoring the discharge pressure when levels reach dangerously high levels. This switch is on the same circuit as the differential pressure cut off switch and the ambient sensor.

TESTING

1. Start the engine and allow to idle. Turn the air conditioner **ON**.
2. Connect an air conditioning manifold gauge to the system. The system should operate at high gauge pressure below 430 psi.
3. Without allowing the engine to overheat, block the flow of air to the condenser with a cover. When the high pressure reaches 450 psi, the clutch should disengage.
4. Remove the cover. When the gauge reading falls below 265 psi, the clutch should cycle back on.
5. Replace the switch, if it does not operate properly.

REMOVAL AND INSTALLATION

1. Disconnect the negative battery cable.
2. Properly discharge the air conditioning system.
3. Disconnect the connector from the switch.
4. Remove the snapring that retains the switch in the compressor.
5. Pull the switch straight from the compressor and discard the O-ring.

To install:

6. Replace the O-ring and lubricate with refrigerant oil before installing.
7. Install the switch to the compressor and secure with a new snapring.
8. Evacuate and recharge the system. Check for leaks.
9. Check the switch for proper operation.

Ambient Temperature Switch

OPERATION

The ambient switch is used in vehicles equipped with a variable displacement compressor and is located behind the grille and in front of condenser. The ambient sensor prevents the compressor clutch from engaging when the ambient temperature is below 50°F (10°C). The ambient switch is a sealed unit and should be replaced, if defective.

TESTING

1. Disconnect the ambient switch connector.
2. Check the continuity across the switch terminals. At ambient temperatures above 50°F (10°C), the circuit should be complete.
3. Chill the switch to below 50°F (10°C) and recheck for continuity. The switch should be open at below the specified temperature.
4. Replace the switch, if it is found to be defective.

REMOVAL AND INSTALLATION

1. Disconnect the switch connector.
2. Check the continuity across the terminals. The switch should be closed at temperatures above 50°F (10°C). If not, replace the switch.
3. Cool the switch with crushed ice. The switch should open shortly after the cool down. If not, replace the switch.

Condenser Fan Control Switch

OPERATION

The condenser fan control switch is used in vehicles with a variable displacement compressor and is located on the discharge line at the compressor. The fan control switch turns the radiator/condenser fan on and off by monitoring the compressor discharge pressure. The radiator top tank sensor can override this switch and cycle the fan any time the engine temperature gets too high.

TESTING

1. Disconnect the fan control switch connector.
2. Connect an air conditioning manifold gauge to the system.
3. Jump across the terminals in the wire connector with a jumper wire.
4. Connect an ohmmeter to the switch terminals.

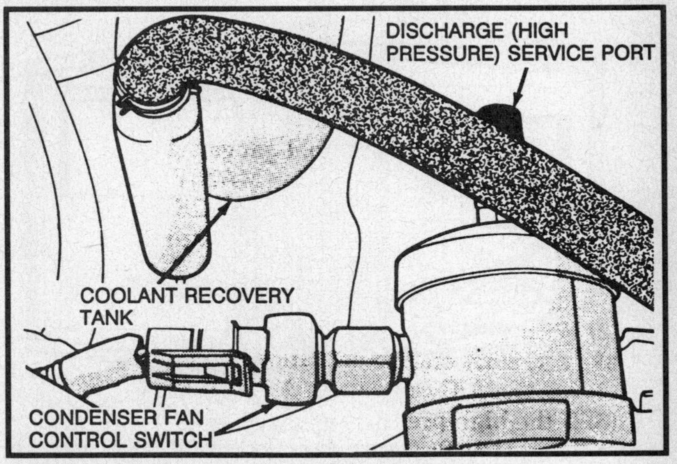
DISCHARGE (HIGH
PRESSURE) SERVICE PORT
COOLANT RECOVERY
TANK
CONDENSER FAN
CONTROL SWITCH

Condenser fan control switch location

5. Start the engine and allow to idle at 1300 rpm. The radiator fan should run constantly.
6. Turn the air conditioner **ON**.
7. If the high pressure reads below 160 psi, the switch should be open.
8. Without allowing the engine to overheat, block the flow of air to the condenser with a cover. When the high pressure reaches 230 psi, the switch should close.
9. Remove the cover. When the pressure drops to below 160 psi, the switch should open again.
10. Replace the switch, if it is defective.

REMOVAL AND INSTALLATION

NOTE: System discharging is not necessary to remove the condenser fan control switch; only a small amount of refrigerant will escape as the switch is being rotated. Take the proper precautions.

1. Disconnect the negative battery cable.
2. Disconnect the connector from the switch.
3. Loosen and quickly rotate the switch counterclockwise.
4. Remove the switch from the high pressure line.
5. The installation is the reverse of the removal procedure.
6. Check the switch for proper operation.

REAR AUXILIARY SYSTEM

Expansion Valve

REMOVAL AND INSTALLATION

Caravan, Voyager and Town & Country

1. Disconnect the negative battery cable.
2. Properly discharge the air conditioning system.
3. Remove the bolt that secures the refrigerant lines to the evaporator sealing plate and separate the parts. Discard the gasket. Cover the exposed ends of the lines to minimize contamination.
4. Remove the middle bench, if equipped. Remove the interior left lower quarter trim panel.
5. Remove the 7 screws that attach the air distribution duct to the floor and unit. Pull the distribution duct straight up to remove.
6. Remove the 6 screws from the top surface of the unit and remove the unit cover.
7. Pull the evaporator and expansion valve straight up in order to clear the extension tube pilots and remove from the vehicle. Cover the exposed ends of the lines to minimize contamination.
8. Remove the Torx® screws and remove the expansion valve from the evaporator. Discard the gasket.

To install:

9. Lubricate the gasket with wax-free refrigerant oil and assemble the expansion valve and evaporator.
10. Lubricate the gasket with wax-free refrigerant oil and install the evaporator and expansion valve assembly to the refrigerant lines and install the bolt.
11. Install the unit cover and air distribution duct.
12. Install the interior trim cover and middle bench.
13. Evacuate and recharge the air conditioning system.
14. Connect the negative battery cable and check the entire climate control system for proper operation and leaks.

Van

1. Disconnect the negative battery cable.
2. Properly discharge the air conditioning system.
3. Raise the vehicle and support safely.
4. Disconnect the refrigerant lines and remove the auxiliary unit lower cover. Cover the exposed ends of the lines to minimize contamination.
5. Disconnect the refrigerant lines from the expansion valve. Disconnect the capillary tube from the refrigerant line and the pull the thermo sensing tube out of the well.
6. The installation is the reverse of the removal procedure.
7. Evacuate and recharge the air conditioning system.
8. Connect the negative battery cable and check the entire climate control system for proper operation and leaks.

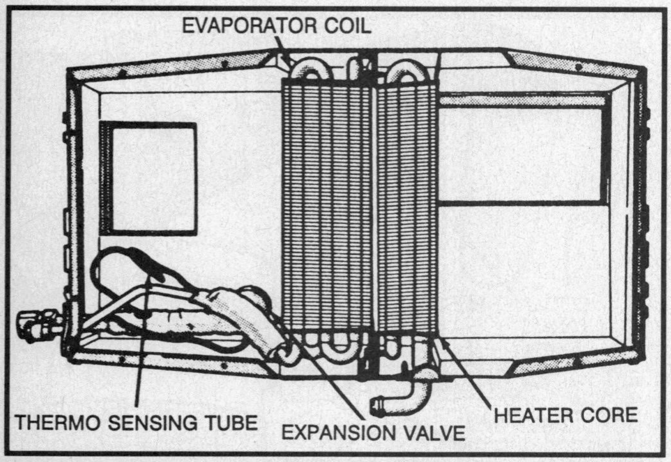
EVAPORATOR COIL
THERMO SENSING TUBE
EXPANSION VALVE
HEATER CORE
Rear air conditioning components—Van

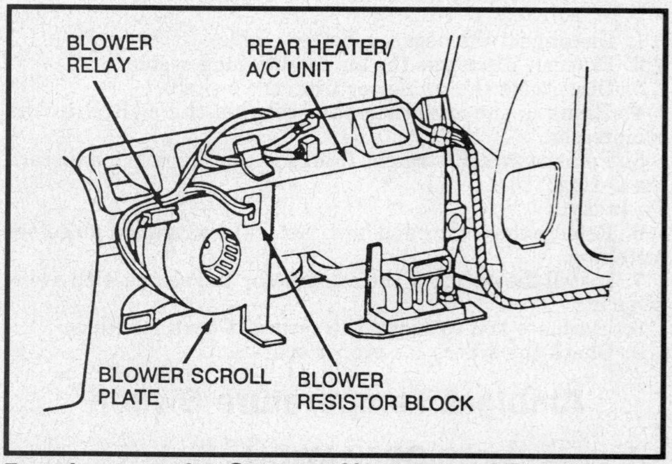
BLOWER RELAY
REAR HEATER/ A/C UNIT
BLOWER SCROLL PLATE
BLOWER RESISTOR BLOCK
Rear heater unit—Caravan, Voyager and Town & Country

Blower Motor

REMOVAL AND INSTALLATION

Caravan, Voyager and Town & Country

1. Disconnect the negative battery cable.
2. Remove the middle bench, if equipped. Remove the left lower quarter trim panel.
3. Remove 1 blower scroll cover to floor screw and 7 scroll to unit screws.
4. Remove the blower relay.
5. Rotate the blower scroll cover from under the unit.
6. Remove the fan from the blower motor, remove the 3 motor attaching screws and remove the motor from the unit.
7. The installation is the reverse of the removal procedure.
8. Connect the negative battery cable and check the blower motor for proper operation.

Van

1. Disconnect the negative battery cable.
2. Disconnect the blower motor connectors.
3. Remove the screws that mount the blower assembly to the floor.
4. Remove the blower assembly.
5. The installation is the reverse of the removal procedure.
6. Connect the negative battery cable and check the blower motor for proper operation.

Blower Motor Resistor

REMOVAL AND INSTALLATION

Caravan, Voyager and Town & Country

1. Disconnect the negative battery cable.
2. Remove the middle bench, if equipped. Remove the left lower quarter trim panel.
3. Disconnect the wiring harness from the resistor.
4. Remove the screws that attach the resistor to the rear unit and remove the resistor.
5. The installation is the reverse of the removal procedure.
6. Connect the negative battery cable and check for proper operation.

Van

1. Disconnect the negative battery cable.
2. Disconnect the blower motor connectors.
3. Remove the screws that mount the blower assembly to the floor.
4. Remove the blower assembly. If possible, disassemble to service the blower resistor.
5. The installation is the reverse of the removal procedure.
6. Connect the negative battery cable and check the blower motor for proper operation.

Heater Core

REMOVAL AND INSTALLATION

Caravan, Voyager and Town & Country

1. Disconnect the negative battery cable. Pinch off the hoses to the rear heater core.
2. Raise the vehicle and support safely. Disconnect the underbody heater hoses from the rear heater core tubes.
3. Remove the middle bench, if equipped. Remove the interior left lower quarter trim panel.
4. Remove the 7 screws that attach the air distribution duct to the floor and unit. Pull the distribution duct straight up to remove.
5. Remove the 6 screws from the top surface of the unit and remove the unit cover.
6. Pull the heater core straight up and out of the unit.
7. The installation is the reverse of the removal procedure.
8. Connect the negative battery cable and check for leaks.

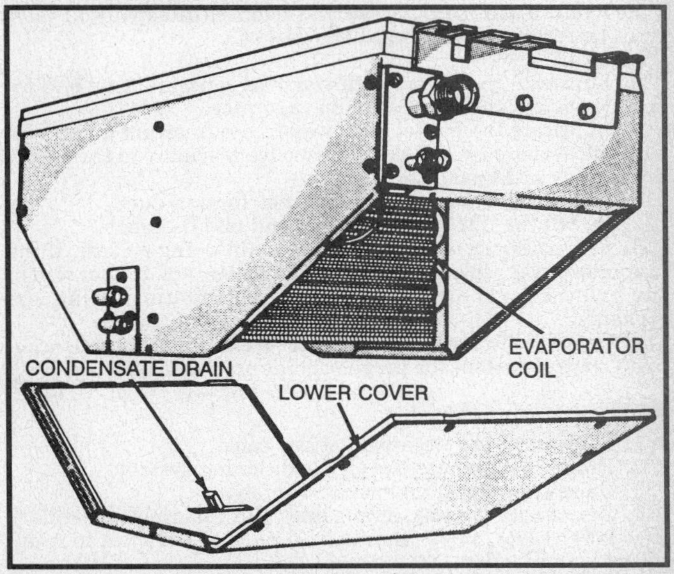
EVAPORATOR COIL
CONDENSATE DRAIN
LOWER COVER

Rear air conditioning housing with cover removed—Van

Van

1. Disconnect the negative battery cable. Pinch off the hoses to the rear heater core.
3. Raise the vehicle and support safely.
4. Remove the auxiliary unit lower cover.
5. Disconnect the hoses from the heater core and remove the core from the unit.
6. The installation is the reverse of the removal procedure.
7. Connect the negative battery cable and check the entire climate control system for proper operation and leaks.

Evaporator

REMOVAL AND INSTALLATION

Caravan, Voyager and Town & Country

1. Disconnect the negative battery cable.
2. Properly discharge the air conditioning system.
3. Remove the bolt that secures the refrigerant lines to the evaporator sealing plate and separate the parts. Discard the gasket. Cover the exposed ends of the lines to minimize contamination.
4. Remove the middle bench, if equipped. Remove the interior left lower quarter trim panel.
5. Remove the 7 screws that attach the air distribution duct to the floor and unit. Pull the distribution duct straight up to remove.
6. Remove the 6 screws from the top surface of the unit and remove the unit cover.
7. Pull the evaporator and expansion valve straight up in order to clear the extension tube pilots and remove from the vehicle. Cover the exposed ends of the lines to minimize contamination.

8. Remove the Torx® screws and remove the expansion valve from the evaporator. Discard the gasket.

To install:

9. Lubricate the gasket with wax-free refrigerant oil and assemble the expansion valve and evaporator.
10. Lubricate the gasket with wax-free refrigerant oil and install the evaporator and expansion valve assembly to the refrigerant lines and install the bolt.
11. Install the unit cover and air distribution duct.
12. Install the interior trim cover and middle bench.
13. Evacuate and recharge the air conditioning system. If the evaporator was replaced, measure the amount of oil that was in the original evaporator and add that amount during the recharge.
14. Connect the negative battery cable and check the entire climate control system for proper operation and leaks.

Van

1. Disconnect the negative battery cable.
2. Properly discharge the air conditioning system.
3. Raise the vehicle and support safely.
4. Disconnect the refrigerant lines and remove the auxiliary unit lower cover. Cover the exposed ends of the lines to minimize contamination.
5. Remove the seal and cover plate. Remove the evaporator from the rear unit.

To install:

6. The installation is the reverse of the removal procedure. Replace the O-rings when installing.
7. Evacuate and recharge the air conditioning system. If the evaporator was replaced, measure the amount of oil that was in the original evaporator and add that amount during the recharge.
8. Connect the negative battery cable and check the entire climate control system for proper operation and leaks.

Refrigerant Lines

REMOVAL AND INSTALLATION

1. Disconnect the negative battery cable.

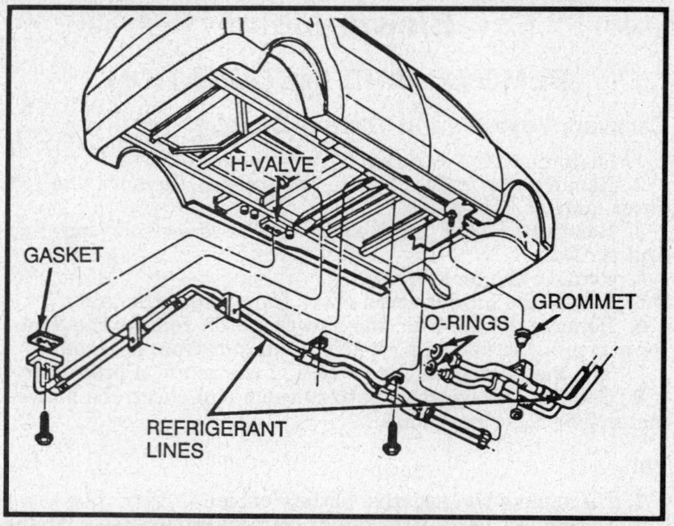
H-VALVE
GASKET
GROMMET
O-RINGS
REFRIGERANT
LINES

Rear air conditioning underbody plumbing – Caravan, Voyager and Town & Country

2. Properly discharge the air conditioning system.
3. Raise the vehicle and support safely.
4. Remove the nuts or bolts that attach the refrigerant line sealing plates to the adjoining components. If the lines are connected with flare nuts, use a back-up wrench when disassembling. Cover the exposed ends of the lines to minimize contamination.
5. Remove the support mount.
6. Remove the lines and discard the gaskets or O-rings.

To install:

7. Coat the new gaskets or O-rings with wax-free refrigerant oil and install. Connect the refrigerant lines to the adjoining components and tighten the nuts or bolts.
8. Install the support mount.
9. Evacuate and recharge the air conditioning system.
10. Connect the negative battery cable and check the entire climate control system for proper operation and leaks.

SYSTEM DIAGNOSIS

Air Conditioning Performance

PERFORMANCE TEST

Air temperature in the testing area must be at least 70°F (21°C) to ensure the accuracy of this test.

1. Connect a manifold gauge set the the system.
2. Set the controls to **RECIRC** or **PANEL** or **MAX A/C**, temperature control level on its COOLEST position and the blower on HIGH.
3. Start the engine and adjust the idle speed to 1000 rpm with the compressor clutch engaged.

AIR CONDITIONING SYSTEM PRESSURES

Ambient Temperature °F (°C)	Air Temperature at Center Panel Vent °F (°C)	Compressor Discharge Pressure PSI (kPa)	Evaporator Suction Pressure PSI (kPa)
70 (21)	35–46 (2–8)	140–210 (965–1448)	10–35 (69–241)
80 (26.5)	39–50 (4–10)	180–235 (1240–1620)	16–38 (110–262)
90 (32)	44–55 (7–13)	210–270 (1448–1860)	20–42 (138–290)
100 (37.5)	50–62 (10–17)	240–310 (1655–2137)	25–48 (172–331)
110 (43)	56–70 (13–21)	280–350 (1930–2413)	30–55 (207–379)

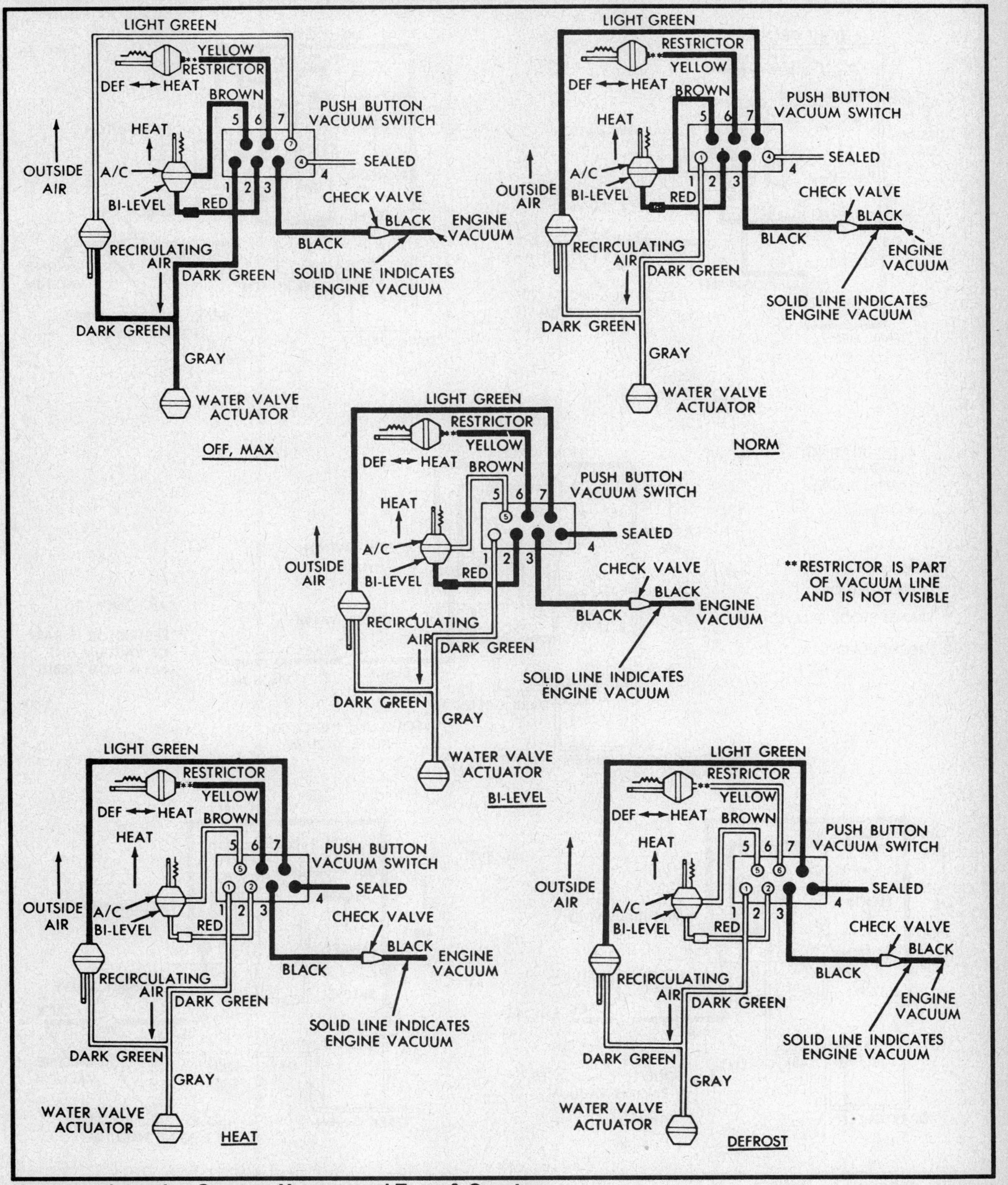
LIGHT GREEN
YELLOW
RESTRICTOR
DEF ↔ HEAT
BROWN
PUSH BUTTON VACUUM SWITCH
HEAT
OUTSIDE AIR
A/C
BI-LEVEL
RED
SEALED
CHECK VALVE
BLACK
ENGINE VACUUM
RECIRCULATING AIR
DARK GREEN
SOLID LINE INDICATES ENGINE VACUUM
GRAY
WATER VALVE ACTUATOR
OFF, MAX
NORM
BI-LEVEL
HEAT
DEFROST
**RESTRICTOR IS PART OF VACUUM LINE AND IS NOT VISIBLE

Vacuum schematic—Caravan, Voyager and Town & Country

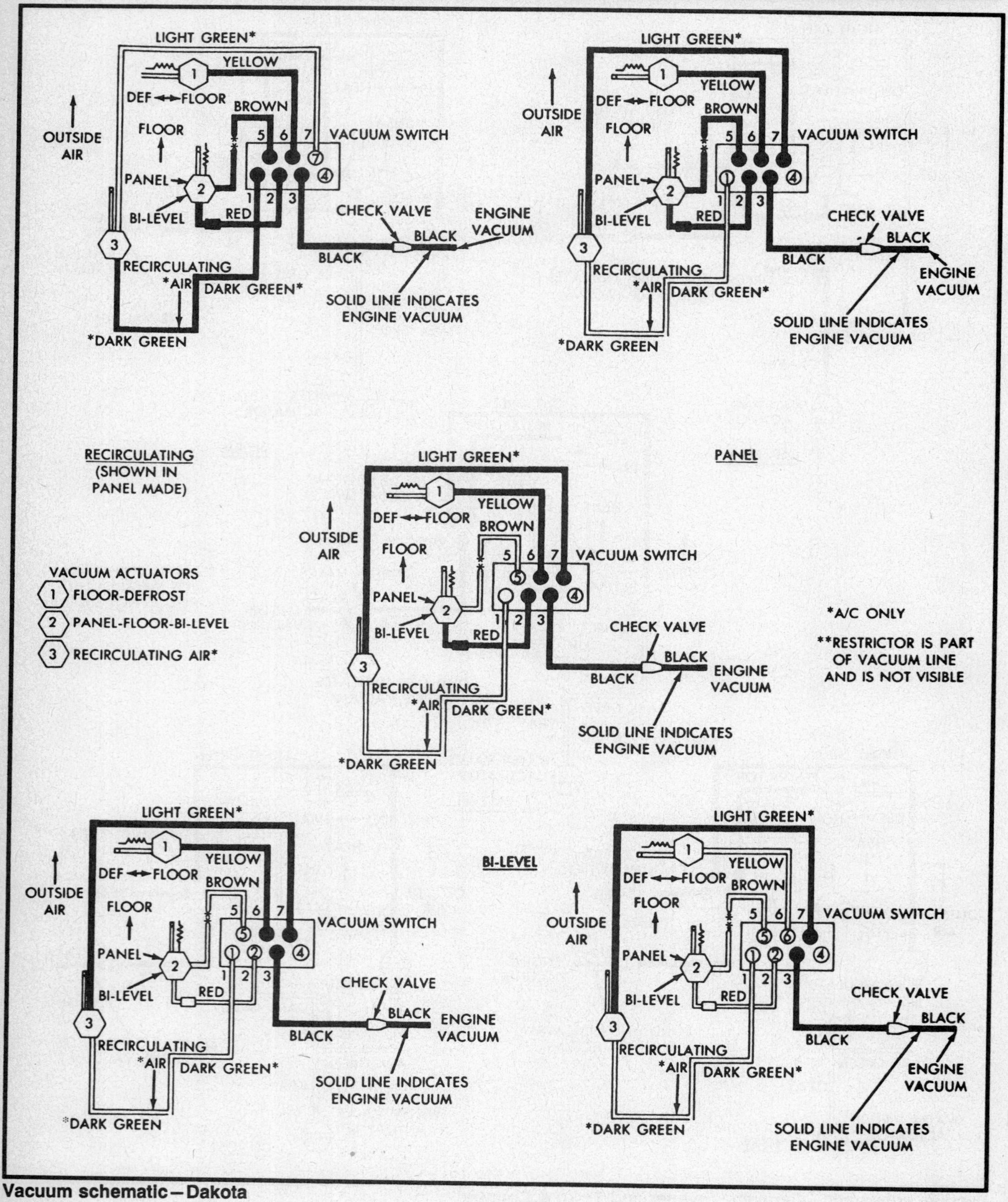
LIGHT GREEN*
YELLOW
DEF ↔ FLOOR
BROWN
OUTSIDE AIR
FLOOR
VACUUM SWITCH
PANEL
BI-LEVEL
RED
CHECK VALVE
ENGINE VACUUM
BLACK
BLACK
RECIRCULATING *AIR
DARK GREEN*
SOLID LINE INDICATES ENGINE VACUUM
*DARK GREEN
RECIRCULATING
(SHOWN IN PANEL MADE)
PANEL
VACUUM ACTUATORS
1 FLOOR-DEFROST
2 PANEL-FLOOR-BI-LEVEL
3 RECIRCULATING AIR*
*A/C ONLY
**RESTRICTOR IS PART OF VACUUM LINE AND IS NOT VISIBLE
BI-LEVEL

Vacuum schematic—Dakota

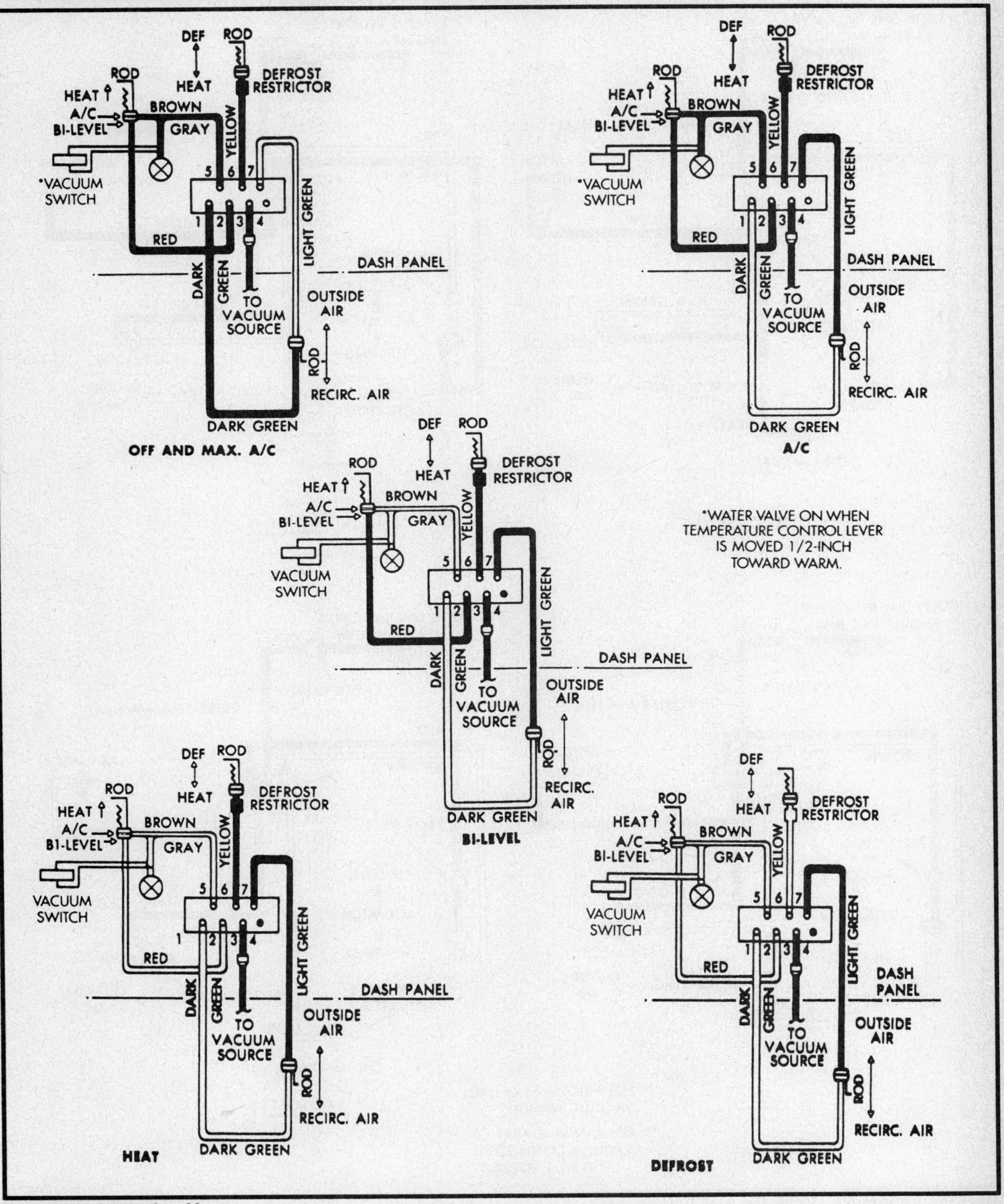
DEF
ROD
HEAT
DEFROST RESTRICTOR
HEAT
A/C
BI-LEVEL
BROWN
GRAY
YELLOW
*VACUUM SWITCH
5 6 7
1 2 3 4
RED
LIGHT GREEN
DASH PANEL
DARK GREEN
TO VACUUM SOURCE
OUTSIDE AIR
RECIRC. AIR
DARK GREEN
OFF AND MAX. A/C
A/C
BI-LEVEL
HEAT
DEFROST
*WATER VALVE ON WHEN TEMPERATURE CONTROL LEVER IS MOVED 1/2-INCH TOWARD WARM.

Vacuum schematic—Van

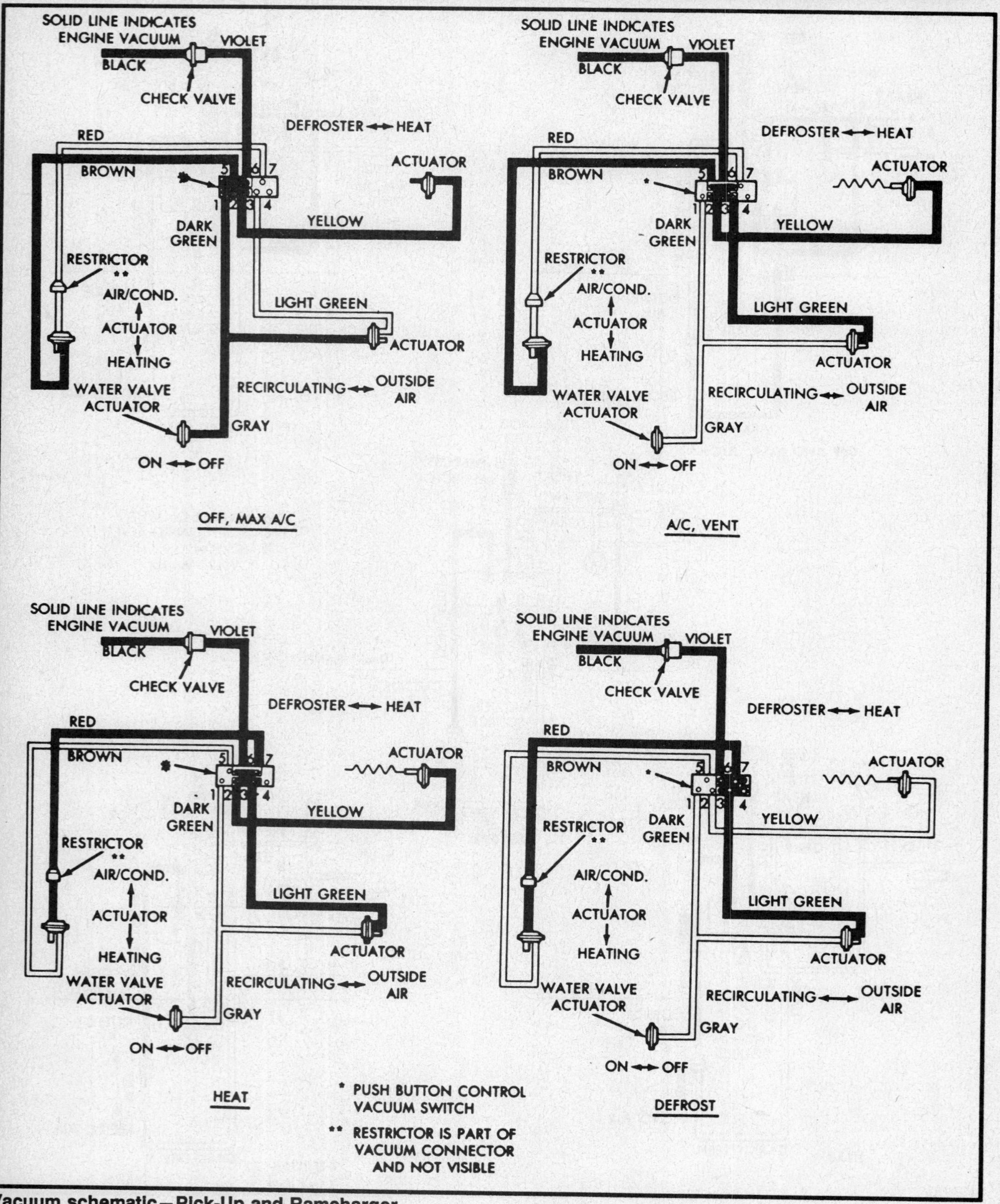
SOLID LINE INDICATES ENGINE VACUUM
VIOLET
BLACK
CHECK VALVE
DEFROSTER ↔ HEAT
RED
BROWN
ACTUATOR
*
5 6 7
1 2 3 4
DARK GREEN
YELLOW
RESTRICTOR **
AIR/COND.
ACTUATOR
HEATING
LIGHT GREEN
ACTUATOR
WATER VALVE ACTUATOR
RECIRCULATING ↔ OUTSIDE AIR
GRAY
ON ↔ OFF
OFF, MAX A/C
SOLID LINE INDICATES ENGINE VACUUM
VIOLET
BLACK
CHECK VALVE
DEFROSTER ↔ HEAT
RED
BROWN
ACTUATOR
*
5 6 7
1 2 3 4
DARK GREEN
YELLOW
RESTRICTOR **
AIR/COND.
ACTUATOR
HEATING
LIGHT GREEN
ACTUATOR
WATER VALVE ACTUATOR
RECIRCULATING ↔ OUTSIDE AIR
GRAY
ON ↔ OFF
A/C, VENT
SOLID LINE INDICATES ENGINE VACUUM
VIOLET
BLACK
CHECK VALVE
DEFROSTER ↔ HEAT
RED
BROWN
ACTUATOR
*
5 6 7
1 2 3 4
DARK GREEN
YELLOW
RESTRICTOR **
AIR/COND.
ACTUATOR
HEATING
LIGHT GREEN
ACTUATOR
WATER VALVE ACTUATOR
RECIRCULATING ↔ OUTSIDE AIR
GRAY
ON ↔ OFF
HEAT
SOLID LINE INDICATES ENGINE VACUUM
VIOLET
BLACK
CHECK VALVE
DEFROSTER ↔ HEAT
RED
BROWN
ACTUATOR
*
5 6 7
1 2 3 4
RESTRICTOR **
DARK GREEN
YELLOW
AIR/COND.
ACTUATOR
HEATING
LIGHT GREEN
ACTUATOR
WATER VALVE ACTUATOR
RECIRCULATING ↔ OUTSIDE AIR
GRAY
ON ↔ OFF
DEFROST
* PUSH BUTTON CONTROL VACUUM SWITCH
** RESTRICTOR IS PART OF VACUUM CONNECTOR AND NOT VISIBLE

Vacuum schematic—Pick-Up and Ramcharger

4. Allow the engine to come to normal operating temperature and keep all doors and windows closed.
5. Insert a thermometer in the left center panel outlet and operate the engine for 5 minutes. The compressor clutch may cycle, depending on the ambient conditions.
6. With the clutch engaged, compare the discharge air temperature to the performance chart.
7. Disconnect and plug the gray vacuum line going to the heater water control valve, if equipped. Observe the valve arm for movement as the line is disconnected. If there is no movement, check the valve for sticking.
8. Operate the air conditioning for 2 additional minutes and observe the discharge air temperature again. If the discharge air temperature increased by more than 5°F, check the blend air door for proper operation. If not, compare the the temperature, suction and discharge pressures to the chart. Reconnect the gary vacuum line.
9. If the values do not meet specifications, check system components for proper operation.

Vacuum Actuating System

INSPECTION

Check the system for proper operation. Air should come from the appropriate vents when the corresponding mode is selected under all driving conditions. If a problem is detected use the flow-charts to check the flow of vacuum.

1. Check the engine for sufficient vacuum and the main supplier hose at the brake booster for leaks or kinks.
3. Check the check valve under the instrument panel for proper operation. It should not hold vacuum when vacuum is applied from the engine side but should when appied from the system side.
4. Check all interior vacuum lines, especially the 7-way connection behind the instrument panel for leaks or kinks.
5. Check the control head for leaky ports or damaged parts.
6. Check all actuators for ability to hold vacuum.

Air Conditioning Compressor

COMPRESSOR NOISE

Noises that develop during air conditioning operation can be misleading. A noise that sounds like serious compressor damage may only be a loose belt, mounting bolt or clutch assembly. Improper belt tension can also emit a noise that can be mistaken for more serious problems. Check and adjust all possible causes of the noise before replacing the compressor.

COMPRESSOR CLUTCH INOPERATIVE

The air conditioning compressor clutch electrical circuit is controlled by the engine controller (SMEC or SBEC) located in the engine compartment. If the compressor clutch does not engage, check the basics and continue on to the diagnostic charts, if the basics check out.

NOTE: Do not use a 12 volt test light to probe wires or damage the on-board computer may result.

Except 1989–90 Vehicles With 2.5L Engine

1. Verify refrigerant charge and charge, as required.
2. Check for battery voltage at the clutch coil connection. If voltage is detected, check the coil.
3. If battery voltage is not detected at the coil, check for voltage at the low pressure or differential cut off switch. If voltage is not detected there either, check fuses etc. If the fuses are good, use the DRB-II or digital voltmeter to determine the location of the problem.

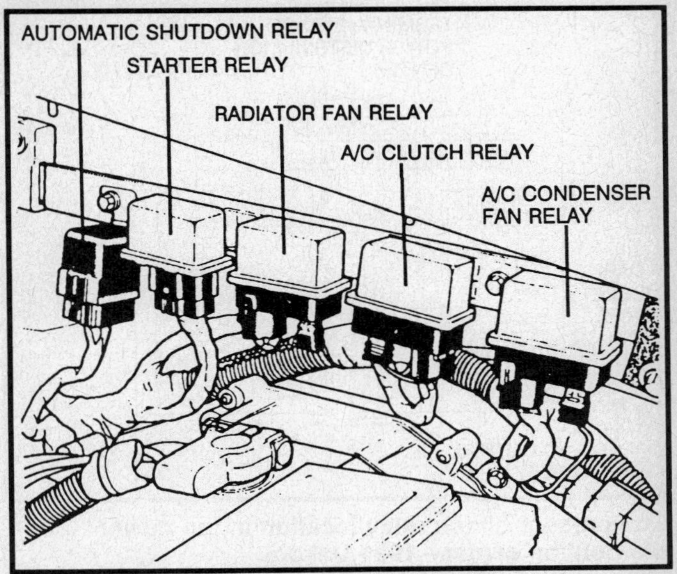
AUTOMATIC SHUTDOWN RELAY
STARTER RELAY
RADIATOR FAN RELAY
A/C CLUTCH RELAY
A/C CONDENSER FAN RELAY

Compressor clutch relay location—1989–90 Caravan, Voyager and Town & Country

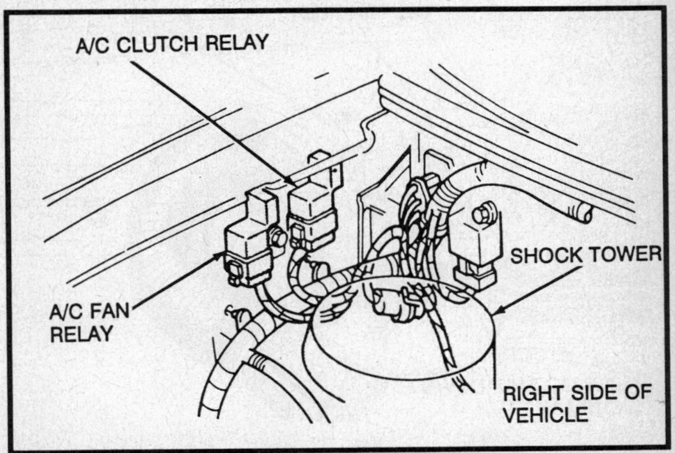
A/C CLUTCH RELAY
SHOCK TOWER
A/C FAN RELAY
RIGHT SIDE OF VEHICLE

Compressor clutch relay location—1991 Caravan, Voyager and Town & Country

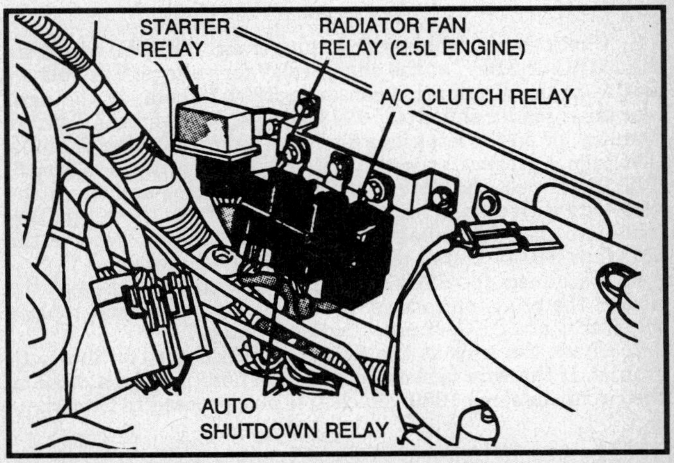
STARTER RELAY
RADIATOR FAN RELAY (2.5L ENGINE)
A/C CLUTCH RELAY
AUTO SHUTDOWN RELAY

Compressor clutch relay location—1989–90 Dakota

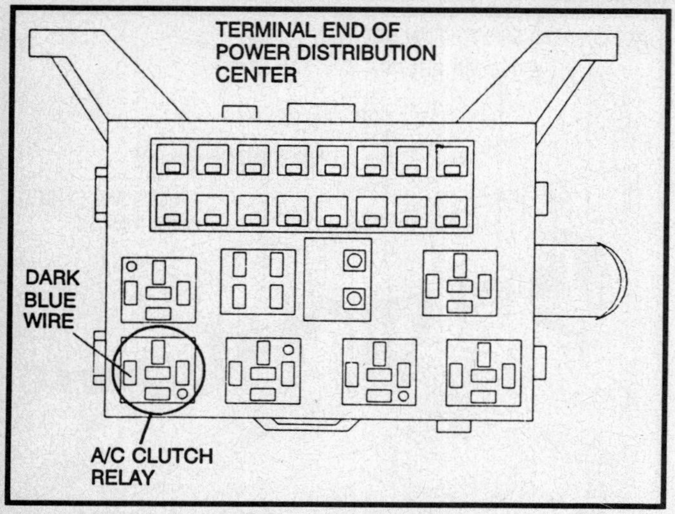
TERMINAL END OF
POWER DISTRIBUTION
CENTER
DARK
BLUE
WIRE
A/C CLUTCH
RELAY

Compressor clutch relay location in the power distribution center—1991 Dakota

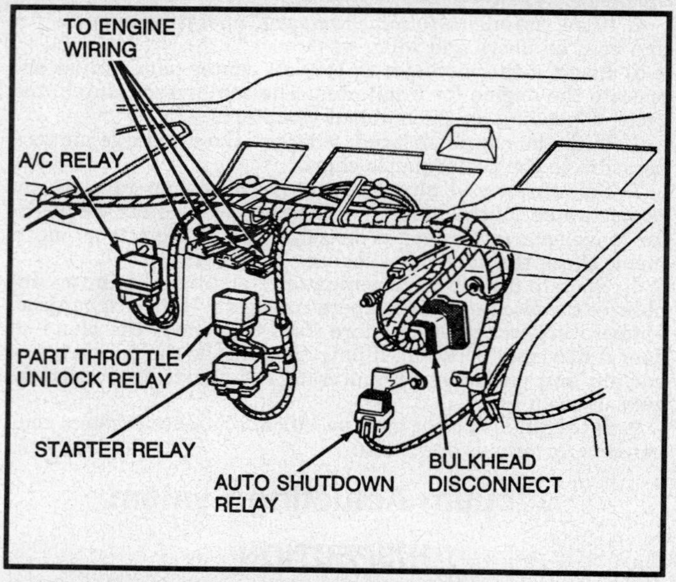
TO ENGINE
WIRING
A/C RELAY
PART THROTTLE
UNLOCK RELAY
STARTER RELAY
AUTO SHUTDOWN
RELAY
BULKHEAD
DISCONNECT

Compressor clutch relay location—Van

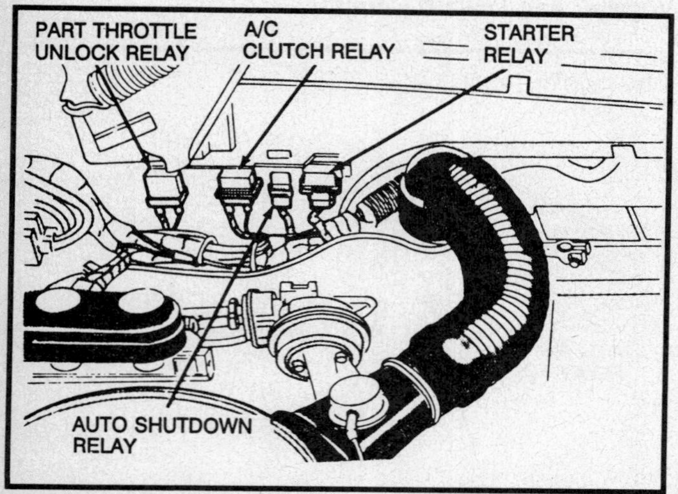
PART THROTTLE
UNLOCK RELAY
A/C
CLUTCH RELAY
STARTER
RELAY
AUTO SHUTDOWN
RELAY

Compressor clutch relay location—Pick-Up and Ramcharger

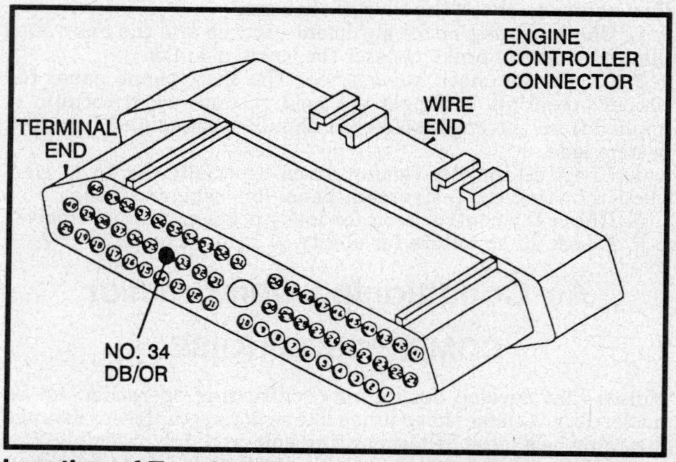
ENGINE
CONTROLLER
CONNECTOR
WIRE
END
TERMINAL
END
NO. 34
DB/OR

Location of Terminal No. 34 on the SMEC or SBEC connector

4. Check the dark blue with orange tracer (DB/OR) wire from the SMEC or SBEC at the clutch relay for voltage. The relay is located in the distribution center on 1991 Dakota, on the right rear inner fender shield on 1991 Caravan, Voyager and Town & Country, or on the left inner fender shield on all other vehicles. If voltage is present, proceed to Step 5. If not, proceed to Step 6.
5. Disconnect the SMEC or SBEC connector and check the dark blue with orange tracer (DB/OR) wire from the relay (Terminal No. 34) for voltage. If voltage is present, replace the SMEC or SBEC. If not, repair the open in the wire.
6. Disconnect the SMEC or SBEC connector and recheck the wire at the relay for voltage. If voltage is now present, replace the SMEC or SBEC. If not, proceed to Step 7.
7. Check the wire at the SMEC or SBEC for continuity to ground. If the wire is shorted, repair. There may be a diode in the circuit in some 1989 vehicles. If not, proceed to Step 8.
8. Check the dark blue wire (hot wire from J2 splice) at the relay for voltage. If voltage is present, replace the clutch relay. If not, repair the open to the harness splice.

1989–90 Vehicles With 2.5L Engine

1. Verify refrigerant charge and charge, as required.
2. Check for battery voltage at the clutch coil connection. If voltage is detected, check the coil.
3. If battery voltage is not detected at the coil, check for voltage at the low pressure or differential cut off switch. If voltage is not detected there either, check fuses etc. If the fuses are good, use the DRB-II or digital voltmeter in conjunction with the charts to determine the location of the problem.

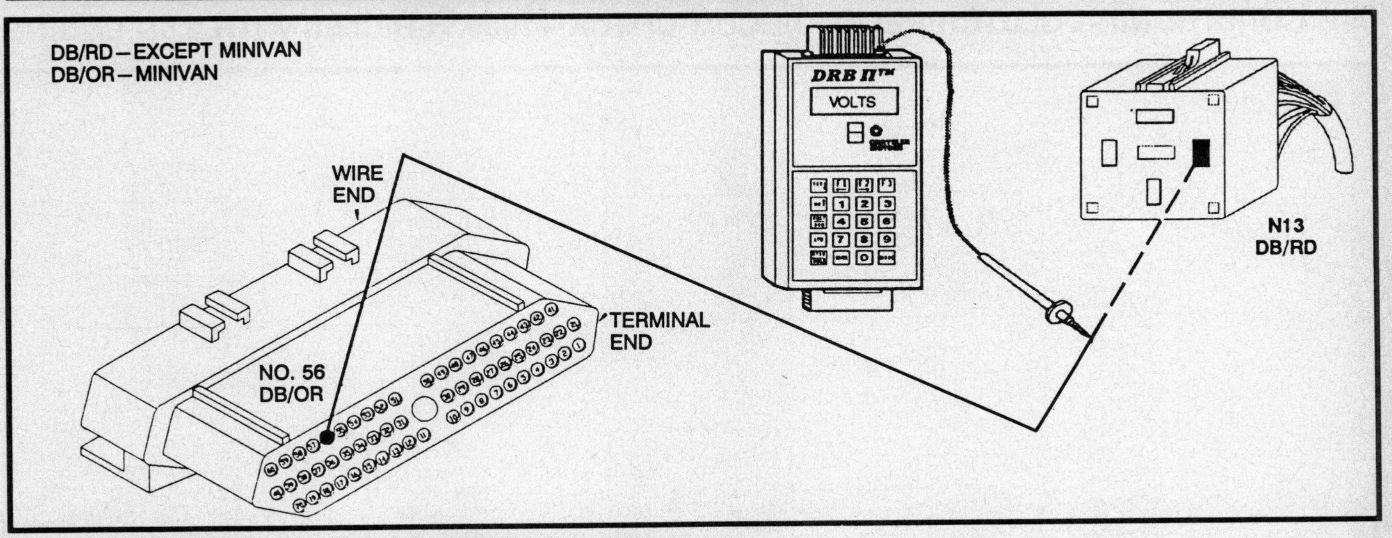
DB/RD—EXCEPT MINIVAN
DB/OR—MINIVAN
WIRE END
NO. 56
DB/OR
TERMINAL END
DRB II™
VOLTS
N13
DB/RD

Checking the DB/OR wire from the SMEC to the relay

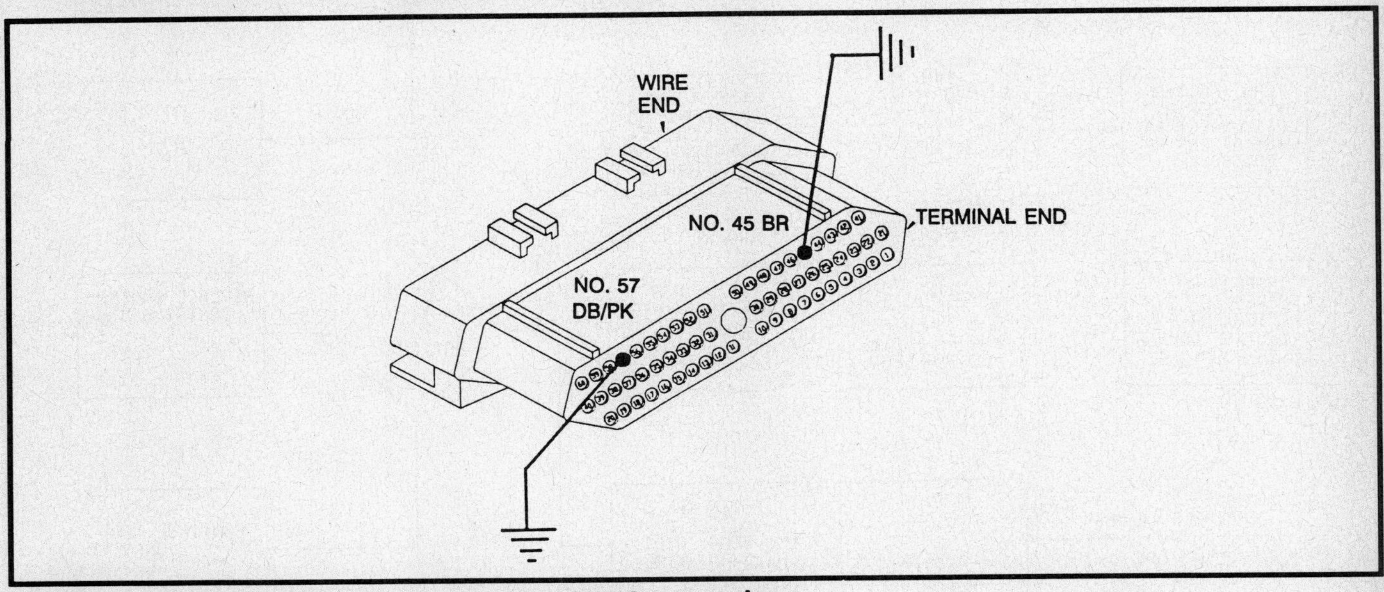
WIRE END
NO. 45 BR
TERMINAL END
NO. 57
DB/PK

Location of Terminals Nos. 45 and 57 on the SMEC connector

AIR CONDITIONING CLUTCH RELAY CIRCUIT CHECK—1989 VEHICLES WITH 2.5L ENGINE

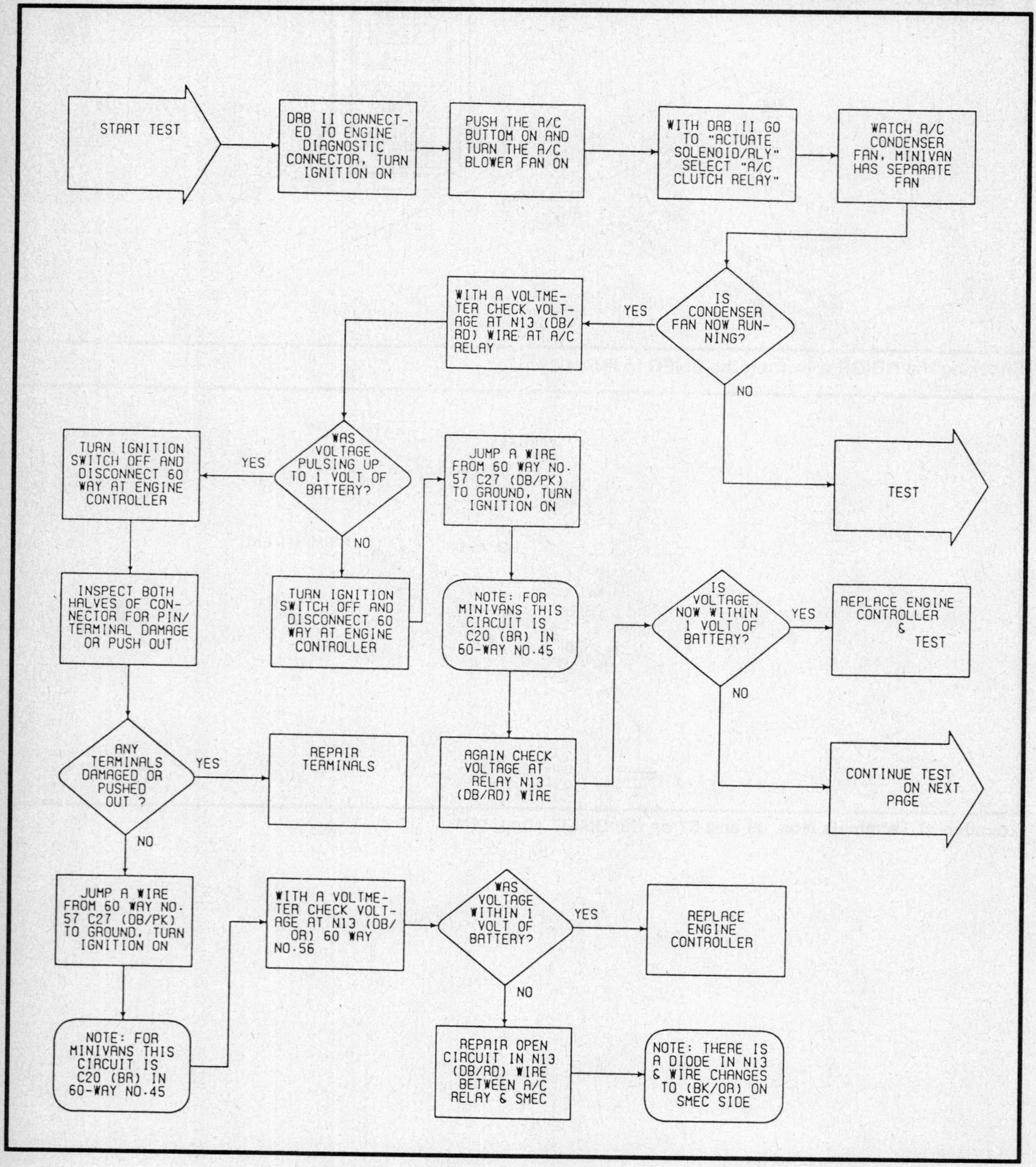
START TEST
DRB II CONNECTED TO ENGINE DIAGNOSTIC CONNECTOR, TURN IGNITION ON
PUSH THE A/C BUTTOM ON AND TURN THE A/C BLOWER FAN ON
WITH DRB II GO TO "ACTUATE SOLENOID/RLY" SELECT "A/C CLUTCH RELAY"
WATCH A/C CONDENSER FAN, MINIVAN HAS SEPARATE FAN
IS CONDENSER FAN NOW RUNNING?
YES
NO
WITH A VOLTMETER CHECK VOLTAGE AT N13 (DB/RD) WIRE AT A/C RELAY
TEST
WAS VOLTAGE PULSING UP TO 1 VOLT OF BATTERY?
YES
NO
TURN IGNITION SWITCH OFF AND DISCONNECT 60 WAY AT ENGINE CONTROLLER
JUMP A WIRE FROM 60 WAY NO. 57 C27 (DB/PK) TO GROUND, TURN IGNITION ON
INSPECT BOTH HALVES OF CONNECTOR FOR PIN/TERMINAL DAMAGE OR PUSH OUT
TURN IGNITION SWITCH OFF AND DISCONNECT 60 WAY AT ENGINE CONTROLLER
NOTE: FOR MINIVANS THIS CIRCUIT IS C20 (BR) IN 60-WAY NO.45
IS VOLTAGE NOW WITHIN 1 VOLT OF BATTERY?
YES
NO
REPLACE ENGINE CONTROLLER & TEST
ANY TERMINALS DAMAGED OR PUSHED OUT ?
YES
NO
REPAIR TERMINALS
AGAIN CHECK VOLTAGE AT RELAY N13 (DB/RD) WIRE
CONTINUE TEST ON NEXT PAGE
JUMP A WIRE FROM 60 WAY NO. 57 C27 (DB/PK) TO GROUND, TURN IGNITION ON
WITH A VOLTMETER CHECK VOLTAGE AT N13 (DB/OR) 60 WAY NO.56
WAS VOLTAGE WITHIN 1 VOLT OF BATTERY?
YES
NO
REPLACE ENGINE CONTROLLER
NOTE: FOR MINIVANS THIS CIRCUIT IS C20 (BR) IN 60-WAY NO.45
REPAIR OPEN CIRCUIT IN N13 (DB/RD) WIRE BETWEEN A/C RELAY & SMEC
NOTE: THERE IS A DIODE IN N13 & WIRE CHANGES TO (BK/OR) ON SMEC SIDE

AIR CONDITIONING CLUTCH RELAY CIRCUIT CHECK—1989 VEHICLES WITH 2.5L ENGINE

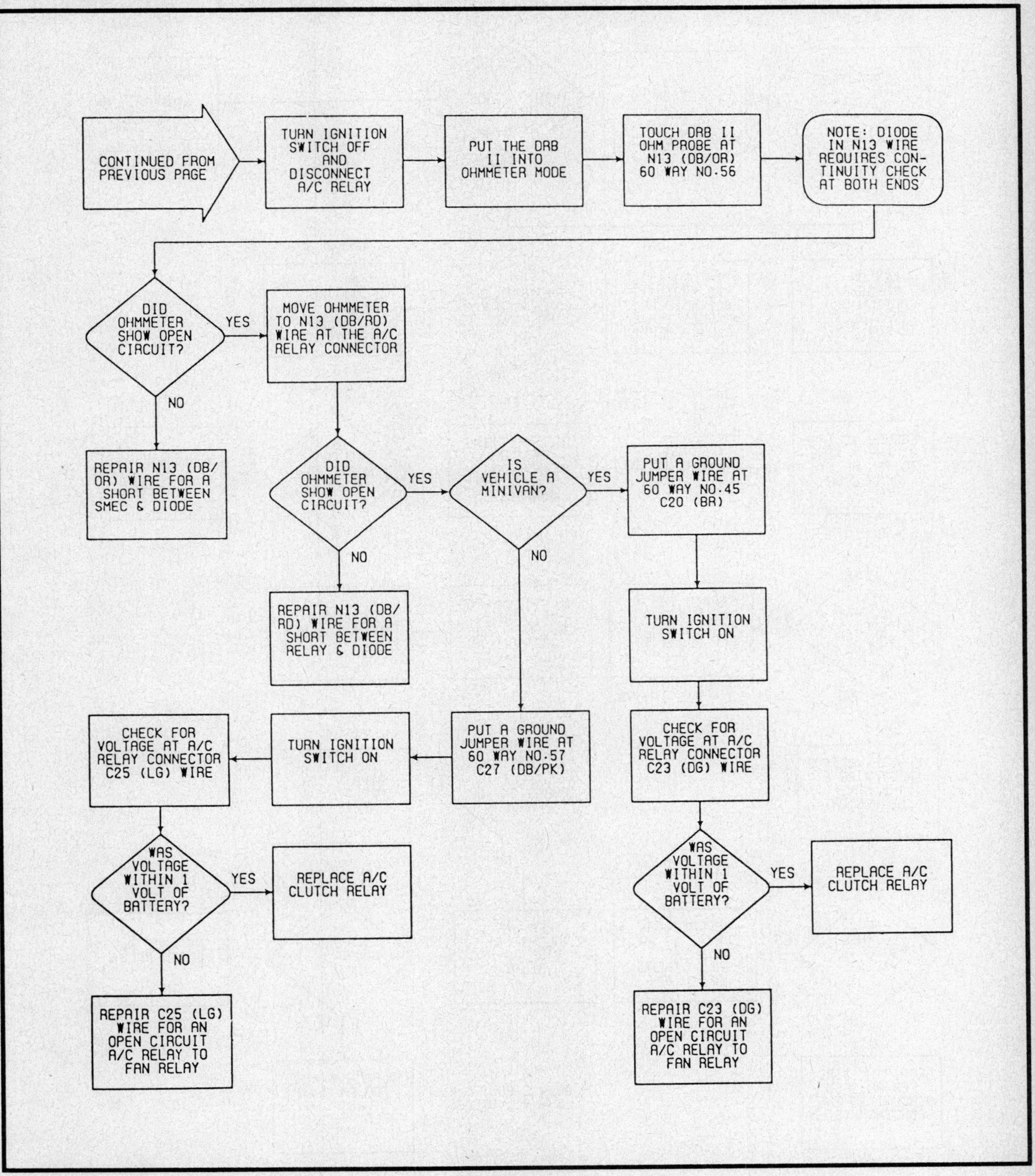
CONTINUED FROM PREVIOUS PAGE
TURN IGNITION SWITCH OFF AND DISCONNECT A/C RELAY
PUT THE DRB II INTO OHMMETER MODE
TOUCH DRB II OHM PROBE AT N13 (DB/OR) 60 WAY NO.56
NOTE: DIODE IN N13 WIRE REQUIRES CONTINUITY CHECK AT BOTH ENDS
DID OHMMETER SHOW OPEN CIRCUIT?
YES
MOVE OHMMETER TO N13 (DB/RD) WIRE AT THE A/C RELAY CONNECTOR
NO
REPAIR N13 (DB/OR) WIRE FOR A SHORT BETWEEN SMEC & DIODE
DID OHMMETER SHOW OPEN CIRCUIT?
YES
IS VEHICLE A MINIVAN?
YES
PUT A GROUND JUMPER WIRE AT 60 WAY NO.45 C20 (BR)
NO
NO
REPAIR N13 (DB/RD) WIRE FOR A SHORT BETWEEN RELAY & DIODE
TURN IGNITION SWITCH ON
CHECK FOR VOLTAGE AT A/C RELAY CONNECTOR C25 (LG) WIRE
TURN IGNITION SWITCH ON
PUT A GROUND JUMPER WIRE AT 60 WAY NO.57 C27 (DB/PK)
CHECK FOR VOLTAGE AT A/C RELAY CONNECTOR C23 (DG) WIRE
WAS VOLTAGE WITHIN 1 VOLT OF BATTERY?
YES
REPLACE A/C CLUTCH RELAY
WAS VOLTAGE WITHIN 1 VOLT OF BATTERY?
YES
REPLACE A/C CLUTCH RELAY
NO
REPAIR C25 (LG) WIRE FOR AN OPEN CIRCUIT A/C RELAY TO FAN RELAY
NO
REPAIR C23 (DG) WIRE FOR AN OPEN CIRCUIT A/C RELAY TO FAN RELAY

AIR CONDITIONING CLUTCH RELAY CIRCUIT CHECK—1990 VEHICLES WITH 2.5L ENGINE

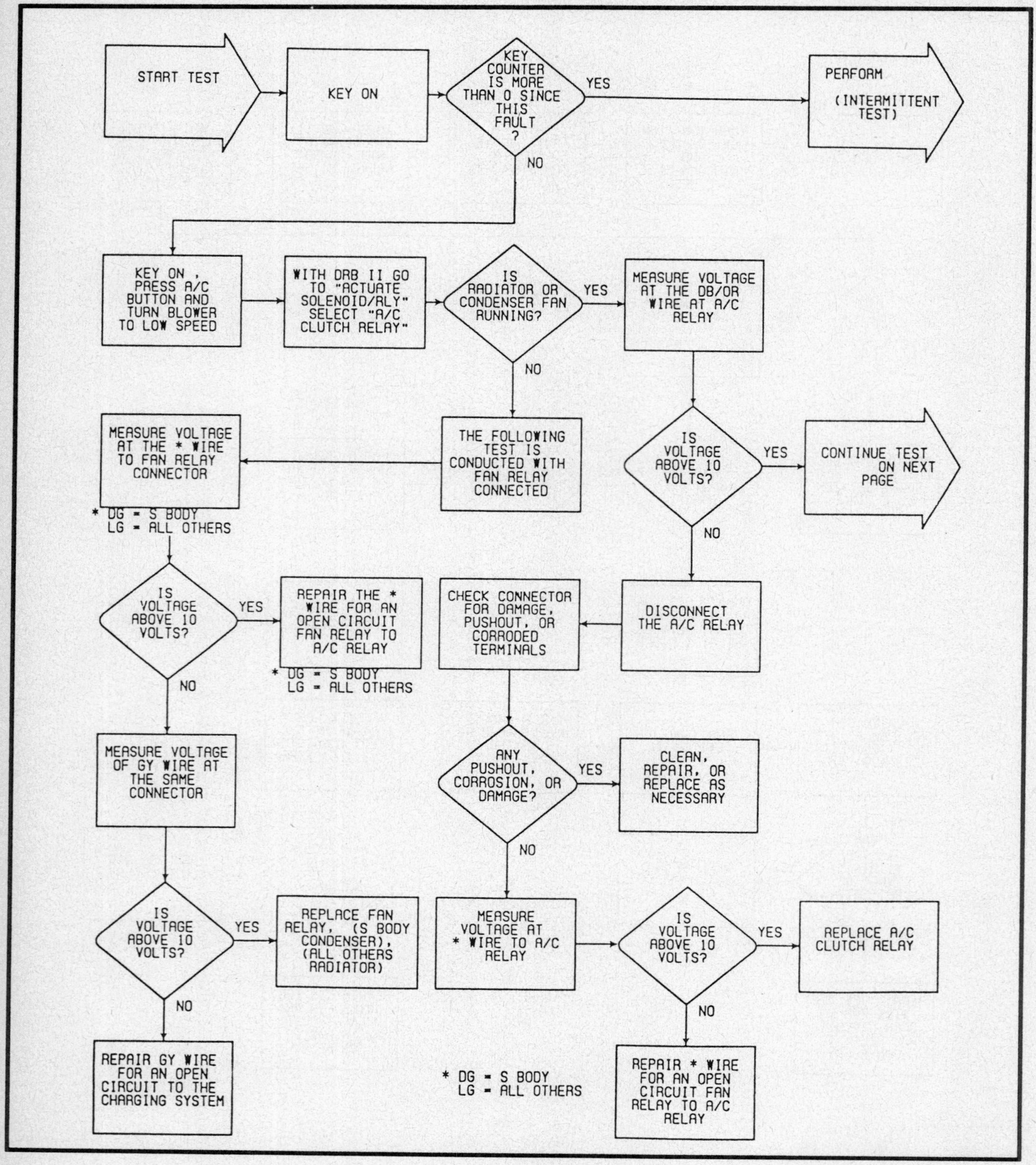
START TEST
KEY ON
KEY COUNTER IS MORE THAN 0 SINCE THIS FAULT ?
YES
PERFORM (INTERMITTENT TEST)
NO
KEY ON , PRESS A/C BUTTON AND TURN BLOWER TO LOW SPEED
WITH DRB II GO TO "ACTUATE SOLENOID/RLY" SELECT "A/C CLUTCH RELAY"
IS RADIATOR OR CONDENSER FAN RUNNING?
YES
MEASURE VOLTAGE AT THE DB/OR WIRE AT A/C RELAY
NO
THE FOLLOWING TEST IS CONDUCTED WITH FAN RELAY CONNECTED
MEASURE VOLTAGE AT THE * WIRE TO FAN RELAY CONNECTOR
* DG = S BODY
LG = ALL OTHERS
IS VOLTAGE ABOVE 10 VOLTS?
YES
CONTINUE TEST ON NEXT PAGE
NO
DISCONNECT THE A/C RELAY
CHECK CONNECTOR FOR DAMAGE, PUSHOUT, OR CORRODED TERMINALS
IS VOLTAGE ABOVE 10 VOLTS?
YES
REPAIR THE * WIRE FOR AN OPEN CIRCUIT FAN RELAY TO A/C RELAY
* DG = S BODY
LG = ALL OTHERS
NO
MEASURE VOLTAGE OF GY WIRE AT THE SAME CONNECTOR
ANY PUSHOUT, CORROSION, OR DAMAGE?
YES
CLEAN, REPAIR, OR REPLACE AS NECESSARY
NO
IS VOLTAGE ABOVE 10 VOLTS?
YES
REPLACE FAN RELAY, (S BODY CONDENSER), (ALL OTHERS RADIATOR)
NO
REPAIR GY WIRE FOR AN OPEN CIRCUIT TO THE CHARGING SYSTEM
MEASURE VOLTAGE AT * WIRE TO A/C RELAY
IS VOLTAGE ABOVE 10 VOLTS?
YES
REPLACE A/C CLUTCH RELAY
NO
REPAIR * WIRE FOR AN OPEN CIRCUIT FAN RELAY TO A/C RELAY
* DG = S BODY
LG = ALL OTHERS

AIR CONDITIONING CLUTCH RELAY CIRCUIT CHECK—1990 VEHICLES WITH 2.5L ENGINE

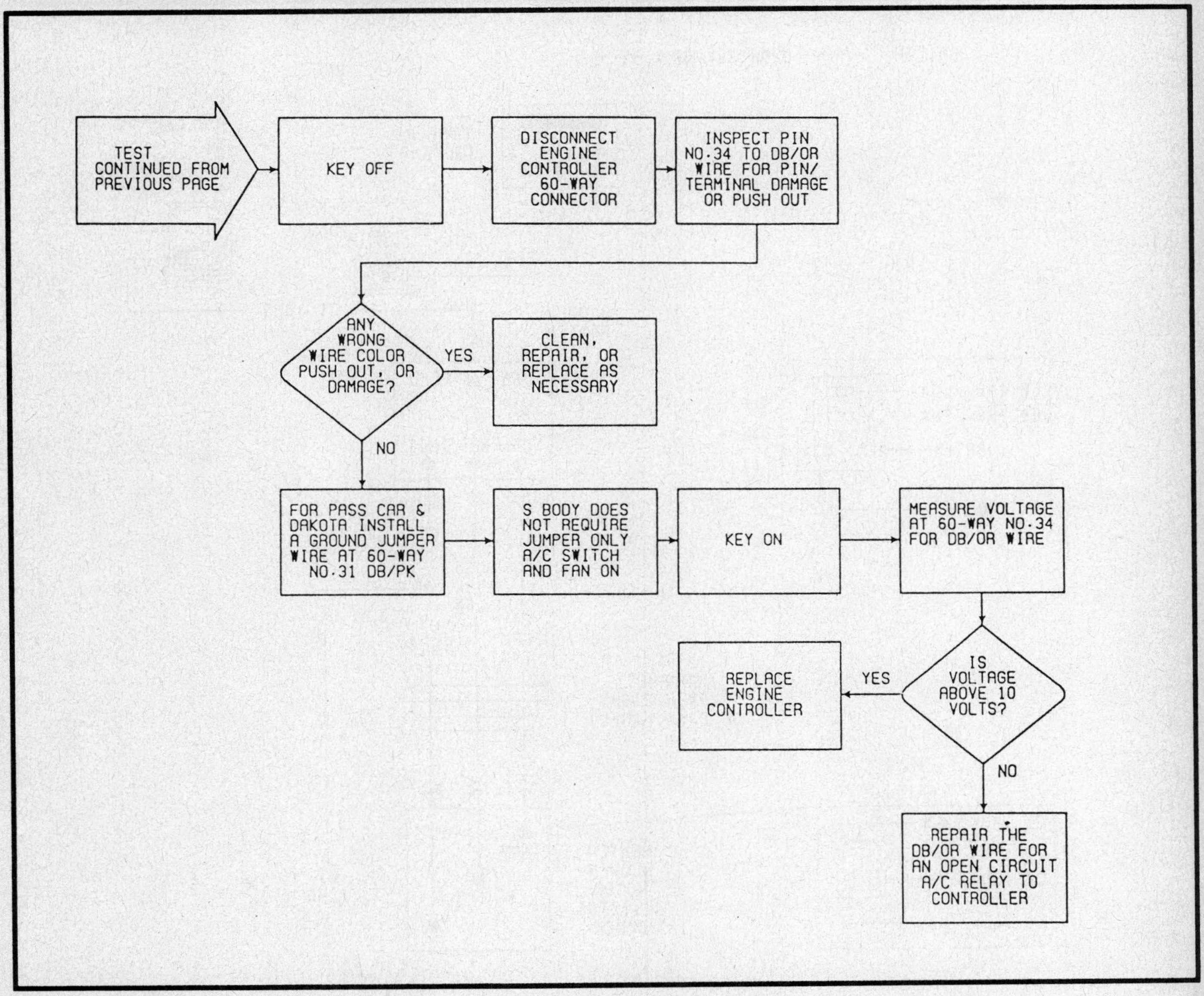
TEST CONTINUED FROM PREVIOUS PAGE
KEY OFF
DISCONNECT ENGINE CONTROLLER 60-WAY CONNECTOR
INSPECT PIN NO.34 TO DB/OR WIRE FOR PIN/ TERMINAL DAMAGE OR PUSH OUT
ANY WRONG WIRE COLOR PUSH OUT, OR DAMAGE?
YES
CLEAN, REPAIR, OR REPLACE AS NECESSARY
NO
FOR PASS CAR & DAKOTA INSTALL A GROUND JUMPER WIRE AT 60-WAY NO.31 DB/PK
S BODY DOES NOT REQUIRE JUMPER ONLY A/C SWITCH AND FAN ON
KEY ON
MEASURE VOLTAGE AT 60-WAY NO.34 FOR DB/OR WIRE
IS VOLTAGE ABOVE 10 VOLTS?
YES
REPLACE ENGINE CONTROLLER
NO
REPAIR THE DB/OR WIRE FOR AN OPEN CIRCUIT A/C RELAY TO CONTROLLER

CLUTCH COIL TESTING

1. Verify the battery state of charge; the indicator should be green.
2. Connect a 0–10 scale ammeter in series with the clutch coil terminal. Use a volt meter with clips to measure the voltage across the battery and clutch coil.
3. Turn the air conditioning **ON** and switch the blower to **LOW** speed. Start the engine and run at normal idle.
4. The compressor clutch should engage immediately and the clutch voltage should be within 2 volts of battery voltage.
5. The clutch coil is considered good if the current draw is 2.0–3.7 amperes at 12 volts at the clutch coil. If the voltage is more than 12.5 volts, add loads by turning on accessories until the voltage drops below 12.5 volts.
6. If the coil current reads 0, the coil is open and should be replaced.
7. If the ammeter reading is 4 or more amps, then the coil is shorted and should be replaced.
8. If the coil voltage is not within 2 volts of battery voltage, test the clutch coil feed circuit for excessive voltage drop.

WIRING SCHEMATICS

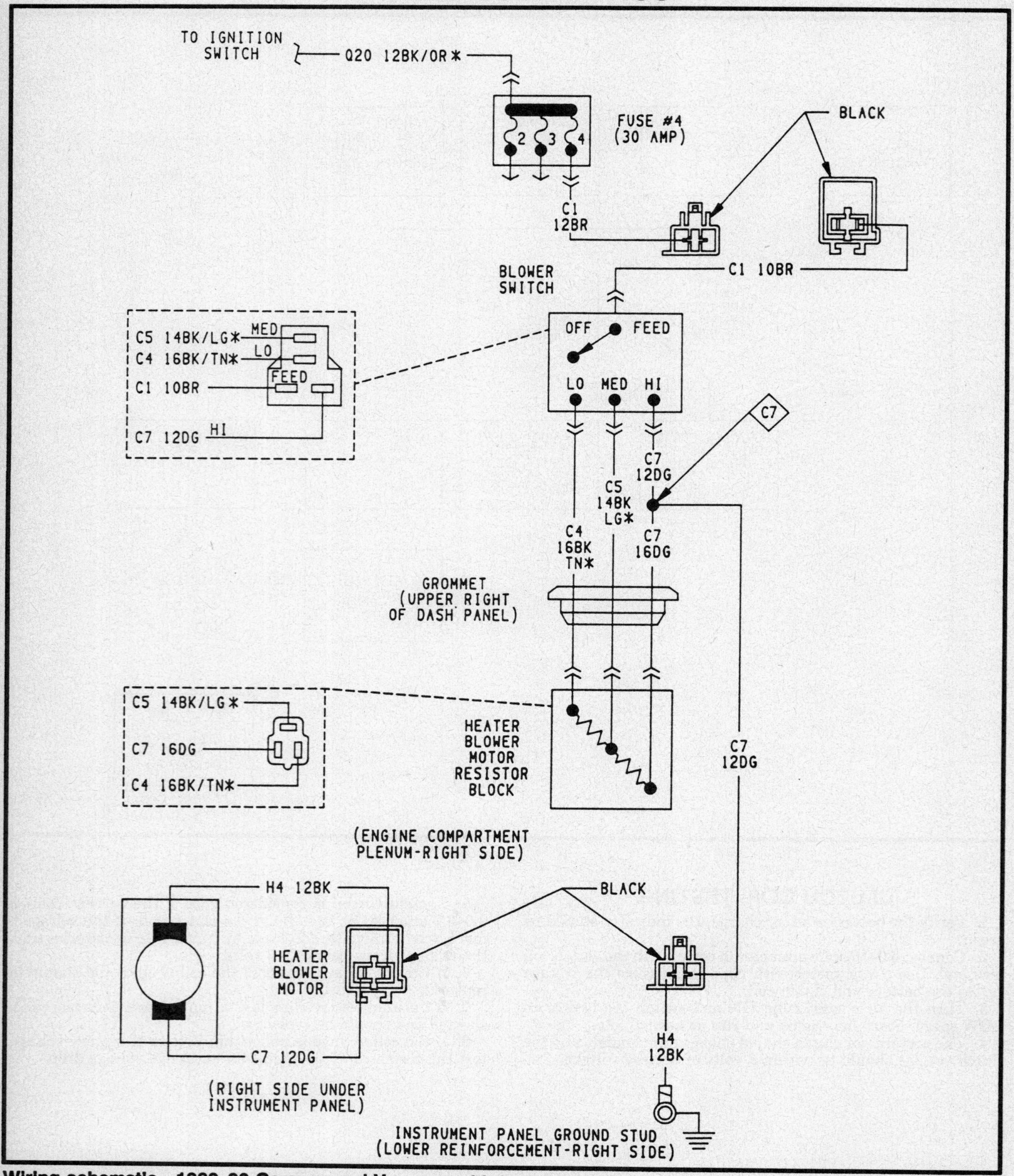
TO IGNITION SWITCH
Q20 12BK/OR*
FUSE #4 (30 AMP)
2
3
4
C1 12BR
BLACK
C1 10BR
BLOWER SWITCH
C5 14BK/LG*
MED
C4 16BK/TN*
LO
FEED
C1 10BR
C7 12DG
HI
OFF
FEED
LO
MED
HI
C7
C7 12DG
C5 14BK LG*
C4 16BK TN*
C7 16DG
GROMMET (UPPER RIGHT OF DASH PANEL)
C5 14BK/LG*
C7 16DG
C4 16BK/TN*
HEATER BLOWER MOTOR RESISTOR BLOCK
C7 12DG
(ENGINE COMPARTMENT PLENUM-RIGHT SIDE)
H4 12BK
BLACK
HEATER BLOWER MOTOR
C7 12DG
(RIGHT SIDE UNDER INSTRUMENT PANEL)
H4 12BK
INSTRUMENT PANEL GROUND STUD (LOWER REINFORCEMENT-RIGHT SIDE)

Wiring schematic—1989–90 Caravan and Voyager with heater only

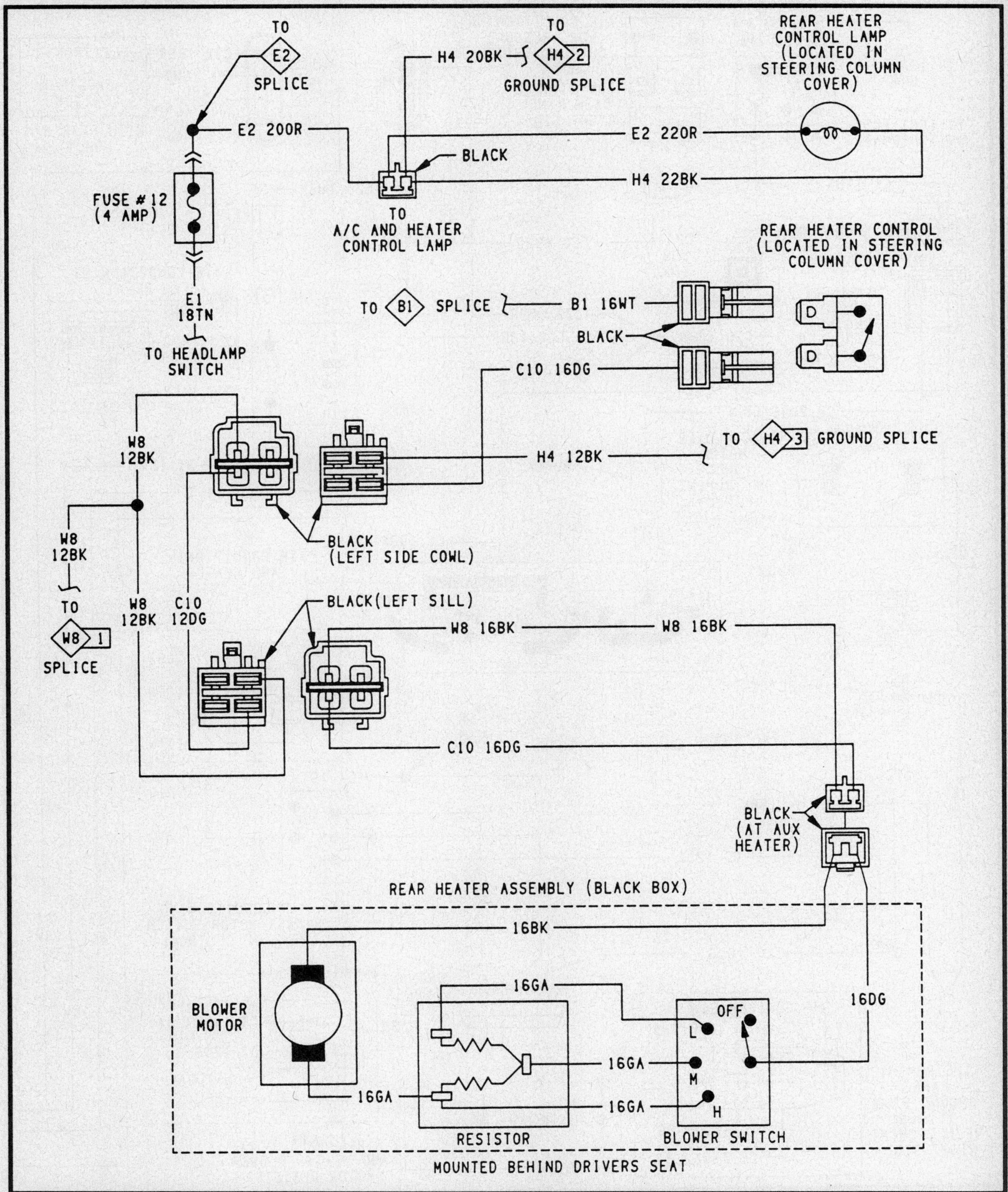
TO
E2
SPLICE
TO
H4 20BK
H4 2
GROUND SPLICE
REAR HEATER
CONTROL LAMP
(LOCATED IN
STEERING COLUMN
COVER)
E2 20OR
E2 22OR
BLACK
H4 22BK
FUSE #12
(4 AMP)
TO
A/C AND HEATER
CONTROL LAMP
REAR HEATER CONTROL
(LOCATED IN STEERING
COLUMN COVER)
TO
B1
SPLICE
B1 16WT
BLACK
E1
18TN
TO HEADLAMP
SWITCH
C10 16DG
W8
12BK
TO
H4 3
GROUND SPLICE
H4 12BK
W8
12BK
BLACK
(LEFT SIDE COWL)
TO
W8 1
SPLICE
W8
12BK
C10
12DG
BLACK(LEFT SILL)
W8 16BK
W8 16BK
C10 16DG
BLACK
(AT AUX
HEATER)
REAR HEATER ASSEMBLY (BLACK BOX)
16BK
BLOWER
MOTOR
16GA
OFF
L
16DG
16GA
M
16GA
16GA
H
RESISTOR
BLOWER SWITCH
MOUNTED BEHIND DRIVERS SEAT

Wiring schematic—1989–90 Caravan and Voyager with rear heater only

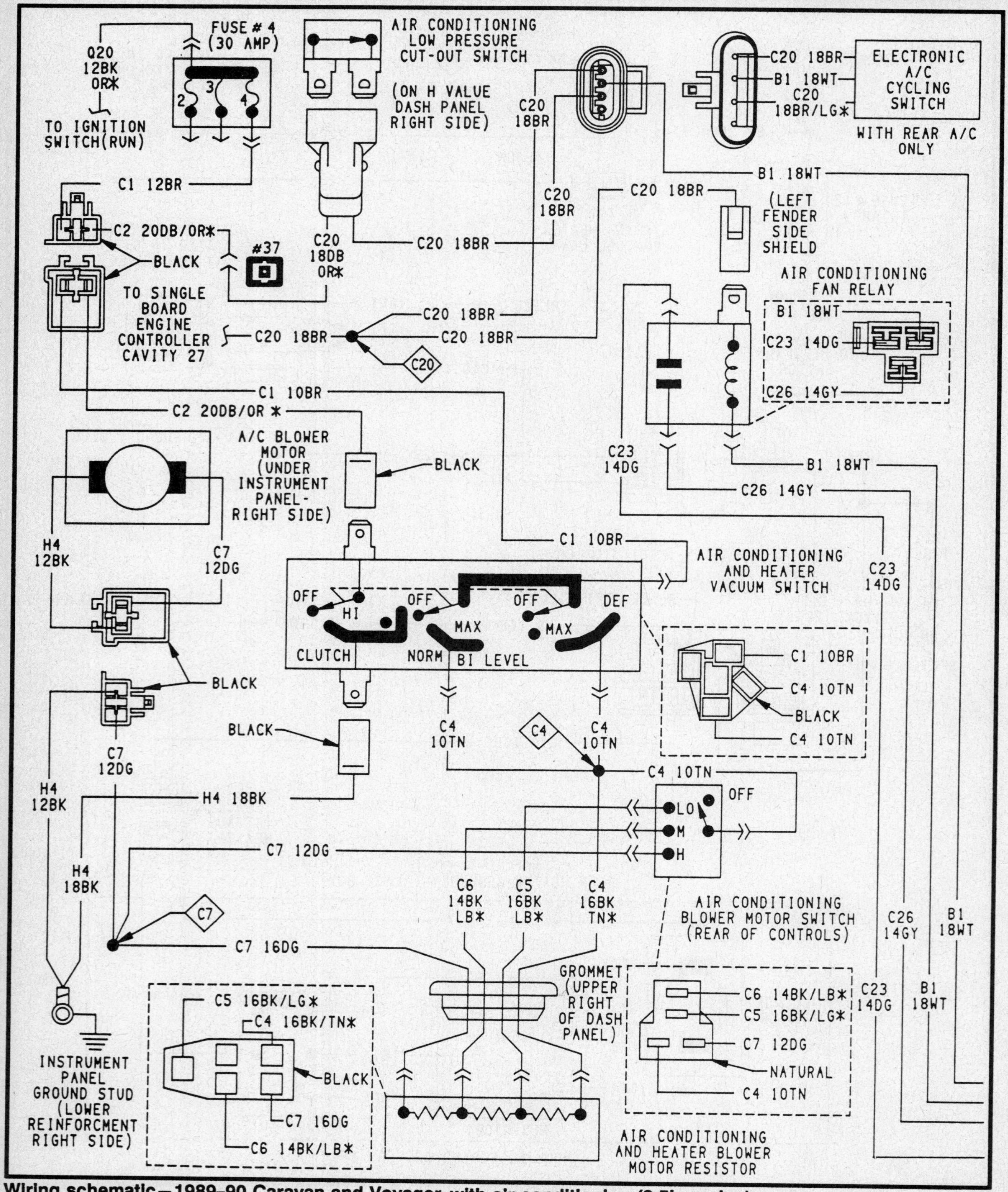
FUSE # 4 (30 AMP)
Q20 12BK OR*
TO IGNITION SWITCH(RUN)
AIR CONDITIONING LOW PRESSURE CUT-OUT SWITCH
(ON H VALUE DASH PANEL RIGHT SIDE)
C20 18BR
C20 18BR
C20 18BR/LG*
B1 18WT
ELECTRONIC A/C CYCLING SWITCH
WITH REAR A/C ONLY
B1 18WT
C1 12BR
C2 20DB/OR*
BLACK
#37
C20 18DB OR*
C20 18BR
C20 18BR
(LEFT FENDER SIDE SHIELD
AIR CONDITIONING FAN RELAY
B1 18WT
C23 14DG
C26 14GY
TO SINGLE BOARD ENGINE CONTROLLER CAVITY 27
C20 18BR
C20 18BR
C20 18BR
C20
C1 10BR
C2 20DB/OR *
A/C BLOWER MOTOR (UNDER INSTRUMENT PANEL-RIGHT SIDE)
BLACK
C23 14DG
B1 18WT
C26 14GY
H4 12BK
C7 12DG
C1 10BR
AIR CONDITIONING AND HEATER VACUUM SWITCH
C23 14DG
OFF
HI
OFF
OFF
DEF
MAX
MAX
CLUTCH
NORM
BI LEVEL
BLACK
C1 10BR
C4 10TN
BLACK
C4 10TN
BLACK
C7 12DG
C4 10TN
C4
C4 10TN
C4 10TN
H4 12BK
H4 18BK
OFF
LO
M
H
C7 12DG
H4 18BK
C6 14BK LB*
C5 16BK LB*
C4 16BK TN*
AIR CONDITIONING BLOWER MOTOR SWITCH (REAR OF CONTROLS)
C26 14GY
B1 18WT
C7
C7 16DG
GROMMET (UPPER RIGHT OF DASH PANEL)
C23 14DG
B1 18WT
C5 16BK/LG*
C4 16BK/TN*
BLACK
C7 16DG
C6 14BK/LB*
INSTRUMENT PANEL GROUND STUD (LOWER REINFORCMENT RIGHT SIDE)
C6 14BK/LB*
C5 16BK/LG*
C7 12DG
NATURAL
C4 10TN
AIR CONDITIONING AND HEATER BLOWER MOTOR RESISTOR

Wiring schematic—1989–90 Caravan and Voyager with air conditioning (2.5L engine)

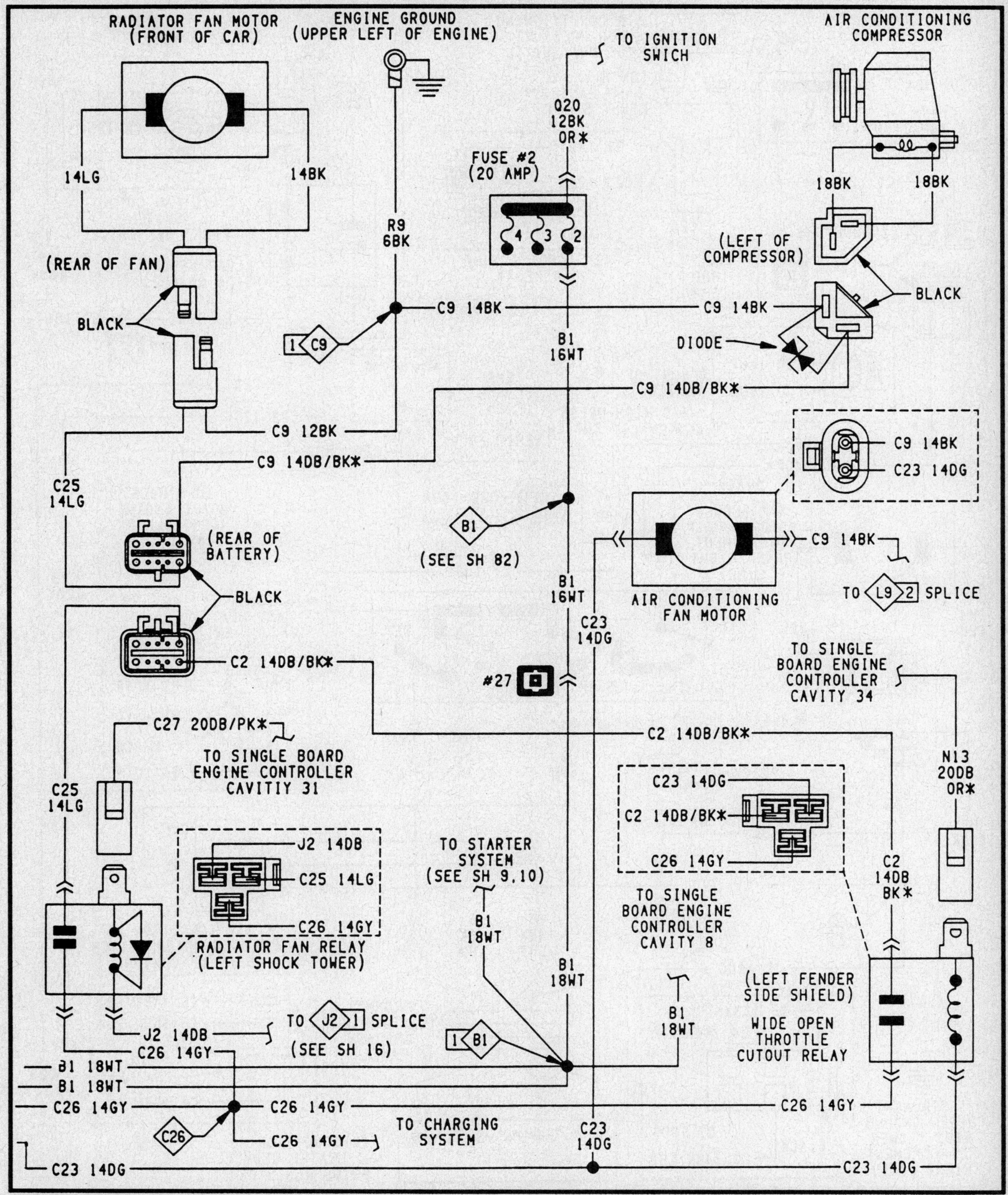
RADIATOR FAN MOTOR (FRONT OF CAR)
ENGINE GROUND (UPPER LEFT OF ENGINE)
TO IGNITION SWICH
AIR CONDITIONING COMPRESSOR
Q20 12BK OR*
FUSE #2 (20 AMP)
14LG
14BK
R9 6BK
18BK
18BK
(LEFT OF COMPRESSOR)
(REAR OF FAN)
BLACK
C9 14BK
C9 14BK
BLACK
1 C9
B1 16WT
DIODE
C9 14DB/BK*
C9 12BK
C9 14DB/BK*
C9 14BK
C23 14DG
C25 14LG
B1
(REAR OF BATTERY)
(SEE SH 82)
C9 14BK
B1 16WT
AIR CONDITIONING FAN MOTOR
TO L9 2 SPLICE
BLACK
C23 14DG
C2 14DB/BK*
#27
TO SINGLE BOARD ENGINE CONTROLLER CAVITY 34
C27 20DB/PK*
C2 14DB/BK*
TO SINGLE BOARD ENGINE CONTROLLER CAVITIY 31
C23 14DG
N13 20DB OR*
C25 14LG
C2 14DB/BK*
J2 14DB
TO STARTER SYSTEM (SEE SH 9,10)
C25 14LG
C26 14GY
C2 14DB BK*
C26 14GY
TO SINGLE BOARD ENGINE CONTROLLER CAVITY 8
B1 18WT
RADIATOR FAN RELAY (LEFT SHOCK TOWER)
B1 18WT
(LEFT FENDER SIDE SHIELD)
B1 18WT
WIDE OPEN THROTTLE CUTOUT RELAY
J2 14DB
TO J2 1 SPLICE
1 B1
C26 14GY
(SEE SH 16)
B1 18WT
B1 18WT
C26 14GY
C26 14GY
C26 14GY
C26
C26 14GY
TO CHARGING SYSTEM
C23 14DG
C23 14DG
C23 14DG

Wiring schematic—1989–90 Caravan and Voyager with air conditioning (2.5L engine)

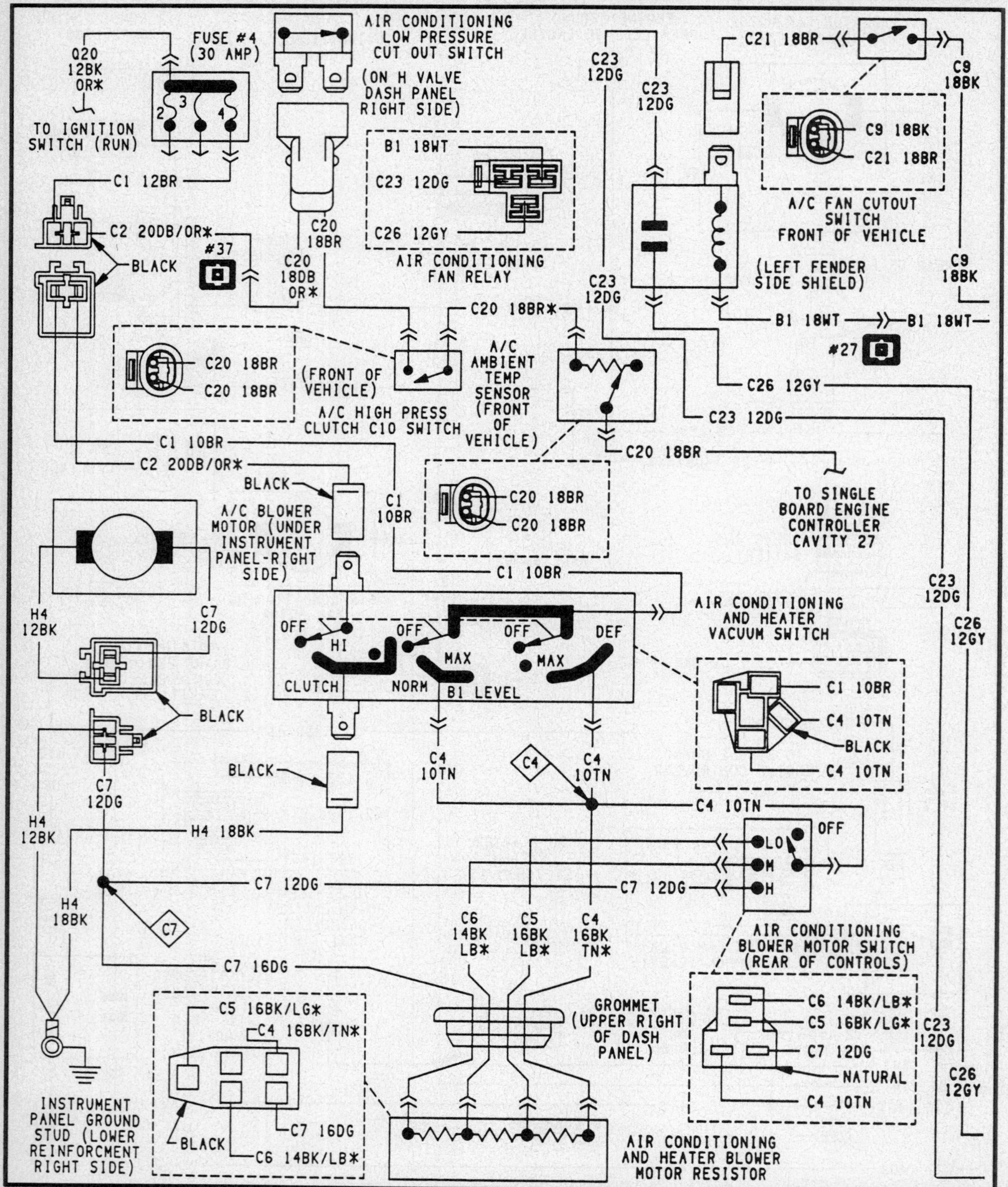
FUSE #4
(30 AMP)
Q20
12BK
OR*
TO IGNITION
SWITCH (RUN)
AIR CONDITIONING
LOW PRESSURE
CUT OUT SWITCH
(ON H VALVE
DASH PANEL
RIGHT SIDE)
B1 18WT
C23 12DG
C26 12GY
AIR CONDITIONING
FAN RELAY
C1 12BR
C2 20DB/OR*
#37
BLACK
C20
18BR
C20
18DB
OR*
C23
12DG
C21 18BR
C9
18BK
C9 18BK
C21 18BR
A/C FAN CUTOUT
SWITCH
FRONT OF VEHICLE
(LEFT FENDER
SIDE SHIELD)
B1 18WT
#27
C20 18BR*
C20 18BR
(FRONT OF
VEHICLE)
A/C HIGH PRESS
CLUTCH C10 SWITCH
A/C
AMBIENT
TEMP
SENSOR
(FRONT
OF
VEHICLE)
C26 12GY
C23 12DG
C1 10BR
C2 20DB/OR*
C20 18BR
TO SINGLE
BOARD ENGINE
CONTROLLER
CAVITY 27
A/C BLOWER
MOTOR (UNDER
INSTRUMENT
PANEL-RIGHT
SIDE)
C1
10BR
H4
12BK
C7
12DG
AIR CONDITIONING
AND HEATER
VACUUM SWITCH
OFF
HI
CLUTCH
OFF
MAX
NORM
B1 LEVEL
OFF
MAX
DEF
C4 10TN
BLACK
C4
C7
H4 18BK
C7 12DG
H4
18BK
C6
14BK
LB*
C5
16BK
LB*
C4
16BK
TN*
LO
M
H
OFF
AIR CONDITIONING
BLOWER MOTOR SWITCH
(REAR OF CONTROLS)
C7 16DG
GROMMET
(UPPER RIGHT
OF DASH
PANEL)
C5 16BK/LG*
C4 16BK/TN*
C7 16DG
C6 14BK/LB*
C6 14BK/LB*
C5 16BK/LG*
C7 12DG
NATURAL
C4 10TN
INSTRUMENT
PANEL GROUND
STUD (LOWER
REINFORCMENT
RIGHT SIDE)
AIR CONDITIONING
AND HEATER BLOWER
MOTOR RESISTOR

Wiring schematic—1989–90 Caravan, Voyager and Town & Country with air conditioning (3.0L and 3.3L engines)

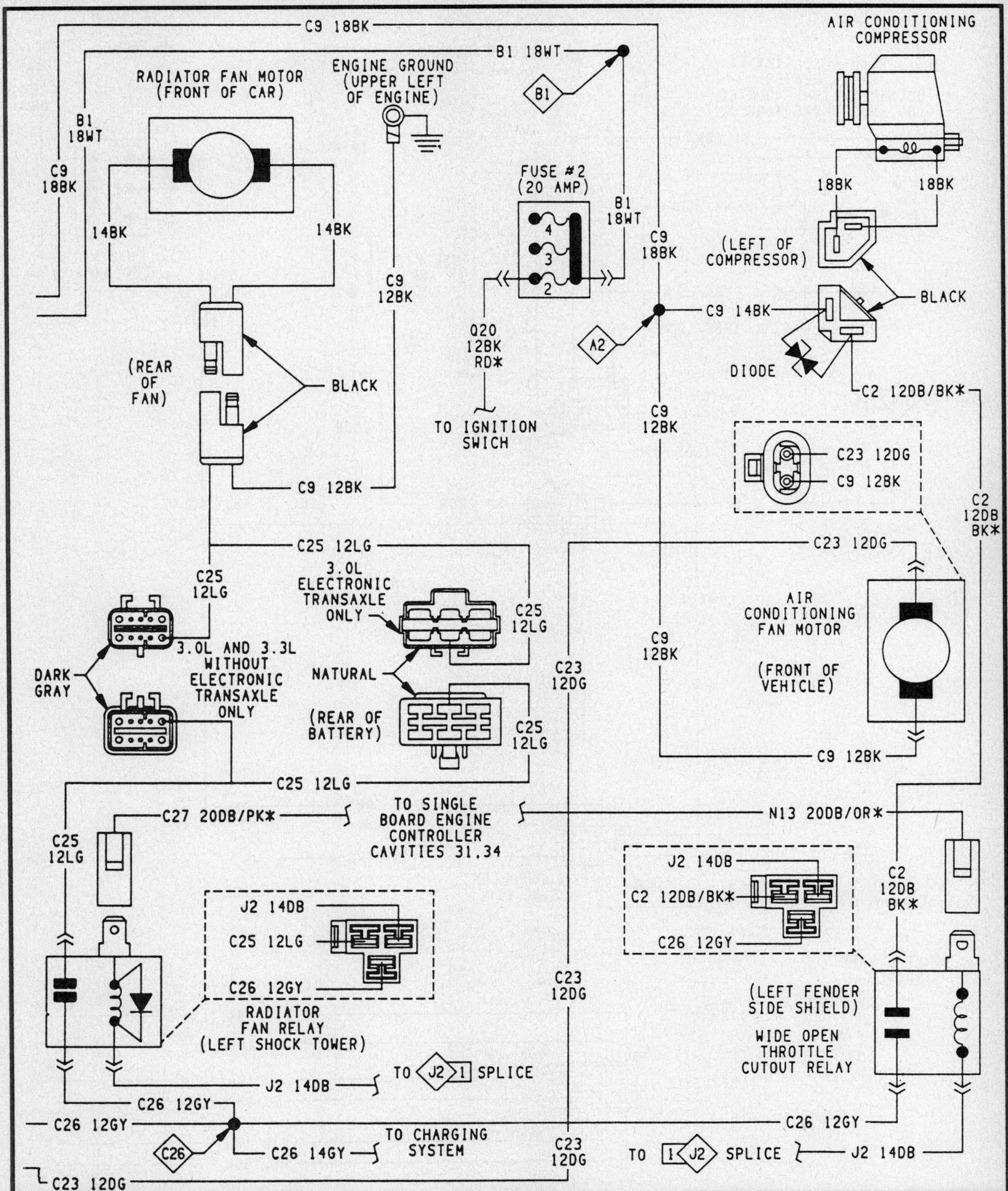
C9 18BK
B1 18WT
RADIATOR FAN MOTOR (FRONT OF CAR)
ENGINE GROUND (UPPER LEFT OF ENGINE)
B1
AIR CONDITIONING COMPRESSOR
B1 18WT
C9 18BK
14BK
14BK
FUSE #2 (20 AMP)
B1 18WT
C9 18BK
18BK
18BK
(LEFT OF COMPRESSOR)
C9 12BK
Q20 12BK RD*
A2
C9 14BK
BLACK
(REAR OF FAN)
BLACK
DIODE
C2 12DB/BK*
TO IGNITION SWICH
C9 12BK
C23 12DG
C9 12BK
C9 12BK
C2 12DB BK*
C25 12LG
C23 12DG
3.0L ELECTRONIC TRANSAXLE ONLY
C25 12LG
AIR CONDITIONING FAN MOTOR
C25 12LG
DARK GRAY
3.0L AND 3.3L WITHOUT ELECTRONIC TRANSAXLE ONLY
NATURAL
C9 12BK
C23 12DG
(FRONT OF VEHICLE)
(REAR OF BATTERY)
C25 12LG
C9 12BK
C25 12LG
C27 20DB/PK*
TO SINGLE BOARD ENGINE CONTROLLER CAVITIES 31,34
N13 20DB/OR*
C25 12LG
J2 14DB
C2 12DB/BK*
C2 12DB BK*
J2 14DB
C26 12GY
C25 12LG
C26 12GY
C23 12DG
(LEFT FENDER SIDE SHIELD)
RADIATOR FAN RELAY (LEFT SHOCK TOWER)
WIDE OPEN THROTTLE CUTOUT RELAY
TO J2 1 SPLICE
J2 14DB
C26 12GY
C26 12GY
C26 12GY
C26
C26 14GY
TO CHARGING SYSTEM
C23 12DG
TO 1 J2 SPLICE
J2 14DB
C23 12DG

Wiring schematic—1989–90 Caravan, Voyager and Town & Country with air conditioning (3.0L and 3.3L engines)

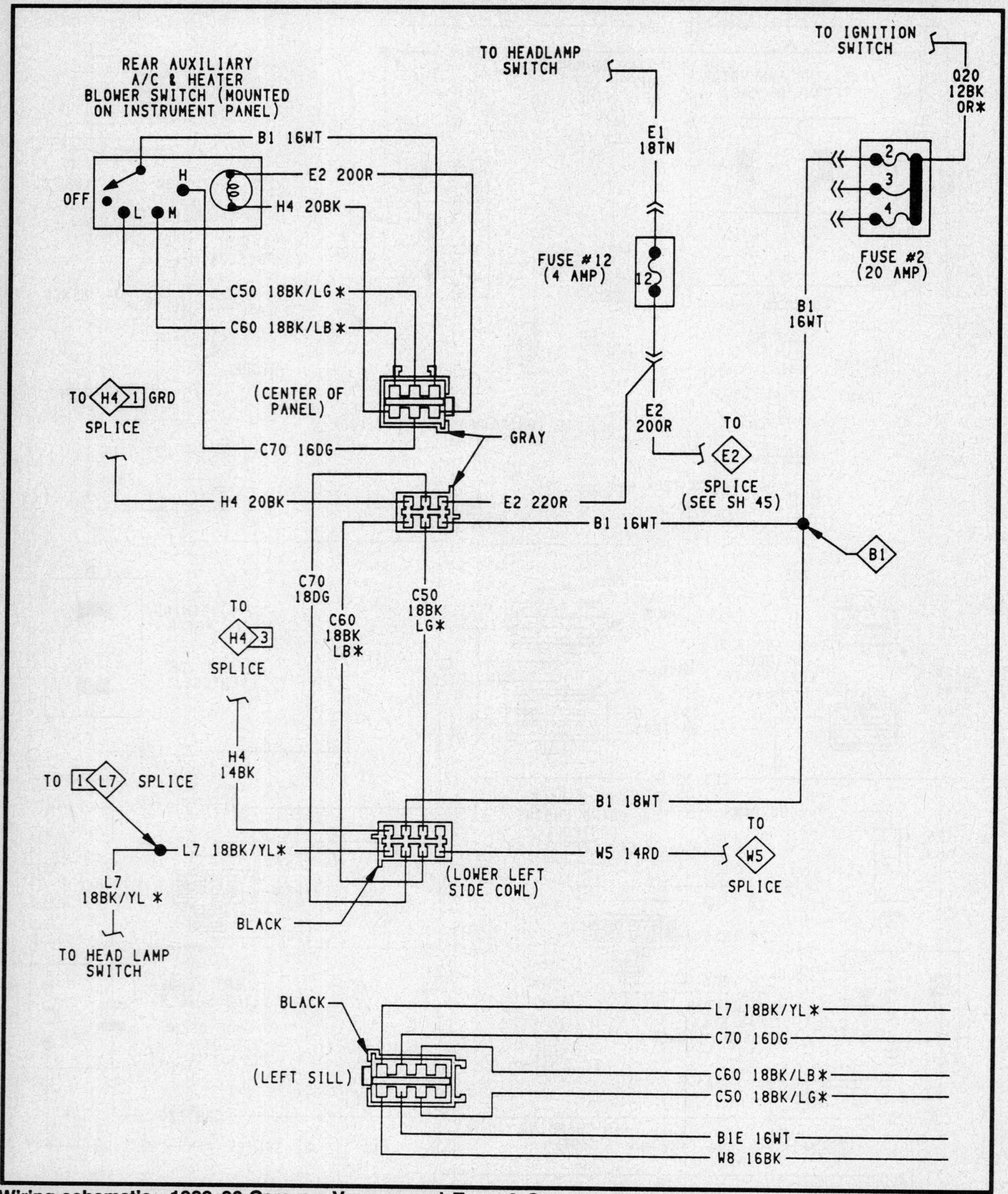
REAR AUXILIARY A/C & HEATER BLOWER SWITCH (MOUNTED ON INSTRUMENT PANEL)
TO HEADLAMP SWITCH
TO IGNITION SWITCH
Q20 12BK OR*
B1 16WT
E2 20OR
H4 20BK
OFF
H
L
M
E1 18TN
FUSE #12 (4 AMP)
12
FUSE #2 (20 AMP)
2
3
4
C50 18BK/LG*
C60 18BK/LB*
B1 16WT
TO H4 1 GRD SPLICE
(CENTER OF PANEL)
E2 20OR
TO E2 SPLICE (SEE SH 45)
C70 16DG
GRAY
H4 20BK
E2 22OR
B1 16WT
B1
C70 18DG
C60 18BK LB*
C50 18BK LG*
TO H4 3 SPLICE
H4 14BK
TO 1 L7 SPLICE
B1 18WT
L7 18BK/YL*
W5 14RD
TO W5 SPLICE
(LOWER LEFT SIDE COWL)
L7 18BK/YL *
TO HEAD LAMP SWITCH
BLACK
BLACK
(LEFT SILL)
L7 18BK/YL*
C70 16DG
C60 18BK/LB*
C50 18BK/LG*
B1E 16WT
W8 16BK

Wiring schematic—1989–90 Caravan, Voyager and Town & Country with rear air conditioning

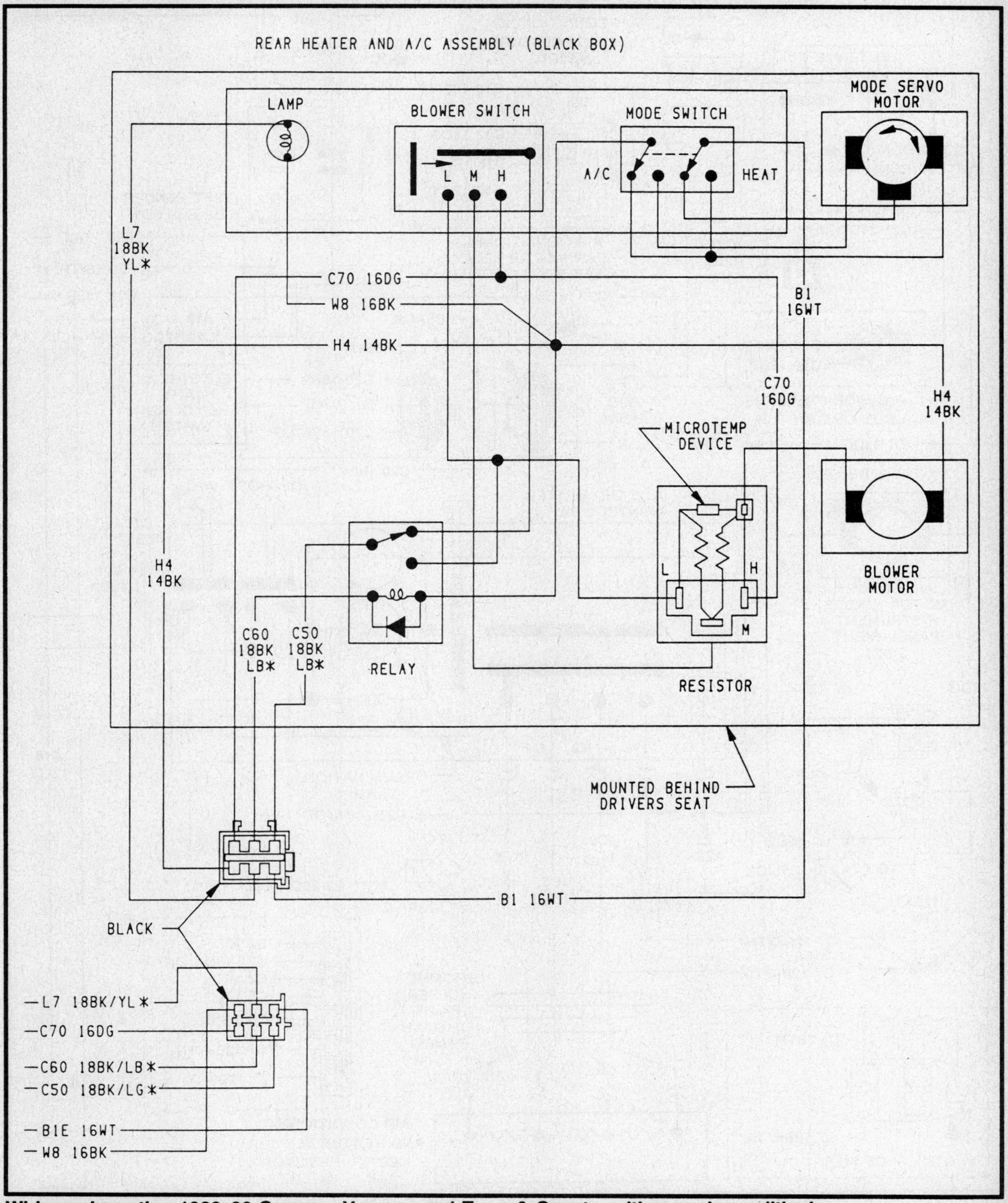
REAR HEATER AND A/C ASSEMBLY (BLACK BOX)
LAMP
BLOWER SWITCH
L M H
MODE SWITCH
A/C
HEAT
MODE SERVO MOTOR
L7 18BK YL*
C70 16DG
W8 16BK
H4 14BK
B1 16WT
C70 16DG
H4 14BK
MICROTEMP DEVICE
L
H
M
BLOWER MOTOR
H4 14BK
C60 18BK LB*
C50 18BK LB*
RELAY
RESISTOR
MOUNTED BEHIND DRIVERS SEAT
B1 16WT
BLACK
L7 18BK/YL*
C70 16DG
C60 18BK/LB*
C50 18BK/LG*
B1E 16WT
W8 16BK

Wiring schematic—1989–90 Caravan, Voyager and Town & Country with rear air conditioning

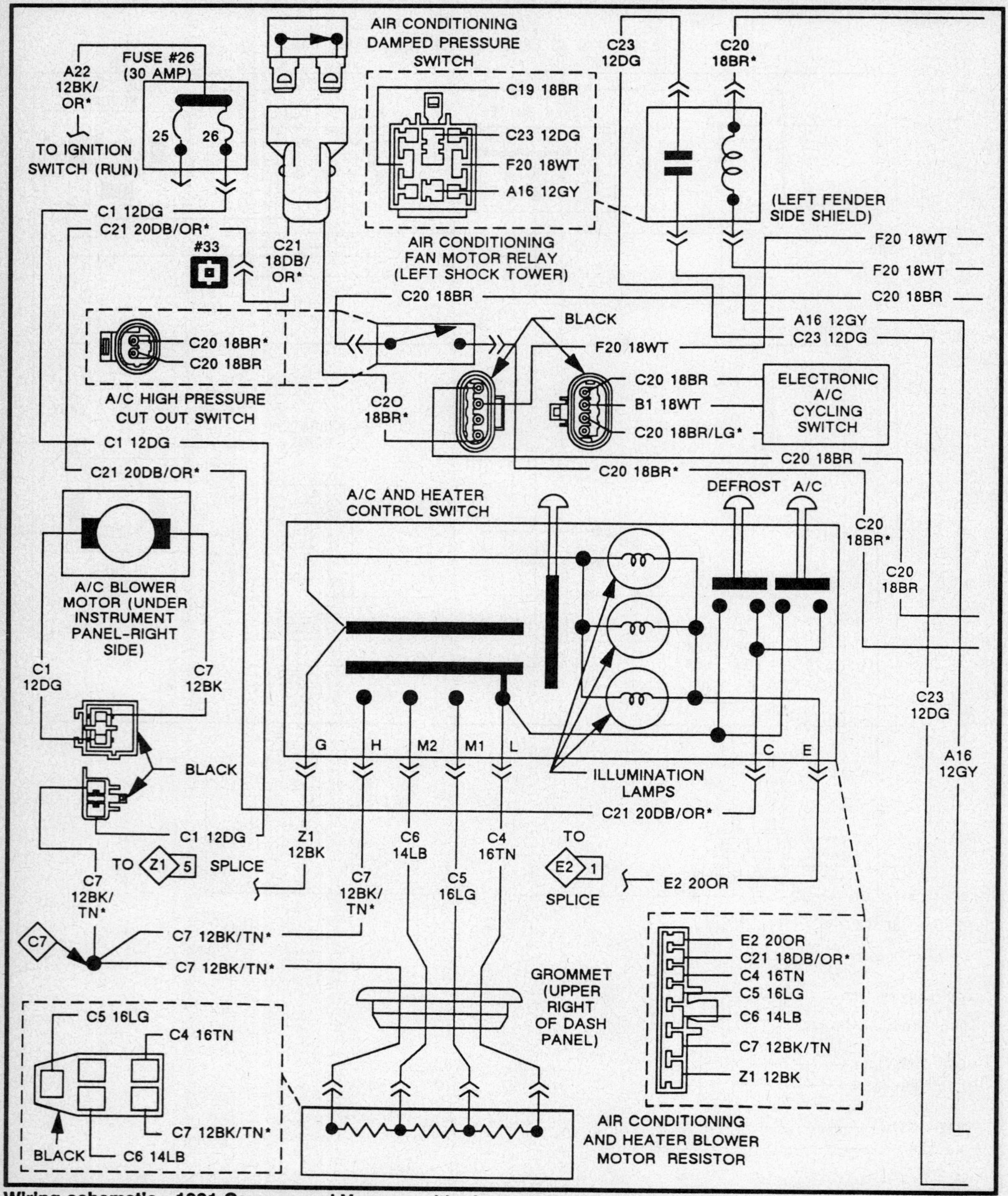
AIR CONDITIONING DAMPED PRESSURE SWITCH
FUSE #26 (30 AMP)
A22 12BK/OR*
25
26
TO IGNITION SWITCH (RUN)
C19 18BR
C23 12DG
F20 18WT
A16 12GY
C23 12DG
C20 18BR*
(LEFT FENDER SIDE SHIELD)
C1 12DG
C21 20DB/OR*
#33
C21 18DB/OR*
AIR CONDITIONING FAN MOTOR RELAY (LEFT SHOCK TOWER)
F20 18WT
F20 18WT
C20 18BR
C20 18BR
BLACK
A16 12GY
C23 12DG
C20 18BR*
C20 18BR
F20 18WT
A/C HIGH PRESSURE CUT OUT SWITCH
C20 18BR
ELECTRONIC A/C CYCLING SWITCH
C2O 18BR*
B1 18WT
C20 18BR/LG*
C1 12DG
C20 18BR
C21 20DB/OR*
C20 18BR*
A/C AND HEATER CONTROL SWITCH
DEFROST
A/C
C20 18BR*
C20 18BR
A/C BLOWER MOTOR (UNDER INSTRUMENT PANEL-RIGHT SIDE)
C1 12DG
C7 12BK
C23 12DG
G
H
M2
M1
L
C
E
A16 12GY
BLACK
ILLUMINATION LAMPS
C21 20DB/OR*
C1 12DG
Z1 12BK
C6 14LB
C4 16TN
TO
TO
Z1
5
SPLICE
E2
1
C7 12BK/TN*
C7 12BK/TN*
C5 16LG
E2 20OR
SPLICE
C7
C7 12BK/TN*
C7 12BK/TN*
GROMMET (UPPER RIGHT OF DASH PANEL)
E2 20OR
C21 18DB/OR*
C4 16TN
C5 16LG
C6 14LB
C7 12BK/TN
Z1 12BK
C5 16LG
C4 16TN
C7 12BK/TN*
BLACK
C6 14LB
AIR CONDITIONING AND HEATER BLOWER MOTOR RESISTOR

Wiring schematic—1991 Caravan and Voyager with air conditioning (2.5L engine)

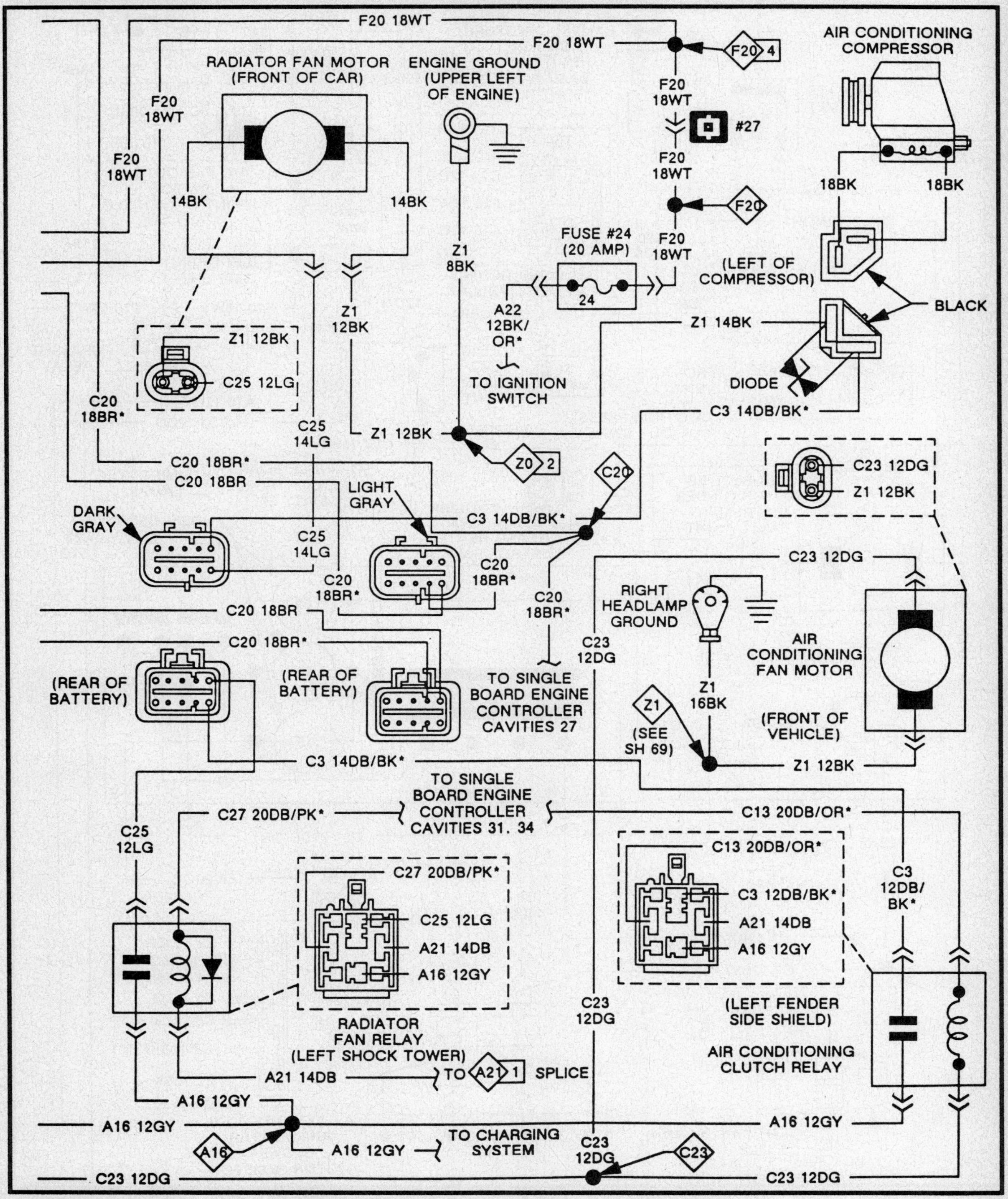
F20 18WT
F20 18WT
F20 4
AIR CONDITIONING COMPRESSOR
RADIATOR FAN MOTOR (FRONT OF CAR)
ENGINE GROUND (UPPER LEFT OF ENGINE)
F20 18WT
F20 18WT
#27
F20 18WT
F20 18WT
F20
F20 18WT
14BK
14BK
18BK
18BK
FUSE #24 (20 AMP)
24
Z1 8BK
(LEFT OF COMPRESSOR)
BLACK
Z1 12BK
A22 12BK/OR*
Z1 14BK
Z1 12BK
C25 12LG
TO IGNITION SWITCH
DIODE
C20 18BR*
C3 14DB/BK*
C25 14LG
Z1 12BK
Z0 2
C23 12DG
Z1 12BK
C20 18BR*
C20
C20 18BR
LIGHT GRAY
DARK GRAY
C3 14DB/BK*
C25 14LG
C20 18BR*
C23 12DG
C20 18BR*
C20 18BR*
RIGHT HEADLAMP GROUND
C20 18BR
C23 12DG
AIR CONDITIONING FAN MOTOR
C20 18BR*
(REAR OF BATTERY)
(REAR OF BATTERY)
TO SINGLE BOARD ENGINE CONTROLLER CAVITIES 27
Z1 16BK
Z1
(SEE SH 69)
(FRONT OF VEHICLE)
C3 14DB/BK*
Z1 12BK
TO SINGLE BOARD ENGINE CONTROLLER CAVITIES 31. 34
C27 20DB/PK*
C13 20DB/OR*
C25 12LG
C13 20DB/OR*
C27 20DB/PK*
C3 12DB/BK*
C3 12DB/BK*
C25 12LG
A21 14DB
A21 14DB
A16 12GY
A16 12GY
C23 12DG
RADIATOR FAN RELAY (LEFT SHOCK TOWER)
(LEFT FENDER SIDE SHIELD)
AIR CONDITIONING CLUTCH RELAY
A21 14DB
TO A21 1 SPLICE
A16 12GY
A16 12GY
A16 12GY
A16
A16 12GY
TO CHARGING SYSTEM
C23 12DG
C23
C23 12DG
C23 12DG

Wiring schematic—1991 Caravan and Voyager with air conditioning (2.5L engine)

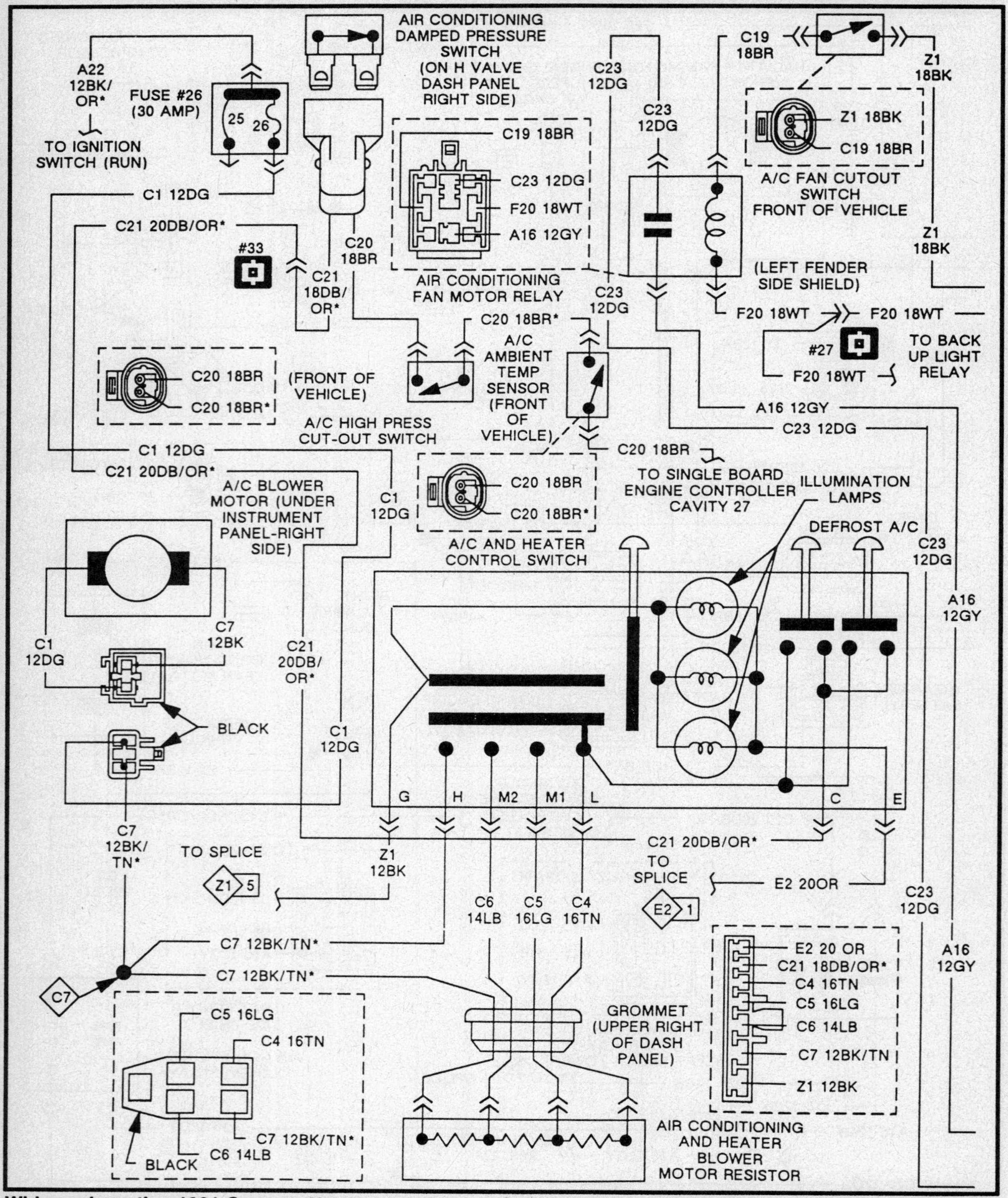
AIR CONDITIONING DAMPED PRESSURE SWITCH (ON H VALVE DASH PANEL RIGHT SIDE)
A22 12BK/OR*
FUSE #26 (30 AMP)
25
26
TO IGNITION SWITCH (RUN)
C1 12DG
C21 20DB/OR*
#33
C21 18DB/OR*
C20 18BR
C19 18BR
C23 12DG
F20 18WT
A16 12GY
AIR CONDITIONING FAN MOTOR RELAY
C23 12DG
C19 18BR
Z1 18BK
A/C FAN CUTOUT SWITCH FRONT OF VEHICLE
(LEFT FENDER SIDE SHIELD)
F20 18WT
#27
TO BACK UP LIGHT RELAY
C20 18BR*
A/C AMBIENT TEMP SENSOR (FRONT OF VEHICLE)
C20 18BR
(FRONT OF VEHICLE)
A/C HIGH PRESS CUT-OUT SWITCH
A16 12GY
C23 12DG
TO SINGLE BOARD ENGINE CONTROLLER CAVITY 27
ILLUMINATION LAMPS
DEFROST A/C
A/C AND HEATER CONTROL SWITCH
A/C BLOWER MOTOR (UNDER INSTRUMENT PANEL-RIGHT SIDE)
C7 12BK
C21 20DB/OR*
BLACK
G H M2 M1 L C E
C7 12BK/TN*
TO SPLICE
Z1 5
Z1 12BK
C6 14LB
C5 16LG
C4 16TN
E2 20OR
E2 1
C7
C5 16LG
C4 16TN
C7 12BK/TN*
C6 14LB
BLACK
GROMMET (UPPER RIGHT OF DASH PANEL)
E2 20 OR
C21 18DB/OR*
C7 12BK/TN
Z1 12BK
AIR CONDITIONING AND HEATER BLOWER MOTOR RESISTOR

Wiring schematic—1991 Caravan, Voyager and Town & Country with air conditioning (3.0L and 3.3L engines)

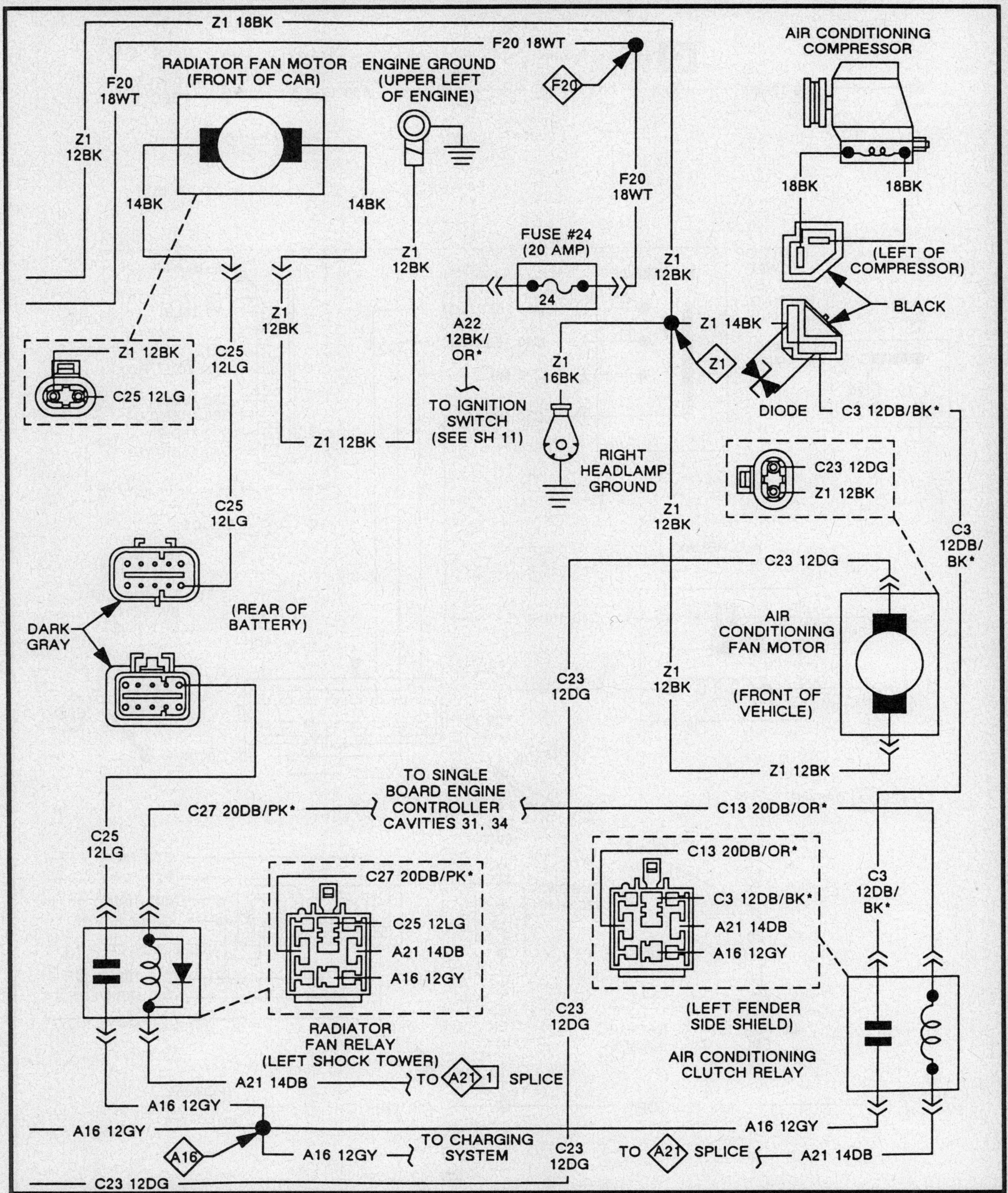
Z1 18BK
F20 18WT
F20 18WT
Z1 12BK
RADIATOR FAN MOTOR (FRONT OF CAR)
ENGINE GROUND (UPPER LEFT OF ENGINE)
F20
AIR CONDITIONING COMPRESSOR
14BK
14BK
F20 18WT
18BK
18BK
FUSE #24 (20 AMP)
24
Z1 12BK
Z1 12BK
Z1 12BK
(LEFT OF COMPRESSOR)
BLACK
Z1 14BK
A22 12BK/OR*
Z1 12BK
C25 12LG
Z1 16BK
Z1
C25 12LG
TO IGNITION SWITCH (SEE SH 11)
DIODE
C3 12DB/BK*
Z1 12BK
RIGHT HEADLAMP GROUND
C23 12DG
Z1 12BK
C25 12LG
Z1 12BK
C3 12DB/BK*
C23 12DG
(REAR OF BATTERY)
DARK GRAY
AIR CONDITIONING FAN MOTOR
C23 12DG
Z1 12BK
(FRONT OF VEHICLE)
Z1 12BK
TO SINGLE BOARD ENGINE CONTROLLER CAVITIES 31, 34
C27 20DB/PK*
C13 20DB/OR*
C25 12LG
C13 20DB/OR*
C27 20DB/PK*
C3 12DB/BK*
C3 12DB/BK*
C25 12LG
A21 14DB
A21 14DB
A16 12GY
A16 12GY
C23 12DG
(LEFT FENDER SIDE SHIELD)
RADIATOR FAN RELAY (LEFT SHOCK TOWER)
AIR CONDITIONING CLUTCH RELAY
A21 14DB
TO A21 1 SPLICE
A16 12GY
A16 12GY
A16 12GY
A16
A16 12GY
TO CHARGING SYSTEM
C23 12DG
TO A21 SPLICE
A21 14DB
C23 12DG

Wiring schematic—1991 Caravan, Voyager and Town & Country with air conditioning (3.0L and 3.3L engines)

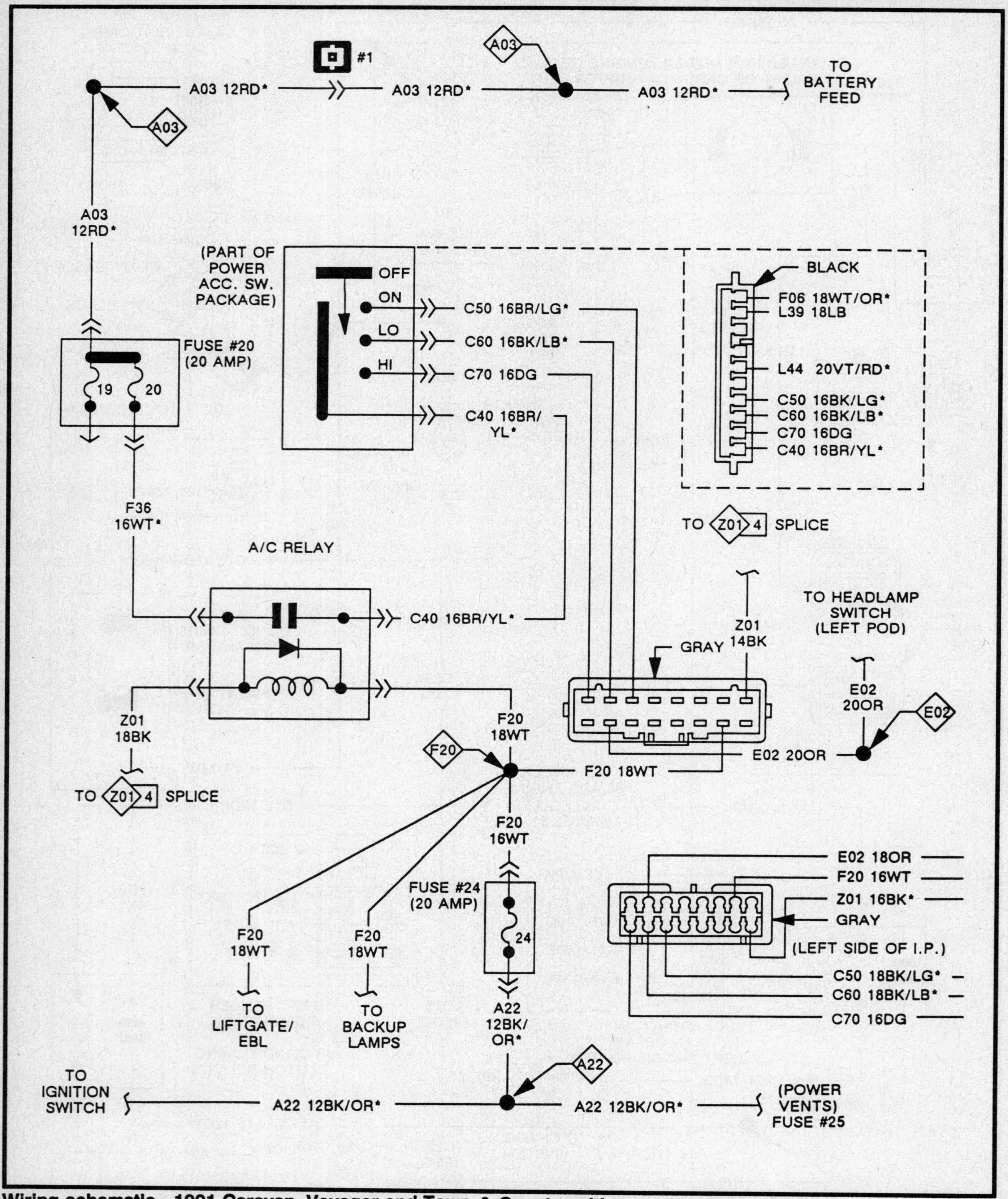
#1
A03
A03 12RD*
TO BATTERY FEED
A03 12RD*
FUSE #20 (20 AMP)
19
20
F36 16WT*
(PART OF POWER ACC. SW. PACKAGE)
OFF
ON
LO
HI
C50 16BR/LG*
C60 16BK/LB*
C70 16DG
C40 16BR/YL*
BLACK
F06 18WT/OR*
L39 18LB
L44 20VT/RD*
C50 16BK/LG*
C60 16BK/LB*
C70 16DG
C40 16BR/YL*
TO Z01 4 SPLICE
A/C RELAY
C40 16BR/YL*
Z01 14BK
GRAY
TO HEADLAMP SWITCH (LEFT POD)
E02 20OR
Z01 18BK
F20 18WT
F20
E02 20OR
F20 18WT
F20 16WT
FUSE #24 (20 AMP)
24
E02 18OR
F20 16WT
Z01 16BK*
GRAY
(LEFT SIDE OF I.P.)
C50 18BK/LG*
C60 18BK/LB*
C70 16DG
TO LIFTGATE/ EBL
TO BACKUP LAMPS
A22 12BK/OR*
A22
TO IGNITION SWITCH
(POWER VENTS) FUSE #25

Wiring schematic—1991 Caravan, Voyager and Town & Country with rear air conditioning

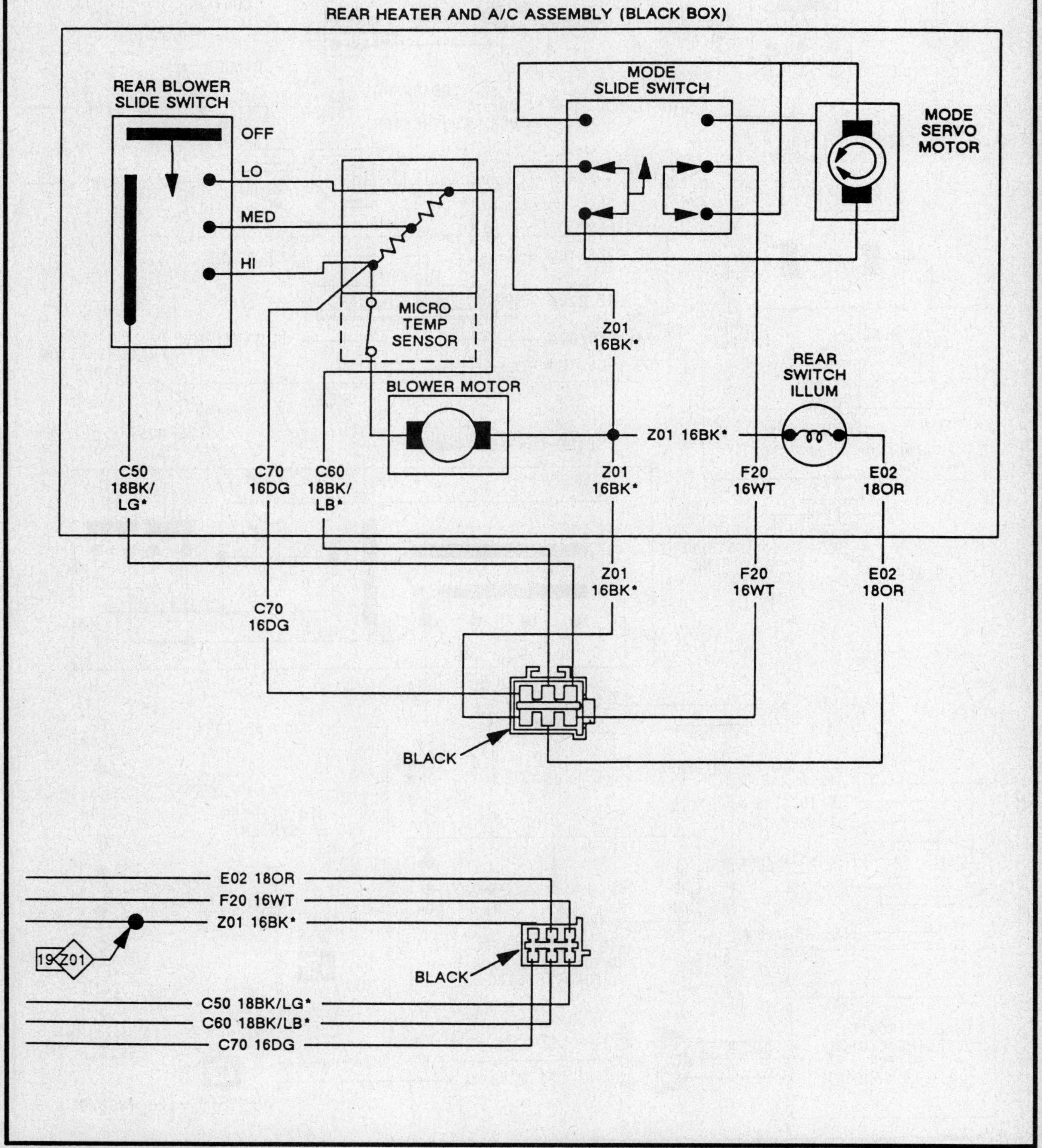
REAR HEATER AND A/C ASSEMBLY (BLACK BOX)
REAR BLOWER SLIDE SWITCH
OFF
LO
MED
HI
MODE SLIDE SWITCH
MODE SERVO MOTOR
MICRO TEMP SENSOR
BLOWER MOTOR
Z01 16BK*
REAR SWITCH ILLUM
Z01 16BK*
C50 18BK/LG*
C70 16DG
C60 18BK/LB*
Z01 16BK*
F20 16WT
E02 18OR
Z01 16BK*
F20 16WT
E02 18OR
C70 16DG
BLACK
E02 18OR
F20 16WT
Z01 16BK*
19 Z01
BLACK
C50 18BK/LG*
C60 18BK/LB*
C70 16DG

Wiring schematic—1991 Caravan, Voyager and Town & Country with rear air conditioning

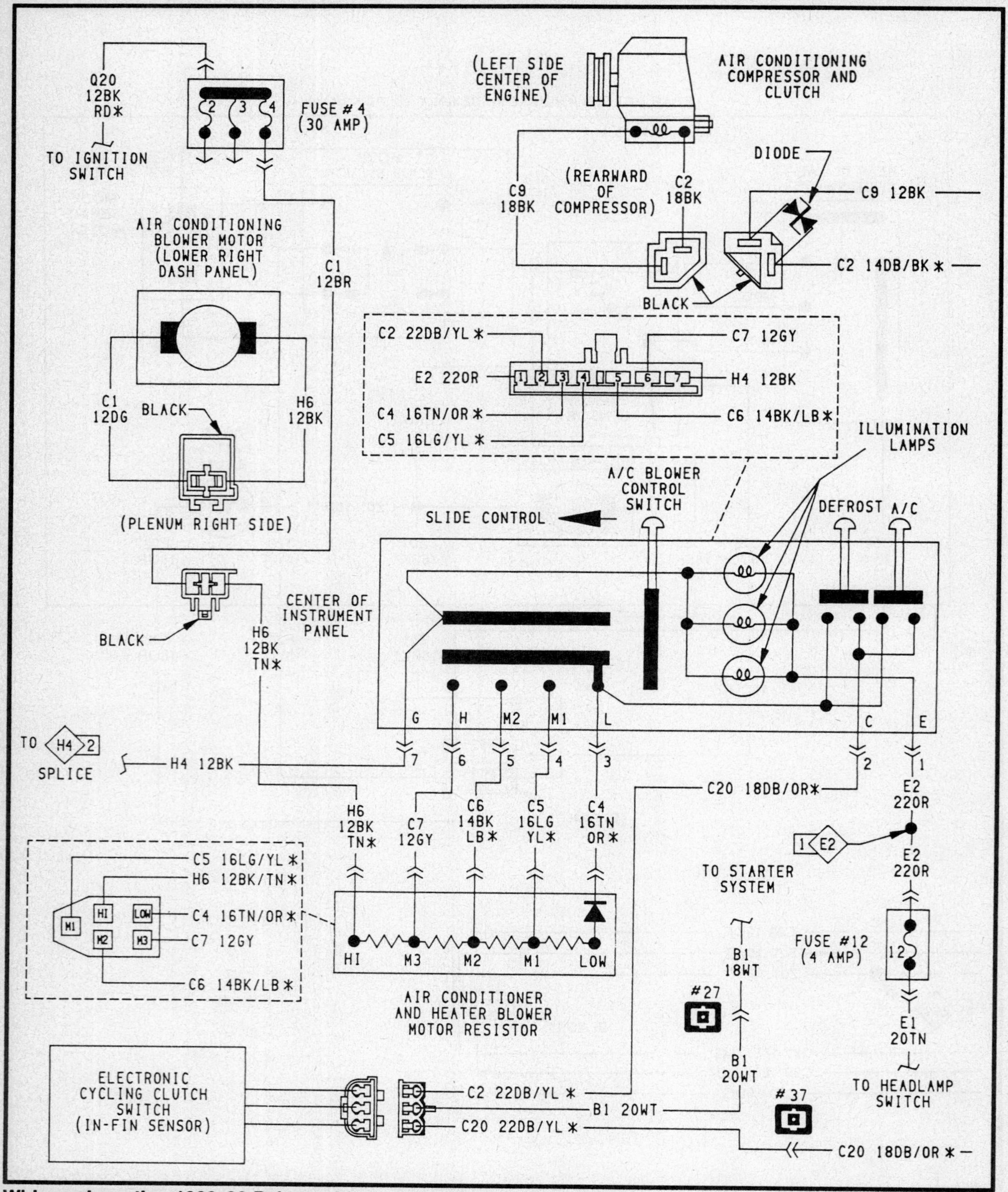
Q20
12BK
RD*
TO IGNITION
SWITCH
FUSE #4
(30 AMP)
(LEFT SIDE
CENTER OF
ENGINE)
AIR CONDITIONING
COMPRESSOR AND
CLUTCH
DIODE
(REARWARD
OF
COMPRESSOR)
C9
18BK
C2
18BK
C9 12BK
C2 14DB/BK *
BLACK
AIR CONDITIONING
BLOWER MOTOR
(LOWER RIGHT
DASH PANEL)
C1
12BR
C2 22DB/YL *
C7 12GY
E2 22OR
H4 12BK
C4 16TN/OR *
C6 14BK/LB *
C5 16LG/YL *
C1
12DG
BLACK
H6
12BK
(PLENUM RIGHT SIDE)
ILLUMINATION
LAMPS
A/C BLOWER
CONTROL
SWITCH
DEFROST
A/C
SLIDE CONTROL
CENTER OF
INSTRUMENT
PANEL
BLACK
H6
12BK
TN*
G
H
M2
M1
L
C
E
TO
H4
SPLICE
H4 12BK
C20 18DB/OR*
E2
22OR
H6
12BK
TN*
C7
12GY
C6
14BK
LB*
C5
16LG
YL*
C4
16TN
OR*
E2
C5 16LG/YL *
H6 12BK/TN *
C4 16TN/OR *
C7 12GY
C6 14BK/LB *
M1
HI
LOW
M2
M3
TO STARTER
SYSTEM
FUSE #12
(4 AMP)
HI
M3
M2
M1
LOW
AIR CONDITIONER
AND HEATER BLOWER
MOTOR RESISTOR
B1
18WT
#27
E1
20TN
TO HEADLAMP
SWITCH
ELECTRONIC
CYCLING CLUTCH
SWITCH
(IN-FIN SENSOR)
C2 22DB/YL *
B1 20WT
C20 22DB/YL *
B1
20WT
#37
C20 18DB/OR *

Wiring schematic—1989–90 Dakota with air conditioning (2.5L engine)

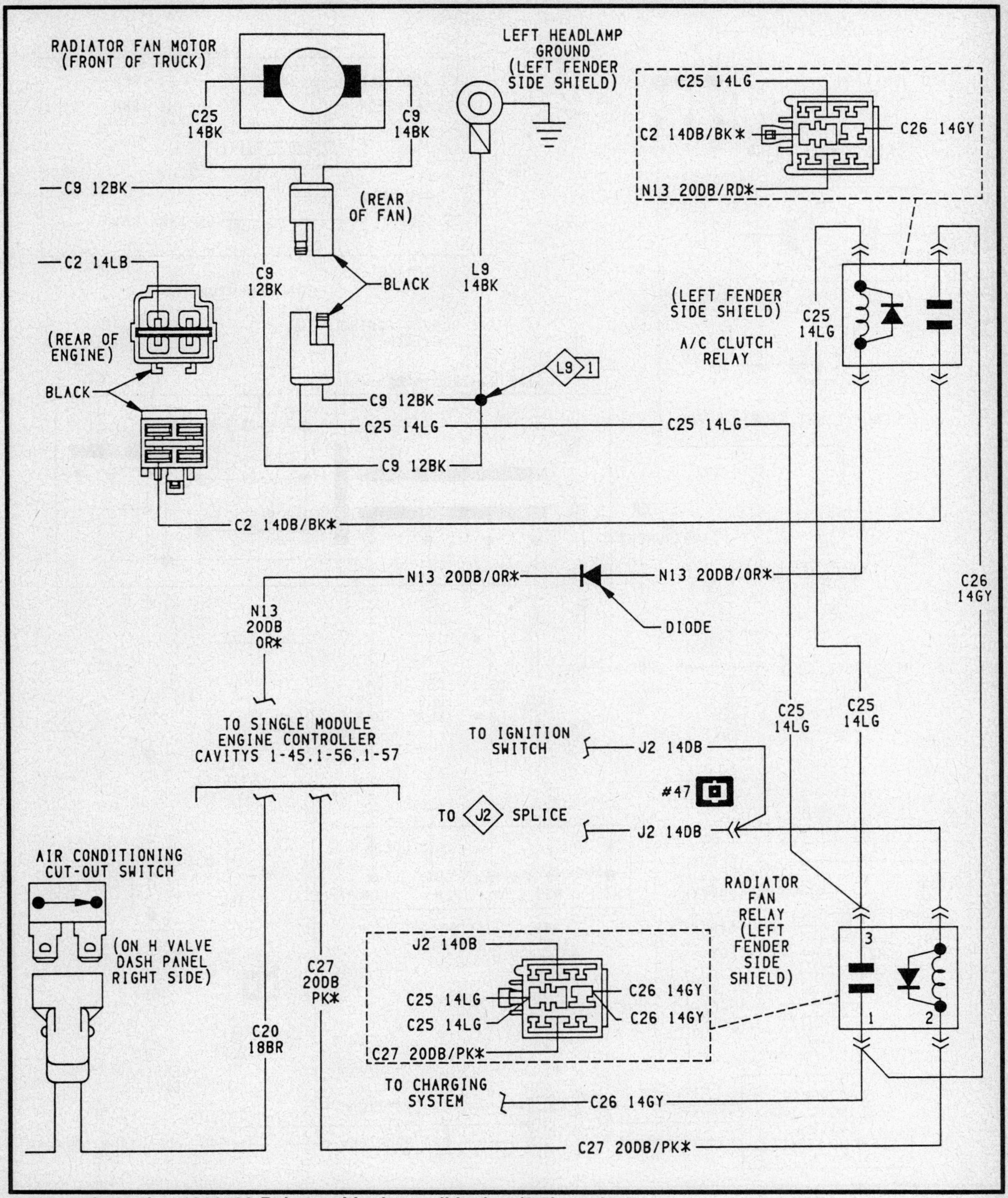
RADIATOR FAN MOTOR (FRONT OF TRUCK)
C25 14BK
C9 14BK
LEFT HEADLAMP GROUND (LEFT FENDER SIDE SHIELD)
C25 14LG
C2 14DB/BK*
C26 14GY
N13 20DB/RD*
C9 12BK
(REAR OF FAN)
C2 14LB
C9 12BK
BLACK
L9 14BK
(REAR OF ENGINE)
BLACK
(LEFT FENDER SIDE SHIELD)
A/C CLUTCH RELAY
C25 14LG
L9 1
C9 12BK
C25 14LG
C25 14LG
C9 12BK
C2 14DB/BK*
N13 20DB/OR*
N13 20DB/OR*
DIODE
N13 20DB OR*
C26 14GY
TO SINGLE MODULE ENGINE CONTROLLER CAVITYS 1-45,1-56,1-57
TO IGNITION SWITCH
J2 14DB
C25 14LG
C25 14LG
#47
TO J2 SPLICE
J2 14DB
AIR CONDITIONING CUT-OUT SWITCH
(ON H VALVE DASH PANEL RIGHT SIDE)
RADIATOR FAN RELAY (LEFT FENDER SIDE SHIELD)
J2 14DB
C27 20DB PK*
C25 14LG
C26 14GY
C25 14LG
C26 14GY
C20 18BR
C27 20DB/PK*
3
1
2
TO CHARGING SYSTEM
C26 14GY
C27 20DB/PK*
Wiring schematic—1989–90 Dakota with air conditioning (2.5L engine)

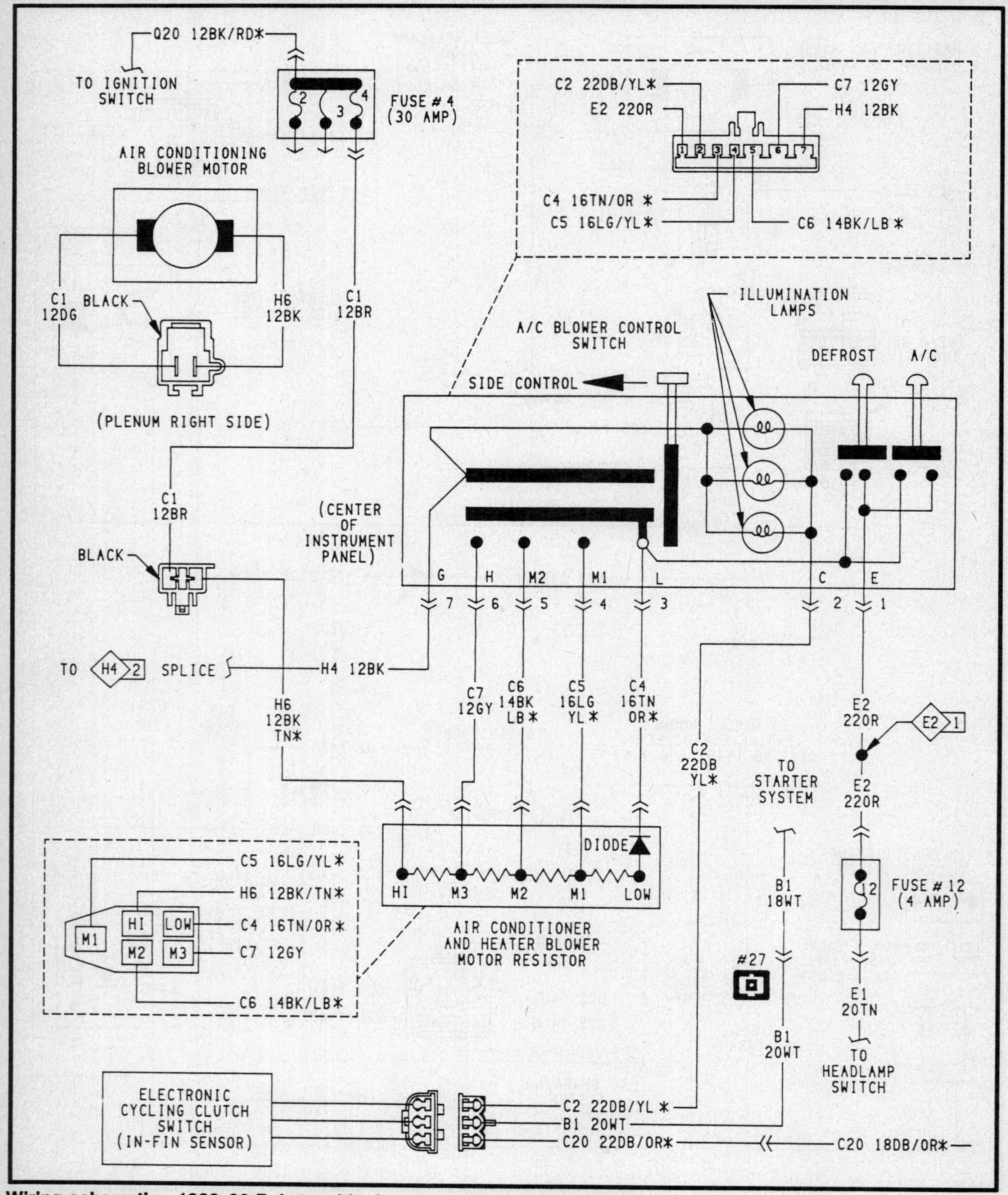
Q20 12BK/RD*
TO IGNITION SWITCH
FUSE # 4 (30 AMP)
AIR CONDITIONING BLOWER MOTOR
C2 22DB/YL*
E2 22OR
C7 12GY
H4 12BK
C4 16TN/OR *
C5 16LG/YL*
C6 14BK/LB *
C1 12DG
BLACK
H6 12BK
C1 12BR
ILLUMINATION LAMPS
A/C BLOWER CONTROL SWITCH
DEFROST
A/C
SIDE CONTROL
(PLENUM RIGHT SIDE)
C1 12BR
(CENTER OF INSTRUMENT PANEL)
BLACK
G H M2 M1 L C E
7 6 5 4 3 2 1
TO H4 2 SPLICE
H4 12BK
H6 12BK TN*
C7 12GY
C6 14BK LB*
C5 16LG YL*
C4 16TN OR*
C2 22DB YL*
TO STARTER SYSTEM
E2 22OR
E2 1
DIODE
HI M3 M2 M1 LOW
AIR CONDITIONER AND HEATER BLOWER MOTOR RESISTOR
C5 16LG/YL*
H6 12BK/TN*
C4 16TN/OR*
C7 12GY
C6 14BK/LB*
M1 HI LOW M2 M3
B1 18WT
#27
FUSE # 12 (4 AMP)
E1 20TN
B1 20WT
TO HEADLAMP SWITCH
ELECTRONIC CYCLING CLUTCH SWITCH (IN-FIN SENSOR)
C2 22DB/YL *
B1 20WT
C20 22DB/OR*
C20 18DB/OR*

Wiring schematic—1989–90 Dakota with air conditioning (3.9L engine)

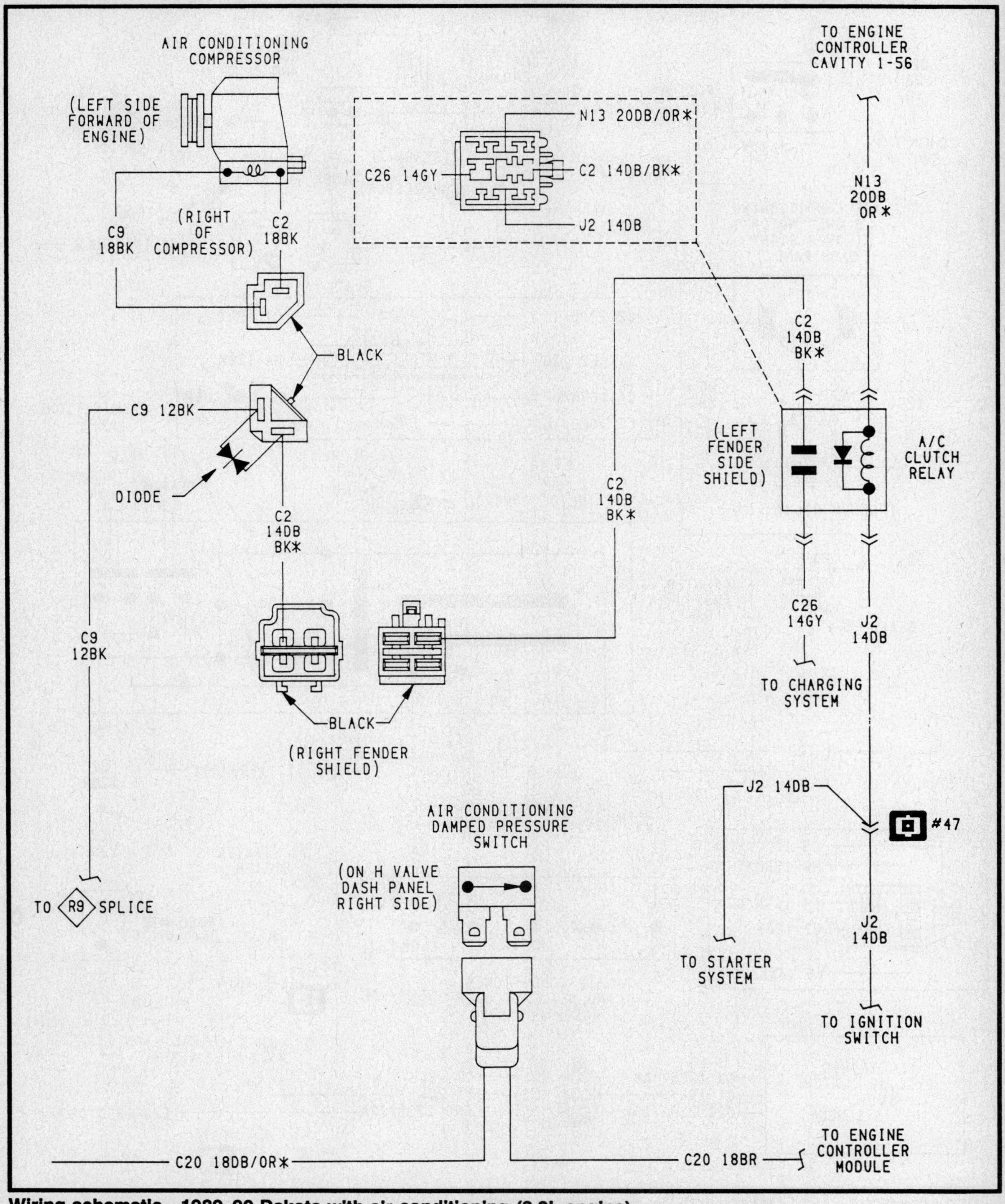
AIR CONDITIONING COMPRESSOR
(LEFT SIDE FORWARD OF ENGINE)
(RIGHT OF COMPRESSOR)
C9 18BK
C2 18BK
C26 14GY
N13 20DB/OR*
C2 14DB/BK*
J2 14DB
TO ENGINE CONTROLLER CAVITY 1-56
N13 20DB OR*
BLACK
C9 12BK
DIODE
C2 14DB BK*
C2 14DB BK*
C2 14DB BK*
(LEFT FENDER SIDE SHIELD)
A/C CLUTCH RELAY
C26 14GY
J2 14DB
TO CHARGING SYSTEM
C9 12BK
BLACK
(RIGHT FENDER SHIELD)
J2 14DB
#47
AIR CONDITIONING DAMPED PRESSURE SWITCH
(ON H VALVE DASH PANEL RIGHT SIDE)
TO R9 SPLICE
J2 14DB
TO STARTER SYSTEM
TO IGNITION SWITCH
C20 18DB/OR*
C20 18BR
TO ENGINE CONTROLLER MODULE

Wiring schematic—1989–90 Dakota with air conditioning (3.9L engine)

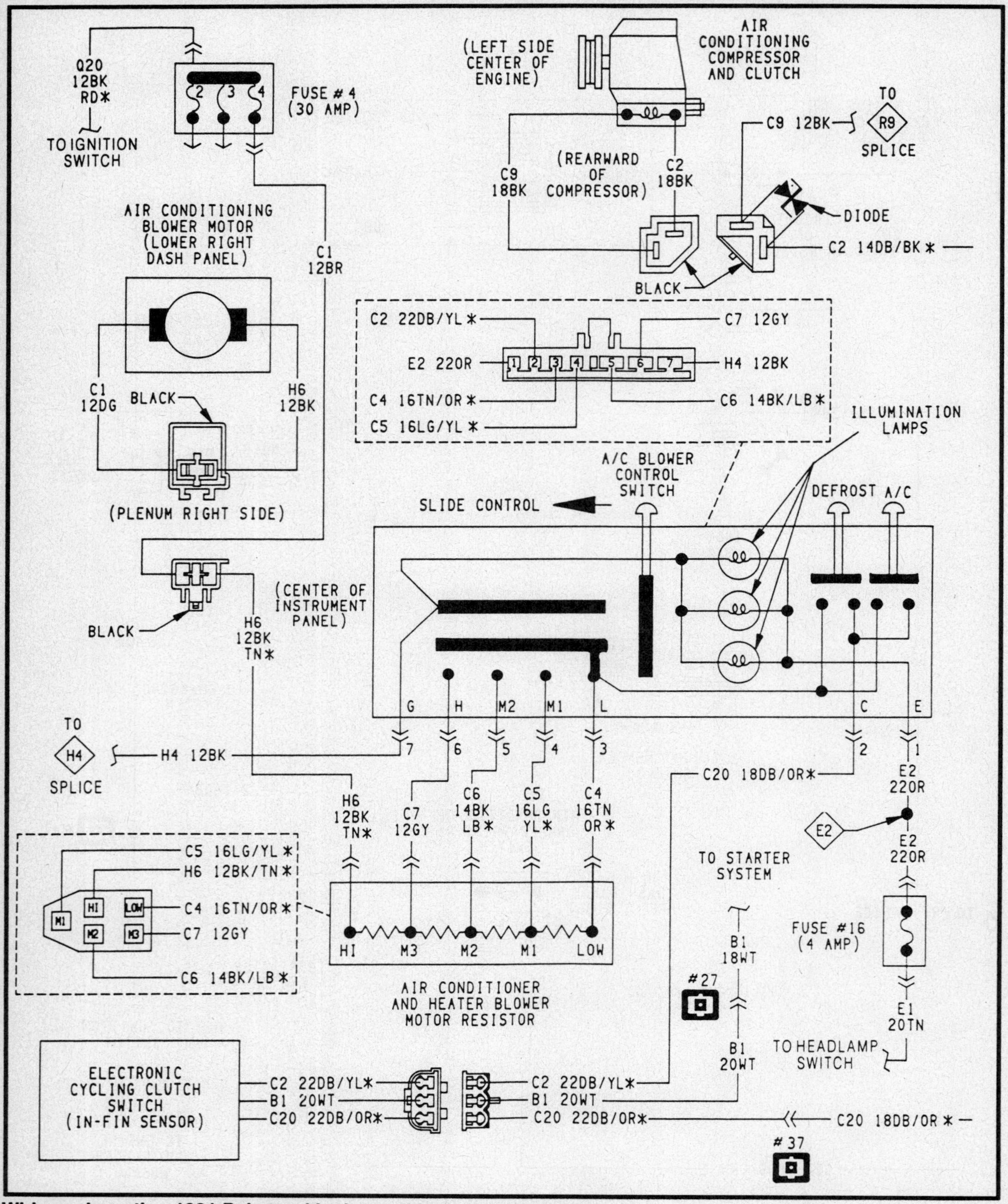
Q20 12BK RD*
TO IGNITION SWITCH
FUSE # 4 (30 AMP)
(LEFT SIDE CENTER OF ENGINE)
AIR CONDITIONING COMPRESSOR AND CLUTCH
TO R9 SPLICE
C9 12BK
(REARWARD OF COMPRESSOR)
C9 18BK
C2 18BK
DIODE
C2 14DB/BK*
BLACK
AIR CONDITIONING BLOWER MOTOR (LOWER RIGHT DASH PANEL)
C1 12BR
C1 12DG
H6 12BK
BLACK
(PLENUM RIGHT SIDE)
C2 22DB/YL*
C7 12GY
E2 22OR
H4 12BK
C4 16TN/OR*
C6 14BK/LB*
C5 16LG/YL*
ILLUMINATION LAMPS
A/C BLOWER CONTROL SWITCH
SLIDE CONTROL
DEFROST
A/C
(CENTER OF INSTRUMENT PANEL)
BLACK
H6 12BK TN*
G H M2 M1 L C E
7 6 5 4 3 2 1
TO H4 SPLICE
H4 12BK
C20 18DB/OR*
E2 22OR
E2
H6 12BK TN*
C7 12GY
C6 14BK LB*
C5 16LG YL*
C4 16TN OR*
C5 16LG/YL*
H6 12BK/TN*
C4 16TN/OR*
C7 12GY
C6 14BK/LB*
M1 HI LOW M2 M3
HI M3 M2 M1 LOW
AIR CONDITIONER AND HEATER BLOWER MOTOR RESISTOR
TO STARTER SYSTEM
B1 18WT
#27
B1 20WT
FUSE #16 (4 AMP)
E1 20TN
TO HEADLAMP SWITCH
ELECTRONIC CYCLING CLUTCH SWITCH (IN-FIN SENSOR)
C2 22DB/YL*
B1 20WT
C20 22DB/OR*
C20 18DB/OR*
#37

Wiring schematic—1991 Dakota with air conditioning (2.5L engine)

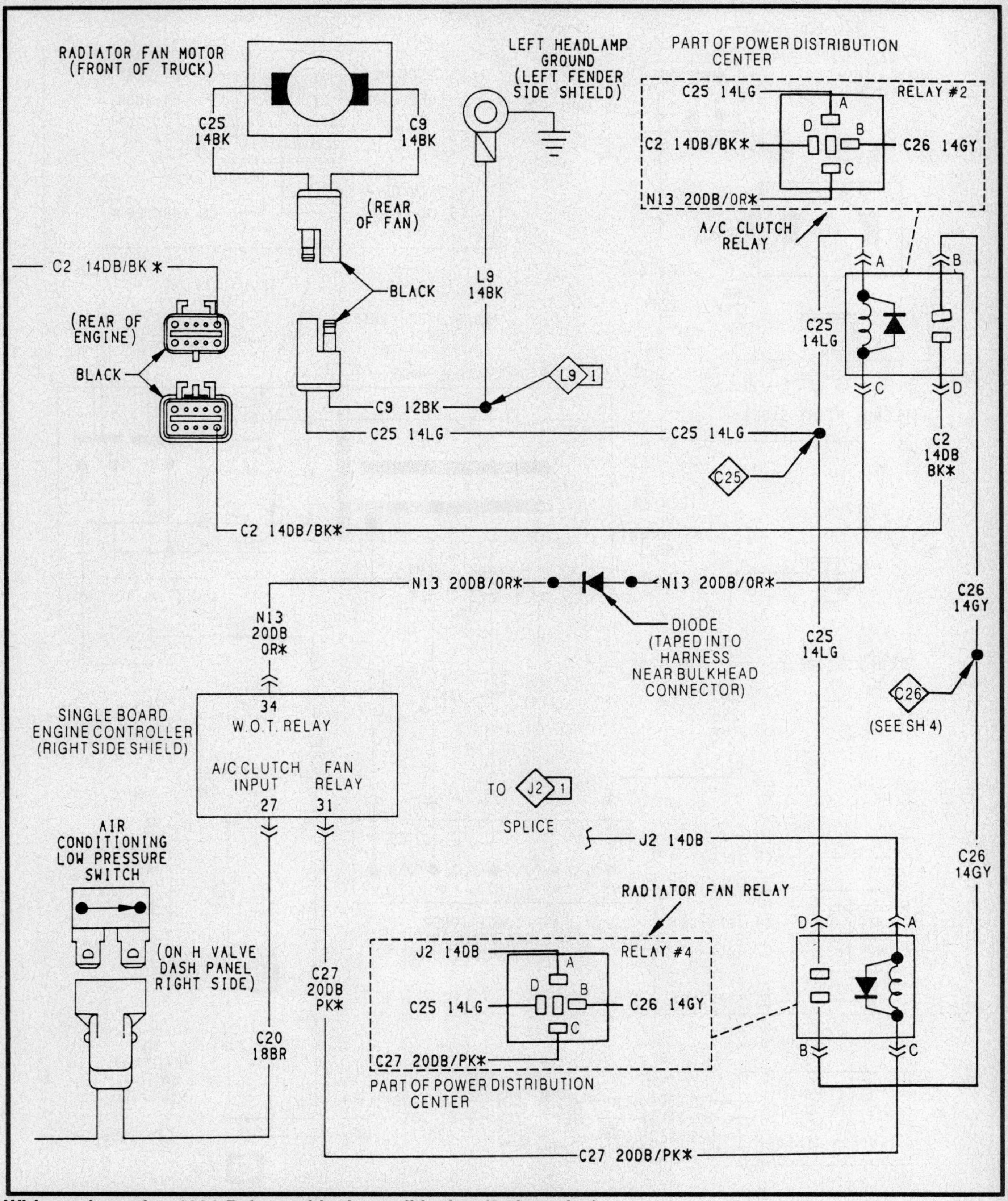
RADIATOR FAN MOTOR (FRONT OF TRUCK)
C25 14BK
C9 14BK
(REAR OF FAN)
LEFT HEADLAMP GROUND (LEFT FENDER SIDE SHIELD)
PART OF POWER DISTRIBUTION CENTER
C25 14LG
RELAY #2
C2 14DB/BK*
C26 14GY
N13 20DB/OR*
A/C CLUTCH RELAY
C2 14DB/BK *
BLACK
L9 14BK
(REAR OF ENGINE)
BLACK
L9 1
C9 12BK
C25 14LG
C25 14LG
C25
C2 14DB BK*
C2 14DB/BK*
N13 20DB/OR*
N13 20DB/OR*
DIODE (TAPED INTO HARNESS NEAR BULKHEAD CONNECTOR)
N13 20DB OR*
C26 14GY
C25 14LG
C26
(SEE SH 4)
SINGLE BOARD ENGINE CONTROLLER (RIGHT SIDE SHIELD)
34 W.O.T. RELAY
A/C CLUTCH INPUT 27
FAN RELAY 31
TO J2 1
SPLICE
J2 14DB
AIR CONDITIONING LOW PRESSURE SWITCH
(ON H VALVE DASH PANEL RIGHT SIDE)
RADIATOR FAN RELAY
C26 14GY
J2 14DB
RELAY #4
C25 14LG
C26 14GY
C27 20DB/PK*
C27 20DB PK*
C20 18BR
PART OF POWER DISTRIBUTION CENTER
C27 20DB/PK*

Wiring schematic—1991 Dakota with air conditioning (2.5L engine)

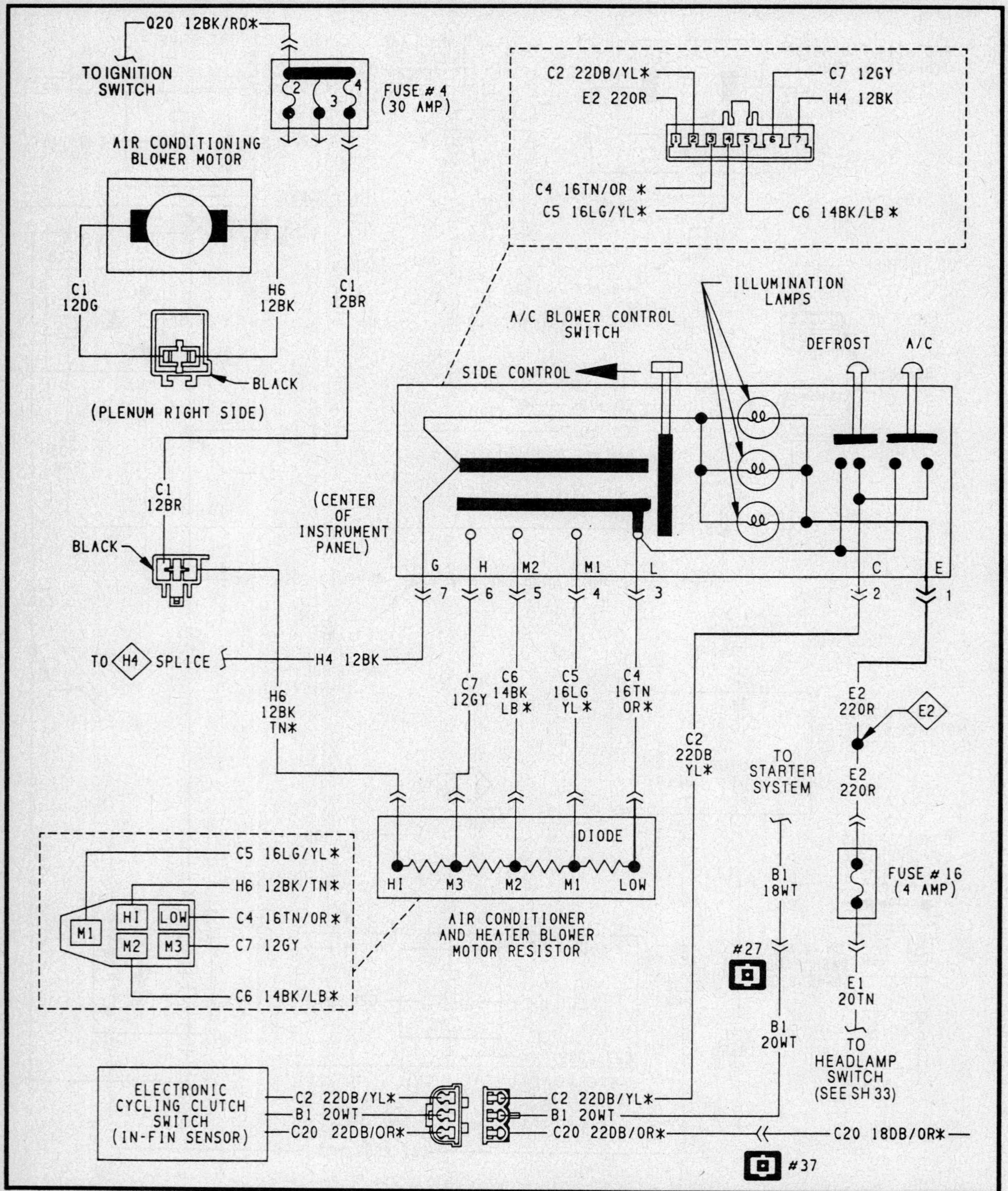
Q20 12BK/RD*
TO IGNITION SWITCH
FUSE # 4 (30 AMP)
AIR CONDITIONING BLOWER MOTOR
C1 12DG
H6 12BK
C1 12BR
BLACK
(PLENUM RIGHT SIDE)
C2 22DB/YL*
E2 220R
C7 12GY
H4 12BK
C4 16TN/OR *
C5 16LG/YL*
C6 14BK/LB*
ILLUMINATION LAMPS
A/C BLOWER CONTROL SWITCH
DEFROST
A/C
SIDE CONTROL
C1 12BR
BLACK
(CENTER OF INSTRUMENT PANEL)
G
H
M2
M1
L
C
E
TO H4 SPLICE
H4 12BK
H6 12BK TN*
C7 12GY
C6 14BK LB*
C5 16LG YL*
C4 16TN OR*
C2 22DB YL*
TO STARTER SYSTEM
E2 220R
E2
E2 220R
FUSE # 16 (4 AMP)
DIODE
HI
M3
M2
M1
LOW
AIR CONDITIONER AND HEATER BLOWER MOTOR RESISTOR
C5 16LG/YL*
H6 12BK/TN*
C4 16TN/OR*
C7 12GY
C6 14BK/LB*
M1
HI
LOW
M2
M3
B1 18WT
#27
B1 20WT
E1 20TN
TO HEADLAMP SWITCH (SEE SH 33)
ELECTRONIC CYCLING CLUTCH SWITCH (IN-FIN SENSOR)
C2 22DB/YL*
B1 20WT
C20 22DB/OR*
C2 22DB/YL*
B1 20WT
C20 22DB/OR*
C20 18DB/OR*
#37

Wiring schematic—1991 Dakota with air conditioning (3.9L and 5.2L engines)

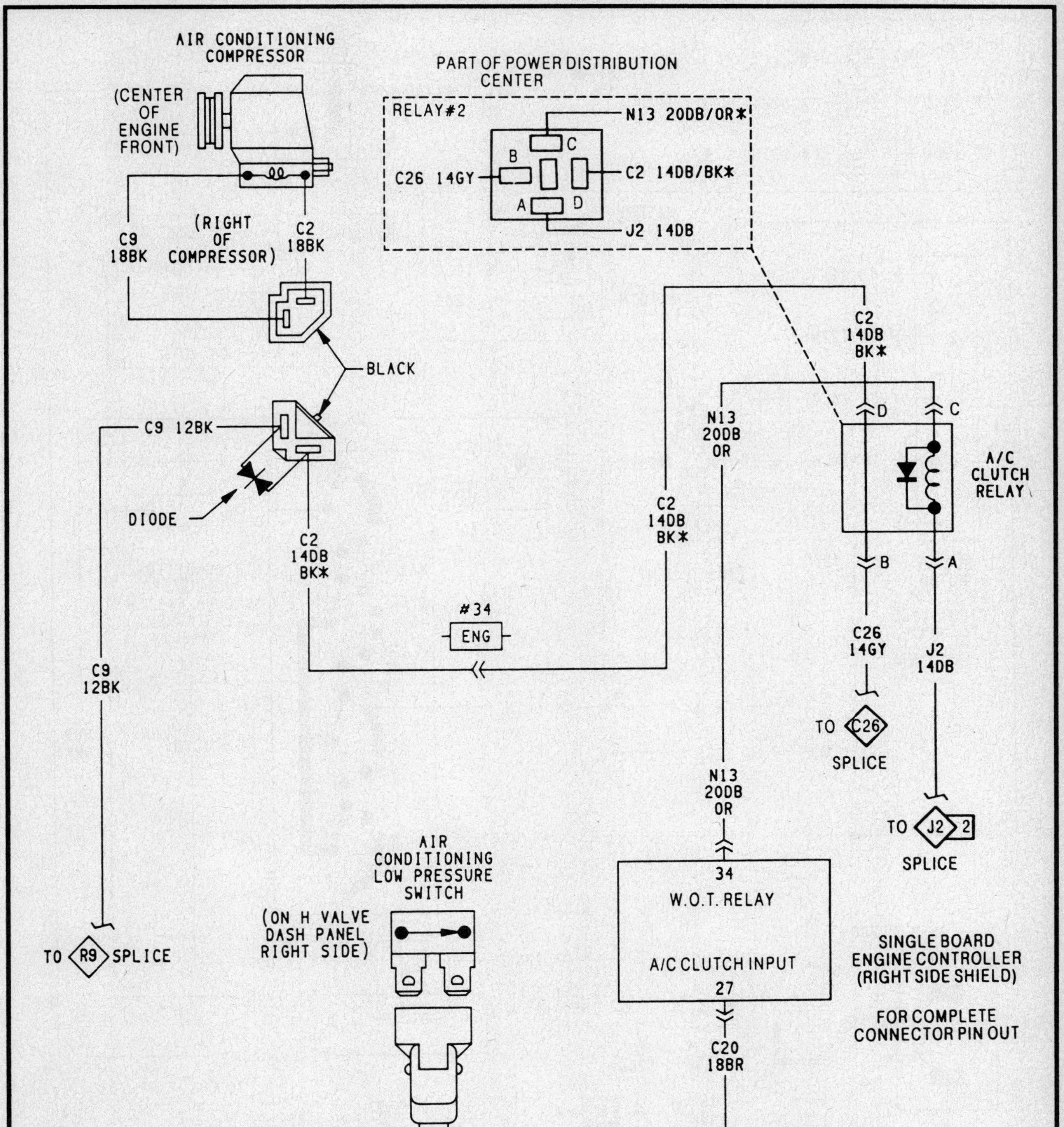
AIR CONDITIONING COMPRESSOR
(CENTER OF ENGINE FRONT)
PART OF POWER DISTRIBUTION CENTER
RELAY#2
N13 20DB/OR*
C
B
C26 14GY
C2 14DB/BK*
A
D
J2 14DB
C9 18BK
(RIGHT OF COMPRESSOR)
C2 18BK
C2 14DB BK*
BLACK
C9 12BK
D
C
N13 20DB OR
A/C CLUTCH RELAY
DIODE
C2 14DB BK*
C2 14DB BK*
B
A
#34
ENG
C9 12BK
C26 14GY
J2 14DB
TO C26 SPLICE
N13 20DB OR
TO J2 2 SPLICE
AIR CONDITIONING LOW PRESSURE SWITCH
(ON H VALVE DASH PANEL RIGHT SIDE)
34
W.O.T. RELAY
A/C CLUTCH INPUT
27
SINGLE BOARD ENGINE CONTROLLER (RIGHT SIDE SHIELD)
FOR COMPLETE CONNECTOR PIN OUT
TO R9 SPLICE
C20 18BR
C20 18DB/OR*
C20 18BR

Wiring schematic—1991 Dakota with air conditioning (3.9L and 5.2L engines)

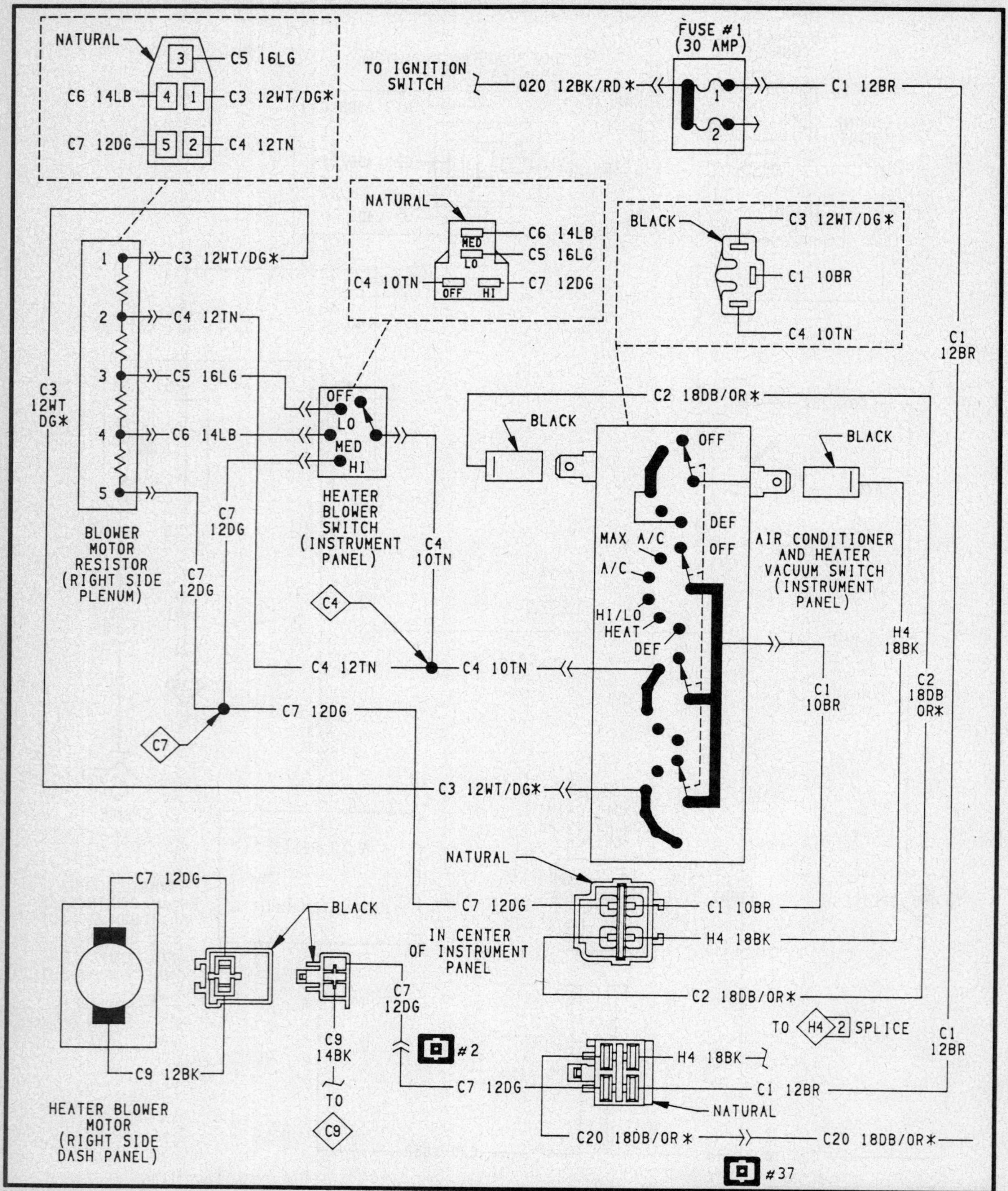
NATURAL
C5 16LG
C6 14LB
C3 12WT/DG*
C7 12DG
C4 12TN
TO IGNITION SWITCH
Q20 12BK/RD*
FUSE #1 (30 AMP)
C1 12BR
NATURAL
C6 14LB
MED
C5 16LG
LO
C4 10TN
OFF
HI
C7 12DG
BLACK
C3 12WT/DG*
C1 10BR
C4 10TN
C3 12WT/DG*
C4 12TN
C5 16LG
C6 14LB
C3 12WT DG*
OFF
LO
MED
HI
C2 18DB/OR*
BLACK
OFF
DEF
OFF
MAX A/C
A/C
HI/LO HEAT
DEF
BLACK
AIR CONDITIONER AND HEATER VACUUM SWITCH (INSTRUMENT PANEL)
C1 12BR
BLOWER MOTOR RESISTOR (RIGHT SIDE PLENUM)
C7 12DG
HEATER BLOWER SWITCH (INSTRUMENT PANEL)
C4 10TN
H4 18BK
C2 18DB OR*
C1 10BR
C4
C4 12TN
C4 10TN
C7
C7 12DG
C3 12WT/DG*
NATURAL
C7 12DG
C1 10BR
H4 18BK
IN CENTER OF INSTRUMENT PANEL
C2 18DB/OR*
BLACK
C9 12BK
C9 14BK
TO
C9
#2
TO H4 2 SPLICE
H4 18BK
C1 12BR
NATURAL
C20 18DB/OR*
C20 18DB/OR*
HEATER BLOWER MOTOR (RIGHT SIDE DASH PANEL)
#37

Wiring schematic—1989 Pick-Up and Ramcharger with air conditioning (3.9L, 5.2L and 5.9L gasoline engines)

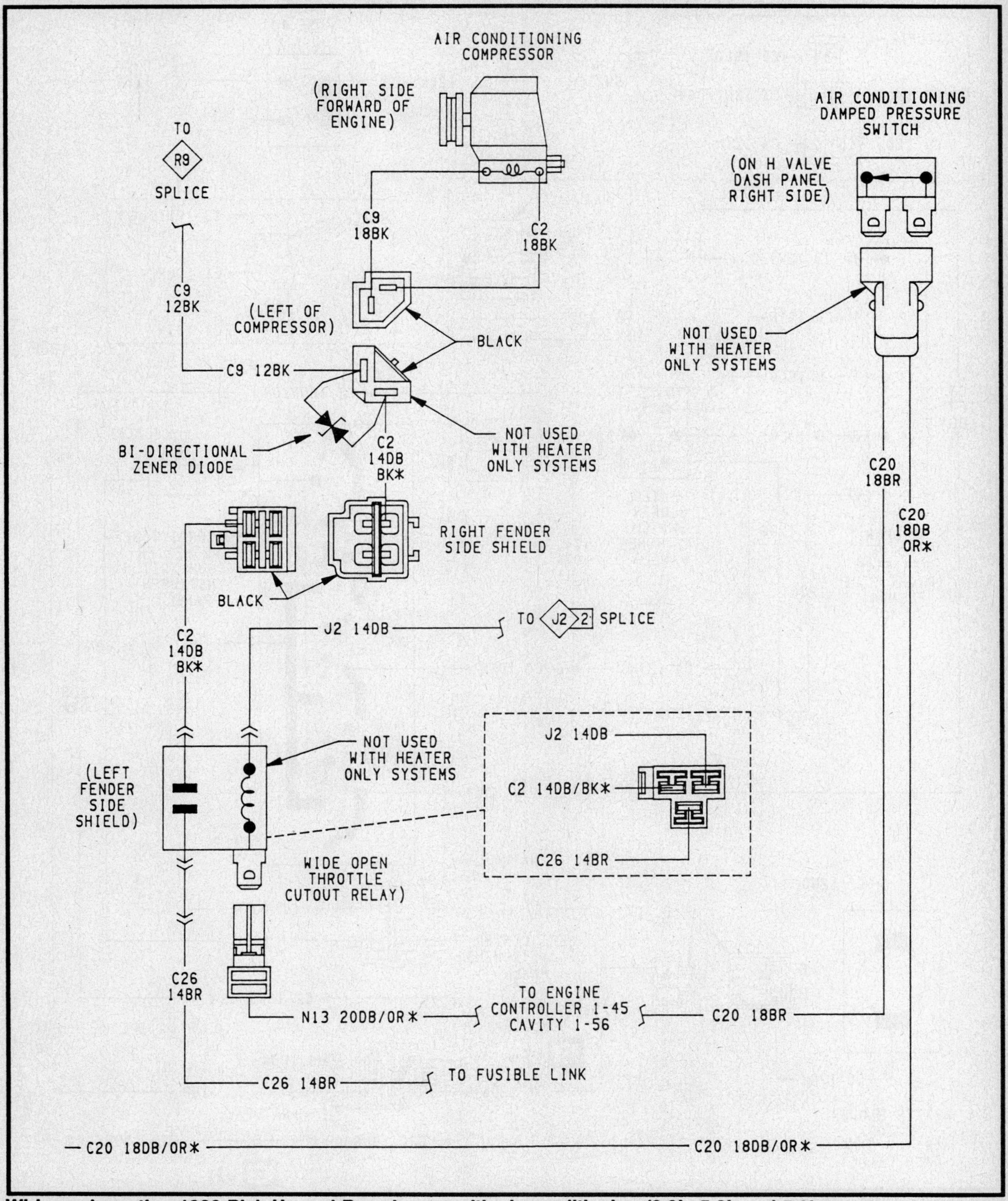
AIR CONDITIONING COMPRESSOR
(RIGHT SIDE FORWARD OF ENGINE)
TO
R9
SPLICE
C9 18BK
C2 18BK
C9 12BK
(LEFT OF COMPRESSOR)
BLACK
C9 12BK
BI-DIRECTIONAL ZENER DIODE
C2 14DB BK*
NOT USED WITH HEATER ONLY SYSTEMS
AIR CONDITIONING DAMPED PRESSURE SWITCH
(ON H VALVE DASH PANEL RIGHT SIDE)
NOT USED WITH HEATER ONLY SYSTEMS
C20 18BR
C20 18DB OR*
RIGHT FENDER SIDE SHIELD
BLACK
C2 14DB BK*
J2 14DB
TO J2 2 SPLICE
(LEFT FENDER SIDE SHIELD)
NOT USED WITH HEATER ONLY SYSTEMS
WIDE OPEN THROTTLE CUTOUT RELAY)
J2 14DB
C2 14DB/BK*
C26 14BR
C26 14BR
N13 20DB/OR*
TO ENGINE CONTROLLER 1-45 CAVITY 1-56
C20 18BR
C26 14BR
TO FUSIBLE LINK
C20 18DB/OR*
C20 18DB/OR*

Wiring schematic—1989 Pick-Up and Ramcharger with air conditioning (3.9L, 5.2L and 5.9L gasoline engines)

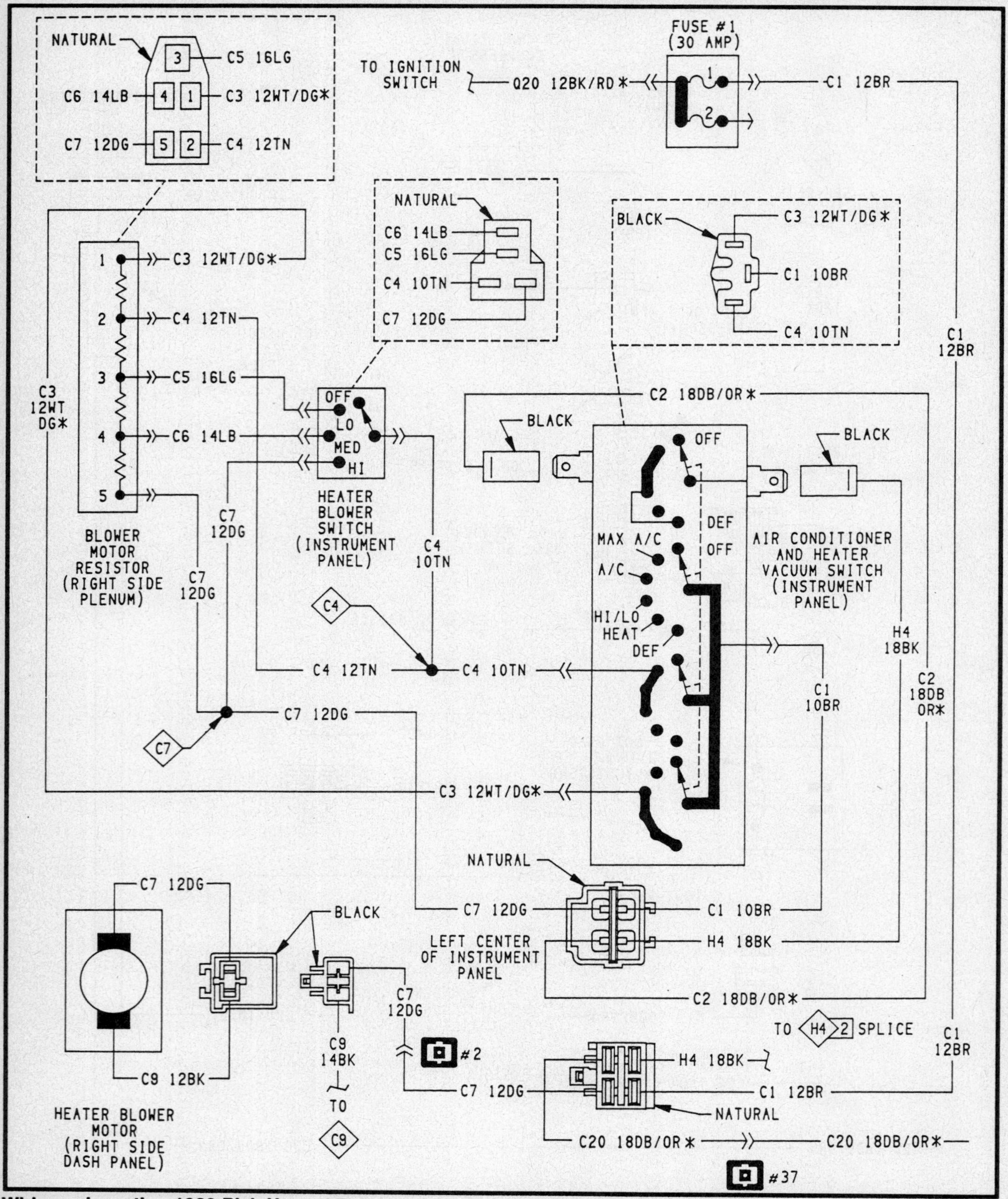
NATURAL
C5 16LG
C6 14LB
C3 12WT/DG*
C7 12DG
C4 12TN
TO IGNITION SWITCH
Q20 12BK/RD*
FUSE #1 (30 AMP)
C1 12BR
NATURAL
C6 14LB
C5 16LG
C4 10TN
C7 12DG
BLACK
C3 12WT/DG*
C1 10BR
C4 10TN
C3 12WT/DG*
C4 12TN
C5 16LG
C6 14LB
OFF
LO
MED
HI
C2 18DB/OR*
BLACK
BLACK
OFF
DEF
OFF
MAX A/C
A/C
HI/LO
HEAT
DEF
BLOWER MOTOR RESISTOR (RIGHT SIDE PLENUM)
HEATER BLOWER SWITCH (INSTRUMENT PANEL)
C4 10TN
C7 12DG
C7 12DG
AIR CONDITIONER AND HEATER VACUUM SWITCH (INSTRUMENT PANEL)
H4 18BK
C2 18DB OR*
C1 10BR
C4 12TN
C4 10TN
C7 12DG
C3 12WT/DG*
NATURAL
C7 12DG
C1 10BR
H4 18BK
LEFT CENTER OF INSTRUMENT PANEL
C2 18DB/OR*
BLACK
C7 12DG
C9 12BK
C7 12DG
C9 14BK
TO C9
#2
TO H4 2 SPLICE
H4 18BK
C1 12BR
C7 12DG
NATURAL
C20 18DB/OR*
C20 18DB/OR*
#37
HEATER BLOWER MOTOR (RIGHT SIDE DASH PANEL)

Wiring schematic—1989 Pick-Up and Ramcharger with air conditioning (5.9L diesel engine)

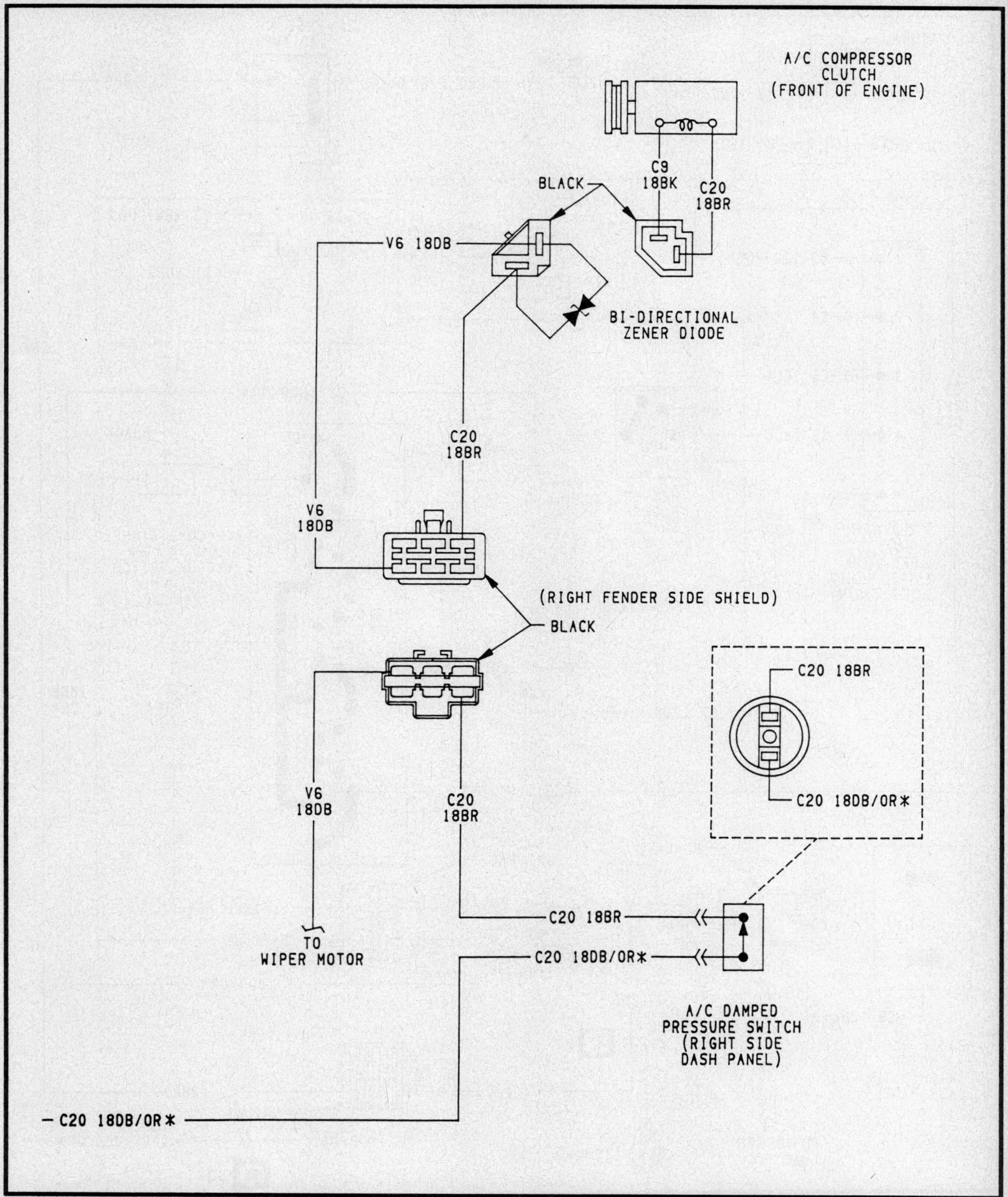
A/C COMPRESSOR
CLUTCH
(FRONT OF ENGINE)
BLACK
C9
18BK
C20
18BR
V6 18DB
BI-DIRECTIONAL
ZENER DIODE
C20
18BR
V6
18DB
(RIGHT FENDER SIDE SHIELD)
BLACK
C20 18BR
C20 18DB/OR*
V6
18DB
C20
18BR
TO
WIPER MOTOR
C20 18BR
C20 18DB/OR*
A/C DAMPED
PRESSURE SWITCH
(RIGHT SIDE
DASH PANEL)
C20 18DB/OR*

Wiring schematic—1989 Pick-Up and Ramcharger with air conditioning (5.9L diesel engine)

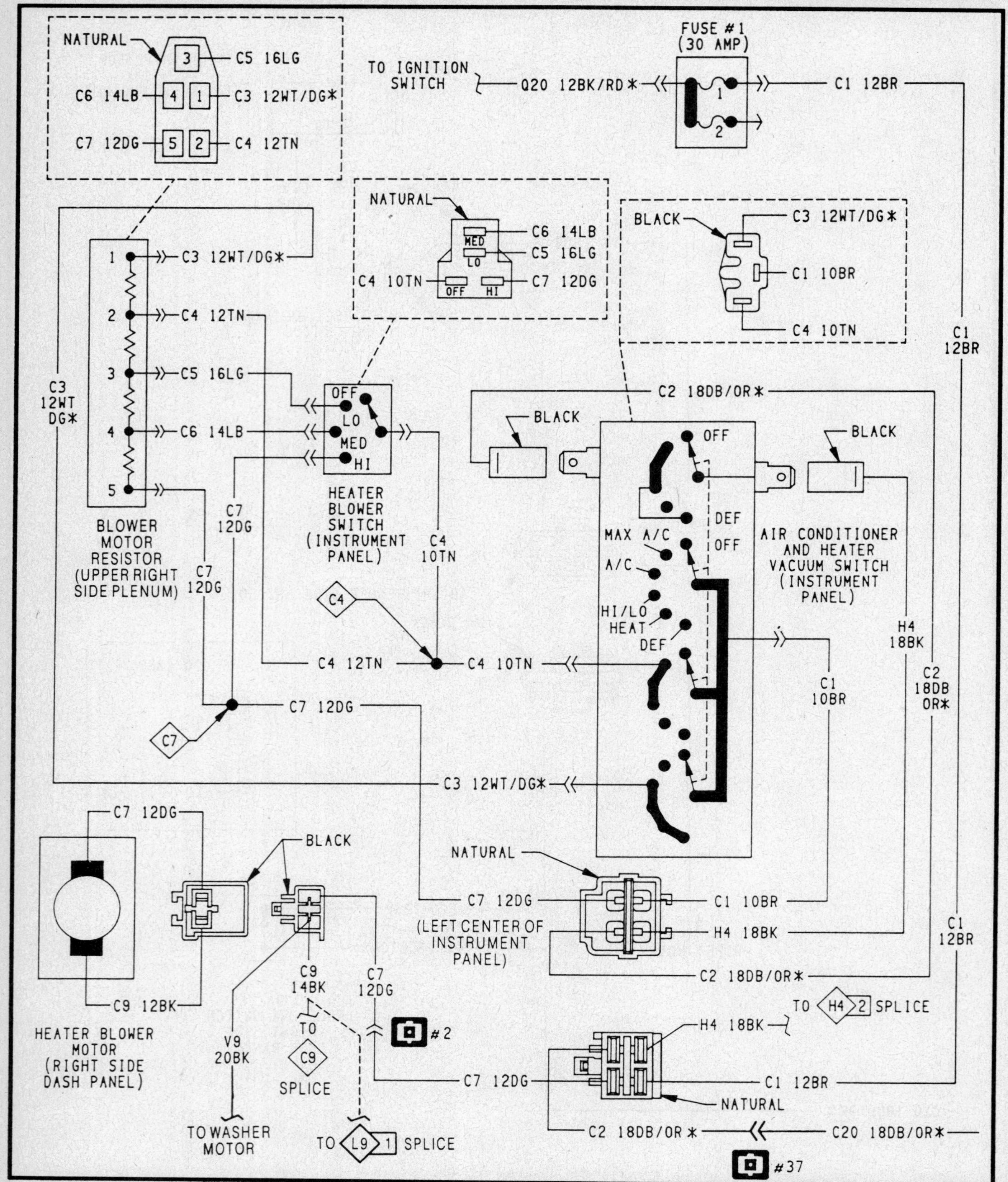
NATURAL
C5 16LG
C6 14LB
C3 12WT/DG*
C7 12DG
C4 12TN
TO IGNITION SWITCH
Q20 12BK/RD*
FUSE #1 (30 AMP)
C1 12BR
NATURAL
C6 14LB
MED
C5 16LG
LO
C4 10TN
OFF
HI
C7 12DG
BLACK
C3 12WT/DG*
C1 10BR
C4 10TN
C3 12WT DG*
C4 12TN
C5 16LG
C6 14LB
C2 18DB/OR*
BLACK
OFF
LO
MED
HI
HEATER BLOWER SWITCH (INSTRUMENT PANEL)
BLOWER MOTOR RESISTOR (UPPER RIGHT SIDE PLENUM)
C7 12DG
C4 10TN
DEF
OFF
MAX A/C
A/C
HI/LO HEAT
DEF
AIR CONDITIONER AND HEATER VACUUM SWITCH (INSTRUMENT PANEL)
H4 18BK
C1 10BR
C2 18DB OR*
C1 12BR
C4
C4 12TN
C4 10TN
C7 12DG
C7
C3 12WT/DG*
C7 12DG
BLACK
NATURAL
C7 12DG
C1 10BR
H4 18BK
(LEFT CENTER OF INSTRUMENT PANEL)
C2 18DB/OR*
C9 12BK
C9 14BK
C7 12DG
HEATER BLOWER MOTOR (RIGHT SIDE DASH PANEL)
V9 20BK
TO C9 SPLICE
#2
TO H4 2 SPLICE
H4 18BK
C7 12DG
C1 12BR
NATURAL
C2 18DB/OR*
C20 18DB/OR*
TO WASHER MOTOR
TO L9 1 SPLICE
#37

Wiring schematic—1990–91 Pick-Up and Ramcharger with air conditioning (3.9L, 5.2L and 5.9L gasoline engines)

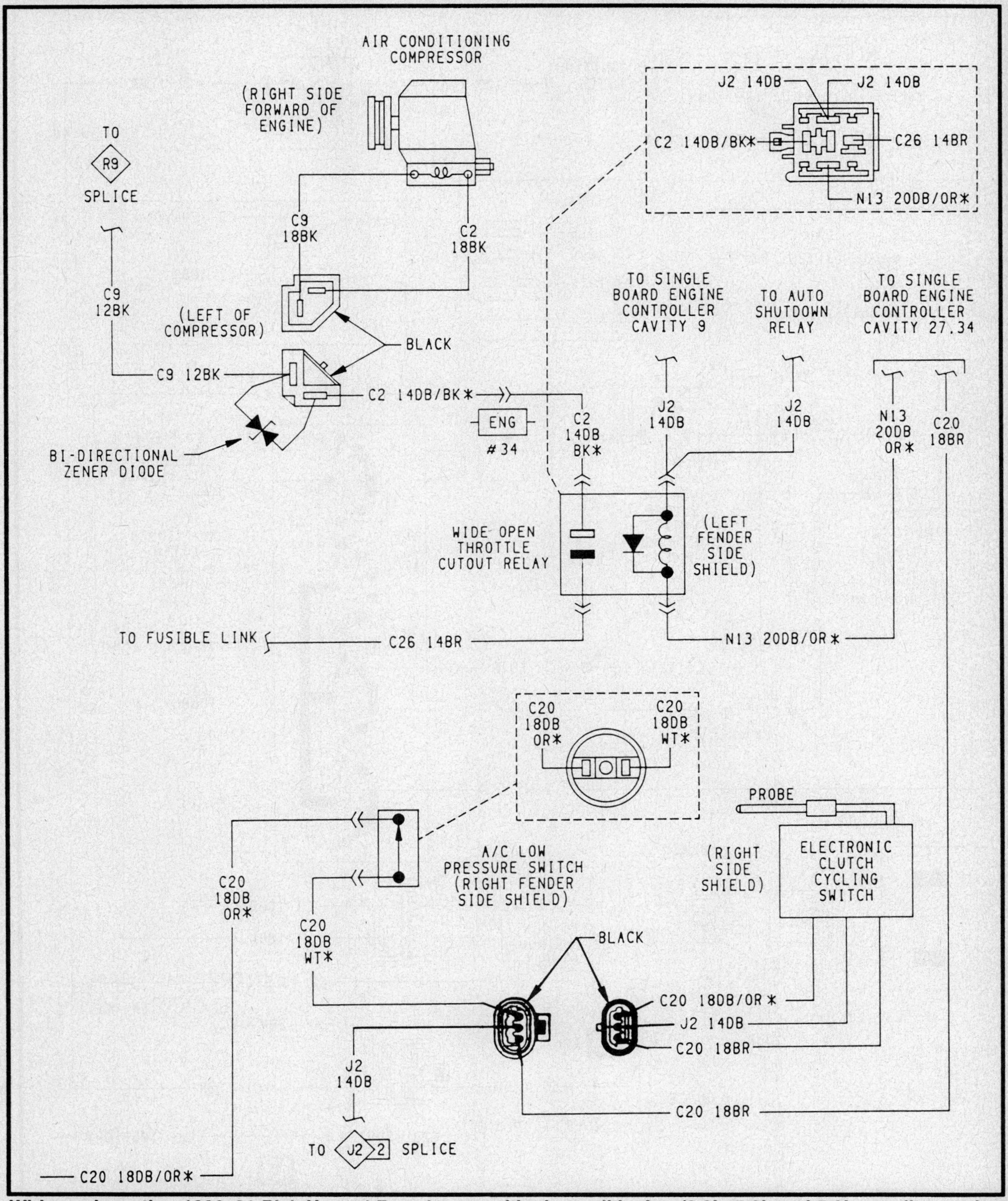
AIR CONDITIONING COMPRESSOR
(RIGHT SIDE FORWARD OF ENGINE)
TO R9 SPLICE
C9 18BK
C2 18BK
C9 12BK
(LEFT OF COMPRESSOR)
BLACK
C9 12BK
C2 14DB/BK*
BI-DIRECTIONAL ZENER DIODE
ENG #34
J2 14DB
J2 14DB
C2 14DB/BK*
C26 14BR
N13 20DB/OR*
TO SINGLE BOARD ENGINE CONTROLLER CAVITY 9
TO AUTO SHUTDOWN RELAY
TO SINGLE BOARD ENGINE CONTROLLER CAVITY 27.34
C2 14DB BK*
J2 14DB
J2 14DB
N13 20DB OR*
C20 18BR
WIDE OPEN THROTTLE CUTOUT RELAY
(LEFT FENDER SIDE SHIELD)
TO FUSIBLE LINK
C26 14BR
N13 20DB/OR*
C20 18DB OR*
C20 18DB WT*
PROBE
A/C LOW PRESSURE SWITCH (RIGHT FENDER SIDE SHIELD)
(RIGHT SIDE SHIELD)
ELECTRONIC CLUTCH CYCLING SWITCH
C20 18DB OR*
C20 18DB WT*
BLACK
C20 18DB/OR*
J2 14DB
C20 18BR
J2 14DB
C20 18BR
TO J2 2 SPLICE
C20 18DB/OR*

Wiring schematic—1990–91 Pick-Up and Ramcharger with air conditioning (3.9L, 5.2L and 5.9L gasoline engines)

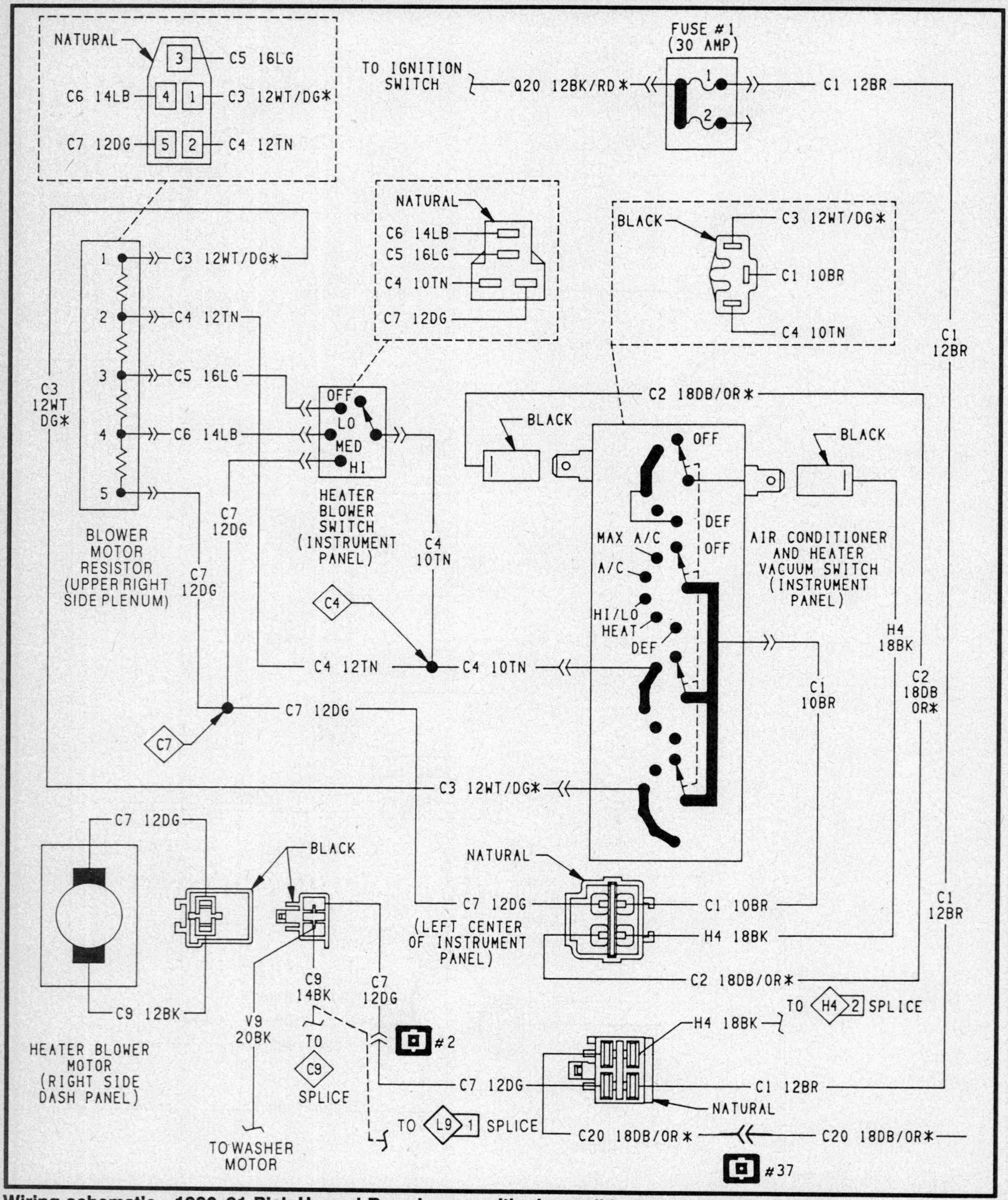
NATURAL
C5 16LG
C6 14LB
C3 12WT/DG*
C7 12DG
C4 12TN
TO IGNITION SWITCH
Q20 12BK/RD*
FUSE #1 (30 AMP)
C1 12BR
NATURAL
C6 14LB
C5 16LG
C4 10TN
C7 12DG
BLACK
C3 12WT/DG*
C1 10BR
C4 10TN
C4 12TN
C5 16LG
C6 14LB
OFF
LO
MED
HI
HEATER BLOWER SWITCH (INSTRUMENT PANEL)
BLOWER MOTOR RESISTOR (UPPER RIGHT SIDE PLENUM)
C2 18DB/OR*
BLACK
OFF
DEF
MAX A/C
A/C
HI/LO HEAT
AIR CONDITIONER AND HEATER VACUUM SWITCH (INSTRUMENT PANEL)
H4 18BK
C1 10BR
C7 12DG
C3 12WT/DG*
NATURAL
(LEFT CENTER OF INSTRUMENT PANEL)
H4 18BK
C2 18DB/OR*
HEATER BLOWER MOTOR (RIGHT SIDE DASH PANEL)
C9 12BK
V9 20BK
C9 14BK
TO C9 SPLICE
#2
TO H4 2 SPLICE
C1 12BR
TO L9 1 SPLICE
C20 18DB/OR*
#37
TO WASHER MOTOR

Wiring schematic—1990–91 Pick-Up and Ramcharger with air conditioning (5.9L diesel engine)

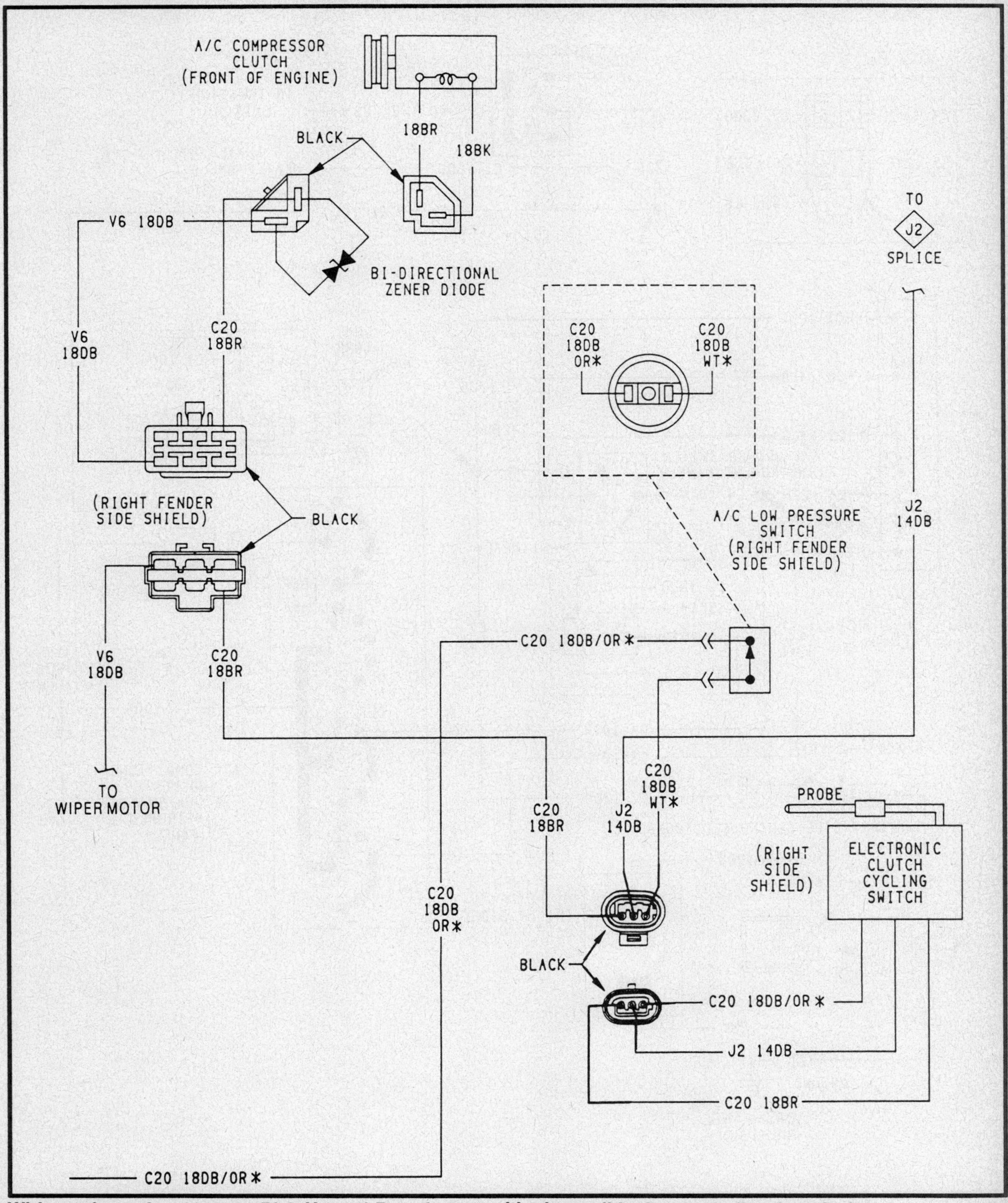
A/C COMPRESSOR CLUTCH (FRONT OF ENGINE)
BLACK
18BR
18BK
V6 18DB
BI-DIRECTIONAL ZENER DIODE
TO J2 SPLICE
C20 18DB OR*
C20 18DB WT*
V6 18DB
C20 18BR
(RIGHT FENDER SIDE SHIELD)
BLACK
A/C LOW PRESSURE SWITCH (RIGHT FENDER SIDE SHIELD)
J2 14DB
C20 18DB/OR*
V6 18DB
C20 18BR
TO WIPER MOTOR
C20 18DB WT*
C20 18BR
J2 14DB
PROBE
(RIGHT SIDE SHIELD)
ELECTRONIC CLUTCH CYCLING SWITCH
C20 18DB OR*
BLACK
C20 18DB/OR*
J2 14DB
C20 18BR
C20 18DB/OR*

Wiring schematic—1990–91 Pick-Up and Ramcharger with air conditioning (5.9L diesel engine)

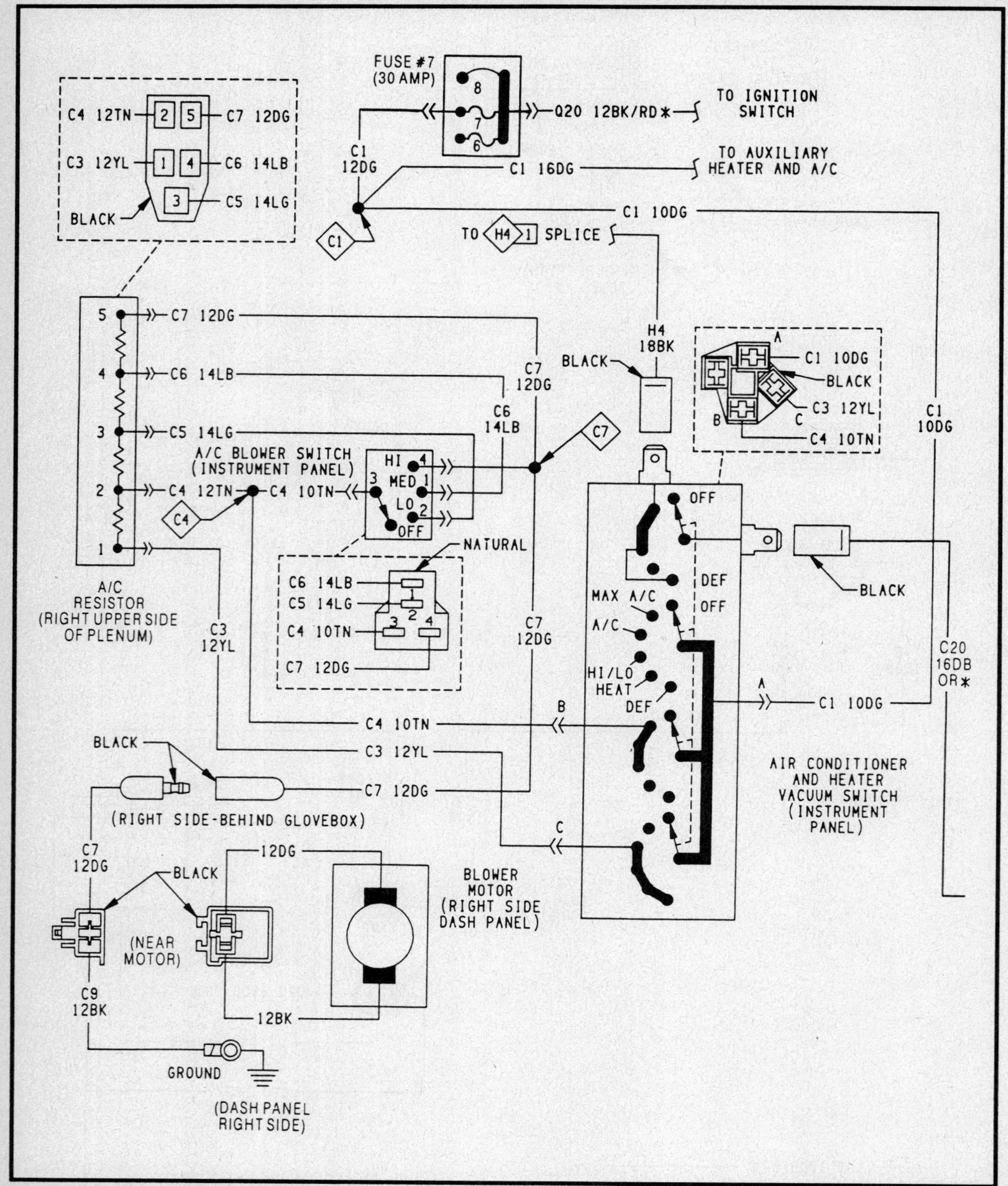
FUSE #7
(30 AMP)
8
7
6
Q20 12BK/RD *
TO IGNITION SWITCH
C1 12DG
C1 16DG
TO AUXILIARY HEATER AND A/C
C1 10DG
C1
TO H4 1 SPLICE
C4 12TN
2
5
C7 12DG
C3 12YL
1
4
C6 14LB
3
C5 14LG
BLACK
5
C7 12DG
4
C6 14LB
3
C5 14LG
2
C4 12TN
C4 10TN
1
C4
A/C RESISTOR
(RIGHT UPPER SIDE OF PLENUM)
A/C BLOWER SWITCH
(INSTRUMENT PANEL)
HI
MED
LO
OFF
C7 12DG
C6 14LB
C7
H4 18BK
BLACK
NATURAL
C6 14LB
C5 14LG
C4 10TN
C7 12DG
C3 12YL
A
C1 10DG
BLACK
C3 12YL
B
C
C4 10TN
C1 10DG
OFF
DEF
OFF
MAX A/C
A/C
HI/LO HEAT
DEF
BLACK
C20 16DB OR *
C1 10DG
C4 10TN
C3 12YL
C7 12DG
AIR CONDITIONER AND HEATER VACUUM SWITCH
(INSTRUMENT PANEL)
BLACK
(RIGHT SIDE-BEHIND GLOVEBOX)
C7 12DG
12DG
BLACK
(NEAR MOTOR)
BLOWER MOTOR
(RIGHT SIDE DASH PANEL)
C9 12BK
12BK
GROUND
(DASH PANEL RIGHT SIDE)

Wiring schematic—Van with air conditioning

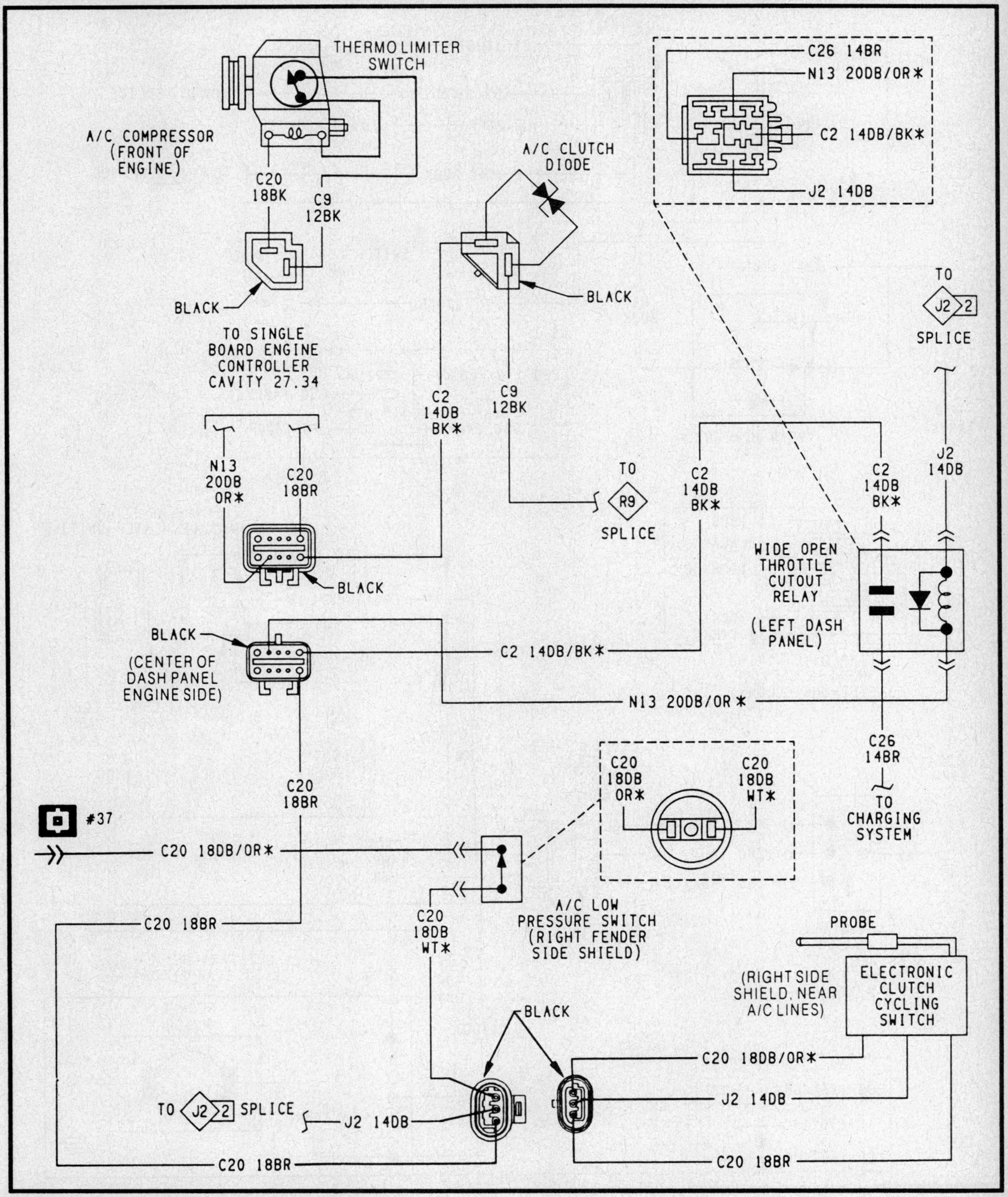
THERMO LIMITER SWITCH
A/C COMPRESSOR (FRONT OF ENGINE)
C20 18BK
C9 12BK
BLACK
TO SINGLE BOARD ENGINE CONTROLLER CAVITY 27.34
A/C CLUTCH DIODE
BLACK
C26 14BR
N13 20DB/OR*
C2 14DB/BK*
J2 14DB
TO
J2 2
SPLICE
C2 14DB BK*
C9 12BK
N13 20DB OR*
C20 18BR
TO
R9
SPLICE
C2 14DB BK*
C2 14DB BK*
J2 14DB
WIDE OPEN THROTTLE CUTOUT RELAY
(LEFT DASH PANEL)
BLACK
BLACK
(CENTER OF DASH PANEL ENGINE SIDE)
C2 14DB/BK*
N13 20DB/OR*
C26 14BR
TO CHARGING SYSTEM
C20 18DB OR*
C20 18DB WT*
C20 18BR
#37
C20 18DB/OR*
C20 18BR
C20 18DB WT*
A/C LOW PRESSURE SWITCH (RIGHT FENDER SIDE SHIELD)
PROBE
(RIGHT SIDE SHIELD, NEAR A/C LINES)
ELECTRONIC CLUTCH CYCLING SWITCH
BLACK
C20 18DB/OR*
J2 14DB
TO J2 2 SPLICE
J2 14DB
C20 18BR
C20 18BR

Wiring schematic—Van with air conditioning

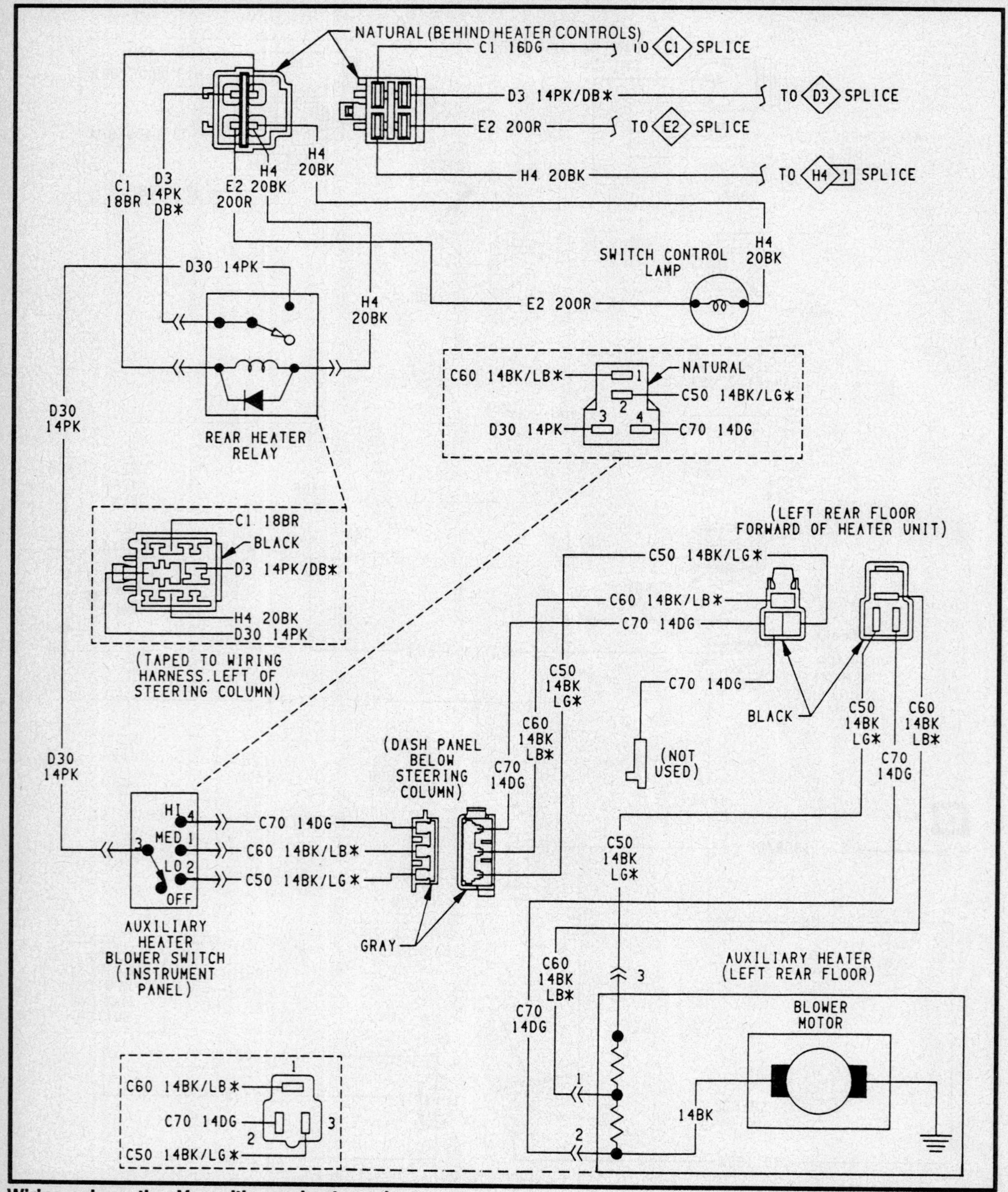
NATURAL (BEHIND HEATER CONTROLS)
C1 16DG
TO C1 SPLICE
D3 14PK/DB*
TO D3 SPLICE
E2 20OR
TO E2 SPLICE
H4 20BK
TO H4 1 SPLICE
C1 18BR
D3 14PK DB*
E2 20OR
H4 20BK
H4 20BK
SWITCH CONTROL LAMP
H4 20BK
D30 14PK
H4 20BK
E2 20OR
D30 14PK
REAR HEATER RELAY
C60 14BK/LB*
NATURAL
C50 14BK/LG*
D30 14PK
C70 14DG
C1 18BR
BLACK
D3 14PK/DB*
H4 20BK
D30 14PK
(TAPED TO WIRING HARNESS.LEFT OF STEERING COLUMN)
(LEFT REAR FLOOR FORWARD OF HEATER UNIT)
C50 14BK/LG*
C60 14BK/LB*
C70 14DG
C50 14BK LG*
C70 14DG
BLACK
C60 14BK LB*
C50 14BK LG*
C60 14BK LB*
(NOT USED)
(DASH PANEL BELOW STEERING COLUMN)
C70 14DG
C70 14DG
D30 14PK
HI 4
MED 1
LO 2
OFF
C70 14DG
C60 14BK/LB*
C50 14BK/LG*
C50 14BK LG*
AUXILIARY HEATER BLOWER SWITCH (INSTRUMENT PANEL)
GRAY
C60 14BK LB*
C70 14DG
AUXILIARY HEATER (LEFT REAR FLOOR)
BLOWER MOTOR
14BK
C60 14BK/LB*
C70 14DG
C50 14BK/LG*

Wiring schematic—Van with rear heater only

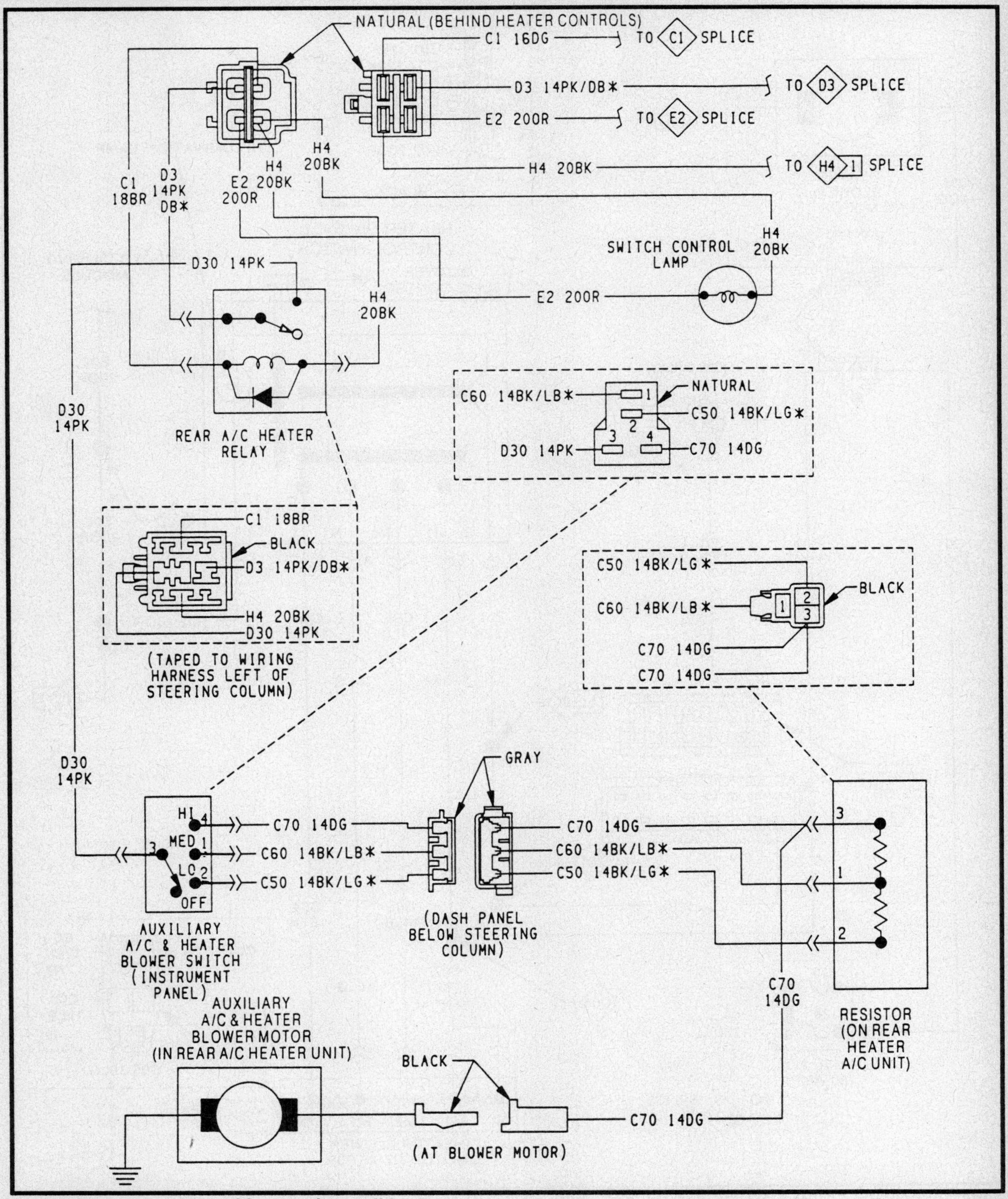
NATURAL (BEHIND HEATER CONTROLS)
C1 16DG
TO C1 SPLICE
D3 14PK/DB*
TO D3 SPLICE
E2 20OR
TO E2 SPLICE
H4 20BK
TO H4 1 SPLICE
C1 18BR
D3 14PK DB*
E2 20OR
H4 20BK
SWITCH CONTROL LAMP
D30 14PK
REAR A/C HEATER RELAY
C60 14BK/LB*
NATURAL
C50 14BK/LG*
D30 14PK
C70 14DG
C1 18BR
BLACK
D3 14PK/DB*
H4 20BK
D30 14PK
(TAPED TO WIRING HARNESS LEFT OF STEERING COLUMN)
C50 14BK/LG*
C60 14BK/LB*
BLACK
C70 14DG
C70 14DG
GRAY
HI
MED
LO
OFF
C70 14DG
C60 14BK/LB*
C50 14BK/LG*
AUXILIARY A/C & HEATER BLOWER SWITCH (INSTRUMENT PANEL)
(DASH PANEL BELOW STEERING COLUMN)
RESISTOR (ON REAR HEATER A/C UNIT)
AUXILIARY A/C & HEATER BLOWER MOTOR (IN REAR A/C HEATER UNIT)
BLACK
(AT BLOWER MOTOR)

Wiring schematic—Van with rear air conditioning

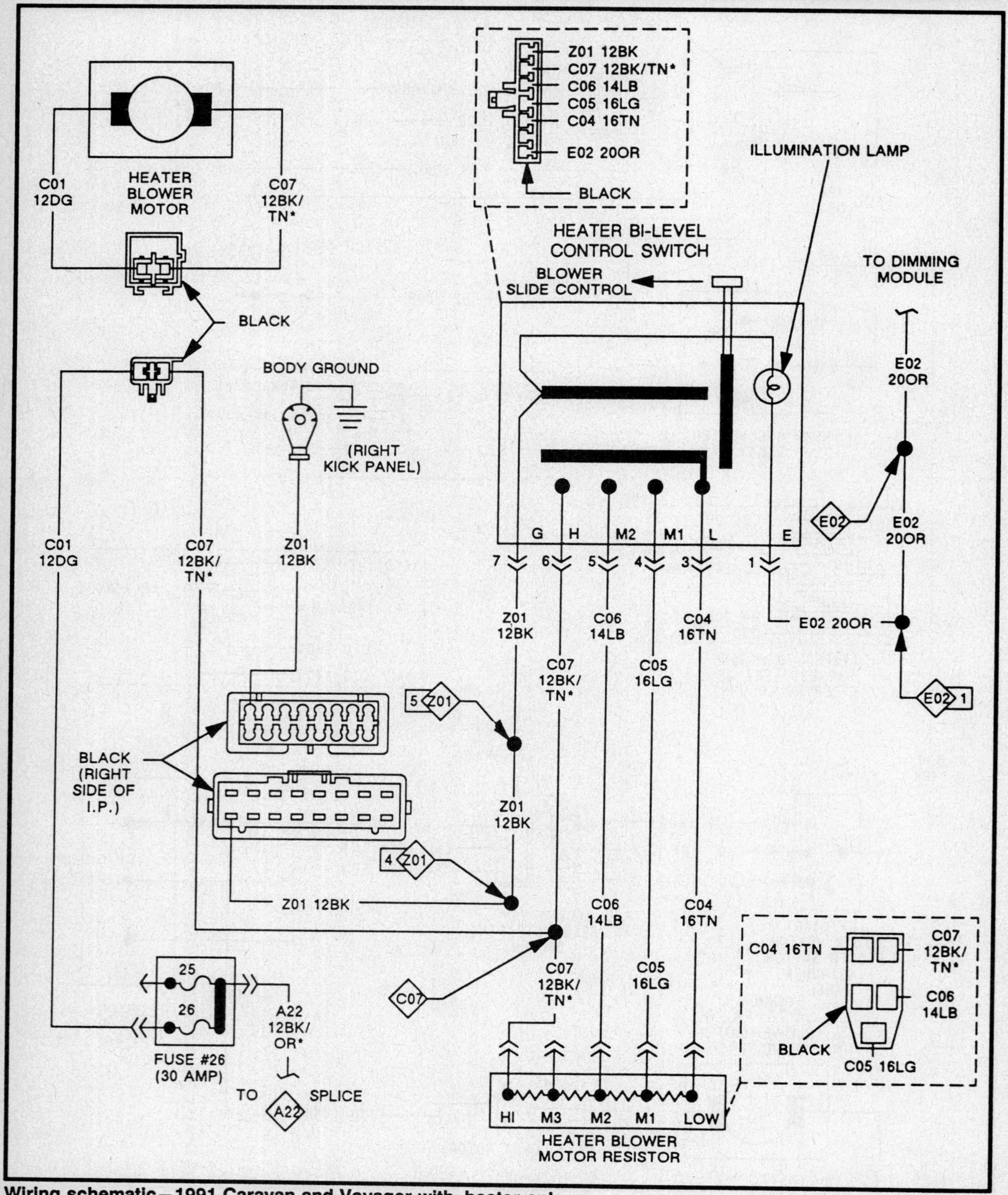
Z01 12BK
C07 12BK/TN*
C06 14LB
C05 16LG
C04 16TN
E02 20OR
BLACK
ILLUMINATION LAMP
HEATER BI-LEVEL CONTROL SWITCH
BLOWER SLIDE CONTROL
TO DIMMING MODULE
C01 12DG
HEATER BLOWER MOTOR
C07 12BK/TN*
BLACK
BODY GROUND
(RIGHT KICK PANEL)
E02 20OR
G H M2 M1 L E
7 6 5 4 3 1
C01 12DG
C07 12BK/TN*
Z01 12BK
Z01 12BK
C06 14LB
C04 16TN
E02 20OR
C07 12BK/TN*
C05 16LG
5 Z01
E02 1
BLACK (RIGHT SIDE OF I.P.)
Z01 12BK
4 Z01
Z01 12BK
C06 14LB
C04 16TN
C04 16TN
C07 12BK/TN*
C07 12BK/TN*
C05 16LG
C06 14LB
25
26
C07
FUSE #26 (30 AMP)
A22 12BK/OR*
BLACK
C05 16LG
TO SPLICE A22
HI M3 M2 M1 LOW
HEATER BLOWER MOTOR RESISTOR

Wiring schematic—1991 Caravan and Voyager with heater only

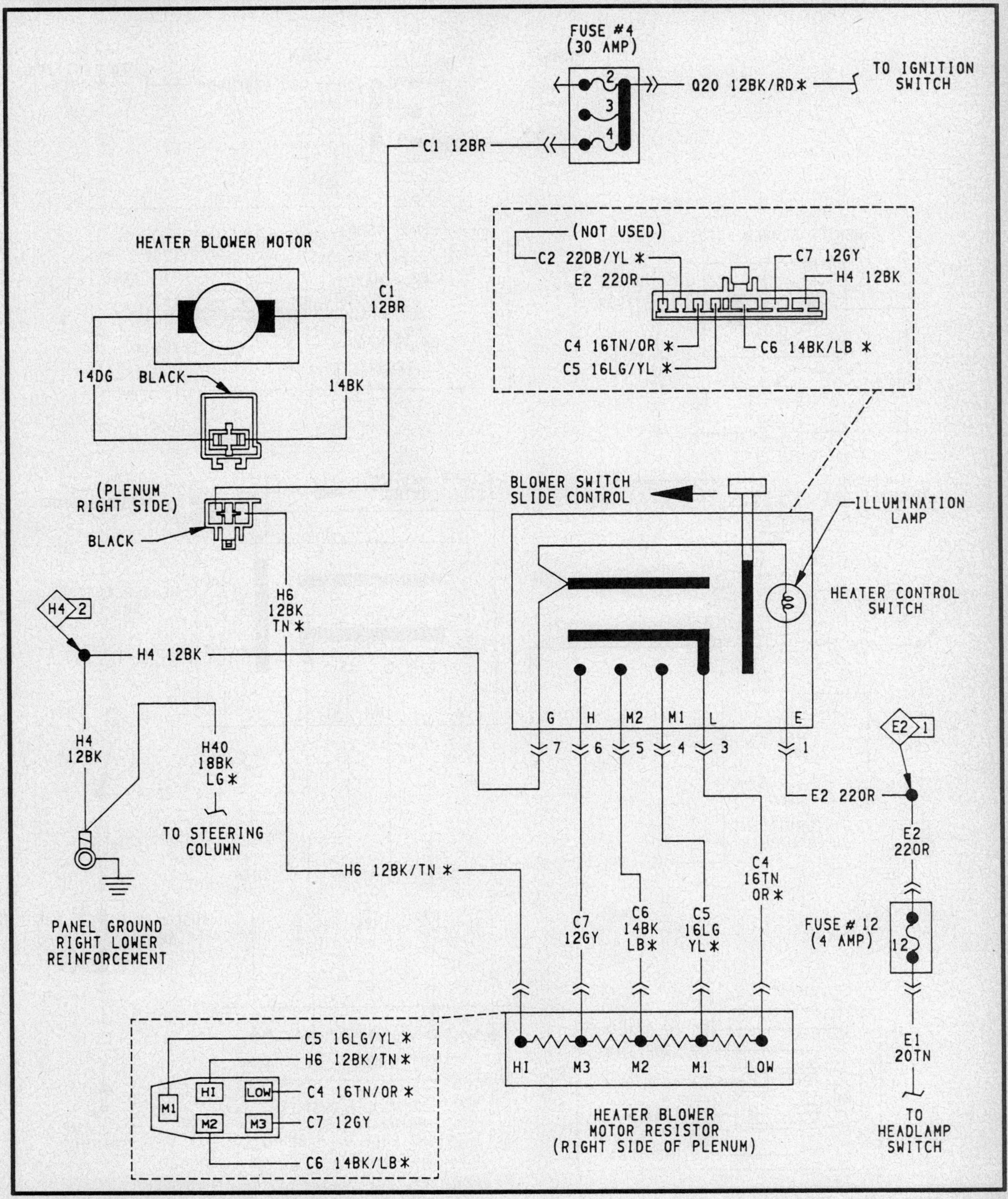
FUSE #4
(30 AMP)
Q20 12BK/RD *
TO IGNITION SWITCH
C1 12BR
(NOT USED)
C2 22DB/YL *
C7 12GY
E2 22OR
H4 12BK
C4 16TN/OR *
C6 14BK/LB *
C5 16LG/YL *
HEATER BLOWER MOTOR
C1
12BR
14DG
BLACK
14BK
(PLENUM
RIGHT SIDE)
BLACK
BLOWER SWITCH
SLIDE CONTROL
ILLUMINATION
LAMP
HEATER CONTROL
SWITCH
H4 2
H4 12BK
H6
12BK
TN *
G H M2 M1 L E
7 6 5 4 3 1
E2 1
E2 22OR
H4
12BK
H40
18BK
LG *
TO STEERING
COLUMN
H6 12BK/TN *
C4
16TN
OR *
E2
22OR
C7
12GY
C6
14BK
LB *
C5
16LG
YL *
FUSE # 12
(4 AMP)
PANEL GROUND
RIGHT LOWER
REINFORCEMENT
C5 16LG/YL *
H6 12BK/TN *
HI
LOW
C4 16TN/OR *
M1
M2
M3
C7 12GY
C6 14BK/LB *
HI M3 M2 M1 LOW
E1
20TN
TO
HEADLAMP
SWITCH
HEATER BLOWER
MOTOR RESISTOR
(RIGHT SIDE OF PLENUM)

Wiring schematic – 1989–90 Dakota with heater only

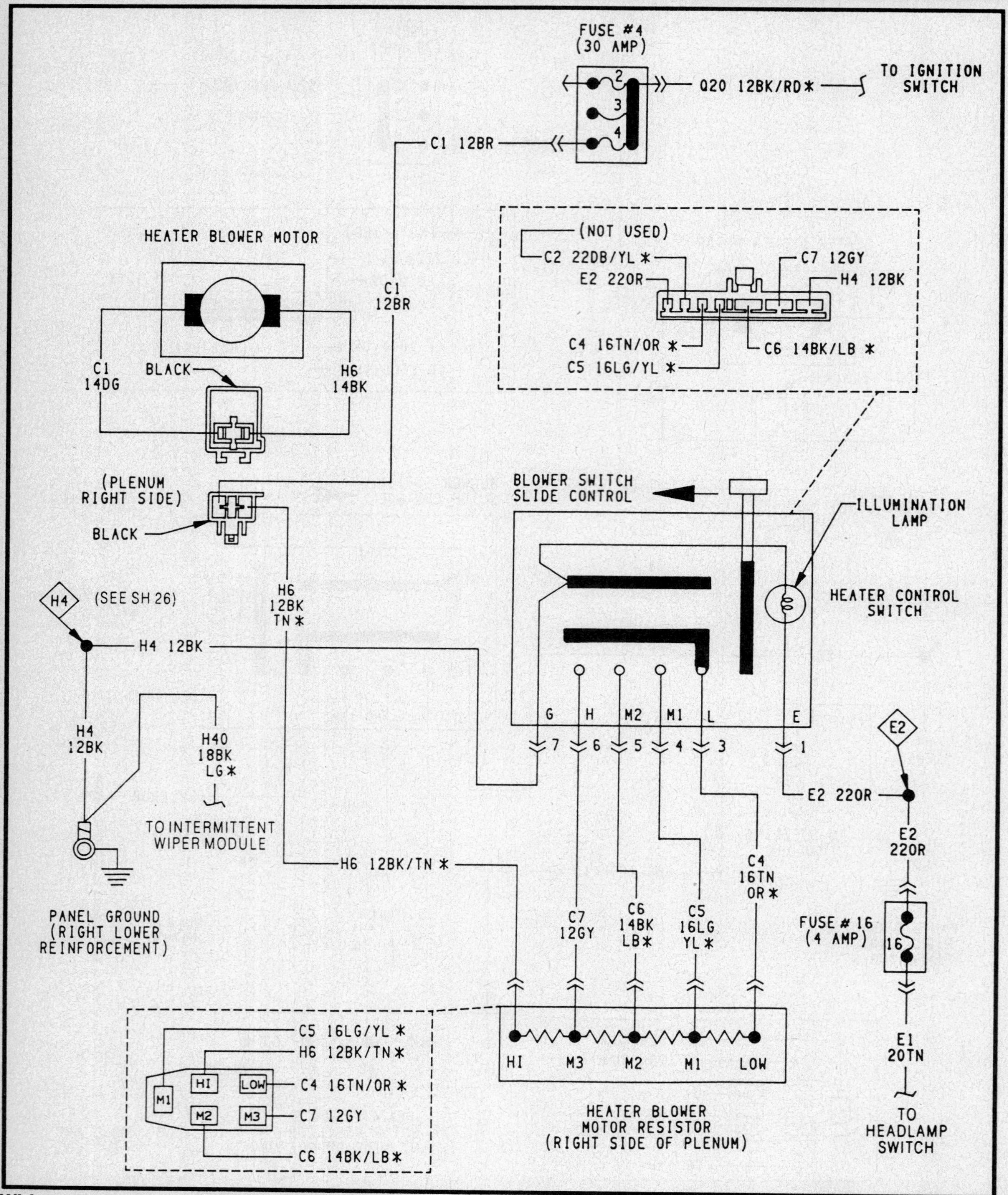
FUSE #4
(30 AMP)
Q20 12BK/RD*
TO IGNITION SWITCH
C1 12BR
HEATER BLOWER MOTOR
C1
12BR
(NOT USED)
C2 22DB/YL*
E2 22OR
C7 12GY
H4 12BK
C4 16TN/OR*
C5 16LG/YL*
C6 14BK/LB*
C1
14DG
BLACK
H6
14BK
(PLENUM
RIGHT SIDE)
BLACK
BLOWER SWITCH
SLIDE CONTROL
ILLUMINATION
LAMP
HEATER CONTROL
SWITCH
H4
(SEE SH 26)
H6
12BK
TN*
H4 12BK
G H M2 M1 L E
7 6 5 4 3 1
E2
E2 22OR
H4
12BK
H40
18BK
LG*
TO INTERMITTENT
WIPER MODULE
E2
22OR
H6 12BK/TN*
C4
16TN
OR*
PANEL GROUND
(RIGHT LOWER
REINFORCEMENT)
C7
12GY
C6
14BK
LB*
C5
16LG
YL*
FUSE #16
(4 AMP)
16
C5 16LG/YL*
H6 12BK/TN*
C4 16TN/OR*
C7 12GY
C6 14BK/LB*
M1 HI LOW M2 M3
HI M3 M2 M1 LOW
E1
20TN
HEATER BLOWER
MOTOR RESISTOR
(RIGHT SIDE OF PLENUM)
TO
HEADLAMP
SWITCH

Wiring schematic—1991 Dakota with heater only

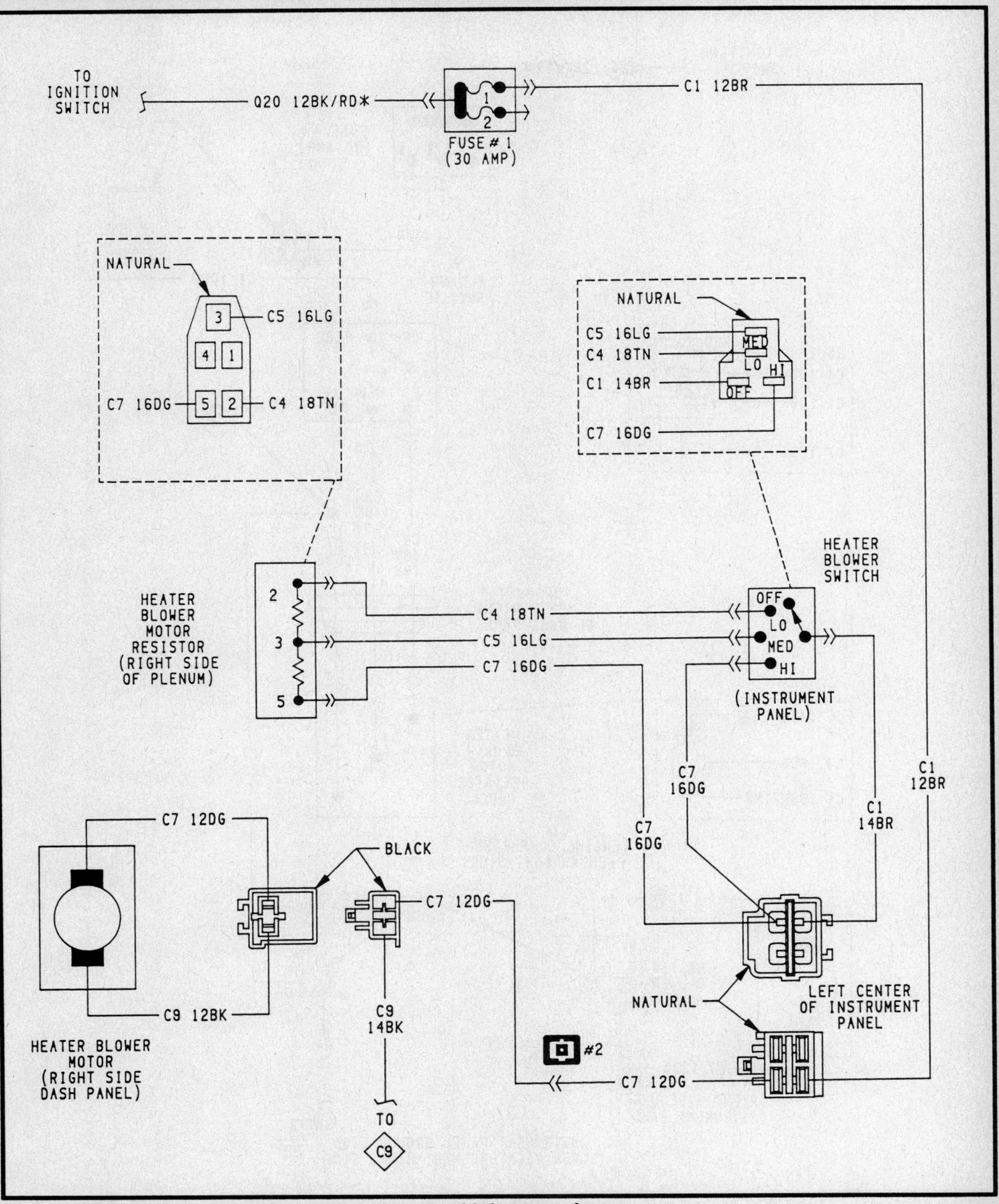
TO IGNITION SWITCH
Q20 12BK/RD*
FUSE # 1 (30 AMP)
C1 12BR
NATURAL
C5 16LG
C7 16DG
C4 18TN
NATURAL
C5 16LG
C4 18TN
C1 14BR
C7 16DG
MED
LO
HI
OFF
HEATER BLOWER SWITCH
HEATER BLOWER MOTOR RESISTOR (RIGHT SIDE OF PLENUM)
C4 18TN
C5 16LG
C7 16DG
OFF
LO
MED
HI
(INSTRUMENT PANEL)
C7 16DG
C7 16DG
C1 14BR
C1 12BR
C7 12DG
BLACK
C7 12DG
C9 12BK
C9 14BK
TO
C9
#2
C7 12DG
NATURAL
LEFT CENTER OF INSTRUMENT PANEL
HEATER BLOWER MOTOR (RIGHT SIDE DASH PANEL)

Wiring schematic—Van, Pick-Up and Ramcharger with heater only

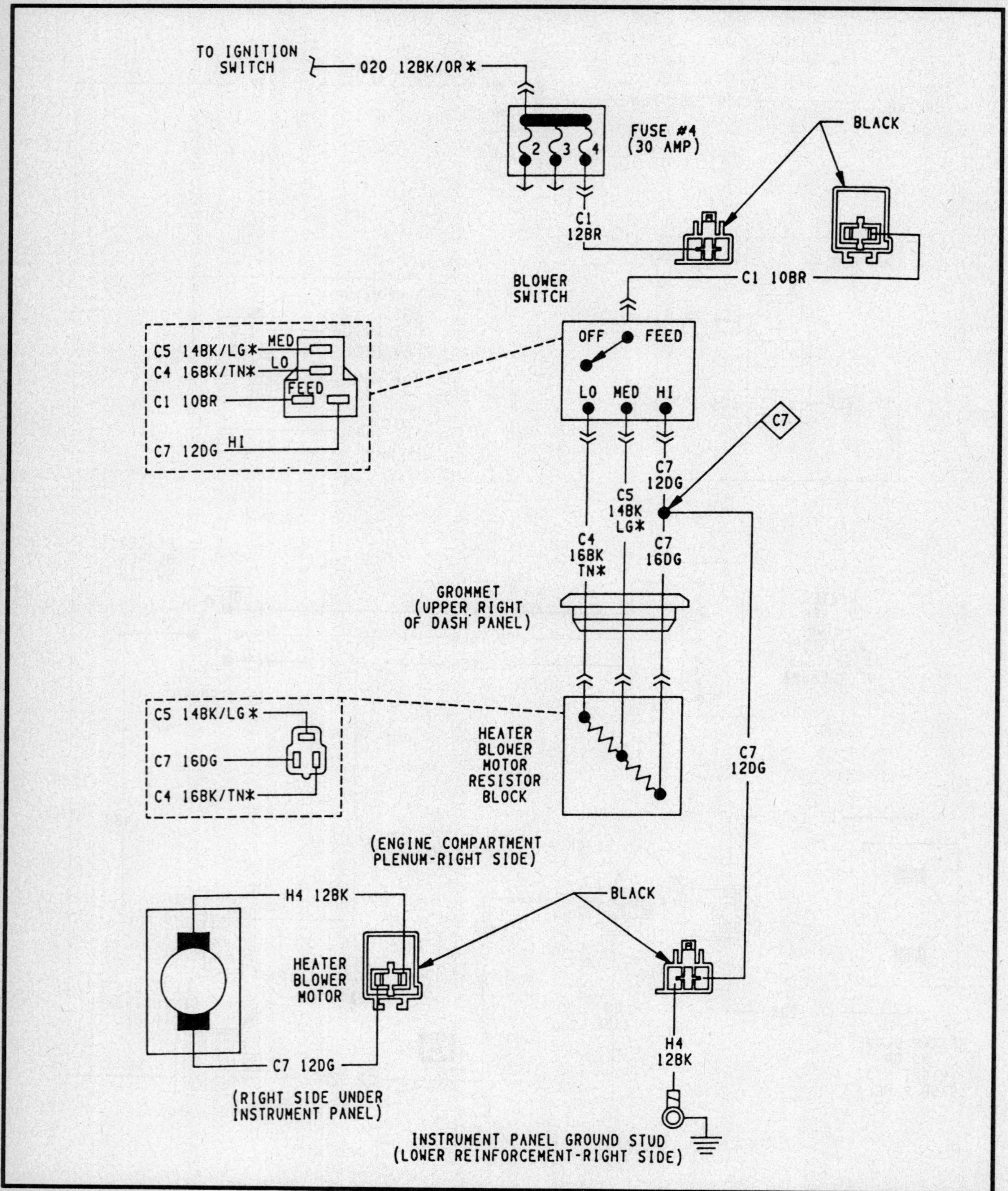
TO IGNITION SWITCH
Q20 12BK/OR*
FUSE #4 (30 AMP)
2
3
4
BLACK
C1 12BR
BLOWER SWITCH
C1 10BR
C5 14BK/LG*
MED
C4 16BK/TN*
LO
FEED
C1 10BR
C7 12DG
HI
OFF
FEED
LO
MED
HI
C7
C7 12DG
C5 14BK LG*
C4 16BK TN*
C7 16DG
GROMMET (UPPER RIGHT OF DASH PANEL)
C5 14BK/LG*
C7 16DG
C4 16BK/TN*
HEATER BLOWER MOTOR RESISTOR BLOCK
C7 12DG
(ENGINE COMPARTMENT PLENUM-RIGHT SIDE)
H4 12BK
BLACK
HEATER BLOWER MOTOR
C7 12DG
H4 12BK
(RIGHT SIDE UNDER INSTRUMENT PANEL)
INSTRUMENT PANEL GROUND STUD (LOWER REINFORCEMENT-RIGHT SIDE)

Wiring schematic – 1989–90 Caravan and Voyager with heater only

9 FORD MOTOR COMPANY 9

F-SERIES • BRONCO • E-SERIES • BRONCO II • RANGER • EXPLORER • AEROSTAR

SPECIFICATIONS

ENGINE IDENTIFICATION

Year	Model	Engine Displacement cu. in. (liter)	Engine Series Identification (VIN)	No. of Cylinders	Engine Type
1989	Aerostar	183 (3.0)	U	6	OHV
	Bronco	300 (4.9)	Y	6	OHV
	Bronco	302 (5.0)	N	8	OHV
	Bronco	351 (5.8)	H	8	OHV
	Bronco II	177 (2.9)	T	6	OHV
	E-150	300 (4.9)	Y	6	OHV
	E-150	302 (5.0)	N	8	OHV
	E-150	351 (5.8)	H	8	OHV
	E-250	300 (4.9)	Y	6	OHV
	E-250	302 (5.0)	N	8	OHV
	E-250	351 (5.8)	H	8	OHV
	E-250	445 (7.3)	M	8	Diesel
	E-250	460 (7.5)	G	8	OHV
	E-350	300 (4.9)	Y	6	OHV
	E-350	351 (5.8)	H	8	OHV
	E-350	445 (7.3)	M	8	Diesel
	E-350	460 (7.5)	G	8	OHV
	F-150	300 (4.9)	Y	6	OHV
	F-150	302 (5.0)	N	8	OHV
	F-150	351 (5.8)	H	8	OHV
	F-250	300 (4.9)	Y	6	OHV
	F-250	302 (5.0)	N	8	OHV
	F-250	351 (5.8)	H	8	OHV
	F-250	445 (7.3)	M	8	Diesel
	F-250	460 (7.5)	G	8	OHV
	F-350	300 (4.9)	Y	6	OHV
	F-350	351 (5.8)	H	8	OHV
	F-350	445 (7.3)	M	8	Diesel
	F-350	460 (7.5)	G	8	OHV
	Ranger	140 (2.3)	A	4	OHC
	Ranger	177 (2.9)	T	6	OHV
1990	Aerostar	183 (3.0)	U	6	OHV
	Aerostar	241 (4.0)	X	6	OHV
	Bronco	300 (4.9)	Y	6	OHV
	Bronco	302 (5.0)	N	8	OHV
	Bronco	351 (5.8)	H	8	OHV
	Bronco II	177 (2.9)	T	6	OHV
	E-150	300 (4.9)	Y	6	OHV
	E-150	302 (5.0)	N	8	OHV
	E-150	351 (5.8)	H	8	OHV
	E-250	300 (4.9)	Y	6	OHV
	E-250	302 (5.0)	N	8	OHV

ENGINE IDENTIFICATION

Year	Model	Engine Displacement cu. in. (liter)	Engine Series Identification (VIN)	No. of Cylinders	Engine Type
1990	E-250	351 (5.8)	H	8	OHV
	E-250	445 (7.3)	M	8	Diesel
	E-250	460 (7.5)	G	8	OHV
	E-350	300 (4.9)	Y	6	OHV
	E-350	351 (5.8)	H	8	OHV
	E-350	445 (7.3)	M	8	Diesel
	E-350	460 (7.5)	G	8	OHV
	F-150	300 (4.9)	Y	6	OHV
	F-150	302 (5.0)	N	8	OHV
	F-150	351 (5.8)	H	8	OHV
	F-250	300 (4.9)	Y	6	OHV
	F-250	302 (5.0)	N	8	OHV
	F-250	351 (5.8)	H	8	OHV
	F-250	445 (7.3)	M	8	Diesel
	F-250	460 (7.5)	G	8	OHV
	F-350	300 (4.9)	Y	6	OHV
	F-350	351 (5.8)	H	8	OHV
	F-350	445 (7.3)	M	8	Diesel
	F-350	460 (7.5)	G	8	OHV
	Ranger	140 (2.3)	A	4	OHC
	Ranger	177 (2.9)	T	6	OHV
	Ranger	241 (4.0)	X	6	OHV
1991	Aerostar	183 (3.0)	U	6	OHV
	Aerostar	241 (4.0)	X	6	OHV
	Bronco	300 (4.9)	Y	6	OHV
	Bronco	302 (5.0)	N	8	OHV
	Bronco	351 (5.8)	H	8	OHV
	Explorer	241 (4.0)	X	6	OHV
	E-150	300 (4.9)	Y	6	OHV
	E-150	302 (5.0)	N	8	OHV
	E-150	351 (5.8)	H	8	OHV
	E-250	300 (4.9)	Y	6	OHV
	E-250	302 (5.0)	N	8	OHV
	E-250	351 (5.8)	H	8	OHV
	E-250	445 (7.3)	M	8	Diesel
	E-250	460 (7.5)	G	8	OHV
	E-350	300 (4.9)	Y	6	OHV
	E-350	351 (5.8)	H	8	OHV
	E-350	445 (7.3)	M	8	Diesel
	E-350	460 (7.5)	G	8	OHV
	F-150	300 (4.9)	Y	6	OHV
	F-150	302 (5.0)	N	8	OHV
	F-150	351 (5.8)	H	8	OHV
	F-250	300 (4.9)	Y	6	OHV

ENGINE IDENTIFICATION

Year	Model	Engine Displacement cu. in. (liter)	Engine Series Identification (VIN)	No. of Cylinders	Engine Type
1991	F-250	302 (5.0)	N	8	OHV
	F-250	351 (5.8)	H	8	OHV
	F-250	445 (7.3)	M	8	Diesel
	F-250	460 (7.5)	G	8	OHV
	F-350	300 (4.9)	Y	6	OHV
	F-350	351 (5.8)	H	8	OHV
	F-350	445 (7.3)	M	8	Diesel
	F-350	460 (7.5)	G	8	OHV
	Ranger	140 (2.3)	A	4	OHV
	Ranger	177 (2.9)	T	6	OHV
	Ranger	241 (4.0)	X	6	OHV

REFRIGERANT CAPACITIES

Year	Model	Freon (oz.)	Oil (fl. oz.)	Type ⑬
1989	Aerostar	①	②	FX15
	Bronco	48–52 ③	7	FX15
	Bronco II	32–36 ④	10	6E171
	E-150	①	②	FX-15
	E-250	①	② ⑤	FX-15 ⑥
	E-350	①	② ⑤	FX-15 ⑥
	F-150	48–52 ③	7	FX-15
	F-250	48–52 ③	7 ⑦	FX-15 ⑥
	F-350	48–52 ③	7 ⑦	FX-15 ⑥
	Ranger	32–36 ④	7 ⑧	FX-15 ⑨
1990	Aerostar	①	②	FX15
	Bronco	48–52 ③	7	FX15
	Bronco II	32–36 ④	10	6E171
	E-150	①	⑩	FS-6
	E-250	①	⑩	FS-6 ⑥
	E-350	①	⑩	FS-6 ⑥
	F-150	48–52 ③	7	FX-15
	F-250	48–52 ③	7 ⑦	FX-15 ⑥
	F-350	48–52 ③	7 ⑦	FX-15 ⑥
	Ranger	32–36 ④	7 ⑧	FX-15 ⑨
1991	Aerostar	①	②	FX15
	Bronco	44	7	FX15
	Explorer	32–36 ④	7	FX-15
	E-150	①	⑩	FS-6
	E-250	①	⑩	FS-6 ⑥
	E-350	①	⑩	FS-6 ⑥
	F-150	44	7	FX-15
	F-250	44	7 ⑦	FX-15 ⑪

REFRIGERANT CAPACITIES

Year	Model	Freon (oz.)	Oil (fl. oz.)	Type ⑬
	F-350	44	7⑦	FX-15⑪
	Ranger	32–36④	7⑧	FX-15⑫

① Front A/C only: 56–60 oz., 56 oz. is preferred
Front and Rear A/C: 68–72 oz., 68 oz. is preferred
② Front A/C only: 7 fl. oz.
Front and Rear A/C: 10 fl. oz.
③ 48 oz. is preferred
④ 32 oz. is preferred
⑤ If equipped with 73.L diesel: 10 fl. oz. with front A/C only, 13 fl. oz. with front and rear A/C
⑥ 6E171 if equipped with 7.3L diesel
⑦ If equipped with 7.3L Diesel: 10 fl. oz.
⑧ If equipped with 2.9L engine: 10 fl. oz.
⑨ 6P148 if equipped with 2.9L engine
⑩ Front A/C only: 10 fl. oz.
Front and Rear A/C: 13 fl. oz.
⑪ FS-6 if equipped with 7.3L Diesel
⑫ FS-6 if equipped with 2.9L engine
⑬ Compressor name

AIR CONDITIONING BELT TENSION CHART

Year	Model	Engine (L)	Belt Type	Specification ①	
				New	Used
1989	Aerostar	3.0	V-Ribbed	150-190	140–160
	Bronco	4.9	V-Ribbed	②	②
	Bronco	5.0	V-Ribbed	②	②
	Bronco	5.8	V-Ribbed	②	②
	Bronco II	2.9	V-Belt	120–160	110–130
	E-150	4.9	V-Ribbed	②	②
	E-150	5.0	V-Ribbed	②	②
	E-150	5.8	V-Ribbed	②	②
	E-250	4.9	V-Ribbed	②	②
	E-250	5.0	V-Ribbed	②	②
	E-250	5.8	V-Ribbed	②	②
	E-250	7.3	V-Belt	140–180	104
	E-250	7.5	V-Ribbed	②	②
	E-350	4.9	V-Ribbed	②	②
	E-350	5.8	V-Ribbed	②	②
	E-350	7.3	V-Belt	140–180	104
	E-350	7.5	V-Ribbed	②	②
	F-150	4.9	V-Ribbed	②	②
	F-150	5.0	V-Ribbed	②	②
	F-150	5.8	V-Ribbed	②	②
	F-250	4.9	V-Ribbed	②	②
	F-250	5.0	V-Ribbed	②	②
	F-250	5.8	V-Ribbed	②	②
	F-250	7.3	V-Belt	140–180	104
	F-250	7.5	V-Ribbed	②	②
	F-350	4.9	V-Ribbed	②	②
	F-350	5.8	V-Ribbed	②	②
	F-350	7.3	V-Belt	140–180	104
	F-350	7.5	V-Ribbed	②	②
	Ranger	2.3	V-Ribbed	150–190	140–160
	Ranger	2.9	V-Belt	120–160	110–130

AIR CONDITIONING BELT TENSION CHART

Year	Model	Engine (L)	Belt Type	Specification ① New	Specification ① Used
1990	Aerostar	3.0	V-Ribbed	150-190	140–160
	Aerostar	4.0	V-Ribbed	②	②
	Bronco	4.9	V-Ribbed	②	②
	Bronco	5.0	V-Ribbed	②	②
	Bronco	5.8	V-Ribbed	②	②
	Bronco II	2.9	V-Belt	120–160	110–130
	E-150	4.9	V-Ribbed	②	②
	E-150	5.0	V-Ribbed	②	②
	E-150	5.8	V-Ribbed	②	②
	E-250	4.9	V-Ribbed	②	②
	E-250	5.0	V-Ribbed	②	②
	E-250	5.8	V-Ribbed	②	②
	E-250	7.3	V-Belt	140–180	95–115
	E-250	7.5	V-Ribbed	②	②
	E-350	4.9	V-Ribbed	②	②
	E-350	5.8	V-Ribbed	②	②
	E-350	7.3	V-Belt	140–180	95–115
	E-350	7.5	V-Ribbed	②	②
	F-150	4.9	V-Ribbed	②	②
	F-150	5.0	V-Ribbed	②	②
	F-150	5.8	V-Ribbed	②	②
	F-250	4.9	V-Ribbed	②	②
	F-250	5.0	V-Ribbed	②	②
	F-250	5.8	V-Ribbed	②	②
	F-250	7.3	V-Belt	140–180	95–115
	F-250	7.5	V-Ribbed	②	②
	F-350	4.9	V-Ribbed	②	②
	F-350	5.8	V-Ribbed	②	②
	F-350	7.3	V-Belt	140–180	95–115
	F-350	7.5	V-Ribbed	②	②
	Ranger	2.3	V-Ribbed	150–190	140–160
	Ranger	2.9	V-Belt	120–160	110–130
	Ranger	4.0	V-Ribbed	②	②
1991	Aerostar	3.0	V-Ribbed	150-190	140–160
	Aerostar	4.0	V-Ribbed	②	②
	Bronco	4.9	V-Ribbed	②	②
	Bronco	5.0	V-Ribbed	②	②
	Bronco	5.8	V-Ribbed	②	②
	Explorer	4.0	V-Ribbed	②	②
	E-150	4.9	V-Ribbed	②	②
	E-150	5.0	V-Ribbed	②	②
	E-150	5.8	V-Ribbed	②	②
	E-250	4.9	V-Ribbed	②	②
	E-250	5.0	V-Ribbed	②	②
	E-250	5.8	V-Ribbed	②	②

AIR CONDITIONING BELT TENSION CHART

Year	Model	Engine (L)	Belt Type	Specification ① New	Specification ① Used
1991	E-250	7.3	V-Belt	140–180	95–115
	E-250	7.5	V-Ribbed	②	②
	E-350	4.9	V-Ribbed	②	②
	E-350	5.8	V-Ribbed	②	②
	E-350	7.3	V-Belt	140–180	95–115
	E-350	7.5	V-Ribbed	②	②
	F-150	4.9	V-Ribbed	②	②
	F-150	5.0	V-Ribbed	②	②
	F-150	5.8	V-Ribbed	②	②
	F-250	4.9	V-Ribbed	②	②
	F-250	5.0	V-Ribbed	②	②
	F-250	5.8	V-Ribbed	②	②
	F-250	7.3	V-Belt	140–180	95–115
	F-250	7.5	V-Ribbed	②	②
	F-350	4.9	V-Ribbed	②	②
	F-350	5.8	V-Ribbed	②	②
	F-350	7.3	V-Belt	140–180	95–115
	F-350	7.5	V-Ribbed	②	②
	Ranger	2.3	V-Ribbed	150–190	140–160
	Ranger	2.9	V-Belt	120–160	110–130
	Ranger	4.0	V-Ribbed	②	②

① Lbs. using a belt tension gauge
② Automatic belt tensioner

SYSTEM DESCRIPTION

General Information

The air conditioning system used on Ford trucks is the fixed orifice tube-cycling clutch type. The system components consist of the compressor, magnetic clutch, condenser, evaporator, suction accumulator/drier and the necessary connecting refrigerant lines. The fixed orifice tube assembly is the restriction between the high and low pressure liquid refrigerant and meters the flow of liquid refrigerant into the evaporator core. Evaporator temperature is controlled by sensing the pressure within the evaporator with the clutch cycling pressure switch. The pressure switch controls compressor operation as necessary to maintain the evaporator pressure within specified limits.

E Series Vans and Aerostar can be equipped with a rear auxiliary system. In addition to the components listed above, vehicles equipped with the rear auxiliary system will also be equipped with an additional evaporator as well as the necessary connecting refrigerant lines.

NOTE: The rear auxiliary air conditioning system on E Series Vans is equipped with an expansion valve instead of a fixed orifice tube, to regulate the flow of refrigerant into the evaporator.

Service Valve Location

The air conditioning system has a high pressure (discharge) and a low pressure (suction) gauge port valve. These are Schrader valves which provide access to both the high and low pressure sides of the system for service hoses and a manifold gauge set so system pressures can be read. The high pressure gauge port valve is located between the compressor and the condenser, in the high pressure vapor (discharge) line. The low pressure gauge port valve is located between the suction accumulator/drier and the compressor, in the low pressure vapor (suction) line, on Bronco, E Series and F Series. On Aerostar, Bronco II, Explorer and Ranger, the low pressure gauge port valve is located on the suction accumulator/drier.

High side adapter set D81L–19703–A or tool YT–354, 355 or equivalent, is required to connect a manifold gauge set or charging station to the high pressure gauge port valve. On Bronco, E Series and F Series, service tee fitting D87P–19703–A, which may be mounted on the clutch cycling pressure switch fitting, is

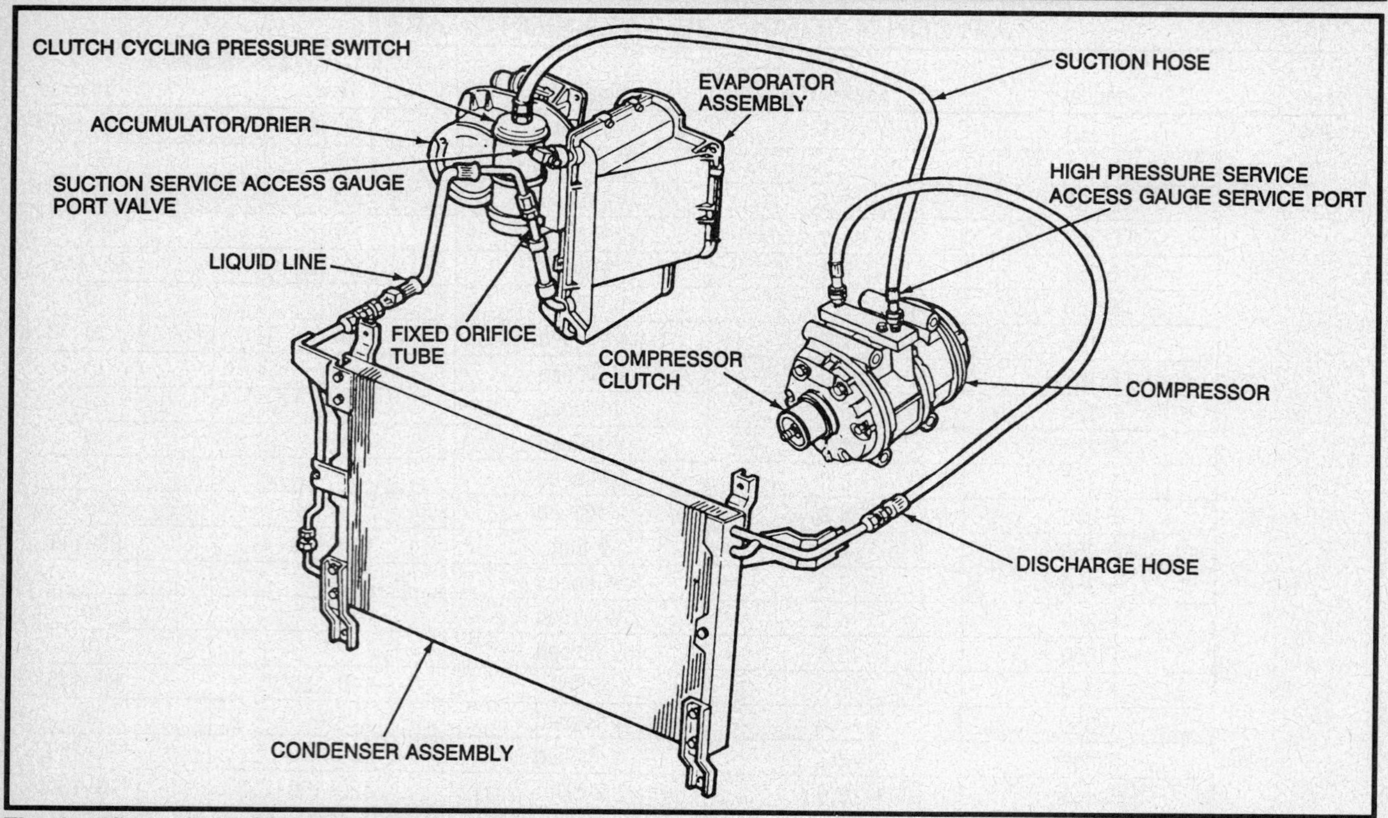
CLUTCH CYCLING PRESSURE SWITCH
SUCTION HOSE
EVAPORATOR ASSEMBLY
ACCUMULATOR/DRIER
SUCTION SERVICE ACCESS GAUGE PORT VALVE
HIGH PRESSURE SERVICE ACCESS GAUGE SERVICE PORT
LIQUID LINE
FIXED ORIFICE TUBE
COMPRESSOR CLUTCH
COMPRESSOR
DISCHARGE HOSE
CONDENSER ASSEMBLY

Fixed orifice tube refrigerant system components— typical

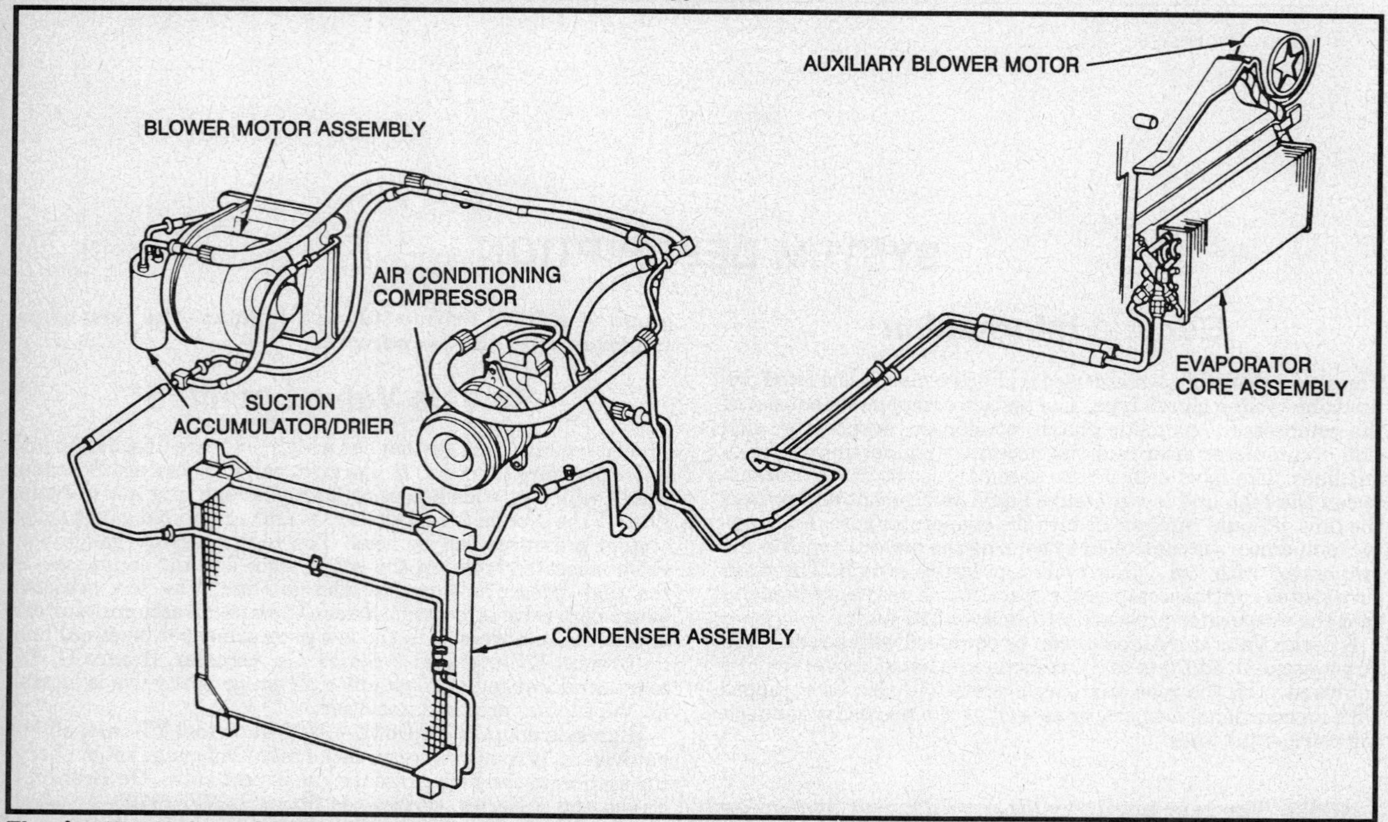
AUXILIARY BLOWER MOTOR
BLOWER MOTOR ASSEMBLY
AIR CONDITIONING COMPRESSOR
SUCTION ACCUMULATOR/DRIER
EVAPORATOR CORE ASSEMBLY
CONDENSER ASSEMBLY

Fixed orifice tube refrigerant system with rear auxiliary system components—typical

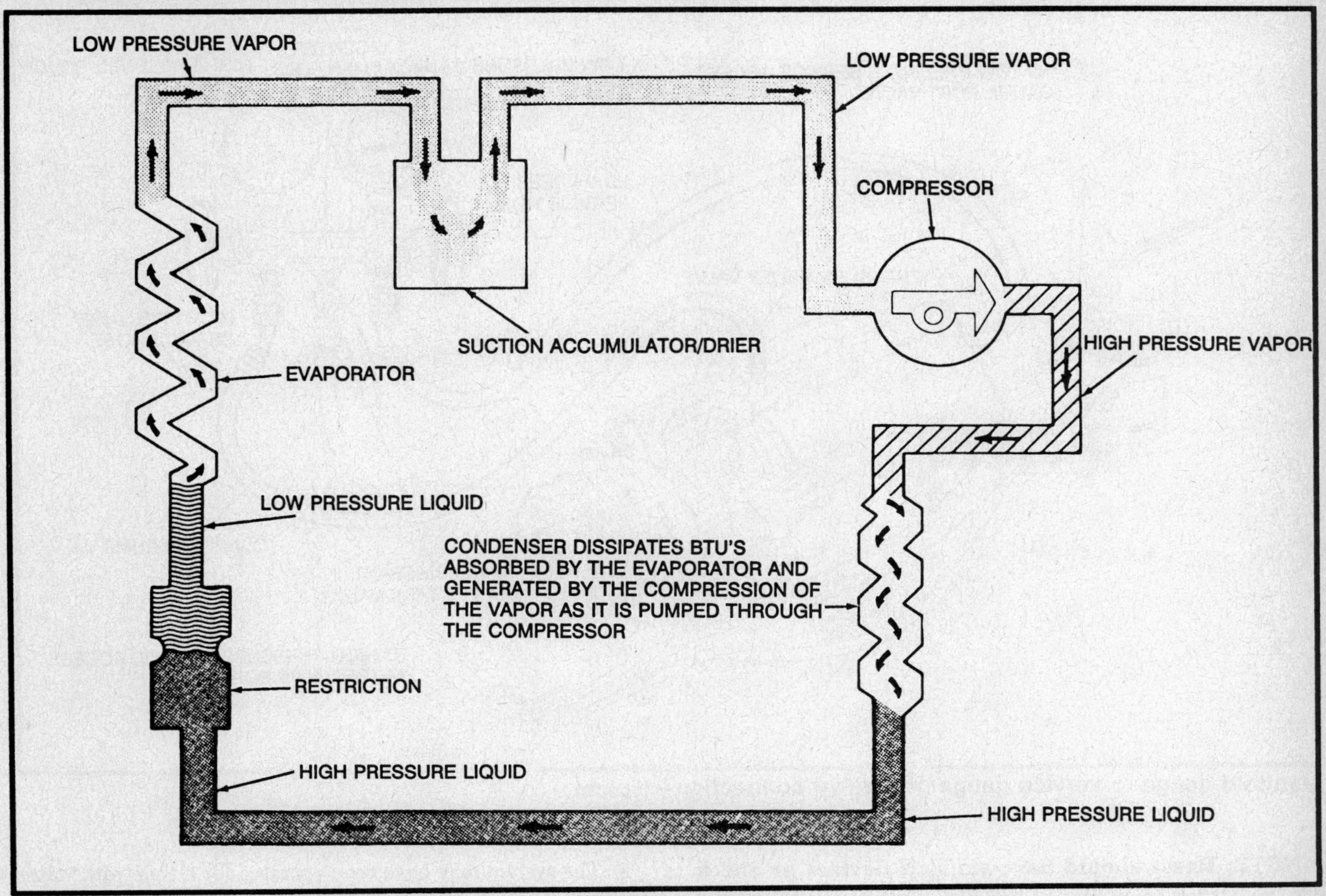
LOW PRESSURE VAPOR
LOW PRESSURE VAPOR
COMPRESSOR
SUCTION ACCUMULATOR/DRIER
HIGH PRESSURE VAPOR
EVAPORATOR
LOW PRESSURE LIQUID
CONDENSER DISSIPATES BTU'S ABSORBED BY THE EVAPORATOR AND GENERATED BY THE COMPRESSION OF THE VAPOR AS IT IS PUMPED THROUGH THE COMPRESSOR
RESTRICTION
HIGH PRESSURE LIQUID
HIGH PRESSURE LIQUID

Refrigerant flow through the fixed orifice tube refrigerant system

available for use in the low pressure side, to be used in place of the low pressure gauge port valve.

System Discharging

WITHOUT RECOVERY SYSTEM

1. Connect a manifold gauge set as follows:
   a. Turn both manifold gauge set valves all the way to the right, to close the high and low pressure hoses to the center manifold and hose.
   b. Remove the caps from the high and low pressure service gauge port valves.
   c. If the manifold gauge set hoses do not have valve depressing pins in them, install fitting adapters T71P–19703–S and R or equivalent, which have pins, on the low and high pressure hoses.
   d. Connect the high and low pressure hoses or adapters, to the respective high and low pressure service gauge port valves. High side adapter set D81L–19703–A or tool YT–354, 355 or equivalent, is required to connect a manifold gauge set or charging station to the high pressure gauge port valve.

NOTE: On Bronco, E Series and F Series, service tee fitting D87P–19703–A, which may be mounted on the clutch cycling pressure switch fitting, is available for use in the low pressure side, to be used in place of the low pressure gauge port valve.

2. Make sure the center hose connection at the manifold gauge set is tight.
3. Place the open end of the center hose in a garage exhaust outlet.
4. Open the low pressure valve of the manifold gauge set a slight amount and let the refrigerant slowly discharge from the system.
5. When the system is nearly discharged, open the high pressure gauge valve slowly, to avoid refrigerant oil loss. This will allow any refrigerant trapped in the compressor and high pressure discharge line to discharge.
6. As soon as the system is completely discharged, close both the high and low pressure valves to prevent moisture from entering the system.

WITH RECOVERY SYSTEM

The use of refrigerant recovery systems and recycling stations makes possible the recovery and reuse of refrigerant after contaminents and moisture have been removed. The reuse of refrigerant will minimize the discharge of ozone depleting chlorofluorocarbons into the atmosphere. If a recovery system or recycling station is used, the following general procedures should be observed, in addition to the operating instructions provided by the equipment manufacturer.

1. Connect the refrigerant recycling station hose(s) to the vehicle air conditioning service ports and the recovery station inlet fitting.

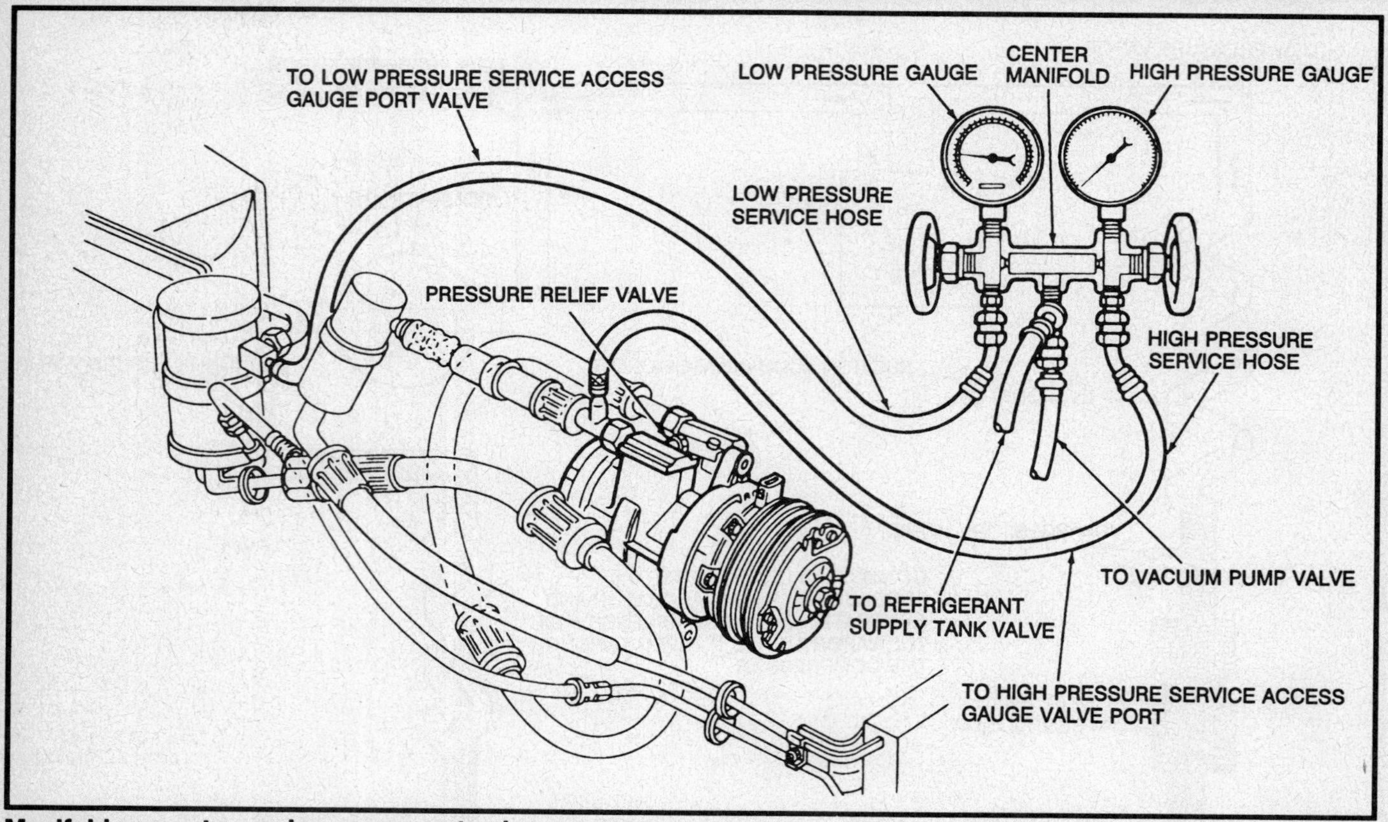
TO LOW PRESSURE SERVICE ACCESS
GAUGE PORT VALVE
LOW PRESSURE GAUGE
CENTER
MANIFOLD
HIGH PRESSURE GAUGE
LOW PRESSURE
SERVICE HOSE
PRESSURE RELIEF VALVE
HIGH PRESSURE
SERVICE HOSE
TO VACUUM PUMP VALVE
TO REFRIGERANT
SUPPLY TANK VALVE
TO HIGH PRESSURE SERVICE ACCESS
GAUGE VALVE PORT

Manifold gauge to service gauge port valve connection—typical

NOTE: Hoses should have shut off devices or check valves within 12 inches of the hose end to minimize the introduction of air into the recycling station and to minimize the amount of refrigerant released when the hose(s) is disconnected.

2. Turn the power to the recycling station **ON** to start the recovery process. Allow the recycling station to pump the refrigerant from the system until the station pressure goes into a vacuum. On some stations the pump will be shut off automatically by a low pressure switch in the electrical system. On other units it may be necessary to manually turn **OFF** the pump.

3. Once the recycling station has evacuated the vehicle air conditioning system, close the station inlet valve, if equipped. Then switch **OFF** the electrical power.

4. Allow the vehicle air conditioning system to remain closed for about 2 minutes. Observe the system vacuum level as shown on the gauge. If the pressure does not rise, disconnect the recycling station hose(s).

5. If the system pressure rises, repeat Steps 2, 3 and 4 until the vacuum level remains stable for 2 minutes.

System Flushing

A refrigerant system can become badly contaminated for a number of reasons:

- The compressor may have failed due to damage or wear.
- The compressor may have been run for some time with a severe leak or an opening in the system.
- The system may have been damaged by a collision and left open for some time.
- The system may not have been cleaned properly after a previous failure.
- The system may have been operated for a time with water or moisture in it.

A badly contaminated system contains water, carbon and other decomposition products. When this condition exists, the system must be flushed with a special flushing agent using equipment designed specially for this purpose.

FLUSHING AGENTS

To be suitable as a flushing agent, a refrigerant must remain in liquid state during the flushing operation in order to wash the inside surfaces of the system components. Refrigerant vapor will not remove contaminent particles. They must be flushed with a liquid.

Some refrigerants are better suited to flushing than others. Neither Refrigerant-12 (R-12) nor Refrigerant-114 (R-114) is suitable for flushing a system because of low vaporization (boiling) points: −21.6°F (−29.8°C) for R-12 and 38.4°F (3.5°C) for R-114. Both these refrigerants would be difficult to use and would not do a sufficient job because of the tendency to vaporize rather than remain in a liquid state, especially in high ambient temperatures.

Refrigerant-11 (R-11) and Refrigerant-113 (R-113) are much better suited for use with special flushing equipment. Both have rather high vaporization points: 74.7°F (23.7°C) for R-11 and 117.6°F (47.5°C) for R-113. Both refrigerants also have low closed container pressures. This reduces the danger of an accidental system discharge due to a ruptured hose or fitting. R-113 will do the best job amd is recommended as a flushing refrigerant. Both R-11 and R-113 require a propellant or pump type flushing equipment due to their low closed container pressures. R-12 can be used as a propellant with either flushing refriger-

REFRIGERANT FLUSHING INFORMATION CHART

Refrigerant	Vaporizes @ °F	Approximate Closed Container Pressure @					Adaptability
		60°F	70°F	80°F	90°F	100°F	
R-12	−21.6°F	57 PSI	70 PSI	84 PSI	100 PSI	117 PSI	Self Propelling
F-114	38.4°F	8 PSI	13 PSI	19 PSI	25 PSI	32 PSI	
F-11	74.7°F	8 in Hg	3 in Hg	1 PSI	5 PSI	9 PSI	Pump Required*
F-113	117.6°F	22 in Hg	19 in Hg	16 in Hg	13 in Hg	8 in Hg	

*F-11 is also available in pressurized containers. This makes it suitable for usage when special flushing equipment is not available. However, it is more toxic than R-12 and F-114.

ant. R-11 is available in pressurized containers. Although not recommended for regular use, it may become necessary to use R-11 if special flushing equipment is not available. R-11 is more toxic than other refrigerants and should be handled with extra care.

SPECIAL FLUSHING EQUIPMENT

Special refrigerant system flushing equipment is available from a number of air conditioning equipment and usually comes in kit form. A flushing kit, such as model 015–00205 or equivalent, consists of a cylinder for the flushing agent, a nozzle to introduce the flushing agent into the system and a connecting hose.

A second type of equipment, which must be connected into the system, allows for the continuous circulation of the flushing agent through the system. Contaminents are trapped by an external filter/drier. If this equipment is used, follow the manufacturer's instructions and observe all safety precautions.

SYSTEM CLEANING AND FLUSHING

NOTE: Use extreme care and adhere to all safety precautions related to the use of refrigerants when flushing a system.

When it is necessary to flush a refrigerant system, the accumulator/drier must be removed and replaced, because it is impossible to clean. Remove the fixed orifice tube and replace it. If a new tube is not available, carefully wash the contaminated tube in flushing refrigerant or mineral spirits and blow it dry. If the tube does not show signs of damage or deterioration, it may be reused. Install new O-rings.

Any moisture in the evaporator core will be removed during leak testing and system evacuation following the cleaning job. Perorm the cleaning procedure carefully as follows:

1. Check the hose connections at the flushing cylinder outlet and flushing nozzle, to make sure they are secure.
2. Make sure the flushing cylinder is filled with approximately 1 pint of R-113 and the valve assembly on top of the cylinder is tightened securely.
3. Connect a can of R-12 to the Schrader valve at the top of the charging cylinder. A refrigerant hose and a special safety-type refrigerant dispensing valve, such as YT–280 refrigerant dispensing valve or equivalent, and a valve retainer are required for connecting the small can to the cylinder. Make sure all connections are secure.
4. Connect a gauge manifold and discharge the system. Disconnect the gauge manifold.
5. Remove and discard the accumulator/drier. Install a new accumulator/drier and connect it to the evaporator. Do not connect it to the suction line from the compressor. Make sure the protective cap is in place on the suction line connection.
6. Replace the fixed orifice tube. Install the protective cap on the evaporator inlet tube as soon as the new orifice tube is in place. The liquid line will be connected later.
7. Remove the compressor from the vehicle for cleaning and service or replacement, whichever is required. If the compressor is cleaned and serviced, add the specified amount of refrigerant oil prior to installing in the vehicle. Place protective caps on the compressor inlet and outlet connections and install it on the mounting brackets in the vehicle. If the compressor is replaced, adjust the oil level. Install the shipping caps on the compressor connections and install the new compressor on the mounting brackets in the vehicle.
8. Back-flush the condenser and liquid line as follows:
   a. Remove the discharge hose from the condenser and clamp a piece of ½ in. i.d. heater hose to the condenser inlet line. Make sure the hose is long enough so the free end can be inserted into a suitable waste container to catch the flushing refrigerant.
   b. Move the flushing equipment into position and open the valve on the can of R-12, fully counterclockwise.
   c. Back-flush the condenser and liquid line by introducing the flushing refrigerant into the supported end of the liquid line with the flushing nozzle. Hold the nozzle firmly against the open end of the liquid line.
   d. After the liquid line and condenser have been flushed, lay the charging cylinder on it's side so the R-12 will not force more flushing refrigerant into the liquid line. Press the nozzle firmly to the liquid line and admit R-12 to force all flushing refrigerant from the liquid line and condenser.
   e. Remove the heater hose and clamp from the condenser inlet connection.
   f. Stand the flushing cylinder upright and flush the compressor discharge hose. Secure it so the flushing refrigerant goes into the waste container.
   g. Close the dispensing valve of the R-12 can, full clockwise. If there is any flushing refrigerant in the cylinder, it may be left there until the next flushing job. Put the flushing kit and R-12 can in a suitable storage location.
9. Connect all refrigerant lines. All connections should be cleaned and new O-rings should be used. Lubricate new O-rings with clean refrigerant oil.
10. Connect a charging station or manifold gauge set and charge the system with 1 lb. of R-12. Do not evacuate the system until after it has been leak tested.
11. Leak test all connections and components with flame-type leak detector 023–00006, electronic leak detector 055–00014 or 055–00015 or equivalent. If no leaks are found, proceed to Step 12. If leaks are found, service as necessary, check the system and then go to Step 12.

CAUTION

Fumes from flame-type leak detectors are noxious, avoid inhaling them or personal injury may result.

NOTE: Good ventilation is necessary in the area where air conditioning leak testing is to be done. If the surrounding air is contaminated with refrigerant gas, the leak detector will indicate this gas all the time. Odors from other chemicals such as anti-freeze, diesel fuel, disc brake cleaner or other cleaning solvents can cause the same problem. A fan, even in a well ventilated area, is very helpful in removing small traces of air contamination that might affect the leak detector.

12. Evacuate and charge the system with the specified amount of R-12. Operate the system to make sure it is cooling properly.

System Evacuating

1. Connect a manifold gauge set as follows:
   a. Turn both manifold gauge set valves all the way to the right, to close the high and low pressure hoses to the center manifold and hose.
   b. Remove the caps from the high and low pressure service gauge port valves.
   c. If the manifold gauge set hoses do not have valve depressing pins in them, install fitting adapters T71P–19703–S and R or equivalent, which have pins, on the low and high pressure hoses.
   d. Connect the high and low pressure hoses or adapters, to the respective high and low pressure service gauge port valves. High side adapter set D81L–19703–A or tool YT–354 or 355 or equivalent is required to connect a manifold gauge set or charging station to the high pressure gauge port valve.

NOTE: On Bronco, E Series and F Series, service tee fitting D87P–19703–A, which may be mounted on the clutch cycling pressure switch fitting, is available for use in the low pressure side, to be used in place of the low pressure gauge port valve.

2. Leak test all connections and components with flame-type leak detector 023–00006, electronic leak detector 055–00014 or 055–00015 or equivalent.

CAUTION

Fumes from flame-type leak detectors are noxious, avoid inhaling them or personal injury may result.

NOTE: Good ventilation is necessary in the area where air conditioning leak testing is to be done. If the surrounding air is contaminated with refrigerant gas, the leak detector will indicate this gas all the time. Odors from other chemicals such as anti-freeze, diesel fuel, disc brake cleaner or other cleaning solvents can cause the same problem. A fan, even in a well ventilated area, is very helpful in removing small traces of air contamination that might affect the leak detector.

3. Properly discharge the refrigerant system according the to proper procedure.
4. Make sure both manifold gauge valves are turned all the way to the right. Make sure the center hose connection at the manifold gauge is tight.
5. Connect the manifold gauge set center hose to a vacuum pump.
6. Open the manifold gauge set valves and start the vacuum pump.
7. Evacuate the system with the vacuum pump until the low pressure gauge reads at least 25 in. Hg vacuum or as close to 30 in. Hg vacuum as possible. Continue to operate the vacuum pump for 15 minutes. If a part of the system has been replaced, continue to operate the vacuum pump for another 20–30 minutes.
8. When evacuation of the system is complete, close the manifold gauge set valves and turn the vacuum pump **OFF**.
9. Observe the low pressure gauge for 5 minutes to ensure that system vacuum is held. If vacuum is held, charge the system. If vacuum is not held for 5 minutes, leak test the system, service the leaks and evacuate the system again.

System Charging

1. Connect a manifold gauge set according to the proper procedure. Properly discharge and evacuate the system.
2. With the manifold gauge set valves closed to the center hose, disconnect the vacuum pump from the manifold gauge set.
3. Connect the center hose of the manifold gauge set to a refrigerant drum or a small can refrigerant dispensing valve tool YT–280, 1034 or equivalent. If a charging station is used, follow the instructions of the manufacturer. If a small can dispensing valve is used, install the small can(s) on the dispensing valve.

NOTE: Use only a safety type dispensing valve.

4. Loosen the center hose at the manifold gauge set and open the refrigerant drum valve or small can dispensing valve. Allow the refrigerant to escape to purge air and moisture from the center hose. Then, tighten the center hose connection at the manifold gauge set.
5. Disconnect the wire harness snap lock connector from the clutch cycling pressure switch and install a jumper wire across the 2 terminals of the connector.
6. Open the manifold gauge set low side valve to allow refrigerant to enter the system. Keep the refrigerant can in an upright position.

CAUTION

Do not open the manifold gauge set high pressure (discharge) gauge valve when charging with a small container. Opening the valve can cause the small refrigerant container to explode, which can result in personal injury.

7. When no more refrigerant is being drawn into the system, start the engine and move the function selector lever to the **NORM/A/C** position on Aerostar, the **VENT/HEAT/A/C** position on Bronco II, Explorer and Ranger or the **MAX A/C** position on Bronco, E Series and F Series. Move the blower switch to **HI** to draw the remaining refrigerant into the system. Continue to add refrigerant to the system until the specified weight of R-12 is in the system. Then close the manifold gauge set low pressure valve and the refrigerant supply valve.
8. Remove the jumper wire from the clutch cycling pressure switch snap lock connector. Connect the connector to the pressure switch.
9. Operate the system until pressures stabilize to verify normal operation and system pressures.
10. In high ambient temperatures, it may be necessary to operate a high volume fan positioned to blow air through the radiator and condenser to aid in cooling the engine and prevent excessive refrigerant system pressures.
11. When charging is completed and system operating pressures are normal, disconnect the manifold gauge set from the vehicle. Install the protective caps on the service gauge port valves.

SYSTEM COMPONENTS

Radiator

REMOVAL AND INSTALLATION

Aerostar, Bronco II, Explorer and Ranger

1. Disconnect the negative battery cable.
2. Drain the cooling system by removing the radiator cap and attaching a ⅜ in. i.d. hose to the draincock nipple, located at the lower rear corner of the radiator tank. Then, open the draincock and allow the coolant to flow through the hose into a suitable container.
3. Remove the rubber overflow tube from the radiator and store it aside.
4. Remove the shroud's or finger guard's 2 upper attaching screws. Lift the shroud out of the lower retaining clips and drape it on the fan.
5. Loosen the upper and lower hose clamps at the radiator and remove the hoses from the radiator connectors.
6. If equipped with an automatic transmission, disconnect the 2 transmission cooling lines from the oil cooler fittings on the radiator. The intermediate flare fittings should remain installed. Disconnect the transmission cooler tube support bracket from the bottom flange of the radiator by removing the screw.
7. Remove the 2 radiator upper attaching screws. Tilt the radiator back approximately 1 in. and lift directly upward, clear of the radiator support and the cooling fan.
8. If either hose is to be replaced, loosen the clamp at the engine end and slip the hose off the connections with a twisting motion.
9. Remove the radiator lower support rubber insulators.

To install:

10. Position the radiator lower support rubber insulators to the lower support.
11. If either hose has been replaced, position the hose on the engine with the index arrow in line with the mark on the fitting at the engine.
12. Position the radiator into the engine compartment to the radiator support, being careful to clear the fan. Make sure the mounting pins on the bottoms of both tanks are inserted into the holes in the lower support rubber insulators and that the radiator is firmly seated on the insulators. Attach the overflow hose to the uppermost nipple on the filler neck.
13. Install the upper attaching bolts to attach the radiator to the radiator support. Tighten to 12–20 ft. lbs. (17–27 Nm).
14. If equipped with an automatic transmission, perform the following procedure:
    a. Loosely connect the 2 transmission cooling lines to the radiator oil cooler fittings.
    b. Connect the transmission cooler tube support bracket to the bottom flange of the radiator with the attaching screw.
    c. Attach the cooler tubes onto the plastic clip on the tube support bracket.
    d. Tighten the cooler tube nuts attachin the cooler tube to the radiator connectors. Tighten the tube nuts to 12–18 ft. lbs. (16–24 Nm).
15. Attach the radiator upper hose to the radiator. Position the hose on the radiator connector so the stripe on the hose is at the 12 o'clock position. Slide the compression clamp into it's installed position.
16. Position the lower hose to the radiator with the stripe on the hose at the 6 o'clock position. Slide the compression clamp into it's installed position.
17. Position the shroud in the lower retainer clips and attach the top of the shroud to the radiator with 2 screw and washer assemblies. Tighten to 4–5 ft. lbs. (5.5–8 Nm).

NOTE: Make sure the overflow hose is attached to the uppermost nipple on the filler neck.

18. Close the radiator draincock and fill the cooling system.
19. Connect the negative battery cable. Operate the engine for 15 minutes and check for leaks. Recheck the coolant level.

Bronco, E Series and F Series

1. Disconnect the negative battery cable.
2. Drain the cooling system by removing the radiator cap and opening the draincock located at the lower rear corner of the radiator tank. To prevent coolant loss, slip a hose on the draincock and drain the coolant into a clean container.
3. Remove the rubber overflow tube from the coolant recovery bottle and detach it from the shroud, if necessary.
4. Remove the shroud's 2 or 4 attaching bolts, lift the shroud back and drape it on the fan.
5. Loosen the upper and lower hose clamps at the radiator and remove the hoses from the radiator connectors.
6. If equipped with an automatic transmission, disconnect the 2 automatic transmission oil cooling lines from the radiator fittings.
7. If equipped with the E4OD automatic transmission, disconnect the heated water bypass hose.
8. On E Series and 7.3L diesel equipped vehicles, remove the 4 radiator attaching bolts. On Bronco and F Series equipped with gasoline engines, remove the 2 radiator upper attaching bolts. Tilt the radiator back approximately 1 in. and lift directly upward, clear of the radiator support.
9. If either hose is to be replaced, loosen the clamp at the engine end and slip the hose off the connection with a twisting motion.
10. On Bronco and F Series equipped with gasoline engines, remove the radiator lower support rubber pads.

To install:

11. On Bronco and F Series equipped with gasoline engines, position the radiator lower support pads to the lower frame.
12. If either hose has been replaced, install on the engine and tighten the clamps to 20–30 inch lbs. (2.25–3.38 Nm).
13. Position the radiator into the engine compartment to the radiator support, being careful to clear the fan. On E Series and 7.3L diesel equipped vehicles, install the 4 mounting bolts and tighten to 10–15 ft. lbs. (14–20 Nm). On Bronco and F Series equipped with gasoline engines, install the 2 upper radiator attaching bolts and tighten to 8–11 ft. lbs. (11–14 Nm).
14. If equipped with an automatic transmission, connect the oil cooling lines to the radiator connectors.
15. Attach the upper and lower radiator hoses and clamps.
16. If equipped with the E4OD automatic transmission, attach the heated water bypass hose.
17. On E Series and 7.3L diesel equipped vehicles, position the shroud to the radiator and attach with 4 bolts. Tighten the bolts to 4–6 ft. lbs. (5.4–8 Nm). On Bronco and F Series equipped with gasoline engines, position the shroud on the lower retainer clips and attach the top of the shroud to the radiator with 2 washer and screw assemblies. Tighten to 4–6 ft. lbs. (5.5–8 Nm).
18. Attach the rubber overflow tube from the coolant recovery bottle to the radiator, if applicable.
19. Close the draincock and fill the cooling system.
20. Connect the negative battery cable. Operate the engine for 15 minutes and check for leaks. Check the coolant level and bring it up to within 1½ in. of the radiator filler neck.

COOLING SYSTEM BLEEDING

When the entire cooling system is drained, the following procedure should be used to remove air from the cooling system and ensure a complete fill.

1. Close the radiator draincock and install the cylinder block drain plug, if removed.
2. Fill the cooling system with a 50/50 mixture of anti-freeze and water. Allow several minutes for trapped air to escape. When filling a cross flow radiator, allow time for the coolant to flow through the radiator tubes to the other end of the tank to ensure the radiator is full.

NOTE: On Bronco, E Series and F Series, disconnect the heater outlet hose at the water pump to bleed or release trapped air in the system. When the coolant begins to escape, connect the heater outlet hose.

3. Install the radiator cap to the pressure relief position by installing the cap to the fully installed position and then backing off to the 1st stop. This will allow any air to escape and will minimize spillage.
4. Slide the heater temperature and mode selection levers to the maximum heat position.
5. Start the engine and allow to operate at fast idle for approximately 3–4 minutes.
6. With the engine shut off, wrap the radiator cap with a thick cloth, carefully remove the cap and add coolant to bring the coolant level up to the filler neck seat on Aerostar, Bronco II, Explorer and Ranger. On Bronco, E Series and F Series, fill the radiator until the coolant is between the cap seal in the filler neck to 1.5 in. below the cap seal.
7. Install the cap to the fully installed position. Then, back off to the 1st stop and operate the engine at fast idle until the thermostat opens and the upper radiator hose is warm. To check the coolant level, shut the engine off, wrap the cap with a thick cloth and cautiously remove the cap. Add additional coolant, if necessary. Install the cap to the fully installed position.

CAUTION

To avoid personal injury from scalding hot coolant or steam blowing out of the radiator, use extreme care when removing the cap from a hot radiator.

8. Fill the coolant recovery reservoir to the proper level with a 50/50 mix of anti-freeze and water.

Condenser

REMOVAL AND INSTALLATION

Aerostar

NOTE: Whenever the condenser is replaced, it will be necessary to replace the suction accumulator/drier.

1. Disconnect the negative battery cable.
2. Discharge the refrigerant from the air conditioning system according to the proper procedure.
3. Disconnect the compressor discharge line and the liquid line from the condenser at the spring-lock couplings using the spring-lock coupling disconnect procedure. Cap the openings to prevent the entry of dirt and moisture.
4. Tilt the top of the radiator rearward after removing the upper radiator bolts, being careful not to damage the cooling fan and/or radiator.
5. Remove the 2 bolts attaching the 2 condenser upper mounting brackets to the rear side of the radiator support. Lift the condenser from the vehicle.

To install:

NOTE: Add 1 oz. (30ml) of clean refrigerant oil to a replacement condenser to maintain the correct total system oil charge.

6. Check the condenser to make sure there is a rubber isolator on each of the lower mounting studs. Replace if worn or missing.
7. Position the condenser to the vehicle with the lower studs in the lower mount holes and with the upper brackets on the rear face of the upper radiator support.
8. Install the 2 bolts attaching the 2 condenser support mounting brackets to the rear side of the radiator support.
9. Move the radiator into the correct installed position and install the 2 upper retaining bolts.
10. Connect the discharge and liquid lines to the condenser using the spring-lock coupling connection procedure.
11. Connect the negative battery cable. Leak test, evacuate and charge the system according to the proper procedure. Observe all safety precautions.
12. Check the system for proper operation.

Bronco II, Explorer and Ranger

NOTE: Whenever the condenser is replaced, it will be necessary to replace the suction accumulator/drier.

1. Disconnect the negative battery cable.
2. Discharge the refrigerant from the air conditioning system according to the proper procedure.
3. Disconnect the compressor discharge line and the liquid line from the condenser at the spring-lock couplings using the spring-lock coupling disconnect procedure. Cap the openings to prevent the entry of dirt and moisture.
4. Working under the vehicle, remove the 2 nuts attaching the 2 lower mounting studs.
5. Tilt the top of the radiator rearward, after removing the upper radiator brackets, being careful not to damage the cooling fan and/or the radiator.
6. Remove the 2 bolts attaching the 2 condenser upper mounting brackets to the rear side of the radiator support and lift the condenser from the vehicle.

To install:

NOTE: Add 1 oz. (30ml) of clean refrigerant oil to a replacement condenser to maintain the correct total system oil charge.

7. Assemble the 2 "J" nuts and studs to the bottom of the condenser to be installed.
8. Position the condenser to the vehicle with the lower studs and upper brackets on the rear face of the radiator support.
9. Install the 2 bolts attaching the 2 condenser upper mounting brackets to the rear side of the radiator support. Working under the vehicle, fasten the 2 nuts to the lower studs.
10. Move the radiator into the correct installed position and install the 2 upper retaining brackets.
11. Connect the discharge and liquid lines to the condenser using the spring-lock coupling connection procedure.
12. Connect the negative battery cable. Leak test, evacuate and charge the system according to the proper procedure. Observe all safety precautions.
13. Check the system for proper operation.

Bronco and F Series

NOTE: Whenever the condenser is replaced, it will be necessary to replace the suction accumulator/drier.

1. Disconnect the negative battery cable.
2. Discharge the refrigerant from the air conditioning system according to the proper procedure.
3. Disconnect the compressor discharge and liquid lines from the condenser. Cap the lines to prevent the entrance of dirt and moisture.
4. Partially drain the radiator and disconnect the upper hose from the radiator.
5. Working under the vehicle, remove the 2 screws attaching the 2 condenser lower mounting brackets to the front radiator support.
6. Remove the bolts from the radiator upper retaining brackets and tilt the radiator rearward.

SPRING-LOCK COUPLING PROCEDURES

TO CONNECT COUPLING

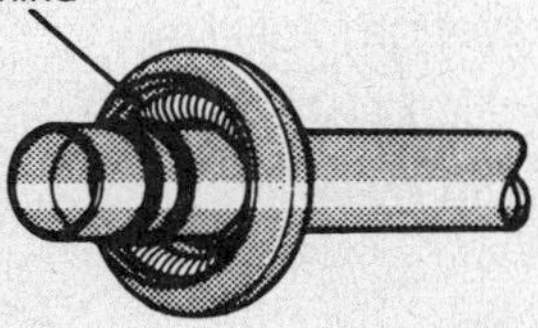
GARTER SPRING

1. CHECK FOR MISSING OR DAMAGED GARTER SPRING — REMOVE DAMAGED SPRING WITH SMALL HOOKED WIRE — INSTALL NEW SPRING IF DAMAGED OR MISSING.

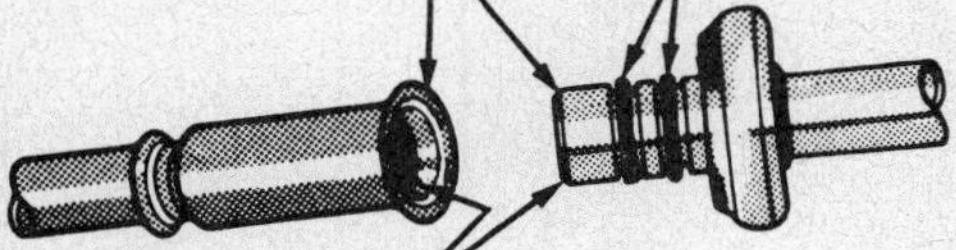
A — CLEAN FITTINGS
B — INSTALL NEW O-RINGS — USE ONLY SPECIFIED O-RINGS
C — LUBRICATE WITH CLEAN REFRIGERANT OIL
D — ASSEMBLE FITTING TOGETHER BY PUSHING WITH A SLIGHT TWISTING MOTION

2. (see A–D above)

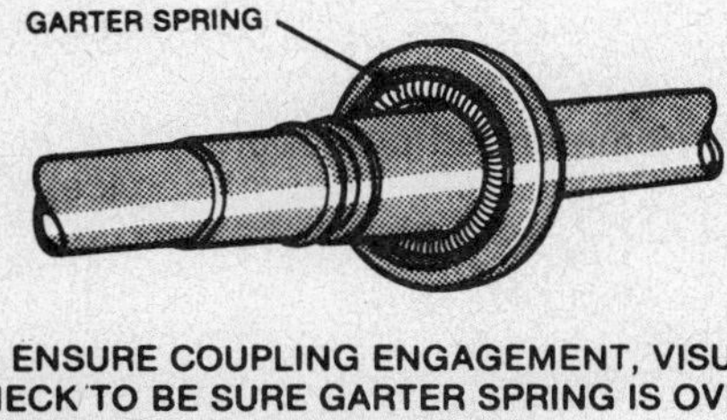
GARTER SPRING

3. TO ENSURE COUPLING ENGAGEMENT, VISUALLY CHECK TO BE SURE GARTER SPRING IS OVER FLARED END OF FEMALE FITTING.

TO DISCONNECT COUPLING

CAUTION — DISCHARGE SYSTEM BEFORE DISCONNECTING COUPLING

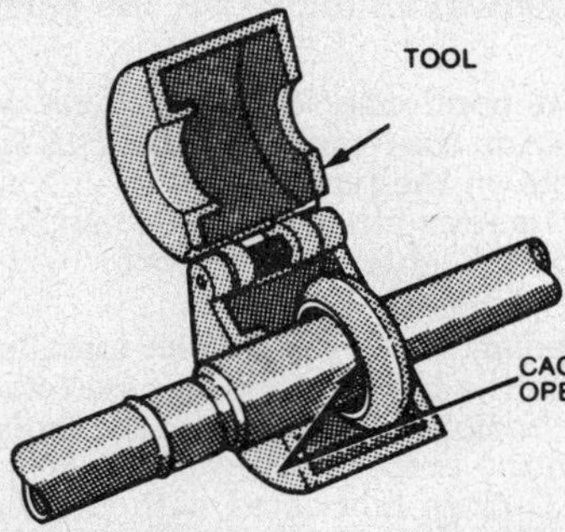
TOOL
CAGE OPENING

(1) FIT TOOL TO COUPLING SO THAT TOOL CAN ENTER CAGE OPENING TO RELEASE THE GARTER SPRING.

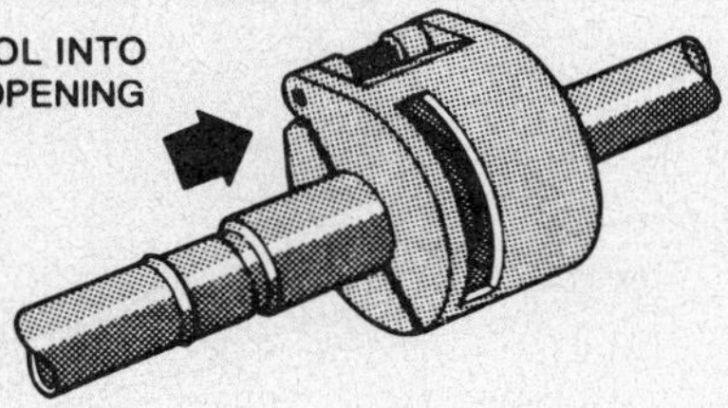
PUSH TOOL INTO CAGE OPENING

(2) PUSH THE TOOL INTO THE CAGE OPENING TO RELEASE THE FEMALE FITTING FROM THE GARTER SPRING.

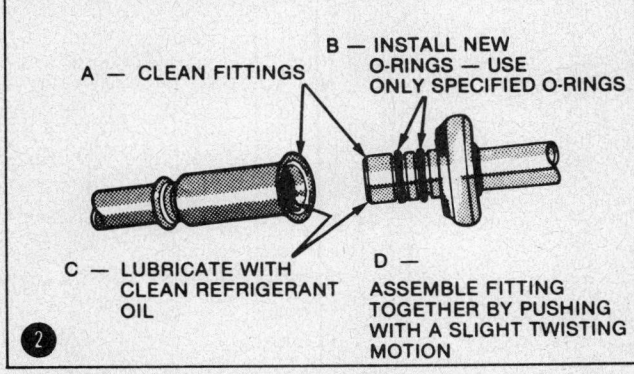

(3) PULL THE COUPLING MALE AND FEMALE FITTINGS APART.

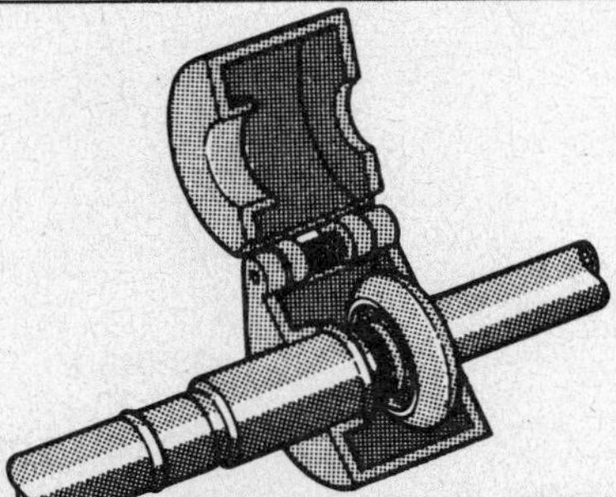

(4) REMOVE THE TOOL FROM THE DISCONNECTED SPRING LOCK COUPLING.

7. Remove the 2 screws attaching the 2 condenser upper mounting brackets to the rear side of the radiator support and lift the condenser from the vehicle.

To install:

NOTE: Add 1 oz. (30ml) of clean refrigerant oil to a replacement condenser to maintain the correct total system oil charge.

8. Position the condenser to the vehicle with the lower mounting brackets on the front side of the radiator support and the upper brackets on the rear side.
9. Install the 4 screws attaching the 4 mounting brackets to the radiator support. Tighten the screws to 10–14 ft. lbs. (13.6–19 Nm).
10. Move the radiator into the correct installed position and install the bolts to the upper retaining brackets.
11. Connect the radiator upper hose to the radiator and fill the cooling system to the proper level.
12. Using new O-rings lubricated with clean refrigerant oil, connect the compressor discharge and liquid lines to the condenser. Tighten the connections to 15–20 ft. lbs. (21–27 Nm).
13. Connect the negative battery cable. Leak test, evacuate and charge the system according to the proper procedure. Observe all safety precautions.
14. Check the system for proper operation.

E Series

NOTE: Whenever the condenser is replaced, it will be necessary to replace the suction accumulator/drier.

1. Disconnect the negative battery cable.
2. Discharge the refrigerant from the air conditioning system according to the proper procedure.
3. Disconnect the compressor discharge line and liquid line from the condenser using the spring-lock coupling disconnect procedure. Cap the refrigerant lines to prevent entry of excessive moisture and dirt.
4. Remove the 2 screws retaining the hood latch to the radiator support and position the hood latch aside.
5. Remove the 9 screws retaining the top edge of the radiator grille to the radiator support.
6. Remove the screw retaining the center area of the grille to the grille center support and the screw retaining the grille center support to the radiator support.

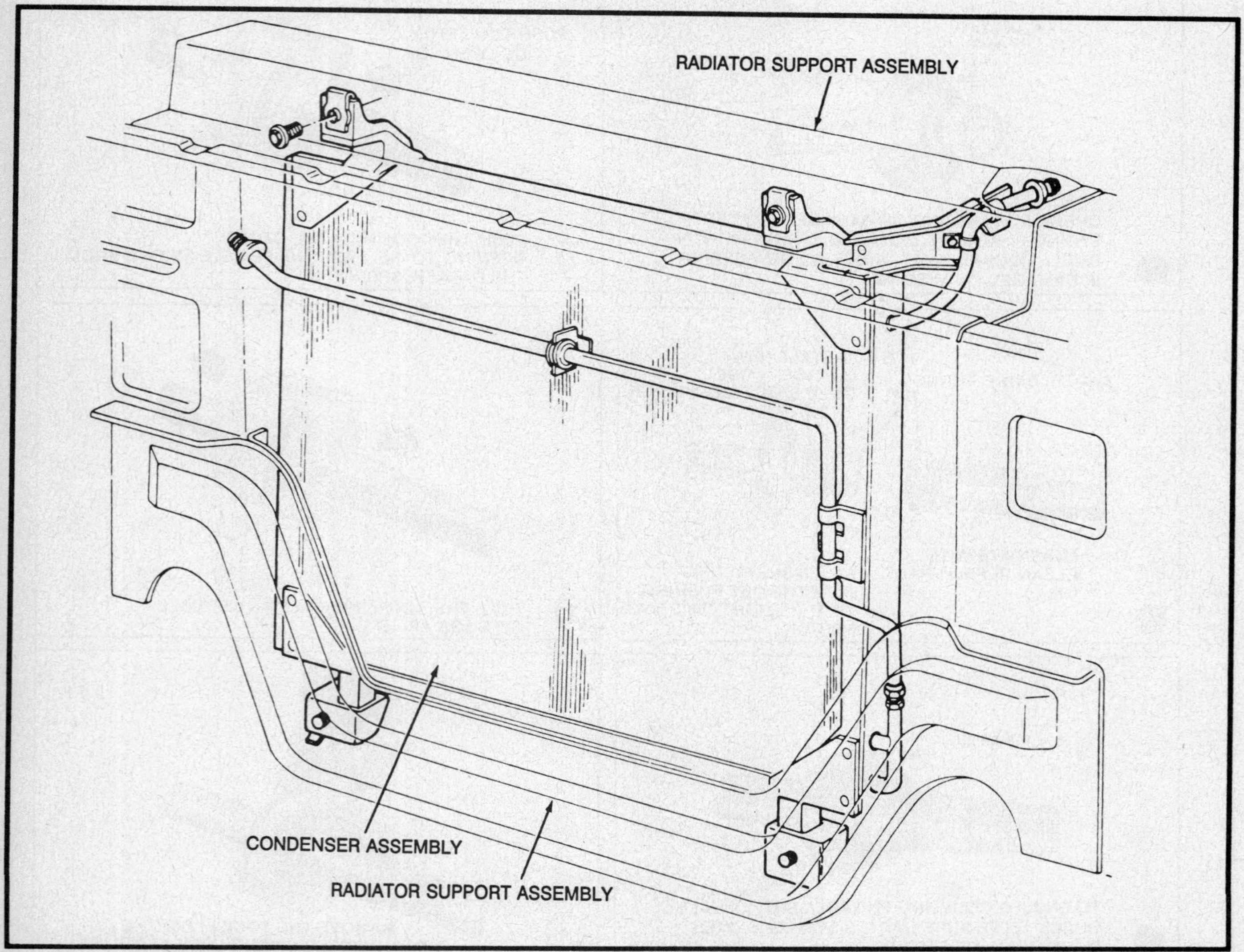
RADIATOR SUPPORT ASSEMBLY
CONDENSER ASSEMBLY
RADIATOR SUPPORT ASSEMBLY

Condenser Installation—E Series

7. Working under the vehicle, reposition the splash shield and remove the 2 condenser lower retaining nuts.
8. Remove the 2 bolts retaining the top of the condenser to the radiator upper support.
9. Remove the 4 bolts retaining each end of the radiator upper support to the radiator side supports.
10. Carefully pull the top edge of the grille forward and remove the radiator upper support.
11. Lift the condenser from the vehicle.

To install:

NOTE: Add 1 oz. (30ml) of clean refrigerant oil to a replacement condenser to maintain the correct total system oil charge.

12. Position the condenser to the vehicle and install 2 condenser lower retaining nuts.
13. Position the radiator upper support to the vehicle using care not to damage the radiator grille.
14. Install the 4 bolts retaining each end of the radiator upper supports to the side supports.
15. Install the 2 bolts retaining the top end of the condenser to the radiator upper support.
16. Install the screw retaining the grille center support to the radiator support.
17. Install the 9 screws retaining the top edge of the grille.
18. Install the screw retaining the center area of the grille to the grille center support.
19. Connect the compressor discharge and liquid lines to the condenser using the spring-lock coupling connection procedure.
20. Install and adjust the hood latch.
21. Connect the negative battery cable. Leak test, evacuate and charge the system according to the proper procedure. Observe all safety precautions.
22. Check the system for proper operation.

Compressor

REMOVAL AND INSTALLATION

NOTE: The suction accumulator/drier and the fixed orifice tube should also be replaced whenever the compressor is replaced.

1. Disconnect the negative battery cable.
2. Discharge the refrigerant from the air conditioning system according to the proper procedure.
3. Disconnect the wire connector from the clutch field coil connector.
4. Loosen and remove the drive belt from the compressor pulley.
5. Disconnect the refrigerant lines from the compressor. Plug the refrigerant lines and compressor ports to prevent the entrance of dirt and moisture.
6. Remove the mounting bolts and the necessary mounting brackets and remove the compressor.

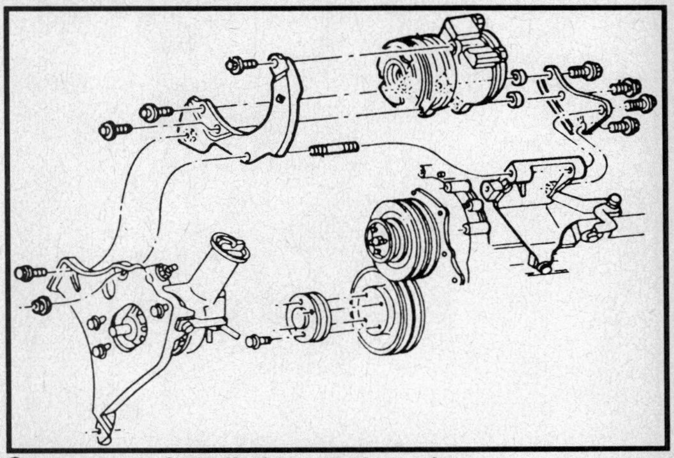

Compressor installation—2.9L engine

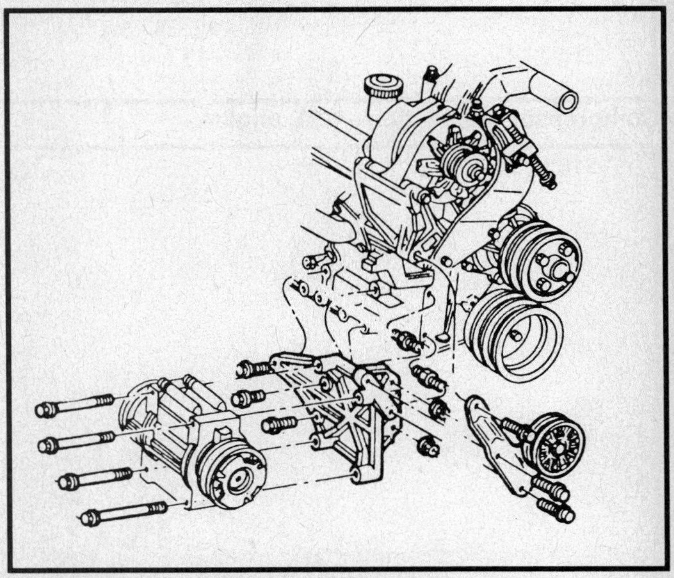

Compressor installation—3.0L engine

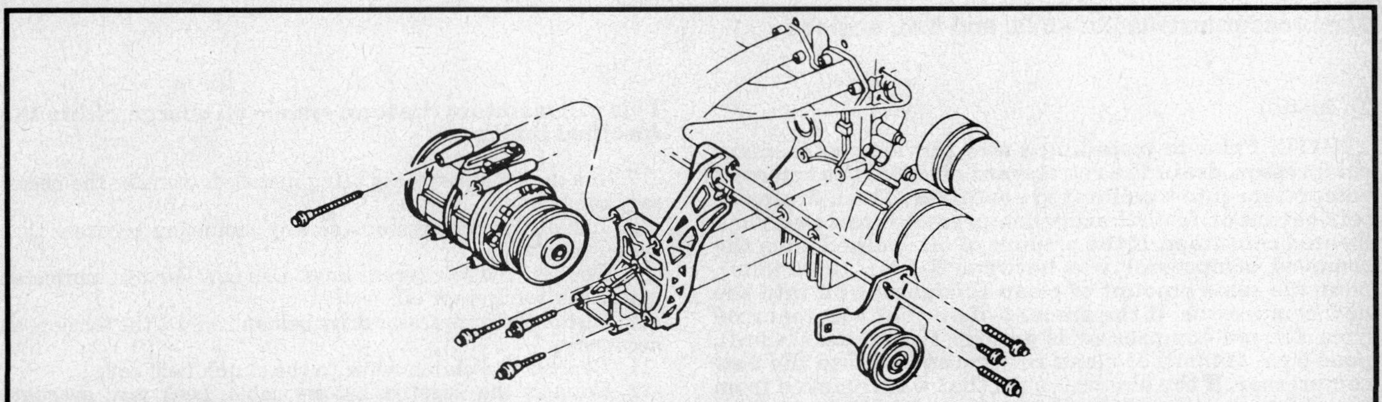

Compressor installation—2.3L engine

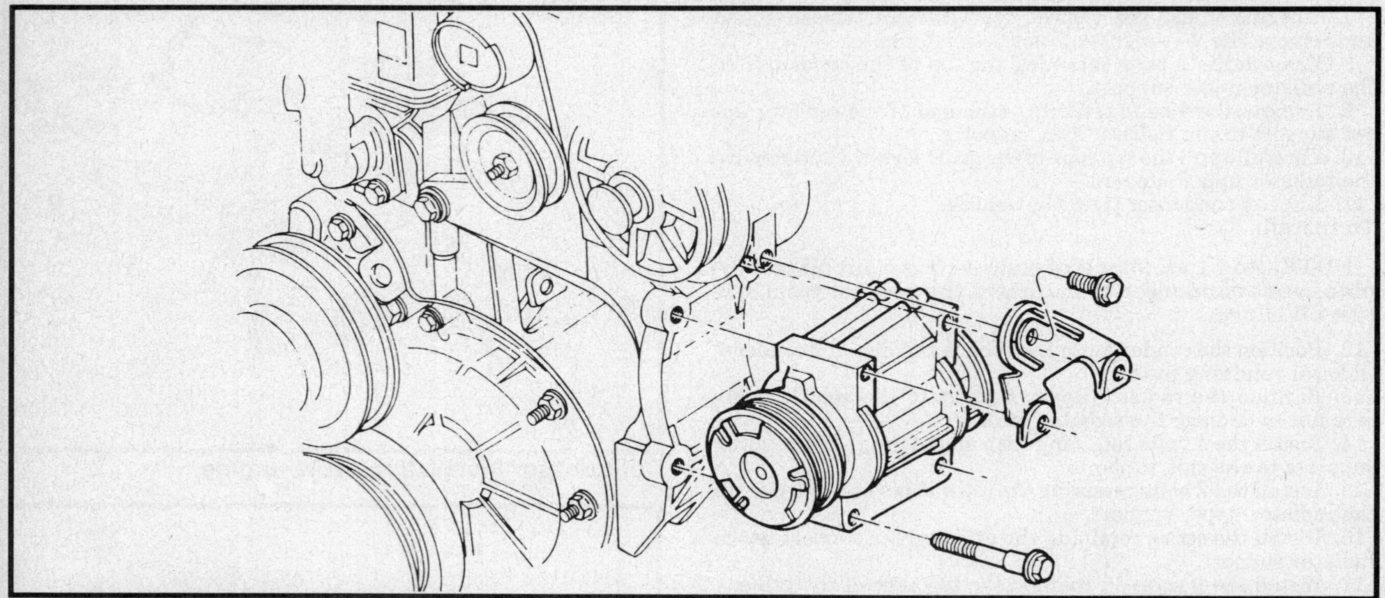

Compressor installation—4.9L engine

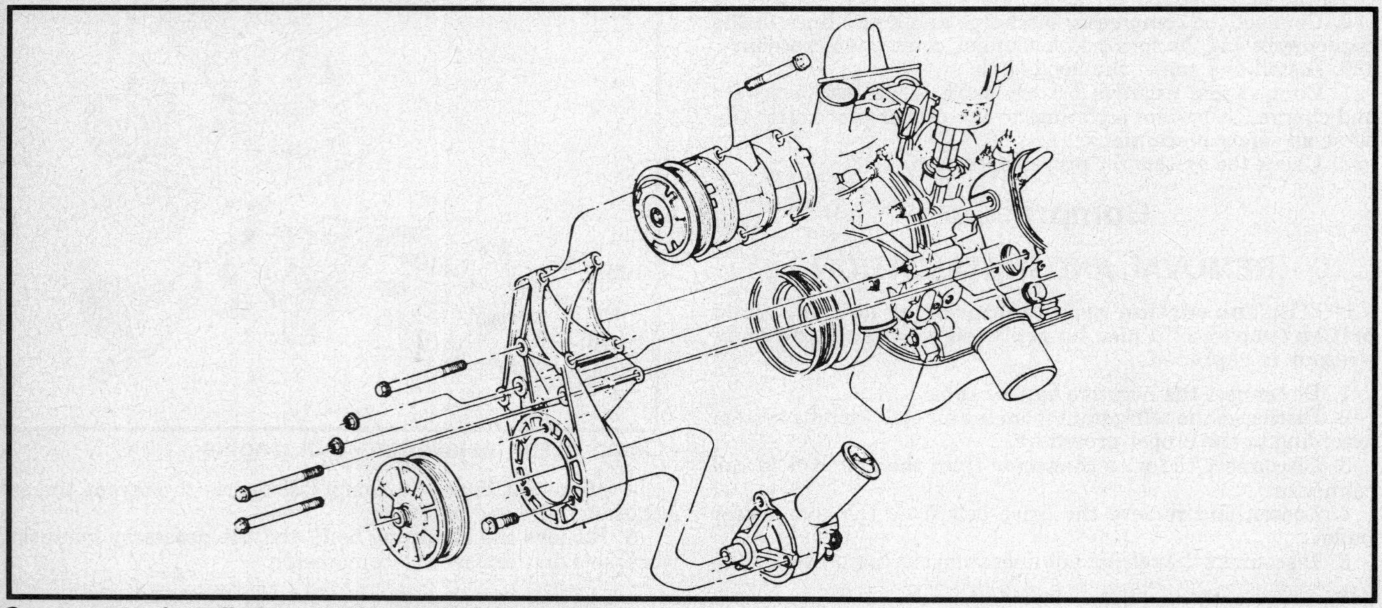

Compressor installation—5.0L and 5.8L engines

To install:

NOTE: Prior to installing a new service replacement compressor, drain the refrigerant oil from the removed compressor into a calibrated container. Then, drain the refrigerant oil from the new compressor into a clean calibrated container. If the amount of oil drained from the removed compressor was between 3–5 oz. (90–148ml), pour the same amount of clean refrigerant oil into the new compressor. If the amount of oil that was removed from the old compressor is greater than 5 oz. (148ml), pour 5 oz. (148ml) of clean refrigerant oil into the new compressor. If the amount of oil that was removed from the old compressor is less than 3 oz. (90ml), pour 3 oz. (90ml) of clean refrigerant oil into the new compressor. This will maintain the total system oil charge within the specified limits.

7. If a new compressor is being installed, transfer the necessary components.
8. Install the compressor and any mounting brackets that were removed.
9. Connect the refrigerant lines. Use new O-rings lubricated with clean refrigerant oil.
10. Install the compressor drive belt and adjust the tension, as necessary.
11. Connect the clutch wires to the clutch field coil.
12. Connect the negative battery cable. Leak test, evacuate and charge the system according to the proper procedure. Observe all safety precautions.

13. Check the system for proper operation.

Accumulator/Drier

REMOVAL AND INSTALLATION

The accumulator/drier should be replaced under the following conditions:

- The accumulator/drier is restricted, plugged or perforated.
- The system has been left open for more than 24 hours.
- There is evidence of moisture in the system: internal corrosion of metal lines or the refrigerant oil is thick and dark.
- A component such as a condenser, evaporator, refrigerant line or a seized compressor is replaced. Flush the system and replace the orifice tube when replacing a seized or damaged compressor.
- There is more than 5 oz. of compressor oil in the accumulator/drier, indicating that the bleed hole is clogged. Be sure to check this before a compressor is replaced for lack of performance or seizure.

NOTE: The accumulator/drier must be replaced whenever a condenser, evaporator core, refrigerant line, seized compressor or damage to some other major component requires opening of the refrigerant system in order to service the difficulty.

Do not replace the accumulator/drier every time if the following conditions exist:

- There is a loss of refrigerant charge.
- A component, except as described above, is changed.
- A dent is found in the outer shell of the accumulator/drier.

Aerostar and E Series

1. Disconnect the negative battery cable.
2. Discharge the refrigerant from the air conditioning system according to the proper procedure.
3. Disconnect the electrical connector from the pressure switch.
4. Remove the pressure switch by unscrewing it from the accumulator/drier.
5. Disconnect the suction line from the accumulator/drier using the spring-lock coupling disconnect procedure.
6. On Aerostar, remove the 2 mounting bands holding the accumulator/drier and remove the clamp around the inlet tube. On E Series, remove the 2 mounting screws retaining the bracket for the accumulator/drier.
7. Using the spring-lock coupling disconnection procedure, disconnect the accumulator/drier from the evaporator outlet tube and remove the accumulator/drier. Cap all open refrigerant connections to prevent the entrance of dirt and moisture.

To install:

8. Install the accumulator/drier on the evaporator outlet tube using the spring-lock coupling connection procedure.
9. On Aerostar, install the 2 mounting bands around the accumulator/drier and install the clamp around the inlet line. Tighten the screws to 15 inch lbs. (1.7 Nm). On E Series, install the 2 mounting screws on the bracket for the accumulator/drier. Tighten the screws to 15 inch lbs. (1.7 Nm).
10. Connect the suction line to the accumulator/drier using the spring-lock coupling connection procedure.
11. Install a new O-ring lubricated with clean refrigerant oil on the pressure switch nipple of the suction accumulator/drier. Then, install the pressure switch and tighten to 5–10 ft. lbs. (7–13 Nm) if the switch has a metal base. Hand tighten only, if the switch has a plastic base.
12. Connect the electrical connector to the pressure switch and connect the negative battery cable.
13. Leak test, evacuate and charge the system according to the proper procedure. Observe all safety precautions.
14. Check the system for proper operation.

Bronco, Bronco II, F Series, Explorer and Ranger

1. Disconnect the negative battery cable.
2. Discharge the refrigerant from the air conditioning system according to the proper procedure.
3. Disconnect the electrical connector from the pressure switch.
4. Remove the pressure switch by unscrewing it from the accumulator/drier.
5. Disconnect the suction hose from the accumulator/drier. On Bronco II, Explorer and Ranger, use the spring-lock coupling disconnect procedure. On Bronco and F Series, use 2 wrenches to prevent component damage. Cap the openings to prevent the entrance of dirt and moisture.
6. Loosen the fitting connecting the accumulator/drier to the evaporator core. Use 2 wrenches to prevent component damage.
7. On Bronco II, Explorer and Ranger, remove the lower forward screw holding the flanges of the case and bracket together and the screw holding the evaporator inlet tube to the accumulator bracket. Disconnect the accumulator/drier from the evaporator core and remove the bracket from the accumulator/drier.
8. On Bronco and F Series, remove the 2 screws attaching the accumulator/drier strap to the evaporator case and clip to the evaporator inlet tube.

To install:

9. On Bronco II, Explorer and Ranger, perform the following procedure:
   a. Position the bracket on the replacement accumulator/drier loosely.
   b. Using a new O-ring lubricated with clean refrigerant oil, connect the accumulator/drier to the evaporator core tube while aligning the bracket to the slot between the case flanges.
   c. Tighten the accumulator/drier to the evaporator core fitting to 26–31 ft. lbs. (32–42 Nm) using a backup wrench. Install the lower forward screw which retains the bracket between the case flanges. Tighten the bracket on the accumulator and reinstall the clip that holds the evaporator inlet tube to the accumulator bracket.
   d. Connect the suction hose to the accumulator/drier using the spring-lock coupling connection procedure.
10. On Bronco and F Series, perform the following procedure:
   a. Using a new O-ring lubricated with clean refrigerant oil, connect the accumulator/drier to the evaporator core tube. Tighten the connection finger-tight.
   b. Position the strap on the accumulator/drier to the evaporator case and clip to the evaporator core inlet tube. Align the strap and clip with the mounting bracket and install the 2 attaching screws. Loosen the connection of the accumulator/drier to the evaporator core if it is necessary to re-position the accumulator/drier to install the strap attaching screws.
   c. Tighten the accumulator/drier-to-evaporator core fitting to 26–31 ft. lbs. (32–42 Nm) using a backup wrench.
11. Install a new O-ring lubricated with clean refrigerant oil on the pressure switch nipple of the accumulator/drier. Install the pressure switch. Tighten the switch to 5–10 ft. lbs. (7–13 Nm) if the switch has a metal base and hand tighten only if the switch has a plastic base.
12. Connect the electrical connector to the pressure switch and connect the negative battery cable.
13. Leak test, evacuate and charge the system according to the proper procedure. Observe all safety precautions.
14. Check the system for proper operation.

Fixed Orifice Tube

REMOVAL AND INSTALLATION

1. Disconnect the negative battery cable.
2. Discharge the refrigerant from the air conditioning system according to the proper procedure.

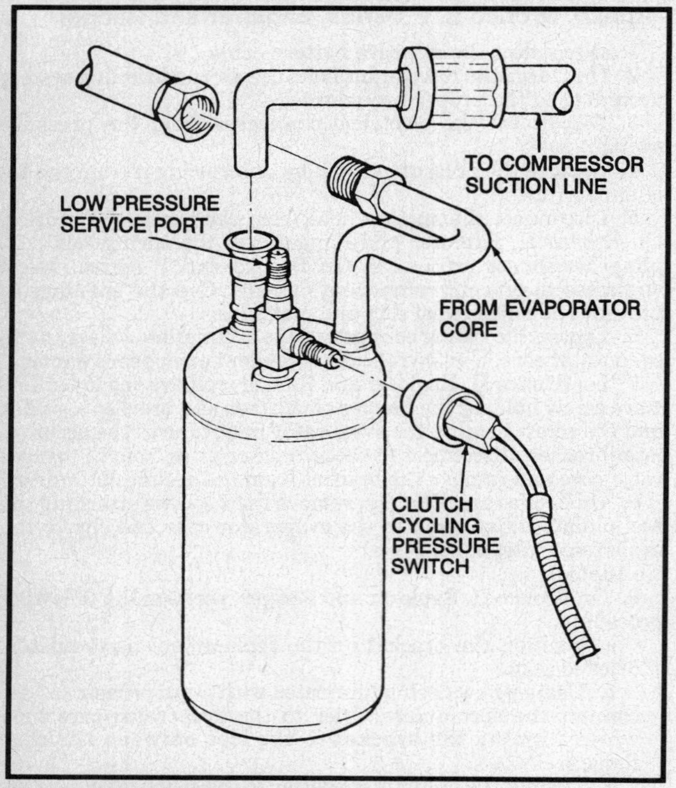
TO COMPRESSOR SUCTION LINE
LOW PRESSURE SERVICE PORT
FROM EVAPORATOR CORE
CLUTCH CYCLING PRESSURE SWITCH

Accumulator/drier—typical

3. Disconnect the liquid line from the evaporator core. Cap the liquid line to prevent the entry of dirt and excessive moisture.

4. Squirt a small amount of clean refrigerant oil into the evaporator core inlet tube to lubricate the tube and orifice O-rings during removal of the fixed orifice tube from the evaporator core tube.

5. Engage fixed orifice tube installer T83–19990–A or equivalent, with the 2 tangs on the fixed orifice tube.

NOTE: Do not attempt to remove the fixed orifice tube with pliers or by twisting the tube. To do so will break the fixed orifice tube body in the evaporator core tube. Use only the recommended tool.

6. Hold the T-handle of the tool to keep it from turning and run the nut on the tool down against the evaporator core tube until the orifice is pulled from the tube.

7. If the fixed orifice tube breaks in the evaporator core tube, it must be removed from the tube with broken orifice tube extractor T83L–19990–B or equivalent.

8. To remove a broken orifice tube, insert the screw end of the extractor into the evaporator core tube and thread the screw end of the tool into the brass tube in the center of the fixed orifice tube. Then, pull the fixed orifice tube from the evaporator core tube.

9. If only the brass center tube is removed during Step 8, insert the screw end of the tool into the evaporator core tube and screw the end of the tool into the fixed orifice tube body. Then, pull the fixed orifice tube body from the evaporator core tube.

To install:

10. Lubricate the O-rings on the fixed orifice tube body liberally with clean refrigerant oil.

11. Place the fixed orifice tube in the fixed orifice tube remover/replacer T83L–19990–A or equivalent, and insert the fixed

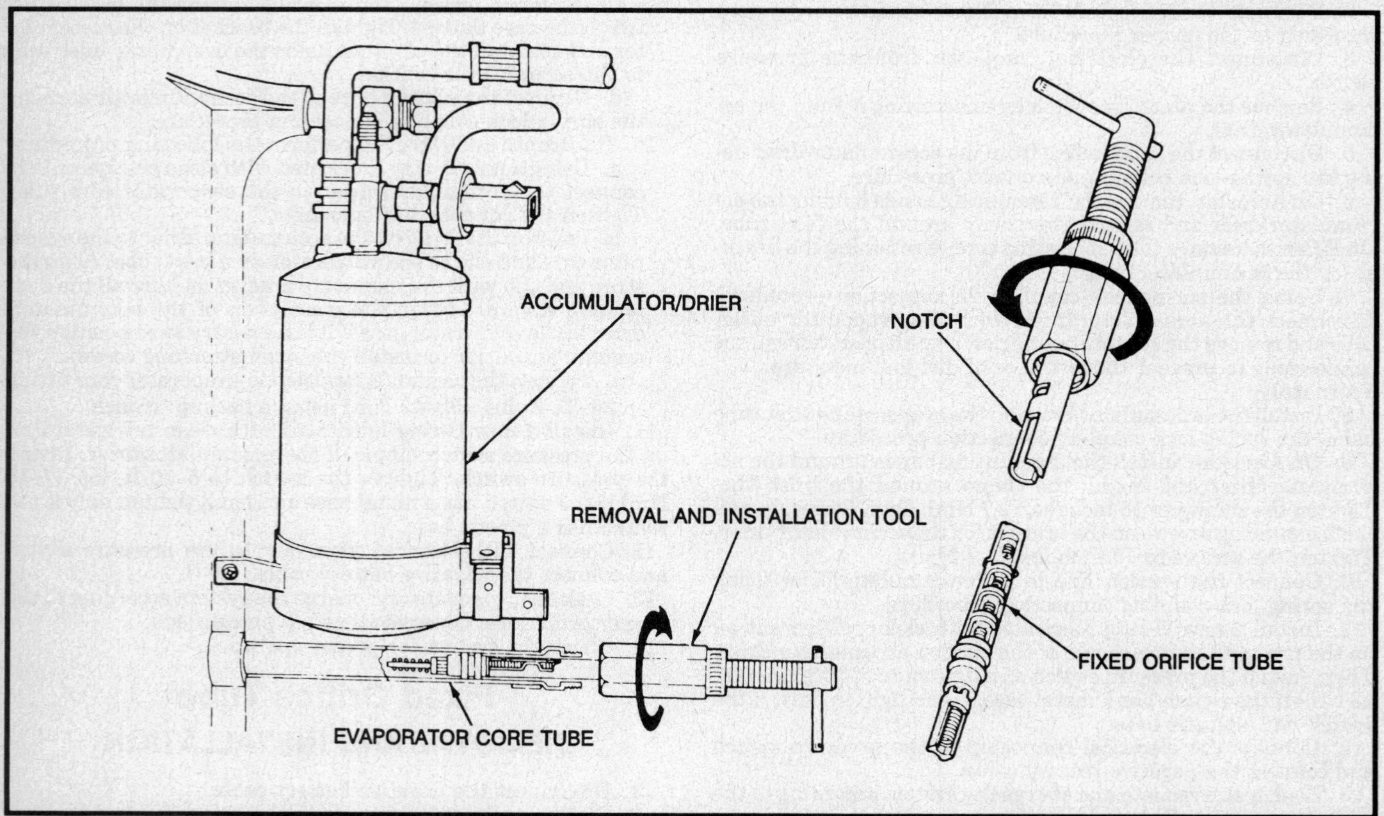
ACCUMULATOR/DRIER
NOTCH
REMOVAL AND INSTALLATION TOOL
FIXED ORIFICE TUBE
EVAPORATOR CORE TUBE

Fixed orifice tube installation—Bronco II, Explorer and Ranger

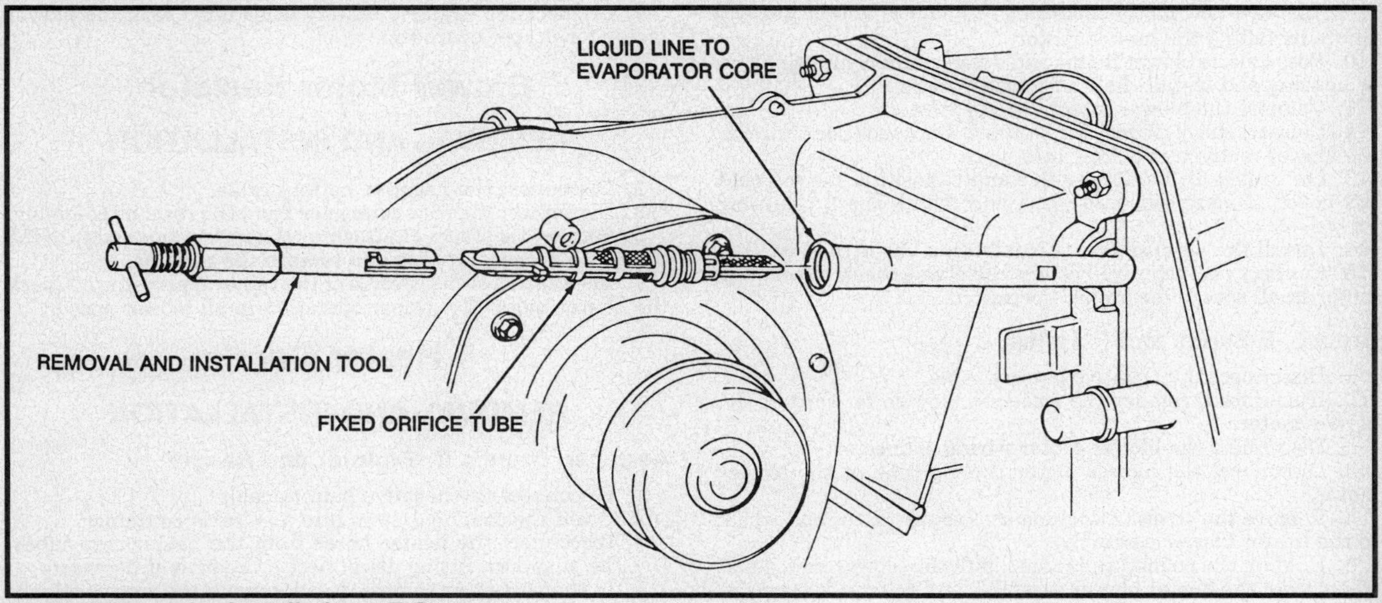
LIQUID LINE TO
EVAPORATOR CORE
REMOVAL AND INSTALLATION TOOL
FIXED ORIFICE TUBE

Fixed orifice tube installation—E Series

orifice tube into the evaporator core tube until the orifice is seated at the top.

12. Remove the tool from the fixed orifice tube.
13. Connect the liquid line to the evaporator core using the spring-lock coupling connection procedure.
14. Leak test, evacuate and charge the system according to the proper procedure. Observe all safety precautions.
15. Check the system for proper operation.

Blower Motor

REMOVAL AND INSTALLATION

Aerostar, Bronco II, Explorer and Ranger

WITHOUT AIR CONDITIONING

1. Disconnect the negative battery cable.
2. Remove the air cleaner or air inlet duct, as necessary.
3. On Aerostar, remove the 2 screws attaching the vacuum reservoir to the blower assembly and remove the reservoir.
4. Disconnect the wire harness connector from the blower motor by pushing down on the connector tabs and pulling the connector off of the motor.
5. Disconnect the blower motor cooling tube at the blower motor.
6. Remove the 3 screws attaching the blower motor and wheel to the heater blower assembly.
7. Holding the cooling tube aside, pull the blower motor and wheel from the heater blower assembly and remove it from the vehicle.
8. Remove the blower wheel push-nut or clamp from the motor shaft and pull the blower wheel from the motor shaft.

To install:

9. Install the blower wheel on the blower motor shaft.
10. Install the hub clamp or push-nut.
11. Holding the cooling tube aside, position the blower motor and wheel on the heater blower assembly and install the 3 attaching screws.
12. Connect the blower motor cooling tube and the wire harness connector.
13. On Aerostar, install the vacuum reservoir on the hoses with the 2 screws.
14. Install the air cleaner or air inlet duct, as necessary.

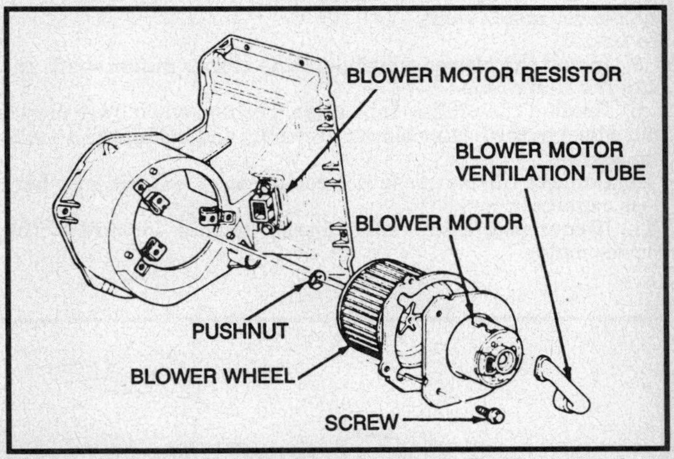
BLOWER MOTOR RESISTOR
BLOWER MOTOR
VENTILATION TUBE
BLOWER MOTOR
PUSHNUT
BLOWER WHEEL
SCREW

Blower motor installation—Bronco II, Explorer and Ranger

15. Connect the negative battery cable and check the system for proper operation.

WITH AIR CONDITIONING

1. Disconnect the negative battery cable.
2. In the engine compartment, disconnect the wire harness from the motor by pushing down on the tab while pulling the connection off at the motor.
3. Remove the air cleaner or air inlet duct, as necessary.
4. On Bronco II, Explorer and Ranger, remove the solenoid box cover retaining bolts and the solenoid box cover, if equipped.
5. Disconnect the blower motor cooling tube from the blower motor.
6. Remove the 3 blower motor mounting plate attaching screws and remove the motor and wheel assembly from the evaporator assembly blower motor housing.
7. Remove the blower motor hub clamp from the motor shaft and pull the blower wheel from the shaft.

To install:

8. Install the blower motor wheel on the blower motor shaft and install a new hub clamp.

9. Install a new motor mounting seal on the blower housing before installing the blower motor.
10. Position the blower motor and wheel assembly in the blower housing and install the 3 attaching screws.
11. Connect the blower motor cooling tube.
12. Connect the electrical wire harness hardshell connector to the blower motor by pushing into place.
13. On Bronco II, Explorer and Ranger, position the solenoid box cover, if equipped, into place and install the 3 retaining screws.
14. Install the air cleaner or air inlet duct, as necessary.
15. Connect the negative battery cable and check the blower motor in all speeds for proper operation.

Bronco, E Series and F Series

1. Disconnect the negative battery cable.
2. If equipped, remove the emission module forward of the blower motor.
3. Disconnect the blower motor wiring connector.
4. Disconnect the blower motor cooling tube at the blower motor.
5. Remove the screws attaching the blower motor and wheel to the heater blower assembly.
6. Holding the cooling tube aside, pull the blower motor and wheel from the heater blower assembly and remove it from the vehicle.
7. Remove the hub clamp and remove the blower wheel from the blower motor shaft.

To install:

8. Install the blower wheel onto the blower motor shaft. Install the hub clamp.
9. Holding the cooling tube aside, position the blower motor and wheel in the heater blower assembly and install the attaching screws.
10. Connect the blower motor cooling tube and the wire harness connector.
11. If equipped, install the emission module forward of the blower motor.
12. Connect the negative battery cable and check the blower motor for proper operation.

Blower Motor Resistor

REMOVAL AND INSTALLATION

1. Disconnect the negative battery cable.
2. Disconnect the wire connector from the resistor assembly.
3. Remove the 2 screws attaching the resistor assembly to the blower or evaporator case and remove the resistor.
4. Installation is the reverse of the removal procedure. Check the blower motor for proper operation in all blower speeds.

Heater Core

REMOVAL AND INSTALLATION

Aerostar, Bronco II, Explorer and Ranger

1. Disconnect the negative battery cable.
2. Drain the cooling system into a suitable container.
3. Disconnect the heater hoses from the heater core tubes. Use the snap-lock fitting disconnect procedure, if necessary.
4. In the passenger compartment, remove the screws attaching the heater core access cover to the plenum assembly. Remove the access cover.
5. Pull the heater core rearward and down, removing it from the plenum assembly.

To install:

6. Position the heater core and seal in the plenum assembly.
7. Install the heater core access cover to the plenum assembly and secure it with the screws.
8. Connect the heater hoses to the heater core tubes. Use the snap-lock fitting connection procedure.
9. Fill the cooling system to the proper level.
10. Connect the negative battery cable and check the system for proper operation and coolant leaks.

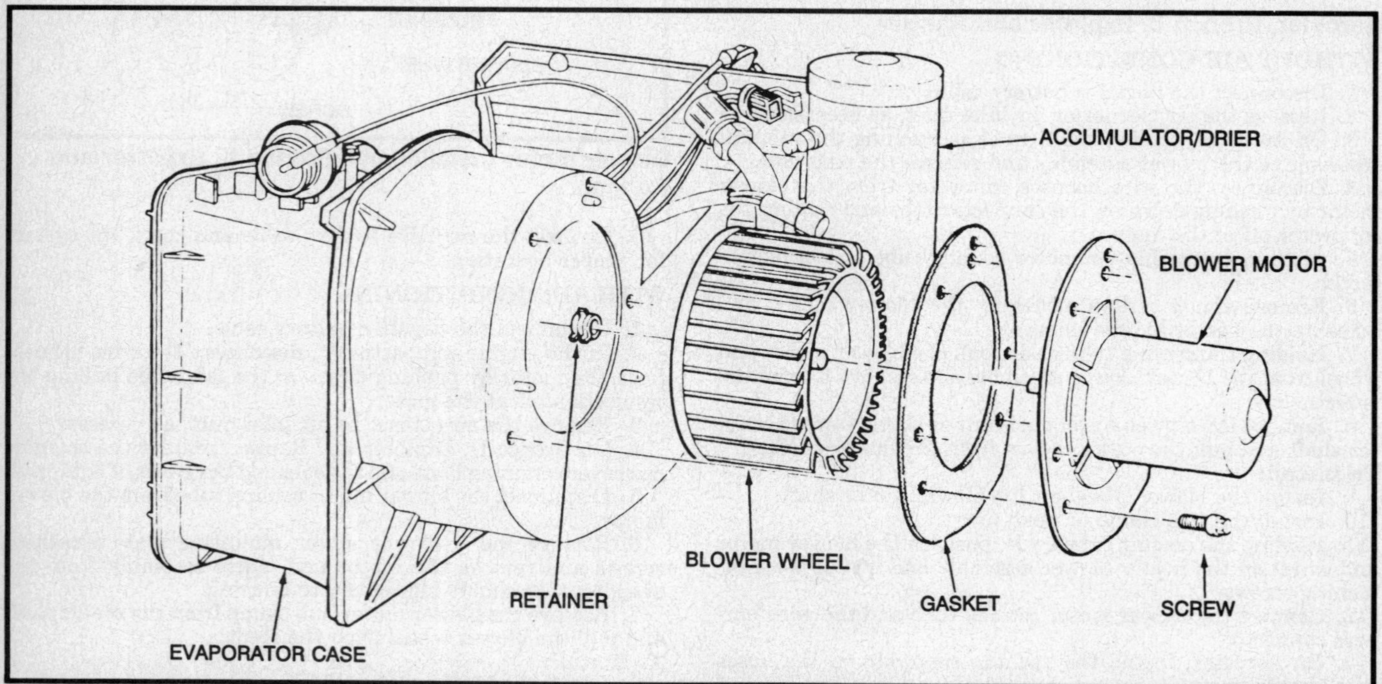
ACCUMULATOR/DRIER
BLOWER MOTOR
BLOWER WHEEL
RETAINER
GASKET
SCREW
EVAPORATOR CASE

Blower motor installation—Bronco and F Series without air conditioning

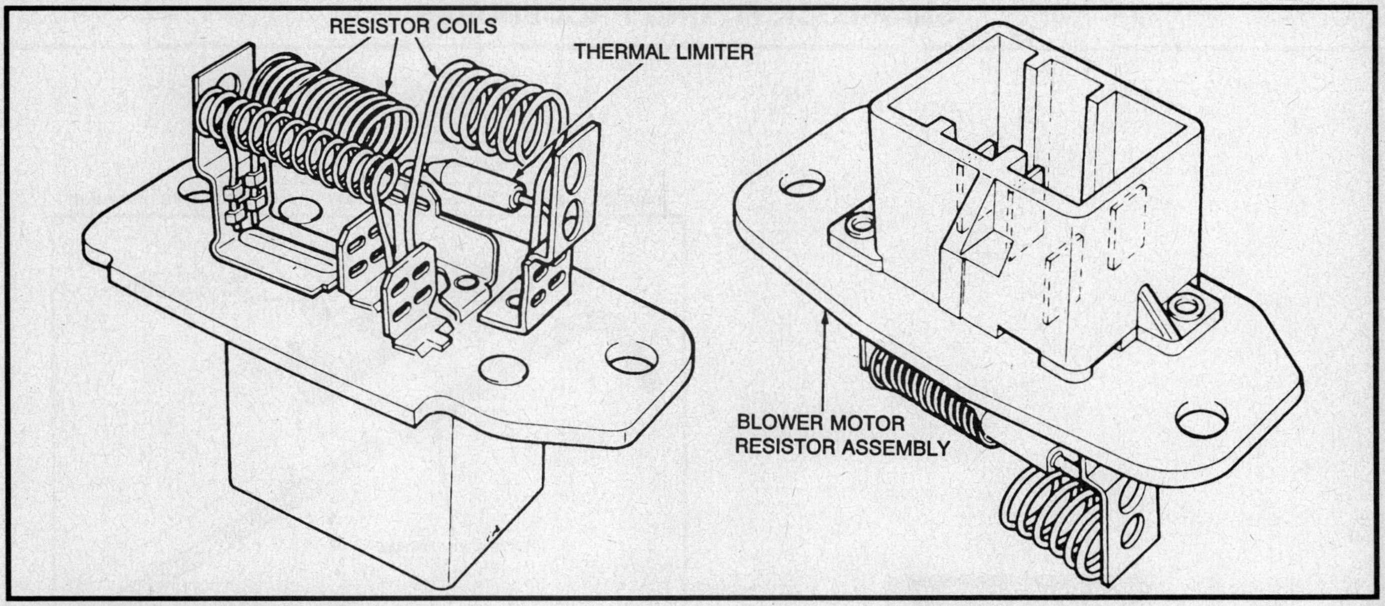
RESISTOR COILS
THERMAL LIMITER
BLOWER MOTOR
RESISTOR ASSEMBLY

Blower motor resistor—typical

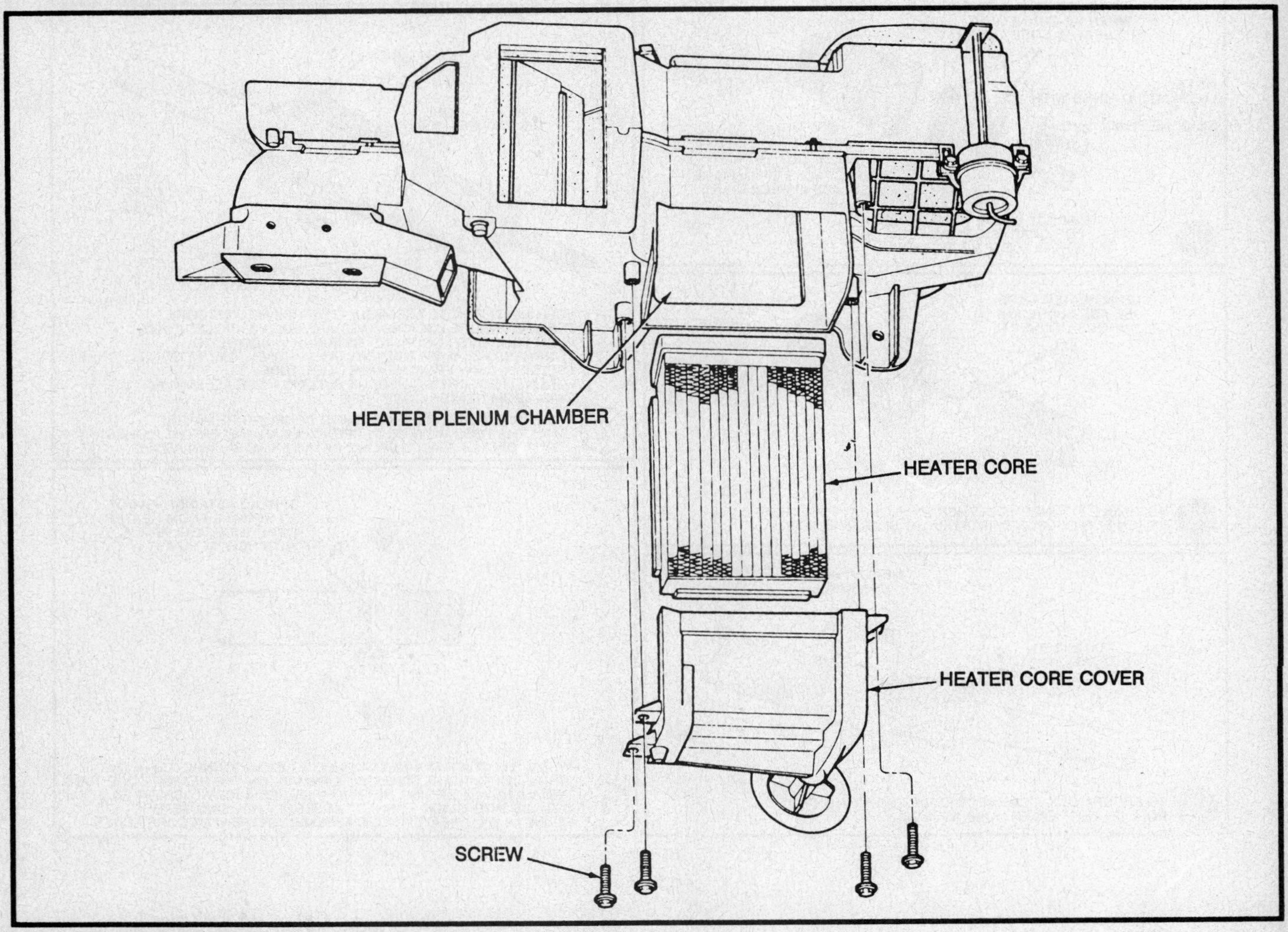
HEATER PLENUM CHAMBER
HEATER CORE
HEATER CORE COVER
SCREW

Heater core installation—Bronco II, Explorer and Ranger

SNAP-LOCK FITTING PROCEDURES

TO DISCONNECT COUPLING

CAUTION — ENGINE SHOULD BE OFF BEFORE DISCONNECTING COUPLING

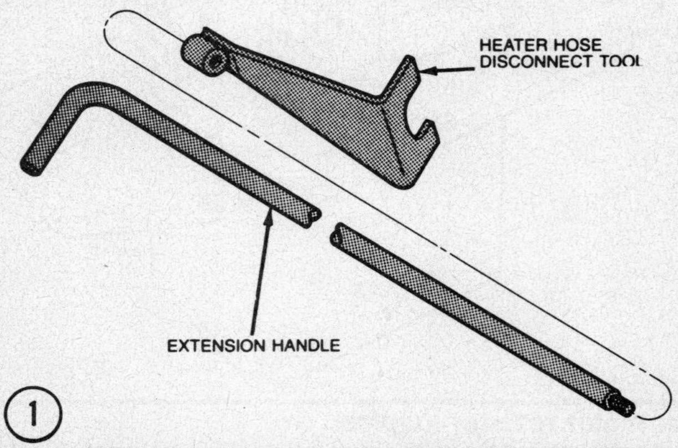
HEATER HOSE
DISCONNECT TOOL
EXTENSION HANDLE

1

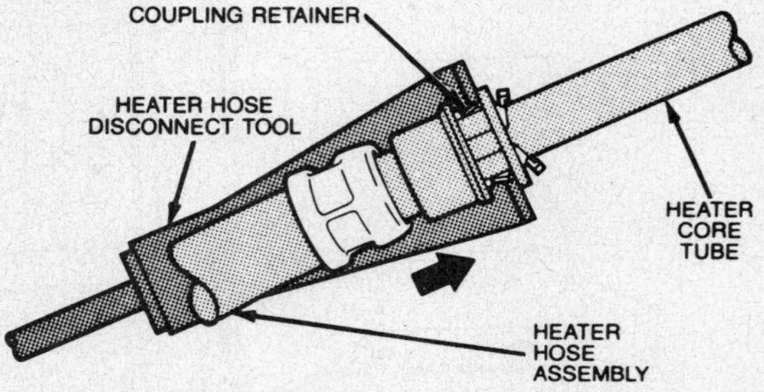
COUPLING RETAINER
HEATER HOSE
DISCONNECT TOOL
HEATER
CORE
TUBE
HEATER
HOSE
ASSEMBLY

2 PUSH HEATER HOSE ASSEMBLY TOWARDS HEATER CORE TUBE TO ENSURE LOCKING TABS ARE FULLY EXPOSED, THEN PUSH TOOL OVER COUPLING RETAINER WINDOWS TO COMPRESS RETAINER LOCKING TABS — THEN PULL HOSE ASSEMBLY AWAY FROM HEATER CORE TUBE.
REMOVE TOOL THEN CONTINUE PULLING HOSE ASSEMBLY AWAY FROM HEATER CORE TUBE.

NOTE: WHEN COMPRESSING WHITE COUPLING RETAINER, THE TOOL MUST BE PERPENDICULAR AND ON THE HIGHEST POINT OF THE COUPLING RETAINER AS SHOWN ABOVE.

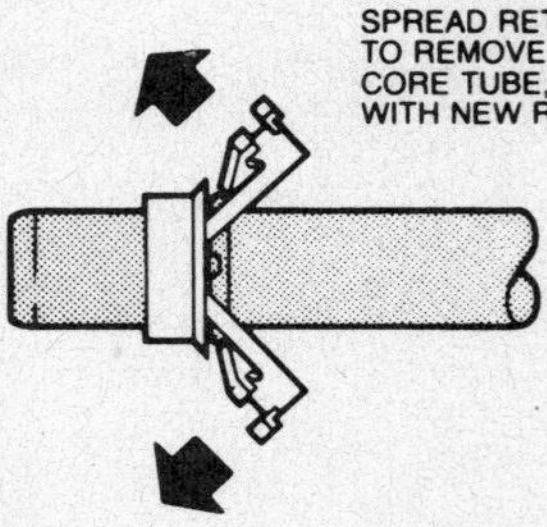
SPREAD RETAINER APART
TO REMOVE FROM HEATER
CORE TUBE, AND REPLACE
WITH NEW RETAINER

3 WHEN THE QUICK CONNECT COUPLING IS DISCONNECTED — THE WHITE COUPLING RETAINER WILL REMAIN ON THE HEATER CORE TUBE. INSTALL NEW COUPLING RETAINER, SPACER & NEW LUBRICATED O-RINGS INTO QUICK CONNECT ASSEMBLY HOUSING BEFORE RE-INSTALLING HEATER HOSE ASSEMBLY TO HEATER CORE TUBES.

TO CONNECT COUPLING

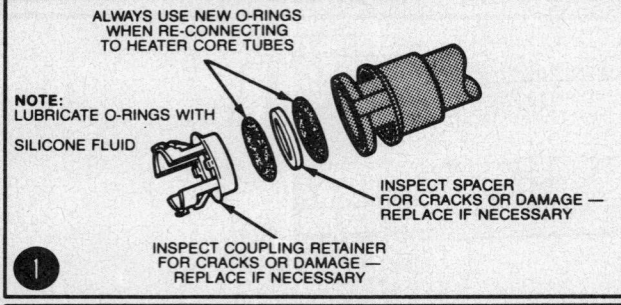

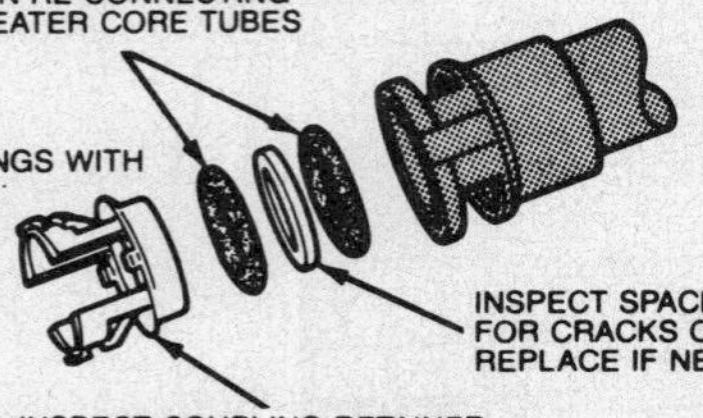
ALWAYS USE NEW O-RINGS
WHEN RE-CONNECTING
TO HEATER CORE TUBES
NOTE:
LUBRICATE O-RINGS WITH
SILICONE FLUID
INSPECT SPACER
FOR CRACKS OR DAMAGE —
REPLACE IF NECESSARY
INSPECT COUPLING RETAINER
FOR CRACKS OR DAMAGE —
REPLACE IF NECESSARY

1

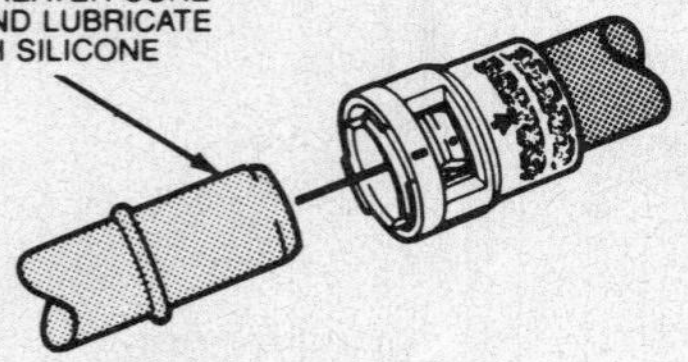
CLEAN HEATER CORE
TUBE AND LUBRICATE
WITH SILICONE

2 ASSEMBLE FITTINGS TOGETHER BY PUSHING TOGETHER — LISTEN FOR COUPLING RETAINER TO SNAP IN PLACE.

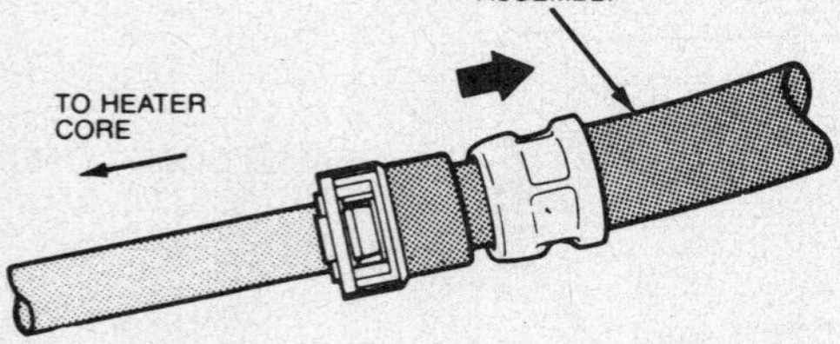
HEATER HOSE
ASSEMBLY
TO HEATER
CORE

3 TO ENSURE QUICK CONNECT ENGAGEMENT, LIGHTLY PULL ON THE HEATER HOSE ASSEMBLY

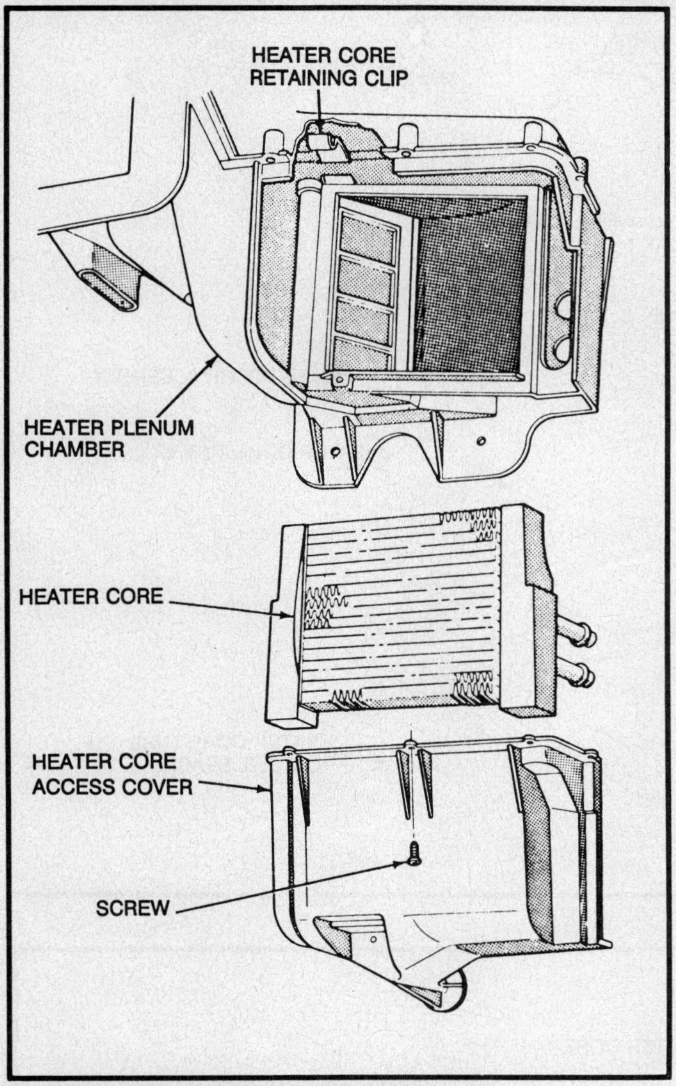
HEATER CORE
RETAINING CLIP
HEATER PLENUM
CHAMBER
HEATER CORE
HEATER CORE
ACCESS COVER
SCREW

Heater core installation—Aerostar

Bronco, E Series and F Series

1. Disconnect the negative battery cable.
2. Drain the cooling system into a suitable container.
3. Disconnect the heater hoses from the heater core in the engine compartment.
4. On E Series, remove the 2 screws retaining the modesty panel to the underside of the instrument panel. Remove the modesty panel.
5. On Bronco and F Series, remove the glove compartment.
6. From inside the passenger compartment, remove the screws from the heater core cover and remove the cover. On Bronco and F Series, disconnect the vacuum source but leave the vacuum harness attached to the cover.
7. On E Series, remove the screw and retaining bracket at the bottom of the heater core.
8. Remove the heater core and seal.

To install:

9. Position the heater core and seal into the heater case or plenum.
10. Position the heater core cover and install the attaching screws.
11. On E Series, install the modesty panel and the retaining screws. On Bronco and F Series, Connect the vacuum harness to it's source connection and install the glove compartment.
12. Connect the heater hoses to the heater core.
13. Fill the cooling system to the proper level.
14. Connect the negative battery cable and check the system for proper operation and coolant leaks.

Evaporator

REMOVAL AND INSTALLATION

Aerostar

1. Disconnect the negative battery cable.
2. Discharge the refrigerant from the air conditioning system according to the proper procedure.
3. Remove the air cleaner and air inlet duct.
4. Disconnect the electrical connectors from the blower motor, blower motor resistor and pressure switch.
5. Disconnect the liquid line from the inlet tube and the suction line from the accumulator/drier, using the spring-lock coupling disconnect procedure. Cap all open refrigerant lines to prevent the entry of dirt and moisture.
6. Disconnect the vacuum harness check valve from the engine source line and disconnect the vacuum line from the vacuum motor.
7. Remove the 2 mounting bands holding the accumulator/drier to the evaporator core and the clamp from around the evaporator inlet tube.
8. Disconnect the accumulator/drier from the evaporator core outlet tube using the spring-lock coupling disconnect procedure. Remove the accumulator/drier. Cap all open refrigerant connections to prevent the entry of dirt and moisture.
9. Remove the 11 screws holding the evaporator case blower housing to the evaporator case assembly. Remove the evaporator case blower housing from the vehicle.
10. Remove the evaporator core from the vehicle.

To install:

NOTE: Add 3 oz. (90ml) of clean refrigerant oil to a new replacement evaporator core to maintain the total system oil charge.

11. Position the evaporator core into the installed evaporator case half.
12. Position the evaporator case blower housing to the evaporator case and install with the 11 screws.
13. Connect the accumulator/drier to the evaporator core outlet tube using the spring-lock coupling connection procedure.
14. Install the 2 mounting bands around the accumulator/drier and install the clamp around the inlet line. Tighten the screws to 15 inch lbs. (1.7 Nm).
15. Connect the liquid and suction lines using the spring-lock coupling connection procedure.
16. Connect the electrical connectors to the blower motor, pressure switch and blower motor resistor.
17. Connect the vacuum line to the vacuum motor. Connect the vacuum source line from the engine to the check valve.
18. Connect the negative battery cable. Leak test, evacuate and charge the system according to the proper procedure. Observe all safety precautions.
19. Check the system for proper operation.

Bronco II, Explorer and Ranger

1. Disconnect the negative battery cable.
2. Discharge the refrigerant from the air conditioning system according to the proper procedure.
3. Disconnect the electrical connector from the pressure switch located on top of the accumulator/drier. Remove the pressure switch.

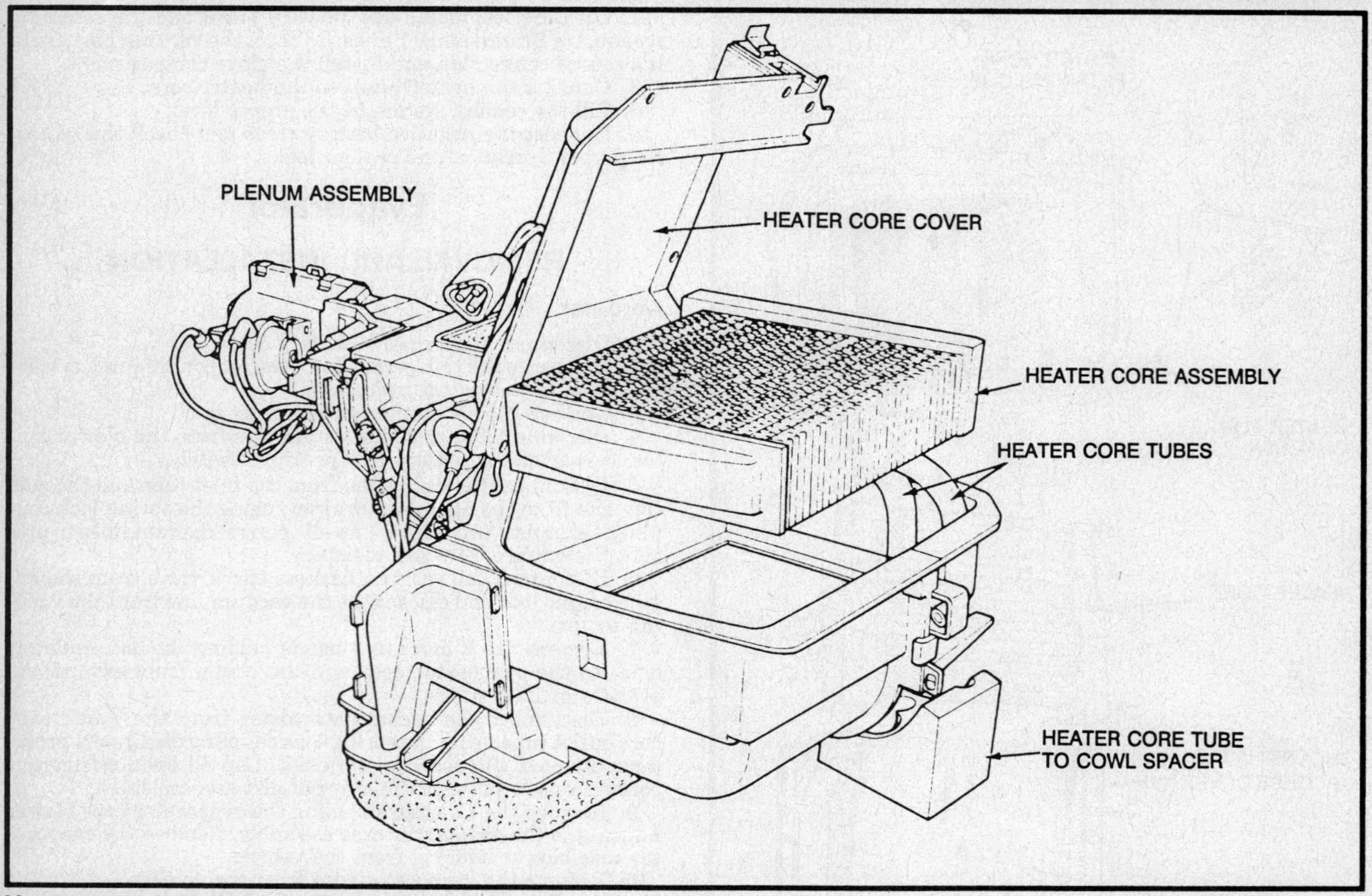
PLENUM ASSEMBLY
HEATER CORE COVER
HEATER CORE ASSEMBLY
HEATER CORE TUBES
HEATER CORE TUBE
TO COWL SPACER

Heater core installation—Bronco and F Series

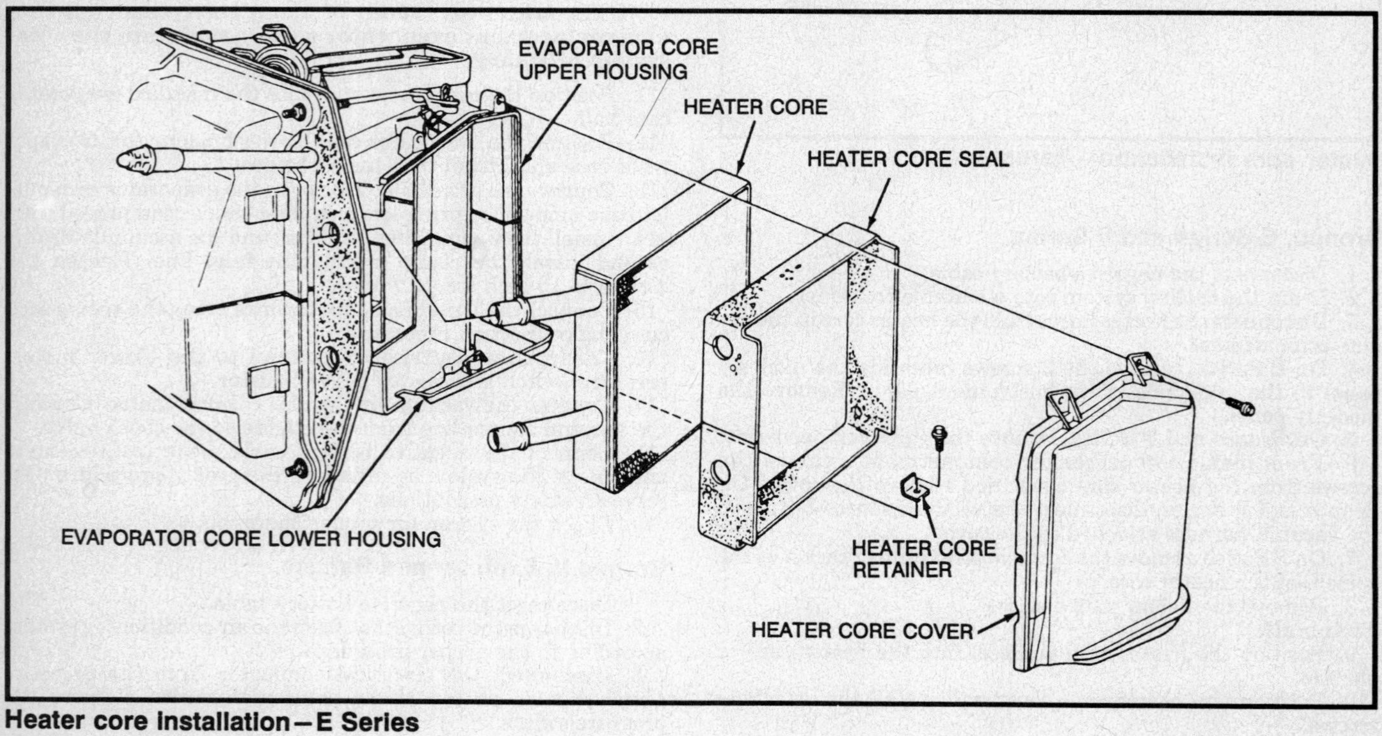
EVAPORATOR CORE
UPPER HOUSING
HEATER CORE
HEATER CORE SEAL
EVAPORATOR CORE LOWER HOUSING
HEATER CORE
RETAINER
HEATER CORE COVER

Heater core installation—E Series

4. Disconnect the suction hose from the accumulator/drier using the spring-lock coupling disconnect procedure. Cap the openings to prevent the entrance of dirt and moisture.
5. Disconnect the liquid line from the evaporator core inlet tube using a backup wrench to loosen the fitting. Cap the openings to prevent the entrance of dirt and moisture.
6. Remove the screws holding the evaporator case service cover and vacuum reservoir to the evaporator case assembly.
7. Store the vacuum reservoir in a secure position to avoid vacuum line damage.
8. Remove the 2 dash panel mounting nuts.
9. Remove the evaporator case service cover from the evaporator case assembly.
10. Remove the evaporator core and accumulator/drier assembly from the vehicle.

To install:

NOTE: Add 3 oz. (90ml) of clean refrigerant oil to a new replacement evaporator core to maintain the total system oil charge.

11. Position the evaporator core and accumulator/drier assembly into the evaporator case out-board half.
12. Position the evaporator case service cover into place on the evaporator case assembly.
13. Install the 2 dash panel mounting nuts.
14. Install the screws holding the evaporator service case half to the evaporator case assembly.
15. Place the vacuum reservoir in it's installed position. Attach the reservoir to the case with 2 screws.
16. Connect the liquid line to the evaporator inlet tube using a backup wrench to tighten the fitting. Use a new O-ring lubricated with clean refrigerant oil.
17. Connect the suction hose to the accumulator/drier according to the spring-lock coupling connection procedure.
18. Install the pressure switch on the accumulator/drier and tighten finger-tight.

NOTE: Do not use a wrench to tighten the pressure switch.

19. Connect the electrical connector to the pressure switch.
20. Connect the negative battery cable. Leak test, evacuate and charge the system according to the proper procedure. Observe all safety precautions.
21. Check the system for proper operation.

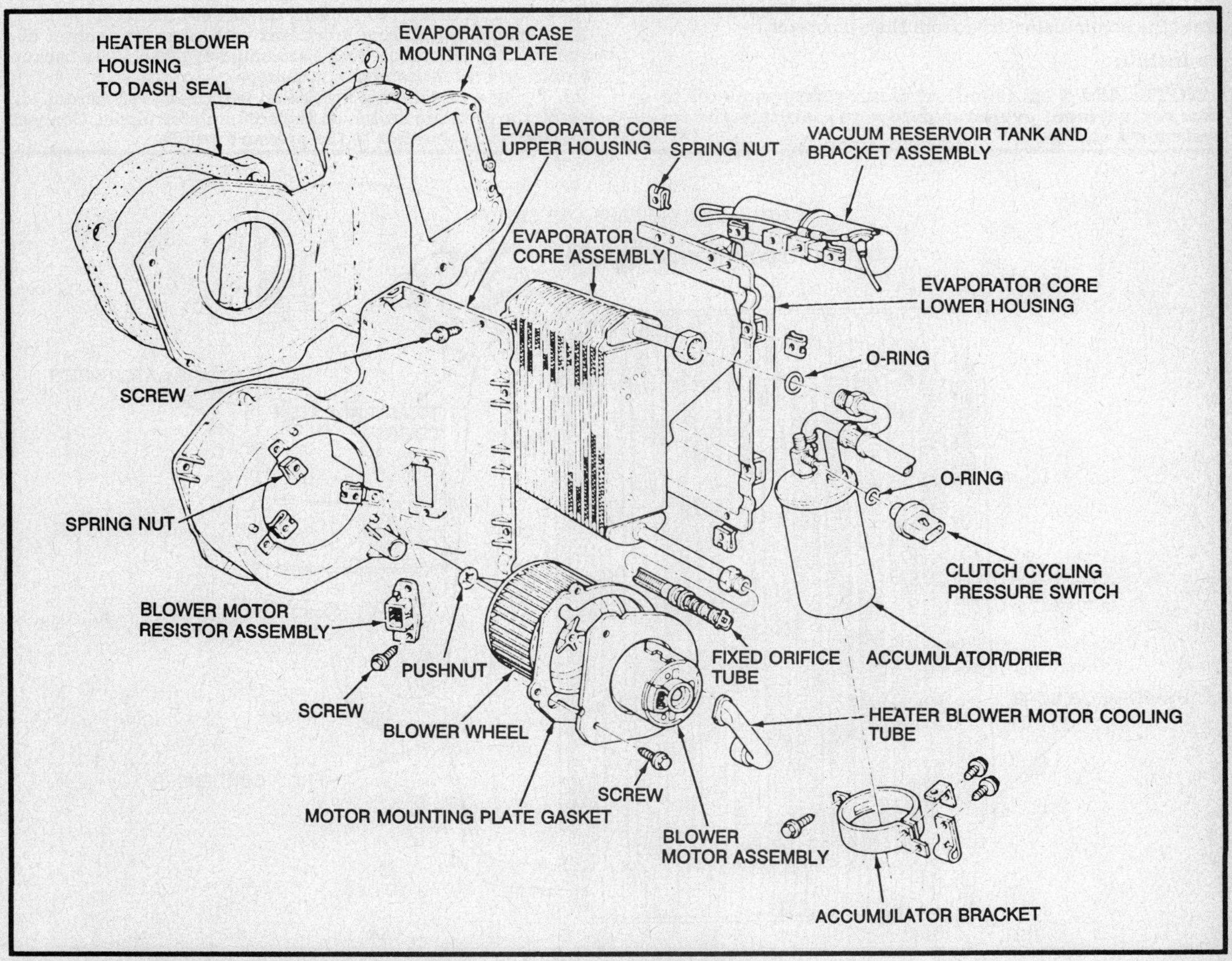
HEATER BLOWER HOUSING TO DASH SEAL
EVAPORATOR CASE MOUNTING PLATE
EVAPORATOR CORE UPPER HOUSING
SPRING NUT
VACUUM RESERVOIR TANK AND BRACKET ASSEMBLY
EVAPORATOR CORE ASSEMBLY
EVAPORATOR CORE LOWER HOUSING
O-RING
SCREW
O-RING
SPRING NUT
CLUTCH CYCLING PRESSURE SWITCH
BLOWER MOTOR RESISTOR ASSEMBLY
PUSHNUT
FIXED ORIFICE TUBE
ACCUMULATOR/DRIER
SCREW
BLOWER WHEEL
HEATER BLOWER MOTOR COOLING TUBE
SCREW
MOTOR MOUNTING PLATE GASKET
BLOWER MOTOR ASSEMBLY
ACCUMULATOR BRACKET

Evaporator assembly exploded view—Bronco II, Explorer and Ranger

Bronco and F Series

1. Disconnect the negative battery cable.
2. Discharge the refrigerant from the air conditioning system according to the proper procedure.
3. Disconnect the electrical connector from the pressure switch on the side of the accumulator/drier. Remove the pressure switch.
4. Disconnect the suction hose from the accumulator/drier. Use a backup wrench to loosen the fitting. Cap the openings to prevent the entrance of dirt and moisture.
5. Disconnect the liquid line from the evaporator core using the spring-lock coupling onnect procedure. Cap the liquid line to prevent the entry of dirt and excessive moisture.
6. On gasoline engine equipped vehicles, remove the nut retaining the MAP sensor bracket to the upper left corner of the evaporator case. Remove the spring clip holding the MAP sensor to the housing and put the MAP sensor aside.
7. Remove the nut retaining the upper left corner of the evaporator case to the dash panel.
8. Remove the 6 screws attaching the left evaporator cover to the evaporator case. Remove the left evaporator cover.
9. Remove the evaporator core and accumulator from the evaporator case.
10. Remove the support straps from the accumulator and separate the accumulator/drier from the evaporator.

To install:

NOTE: Add 3 oz. (90ml) of clean refrigerant oil to a new replacement evaporator core to maintain the total system oil charge.

11. Transfer the accumulator support straps and spring nuts to the replacement evaporator core.
12. Install the evaporator core in the evaporator case.
13. Position the evaporator cover to the evaporator case and install the 6 attaching screws.
14. Install the nut to retain the upper left corner of the case to the dash panel.
15. Install the spring clip to the rib on the evaporator case and push into position.
16. Install the nut to retain the upper left corner of the MAP sensor bracket to the upper left corner of the evaporator case.
17. In the passenger compartment, install the screw to attach the lower edge of the plenum and bottom of the evaporator case to the dash panel.
18. Remove the cap from the evaporator core liquid line connection and install a new fixed orifice tube in the evaporator core tube.
19. Using a new O-ring lubricated with clean refrigerant oil, connect the liquid line to the evaporator core. Use the spring-lock coupling connection procedure.
20. Using a new O-ring lubricated with clean refrigerant oil, connect the accumulator/drier to the evaporator core.
21. Install the accumulator support straps. Tighten the accumulator-to-evaporator core fitting to 15–20 ft. lbs. (21–27 Nm). Use a backup wrench to prevent component damage.
22. Using a new O-ring lubricated with clean refrigerant oil, connect the suction hose to the accumulator/drier. Use a backup wrench to prevent component damage.
23. Using a new O-ring lubricated with clean refrigerant oil, install the pressure switch on the accumulator nipple. Connect the electrical connector to the pressure switch.

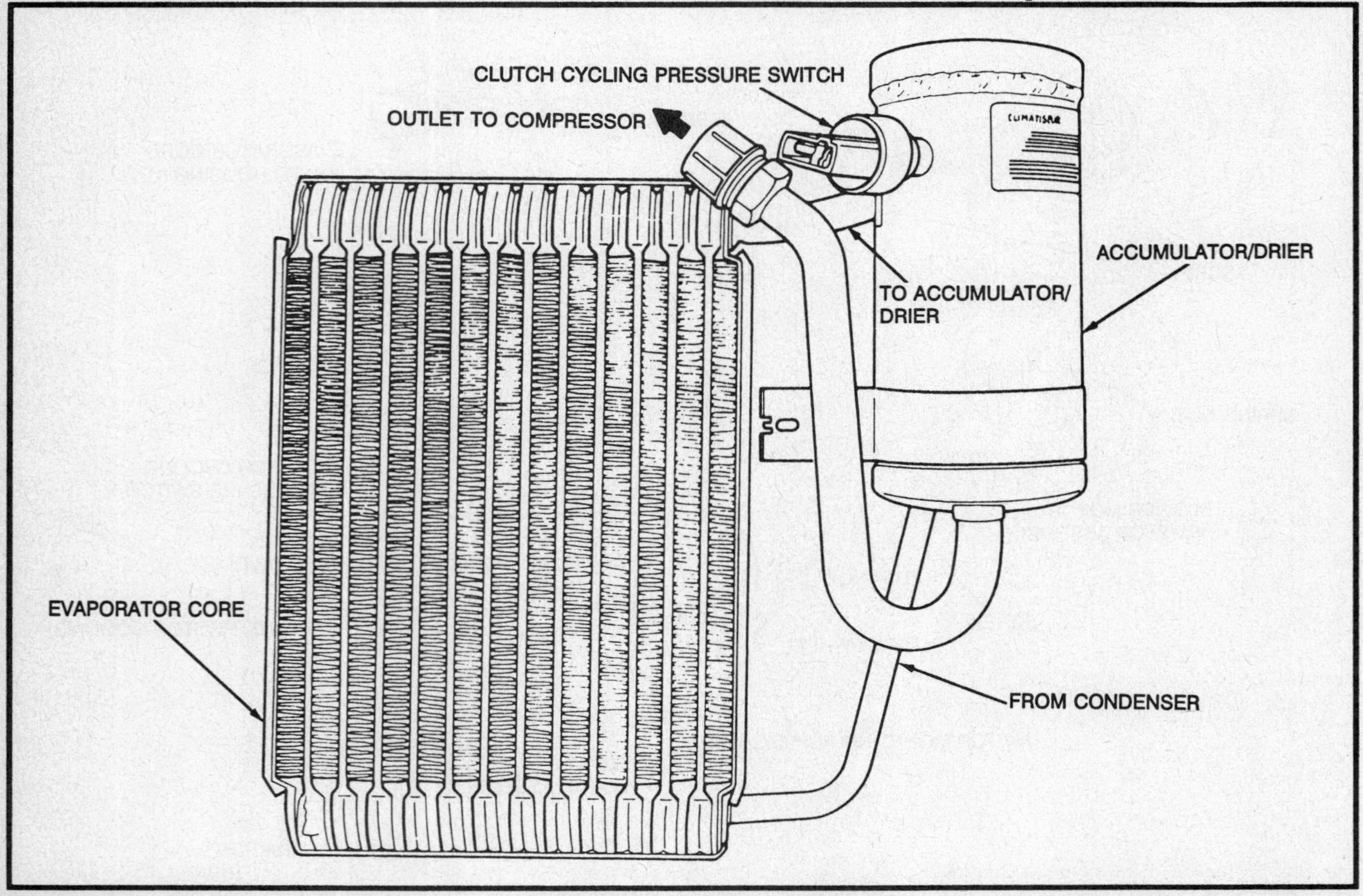
CLUTCH CYCLING PRESSURE SWITCH
OUTLET TO COMPRESSOR
ACCUMULATOR/DRIER
TO ACCUMULATOR/
DRIER
EVAPORATOR CORE
FROM CONDENSER

Evaporator core and accumulator/drier assembly— Bronco and F Series

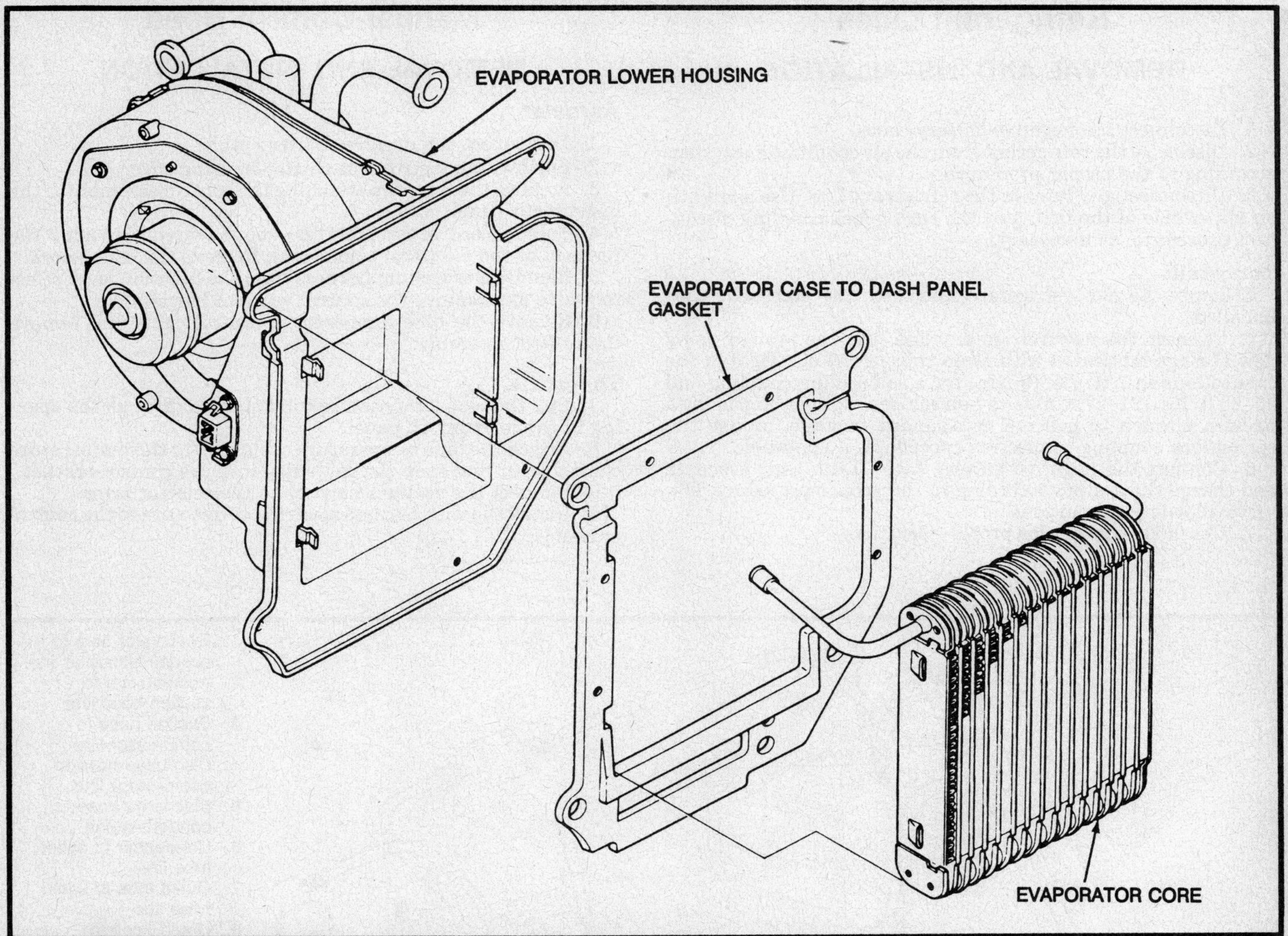
EVAPORATOR LOWER HOUSING
EVAPORATOR CASE TO DASH PANEL GASKET
EVAPORATOR CORE

Evaporator assembly—E Series

24. Leak test, evacuate and charge the system according to the proper procedure. Observe all safety precautions.
25. Check the system for proper operation.

E Series

1. Disconnect the battery cables and remove the battery.
2. Drain the coolant from the radiator into a suitable container.
3. Discharge the refrigerant from the air conditioning system according to the proper procedure.
4. Disconnect the electrical connector from the resistor on the evaporator case and from the pressure switch on the accumulator.
5. Disconnect the EEC-IV harness.
6. Disconnect the heater hoses from the heater core.
7. Disconnect the suction line from the accumulator/drier and the liquid line from the evaporator core.
8. Remove the 5 nuts retaining the evaporator assembly to the dash and remove the evaporator assembly.
9. Remove the 2 screws retaining the accumulator/drier to the case. Disconnect the accumulator from the evaporator case.
10. Remove the evaporator core and seal assembly by pulling back the retaining tab in the housing.

To install:

NOTE: Add 3 oz. (90ml) of clean refrigerant oil to a new replacement evaporator core to maintain the total system oil charge.

11. Position the evaporator core and seal assembly on the evaporator assembly and snap it into the 4 retaining tabs.
12. Using a new O-ring lubricated with clean refrigerant oil, install the accumulator/drier on the evaporator core.
13. Install the 2 screws that retain the accumulator to the case.
14. Position the evaporator assembly against the dash and secure with the 5 nuts.
15. Using new O-rings lubricated with clean refrigerant oil, connect the suction line to the accumulator/drier and the liquid line to the evaporator core.
16. Connect the EEC-IV harness and the connectors to the resistor and pressure switch.
17. Connect the heater hoses to the heater core and fill the cooling system to the proper level.
18. Install the battery and connect the battery cables.
19. Leak test, evacuate and charge the system according to the proper procedure. Observe all safety precautions.
20. Check the system for proper operation.

Refrigerant Lines

REMOVAL AND INSTALLATION

1. Disconnect the negative battery cable.
2. Discharge the refrigerant from the air conditioning system according to the proper procedure.
3. Disconnect and remove the refrigerant line. Use a wrench on either side of the fitting or the spring-lock coupling disconnect procedure, as necessary.

To install:

4. Route the new refrigerant line, with the protective caps installed.
5. Connect the new refrigerant line into the system using new O-rings lubricated with clean refrigerant oil. Tighten the connections to 7 ft. lbs. (9 Nm) for a self-sealing coupling and 15–20 ft. lbs. (21–27 Nm) for a non self-sealing coupling, using a backup wrench to prevent component damage, or use the spring-lock coupling connection procedure, if applicable.
6. Connect the negative battery cable. Leak test, evacuate and charge the system according to the proper procedure. Observe all safety precautions.
7. Check the system for proper operation.

Manual Control Head

REMOVAL AND INSTALLATION

Aerostar

1. Disconnect the negative battery cable.
2. Remove the instrument cluster housing cover.
3. Remove the 3 screws attaching the control assembly to the instrument panel.
4. Pull the control assembly far enough rearward to allow the removal of the electrical connectors. Remove the connectors.
5. Remove the vacuum harness from the function lever selector valve and remove the control vacuum harness.
6. Remove the blue temperature control cable and remove the control assembly.

To install:

7. Pull the blue temperature control cable through the opening in the instrument panel.
8. Attach the blue temperature cable wire to the temperature control lever and snap the cable flag into the control bracket.
9. Connect the vacuum harness to the selector lever.
10. Install the wire harness electrical connectors to the control assembly.

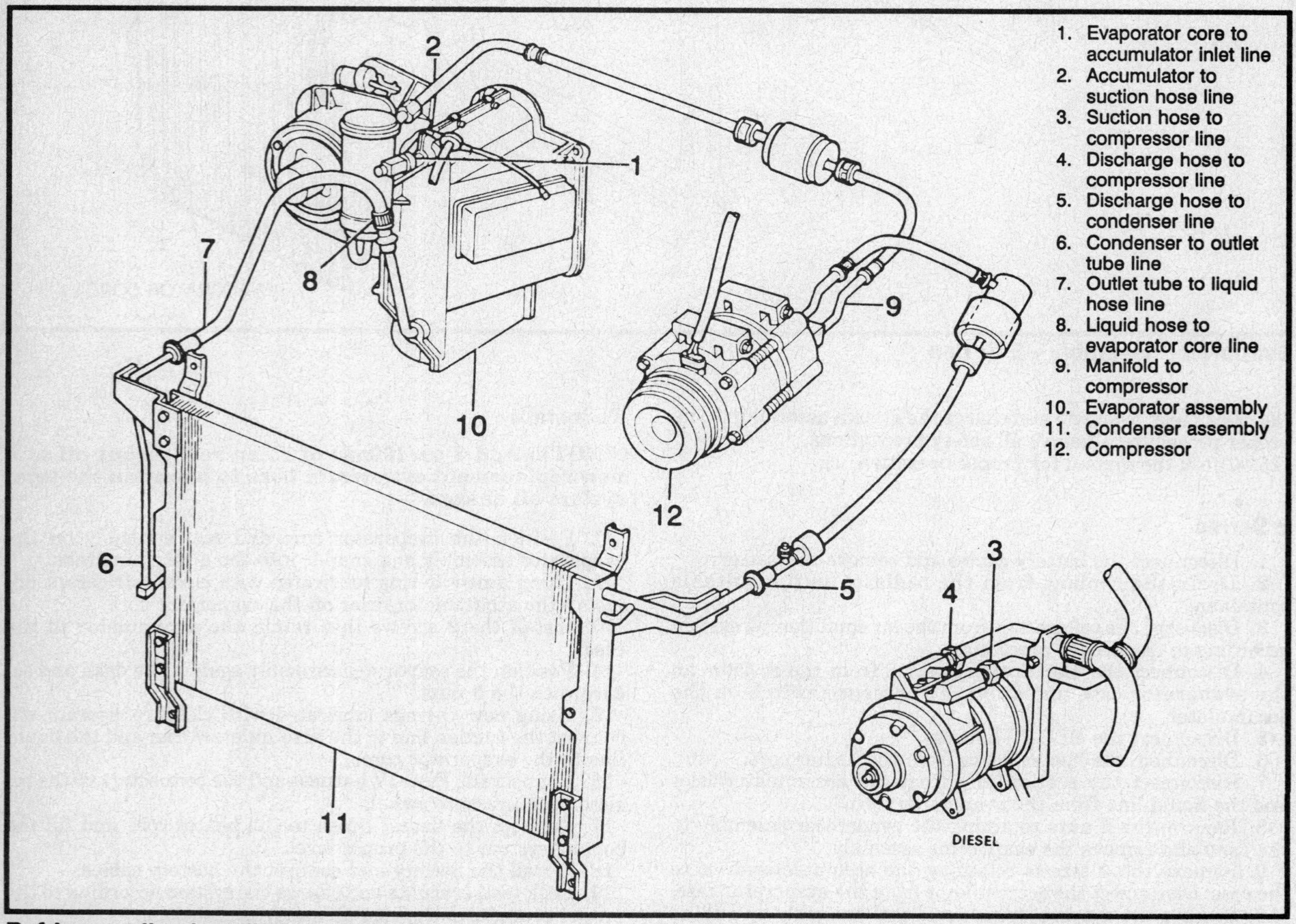
1
2
3
4
5
6
7
8
9
10
11
12
DIESEL
1. Evaporator core to accumulator inlet line
2. Accumulator to suction hose line
3. Suction hose to compressor line
4. Discharge hose to compressor line
5. Discharge hose to condenser line
6. Condenser to outlet tube line
7. Outlet tube to liquid hose line
8. Liquid hose to evaporator core line
9. Manifold to compressor
10. Evaporator assembly
11. Condenser assembly
12. Compressor

Refrigerant line installation—typical

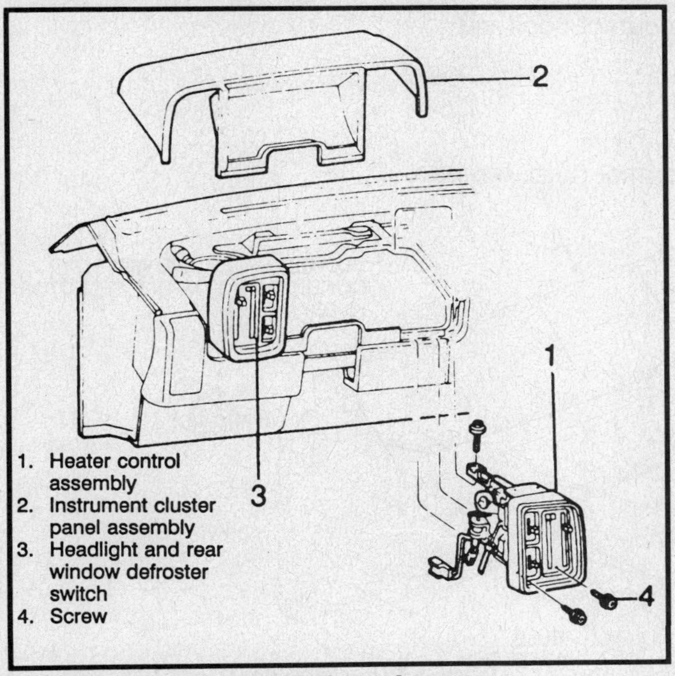
2
1
3
4
1. Heater control assembly
2. Instrument cluster panel assembly
3. Headlight and rear window defroster switch
4. Screw

Control assembly installation—Aerostar

11. Position the control assembly to the instrument panel and install the 3 attaching screws.
12. Install the instrument cluster housing cover.
13. Connect the negative battery cable and check the controls for proper operation.

Bronco II, Explorer and Ranger

1. Disconnect the negative battery cable.
2. Open the ash tray and remove the 2 screws that hold the ash tray drawer slide to the instrument panel. Remove the ash tray and drawer slide bracket from the instrument panel.
3. Gently pull the finish panel away from the instrument panel and the cluster. The finish panel pops straight back for approximately 1 in., then up to remove. Be careful not to trap the finish panel around the steering column.

NOTE: If equipped with the electronic 4×4 shift-on-the-fly module, disconnect the wire from the rear of the 4×4 transfer switch before trying to remove the finish panel from the instrument panel.

4. Remove the 4 screws attaching the control assembly to the instrument panel.
5. Pull the control through the instrument panel opening far enough to allow removal of the electrical connections from the blower switch and control assembly illumination lamp. Using a suitable tool, remove the 2 hose vacuum harness from the vacuum switch on the side of the control.
6. At the rear of the control, using a suitable tool, release the temperature and function cable snap-in flags from the white control bracket.
7. On the bottom side of the control, remove the temperature cable from the control by rotating the cable until the T-pin releases the cable. The temperature cable is black with a blue snap-in flag.
8. Pull enough cable through the instrument panel opening until the function cable can be held vertical to the control, then remove the control cable from the function lever. The function cable is white with a black snap-in flag.
9. Remove the control assembly from the instrument panel.

To install:

10. Pull the control cables through the control assembly opening in the instrument panel for a distance of approximately 8 in. (203mm).
11. Hold the control assembly up to the instrument panel with it's face directed toward the floor of the vehicle. This will locate the face of the control in a position that is 90 degrees out of it's installed position.
12. Carefully bend and attach the function cable that has a white color code and a black snap-in terminal to the white plastic lever on the control assembly. Rotate the control assembly back to it's normal position for installation, then snap the black cable flag into the control assembly bracket.
13. On the opposite side of the control assembly, attach the black temperature control cable with the blue plastic snap-in flag to the blue plastic lever on the control. Make sure the end of the cable is seated securely with the T-top pin on the control. Rotate the cable to it's operating position and snap the blue cable flag into the control assembly bracket.
14. Connect the wiring harness to the blower switch and the illumination lamp to it's receptacle on the control assembly. Connect the dual terminal on the vacuum hose to the vacuum switch on the control assembly.
15. Position the control assembly into the instrument panel opening and install the 4 mounting screws.
16. If equipped, reconnect the 4×4 electric shift harness on the rear of the cluster finish panel.
17. Install the cluster finish panel with integral push-pins. Make sure that all pins are fully seated around the rim of the panel.
18. Reinsert the ash tray slide bracket and reconnect the illumination connection circuit. Reinstall the 2 screws that retain the ash tray retainer bracket and the finish panel.
19. Replace the ash tray and reconnect the cigarette lighter.
20. Connect the negative battery cable and check the heater system for proper control assembly operation.

Bronco and F Series

1. Disconnect the negative battery cable.
2. Pull the center finish panel away from the instrument panel to gain access to the 4 screws that attach the control assembly to the instrument panel.
3. Remove the 4 screws. Then, pull the control assembly far enough through the opening in the panel to allow disengagement of the electrical connectors for the blower switch and control illumination lamp.
4. Disconnect the vacuum harness connector from the vacuum selector valve on the control assembly.
5. Disconnect the vacuum harness from the plenum assembly connector.
6. Using a suitable tool, carefully release the temperature control snap-in flange from the underside of the control assembly.
7. Rotate the control assembly 90 degrees and disconnect the temperature control cable from the temperature control lever.
8. Move the control assembly away from the instrument panel.

To install:

9. Pull the temperature control cable through the control assembly opening in the instrument panel for a distance of approximately 8 in. (203mm).
10. Hold the control assembly against the instrument panel with the face of the control directed toward the roof of the vehicle. Attach the temperature cable to it's control lever.
11. Rotate the control assembly to position it into the instrument panel opening. Snap the cable flag into the control bracket. Be sure the flag is firmly seated.
12. Connect the wire harness to the blower switch and control illumination lamp. Attach the vacuum harness to the vacuum selector valve and plenum.

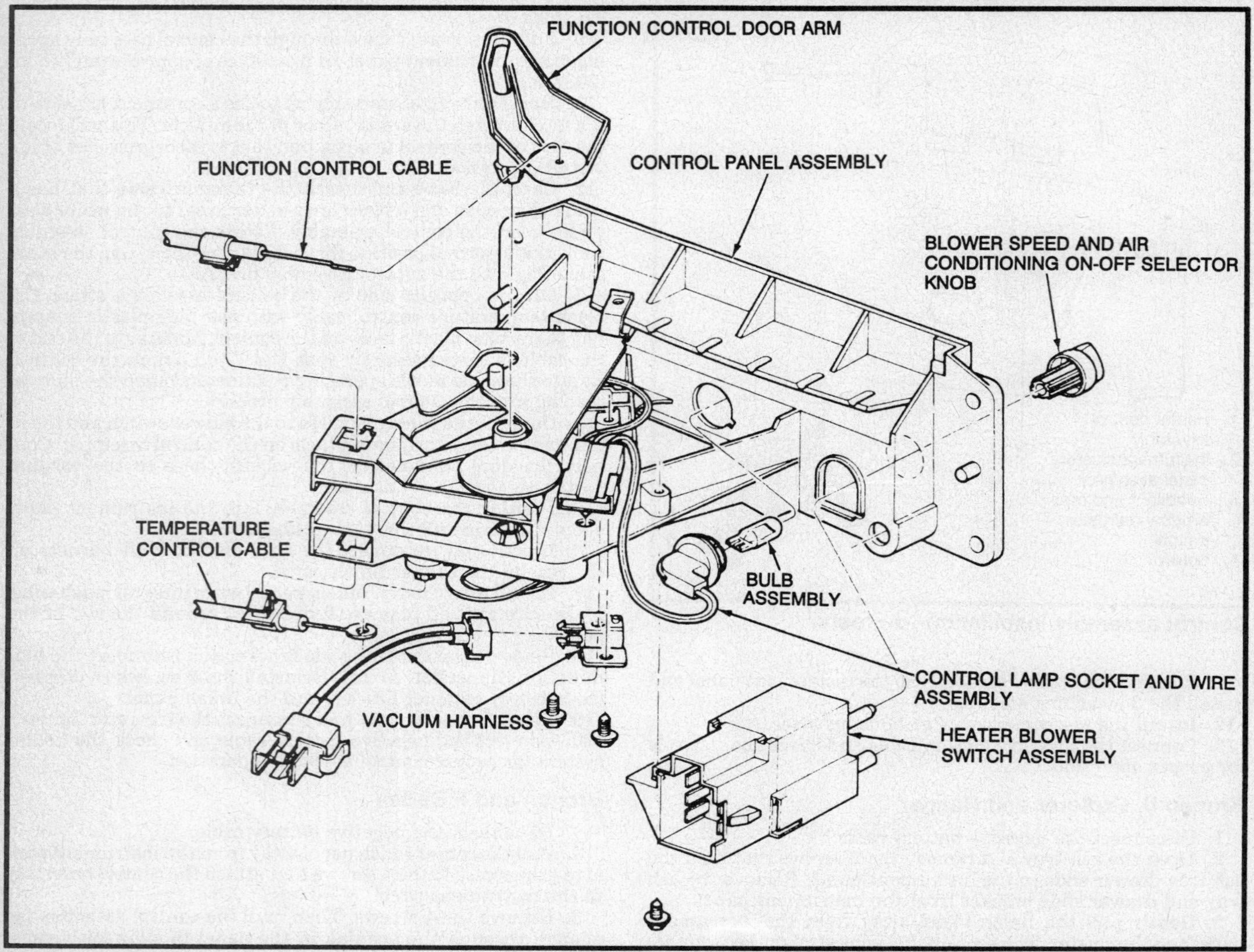
FUNCTION CONTROL DOOR ARM
FUNCTION CONTROL CABLE
CONTROL PANEL ASSEMBLY
BLOWER SPEED AND AIR CONDITIONING ON-OFF SELECTOR KNOB
TEMPERATURE CONTROL CABLE
BULB ASSEMBLY
CONTROL LAMP SOCKET AND WIRE ASSEMBLY
VACUUM HARNESS
HEATER BLOWER SWITCH ASSEMBLY

Control assembly rear view—Bronco II, Explorer and Ranger

13. Position the control assembly into it's instrument panel opening while being careful that the vacuum and electrical harness are properly stowed.
14. Install the finish panel.
15. Connect the negative battery cable and check the system for proper operation.

E Series

1. Disconnect the negative battery cable.
2. Remove the trim applique.
3. Remove the 4 screws retaining the control assembly to the mounting bracket.
4. Carefully pull the control assembly from the opening in the mounting bracket.
5. Disconnect the electrical wiring connector from the blower switch, vacuum selector and illumination bulb.
6. Remove the push-on vacuum harness retaining clips from the vacuum selector. Disconnect the vacuum harness from the vacuum selector.
7. Remove the temperature control cable from the control assembly. Disconnect the bullet-type cable retainer from the bracket using control cable removal tool T83P-18532-AH, or needle-nose pliers to compress the retaining ears. Both cable "S" bends are removed from the bottom side of the levers by rotating the cable wire 90 degrees to the lever.

To install:

8. Connect the temperature and function control cables to the control assembly.
9. Connect the vacuum harness to the vacuum selector and retain it with the 2 push-on clips.
10. Connect the electrical wiring connector to the blower switch, vacuum selector valve and illumination bulb wire and socket assembly.
11. Carefully position the control assembly on it's mounting bracket and install the attaching screws.
12. Install the applique and adjust the control cables.
13. Connect the negative battery cable and check the system for proper operation.

Manual Control Cables

ADJUSTMENT

Aerostar

TEMPERATURE CONTROL CABLE

To check the temperature control cable adjustment, move the

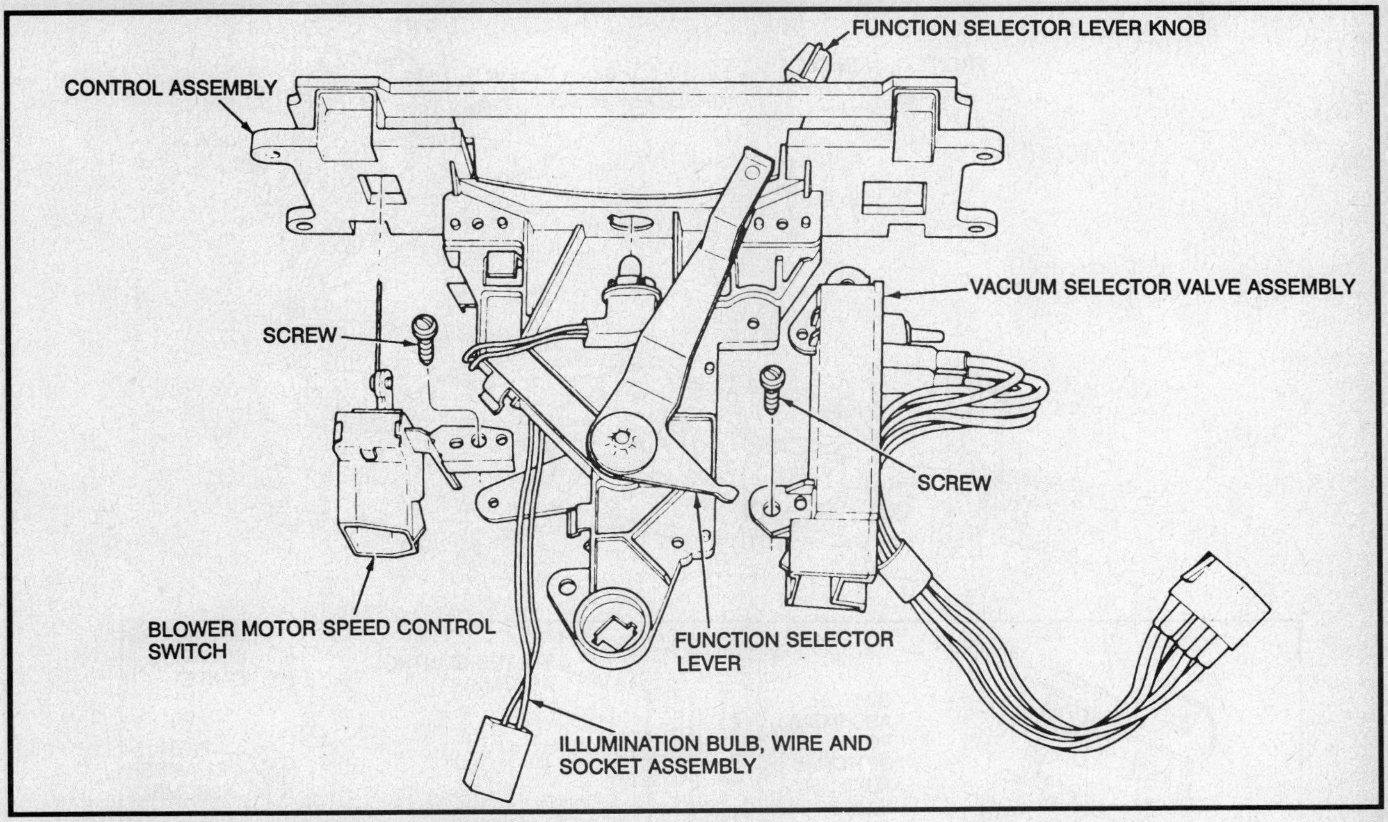
FUNCTION SELECTOR LEVER KNOB
CONTROL ASSEMBLY
VACUUM SELECTOR VALVE ASSEMBLY
SCREW
SCREW
BLOWER MOTOR SPEED CONTROL SWITCH
FUNCTION SELECTOR LEVER
ILLUMINATION BULB, WIRE AND SOCKET ASSEMBLY

Control assembly rear view—Bronco and F Series

temperature control lever back and forth, checking for the sound of the temperature blend door seating against the stop. The temperature control lever should have an equal amount of travel at each end and should not bottom out at either end of the slot. If these conditions are not met, the temperature control cable may not be adjusted properly or may not be connected. To adjust the temperature control cable, proceed as follows:

1. Remove the instrument panel upper finish panel.
2. Set the function control lever at mid-position, between **VENT** and **HEAT** and the temperature control lever at the **COOL** position.
3. Working through the opening, remove the cable housing from the metal clip on top of the plenum by depressing the clip tab and pulling the cable up. The cable wire end loop should remain attached to the control cam on the plenum.
4. To adjust the temperature control cable, rotate the temperature cam clockwise until the temperature blend door seats. Check that the temperature control lever is in the **COOL** position, then install the cable housing to the retaining clip by pushing it from the top until it snaps in place.
5. Turn the blower to **HIGH** and actuate the levers, checking for proper cable adjustment and function. Readjust, as necessary.
6. Install the instrument panel upper finish panel.

Bronco II, Explorer and Ranger

FUNCTION SELECTOR AND TEMPERATURE SELECTOR CONTROL CABLE

To check the temperature cable adjustment, move the temperature control lever all the way to the left, then move it all the way to the right. At the extreme ends of lever travel, the door should be heard to firmly seat, indicated by a loud thumping sound, allowing either maximum or no air flow through the heater core. To check the function cable adjustment, see that the function lever will reach the detents at the far left and right of it's travel. In addition, check that the air flow is correct when the function lever is moved through each detent provided in the control assembly. If cable adjustment is needed, proceed as follows:

1. Disengage the glove compartment door by squeezing it's sides together. Allow the door to hang free.
2. Working through the glove compartment opening, remove the cable jacket from the metal attaching clip on the top of the plenum by depressing the clip tab and pulling the cable out of the clip.

NOTE: The cable end should remain attached to the door cams.

3. To adjust the temperature control cable, set the temperature lever at **COOL** and hold. With the cable end attached to the temperature door cam, push gently on the cable jacket to seat the blend door. Push until resistance is felt. Reinstall the cable to the clip by pushing the cable jacket into the clip from the top until it snaps in.
4. To adjust the function control cable, set the function selector lever in the **DEFROST** detent and hold. With the cable end attached to the function cam, pull on the cam jacket until cam travel stops. Reinstall the cable to the clip by pushing the cable jacket into the clip from the top until it snaps in place.
5. Install the glove compartment.
6. Run the system blower on **HIGH** and actuate the levers, checking for proper adjustment.

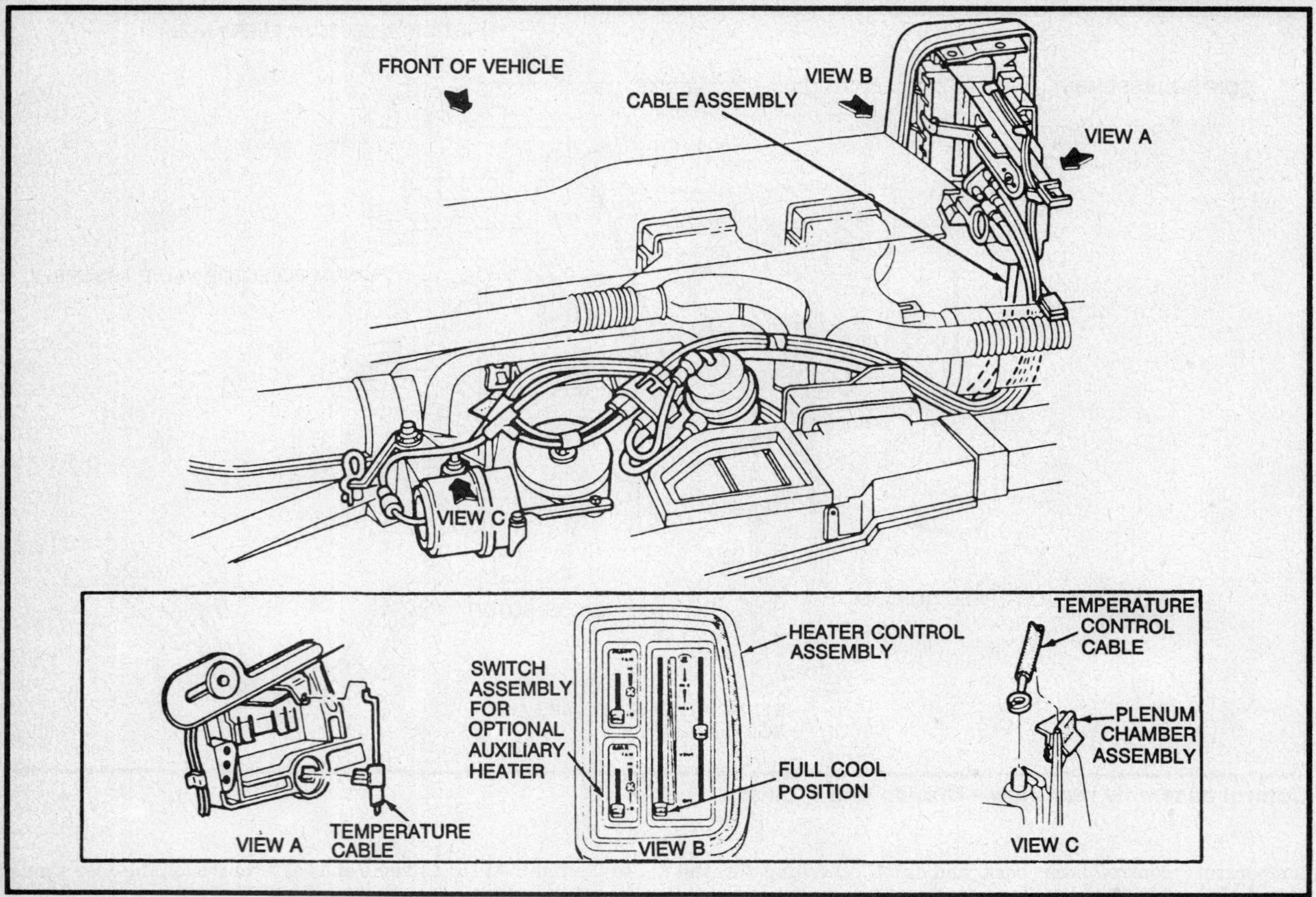
FRONT OF VEHICLE
VIEW B
CABLE ASSEMBLY
VIEW A
VIEW C
SWITCH ASSEMBLY FOR OPTIONAL AUXILIARY HEATER
HEATER CONTROL ASSEMBLY
TEMPERATURE CONTROL CABLE
PLENUM CHAMBER ASSEMBLY
FULL COOL POSITION
VIEW A
TEMPERATURE CABLE
VIEW B
VIEW C

Temperature control cable—Aerostar

Bronco and F Series

TEMPERATURE CONTROL CABLE

To check the temperature control cable adjustment, move the temperature control lever back and forth, checking for the sound of the temperature blend door seating against the stop. If the sound of the door seating is not heard before the lever reaches it's limit of travel, the temperature control cable may be misadjusted or not connected. To adjust the temperature control cable, proceed as follows:

1. Disengage the glove compartment door by squeezing the side with the stop and removing the pin holding the check strap from the opposite side. Allow the door to hang free.
2. Working through the glove compartment opening, remove the cable jacket from the metal attaching clip on top of the plenum by depressing the clip tab and pulling the cable up.

NOTE: The cable end should remain attached to the door cam and/or crank arm.

3. Set the temperature control lever to **COOL** and hold firmly.
4. With the cable end attached to the temperature door cam, push gently on the cable jacket to seat the blend door. Push until resistance is felt. Install the cable into the clip by pushing the cable jacket into the clip from the top intil it snaps into place.
5. Operate the system to check temperature control.

E Series

TEMPERATURE CONTROL CABLE

1. Set the temperature control lever on the **COOL** position.
2. Remove the cable from the retaining clip on top of the evaporator-heater case. Leave the cable attached to the yellow crank.
3. Rotate the yellow crank counterclockwise until the temperature blend door seats.
4. Check again to be sure the temperature lever is in the **COOL** position, then install the cable housing in it's retaining clip by pushing it from the top until it snaps into place.
5. Turn the blower switch to **HI** and move the temperature lever through it's range of travel to check for proper cable adjustment. Readjust, if necessary.

REMOVAL AND INSTALLATION

Aerostar

TEMPERATURE CONTROL CABLE

1. Disconnect the negative battery cable.
2. Remove the instrument panel upper finish panel and the instrument cluster housing assembly.
3. Remove the radio.
4. Working through the opening on the instrument panel top, remove the cable housing from the metal clips on top of the plenum. Disconnect the cable wire end loop from the cam.
5. Remove the control assembly.

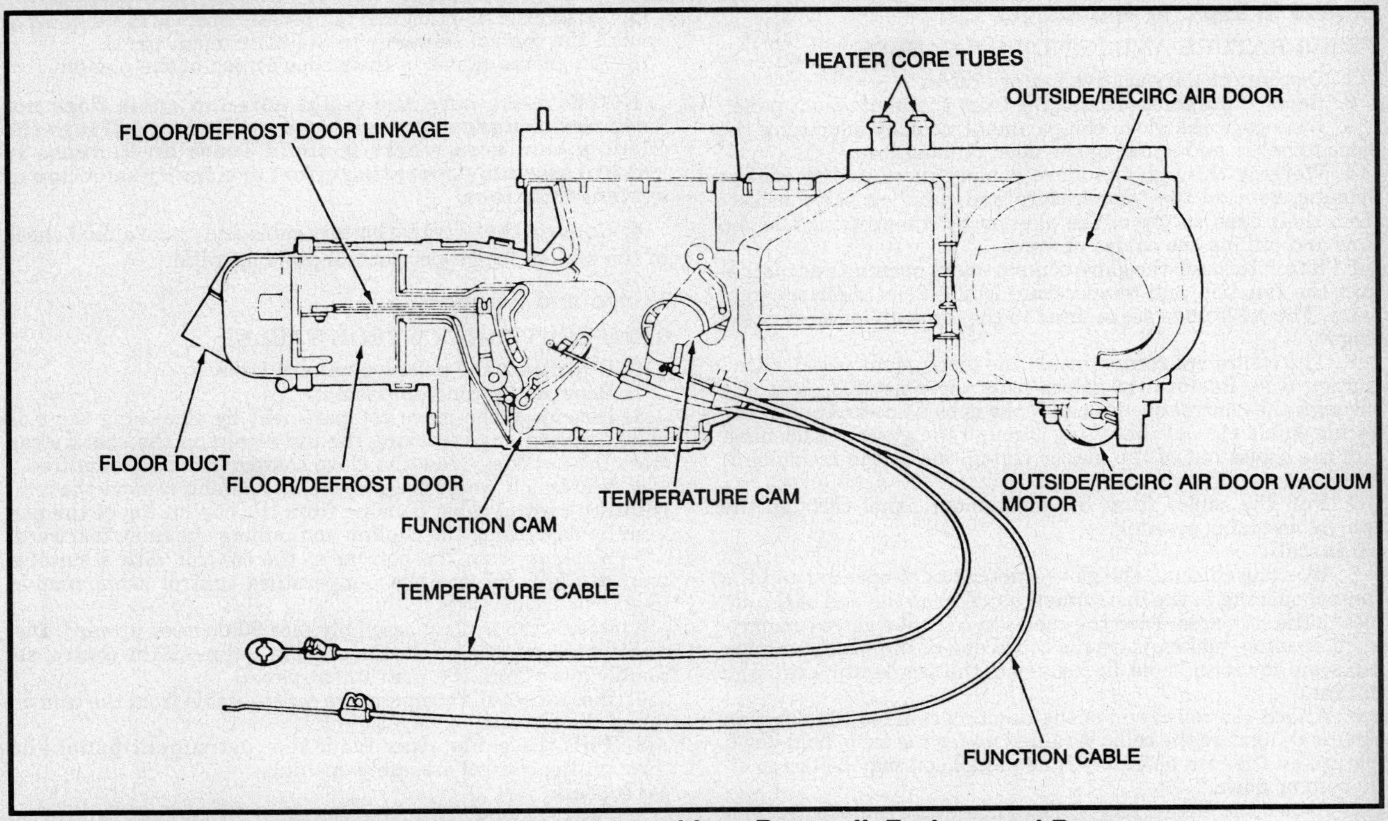
HEATER CORE TUBES
OUTSIDE/RECIRC AIR DOOR
FLOOR/DEFROST DOOR LINKAGE
FLOOR DUCT
FLOOR/DEFROST DOOR
TEMPERATURE CAM
FUNCTION CAM
OUTSIDE/RECIRC AIR DOOR VACUUM MOTOR
TEMPERATURE CABLE
FUNCTION CABLE

Function selector and temperature selector control cables—Bronco II, Explorer and Ranger

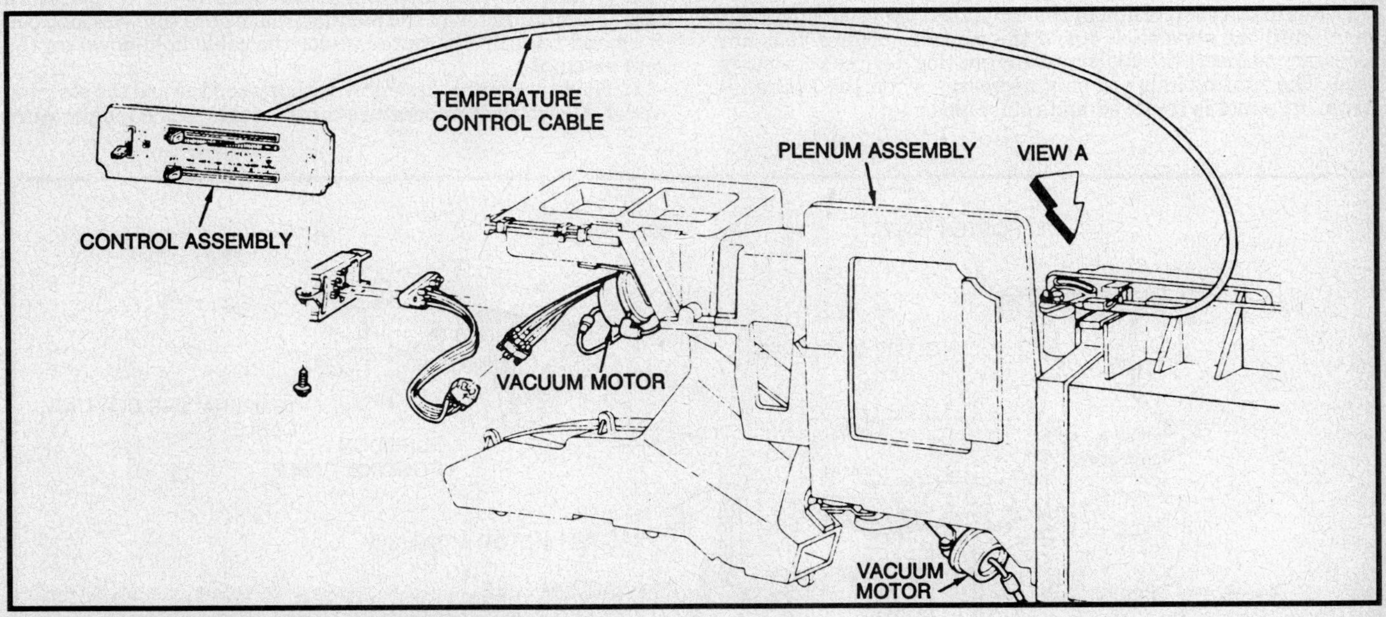
TEMPERATURE CONTROL CABLE
PLENUM ASSEMBLY
VIEW A
CONTROL ASSEMBLY
VACUUM MOTOR
VACUUM MOTOR

Temperature control cable—Bronco and F Series

6. Remove the cable from the instrument panel.

To install:

7. Install the cable into the instrument panel and connect the cable wire end loop to the cam.
8. Install the control assembly.
9. Adjust the cable.
10. Install the radio.
11. Install the instrument cluster housing assembly and the instrument panel upper finish panel.
12. Connect the negative battery cable and check the system for proper operation.

Bronco II, Explorer and Ranger

TEMPERATURE AND FUNCTION CABLES

1. Disconnect the negative battery cable.
2. Remove the control assembly from the instrument panel.
3. Disengage the glove compartment door by squeezing the sides together and allowing the door to hang free.
4. Working through the glove compartment and/or control opening, remove the temperature and function cable jackets from their clips on top of the plenum by compressing the clip tans and pulling the cables upward.
5. Reach through the glove compartment opening and disconnect the function and temperature cables from their separate cams. The cable ends are secured to the cams under a retention finger.
6. The cables are routed inside the instrument panel with 2 routing aids. Remove the cables from these devices. Reaching through the control opening, pull the cables upward out of the wiring shield cut-out. Reaching through the glove box opening, pull the cables out of the plastic clip up inside the instrument panel.
7. Pull the cables from the instrument panel through the control assembly opening.

To install:

8. Working through the glove compartment opening and the control opening in the instrument panel, feed the end of the cables to the cam area. Feed the cables in from the glove compartment opening, making sure the coiled end of the white function cable and the round hole diecast end of the temperature cable go in first.
9. Attach the coiled end of the function cable to the function cam, making sure the cable is routed under the cable hold-down feature on the cam assembly. The pigtail coil may be facing either up or down.
10. Attach the diecast end of the temperature cable to the temperature cam making sure the cable is routed under the cable hold-down feature on the cam assembly.
11. Route the control end of the cable through the instrument panel until the ends stick out of the control opening. It is not necessary to insert the cable into any routing devices previously used. The routing aids are only necessary when the entire instrument panel is removed and reinstalled.
12. Attach the function and temperature cables to the control. Install the control assembly in the instrument panel.
13. Adjust the cables in their clips on top of the plenum.

NOTE: Make sure the radio antenna cable does not become disengaged from it's mounting and fall into the plenum cam area where it could cause an increase in control assembly operating effort or a faulty selection of system functions.

14. Connect the negative battery cable and make a final check of the system for proper control cable operation.

Bonco and F Series

TEMPERATURE CONTROL CABLE

1. Disconnect the negative battery cable.
2. Remove the control assembly.
3. Disengage the glove compartment by squeezing the side with the stop and removing the pin retaining the check strap from the outside. Allow the glove compartment to hang free.
4. Working through the glove compartment, remove the temperature control cable housing from the clip on top of the plenum by depressing the clip tab and pulling the cable rearward.
5. Working from the bottom of the control with a suitable tool, carefully release the temperature control cable snap-in flag.
6. Rotate the control assembly face 90 degrees upward. Disconnect the temperature control cable and move the control assembly away from the instrument panel.
7. Disconnect the temperature control cable from the cam on top of the plenum.
8. Pull the cable away from the instrument panel and through the control assembly opening.

To install:

9. Feed the wire loop end of the cable through the control assembly opening in the instrument panel.
10. Attach the wire loop end of the cable to the temperature cam assembly on top of the plenum. Make sure the wire loop coil is up and the cable is routed under the cable hold-down on the cam assembly.
11. Hold the control assembly with it's top toward the steering wheel. Attach the temperature control cable to the temperature

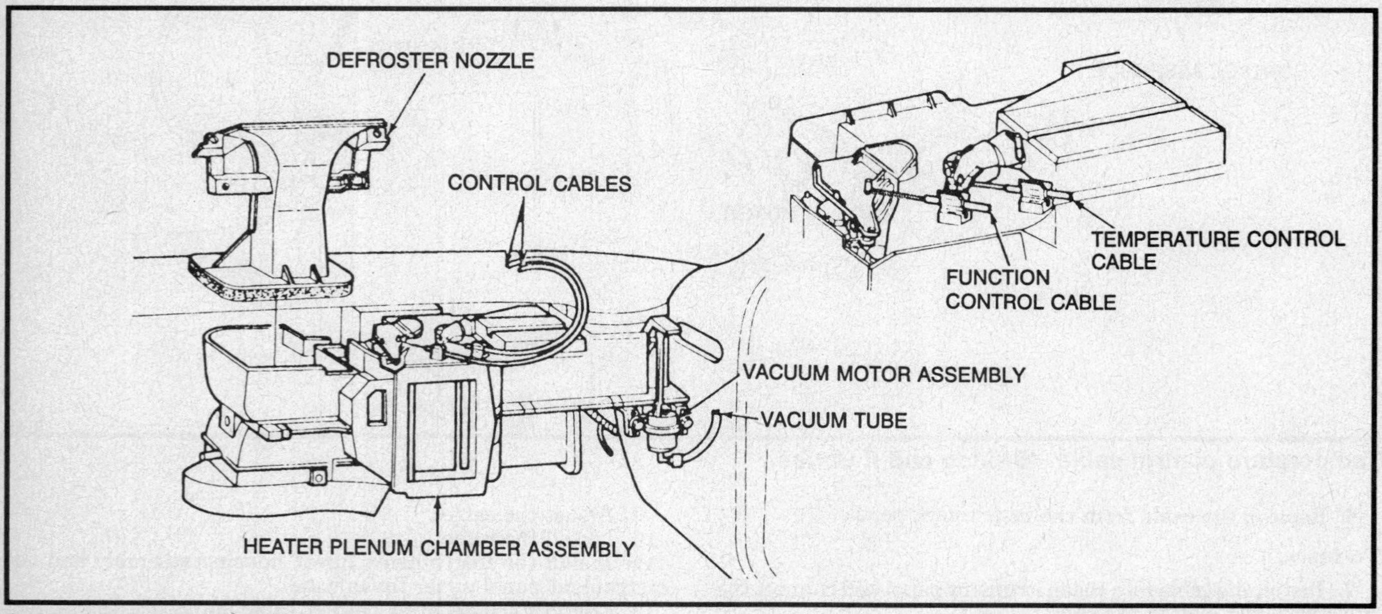
DEFROSTER NOZZLE
CONTROL CABLES
TEMPERATURE CONTROL CABLE
FUNCTION CONTROL CABLE
VACUUM MOTOR ASSEMBLY
VACUUM TUBE
HEATER PLENUM CHAMBER ASSEMBLY

Control cables—Bronco II, Explorer and Ranger

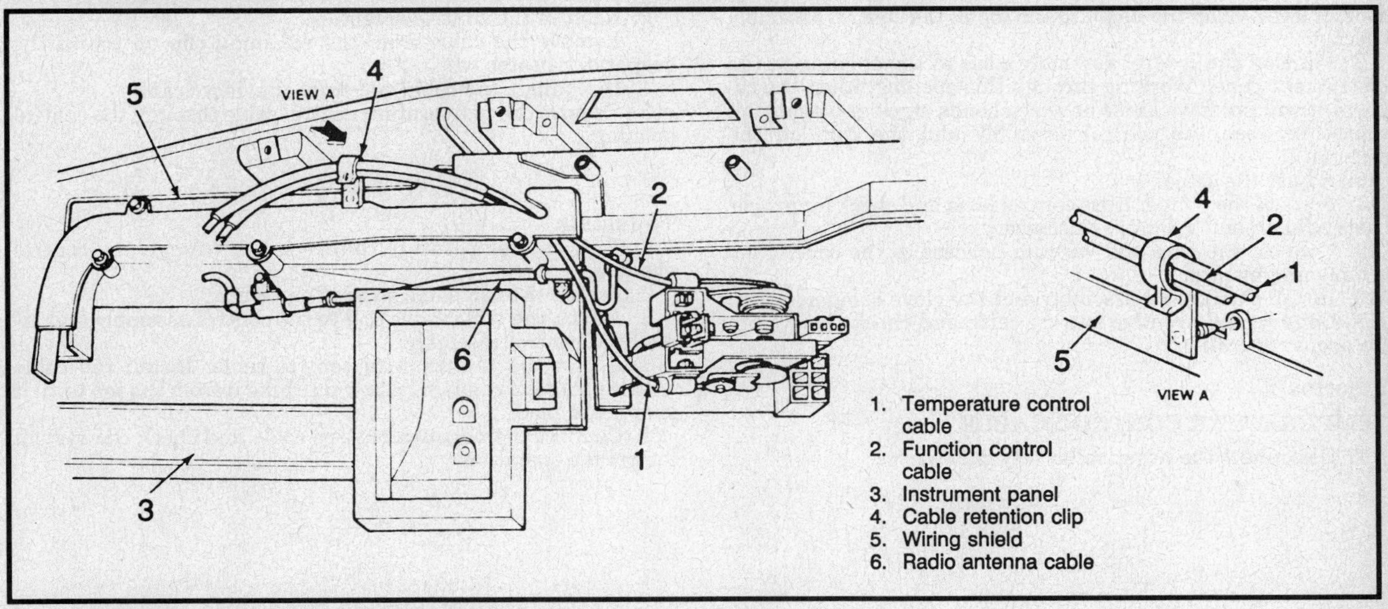
VIEW A
5
4
2
6
1
3
4
2
1
5
VIEW A
1. Temperature control cable
2. Function control cable
3. Instrument panel
4. Cable retention clip
5. Wiring shield
6. Radio antenna cable

Control cables—Bronco II, Explorer and Ranger

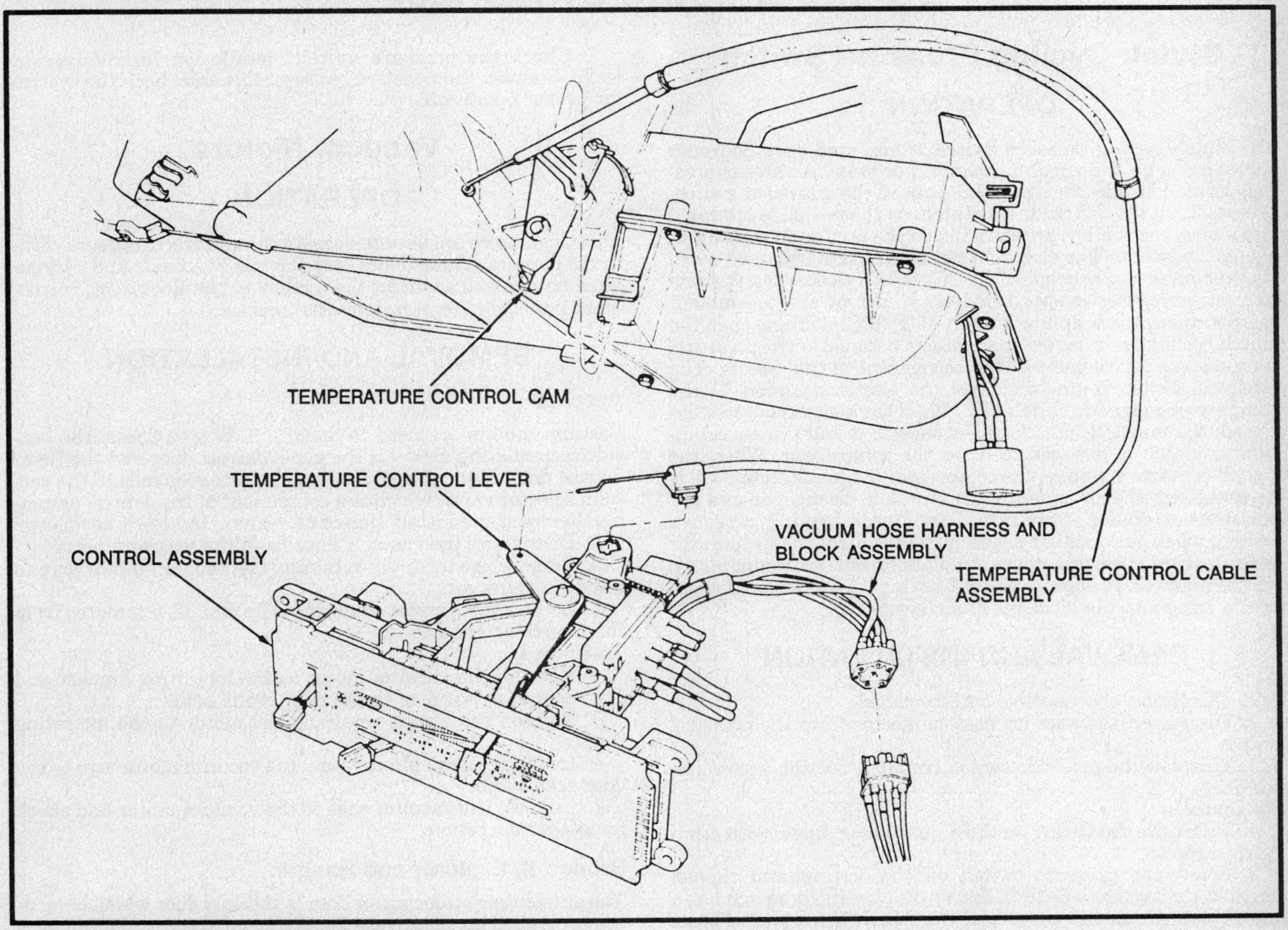
TEMPERATURE CONTROL CAM
TEMPERATURE CONTROL LEVER
CONTROL ASSEMBLY
VACUUM HOSE HARNESS AND BLOCK ASSEMBLY
TEMPERATURE CONTROL CABLE ASSEMBLY

Temperature control cable—Bronco and F Series

control lever. Snap the flag into the top of the control assembly bracket.

12. Position the control assembly close to the opening in the instrument panel. Working through this opening, route the cable so it will not have kinks or sharp bends anywhere along it's course between the control assembly and the cam on the plenum.

13. Adjust the cable.

14. Actuate the temperature control lever and check for proper cable adjustment. Adjust, as necessary.

15. Connect the wire and vacuum harness to the control assembly and plenum.

16. Install the control assembly and the glove compartment.

17. Connect the negative battery cable and check the system for proper operation.

E Series

TEMPERATURE CONTROL CABLE

1. Disconnect the negative battery cable.

2. Remove the control assembly.

3. Remove the cable from the retaining clip on top of the evaporator-heater case.

4. Disconnect the cable end from the door crank.

5. Remove the temperature control cable through the control opening.

To install:

6. Feed the temperature control cable through the control opening.

7. Attach the cable end to the door crank.

8. Attach the other cable end to the control assembly and install the control assembly.

9. Adjust the temperature control cable. Install the cable housing into it's retaining clip by pushing it from the top until it snaps into place.

10. Connect the negative battery cable and check the system for proper operation.

SENSORS AND SWITCHES

Clutch Cycling Pressure Switch

OPERATION

The clutch cycling pressure switch is mounted on a Schrader valve fitting on the suction accumulator/drier. A valve depressor, located inside the threaded end of the pressure switch, presses in on the Schrader valve stem as the switch is mounted and allows the suction pressure inside the accumulator/drier to act on the switch. The electrical switch contacts will open when the suction pressure drops to 23–26 psi. and close when the suction pressure rises to approximately 45 psi. or above. Ambient temperatures below approximately 45°F (9°C) will also open the clutch cycling pressure switch contacts because of the pressure/temperature relationship of the refrigerant in the system. The electrical switch contacts control the electrical circuit to the compressor magnetic clutch coil. When the switch contacts are closed, the magnetic clutch coil is energized and the air conditioning clutch is engaged to drive the compressor. When the switch contacts are open, the compressor magnetic clutch coil is de-energized, the air conditioning clutch is disengaged and the compressor does not operate. The clutch cycling pressure switch, when functioning properly, will control the evaporator core pressure at a point where the plate/fin surface temperature will be maintained slightly above freezing which prevents evaporator icing and the blockage of airflow.

REMOVAL AND INSTALLATION

1. Disconnect the negative battery cable.

2. Disconnect the wire harness connector from the pressure switch.

3. Unscrew the pressure switch from the suction accumulator/drier.

To install:

4. Lubricate the O-ring on the accumulator nipple with clean refrigerant oil.

5. Screw the pressure switch on the accumulator nipple. Tighten the switch to 5–10 ft. lbs. (7–13 Nm) if the switch has a metal base. Hand tighten only if the switch has a plastic base.

6. Connect the wire connector to the pressure switch.

7. Check the pressure switch installation for refrigerant leaks. Connect the negative battery cable and check the system for proper operation.

Vacuum Motors

OPERATION

Vacuum motors are used to operate the air directing doors within the plenum. These doors vary the mix of outside and recirculated air, as well as direct the airflow to the floor duct, instrument panel registers or defroster nozzles.

REMOVAL AND INSTALLATION

Aerostar

Vacuum motors are used to operate 3 damper doors: the outside/recirculating air door, the panel/defrost door and the floor/defrost door. Each of these vacuum motors responds to the vacuum selector valve, which is a component of the control assembly. Removal and installation of all vacuum motors is as follows:

1. Disconnect the vacuum hose from the vacuum motor.

2. Remove the push pin retaining the vacuum motor arm to the door crank arm.

3. Loosen the 2 motor retaining nuts and lift the motor from the mounting bracket.

To install:

4. Position the vacuum motor to the mounting bracket and the vacuum motor arm to the door crank arm.

5. Tighten the 2 nuts retaining the motor to the mounting bracket.

6. Install the push pin to retain the vacuum motor arm to the door crank arm.

7. Connect the vacuum hose to the vacuum motor and check for proper operation.

Bronco II, Explorer and Ranger

The outside/recirculating air door is the only door which is vacuum controlled on these vehicles. Removal and installation is as follows:

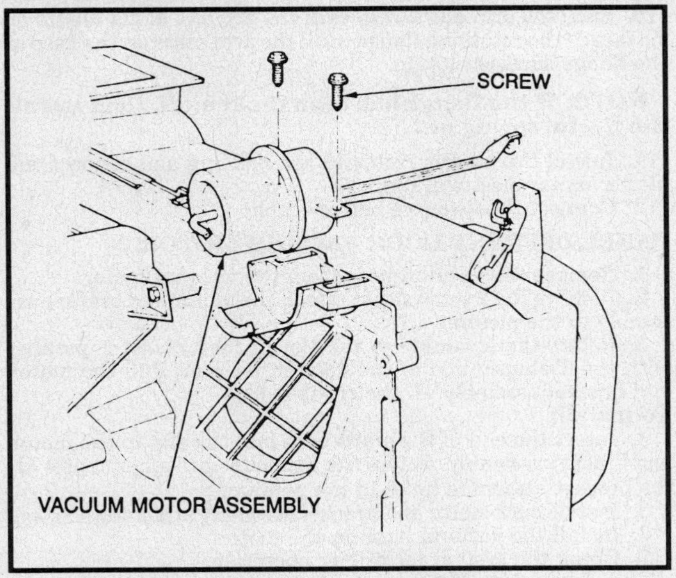
SCREW
VACUUM MOTOR ASSEMBLY

Outside/recirculating air door vacuum motor installation—Bronco II, Explorer and Ranger

1. Open the glove compartment and remove the contents. Press in the sides of the glove compartment and pull back so it hangs down. The vacuum motor should be visible on the right side of the plenum.
2. Disconnect the vacuum hose from the vacuum motor nipple.
3. Remove the 2 screws attaching the vacuum motor to the plenum.
4. Swing the vacuum motor rearward and disconnect the vacuum motor arm from the shaft on the plenum by sliding the motor arm to the left.

To install:

5. Position the vacuum motor arm so the shaft on the plenum protrudes through the hole in the vacuum motor.
6. Swing the vacuum motor forward and install 2 screws attaching the vacuum motor to the plenum.
7. Connect the vacuum hose to the vacuum motor nipple.
8. Push the sides of the glove compartment and install to the latched position.
9. Start the engine and move the function lever forward in the control assembly to verify that the vacuum motor functions properly.

Bronco and F Series

Vacuum motors are used to operate 3 damper doors: the outside/recirculating air door, the panel/defrost door and the floor/defrost door. Each of these vacuum motors responds to the vac-

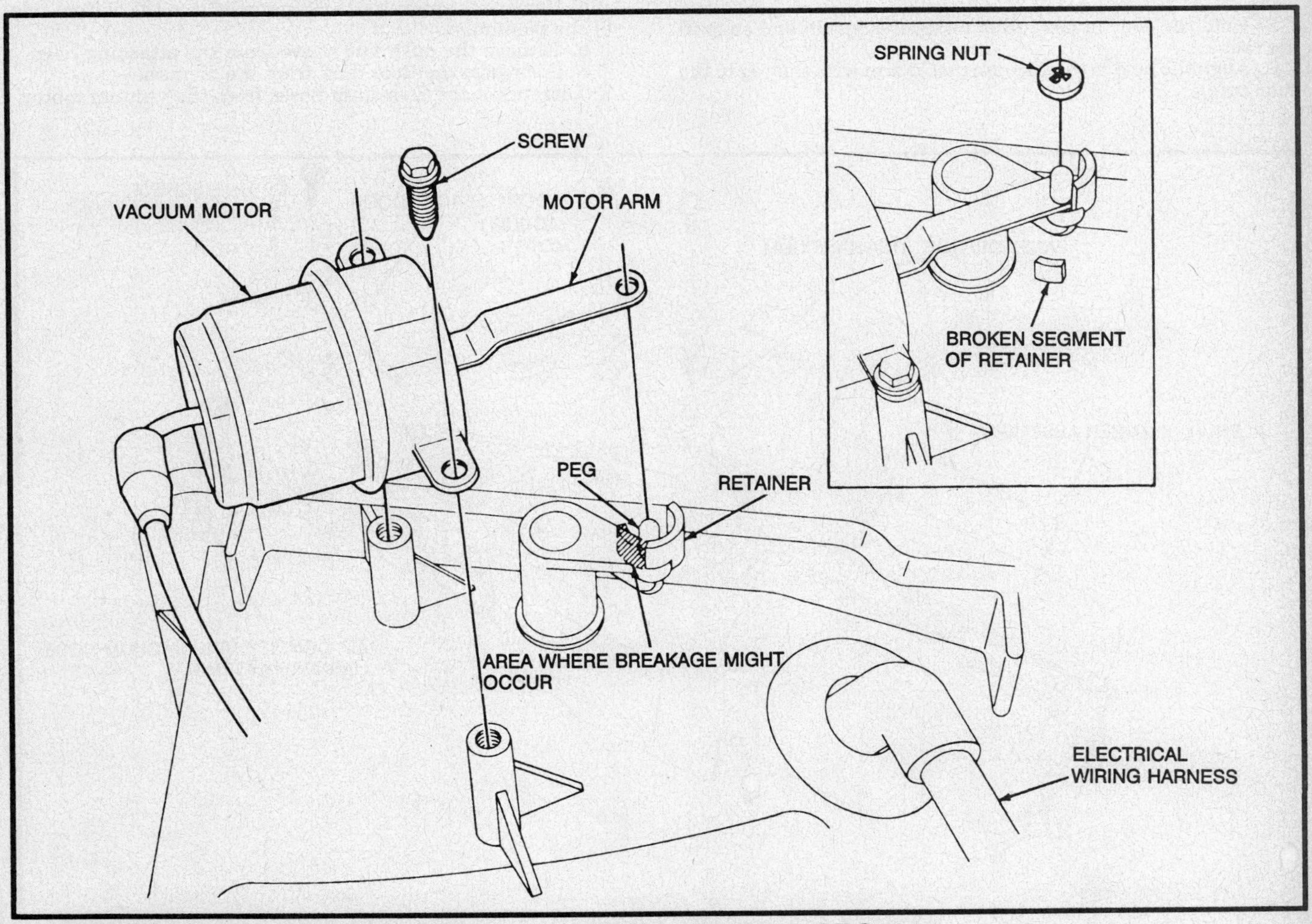
SPRING NUT
BROKEN SEGMENT
OF RETAINER
SCREW
VACUUM MOTOR
MOTOR ARM
PEG
RETAINER
AREA WHERE BREAKAGE MIGHT
OCCUR
ELECTRICAL
WIRING HARNESS

Outside/recirculating air door vacuum motor Installation—Bronco and F Series

uum selector valve, which is a component of the control assembly. Removal and installation is as follows:

OUTSIDE/RECIRCULATING AIR DOOR VACUUM MOTOR

1. Disconnect the negative battery cable.
2. Disconnect the blower motor connector and remove the blower motor.
3. If only the vacuum motor is to be removed, disconnect the 2 screws that attach the motor to the upper surface of the outside door duct.
4. Pry the motor and arm assembly upward at the arm end to free it from it's mounting peg.

NOTE: A retaining flange that is an integral part of the crank, peg and flange component may partially obstruct the motor arm in it's upward movement along the peg. If this retaining flange should break off when forcing the motor arm upward, a $^3/_{16}$ in. spring nut must be used to retain the motor arm when the same or a replacement motor is installed.

5. Look through the blower motor opening in the case and use a suitable tool to depress the snap-on door crank while pulling up on the door shaft to release the crank from the door.
6. Remove the door through the blower motor opening.

To install:

7. Insert the door through the blower motor opening. Seat the bottom door pivot first, then swing the top door pivot into place.
8. Hold the door in the full outside air position and snap in the crank.
9. Align the hole in the vacuum motor arm with the peg in the door crank.
10. Slide the arm downward over the peg and along the inner surface of the retaining flange until the arm seats on the base of the flange surface.

NOTE: If the flange has been broken off, then install the $^3/_{16}$ in. spring nut.

11. Install the blower motor in the housing and connect the blower motor electrical harness.
12. Connect the negative battery cable.

PANEL/DEFROST DOOR VACUUM MOTOR

1. Remove the vacuum hose from the vacuum motor.
2. Remove the 2 screws that attach the motor and bracket assembly to the plenum.
3. Rotate the assembly so the slot in the bracket is parallel with the T-shaped end of the door crank arm. Pull the motor and bracket assembly off the crank arm.

To install:

4. Insert the end of the crank arm into the slot in the motor and bracket assembly. Rotate the assembly into alignment with the bracket attaching holes in the plenum.
5. Install the 2 motor and bracket assembly attaching screws.
6. Install the vacuum hose on the motor.
7. Check the system for proper operation.

FLOOR/DEFROST DOOR VACUUM MOTOR

1. Remove the floor duct as follows:
   a. Remove the plastic attaching screw from the bottom side of the plenum.
   b. Remove the push nut sleeve from the attaching hole.
   c. Disengage the floor duct from the plenum.
2. Disconnect the 2 vacuum hoses from the vacuum motor.

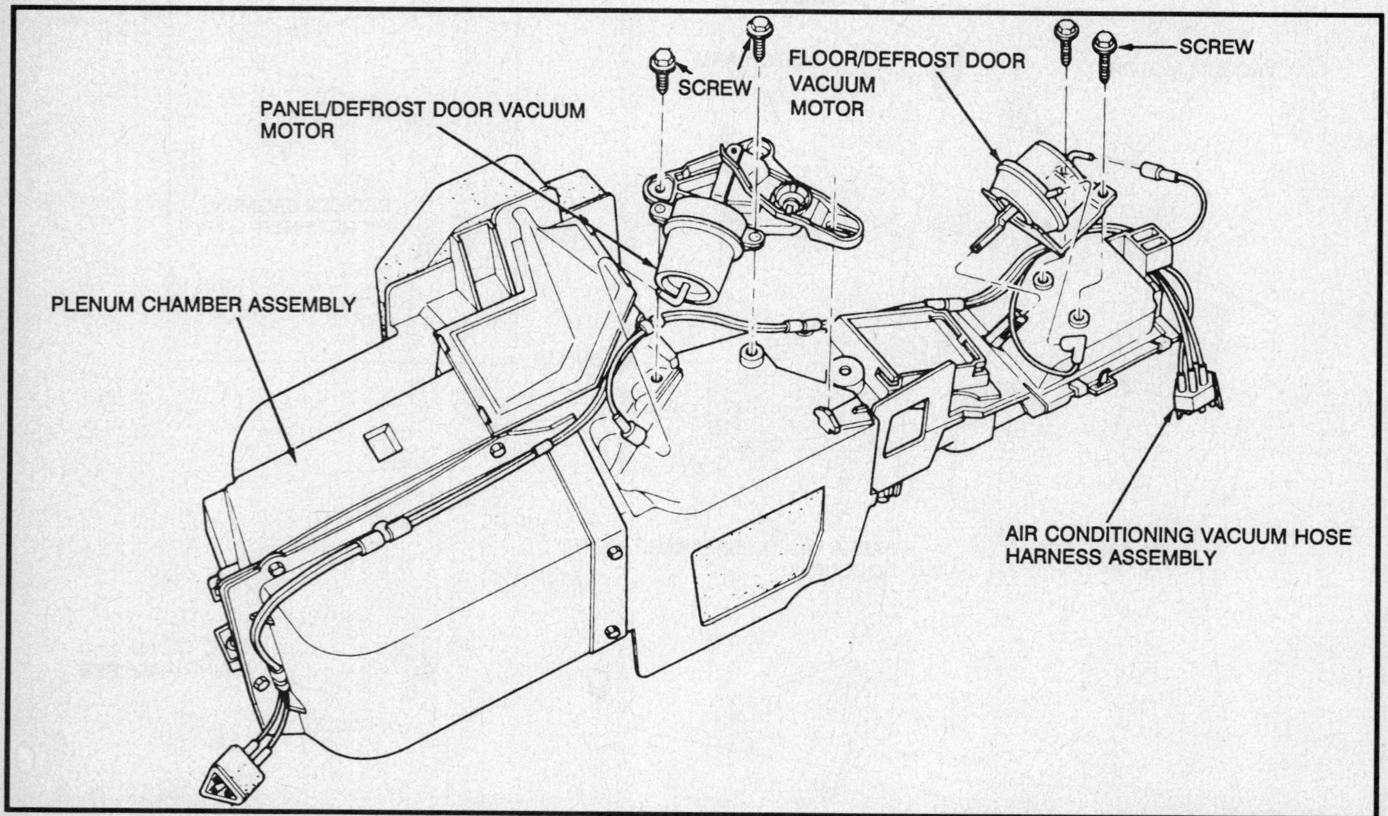
SCREW
SCREW
FLOOR/DEFROST DOOR VACUUM MOTOR
PANEL/DEFROST DOOR VACUUM MOTOR
PLENUM CHAMBER ASSEMBLY
AIR CONDITIONING VACUUM HOSE HARNESS ASSEMBLY

Panel/defrost and floor/defrost door vacuum motor installation—Bronco and F Series

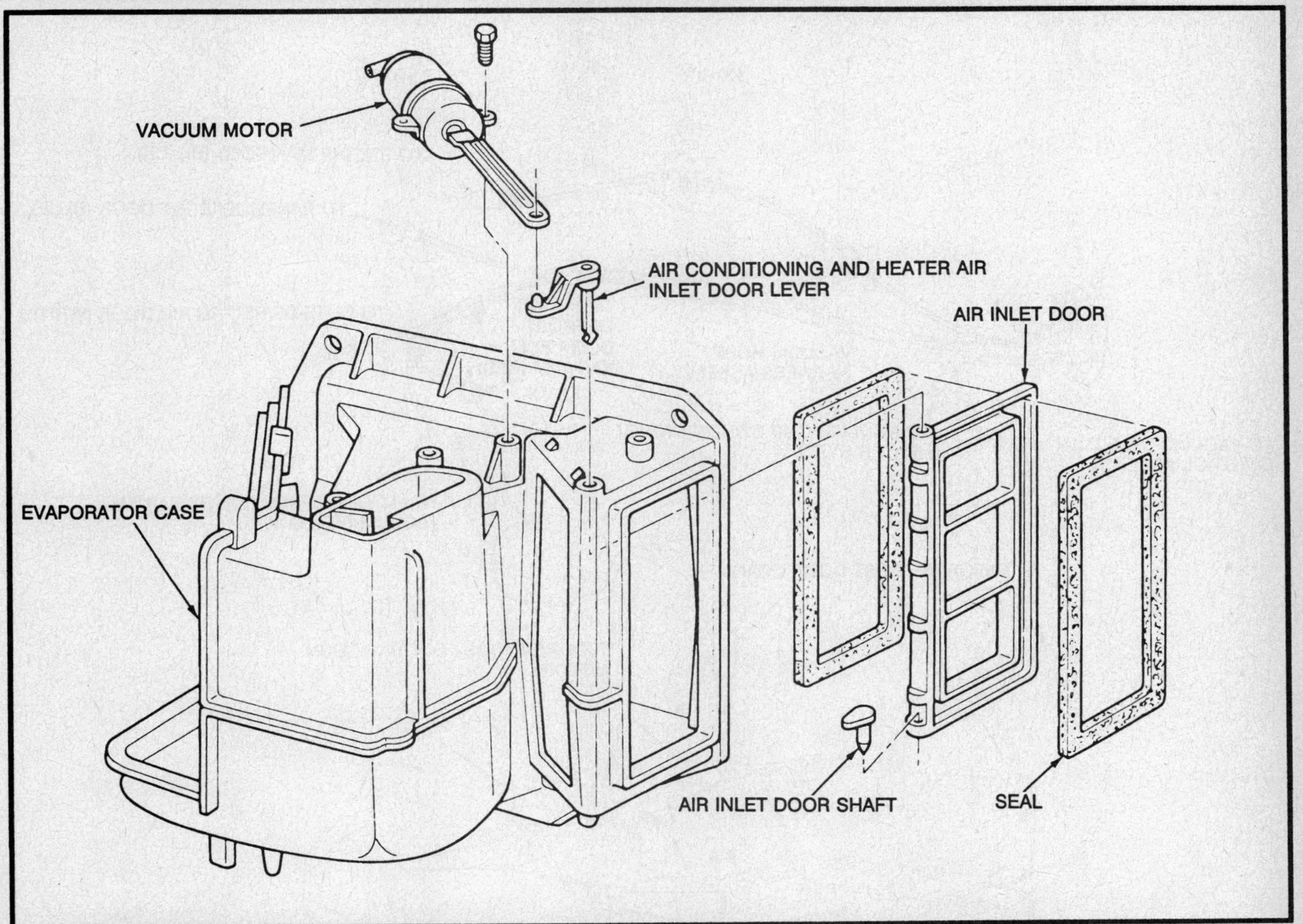
VACUUM MOTOR
AIR CONDITIONING AND HEATER AIR INLET DOOR LEVER
AIR INLET DOOR
EVAPORATOR CASE
AIR INLET DOOR SHAFT
SEAL

Outside/recirculating air door vacuum motor and door assembly exploded view—E Series

3. Remove the 2 screws that secure the motor and bracket assembly to the plenum.
4. Using a suitable tool, depress the tang on the side of the door operating lever and pull the motor arm out of the lever.

To install:

5. Slide the motor arm into the door lever until the locking tang engages.
6. Attach the 2 vacuum hoses.
7. Install the 2 motor and bracket attaching screws.
8. Install the floor duct as follows:
   a. Position the duct on the plenum and engage the lugs inside the duct with their mating slots in the plenum. Tilt the duct into place, then push in to secure engagement.
   b. Start the plastic screw into the push nut sleeve. Then, install through the floor duct flange and into the attaching hole in the plenum. Make sure the attachment is secure.
9. Check the system for proper operation.

E Series

Vacuum motors are used to operate 3 damper doors: the outside/recirculating air door, the panel/defrost door and the floor/defrost door. Each of these vacuum motors responds to the vacuum selector valve, which is a component of the control assembly. Removal and installation of all vacuum motors is as follows:

1. Remove the 2 screws retaining the motor to the plenum case.
2. Carefully pry the vacuum motor arm off the rosebud clip on the door crank.
3. Disconnect the vacuum hose from the vacuum motor and remove the motor and bracket.

To install:

4. Snap the vacuum motor arm over the rosebud clip on the crank.
5. Connect the vacuum hose to the vacuum motor and position the motor and bracket to the plenum case.
6. Install the 2 screws retaining the vacuum motor.
7. If necessary, install a new pushnut to retain the motor arm on the door crank arm.
8. Check the system for proper operation.

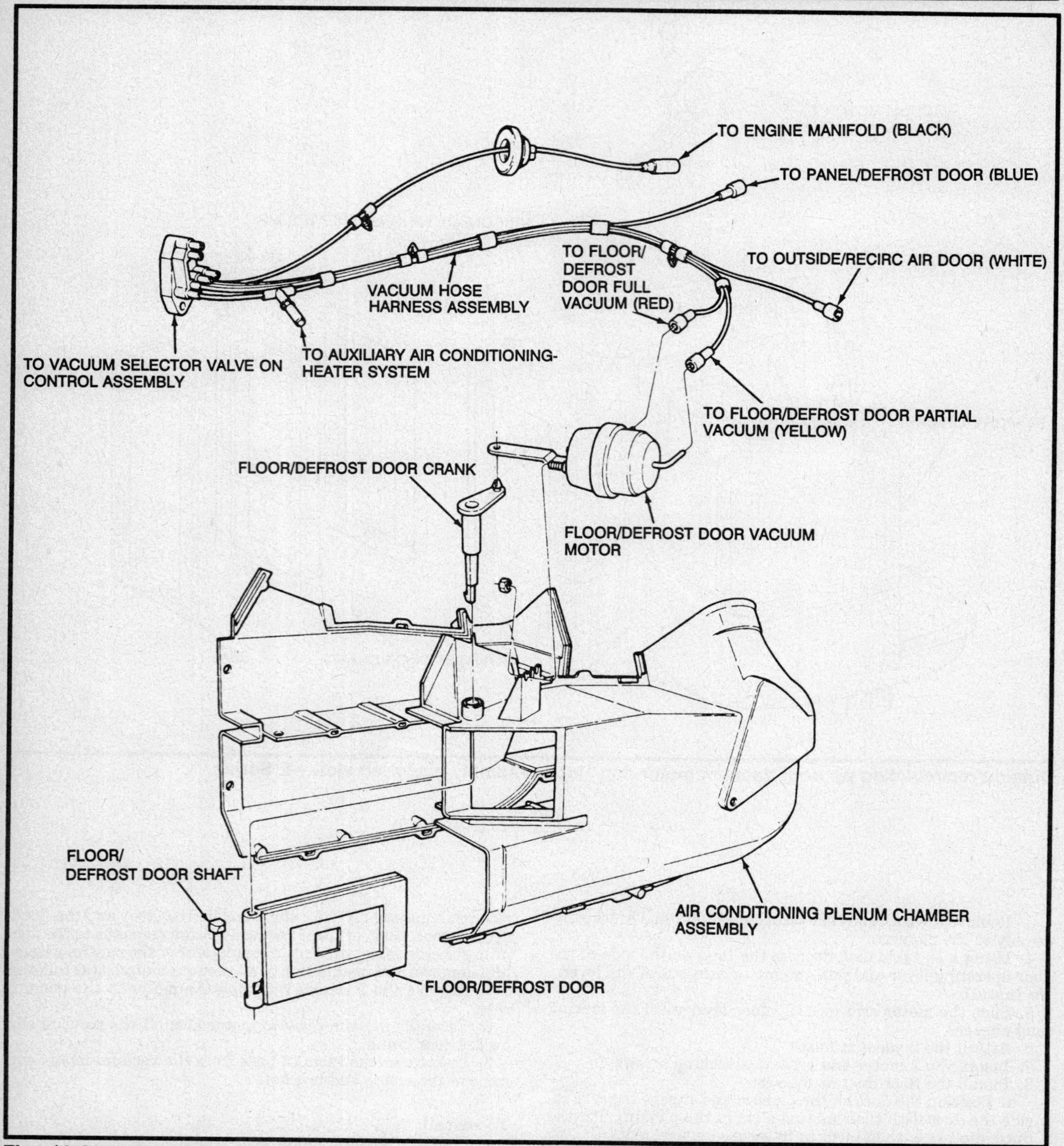
TO ENGINE MANIFOLD (BLACK)
TO PANEL/DEFROST DOOR (BLUE)
TO OUTSIDE/RECIRC AIR DOOR (WHITE)
TO FLOOR/
DEFROST
DOOR FULL
VACUUM (RED)
VACUUM HOSE
HARNESS ASSEMBLY
TO VACUUM SELECTOR VALVE ON
CONTROL ASSEMBLY
TO AUXILIARY AIR CONDITIONING-
HEATER SYSTEM
TO FLOOR/DEFROST DOOR PARTIAL
VACUUM (YELLOW)
FLOOR/DEFROST DOOR CRANK
FLOOR/DEFROST DOOR VACUUM
MOTOR
FLOOR/
DEFROST DOOR SHAFT
AIR CONDITIONING PLENUM CHAMBER
ASSEMBLY
FLOOR/DEFROST DOOR

Floor/defrost door vacuum motor, plenum chamber assembly and vacuum hose harness—E Series

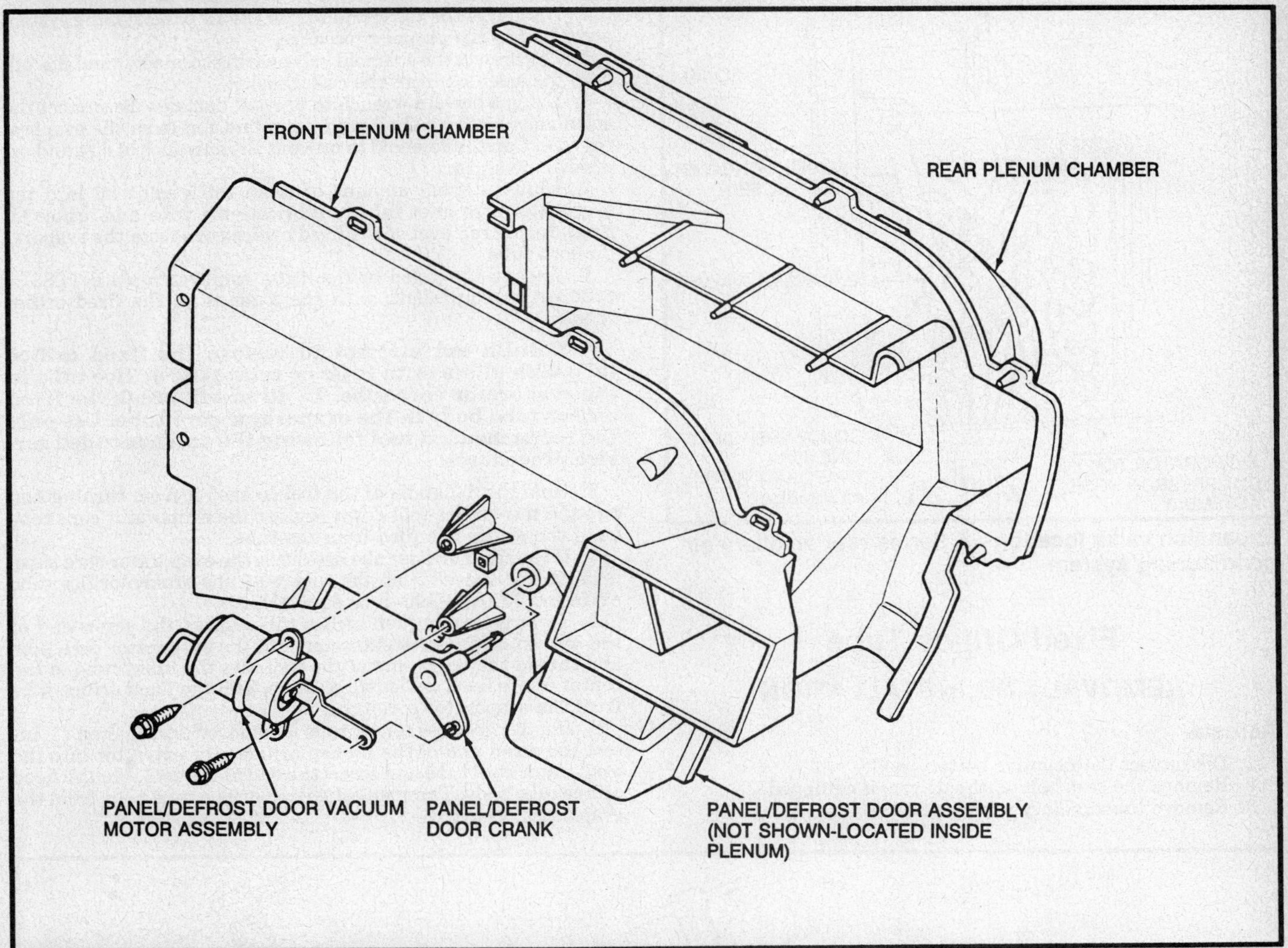
FRONT PLENUM CHAMBER
REAR PLENUM CHAMBER
PANEL/DEFROST DOOR VACUUM MOTOR ASSEMBLY
PANEL/DEFROST DOOR CRANK
PANEL/DEFROST DOOR ASSEMBLY (NOT SHOWN-LOCATED INSIDE PLENUM)

Panel/defrost door vacuum motor and plenum assembly exploded view—E Series

REAR AUXILIARY SYSTEM

Expansion Valve

REMOVAL AND INSTALLATION

E Series

1. Remove the first bench seat, if equipped.
2. Remove the auxiliary air conditioner cover assembly.
3. Discharge the refrigerant from the air conditioning system according to the proper procedure.
4. Disconnect the liquid line from the expansion valve. Use a backup wrench to prevent component damage. Cap the line to prevent the entrance of dirt and moisture.
5. Remove the insulating tape from the evaporator core outlet tube. Then, remove the clamp and expansion valve capillary bulb from the outlet tube of the evaporator core.
6. Using a backup wrench, remove the expansion valve from the evaporator core inlet tube. Cap the inlet tube to prevent the entrance of dirt and moisture.

To install:

7. Connect the expansion valve to the evaporator core inlet tube using a new O-ring lubricated with clean refrigerant oil. Tighten the connection only finger-tight at this time.
8. Connect the liquid line to the expansion valve using a new O-ring lubricated with clean refrigerant oil.
9. Using a backup wrench, tighten the liquid line to the expansion valve fitting to 10–15 ft. lbs. (14–20 Nm). Tighten the expansion valve to the evaporator core fitting to 15–20 ft. lbs. (21–27 Nm).
10. Clamp the expansion valve capiliary tube bulb to the evaporator core outlet tube. Clean both surfaces. The bulb must make good contact with the outlet tube.
11. Wrap the evaporator core outlet tube and capillary tube bulb with insulating tape.
12. Leak test, evacuate and charge the system according to the proper procedure. Observe all safety precautions.
13. Install the auxiliary air conditioner cover assembly.
14. Install the first bench seat, if equipped.

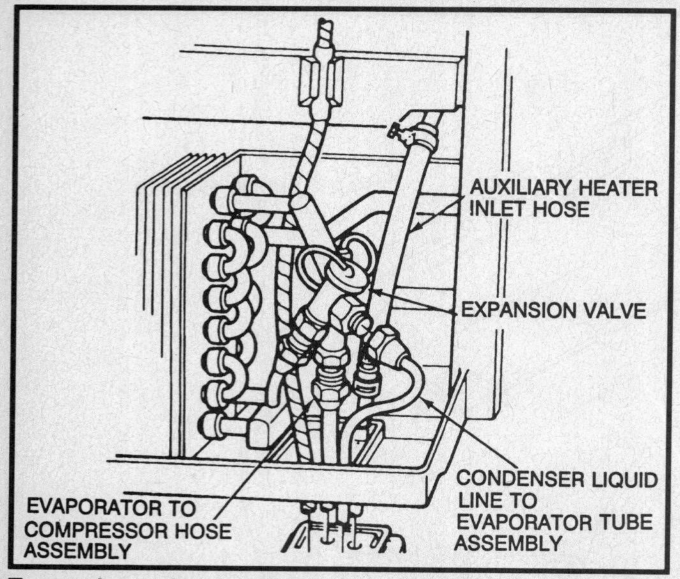
AUXILIARY HEATER INLET HOSE
EXPANSION VALVE
CONDENSER LIQUID LINE TO EVAPORATOR TUBE ASSEMBLY
EVAPORATOR TO COMPRESSOR HOSE ASSEMBLY

Expansion valve location – E Series rear auxiliary air conditioning system

Fixed Orifice Tube

REMOVAL AND INSTALLATION

Aerostar

1. Disconnect the negative battery cable.
2. Remove the seat behind the driver, if equipped.
3. Remove the auxiliary service cover.
4. Discharge the refrigerant from the air conditioning system according to the proper procedure.
5. Disconnect the solenoid valve wiring connector and disconnect the solenoid from the case bracket.
6. Using a backup wrench to prevent damage, disconnect the solenoid valve from the liquid jump line and from the evaporator core. Cap the solenoid to prevent the entrance of dirt and excessive moisture.
7. Squirt a small amount of clean refrigerant oil into the evaporator core inlet tube to lubricate the tube and orifice O-rings during removal of the fixed orifice tube from the evaporator core tube.
8. Engage the fixed orifice tube remover/replacer T83L–19990–A or equivalent, with the 2 tangs on the fixed orifice tube.

NOTE: Do not attempt to remove the fixed orifice tube with pliers or to twist or rotate the orifice tube in the evaporator core tube. To do so will break the fixed orifice tube body in the evaporator core tube. Use only the recommended tool following the recommended service procedures.

9. Hold the T-handle of the tool to keep it from turning and run the nut on the tool down against the evaporator core tube until the orifice is pulled from the tube.
10. If the fixed orifice tube breaks in the evaporator core tube, it must be removed from the tube with the broken orifice tube extractor T83L–19990–B or equivalent.
11. To remove a broken orifice tube, insert the screw end of the broken orifice tube extractor into the evaporator core tube and thread the screw end of the tool into the brass tube in the center of the fixed orifice tube. Then, pull the fixed orifice tube from the evaporator core tube.
12. If only the brass center tube is removed during Step 11, insert the screw end of the broken orifice tube extractor into the evaporator core tube and screw the end of the tool into the fixed orifice tube body. Then, pull the fixed orifice tube body from the evaporator core tube.

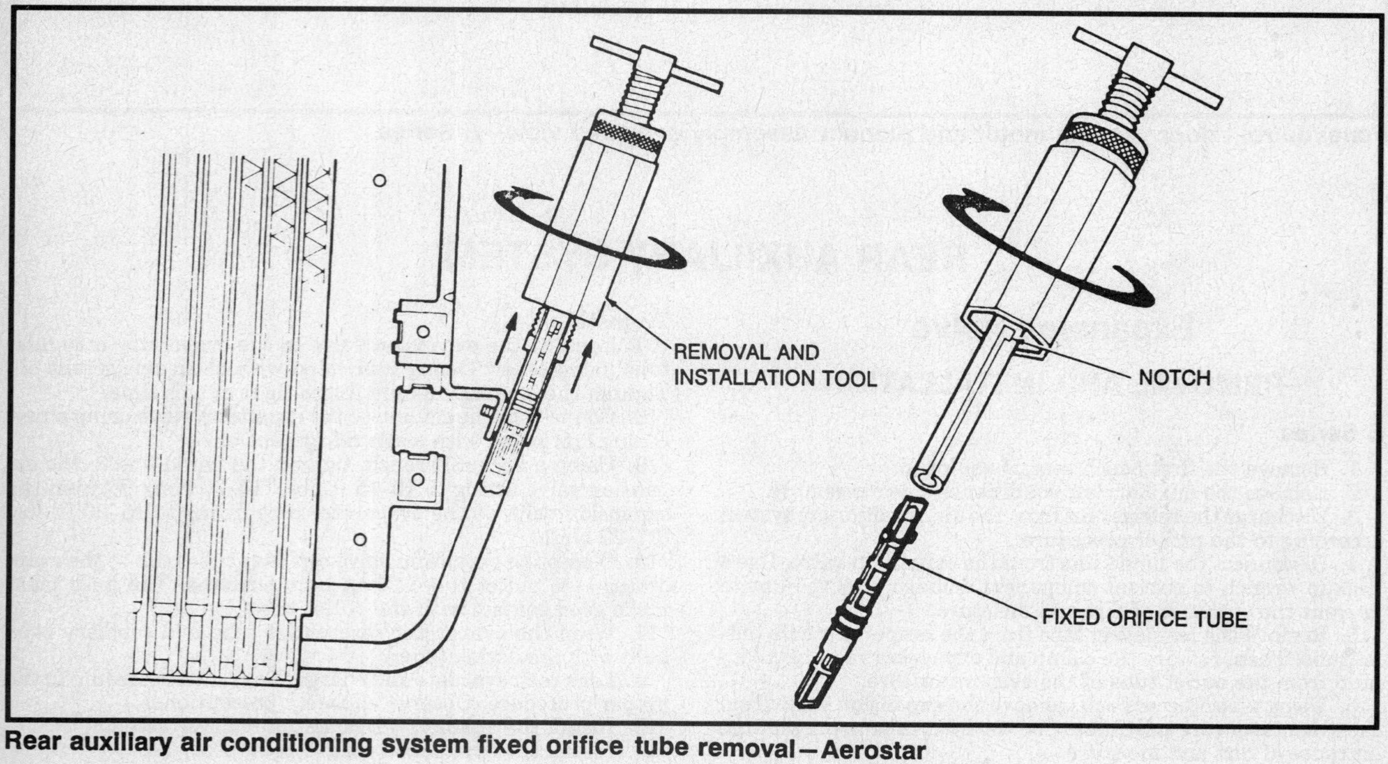
REMOVAL AND INSTALLATION TOOL
NOTCH
FIXED ORIFICE TUBE

Rear auxiliary air conditioning system fixed orifice tube removal – Aerostar

To install:

13. Lubricate the O-rings and the fixed orifice tube body liberally with clean refrigerant oil.
14. Place the fixed orifice tube in the fixed orifice tube remover/replacer T83L–19990–A or equivalent, and insert the fixed orifice tube into the evaporator core tube until the orifice is seated at the stop. The orifice tube used in the rear auxiliary system is color coded brown.
15. Remove the tool from the fixed orifice tube.
16. Using a new O-ring lubricated with clean refrigerant oil, connect the solenoid to the evaporator core tube. Tighten the fitting to 15–20 ft. lbs. (21–27 Nm) using a backup wrench.
17. Connect the solenoid electrical connector to the harness and attach to the bracket.
18. Connect the negative battery cable. Leak test, evacuate and charge the system according to the proper procedure. Observe all safety precautions.
19. Install the service cover and passenger seat.

Blower Motor

REMOVAL AND INSTALLATION

Aerostar

1. Disconnect the negative battery cable.
2. Remove the seat behind the driver and remove the service panel.
3. Remove the 3 screws from the solenoid bracket and disconnect the motor connector.
4. Disconnect the blower motor air cooling tube from the motor.
5. Remove the remaining 2 screws from the motor mounting plate and remove the motor and wheel assembly from the housing.
6. Remove the hub clamp spring from the blower wheel hub and the retainer from the motor shaft. Remove the blower wheel from the motor shaft.
7. Remove the nuts holding the motor to the motor mounting plate.

To install:

8. Install a new motor mounting plate using 2 nuts and tighten to 13–17 inch lbs. (1.5–2.0 Nm).

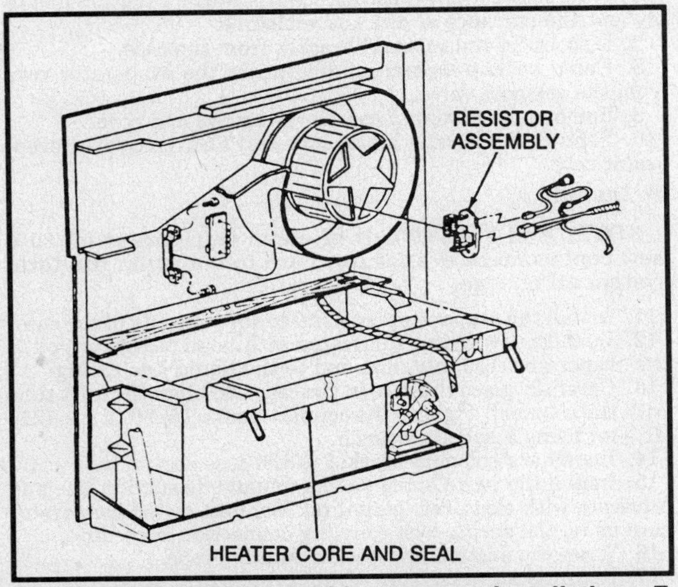
RESISTOR ASSEMBLY
HEATER CORE AND SEAL

Blower motor resistor and heater core installation—E Series rear auxiliary heater/air conditioning system

9. Position the blower wheel on the blower shaft. Being careful to match the flat surfaces exactly, push the wheel down until it stops against the motor. Install a new hub clamp spring on the blower hub.
10. Install a new motor mounting seal on the blower motor flange.
11. Position the blower motor and wheel assembly in the housing and attach with the upper attaching screws.
12. Install the solenoid bracket with the 3 attaching screws.
13. Install the blower motor cooling tube and connect the blower motor connector.
14. Connect the negative battery cable and check the blower motor for proper operation.
15. Install the service cover and passenger seat.

E Series

1. Disconnect the negative battery cable.
2. Remove the first bench seat, if equipped.
3. Remove the auxiliary heater and/or air conditioner cover assembly attaching screws and remove the cover.
4. Remove the blower motor mounting plate and remove the blower motor.
5. Installation is the reverse of the removal procedure.

Blower Motor Resistor

REMOVAL AND INSTALLATION

1. Disconnect the negative battery cable.
2. Remove the first bench seat, if equipped.
3. Remove the auxiliary heater/air conditioner service cover attaching screws and remove the cover.
4. Disconnect the wire connector from the resistor assembly.
5. Remove the 2 resistor retaining screws and remove the resistor assembly.

To install:

6. Position the resistor to the housing and install the 2 retaining screws.
7. Connect the wire connector to the resistor assembly and connect the negative battery cable.
8. Hold the auxiliary unit cover in place and check the operation of the blower at each blower speed. Do not touch the resistor during or after operation of the blower motor.
9. Install the auxiliary service cover and install the bench seat, if equipped.

Heater Core

REMOVAL AND INSTALLATION

Aerostar

1. Remove the first seat behind the driver, if equipped.
2. Remove the auxiliary heater/air conditioner cover attaching screws and remove the cover.
3. Remove the auxiliary unit floor duct by removing 1 or 2 attaching screws, as required and rotating the duct gently downward.
4. Remove the remaining 16 screws from the cover and remove the cover from the case.
5. Remove the heater hoses from the auxiliary heater core and plug the hoses with suitable 5/8 in. plugs.
6. Slide the heater core and seal assembly out of the housing slot.

To install:

7. Slide the heater core and seal assembly into the housing slot.
8. Connect the heater hoses to the heater core tubes.
9. Fill the cooling system to the proper level and check for coolant leaks.

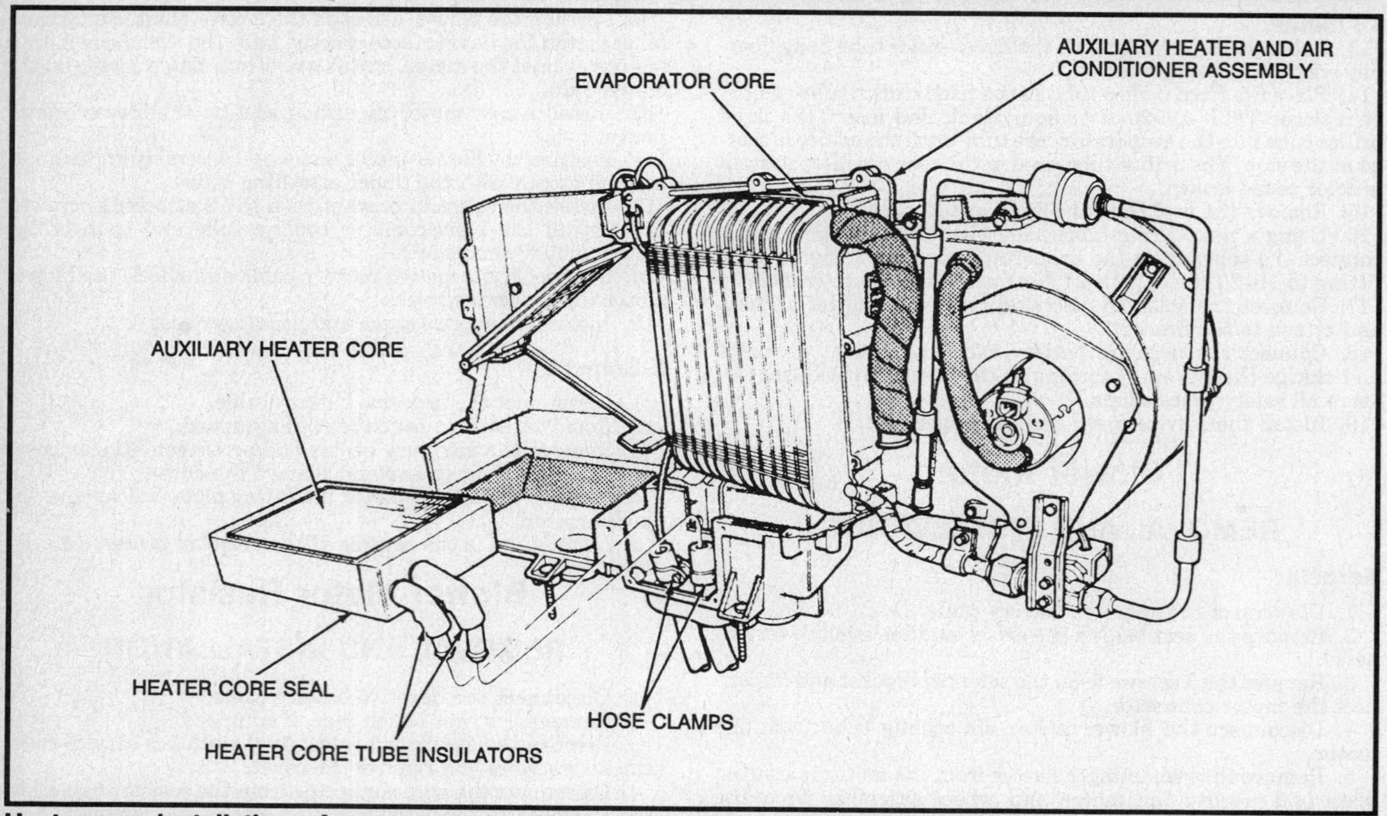
AUXILIARY HEATER AND AIR CONDITIONER ASSEMBLY
EVAPORATOR CORE
AUXILIARY HEATER CORE
HEATER CORE SEAL
HOSE CLAMPS
HEATER CORE TUBE INSULATORS

Heater core installation—Aerostar rear auxiliary heater and/or air conditiong system

10. Install the auxiliary heater/air conditioner cover.
11. Install the floor duct.
12. Install the service cover and passenger seat.

E Series

1. Remove the first bench seat, if equipped.
2. Remove the auxiliary heater and/or air conditioner cover attaching screws and remove the cover.
3. Remove and discard the strap retaining the heater core in the auxiliary system case.
4. Remove the heater hoses from the auxiliary heater core and plug the hoses with suitable ⅝ in. plugs.
5. Disengage the wire assembly from the heater core seal.
6. Slide the heater core and seal assembly out of the housing slot.

To install:

7. Position the wire assembly to one side and slide the heater core and seal assembly into the housing slot.
8. Remove the plugs from the heater hose and connect the hoses to the heater core tubes. Tighten the clamps.
9. Fill the cooling system to the proper level and check for coolant leaks.
10. Install a new strap to retain the heater core in the case assembly.
11. Install the auxiliary heater and/or air conditioner cover.
12. Install the bench seat, if equipped. Tighten the retaining bolts to 25–45 ft. lbs. (34–61 Nm).

Evaporator

REMOVAL AND INSTALLATION

Aerostar

1. Disconnect the negative battery cable.
2. Remove the first seat behind the driver, if equipped.
3. Remove the auxiliary air conditioner service cover attaching screws and remove the cover.
4. Discharge the refrigerant from the air conditioning system according to the proper procedure.
5. Remove the floor duct.
6. Disconnect the suction line from the evaporator core using the spring-lock coupling disconnect procedure. Plug the line to prevent the entrance of dirt and moisture.
7. Disconnect the solenoid bracket from the case.
8. Using backup wrenches, disconnect the evaporator core from the solenoid valve.
9. Remove the auxiliary case cover screws and cover.
10. Remove the resistor block connector and remove the evaporator core.

To install:

NOTE: Add 3 oz. (90ml) of clean refrigerant oil to a new replacement evaporator core to maintain the total system oil charge.

11. Install the evaporator core seal to the tube end of the core.
12. Install a new O-ring lubricated with clean refrigerant oil to the evaporator core inlet line and to the liquid line fitting.
13. Carefully place the core in the case and align the inlet tube with the solenoid. Tighten the connections to 15–20 ft. lbs. (21–27 Nm) using a backup wrench.
14. Install the solenoid bracket to the case assembly.
15. Install the new O-ring on the underbody suction line and lubricate with clean refrigerant oil. Connect to the evaporator core using the spring-lock coupling connection procedure.
16. Wrap the suction line with insulating tape.
17. Reconnect the resistor wiring connector.
18. Install the case cover and the floor duct.
19. Connect the negative battery cable. Leak test, evacuate

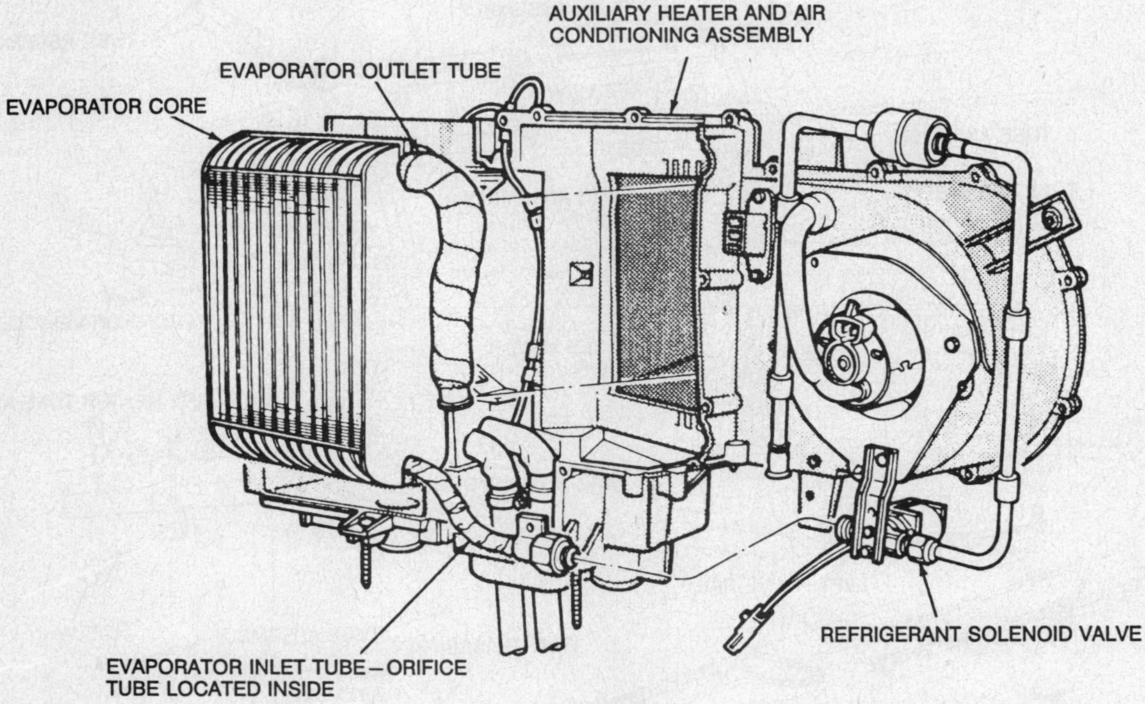
AUXILIARY HEATER AND AIR CONDITIONING ASSEMBLY
EVAPORATOR OUTLET TUBE
EVAPORATOR CORE
REFRIGERANT SOLENOID VALVE
EVAPORATOR INLET TUBE—ORIFICE TUBE LOCATED INSIDE

Evaporator core installation—Aerostar auxiliary air conditioning system.

and charge the system according to the proper procedure. Observe all safety precautions.

20. Install the service cover and the passenger seat.

E Series

NOTE: Whenever a refrigerant line, expansion valve or evaporator core in the auxiliary system is replaced, it will be necessary to replace the suction accumulator/drier in the main system.

1. Disconnect the negative battery cable.
2. Remove the first bench seat, if equipped.
3. Remove the auxiliary air conditioner cover assembly retaining screws and remove the cover assembly.
4. Discharge the refrigerant from the air conditioning system according to the proper procedure.
5. Using backup wrenches to prevent component damage, disconnect the suction line from the evaporator core and the liquid line from the expansion valve. Cap all open refrigerant line connections to prevent the entrance of dirt and moisture.
6. Disconnect the heater hoses, if equipped with an auxiliary heater, from the auxiliary heater core. Plug the hoses with suitable ⅝ in. plugs.
7. Remove the 4 screws retaining the evaporator core and mounting bracket to the auxiliary case assembly.
8. Remove the evaporator core, expansion valve and core mounting plate from the case assembly.
9. Remove the expansion valve and mounting plate from the evaporator core.

To install:

NOTE: Add 3 oz. (90ml) of clean refrigerant oil to a new replacement evaporator core to maintain the total system oil charge.

10. Connect the expansion valve to the evaporator core inlet tube using a new O-ring lubricated with clean refrigerant oil. Tighten the connection to 15–20 ft. lbs. (21–27 Nm) using a backup wrench.
11. Clamp the expansion valve capiliary bulb to the evaporator core outlet tube making sure the bulb makes good contact with the outlet tube. Clean both surfaces. Wrap the capillary bulb and outlet tube with insulating tape.
12. Wrap the ends of the evaporator core with insulating tape.
13. Attach the mounting plate to the expansion valve end of the evaporator core with 2 screws.
14. Carefully position the evaporator core to the case and refrigerant lines. Use new O-rings lubricated with clean refrigerant oil at the refrigerant line connections.
15. Tighten the suction line to evaporator core connection to 30–35 ft. lbs. (41–47 Nm) and the liquid line to expansion valve connection to 10–15 ft. lbs. (14–20 Nm). Use a backup wrench to prevent component damage.
16. Install the 4 screws that retain the evaporator core mounting brackets to the evaporator case.
17. Remove the plugs from the heater hoses and connect the hoses to the heater core. Tighten the hose clamps.
18. Fill the radiator to the proper level.
19. Connect the negative battery cable. Leak test, evacuate and charge the system according to the proper procedure. Observe all safety precautions.
20. Install the auxiliary air conditioner cover assembly.
21. Install the bench seat, if equipped and tighten the retaining bolts to 25–45 ft. lbs. (34–61 Nm).

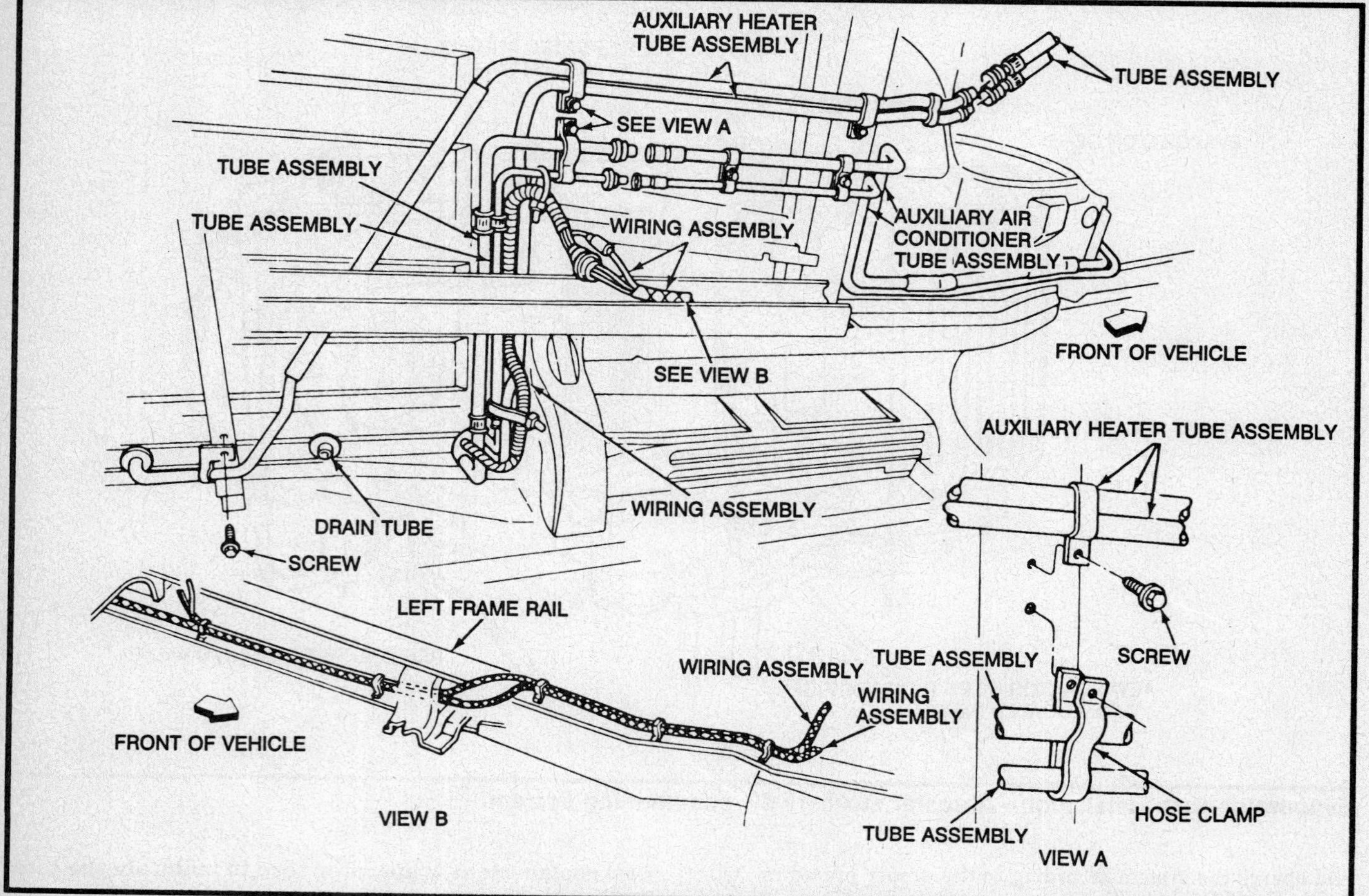
AUXILIARY HEATER
TUBE ASSEMBLY
TUBE ASSEMBLY
SEE VIEW A
TUBE ASSEMBLY
TUBE ASSEMBLY
WIRING ASSEMBLY
AUXILIARY AIR
CONDITIONER
TUBE ASSEMBLY
FRONT OF VEHICLE
SEE VIEW B
AUXILIARY HEATER TUBE ASSEMBLY
WIRING ASSEMBLY
DRAIN TUBE
SCREW
LEFT FRAME RAIL
WIRING ASSEMBLY
TUBE ASSEMBLY
SCREW
WIRING
ASSEMBLY
FRONT OF VEHICLE
VIEW B
HOSE CLAMP
TUBE ASSEMBLY
VIEW A

Typical underbody routing of air conditioner/heater hoses and tubes between main and auxiliary systems—E Series

Refrigerant Lines

REMOVAL AND INSTALLATION

1. Disconnect the negative battery cable.
2. Discharge the refrigerant from the air conditioning system according to the proper procedure.
3. Disconnect and remove the refrigerant line. Use a wrench on either side of the fitting or the spring-lock coupling disconnect procedure, as necessary.

To install:

4. Route the new refrigerant line, with the protective caps installed.
5. Connect the new refrigerant line into the system using new O-rings lubricated with clean refrigerant oil. Tighten the connections using a backup wrench to prevent component damage, or use the spring-lock coupling connection procedure, if applicable.
6. Connect the negative battery cable. Leak test, evacuate and charge the system according to the proper procedure. Observe all safety precautions.
7. Check the system for proper operation.

SENSORS AND SWITCHES

Solenoid Valve

OPERATION

The solenoid valve is used on Aerostar. It's function is to shut off the flow of refrigerant into the rear evaporator, when the rear blower is shut off.

REMOVAL AND INSTALLATION

1. Disconnect the negative battery cable.
2. Remove the first seat behind the driver, if equipped.
3. Remove the auxiliary service cover.
4. Discharge the refrigerant from the air conditioning system according to the proper procedure.

5. Disconnect the wiring connector from the solenoid and the solenoid from the case bracket.
6. Using a backup wrench to prevent damage, disconnect the solenoid valve from the liquid jump line and from the evaporator core. Cap the liquid line and core to prevent the entrance fo dirt and moisture.
7. Remove the solenoid.

To install:

8. Install new O-rings lubricated with clean refrigerant oil to the liquid jump line and the evaporator core.
9. Install the solenoid to both lines, tightening the connections only finger-tight at this time.
10. Attach the solenoid to the bracket and tighten the screws.
11. Using a backup wrench, tighten the liquid jump line to the solenoid to 10–15 ft. lbs. (14–20 Nm) and the solenoid to the evaporator core to 15–20 ft. lbs. (21–27 Nm).
12. Connect the solenoid electrical connector to the harness and attach to the bracket.
13. Connect the negative battery cable. Leak test, evacuate and charge the system according to the proper procedure. Observe all safety precautions.
14. Install the service panel and passenger seat.

Vacuum Motor

OPERATION

Vacuum is used to control the operation of the function door on the auxiliary unit on Aerostar. If the front control is in the **HEAT, MIX** or **DEFROST** position, the vacuum motor operated function door in the rear unit will deliver heated air through the floor outlets. If the front control is in the **VENT** position, the door in the rear unit will provide recirculated air which is delivered through the overhead and belt line registers. If the front control is set for air conditioning and there is an air conditioning unit in the rear system, that unit will deliver air conditioning through the overhead and belt line registers. However, if there is no rear air conditioning unit, the rear unit will function as if the front unit were set in the **VENT** position.

REMOVAL AND INSTALLATION

1. Remove the first seat behind the driver.
2. Remove the auxiliary service panel.
3. Remove the floor duct.
4. Remove the auxiliary cover.
5. Remove the push pin from the crank arm using a suitable tool.

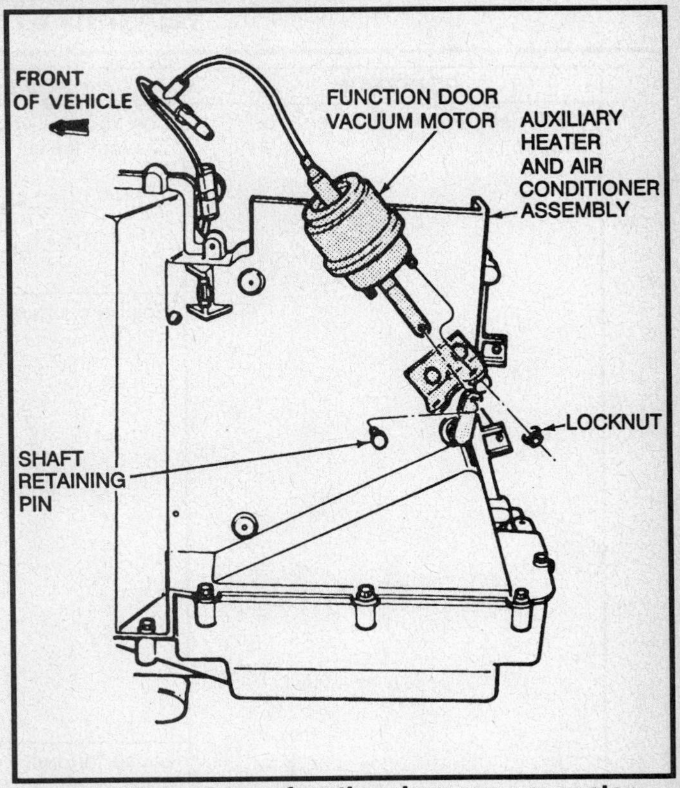
FRONT OF VEHICLE
FUNCTION DOOR VACUUM MOTOR
AUXILIARY HEATER AND AIR CONDITIONER ASSEMBLY
LOCKNUT
SHAFT RETAINING PIN

Rear auxiliary system function door vacuum motor installation—Aerostar

6. Remove the nuts from the studs just above the function door.
7. Disconnect the vacuum line from the vacuum motor and remove the vacuum motor.

To install:

8. Attach the vacuum line to the motor and install the motor on the case. Tighten the nuts to 10–13 inch lbs.
9. Attach the vacuum motor shaft to the mode door crank using the push pin.
10. Install the cover and the floor duct.
11. Install the service cover and passenger seat.

SYSTEM DIAGNOSIS

Heating System

BLOWER MOTOR TESTING

Visual Check

Check to see that all blower motor connections are correct including proper ground of the system. Check the resistor connection at the heater case and the heater fuse. Also check the connection at the rear of the blower switch.

Loose Blower Wheel Test

Place the blower switch in the **HIGH** position. If airflow is not evident but the motor can be heard, the blower wheel may not be secured to the motor shaft. Do not replace the blower motor unless the unit fails the current draw test.

Blower Motor Current Draw Test

EXCEPT E SERIES AND REAR AUXILIARY SYSTEMS

1. Disconnect the blower motor electrical wire harness.
2. Connect an ammeter between the positive terminal on the motor and the corresponding terminal of the wire harness connector. Connect a jumper wire between the ground terminal on the motor and the corresponding terminal of the wire harness connector.
3. Place the temperature control lever in the mid-range position, halfway between **COOL** and **WARM**. Place the function control lever in the **PANEL** position on Bronco, Bronco II, Ex-

HEATING SYSTEM DIAGNOSIS

CONDITION	POSSIBLE CAUSE	RESOLUTION
Insufficient, erratic, or no heat or defrost.	Low radiator coolant level due to: Coolant leaks.	Check radiator cap pressure. Replace if below minimum pressure. Fill to specified coolant level. Pressure test for engine cooling system and heater system leaks. Service as required.
	Engine overheating.	Check radiator cap. Replace if below minimum pressure. Remove bugs, leaves, etc. from radiator or condenser fins. Check for: Loose fan belt Sticking thermostat Incorrect ignition timing Water pump impeller damage Restricted cooling system Service as required.
	Loose fan belt.	Replace if cracked or worn and/or adjust belt tension.
	Thermostat.	Check coolant temperature at radiator filler neck. If under 170°F, replace thermostat.
	Plugged or partially plugged heater core.	Clean and backflush engine cooling system and heater core.
	Loose or improperly adjusted control cables.	Adjust to specifications.
	Kinked, clogged, collapsed, soft, swollen, or decomposed engine cooling system or heater system hoses.	Replace damaged hoses and backflush engine cooling system, then heater system, until all particles have been removed.
	Blocked air inlet.	Check cowl air inlet for leaves, foreign material, etc. Remove as required. Check internal blower inlet screen (on vehicles so equipped) for leaves and foreign material.

plorer, F Series and Ranger or in the **VENT** position on Aerostar.

4. With the battery fully charged, start the engine and operate the blower in all speeds. Record the current draw for each blower speed.
5. The current draw for each blower speed should be within the proper limits.
6. Disconnect the ammeter and jumper wire and reconnect the harness connector to the blower motor.
7. Check the blower system for proper operation.

E SERIES

1. Separate the blower motor ground wire at the blower motor resistor.
2. Connect the positive lead of an ammeter to the female spade connector and the negative lead of the ammeter to the resistor terminal.
3. Place the temperature selector lever in the mid-position and the function lever in the **HEAT** position to turn the blower on.

HEATING SYSTEM DIAGNOSIS

CONDITION	POSSIBLE CAUSE	RESOLUTION
Blower does not operate properly. Check fuse.	Blower motor.	Connect a #10 gauge (or larger diameter) jumper wire directly from the positive battery terminal to the positive lead (orange wire) of the blower motor. If the motor runs, the problem must be external to the motor. If the motor will not run, connect a #10 gauge (or larger diameter) jumper wire from the motor black lead to a good ground. If the motor runs, the trouble is in the ground circuit. On vehicles with ground side switching, check the blower resistor, the blower switch and the harness connections. Service as required. If motor still will not run, the motor is inoperative and should be replaced.
	Blower resistor.	Check continuity of resistors for opens or shorts (self-powered test lamp). Service or replace as required.
	Blower wire harness.	Check for proper installation of harness connector terminal connectors. Check wire-to-terminal continuity. Check continuity of wires in harness for shorts, opens, abrasion, etc. Service as required.
	Blower switch(es).	Check blower switch(es) for proper contact. Replace switch(es) as required.
Vacuum motor system	Vacuum leak. Loose or disconnected vacuum hose. Damaged vacuum motor. Misrouted vacuum connections	Repair or repair system components, as required.

4. Turn the ignition switch to the **ON** position.
5. With a fully charged battery, check the blower motor current draw in each blower speed.
6. The current draw for each blower speed should be within the proper limits.
7. Disconnect the ammeter and connect the blower motor ground wire at the blower motor resistor.

AEROSTAR AUXILIARY HEATING SYSTEM

1. Disconnect the harness connector wire from the motor connector near the blower motor.
2. Connect an ammeter between the positive orange wire terminal of the motor connector and the corresponding brown-orange wire terminal. Connect a jumper wire between the 2 negative terminals, the black wire on the blower motor connector and the orange-black connector on the harness connector.
3. Place the temperature control lever in the **MAX HEAT** position and the function control lever in the **HEAT** position.
4. With the battery fully charged, turn the switch **ON** and operate the blower in all blower speeds. Record the current draw for each blower speed.
5. The current draw for each blower speed should be within the specified limits.
6. Disconnect the ammeter and connect the blower motor wire to the harness at the connectors.

E SERIES AUXILIARY HEATING SYSTEM

1. Separate the blower motor ground wire from the blower motor resistor.
2. Connect the positive lead of an ammeter to the female spade connector on the motor wire and the negative lead to the blower motor resistor.
3. With a fully charged battery, operate the blower in each switch position and record the current draw.
4. The current draw for each switch position should be within the proper limits.
5. Disconnect the ammeter and connect the blower motor ground wire.

BLOWER MOTOR CURRENT DRAW AND VOLTAGE DROP—HEATING SYSTEM

Switch Position	Aerostar Amps	Aerostar Volts	Bronco II Explorer/Ranger Amps	Bronco II Explorer/Ranger Volts	1989 Bronco/F Series Amps	1989 Bronco/F Series Volts	1990-91 Bronco/F Series Amps	1990-91 Bronco/F Series Volts	E Series Amps	E Series Volts
Off	0	0	0	0	0	0	—	—	—	—
Low	3.2	4.1–5.6	3.5–5.5	5	4	5	3–5	3–4	4.0	4.0
Medium Low	6.0	6.4–7.9	5–7.5	8	—	—	6–8	5–7	7.3	6.0
Medium	—	—	—	—	6	8	—	—	—	—
Medium High	9.5	8.7–10.2	7–9.5	10	—	—	10–14	7–10	13.8	9.0
High	13.5	11.3–12.8	9.5–11.5	12	9	12	15–22	11–14	23.0	12.8

Blower Motor Voltage Test

EXCEPT REAR AUXILIARY HEATER SYSTEM

1. On all except E Series, place the temperature selector lever in the mid-range position, halfway between **COOL** and **WARM**. On E Series, place the temperature selector lever in the **WARM** position.
2. On Bronco, Bronco II, Explorer, F Series and Ranger, place the function control lever in the **PANEL** position. On Aerostar, place the function control lever in the **VENT** position. On E Series, place the function control lever in the **FLOOR** position.
3. Insert the probes of a voltmeter into the connector at the rear of the blower motor and make contact with the wire terminals. With the engine running, measure the voltage drop across the motor.
4. With the engine running and battery voltage approximately 14.2 volts, the voltage reading should be within the specified range.
5. Disconnect the voltmeter from the connector.

AEROSTAR AND E SERIES AUXILIARY HEATER SYSTEMS

1. Insert the probes of a voltmeter into the wire holes of the blower motor connectors and make contact with the wire terminals.
2. Measure the voltage drop across the motor.
3. With the engine running and battery voltage approximately 14.2 volts, the voltage reading should be within the range specified.

Blower Switch Continuity Test

Check for continuity between the connected terminals indicated on the schematic. Check the terminal continuity at every lever position. The light should go on for each connected pair of terminals.

HEATER CORE TESTING

Bleeding Air From the Heater Core

EXCEPT AEROSTAR

NOTE: On Aerostar, the heater core is self purging at an engine rpm of 2000.

Remove the hose at the outlet connection of the heater core; the hose that leads to the water pump. Allow any trapped air to flow out. When a continuous flow of coolant is obtained, connect the hose to the core. Do not overtighten the hose clamps.

Heater Core Leak Test

EXCEPT AEROSTAR

1. Inspect for visible evidence of coolant leakage at the hose to the heater core attachments. A coolant leak at the hose could follow the heater core tube to the core and appear as a leak in the heater core.
2. Check the system for loose heater hose clamps. The clamps should be tightened to 16–22 inch lbs. (1.81–2.49 Nm).
3. If leakage is found and the hose clamps are tight, check the heater tubes for distortion. Severe distortion of the tubes could cause leakage at the hose connection.

AEROSTAR

1. Inspect for visible evidence of coolant leakage at the hose to the heater core attachments. A coolant leak at the hose could follow the heater core tube to the core and appear as a leak in the heater core.
2. For the front unit core, remove the hoses at the core using the snap-lock fitting disconnect procedure. Check for damaged or missing O-rings. Replace if necessary and install the hoses by pushing the hose on the tube until the connector snaps in place over the white plastic snap tabs. Check the core tubes for damage. Replace the core, if necessary.
3. For the auxiliary core, check the system for loose heater hose clamps. The clamps should be tightened to 22–30 inch lbs. (2.4–3.3 Nm). If the clamps are tight and leakage is found, check the heater core tubes for distortion. Severe distortion of the tubes could cause leakage at the hose connection. Replace the core, if necessary.

Pressure Test

1. Drain the cooling system.
2. Disconnect the heater hoses from the heater core tubes.
3. Install a short piece of heater hose, approximately 4 in. long onto each heater core tube.
4. Fill the heater core and hoses with water and install a plug in the end of one hose. In the other hose end, install an adapter suitable to connect with a radiator pressure tester. Secure the hoses to the heater core, plug and adapter with hose clamps.
5. Attach the radiator pressure tester to the adapter. Close the bleed valve at the base of the gauge and pump 30 psi of air pressure into the heater core.

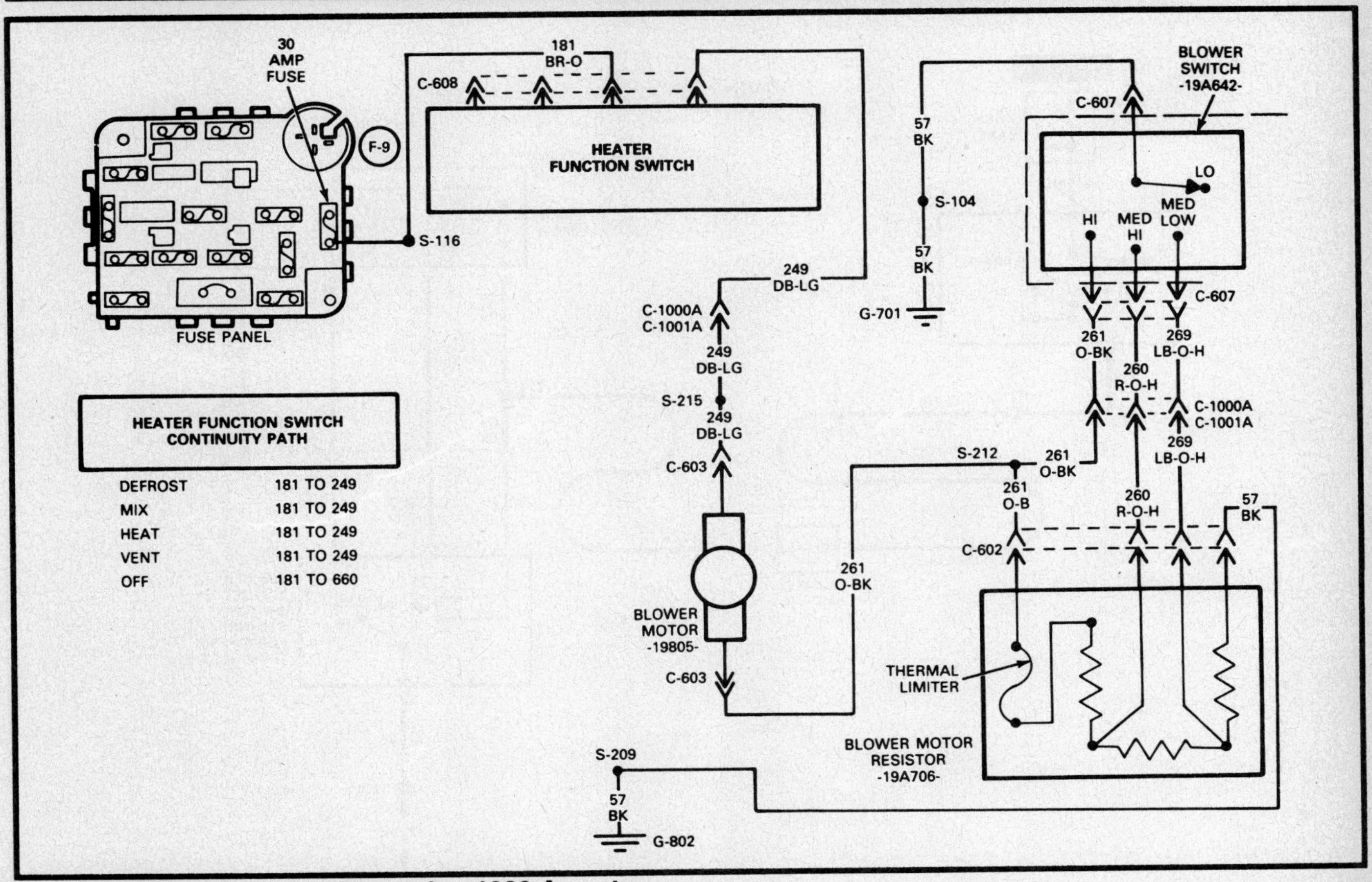
30 AMP FUSE
F-9
FUSE PANEL
S-116
C-608
181 BR-O
HEATER FUNCTION SWITCH
249 DB-LG
C-1000A
C-1001A
249 DB-LG
S-215
249 DB-LG
C-603
BLOWER MOTOR -19805-
C-603
HEATER FUNCTION SWITCH CONTINUITY PATH
DEFROST 181 TO 249
MIX 181 TO 249
HEAT 181 TO 249
VENT 181 TO 249
OFF 181 TO 660
57 BK
S-104
57 BK
G-701
BLOWER SWITCH -19A642-
C-607
LO
MED LOW
MED HI
HI
C-607
261 O-BK
260 R-O-H
269 LB-O-H
C-1000A
C-1001A
269 LB-O-H
S-212
261 O-BK
261 O-B
260 R-O-H
57 BK
C-602
261 O-BK
THERMAL LIMITER
BLOWER MOTOR RESISTOR -19A706-
S-209
57 BK
G-802
Heating system electrical schematic—1989 Aerostar

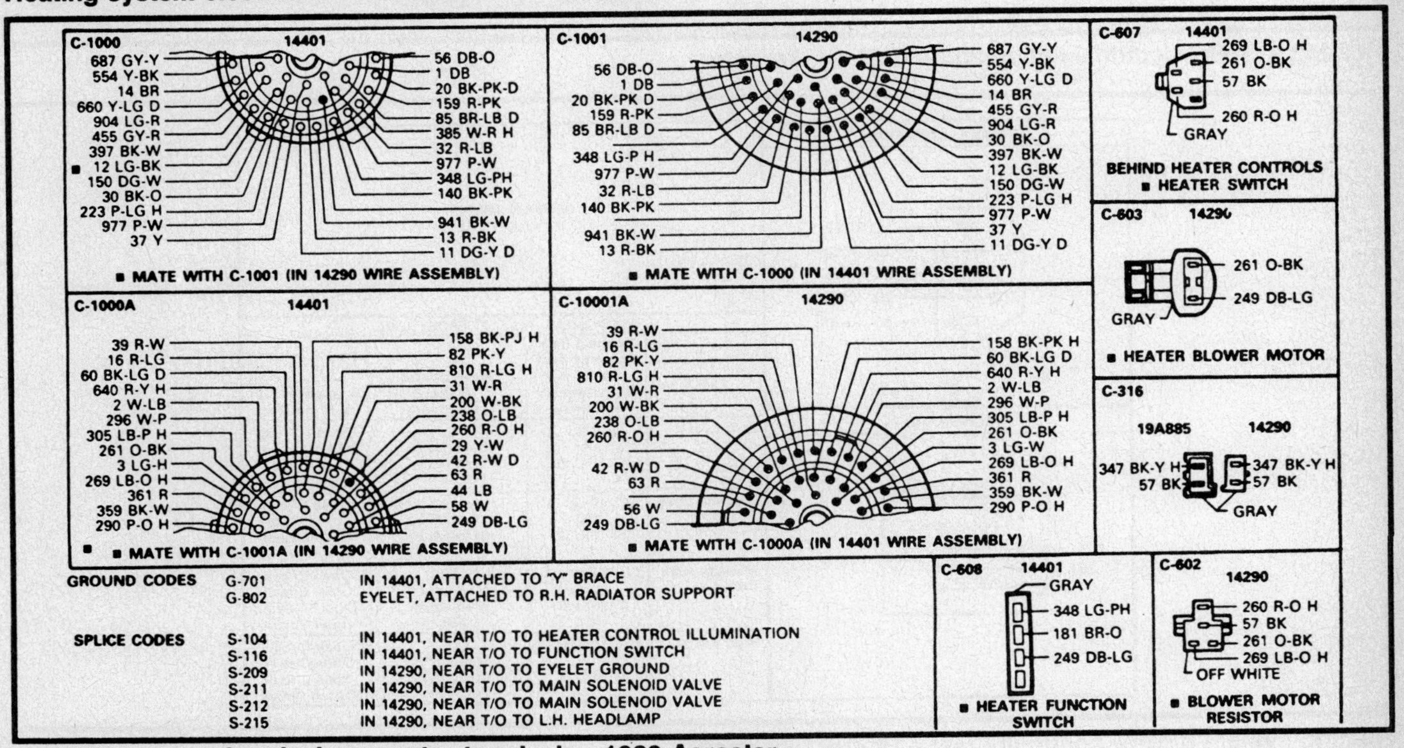
C-1000 14401
687 GY-Y
554 Y-BK
14 BR
660 Y-LG D
904 LG-R
455 GY-R
397 BK-W
12 LG-BK
150 DG-W
30 BK-O
223 P-LG H
977 P-W
37 Y
56 DB-O
1 DB
20 BK-PK-D
159 R-PK
85 BR-LB D
385 W-R H
32 R-LB
977 P-W
348 LG-PH
140 BK-PK
941 BK-W
13 R-BK
11 DG-Y D
■ MATE WITH C-1001 (IN 14290 WIRE ASSEMBLY)
C-1001 14290
56 DB-O
1 DB
20 BK-PK D
159 R-PK
85 BR-LB D
348 LG-P H
977 P-W
32 R-LB
140 BK-PK
941 BK-W
13 R-BK
687 GY-Y
554 Y-BK
660 Y-LG D
14 BR
455 GY-R
904 LG-R
30 BK-O
397 BK-W
12 LG-BK
150 DG-W
223 P-LG H
977 P-W
37 Y
11 DG-Y D
■ MATE WITH C-1000 (IN 14401 WIRE ASSEMBLY)
C-607 14401
269 LB-O H
261 O-BK
57 BK
260 R-O H
GRAY
BEHIND HEATER CONTROLS
■ HEATER SWITCH
C-1000A 14401
39 R-W
16 R-LG
60 BK-LG D
640 R-Y H
2 W-LB
296 W-P
305 LB-P H
261 O-BK
3 LG-H
269 LB-O H
361 R
359 BK-W
290 P-O H
158 BK-PJ H
82 PK-Y
810 R-LG H
31 W-R
200 W-BK
238 O-LB
260 R-O H
29 Y-W
42 R-W D
63 R
44 LB
58 W
249 DB-LG
■ MATE WITH C-1001A (IN 14290 WIRE ASSEMBLY)
C-10001A 14290
39 R-W
16 R-LG
82 PK-Y
810 R-LG H
31 W-R
200 W-BK
238 O-LB
260 R-O H
42 R-W D
63 R
56 W
249 DB-LG
158 BK-PK H
60 BK-LG D
640 R-Y H
2 W-LB
296 W-P
305 LB-P H
261 O-BK
3 LG-W
269 LB-O H
361 R
359 BK-W
290 P-O H
■ MATE WITH C-1000A (IN 14401 WIRE ASSEMBLY)
C-603 14290
261 O-BK
249 DB-LG
GRAY
■ HEATER BLOWER MOTOR
C-316
19A885
14290
347 BK-Y H
57 BK
347 BK-Y H
57 BK
GRAY
GROUND CODES G-701 IN 14401, ATTACHED TO "Y" BRACE
G-802 EYELET, ATTACHED TO R.H. RADIATOR SUPPORT
SPLICE CODES S-104 IN 14401, NEAR T/O TO HEATER CONTROL ILLUMINATION
S-116 IN 14401, NEAR T/O TO FUNCTION SWITCH
S-209 IN 14290, NEAR T/O TO EYELET GROUND
S-211 IN 14290, NEAR T/O TO MAIN SOLENOID VALVE
S-212 IN 14290, NEAR T/O TO MAIN SOLENOID VALVE
S-215 IN 14290, NEAR T/O TO L.H. HEADLAMP
C-608 14401
GRAY
348 LG-PH
181 BR-O
249 DB-LG
■ HEATER FUNCTION SWITCH
C-602 14290
260 R-O H
57 BK
261 O-BK
269 LB-O H
OFF WHITE
■ BLOWER MOTOR RESISTOR
Heating system electrical connector terminals—1989 Aerostar

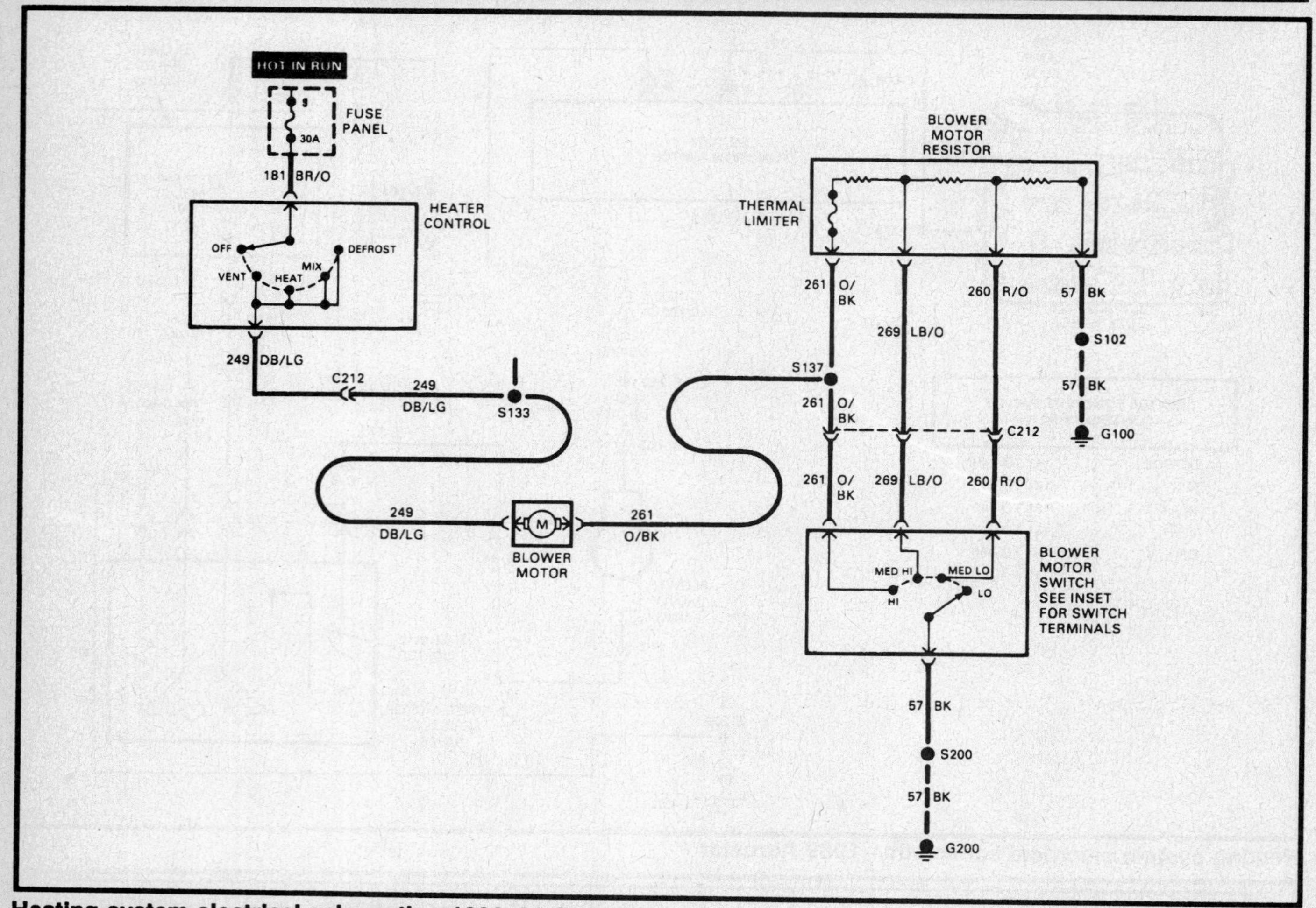
HOT IN RUN
FUSE PANEL
30A
181 BR/O
HEATER CONTROL
OFF
DEFROST
VENT
HEAT
MIX
249 DB/LG
C212
249 DB/LG
S133
249 DB/LG
BLOWER MOTOR
261 O/BK
BLOWER MOTOR RESISTOR
THERMAL LIMITER
261 O/BK
269 LB/O
260 R/O
57 BK
S102
57 BK
G100
S137
261 O/BK
C212
261 O/BK
269 LB/O
260 R/O
BLOWER MOTOR SWITCH SEE INSET FOR SWITCH TERMINALS
MED HI
MED LO
HI
LO
57 BK
S200
57 BK
G200

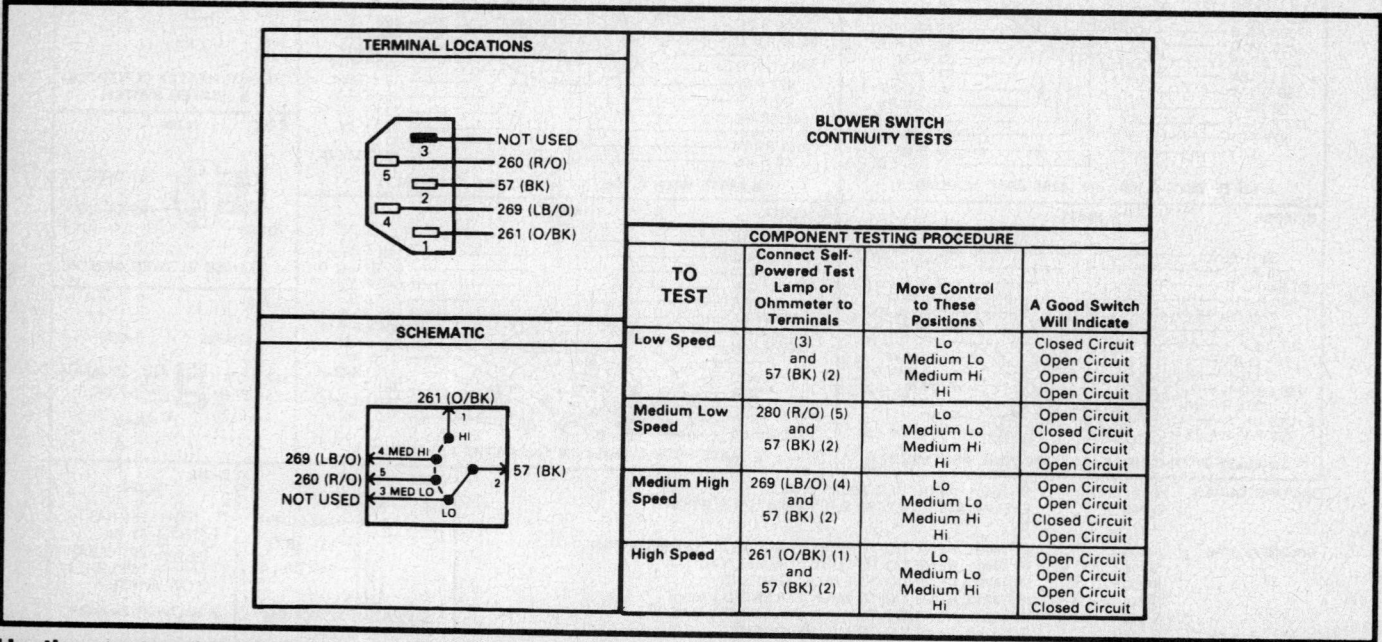

Heating system electrical schematic—1990–91 Aerostar

TERMINAL LOCATIONS

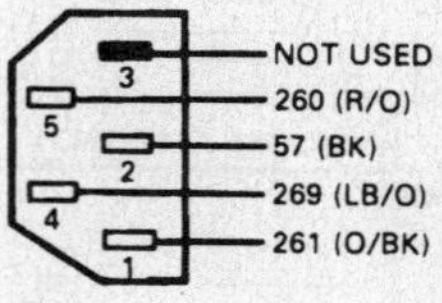
NOT USED
260 (R/O)
57 (BK)
269 (LB/O)
261 (O/BK)
3
5
2
4
1

SCHEMATIC

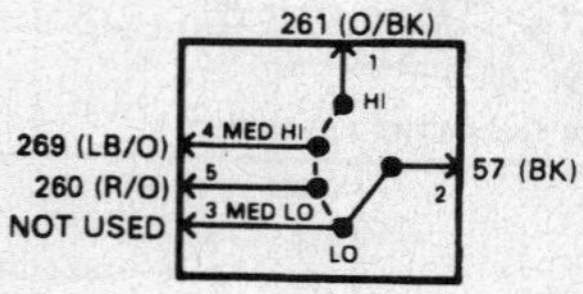
261 (O/BK)
HI
269 (LB/O)
4 MED HI
260 (R/O)
5
NOT USED
3 MED LO
LO
57 (BK)
2

BLOWER SWITCH CONTINUITY TESTS

COMPONENT TESTING PROCEDURE

TO TEST	Connect Self-Powered Test Lamp or Ohmmeter to Terminals	Move Control to These Positions	A Good Switch Will Indicate
Low Speed	(3) and 57 (BK) (2)	Lo Medium Lo Medium Hi Hi	Closed Circuit Open Circuit Open Circuit Open Circuit
Medium Low Speed	280 (R/O) (5) and 57 (BK) (2)	Lo Medium Lo Medium Hi Hi	Open Circuit Closed Circuit Open Circuit Open Circuit
Medium High Speed	269 (LB/O) (4) and 57 (BK) (2)	Lo Medium Lo Medium Hi Hi	Open Circuit Open Circuit Closed Circuit Open Circuit
High Speed	261 (O/BK) (1) and 57 (BK) (2)	Lo Medium Lo Medium Hi Hi	Open Circuit Open Circuit Open Circuit Closed Circuit

Heating system blower continuity test—1990–91 Aerostar

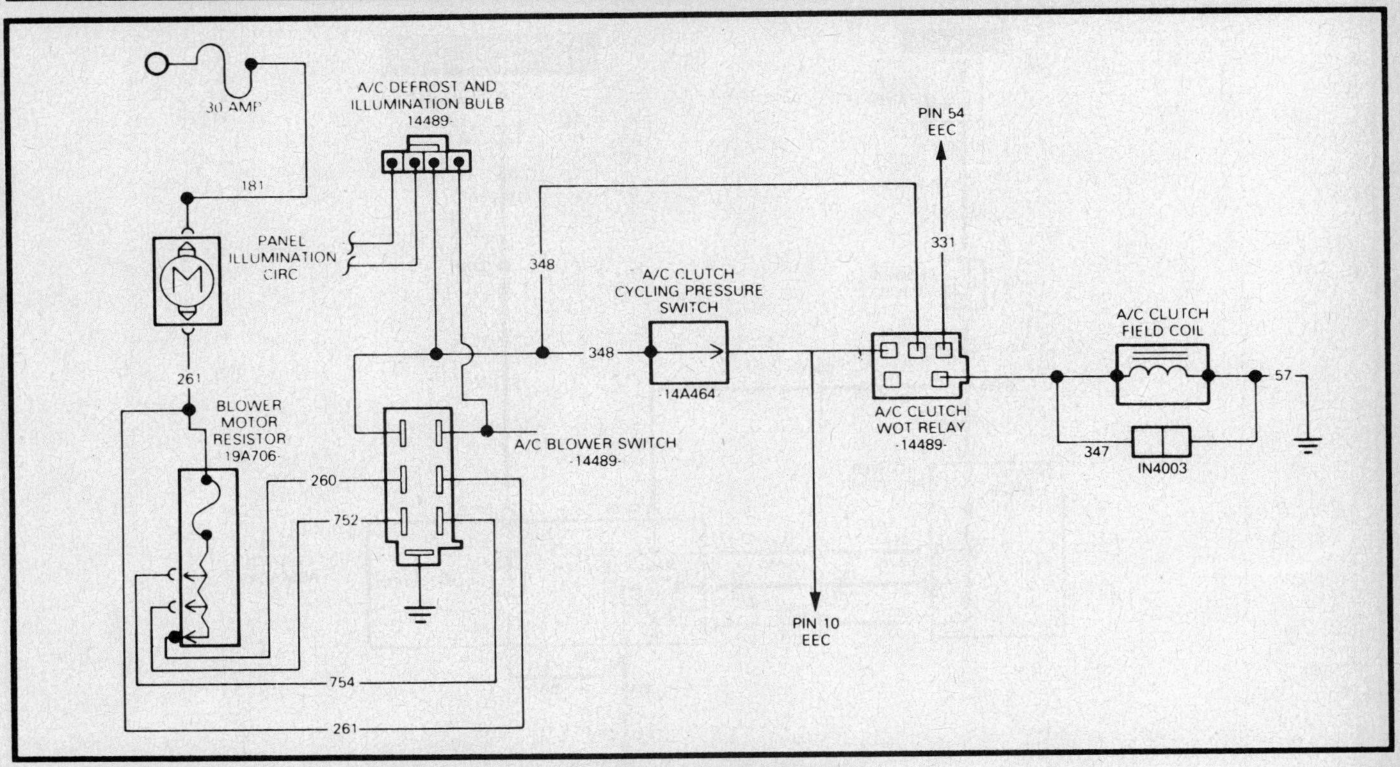
30 AMP
181
A/C DEFROST AND ILLUMINATION BULB 14489-
PANEL ILLUMINATION CIRC
PIN 54 EEC
331
348
A/C CLUTCH CYCLING PRESSURE SWITCH
348
14A464
A/C CLUTCH FIELD COIL
57
261
BLOWER MOTOR RESISTOR 19A706-
A/C BLOWER SWITCH -14489-
A/C CLUTCH WOT RELAY -14489-
347
IN4003
260
752
PIN 10 EEC
754
261

Heating system electrical schematic—1989–90 Bronco II and Ranger

6. Observe the pressure gauge for a minimum of 3 minutes. The pressure should not drop.
7. If the pressure does not drop, no leaks are indicated.
8. If the pressure drops, check the hose connections at the core tubes for leaks. If the hoses do not leak, remove the heater core from the vehicle and bench test the core.

Bench Test

1. Drain all coolant from the heater core.
2. Connect the test hoses with the plug and adapter to the core tubes. Tighten the clamps and connect the pressure tester to the adapter.
3. Apply 30 psi of air pressure to the heater core with the radiator pressure tester and submerge the core in water.
4. If a leak is observed, repair or replace the heater core, as necessary.

Air Conditioning System

BLOWER MOTOR TESTING

Blower Motor Current Draw Test

EXCEPT E SERIES AND REAR AUXILIARY SYSTEMS

1. Disconnect the blower motor electrical wire harness.
2. Connect an ammeter between the positive terminal on the motor and the corresponding terminal of the wire harness connector. Connect a jumper wire between the ground terminal on the motor and the corresponding terminal of the wire harness connector.
3. Place the temperature control lever in the mid-range position, halfway between **COOL** and **WARM**. Place the function control lever in the **PANEL** position on Bronco, Bronco II, Explorer, F Series and Ranger or in the **MAX A/C** position on Aerostar.

TERMINAL LOCATION ON SWITCH	COMPONENT TESTING PROCEDURE		
SCHEMATIC OF SWITCH	CONNECT SELF-POWERED LIGHT OR OHMMETER TO TERMINALS	MOVE CONTROL TO EACH POSITION	A GOOD SWITCH WILL INDICATE A CIRCUIT THAT IS:
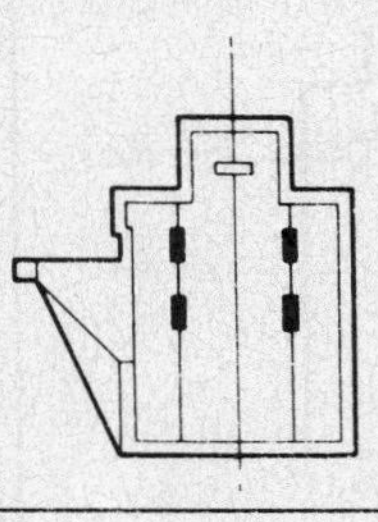	260 R/O (E) AND 234 DB/W (A)	OFF LO MEDIUM 2 MEDIUM 1 HI	OPEN CLOSED OPEN OPEN OPEN
	754 LG/W(B) AND 234 DB/W(A)	OFF LO MEDIUM 2 MEDIUM 1 HI	OPEN OPEN CLOSED OPEN OPEN
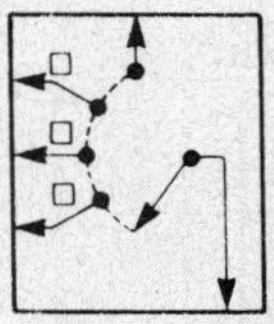	752 Y/R (C) AND 234 DB/W(A)	OFF LO MEDIUM 2 MEDIUM 1 HI	OPEN OPEN OPEN CLOSED OPEN
	261 O/BK (D) AND 234 DB/W (A)	OFF LO MEDIUM 2 MEDIUM 1 HI	OPEN OPEN OPEN OPEN CLOSED

Heating system blower continuity test—1989–90 Bronco II and Ranger

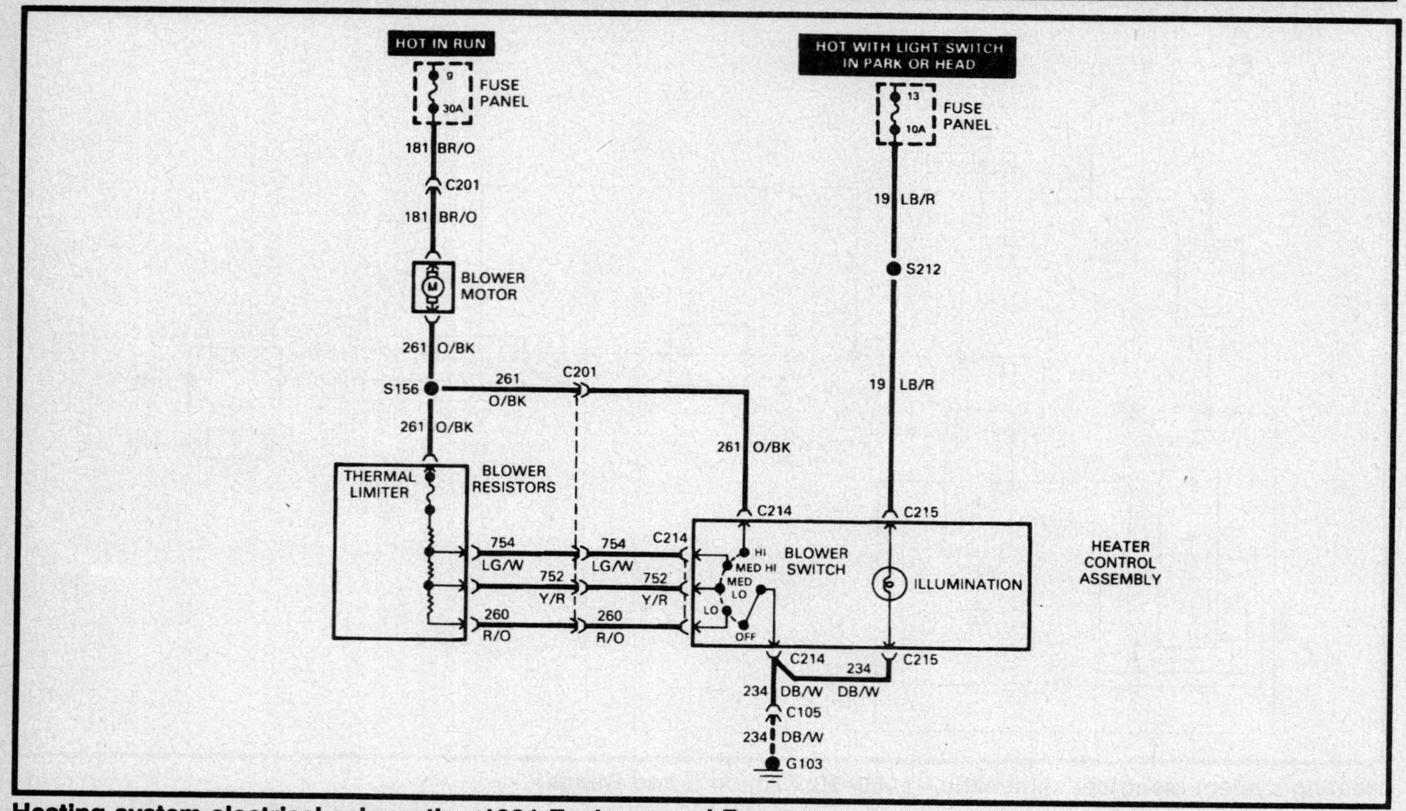
HOT IN RUN
9
30A
FUSE PANEL
181 BR/O
C201
181 BR/O
BLOWER MOTOR
261 O/BK
S156
261 O/BK
C201
261 O/BK
261 O/BK
THERMAL LIMITER
BLOWER RESISTORS
754 LG/W
752 Y/R
260 R/O
754 LG/W
752 Y/R
260 R/O
C214
C214
HI
MED HI
MED LO
LO
OFF
BLOWER SWITCH
ILLUMINATION
HOT WITH LIGHT SWITCH IN PARK OR HEAD
13
10A
FUSE PANEL
19 LB/R
S212
19 LB/R
C215
HEATER CONTROL ASSEMBLY
C214
234
C215
234 DB/W DB/W
C105
234 DB/W
G103

Heating system electrical schematic—1991 Explorer and Ranger

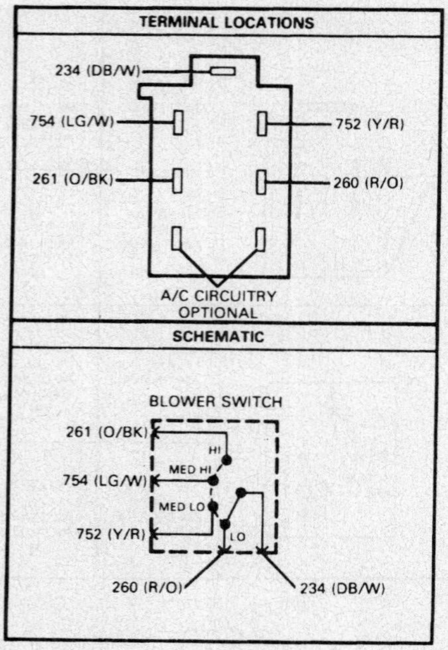
TERMINAL LOCATIONS
234 (DB/W)
754 (LG/W)
752 (Y/R)
261 (O/BK)
260 (R/O)
A/C CIRCUITRY OPTIONAL
SCHEMATIC
BLOWER SWITCH
261 (O/BK)
HI
MED HI
754 (LG/W)
MED LO
752 (Y/R)
LO
260 (R/O)
234 (DB/W)

COMPONENT TESTING PROCEDURE

TO TEST	Connect Self-Powered Test Light or Ohmmeter to Terminals	Move Switch to These Positions	A Good Switch Will Indicate
Low Speed	260 R/O and 234 DB/W	Lo Medium Lo Medium Hi Hi	Closed Circuit Open Circuit Open Circuit Open Circuit
Medium Low Speed	752 Y/R and 234 DB/W	Lo Medium Lo Medium Hi Hi	Open Circuit Closed Circuit Open Circuit Open Circuit
Medium Hi Speed	754 LG/W and 234 DB/W	Lo Medium Lo Medium Hi Hi	Open Circuit Open Circuit Closed Circuit Open Circuit
High Speed	261 O/BK and 234 DB/W	Lo Medium Lo Medium Hi Hi	Open Circuit Open Circuit Open Circuit Closed Circuit

WIRE COLOR CODES
BR/O - BROWN/ORANGE
DB/W - DARK BLUE/WHITE
LB/R - LIGHT BLUE/RED
LG/W - LIGHT GREEN/WHITE
O/BK - ORANGE/BLACK
R/O - RED/ORANGE
Y/R - YELLOW/RED

Heating system blower continuity test—1991 Explorer and Ranger

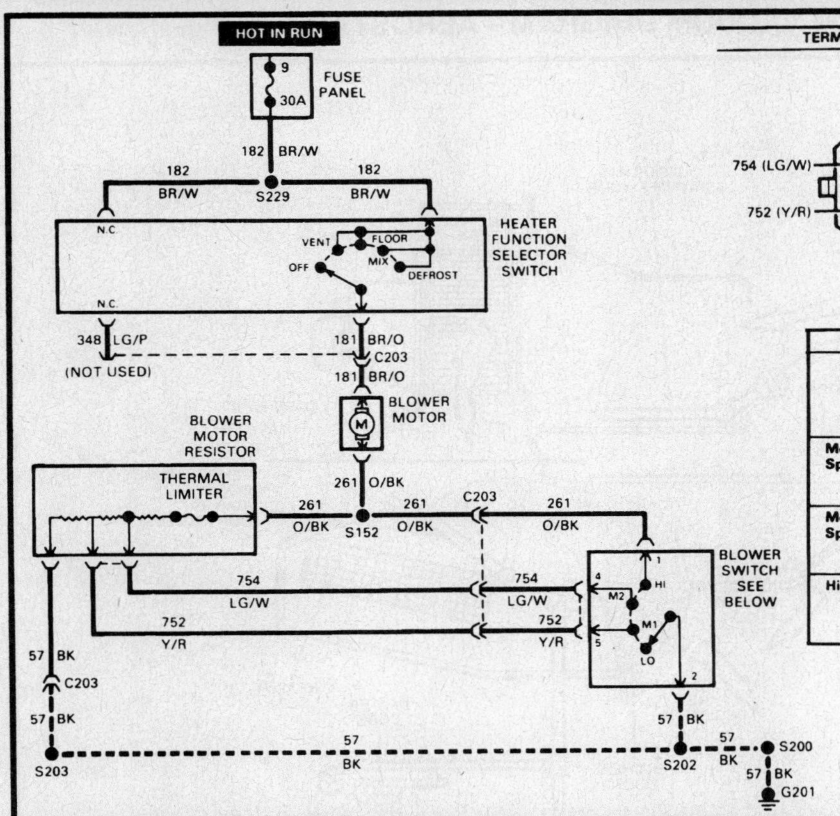
HOT IN RUN
9
30A
FUSE PANEL
182 BR/W
182 BR/W
S229
182 BR/W
N.C.
VENT
FLOOR
OFF
MIX
DEFROST
HEATER FUNCTION SELECTOR SWITCH
N.C.
348 LG/P
(NOT USED)
181 BR/O
C203
181 BR/O
BLOWER MOTOR
BLOWER MOTOR RESISTOR
THERMAL LIMITER
261 O/BK
261 O/BK
S152
261 O/BK
C203
261 O/BK
754 LG/W
754 LG/W
752 Y/R
752 Y/R
BLOWER SWITCH SEE BELOW
HI
M2
M1
LO
57 BK
C203
57 BK
S203
57 BK
57 BK
S202
57 BK
S200
57 BK
G201

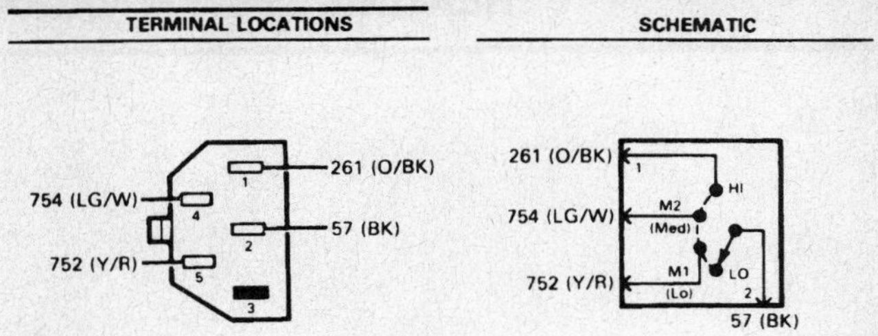
TERMINAL LOCATIONS
261 (O/BK)
754 (LG/W)
57 (BK)
752 (Y/R)
SCHEMATIC
261 (O/BK)
HI
M2 (Med)
754 (LG/W)
M1 (Lo)
LO
752 (Y/R)
57 (BK)

COMPONENT TESTING PROCEDURE			
TO TEST	**Connect Self-Powered Test Lamp or Ohmmeter to Terminals**	**Move Switch to These Positions**	**A Good Switch Will Indicate**
Medium-Low Speed	57 (BK) 2 and 752 (Y/R) 5	Lo M1 M2 Hi	Open circuit Closed circuit Open circuit Open circuit
Medium Speed	57 (BK) 2 and 754 (LG/W) 4	Lo M1 M2 Hi	Open circuit Open circuit Closed circuit Open circuit
High Speed	57 (BK) 2 and 261 (O/BK) 1	Lo M1 M2 Hi	Open circuit Open circuit Open circuit Closed circuit

Heating system electrical schematic—Bronco and F Series

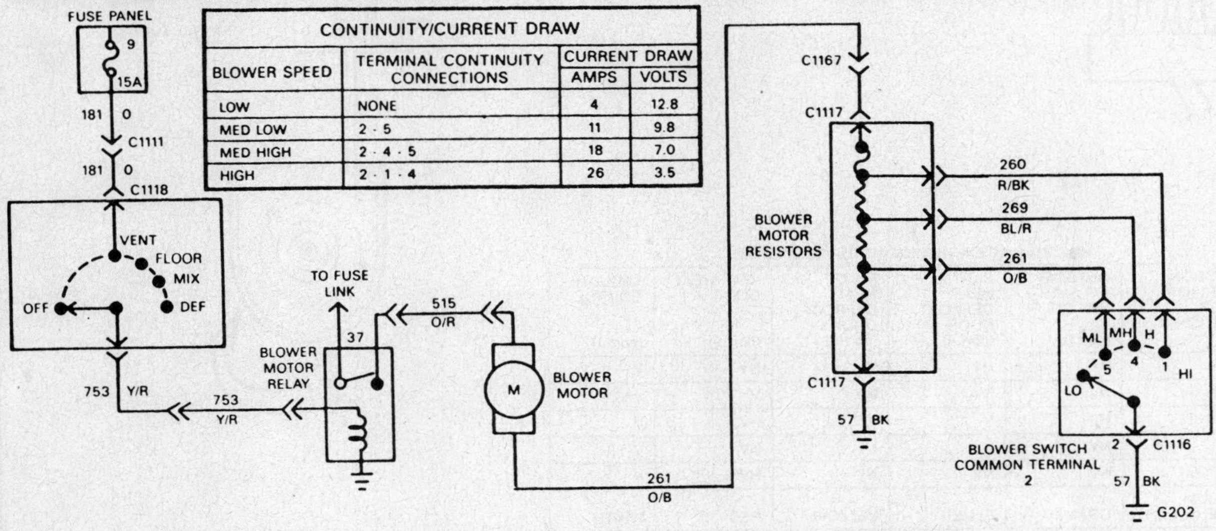
FUSE PANEL
9
15A
181 O
C1111
181 O
C1118
VENT
FLOOR
MIX
OFF
DEF
753 Y/R
753 Y/R
TO FUSE LINK
37
515 O/R
BLOWER MOTOR RELAY
BLOWER MOTOR
261 O/B
C1167
C1117
BLOWER MOTOR RESISTORS
260 R/BK
269 BL/R
261 O/B
ML
MH
H
5
4
1
HI
LO
C1117
57 BK
2
C1116
BLOWER SWITCH COMMON TERMINAL 2
57 BK
G202

CONTINUITY/CURRENT DRAW			
BLOWER SPEED	TERMINAL CONTINUITY CONNECTIONS	CURRENT DRAW	
		AMPS	VOLTS
LOW	NONE	4	12.8
MED LOW	2 - 5	11	9.8
MED HIGH	2 - 4 - 5	18	7.0
HIGH	2 - 1 - 4	26	3.5

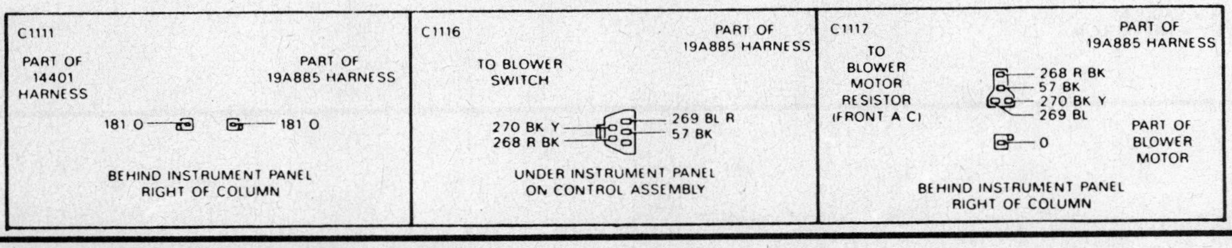
C1111
PART OF 14401 HARNESS
PART OF 19A885 HARNESS
181 O
181 O
BEHIND INSTRUMENT PANEL RIGHT OF COLUMN
C1116
TO BLOWER SWITCH
PART OF 19A885 HARNESS
270 BK Y
268 R BK
269 BL R
57 BK
UNDER INSTRUMENT PANEL ON CONTROL ASSEMBLY
C1117
TO BLOWER MOTOR RESISTOR (FRONT A C)
PART OF 19A885 HARNESS
268 R BK
57 BK
270 BK Y
269 BL
O
PART OF BLOWER MOTOR
BEHIND INSTRUMENT PANEL RIGHT OF COLUMN

Heating system electrical schematic—E Series

HEATING SYSTEM VACUUM DIAGRAM—AEROSTAR

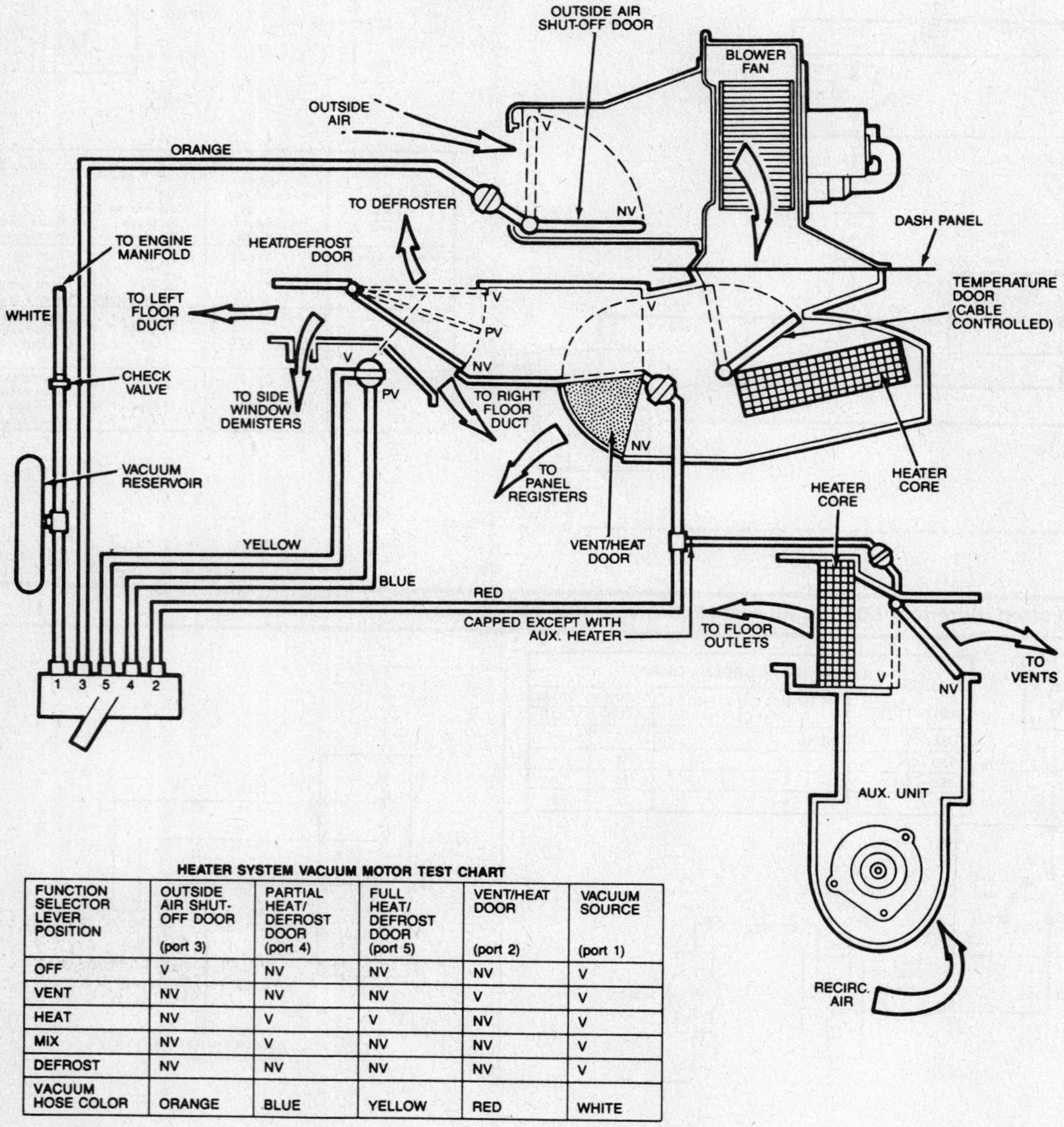
OUTSIDE AIR SHUT-OFF DOOR
BLOWER FAN
OUTSIDE AIR
V
ORANGE
TO DEFROSTER
NV
DASH PANEL
TO ENGINE MANIFOLD
HEAT/DEFROST DOOR
V
TEMPERATURE DOOR (CABLE CONTROLLED)
TO LEFT FLOOR DUCT
WHITE
V
PV
V
NV
CHECK VALVE
PV
TO SIDE WINDOW DEMISTERS
TO RIGHT FLOOR DUCT
NV
TO PANEL REGISTERS
HEATER CORE
HEATER CORE
VACUUM RESERVOIR
VENT/HEAT DOOR
YELLOW
BLUE
RED
CAPPED EXCEPT WITH AUX. HEATER
TO FLOOR OUTLETS
TO VENTS
V
NV
1 3 5 4 2
AUX. UNIT
RECIRC. AIR

HEATER SYSTEM VACUUM MOTOR TEST CHART

FUNCTION SELECTOR LEVER POSITION	OUTSIDE AIR SHUT-OFF DOOR (port 3)	PARTIAL HEAT/ DEFROST DOOR (port 4)	FULL HEAT/ DEFROST DOOR (port 5)	VENT/HEAT DOOR (port 2)	VACUUM SOURCE (port 1)
OFF	V	NV	NV	NV	V
VENT	NV	NV	NV	V	V
HEAT	NV	V	V	NV	V
MIX	NV	V	NV	NV	V
DEFROST	NV	NV	NV	NV	V
VACUUM HOSE COLOR	ORANGE	BLUE	YELLOW	RED	WHITE

V = VACUUM
NV = NO VACUUM

HEATING SYSTEM VACUUM DIAGRAM—BRONCO AND F SERIES

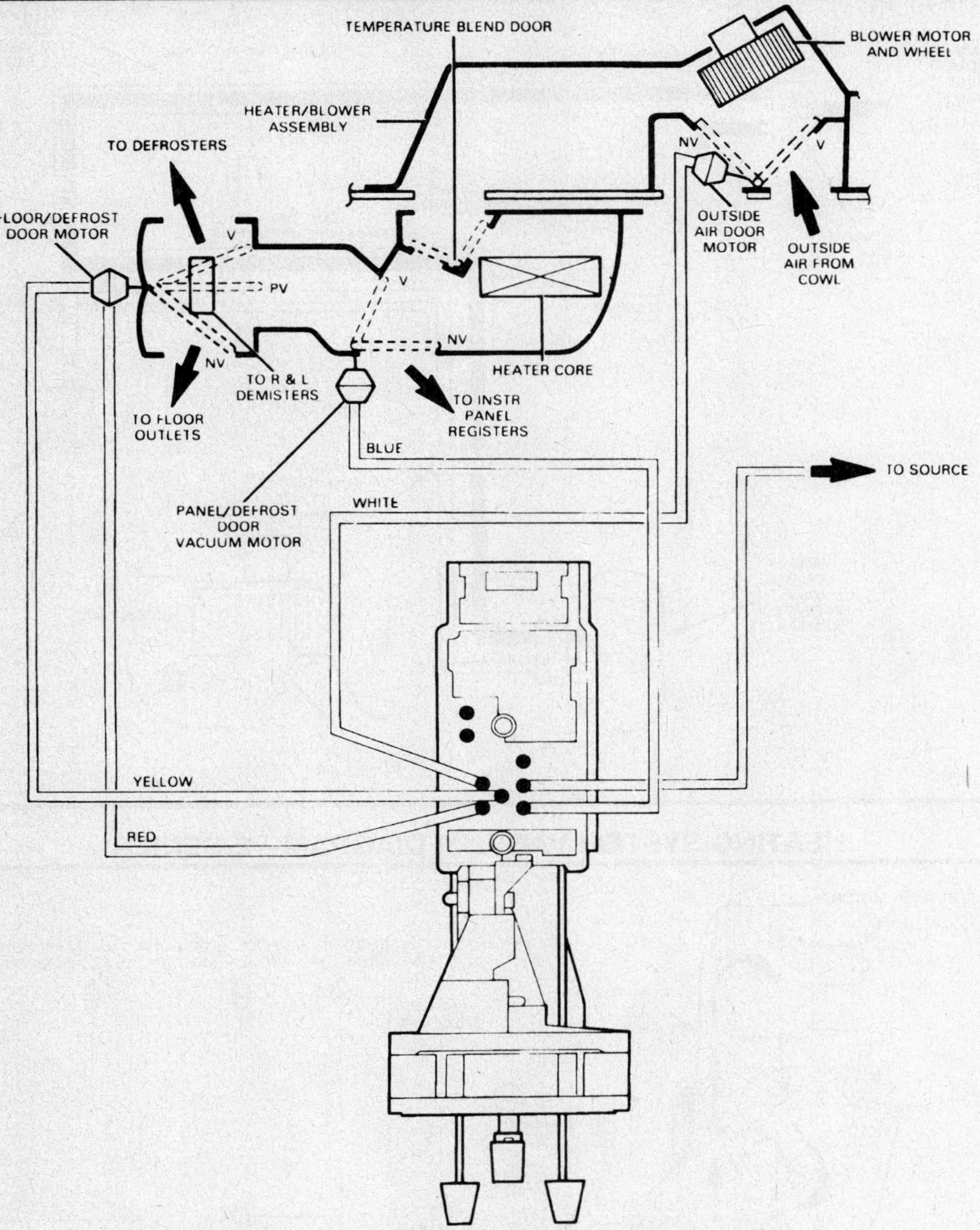
TEMPERATURE BLEND DOOR
BLOWER MOTOR AND WHEEL
HEATER/BLOWER ASSEMBLY
TO DEFROSTERS
NV
V
FLOOR/DEFROST DOOR MOTOR
V
PV
V
OUTSIDE AIR DOOR MOTOR
OUTSIDE AIR FROM COWL
NV
NV
HEATER CORE
TO R & L DEMISTERS
TO FLOOR OUTLETS
TO INSTR PANEL REGISTERS
BLUE
TO SOURCE
PANEL/DEFROST DOOR VACUUM MOTOR
WHITE
YELLOW
RED

PORT	FUNCTION	LEVER POSITION					HOSE COLOR
		OFF	VENT	FLR	FLR/DEF	DEF	
1	OUTSIDE AIR	V	NV	NV	NV	NV	WHITE
2	PANEL/ DEFROST	NV	V	NV	NV	NV	BLUE
3	FLOOR	V	V	V	NV	NV	RED
4	FLOOR/ DEFROST	V	V	V	V	NV	YELLOW
7	SOURCE	V	V	V	V	V	BLACK

HEATING SYSTEM VACUUM DIAGRAM—BRONCO II, EXPLORER AND RANGER

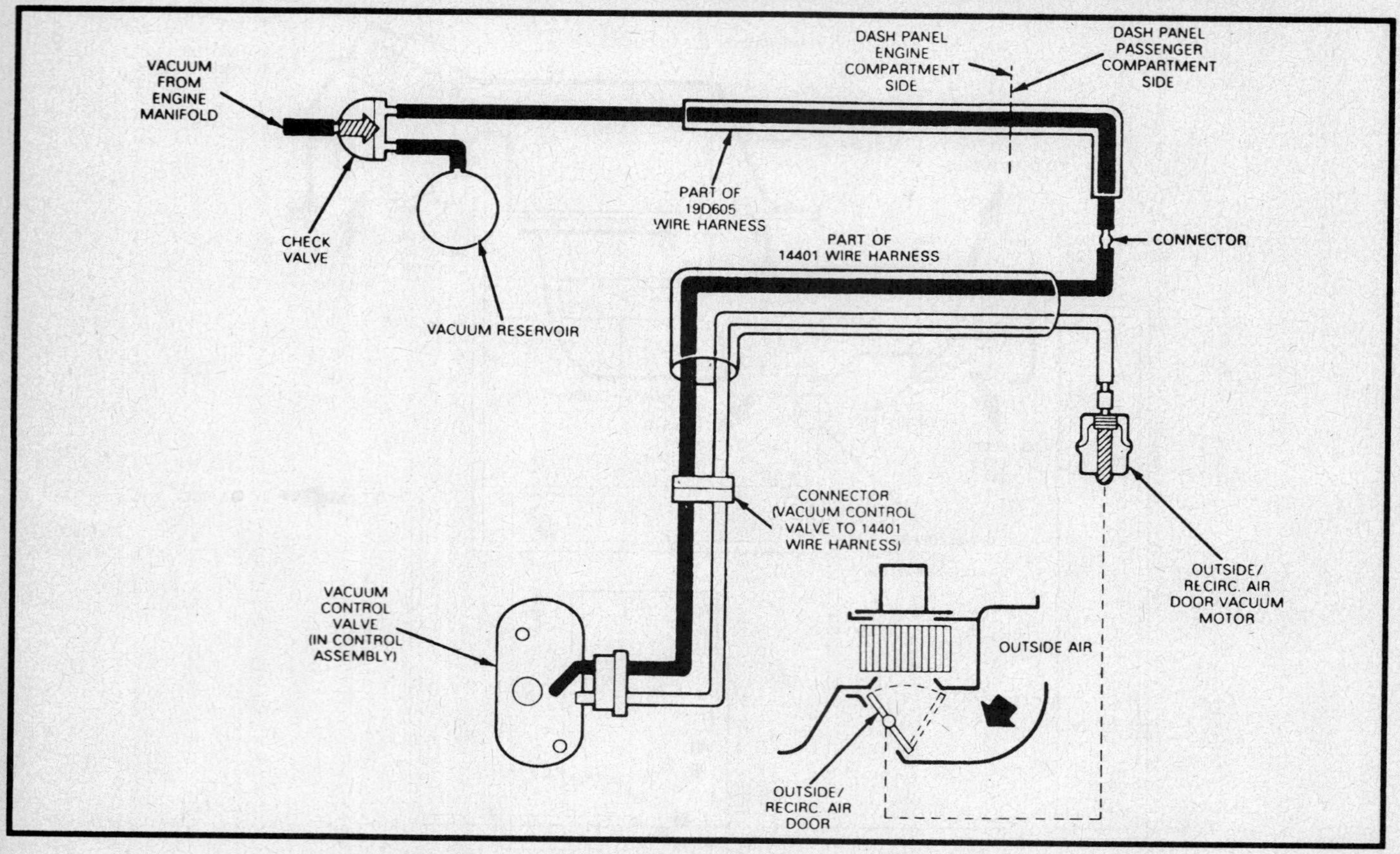
VACUUM FROM ENGINE MANIFOLD
CHECK VALVE
VACUUM RESERVOIR
PART OF 19D605 WIRE HARNESS
DASH PANEL ENGINE COMPARTMENT SIDE
DASH PANEL PASSENGER COMPARTMENT SIDE
CONNECTOR
PART OF 14401 WIRE HARNESS
CONNECTOR (VACUUM CONTROL VALVE TO 14401 WIRE HARNESS)
VACUUM CONTROL VALVE (IN CONTROL ASSEMBLY)
OUTSIDE/ RECIRC. AIR DOOR VACUUM MOTOR
OUTSIDE AIR
OUTSIDE/ RECIRC. AIR DOOR

HEATING SYSTEM VACUUM DIAGRAM—E SERIES

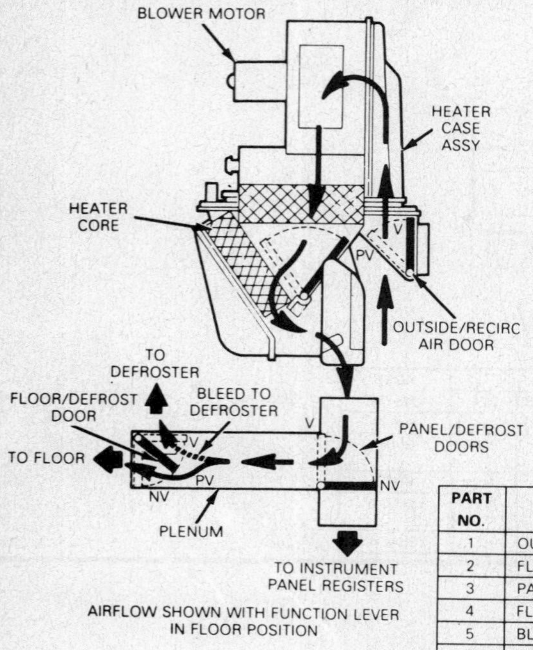
BLOWER MOTOR
HEATER CASE ASSY
HEATER CORE
V
PV
OUTSIDE/RECIRC AIR DOOR
TO DEFROSTER
FLOOR/DEFROST DOOR
BLEED TO DEFROSTER
TO FLOOR
PV
NV
PLENUM
V
NV
PANEL/DEFROST DOORS
TO INSTRUMENT PANEL REGISTERS
AIRFLOW SHOWN WITH FUNCTION LEVER IN FLOOR POSITION

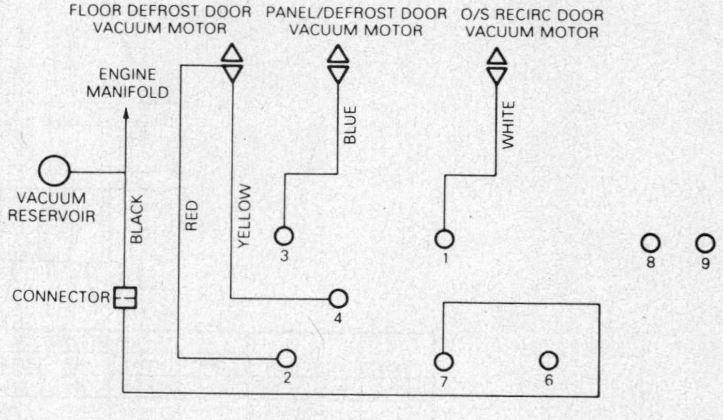
FLOOR DEFROST DOOR VACUUM MOTOR
PANEL/DEFROST DOOR VACUUM MOTOR
O/S RECIRC DOOR VACUUM MOTOR
ENGINE MANIFOLD
VACUUM RESERVOIR
BLACK
RED
YELLOW
BLUE
WHITE
CONNECTOR
3
1
8
9
4
2
7
6

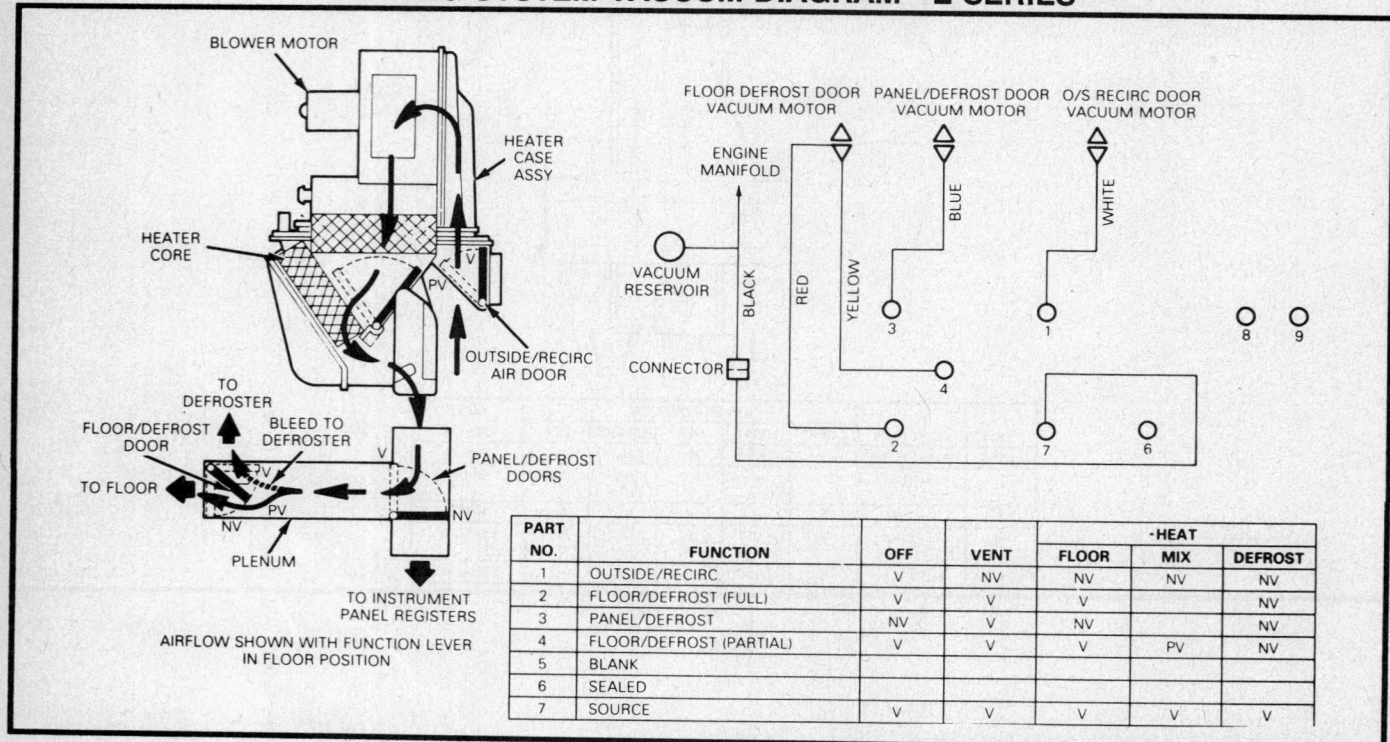

PART NO.	FUNCTION	OFF	VENT	-HEAT FLOOR	MIX	DEFROST
1	OUTSIDE/RECIRC.	V	NV	NV	NV	NV
2	FLOOR/DEFROST (FULL)	V	V	V		NV
3	PANEL/DEFROST	NV	V	NV		NV
4	FLOOR/DEFROST (PARTIAL)	V	V	V	PV	NV
5	BLANK					
6	SEALED					
7	SOURCE	V	V	V	V	V

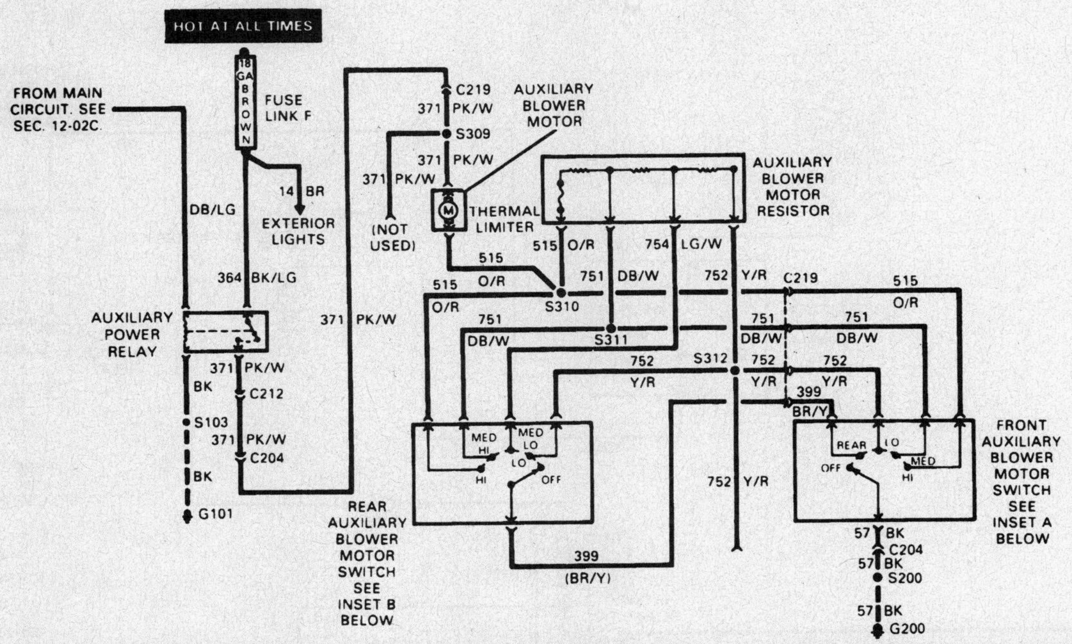
HOT AT ALL TIMES
18 GA BROWN
FUSE LINK F
FROM MAIN CIRCUIT. SEE SEC. 12-02C.
DB/LG
14 BR
EXTERIOR LIGHTS
364 BK/LG
AUXILIARY POWER RELAY
371 PK/W
BK
C212
S103
371 PK/W
C204
BK
G101
C219
371 PK/W
S309
371 PK/W
371 PK/W
AUXILIARY BLOWER MOTOR
THERMAL LIMITER
(NOT USED)
AUXILIARY BLOWER MOTOR RESISTOR
515 O/R
754 LG/W
515
O/R
S310
751 DB/W
752 Y/R
C219
S311
S312
751 DB/W
752 Y/R
399 BR/Y
REAR AUXILIARY BLOWER MOTOR SWITCH SEE INSET B BELOW
399 (BR/Y)
FRONT AUXILIARY BLOWER MOTOR SWITCH SEE INSET A BELOW
57 BK
C204
S200
G200
MED HI
MED LO
LO
HI
OFF
REAR

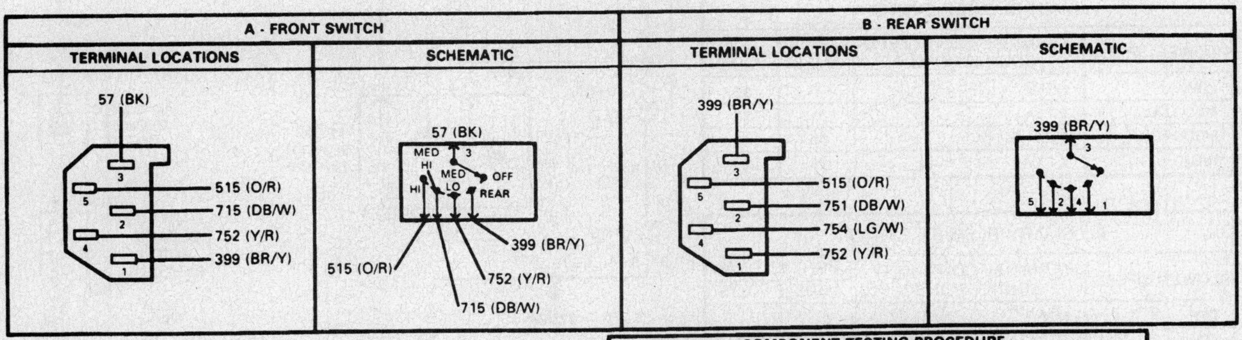
A - FRONT SWITCH
TERMINAL LOCATIONS
SCHEMATIC
57 (BK)
515 (O/R)
715 (DB/W)
752 (Y/R)
399 (BR/Y)
MED HI
MED LO
OFF
REAR
HI
B - REAR SWITCH
TERMINAL LOCATIONS
SCHEMATIC
399 (BR/Y)
515 (O/R)
751 (DB/W)
754 (LG/W)
752 (Y/R)

COMPONENT TESTING PROCEDURE

TO TEST	Connect Self-Powered Test Lamp or Ohmmeter to Terminals	Move Control to These Positions	A Good Switch Will Indicate
Rear Select	399 (BR/Y) and 57 (BK) (3)	Off Rear Lo Medium Hi	Open Circuit Closed Circuit Open Circuit Open Circuit Open Circuit
Low Speed	752 (Y/R) (4) and 57 (BK) (3)	Off Rear Lo Medium Hi	Open Circuit Open Circuit Closed Circuit Open Circuit Open Circuit
Medium Speed	715 (DB/W) (2) and 57 (BK) (3)	Off Rear Lo Medium Hi	Open Circuit Open Circuit Open Circuit Closed Circuit Open Circuit
High Speed	515 (O/R) (5) and 57 (BK) (3)	Off Rear Lo Medium Hi	Open Circuit Open Circuit Open Circuit Open Circuit Closed Circuit

COMPONENT TESTING PROCEDURE

TO TEST	Connect Self-Powered Test Lamp or Ohmmeter to Terminals	Move Control to These Positions	A Good Switch Will Indicate
Low Speed	752 (Y/R) (1) and 399 (BR/Y) (3)	Off Lo Medium Lo Medium Hi Hi	Open Circuit Closed Circuit Open Circuit Open Circuit Open Circuit
Medium Low Speed	754 (LG/W) (4) and 399 (BR/Y) (3)	Off Lo Medium Lo Medium Hi Hi	Open Circuit Open Circuit Closed Circuit Open Circuit Open Circuit
Medium High Speed	751 (DB/W) (2) and 399 (BR/Y) (3)	Off Lo Medium Lo Medium Hi Hi	Open Circuit Open Circuit Open Circuit Closed Circuit Open Circuit
High Speed	515 (O/R) (5) and 399 (BR/Y) (3)	Off Lo Medium Lo Medium Hi Hii	Open Circuit Open Circuit Open Circuit Open Circuit Closed Circuit

Heating system electrical schematic—1990–91 Aerostar with auxiliary heating system

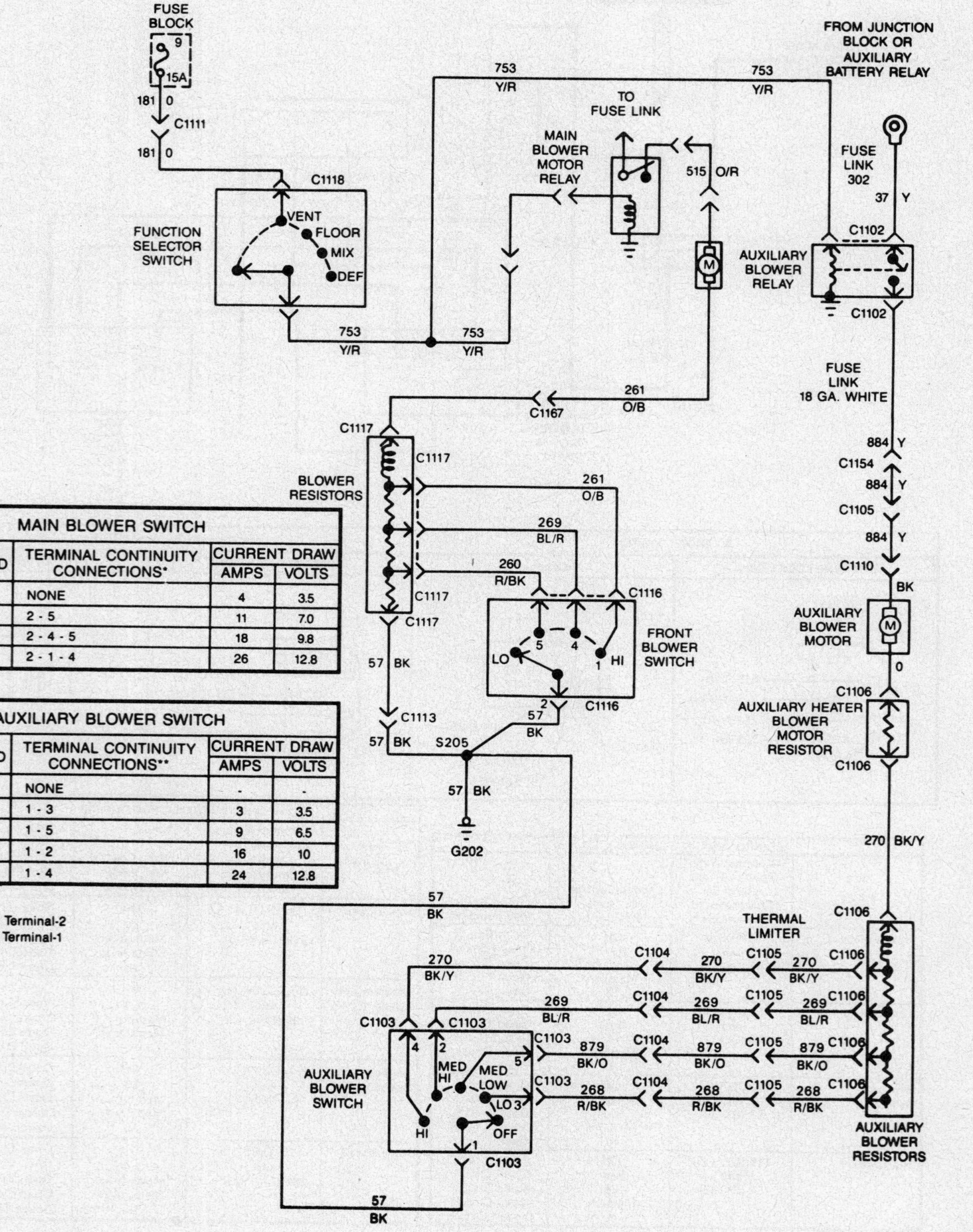
FUSE BLOCK
9
15A
181 0
C1111
181 0
C1118
FUNCTION SELECTOR SWITCH
VENT
FLOOR
MIX
DEF
753 Y/R
753 Y/R
753 Y/R
753 Y/R
TO FUSE LINK
MAIN BLOWER MOTOR RELAY
515 O/R
FROM JUNCTION BLOCK OR AUXILIARY BATTERY RELAY
FUSE LINK 302
37 Y
C1102
AUXILIARY BLOWER RELAY
C1102
FUSE LINK 18 GA. WHITE
261 O/B
C1167
C1117
BLOWER RESISTORS
C1117
261 O/B
269 BL/R
260 R/BK
C1117
C1116
C1117
FRONT BLOWER SWITCH
LO
5
4
1
HI
2
C1116
57 BK
57 BK
C1113
57 BK
S205
57 BK
G202
884 Y
C1154
884 Y
C1105
884 Y
C1110
BK
AUXILIARY BLOWER MOTOR
0
C1106
AUXILIARY HEATER BLOWER MOTOR RESISTOR
C1106
270 BK/Y
C1106
THERMAL LIMITER
57 BK
270 BK/Y
C1104
270 BK/Y
C1105
270 BK/Y
C1106
269 BL/R
C1104
269 BL/R
C1105
269 BL/R
C1106
C1103
C1103
879 BK/O
C1104
879 BK/O
C1105
879 BK/O
C1106
C1103
268 R/BK
C1104
268 R/BK
C1105
268 R/BK
C1106
AUXILIARY BLOWER SWITCH
4
2
MED HI
MED LOW
5
LO 3
HI
OFF
1
C1103
57 BK
AUXILIARY BLOWER RESISTORS

MAIN BLOWER SWITCH

BLOWER SPEED	TERMINAL CONTINUITY CONNECTIONS*	CURRENT DRAW AMPS	CURRENT DRAW VOLTS
LOW	NONE	4	3.5
MED LOW	2 - 5	11	7.0
MED HIGH	2 - 4 - 5	18	9.8
HIGH	2 - 1 - 4	26	12.8

AUXILIARY BLOWER SWITCH

BLOWER SPEED	TERMINAL CONTINUITY CONNECTIONS**	CURRENT DRAW AMPS	CURRENT DRAW VOLTS
OFF	NONE	-	-
LOW	1 - 3	3	3.5
MED LOW	1 - 5	9	6.5
MED HIGH	1 - 2	16	10
HIGH	1 - 4	24	12.8

(*) Common Terminal-2
(**) Common Terminal-1

Heating system electrical schematic—1989 E Series with auxiliary heating system

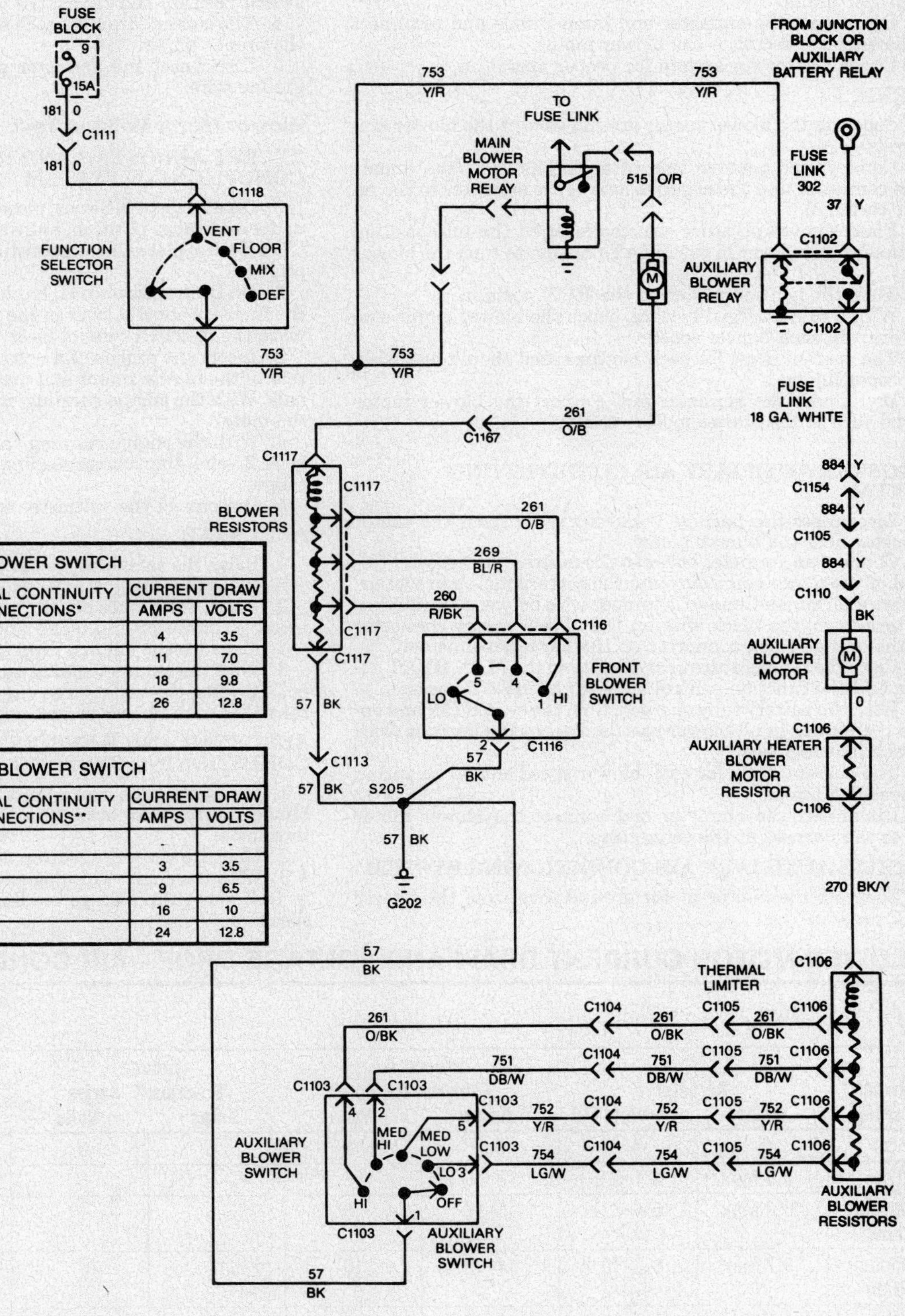
FUSE BLOCK
9
15A
181 0
C1111
181 0
C1118
FUNCTION SELECTOR SWITCH
VENT
FLOOR
MIX
DEF
753 Y/R
753 Y/R
753 Y/R
753 Y/R
TO FUSE LINK
MAIN BLOWER MOTOR RELAY
515 O/R
FROM JUNCTION BLOCK OR AUXILIARY BATTERY RELAY
FUSE LINK 302
37 Y
C1102
AUXILIARY BLOWER RELAY
C1102
FUSE LINK 18 GA. WHITE
261 O/B
C1167
C1117
BLOWER RESISTORS
C1117
261 O/B
269 BL/R
260 R/BK
C1117
C1116
C1117
FRONT BLOWER SWITCH
LO
5
4
1
HI
2
C1116
57 BK
C1113
57 BK
S205
57 BK
57 BK
G202
884 Y
C1154
884 Y
C1105
884 Y
C1110
BK
AUXILIARY BLOWER MOTOR
0
C1106
AUXILIARY HEATER BLOWER MOTOR RESISTOR
C1106
270 BK/Y
C1106
THERMAL LIMITER
57 BK
261 O/BK
C1104
261 O/BK
C1105
261 O/BK
C1106
751 DB/W
C1104
751 DB/W
C1105
751 DB/W
C1106
C1103
C1103
752 Y/R
C1104
752 Y/R
C1105
752 Y/R
C1106
754 LG/W
C1104
754 LG/W
C1105
754 LG/W
C1106
AUXILIARY BLOWER SWITCH
MED HI
MED LOW
LO 3
HI
OFF
C1103
AUXILIARY BLOWER SWITCH
AUXILIARY BLOWER RESISTORS
57 BK

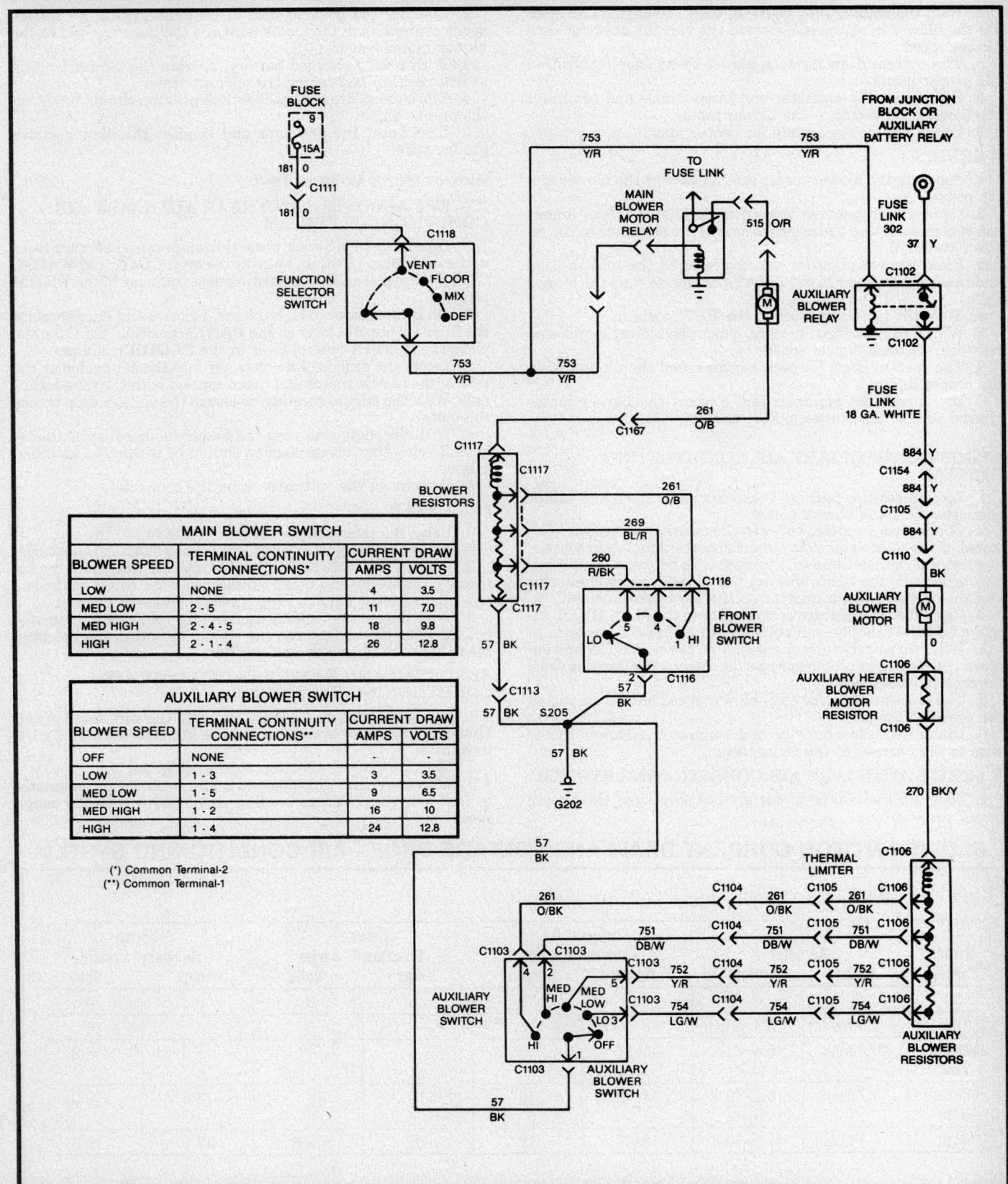

MAIN BLOWER SWITCH			
BLOWER SPEED	TERMINAL CONTINUITY CONNECTIONS*	CURRENT DRAW	
		AMPS	VOLTS
LOW	NONE	4	3.5
MED LOW	2 - 5	11	7.0
MED HIGH	2 - 4 - 5	18	9.8
HIGH	2 - 1 - 4	26	12.8

AUXILIARY BLOWER SWITCH			
BLOWER SPEED	TERMINAL CONTINUITY CONNECTIONS**	CURRENT DRAW	
		AMPS	VOLTS
OFF	NONE	-	-
LOW	1 - 3	3	3.5
MED LOW	1 - 5	9	6.5
MED HIGH	1 - 2	16	10
HIGH	1 - 4	24	12.8

(*) Common Terminal-2
(**) Common Terminal-1

Heating system electrical schematic—1990–91 E Series with auxiliary heating system

4. With the battery fully charged, start the engine and operate the blower in all speeds. Record the current draw for each blower speed.
5. The current draw for each blower speed should be within the proper limits.
6. Disconnect the ammeter and jumper wire and reconnect the harness connector to the blower motor.
7. Check the blower system for proper operation.

E SERIES

1. Separate the blower motor ground wire at the blower motor resistor.
2. Connect the positive lead of an ammeter to the female spade connector and the negative lead of the ammeter to the resistor terminal.
3. Place the temperature selector lever in the mid-position and the function lever in the **HEAT** position to turn the blower on.
4. Turn the ignition switch to the **RUN** position.
5. With a fully charged battery, check the blower motor current draw in each blower speed.
6. The current draw for each blower speed should be within the proper limits.
7. Disconnect the ammeter and connect the blower motor ground wire at the blower motor resistor.

AEROSTAR AUXILIARY AIR CONDITIONING SYSTEM

1. Disconnect the harness connector wire from the motor connector near the blower motor.
2. Connect an ammeter between the positive orange wire terminal of the motor connector and the corresponding brown-orange wire terminal. Connect a jumper wire between the 2 negative terminals, the black wire on the blower motor connector and the orange-black connector on the harness connector.
3. Place the temperature control lever in the **MAX HEAT** position and the function control lever in the **HEAT** position.
4. With the battery fully charged, turn the switch **ON** and operate the blower in all blower speeds. Record the current draw for each blower speed.
5. The current draw for each blower speed should be within the specified limits.
6. Disconnect the ammeter and connect the blower motor wire to the harness at the connectors.

E SERIES AUXILIARY AIR CONDITIONING SYSTEM

1. Separate the blower motor ground wire from the blower motor resistor.
2. Connect the positive lead of an ammeter to the female spade connector on the motor wire and the negative lead to the blower motor resistor.
3. With a fully charged battery, operate the blower in each switch position and record the current draw.
4. The current draw for each switch position should be within the proper limits.
5. Disconnect the ammeter and connect the blower motor ground wire.

Blower Motor Voltage Test

EXCEPT AEROSTAR AND REAR AUXILIARY AIR CONDITIONING SYSTEM

1. On all except E Series, place the temperature selector lever in the mid-range position, halfway between **COOL** and **WARM**. On E Series, place the temperature selector lever in the **WARM** position.
2. On Bronco, Bronco II, Explorer, F Series and Ranger, place the function control lever in the **PANEL** position. On E Series, place the function control lever in the **FLOOR** position.
3. Insert the probes of a voltmeter into the connector at the rear of the blower motor and make contact with the wire terminals. With the engine running, measure the voltage drop across the motor.
4. With the engine running and battery voltage approximately 14.2 volts, the voltage reading should be within the specified range.
5. Disconnect the voltmeter from the connector.

AEROSTAR

1. Raise the temperature selector to the top of the slot.
2. Place the function selector lever in the **MAX A/C** position.
3. Insert the probes of a voltmeter into the wire holes on the motor's connector and make contact with the wire terminals.
4. Measure the voltage drop across the blower motor.
5. With the engine running and battery voltage approximately 14.2 volts, the voltage reading should be within the specified range for each blower switch position.

AEROSTAR AND E SERIES AUXILIARY AIR CONDITIONING SYSTEMS

1. Insert the probes of a voltmeter into the wire holes of the blower motor connectors and make contact with the wire terminals.
2. Measure the voltage drop across the motor.
3. With the engine running and battery voltage approximately 14.2 volts, the voltage reading should be within the range specified.

BLOWER MOTOR CURRENT DRAW AND VOLTAGE DROP—AIR CONDITIONING SYSTEM

Switch Position	Aerostar Amps	Aerostar Volts	Bronco II/Explorer/Ranger Amps	Bronco II/Explorer/Ranger Volts	Bronco/E Series/F Series Amps	Bronco/E Series/F Series Volts	E Series Auxiliary System Amps	E Series Auxiliary System Volts
Off	0	0	0	0	0	0	0	0
Low	3.6 Max	4.1–5.6	9–11.5	5	6	5	4	4
Medium Low	6.3 Max	6.4–7.9	11.5–14	8	8	7	7.3	6.0
Medium High	9.7 Max	8.7–10.2	14–16.5	10	15	10	13.8	9.0
High	14.1 Max	11.3–12.8	16–18.5	12	25	12.8	23.0	12.8

REFRIGERANT SYSTEM TESTING

Visual Inspection

Obstructed air passages, broken belts, disconnected or broken wires, loose clutch, loose or broken mounting brackets and many refrigerant leaks may be determined by visual inspection.

A refrigerant leak will usually appear as an oily residue at the leakage point in the system. The oily residue soon picks up dust or dirt particles from the surrounding air and appears greasy. Through time, this will build up and appear to be heavy dirt impregnated grease.

Most common leaks are caused by damaged or missing O-ring seals at the various hose and component connections. When these O-rings are replaced, the new O-rings should be lubricated with refrigerant oil and care should be taken to keep lint from shop towels or rags from contaminating the internal surfaces of the connection.

Another type of leak may appear at the internal schrader valve core in the service access gauge port valve fittings. If tightening the valve core does not stop the leak, it should be replaced with a new 19D701 or equivalent, air conditioning charging valve core.

Missing service access gauge port valve caps, 19D702 or equivalent, can also cause a refrigerant leak. If this important primary seal is missing, dirt will enter the area of the air conditioning charging valve core. When the service hose is attached, the valve depressor in the end of the service hose forces the dirt into the valve seat area and the dirt will destroy the sealing surface of the air conditioning charging valve core. When a service access gauge port valve cap is missing, the protected area of the air conditioning charging valve core should be cleaned and a new 19D702 service access gauge port valve cap should be installed.

NOTE: Service access gauge port valve caps must be installed finger-tight. If tightened with pliers, the sealing surface of the service access gauge port valve may be damaged.

Performance Testing

The best way to diagnose a problem in the refrigerant system is to note the system pressures, shown by the manifold gauges, and the clutch cycle rate and times. Then, compare the findings with the clutch cycle rate and time charts. Remember when testing:

- System pressures are lower in the suction portion of a cycle and higher in the discharge portion of that cycle.
- A clutch cycle is the time the clutch is engaged plus the time it is disengaged, time on plus time off.
- Clutch cycle times are the lengths of time, in seconds, that the clutch is ON and OFF.

The following procedure is recommended to obtain an accurate diagnosis in the least amount of time.

1. Connect a manifold gauge set to the system. Purge the air from the red and blue hoses by loosening the hose fittings at the gauge set to allow air to be pushed out by system pressure.

NOTE: The test conditions specified in each chart must be met to obtain accurate test results.

2. Start the engine and turn on the air conditioning as soon as the system is stabilized. Record the high and low pressures, as shown by the manifold gauges. The low pressure should cycle between an approximate 25–45 psi. As the low pressure is dropping, the high pressure should increase. When the clutch disengages, the low side should increase and the high side should decrease.
3. Determine the clutch cycle rate per minute. The clutch on time plus off time is a cycle.
4. Record the clutch off time in seconds.
5. Record the clutch on time in seconds.
6. Record the center register discharge temperature.
7. Determine and record ambient temperatures.
8. Compare test readings with the applicable chart.
9. Plot a vertical line for the recorded ambient temperature from the scale at the bottom of each chart to the top of each chart. Plot a horizontal line for each of the other test readings from the scale at the left side of the appropriate chart.
10. If the point where the 2 lines cross on each of the charts falls within the dark band, the system is operating normally. If the lines cross outside the dark band on one or more of the charts, there is a problem and the specific cause must be determined. This is done by using the refrigerant system and clutch cycle timing evaluation chart.
11. After servicing and correcting a refrigerant system problem, take additional pressure readings and observe the clutch cycle rate while meeting the conditional requirements to make sure the problem has been corrected.

In ambient temperature above 100°F (38°C), the compressor clutch will not normally cycle off and in many instances, the clutch will not cycle off when temperatures are above 90°F (32°C). This will depend on local conditions and engine/vehicle speed. Also, clutch cycling will normally not occur when the engine is operating at curb idle speed.

If the system contains no refrigerant or is extremely low on refrigerant, the clutch will not engage for compressor operation. A rapid cycling compressor clutch is usually an indication that the system is low on refrigerant.

The following test conditions must be established to obtain accurate pressure readings:

- Run engine at 1500 rpm for 10 minutes.
- Operate the air conditioning system on max air conditioning, recirculating air.
- Run the blower at maximum speed.
- Stabilize in vehicle temperature at 70–80°F (21–27°C).

AIR CONDITIONING TROUBLESHOOTING FLOWCHART

INSUFFICIENT A/C COOLING

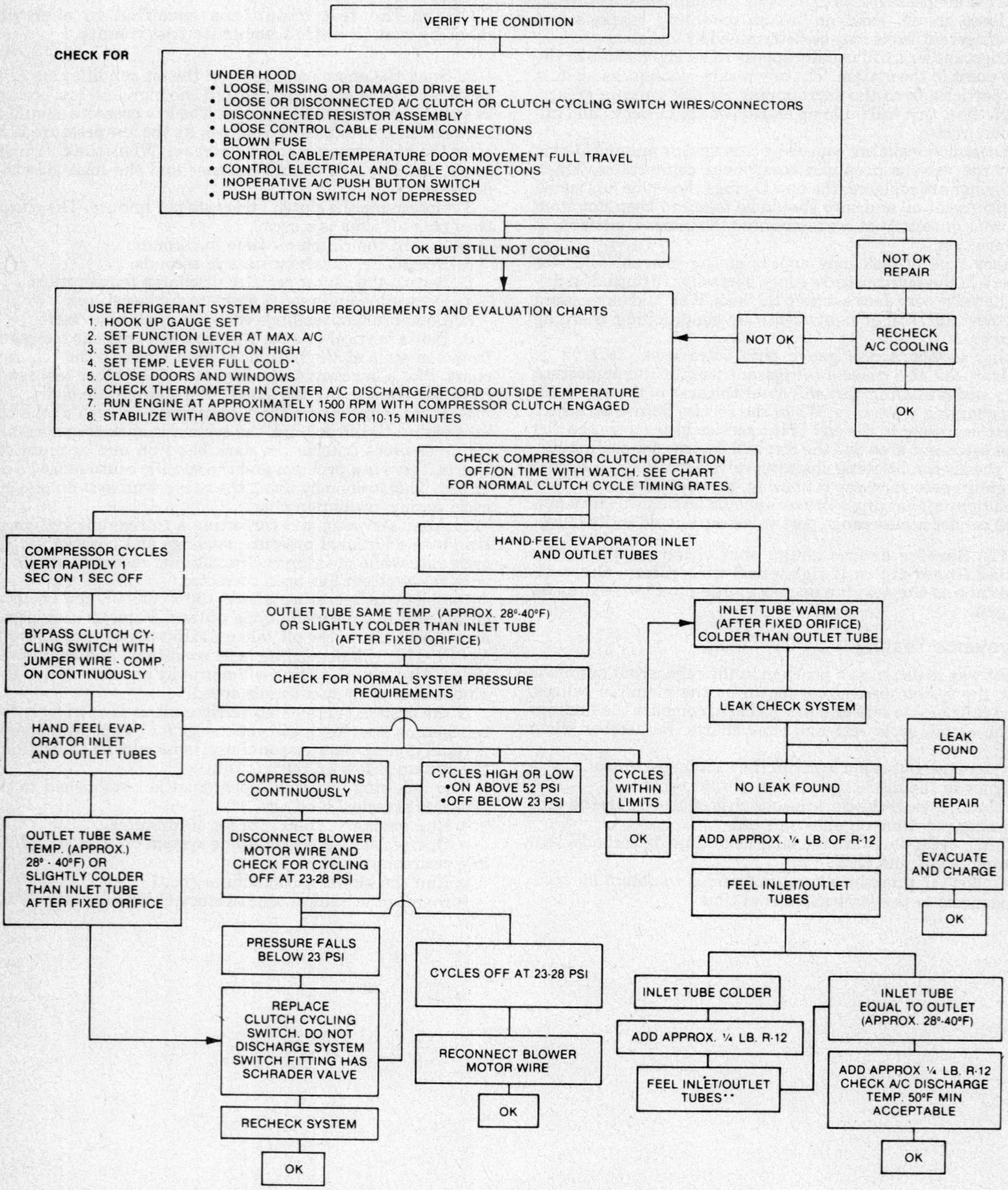
VERIFY THE CONDITION
CHECK FOR
UNDER HOOD
• LOOSE, MISSING OR DAMAGED DRIVE BELT
• LOOSE OR DISCONNECTED A/C CLUTCH OR CLUTCH CYCLING SWITCH WIRES/CONNECTORS
• DISCONNECTED RESISTOR ASSEMBLY
• LOOSE CONTROL CABLE PLENUM CONNECTIONS
• BLOWN FUSE
• CONTROL CABLE/TEMPERATURE DOOR MOVEMENT FULL TRAVEL
• CONTROL ELECTRICAL AND CABLE CONNECTIONS
• INOPERATIVE A/C PUSH BUTTON SWITCH
• PUSH BUTTON SWITCH NOT DEPRESSED
OK BUT STILL NOT COOLING
NOT OK REPAIR
RECHECK A/C COOLING
NOT OK
OK
USE REFRIGERANT SYSTEM PRESSURE REQUIREMENTS AND EVALUATION CHARTS
1. HOOK UP GAUGE SET
2. SET FUNCTION LEVER AT MAX. A/C
3. SET BLOWER SWITCH ON HIGH
4. SET TEMP. LEVER FULL COLD*
5. CLOSE DOORS AND WINDOWS
6. CHECK THERMOMETER IN CENTER A/C DISCHARGE/RECORD OUTSIDE TEMPERATURE
7. RUN ENGINE AT APPROXIMATELY 1500 RPM WITH COMPRESSOR CLUTCH ENGAGED
8. STABILIZE WITH ABOVE CONDITIONS FOR 10-15 MINUTES
CHECK COMPRESSOR CLUTCH OPERATION OFF/ON TIME WITH WATCH. SEE CHART FOR NORMAL CLUTCH CYCLE TIMING RATES.
COMPRESSOR CYCLES VERY RAPIDLY 1 SEC ON 1 SEC OFF
BYPASS CLUTCH CYCLING SWITCH WITH JUMPER WIRE - COMP. ON CONTINUOUSLY
HAND FEEL EVAPORATOR INLET AND OUTLET TUBES
OUTLET TUBE SAME TEMP. (APPROX.) 28° - 40°F) OR SLIGHTLY COLDER THAN INLET TUBE AFTER FIXED ORIFICE
HAND-FEEL EVAPORATOR INLET AND OUTLET TUBES
OUTLET TUBE SAME TEMP. (APPROX. 28°-40°F) OR SLIGHTLY COLDER THAN INLET TUBE (AFTER FIXED ORIFICE)
CHECK FOR NORMAL SYSTEM PRESSURE REQUIREMENTS
INLET TUBE WARM OR (AFTER FIXED ORIFICE) COLDER THAN OUTLET TUBE
LEAK CHECK SYSTEM
LEAK FOUND
REPAIR
EVACUATE AND CHARGE
OK
NO LEAK FOUND
ADD APPROX. ¼ LB. OF R-12
FEEL INLET/OUTLET TUBES
COMPRESSOR RUNS CONTINUOUSLY
CYCLES HIGH OR LOW
•ON ABOVE 52 PSI
•OFF BELOW 23 PSI
CYCLES WITHIN LIMITS
OK
DISCONNECT BLOWER MOTOR WIRE AND CHECK FOR CYCLING OFF AT 23-28 PSI
PRESSURE FALLS BELOW 23 PSI
CYCLES OFF AT 23-28 PSI
REPLACE CLUTCH CYCLING SWITCH. DO NOT DISCHARGE SYSTEM SWITCH FITTING HAS SCHRADER VALVE
RECONNECT BLOWER MOTOR WIRE
OK
RECHECK SYSTEM
OK
INLET TUBE COLDER
ADD APPROX. ¼ LB. R-12
FEEL INLET/OUTLET TUBES**
INLET TUBE EQUAL TO OUTLET (APPROX. 28°-40°F)
ADD APPROX ¼ LB. R-12 CHECK A/C DISCHARGE TEMP. 50°F MIN ACCEPTABLE
OK

*ON ATC SYSTEMS APPLY 15 INCHES VACUUM DIRECTLY TO SERVO VACUUM MOTOR

**CONTINUE TO ADD R-12 IN APPROX. ¼ LB. INCREMENTS UNTIL TUBES FEEL EQUAL IN TEMPERATURE AND APPROX. 28°-40°F

COMPRESSOR CLUTCH CIRCUIT DIAGNOSIS—BRONCO, E SERIES AND F SERIES

TEST STEP	RESULT ▶	ACTION TO TAKE
A1 CHECK SYSTEM OPERATION		
• Turn blower switch On. • Turn ignition switch to Run position. • Compressor clutch should engage.	Clutch operates ▶ Clutch does not operate ▶	System OK. GO to **A2**.
A2 CHECK FOR VOLTAGE		
• Check for voltage at circuit wire at the clutch cycling pressure switch connector or A/C control switch (E-150 — E-350).	Voltage present ▶ No voltage ▶	GO to **A3**. GO to **A9**.
A3 BY-PASS PRESSURE SWITCH		
• Disconnect connector at clutch cycling pressure switch or control switch (E-150 — E-350). • Jumper connector pins or control switch. • Clutch snould engage.	OK ▶ No OK ▶ (NOT OK)	GO to **A4**. GO to **A5**.
A4 CHECK SYSTEM PRESSURE		
• Connect manifold gauge set and check system pressure.	Pressure above 55 psi ▶ Pressure below 55 psi (ambient temperature above 50°F) ▶	REPIACE clutch cycling pressure switch. GO to **A1**. CHECK refrigerant system for leaks. REPAIR and CHARGE system as necessary. GO to **A1**.
A5 CHECK VOLTAGE AT CLUTCH		
• Check for voltage at clutch field coil.	Voltage present ▶ No voltage ▶	GO to **A8**. GO to **A7**.
A6 CHECK CLUTCH GROUND		
• Jumper ground terminal of clutch field coil to ground. • Clutch should engage.	OK ▶ NOT OK ▶	SERVICE open in ground wire. GO to **A1**. REPLACE clutch field coil. GO to **A1**.
A7 CHECK FUSE		
• Check Fuse 17 in fuse panel for continuity.	OK ▶ NOT OK ▶	GO to **A8**. CHECK for short. SERVICE as necessary. REPLACE fuse. GO to **A1**.
A8 CHECK A/C CONTROLS		
• Move Function selector lever to DEFROST position. • Check for voltage at circuit wire at the clutch cycling pressure switch connector.	Voltage present ▶ No voltage ▶	GO to **A10**. GO to **A9**.

COMPRESSOR CLUTCH CIRCUIT DIAGNOSIS—BRONCO, E SERIES AND F SERIES

TEST STEP		RESULT	ACTION TO TAKE
A9	CHECK CIRCUIT 294		
	• Remove connector from A/C push-button switch. • Check for voltage at circuit.	Voltage present ▶	GO to **A10**.
		No voltage ▶	CHECK for open in Circuit 294. SERVICE as necessary. GO to **A1**.
A10	CHECK A/C CONTROLS		
	• Check A/C push button switch and Function switch for continuity. **NOTE: A/C push-button switch must be depressed. Function switch must be in DEFROST position.**	Continuity through Function switch only ▶	REPLACE A/C pushbutton switch. GO to **A1**.
		Continuity through A/C pushbutton switch only ▶	REPLACE Function switch. GO to **A1**.
		Continuity through both switches ▶	CHECK for open in circuit between control assembly and clutch cycling pressure switch. SERVICE as necessary. GO to **A1**.

CLUTCH CYCLE TIMING EVALUATION CHART

THESE CONDITIONAL REQUIREMENTS FOR THE FIXED ORIFICE TUBE CYCLING CLUTCH SYSTEM TESTS MUST BE SATISFIED TO OBTAIN ACCURATE PRESSURE READINGS.

- Stabilized in Car Temperatures @ 70°F to 80°F (21°C to 27°C)
- Maximum A/C (Recirculating Air)
- Maximum Blower Speed
- 1500 Engine RPM For 10 Minutes

NORMAL CLUTCH CYCLE RATE PER MINUTE

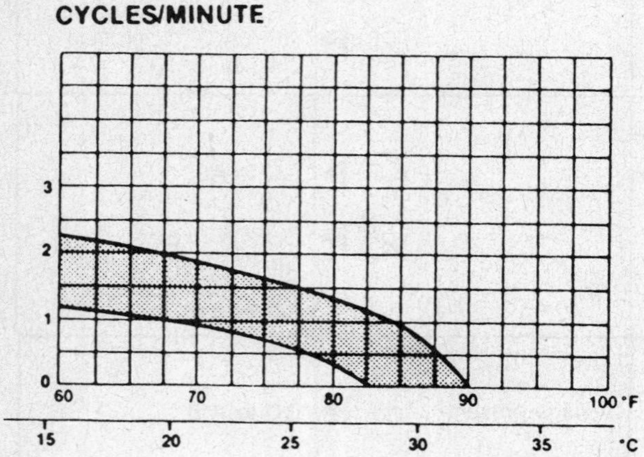
CYCLES/MINUTE
3
2
1
0
60
70
80
90
100 °F
15
20
25
30
35
°C

NORMAL FIXED ORIFICE TUBE CYCLING CLUTCH REFRIGERANT SYSTEM PRESSURES

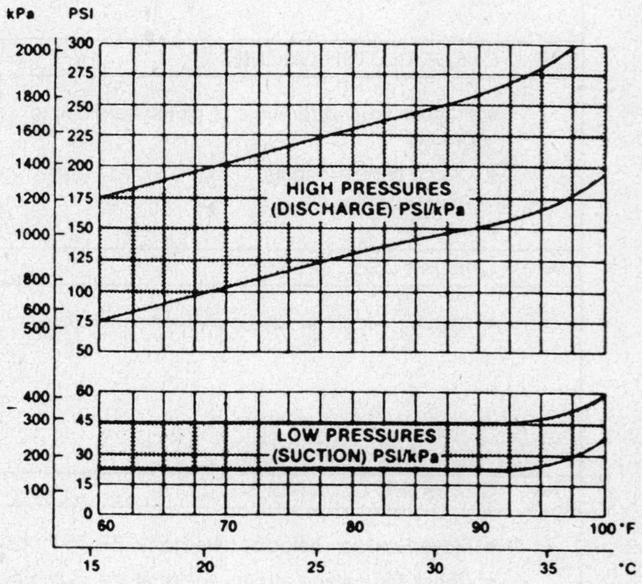
kPa
PSI
2000
1800
1600
1400
1200
1000
800
600
500
300
275
250
225
200
175
150
125
100
75
50
HIGH PRESSURES
(DISCHARGE) PSI/kPa
400
300
200
100
60
45
30
15
0
LOW PRESSURES
(SUCTION) PSI/kPa
60
70
80
90
100 °F
15
20
25
30
35
°C

AMBIENT TEMPERATURES

CLUTCH CYCLE TIMING EVALUATION CHART

THESE CONDITIONAL REQUIREMENTS FOR THE FIXED ORIFICE TUBE CYCLING CLUTCH SYSTEM TESTS MUST BE SATISFIED TO OBTAIN ACCURATE CLUTCH CYCLE TIMING

- Stabilized in Car Temperatures @ 70°F to 80°F (21°C to 27°C)
- Maximum A/C (Recirculating Air)
- Maximum Blower Speed
- 1500 Engine RPM For 10 Minutes

NORMAL CENTER REGISTER DISCHARGE TEMPERATURES

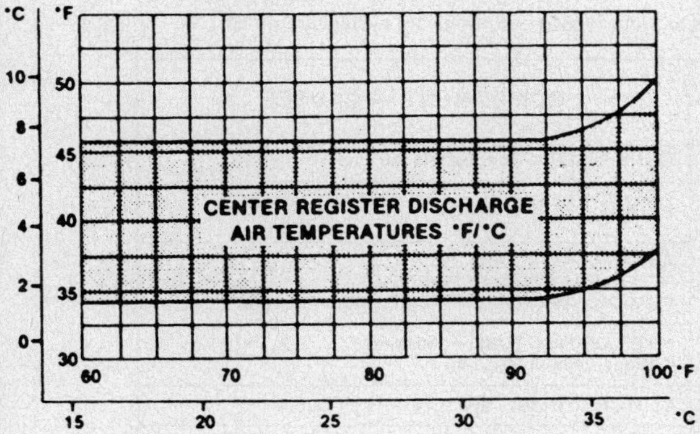
°C
°F
10
8
6
4
2
0
50
45
40
35
30
CENTER REGISTER DISCHARGE
AIR TEMPERATURES °F/°C
60
70
80
90
100 °F
15
20
25
30
35
°C

AMBIENT TEMPERATURES

SECONDS TOTAL CLUTCH CYCLE TIME — SECONDS

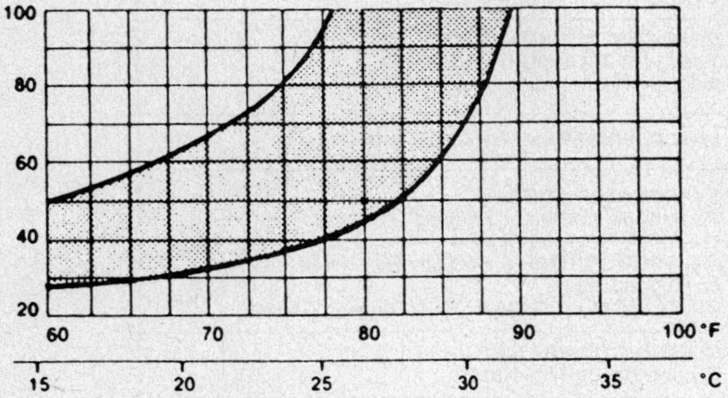
100
80
60
40
20
60
70
80
90
100 °F
15
20
25
30
35
°C

AMBIENT TEMPERATURES

SECONDS NORMAL CLUTCH ON TIME — SECONDS

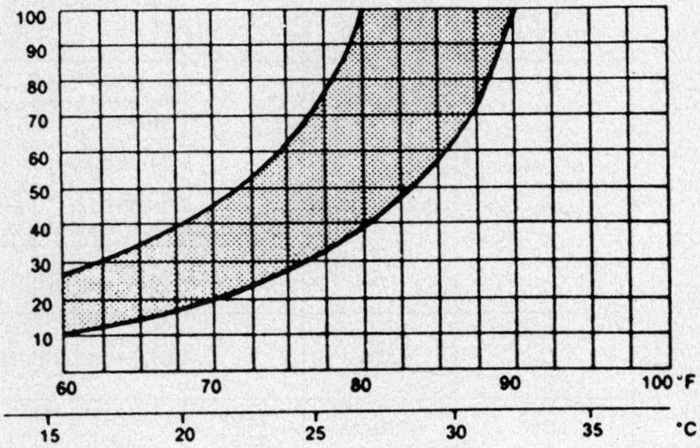
100
90
80
70
60
50
40
30
20
10
60
70
80
90
100 °F
15
20
25
30
35
°C

AMBIENT TEMPERATURES

SECONDS NORMAL CLUTCH OFF TIME — SECONDS

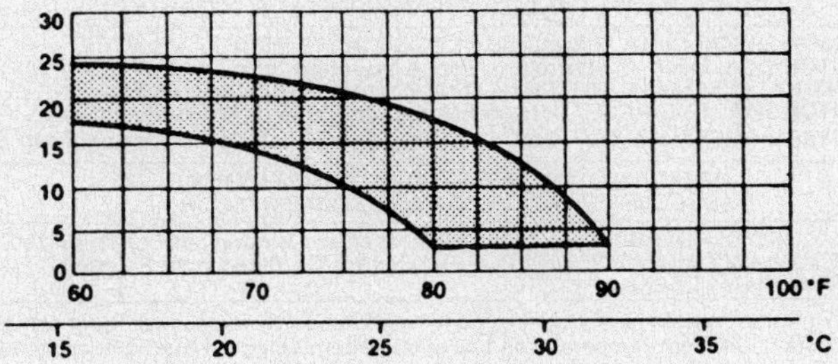
30
25
20
15
10
5
0
60
70
80
90
100 °F
15
20
25
30
35
°C

AMBIENT TEMPERATURES

CLUTCH CYCLE TIMING EVALUATION CHART

REFRIGERANT SYSTEM PRESSURE AND CLUTCH CYCLE TIMING EVALUATION CHART FOR FIXED ORIFICE TUBE CYCLING CLUTCH SYSTEMS

NOTE: Normal system conditional requirements must be maintained to properly evaluate refrigerant system pressures. Refer to charts applicable to system under test.

HIGH (DISCHARGE) PRESSURE	LOW (SUCTION) PRESSURE	CLUTCH CYCLE TIME			COMPONENT — CAUSES
		RATE	ON	OFF	
HIGH	HIGH	CONTINUOUS RUN			CONDENSER — Inadequate Airflow
HIGH	NORMAL TO HIGH				ENGINE OVERHEATING
NORMAL TO HIGH	NORMAL				AIR IN REFRIGERANT. REFRIGERANT OVERCHARGE (a) HUMIDITY OR AMBIENT TEMP. VERY HIGH (b).
NORMAL	HIGH				FIXED ORIFICE TUBE — Missing. O-Rings Leaking/Missing
NORMAL	HIGH	SLOW	LONG	LONG	CLUTCH CYCLING SWITCH — High Cut-In
NORMAL	NORMAL	SLOW OR NO CYCLE	LONG OR CONTINUOUS	NORMAL OR NO CYCLE	MOISTURE IN REFRIGERANT SYSTEM. EXCESSIVE REFRIGERANT OIL
		FAST	SHORT	SHORT	CLUTCH CYCLING SWITCH — Low Cut-In or High Cut-Out
NORMAL	LOW	SLOW	LONG	LONG	CLUTCH CYCLING SWITCH — Low Cut-Out
NORMAL TO LOW	HIGH	CONTINUOUS RUN			Compressor — Low Performance
NORMAL TO LOW	NORMAL TO HIGH				A/C SUCTION LINE — Partially Restricted or Plugged (c)
NORMAL TO LOW	NORMAL	FAST	SHORT	NORMAL	EVAPORATOR — Low Airflow
			SHORT TO VERY SHORT	NORMAL TO LONG	CONDENSER, FIXED ORIFICE TUBE, OR A/C LIQUID LINE — Partially Restricted or Plugged
			SHORT TO VERY SHORT	SHORT TO VERY SHORT	LOW REFRIGERANT CHARGE
			SHORT TO VERY SHORT	LONG	EVAPORATOR CORE — Partially Restricted or Plugged
NORMAL TO LOW	LOW	CONTINUOUS RUN			A/C SUCTION LINE — Partially Restricted or Plugged. (d) CLUTCH CYCLING SWITCH — Sticking Closed
LOW	NORMAL	VERY FAST	VERY SHORT	VERY SHORT	CLUTCH CYCLING SWITCH — Cycling Range Too Close
ERRATIC OPERATION OR COMPRESSOR NOT RUNNING		—	—	—	CLUTCH CYCLING SWITCH — Dirty Contacts or Sticking Open. POOR CONNECTION AT A/C CLUTCH CONNECTOR OR CLUTCH CYCLING SWITCH CONNECTOR. A/C ELECTRICAL CIRCUIT ERRATIC

ADDITIONAL POSSIBLE CAUSE COMPONENTS ASSOCIATED WITH INADEQUATE COMPRESSOR OPERATION

- COMPRESSOR CLUTCH Slipping • LOOSE DRIVE BELT
- CLUTCH COIL Open — Shorted, or Loose Mounting
- CONTROL ASSEMBLY SWITCH — Dirty Contacts or Sticking Open
- CLUTCH WIRING CIRCUIT — High Resistance, Open or Blown Fuse
- A/C HIGH PRESSURE CUT-OUT SWITCH—Dirty Contacts or Sticking Open (If So Equipped)

ADDITIONAL POSSIBLE CAUSE COMPONENTS ASSOCIATED WITH A DAMAGED COMPRESSOR

- CLUTCH CYCLING SWITCH — Sticking Closed or Compressor Clutch Seized
- SUCTION ACCUMULATOR DRIER — Refrigerant Oil Bleed Hole Plugged
- REFRIGERANT LEAKS

(a) Compressor may make noise on initial run. This is slugging condition caused by excessive liquid refrigerant.
(b) Compressor clutch may not cycle in ambient temperatures above 80°F depending on humidity conditions.
(c) Low pressure reading will be **normal to high** if pressure is taken at accumulator and if restriction is downstream of service access valve.
(d) Low pressure reading will be **low** if pressure is taken near the compressor and restriction is upstream of service access valve.

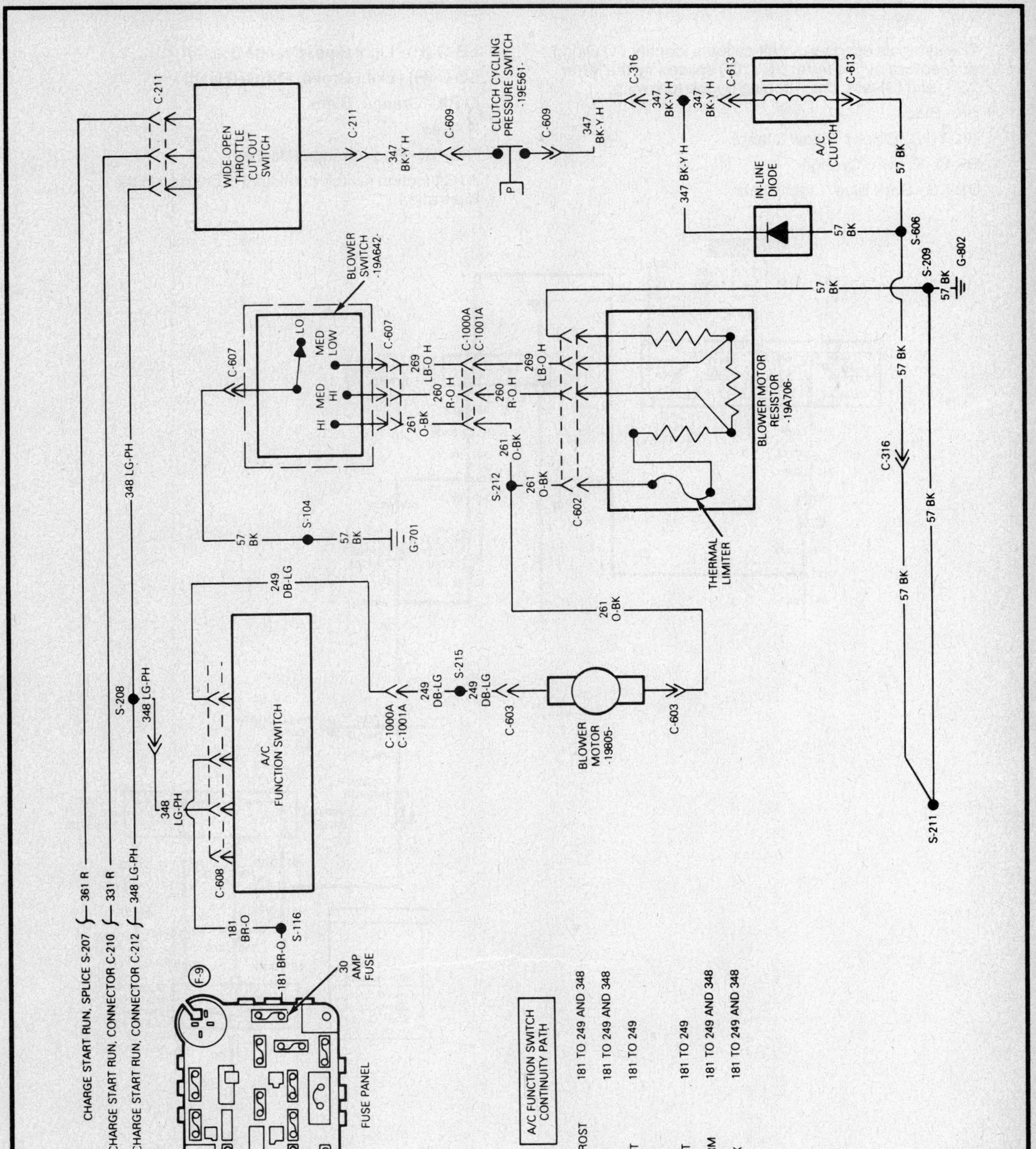
WIDE OPEN THROTTLE CUT-OUT SWITCH
C-211
347 BK-Y H
C-609
CLUTCH CYCLING PRESSURE SWITCH -19E561-
C-316
C-613
A/C CLUTCH
57 BK
IN-LINE DIODE
347 BK-Y H
S-606
S-209
G-802
BLOWER SWITCH -19A642-
LO
MED LOW
MED HI
HI
C-607
269 LB-O H
260 R-O H
261 O-BK
C-1000A C-1001A
S-212
C-602
BLOWER MOTOR RESISTOR -19A706-
THERMAL LIMITER
57 BK
S-104
G-701
249 DB-LG
348 LG-PH
S-208
A/C FUNCTION SWITCH
S-215
C-603
BLOWER MOTOR -19805-
S-211
C-608
181 BR-O
S-116
CHARGE START RUN, SPLICE S-207
361 R
CHARGE START RUN, CONNECTOR C-210
331 R
CHARGE START RUN, CONNECTOR C-212
F-9
30 AMP FUSE
FUSE PANEL
A/C FUNCTION SWITCH CONTINUITY PATH
DEFROST 181 TO 249 AND 348
MIX 181 TO 249 AND 348
HEAT 181 TO 249
OFF
VENT 181 TO 249
NORM 181 TO 249 AND 348
MAX 181 TO 249 AND 348

Air conditioning system electrical schematic—1989 Aerostar

The symbols used as circuit callouts identify (1) wiring connectors by the letter "C", (2) splices by the letter "S", and (3) wire color coding by the following:

BK - Black

BK-Y(H) - Black / Yellow (Hash)

BR-O - Brown / Orange

DB-LG - Dark Blue / Light Green

LB-O-(H) - Light Blue / Orange (Hash)

LG-P-(H) - Light Green / Purple (Hash)

O-BK - Orange / Black

R - Red

R-O-(H) - Red / Orange (Hash)

A / C function switch continuity is charted in the illustration.

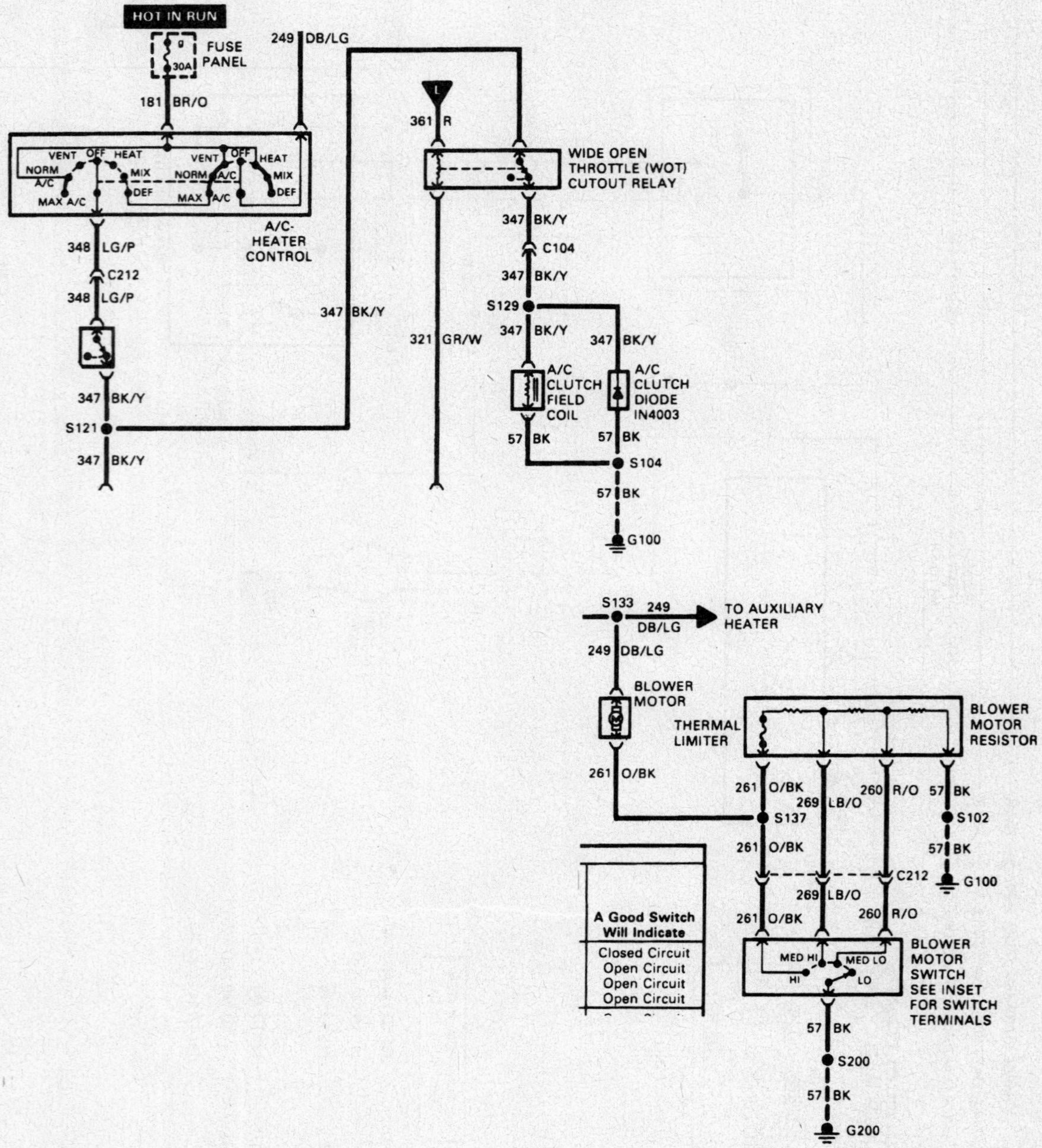
HOT IN RUN
FUSE PANEL
30A
181 BR/O
249 DB/LG
VENT OFF HEAT
NORM MIX
A/C DEF
MAX A/C
A/C-HEATER CONTROL
348 LG/P
C212
347 BK/Y
S121
361 R
WIDE OPEN THROTTLE (WOT) CUTOUT RELAY
C104
S129
321 GR/W
A/C CLUTCH FIELD COIL
A/C CLUTCH DIODE IN4003
57 BK
S104
G100
S133
TO AUXILIARY HEATER
BLOWER MOTOR
THERMAL LIMITER
BLOWER MOTOR RESISTOR
261 O/BK
269 LB/O
260 R/O
S137
S102
MED HI
MED LO
HI
LO
BLOWER MOTOR SWITCH SEE INSET FOR SWITCH TERMINALS
S200
G200
A Good Switch Will Indicate
Closed Circuit
Open Circuit
Open Circuit
Open Circuit

Air conditioning system electrical schematic—1990–91 Aerostar

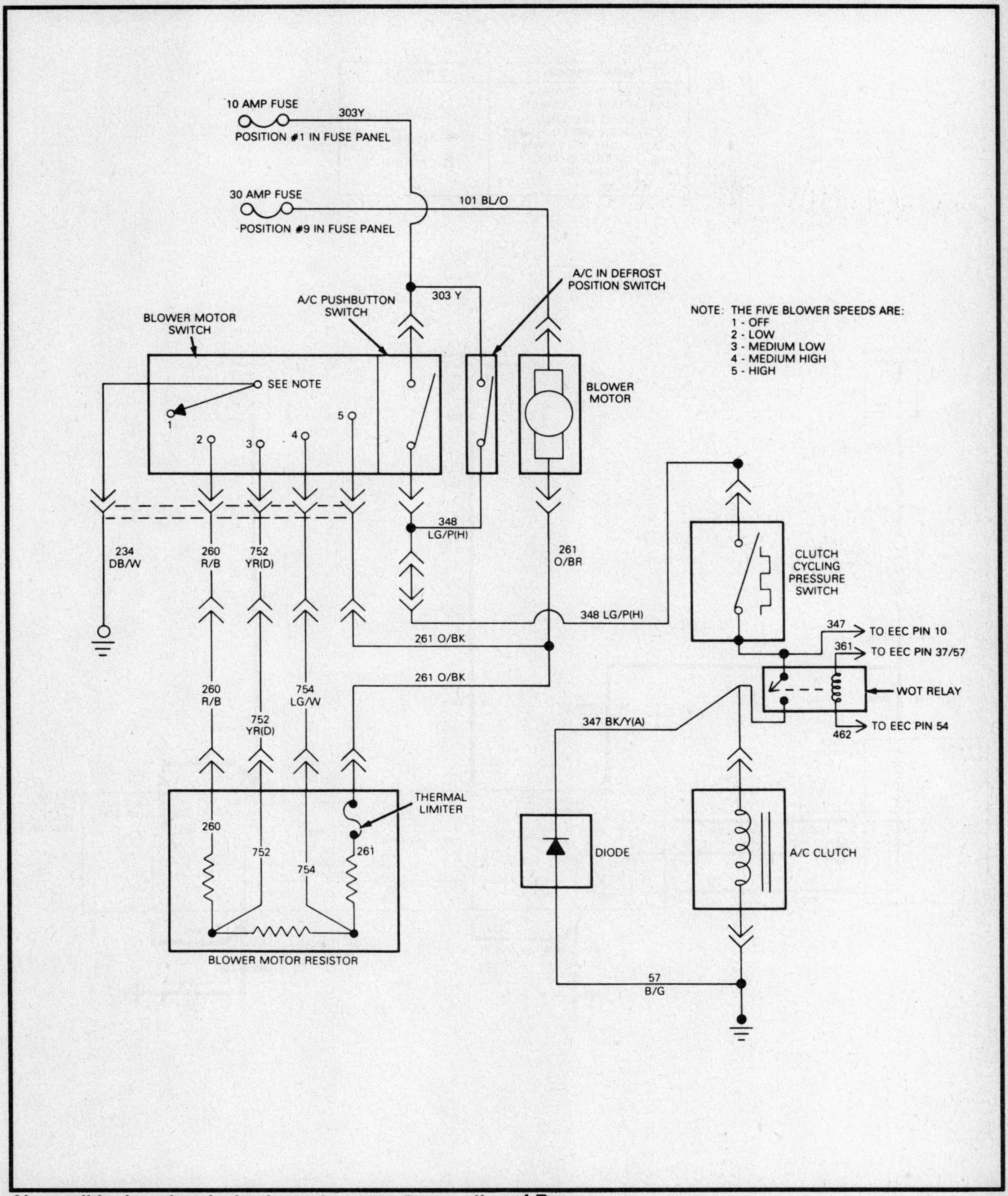
10 AMP FUSE
303Y
POSITION #1 IN FUSE PANEL
30 AMP FUSE
101 BL/O
POSITION #9 IN FUSE PANEL
A/C IN DEFROST
POSITION SWITCH
303 Y
A/C PUSHBUTTON
SWITCH
BLOWER MOTOR
SWITCH
NOTE: THE FIVE BLOWER SPEEDS ARE:
1 - OFF
2 - LOW
3 - MEDIUM LOW
4 - MEDIUM HIGH
5 - HIGH
SEE NOTE
1
2
3
4
5
BLOWER
MOTOR
348
LG/P(H)
234
DB/W
260
R/B
752
YR(D)
261
O/BR
CLUTCH
CYCLING
PRESSURE
SWITCH
348 LG/P(H)
261 O/BK
347
TO EEC PIN 10
361
TO EEC PIN 37/57
261 O/BK
WOT RELAY
260
R/B
754
LG/W
752
YR(D)
347 BK/Y(A)
TO EEC PIN 54
462
THERMAL
LIMITER
260
752
261
754
DIODE
A/C CLUTCH
BLOWER MOTOR RESISTOR
57
B/G

Air conditioning electrical schematic—1989 Bronco II and Ranger

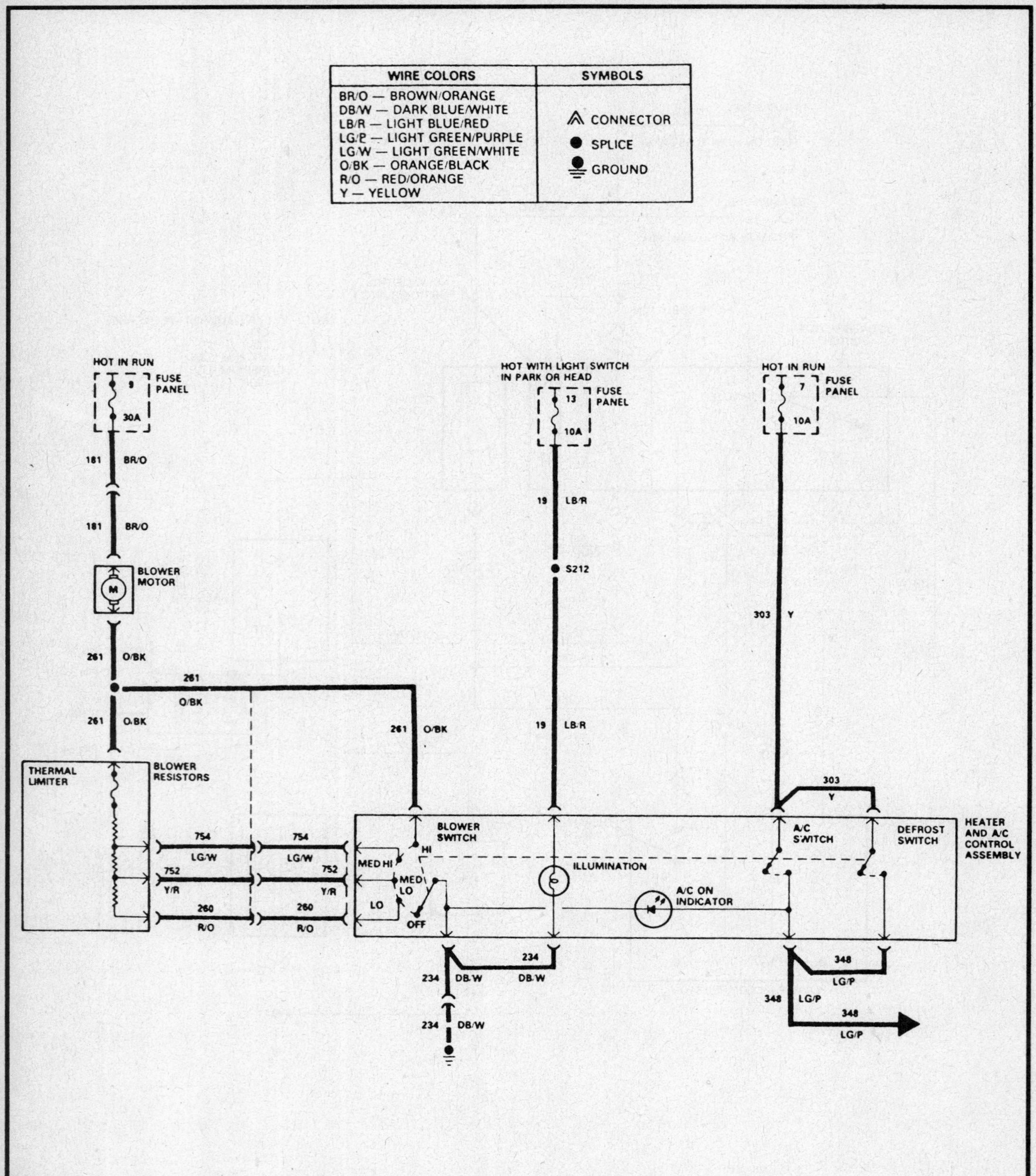
WIRE COLORS
BR/O — BROWN/ORANGE
DB/W — DARK BLUE/WHITE
LB/R — LIGHT BLUE/RED
LG/P — LIGHT GREEN/PURPLE
LG/W — LIGHT GREEN/WHITE
O/BK — ORANGE/BLACK
R/O — RED/ORANGE
Y — YELLOW
SYMBOLS
CONNECTOR
SPLICE
GROUND
HOT IN RUN
FUSE PANEL
9
30A
181 BR/O
BLOWER MOTOR
M
261 O/BK
THERMAL LIMITER
BLOWER RESISTORS
754 LG/W
752 Y/R
260 R/O
HOT WITH LIGHT SWITCH IN PARK OR HEAD
13
10A
19 LB/R
S212
7
303 Y
BLOWER SWITCH
HI
MED HI
MED LO
LO
OFF
ILLUMINATION
A/C ON INDICATOR
A/C SWITCH
DEFROST SWITCH
HEATER AND A/C CONTROL ASSEMBLY
234 DB/W
348 LG/P

Air conditioning electrical schematic—1990 Bronco II, 1991 Explorer and 1990–91 Ranger

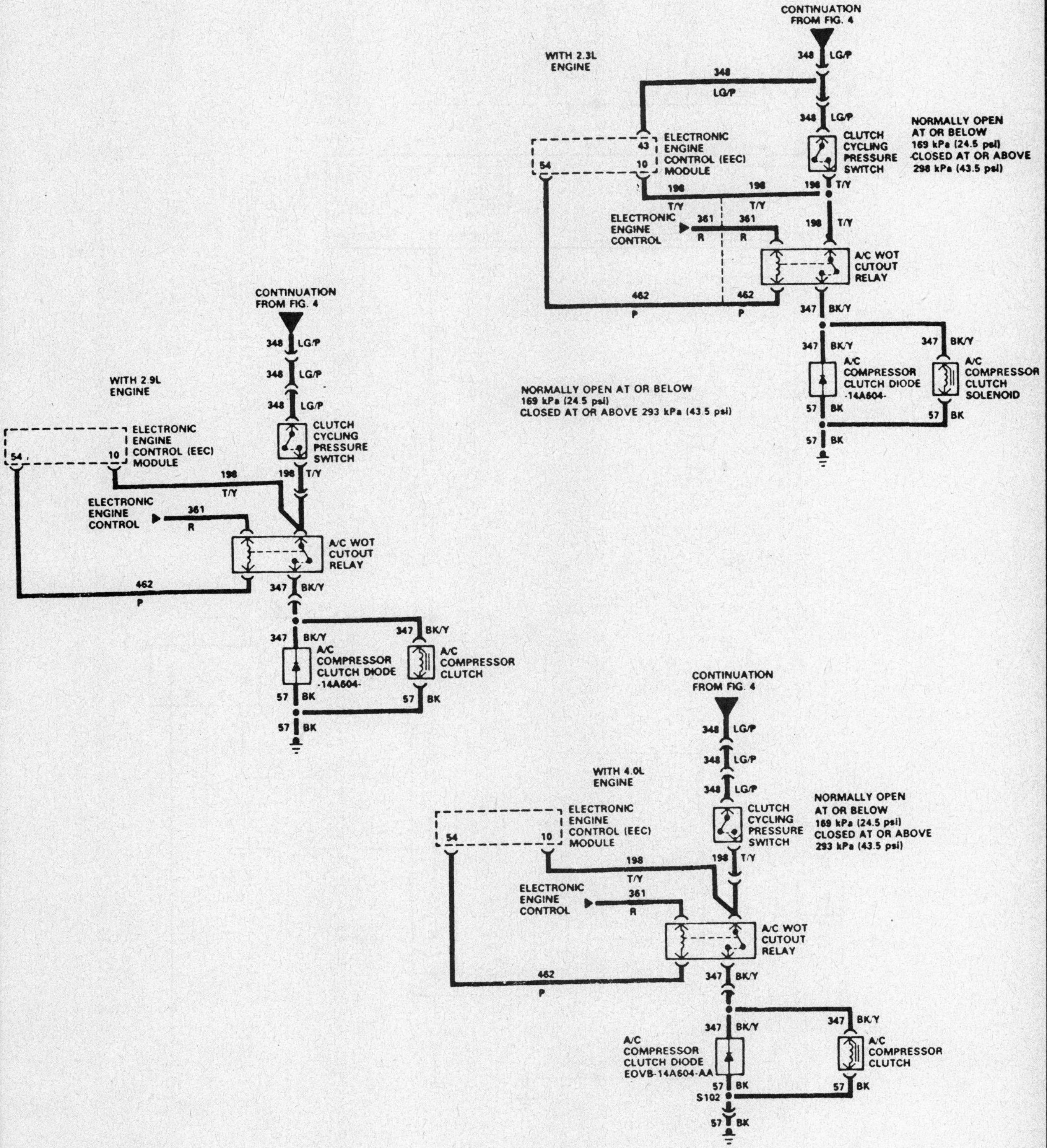
CONTINUATION FROM FIG. 4
WITH 2.3L ENGINE
348 LG/P
ELECTRONIC ENGINE CONTROL (EEC) MODULE
43
10
54
CLUTCH CYCLING PRESSURE SWITCH
NORMALLY OPEN AT OR BELOW 169 kPa (24.5 psi) CLOSED AT OR ABOVE 293 kPa (43.5 psi)
198 T/Y
ELECTRONIC ENGINE CONTROL
361 R
A/C WOT CUTOUT RELAY
462 P
347 BK/Y
A/C COMPRESSOR CLUTCH DIODE -14A604-
A/C COMPRESSOR CLUTCH SOLENOID
57 BK
CONTINUATION FROM FIG. 4
WITH 2.9L ENGINE
348 LG/P
ELECTRONIC ENGINE CONTROL (EEC) MODULE
54
10
CLUTCH CYCLING PRESSURE SWITCH
198 T/Y
ELECTRONIC ENGINE CONTROL
361 R
A/C WOT CUTOUT RELAY
462 P
347 BK/Y
A/C COMPRESSOR CLUTCH DIODE -14A604-
A/C COMPRESSOR CLUTCH
57 BK
NORMALLY OPEN AT OR BELOW 169 kPa (24.5 psi) CLOSED AT OR ABOVE 293 kPa (43.5 psi)
CONTINUATION FROM FIG. 4
WITH 4.0L ENGINE
348 LG/P
ELECTRONIC ENGINE CONTROL (EEC) MODULE
54
10
CLUTCH CYCLING PRESSURE SWITCH
NORMALLY OPEN AT OR BELOW 169 kPa (24.5 psi) CLOSED AT OR ABOVE 293 kPa (43.5 psi)
198 T/Y
ELECTRONIC ENGINE CONTROL
361 R
A/C WOT CUTOUT RELAY
462 P
347 BK/Y
A/C COMPRESSOR CLUTCH DIODE E0VB-14A604-AA
A/C COMPRESSOR CLUTCH
57 BK
S102

Air conditioning electrical schematic continued— 1990 Bronco II, 1991 Explorer and 1990–91 Ranger

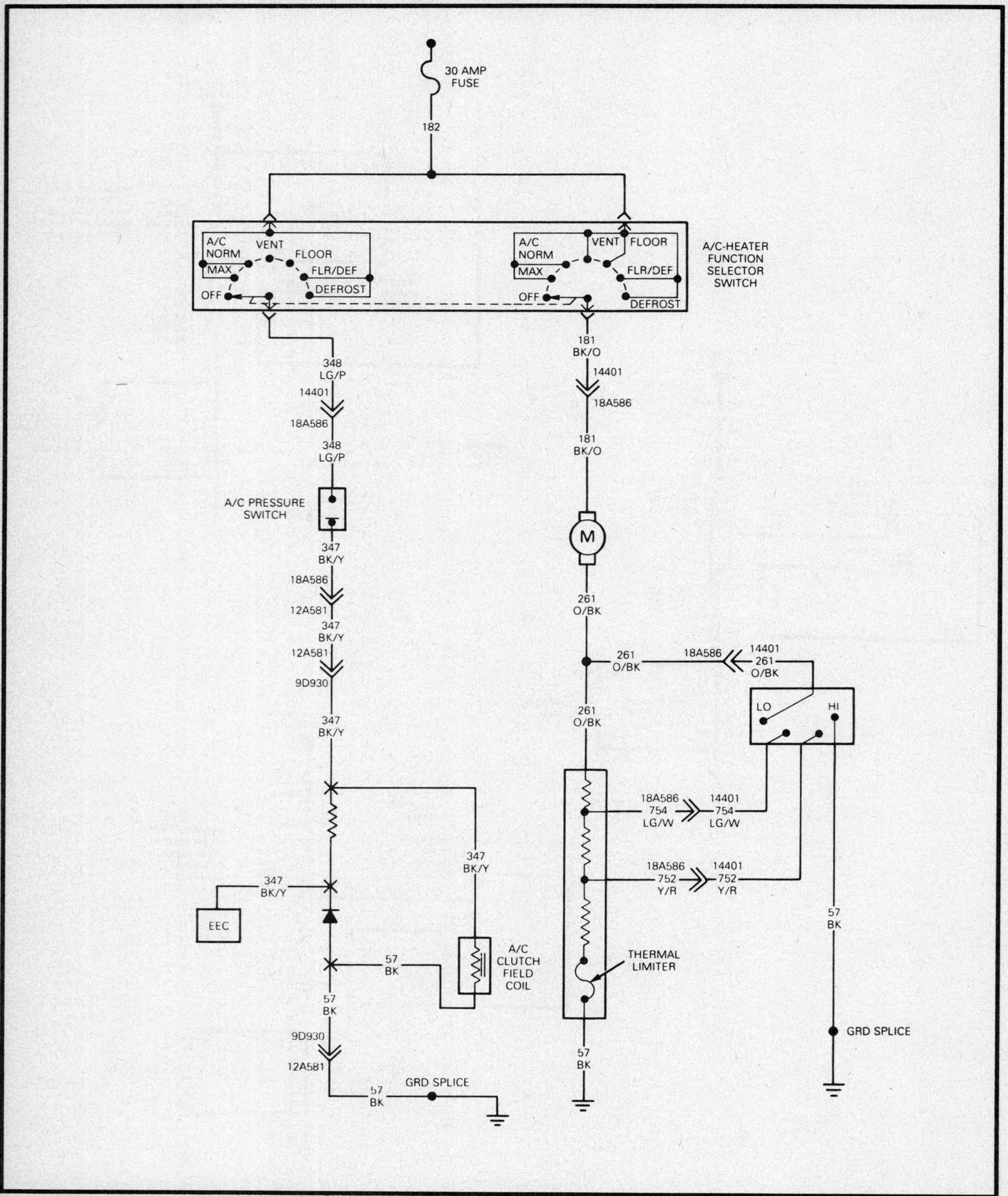
30 AMP FUSE
182
A/C NORM
VENT
FLOOR
MAX
FLR/DEF
OFF
DEFROST
A/C-HEATER FUNCTION SELECTOR SWITCH
348 LG/P
14401
18A586
181 BK/O
A/C PRESSURE SWITCH
347 BK/Y
12A581
9D930
M
261 O/BK
LO
HI
754 LG/W
752 Y/R
57 BK
EEC
A/C CLUTCH FIELD COIL
THERMAL LIMITER
GRD SPLICE

Air conditioning electrical schematic—1989–90 Bronco and F Series

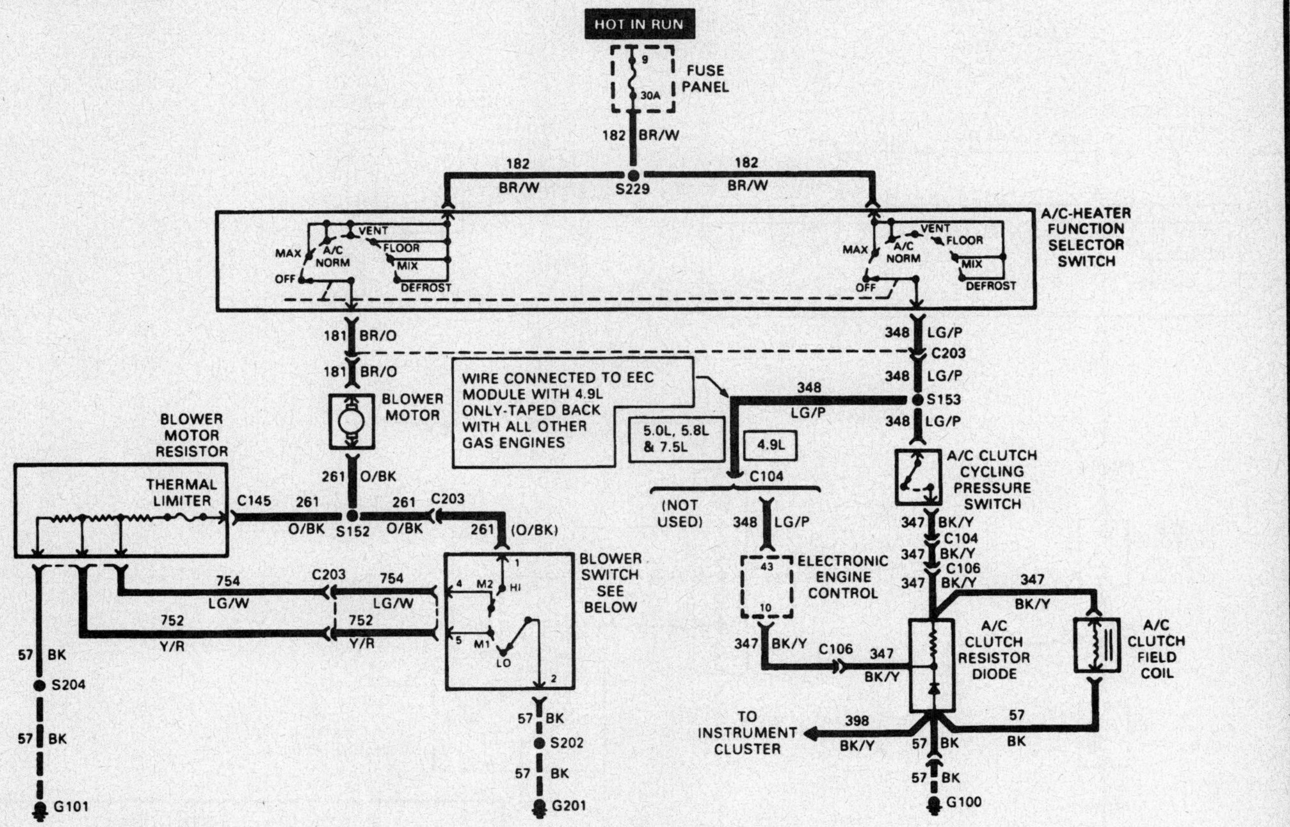
HOT IN RUN
9
30A
FUSE PANEL
182 BR/W
182 BR/W
S229
182 BR/W
A/C-HEATER FUNCTION SELECTOR SWITCH
MAX
A/C NORM
OFF
VENT
FLOOR
MIX
DEFROST
181 BR/O
181 BR/O
BLOWER MOTOR
348 LG/P
C203
348 LG/P
S153
348 LG/P
WIRE CONNECTED TO EEC MODULE WITH 4.9L ONLY-TAPED BACK WITH ALL OTHER GAS ENGINES
5.0L, 5.8L & 7.5L
4.9L
C104
(NOT USED)
348 LG/P
ELECTRONIC ENGINE CONTROL
A/C CLUTCH CYCLING PRESSURE SWITCH
347 BK/Y
C104
C106
BLOWER MOTOR RESISTOR
THERMAL LIMITER
C145
261 O/BK
S152
261 O/BK
C203
261 (O/BK)
BLOWER SWITCH SEE BELOW
M2 HI
M1 LO
754 LG/W
752 Y/R
57 BK
S204
G101
S202
G201
A/C CLUTCH RESISTOR DIODE
A/C CLUTCH FIELD COIL
TO INSTRUMENT CLUSTER
398 BK/Y
57 BK
G100

TERMINAL LOCATIONS	SCHEMATIC
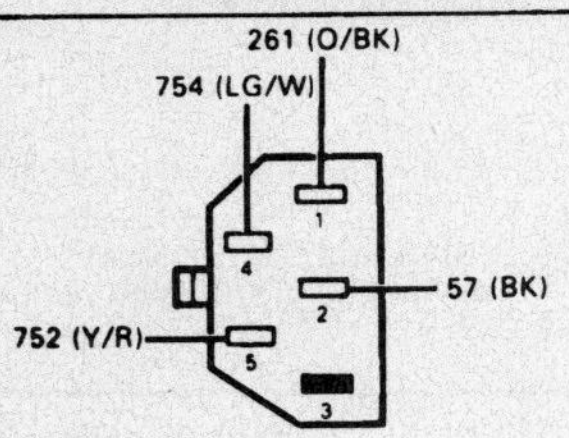	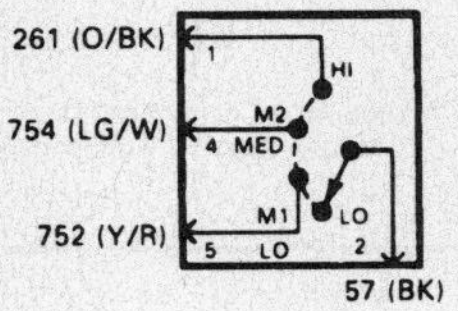

261 (O/BK)
754 (LG/W)
57 (BK)
752 (Y/R)
1
2
3
4
5

261 (O/BK)
754 (LG/W)
752 (Y/R)
57 (BK)
HI
M2
MED
M1
LO

COMPONENT TESTING PROCEDURE

TO TEST	Connect Self-Powered Test Lamp or Ohmmeter to Terminals	Move Switch to These Positions	A Good Switch Will Indicate
Medium-Low Speed	57 (BK) 2 and 752 (Y/R) 5	Lo M1 M2 Hi	Open circuit Closed circuit Open circuit Open circuit
Medium Speed	57 (BK) 2 and 754 (LG/W)	Lo M1 M2 Hi	Open circuit Open circuit Closed circuit Open circuit
High Speed	57 (BK) 2 and 261 (O/BK) 1	Lo M1 M2 Hi	Open circuit Open circuit Open circuit Closed circuit

Air conditioning electrical schematic—1991 Bronco and F Series

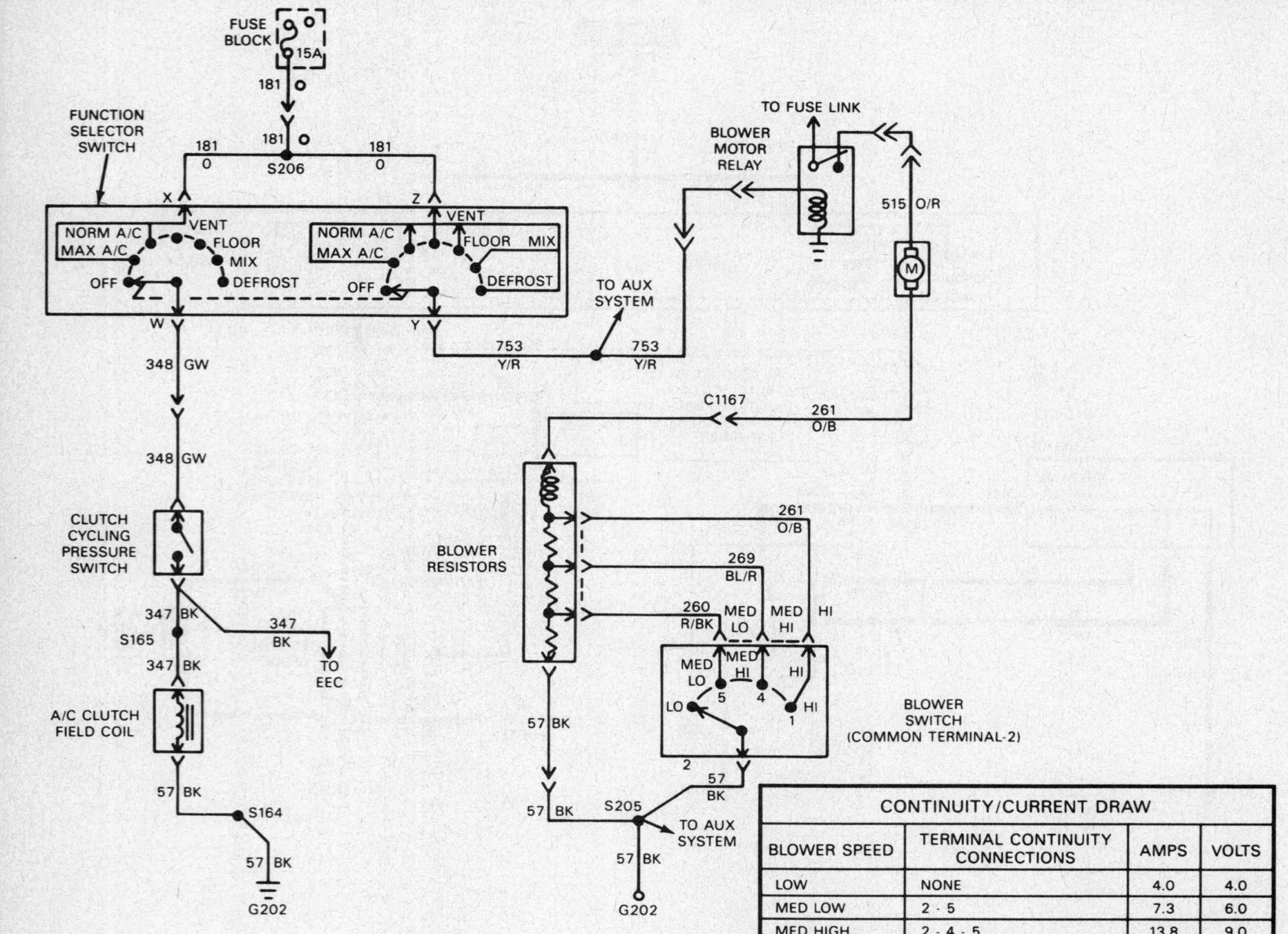
FUSE BLOCK
15A
181 O
FUNCTION SELECTOR SWITCH
181 O
S206
X
Z
VENT
NORM A/C
MAX A/C
FLOOR
MIX
OFF
DEFROST
W
Y
348 GW
753 Y/R
TO AUX SYSTEM
TO FUSE LINK
BLOWER MOTOR RELAY
515 O/R
C1167
261 O/B
CLUTCH CYCLING PRESSURE SWITCH
347 BK
S165
TO EEC
A/C CLUTCH FIELD COIL
57 BK
S164
G202
BLOWER RESISTORS
269 BL/R
260 R/BK
MED LO
MED HI
HI
LO
BLOWER SWITCH (COMMON TERMINAL-2)
S205
TO AUX SYSTEM

CONTINUITY/CURRENT DRAW			
BLOWER SPEED	TERMINAL CONTINUITY CONNECTIONS	AMPS	VOLTS
LOW	NONE	4.0	4.0
MED LOW	2 - 5	7.3	6.0
MED HIGH	2 - 4 - 5	13.8	9.0
HIGH	2 - 1 - 4	23.0	12.8

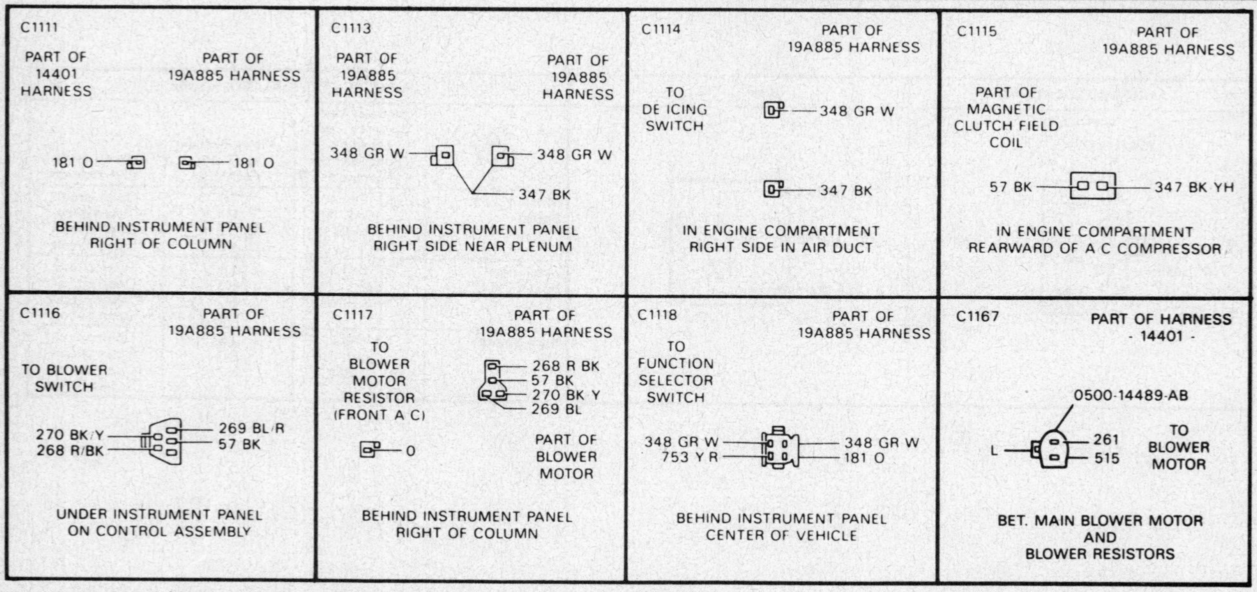
C1111
PART OF 14401 HARNESS
PART OF 19A885 HARNESS
181 O
181 O
BEHIND INSTRUMENT PANEL RIGHT OF COLUMN
C1113
PART OF 19A885 HARNESS
PART OF 19A885 HARNESS
348 GR W
348 GR W
347 BK
BEHIND INSTRUMENT PANEL RIGHT SIDE NEAR PLENUM
C1114
PART OF 19A885 HARNESS
TO DE ICING SWITCH
348 GR W
347 BK
IN ENGINE COMPARTMENT RIGHT SIDE IN AIR DUCT
C1115
PART OF 19A885 HARNESS
PART OF MAGNETIC CLUTCH FIELD COIL
57 BK
347 BK YH
IN ENGINE COMPARTMENT REARWARD OF A C COMPRESSOR
C1116
PART OF 19A885 HARNESS
TO BLOWER SWITCH
270 BK/Y
268 R/BK
269 BL/R
57 BK
UNDER INSTRUMENT PANEL ON CONTROL ASSEMBLY
C1117
PART OF 19A885 HARNESS
TO BLOWER MOTOR RESISTOR (FRONT A C)
268 R BK
57 BK
270 BK Y
269 BL
O
PART OF BLOWER MOTOR
BEHIND INSTRUMENT PANEL RIGHT OF COLUMN
C1118
PART OF 19A885 HARNESS
TO FUNCTION SELECTOR SWITCH
348 GR W
753 Y R
348 GR W
181 O
BEHIND INSTRUMENT PANEL CENTER OF VEHICLE
C1167
PART OF HARNESS - 14401 -
0500-14489-AB
L
261
515
TO BLOWER MOTOR
BET. MAIN BLOWER MOTOR AND BLOWER RESISTORS

Air conditioning electrical schematic—1989 E Series

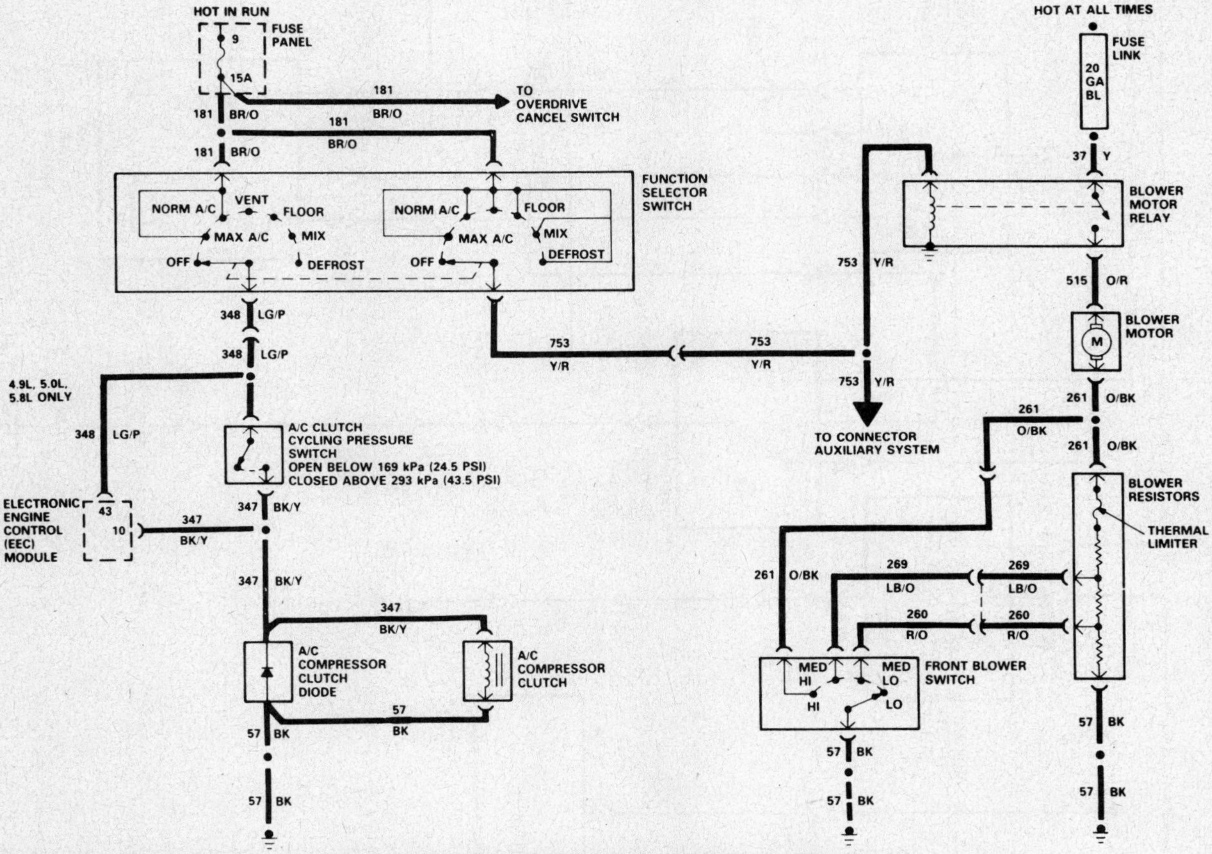
HOT IN RUN
FUSE PANEL
9
15A
181 BR/O
TO OVERDRIVE CANCEL SWITCH
FUNCTION SELECTOR SWITCH
NORM A/C
VENT
FLOOR
MAX A/C
MIX
OFF
DEFROST
348 LG/P
4.9L, 5.0L, 5.8L ONLY
A/C CLUTCH CYCLING PRESSURE SWITCH
OPEN BELOW 169 kPa (24.5 PSI)
CLOSED ABOVE 293 kPa (43.5 PSI)
ELECTRONIC ENGINE CONTROL (EEC) MODULE
43
10
347 BK/Y
A/C COMPRESSOR CLUTCH DIODE
A/C COMPRESSOR CLUTCH
57 BK
753 Y/R
HOT AT ALL TIMES
FUSE LINK
20 GA BL
37 Y
BLOWER MOTOR RELAY
515 O/R
BLOWER MOTOR
M
TO CONNECTOR AUXILIARY SYSTEM
261 O/BK
BLOWER RESISTORS
THERMAL LIMITER
269 LB/O
260 R/O
MED HI
MED LO
HI
LO
FRONT BLOWER SWITCH

WIRE COLORS	WIRE COLORS (CONT.)	SYMBOLS
BK — BLACK	O/BK — ORANGE/BLACK	CONNECTOR
BK/Y — BLACK/YELLOW	O/R — ORANGE/RED	SPLICE
BR/O — BROWN/ORANGE	R/O — RED/ORANGE	GROUND
LB/O — LIGHT BLUE/ORANGE	Y — YELLOW	
LG/P — LIGHT GREEN/PURPLE	Y/R — YELLOW/RED	

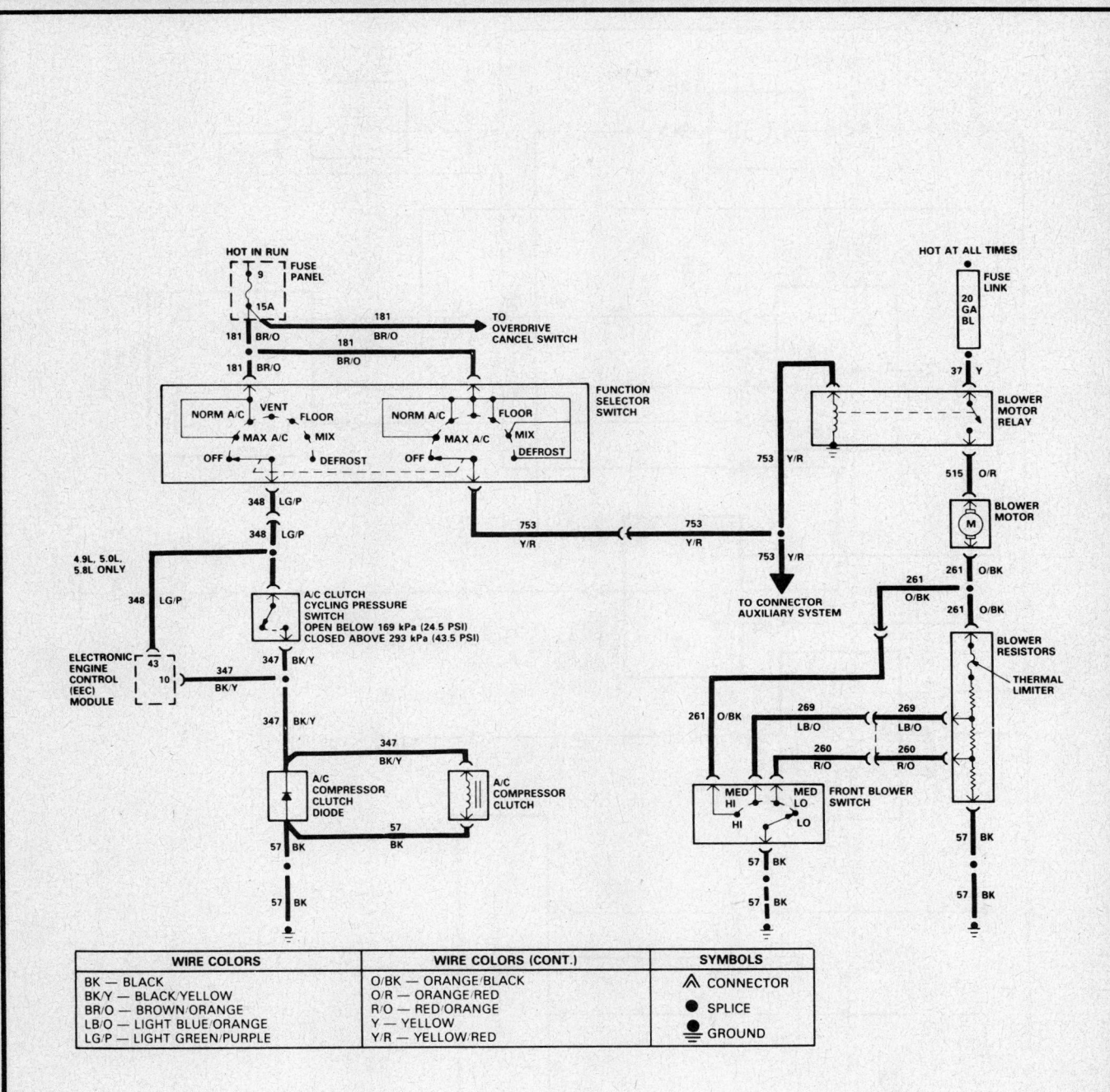

Air conditioning electrical schematic—1990–91 E Series

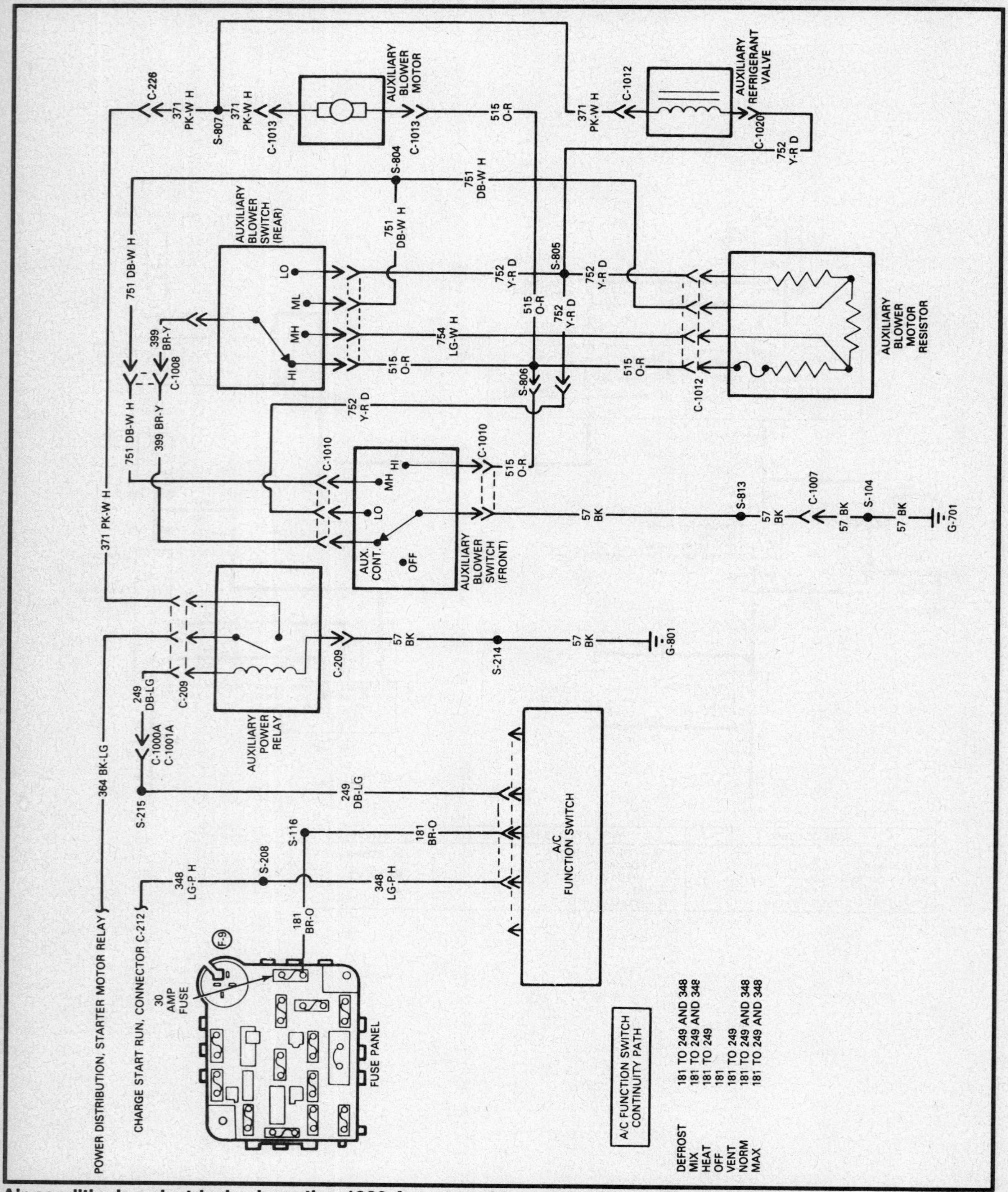
AUXILIARY BLOWER MOTOR
AUXILIARY REFRIGERANT VALVE
AUXILIARY BLOWER SWITCH (REAR)
AUXILIARY BLOWER MOTOR RESISTOR
AUXILIARY BLOWER SWITCH (FRONT)
AUX. CONT.
OFF
AUXILIARY POWER RELAY
A/C FUNCTION SWITCH
FUSE PANEL
30 AMP FUSE
F-9
POWER DISTRIBUTION, STARTER MOTOR RELAY
CHARGE START RUN, CONNECTOR C-212
A/C FUNCTION SWITCH CONTINUITY PATH
DEFROST 181 TO 249 AND 348
MIX 181 TO 249 AND 348
HEAT 181 TO 249
OFF 181
VENT 181 TO 249
NORM 181 TO 249 AND 348
MAX 181 TO 249 AND 348

Air conditioning electrical schematic – 1989 Aerostar with auxiliary air conditioning system

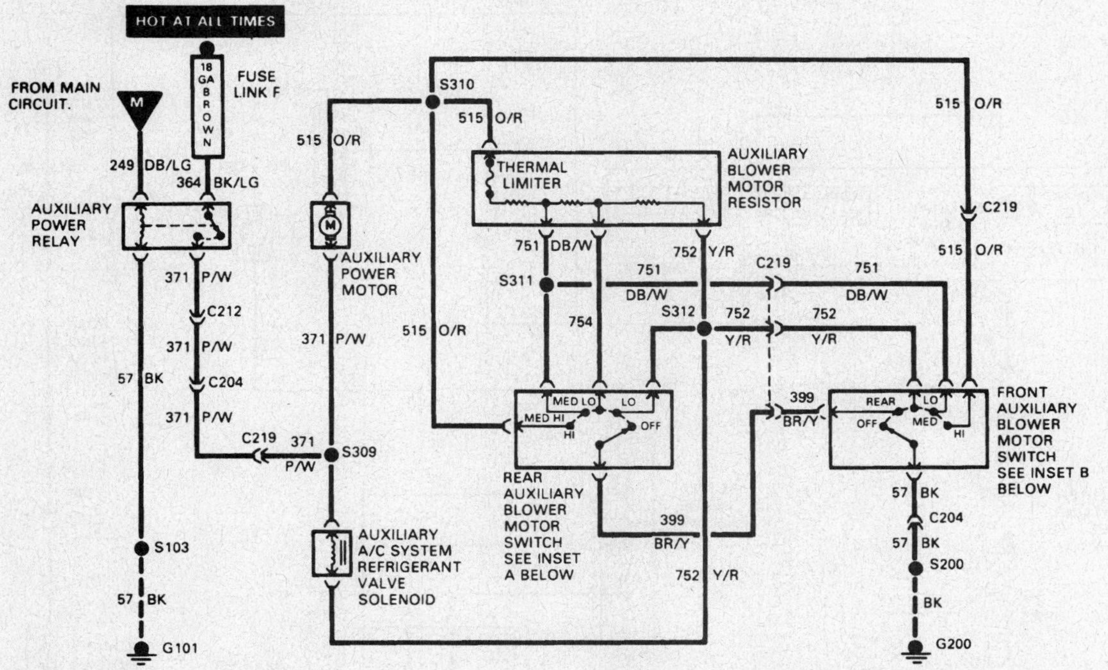
HOT AT ALL TIMES
18 GA BROWN
FUSE LINK F
FROM MAIN CIRCUIT.
M
249 DB/LG
364 BK/LG
AUXILIARY POWER RELAY
371 P/W
C212
371 P/W
57 BK
C204
371 P/W
C219 371 P/W
S309
S103
57 BK
G101
S310
515 O/R
515 O/R
515 O/R
AUXILIARY POWER MOTOR
371 P/W
AUXILIARY A/C SYSTEM REFRIGERANT VALVE SOLENOID
THERMAL LIMITER
AUXILIARY BLOWER MOTOR RESISTOR
751 DB/W
752 Y/R
S311
751 DB/W
754
S312
752 Y/R
C219
751 DB/W
752 Y/R
C219
515 O/R
MED LO
LO
MED HI
HI
OFF
REAR AUXILIARY BLOWER MOTOR SWITCH SEE INSET A BELOW
399 BR/Y
752 Y/R
399 BR/Y
REAR
LO
OFF
MED
HI
FRONT AUXILIARY BLOWER MOTOR SWITCH SEE INSET B BELOW
57 BK
C204
57 BK
S200
BK
G200

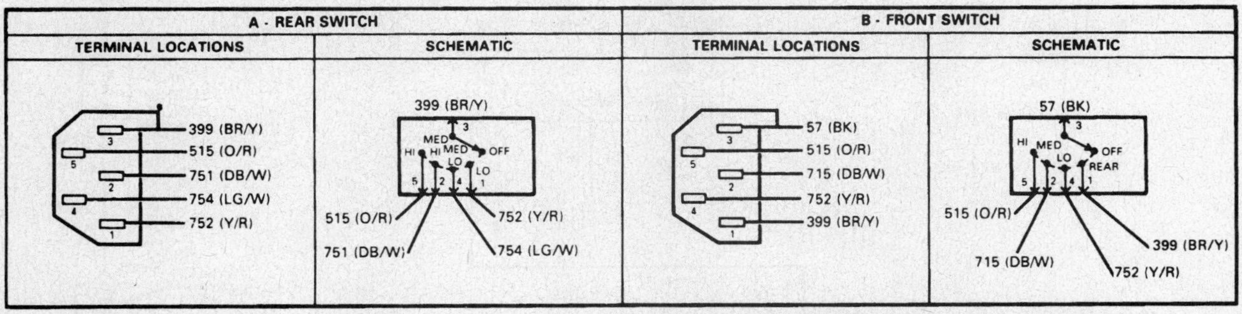
A - REAR SWITCH
TERMINAL LOCATIONS
SCHEMATIC
399 (BR/Y)
515 (O/R)
751 (DB/W)
754 (LG/W)
752 (Y/R)
HI
MED HI
MED LO
LO
OFF
515 (O/R)
751 (DB/W)
752 (Y/R)
754 (LG/W)
B - FRONT SWITCH
TERMINAL LOCATIONS
SCHEMATIC
57 (BK)
515 (O/R)
715 (DB/W)
752 (Y/R)
399 (BR/Y)
HI
MED
LO
OFF
REAR
515 (O/R)
715 (DB/W)
752 (Y/R)
399 (BR/Y)

COMPONENT TESTING PROCEDURE

TO TEST	Connect Self-Powered Test Lamp or Ohmmeter to Terminals	Move Control to These Positions	A Good Switch Will Indicate
Rear Select	399 (BR/Y) and 57 (BK) (3)	Off Rear Lo Medium Hi	Open Circuit Closed Circuit Open Circuit Open Circuit Open Circuit
Low Speed	752 (Y/R) (4) and 57 (BK) (3)	Off Rear Lo Medium Hi	Open Circuit Open Circuit Closed Circuit Open Circuit Open Circuit
Medium Speed	715 (DB/W) (2) and 57 (BK) (3)	Off Rear Lo Medium Hi	Open Circuit Open Circuit Open Circuit Closed Circuit Open Circuit
High Speed	515 (O/R) (5) and 57 (BK) (3)	Off Rear Lo Medium Hi	Open Circuit Open Circuit Open Circuit Open Circuit Closed Circuit

COMPONENT TESTING PROCEDURE

TO TEST	Connect Self-Powered Test Lamp or Ohmmeter to Terminals	Move Control to These Positions	A Good Switch Will Indicate
Low Speed	752 (Y R) (1) and 399 (BR Y) (3)	Off Lo Medium Lo Medium Hi Hi	Open Circuit Closed Circuit Open Circuit Open Circuit Open Circuit
Medium Low Speed	754 (LG W) (4) and 399 (BR Y) (3)	Off Lo Medium Lo Medium Hi Hi	Open Circuit Open Circuit Closed Circuit Open Circuit Open Circuit
Medium High Speed	751 (DB W) (2) and 399 (BR Y) (3)	Off Lo Medium Lo Medium Hi Hi	Open Circuit Open Circuit Open Circuit Closed Circuit Open Circuit
High Speed	515 (O R) (5) and 399 (BR Y) (3)	Off Lo Medium Lo Medium Hi Hi	Open Circuit Open Circuit Open Circuit Open Circuit Closed Circuit

Air conditioning electrical schematic—1990–91 Aerostar auxiliary system

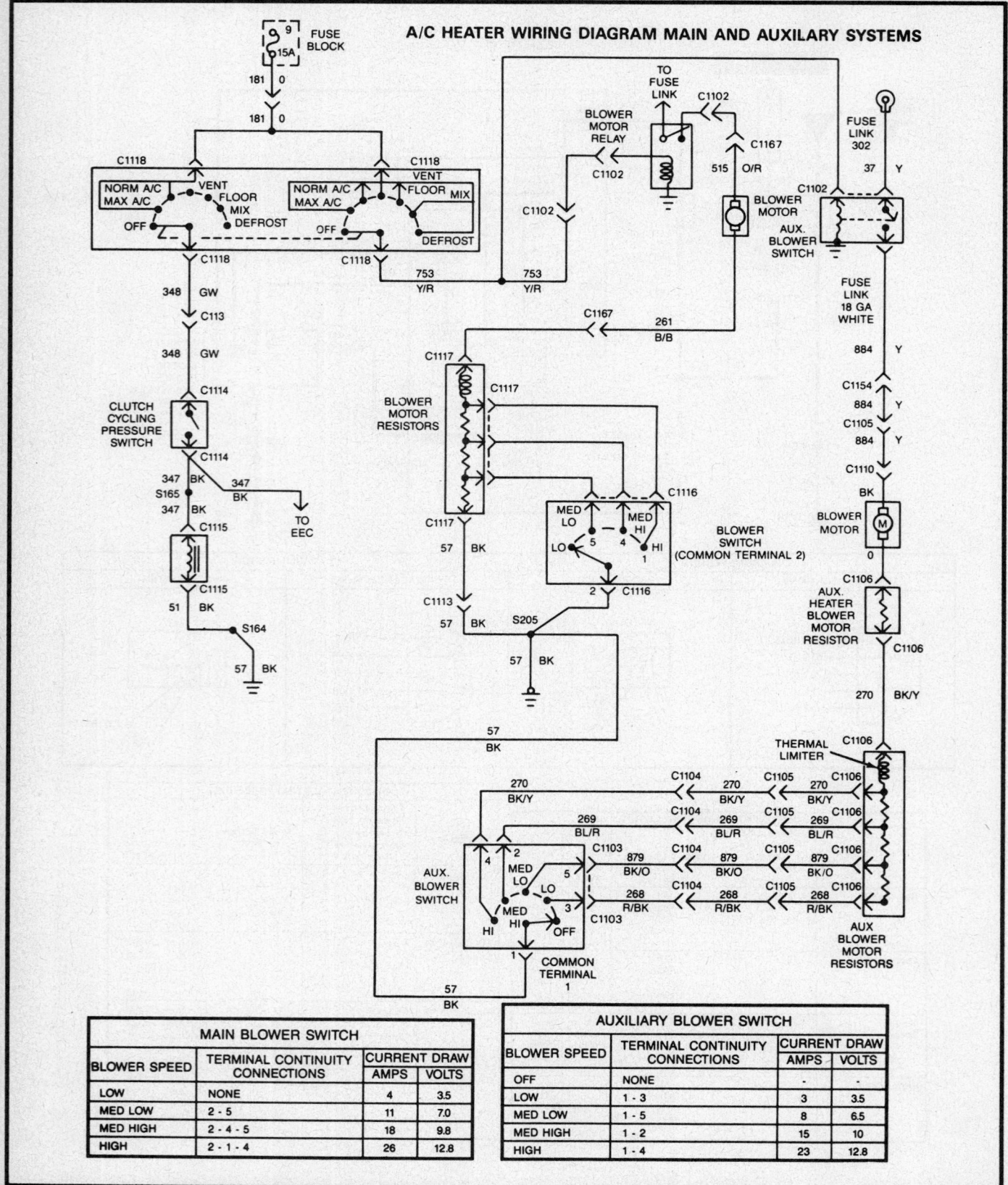

A/C HEATER WIRING DIAGRAM MAIN AND AUXILARY SYSTEMS

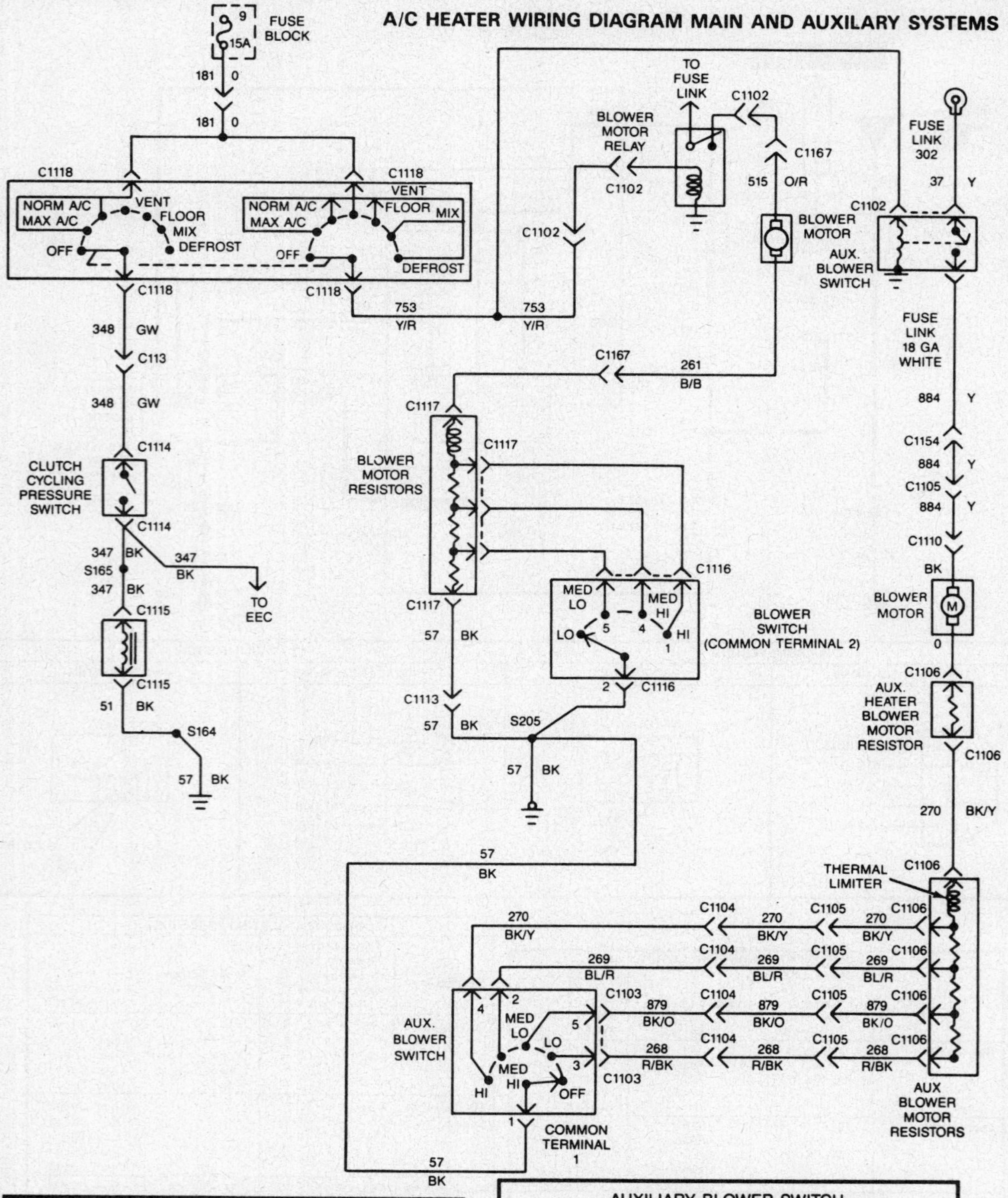
FUSE BLOCK
9
15A
181 O
C1118
VENT
FLOOR
MIX
DEFROST
NORM A/C
MAX A/C
OFF
348 GW
C113
C1114
CLUTCH CYCLING PRESSURE SWITCH
347 BK
S165
TO EEC
C1115
51 BK
S164
57 BK
753 Y/R
TO FUSE LINK
C1102
BLOWER MOTOR RELAY
C1167
515 O/R
BLOWER MOTOR
261 B/B
C1117
BLOWER MOTOR RESISTORS
C1116
MED LO
MED HI
LO
HI
BLOWER SWITCH (COMMON TERMINAL 2)
C1113
S205
FUSE LINK 302
37 Y
AUX. BLOWER SWITCH
FUSE LINK 18 GA WHITE
884 Y
C1154
C1105
C1110
C1106
AUX. HEATER BLOWER MOTOR RESISTOR
270 BK/Y
THERMAL LIMITER
C1104
269 BL/R
C1103
879 BK/O
268 R/BK
OFF
COMMON TERMINAL 1
AUX BLOWER MOTOR RESISTORS

MAIN BLOWER SWITCH			
BLOWER SPEED	TERMINAL CONTINUITY CONNECTIONS	CURRENT DRAW	
		AMPS	VOLTS
LOW	NONE	4	3.5
MED LOW	2 - 5	11	7.0
MED HIGH	2 - 4 - 5	18	9.8
HIGH	2 - 1 - 4	26	12.8

AUXILIARY BLOWER SWITCH			
BLOWER SPEED	TERMINAL CONTINUITY CONNECTIONS	CURRENT DRAW	
		AMPS	VOLTS
OFF	NONE	-	-
LOW	1 - 3	3	3.5
MED LOW	1 - 5	8	6.5
MED HIGH	1 - 2	15	10
HIGH	1 - 4	23	12.8

Air conditioning electrical schematic – 1989 E Series with auxillary air conditioning

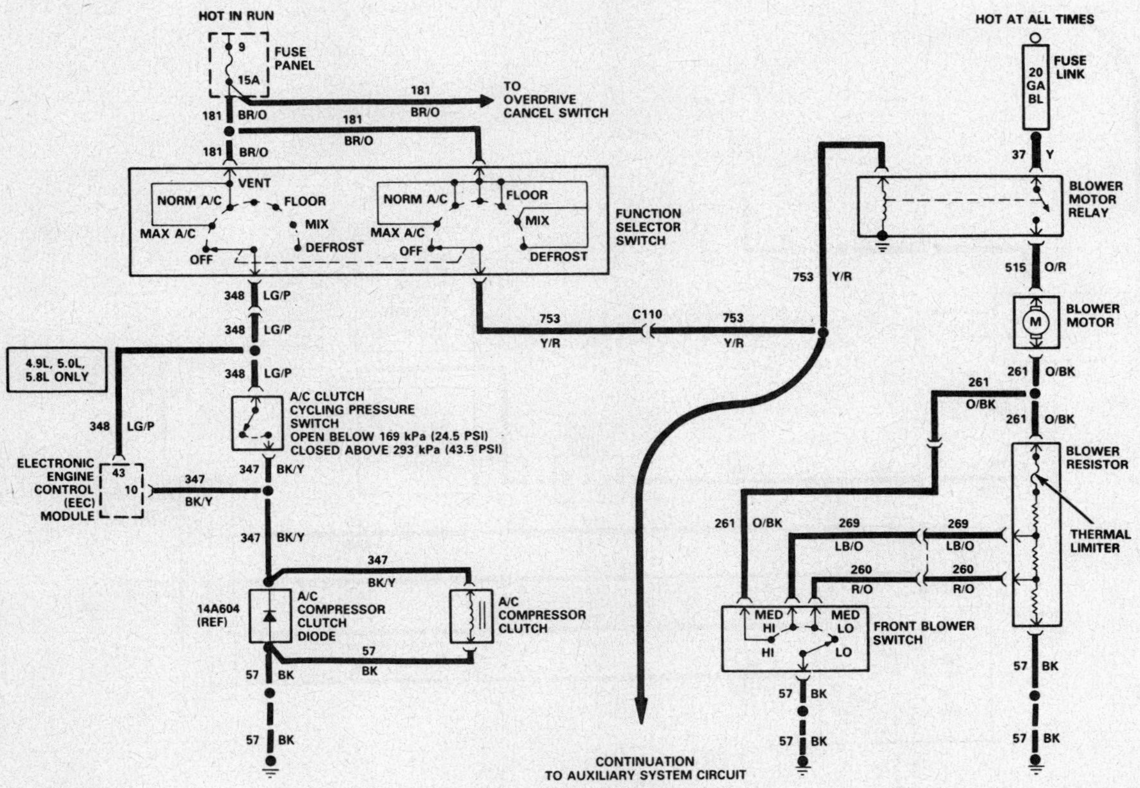
HOT IN RUN
9
15A
FUSE PANEL
181
BR/O
TO OVERDRIVE CANCEL SWITCH
VENT
NORM A/C
FLOOR
MIX
MAX A/C
DEFROST
OFF
FUNCTION SELECTOR SWITCH
348
LG/P
4.9L, 5.0L, 5.8L ONLY
A/C CLUTCH CYCLING PRESSURE SWITCH
OPEN BELOW 169 kPa (24.5 PSI)
CLOSED ABOVE 293 kPa (43.5 PSI)
ELECTRONIC ENGINE CONTROL (EEC) MODULE
43
10
347
BK/Y
14A604 (REF)
A/C COMPRESSOR CLUTCH DIODE
A/C COMPRESSOR CLUTCH
57
BK
753
Y/R
C110
CONTINUATION TO AUXILIARY SYSTEM CIRCUIT
HOT AT ALL TIMES
FUSE LINK
20 GA BL
37
Y
BLOWER MOTOR RELAY
515
O/R
BLOWER MOTOR
M
261
O/BK
BLOWER RESISTOR
THERMAL LIMITER
269
LB/O
260
R/O
MED HI
MED LO
HI
LO
FRONT BLOWER SWITCH

WIRE COLORS	WIRE COLORS (CONT.)	SYMBOLS
BK — BLACK	O/BK — ORANGE/BLACK	CONNECTOR
BK/Y — BLACK/YELLOW	O/R — ORANGE/RED	SPLICE
BR/O — BROWN/ORANGE	R/O — RED/ORANGE	GROUND
LB/O — LIGHT BLUE/ORANGE	Y — YELLOW	
LG/P — LIGHT GREEN/PURPLE	Y/R — YELLOW/RED	

Air conditioning electrical schematic—1990–91 E Series with auxiliary air conditioning

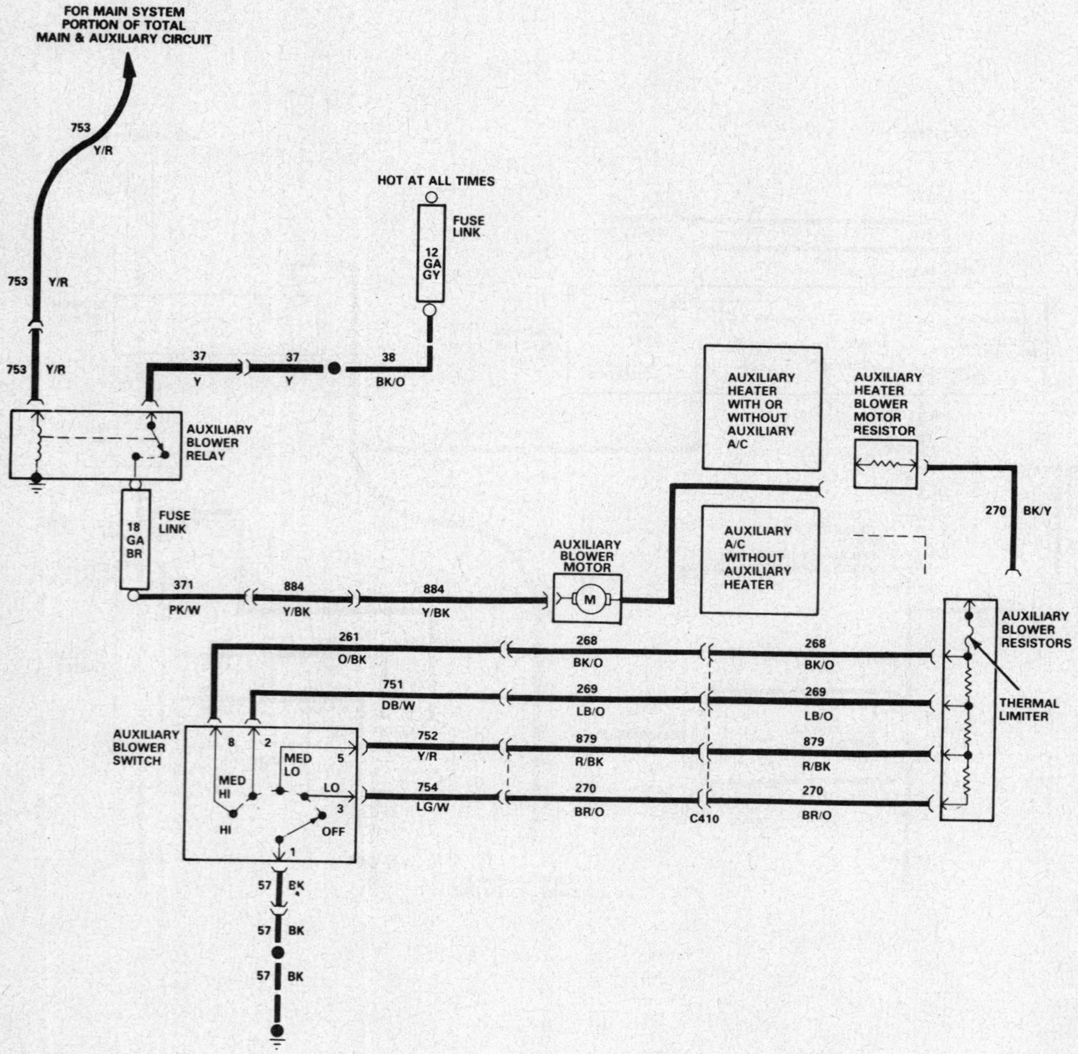
FOR MAIN SYSTEM
PORTION OF TOTAL
MAIN & AUXILIARY CIRCUIT
753
Y/R
HOT AT ALL TIMES
FUSE
LINK
12
GA
GY
37
Y
38
BK/O
AUXILIARY
BLOWER
RELAY
18
GA
BR
371
PK/W
884
Y/BK
AUXILIARY
BLOWER
MOTOR
AUXILIARY
HEATER
WITH OR
WITHOUT
AUXILIARY
A/C
AUXILIARY
A/C
WITHOUT
AUXILIARY
HEATER
AUXILIARY
HEATER
BLOWER
MOTOR
RESISTOR
270
BK/Y
261
O/BK
268
BK/O
751
DB/W
269
LB/O
752
Y/R
879
R/BK
754
LG/W
270
BR/O
C410
AUXILIARY
BLOWER
RESISTORS
THERMAL
LIMITER
AUXILIARY
BLOWER
SWITCH
MED
HI
MED
LO
LO
HI
OFF
57
BK

WIRE COLORS	WIRE COLORS (CONT.)	SYMBOLS
BK — BLACK BK/Y — BLACK/YELLOW BR/O — BROWN/ORANGE LB/O — LIGHT BLUE/ORANGE LG/P — LIGHT GREEN/PURPLE	O/BK — ORANGE/BLACK O/R — ORANGE/RED R/O — RED/ORANGE Y — YELLOW Y/R — YELLOW/RED	CONNECTOR SPLICE GROUND

Air conditioning electrical schematic—1990–91 E Series with auxiliary air conditioning

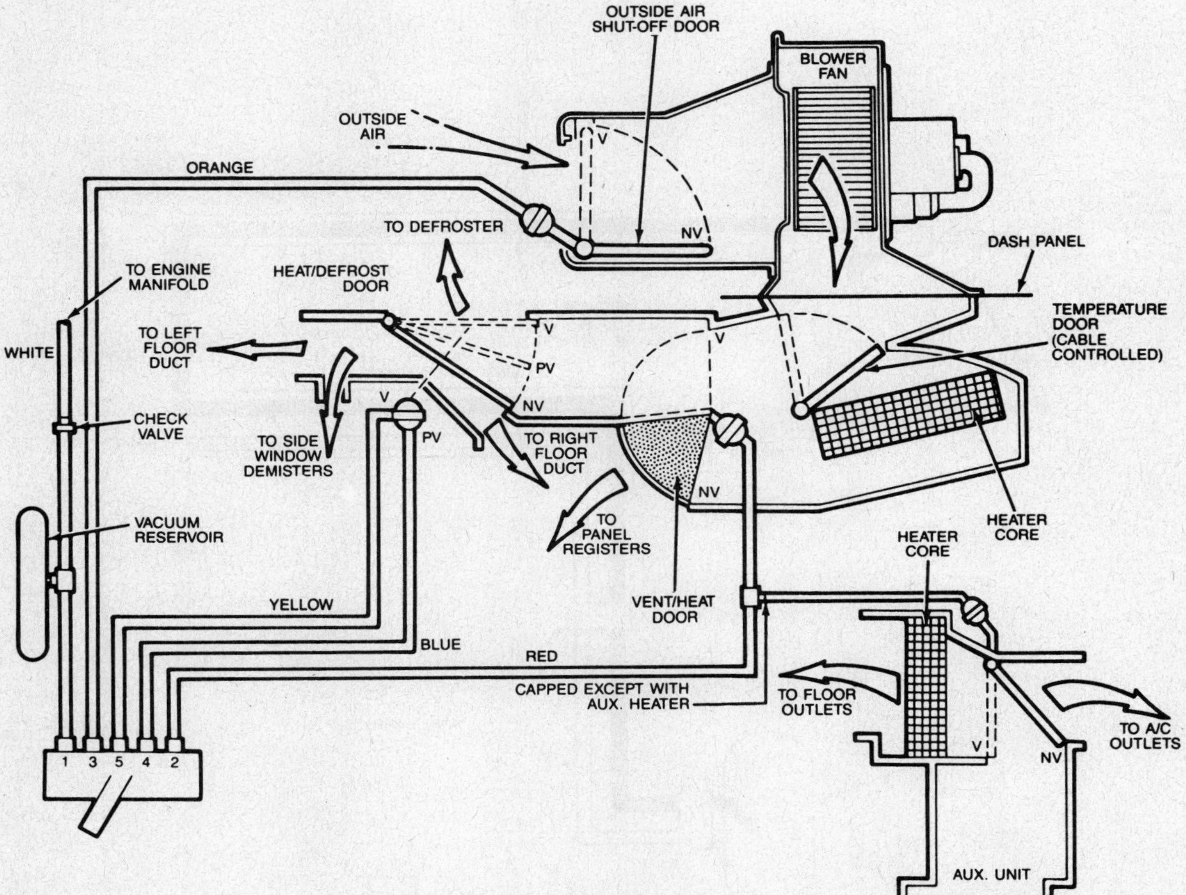
OUTSIDE AIR SHUT-OFF DOOR
BLOWER FAN
OUTSIDE AIR
V
ORANGE
TO DEFROSTER
NV
DASH PANEL
TO ENGINE MANIFOLD
HEAT/DEFROST DOOR
TEMPERATURE DOOR (CABLE CONTROLLED)
WHITE
TO LEFT FLOOR DUCT
V
PV
V
NV
CHECK VALVE
V
PV
TO SIDE WINDOW DEMISTERS
TO RIGHT FLOOR DUCT
NV
TO PANEL REGISTERS
VACUUM RESERVOIR
HEATER CORE
HEATER CORE
YELLOW
VENT/HEAT DOOR
BLUE
RED
CAPPED EXCEPT WITH AUX. HEATER
TO FLOOR OUTLETS
TO A/C OUTLETS
V
NV
1 3 5 4 2
AUX. UNIT
RECIRC. AIR

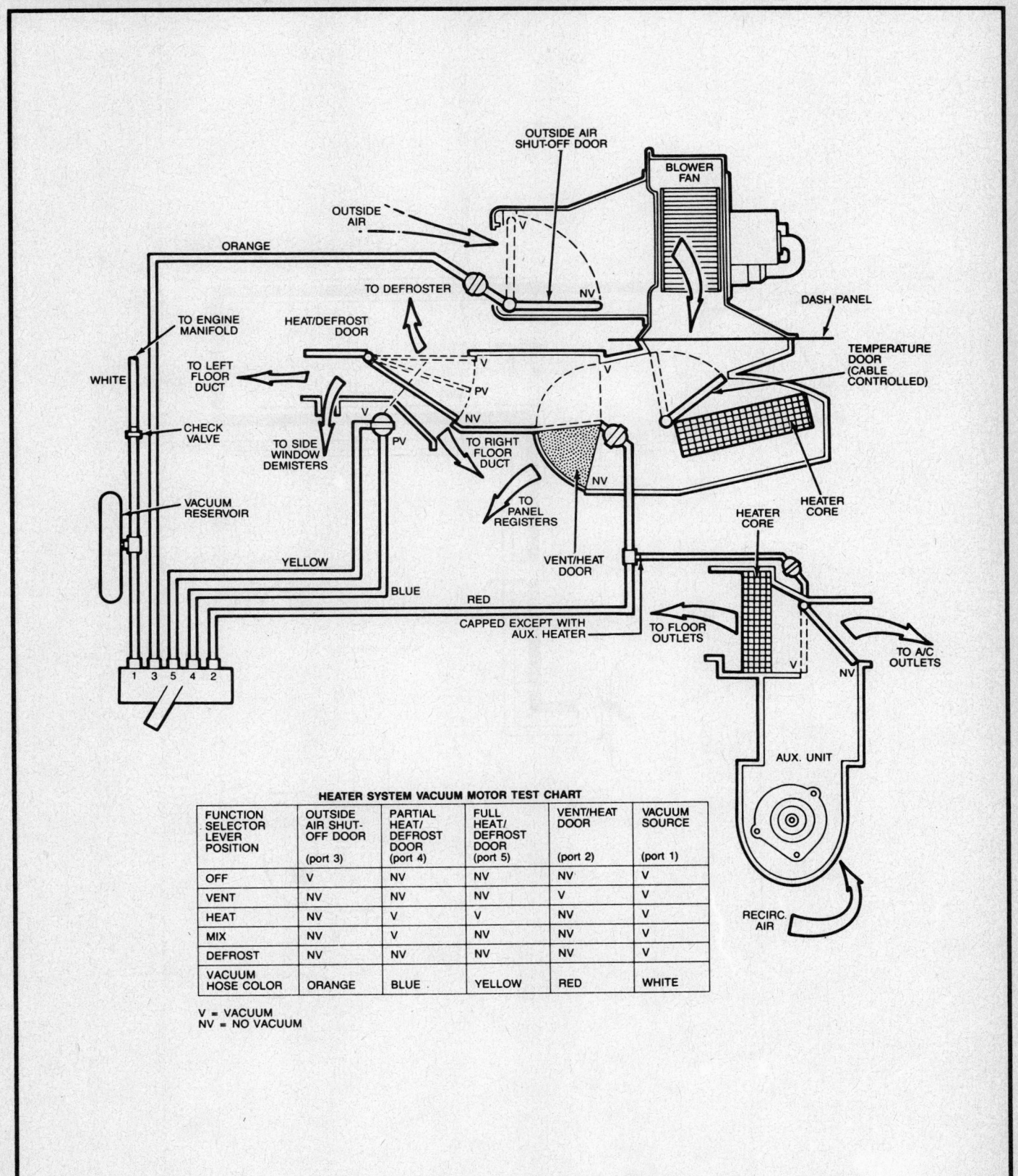

HEATER SYSTEM VACUUM MOTOR TEST CHART

FUNCTION SELECTOR LEVER POSITION	OUTSIDE AIR SHUT-OFF DOOR (port 3)	PARTIAL HEAT/ DEFROST DOOR (port 4)	FULL HEAT/ DEFROST DOOR (port 5)	VENT/HEAT DOOR (port 2)	VACUUM SOURCE (port 1)
OFF	V	NV	NV	NV	V
VENT	NV	NV	NV	V	V
HEAT	NV	V	V	NV	V
MIX	NV	V	NV	NV	V
DEFROST	NV	NV	NV	NV	V
VACUUM HOSE COLOR	ORANGE	BLUE	YELLOW	RED	WHITE

V = VACUUM
NV = NO VACUUM

Air conditioning system vacuum diagram—Aerostar

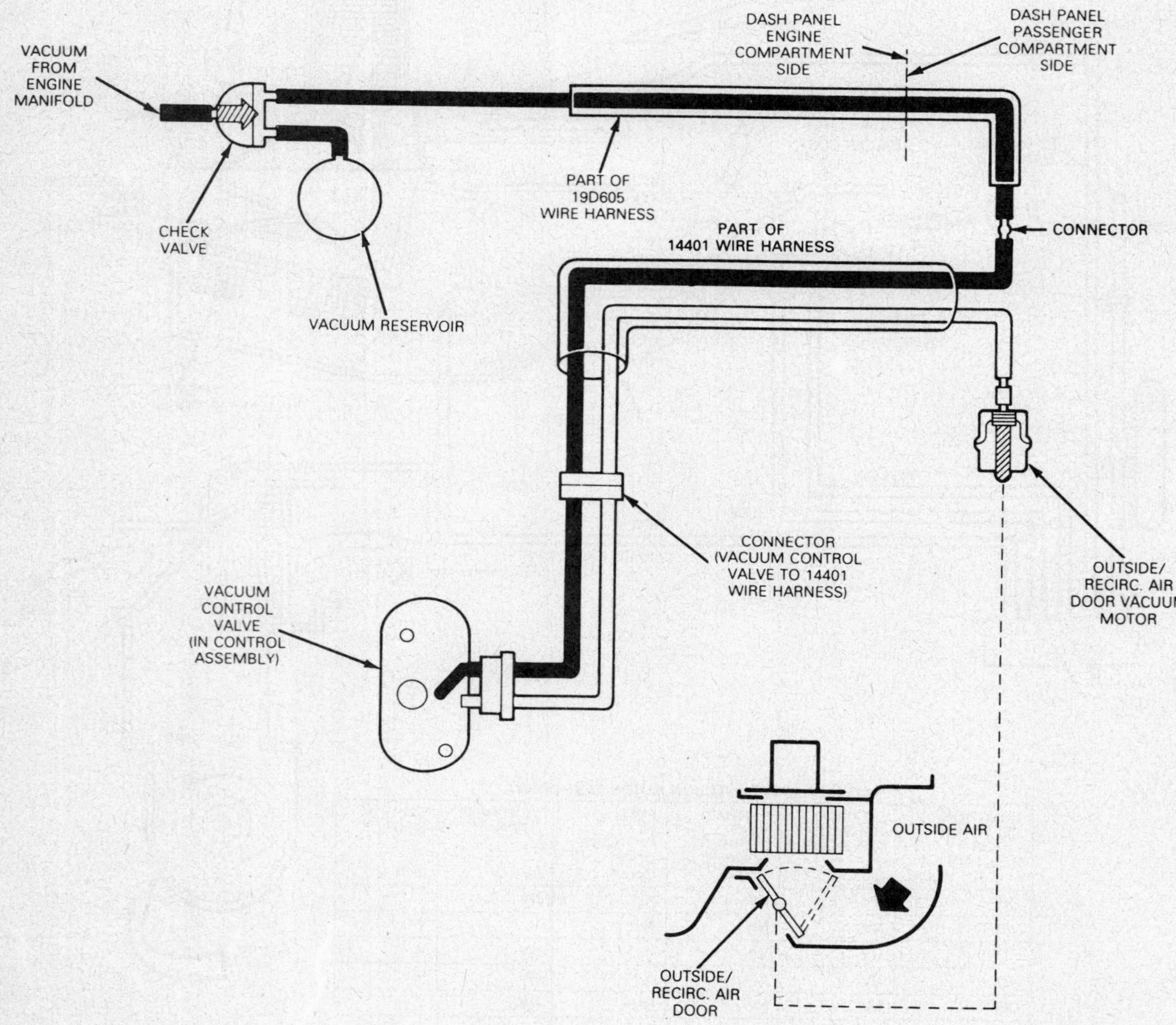
VACUUM FROM ENGINE MANIFOLD
CHECK VALVE
VACUUM RESERVOIR
PART OF 19D605 WIRE HARNESS
DASH PANEL ENGINE COMPARTMENT SIDE
DASH PANEL PASSENGER COMPARTMENT SIDE
CONNECTOR
PART OF 14401 WIRE HARNESS
CONNECTOR (VACUUM CONTROL VALVE TO 14401 WIRE HARNESS)
OUTSIDE/ RECIRC. AIR DOOR VACUUM MOTOR
VACUUM CONTROL VALVE (IN CONTROL ASSEMBLY)
OUTSIDE AIR
OUTSIDE/ RECIRC. AIR DOOR

Air conditioning system vacuum diagram—Bronco II, Explorer and Ranger

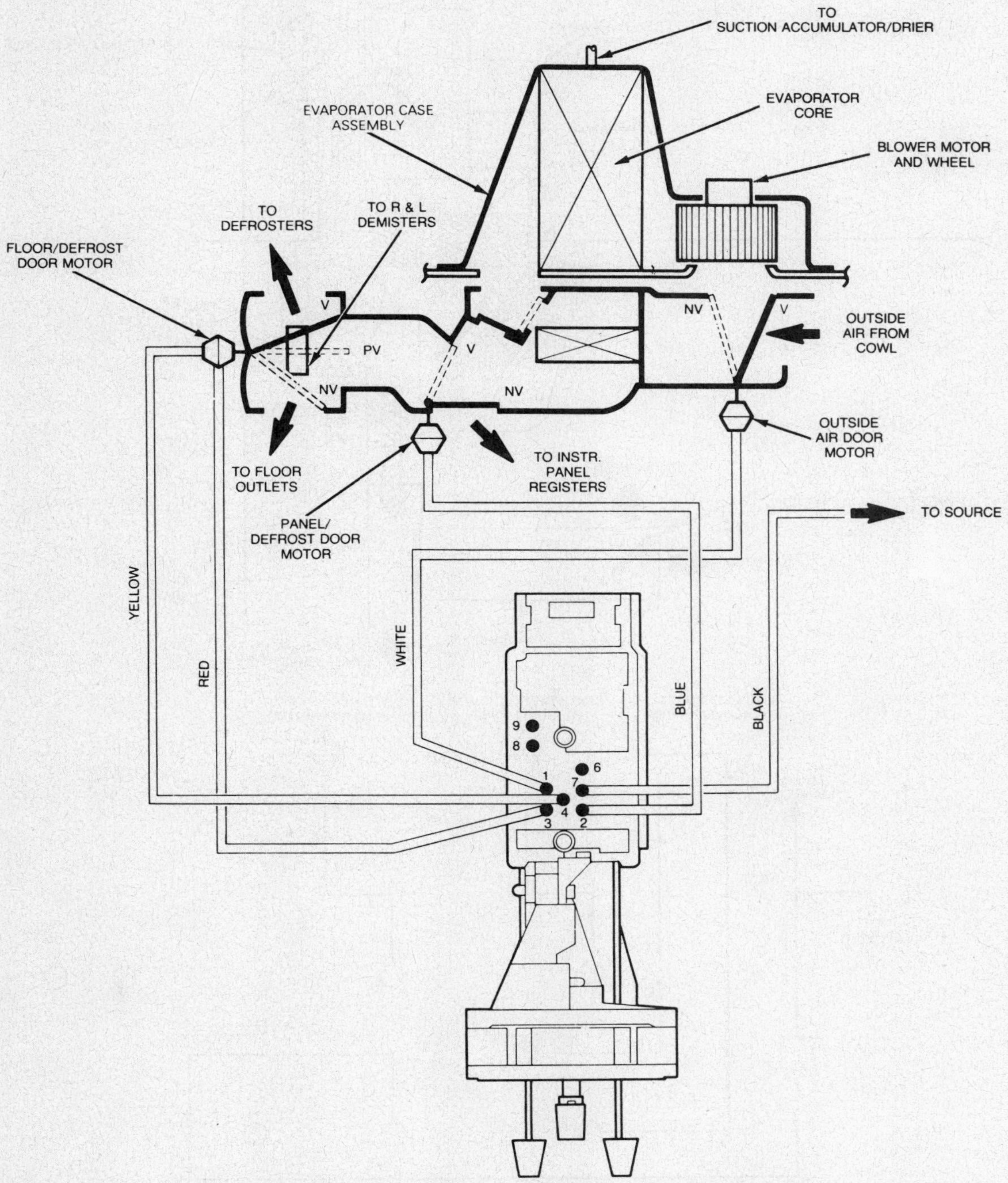
TO
SUCTION ACCUMULATOR/DRIER
EVAPORATOR CASE
ASSEMBLY
EVAPORATOR
CORE
BLOWER MOTOR
AND WHEEL
TO
DEFROSTERS
TO R & L
DEMISTERS
FLOOR/DEFROST
DOOR MOTOR
V
PV
NV
V
NV
NV
V
OUTSIDE
AIR FROM
COWL
OUTSIDE
AIR DOOR
MOTOR
TO FLOOR
OUTLETS
TO INSTR.
PANEL
REGISTERS
PANEL/
DEFROST DOOR
MOTOR
TO SOURCE
YELLOW
RED
WHITE
BLUE
BLACK
9
8
6
1
7
4
3
2

PORT	FUNCTION	LEVER POSITION						HOSE COLOR
		OFF	MAX A/C	NORM A/C	FLR	FLR/DEF	DEF	
1	O/S RECIRC. AIR	V	V	NV	NV	NV	NV	WHITE
2	PNL/DEF	NV	V	V	NV	NV	NV	BLUE
3	FLOOR	V	V	V	V	NV	NV	RED
4	FLR/DEF	V	V	V	V	PV	NV	YELLOW
7	SOURCE	V	V	V	V	V	V	BLACK

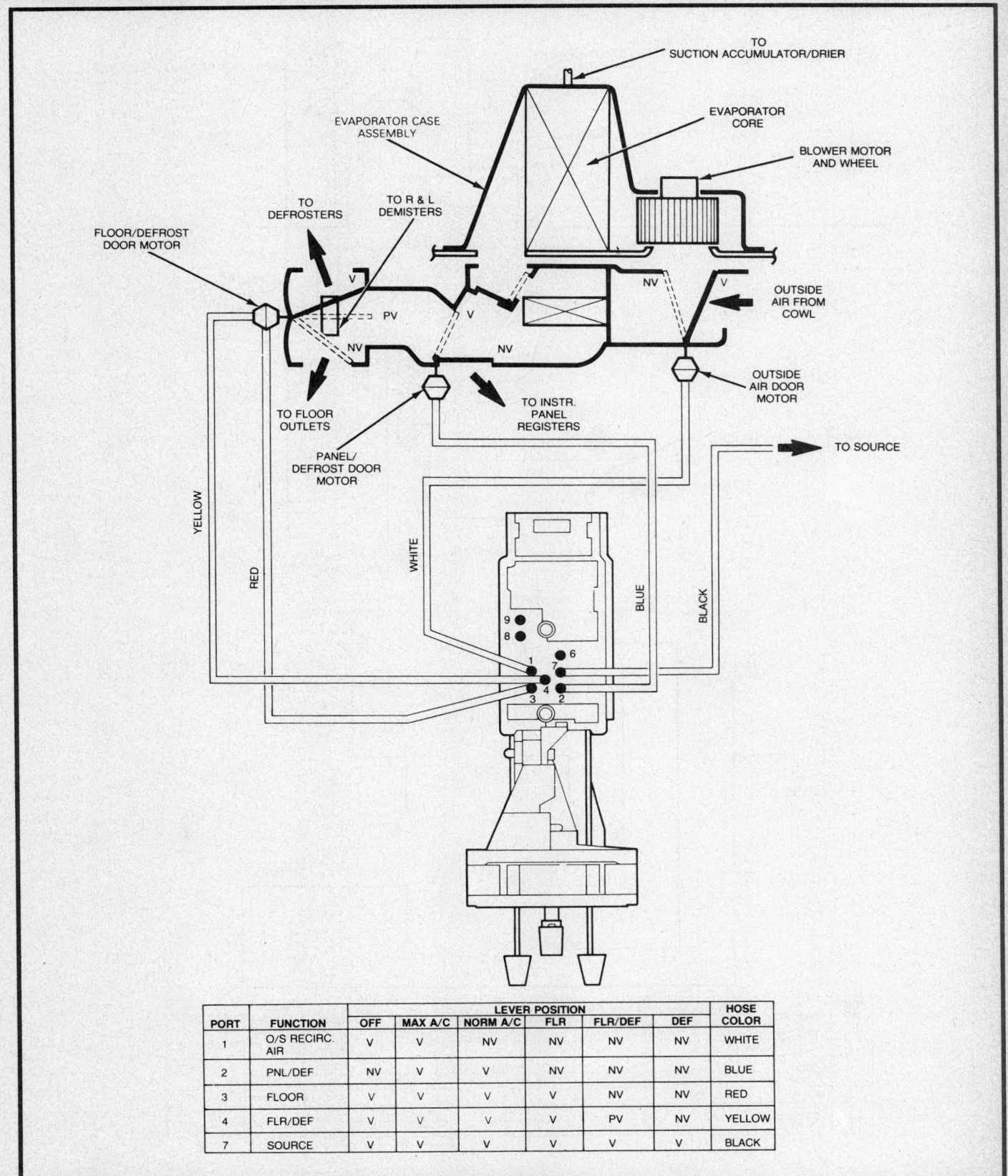

Air conditioning system vacuum diagram—Bronco and F Series

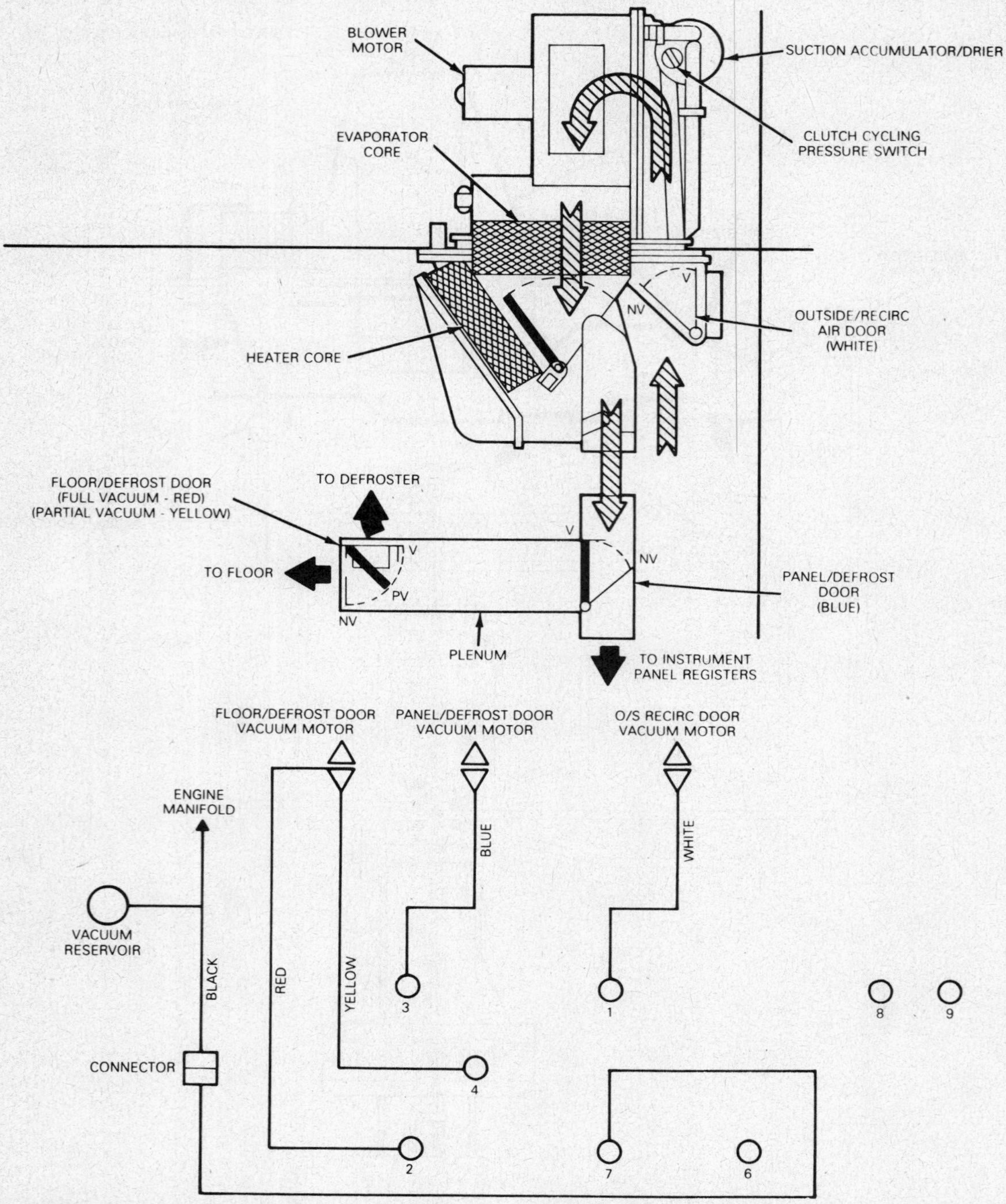
BLOWER MOTOR
SUCTION ACCUMULATOR/DRIER
EVAPORATOR CORE
CLUTCH CYCLING PRESSURE SWITCH
V
NV
OUTSIDE/RECIRC AIR DOOR (WHITE)
HEATER CORE
FLOOR/DEFROST DOOR (FULL VACUUM - RED) (PARTIAL VACUUM - YELLOW)
TO DEFROSTER
V
V
TO FLOOR
PV
NV
NV
PANEL/DEFROST DOOR (BLUE)
PLENUM
TO INSTRUMENT PANEL REGISTERS
FLOOR/DEFROST DOOR VACUUM MOTOR
PANEL/DEFROST DOOR VACUUM MOTOR
O/S RECIRC DOOR VACUUM MOTOR
ENGINE MANIFOLD
BLUE
WHITE
VACUUM RESERVOIR
BLACK
RED
YELLOW
3
1
8
9
CONNECTOR
4
2
7
6

PORT NO	FUNCTION	OFF	A/C		VENT	HEAT		
			MAX	NORM		FLOOR	FLR/DEF	DEFROST
1	OUTSIDE - RECIRC	V	V	NV	NV	NV	NV	NV
2	FLOOR - DEFROST (FULL)	V	V	V	V	V	-	NV
3	PANEL - DEFROST	NV	V	V	V	NV	-	NV
4	FLOOR - DEFROST (PARTIAL)	V	V	V	V	V	PV	NV
5	BLANK	-	-	-	-	-	-	
6	SEALED	-	-	-	-	-	-	
7	SOURCE	V	V	V	V	V	V	V

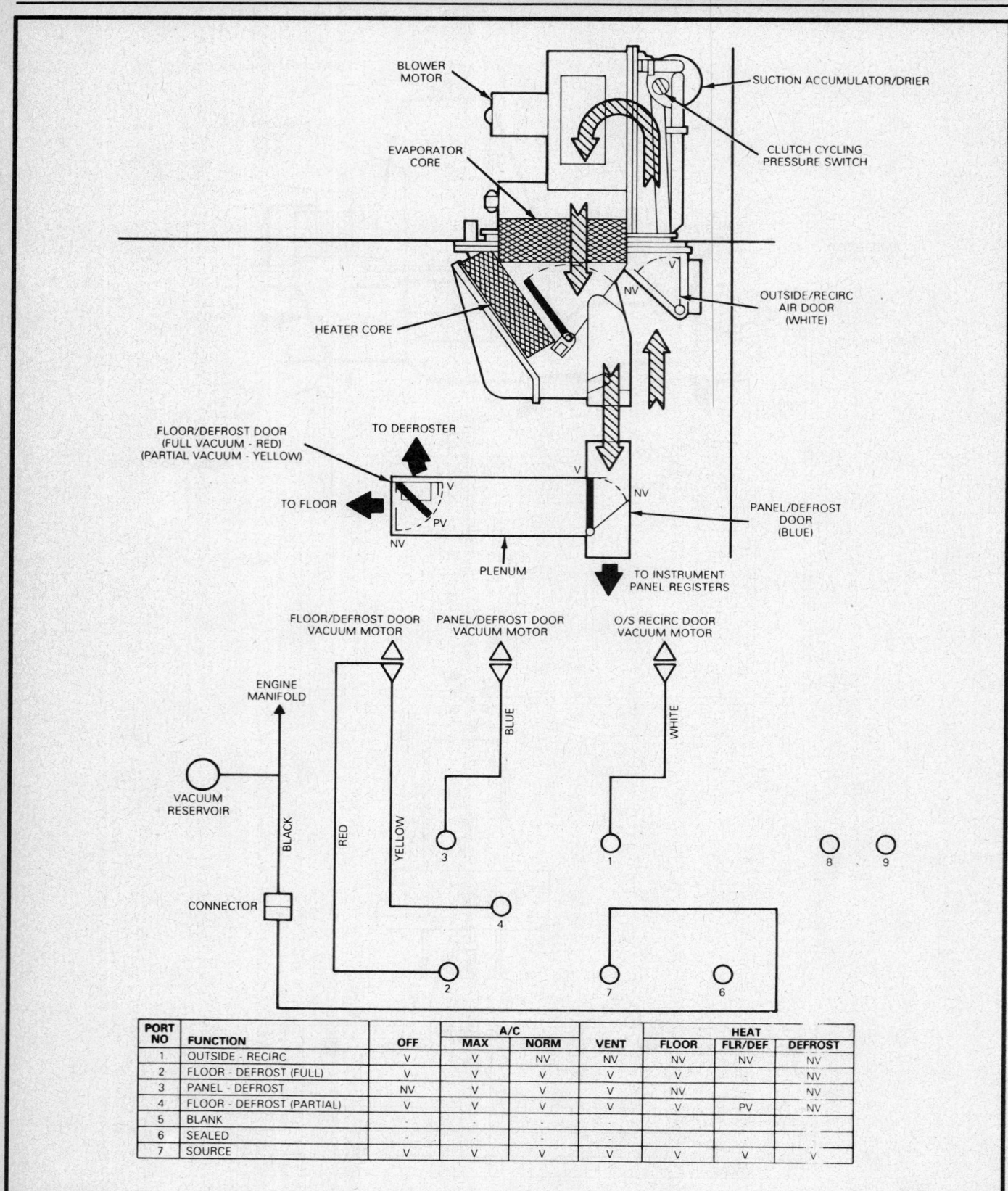

Air conditioning system vacuum diagram—E Series

10 GENERAL MOTORS CORPORATION 10

C/K SERIES (PICK-UP) • BLAZER/JIMMY • SUBURBAN • G SERIES (VAN) • ASTRO/SAFARI
S/T SERIES • S10 BLAZER/S15 JIMMY/BRAVADA • LUMINA APV • SILHOUETTE • TRANS SPORT

SPECIFICATIONS

VEHICLE IDENTIFICATION CHART

It is important for servicing and ordering parts to be certain of the vehicle and engine identification. The VIN (vehicle identification number) is a 17 digit number visible through the windshield on the driver's side of the dash and contains the vehicle and engine identification codes. The tenth digit indicates model year, and the eighth digit indicates engine code. It can be interpreted as follows:

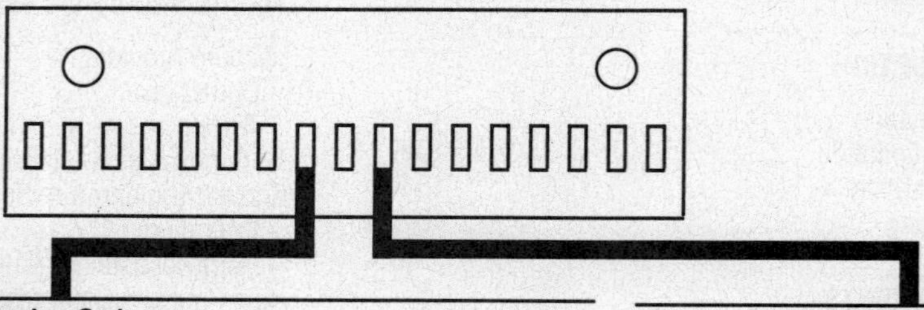

Engine Code

Code	Cu. In.	Liters	Cyl.	Fuel Sys.	Eng. Mfg.
E	151	2.5	4	TBI	CPC—North
R	173	2.8	6	TBI	CPC
D	191	3.1	6	TBI	CPC
8	262	4.3	6	TBI	CPC
B	262	4.3HO	6	TBI	CPC
H	305	5.0	8	TBI	CPC
K	350	5.7	8	TBI	CPC
C	379	6.2	8	Diesel	CPC
J	379	6.2	8	Diesel	CPC
N	454	7.4	8	TBI	CPC

Model Year

Code	Year
K	1989
L	1990
M	1991

REFRIGERANT CAPACITIES

Year	Model	Freon (oz.)	Oil (fl. oz.)	Type ⑯
1989	C/K Series (Pick-Up)	40	6	R-4
	Blazer and Jimmy	52	8	HR-6
		52	6	R-4
	Suburban	52 ①	8 ②	HR-6
		52 ①	6 ③	R-4
	G Series (Van)	56 ④ ⑤	10 ⑥	A-6
		56 ④ ⑤	6 ⑥	R-4
	S Series (Blazer and Pick-Up)	40	10	R-4
		40	10	V-5
	Astro and Safari	36 ⑦	6	R-4
		36 ⑦	8	V-5
1990	C/K Series (Pick-Up)	40	6	R-4
	Blazer and Jimmy	50	6	R-4
	Suburban	50 ⑧	6 ⑨	R-4
	G Series (Van)	48 ⑩ ⑪	10 ⑥	A-6
		48 ⑩ ⑪	6 ⑥	R-4
	S Series (Blazer and Pick-Up)	40	10	R-4
		40	10	V-5

REFRIGERANT CAPACITIES

Year	Model	Freon (oz.)	Oil (fl. oz.)	Type ⑯
1990	Astro and Safari	48 ⑦	8	HR-6
		48 ⑦	8	V-5
	Lumina APV, Silhouette and Trans Sport	50	8	V-5
1991	C/K Series (Pick-Up)	40	6	R-4
	Blazer and Jimmy	48	8	HR-6
		48	6	R-4
	Suburban	36 ⑫	8 ⑬	HR-6
		36 ⑫	6 ⑭	R-4
	G Series (Van)	48 ⑩ ⑪	10 ⑥	A-6
		48 ⑩ ⑪	6 ⑥	R-4
	S Series (Blazer and Pick-Up)	40	6	R-4
		40	9	V-5
	Astro and Safari	36 ⑦	8 ⑮	HR-6
	Lumina APV, Silhouette and Trans Sport	50	8	V-5
	Bravada	45	6	R-4

① Rear system—84
② Rear system—11
③ Rear system—9
④ Except 7.4L engine, Rear system—72
⑤ 7.4L engine Front—44
Rear—64
⑥ Rear system A-6 13
R-4 9
⑦ Rear system—60
⑧ Rear system—82
⑨ Rear system—9
⑩ Except 7.4L engine, rear system—69
⑪ 7.4L engine Front—40
Rear—64
⑫ Rear system—72
⑬ Rear system—8
⑭ Rear system—9
⑮ Rear system—10.5
⑯ Compressor

AIR CONDITIONING BELT TENSION CHART

Year	Model	Engine (L)	Belt Type	Specification New	Specification Used
1989	C/K Series (Pick-Up)	4.3L	Serpentine	①	①
		5.7L	Serpentine	①	①
		6.2L	Serpentine	①	①
		7.4L	Serpentine	①	①
	Suburban, Blazer and Jimmy	5.7L	Serpentine	①	①
		6.2L	Serpentine	①	①
		7.4L	Serpentine	①	①
	G Series (Van)	4.3L	Serpentine	①	①
		5.0L	Serpentine	①	①
		5.7L	Serpentine	①	①
		6.2L	Serpentine	①	①
		7.4L	Serpentine	①	①
	S Series (Blazer, Jimmy and Pick-Up)	2.5L	Serpentine	①	①
		2.8L	Serpentine	①	①
		4.3L	Serpentine	①	①
	Astro and Safari	2.5L	Serpentine	①	①
		4.3L	Serpentine	①	①
1990	C/K Series (Pick-Up)	4.3L	Serpentine	①	①
		5.0L	Serpentine	①	①
		5.7L	Serpentine	①	①
		6.2L	Serpentine	①	①
		7.4L	Serpentine	①	①

AIR CONDITIONING BELT TENSION CHART

Year	Model	Engine (L)	Belt Type	Specification New	Specification Used
1990	Suburban, Blazer and Jimmy	5.7L	Serpentine	①	①
		6.2L	Serpentine	①	①
		7.4L	Serpentine	①	①
	G Series (Van)	4.3L	Serpentine	①	①
		5.0L	Serpentine	①	①
		5.7L	Serpentine	①	①
		6.2L	Serpentine	①	①
		7.4L	Serpentine	①	①
	S Series (Blazer, Jimmy and Pick-Up)	2.5L	Serpentine	①	①
		2.8L	Serpentine	①	①
		4.3L	Serpentine	①	①
	Astro and Safari	2.5L	Serpentine	①	①
		4.3L	Serpentine	①	①
	Lumina APV, Silhouette and Trans Sport	3.1L	Serpentine	①	①
1991	C/K Series (Pick-Up)	4.3L	Serpentine	①	①
		5.0L	Serpentine	①	①
		5.7L	Serpentine	①	①
		6.2L	Serpentine	①	①
		7.4L	Serpentine	①	①
	Suburban, Blazer and Jimmy	5.7L	Serpentine	①	①
		6.2L	Serpentine	①	①
		7.4L	Serpentine	①	①
	G Series (Van)	4.3L	Serpentine	①	①
		5.0L	Serpentine	①	①
		5.7L	Serpentine	①	①
		6.2L	Serpentine	①	①
		7.4L	Serpentine	①	①
	S Series (Blazer, Jimmy and Pick-Up)	2.5L	Serpentine	①	①
		2.8L	Serpentine	①	①
		4.3L	Serpentine	①	①
	Astro and Safari	4.3L	Serpentine	①	①
	Lumina APV. Silhouette and Trans Sport	3.1L	Serpentine	①	①
	Bravada	4.3L	Serpentine	①	①

① Automatic Tensioner—No adjustment necessary

SYSTEM DESCRIPTION

General Information

The heater and air conditioning systems are controlled manually. The manual system controls can be cable-actuated or actuated through a vacuum switching valve and vacuum actuators.

The heating system provides heating, ventilation and defrosting for the windshield and, on some vehicles, the side windows. The heater core is a heat exchanger supplied with coolant from the engine cooling system. Temperature is controlled by the temperature valve which moves an air door that directs air flow through the heater core for more heat or bypasses the heater core for less heat.

The mode doors may be cable operated or controlled by vacuum actuators. On the vacuum controlled system, the mode selector on the control panel directs engine vacuum to the actuators. The position of the mode doors determines whether air flows from the floor, panel, defrost or panel and defrost ducts (bi-level mode).

There are 2 basic air conditioning refrigerant systems, employing 4 types of compressors used on General Motors Pick-Up and Van air conditioning sytems. The R-4, HR-6 and A-6 compressors, are used on Cycling Clutch Orifice Tube (CCOT) systems. On CCOT systems, the compressor cycles on and off according to system demands. The compressor driveshaft is driven by the serpentine belt when the electro-magnetic clutch is engaged. System pressure is controlled by the pressure cycling switch. The R-4 compressor uses a 4 cylinder radial opposed design. The HR-6 compressor is a fixed displacement axial compressor consisting of 3 double-ended pistons actuated by a swash plate shaft assembly. The A-6 compressor uses a 6 cylinder axial configuration.

The V-5 compressor, used on the Variable Displacement Orifice Tube (VDOT) system, is designed to meet the demands of the air conditioning system without cycling. The compressor employs a variable angle wobble plate controlling the displacement of 5 axially oriented cylinders. Displacement is controlled by a bellows actuated control valve located in the rear head of the compressor. The electro-magnetic compressor clutch connects the compressor shaft to the serpentine drive belt when the coil is energized.

Service Valve Locations

The high-side fitting is normally located in the refrigerant line near the compressor.

The low-side fitting is normally located on the accumulator or in the condenser-to-evaporator refrigerant line.

System Discharging

R-12 refrigerant is a chlorofluorocarbon which, when released into the atmosphere, can contribute to the depletion on the ozone layer in the upper atmosphere. Ozone filters out harmful radiation from the sun. In order to protect the ozone layer, an approved R-12 Recovery/Recycling machine that meets SAE standards should be employed when discharging the system. Follow the operating instructions provided with the approved equipment exactly to properly discharge the system.

System Evacuating

If the air conditioning system has been opened to the atmosphere, it should be air and moisture free before being recharged with refrigerant. Moisture and air mixed with refrigerant will raise the compressor head pressure, possibly damage the system's components and will reduce the performance of the system. In addition, air and moisture in the system can lead to internal corrosion of the system components. Moisture will boil at normal room temperature when exposed to a vacuum. To evacuate or rid the system of air and moisture:

1. Leak test the system and repair any leaks found.
2. Connect an approved charging station, recovery/recycling machine or manifold gauge set and vacuum pump to the discharge and suction ports. The red hose is normally connected to the discharge (high pressure) line. The blue hose is connected to the suction (low pressure) line. If using a manifold gauge set, the center (usually yellow) hose is connected to the charging station or recovery/recycling machine.
3. Open the discharge and suction ports and start the vacuum pump. If the pump is not able to pull at least 26 in. Hg of vacuum there is a leak that must be repaired before evacuation can occur.
4. Once the system has reached at least 26 in. Hg of vacuum, allow the system to evacuate for at least 10 minutes. The longer the system is evacuated, the more moisture will be removed.
5. Close all valves and turn the pump off. If the system loses more than 2 in. Hg of vacuum after 15 minutes, there is a leak that should be repaired.

System Charging

1. Connect an approved charging station, recovery/recycling machine or manifold gauge set to the discharge and suction ports. The red hose is normally connected to the discharge (high pressure) line, and the blue hose is connected to the suction (low pressure) line. If using a manifold gauge set, the center (usually yellow) hose is connected to the charging station or recovery/recycling machine.
2. Follow the instructions provided with the equipment and charge the system with the specified amount of refrigerant.

SYSTEM COMPONENTS

Radiator

REMOVAL AND INSTALLATION

Except G Series Van With 6.2L Diesel Engine and Lumina APV, Silhouette and Trans Sport

1. Disconnect the negative battery cable.
2. Drain the engine coolant into a clean container for reuse.
3. Remove the upper and lower fan shrouds.
4. Remove the upper insulators.
5. Disconnect the radiator inlet and outlet hoses.
6. If equipped with an automatic transmission, disconnect the transmission fluid cooler lines from the radiator.
7. If equipped, disconnect the engine oil cooler lines.
8. Disconnect the coolant overflow hose from the filler neck.
9. Remove the radiator from the vehicle.
10. Remove the lower insulators, as required.

To install:

11. If removed, install the lower radiator insulators.
12. Install the radiator in the vehicle.
13. If equipped, connect the engine oil cooler lines.
14. If equipped with an automatic transmission, connect the transmission fluid cooler lines to the radiator.
15. Connect the radiator inlet and outlet hoses.
16. Install the upper insulators.
17. Install the lower and upper fan shrouds.
18. Connect the coolant overflow hose to the filler neck.
19. Connect the negative battery cable.
20. Fill cooling system and check for leaks. Start the engine and allow to come to normal operating temperature. Recheck for leaks. Top-up coolant.

G Series Van With 6.2L Diesel Engine

1. Disconnect the negative battery cable.
2. Drain the engine coolant into a clean container for reuse.
3. Remove the air intake snorkel.
4. Remove the windshield washer bottle.
5. Disconnect the hood release cable.
6. Remove the upper fan shroud.
7. Disconnect the upper radiator hose from the radiator.
8. Disconnect the transmission cooler lines from the radiator.
9. Disconnect the low coolant sensor electrical connector.
10. Disconnect the overflow hose from the radiator.

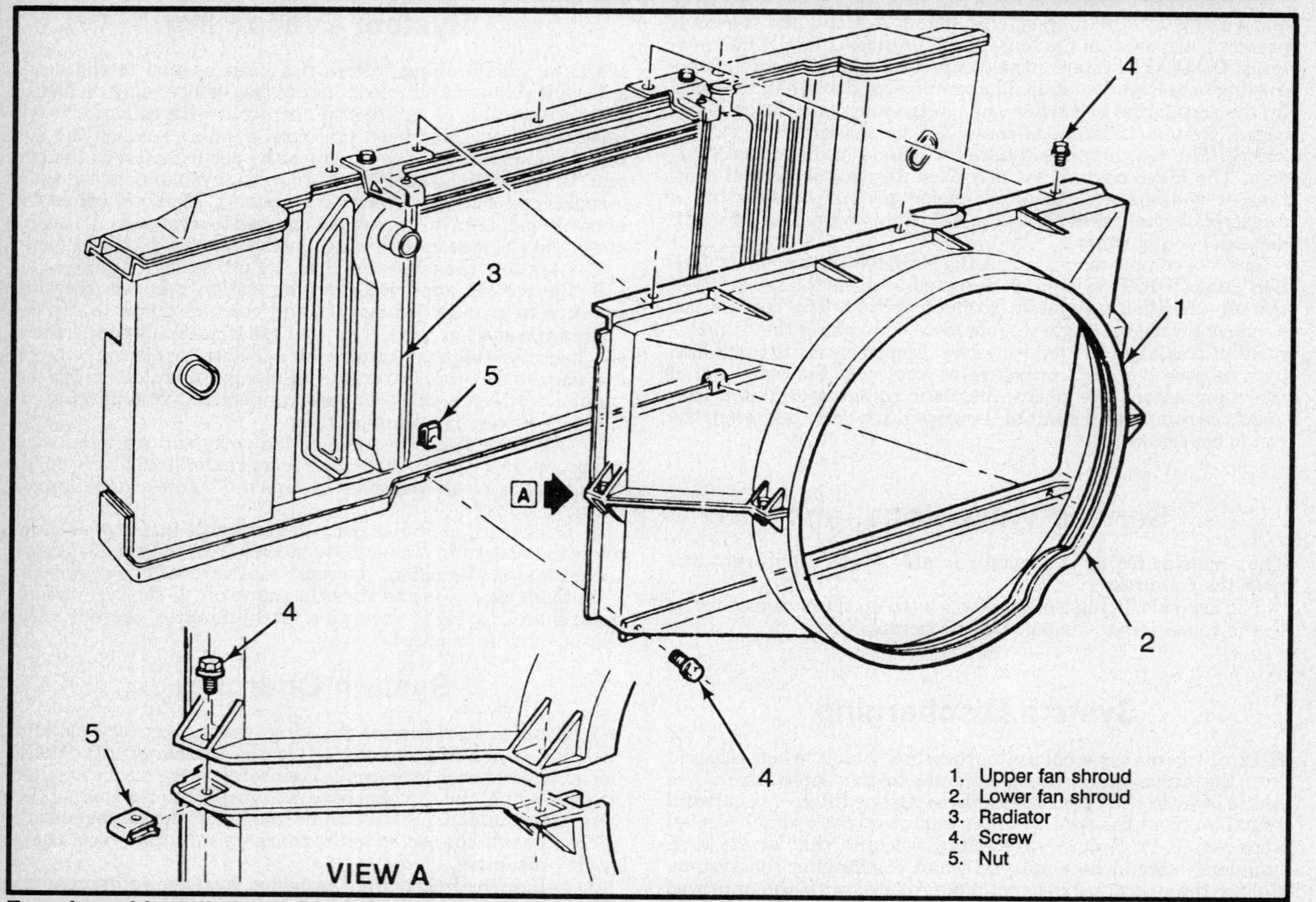
4
3
1
5
A
4
2
5
4
VIEW A
1. Upper fan shroud
2. Lower fan shroud
3. Radiator
4. Screw
5. Nut

Fan shroud installation – C/K Pick-Up with 6.2L or 7.4L engine shown

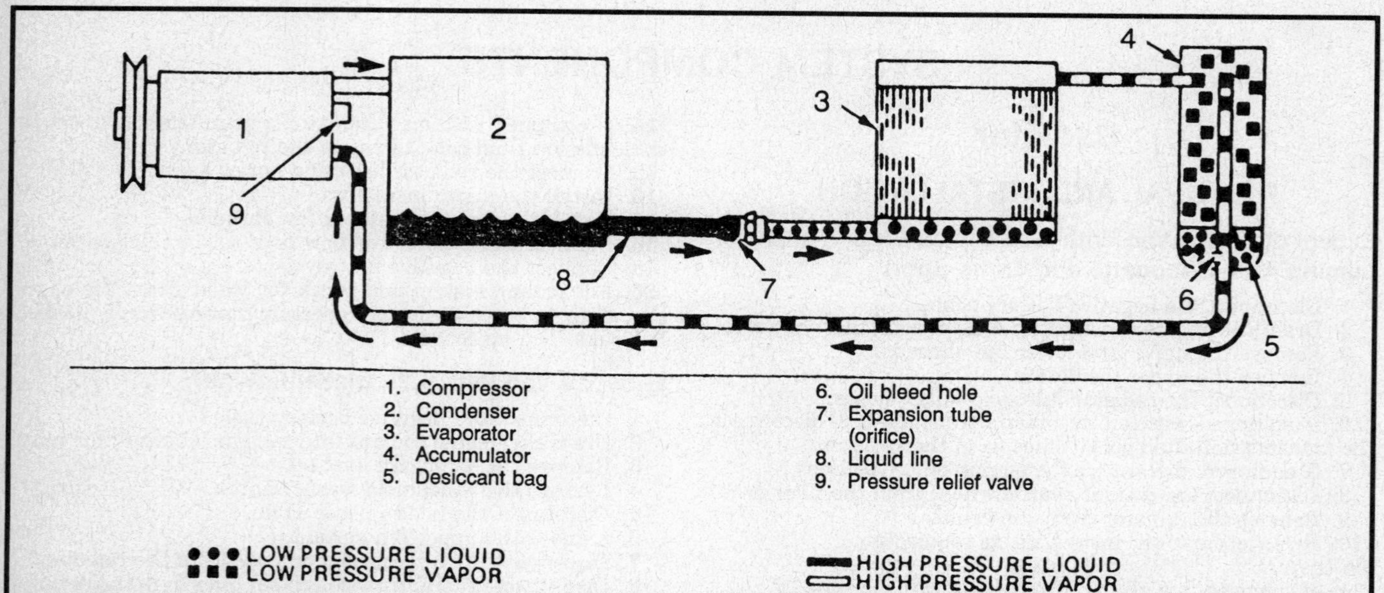
1
2
3
4
9
8
7
6
5
1. Compressor
2. Condenser
3. Evaporator
4. Accumulator
5. Desiccant bag
6. Oil bleed hole
7. Expansion tube (orifice)
8. Liquid line
9. Pressure relief valve
LOW PRESSURE LIQUID
LOW PRESSURE VAPOR
HIGH PRESSURE LIQUID
HIGH PRESSURE VAPOR

Air conditioning system refrigerant cycle

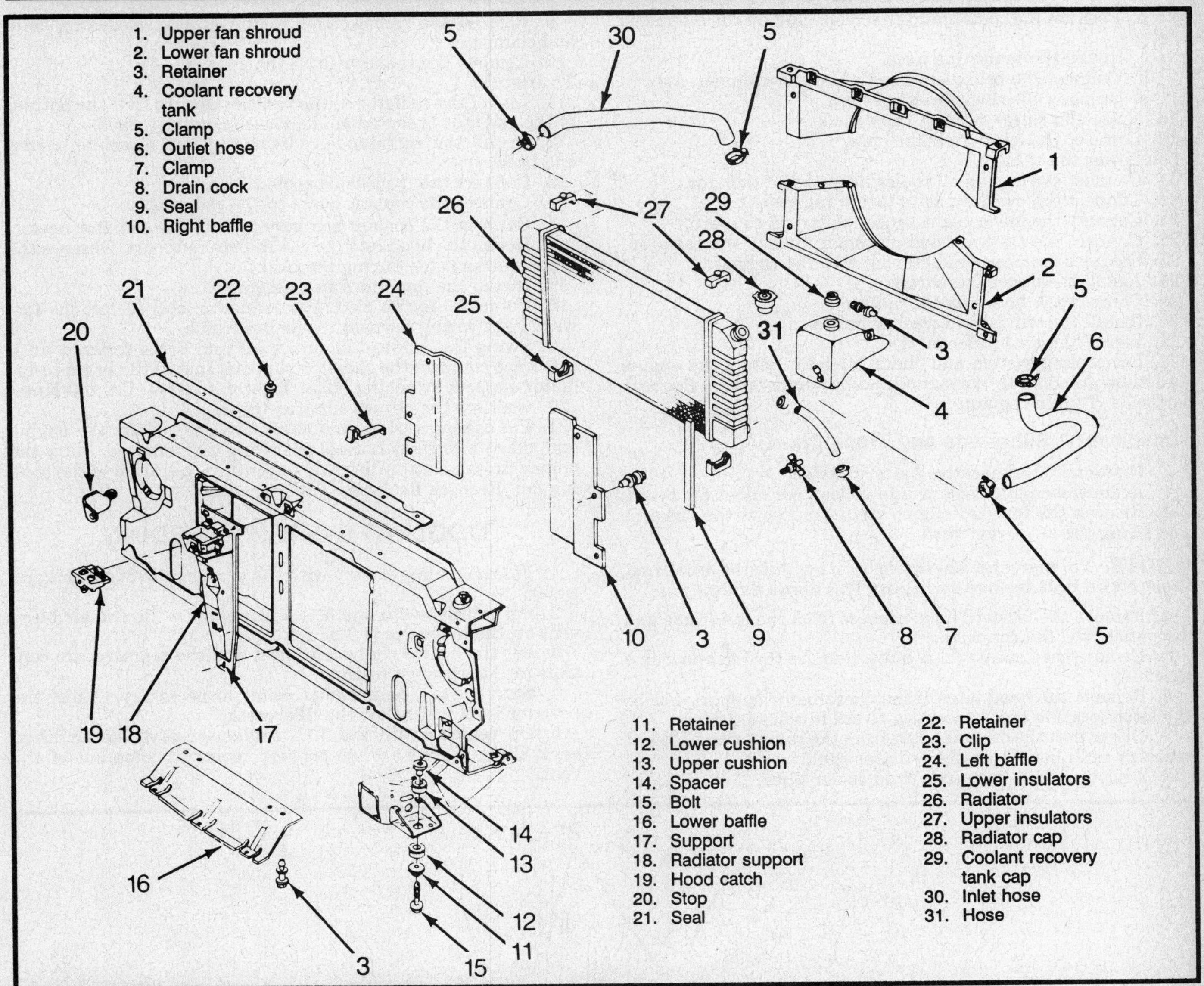
1. Upper fan shroud
2. Lower fan shroud
3. Retainer
4. Coolant recovery tank
5. Clamp
6. Outlet hose
7. Clamp
8. Drain cock
9. Seal
10. Right baffle
11. Retainer
12. Lower cushion
13. Upper cushion
14. Spacer
15. Bolt
16. Lower baffle
17. Support
18. Radiator support
19. Hood catch
20. Stop
21. Seal
22. Retainer
23. Clip
24. Left baffle
25. Lower insulators
26. Radiator
27. Upper insulators
28. Radiator cap
29. Coolant recovery tank cap
30. Inlet hose
31. Hose

Radiator and related components—S Series and Bravada shown

11. Raise and safely support the vehicle.
12. Disconnect the lower radiator hose from the radiator.
13. Lower the vehicle.
14. Remove the master cylinder from the brake booster by performing the following:
    a. Disconnect the brake lines from the master cylinder.

NOTE: Cover the ends of the brake lines and the brake line fittings on the master cylinder to prevent the entry of dirt and the excess loss of brake fluid.

    b. Remove the master cylinder mounting nuts.
    c. Position the combination valve bracket aside.
    d. Remove the master cylinder from the vehicle.
15. Remove the radiator from the vehicle.

To install:

16. Position the radiator in the vehicle.
17. Install the master cylinder on the brake booster by performing the following:
    a. Place the master cylinder in position.

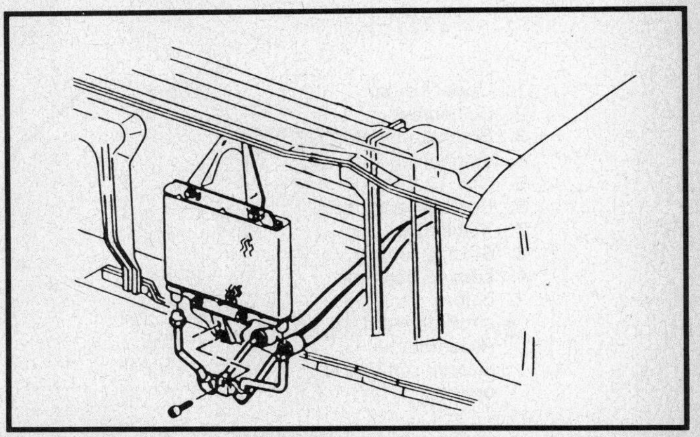

Auxiliary engine oil cooler

b. Position the combination valve bracket on the mounting studs.
c. Install the mounting nuts.
d. Connect the brake lines to the master cylinder.
e. Properly bleed the brake system.
18. Raise and safely support the vehicle.
19. Connect the lower radiator hose.
20. Lower the vehicle.
21. Connect the engine oil cooler lines to the radiator.
22. Connect the overflow hose to the radiator.
21. Connect the low coolant sensor electrical connector.
22. Connect the transmission oil cooler lines to the radiator.
23. Connect the upper radiator hose to the radiator.
24. Install the upper fan shroud.
25. Connect the hood release cable.
26. Install the windshield washer bottle.
27. Install the air intake snorkel.
28. Fill cooling system and check for leaks. Start the engine and allow to come to normal operating temperature. Recheck for leaks. Top-up coolant.

Lumina APV, Silhouette and Trans Sport

1. Disconnect the negative battery cable.
2. Drain the engine coolant into a clean container for reuse.
3. Remove the forward engine strut bracket at the radiator and swing the strut rearward.

NOTE: To prevent shearing of the rubber bushing, loosen the bolt before swinging the strut aside.

4. Remove the forward light harness from the fan frame and disconnect the fan connector.
5. Remove the fan attaching bolts. Remove the fan and frame assembly.
6. Remove the hood latch from the radiator support. Scribe the latch location before removal to aid in reinstallation.
7. Disconnect the coolant hoses from the radiator and coolant recovery tank hose from the radiator neck.
8. Disconnect the transaxle fluid cooler lines.
9. Remove the radiator-to-radiator support attaching bolts and clamps.
10. Remove the radiator from the vehicle.

To install:

11. Install the radiator in the vehicle. Ensure that the bottom of the radiator is seated in the lower mounting pads.
12. Install the radiator-to-radiator support attaching clamp and bolts.
13. Connect the transaxale cooler lines.
14. Connect the coolant hoses to the radiator.
15. Connect the coolant recovery hose to the radiator neck.
16. Install the hood latch to the radiator support. Observe the matchmarks made during removal.
17. Install the fan and frame assembly.
18. Connect the fan electrical connector and install the forward light wiring harness to the fan frame.
19. Swing the forward engine strut and brace forward until the brace contacts the radiator support. Install the brace-to-radiator support attaching bolts. Tighten to 37 ft. lbs. (50 Nm).
20. Connect the negative battery cable.
21. Fill cooling system and check for leaks. Start the engine and allow to come to normal operating temperature. Allow the engine to warm up sufficiently to confirm operation of the cooling fan. Recheck for leaks. Top-up coolant.

COOLING SYSTEM BLEEDING

1. Fill the cooling system with the proper ratio of coolant and water.
2. On vehicles with the 3.1L engine, open the the air bleed vent on the bypass pipe 2 or 3 turns.
3. Set the heater controls to heat and the temperature controls to the warmest setting.
4. Start the engine and add coolant, as necessary, to keep the radiator level just below the filler neck.
5. On vehicles with the 3.1L engine, observe the air bleed vent. Close the vent when coolant begins to come out of the vent.

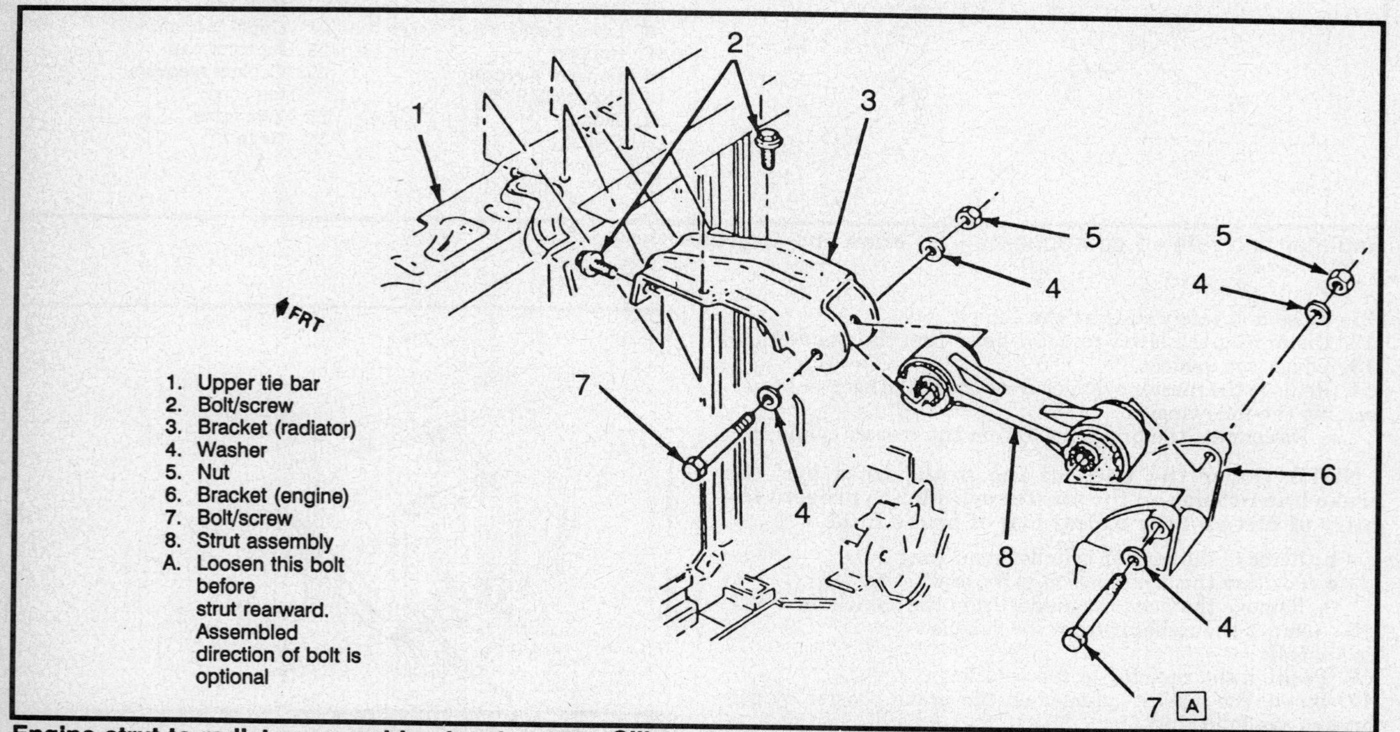
1
2
3
4
5
6
7
8
FRT
1. Upper tie bar
2. Bolt/screw
3. Bracket (radiator)
4. Washer
5. Nut
6. Bracket (engine)
7. Bolt/screw
8. Strut assembly
A. Loosen this bolt before strut rearward. Assembled direction of bolt is optional
A

Engine strut-to-radiator assembly—Lumina APV, Silhouette and Trans Sport

6. Allow the engine to come to normal operating temperature; indicated by the upper radiator hose becoming hot.
7. The air coming out of the heater should be getting hot.
8. Check the coolant level in the radiator and coolant reservoir. Install the radiator cap, turning it until the arrows align with the overflow tube.

Electric Cooling Fan

TESTING

Lumina APV, Silhouette and Trans Sport

1. Check fuse or circuit breaker for power to cooling fan motor.
2. Remove connector(s) at cooling fan motor(s). Connect jumper wire and apply battery voltage to the positive terminal of the cooling fan motor.
3. Using an ohmmeter, check for continuity in cooling fan motor.

NOTE: Remove the cooling fan connector at the fan motor before performing continuity checks. Perform continuity check of the motor windings only. The cooling fan control circuit is connected electrically to the ECM through the cooling fan relay. Ohmmeter battery voltage must not be applied to the ECM.

4. Ensure proper continuity of cooling fan motor ground circuit at chassis ground connector.

REMOVAL AND INSTALLATION

Lumina APV, Silhouette and Trans Sport

1. Disconnect the negative battery cable.
2. Remove the forward engine strut bracket at the radiator and swing the strut rearward.

NOTE: To prevent shearing of the rubber bushing, loosen the bolt before swinging the strut aside.

3. Remove the forward light harness from the fan frame and disconnect the fan connector.
4. Remove the fan attaching bolts and remove the fan and frame assembly.

To install:

5. Install the fan and frame assembly.
6. Connect the fan electrical connector and install the forward light wiring harness to the fan frame.
7. Swing the forward engine strut and brace forward until the brace contacts the radiator support. Install the brace-to-radiator support attaching bolts. Tighten to 37 ft. lbs. (50 Nm).
8. Connect the negative battery cable.

Condenser

REMOVAL AND INSTALLATION

C/K Series Pick-Up and 1989–90 Suburban, Blazer and Jimmy

1. Disconnect the negative battery cable.
2. Properly discharge and recover the air conditioning system refrigerant.
3. Remove the grille assembly.
4. Remove the radiator grille center support.
5. Remove the left side grille-to-upper fender support screws, as required.
6. Disconnect the condenser inlet and outlet fitting connections.

NOTE: Use a backup wrench on the condenser fittings when disconnecting the refrigerant lines.

7. Discard the O-rings.

NOTE: Cap the refrigerant lines when opening the system to prevent the entry of dirt and moisture and the loss of refrigerant lubricant.

8. Remove the condenser-to-radiator support screws.
9. Remove the condenser support brackets.
10. Remove the upper condenser insulators.
11. Remove the condenser from the vehicle by pulling it forward. Bend the left side grille support outboard to gain clearance for the removal of the condenser.
12. Remove the lower condenser insulators, as required.

To install:

13. If removed, install the lower condenser insulators.
14. Add 1 oz. of refrigerant lubricant to the system.
15. Place the condenser in position. Ensure that the condenser is properly seated in the lower condenser insulators.
16. Install the upper condenser insulators.
17. Install the condenser brackets.
18. Install the condenser-to-radiator support screws.
19. Replace the condenser fitting O-rings. Lubricate the O-rings with refrigerant oil.
20. Connect the condenser inlet and outlet fitting connections.

NOTE: Use a backup wrench on the condenser fittings when connecting the refrigerant lines.

21. If removed, install the left side grille support-to-upper fender support screws.
22. Install the radiator grille center support.
23. Install the grille assembly.
24. Connect the negative battery cable.
25. Evacuate, recharge and leak test the air conditioning system.

1991 Suburban, Blazer and Jimmy

1. Disconnect the negative battery cable.
2. Properly discharge and recover the air conditioning system refrigerant.
3. Remove the fan.
4. Remove the fan shroud.

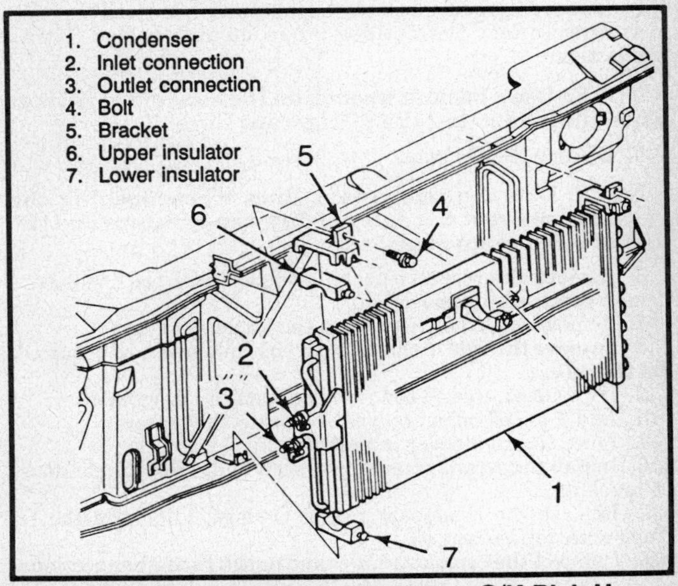
1. Condenser
2. Inlet connection
3. Outlet connection
4. Bolt
5. Bracket
6. Upper insulator
7. Lower insulator
5
4
6
2
3
1
7

Condenser and related components—C/K Pick-Up shown

5. Remove the radiator mounting bolts. Position the radiator rearward.
6. Disconnect the condenser inlet and outlet fitting connections.

NOTE: Use a backup wrench on the condenser fittings when disconnecting the refrigerant lines.

7. Discard the O-rings.

NOTE: Cap the refrigerant lines when opening the system to prevent the entry of dirt and moisture and the loss of refrigerant lubricant.

8. Remove the condenser-to-radiator support screws.
9. Remove the condenser support brackets.
10. Remove the upper condenser insulators.
11. Remove the condenser from the vehicle by pulling it forward. Bend the left side grille support outboard to gain clearance for the removal of the condenser.
12. Remove the lower condenser insulators, as required.

To install:

13. If removed, install the lower condenser insulators.
14. Add 1 oz. of refrigerant lubricant to the system.
15. Place the condenser in position. Ensure that the condenser is properly seated in the lower condenser insulators.
16. Install the upper condenser insulators.
17. Install the condenser brackets.
18. Install the condenser-to-radiator support screws.
19. Replace the condenser fitting O-rings. Lubricate the O-rings with refrigerant oil.
20. Connect the condenser inlet and outlet fitting connections.

NOTE: Use a backup wrench on the condenser fittings when connecting the refrigerant lines.

21. Install the fan shroud.
22. Install the fan.
23. Connect the negative battery cable.
24. Evacuate, recharge and leak test the air conditioning system.

G Series Van

1. Disconnect the negative battery cable.
2. Properly discharge and recover the air conditioning system refrigerant.
3. Remove the grille, hood lock and center hood lock support.
4. Disconnect the condenser inlet and outlet fitting connections.

NOTE: Use a backup wrench on the condenser fittings when disconnecting the refrigerant lines.

5. Discard the O-rings.

NOTE: Cap the refrigerant lines when opening the system to prevent the entry of dirt and moisture and the loss of refrigerant lubricant.

6. Remove the screws attaching the left and right side condenser brackets to the radiator.
7. Remove the condenser from the vehicle.
8. Remove the side brackets from the condenser, as required.

To install:

9. If removed, install the side brackets to the condenser.
10. Add 1 oz. of refrigerant lubricant to the system.
11. Place the condenser in position.
12. Install the screws attaching the left and right side condenser brackets.
13. Replace the condenser fitting O-rings. Lubricate the O-rings with refrigerant oil.
14. Connect the condenser inlet and outlet fitting connections.

NOTE: Use a backup wrench on the condenser fittings when connecting the refrigerant lines.

15. Install the grille, hood lock and center hood lock support.
16. Connect the negative battery cable.
17. Properly discharge and recover the air conditioning system refrigerant.

S Series and Bravada

1. Disconnect the negative battery cable.
2. Properly discharge and recover the air conditioning system refrigerant.
3. Remove the upper fan shroud.
4. Remove the radiator.
5. Remove the shields at either side of the radiator support.
6. Remove the condenser retainers and insulators.
7. Disconnect the condenser inlet and outlet fitting connections.

NOTE: Use a backup wrench on the condenser fittings when disconnecting the refrigerant lines.

8. Discard the O-rings.

NOTE: Cap the refrigerant lines when opening the system to prevent the entry of dirt and moisture and the loss of refrigerant lubricant.

9. Remove the condenser attaching bolts and remove the condenser from the vehicle.

To install:

10. Add 1 oz. of refrigerant lubricant to the system.
11. Place the condenser in position. Ensure that the condenser is properly seated in the lower condenser insulators.
12. Install the condenser retainers and mounting bolts.
13. Replace the condenser fitting O-rings. Lubricate the O-rings with refrigerant oil.
14. Connect the condenser inlet and outlet fitting connections.

NOTE: Use a backup wrench on the condenser fittings when connecting the refrigerant lines.

15. Install the radiator.
16. Install the upper fan shroud.
17. Connect the negative battery cable.
18. Evacuate, recharge and leak test the air conditioning system.

Astro and Safari

1. Disconnect the negative battery cable.
2. Properly discharge and recover the air conditioning system refrigerant.
3. Remove the grille and front-end panel.
4. Remove the radiator bar support.
5. Disconnect the condenser inlet and outlet fitting connections.

NOTE: Use a backup wrench on the condenser fittings when disconnecting the refrigerant lines.

6. Discard the O-rings.

NOTE: Cap the refrigerant lines when opening the system to prevent the entry of dirt and moisture and the loss of refrigerant lubricant.

7. Remove the condenser attaching bolts and insulators. Remove the condenser from the vehicle.

To install:

8. Add 1 oz. of refrigerant lubricant to the system.
9. Place the condenser in position. Ensure that the condenser is properly seated in the lower condenser mounts.
10. Install the condenser insulators, retainers and mounting bolts.
11. Replace the condenser fitting O-rings. Lubricate the O-rings with refrigerant oil.
12. Connect the condenser inlet and outlet fitting connections.

NOTE: Use a backup wrench on the condenser fittings when connecting the refrigerant lines.

13. Install the radiator bar support.
14. Install the grille and front-end panel.
15. Connect the negative battery cable.
16. Evacuate, recharge and leak test the air conditioning system.

Lumina APV, Silhouette and Trans Sport

1. Disconnect the negative battery cable.
2. Properly discharge and recover the air conditioning system refrigerant.
3. Disconnect the condenser inlet and outlet fitting connections.

NOTE: Use a backup wrench on the condenser fittings when disconnecting the refrigerant lines.

4. Discard the O-rings.

NOTE: Cap the refrigerant lines when opening the system to prevent the entry of dirt and moisture and the loss of refrigerant lubricant.

5. Remove the center support grille.
6. Remove the upper and lower air deflectors.
7. Disengage the the upper and lower condenser insulators.
8. Remove the upper condenser seal from the front engine compartment panel assembly.
9. Remove the condenser from the vehicle.

To install:

10. Add 1 oz. of refrigerant lubricant to the system.
11. Place the condenser in position. Ensure that the condenser is properly seated in the lower condenser insulators.
12. Install the upper condenser seal to the front engine compartment panel assembly.
13. Align the seal left and right side retainers to the holes in the panel. Apply pressure to secure the seal to the panel.
14. Install the upper and lower insulators. Ensure that the tab points forward.
15. Install the condenser with the insulators installed to the front engine compartment assembly.
16. Align the upper insulator tabs to the holes in the retainers.
17. Install the retainer to the lower tie bar aligning the retainer over the stud and engage the tab of the lower insulator.
18. Start the inboard screws in the tie bar before installing the nuts.
19. Install the retaining nuts.
20. Replace the condenser fitting O-rings. Lubricate the O-rings with refrigerant oil.
21. Connect the condenser inlet and outlet fitting connections.

NOTE: Use a backup wrench on the condenser fittings when connecting the refrigerant lines.

22. Install the upper and lower air deflectors.
23. Install the center grille support.
24. Connect the negative battery cable.
25. Evacuate, recharge and leak test the air conditioning system.

Compressor

REMOVAL AND INSTALLATION

C/K Series Pick-Up, Suburban, Blazer, Jimmy, S Series and Bravada

1. Disconnect the negative battery cable.
2. Properly discharge and recover the air conditioning system refrigerant.
3. Remove the compressor drive belt.
4. Remove the refrigerant line coupler assembly retaining bolt from the rear of the compressor. Disconnect the refrigerant line coupler assembly. Discard the O-rings.

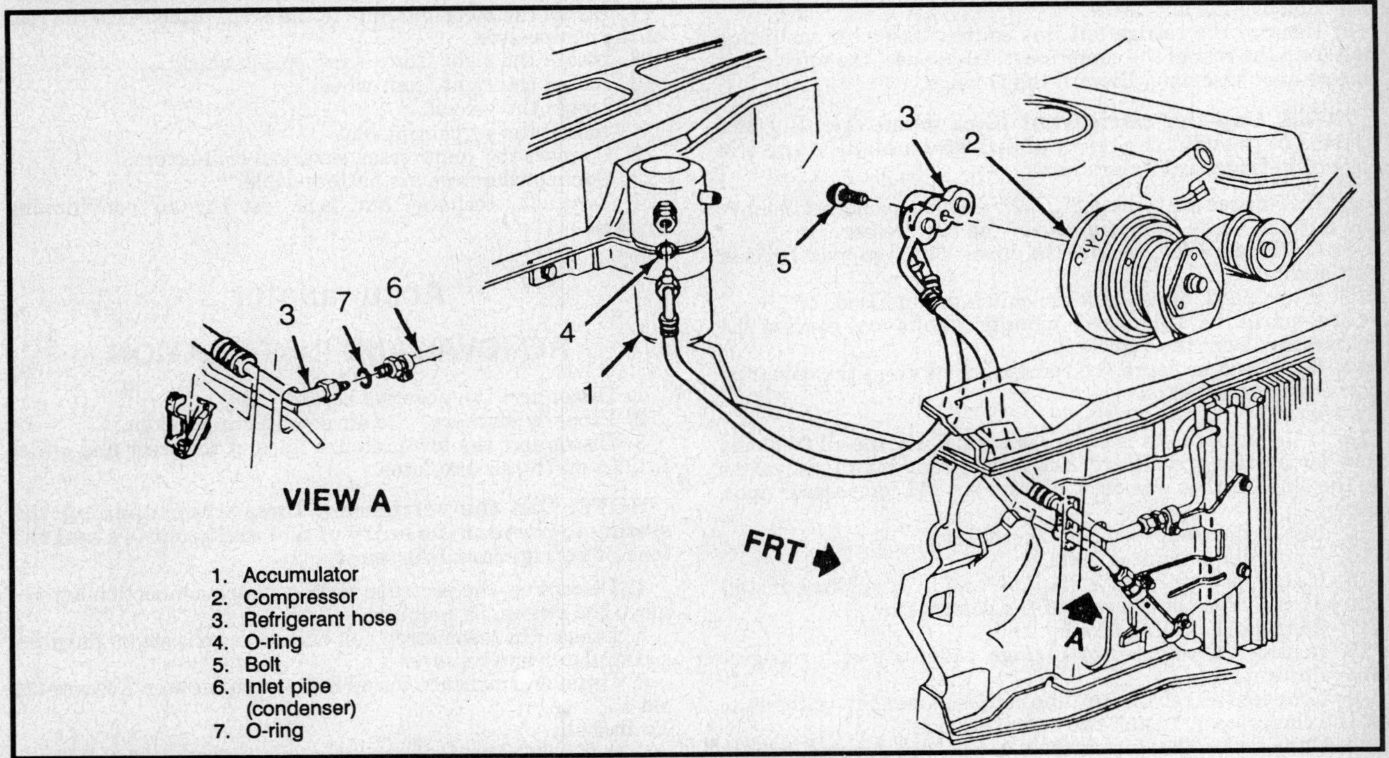
3
2
5
4
1
3
7
6
VIEW A
FRT
A
1. Accumulator
2. Compressor
3. Refrigerant hose
4. O-ring
5. Bolt
6. Inlet pipe (condenser)
7. O-ring

Refrigerant hose assembly and related components—C/K Pick-Up shown

NOTE: Cap the refrigerant lines when opening the system to prevent the entry of dirt and moisture and the loss of refrigerant lubricant.

5. Disconnect the compressor electrical connector.
6. On C/K models with 4.3L, 5.0L and 5.7L engines, remove the nut and brace from the rear of the compressor.
7. Remove the compressor mounting bolts.
8. Remove the compressor from the vehicle.
9. Drain and measure the refrigerant oil from the compressor. Discard the old oil.

To install:

10. If the compressor is to be replaced, drain the oil from the new compressor and discard. Add new refrigerant oil equivalent to the amount that was drained from the old compressor upon removal.
11. Install the compressor in the vehicle.
12. Install the mounting bolts.
13. On C/K models with 4.3L, 5.0L and 5.7L engines, install the nut and brace at the rear of the compressor.
14. Connect the compressor electrical connector.
15. Replace the compressor O-rings. Lubricate with refrigerant lubricant.
16. Connect the refrigerant line coupler assembly to the rear of the compressor. Install the retaining bolt.
17. Install the compressor drive belt.
18. Connect the negative battery cable.
19. Evacuate, recharge and leak test the air conditioning system.

G Series Van, Astro and Safari

1. Disconnect the negative battery cable.
2. Properly discharge and recover the air conditioning system refrigerant.
3. Disconnect the compressor electrical connector.
4. Remove the compressor drive belt.
5. Remove the engine cover.
6. Remove the air cleaner.
7. Remove the refrigerant line coupler assembly mounting bolt from the rear of the compressor. Disconnect the refrigerant line coupler assembly. Discard the O-rings.

NOTE: Cap the refrigerant lines when opening the system to prevent the entry of dirt and moisture and the loss of refrigerant lubricant.

8. If equipped with the 4.3L, 5.0L and 5.7L engines, remove the nut and brace from the rear of the compressor.
9. On G series Van, remove the dipstick tube support bracket bolt and nut.
10. If equipped, disconnect the clutch ground lead.
11. Remove the compressor mounting bolts and remove the compressor from the vehicle.
12. Drain and measure the refrigerant oil from the compressor. Discard the old oil.

To install:

13. If the compressor is to be replaced, drain the oil from the new compressor and discard. Add new refrigerant oil equivalent to the amount that was drained from the old compressor upon removal.
14. Install the compressor in the vehicle.
15. Install the mounting bolts.
16. If equipped with the 4.3L, 5.0L and 5.7L engines, install the nut and brace at the rear of the compressor.
17. Connect the clutch ground lead.
18. Replace the compressor O-rings. Lubricate with refrigerant lubricant.
19. Connect the refrigerant line coupler assembly to the rear of the compressor. Install the mounting bolt.
20. On G series Van, install the dipstick tube support bracket bolt and nut.
21. Install the air cleaner.
22. Install the engine cover.
23. Install the compressor drive belt.
24. Connect the compressor electrical connector.
25. Connect the negative battery cable.
26. Evacuate, recharge and leak test the air conditioning system.

Lumina APV, Silhouette and Trans Sport

1. Disconnect the negative battery cable.
2. Properly discharge and recover the air conditioning system refrigerant.
3. Disconnect the compressor electrical connectors.
4. Remove the serpentine belt.
5. Raise and safely support the vehicle.
6. Remove the right front wheel to provide access to the compressor.
7. Remove the right front wheel splash shield.
8. Remove the bolts and nuts from the brace attached to the rear of the compressor.
9. Remove the bolts from the front engine bracket securing the compressor.
10. Remove the engine block stud nut securing the compressor brace.
11. Remove the compressor from the vehicle.
12. Drain and measure the refrigerant oil from the compressor. Discard the old oil.

To install:

13. If the compressor is to be replaced, drain the oil from the new compressor and discard. Add new refrigerant oil equivalent to the amount that was drained from the old compressor upon removal.
14. Install the compressor in the vehicle.
15. Install the engine block stud nut securing the compressor brace.
16. Install the bolts to the front engine bracket securing the compressor.
17. Install the bolts and nuts to the brace attached to the rear of the compressor.
18. Install the right front wheel splash shield.
19. Install the right front wheel.
20. Lower the vehicle.
21. Install the serpentine belt.
22. Connect the compressor electrical connectors.
23. Connect the negative battery cable.
24. Evacuate, recharge and leak test the air conditioning system.

Accumulator

REMOVAL AND INSTALLATION

1. Disconnect the negative battery cable.
2. Properly discharge the air conditioning system.
3. Disconnect the low-pressure lines at the inlet and outlet fittings on the accumulator.

NOTE: Cap the refrigerant lines when opening the system to prevent the entry of dirt and moisture and the loss of refrigerant lubricant.

4. Disconnect the pressure cycling switch connection and remove the switch, as required.
5. Loosen the lower strap bolt and spread the strap. Turn the accumulator and remove.
6. Drain and measure the oil in the accumulator. Discard the old oil.

To install:

7. Add new oil equivalent to the amount drained from the old accumulator. Add an additional 2–3 oz. (60–90ml) of oil to com-

pensate for the oil retained by the accumulator dessicant.

8. Position the accumulator in the securing bracket and tighten the clamp bolt.
9. Install new O-rings at the inlet and outlet connections on the accumulator. Lubricate the O-rings with refrigerant oil.
10. Connect the low-pressure inlet and outlet lines.
11. Evacuate, charge and leak test the system.
12. Connect the negative battery cable.

Fixed Orifice Tube

REMOVAL AND INSTALLATION

1. Properly discharge the air conditioning system.
2. Loosen the fitting at the liquid line outlet on the condenser or evaporator inlet pipe and disconnect. Discard the O-ring.

NOTE: Use a backup wrench on the condenser outlet fitting when loosening the lines.

3. Carefully, remove the fixed orifice tube from the tube fitting in the evaporator inlet line.
4. In the event that the restricted or plugged orifice tube is difficult to remove, perform the following:
   a. Remove as much of the impacted residue as possible.
   b. Using a hair dryer, epoxy drier or equivalent, carefully apply heat approximately ¼ in. from the dimples on the inlet pipe. Do not overheat the pipe.

NOTE: If the system has a pressure switch near the orifice tube, it should be removed prior to heating the pipe to avoid damage to the switch.

   c. While applying heat, use special tool J 26549-C or equivalent to grip the orifice tube. Use a turning motion along with a push-pull motion to loosen the impacted orifice tube and remove it.
5. Swab the inside of the evaporator inlet pipe with solvent to remove any remaining residue.

To install:

6. Add 1 oz. of 525 viscosity refrigerant oil to the system.
7. Lubricate the new O-ring and orifice tube with refrigerant oil and insert into the inlet pipe.

NOTE: Ensure that the new orifice tube is inserted in the inlet tube with the smaller screen end first.

8. Connect the evaporator inlet pipe with the condenser outlet fitting.

NOTE: Use a backup wrench on the condenser outlet fitting when tightening the lines.

9. Evacuate, recharge and leak test the system.

Blower Motor

REMOVAL AND INSTALLATION

C/K Series Pick-Up

1989–90

1. Disconnect the negative battery cable.
2. Disconnect the blower motor electrical connector.
3. Remove the blower motor flange screws.
4. Remove the blower motor.

To install:

5. Install the blower motor.
6. Install the blower motor flange screws.
7. Connect the blower motor electrical connector.
8. Connect the negative battery cable.
9. Operate the blower motor to ensure that it functions on all speeds.

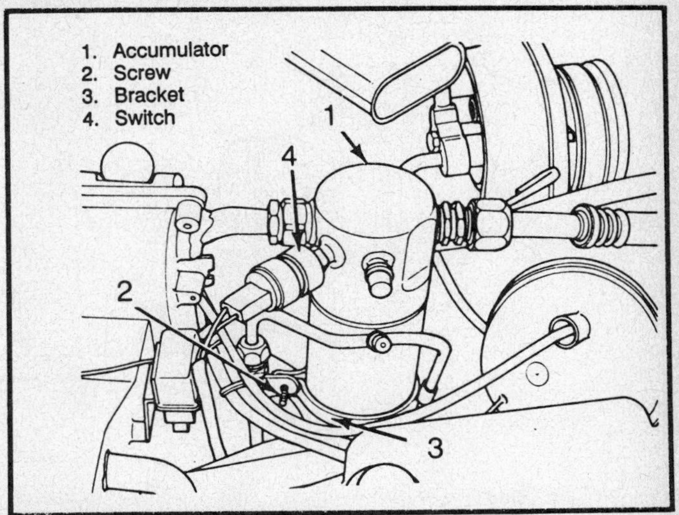
1. Accumulator
2. Screw
3. Bracket
4. Switch
1
4
2
3

Accumulator replacement—4.3L engine shown

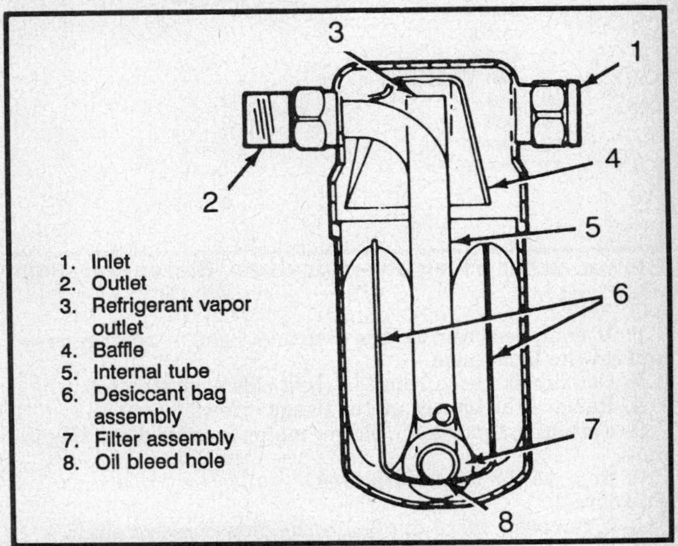
3
1
4
2
5
6
7
8
1. Inlet
2. Outlet
3. Refrigerant vapor outlet
4. Baffle
5. Internal tube
6. Desiccant bag assembly
7. Filter assembly
8. Oil bleed hole

Accumulator internal components

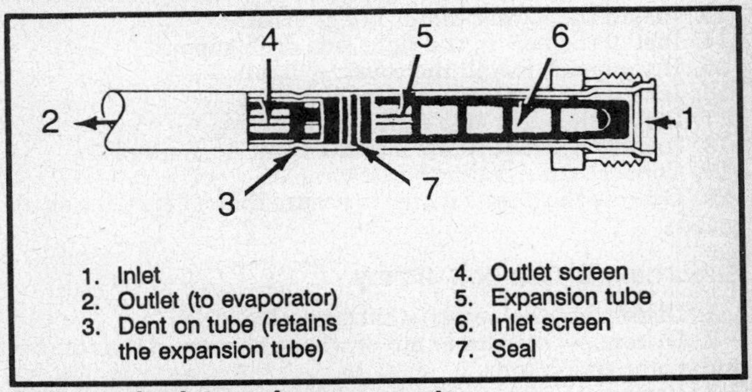
4
5
6
2
1
3
7
1. Inlet
2. Outlet (to evaporator)
3. Dent on tube (retains the expansion tube)
4. Outlet screen
5. Expansion tube
6. Inlet screen
7. Seal

Orifice tube internal components

1991

1. Disconnect the negative battery cable.
2. Remove the front screw from the right door sill plate.
3. Remove the right side cowl kick panel.
4. Disconnect the electrical connector from the blower motor.
5. Remove the blower motor cooling tube.

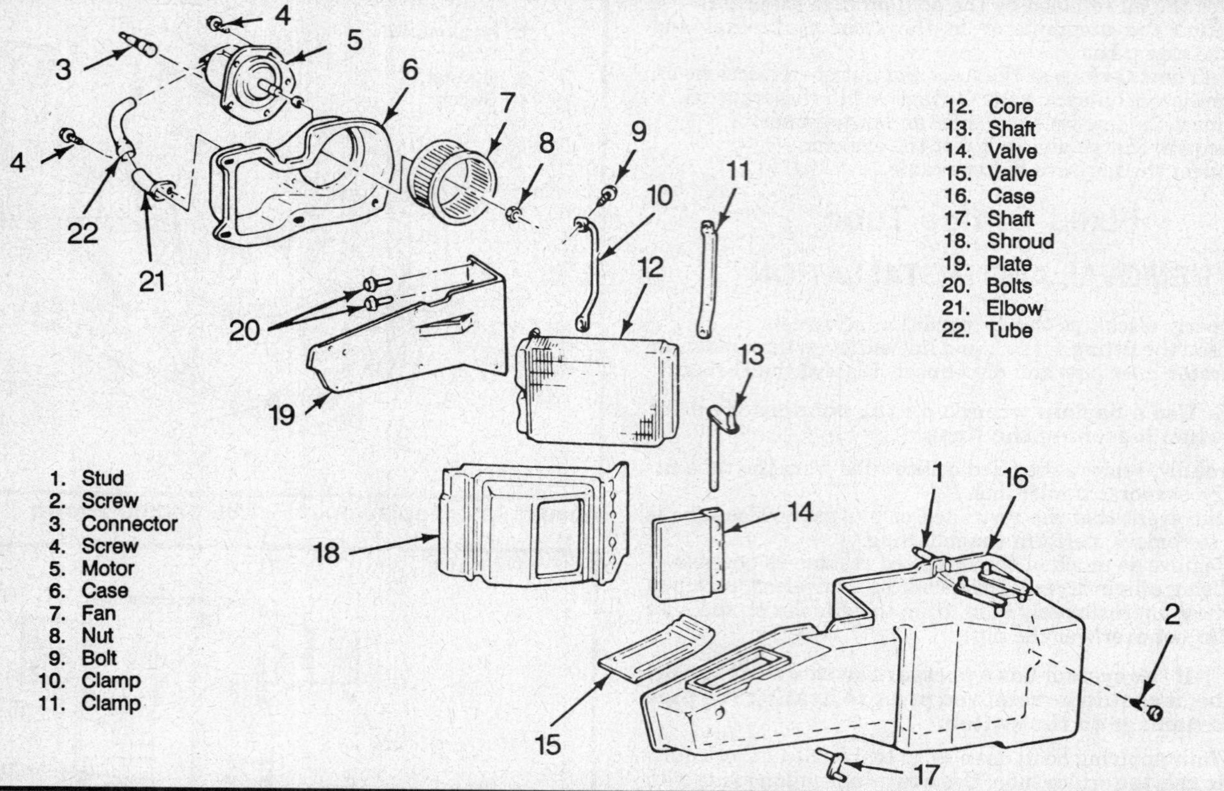
1. Stud
2. Screw
3. Connector
4. Screw
5. Motor
6. Case
7. Fan
8. Nut
9. Bolt
10. Clamp
11. Clamp
12. Core
13. Shaft
14. Valve
15. Valve
16. Case
17. Shaft
18. Shroud
19. Plate
20. Bolts
21. Elbow
22. Tube

Blower motor assembly—Suburban, Blazer and Jimmy

6. If equipped, remove the courtesy light attaching screws and set the light aside.
7. Remove the bolt from the right side dash support.
8. Remove the blower motor flange screws.
9. Carefully, remove the blower motor to avoid distorting the fan.
10. Remove the fan, as required.

To install:

11. If removed, instll the fan to the blower motor shaft.
12. Carefully, guide the blower motor and blower fan assembly into position.
13. Install the blower motor flange screws.
14. Install the bolt to the right side dash support.
15. If equipped, install the courtesy light.
16. Install the blower motor cooling tube.
17. Install the right side cowl kick panel.
18. Install the front screw into the front door sill plate.
19. Connect the negative battery cable.
20. Operate the blower motor to ensure that it functions on all speeds.

Suburban, Blazer and Jimmy

1. Disconnect the negative battery cable.
2. Disconnect the blower motor wiring harness at the resistor and motor connectors.
3. Remove the 5 motor mounting screws.
4. Carefully, pry on the blower motor flange to separate the flange from the sealer.
5. Remove the blower motor shaft nut.
6. Remove the fan from the motor shaft.
7. Remove the nut from the the motor.

To install:

8. Install the nut to the motor.
9. Install the fan to the motor shart. Ensure that the open end of the fan wheel faces away from the blower motor.
10. Install the shaft nut.
11. Apply a new bead of permagum sealer to the case mounting flange.
12. Install the motor and fan assembly to the case.
13. Install the 5 mounting screws.
14. Connect the blower motor resistor and motor connectors.
15. Connect the negative battery cable.
16. Operate the blower motor to ensure that it functions on all speeds.

G Series Van, Astro and Safari

1. Disconnect the negative battery cable.
2. Disconnect the coolant overflow hose from the coolant recovery bottle.
3. Remove the recovery bottle fasteners. Remove the recovery bottle from the vehicle.
4. On Astro and Safari, Disconnect the windshield washer hose and electrical connector. Remove the windshield washer fluid bottle.
5. Disconnect the blower motor wiring harness.
6. Remove the blower motor cooling tube, as required.
7. Remove the 5 motor mounting screws.
8. Remove the motor and fan assembly. Carefully pry on the blower flange to separate the blower flange from the sealer.
9. Remove the blower motor shaft nut.
10. Remove the fan from the motor.

To install:

11. Install the fan to the motor shaft. Ensure that the open end of the fan wheel faces away from the blower motor.
12. Install the nut on the blower motor shaft.
13. Apply a bead of permagum sealer to the mounting flange.

14. Install the blower motor and fan assemlby to the case. Install the 5 mounting screws.
15. Connect the blower motor wiring harness.
16. If disconnected, connect the blower motor cooling tube.
17. Install the coolant recovery bottle.
18. Connect the coolant hose to the recovery bottle.
19. Disconnect the blower motor wiring harness.
20. On Astro and Safari, Disconnect the windshield washer hose and electrical connector. Remove the windshield washer fluid bottle.
21. Connect the negative battery cable.
22. Operate the blower motor to ensure that it functions on all speeds.

S Series and Bravada

1. Disconnect the negative battery cable.
2. Disconnect the blower motor electrical connector.
3. Remove the blower motor flange screws.
4. Disconnect the blower motor cooling tube.
5. Remove the blower motor.

To install:

6. Install the blower motor.
7. Connect the blower motor cooling tube.
8. Install the blower motor flange screws.
9. Connect the blower motor electrical connector.
10. Connect the negative battery cable.
11. Operate the blower motor to ensure that it functions on all speeds.

Lumina APV, Silhouette and Trans Sport

1. Disconnect the negative battery cable.
2. Remove the engine air cleaner.
3. Remove the left side windshield wiper transmission arm link.
4. Disconnect the blower motor electrical connector.
5. Remove the blower motor retaining screws. Remove the blower motor.

To install:

6. Install the blower motor and retaining screws.
7. Connect the blower motor electrical connector.
8. Install the left side windshield wiper transmission arm link.
9. Install the air cleaner.
10. Connect the negative battery cable.
11. Operate the blower motor to ensure that it functions on all speeds.

Blower Motor Resistor

REMOVAL AND INSTALLATION

1. Disconnect the negative battery cable.
2. Disconnect the electrical connector at the resistor.
3. Remove the resistor attaching screws.
4. Remove the resistor from the evaporator case.

To install:

5. Position the resistor in the evaporator case. Install the attaching screws.
6. Connect the electrical connector.
7. Connect the negative battery cable.

Heater Core

REMOVAL AND INSTALLATION

C/K Series Pick-Up

1. Disconnect the negative battery cable.
2. Drain the engine coolant into a clean container for reuse.
3. Remove the coolant overflow bottle, as required, for access.
4. Disconnect the heater hoses from the heater core tubes.
5. Remove the 7 screws that hold the heater case bottom cover. Remove the cover.
6. Remove the screws and brackets that hold the core to the case.
7. Remove the heater core.

To install:

8. Install the heater core.
9. Install the screws and brackets that hold the core to the case.
10. Install the heater case bottom cover. Install the 7 screws that hold the bottom cover in place.
11. Connect the heater hoses to the heater core tubes.
12. If removed, install the coolant overflow bottle.
13. Connect the negative battery cable.
14. Fill cooling system and check for leaks. Start the engine and allow to come to normal operating temperature. Recheck for leaks. Top-up coolant.

Suburban, Blazer and Jimmy

1. Disconnect the negative battery cable.
2. Drain the engine coolant into a clean container for reuse.
3. Disconnect the heater hoses at the heater core tubes. Plug the heater core tubes to prevent spillage during removal.
4. Remove the screws and nuts from the studs that project into the engine compartment.
5. Remove the glove box.
6. Disconnect the defroster and temperature cables.
7. Remove the floor outlet.
8. Remove the screw that holds the defroster duct to the heater distributor.
9. Pull the heater assembly rearward to reach the wiring harness. Disconnect the harness.
10. Remove the heater case.
11. Remove the heater core retaining clamps.
12. Remove the heater core.

To install:

13. Position the heater core in the case.
14. Install the heater core retaining clamps.
15. Position the heater case in the vehicle.
16. Install the screws and nuts to the studs.
17. Connect the wiring harness.
18. Install the screw that holds the defroster duct to the heater distributor.
19. Install the floor outlet.
20. Connect the defroster and temperature cables.
21. Install the glove box.
22. Connect the heater hoses to the heater core tubes.
23. Connect the negative battery cable.
24. Fill cooling system and check for leaks. Start the engine and allow to come to normal operating temperature. Recheck for leaks. Top-up coolant.

G Series Van

1. Disconnect the negative battery cable.
2. Drain the engine coolant into a clean container for reuse.
3. Remove the coolant recovery tank, as required.
4. Disconnect the heater hoses from the heater core tubes. Plug the tubes to prevent spillage during removal.
5. Remove the screws that hold the distributor duct to the distributor case and the distributor duct to the engine cover.
6. Remove the engine housing cover.
7. Loosen the instrument panel, as required, to aid in removal of the heater case.
8. Lower the steering column.
9. Remove the screws attaching the defroster duct to the distributor case.
10. Remove the distributor to heater case screws.
11. Disconnect the temperature door cable and set aside.

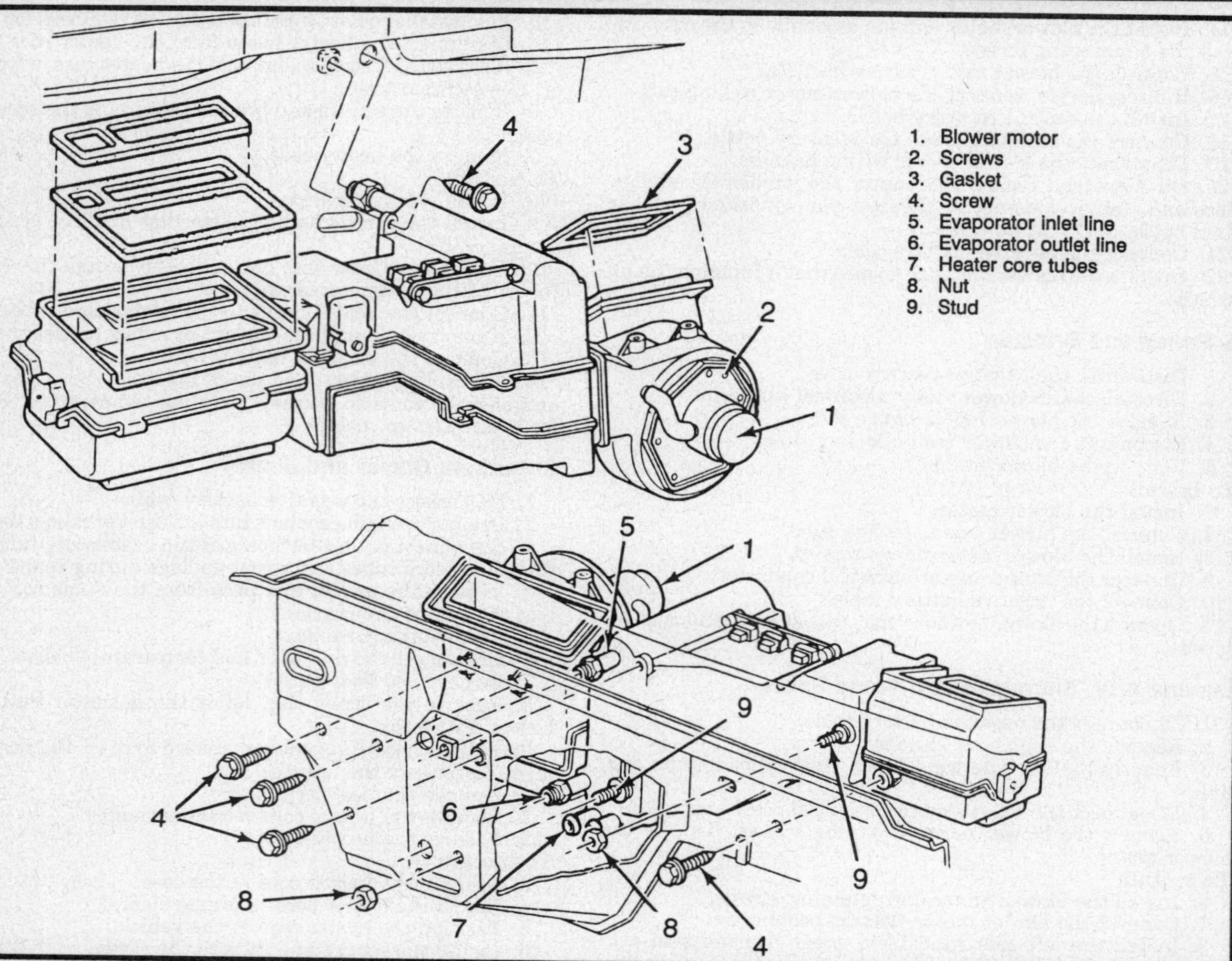
1. Blower motor
2. Screws
3. Gasket
4. Screw
5. Evaporator inlet line
6. Evaporator outlet line
7. Heater core tubes
8. Nut
9. Stud

Heater case assembly—C/K Pick-Up

12. Remove the 3 nuts on the engine compartment side of the distributor case and 1 screw on the passenger compartment side.
13. Tilt the case assembly to the rear at the top and lift until the core tubes clear the dash openings.
14. Remove the heater core retaining straps.
15. Remove the heater core.

To install:

16. Apply a bead of permagum sealer between the core and the case.
17. Position the heater core in the heater case.
18. Install the core retaining straps.
19. Apply a bead of permagum sealer between the heater case and the opening in the vehicle.
20. Install the heater case in the vehicle by tilting the case until the core tubes clear the cowl opening.
21. Connect the temperature cable to the heater case.
22. Install the distributor duct to the heater case.
23. Install the defroster duct to the heater case.
24. Install the instrument panel screws that were loosened during removal.
25. Tighten the steering column retaining bolts.
26. Install the engine housing cover.
27. Connect the heater core hoses.
28. If removed, install the coolant recovery tank.
29. Connect the negative battery cable.
30. Fill cooling system and check for leaks. Start the engine and allow to come to normal operating temperature. Recheck for leaks. Top-up coolant.

S Series and Bravada

1. Disconnect the negative battery cable.
2. Drain the engine coolant into a clean container for reuse.
3. Disconnect the heater hoses from the heater core tubes. Plug the hoses to prevent spillage during removal.
4. Remove the rear heater core cover.
5. Remove the heater core brackets.
6. Remove the heater core.

To install:

7. Install the heater core.
8. Install the heater core brackets.
9. Install the rear heater core cover.
10. Connect the heater hoses to the heater core tubes.
11. Connect the negative battery cable.
12. Fill cooling system and check for leaks. Start the engine and allow to come to normal operating temperature. Recheck for leaks. Top-up coolant.

Astro and Safari

1. Disconnect the negative battery cable.
2. Drain the engine coolant into a clean container for reuse.
3. Disconnect the heater hoses from the heater core tubes.

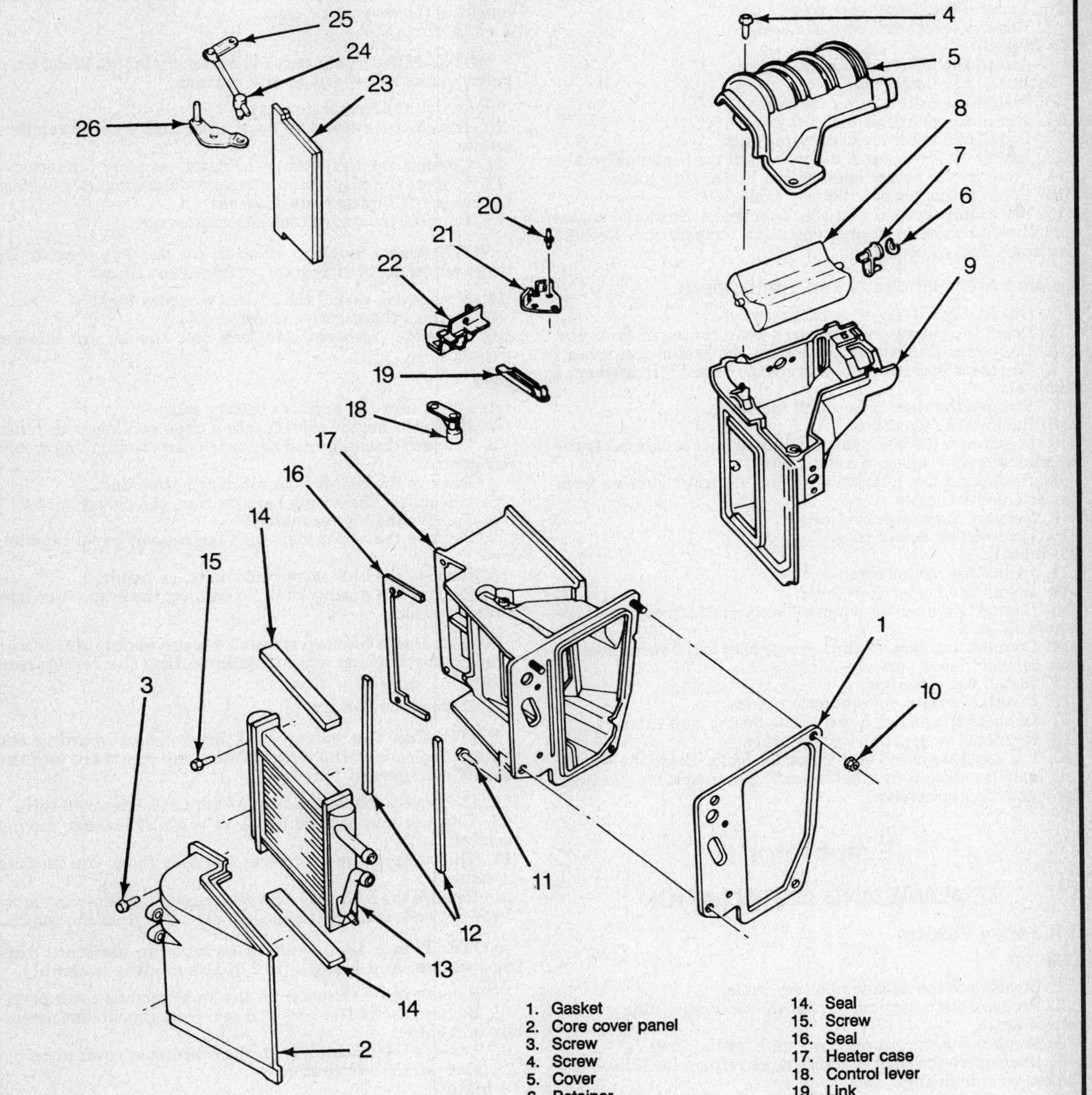
25
24
23
26
20
21
22
19
18
17
16
14
15
3
4
5
8
7
6
9
1
10
11
12
13
14
2

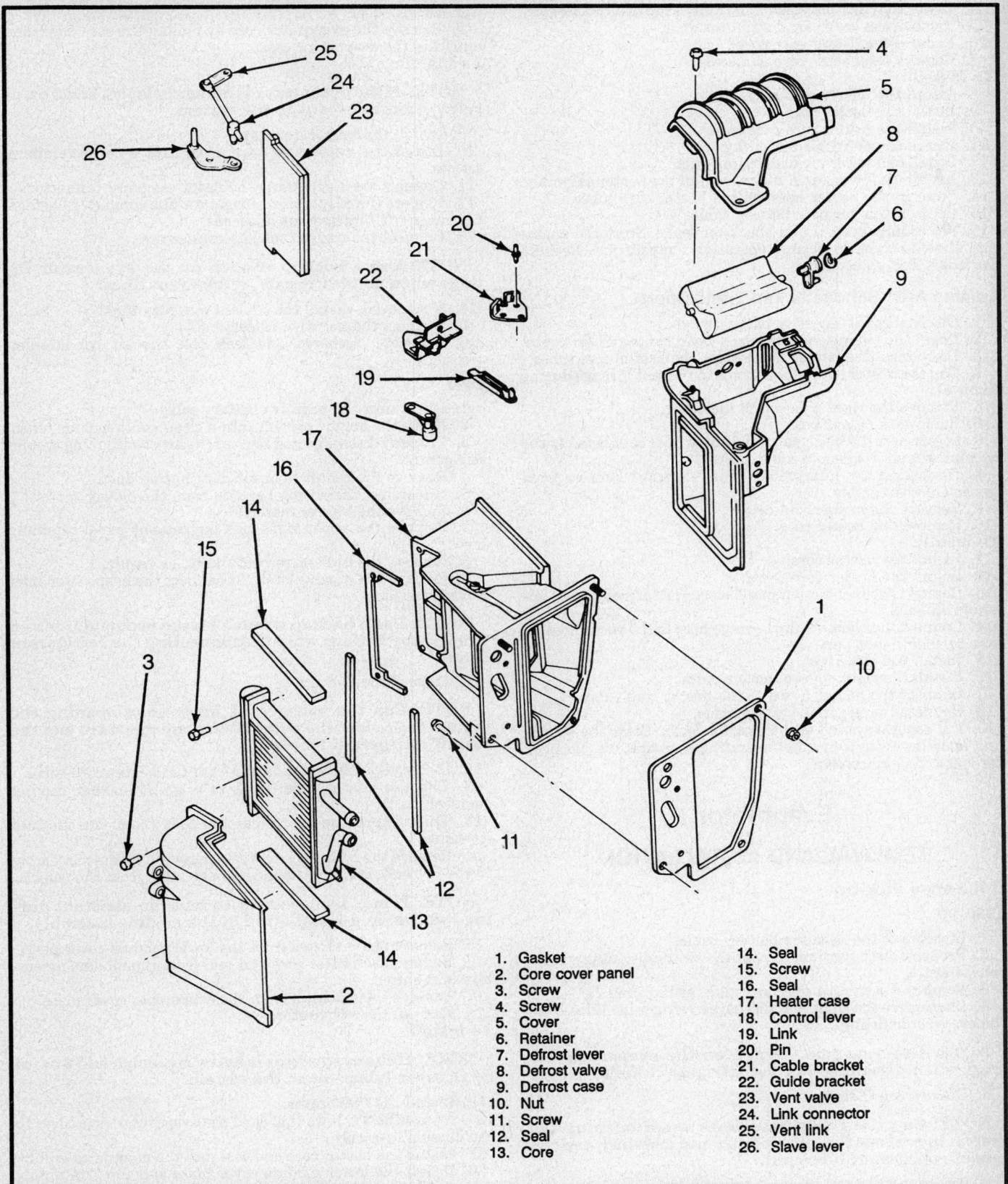

1. Gasket
2. Core cover panel
3. Screw
4. Screw
5. Cover
6. Retainer
7. Defrost lever
8. Defrost valve
9. Defrost case
10. Nut
11. Screw
12. Seal
13. Core
14. Seal
15. Screw
16. Seal
17. Heater case
18. Control lever
19. Link
20. Pin
21. Cable bracket
22. Guide bracket
23. Vent valve
24. Link connector
25. Vent link
26. Slave lever

Heater assembly components—Astro and Safari

4. Lower the filler panel from in front of the heater assembly.
5. Remove the lower air distributor duct.
6. Remove the heater case cover.
7. Remove the heater core and seals.

To install:

8. Install the heater core seals.
9. Install the heater core.
10. Install the heater core case cover.
11. Install the defroster outlet duct.
12. Install the lower air distributor duct.
13. Install the lower panel to the front of the heater assembly.
14. Connect the heater hoses to the heater core tubes.
15. Connect the negative battery cable.
16. Fill cooling system and check for leaks. Start the engine and allow to come to normal operating temperature. Recheck for leaks. Top-up coolant.

Lumina APV, Silhouette and Trans Sport

1. Disconnect the negative battery cable.
2. Drain the engine coolant into a clean container for reuse.
3. Disconnect the heater hoses from the heater core tubes.
4. Cap the heater core tube fittings to prevent leakage during removal.
5. Remove the right side sound insulator.
6. Remove the glove box.
7. Disconnect the black vacuum source hose connected to the vacuum actuator solenoid input port.
8. Disconnect the instrument panel electrical harness from the solenoid assembly.
9. Remove the heater core cover.
10. Remove the heater core.

To install:

11. Install the heater core.
12. Install the heater core cover.
13. Connect the instrument panel electrical harness to the solenoid assembly.
14. Connect the black vacuum source hose to the vacuum actuator solenoid input port.
15. Install the glove box.
16. Install the right side sound insulator.
17. Connect the heater hoses to the heater core tubes.
18. Connect the negative battery cable.
19. Fill cooling system and check for leaks. Start the engine and allow to come to normal operating temperature. Recheck for leaks. Top-up coolant.

Evaporator

REMOVAL AND INSTALLATION

C/K Series Pick-Up

1989–90

1. Disconnect the negative battery cable.
2. Properly discharge and recover the air conditioning system refrigerant.
3. Remove the coolant overflow tank, as required.
4. Disconnect the inlet and discharge refrigerant lines from the evaporator fittings.

NOTE: Use a backup wrench on the evaporator fittings when disconnecting the refrigerant lines.

5. Discard the O-rings.

NOTE: Cap the refrigerant lines when opening the system to prevent the entry of dirt and moisture and the loss of refrigerant lubricant.

6. Disconnect the temperature actuator electrical connector.
7. Remove the 4 screws from the evaporator core cover and remove the cover.
8. Remove the evaporator core by pulling the core down and out from the evaporator case.

To install:

NOTE: If the evaporator is being replaced, add 3 oz. of refrigerant lubricant to the system.

9. Install the evaporator core.
10. Install the evaporator core cover and 4 cover retaining screws.
11. Connect the temperature actuator electrical connector.
12. Replace the evaporator refrigerant line connector O-rings. Lubricate with refrigerant lubricant.
13. Connect the refrigerant line connectors.

NOTE: Use a backup wrench on the evaporator fittings when connecting the refrigerant lines.

14. If removed, install the coolant overflow tank.
15. Connect the negative battery cable.
16. Evacuate, recharge and leak test the air conditioning system.

1991

1. Disconnect the negative battery cable.
2. Drain the engine coolant into a clean container for reuse.
3. Properly discharge and recover the air conditioning system refrigerant.
4. Remove the center floor air distribution duct.
5. Disconnect the wiring harness from the blower motor.
6. Remove the blower motor.
7. Remove the upper right side instrument panel retaining bolt.
8. Remove the coolant recovery tank, as required.
9. Remove the accumulator. Disconnect the evaporator inlet refrigerant line.

NOTE: Use a backup wrench on the accumulator and evaporator fittings when disconnecting the refrigerant lines.

10. Discard the O-rings.

NOTE: Cap the refrigerant lines when opening the system to prevent the entry of dirt and moisture and the loss of refrigerant lubricant.

11. Disconnect the heater hoses from the heater core tubes.
12. Cap the heater core tubes to prevent leakage during removal.
13. Disconnect the electrical harness from the module assembly.
14. Remove the bolts and nuts attaching the module assembly to the firewall. Remove the module assembly from the vehicle.

NOTE: It may be necessary to have an assistant during removal and installation of the module assembly.

15. Remove the 7 screws from the lower module cover plate.
16. Remove the heater core and seal from the module assembly, as required.
17. Remove the 4 screws from the evaporator cover plate.
18. Remove the evaporator.

To install:

NOTE: If the evaporator is being replaced, add 3 oz. of refrigerant lubricant to the system.

19. Install the evaporator.
20. Install the 4 screws that hold the evaporator case cover to the module assembly.
21. Install the heater core and seal into the module assembly.
22. Install the lower module cover plate and the 7 retaining screws.
23. Install the module assembly in the vehicle. Install the bolts

and nuts attaching the module assembly to the firewall.
24. Connect the electrical harness to the module assembly.
25. Connect the heater hoses to the heater core tubes.
26. Replace the accumulator and evaporator inlet line fitting O-rings. Lubricate with refrigerant lubricant.
27. Install the accumulator. Install the evaporator inlet refrigerant lines.

NOTE: Use a backup wrench on the accumulator and evaporator fittings when connecting the refrigerant lines.

28. If removed, install the coolant recovery tank.
29. Install the upper right bolt to the instrument panel assembly.
30. Install the blower motor. Connect the blower motor electrical connector.
31. Install the center floor air distribution duct.
32. Connect the negative battery cable.
33. Fill cooling system and check for leaks. Start the engine and allow to come to normal operating temperature. Recheck for leaks. Top-up coolant.
34. Evacuate, recharge and leak test the air conditioning system.

Suburban, Blazer and Jimmy

EXCEPT 6.2L DIESEL ENGINE

1. Disconnect the negative battery cable.
2. Properly discharge and recover the air conditioning system refrigerant.
3. Remove the nuts from the selector duct studs projecting through the dash panel.
4. Remove the evaporator case cover.
5. Disconnect the evaporator refrigerant lines.

NOTE: Use a backup wrench on the evaporator fittings when disconnecting the refrigerant lines.

6. Discard the O-rings.

NOTE: Cap the refrigerant lines when opening the system to prevent the entry of dirt and moisture and the loss of refrigerant lubricant.

7. Remove the orifice tube from the evaporator inlet refrigerant line fitting.
8. Remove the 8 evaporator core assembly retaining bolts and remove the assembly.

To install:

NOTE: If the evaporator core is being replaced, add 3 oz. of refrigerant lubricant to the system.

9. Install the evaporator core assembly and install the 8 attaching bolts.
10. Install the orifice tube.
11. Replace the refrigerant line O-rings. Lubricate with refrigerant lubricant.
12. Connect the evaporator refrigerant lines.

NOTE: Use a backup wrench on the evaporator fittings when connecting the refrigerant lines.

13. Connect the negative battery cable.
14. Evacuate, recharge and leak test the air conditioning system.

6.2L DIESEL ENGINE

1. Disconnect the negative battery cable.
2. Properly discharge and recover the air conditioning system refrigerant.
3. Drain the engine coolant into a clean container for reuse.
4. Remove the air cleaner and resonator.
5. Remove the accumulator.

NOTE: Use a backup wrench on the accumulator fittings when disconnecting the refrigerant lines.

6. Discard the O-rings.

NOTE: Cap the refrigerant lines when opening the system to prevent the entry of dirt and moisture and the loss of refrigerant lubricant.

7. Remove the fuel filter retaining bolt from the firewall and set the fuel filter aside.
8. Remove the relay and resistors from the heater case.
9. Disconnect the heater hoses from the heater core tubes. Cap the heater core tubes to prevent leakage during removal.
10. Remove the inner fender well bolts, including the jack assembly. Lower the fender slightly.
11. Remove the 2 nuts from the studs in the firewall at the top of the insulator.
12. Remove the screw in the bottom of the insulator.
13. Remove the inlet refrigerant line retaining bolt.
14. Disconnect the inlet refrigerant line from the evaporator.

NOTE: Use a backup wrench on the evaporator fittings when disconnecting the refrigerant lines.

15. Discard the O-rings.

NOTE: Cap the refrigerant lines when opening the system to prevent the entry of dirt and moisture and the loss of refrigerant lubricant.

16. Remove the insulator cover from the evaporator.
17. Remove the 8 bolts holding the evaporator case together. Two of the bolts are in the firewall. Separate the case.
18. Remove the evaporator.

To install:

NOTE: If the evaporator is being replaced, add 3 oz. of refrigerant lubricant to the system.

19. Install the evaporator core.
20. Install the case cover and the 8 bolts that hold the case together.
21. Install the insulator cover over the evaportor case.
22. Replace the evaporator inlet line O-rings. Lubricate with refrigerant lubricant.
23. Connect the evaporator inlet refrigerant line.

NOTE: Use a backup wrench on the condenser fittings when connecting the refrigerant lines.

24. Install the evaporator inlet line retaining bolt.
25. Install the 2 nuts and 1 screw that hold the insulator to the firewall.
26. Install the inner fender well bolts and jack assembly.
27. Connect the heater hoses.
28. Install the relay and resistor.
29. Install the fuel filter retaining bolt.
30. Replace the accumulator O-rings. Lubricate with refrigerant lubricant.
31. Install the accumulator.

NOTE: Use a backup wrench on the accumulator fittings when connecting the refrigerant lines.

32. Install the air cleaner and resonator.
33. Connect the negative battery cable.
34. Fill cooling system and check for leaks. Start the engine and allow to come to normal operating temperature. Recheck for leaks. Top-up coolant.
35. Evacuate, recharge and leak test the air conditioning system.

G Series Van

EXCEPT 6.2L DIESEL ENGINE

1. Disconnect the negative battery cable.
2. Properly discharge and recover the air conditioning system refrigerant.
3. Remove the coolant recovery tank and bracket.
4. Disconnect the electrical connectors from the core case assembly.
5. Remove the bracket from the evaporator case.
6. Remove the right side marker light, as required, for access.
7. Disconnect the accumulator and evaporator refrigerant line fittings.

NOTE: Use a backup wrench on the condenser fittings when disconnecting the refrigerant lines.

8. Discard the O-rings.

NOTE: Cap the refrigerant lines when opening the system to prevent the entry of dirt and moisture and the loss of refrigerant lubricant.

9. Remove the accumulator from the evaporator case.
10. Remove the 3 nuts and 1 screw attaching the ECM to the dash panel.
11. Remove the evaporator core case and housing assembly from the vehicle.
12. Remove the screws and separate the case sections.
13. Remove the evaporator core.

To install:

NOTE: If the evaporator core is being replaced, add 3 oz. of refrigerant lubricant to the system.

14. Install the evaporator core into the case.
15. Mate the case sections and install the screws.
16. Install the evaporator case and housing assembly to the vehicle.
17. Position the ECM to the dash panel and install the 3 retaining nuts and 1 screw.
18. Replace the evaporator and accumulator O-rings. Lubricate with refrigerant lubricant.
19. Connect the evaporator and accumulator refrigerant lines.

NOTE: Use a backup wrench on the evaporator and accumulator fittings when connecting the refrigerant lines.

20. Install the accumulator to the evaporator case.
21. If removed, install the right side marker light.
22. Install the bracket to the evaporator case.
23. Connect the electrical connectors.
24. Install the coolant recovery tank and bracket.
25. Connect the negative battery cable.
26. Evacuate, recharge and leak test the air conditioning system.

6.2L DIESEL ENGINE

1. Disconnect the negative battery cable.
2. Properly discharge and recover the air conditioning system refrigerant.
3. Remove the cold air intake.
4. Remove the hood latch assembly and cable retainer and set aside.
5. Remove the windshield solvent tank.
6. Disconnect the accumulator and evaporator refrigerant lines.

NOTE: Use a backup wrench on the condenser fittings when disconnecting the refrigerant lines.

7. Discard the O-rings.

NOTE: Cap the refrigerant lines when opening the system to prevent the entry of dirt and moisture and the loss of refrigerant lubricant.

8. Remove the accumulator.
9. Disconnect the blower motor relay and resistor electrical connectors.
10. Remove the blower motor relay and resistor.
11. Remove the upper half of the fan shroud.
12. Remove the radiator.
13. Remove the heater valve assembly bracket and set aside.
14. Remove the upper screws of the lower evaporator core insulation. Push the insulation down and out of the way.
15. Remove the blower motor and evaporator core insulation.
16. Remove the coolant recovery tank and bracket.
17. Disconnect the core case assembly electrical connectors.
18. Remove the bracket at the evaporator case.
19. Remove the right side marker light, as required, for access.
20. Remove the 3 nuts and 1 screw attaching the ECM to the dash panel.
21. Remove the evaporator core case and housing assembly from the vehicle.
22. Remove the screws and separated the case sections.
23. Remove the evaporator core.

To install:

NOTE: If replacing the evaporator, add 3 oz. of refrigerant lubricant to the system.

24. Position the evaporator core in the case.
25. Mate the case sections and istall the retaining screws.
26. Install the core case and housing assembly in the vehicle.
27. Install the ECM to the dash panel using the 3 nuts and 1 screws.
28. Replace the evaporator inlet line O-rings. Lubricate with refrigerant lubricant.
29. Connect the evaporator inlet line.

NOTE: Use a backup wrench on the evaporator fittings when connecting the refrigerant lines.

30. Install the right side marker light.
31. Install the bracket to the evaporator case.
32. Connect the core case assembly electrical connectors.
33. Install the recovery tank and bracket.
34. Install the blower motor and evaporator core insulation.
35. Raise the lower evaporator insulation into position and install the upper screws.
36. Install the heater valve assembly bracket.
37. Install the radiator.
38. Install the upper half of the fan shroud.
39. Install the blower motor relay and resistor. Connect the blower motor relay and resistor electrical connectors.
40. Install the accumulator.
41. Replace the accumulator O-rings. Lubricate with refrigerant lubricant.
42. Connect the accumulator refrigerant line.

NOTE: Use a backup wrench on the accumulator fittings when connecting the refrigerant lines.

43. Install the windshield solvent tank.
44. Install the hood latch assembly and cable retainer.
45. Install the cold air intake.
46. Connect the negative battery cable.
47. Evacuate, recharge and leak test the air conditioning system.

S Series and Bravada

1. Disconnect the negative battery cable.
2. Properly discharge and recover the air conditioning system refrigerant.

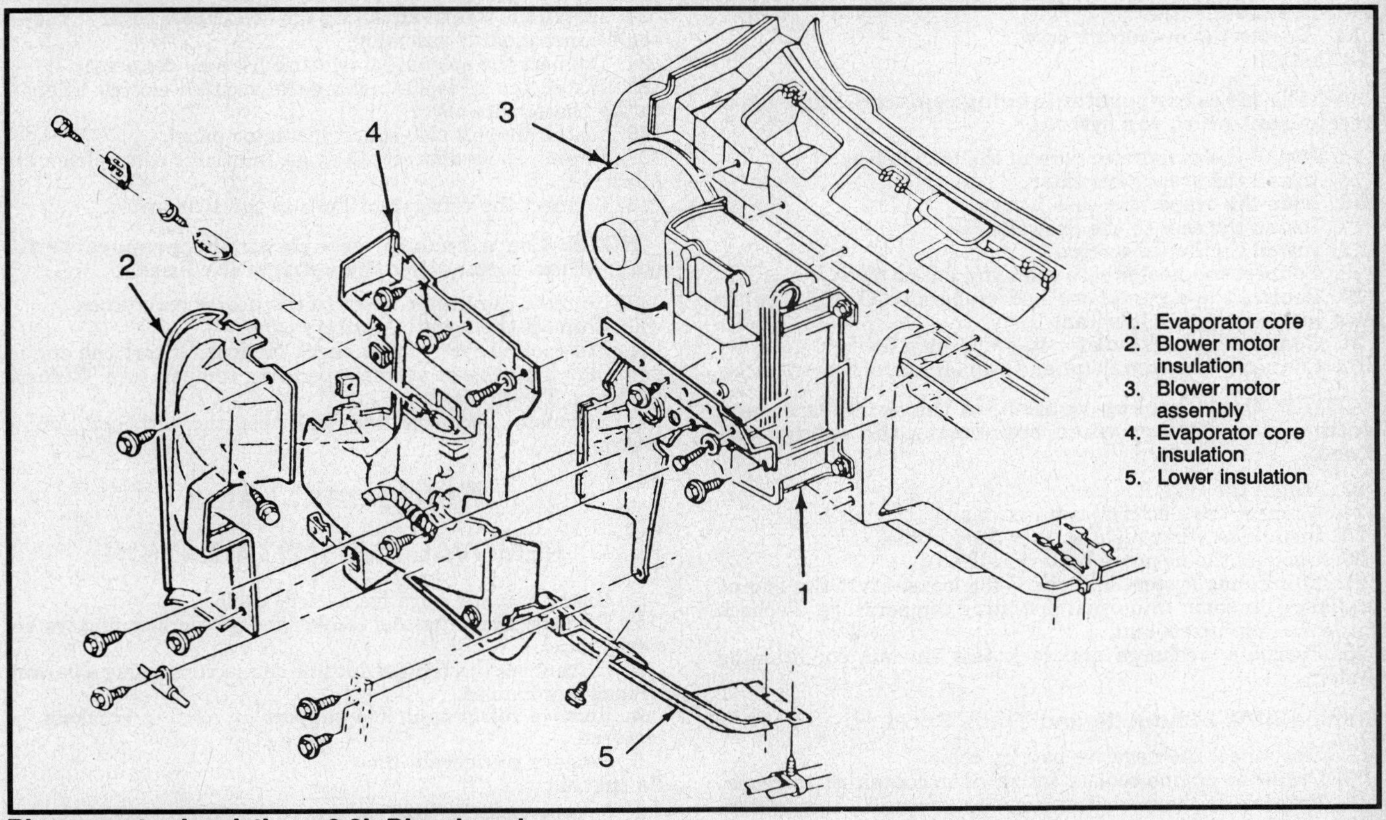
1
2
3
4
5
1. Evaporator core
2. Blower motor insulation
3. Blower motor assembly
4. Evaporator core insulation
5. Lower insulation

Blower motor insulation—6.2L Diesel engine

3. Remove the blower motor resistor and set aside. Leave resistor connected.
4. Disconnect the blower motor electrical connector.
5. Disconnect the refrigerant lines from the evaporator, accumulator and disconnect the accumulator from the evaporator.

NOTE: Use a backup wrench on the accumulator and evaporator fittings when disconnecting the refrigerant lines.

6. Discard the O-rings.

NOTE: Cap the refrigerant lines when opening the system to prevent the entry of dirt and moisture and the loss of refrigerant lubricant.

7. Remove the accumulator bracket.
8. Remove the blower motor assembly.
9. Remove the screws retaining the evaporator case and remove the case.
10. Remove the evaporator core.

To install:

NOTE: If replacing the evaporator, add 2 oz. of refrigerant lubricant to the system.

11. Install the evaporator core into the case.
12. Install the case to the firewall.
13. Install the accumulator bracket.
14. Replace the accumulator and evaporator O-rings. Lubricate with refrigerant lubricant.
15. Connect the accumulator-to-evaporator refrigerant connection.
16. Connect the accumulator and condenser refrigerant lines.

NOTE: Use a backup wrench on the accumulator and evaporator fittings when connecting the refrigerant lines.

17. Install the blower motor assembly.
18. Connect the blower motor electrical connector.
19. Install the blower motor resistor.
20. Connect the negative battery cable.
21. Evacuate, recharge and leak test the air conditioning system.

Astro and Safari

1. Disconnect the negative battery cable.
2. Properly discharge and recover the air conditioning system refrigerant.
3. Drain the engine coolant into a clean container for reuse.
4. Remove the windshield washer fluid bottle.
5. Disconnect the electrical connectors.
6. Disconnect the heater hoses from the heater core tubes. Cap the heater core tubes to prevent leakage during removal.
7. Disconnect the refrigerant lines from the evaporator and accumulator.

NOTE: Use a backup wrench on the evaporator and accumulator fittings when disconnecting the refrigerant lines.

8. Discard the O-rings.

NOTE: Cap the refrigerant lines when opening the system to prevent the entry of dirt and moisture and the loss of refrigerant lubricant.

9. Remove the relay bracket.
10. Remove the case flange nuts.
11. Remove the blower case. Separate the case halves.

12. Remove the filter.
13. Remove the evaporator core.

To install:

NOTE: If the evaporator is being replaced, add 3 oz. of refrigerant oil to the system.

14. Install the evaporator core in the case halves.
15. Install the evaporator filter.
16. Mate the evaporator case halves.
17. Install the case to the firewall.
18. Install the flange screws.
19. Connect the heater core inlet and outlet pipes.
20. Replace the accumulator and evaporator O-rings. Lubricate with refrigerant lubricant.
21. Connect the accumulator-to-evaporator fittings.
22. Connect the accumulator and evaporator refrigerant lines.

NOTE: Use a backup wrench on the evaporator and accumulator fittings when connecting the refrigerant lines.

23. Install the relay bracket.
24. Connect the electrical connections.
25. Install the windshield washer fluid bttole.
26. Connect the negative battery cable.
27. Fill cooling system and check for leaks. Start the engine and allow to come to normal operating temperature. Recheck for leaks. Top-up coolant.
28. Evacuate, recharge and leak test the air conditioning system.

Lumina APV, Silhouette and Trans Sport

1. Disconnect the negative battery cable.
2. Drain the engine coolant into a clean container for reuse.
3. Properly discharge and recover the air conditioning system refrigerant.
4. Disconnect the heater hoses from the heater core tubes. Cap the heater core tubes to prevent leakage during removal.
5. Disconnect the refrigerant lines from the evaporator.

NOTE: Use a backup wrench on the evaporator fittings when disconnecting the refrigerant lines.

6. Discard the O-rings.

NOTE: Cap the refrigerant lines when opening the system to prevent the entry of dirt and moisture and the loss of refrigerant lubricant.

7. Remove the left side sound insulator panel.
8. Remove the screws attaching the vacuum electric solenoid to the heater core cover.
9. Disconnect the solenoid-to-electric harness connector.
10. Remove the screws attaching the heater core cover to the air conditioner module assembly.
11. Remove the heater core.
12. Remove the upper instrument panel trim pad assembly.
13. Disconnect the temperature motor harness connector.
14. Remove the screws attaching the temperature door/slave door housing.
15. Remove, from the engine compartment side of the cowl, the bolts that attach the evaporator core to the evaporator cover.
16. Remove the evaporator.

To install:

17. Install the evaporator.
18. Install, from the engine compartment side of the cowl, the bolts that attach the evaporator core to the evaporator cover.
19. Install the screws attaching the temperature door/slave door housing.
20. Connect the temperature motor harness connector.
21. Install the upper instrument panel trim pad assembly.
22. Install the heater core.
23. Install the screws attaching the heater core cover to the air conditioner module assembly.
24. Connect the solenoid-to-electric harness connector.
25. Install the screws attaching the vacuum electric solenoid to the heater core cover.
26. Install the left side sound insulator panel.
27. Replace the evaporator O-rings. Lubricate with refrigerant lubricant.
28. Connect the refrigerant lines to the evaporator.

NOTE: Use a backup wrench on the evaporator fittings when connecting the refrigerant lines.

29. Connect the heater hoses to the heater core tubes.
30. Connect the negative battery cable.
31. Fill cooling system and check for leaks. Start the engine and allow to come to normal operating temperature. Recheck for leaks. Top-up coolant.
32. Evacuate, recharge and leak test the air conditioning system.

Refrigerant Lines

REMOVAL AND INSTALLATION

1. Disconnect the negative battery cable.
2. Properly discharge and recover the air conditioning system refrigerant.
3. Disconnect the refrigerant line connectors, using a backup wrench as required.
4. Remove refrigerant line support or routing brackets, as required.
5. Remove refrigerant line.

To install:

6. Position new refrigerant line in place, leaving protective caps installed until ready to connect.
7. Install new O-rings on refrigerant line connector fittings. Lubricate with refrigerant oil.
8. Connect refrigerant line, using a backup wrench, as required.
9. Install refrigerant line support or routing brackets, as required.
10. Evacuate, recharge and leak test the system.
11. Connect the negative battery cable.

Manual Control Head

REMOVAL AND INSTALLATION

C/K Series Pick-Up, S Series, Bravada, Astro and Safari

1. Disconnect the negative battery cable.
2. Remove the instrument panel bezel or fascia.
3. Remove the control assembly mounting screws.
4. Pull the control assembly out far enough to reach the cables and electrical connectors.
5. Disconnect the control cables.
6. Disconnect the electrical connectors.
7. If equipped, disconnect the vacuum harness.
8. Remove the blower switch, as required.
9. Remove the control assembly.

To install:

10. Install the control assembly.
11. If removed, install the blower switch.
12. If equipped, connect the vacuum harness.
13. Connect the electrical connectors.
14. Connect the control cables.
15. Place the control assembly into position and install the mounting screws.

16. Install the instrument panel bezel or fascia.
17. Connect the negative battery cable.

Suburban, Blazer and Jimmy

WITHOUT AIR CONDITIONING

1. Disconnect the negative battery cable.
2. Remove the instrument panel bezel or fascia.
3. Remove the control assembly mounting screws.
4. Pull the control assembly out far enough to reach the cables and electrical connectors.
5. Disconnect the control cables.
6. Disconnect the electrical connectors.
7. Remove the blower switch, as required.
8. Remove the control assembly.

To install:

9. Install the control assembly.
10. If removed, install the blower switch.
11. Connect the electrical connectors.
12. Connect the control cables.
13. Place the control assembly into position and install the mounting screws.
14. Install the instrument panel bezel or fascia.
15. Connect the negative battery cable.

WITH AIR CONDITIONING

1. Disconnect the negative battery cable.
2. On 1989–90 vehicles, remove the radio, as required.
3. On 1991 vehicles, remove the lower steering column bezel.
4. Remove the instrument panel bezel or fascia.
5. Remove the control assembly mounting screws.
6. Pull the control assembly out far enough to reach the cables and electrical connectors.
7. Disconnect the control cables.
8. Disconnect the vacuum harness hose.
9. Disconnect the electrical connectors.
10. Remove the blower switch, as required.
11. Remove the control assembly.

To install:

12. Install the control assembly.
13. If removed, install the blower switch.
14. Connect the electrical connectors.
15. Connect the vacuum harness hose.
16. Connect the control cables.
17. Place the control assembly into position and install the mounting screws.
18. Install the instrument panel bezel or fascia.
19. On 1989–90 vehicles, install the radio, as required.
20. On 1991 vehicles, install the lower steering column bezel.
21. Connect the negative battery cable.

G Series Van

1. Disconnect the negative battery cable.
2. If equipped with air conditioning, remove the headlight switch control knob.
3. Remove the instrument panel bezel or fascia.
4. Remove the control assembly mounting screws.
5. Pull the control assembly out far enough to reach the cables and electrical connectors.
6. Disconnect the control cables.
7. Disconnect the electrical connectors.
8. If equipped, disconnect the vacuum harness.
9. Remove the blower switch, as required.
10. Remove the control assembly.

To install:

11 Install the control assembly.
12. If removed, install the blower switch.
13. If equipped, connect the vacuum harness.
14. Connect the electrical connectors.
15. Connect the control cables.
16. Place the control assembly into position and install the mounting screws.
17. Install the instrument panel bezel or fascia.
18. If equipped with air conditioning, install the headlight switch control knob.
19. Connect the negative battery cable.

Lumina APV, Silhouette and Trans Sport

1. Disconnect the negative battery cable.
2. Remove the lower steering column trim cover to expose the left side accessory trim plate mounting screws.
3. Lower the glove box door to expose the right side accessory trim plate mounting screws.
4. Remove the accessory trim plate mounting screws and remove the accessory trim plate.
5. Loosen the screws retaining the heater-HVAC control assembly to the seft side of the accessory mounting bracket.
6. Slide the control assembly out from the bracket.
7. Disconnect the instrument panel electrical harness connectors attached to the rear of the control assembly.
8. Remove the control assembly.

To install:

9. Install the control assembly
10. Connect the instrument panel harness connectors to the control assembly.
11. Slide the heater-HVAC control assembly into the accessory housing bracket and install the mounting screws.
12. Install the accessory trim plate and mounting screws.
13. Close the glove box door and install the lower steering column trim cover.
14. Connect the negative battery cable.

Manual Control Cables

ADJUSTMENT

1. Remove the retainer from the lever.
2. Remove the cable.
3. Bend the cable to lengthen or shorten.
4. Reattach the cable to the lever and move the control lever in the full range of its travel and listen for the door opening and closing. Readjust the cable, as necessary.
5. Install the retainer.

REMOVAL AND INSTALLATION

1. Remove the trim panels or bezels.
2. Remove the control assembly and pull out far enough to disconnect the control cable.
3. Remove the retainer at the actuator lever and remove the cable from the actuator lever.
4. Remove the routing and mounting brackets or loosen enough to slide the cable through.
5. Remove the cable.

To install:

6. Feed the cable through the brackets and into position.
7. Attach the cable at both ends and install the retainers.
8. Check cable adjustment.

SENSORS AND SWITCHES

Vacuum Actuator

OPERATION

Used on certain heating and air conditioning systems, the vacuum actuators operate the air doors determining the different modes. The actuator consists of a spring loaded diaphragm connected to a lever. When vacuum is applied to the diaphragm, the lever moves the control door to its appropriate position. When the lever on the control panel is moved to another position, vacuum is cut off and the spring returns the actuator lever to its normal position.

TESTING

1. Disconnect the vacuum line from the actuator.
2. Attach a hand-held vacuum pump to the actuator.
3. Apply vacuum to the actuator.
4. The actuator lever should move to its engaged position and remain there while vacuum is applied.
5. When vacuum is released it should move back to its normal position.
6. The lever should operate smoothly and not bind.

REMOVAL AND INSTALLATION

1. Remove the vacuum lines from the actuator.
2. Disconnect the linkage from the actuator.
3. Remove the hardware attaching the actuator.
4. Remove the actuator.

To install:

5. Install the actuator and attaching hardware.
6. Connect the linkage to the actuator.
7. Connect the vacuum lines to the actuator.
8. Test system to confirm proper functioning of the actuator.

Coolant Temperature Sensor

OPERATION

The coolant temperature sensor provides an engine temperature signal to the ECM. The ECM controls the operation of the electric cooling fans, if equipped, and in cases of high engine temperature, deengergizes the compressor clutch. The coolant temperature sensor is located in the front of the engine, usually mounted on or near the thermostat housing.

REMOVAL AND INSTALLATION

1. Disconnect the negative battery cable.
2. Drain the cooling system into a clean container for reuse.
3. Disconnect the electrical connector from the coolant temperature sensor.
4. Remove the coolant temperature sensor.

To install:

5. Install the coolant temperature sensor.
6. Connect the electrical connector.
7. Fill the cooling system.
8. Connect the negative battery cable.
9. Start the engine and check for leaks.

High-Pressure Compressor Cut-Off Switch

OPERATION

Used on Lumina APV, Silhouette and Trans Sport, the function of the switch is to protect the compressor in the event of excessively high compressor head pressure and to deenergize the compressor clutch before the high pressure relief valve discharge pressure is reached. The high-pressure switch is mounted on the back of the compressor on a Schrader-type valve and does not require discharging the system to be serviced.

REMOVAL AND INSTALLATION

1. Disconnect the negative battery cable.
2. Disconnect the electrical connector.
3. Remove the switch from the coupled hose assembly. Discard the O-ring.

To install:

4. Lubricate a new O-ring with refrigerant oil.
5. Install the O-ring on the switch and install the switch.
6. Connect the electrical connector.
7. Connect the negative battery cable.

Low-Pressure Compressor Cut-Off Switch

OPERATION

Used on Lumina APV, Silhouette and Trans Sport, the function of the switch is to deenergize the compressor in the event of a low-charge condition. The switch also prevents the compressor from running in excessively cold weather. The switch is mounted at the back of the compressor. Servicing the valve requires discharging the system.

REMOVAL AND INSTALLATION

1. Disconnect the negative battery cable.
2. Properly discharge and recover the air conditioning system refrigerant.
3. Disconnect the electrical connector(s).
4. Remove the switch. Discard the O-ring.

To install:

5. Replace the O-ring. Lubricate the new O-ring with refrigerant oil.
6. Install the switch.
7. Connect the electrical connector(s).
8. Evacuate, charge and leak test the system.
9. Connect the negative battery cable.

Pressure Cycling Switch

OPERATION

The pressure cycling switch controls the refrigeration cycle by sensing low-side pressure as an indicator of evaporator temperature. The pressure cycling switch is the freeze-protection device in the system and senses refrigerant pressure on the suction side. The pressure cycling switch is not used with V-5 compressors since Variable Displacement Orifice Tube (VDOT) system does not cycle.

REMOVAL AND INSTALLATION

NOTE: The switch is mounted on a Schrader valve on the accumulator. The system need not be discharged to remove the pressure cycling switch.

1. Disconnect the negative battery cable.
2. Disconnect the electrical connector.
3. Remove the switch and O-ring seal. Discard the O-ring.

To install:

4. Install a new O-ring. Lubricate with refrigerant oil.
5. Install the switch to the accumulator.
6. Connect the electrical connector.
7. Connect the negative battery cable.

REAR AUXILIARY SYSTEM

Expansion Valve

REMOVAL AND INSTALLATION

Surburban and G Series Van

1. Disconnect the negative battery cable.
2. Properly discharge and recover the air conditioning system refrigerant.
3. Remove the rear duct work.
4. Disconnect the blower motor harness connector.
5. Disconnect the ground wire.

NOTE: Support the lower case and motor assemblies.

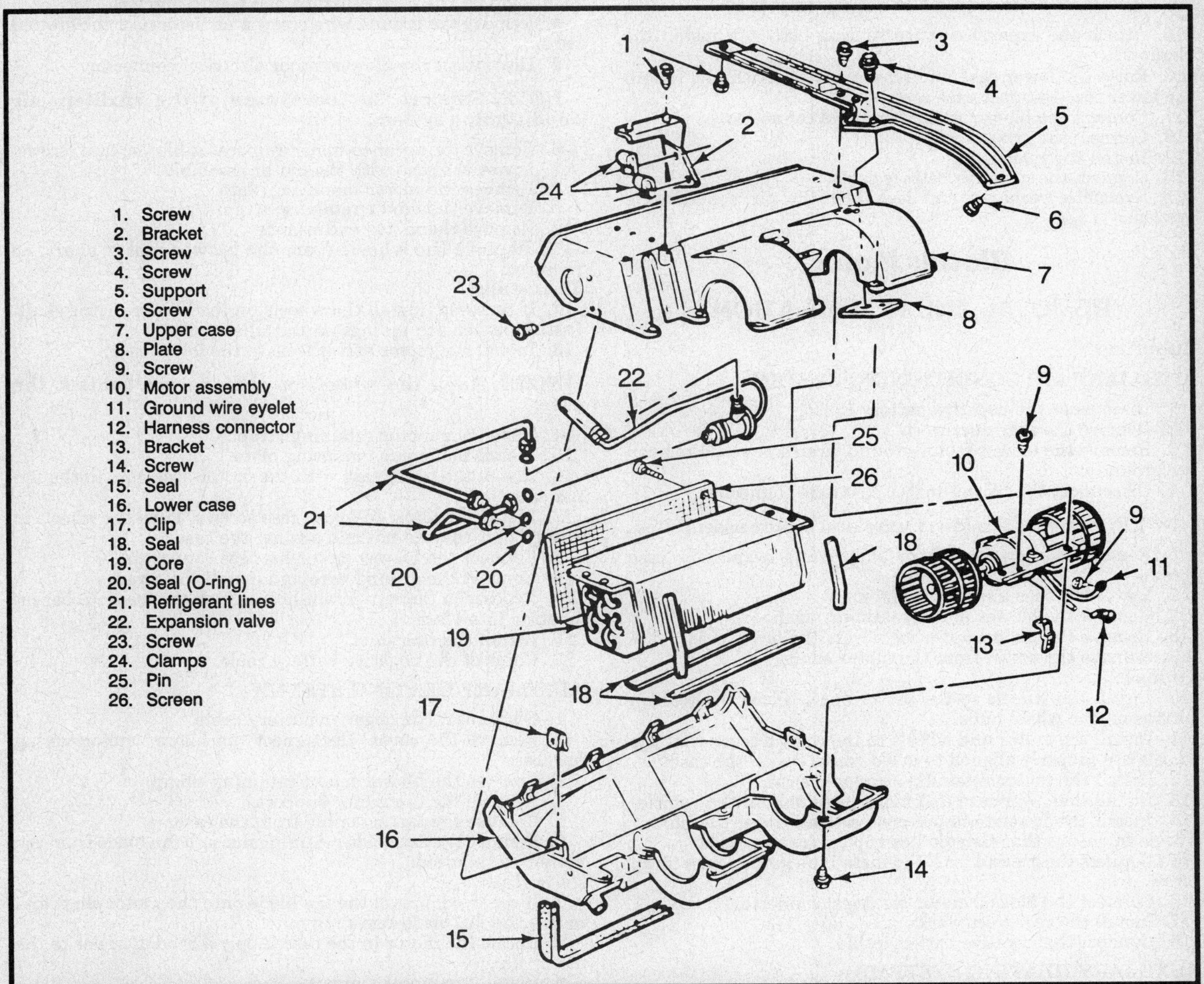
1. Screw
2. Bracket
3. Screw
4. Screw
5. Support
6. Screw
7. Upper case
8. Plate
9. Screw
10. Motor assembly
11. Ground wire eyelet
12. Harness connector
13. Bracket
14. Screw
15. Seal
16. Lower case
17. Clip
18. Seal
19. Core
20. Seal (O-ring)
21. Refrigerant lines
22. Expansion valve
23. Screw
24. Clamps
25. Pin
26. Screen

Rear interior roof-mounted evaporator and related components—Suburban

6. Remove the lower-to-upper blower and evaporator case screws.
7. Lower the case with the motor assembly.
8. Remove the expansion valve sensing bulb clamps.
9. Disconnect the expansion valve refrigerant lines.

NOTE: Use a backup wrench on the expansion valve fittings when disconnecting the refrigerant lines.

10. Discard the O-rings.

NOTE: Cap the refrigerant lines when opening the system to prevent the entry of dirt and moisture and the loss of refrigerant lubricant.

11. Remove the expansion valve assembly.

To install:

12. Place the expansion valve in position.
13. Replace the expansion valve O-rings. Lubricate with refrigerant lubricant.
14. Connect the expansion valve refrigerant lines.

NOTE: Use a backup wrench on the expansion valve fittings when connecting the refrigerant lines.

15. Attach the expansion valve sensing bulb and install the clamps.
16. Raise the lower case and blower motor assembly. Install the lower case-to-upper case screws.
17. Connect the blower motor electrical connector.
18. Connect the ground wire.
19. Install the rear duct.
20. Connect the negative battery cable.
21. Evacuate, recharge and leak test the air conditioning system.

Blower Motor

REMOVAL AND INSTALLATION

Suburban

AUXILIARY AIR CONDITIONING SYSTEM

1. Disconnect the negative battery cable.
2. Remove the rear duct work.
3. Remove the blower motor ground strap screw and remove the ground strap.
4. Disconnect the blower motor electrical connector.

NOTE: Support the lower case and motor assemblies.

5. Remove the lower-to-upper blower and evaporator case screws.
6. Lower the case and motor assembly.
7. Remove the blower motor retaining strap.
8. Remove the motor and wheels from the lower case.
9. Remove the wheel from the motor shaft.

To install:

10. Install the wheels to the motor shaft. Place the tension springs on the wheel hubs.
11. Install the motor and wheels to the case. Ensure that the wheels are properly aligned to avoid contact with the case.
12. Install the motor retaining strap and foam.
13. Install the lower case and motor assembly in the vehicle.
14. Install the lower-to-upper case screws. Turn the blower wheels to ensure that they do not rub against the case.
15. Connect the ground wire and install the ground wire strap screw.
16. Connect the blower motor electrical connector.
17. Install the rear duct work.
18. Connect the negative battery cable.

AUXILIARY HEATING SYSTEM

1. Disconnect the negative battery cable.
2. Disconnect the blower motor wiring harness.
3. Remove the blower motor retaining clamp.
4. Remove the fan motor support.
5. Remove the fan assembly from the case.
6. Remove the fan blade retaining nut and fan blade from the motor, as required.

To install:

7. If removed, install the fan blade onto the motor shaft and install the fan blade retaining nut.
8. Install the motor in the case.
9. Install the motor support.
10. Install the lower motor retaining clamp.
11. Connect the blower mtor wiring harness.
12. Connect the negative battery cable.

G Series Van

AUXILIARY AIR CONDITIONING SYSTEM

1. Disconnect the negative battery cable.
2. Remove the rear duct work.
3. Place the refrigerant lines aside. Pull back the foam rubber insulation on the high pressure line before moving.
4. Remove the ground wire screw and disconnect the ground wire.
5. Disconnect the blower motor electrical connector.

NOTE: Support the lower case of the auxiliary air conditioning system.

6. Remove the lower-to-upper evaporator-blower case screws.
7. Lower the case with the motor assembly.
8. Remove the motor mounting plate.
9. Remove the motor retaining strap.
10. Remove the motor and wheels.
11. Remove the wheels from the blower motor shaft, as required.

To install:

12. If removed, install the wheels on the blower motor shaft. Install the tension springs on the wheel hubs.
13. Install the motor and wheels to the lower case.

NOTE: Align the wheels so they do not contact the case.

14. Install the motor retaining strap.
15. Install the motor mounting plate.
16. Install the lower case with the motor assembly to the upper case.
17. Install the lower-to-upper case screws. Turn the wheels to ensure that they do not rub against the case.
18. Connect the blower motor harness connector.
19. Connect the ground wire and install the screw.
20. Reposition the refrigerant hoses. Push the foam rubber insulation into place.
21. Install the rear duct.
22. Connect the negative battery cable.

AUXILIARY HEATING SYSTEM

1. Disconnect the negative battery cable.
2. Remove the cover. Disconnect the blower motor wiring harness.
3. Remove the blower motor retaining clamp.
4. Remove the fan motor support.
5. Remove the fan assembly from the case.
6. Remove the fan blade retaining nut and fan blade from the motor, as required.

To install:

7. If removed, install the fan blade onto the motor shaft and install the fan blade retaining nut.
8. Install the motor in the case. Apply a bead of sealer to the motor flange.
9. Install the motor support.
10. Install the lower motor retaaining clamp.

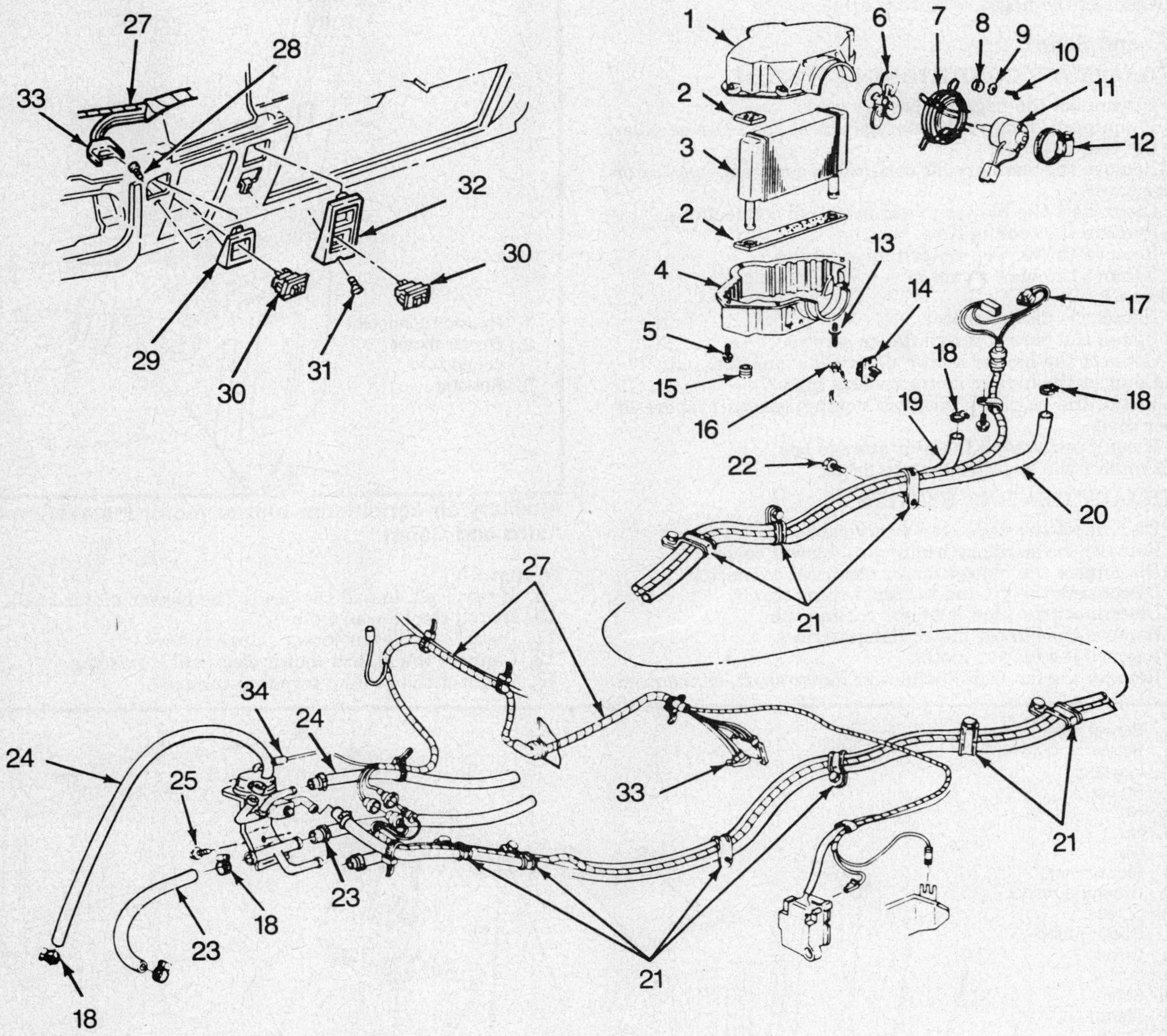
27
28
33
32
30
29
30
31
1
2
3
2
4
5
15
16
13
14
6
7
8
9
10
11
12
17
18
19
18
22
20
21
27
34
24
24
25
33
23
18
23
18
21
21

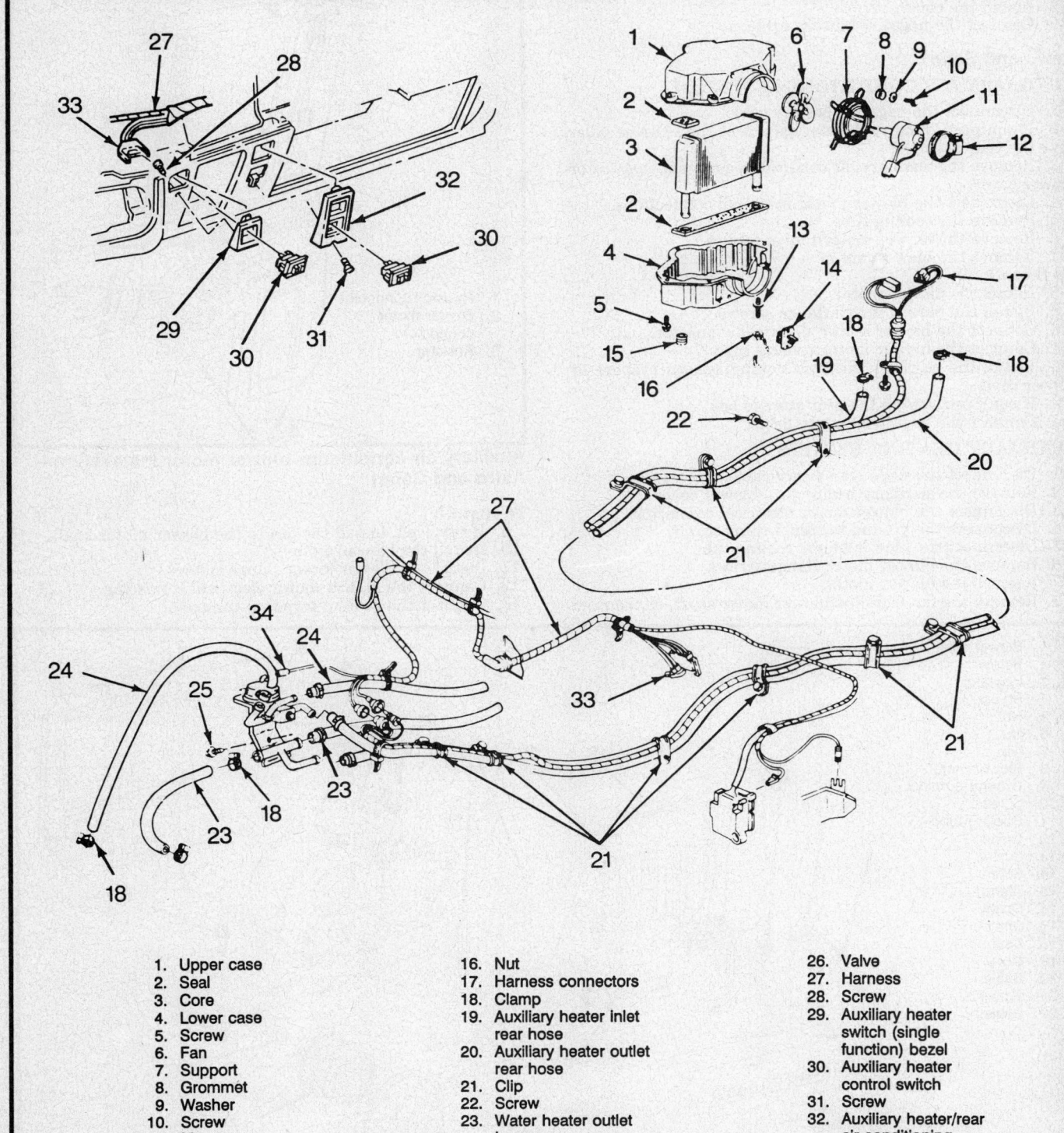

1. Upper case
2. Seal
3. Core
4. Lower case
5. Screw
6. Fan
7. Support
8. Grommet
9. Washer
10. Screw
11. Motor
12. Clamp
13. Stud
14. Resistor
15. Seal
16. Nut
17. Harness connectors
18. Clamp
19. Auxiliary heater inlet rear hose
20. Auxiliary heater outlet rear hose
21. Clip
22. Screw
23. Water heater outlet hose
24. Water heater inlet hose
25. Screw
26. Valve
27. Harness
28. Screw
29. Auxiliary heater switch (single function) bezel
30. Auxiliary heater control switch
31. Screw
32. Auxiliary heater/rear air conditioning control switch (dual function)
33. Connector
34. Vacuum line

Auxiliary heating system—Suburban

11. Connect the blower mtor wiring harness.
12. Install the cover.
13. Connect the negative battery cable.

Astro and Safari

AUXILIARY AIR CONDITIONING SYSTEM

1. Disconnect the negative battery cable.
2. If equipped, remove the storage box at the left side pillar, near the rear door.
3. Remove the auxiliary air conditioning system evaporator-blower cover.
4. Disconnect the blower motor electrical connections.
5. Remove the cooling tube.
6. Remove the blower motor flange screws.
7. Remove the blower motor.

To install:

8. Install the blower motor.
9. Install the blower motor flange screws.
10. Connect the blower motor electrical connector.
11. Connect the blower motor cooling tube.
12. Install the auxiliary air conditioning system evaporator-blower cover.
13. If equipped, install the rear storage box.
14. Connect the negative battery cable.

AUXILIARY HEATING SYSTEM

1. Disconnect the negative battery cable.
2. Remove the auxiliary heater core-blower cover.
3. Disconnect the blower motor electrical connector.
4. Disconnect the ground terminal connector.
5. Disconnect the blower motor cooling tube.
6. Remove the blower motor flange screws.
7. Remove the blower motor.
8. Remove the fan from the blower motor shaft, as required.

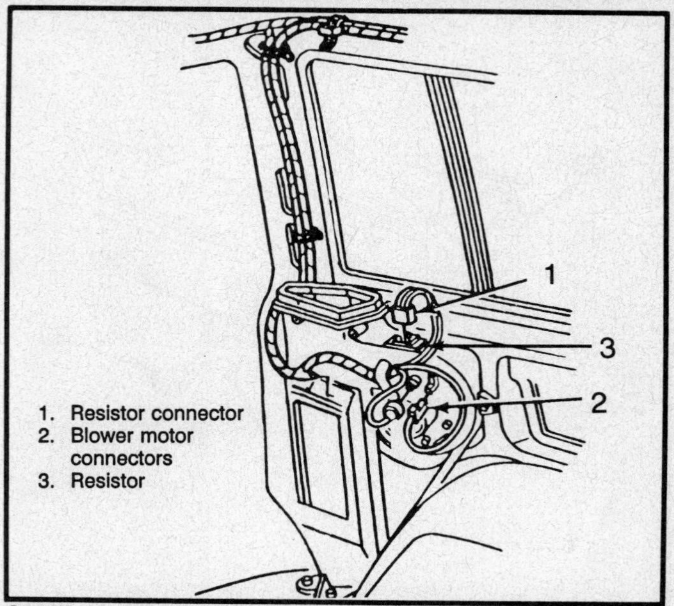
1. Resistor connector
2. Blower motor connectors
3. Resistor
1
3
2

Auxiliary air conditioner blower motor installation—Astro and Safari

To install:

9. If removed, install the fan to the blower motor shaft.
10. Install the blower motor.
11. Install the blower motor flange screws.
12. Connect the blower motor electrical connector.
13. Connect the ground terminal connector.

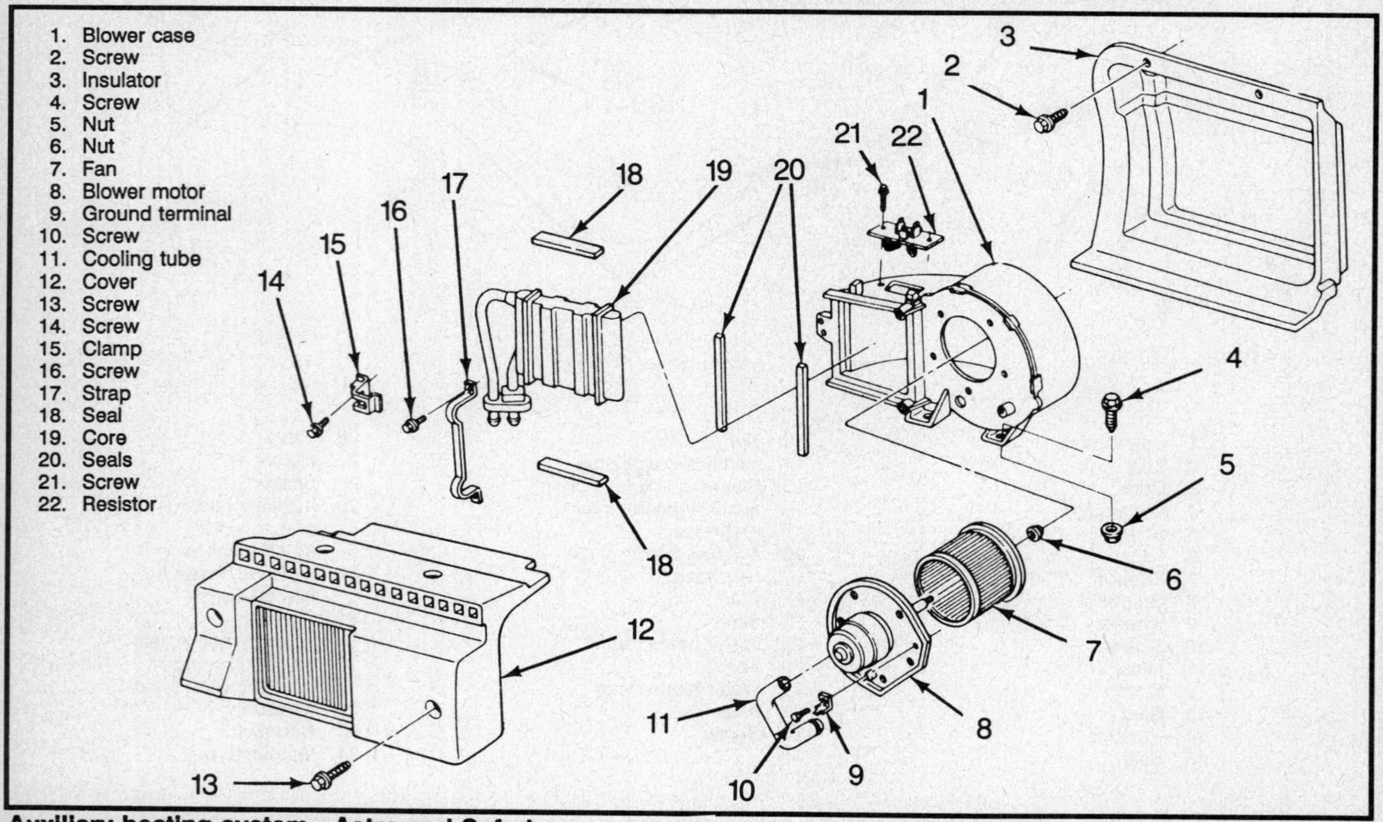
1. Blower case
2. Screw
3. Insulator
4. Screw
5. Nut
6. Nut
7. Fan
8. Blower motor
9. Ground terminal
10. Screw
11. Cooling tube
12. Cover
13. Screw
14. Screw
15. Clamp
16. Screw
17. Strap
18. Seal
19. Core
20. Seals
21. Screw
22. Resistor

Auxiliary heating system—Astro and Safari

14. Connect the blower motor cooling tube.
15. Install the auxiliary heater core-blower cover.
16. Connect the negative battery cable.

Lumina APV, Silhouette and Trans Sport

1. Disconnect the negative battery cable.
2. Remove the left front quarter trim panel.
3. Remove the motor housing-to-case screws.
4. Remove the motor housing assembly.
5. Remove the fan retaining nut.
6. Remove the fan.

To install:

7. Install the fan.
8. Install the fan retaining nut.
9. Install the motor housing assembly.
10. Install the motor housing-to-case screws.
11. Install the left front quarter panel trim.
12. Connect the negative battery cable.

Blower Motor Resistor

REMOVAL AND INSTALLATION

1. Disconnect the negative battery cable.
2. Disconnect the electrical connector at the resistor.
3. Remove the resistor attaching screws.
4. Remove the resistor from the evaporator case.

To install:

5. Position the resistor in the evaporator case. Install the attaching screws.
6. Connect the electrical connector.
7. Connect the negative battery cable.

Heater Core

REMOVAL AND INSTALLATION

Suburban and G Series Van

1. Disconnect the negative battery cable.
2. Drain the engine coolant into a clean container for reuse.
3. Disconnect the heater hoses from the heater core tubes. Cap the heater core tubes to prevent leakage during removal.
4. Disconnect the blower motor electrical connector.
5. Remove the the blower motor retaining clamp.
6. Remove the blower motor, support and fan as an assembly.
7. Remove the upper case.
8. Remove the heater core seal.
9. Remove the heater core.

To install:

10. Install the heater core.
11. Install the seal.
12. Install the upper case.
13. Install the motor, support and fan assembly.
14. Install the blower motor retaining clamp.
15. Connect the blower motor electrical connector.
16. Connect the heater core hoses.
17. Connect the negative battery cable.
18. Fill cooling system and check for leaks. Start the engine and allow to come to normal operating temperature. Recheck for leaks. Top-up coolant.

Astro and Safari

1. Disconnect the negative battery cable.
2. Drain the engine coolant into a clean container for reuse.
3. Disconnect the heater hoses from the auxiliary heater core tubes. Cap the heater core tubes to prevent leakage during removal.
4. Remove the auxiliary heating core-blower cover.

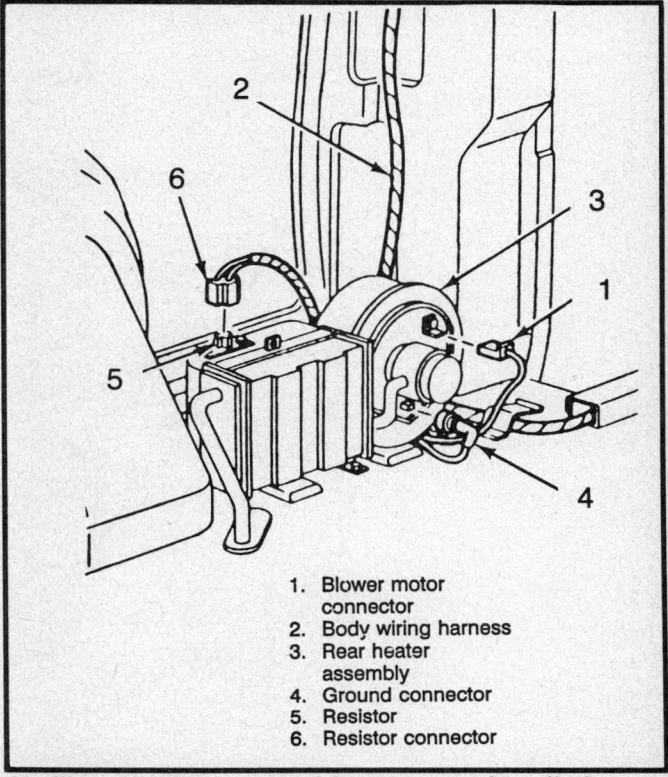

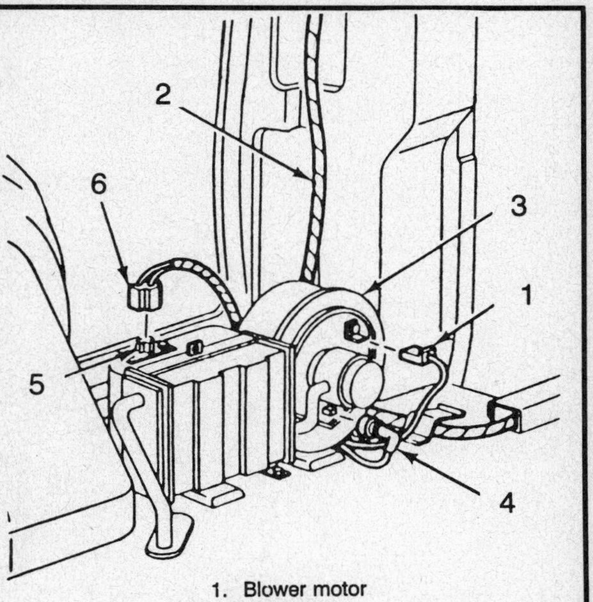
2
6
3
1
5
4
1. Blower motor connector
2. Body wiring harness
3. Rear heater assembly
4. Ground connector
5. Resistor
6. Resistor connector

Auxiliary heating system blower motor installation—Astro and Safari

5. Remove the heater core retaining screws.
6. Remove the heater core mounting strap and clamp.
7. Remove the heater core.
8. Remove the seals from the heater core.

To install:

9. Install the seals to the heater core.
10. Install the heater core.
11. Install the mounting strap and clamp.
12. Install the heater core retaining screws.
13. Install the auxiliary heating core-blower cover.
14. Connect the heater hoses to the auxiliary heater core tubes.
15. Connect the negative battery cable.
16. Fill cooling system and check for leaks. Start the engine and allow to come to normal operating temperature. Recheck for leaks. Top-up coolant.

Evaporator

REMOVAL AND INSTALLATION

Suburban and G Series Van

1. Disconnect the negative battery cable.
2. Properly discharge and recover the air conditioning system refrigerant.
3. Remove the rear duct work.
4. Disconnect the blower motor harness connector.
5. Disconnect the ground wire.
6. Disconnect the refrigerant lines at the rear of the blower-evaporator assembly.

NOTE: Use a backup wrench on the evaporator fittings when disconnecting the refrigerant lines.

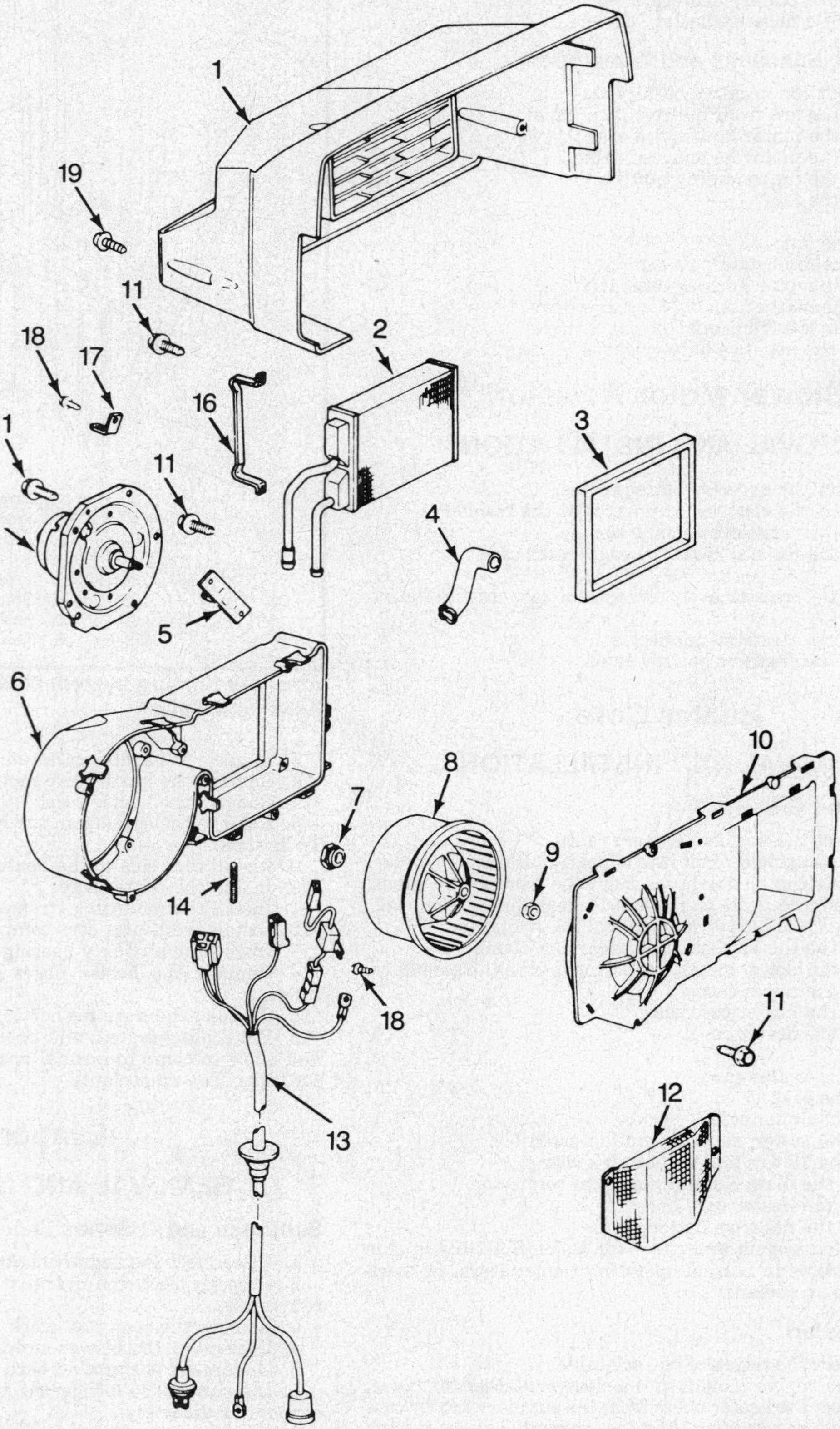
1
2
3
4
5
6
7
8
9
10
11
11
11
11
12
13
14
15
16
17
18
18
19

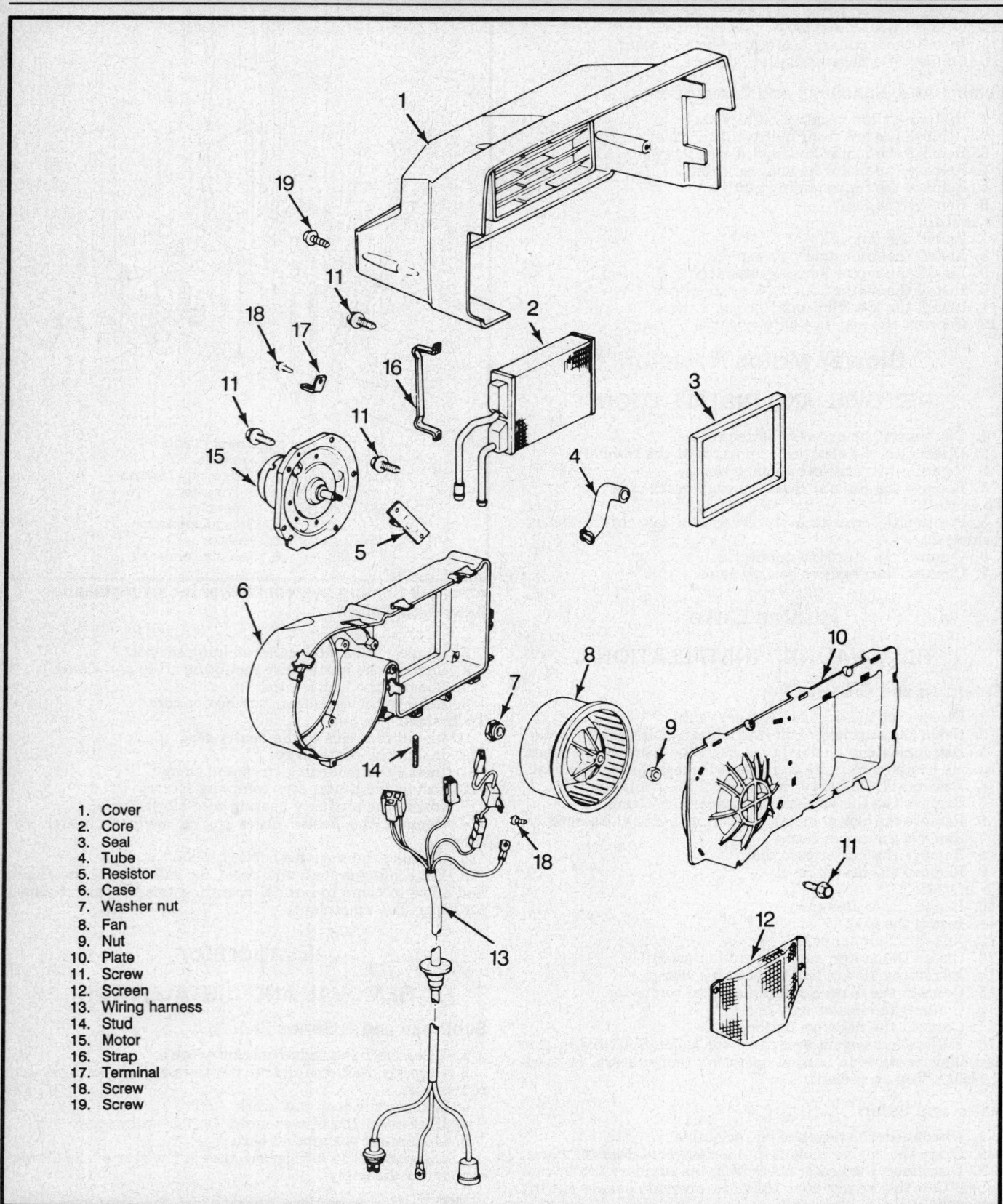

1. Cover
2. Core
3. Seal
4. Tube
5. Resistor
6. Case
7. Washer nut
8. Fan
9. Nut
10. Plate
11. Screw
12. Screen
13. Wiring harness
14. Stud
15. Motor
16. Strap
17. Terminal
18. Screw
19. Screw

Auxiliary heating system—G Series Van

7. Discard the O-rings.

NOTE: Cap the refrigerant lines when opening the system to prevent the entry of dirt and moisture and the loss of refrigerant lubricant.

8. Remove the blower-evaporator support-to-roof rail screws.
9. Remove the blower and evaporator core from the vehicle.
10. Invert the blower and evaporator core unit and place on a work bench.
11. Remove the lower case assembly.
12. Remove the upper case and supports from the evaporator core.
13. Disconnect the expansion valve refrigerant lines.

NOTE: Use a backup wrench on the expansion valve fittings when disconnecting the refrigerant lines.

14. Discard the O-rings.

NOTE: Cap the refrigerant lines when opening the system to prevent the entry of dirt and moisture and the loss of refrigerant lubricant.

15. Disconnect the expansion valve sensing bulb from the evaporator outlet line.
16. Remove the expansion valve.
17. Remove the plastic pins that hold the screen to the evaporator core.
18. Remove the wire screen.

To install:

NOTE: If the evaporator core is being replaced, add 3 oz. of refrigerant lubricant to the system.

19. Install the wire screen to the front of the evaporator core.
20. Install the plastic pins.
21. Replace the expansion valve O-rings. Lubricate with refrigerant lubricant.
22. Install the expansion valve.

NOTE: Use a backup wrench on the expansion valve fittings when connecting the refrigerant lines.

23. Attach the sensing bulb to the evaporator outlet line.

NOTE: The sensing bulb must make good contact with the line.

24. Install the upper case and supports to the core.
25. Install the lower core case and blower assembly.
26. Install the blower-evaporator assembly to the roof.
27. Install the support-to-roof rail screws.
28. Replace the evaporator O-rings. Lubricate with refrigerant lubricant.
29. Connect the refrigerant lines to the rear of the blower-evaporator unit.

NOTE: Use a backup wrench on the evaporator fittings when connecting the refrigerant lines.

30. Connect the blower motor electrical connector.
31. Connect the ground wire.
32. Install the rear duct work.
33. Connect the negative battery cable.
34. Evacuate, recharge and leak test the air conditioning system.

Astro and Safari

1. Disconnect the negative battery cable.
2. Properly discharge and recover the air conditioning system refrigerant.
3. If equipped, remove the storage box at the left side pillar, near the rear door.
4. Remove the auxiliary air conditioning system evaporator-blower cover.

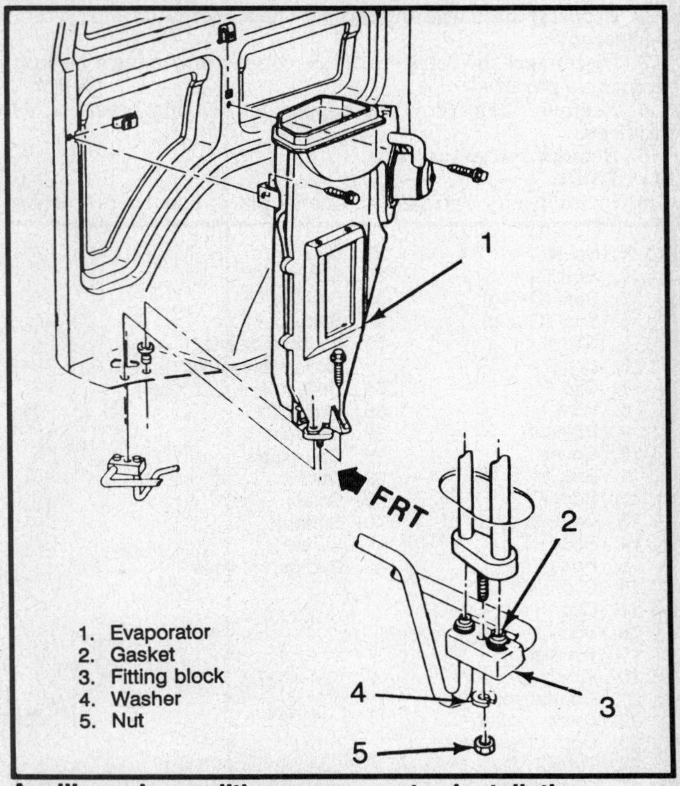
FRT
1
2
3
4
5
1. Evaporator
2. Gasket
3. Fitting block
4. Washer
5. Nut

Auxiliary air conditioner evaporator installation—Astro and Safari

5. Disconnect the electrical connector(s), as required.
6. Disconnect the tube fitting block. Discard the O-rings.

NOTE: Cap the refrigerant lines when opening the system to prevent the entry of dirt and moisture and the loss of refrigerant lubricant.

7. Remove the screws attaching the blower motor and evaporator case assembly. Remove the assembly.
8. Separate the case halves.
9. Remove the evaporator core seal.
10. Remove the evaporator.

To install:

11. Install the evaporator core.
12. Install the evaporator core seal.
13. Reassemble the case halves.
14. Install the blower motor and evaporator case assembly in the vehicle. Install the retaining screws.
15. Replace the tube fitting O-rings. Lubricate with refrigerant lubricant.
16. Connect the tube fitting block. Tighten to 18 ft. lbs. (25 Nm).
17. If disconnected, connect the electrical connector(s).
18. Install the auxiliary air conditioning system evaporator-blower cover.
19. If equipped, install the rear storage box.
20. Connect the negative battery cable.
21. Evacuate, recharge and leak test the air conditioning system.

Refrigerant Lines

REMOVAL AND INSTALLATION

1. Disconnect the negative battery cable.

2. Properly discharge and recover the air conditioning system refrigerant.
3. Disconnect the refrigerant line connectors, using a backup wrench as required.
4. Remove refrigerant line support or routing brackets, as required.
5. Remove refrigerant line.

To install:

6. Position new refrigerant line in place, leaving protective caps installed until ready to connect.
7. Install new O-rings on refrigerant line connector fittings. Lubricate with refrigerant oil.
8. Connect refrigerant line, using a backup wrench, as required.
9. Install refrigerant line support or routing brackets, as required.
10. Evacuate, recharge and leak test the system.
11. Connect the negative battery cable.

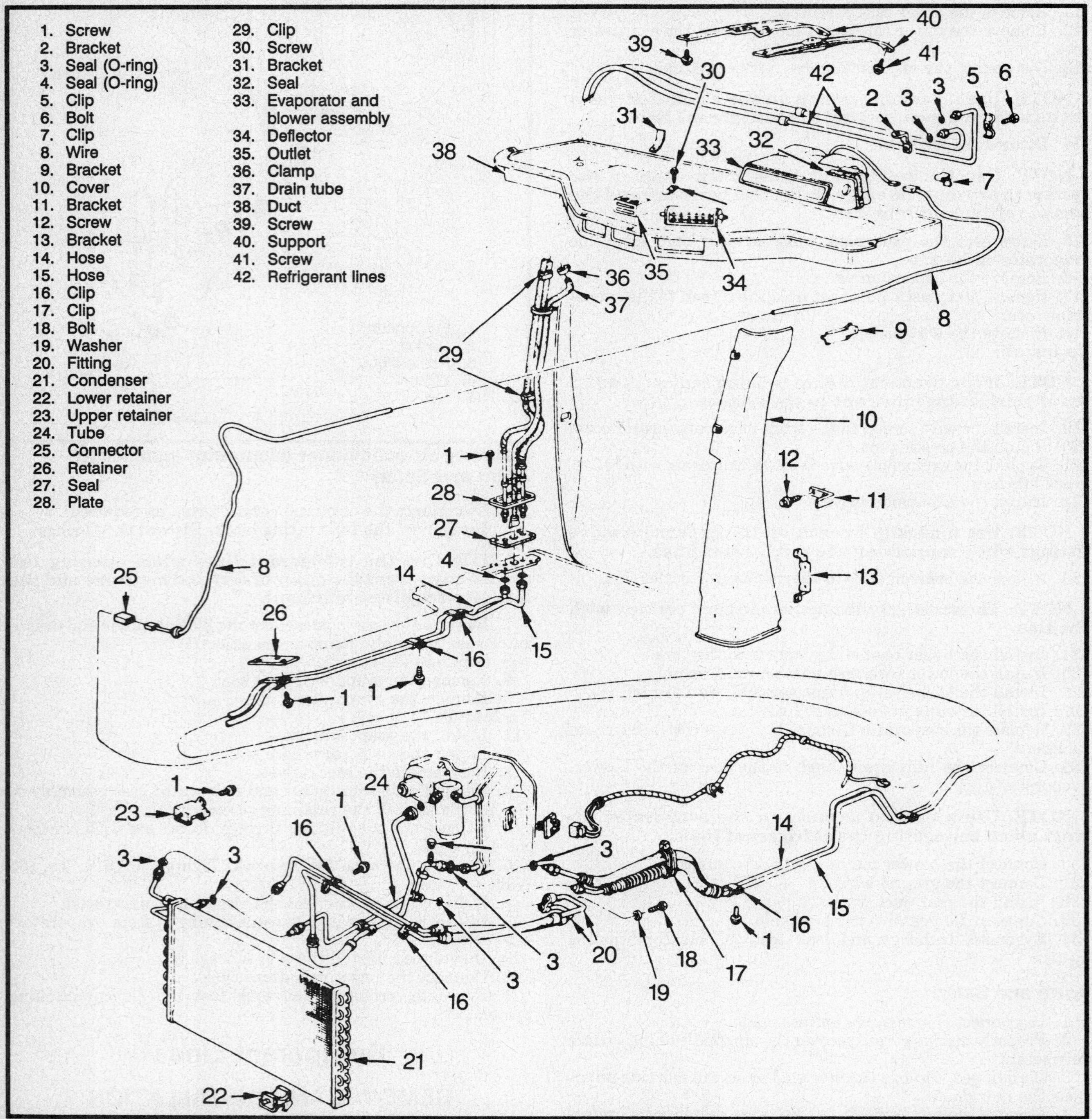
1. Screw
2. Bracket
3. Seal (O-ring)
4. Seal (O-ring)
5. Clip
6. Bolt
7. Clip
8. Wire
9. Bracket
10. Cover
11. Bracket
12. Screw
13. Bracket
14. Hose
15. Hose
16. Clip
17. Clip
18. Bolt
19. Washer
20. Fitting
21. Condenser
22. Lower retainer
23. Upper retainer
24. Tube
25. Connector
26. Retainer
27. Seal
28. Plate
29. Clip
30. Screw
31. Bracket
32. Seal
33. Evaporator and blower assembly
34. Deflector
35. Outlet
36. Clamp
37. Drain tube
38. Duct
39. Screw
40. Support
41. Screw
42. Refrigerant lines

Auxiliary air conditioner refrigerant lines—Suburban

HEATING SYSTEM DIAGNOSIS—EXCEPT LUMINA APV, SILHOUETTE AND TRANS SPORT

PROBLEM	POSSIBLE CAUSE	CORRECTION
No Heat	1. Low coolant level. 2. Door(s) which control the air flow are not operating correctly. (Move the control levers rapidly back and forth. Listen for the door to hit the housing. If the door is heard hitting the housing, its operation is OK.) a. Cable end retaining screws are loose or missing. b. Broken or unhooked cable ends. c. Pivot shaft of door is out of its seating. d. Door blockage. 3. Blower motor does not turn. a. Blown fuse. b. Poor ground. c. Faulty lead connection to motor. d. Faulty blower motor resistor. e. Faulty fan switch. f. Shorted or open circuit between switch and resistor, or between resistor and motor. 4. No air flow, air intake tube blocked. a. Blower motor does not work. b. Plugged ducts. c. Door(s) which control air flow are not operating correctly. 5. Plugged heater core and/or hoses. 6. Engine cooling system will not warm up. 7. Faulty heater core. 8. Faulty pulleys or improper water pump belt tension.	1. Fill the cooling system. 2. Determine and correct cause of malfunction. a. Tighten or install screws. b. Replace the cable or secure with a new push nut. c. Seat the pivot shaft correctly. d. Remove the blockage. 3. Repair or replace blower motor. a. Locate and repair the short. b. Repair the ground. c. Restore the proper connection. d. Replace the resistor. e. Replace the switch. f. Locate the point of the open or shorted circuit and repair. 4. Restore the air flow, clean the screen. a. See number 3, above. b. Remove the blockage. c. See number 2, above. 5. Remove the hoses from the engine and water pump. Reverse flush. 6. Check engine thermostat and radiator cap. 7. Replace the core. 8. Replace the pulleys or tighten the belts.
Poor Removal of Fog or Frost	1. Air control doors are not functioning properly. 2. Blower motor does not spin. 3. Plugged defroster outlets or ducts. 4. Operation of defroster with "AIR" lever in the "BLUE" (cold) position.	1. See "NO HEAT." 2. See "NO HEAT." 3. Remove blockage. 4. Put "AIR" lever in the "RED" (hot) position.
Too Warm in Cab	1. Temperature door not operating correctly. 2. Overheated engine. 3. Blower motor operating only on high speed (faulty resistor).	1. See "NO HEAT." 2. Perform Cooling System Diagnosis. 3. Replace the blower motor resistor.
Heater Gurgle	1. Low coolant level. 2. Plugged heater core and/or hoses.	1. Fill the cooling system. 2. Disconnect the coolant lines of the heater core at the engine water jacket and water pump. Reverse flush.

Problem	Possible Cause	Correction
Temperature of Heater Air at the Outlets Is Too Low to Heat Up Passenger Compartment	Refer to "Insufficient Heat Diagnosis."	Refer to "Insufficient Heat Diagnosis."
Temperature of Heater Air at the Outlets Is Adequate but the Vehicle Will Not Build Up Sufficient Heat	1. Floor side kick pad ventilators partially open. 2. Leaking grommets in dash. 3. Leaking welded seams along the rocker panel and windshield. 4. Leaks through the access holes and screw holes. 5. Leaking rubber molding around the door and windows. 6. Leaks between the sealing edge of blower and the air inlet assembly and cowl, and between the sealing edge of the heater distributor assembly and cowl.	1. Check and adjust. 2. Reseal or replace. 3. Clean and rewash. 4. Reseal or replace. 5. Reseal or replace. 6. Reseal or replace.
Inadequate Defrosting Action	1. Check that the DEFROST lever completely opens the defroster door in the DEF position. 2. Insure that the temperature and air doors open fully. 3. Look for obstructions in the defroster ducts. 4. Check for air leak in the ducting between the defroster outlet on heater assembly and the defroster duct under the instrument panel. 5. Check the position of the bottom of the nozzle to the heater locating tab. 6. Check the position of the defroster nozzle openings relative to instrument panel openings. Mounting tabs provide positive position if properly installed.	1. Adjust if necessary. 2. Adjust. 3. Remove any obstructions. 4. Seal area as necessary. 5. Adjust. 6. Adjust the defroster nozzle openings.
Inadequate Circulation of Heated Air Through the Vehicle	1. Check the heater outlet for correct installation. 2. Inspect the floor carpet to insure that the carpet lies flat under the front seat and does not obstruct air flow. Also inspect around the outlet ducts to insure that the carpet is well fastened to floor to prevent cupping of the air flow.	1. Remove and install. 2. Correct as necessary.
Erratic Heater Operation	1. Check the coolant level. 2. Check for kinked heater hoses. 3. Check the operation of all bowden cables and doors. 4. Sediment in the heater lines and radiator causing the engine thermostat to stick open. 5. Partially plugged heater core.	1. Fill to the proper level. 2. Relieve kinks or replace hoses. 3. Adjust as necessary. 4. Flush the system and clean or replace thermostat as necessary. 5. Backflush core as necessary.
Hard Operating or Broken Controls	1. Check for loose cable tab screws or misadjusted, misrouted or kinked cables. 2. Check for sticking heater system door(s).	1. Correct as required. 2. Lubricate as required using a silicone spray.

INSUFFICIENT HEAT DIAGNOSIS—EXCEPT LUMINA APV, SILHOUETTE AND TRANS SPORT

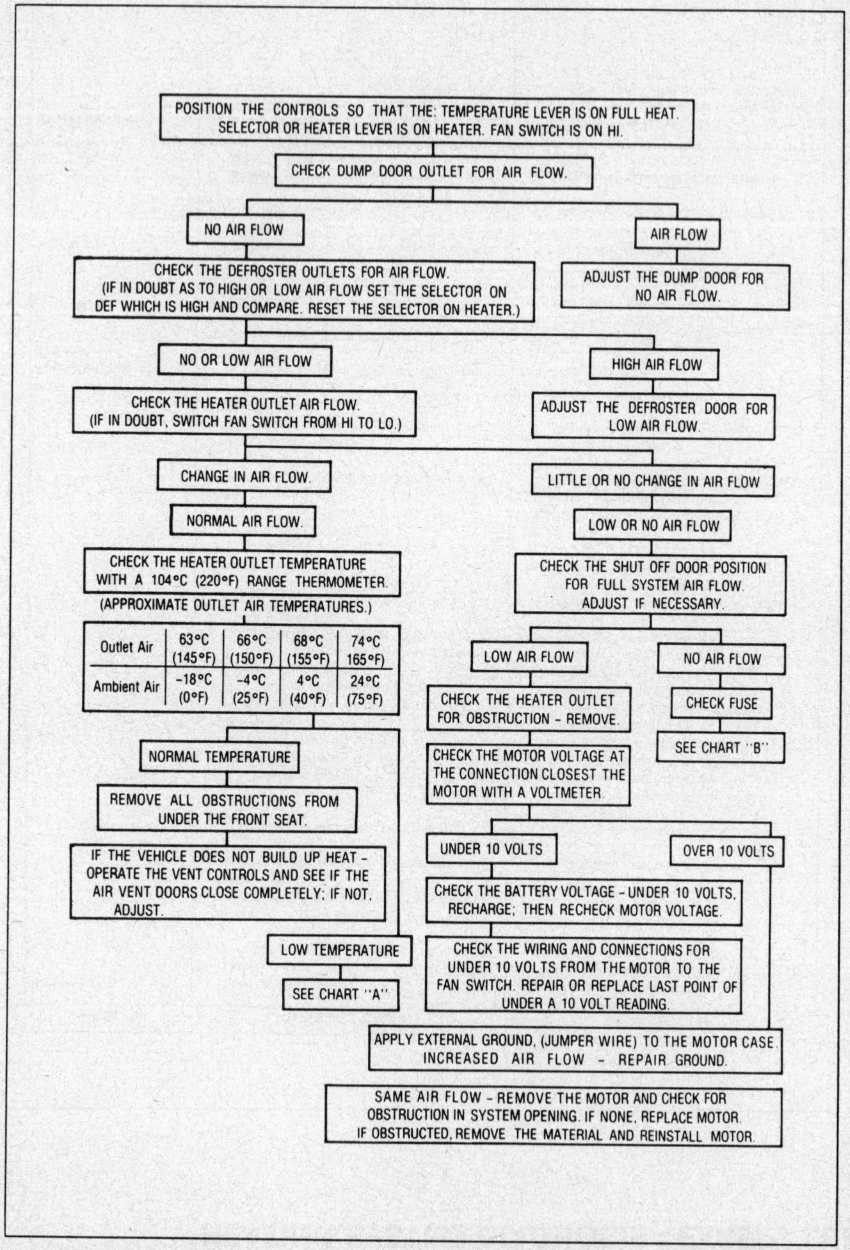
POSITION THE CONTROLS SO THAT THE: TEMPERATURE LEVER IS ON FULL HEAT. SELECTOR OR HEATER LEVER IS ON HEATER. FAN SWITCH IS ON HI.
CHECK DUMP DOOR OUTLET FOR AIR FLOW.
NO AIR FLOW
AIR FLOW
CHECK THE DEFROSTER OUTLETS FOR AIR FLOW. (IF IN DOUBT AS TO HIGH OR LOW AIR FLOW SET THE SELECTOR ON DEF WHICH IS HIGH AND COMPARE. RESET THE SELECTOR ON HEATER.)
ADJUST THE DUMP DOOR FOR NO AIR FLOW.
NO OR LOW AIR FLOW
HIGH AIR FLOW
CHECK THE HEATER OUTLET AIR FLOW. (IF IN DOUBT, SWITCH FAN SWITCH FROM HI TO LO.)
ADJUST THE DEFROSTER DOOR FOR LOW AIR FLOW.
CHANGE IN AIR FLOW.
LITTLE OR NO CHANGE IN AIR FLOW
NORMAL AIR FLOW.
LOW OR NO AIR FLOW
CHECK THE HEATER OUTLET TEMPERATURE WITH A 104°C (220°F) RANGE THERMOMETER.
(APPROXIMATE OUTLET AIR TEMPERATURES.)
Outlet Air 63°C (145°F) 66°C (150°F) 68°C (155°F) 74°C 165°F)
Ambient Air −18°C (0°F) −4°C (25°F) 4°C (40°F) 24°C (75°F)
CHECK THE SHUT OFF DOOR POSITION FOR FULL SYSTEM AIR FLOW. ADJUST IF NECESSARY.
LOW AIR FLOW
NO AIR FLOW
CHECK THE HEATER OUTLET FOR OBSTRUCTION - REMOVE.
CHECK FUSE
SEE CHART "B"
NORMAL TEMPERATURE
CHECK THE MOTOR VOLTAGE AT THE CONNECTION CLOSEST THE MOTOR WITH A VOLTMETER.
REMOVE ALL OBSTRUCTIONS FROM UNDER THE FRONT SEAT.
IF THE VEHICLE DOES NOT BUILD UP HEAT - OPERATE THE VENT CONTROLS AND SEE IF THE AIR VENT DOORS CLOSE COMPLETELY; IF NOT, ADJUST.
UNDER 10 VOLTS
OVER 10 VOLTS
CHECK THE BATTERY VOLTAGE - UNDER 10 VOLTS, RECHARGE; THEN RECHECK MOTOR VOLTAGE.
LOW TEMPERATURE
SEE CHART "A"
CHECK THE WIRING AND CONNECTIONS FOR UNDER 10 VOLTS FROM THE MOTOR TO THE FAN SWITCH. REPAIR OR REPLACE LAST POINT OF UNDER A 10 VOLT READING.
APPLY EXTERNAL GROUND, (JUMPER WIRE) TO THE MOTOR CASE. INCREASED AIR FLOW - REPAIR GROUND.
SAME AIR FLOW - REMOVE THE MOTOR AND CHECK FOR OBSTRUCTION IN SYSTEM OPENING. IF NONE, REPLACE MOTOR. IF OBSTRUCTED, REMOVE THE MATERIAL AND REINSTALL MOTOR.

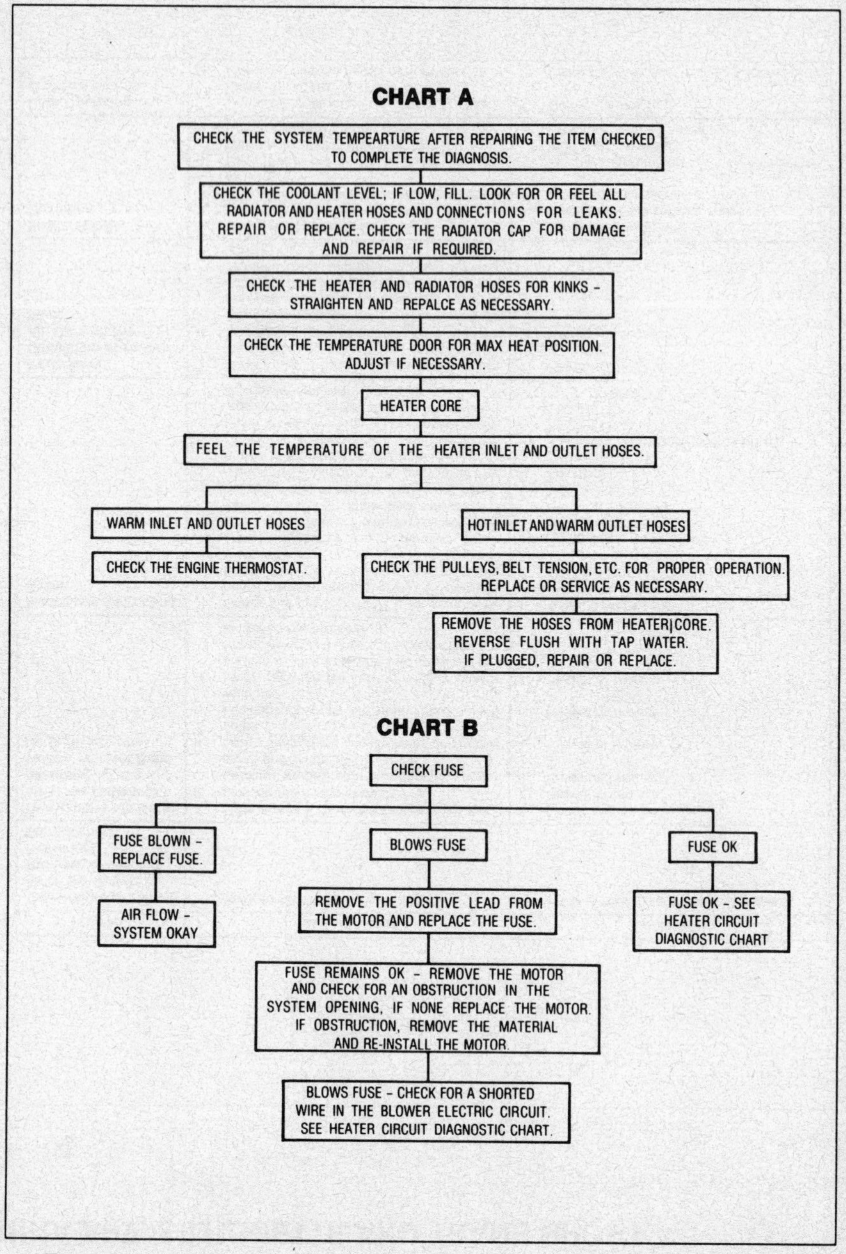
CHART A
CHECK THE SYSTEM TEMPEARTURE AFTER REPAIRING THE ITEM CHECKED TO COMPLETE THE DIAGNOSIS.
CHECK THE COOLANT LEVEL; IF LOW, FILL. LOOK FOR OR FEEL ALL RADIATOR AND HEATER HOSES AND CONNECTIONS FOR LEAKS. REPAIR OR REPLACE. CHECK THE RADIATOR CAP FOR DAMAGE AND REPAIR IF REQUIRED.
CHECK THE HEATER AND RADIATOR HOSES FOR KINKS - STRAIGHTEN AND REPALCE AS NECESSARY.
CHECK THE TEMPERATURE DOOR FOR MAX HEAT POSITION. ADJUST IF NECESSARY.
HEATER CORE
FEEL THE TEMPERATURE OF THE HEATER INLET AND OUTLET HOSES.
WARM INLET AND OUTLET HOSES
HOT INLET AND WARM OUTLET HOSES
CHECK THE ENGINE THERMOSTAT.
CHECK THE PULLEYS, BELT TENSION, ETC. FOR PROPER OPERATION. REPLACE OR SERVICE AS NECESSARY.
REMOVE THE HOSES FROM HEATER CORE. REVERSE FLUSH WITH TAP WATER. IF PLUGGED, REPAIR OR REPLACE.
CHART B
CHECK FUSE
FUSE BLOWN - REPLACE FUSE.
BLOWS FUSE
FUSE OK
AIR FLOW - SYSTEM OKAY
REMOVE THE POSITIVE LEAD FROM THE MOTOR AND REPLACE THE FUSE.
FUSE OK - SEE HEATER CIRCUIT DIAGNOSTIC CHART
FUSE REMAINS OK - REMOVE THE MOTOR AND CHECK FOR AN OBSTRUCTION IN THE SYSTEM OPENING, IF NONE REPLACE THE MOTOR. IF OBSTRUCTION, REMOVE THE MATERIAL AND RE-INSTALL THE MOTOR.
BLOWS FUSE - CHECK FOR A SHORTED WIRE IN THE BLOWER ELECTRIC CIRCUIT. SEE HEATER CIRCUIT DIAGNOSTIC CHART.

HEATER CIRCUIT DIAGNOSIS—EXCEPT LUMINA APV, SILHOUETTE AND TRANS SPORT

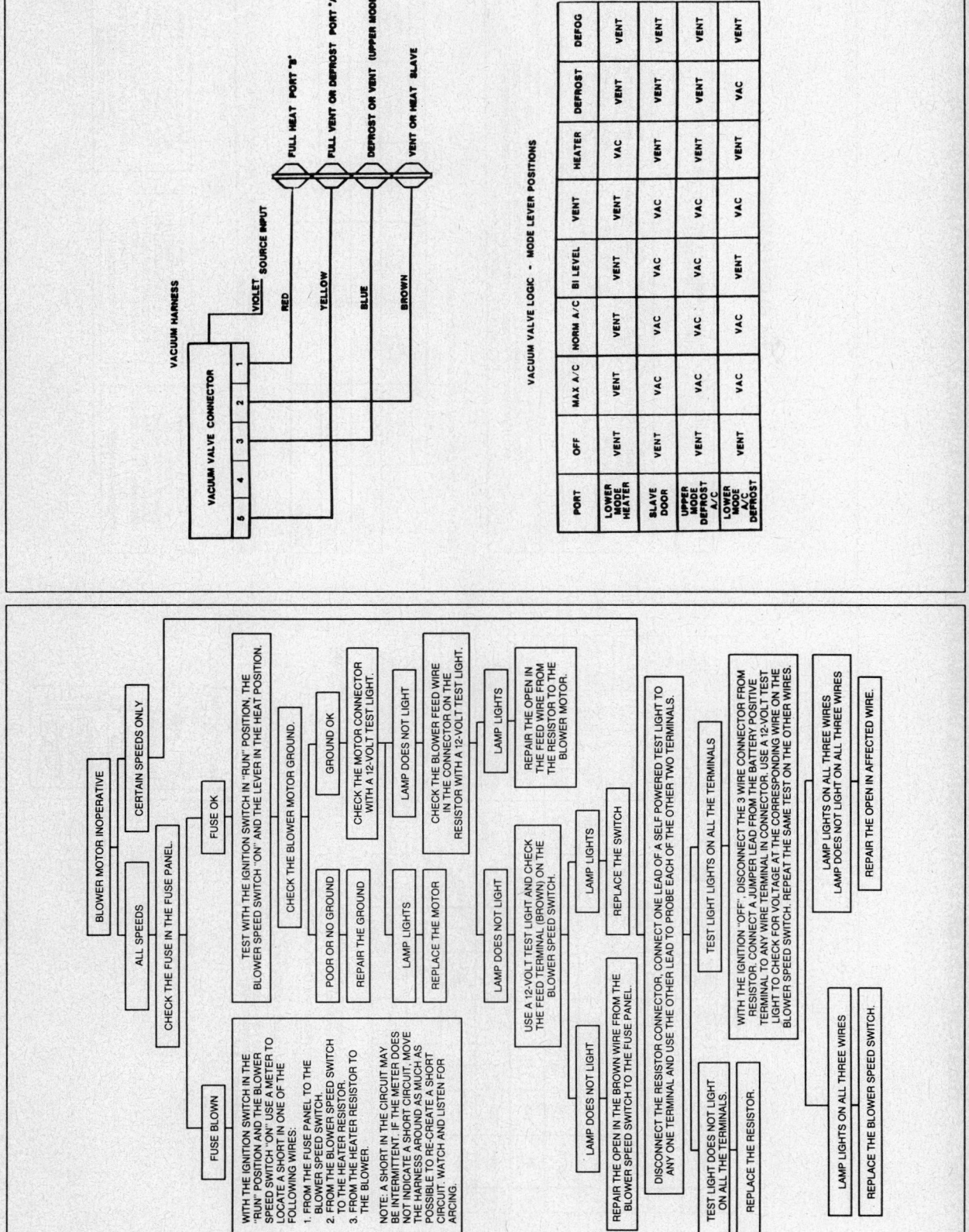

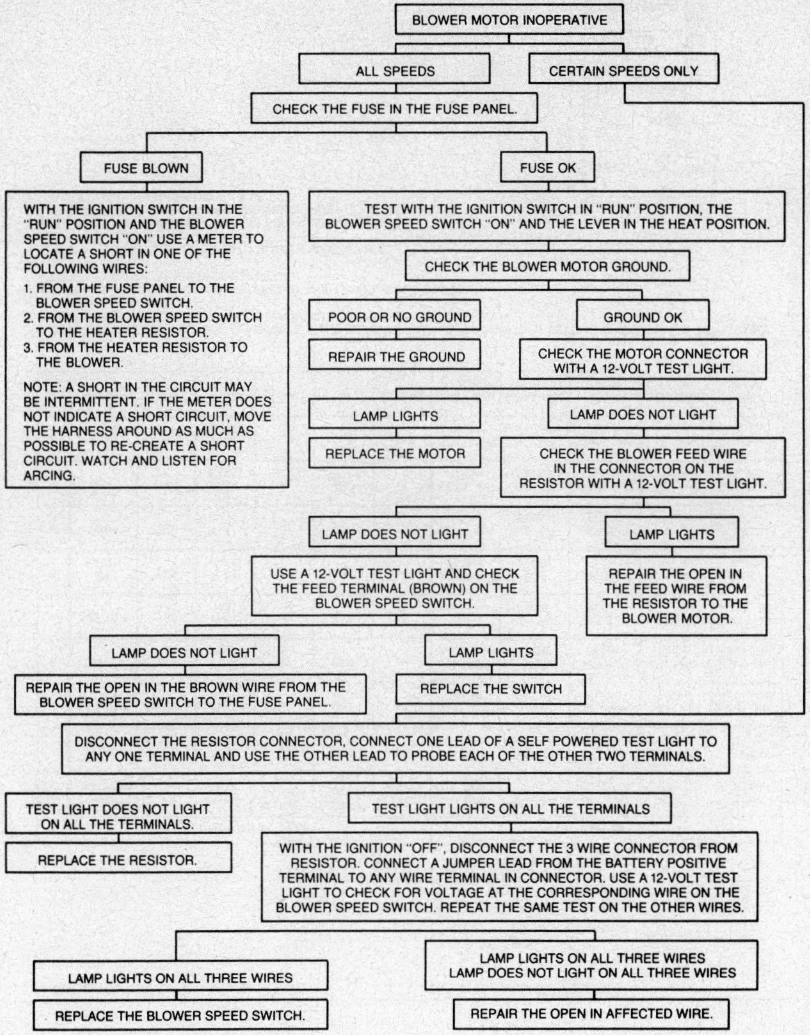
BLOWER MOTOR INOPERATIVE
ALL SPEEDS
CERTAIN SPEEDS ONLY
CHECK THE FUSE IN THE FUSE PANEL.
FUSE BLOWN
FUSE OK
WITH THE IGNITION SWITCH IN THE "RUN" POSITION AND THE BLOWER SPEED SWITCH "ON" USE A METER TO LOCATE A SHORT IN ONE OF THE FOLLOWING WIRES:
1. FROM THE FUSE PANEL TO THE BLOWER SPEED SWITCH.
2. FROM THE BLOWER SPEED SWITCH TO THE HEATER RESISTOR.
3. FROM THE HEATER RESISTOR TO THE BLOWER.
NOTE: A SHORT IN THE CIRCUIT MAY BE INTERMITTENT. IF THE METER DOES NOT INDICATE A SHORT CIRCUIT, MOVE THE HARNESS AROUND AS MUCH AS POSSIBLE TO RE-CREATE A SHORT CIRCUIT. WATCH AND LISTEN FOR ARCING.
TEST WITH THE IGNITION SWITCH IN "RUN" POSITION, THE BLOWER SPEED SWITCH "ON" AND THE LEVER IN THE HEAT POSITION.
CHECK THE BLOWER MOTOR GROUND.
POOR OR NO GROUND
GROUND OK
REPAIR THE GROUND
CHECK THE MOTOR CONNECTOR WITH A 12-VOLT TEST LIGHT.
LAMP LIGHTS
LAMP DOES NOT LIGHT
REPLACE THE MOTOR
CHECK THE BLOWER FEED WIRE IN THE CONNECTOR ON THE RESISTOR WITH A 12-VOLT TEST LIGHT.
LAMP DOES NOT LIGHT
LAMP LIGHTS
USE A 12-VOLT TEST LIGHT AND CHECK THE FEED TERMINAL (BROWN) ON THE BLOWER SPEED SWITCH.
REPAIR THE OPEN IN THE FEED WIRE FROM THE RESISTOR TO THE BLOWER MOTOR.
LAMP DOES NOT LIGHT
LAMP LIGHTS
REPAIR THE OPEN IN THE BROWN WIRE FROM THE BLOWER SPEED SWITCH TO THE FUSE PANEL.
REPLACE THE SWITCH
DISCONNECT THE RESISTOR CONNECTOR, CONNECT ONE LEAD OF A SELF POWERED TEST LIGHT TO ANY ONE TERMINAL AND USE THE OTHER LEAD TO PROBE EACH OF THE OTHER TWO TERMINALS.
TEST LIGHT DOES NOT LIGHT ON ALL THE TERMINALS.
TEST LIGHT LIGHTS ON ALL THE TERMINALS
REPLACE THE RESISTOR.
WITH THE IGNITION "OFF", DISCONNECT THE 3 WIRE CONNECTOR FROM RESISTOR. CONNECT A JUMPER LEAD FROM THE BATTERY POSITIVE TERMINAL TO ANY WIRE TERMINAL IN CONNECTOR. USE A 12-VOLT TEST LIGHT TO CHECK FOR VOLTAGE AT THE CORRESPONDING WIRE ON THE BLOWER SPEED SWITCH. REPEAT THE SAME TEST ON THE OTHER WIRES.
LAMP LIGHTS ON ALL THREE WIRES
LAMP LIGHTS ON ALL THREE WIRES LAMP DOES NOT LIGHT ON ALL THREE WIRES
REPLACE THE BLOWER SPEED SWITCH.
REPAIR THE OPEN IN AFFECTED WIRE.

HEATER SYSTEM CONTROL LOGIC—LUMINA APV, SILHOUETTE AND TRANS SPORT

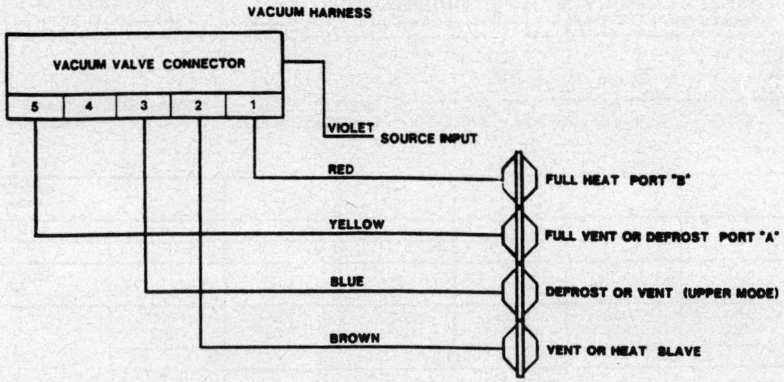
VACUUM HARNESS
VACUUM VALVE CONNECTOR
5
4
3
2
1
VIOLET
SOURCE INPUT
RED
YELLOW
BLUE
BROWN
FULL HEAT PORT "B"
FULL VENT OR DEFROST PORT "A"
DEFROST OR VENT (UPPER MODE)
VENT OR HEAT SLAVE

VACUUM VALVE LOGIC - MODE LEVER POSITIONS

PORT	OFF	MAX A/C	NORM A/C	BI LEVEL	VENT	HEATER	DEFROST	DEFOG
LOWER MODE HEATER	VENT	VENT	VENT	VENT	VENT	VAC	VENT	VENT
SLAVE DOOR	VENT	VAC	VAC	VAC	VAC	VENT	VENT	VENT
UPPER MODE DEFROST A/C	VENT	VAC	VAC	VAC	VAC	VENT	VENT	VENT
LOWER MODE A/C DEFROST	VENT	VAC	VAC	VENT	VAC	VENT	VAC	VENT

HEATER FUNCTIONAL TEST

STEP	CONTROL SETTINGS						SYSTEM RESPONSE				
	MODE BUTTON	LITE ON	TEMP SETT.	BLOWER FAN SW FRT	BLOWER FAN SW RR	BLOWER SPEED	RR. OPT. AUX. DUCT.	HEATER OUTLETS	A C I P OUTLETS	DEF. OUTLETS	SIDE WDO DEF.
1	OFF	YES	FULL HOT	HI	OFF	OFF	NO AIR FLOW	NO AIR FLOW	NO AIR FLOW	NO AIR FLOW	NO AIR FLOW
2	DEFR.	YES	FULL HOT	HI	OFF	HI	NO AIR FLOW	AIR FLOW	NO AIR FLOW	HOT AIR FLOW	SOME HOT AIR FLOW
3	MIX	YES	FULL HOT	HI	OFF	HI	SOME AIR FLOW	HOT AIR FLOW	NO AIR FLOW	HOT AIR FLOW	SOME HOT AIR FLOW
4	HEATER	YES	FULL HOT	HI	OFF	HI	AIR FLOW	HOT AIR FLOW	NO AIR FLOW	SOME AIR FLOW	SOME HOT AIR FLOW
5	BI-LEVEL	YES	FULL COLD	HI	OFF	HI	SOME AIR FLOW	AIR FLOW	COOL AIR FLOW	SOME AIR FLOW	SOME AIR FLOW
6	VENT	YES	FULL HOT	HI	OFF	HI	SOME AIR FLOW	NO AIR FLOW	HOT AIR FLOW	NO AIR FLOW	SOME AIR FLOW
7	VENT	YES	FULL COLD	HI	OFF	HI	SOME AIR FLOW	NO AIR FLOW	COOL AIR FLOW	NO AIR FLOW	SOME AIR FLOW
.8	VENT	YES	FULL COLD	LOW	OFF	LOW	SOME AIR FLOW	NO AIR FLOW	COOL AIR FLOW	NO AIR FLOW	SOME AIR FLOW
9	HEATER	YES	FULL HOT	LOW	HI	LOW/HI	HOT AIR FLOW	SOME HOT AIR FLOW	NO AIR FLOW	SOME AIR FLOW	SOME AIR FLOW

- TEMPERATURE DOOR ACTUATOR MOTOR SHOULD BE HEARD DURING TEMPERATURE SETTING CHANGES, AND NOTICEABLE BLOWER SPEED INCREASE MUST OCCUR FROM LOW TO MID, TO MID, AND HIGH.
- CHECK TEMPERATURE LEVER FOR EFFORT AND TRAVEL (COLD TO HOT). (TEMPERATURE CHANGE SHOULD OCCUR).
- CHECK FOR AIR FLOW AS DEFINED IN SYSTEM RESPONSE.
- ALL I/P OUTLETS MUST BE CHECKED FOR: 1) BARREL ROTATION, 2) VANE OPERATION, 3) BARREL AND VANES MUST HOLD PRESENT POSITION IN HI BLOWER OPERATION.

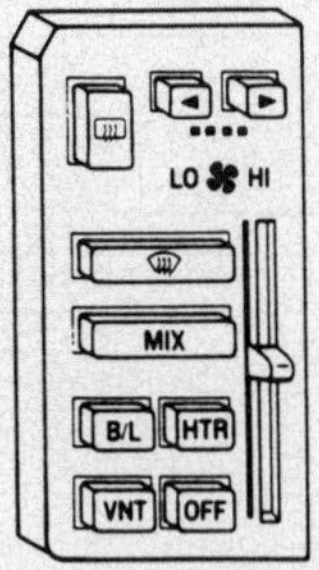
LO HI
MIX
B/L
HTR
VNT
OFF

④ BLOWER NOISE

CHECK ALL ELECTRICAL CONNECTIONS AND GROUNDS FOR PROPER CONNECTION. REFER TO SECTION 8A.

SIT IN THE VEHICLE WITH THE DOORS AND WINDOWS CLOSED. WITH THE IGNITION ON AND THE ENGINE OFF, START WITH THE BLOWER ON HIGH, IN VENT MODE AND THE TEMPERATURE LEVER ON FULL COLD. CYCLE THROUGH BLOWER SPEEDS, MODES AND TEMPERATURE VALVE POSITIONS TO FIND WHERE THE NOISE OCCURS AND WHERE THE NOISE DOES NOT OCCUR. TRY TO DEFINE THE TYPE OF NOISE: AIR RUSH, WHINE, TICK/CLICK, SQUEAL/SCREECH, FLUTTER, RUMBLE OR SCRAPING NOISE. CHART BELOW SHOULD BE COMPLETELY FILLED IN AT COMPLETION.

A CONSTANT AIR RUSH NOISE IS TYPICAL OF ALL SYSTEMS ON HIGH BLOWER. SOME SYSTEMS AND MODES (USUALLY DEFROSTER) MAY BE WORSE THAN OTHERS. CHECK ANOTHER VEHICLE IF POSSIBLE (SAME MODEL) TO DETERMINE IF THE NOISE IS TYPICAL OF THE SYSTEM AS DESIGNED.

INDICATE THE TYPE OF NOISE AND WHERE IT OCCURS:

	VENT		HEATER		DEFROST	
	FULL COLD	FULL HOT	FULL COLD	FULL HOT	FULL COLD	FULL HOT
LOW BLOWER						
M2						
M3						
HIGH BLOWER						

A — WHINE, B — CLICK/TICK, C — SQUEAL/SCREECH, D — FLUTTER, E — RUMBLE,
F — SCRAPING, G — AIR RUSH, H — OTHER, DESCRIBE ______

1. NOISE IS CONSTANT BUT LESSENS WITH BLOWER SPEED REDUCTION. TYPICAL NOISES ARE WHINE, TICK/CLICK, FLUTTER OR SCRAPING NOISE.

2. NOISE IS AT START-UP ONLY OR IS INTERMITTANT. MAY OCCUR AT COLD AMBIENTS AND LOW BLOWER SPEEDS. TYPICAL NOISE IS AN OBJECTIONABLE SQUEAL/SCREECH.

(L)

3. NOISE IS CONSTANT AT HIGH BLOWER SPEEDS WITH SOME DOOR COMBINATIONS BUT CAN BE ELIMINATED AT LOWER BLOWER SPEEDS OR WITH OTHER VALVE COMBINATIONS. TYPICAL NOISES ARE FLUTTER OR RUMBLE.

(M)

HEATER SYSTEM DIAGNOSIS—LUMINA APV, SILHOUETTE AND TRANS SPORT (CONT'D)

4 BLOWER NOISE

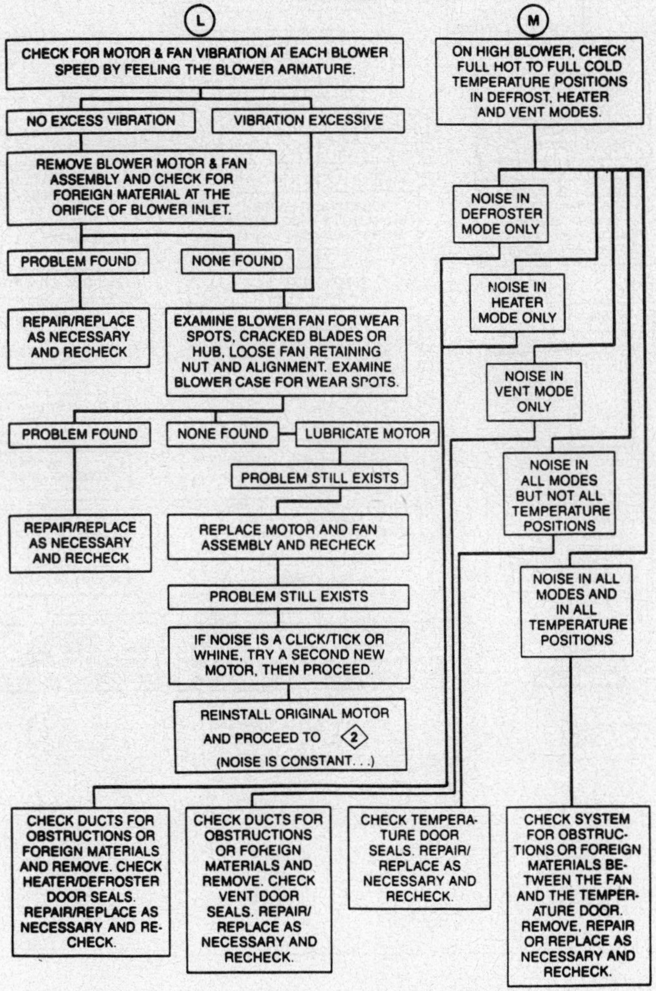
L
CHECK FOR MOTOR & FAN VIBRATION AT EACH BLOWER SPEED BY FEELING THE BLOWER ARMATURE.
NO EXCESS VIBRATION
VIBRATION EXCESSIVE
REMOVE BLOWER MOTOR & FAN ASSEMBLY AND CHECK FOR FOREIGN MATERIAL AT THE ORIFICE OF BLOWER INLET.
PROBLEM FOUND
NONE FOUND
REPAIR/REPLACE AS NECESSARY AND RECHECK
EXAMINE BLOWER FAN FOR WEAR SPOTS, CRACKED BLADES OR HUB, LOOSE FAN RETAINING NUT AND ALIGNMENT. EXAMINE BLOWER CASE FOR WEAR SPOTS.
PROBLEM FOUND
NONE FOUND
LUBRICATE MOTOR
PROBLEM STILL EXISTS
REPAIR/REPLACE AS NECESSARY AND RECHECK
REPLACE MOTOR AND FAN ASSEMBLY AND RECHECK
PROBLEM STILL EXISTS
IF NOISE IS A CLICK/TICK OR WHINE, TRY A SECOND NEW MOTOR, THEN PROCEED.
REINSTALL ORIGINAL MOTOR AND PROCEED TO 2 (NOISE IS CONSTANT. . .)
M
ON HIGH BLOWER, CHECK FULL HOT TO FULL COLD TEMPERATURE POSITIONS IN DEFROST, HEATER AND VENT MODES.
NOISE IN DEFROSTER MODE ONLY
NOISE IN HEATER MODE ONLY
NOISE IN VENT MODE ONLY
NOISE IN ALL MODES BUT NOT ALL TEMPERATURE POSITIONS
NOISE IN ALL MODES AND IN ALL TEMPERATURE POSITIONS
CHECK DUCTS FOR OBSTRUCTIONS OR FOREIGN MATERIALS AND REMOVE. CHECK HEATER/DEFROSTER DOOR SEALS. REPAIR/REPLACE AS NECESSARY AND RE-CHECK.
CHECK DUCTS FOR OBSTRUCTIONS OR FOREIGN MATERIALS AND REMOVE. CHECK VENT DOOR SEALS. REPAIR/ REPLACE AS NECESSARY AND RECHECK.
CHECK TEMPERA-TURE DOOR SEALS. REPAIR/ REPLACE AS NECESSARY AND RECHECK.
CHECK SYSTEM FOR OBSTRUC-TIONS OR FOREIGN MATERIALS BE-TWEEN THE FAN AND THE TEMPER-ATURE DOOR. REMOVE, REPAIR OR REPLACE AS NECESSARY AND RECHECK.

1 INSUFFICIENT HEATING OR DEFROSTING

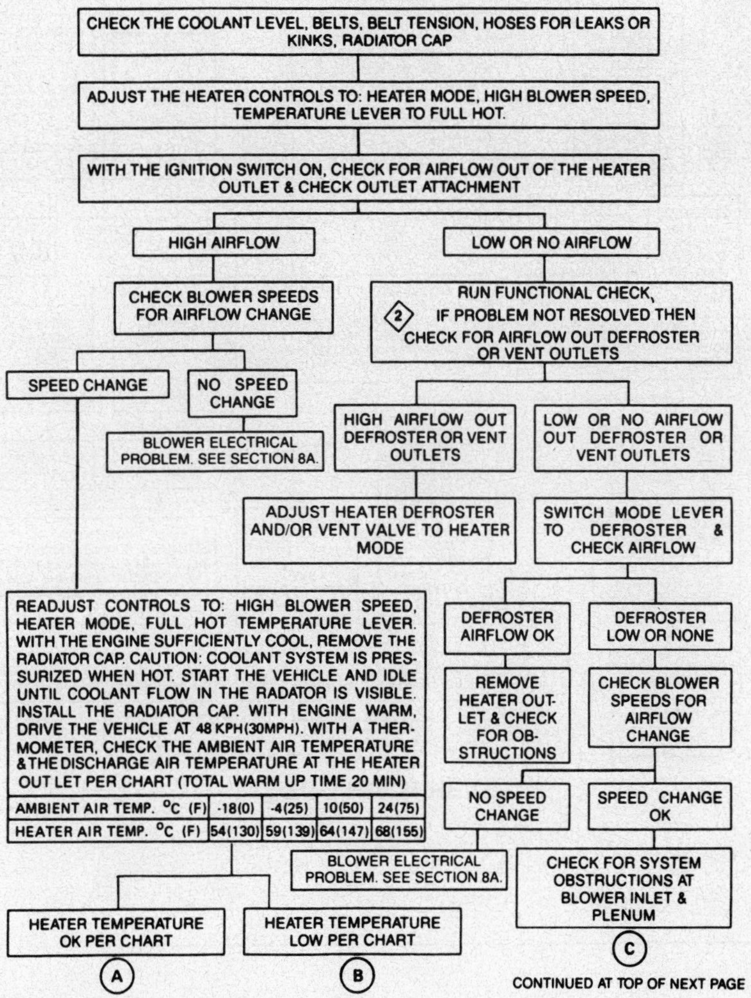
CHECK THE COOLANT LEVEL, BELTS, BELT TENSION, HOSES FOR LEAKS OR KINKS, RADIATOR CAP
ADJUST THE HEATER CONTROLS TO: HEATER MODE, HIGH BLOWER SPEED, TEMPERATURE LEVER TO FULL HOT.
WITH THE IGNITION SWITCH ON, CHECK FOR AIRFLOW OUT OF THE HEATER OUTLET & CHECK OUTLET ATTACHMENT
HIGH AIRFLOW
LOW OR NO AIRFLOW
CHECK BLOWER SPEEDS FOR AIRFLOW CHANGE
RUN FUNCTIONAL CHECK, 2 IF PROBLEM NOT RESOLVED THEN CHECK FOR AIRFLOW OUT DEFROSTER OR VENT OUTLETS
SPEED CHANGE
NO SPEED CHANGE
BLOWER ELECTRICAL PROBLEM. SEE SECTION 8A.
HIGH AIRFLOW OUT DEFROSTER OR VENT OUTLETS
LOW OR NO AIRFLOW OUT DEFROSTER OR VENT OUTLETS
ADJUST HEATER DEFROSTER AND/OR VENT VALVE TO HEATER MODE
SWITCH MODE LEVER TO DEFROSTER & CHECK AIRFLOW
READJUST CONTROLS TO: HIGH BLOWER SPEED, HEATER MODE, FULL HOT TEMPERATURE LEVER. WITH THE ENGINE SUFFICIENTLY COOL, REMOVE THE RADIATOR CAP. CAUTION: COOLANT SYSTEM IS PRES-SURIZED WHEN HOT. START THE VEHICLE AND IDLE UNTIL COOLANT FLOW IN THE RADIATOR IS VISIBLE. INSTALL THE RADIATOR CAP. WITH ENGINE WARM, DRIVE THE VEHICLE AT 48 KPH(30MPH). WITH A THER-MOMETER, CHECK THE AMBIENT AIR TEMPERATURE & THE DISCHARGE AIR TEMPERATURE AT THE HEATER OUT LET PER CHART (TOTAL WARM UP TIME 20 MIN)
AMBIENT AIR TEMP. °C (F) -18(0) -4(25) 10(50) 24(75)
HEATER AIR TEMP. °C (F) 54(130) 59(139) 64(147) 68(155)
DEFROSTER AIRFLOW OK
DEFROSTER LOW OR NONE
REMOVE HEATER OUT-LET & CHECK FOR OB-STRUCTIONS
CHECK BLOWER SPEEDS FOR AIRFLOW CHANGE
NO SPEED CHANGE
SPEED CHANGE OK
BLOWER ELECTRICAL PROBLEM. SEE SECTION 8A.
CHECK FOR SYSTEM OBSTRUCTIONS AT BLOWER INLET & PLENUM
HEATER TEMPERATURE OK PER CHART
HEATER TEMPERATURE LOW PER CHART
A
B
C

CONTINUED AT TOP OF NEXT PAGE

HEATER SYSTEM DIAGNOSIS—LUMINA APV, SILHOUETTE AND TRANS SPORT (CONT'D)

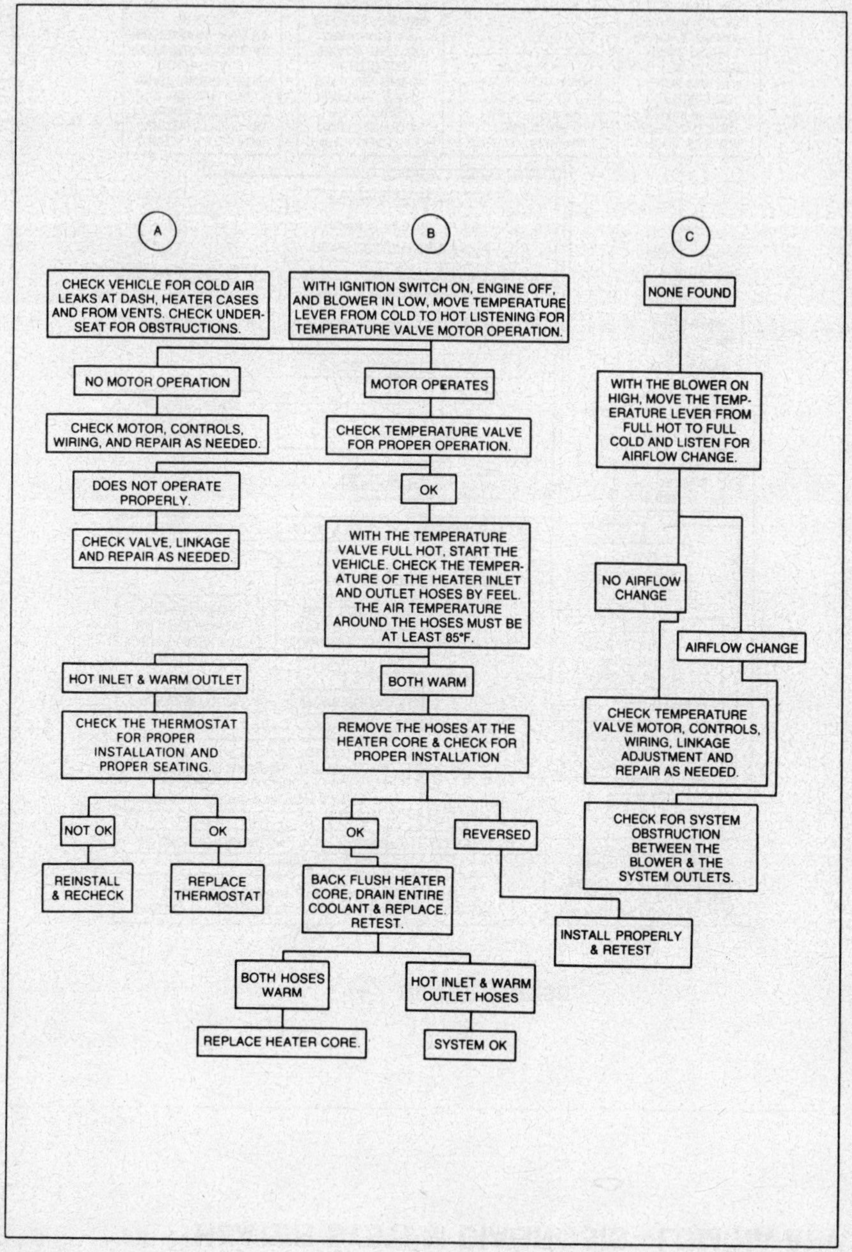
A
CHECK VEHICLE FOR COLD AIR LEAKS AT DASH, HEATER CASES AND FROM VENTS. CHECK UNDER-SEAT FOR OBSTRUCTIONS.
B
WITH IGNITION SWITCH ON, ENGINE OFF, AND BLOWER IN LOW, MOVE TEMPERATURE LEVER FROM COLD TO HOT LISTENING FOR TEMPERATURE VALVE MOTOR OPERATION.
NO MOTOR OPERATION
CHECK MOTOR, CONTROLS, WIRING, AND REPAIR AS NEEDED.
MOTOR OPERATES
CHECK TEMPERATURE VALVE FOR PROPER OPERATION.
DOES NOT OPERATE PROPERLY.
CHECK VALVE, LINKAGE AND REPAIR AS NEEDED.
OK
WITH THE TEMPERATURE VALVE FULL HOT, START THE VEHICLE. CHECK THE TEMPERATURE OF THE HEATER INLET AND OUTLET HOSES BY FEEL. THE AIR TEMPERATURE AROUND THE HOSES MUST BE AT LEAST 85°F.
HOT INLET & WARM OUTLET
CHECK THE THERMOSTAT FOR PROPER INSTALLATION AND PROPER SEATING.
NOT OK
REINSTALL & RECHECK
OK
REPLACE THERMOSTAT
BOTH WARM
REMOVE THE HOSES AT THE HEATER CORE & CHECK FOR PROPER INSTALLATION
OK
BACK FLUSH HEATER CORE, DRAIN ENTIRE COOLANT & REPLACE. RETEST.
BOTH HOSES WARM
REPLACE HEATER CORE.
HOT INLET & WARM OUTLET HOSES
SYSTEM OK
REVERSED
INSTALL PROPERLY & RETEST
C
NONE FOUND
WITH THE BLOWER ON HIGH, MOVE THE TEMPERATURE LEVER FROM FULL HOT TO FULL COLD AND LISTEN FOR AIRFLOW CHANGE.
NO AIRFLOW CHANGE
CHECK TEMPERATURE VALVE MOTOR, CONTROLS, WIRING, LINKAGE ADJUSTMENT AND REPAIR AS NEEDED.
AIRFLOW CHANGE
CHECK FOR SYSTEM OBSTRUCTION BETWEEN THE BLOWER & THE SYSTEM OUTLETS.

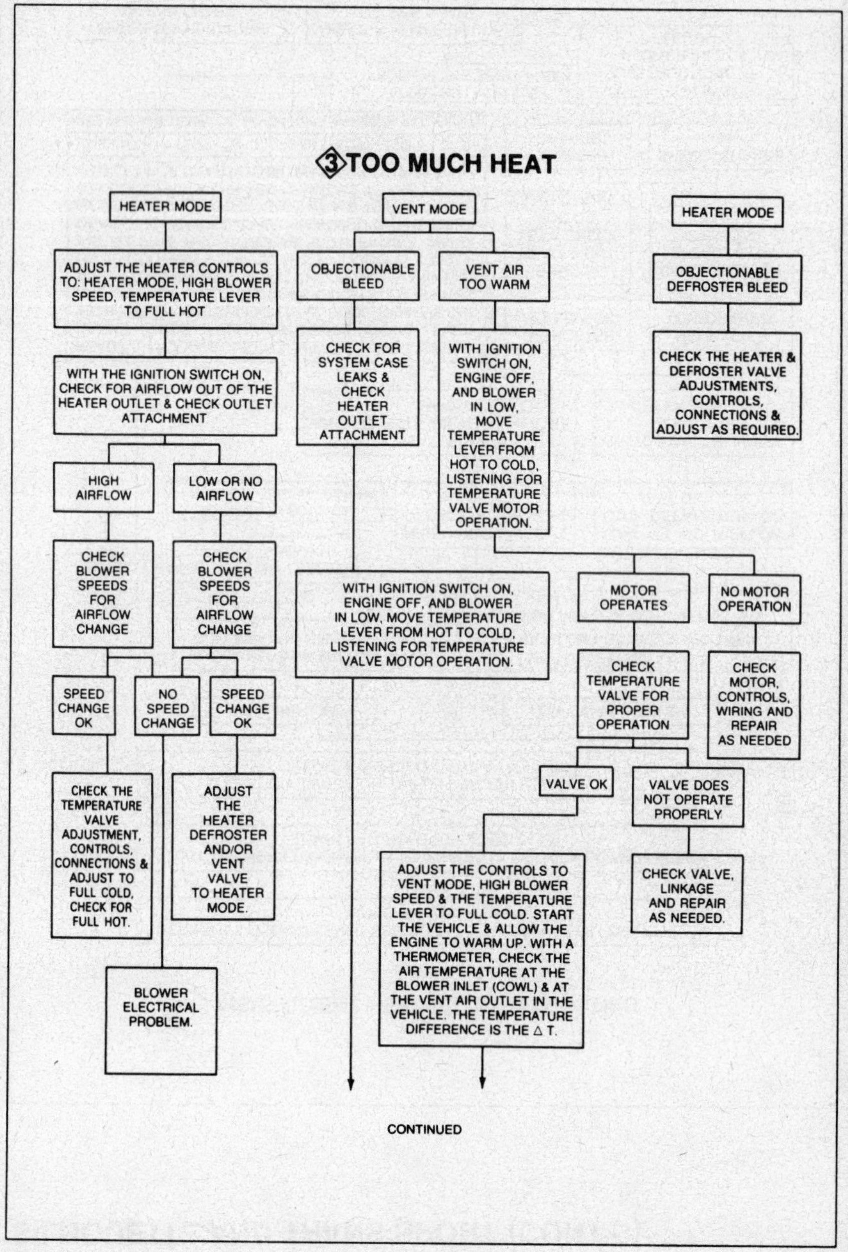
3 TOO MUCH HEAT
HEATER MODE
ADJUST THE HEATER CONTROLS TO: HEATER MODE, HIGH BLOWER SPEED, TEMPERATURE LEVER TO FULL HOT
WITH THE IGNITION SWITCH ON, CHECK FOR AIRFLOW OUT OF THE HEATER OUTLET & CHECK OUTLET ATTACHMENT
HIGH AIRFLOW
CHECK BLOWER SPEEDS FOR AIRFLOW CHANGE
LOW OR NO AIRFLOW
CHECK BLOWER SPEEDS FOR AIRFLOW CHANGE
SPEED CHANGE OK
CHECK THE TEMPERATURE VALVE ADJUSTMENT, CONTROLS, CONNECTIONS & ADJUST TO FULL COLD, CHECK FOR FULL HOT.
NO SPEED CHANGE
BLOWER ELECTRICAL PROBLEM.
SPEED CHANGE OK
ADJUST THE HEATER DEFROSTER AND/OR VENT VALVE TO HEATER MODE.
VENT MODE
OBJECTIONABLE BLEED
CHECK FOR SYSTEM CASE LEAKS & CHECK HEATER OUTLET ATTACHMENT
VENT AIR TOO WARM
WITH IGNITION SWITCH ON, ENGINE OFF, AND BLOWER IN LOW, MOVE TEMPERATURE LEVER FROM HOT TO COLD, LISTENING FOR TEMPERATURE VALVE MOTOR OPERATION.
WITH IGNITION SWITCH ON, ENGINE OFF, AND BLOWER IN LOW, MOVE TEMPERATURE LEVER FROM HOT TO COLD, LISTENING FOR TEMPERATURE VALVE MOTOR OPERATION.
MOTOR OPERATES
CHECK TEMPERATURE VALVE FOR PROPER OPERATION
VALVE OK
ADJUST THE CONTROLS TO VENT MODE, HIGH BLOWER SPEED & THE TEMPERATURE LEVER TO FULL COLD. START THE VEHICLE & ALLOW THE ENGINE TO WARM UP. WITH A THERMOMETER, CHECK THE AIR TEMPERATURE AT THE BLOWER INLET (COWL) & AT THE VENT AIR OUTLET IN THE VEHICLE. THE TEMPERATURE DIFFERENCE IS THE △ T.
VALVE DOES NOT OPERATE PROPERLY
CHECK VALVE, LINKAGE AND REPAIR AS NEEDED.
NO MOTOR OPERATION
CHECK MOTOR, CONTROLS, WIRING AND REPAIR AS NEEDED
HEATER MODE
OBJECTIONABLE DEFROSTER BLEED
CHECK THE HEATER & DEFROSTER VALVE ADJUSTMENTS, CONTROLS, CONNECTIONS & ADJUST AS REQUIRED.
CONTINUED

HEATER SYSTEM DIAGNOSIS—LUMINA APV, SILHOUETTE AND TRANS SPORT (CONT'D)

3 TOO MUCH HEAT (Continued)

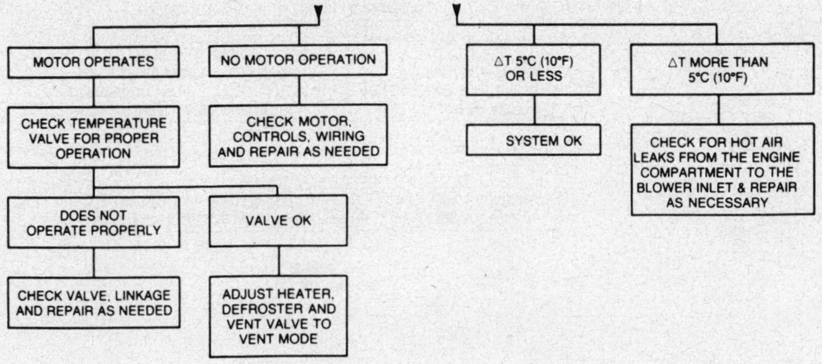
MOTOR OPERATES
NO MOTOR OPERATION
CHECK TEMPERATURE VALVE FOR PROPER OPERATION
CHECK MOTOR, CONTROLS, WIRING AND REPAIR AS NEEDED
DOES NOT OPERATE PROPERLY
VALVE OK
CHECK VALVE, LINKAGE AND REPAIR AS NEEDED
ADJUST HEATER, DEFROSTER AND VENT VALVE TO VENT MODE
ΔT 5°C (10°F) OR LESS
ΔT MORE THAN 5°C (10°F)
SYSTEM OK
CHECK FOR HOT AIR LEAKS FROM THE ENGINE COMPARTMENT TO THE BLOWER INLET & REPAIR AS NECESSARY

AIR CONDITIONING SYSTEM DIAGNOSIS INSUFFICIENT COOLING

INSUFFICIENT COOLING—A/C SYSTEMS WITH CYCLING CLUTCH—EXPANSION TUBE (PRESSURE SENSING)

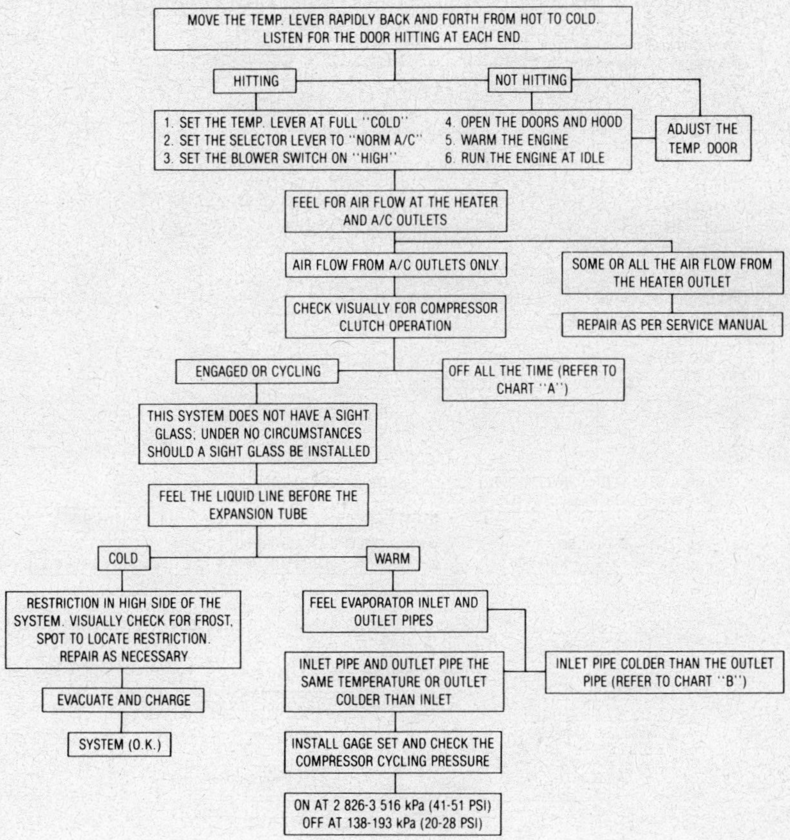
MOVE THE TEMP. LEVER RAPIDLY BACK AND FORTH FROM HOT TO COLD. LISTEN FOR THE DOOR HITTING AT EACH END.
HITTING
NOT HITTING
1. SET THE TEMP. LEVER AT FULL "COLD"
2. SET THE SELECTOR LEVER TO "NORM A/C"
3. SET THE BLOWER SWITCH ON "HIGH"
4. OPEN THE DOORS AND HOOD
5. WARM THE ENGINE
6. RUN THE ENGINE AT IDLE
ADJUST THE TEMP. DOOR
FEEL FOR AIR FLOW AT THE HEATER AND A/C OUTLETS
AIR FLOW FROM A/C OUTLETS ONLY
SOME OR ALL THE AIR FLOW FROM THE HEATER OUTLET
CHECK VISUALLY FOR COMPRESSOR CLUTCH OPERATION
REPAIR AS PER SERVICE MANUAL
ENGAGED OR CYCLING
OFF ALL THE TIME (REFER TO CHART "A")
THIS SYSTEM DOES NOT HAVE A SIGHT GLASS; UNDER NO CIRCUMSTANCES SHOULD A SIGHT GLASS BE INSTALLED
FEEL THE LIQUID LINE BEFORE THE EXPANSION TUBE
COLD
WARM
RESTRICTION IN HIGH SIDE OF THE SYSTEM. VISUALLY CHECK FOR FROST, SPOT TO LOCATE RESTRICTION. REPAIR AS NECESSARY
FEEL EVAPORATOR INLET AND OUTLET PIPES
EVACUATE AND CHARGE
INLET PIPE AND OUTLET PIPE THE SAME TEMPERATURE OR OUTLET COLDER THAN INLET
INLET PIPE COLDER THAN THE OUTLET PIPE (REFER TO CHART "B")
SYSTEM (O.K.)
INSTALL GAGE SET AND CHECK THE COMPRESSOR CYCLING PRESSURE
ON AT 2 826-3 516 kPa (41-51 PSI)
OFF AT 138-193 kPa (20-28 PSI)

CONTINUED ON FOLLOWING PAGE

AIR CONDITIONING SYSTEM DIAGNOSIS—INSUFFICIENT COOLING (CONT'D)

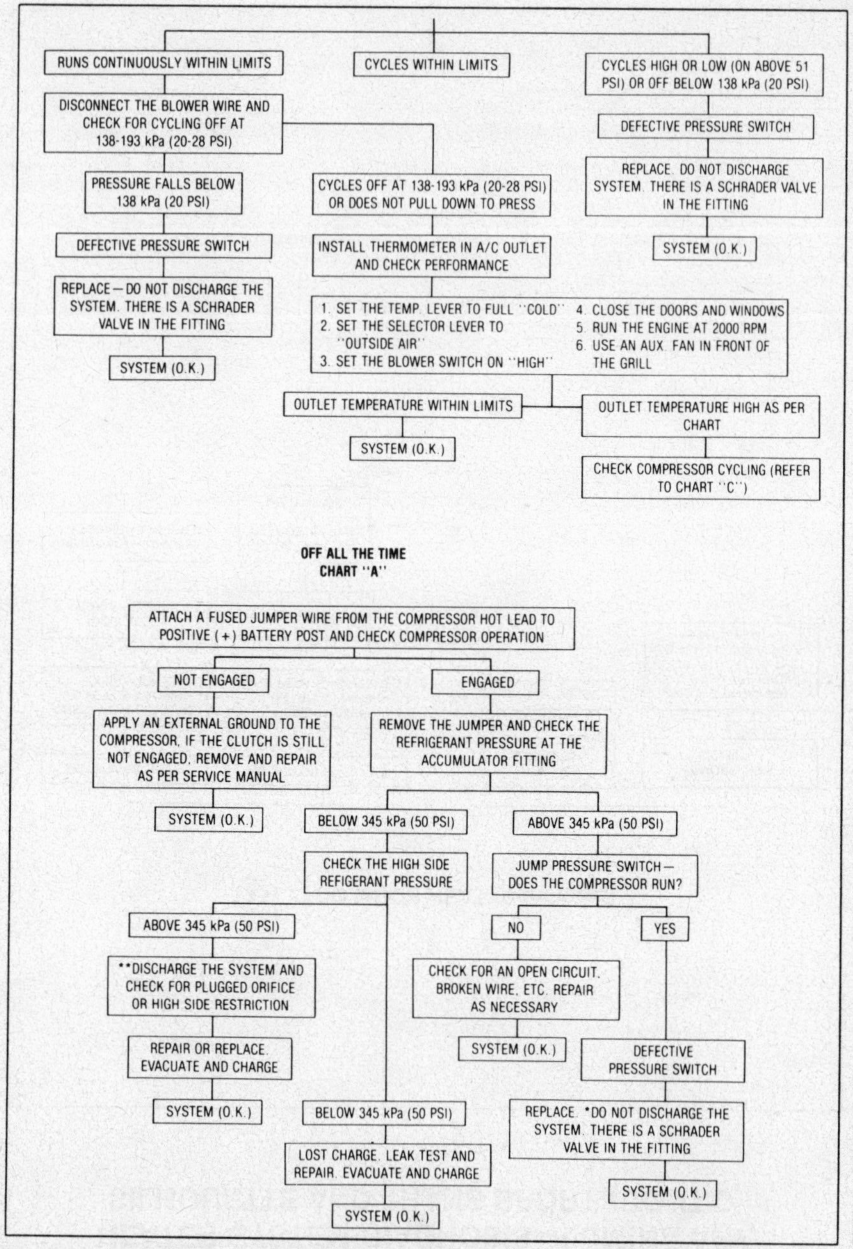
RUNS CONTINUOUSLY WITHIN LIMITS
CYCLES WITHIN LIMITS
CYCLES HIGH OR LOW (ON ABOVE 51 PSI) OR OFF BELOW 138 kPa (20 PSI)
DISCONNECT THE BLOWER WIRE AND CHECK FOR CYCLING OFF AT 138-193 kPa (20-28 PSI)
DEFECTIVE PRESSURE SWITCH
PRESSURE FALLS BELOW 138 kPa (20 PSI)
CYCLES OFF AT 138-193 kPa (20-28 PSI) OR DOES NOT PULL DOWN TO PRESS
REPLACE. DO NOT DISCHARGE SYSTEM. THERE IS A SCHRADER VALVE IN THE FITTING
DEFECTIVE PRESSURE SWITCH
INSTALL THERMOMETER IN A/C OUTLET AND CHECK PERFORMANCE
SYSTEM (O.K.)
REPLACE—DO NOT DISCHARGE THE SYSTEM. THERE IS A SCHRADER VALVE IN THE FITTING
1. SET THE TEMP. LEVER TO FULL "COLD"
2. SET THE SELECTOR LEVER TO "OUTSIDE AIR"
3. SET THE BLOWER SWITCH ON "HIGH"
4. CLOSE THE DOORS AND WINDOWS
5. RUN THE ENGINE AT 2000 RPM
6. USE AN AUX. FAN IN FRONT OF THE GRILL
SYSTEM (O.K.)
OUTLET TEMPERATURE WITHIN LIMITS
OUTLET TEMPERATURE HIGH AS PER CHART
SYSTEM (O.K.)
CHECK COMPRESSOR CYCLING (REFER TO CHART "C")
OFF ALL THE TIME
CHART "A"
ATTACH A FUSED JUMPER WIRE FROM THE COMPRESSOR HOT LEAD TO POSITIVE (+) BATTERY POST AND CHECK COMPRESSOR OPERATION
NOT ENGAGED
ENGAGED
APPLY AN EXTERNAL GROUND TO THE COMPRESSOR. IF THE CLUTCH IS STILL NOT ENGAGED, REMOVE AND REPAIR AS PER SERVICE MANUAL
REMOVE THE JUMPER AND CHECK THE REFRIGERANT PRESSURE AT THE ACCUMULATOR FITTING
SYSTEM (O.K.)
BELOW 345 kPa (50 PSI)
ABOVE 345 kPa (50 PSI)
CHECK THE HIGH SIDE REFIGERANT PRESSURE
JUMP PRESSURE SWITCH—DOES THE COMPRESSOR RUN?
ABOVE 345 kPa (50 PSI)
NO
YES
**DISCHARGE THE SYSTEM AND CHECK FOR PLUGGED ORIFICE OR HIGH SIDE RESTRICTION
CHECK FOR AN OPEN CIRCUIT, BROKEN WIRE, ETC. REPAIR AS NECESSARY
REPAIR OR REPLACE. EVACUATE AND CHARGE
SYSTEM (O.K.)
DEFECTIVE PRESSURE SWITCH
SYSTEM (O.K.)
BELOW 345 kPa (50 PSI)
REPLACE. *DO NOT DISCHARGE THE SYSTEM. THERE IS A SCHRADER VALVE IN THE FITTING
LOST CHARGE. LEAK TEST AND REPAIR. EVACUATE AND CHARGE
SYSTEM (O.K.)
SYSTEM (O.K.)

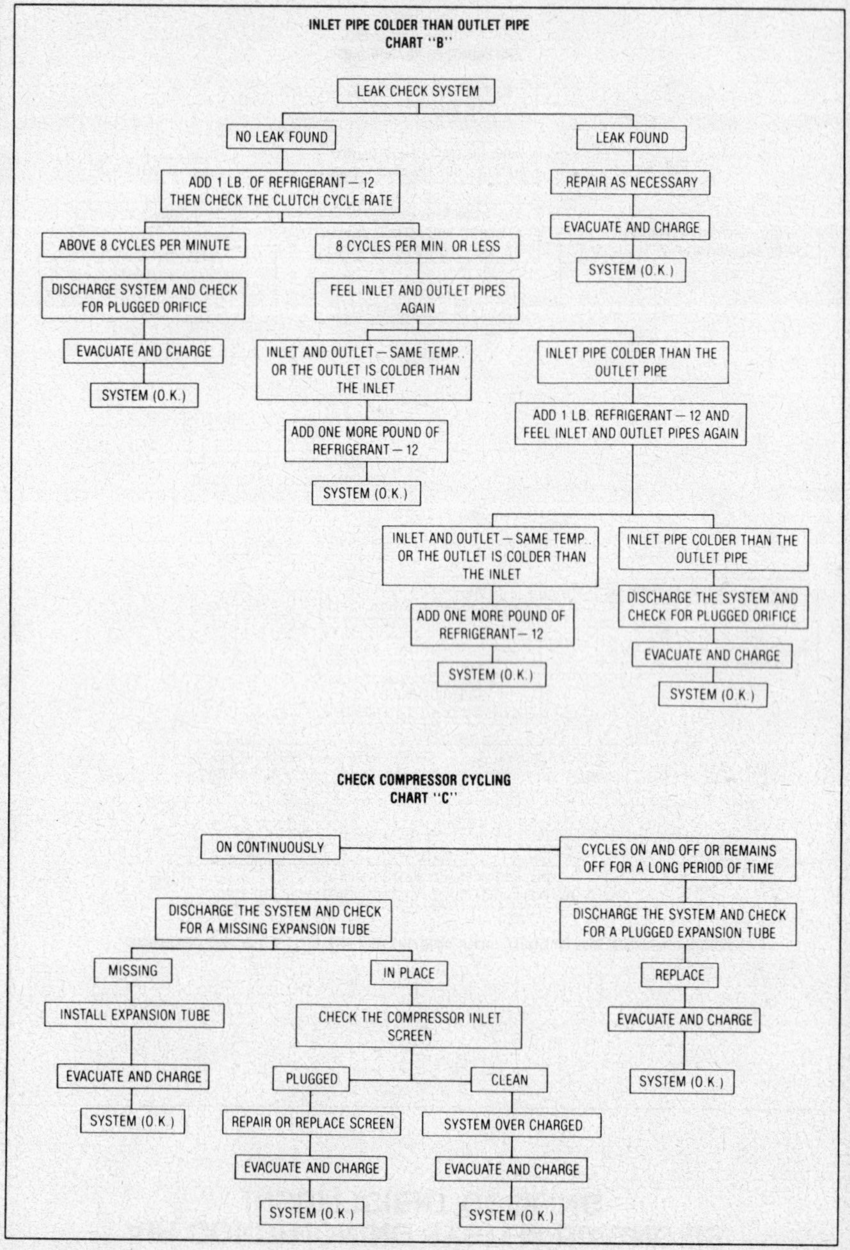
INLET PIPE COLDER THAN OUTLET PIPE
CHART "B"
LEAK CHECK SYSTEM
NO LEAK FOUND
LEAK FOUND
ADD 1 LB. OF REFRIGERANT—12 THEN CHECK THE CLUTCH CYCLE RATE
REPAIR AS NECESSARY
EVACUATE AND CHARGE
ABOVE 8 CYCLES PER MINUTE
8 CYCLES PER MIN. OR LESS
SYSTEM (O.K.)
DISCHARGE SYSTEM AND CHECK FOR PLUGGED ORIFICE
FEEL INLET AND OUTLET PIPES AGAIN
EVACUATE AND CHARGE
INLET AND OUTLET—SAME TEMP., OR THE OUTLET IS COLDER THAN THE INLET
INLET PIPE COLDER THAN THE OUTLET PIPE
SYSTEM (O.K.)
ADD ONE MORE POUND OF REFRIGERANT—12
ADD 1 LB. REFRIGERANT—12 AND FEEL INLET AND OUTLET PIPES AGAIN
SYSTEM (O.K.)
INLET AND OUTLET—SAME TEMP., OR THE OUTLET IS COLDER THAN THE INLET
INLET PIPE COLDER THAN THE OUTLET PIPE
ADD ONE MORE POUND OF REFRIGERANT—12
DISCHARGE THE SYSTEM AND CHECK FOR PLUGGED ORIFICE
SYSTEM (O.K.)
EVACUATE AND CHARGE
SYSTEM (O.K.)
CHECK COMPRESSOR CYCLING
CHART "C"
ON CONTINUOUSLY
CYCLES ON AND OFF OR REMAINS OFF FOR A LONG PERIOD OF TIME
DISCHARGE THE SYSTEM AND CHECK FOR A MISSING EXPANSION TUBE
DISCHARGE THE SYSTEM AND CHECK FOR A PLUGGED EXPANSION TUBE
MISSING
IN PLACE
REPLACE
INSTALL EXPANSION TUBE
CHECK THE COMPRESSOR INLET SCREEN
EVACUATE AND CHARGE
EVACUATE AND CHARGE
PLUGGED
CLEAN
SYSTEM (O.K.)
SYSTEM (O.K.)
REPAIR OR REPLACE SCREEN
SYSTEM OVER CHARGED
EVACUATE AND CHARGE
EVACUATE AND CHARGE
SYSTEM (O.K.)
SYSTEM (O.K.)

AIR CONDITIONING SYSTEM DIAGNOSIS COMPRESSOR

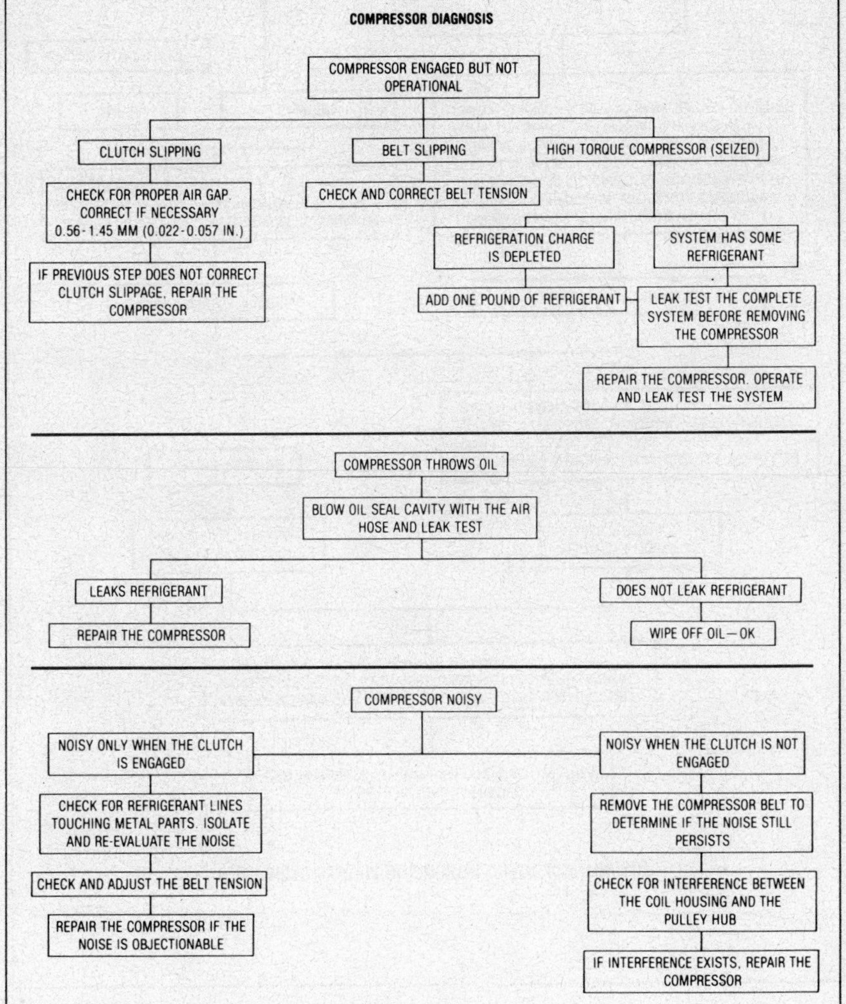
COMPRESSOR DIAGNOSIS
COMPRESSOR ENGAGED BUT NOT OPERATIONAL
CLUTCH SLIPPING
CHECK FOR PROPER AIR GAP. CORRECT IF NECESSARY 0.56-1.45 MM (0.022-0.057 IN.)
IF PREVIOUS STEP DOES NOT CORRECT CLUTCH SLIPPAGE, REPAIR THE COMPRESSOR
BELT SLIPPING
CHECK AND CORRECT BELT TENSION
HIGH TORQUE COMPRESSOR (SEIZED)
REFRIGERATION CHARGE IS DEPLETED
ADD ONE POUND OF REFRIGERANT
SYSTEM HAS SOME REFRIGERANT
LEAK TEST THE COMPLETE SYSTEM BEFORE REMOVING THE COMPRESSOR
REPAIR THE COMPRESSOR. OPERATE AND LEAK TEST THE SYSTEM
COMPRESSOR THROWS OIL
BLOW OIL SEAL CAVITY WITH THE AIR HOSE AND LEAK TEST
LEAKS REFRIGERANT
REPAIR THE COMPRESSOR
DOES NOT LEAK REFRIGERANT
WIPE OFF OIL—OK
COMPRESSOR NOISY
NOISY ONLY WHEN THE CLUTCH IS ENGAGED
CHECK FOR REFRIGERANT LINES TOUCHING METAL PARTS. ISOLATE AND RE-EVALUATE THE NOISE
CHECK AND ADJUST THE BELT TENSION
REPAIR THE COMPRESSOR IF THE NOISE IS OBJECTIONABLE
NOISY WHEN THE CLUTCH IS NOT ENGAGED
REMOVE THE COMPRESSOR BELT TO DETERMINE IF THE NOISE STILL PERSISTS
CHECK FOR INTERFERENCE BETWEEN THE COIL HOUSING AND THE PULLEY HUB
IF INTERFERENCE EXISTS, REPAIR THE COMPRESSOR

AIR CONDITIONING SYSTEM DIAGNOSIS ELECTRICAL SYSTEM

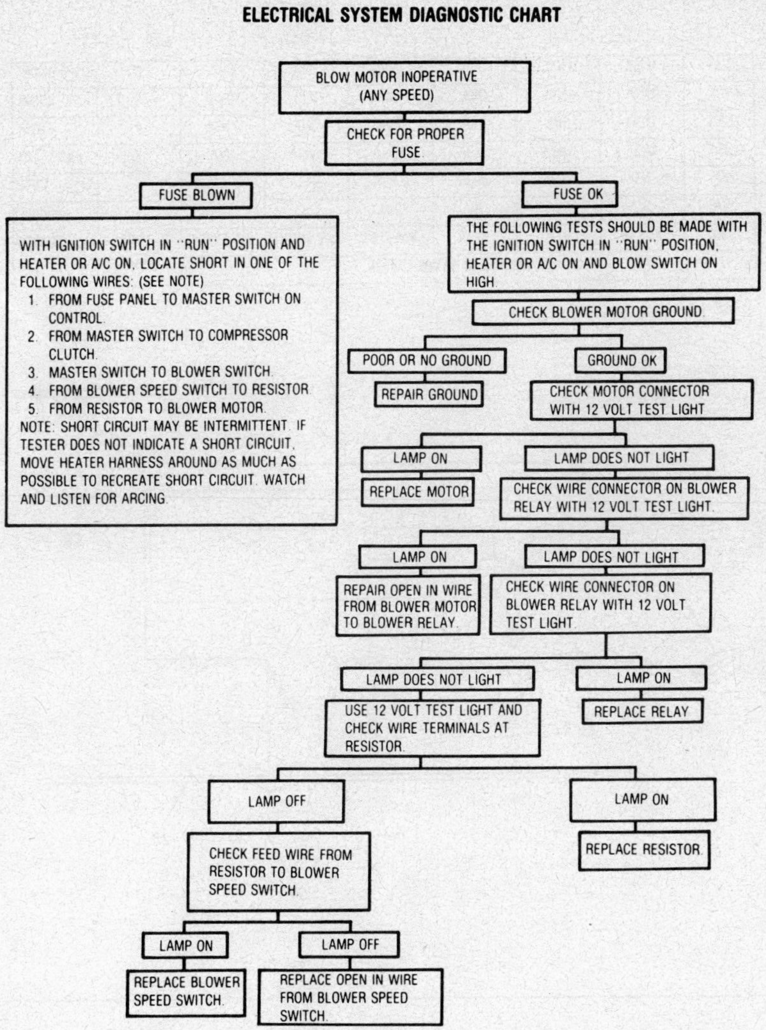
ELECTRICAL SYSTEM DIAGNOSTIC CHART
BLOW MOTOR INOPERATIVE (ANY SPEED)
CHECK FOR PROPER FUSE
FUSE BLOWN
WITH IGNITION SWITCH IN "RUN" POSITION AND HEATER OR A/C ON, LOCATE SHORT IN ONE OF THE FOLLOWING WIRES: (SEE NOTE)
1. FROM FUSE PANEL TO MASTER SWITCH ON CONTROL.
2. FROM MASTER SWITCH TO COMPRESSOR CLUTCH.
3. MASTER SWITCH TO BLOWER SWITCH.
4. FROM BLOWER SPEED SWITCH TO RESISTOR
5. FROM RESISTOR TO BLOWER MOTOR.
NOTE: SHORT CIRCUIT MAY BE INTERMITTENT. IF TESTER DOES NOT INDICATE A SHORT CIRCUIT, MOVE HEATER HARNESS AROUND AS MUCH AS POSSIBLE TO RECREATE SHORT CIRCUIT. WATCH AND LISTEN FOR ARCING.
FUSE OK
THE FOLLOWING TESTS SHOULD BE MADE WITH THE IGNITION SWITCH IN "RUN" POSITION, HEATER OR A/C ON AND BLOW SWITCH ON HIGH
CHECK BLOWER MOTOR GROUND.
POOR OR NO GROUND
REPAIR GROUND
GROUND OK
CHECK MOTOR CONNECTOR WITH 12 VOLT TEST LIGHT
LAMP ON
REPLACE MOTOR
LAMP DOES NOT LIGHT
CHECK WIRE CONNECTOR ON BLOWER RELAY WITH 12 VOLT TEST LIGHT.
LAMP ON
REPAIR OPEN IN WIRE FROM BLOWER MOTOR TO BLOWER RELAY.
LAMP DOES NOT LIGHT
CHECK WIRE CONNECTOR ON BLOWER RELAY WITH 12 VOLT TEST LIGHT.
LAMP DOES NOT LIGHT
USE 12 VOLT TEST LIGHT AND CHECK WIRE TERMINALS AT RESISTOR.
LAMP ON
REPLACE RELAY
LAMP OFF
CHECK FEED WIRE FROM RESISTOR TO BLOWER SPEED SWITCH.
LAMP ON
REPLACE BLOWER SPEED SWITCH.
LAMP OFF
REPLACE OPEN IN WIRE FROM BLOWER SPEED SWITCH.
LAMP ON
REPLACE RESISTOR.

AIR CONDITIONING SYSTEM DIAGNOSIS ELECTRICAL SYSTEM (CONT'D)

ELECTRICAL SYSTEM DIAGNOSTIC CHART (CONTINUED)

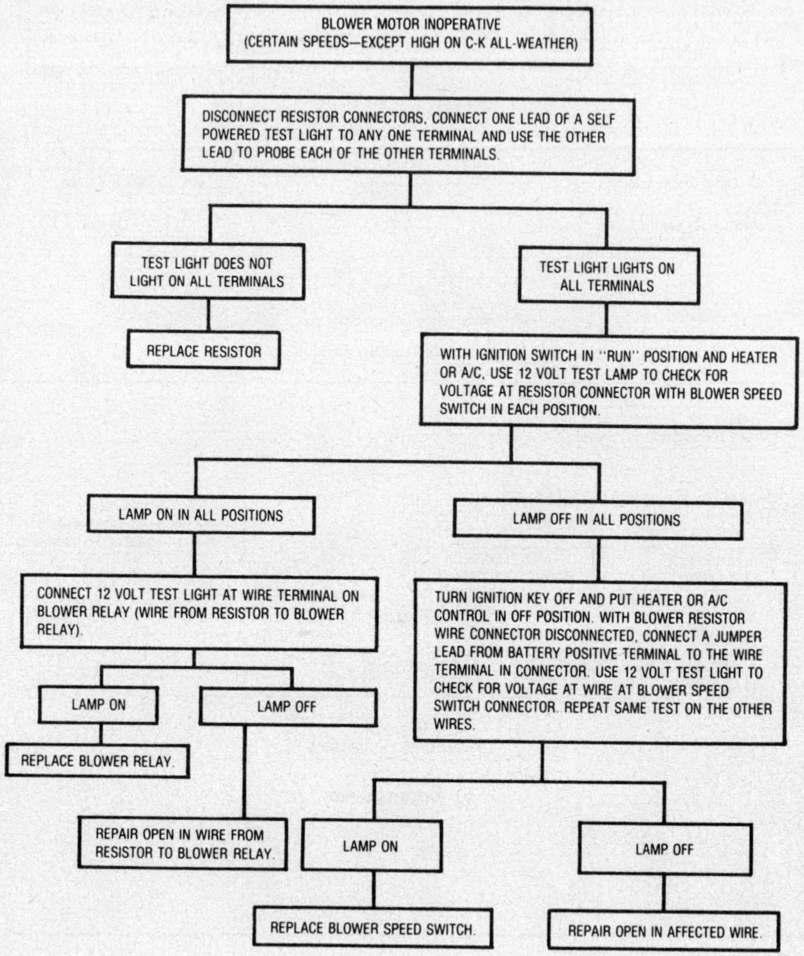
BLOWER MOTOR INOPERATIVE (CERTAIN SPEEDS—EXCEPT HIGH ON C-K ALL-WEATHER)
DISCONNECT RESISTOR CONNECTORS, CONNECT ONE LEAD OF A SELF POWERED TEST LIGHT TO ANY ONE TERMINAL AND USE THE OTHER LEAD TO PROBE EACH OF THE OTHER TERMINALS.
TEST LIGHT DOES NOT LIGHT ON ALL TERMINALS
REPLACE RESISTOR
TEST LIGHT LIGHTS ON ALL TERMINALS
WITH IGNITION SWITCH IN "RUN" POSITION AND HEATER OR A/C, USE 12 VOLT TEST LAMP TO CHECK FOR VOLTAGE AT RESISTOR CONNECTOR WITH BLOWER SPEED SWITCH IN EACH POSITION.
LAMP ON IN ALL POSITIONS
CONNECT 12 VOLT TEST LIGHT AT WIRE TERMINAL ON BLOWER RELAY (WIRE FROM RESISTOR TO BLOWER RELAY).
LAMP ON
REPLACE BLOWER RELAY.
LAMP OFF
REPAIR OPEN IN WIRE FROM RESISTOR TO BLOWER RELAY.
LAMP OFF IN ALL POSITIONS
TURN IGNITION KEY OFF AND PUT HEATER OR A/C CONTROL IN OFF POSITION. WITH BLOWER RESISTOR WIRE CONNECTOR DISCONNECTED, CONNECT A JUMPER LEAD FROM BATTERY POSITIVE TERMINAL TO THE WIRE TERMINAL IN CONNECTOR. USE 12 VOLT TEST LIGHT TO CHECK FOR VOLTAGE AT WIRE AT BLOWER SPEED SWITCH CONNECTOR. REPEAT SAME TEST ON THE OTHER WIRES.
LAMP ON
REPLACE BLOWER SPEED SWITCH.
LAMP OFF
REPAIR OPEN IN AFFECTED WIRE.

AIR CONDITIONING SYSTEM DIAGNOSIS VACUUM SCHEMATIC

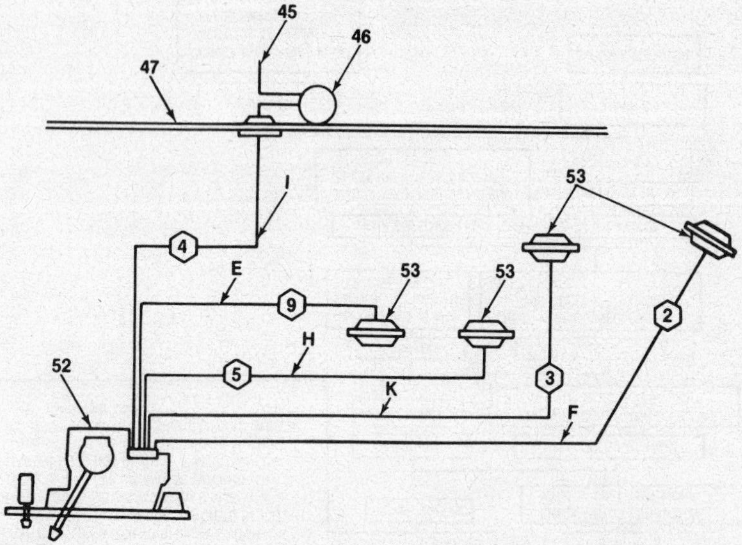
45
46
47
53
I
E
H
K
F
52
4
9
5
3
2

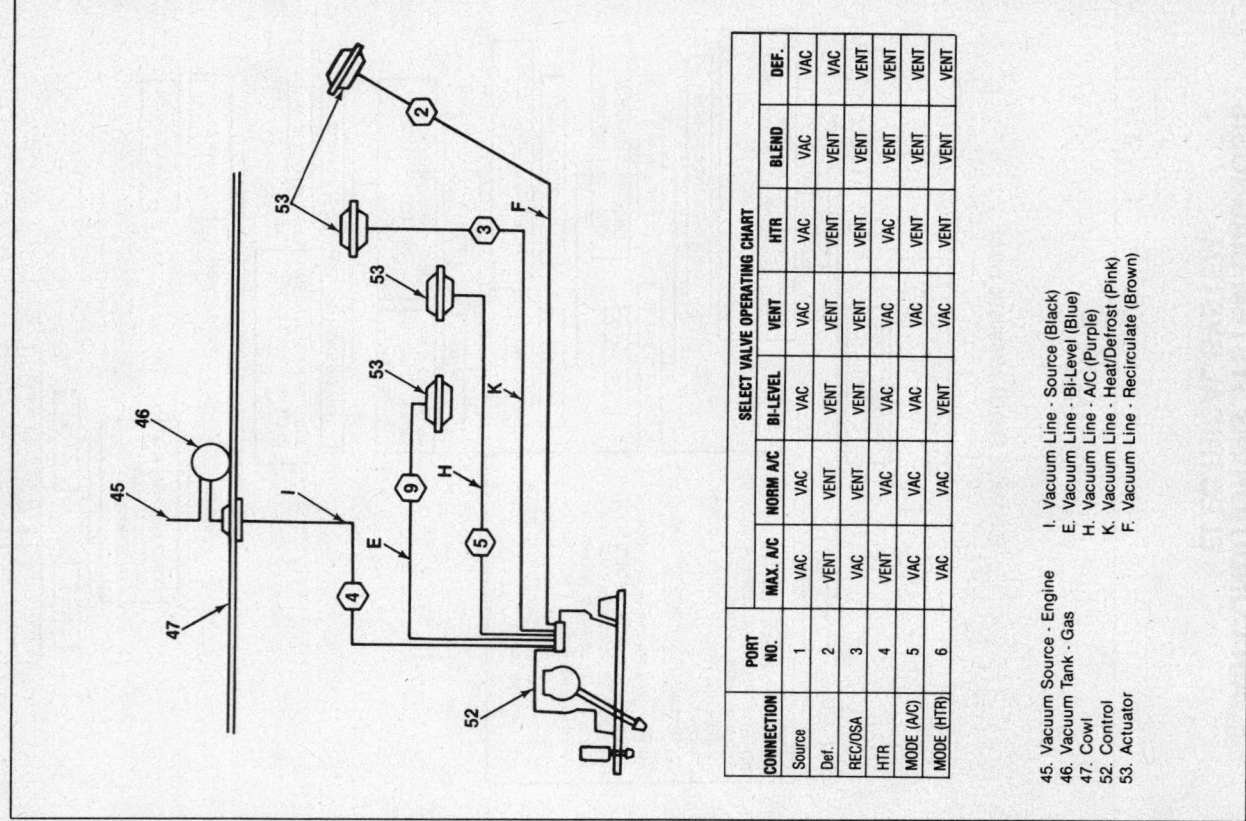

CONNECTION	PORT NO.	SELECT VALVE OPERATING CHART						
		MAX. A/C	NORM A/C	BI-LEVEL	VENT	HTR	BLEND	DEF.
Source	1	VAC	VAC	VAC	VAC	VAC	VAC	VAC
Def.	2	VENT	VENT	VENT	VENT	VENT	VENT	VAC
REC/OSA	3	VAC	VENT	VENT	VENT	VENT	VENT	VENT
HTR	4	VENT	VAC	VAC	VAC	VAC	VENT	VENT
MODE (A/C)	5	VAC	VAC	VAC	VAC	VENT	VENT	VENT
MODE (HTR)	6	VAC	VAC	VENT	VAC	VENT	VENT	VENT

45. Vacuum Source - Engine
46. Vacuum Tank - Gas
47. Cowl
52. Control
53. Actuator

I. Vacuum Line - Source (Black)
E. Vacuum Line - Bi-Level (Blue)
H. Vacuum Line - A/C (Purple)
K. Vacuum Line - Heat/Defrost (Pink)
F. Vacuum Line - Recirculate (Brown)

AIR CONDITIONING SYSTEM DIAGNOSIS
VACUUM ACTUATED CONTROL ASSEMBLY

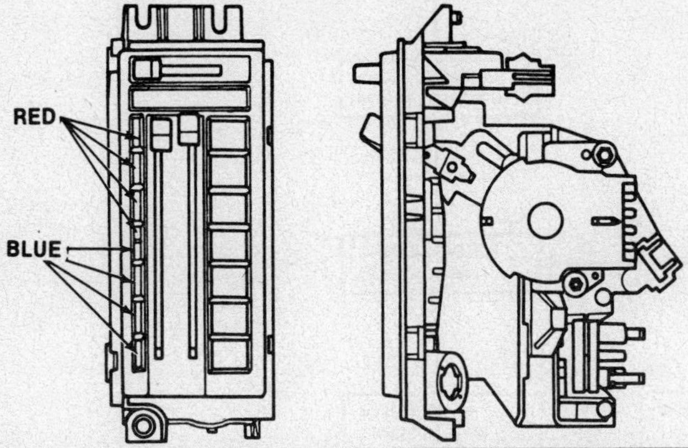
RED
BLUE

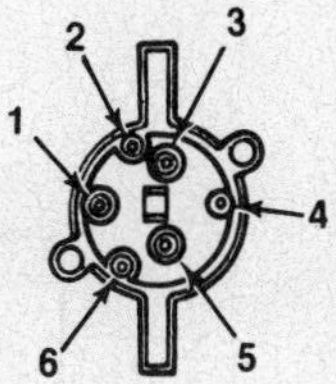
1
2
3
4
5
6

CONNECTION	PORT NO.	SELECT VALVE OPERATING CHART						
		MAX. A/C	NORM A/C	BI-LEVEL	VENT	HTR	BLEND	DEF.
Source	1	VAC	VAC	VAC	VAC	VAC	VAC	VAC
Def.	2	VENT	VENT	VENT	VENT	VENT	VENT	VAC
REC/OSA	3	VAC	VENT	VENT	VENT	VENT	VENT	VENT
HTR	4	VENT	VAC	VAC	VAC	VAC	VENT	VENT
MODE (A/C)	5	VAC	VAC	VAC	VAC	VENT	VENT	VENT
MODE (HTR)	6	VAC	VAC	VENT	VAC	VENT	VENT	VENT

BLOWER SWITCH				
	POSITION			
TERM	OFF	M_1	M_2	HI
B+	No Continuity	Conn. To M_1	Conn. To M_2	Conn. To H
H	No Continuity	No Continuity	No Continuity	Conn. to B+
M_1	No Continuity	Conn. To B+	Continuity Optional	No Continuity
M_2	No Continuity	No Continuity	Conn. To B+	Continuity Optional

CONNECTION	TERM NO.	SELECT VALVE OPERATING CHART						
		MAX. A/C	NORM A/C	BI-LEVEL	VENT	HEAT	BLEND	DEFROST
Compressor	1	Conn. 3,5	Conn. 3,5	Conn. 3,5	No Conn.	No Conn.	Conn. 3,5	Conn. 3,5
No Used	2				No Conn.			
B+	3	Conn. 1,5	Conn. 1,5	Conn. 1,5	No Conn.	No Conn.	Conn. 1,5	Conn. 1,5
No Used	4				No Conn.			
Compressor	5	Conn. 1,3	Conn. 1,3	Conn. 1,3	No Conn.	No Conn.	Conn. 1,3	Conn. 1,3

AIR CONDITIONING SYSTEM DIAGNOSIS
VDOT SYSTEM

STEP 1

A/C FUNCTIONAL TEST

STEP	CONTROL SETTINGS						SYSTEM RESPONSE					
	MODE BUTTON	LITE ON	TEMP SETT.	FAN SW FRT	FAN SW RR	FAN SPEED	RR. OPT. AUX. DUCT.	HEATER OUTLETS	A/C I/P OUTLETS	DEF. OUTLETS	SIDE WDO DEF.	A/C COMPR.
1	OFF	YES	FULL HOT	HI	OFF	OFF	NO AIR FLOW	NO AIR FLOW	NO AIR FLOW	NO AIR FLOW	NO AIR FLOW	OFF
2	DEFR.	YES	FULL HOT	HI	OFF	HI	SOME AIR FLOW	SOME AIR FLOW	NO AIR FLOW	HOT AIR FLOW	SOME HOT AIR FLOW	ON
3	MIX	YES	FULL HOT	HI	OFF	HI	SOME AIR FLOW	AIR FLOW	NO AIR FLOW	HOT AIR FLOW	SOME HOT AIR FLOW	ON
4	HEATER	YES	FULL HOT	HI	OFF	HI	AIR FLOW	HOT AIR FLOW	NO AIR FLOW	SOME AIR FLOW	SOME HOT AIR FLOW	OFF
5	VENT	YES	FULL HOT	HI	OFF	HI	SOME AIR FLOW	NO AIR FLOW	HOT AIR FLOW	NO AIR FLOW	SOME AIR FLOW	OFF
6	BI-LEVEL	YES	FULL COLD	HI	OFF	HI	SOME AIR FLOW	AIR FLOW	COLD AIR FLOW	SOME AIR FLOW	SOME AIR FLOW	ON
7	NORMAL	YES	FULL COLD	LOW	OFF	HI	SOME AIR FLOW	NO AIR FLOW	COLD AIR FLOW	NO AIR FLOW	SOME AIR FLOW	ON
8	NORMAL	YES	FULL COLD	HI	OFF	LOW	SOME AIR FLOW	NO AIR FLOW	COLD AIR FLOW	NO AIR FLOW	SOME AIR FLOW	ON
9	MAX.	YES	FULL COLD	HI	OFF	HI	SOME AIR FLOW	NO AIR FLOW	COLD AIR FLOW	NO AIR FLOW	SOME AIR FLOW	ON
10	MAX.	YES	FULL COLD	LOW	OFF	LOW	SOME AIR FLOW	NO AIR FLOW	COLD AIR FLOW	NO AIR FLOW	SOME AIR FLOW	ON
11	HEATER	YES	FULL HOT	LOW	HI	LOW/HI	HOT AIR FLOW	SOME AIR FLOW	NO AIR FLOW	SOME AIR FLOW	SOME AIR FLOW	OFF

- TEMPERATURE DOOR ACTUATOR MOTOR SHOULD BE HEARD DURING TEMPERATURE SETTING CHANGES, AND NOTICEABLE BLOWER SPEED INCREASE MUST OCCUR FROM LOW TO MID, TO MID, AND HIGH
- CHECK TEMPERATURE LEVER FOR EFFORT AND TRAVEL (COLD TO HOT) (TEMPERATURE CHANGE SHOULD OCCUR).
- CHECK FOR AIR FLOW AS DEFINED IN SYSTEM RESPONSE
- ALL I/P OUTLETS MUST BE CHECKED FOR: 1) BARREL ROTATION. 2) VANE OPERATION, 3) BARREL AND VANES MUST HOLD PRESENT POSITION IN HI BLOWER OPERATION.

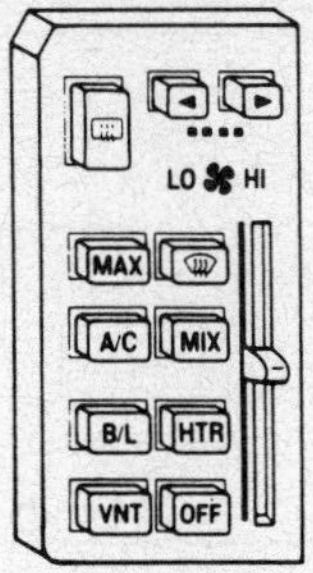
LO
HI
MAX
A/C
MIX
B/L
HTR
VNT
OFF

AIR CONDITIONING SYSTEM DIAGNOSIS—VDOT SYSTEM (CONT'D)

STEP 2--*Checking Refrigerant Charge*

Note: Before proceeding with this step, pressure gauges must be properly calibrated, the ambient air temperature must be 60°F or above, and the engine must be warmed to operating temperature.

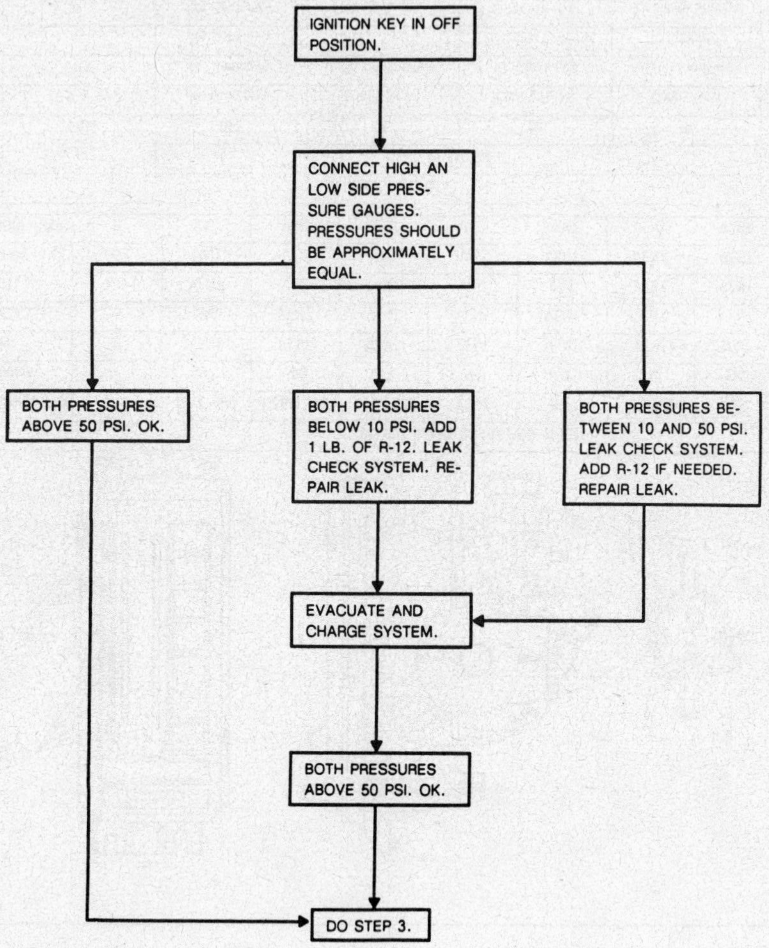
IGNITION KEY IN OFF POSITION.
CONNECT HIGH AN LOW SIDE PRESSURE GAUGES. PRESSURES SHOULD BE APPROXIMATELY EQUAL.
BOTH PRESSURES ABOVE 50 PSI. OK.
BOTH PRESSURES BELOW 10 PSI. ADD 1 LB. OF R-12. LEAK CHECK SYSTEM. REPAIR LEAK.
BOTH PRESSURES BETWEEN 10 AND 50 PSI. LEAK CHECK SYSTEM. ADD R-12 IF NEEDED. REPAIR LEAK.
EVACUATE AND CHARGE SYSTEM.
BOTH PRESSURES ABOVE 50 PSI. OK.
DO STEP 3.

STEP 3--*Checking Compressor Clutch Engagement*

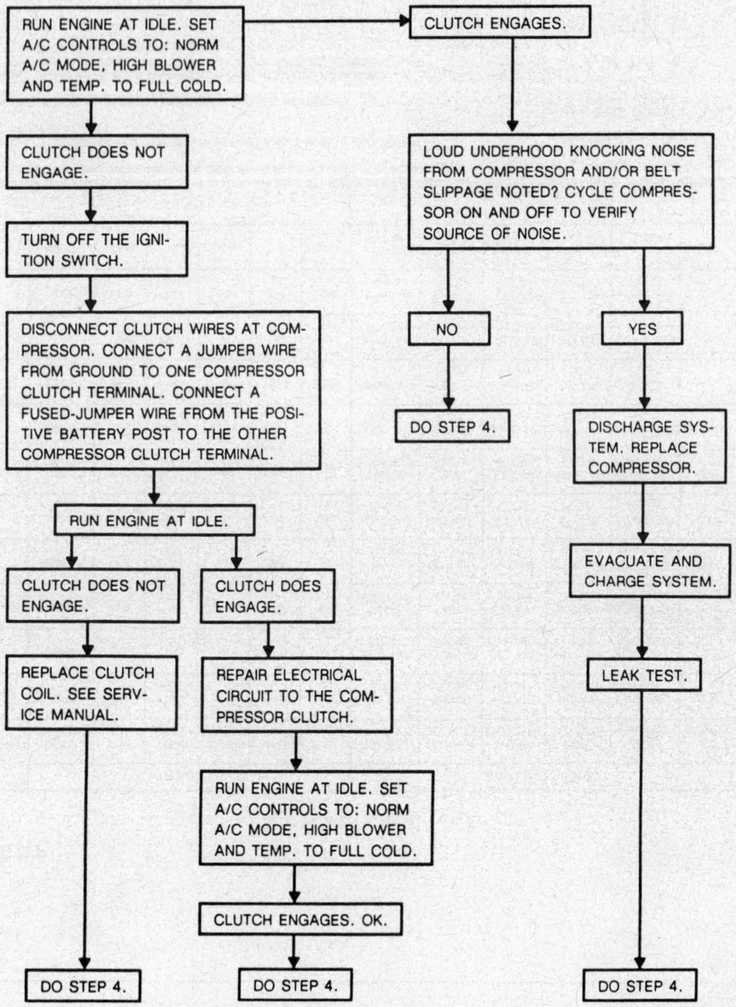
RUN ENGINE AT IDLE. SET A/C CONTROLS TO: NORM A/C MODE, HIGH BLOWER AND TEMP. TO FULL COLD.
CLUTCH ENGAGES.
LOUD UNDERHOOD KNOCKING NOISE FROM COMPRESSOR AND/OR BELT SLIPPAGE NOTED? CYCLE COMPRESSOR ON AND OFF TO VERIFY SOURCE OF NOISE.
NO
DO STEP 4.
YES
DISCHARGE SYSTEM. REPLACE COMPRESSOR.
EVACUATE AND CHARGE SYSTEM.
LEAK TEST.
DO STEP 4.
CLUTCH DOES NOT ENGAGE.
TURN OFF THE IGNITION SWITCH.
DISCONNECT CLUTCH WIRES AT COMPRESSOR. CONNECT A JUMPER WIRE FROM GROUND TO ONE COMPRESSOR CLUTCH TERMINAL. CONNECT A FUSED-JUMPER WIRE FROM THE POSITIVE BATTERY POST TO THE OTHER COMPRESSOR CLUTCH TERMINAL.
RUN ENGINE AT IDLE.
CLUTCH DOES NOT ENGAGE.
REPLACE CLUTCH COIL. SEE SERVICE MANUAL.
DO STEP 4.
CLUTCH DOES ENGAGE.
REPAIR ELECTRICAL CIRCUIT TO THE COMPRESSOR CLUTCH.
RUN ENGINE AT IDLE. SET A/C CONTROLS TO: NORM A/C MODE, HIGH BLOWER AND TEMP. TO FULL COLD.
CLUTCH ENGAGES. OK.
DO STEP 4.

AIR CONDITIONING SYSTEM DIAGNOSIS—VDOT SYSTEM (CONT'D)

STEP 4--*Checking System Performance*

IMPORTANT
THIS TEST WAS DESIGNED FOR TYPICAL GARAGE CONDITIONS: 70-90°F AND NO SUN LOAD. NORMAL DISCHARGE AIR TEMPERATURE IS TYPICALLY AT LEAST 20°F COOLER THAN AMBIENT TEMPERATURE. FOLLOW THIS TEST PROCEDURE EXACTLY. IT IS DESIGNED TO CREATE ENOUGH COOLING LOAD TO CAUSE THE V5 COMPRESSOR TO OPERATE AT FULL STROKE. THIS IS ABSOLUTELY NECESSARY FOR ACCURATE TEST RESULTS.

CLOSE ALL VEHICLE WINDOWS AND DOORS. SET A/C CONTROLS TO: NORM A/C MODE, HIGH BLOWER AND TEMP. TO FULL COLD. RUN ENGINE AT IDLE FOR 5 MINUTES.

FEEL LIQUID LINE ON BOTH SIDES OF ORIFICE (EXPANSION) TUBE.

SAME TEMPERATURE. DISCHARGE SYSTEM.

ORIFICE (EXPANSION) TUBE MISSING.

INSTALL ORIFICE (EXPANSION) TUBE.

EVACUATE AND CHARGE SYSTEM.

LEAK TEST.

NOTE DISCHARGE AIR TEMPERATURE. IS IT WITHIN SPECIFICATIONS?

YES → END

NO → FOLLOW STEP 4 AGAIN.

NOTICEABLE TEMPERATURE DIFFERENCE.

RECORD LOW AND HIGH SIDE PRESSURES AFTER A/C SYSTEM HAS BEEN OPERATING FOR 5 MINUTES OR MORE. ON ENGINES WITH COOLING FANS THAT CYCLE, TAKE PRESSURE READINGS WITH ENGINE COOLING FAN ON.

LOCATE THE INTERSECTION OF THE LOW AND HIGH SIDE PRESSURES ON THE DIAGNOSTIC CHART (FIGURE 1).

CONTINUE TESTING WITH NEXT CHART.

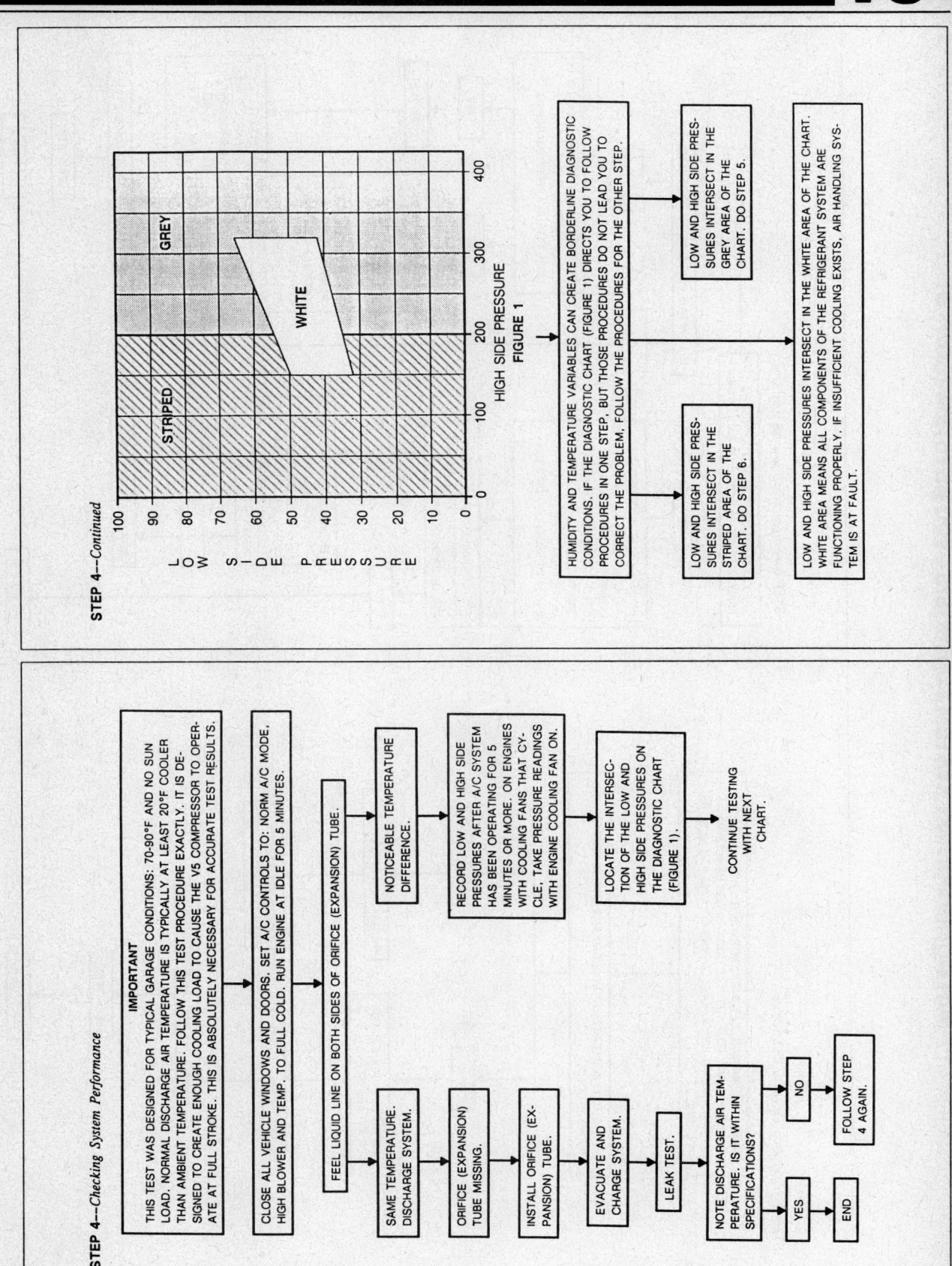

STEP 4--*Continued*

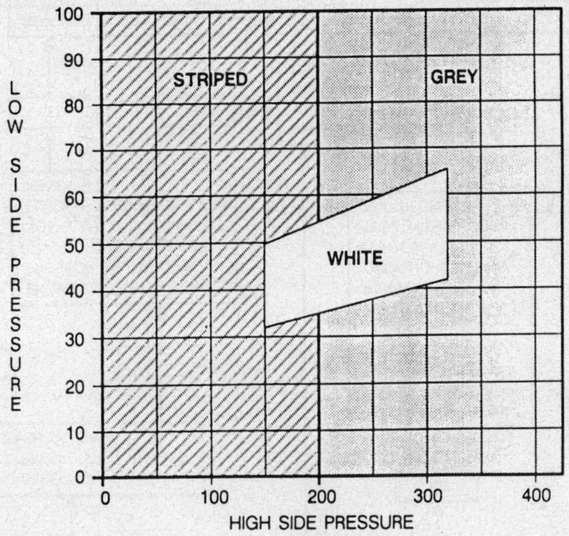
LOW SIDE PRESSURE
100
90
80
70
60
50
40
30
20
10
0
STRIPED
GREY
WHITE
0
100
200
300
400
HIGH SIDE PRESSURE

FIGURE 1

HUMIDITY AND TEMPERATURE VARIABLES CAN CREATE BORDERLINE DIAGNOSTIC CONDITIONS. IF THE DIAGNOSTIC CHART (FIGURE 1) DIRECTS YOU TO FOLLOW PROCEDURES IN ONE STEP, BUT THOSE PROCEDURES DO NOT LEAD YOU TO CORRECT THE PROBLEM, FOLLOW THE PROCEDURES FOR THE OTHER STEP.

LOW AND HIGH SIDE PRESSURES INTERSECT IN THE STRIPED AREA OF THE CHART. DO STEP 6.

LOW AND HIGH SIDE PRESSURES INTERSECT IN THE GREY AREA OF THE CHART. DO STEP 5.

LOW AND HIGH SIDE PRESSURES INTERSECT IN THE WHITE AREA OF THE CHART. WHITE AREA MEANS ALL COMPONENTS OF THE REFRIGERANT SYSTEM ARE FUNCTIONING PROPERLY. IF INSUFFICIENT COOLING EXISTS, AIR HANDLING SYSTEM IS AT FAULT.

AIR CONDITIONING SYSTEM DIAGNOSIS—VDOT SYSTEM (CONT'D)

STEP 5--*Grey Area Diagnosis And Service*

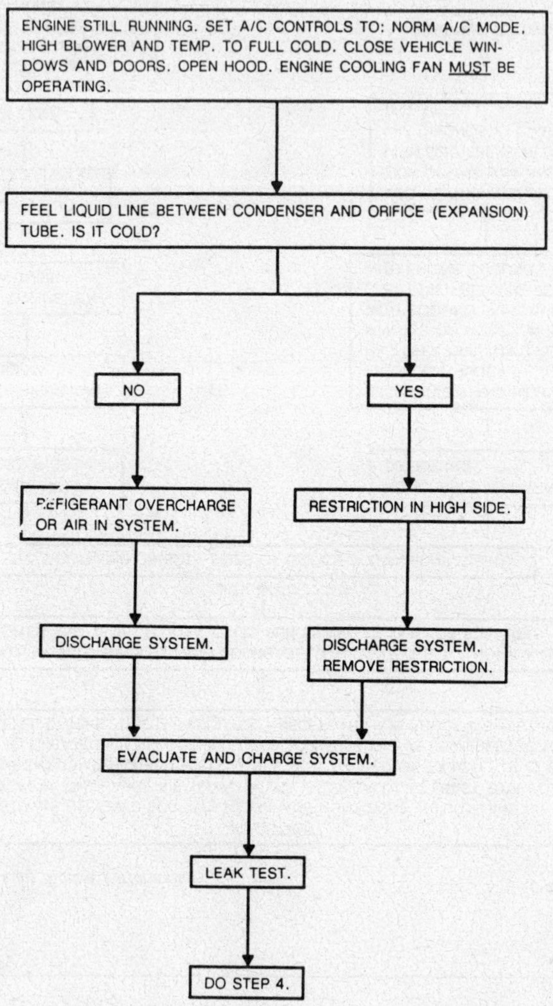
ENGINE STILL RUNNING. SET A/C CONTROLS TO: NORM A/C MODE, HIGH BLOWER AND TEMP. TO FULL COLD. CLOSE VEHICLE WINDOWS AND DOORS. OPEN HOOD. ENGINE COOLING FAN MUST BE OPERATING.
FEEL LIQUID LINE BETWEEN CONDENSER AND ORIFICE (EXPANSION) TUBE. IS IT COLD?
NO
YES
REFIGERANT OVERCHARGE OR AIR IN SYSTEM.
RESTRICTION IN HIGH SIDE.
DISCHARGE SYSTEM.
DISCHARGE SYSTEM. REMOVE RESTRICTION.
EVACUATE AND CHARGE SYSTEM.
LEAK TEST.
DO STEP 4.

STEP 6--*Striped Area Diagnosis And Service*

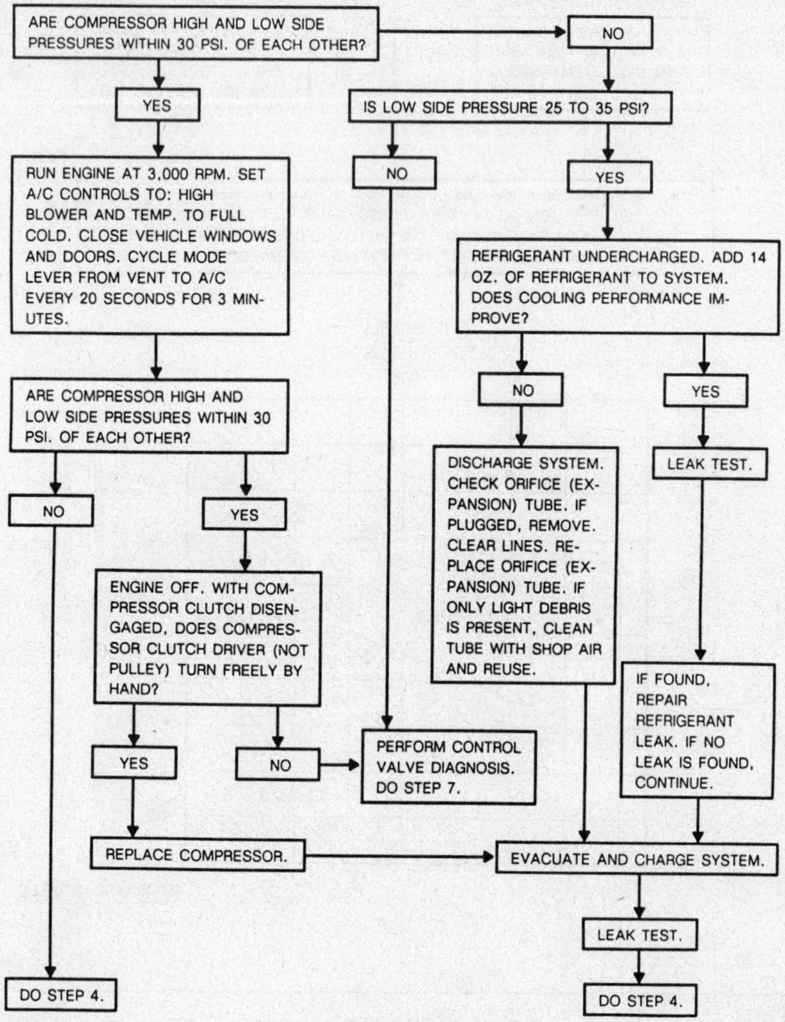
ARE COMPRESSOR HIGH AND LOW SIDE PRESSURES WITHIN 30 PSI. OF EACH OTHER?
NO
YES
IS LOW SIDE PRESSURE 25 TO 35 PSI?
RUN ENGINE AT 3,000 RPM. SET A/C CONTROLS TO: HIGH BLOWER AND TEMP. TO FULL COLD. CLOSE VEHICLE WINDOWS AND DOORS. CYCLE MODE LEVER FROM VENT TO A/C EVERY 20 SECONDS FOR 3 MINUTES.
NO
YES
REFRIGERANT UNDERCHARGED. ADD 14 OZ. OF REFRIGERANT TO SYSTEM. DOES COOLING PERFORMANCE IMPROVE?
ARE COMPRESSOR HIGH AND LOW SIDE PRESSURES WITHIN 30 PSI. OF EACH OTHER?
NO
YES
DISCHARGE SYSTEM. CHECK ORIFICE (EXPANSION) TUBE. IF PLUGGED, REMOVE. CLEAR LINES. REPLACE ORIFICE (EXPANSION) TUBE. IF ONLY LIGHT DEBRIS IS PRESENT, CLEAN TUBE WITH SHOP AIR AND REUSE.
LEAK TEST.
NO
YES
ENGINE OFF. WITH COMPRESSOR CLUTCH DISENGAGED, DOES COMPRESSOR CLUTCH DRIVER (NOT PULLEY) TURN FREELY BY HAND?
IF FOUND, REPAIR REFRIGERANT LEAK. IF NO LEAK IS FOUND, CONTINUE.
YES
NO
PERFORM CONTROL VALVE DIAGNOSIS. DO STEP 7.
REPLACE COMPRESSOR.
EVACUATE AND CHARGE SYSTEM.
LEAK TEST.
DO STEP 4.
DO STEP 4.

AIR CONDITIONING SYSTEM DIAGNOSIS VDOT SYSTEM (CONT'D)

STEP 7--*Control Valve Diagnosis*

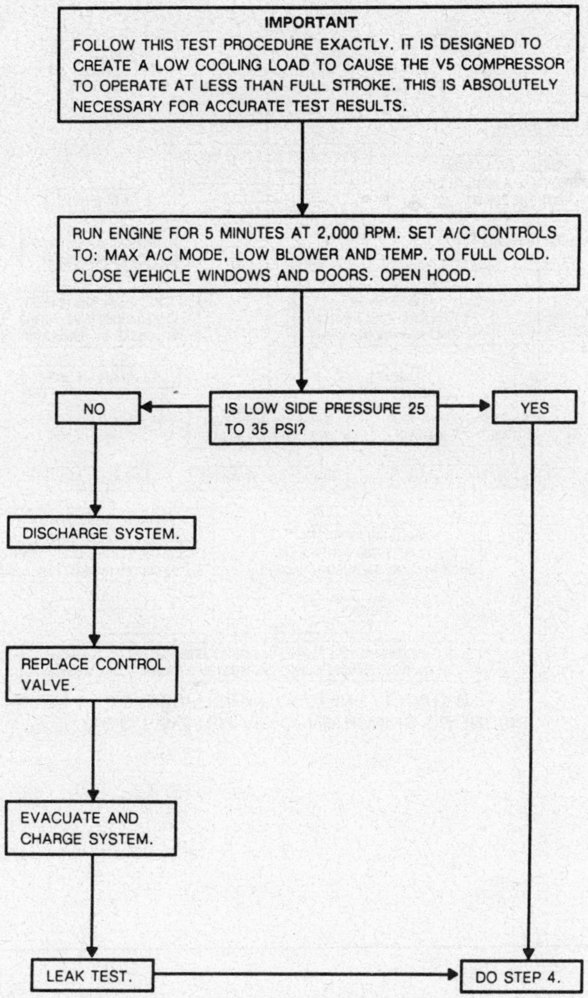
IMPORTANT
FOLLOW THIS TEST PROCEDURE EXACTLY. IT IS DESIGNED TO CREATE A LOW COOLING LOAD TO CAUSE THE V5 COMPRESSOR TO OPERATE AT LESS THAN FULL STROKE. THIS IS ABSOLUTELY NECESSARY FOR ACCURATE TEST RESULTS.
RUN ENGINE FOR 5 MINUTES AT 2,000 RPM. SET A/C CONTROLS TO: MAX A/C MODE, LOW BLOWER AND TEMP. TO FULL COLD. CLOSE VEHICLE WINDOWS AND DOORS. OPEN HOOD.
IS LOW SIDE PRESSURE 25 TO 35 PSI?
NO
YES
DISCHARGE SYSTEM.
REPLACE CONTROL VALVE.
EVACUATE AND CHARGE SYSTEM.
LEAK TEST.
DO STEP 4.

AIR CONDITIONING SYSTEM DIAGNOSIS CCOT SYSTEM

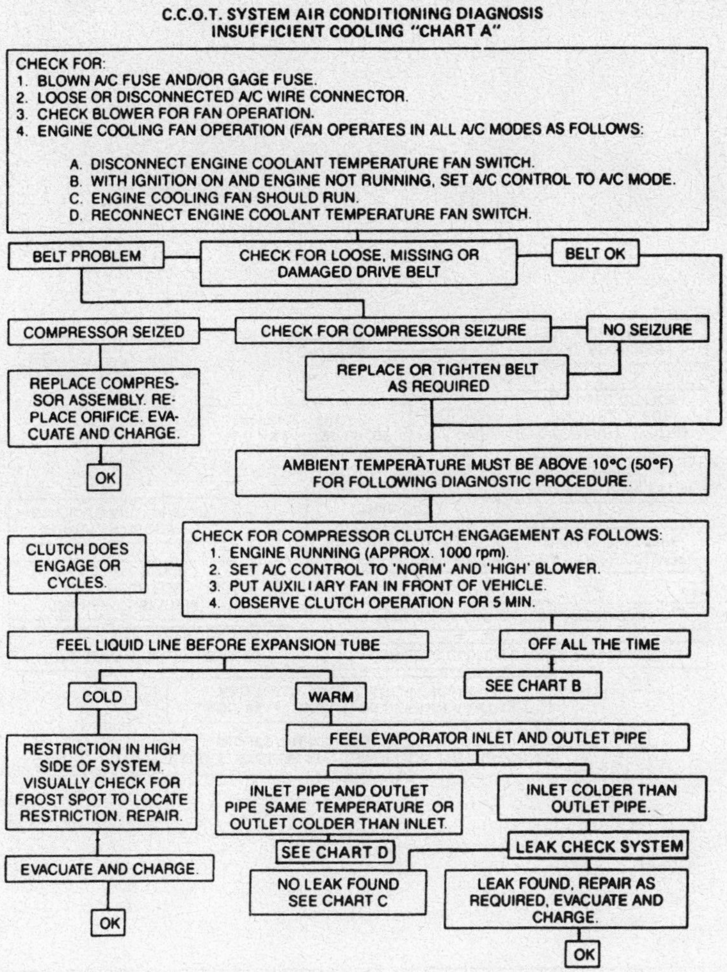
C.C.O.T. SYSTEM AIR CONDITIONING DIAGNOSIS
INSUFFICIENT COOLING "CHART A"
CHECK FOR:
1. BLOWN A/C FUSE AND/OR GAGE FUSE.
2. LOOSE OR DISCONNECTED A/C WIRE CONNECTOR.
3. CHECK BLOWER FOR FAN OPERATION.
4. ENGINE COOLING FAN OPERATION (FAN OPERATES IN ALL A/C MODES AS FOLLOWS:
A. DISCONNECT ENGINE COOLANT TEMPERATURE FAN SWITCH.
B. WITH IGNITION ON AND ENGINE NOT RUNNING, SET A/C CONTROL TO A/C MODE.
C. ENGINE COOLING FAN SHOULD RUN.
D. RECONNECT ENGINE COOLANT TEMPERATURE FAN SWITCH.
BELT PROBLEM
CHECK FOR LOOSE, MISSING OR DAMAGED DRIVE BELT
BELT OK
COMPRESSOR SEIZED
CHECK FOR COMPRESSOR SEIZURE
NO SEIZURE
REPLACE COMPRESSOR ASSEMBLY. REPLACE ORIFICE. EVACUATE AND CHARGE.
REPLACE OR TIGHTEN BELT AS REQUIRED
OK
AMBIENT TEMPERATURE MUST BE ABOVE 10°C (50°F) FOR FOLLOWING DIAGNOSTIC PROCEDURE.
CLUTCH DOES ENGAGE OR CYCLES.
CHECK FOR COMPRESSOR CLUTCH ENGAGEMENT AS FOLLOWS:
1. ENGINE RUNNING (APPROX. 1000 rpm).
2. SET A/C CONTROL TO 'NORM' AND 'HIGH' BLOWER.
3. PUT AUXILIARY FAN IN FRONT OF VEHICLE.
4. OBSERVE CLUTCH OPERATION FOR 5 MIN.
FEEL LIQUID LINE BEFORE EXPANSION TUBE
OFF ALL THE TIME
SEE CHART B
COLD
WARM
FEEL EVAPORATOR INLET AND OUTLET PIPE
RESTRICTION IN HIGH SIDE OF SYSTEM. VISUALLY CHECK FOR FROST SPOT TO LOCATE RESTRICTION. REPAIR.
INLET PIPE AND OUTLET PIPE SAME TEMPERATURE OR OUTLET COLDER THAN INLET.
INLET COLDER THAN OUTLET PIPE.
SEE CHART D
LEAK CHECK SYSTEM
EVACUATE AND CHARGE.
NO LEAK FOUND SEE CHART C
LEAK FOUND, REPAIR AS REQUIRED, EVACUATE AND CHARGE.
OK
OK

AIR CONDITIONING SYSTEM DIAGNOSIS—CCOT SYSTEM (CONT'D)

C.C.O.T SYSTEM AIR CONDITIONING DIAGNOSIS
INSUFFICIENT COOLIING "CHART B"

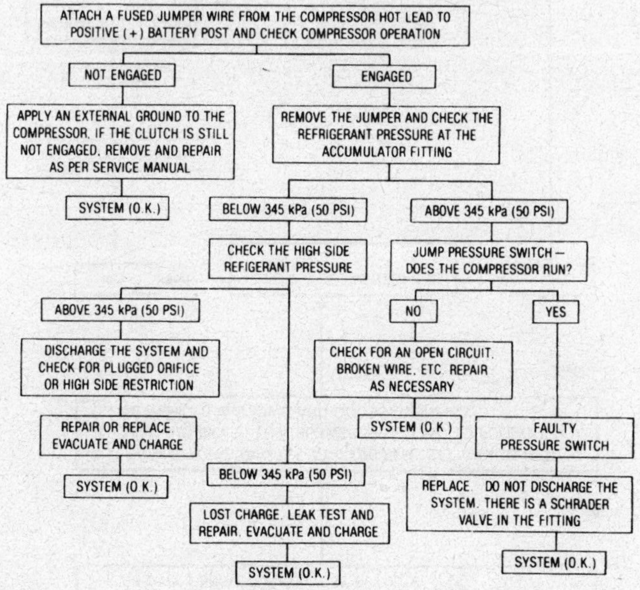
ATTACH A FUSED JUMPER WIRE FROM THE COMPRESSOR HOT LEAD TO POSITIVE (+) BATTERY POST AND CHECK COMPRESSOR OPERATION
NOT ENGAGED
ENGAGED
APPLY AN EXTERNAL GROUND TO THE COMPRESSOR. IF THE CLUTCH IS STILL NOT ENGAGED, REMOVE AND REPAIR AS PER SERVICE MANUAL
SYSTEM (O.K.)
REMOVE THE JUMPER AND CHECK THE REFRIGERANT PRESSURE AT THE ACCUMULATOR FITTING
BELOW 345 kPa (50 PSI)
ABOVE 345 kPa (50 PSI)
CHECK THE HIGH SIDE REFIGERANT PRESSURE
JUMP PRESSURE SWITCH — DOES THE COMPRESSOR RUN?
ABOVE 345 kPa (50 PSI)
NO
YES
DISCHARGE THE SYSTEM AND CHECK FOR PLUGGED ORIFICE OR HIGH SIDE RESTRICTION
CHECK FOR AN OPEN CIRCUIT. BROKEN WIRE, ETC. REPAIR AS NECESSARY
SYSTEM (O.K.)
FAULTY PRESSURE SWITCH
REPAIR OR REPLACE. EVACUATE AND CHARGE
SYSTEM (O.K.)
BELOW 345 kPa (50 PSI)
REPLACE. DO NOT DISCHARGE THE SYSTEM. THERE IS A SCHRADER VALVE IN THE FITTING
LOST CHARGE. LEAK TEST AND REPAIR. EVACUATE AND CHARGE
SYSTEM (O.K.)
SYSTEM (O.K.)

C.C.O.T. SYSTEM AIR CONDITIONING DIAGNOSIS
INSUFFICIENT COOLING "CHART C"

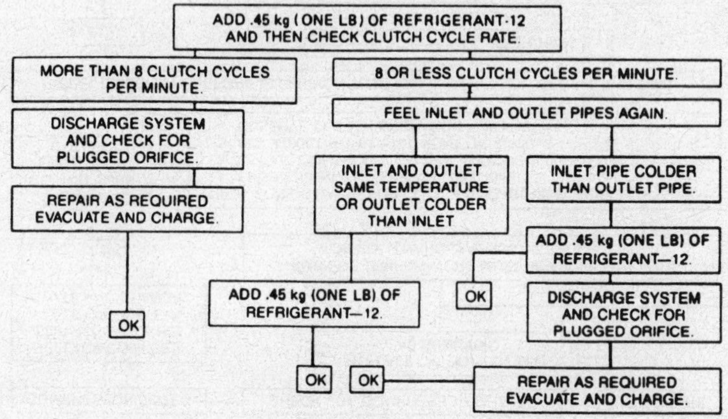
ADD .45 kg (ONE LB) OF REFRIGERANT-12 AND THEN CHECK CLUTCH CYCLE RATE.
MORE THAN 8 CLUTCH CYCLES PER MINUTE.
8 OR LESS CLUTCH CYCLES PER MINUTE.
DISCHARGE SYSTEM AND CHECK FOR PLUGGED ORIFICE.
FEEL INLET AND OUTLET PIPES AGAIN.
REPAIR AS REQUIRED EVACUATE AND CHARGE.
INLET AND OUTLET SAME TEMPERATURE OR OUTLET COLDER THAN INLET
INLET PIPE COLDER THAN OUTLET PIPE.
ADD .45 kg (ONE LB) OF REFRIGERANT—12.
OK
ADD .45 kg (ONE LB) OF REFRIGERANT—12.
OK
DISCHARGE SYSTEM AND CHECK FOR PLUGGED ORIFICE.
OK
OK
REPAIR AS REQUIRED EVACUATE AND CHARGE.

AIR CONDITIONING SYSTEM DIAGNOSIS—CCOT SYSTEM (CONT'D)

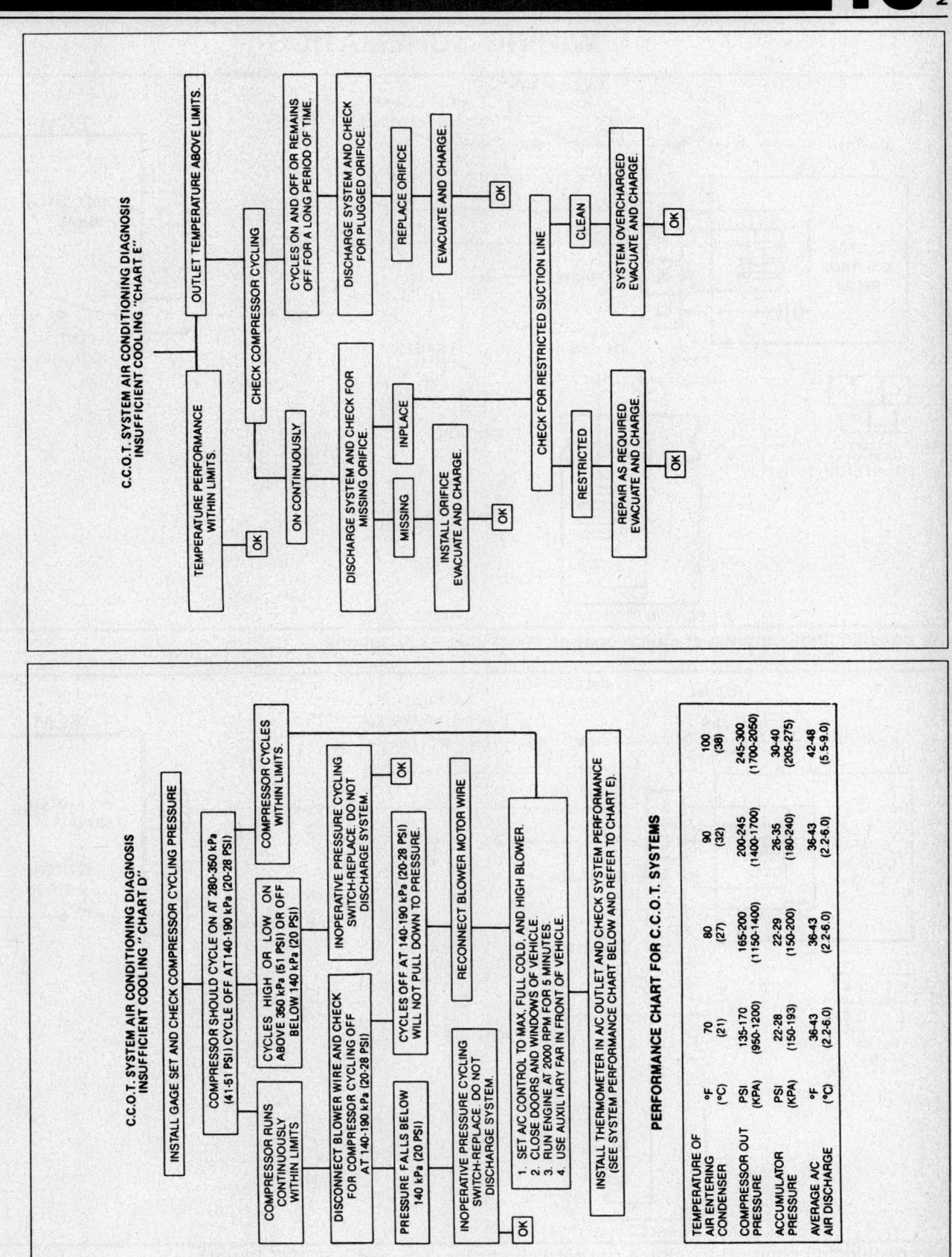

C.C.O.T. SYSTEM AIR CONDITIONING DIAGNOSIS
INSUFFICIENT COOLING "CHART D"

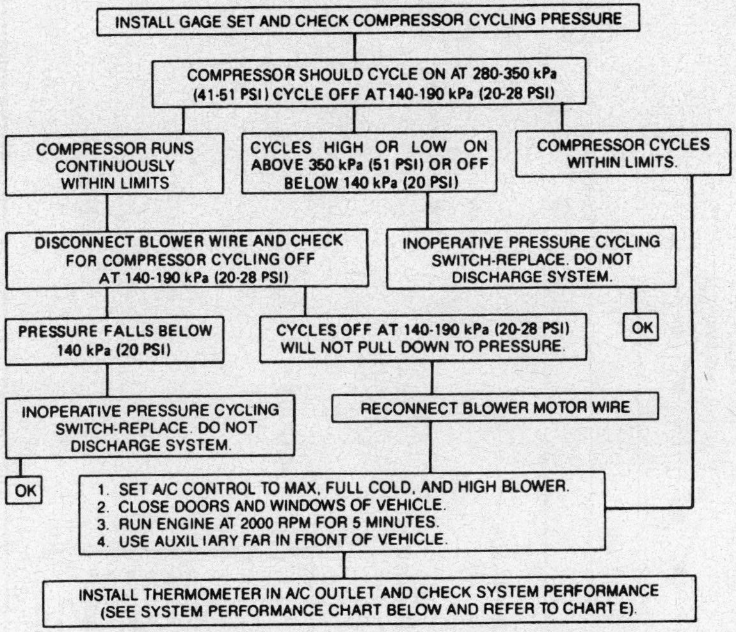
INSTALL GAGE SET AND CHECK COMPRESSOR CYCLING PRESSURE
COMPRESSOR SHOULD CYCLE ON AT 280-350 kPa (41-51 PSI) CYCLE OFF AT 140-190 kPa (20-28 PSI)
COMPRESSOR RUNS CONTINUOUSLY WITHIN LIMITS
CYCLES HIGH OR LOW ON ABOVE 350 kPa (51 PSI) OR OFF BELOW 140 kPa (20 PSI)
COMPRESSOR CYCLES WITHIN LIMITS.
DISCONNECT BLOWER WIRE AND CHECK FOR COMPRESSOR CYCLING OFF AT 140-190 kPa (20-28 PSI)
INOPERATIVE PRESSURE CYCLING SWITCH-REPLACE. DO NOT DISCHARGE SYSTEM.
OK
PRESSURE FALLS BELOW 140 kPa (20 PSI)
CYCLES OFF AT 140-190 kPa (20-28 PSI) WILL NOT PULL DOWN TO PRESSURE.
INOPERATIVE PRESSURE CYCLING SWITCH-REPLACE. DO NOT DISCHARGE SYSTEM.
RECONNECT BLOWER MOTOR WIRE
OK
1. SET A/C CONTROL TO MAX, FULL COLD, AND HIGH BLOWER.
2. CLOSE DOORS AND WINDOWS OF VEHICLE.
3. RUN ENGINE AT 2000 RPM FOR 5 MINUTES.
4. USE AUXIL IARY FAR IN FRONT OF VEHICLE.
INSTALL THERMOMETER IN A/C OUTLET AND CHECK SYSTEM PERFORMANCE (SEE SYSTEM PERFORMANCE CHART BELOW AND REFER TO CHART E).

PERFORMANCE CHART FOR C.C.O.T. SYSTEMS

TEMPERATURE OF AIR ENTERING CONDENSER	°F (°C)	70 (21)	80 (27)	90 (32)	100 (38)
COMPRESSOR OUT PRESSURE	PSI (KPA)	135-170 (950-1200)	165-200 (1150-1400)	200-245 (1400-1700)	245-300 (1700-2050)
ACCUMULATOR PRESSURE	PSI (KPA)	22-28 (150-193)	22-29 (150-200)	26-35 (180-240)	30-40 (205-275)
AVERAGE A/C AIR DISCHARGE	°F (°C)	36-43 (2.2-6.0)	36-43 (2.2-6.0)	36-43 (2.2-6.0)	42-48 (5.5-9.0)

C.C.O.T. SYSTEM AIR CONDITIONING DIAGNOSIS
INSUFFICIENT COOLING "CHART E"

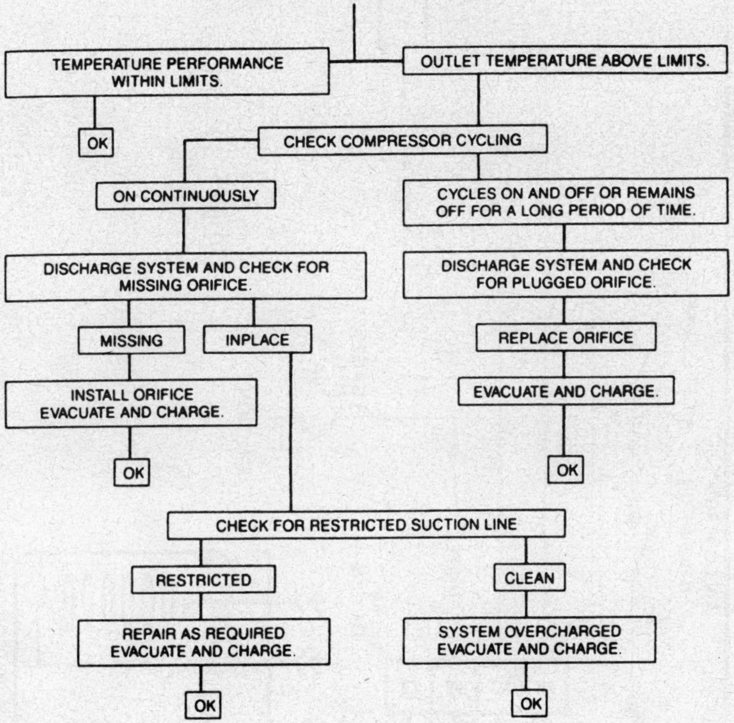
TEMPERATURE PERFORMANCE WITHIN LIMITS.
OUTLET TEMPERATURE ABOVE LIMITS.
OK
CHECK COMPRESSOR CYCLING
ON CONTINUOUSLY
CYCLES ON AND OFF OR REMAINS OFF FOR A LONG PERIOD OF TIME.
DISCHARGE SYSTEM AND CHECK FOR MISSING ORIFICE.
DISCHARGE SYSTEM AND CHECK FOR PLUGGED ORIFICE.
MISSING
INPLACE
REPLACE ORIFICE
INSTALL ORIFICE EVACUATE AND CHARGE.
EVACUATE AND CHARGE.
OK
OK
CHECK FOR RESTRICTED SUCTION LINE
RESTRICTED
CLEAN
REPAIR AS REQUIRED EVACUATE AND CHARGE.
SYSTEM OVERCHARGED EVACUATE AND CHARGE.
OK
OK

WIRING SCHEMATICS

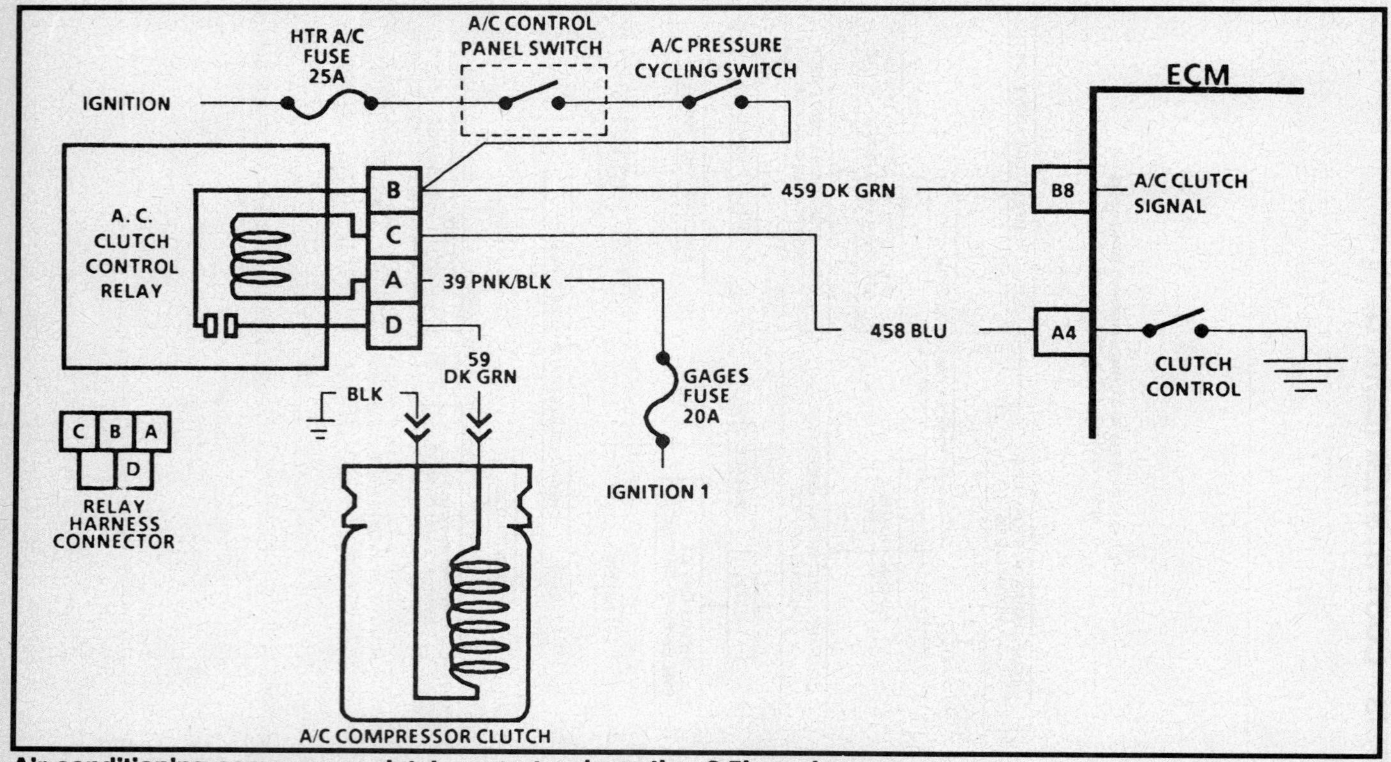
HTR A/C FUSE 25A
A/C CONTROL PANEL SWITCH
A/C PRESSURE CYCLING SWITCH
ECM
IGNITION
A. C. CLUTCH CONTROL RELAY
B
C
A
D
459 DK GRN
B8
A/C CLUTCH SIGNAL
39 PNK/BLK
458 BLU
A4
CLUTCH CONTROL
59 DK GRN
BLK
GAGES FUSE 20A
IGNITION 1
C B A D
RELAY HARNESS CONNECTOR
A/C COMPRESSOR CLUTCH

Air conditioning compressor clutch control schematic – 2.5L engine

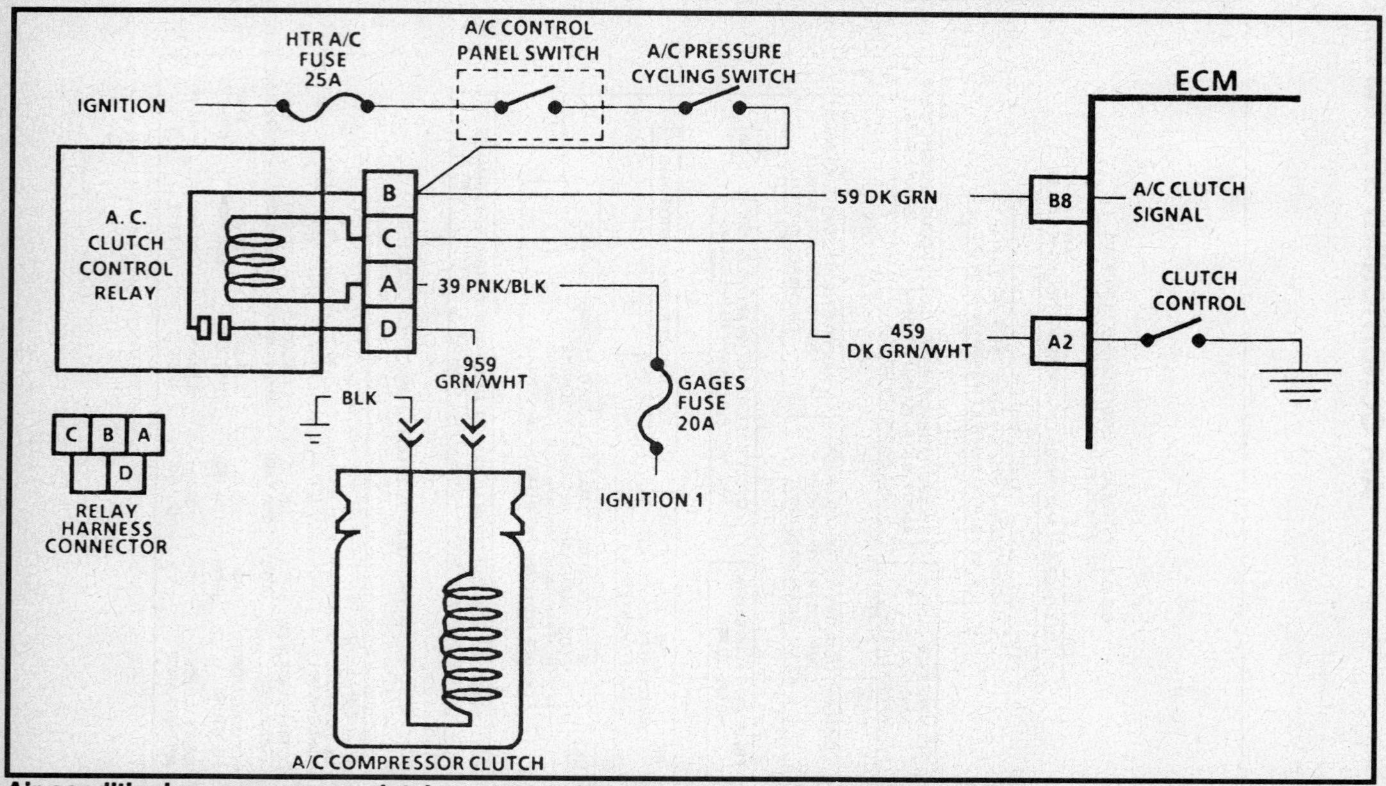
HTR A/C FUSE 25A
A/C CONTROL PANEL SWITCH
A/C PRESSURE CYCLING SWITCH
ECM
IGNITION
A. C. CLUTCH CONTROL RELAY
B
C
A
D
59 DK GRN
B8
A/C CLUTCH SIGNAL
CLUTCH CONTROL
39 PNK/BLK
459 DK GRN/WHT
A2
959 GRN/WHT
BLK
GAGES FUSE 20A
IGNITION 1
C B A D
RELAY HARNESS CONNECTOR
A/C COMPRESSOR CLUTCH

Air conditioning compressor clutch control schematic – 2.8L and 4.3L (S/T Series)

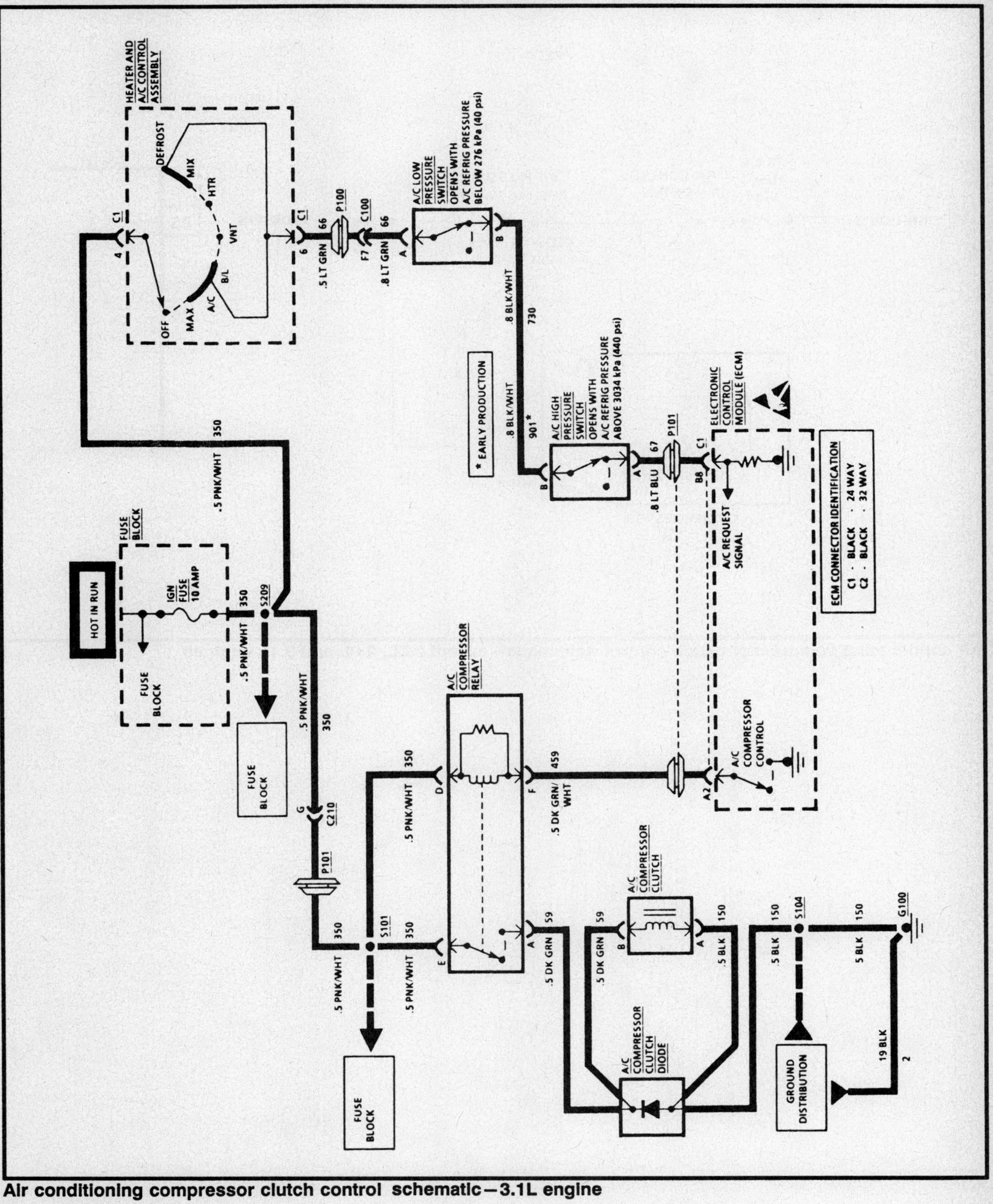
HEATER AND A/C CONTROL ASSEMBLY
DEFROST
MIX
HTR
VNT
B/L
A/C
MAX
OFF
A/C LOW PRESSURE SWITCH
OPENS WITH A/C REFRIG PRESSURE BELOW 276 kPa (40 psi)
A/C HIGH PRESSURE SWITCH
OPENS WITH A/C REFRIG PRESSURE ABOVE 3034 kPa (440 psi)
* EARLY PRODUCTION
ELECTRONIC CONTROL MODULE (ECM)
A/C REQUEST SIGNAL
ECM CONNECTOR IDENTIFICATION
C1 - BLACK - 24 WAY
C2 - BLACK - 32 WAY
HOT IN RUN
FUSE BLOCK
IGN FUSE 10 AMP
A/C COMPRESSOR RELAY
COMPRESSOR CONTROL
A/C COMPRESSOR CLUTCH
A/C COMPRESSOR CLUTCH DIODE
GROUND DISTRIBUTION
.5 PNK/WHT
.5 LT GRN
.8 LT GRN
.8 BLK/WHT
.8 LT BLU
.5 DK GRN/WHT
.5 DK GRN
.5 BLK
19 BLK

Air conditioning compressor clutch control schematic—3.1L engine

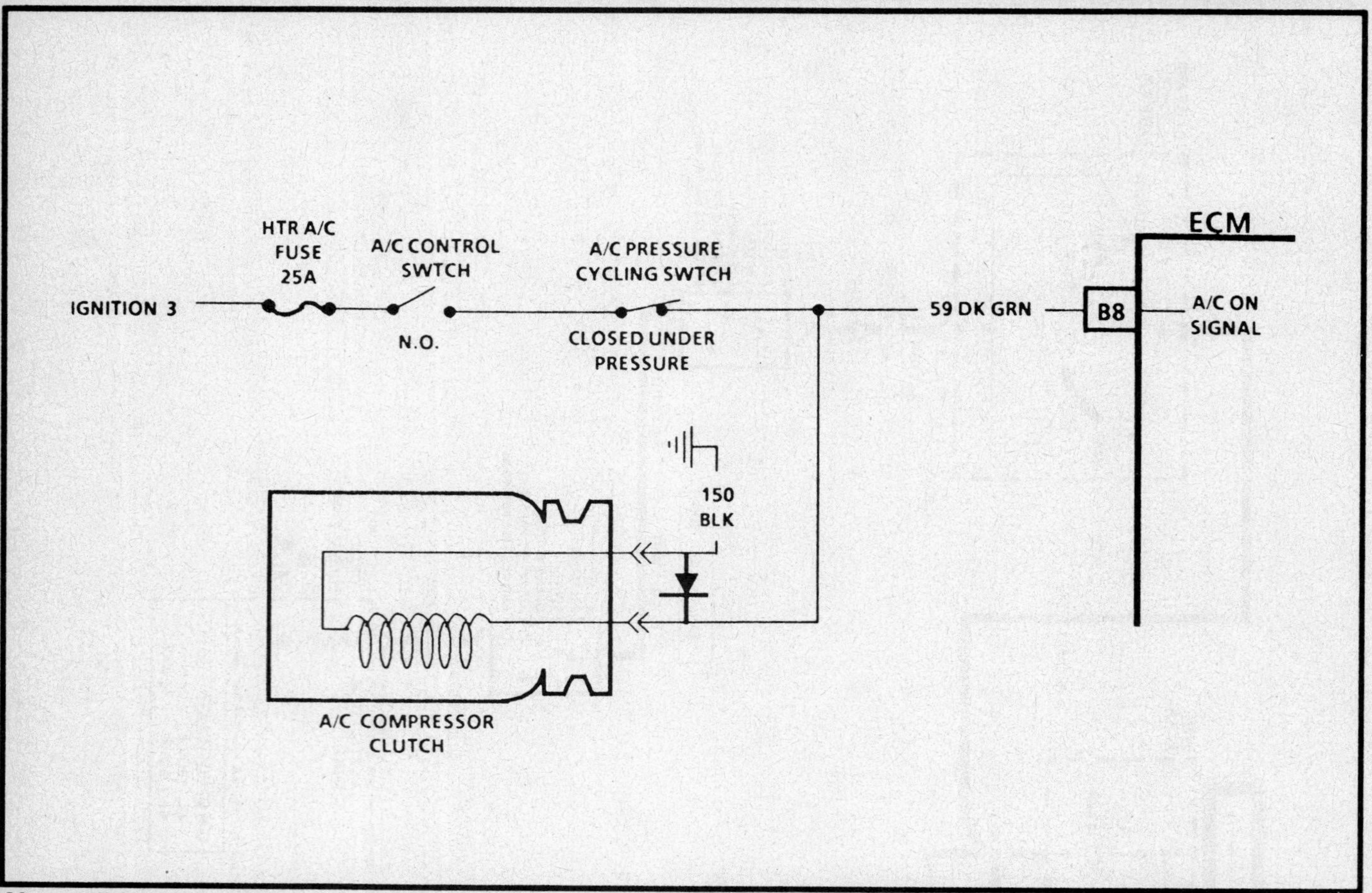
HTR A/C
FUSE
25A
A/C CONTROL
SWTCH
A/C PRESSURE
CYCLING SWTCH
ECM
IGNITION 3
59 DK GRN
B8
A/C ON
SIGNAL
N.O.
CLOSED UNDER
PRESSURE
150
BLK
A/C COMPRESSOR
CLUTCH

Air conditioning compressor clutch control schematic—except 2.5L, 2.8L and 3.1L engines

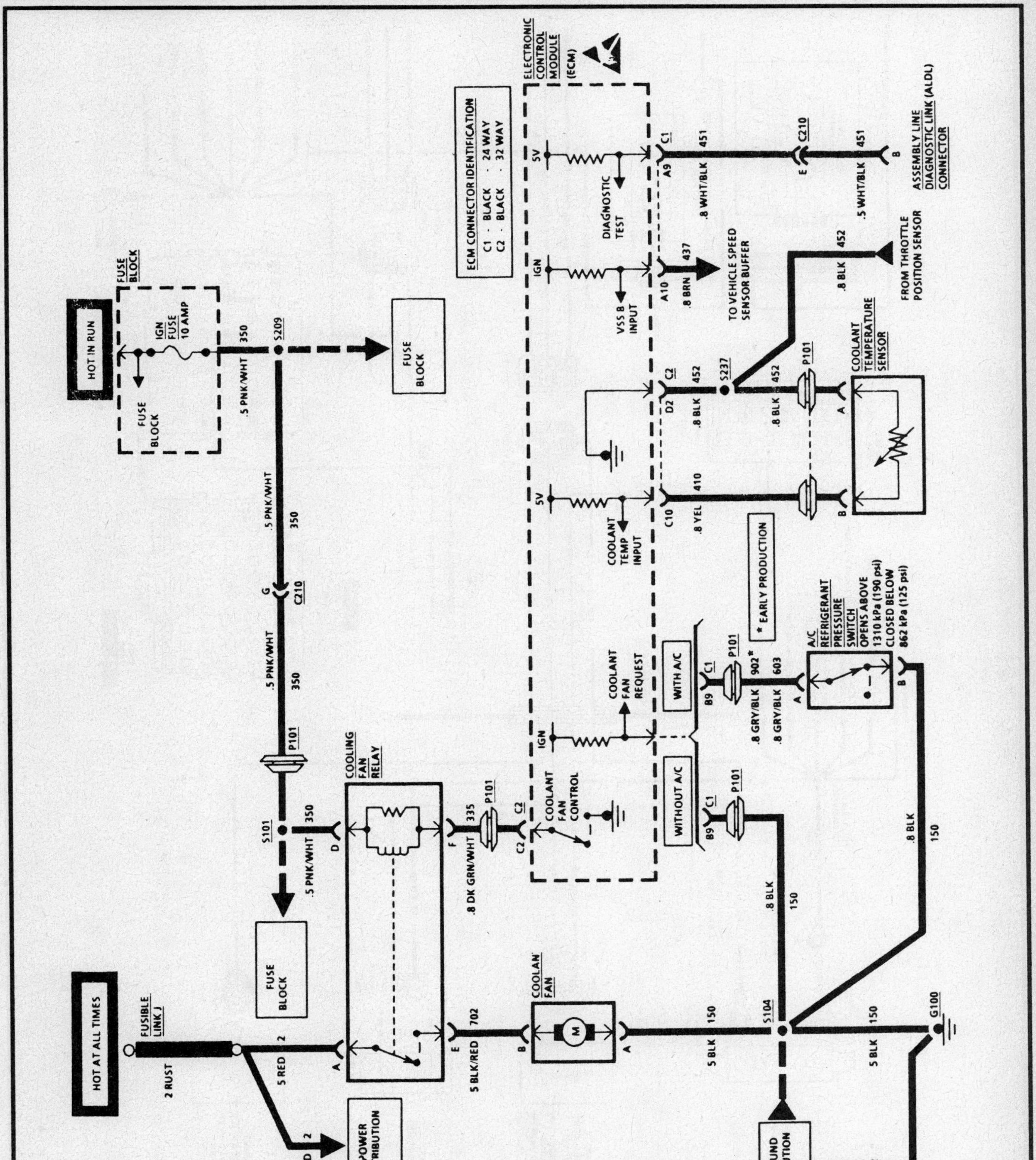
HOT IN RUN
FUSE BLOCK
IGN FUSE 10 AMP
350
S209
.5 PNK/WHT
FUSE BLOCK
HOT AT ALL TIMES
FUSIBLE LINK J
2 RUST
5 RED
2
POWER DISTRIBUTION
C210
G
P101
S101
COOLING FAN RELAY
335
.8 DK GRN/WHT
702
5 BLK/RED
COOLANT FAN
150
5 BLK
S104
G100
GROUND DISTRIBUTION
19 BLK
.8 BLK
ELECTRONIC CONTROL MODULE (ECM)
ECM CONNECTOR IDENTIFICATION
C1 - BLACK - 24 WAY
C2 - BLACK - 32 WAY
5V
IGN
DIAGNOSTIC TEST
VSS B INPUT
COOLANT TEMP INPUT
COOLANT FAN REQUEST
COOLANT FAN CONTROL
451
.8 WHT/BLK
.5 WHT/BLK
ASSEMBLY LINE DIAGNOSTIC LINK (ALDL) CONNECTOR
437
.8 BRN
TO VEHICLE SPEED SENSOR BUFFER
452
.8 BLK
FROM THROTTLE POSITION SENSOR
S237
COOLANT TEMPERATURE SENSOR
410
.8 YEL
* EARLY PRODUCTION
WITH A/C
WITHOUT A/C
902*
603
.8 GRY/BLK
A/C REFRIGERANT PRESSURE SWITCH
OPENS ABOVE 1310 kPa (190 psi)
CLOSED BELOW 862 kPa (125 psi)

Coolant fan schematic—Lumina APV, Silhouette and Trans Sport

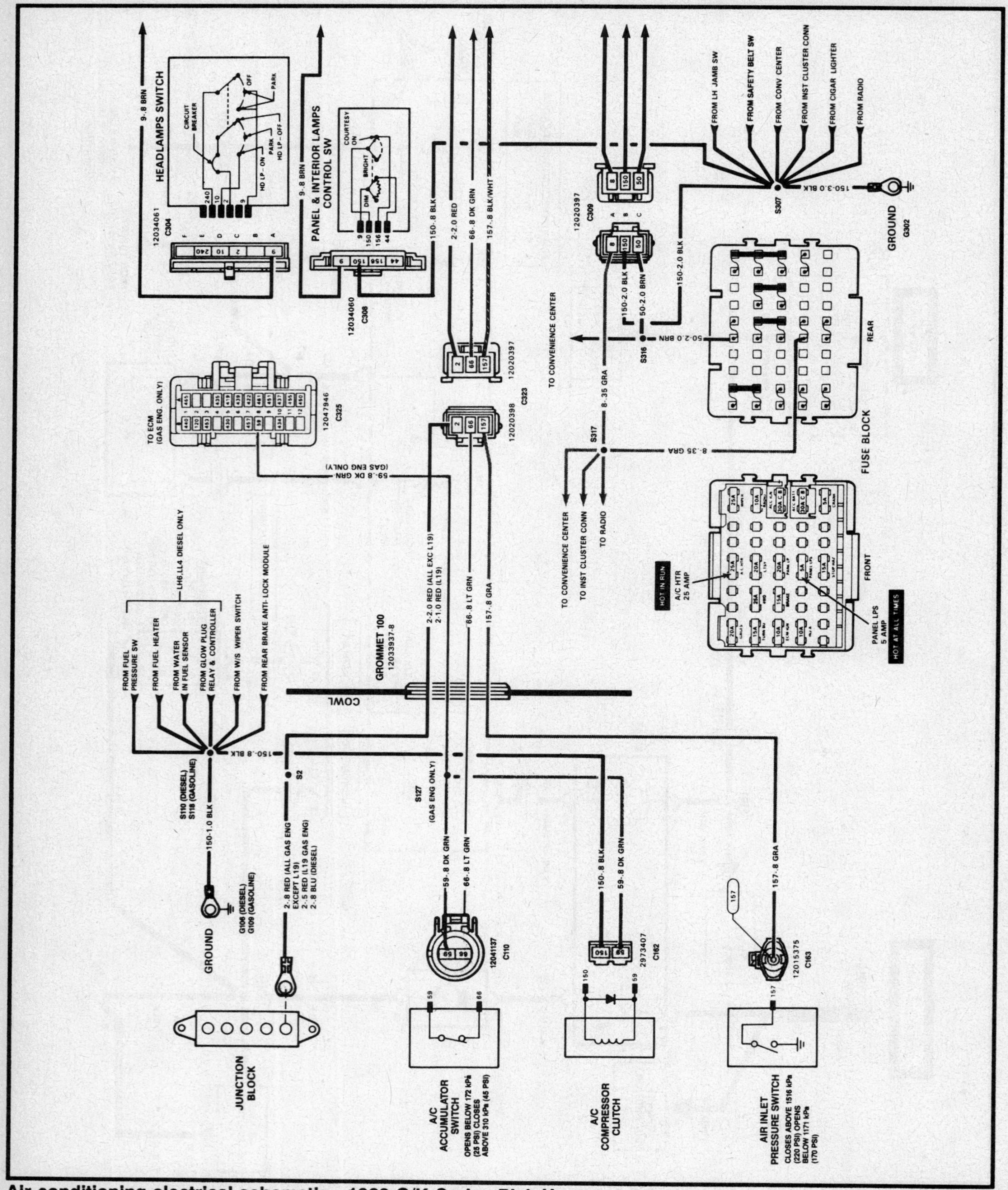
HEADLAMPS SWITCH
PANEL & INTERIOR LAMPS CONTROL SW
FUSE BLOCK
REAR
FRONT
GROUND
G302
S307
S316
S317
C309
C323
C325
TO ECM (GAS ENG. ONLY)
TO CONVENIENCE CENTER
TO INST CLUSTER CONN
TO RADIO
FROM LH JAMB SW
FROM SAFETY BELT SW
FROM CONV CENTER
FROM INST CLUSTER CONN
FROM CIGAR LIGHTER
FROM RADIO
A/C HTR 25 AMP
PANEL LPS 5 AMP
HOT IN RUN
HOT AT ALL TIMES
GROMMET 100
COWL
FROM FUEL PRESSURE SW
FROM FUEL HEATER
FROM WATER IN FUEL SENSOR
FROM GLOW PLUG RELAY & CONTROLLER
FROM W/S WIPER SWITCH
FROM REAR BRAKE ANTI-LOCK MODULE
LH6, LL4 DIESEL ONLY
JUNCTION BLOCK
A/C ACCUMULATOR SWITCH
OPENS BELOW 172 kPa (25 PSI) CLOSES ABOVE 310 kPa (45 PSI)
A/C COMPRESSOR CLUTCH
AIR INLET PRESSURE SWITCH
CLOSES ABOVE 1516 kPa (220 PSI) OPENS BELOW 1171 kPa (170 PSI)

Air conditioning electrical schematic—1989 C/K Series Pick-Up

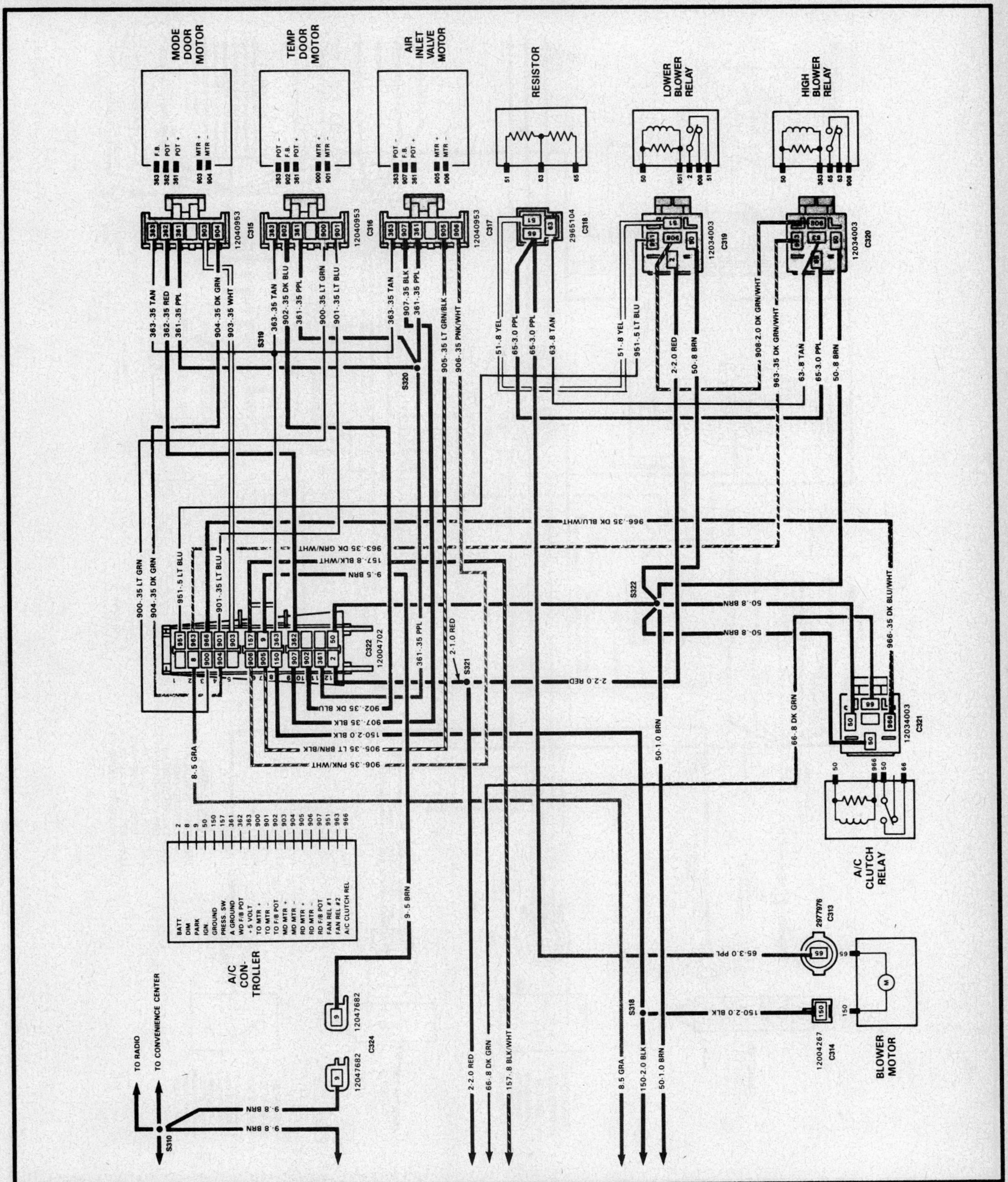
MODE DOOR MOTOR
TEMP DOOR MOTOR
AIR INLET VALVE MOTOR
RESISTOR
LOWER BLOWER RELAY
HIGH BLOWER RELAY
A/C CLUTCH RELAY
BLOWER MOTOR
A/C CON-TROLLER
TO RADIO
TO CONVENIENCE CENTER

Air conditioning electrical schematic—1989 C/K Series Pick-Up (cont'd)

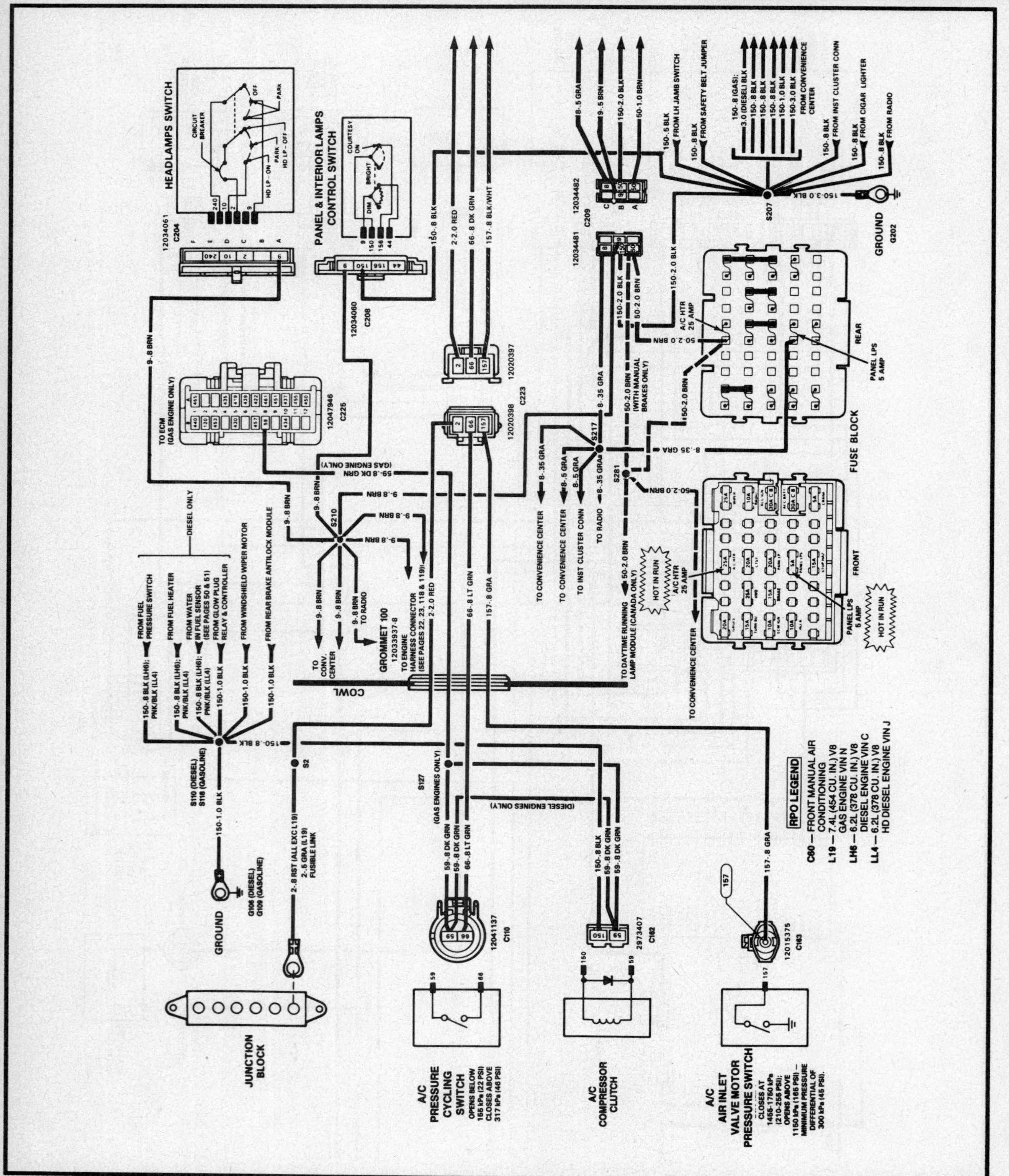
HEADLAMPS SWITCH
PANEL & INTERIOR LAMPS CONTROL SWITCH
FUSE BLOCK
GROUND
JUNCTION BLOCK
A/C PRESSURE CYCLING SWITCH
A/C COMPRESSOR CLUTCH
A/C INLET VALVE MOTOR PRESSURE SWITCH
COWL
GROMMET 100
RPO LEGEND
C60 — FRONT MANUAL AIR CONDITIONING
L19 — 7.4L (454 CU. IN.) V8 GAS ENGINE VIN N
LH6 — 6.2L (378 CU. IN.) V8 DIESEL ENGINE VIN C
LL4 — 6.2L (378 CU. IN.) V8 HD DIESEL ENGINE VIN J

Air conditioning electrical schematic—1990 C/K Series Pick-Up

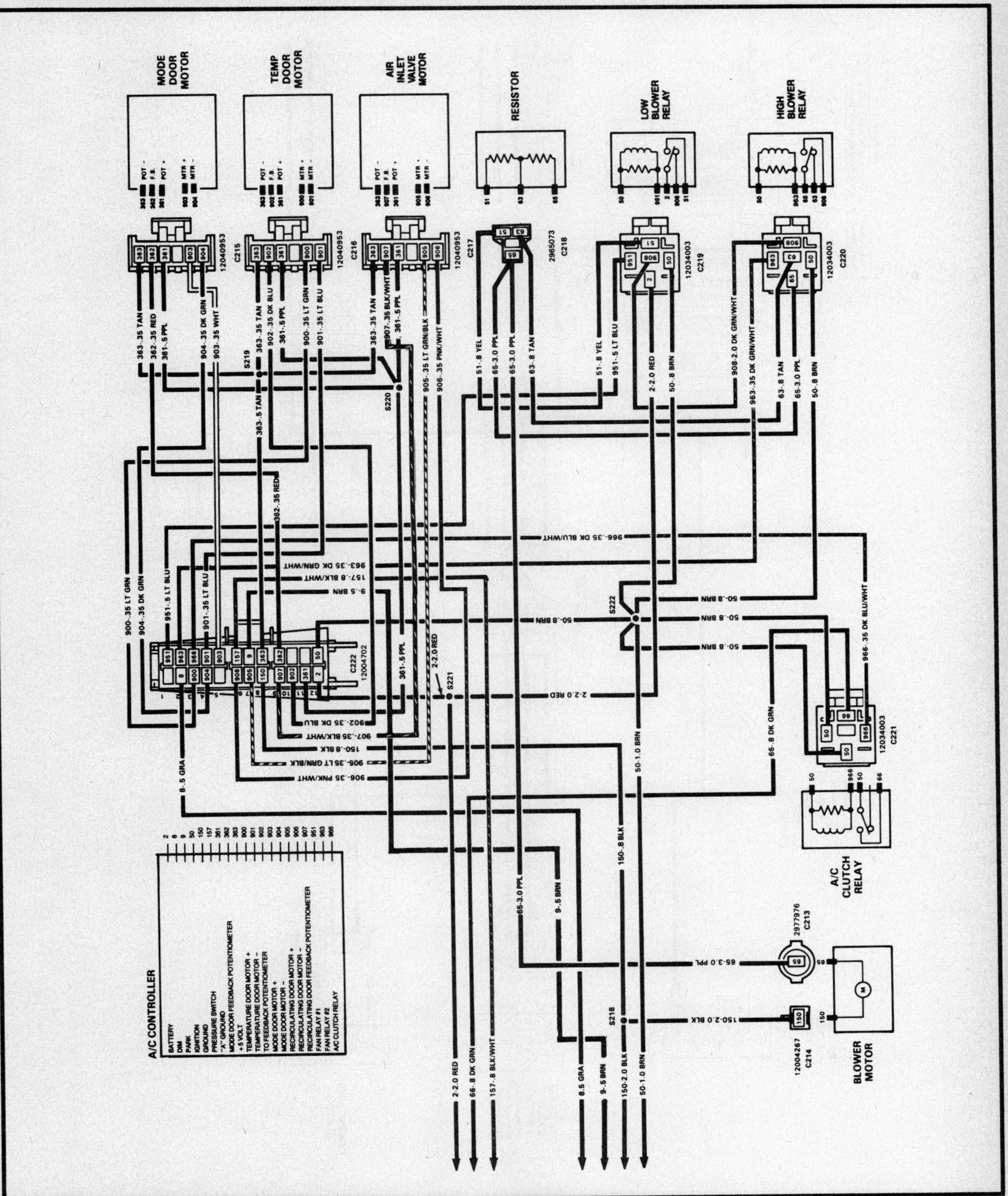
MODE DOOR MOTOR
TEMP DOOR MOTOR
AIR INLET VALVE MOTOR
RESISTOR
LOW BLOWER RELAY
HIGH BLOWER RELAY
A/C CLUTCH RELAY
BLOWER MOTOR
A/C CONTROLLER
BATTERY
DIM
PARK
IGNITION
GROUND
PRESSURE SWITCH
"A" GROUND
MODE DOOR FEEDBACK POTENTIOMETER
+5 VOLT
TEMPERATURE DOOR MOTOR +
TEMPERATURE DOOR MOTOR -
TO FEEDBACK POTENTIOMETER
MODE DOOR MOTOR +
MODE DOOR MOTOR -
RECIRCULATING DOOR MOTOR +
RECIRCULATING DOOR MOTOR -
RECIRCULATING DOOR FEEDBACK POTENTIOMETER
FAN RELAY #1
FAN RELAY #2
A/C CLUTCH RELAY

Air conditioning electrical schematic—1990 C/K Series Pick-Up (cont'd)

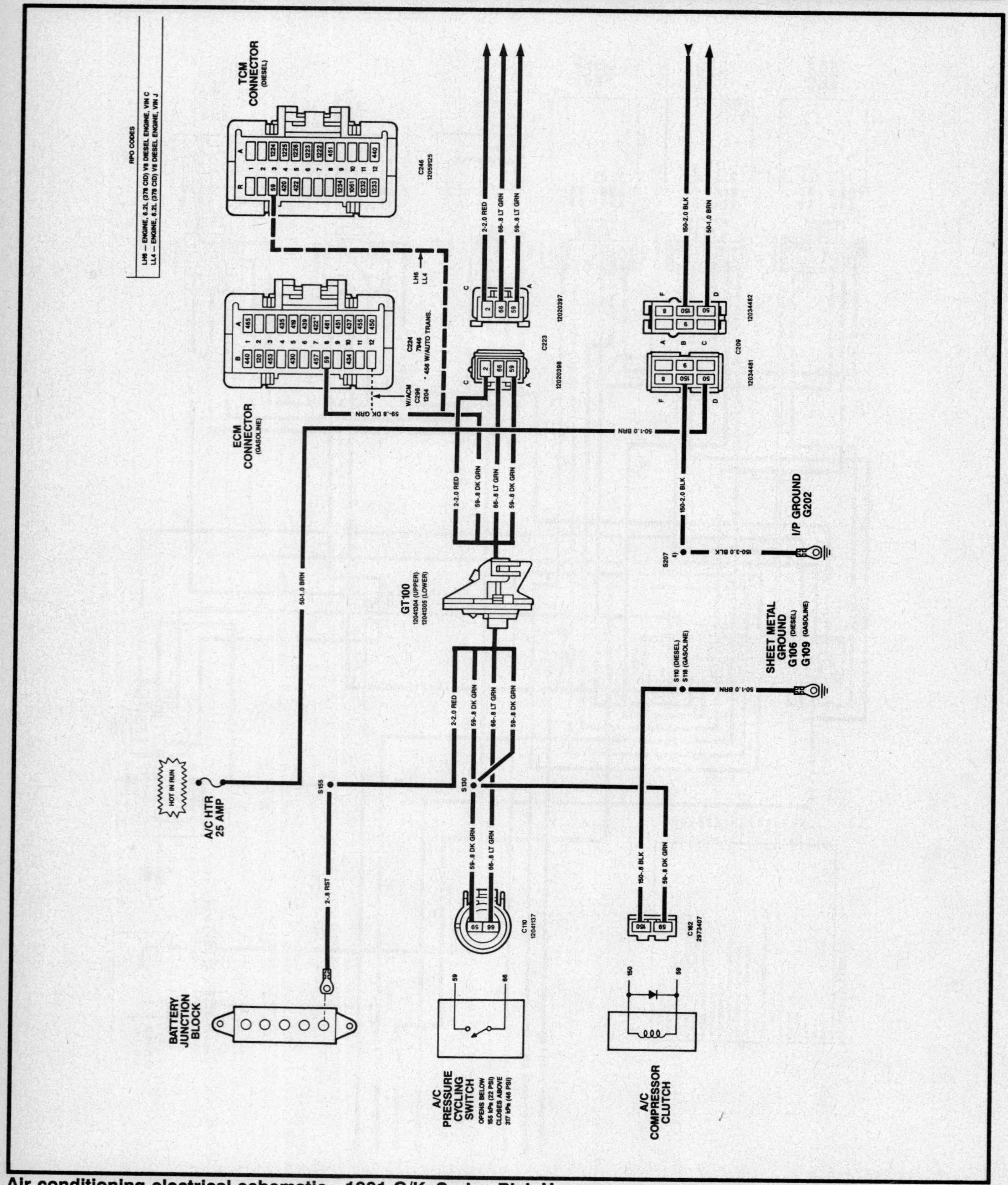
TCM CONNECTOR (DIESEL)
ECM CONNECTOR (GASOLINE)
GT100
I/P GROUND G202
SHEET METAL GROUND G106 (DIESEL) G109 (GASOLINE)
A/C HTR 25 AMP
HOT IN RUN
BATTERY JUNCTION BLOCK
A/C PRESSURE CYCLING SWITCH
A/C COMPRESSOR CLUTCH

Air conditioning electrical schematic—1991 C/K Series Pick-Up

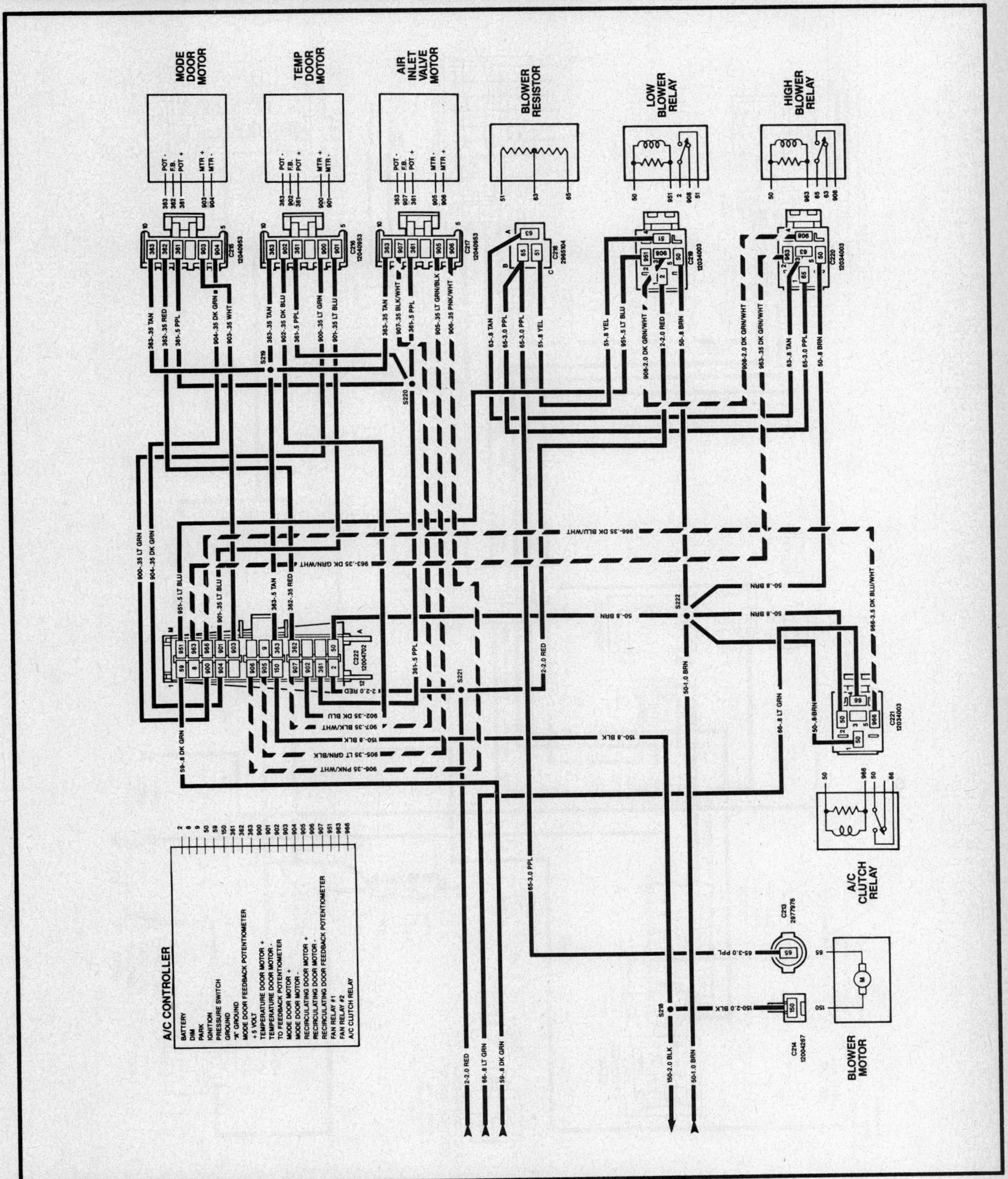
MODE DOOR MOTOR
TEMP DOOR MOTOR
AIR INLET VALVE MOTOR
BLOWER RESISTOR
LOW BLOWER RELAY
HIGH BLOWER RELAY
A/C CONTROLLER
A/C CLUTCH RELAY
BLOWER MOTOR

Air conditioning electrical schematic—1991 C/K Series Pick-Up (cont'd)

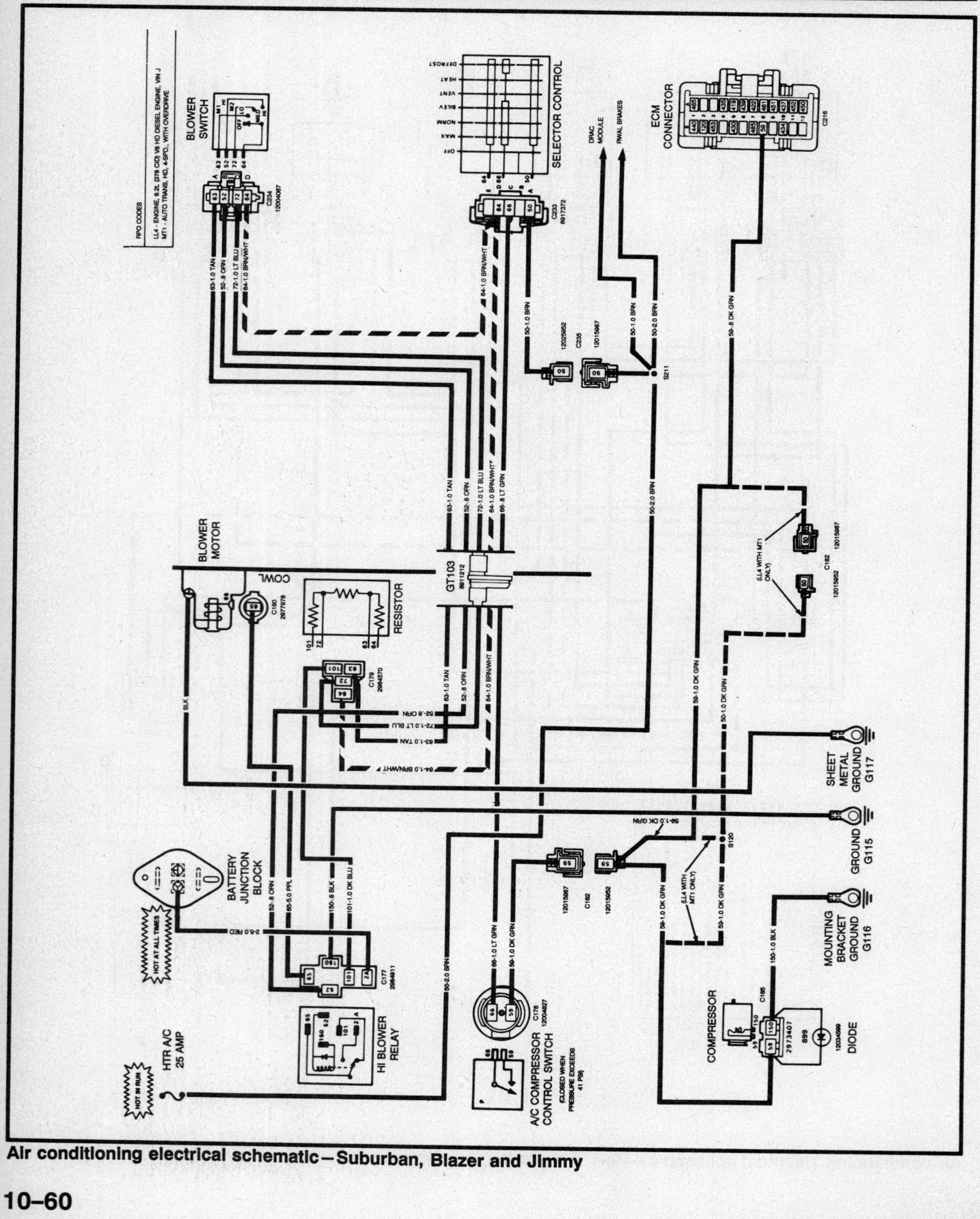
BLOWER SWITCH
SELECTOR CONTROL
ECM CONNECTOR
BLOWER MOTOR
COWL
RESISTOR
GT103
BATTERY JUNCTION BLOCK
HI BLOWER RELAY
HTR A/C 25 AMP
A/C COMPRESSOR CONTROL SWITCH
COMPRESSOR
DIODE
SHEET METAL GROUND G117
GROUND G115
MOUNTING BRACKET GROUND G116

Air conditioning electrical schematic—Suburban, Blazer and Jimmy

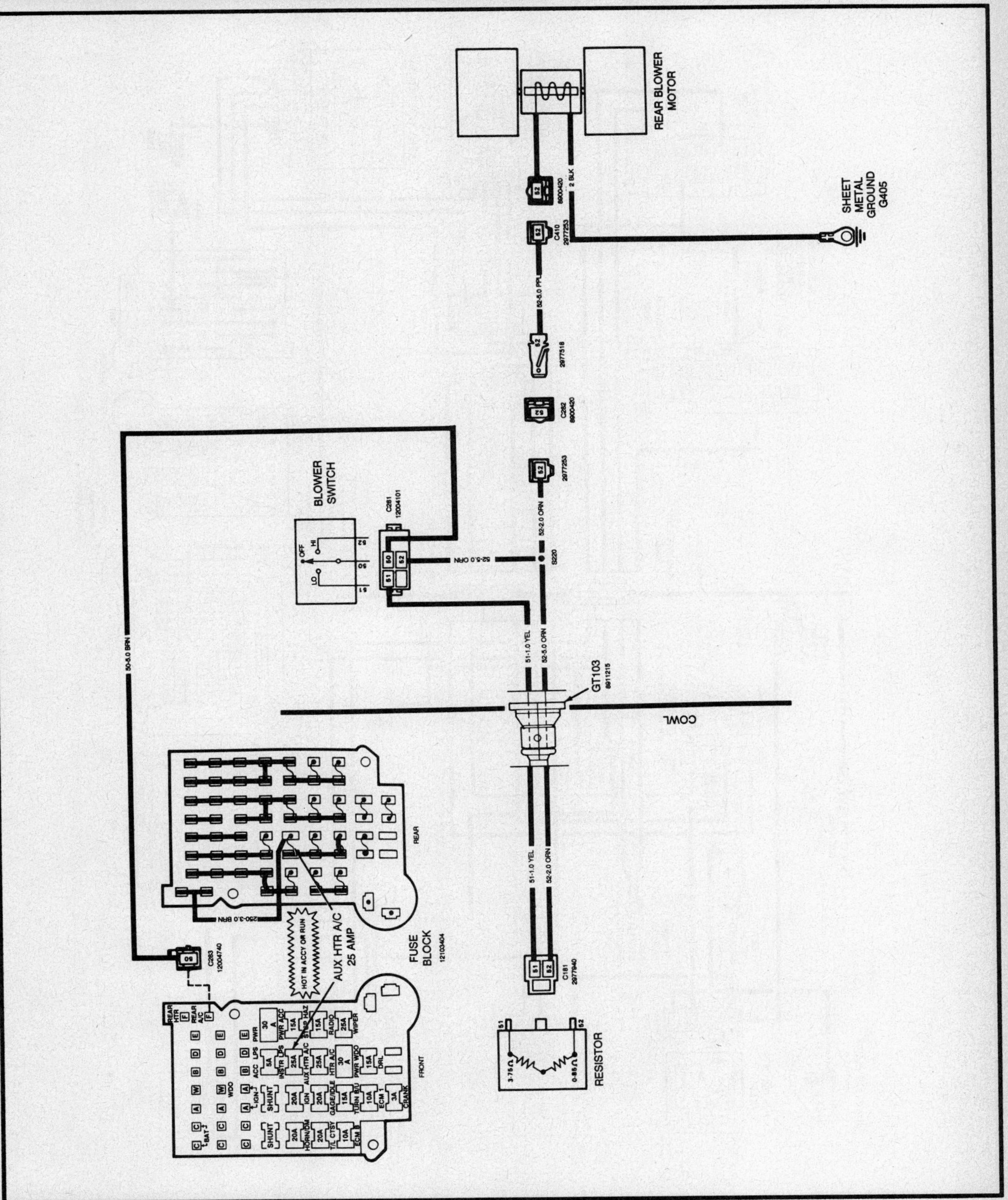
REAR BLOWER MOTOR
SHEET METAL GROUND G405
BLOWER SWITCH
COWL
GT103
AUX HTR A/C 25 AMP
HOT IN ACCY OR RUN
FUSE BLOCK
RESISTOR

Auxiliary air conditioning electrical schematic— Suburban, Blazer and Jimmy

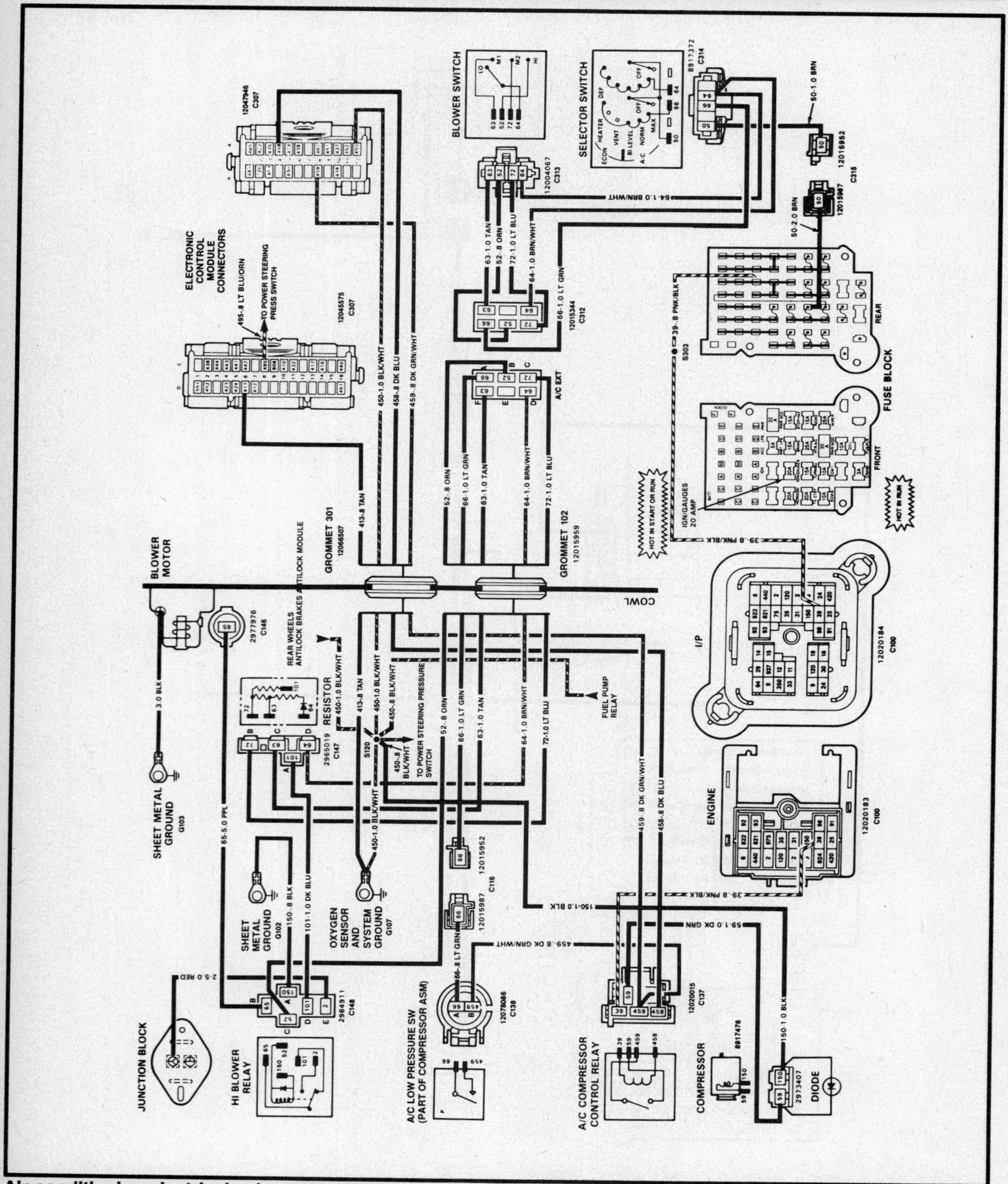
BLOWER SWITCH
SELECTOR SWITCH
ELECTRONIC CONTROL MODULE CONNECTORS
TO POWER STEERING PRESS SWITCH
BLOWER MOTOR
GROMMET 301
GROMMET 102
COWL
FUSE BLOCK
REAR
FRONT
HOT IN START OR RUN
HOT IN RUN
IGN/GAUGES 20 AMP
I/P
ENGINE
SHEET METAL GROUND G103
RESISTOR
REAR WHEELS ANTILOCK BRAKES
FUEL PUMP RELAY
SHEET METAL GROUND G102
OXYGEN SENSOR AND SYSTEM GROUND G107
JUNCTION BLOCK
HI BLOWER RELAY
A/C LOW PRESSURE SW (PART OF COMPRESSOR ASM)
A/C COMPRESSOR CONTROL RELAY
COMPRESSOR
DIODE
A/C EXT

Air conditioning electrical schematic—S/T Series Pick-Up, Blazer and Jimmy with 2.5L engine

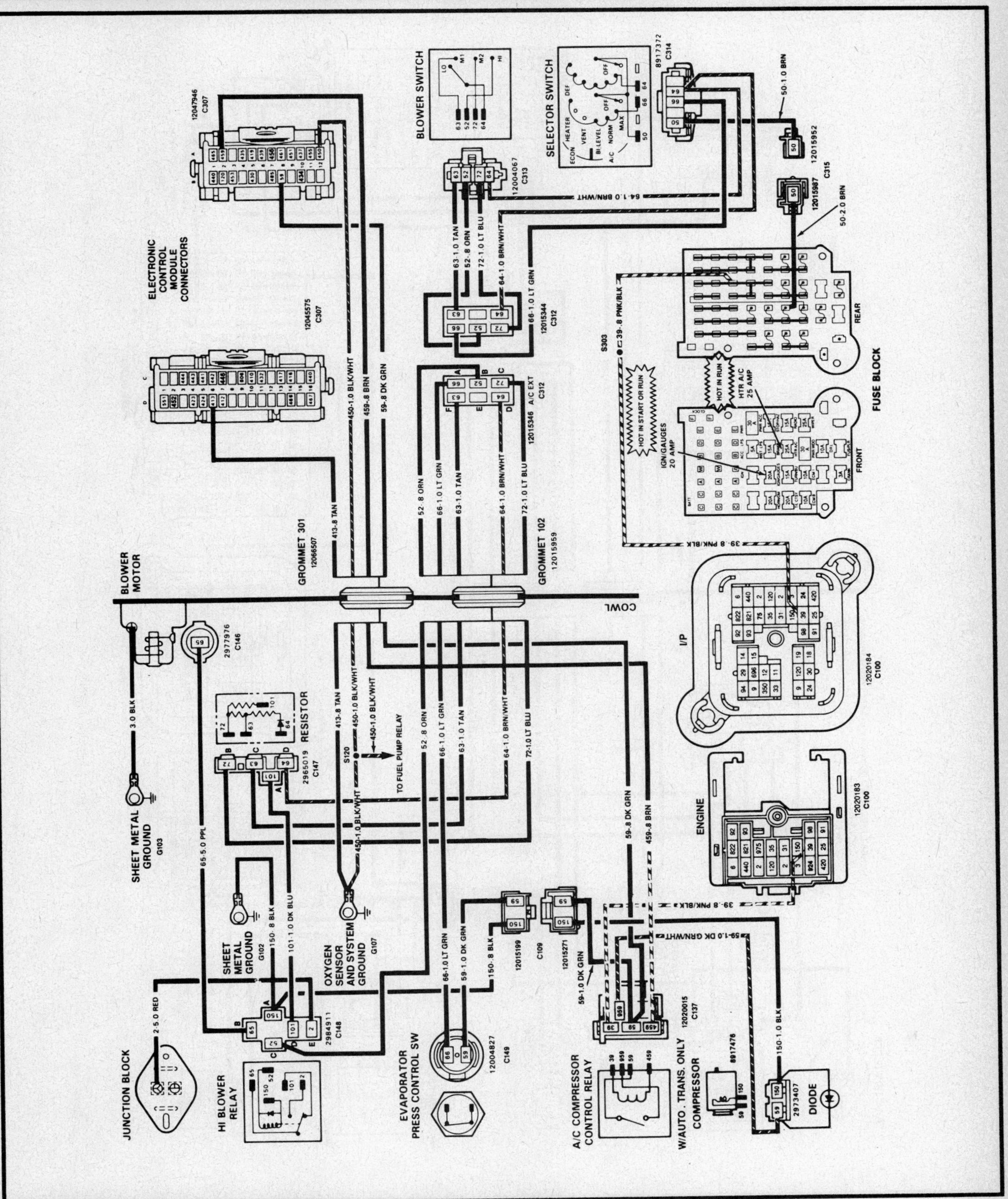
BLOWER SWITCH
SELECTOR SWITCH
ELECTRONIC CONTROL MODULE CONNECTORS
FUSE BLOCK
REAR
FRONT
HOT IN START OR RUN
HOT IN RUN
HTR A/C 25 AMP
IGN/GAUGES 20 AMP
BLOWER MOTOR
GROMMET 301
GROMMET 102
COWL
I/P
ENGINE
RESISTOR
TO FUEL PUMP RELAY
SHEET METAL GROUND
OXYGEN SENSOR AND SYSTEM GROUND
JUNCTION BLOCK
HI BLOWER RELAY
EVAPORATOR PRESS CONTROL SW
A/C COMPRESSOR CONTROL RELAY
W/AUTO. TRANS. ONLY COMPRESSOR
DIODE

Air conditioning electrical schematic—S/T Series Pick-Up, Blazer and Jimmy with 2.8L engine

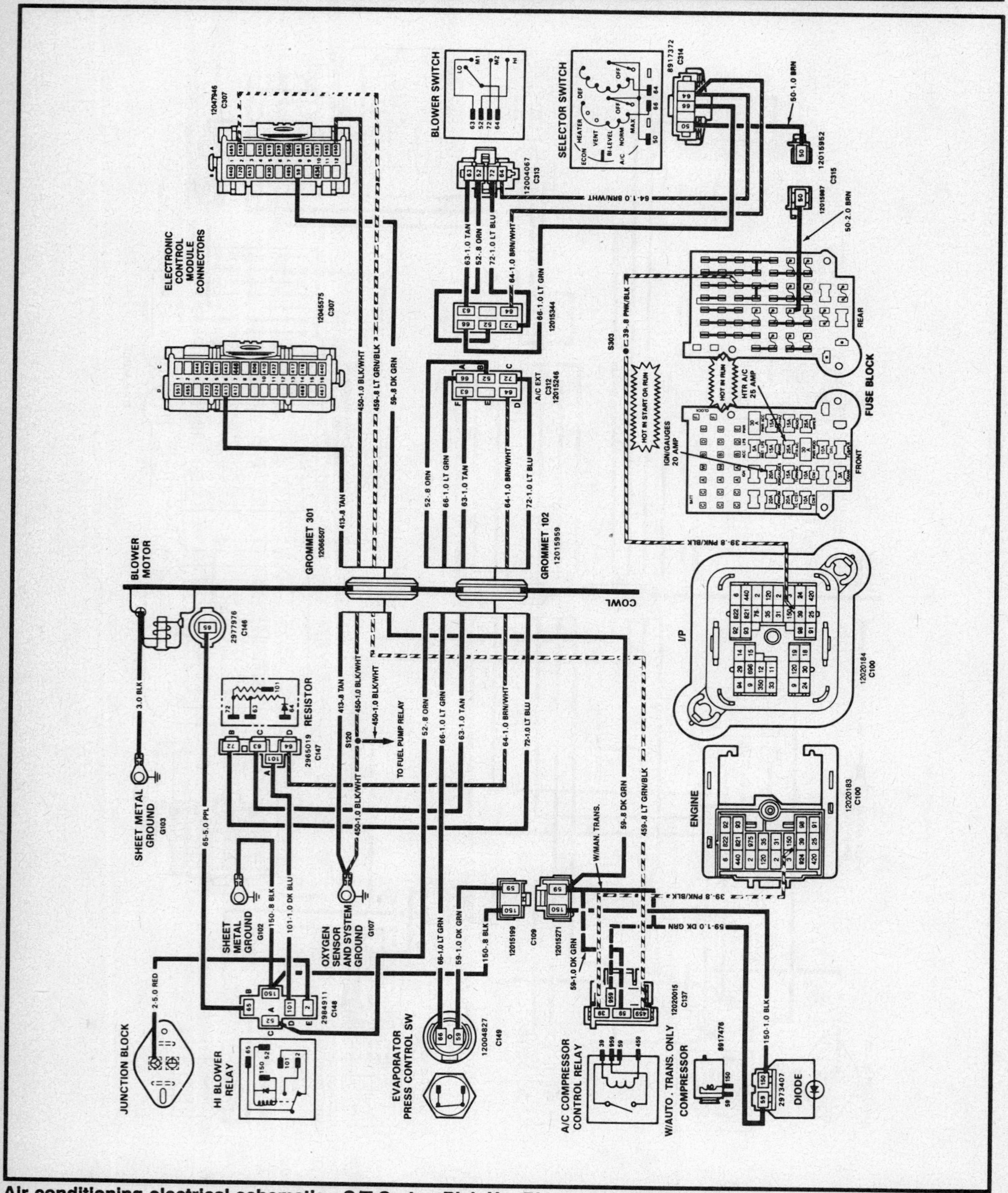
ELECTRONIC CONTROL MODULE CONNECTORS
BLOWER SWITCH
SELECTOR SWITCH
FUSE BLOCK
REAR
FRONT
BLOWER MOTOR
GROMMET 301
GROMMET 102
COWL
RESISTOR
TO FUEL PUMP RELAY
SHEET METAL GROUND
OXYGEN SENSOR AND SYSTEM GROUND
ENGINE
W/MAN. TRANS.
JUNCTION BLOCK
HI BLOWER RELAY
EVAPORATOR PRESS CONTROL SW
A/C COMPRESSOR CONTROL RELAY
W/AUTO. TRANS. ONLY COMPRESSOR
DIODE

Air conditioning electrical schematic – S/T Series Pick-Up, Blazer and Jimmy with 4.3L engine

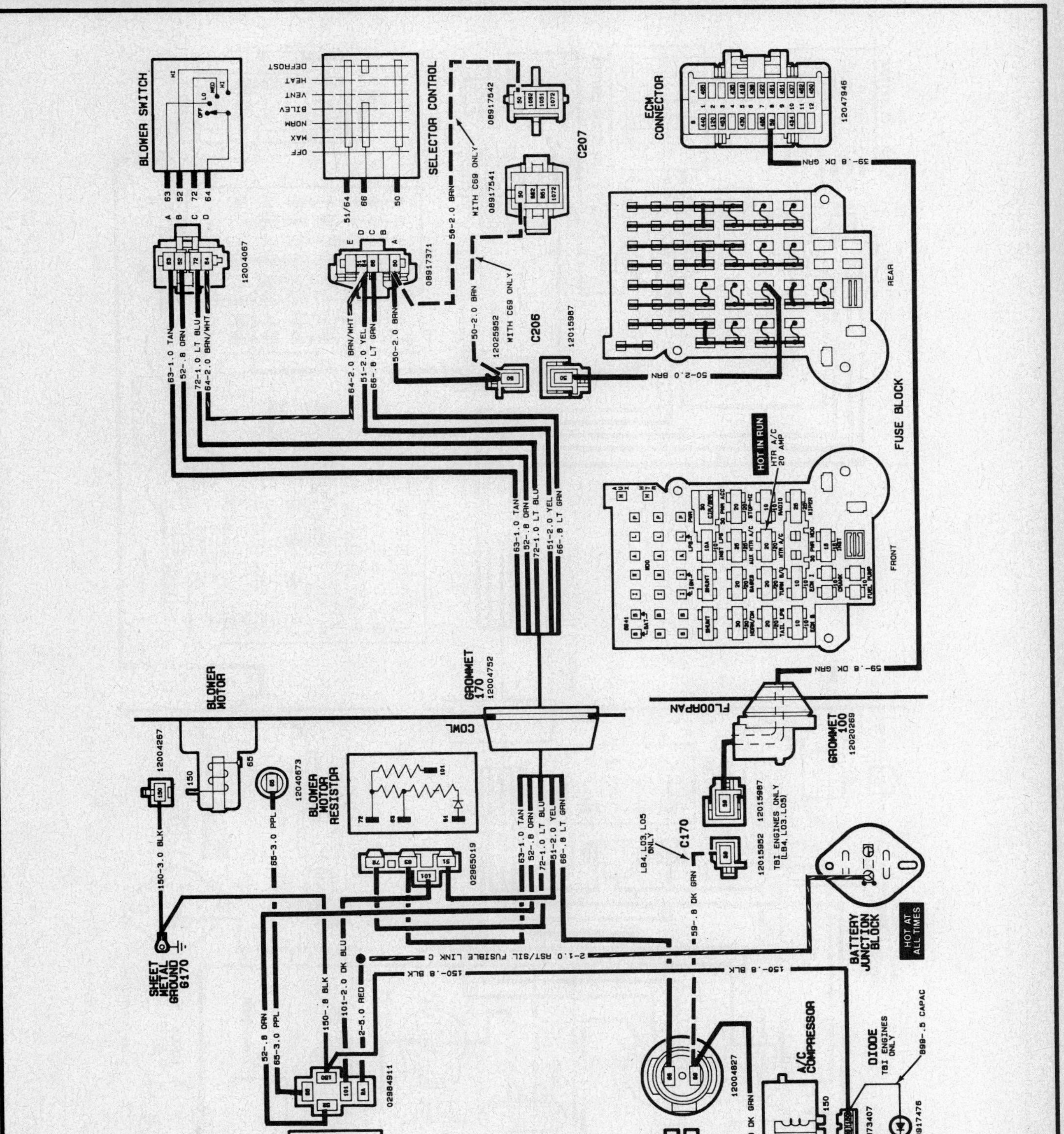
BLOWER SWITCH
SELECTOR CONTROL
ECM CONNECTOR
C207
C206
FUSE BLOCK
HOT IN RUN
BLOWER MOTOR
GROMMET 170
COWL
FLOORPAN
GROMMET 100
BLOWER MOTOR RESISTOR
C170
BATTERY JUNCTION BLOCK
HOT AT ALL TIMES
SHEET METAL GROUND G170
HI BLOWER RELAY
A/C COMPRESSOR
DIODE
EVAPORATOR PRESSURE CONTROL SWITCH

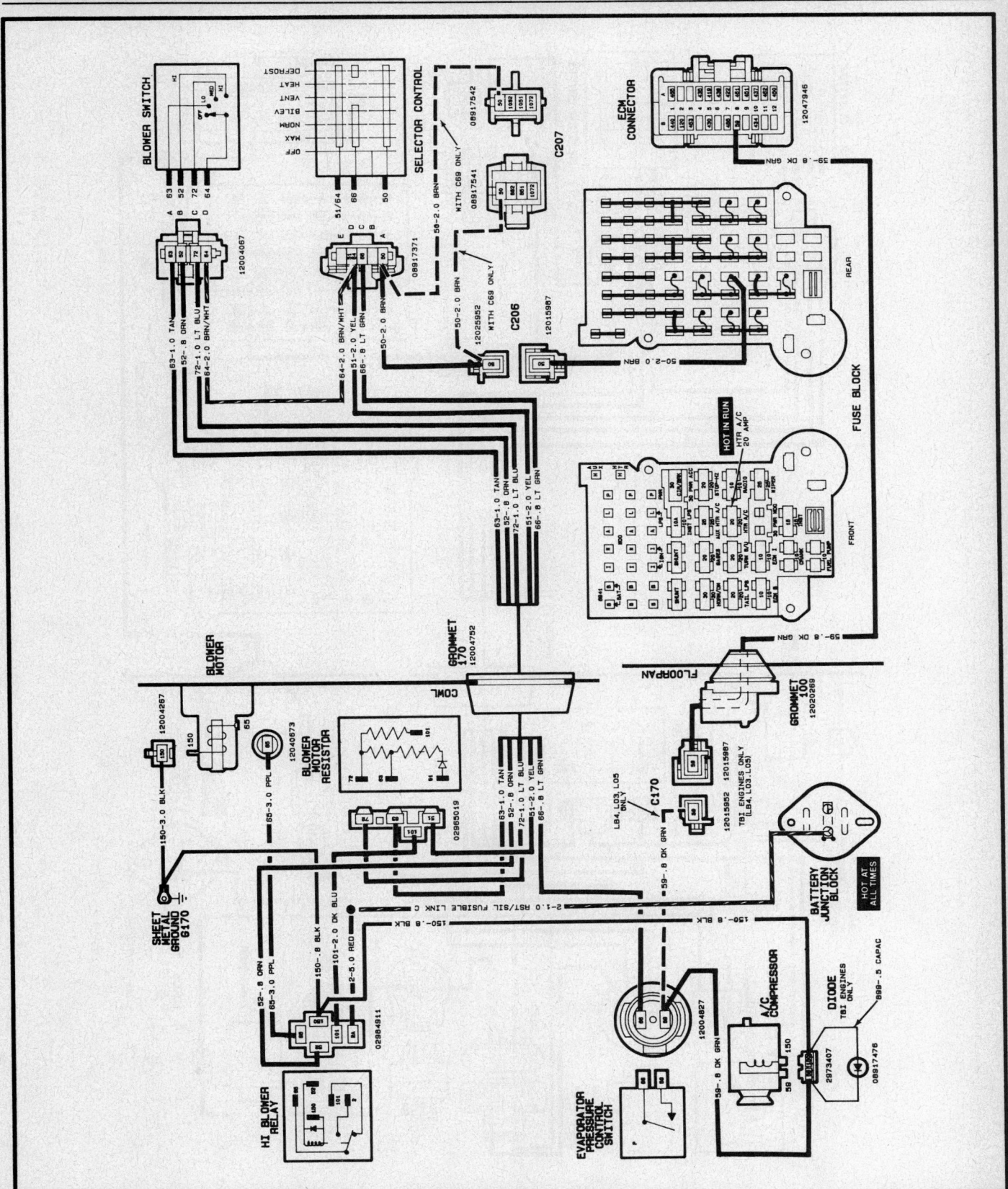

Air conditioning electrical schematic – G Series Van (except 7.4L engine)

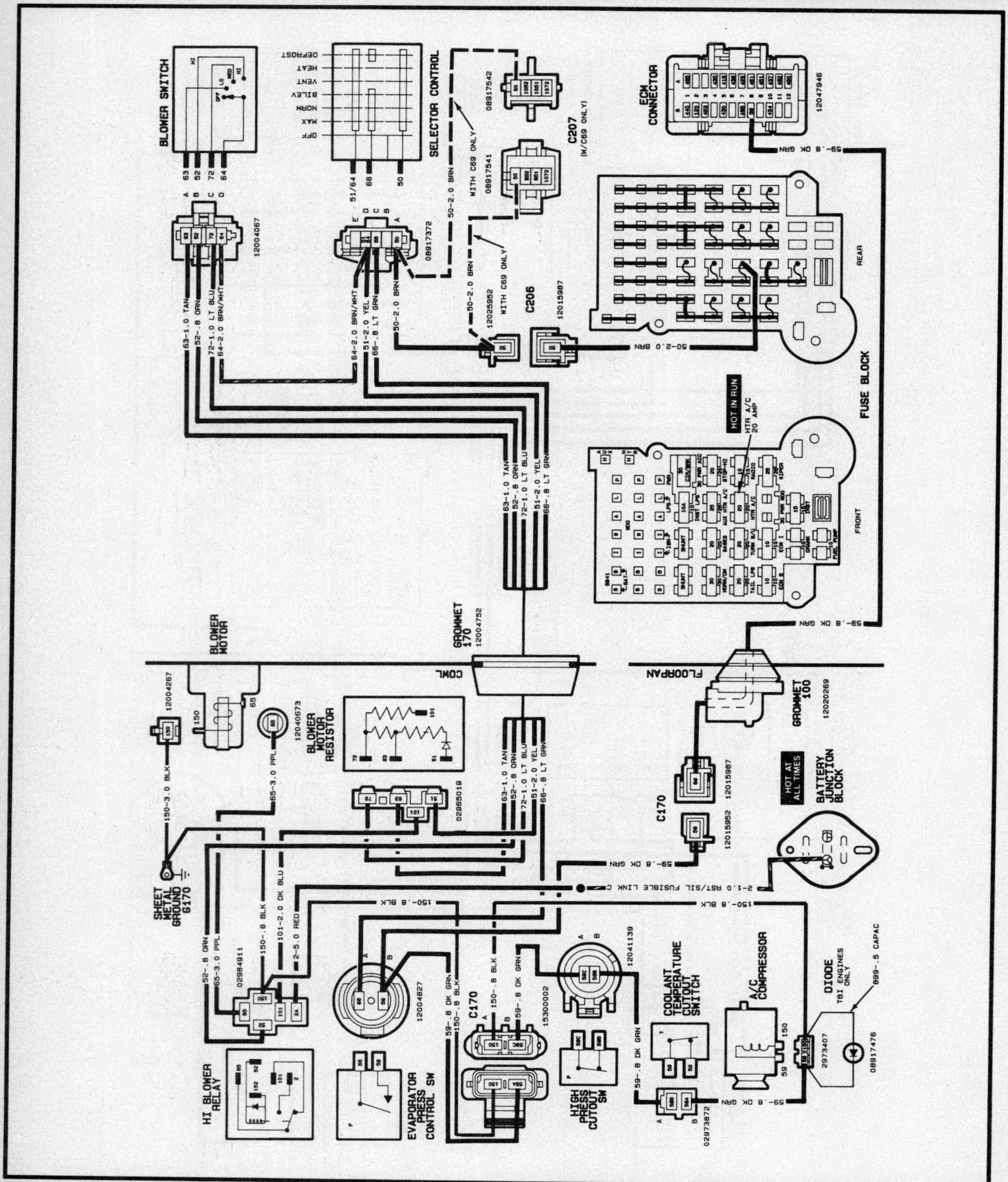
BLOWER SWITCH
SELECTOR CONTROL
OFF
MAX
NORM
BILEV
VENT
HEAT
DEFROST
C207
C206
ECM CONNECTOR
FUSE BLOCK
REAR
FRONT
HOT IN RUN
HTR A/C 20 AMP
GROMMET 170
COWL
FLOORPAN
GROMMET 100
BLOWER MOTOR
BLOWER MOTOR RESISTOR
SHEET METAL GROUND G170
HOT AT ALL TIMES
BATTERY JUNCTION BLOCK
C170
HI BLOWER RELAY
EVAPORATOR PRESS CONTROL SW
HIGH PRESS CUTOUT SW
COOLANT TEMPERATURE CUTOUT SWITCH
A/C COMPRESSOR
DIODE
TBI ENGINES ONLY

Air conditioning electrical schematic—G Series Van with 7.4L engine

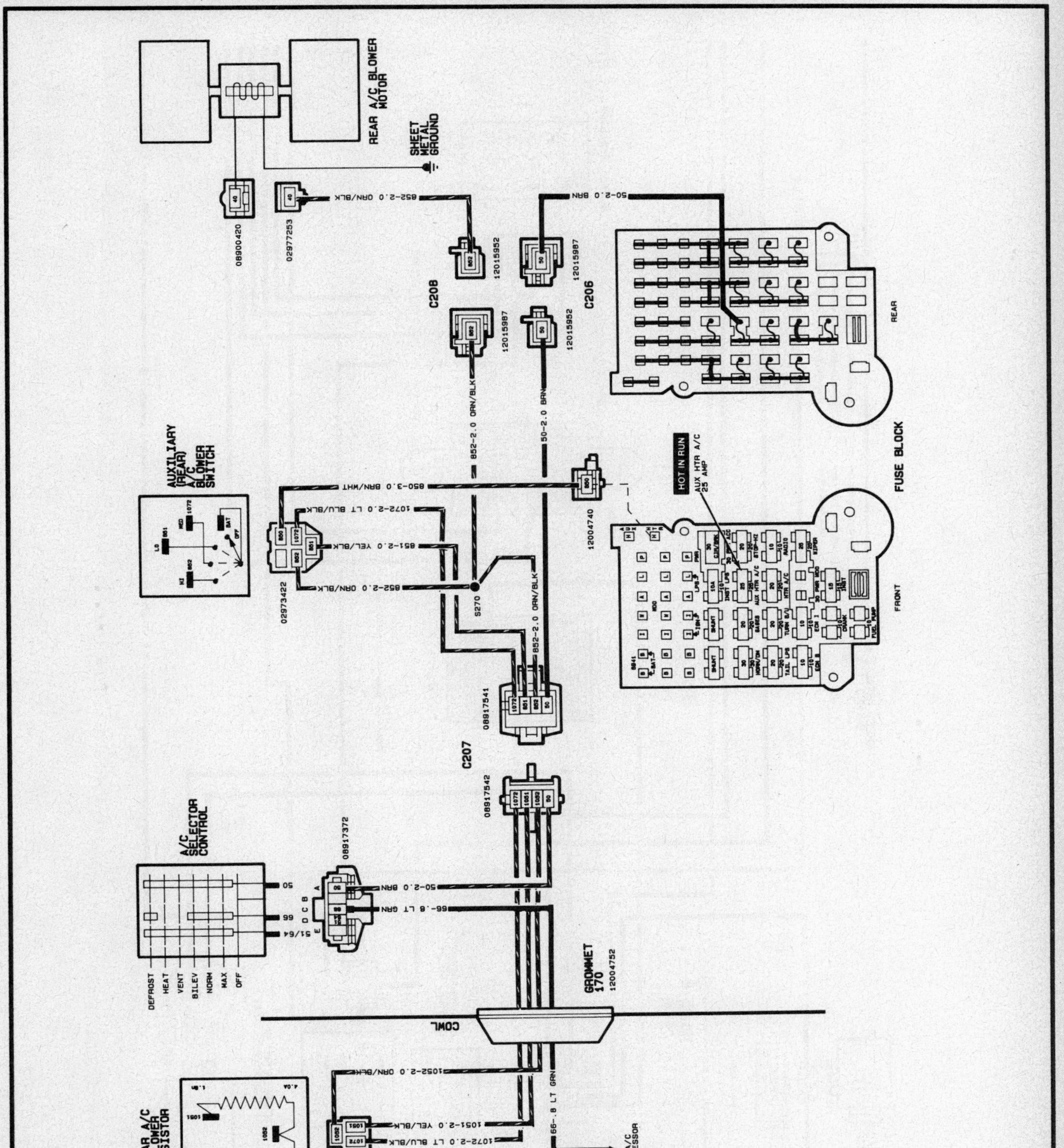
REAR A/C BLOWER MOTOR
SHEET METAL GROUND
08900420
02977253
852-2.0 ORN/BLK
50-2.0 BRN
12015952
12015987
C208
C206
12015987
12015952
852-2.0 ORN/BLK
50-2.0 BRN
REAR
FUSE BLOCK
HOT IN RUN
AUX HTR A/C 25 AMP
12004740
850-3.0 BRN/WHT
1072-2.0 LT BLU/BLK
851-2.0 YEL/BLK
852-2.0 ORN/BLK
AUXILIARY (REAR) A/C BLOWER SWITCH
02973422
S270
852-2.0 ORN/BLK
FRONT
08917541
C207
08917542
A/C SELECTOR CONTROL
08917372
50-2.0 BRN
66-.8 LT GRN
DEFROST
HEAT
VENT
BILEV
NORM
MAX
OFF
GROMMET 170
12004752
COWL
1052-2.0 ORN/BLK
1051-2.0 YEL/BLK
1072-2.0 LT BLU/BLK
66-.8 LT GRN
TO A/C COMPRESSOR
REAR A/C BLOWER RESISTOR
02977940

Auxiliary air conditioning electrical schematic—G Series Van

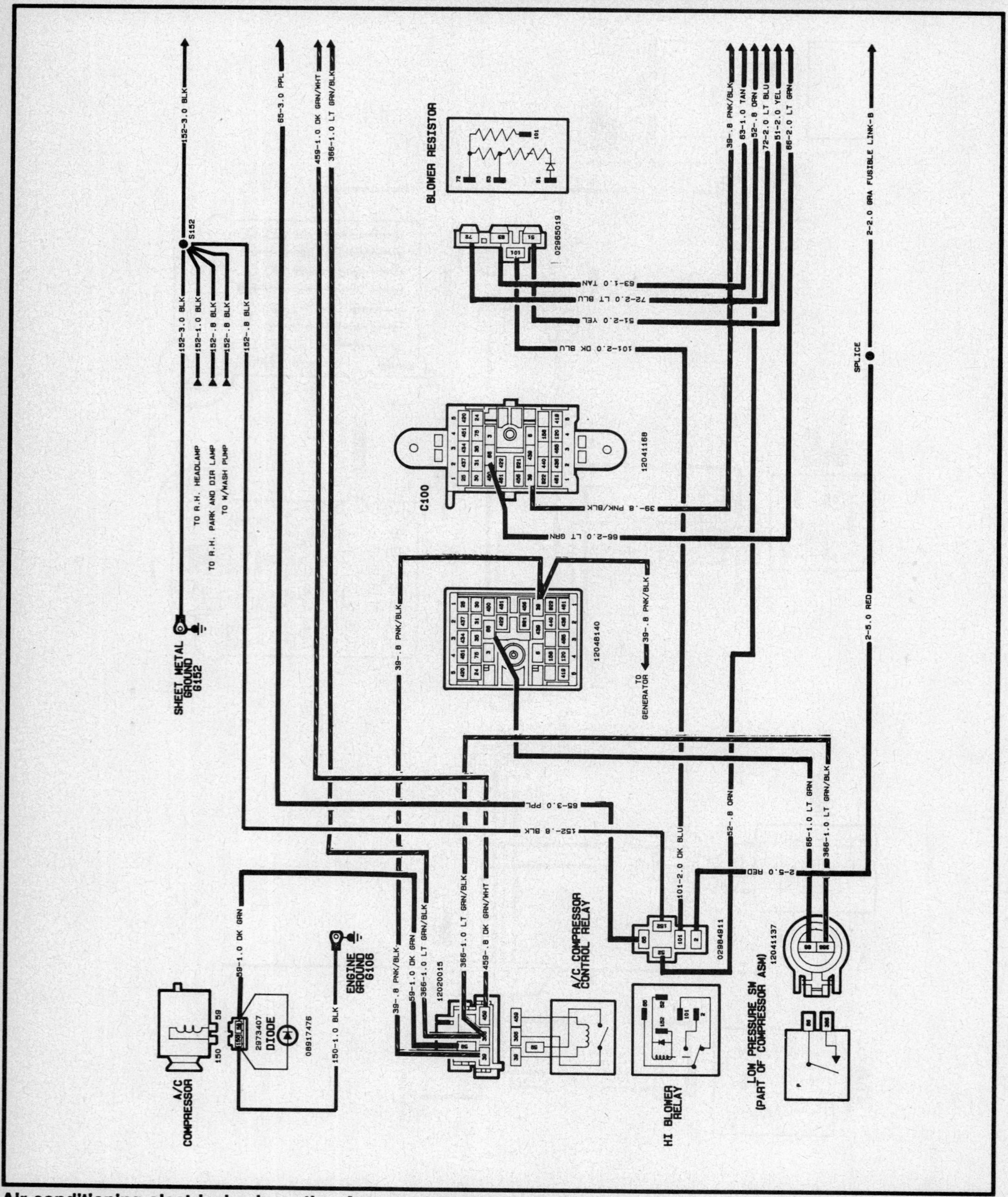
BLOWER RESISTOR
02965019
63-1.0 TAN
72-2.0 LT BLU
51-2.0 YEL
101-2.0 DK BLU
39-.8 PNK/BLK
63-1.0 TAN
52-.8 ORN
72-2.0 LT BLU
51-2.0 YEL
66-2.0 LT GRN
2-2.0 GRA FUSIBLE LINK-B
SPLICE
2-5.0 RED
C100
12041168
66-2.0 LT GRN
12048140
TO GENERATOR
152-3.0 BLK
S152
152-1.0 BLK
152-.8 BLK
TO R.H. HEADLAMP
TO R.H. PARK AND DIR LAMP
TO W/WASH PUMP
SHEET METAL GROUND G152
65-3.0 PPL
459-1.0 DK GRN/WHT
366-1.0 LT GRN/BLK
152-.8 BLK
52-.8 ORN
101-2.0 DK BLU
66-1.0 LT GRN
366-1.0 LT GRN/BLK
59-1.0 DK GRN
150-1.0 BLK
A/C COMPRESSOR
2973407
DIODE
08917476
ENGINE GROUND G106
39-.8 PNK/BLK
59-1.0 DK GRN
366-1.0 LT GRN/BLK
12020015
366-1.0 LT GRN/BLK
459-.8 DK GRN/WHT
A/C COMPRESSOR CONTROL RELAY
02984911
HI BLOWER RELAY
LOW PRESSURE SW (PART OF COMPRESSOR ASM)
12041137

Air conditioning electrical schematic—Astro and Safari with 2.5L engine

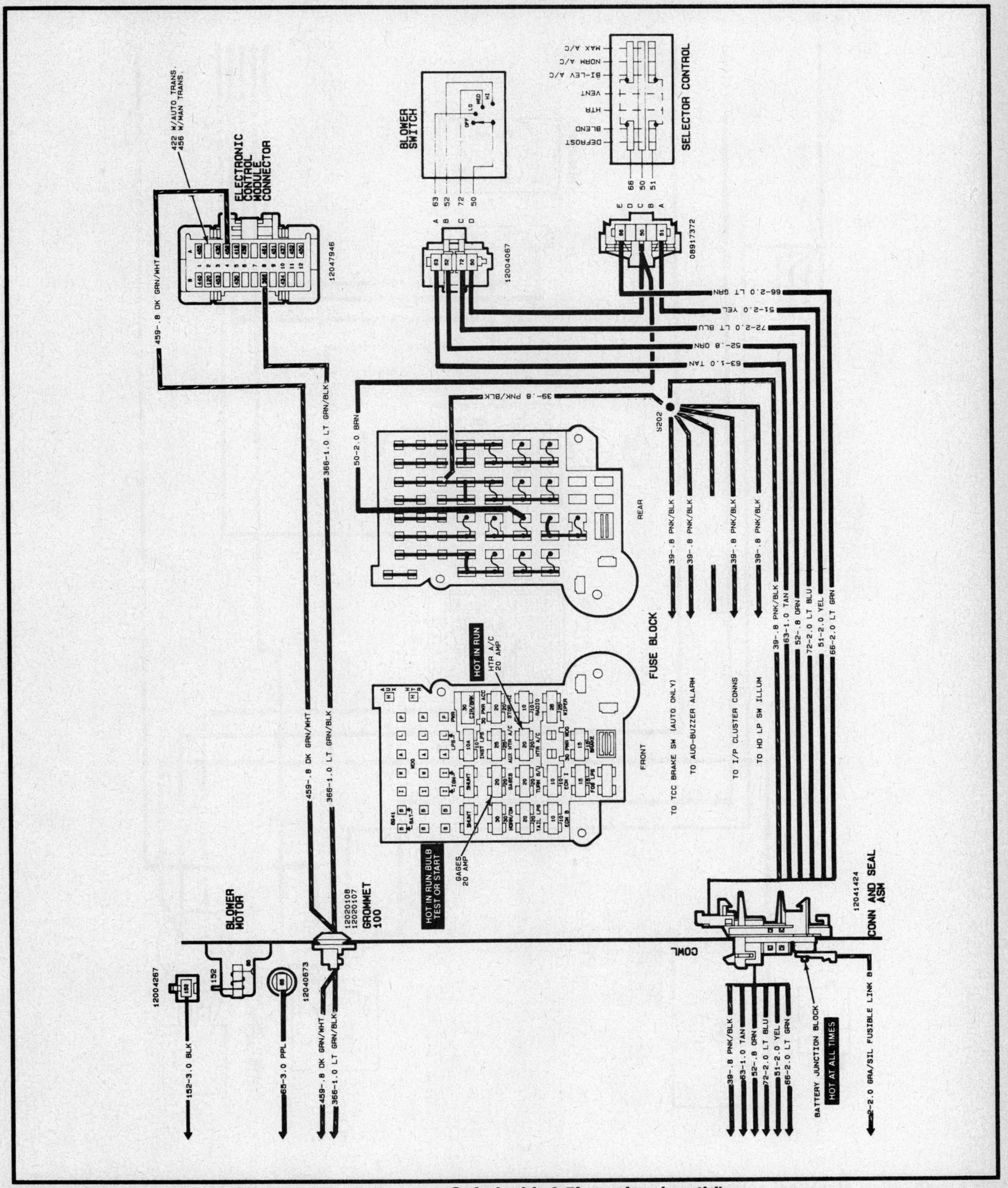
BLOWER MOTOR
GROMMET 100
ELECTRONIC CONTROL MODULE CONNECTOR
BLOWER SWITCH
SELECTOR CONTROL
FUSE BLOCK
CONN AND SEAL ASM
COWL
BATTERY JUNCTION BLOCK
HOT AT ALL TIMES
HOT IN RUN
HOT IN RUN, BULB TEST OR START
FRONT
REAR
TO TCC BRAKE SW (AUTO ONLY)
TO AUD-BUZZER ALARM
TO I/P CLUSTER CONNS
TO HD LP SW ILLUM

Air conditioning electrical schematic—Astro and Safari with 2.5L engine (cont'd)

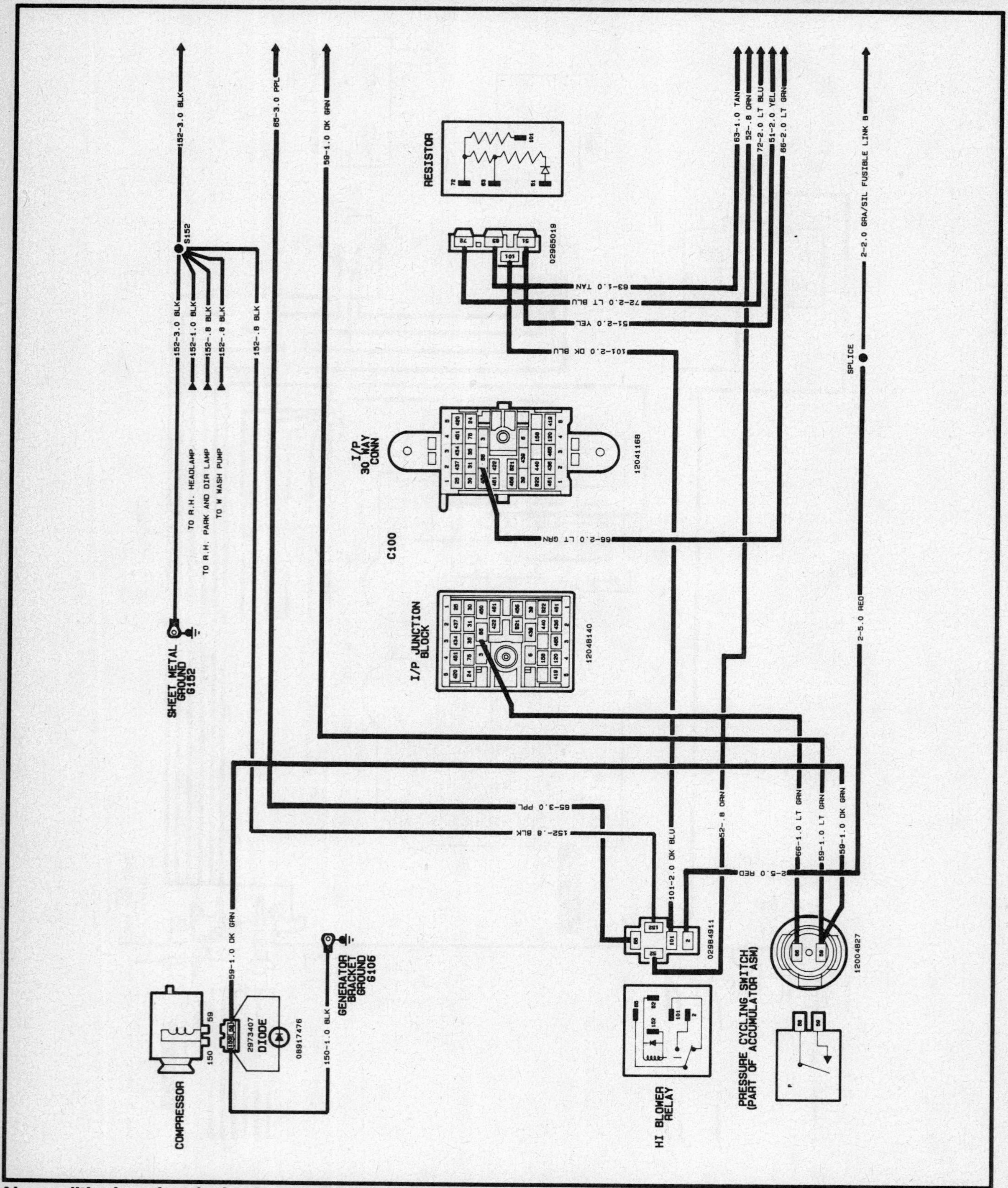
152-3.0 BLK
65-3.0 PPL
59-1.0 DK GRN
RESISTOR
63-1.0 TAN
52-.8 ORN
72-2.0 LT BLU
51-2.0 YEL
66-2.0 LT GRN
2-2.0 GRA/SIL FUSIBLE LINK B
S152
02965019
72-2.0 LT BLU
51-2.0 YEL
101-2.0 DK BLU
SPLICE
152-1.0 BLK
152-.8 BLK
TO R.H. HEADLAMP
TO R.H. PARK AND DIR LAMP
TO W WASH PUMP
I/P 30 WAY CONN
12041168
66-2.0 LT GRN
C100
I/P JUNCTION BLOCK
12048140
SHEET METAL GROUND G152
2-5.0 RED
65-3.0 PPL
152-.8 BLK
66-1.0 LT GRN
59-1.0 LT GRN
59-1.0 DK GRN
2-5.0 RED
02984911
12004827
COMPRESSOR
2973407
DIODE
08917476
150-1.0 BLK
GENERATOR BRACKET GROUND G106
HI BLOWER RELAY
PRESSURE CYCLING SWITCH (PART OF ACCUMULATOR ASM)

Air conditioning electrical schematic—Astro and Safari with 4.3L engine

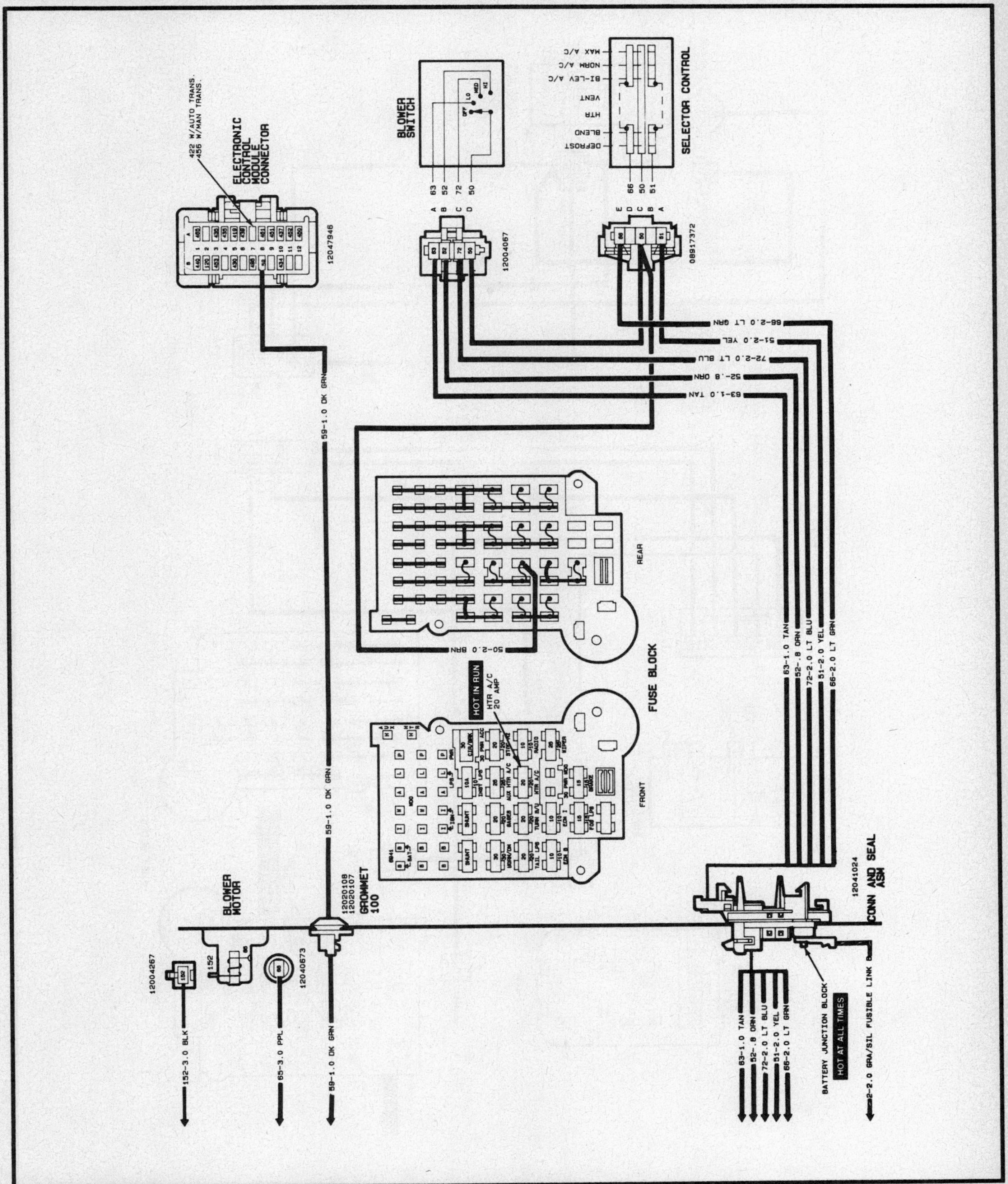
ELECTRONIC CONTROL MODULE CONNECTOR
422 W/AUTO TRANS.
456 W/MAN TRANS.
12047946
BLOWER SWITCH
12004067
SELECTOR CONTROL
DEFROST
BLEND
HTR
VENT
BI-LEV A/C
NORM A/C
MAX A/C
08917372
66-2.0 LT GRN
51-2.0 YEL
72-2.0 LT BLU
52-.8 ORN
63-1.0 TAN
59-1.0 DK GRN
50-2.0 BRN
REAR
FRONT
FUSE BLOCK
HOT IN RUN
HTR A/C
20 AMP
BLOWER MOTOR
12004267
12040673
GROMMET 100
12020108
12020107
12041024
CONN AND SEAL ASM
152-3.0 BLK
65-3.0 PPL
BATTERY JUNCTION BLOCK
HOT AT ALL TIMES
2-2.0 GRA/SIL FUSIBLE LINK

Air conditioning electrical schematic—Astro and Safari with 4.3L engine (cont'd)

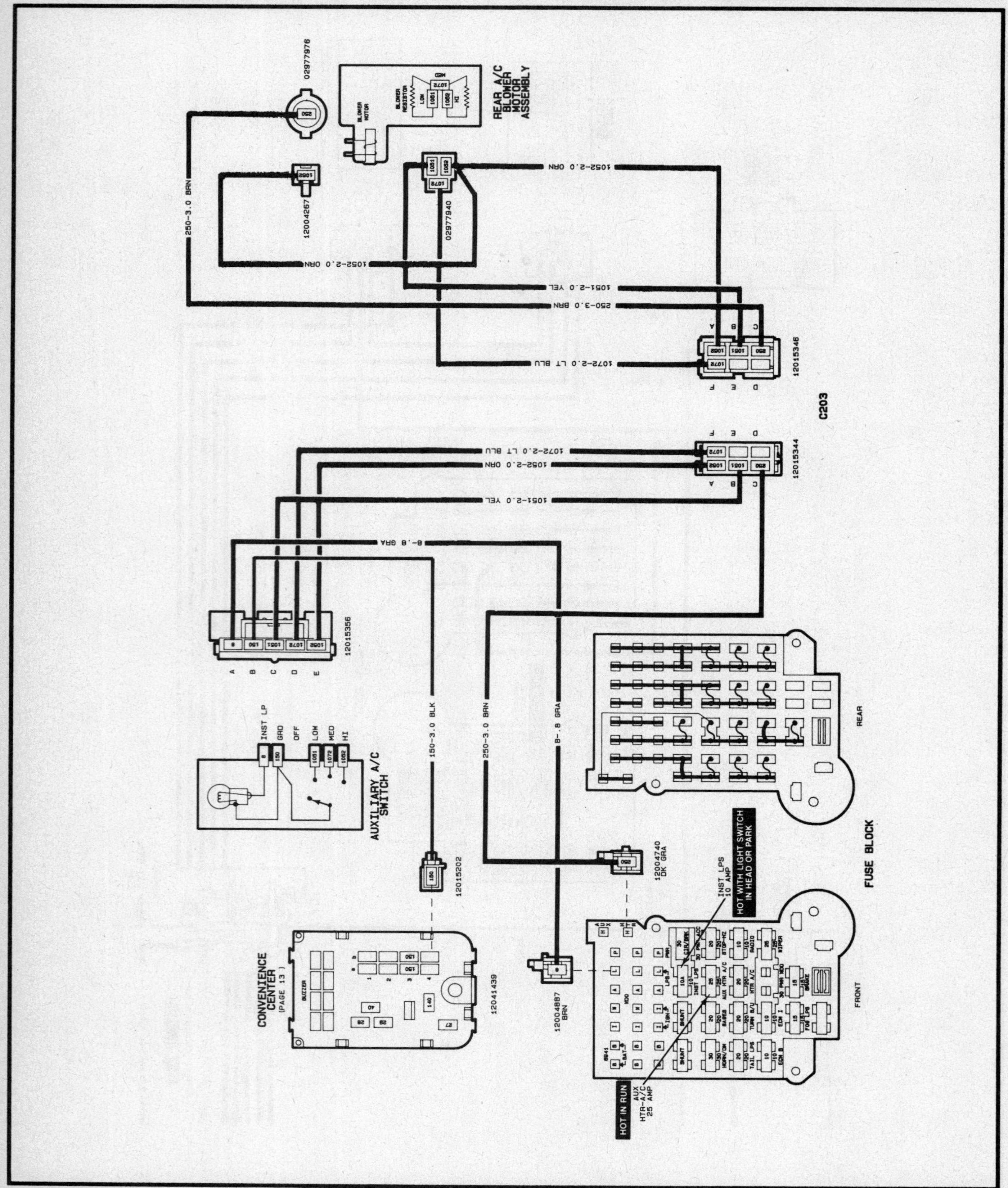
REAR A/C BLOWER MOTOR ASSEMBLY
02977976
12004267
02977940
1052-2.0 ORN
1051-2.0 YEL
250-3.0 BRN
1072-2.0 LT BLU
12015346
C203
12015344
8-.8 GRA
12015356
AUXILIARY A/C SWITCH
INST LP
GRD
OFF
LOW
MED
HI
150-3.0 BLK
12015202
CONVENIENCE CENTER (PAGE 13)
12041439
12004740 DK GRA
12004887 BRN
FUSE BLOCK
REAR
FRONT
INST LPS 10 AMP
HOT WITH LIGHT SWITCH IN HEAD OR PARK
HOT IN RUN
AUX HTR-A/C 25 AMP

Auxiliary air conditioning electrical schematic—1989 Astro and Safari

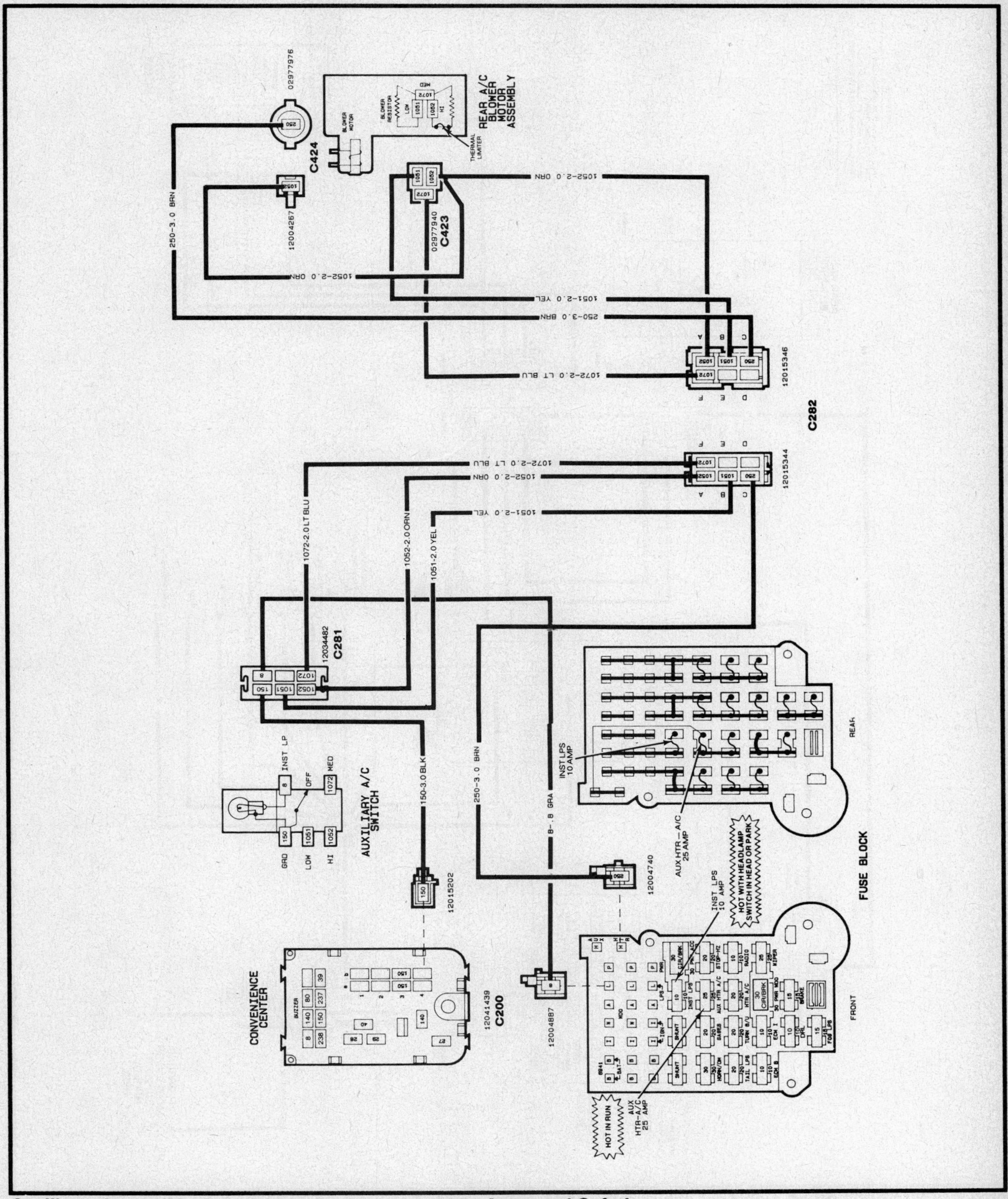

REAR A/C BLOWER MOTOR ASSEMBLY
BLOWER MOTOR
BLOWER RESISTOR
THERMAL LIMITER
LOW
MED
HI
02977976
C424
12004267
C423
02977940
250-3.0 BRN
1052-2.0 ORN
1051-2.0 YEL
1072-2.0 LT BLU
12015346
C282
12015344
1072-2.0 LT BLU
1052-2.0 ORN
1051-2.0 YEL
C281
12034482
AUXILIARY A/C SWITCH
INST LP
OFF
GRD
LOW
MED
HI
150-3.0 BLK
250-3.0 BRN
8-.8 GRA
12015202
12004740
12004887
CONVENIENCE CENTER
12041439
C200
BUZZER
INST LPS 10 AMP
AUX HTR—A/C 25 AMP
HOT WITH HEADLAMP SWITCH IN HEAD OR PARK
HOT IN RUN
REAR
FRONT
FUSE BLOCK

Auxiliary air conditioning electrical schematic—1990 Astro and Safari

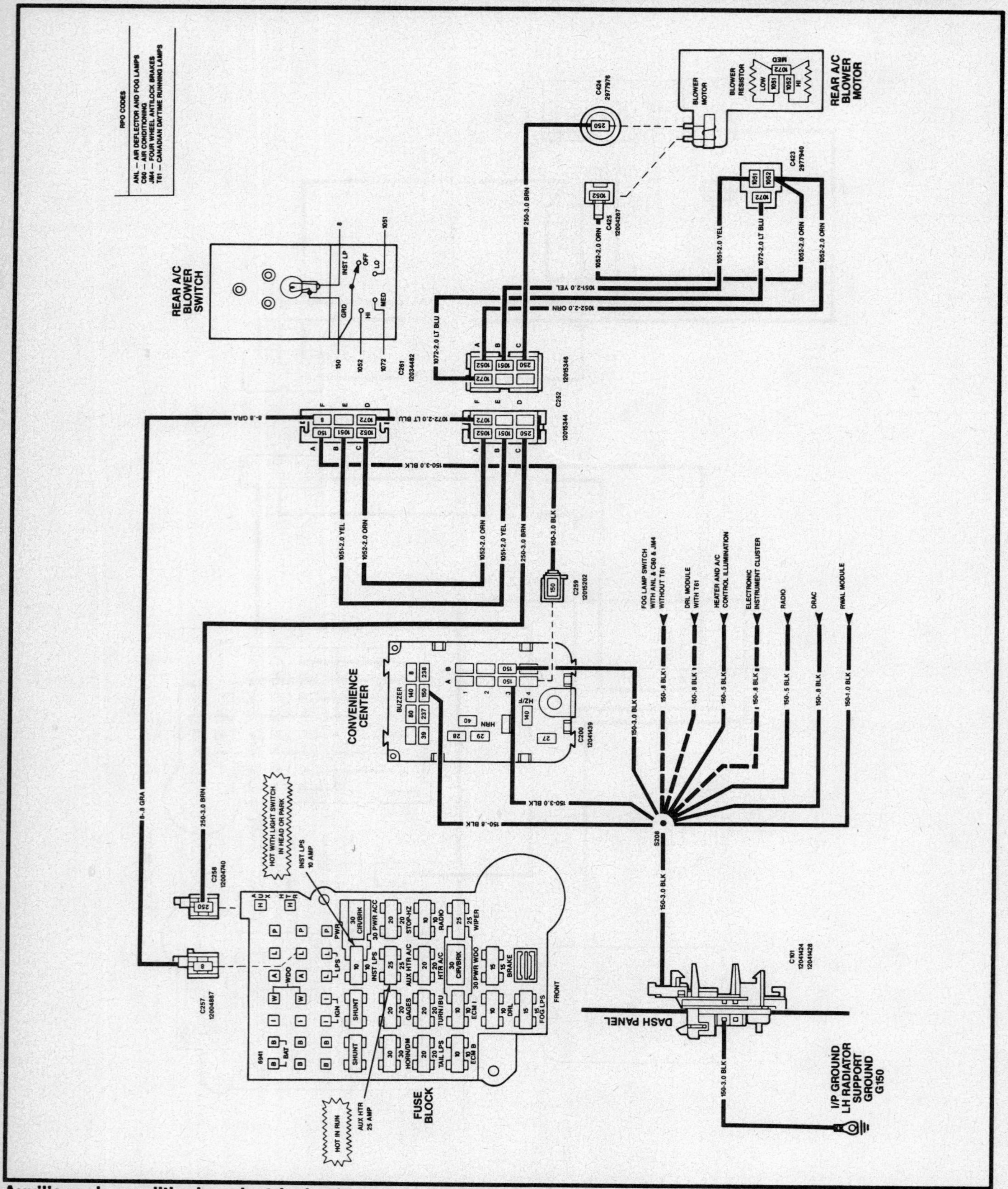
RPO CODES
REAR A/C BLOWER MOTOR
REAR A/C BLOWER SWITCH
CONVENIENCE CENTER
FUSE BLOCK
DASH PANEL
I/P GROUND LH RADIATOR SUPPORT GROUND G150

Auxiliary air conditioning electrical schematic—1991 Astro and Safari

11 JEEP 11

COMANCHE • CHEROKEE • GRAND WAGONEER • WAGONEER • WRANGLER

SPECIFICATIONS

ENGINE IDENTIFICATION

Year	Model	Engine Displacement cu. in. (liter)	Engine Series Identification (VIN)	No. of Cylinders	Engine Type
1989	Comanche	150 (2.5)	E	4	OHV
	Comanche	243 (4.0)	L	6	OHV
	Wrangler	150 (2.5)	E	4	OHV
	Wrangler	258 (4.2)	M	6	OHV
	Cherokee	150 (2.5)	E	4	OHV
	Cherokee	243 (4.0)	L	6	OHV
	Wagoneer	243 (4.0)	L	6	OHV
	Grand Wagoneer	360 (5.9)	7	8	OHV
1990	Comanche	150 (2.5)	E	4	OHV
	Comanche	243 (4.0)	L	6	OHV
	Wrangler	150 (2.5)	E	4	OHV
	Wrangler	258 (4.2)	M	6	OHV
	Cherokee	150 (2.5)	E	4	OHV
	Cherokee	243 (4.0)	L	6	OHV
	Wagoneer	243 (4.0)	L	6	OHV
	Grand Wagoneer	360 (5.9)	7	8	OHV
1991	Comanche	150 (2.5)	P	4	OHV
	Comanche	243 (4.0)	S	6	OHV
	Wrangler	150 (2.5)	P	4	OHV
	Cherokee	150 (2.5)	P	4	OHV
	Cherokee	243 (4.0)	S	6	OHV
	Grand Wagoneer	360 (5.9)	7	8	OHV

REFRIGERANT CAPACITIES

Year	Model	Freon (oz.)	Oil (fl. oz.)	Type ①
1989	Comanche	32	6.0	SD-508
	Wrangler	32	6.0	SD-508
	Cherokee	32	6.0	SD-508
	Wagoneer	32	6.0	SD-508
	Grand Wagoneer	32	4.6	SD-709
1990	Comanche	38	6.0	SD-508
	Wrangler	32	6.0	SD-508
	Cherokee	38	6.0	SD-508
	Wagoneer	38	6.0	SD-508
	Grand Wagoneer	32	4.6	SD-709
1991	Comanche	38	4.6	SD-709
	Wrangler	32	4.6	SD-709
	Cherokee	38	4.6	SD-709
	Grand Wagoneer	32	4.6	SD-709

① Compressor

AIR CONDITIONING BELT TENSION CHART

Year	Model	Engine (L)	Belt Type	Specification New	Specification Used
1989	Comanche	150 (2.5)	Serpentine	180–200	140–160
	Comanche	243 (4.0)	Serpentine	180–200	140–160
	Wrangler	150 (2.5)	Serpentine	180–200	140–160
	Wrangler	258 (4.2)	Serpentine	180–200	140–160
	Cherokee	150 (2.5)	Serpentine	180–200	140–160
	Cherokee	243 (4.0)	Serpentine	180–200	140–160
	Wagoneer	243 (4.0)	Serpentine	180–200	140–160
	Grand Wagoneer	360 (5.9)	V-belt	120–160	90–115
1989	Comanche	150 (2.5)	Serpentine	180–200	140–160
	Comanche	243 (4.0)	Serpentine	180–200	140–160
	Wrangler	150 (2.5)	Serpentine	180–200	140–160
	Wrangler	258 (4.2)	Serpentine	180–200	140–160
	Cherokee	150 (2.5)	Serpentine	180–200	140–160
	Cherokee	243 (4.0)	Serpentine	180–200	140–160
	Wagoneer	243 (4.0)	Serpentine	180–200	140–160
	Grand Wagoneer	360 (5.9)	V-belt	120–160	90–115
1991	Comanche	150 (2.5)	Serpentine	180–200	140–160
	Comanche	243 (4.0)	Serpentine	180–200	140–160
	Wrangler	150 (2.5)	Serpentine	180–200	140–160
	Cherokee	150 (2.5)	Serpentine	180–200	140–160
	Cherokee	243 (4.0)	Serpentine	180–200	140–160
	Grand Wagoneer	360 (5.9)	V-belt	120–160	90–115

SYSTEM DESCRIPTION

General Information

Comanche, Cherokee and Wagoneer

The climate control system is an integrated assembly combining air conditioning, heating and fresh air ventilating. Vehicles without air conditioning use a similar assembly minus the air conditioning components. Both systems basically consist of the blower and air inlet assembly and the heater core and air distribution assembly, which may be removed and serviced separately.

The heater system is a blend air type in which fresh air is heated and blended with cooler outside air in varying amounts to produce the desired temperature. The heater coolant valve provides variable coolant flow to the heater core for differing climate conditions.

The air conditioning system adds an evaporator for cooling and dehumidifying. The evaporator does not operate at ambient temperatures below 30°F (−1°C). Evaporator temperature is determined by a fixed setting thermostat switch which cycles the compressor clutch to avoid evaporator freezing. The blower automatically operates except in the **OFF** mode, in which case the blower and outside air are shut off.

Wrangler

A blend air heater system is used, providing constant coolant flow through the heater core. The temperature of heated air entering the passenger compartment is controlled by regulating the amount of air that flows through the heater core. The air control lever operates a door in the fresh air intake duct which controls the amount of air flow into the heater housing. The temperature control lever determines air flow through the heater core by operating the heater housing blend air door.

The air conditioning system is a dual flow unit. Cooling air can be drawn from outside the vehicle or recirculated from inside. The evaporator, blower fan and motor, thermostat, expansion valve, capillary tube, air outlets and system control are located in the evaporator housing. A rotary type compressor and magnetically operated clutch pulley is used for the system.

Grand Wagoneer

The Grand Wagoneer also uses a blend air type system, similar in operation as previous vehicles. An electric control module is used to control air conditioning compressor operation. The module is located on the air conditoning duct under the instrument panel above the accelerator panel. Input signals to the control module are from a thermistor located in the evaporator housing and a potentiometer actuated by the temperature control lever. The control module energizes the clutch while the potentiometer regulates the output of the system. The thermistor monitors evaporator temperature. Thermistor signals are relayed to the module which energizes or de-energizes the clutch as needed.

A relay is used to activate the blower motor in the heat/defrost or air conditioning modes. The relay is taped to the wiring harness behind the air conditioning housing.

The temperature control lever operates the blend air door in the heater core housing to regulate heat while in the heat or defrost mode. When in the air conditioning mode, the lever activates the potentiometer.

Service Valve Location

The service valve are located on the rear of the compressor on both the SD-508 and SD-709 compressors.

System Discharging

R-12 refrigerant is a chlorofluorocarbon which, when mishandled, can contribute to the depletion on the ozone layer in the upper atmosphere. Ozone filters out harmful radiation from the sun. In order to protect the ozone layer, an approved R-12 Recovery/Recycling machine that meets SAE standard J1991 should be employed when discharging the system. Follow the operating instructions provided with the approved equipment exactly to properly discharge the system.

NOTE: It is not necessary to discharge the air conditioning system for compressor removal. The compressor can be isolated from the remainder of the system, thereby eliminating the need for recharging when assembling.

System Evacuating

If the air conditioning system has been opened to the atmosphere, it should be air and moisture free before being recharged with refrigerant. Moisture and air mixed with refrigerant will raise the compressor head pressure, possibly damage the system's components and will reduce the performance of the system. Moisture will boil at normal room temperature when exposed to a vacuum. To evacuate the system, perform the following procedure:

1. Leak test the system and repair any leaks found.
2. Connect an approved charging station, Recovery/Recycling machine or manifold gauge set and vacuum pump to the discharge and suction ports. The red hose is normally connected to the discharge (high pressure) line and the blue hose is connected to the suction (low pressure) line.
3. Open the discharge and suction ports and start the vacuum pump. If the pump is not able to pull at least 26 in. Hg of vacuum, there is a leak that must be repaired before evacuation can occur.
4. Once the system has reached at least 26 in. Hg of vacuum, allow the system to evacuate for at least 10 minutes. The longer the system is evacuated, the more contaminants will be removed.
5. Close all valves and turn the pump off. If the system loses more than 2 in. Hg of vacuum after 15 minutes, there is a leak that should be repaired.

System Charging

1. Connect an approved charging station, Recovery/Recycling machine or manifold gauge set to the discharge and suction ports. The red hose is normally connected to the discharge (high pressure) line and the blue hose is connected to the suction (low pressure) line.
2. Follow the instructions provided with the equipment and charge the system with the specified amount of refrigerant.
3. Perform a leak test.

SYSTEM COMPONENTS

Radiator

REMOVAL AND INSTALLATION

1. Disconnect the negative battery cable.
2. Drain the coolant. Grille removal may be necessary.
3. Remove the upper and lower hoses and coolant reserve tank hose from the radiator.
4. Remove the alignment dowel E-clip from the lower radiator mounting bracket.
5. Disconnect the overflow tube from the radiator. Remove the electric cooling fan or fan shroud mounting bolts and pull the fan shroud back to the engine.
6. If equipped, disconnect and plug the transmission cooler lines.
7. Remove the top radiator mounting bolts and remove the grille mounting screws.
8. If equipped, remove the condenser to radiator mounting bolts and remove the radiator from the vehicle.

To install:

9. Slide the radiator into position behind the condenser, if equipped. Align the dowel pin with the bottom mounting bracket and install the E-clip.
10. Tighten the condenser-to-radiator bolts to 55 inch lbs. (6.2 Nm).
11. Install the grille. Install and tighten the radiator mounting bolts.
12. Connect the transmission cooler lines, if equipped. Install the fan shroud or electric cooling fan.
13. Connect the radiator hoses and fill with coolant.
14. Connect the negative battery cable and check for leaks.

COOLING SYSTEM BLEEDING

Air trapped in the system will prevent proper filling and leave the radiator coolant level low, causing a risk of overheating.

1. To bleed the system, start with the system cool, the radiator cap off and the radiator filled to about an inch below the filler neck.
2. Start the engine and run it at slightly above normal idle speed. This will ensure adequate circulation. If air bubbles appear and the coolant level drops, fill the system with coolant to bring the level back to the proper level.
3. Run the engine until the thermostat opens; coolant will move abruptly across the top of the radiator and the temperature of the radiator will suddenly rise.
4. At this point, air is expelled and the level may drop. Keep refilling the system until the level is near the top of the radiator and remains constant.

5. If the vehicle has an overflow tank, fill the radiator right up to the filler neck. Replace the radiator filler cap.

Electric Cooling Fan

Comanche, Cherokee and Wagoneer with 4.0L engine and air conditioning and/or heavy duty cooling are equipped with an auxiliary electric fan.

TESTING

1. Remove the fan relay, mounted on the left inner fender panel.
2. Using a jumper wire, with an in-line 25 amp fuse, supply battery voltage to the the No. 4 terminal of the relay connector.
3. If the fan operates, the motor is good. If the motor does not operate, check the continuity between the No. 4 terminal and the body ground connections on the fender panel. If continuity exists, replace the fan motor. If there is no continuity, repair the open circuit and retest.

REMOVAL AND INSTALLATION

1. Disconnect the negative battery cable.
2. Disconnect the electrical lead from the fan assembly.
3. Remove the fan mounting bolts and remove the fan assembly from the shroud and radiator.
4. The installation is the reverse of the removal procedure.

Condenser

REMOVAL AND INSTALLATION

Comanche, Cherokee and Wagoneer

1. Disconnect the negative battery cable.
2. Properly discharge the air conditioning system. Drain the coolant.
3. Disconnect the fan shroud, radiator hoses and automatic transmission cooler lines, if equipped. Unplug the low pressure switch.
4. Disconnect the refrigerant lines from the condenser. Cover the exposed ends of the lines to minimize contamination.
5. Remove the condenser and radiator as an assembly and disassemble on a workbench.

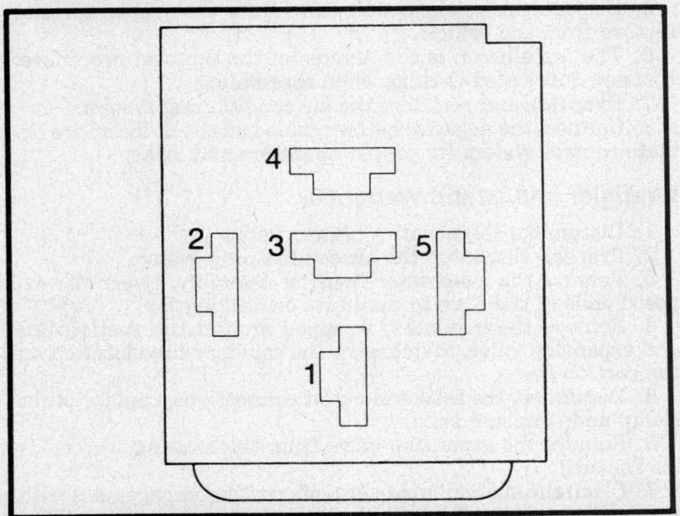
4
2
3
5
1

Auxiliary electric cooling fan connector terminal identification

6. The installation is the reverse of the removal procedure. Use new lubricated O-rings when assembling.
7. Evacuate and recharge the air conditioning system. If the condenser was replaced, add 1 oz. of refrigerant oil during the recharge.
8. Connect the negative battery cable and check the entire climate control system for proper operation and leaks.

Wrangler and Grand Wagoneer

1. Disconnect the negative battery cable.
2. Properly discharge the air conditioning system.
3. Drain the coolant and remove the radiator.
4. Disconnect the pressure line from the condenser. Cover the exposed end of the line to minimize contamination. Remove the mounting screws and tilt the bottom of the condenser toward the engine.
5. From the underside of the vehicle, disconnect the evaporator line from the receiver/drier.
6. Remove the condenser and receiver/drier and disassemble on a worbench.
7. The installation is the reverse of the removal procedure. Use new lubricated O-rings when assembling.
8. Evacuate and recharge the air conditioning system. If the condenser was replaced, add 1 oz. of refrigerant oil during the recharge.
9. Connect the negative battery cable and check the entire climate control system for proper operation and leaks.

Compressor

COMPRESSOR ISOLATION

It is not necessary to discharge the air conditioning system for

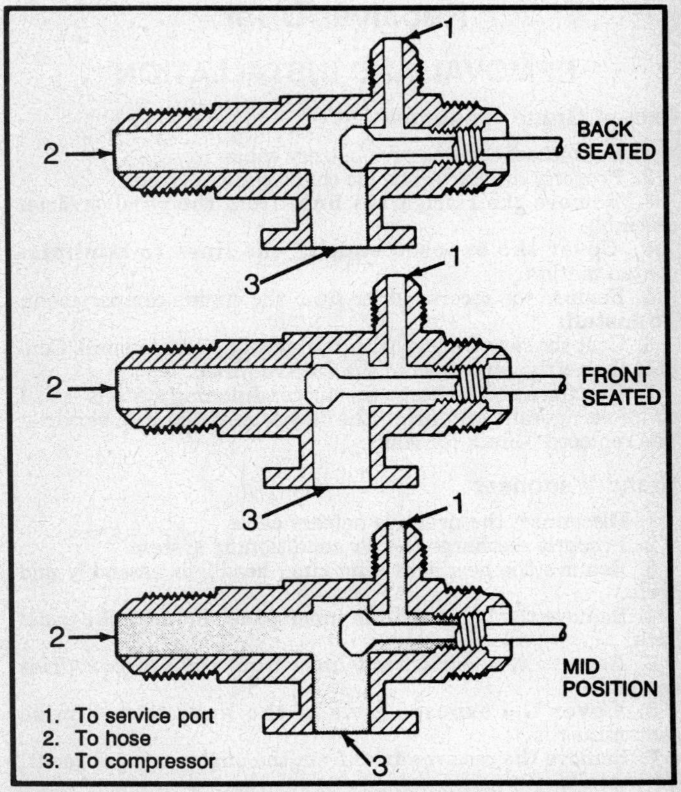
BACK SEATED
FRONT SEATED
MID POSITION
1. To service port
2. To hose
3. To compressor

Service valve seating positions for compressor isolation

compressor removal. The compressor can be isolated from the remainder of the system, thereby eliminating the need for recharging when assembling.

1. Connect a manifold gauge set with hand valves closed.
2. Place both service valves at mid-position.
3. Start the engine and operate the air conditioning system.
4. Turn the suction service valve (the valve below the larger line) slowly clockwise toward the front-seated position.
5. When the pressure drops to zero, stop the engine and quickly front-seat the suction valve completely.
6. Front-seat the discharge valve.
7. To complete the isolation, slowly loosen the oil level check plug located on top of the compressor body to release residual pressure inside the compressor.

REMOVAL AND INSTALLATION

1. Disconnect the negative battery cable.
2. Isolate the compressor.
3. Disconnect the refrigerant lines from the compressor. Cover the exposed ends of the lines to minimize contamination.
4. Remove the drive belt(s) by loosening the alternator or power steering pump.
5. Remove the mounting bolts and remove the compressor from the vehicle.

To install:

6. If a replacement compressor is being installed, check the oil level using the proper procedure.
7. Install the compressor to the bracket and install the bolts.
8. Install the belt(s) and adjust the specification.
9. Connect the refrigerant lines to the compressor. Use new lubricated O-rings when assembling.
10. Connect the negative battery cable and check the entire climate control system for proper operation and leaks.

Receiver/Drier

REMOVAL AND INSTALLATION

Except Grand Wagoneer

1. Disconnect the negative battery cable.
2. Properly discharge the air conditioning system.
3. Remove the refrigerant lines from the receiver/drier assembly.
4. Cover the exposed ends of the lines to minimize contamination.
5. Remove the receiver/drier from the engine compartment.

To install:

6. Coat the new O-rings with refrigerant oil and install. Connect the refrigerant lines to the receiver/drier.
7. Evacuate and recharge the air conditioning system. Add 1 oz. of refrigerant oil during the recharge if the receiver/drier was replaced. Check for leaks.

Grand Wagoneer

1. Disconnect the negative battery cable.
2. Properly discharge the air conditioning system.
3. Remove the headlight trim ring, headlight assembly and grille.
4. Remove the bolt from the inner panel and pull the panel back.
5. Remove the refrigerant lines from the receiver/drier assembly.
6. Cover the exposed ends of the lines to minimize contamination.
7. Remove the receiver/drier from the engine compartment.

To install:

8. Coat the new O-rings with refrigerant oil and install. Connect the refrigerant lines to the receiver/drier.

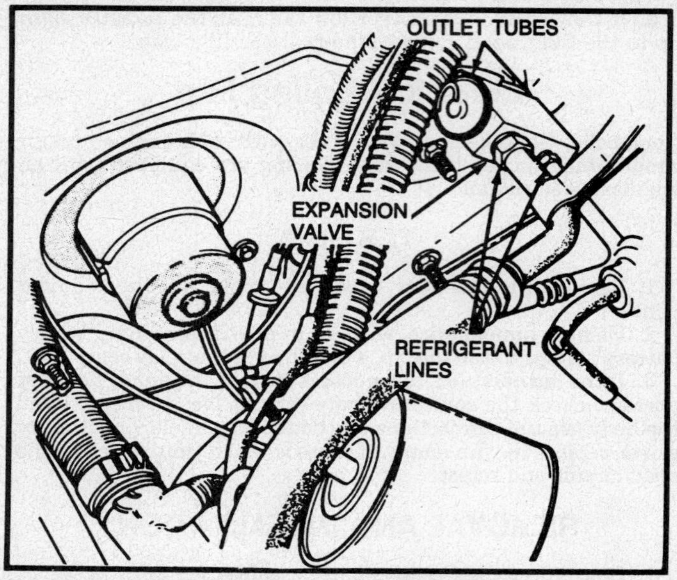
OUTLET TUBES
EXPANSION VALVE
REFRIGERANT LINES

Expansion valve location—Comanche, Cherokee and Wagoneer

9. Install the panel and bolt. Install the front end parts.
10. Evacuate and recharge the air conditioning system. If the receiver/drier was replaced, add 1 oz. of refrigerant oil during the recharge. Check for leaks.

Expansion Valve

REMOVAL AND INSTALLATION

Comanche, Cherokee and Wagoneer

1. Disconnect the negative battery cable.
2. Properly discharge the air conditioning system.
3. Remove the coolant reservoir and bracket.
4. Disconnect the refrigerant lines from the expansion valve, located on the firewall near the blower motor. Cover the exposed ends of the lines to minimize contamination.
5. Disconnect the expansion valve from the evaporator and remove from the vehicle.
6. The installation is the reverse of the removal procedure. Use new lubricated O-rings when assembling.
7. Evacuate and recharge the air conditioning system.
8. Connect the negative battery cable and check the entire climate control system for proper operation and leaks.

Wrangler and Grand Wagoneer

1. Disconnect the negative battery cable.
2. Properly discharge the air conditioning system.
3. Remove the evaporator housing assembly. Cover the exposed ends of the lines to minimize contamination.
4. Remove the insulation wrapped around the suction line and expansion valve. Matchmark the capillary tube location on the suction line.
5. Disconnect the inlet and outlet connections, capillary tube clamp and equalizer tube.
6. Remove the expansion valve from the housing.

To install:

7. Clean the suction line to provide positive engagement with the replacement expansion valve's capillary tube.
8. Connect the inlet and outlet connections. Clamp the capillary tube at the marked position and connect the equalizer tube.

Make sure the capillary tube is clamped securely so firm contact with the suction line is achieved.
9. Wrap the expansion valve and suction line with the insulation.
10. Install the evaporator housing.
11. Evacuate and recharge the air conditioning system.
12. Connect the negative battery cable and check the entire climate control system for proper operation and leaks.

Blower Motor

REMOVAL AND INSTALLATION

Comanche, Cherokee and Wagoneer

2.5L ENGINE

1. Disconnect the negative battery cable.
2. Disconnect the blower motor wiring, located near the firewall.
3. Remove the blower motor mounting screws.
4. Remove the blower and fan assembly.
5. Remove the fan from the motor shaft to gain access to the motor attaching nuts.
6. The installation is the reverse of the removal procedure.
7. Connect the negative battery cable and check the blower for proper operation.

4.0L ENGINE

1. Disconnect the negative battery cable.
2. Remove the coolant reservoir strap, move the reservoir aside and remove the bracket.
3. If equipped with anti-lock brakes, remove the brake pump and bracket together and position aside.
4. Disconnect the blower motor wiring.
5. Remove the blower motor mounting screws.
6. Remove the blower and fan assembly.
7. Remove the fan from the motor shaft to gain access to the motor attaching nuts.

To install:

8. Assemble the motor and fan. The 2 ears of the retainer clip must be positioned over the flat surface of the motor shaft.
9. Install the motor assembly to the firewall and connect the wiring.
10. Install the anti-lock brake and coolant reservoir components.
11. Connect the negative battery cable and check the blower for proper operation.

Wrangler

1. Disconnect the negative battery cable.
2. If equipped with air conditioning, lower the evaporator housing. If not, remove the heater housing.
3. Remove the blower to housing attaching screws and remove the blower from the housing.
4. The installation is the reverse of the removal procedure.
5. Connect the negative battery cable and check the entire climate control system for proper operation.

Grand Wagoneer

1. Disconnect the negative battery cable.
2. Disconnect the electrical lead.
3. Remove the blower to housing attaching screws and remove the blower from the housing.
4. The installation is the reverse of the removal procedure.
5. Connect the negative battery cable and check the entire climate control system for proper operation.

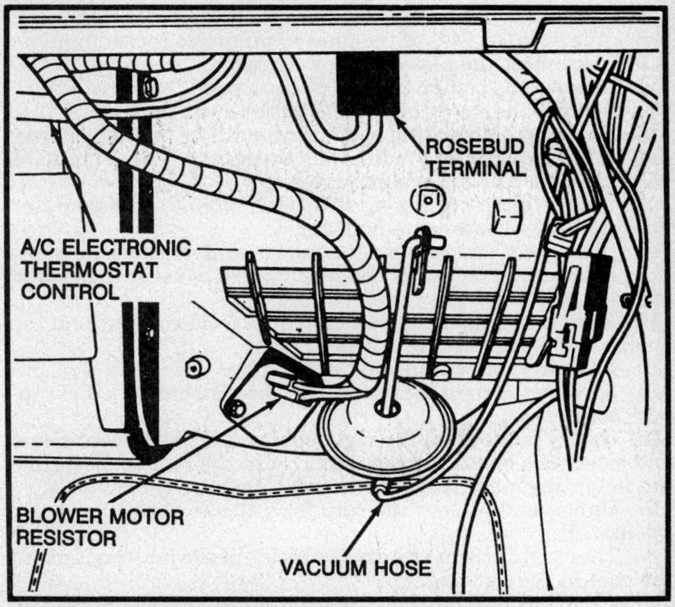
ROSEBUD
TERMINAL
A/C ELECTRONIC
THERMOSTAT
CONTROL
BLOWER MOTOR
RESISTOR
VACUUM HOSE

Blower motor resistor location—Comanche, Cherokee and Wagoneer

Blower Motor Resistor

REMOVAL AND INSTALLATION

Comanche, Cherokee and Wagoneer

1. Disconnect the negative battery cable.
2. Remove the vacuum motor cover.
3. Disconnect the resistor connector and remove the resistor.
4. The installation is the reverse of the removal procedure.
5. Connect the negative battery cable and check the system for proper operation.

Grand Wagoneer

1989 vehicles are equipped with separate identical resistors for the heater and air conditioning systems. The heater resistor is located on the heater core housing in the engine compartment. The air conditioning resistor is located on the evaporator housing to the left of the steering column.

1990–91 vehicles are equipped with 1 resistor for both systems, which is located in the cowl plenum chamber adjacent to the power brake booster/master cylinder.

1. Disconnect the negative battery cable.
2. Disconnect the resistor connector.
3. Remove the resistor.
4. The installation is the reverse of the removal procedure.
5. Connect the negative battery cable and check the system for proper operation.

Heater Core

REMOVAL AND INSTALLATION

Comanche, Cherokee and Wagoneer

1. Disconnect the negative battery cable. Drain the coolant.
2. Disconnect the heater hoses at the core tubes.
3. If equipped with air conditioning, discharge the refrigerant.

4. Disconnect the refrigerant lines from the expansion valve. Cover the exposed ends of the lines to minimize contamination.
5. Disconnect the blower motor wires and vent tube.
6. Remove the center console, if equipped.
7. Remove the lower half of the instrument panel.
8. Disconnect the wiring at the air conditioning relay, blower motor resistors and air conditioning thermostat. Disconnect the vacuum hoses at the vacuum motor.
9. Cut the plastic retaining strap that retains the evaporator housing to the heater core housing.
10. Disconnect and remove the heater control cable.
11. Remove the 3 clips at the rear blower housing flange and remove the retaining screws.
12. Remove the housing attaching nuts from the studs on the engine compartment side of the firewall.
13. Remove the condensation drain tube.
14. Remove the right kick panel and the instrument panel support bolt.
15. Gently pull out on the right side of the instrument panel and rotate the housing down and toward the rear to disengage the mounting studs from the firewall. Remove the housing.
16. Unbolt and remove the core from the housing.

To install:

17. Thoroughly clean and dry the inside of the housing. Install the core in the housing.
18. Position the housing on the mounting studs on the firewall.
19. Install the right kick panel and the instrument panel support bolt.
20. Install the condensation drain tube.
21. Install the housing attaching nuts from the studs on the engine compartment side of the firewall.
22. Install the 3 clips at the rear blower housing flange and install the retaining screws.
23. Connect the heater control cable.
24. Install a new plastic retaining strap that retains the evaporator housing to the heater core housing.
25. Connect the wiring at the relay, blower motor resistors and thermostat.
26. Connect the vacuum hoses to the vacuum motor.
27. Install the lower half of the instrument panel.
28. Install the center console, if equipped.
29. Connect the blower motor wires and vent tube.
30. Connect the refrigerant lines to the expansion valve.
31. Connect the heater hoses to the core tubes.
32. Fill the cooling system.
33. Evacuate and recharge the air conditioning system.
34. Connect the negative battery cable and check the entire climate control system for proper operation and leaks.

Wrangler

1. Disconnect the negative battery cable.
2. Drain the coolant.
3. Disconnect the heater hoses from the core tubes.
4. Disconnect the vent door cables.
5. Disconnect the blower motor wiring.
6. Disconnect the defroster duct.
7. Remove the nuts that attach the heater housing studs to the engine compartment side of the firewall.
8. To remove the heater housing assembly, tilt it downward to disengage it from the defroster duct, and pull it rearward and out from beneath the instrument panel.
9. Remove the cover from the housing and remove the heater core from the housing.

To install:

10. Thoroughly clean and dry the inside of the housing. Install the core in the housing and install the cover.

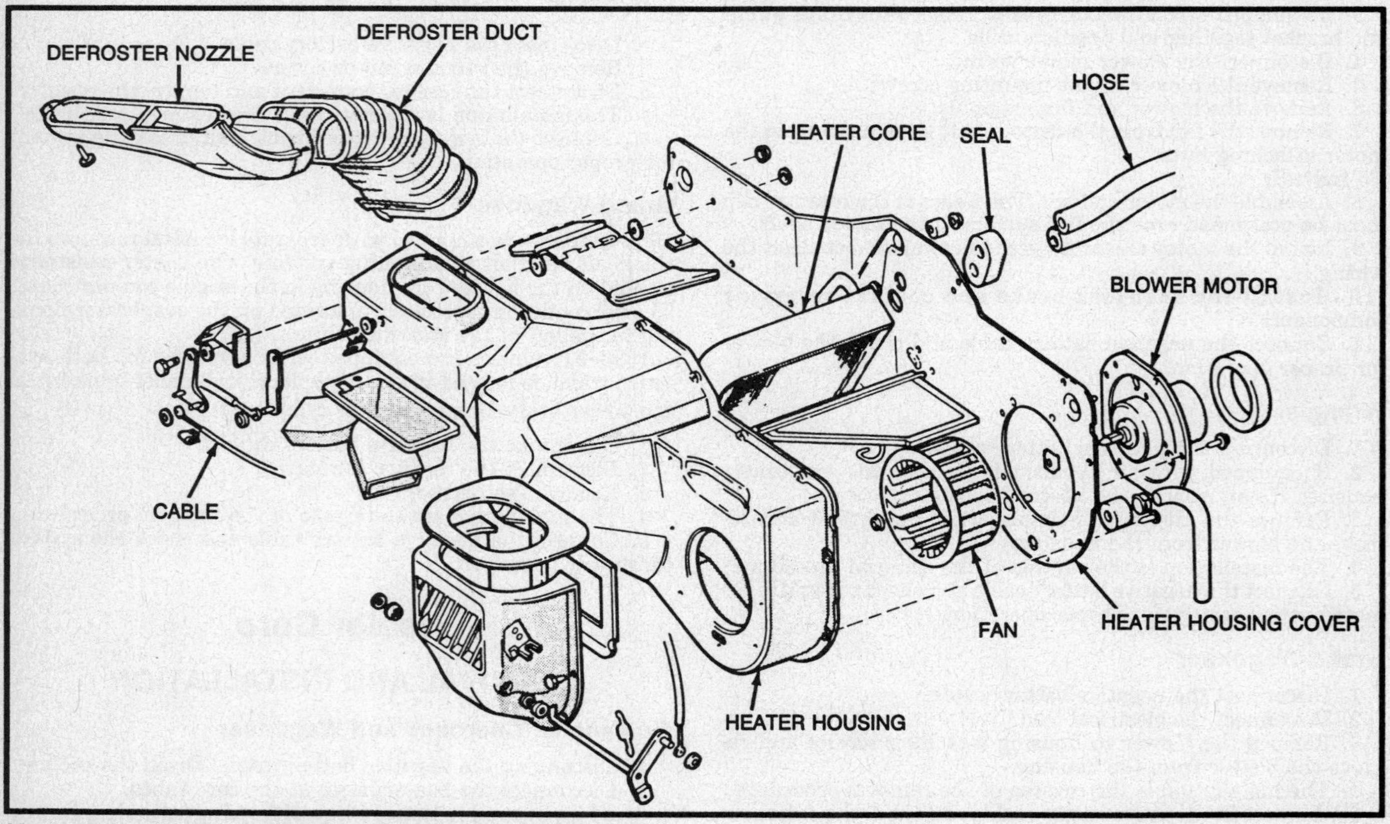
DEFROSTER DUCT
DEFROSTER NOZZLE
HOSE
HEATER CORE
SEAL
BLOWER MOTOR
CABLE
FAN
HEATER HOUSING COVER
HEATER HOUSING

Heater housing and related components – Wrangler

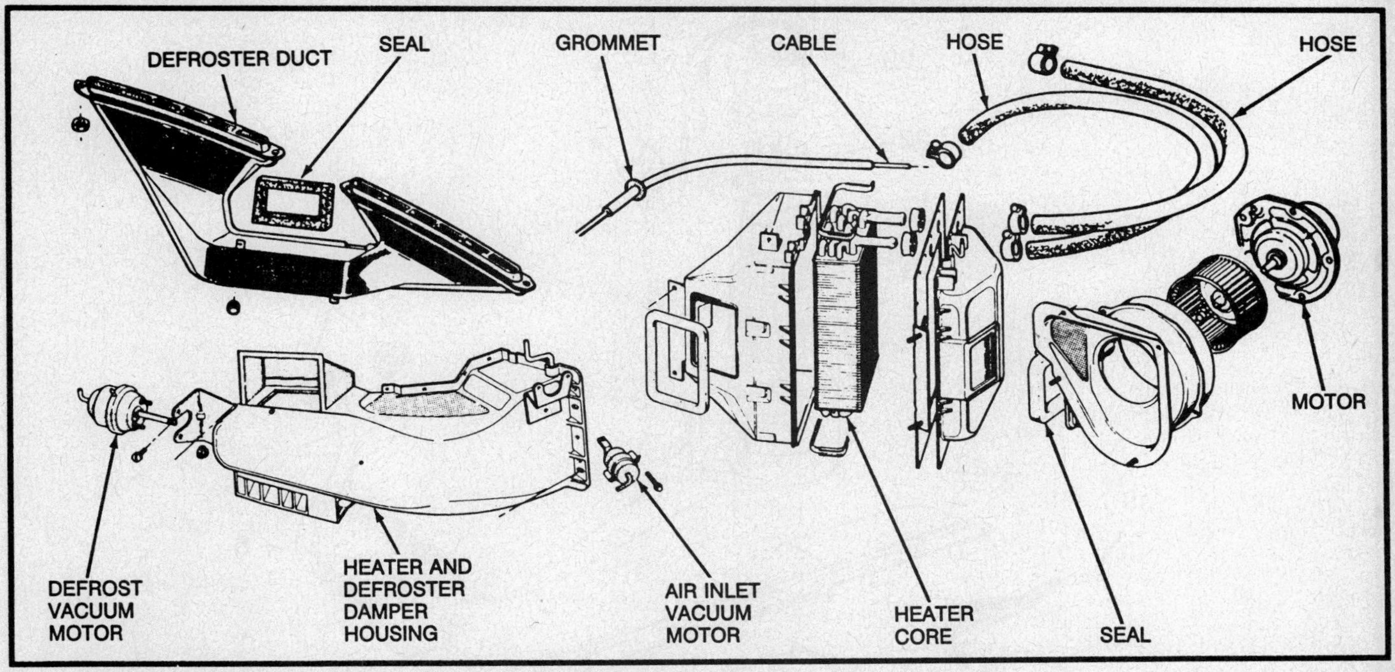
DEFROSTER DUCT
SEAL
GROMMET
CABLE
HOSE
HOSE
MOTOR
DEFROST VACUUM MOTOR
HEATER AND DEFROSTER DAMPER HOUSING
AIR INLET VACUUM MOTOR
HEATER CORE
SEAL

Heater housing and related components—Grand Wagoneer

11. Install the seals on the heater core tubes and over the blower motor housing.
12. Install the housing to the dash panel. Make sure all studs extend through the sheet metal.
13. Install the attaching nuts to the studs.
14. Connect the defroster duct.
15. Connect the blower motor wiring and vent door cables.
16. Connect the heater hoses to the core tubes.
17. Fill the cooling system.
18. Connect the negative battery cable and check the entire climate control system for proper operation and leaks.

Grand Wagoneer

1. Disconnect the negative battery cable.
2. Drain the coolant.
3. Disconnect the heater hoses from the core tubes.
4. Disconnect the temperature control cable from the blend air door.
5. Remove the nuts that attach the heater housing studs to the firewall.
6. Remove the housing and disassemble on a workbench.
7. Remove the heater core from the housing.

To install:

8. Thoroughly clean and dry the inside of the housing.
9. Install the heater core to the housing and assemble.
10. Install the housing to the vehicle and install the nuts.
11. Connect the temperature control cable to the blend air door.
12. Connect the heater hoses to the core tubes.
13. Fill the cooling system.
14. Connect the negative battery cable and check the entire climate control system for proper operation and leaks.

Evaporator

REMOVAL AND INSTALLATION

Comanche, Cherokee and Wagoneer

1. Disconnect the negative battery cable. Drain the coolant.
2. Disconnect the heater hoses at the core tubes.
3. Discharge the refrigerant.
4. Disconnect the refrigerant lines from the expansion valve. Cover the exposed ends of the lines to minimize contamination.
5. Disconnect the blower motor wires and vent tube.
6. Remove the center console, if equipped.
7. Remove the lower half of the instrument panel.
8. Disconnect the wiring at the air conditioning relay, blower motor resistors and air conditioning thermostat. Disconnect the vacuum hoses at the vacuum motor.
9. Cut the plastic retaining strap that retains the evaporator housing to the heater core housing.
10. Disconnect and remove the heater control cable.
11. Remove the 3 clips at the rear blower housing flange and remove the retaining screws.
12. Remove the housing attaching nuts from the studs on the engine compartment side of the firewall.
13. Remove the condensation drain tube.
14. Remove the right kick panel and the instrument panel support bolt.
15. Gently pull out on the right side of the instrument panel and rotate the housing down and toward the rear to disengage the mounting studs from the firewall. Remove the housing.
16. Unbolt and remove the evaporator from the housing.

To install:

17. Thoroughly clean and dry the inside of the housing. Install the evaporator in the housing.
18. Position the housing on the mounting studs on the firewall.
19. Install the right kick panel and the instrument panel support bolt.
20. Install the condensation drain tube.
21. Install the housing attaching nuts from the studs on the engine compartment side of the firewall.
22. Install the 3 clips at the rear blower housing flange and install the retaining screws.
23. Connect the heater control cable.
24. Install a new plastic retaining strap that retains the evaporator housing to the heater core housing.

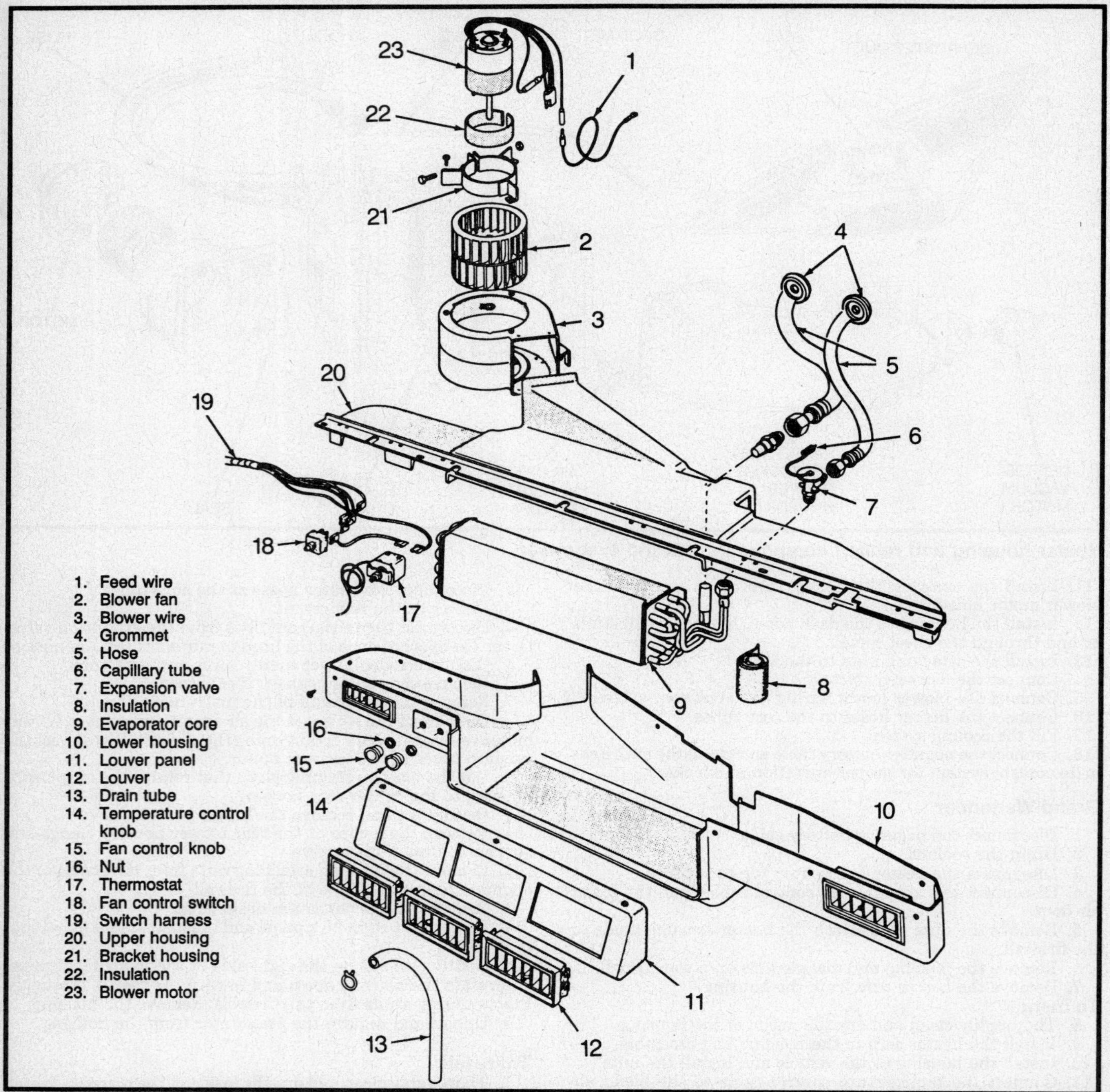
23
1
22
21
2
4
3
5
20
19
6
7
18
17
8
9
16
15
14
10
11
13
12
1. Feed wire
2. Blower fan
3. Blower wire
4. Grommet
5. Hose
6. Capillary tube
7. Expansion valve
8. Insulation
9. Evaporator core
10. Lower housing
11. Louver panel
12. Louver
13. Drain tube
14. Temperature control knob
15. Fan control knob
16. Nut
17. Thermostat
18. Fan control switch
19. Switch harness
20. Upper housing
21. Bracket housing
22. Insulation
23. Blower motor

Evaporator housing and related components – Wrangler

25. Connect the wiring at the relay, blower motor resistors and thermostat.
26. Connect the vacuum hoses to the vacuum motor.
27. Install the lower half of the instrument panel.
28. Install the center console, if equipped.
29. Connect the blower motor wires and vent tube.
30. Connect the refrigerant lines to the expansion valve.
31. Connect the heater hoses to the core tubes.
32. Fill the cooling system.
33. Evacuate and recharge the air conditioning system. If the evaporator was replaced, add 1 oz. of refrigerant oil during the recharge.
34. Connect the negative battery cable and check the entire climate control system for proper operation and leaks.

Wrangler and Grand Wagoneer

1. Disconnect the negative battery cable.

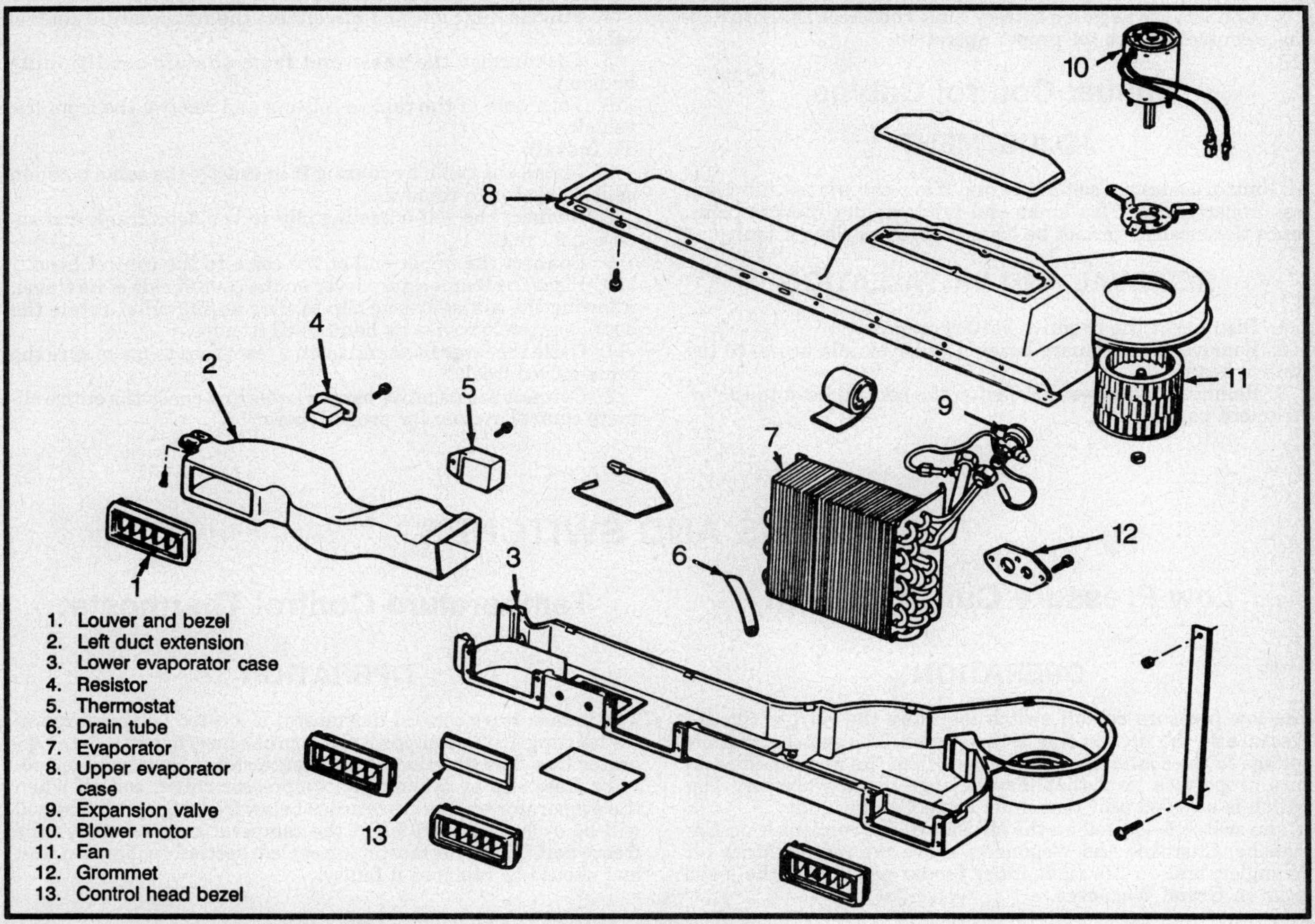
10
8
4
2
5
9
7
11
12
3
6
1
13
1. Louver and bezel
2. Left duct extension
3. Lower evaporator case
4. Resistor
5. Thermostat
6. Drain tube
7. Evaporator
8. Upper evaporator case
9. Expansion valve
10. Blower motor
11. Fan
12. Grommet
13. Control head bezel

Evaporator housing and related components—Grand Wagoneer

2. Properly discharge the air conditioning system.
3. Disconnect the refrigerant lines.
4. Remove the hose clamps and dash grommet retaining screws.
5. Remove the evaporator mounting screws and bracket. Lower the evaporator housing and pull the hose grommet through the dash opening.
6. Disassemble the housing and remove the evaporator.

To install:

7. Thoroughly clean and dry the inside of the housing.
8. Install the evaporator to the housing and assemble.
9. Install the housing to the vehicle and install the mounting screws.
10. Install the dash grommet retaining screw and hose clamp.
11. Connect the refrigerant lines.
12. Evacuate and recharge the air conditioning system. Add 1 oz. of refrigerant oil during the recharge if the evaporator was replaced.
13. Connect the negative battery cable and check the entire climate control system for proper operation and leaks.

Refrigerant Lines

REMOVAL AND INSTALLATION

1. Disconnect the negative battery cable.
2. Properly discharge the air conditioning system.
3. Unscrew the desired line from its adjoining component. If the lines are connected with flare nuts, use a back-up wrench when disassembling. Cover the exposed ends of the lines to minimize contamination.
4. Remove the lines and discard the O-rings.

To install:

5. Coat the O-rings with refrigerant oil and install. Connect the refrigerant lines to the adjoining components and tighten.
6. Evacuate and recharge the air conditioning system.
7. Connect the negative battery cable and check the entire climate control system for proper operation and leaks.

Manual Control Head

REMOVAL AND INSTALLATION

1. Disconnect the negative battery cable.
2. Remove the instrument panel bezel.
3. On Comanche, Cherokee and Wagoneer, remove the radio.
4. Remove the manual control head retaining screws and pull the unit out of the instrument panel.
5. Disconnect all electrical connections, actuating cables and vacuum hoses from the unit and remove from the instrument panel.
6. The installation is the reverse of the removal procedure.

7. Connect the negative battery cable and check the entire climate control system for proper operation.

Manual Control Cables

ADJUSTMENT

All control cables are self-adjusting. If any cable is not functioning properly, check for kinks and lubricate dry moving parts. Since these cables cannot be disassembled, replace if faulty.

REMOVAL AND INSTALLATION

1. Disconnect the negative battery cable.
2. Remove the necessary bezel in order to gain access to the control head.
3. Remove the screws that fasten the control head to the instrument panel.
4. Pull the unit out and disconnect the temperature control cable.
5. Disconnect the cable end from the air conditioning housing.
6. Take note of the cable's routing and remove the from the vehicle.

To install:

7. Install the cable by routing it in exactly the same position as it was prior to removal.
8. Connect the self-adjusting clip to the door crank and secure the cable.
9. Connect the upper end of the cable to the control head.
10. Place the temperature lever on the coolest side of its travel. Allowing the self-adjusting clip to slide on the cable, rotate the door counterclockwise by hand until it stops.
11. Cycle the lever back and forth a few times to make sure the cable moves freely.
12. Connect the negative battery cable and check the entire climate control system for proper operation.

SENSORS AND SWITCHES

Low Pressure Cut Off Switch

OPERATION

The low pressure cut off switch monitors the refrigerant gas pressure on the suction side of the system. The switch turns off voltage to the compressor clutch coil when the monitored pressure drops to a level that may damage the compressor. The switch is a sealed unit that must be replaced if faulty.

The switch is located on the left side of the condenser on Comanche, Cherokee and Wagoneer; above the receiver/drier on Wrangler; and on the right inner fender panel near the sight glass on Grand Wagoneer.

TESTING

1. If the system is low on refrigerant and the compressor clutch does not engage, unplug the switch and jump the terminals. If the clutch engages, the switch is operating properly.
2. If the system pressures are nominal and the compressor clutch does not engage, unplug the switch and jump the terminals. If the compressor engages, the switch is faulty and should be replaced. If the compressor clutch still does not engage, check the terminals for battery voltage and/or a possible open circuit.
3. If possible, the expansion valve head can be frozen in order to attain low suction pressure. This should engage the switch and stop the flow of voltage.

REMOVAL AND INSTALLATION

1. Disconnect the negative battery cable.
2. Properly discharge the air conditioning system.
3. Unplug the connector from the switch.
4. Unscrew the switch from the component on which it is mounted.

To install:

5. Seal the threads of the new switch with teflon tape.
6. Install the switch and connect the connector.
7. Evacuate and recharge the system. Check for leaks.
8. Check the switch for proper operation.

Temperature Control Thermostat

OPERATION

The temperature control thermostat is located on the evaporator housing and is equipped with a probe inserted into the evaporator fins. The function of the thermostat is to prevent evaporator freeze-up by cycling the compressor clutch coil off when the evaporator temperature drops below freezing point. The coil will be cycled back on when the temperature rises above the freeze point. The thermostat is a sealed, specially calibrated unit and should be replaced if faulty.

TESTING

1. Test the switch in an area with ambient temperature of at least 70°F (21°C).
2. Turn the ignition switch to the **RUN** position. Turn the air conditioning and blower switches **ON**.
3. Measure the voltage at terminal A of the thermostat connector. If no voltage is detected, repair the open from the blower switch.
4. If 12 volts was detected, measure the voltage at the other terminal. If voltage is not detected, replace the thermostat.
5. If 12 volts was detected, measure the voltage at the low pressure cut off switch connector. If no voltage was detected, repair the open.

REMOVAL AND INSTALLATION

Comanche, Cherokee and Wagoneer

1. Disconnect the negative battery cable.
2. Remove the center console, if equipped.
3. Remove the lower instrument panel assembly.
4. Pull the rosebud terminal out of the housing.
5. Disconnect the electrical connector from the thermostat.
6. Remove the wires from the retaining clip.
7. Carefully remove the thermostat probe/thermostat electric cycling switch from the tube guide hole.

To install:

8. Carefully insert the thermostat probe into the tube guide

hole until the thermostat electric cycling switch body contacts the housing.

9. Connect the rosebud terminal and snap into the hole in the housing.

10. Connect the wiring and secure the wires with the retaining clip.

11. Install the lower instrument panel and center console.

12. Connect the negative battery cable and check the entire climate control system for proper operation.

Wrangler

1. Disconnect the negative battery cable.
2. Lower the evaporator housing.
3. Remove the attaching screws holding the 2 halves of the housing together and separate the housings.
4. Remove the thermostat from the evaporator housing.

To install:

5. Install the thermostat. Be sure to insert the probe at least 2 in. into the evaporator coil. Do not bend or kink the tube excessively when installing.
6. Assemble the evaporator housing and install.
7. Connect the negative battery cable and check the entire climate control system for proper operation.

Thermistor

OPERATION

On Grand Wagoneer, the thermistor monitors the temperature of the evaporator and relays the signals to the electronic control module in order to prevent evaporator freeze-up. The control module will energize or de-energize the compressor clutch accordingly.

TESTING

1. Locate the air conditioning control module under the instrument panel.
2. Connect an ohmmeter across the green with white tracer and green thermistor wires at the end of the module connector.
3. Check the resistance of the thermistor with the values below:
   30°F (−1°C)—17,000 ohms
   35°F (2°C)—15,000 ohms
   70°F (21°C)—6000 ohms
   75°F (24°C)—5250 ohms
   80°F (27°C)—4500 ohms
   85°F (30°C)—4000 ohms
   90°F (32°C)—3500 ohms
4. If the resistance value does not agree with the chart, replace the thermistor.

REMOVAL AND INSTALLATION

1. Disconnect the negative battery cable.
2. Lower the 4WD selector switch.
3. Remove the lower evaporator housing housing mounting screws and ground wire screw.
4. Remove the insulation material.
5. Remove the housing cover mounting screws.

NOTE: Perform the following steps slowly and carefully. Be very careful not to damage the evaporator when drilling.

6. Place a piece of sheet metal between the evaporator and front of the housing. This will protect the evaporator.
7. Drill a 1¼ in. hole through the front of the evaporator housing. Place the hole so its outer edge is within ⅛ in. of the black metal bracket and left vertical indentation.

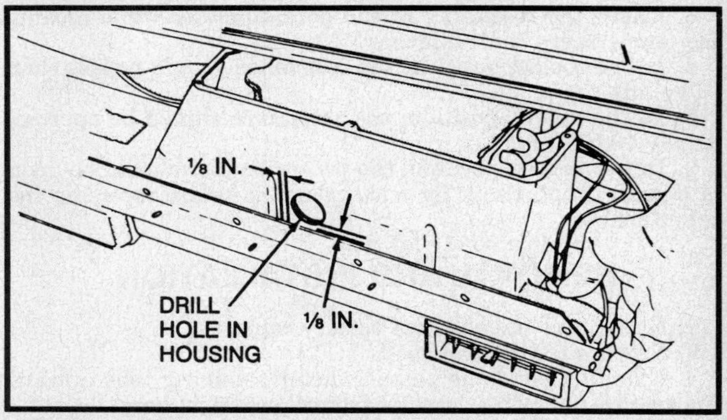
⅛ IN.
DRILL
HOLE IN
HOUSING
⅛ IN.

Drill the hole in the indicated position for thermistor probe removal—Grand Wagoneer

8. Trim the edges of the hole to protect the thermistor probe from damage.
9. Remove the blower motor mounting screws and remove the blower.
10. Disconnect the thermistor wiring.
11. Remove the evaporator core mounting screws and lift the evaporator up to allow access to the thermistor probe.
12. Remove the thermistor probe through the hole that was drilled earlier.

To install:

13. Install the thermistor probe through the drilled hole and insert into the hole vacated by the old probe. If this is not possible, position the probe into the evaporator housing as low and far to the left as possible.
14. Lower the evaporator core into the housing.
15. Route the wiring between the evaporator housing and evaporator core.
16. Push the end of the thermistor probe through the hole and bring toward the blower motor.
17. Connect the thermistor wiring.
18. Slit the plastic grommet and install into the drilled hole.
19. Position the evaporator core and install its mounting screws.
20. Install the evaporator housing cover and insulation material.
21. Raise the housing into position and install the mounting screws. Attach the ground wire.
22. Install the 4WD selector switch.
23. Connect the negative battery cable and check the entire climate control system for proper operation.

Potentiometer

OPERATION

On Grand Wagoneer, the potentiometer, located in the control head and actuated by the temperature control lever, relays the position of the lever to the electronic control unit. The control unit will process this information and regulate air conditioning output accordingly.

TESTING

1. Locate the air conditioning control module under the instrument panel.
2. Connect an ohmmeter across the brown with white tracer and brown potentiometer wires at the end of the module connector.

3. Check the resistance of the potentiometer while moving the temperature control lever.
4. In the coolest position, the resistance should be less than 100 ohms.
5. In the middle position, the resistance should be approximately 10,000 ohms.
6. In the hottest position, the potentiometer should be open (∞ ohms). If not, check for a short circuit before replacing the potentiometer.

REMOVAL AND INSTALLATION

1. Disconnect the negative battery cable.
2. Remove the control head.
3. Carefully bend the potentiometer retaining tabs upward and remove the potentiometer from the control head.
4. The installation is the reverse of the removal procedure.
5. Connect the negative battery cable and check the entire climate control system for proper operation.

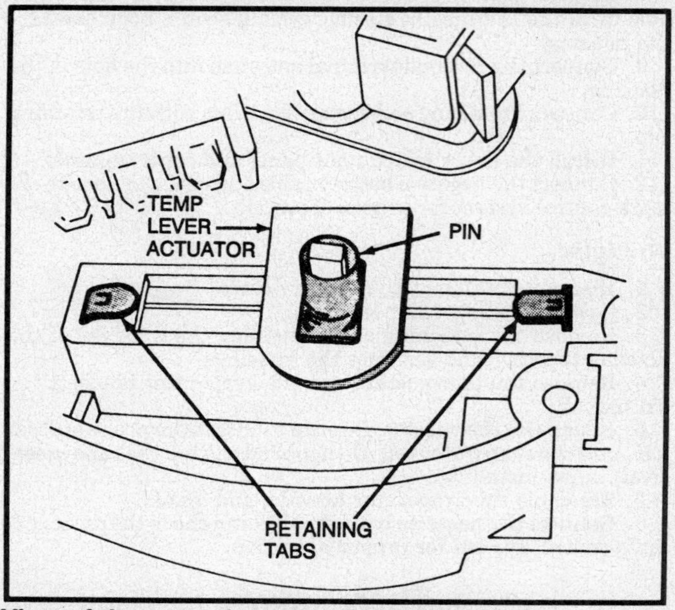
TEMP
LEVER
ACTUATOR
PIN
RETAINING
TABS
View of the potentiometer—Grand Wagoneer

Electronic Control Module

OPERATION

On Grand Wagoneer, the electronic control unit, located on the ductwork above the accelerator pedal, is used to control compressor operation. The module processes information received from the thermistor and potentiometer and energized or de-energizes the compressor clutch accordingly.

TESTING

1. Check all other system components for proper operation.
2. Check all wiring and connectors for possible problems.
3. If everything is satisfactory, substitute the control module with a known good test unit.

REMOVAL AND INSTALLATION

1. Disconnect the negative battery cable.
2. Locate the control module above the accelerator pedal.
3. Disconnect the connector from the module and remove from under the instrument panel.
4. The installation is the reverse of the removal procedure.
5. Connect the negative battery cable and check the entire climate control system for proper operation.

SYSTEM DIAGNOSIS

Air Conditioning Circuit

QUICK CHECK

Grand Wagoneer

1. Disconnect the wiring harness from the control module.
2. Connect the harness from tester AMGN 19-010 to the control module.
3. Connect the wiring harness to the tester.
4. Turn the ignition switch to the **ON** position.
5. Turn the air conditioning **ON** and place the temperature control lever in its coldest position.
6. Turn the tester knob to to the desired position to test the components. If the light fails to illuminate in any of the test positions, inspect the component(s) individually.

Air Conditioning Compressor

COMPRESSOR NOISE

Noises that develop during air conditioning operation can be misleading. A noise that sounds like serious compressor damage may only be a loose belt, mounting bolt or clutch assembly. Improper belt tension can also emit a noise that can be mistaken for more serious problems. Check and adjust all possible causes of the noise, including oil level, before replacing the compressor.

COMPRESSOR OIL LEVEL CHECK

Compressor Replacement

When replacing a compressor, use the following procedure to adjust the oil level of the replacement compressor to the proper level.

1. Remove the oil filler plug and service ports from both the original and replacement compressors.
2. Drain the oil from the replacement compressor through the oil fill plug into a clean container. Then rotate the clutch plate and drain any remaining oil through the discharge port.
3. Repeat Step 2 for the original compressor.
4. Fill the replacement compressor with the same amount of oil drained from the original compressor plus 1 oz.

Periodic Checking Procedure

1. Start the engine and run the air conditioning system for 10 minutes.
2. Stop the engine and disconnect the negative battery cable. Disconnect the compressor clutch connector.
3. Front seat the service valves.
4. To determine the mounting angle, position an angle gauge across the flat surfaces of the 2 front mounting ears and center the bubble. Read the mounting angle to the closest degree. Comanche, Cherokee, Wagoneer and Wrangler should have a 0 degree mounting angle. Grand Wagoneer should have a 65 degree angle.

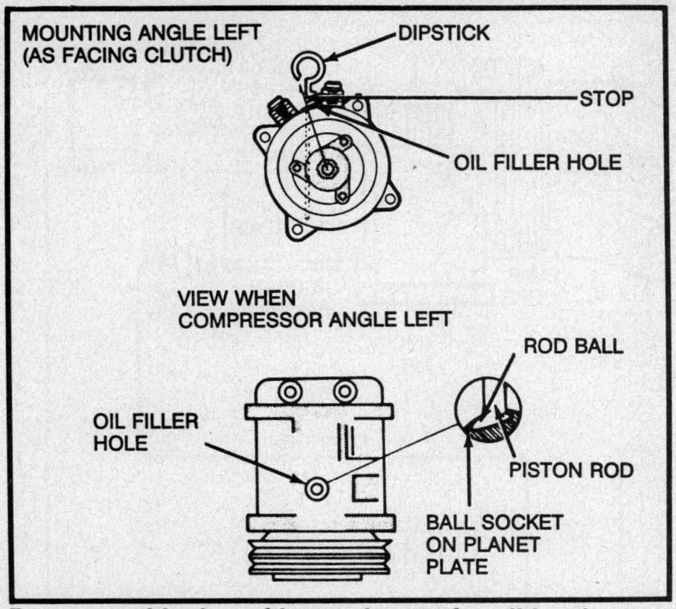
MOUNTING ANGLE LEFT
(AS FACING CLUTCH)
DIPSTICK
STOP
OIL FILLER HOLE
VIEW WHEN
COMPRESSOR ANGLE LEFT
ROD BALL
OIL FILLER
HOLE
PISTON ROD
BALL SOCKET
ON PLANET
PLATE

Proper positioning of internal parts for oil level check—SD-508 compressor

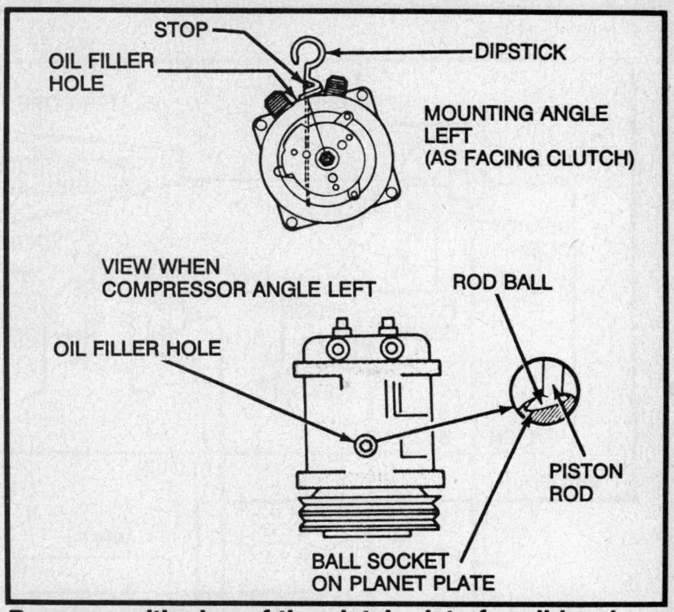
STOP
OIL FILLER
HOLE
DIPSTICK
MOUNTING ANGLE
LEFT
(AS FACING CLUTCH)
VIEW WHEN
COMPRESSOR ANGLE LEFT
ROD BALL
OIL FILLER HOLE
PISTON
ROD
BALL SOCKET
ON PLANET PLATE

Proper positioning of the clutch plate for oil level check—SD-709 compressor

5. Remove the oil filler plug.
6. For the SD-508 compressor, look through the oil filter plug hole and rotate the clutch front plate to position the internal parts out of the way of the path of the dipstick. For the SD-708 compressor, position the internal parts by rotating the clutch plate counterweight to a 30 degree angle.
7. Insert the dipstick tool J-29642-12 or equivalent, to its **STOP** position. The stop is the angle near the top of the dipstick. The bottom surface of the angle must be flush with the surface of the oil filler hole.
8. Remove the dipstick and count the number of increments (grooves) covered with oil.

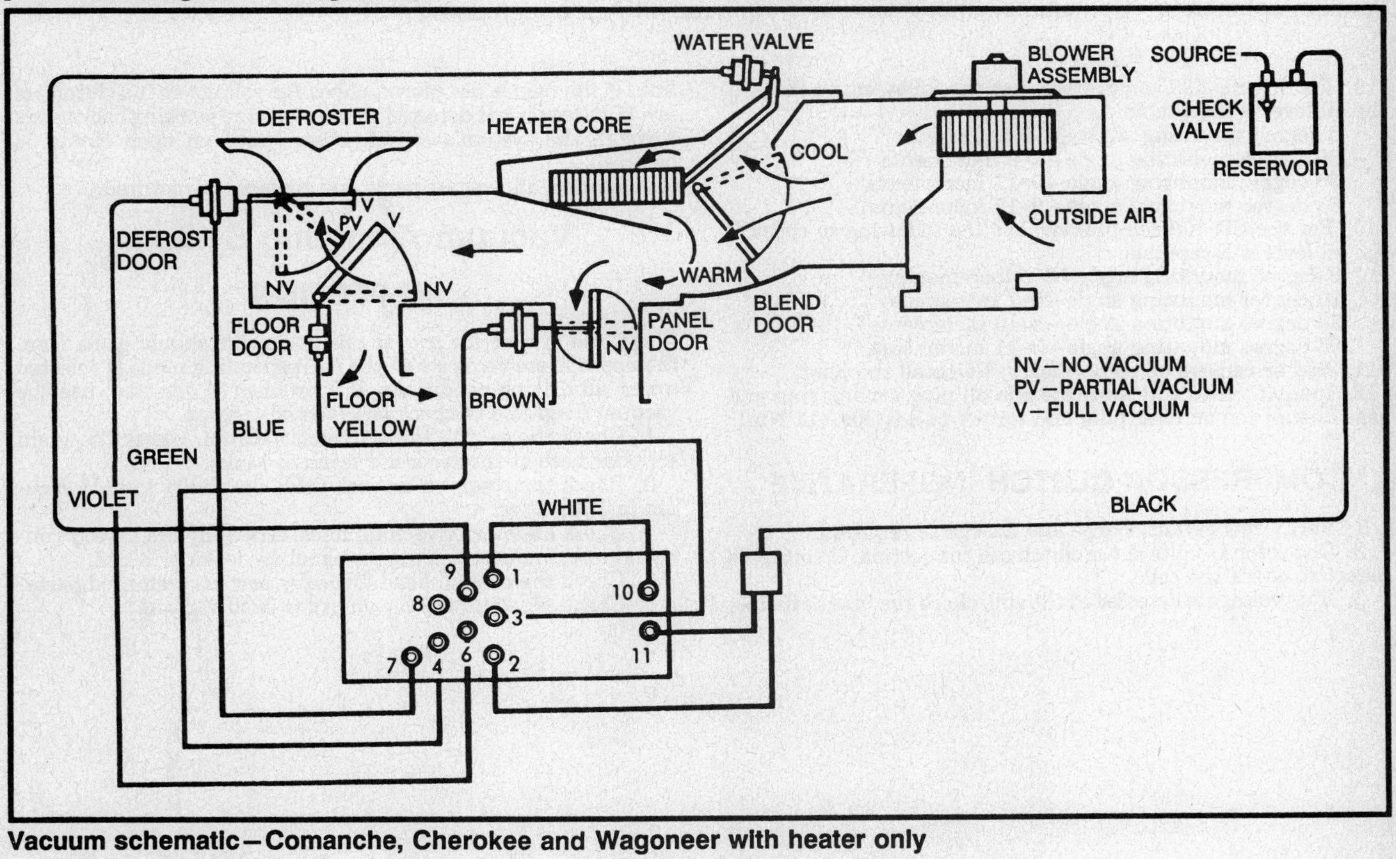
WATER VALVE
BLOWER
ASSEMBLY
SOURCE
CHECK
VALVE
RESERVOIR
DEFROSTER
HEATER CORE
COOL
OUTSIDE AIR
DEFROST
DOOR
V
PV
V
NV
NV
WARM
BLEND
DOOR
FLOOR
DOOR
PANEL
DOOR
NV
FLOOR
BROWN
BLUE
YELLOW
GREEN
VIOLET
WHITE
BLACK
NV—NO VACUUM
PV—PARTIAL VACUUM
V—FULL VACUUM
1
2
3
4
6
7
8
9
10
11

Vacuum schematic—Comanche, Cherokee and Wagoneer with heater only

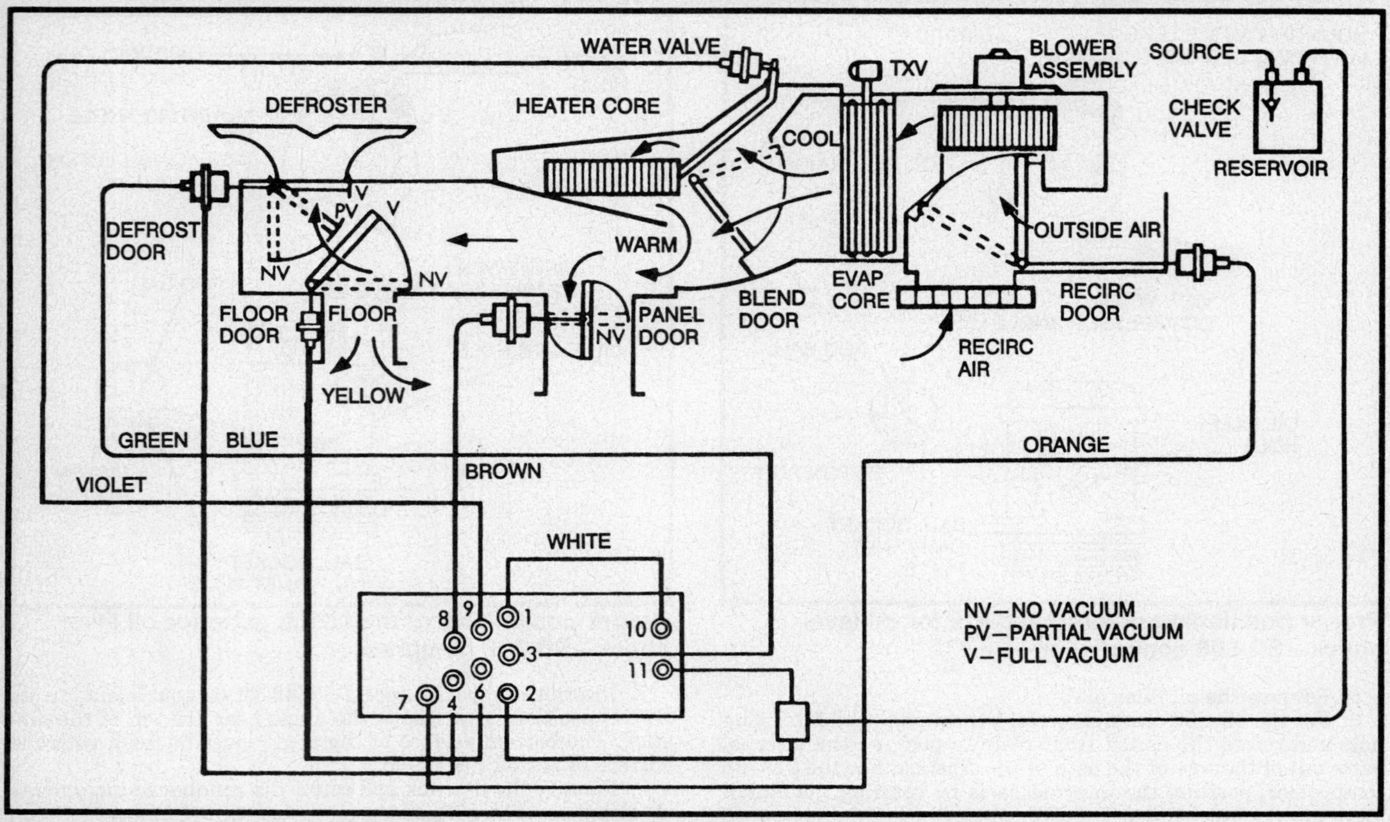
WATER VALVE
TXV
BLOWER ASSEMBLY
SOURCE
CHECK VALVE
RESERVOIR
DEFROSTER
HEATER CORE
COOL
DEFROST DOOR
V
PV
V
NV
NV
WARM
OUTSIDE AIR
FLOOR DOOR
FLOOR
PANEL DOOR
NV
BLEND DOOR
EVAP CORE
RECIRC DOOR
RECIRC AIR
YELLOW
GREEN
BLUE
VIOLET
BROWN
ORANGE
WHITE
NV—NO VACUUM
PV—PARTIAL VACUUM
V—FULL VACUUM

Vacuum schematic—Comanche, Cherokee and Wagoneer with air conditioning

9. For the SD-508 compressor, use the following to check if the oil level is acceptable:
   0 degree mounting angle—4–6 increments
   20 degree mounting angle—7–9 increments
   50 degree mounting angle—9–11 increments
   65 degree mounting angle—9–12 increments
10. For the SD-709 compressor, use the following to check if the oil level is acceptable:
   0 degree mounting angle—3–5 increments
   20 degree mounting angle—5–7 increments
   50 degree mounting angle—8–10 increments
   65 degree mounting angle—9–11 increments
11. Add or remove oil as necessary. Reinstall the plug.
12. Inspect, clean and lubricate the oil plug sealing ring and seat. Install the oil filler plug and torque to 8 ft. lbs. (11 Nm).

COMPRESSOR CLUTCH INOPERATIVE

1. Verify refrigerant charge and charge as required.
2. Check for 12 volts at the clutch coil connection. If voltage is detected, check the coil.
3. If no voltage is detected at the coil, check the fuse or fusible link. If the fuse is not blown, check for voltage at the clutch relay. If voltage is not detected there, continue working backwards through the system's switches, etc. until an open circuit is detected.
4. Inspect all suspect parts and replace, as required.

Vacuum Actuating System

INSPECTION

Check the system for proper operation. Air should come from the appropriate vents when the corresponding mode is selected under all driving conditions. If a problem is detected, use the vacuum diagrams to check the flow of vacuum.

1. Check the engine for sufficient vacuum. Check the main supplier hose at the reservoir leaks or kinks.
3. Check the reservoir's check valve for ability to hold vacuum in 1 direction.
4. Check all interior vacuum lines, especially the 11-way connection behind the instrument panel for leaks or kinks.
5. Check the control head for leaky ports or damaged parts.
6. Check all actuators for ability to hold vacuum.

WIRING SCHEMATICS

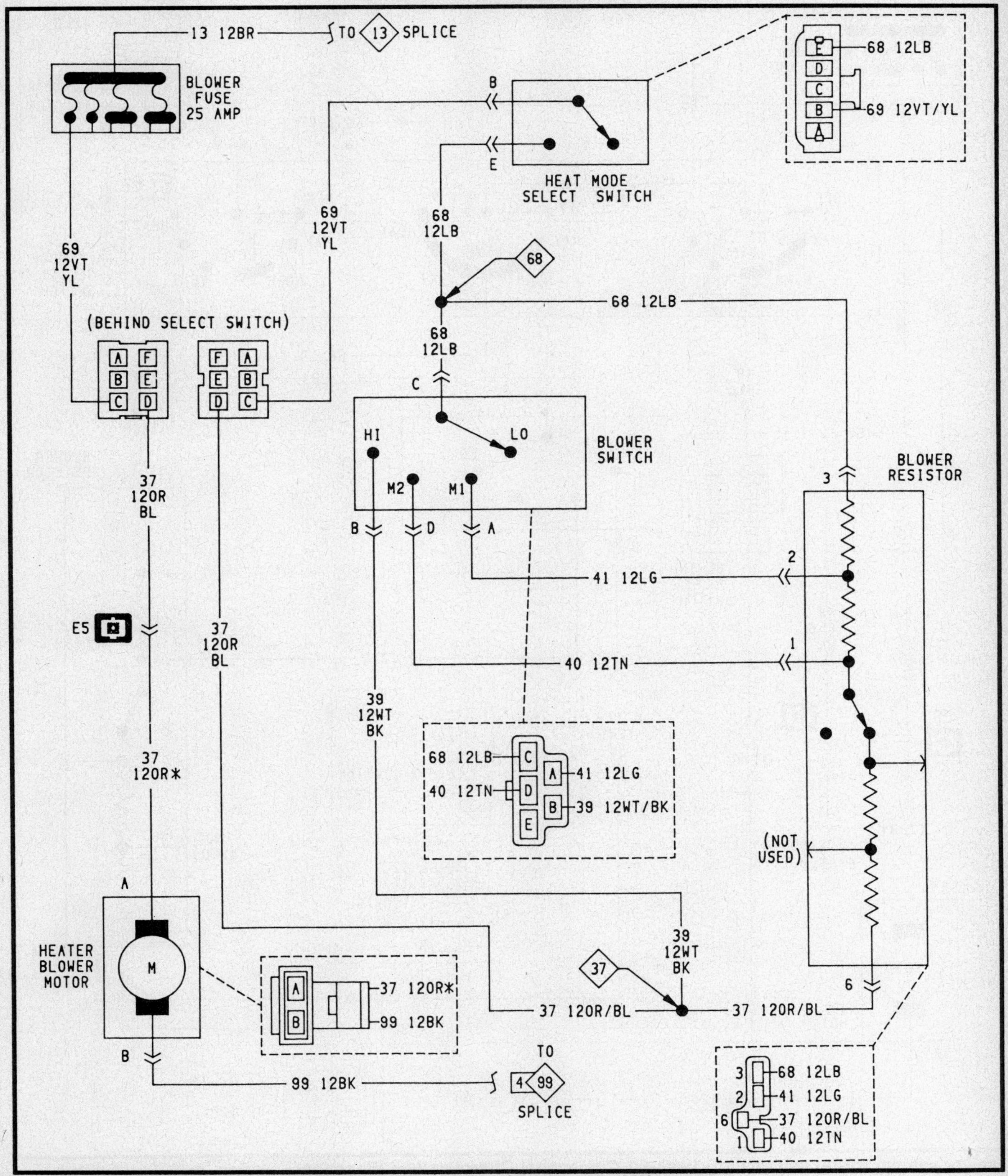
13 12BR
TO 13 SPLICE
BLOWER FUSE 25 AMP
B
E
HEAT MODE SELECT SWITCH
68 12LB
D
C
B
A
69 12VT/YL
69 12VT YL
69 12VT YL
68 12LB
68
68 12LB
68 12LB
(BEHIND SELECT SWITCH)
C
HI
LO
BLOWER SWITCH
M2
M1
B
D
A
BLOWER RESISTOR
3
2
41 12LG
1
40 12TN
37 12OR BL
37 12OR BL
E5
39 12WT BK
68 12LB
40 12TN
41 12LG
39 12WT/BK
(NOT USED)
37 12OR*
A
HEATER BLOWER MOTOR
M
37 12OR*
99 12BK
39 12WT BK
37
6
37 12OR/BL
37 12OR/BL
B
99 12BK
TO
4 99
SPLICE
3 68 12LB
2 41 12LG
6 37 12OR/BL
1 40 12TN

Heater system wiring schematic—1989–90 Comanche, Cherokee and Wagoneer

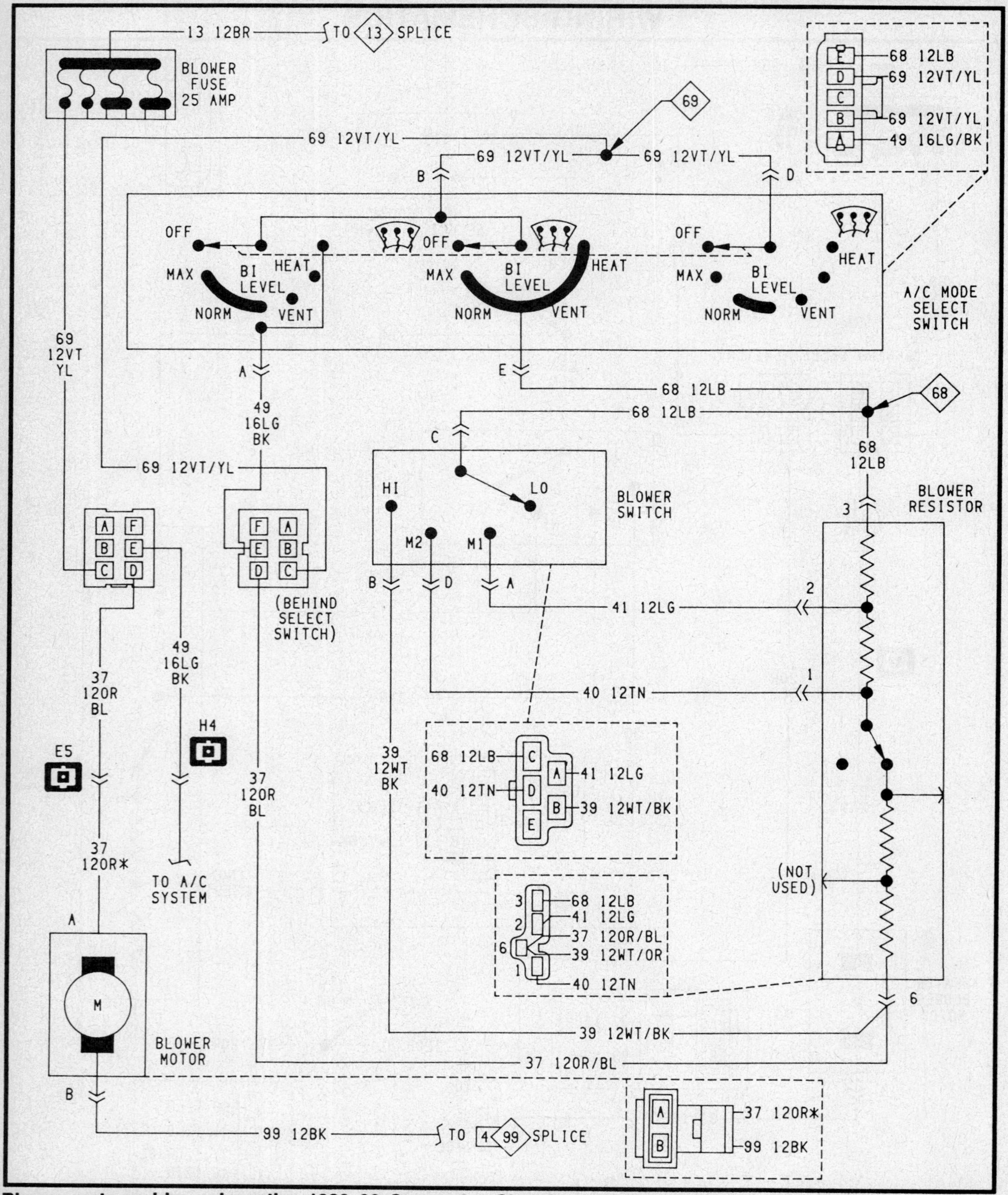
13 12BR
TO 13 SPLICE
BLOWER FUSE 25 AMP
69 12VT/YL
69
69 12VT/YL
69 12VT/YL
B
D
68 12LB
69 12VT/YL
69 12VT/YL
49 16LG/BK
OFF
MAX
BI LEVEL
HEAT
NORM
VENT
OFF
MAX
BI LEVEL
HEAT
NORM
VENT
OFF
MAX
BI LEVEL
HEAT
NORM
VENT
A/C MODE SELECT SWITCH
69 12VT YL
A
49 16LG BK
E
68 12LB
68
68 12LB
C
68 12LB
69 12VT/YL
HI
LO
M2
M1
BLOWER SWITCH
BLOWER RESISTOR
3
B
D
A
(BEHIND SELECT SWITCH)
41 12LG
2
40 12TN
1
37 12OR BL
49 16LG BK
H4
E5
37 12OR*
TO A/C SYSTEM
39 12WT BK
37 12OR BL
68 12LB
41 12LG
40 12TN
39 12WT/BK
68 12LB
41 12LG
37 12OR/BL
39 12WT/OR
40 12TN
(NOT USED)
6
A
M
BLOWER MOTOR
39 12WT/BK
37 12OR/BL
B
99 12BK
TO 4 99 SPLICE
37 12OR*
99 12BK

Blower system wiring schematic—1989–90 Comanche, Cherokee and Wagoneer

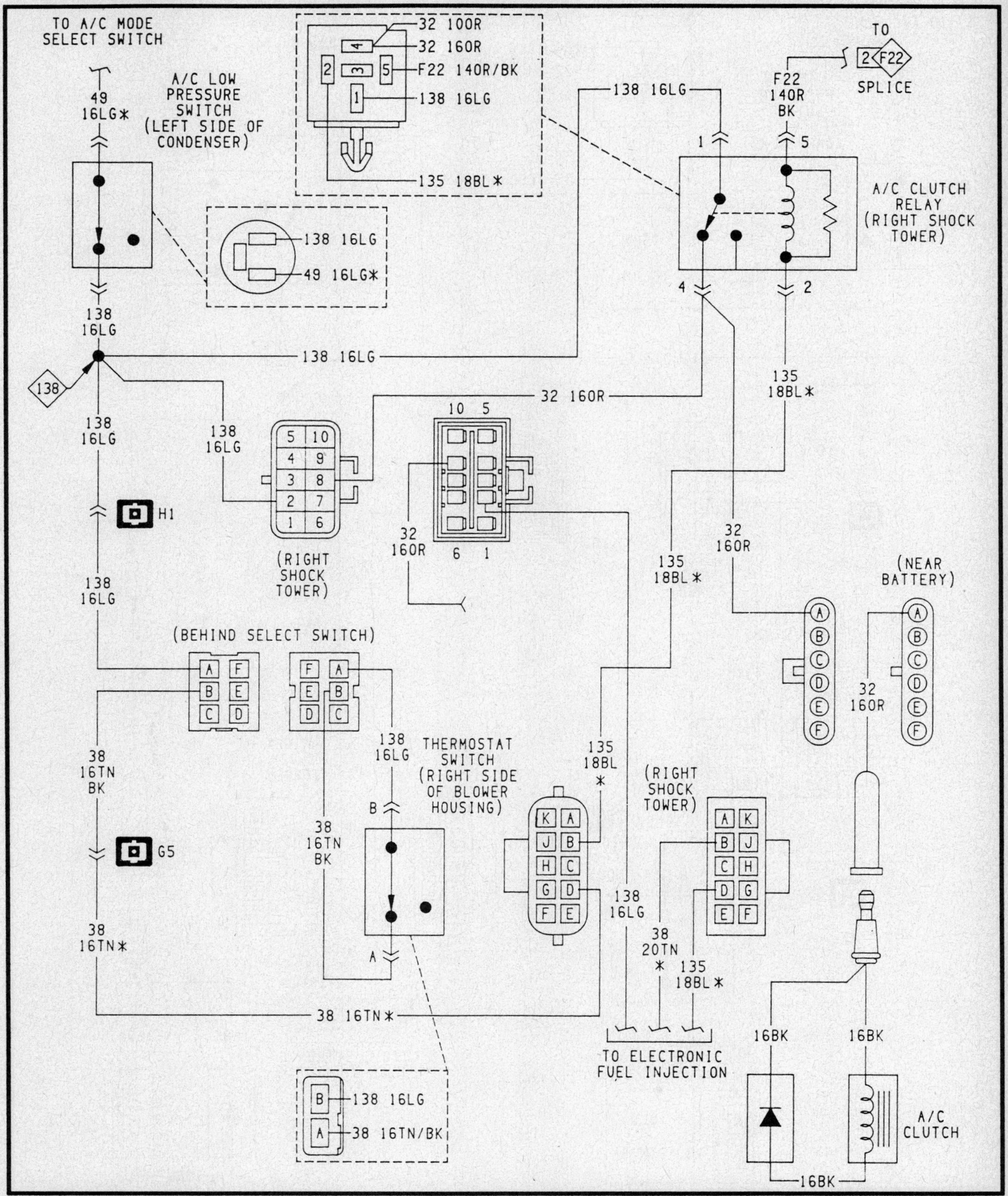
TO A/C MODE SELECT SWITCH
49 16LG*
A/C LOW PRESSURE SWITCH (LEFT SIDE OF CONDENSER)
32 10OR
32 16OR
F22 14OR/BK
138 16LG
135 18BL*
138 16LG
49 16LG*
TO
2 F22
SPLICE
F22 14OR BK
138 16LG
A/C CLUTCH RELAY (RIGHT SHOCK TOWER)
138 16LG
138
138 16LG
32 16OR
135 18BL*
138 16LG
H1
(RIGHT SHOCK TOWER)
32 16OR
135 18BL*
32 16OR
(NEAR BATTERY)
(BEHIND SELECT SWITCH)
38 16TN BK
138 16LG
THERMOSTAT SWITCH (RIGHT SIDE OF BLOWER HOUSING)
G5
38 16TN BK
135 18BL *
(RIGHT SHOCK TOWER)
32 16OR
38 16TN*
138 16LG
38 20TN *
135 18BL*
38 16TN*
TO ELECTRONIC FUEL INJECTION
16BK
16BK
138 16LG
38 16TN/BK
A/C CLUTCH
16BK

Air conditioning system wiring schematic—1989–90 Comanche, Cherokee and Wagoneer with 2.5L engine

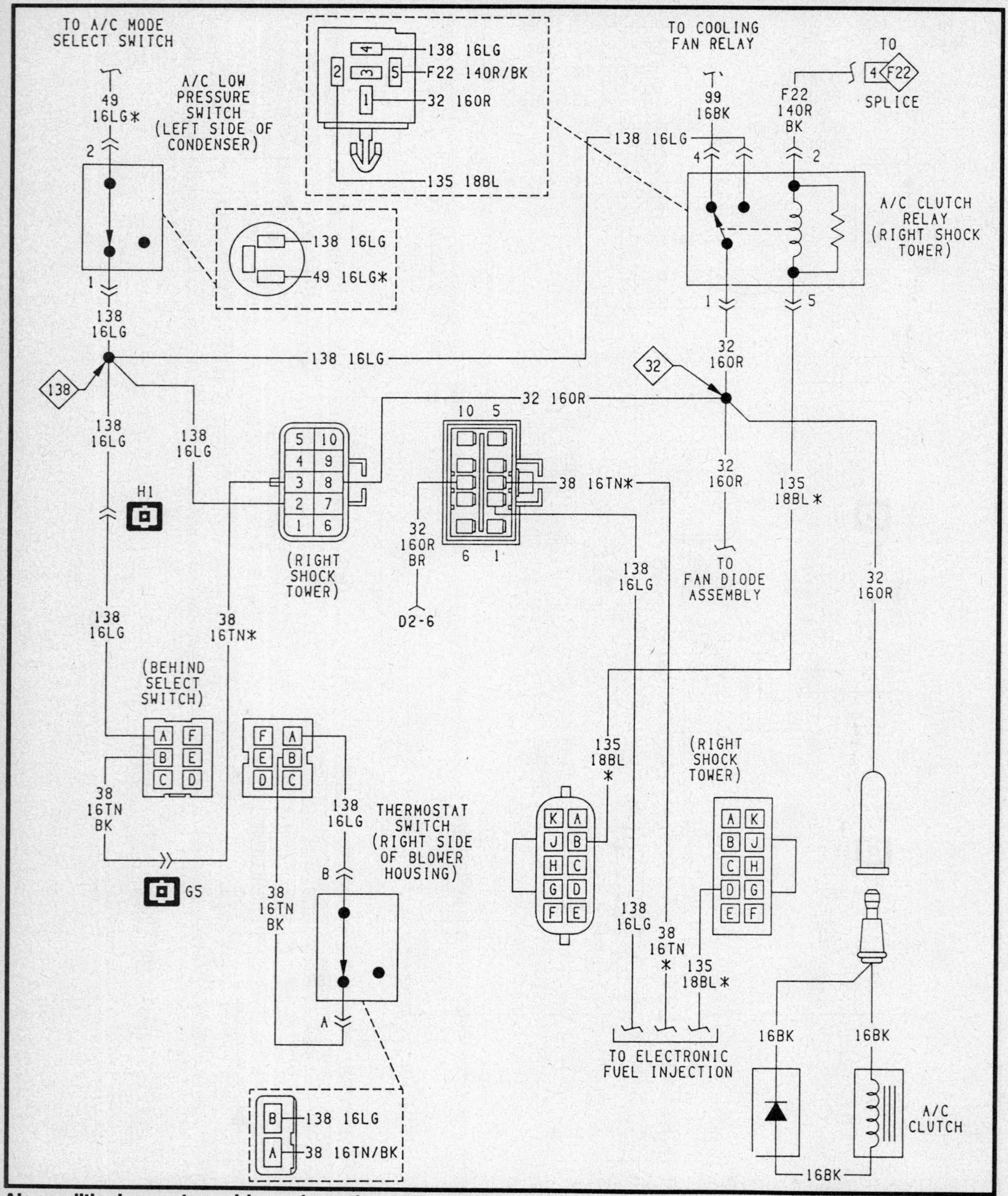
TO A/C MODE SELECT SWITCH
A/C LOW PRESSURE SWITCH (LEFT SIDE OF CONDENSER)
49 16LG*
138 16LG
TO COOLING FAN RELAY
99 16BK
F22 140R BK
TO
4 F22
SPLICE
32 160R
135 18BL
F22 140R/BK
A/C CLUTCH RELAY (RIGHT SHOCK TOWER)
(RIGHT SHOCK TOWER)
38 16TN*
D2-6
32 160R BR
TO FAN DIODE ASSEMBLY
135 18BL*
H1
G5
(BEHIND SELECT SWITCH)
38 16TN BK
THERMOSTAT SWITCH (RIGHT SIDE OF BLOWER HOUSING)
38 16TN/BK
TO ELECTRONIC FUEL INJECTION
16BK
A/C CLUTCH

Air conditioning system wiring schematic—1989–90 Comanche, Cherokee and Wagoneer with 4.0L engine

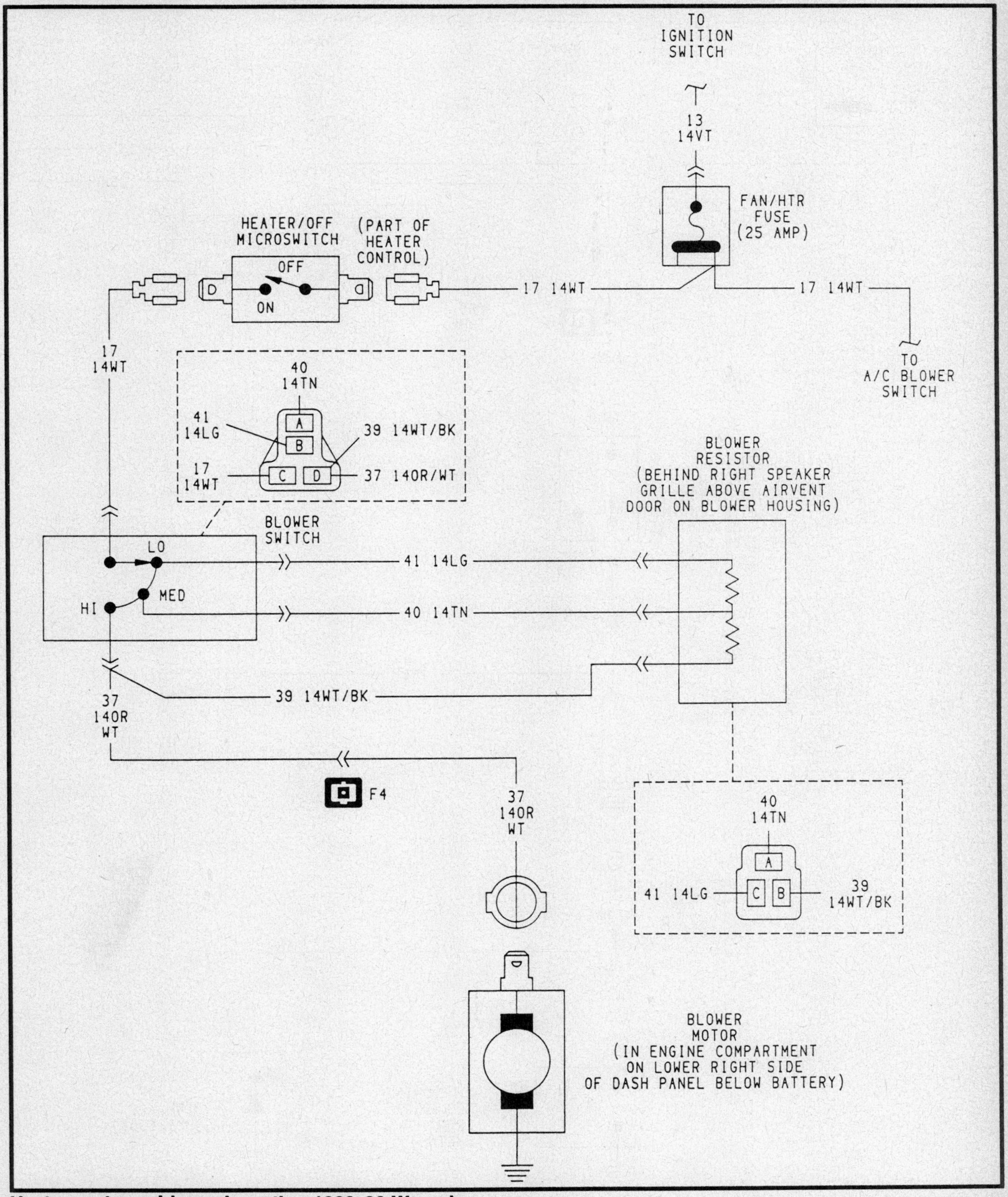
TO
IGNITION
SWITCH
13
14VT
FAN/HTR
FUSE
(25 AMP)
HEATER/OFF
MICROSWITCH
(PART OF
HEATER
CONTROL)
OFF
ON
17 14WT
17 14WT
TO
A/C BLOWER
SWITCH
17
14WT
40
14TN
41
14LG
A
B
39 14WT/BK
17
14WT
C
D
37 14OR/WT
BLOWER
RESISTOR
(BEHIND RIGHT SPEAKER
GRILLE ABOVE AIRVENT
DOOR ON BLOWER HOUSING)
BLOWER
SWITCH
LO
MED
HI
41 14LG
40 14TN
39 14WT/BK
37
14OR
WT
F4
37
14OR
WT
40
14TN
A
41 14LG
C
B
39
14WT/BK
BLOWER
MOTOR
(IN ENGINE COMPARTMENT
ON LOWER RIGHT SIDE
OF DASH PANEL BELOW BATTERY)

Heater system wiring schematic—1989–90 Wrangler

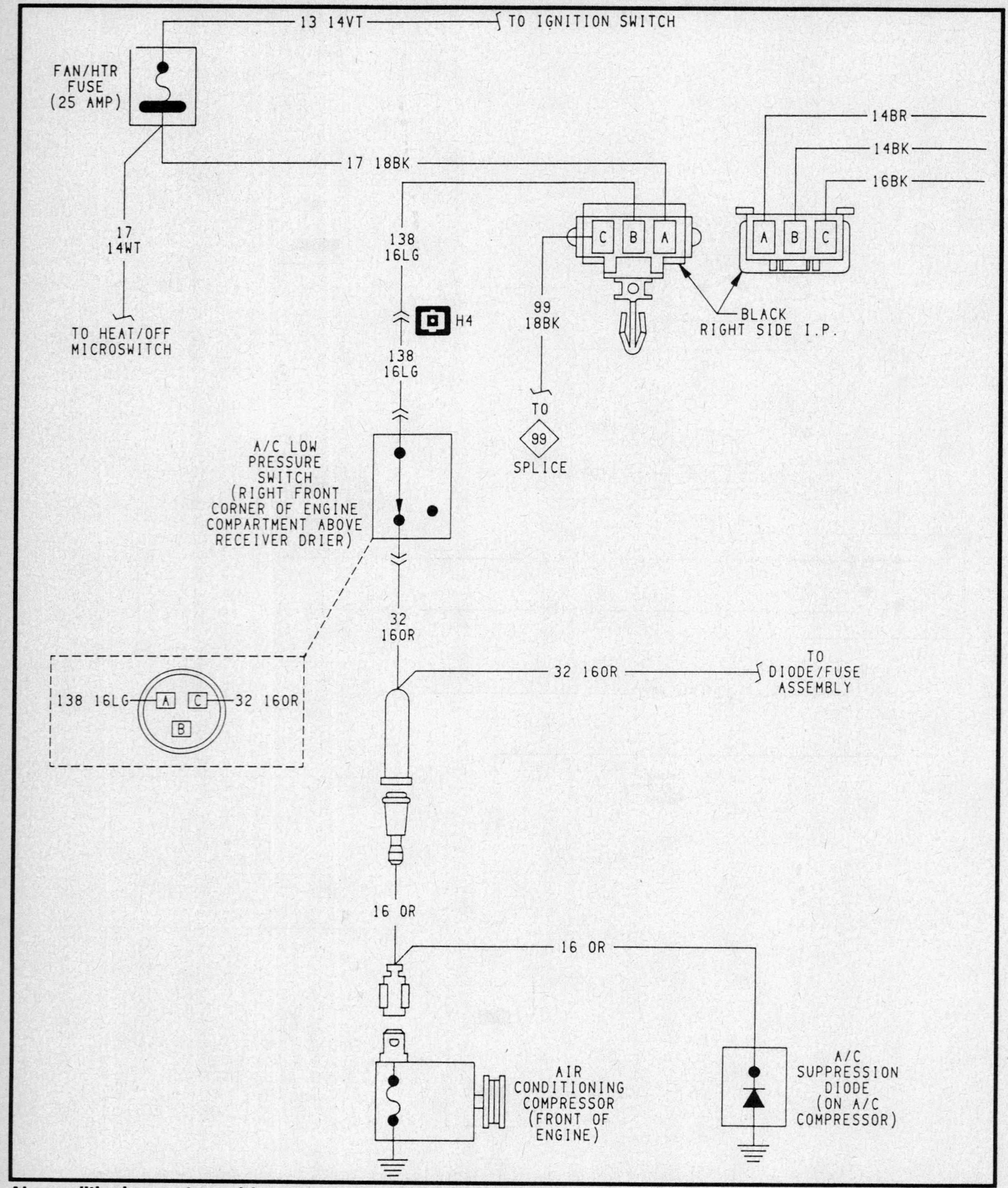
13 14VT
TO IGNITION SWITCH
FAN/HTR FUSE (25 AMP)
17 18BK
14BR
14BK
16BK
17 14WT
138 16LG
C B A
A B C
99 18BK
BLACK RIGHT SIDE I.P.
H4
TO HEAT/OFF MICROSWITCH
138 16LG
TO
99
SPLICE
A/C LOW PRESSURE SWITCH (RIGHT FRONT CORNER OF ENGINE COMPARTMENT ABOVE RECEIVER DRIER)
32 16OR
32 16OR
TO DIODE/FUSE ASSEMBLY
138 16LG
A
C
32 16OR
B
16 OR
16 OR
AIR CONDITIONING COMPRESSOR (FRONT OF ENGINE)
A/C SUPPRESSION DIODE (ON A/C COMPRESSOR)

Air conditioning system wiring schematic—1989–90 Wrangler

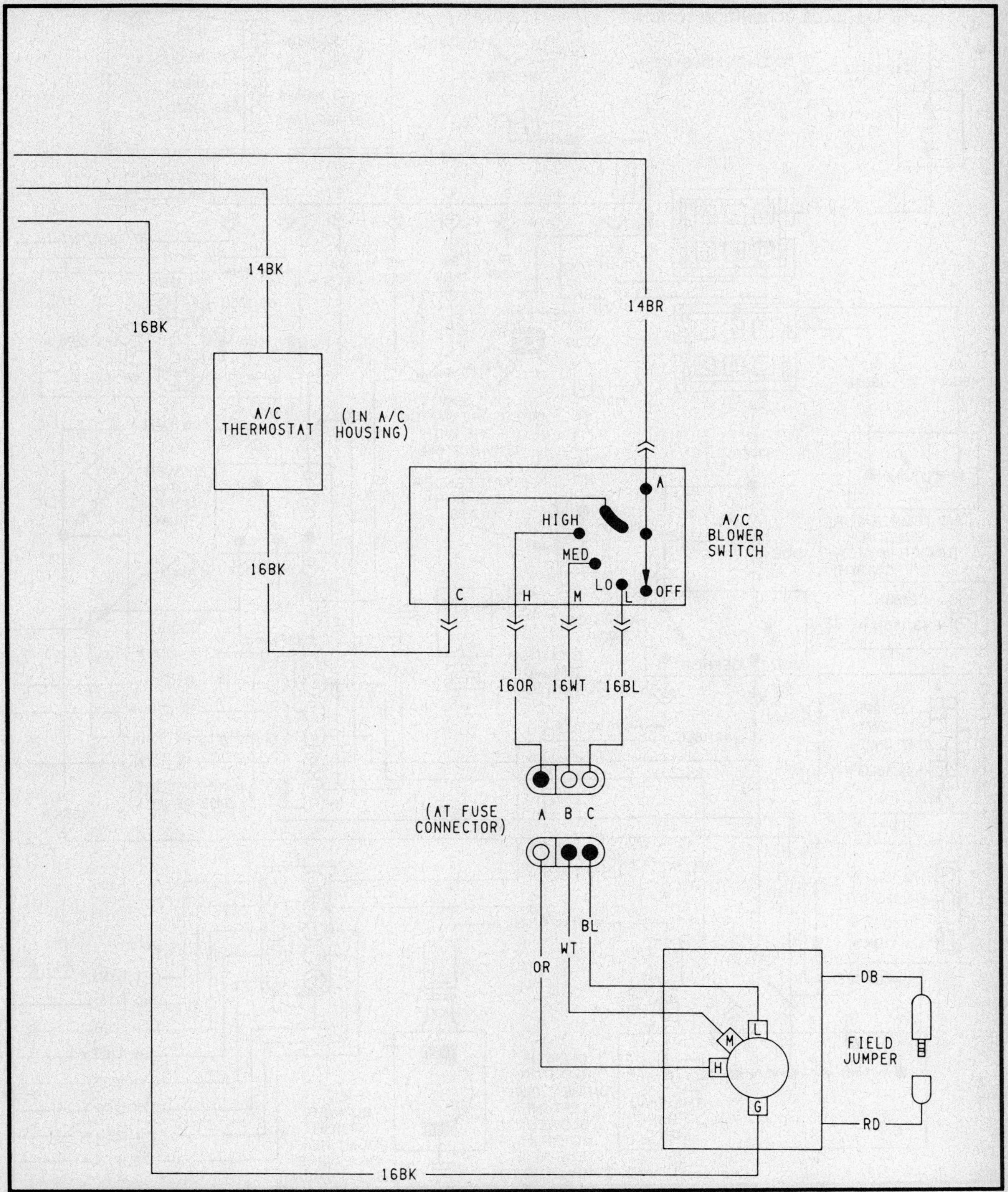
14BK
16BK
14BR
A/C THERMOSTAT
(IN A/C HOUSING)
16BK
A
HIGH
MED
LO
OFF
A/C BLOWER SWITCH
C
H
M
L
16OR
16WT
16BL
(AT FUSE CONNECTOR)
A
B
C
BL
WT
OR
DB
M
L
H
G
FIELD JUMPER
RD
16BK

Air conditioning system wiring schematic—1989–90 Wrangler

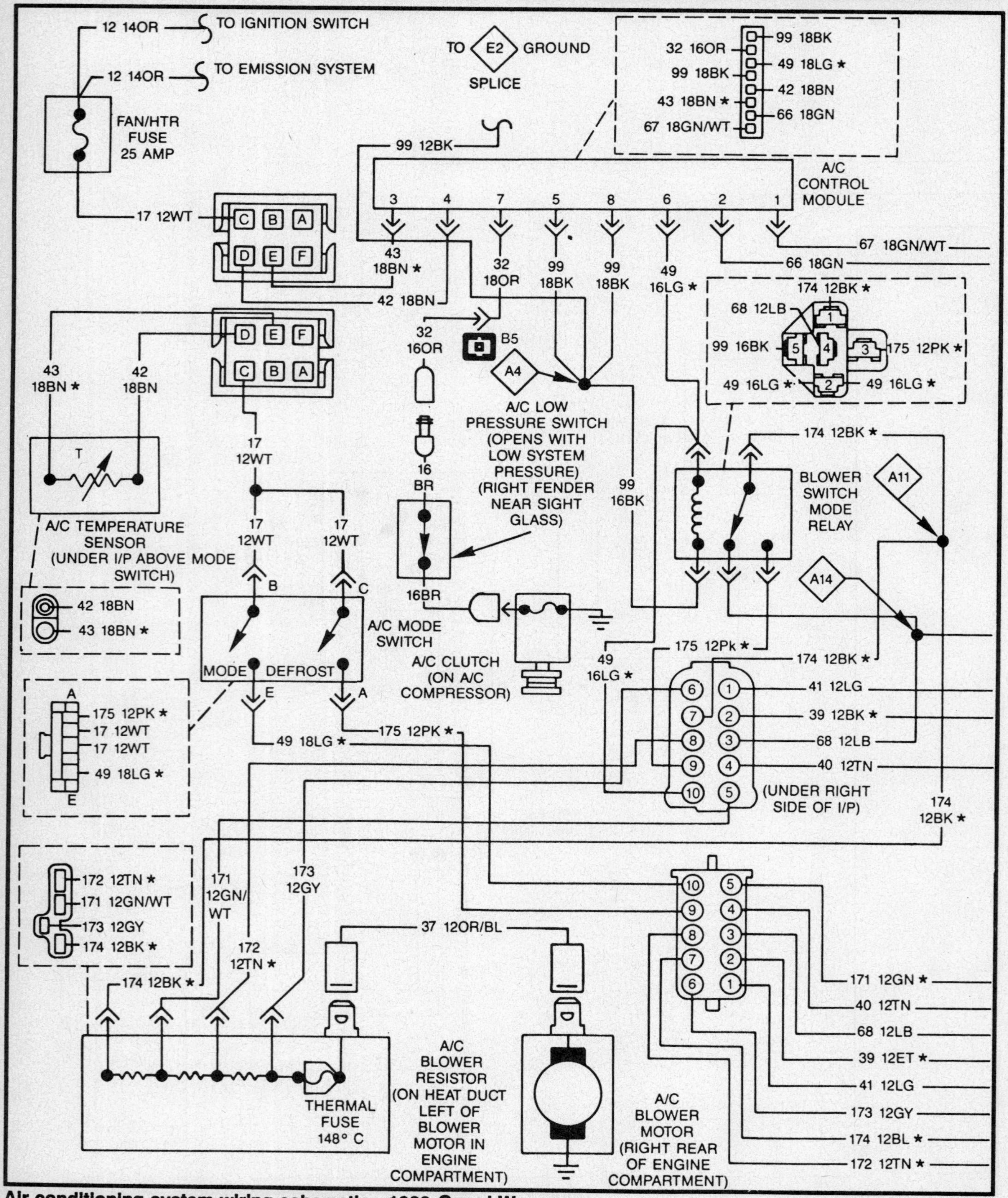
12 14OR
TO IGNITION SWITCH
12 14OR
TO EMISSION SYSTEM
FAN/HTR FUSE 25 AMP
TO E2 GROUND SPLICE
32 16OR
99 18BK
43 18BN ★
67 18GN/WT
99 18BK
49 18LG ★
42 18BN
66 18GN
99 12BK
A/C CONTROL MODULE
17 12WT
43 18BN ★
32 18OR
99 18BK
99 18BK
49 16LG ★
67 18GN/WT
66 18GN
42 18BN
174 12BK ★
68 12LB
99 16BK
175 12PK ★
49 16LG ★
49 16LG ★
43 18BN ★
42 18BN
32 16OR
B5
A4
A/C LOW PRESSURE SWITCH (OPENS WITH LOW SYSTEM PRESSURE) (RIGHT FENDER NEAR SIGHT GLASS)
16 BR
99 16BK
17 12WT
174 12BK ★
BLOWER SWITCH MODE RELAY
A11
A/C TEMPERATURE SENSOR (UNDER I/P ABOVE MODE SWITCH)
17 12WT
17 12WT
42 18BN
43 18BN ★
16BR
A14
A/C MODE SWITCH
MODE
DEFROST
A/C CLUTCH (ON A/C COMPRESSOR)
175 12Pk ★
174 12BK ★
49 16LG ★
41 12LG
39 12BK ★
68 12LB
40 12TN
175 12PK ★
17 12WT
17 12WT
49 18LG ★
49 18LG ★
175 12PK ★
(UNDER RIGHT SIDE OF I/P)
174 12BK ★
172 12TN ★
171 12GN/WT
173 12GY
174 12BK ★
171 12GN/WT
173 12GY
37 12OR/BL
172 12TN ★
174 12BK ★
171 12GN ★
40 12TN
68 12LB
39 12ET ★
41 12LG
173 12GY
174 12BL ★
172 12TN ★
THERMAL FUSE 148° C
A/C BLOWER RESISTOR (ON HEAT DUCT LEFT OF BLOWER MOTOR IN ENGINE COMPARTMENT)
A/C BLOWER MOTOR (RIGHT REAR OF ENGINE COMPARTMENT)

Air conditioning system wiring schematic—1989 Grand Wagoneer

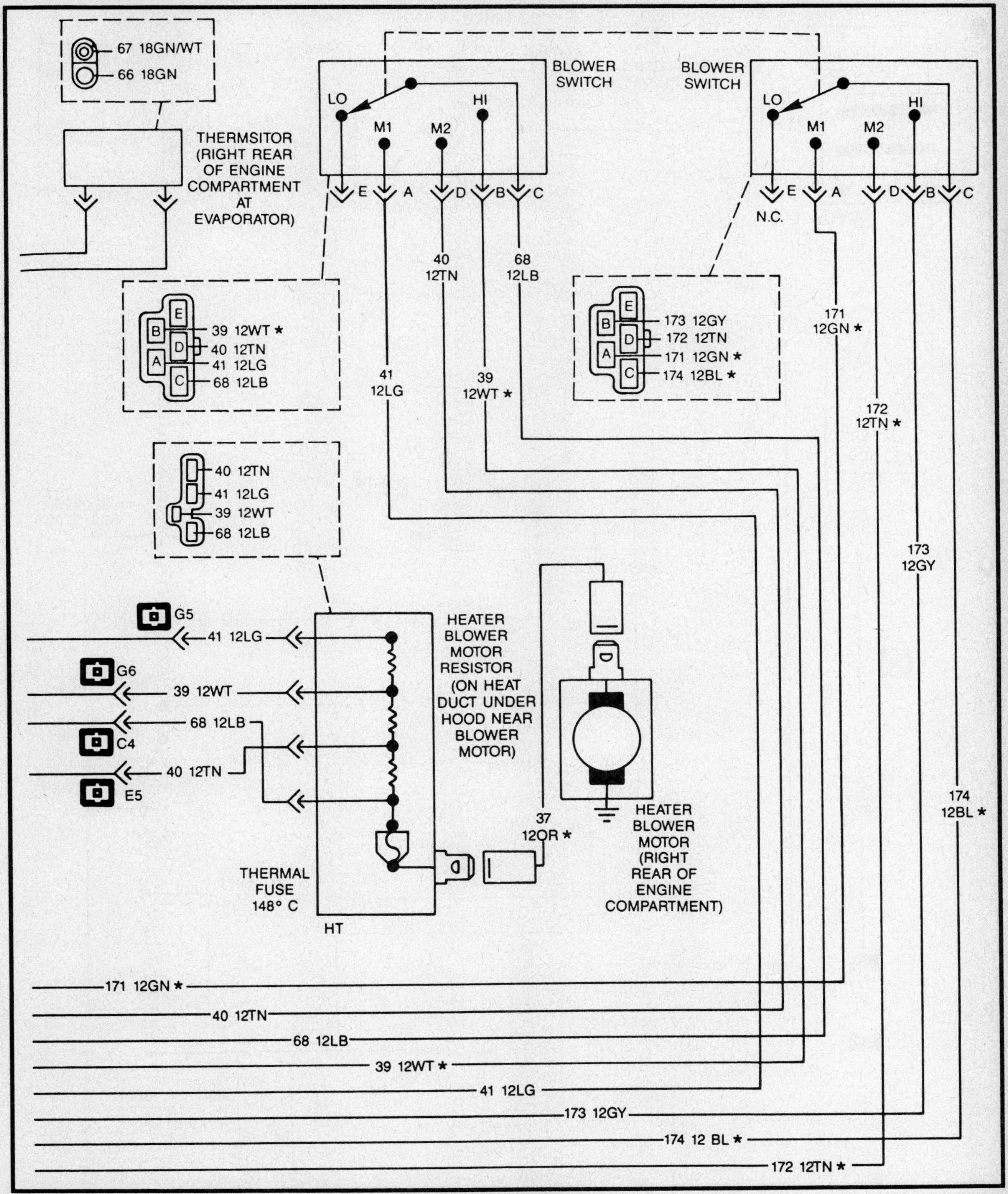
67 18GN/WT
66 18GN
THERMSITOR (RIGHT REAR OF ENGINE COMPARTMENT AT EVAPORATOR)
BLOWER SWITCH
LO
HI
M1
M2
E
A
D
B
C
40 12TN
68 12LB
41 12LG
39 12WT *
BLOWER SWITCH
N.C.
171 12GN *
172 12TN *
173 12GY
174 12BL *
39 12WT *
40 12TN
41 12LG
68 12LB
173 12GY
172 12TN
171 12GN *
174 12BL *
40 12TN
41 12LG
39 12WT
68 12LB
G5
G6
C4
E5
41 12LG
39 12WT
68 12LB
40 12TN
HEATER BLOWER MOTOR RESISTOR (ON HEAT DUCT UNDER HOOD NEAR BLOWER MOTOR)
37 12OR *
HEATER BLOWER MOTOR (RIGHT REAR OF ENGINE COMPARTMENT)
THERMAL FUSE 148° C
HT
171 12GN *
40 12TN
68 12LB
39 12WT *
41 12LG
173 12GY
174 12 BL *
172 12TN *

Air conditioning system wiring schematic—1989 Grand Wagoneer

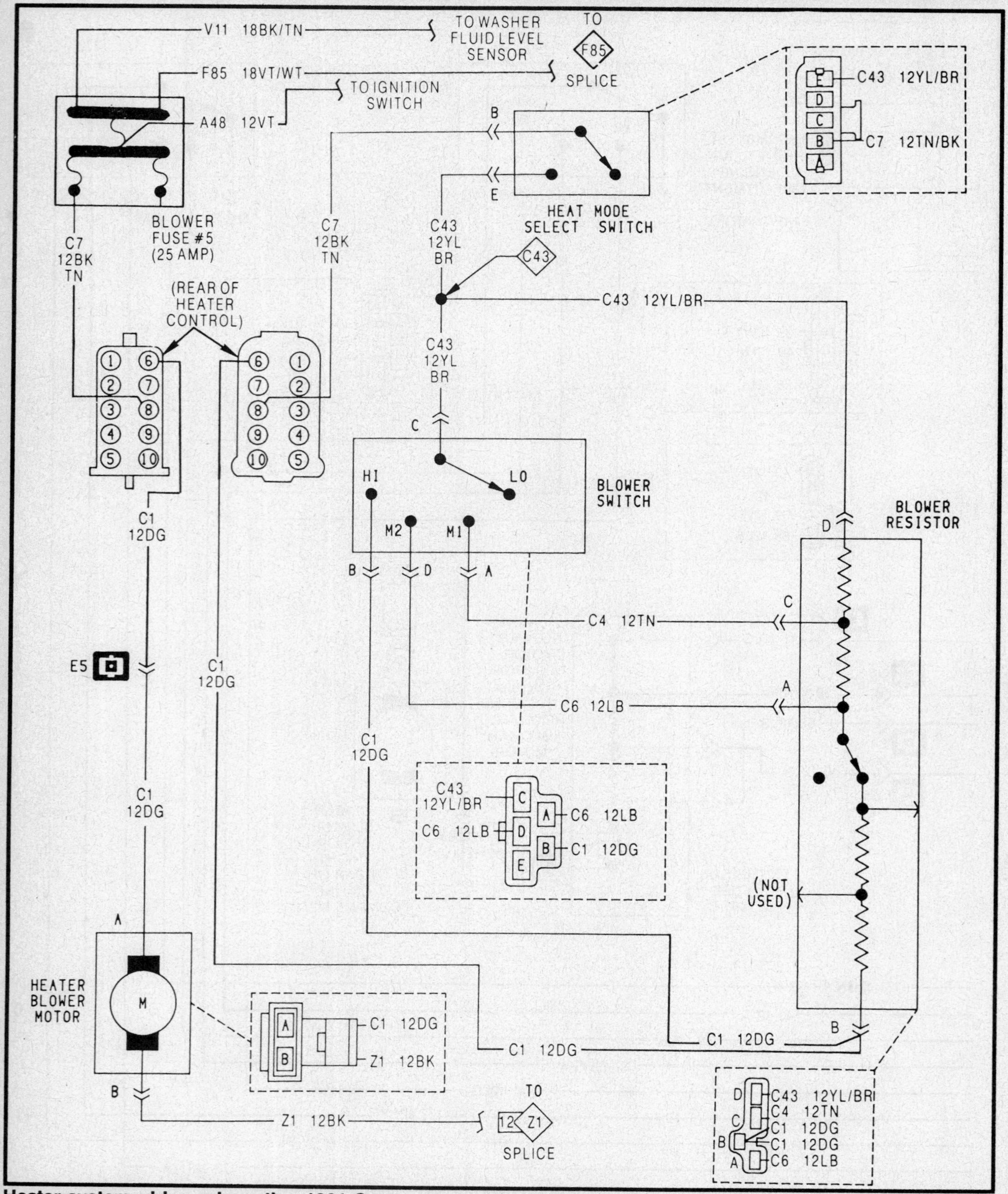
V11 18BK/TN
TO WASHER FLUID LEVEL SENSOR
F85 18VT/WT
TO F85 SPLICE
TO IGNITION SWITCH
A48 12VT
B
E
HEAT MODE SELECT SWITCH
C43 12YL/BR
C7 12TN/BK
BLOWER FUSE #5 (25 AMP)
C7 12BK TN
C43 12YL BR
(REAR OF HEATER CONTROL)
BLOWER SWITCH
HI
LO
M2
M1
C1 12DG
E5
C4 12TN
C6 12LB
BLOWER RESISTOR
(NOT USED)
HEATER BLOWER MOTOR
M
Z1 12BK
TO Z1 SPLICE

Heater system wiring schematic—1991 Comanche and Cherokee

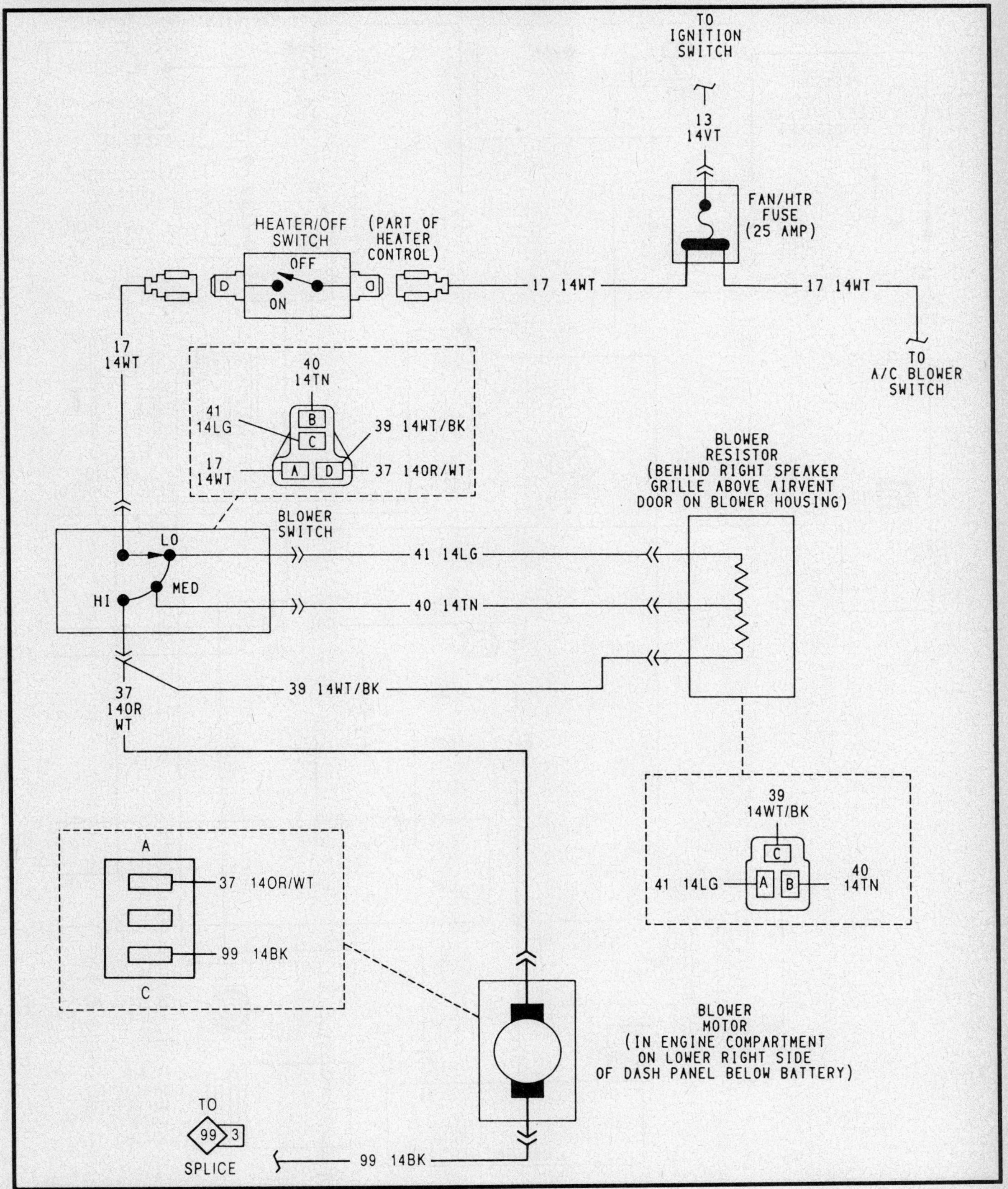
TO
IGNITION
SWITCH
13
14VT
FAN/HTR
FUSE
(25 AMP)
HEATER/OFF
SWITCH
(PART OF
HEATER
CONTROL)
OFF
ON
D
17 14WT
17 14WT
TO
A/C BLOWER
SWITCH
17
14WT
40
14TN
41
14LG
B
C
39 14WT/BK
17
14WT
A
D
37 14OR/WT
BLOWER
SWITCH
LO
MED
HI
41 14LG
40 14TN
39 14WT/BK
BLOWER
RESISTOR
(BEHIND RIGHT SPEAKER
GRILLE ABOVE AIRVENT
DOOR ON BLOWER HOUSING)
37
14OR
WT
39
14WT/BK
C
41 14LG
A
B
40
14TN
A
37 14OR/WT
99 14BK
C
BLOWER
MOTOR
(IN ENGINE COMPARTMENT
ON LOWER RIGHT SIDE
OF DASH PANEL BELOW BATTERY)
TO
99
3
SPLICE
99 14BK

Heater system wiring schematic—1991 Wrangler

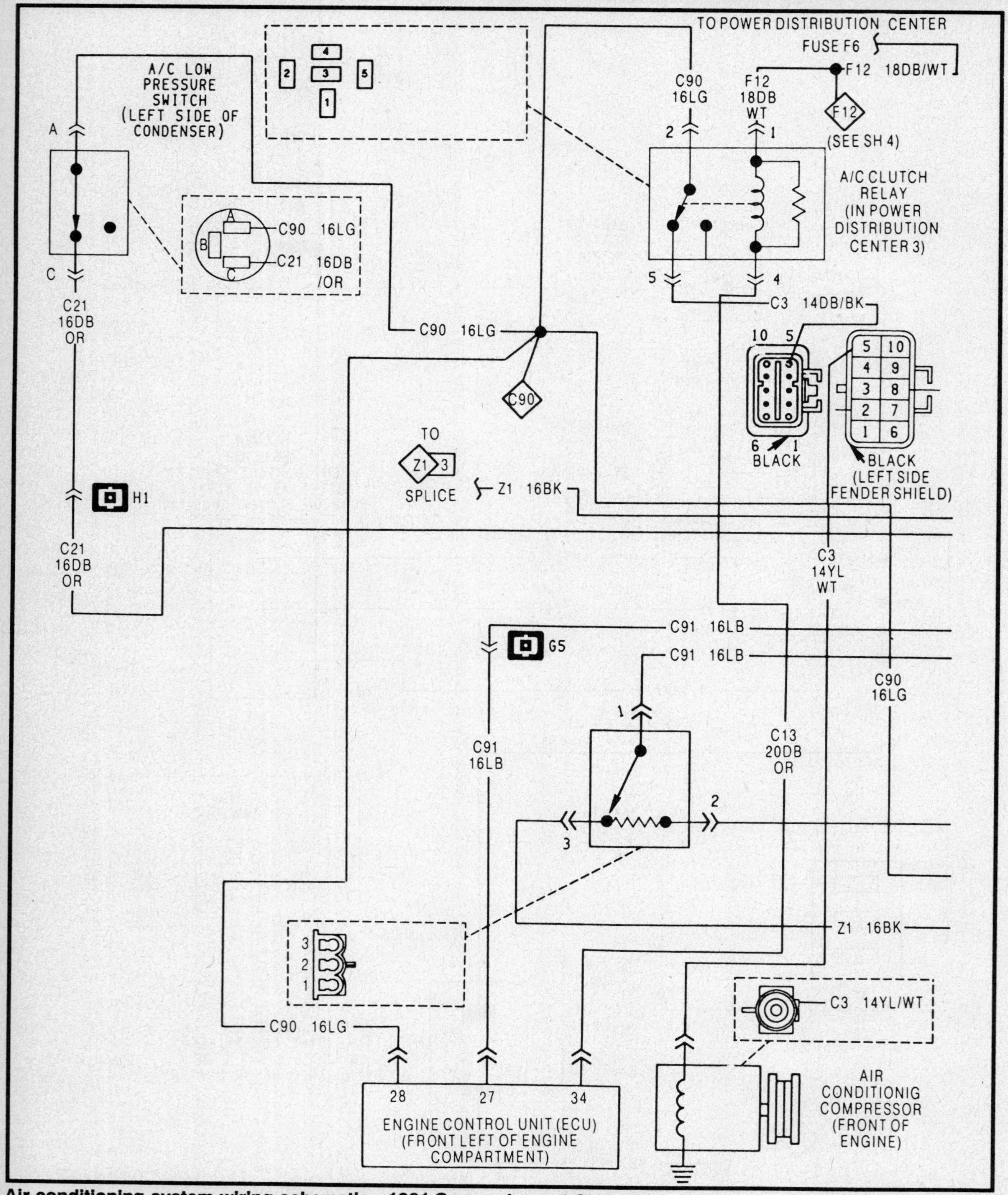
TO POWER DISTRIBUTION CENTER
FUSE F6
F12 18DB/WT
A/C LOW PRESSURE SWITCH (LEFT SIDE OF CONDENSER)
C90 16LG
F12 18DB WT
F12
(SEE SH 4)
A/C CLUTCH RELAY (IN POWER DISTRIBUTION CENTER 3)
C90 16LG
C21 16DB /OR
C21 16DB OR
C90 16LG
C3 14DB/BK
C90
BLACK
BLACK (LEFT SIDE FENDER SHIELD)
TO Z1 3 SPLICE
Z1 16BK
H1
C21 16DB OR
C3 14YL WT
C91 16LB
G5
C91 16LB
C90 16LG
C91 16LB
C13 20DB OR
Z1 16BK
C3 14YL/WT
C90 16LG
28 27 34
ENGINE CONTROL UNIT (ECU) (FRONT LEFT OF ENGINE COMPARTMENT)
AIR CONDITIONIG COMPRESSOR (FRONT OF ENGINE)

Air conditioning system wiring schematic—1991 Comanche and Cherokee

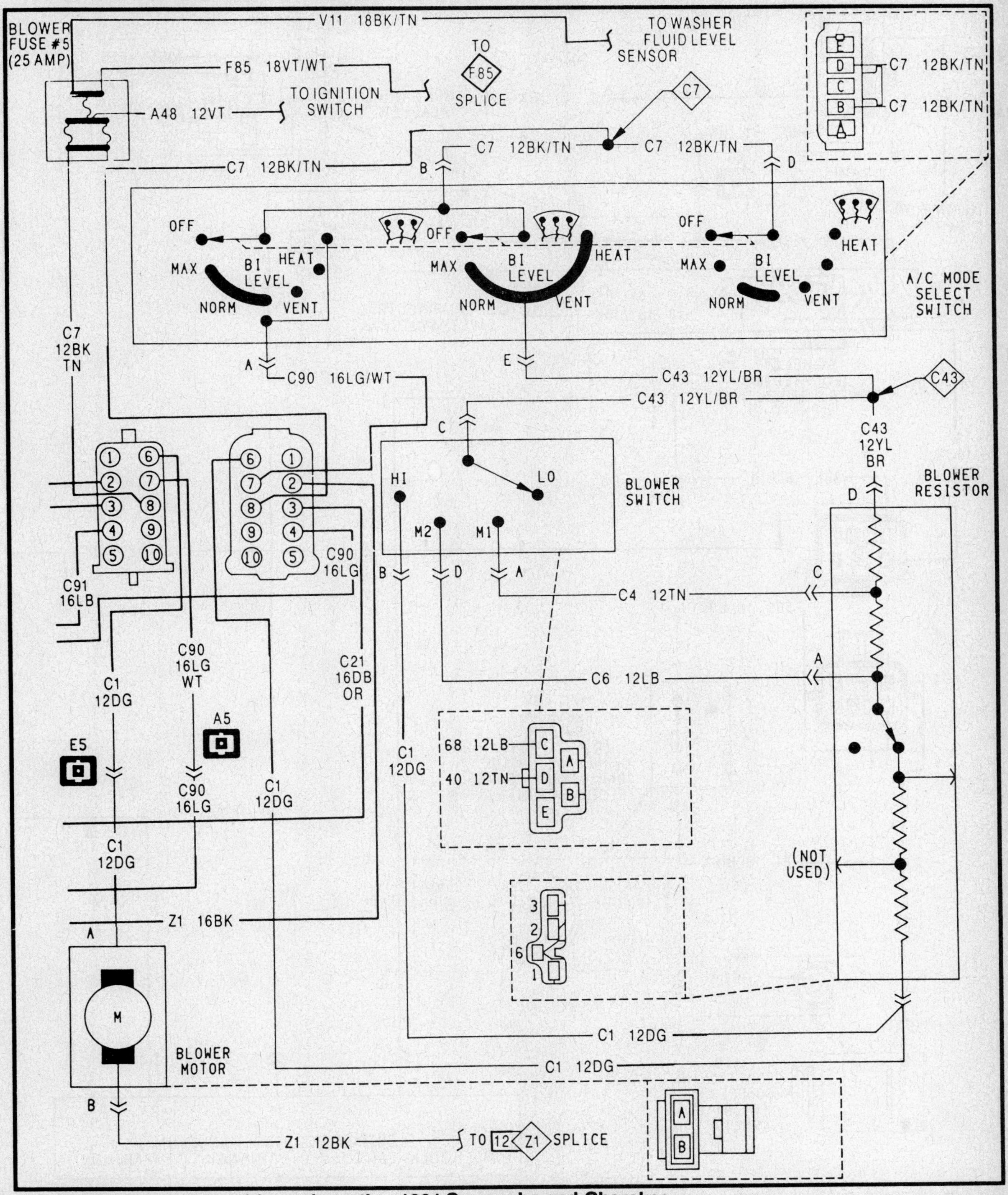
BLOWER FUSE #5 (25 AMP)
V11 18BK/TN
TO WASHER FLUID LEVEL SENSOR
F85 18VT/WT
TO F85 SPLICE
A48 12VT
TO IGNITION SWITCH
C7
C7 12BK/TN
C7 12BK/TN
C7 12BK/TN
C7 12BK/TN
C7 12BK/TN
OFF
MAX
BI LEVEL
HEAT
NORM
VENT
A/C MODE SELECT SWITCH
C7 12BK TN
C90 16LG/WT
C43 12YL/BR
C43 12YL/BR
C43
C43 12YL BR
BLOWER RESISTOR
HI
LO
M2
M1
BLOWER SWITCH
C90 16LG
C91 16LB
C4 12TN
C6 12LB
C90 16LG WT
C21 16DB OR
C1 12DG
E5
A5
C90 16LG
C1 12DG
68 12LB
40 12TN
(NOT USED)
C1 12DG
Z1 16BK
C1 12DG
C1 12DG
BLOWER MOTOR
M
Z1 12BK
TO 12 Z1 SPLICE

Air conditioning system wiring schematic—1991 Comanche and Cherokee

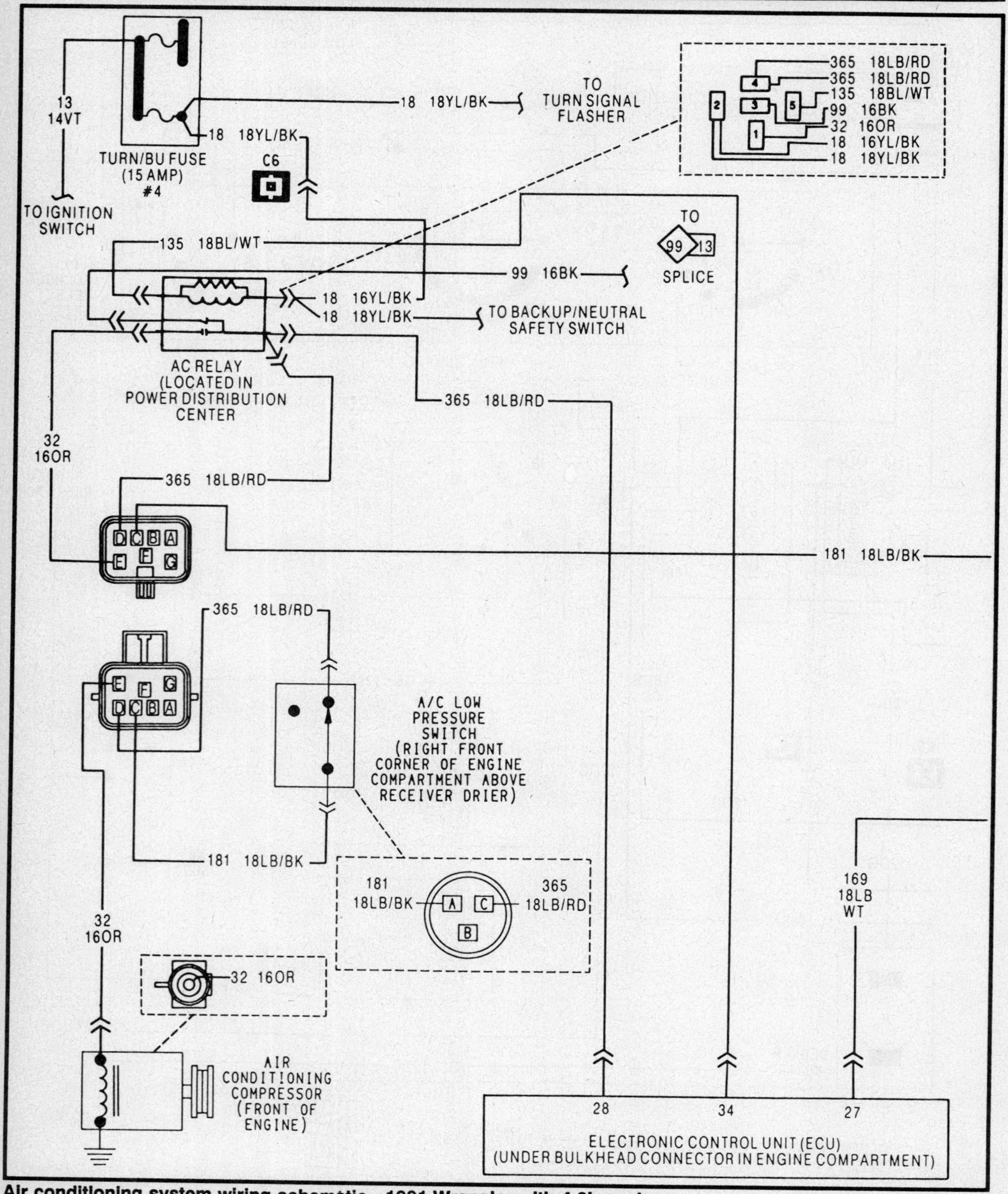
13
14VT
TURN/BU FUSE
(15 AMP)
#4
TO IGNITION SWITCH
18 18YL/BK
TO TURN SIGNAL FLASHER
18 18YL/BK
C6
365 18LB/RD
365 18LB/RD
135 18BL/WT
99 16BK
32 16OR
18 16YL/BK
18 18YL/BK
135 18BL/WT
99 16BK
TO
99 13
SPLICE
18 16YL/BK
18 18YL/BK
TO BACKUP/NEUTRAL SAFETY SWITCH
AC RELAY (LOCATED IN POWER DISTRIBUTION CENTER
365 18LB/RD
32
16OR
365 18LB/RD
181 18LB/BK
365 18LB/RD
A/C LOW PRESSURE SWITCH (RIGHT FRONT CORNER OF ENGINE COMPARTMENT ABOVE RECEIVER DRIER)
181 18LB/BK
181
18LB/BK
365
18LB/RD
32
16OR
32 16OR
169
18LB
WT
AIR CONDITIONING COMPRESSOR (FRONT OF ENGINE)
28
34
27
ELECTRONIC CONTROL UNIT (ECU)
(UNDER BULKHEAD CONNECTOR IN ENGINE COMPARTMENT)

Air conditioning system wiring schematic – 1991 Wrangler with 4.0L engine

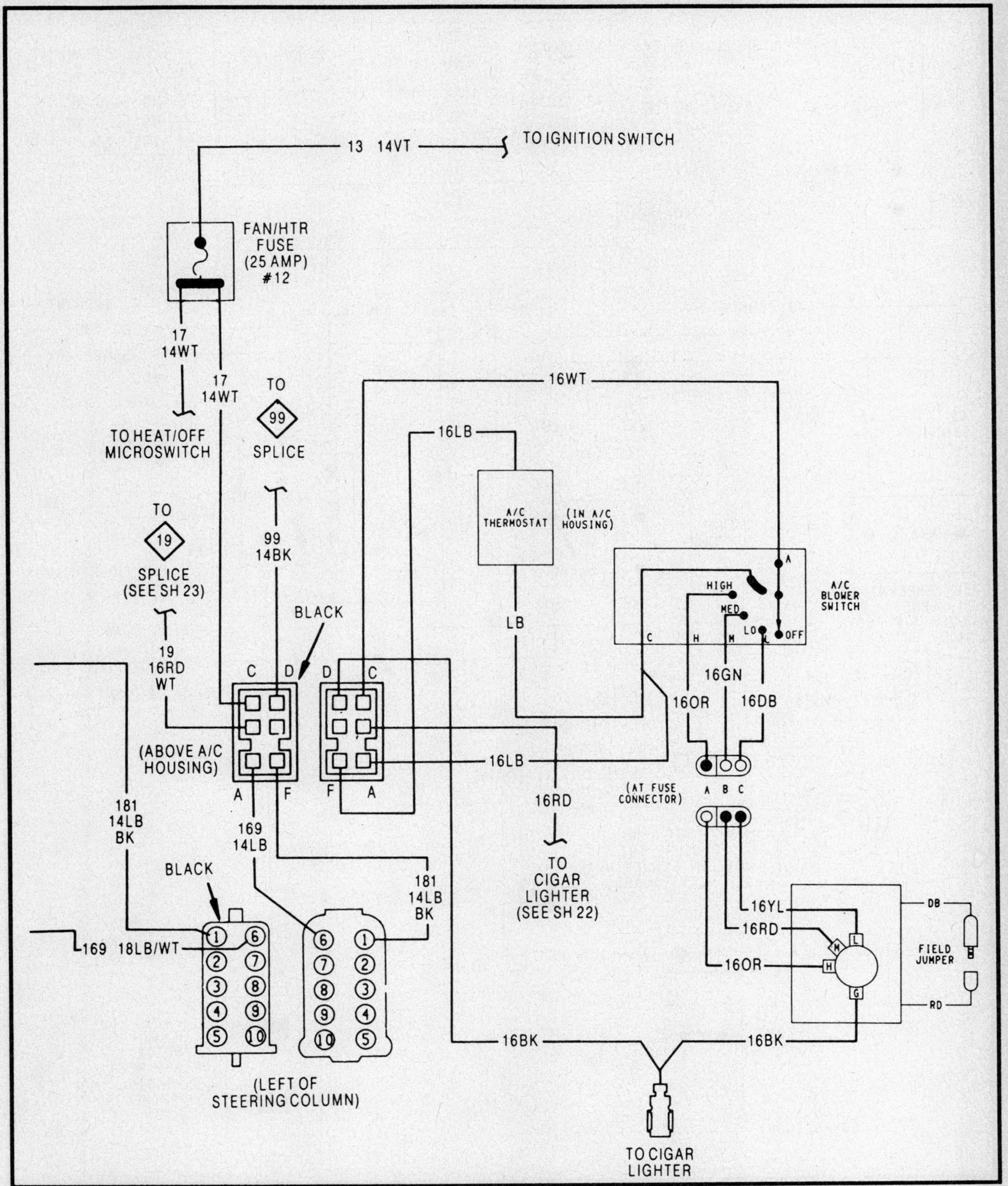
13 14VT
TO IGNITION SWITCH
FAN/HTR
FUSE
(25 AMP)
#12
17
14WT
TO HEAT/OFF
MICROSWITCH
17
14WT
TO
99
SPLICE
99
14BK
TO
19
SPLICE
(SEE SH 23)
19
16RD
WT
BLACK
C
D
D
C
(ABOVE A/C
HOUSING)
A
F
F
A
16WT
16LB
A/C
THERMOSTAT
(IN A/C
HOUSING)
LB
HIGH
MED
LO
OFF
A/C
BLOWER
SWITCH
C
H
M
L
16GN
16OR
16DB
16LB
16RD
TO
CIGAR
LIGHTER
(SEE SH 22)
(AT FUSE
CONNECTOR)
A B C
181
14LB
BK
169
14LB
181
14LB
BK
BLACK
169 18LB/WT
(LEFT OF
STEERING COLUMN)
16YL
16RD
16OR
DB
FIELD
JUMPER
RD
16BK
16BK
TO CIGAR
LIGHTER

Air conditioning system wiring schematic—1991 Wrangler with 4.0L engine

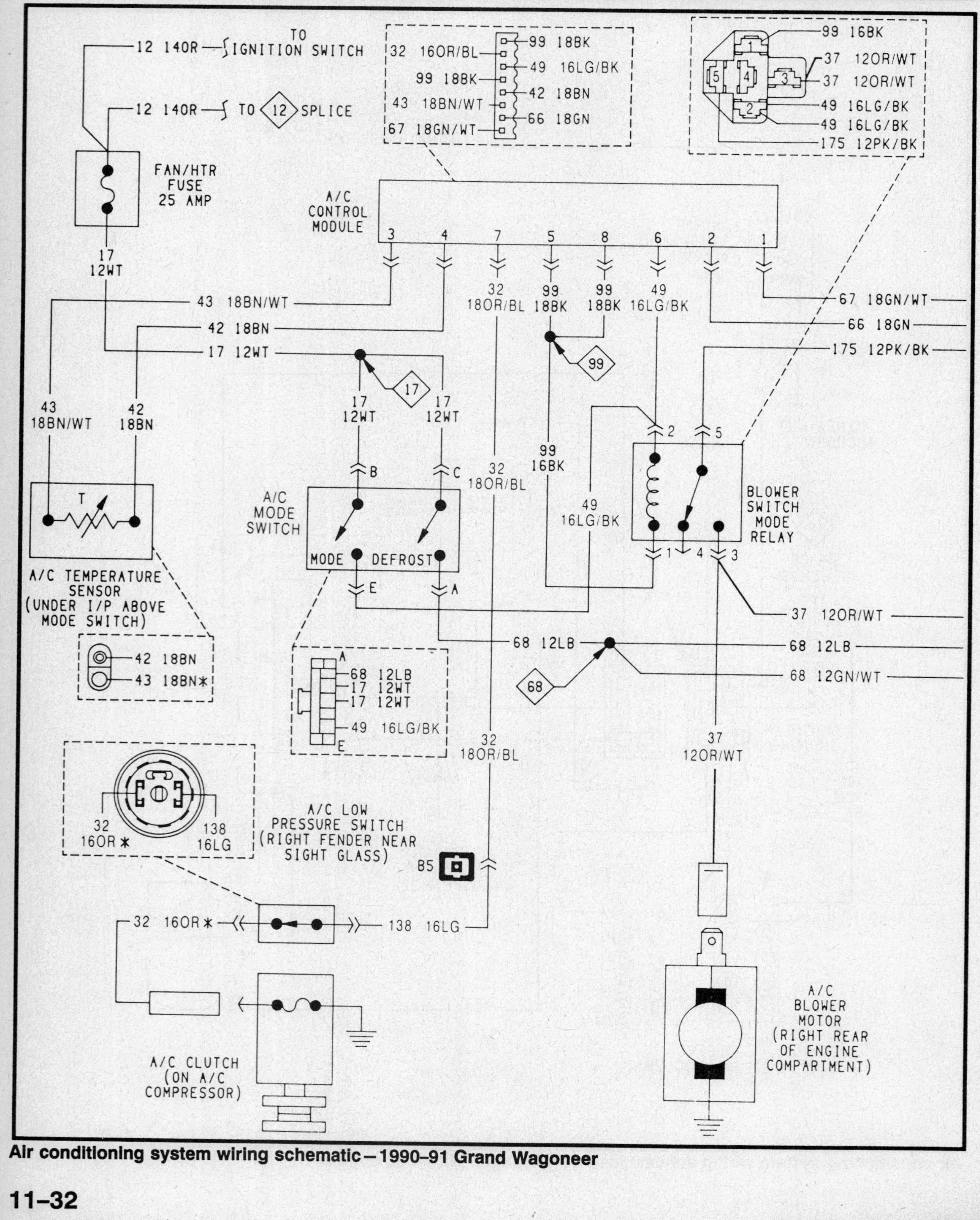
12 14OR
TO IGNITION SWITCH
12 14OR
TO 12 SPLICE
FAN/HTR FUSE 25 AMP
17 12WT
32 16OR/BL
99 18BK
43 18BN/WT
67 18GN/WT
99 18BK
49 16LG/BK
42 18BN
66 18GN
99 16BK
37 12OR/WT
37 12OR/WT
49 16LG/BK
49 16LG/BK
175 12PK/BK
A/C CONTROL MODULE
3 4 7 5 8 6 2 1
43 18BN/WT
42 18BN
17 12WT
32 18OR/BL
99 18BK
99 18BK
49 16LG/BK
67 18GN/WT
66 18GN
175 12PK/BK
99
17
17 12WT
17 12WT
43 18BN/WT
42 18BN
99 16BK
32 18OR/BL
49 16LG/BK
A/C MODE SWITCH
MODE
DEFROST
B C E A
BLOWER SWITCH MODE RELAY
2 5 1 4 3
A/C TEMPERATURE SENSOR (UNDER I/P ABOVE MODE SWITCH)
42 18BN
43 18BN*
68 12LB
68 12LB
68 12GN/WT
37 12OR/WT
68
A
68 12LB
17 12WT
17 12WT
49 16LG/BK
E
32 18OR/BL
37 12OR/WT
32 16OR*
138 16LG
A/C LOW PRESSURE SWITCH (RIGHT FENDER NEAR SIGHT GLASS)
B5
32 16OR*
138 16LG
A/C CLUTCH (ON A/C COMPRESSOR)
A/C BLOWER MOTOR (RIGHT REAR OF ENGINE COMPARTMENT)

Air conditioning system wiring schematic—1990–91 Grand Wagoneer

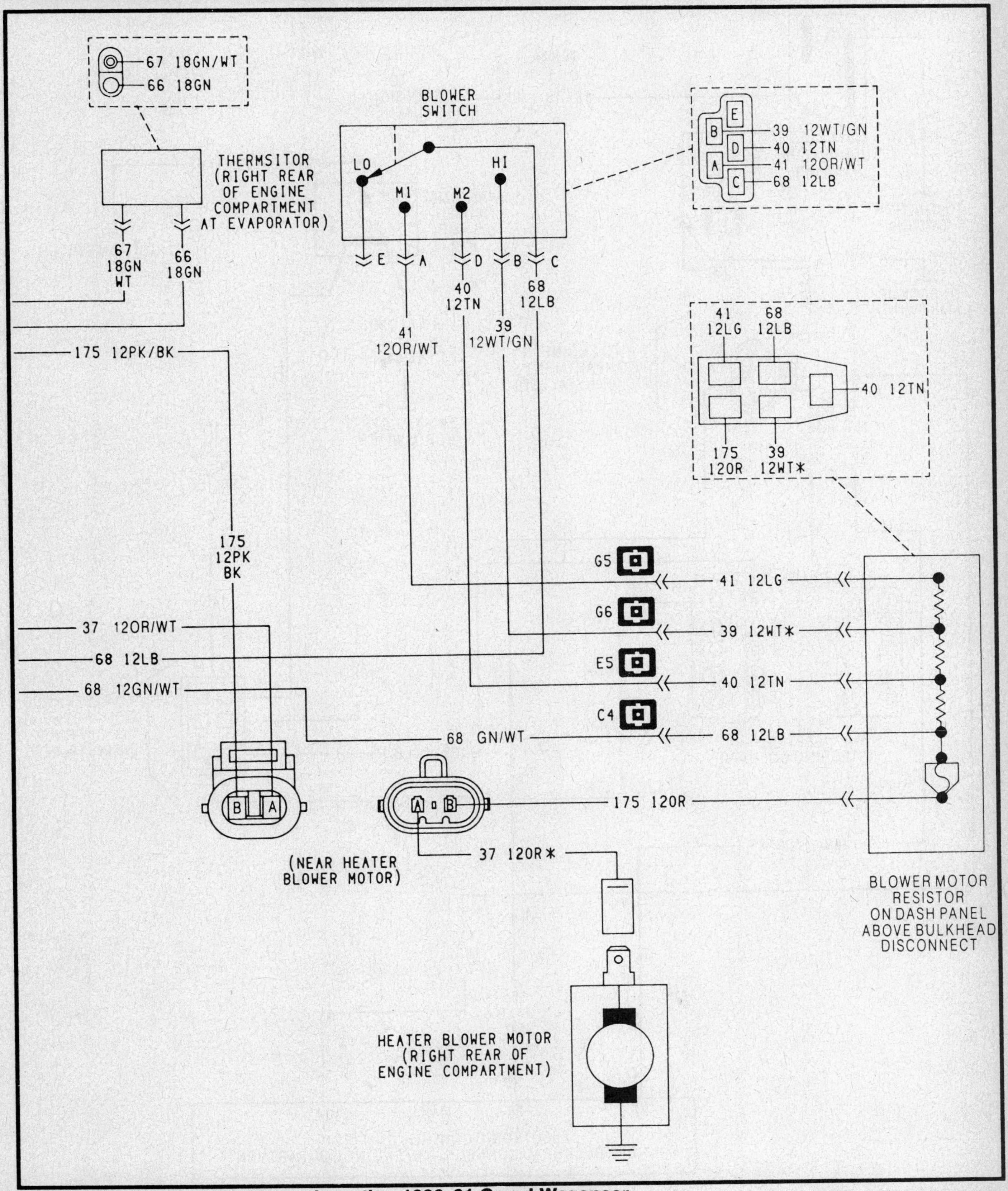
67 18GN/WT
66 18GN
BLOWER SWITCH
THERMSITOR (RIGHT REAR OF ENGINE COMPARTMENT AT EVAPORATOR)
LO
HI
M1
M2
39 12WT/GN
40 12TN
41 12OR/WT
68 12LB
E A D B C
67 18GN WT
66 18GN
40 12TN
68 12LB
41 12OR/WT
39 12WT/GN
41 12LG
68 12LB
40 12TN
175 12OR
39 12WT*
175 12PK/BK
175 12PK BK
G5
G6
E5
C4
41 12LG
39 12WT*
40 12TN
68 12LB
37 12OR/WT
68 12LB
68 12GN/WT
68 GN/WT
175 12OR
37 12OR*
(NEAR HEATER BLOWER MOTOR)
BLOWER MOTOR RESISTOR ON DASH PANEL ABOVE BULKHEAD DISCONNECT
HEATER BLOWER MOTOR (RIGHT REAR OF ENGINE COMPARTMENT)

Air conditioning system wiring schematic—1990–91 Grand Wagoneer

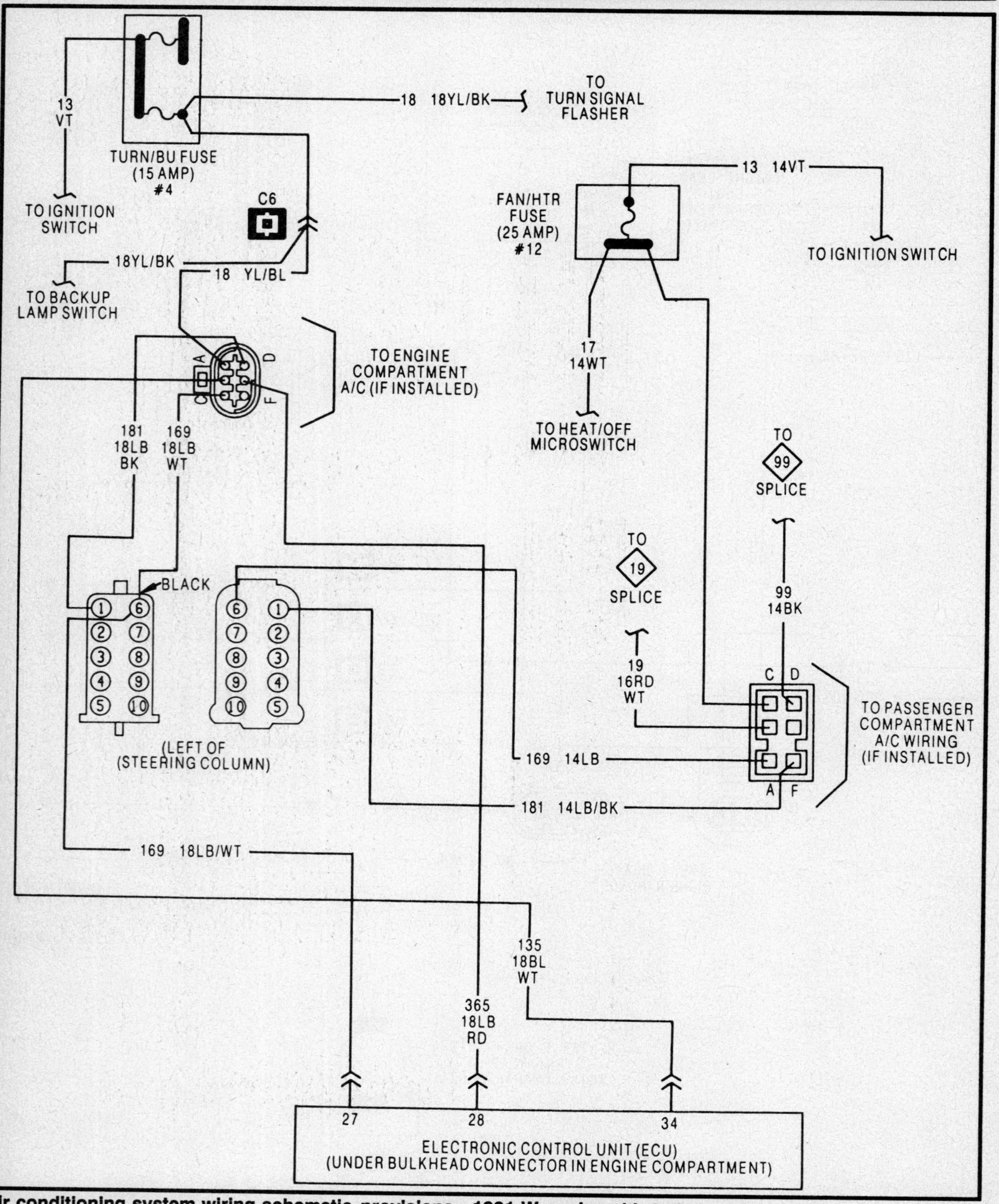
13
VT
TO IGNITION
SWITCH
TURN/BU FUSE
(15 AMP)
#4
18 18YL/BK
TO
TURN SIGNAL
FLASHER
C6
18YL/BK
TO BACKUP
LAMP SWITCH
18 YL/BL
A
D
C
F
TO ENGINE
COMPARTMENT
A/C (IF INSTALLED)
181
18LB
BK
169
18LB
WT
BLACK
(LEFT OF
(STEERING COLUMN)
13 14VT
FAN/HTR
FUSE
(25 AMP)
#12
TO IGNITION SWITCH
17
14WT
TO HEAT/OFF
MICROSWITCH
TO
99
SPLICE
TO
19
SPLICE
99
14BK
19
16RD
WT
C D
A F
TO PASSENGER
COMPARTMENT
A/C WIRING
(IF INSTALLED)
169 14LB
181 14LB/BK
169 18LB/WT
135
18BL
WT
365
18LB
RD
27
28
34
ELECTRONIC CONTROL UNIT (ECU)
(UNDER BULKHEAD CONNECTOR IN ENGINE COMPARTMENT)

Air conditioning system wiring schematic provisions—1991 Wrangler with 2.5L engine

12 ACURA/STERLING 12

INTEGRA • LEGEND • 825 • 827

SPECIFICATIONS

ENGINE IDENTIFICATION

Year	Model	Engine Displacement cu. in. (cc/liter)	Engine Series Identification	No. of Cylinders	Engine Type
1989	Integra	97 (1590/1.6)	D16A1	4	DOHC
	Legend	163 (2675/2.7)	C27A1	6	OHC
	Legend Coupe	163 (2675/2.7)	C27A1	6	OHC
	825	163 (2675/2.5)	C27A1	6	OHC
1990	Integra	112 (1834/1.8)	B18A1	4	DOHC
	Legend	163 (2675/2.7)	C27A1	6	OHC
	Legend Coupe	163 (2675/2.7)	C27A1	6	OHC
	827	163 (2675/2.5)	C27A1	6	OHC
1991	Integra	112 (1834/1.8)	B18A1	4	DOHC
	Legend	196 (3206/3.2)	NA	6	OHC
	Legend Coupe	196 (3206/3.2)	NA	6	OHC
	827	163 (2675/2.7)	C27A1	6	OHC

NA—Not available

REFRIGERANT CAPACITIES

Year	Model	Freon (oz.)	Oil (fl. oz.)	Type
1989	Integra	30–33	2.0 ①	R-12
	Legend	30–33	3.6 ②	R-12
	Legend Coupe	30–33	3.6 ②	R-12
	Sterling	36	5.0	R-12
1990	Integra	30–34	2.0 ①	R-12
	Legend	30–33	3.6 ②	R-12
	Legend Coupe	30–33	3.6 ②	R-12
	Sterling	36	5.6	R-12
1991	Integra	30–34	2.0 ①	R-12
	Legend	NA	NA	NA
	Legend Coupe	NA	NA	NA
	Sterling	NA	NA	NA

① Quantity listed is less the compressor. When replacing the compressor, subtract the volume of oil drained from the removed compressor from 3 ounces and drain the calculated volume of oil from the new compressor.

② Quantity listed is less the compressor. When a new compressor is installed, drain 1 ounce of oil from the suction fitting on the compressor.

NA—Not available.

AIR CONDITIONING BELT TENSION CHART

Year	Model	Engine Displacement cu. in. (cc/liter)	Belt Type	New	Used
1989	Integra	97 (1590/1.6)	5-ribbed	NA	9/32–23/32 ①
	Legend	163 (2675/2.7)	5-ribbed	NA	9/32–11/32 ①
	Legend Coupe	163 (2675/2.7)	5-ribbed	NA	9/32–11/32 ①
	Sterling	163 (2675/2.7)	5-ribbed	NA	9/32–11/32 ①

AIR CONDITIONING BELT TENSION CHART

Year	Model	Engine Displacement cu. in. (cc/liter)	Belt Type	New	Used
1990	Integra	112 (1834/1.8)	5-ribbed	3/16–1/4 ①	9/32–11/32 ①
	Legend	163 (2675/2.7)	5-ribbed	NA	9/32–11/32 ①
	Legend Coupe	163 (2675/2.7)	5-ribbed	NA	9/32–11/32 ①
	Sterling	163 (2675/2.7)	5-ribbed	NA	9/32–11/32 ①
1991	Integra	112 (1834/1.8)	5-ribbed	3/16–1/4 ①	9/32–11/32 ①
	Legend	196 (3206/3.2)	5-ribbed	NA	9/32–11/32 ①
	Legend Coupe	196 (3206/3.2)	5-ribbed	NA	9/32–11/32 ①
	Sterling	163 (2675/2.7)	5-ribbed	NA	9/32–11/32 ①

① Deflection in inches at 22 lbs. force, at midway point of belt.
NA—Not available.

SYSTEM DESCRIPTION

General Information

HEATING SYSTEM

A rotary dial on the control panel regulates both the air mix door and the flow of the engine coolant to the heater core. Through a gear reduction and cam lever mechanism, rotating the dial moves the heat control cable. Through a dial indicator at the heater core, the cable moves the air mix door and a vacuum control valve. The control valve, in turn, regulates the vacuum to a diaphragm controlled engine coolant valve. Rotating the dial from the **MAX COOL** position toward the **HOT** position sends a proportionate amount of heated engine coolant to the heater core and air through the core, to heat the vehicle.

The blower motor, fan and recirculation control door that switches fresh air ventilation/recirculation, are inside the blower motor housing. On the bottom of the case, there is a power transistor to change the motor speed activated by the heater fan switch. A servo motor above the fan activates the recirculation control doors.

AIR CONDITIONING SYSTEM

The air conditioning system provides the means of supplying cooled and dehumidified, fresh or recirculated air to the interior of the vehicle. The cooling effect is obtained by blowing air through the matrix of the evaporator unit and when required, mixing the air with heated air by means of the heater distribution and blend unit, to provide the conditions required inside the vehicle. The volume of conditioned air being supplied is controlled by a variable speed fan.

A sealed system, charged with freon refrigerant R–12, together with a fan unit, blend unit and control system combine to achieve the cooled air condition. The sealed system is made up of the compressor, condenser, receiver/drier, thermostatic expansion valve and evaporator assembly.

The radial compressor is belt driven from the crankshaft pulley, pressurizes and circulates the refrigerant through the system. Mounted on the compressor, an electro mechanical clutch maintains the correct temperature and pressure by engaging and disengaging to support the system's requirements. The clutch action is normally controlled by a thermistor located on the evaporator.

Should the temperature at the evaporator fall low enough for ice to begin to form on the fins, the thermistor signals the computer to disengage the clutch and also isolates the cooling fan relays. When the temperature at the evaporator rises to the control temperature, the system is reactivated.

Should the system pressure become excessive or drop sufficiently to cause damage to the compressor, a dual pressure switch, located in the high pressure line, signals the computer to disengage the clutch. Excessive pressure also activates the high pressure switch and the cooling fans are operated at high speed.

Automatic Climate Control

The automatic climate control system used on 1987–90 Legend and Legend Coupe, has a built in self-diagnosis feature. If a problem is suspected, turn the ignition switch to the **OFF** position for at least 1 minute. Then turn the ignition switch to the **ON** position and push both the **AUTO** and **OFF** buttons on the control panel at the same time. Any problems in the air conditioning circuits will be indicated by the respective **LED** light coming on.

The climate control unit does not memorize the self-diagnosis indicator lights. If the ignition is turned **OFF** for approximately 1 minute or more, the indicator light memory will be lost.

Before replacing any components, recheck that all connector terminals and wires are secure. The term intermittent failure means a system may have had a failure but checks out good through all the test. If may be necessary to road test the vehicle to reproduce the intermittent failure or if the problem was a loose connection, it may have been already solved while performing these tests.

NOTE: The Sterling is also equipped with a automatic climate control system. The only way to diagnosis the air conditioning circuit in this system is by using the Sterling air conditioning fast check tester. It is recommended that the manufacturers instructions incorporated with the fast check tester be used to diagnosis the air conditioning system.

Service Valve Locations

The service valves for charging and discharging the air conditioning system are schrader type valves, with one being located

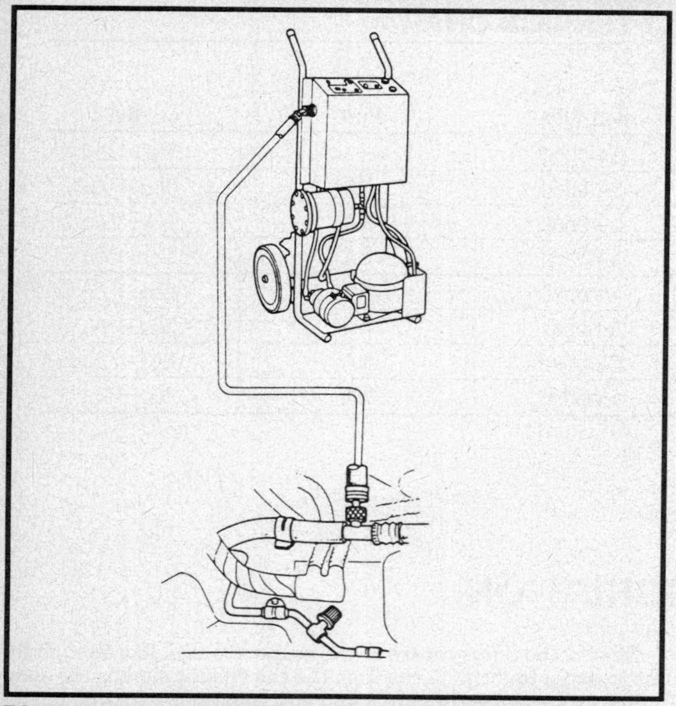

Discharging the system using a typical refrigerant recovery/recycle system.

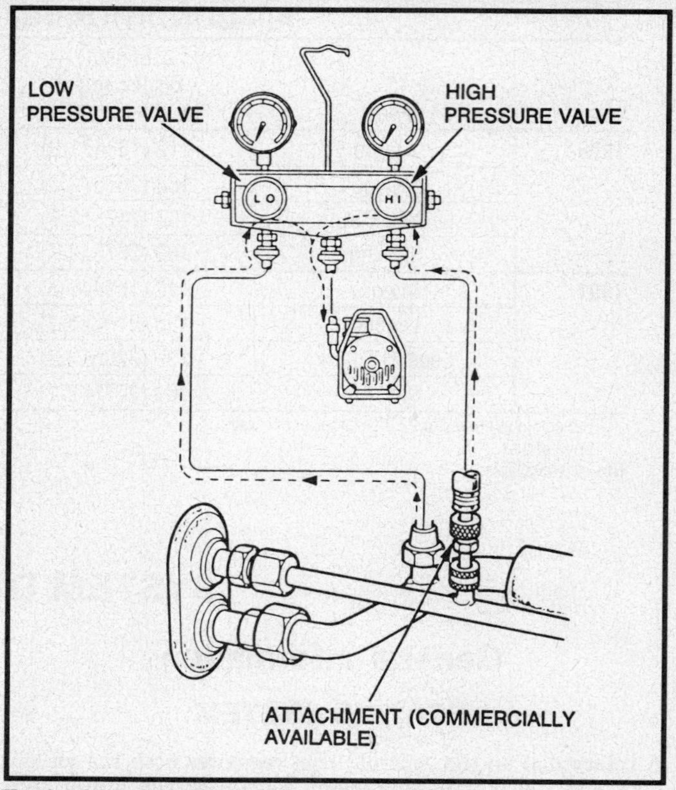
LOW
PRESSURE VALVE
HIGH
PRESSURE VALVE
LO
HI
ATTACHMENT (COMMERCIALLY
AVAILABLE)

Typical hookup for system evacuation

on the rear of the high pressure air conditioning refrigerant line and the other is located the rear of the low pressure air conditioning line. Depending on the type of gauges and charging equipment being used, it may be necessary to use some type of adaptors to make a good clean, solid connection to the air conditioning pressure line schrader valves.

System Discharging

Connect a refrigerant recovery/recycle system to the vehicle's air conditioning system and operate as instructed by the refrigerant recovery/recycle system manufacturer.

System Evacuating

Any time the air conditioning system has been exposed to the atmosphere, such as during a repair or installation. The system must be evacuated using a vacuum pump. If the system has been opened for several days, the receiver/drier should be replaced.

Integra and Legend

1. Connect the gauge set to the appropriate high and low side fittings and connect the center hose to the vacuum pump inlet.
2. Start the pump and open both gauge valves. Run the pump for 15 minutes. Close the valves and stop the pump. The low pressure gauge should read above 27 in. Hg vacuum and remain steady with the valve closed.

NOTE: If the low pressure gauge does not reach more than 27 in. Hg vacuum in 15 minutes, there is probably a leak in the air conditioning system. Check and repair as necessary.

3. If there are no leaks, open the valve and continue to pump for at least another 15 minutes, then close the valves, stop the pump and disconnect the center charging hose.

Sterling

1. Connect the gauge set to the appropriate high and low side fittings and connect the center hose to the vacuum pump inlet.
2. Start the pump and open both gauge valves. Run the pump for 15 minutes. Close the valves and stop the pump. The low pressure gauge should read above 30 in. Hg vacuum and remain steady for 10 minutes.

NOTE: If the low pressure gauge does not reach more than 27 in. Hg vacuum in 15 minutes, there is probably a leak in the air conditioning system. Check and repair as necessary.

3. If there are no leaks, open the valve and continue to pump for at least another 15 minutes, then close the valves, stop the pump and disconnect the center charging hose.

System Charging

Always wear eye protection and gloves while charging the air conditioning system. The air conditioning system may be charged with refrigerant by either vapor or liquid methods. If the system is overcharged, the compressor will be damaged.

Do not use disposable cans to liquid charge through the high pressure side of the system. The system pressure could transfer into the can causing it to explode. Use only the bulk supply of the refrigerant from the charging station. Do not run the engine during liquid charge as running the engine will damage the compressor.

Liquid charging may only be performed with a charging station, following the manufacturer's instructions.

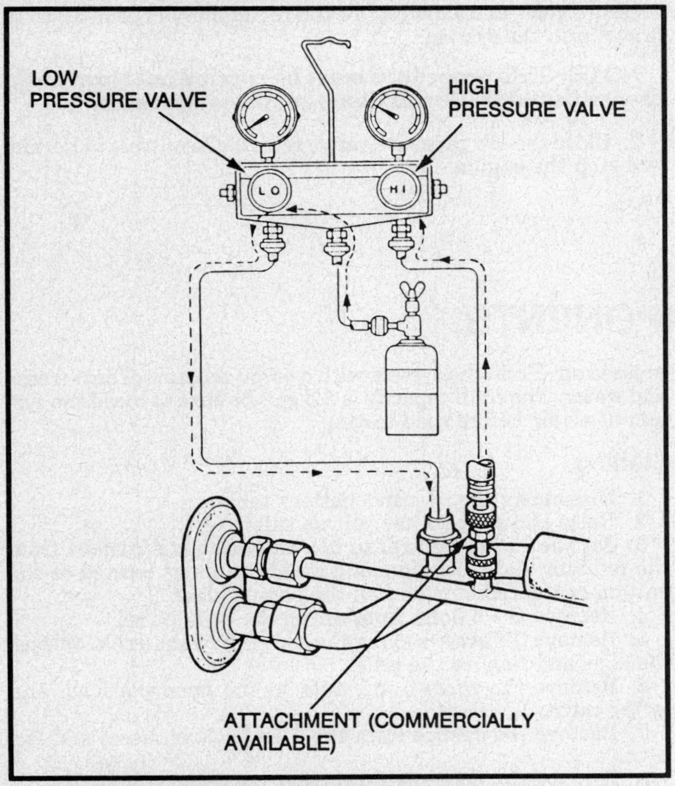
LOW PRESSURE VALVE
HIGH PRESSURE VALVE
LO
HI
ATTACHMENT (COMMERCIALLY AVAILABLE)

Typical hookup for system charging

Integra

1989

1. After the system has been evacuated, connect the gauge set to the appropriate high and low side fittings and connect the center hose to the R–12 refrigerant line.
2. With the refrigerant can in the upright position, the gauge valves should be in the closed position. Purge the air from the charging hose by opening the refrigerant valve and loosening the center hose connector at the gauge manifold, letting it hiss for a few seconds and then retighten the connector.
3. Open and adjust the low pressure gauge valve to keep the pressure from exceeding 60 psi while charging.
4. Start the engine (run it below 1500 rpm) and switch the air conditioner blower to the **HIGH** position.
5. Keep the refrigerant can right side up. Charge the system with the required amount of refrigerant, until the sight glass is free of bubbles, indicating a full charge.
6. When fully charged, close the gauge valves, then the valve on the refrigerant can. Slowly disconnect the refrigerant hose from the center gauge connection to allow excess refrigerant to escape. Quickly remove the gauges from the system to minimize refrigerant loss.

1990-91

1. After the system has been evacuated, connect the gauge set to the appropriate high and low side fittings and connect the center hose to the R–12 refrigerant line.
2. With the refrigerant can in the upright position, the gauge valves should be in the closed position. Purge the air from the charging hose by opening the refrigerant valve and loosening the center hose connector at the gauge manifold, letting it hiss for a few seconds and then retighten the connector.
3. Open the high gauge valve and charge with approximately 10.5 oz. of refrigerent.

NOTE: Do not start the engine with the high gauge valve open and do not open the low gauge valve.

4. After charging, start the engine and close the high gauge valve.
5. Start the engine and turn **ON** the air conditioning switch and heater fan switch and turn the air mix lever to **COLD**.
6. Run the engine at 1500–2000 rpm, engage the compressor clutch and check that the low gauge pressure suddenly drops.
7. If the low pressure does not drop, raise the engine speed to 2500 rpm and turn the air conditioning switch **ON** and **OFF**.
8. If the pressure does not drop, turn the ignition switch **OFF** and wait 1–2 minutes, then restart the engine and raise to 2500 rpm and turn the air conditioning switch **ON** and **OFF**.
9. If the pressure still does not drop, stop the engine and close the low gauge valve and recharge with an additional 3.5 oz. of refrigerent and repeat Step 7.
10. If the low pressure still does not drop after repeating the procedure in Step 7 several times, stop the engine, evacuate the system and repeat Steps 1–11.
11. Open the low gauge valve and charge refrigerent with the engine running at 2500 rpm.

NOTE: Do not open the high gauge valve and keep the refrigerent can right side up.

12. Charge the system with an additional 19–23 oz. of refrigerent to complete the charge.
13. When fully charged, close the gauge valves, then the valve on the can. Slowly disconnect the refrigerant hose from the center gauge connection to allow the excess refrigerent to escape. Quickly remove the gauges from the system to minimize refrigerant loss.

Legend

1. After the system has been evacuated, connect the gauge set to the appropriate high and low side fittings and connect the center hose to the R–12 refrigerant line.
2. With the refrigerant can in the upright position, the gauge valves should be in the closed position. Purge the air from the charging hose by opening the refrigerant valve and loosening the center hose connector at the gauge manifold, letting it hiss for a few seconds and then retighten the connector.
3. Open and adjust the low pressure gauge valve to keep the pressure from exceeding 40 psi while charging.
4. Start the engine (run it below 1500 rpm) and switch the air conditioner fan on **MAX** position.
5. Keep the refrigerant can right side up. Charge the system with the required amount of refrigerant, until the sight glass is free of bubbles, indicating a full charge.
6. When fully charged, close the gauge valves, then the valve on the refrigerant can. Slowly disconnect the refrigerant hose from the center gauge connection to allow excess refrigerant to escape. Quickly remove the gauges from the system to minimize refrigerant loss.

Sterling

1. After the system has been evacuated, connect the gauge set to the appropriate high and low side fittings and connect the center hose to the R–12 refrigerant line.
2. With the refrigerant can in the upright position, the gauge valves should be in the closed position. Purge the air from the charging hose by opening the refrigerant valve and loosening the center hose connector at the gauge manifold, letting it hiss for a few seconds and then retighten the connector.
3. Slowly open the high gauge valve and charge the system. If bubbles appear, reduce the rate of charge and watch for the level in the charging cylinder to stop falling.
4. Close the high pressure valve when charged with the correct amount.

NOTE: If a full charge of 36 oz. has not been accepted, continue the procedure with the engine running.

5. Start the engine and run it at 1500 rpm. Close doors and windows, switch on the air conditioning system with the temperature lever on **COLD** and the blower motor at the maximum speed.
6. Select the vent mode on the switch panel, open the low pressure valve and slowly allow the remainder of the R–12 to be drawn into the system.

NOTE: This procedure must be carried out slowly otherwise liquid R–12 will damage the compressor.

7. Close the low pressure valve, return all controls to normal and stop the engine.

SYSTEM COMPONENTS

Radiator

REMOVAL AND INSTALLATION

Integra

1. Disconnect the negative battery cable and drain the coolant from the radiator by using the drain plug located at the bottom of the radiator.
2. Remove the top and bottom radiator hoses. Remove the coolant reserve tank.
3. Disconnect the fan motor wire connection and remove the fan motor shroud retaining bolts. Remove the fan motor shroud along with the fan motor assembly.
4. Remove the coolant line and electrical connection to the thermo-sensor located in the bottom of the radiator.
5. Remove the radiator support bolts and bushings from the top sides of the radiator.
6. Slowly lift the radiator out of the vehicle.

To install:

7. Installation is the reverse order of the removal procedure. Be sure to check the cooling system hoses for damage, leaks or deterioration and replace, if necessary. Use new O-rings whenever reassembling. Inspect all soldered joints and seams for leaks. Blow the dirt out from between the core fins with compressed air. Refill the system with a 50/50 mixture of anti-freeze and water. The refill capacity is 1.5 gal. Be sure to bleed the system of all air before road testing.

Legend and Legend Coupe

1989–90

1. Disconnect the negative battery cable and drain the coolant from the radiator by using the drain plug located at the bottom of the radiator.
2. Remove the top and bottom radiator hoses. Remove the coolant reserve tank.
3. Disconnect the fan motor wire connections and remove the fan motor shroud(s) retaining bolts. Remove the fan motor shroud(s) along with the fan motor assembly.

NOTE: If it is necessary to remove the fan assembly first, remove the fan retaining bolts and fan resistors from the fans and remove the fans from their prospective fan shrouds.

4. Remove the coolant line and electrical connection to the thermo-sensor located in the bottom of the radiator.
5. Remove the radiator support bolts and bushings from the top sides of the radiator.
6. Slowly lift the radiator out of the vehicle.
7. Installation is the reverse order of the removal procedure. Be sure to check the cooling system hoses for damage, leaks or deterioration and replace, if necessary. Use new O-rings whenever reassembling. Inspect all soldered joints and seams for leaks. Blow the dirt out from between the core fins with compressed air. Refill the system with a 50/50 mixture of anti-freeze and water. The refill capacity is 2.3 gal. Be sure to bleed the system of all air before road testing.

Sterling

1. Disconnect the negative battery cable.
2. Raise and support the vehicle safely.
3. Set the heater control to hot and drain the coolant from the radiator and block by using the drain plugs located at the bottom of the radiator and on the engine block.
4. Remove the 5 bolts from under the body panel.
5. Remove the screws along the top edge of the grille, release the clips and remove the grille.
6. Remove the screws and nuts to the hood platform and saftey catch.
7. Remove the clamps from the release cable, hoses and fan cowl.
8. Remove the hood platform from the body.
9. Remove the top and bottom radiator hoses. Remove the coolant reserve tank.
10. Disconnect the fan motor wire connections and remove the fan motor shroud(s) retaining bolts. Remove the fan motor shroud(s) along with the fan motor assembly.
11. Disconnect all electrical connectors to the sensors and switches installed in the radiator.
12. Remove the radiator retaining rings and bushings from the top sides of the radiator.
13. Slowly lift the radiator out of the vehicle.

To install:

14. Installation is the reverse order of the removal procedure. Be sure to check the cooling system hoses for damage, leaks or deterioration and replace, if necessary. Use new O-rings whenever reassembling. Inspect all soldered joints and seams for leaks. Blow the dirt out from between the core fins with compressed air. Refill the system with a 50/50 mixture of anti-freeze and water. The refill capacity is 2.3 gal. Be sure to bleed the system of all air before road test.

Electric Cooling Fan

REMOVAL AND INSTALLATION

1. Disconnect the negative battery cable or remove the front fuse in the engine compartment to prevent the fan from operating, if the engine is hot.
2. Raise and support the vehicle safely.
3. Remove the 5 retaining bolts from under the hood platform front panel and remove the hood platform.
4. Release the top hose clip and move the hose aside.
5. Disconnect the fan cowl nuts, and the electrical connector and remove the fan and cowl assembly from the vehicle.
6. Installation is the reverse of removal.

NOTE: The fan and cowl assembly are a balanced assembly.

COOLING SYSTEM BLEEDING

1. Set the heater temperature lever to obtain maximum heat.
2. When the radiator is cool, remove the radiator cap and drain plug, and drain the radiator.
3. Reinstall the radiator drain plug and tighten it securely.
4. Remove, drain and reinstall the reserve tank. Fill the tank halfway to the **MAX** mark with water then up to the **MAX** mark with coolant.
5. Mix the recommended anti-freeze with an equal amount of water, in a clean container.

NOTE: Use only Acura recomended anti-freeze coolant. For best corrosion protection, the coolant concentration must be maintained year-round at 50 percent minimum. Coolant concentrations less than 50 percent may not provide sufficient protection against corrosion or freezing. Coolant concentrations greater than 60 percent will impair cooling efficiency and are not recommended. Do not mix different brand anti-freeze/coolants. Do not use additional rust inhibitors or anti-rust products, they may not be compatible with the recommended coolant.

6. Loosen the air bleed bolt located in the coolant outlet. Fill the radiator to the bottom of the fill neck with the proper anti-freeze mixture. Tighten the bleed bolt as soon as the coolant flows in a steady stream without any bubbles.
7. With the radiator cap off, start the engine and run it until it reaches normal operating temperature, the coolant fan will come on twice. Then, if necessary, add more coolant to the radiator to bring the level back up to the bottom of the radiator fill neck.
8. Put the radiator cap on and run the engine. Check for leaks and repair, as necessary.

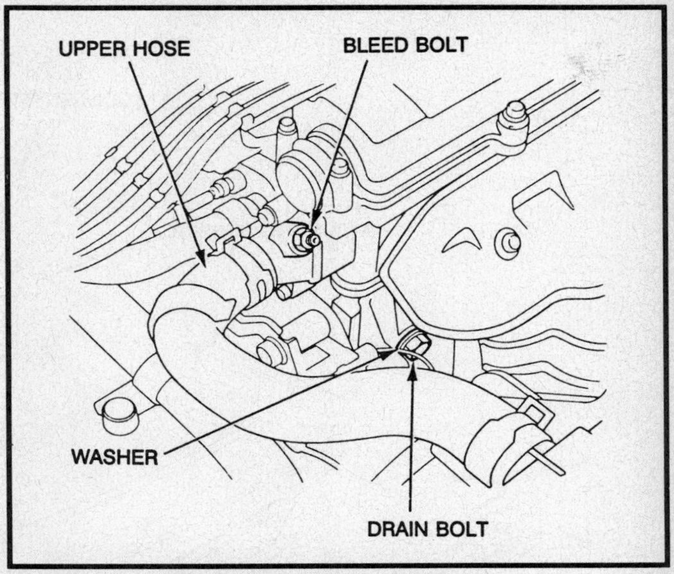
UPPER HOSE
BLEED BOLT
WASHER
DRAIN BOLT

Coolant air bleed bolt—1990–91 Integra

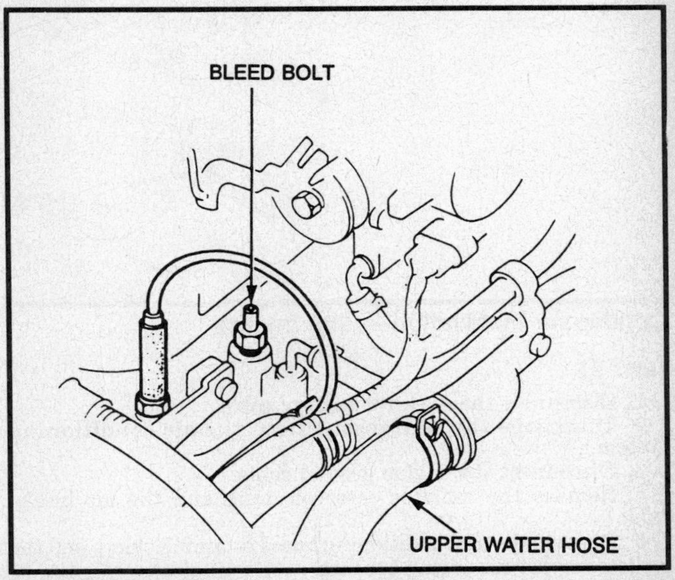
BLEED BOLT
UPPER WATER HOSE

Coolant air bleed bolt—1989–90 Legend and Legend Coupe

Condenser

REMOVAL AND INSTALLATION

Integra

1989

1. Disconnect the negative battery cable.

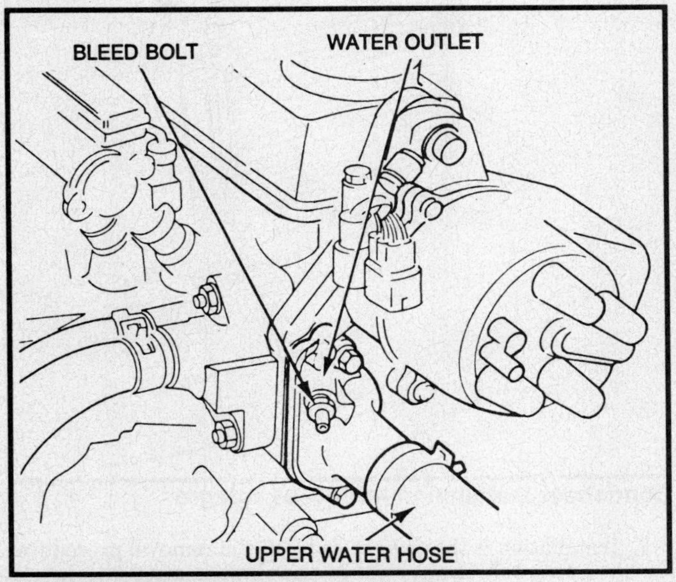
BLEED BOLT
WATER OUTLET
UPPER WATER HOSE

Coolant air bleed bolt—1989 Integra

2. Discharge the refrigerant from the air conditioning system.
3. Remove the front bumper. Remove the front bulkhead bracket retaining bolts and remove the front bulkhead bracket.
4. Disconnect the condensor pipe.
5. Remove the front bulkhead stay retaining bolts and remove the front bulkhead stay.
6. Remove the open wire clip for the stay and condenser pipe clamp.
7. Disconnect the condensor line and discharge line from the condensor. Be sure to cap the lines immediately to keep moisture and dirt out of the system.
8. Remove the condensor mounting bolts and lift the condenser up and out of the vehicle.
9. Installation is the reverse order of the removal procedure. Be sure to evacuate the system before recharging it with fresh freon.

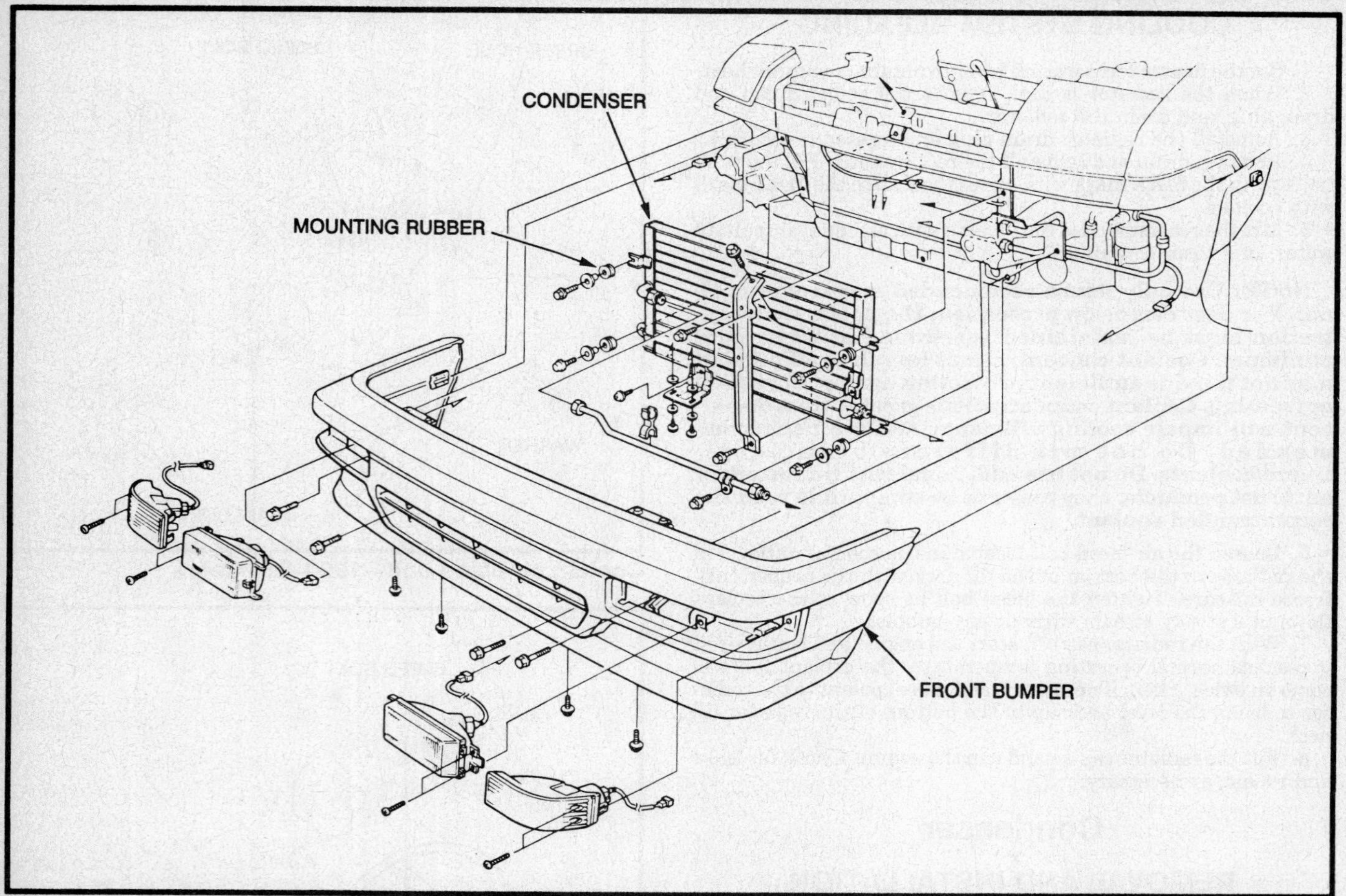
CONDENSER
MOUNTING RUBBER
FRONT BUMPER

Condenser Installation—1989 Integra

1990–91

1. Disconnect the negative battery cable.
2. Discharge the refrigerant from the air conditioning system.
3. Disconnect the engine ground cable.
4. Remove the radiator reservoir tank and the air intake tube.
5. Remove the air conditioning hoses retaining clamp and the radiator upper mounting bracket.
6. Disconnect and cap the condenser pipe and discharge pipe from the condenser.
7. Remove the mounting bolts and remove the condenser.
8. Installation is the reverse order of the removal procedure. Evacuate and charge the system.

Legend and Legend Coupe

1989–90

1. Disconnect the negative battery cable.
2. Discharge the refrigerant from the air conditioning system.
3. Remove the front grille assembly.
4. Disconnect the condensor line and discharge line from the condensor. Be sure to cap the lines immediately to keep moisture and dirt out of the system.
5. Remove the condensor mounting bolts.
6. Remove the front bulkhead retaining bolts and remove the front bulkhead and condensor up and out of the vehicle.

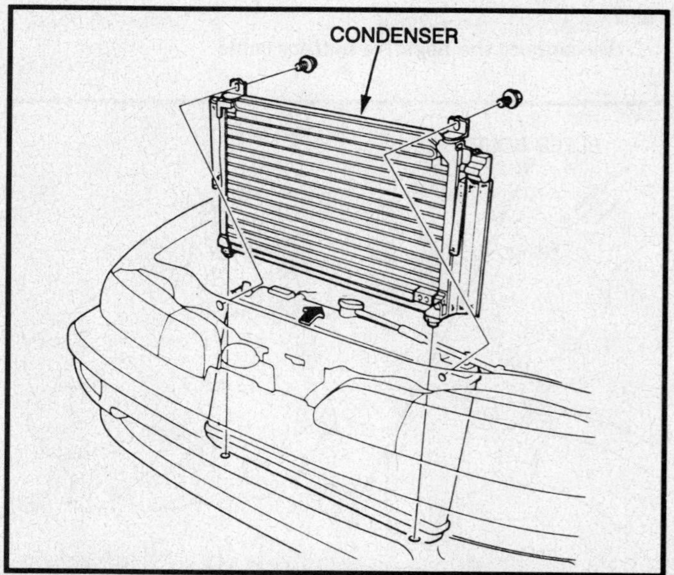
CONDENSER

Condenser Installation—1990–91 Integra

7. Installation is the reverse order of the removal procedure. Be sure to push the 2 rubber insulators onto the lower condensor mounts, then set the condensor in place in front of

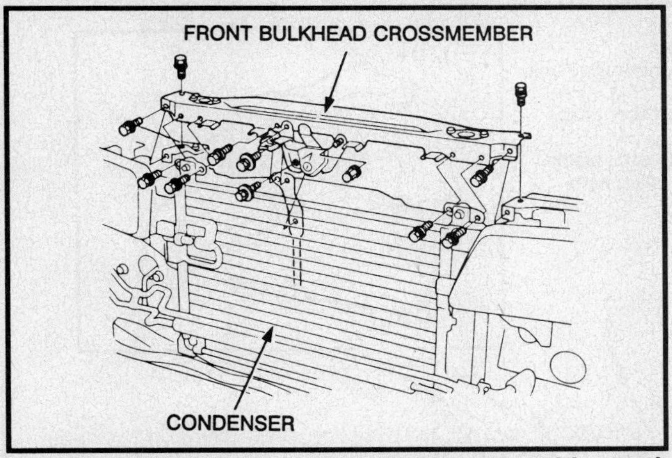
FRONT BULKHEAD CROSSMEMBER
CONDENSER

Condenser Installation — 1989–90 Legend and Legend Coupe

the radiator. Be sure to evacuate the system before recharging it with fresh freon. Do not forget to install the ground cable back onto the front bulkhead with a mounting bolt.

Sterling

1. Disconnect the negative battery cable.
2. Discharge the refrigerant from the air conditioning system.
3. Remove the front grille assembly.
4. Disconnect the condensor line and discharge line from the condensor. Always use a back-up wrench when breaking the air conditioning line unions apart to prevent the pipes from distorting. Make sure to get the O-rings out of the fitting and to cap the lines immediately to keep moisture and dirt out of the system.
5. Remove the condensor mounting nuts.
6. Remove the front hood platform retaining bolts and remove the front hood platform.
7. Lift the condenser up and out of the vehicle.
8. Installation is the reverse order of the removal procedure. Be sure to push the 2 rubber insulators onto the lower condensor mounts, then set the condensor in place in front of the radiator. Be sure to evacuate the system before recharging it with fresh freon.

Compressor

REMOVAL AND INSTALLATION

Integra and Sterling

1. If the compressor still works, run the engine at idle speed and turn the air conditioning for a few minutes.
2. Remove the intake air duct bolt and air duct assembly.
3. Raise and support the vehicle safely. Remove the front under cover from the bottom of the engine compartment.
4. Discharge the refrigerant system. Disconnect the compressor clutch wire and remove the connector from the holder.
5. Disconnect the suction and discharge hose from the compressor. Be sure to cap the open fittings immediately to keep dirt and moisture out of the system.
6. Remove the suction hose clamps and discharge hose holder.
7. On the 1990–91 Integra, remove the 2 mounting bolts, the power steering pump belt and the power steering pump.
8. Loosen the compressor mounting bolts and the compressor belt adjusting nuts and bolt. Remove the compressor belt.
9. Remove the compressor mounting bolts and remove the compressor. Remove the compressor mounting bracket if necessary.

To install:

10. Installation is the reverse order of the removal procedure. If a new compressor was installed, be sure to drain 1 fluid oz. of refrigerant oil through the suction fitting on the compressor. Adjust the belt and apply the proper belt tension to the belt. The belt deflection should be $^{9}/_{32}$–$^{11}/_{32}$ in. with 22 lbs. of force between the 2 pulleys. Torque the compressor belt adjusting bolt to 33 ft. lbs. Evacuate and recharge the system properly.

Legend and Legend Coupe

1989–90

1. If the compressor still works, run the engine at idle speed and turn the air conditioning **ON** for a few minutes.
2. Raise and support the vehicle safely. Remove the front grille, spoiler bumper and right wheel. Remove the front under cover from the bottom of the engine compartment.
3. Remove the right radius rod from under the vehicle.
4. Discharge the refrigerant system. Disconnect the compressor clutch wire and remove the connector from the holder.
5. Disconect the suction and discharge hose from the compressor. Be sure to cap the open fittings immediately to keep dirt and moisture out of the system.

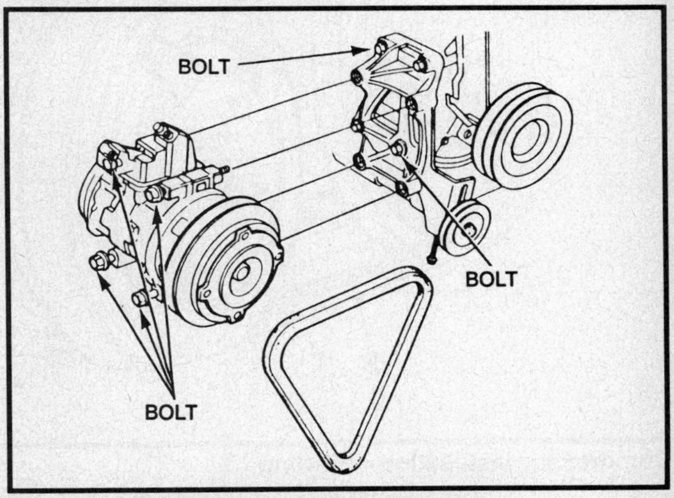
BOLT
BOLT
BOLT

Compressor Installation — 1989 Integra

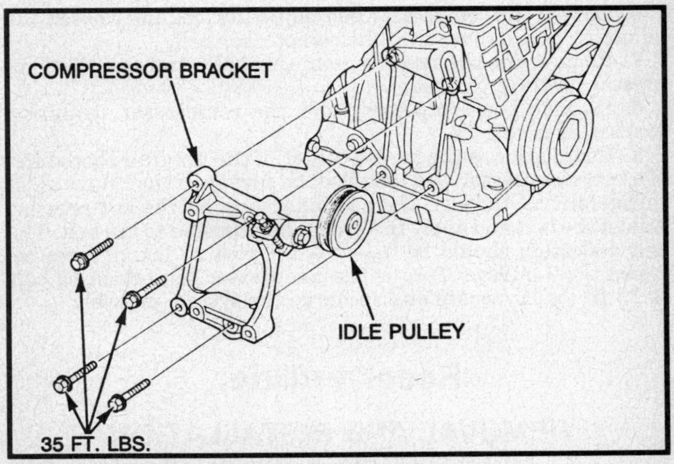
COMPRESSOR BRACKET
IDLE PULLEY
35 FT. LBS.

Compressor Installation — 1990–91 Integra

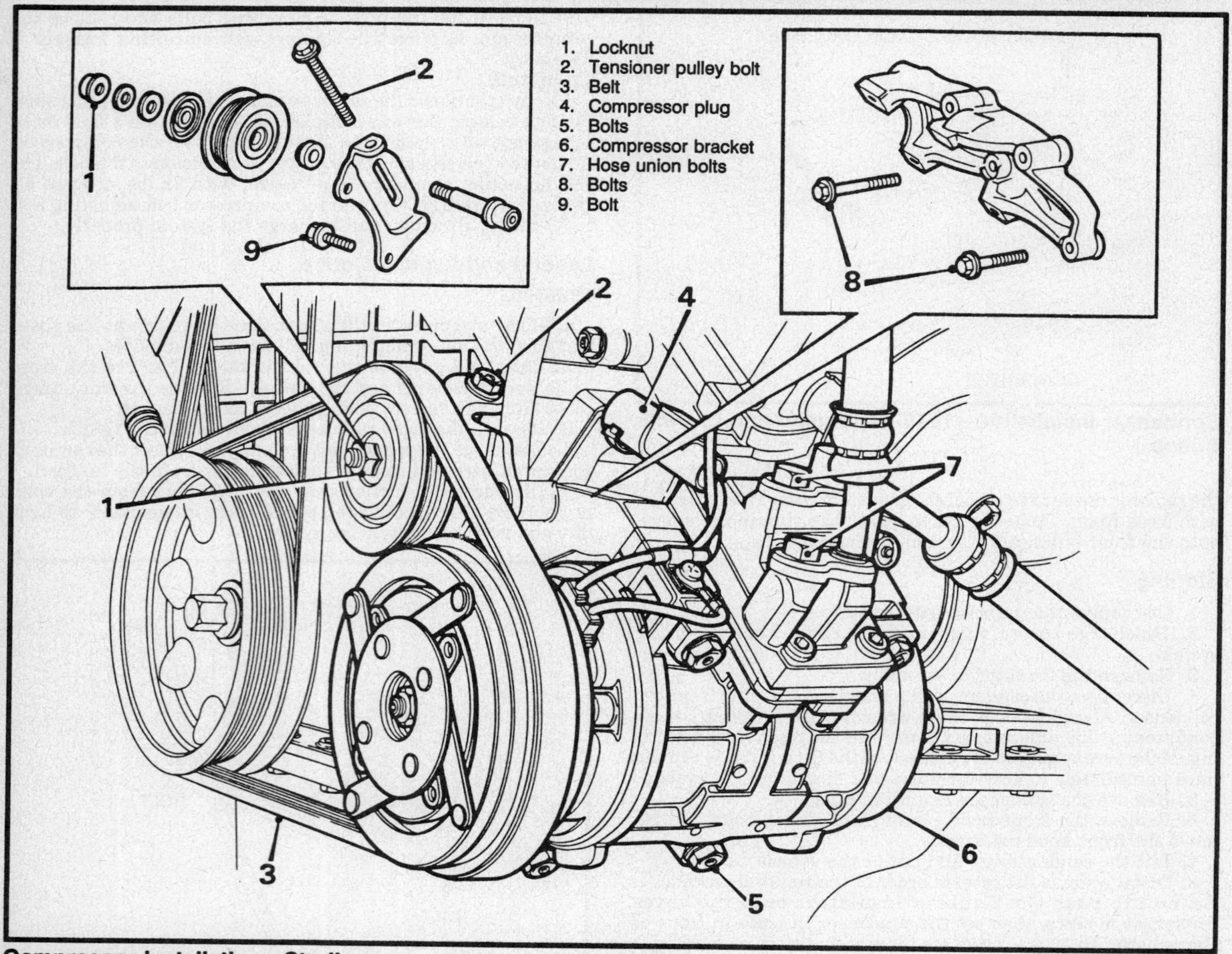
1. Locknut
2. Tensioner pulley bolt
3. Belt
4. Compressor plug
5. Bolts
6. Compressor bracket
7. Hose union bolts
8. Bolts
9. Bolt
1
2
3
4
5
6
7
8
9

Compressor installation—Sterling

6. Loosen the compressor belt adjusting lock nut, loosen the adjusting bolt and remove the compressor belt.
7. Remove the compressor mounting bolts and rest the compressor on the front beam.
8. Remove the compressor and the compressor mounting bracket, if necessary.
9. Installation is the reverse order of the removal procedure. If a new compressor was installed, be sure to drain 1 fluid oz. of refrigerant oil through the suction fitting on the compressor. Adjust the belt and apply the proper belt tension to the belt. The belt deflection should be $^{9}/_{32}$–$^{11}/_{32}$ in. with 22 lbs. of force between the 2 pulleys. Torque the compressor belt adjusting bolt to 33 ft. lbs. Evacuate and recharge the system properly.

Receiver/Drier

REMOVAL AND INSTALLATION

1. Disconnect the negative battery cable.

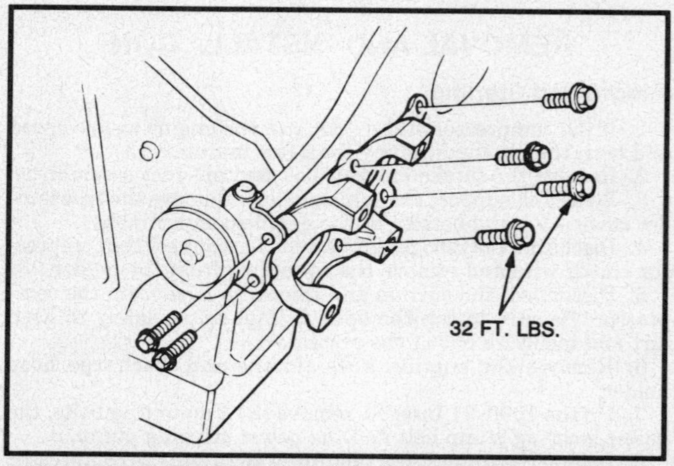
32 FT. LBS.

Compressor installation—Legend and Legend Coupe

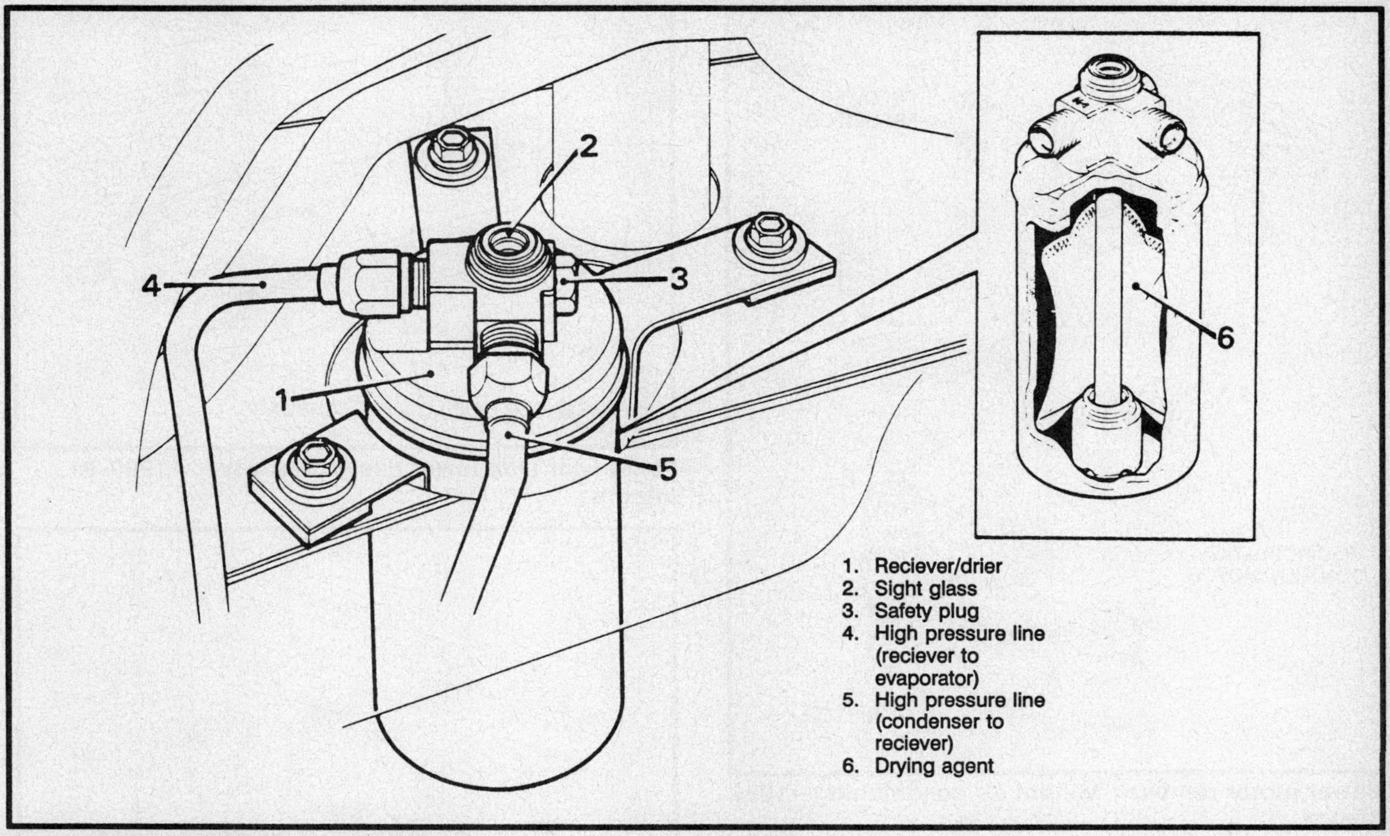
1
2
3
4
5
6
1. Reciever/drier
2. Sight glass
3. Safety plug
4. High pressure line (reciever to evaporator)
5. High pressure line (condenser to reciever)
6. Drying agent

Reciever/drier Installation—Sterling

2. Discharge the refrigerant from the air conditioning system.
3. Disconnect the receiver/drier air conditioning line and discharge line from the receiver/drier. Always use a back-up wrench when breaking the air conditioning line unions apart to prevent the pipes from distorting. Make sure to get the O-rings out of the fitting and to cap the lines immediately to keep moisture and dirt out of the system.
4. Remove the bolts attaching the reciever/drier to the vehicle and remove the receiver/drier.
5. Installation is the reverse order of the removal procedure. Be sure to use new O-rings where they are called for and to evacuate the system before recharging it with fresh freon.

Blower Motor

REMOVAL AND INSTALLATION

Integra Without Air Condtioning

1989

1. Disconnect the negative battery cable.
2. Remove the glove box. Remove the glove box frame.
3. Remove the blower duct assembly. Disconnect the wire connections from the blower motor.
4. Remove the blower retaining bolts. Remove the blower motor from the blower motor housing.
5. Installation is the reverse order of the removal procedure. Make sure when installation is complete, there is no air leakage.

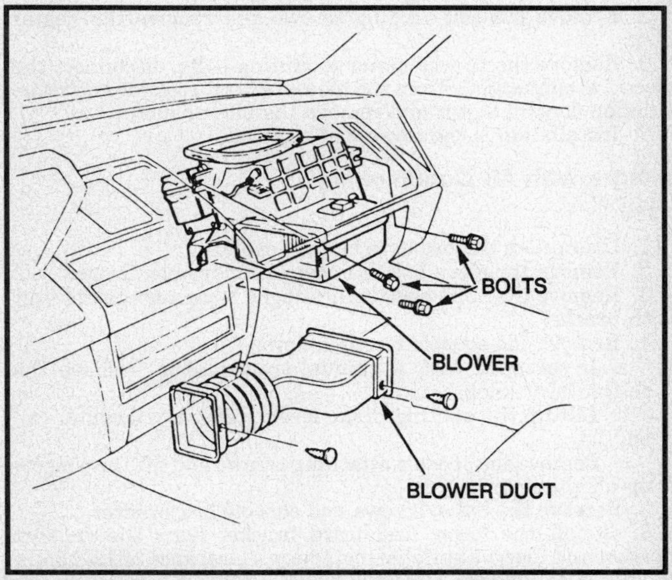
BOLTS
BLOWER
BLOWER DUCT

Blower motor and housing removal, without air conditioning—1989 Integra

1990–91

1. Disconnect the negative battery cable.
2. Remove the passenger side lower dashboard cover.

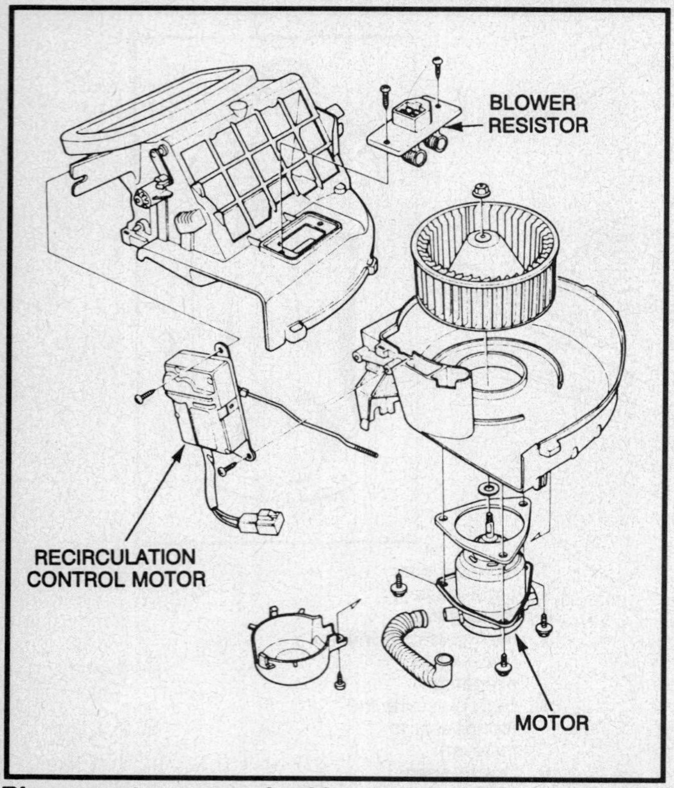
BLOWER
RESISTOR
RECIRCULATION
CONTROL MOTOR
MOTOR

Blower motor removal, without air conditioning – 1989 Integra

3. Remove the glove box and the front console.
4. Remove the passenger side knee bolster.
5. Remove the self tapping screws and remove the heater duct.
6. Remove the blower motor mounting bolts, disconnect the electrical connections from the blower motor, resistor and recirculation control motor and remove the blower motor.
7. Installation is the reverse of removal.

Integra With Air Conditioning

1989

1. Disconnect the negative battery cable.
2. Remove the glove box. Remove the glove box frame.
3. Remove the bolts and the headlight retractor control unit with bracket.
4. Remove the console box as follows:
   a. If equipped with a manual transmission, remove the shifter lever knob.
   b. Lift up the parking brake lever. Remove the center cap and lid.
   c. Remove the console attaching screws and lift the console up off the floor boards.
5. Remove the bolts, screws and console box bracket.
6. Unbolt the lower dashboard bracket from the support bracket and insert a suitable tool to pry a clearance of 12–15mm to ease in the blower removal.
7. Remove the blower duct assembly. Disconnect the wire connections from the blower motor.
8. Remove the blower retaining bolts. Remove the blower motor from the blower motor housing.
9. Installation is the reverse order of the removal procedure. Make sure when installation is complete, there is no air leakage.

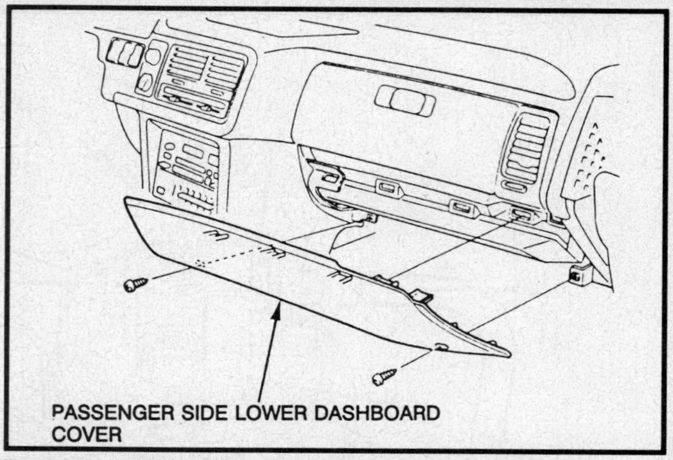
PASSENGER SIDE LOWER DASHBOARD
COVER

Passenger side lower dashboard cover – 1990–91 Integra

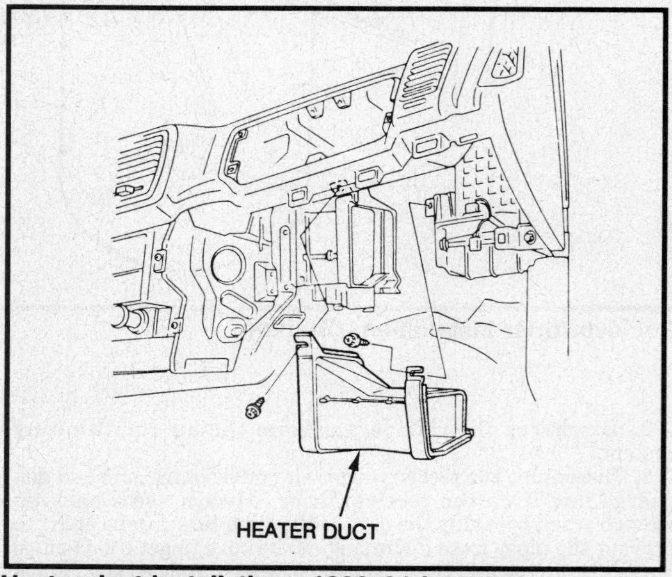
HEATER DUCT

Heater duct installation – 1990–91 Integra

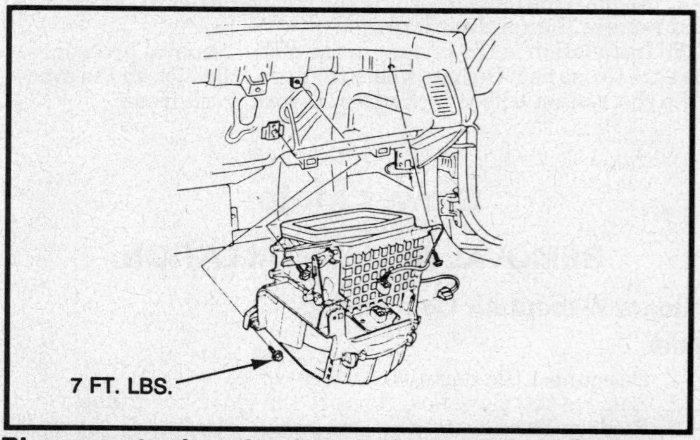
7 FT. LBS.

Blower motor housing installation – 1990–91 Integra

1990–91

1. Disconnect the negative battery cable.
2. Remove the passenger side lower dashboard cover.

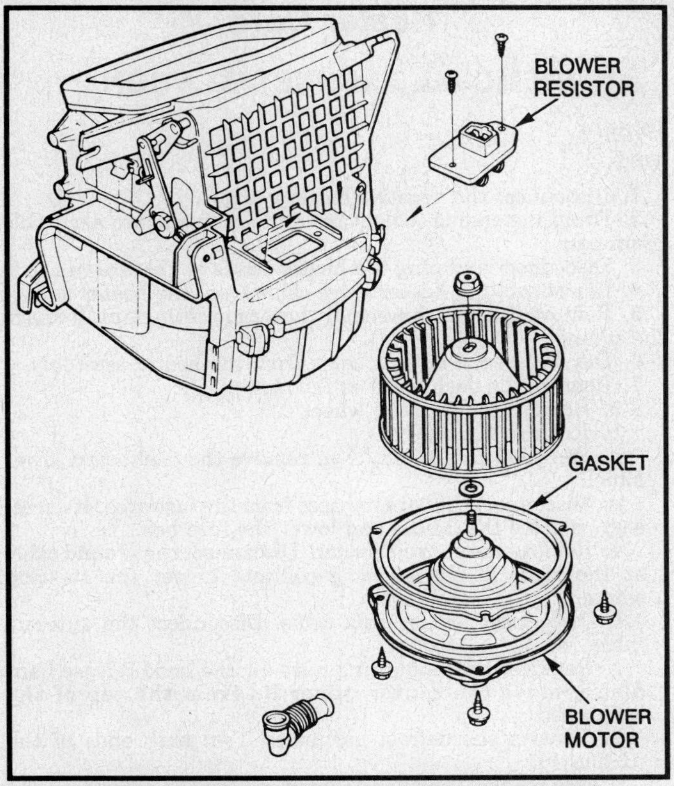
BLOWER
RESISTOR
GASKET
BLOWER
MOTOR

Blower motor and housing installation—1990–91 Integra

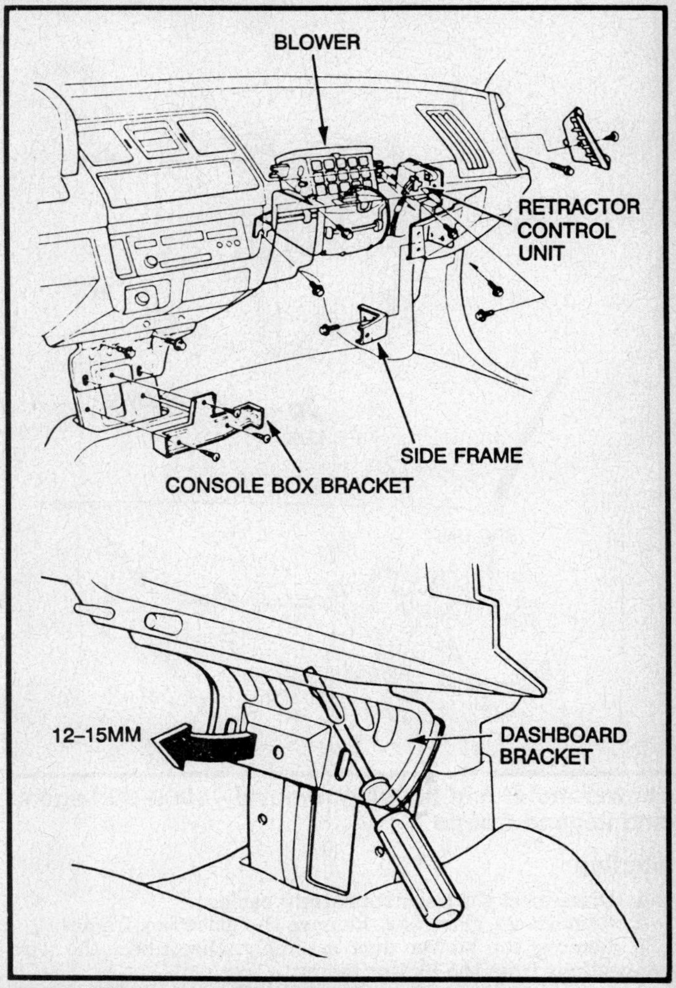
BLOWER
RETRACTOR
CONTROL
UNIT
SIDE FRAME
CONSOLE BOX BRACKET
12–15MM
DASHBOARD
BRACKET

Blower motor and housing removal, with air conditioning—1989 Integra

3. Remove the glove box and the front console.
4. Remove the passenger side knee bolster.
5. Remove the self tapping screws and remove the heater duct.
6. Remove the blower motor mounting bolts, disconnect the electrical connections from the blower motor, resistor and recirculation control motor and remove the blower motor.
7. Installation is the reverse of removal.

Legend and Legend Coupe

1989–90

1. Disconnect the negative battery cable.
2. Remove the lower glove box cover retaining screws and remove the lower cover.
3. Remove the glove box retaining screws and remove the glove box.
4. Remove the screws, tapping screws and remove the glove box frame, clips and side heater duct.
5. Discharge the freon from the air conditioning system slowly.
6. Remove the evaporator assembly case.
7. Remove the blower duct assembly. Disconnect the wire connections from the blower motor.
8. Remove the blower retaining bolts. Remove the blower motor from the blower motor housing.
9. Installation is the reverse order of the removal procedure. Make sure when installation is complete, there is no air leakage.

NOTE: When installing the blower motor assembly, adjust the control rod by reconnecting the REC control motor connector to the main wire harness, push the FRESH/REC switch to FRESH and open the air doors. Then connect the control rod to the arm while holding the air doors open.

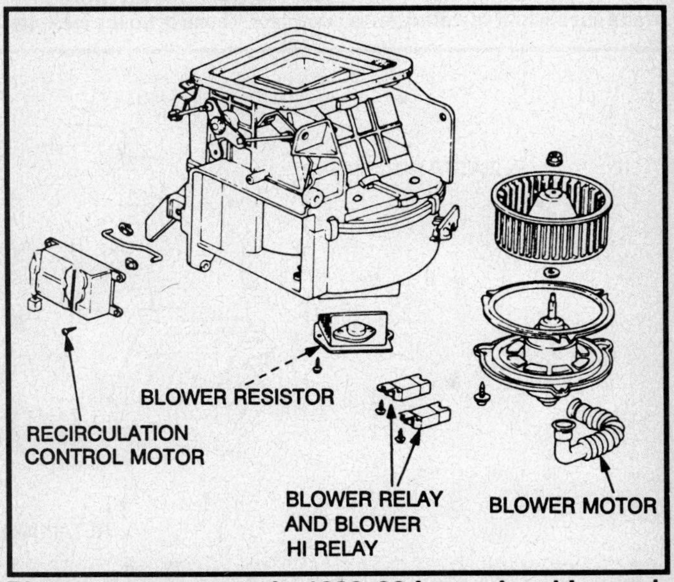
BLOWER RESISTOR
RECIRCULATION
CONTROL MOTOR
BLOWER RELAY
AND BLOWER
HI RELAY
BLOWER MOTOR

Blower motor removal—1989–90 Legend and Legend Coupe

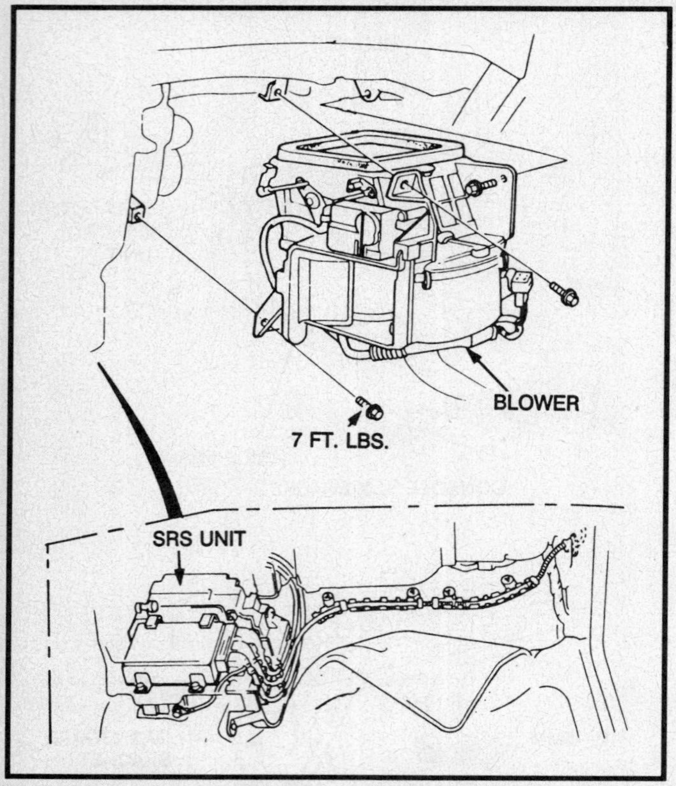
BLOWER
7 FT. LBS.
SRS UNIT

Blower motor and housing removal – 1989–90 Legend and Legend Coupe

Sterling

1. Disconnect the negative battery cable.
2. Remove the glove box. Remove the glove box frame.
3. Remove the blower duct assembly. Disconnect the wire connections from the blower motor.
4. Remove the blower retaining bolts. Remove the blower motor from the blower motor housing.
5. Installation is the reverse order of the removal procedure. Make sure when installation is complete, there is no air leakage.

Heater Core

REMOVAL AND INSTALLATION

Integra

1989

1. Disconnect the negative battery cable.
2. Drain the engine coolant from the radiator into a suitable drain pan.
3. Disconnect and plug the heater hoses at the firewall.
4. Disconnect the heater valve cable from the heater valve.
5. Remove the heater assembly lower mounting nut. Remove the console.
6. Disconnect the air mix cable from the heater assembly.
7. Remove the dashboard as follows:
   a. Remove the steering wheel.
   b. Remove the console.
   c. Remove the fuse lid, then remove the dashboard lower panel.
   d. Disconnect the wire harness from the fuse area. If necessary, remove the 2 nuts and lower the fuse box.
   e. Remove the sunroof switch. Disconnect the ground cable at the right of the steering column. Lower the steering column.
   f. Disconnect the air mix cable. Disconnect the antenna cable.
   g. Remove the 2 mounting nuts for the hood release handle. Remove the center upper lid from the top of the dashboard.
   h. Remove the defrost garnishes from both ends of the dashboard.
   i. Remove the 7 bolts and screws and lift the dashboard out far enough to disconnect the speedometer cable.
   j. Remove the dashboard.
8. Disconnect the wire harness connector. Remove the heater assembly mounting bolts and pull the heater assembly away from the body and out of the vehicle.
9. Remove the self tapping retaining screws from the heater assembly case and the retaining plate.
10. Remove the heater core from the heater assembly case.

To install:

11. Installation is the reverse order of the removal procedure, except for the following:
    a. Apply a suitable sealant to the grommets.

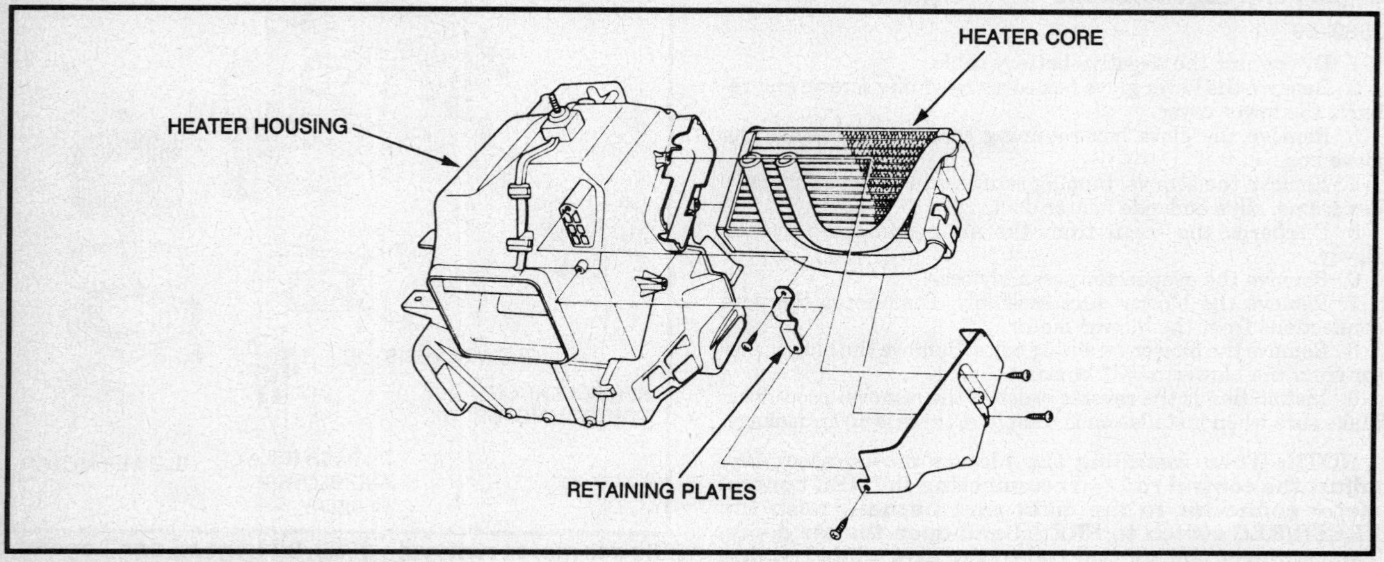
HEATER CORE
HEATER HOUSING
RETAINING PLATES

Heater core removal – 1989 Integra

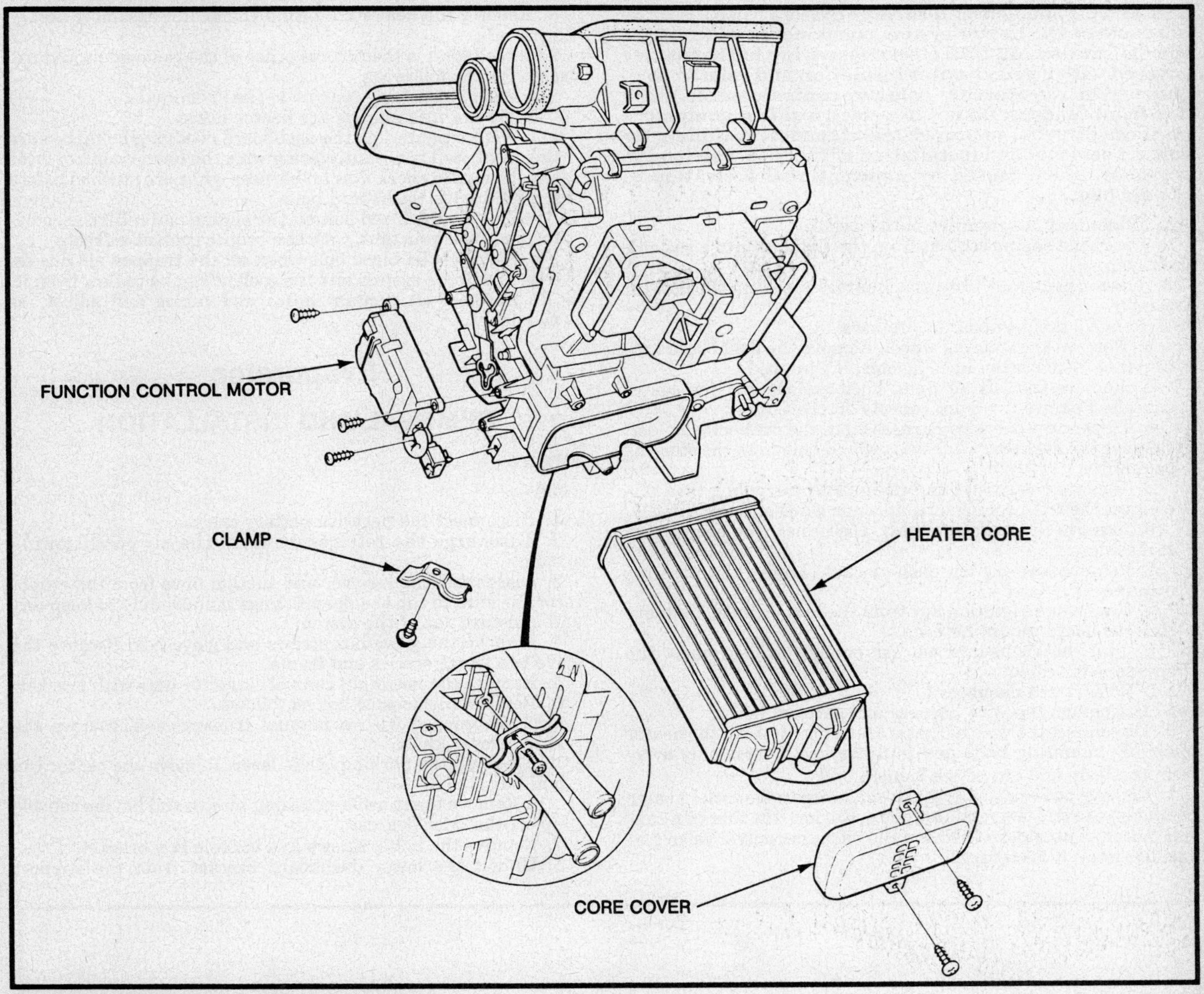
FUNCTION CONTROL MOTOR
CLAMP
HEATER CORE
CORE COVER

Heater core removal – 1990–91 Integra

b. Do not interchange the heater hoses.

c. Before tightening the dashboard retaining bolts, be sure the dashboard is not interfering with the heater control lever or cables. Also check that no harness wires are pinched before tightening the dashboard bolts.

d. Loosen the bleed bolt on the engine and refill the radiator and reservoir tank with the proper coolant mixture.

e. Tighten the bleed bolt when all the trapped air has escaped from the system and the coolant begins to flow from it.

f. Connect all cables and adjust, as necessary.

1990–91

1. Disconnect the negative battery cable.
2. Drain the engine coolant from the radiator into a suitable drain pan.
3. Disconnect and plug the heater hoses at the firewall.
4. Disconnect the heater valve cable from the heater valve.
5. Remove the dashboard, heater duct and the heater lower mounting nut.
6. Remove the heater mounting bolts, disconnect the wire harness connector from the control motor and remove the heater assembly.

To install:

7. Installation is the reverse order of the removal procedure, except for the following.

a. Apply a suitable sealant to the grommets.

b. Do not interchange the heater hoses.

c. Loosen the bleed bolt on the engine and refill the radiator and reservoir tank with the proper coolant mixture.

d. Tighten the bleed bolt when all the trapped air has escaped from the system and the coolant begins to flow from it.

e. Connect all cables and adjust, as necessary.

Legend and Legend Coupe

1989–90

NOTE: The Legend and Legend Coupe includes a driver's side air bag, located in the steering wheel hub as

part of a Supplemental Restraint System (SRS). Servicing some of the heater system components will require special caution. All SRS electrical wiring harnesses are covered with a yellow outer insulation and related components in the steering column, center console, dash and front fenders. Do not use electrical test equipment on these circuits. Improper maintenance, including incorrect removal and installation of the SRS, can lead to personal injury caused by unintentional activation of the air bag.

1. Disconnect the negative battery cable.
2. Drain the engine coolant from the radiator into a suitable drain pan.
3. Disconnect and plug the heater hoses at the heater assembly.
4. Remove the dashboard as follows:
   a. Remove the steering wheel. Remove the dashboard lower panel. Remove the knee bolster, if equipped.
   b. Remove the left air duct, hood release and the center console. Remove the front console on the Coupe.
   c. Disconnect the wire harness from the connector holder. Remove the dashboard harness ground bolt from the steering column.
   d. Remove the screws and radio panel assembly, then disconnect the wire, connectors, antenna cable and the wire tie.
   e. Remove the radio assembly. Disconnect the heater control cable.
   f. Remove the center dash pocket. Lower the steering column.
   g. Remove the ignition key from the lock cylinder. Remove the dashboard mounting nuts.
   h. Pull the dashboard out far enough to disconnect the speedometer cable.
   i. Remove the dashboard.
5. Disconnect the wire harness and vacuum hoses.
6. Disconnect the wire harness connector. Remove the heater assembly mounting bolts and pull the heater assembly away from the body and out of the vehicle.
7. Remove the self tapping retaining screws from the heater assembly case and the retaining plate. Remove the function control motor, if necessary. Remove the vacuum control valve and vacuum joint, if necessary.
8. Remove the heater core from the heater assembly case.

To install:

9. Installation is the reverse order of the removal procedure, except for the following:
   a. Apply a suitable sealant to the grommets.
   b. Do not interchange the heater hoses.
   c. Before tightening the dashboard retaining bolts, be sure the dashboard is not interfering with the heater control lever or cables. Also check that no harness wires are pinched before tightening the dashboard bolts.
   d. Loosen the bleed bolt on the engine and refill the radiator and reservoir tank with the proper coolant mixture.
   e. Tighten the bleed bolt when all the trapped air has escaped from the system and the coolant begins to flow from it.
   f. Connect all vacuum hoses and cables and adjust, as necessary.

Evaporator

REMOVAL AND INSTALLATION

Integra

1989

1. Disconnect the negative battery cable.
2. Discharge the refrigerant from the air conditioning system.
3. Disconnect the receiver and suction lines from the evaporator. Be sure to cap the open fittings immediately to keep dirt and moisture out of the system.
4. Remove the glove box screws and glove box. Remove the glove box frame screws and frame.
5. Remove the headlight control retractor unit with bracket.
6. Remove the console box as follows:
   a. If equipped with a manual transmission, remove the shifter lever knob.
   b. Lift up the parking brake lever. Remove the center cap and lid.
   c. Remove the console attaching screws and lift the console up off the floor boards.
7. Remove the bolts, screws and console box bracket.
8. Unbolt the lower dashboard bracket from the support

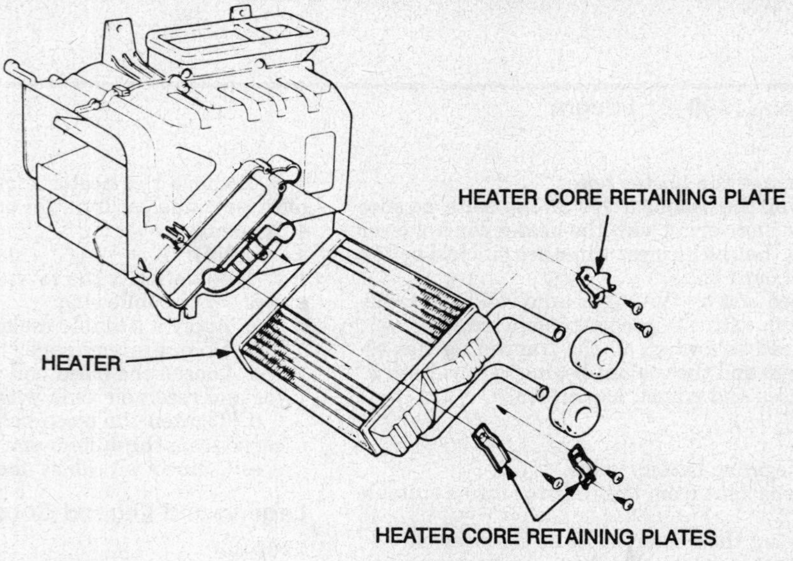
HEATER CORE RETAINING PLATE
HEATER
HEATER CORE RETAINING PLATES

Heater core removal—1989–90 Legend and Legend Coupe

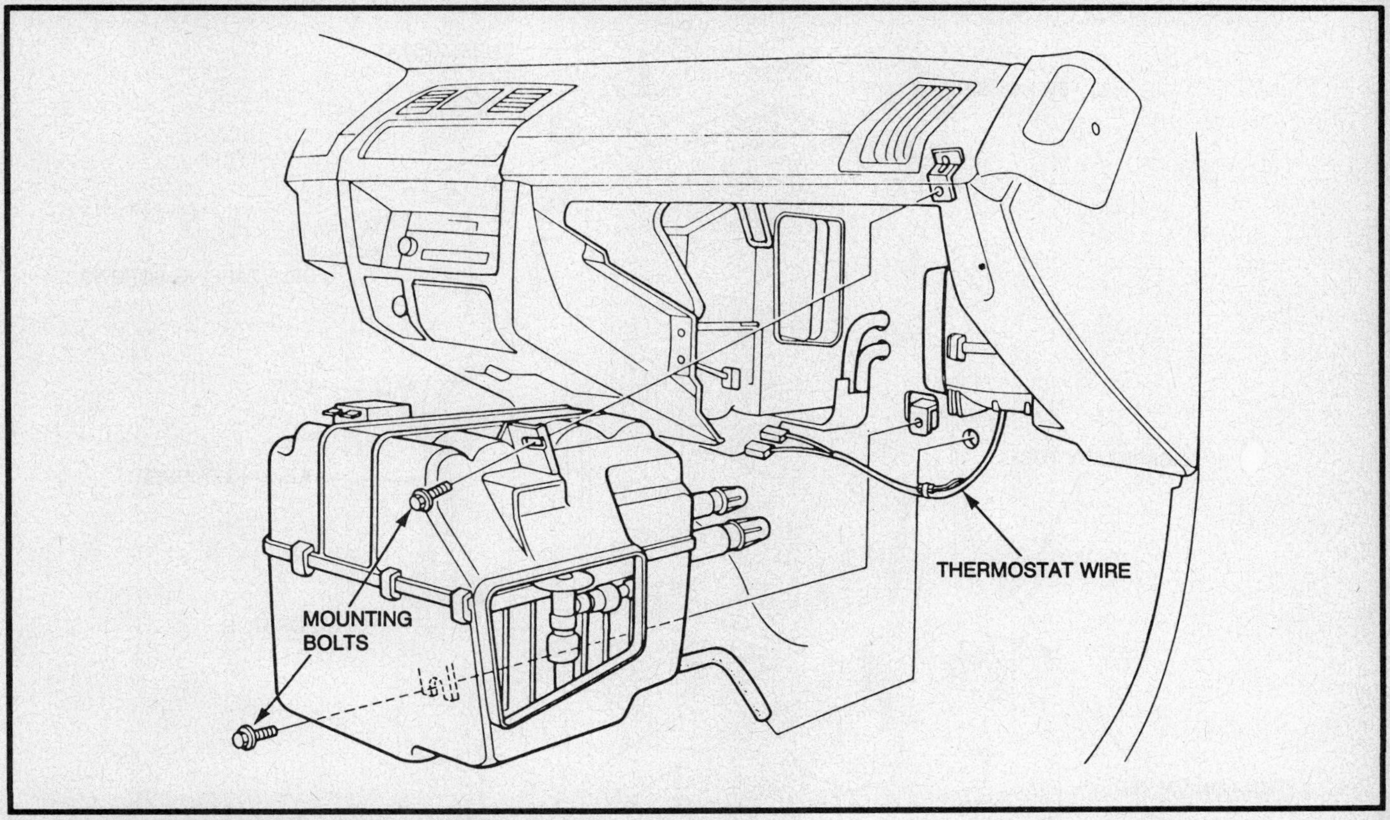
THERMOSTAT WIRE
MOUNTING
BOLTS

Evaporator and housing removal—1989 Integra

bracket and insert a suitable tool to pry a clearance of 12–15mm to ease in the blower removal.

9. Loosen the sealing band. Remove the lower bolt and loosen the upper bolt for the blower motor.
10. Slide the blower motor to the right as far as possible. Disconnect the drain hose from the lower evaporator housing.
11. Remove the evaporator housing retaining bolts and remove the evaporator case from under the dashboard.
12. Disconnect the thermostat wire and pull the wire out of the clamp at the top of the evaporator case.
13. Pull the evaporator sensor out from the evaporator fins. Remove the tapping screws and clips from the housing.
14. Carefully separate the housing and remove the evaporator covers.
15. Remove the evaporator from the case and remove the expansion valve, if necessary.

To install:

16. Installation is the reverse order of the removal procedures. Install the expansion valve capillary tube against the suction line and wrap it with tape. Reassemble the upper and lower housings with clips, making sure there are no caps between them. Reinstall the evaporator sensor in its original position. Be sure to apply sealant to the grommets and make sure there is no air leakage after the installation is complete. Evacuate and recharge the system properly.

1990–91

1. Disconnect the negative battery cable.
2. Discharge the refrigerant from the air conditioning system.
3. Disconnect the receiver and suction lines from the evaporator. Be sure to cap the open fittings immediately to keep dirt and moisture out of the system.
4. Remove the passenger side and driver side lower dashboard cover.
5. Remove the glove box and the front console.
6. Remove the passenger side knee bolster.
7. Remove the 2 screws retaining the evaporator holding brackets, disconnect the connector from the thermostat switch and pull of the wire harness from the clamps.
8. Remove the evaporator from the vehicle.
9. Installation is the reverse of removal. Evacuate and charge the system.

Legend and Legend Coupe

1989–90

1. Disconnect the negative battery cable.
2. Discharge the refrigerant from the air conditioning system.
3. Disconnect the receiver and suction lines from the evaporator. Be sure to cap the open fittings immediately to keep dirt and moisture out of the system.
4. Remove the glove box lower cover and glove box. Remove the glove box and side duct.
5. Disconnect the wire connector from the evaporator sensor connector and the thermostat switch connector, if equipped.
6. Remove the tapping screws and retaining bolts attaching the evaporator assembly to the body of the vehicle. Remove the evaporator assembly case from the upper floor boards of the vehicle.
7. Pull the evaporator sensor out from the evaporator fins. Remove the tapping screws and clips from the housing.
8. Carefully separate the housing and remove the evaporator covers.
9. Remove the evaporator from the case and remove the expansion valve, if necessary.

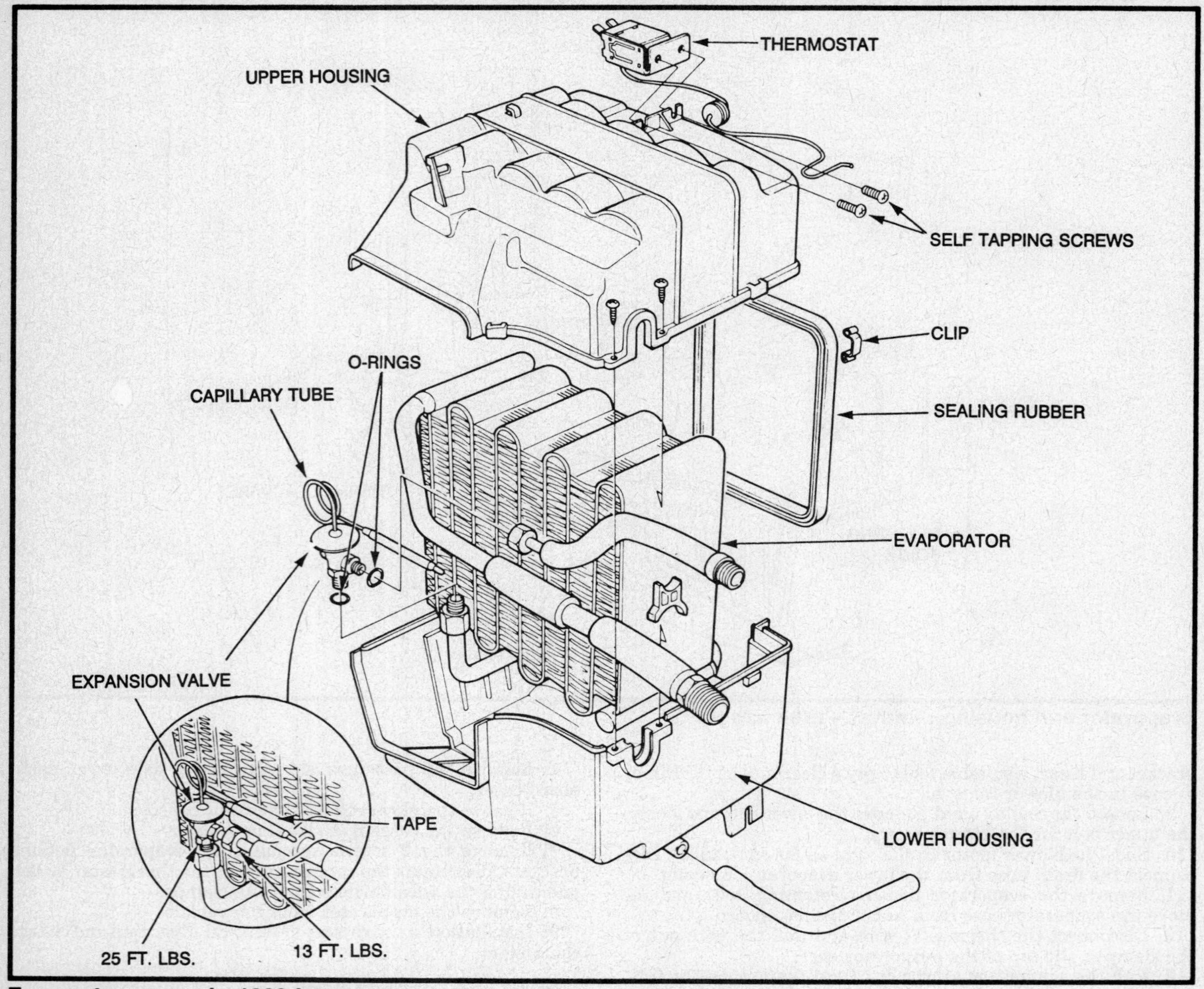
THERMOSTAT
UPPER HOUSING
SELF TAPPING SCREWS
CLIP
O-RINGS
CAPILLARY TUBE
SEALING RUBBER
EVAPORATOR
EXPANSION VALVE
TAPE
LOWER HOUSING
25 FT. LBS.
13 FT. LBS.

Evaporator removal—1989 Integra

To install:

10. Installation and assembly are the reverse order of the disassembly and removal procedures. Install the expansion valve capillary tube against the suction line and wrap it with tape. Reassemble the upper and lower housings with clips, making sure there are no caps between them. Reinstall the evaporator sensor in its original position. Be sure to apply sealant to the grommets and make sure there is no air leakage after the installation is complete. Evacuate and recharge the system properly.

Sterling

1. Disconnect the negative battery cable.
2. Discharge the refrigerant from the air conditioning system.
3. Disconnect the receiver and suction lines from the evaporator. Be sure to cap the open fittings immediately to keep dirt and moisture out of the system.
4. Remove the glove box lower cover and glove box.
5. Remove the radio cassette player, clock and trip computer. Remove the glove compartment support bar.
6. Disconnect all electrical connections to the evaporator assembly and disconnect and cap all the pipe unions to the evaporator assembly
7. Remove the screws from the thermistor and the evaporator assembly. Remove the evaporator assembly from the bulkhead.
8. Pull the thermistor out from the evaporator fins. Remove the tapping screws and clips from the housing.
9. Carefully separate the housing and remove the evaporator covers.
10. Remove the evaporator from the case and remove the expansion valve, if necessary.

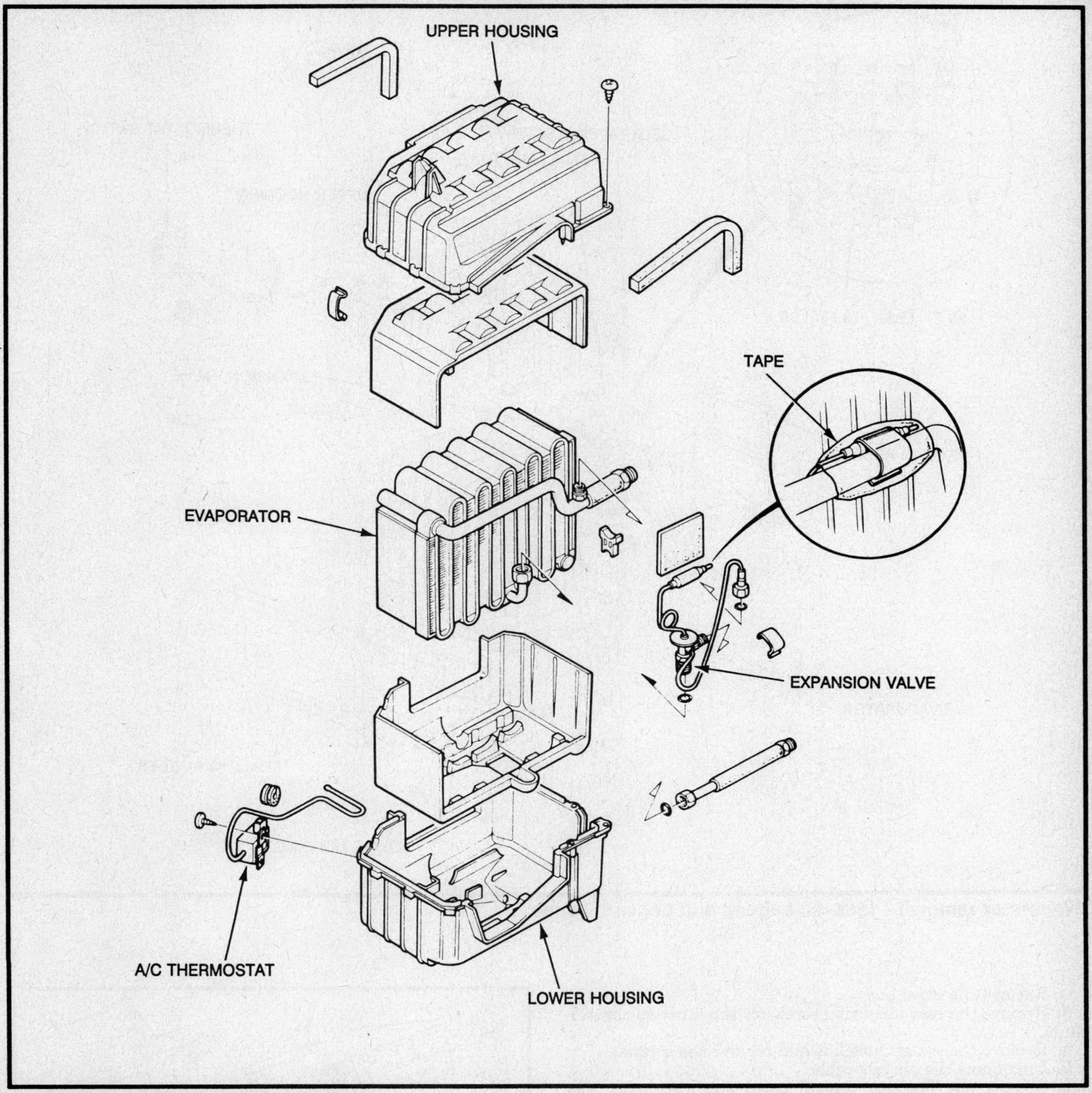
UPPER HOUSING
TAPE
EVAPORATOR
EXPANSION VALVE
A/C THERMOSTAT
LOWER HOUSING

Evaporator removal—1990–91 Integra

To install:

11. Installation is the reverse of removal procedures. Install the expansion valve capillary tube against the suction line and wrap it with tape. Reassemble the upper and lower housings with clips, making sure there are no caps between them. Reinstall the evaporator sensor in its original position. Be sure to apply sealant to the grommets and make sure there is no air leakage after the installation is complete. Evacuate and recharge the system properly.

Manual Control Head

REMOVAL AND INSTALLATION

Integra

1989

1. Disconnect the negative battery cable.

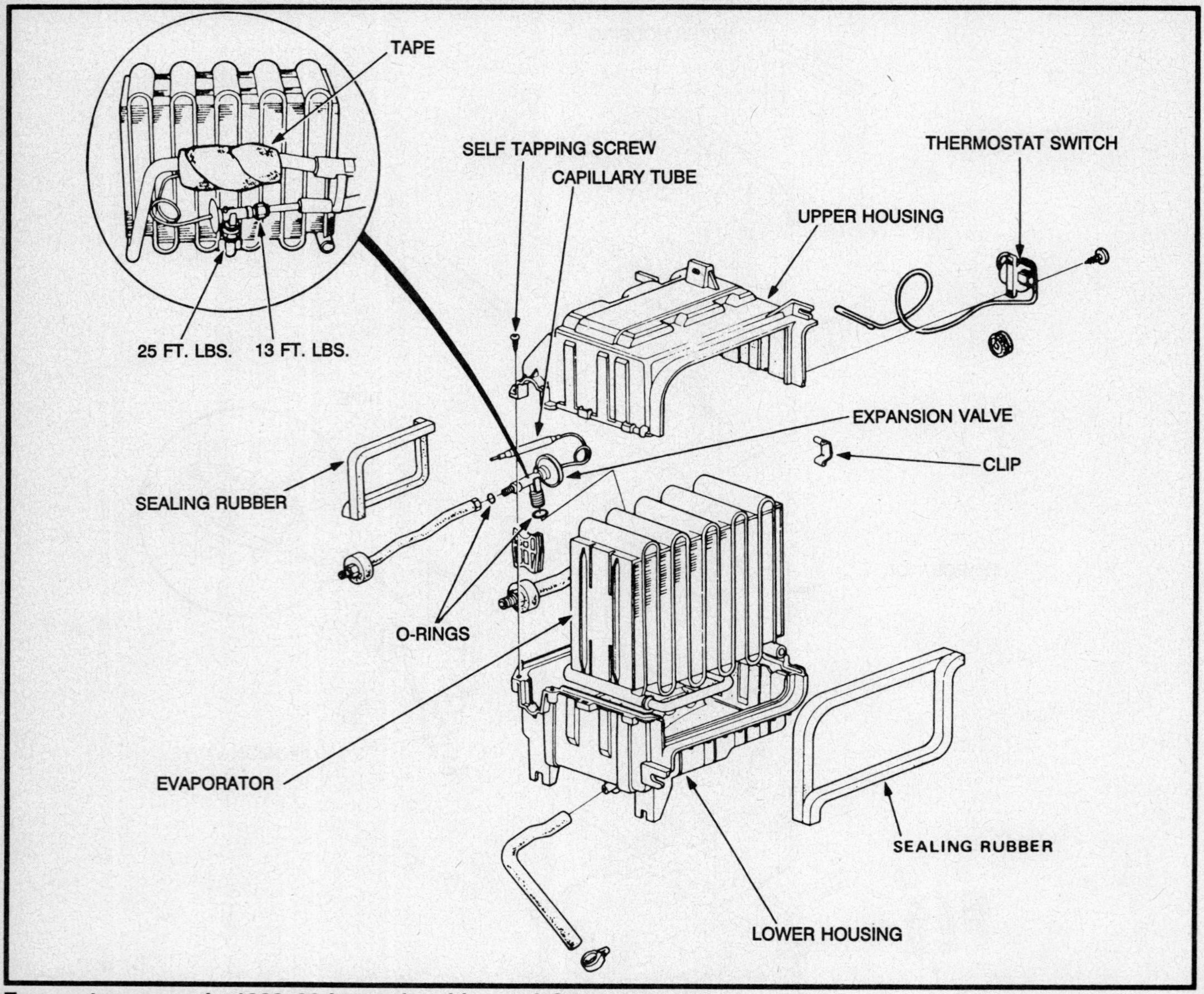
TAPE
SELF TAPPING SCREW
CAPILLARY TUBE
THERMOSTAT SWITCH
UPPER HOUSING
25 FT. LBS.
13 FT. LBS.
EXPANSION VALVE
CLIP
SEALING RUBBER
O-RINGS
EVAPORATOR
SEALING RUBBER
LOWER HOUSING

Evaporator removal—1989–90 Legend and Legend Coupe

2. Remove the glove box.
3. Remove the rear mounting screw for the function control panel.
4. Remove the switch hole lids and remove the screws.
5. Disconnect the air mix cable.
6. Remove the function control panel and disconnect the connectors.
7. Installation is the reverse order of the removal procedure.

1990–91

1. Disconnect the negative battery cable.
2. Remove the instrument panel.
3. Remove the radio/cassette player.
4. Disconnect the air/mix cable at the heater assembly.

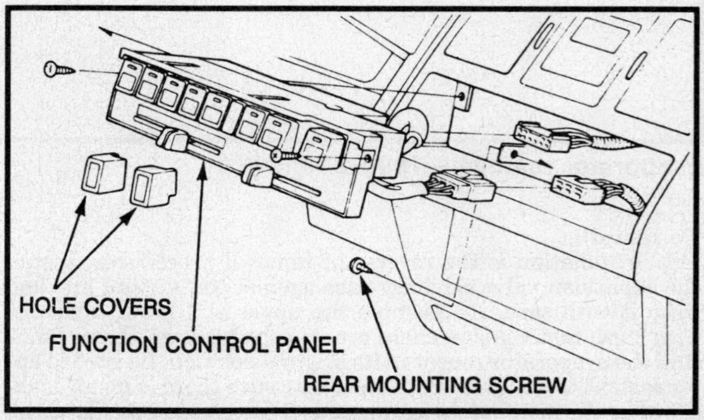
HOLE COVERS
FUNCTION CONTROL PANEL
REAR MOUNTING SCREW

Manual control head—1989 Integra

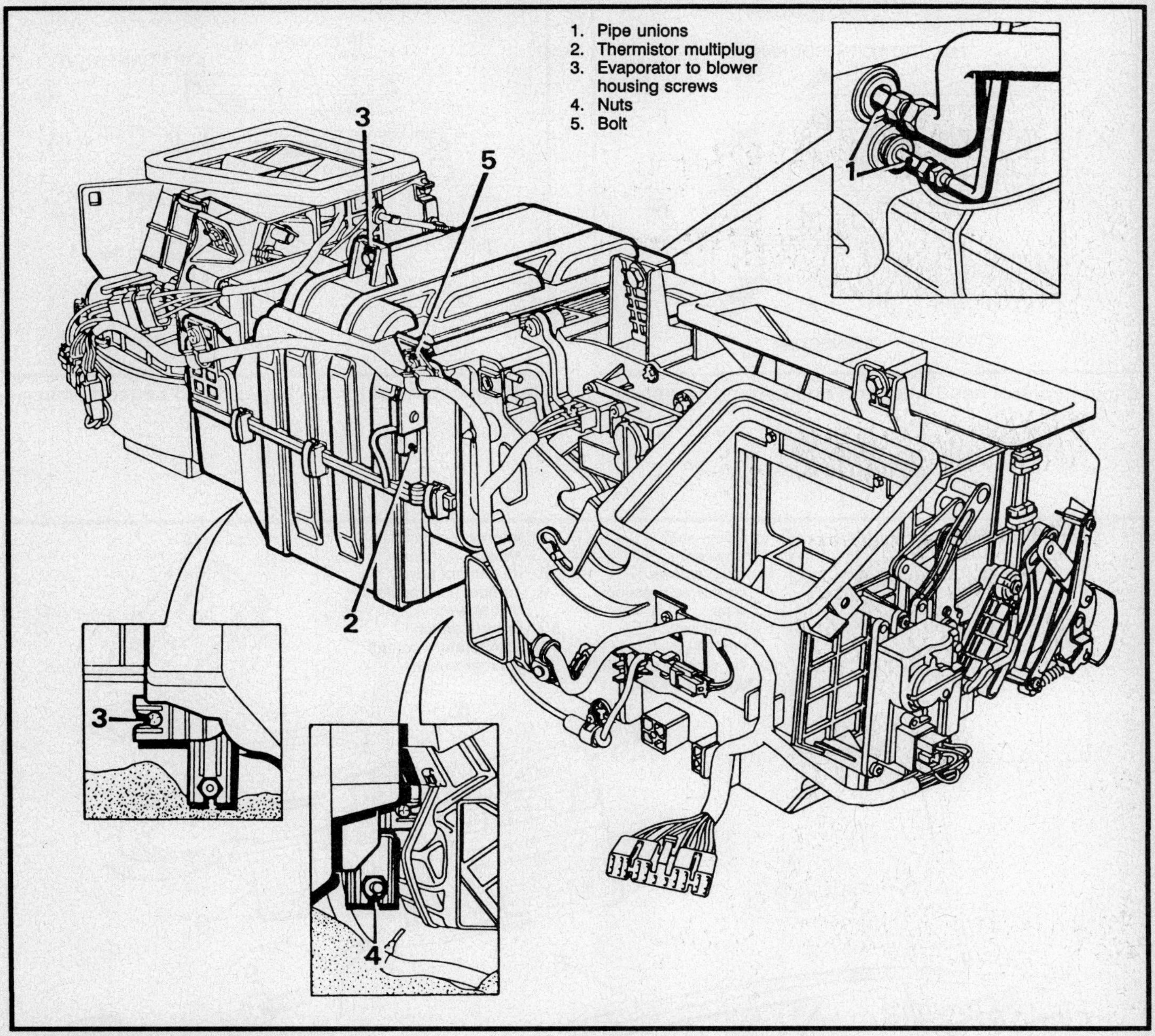
1. Pipe unions
2. Thermistor multiplug
3. Evaporator to blower housing screws
4. Nuts
5. Bolt
3
5
1
2
3
4

Evaporator removal – Sterling

5. Remove the 4 bracket retaining screws then disconnect the wire harness connectors and cables and remove the heater control head.

Legend and Legend Coupe

1989–90

1. Disconnect the negative battery cable.
2. Remove the front console retaining screws and remove the front console.
3. Remove the radio/cassette player.
4. Remove the heater control cable from the heater.
5. Remove the function control panel retaining screws. Disconnect the connector and remove the function control panel.
6. Installation is the reverse order of the removal procedure.

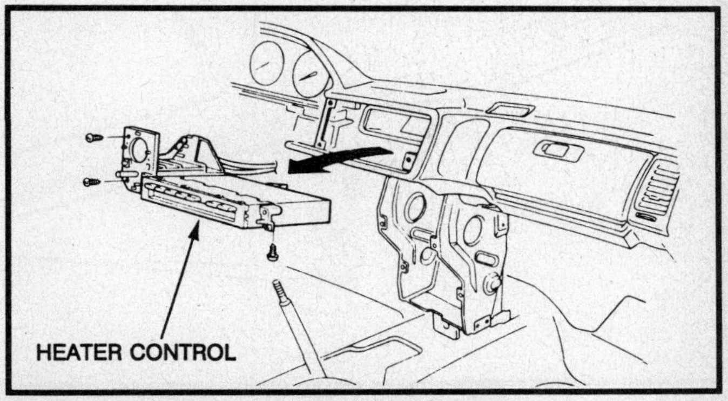
HEATER CONTROL

Manual control head – 1990–91 Integra

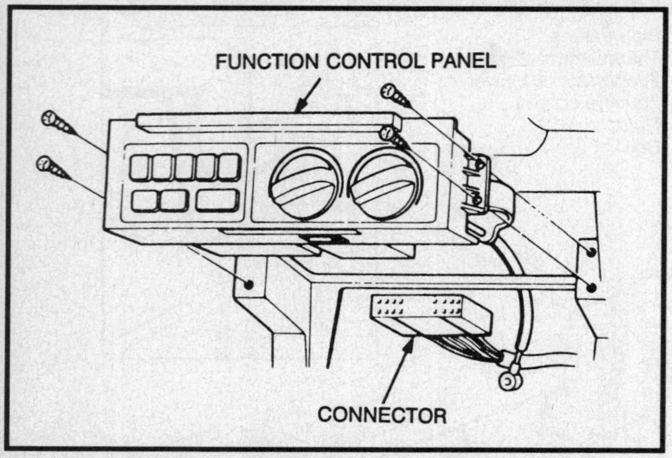
FUNCTION CONTROL PANEL
CONNECTOR

Manual control head—Legend and Legend Coupe

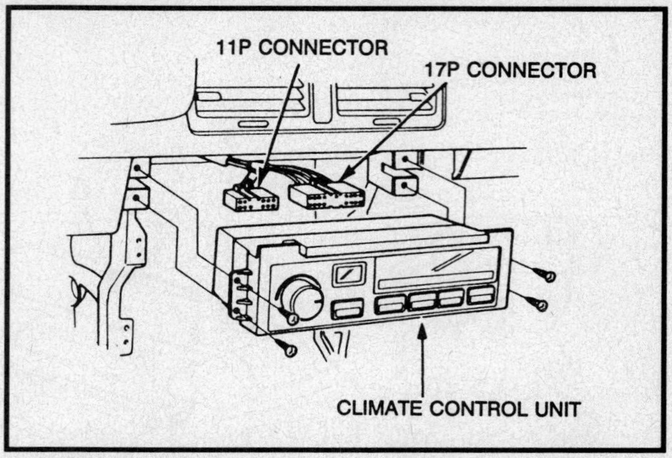
11P CONNECTOR
17P CONNECTOR
CLIMATE CONTROL UNIT

Electronic control head—Legend and Legend Coupe

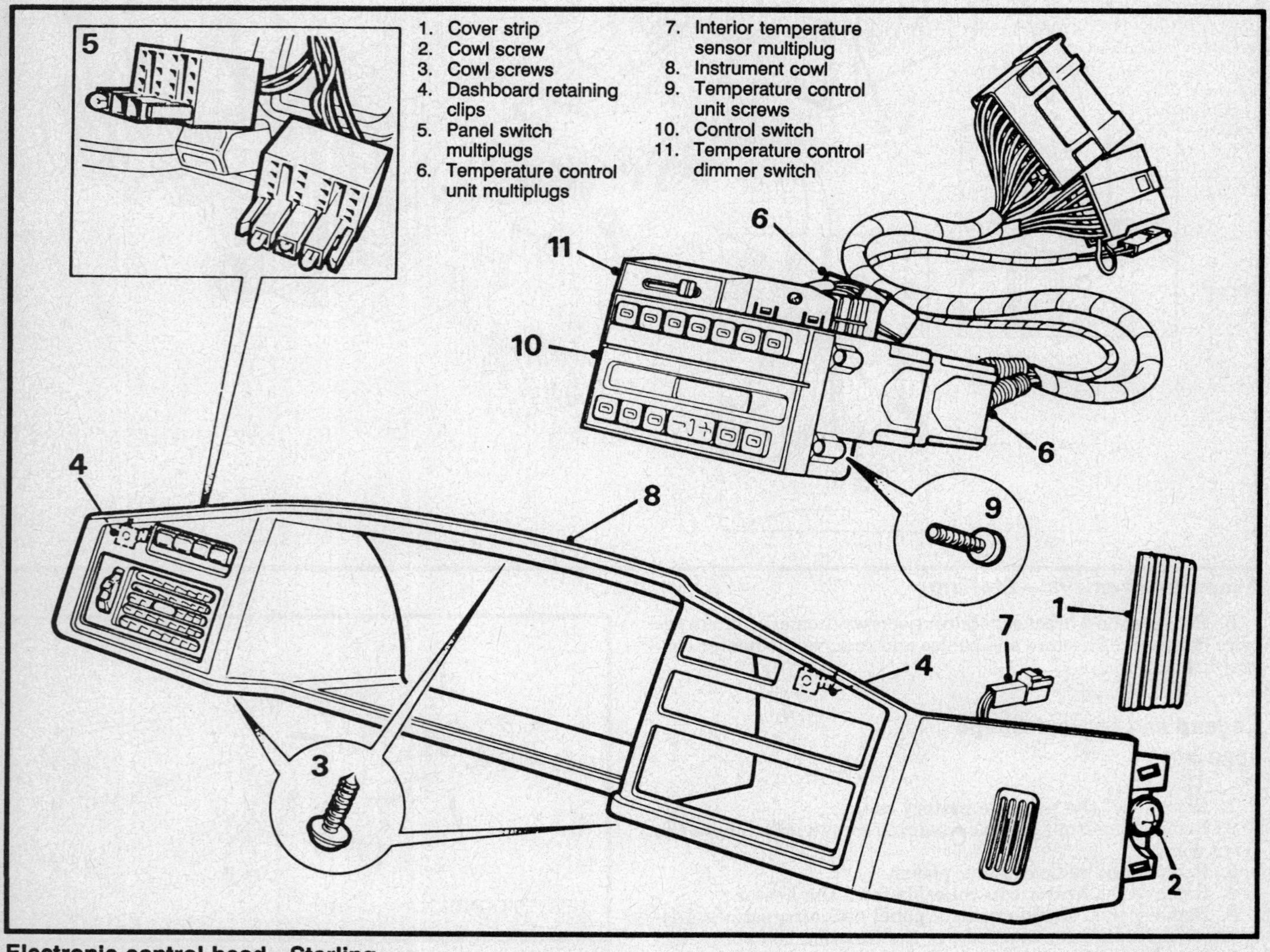
1. Cover strip
2. Cowl screw
3. Cowl screws
4. Dashboard retaining clips
5. Panel switch multiplugs
6. Temperature control unit multiplugs
7. Interior temperature sensor multiplug
8. Instrument cowl
9. Temperature control unit screws
10. Control switch
11. Temperature control dimmer switch

Electronic control head—Sterling

Electronic Control Head

REMOVAL AND INSTALLATION

Legend and Legend Coupe

1989–90

NOTE: The air bag wire harness, identified by yellow harness and connectors, is near the console. Use care not to damage the wire harness and do not use electrical test equipment on this circuit.

1. Disconnect the negative battery cable.
2. Remove the console retaining screws and remove the front console.
3. Remove the 4 screws and pull out the control head.
4. Disconnect the wiring connector and remove the control head.
5. Installation is the reverse of removal.

Sterling

1. Disconnect the negative battery cable.
2. Lift the steering column release lever and lower the column fully.
3. Remove the cover strip retaining screw, located adjacent to the insert on the dashboard shelf.
4. Remove the dashboard cowl retaining screws, pull the clips off, then tag and disconnect the multi-plugs from the panel switch, temperature control unit and interior temperature sensor.
5. Remove the cowl then remove the control unit retaining screws.
6. Installation is the reverse of removal.

Air Mix Cable

ADJUSTMENT

Integra

1. Slide the air temperature control lever to the **HOT** position.
2. On 1989 models, open the air mix door in front of the heater core. Connect the end of the cable to the arm.

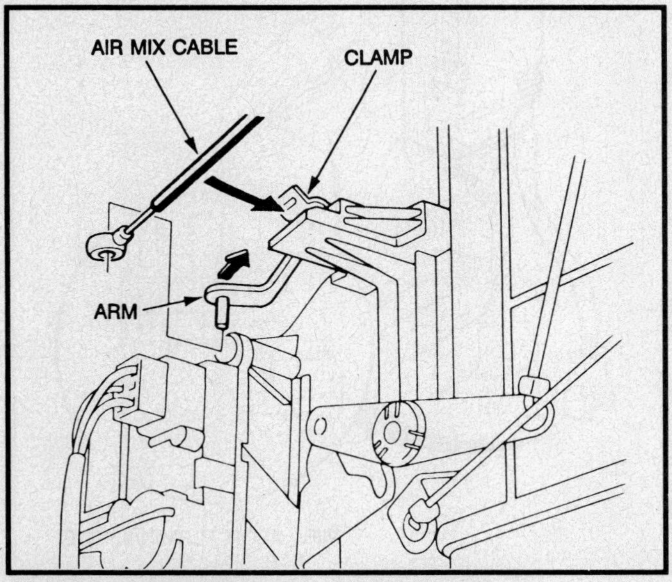
AIR MIX CABLE
CLAMP
ARM
Air mix cable adjustment—1989 Integra

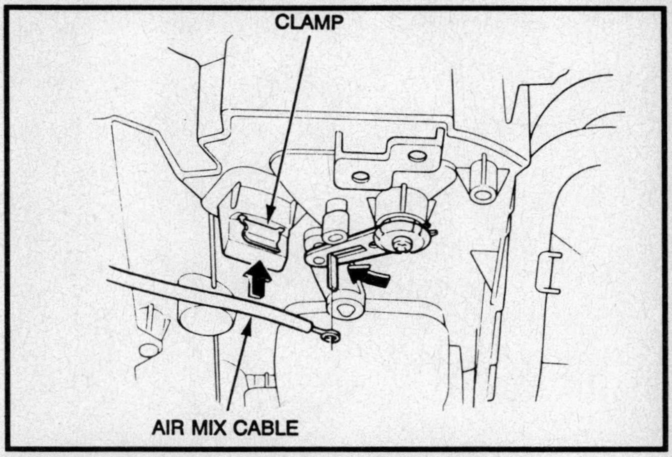
CLAMP
AIR MIX CABLE
Air mix cable adjustment—1990–91 Integra

3. On 1990–91 models, turn the air mix door shaft to the left and connect the end of the cable to the arm.
4. Gently slide the cable housing back from the end enough to take up the slack in the cable but not enough to make the dashboard lever move. Snap the cable housing into the clamp.
5. After the adjustment, make sure the heater valve cable is properly adjusted.

Heater Valve Cable

ADJUSTMENT

Integra

1989

1. Slide the air temperature control lever to the **COLD** position.
2. Close the heater valve fully, connect the end of the heater cable to the valve arm and secure the cable housing with the clamp.

1990–91

1. Slide the air temperature control lever to the **HOT** position.
2. Gently slide the cable housing back from the end enough to take up any slack in the cable but not enough to make the temperature control lever move, then hold the cable housing and snap in the clamp.

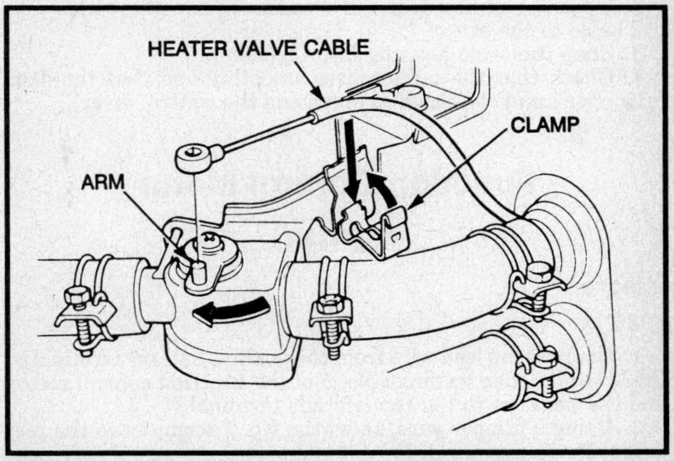
HEATER VALVE CABLE
CLAMP
ARM
Heater valve cable adjustment—1989 Integra

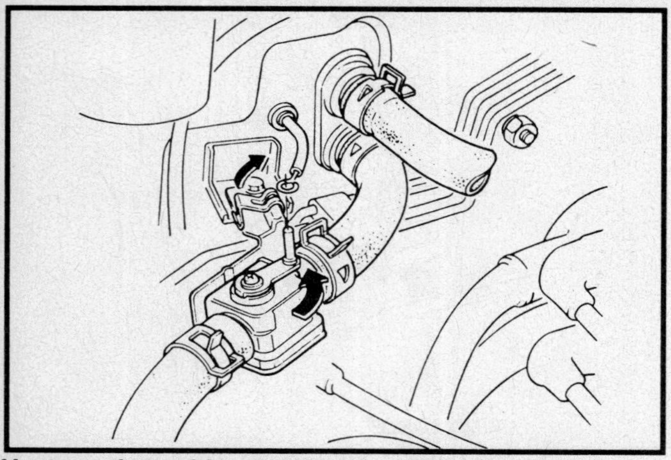

Heater valve cable adjustment—1990–91 Integra

NOTE: The air mix cable should be adjusted if the heater valve cable has been disconnected.

Cool Vent Cable

ADJUSTMENT

Legend and Legend Coupe

1989–90

1. Slide the cool vent control lever to the shut position.
2. Close the cool vent door fully and connect the end of the cool vent cable to the door arm.
3. Snap the cable housing into the clamp.
4. Check that the cable moves smoothly and that the door fully opens and closes when operating the control lever.

Heat Control Cable

ADJUSTMENT

Legend and Legend Coupe

1989–90

1. Turn the temperature control dial to the max **HOT** position.
2. Open the air mix door and connect the end of the heat control cable to the arm.
3. Snap the cable housing into the clamp.
4. Check that the cable moves smoothly and that the door fully opens and closes when operating the control lever.

Function Control Motor

TESTING

Integra

1989

1. Connect the lead wire from the positive battery terminal to the lower left side terminal No. 5 of the function control motor and the negative to the top left side terminal No. 1.
2. Using a jumper wire, short the No. 1 terminal to the rest except for terminal No. 5.
3. The motor should run each time a short circuit is made.

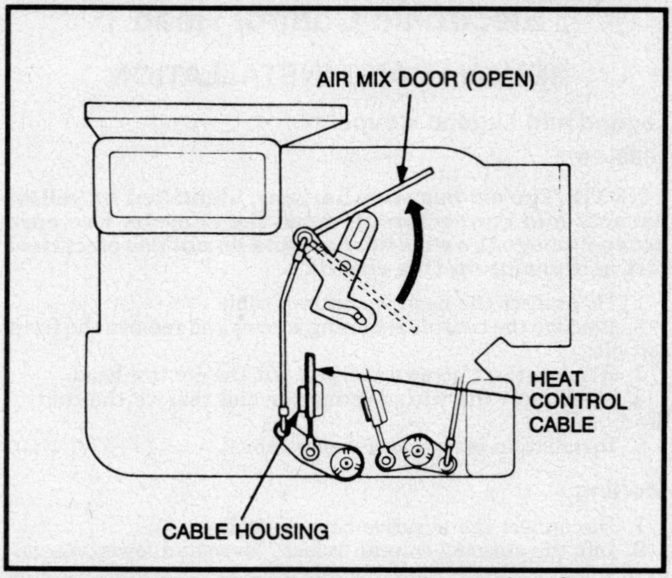
AIR MIX DOOR (OPEN)
HEAT CONTROL CABLE
CABLE HOUSING

Heater control cable adjustment—Legend and Legend Coupe

Legend and Legend Coupe

1989–90

With Manual Air Conditioning

1. Connect the lead wire from the positive battery terminal to the lower left side terminal No. 5 of the function control motor and the negative to the top left side terminal No. 1.

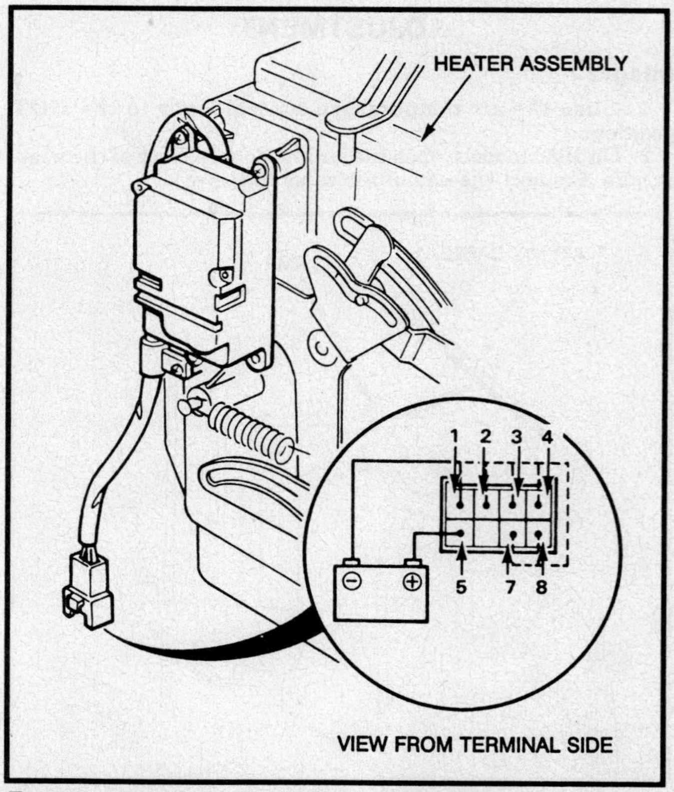
HEATER ASSEMBLY
1 2 3 4
5 7 8
VIEW FROM TERMINAL SIDE

Function control motor test—1989 Integra

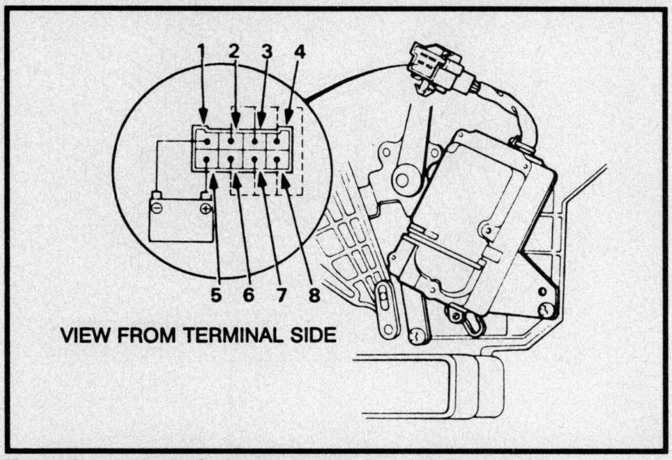
1 2 3 4
5 6 7 8
VIEW FROM TERMINAL SIDE

Function control motor test—Legend and Legend Coupe with manual air conditioning

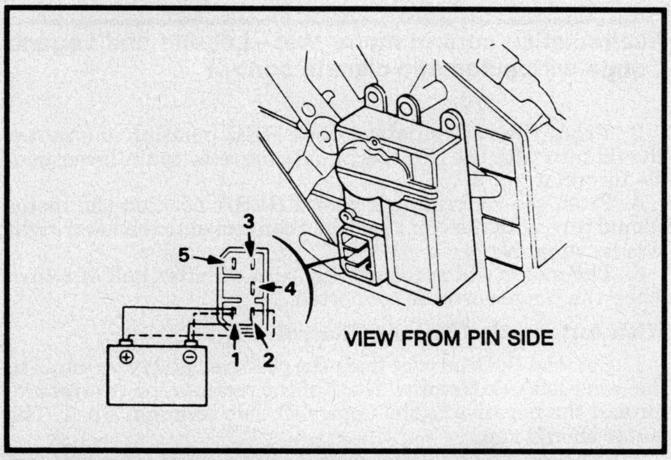
3
5
4
1 2
VIEW FROM PIN SIDE

Function control motor test—Legend and Legend Coupe with automatic climate control

2. Using a jumper wire, short the No. 2 terminal to the rest except for terminal No. 5.
3. The motor should run each time a short circuit is made.

With Automatic Climate Control

1. Using a suitable ohmmeter, measure the resistance between the top No. 3 right side terminal and top left side terminal No. 5 on the function control motor connector. The resistance should be 4 k-ohms.
2. Check the motor operation by connecting a wire from the battery positive terminal to the lower right side terminal No. 2 and the negative to the lower left side terminal No. 1. Reverse the wires to make sure the motor will run in both directions.

NOTE: Be sure to disconnect the battery from the motor as soon as the motor starts to run. Failure to do so will damage the motor.

3. Connect a battery to the motor terminal No. 2 and No. 1 and measure the resistance between terminal No. 5 and the middle right side terminal No. 4. The motor is normal if the resistance is any where between 1.2 k-ohms at **VENT** and 4 k-ohms at **DEF**.
4. Also check the resistance with the battery polarity reversed.

Recirculation Control Motor

TESTING

Integra

1989

1. Connect the lead wire from the positive battery terminal to the lower left side terminal No. 4 of the recirculation control motor and the negative to the top left side terminal No. 1.
2. Using a jumper wire, short the No. 1 terminal to the rest except for terminal No. 4.
3. From the recirculation door **REC** position the motor should turn with the No. 1 terminal connected to the lower right side terminal No. 6.
4. From the recirculation door **FRESH** position the motor should turn with the No. 1 terminal connected to the lower middle terminal No. 5.
5. The motor will automatically turn off after a half of turn when the jumper wire is connected.

1990–91

1. Connect the lead wire from the positive battery terminal to the No. 3 terminal of the recirculation control motor connector and the negative to the No. 2 terminal.
2. Using a jumper wire, connect the No. 2 terminal to the No. 1 or No. 4 terminal.
3. From the recirculation door **REC** position the motor should turn with the No. 2 terminal connected to the terminal No. 1.
4. From the recirculation door **FRESH** position the motor should turn with the No. 2 terminal connected to the terminal No. 4.
5. The motor will automatically turn off after a half of turn when the jumper wire is connected.

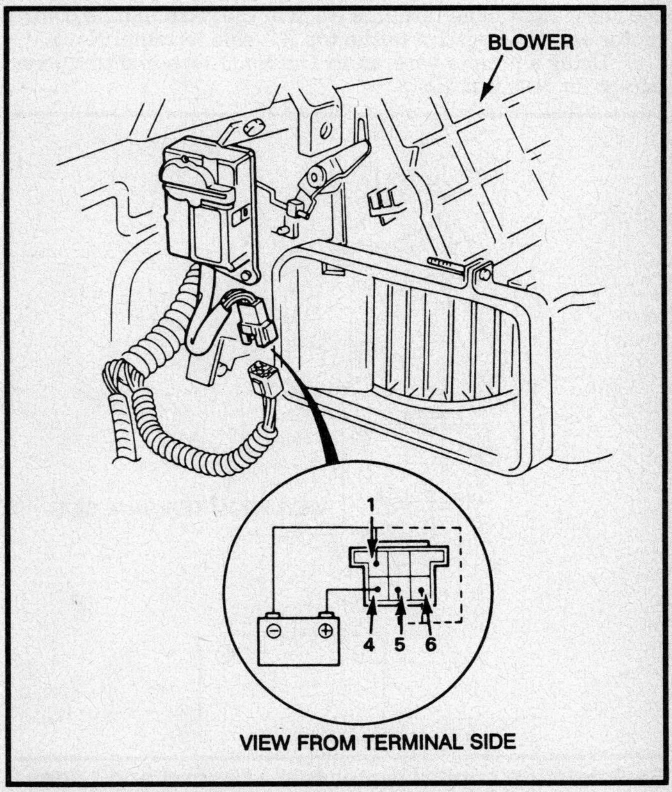
BLOWER
1
4 5 6
VIEW FROM TERMINAL SIDE

Recirculation control motor test—1989 Integra

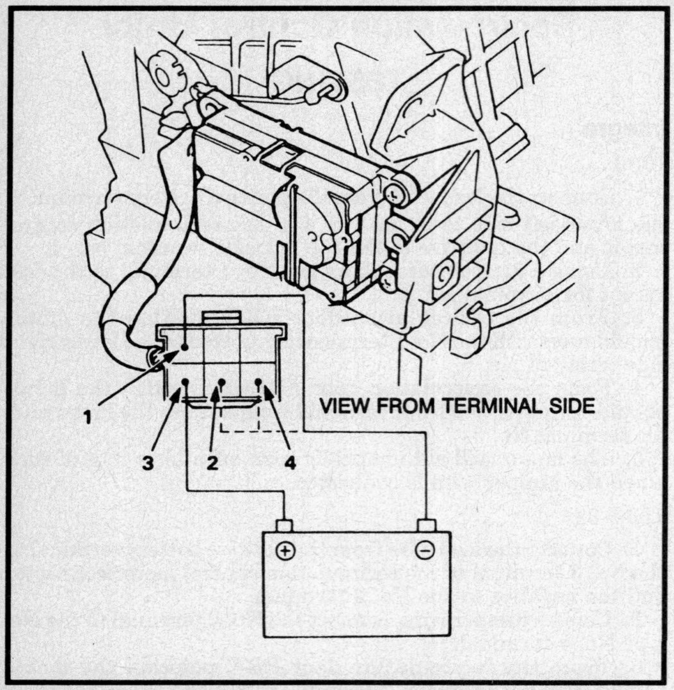
1
3
2
4
VIEW FROM TERMINAL SIDE

Recirculation control motor test—1990–91 Integra

Legend and Legend Coupe

1989–90

With Manual Air Conditioning

1. Connect the lead wire from the positive battery terminal to the lower right hand terminal No. 3 of the recirculation control motor and the negative to the top left side terminal No. 1.
2. Using a jumper wire, short the No. 1 terminal to the rest except for terminal No. 3.

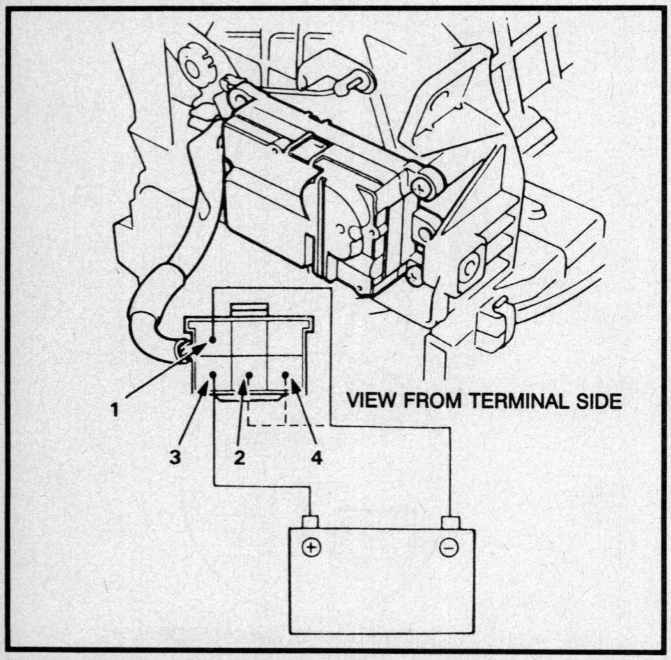
1
3
2
4
VIEW FROM TERMINAL SIDE

Recirculation control motor test—Legend and Legend Coupe with manual air conditioning

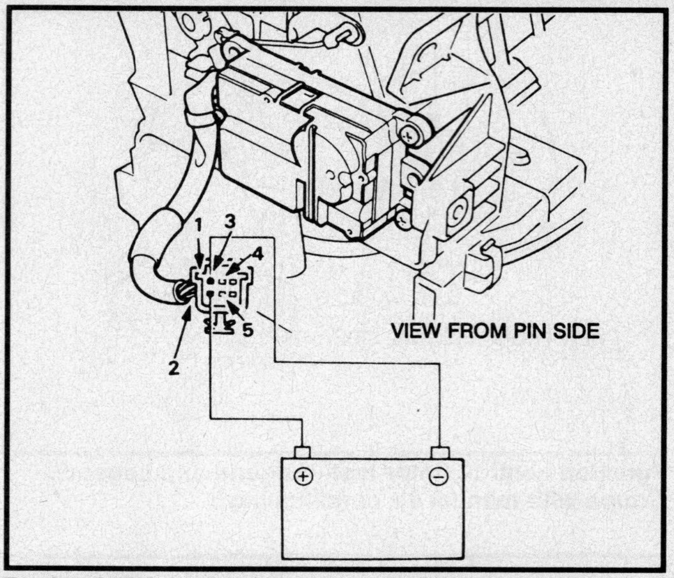
1
3
4
5
2
VIEW FROM PIN SIDE

Recirculation control motor test—Legend and Legend Coupe with automatic climate control

3. From the recirculation door **REC** position the motor should turn with the No. 1 terminal connected to the lower middle terminal No. 2.
4. From the recirculation door **FRESH** position the motor should turn with the No. 1 terminal connected to the lower right side terminal No. 4.
5. The motor will automatically turn off after half of a turn when the jumper wire is connected.

With Automatic Climate Control

1. Connect the lead wire from the positive battery terminal to the lower left side terminal No. 2 of the reciculation control motor and the negative to the upper left side terminal No. 1. The motor should run.
2. Connect the ohmmeter probes to the upper right side terminal No. 4 and the lower right side terminal No. 5.
3. The ohmmeter should continue to cycle back and fourth but hesitate slightly longer when indicating continuity.
4. Connect the ohmmeter probes to the lower right side terminal No. 5 and the upper middle terminal No. 3.
5. The ohmmeter should continue to cycle back and fourth but hesitate slightly longer when indicating continuity.

Air Mix Control Motor

TESTING

Legend and Legend Coupe

1989–90

With Automatic Climate Control

1. Using a suitable ohmmeter, measure the resistance between the top No. 3 and bottom No. 5 terminals on the left side of the air mix control motor connector. The resistance should be 4 k-ohms.
2. Connect the lead wire from the positive battery terminal to the upper right side terminal No. 2 of the air mix control motor and the negative to the lower right side side terminal No. 1.
3. Measure the resistance between the top middle terminal No. 4 and terminal No. 5.
4. The resistance should be approximately 1.2 k-ohms at the **COOL** and 4.0 k-ohms **HOT**.

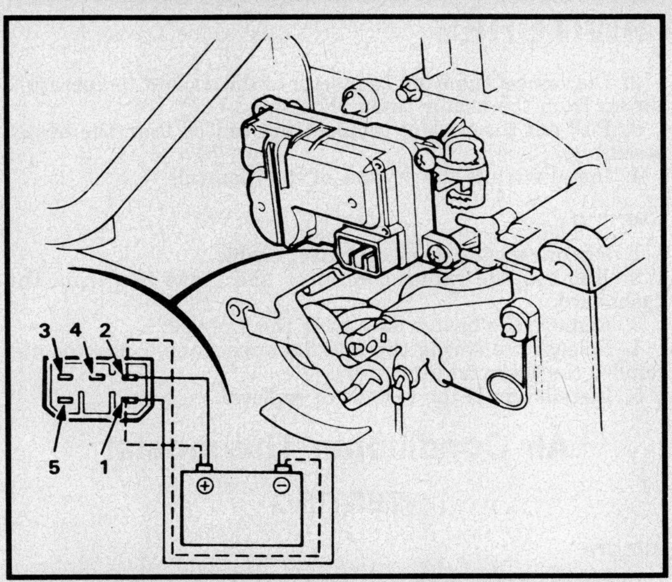
3
4
2
5
1
Air mix control motor test—Legend and Legend Coupe with automatic climate control

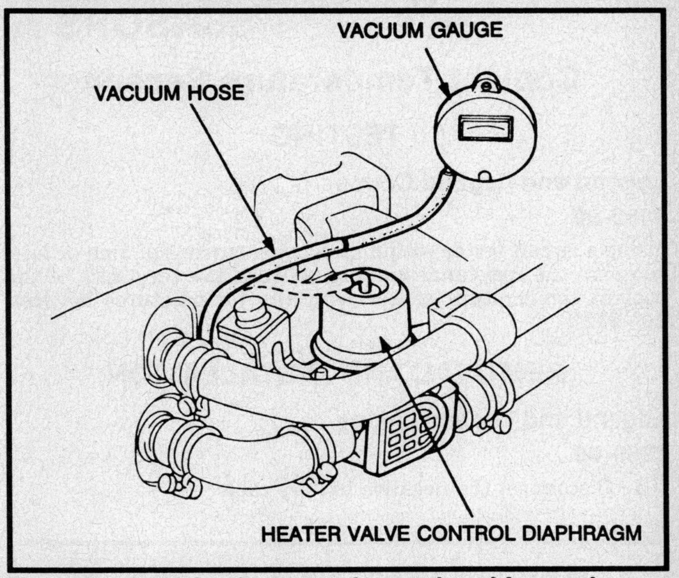
VACUUM GAUGE
VACUUM HOSE
HEATER VALVE CONTROL DIAPHRAGM
Vacuum control valve test—Legend and Legend Coupe with manual air conditioning

5. Also check the resistances with the battery polarity reserved.

Vacuum Control Valve

TESTING

Legend and Legend Coupe

1989–90

1. Check that the vacuum hoses are properly routed and the heat control cable is adjusted properly.
2. Start the engine and let it idle.
3. Disconnect the vacuum hose from the heater valve control diaphragm and connect a vacuum gauge to the hose.
4. Turn the air temperature dial right and left and check for vacuum. There should be vacuum with the temperature lever in the **MAX COOL** position. There should be no vacuum with the temperature lever in the **HOT** position.
5. If there is vacuum when there is not supposed to be or no vacuum when it is supposed to be, inspect the vacuum hose for pinching, disconnected, bending or breakage. Replace the control valve and retest.

Sterling

1. Check that the vacuum hoses are properly routed and the heat control cable is adjusted properly.
2. Start the engine and let it idle.
3. Disconnect the vacuum hose from the heater valve control diaphragm and connect a vacuum gauge to the hose.
4. Turn the air temperature dial right and left and check for vacuum. There should be vacuum with the temperature lever in the **MAX COOL** position. There should be no vacuum with the temperature lever in the **HOT** position.
5. If there is vacuum when there is not supposed to be or no vacuum when it is supposed to be, inspect the vacuum hose for pinching, disconnected, bending or breakage. Replace the control valve and retest.

Heater Control Valve Diaphragm

TESTING

Legend and Legend Coupe

1989–90

1. Disconnect the vacuum hose from the heater control valve diaphragm and install a vacuum pump.
2. Apply vacuum and make sure the diaphragm rod moves smoothly and the vacuum remains steady.
3. If the rod does not move smoothly or vacuum does not remain steady, replace the diaphragm.

Sterling

1. Disconnect the vacuum hose from the heater control valve diaphragm and install a vacuum pump.
2. Apply vacuum and make sure the diaphragm rod moves smoothly and the vacuum remains steady.
3. If the rod does not move smoothly or vacuum does not remain steady, replace the diaphragm.

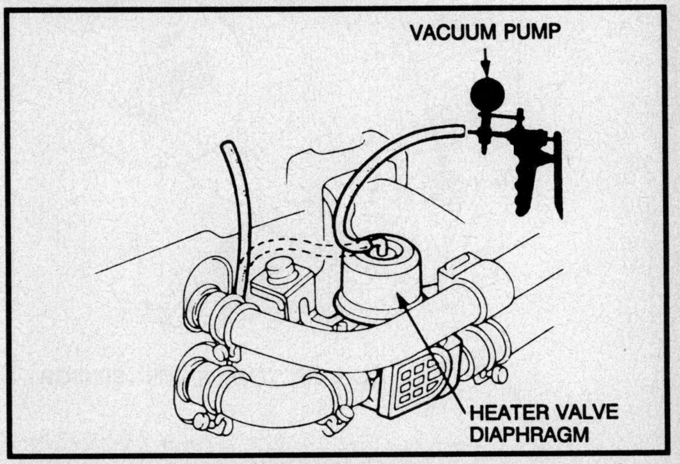
VACUUM PUMP
HEATER VALVE
DIAPHRAGM
Heater valve control diaphragm test—Legend and Legend Coupe with manual air conditioning

SENSORS AND SWITCHES

Coolant Temperature Sensor

TESTING

Legend and Legend Coupe

1989–90

Using a circuit tester with a measuring current of 1ma or less, compare the resistance reading between the terminals of the coolant temperature sensor with the temperatures between 50°–212°F.

REMOVAL AND INSTALLATION

Legend and Legend Coupe

1989–90

1. Disconnect the negative battery cable.

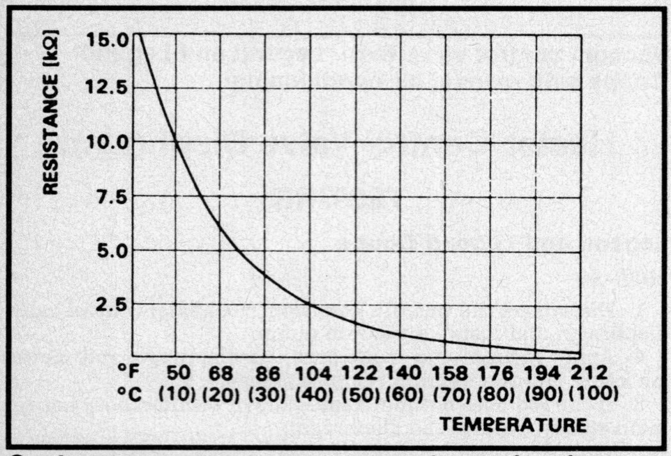
RESISTANCE [kΩ]
15.0
12.5
10.0
7.5
5.0
2.5
°F 50 68 86 104 122 140 158 176 194 212
°C (10) (20) (30) (40) (50) (60) (70) (80) (90) (100)
TEMPERATURE

Coolant temperature sensor test—Legend and Legend Coupe

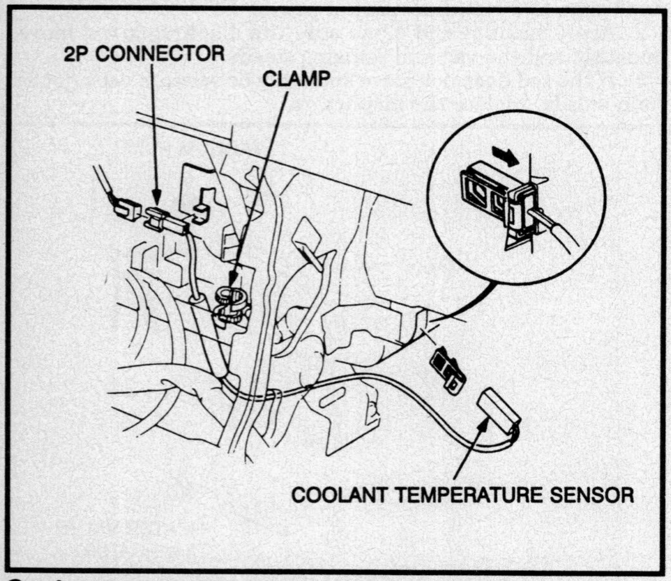
2P CONNECTOR
CLAMP
COOLANT TEMPERATURE SENSOR

Coolant temperature sensor removal—Legend and Legend Coupe

2. Disconnect the 2 pin connector of the coolant temperature sensor from the heater assembly clamp.
3. Pull out the coolant temperature sensor from the heater assembly.
4. Installation is the reverse of the removal.

Sterling

1. Disconnect the negative battery cable.
2. Remove the radio, computer and glove box from the dashboard.
3. Remove the heater duct from the footwell.
4. Release the spring clip and disconnect the connector and remove the thermistor (sensor).
5. Installation is the reverse of removal.

Air Conditioner Thermostat

TESTING

Integra

1. Dip the thermostst capillary tube into a pan filled with ice water and using an ohmmeter, check for continuity.
2. The thermostat should cut off at 33–35°F.
3. The thermostat should cut in at 37–41°F.
4. The cut off and cut in of the thermostat must not be gradual but sudden.
5. If the thermostat fails any part of this test, replace it with a new one.

Air Conditioning Relays

TESTING

All the air conditioning relays are similar and should be tested in the same way as follows:

1. Using a suitable ohmmeter, check for continuity between the top and the bottom terminal on the right side of the connector.
2. There should be no continuity between those 2 terminals.
3. Connect a 12 volt power source across the top and bottom terminals on the left side of the connector.
4. There should now be continuity between the first set of terminals checked.
5. If the relay fails any part of this test, replace it with a new one.

Heater Relay

TESTING

Legend and Legend Coupe

1989–90

1. Using a suitable ohmmeter, check for continuity between the top left side terminal No. 4 and the lower left side terminal (No.3).
2. Connect a 12 volt power source across the top right side terminal No. 2 and the lower right side terminal No. 1.
3. There should be continuity between terminals No. 3 and No. 4.

Diode

TESTING

The diodes are designed to pass current in one direction and

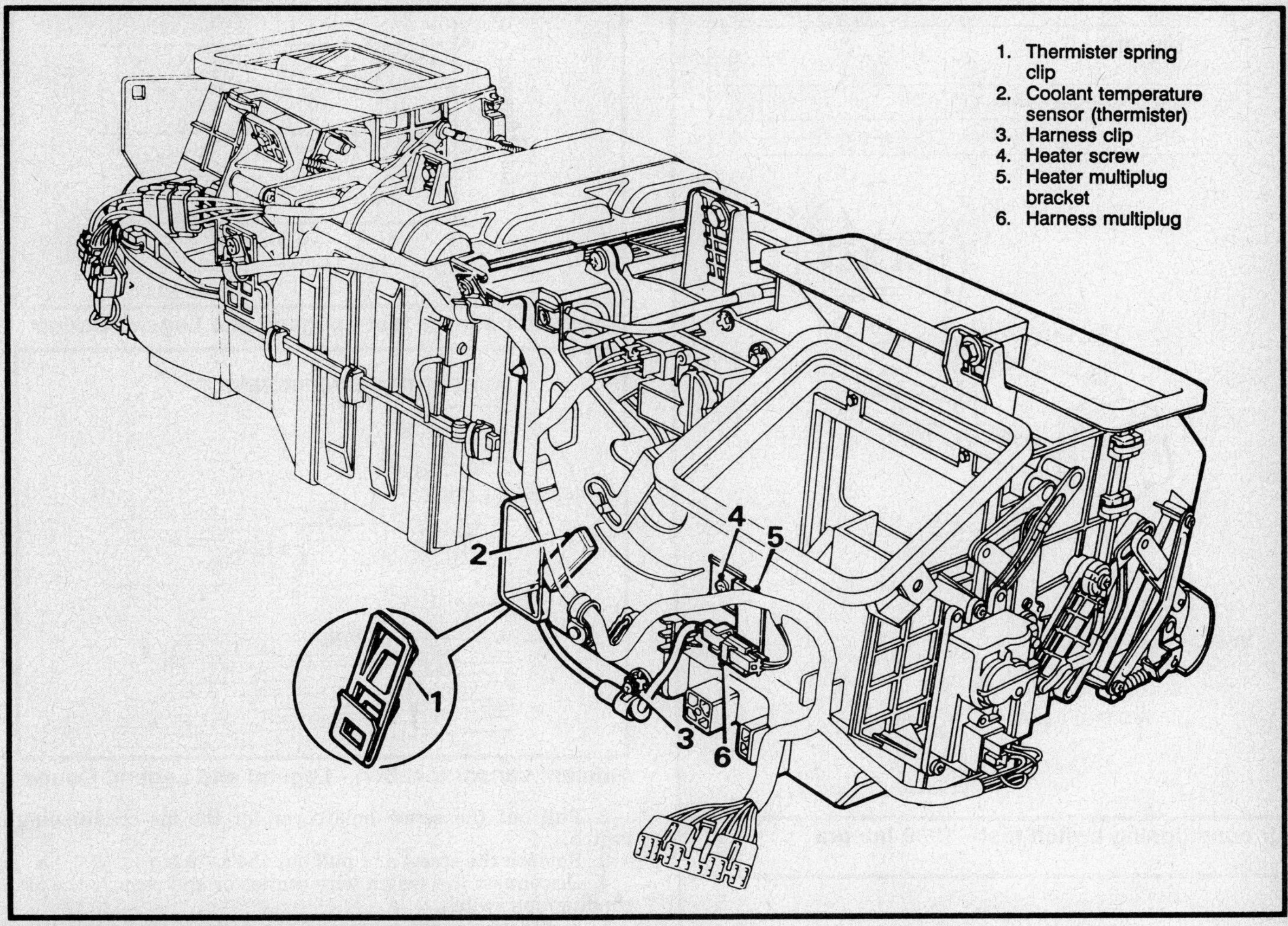
1. Thermister spring clip
2. Coolant temperature sensor (thermister)
3. Harness clip
4. Heater screw
5. Heater multiplug bracket
6. Harness multiplug
1
2
3
4
5
6

Coolant temperature sensor removal—Sterling

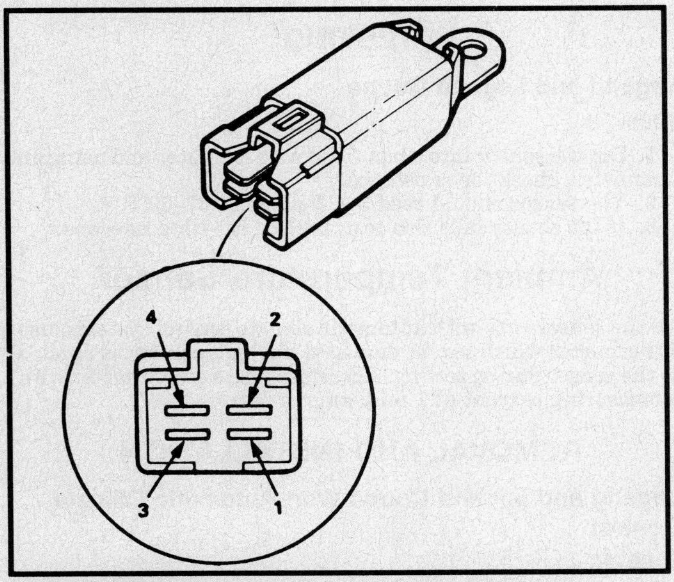
4
2
3
1

Heater relay test—Legend and Legend Coupe

block current in the opposite direction.

1. Using a suitable ohmmeter, check the diodes for continuity.
2. Check for continuity in both directions between the top 2 terminals and the bottom 2 terminals.
3. There should be continuity in only one direction.
4. If the diode fails any part of this test, replace it with a new one.

Air Conditioning Switch

TESTING

Integra

1989

1. Using a suitable ohmmeter, check the switch for continuity.
2. With the switch in the **OFF** position there should be continuity between the first 2 terminals on the left side of the connector.
3. With the switch in the **ON** position there should be continuity between the first 2 terminals on the left side of the connector. There should be no continuity between the last 3 terminals on the connector.

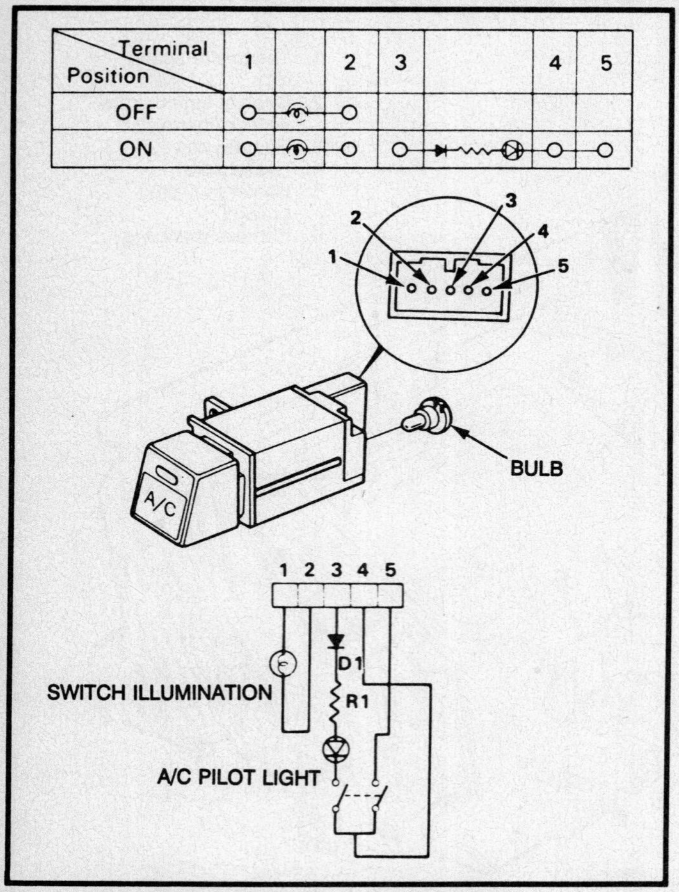
Terminal
Position
1
2
3
4
5
OFF
ON
1
2
3
4
5
A/C
BULB
1 2 3 4 5
D1
R1
SWITCH ILLUMINATION
A/C PILOT LIGHT

Air conditioning switch test—1989 Integra

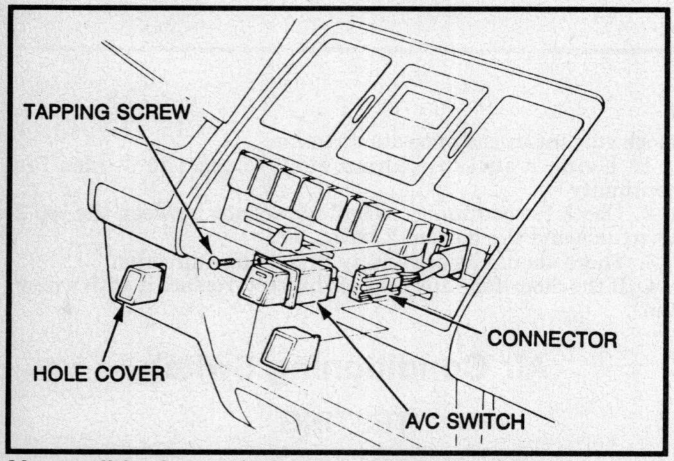
TAPPING SCREW
CONNECTOR
HOLE COVER
A/C SWITCH

Air conditioning switch removal—1989 Integra

4. If the switch fails any part of this test, replace it with a new one.

REMOVAL AND INSTALLATION

Integra

1989

1. Disconnect the negative battery cable.

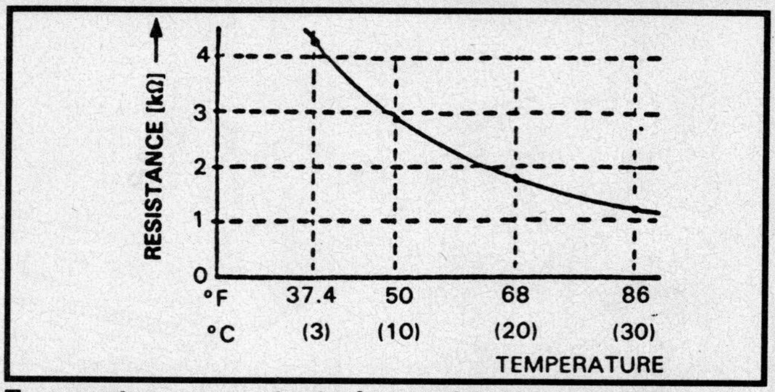
RESISTANCE [kΩ]
4
3
2
1
0
°F
37.4
50
68
86
°C
(3)
(10)
(20)
(30)
TEMPERATURE

Evaporator sensor test—Legend and Legend Coupe

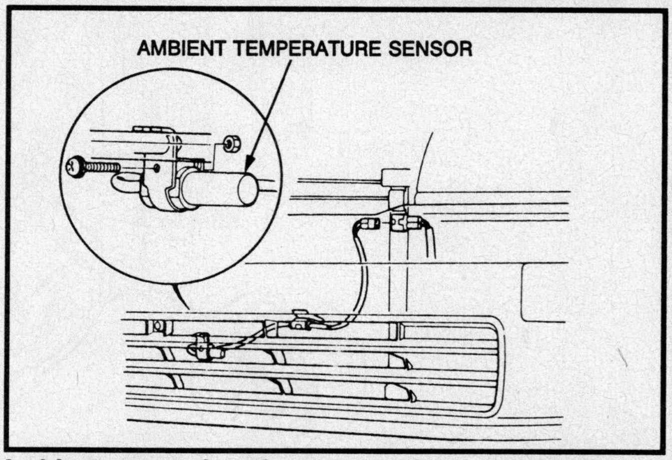
AMBIENT TEMPERATURE SENSOR

Ambient sensor location—Legend and Legend Coupe

2. Pull out the screw hole cover for the air conditioning switch.
3. Remove the screw and pull out the switch.
4. Disconnect the switch wire connector and remove the air conditioning switch.
5. Installation is the reverse of removal.

Evaporator Sensor

TESTING

Legend and Legend Coupe

1989–90

1. Dip the sensor into a pan filled with ice water and using an ohmmeter, check for resistance.
2. The sensor should read 3–4 k-ohms at 37–50°F.
3. If the sensor fails this test, replace it with a new one.

Ambient Temperature Sensor

All the sensors use with automatic climate control systems, use a thermistor which can be damaged if a high current is applied to the sensor during testing. Therefore, use a circuit tester with a measuring current of 1 milli-amp or less.

REMOVAL AND INSTALLATION

Legend and Legend Coupe With Automatic Climate Control

1989–90

1. Disconnect the negative battery cable.

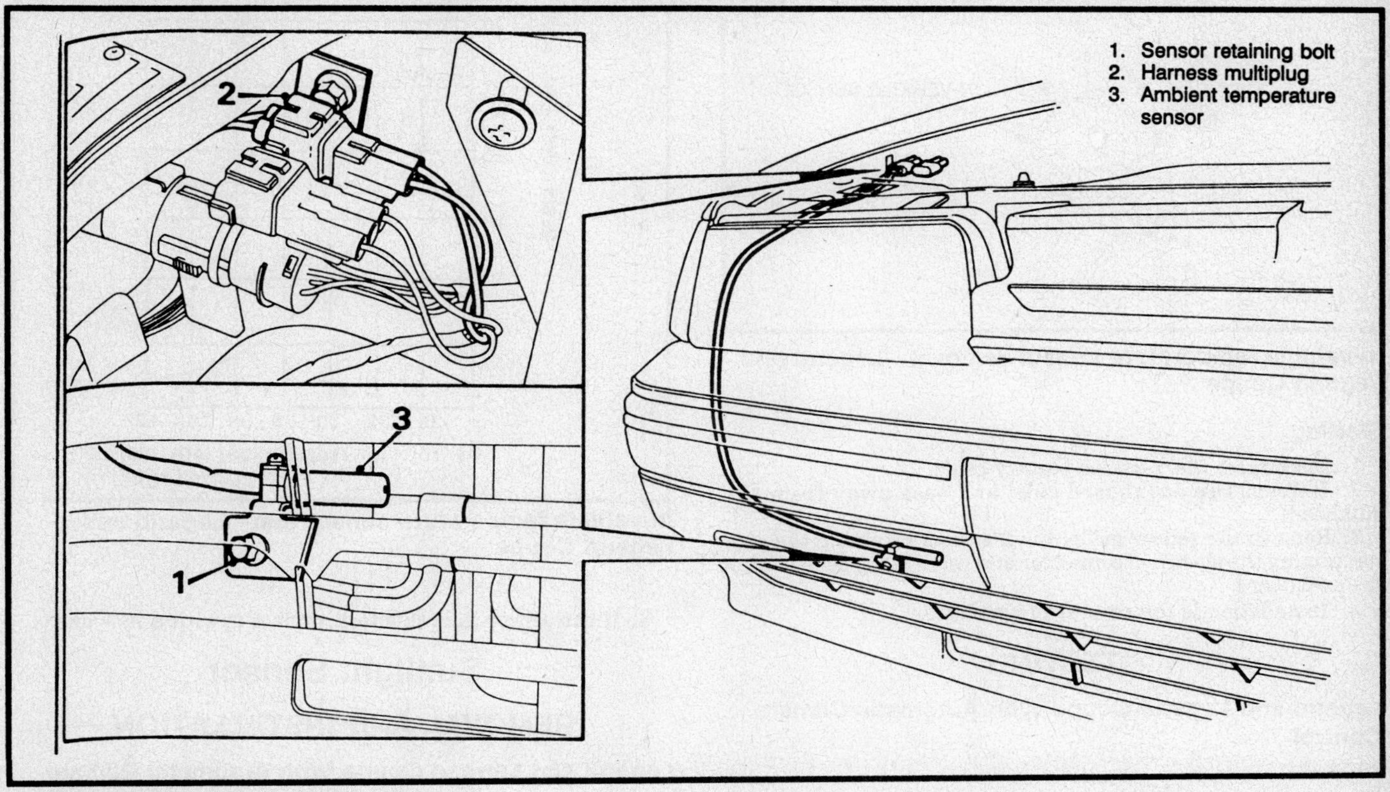
1. Sensor retaining bolt
2. Harness multiplug
3. Ambient temperature sensor
1
2
3

Ambient sensor location—Sterling

2. Remove the front grille.
3. Remove the screw retaining the sensor to the vehicle and disconnect the wire harness.
4. Installation is the reverse of removal.

Sterling

1. Disconnect the negative battery cable.
2. Remove the right side headlight and safely raise and support the vehicle.
3. Remove the ambient temperature sensor retaining bolt, disconnect the electrical connector and remove the sensor from inside the front bumper.
4. Installation is the reverse of removal.

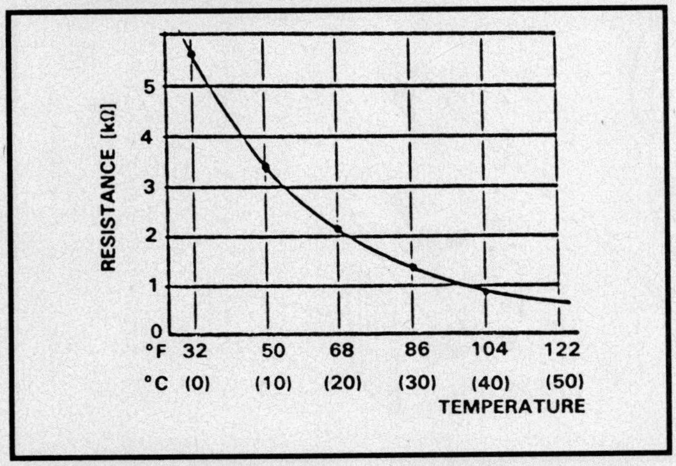
RESISTANCE [kΩ]
5
4
3
2
1
0
°F 32 50 68 86 104 122
°C (0) (10) (20) (30) (40) (50)
TEMPERATURE

Ambient sensor test—Legend and Legend Coupe

TESTING

Legend and Legend Coupe With Automatic Climate Control

1989–90

1. Using a suitable ohmmeter, check the resistance between the terminals of the ambient sensor.
2. The resistance should be 5–0 k-ohms with the temperature between 32–122°F.

NOTE: The way to read the resistance specifications is when the sensor is at 32°F there should be 5 k-ohms and 0 k-ohms at 122°F.

3. If the sensor fails this test, replace it with a new one.

In-Vehicle Temperature Sensor

REMOVAL AND INSTALLATION

Legend and Legend Coupe With Automatic Climate Control

1989–90

The in-vehicle temperature sensor incorporates a small fan to draw in air past the sensor.

1. Disconnect the negative battery cable.
2. Remove the console.
3. Remove the mounting screws retaining the sensor to the vehicle and disconnect the wire harness.
4. Installation is the reverse of removal.

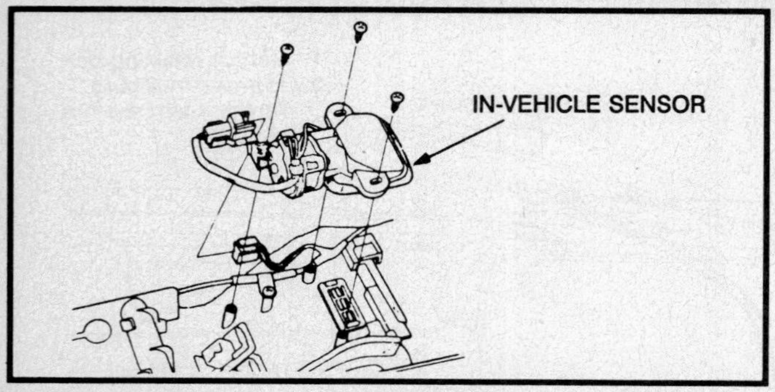
IN-VEHICLE SENSOR

In-vehicle temperature sensor removal—Legend and Legend Coupe

Sterling

1. Disconnect the negative battery cable.
2. Release the dashboard cowl and ease away from the bulkhead.
3. Remove the sensor grille, the 2 screws retaining the sensor, unplug the electrical connector and remove the sensor from the dashboard.
4. Installation is the reverse of removal.

TESTING

Legend and Legend Coupe With Automatic Climate Control

1989–90

1. Using a suitable ohmmeter, check the resistance between the terminals of the in-car sensor.
2. The resistance should be 30–0 k-ohms with the temperature between 32–122°F.

NOTE: The way to read the resistance specifications is when the sensor is at 32°F there should be 30 kilo-ohms and 0 k-ohms at 122°F.

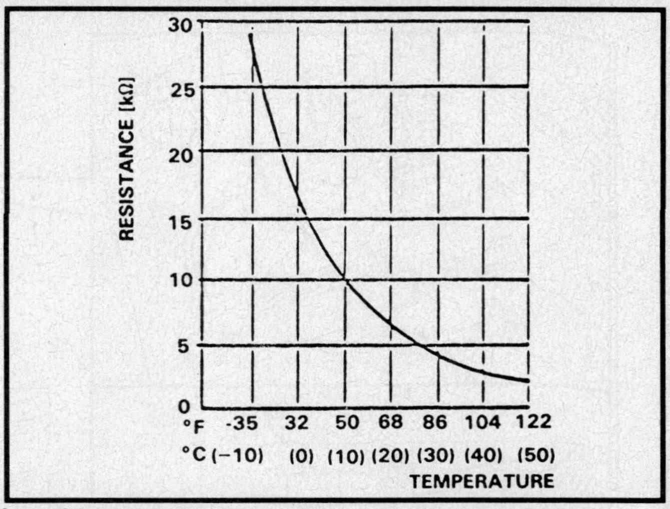
RESISTANCE [kΩ]
30
25
20
15
10
5
0
°F -35 32 50 68 86 104 122
°C (−10) (0) (10) (20) (30) (40) (50)
TEMPERATURE

In-vehicle temperature sensor test—Legend and Legend Coupe

3. If the sensor fails this test, replace it with a new one.

Sunlight Sensor

REMOVAL AND INSTALLATION

Legend and Legend Coupe With Automatic Climate Control

1989–90

1. Disconnect the negative battery cable.
2. Remove the dashboard and unscrew the sensor retaining nut under the dasboard.
3. Disconnect the wire harness and remove the sensor.
4. Installation is the reverse of removal.

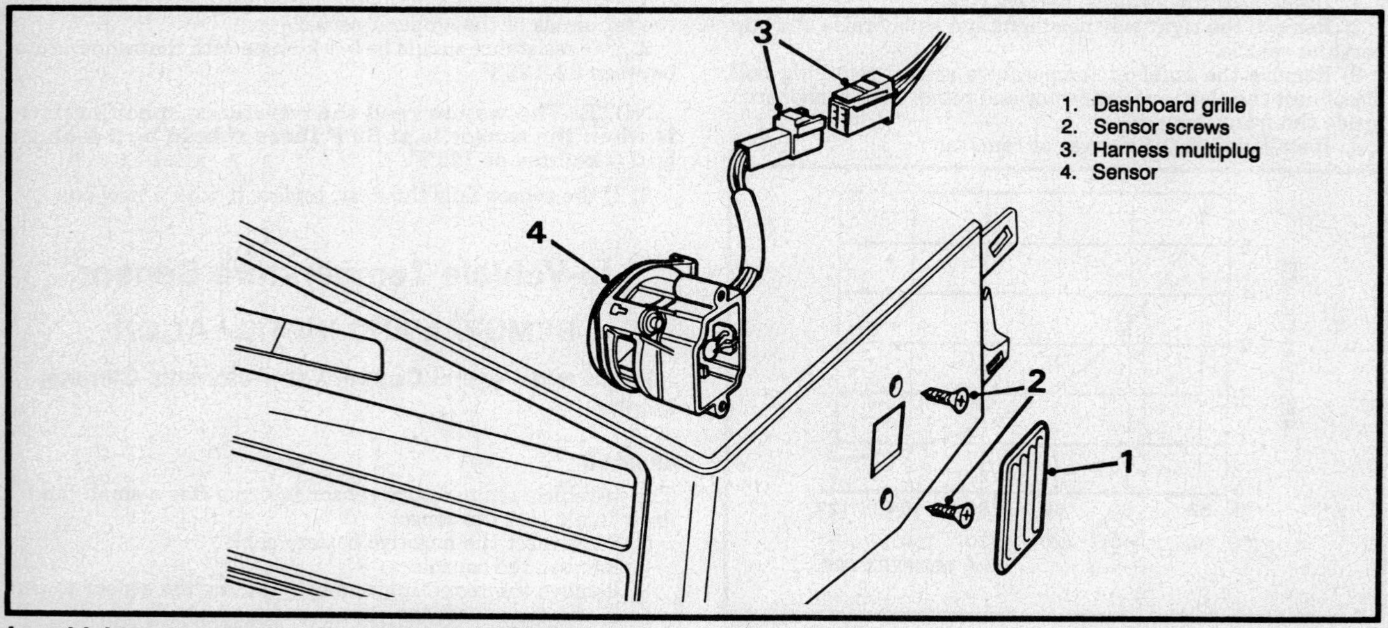
1. Dashboard grille
2. Sensor screws
3. Harness multiplug
4. Sensor
1
2
3
4

In-vehicle temperature sensor removal—Sterling

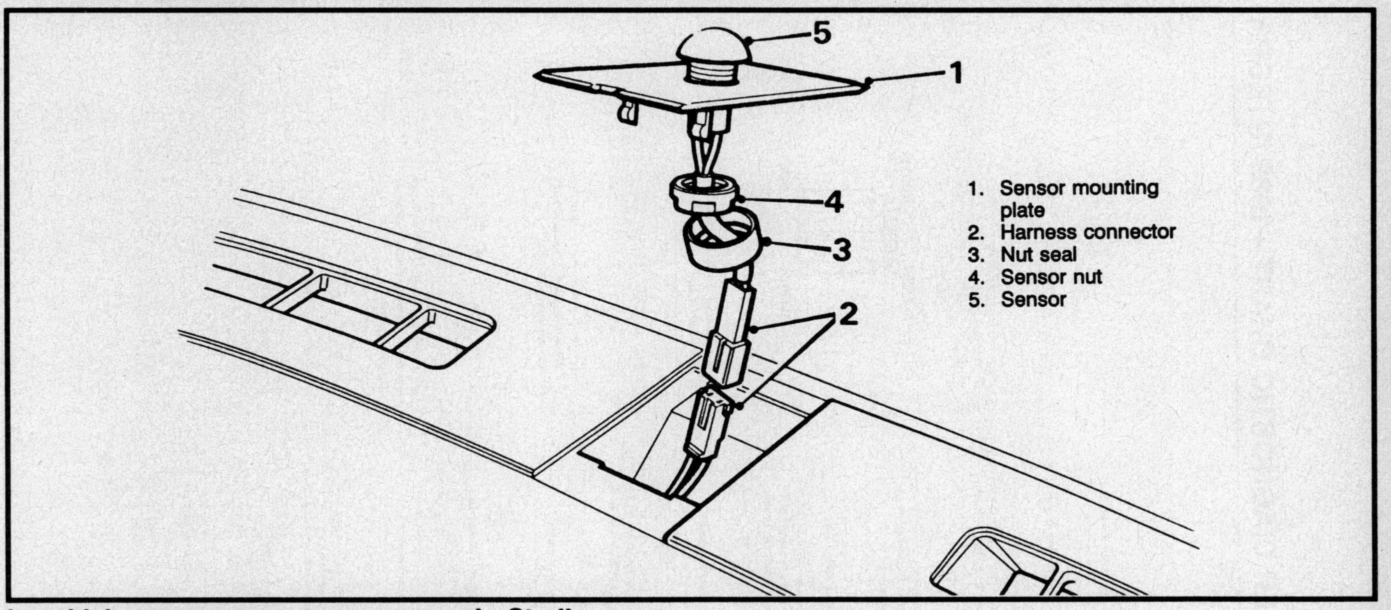
5
1
4
3
2
1. Sensor mounting plate
2. Harness connector
3. Nut seal
4. Sensor nut
5. Sensor

In-vehicle temperature sensor removal—Sterling

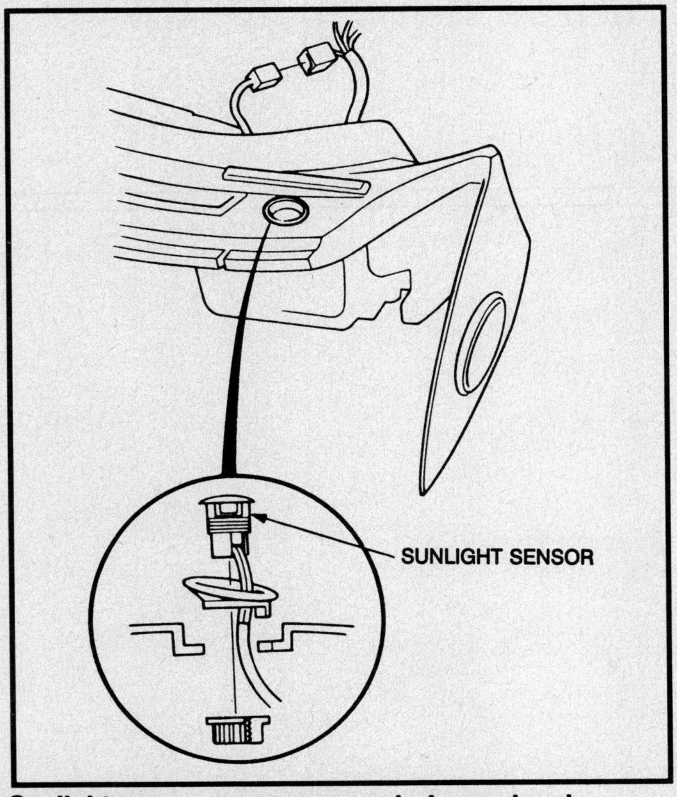
SUNLIGHT SENSOR

Sunlight sensor sensor removal—Legend and Legend Coupe

Sterling

1. Disconnect the negative battery cable.
2. Remove the sensor mounting plate from the dashboard.
3. Release the nut seal, remove the nut, disconnect the electrical connector and remove the sensor from the dashboard.
4. Installation is the reverse of removal.

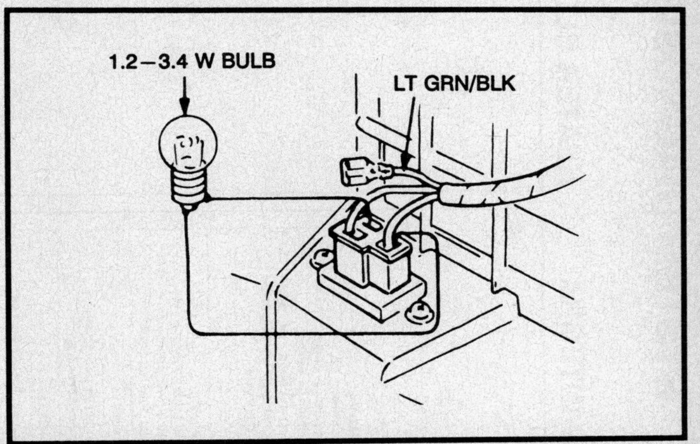
1.2–3.4 W BULB
LT GRN/BLK

Power transistor test—Legend and Legend Coupe

POWER TRANSISTOR

Testing

LEGEND AND LEGEND COUPE

1989–90

1. Check the blower motor and its wire harness, replace or repair, as necessary.
2. Disconnect the wire harness from the power transistor. Pull out the light green wire with the black tracer from the connector and connect a 1.2–3.4 watt bulb. Reconnect the wire harness to the transistor.
3. Turn the ignition to the **ON** position. If the blower motor now operates, the controller is faulty and must be replaced.
4. If the blower motor still does not operate, the power transistor is faulty and must be replaced.

NOTE: To avoid a loose or disconnected terminal, be careful not to damage the locking tab when disconnecting and connecting the terminal. Insulate the light green wire with the black tracer from the body until the testing is completed.

SYSTEM DIAGNOSIS

HEATER DIAGNOSTIC CHART—1989 INTEGRA

SYMPTOM		REMEDY
No hot air flow	Blower motor does not run	See flow chart
	Blower motor runs	Check following: · Clogged heater duct · Clogged blower outlet · Clogged heater valve · Faulty air mix door · Air mix cable out of adjustment · Faulty thermostat
Hot air flow is low	Blower speed does not change	See flow chart
	Blower runs properly	Check following: · Clogged heater duct · Clogged blower outlet · Incorrect door position
Function does not change	Function control motor does not run	See flow chart
	Function control motor runs	Check the heater door linkage and cable adjustments.
Recirculation door does not change	Recirculation motor does not run	See flow chart
	Recirculation motor runs	Check the door linkage then see flow chart

HEATER BLOWER DIAGNOSTIC CHART—1989 INTEGRA

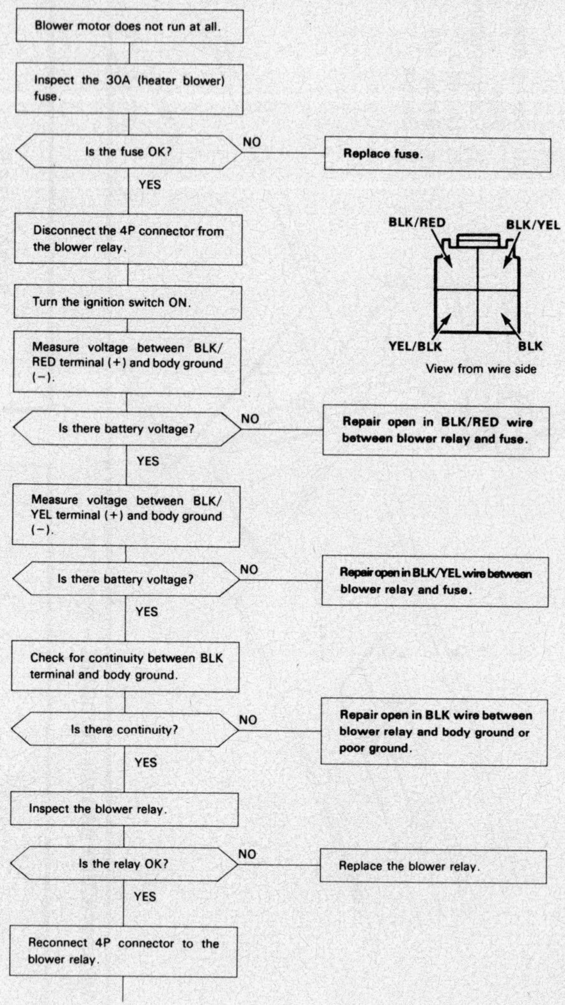
Blower motor does not run at all.
Inspect the 30A (heater blower) fuse.
Is the fuse OK?
NO
Replace fuse.
YES
Disconnect the 4P connector from the blower relay.
BLK/RED
BLK/YEL
YEL/BLK
BLK
View from wire side
Turn the ignition switch ON.
Measure voltage between BLK/RED terminal (+) and body ground (−).
Is there battery voltage?
NO
Repair open in BLK/RED wire between blower relay and fuse.
YES
Measure voltage between BLK/YEL terminal (+) and body ground (−).
Is there battery voltage?
NO
Repair open in BLK/YEL wire between blower relay and fuse.
YES
Check for continuity between BLK terminal and body ground.
Is there continuity?
NO
Repair open in BLK wire between blower relay and body ground or poor ground.
YES
Inspect the blower relay.
Is the relay OK?
NO
Replace the blower relay.
YES
Reconnect 4P connector to the blower relay.

HEATER BLOWER DIAGNOSTIC CHART CONT.—1989 INTEGRA

Disconnect 2P connector from the blower motor.

Measure voltage between YEL/BLK terminal (+) and body ground (−).

Is there battery voltage? — NO → **Repair open in YEL/BLK wire between blower relay and blower motor.**

YES

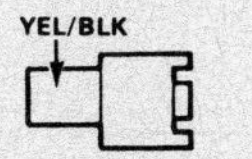
YEL/BLK

View from wire side

Reconnect 2P connector to the blower motor.

Connect a jumper wire between BLU/BLK terminal and body ground.

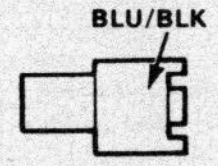
BLU/BLK

View from wire side

Does blower motor run? — NO → **Replace the blower motor.**

YES

Remove the jumper wire.

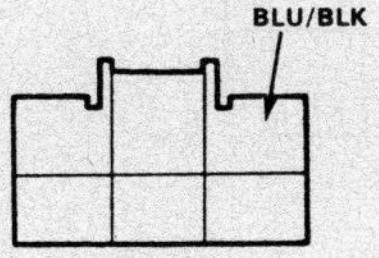
BLU/BLK

View from wire side

Disconnect the 6P connector from blower fan switch.

Connect a jumper wire between BLU/BLK terminal and body ground.

Does the blower motor run? — NO → **Repair open in BLU / BLK wire between blower motor and blower fan switch.**

YES

Remove the jumper wire.

Inspect the blower fan switch?

Is the blower fan switch OK? — NO → **Replace the blower fan switch.**

YES

Repair open in BLK wire between blower fan switch and body ground or poor ground.

Blower motor running speed does not change.

Disconnect 4P connector from the blower resistor.

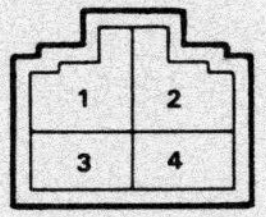
1
2
3
4

View from wire side

Check for resistance between No. 2 and No.4 terminals of the resister.

Is there approximately 3Ω? — NO → **Replace the resistor.**

YES

Reconnect the 4P connector to the resistor.

Disconnect the 6P connector from blower fan switch.

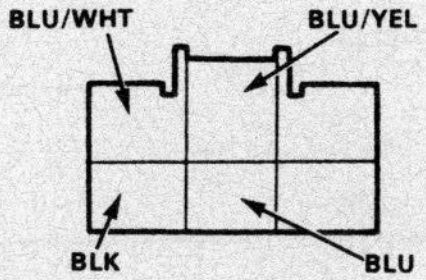
BLU/WHT
BLU/YEL
BLK
BLU

View from terminal side

Turn the ignition switch ON.

Measure voltage between:
- BLU/YEL terminal and body ground.
- BLU/WHT terminal and body ground.
- Bu terminal and body ground.

Is there battery voltage? — NO → **Repair open in BLU/YEL, BLU/WHT and/or BLU wire (s) between blower fan switch and resistor.**

YES

Check for contisuity from BLK terminal to body ground.

Is there continuity? — NO → **Repair open in BLK wire between blower fan switch and body ground or poor ground (G8).**

YES

Replace the blower fan switch.

HEATER FUNCTION CONTROL MOTOR DIAGNOSTIC CHART—1989 INTEGRA

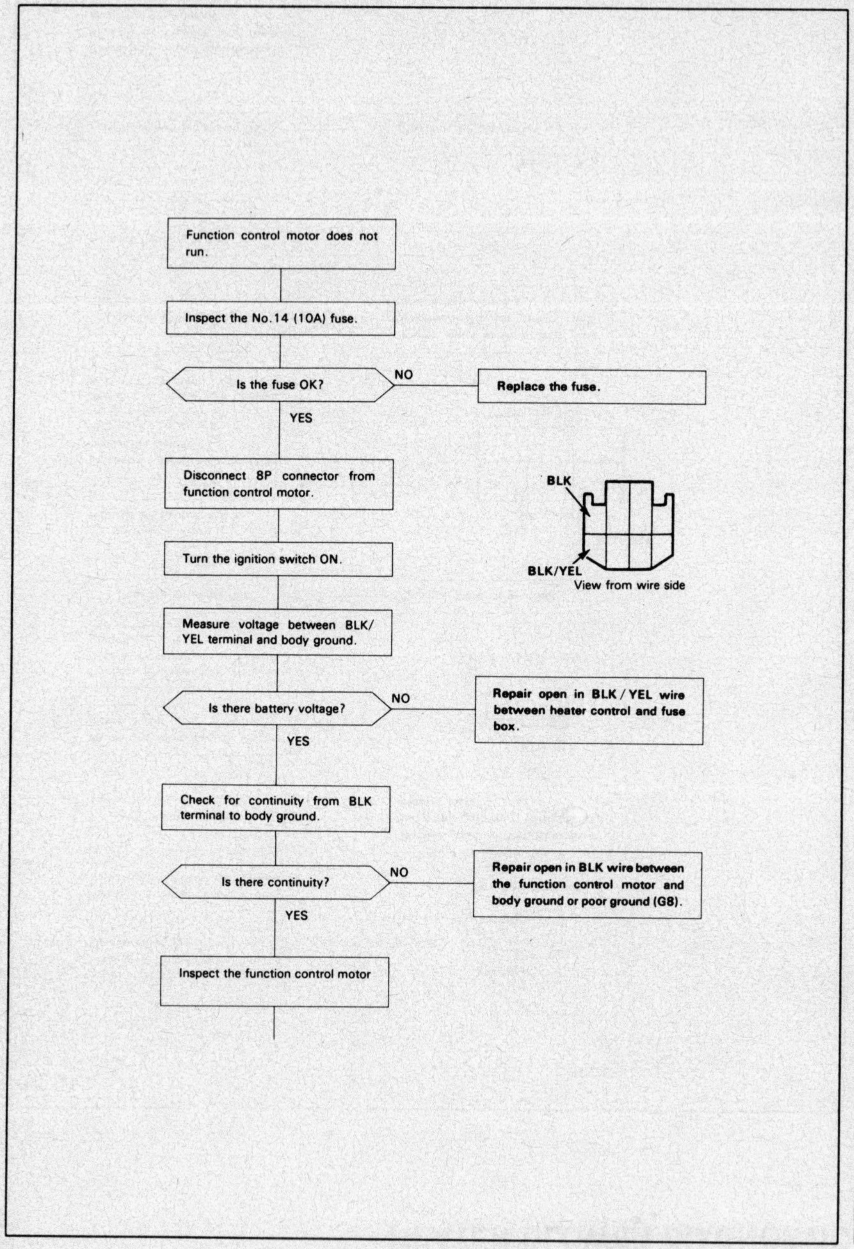
Function control motor does not run.
Inspect the No.14 (10A) fuse.
Is the fuse OK?
NO
Replace the fuse.
YES
Disconnect 8P connector from function control motor.
BLK
BLK/YEL
View from wire side
Turn the ignition switch ON.
Measure voltage between BLK/YEL terminal and body ground.
Is there battery voltage?
NO
Repair open in BLK / YEL wire between heater control and fuse box.
YES
Check for continuity from BLK terminal to body ground.
Is there continuity?
NO
Repair open in BLK wire between the function control motor and body ground or poor ground (G8).
YES
Inspect the function control motor

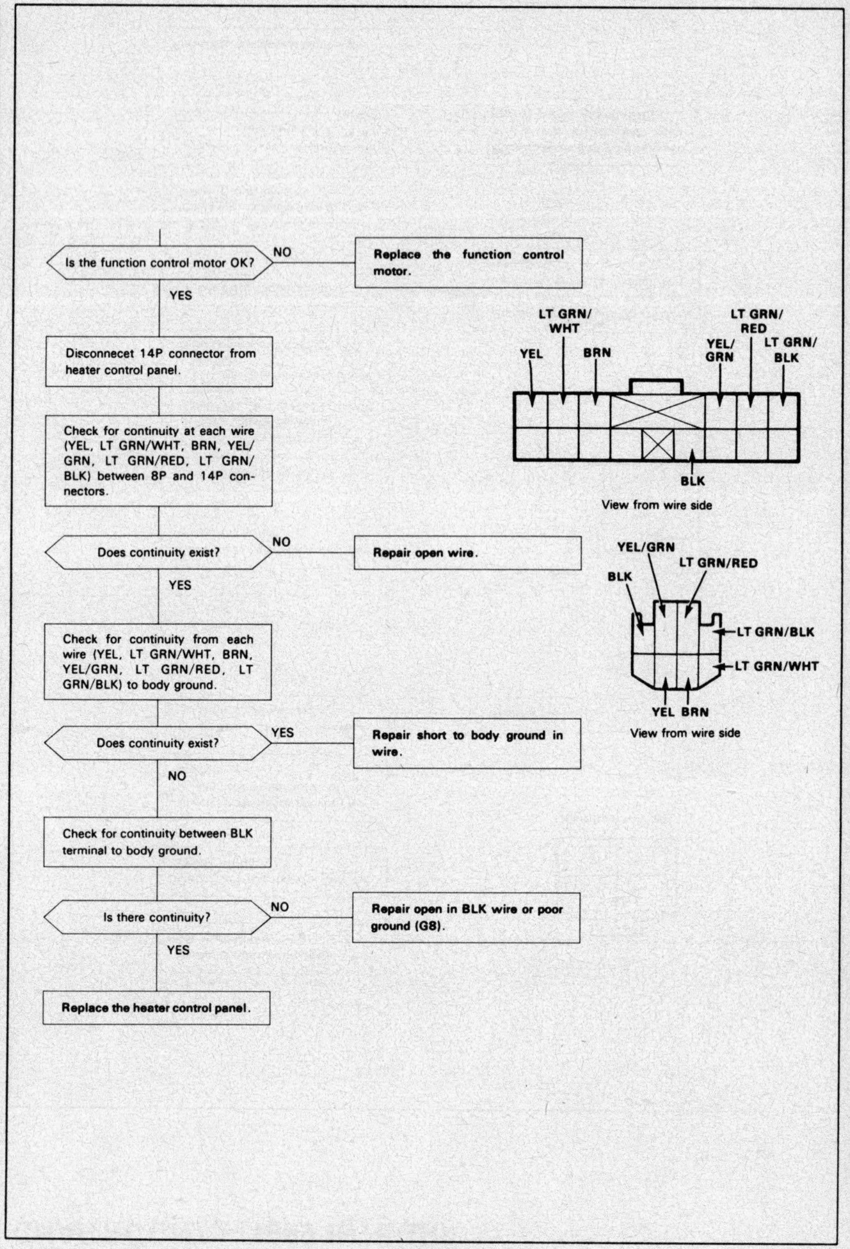
Is the function control motor OK?
NO
Replace the function control motor.
YES
Disconnecet 14P connector from heater control panel.
YEL
LT GRN/WHT
BRN
YEL/GRN
LT GRN/RED
LT GRN/BLK
BLK
View from wire side
Check for continuity at each wire (YEL, LT GRN/WHT, BRN, YEL/GRN, LT GRN/RED, LT GRN/BLK) between 8P and 14P connectors.
Does continuity exist?
NO
Repair open wire.
YES
YEL/GRN
LT GRN/RED
BLK
LT GRN/BLK
LT GRN/WHT
YEL BRN
View from wire side
Check for continuity from each wire (YEL, LT GRN/WHT, BRN, YEL/GRN, LT GRN/RED, LT GRN/BLK) to body ground.
Does continuity exist?
YES
Repair short to body ground in wire.
NO
Check for continuity between BLK terminal to body ground.
Is there continuity?
NO
Repair open in BLK wire or poor ground (G8).
YES
Replace the heater control panel.

HEATER RECIRCULATION MOTOR DIAGNOSTIC CHART – 1989 INTEGRA

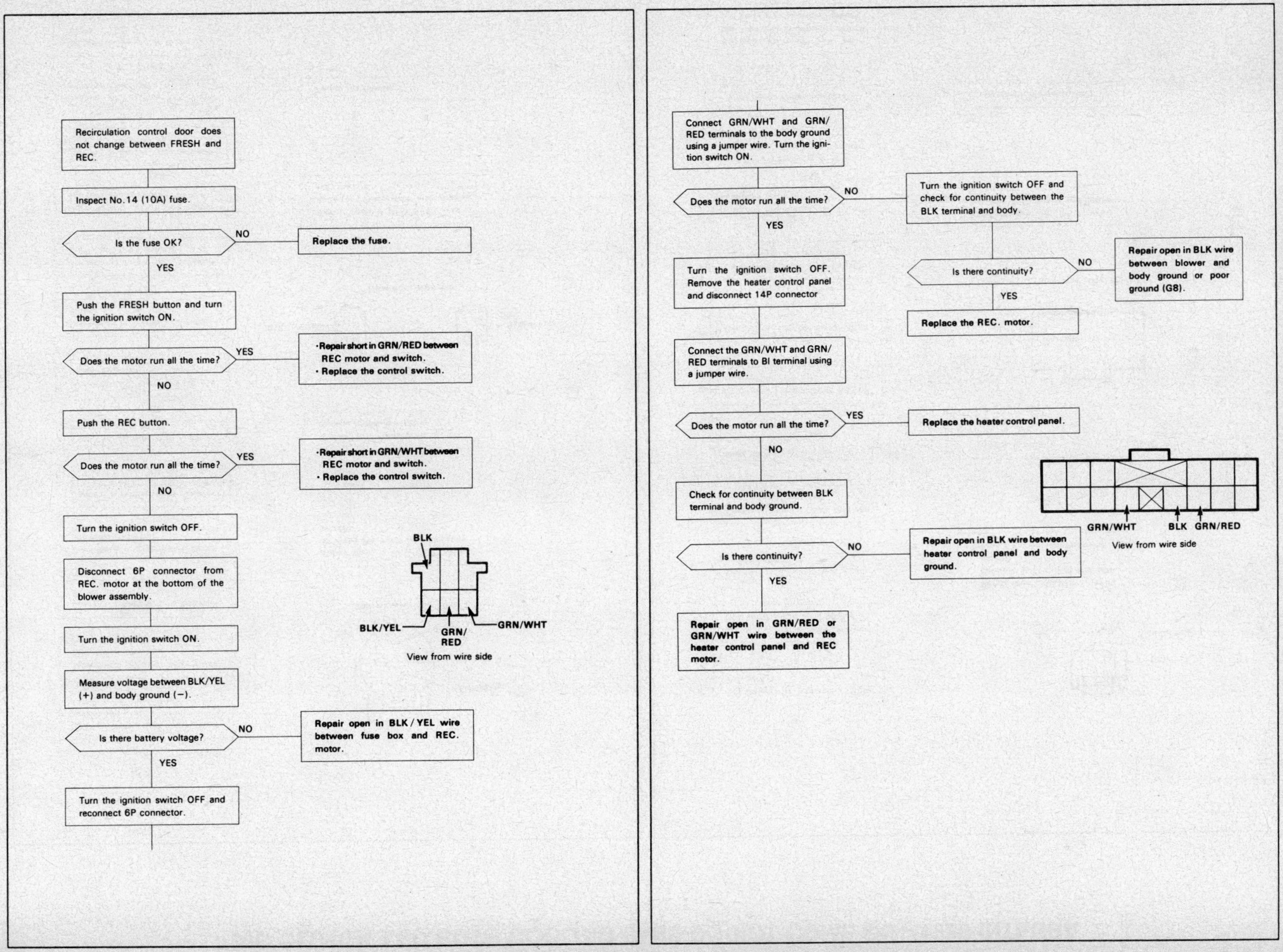
Recirculation control door does not change between FRESH and REC.
Inspect No.14 (10A) fuse.
Is the fuse OK?
NO
Replace the fuse.
YES
Push the FRESH button and turn the ignition switch ON.
Does the motor run all the time?
YES
· Repair short in GRN/RED between REC motor and switch.
· Replace the control switch.
NO
Push the REC button.
Does the motor run all the time?
YES
· Repair short in GRN/WHT between REC motor and switch.
· Replace the control switch.
NO
Turn the ignition switch OFF.
Disconnect 6P connector from REC. motor at the bottom of the blower assembly.
Turn the ignition switch ON.
Measure voltage between BLK/YEL (+) and body ground (−).
Is there battery voltage?
NO
Repair open in BLK / YEL wire between fuse box and REC. motor.
YES
Turn the ignition switch OFF and reconnect 6P connector.
BLK
BLK/YEL
GRN/RED
GRN/WHT
View from wire side
Connect GRN/WHT and GRN/RED terminals to the body ground using a jumper wire. Turn the ignition switch ON.
Does the motor run all the time?
NO
Turn the ignition switch OFF and check for continuity between the BLK terminal and body.
Is there continuity?
NO
Repair open in BLK wire between blower and body ground or poor ground (G8).
YES
Replace the REC. motor.
YES
Turn the ignition switch OFF. Remove the heater control panel and disconnect 14P connector
Connect the GRN/WHT and GRN/RED terminals to BI terminal using a jumper wire.
Does the motor run all the time?
YES
Replace the heater control panel.
NO
Check for continuity between BLK terminal and body ground.
Is there continuity?
NO
Repair open in BLK wire between heater control panel and body ground.
YES
Repair open in GRN/RED or GRN/WHT wire between the heater control panel and REC motor.
GRN/WHT
BLK
GRN/RED
View from wire side

A/C CLUTCH AND BOTH COOLING FANS DO NOT COME ON—1989 INTEGRA

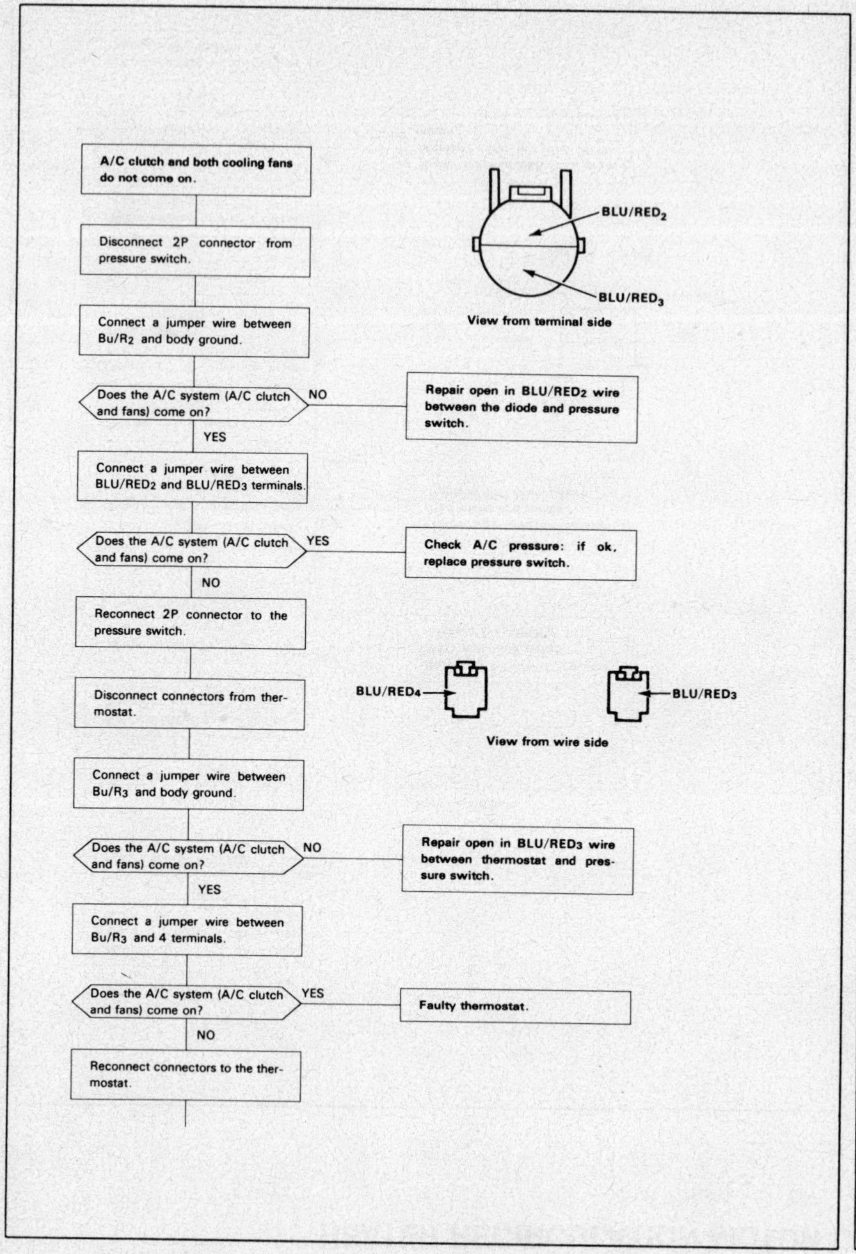
A/C clutch and both cooling fans do not come on.
Disconnect 2P connector from pressure switch.
Connect a jumper wire between Bu/R2 and body ground.
Does the A/C system (A/C clutch and fans) come on?
NO
Repair open in BLU/RED2 wire between the diode and pressure switch.
YES
Connect a jumper wire between BLU/RED2 and BLU/RED3 terminals.
Does the A/C system (A/C clutch and fans) come on?
YES
Check A/C pressure: if ok, replace pressure switch.
NO
Reconnect 2P connector to the pressure switch.
Disconnect connectors from thermostat.
Connect a jumper wire between Bu/R3 and body ground.
Does the A/C system (A/C clutch and fans) come on?
NO
Repair open in BLU/RED3 wire between thermostat and pressure switch.
YES
Connect a jumper wire between Bu/R3 and 4 terminals.
Does the A/C system (A/C clutch and fans) come on?
YES
Faulty thermostat.
NO
Reconnect connectors to the thermostat.
BLU/RED2
BLU/RED3
View from terminal side
BLU/RED4
BLU/RED3
View from wire side

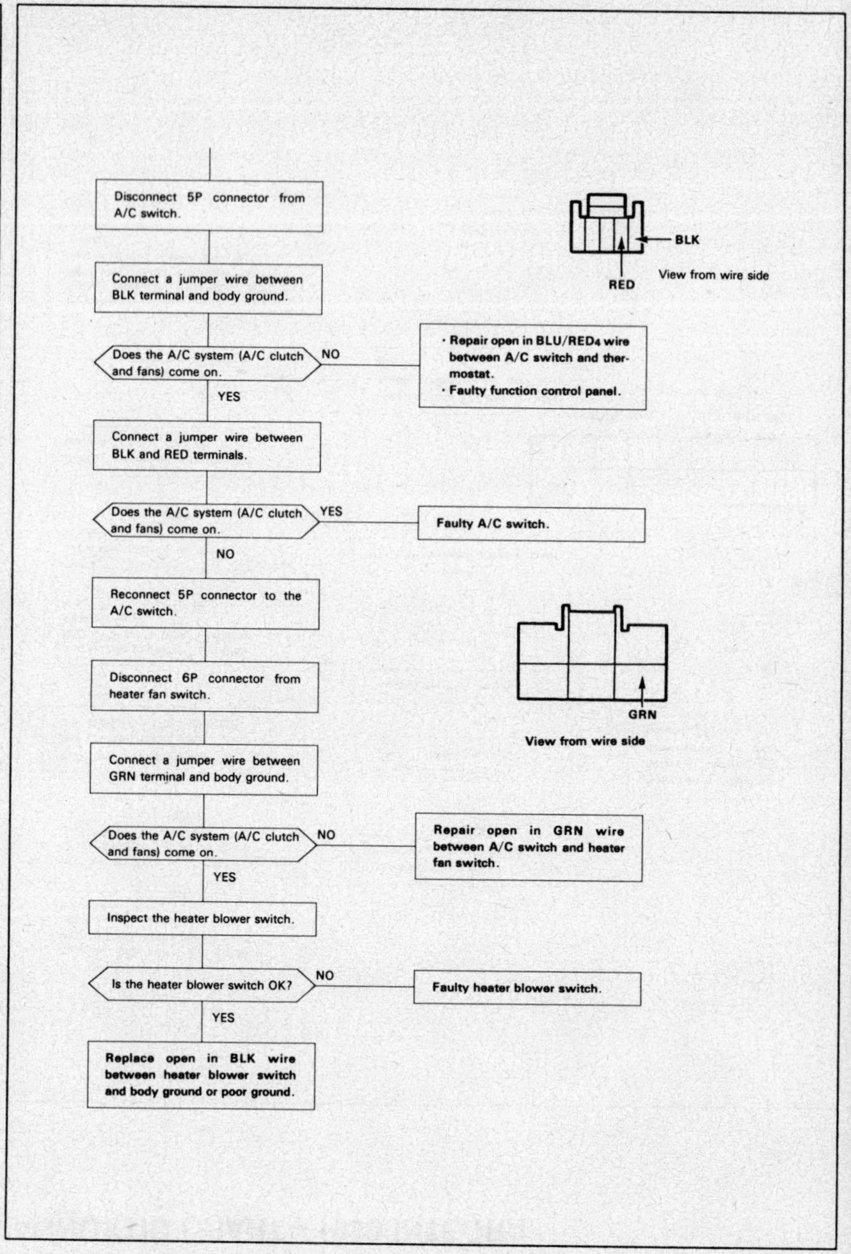
Disconnect 5P connector from A/C switch.
Connect a jumper wire between BLK terminal and body ground.
Does the A/C system (A/C clutch and fans) come on.
NO
· Repair open in BLU/RED4 wire between A/C switch and thermostat.
· Faulty function control panel.
YES
Connect a jumper wire between BLK and RED terminals.
Does the A/C system (A/C clutch and fans) come on.
YES
Faulty A/C switch.
NO
Reconnect 5P connector to the A/C switch.
Disconnect 6P connector from heater fan switch.
Connect a jumper wire between GRN terminal and body ground.
Does the A/C system (A/C clutch and fans) come on.
NO
Repair open in GRN wire between A/C switch and heater fan switch.
YES
Inspect the heater blower switch.
Is the heater blower switch OK?
NO
Faulty heater blower switch.
YES
Replace open in BLK wire between heater blower switch and body ground or poor ground.
BLK
RED
View from wire side
GRN
View from wire side

A/C CLUTCH DOES NOT COME ON—1989 INTEGRA

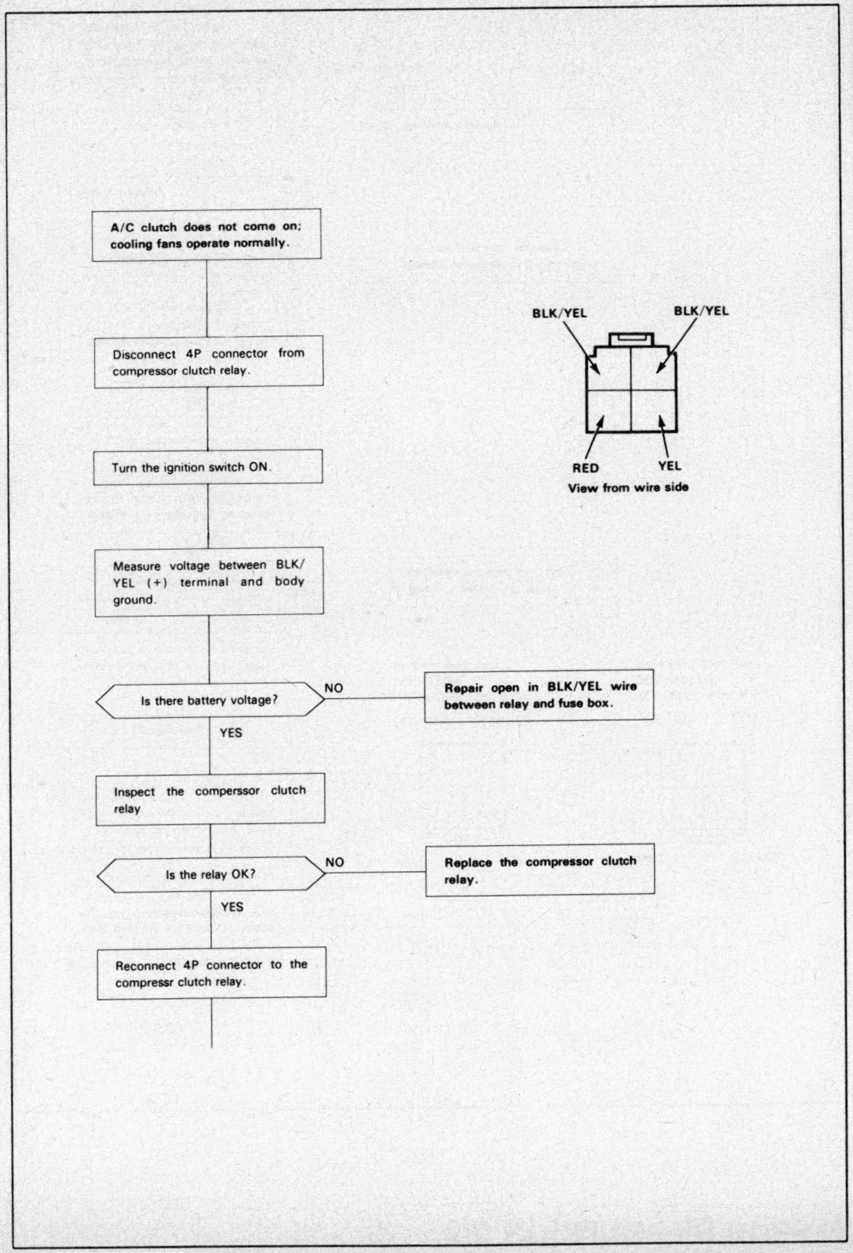
A/C clutch does not come on; cooling fans operate normally.
Disconnect 4P connector from compressor clutch relay.
Turn the ignition switch ON.
Measure voltage between BLK/YEL (+) terminal and body ground.
Is there battery voltage?
NO
Repair open in BLK/YEL wire between relay and fuse box.
YES
Inspect the compersson clutch relay
Is the relay OK?
NO
Replace the compressor clutch relay.
YES
Reconnect 4P connector to the compressr clutch relay.
BLK/YEL
BLK/YEL
RED
YEL
View from wire side

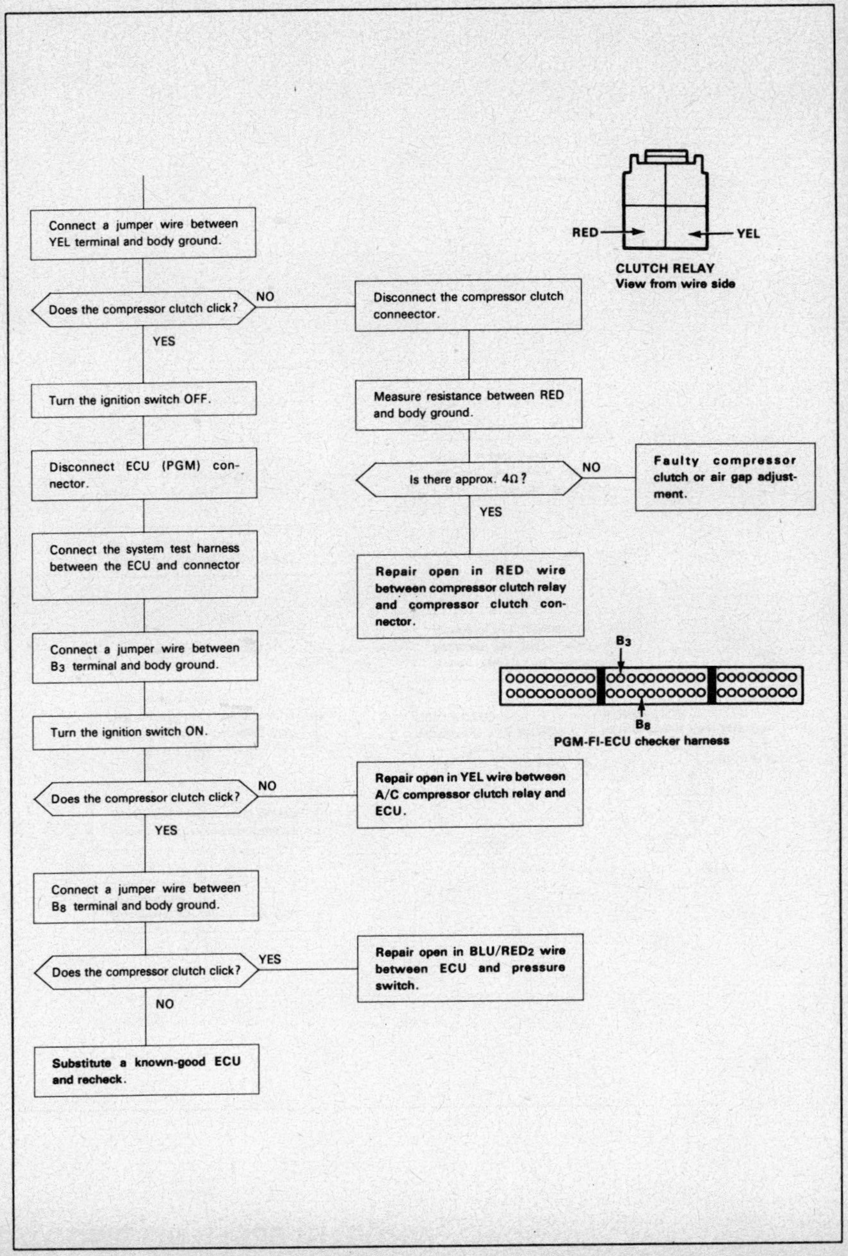
Connect a jumper wire between YEL terminal and body ground.
Does the compressor clutch click?
NO
Disconnect the compressor clutch conneector.
Measure resistance between RED and body ground.
Is there approx. 4Ω?
NO
Faulty compressor clutch or air gap adjustment.
YES
Repair open in RED wire between compressor clutch relay and compressor clutch connector.
YES
Turn the ignition switch OFF.
Disconnect ECU (PGM) connector.
Connect the system test harness between the ECU and connector
Connect a jumper wire between B3 terminal and body ground.
Turn the ignition switch ON.
Does the compressor clutch click?
NO
Repair open in YEL wire between A/C compressor clutch relay and ECU.
YES
Connect a jumper wire between B8 terminal and body ground.
Does the compressor clutch click?
YES
Repair open in BLU/RED2 wire between ECU and pressure switch.
NO
Substitute a known-good ECU and recheck.
RED
YEL
CLUTCH RELAY
View from wire side
B3
B8
PGM-FI-ECU checker harness

A/C COOLING FAN DOES NOT COME ON—1989 INTEGRA

- Check for No. 20, No. 21, and No. 13 fuses.

One cooling fan does not come on; A/C clutch operates normally with the A/C switch.

Disconnect 4P connector from (not running) radiator or condenser fan relay.

Turn the ignition switch ON.

Measure voltage between WHT terminal (+) and body ground.

Is there battery voltage?
- NO → Repair open in WHT wire between the fuse and relay.
- YES → Connect a jumper wire between WHT (+) and BLU/BLK terminals.

Does the condensor (or radiator) fan motor come on.
- NO → (continued on right side)
- YES → Measure voltage between BLK/YEL wire (+) and body ground.

Is there battery voltage?
- NO → Repair open in BLK/YEL wire between the fuse and relay.
- YES → Check the relay

Is the relay OK?
- NO → Replace the relay.
- YES → Faulty diode or repair open in BLU / RED (or BLU) wire between the relay and diode.

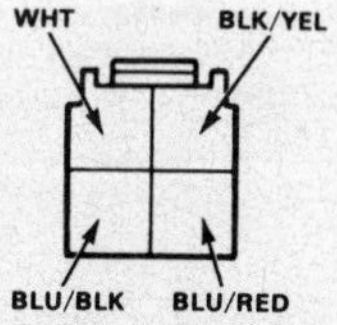
WHT
BLK/YEL
BLU/BLK
BLU/RED
CONDENSOR FAN RELAY CONNECTOR
View from wire side.

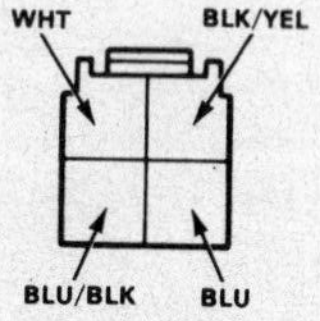
WHT
BLK/YEL
BLU/BLK
BLU
RADIATOR FAN RELAY CONNECTOR
View from wire side.

Disconnect the jumper wire from 4P connector.

Disconnect 2P connector from the (not running) condenser or radiator fan motor.

Measure voltage between BLU/BLK terminal and body ground.

Is there battery voltage?
- NO → Repair open in BLU/BLK wire between fan motor and body ground or poor ground.
- YES → Check for continuity between BLK terminal and body ground.

Is the continuity OK?
- NO → Repair open in BLK wire between fan motor and body ground or poor ground.
- YES → Faulty fan motor.

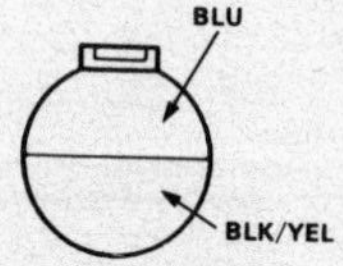
BLU
BLK/YEL
RADIATOR FAN MOTOR CONNECTOR

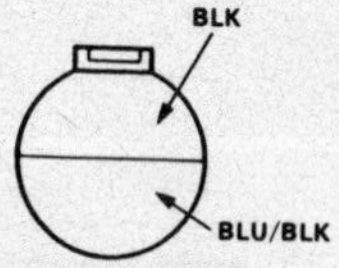
BLK
BLU/BLK
CONDENSER FAN MOTOR CONNECTOR

BOTH A/C COOLING FAN DO NOT COME ON—1989 INTEGRA

- Check No.20, No.21, No.14 and No.13 fuses.

Both cooling fans do not come on; A/C clutch operates normally with A/C switch.

Disconnect 3P connector from diode.

Connect a jumper wire between:
- BLU/RED1 terminal and body ground.
- BLU terminal and body ground.

Do both fans run?
- YES → **Faulty diode.**
- NO ↓

Inspect the radiator and condenser fan relays.

Are the relays OK?
- NO → **Faulty relay(s).**
- YES ↓

Reconnect 4P connector to the radiator and condenser fan relays.

Connect a jumper wire between:
- BLU/RED terminal and body ground.
- BLU terminal and body ground.

Do the fan motors run?
- YES → **Repair open in BLU and/or BLU/RED1 wire between fan relay and diode.**
- NO ↓

Disconnect 2P connector from radiator and condenser fan motors.

Reconnect 3P connector to the diode.

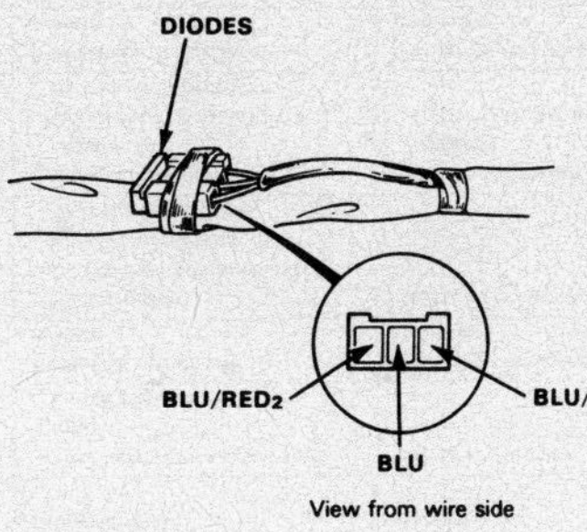
DIODES
BLU/RED2
BLU
BLU/RED1
View from wire side

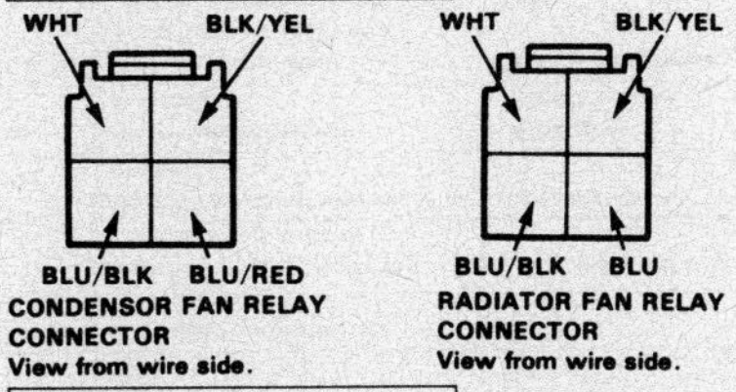
WHT
BLK/YEL
BLU/BLK
BLU/RED
CONDENSOR FAN RELAY CONNECTOR
View from wire side.
WHT
BLK/YEL
BLU/BLK
BLU
RADIATOR FAN RELAY CONNECTOR
View from wire side.

Measure voltage between BLU/BLK terminal and body ground.

Is there battery voltage?
- NO → **Repair open in BLU/BLK wire (s) between fan motor and relay.**
- YES ↓

Check for continuity BLK terminals between fan motor conectors and body ground.

Is there continuity?
- YES → **Faulty fan motor(s).**
- NO ↓

Repair open in BLK wire between fan motor and body ground or poor ground.

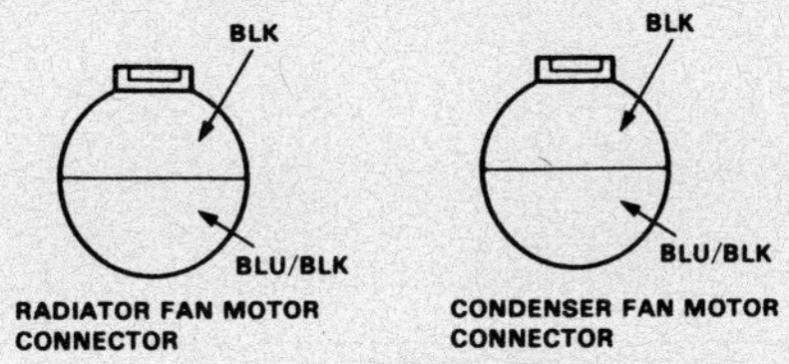
BLK
BLU/BLK
RADIATOR FAN MOTOR CONNECTOR
BLK
BLU/BLK
CONDENSER FAN MOTOR CONNECTOR

A/C SYSTEM DIAGNOSTIC CHART—1989 INTEGRA

TEST RESULTS	RELATED SYMPTOMS	PROBABLE CAUSE	REMEDY
Discharge (high) pressure abnormally high	After stopping compressor, pressure drops to about 196 kPa (28 psi) quickly, and then falls gradually	Air in system	Evacuate system; then recharge
	No bubbles in sight glass when condenser is cooled by water	Excessive refrigerant in system	Discharge refrigerant as required
	Reduced or no air flow through condenser.	· Clogged condenser or radiater fins · Condenser or radiator fan not working properly	· Clean · Check voltage and fan rpm
	Line to condenser is excessively hot	Restricted flow of refrigerant in system	Expansion valve
Discharge pressure abnormally low	Excessive bubbles in sight glass; condenser is not hot	Insufficient refrigerant in system	· Charge system · Check for leak
	High and low pressures are balanced soon after stopping compressor	· Faulty compressor discharge or inlet valve · Faulty compressor seal	Replace compressor Repair
	Outlet of expansion valve is not frosted, low pressure gauge indicates vacuum	· Faulty expansion valve	Repair or Replace
Suction (low) pressure abnormally low	Excessive bubbles in sight glass; condenser is not hot Expansion valve is not frosted and low pressure line is not cold. Low pressure gauge indicates vacuum.	Insufficient refrigerant · Frozen expansion valve · Faulty expansion valve	Check for leaks. Charge as required. Replace expansion valve
	Discharge temperature is low and the air flow from vents is restricted	Frozen evaporator	Run the fan with compressor off then check the thermostat and capillary tube.
	Expansion valve frosted	Clogged expansion valve	Clean or Replace
	Receiver dryer is cool (should be warm during opration)	Clogged receiver dryer	Replace
Suction pressure abnormally high	Low pressure hose and check joint are cooler than around evaporator	· Expansion valve open too long · Loose expansion valve	Repair or Replace
	Suction pressure is lowered when condenser is cooled by water	Excessive refrigerant in system	Discharge refrigerant as necessary
	High and low pressure are equalized as soon as the compressor is stopped	· Faulty gasket · Faulty high pressure valve · Foreign particle stuck in high pressure valve	Replace compressor
Suction and discharge pressures abnormally high	Reduced air flow through condenser	· Clogged condenser or radiator fins · Condenser or radiator fan not working properly	· Clean condenser and radiator · Check voltage and fan rpm
	No bubbles in sight glass when condenser is cooled by water	Excessive refrigerant in system	Discharge refrigerant as necessary.
Suction and discharge pressure abnormally low	Low pressure hose and metal end areas are cooler than evaporator	Clogged or kinked low pressure hose parts	Repair or Replace
	Temperature around expansion valve is too low compared with that around receiver-driver.	Clogged high pressure line	Repair or Replace
Refrigerant leaks	Compressor clutch is dirty	Compressor shaft seal leaking	Replace compressor shaft seal
	Compressor bolt(s) are dirty	Leaking around bolt(s)	Replace compressor
	Compressor gasket is wet with oil	Gasket leaking	Replace compressor

HEATER DIAGNOSTIC CHART—1990–91 INTEGRA

SYMPTOM		REMEDY
No hot air flow	Blower motor does not run	Perform the flowchart
	Blower motor runs	Check following: · Clogged heater duct · Clogged blower outlet · Clogged heater valve · Faulty air mix door · Air mix cable adjustment · Faulty thermostat
Hot air flow is low	Blower speed does not change	Perform flow chart
	Blower runs properly	Check following: · Clogged heater duct · Clogged blower outlet · Incorrect door position

HEATER BLOWER DIAGNOSTIC CHART—1990-91 INTEGRA

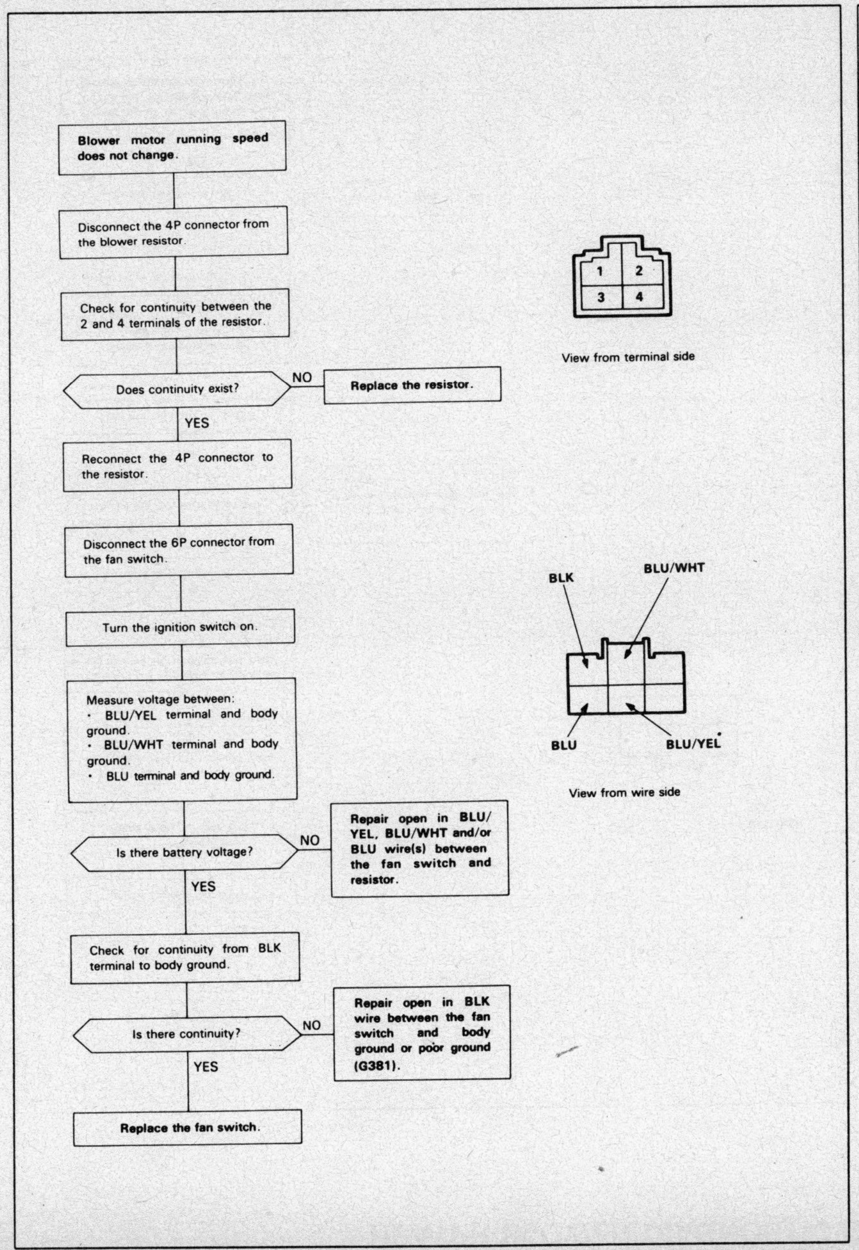
Blower motor running speed does not change.
Disconnect the 4P connector from the blower resistor.
Check for continuity between the 2 and 4 terminals of the resistor.
Does continuity exist?
NO
Replace the resistor.
YES
Reconnect the 4P connector to the resistor.
Disconnect the 6P connector from the fan switch.
Turn the ignition switch on.
Measure voltage between:
· BLU/YEL terminal and body ground.
· BLU/WHT terminal and body ground.
· BLU terminal and body ground.
Is there battery voltage?
NO
Repair open in BLU/YEL, BLU/WHT and/or BLU wire(s) between the fan switch and resistor.
YES
Check for continuity from BLK terminal to body ground.
Is there continuity?
NO
Repair open in BLK wire between the fan switch and body ground or poor ground (G381).
YES
Replace the fan switch.
1
2
3
4
View from terminal side
BLK
BLU/WHT
BLU
BLU/YEL
View from wire side

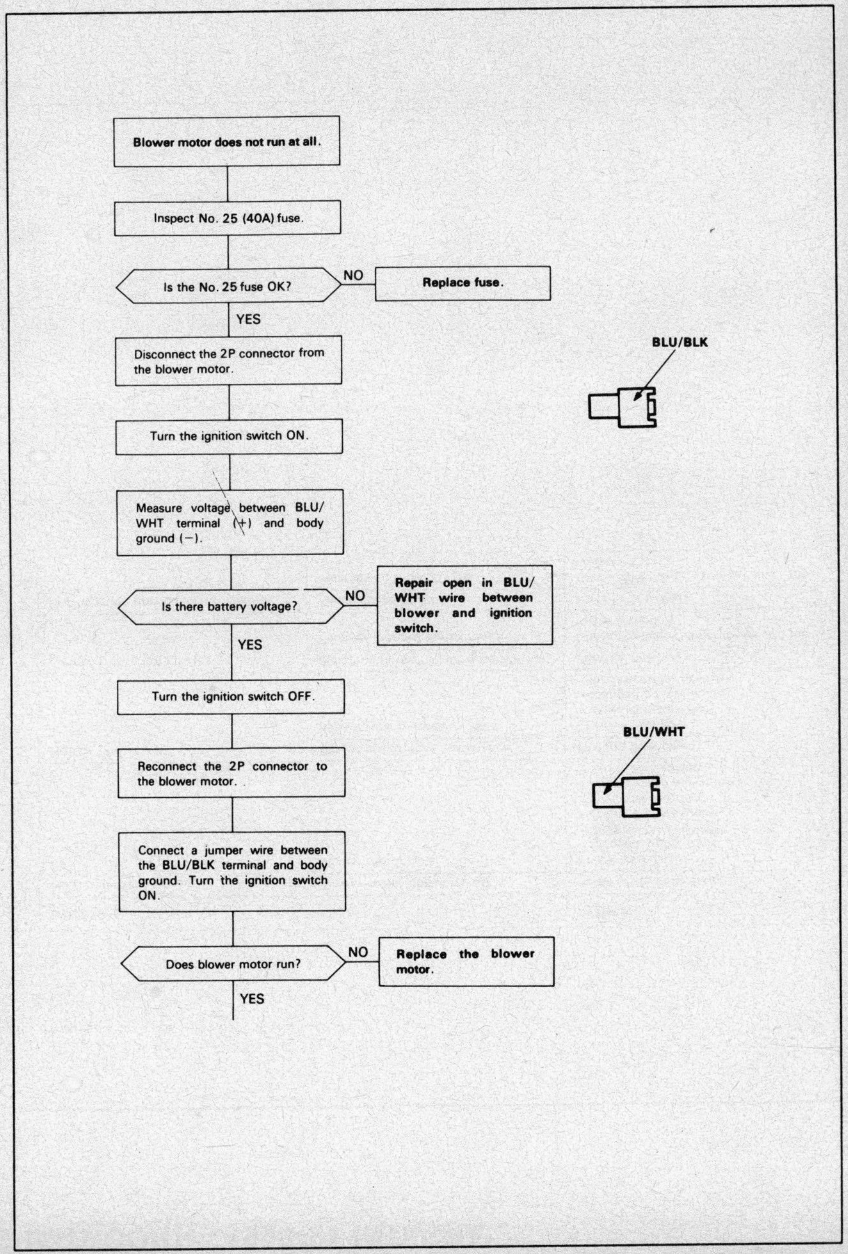
Blower motor does not run at all.
Inspect No. 25 (40A) fuse.
Is the No. 25 fuse OK?
NO
Replace fuse.
YES
Disconnect the 2P connector from the blower motor.
Turn the ignition switch ON.
Measure voltage between BLU/WHT terminal (+) and body ground (−).
Is there battery voltage?
NO
Repair open in BLU/WHT wire between blower and ignition switch.
YES
Turn the ignition switch OFF.
Reconnect the 2P connector to the blower motor.
Connect a jumper wire between the BLU/BLK terminal and body ground. Turn the ignition switch ON.
Does blower motor run?
NO
Replace the blower motor.
YES
BLU/BLK
BLU/WHT

HEATER BLOWER DIAGNOSTIC CHART CONT.—1990–91 INTEGRA

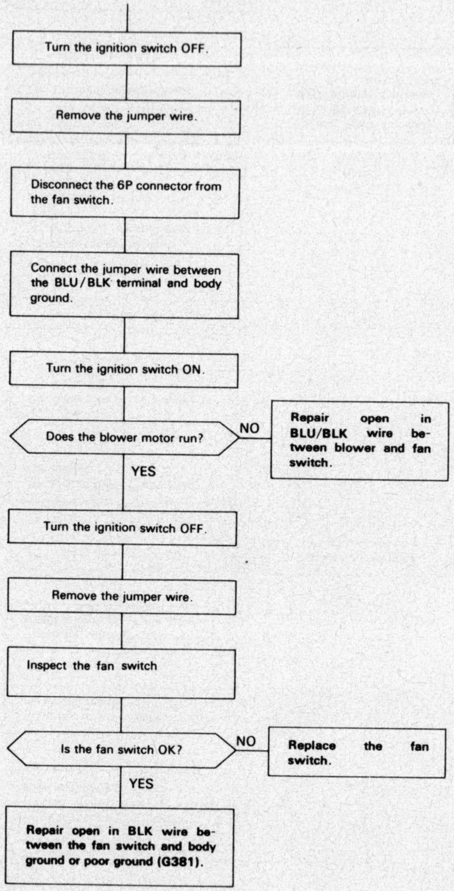
Turn the ignition switch OFF.
Remove the jumper wire.
Disconnect the 6P connector from the fan switch.
Connect the jumper wire between the BLU/BLK terminal and body ground.
Turn the ignition switch ON.
Does the blower motor run?
NO
Repair open in BLU/BLK wire between blower and fan switch.
YES
Turn the ignition switch OFF.
Remove the jumper wire.
Inspect the fan switch
Is the fan switch OK?
NO
Replace the fan switch.
YES
Repair open in BLK wire between the fan switch and body ground or poor ground (G381).

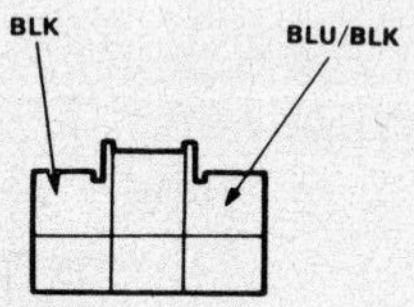
BLK
BLU/BLK

View from wire side

SYMPTOM		REMEDY
No hot air flow	Blower motor does not run	Perform the flowchart
	Blower motor runs	Check following: · Clogged heater duct · Clogged blower outlet · Clogged heater valve · Faulty air mix door · Air mix cable adjustment · Faulty thermostat
Hot air flow is low	Blower speed does not change	Perform flow chart
	Blower runs properly	Check following: · Clogged heater duct · Clogged blower outlet · Incorrect door position
Function does not change	Function control motor does not run	Perform flowchart
	Function control motor runs	Check the heater door linkage and the heater assembly.
Recirculation door does not change	Recirculation motor does not run	Perform flowchart
	Recirculation motor runs	Check the door linkage and the blower.

HEATER RECIRCULATION MOTOR DIAGNOSTIC CHART—1990–91 INTEGRA

NOTE: Check blower side link and recirc. door.

Recirculation control door does not change between FRESH and REC.

Inspect No. 17 fuse.

Is the No. 17 fuse OK?
- NO → **Replace the No. 17 fuse.**
- YES ↓

Push the FRESH button and turn the ignition switch ON.

Does the motor run all the time?
- YES → **· Repair short in GRN/RED wire between recirc. motor and switch.**
  · Replace the control switch.
- NO ↓

Turn off the ignition switch.

Push the REC button and turn the ignition switch ON.

Does the motor run all the time?
- YES → **· Repair short in GRN/WHT wire between recirc. motor and switch.**
  · Replace the control switch.
- NO ↓

Turn off the ignition switch.

Disconnect the 4P connector from the recirc. motor at the bottom of the blower assembly.

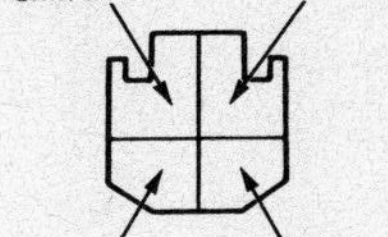
GRN/WHT
BLK
BLK/YEL
GRN/RED

View from wire side

Turn the ignition switch on.

Measure the voltage between the BLK/YEL (+) and body ground (−).

Is there battery voltage?
- NO → **Repair open in BLK/YEL wire between the fuse box and recirc. motor.**
- YES ↓

Turn the ignition switch off.

Check for continuity between the BLK terminal and body ground.

Is there continuity?
- NO → **Repair the poor ground (G381) or open in BLK wire between the heater control panel and blower.**
- YES ↓

Check GRN/WHT for continuity to body ground in FRESH position.

Is there continuity?
- NO → **· Repair open in GRN/WHT wire between recirc. motor and control panel.**
  · Check the heater control panel.
- YES ↓

Check GRN/RED for continuity to body ground in REC position.

Is there continuity?
- NO → **· Repair open in GRN/RED wire between recirc. motor and control panel.**
  · Check the heater control panel.
- YES ↓

Replace the recirculation control motor.

HEATER FUNCTION CONTROL MOTOR DIAGNOSTIC CHART—1990–91 INTEGRA

- Function control motor does not run.
- Inspect No.17 fuse.
- Is the No. 17 fuse OK?
  - NO: Replace the fuse.
  - YES:
- Disconnect the 8P connector from the function control motor.

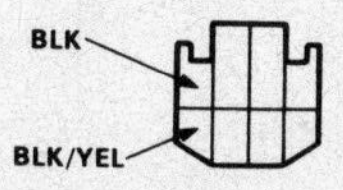
BLK
BLK/YEL
View from wire side

- Turn the ignition switch ON.
- Measure voltage between BLK/YEL terminal and body ground.
- Is there battery voltage?
  - NO: Repair open in BLK/YEL wire between heater control panel and fuse box.
  - YES:
- Turn the ignition switch OFF.
- Check for continuity from BLK terminal to body ground.
- Is there continuity?
  - NO: Repair open in BLK wire between the function control motor and body ground or poor ground (G381).
  - YES:
- Inspect the function control motor
- Is the function control motor OK?
  - NO: Replace the function control motor.
  - YES:
- Disconnect the 13P connector from the heater control panel.

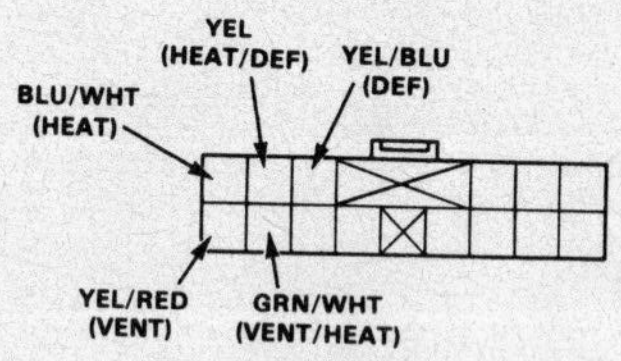
YEL (HEAT/DEF)
YEL/BLU (DEF)
BLU/WHT (HEAT)
YEL/RED (VENT)
GRN/WHT (VENT/HEAT)
View from wire side

- Check for continuity at each wire (BLU/WHT, GRN/WHT, YEL, YEL/RED, YEL/BLU) between the 8P and 13P connectors.
- Is there continuity?
  - NO: Repair open wire.
  - YES:
- Check for continuity from each wire (BLU/WHT, GRN/WHT, YEL/RED, YEL/BLU, YEL) to body ground.

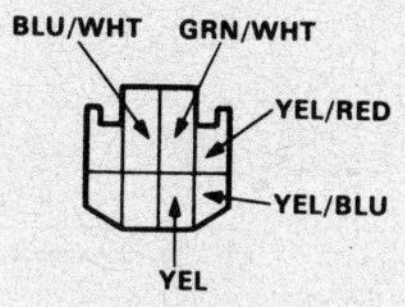
BLU/WHT
GRN/WHT
YEL/RED
YEL/BLU
YEL
View from wire side

- Is there continuity?
  - YES: Repair short to body ground in problem wire.
  - NO:
- Check for continuity between BLK terminal and body ground.
- Is there continuity?
  - NO: Repair open in BLK wire or poor ground (G381).
  - YES:
- Replace the heater control panel.

NOTE: If any of the wires are shorted to ground, the function control motor will not change positions.

AIR CONDITIONER DIAGNOSIS CHART – 1990–91 INTEGRA

NOTE: A/C compressor clutch will not come on without the engine running.

A/C System does not come on.

Turn ignition OFF.

Disconnect the 2P connector from the pressure switch.

Turn the heater fan, A/C switch ON and start the engine.

Connect a jumper wire between the BLU/RED1 terminal and body ground.

Do both fans and the compressor run?

- NO → Repair open in BLU/RED1 wire between pressure switch and diodes.
- YES ↓

Connect a jumper wire between the BLU/RED 1 and 2 terminals.

Do both fans and the compressor run?

- YES → Check refrigerant pressure. If pressure good, replace A/C pressure switch.
- NO ↓

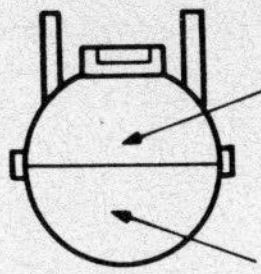
BLU/RED1
BLU/RED2

View from terminal side

Reconnect the 2P connector to the pressure switch.

Disconnect the 2P connector from the thermostat switch.

Connect a jumper wire between the BLU/RED2 terminal and body ground.

Do both fans and the compressor run?

- NO → Repair open in BLU/RED2 wire between pressure and thermostat switches.
- YES ↓

Connect a jumper wire between the BLU/RED2 and 3 terminals.

Do both fans and the compressor run?

- YES → Check evaporator temperature. If temperature is above 41°F, replace A/C thermostat.
- NO ↓

Turn the ignition switch OFF.

Reconnect the 2P connector to the thermostat switch.

Disconnect the 6P connector from the A/C switch.

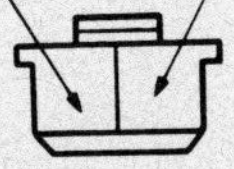
(Thermostat)
BLU/RED3
(Pressure switch)
BLU/RED2

View from wire side

AIR CONDITIONER DIAGNOSIS CHART CONT. 1990–91 INTEGRA

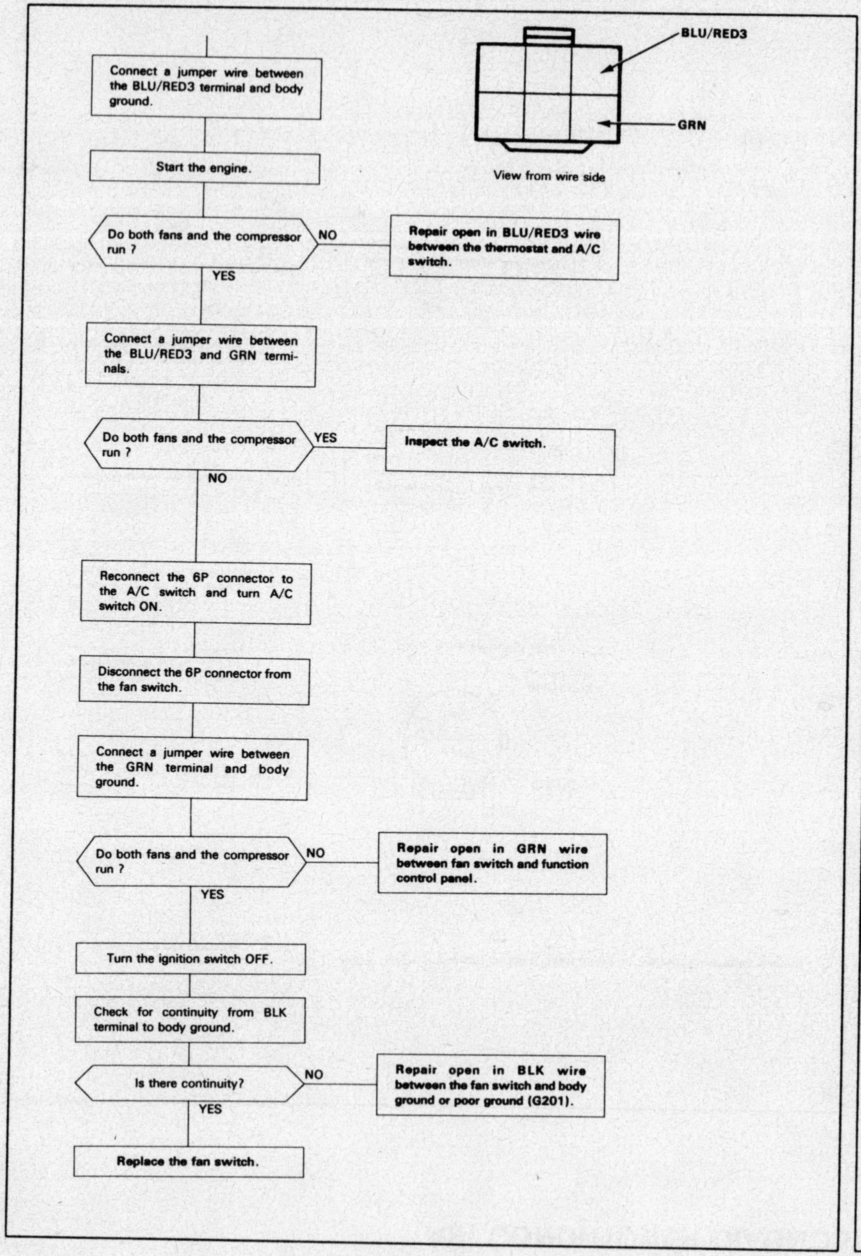
Connect a jumper wire between the BLU/RED3 terminal and body ground.
Start the engine.
Do both fans and the compressor run ?
NO
Repair open in BLU/RED3 wire between the thermostat and A/C switch.
YES
Connect a jumper wire between the BLU/RED3 and GRN terminals.
Do both fans and the compressor run ?
YES
Inspect the A/C switch.
NO
Reconnect the 6P connector to the A/C switch and turn A/C switch ON.
Disconnect the 6P connector from the fan switch.
Connect a jumper wire between the GRN terminal and body ground.
Do both fans and the compressor run ?
NO
Repair open in GRN wire between fan switch and function control panel.
YES
Turn the ignition switch OFF.
Check for continuity from BLK terminal to body ground.
Is there continuity?
NO
Repair open in BLK wire between the fan switch and body ground or poor ground (G201).
YES
Replace the fan switch.
BLU/RED3
GRN
View from wire side

AIR CONDITIONER COMPRESSOR DIAGNOSTIC CHART 1990–91 INTEGRA

NOTE: A/C compressor clutch will not come on without the engine running.

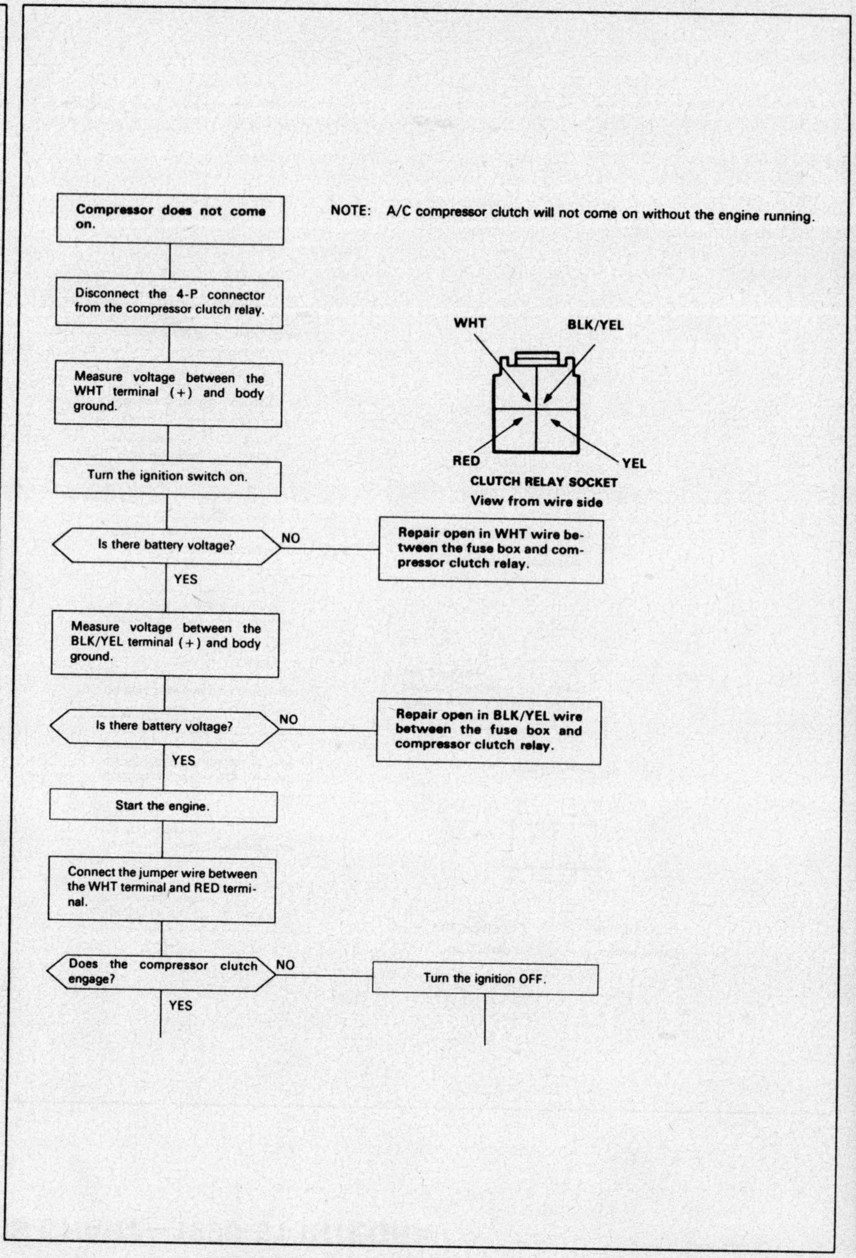
Compressor does not come on.
Disconnect the 4-P connector from the compressor clutch relay.
Measure voltage between the WHT terminal (+) and body ground.
Turn the ignition switch on.
Is there battery voltage?
NO
Repair open in WHT wire between the fuse box and compressor clutch relay.
YES
Measure voltage between the BLK/YEL terminal (+) and body ground.
Is there battery voltage?
NO
Repair open in BLK/YEL wire between the fuse box and compressor clutch relay.
YES
Start the engine.
Connect the jumper wire between the WHT terminal and RED terminal.
Does the compressor clutch engage?
NO
Turn the ignition OFF.
YES
WHT
BLK/YEL
RED
YEL
CLUTCH RELAY SOCKET
View from wire side

AIR CONDITIONER COMPRESSOR DIAGNOSTIC CHART CONT.—1990–91 INTEGRA

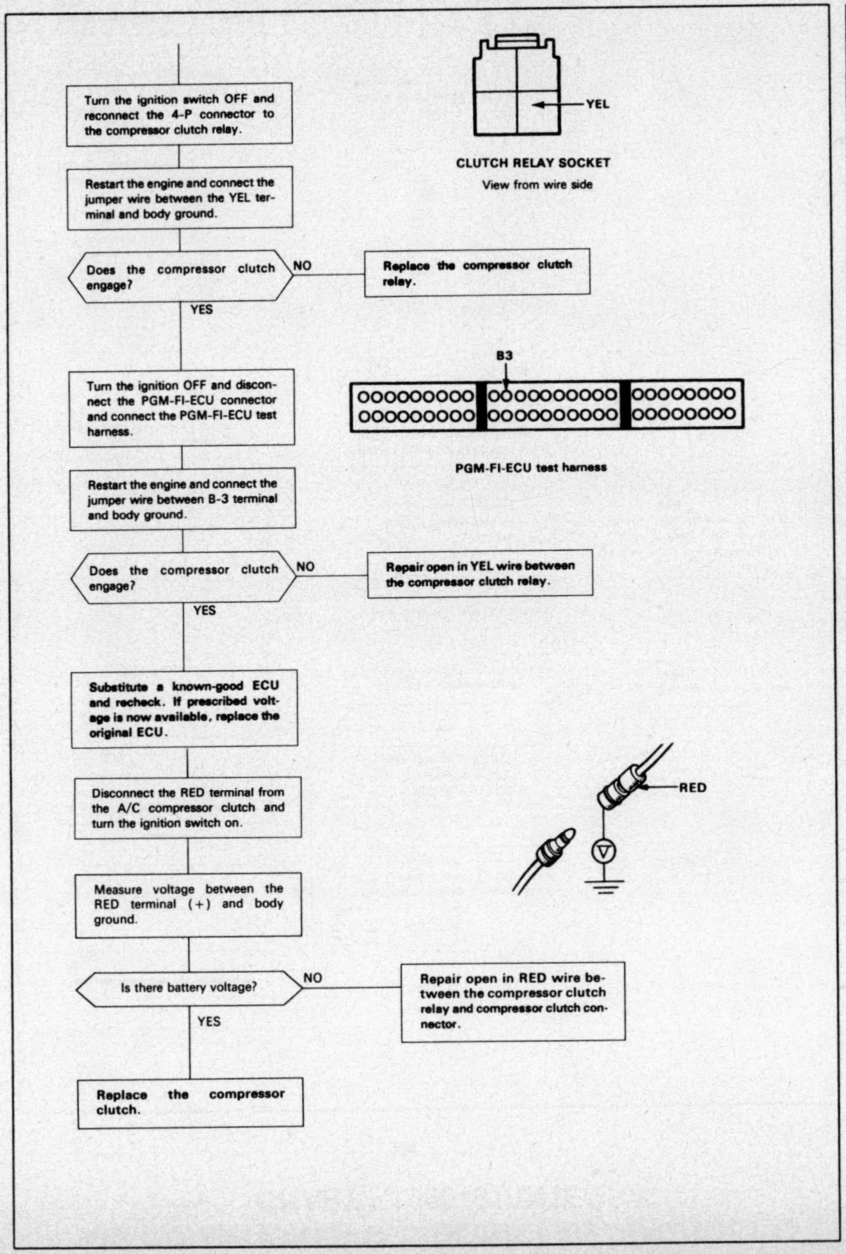
Turn the ignition switch OFF and reconnect the 4-P connector to the compressor clutch relay.
Restart the engine and connect the jumper wire between the YEL terminal and body ground.
Does the compressor clutch engage?
NO
Replace the compressor clutch relay.
YES
Turn the ignition OFF and disconnect the PGM-FI-ECU connector and connect the PGM-FI-ECU test harness.
Restart the engine and connect the jumper wire between B-3 terminal and body ground.
Does the compressor clutch engage?
NO
Repair open in YEL wire between the compressor clutch relay.
YES
Substitute a known-good ECU and recheck. If prescribed voltage is now available, replace the original ECU.
Disconnect the RED terminal from the A/C compressor clutch and turn the ignition switch on.
Measure voltage between the RED terminal (+) and body ground.
Is there battery voltage?
NO
Repair open in RED wire between the compressor clutch relay and compressor clutch connector.
YES
Replace the compressor clutch.
YEL
CLUTCH RELAY SOCKET
View from wire side
B3
PGM-FI-ECU test harness
RED

AIR CONDITIONER CONDENSER FAN DIAGNOSTIC CHART—1990–91 INTEGRA

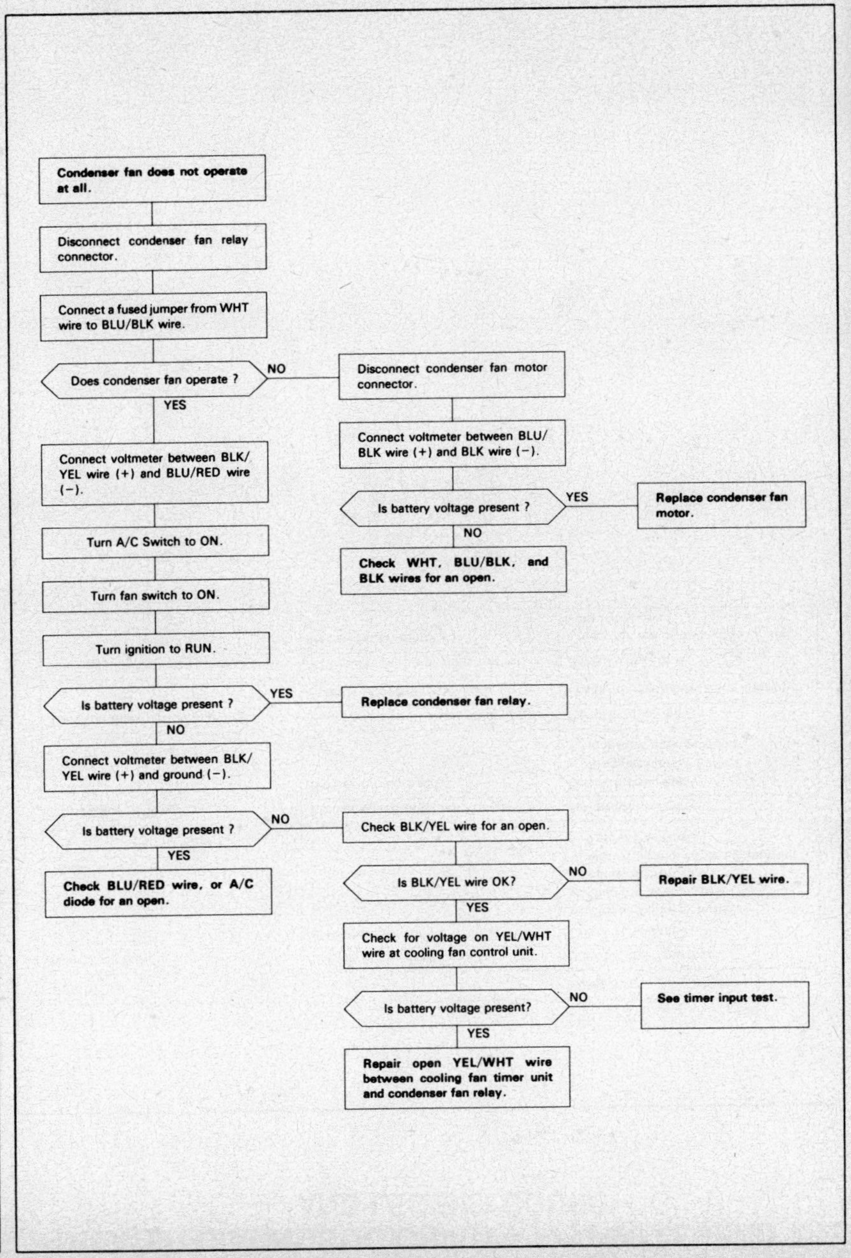
Condenser fan does not operate at all.
Disconnect condenser fan relay connector.
Connect a fused jumper from WHT wire to BLU/BLK wire.
Does condenser fan operate ?
NO
Disconnect condenser fan motor connector.
Connect voltmeter between BLU/BLK wire (+) and BLK wire (−).
Is battery voltage present ?
YES
Replace condenser fan motor.
NO
Check WHT, BLU/BLK, and BLK wires for an open.
YES
Connect voltmeter between BLK/YEL wire (+) and BLU/RED wire (−).
Turn A/C Switch to ON.
Turn fan switch to ON.
Turn ignition to RUN.
Is battery voltage present ?
YES
Replace condenser fan relay.
NO
Connect voltmeter between BLK/YEL wire (+) and ground (−).
Is battery voltage present ?
NO
Check BLK/YEL wire for an open.
Is BLK/YEL wire OK?
NO
Repair BLK/YEL wire.
YES
Check for voltage on YEL/WHT wire at cooling fan control unit.
Is battery voltage present?
NO
See timer input test.
YES
Repair open YEL/WHT wire between cooling fan timer unit and condenser fan relay.
YES
Check BLU/RED wire, or A/C diode for an open.

AIR CONDITIONER COOOLING FAN DIAGNOSTIC CHART – 1990–91 INTEGRA

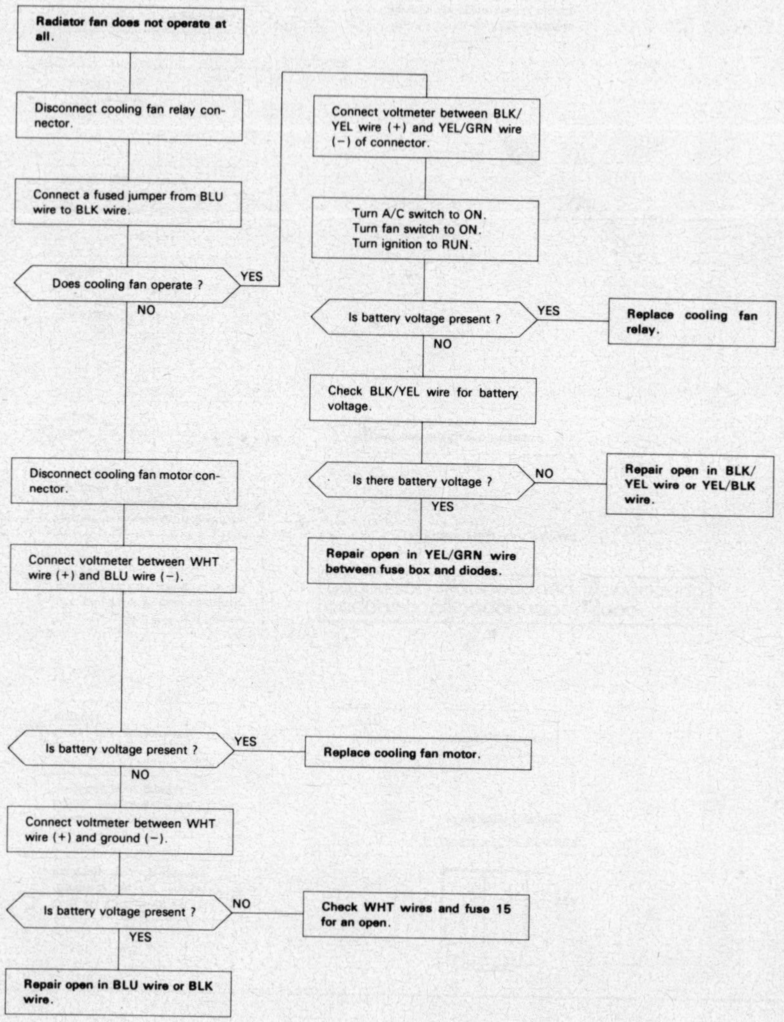
Radiator fan does not operate at all.
Disconnect cooling fan relay connector.
Connect a fused jumper from BLU wire to BLK wire.
Does cooling fan operate ?
YES
NO
Connect voltmeter between BLK/YEL wire (+) and YEL/GRN wire (−) of connector.
Turn A/C switch to ON.
Turn fan switch to ON.
Turn ignition to RUN.
Is battery voltage present ?
YES
Replace cooling fan relay.
NO
Check BLK/YEL wire for battery voltage.
Is there battery voltage ?
NO
Repair open in BLK/YEL wire or YEL/BLK wire.
YES
Repair open in YEL/GRN wire between fuse box and diodes.
Disconnect cooling fan motor connector.
Connect voltmeter between WHT wire (+) and BLU wire (−).
Is battery voltage present ?
YES
Replace cooling fan motor.
NO
Connect voltmeter between WHT wire (+) and ground (−).
Is battery voltage present ?
NO
Check WHT wires and fuse 15 for an open.
YES
Repair open in BLU wire or BLK wire.

HEATER DIAGNOSTIC CHART – 1989–90 LEGEND AND LEGEND COUPE

SYMPTOM		REMEDY
No hot air flow	Blower motor does not run	Perform the flowchart
	Blower motor runs	Check followings: • Clogged blower outlet • Clogged heater valve • Faulty air mix door • Out of air mix cable adjustment • Faulty thermostat
Hot air flow is low	Blower speed does not change	Perform flow chart
	Blower runs properly	Check followings: • Clogged blower outlet • Incorrect door position
Function does not change	Function control motor does not run	Perform flow chart
	Function control motor runs	Check for the heater door linkage.
Recirculation door does not change	Recirculation motor does not run	Perform flow chart
	Recirculation motor run	Check for the door linkage or perform flow chart

HEATER BLOWER DIAGNOSTIC CHART--1989–90 LEGEND AND LEGEND COUPE

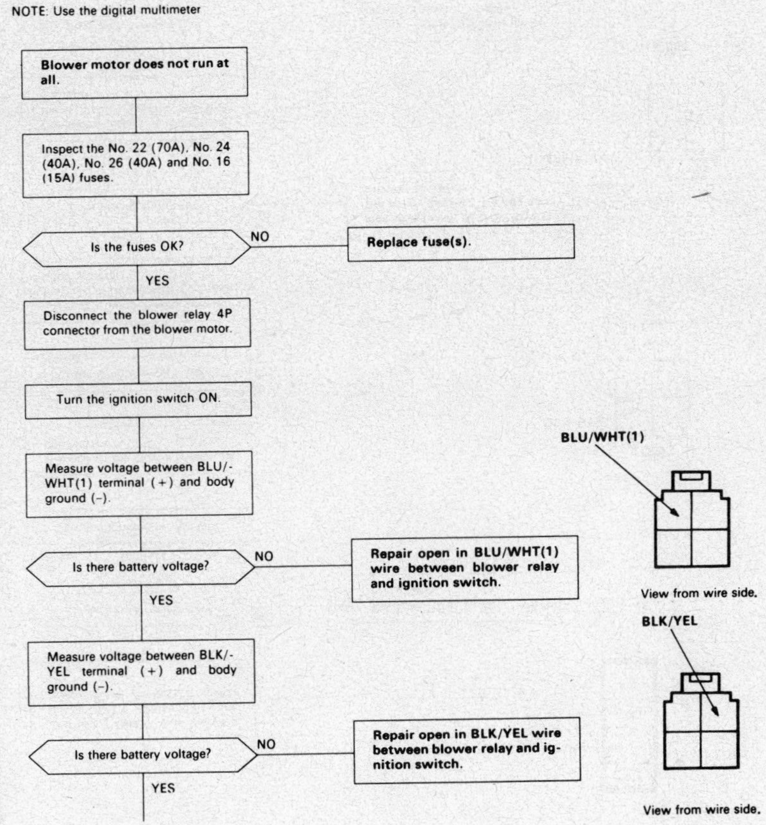
NOTE: Use the digital multimeter
Blower motor does not run at all.
Inspect the No. 22 (70A), No. 24 (40A), No. 26 (40A) and No. 16 (15A) fuses.
Is the fuses OK?
NO
Replace fuse(s).
YES
Disconnect the blower relay 4P connector from the blower motor.
Turn the ignition switch ON.
Measure voltage between BLU/-WHT(1) terminal (+) and body ground (–).
Is there battery voltage?
NO
Repair open in BLU/WHT(1) wire between blower relay and ignition switch.
YES
Measure voltage between BLK/-YEL terminal (+) and body ground (–).
Is there battery voltage?
NO
Repair open in BLK/YEL wire between blower relay and ignition switch.
YES
BLU/WHT(1)
View from wire side.
BLK/YEL
View from wire side.

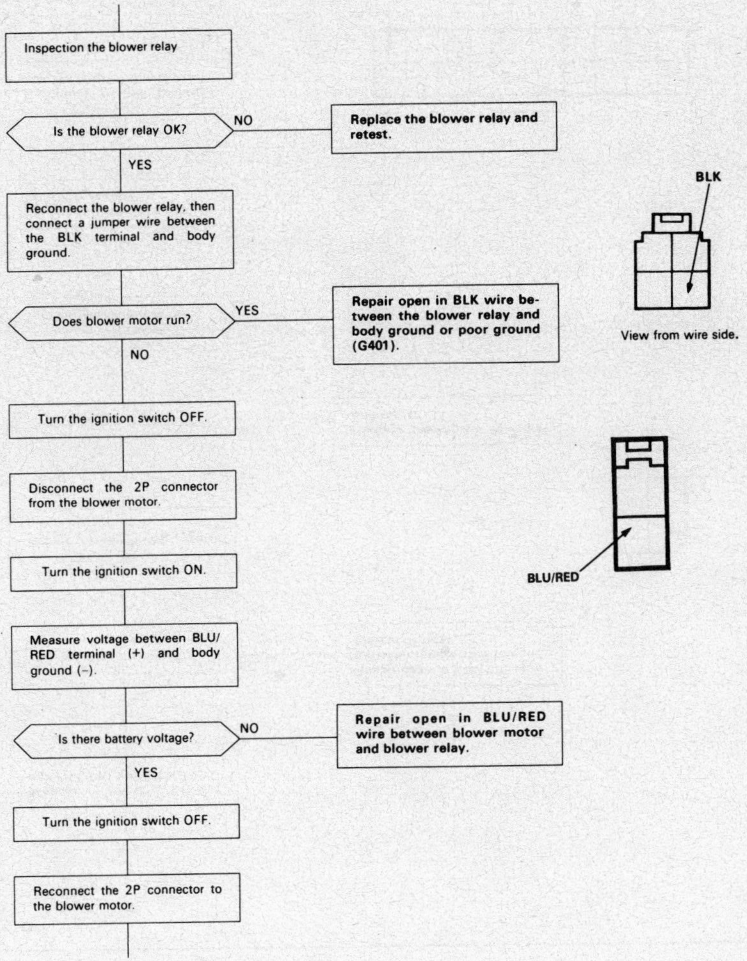
Inspection the blower relay
Is the blower relay OK?
NO
Replace the blower relay and retest.
YES
Reconnect the blower relay, then connect a jumper wire between the BLK terminal and body ground.
Does blower motor run?
YES
Repair open in BLK wire between the blower relay and body ground or poor ground (G401).
NO
Turn the ignition switch OFF.
Disconnect the 2P connector from the blower motor.
Turn the ignition switch ON.
Measure voltage between BLU/RED terminal (+) and body ground (–).
Is there battery voltage?
NO
Repair open in BLU/RED wire between blower motor and blower relay.
YES
Turn the ignition switch OFF.
Reconnect the 2P connector to the blower motor.
BLK
View from wire side.
BLU/RED

HEATER BLOWER DIAGNOSTIC CHART CONT.—1989–90 LEGEND AND LEGEND COUPE

Connect a jumper wire between the BLU/BLK terminal and body ground. Turn the ignition switch ON.

Does blower motor run? — NO → Replace the blower motor and retest.

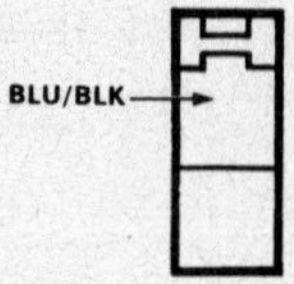
BLU/BLK

YES ↓

Turn the ignition switch OFF.

Disconnect the blower hi relay 4P connector.

BLU/BLK

View from wire side.

Turn the ignition switch ON.

Connect a jumper wire between the BLU/BLK terminal (+) and body ground.

Does blower motor run? — NO → Repair open in BLU/BLK wire between blower motor and blower hi-relay.

YES ↓

Connect a jumper wire between the BLU/BLK terminal and BLK terminal.

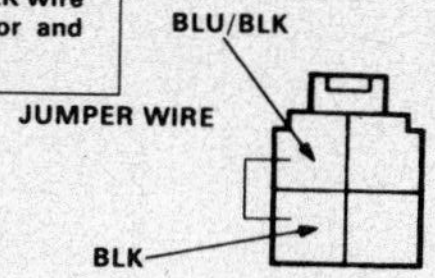
BLU/BLK
JUMPER WIRE
BLK

View from wire side.

Does blower motor run? — NO → Repair open in BLK wire between blower hi-relay and body ground or poor ground (G401).

YES ↓

Measure voltage between BLK/YEL (+) terminal and body ground.

Is the battery voltage? — NO → Repair open in BLK/YEL wire between ignition switch and blower hi-relay.

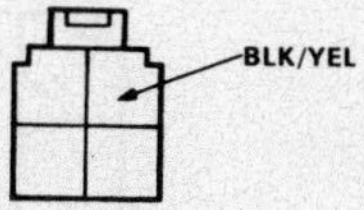
BLK/YEL

View from wire side.

YES ↓

Inspect blower hi-relay (page

Is the blower hi-relay OK? — NO → Replace the blower hi-relay and retest.

YES ↓

Turn the ignition switch OFF.

Reconnect the 4P connector to the blower hi-relay.

Disconnect the 16P connector from the function control panel.

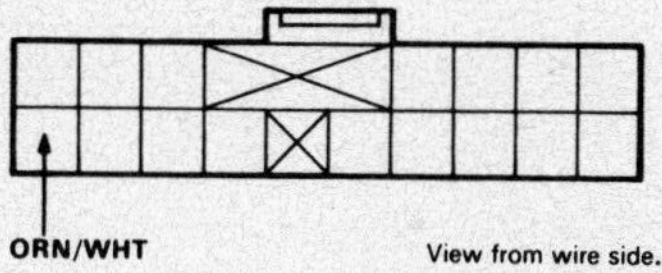
ORN/WHT

View from wire side.

Connect a jumper wire between the ORN/WHT terminal and body ground.

HEATER BLOWER DIAGNOSTIC CHART CONT.–1989–90 LEGEND AND LEGEND COUPE

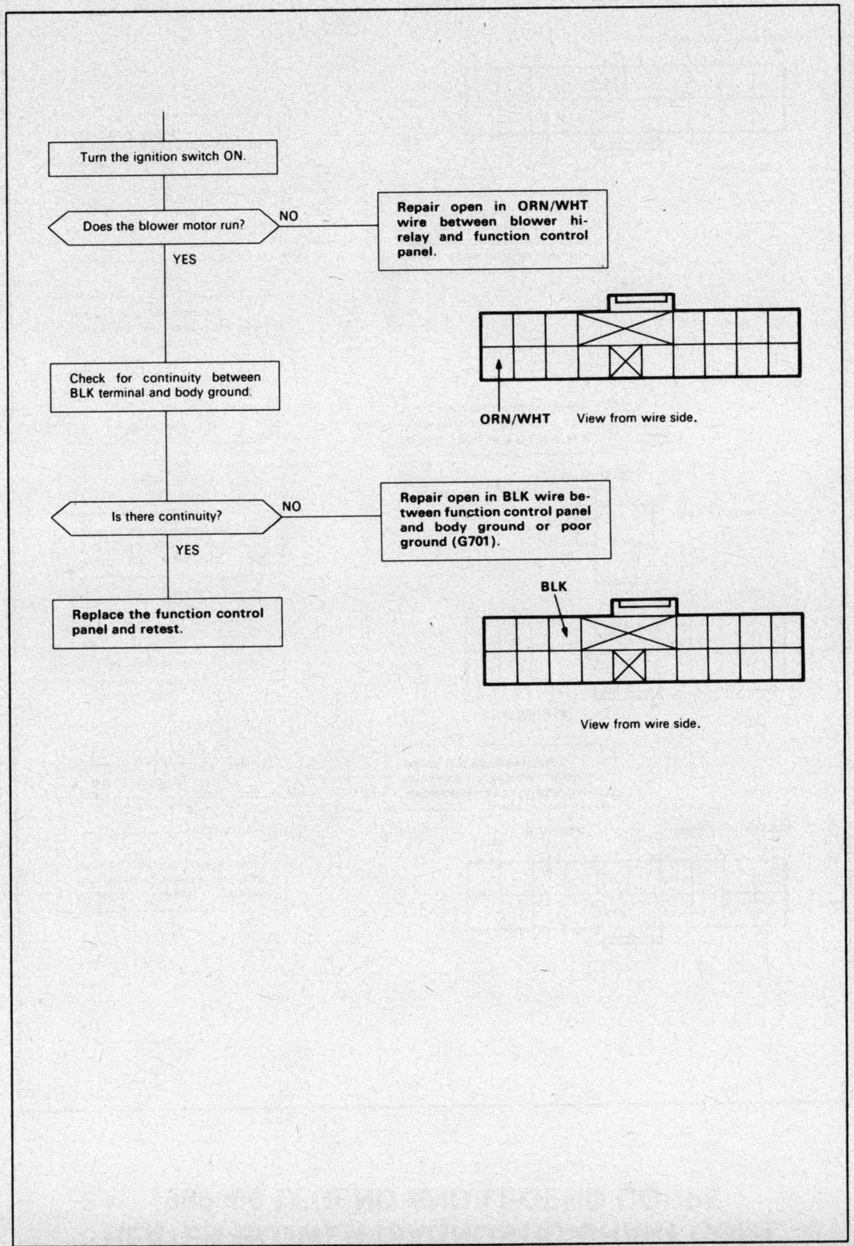
Turn the ignition switch ON.
Does the blower motor run?
NO
Repair open in ORN/WHT wire between blower hi-relay and function control panel.
YES
Check for continuity between BLK terminal and body ground.
ORN/WHT
View from wire side.
Is there continuity?
NO
Repair open in BLK wire between function control panel and body ground or poor ground (G701).
YES
Replace the function control panel and retest.
BLK
View from wire side.

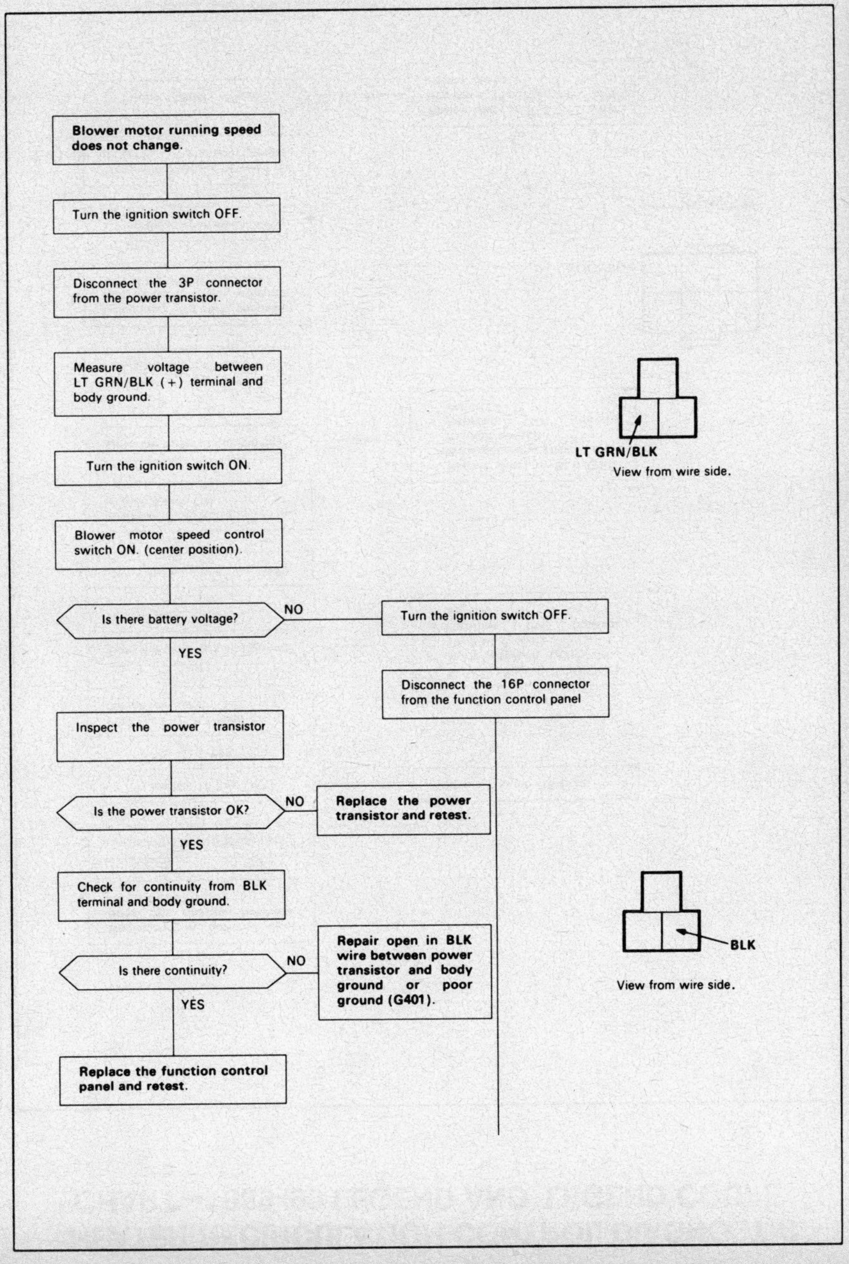
Blower motor running speed does not change.
Turn the ignition switch OFF.
Disconnect the 3P connector from the power transistor.
Measure voltage between LT GRN/BLK (+) terminal and body ground.
LT GRN/BLK
View from wire side.
Turn the ignition switch ON.
Blower motor speed control switch ON. (center position).
Is there battery voltage?
NO
Turn the ignition switch OFF.
Disconnect the 16P connector from the function control panel
YES
Inspect the power transistor
Is the power transistor OK?
NO
Replace the power transistor and retest.
YES
Check for continuity from BLK terminal and body ground.
BLK
View from wire side.
Is there continuity?
NO
Repair open in BLK wire between power transistor and body ground or poor ground (G401).
YES
Replace the function control panel and retest.

HEATER BLOWER DIAGNOSTIC CHART CONT. 1989–90 LEGEND AND LEGEND COUPE

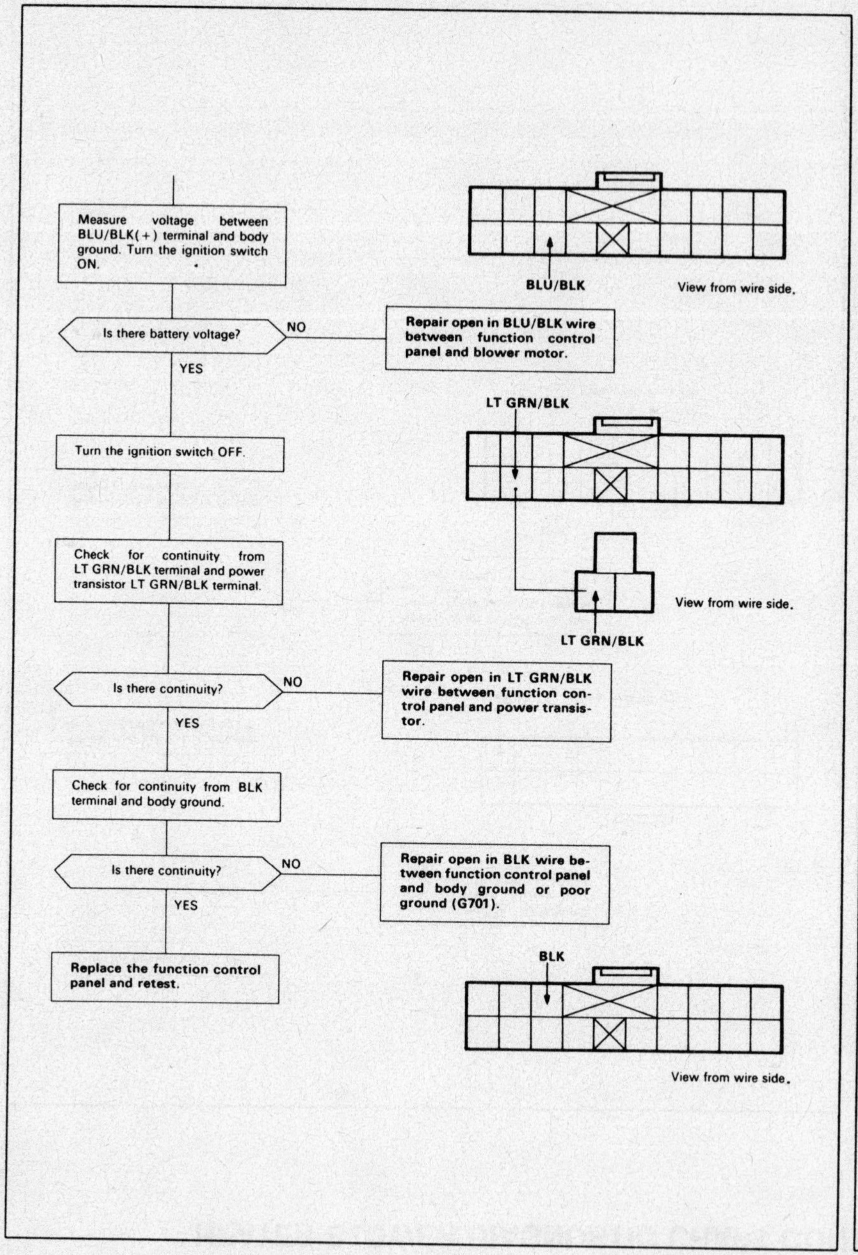
Measure voltage between BLU/BLK(+) terminal and body ground. Turn the ignition switch ON.
Is there battery voltage?
NO
Repair open in BLU/BLK wire between function control panel and blower motor.
YES
Turn the ignition switch OFF.
Check for continuity from LT GRN/BLK terminal and power transistor LT GRN/BLK terminal.
Is there continuity?
NO
Repair open in LT GRN/BLK wire between function control panel and power transistor.
YES
Check for continuity from BLK terminal and body ground.
Is there continuity?
NO
Repair open in BLK wire between function control panel and body ground or poor ground (G701).
YES
Replace the function control panel and retest.
BLU/BLK
View from wire side.
LT GRN/BLK
View from wire side.
LT GRN/BLK
BLK
View from wire side.

HEATER RECIRCULATION CONTROL DIAGNOSTIC CHART—1989–90 LEGEND AND LEGEND COUPE

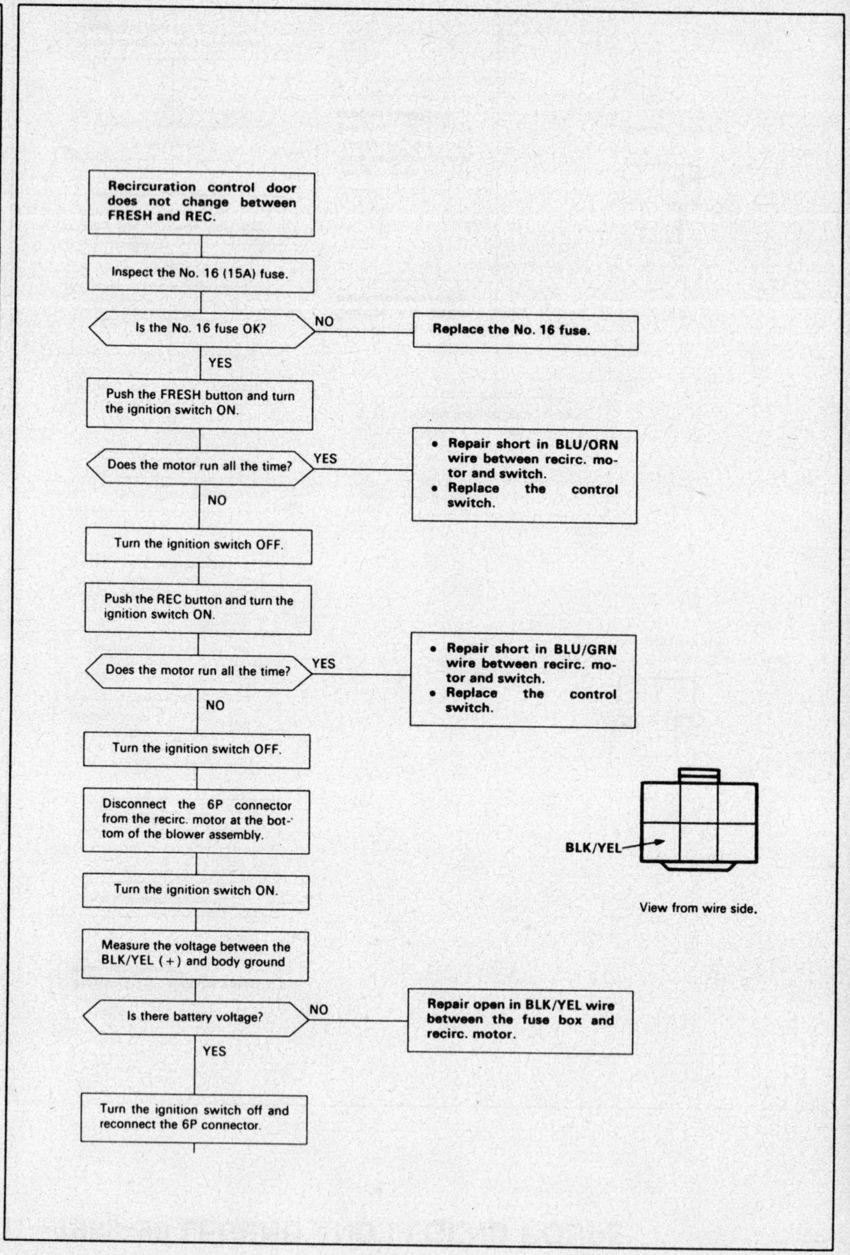
Recircuration control door does not change between FRESH and REC.
Inspect the No. 16 (15A) fuse.
Is the No. 16 fuse OK?
NO
Replace the No. 16 fuse.
YES
Push the FRESH button and turn the ignition switch ON.
Does the motor run all the time?
YES
• Repair short in BLU/ORN wire between recirc. motor and switch.
• Replace the control switch.
NO
Turn the ignition switch OFF.
Push the REC button and turn the ignition switch ON.
Does the motor run all the time?
YES
• Repair short in BLU/GRN wire between recirc. motor and switch.
• Replace the control switch.
NO
Turn the ignition switch OFF.
Disconnect the 6P connector from the recirc. motor at the bottom of the blower assembly.
Turn the ignition switch ON.
Measure the voltage between the BLK/YEL (+) and body ground
Is there battery voltage?
NO
Repair open in BLK/YEL wire between the fuse box and recirc. motor.
YES
Turn the ignition switch off and reconnect the 6P connector.
BLK/YEL
View from wire side.

HEATER RECIRCULATION CONTROL DIAGNOSTIC CHART CONT.—1989–90 LEGEND AND LEGEND COUPE

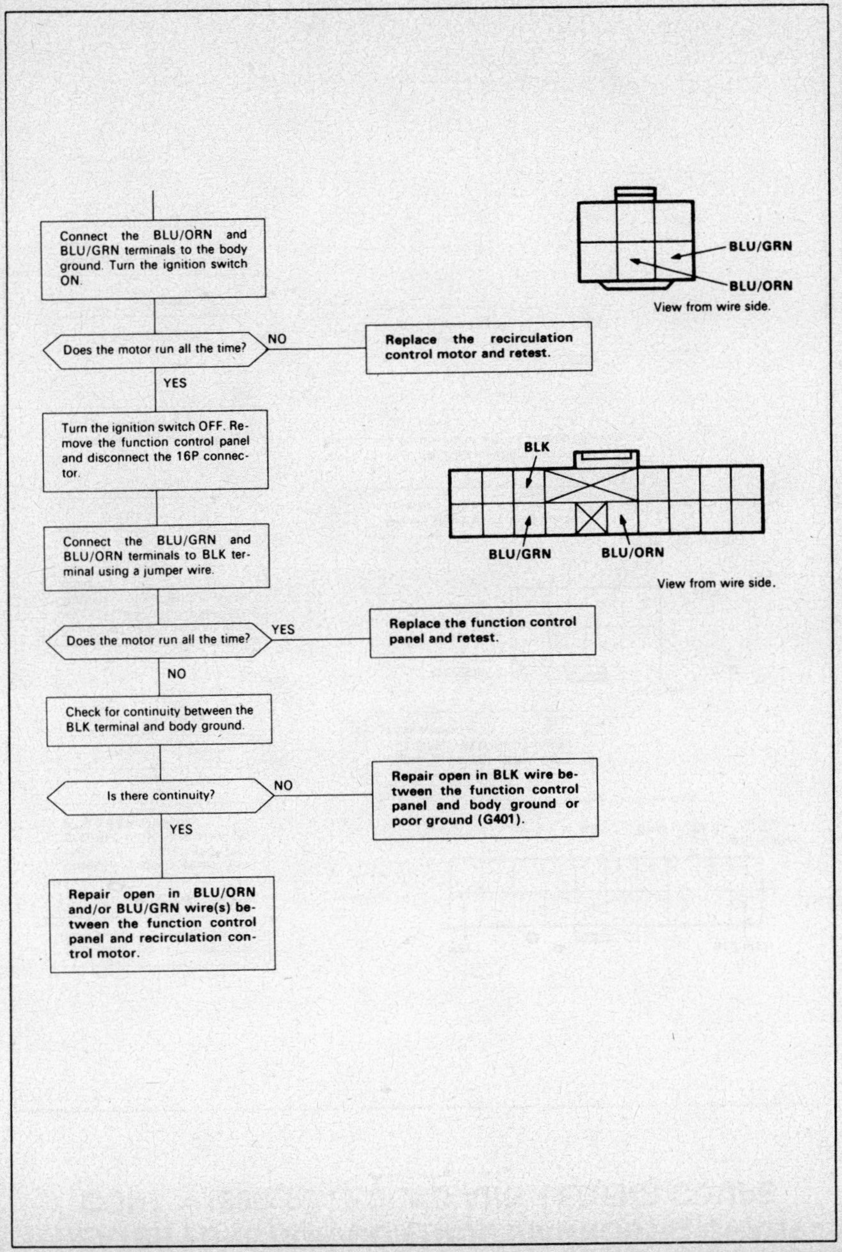
Connect the BLU/ORN and BLU/GRN terminals to the body ground. Turn the ignition switch ON.
Does the motor run all the time?
NO
Replace the recirculation control motor and retest.
YES
Turn the ignition switch OFF. Remove the function control panel and disconnect the 16P connector.
Connect the BLU/GRN and BLU/ORN terminals to BLK terminal using a jumper wire.
Does the motor run all the time?
YES
Replace the function control panel and retest.
NO
Check for continuity between the BLK terminal and body ground.
Is there continuity?
NO
Repair open in BLK wire between the function control panel and body ground or poor ground (G401).
YES
Repair open in BLU/ORN and/or BLU/GRN wire(s) between the function control panel and recirculation control motor.
BLU/GRN
BLU/ORN
View from wire side.
BLK
BLU/GRN
BLU/ORN
View from wire side.

HEATER FUNCTION CONTROL DIAGNOSTIC CHART 1989–90 LEGEND AND LEGEND COUPE

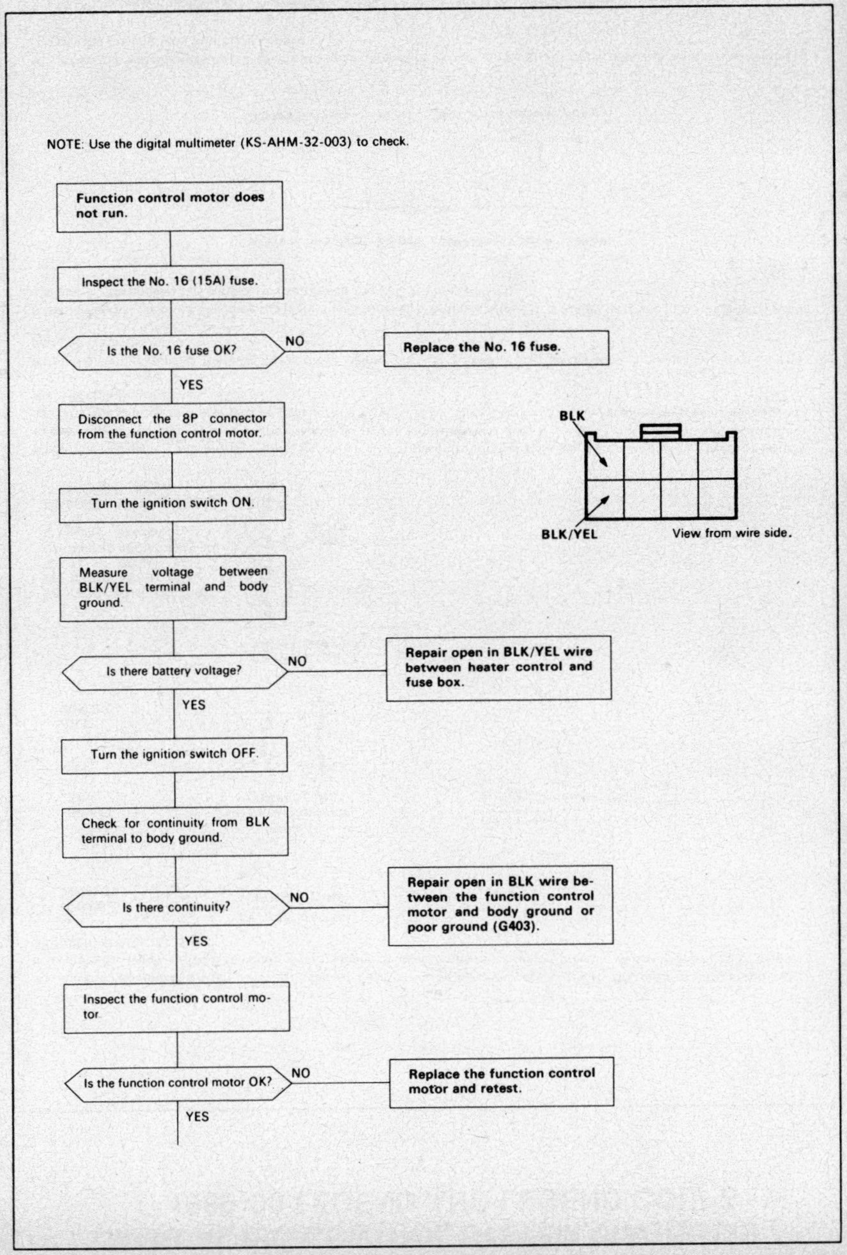
NOTE: Use the digital multimeter (KS-AHM-32-003) to check.
Function control motor does not run.
Inspect the No. 16 (15A) fuse.
Is the No. 16 fuse OK?
NO
Replace the No. 16 fuse.
YES
Disconnect the 8P connector from the function control motor.
Turn the ignition switch ON.
Measure voltage between BLK/YEL terminal and body ground.
Is there battery voltage?
NO
Repair open in BLK/YEL wire between heater control and fuse box.
YES
Turn the ignition switch OFF.
Check for continuity from BLK terminal to body ground.
Is there continuity?
NO
Repair open in BLK wire between the function control motor and body ground or poor ground (G403).
YES
Inspect the function control motor.
Is the function control motor OK?
NO
Replace the function control motor and retest.
YES
BLK
BLK/YEL
View from wire side.

HEATER FUNCTION CONTROL DIAGNOSTIC CHART CONT.—1989–90 LEGEND AND LEGEND COUPE

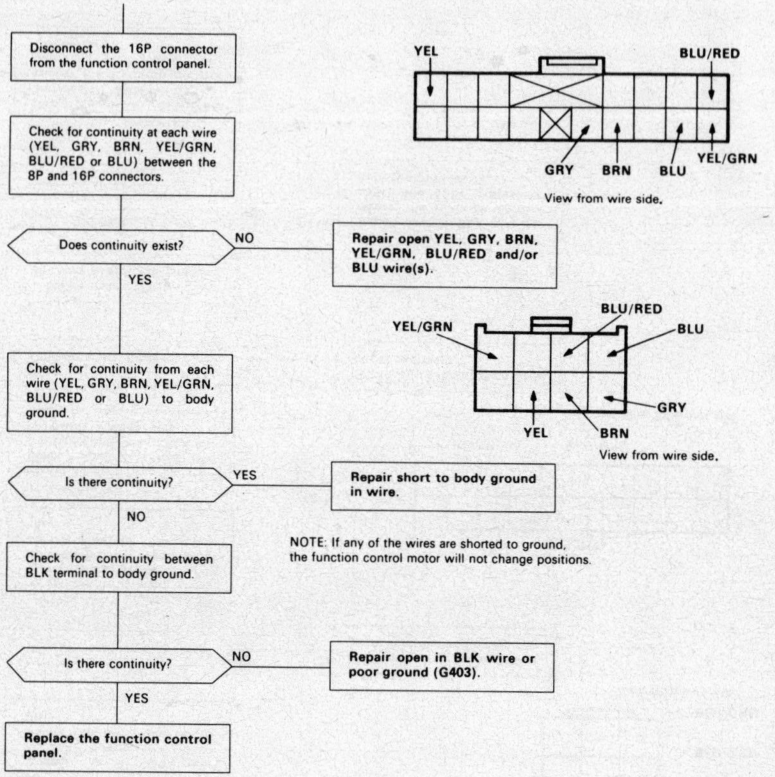
Disconnect the 16P connector from the function control panel.
Check for continuity at each wire (YEL, GRY, BRN, YEL/GRN, BLU/RED or BLU) between the 8P and 16P connectors.
Does continuity exist?
NO
Repair open YEL, GRY, BRN, YEL/GRN, BLU/RED and/or BLU wire(s).
YES
Check for continuity from each wire (YEL, GRY, BRN, YEL/GRN, BLU/RED or BLU) to body ground.
Is there continuity?
YES
Repair short to body ground in wire.
NO
Check for continuity between BLK terminal to body ground.
Is there continuity?
NO
Repair open in BLK wire or poor ground (G403).
YES
Replace the function control panel.
YEL
BLU/RED
GRY
BRN
BLU
YEL/GRN
View from wire side.
BLU/RED
YEL/GRN
BLU
GRY
YEL
BRN
View from wire side.
NOTE: If any of the wires are shorted to ground, the function control motor will not change positions.

MANUAL A/C CONTROL SYSTEM DIAGNOSIS 1989–90 LEGEND AND LEGEND COUPE

Air conditioner control system consists of the A/C switch in the function control panel, A/C control unit, evaporator, dual pressure switch, radiator fan control unit, engine coolant temperature sensor, pressure switch, PGM-FI ECU, magnetic clutch, and the clutch relay.

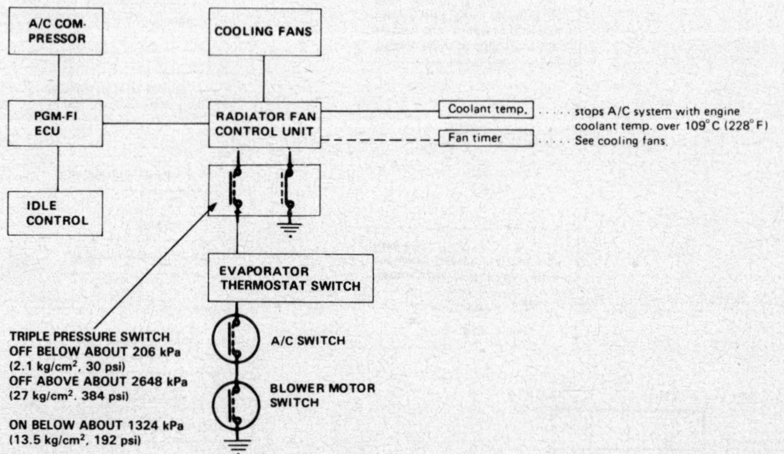
A/C COMPRESSOR
COOLING FANS
PGM-FI ECU
RADIATOR FAN CONTROL UNIT
Coolant temp.
Fan timer
..... stops A/C system with engine coolant temp. over 109°C (228°F)
..... See cooling fans.
IDLE CONTROL
EVAPORATOR THERMOSTAT SWITCH
TRIPLE PRESSURE SWITCH
OFF BELOW ABOUT 206 kPa (2.1 kg/cm², 30 psi)
OFF ABOVE ABOUT 2648 kPa (27 kg/cm², 384 psi)
ON BELOW ABOUT 1324 kPa (13.5 kg/cm², 192 psi)
A/C SWITCH
BLOWER MOTOR SWITCH

When the A/C switch and blower motor switch ON, the A/C control unit sends a signal through the dual pressure switch to the radiator fan control unit. If the evaporator sensor temperature is over 4°C (39°F), the radiator fan control unit activates the cooling fans and sends a signal to the PGM-FI ECU. The ECU then increases engine idle speed and energizes the A/C compressor clutch.

When the temperature at the evaporator drops below 3°C (37°F) the sensor signals the control unit to turn off the fans and compressor.

If the refrigerant pressure becomes too high (due to blockage) or too low (due to leakage) teh triple pressure switch sends a signal to the cooling fan control unit to preven the A/C from operating.

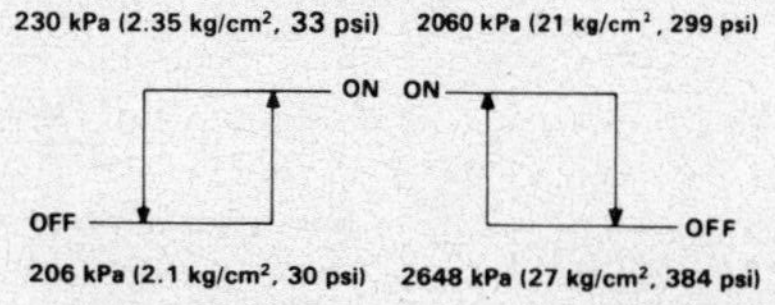
230 kPa (2.35 kg/cm², 33 psi)
2060 kPa (21 kg/cm², 299 psi)
ON
ON
OFF
OFF
206 kPa (2.1 kg/cm², 30 psi)
2648 kPa (27 kg/cm², 384 psi)

- When the system pressure is high (due to heavy operation in high temperature), triple pressure switch is activated to run the cooling fans at a higher speed.
- If engine coolant temperature reaches 109°C (228°F) at the coolant temperature sensor, the A/C is shut off.

MANUAL A/C SYSTEM DIAGNOSIS 1989–90 LEGEND AND LEGEND COUPE

1. With A/C and blower switches on, A/C clutch and fans do not operate: –SEE FLOW CHART "A"
2. With A/C and blower switches on, A/C clutch operates but both fans do not: –PERFORM RADIATOR FAN CONTROL UNIT INPUT TEST
3. With A/C and blower switches on, fans operate but A/C clutch does not engage: –SEE FLOW CHART "C"
4. With A/C and blower switches on, fan does not operate at the correct speed: –PERFORM RADIATOR FAN CONTROL UNIT INPUT TEST
5. With A/C and blower switches on, A/C clutch engages but only one fan runs:–PERFORM RADIATOR FAN CONTROL UNIT INPUT TEST
6. With A/C and blower switches off, cooling fans do not come on even with high coolant temperature: –PERFORM RADIATOR FAN CONTROL UNIT INPUT TEST
7. When engine is turned off and oil temp is above 220°F the condenser fan does not come on: –PERFORM FAN TIMER INPUT TEST

MANUAL A/C RADIATOR FAN CONTROL UNIT INPUT TEST–1989–90 LEGEND AND LEGEND COUPE

NOTE: Before performing input test, do the following:

1. Check fuse No. 24 (40A), 26 (40A), 35 (15A), 39 (20A) and No. 40 (20A) in the Under Hood Relay Box and fuse No. 9 (10A) and 17 (10A) in the Under Dash Fuse Box.
2. Disconnect 10P connector from Radiator Fan Control Unit and turn ignition switch ON.

NOTE:
- Any abnormality found during input test must be corrected before continuing.
- If all tests produce desired result substitute a known good radiator fan control unit.

Wire	Position	Test Condition	Desired Results	Corrective Action
BLK	9	Check for continuity to body ground	Should have continuity to body ground	Repair open in BLK wire between rad fan control and body ground
YEL/BLK	4	Check for battery voltage	Should have battery voltage	Check for open in YEL/BLK wire between rad fan control and No. 17 fuse.
BLU	8	Using a jumper lead connect to body ground	Both fans should run full speed	See flow chart "B"
BLU/BLK	2	Using a jumper lead connect to body ground	A/C compressor clutch should engage	See flow chart "C"
BLU/YEL	5	Using a jumper lead connect to body ground	Radiator fan should run at low speed	See flow chart "D"
		Using a jumper lead connect to YEL/BLK wire	Condensor fan should run at low speed	See flow chart "E"
LT BLU	7	Check for continuity to body ground	Should have continuity to body ground	See flow chart "A"
RED/BLU	10	Check for continuity to body ground	Should have continuity to body ground	Test for open in RED/BLU wire between rad fan control and triple pressure switch abnormal A/C pressure or faulty triple pressure switch
BLU/WHT and BLU/GRN	1 6	Using an ohmmeter on the 20 k scale check for continuity between the BLU/WHT and BLU/GRN wires	Depending on coolant temperature it should be between 0.5 kΩ to 1.2 kΩ	See flow chart "F"

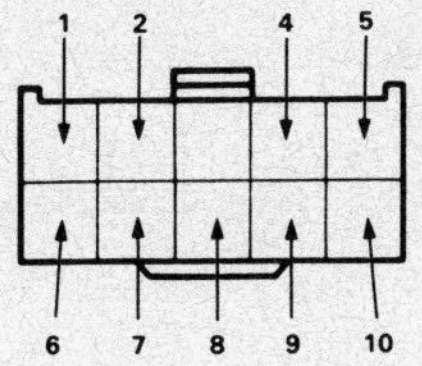
1
2
4
5
6
7
8
9
10
View from wire side

MANUAL A/C FAN TIMER INPUT TEST 1989–90 LEGEND AND LEGEND COUPE

Before performing the fan timer input test do the following:

1. Check fuse No. 26 (40A), 35 (15A), 39 (20A) and 40 (20A) in the under hood relay box and fuse No. 9 (10A) and 17 (10A) in the under dash fuse box.
2. Remove the 7P connector from the Fan timer unit and turn the ignition ON.

NOTE:
- Any abnormality found during input test must be conrrected before continuing.
- If all tests produce desired result substitute a known good fan timer.

Wire	Position	Test Condition	Desired Results	Corrective action if Desired Results or not obtained
BLK	3	Test for continuity to body ground.	Should have continuity.	Repair open in BLK wire between fan timer unit and body ground.
BLK/YEL	6	Test for Battery Voltage with ignitor switch on.	Should have Battery Voltage	Repair open in BLK/YEL between fan timer unit and fuse.
YEL/BLK	5	Test for Battery Voltage at all times (key on or off)	Should have Battery Voltage	Repair open in YEL/BLK wire between fan timer unit and fuse
BLU/YEL	2	Test for 12 volt	Should have 12 V.	Test for open in BLU/YEL wire between fan timer unit and rad fan control unit or faulty rad fan control unit see input test.
ORN	4	Using an ohmmeter on the 20 k scale test for continuity to body ground	There should be to 105°C (221°F)	Test for open, short to ground or faulty oil temp. sensor.
BLU/RED and GRN	1 7	Test for continuity between BLU/RED and GRN wires.	The should be 90 to 120 Ω.	See flow chart "E"

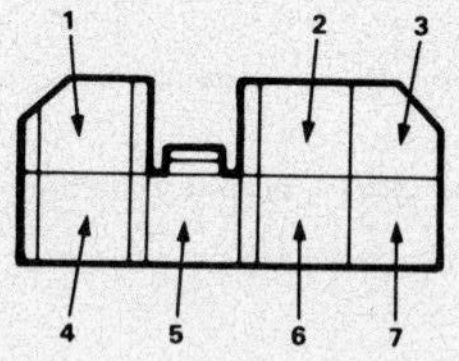
1
2
3
4
5
6
7

MANUAL A/C DIAGNOSTIC CHART A 1989–90 LEGEND AND LEGEND COUPE

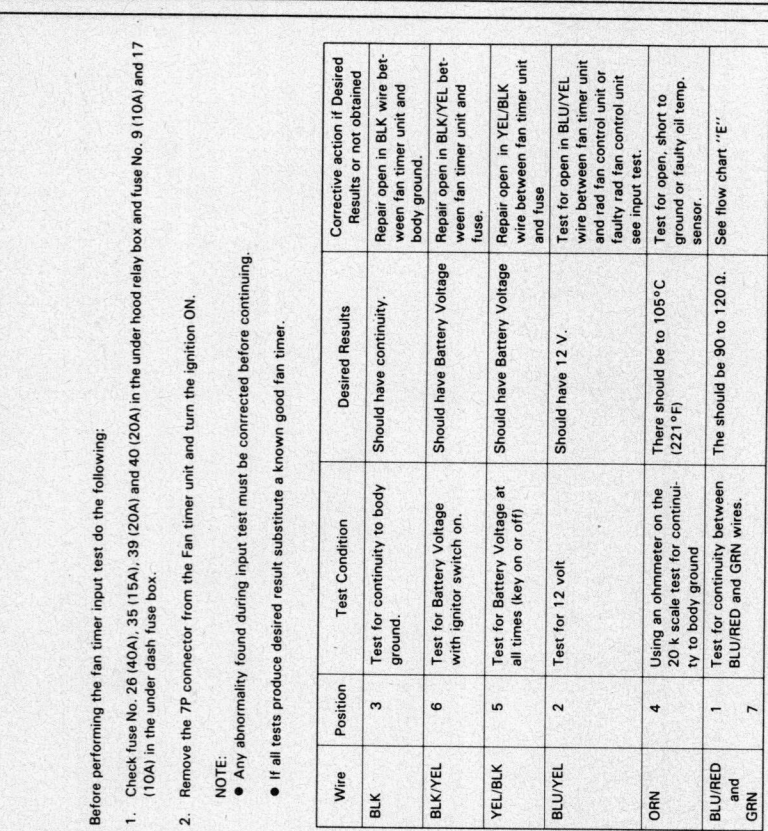

NOTE: Use the digital multimeter (KA-AHM-003) to check.

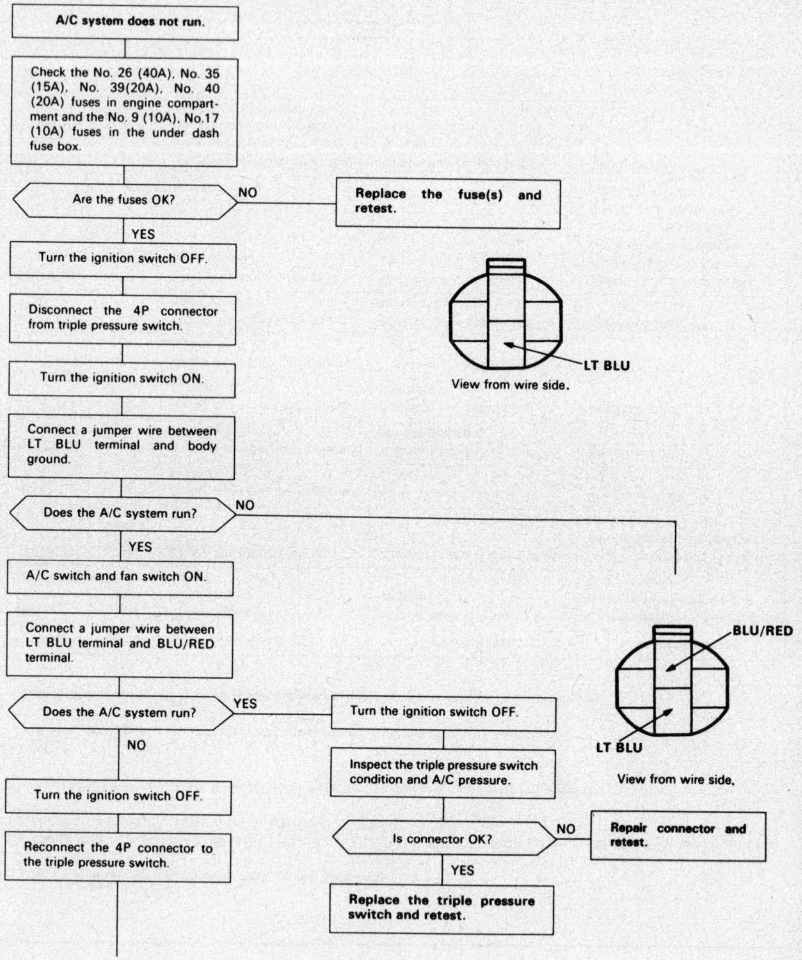
A/C system does not run.
Check the No. 26 (40A), No. 35 (15A), No. 39(20A), No. 40 (20A) fuses in engine compartment and the No. 9 (10A), No.17 (10A) fuses in the under dash fuse box.
Are the fuses OK?
NO
Replace the fuse(s) and retest.
YES
Turn the ignition switch OFF.
Disconnect the 4P connector from triple pressure switch.
LT BLU
View from wire side.
Turn the ignition switch ON.
Connect a jumper wire between LT BLU terminal and body ground.
Does the A/C system run?
NO
YES
A/C switch and fan switch ON.
Connect a jumper wire between LT BLU terminal and BLU/RED terminal.
BLU/RED
LT BLU
View from wire side.
Does the A/C system run?
YES
Turn the ignition switch OFF.
Inspect the triple pressure switch condition and A/C pressure.
Is connector OK?
NO
Repair connector and retest.
YES
Replace the triple pressure switch and retest.
NO
Turn the ignition switch OFF.
Reconnect the 4P connector to the triple pressure switch.

MANUAL A/C DIAGNOSTIC CHART A CONT.—1989–90 LEGEND AND LEGEND COUPE

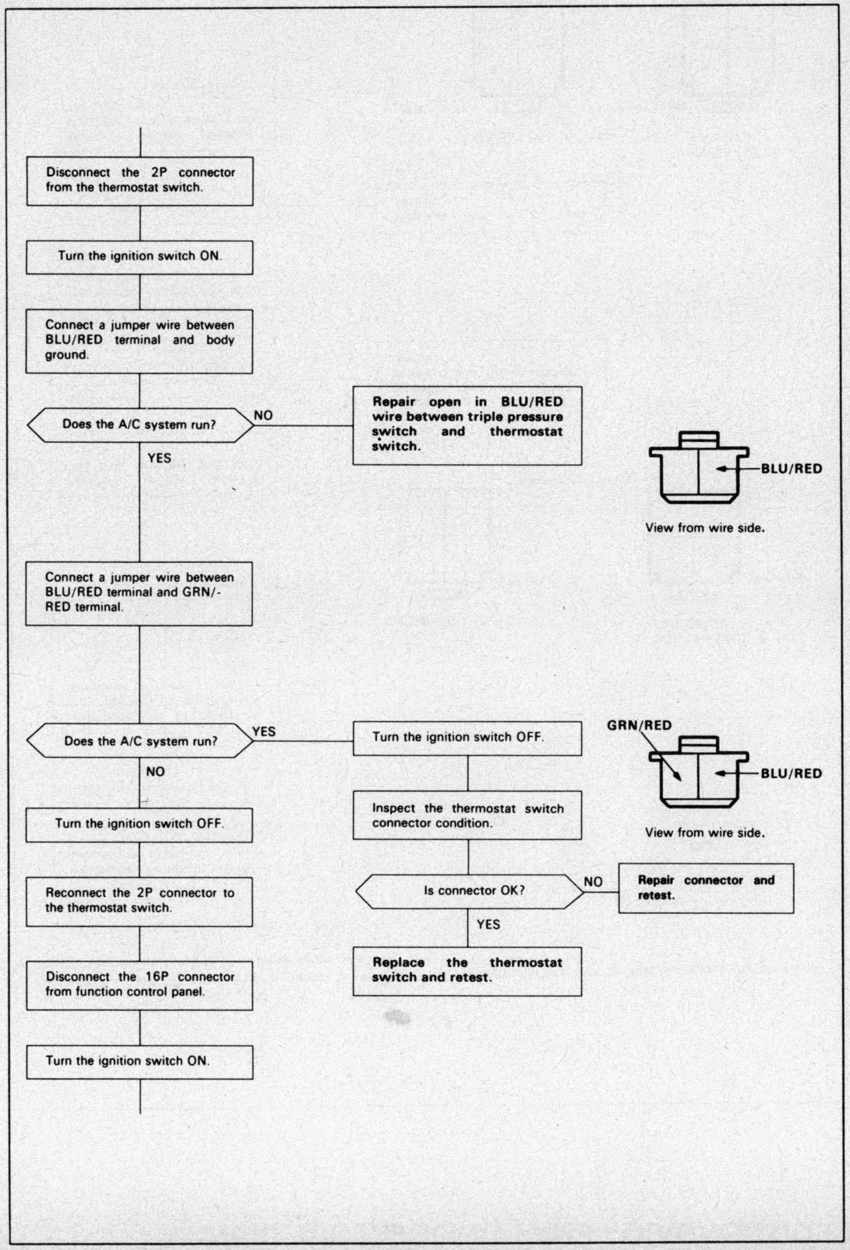
Disconnect the 2P connector from the thermostat switch.
Turn the ignition switch ON.
Connect a jumper wire between BLU/RED terminal and body ground.
Does the A/C system run?
NO
Repair open in BLU/RED wire between triple pressure switch and thermostat switch.
YES
BLU/RED
View from wire side.
Connect a jumper wire between BLU/RED terminal and GRN/-RED terminal.
Does the A/C system run?
YES
Turn the ignition switch OFF.
Inspect the thermostat switch connector condition.
Is connector OK?
NO
Repair connector and retest.
YES
Replace the thermostat switch and retest.
GRN/RED
BLU/RED
View from wire side.
NO
Turn the ignition switch OFF.
Reconnect the 2P connector to the thermostat switch.
Disconnect the 16P connector from function control panel.
Turn the ignition switch ON.

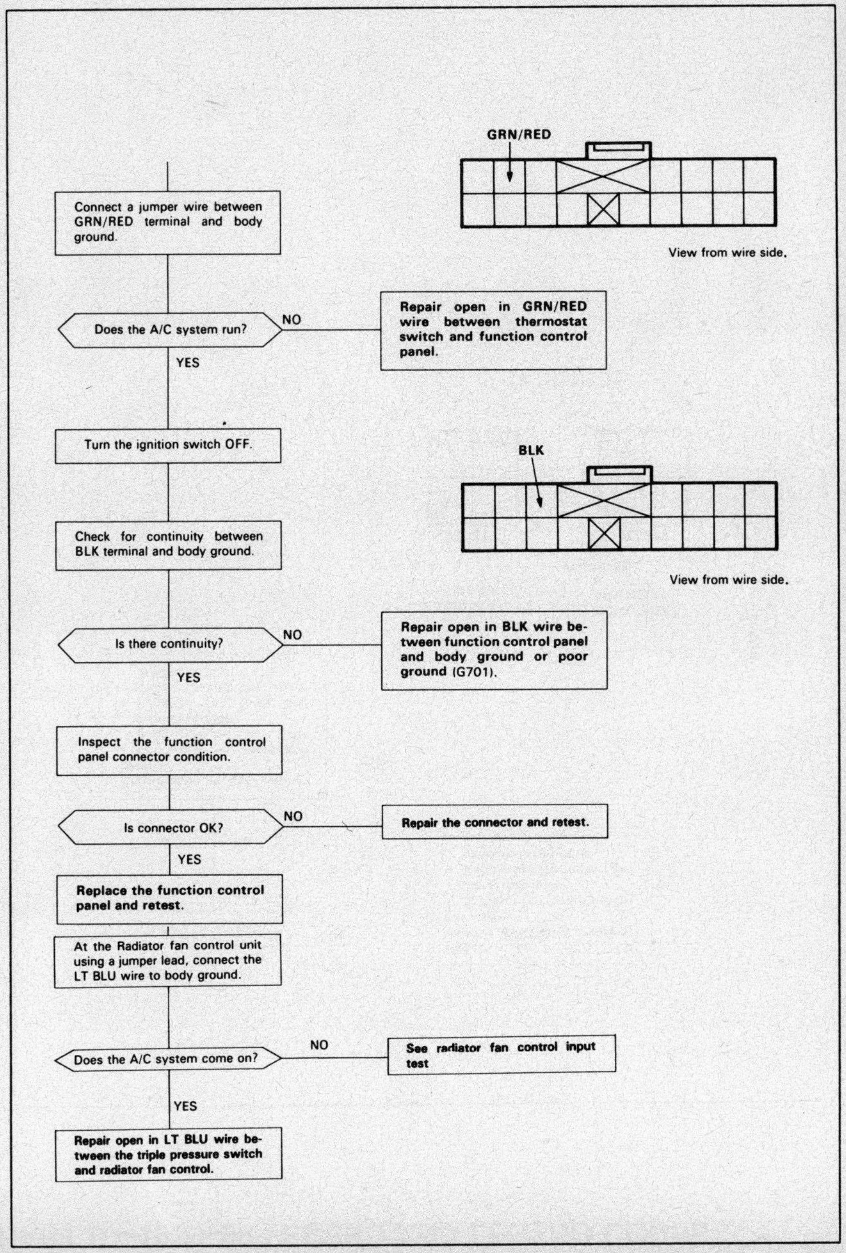
Connect a jumper wire between GRN/RED terminal and body ground.
GRN/RED
View from wire side.
Does the A/C system run?
NO
Repair open in GRN/RED wire between thermostat switch and function control panel.
YES
Turn the ignition switch OFF.
BLK
View from wire side.
Check for continuity between BLK terminal and body ground.
Is there continuity?
NO
Repair open in BLK wire between function control panel and body ground or poor ground (G701).
YES
Inspect the function control panel connector condition.
Is connector OK?
NO
Repair the connector and retest.
YES
Replace the function control panel and retest.
At the Radiator fan control unit using a jumper lead, connect the LT BLU wire to body ground.
Does the A/C system come on?
NO
See radiator fan control input test
YES
Repair open in LT BLU wire between the triple pressure switch and radiator fan control.

MANUAL A/C COOLING FANS—DIAGNOSTIC CHART B—1989–90 LEGEND AND LEGEND COUPE

If one fan runs and the other doesn't, switch the relays. If the problem changes with the relays, replace the defective one. If the problem remains unchanged, start with step 1.

NOTE: Use the digital multimeter (KS-AHM-32-003) to check.

Cooling fans do not run with BLU wire shorted to ground.

1. Turn the ignition switch OFF.
2. Disconnect the 4P connectors from the radiator fan relay and condenser fan relay.
3. Turn the ignition switch ON.

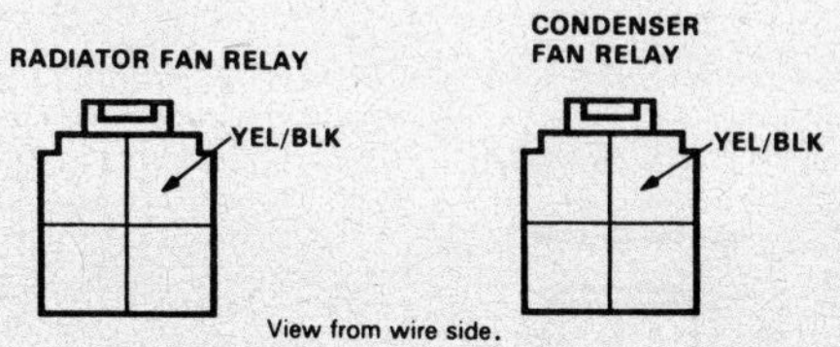
RADIATOR FAN RELAY
YEL/BLK
CONDENSER FAN RELAY
YEL/BLK

View from wire side.

4. Measure voltage between YEL/BLK terminals and body ground.
5. Is there battery voltage?
   - NO: **Repair open in YEL/BLK wire(s) between ignition switch and relay connector(s).**
   - YES: Inspect the radiator and condenser fan relays.
6. Are the relays OK?
   - NO: **Replace the relay(s) and retest.**
   - YES: Measure voltage between WHT/BLU, WHT/GRN terminals and body ground.

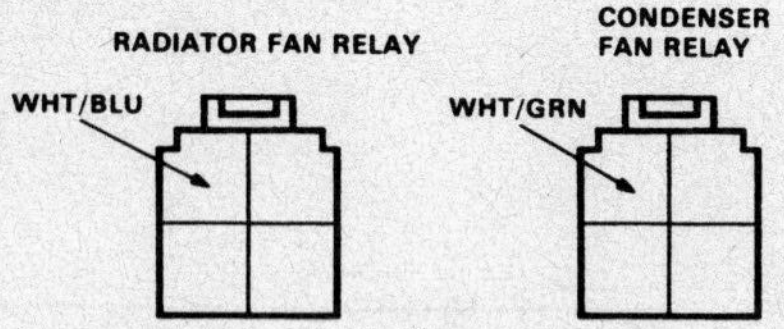
RADIATOR FAN RELAY
WHT/BLU
CONDENSER FAN RELAY
WHT/GRN

View from wire side.

7. Is there battery voltage?
   - NO: **Repair open in WHT/BLU and/or WHT/GRN wire(s) between:**
     - **Radiator fan motor and radiator fan relay.**
     - **Condenser fan motor and condenser fan relay.**
   - YES: **Repair open in BLK wire(s) between:**
     - **Condenser fan relay and body ground or poor ground (G203).**
     - **Radiator fan relay and body ground or poor ground (G203).**

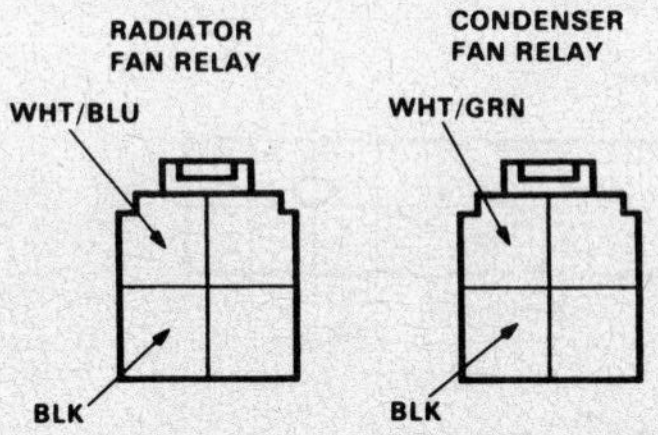
RADIATOR FAN RELAY
WHT/BLU
BLK
CONDENSER FAN RELAY
WHT/GRN
BLK

View from wire side.

MANUAL A/C COMPRESSOR CLUTCH—DIAGNOSTIC CHART C—1989–90 LEGEND AND LEGEND COUPE

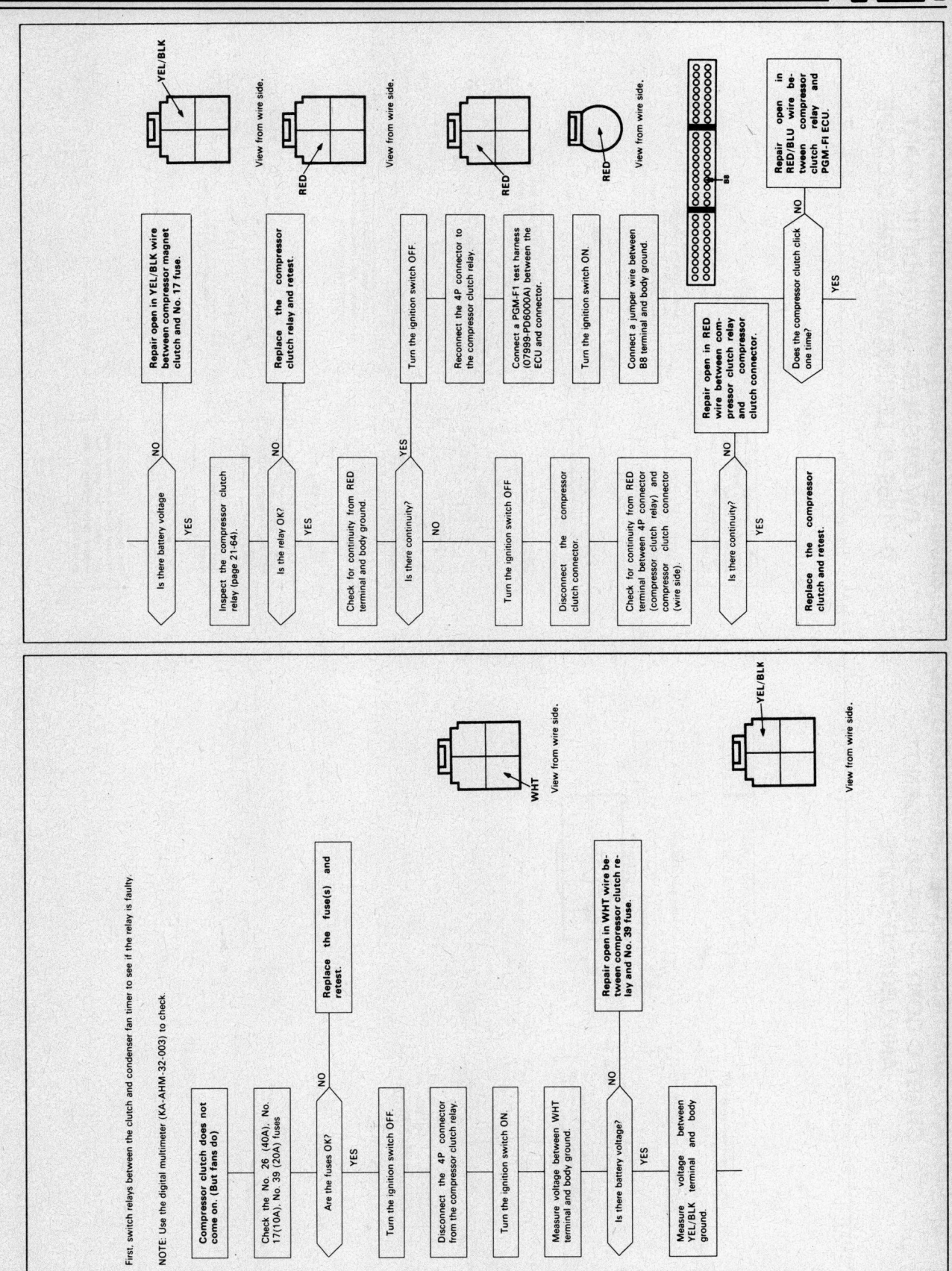

First, switch relays between the clutch and condenser fan timer to see if the relay is faulty.

NOTE: Use the digital multimeter (KA-AHM-32-003) to check.

Compressor clutch does not come on. (But fans do)

Check the No. 26 (40A), No. 17(10A), No. 39 (20A) fuses

Are the fuses OK? — NO → **Replace the fuse(s) and retest.**

YES

Turn the ignition switch OFF.

Disconnect the 4P connector from the compressor clutch relay.

Turn the ignition switch ON.

Measure voltage between WHT terminal and body ground.

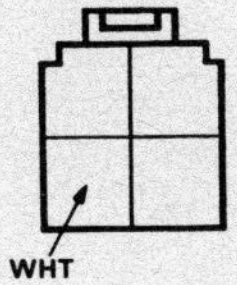
WHT
View from wire side.

Is there battery voltage? — NO → **Repair open in WHT wire between compressor clutch relay and No. 39 fuse.**

YES

Measure voltage between YEL/BLK terminal and body ground.

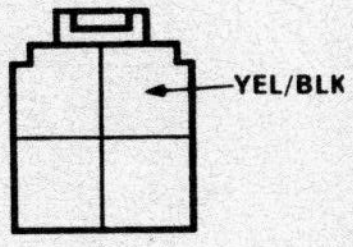
YEL/BLK
View from wire side.

Is there battery voltage — NO → **Repair open in YEL/BLK wire between compressor magnet clutch and No. 17 fuse.**

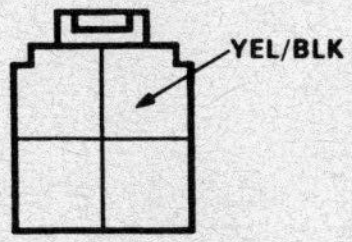
YEL/BLK
View from wire side.

YES

Inspect the compressor clutch relay (page 21-64).

Is the relay OK? — NO → **Replace the compressor clutch relay and retest.**

RED
View from wire side.

YES

Check for continuity from RED terminal and body ground.

Is there continuity? — YES → Turn the ignition switch OFF.

Reconnect the 4P connector to the compressor clutch relay.

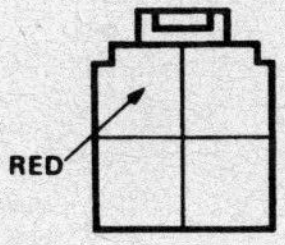
RED

Connect a PGM-F1 test harness (07999-PD6000A) between the ECU and connector.

Turn the ignition switch ON.

RED
View from wire side.

Connect a jumper wire between B8 terminal and body ground.

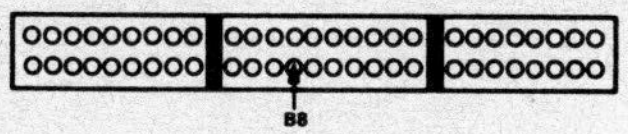
B8

Does the compressor clutch click one time? — NO → **Repair open in RED/BLU wire between compressor clutch relay and PGM-FI ECU.**

YES

Is there continuity? — NO

Turn the ignition switch OFF

Disconnect the compressor clutch connector.

Check for continuity from RED terminal between 4P connector (compressor clutch relay) and compressor clutch connector (wire side).

Is there continuity? — NO → **Repair open in RED wire between compressor clutch relay and compressor clutch connector.**

YES

Replace the compressor clutch and retest.

MANUAL A/C COMPRESSOR CLUTCH—DIAGNOSTIC CHART C CONT.—1989–90 LEGEND AND LEGEND COUPE

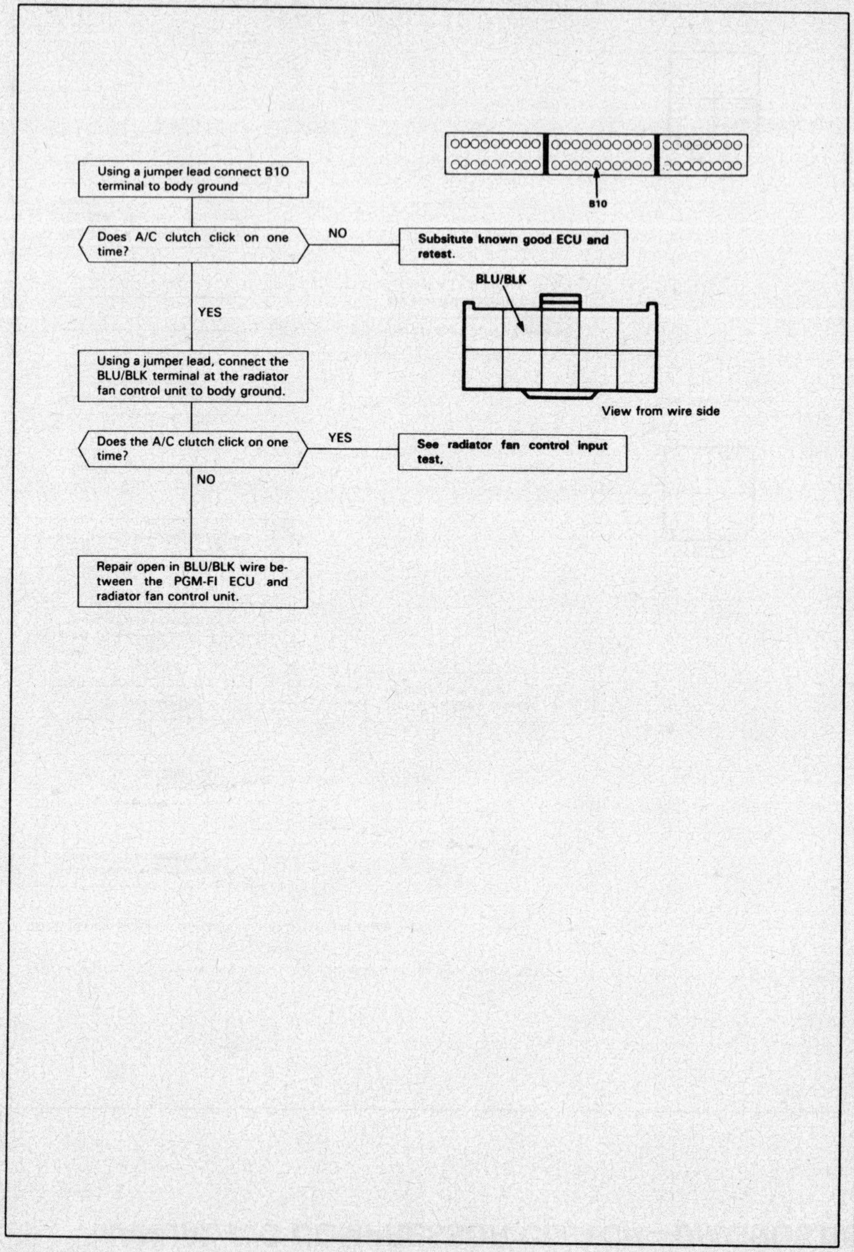
Using a jumper lead connect B10 terminal to body ground
Does A/C clutch click on one time?
NO
Subsitute known good ECU and retest.
YES
Using a jumper lead, connect the BLU/BLK terminal at the radiator fan control unit to body ground.
Does the A/C clutch click on one time?
YES
See radiator fan control input test.
NO
Repair open in BLU/BLK wire between the PGM-FI ECU and radiator fan control unit.
B10
BLU/BLK
View from wire side

MANUAL A/C RADIATOR FAN DOES NOT RUN AT LOW ON SPEED—DIAGNOSTIC CHART D—1989–90 LEGEND AND LEGEND COUPE

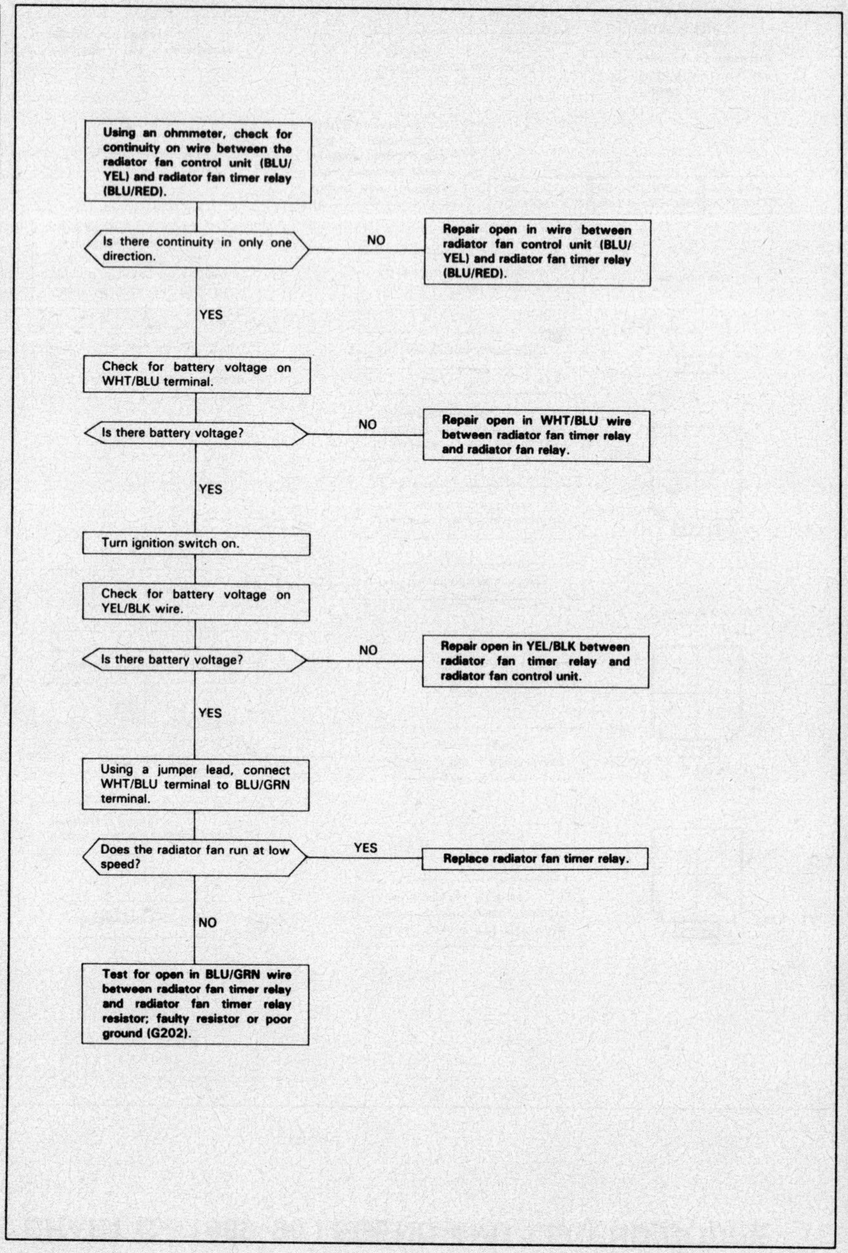
Using an ohmmeter, check for continuity on wire between the radiator fan control unit (BLU/YEL) and radiator fan timer relay (BLU/RED).
Is there continuity in only one direction.
NO
Repair open in wire between radiator fan control unit (BLU/YEL) and radiator fan timer relay (BLU/RED).
YES
Check for battery voltage on WHT/BLU terminal.
Is there battery voltage?
NO
Repair open in WHT/BLU wire between radiator fan timer relay and radiator fan relay.
YES
Turn ignition switch on.
Check for battery voltage on YEL/BLK wire.
Is there battery voltage?
NO
Repair open in YEL/BLK between radiator fan timer relay and radiator fan control unit.
YES
Using a jumper lead, connect WHT/BLU terminal to BLU/GRN terminal.
Does the radiator fan run at low speed?
YES
Replace radiator fan timer relay.
NO
Test for open in BLU/GRN wire between radiator fan timer relay and radiator fan timer relay resistor; faulty resistor or poor ground (G202).

MANUAL A/C CONDENSER FAN SHOULD RUN AT LOW ON SPEED—DIAGNOSTIC CHART E—1989–90 LEGEND AND LEGEND COUPE

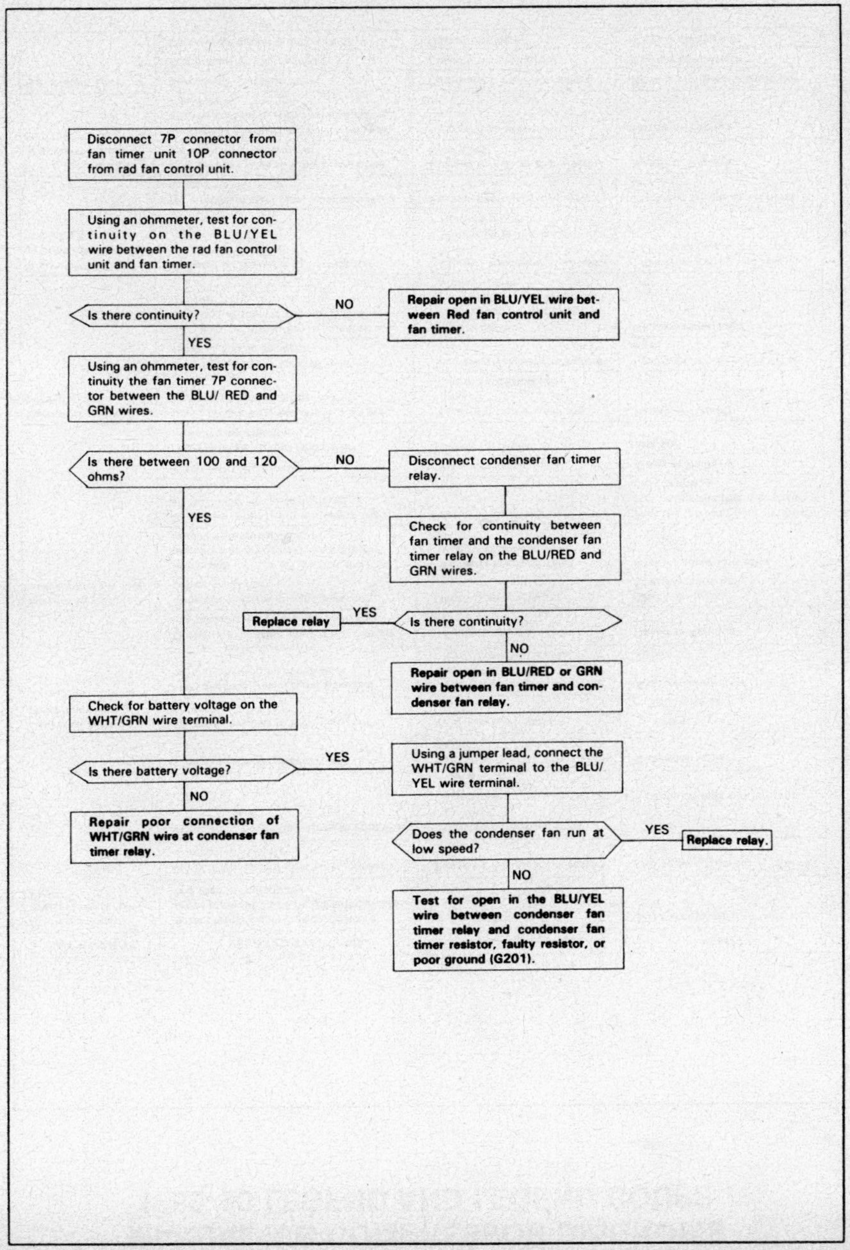
Disconnect 7P connector from fan timer unit 10P connector from rad fan control unit.
Using an ohmmeter, test for continuity on the BLU/YEL wire between the rad fan control unit and fan timer.
Is there continuity?
NO
Repair open in BLU/YEL wire between Red fan control unit and fan timer.
YES
Using an ohmmeter, test for continuity the fan timer 7P connector between the BLU/ RED and GRN wires.
Is there between 100 and 120 ohms?
NO
Disconnect condenser fan timer relay.
Check for continuity between fan timer and the condenser fan timer relay on the BLU/RED and GRN wires.
Is there continuity?
YES
Replace relay
NO
Repair open in BLU/RED or GRN wire between fan timer and condenser fan relay.
YES
Check for battery voltage on the WHT/GRN wire terminal.
Is there battery voltage?
YES
Using a jumper lead, connect the WHT/GRN terminal to the BLU/ YEL wire terminal.
Does the condenser fan run at low speed?
YES
Replace relay.
NO
Test for open in the BLU/YEL wire between condenser fan timer relay and condenser fan timer resistor, faulty resistor, or poor ground (G201).
NO
Repair poor connection of WHT/GRN wire at condenser fan timer relay.

MANUAL A/C RADIATOR FAN TEMPERATURE SENSOR DIAGNOSTIC CHART F—1989–90 LEGEND AND LEGEND COUPE

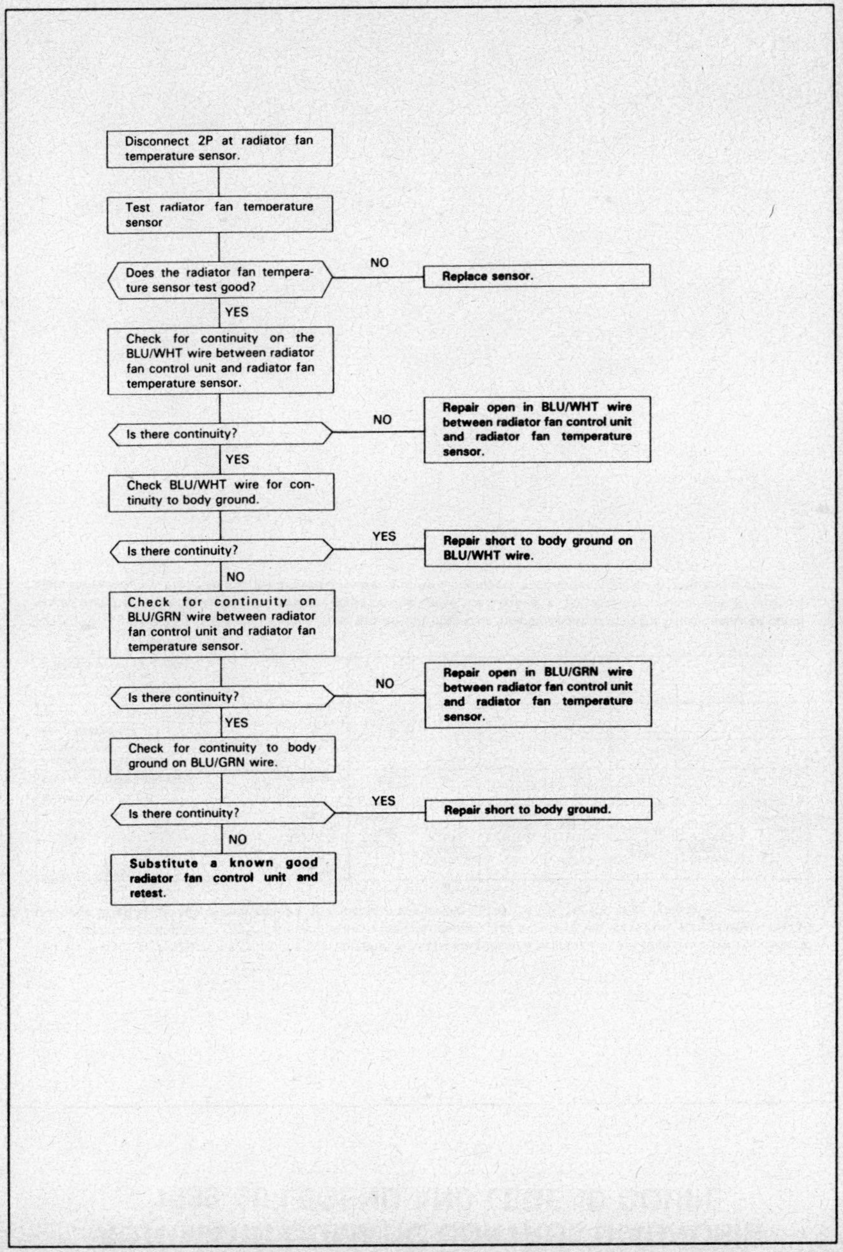
Disconnect 2P at radiator fan temperature sensor.
Test radiator fan temperature sensor
Does the radiator fan temperature sensor test good?
NO
Replace sensor.
YES
Check for continuity on the BLU/WHT wire between radiator fan control unit and radiator fan temperature sensor.
Is there continuity?
NO
Repair open in BLU/WHT wire between radiator fan control unit and radiator fan temperature sensor.
YES
Check BLU/WHT wire for continuity to body ground.
Is there continuity?
YES
Repair short to body ground on BLU/WHT wire.
NO
Check for continuity on BLU/GRN wire between radiator fan control unit and radiator fan temperature sensor.
Is there continuity?
NO
Repair open in BLU/GRN wire between radiator fan control unit and radiator fan temperature sensor.
YES
Check for continuity to body ground on BLU/GRN wire.
Is there continuity?
YES
Repair short to body ground.
NO
Substitute a known good radiator fan control unit and retest.

MANUAL A/C COMPRESSOR DIAGNOSIS
1989–90 LEGEND AND LEGEND COUPE

TEST RESULTS	RELATED SYMPTOMS	PROBABLE CAUSE	REMEDY
Discharge (high) pressure abnormally high	After stopping compressor, pressure drops to about 196 kPa (28 psi) quickly, and then falls gradually	Air in system	Evacuate system; then recharge 52
	No bubbles in sight glass when condenser is cooled by water	Excessive refrigerant in system	Discharge refrigerant as required
	Reduced or no air flow through condenser.	· Clogged condenser or radiator fins · Condenser or radiator fan not working properly.	· Clean · Check voltage and fan rpm
	Line to condenser is excessively hot	Restricted flow of refrigerant in system	Expansion valve
Discharge pressure abnormally low	Excessive bubbles in sight glass; condenser is not hot	Insufficient refrigerant	· Charge system · Check for leak
	High and low pressures are balanced soon after stopping compressor	· Faulty compressor discharge or inlet valve · Faulty compressor seal	Replace compressor Repair
	Outlet of expansion valve is not frosted, low pressure gauge indicates vacuum	· Faulty expansion valve	Repair or Replace
Suction (low) pressure abnormally low	Excessive bubbles in sight glass; condenser is not hot	Insufficient refrigerant	Check for leaks. Charge as required.
	Expansion valve is not frosted and low pressure line is not cold. Low pressure gauge indicates vacuum.	· Frozen expansion valve · Faulty expansion valve	Replace expansion valve
	Discharge temperature is low and the air flow from vents is restricted	Frozen evaporator	Run the fan with compressor off then check the thermostat and capillary tube.
	Expansion valve frosted	Clogged expansion valve	Clean or Replace
	Receiver dryer is cool (should be warm during operation)	Clogged receiver drier	Replace
Suction pressure abnormally high	Low pressure hose and check joint are cooler than around evaporator	· Expansion valve open too long · Loose expansion valve	Repair or Replace
	Suction pressure is lowered when condenser is cooled by water	Excessive refrigerant in system	Discharge refrigerant as necessary
	High and low pressures are balanced too equalized as soon as the compressor is stopped	· Faulty gasket · Faulty high pressure valve · Foreign particle stuck in high pressure valve	Replace compressor
Suction and discharge pressures abnormally high	Reduced air flow through condenser	· Clogged condenser or radiator fins · Condenser or radiator fan not working properly	· Clean condenser and radiator · Check voltage and fan rpm
	No bubbles in sight glass when condenser is cooled by water	Excessive refrigerant in system	Discharge refrigerant as necessary.
Suction and discharge pressures abnormally low	Low pressure hose and metal end areas are cooler than around evaporator	Clogged or kinked low pressure hose parts	Repair or Replace
	Temperature around expansion valve is too low compared with that around receiver-dryer.	Clogged high pressure line	Repair or Replace
Refrigerant leaks	Compressor clutch is dirty	Compressor shaft seal leaking	Replace compressor shaft seal
	Compressor bolt(s) are dirty	Leaking around bolt(s)	Replace compressor
	Compressor gasket is wet with oil	Gasket leaking	Replace compressor

AUTOMATIC CLIMATIC CONTROL DIAGNOSIS
1989–90 LEGEND AND LEGEND COUPE

NOTE: Across each row in the chart, the systems that could be sources of a system are ranked in the order they should be inspected, starting with ①. Find the symptom in the left column, read across to the most likey source, then refer to the page listed at the top of that column. If inspection shows the system is OK, try the next system ②, etc.

SYSTEM / SYMPTOM	POWER CIRCUITS TO CLIMATE CONTROL UNIT	EVAPORATOR TEMPERATURE SENSOR	COOLANT TEMPERATURE SENSOR	AIR MIX CONTROL MOTOR	FUNCTION CONTROL MOTOR	SUNLIGHT SENSOR	IN-CAR TEMPERATURE SENSOR	AMBIENT TEMPERATURE SENSOR
SELF-DIAGNOSIS INDICATOR	(None)	A	B	C	D	E	F	G
Climate control system does not work at all.	①							
No air from blower.	①							
No cold air from blower.		③					①	②
No hot air from blower.				①			②	
Actual temperature is different from set temperatue	②						③	①

NOTE: If you have one of the above symptoms, but no self-diagnosis indicator light, one of the basic heater/air conditioner components controlled by the system could be the cause, i.e., blower motor, A/C compressor clutch, recirculation control motor, etc. Refer to the standard Heater and Air Conditioner section for troubleshooting and testing.

AUTOMATIC CLIMATIC CONTROL—SELF DIAGNOSIS INDICATORS—1989–90 LEGEND AND LEGEND COUPE

The Automatic Climate Control System has a built-in self-diagnosis feature.
If a problem is suspected, turn the ignition switch OFF for at least one minute. Then turn the ignition switch ON and push both the AUTO and OFF buttons on the control panel at the same time. Any problems in circuits A-G will be indicated by the respective LED coming on.
The climate control unit does not memorize the Self -diagnosis indicator lights. If the ignition switch is turned OFF for approximately one minute or more, the indicator light memory will be lost.

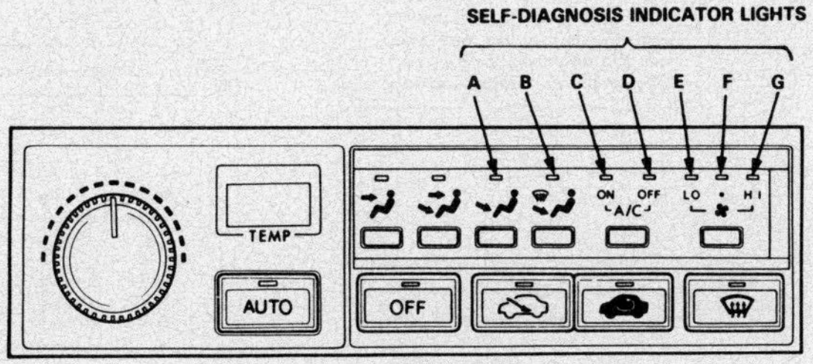
SELF-DIAGNOSIS INDICATOR LIGHTS
A B C D E F G
TEMP
AUTO
OFF
ON OFF A/C
LO HI

Control Panel

NOTE:
- Before replacing any component, recheck that all connector terminals and wires are secure.
- The term ''Intermittent Falure'' means a system may have had a falure, but it checks out OK through all your tests. You may need to road test the car to reproduce the failure, or, if the problem was a loose connection, you may have unknowingly solved it while doing the tests.

AUTOMATIC CLIMATIC CONTROL—SYSTEM AND CONTROL UNIT DIAGNOSIS—1989–90 LEGEND AND LEGEND COUPE

The climate control unit receives the input data sent by the sensors, the temperature setting dial and the potentiometers to decide the outlet air temperature, volume and direction.

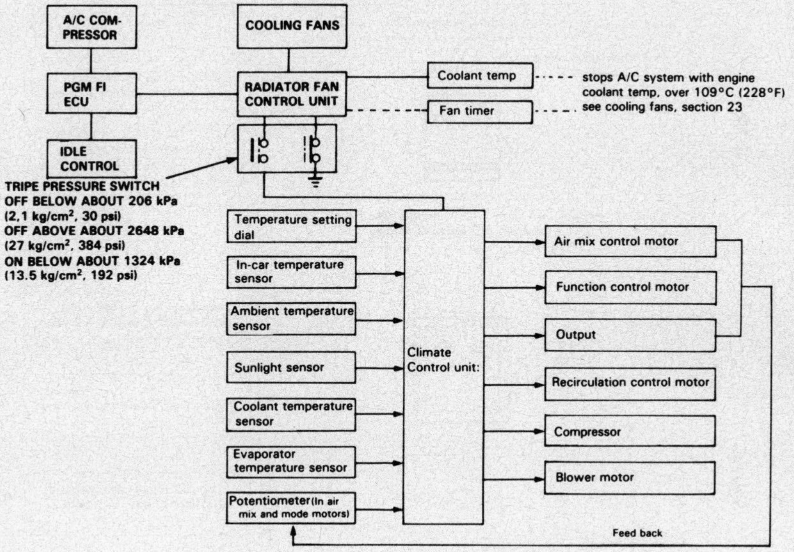
A/C COMPRESSOR
PGM FI ECU
IDLE CONTROL
COOLING FANS
RADIATOR FAN CONTROL UNIT
Coolant temp
Fan timer
stops A/C system with engine coolant temp. over 109°C (228°F) see cooling fans, section 23
TRIPE PRESSURE SWITCH
OFF BELOW ABOUT 206 kPa (2.1 kg/cm², 30 psi)
OFF ABOVE ABOUT 2648 kPa (27 kg/cm², 384 psi)
ON BELOW ABOUT 1324 kPa (13.5 kg/cm², 192 psi)
Temperature setting dial
In-car temperature sensor
Ambient temperature sensor
Sunlight sensor
Coolant temperature sensor
Evaporator temperature sensor
Potentiometer (In air mix and mode motors)
Climate Control unit:
Air mix control motor
Function control motor
Output
Recirculation control motor
Compressor
Blower motor
Feed back

Control Panel:

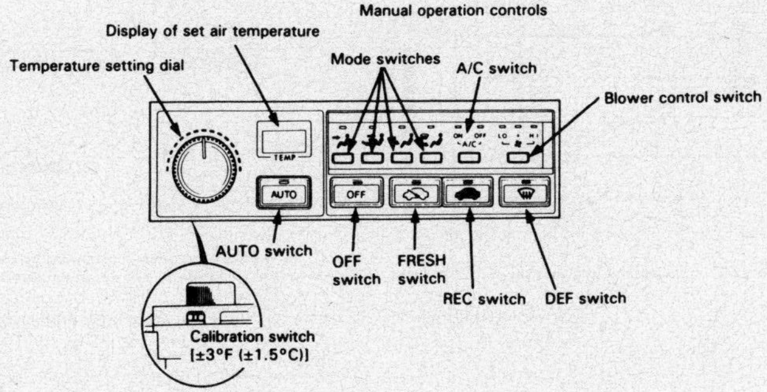
Manual operation controls
Display of set air temperature
Temperature setting dial
Mode switches
A/C switch
Blower control switch
AUTO switch
OFF switch
FRESH switch
REC switch
DEF switch
Calibration switch [±3°F (±1.5°C)]

NOTE:
- The calibration switch can raise or lower the set temperature by ±3°F (1.5°C) in relation to the digitally-displayed temperature.
- Use of the DEF switch:
  If the DEF switch is pushed in the AUTO mode, the control unit selects the FRESH position, turns on the A/C system and regulates the blower speed automatically.
  If the DEF switch is pushed in the OFF mode, the blower speed must be regulated manually.

AUTOMATIC CLIMATIC CONTROL—POWER CIRCUITS TO CONTROL UNIT DIAGNOSIS—1989–90 LEGEND AND LEGEND COUPE

NOTE: Use the digital multimeter (KS-AHM-32-003) to check.

No heater or A/C in either manual or AUTO modes.

Remove the climate control unit

Turn the ignition switch ON.

Measure voltage between No.2 (+) terminal and No.13 (–) terminal.

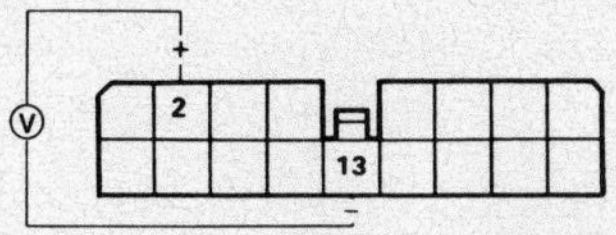
+
2
13
–

View from wire side.

Is there battery voltage?
- NO: **Repair open in WHT/YEL (No.2) wire between control unit and No.1 fuse.**
- YES: Measure voltage between No.1 (+) terminal and No.13 (–) terminal.

Is there battery voltage?
- NO: **Repair open in BLK/YEL (No.1) wire between control unit and No.16 fuse, or between No.16 fuse and ignition switch.**
- YES: **Faulty control unit.**

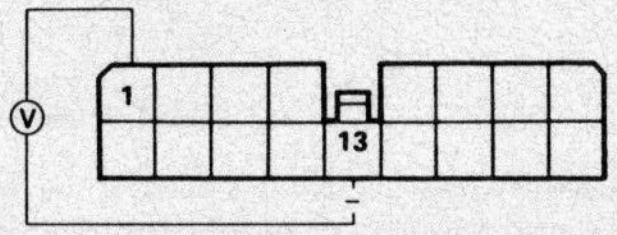
1
13
–

View from wire side.

AUTOMATIC CLIMATIC CONTROL—EVAPORATOR TEMPERATURE SENSOR DIAGNOSIS—1989–90 LEGEND AND LEGEND COUPE

Self-diagnosis indicator light A comes on: Indicates a problem in the Evaporator Sensor circuit.

The evaporator temperature sensor is a temperature dependant resistor (thermistor). The resistance of the thermistor decreases as the evaporator outlet air temperature increases, as shown below.

NOTE: Use the digital multimeter (KS-AHM-32-003) to check.

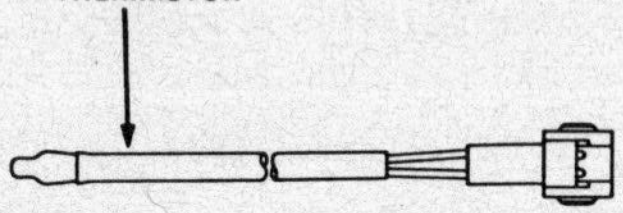
THERMISTOR

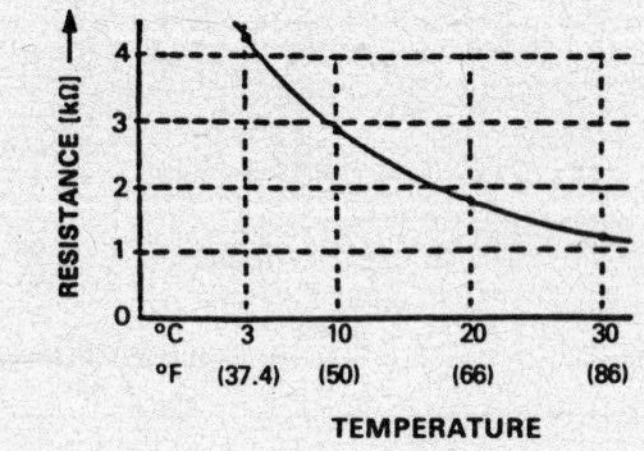
RESISTANCE [kΩ]
4
3
2
1
0
°C 3 10 20 30
°F (37.4) (50) (66) (86)
TEMPERATURE

Problem in the evaporator temperature sensor circuit.

Disconnect the 2-P connector from the evaporator temperature sensor.

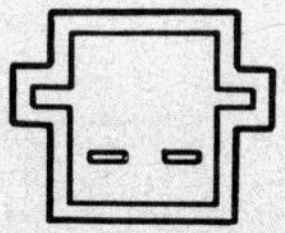

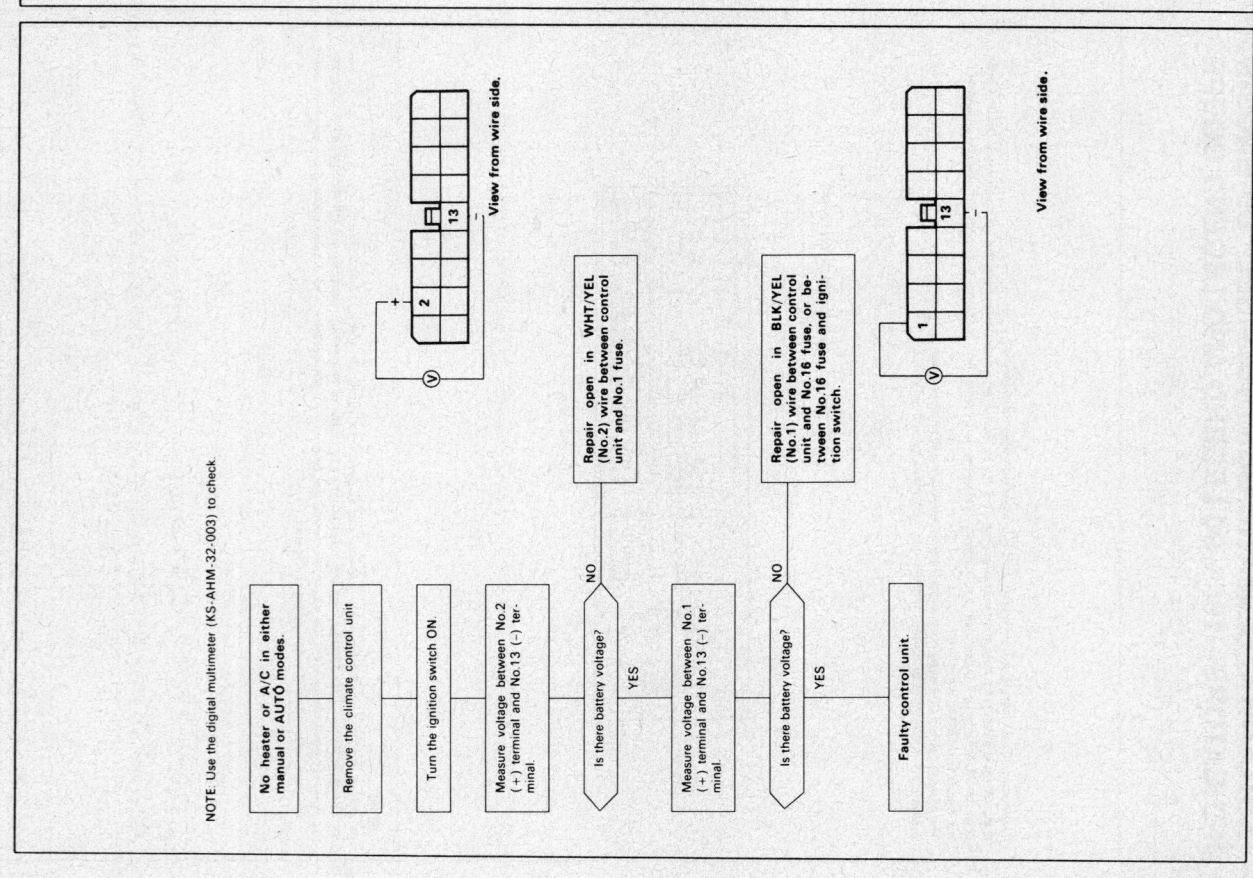

Measure resistance between the 2 terminals on the evaporator temperature sensor.

Is there 1-3 kΩ?
- NO: **Replace evaporator temperature sensor.**
- YES: Turn the ignition switch ON.

BRN
BLK

View from wire side.

Measure voltage between BRN (+) terminal and body ground.

Is there approx. 5V?
- NO: Turn the ignition switch OFF. → Remove the climate control unit → Turn the ignition switch ON. → (B)
- YES: Measure voltage between BRN (+) terminal and BLK (–) terminal. → (A)

AUTOMATIC CLIMATIC CONTROL—EVAPORATOR TEMPERATURE SENSOR DIAGNOSIS CONT.—1989–90 LEGEND AND LEGEND COUPE

(A)

Is there approx. 5V?

- NO: **Repair open in BLK wire between control unit and evaporator temperature sensor.**
- YES: **Substitute a known-good control unit and recheck. If symptom/indication goes away, replace the original control unit.**

(B)

Measure voltage between No.16 (+) terminal and No.5 (–) terminal

Is there approx. 5V?

- YES: **Repair open in BRN wire between control unit (No.16) and evaporator temperature sensor.**
- NO: Disconnect connector from the control unit.

Measure resistance between No.16 (+) terminal and body ground.

Is there less than 100 Ω?

- YES: **Repair short in BRN wire between control unit (No.16) and evaporator temperature sensor.**
- NO: **Substitute a know-good control unit and recheck. If symptom/indication goes away, replace the original control unit.**

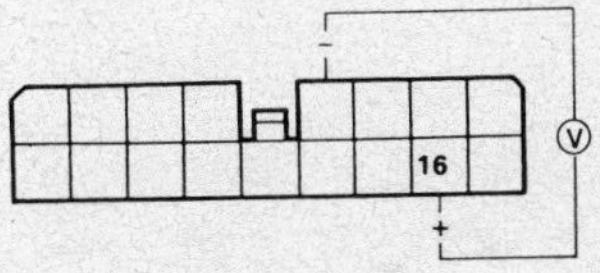
16
V
–
+

View from wire side.

AUTOMATIC CLIMATIC CONTROL—COOLANT TEMPERATURE SENSOR DIAGNOSIS—1989–90 LEGEND AND LEGEND COUPE

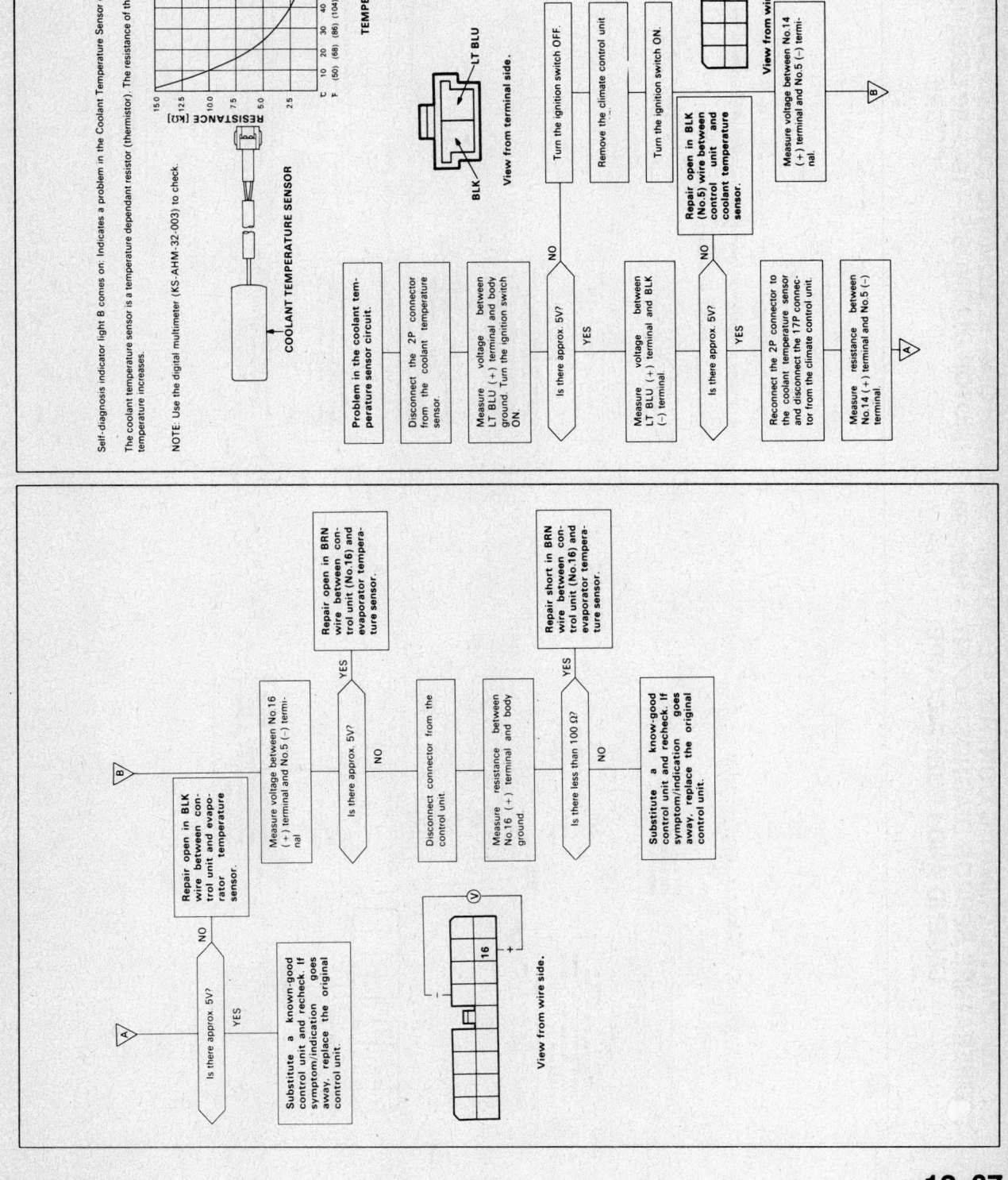

Self-diagnosis indicator light B comes on: Indicates a problem in the Coolant Temperature Sensor circuit.

The coolant temperature sensor is a temperature dependant resistor (thermistor). The resistance of the thermister decreases as the coolant temperature increases.

NOTE: Use the digital multimeter (KS-AHM-32-003) to check.

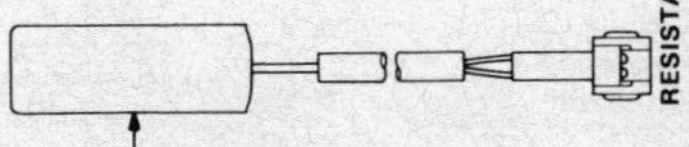

COOLANT TEMPERATURE SENSOR

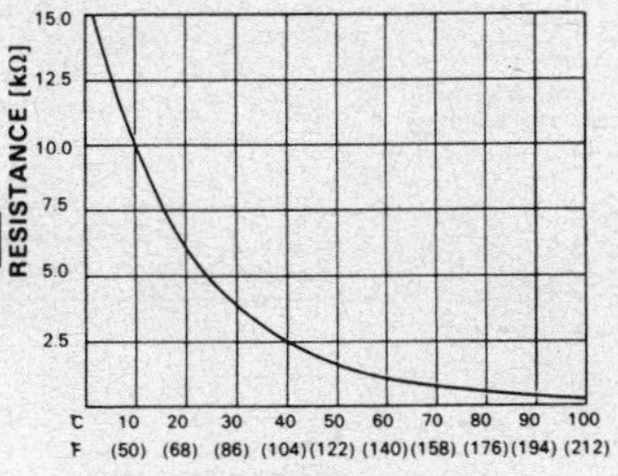
RESISTANCE [kΩ]
15.0
12.5
10.0
7.5
5.0
2.5
℃ 10 20 30 40 50 60 70 80 90 100
℉ (50) (68) (86) (104) (122) (140) (158) (176) (194) (212)

TEMPERATURE

Problem in the coolant temperature sensor circuit.

Disconnect the 2P connector from the coolant temperature sensor.

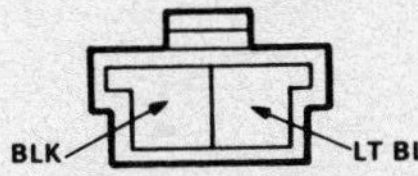
BLK
LT BLU

View from terminal side.

Measure voltage between LT BLU (+) terminal and body ground. Turn the ignition switch ON.

Is there approx. 5V?

- NO: Turn the ignition switch OFF. → Remove the climate control unit → Turn the ignition switch ON. → Measure voltage between No.14 (+) terminal and No.5 (–) terminal. → **(B)**
- YES: Measure voltage between LT BLU (+) terminal and BLK (–) terminal.

Is there approx. 5V?

- NO: **Repair open in BLK (No.5) wire between control unit and coolant temperature sensor.**
- YES: Reconnect the 2P connector to the coolant temperature sensor and disconnect the 17P connector from the climate control unit.

Measure resistance between No.14 (+) terminal and No.5 (–) terminal.

(A)

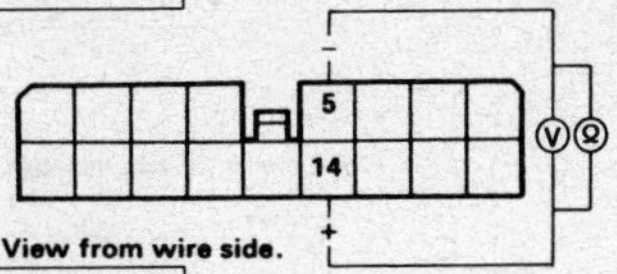
5
14
V Ω
–
+

View from wire side.

AUTOMATIC CLIMATIC CONTROL—COOLANT TEMPERATURE SENSOR DIAGNOSIS CONT.—1989–90 LEGEND AND LEGEND COUPE

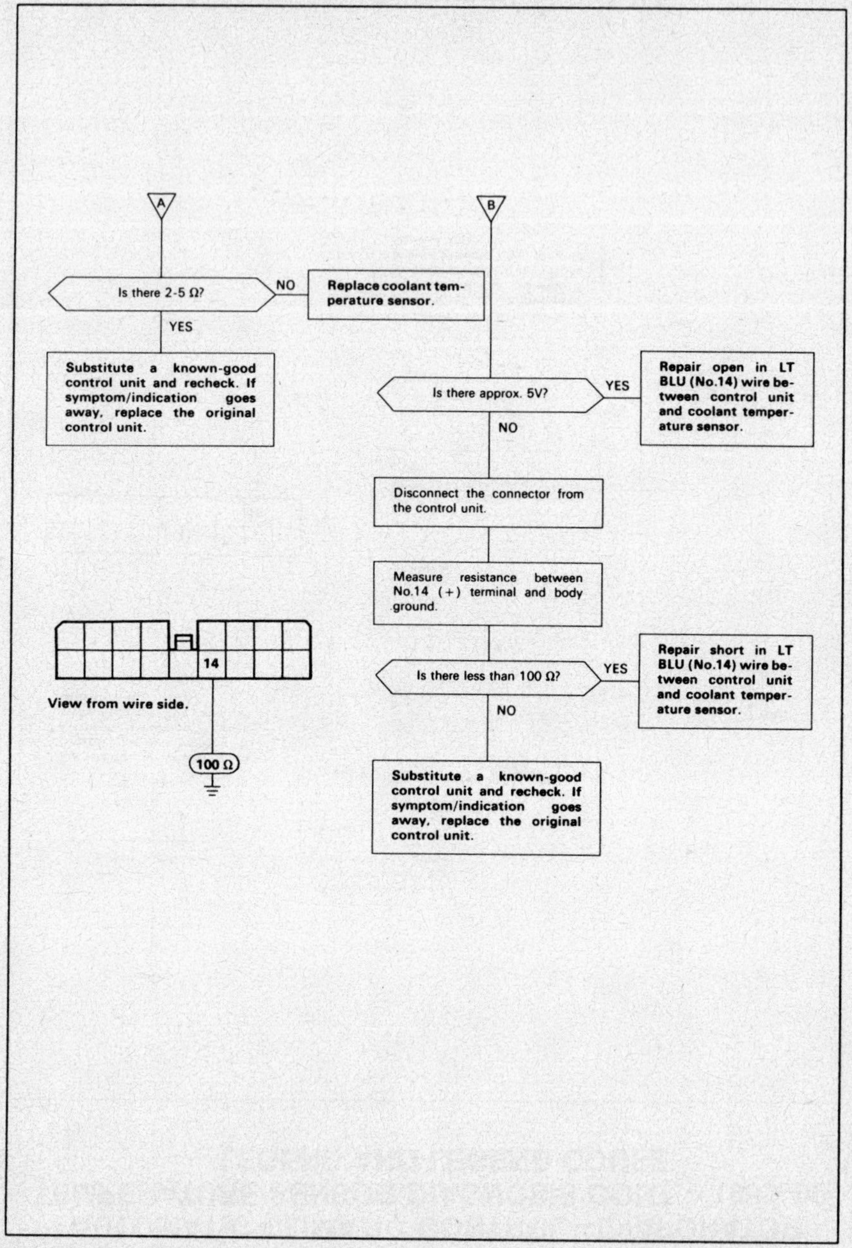
A
Is there 2-5 Ω?
NO
Replace coolant temperature sensor.
YES
Substitute a known-good control unit and recheck. If symptom/indication goes away, replace the original control unit.
14
View from wire side.
100 Ω
B
Is there approx. 5V?
YES
Repair open in LT BLU (No.14) wire between control unit and coolant temperature sensor.
NO
Disconnect the connector from the control unit.
Measure resistance between No.14 (+) terminal and body ground.
Is there less than 100 Ω?
YES
Repair short in LT BLU (No.14) wire between control unit and coolant temperature sensor.
NO
Substitute a known-good control unit and recheck. If symptom/indication goes away, replace the original control unit.

AUTOMATIC CLIMATIC CONTROL—AIR MIX CONTROL MOTOR DIAGNOSIS—1989–90 LEGEND AND LEGEND COUPE

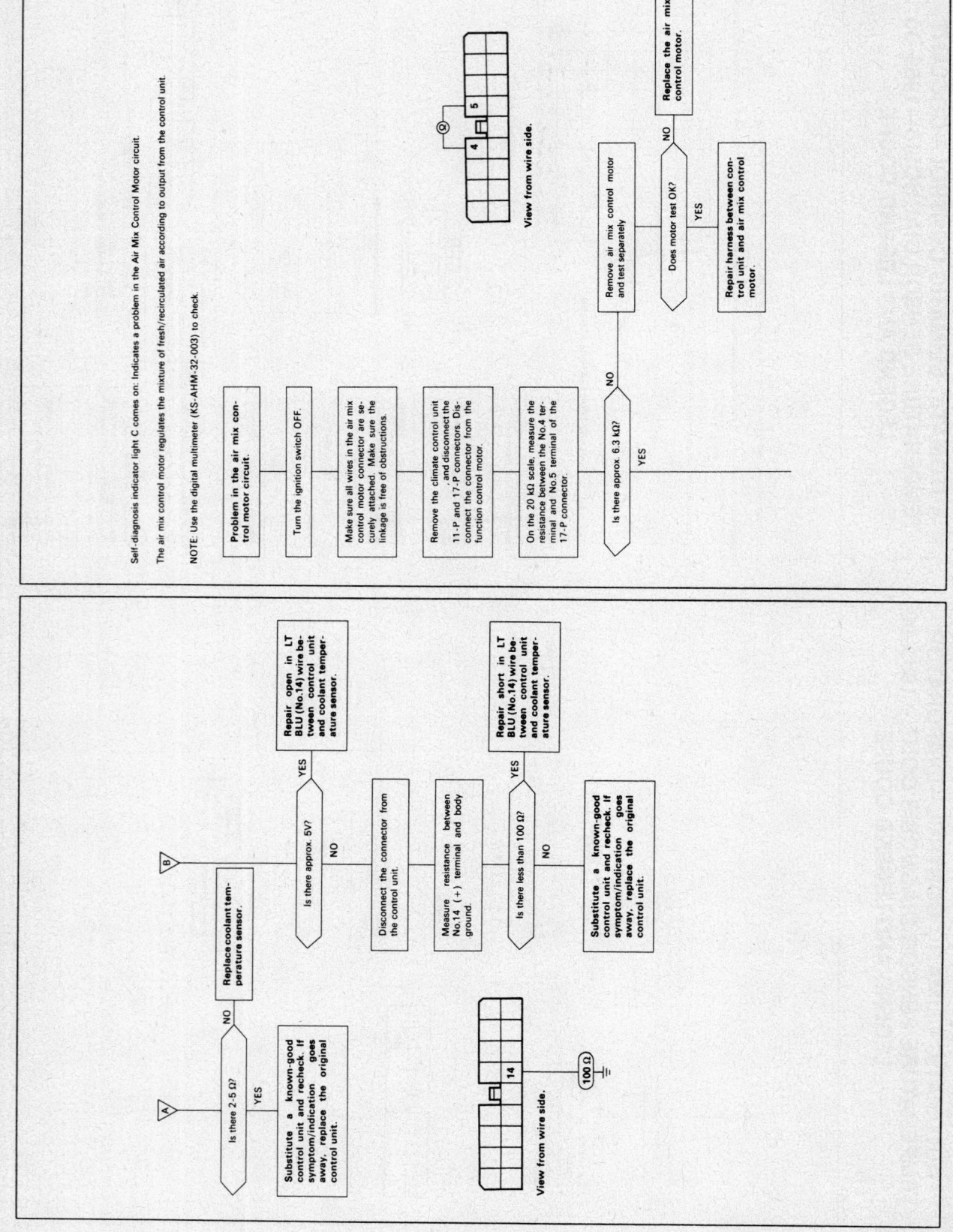

Self-diagnosis indicator light C comes on: Indicates a problem in the Air Mix Control Motor circuit.

The air mix control motor regulates the mixture of fresh/recirculated air according to output from the control unit.

NOTE: Use the digital multimeter (KS-AHM-32-003) to check.

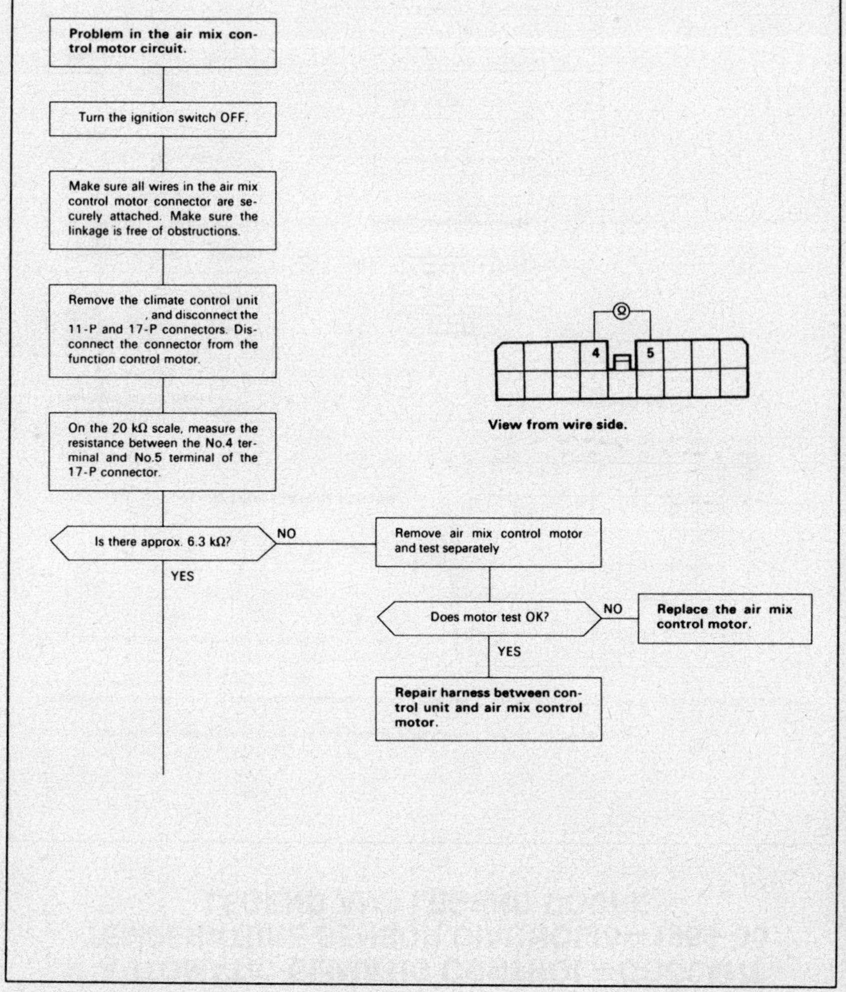
Problem in the air mix control motor circuit.
Turn the ignition switch OFF.
Make sure all wires in the air mix control motor connector are securely attached. Make sure the linkage is free of obstructions.
Remove the climate control unit , and disconnect the 11-P and 17-P connectors. Disconnect the connector from the function control motor.
On the 20 kΩ scale, measure the resistance between the No.4 terminal and No.5 terminal of the 17-P connector.
Is there approx. 6.3 kΩ?
NO
Remove air mix control motor and test separately
Does motor test OK?
NO
Replace the air mix control motor.
YES
Repair harness between control unit and air mix control motor.
YES
Ω
4
5
View from wire side.

AUTOMATIC CLIMATIC CONTROL—AIR MIX CONTROL MOTOR DIAGNOSIS CONT.—1989–90 LEGEND AND LEGEND COUPE

CAUTION: Disconnect the battery as soon as the motor has stoppec Failure to do SO will damage the motor.

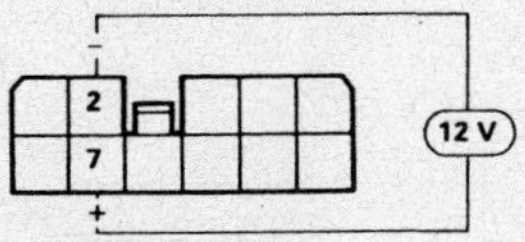

2
7
–
+
12 V

View from wire side.

Check the air mix control motor operation by briefly connecting battery (12V) positive to the No.7 terminal and negative to the No.2 terminal of the 11-P connector. Reverse the wires to be sure the motor will run in both directions.

Does the motor run smoothly in both directions?

- NO → Remove air mix control motor and test separately
  - Does the motor test OK?
    - NO → **Replace air mix control motor.**
    - YES → **Repair harness between control unit and air mix control motor.**
- YES → Measure resistance between No.4 terminal and No.8 terminal of the 17-P connector.

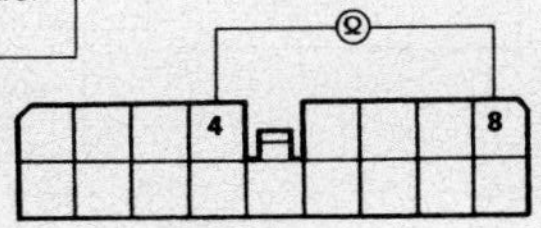

4
8
Ω

View from wire side.

Is there approx. 1.4 kΩ at the HOT position and approx. 5.3 kΩ at the COLD position of the motor?

- NO → Remove air mix control motor and test separately
  - Does motor test OK?
    - NO → **Replace air mix control motor.**
    - YES → **Repair harness between control unit and air mix control motor.**
- YES → **Substitute a known-good control unit and recheck. If symptom/indication goes away, replace the original control unit.**

AUTOMATIC CLIMATIC CONTROL—FUNCTION CONTROL MOTOR DIAGNOSIS—1989–90 LEGEND AND LEGEND COUPE

Self-diagnosis indicator light D comes on: Indicates a problem in the Function Control Motor Circuit.

The function control motor controls the outlet air direction and volume according to output from the control unit.

NOTE: Use the digital multimeter (KS-AHM-32-003) to check.

Problem in the function control motor circuit.

Turn the ignition switch ON.

Make sure all wires in the function control motor connector are securely attached. Make sure the linkage is free of obstructions.

Remove the climate control unit and disconnect the 11-P and 17-P connectors. Disconnect the connector from the air mix control motor.

On the 20 kΩ scale, measure the resistance between the No.5 terminal and No.4 terminal of the 17-P connector.

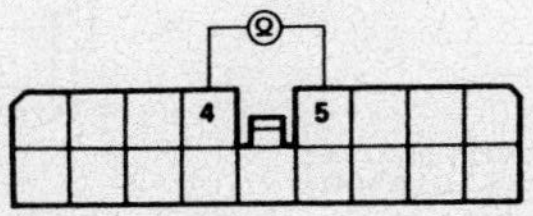

4
5
Ω

View from wire side.

Is there approx. 4 kΩ?

- NO → Remove function control motor and test separately
  - Does motor test OK?
    - NO → **Replace function control motor.**
    - YES → **Repair harness between control unit and function control motor.**
- YES

AUTOMATIC CLIMATIC CONTROL—FUNCTION CONTROL MOTOR DIAGNOSIS CONT.—1989–90 LEGEND AND LEGEND COUPE

CAUTION: Disconnect the battery as soon as the motor has stopped Failure to do so will damage the motor.

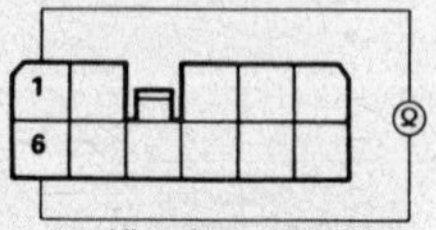
1
6

View from wire side.

Check the function control motor operation by briefly connecting battery (12V) positive to the No.6 terminal and negative to the No.1 terminal of the 11-P connector. Reverse the wires to be sure the motor will run in both direction.

Does the motor run smoothly in both direction?

- NO → Remove function control motor and test separately (page 22-33).
  - Does the motor test OK?
    - NO → **Replace function control motor.**
    - YES → **Repair harness between control unit and function control motor.**
- YES → Measure resistance between No.4 terminal and No.17 terminal of the 17-P connector.

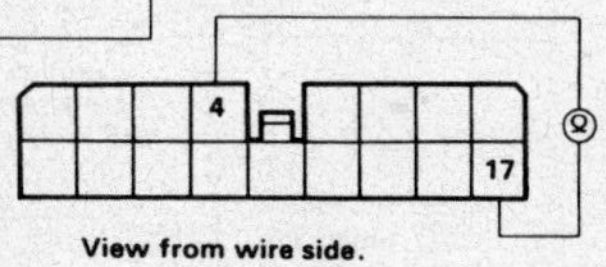
4
17

View from wire side.

Is there approx. 1.2 kΩ at the VENT position and approx. 4.0 kΩ at the DEF position of the motor.

- NO → Remove function control motor and test separately
  - Does motor test OK?
    - NO → **Replace function control motor.**
    - YES → **Repair harness between control unit and function control motor.**
- YES → **Substitute a known-good control unit and recheck. If symptom/indication goes away, replace the original control unit.**

AUTOMATIC CLIMATIC CONTROL—SUNLIGHT SENSOR DIAGNOSIS—1989–90 LEGEND AND LEGEND COUPE

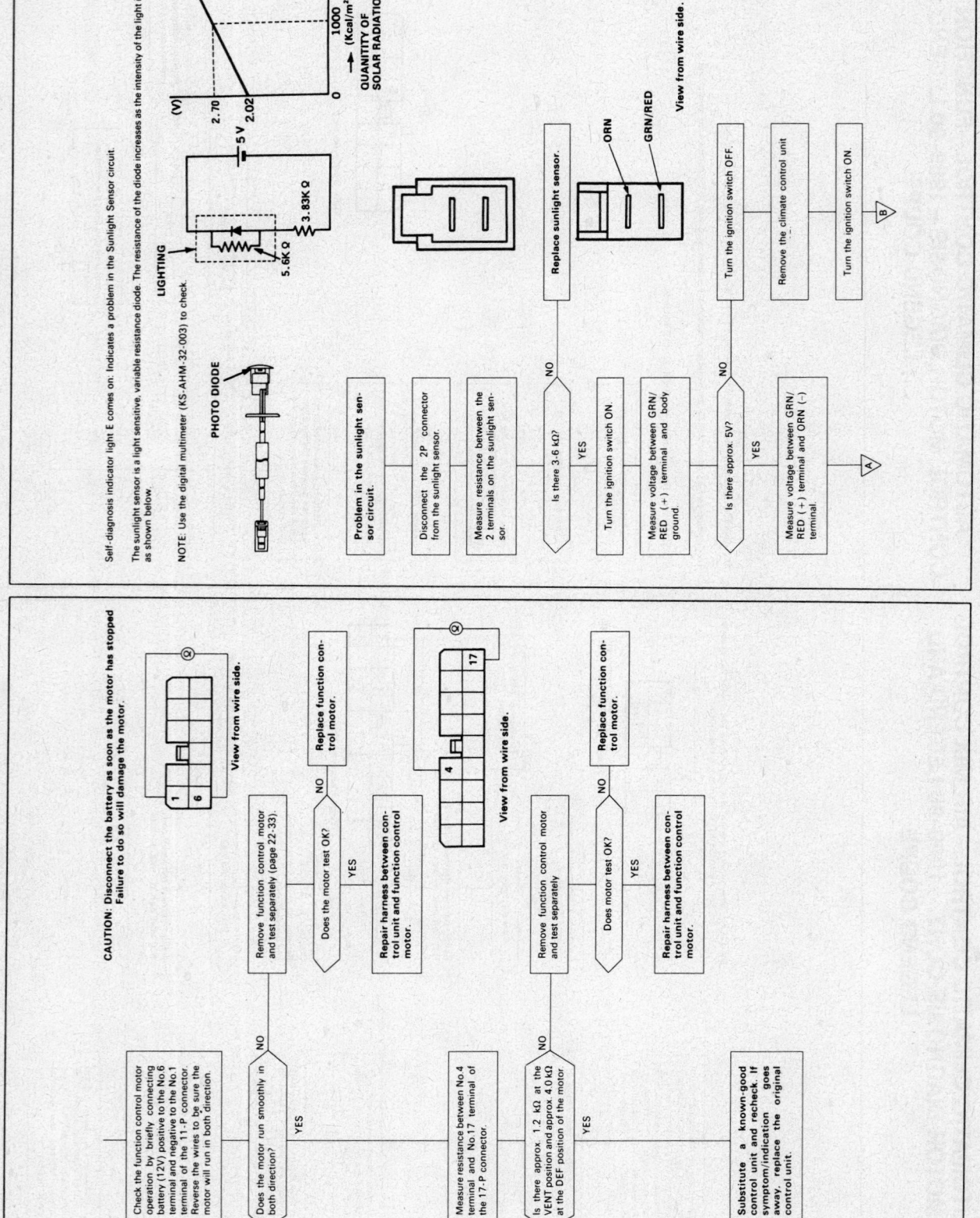

Self-diagnosis indicator light E comes on: Indicates a problem in the Sunlight Sensor circuit.

The sunlight sensor is a light sensitive, variable resistance diode. The resistance of the diode increases as the intensity of the light increases, as shown below.

NOTE: Use the digital multimeter (KS-AHM-32-003) to check.

PHOTO DIODE

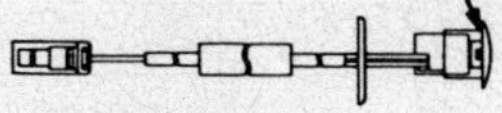

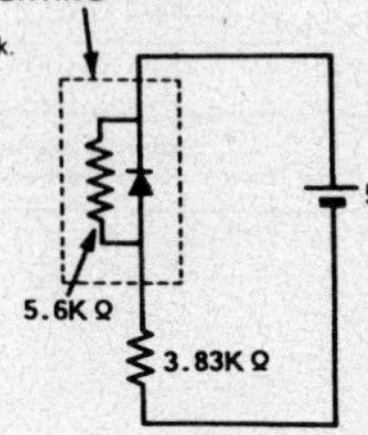
LIGHTING
5 V
5.6K Ω
3.83K Ω

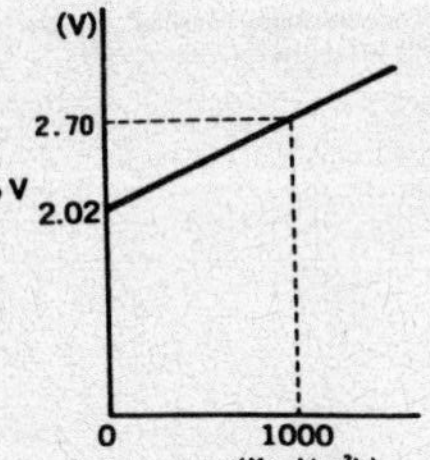
(V)
2.70
2.02
0
1000
(Kcal/m²h)
QUANITITY OF
SOLAR RADIATION

Problem in the sunlight sensor circuit.

Disconnect the 2P connector from the sunlight sensor.

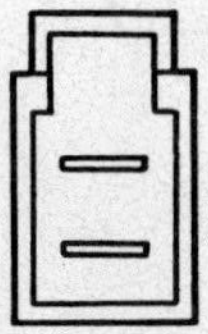

Measure resistance between the 2 terminals on the sunlight sensor.

Is there 3-6 kΩ?

- NO → **Replace sunlight sensor.**
- YES → Turn the ignition switch ON.

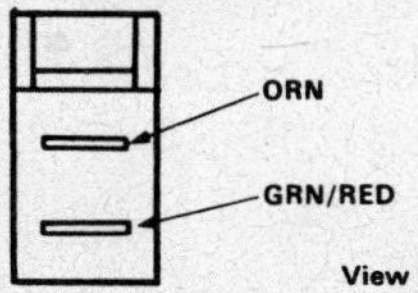
ORN
GRN/RED

View from wire side.

Measure voltage between GRN/RED (+) terminal and body ground.

Is there approx. 5V?

- NO → Turn the ignition switch OFF. → Remove the climate control unit → Turn the ignition switch ON. → (B)
- YES → Measure voltage between GRN/RED (+) terminal and ORN (−) terminal. → (A)

AUTOMATIC CLIMATIC CONTROL—SUNLIGHT SENSOR DIAGNOSIS CONT.—1989–90 LEGEND AND LEGEND COUPE

(A) Is there approx. 5V?

- NO: **Repair open in ORN (-) wire between control unit and sunlight sensor.**
  - (B) Measure voltage between No.4 (+) terminal and No.7 (-) terminal.
    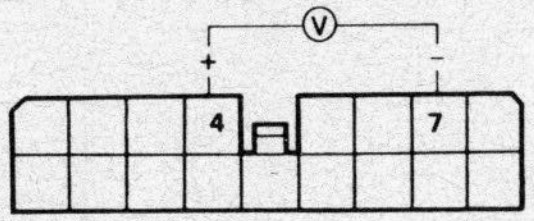
    V
+
−
4
7
    View from wire side.
  - Is there approx. 5V?
    - YES: **Repair open in GRN/RED (No.4) wire between control unit and sunlight sensor.**
    - NO: Disconnect the 17P connector from the climate control unit.
  - Measure resistance between No.4 (+) terminal and body ground.
    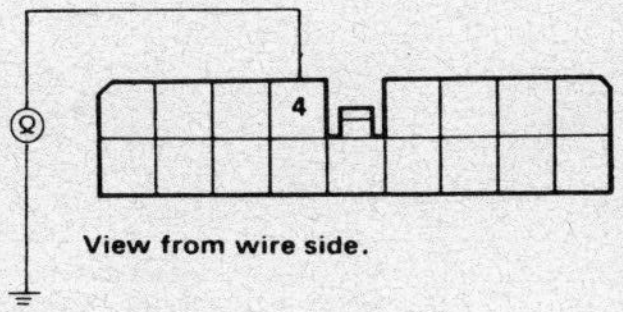
    Ω
4
    View from wire side.
  - Is there less than 100 Ω?
    - NO: **Repair short in GRN/RED (No.4) wire between control unit and sunlight sensor.**
    - YES: **Substitute a known-good control unit and recheck. If symptom/indication goes away, replace the original control unit.**
- YES: **Substitute a known-good control unit and recheck. If symptom/indication goes away, replace the original control unit.**

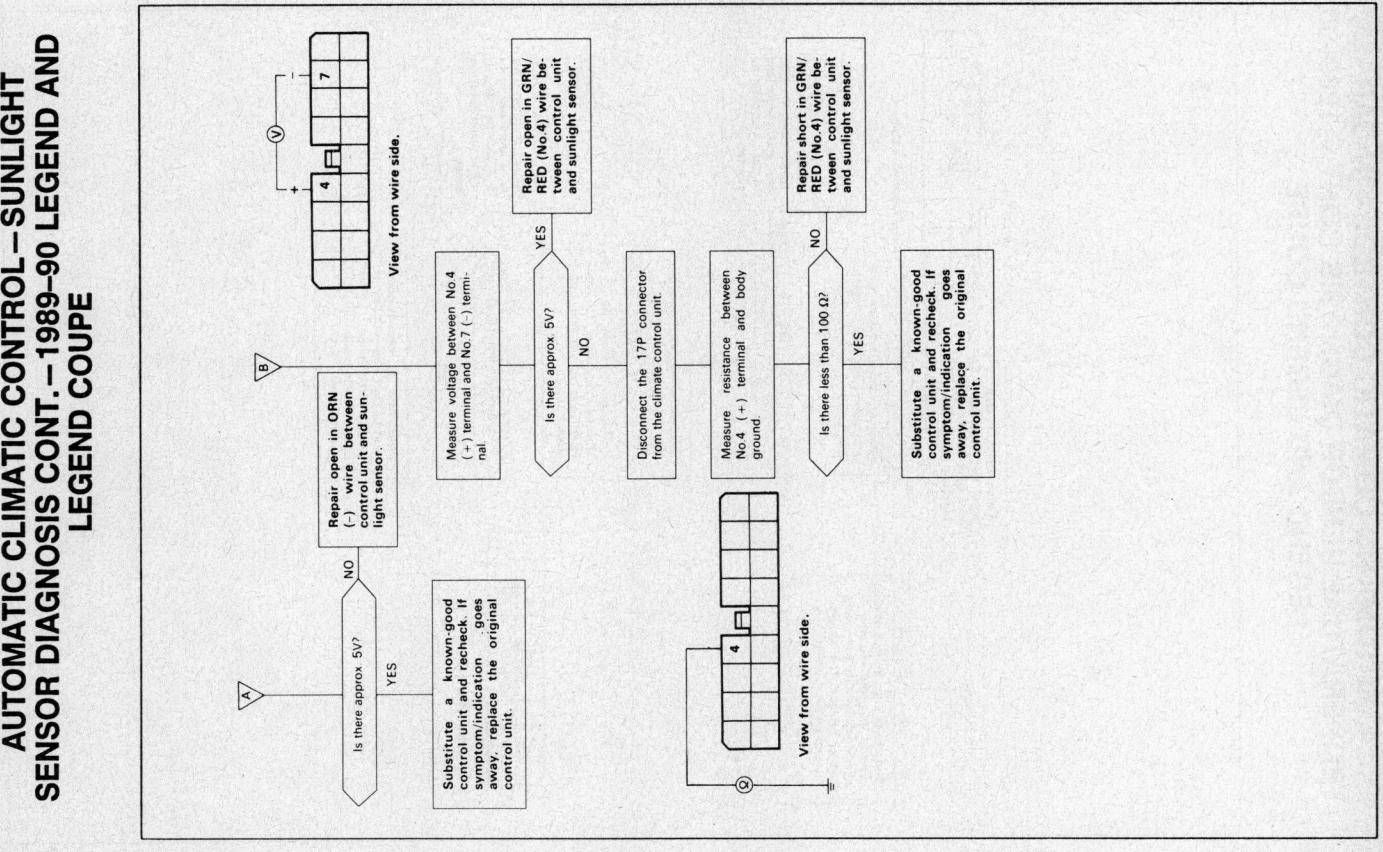

AUTOMATIC CLIMATIC CONTROL—IN-CAR TEMPERATURE SENSOR DIAGNOSIS—1989–90 LEGEND AND LEGEND COUPE

Self-diagnosis indicator light F comes on: Indicates a problem in the In-car Temperature Sensor circuit.

The in-car temperature sensor is a temperature dependant resistor (thermistor). The resistance of the thermistor decreases as the temperature inside the car increases.

NOTE: Use the digital multimeter (KS-AHM-32-003) to check.

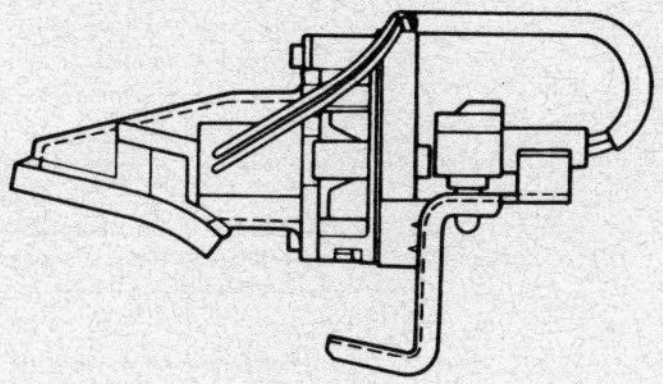

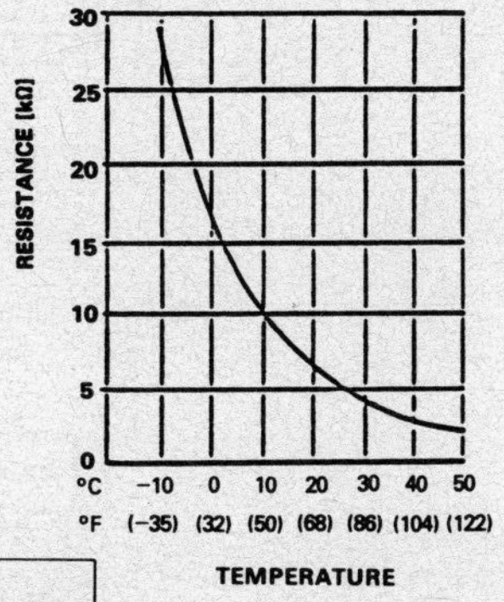
RESISTANCE [kΩ]
30
25
20
15
10
5
0
°C −10 0 10 20 30 40 50
°F (−35) (32) (50) (68) (86) (104) (122)
TEMPERATURE

Problem in the in-car temperature sensor circuit.

Disconnect the 2-P connector from the in-car temperature sensor.

Measure resistance between the 2 terminals on the in-car temperature sensor.

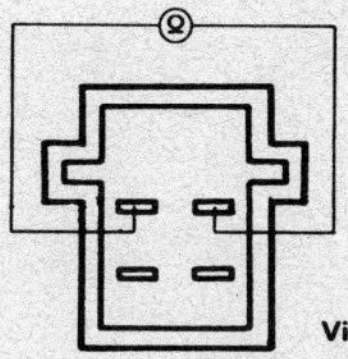
Ω

View from wire side.

Is there 1-3 kΩ ?

- NO: **Replace in-car temperature sensor.**
- YES: Turn the ignition switch ON.

Measure voltage between GRN1 (+) terminal and body ground.

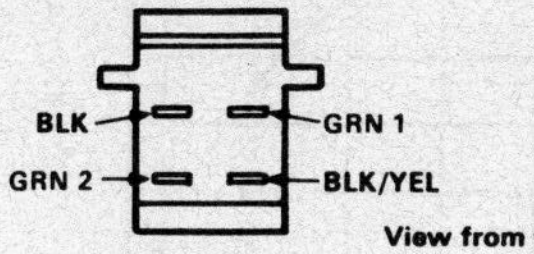
BLK
GRN 2
GRN 1
BLK/YEL

View from wire side.

Is there approx. 5V?

- NO: Turn the ignition switch OFF. → Remove the climate control unit → Turn the ignition switch ON. → (B)
- YES: Measure voltage between GRN1 (+) terminal and BLK (-) terminal. → (A)

AUTOMATIC CLIMATIC CONTROL—IN-CAR TEMPERATURE SENSOR DIAGNOSIS CONT.—1989–90 LEGEND AND LEGEND COUPE

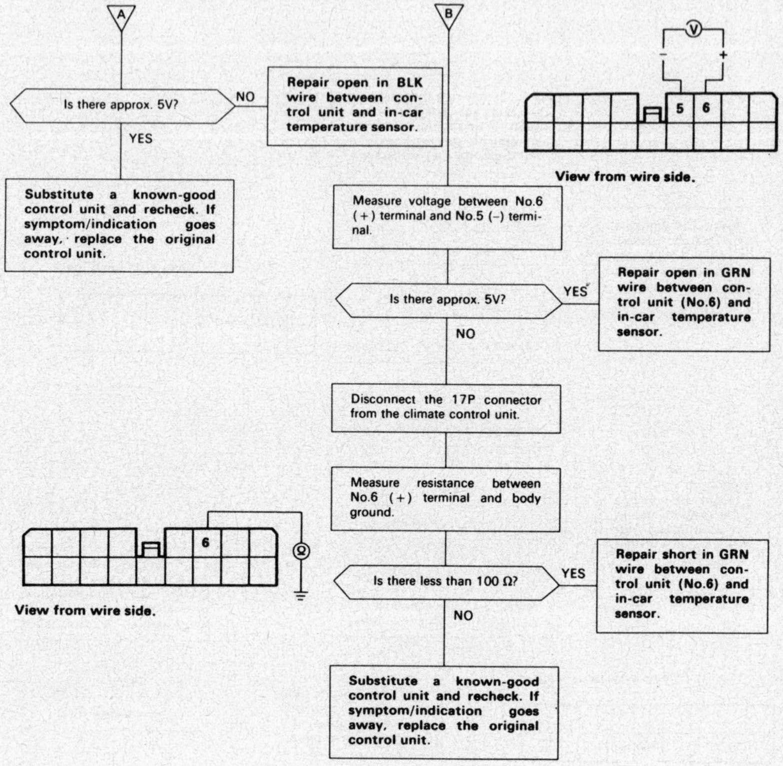
A
Is there approx. 5V?
NO
Repair open in BLK wire between control unit and in-car temperature sensor.
YES
Substitute a known-good control unit and recheck. If symptom/indication goes away, replace the original control unit.
B
Measure voltage between No.6 (+) terminal and No.5 (–) terminal.
Is there approx. 5V?
YES
Repair open in GRN wire between control unit (No.6) and in-car temperature sensor.
NO
Disconnect the 17P connector from the climate control unit.
Measure resistance between No.6 (+) terminal and body ground.
Is there less than 100 Ω?
YES
Repair short in GRN wire between control unit (No.6) and in-car temperature sensor.
NO
Substitute a known-good control unit and recheck. If symptom/indication goes away, replace the original control unit.
5
6
View from wire side.
6
View from wire side.

AUTOMATIC CLIMATIC CONTROL—AMBIENT TEMPERATURE SENSOR DIAGNOSIS—1989–90 LEGEND AND LEGEND COUPE

Self-diagnosis indicator light G comes on: Indicates a problem in the Ambient Temperature Sensor circuit.

The ambient temperature sensor is a temperature dependant resistor (thermistor). The resistance of the thermistor decreases as the temperature outside the car increases.

NOTE: Use the digital multimeter (KS-AHM-32-003) to check.

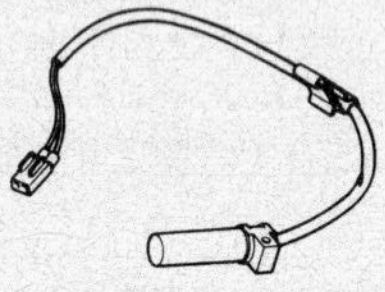

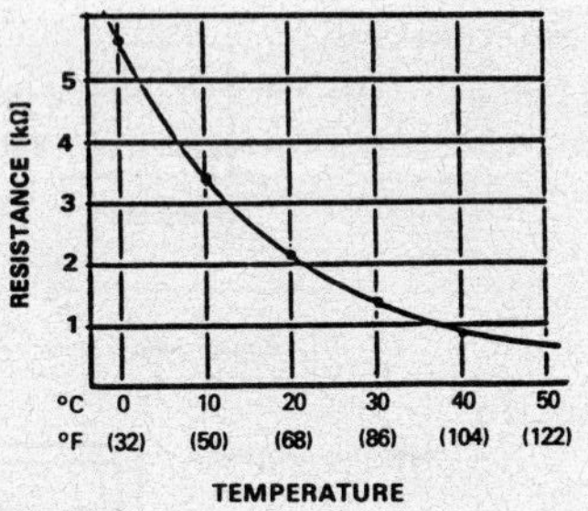
RESISTANCE [kΩ]
5
4
3
2
1
°C 0 10 20 30 40 50
°F (32) (50) (68) (86) (104) (122)
TEMPERATURE

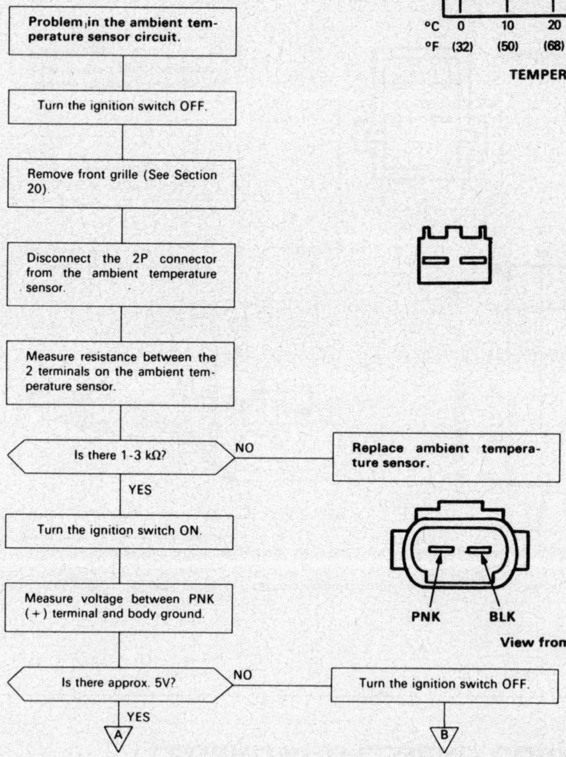
Problem in the ambient temperature sensor circuit.
Turn the ignition switch OFF.
Remove front grille (See Section 20).
Disconnect the 2P connector from the ambient temperature sensor.
Measure resistance between the 2 terminals on the ambient temperature sensor.
Is there 1-3 kΩ?
NO
Replace ambient temperature sensor.
YES
Turn the ignition switch ON.
Measure voltage between PNK (+) terminal and body ground.
Is there approx. 5V?
NO
Turn the ignition switch OFF.
B
YES
A

PNK
BLK
View from terminal side.

AUTOMATIC CLIMATIC CONTROL—AMBIENT TEMPERATURE SENSOR DIAGNOSIS CONT.—1989–90 LEGEND AND LEGEND COUPE

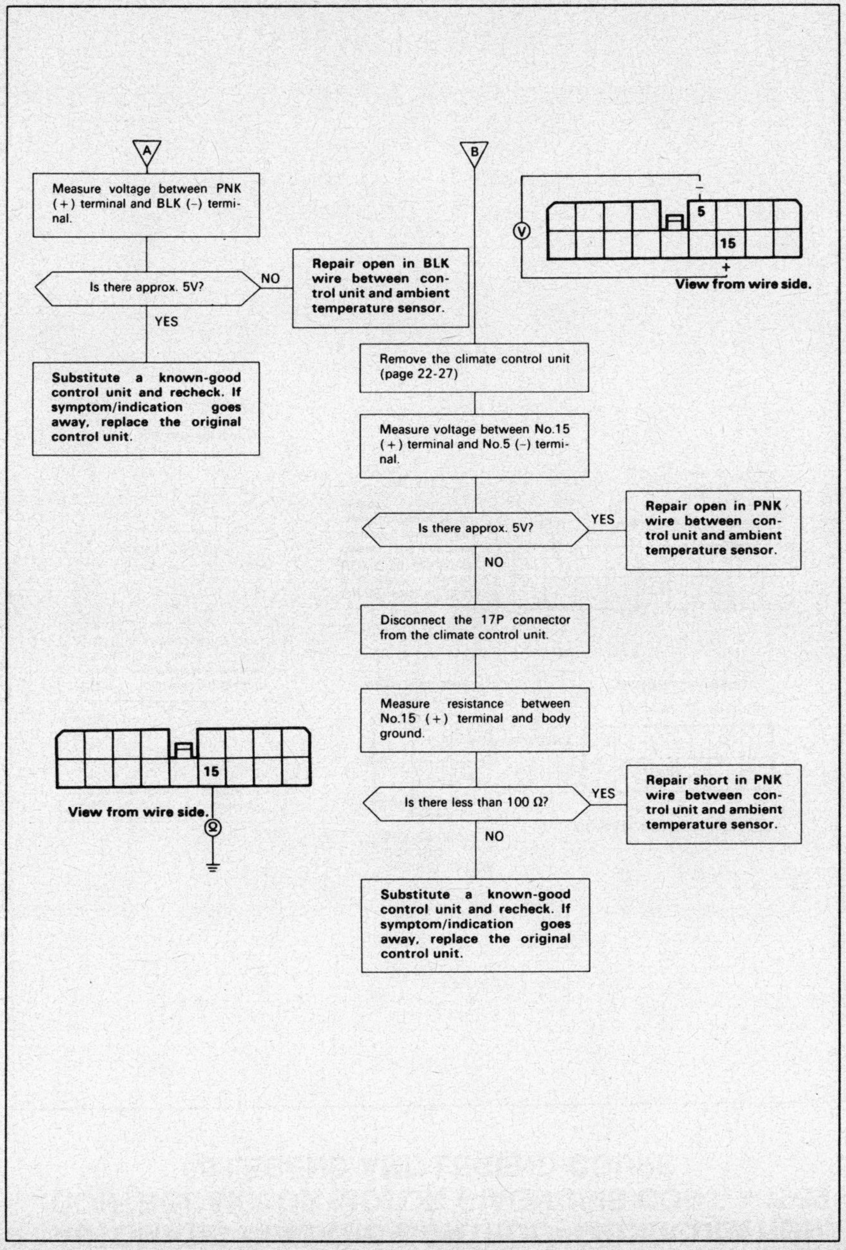
A
Measure voltage between PNK (+) terminal and BLK (–) terminal.
Is there approx. 5V?
NO
Repair open in BLK wire between control unit and ambient temperature sensor.
YES
Substitute a known-good control unit and recheck. If symptom/indication goes away, replace the original control unit.
B
Remove the climate control unit (page 22-27)
Measure voltage between No.15 (+) terminal and No.5 (–) terminal.
5
15
View from wire side.
Is there approx. 5V?
YES
Repair open in PNK wire between control unit and ambient temperature sensor.
NO
Disconnect the 17P connector from the climate control unit.
Measure resistance between No.15 (+) terminal and body ground.
Is there less than 100 Ω?
YES
Repair short in PNK wire between control unit and ambient temperature sensor.
NO
Substitute a known-good control unit and recheck. If symptom/indication goes away, replace the original control unit.
15
View from wire side.

AUTOMATIC CLIMATIC CONTROL—RECIRCULATION CONTROL MOTOR MOTOR DIAGNOSIS—1989–90 LEGEND AND LEGEND COUPE

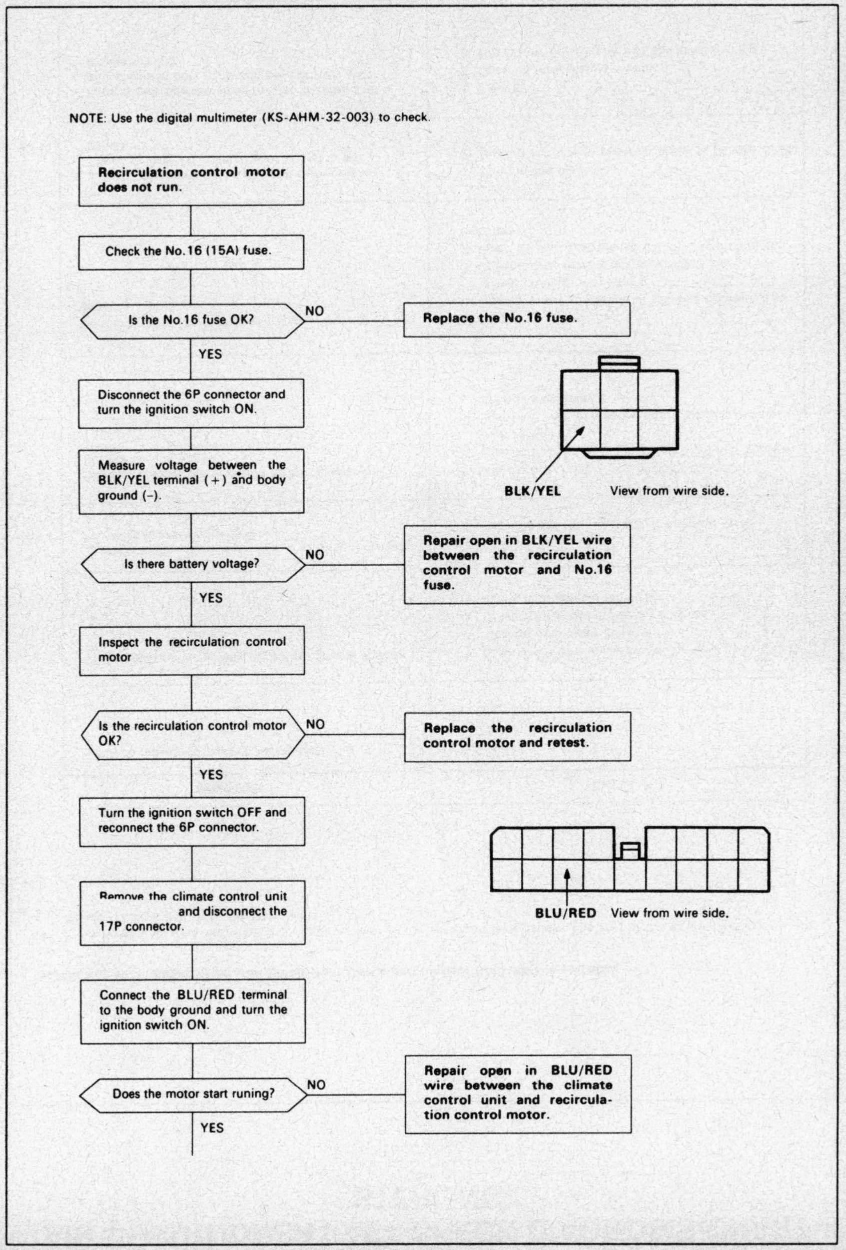
NOTE: Use the digital multimeter (KS-AHM-32-003) to check.
Recirculation control motor does not run.
Check the No.16 (15A) fuse.
Is the No.16 fuse OK?
NO
Replace the No.16 fuse.
YES
Disconnect the 6P connector and turn the ignition switch ON.
BLK/YEL
View from wire side.
Measure voltage between the BLK/YEL terminal (+) and body ground (–).
Is there battery voltage?
NO
Repair open in BLK/YEL wire between the recirculation control motor and No.16 fuse.
YES
Inspect the recirculation control motor
Is the recirculation control motor OK?
NO
Replace the recirculation control motor and retest.
YES
Turn the ignition switch OFF and reconnect the 6P connector.
Remove the climate control unit and disconnect the 17P connector.
BLU/RED
View from wire side.
Connect the BLU/RED terminal to the body ground and turn the ignition switch ON.
Does the motor start runing?
NO
Repair open in BLU/RED wire between the climate control unit and recirculation control motor.
YES

AUTOMATIC CLIMATIC CONTROL—RECIRCULATION CONTROL MOTOR MOTOR DIAGNOSIS CONT.—1989 90 LEGEND AND LEGEND COUPE

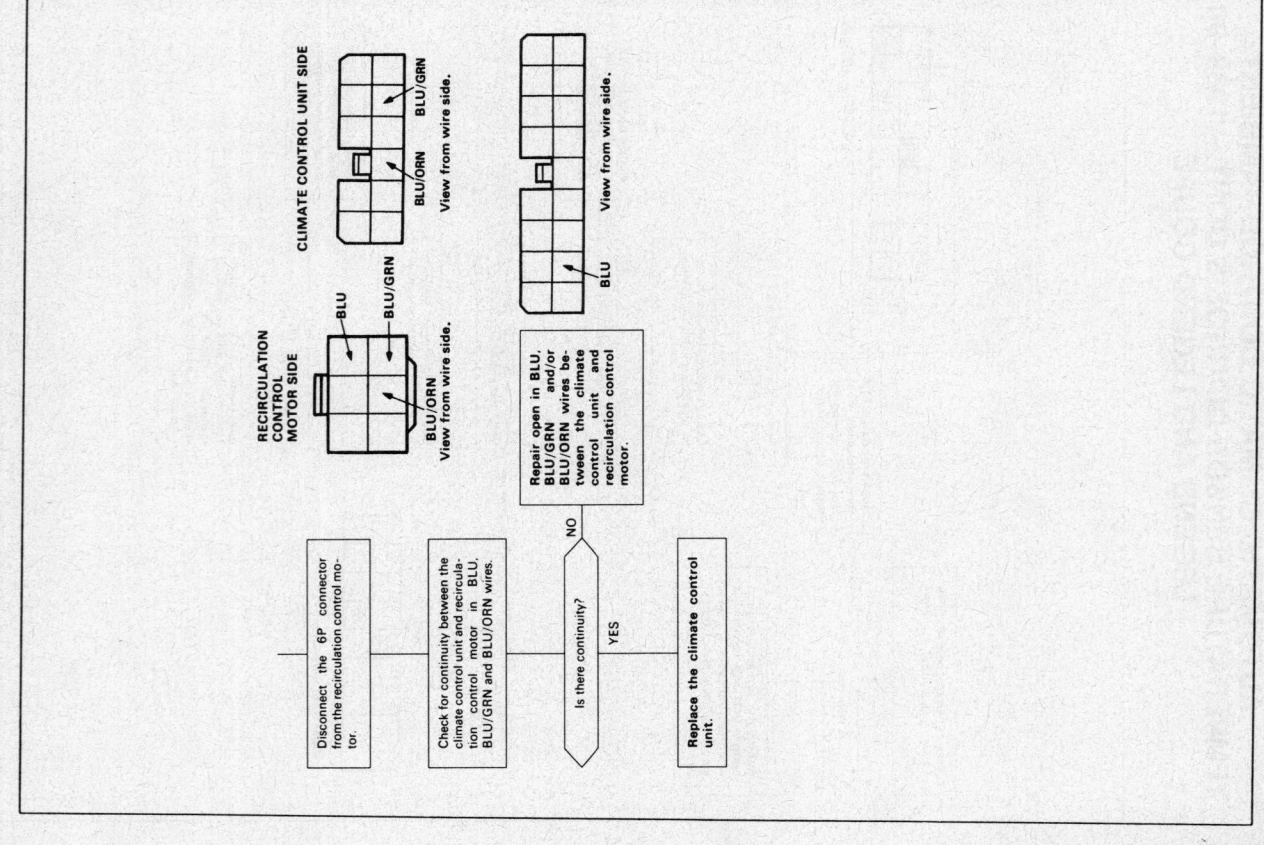

Disconnect the 6P connector from the recirculation control motor.

Check for continuity between the climate control unit and recirculation control motor in BLU, BLU/GRN and BLU/ORN wires.

Is there continuity?

NO — Repair open in BLU, BLU/GRN and/or BLU/ORN wires between the climate control unit and recirculation control motor.

YES — Replace the climate control unit.

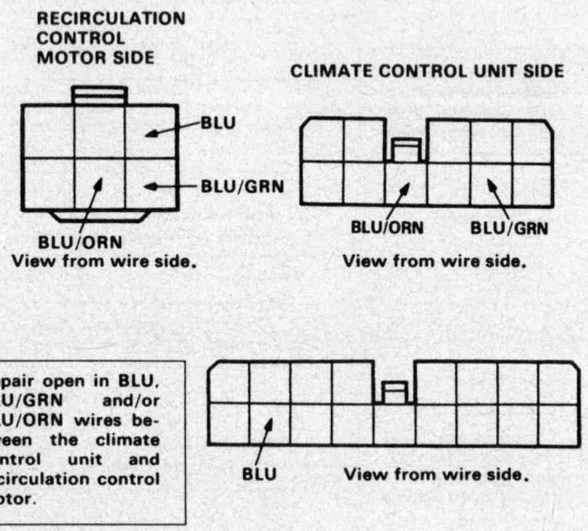
RECIRCULATION CONTROL MOTOR SIDE
BLU
BLU/GRN
BLU/ORN
View from wire side.
CLIMATE CONTROL UNIT SIDE
BLU/ORN
BLU/GRN
View from wire side.
BLU
View from wire side.

AIR CONDITIONER FAST CHECK DIAGNOSIS CHART—STERLING

NOTE: For initial diagnosis on this circuit, Fast Check part number SMD 4063 is available.

- If the cooling fans are not operating properly, refer to the symptom table below. The rest of the air conditioning system should be diagnosed with the fast check.

SYMPTOM	CHECK FOR
Fans do not run at high or low speeds.	1. Fuse 16. 2. Open in B wires or at G100. 3. Open in GY wire between Fuse 16 and splice S106.
With engine running, fans do not run in low speed. Fans run at high speed only.	1. Open in SP wire between change over relay 1 and change over relay 2. 2. Open change over relay 2 contacts. 3. Low speed coolant fan switch.
Radiator coolant fan does not run at all, condensor fan runs at high speed only.	1. Fuse Y. 2. Main coolant fan relay coil or contacts open.
Radiator coolant fan operates at low speed, but not at high speed.	1. Change over relay 1 coil or contacts open. 2. Open in UY wire between splice S120 and change over relay 1. 3. Open in B wire between splice S102 and radiator change over relay 1.
Condensor fan operates at low speed, but not in high speed.	1. Fuse X. 2. Open or short to ground in NO wire between fuse X and change over relay 2. 3. Change over relay 2 coil or contacts open. 4. Open UY wire between splice S120 and change over relay 2.
Fans do not come on when air conditioning is turned on and A/C compressor clutch is engaged.	1. Open in-line diode Q. 2. Open U or UR wire between splice S204 and S124.
Fans do not operate when ignition is turned off and engine is hot. Fans operate normally with engine running.	1. Fuse 5. 2. Open oil temperature switch. 3. Hot restart control unit and associated wiring.

NO COOLED INSIDE AIR WITH AIR CONDITIONER ON DIAGNOSIS CHART—STERLING

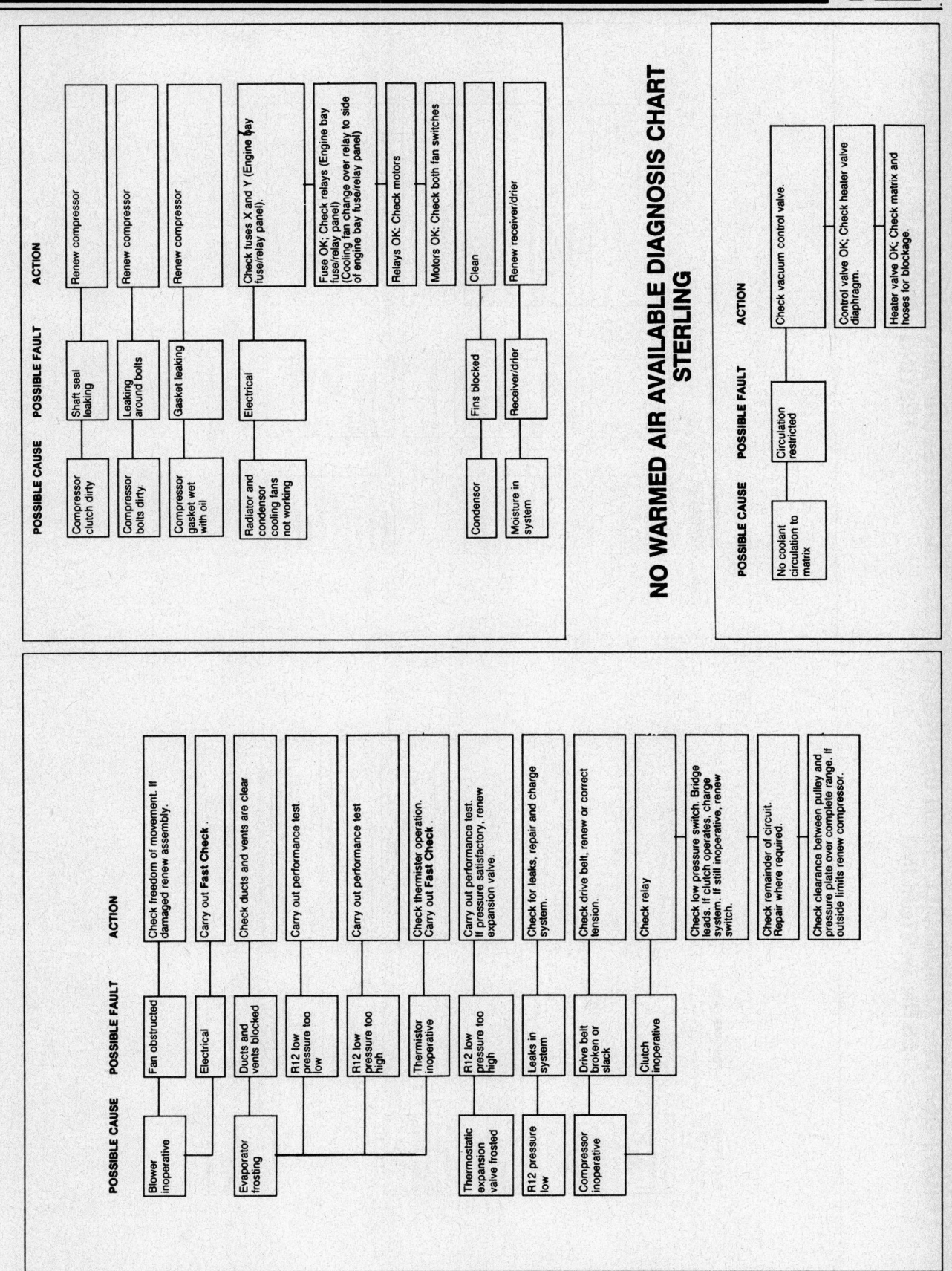

POSSIBLE CAUSE	POSSIBLE FAULT	ACTION
Blower inoperative	Fan obstructed	Check freedom of movement. If damaged renew assembly.
	Electrical	Carry out **Fast Check** .
Evaporator frosting	Ducts and vents blocked	Check ducts and vents are clear
	R12 low pressure too low	Carry out performance test.
	R12 low pressure too high	Carry out performance test
	Thermistor inoperative	Check thermister operation. Carry out **Fast Check** .
Thermostatic expansion valve frosted	R12 low pressure too high	Carry out performance test. If pressure satisfactory, renew expansion valve.
R12 pressure low	Leaks in system	Check for leaks, repair and charge system.
Compressor inoperative	Drive belt broken or slack	Check drive belt, renew or correct tension.
	Clutch inoperative	Check relay
		Check low pressure switch. Bridge leads. If clutch operates, charge system. If still inoperative, renew switch.
		Check remainder of circuit. Repair where required.
		Check clearance between pulley and pressure plate over complete range. If outside limits renew compressor.

POSSIBLE CAUSE	POSSIBLE FAULT	ACTION
Compressor clutch dirty	Shaft seal leaking	Renew compressor
Compressor bolts dirty	Leaking around bolts	Renew compressor
Compressor gasket wet with oil	Gasket leaking	Renew compressor
Radiator and condensor cooling fans not working	Electrical	Check fuses X and Y (Engine bay fuse/relay panel).
		Fuse OK; Check relays (Engine bay fuse/relay panel) (Cooling fan change over relay to side of engine bay fuse/relay panel)
		Relays OK: Check motors
		Motors OK: Check both fan switches
Condensor	Fins blocked	Clean
Moisture in system	Receiver/drier	Renew receiver/drier

NO WARMED AIR AVAILABLE DIAGNOSIS CHART STERLING

POSSIBLE CAUSE	POSSIBLE FAULT	ACTION
No coolant circulation to matrix	Circulation restricted	Check vacuum control valve.
		Control valve OK; Check heater valve diaphragm.
		Heater valve OK; Check matrix and hoses for blockage.

HIGH PRESSURE ABNORMALLY HIGH DURING TESTING—STERLING

CONDITIONS DURING TEST	POSSIBLE FAULT	ACTION
Pressure drops to about 1.9 kgf/cm², 28.5 lbf/in² quickly then falls slowly when compressor stopped	Air in system	Evacuate system. Recharge.
No bubbles in sight glass when condensor is cooled with water	Excessive R12 in system	Discharge R12 as required.
Reduced or no airflow through condensor	Clogged condenser	Clean.
	Clogged radiator fins	Clean
	Cooling fans inoperative	Check
Line to condensor excessively hot	Restricted flow of R12 in system	Renew thermostatic expansion valve.

HIGH PRESSURE ABNORMALLY LOW DURING TESTING—STERLING

CONDITIONS DURING TEST	POSSIBLE FAULT	ACTION
Excessive bubbles in sight glass; condensor not hot	Insufficient R12	Charge system.
		Check for leaks.
High and low pressures are balanced soon after stopping compressor	Faulty compressor discharge or inlet valve	Renew compressor
	Faulty compressor seal	Renew compressor.
Outlet of thermostatic expansion valve not frosted; low pressure gauge indicates vacuum	Faulty thermostatic expansion valve	Renew thermostatic expansion valve.

HIGH AND LOW PRESSURE ABNORMALLY LOW DURING TESTING—STERLING

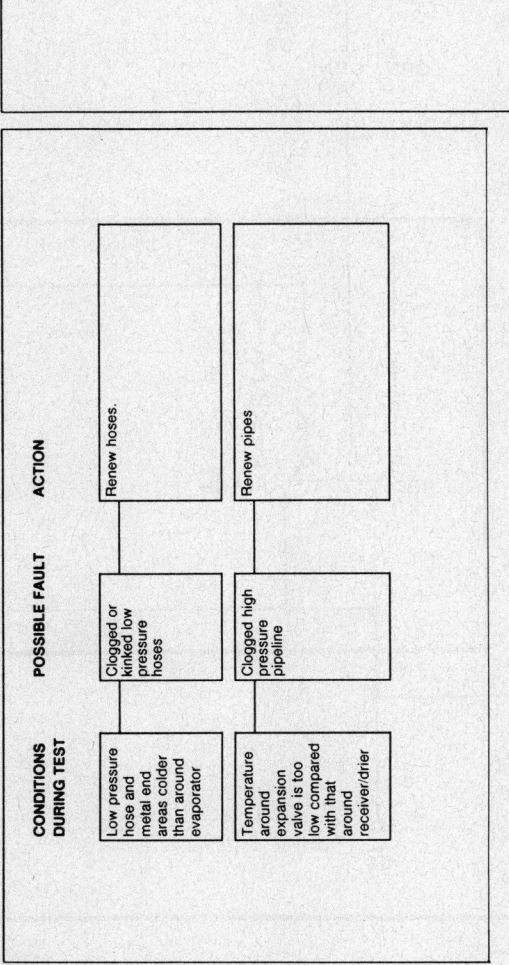

CONDITIONS DURING TEST	POSSIBLE FAULT	ACTION
Low pressure hose and metal end areas colder than around evaporator	Clogged or kinked low pressure hoses	Renew hoses.
Temperature around expansion valve is too low compared with that around receiver/drier	Clogged high pressure pipeline	Renew pipes

HIGH AND LOW PRESSURE ABNORMALLY HIGH DURING TESTING—STERLING

CONDITIONS DURING TEST	POSSIBLE FAULT	ACTION
Reduced air flow through condensor	Clogged condensor	Clean
	Clogged radiator	Clean.
	Cooling fans inoperative	Check
No bubbles in sight glass when condensor is cooled by water	Excessive R12	Discharge R12 as required.

LOW PRESSURE ABNORMALLY HIGH DURING TESTING—STERLING

CONDITIONS DURING TEST	POSSIBLE FAULT	ACTION
Low pressure hose and test connection are colder than around evaporator	Expansion valve open too long	Renew valve.
	Loose expansion valve	Renew valve
Low pressure is lowered when condensor is cooled by water.	Excessive R12	Discharge R12 as required.
High and low pressures are balanced as soon as the compressor is stopped	Faulty gasket	Renew compressor.
	Faulty high pressure valve	Renew compressor.
	Dirt stuck in high pressure valve	Renew compressor.

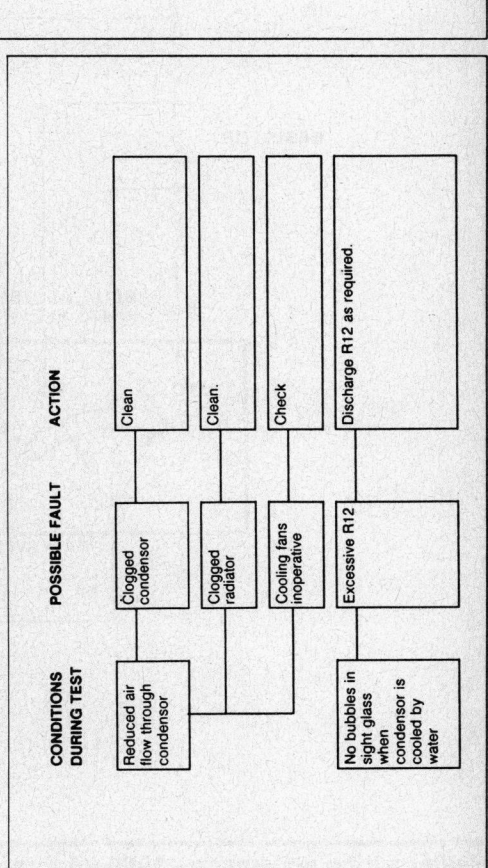

WIRING SCHEMATICS

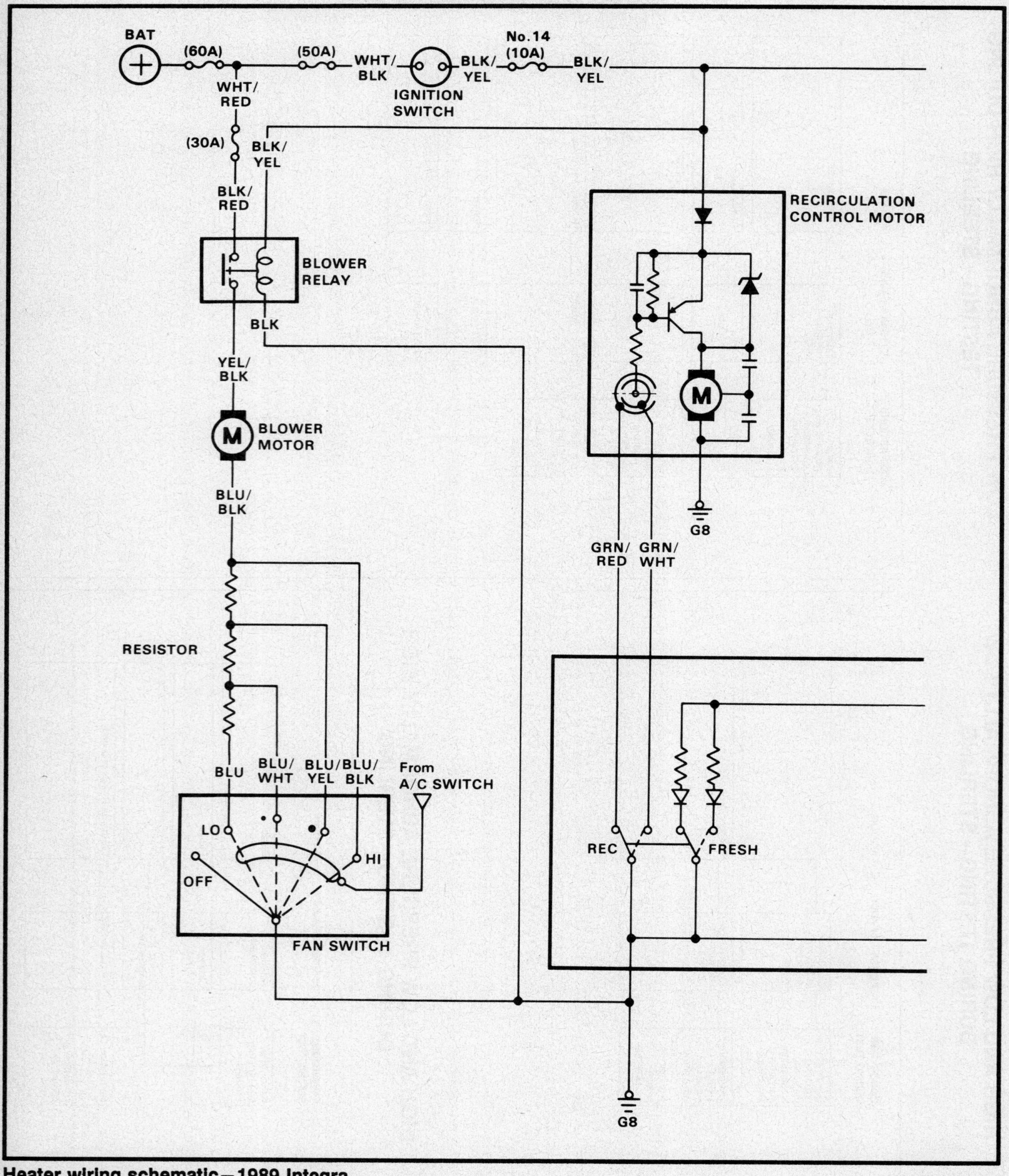
BAT
(60A)
(50A)
WHT/ BLK
IGNITION SWITCH
BLK/ YEL
No.14 (10A)
BLK/ YEL
WHT/ RED
(30A)
BLK/ YEL
BLK/ RED
BLOWER RELAY
BLK
YEL/ BLK
BLOWER MOTOR
BLU/ BLK
RESISTOR
BLU
BLU/ WHT
BLU/ YEL
BLU/ BLK
From A/C SWITCH
LO
HI
OFF
FAN SWITCH
RECIRCULATION CONTROL MOTOR
M
G8
GRN/ RED
GRN/ WHT
REC
FRESH
G8

Heater wiring schematic—1989 Integra

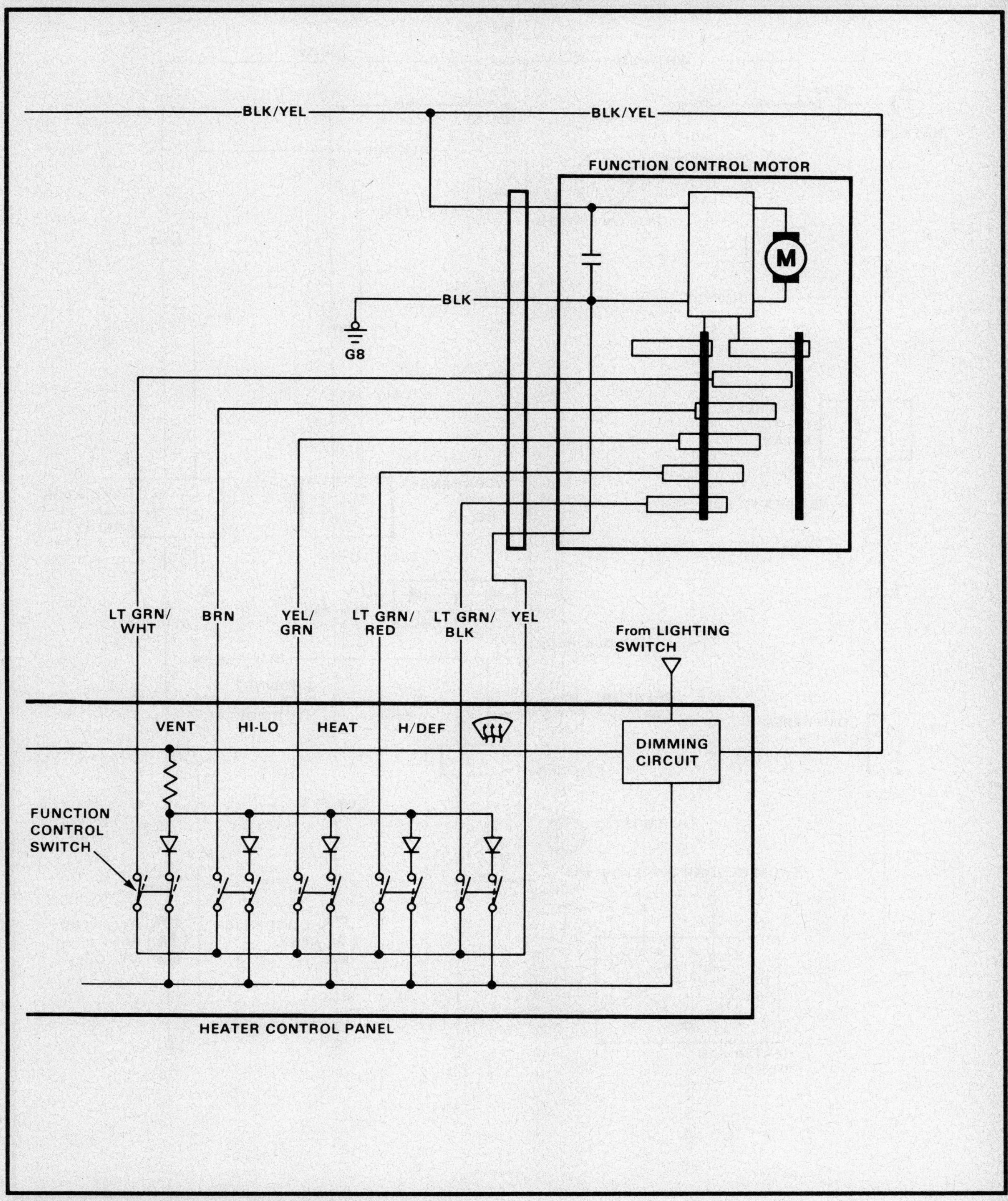
BLK/YEL
BLK/YEL
FUNCTION CONTROL MOTOR
M
BLK
G8
LT GRN/
WHT
BRN
YEL/
GRN
LT GRN/
RED
LT GRN/
BLK
YEL
From LIGHTING
SWITCH
VENT
HI-LO
HEAT
H/DEF
DIMMING
CIRCUIT
FUNCTION
CONTROL
SWITCH
HEATER CONTROL PANEL

Heater wiring schematic—1989 Integra—continued

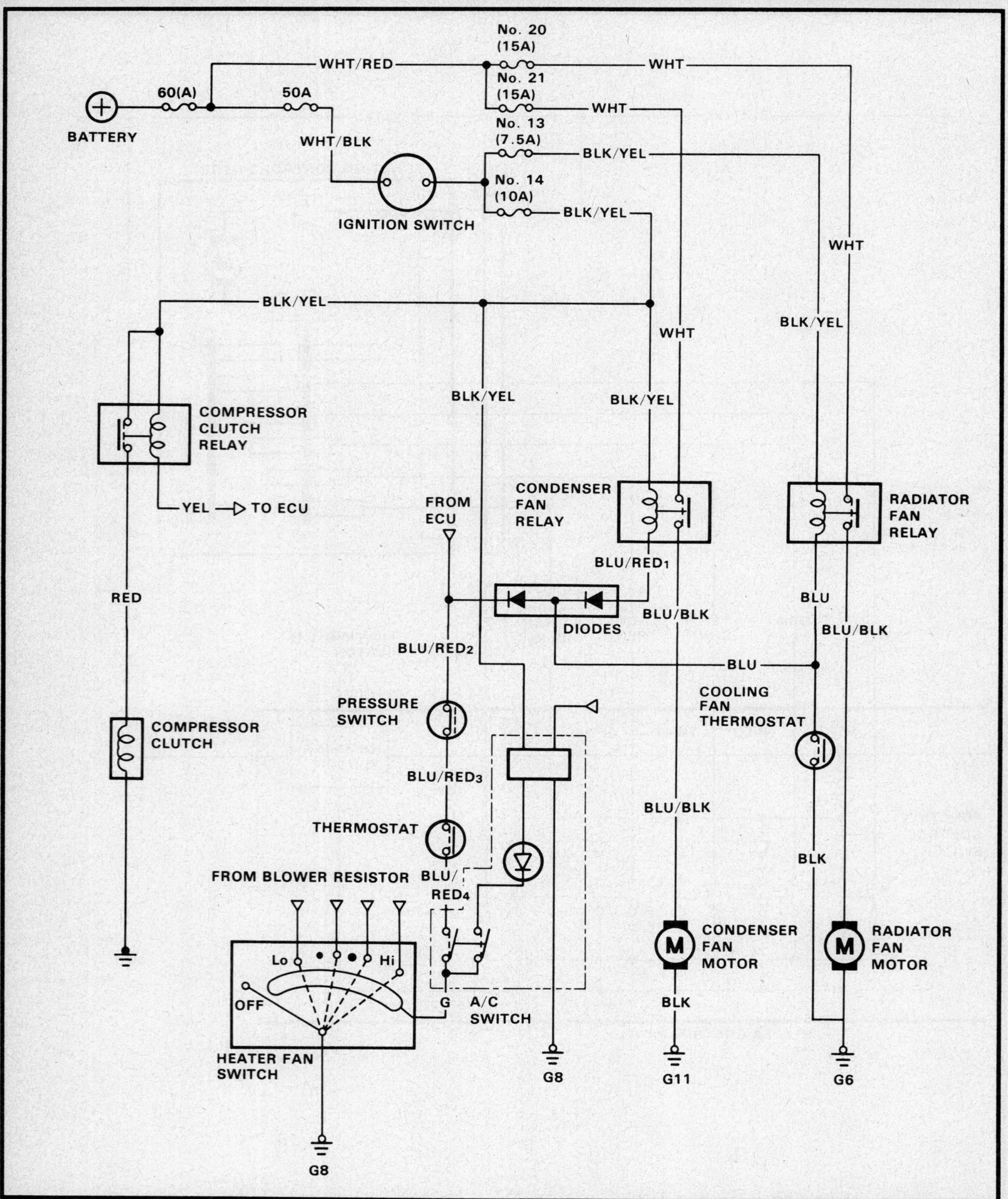
No. 20
(15A)
WHT/RED
WHT
60(A)
50A
No. 21
(15A)
WHT
BATTERY
No. 13
(7.5A)
WHT/BLK
BLK/YEL
No. 14
(10A)
BLK/YEL
IGNITION SWITCH
WHT
BLK/YEL
BLK/YEL
WHT
BLK/YEL
BLK/YEL
BLK/YEL
COMPRESSOR
CLUTCH
RELAY
CONDENSER
FAN
RELAY
RADIATOR
FAN
RELAY
YEL
TO ECU
FROM
ECU
BLU/RED1
RED
BLU
BLU/BLK
DIODES
BLU/BLK
BLU/RED2
BLU
COOLING
FAN
THERMOSTAT
PRESSURE
SWITCH
COMPRESSOR
CLUTCH
BLU/RED3
BLU/BLK
THERMOSTAT
BLK
FROM BLOWER RESISTOR
BLU/
RED4
CONDENSER
FAN
MOTOR
RADIATOR
FAN
MOTOR
Lo
Hi
OFF
G
A/C
SWITCH
BLK
HEATER FAN
SWITCH
G8
G11
G6
G8

Air conditioner wiring schematic—1989 Integra

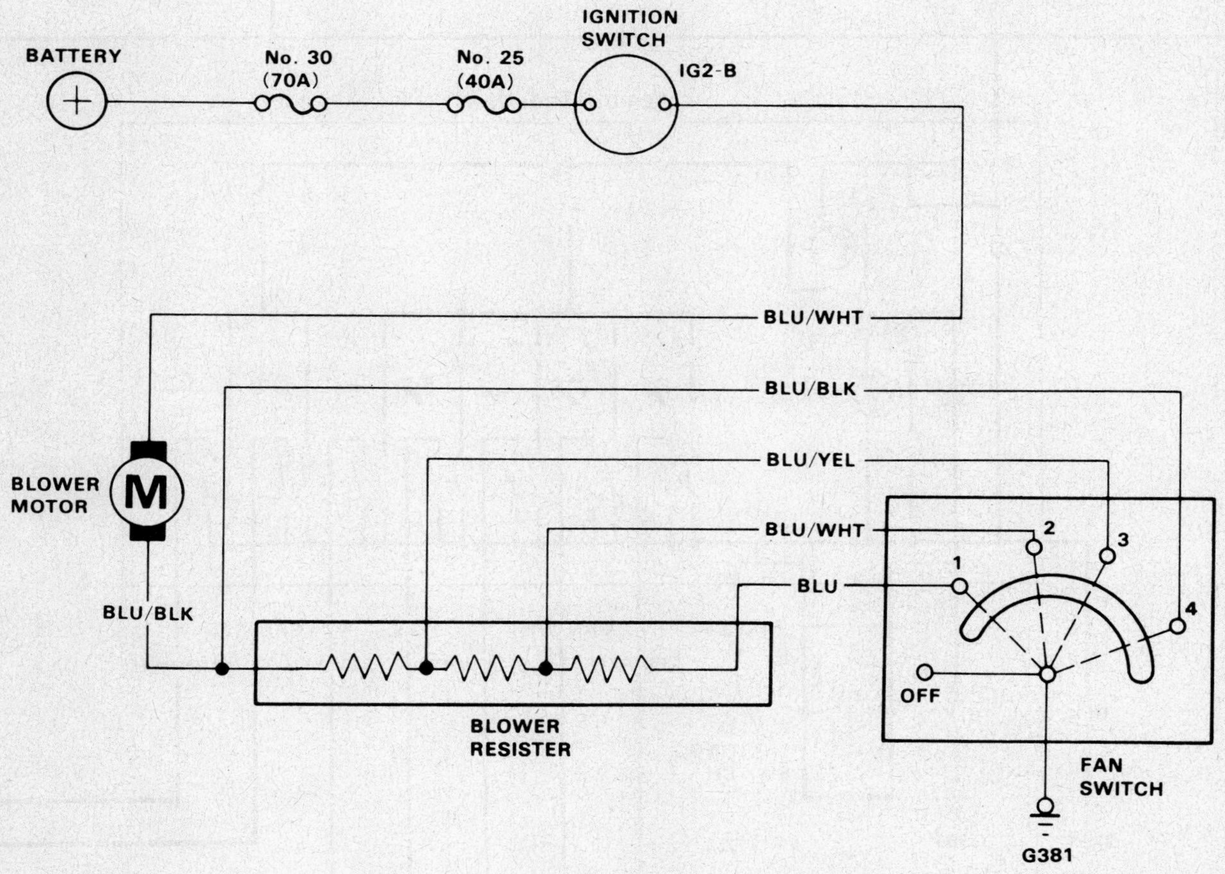
IGNITION SWITCH
BATTERY
No. 30 (70A)
No. 25 (40A)
IG2-B
BLU/WHT
BLU/BLK
BLU/YEL
BLOWER MOTOR
M
BLU/WHT
2
3
1
BLU
4
BLU/BLK
OFF
BLOWER RESISTER
FAN SWITCH
G381

Heater wiring schematic—1990–91 Integra

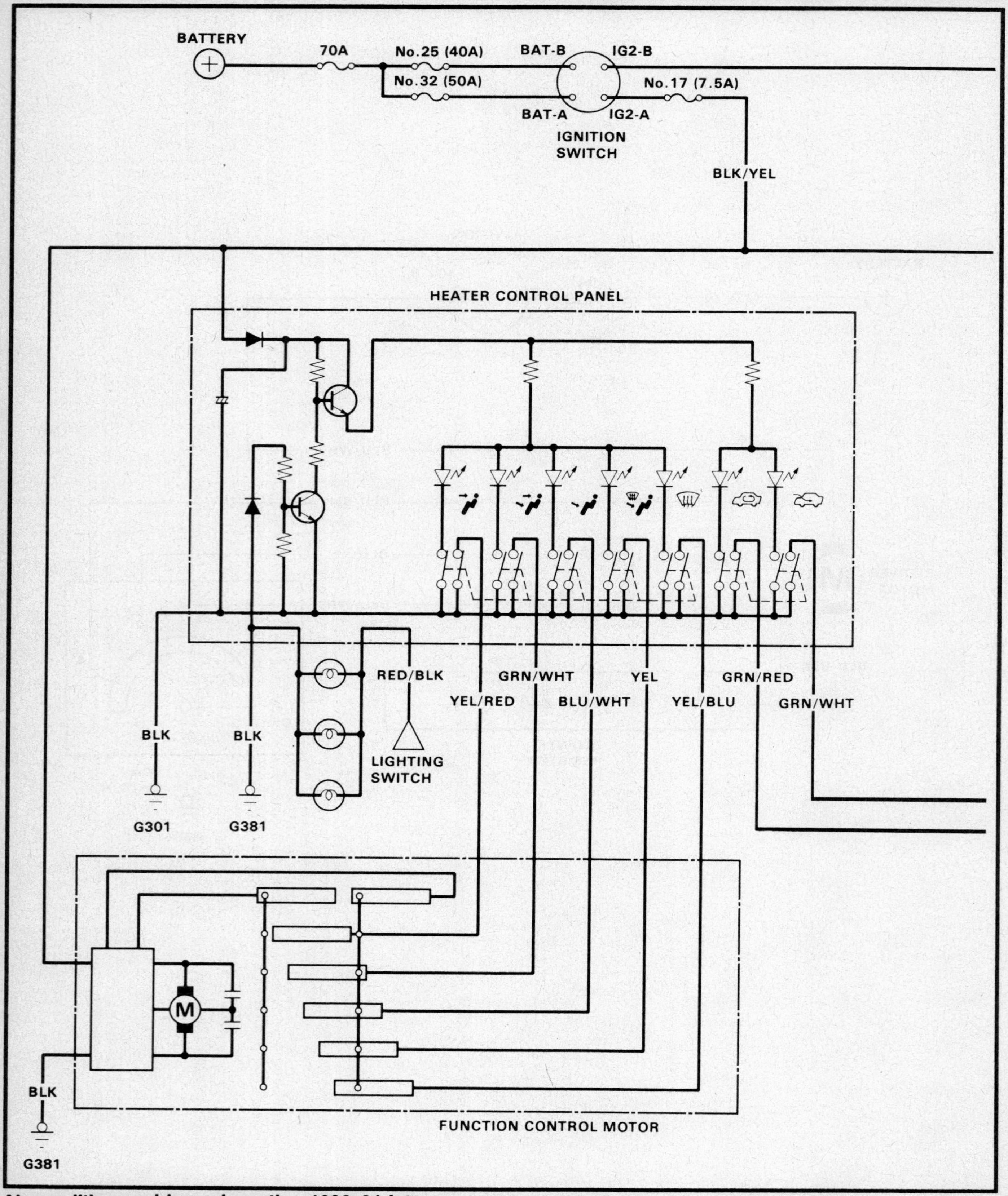
BATTERY
70A
No.25 (40A)
No.32 (50A)
BAT-B
IG2-B
BAT-A
IG2-A
IGNITION SWITCH
No.17 (7.5A)
BLK/YEL
HEATER CONTROL PANEL
RED/BLK
LIGHTING SWITCH
GRN/WHT
YEL/RED
BLU/WHT
YEL
YEL/BLU
GRN/RED
GRN/WHT
BLK
BLK
G301
G381
M
BLK
G381
FUNCTION CONTROL MOTOR

Air conditioner wiring schematic—1990–91 Integra

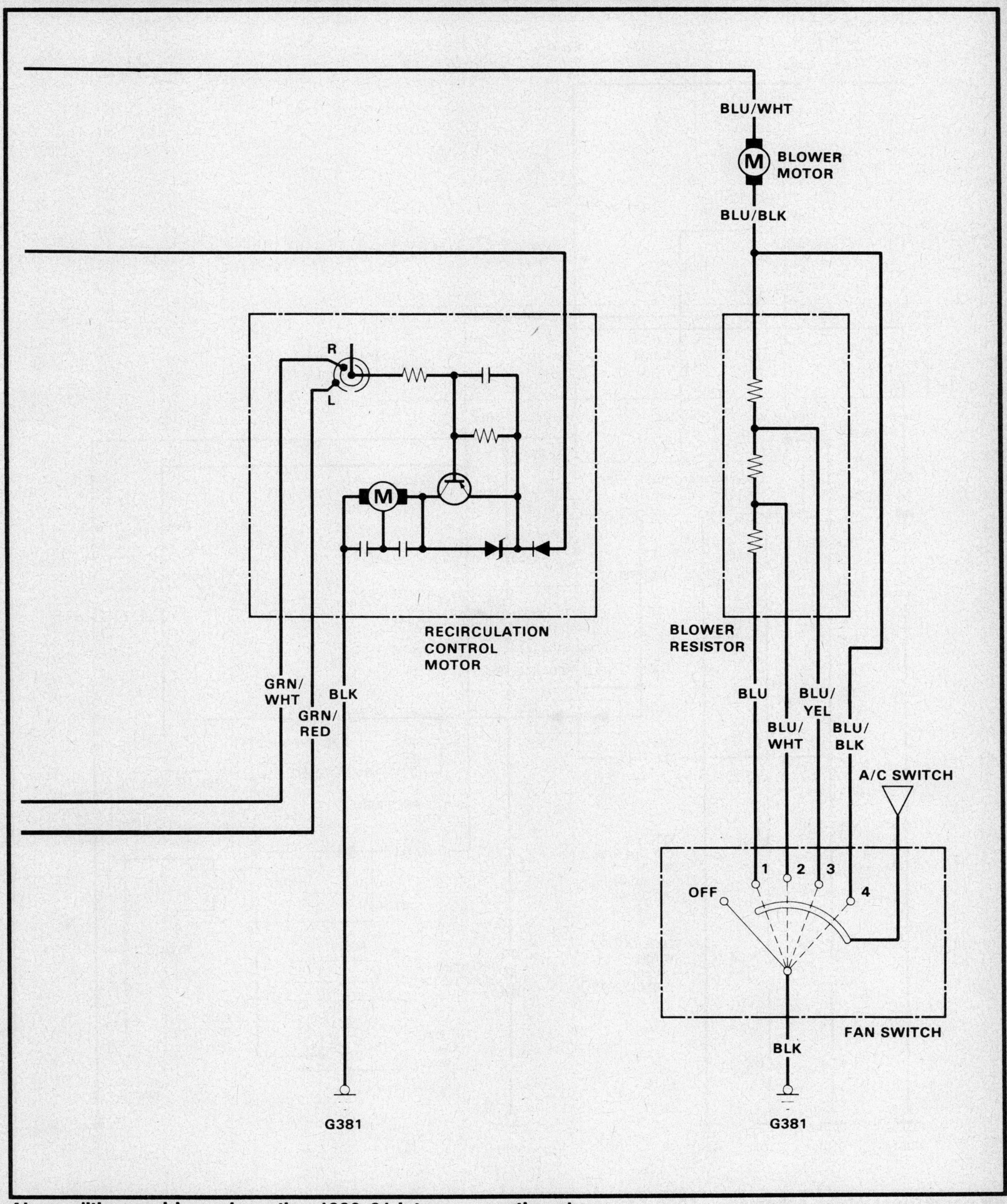
BLU/WHT
BLOWER MOTOR
BLU/BLK
R
L
RECIRCULATION CONTROL MOTOR
BLOWER RESISTOR
GRN/WHT
BLK
GRN/RED
BLU
BLU/YEL
BLU/WHT
BLU/BLK
A/C SWITCH
1
2
3
4
OFF
FAN SWITCH
BLK
G381
G381

Air conditioner wiring schematic—1990–91 Integra—continued

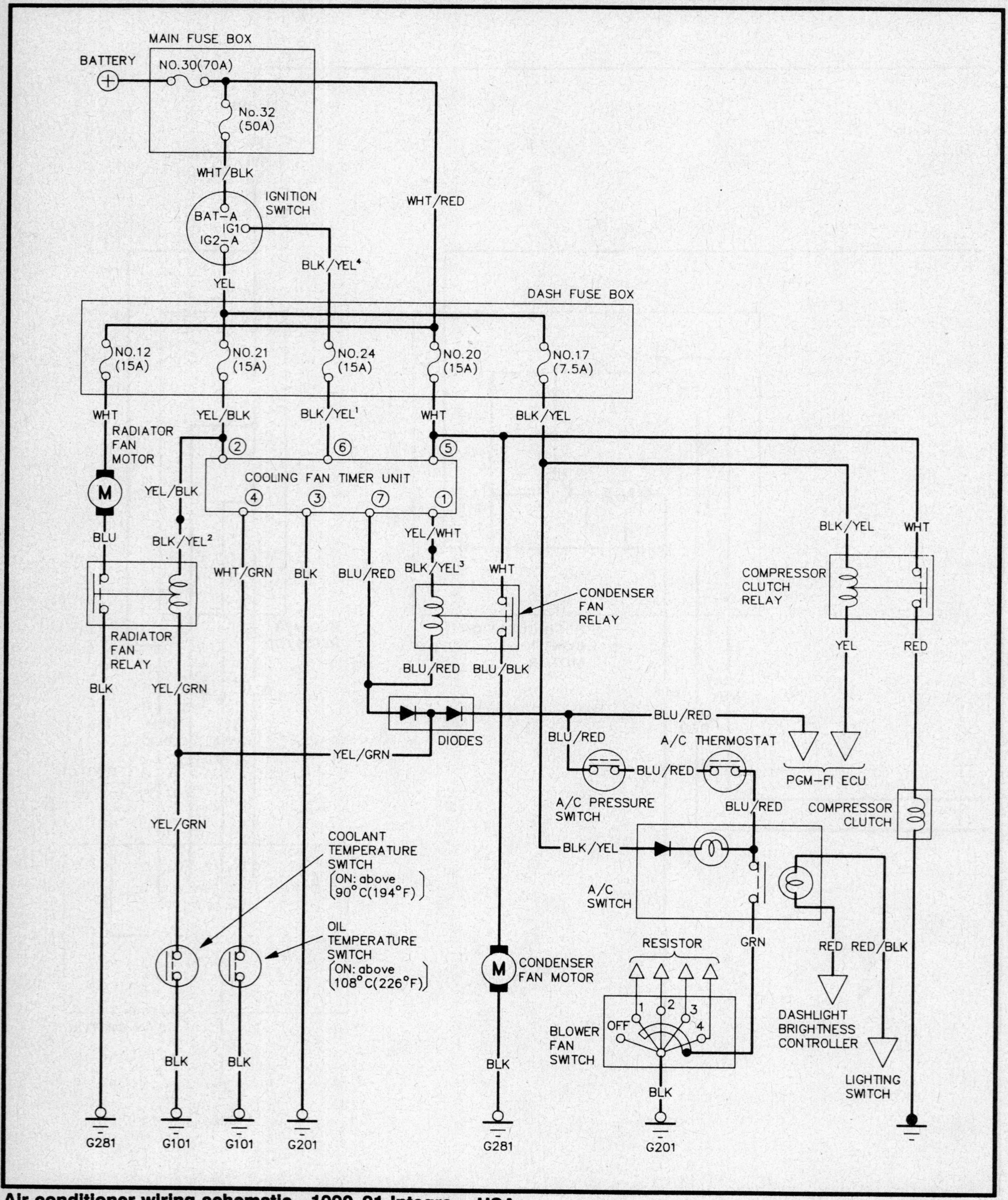
MAIN FUSE BOX
BATTERY
NO.30(70A)
No.32 (50A)
WHT/BLK
IGNITION SWITCH
BAT–A
IG1
IG2–A
WHT/RED
BLK/YEL⁴
YEL
DASH FUSE BOX
NO.12 (15A)
NO.21 (15A)
NO.24 (15A)
NO.20 (15A)
NO.17 (7.5A)
WHT
YEL/BLK
BLK/YEL¹
WHT
BLK/YEL
RADIATOR FAN MOTOR
COOLING FAN TIMER UNIT
YEL/BLK
BLU
BLK/YEL²
WHT/GRN
BLK
BLU/RED
YEL/WHT
BLK/YEL³
WHT
CONDENSER FAN RELAY
BLK/YEL
WHT
COMPRESSOR CLUTCH RELAY
RADIATOR FAN RELAY
YEL
RED
BLK
YEL/GRN
BLU/RED
BLU/BLK
DIODES
BLU/RED
BLU/RED
A/C THERMOSTAT
YEL/GRN
BLU/RED
PGM–FI ECU
A/C PRESSURE SWITCH
BLU/RED
COMPRESSOR CLUTCH
YEL/GRN
BLK/YEL
COOLANT TEMPERATURE SWITCH (ON: above 90°C(194°F))
A/C SWITCH
OIL TEMPERATURE SWITCH (ON: above 108°C(226°F))
RESISTOR
GRN
RED
RED/BLK
CONDENSER FAN MOTOR
DASHLIGHT BRIGHTNESS CONTROLLER
BLOWER FAN SWITCH
OFF
1
2
3
4
BLK
BLK
BLK
BLK
LIGHTING SWITCH
G281
G101
G101
G201
G281
G201

Air conditioner wiring schematic—1990–91 Integra—USA

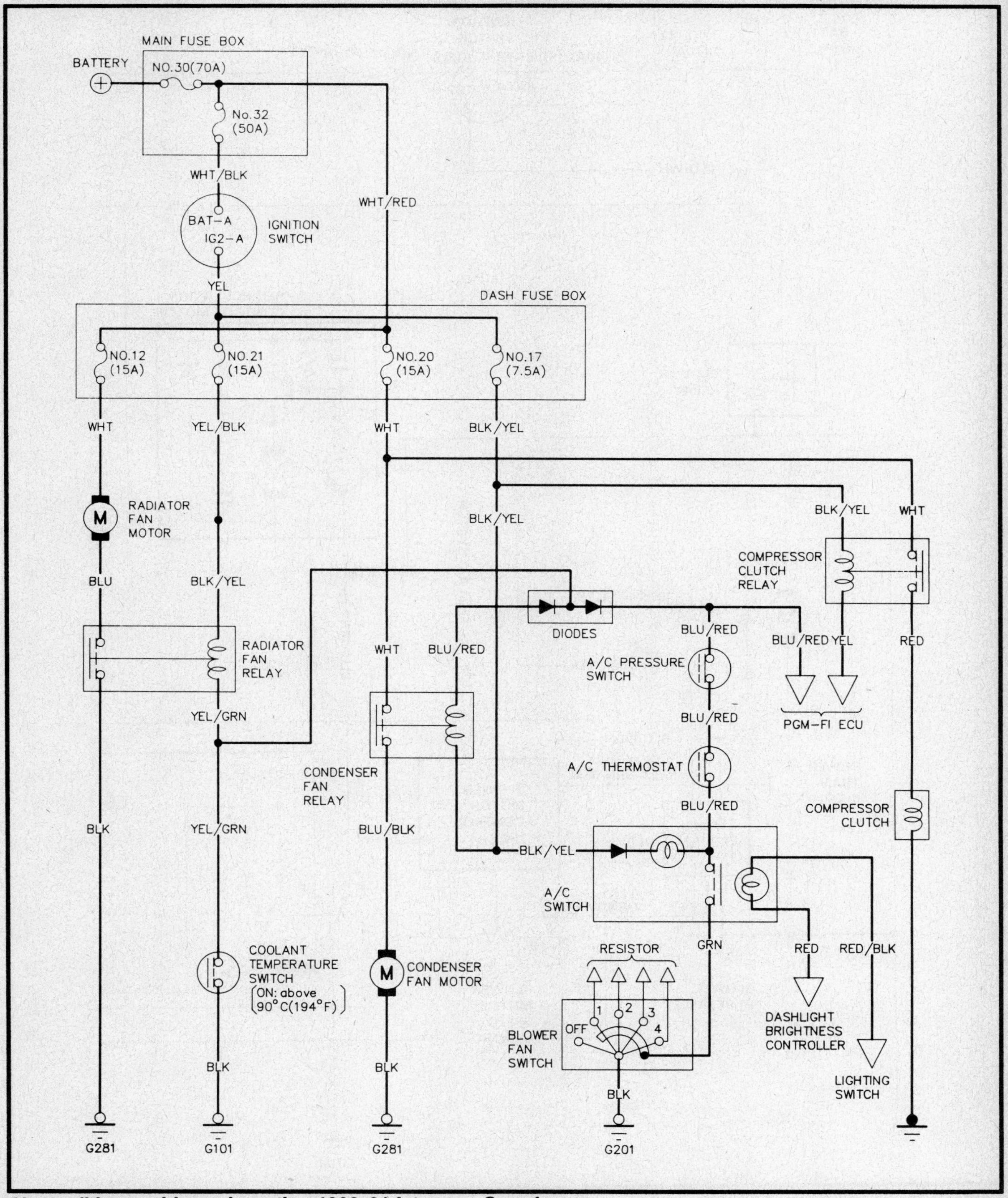
MAIN FUSE BOX
BATTERY
NO.30(70A)
No.32 (50A)
WHT/BLK
BAT-A
IG2-A
IGNITION SWITCH
WHT/RED
YEL
DASH FUSE BOX
NO.12 (15A)
NO.21 (15A)
NO.20 (15A)
NO.17 (7.5A)
WHT
YEL/BLK
WHT
BLK/YEL
RADIATOR FAN MOTOR
BLK/YEL
BLK/YEL
WHT
COMPRESSOR CLUTCH RELAY
BLU
BLK/YEL
RADIATOR FAN RELAY
DIODES
BLU/RED
WHT
BLU/RED
A/C PRESSURE SWITCH
BLU/RED
YEL
RED
YEL/GRN
BLU/RED
PGM-FI ECU
CONDENSER FAN RELAY
A/C THERMOSTAT
BLU/RED
COMPRESSOR CLUTCH
BLK
YEL/GRN
BLU/BLK
BLK/YEL
A/C SWITCH
RESISTOR
GRN
RED
RED/BLK
COOLANT TEMPERATURE SWITCH
(ON: above 90°C(194°F))
CONDENSER FAN MOTOR
1
2
3
4
OFF
BLOWER FAN SWITCH
DASHLIGHT BRIGHTNESS CONTROLLER
LIGHTING SWITCH
BLK
BLK
BLK
G281
G101
G281
G201

Air conditioner wiring schematic—1990–91 Integra— Canada

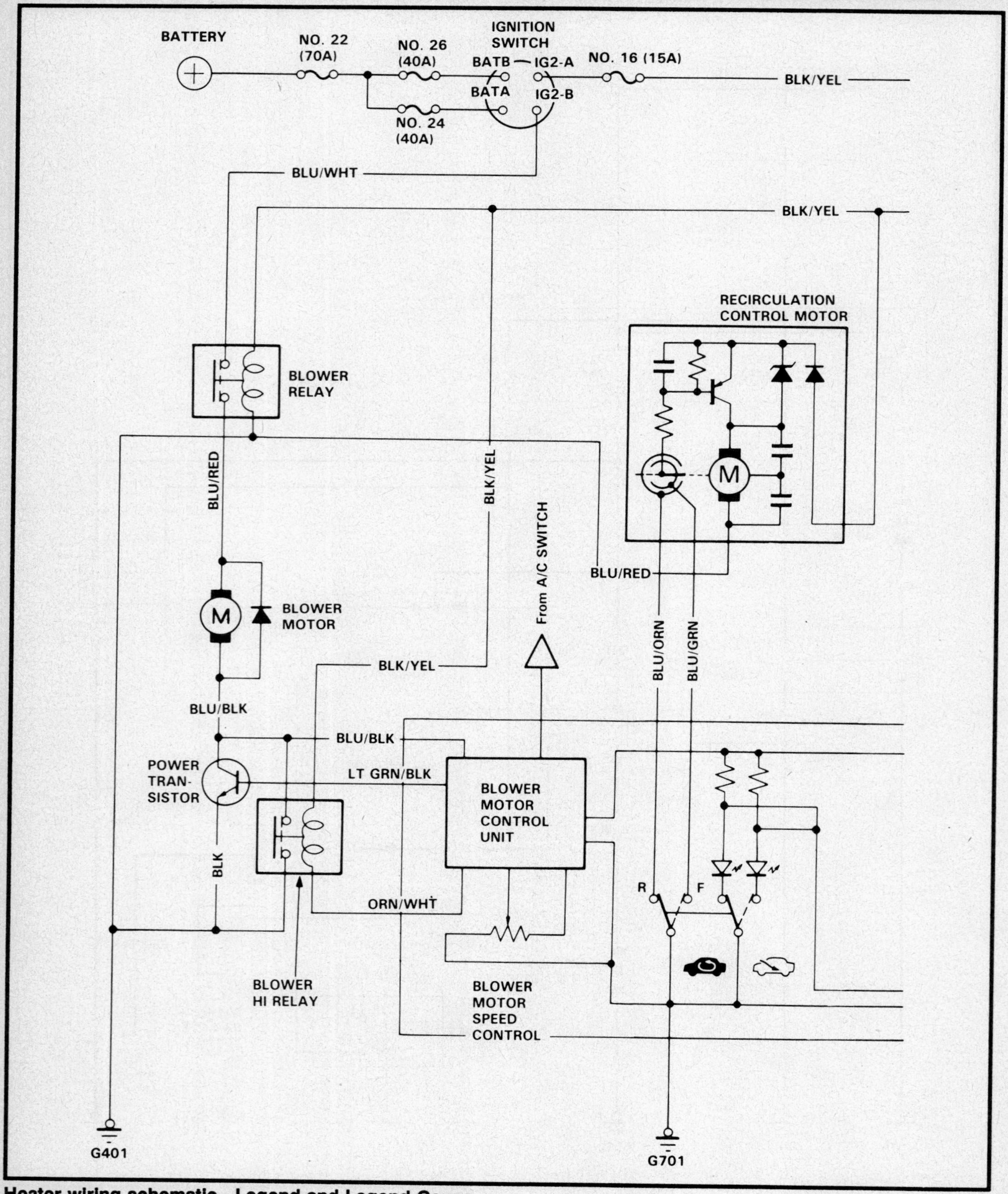
BATTERY
NO. 22 (70A)
NO. 26 (40A)
IGNITION SWITCH
BATB
IG2-A
BATA
IG2-B
NO. 24 (40A)
NO. 16 (15A)
BLK/YEL
BLU/WHT
BLK/YEL
RECIRCULATION CONTROL MOTOR
BLOWER RELAY
BLU/RED
BLK/YEL
From A/C SWITCH
BLU/RED
BLOWER MOTOR
BLU/ORN
BLU/GRN
BLK/YEL
BLU/BLK
BLU/BLK
POWER TRAN-SISTOR
LT GRN/BLK
BLOWER MOTOR CONTROL UNIT
BLK
R
F
ORN/WHT
BLOWER HI RELAY
BLOWER MOTOR SPEED CONTROL
G401
G701

Heater wiring schematic—Legend and Legend Coupe

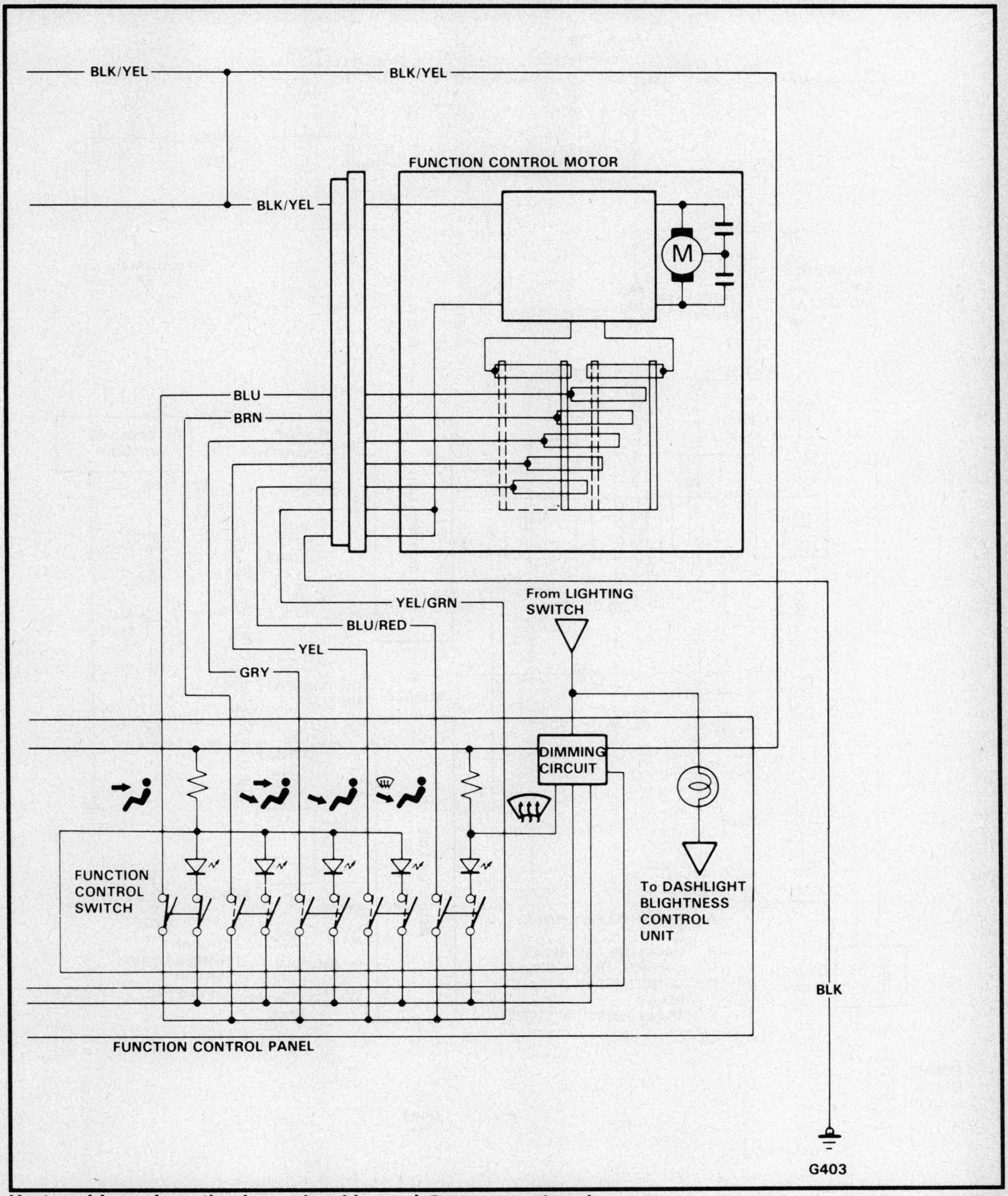
BLK/YEL
BLK/YEL
FUNCTION CONTROL MOTOR
BLK/YEL
M
BLU
BRN
YEL/GRN
From LIGHTING SWITCH
BLU/RED
YEL
GRY
DIMMING CIRCUIT
FUNCTION CONTROL SWITCH
To DASHLIGHT BLIGHTNESS CONTROL UNIT
BLK
FUNCTION CONTROL PANEL
G403

Heater wiring schematic—Legend and Legend Coupe—continued

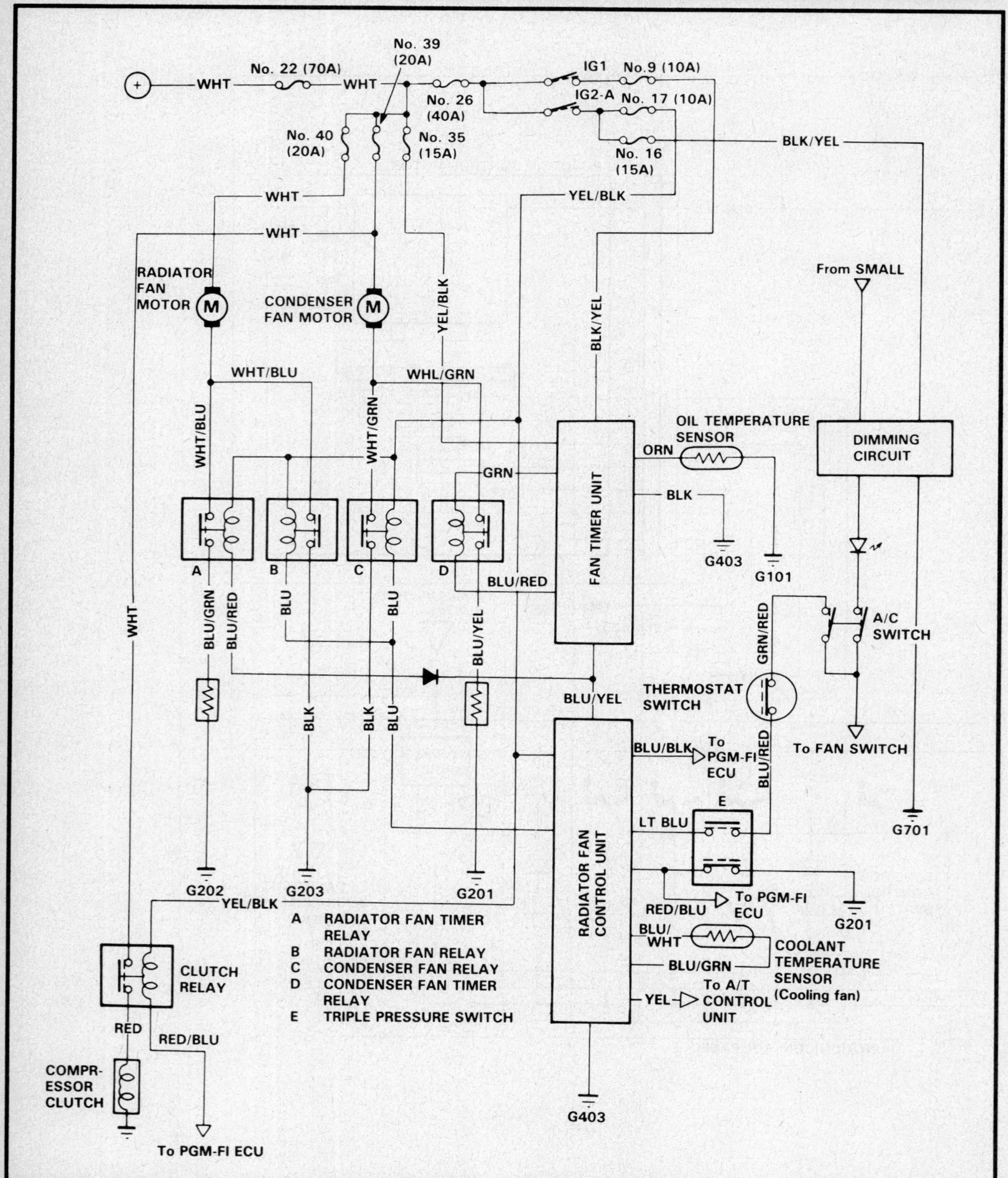
WHT
No. 22 (70A)
WHT
No. 39 (20A)
No. 26 (40A)
IG1
No.9 (10A)
IG2-A
No. 17 (10A)
No. 40 (20A)
No. 35 (15A)
No. 16 (15A)
BLK/YEL
WHT
YEL/BLK
WHT
RADIATOR FAN MOTOR
M
CONDENSER FAN MOTOR
M
YEL/BLK
BLK/YEL
From SMALL
WHT/BLU
WHL/GRN
WHT/BLU
WHT/GRN
GRN
FAN TIMER UNIT
OIL TEMPERATURE SENSOR
ORN
BLK
G403
G101
DIMMING CIRCUIT
A
B
C
D
BLU/RED
WHT
BLU/GRN
BLU/RED
BLU
BLU
BLU/YEL
GRN/RED
A/C SWITCH
THERMOSTAT SWITCH
BLU/YEL
BLK
BLK
BLU
RADIATOR FAN CONTROL UNIT
BLU/BLK
To PGM-FI ECU
BLU/RED
To FAN SWITCH
E
LT BLU
G701
G202
G203
G201
YEL/BLK
RED/BLU
To PGM-FI ECU
G201
BLU/WHT
BLU/GRN
COOLANT TEMPERATURE SENSOR (Cooling fan)
CLUTCH RELAY
YEL
To A/T CONTROL UNIT
RED
RED/BLU
COMPR-ESSOR CLUTCH
To PGM-FI ECU
G403
A RADIATOR FAN TIMER RELAY
B RADIATOR FAN RELAY
C CONDENSER FAN RELAY
D CONDENSER FAN TIMER RELAY
E TRIPLE PRESSURE SWITCH

Manual air conditioning wiring schematic – Legend and Legend Coupe

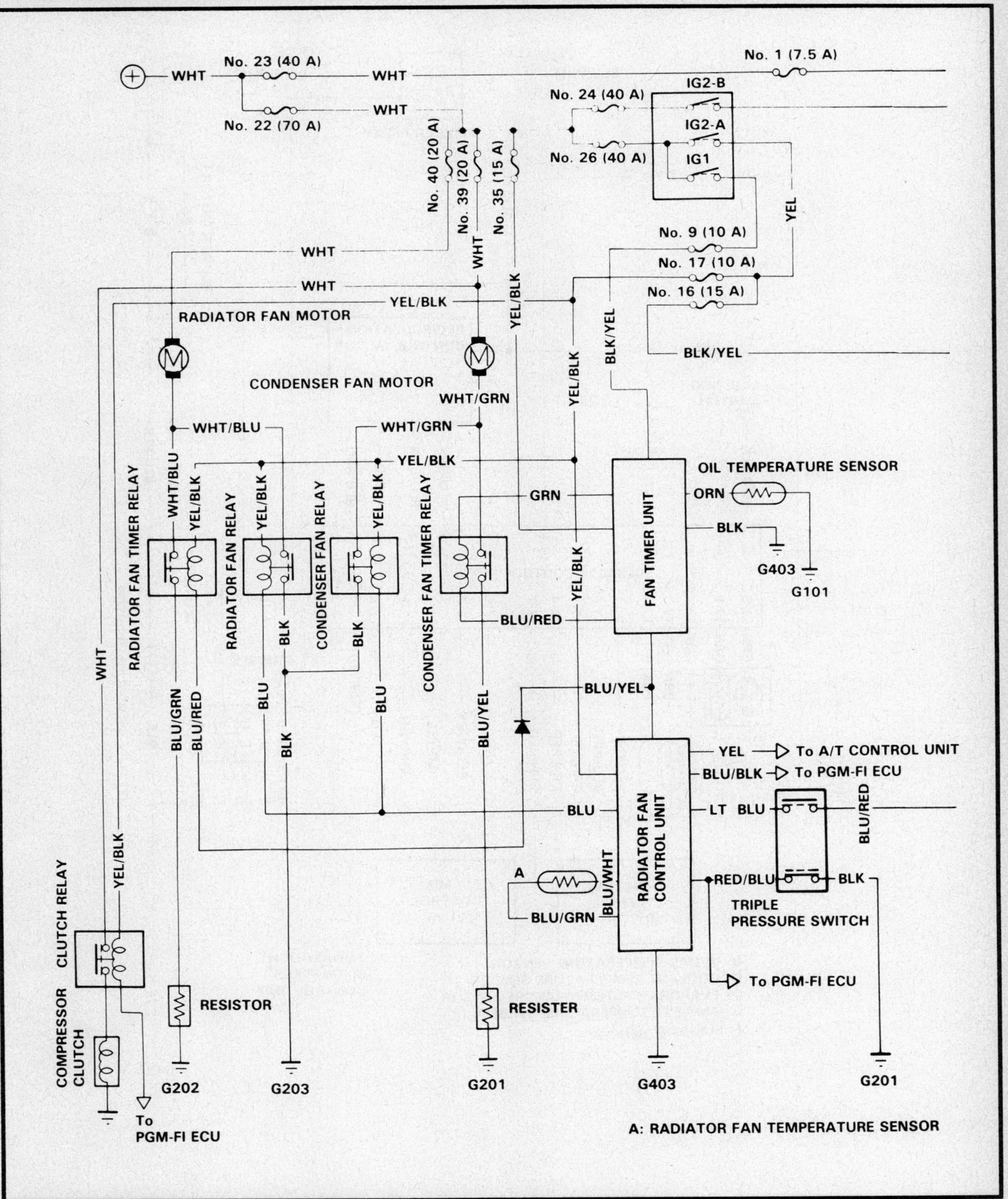
No. 23 (40 A)
WHT
No. 22 (70 A)
No. 1 (7.5 A)
No. 24 (40 A)
IG2-B
IG2-A
IG1
No. 26 (40 A)
No. 40 (20 A)
No. 39 (20 A)
No. 35 (15 A)
YEL
No. 9 (10 A)
No. 17 (10 A)
No. 16 (15 A)
YEL/BLK
BLK/YEL
RADIATOR FAN MOTOR
CONDENSER FAN MOTOR
WHT/GRN
WHT/BLU
OIL TEMPERATURE SENSOR
ORN
BLK
GRN
FAN TIMER UNIT
G403
G101
RADIATOR FAN TIMER RELAY
RADIATOR FAN RELAY
CONDENSER FAN RELAY
CONDENSER FAN TIMER RELAY
BLU/RED
BLU/YEL
BLU/GRN
BLU
YEL
To A/T CONTROL UNIT
BLU/BLK
To PGM-FI ECU
LT BLU
RADIATOR FAN CONTROL UNIT
BLU/WHT
RED/BLU
TRIPLE PRESSURE SWITCH
A
CLUTCH RELAY
COMPRESSOR CLUTCH
RESISTOR
RESISTER
G202
G203
G201
To PGM-FI ECU
A: RADIATOR FAN TEMPERATURE SENSOR

Automatic climate control wiring schematic—Legend and Legend Coupe

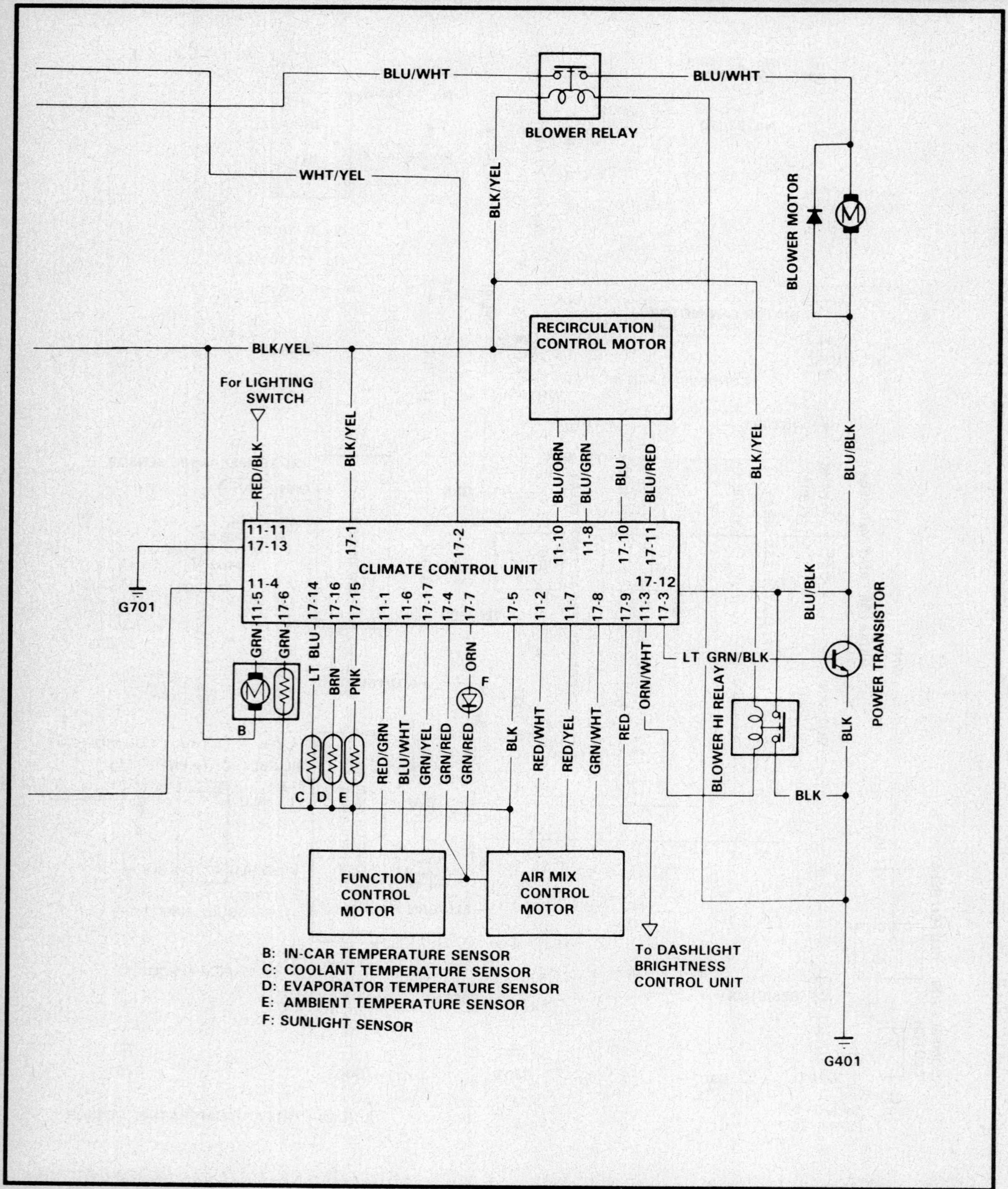
BLU/WHT
BLU/WHT
BLOWER RELAY
WHT/YEL
BLK/YEL
BLOWER MOTOR
RECIRCULATION CONTROL MOTOR
BLK/YEL
For LIGHTING SWITCH
RED/BLK
BLK/YEL
BLU/ORN
BLU/GRN
BLU
BLU/RED
BLK/YEL
BLU/BLK
11-11
17-13
17-1
17-2
11-10
11-8
17-10
17-11
CLIMATE CONTROL UNIT
11-4
17-12
G701
11-5
17-6
17-14
17-16
17-15
11-1
11-6
17-17
17-4
17-7
17-5
11-2
11-7
17-8
17-9
11-3
17-3
BLU/BLK
POWER TRANSISTOR
GRN
GRN
LT BLU
BRN
PNK
ORN
F
LT GRN/BLK
ORN/WHT
BLOWER HI RELAY
B
RED/GRN
BLU/WHT
GRN/YEL
GRN/RED
GRN/RED
BLK
RED/WHT
RED/YEL
GRN/WHT
RED
BLK
BLK
C
D
E
FUNCTION CONTROL MOTOR
AIR MIX CONTROL MOTOR
To DASHLIGHT BRIGHTNESS CONTROL UNIT
B: IN-CAR TEMPERATURE SENSOR
C: COOLANT TEMPERATURE SENSOR
D: EVAPORATOR TEMPERATURE SENSOR
E: AMBIENT TEMPERATURE SENSOR
F: SUNLIGHT SENSOR
G401

Automatic climate control wiring schematic—Legend and Legend Coupe

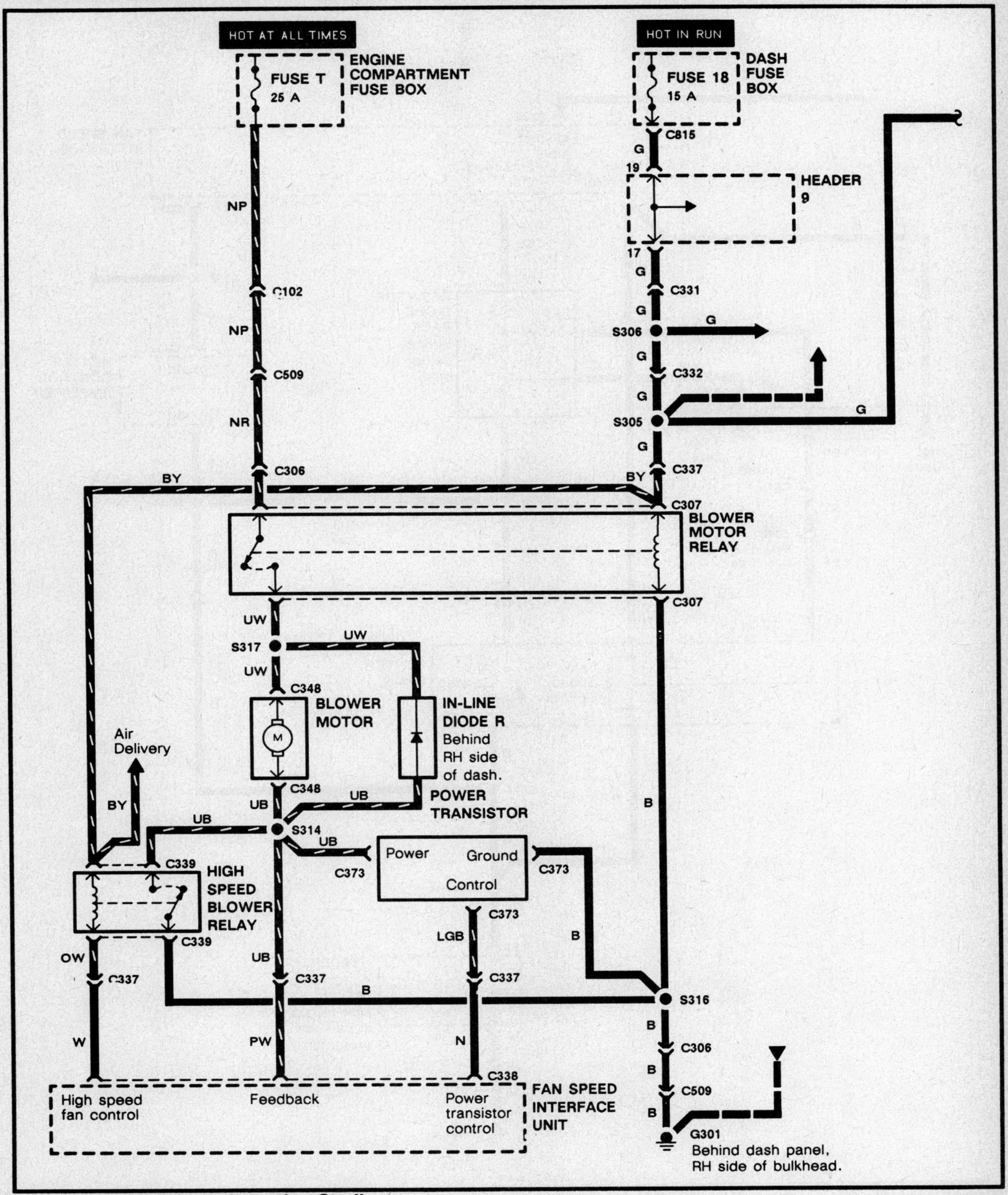
HOT AT ALL TIMES
FUSE T 25 A
ENGINE COMPARTMENT FUSE BOX
HOT IN RUN
FUSE 18 15 A
DASH FUSE BOX
C815
G
19
HEADER 9
17
NP
C102
NP
C509
NR
C306
C331
S306
C332
S305
C337
BY
C307
BLOWER MOTOR RELAY
UW
S317
C348
BLOWER MOTOR
IN-LINE DIODE R
Behind RH side of dash.
UB
POWER TRANSISTOR
Air Delivery
S314
C373
Power
Ground
Control
C339
HIGH SPEED BLOWER RELAY
OW
C337
LGB
B
S316
W
PW
N
C338
C306
C509
High speed fan control
Feedback
Power transistor control
FAN SPEED INTERFACE UNIT
G301
Behind dash panel, RH side of bulkhead.

Blower control wiring schematic—Sterling

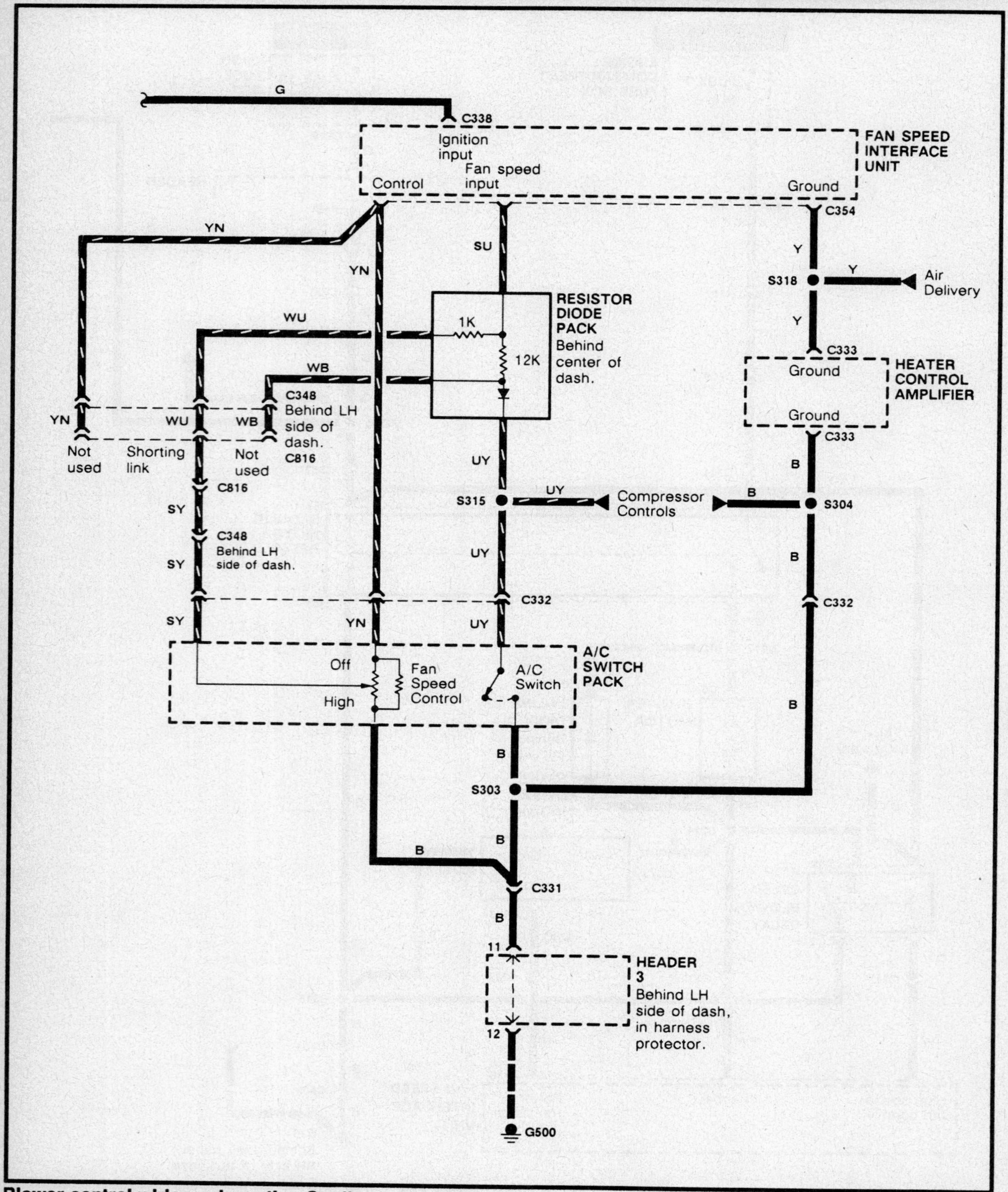
G
C338
Ignition input
Fan speed input
Control
Ground
FAN SPEED INTERFACE UNIT
C354
YN
SU
Y
S318
Y
Air Delivery
YN
Y
RESISTOR DIODE PACK
Behind center of dash.
1K
12K
WU
WB
C333
Ground
HEATER CONTROL AMPLIFIER
Ground
C333
C348
Behind LH side of dash.
C816
YN
WU
WB
Not used
Shorting link
Not used
C816
SY
C348
Behind LH side of dash.
SY
SY
UY
S315
UY
Compressor Controls
B
S304
B
UY
C332
YN
UY
C332
Off
High
Fan Speed Control
A/C Switch
A/C SWITCH PACK
B
B
S303
B
B
C331
B
11
HEADER 3
Behind LH side of dash, in harness protector.
12
G500

Blower control wiring schematic—Sterling—continued

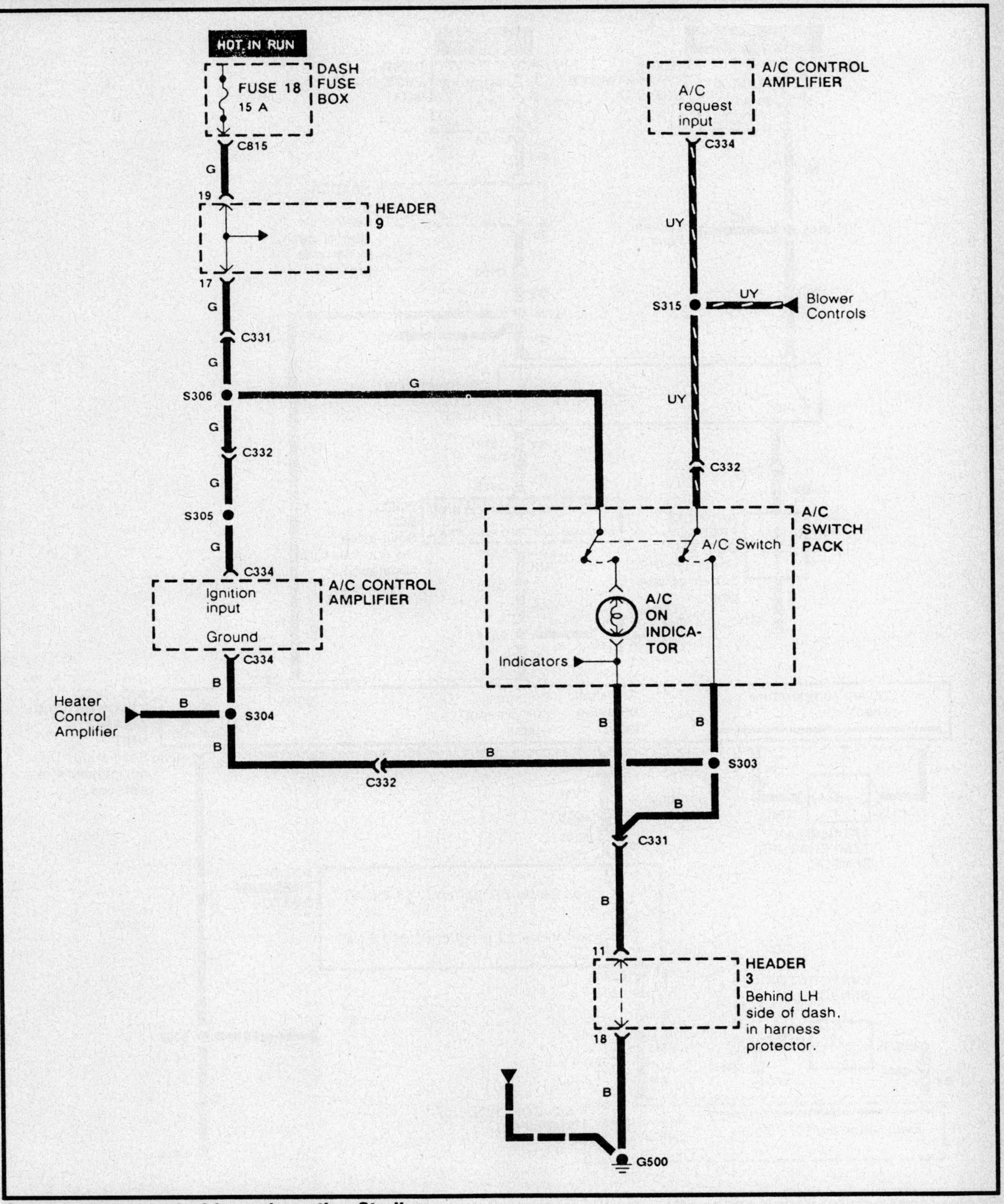
HOT IN RUN
FUSE 18
15 A
DASH FUSE BOX
C815
G
19
HEADER 9
17
G
C331
G
S306
G
G
C332
G
S305
G
C334
Ignition input
Ground
A/C CONTROL AMPLIFIER
C334
B
Heater Control Amplifier
B
S304
B
C332
B
A/C CONTROL AMPLIFIER
A/C request input
C334
UY
S315
UY
Blower Controls
UY
C332
A/C SWITCH PACK
A/C Switch
A/C ON INDICATOR
Indicators
B
B
S303
B
C331
B
11
HEADER 3
Behind LH side of dash, in harness protector.
18
B
G500

Compressor control wiring schematic—Sterling

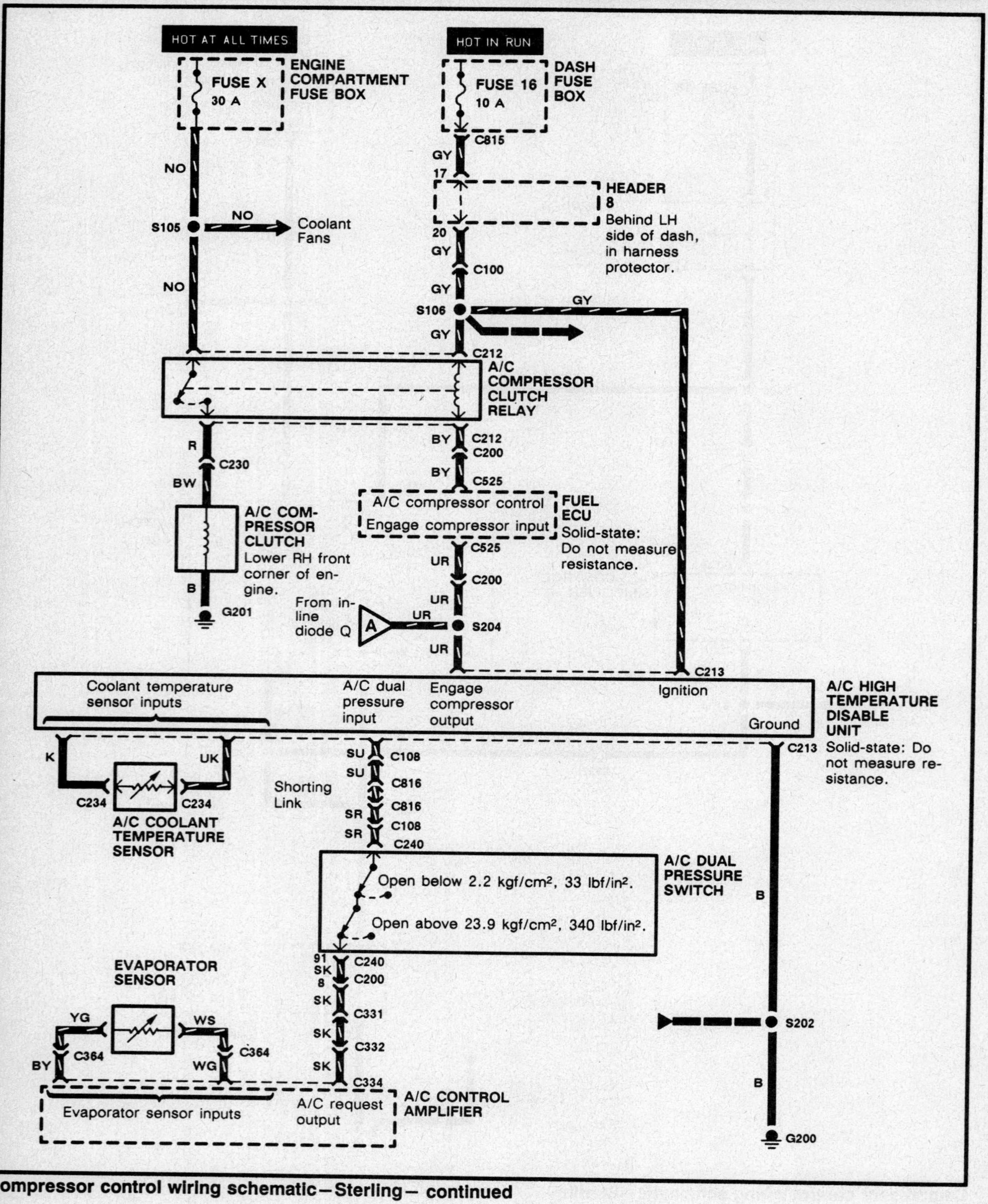
HOT AT ALL TIMES
FUSE X 30 A
ENGINE COMPARTMENT FUSE BOX
HOT IN RUN
FUSE 16 10 A
DASH FUSE BOX
C815
GY
17
HEADER 8
Behind LH side of dash, in harness protector.
20
GY
C100
GY
S106
GY
NO
S105
NO
Coolant Fans
NO
GY
C212
A/C COMPRESSOR CLUTCH RELAY
R
C230
BW
A/C COMPRESSOR CLUTCH
Lower RH front corner of engine.
B
G201
BY
C212
C200
BY
C525
A/C compressor control
Engage compressor input
FUEL ECU
Solid-state: Do not measure resistance.
C525
UR
C200
UR
From in-line diode Q
A
UR
S204
UR
C213
Coolant temperature sensor inputs
A/C dual pressure input
Engage compressor output
Ignition
Ground
A/C HIGH TEMPERATURE DISABLE UNIT
Solid-state: Do not measure resistance.
C213
K
UK
C234
C234
A/C COOLANT TEMPERATURE SENSOR
SU
C108
SU
C816
Shorting Link
C816
SR
C108
SR
C240
A/C DUAL PRESSURE SWITCH
Open below 2.2 kgf/cm², 33 lbf/in².
Open above 23.9 kgf/cm², 340 lbf/in².
B
91
C240
SK
8
C200
SK
C331
SK
C332
SK
C334
EVAPORATOR SENSOR
YG
WS
C364
C364
BY
WG
Evaporator sensor inputs
A/C request output
A/C CONTROL AMPLIFIER
S202
B
G200

Compressor control wiring schematic—Sterling—continued

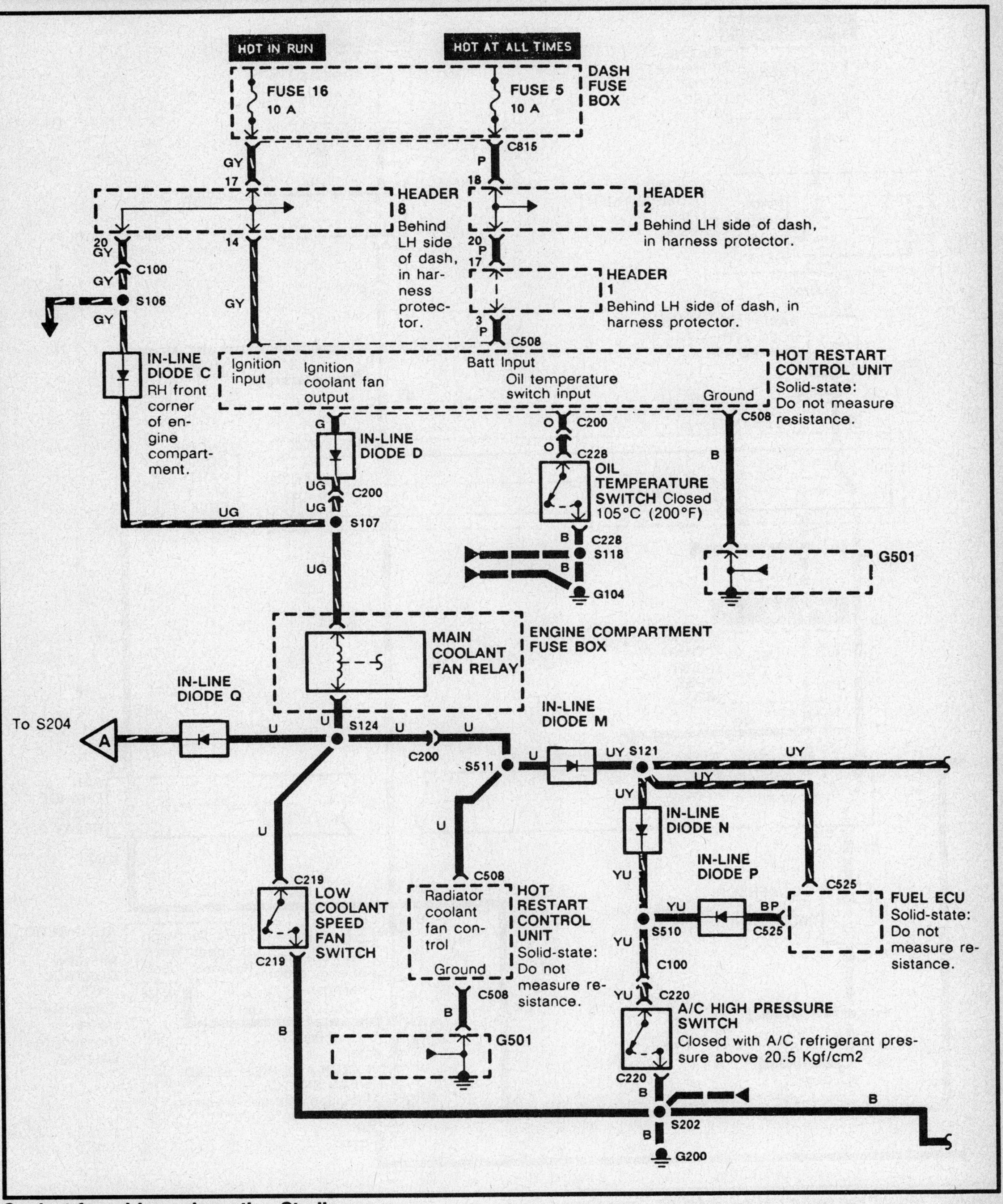
HOT IN RUN
HOT AT ALL TIMES
FUSE 16 10 A
FUSE 5 10 A
DASH FUSE BOX
C815
GY
P
HEADER 8 Behind LH side of dash, in harness protector.
HEADER 2 Behind LH side of dash, in harness protector.
HEADER 1 Behind LH side of dash, in harness protector.
C100
S106
C508
IN-LINE DIODE C RH front corner of engine compartment.
Ignition input
Ignition coolant fan output
Batt Input
Oil temperature switch input
Ground
HOT RESTART CONTROL UNIT Solid-state: Do not measure resistance.
IN-LINE DIODE D
C200
C228
OIL TEMPERATURE SWITCH Closed 105°C (200°F)
UG
S107
S118
G104
G501
ENGINE COMPARTMENT FUSE BOX
MAIN COOLANT FAN RELAY
IN-LINE DIODE Q
To S204
A
S124
IN-LINE DIODE M
S511
UY S121
IN-LINE DIODE N
IN-LINE DIODE P
C219
LOW COOLANT SPEED FAN SWITCH
Radiator coolant fan control
HOT RESTART CONTROL UNIT Solid-state: Do not measure resistance.
C525
FUEL ECU Solid-state: Do not measure resistance.
S510
A/C HIGH PRESSURE SWITCH Closed with A/C refrigerant pressure above 20.5 Kgf/cm2
C220
S202
G200

Coolant fan wiring schematic—Sterling

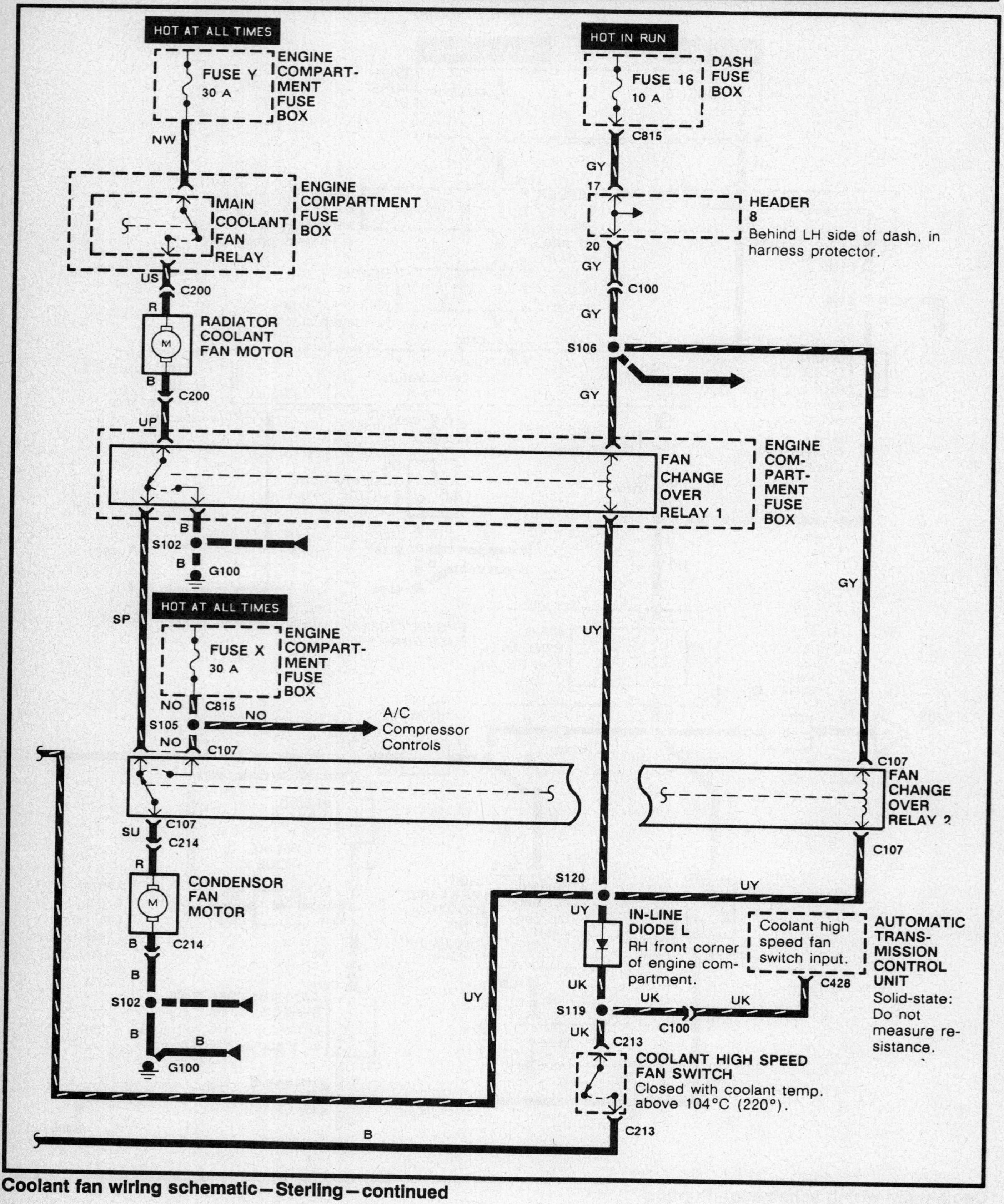
HOT AT ALL TIMES
FUSE Y
30 A
ENGINE COMPARTMENT FUSE BOX
NW
ENGINE COMPARTMENT FUSE BOX
MAIN COOLANT FAN RELAY
US
C200
R
RADIATOR COOLANT FAN MOTOR
B
C200
UP
HOT IN RUN
FUSE 16
10 A
DASH FUSE BOX
C815
GY
17
HEADER 8
Behind LH side of dash, in harness protector.
20
GY
C100
GY
S106
GY
FAN CHANGE OVER RELAY 1
ENGINE COMPARTMENT FUSE BOX
B
S102
B
G100
SP
HOT AT ALL TIMES
FUSE X
30 A
ENGINE COMPARTMENT FUSE BOX
NO
C815
NO
S105
A/C Compressor Controls
NO
C107
UY
GY
C107
FAN CHANGE OVER RELAY 2
C107
SU
C107
C214
R
CONDENSOR FAN MOTOR
B
C214
B
S102
B
B
G100
S120
UY
UY
IN-LINE DIODE L
RH front corner of engine compartment.
UK
Coolant high speed fan switch input.
AUTOMATIC TRANSMISSION CONTROL UNIT
Solid-state: Do not measure resistance.
C428
UY
UK
UK
S119
C100
UK
C213
COOLANT HIGH SPEED FAN SWITCH
Closed with coolant temp. above 104°C (220°).
C213
B

Coolant fan wiring schematic—Sterling—continued

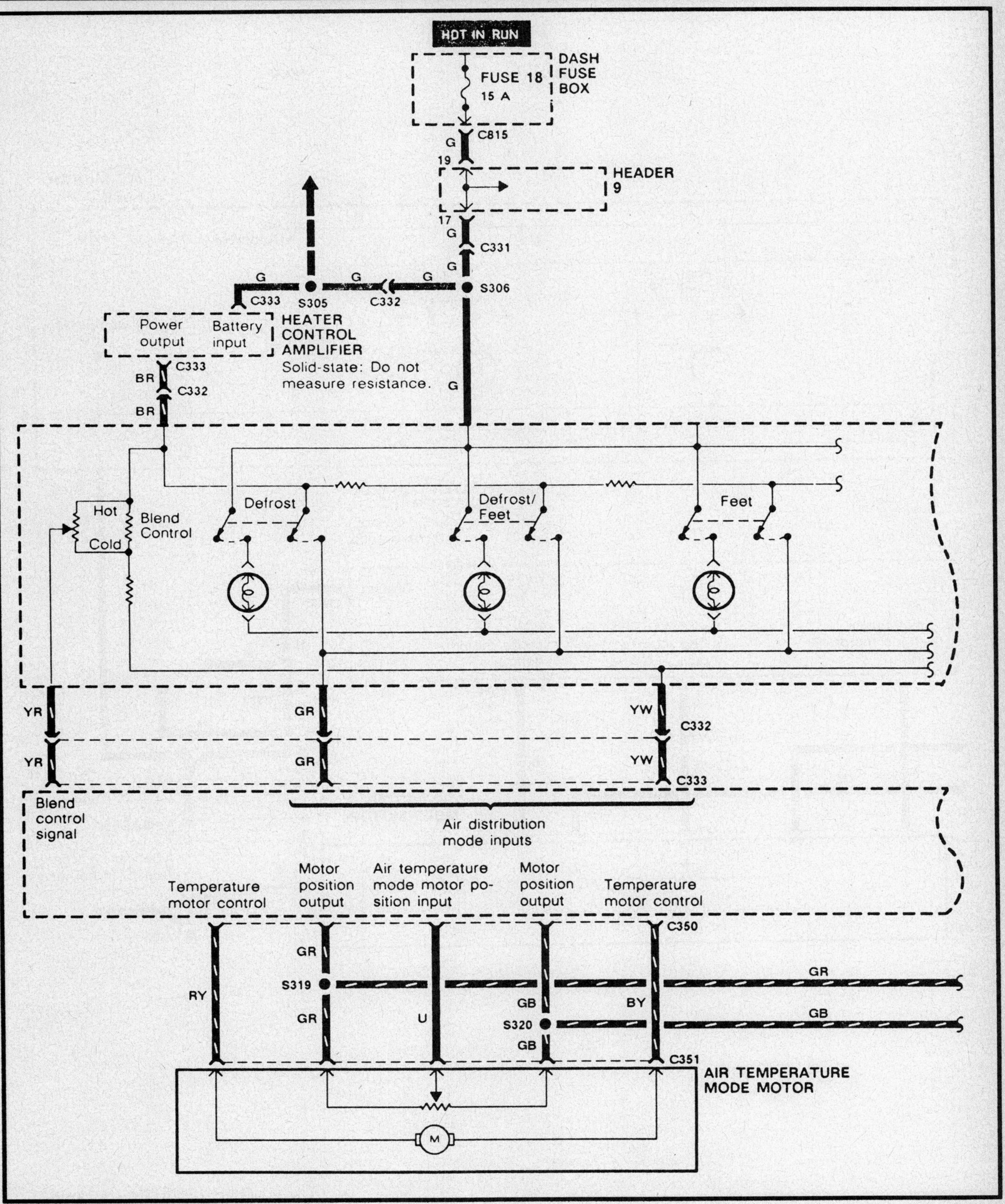
HOT IN RUN
FUSE 18
15 A
DASH FUSE BOX
G
C815
19
HEADER 9
17
G
C331
G
S306
G
G
G
C333
S305
C332
Power output
Battery input
HEATER CONTROL AMPLIFIER
Solid-state: Do not measure resistance.
G
BR
C333
C332
BR
Hot
Cold
Blend Control
Defrost
Defrost/ Feet
Feet
YR
YR
GR
GR
YW
YW
C332
C333
Blend control signal
Air distribution mode inputs
Temperature motor control
Motor position output
Air temperature mode motor position input
Motor position output
Temperature motor control
C350
GR
S319
GR
RY
U
GB
S320
GB
BY
GR
GB
C351
AIR TEMPERATURE MODE MOTOR
M

Air delivery wiring schematic—Sterling

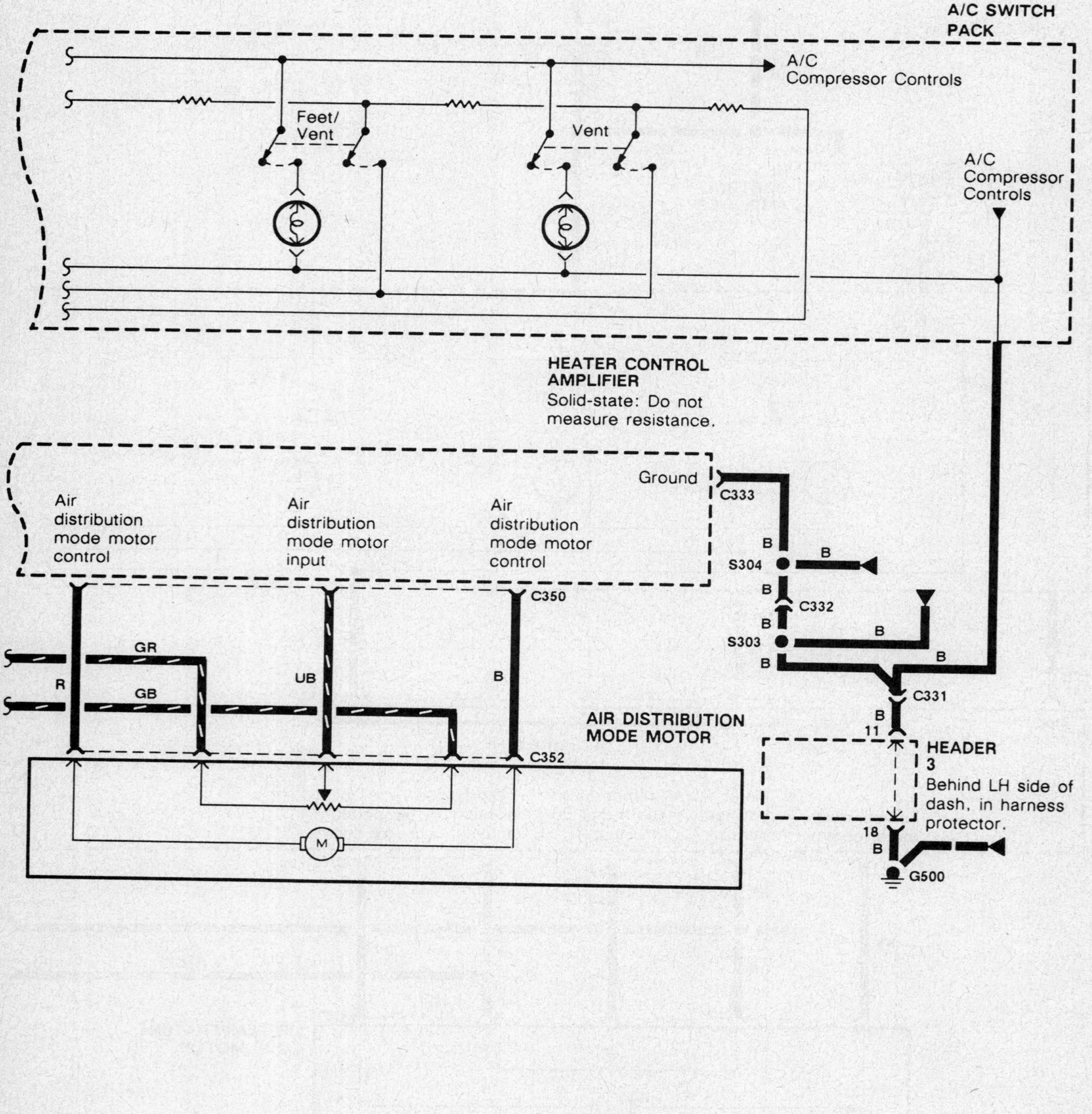
A/C SWITCH PACK
A/C Compressor Controls
Feet/ Vent
Vent
A/C Compressor Controls
HEATER CONTROL AMPLIFIER
Solid-state: Do not measure resistance.
Ground
C333
Air distribution mode motor control
Air distribution mode motor input
Air distribution mode motor control
B
S304
B
B
C332
B
S303
B
B
B
C350
GR
R
GB
UB
B
C331
B
11
AIR DISTRIBUTION MODE MOTOR
C352
HEADER 3
Behind LH side of dash, in harness protector.
18
B
G500
M

Air delivery wiring schematic – Sterling – continued

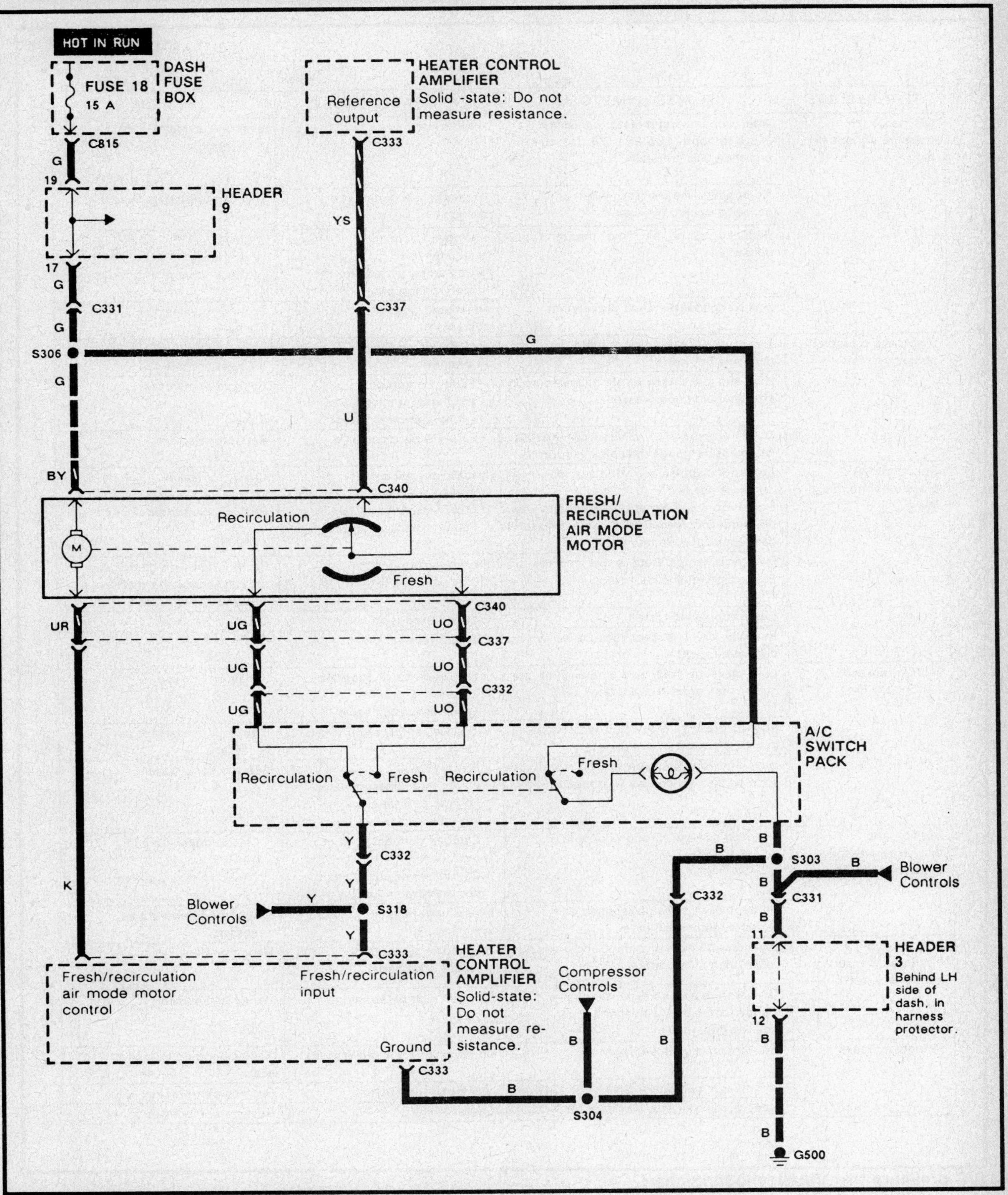
HOT IN RUN
FUSE 18
15 A
DASH FUSE BOX
C815
G
19
HEADER 9
17
G
C331
G
S306
G
BY
HEATER CONTROL AMPLIFIER
Solid -state: Do not measure resistance.
Reference output
C333
YS
C337
U
C340
FRESH/ RECIRCULATION AIR MODE MOTOR
Recirculation
M
Fresh
UR
UG
UO
C340
C337
C332
A/C SWITCH PACK
Recirculation
Fresh
Recirculation
Fresh
Y
C332
Y
Blower Controls
S318
C333
K
HEATER CONTROL AMPLIFIER
Solid-state: Do not measure re- sistance.
Fresh/recirculation air mode motor control
Fresh/recirculation input
Ground
C333
B
S304
Compressor Controls
B
C332
S303
Blower Controls
C331
11
HEADER 3
Behind LH side of dash, in harness protector.
12
G500

Air delivery wiring schematic—Sterling—continued

TEST RESULTS	RELATED SYMPTOMS	PROBABLE CAUSE	REMEDY
Discharge (high) pressure abnormally high	After stopping compressor, pressure drops to about 196 kPa (28 psi) quickly, and then falls gradually	Air in system	Evacuate system; then recharge
	No bubbles in sight glass when condenser is cooled by water	Excessive refrigerant in system	Discharge refrigerant as required
	Reduced or no air flow through condenser.	· Clogged condenser or radiater fins · Condenser or radiator fan not working properly	· Clean · Check voltage and fan rpm
	Line to condenser is excessively hot	Restricted flow of refrigerant in system	Expansion valve
Discharge pressure abnormally low	Excessive bubbles in sight glass; condenser is not hot	Insufficient refrigerant in system	· Charge system · Check for leak
	High and low pressures are balanced soon after stopping compressor	· Faulty compressor discharge or inlet valve · Faulty compressor seal	Replace compressor Repair
	Outlet of expansion valve is not frosted, low pressure gauge indicates vacuum	· Faulty expansion valve	Repair or Replace
Suction (low) pressure abnormally low	Excessive bubbles in sight glass; condenser is not hot Expansion valve is not frosted and low pressure line is not cold. Low pressure gauge indicates vacuum.	Insufficient refrigerant · Frozen expansion valve · Faulty expansion valve	Check for leaks. Charge as required. Replace expansion valve
	Discharge temperature is low and the air flow from vents is restricted	Frozen evaporator	Run the fan with compressor off then check the thermostat and capillary tube.
	Expansion valve frosted	Clogged expansion valve	Clean or Replace
	Receiver dryer is cool (should be warm during opration)	Clogged receiver dryer	Replace
Suction pressure abnormally high	Low pressure hose and check joint are cooler than around evaporator	· Expansion valve open too long · Loose expansion valve	Repair or Replace
	Suction pressure is lowered when condenser is cooled by water	Excessive refrigerant in system	Discharge refrigerant as necessary
	High and low pressure are equalized as soon as the compressor is stopped	· Faulty gasket · Faulty high pressure valve · Foreign particle stuck in high pressure valve	Replace compressor
Suction and discharge pressures abnormally high	Reduced air flow through condenser	· Clogged condenser or radiator fins · Condenser or radiator fan not working properly	· Clean condenser and radiator · Check voltage and fan rpm
	No bubbles in sight glass when condenser is cooled by water	Excessive refrigerant in system	Discharge refrigerant as necessary.
Suction and discharge pressure abnormally low	Low pressure hose and metal end areas are cooler than evaporator	Clogged or kinked low pressure hose parts	Repair or Replace
	Temperature around expansion valve is too low compared with that around receiver-driver.	Clogged high pressure line	Repair or Replace
Refrigerant leaks	Compressor clutch is dirty	Compressor shaft seal leaking	Replace compressor shaft seal
	Compressor bolt(s) are dirty	Leaking around bolt(s)	Replace compressor
	Compressor gasket is wet with oil	Gasket leaking	Replace compressor

A/C pressure test troubleshooting chart

13 BMW 13

3-SERIES • 5-SERIES • 6-SERIES • 7-SERIES

SPECIFICATIONS

ENGINE IDENTIFICATION

Year	Model	Engine Displacement cu. in. (cc/liter)	Engine Series Identification	No. of Cylinders	Engine Type
1989	325	165 (2693/2.7)	M20B27	6	OHC
	325i	152 (2494/2.5)	M20B25	6	OHC
	325iS	152 (2494/2.5)	M20B25	6	OHC
	325iX	152 (2494/2.5)	M20B25	6	OHC
	525	152 (2494/2.5)	M20B25	6	OHC
	535i	209 (3428/3.4)	M30B34	6	OHC
	635CSi	209 (3428/3.4)	M30B35MZ	6	OHC
	L6	209 (3428/3.4)	M30B35MZ	6	OHC
	735i	209 (3428/3.4)	M30B35MZ	6	OHC
	735iL	209 (3428/3.4)	M30B35MZ	6	OHC
	M3	140.4 (2302/2.3)	S14B23	4	DOHC
	M5	210.6 (3453/3.5)	S38Z	6	DOHC
	M6	210.6 (3453/3.5)	S38Z	6	DOHC
	750iL	304.4 (4988/5.0)	M70B50M	12	OHC
1990	318i	109.6 (1796/1.8)	M42	4	OHC
	318iS	109.6 (1796/1.8)	M42	4	OHC
	325i	152 (2494/2.5)	M20B25	6	OHC
	325iS	152 (2494/2.5)	M20B25	6	OHC
	325iX	152 (2494/2.5)	M20B25	6	OHC
	M3	140 (2302/2.3)	S14B23	4	DOHC
	525i	152 (2494/2.5)	M30B25L	6	OHC
	535i	209 (3430/3.5)	M30B35M	6	OHC
	M5	216 (3535/3.6)	S38Z	6	DOHC
	735i	209 (3430/3.5)	M30B35M	6	OHC
	735iL	209 (3430/3.5)	M30B35M	6	OHC
	750iL	304 (4988/5.0)	M70B50M	12	OHC
	850i	304 (4988/5.0)	M70B50M	12	OHC
1991	318i	110 (1796/1.8)	M42	4	DOHC
	318iS	110 (1796/1.8)	M42	4	DOHC
	325i	152 (2494/2.5)	M20B25	6	OHC
	325iX	152 (2494/2.5)	M20B25	6	OHC
	M3	140 (2302/2.3)	S14B23	4	DOHC
	525i	152 (2494/2.5)	M30B25L	6	DOHC
	535i	209 (3430/3.5)	M30B35M	6	OHC
	M5	216 (3535/3.6)	S38Z	6	DOHC
	735i	209 (3430/3.5)	M30B35M	6	OHC
	735iL	209 (3430/3.5)	M30B35M	6	OHC
	750iL	304 (4988/5.0)	M70B50M	12	OHC
	850i	304 (4988/5.0)	M70B50M	12	OHC

OHC—Overhead Cam
DOHC—Dual Overhead Cam

REFRIGERANT CAPACITIES

Year	Model	Freon (oz.)	Oil (fl. oz.)	Refrigerant Type
1989	325	33–35	②	R-12
	325i	33–35	②	R-12
	325iS	33–35	②	R-12
	325iX	33–35	②	R-12
	M3	30–32	②	R-12
	525	52–54 ①	②	R-12
	535i	52–54 ①	②	R-12
	M5	52–54 ①	②	R-12
	635CSi	39	②	R-12
	L6	39	②	R-12
	M6	39	②	R-12
	735i	52–54 ①	②	R-12
	735iL	52–54 ①	②	R-12
	750iL	52–54 ①	②	R-12
1990	318i	33–35	②	R-12
	318iS	33–35	②	R-12
	325i	33–35	②	R-12
	325iS	33–35	②	R-12
	325iX	33–35	②	R-12
	M3	30–32	②	R-12
	525i	52–54 ①	②	R-12
	535i	52–54 ①	②	R-12
	M5	52–54 ①	②	R-12
	735i	52–54 ①	②	R-12
	735iL	52–54 ①	②	R-12
	750iL	52–54 ①	②	R-12
	850i	52–54 ①	②	R-12
1991	318i	33–35	②	R-12
	318iS	33–35	②	R-12
	325i	33–35	②	R-12
	325iX	33–35	②	R-12
	M3	30–32	②	R-12
	525i	52–54 ①	②	R-12
	535i	52–54 ①	②	R-12
	M5	52–54 ①	②	R-12
	735i	52–54 ①	②	R-12
	735iL	52–54 ①	②	R-12
	750iL	52–54 ①	②	R-12
	850i	52–54 ①	②	R-12

① With 22.5 in. wide condenser 67–69 oz.
② Vane Type Compressor—6.7 fl. oz.
Swash Plate Type Compressor—10.1 fl. oz.

AIR CONDITIONING BELT TENSION CHART

Year	Model	Engine Displacement cu. in. (cc/liter)	Belt Type	New	Used
1989	325	165 (2693/2.7)	V-belt	①	①
	325i	152 (2494/2.5)	V-belt	①	①
	325iS	152 (2494/2.5)	V-belt	①	①
	325iX	152 (2494/2.5)	V-belt	①	①
	M3	140 (3202/2.3)	V-belt	①	①
	525	152 (2494/2.5)	V-belt	①	①
	535i	209 (3428/3.4)	V-belt	①	①
	M5	210 (3453/3.5)	V-belt	①	①
	635CSi	209 (3428/3.4)	V-belt	①	①
	L6	209 (3428/3.4)	V-belt	①	①
	M6	210 (3453/3.5)	V-belt	①	①
	735i	209 (3428/3.4)	Ribbed	②	②
	735iL	209 (3428/3.4)	Ribbed	②	②
	750iL	304 (4988/5.0)	Ribbed	②	②
1990	318i	109.6 (1796/1.8)	V-belt	①	①
	318iS	109.6 (1796/1.8)	V-belt	①	①
	325i	152 (2494/2.5)	V-belt	①	①
	325iS	152 (2494/2.5)	V-belt	①	①
	325iX	152 (2494/2.5)	V-belt	①	①
	M3	140 (3202/2.3)	V-belt	①	①
	525i	152 (2494/2.5)	V-belt	①	①
	535i	209 (3430/3.5)	V-belt	①	①
	M5	216 (3435/3.6)	V-belt	①	①
	735i	209 (3430/3.5)	Ribbed	②	②
	735iL	209 (3430/3.5)	Ribbed	②	②
	750iL	304 (4988/5.0)	Ribbed	②	②
	850i	304 (4988/5.0)	Ribbed	②	②
1991	318i	110 (1796/1.8)	V-belt	①	①
	318iS	110 (1796/1.8)	V-belt	①	①
	325i	152 (2494/2.5)	V-belt	①	①
	325iX	152 (2494/2.5)	V-belt	①	①
	M3	140 (3202/2.3)	V-belt	①	①
	525i	152 (2494/2.5)	V-belt	①	①
	535i	209 (3430/3.5)	V-belt	①	①
	M5	216 (3535/3.6)	V-belt	①	①
	735i	209 (3430/3.5)	Ribbed	②	②
	735iL	209 (3430/3.5)	Ribbed	②	②
	750iL	304 (4988/5.0)	Ribbed	②	②
	850i	304 (4988/5.0)	Ribbed	②	②

① Use the standard deflection method to adjust. The belt should deflect no more than 1/2 in., under moderate pressure, at the longest span between 2 pulleys.
② Automatic belt tensioning

SYSTEM DESCRIPTION

General Information

The heating system is an air side controlled unit, where the temperature is regulated by the mixing of cold and warm air using a mixing flap. All outlets can be heated using cable operated flaps. The water flow rate through the heater is regulated by an electromagnetic water valve in the water return circuit. The water valve is switched on and off by the temperature control. The valve will be closed when the temperature is set to less than 68°F. The valve is open without electric power.

With air conditioning the refrigerant is injected through an expansion valve, which is located in the right side of the housing. The system uses a mechanical thermostatic switch, located on the left side of the air conditioning/heater housing, which prevents the system from freezing.

The control flaps are located in front of both of the blower motors and are controlled by 2 positioning motors.

As part of the air conditioning system, a 2 speed auxiliary fan is included, to aid in system cooling. The fan always runs in the first speed, when the air conditioning is switched on. Regardless of air conditioner operation, the first speed of the auxiliary fan, is switched on when the coolant temperature is 192–199°F, as determined by the coolant temperature sensor. The fan is switched off at a coolant temperature of 180–187°F.

The second speed of the auxiliary fan, regardless of air conditioner operation, is activated at a coolant temperature range of 207–214°F. It is turned off at a coolant temperature of 194–201°F.

The system is equipped with both a high and low pressure cutoff switch, located at the receiver/drier. The high pressure switch stops the compressor when the refrigerant pressure reaches 252–363 psi. and switches the compressor back on when the pressure drops to 284–320 psi. The low pressure switch stops the compressor when the refrigerant pressure drops to 24–32 psi. and switches the compressor on when the pressure rises to 28–34 psi.

System Controls

All vehicles can be equipped with either an manual or automatic climate control system. The manual system is controlled by a combination of button, slide and rotary controls. The automatic system is controlled by a combination of rotary dials and push buttons.

5, 6, 7 and 8 Series vehicles equipped with automatic climate control also have a separate control for the passenger compartment. This control operates independent of the main control head. 6 Series vehicles also have separate controls for the rear passenger compartment.

As an option 5, 7 and 8 Series vehicles have an extra ventilation system. This system can be programmed to vent the passenger compartment when the vehicle is parked. The ventilation is controlled by a timer in conjunction with the automatic climate control system. It shares components with the climate control system in addition to it's own timer and relays. It operates the blower at low speed and controls the position of the vent flaps, all dependent on interior temperature.

Service Valve Location

The service valves for both the high and low pressure sides of the air conditioning system, are located in the pressure lines. They can be either at the compressor or the drier. The thinner of the 2 pressure lines is the high pressure side.

System Discharging

R-12 refrigerant is a chloroflourocarbon which, when mishandled, can contribute to the depletion of the ozone layer in the upper atmosphere. Ozone filters out harmful radiation from the sun. In order to protect the ozone layer, an approved R-12 Recovery/Recycling machine that meets SAE standard J1991 should be employed when discharging the system. Follow the operating instructions provided with the approved equipment exactly to properly discharge the system.

System Evacuating

If the air conditioning system has been opened to the atmosphere, it should be air and moisture free before being recharged with refrigerant. Moisture and air mixed with refrigerant will raise the compressor head pressure, possibly damaging the system's components and will reduce the performance of the system. Moisture will boil at normal room temperature when exposed to a vacuum. To evacuate or rid the system of air and moisture, perform the following procedure:

1. Leak test the system and repair any leaks found.
2. Connect an approved charging station, Recovery/Recycling machine or manifold gauge set and vacuum pump to the discharge and suction ports. The red hose is normally connected to the discharge (high pressure) line and the blue hose is connected to the suction (low pressure) line.
3. Open the discharge and suction ports and start the vacuum pump. If the pump is not able to pull at least 26 in. Hg vacuum, there is a leak that must be repaired before evacuation can occur.
4. Once the system has reached at least 26 in. Hg vacuum, allow the system to evacuate for at least 15 minutes. The longer the system is evacuated, the more contaminants will be removed.
5. Close all valves and turn the pump off. If the system loses more than 2 in. Hg vacuum after 15 minutes, there is a leak that should be repaired.

System Charging

1. Connect an approved charging station, Recovery/Recycling machine or manifold gauge set to the discharge and suction ports. The red hose is normally connected to the discharge (high pressure) line and the blue hose is connected to the suction (low pressure) line.
2. Follow the instructions provided with the equipment and charge the system with the specified amount of refrigerant.
3. Perform a leak test.

SYSTEM COMPONENTS

Radiator

REMOVAL AND INSTALLATION

1. Disconnect the negative battery cable. Drain the cooling system. On some engines, this requires removing the plug from the bottom radiator tank.
2. If equipped with a coolant expansion tank, remove the cap, disconnect the hose at the radiator and drain the coolant into a clean container. If equipped with a splash guard, remove it.
3. Remove the coolant hoses and disconnect the automatic transmission oil cooler lines and plug their openings as well as the openings in the cooler.
4. Disconnect any of the temperature switch wire connectors.
5. Remove the shroud from the radiator. On some vehicles, this is done by simply pressing the release tabs toward the rear of the vehicle. On others, there are metal slips that must be pulled upward and off to free the shroud from the radiator. The shroud will remain in the vehicle, resting on the fan on most vehicles. On the 7 and 8 Series, remove the fan and shroud together. Make sure to store the fan in a vertical position. The fan must be held stationary with some sort of flat blade cut to fit over the hub and drilled to fit over 2 of the studs on the front of the pulley. Then, unscrew the retaining nut at the center of the fluid drive hub turning it clockwise to remove, because it has left hand threads.
6. If equipped with the M30 B35 engine, remove the fan and shroud; then, spread the retaining clip and pull the oil cooler out to the right. Remove the radiator retaining bolt(s) and lift the radiator from the vehicle.
7. The radiator is installed in the reverse order of removal. Fill and bleed the cooling system.

NOTE: On the M3, there are rubber washers that go on either side of the mounting brackets at the top and the bottom of the unit is suspended by rubber bushings into which prongs located on the bottom tank will fit. Make sure all parts fit right when the unit is installed.

8. Check that rubber mounts are located so as to effectively isolate the radiator from the chassis, as this will help ensure reliable radiator performance. If the vehicle uses plastic upper and lower radiator tanks and has a radiator drain plug, be careful not to over torque the plugs.
9. Torque engine oil cooler pipes to 18–21 ft. lbs. and transmission cooler pipes to 13–15 ft. lbs.
10. Torque the thermostatic fan hub on the 7 and 8 Series to 29–36 ft. lbs.

Bleeder screw location—5, 6 and 7 Series

COOLING SYSTEM BLEEDING

With Bleeder Screw on Thermostat Housing

Set the heat valve in the **WARM** position, start the engine and bring it to normal operating temperature. Run the engine at fast idle and open the venting screw on the thermostat housing until the coolant comes out free of air bubbles. Close the bleeder screw and refill the cooling system.

Without Bleeder Screw

Fill the cooling system, place the heater valve in the **WARM** position, close the pressure cap to the second (fully closed) position. Start the engine and bring to normal operating temperature. Carefully release the pressure cap to the first position and squeeze the upper and lower radiator hoses in a pumping action to allow trapped air to escape through the radiator. Recheck the coolant level and close the pressure cap to its second position.

Electric Cooling Fan

TESTING

CAUTION

Make sure the key is in the OFF position when checking the electric cooling fan. If not, the fan could turn ON at any time, causing serious personal injury.

1. Disconnect the negative battery cable. Unplug the fan connector.
2. Using a jumper wire, connect the female terminal of the fan connector to the negative battery terminal.
3. The fan should turn on when the male terminal is connected to the positive battery terminal.
4. If not, the fan is defective and should be replaced.

REMOVAL AND INSTALLATION

1. Disconnect the negative battery cable.
2. Remove the bolts retaining the center front grille.
3. Remove the center grille.
4. Raise and safely support the vehicle, remove the splash shield.
5. Disconnect the cooling fan connector through the grille opening.
6. Lower the vehicle slightly and remove the fan assembly mounting bolts.
7. Lower the fan assembly from the vehicle.
8. Installation is the reverse of the removal procedure. After installation, check the operation of the cooling fan.

Condenser

REMOVAL AND INSTALLATION

1. Disconnect the negative battery cable.
2. Properly discharge the air conditioning system.
3. Drain the cooling system. Remove the radiator from the vehicle.
4. Remove the bolts retaining the right and center grille, remove the grilles.
5. Disconnect and plug the refrigerant lines at the condenser, through the right side grille opening.
6. Disconnect the auxiliary cooling fan connector. Remove the cooling fan from the condenser.
7. Remove the condenser mounting bolts and remove the condenser upward.

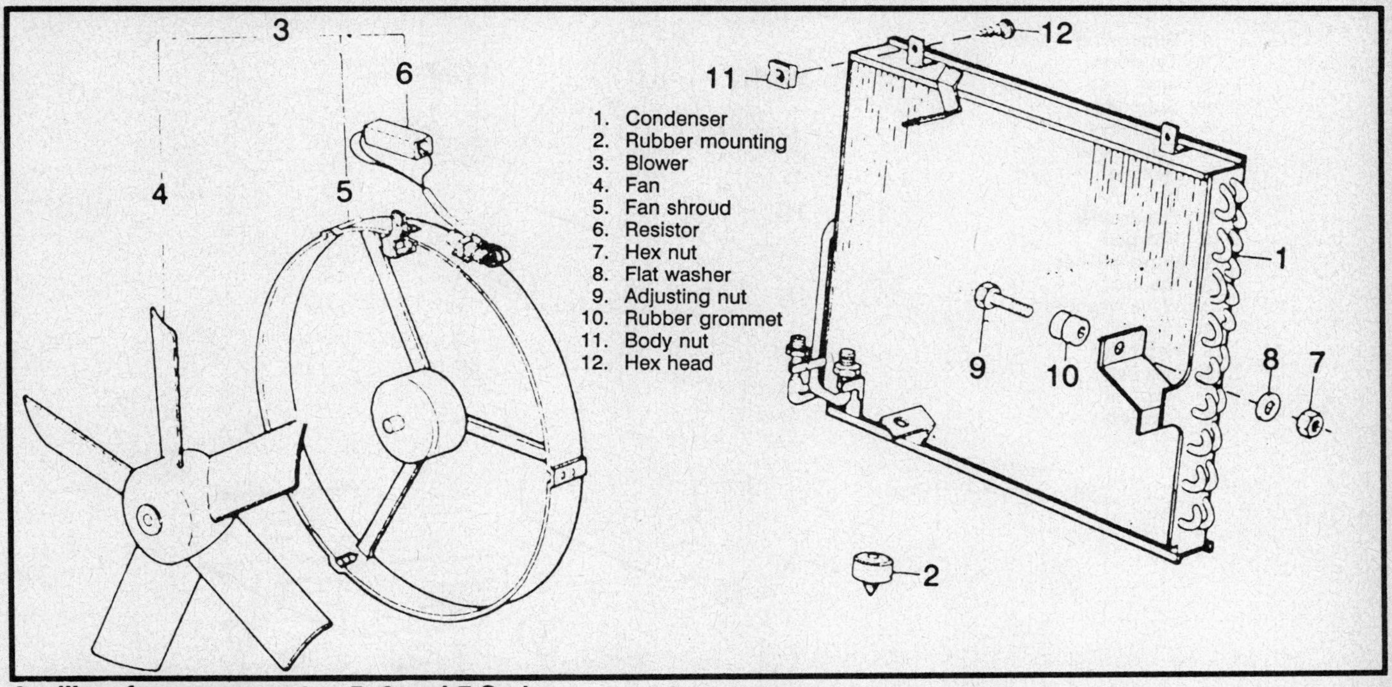
1. Condenser
2. Rubber mounting
3. Blower
4. Fan
5. Fan shroud
6. Resistor
7. Hex nut
8. Flat washer
9. Adjusting nut
10. Rubber grommet
11. Body nut
12. Hex head

Auxiliary fan components—5, 6 and 7 Series

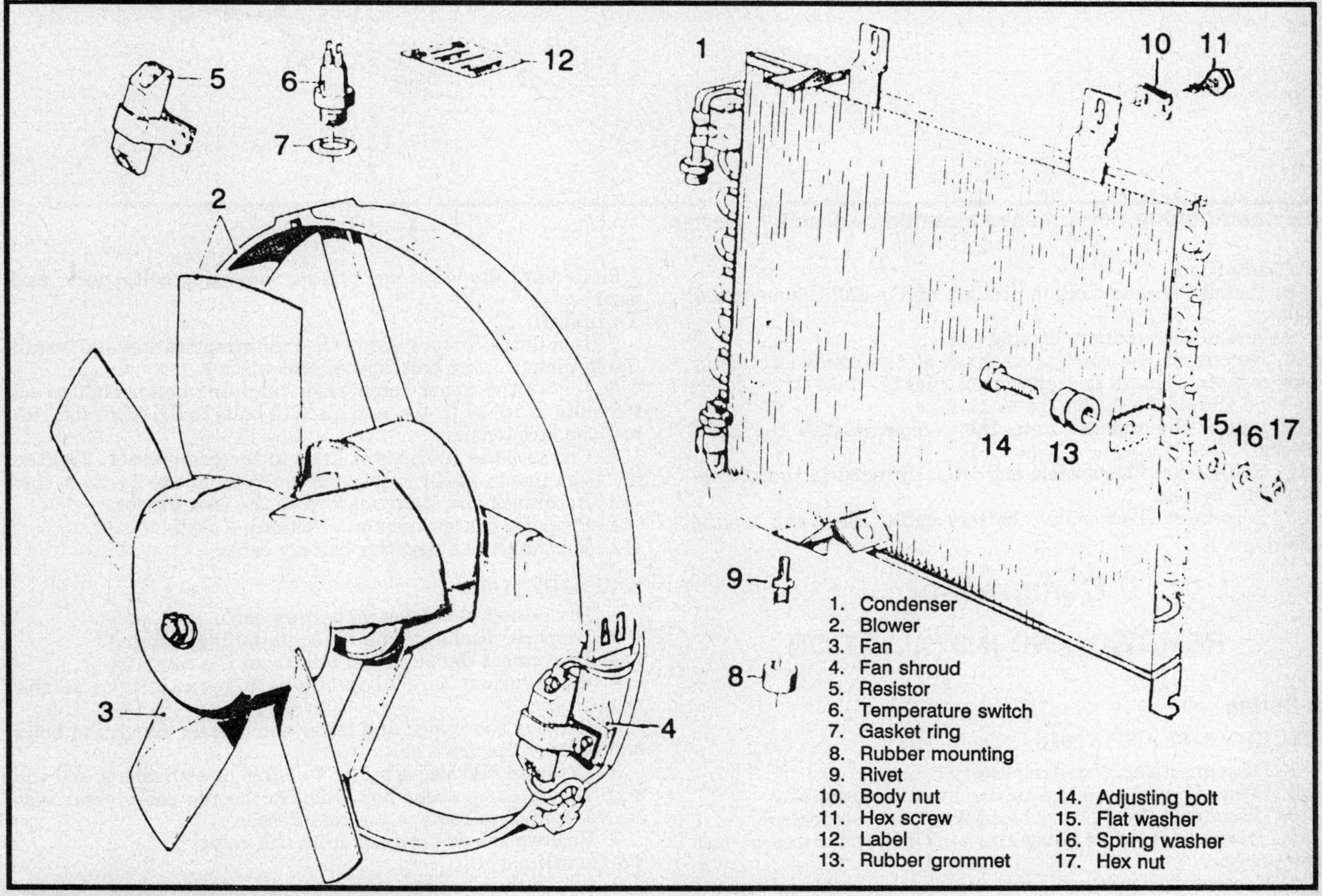
1. Condenser
2. Blower
3. Fan
4. Fan shroud
5. Resistor
6. Temperature switch
7. Gasket ring
8. Rubber mounting
9. Rivet
10. Body nut
11. Hex screw
12. Label
13. Rubber grommet
14. Adjusting bolt
15. Flat washer
16. Spring washer
17. Hex nut

Auxiliary fan components—3 Series

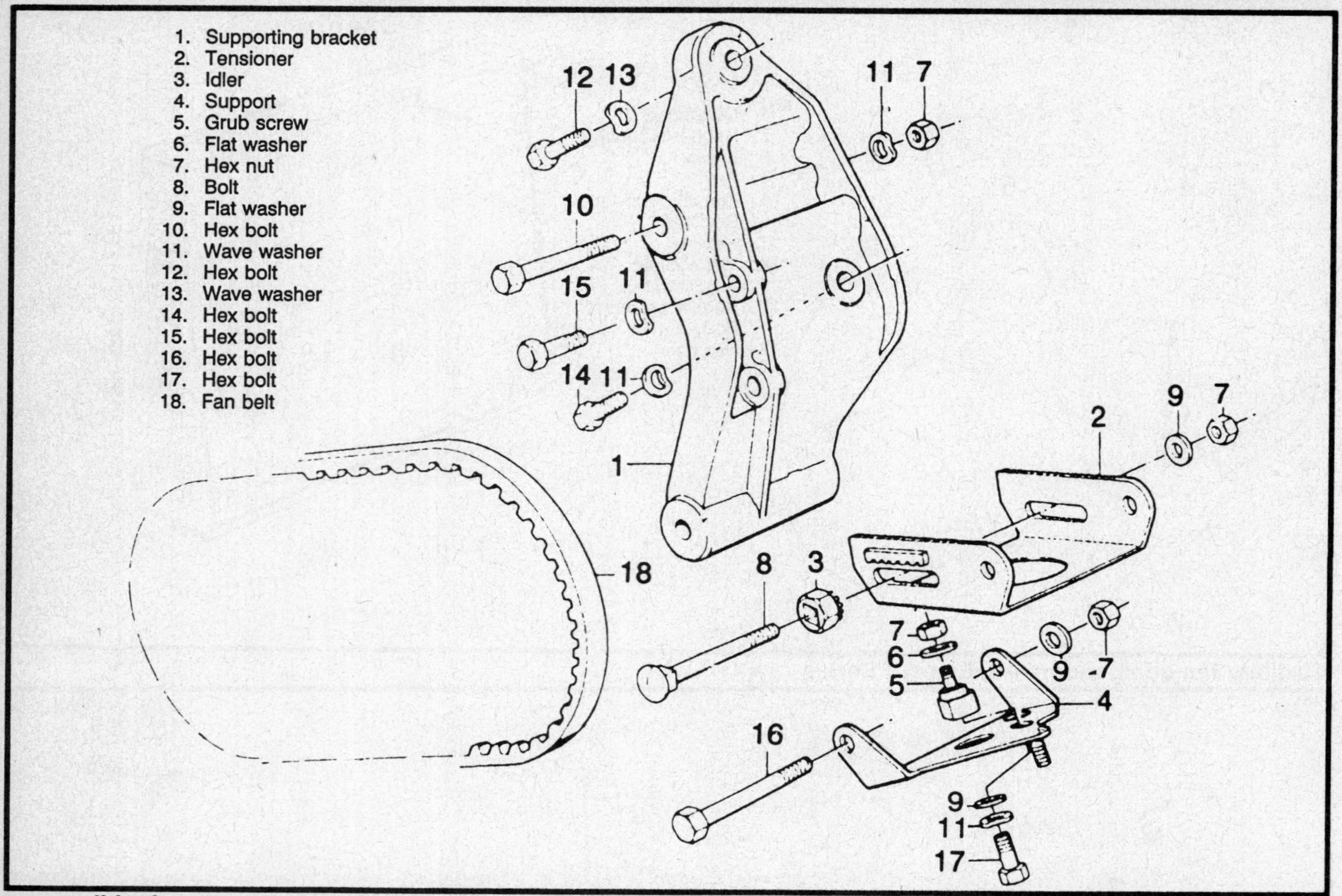
1. Supporting bracket
2. Tensioner
3. Idler
4. Support
5. Grub screw
6. Flat washer
7. Hex nut
8. Bolt
9. Flat washer
10. Hex bolt
11. Wave washer
12. Hex bolt
13. Wave washer
14. Hex bolt
15. Hex bolt
16. Hex bolt
17. Hex bolt
18. Fan belt

Air conditioning compressor mounting—5 and 7 Series

To install:

8. Install the condenser in position and install the mounting bolts.
9. Install the auxiliary cooling fan.
10. Reconnect the refrigerant lines at the condenser, using new gaskets. Tighten the refrigerant lines to 10–14 ft. lbs. for ⅝ in. pipe and 24–28 ft. lbs. for ¾ in. pipe.
11. Install the radiator into the vehicle. Install the grille pieces.
12. Refill the cooling system and properly recharge the air conditioning system.
13. Reconnect the negative battery cable. Bleed the cooling system.

Compressor

REMOVAL AND INSTALLATION

3 Series

EXCEPT 318I AND 318IS

1. Disconnect the negative battery cable.
2. Properly discharge the air conditioning system.
3. Disconnect the electrical lead from the compressor.
4. Disconnect and plug the refrigerant lines at the compressor.
5. Remove the upper compressor mounting bolts and remove the drive belt.
6. Remove the lower compressor mounting bolt, spacer and washer.

To install:

7. Install the compressor in the mounting bracket and install the lower retaining bolt, spacer and washer.
8. Install the upper compressor retaining bolts. Tighten all M8 bolts to 16–17 ft. lbs. and all M10 bolts to 31–35 ft. lbs. Adjust the belt tension.
9. Connect the refrigerant lines to the compressor. Tighten the ⅝ in. line to 10–14 ft. lbs. and the ¾ in. line to 24–28 ft. lbs.
10. Reconnect the electrical lead to the compressor.
11. Properly charge the air conditioning system.
12. Reconnect the negative battery cable.

318I AND 318IS

1. Disconnect the negative battery cable.
2. Properly discharge the air conditioning system.
3. Disconnect the electrical lead from the compressor.
4. Disconnect and plug the refrigerant lines at the compressor.
5. Remove the upper and lower compressor mounting bolts and remove the drive belt.
6. Using special sleeve puller 64 5 070 or equivalent, and the original top compressor bolt, remove the top compressor bolt sleeve enough to remove the compressor.
7. Remove the compressor from the vehicle.

To install:

8. Install the compressor in position and tighten the top compressor bolt sleeve.

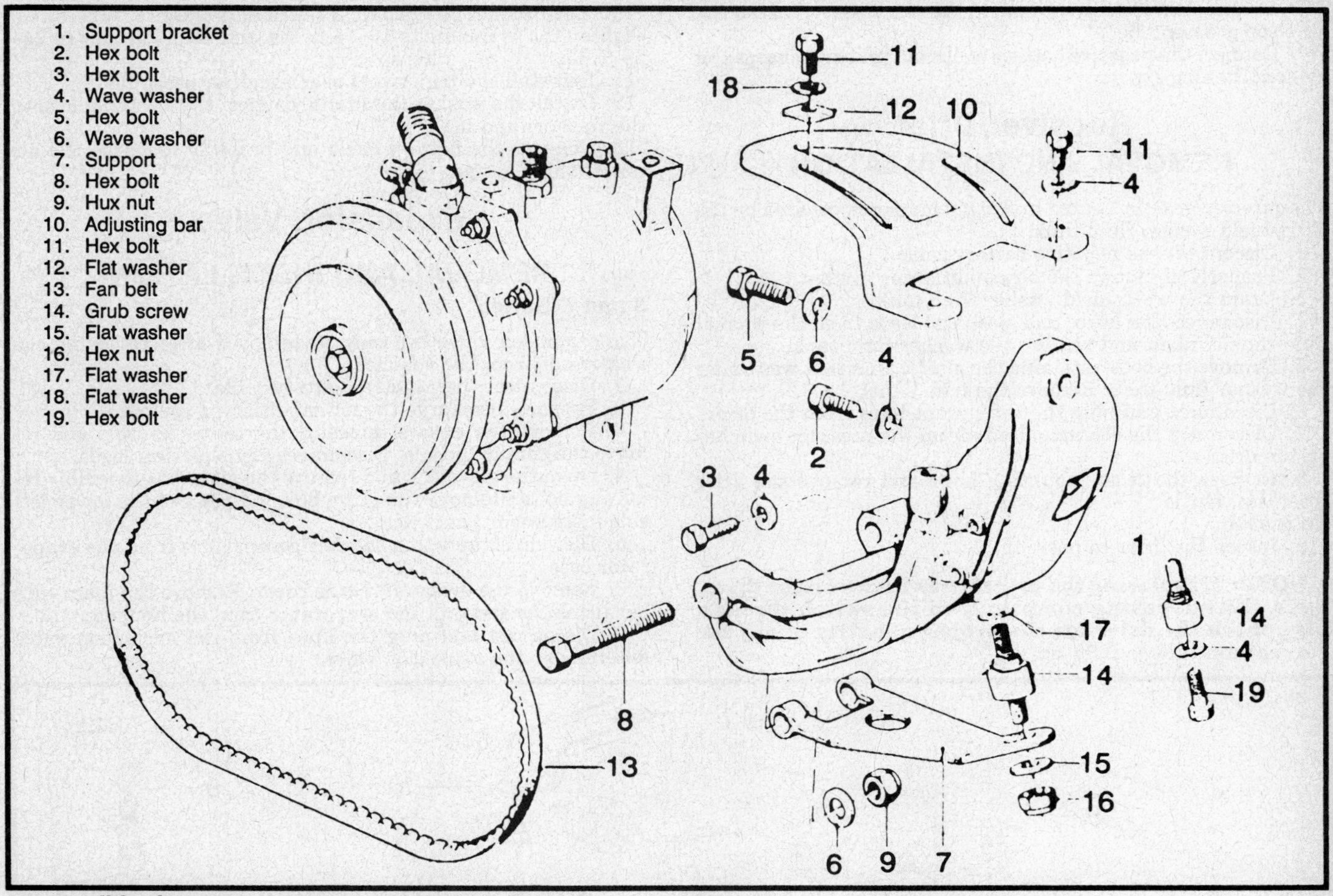
1. Support bracket
2. Hex bolt
3. Hex bolt
4. Wave washer
5. Hex bolt
6. Wave washer
7. Support
8. Hex bolt
9. Hux nut
10. Adjusting bar
11. Hex bolt
12. Flat washer
13. Fan belt
14. Grub screw
15. Flat washer
16. Hex nut
17. Flat washer
18. Flat washer
19. Hex bolt

Air conditioning compressor mounting – 6 Series

9. Install the upper and lower compressor bolts. Tighten all M8 bolts to 16–17 ft. lbs. and all M10 bolts to 31–35 ft. lbs. Adjust the belt tension.
10. Connect the refrigerant lines to the compressor. Tighten the ⅝ in. line to 10–14 ft. lbs. and the ¾ in. line to 24–28 ft. lbs.
11. Reconnect the electrical lead to the compressor. Properly charge the air conditioning system. Check the system operation.

5, 6, 7 and 8 Series

1. Disconnect the negative battery cable.
2. Properly discharge the air conditioning system.
3. Remove the air cleaner inlet hose and remove the air cleaner assembly.
4. Cut the straps retaining the compressor electrical lead and disconnect the lead.
5. Disconnect and plug the refrigerant lines at the compressor.
6. Raise and safely support the vehicle.
7. Remove the bolts retaining the splash shield and remove the splash shield.
8. Loosen the lower compressor mounting and belt tensioner bolts, remove the drive belt from the compressor pulley.
9. Remove the compressor mounting bolts, remove the compressor. On the 6 Series vehicles, remove the upper compressor retaining bolt.

To install:

10. Install the compressor in position under the vehicle and install the retaining bolts.
11. On 6 Series vehicles, install the upper retaining bolt.
12. Install the accessory drive belt and tighten the mounting bolts. Adjust the belt tensioner to the stop and tighten the tensioner bolt. Tighten all M8 bolts to 16–17 ft. lbs. and all M10 bolts to 31–35 ft. lbs.
13. Install the splash shield and lower the vehicle.
14. Connect the refrigerant lines to the compressor. Tighten the ⅝ in. line to 10–14 ft. lbs. and the ¾ in. line to 24–28 ft. lbs.

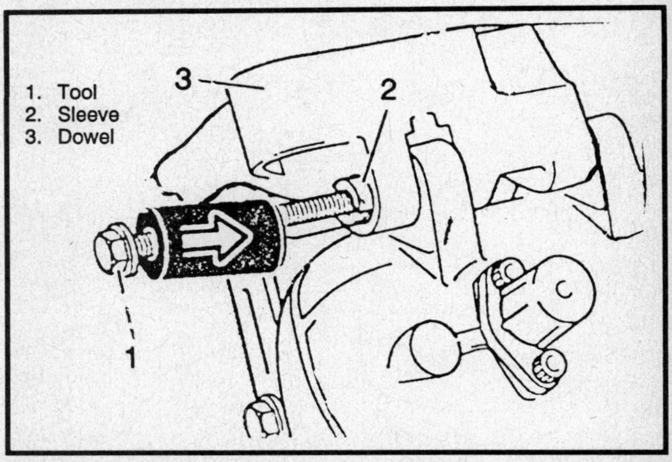
1. Tool
2. Sleeve
3. Dowel

Removing the dowel sleeve from the air conditioning compressor mounting – 3 Series

15. Reconnect the electrical lead to the compressor. Install the air cleaner assembly.
16. Connect the negative battery cable and properly charge the air conditioning system.

Receiver/Drier

REMOVAL AND INSTALLATION

The receiver drier is located under a trim panel, covered by the windshield washer fluid tank.

1. Disconnect the negative battery cable.
2. Properly discharge the air conditioning system.
3. Drain the windshield washer fluid tank.
4. Disconnect the hoses and electrical leads from the washer fluid tank. Unbolt and remove the washer fluid tank.
5. Remove the bolts retaining the plastic trim that was under the washer fluid tank. Remove the trim panel.
6. Disconnect and plug the refrigerant lines from the drier.
7. Disconnect the electrical leads from the pressure switches on the drier.
8. Remove the drier mounting bolts and remove the drier from the vehicle.

To install:

9. Install the drier in position.

NOTE: If replacing the pressure switches on the drier, use a thread locking compound on the switch threads. Also check the drier for the proper quantity of oil, the correct amount is 0.35 oz.

10. Reconnect the electrical leads and the pressure lines. Tighten the ⅝ in. line to 10–14 ft. lbs. and the ¾ in. line to 24–28 ft. lbs.
11. Reinstall the trim panel over the drier assembly.
12. Install the washer fluid tank, connect the electrical lead to the washer fluid tank.
13. Connect the battery cable and properly recharge the air conditioning system.

Expansion Valve

REMOVAL AND INSTALLATION

3 and 6 Series

The expansion valve can only be removed after removing the evaporator from the vehicle.

1. Disconnect the negative battery cable.
2. Properly discharge the air conditioning system.
3. Remove the screws retaining the center console and remove the center console. Disconnect any electrical leads.
4. Open the glove box and remove the glove box assembly retaining bolts. Remove the glove box and remove the lower left side instrument panel trim.
5. Disconnect and plug the refrigerant lines from the evaporator case.
6. Remove the evaporator case cover. Remove the foam rubber insulator and pull the evaporator from the housing.
7. Disconnect and plug the lines from the expansion valve and remove the expansion valve.

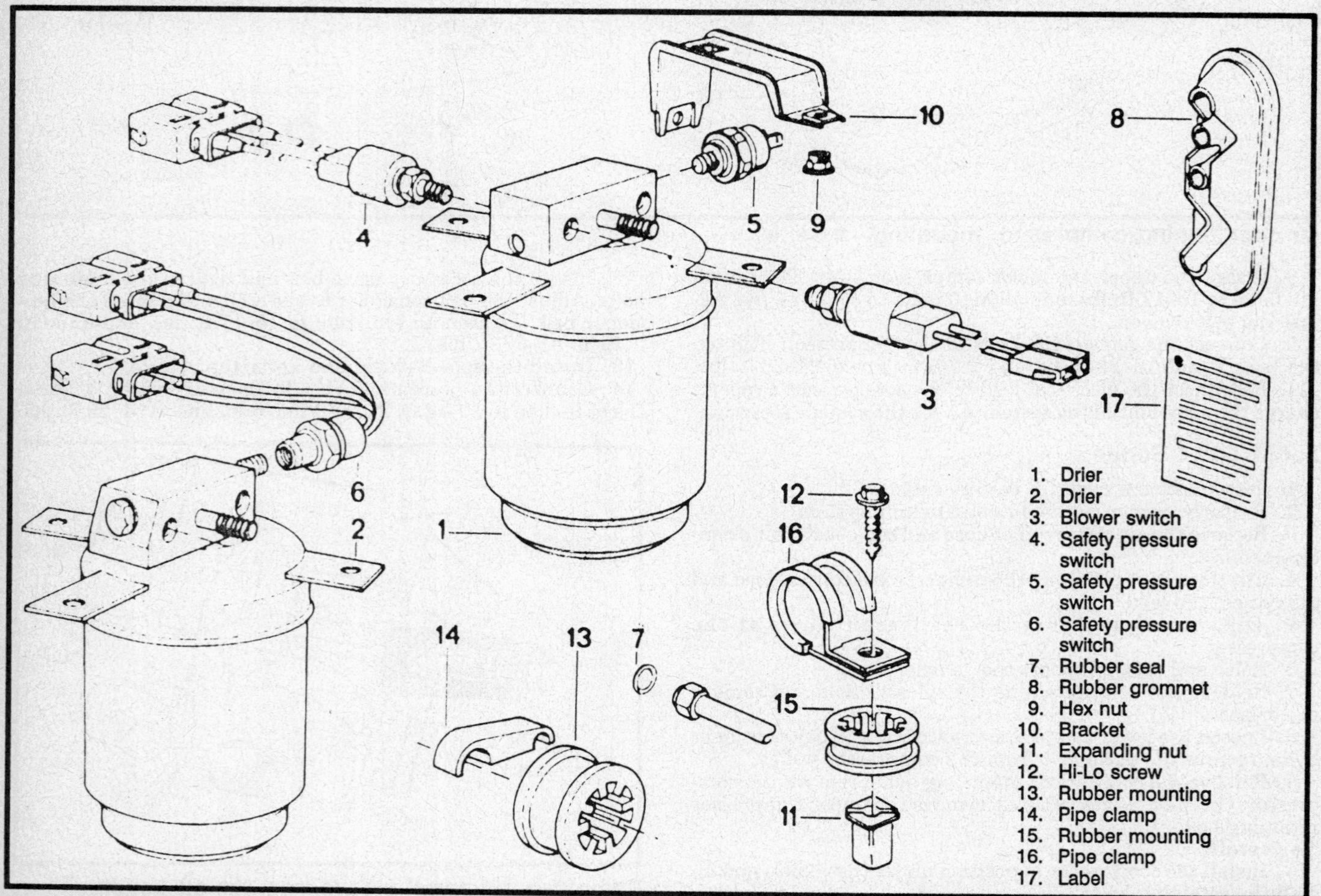
10
8
4
5
9
3
17
6
2
1
12
16
14
13
7
15
11
1. Drier
2. Drier
3. Blower switch
4. Safety pressure switch
5. Safety pressure switch
6. Safety pressure switch
7. Rubber seal
8. Rubber grommet
9. Hex nut
10. Bracket
11. Expanding nut
12. Hi-Lo screw
13. Rubber mounting
14. Pipe clamp
15. Rubber mounting
16. Pipe clamp
17. Label

Receiver/drier components

To install:

8. Install the expansion valve on the evaporator assembly, connecting the refrigerant lines. Tighten the ⅝ in. line to 10–14 ft. lbs. and the ¾ in. line to 24–28 ft. lbs.

NOTE: Before installing the evaporator into the housing, make sure the fins on the evaporator are not bent. If any fins are bent, use a fin comb or equivalent, to straighten them.

9. Install the evaporator into the housing. Install the foam cover and the plastic cover over the evaporator.
10. Connect the refrigerant lines to the evaporator. Tighten the ⅝ in. line to 10–14 ft. lbs. and the ¾ in. line to 24–28 ft. lbs.
11. Install the instrument panel trim and the glove box.
12. Install the center console, connecting any electrical leads.
13. Connect the negative battery cable. Properly recharge the air conditioning system.

5, 7 and 8 Series

The expansion valve can only be removed after removing the evaporator case.

1. Disconnect the negative battery cable.
2. Properly discharge the air conditioning system.
3. If equipped with an automatic transmission, remove the screw retaining the shift lever T-handle. On manual transmission equipped vehicles, remove the shifter knob.
4. Remove the shift lever cover and pull the window switches out of the console.
5. Remove the center console retaining screws, disconnect all electrical leads and remove the console.
6. Open the glove box and remove the glove box door assembly.
7. Remove the left and right "A" pillar trim. Remove the left and right kick panel trim.

CAUTION

When removing the steering wheel on airbag equipped vehicles, use extreme caution handling the air bag assembly. Store the steering wheel with the airbag assembly facing up, to avoid injury in case of accidental deployment. Replace damaged airbag assemblies. Do not try to repair or reuse deployed airbag assemblies.

8. Remove the lower instrument panel trim pads. Remove the steering wheel.
9. Remove the steering column trim.
10. Remove the instrument panel "A" pillar retaining bolts. Remove the lower instrument panel retaining bolts at the kick panels.
11. Remove the instrument cluster retaining screws and remove the instrument cluster. Disconnect all instrument cluster electrical leads.
12. Remove the radio assembly and radio trim.
13. Remove the ventilation control head.
14. Remove the upper instrument panel retaining screws and pull the instrument panel away from the firewall.
15. Disconnect all electrical multi-plugs and pull the instrument panel out of the vehicle.
16. Remove the cowl cover from in the engine compartment. Disconnect the electrical leads at the blower.
17. Inside the vehicle, remove the evaporator cover. Remove the refrigerant line retaining bolt. Disconnect the refrigerant lines from the expansion valve and remove the expansion valve from the evaporator.

To install:

18. Install the expansion valve on the evaporator and connect the refrigerant lines.
19. Install the evaporator cover. Connect the refrigerant lines. Insall the cowl cover in the engine compartment. Reconnect the blower electrical leads.
20. Install the instrument panel in position and connect the electrical leads.
21. Install the instrument panel retaining screws. Install the ventilation control head and the radio assembly.
22. Install the instrument cluster.
23. Install the "A" pillar trim and the kick panel trim.
24. Install the steering column trim and the steering wheel.
25. Install the lower instrument panel trim and the glove box assembly.
26. Install the center console and the shift lever.
27. Connect the negative battery cable.
28. Properly charge the air conditioning system. Check the system operation.

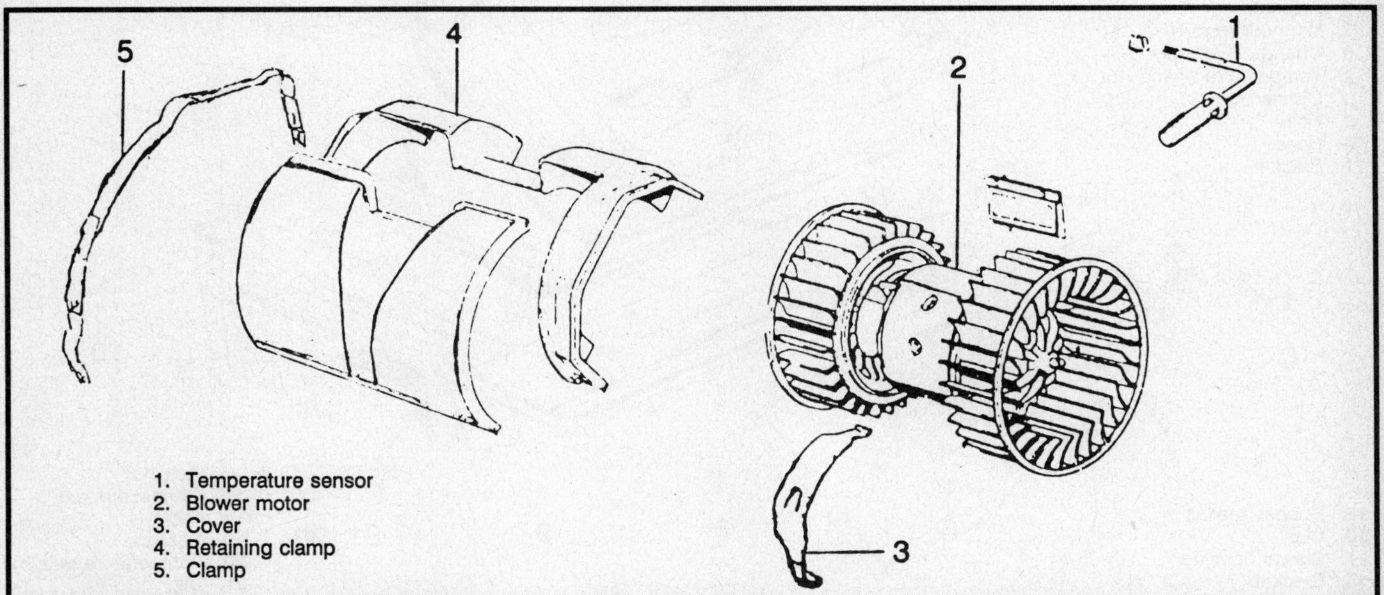
1
2
3
4
5
1. Temperature sensor
2. Blower motor
3. Cover
4. Retaining clamp
5. Clamp

Blower motor and upper housing cover—3 Series, others similar

Blower Motor

REMOVAL AND INSTALLATION

The blower motor assembly on all of the vehicles is accessible through the engine compartment. There is a plastic cover over the top of the motor assembly, which is located in the cowl.

1. Disconnect the negative battery cable.
2. Remove the rubber hood gasket at the cowl.
3. Remove any wires that are strapped to the top of the cowl cover.
4. On 5, 7 and 8 Series vehicles, remove the coolant expansion tank from the firewall. Position it aside, being careful not to bend the coolant return hose.
5. Remove the cowl cover retaining bolts. Remove the cowl cover.
6. Disconnect the blower housing top cover. On 3 Series vehicles disconnect the 2 retaining straps. On 5, 6, 7 and 8 Series vehicles, open the center retaining clip. Remove the cover from the vehicle.

NOTE: The cover will separate into 2 pieces.

7. Disconect the blower motor wire connectors.
8. Release the metal retaining strap from the blower motor and pull the motor out of the housing.

NOTE: The blower motor cages are balanced on the motor shaft and should not be removed from the motor assembly. If the motor is being replaced, it is replaced as a complete assembly with cages.

9. Remove the housing gasket.

To install:

10. Install the blower motor assembly into the housing. Connect the electrical leads.

NOTE: The motor can only be positioned one way in the housing. This is determined by the shape of the motor itself. Do not try to force the motor into position.

11. Latch the blower motor retaining strap into place.
12. Install the housing gasket.
13. Install the housing cover assembly, position the retaining strap(s) and secure the cover.
14. Install the cowl cover in position.
15. On 5, 7 and 8 Series vehicles, install the coolant expansion tank. Reposition any electrical leads along the cowl cover.
16. Reattach the rubber cowl gasket. Connect the negative battery cable. Check the operation of the blower.

Heater Core

REMOVAL AND INSTALLATION

The heater case assembly must be removed to remove the heater core on all 3 Series vehicles.

3 Series

1. Disconnect the negative battery cable.
2. Drain the cooling system and properly discharge the air conditioning system.
3. If equipped with an automatic transmission, remove the screw retaining the shift lever T-handle. On manual transmission equipped vehicles, remove the shifter knob.

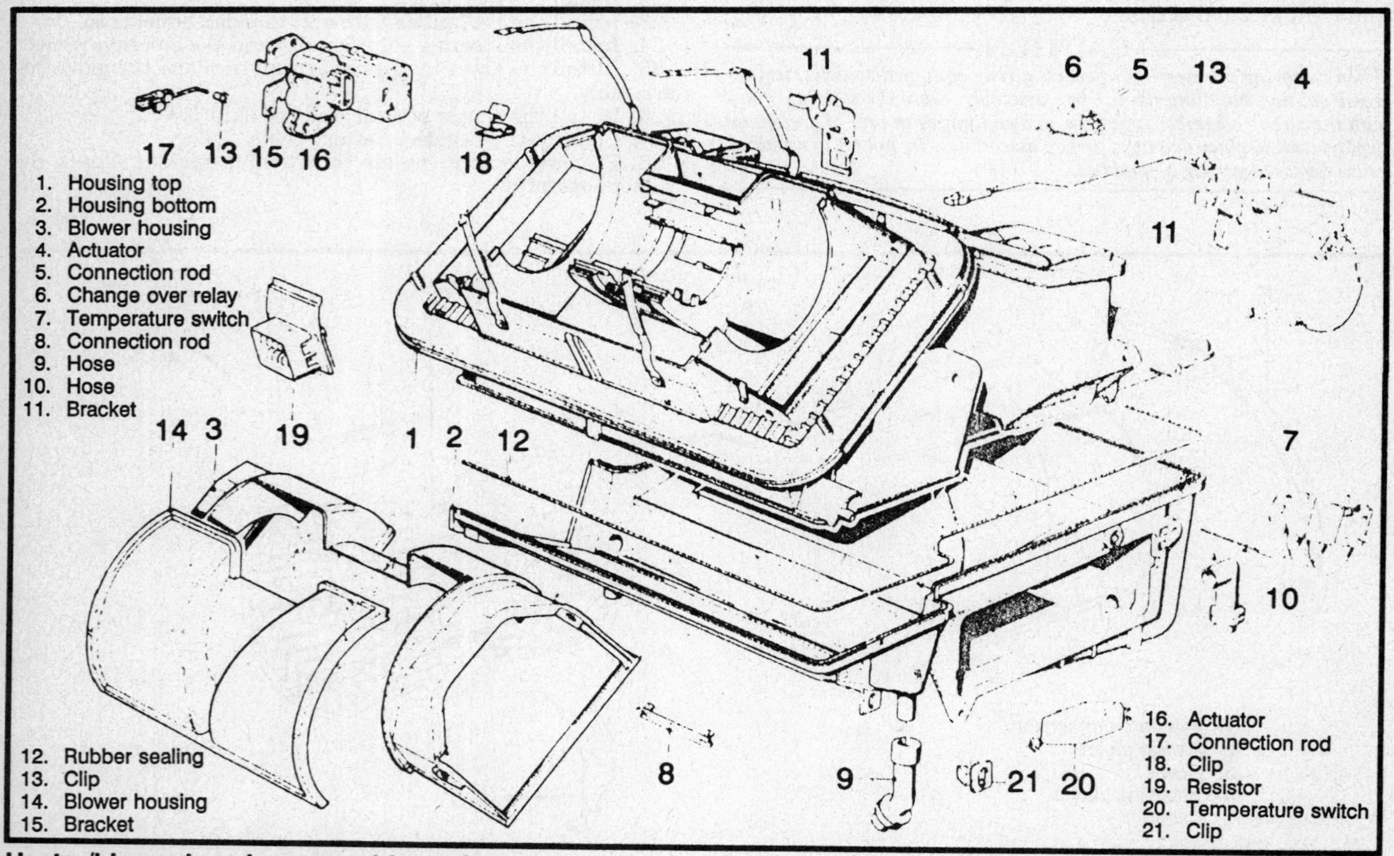
1. Housing top
2. Housing bottom
3. Blower housing
4. Actuator
5. Connection rod
6. Change over relay
7. Temperature switch
8. Connection rod
9. Hose
10. Hose
11. Bracket
12. Rubber sealing
13. Clip
14. Blower housing
15. Bracket
16. Actuator
17. Connection rod
18. Clip
19. Resistor
20. Temperature switch
21. Clip

Heater/blower housing assembly—3 Series

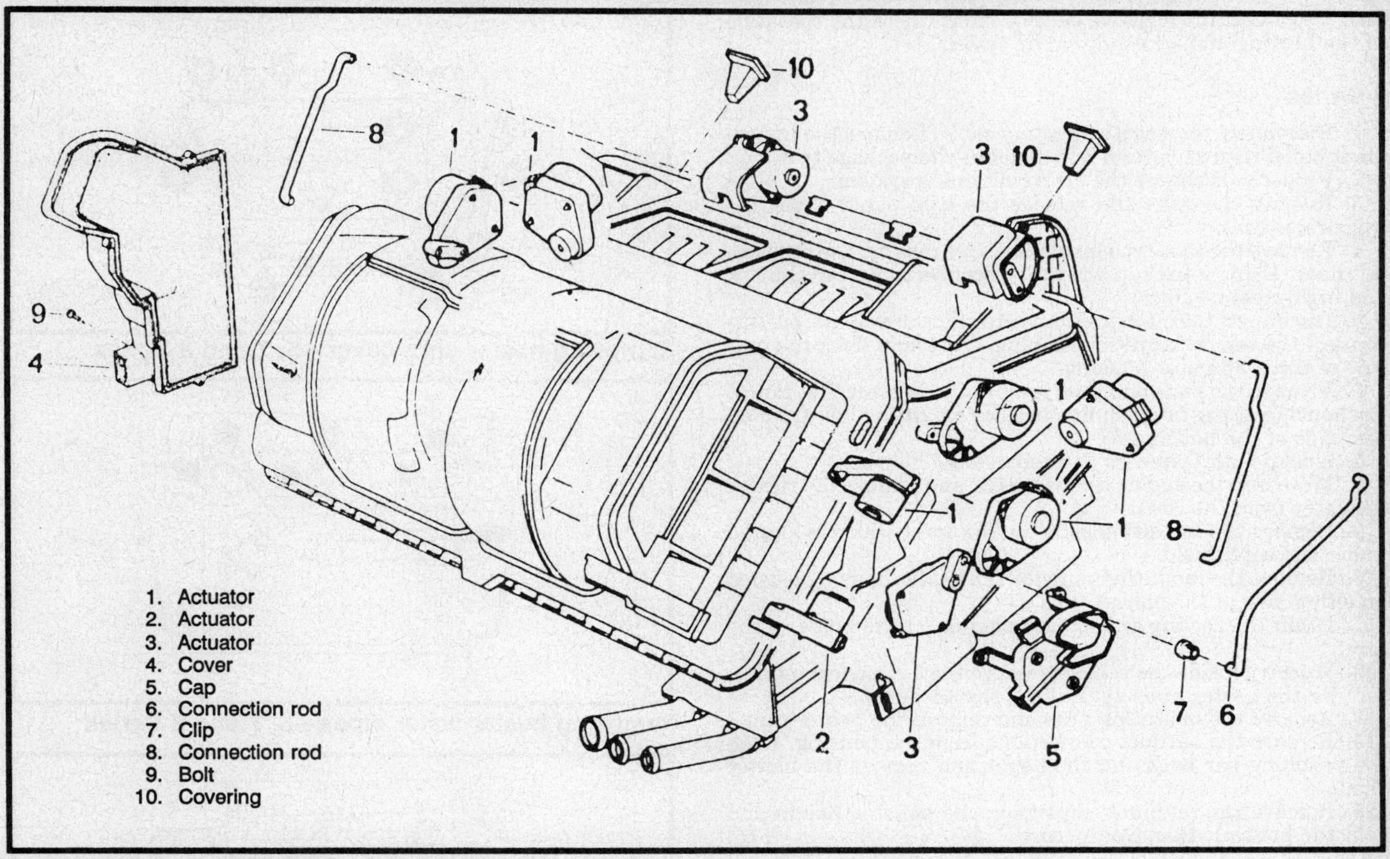
10
3
8
1
1
3
10
9
4
1
1
1
1
8
2
3
5
7
6
1. Actuator
2. Actuator
3. Actuator
4. Cover
5. Cap
6. Connection rod
7. Clip
8. Connection rod
9. Bolt
10. Covering

Heater/blower housing assembly—5, 6 and 7 Series

4. Remove the shift lever cover and pull the window switches out of the console.
5. Remove the center console retaining screws, disconnect all electrical leads and remove the console.
6. Open the glove box and remove the glove box door assembly.
7. Remove the left and right "A" pillar trim. Remove the left and right kick panel trim.
8. Remove the lower instrument panel trim pads. Remove the steering wheel.

CAUTION

When removing the steering wheel on airbag equipped vehicles, use extreme caution handling the air bag assembly. Store the airbag with the airbag facing up, to avoid injury in case of accidental deployment. Replace damamged airbag assemblies. Do not try to repair or reuse deployed airbag assemblies.

9. Remove the steering column trim.
10. Remove the instrument panel "A" pillar retaining bolts. Remove the lower instrument panel retaining bolts at the kick panels.
11. Remove the instrument cluster retaining screws and remove the instrument cluster. Disconnect all instrument cluster electrical leads.
12. Remove the radio assembly and radio trim.
13. Remove the ventilation control head.
14. Remove the upper instrument panel retaining screws and pull the instrument panel away from the firewall.
15. Disconnect all electrical multi-plugs and pull the instrument panel out of the vehicle.
16. Disconnect the refrigerant lines from the evaporator.
17. Remove the cowl cover from in the engine compartment. Disconnect the coolant lines from the heater core.
18. Disconnect the electrical leads from the blower.
19. Disconnect the air ducts from the heater case.
20. Remove the heater case retaining bolts from the engine compartment side and the retaining bolts from the interior side. Check to make sure the flaps in the heater case are all closed.
21. Remove the case assembly from the vehicle.
22. Remove the clips retaining the case halves and remove the blower motor cover and motor.
23. Remove the heater core from the case.

To install:

24. Install the core in the case. Make sure the gasket is properly positioned.
25. Assemble the case halves and attach the blower cover, install the blower.
26. Install the heater case in position in the vehicle. Re-attach the air ducts.
27. Reconnect the refrigerant lines and coolant hoses. Connect the electrical leads.
28. Reposition the instrument panel into the vehicle and connect the electrical multi-plugs. Be sure the instrument panel is properly positioned and install all retaining bolts.
29. Install the ventilation control head, the radio and the glove box assembly.
30. Install the "A" pillar trim and the kick panel trim plates.
31. Install the lower instrument panel trim pieces.
32. Install the steering column trim and the steering wheel.
33. Install the center console and the shift lever cover. Install the shifter knob or handle.
34. Refill the cooling system and properly charge the air conditioning system.

35. Reconnect the negative battery cable. Check the operation of the heating and air conditioning system.

6 Series

1. Disconnect the negative battery cable. Remove the instrument panel trim at bottom left. Remove the package tray.
2. Properly discharge the air conditioning system.
3. Remove the bolts and remove the trim panel under the evaporator unit.
4. Remove the tape type insulation. Get caps for the refrigerant lines. Using a backup wrench, disconnect and cap the low and high pressure lines.
5. Disconnect the electrical connector for the evaporator. Disconnect the temperature sensor plug, accessible from the outside of the evaporator housing.
6. Remove the bolts and then remove the bracket that braces the housing at the firewall. Remove the mounting bolt from either side of the housing.
7. Unclip both fasteners and remove the housing.
8. Move into the engine compartment and remove the rubber insulator from the cowl.
9. Remove the mounting bolts for the cover which is located under the windshield.
10. Remove the mounting nuts for the heater housing located on either side of the blower.
11. Drain the cooling system and disconnect the hoses at the core.
12. Working inside the vehicle, remove the 3 electrical connectors for the heater housing. Pull off the air ducts.
13. Remove the mounting nuts and remove the heater unit.
14. Remove the air duct connections from the housing. Push the retaining bar back and then split and remove the blower shells.
15. Remove the retaining clips from the housing halves and split the housing. Remove the core.

To install:

16. Install the core in the case. Assemble the housing halves.
17. Install the blower shells. Install the heater unit and mounting nuts.
18. Connect the electrical connections to the heater.
19. Connect the air ducts. Install the cover under the windshiled and install the rubber insulator to the cowl.
20. Install the bracket at the firewall and install the mounting bolts.
21. Connect the electrical leads at the evaporator and reconnect the refrigerant lines.
22. Install the trim panels under the evaporator. Install the instrument panel trim and the package tray.
23. Properly charge the air conditioning system and connect the negative battery cable.

5, 7 and 8 Series

1. Disconnect the negative battery cable.
2. Drain the cooling system.
3. Remove the screws retaining the center console. Remove the ashtray assembly.
4. Remove the glove box door assembly.
5. Remove the right side heater case cover screws and remove the cover.
6. Remove the front vent drive motor. Disconnect the plug from the inside temperature sensor.
7. Remove the heater core cover retaining screws. Remove the cover clips and straps.
8. Remove the cover and gasket. Disconnect the coolant hoses from the heater core.
9. Remove the heater pipe-to-heater core retaining bolts. Remove the heater pipes.
10. Remove the heater core retaining bolts. Remove the heater core by tilting it aside.

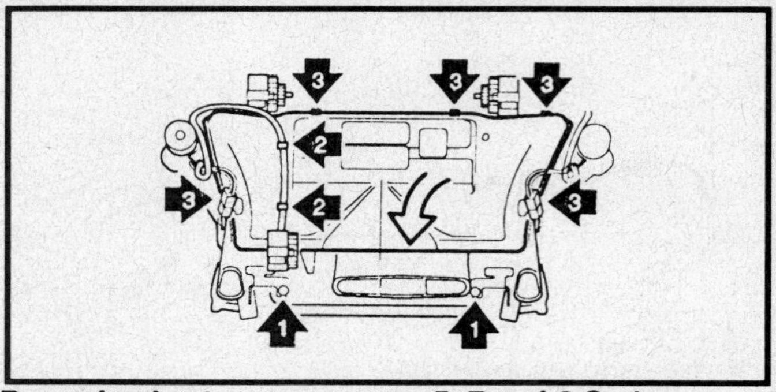
3
3
3
2
2
3
3
1
1

Removing heater core cover – 5, 7 and 8 Series

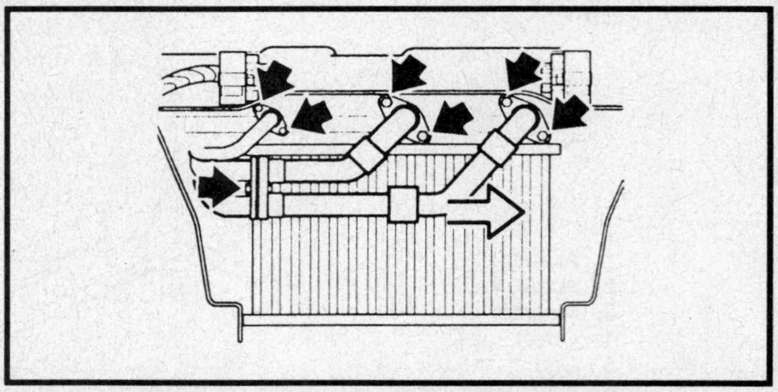

Removing heater water pipes – 5, 7 and 8 Series

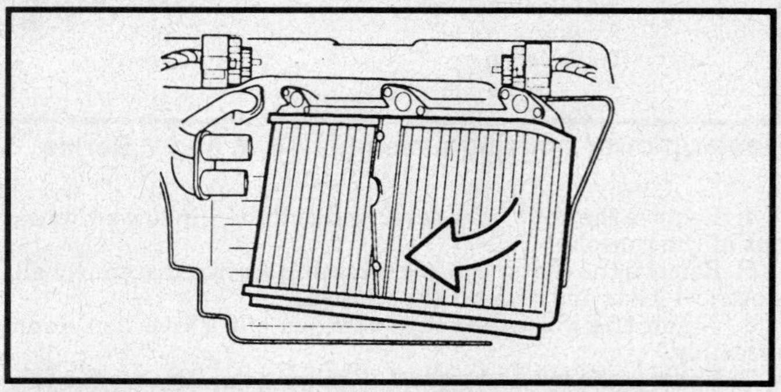

Remove the heater core by pulling it out to the right – 5, 7 and 8 Series

To install:

11. Install the heater core in the heater case. Install the heater core retaining bolts.
12. Install the heater pipes to the heater core. Tighten M6 bolts to 6–7 ft. lbs. and M8 bolts to 16–17 ft. lbs. Connect the heater hoses.

NOTE: Check the O-rings in the heater pipes and replace them if they are damaged.

13. Install the heater case cover and retaining clips. Install the cover retaining screws. Make sure the cover gasket is properly positioned.
14. Install the front vent drive motor. Install the right heater case cover.
15. Connect the inside temperature sensor. Install the glove box door assembly.
16. Install the center console and the ashtray.
17. Fill the cooling system and connect the negative battery cable.
18. Check the operation of the heater.

Evaporator

REMOVAL AND INSTALLATION

3 and 6 Series

1. Disconnect the negative battery cable.
2. Properly discharge the air conditioning system.
3. Remove the screws retaining the center console and remove the center console. Disconnect any electrical leads.
4. Open the glove box and remove the glove box assembly retaining bolts. Remove the glove box and remove the lower left side instrument panel trim.
5. Disconnect and plug the refrigerant lines from the evaporator.
6. Remove the evaporator case cover. Remove the foam rubber insulator and pull the evaporator from the housing.
7. Remove the expansion valve if replacing the evaporator.

To install:

8. Install the expansion valve on the evaporator assembly, connecting the refrigerant lines. Tighten the 5/8 in. line to 10–14 ft. lbs. and the 3/4 in. line to 24–28 ft. lbs.

NOTE: Before installing the evaporator into the housing, make sure the fins on the evaporator are not bent. If any fins are bent, use a fin comb or equivalent, to straighten them.

9. Install the evaporator into the housing. Install the foam cover and the plastic cover over the evaporator.
10. Connect the refrigerant lines to the evaporator. Tighten the 5/8 in. line to 10–14 ft. lbs. and the 3/4 in. line to 24–28 ft. lbs.
11. Install the instrument panel trim and the glove box.
12. Install the center console, connecting any electrical leads.
13. Connect the negative battery cable. Properly recharge the air conditioning system.

5, 7 and 8 Series

The evaporator can only be removed after removing the evaporator case.

1. Disconnect the negative battery cable.
2. Properly discharge the air conditioning system.
3. If equipped with an automatic transmission, remove the screw retaining the shift lever T-handle. On manual transmission equipped vehicles, remove the shifter knob.
4. Remove the shift lever cover and pull the window switches out of the console.
5. Remove the center console retaining screws, disconnect all electrical leads and remove the console.
6. Open the glove box and remove the glove box door assembly.
7. Remove the left and right "A" pillar trim. Remove the left and right kick panel trim.
8. Remove the lower instrument panel trim pads. Remove the steering wheel.

CAUTION

When removing the steering wheel on airbag equipped vehicles, use extreme caution handling the air bag assembly. Store the airbag with the airbag facing up, to avoid injury in case of accidental deployment. Replace damaged airbag assemblies. Do not try to repair or reuse deployed airbag assemblies.

9. Remove the steering column trim.
10. Remove the instrument panel "A" pillar retaining bolts. Remove the lower instrument panel retaining bolts at the kick panels.
11. Remove the instrument cluster retaining screws and remove the instrument cluster. Disconnect all instrument cluster electrical leads.
12. Remove the radio assembly and radio trim.
13. Remove the ventilation control head.
14. Remove the upper instrument panel retaining screws and pull the instrument panel away from the firewall.
15. Disconnect all electrical multi-plugs and pull the instrument panel out of the vehicle.
16. Remove the cowl cover from in the engine compartment. Disconnect the electrical leads at the blower.
17. Inside the vehicle, remove the evaporator cover. Remove the refrigerant line retaining bolt. Disconnect the refrigerant lines from the expansion valve and remove the expansion valve from the evaporator.

To install:

18. Install the expansion valve on the evaporator and connect the refrigerant lines.
19. Install the evaporator cover. Connect the refrigerant lines. Install the cowl cover in the engine compartment. Reconnect the blower electrical leads.
20. Install the instrument panel in position and connect the electrical leads.
21. Install the instrument panel retaining screws. Install the ventilation control head and the radio assembly.
22. Install the instrument cluster.
23. Install the "A" pillar trim and the kick panel trim.
24. Install the steering column trim and the steering wheel.
25. Install the lower instrument panel trim and the glove box assembly.
26. Install the center console and the shift lever.
27. Connect the negative battery cable.
28. Properly charge the air conditioning system. Check the system operation.

Refrigerant Lines

REMOVAL AND INSTALLATION

1. Disconnect the negative battery cable.
2. Properly discharge the air conditioning system.
3. Remove the nuts or bolts that attach the refrigerant line sealing plates to the adjoining components. If the lines are connected with flare nuts, use a back-up wrench when disassembling. Cover the exposed ends of the lines to minimize contamination.
4. Remove the lines and discard the gaskets or O-rings.

To install:

5. Coat the new gaskets or O-rings with wax-free refrigerant oil and install. Connect the refrigerant lines to the adjoining components and tighten the nuts or bolts.
6. Evacuate and recharge the air conditioning system.
7. Connect the negative battery cable and check the entire climate control system for proper operation and leaks.

Manual Control Head

REMOVAL AND INSTALLATION

3 Series

1. Disconnect the negative battery cable.
2. Remove the radio from the instrument panel.
3. Remove the switches from above the radio opening, the switches can be removed by prying them out and disconnecting the leads.
4. Remove the top 2 control panel retaining screws, through the radio opening. Remove the bottom 2 control panel retaining screws from under the panel.
5. Remove the rotary knobs from the control panel, by pulling them off.
6. Remove the knobs from the slide controls.
7. Pull the panel outward and disconnect the electrical leads from the back. Disconnect the selector cable clamps and remove the selector cables from the control head.

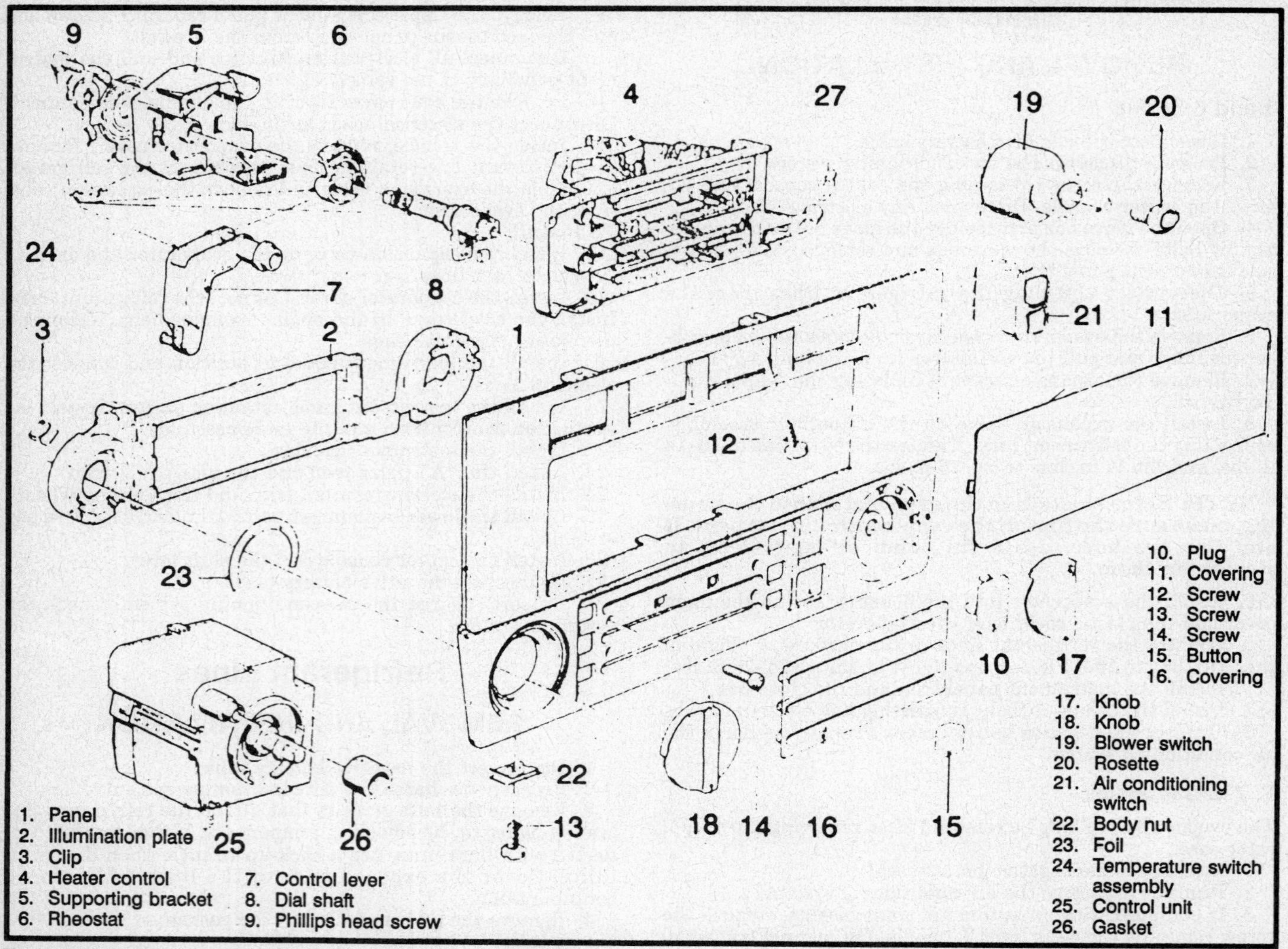
1. Panel
2. Illumination plate
3. Clip
4. Heater control
5. Supporting bracket
6. Rheostat
7. Control lever
8. Dial shaft
9. Phillips head screw
10. Plug
11. Covering
12. Screw
13. Screw
14. Screw
15. Button
16. Covering
17. Knob
18. Knob
19. Blower switch
20. Rosette
21. Air conditioning switch
22. Body nut
23. Foil
24. Temperature switch assembly
25. Control unit
26. Gasket

Exploded view of control head components—3 Series

8. Remove the control head from the control panel.

To install:

9. Insert the control head into the control panel.
10. Reconnect the control cables to the control head, tighten the clamps when the cables are butted against the stop.
11. Reconnect the electrical leads to the control head.
12. Attach the control panel to the instrument panel. Install the upper and lower retaining screws.
13. Install the control knobs. Install the radio and the switches, connecting all electrical leads.
14. Connect the negative battery cable and check the operation of the system.

5 Series

1. Disconnect the negative battery cable.
2. Remove the radio assembly from the vehicle.
3. Remove the rear defogger switch, by prying it outward from the side.
4. Through the rear defogger switch opening, press the control head retaining tab.
5. With the tab pressed push the control head outward and disconnect the electrical leads.
6. Press the clip retaining the control cable and disconnect the control cable.
7. Remove the control head from the vehicle.

To install:

8. Connect the control cable to the rear of the control head. Push the cable until it is seated in the retainer.
9. Reconnect the electrical leads to the control head.
10. Push the control head into the instrument panel until it clicks into position.
11. Install the rear defogger switch. Install the radio assembly.
12. Connect the negative battery cable and check the operation of the system.

6 Series

1. Disconnect the negative battery cable.
2. Pry out the thin trim plate along the left side of the control panel.
3. Remove the rear defroster switch, the hazard light switch and the switch plate cover from the control panel. All of these can be removed by carefully prying them out and disconnecting the electrical leads.
4. Pull of the rotary control and the slide control knobs.
5. Remove the 2 left side, control head retaining screws.
6. Remove the 2 screws through the right side switch openings.

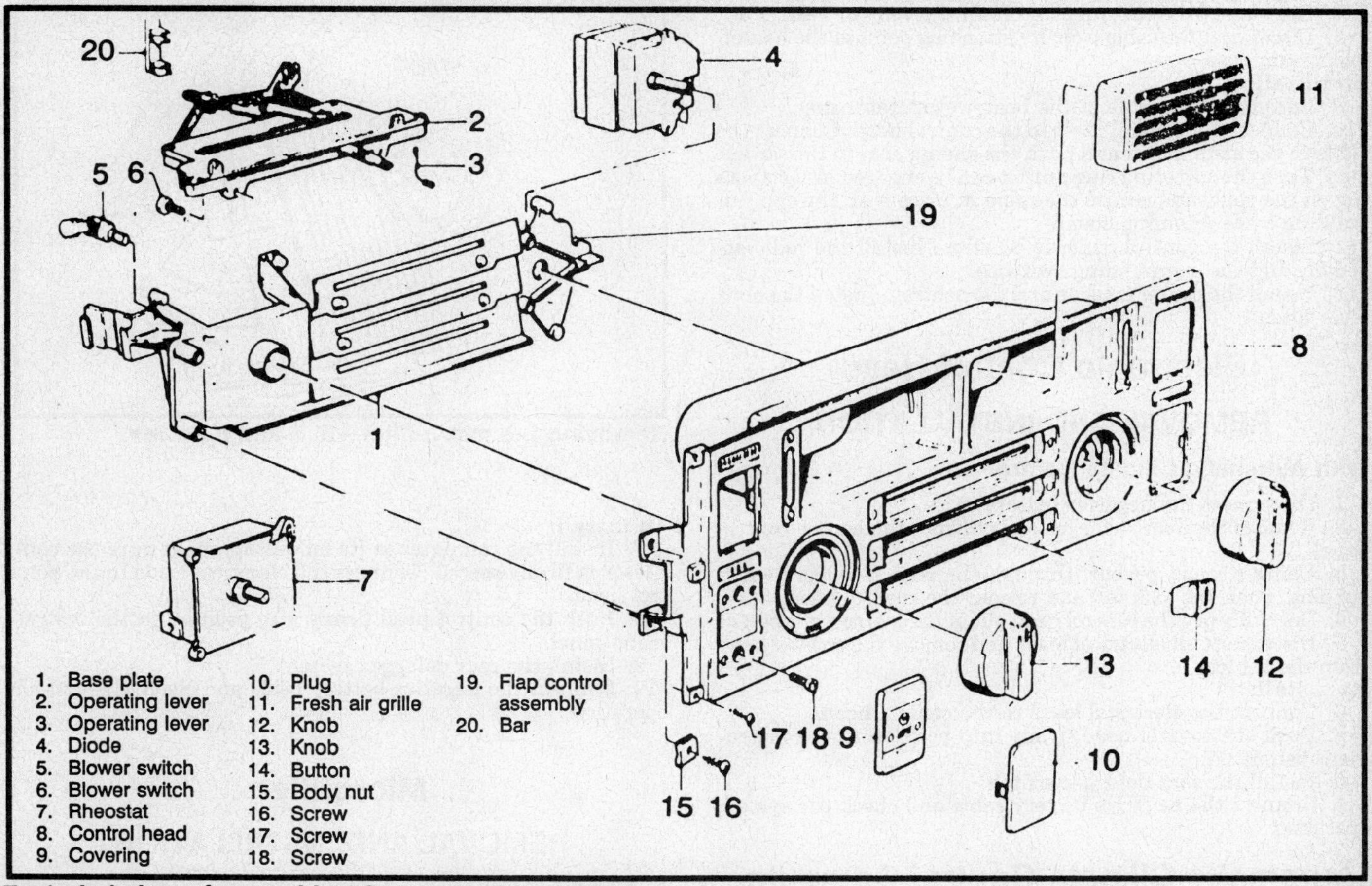
1. Base plate
2. Operating lever
3. Operating lever
4. Diode
5. Blower switch
6. Blower switch
7. Rheostat
8. Control head
9. Covering
10. Plug
11. Fresh air grille
12. Knob
13. Knob
14. Button
15. Body nut
16. Screw
17. Screw
18. Screw
19. Flap control assembly
20. Bar

Exploded view of control head components – 6 Series

7. Remove the 2 screws from the right side, rotary knob opening.
8. Remove the 2 screws from the hazard switch opening.
9. Tilt the control plate forward and disconnect the electrical leads.
10. Remove the clamps and disconnect the control cables. Remove the control panel from the vehicle.

To install:

11. Connect the control cables to the control head. Connect the cables to the sliding arm and push the sliding arm to the far left stop. Turn the adjusting ring until it can be engaged in the opening on the cable and secure the cable in place with the clip. Install the cable retaining clamp.
12. Reconnect the electrical leads and position the control head on the instrument panel.
13. Install all of the retaining screws and reinstall the control knobs.
14. Connect the electrical lead to each of the switches removed and push the switch into it's opening in the control head.
15. Install the small trim panel on the left side of the control head.
16. Connect the negative battery cable.

7 Series

1. Disconnect the negative battery cable.
2. Remove the rear defogger switch from the center control panel.
3. Using a small prybar, through the rear defogger switch opening, push the lock tab and release the control head.
4. Carefully pry the control head out of the instrument panel.
5. Disconnect all electrical leads and remove the control head from the vehicle.

To install:

6. Connect the electrical leads to the control head.
7. Push the control head firmly into position in the instrument panel.
8. Install the rear defogger switch.
9. Connect the negative battery cable and check the system operation.

Manual Control Cables

REMOVAL AND INSTALLATION

3 Series

There are 4 replaceable cables used in the 3 Series vehicles; footwell ventilation, window ventilation, temperature mixing flap and the fresh air flap. Each cable is hooked at the control head and on the heater/evaporator case.

1. Disconnect the negative battery cable.
2. Remove the lower left side instrument panel trim.
3. Remove the shift lever knob. Remove the ashtray assembly.
4. Remove the center console retaining screws and remove the center console.
5. Remove the radio assembly and the surrounding control switches from the control panel.
6. Remove the control panel retaining screws and pull the control panel forward.

7. Disconnect the control cable from the control head.
8. Disconnect the cable from its attaching point at the heater/evaporator case.

To install:

9. Reconnect the cable at the heater/evaporator case.
10. Connect the control cable to the control head. Connect the cable to the sliding arm and push the sliding arm to the far left stop. Turn the adjusting ring until it can be engaged in the opening on the cable and secure the cable in place with the clip. Install the cable retaining clamp.
11. Install the control panel in position. Install the radio assembly and the surrounding switches.
12. Install the center console and the ashtray. Install the shift lever knob.

Electronic Control Head

REMOVAL AND INSTALLATION

With Automatic Climate Control

1. Disconnect the negative battery cable.
2. Remove the rear defogger switch from the center control panel.
3. Using a small prybar, through the rear defogger switch opening, push the lock tab and release the control head.
4. Carefully pry the control head out of the instrument panel.
5. Disconnect all electrical leads and remove the control head from the vehicle.

To install:

6. Connect the electrical leads to the control head.
7. Push the control head firmly into position in the instrument panel.
8. Install the rear defogger switch.
9. Connect the negative battery cable and check the system operation.

Automatic Climate Control Computer

REMOVAL AND INSTALLATION

5, 7 and 8 Series

The climate control computer is attached to the instrument panel, behind the ventilation control head.

1. Disconnect the negative battery cable.
2. Remove the rear defogger switch from the center control panel.
3. Using a small prybar, through the rear defogger switch opening, push the lock tab and release the control head.
4. Carefully pry the control head out of the instrument panel.
5. Disconnect all electrical leads and remove the control head from the vehicle.
6. Reach through the control head opening and release the computer retaining clip. Pull the computer out of its mounting and release the wire connector from it.

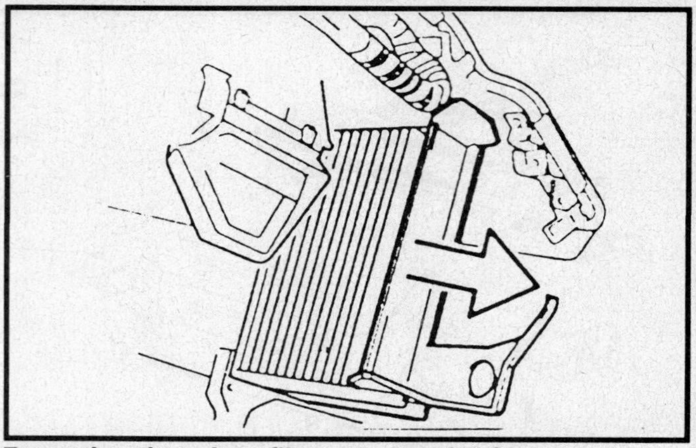

Removing the micro-filter—5, 7 and 8 Series

To install:

7. Install the computer in its mounting, make sure the connector is firmly seated. Connect the electrical leads to the control head.
8. Push the control head firmly into position in the instrument panel.
9. Install the rear defogger switch.
10. Connect the negative battery cable and check the system operation.

Microfilter

REMOVAL AND INSTALLATION

5, 7 and 8 Series

The fresh air microfilter is located in the right lower side of the evaporator housing.

1. Disconnect the negative battery cable.
2. Remove the trim on the right side of the center console.
3. Open the glove box and remove the screws on the ventilation duct behind it.
4. Fold the ventilation duct down. Disconnect the blower lead from under the instrument panel.
5. Remove the screws retaining the microfilter cover and the microfilter.
6. Slide the microfilter out of the case.

To install:

7. Install the new microfilter in the case and install the retaining bolts.
8. Install the ventilation duct and retaining screws.
9. Install the center console trim.
10. Connect the negative battery cable.

SENSORS AND SWITCHES

Water Shut-Off Solenoid

OPERATION

3 and 6 Series

The Water Shut-Off solenoid is located on the left side of the evaporator housing on 3 Series vehicles.

The water Shut-Off solenoid controls the flow of engine coolant through the heater core. When the solenoid is activated, coolant flow is shut off to allow maximum cooling from the air conditioning system. The solenoid is controlled by the Hot Water Cut-Off switch which is part of the air conditioning control panel TEMP control.

Battery voltage is applied through fuse 20 to the Hot Water Cut-Off switch when the ignition switch is in the **RUN** position.

The Hot Water Cut-Off switch is closed when the TEMP control is rotated fully counterclockwise, to the coldest position and is open when the the control is rotated more than 20 degress clockwise. When the switch is closed, battery voltage is applied through the to the Water Shut-Off solenoid and coolant flow is restricted.

On 6 Series vehicles a Heater Regulator controls the operation of the Water Shut-Off valve. The regulator opens and closes the shut-off valve at about 4 second intervals.

TESTING

3 and 6 Series

WATER SHUT-OFF SOLENOID TEST 1–3 SERIES

Measure: VOLTAGE
At: WATER SHUT-OFF SOLENOID CONNECTOR (Disconnected)
Conditions:
- Ignition Switch: RUN
- A/C Control Panel TEMP Control: FULLY COUNTERCLOCKWISE

Measure Between	Correct Voltage	For Diagnosis
BU & Ground	Battery	See 1
BU & or BR	Battery	See 2
• Rotate A/C Control Panel TEMP Control to Mid-Position		
BU & Ground	0 Volts	See 3

- If all voltages are correct, replace the Water Shut-Off Solenoid.

1. Check the BU wire and A/C In-Line Fuse for an open. If wire and Fuse are good, go to Table 2.
2. Check the BR wire for an open to ground. Check that connector C204 is properly mated.
3. Check BU wire for a wire-to-wire short to voltage. If wire is good, replace the A/C Control Panel TEMP Control.

WATER SHUT-OFF SOLENOID TEST 2–3 SERIES

Measure: VOLTAGE
At: HOT WATER CUT-OFF SWITCH CONNECTOR (Disconnected)
Conditions:
- Ignition Switch: RUN
- Water Shut-Off Solenoid: CONNECTED

Measure Between	Correct Voltage	For Diagnosis
GN/BR & Ground	Battery	See 1
GN/BR & BU	Battery	See 2

- If both voltages are correct, replace the A/C Control Panel TEMP Control.

1. Check the GN/BR wire for an open back to Fuse 20.
2. Check the BU wire for an open.

A: HEATER REGULATOR TEST 1–3 SERIES

Measure: VOLTAGE
At: HEATER REGULATOR CONNECTOR (Disconnected)
Conditions:
- Ignition Switch: RUN
- A/C Selector Switch: OFF

Measure Between	Correct Voltage	For Diagnosis
2 & Ground	Battery	See 1
2 & 3	Battery	See 2
1 & 3	Battery	See 3
4 & 3	0 Volts	See 4
• A/C Selector Switch: ON		
4 & 3	Battery	See 5

- If all voltages are correct, go to Table 2.

1. Check the associated wire for an open
2. Check the associated wire for an open to ground G200
3. Check that Water Shut-Off Valve connector is firmly seated. Check the wires at the Water Shut-Off Valve for an open. If wires and connector are good, replace the Water Shut-Off Valve.
4. Check the wire at terminal 4 for a wire to wire short to voltage. If wire is good, do Test F.

A: HEATER REGULATOR TEST 2–3 SERIES

Measure: RESISTANCE
At: HEATER REGULATOR CONNECTOR (Disconnected)
Conditions:
- Ignition Switch: OFF
- Negative Battery Terminal: DISCONNECTED

Measure Between	Correct Resistance	For Diagnosis
6 & Ground	Approximately 11K ohms at 70°F (21°C)	See 1
7 & Ground	Approximately 11K ohms at 70°F (21°C)	See 2

- If all resistances are correct, go to Test B.

1. Check the wire at terminal 6 for an open or short to ground. Check the wire at terminal 3 of the Interior Temperature Sensor for an open If wires are good, replace the Interior Temperature Sensor.
2. Check the wire at terminal 7 for an open or short to ground (see schematic). Check the wire at terminal 1 of the Heater Temperature Sensor for an open If wires are good, replace the Heater Temperature Sensor.

B: WATER SHUT-OFF VALVE TEST 1–3 SERIES

Measure: VOLTAGE
At: WATER SHUT-OFF VALVE CONNECTOR (Disconnected)
Condition:
- Ignition Switch: RUN

Measure Between	Correct Voltage	For Diagnosis
Wire from Fuse 19 & Ground (see schematic)	Battery	See 1

- If the voltage is correct, go to Table 2.

1. Check the associated wire for an open to Fuse 19

B: WATER SHUT-OFF VALVE TEST 2–3 SERIES

Connect: TEST LAMP
At: WATER SHUT-OFF VALVE CONNECTOR (Disconnected)
Conditions:
- Ignition Switch: RUN
- Engine at operating temperature
- Blower Speed Control: FAST
- A/C Selector Switch: OFF
- Temp Select Control: Fully Counterclockwise

Connect Between	Correct Result	For Diagnosis
Water Shut-Off Valve Terminals	Test Lamp lights	See 1
• Temp Select Control fully clockwise		
Water Shut-Off Valve Terminals	Test Lamp does not light	See 1
• Temp Select Control at same temperature setting as existing in-car temperature		
Water Shut-Off Valve Terminals	Test Lamp flashes on and off at approximately 4-second intervals	See 1
• Temp Select Control fully clockwise		
Water Shut-Off Valve Terminals	Test Lamp stays off	See 1

- If all results are correct, Heater Regulator is operating normally. If warm air is not generated in heat mode, replace the Heater Shut-Off Valve.

1. Replace Heater Regulator.

Blower Control Switches

OPERATION

3 and 6 Series

With the ignition switch in the **RUN** position, battery voltage is applied to the control switches and the blower speed control. If either the A/C SELECT switch or the FRESH/RECIRC switch are **ON** or the blower speed control is in the **1** position, battery voltage is applied through the blower resistor to the blower motor.

The blower motor is a variable speed motor which runs proportional to the voltage applied to it.

TESTING

3 and 6 Series

A: CONTROL SWITCH VOLTAGE TEST 3 SERIES

Measure: VOLTAGE
At: CONTROL SWITCHES CONNECTOR (Disconnected)
Conditions: • Ignition Switch: RUN
• Blower Speed Control: OFF

Measure Between	Correct Voltage	For Diagnosis
1 (GN/BR) & Ground	Battery	See 1
1 (GN/BR) & 3 (YL)	Battery	See 2 & 4
7 (GN/BR) & Ground	Battery	See 1
7 (GN/BR) & 5 (YL)	Battery	See 2 & 4
7 (GN/BR) & 6 (BR/WT)	Battery	See 3

- If all voltages are correct, do Test B.

1. Check the GN/BR wire for an open.
2. Check the YL wire for an open.
3. Check the BR/WT wire for an open.
4. If voltage is not present between the GN/BR wire and both the YL wires (terminals 3 and 5), do Test B.

C: BLOWER MOTOR TEST 3 SERIES

Measure: VOLTAGE
At: BLOWER MOTOR CONNECTOR
Conditions: • Ignition Switch: RUN
• A/C Select Switch: ON
• Blower Speed Control: HIGH

Measure Between	Correct Voltage	For Diagnosis
BU & Ground	Battery	See 1
BU & BR	Battery	See 2

- If both voltages are correct, replace the Blower Motor.

1. Check the BU wire for an open. If wire is good, recheck Test B.
2. Check the BR wire to ground G200 for an open.

B: BLOWER SPEED CONTROL TEST 3 SERIES

Measure: VOLTAGE
AT: BLOWER SPEED CONTROL CONNECTOR (Disconnected)
Conditions:
- Ignition Switch: RUN
- A/C Select Switch: ON (Depressed)
- Fresh/Recirculating Air Switch: FRESH (Not Depressed)

Measure Between	Correct Voltage	For Diagnosis
4 (GN/BR) & Ground	Battery	See 1
7 (YL) & Ground	Battery	See 2
• A/C Select Switch: OFF (Not Depressed)		
7 (YL) & Ground	0 Volts	See 3
4 (GN/BR) & 7 (YL)	Battery	See 4, 8, 9, & 10
4 (GN/BR) & 1 (BK)	Battery	See 5, 8, 9, & 10
4 (GN/BR) & 2 (GN)	Battery	See 6, 8, 9, & 10
4 (GN/BR) & 3 (BU)	Battery	See 7 & 10

- If all voltages are correct, replace the Blower Motor.

1. Check the GN/BR wire for an open.
2. Check the YL wire for an open between Blower Speed Control and splice S231.
3. Check the YL wire for a wire to wire short to voltage.
4. Check the YL wire for an open between splice S231 and the Blower Resistors.
5. Check the BK wire for an open.
6. Check the GN wire for an open.
7. Check the BU wire for an open.
8. If voltage is not present at the YL wire, but is present at the GN wire or BK wire, replace the Blower Resistors.
9. If voltage is not present at the YL, BK or GN wires, check for an open Blower Resistors' Safety Switch.
10. If voltage is not present at the YL, BK, GN and BU wires, do Test C.

F: A/C SELECTOR SWITCH VOLTAGE TEST—6 SERIES

Measure: VOLTAGE
At: A/C SELECTOR SWITCH CONNECTOR (Disconnected)
Conditions: • Ignition Switch: RUN
• Blower Speed Control: 3

Measure Between	Correct Voltage	For Diagnosis
4 & Ground	Battery	See 1
4 & 6	Battery	See 2
4 & 2	Battery	See 3
4 & 7	Battery	See 4

- If all voltages are correct but A/C Selector Switch does not operate normally, replace

1. Check the associated wire for an open
   If wire is good, check Fuse 19.
2. Check the wire at terminal 6 for an open
3. Check the wire at terminal 2 for an open
4. Check the wire at terminal 7 for an open

G: BLOWER SPEED CONTROL VOLTAGE TEST 1—6 SERIES

Measure: VOLTAGE
At: BLOWER SPEED CONTROL CONNECTOR (Disconnected)
Conditions: • Ignition Switch: RUN
• Blower Speed Control: MIN
• A/C Selector Switch: OFF

Measure Between	Correct Voltage	For Diagnosis
C1/3 & Ground	Battery	See 1
C1/3 & C1/4	Battery	See 2
C2 & Ground	Battery	See 3
C1/2 & Ground	0 Volts	See 4
• A/C Selector Switch: ON		
C1/2 & Ground	Battery	See 3

- If all voltages are correct but Speed Control setting will not vary blower speed, go to Table 2.

1. Check the associated wire for an open back to Fuse 20
2. Check the wire to terminal 4 for an open to ground G200
3. Check the associated wire for an open
4. Check the associated wire for a wire-to-wire short to voltage

G: BLOWER SPEED CONTROL VOLTAGE TEST 2—6 SERIES

Measure: VOLTAGE
At: A/C SELECTOR SWITCH CONNECTOR (Disconnected)
Conditions:
• Ignition Switch: RUN
• Blower Speed Control: SLOW
• Blower Speed Control: CONNECTED

Measure Between	Correct Voltage	For Diagnosis
5 & Ground	Less than 0.5 Volts	See 1
• Blower Speed: FAST		
5 & Ground	Approximately 10 Volts	See 2
• A/C Selector Switch Connector: Reconnected • A/C Selector Switch: OFF		
1 & Ground	Approximately 10 Volts	See 3
• A/C Selector Switch: ON		
3 & Ground	Approximately 10 Volts	See 4
• Blower Speed: SLOW		
3 & Ground	Approximately 3 Volts	See 5

- If all voltages are correct but blower motors do not operate normally, do Test H or I.

1. If the voltage is greater than 0.5 volts, replace the Blower Speed Control.
2. Check the associated wire for an open
   If the wire is good, replace the Blower Speed Control.
3. Check the associated wire for a short to ground (see schematic). If the wire is good, do Test H.
4. Check the associated wire for a short to ground . If the wire is good, do Test I.
5. Replace the Blower Speed Control.

J: BLOWER SELECT RELAY VOLTAGE TEST 6 SERIES

Measure: VOLTAGE
At: BLOWER SELECT RELAY (Disconnected)
Conditions:
- Ignition Switch: RUN
- Blower Speed Control: FAST
- A/C Selector Switch: Depressed (ON)

Measure Between	Correct Voltage	For Diagnosis
86 & Ground	Battery	See 1
86 & 85	Battery	See 2
87 & Ground	Battery	See 3
87a & Ground	Battery	See 4

- If all voltages are correct but either the A/C Blower or Heater Blower will not operate with Blower Speed at FAST, replace the Blower Select Relay.

1. Check the associated wire for an open to splice S226 If wire is good, do Test F.
2. Check the wire at terminal 85 for an open to ground G200
3. Check the associated wire for an open back to terminal 1 of the A/C Blower Housing
4. Check the associated wire for an open back to terminal 1 of the Heater Blower Housing

FRESH/RECIRC Air Flap Motor

OPERATION

3 and 6 Series

The FRESH/RECIRC door flap motors are located on either side of the evaporator housng.

With the ignition switch in the **RUN** position, battery voltage is applied to terminal **7** of the control switches, the normally open contacts of the left fresh air/recirculating air relay and the normally closed contacts of the right fresh air/recirculating air relay. Depending on the switch position, the air flaps are either opened or closed and the voltage is shifted left to right at the relays as the contacts are opened and closed.

Both of the flap control motors remain energized constantly, stalling when the doors reach full travel, to hold them in position.

TESTING

3 and 6 Series

A: FRESH/RECIRCULATING AIR FLAP DOOR MOTOR VOLATGE TEST—3 SERIES

Measure: VOLTAGE
At: FRESH/RECIRCULATING AIR FLAP DOOR MOTOR PIGTAIL CONNECTORS (Disconnected)
Conditions:
- Ignition Switch: RUN
- Fresh/Recirculating Air Switch: RELEASED (FRESH)

Measure Between	Correct Voltage	For Diagnosis
WT and Ground	Battery	See 1
WT and YL	Battery	See 2
• Fresh/Recirculating Air Switch: DEPRESSED (RECIRCULATING)		
YL and Ground	Battery	See 3
YL and WT	Battery	See 3

- If all voltages are correct, replace the inoperative motor.

1. Check the WT wire for an open. If wire is good, do Test B for RH Air Relay.
2. Check the YL wire for an open. If wire is good, do Test B for LH Air Relay.
3. Do Test B for both Air Relays.

B: FRESH/RECIRCULATING AIR RELAY VOLTAGE TEST—3 SERIES

Measure: VOLTAGE
At: FRESH/RECIRCULATING AIR RELAY CONNECTOR (Disconnected)
Conditions:
- Ignition Switch: RUN
- Fresh/Recirculating Air Switch: DEPRESSED (RECIRCULATING)
- Fresh/Recirculating Air Flap Door Motor Connectors: CONNECTED

Measure Between	Correct Voltage	For Diagnosis
87 (GN/BR) and Ground	Battery	See 1
86 (GN) and Ground	Battery	See 2
86 (GN) and 85 (BR)	Battery	See 3

B: FRESH/RECIRCULATING AIR RELAY VOLTAGE TEST—3 SERIES CONTINUED

86 (GN) and 87a (BR)	Battery	See 3

- If all voltages are correct, replace the suspect Fresh/Recirculating Air Relay.

1. Check the GN/BR wire for an open.
2. Check the GN wire back to the Control Switches for an open. If wire is good, do Test C.
3. Check the BR wire for an open.

C: CONTROL SWITCHES VOLTAGE TEST—3 SERIES

Measure: VOLTAGE
At: CONTROL SWITCHES CONNECTOR (Disconnected)
Condition:
- Ignition Switch: RUN

Measure Between	Correct Voltage	For Diagnosis
7 (GN/BR) & Ground	Battery	See 1
7 (GN/BR) & 8 (GN)	Battery	See 2

- If both voltages are correct, replace the Control Switches.

1. Check the GN/BR wire for an open. If wire is good, check that connector C204 is properly mated.
2. Check the GN wire for an open between the Control Switches and the LH and RH Fresh/Recirculating Air Relays.

K: FRESH AIR DOOR CONTROL UNIT VOLTAGE TEST 1—6 SERIES

Measure: VOLTAGE
At: FRESH AIR DOOR CONTROL UNIT CONNECTOR (Disconnected)
Conditions:
- Ignition Switch: RUN
- A/C Selector Switch: Not Depressed (OFF)

Measure Between	Correct Voltage	For Diagnosis
5 & Ground	Battery	See 1

K: FRESH AIR DOOR CONTROL UNIT VOLTAGE TEST 1—6 SERIES CONTINUED

Measure Between	Correct Voltage	For Diagnosis
5 & 6	Battery	See 2
1 & 6	0 Volts	See 3
• A/C Selector Switch: Depressed (ON)		
1 & 6	Battery	See 4

- If all voltages are correct, go to Table 2.

1. Check the associated wire for an open
   If wire is good, check Fuse 19.
2. Check the associated wire for an open between terminal 6 and ground G200
3. If voltage is present, check the wire at terminal 1 for a wire-to-wire short to voltage. If the wire is good, replace the A/C Selector Switch.
4. Check the wire at terminal 1 for an open to splice S226

K: FRESH AIR DOOR CONTROL UNIT VOLTAGE TEST 2—6 SERIES

Measure: RESISTANCE
At: FRESH AIR DOOR CONTROL UNIT CONNECTOR (Disconnected)
Conditions:
- Ignition Switch: OFF
- Negative Battery Terminal: DISCONNECTED
- Center Slide Lever at extreme left

Measure Between	Correct Resistance	For Diagnosis
2 & Ground	10K ohms ± 1K ohm	See 1
3 & Ground	10K ohms ± 1K ohm	See 2
• Center Slide Lever at extreme right		
3 & Ground	Less than 500 Ohms	See 3
4 & 7	60 to 70 Ohms	See 4

- If all resistances are correct but Fresh Air Door does not operate, replace the Fresh Air Door Control Unit.

1. Check the associated wire and the wire at terminal 3 of the Fresh Air Door Control Potentiometer for an open
   If the wires are good, replace the Fresh Air Door Control Potentiometer.
2. Check the associated wire for an open
   If the wire is good, replace the Fresh Air Door Control Potentiometer.
3. Replace the Fresh Air Door Control Potentiometer.
4. Check the wires at terminals 4 and 7 for an open or wire-to-wire short
   If the wires are good, replace the Stepping Motor.

REMOVAL AND INSTALLATION

3 and 6 Series

1. Disconnect the negative battery cable.
2. Remove the shift lever knob.
3. Remove the ashtray and the radio assembly.
4. Remove the center console retaining screws and remove the center console.
5. Remove the ventilation control head.
6. Disconnect the air control cable.
7. Disconnect the electrical leads from the motor assembly.
8. Disconnect the motor operating rod. Remove the motor holder retaining bolts from the case and remove the holder.
9. Remove the motor from the holder.

To install:

10. Insert the motor in the holder and attach the assembly to the case.
11. Connect the operating rod to the motor and connect the electrical lead.
12. Connect the air control cable.
13. Install the ventilation control head.
14. Install the center console, ashtray and radio.
15. Install the shift lever. Connect the negative battery cable. Check the operation of the system.

Evaporator Temperature Regulator/Sensor

OPERATION

3 and 6 Series

The evaporator temperature regulator and the evaporator temperature sensor are both located on the left side of the evaporator housing.

When the igntion switch is in the **RUN** position, battery voltage is applied to the air conditioning select switch. When the switch is pressed, voltage is applied to terminal **3** of the evaporator temperature regulator. The evaporator temperature regulator applies voltage from terminal **2** to the compressor clutch through the high pressure cut-out switch and the low pressure cut-out switch.

The high pressure cut-out switch will disengage the compressor clutch when the refrigerant pressure rises above 385 psi. The evaporator temperature regulator will detect the high pressure cut-out switch opening at terminal **5** and will turn off the output voltage at the compressor control terminal. The temperature regulator will not allow the compressor clutch to be turned on again until circuit continuity has been restored between terminals **5** and **2**.

Whenever the compressor clutch is de-energized, the collapsing magnetic field induces a voltage in the winding. The clutch diode provides a path for the resulting current.

When the compressor clutch is turned on, voltage is applied to terminal **29** of the Motronic Control Unit. The control unit uses this signal to increase the idle speed to compensate for the increased engine load from the compressor.

TESTING

3 and 6 Series

A: A/C ISOLATION TEST 1—3 SERIES

Measure: VOLTAGE
At: EVAPORATOR TEMPERATURE REGULATOR (Disconnected)
Conditions:
- Ignition Switch: RUN (Engine need not be running)
- A/C Selector Switch: ON (Depressed)

Measure Between	Correct Voltage	For Diagnosis
3 & Ground	Battery	See 1

- If voltage is correct, go to Table 2.

1. Go to Test E.

A: A/C ISOLATION TEST 2—3 SERIES

Connect: FUSED JUMPER
At: EVAPORATOR TEMPERATURE REGULATOR (Disconnected)
Conditions:
- Ignition Switch: RUN
- A/C Selector Switch: ON (Depressed)

Connect Across	Correct Result	For Diagnosis
2 & 3	Compressor Clutch Engages	See 1

- If result is correct go to Test C.

1. Go to Test B.

B: PRESSURE SWITCH TEST—3 SERIES

Measure: RESISTANCE
At: EVAPORATOR TEMPERATURE REGULATOR CONNECTOR (Disconnected)
Conditions:
- Ignition Switch: OFF
- Negative Battery Terminal: DISCONNECTED

Measure Between	Correct Resistance	For Diagnosis
2 & Ground	Approx 3 to 4 ohms	See 1

- If measurement is correct replace the Evaporator Temperature Regulator.

1. Check for an open Low Pressure Cut-Out Switch, High Pressure Cut-Out Switch, A/C Temperature Switch, or associated wiring. If High Pressure Cut-Out Switch is open, check refrigerant pressure to be sure it is normal before replacing the switch. If the switch and related wiring is OK, replace the Compressor Clutch.

C: EVAPORATOR TEMPERATURE REGULATOR VOLTAGE AND RESISTANCE TEST—3 SERIES

Measure: RESISTANCE
At: EVAPORATOR TEMPERATURE REGULATOR CONNECTOR (Disconnected)
Conditions:
- Ignition Switch: OFF
- Negative Battery Terminal: DISCONNECTED

Measure Between	Correct Resistance	For Diagnosis
1 & Ground	Approximately 3.5K to 4.5K ohms at 70°F (21°C)	See 1
4 & Ground	Less than 0.5 ohms	See 2
6 & Ground	Less than 0.5 ohms	See 2
5 & 2	Less than 0.5 ohms	See 3

- If all resistances are correct but Compressor Clutch does not operate normally, replace the Evaporator Temperature Regulator.

1. Check the BK/WT wire for an open or a short to ground Check the BR wire for an open If wires are good, replace the Evaporator Temperature Sensor.
2. Check the BR wire for an open
3. Check BK/YL for an open between terminal 5 and the Low Pressure Cut-Out Switch.

D: IDLE SPEED CONTROL VOLTAGE TEST—3 SERIES

Measure: VOLTAGE
At: MOTRONIC CONTROL UNIT CONNECTOR (Connected — Universal Adapter)
Conditions:
- Ignition Switch: RUN
- A/C Control Panel: A/C ON
- Temperature Outside Car: Above 60 degrees F (16 degrees C)

Measure Between	Correct Voltage	For Diagnosis
40 (BK/GY) & Ground	Battery	See 1
41 (VI/GY) & Ground	Battery	See 2

- If the voltage is correct, repair/replace the Motronic Control Unit.

1. Check for an open in the BL/WT and BK/RD wires.
2. Check for an open in the VI/GY and BK/VI wires.

E: A/C SELECT SWITCH VOLTAGE TEST—3 SERIES

Measure: VOLTAGE
At: CONTROL SWITCHES CONNECTOR (Connected)
Conditions:
- Ignition Switch: RUN
- A/C Control Panel: A/C ON
- Temperature Outside Car: Above 60 degrees F (16 degrees C)

Measure Between	Correct Voltage	For Diagnosis
4 (WT) & Ground	Battery	See 1
2 (BK/VI) & Ground	Battery	See 2

- If both voltages are correct, check connections at Evaporator Temperature Regulator.

1. Check for an open in the WT and GN/BR wires.
2. Replace the A/C Select Switch.

C: A/C ISOLATION TEST 1—6 SERIES

Measure: VOLTAGE
At: HIGH PRESSURE CUT-OUT SWITCH HARNESS CONNECTOR C108 (Disconnected)
Conditions:
- Ignition Switch: RUN (Engine need not be running)
- Temp Select Control: 61°F (Fully Counterclockwise)
- A/C Selector Switch: Depressed (ON)

Measure Between	Correct Voltage	For Diagnosis
Wire to C102 & Ground	Battery	See 1

- If the voltage is correct, go to Table 2.

1. Do Test E.

C: A/C ISOLATION TEST 2—6 SERIES

Connect: FUSED JUMPER
At: HIGH PRESSURE CUT-OUT SWITCH HARNESS CONNECTOR (Disconnected)
Conditions:
- Ignition Switch: RUN
- Temp Select Control: 61°F (Fully Counterclockwise)
- A/C Selector Switch: ON

Connect Between	Correct Result	For Diagnosis
High Pressure Cut-Out Switch Terminals	Compressor Clutch engages	See 1

- If the result is correct, check that High Pressure Cut-Out Switch is closed. If the switch is open, replace it.

1. Do Test D.

D: COMPRESSOR CLUTCH VOLTAGE TEST—6 SERIES

Measure: VOLTAGE
At: COMPRESSOR CLUTCH HARNESS CONNECTOR (Disconnected)
Conditions:
- Ignition Switch: RUN (Engine need not be running)
- Temp Select Control: 61°F (Fully Counterclockwise)
- A/C Selector Switch: ON

Measure Between	Correct Voltage	For Diagnosis
Wire & Ground	Battery	See 1

- If the voltage is correct and the refrigerant charge is normal, but Compressor Clutch does not engage, replace the Compressor Clutch.

1. Check the wire for an open. Check that the A/C Temperature Switch is closed. Repair/replace as necessary.

E: EVAPORATOR TEMPERATURE REGULATOR VOLTAGE AND RESISTANCE TEST 1—6 SERIES

Measure: VOLTAGE
At: EVAPORATOR TEMPERATURE REGULATOR CONNECTOR (Disconnected)
Conditions:
- Ignition Switch: RUN
- Temp Select Control: 61°F (Fully Counterclockwise)
- A/C Selector Switch: ON

Measure Between	Correct Voltage	For Diagnosis
4 & Ground	Battery	See 1
4 & 1	Battery	See 2
3 & Ground	Less than 0.5 Volts	See 3
• Turn Temp Select Control to 87°F (Fully Clockwise)		
3 & Ground	Approximately 8 Volts	See 4
• A/C Selector Switch: OFF		
4 & Ground	0 Volts	See 5

E: EVAPORATOR TEMPERATURE REGULATOR VOLTAGE AND RESISTANCE TEST 1—6 SERIES CONTINUED

- If all voltages are correct, go to Table 2.

1. Check the associated wire for an open If wire is good, do Test F.
2. Check the wire at terminal 1 for an open to splice S225.
3. If higher voltage is present, replace Heater Regulator.
4. Voltage should increase smoothly to 8 volts as Temp Select Control is turned clockwise. If no voltage is present, check associated wire for an open If wire is good or voltage does not increase uniformly, replace the Heater Regulator.
5. Check the associated wire for a wire-to-wire short to voltage. If wire is good, replace the A/C Selector Switch.

REMOVAL AND INSTALLATION

3 and 6 Series

The evaporator temperature sensor is located on the right side of the evaporator case.

1. Disconnect the negative battery cable.
2. Remove the lower right instrument panel trim.
3. Disconnect the electrical lead from the sensor.
4. Remove the sensor from the housing by pulling it out.
5. Install the sensor in position in the case and push it in firmly to seat it.
6. Install the right instrument panel trim. Connect the negative battery cable.

E: EVAPORATOR TEMPERATURE REGULATOR VOLTAGE AND RESISTANCE TEST 2—6 SERIES

Measure: RESISTANCE
At: EVAPORATOR TEMPERATURE REGULATOR CONNECTOR (Disconnected)
Conditions: • Ignition Switch: OFF
• Negative Battery Terminal: DISCONNECTED

Measure Between	Correct Voltage	For Diagnosis
5 & Ground	Approximately 3 to 4 ohms	See 1
5 & 2	Less than 0.5 ohms	See 3
6 & Ground	Approximately 3.5K to 4.5K ohms at 70°F (21°C)	See 2

- If both resistances are correct, but Compressor Clutch does not operate normally, replace the Evaporator Temperature Regulator.

1. Check the associated wire for an open between the Evaporator Temperature Regulator terminal 5 and High Pressure Cut-Out Switch
2. Check the associated wire for an open or a short to ground (see schematic). Check the associated wire from terminal 1 to splice S225 for an open If wires are good, replace the Evaporator Temperature Sensor.
3. Check wire at Terminal 2 for an open between Terminal 2 and connector C106.

AUXILIARY AIR CONDITIONING SYSTEM

General Information

The 6 Series is offered with an auxiliary air conditioning system for rear seat occupants. This system has a separate blower motor, evaporator, exspansion valve and evaporator temperature sensor from the main air conditioning system. Temperature is controlled by individual controls in the rear console of the vehicle.

Rear Control Panel

REMOVAL AND INSTALLATION

6 Series

The rear control panel consists of a temperature selector and a blower speed switch.

1. Disconnect the negative battery cable.

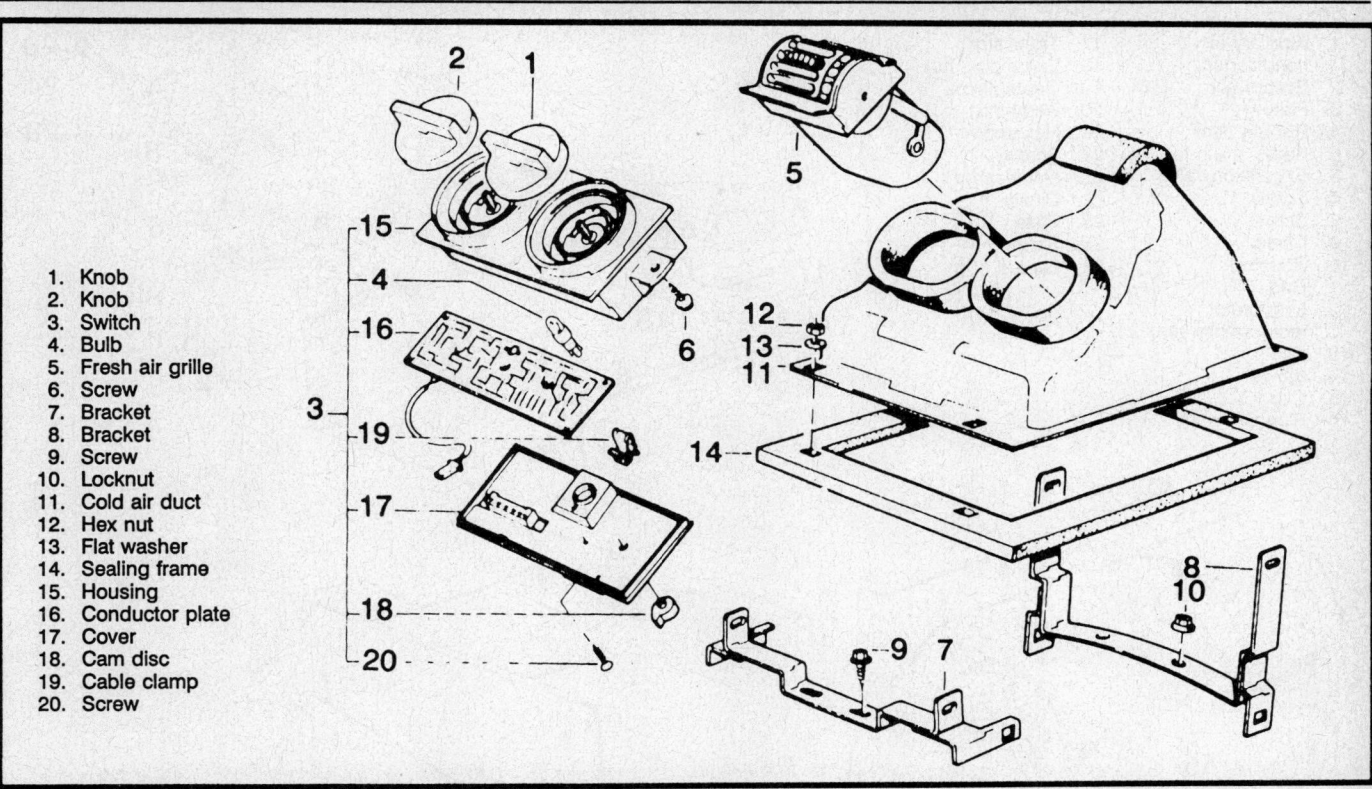

1. Knob
2. Knob
3. Switch
4. Bulb
5. Fresh air grille
6. Screw
7. Bracket
8. Bracket
9. Screw
10. Locknut
11. Cold air duct
12. Hex nut
13. Flat washer
14. Sealing frame
15. Housing
16. Conductor plate
17. Cover
18. Cam disc
19. Cable clamp
20. Screw

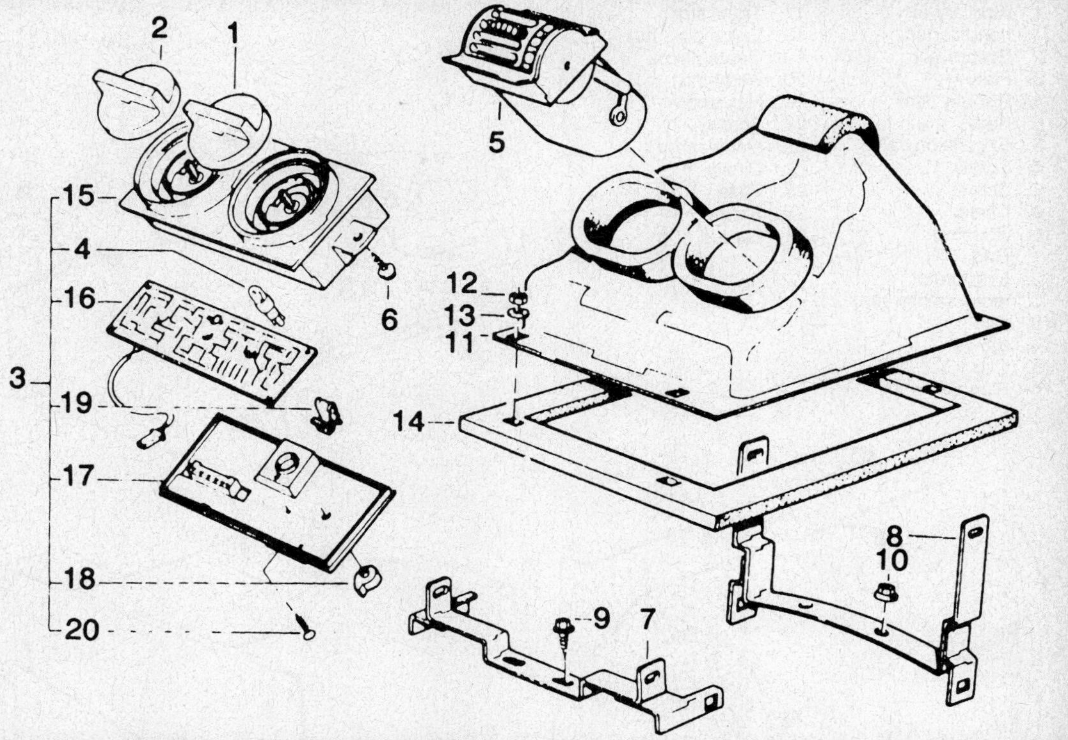
2
1
5
15
4
16
3
19
17
18
20
6
12
13
11
14
8
10
9
7

Rear blower control and air duct assembly—6 Series

P: IDLE SPEED CONTROL VOLTAGE TEST—6 SERIES

Measure: VOLTAGE
At: MOTRONIC CONTROL UNIT CONNECTOR (Connected — Universal Adapter)
Conditions:
- Ignition Switch: RUN
- A/C Control Panel: A/C On
- Temperature Outside Car: Above 60 degrees F (16 degrees C)

Measure Between	Correct Voltage	For Diagnosis
40 & Ground	Battery	See 1
41 & Ground	Battery	See 2

- If the voltage is correct, check connections at Motronic Control Unit.

1. Check BK/GY and BK wires to Evaporator Temperature Regulator for an open (see schematic). Repair/replace as necessary.
2. Check VI/GY and GN/YL wires to A/C Selector Switch for an open Repair/replace as necessary.

L: REAR A/C CONTROL VOLTAGE TEST—6 SERIES

Measure: VOLTAGE
At: REAR A/C CONTROL CONNECTOR (Disconnected)
Conditions:
- Ignition Switch: RUN
- Front A/C Selector Switch: ON

Measure Between	Correct Voltage	For Diagnosis
1 & Ground	Battery	See 1
1 & 2	Battery	See 2
3 & Ground	Battery	See 3

- If all voltages are correct but air flow is not cooled, go to Test M.

1. Check the associated wire for an open back to splice S202 Check that connector C220 is properly mated.
2. Check the wire at terminal 2 for an open to ground G302
3. Check the associated wire for an open If the wire is good, do Test M.

1. Auxiliary air conditioner
2. Evaporator
3. Plate
4. Rubber seal
5. Seal
6. Expansion valve
7. Screw
8. Screw
9. Circlip
10. Housing
11. Grid
12. Evaporator temperature sensor
13. Clip
14. Blower
15. Clip
16. Pipe
17. Transistor
18. Expanding nut
19. Cable clamp
20. Body nut
21. Hex screw
22. Screw
23. Flat washer
24. Circlip
25. Plate
26. Screw
27. Gasket ring

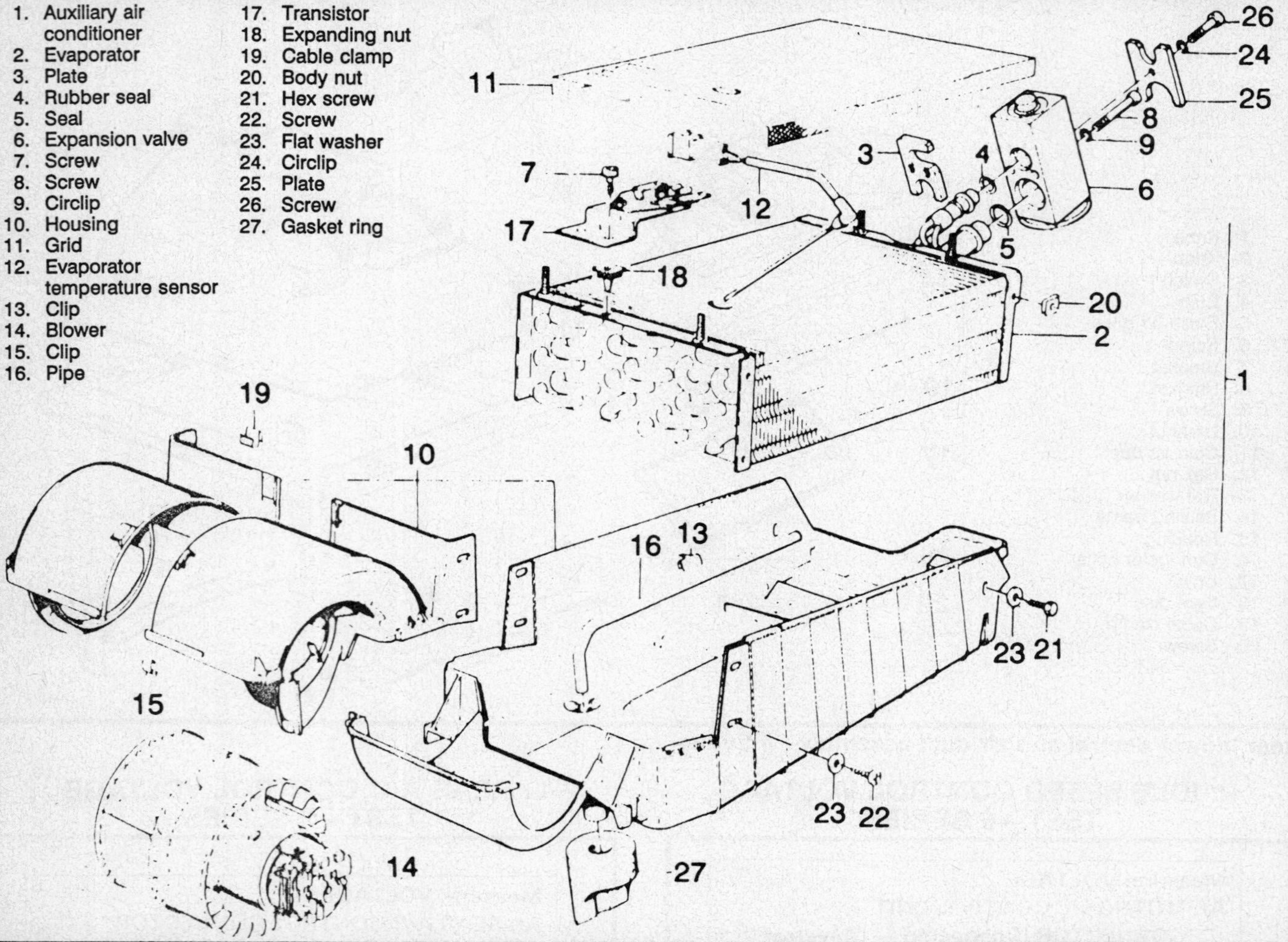
26
24
25
11
8
9
3
4
6
7
12
17
5
18
20
2
1
19
10
16
13
23
21
15
23
22
14
27

Auxiliary air conditioning system components – 6 Series

2. Remove the rear armrest storage box.
3. Remove the side trim panels from the console.
4. Remove the screws that retain the armrest lid. Pull the temperature control and fan control knobs off.
5. Remove the console retaining screws and lift the top off the console.
6. Disconnect the electrical lead from the console top.
7. Remove the control head retaining screws from the console and remove the control head.

To install:

8. Install the control head in the console.
9. Connect the electrical lead to the control head.
10. Install the console top and the armrest lid. Install the control knobs.
11. Install the trim panels on the console.
12. Install the armrest storage box.
13. Connect the negative battery cable and check the system operation.

Expansion Valve

REMOVAL AND INSTALLATION

6 Series

1. Disconnect the negative battery cable. Properly discharge the air conditioning system.

M: REAR AUXILIARY REFRIGERANT VALVE VOLTAGE TEST 1 – 6 SERIES

Measure: VOLTAGE
At: REAR AUXILIARY REFRIGERANT VALVE (Disconnected)
Conditions:
- Ignition Switch: RUN
- Rear A/C Control Connector: CONNECTED

Measure Between	Correct Voltage	For Diagnosis
1 & Ground	Battery	See 1

- If the voltage is correct, go to Table 2.

1. Check the associated wire for an open to Fuse 19.

M: REAR AUXILIARY REFRIGERANT VALVE VOLTAGE TEST 2–6 SERIES

Connect: TEST LAMP
At: REAR AUXILIARY REFRIGERANT VALVE (Disconnected)
Conditions:
- Ignition Switch: RUN
- Front A/C Selector Switch: ON
- Rear Blower Control: FAST
- Rear Temperature Control: Fully Counterclockwise

Connect Between	Correct Result	For Diagnosis
1 & 2	Test Lamp lights	See 1
• Rear Temperature Control: Fully Clockwise		
1 & 2	Test lamp does not light	See 1

- If both results are correct, Rear Temperature Control is operating normally. If cold air is not generated in cooling mode, replace the Rear Auxiliary Refrigerant Valve.

1. Replace the Rear A/C Control.

2. Remove the rear armrest storage box.
3. Remove the side trim panels from the console.
4. Remove the screws that retain the armrest lid. Pull the temperature control and fan control knobs off.
5. Remove the console retaining screws and lift the top off the console.
6. Disconnect the electrical lead from the console top.
7. Remove the rear seat assemblies. Remove the remaining console trim pieces.
8. Remove the screws that retain the air duct to to the evaporator housing.
9. Disconnect the refrigerant lines from the expansion valve.
10. Disconnect the expansion valve from the evaporator.

To install:

11. Install the expansion valve on the evaporator, using new O-rings.
12. Connect the refrigerant lines to the expansion valve.
13. Install the air duct to the evaporator housing.
14. Install the rear seat assemblies. Install the console trim. Connect the electrical leads to the control head and install the console top.
15. Install the armrest assembly and the storage box.
16. Connect the negative battery cable and properly charge the air conditioning system. Check the system operation.

Rear Blower Motor

REMOVAL AND INSTALLATION

6 Series

1. Disconnect the negative battery cable.
2. Remove the rear armrest storage box.

N: REAR BLOWER MOTOR TEST 1–6 SERIES

Measure: VOLTAGE
At: REAR A/C CONTROL CONNECTOR C2 (Disconnected)
Conditions:
- Ignition Switch: RUN
- A/C Selector Switch: COOL

Measure Between	Correct Voltage	For Diagnosis
GN/YL & Ground	Battery	See 1

- If voltage is correct, go to Table 2.

1. Check GN/YL wire for an open

N: REAR BLOWER MOTOR TEST 2–6 SERIES

Connect: FUSED JUMPER
At: REAR A/C CONTROL CONNECTORS C2 & C3 (Disconnected)
Conditions:
- Ignition Switch: RUN
- A/C Selector Switch: COOL

Connect Between	Correct Result	If Result Is Incorrect
GN/YL & BU/BK	Rear Blower Motor runs	See 1

- If result is correct, replace Rear A/C Control.

1. Check BU/BK wire for an open

O: REAR BLOWER MOTOR VOLTAGE TEST 6 SERIES

Measure: VOLTAGE
At: REAR BLOWER MOTOR CONNECTOR (Disconnected)
Conditions:
- Ignition Switch: RUN
- A/C Selector Switch: COOL
- Rear A/C Control: MAX Blower Speed

Measure Between	Correct Voltage	If Voltage Is Incorrect
BU/BK & Ground	Battery	See 1
BU/BK & BR	Battery	See 2

- If all voltages are correct, replace Rear Blower Motor.

1. Reconnect Rear Blower Motor connector and go to Test N.
2. Check BR wire to ground for an open

3. Remove the seat assemblies. Remove the side trim panels from the console.
4. Remove the screws that retain the armrest lid. Pull the temperature control and fan control knobs off.
5. Remove the console retaining screws and lift the top off the console.
6. Disconnect the electrical lead from the console top.
7. Remove the remaining console trim pieces.
8. Disconnect the electrical lead from the blower motor.
9. Remove the upper blower case mounting bolts. Remove the blower case retaining clips and separate the blower case.
10. Remove the blower motor assembly from the blower case.

NOTE: The blower motor and cages are assembled as an balanced component. Do not try to remove the cages from the motor. The motor and cages can only be replaced as an assembly.

To install:

11. Install the blower motor into the lower case and install the upper case half.
12. Connect the electrical lead to the blower motor.
13. Install the seat assemblies. Install the console trim pieces. Connect the electrical lead to the control head and install the console top.
14. Install the armrest assembly, storage box and the control knobs.
15. Connect the negative battery cable and check the system operation.

Evaporator

REMOVAL AND INSTALLATION

6 Series

1. Disconnect the negative battery cable. Properly discharge the air conditioning system.
2. Remove the rear armrest storage box.
3. Remove the seat assemblies. Remove the side trim panels from the console.
4. Remove the screws that retain the armrest lid. Pull the temperature control and fan control knobs off.
5. Remove the console retaining screws and lift the top off the console.
6. Disconnect the electrical lead from the console top.
7. Remove the remaining console trim pieces. Disconnect the electrical leads to the blower motor.
8. Remove the screws that retain the air duct to to the evaporator housing.
9. Disconnect the refrigerant lines from the expansion valve.
10. Disconnect the expansion valve from the evaporator.
11. Remove the evaporator housing retaining bolts and remove the entire assembly from the vehicle.
12. Disconnect the pressure regulator. Remove the evaporator from the housing assembly.

To install:

13. Reconnect the pressure regulator and install the evaporator in the housing.
14. Install the evaporator housing in the vehicle, be sure to use a new gasket on the housing drain.
15. Reconnect the expansion valve to the evaporator, use new O-rings.
16. Connect the refrigerant lines to the expansion valve.
17. Install the air duct to the evaporator housing. Connect the electrical lead to the blower motor.
18. Install the seat assemblies. Install the console trim. Connect the electrical leads to the control head and install the console top.
19. Install the armrest assembly and the storage box.
20. Connect the negative battery cable and properly charge the air conditioning system. Check the system operation.

SYSTEM DIAGNOSIS

Integrated Automatic Climate Control System (IHKA/IHKR)

The IHKR/IHKA climate control system is controlled by a microprocessor. The climate control computer has the ability to store defect codes in the case of system difficulty. The control unit monitors various parts of the vehicle, including the ignition system.

All stored fault codes can be read and used to determine the system problem. Codes can be read only by using the BMW Diagnostic Service Tester, or equivalent.

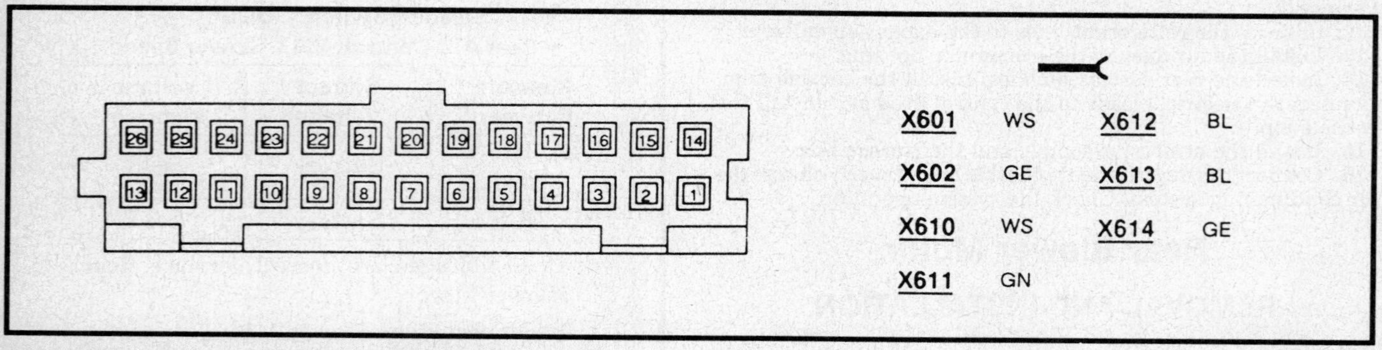
26 25 24 23 22 21 20 19 18 17 16 15 14
13 12 11 10 9 8 7 6 5 4 3 2 1
X601 WS
X612 BL
X602 GE
X613 BL
X610 WS
X614 GE
X611 GN

Terminal locations—7 Series IHKA/R control unit

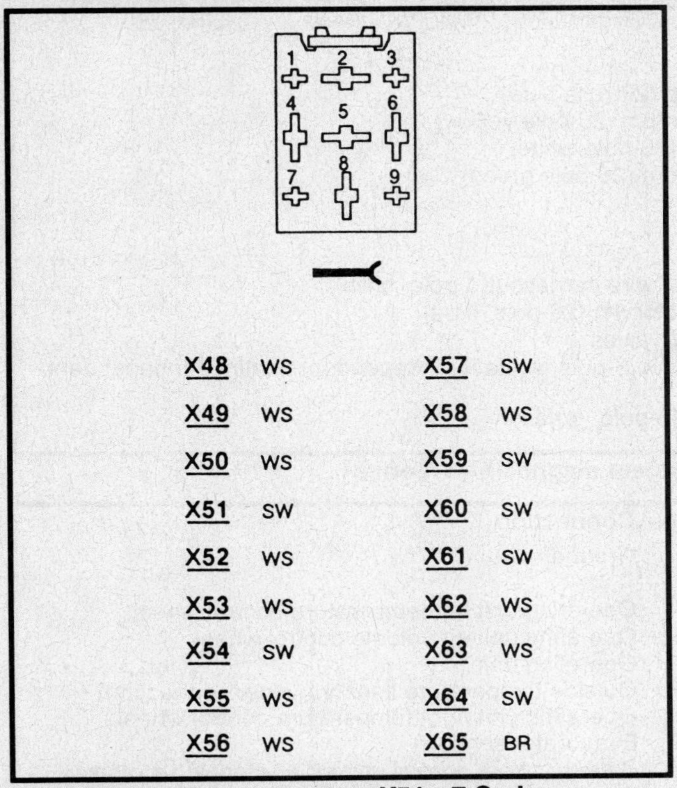
1
2
3
4
5
6
7
8
9
X48 WS
X49 WS
X50 WS
X51 SW
X52 WS
X53 WS
X54 SW
X55 WS
X56 WS
X57 SW
X58 WS
X59 SW
X60 SW
X61 SW
X62 WS
X63 WS
X64 SW
X65 BR

Terminal locations, connector X51—7 Series

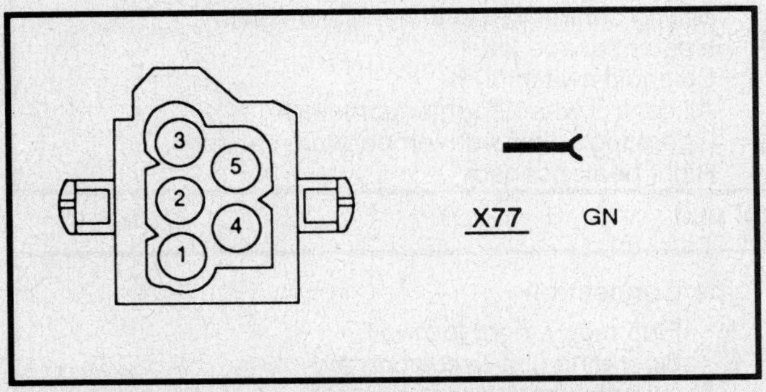
1
2
3
4
5
X77 GN

Terminal locations, connector X77—7 Series

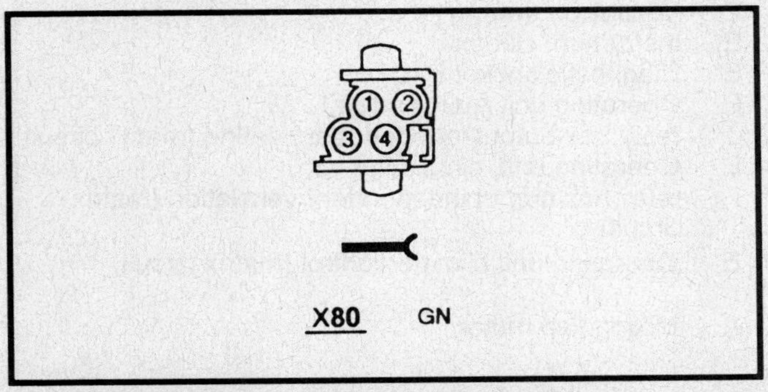
1
2
3
4
X80 GN

Terminal locations, connector X80—7 Series

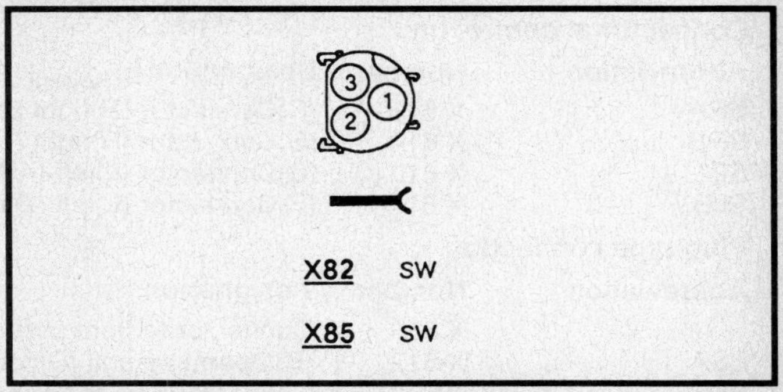
1
2
3
X82 SW
X85 SW

Terminal locations, connector X82/X85—7 Series

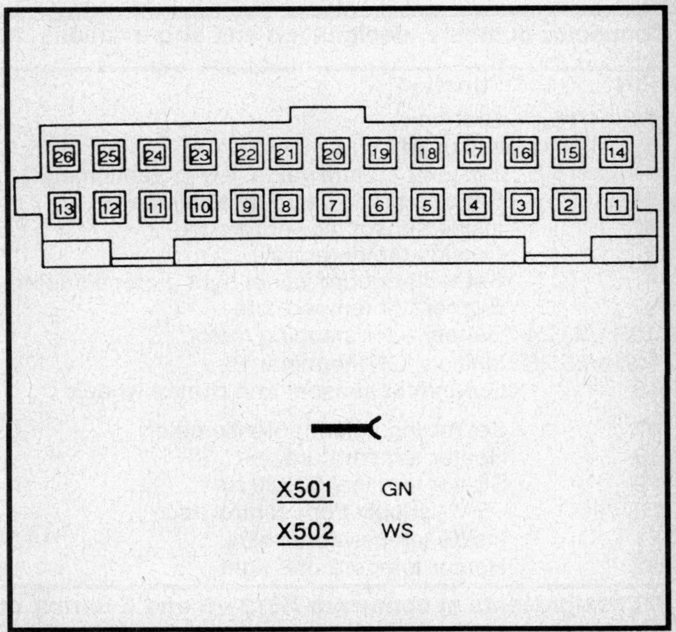
26 25 24 23 22 21 20 19 18 17 16 15 14
13 12 11 10 9 8 7 6 5 4 3 2 1
X501 GN
X502 WS

Terminal locations, connector X501/X502—7 Series

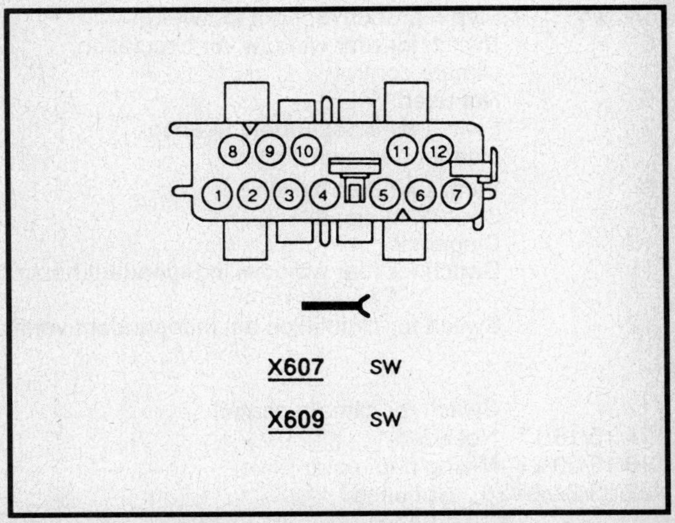
8 9 10 11 12
1 2 3 4 5 6 7
X607 SW
X609 SW

Terminal locations, connector X607/X609—7 Series

Connector at control unit

Abbreviation	Number	Designation
SRA	X 613	(S)Connector (R)right (A)top (26-pole blue)
SRB	X 614	(S)Connector (R)right (B)bottom (26-pole yellow)
SLA	X 610	(S)Connector (L)left (A)top (26-pole white)
SLB	X 611	(S)Connector (L)left (B)bottom (26-pole green)

Plug-type connection

Abbreviation	Number	Designation
	X 35	Connector to front section of wire harness (21-pole, black)
BSA	X 612	(B)Operating unit (S)connector (A) (26-pole, blue)
BSB	X 693	Connector plus to the water valves
BSC	X 682	Connector from operating unit (3-pole, white for independent heating / independent ventilation) to relay box
	X 671	Connector to output stage (5-pole, green)

Connector numbers, designation and abbreviations for system diagnosis—7 Series

PIN	Function	Type	Connection
1/2/14/15	Ground	E	Ground
3	Not used		
4	Set temperature value, left (potentiometer)	E	Operating unit left temperature control wheel
5	Set air volume value (potentiometer)	E	Operating unit air volume control wheel
6	Inside sensor blower (ground)	A	Operating unit
7	Outside temperature	A/E	Outside temperature sensor (solder connection)
8	Set temperature value, right (potentiometer)	E	Operating unit right temperature control wheel
9	Evaporator temperature	A/E	Evaporator sensor
10/11/23/24	Battery + for stepping motor	A	Battery + from control unit for all stepping motors
12/13/25/26	Ignition "ON" terminal 15	E	Terminal 15
16	Ground for sensors and control wheels	A	Ground from control unit for all sensors and control wheels
17	Set mixing value (potentiometer)	E	Mixing control wheel in ventilation grille
18	Heater temperature, left	A/E	Heater sensor, left
19	Starter terminal 50 (30 h)	E	Solenoid switch 30 h
20	+5 V - supply from control unit	A	All control wheels (potentiometer)
21	Inside temperature value	A/E	Operating unit inside temperature sensor
22	Heater temperature, right	A/E	Right heater sensor

Pin assignments at connector X613—5 and 7 Series control unit

PIN	Function	Type	Connection
1/2/3/4	Flap motor drive, right footwell	A	Flap motor, right footwell
5	Switch for rear window, air circulation, climate control	E	Operating unit circulation air, climate control, rear window
6	Not used		
7	Switch for independent heating, independent ventilation	E	Relay box output independent heating / independent ventilation (matrix circuit)
8	Ventilation flap switch	E	Ventilation switch
9	Speed "A" signal	E	Instrument cluster
10	Diagnosis	E	Diagnostic socket RxD
11	Switch for rear window, independent heating	E	Operating unit rear window, relay box output independent heating (matrix circuit
12	Switch for circulation air, independent ventilation	E	Operating unit, circulation air, relay box output independent ventilation (matrix circuit)
13	Switch for climate control	E	Operating unit climate control (matrix circuit)
14/15/16/17	Not used		
18/19/20/21	Mixing flap motor drive	A	Mixing flap motor
22/23/24/25/26	Not used		

Pin assignments at connector X614—5 and 7 Series control unit

PIN	Function	Type	Connection
1/2/3/4	Not used		
5	Blower output stage drive	A	Blower output stage
6	Auxiliary fan relay drive (= A/C motronic relay - DME)	A	Air conditioning system/motronic relay
7	Rear defogger relay drive	A	Rear defogger relay
8	Climate control relay drive, auxiliary fan stage 1	A	Climate control relay, auxiliary fan relay stage I
9/10/11/	Not used		
12/13/25/26	Continuous plus supply terminal 30	E	Front power distributor
14/15/16/17	Flap motor drive, circulation air	A	Circulation air flap motor
18	Function light drive A/C circulation air	A	Operating unit
19	Rear window function light drive	A	Operating unit
20	Diagnosis	A	Diagnostic connector TxD
21	Left water valve drive	A	Water valve
22	Auxiliary water pump relay drive	A	Auxiliary water pump relay K8
23	Right water valve drive	A	Water valve
24	Footwell slide control	E	Operating unit footwell slide control (potentiometer)

Pin assignments at connector X610—5 and 7 Series control unit

PIN	Function	Type	Connection
1/14/15/16	Flap motor drive, left footwell	A	Left footwell flap motor
2/3/4/5	Not used		
6/7/8/9	Fresh air flap motor drive	A	Fresh air flap motor
10/11/12/13	Not used		
17/18/19/20	Not used		
21/22/23/24	Not used		
25/26	Not used		

Pin assignments at connector X611—5 and 7 Series control unit

PIN	Function	Type	Connection
1/2	Not used		
3	Switch for rear window, independent heating	A/E	Control unit connector X 614 pin 11
4	Switch for independent heating, independent ventilation	A	Control unit connector X 614 pin 7
5	Switch for circulation air, independent ventilation	A/E	Control unit connector X 614 pin 12
6	Switch for rear window, circulation air, climate control	A	Control unit connector X 614 pin 5
7	Rear window function light drive	E	Control unit connector X 610 pin 19
8/9/10/11/12	Not used		
13	Inside temperature value	A/E	Control unit connector X 613 pin 21
14	+5 V supply from control unit	E	Control unit connector X 613 pin 20
15	Ground for sensors and control wheels	E	Control unit connector X 613 pin 16
16	Function light drive	E	Control unit connector X 610 pin 18
17	Air volume control wheel switch Max position	E	Ignition switch terminal 15
18	Footwell slide control	A	Control unit connector X 610 pin 24
19	Operating unit lighting	E	Dimmer for instrument lighting
20	Ground for function and operating unit lighting	E	Ground
21	Set temperature value, right (potentiometer)	A	Control unit connector X 613 pin 8
22	Set temperature value, left (potentiometer)	A	Control unit connector X 613 pin 4
23	Air volume value (potentiometer)	A	Control unit connector X 613 pin 5
24	Switch for heating, climate control, circulation air	A	Control unit connector X 614 pin 13
25	Air volume control wheel switch in MAX position	A	Output stage connector X 671 pin 3
26	Inside sensor blower (ground)	E	Control unit connector X 613 pin 6

Pin assignments at connector X612—5 and 7 Series operating unit

D 900 Defect code memory – stored defect codes:

Defect code No.	Defect location	Connector	Pin
01	Right temperature control wheel	blue	8
04	Right heater sensor	blue	22
07	Evaporator sensor	blue	9
10	Outside temperature sensor	blue	7
13	Inside temperature sensor	blue	21
16	Blower inside sensor	blue	6
22	Auxiliary fan relay (= A/C Motronic relay - DME)	white	6
25	Left temperature control wheel	blue	4
28	Left heater sensor	blue	18
31	Air volume control wheel	blue	5
32	Footwell slide control	white	24
34	Mixing control wheel	blue	16,17,20
38	Auxiliary water pump relay	white	22
40	Left water valve	white	21
44	A/C relay	white	8
46	Right water valve	white	23
48	Rear window defogger relay	white	7
52	Fresh air flap motor	green	6,7,8,9
55	Circulation air flap motor	white	14,15,16,17
61	Mixing flap motor	yellow	18,19,20,21
70	Left footwell flap motor	green	1,14,15,16
73	Right footwell flap motor	yellow	1,2,3,4

Defect code table—5 Series

Fuse	Fault when the fuse is defective
No. F09	Auxiliary water pump relay (working circuit) Compressor clutch relay - auxiliary fan stage I (working circuit)
No. F19	Blower motor does not operate (also in maximum air volume control wheel position)
No. F20	IHKR control unit (defect storage not possible)
No. F24	IHKR control unit (diagnostic procedure not possible) both water valves, inside sensor blower (IHKA) Function lighting (operating unit IHKA)
No. F25	Air conditioning system relay ON signal to DME (working circuit) Auxiliary fan relay stage 2 (working circuit)
No. F29	Compressor clutch relay - auxiliary fan relay stage 1 (control circuit) auxiliary water pump relay (control circuit) air conditioning system relay ON signal to DME (control circuit) auxiliary fan relay stage 2 (control circuit) Rear window defogger (control circuit)
No. F46	Rear defogger (working circuit)

Climate control system fuses and related fault codes

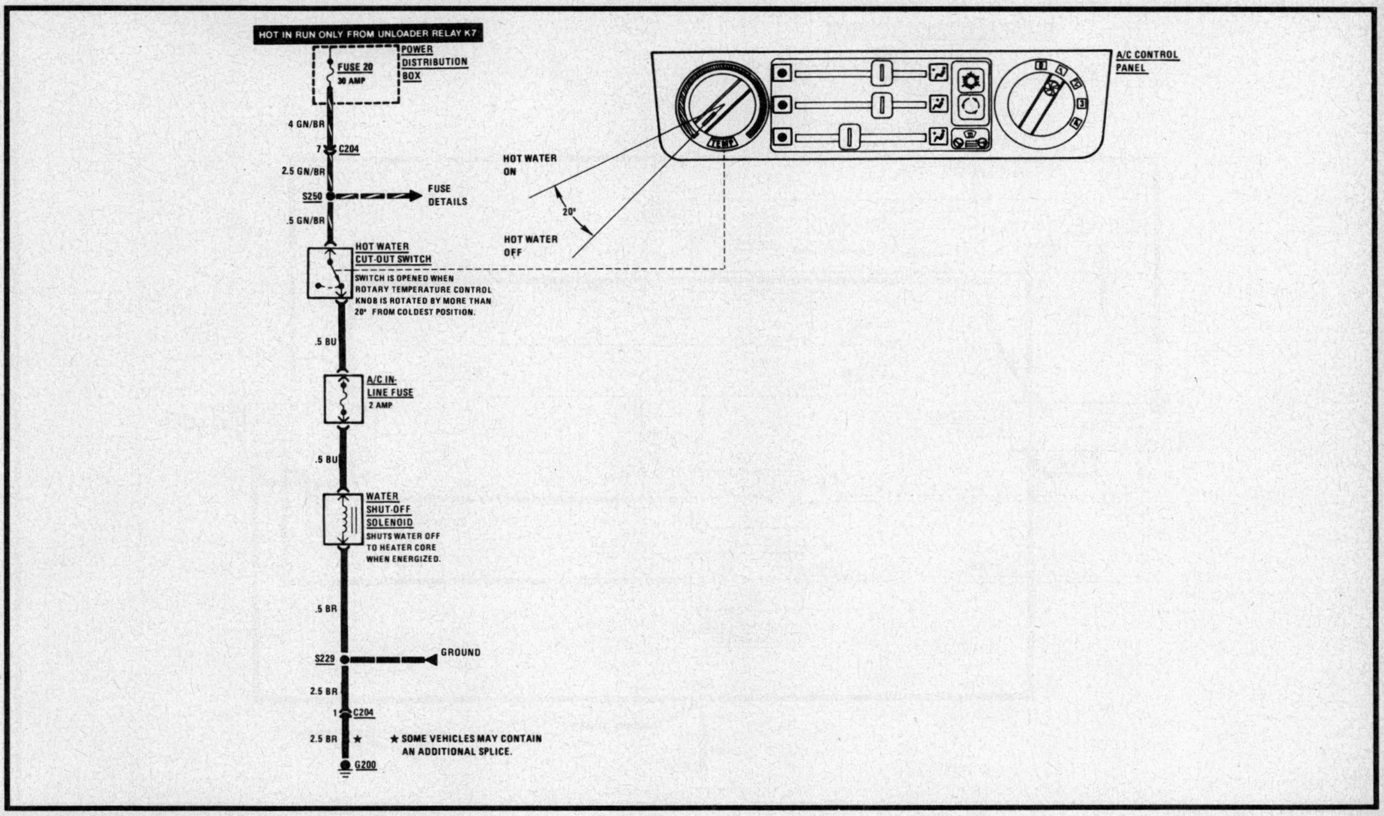
HOT IN RUN ONLY FROM UNLOADER RELAY K7
FUSE 20
30 AMP
POWER DISTRIBUTION BOX
4 GN/BR
C204
2.5 GN/BR
S250
FUSE DETAILS
.5 GN/BR
HOT WATER CUT-OUT SWITCH
SWITCH IS OPENED WHEN ROTARY TEMPERATURE CONTROL KNOB IS ROTATED BY MORE THAN 20° FROM COLDEST POSITION.
.5 BU
A/C IN-LINE FUSE
2 AMP
.5 BU
WATER SHUT-OFF SOLENOID
SHUTS WATER OFF TO HEATER CORE WHEN ENERGIZED.
.5 BR
S229
GROUND
2.5 BR
C204
2.5 BR
★ SOME VEHICLES MAY CONTAIN AN ADDITIONAL SPLICE.
G200
HOT WATER ON
20°
HOT WATER OFF
TEMP
A/C CONTROL PANEL

Hot water control circuit—3 Series

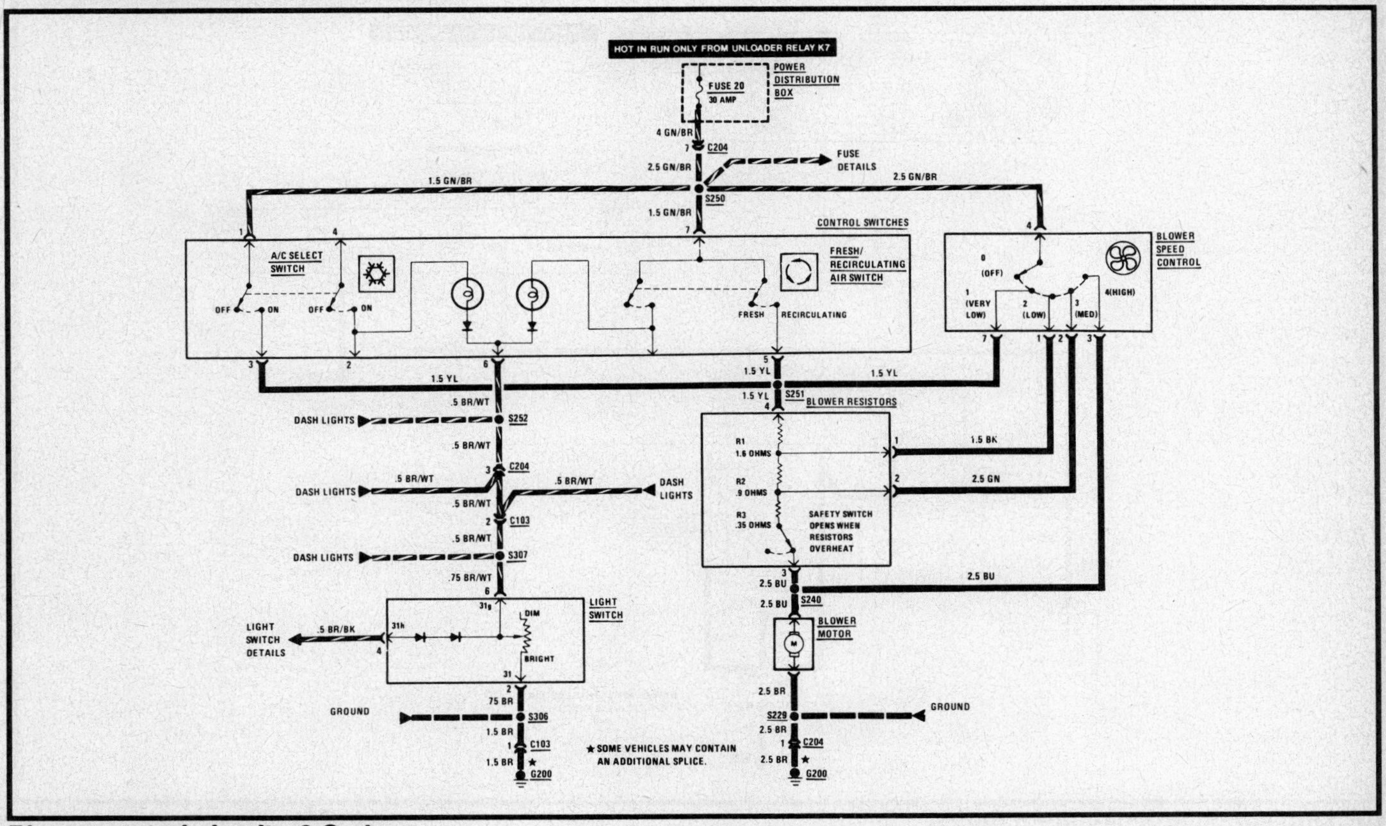
HOT IN RUN ONLY FROM UNLOADER RELAY K7
FUSE 20
30 AMP
POWER DISTRIBUTION BOX
4 GN/BR
C204
2.5 GN/BR
FUSE DETAILS
1.5 GN/BR
2.5 GN/BR
S250
1.5 GN/BR
CONTROL SWITCHES
A/C SELECT SWITCH
OFF
ON
FRESH/RECIRCULATING AIR SWITCH
FRESH
RECIRCULATING
BLOWER SPEED CONTROL
0 (OFF)
1 (VERY LOW)
2 (LOW)
3 (MED)
4(HIGH)
1.5 YL
.5 BR/WT
S252
DASH LIGHTS
C204
C103
S307
.75 BR/WT
S251
BLOWER RESISTORS
R1 1.6 OHMS
R2 .9 OHMS
R3 .35 OHMS
SAFETY SWITCH OPENS WHEN RESISTORS OVERHEAT
1.5 BK
2.5 GN
2.5 BU
S240
BLOWER MOTOR
LIGHT SWITCH
LIGHT SWITCH DETAILS
.5 BR/BK
DIM
BRIGHT
GROUND
.75 BR
S306
1.5 BR
C103
G200
★ SOME VEHICLES MAY CONTAIN AN ADDITIONAL SPLICE.
2.5 BR
S229
C204

Blower control circuit—3 Series

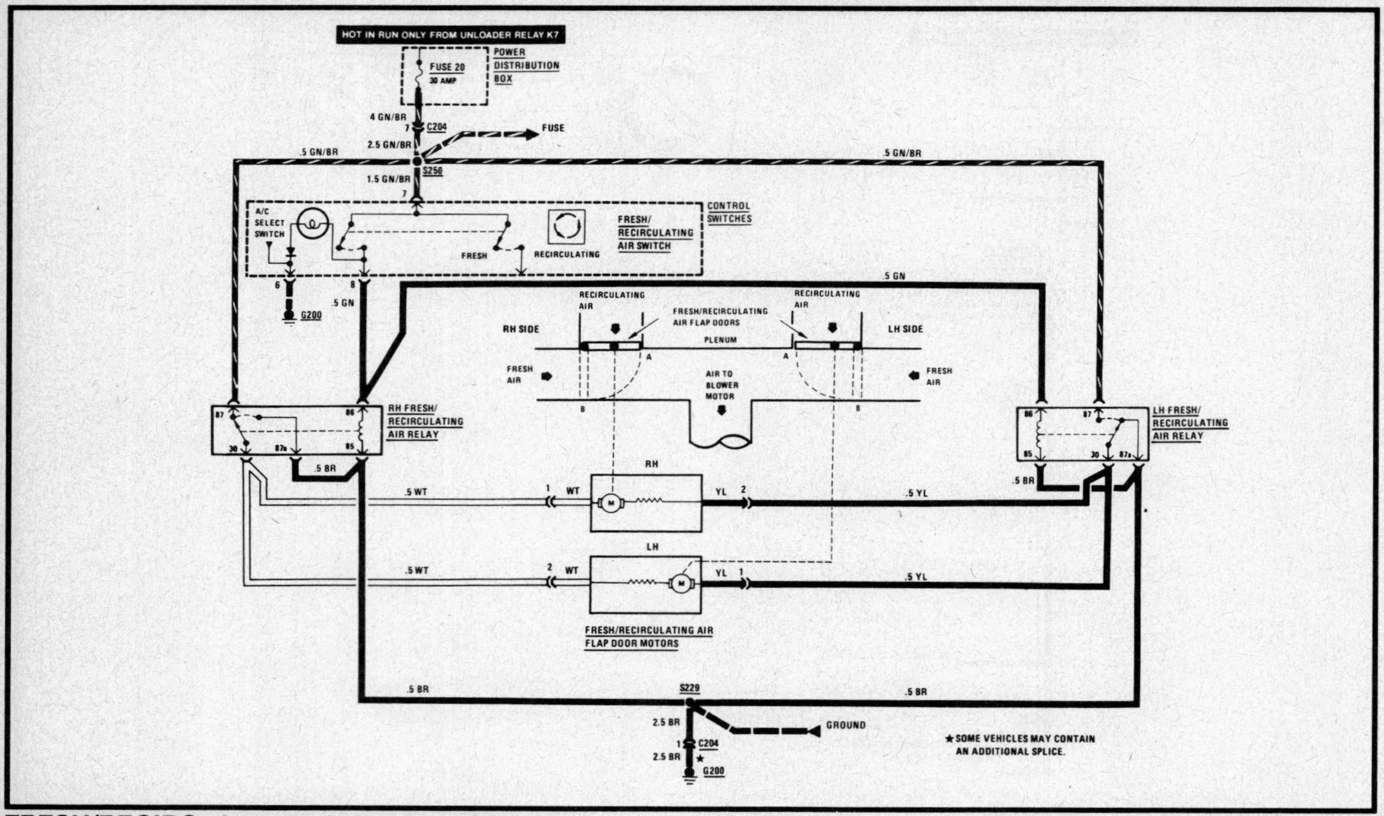
HOT IN RUN ONLY FROM UNLOADER RELAY K7
FUSE 20
30 AMP
POWER DISTRIBUTION BOX
4 GN/BR
C204
2.5 GN/BR
FUSE
.5 GN/BR
S250
1.5 GN/BR
.5 GN/BR
A/C SELECT SWITCH
FRESH
RECIRCULATING
FRESH/ RECIRCULATING AIR SWITCH
CONTROL SWITCHES
G200
.5 GN
.5 GN
RECIRCULATING AIR
FRESH/RECIRCULATING AIR FLAP DOORS
RECIRCULATING AIR
RH SIDE
PLENUM
LH SIDE
FRESH AIR
AIR TO BLOWER MOTOR
FRESH AIR
RH FRESH/ RECIRCULATING AIR RELAY
LH FRESH/ RECIRCULATING AIR RELAY
.5 BR
RH
.5 WT
WT
YL
.5 YL
.5 BR
LH
.5 WT
WT
YL
.5 YL
FRESH/RECIRCULATING AIR FLAP DOOR MOTORS
.5 BR
S229
.5 BR
2.5 BR
GROUND
C204
2.5 BR
G200
★SOME VEHICLES MAY CONTAIN AN ADDITIONAL SPLICE.

FRESH/RECIRC air control circuit—3 Series

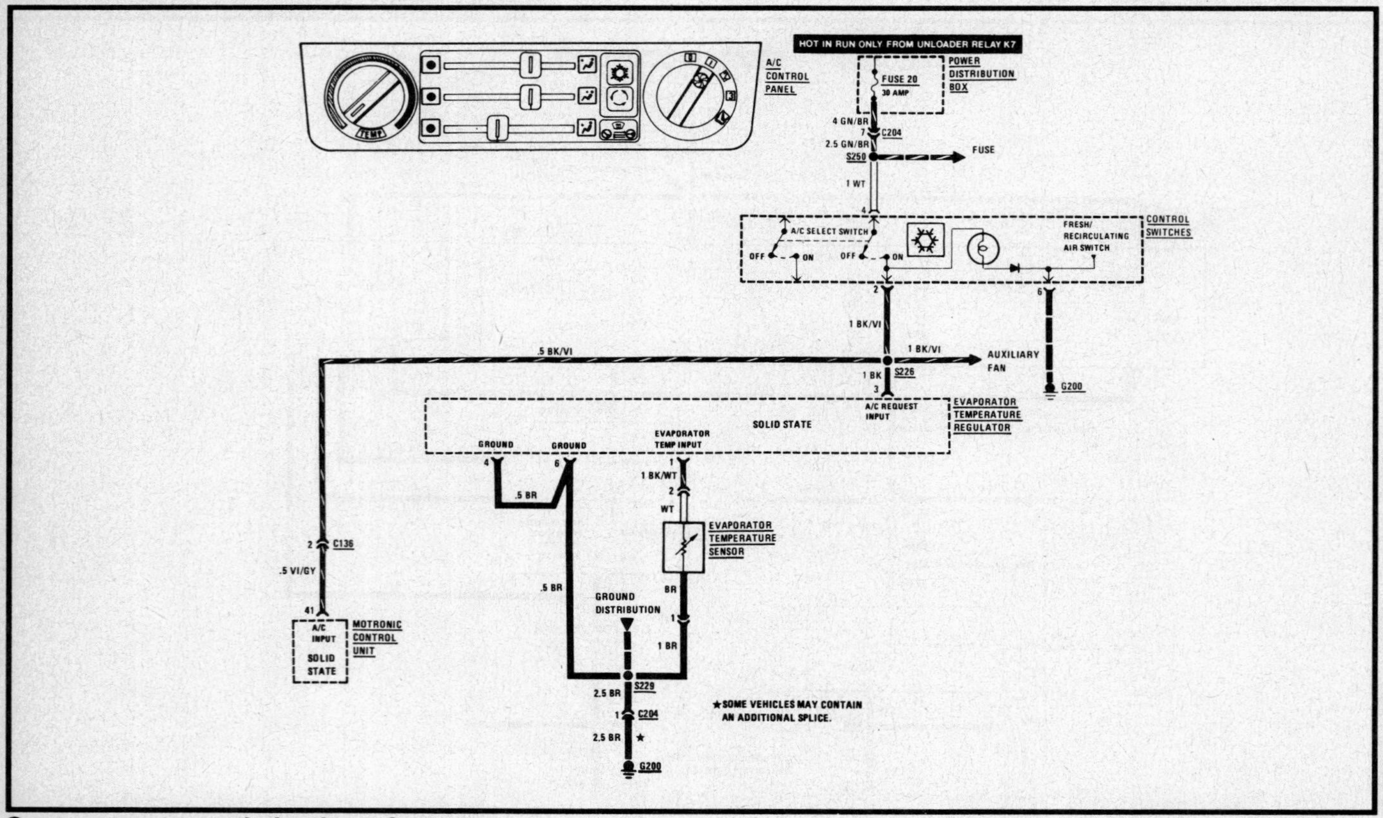
TEMP
A/C CONTROL PANEL
HOT IN RUN ONLY FROM UNLOADER RELAY K7
FUSE 20
30 AMP
POWER DISTRIBUTION BOX
4 GN/BR
C204
2.5 GN/BR
S250
FUSE
1 WT
A/C SELECT SWITCH
OFF
ON
OFF
ON
FRESH/ RECIRCULATING AIR SWITCH
CONTROL SWITCHES
1 BK/VI
.5 BK/VI
1 BK/VI
AUXILIARY FAN
1 BK
S226
G200
A/C REQUEST INPUT
SOLID STATE
EVAPORATOR TEMPERATURE REGULATOR
GROUND
GROUND
EVAPORATOR TEMP INPUT
.5 BR
1 BK/WT
WT
EVAPORATOR TEMPERATURE SENSOR
C136
.5 VI/GY
.5 BR
GROUND DISTRIBUTION
BR
1 BR
A/C INPUT
SOLID STATE
MOTRONIC CONTROL UNIT
2.5 BR
S229
C204
2.5 BR
G200
★SOME VEHICLES MAY CONTAIN AN ADDITIONAL SPLICE.

Compressor control circuit—3 Series

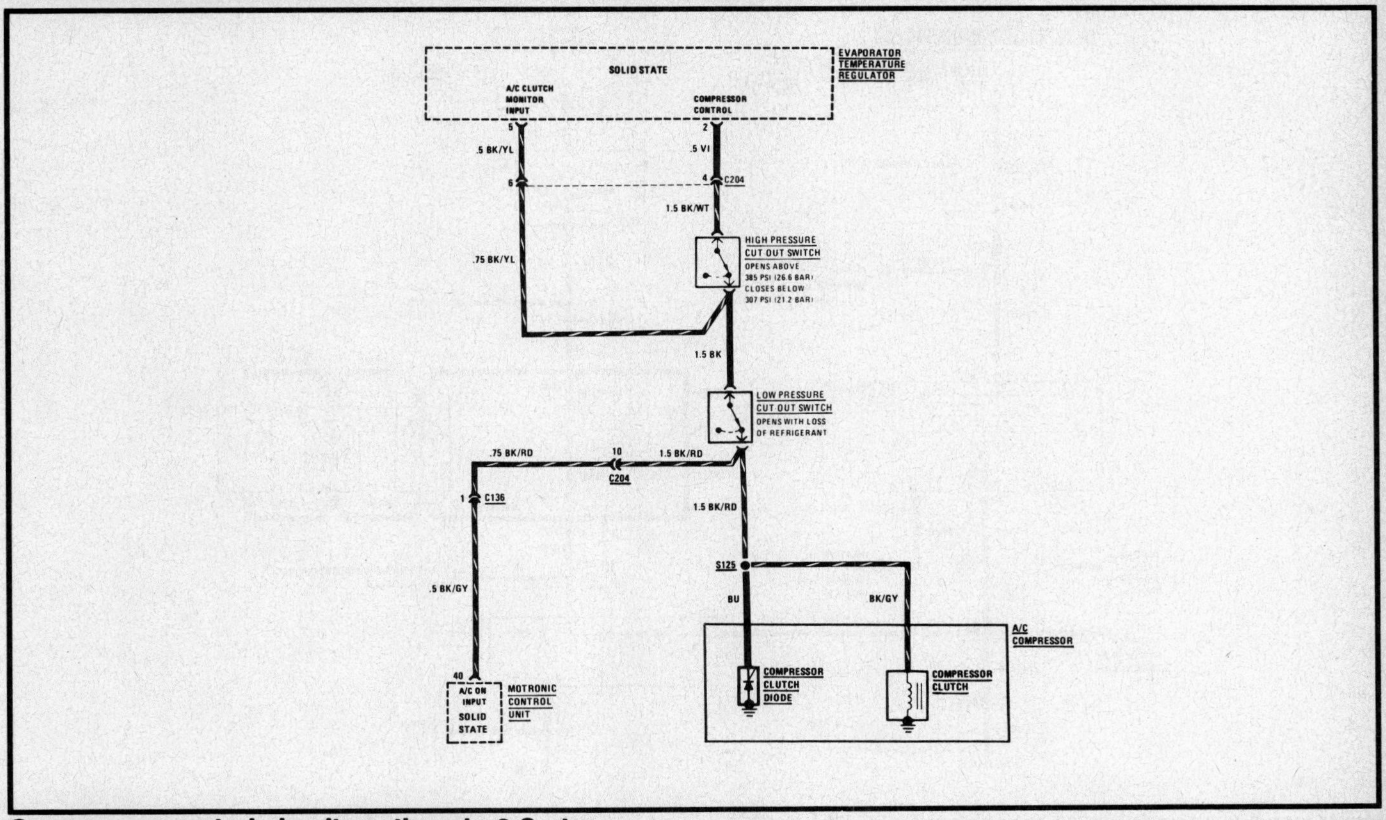
EVAPORATOR TEMPERATURE REGULATOR
SOLID STATE
A/C CLUTCH MONITOR INPUT
COMPRESSOR CONTROL
.5 BK/YL
.5 VI
C204
1.5 BK/WT
.75 BK/YL
HIGH PRESSURE CUT OUT SWITCH
OPENS ABOVE 385 PSI (26.6 BAR)
CLOSES BELOW 307 PSI (21.2 BAR)
1.5 BK
LOW PRESSURE CUT OUT SWITCH
OPENS WITH LOSS OF REFRIGERANT
.75 BK/RD
1.5 BK/RD
C204
C136
1.5 BK/RD
S125
BU
BK/GY
.5 BK/GY
A/C COMPRESSOR
COMPRESSOR CLUTCH DIODE
COMPRESSOR CLUTCH
A/C ON INPUT
SOLID STATE
MOTRONIC CONTROL UNIT

Compressor control circuit continued – 3 Series

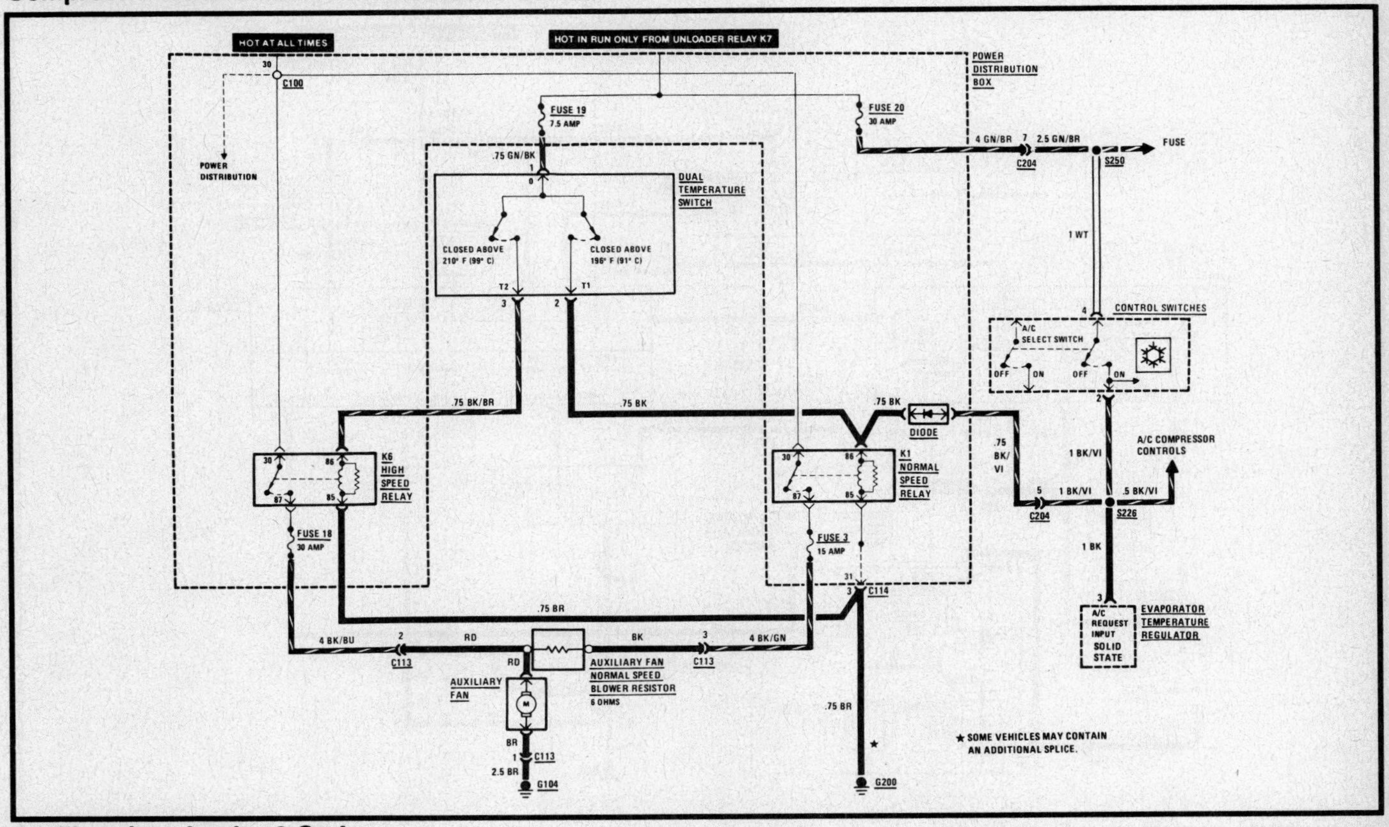
HOT AT ALL TIMES
HOT IN RUN ONLY FROM UNLOADER RELAY K7
POWER DISTRIBUTION BOX
C100
POWER DISTRIBUTION
FUSE 19
7.5 AMP
FUSE 20
30 AMP
4 GN/BR
2.5 GN/BR
C204
S250
FUSE
.75 GN/BK
DUAL TEMPERATURE SWITCH
CLOSED ABOVE 210° F (99° C)
CLOSED ABOVE 196° F (91° C)
T2
T1
1 WT
CONTROL SWITCHES
A/C SELECT SWITCH
OFF
ON
.75 BK/BR
.75 BK
.75 BK
DIODE
.75 BK/VI
A/C COMPRESSOR CONTROLS
1 BK/VI
K6 HIGH SPEED RELAY
K1 NORMAL SPEED RELAY
1 BK/VI
.5 BK/VI
C204
S226
FUSE 18
30 AMP
FUSE 3
15 AMP
1 BK
C114
.75 BR
EVAPORATOR TEMPERATURE REGULATOR
A/C REQUEST INPUT
SOLID STATE
4 BK/BU
RD
BK
4 BK/GN
C113
C113
AUXILIARY FAN NORMAL SPEED BLOWER RESISTOR
6 OHMS
AUXILIARY FAN
.75 BR
BR
C113
2.5 BR
G104
G200
★ SOME VEHICLES MAY CONTAIN AN ADDITIONAL SPLICE.

Auxiliary fan circuit – 3 Series

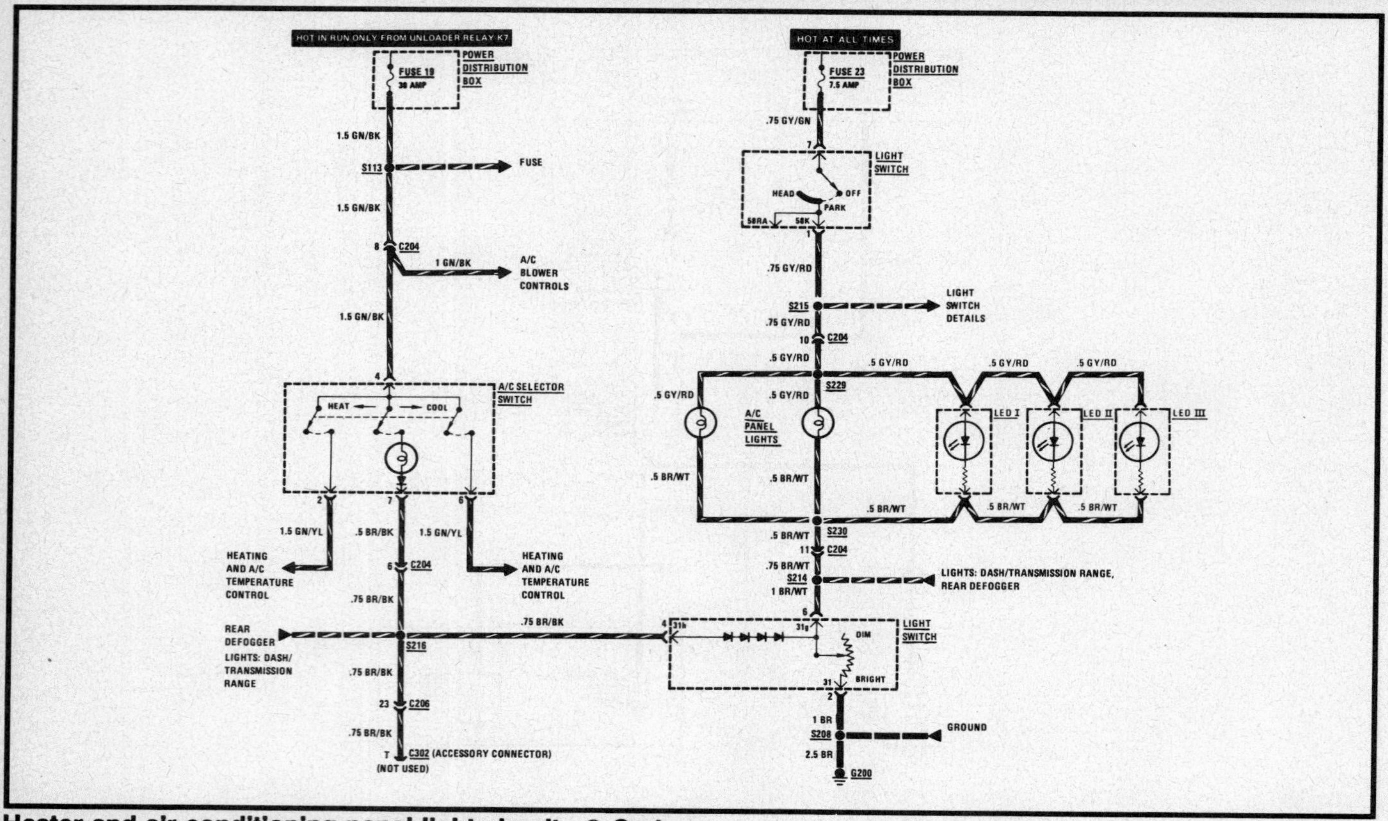
HOT IN RUN ONLY FROM UNLOADER RELAY K7
FUSE 19 30 AMP
POWER DISTRIBUTION BOX
1.5 GN/BK
S113
FUSE
C204
1 GN/BK
A/C BLOWER CONTROLS
A/C SELECTOR SWITCH
HEAT
COOL
1.5 GN/YL
.5 BR/BK
HEATING AND A/C TEMPERATURE CONTROL
.75 BR/BK
REAR DEFOGGER LIGHTS: DASH/ TRANSMISSION RANGE
S216
C206
C302 (ACCESSORY CONNECTOR) (NOT USED)
HOT AT ALL TIMES
FUSE 23 7.5 AMP
.75 GY/GN
LIGHT SWITCH
HEAD
OFF
PARK
58RA
58K
.75 GY/RD
S215
LIGHT SWITCH DETAILS
.5 GY/RD
S229
A/C PANEL LIGHTS
LED I
LED II
LED III
.5 BR/WT
S230
.75 BR/WT
S214
1 BR/WT
LIGHTS: DASH/TRANSMISSION RANGE, REAR DEFOGGER
DIM
BRIGHT
1 BR
S208
GROUND
2.5 BR
G200

Heater and air conditioning panel light circuit – 6 Series

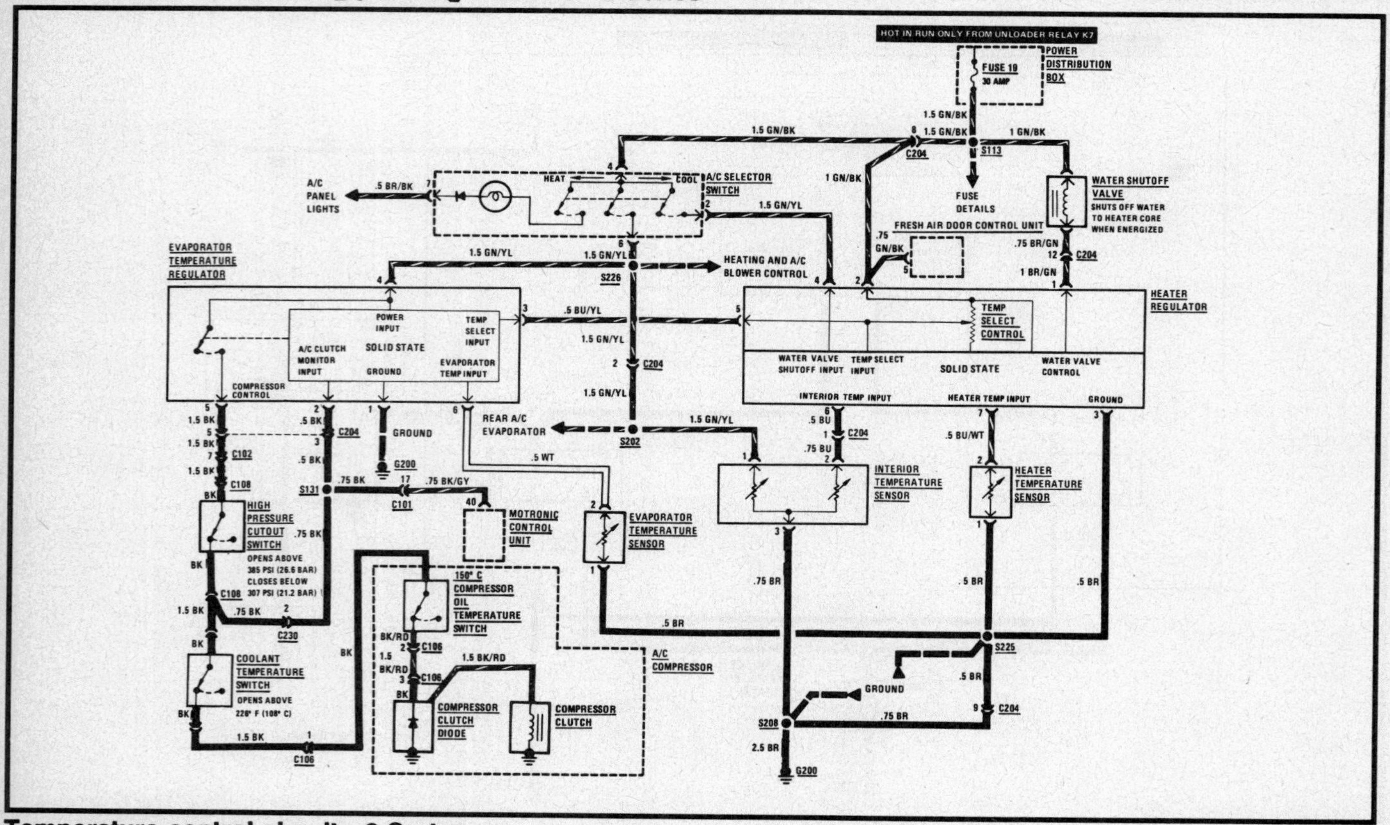
HOT IN RUN ONLY FROM UNLOADER RELAY K7
FUSE 19 30 AMP
POWER DISTRIBUTION BOX
1.5 GN/BK
1 GN/BK
C204
S113
FUSE DETAILS
WATER SHUTOFF VALVE
SHUTS OFF WATER TO HEATER CORE WHEN ENERGIZED
A/C PANEL LIGHTS
.5 BR/BK
A/C SELECTOR SWITCH
HEAT
COOL
1.5 GN/YL
FRESH AIR DOOR CONTROL UNIT
.75 GN/BK
.75 BR/GN
1 BR/GN
EVAPORATOR TEMPERATURE REGULATOR
HEATING AND A/C BLOWER CONTROL
S226
POWER INPUT
TEMP SELECT INPUT
A/C CLUTCH MONITOR INPUT
SOLID STATE
GROUND
EVAPORATOR TEMP INPUT
COMPRESSOR CONTROL
.5 BU/YL
HEATER REGULATOR
TEMP SELECT CONTROL
WATER VALVE SHUTOFF INPUT
TEMP SELECT INPUT
WATER VALVE CONTROL
INTERIOR TEMP INPUT
HEATER TEMP INPUT
GROUND
1.5 BK
.5 BK
C102
C108
REAR A/C EVAPORATOR
S202
.5 BU
.75 BU
.5 BU/WT
G200
S131
.75 BK
.75 BK/GY
C101
.5 WT
HIGH PRESSURE CUTOUT SWITCH
OPENS ABOVE 385 PSI (26.6 BAR) CLOSES BELOW 307 PSI (21.2 BAR)
MOTRONIC CONTROL UNIT
EVAPORATOR TEMPERATURE SENSOR
INTERIOR TEMPERATURE SENSOR
HEATER TEMPERATURE SENSOR
150° C COMPRESSOR OIL TEMPERATURE SWITCH
C230
C106
BK/RD
1.5 BK/RD
A/C COMPRESSOR
.75 BR
.5 BR
S225
COOLANT TEMPERATURE SWITCH
OPENS ABOVE 228° F (108° C)
COMPRESSOR CLUTCH DIODE
COMPRESSOR CLUTCH
GROUND
S208
2.5 BR

Temperature control circuit – 6 Series

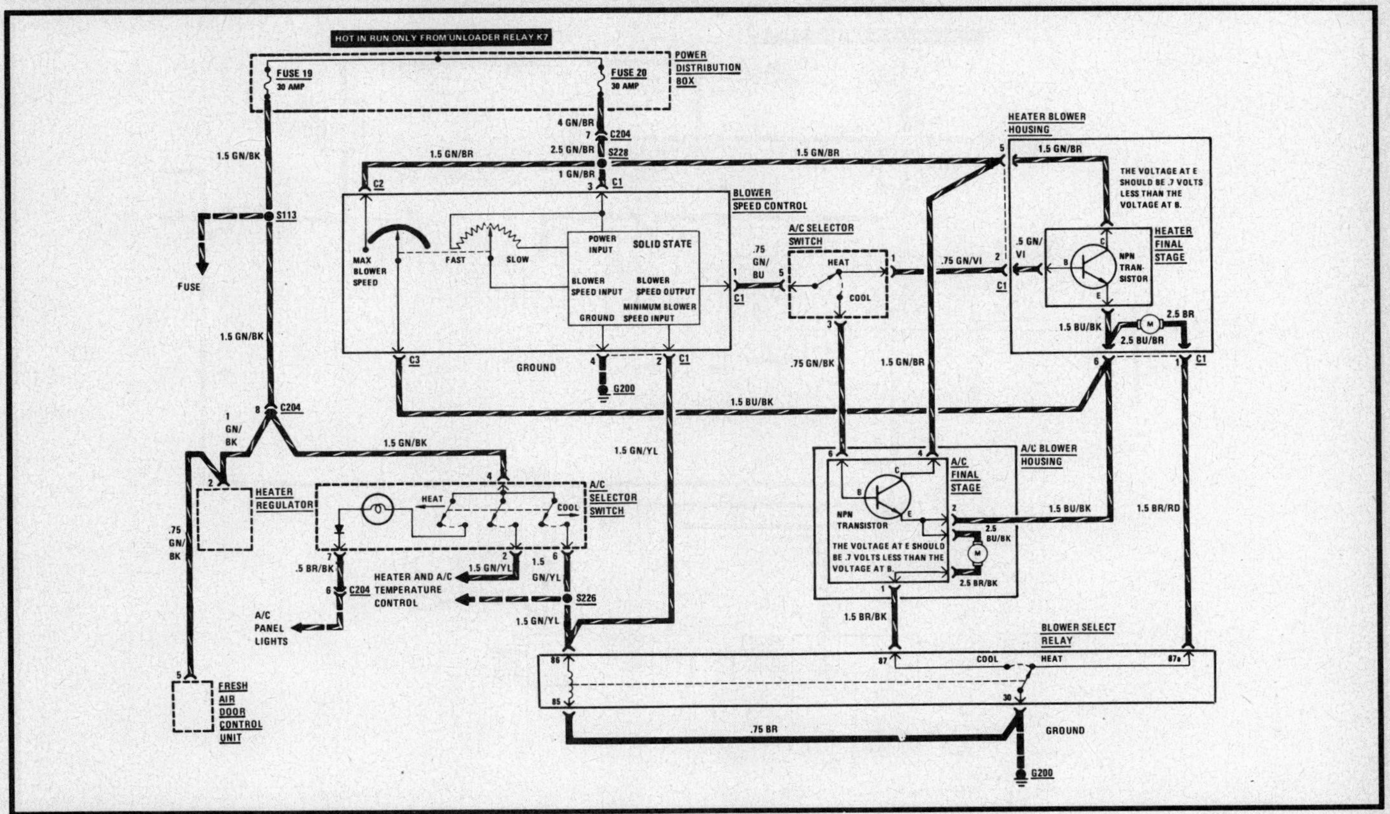
HOT IN RUN ONLY FROM UNLOADER RELAY K7
FUSE 19 30 AMP
FUSE 20 30 AMP
POWER DISTRIBUTION BOX
4 GN/BR
C204
2.5 GN/BR
S228
1 GN/BR
C1
1.5 GN/BK
1.5 GN/BR
C2
HEATER BLOWER HOUSING
THE VOLTAGE AT E SHOULD BE .7 VOLTS LESS THAN THE VOLTAGE AT B.
BLOWER SPEED CONTROL
S113
FUSE
MAX BLOWER SPEED
FAST
SLOW
POWER INPUT
SOLID STATE
BLOWER SPEED INPUT
BLOWER SPEED OUTPUT
MINIMUM BLOWER SPEED INPUT
GROUND
A/C SELECTOR SWITCH
HEAT
COOL
.75 GN/BU
.75 GN/VI
.5 GN/VI
HEATER FINAL STAGE
NPN TRANSISTOR
1.5 BU/BK
2.5 BR
2.5 BU/BR
C3
G200
.75 GN/BK
1.5 BU/BK
C204
1 GN/BK
1.5 GN/YL
A/C BLOWER HOUSING
A/C FINAL STAGE
HEATER REGULATOR
A/C SELECTOR SWITCH
NPN TRANSISTOR
THE VOLTAGE AT E SHOULD BE .7 VOLTS LESS THAN THE VOLTAGE AT B.
2.5 BU/BK
2.5 BR/BK
1.5 BR/RD
.75 GN/BK
.5 BR/BK
1.5 GN/YL
HEATER AND A/C TEMPERATURE CONTROL
S226
A/C PANEL LIGHTS
1.5 BR/BK
BLOWER SELECT RELAY
COOL
HEAT
FRESH AIR DOOR CONTROL UNIT
.75 BR
GROUND
G200

Blower control circuit—6 Series

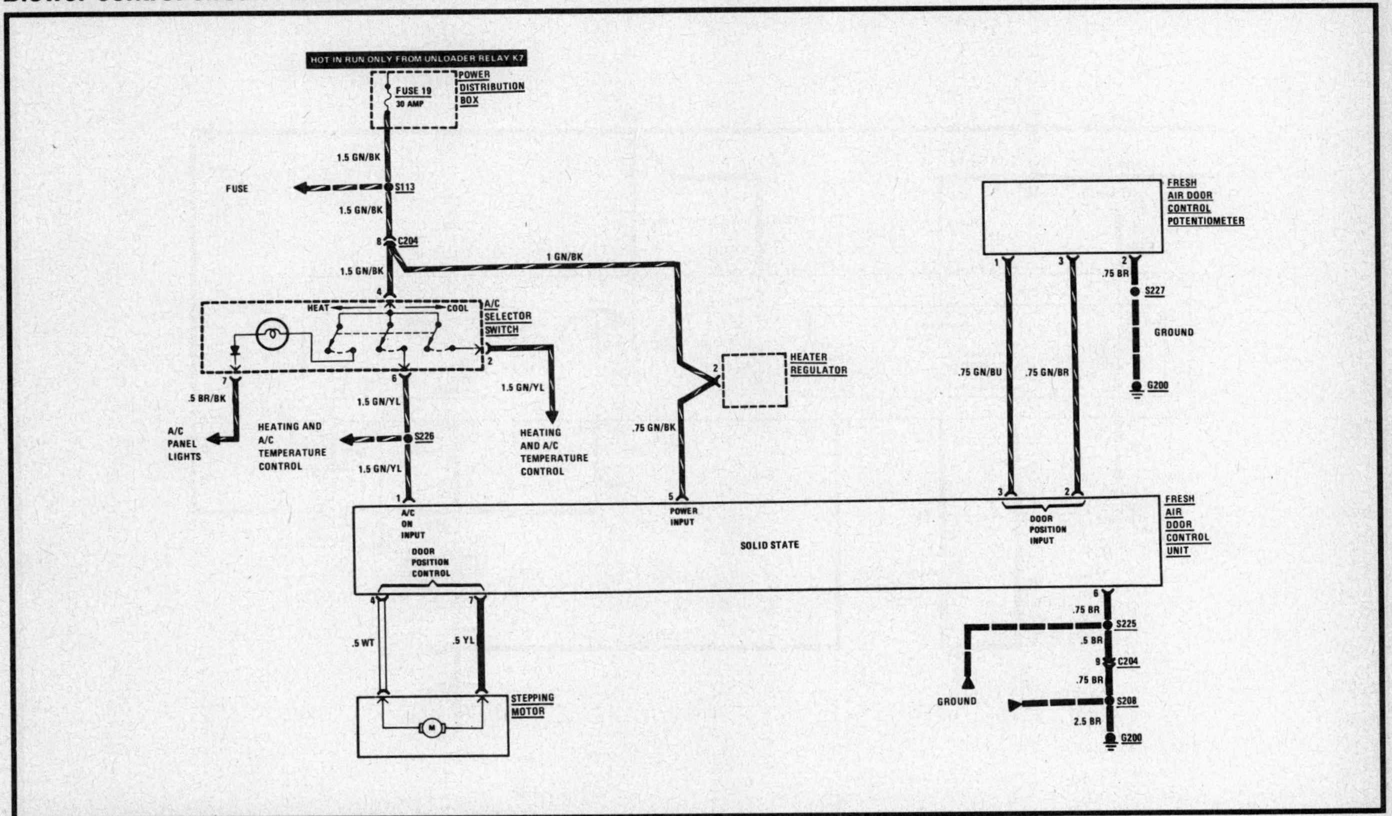
HOT IN RUN ONLY FROM UNLOADER RELAY K7
FUSE 19 30 AMP
POWER DISTRIBUTION BOX
1.5 GN/BK
FUSE
S113
C204
1 GN/BK
FRESH AIR DOOR CONTROL POTENTIOMETER
.75 BR
S227
GROUND
G200
HEAT
COOL
A/C SELECTOR SWITCH
HEATER REGULATOR
.5 BR/BK
1.5 GN/YL
.75 GN/BU
.75 GN/BR
A/C PANEL LIGHTS
HEATING AND A/C TEMPERATURE CONTROL
S226
.75 GN/BK
A/C ON INPUT
POWER INPUT
SOLID STATE
DOOR POSITION INPUT
DOOR POSITION CONTROL
FRESH AIR DOOR CONTROL UNIT
.75 BR
S225
.5 BR
C204
S208
2.5 BR
G200
GROUND
.5 WT
.5 YL
STEPPING MOTOR

Blower control circuit continued—6 Series

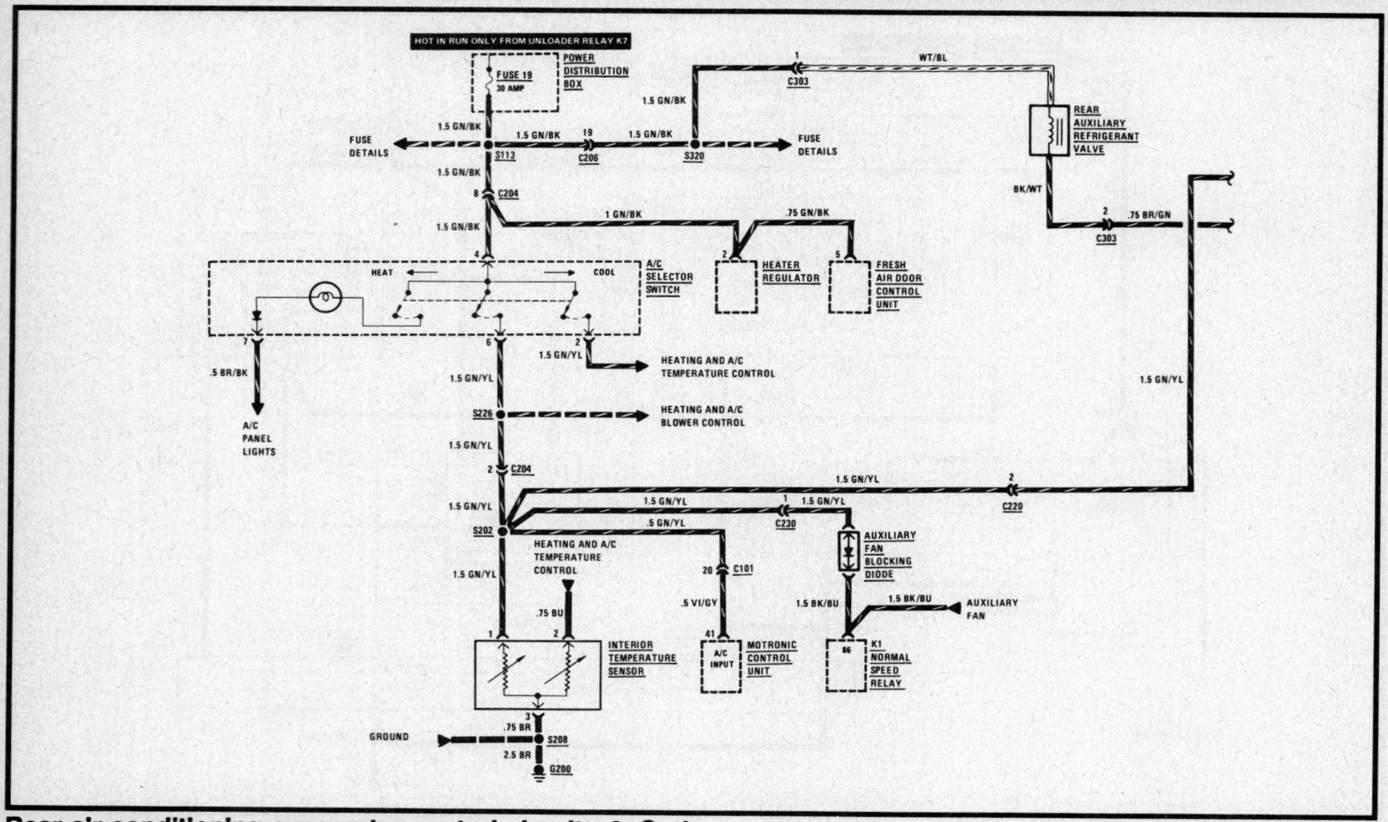
HOT IN RUN ONLY FROM UNLOADER RELAY K7
FUSE 19 30 AMP
POWER DISTRIBUTION BOX
1.5 GN/BK
FUSE DETAILS
S113
1.5 GN/BK
19
C206
S320
FUSE DETAILS
WT/BL
C303
REAR AUXILIARY REFRIGERANT VALVE
BK/WT
C204
1 GN/BK
.75 GN/BK
HEATER REGULATOR
FRESH AIR DOOR CONTROL UNIT
.75 BR/GN
HEAT
COOL
A/C SELECTOR SWITCH
.5 BR/BK
A/C PANEL LIGHTS
1.5 GN/YL
HEATING AND A/C TEMPERATURE CONTROL
S226
HEATING AND A/C BLOWER CONTROL
C220
C230
S202
.5 GN/YL
AUXILIARY FAN BLOCKING DIODE
C101
.5 VI/GY
1.5 BK/BU
AUXILIARY FAN
.75 BU
INTERIOR TEMPERATURE SENSOR
A/C INPUT
MOTRONIC CONTROL UNIT
K1 NORMAL SPEED RELAY
GROUND
.75 BR
S208
2.5 BR
G200

Rear air conditioning evaporator control circuit—6 Series

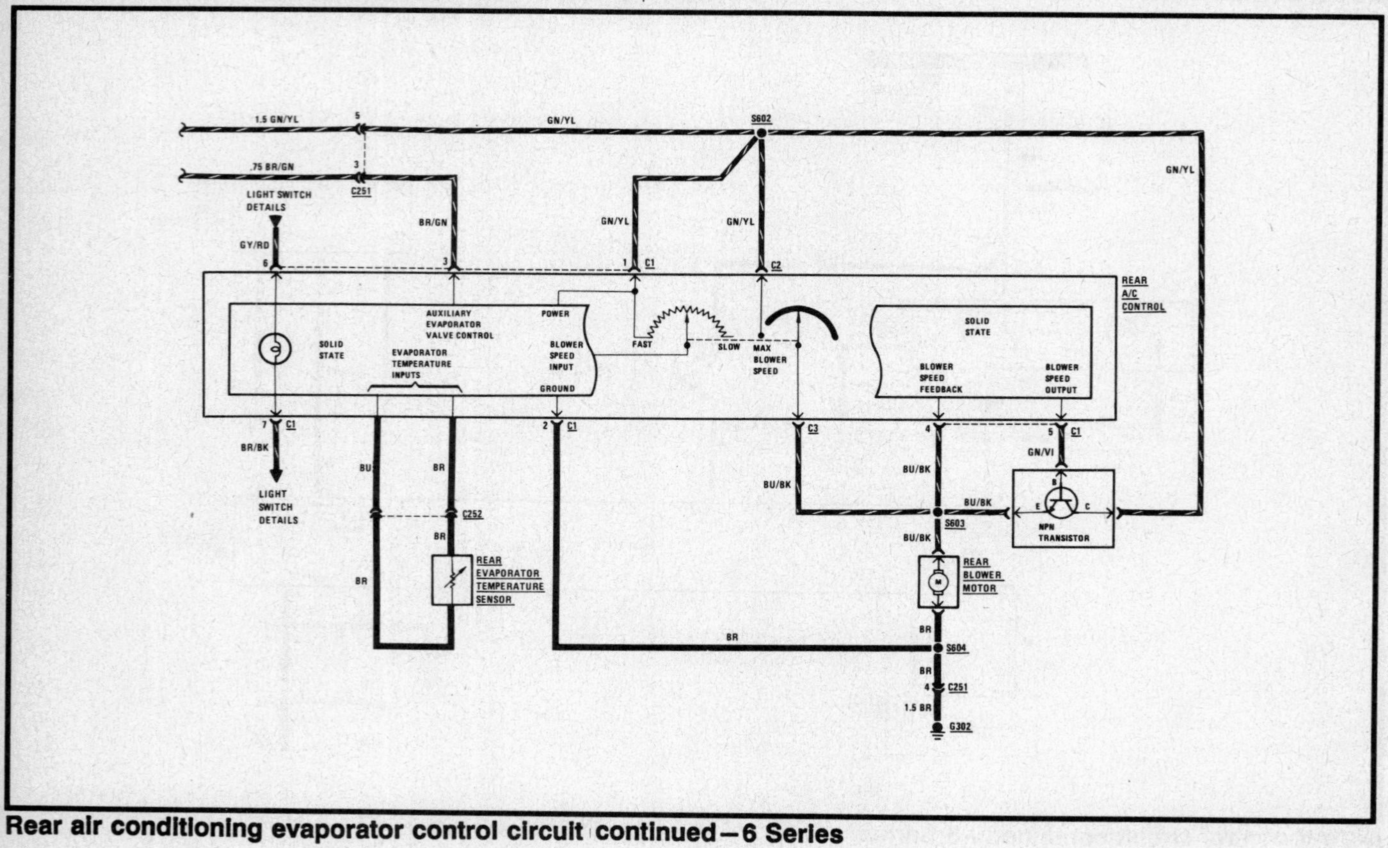
1.5 GN/YL
GN/YL
S602
.75 BR/GN
C251
LIGHT SWITCH DETAILS
BR/GN
GY/RD
C1
C2
REAR A/C CONTROL
SOLID STATE
AUXILIARY EVAPORATOR VALVE CONTROL
EVAPORATOR TEMPERATURE INPUTS
POWER
BLOWER SPEED INPUT
GROUND
FAST
SLOW
MAX BLOWER SPEED
BLOWER SPEED FEEDBACK
BLOWER SPEED OUTPUT
BR/BK
LIGHT SWITCH DETAILS
BU
BR
C3
BU/BK
GN/VI
C252
REAR EVAPORATOR TEMPERATURE SENSOR
S603
NPN TRANSISTOR
REAR BLOWER MOTOR
S604
1.5 BR
G302

Rear air conditioning evaporator control circuit continued—6 Series

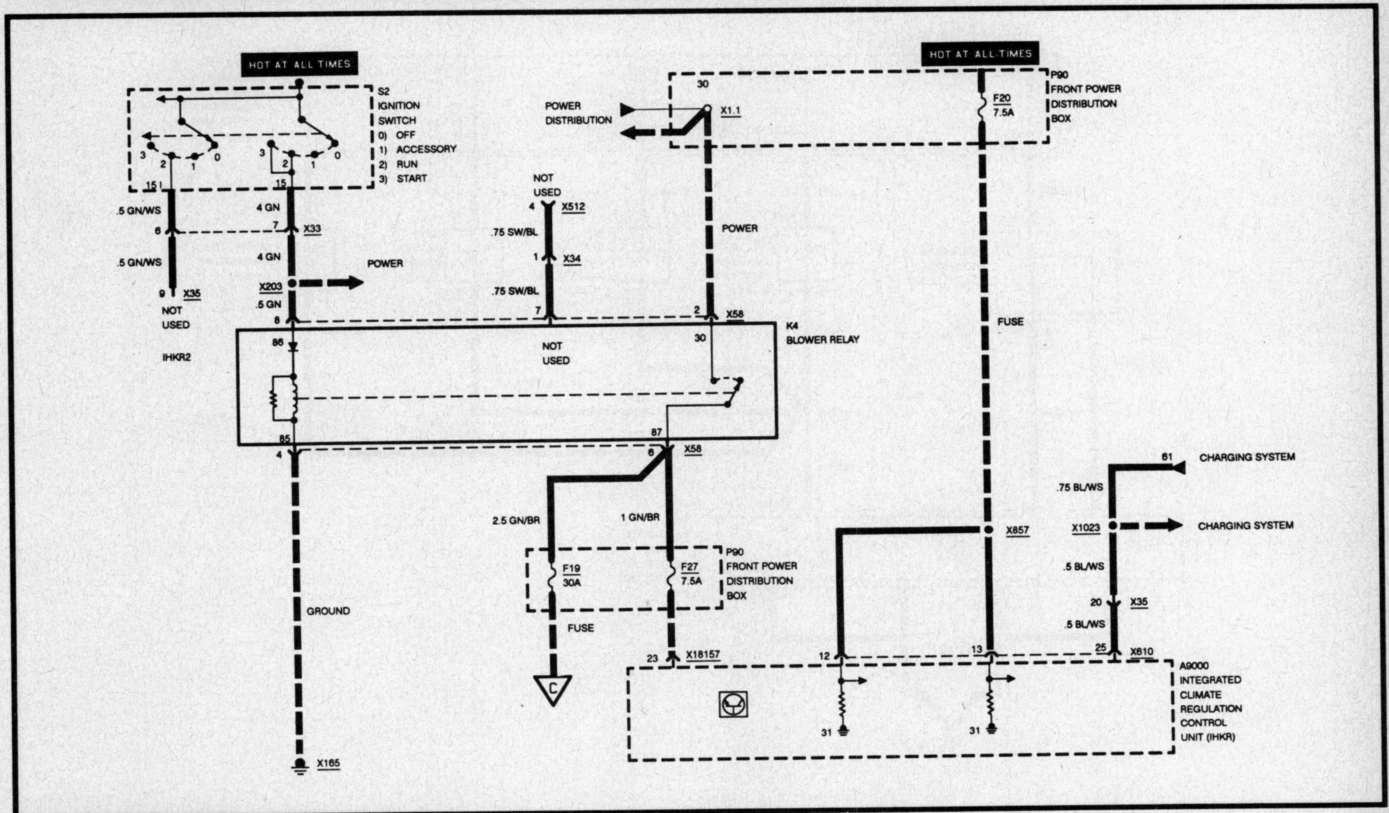
HOT AT ALL TIMES
S2
IGNITION
SWITCH
0) OFF
1) ACCESSORY
2) RUN
3) START
.5 GN/WS
4 GN
X33
X35
NOT
USED
IHKR2
X203
.5 GN
POWER
POWER
DISTRIBUTION
X1.1
NOT
USED
X512
.75 SW/BL
X34
X58
K4
BLOWER RELAY
HOT AT ALL TIMES
P90
FRONT POWER
DISTRIBUTION
BOX
F20
7.5A
FUSE
2.5 GN/BR
1 GN/BR
F19
30A
F27
7.5A
GROUND
X165
X18157
X857
X1023
CHARGING SYSTEM
CHARGING SYSTEM
.75 BL/WS
.5 BL/WS
X610
A9000
INTEGRATED
CLIMATE
REGULATION
CONTROL
UNIT (IHKR)

Power circuit – 5 Series

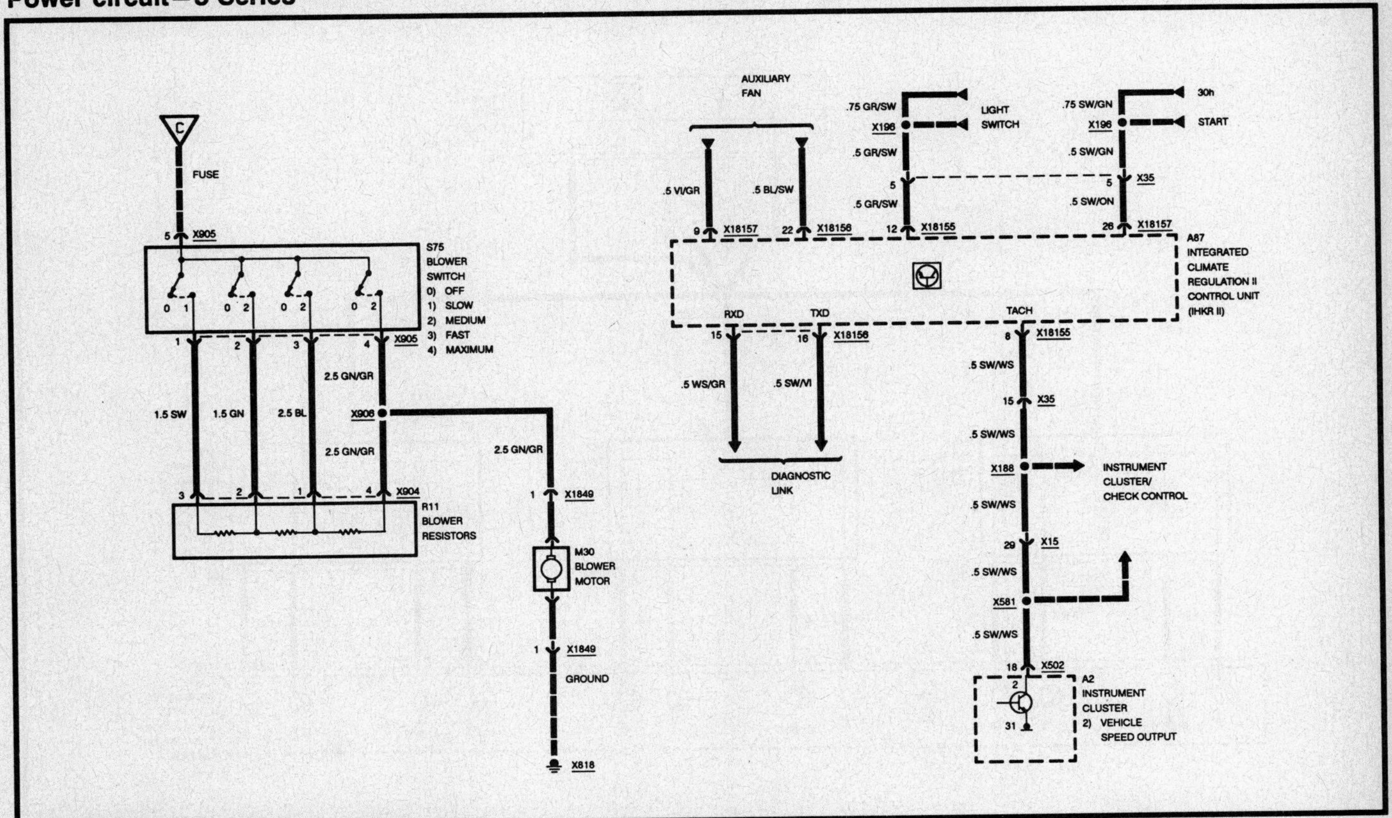
FUSE
X905
S75
BLOWER
SWITCH
0) OFF
1) SLOW
2) MEDIUM
3) FAST
4) MAXIMUM
1.5 SW
1.5 GN
2.5 BL
2.5 GN/GR
X906
X904
R11
BLOWER
RESISTORS
X1849
M30
BLOWER
MOTOR
GROUND
X818
AUXILIARY
FAN
.5 VI/GR
.5 BL/SW
.75 GR/SW
X196
LIGHT
SWITCH
.5 GR/SW
.75 SW/GN
30h
START
.5 SW/GN
X35
X18157
X18156
X18155
A87
INTEGRATED
CLIMATE
REGULATION II
CONTROL UNIT
(IHKR II)
RXD
TXD
TACH
.5 WS/GR
.5 SW/VI
DIAGNOSTIC
LINK
.5 SW/WS
X188
INSTRUMENT
CLUSTER/
CHECK CONTROL
X15
X581
X502
A2
INSTRUMENT
CLUSTER
2) VEHICLE
SPEED OUTPUT

Power circuit continued – 5 Series

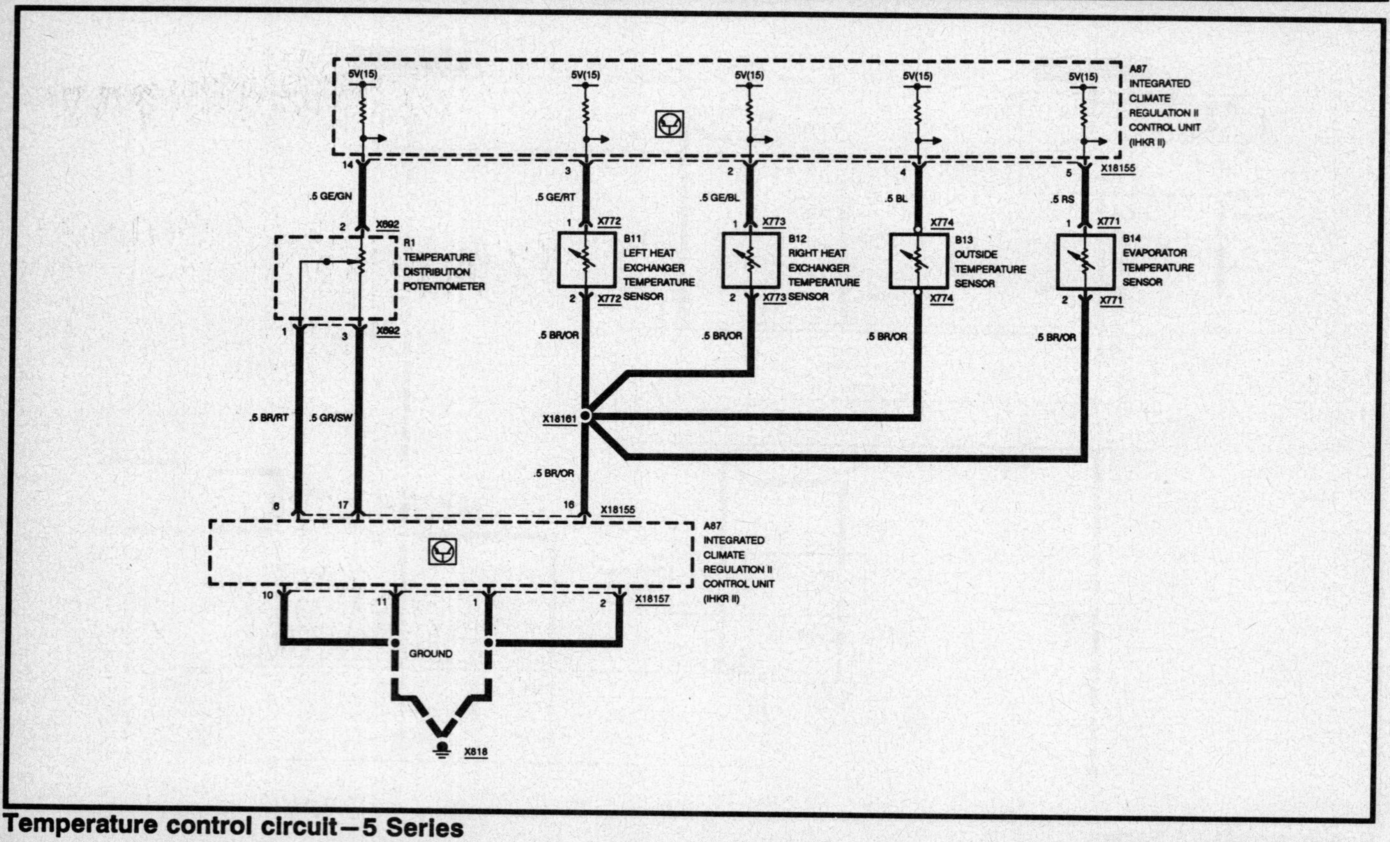
5V(15)
A87
INTEGRATED
CLIMATE
REGULATION II
CONTROL UNIT
(IHKR II)
X18155
.5 GE/GN
.5 GE/RT
.5 GE/BL
.5 BL
.5 RS
X692
R1
TEMPERATURE
DISTRIBUTION
POTENTIOMETER
X772
B11
LEFT HEAT
EXCHANGER
TEMPERATURE
SENSOR
X773
B12
RIGHT HEAT
EXCHANGER
TEMPERATURE
SENSOR
X774
B13
OUTSIDE
TEMPERATURE
SENSOR
X771
B14
EVAPORATOR
TEMPERATURE
SENSOR
.5 BR/OR
.5 BR/RT
.5 GR/SW
X18161
X18157
GROUND
X818

Temperature control circuit—5 Series

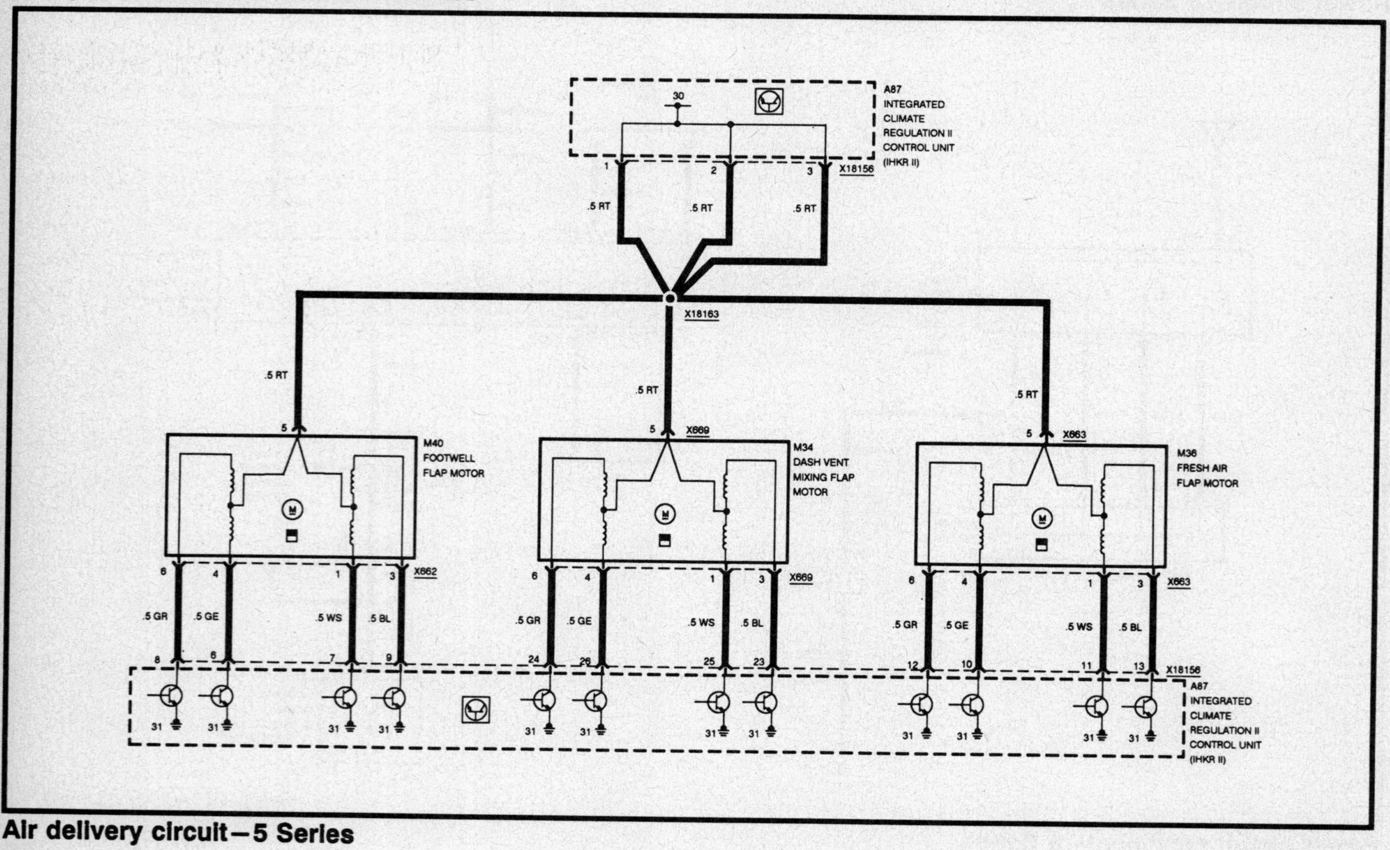
30
A87
INTEGRATED
CLIMATE
REGULATION II
CONTROL UNIT
(IHKR II)
X18156
.5 RT
X18163
M40
FOOTWELL
FLAP MOTOR
X669
M34
DASH VENT
MIXING FLAP
MOTOR
X663
M36
FRESH AIR
FLAP MOTOR
X662
.5 GR
.5 GE
.5 WS
.5 BL
31

Air delivery circuit—5 Series

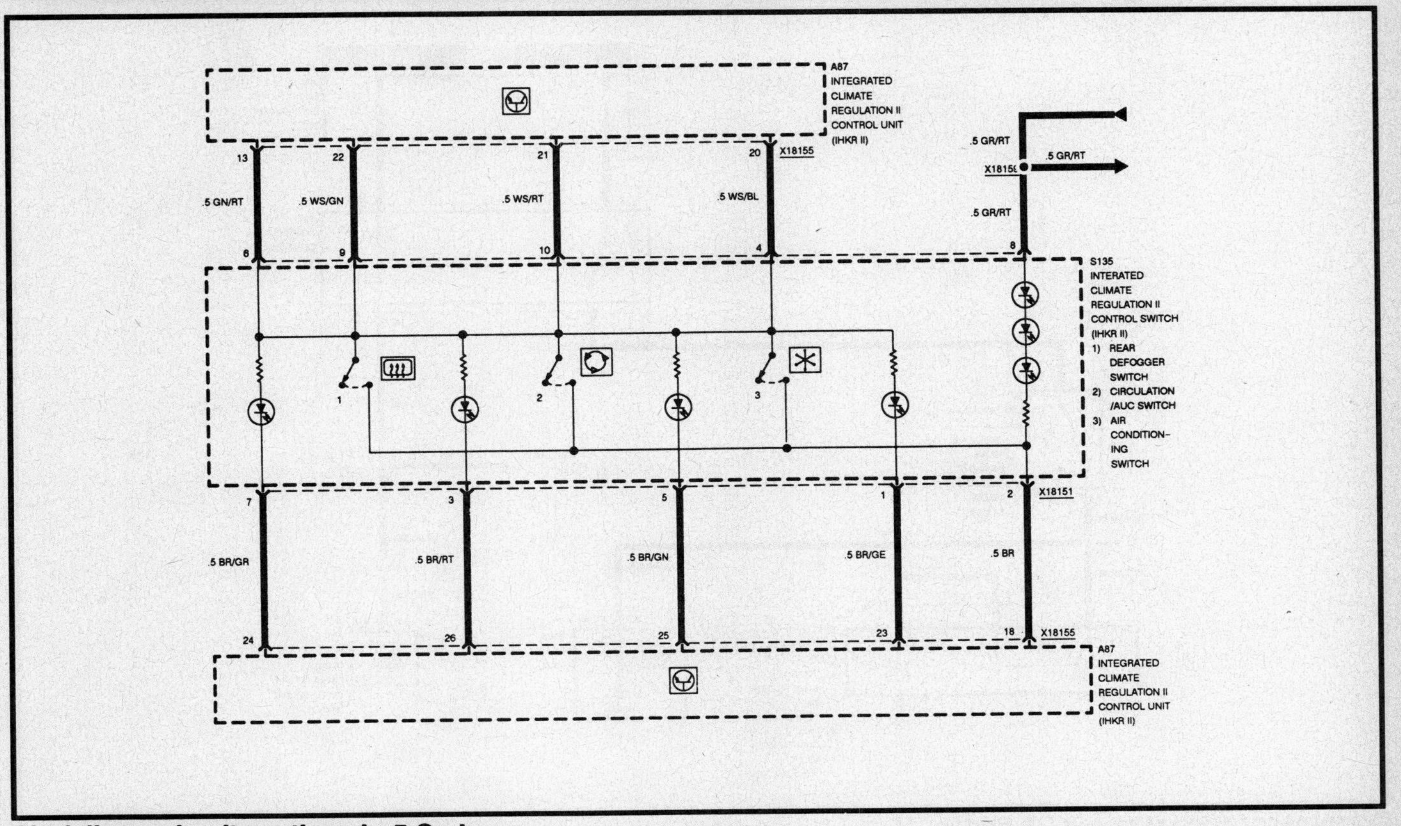
A87
INTEGRATED
CLIMATE
REGULATION II
CONTROL UNIT
(IHKR II)
X18155
.5 GN/RT
.5 WS/GN
.5 WS/RT
.5 WS/BL
.5 GR/RT
X18159
S135
INTERATED
CLIMATE
REGULATION II
CONTROL SWITCH
(IHKR II)
1) REAR DEFOGGER SWITCH
2) CIRCULATION /AUC SWITCH
3) AIR CONDITION-ING SWITCH
X18151
.5 BR/GR
.5 BR/RT
.5 BR/GN
.5 BR/GE
.5 BR
X18155
A87
INTEGRATED
CLIMATE
REGULATION II
CONTROL UNIT
(IHKR II)

Air delivery circuit continued—5 Series

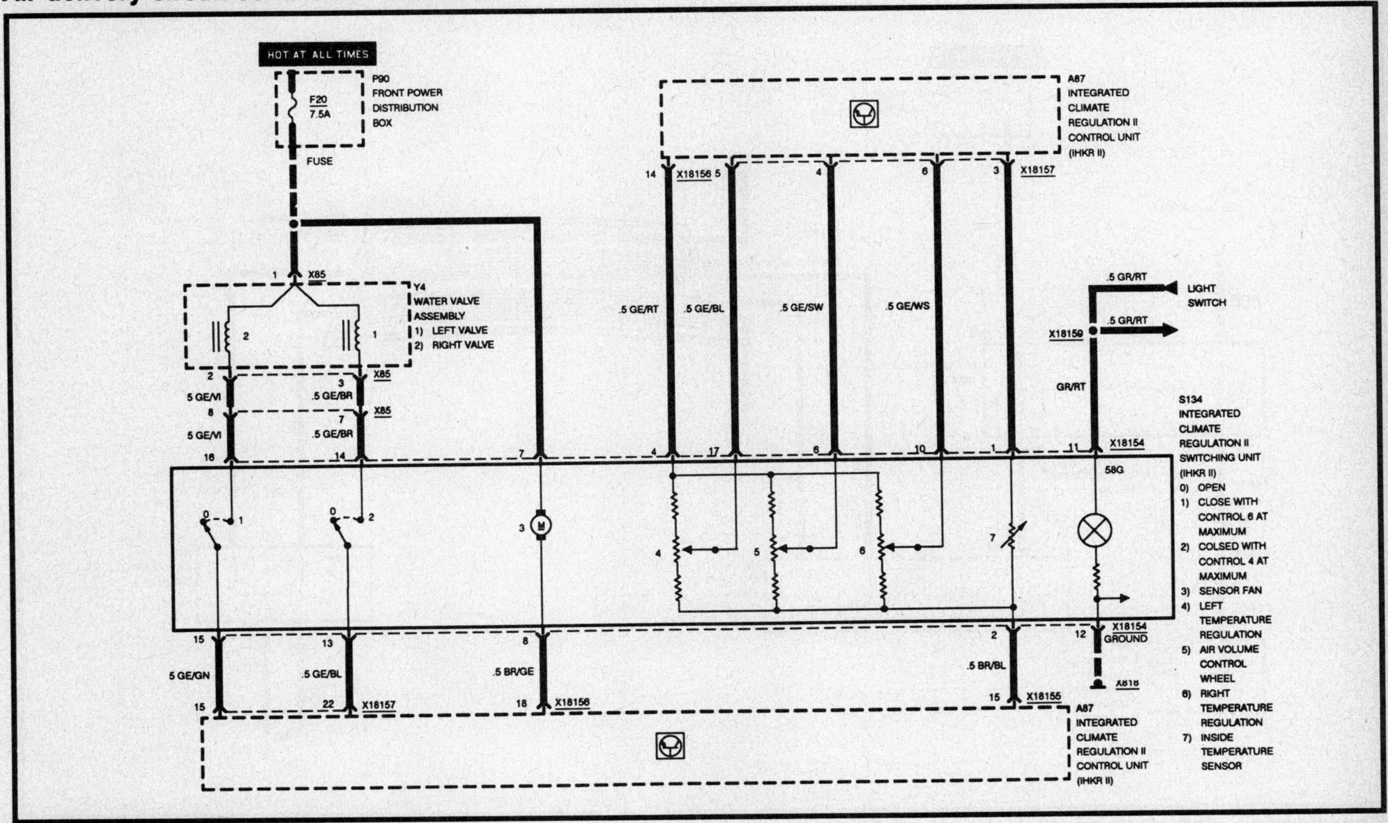
HOT AT ALL TIMES
F20
7.5A
P90
FRONT POWER
DISTRIBUTION
BOX
FUSE
A87
INTEGRATED
CLIMATE
REGULATION II
CONTROL UNIT
(IHKR II)
X18156
X18157
X85
Y4
WATER VALVE
ASSEMBLY
1) LEFT VALVE
2) RIGHT VALVE
5 GE/VI
.5 GE/BR
.5 GE/RT
.5 GE/BL
.5 GE/SW
.5 GE/WS
.5 GR/RT
LIGHT
SWITCH
X18159
GR/RT
X18154
58G
S134
INTEGRATED
CLIMATE
REGULATION II
SWITCHING UNIT
(IHKR II)
0) OPEN
1) CLOSE WITH CONTROL 6 AT MAXIMUM
2) COLSED WITH CONTROL 4 AT MAXIMUM
3) SENSOR FAN
4) LEFT TEMPERATURE REGULATION
5) AIR VOLUME CONTROL WHEEL
6) RIGHT TEMPERATURE REGULATION
7) INSIDE TEMPERATURE SENSOR
GROUND
5 GE/GN
.5 GE/BL
.5 BR/GE
.5 BR/BL
X818
X18157
X18156
X18155
A87
INTEGRATED
CLIMATE
REGULATION II
CONTROL UNIT
(IHKR II)

Air delivery circuit continued—5 Series

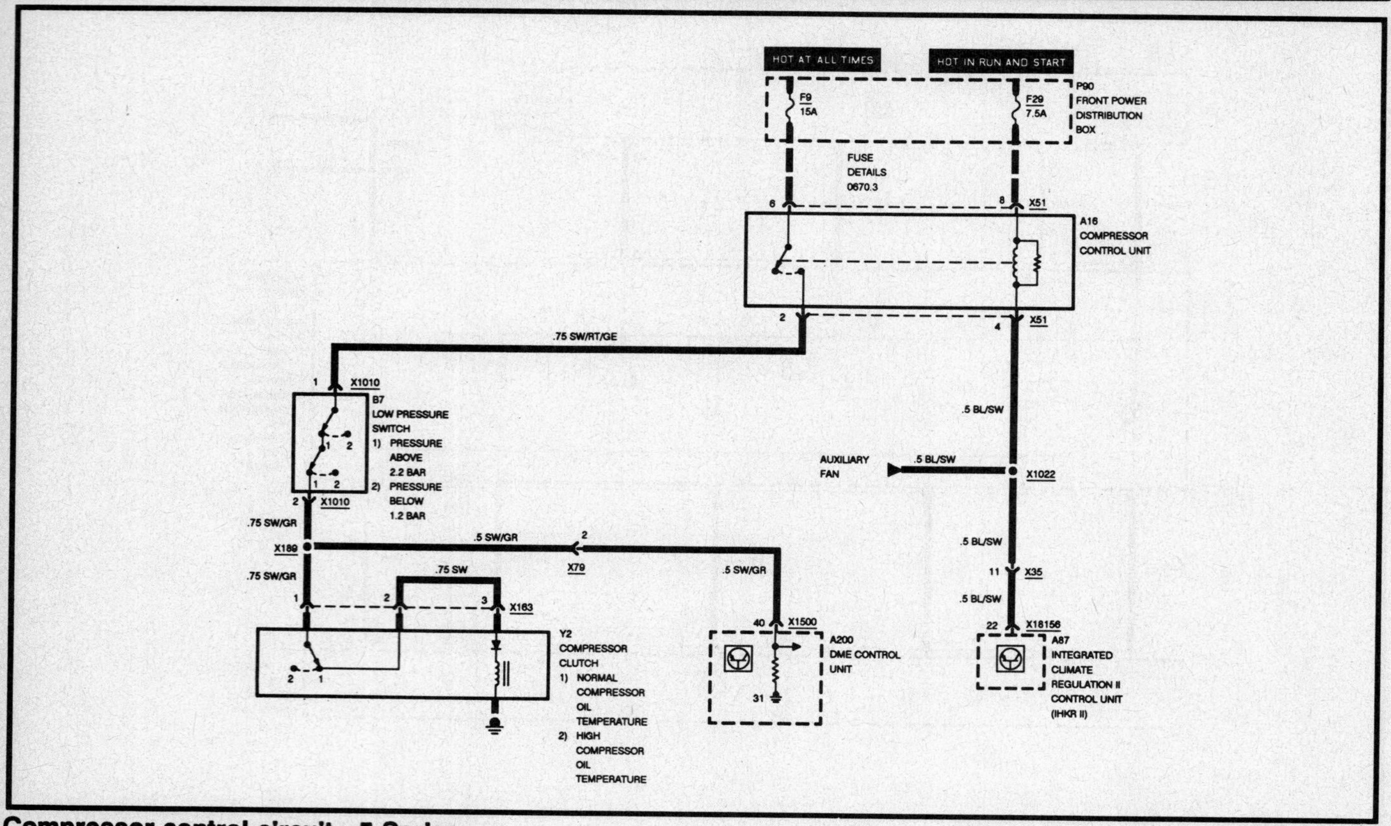
HOT AT ALL TIMES
HOT IN RUN AND START
F9
15A
F29
7.5A
P90
FRONT POWER
DISTRIBUTION
BOX
FUSE
DETAILS
0670.3
X51
A16
COMPRESSOR
CONTROL UNIT
.75 SW/RT/GE
X1010
B7
LOW PRESSURE
SWITCH
1) PRESSURE
ABOVE
2.2 BAR
2) PRESSURE
BELOW
1.2 BAR
.5 BL/SW
AUXILIARY
FAN
X1022
.75 SW/GR
X189
.5 SW/GR
X79
.75 SW
X163
X35
X1500
X18156
Y2
COMPRESSOR
CLUTCH
1) NORMAL
COMPRESSOR
OIL
TEMPERATURE
2) HIGH
COMPRESSOR
OIL
TEMPERATURE
A200
DME CONTROL
UNIT
A87
INTEGRATED
CLIMATE
REGULATION II
CONTROL UNIT
(IHKR II)

Compressor control circuit—5 Series

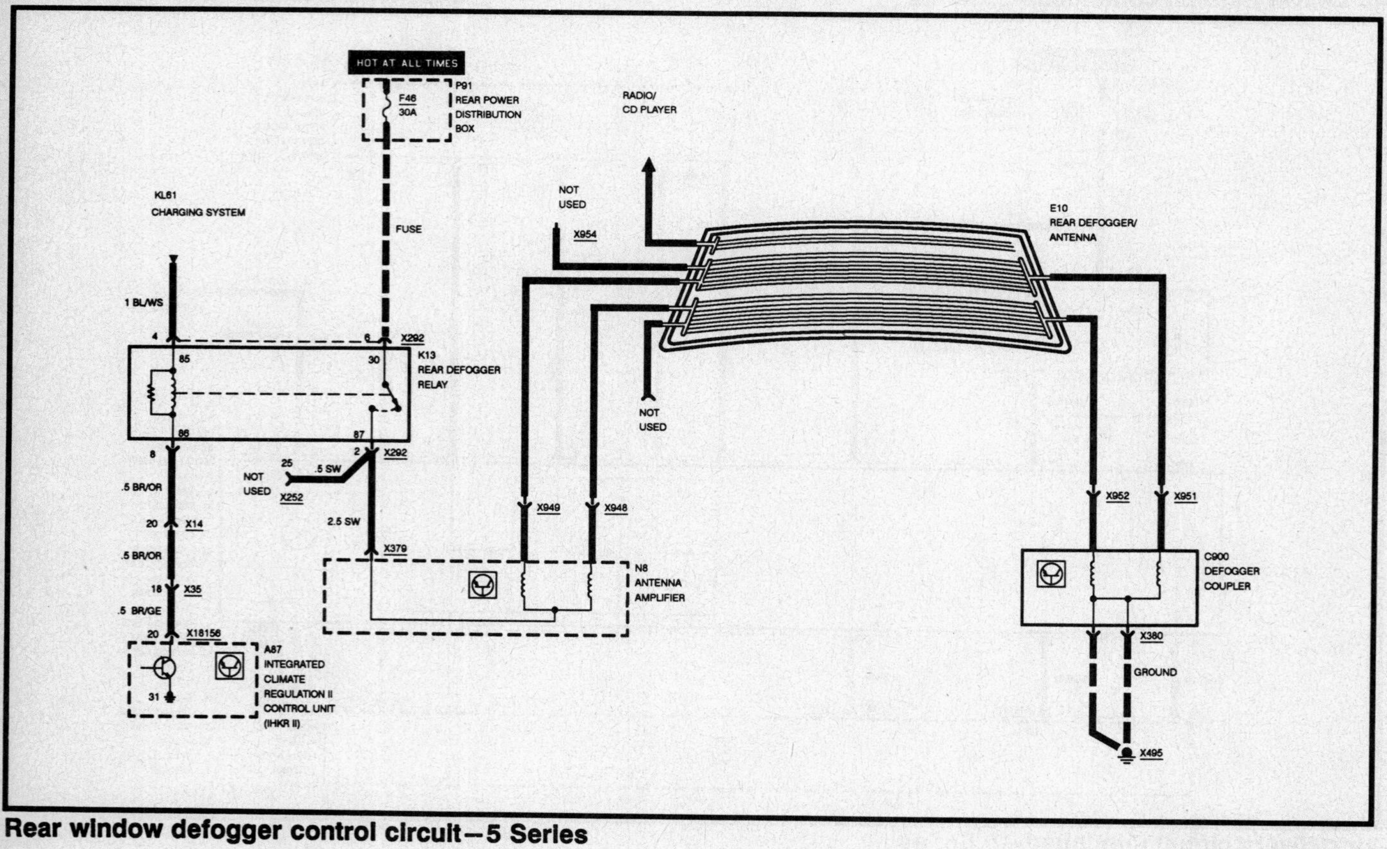
HOT AT ALL TIMES
F46
30A
P91
REAR POWER
DISTRIBUTION
BOX
RADIO/
CD PLAYER
KL61
CHARGING SYSTEM
FUSE
NOT
USED
X954
E10
REAR DEFOGGER/
ANTENNA
1 BL/WS
X292
K13
REAR DEFOGGER
RELAY
NOT
USED
X252
.5 SW
.5 BR/OR
X14
2.5 SW
X379
X949
X948
X952
X951
X35
.5 BR/GE
X18156
N8
ANTENNA
AMPLIFIER
C900
DEFOGGER
COUPLER
X380
GROUND
X495
A87
INTEGRATED
CLIMATE
REGULATION II
CONTROL UNIT
(IHKR II)

Rear window defogger control circuit—5 Series

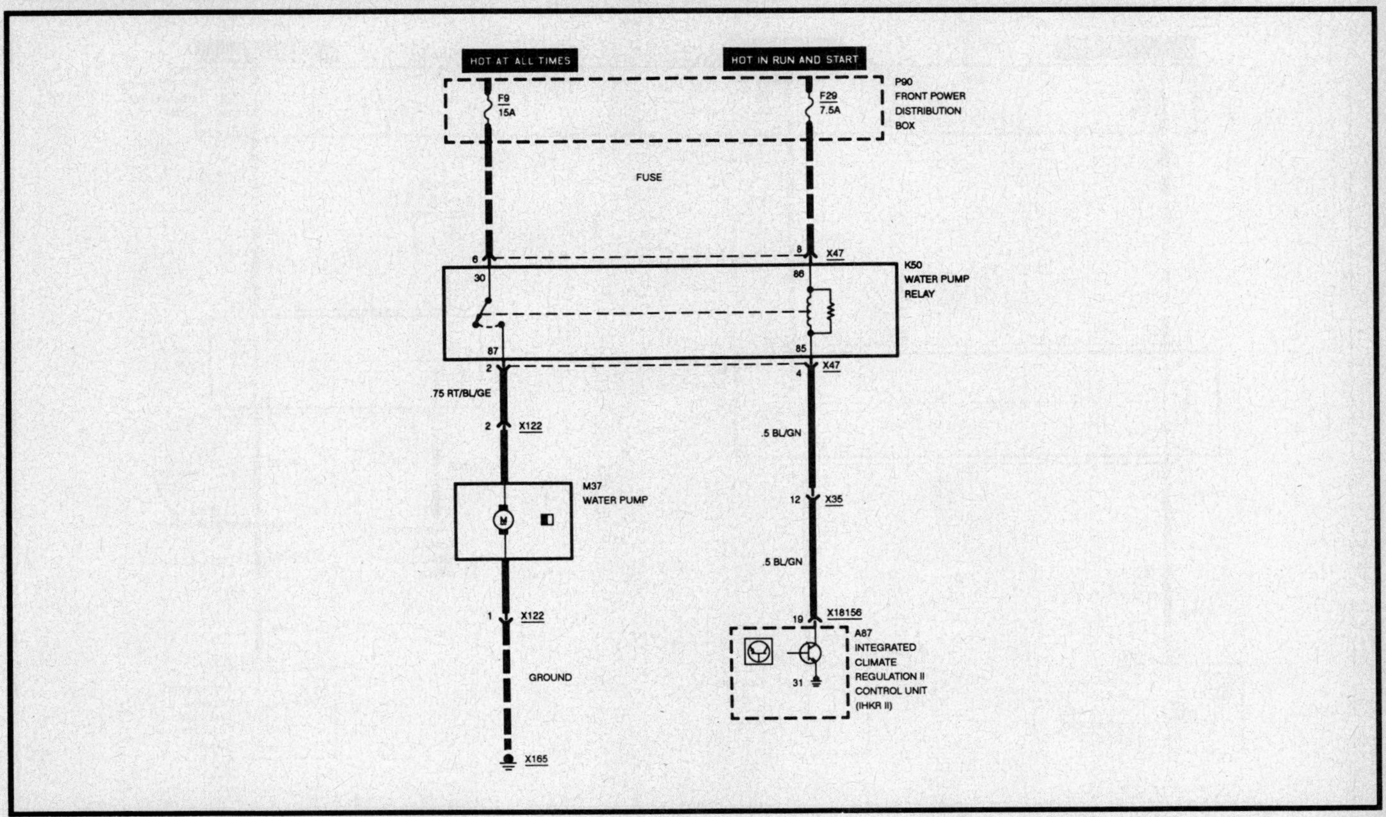
HOT AT ALL TIMES
HOT IN RUN AND START
F9
15A
F29
7.5A
P90
FRONT POWER
DISTRIBUTION
BOX
FUSE
X47
K50
WATER PUMP
RELAY
.75 RT/BL/GE
X122
.5 BL/GN
M37
WATER PUMP
X35
X18156
A87
INTEGRATED
CLIMATE
REGULATION II
CONTROL UNIT
(IHKR II)
GROUND
X165

Auxiliary water pump circuit—5 Series

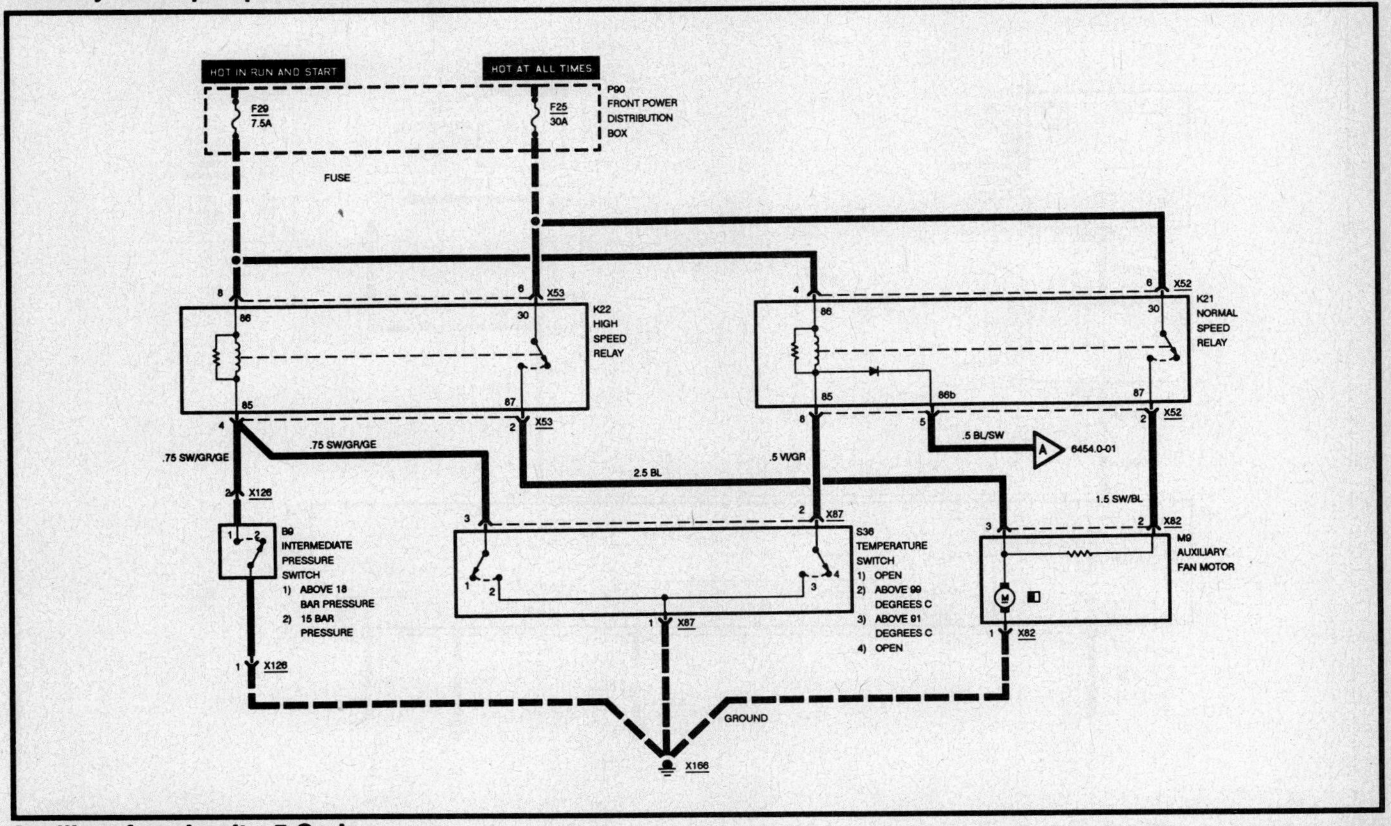
HOT IN RUN AND START
HOT AT ALL TIMES
F29
7.5A
F25
30A
P90
FRONT POWER
DISTRIBUTION
BOX
FUSE
X53
K22
HIGH
SPEED
RELAY
X52
K21
NORMAL
SPEED
RELAY
.75 SW/GR/GE
.5 W/GR
2.5 BL
.5 BL/SW
6454.0-01
1.5 SW/BL
X126
B9
INTERMEDIATE
PRESSURE
SWITCH
1) ABOVE 18
BAR PRESSURE
2) 15 BAR
PRESSURE
X87
S36
TEMPERATURE
SWITCH
1) OPEN
2) ABOVE 99
DEGREES C
3) ABOVE 91
DEGREES C
4) OPEN
X82
M9
AUXILIARY
FAN MOTOR
GROUND
X166

Auxiliary fan circuit—5 Series

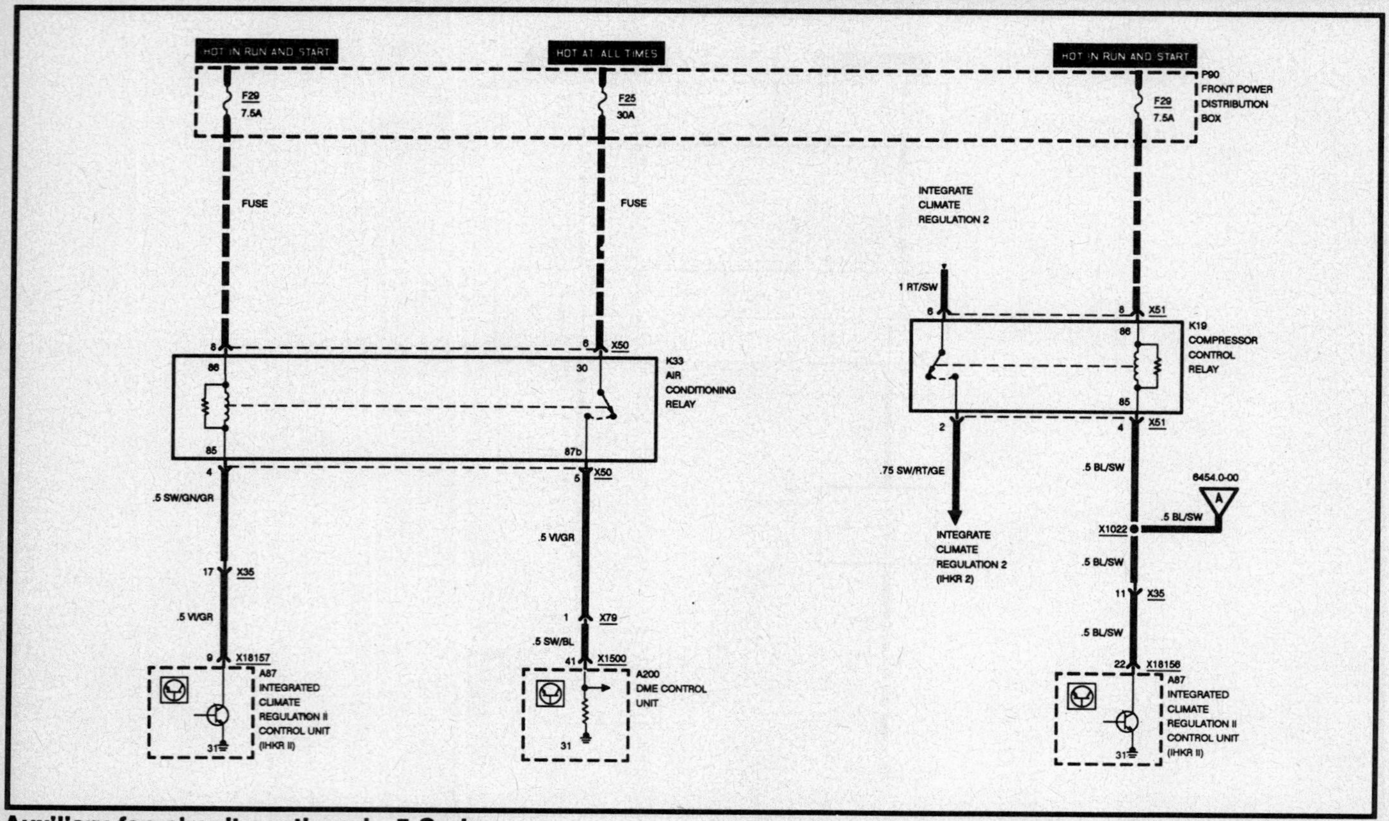
HOT IN RUN AND START
HOT AT ALL TIMES
HOT IN RUN AND START
F29
7.5A
F25
30A
F29
7.5A
P90
FRONT POWER
DISTRIBUTION
BOX
FUSE
FUSE
INTEGRATE
CLIMATE
REGULATION 2
1 RT/SW
X50
K33
AIR
CONDITIONING
RELAY
86
30
85
87b
X51
K19
COMPRESSOR
CONTROL
RELAY
.5 SW/GN/GR
.5 VI/GR
X35
.5 VI/GR
X79
.5 SW/BL
X1500
X18157
A87
INTEGRATED
CLIMATE
REGULATION II
CONTROL UNIT
(IHKR II)
A200
DME CONTROL
UNIT
.75 SW/RT/GE
INTEGRATE
CLIMATE
REGULATION 2
(IHKR 2)
.5 BL/SW
6454.0-00
X1022
.5 BL/SW
.5 BL/SW
.5 BL/SW
X18156
A87
INTEGRATED
CLIMATE
REGULATION II
CONTROL UNIT
(IHKR II)

Auxiliary fan circuit continued—5 Series

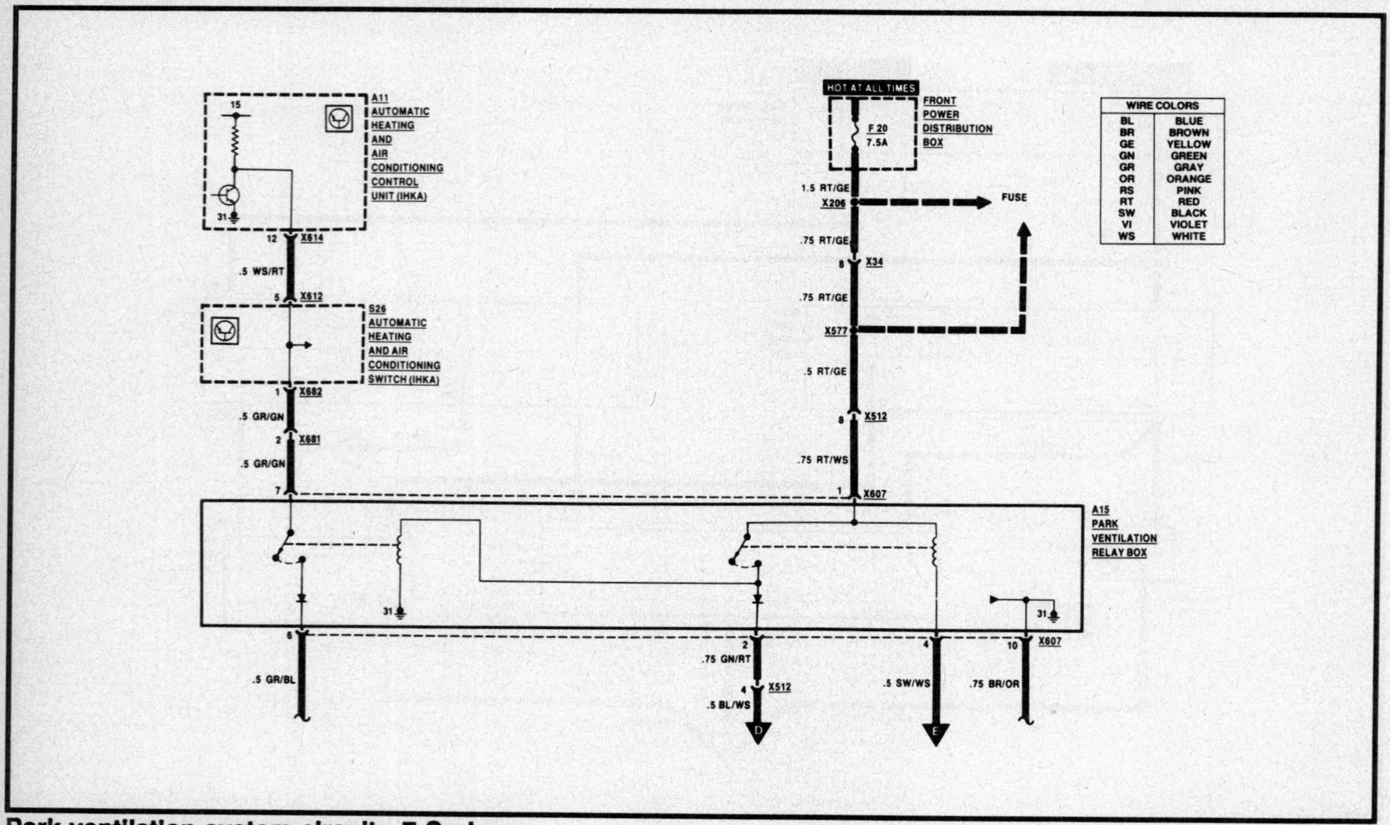
A11
AUTOMATIC
HEATING
AND
AIR
CONDITIONING
CONTROL
UNIT (IHKA)
X614
.5 WS/RT
X612
S26
AUTOMATIC
HEATING
AND AIR
CONDITIONING
SWITCH (IHKA)
X682
.5 GR/GN
X681
.5 GR/GN
HOT AT ALL TIMES
F 20
7.5A
FRONT
POWER
DISTRIBUTION
BOX
1.5 RT/GE
X206
FUSE
.75 RT/GE
X34
.75 RT/GE
X577
.5 RT/GE
X512
.75 RT/WS
X607
A15
PARK
VENTILATION
RELAY BOX
.5 GR/BL
.75 GN/RT
X512
.5 BL/WS
.5 SW/WS
.75 BR/OR
X607

WIRE COLORS	
BL	BLUE
BR	BROWN
GE	YELLOW
GN	GREEN
GR	GRAY
OR	ORANGE
RS	PINK
RT	RED
SW	BLACK
VI	VIOLET
WS	WHITE

Park ventilation system circuit—7 Series

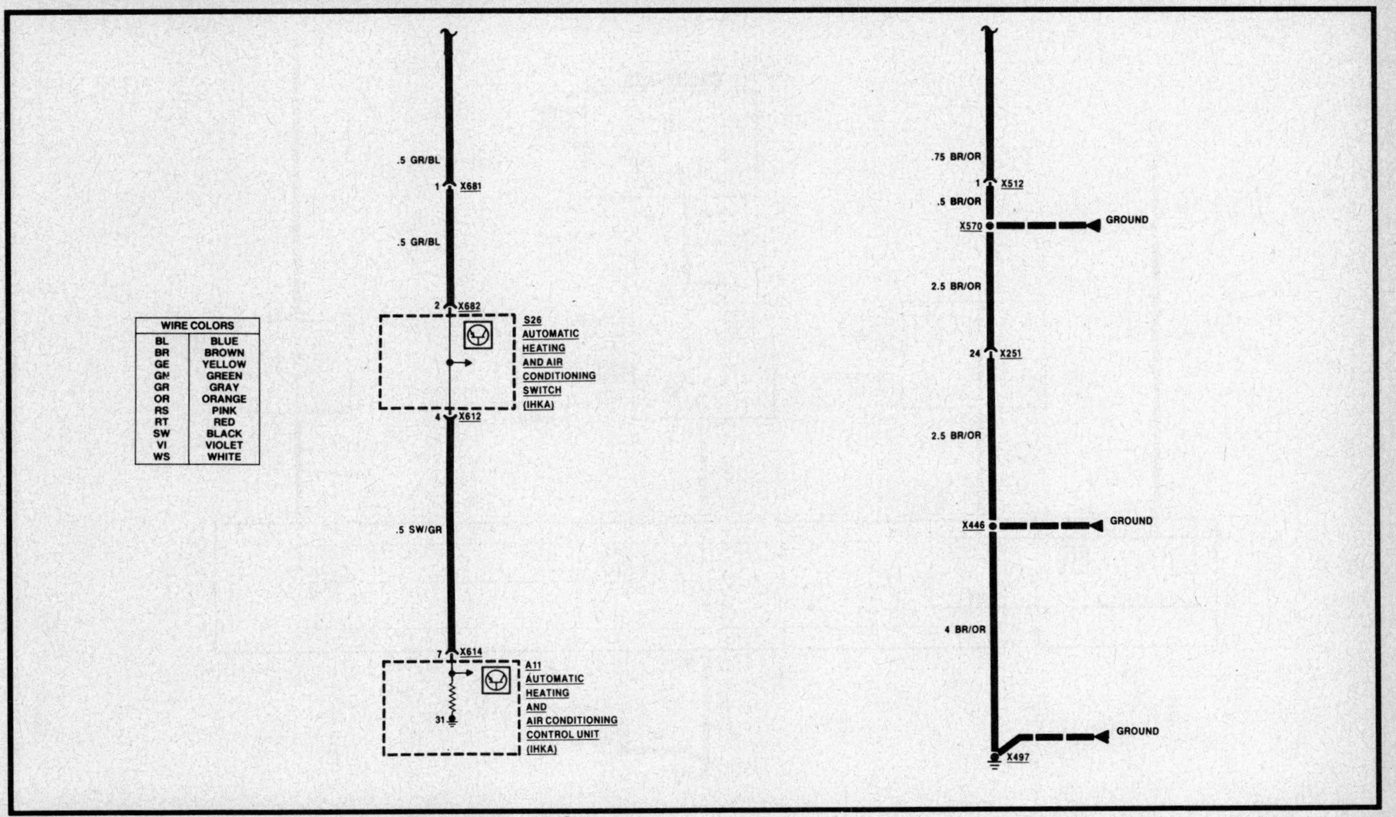
WIRE COLORS
BL BLUE
BR BROWN
GE YELLOW
GN GREEN
GR GRAY
OR ORANGE
RS PINK
RT RED
SW BLACK
VI VIOLET
WS WHITE
.5 GR/BL
1 X681
.5 GR/BL
2 X682
S26
AUTOMATIC HEATING AND AIR CONDITIONING SWITCH (IHKA)
4 X612
.5 SW/GR
7 X614
A11
AUTOMATIC HEATING AND AIR CONDITIONING CONTROL UNIT (IHKA)
31
.75 BR/OR
1 X512
.5 BR/OR
X570
GROUND
2.5 BR/OR
24 X251
2.5 BR/OR
X446
GROUND
4 BR/OR
GROUND
X497

Park ventilation system circuit continued – 7 Series

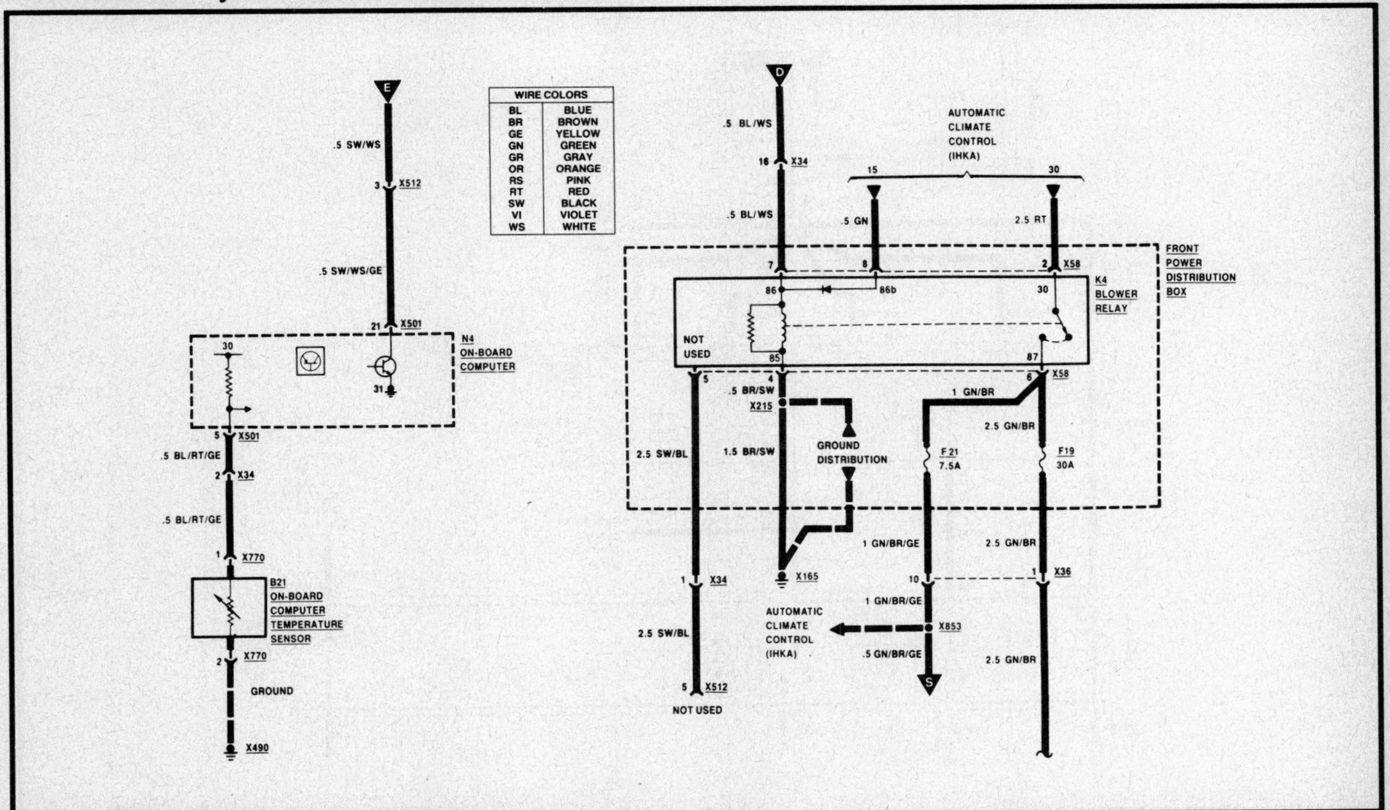
E
.5 SW/WS
3 X512
.5 SW/WS/GE
21 X501
N4
ON-BOARD COMPUTER
30
31
5 X501
.5 BL/RT/GE
2 X34
.5 BL/RT/GE
1 X770
B21
ON-BOARD COMPUTER TEMPERATURE SENSOR
2 X770
GROUND
X490
WIRE COLORS
BL BLUE
BR BROWN
GE YELLOW
GN GREEN
GR GRAY
OR ORANGE
RS PINK
RT RED
SW BLACK
VI VIOLET
WS WHITE
D
.5 BL/WS
16 X34
.5 BL/WS
AUTOMATIC CLIMATE CONTROL (IHKA)
15
30
.5 GN
2.5 RT
7
8
2 X58
FRONT POWER DISTRIBUTION BOX
86
86b
30
K4
BLOWER RELAY
NOT USED
85
87
5
4
6 X58
.5 BR/SW
X215
1 GN/BR
2.5 GN/BR
GROUND DISTRIBUTION
2.5 SW/BL
1.5 BR/SW
F 21
7.5A
F19
30A
1 GN/BR/GE
2.5 GN/BR
1 X34
X165
10
1 X36
1 GN/BR/GE
AUTOMATIC CLIMATE CONTROL (IHKA)
X853
2.5 SW/BL
.5 GN/BR/GE
2.5 GN/BR
5 X512
NOT USED
S

Park ventilation system circuit continued – 7 Series

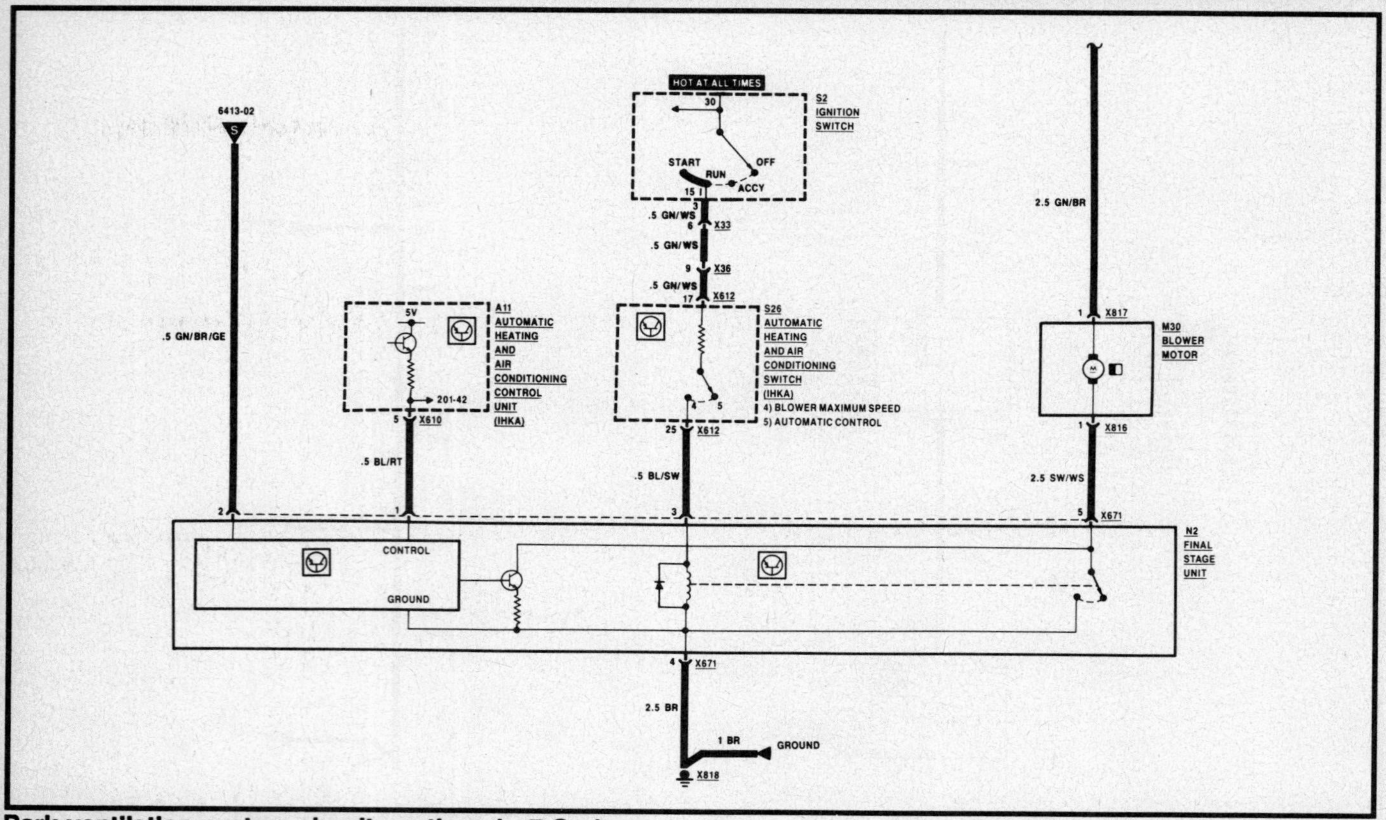
HOT AT ALL TIMES
S2 IGNITION SWITCH
START RUN OFF ACCY
6413-02
.5 GN/BR/GE
A11 AUTOMATIC HEATING AND AIR CONDITIONING CONTROL UNIT (IHKA)
S26 AUTOMATIC HEATING AND AIR CONDITIONING SWITCH (IHKA)
4) BLOWER MAXIMUM SPEED
5) AUTOMATIC CONTROL
2.5 GN/BR
M30 BLOWER MOTOR
.5 BL/RT
.5 BL/SW
2.5 SW/WS
N2 FINAL STAGE UNIT
CONTROL
GROUND
2.5 BR
1 BR
GROUND

Park ventilation system circuit continued – 7 Series

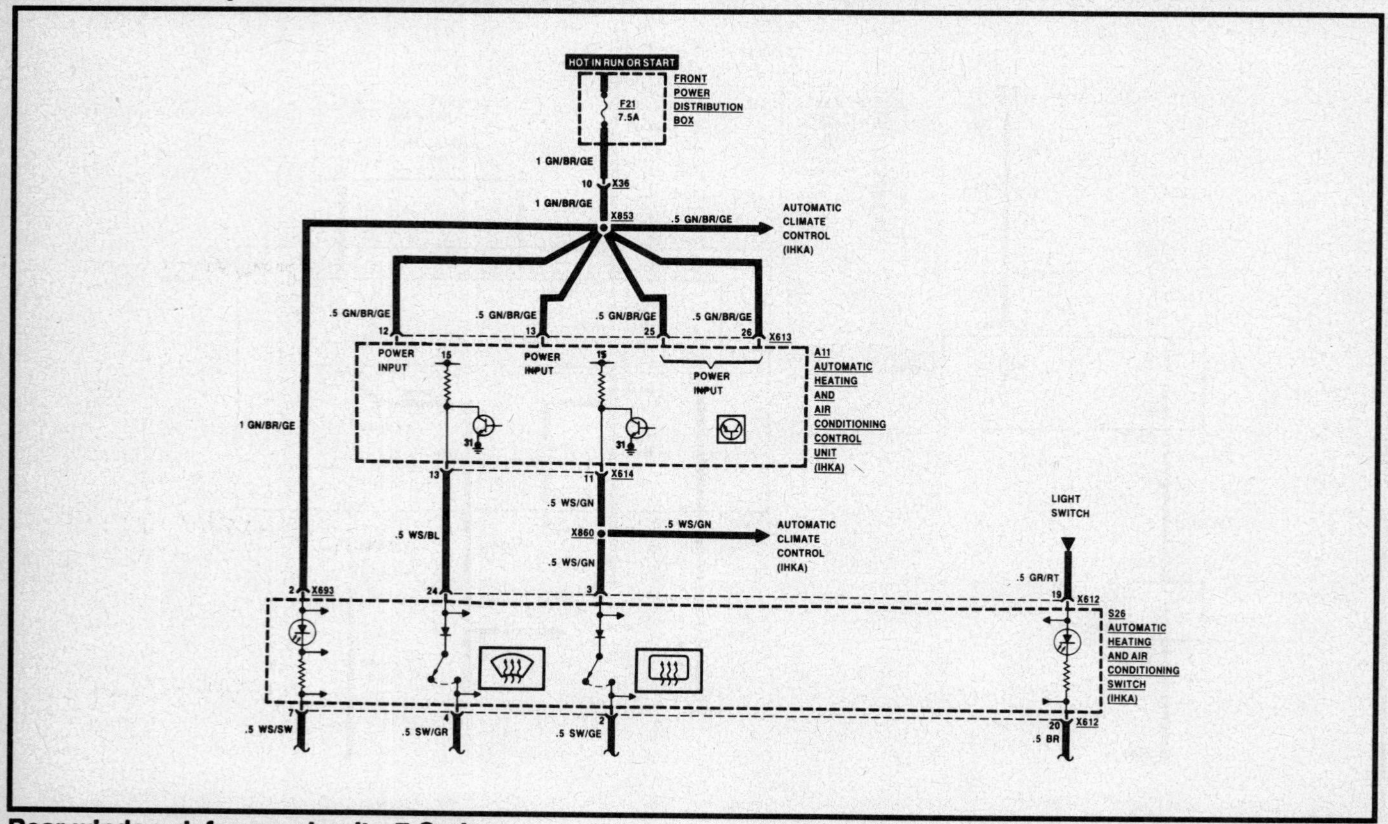
HOT IN RUN OR START
FRONT POWER DISTRIBUTION BOX
F21 7.5A
1 GN/BR/GE
.5 GN/BR/GE
AUTOMATIC CLIMATE CONTROL (IHKA)
POWER INPUT
A11 AUTOMATIC HEATING AND AIR CONDITIONING CONTROL UNIT (IHKA)
.5 WS/GN
.5 WS/BL
LIGHT SWITCH
.5 GR/RT
S26 AUTOMATIC HEATING AND AIR CONDITIONING SWITCH (IHKA)
.5 WS/SW
.5 SW/GR
.5 SW/GE
.5 BR

Rear window defogger circuit – 7 Series

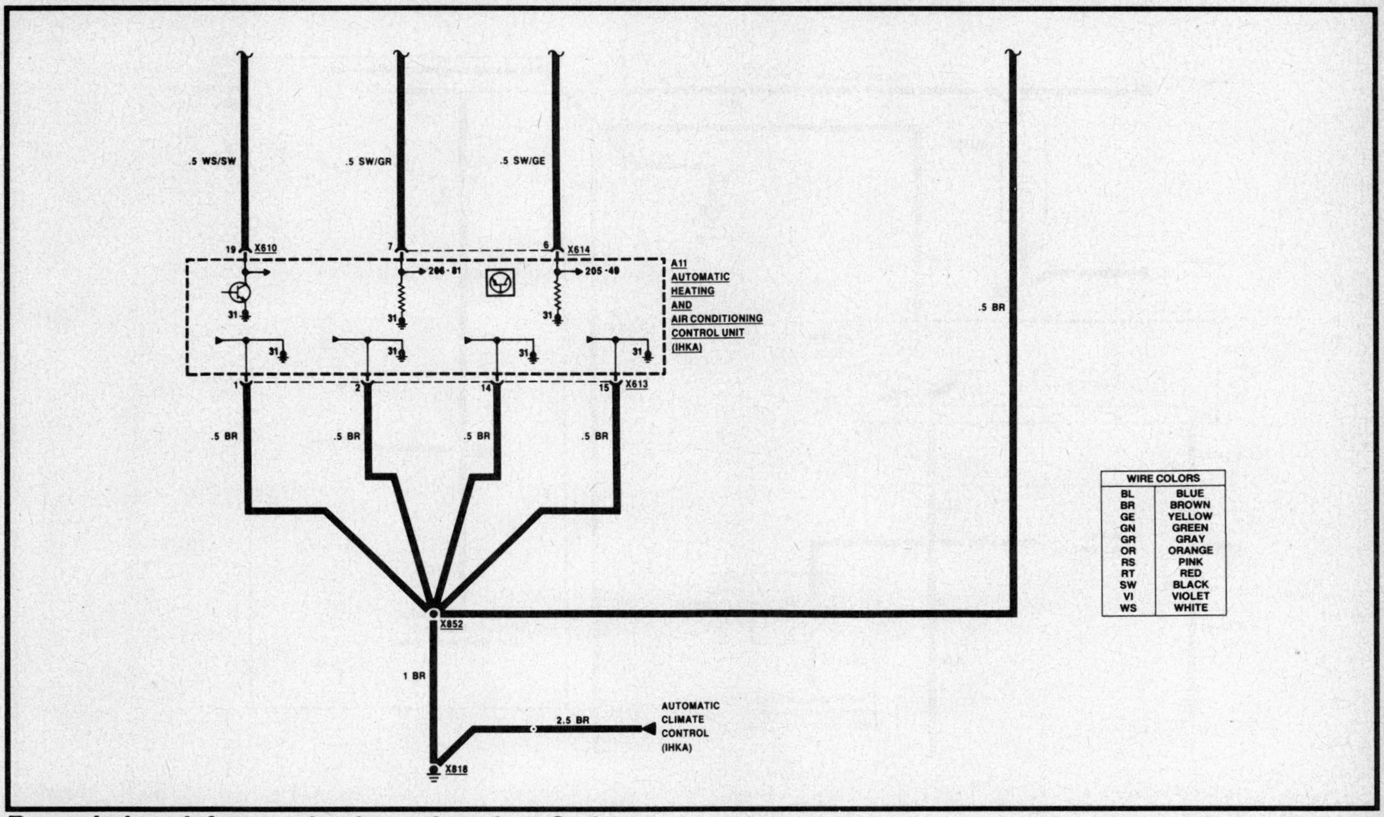
.5 WS/SW
.5 SW/GR
.5 SW/GE
X610
X614
206-81
205-49
A11
AUTOMATIC
HEATING
AND
AIR CONDITIONING
CONTROL UNIT
(IHKA)
.5 BR
X613
.5 BR
.5 BR
.5 BR
.5 BR
WIRE COLORS
BL BLUE
BR BROWN
GE YELLOW
GN GREEN
GR GRAY
OR ORANGE
RS PINK
RT RED
SW BLACK
VI VIOLET
WS WHITE
X852
1 BR
2.5 BR
AUTOMATIC
CLIMATE
CONTROL
(IHKA)
X818

Rear window defogger circuit continued—7 Series

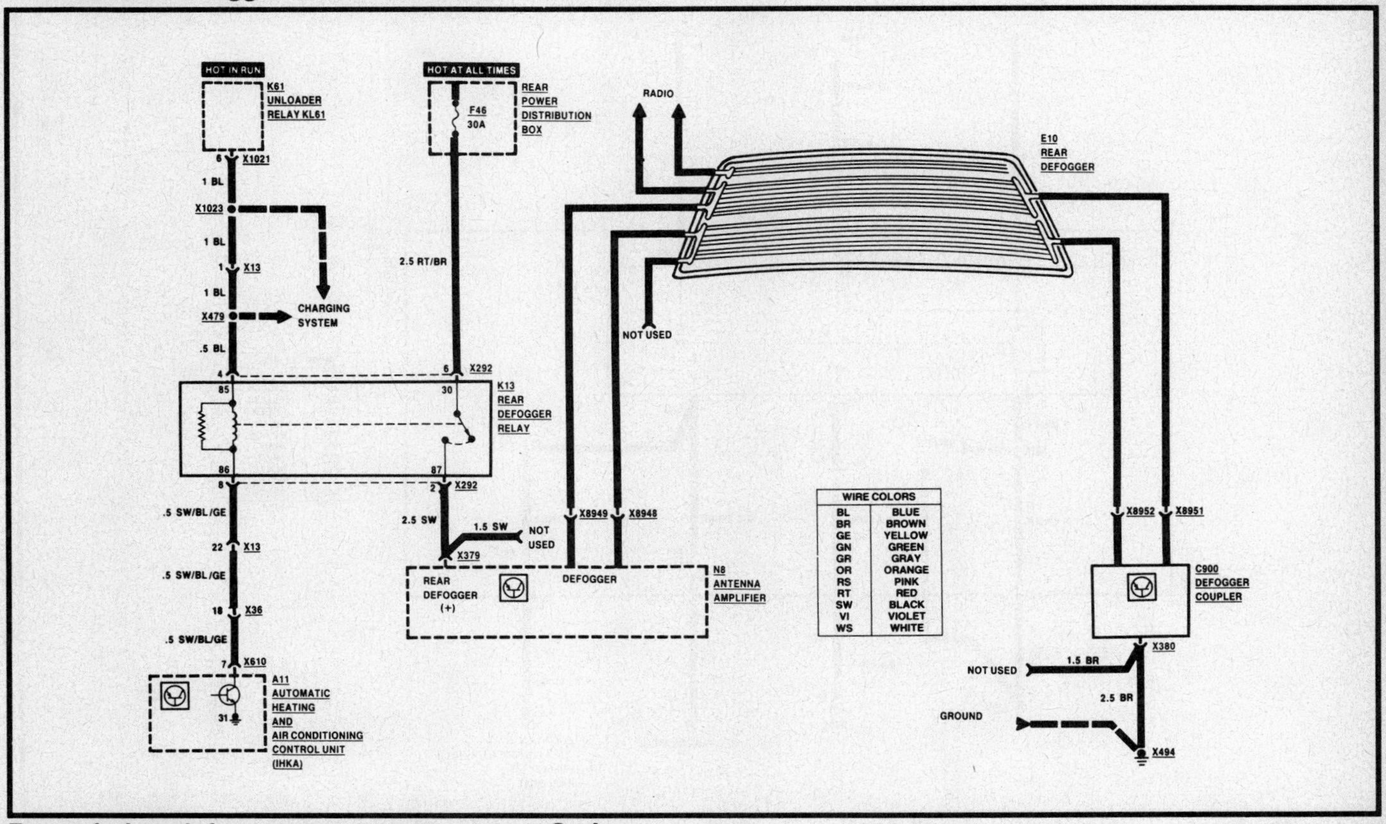
HOT IN RUN
K61
UNLOADER
RELAY KL61
X1021
1 BL
X1023
1 BL
X13
1 BL
X479
CHARGING
SYSTEM
.5 BL
HOT AT ALL TIMES
F46
30A
REAR
POWER
DISTRIBUTION
BOX
2.5 RT/BR
RADIO
E10
REAR
DEFOGGER
NOT USED
X292
K13
REAR
DEFOGGER
RELAY
X292
.5 SW/BL/GE
X13
.5 SW/BL/GE
X36
.5 SW/BL/GE
X610
A11
AUTOMATIC
HEATING
AND
AIR CONDITIONING
CONTROL UNIT
(IHKA)
2.5 SW
1.5 SW
NOT
USED
X379
REAR
DEFOGGER
(+)
DEFOGGER
X8949
X8948
N8
ANTENNA
AMPLIFIER
WIRE COLORS
BL BLUE
BR BROWN
GE YELLOW
GN GREEN
GR GRAY
OR ORANGE
RS PINK
RT RED
SW BLACK
VI VIOLET
WS WHITE
X8952
X8951
C900
DEFOGGER
COUPLER
X380
NOT USED
1.5 BR
2.5 BR
GROUND
X494

Rear window defogger circuit continued—7 Series

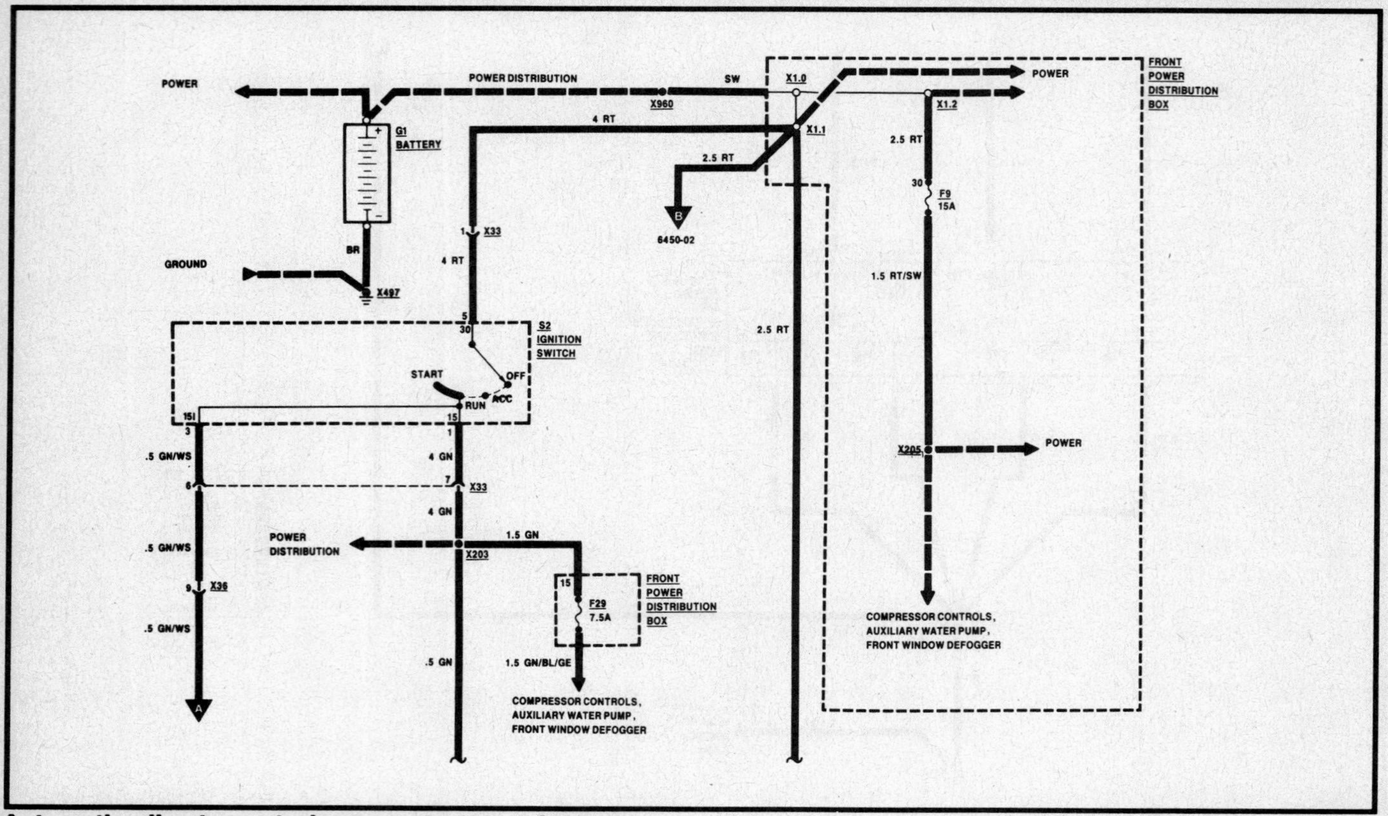
POWER
POWER DISTRIBUTION
SW
X960
4 RT
G1 BATTERY
X1.0
X1.1
X1.2
POWER
FRONT POWER DISTRIBUTION BOX
2.5 RT
B
6450-02
2.5 RT
30
F9 15A
BR
GROUND
X497
1
X33
4 RT
1.5 RT/SW
5
30
S2 IGNITION SWITCH
START
OFF
ACC
RUN
2.5 RT
15I
15
3
1
.5 GN/WS
4 GN
6
7
X33
4 GN
X205
POWER
POWER DISTRIBUTION
X203
1.5 GN
.5 GN/WS
15
F29 7.5A
FRONT POWER DISTRIBUTION BOX
9
X36
.5 GN/WS
.5 GN
1.5 GN/BL/GE
COMPRESSOR CONTROLS, AUXILIARY WATER PUMP, FRONT WINDOW DEFOGGER
COMPRESSOR CONTROLS, AUXILIARY WATER PUMP, FRONT WINDOW DEFOGGER
A

Automatic climate control power circuit—7 Series

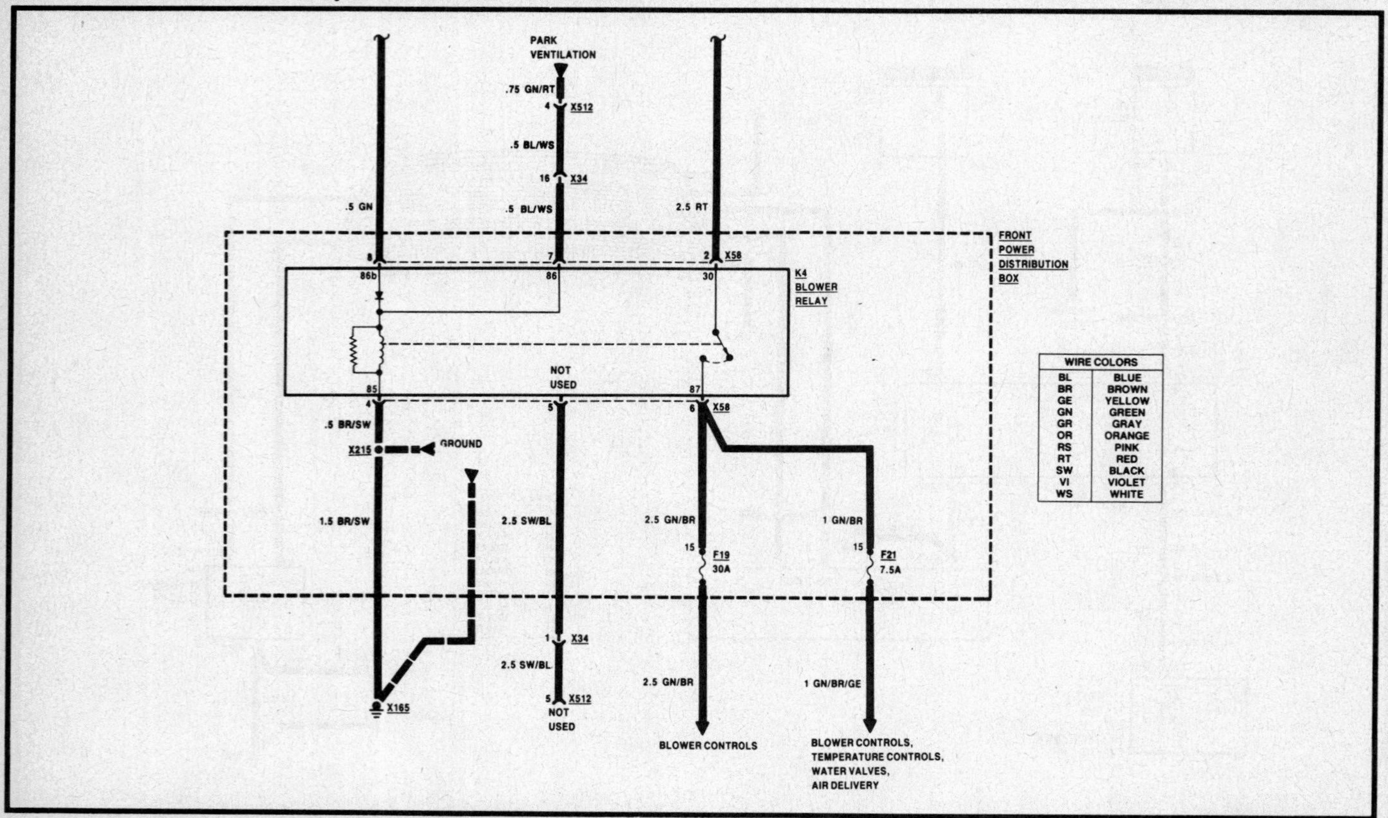
PARK VENTILATION
.75 GN/RT
4
X512
.5 BL/WS
16
X34
.5 GN
.5 BL/WS
2.5 RT
FRONT POWER DISTRIBUTION BOX
8
7
2
X58
86b
86
30
K4 BLOWER RELAY
NOT USED
85
87
4
5
6
X58
.5 BR/SW
X215
GROUND
1.5 BR/SW
2.5 SW/BL
2.5 GN/BR
1 GN/BR
15
F19 30A
15
F21 7.5A
1
X34
2.5 SW/BL
5
X512
NOT USED
2.5 GN/BR
1 GN/BR/GE
X165
BLOWER CONTROLS
BLOWER CONTROLS, TEMPERATURE CONTROLS, WATER VALVES, AIR DELIVERY
WIRE COLORS
BL BLUE
BR BROWN
GE YELLOW
GN GREEN
GR GRAY
OR ORANGE
RS PINK
RT RED
SW BLACK
VI VIOLET
WS WHITE

Automatic climate control power circuit continued—7 Series

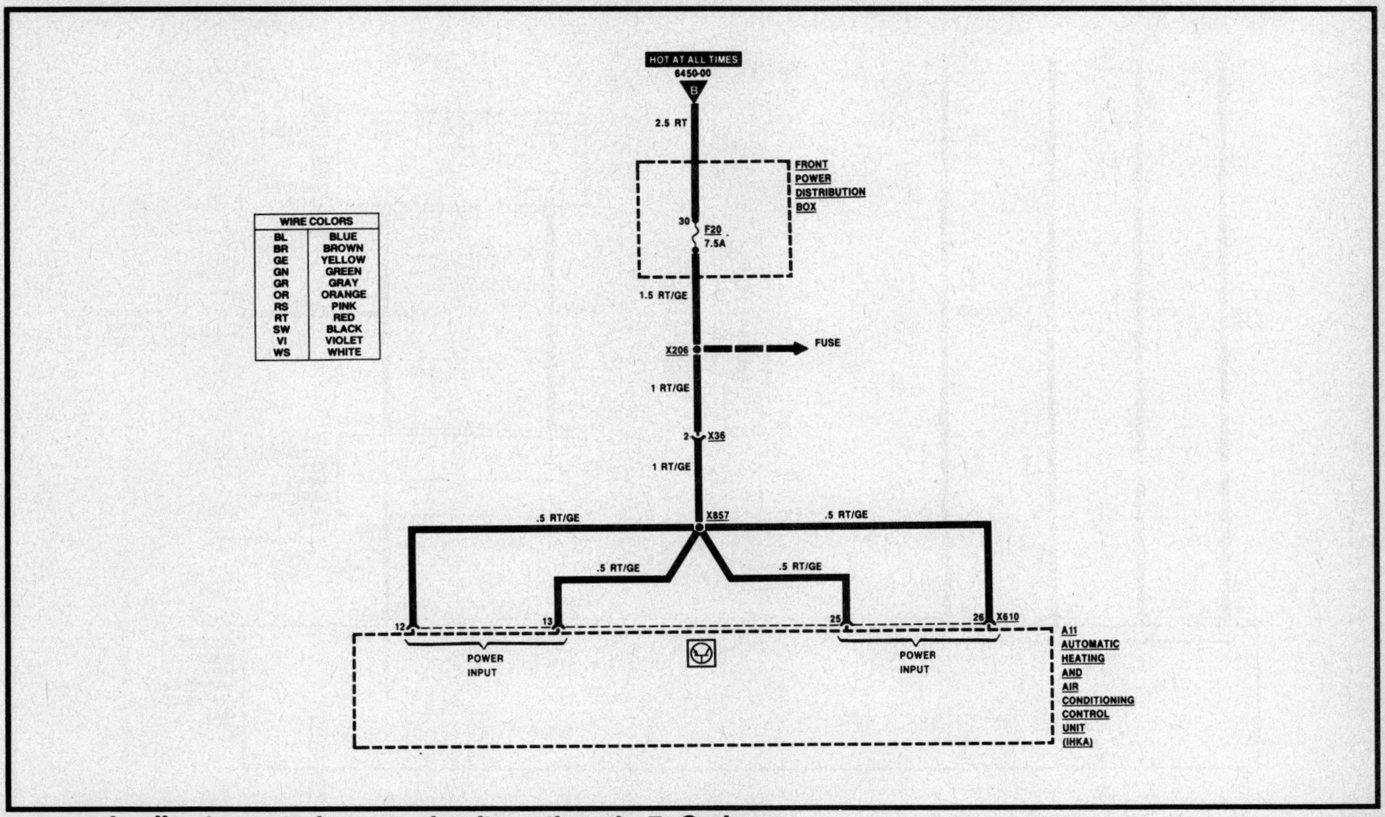
HOT AT ALL TIMES
6450-00
B
2.5 RT
FRONT POWER DISTRIBUTION BOX
30
F20 7.5A
1.5 RT/GE
X206
FUSE
1 RT/GE
2
X36
1 RT/GE
.5 RT/GE
X857
.5 RT/GE
.5 RT/GE
.5 RT/GE
12
13
25
26
X610
POWER INPUT
POWER INPUT
A11 AUTOMATIC HEATING AND AIR CONDITIONING CONTROL UNIT (IHKA)

WIRE COLORS	
BL	BLUE
BR	BROWN
GE	YELLOW
GN	GREEN
GR	GRAY
OR	ORANGE
RS	PINK
RT	RED
SW	BLACK
VI	VIOLET
WS	WHITE

Automatic climate control power circuit continued—7 Series

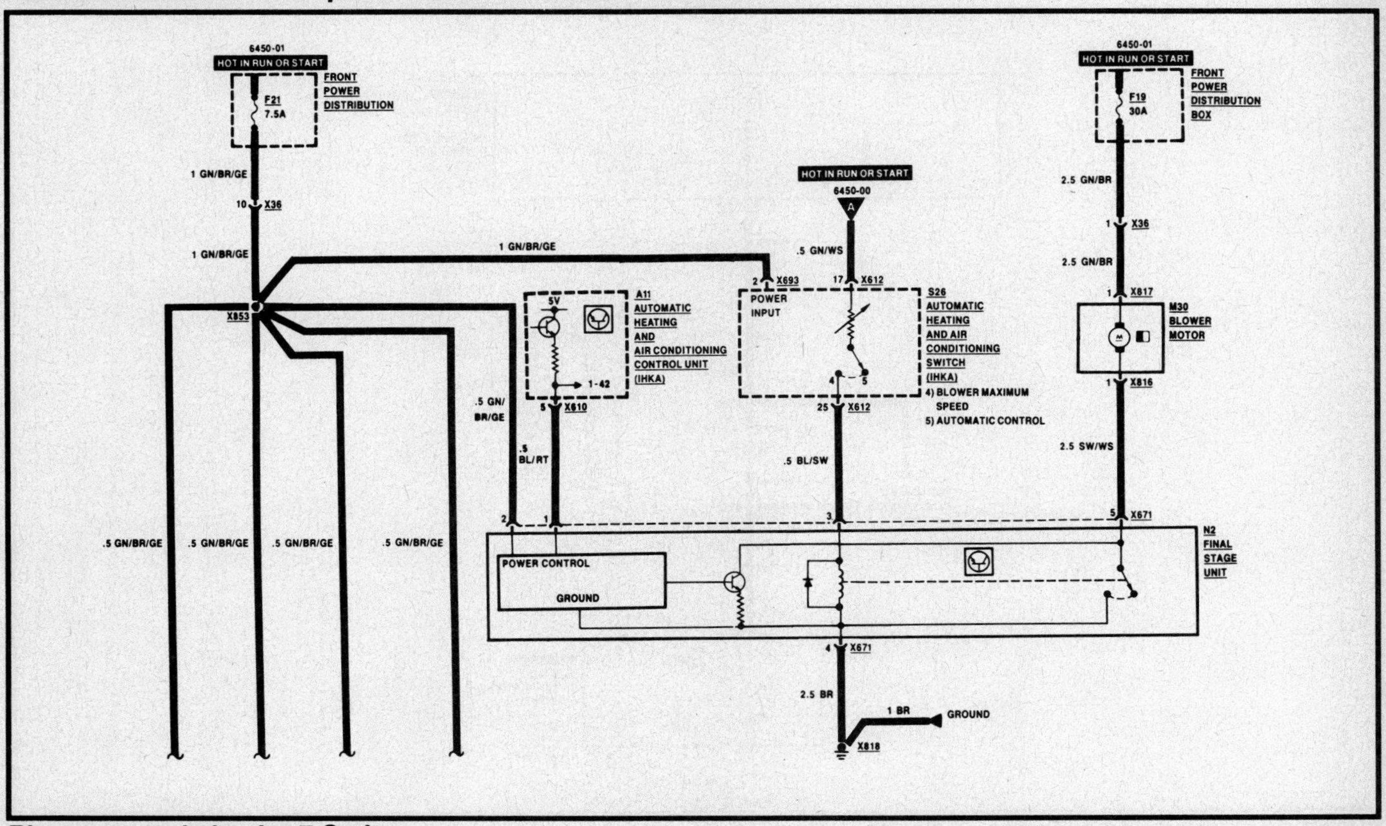
6450-01
HOT IN RUN OR START
F21 7.5A
FRONT POWER DISTRIBUTION
1 GN/BR/GE
10
X36
1 GN/BR/GE
1 GN/BR/GE
X853
5V
A11 AUTOMATIC HEATING AND AIR CONDITIONING CONTROL UNIT (IHKA)
1-42
.5 GN/ BR/GE
5
X610
.5 BL/RT
HOT IN RUN OR START
6450-00
A
.5 GN/WS
2
X693
17
X612
POWER INPUT
S26 AUTOMATIC HEATING AND AIR CONDITIONING SWITCH (IHKA)
4) BLOWER MAXIMUM SPEED
5) AUTOMATIC CONTROL
4
5
25
X612
.5 BL/SW
6450-01
HOT IN RUN OR START
F19 30A
FRONT POWER DISTRIBUTION BOX
2.5 GN/BR
1
X36
2.5 GN/BR
1
X817
M30 BLOWER MOTOR
1
X816
2.5 SW/WS
.5 GN/BR/GE
.5 GN/BR/GE
.5 GN/BR/GE
.5 GN/BR/GE
2
1
3
5
X671
POWER CONTROL
GROUND
N2 FINAL STAGE UNIT
4
X671
2.5 BR
1 BR
GROUND
X818

Blower control circuit—7 Series

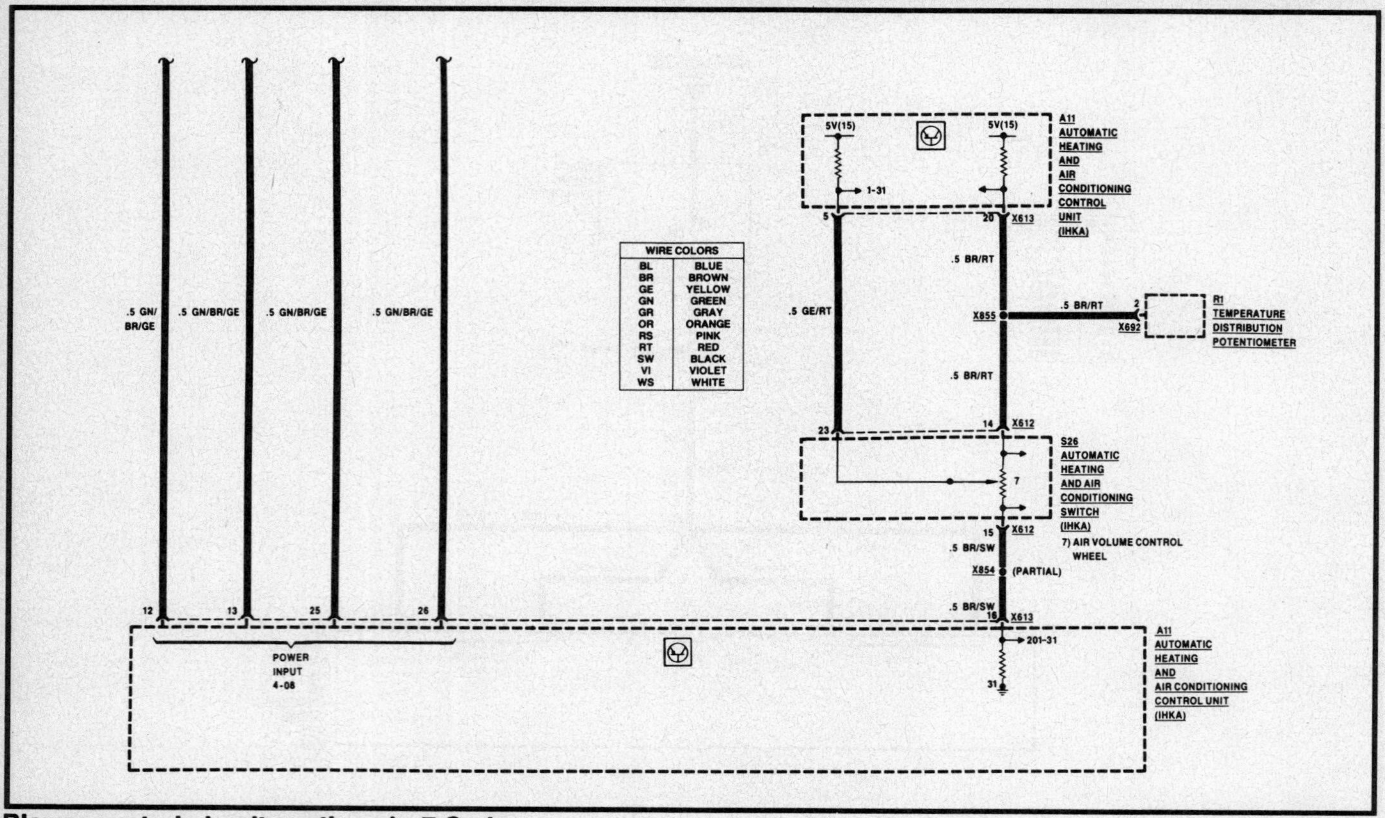
.5 GN/
BR/GE
.5 GN/BR/GE
.5 GN/BR/GE
.5 GN/BR/GE
12
13
25
26
POWER
INPUT
4-08
WIRE COLORS
BL BLUE
BR BROWN
GE YELLOW
GN GREEN
GR GRAY
OR ORANGE
RS PINK
RT RED
SW BLACK
VI VIOLET
WS WHITE
5V(15)
5V(15)
1-31
A11
AUTOMATIC
HEATING
AND
AIR
CONDITIONING
CONTROL
UNIT
(IHKA)
5
20
X613
.5 BR/RT
.5 GE/RT
X855
.5 BR/RT
2
X692
R1
TEMPERATURE
DISTRIBUTION
POTENTIOMETER
.5 BR/RT
23
14
X612
S26
AUTOMATIC
HEATING
AND AIR
CONDITIONING
SWITCH
(IHKA)
7
15
X612
7) AIR VOLUME CONTROL
WHEEL
.5 BR/SW
X854
(PARTIAL)
.5 BR/SW
16
X613
201-31
31
A11
AUTOMATIC
HEATING
AND
AIR CONDITIONING
CONTROL UNIT
(IHKA)

Blower control circuit continued—7 Series

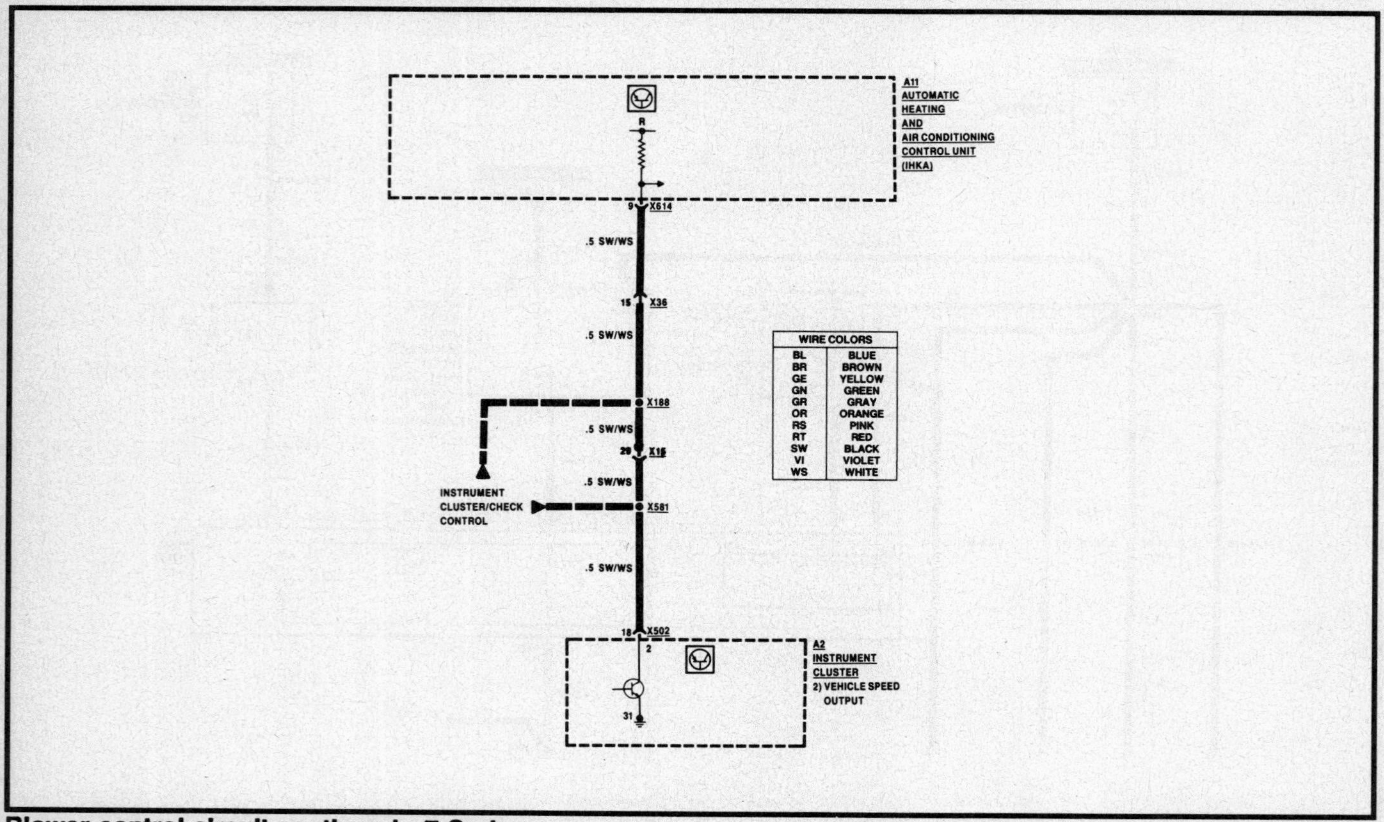
R
A11
AUTOMATIC
HEATING
AND
AIR CONDITIONING
CONTROL UNIT
(IHKA)
9
X614
.5 SW/WS
15
X36
.5 SW/WS
WIRE COLORS
BL BLUE
BR BROWN
GE YELLOW
GN GREEN
GR GRAY
OR ORANGE
RS PINK
RT RED
SW BLACK
VI VIOLET
WS WHITE
X188
.5 SW/WS
29
.5 SW/WS
INSTRUMENT
CLUSTER/CHECK
CONTROL
X581
.5 SW/WS
18
X502
2
31
A2
INSTRUMENT
CLUSTER
2) VEHICLE SPEED
OUTPUT

Blower control circuit continued—7 Series

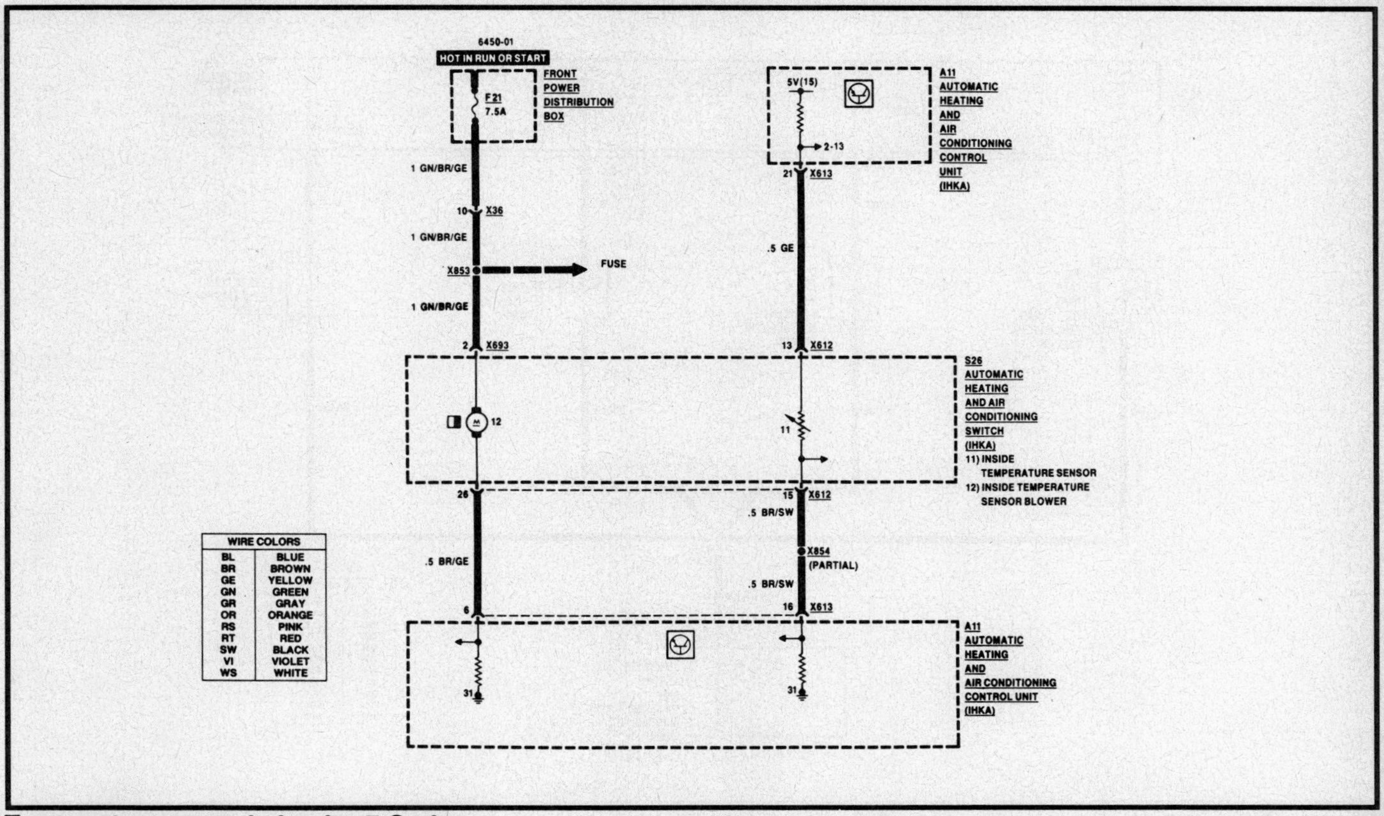
6450-01
HOT IN RUN OR START
F21 7.5A
FRONT POWER DISTRIBUTION BOX
1 GN/BR/GE
10 X36
1 GN/BR/GE
X853
FUSE
1 GN/BR/GE
2 X693
12
26
.5 BR/GE
6
31
5V(15)
2-13
A11 AUTOMATIC HEATING AND AIR CONDITIONING CONTROL UNIT (IHKA)
21 X613
.5 GE
13 X612
11
S26 AUTOMATIC HEATING AND AIR CONDITIONING SWITCH (IHKA)
11) INSIDE TEMPERATURE SENSOR
12) INSIDE TEMPERATURE SENSOR BLOWER
15 X612
.5 BR/SW
X854 (PARTIAL)
.5 BR/SW
16 X613
31
A11 AUTOMATIC HEATING AND AIR CONDITIONING CONTROL UNIT (IHKA)

WIRE COLORS	
BL	BLUE
BR	BROWN
GE	YELLOW
GN	GREEN
GR	GRAY
OR	ORANGE
RS	PINK
RT	RED
SW	BLACK
VI	VIOLET
WS	WHITE

Temperature control circuit—7 Series

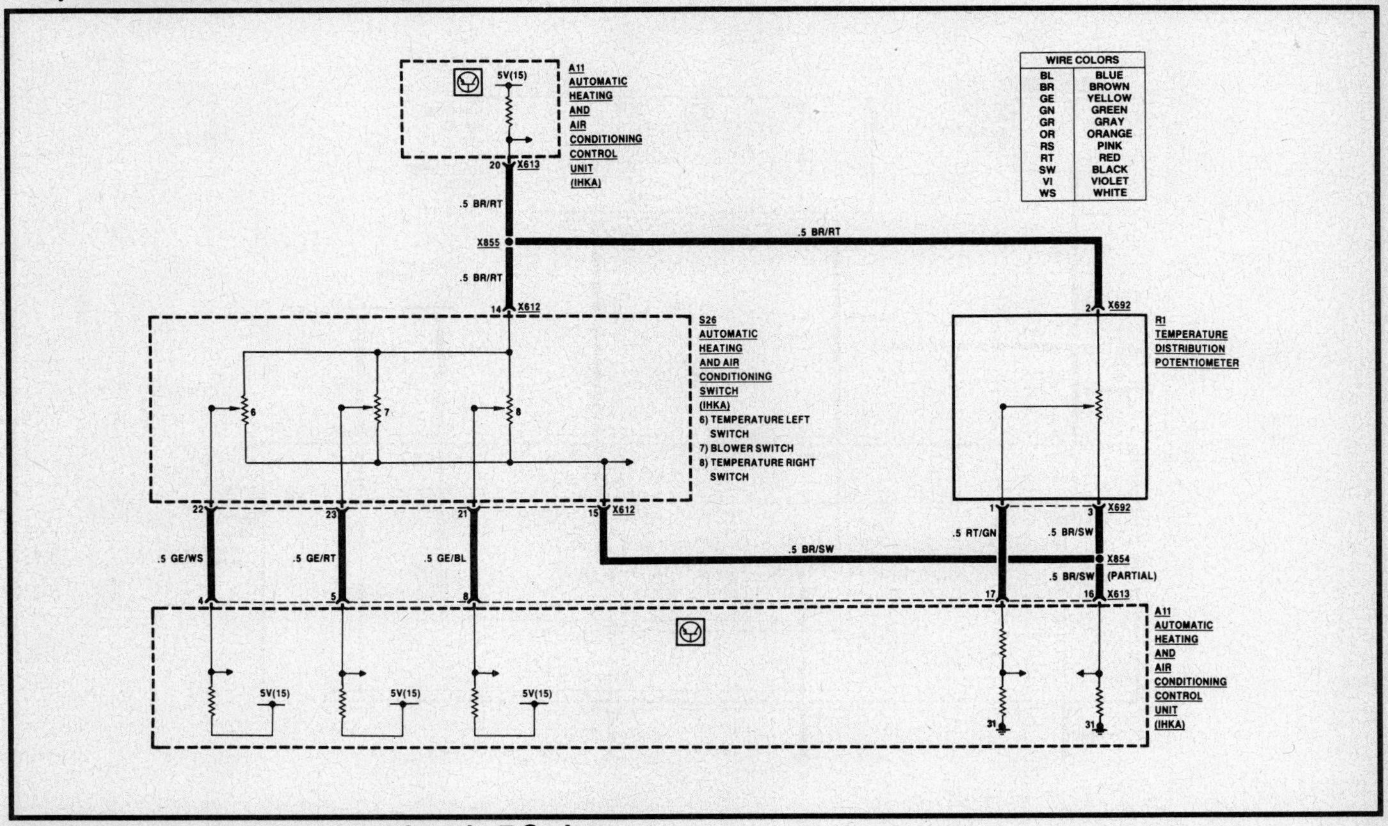
5V(15)
A11 AUTOMATIC HEATING AND AIR CONDITIONING CONTROL UNIT (IHKA)
20 X613
.5 BR/RT
X855
.5 BR/RT
.5 BR/RT
14 X612
6
7
8
S26 AUTOMATIC HEATING AND AIR CONDITIONING SWITCH (IHKA)
6) TEMPERATURE LEFT SWITCH
7) BLOWER SWITCH
8) TEMPERATURE RIGHT SWITCH
22
23
21
15 X612
.5 GE/WS
.5 GE/RT
.5 GE/BL
.5 BR/SW
4
5
8
5V(15)
5V(15)
5V(15)
2 X692
R1 TEMPERATURE DISTRIBUTION POTENTIOMETER
1
3 X692
.5 RT/GN
.5 BR/SW
X854
.5 BR/SW (PARTIAL)
17
16 X613
31
31
A11 AUTOMATIC HEATING AND AIR CONDITIONING CONTROL UNIT (IHKA)

WIRE COLORS	
BL	BLUE
BR	BROWN
GE	YELLOW
GN	GREEN
GR	GRAY
OR	ORANGE
RS	PINK
RT	RED
SW	BLACK
VI	VIOLET
WS	WHITE

Temperature control circuit continued—7 Series

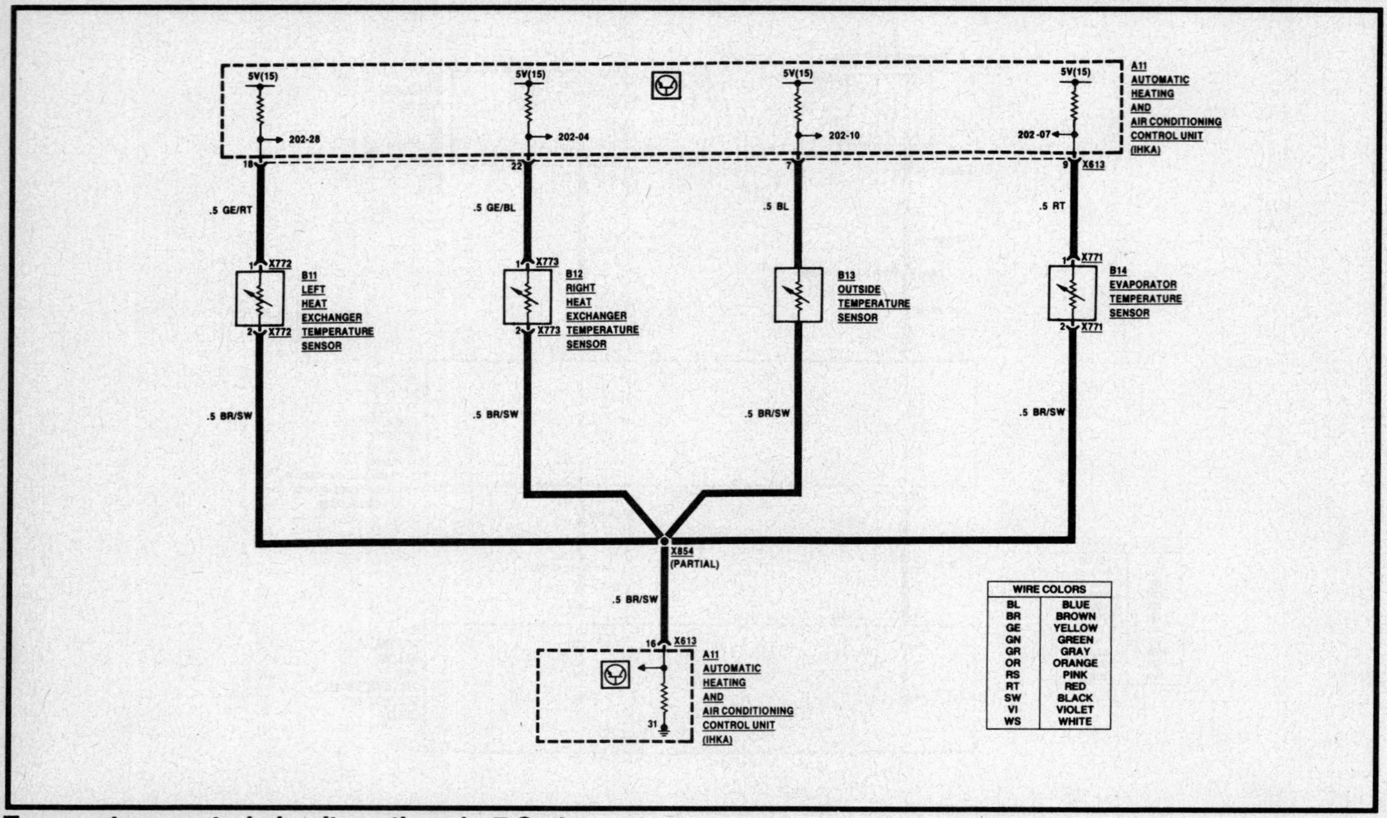
5V(15)
202-28
202-04
202-10
202-07
A11
AUTOMATIC
HEATING
AND
AIR CONDITIONING
CONTROL UNIT
(IHKA)
X613
.5 GE/RT
.5 GE/BL
.5 BL
.5 RT
X772
X773
X771
B11
LEFT
HEAT
EXCHANGER
TEMPERATURE
SENSOR
B12
RIGHT
HEAT
EXCHANGER
TEMPERATURE
SENSOR
B13
OUTSIDE
TEMPERATURE
SENSOR
B14
EVAPORATOR
TEMPERATURE
SENSOR
.5 BR/SW
X854
(PARTIAL)
X613
A11
AUTOMATIC
HEATING
AND
AIR CONDITIONING
CONTROL UNIT
(IHKA)

WIRE COLORS	
BL	BLUE
BR	BROWN
GE	YELLOW
GN	GREEN
GR	GRAY
OR	ORANGE
RS	PINK
RT	RED
SW	BLACK
VI	VIOLET
WS	WHITE

Temperature control circuit continued—7 Series

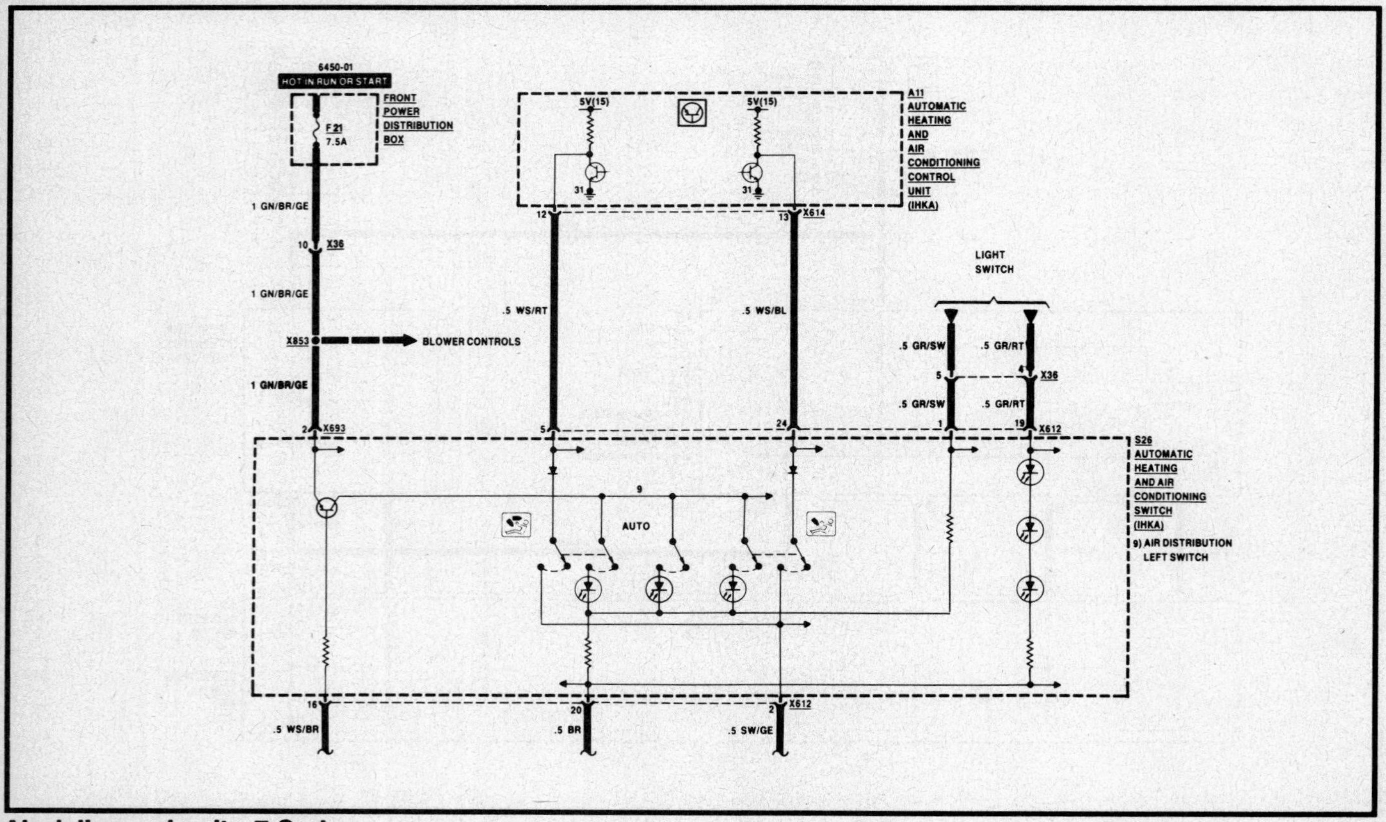
6450-01
HOT IN RUN OR START
F21
7.5A
FRONT
POWER
DISTRIBUTION
BOX
1 GN/BR/GE
X36
X853
BLOWER CONTROLS
X693
A11
AUTOMATIC
HEATING
AND
AIR
CONDITIONING
CONTROL
UNIT
(IHKA)
5V(15)
X614
.5 WS/RT
.5 WS/BL
LIGHT
SWITCH
.5 GR/SW
.5 GR/RT
X36
X612
AUTO
S26
AUTOMATIC
HEATING
AND AIR
CONDITIONING
SWITCH
(IHKA)
9) AIR DISTRIBUTION
LEFT SWITCH
X612
.5 WS/BR
.5 BR
.5 SW/GE

Air delivery circuit—7 Series

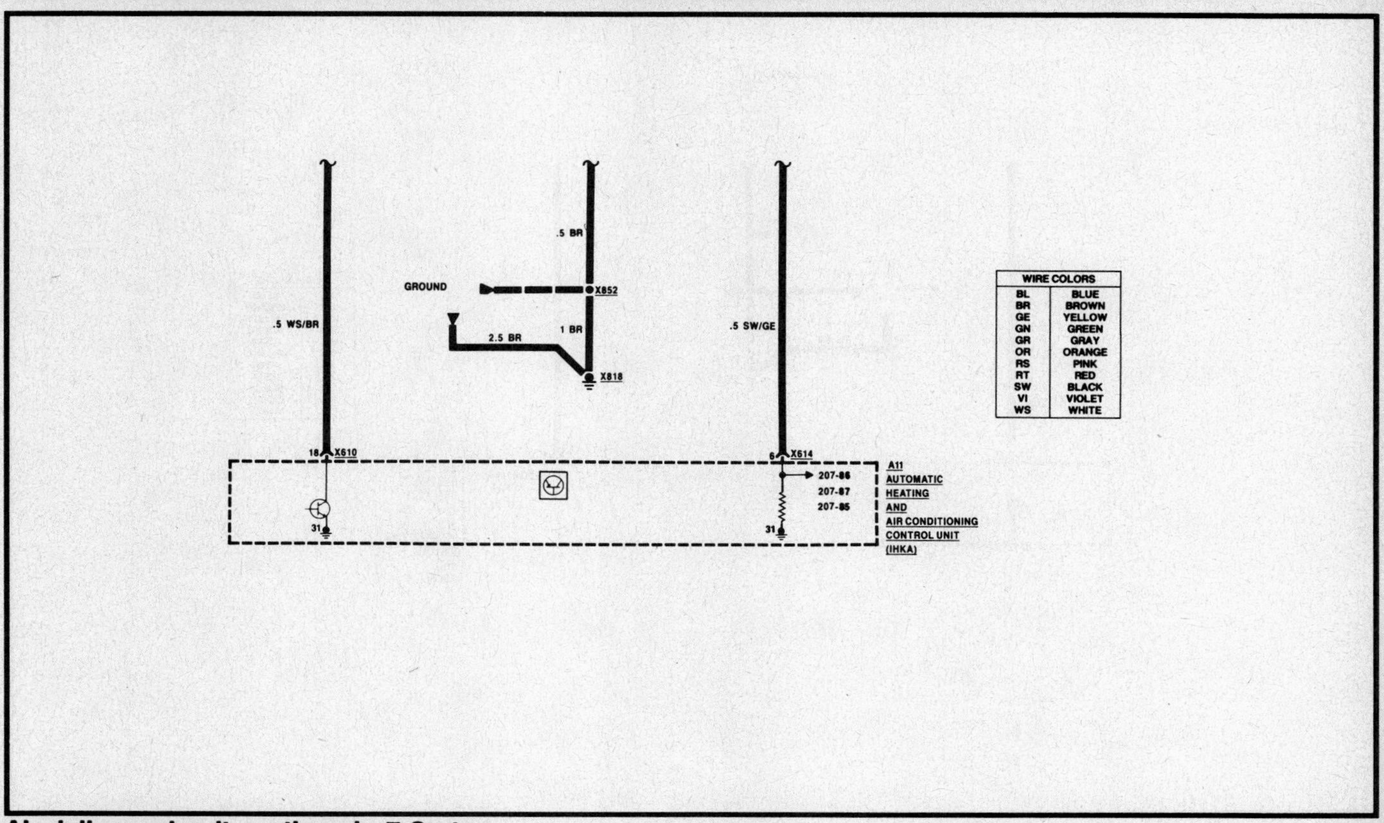
.5 BR
GROUND
X852
.5 WS/BR
2.5 BR
1 BR
X818
.5 SW/GE
WIRE COLORS
BL BLUE
BR BROWN
GE YELLOW
GN GREEN
GR GRAY
OR ORANGE
RS PINK
RT RED
SW BLACK
VI VIOLET
WS WHITE
18 X610
6 X614
207-86
207-87
207-85
31
A11 AUTOMATIC HEATING AND AIR CONDITIONING CONTROL UNIT (IHKA)

Air delivery circuit continued—7 Series

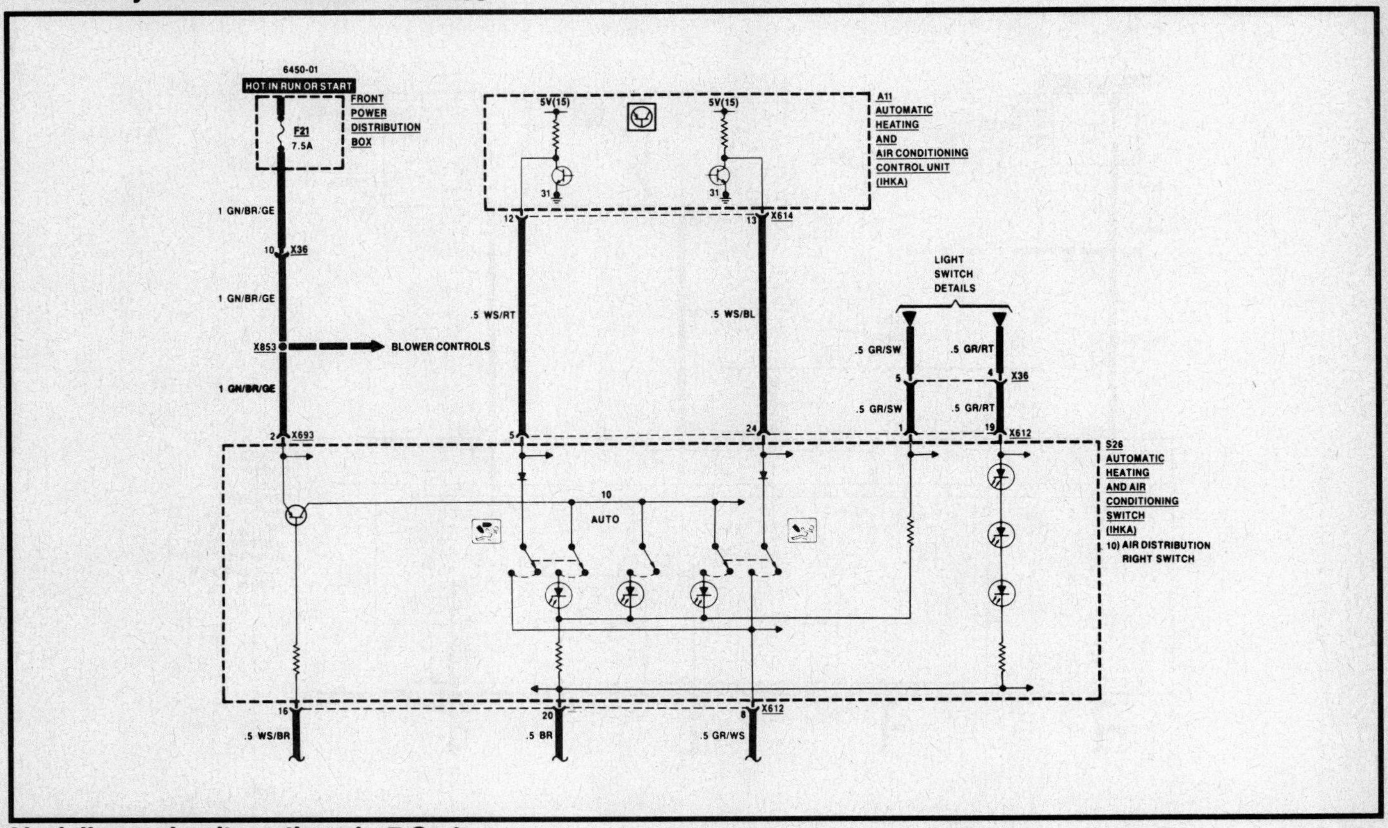
6450-01
HOT IN RUN OR START
FRONT POWER DISTRIBUTION BOX
F21 7.5A
1 GN/BR/GE
10 X36
X853
BLOWER CONTROLS
2 X693
5V(15)
A11 AUTOMATIC HEATING AND AIR CONDITIONING CONTROL UNIT (IHKA)
12
13 X614
.5 WS/RT
.5 WS/BL
LIGHT SWITCH DETAILS
.5 GR/SW
.5 GR/RT
5
4 X36
24
1
19 X612
S26 AUTOMATIC HEATING AND AIR CONDITIONING SWITCH (IHKA)
10) AIR DISTRIBUTION RIGHT SWITCH
10
AUTO
16
20
8 X612
.5 WS/BR
.5 BR
.5 GR/WS

Air delivery circuit continued—7 Series

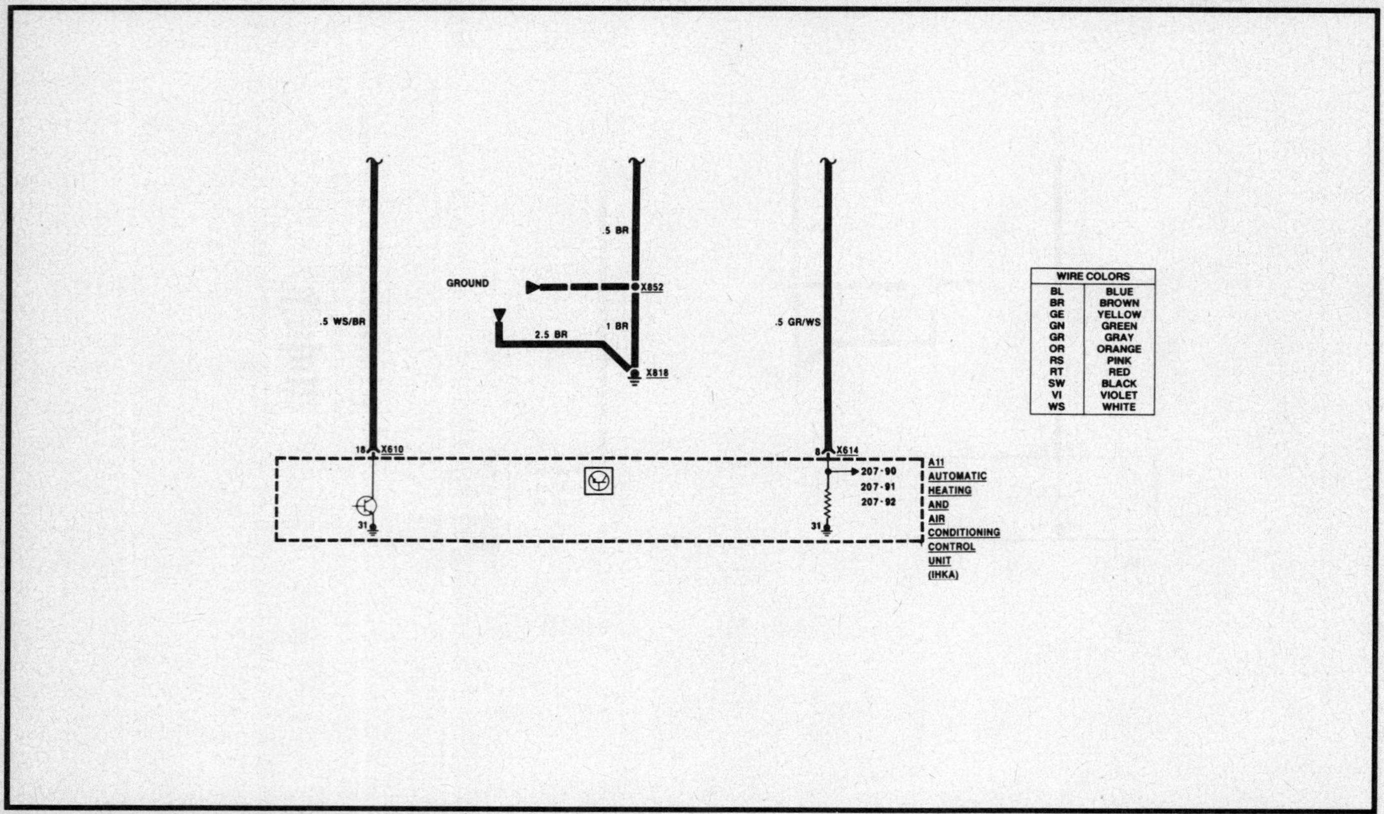
GROUND
.5 BR
X852
.5 WS/BR
2.5 BR
1 BR
X818
.5 GR/WS
WIRE COLORS
BL BLUE
BR BROWN
GE YELLOW
GN GREEN
GR GRAY
OR ORANGE
RS PINK
RT RED
SW BLACK
VI VIOLET
WS WHITE
X610
X614
207-90
207-91
207-92
A11
AUTOMATIC
HEATING
AND
AIR
CONDITIONING
CONTROL
UNIT
(IHKA)

Air delivery circuit continued—7 Series

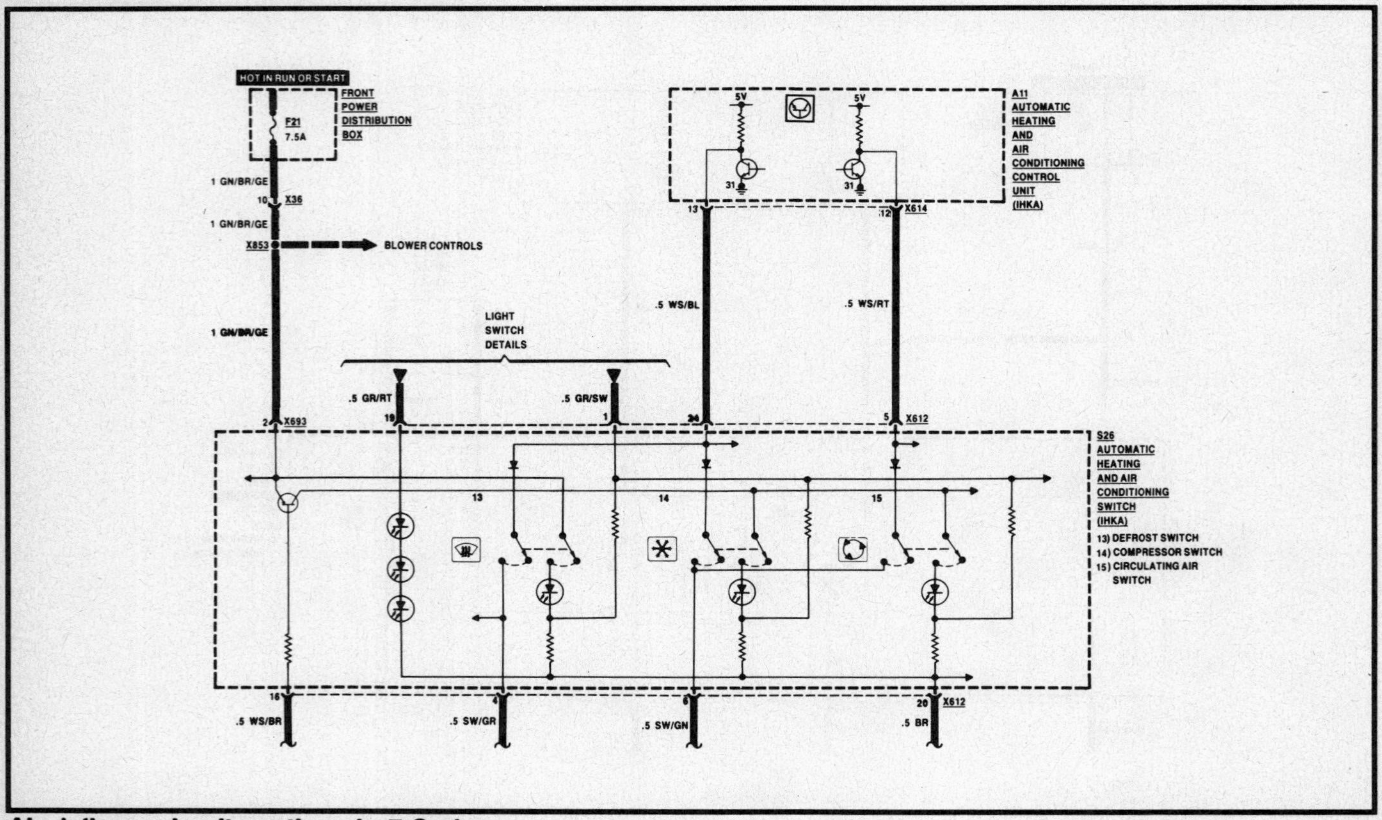
HOT IN RUN OR START
F21
7.5A
FRONT
POWER
DISTRIBUTION
BOX
1 GN/BR/GE
X36
1 GN/BR/GE
X853
BLOWER CONTROLS
1 GN/BR/GE
LIGHT
SWITCH
DETAILS
.5 GR/RT
.5 GR/SW
X693
A11
AUTOMATIC
HEATING
AND
AIR
CONDITIONING
CONTROL
UNIT
(IHKA)
5V
X614
.5 WS/BL
.5 WS/RT
X612
S26
AUTOMATIC
HEATING
AND AIR
CONDITIONING
SWITCH
(IHKA)
13) DEFROST SWITCH
14) COMPRESSOR SWITCH
15) CIRCULATING AIR
SWITCH
.5 WS/BR
.5 SW/GR
.5 SW/GN
.5 BR
X612

Air delivery circuit continued—7 Series

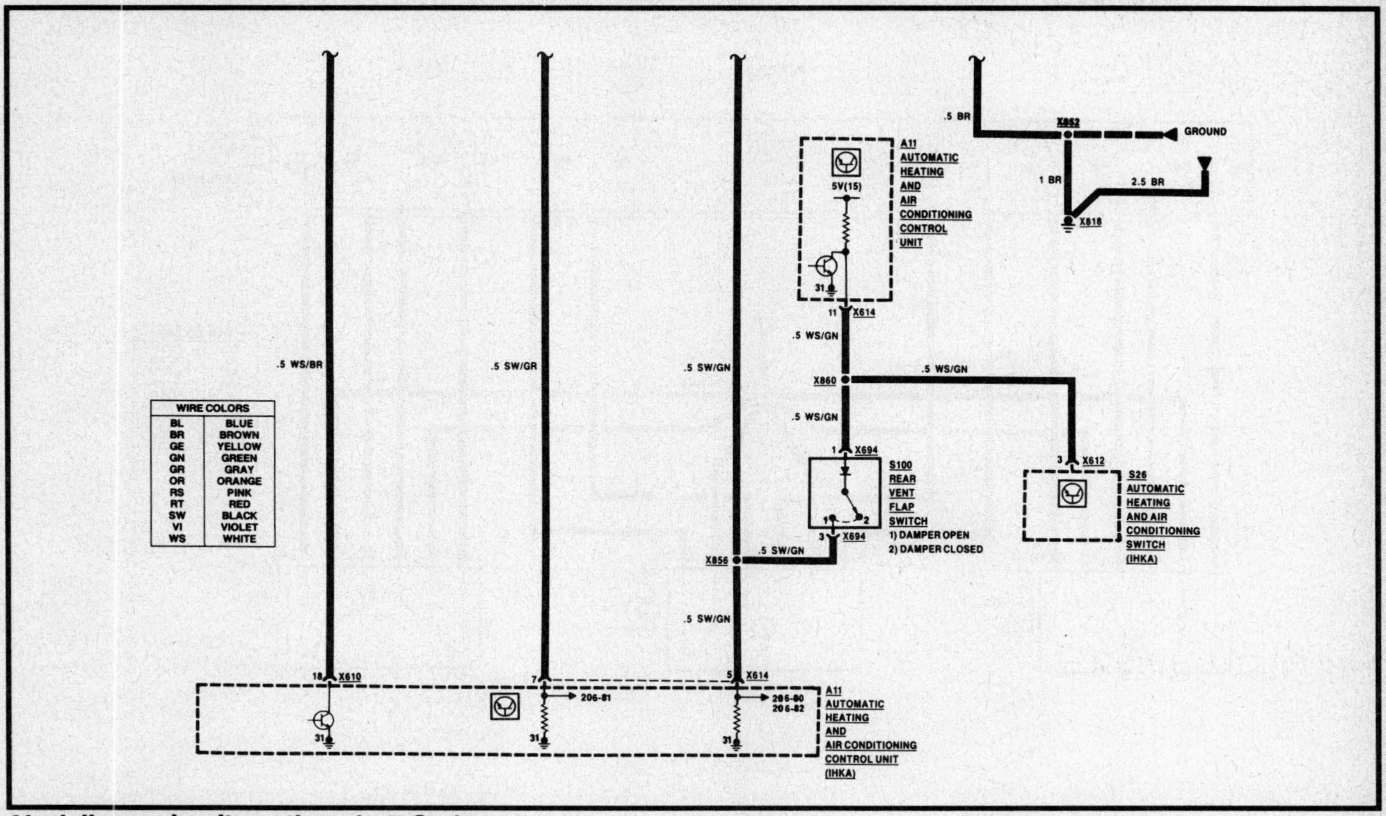
.5 BR
X862
GROUND
1 BR
2.5 BR
X818
A11
AUTOMATIC
HEATING
AND
AIR
CONDITIONING
CONTROL
UNIT
5V(15)
31
11 X614
.5 WS/GN
.5 WS/BR
.5 SW/GR
.5 SW/GN
X860
.5 WS/GN
.5 WS/GN
1 X694
S100
REAR
VENT
FLAP
SWITCH
1) DAMPER OPEN
2) DAMPER CLOSED
3 X694
X856
.5 SW/GN
3 X612
S26
AUTOMATIC
HEATING
AND AIR
CONDITIONING
SWITCH
(IHKA)
WIRE COLORS
BL BLUE
BR BROWN
GE YELLOW
GN GREEN
GR GRAY
OR ORANGE
RS PINK
RT RED
SW BLACK
VI VIOLET
WS WHITE
.5 SW/GN
18 X610
7
5 X614
206-81
206-80
206-82
31
A11
AUTOMATIC
HEATING
AND
AIR CONDITIONING
CONTROL UNIT
(IHKA)

Air delivery circuit continued—7 Series

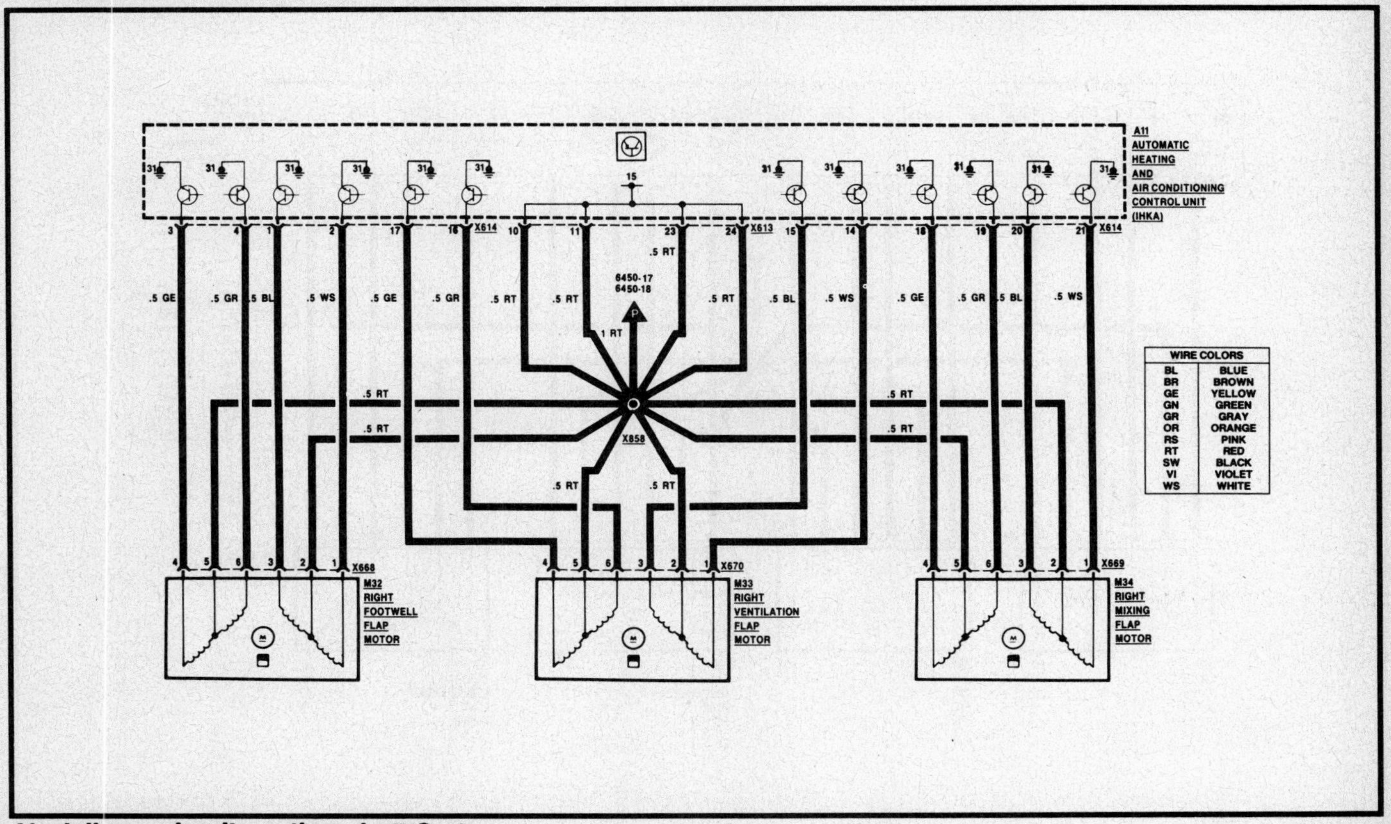
A11
AUTOMATIC
HEATING
AND
AIR CONDITIONING
CONTROL UNIT
(IHKA)
31
15
3 4 1 2 17 16 X614 10 11 23 24 X613 15 14 18 19 20 21 X614
.5 RT
6450-17
6450-18
.5 GE .5 GR .5 BL .5 WS .5 GE .5 GR .5 RT .5 RT .5 RT .5 BL .5 WS .5 GE .5 GR .5 BL .5 WS
1 RT
.5 RT
.5 RT
X858
WIRE COLORS
BL BLUE
BR BROWN
GE YELLOW
GN GREEN
GR GRAY
OR ORANGE
RS PINK
RT RED
SW BLACK
VI VIOLET
WS WHITE
4 5 6 3 2 1 X668
M32
RIGHT
FOOTWELL
FLAP
MOTOR
4 5 6 3 2 1 X670
M33
RIGHT
VENTILATION
FLAP
MOTOR
4 5 6 3 2 1 X669
M34
RIGHT
MIXING
FLAP
MOTOR

Air delivery circuit continued—7 Series

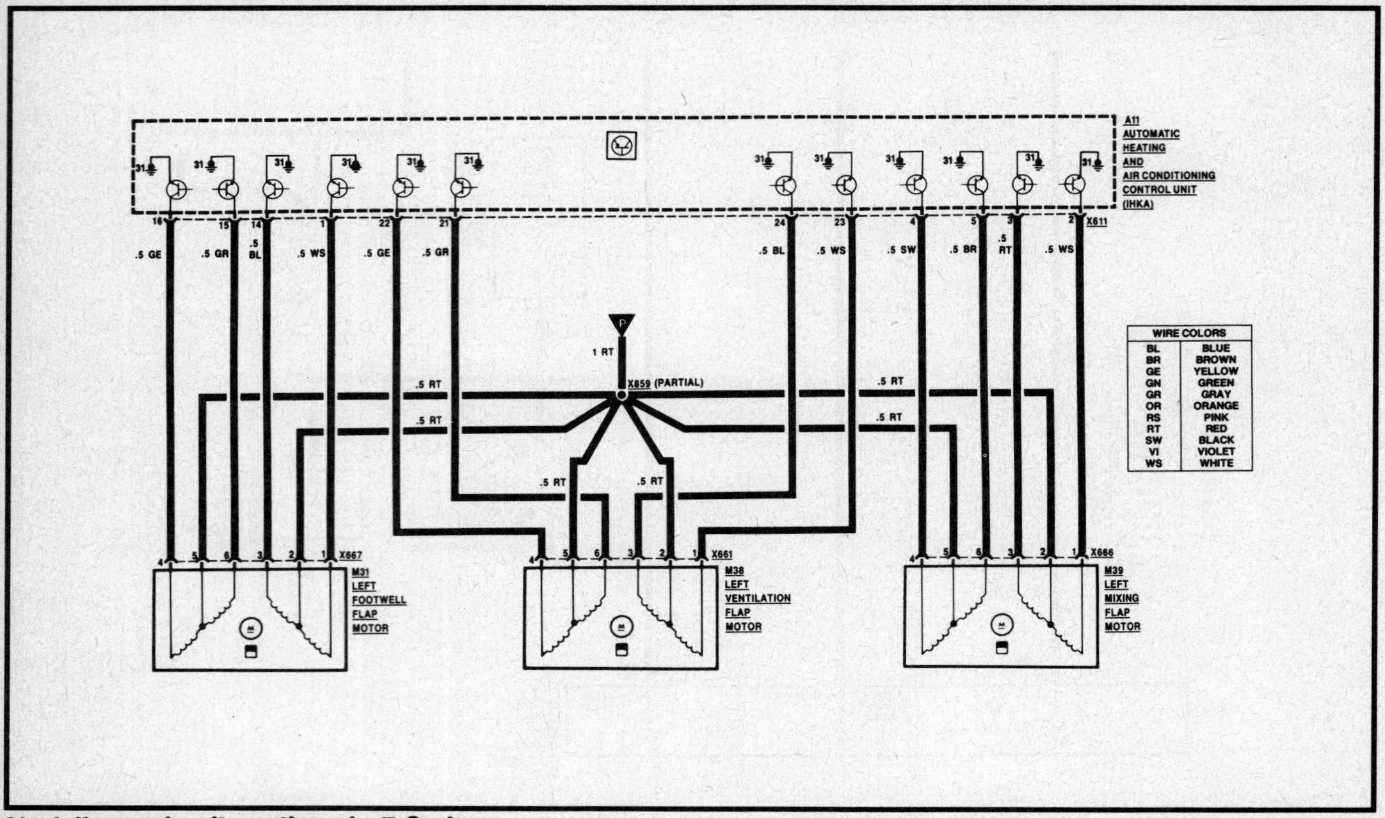
A11 AUTOMATIC HEATING AND AIR CONDITIONING CONTROL UNIT (IHKA)
X611
X859 (PARTIAL)
1 RT
.5 RT
.5 GE
.5 GR
.5 BL
.5 WS
.5 SW
.5 BR
.5 RT
X667
X661
X666
M31 LEFT FOOTWELL FLAP MOTOR
M38 LEFT VENTILATION FLAP MOTOR
M39 LEFT MIXING FLAP MOTOR
WIRE COLORS
BL BLUE
BR BROWN
GE YELLOW
GN GREEN
GR GRAY
OR ORANGE
RS PINK
RT RED
SW BLACK
VI VIOLET
WS WHITE

Air delivery circuit continued—7 Series

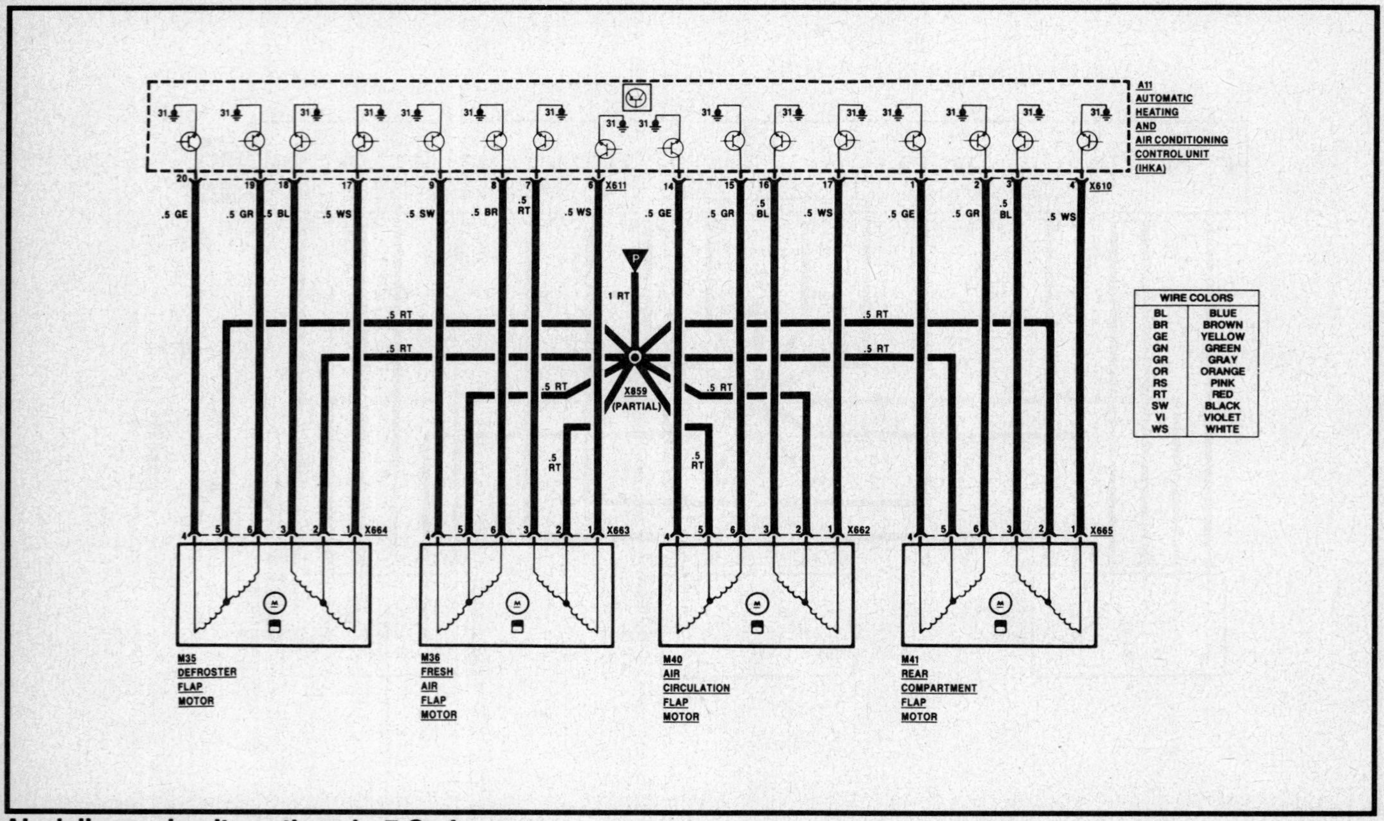
A11 AUTOMATIC HEATING AND AIR CONDITIONING CONTROL UNIT (IHKA)
X611
X610
X859 (PARTIAL)
1 RT
.5 RT
X664
X663
X662
X665
M35 DEFROSTER FLAP MOTOR
M36 FRESH AIR FLAP MOTOR
M40 AIR CIRCULATION FLAP MOTOR
M41 REAR COMPARTMENT FLAP MOTOR
WIRE COLORS
BL BLUE
BR BROWN
GE YELLOW
GN GREEN
GR GRAY
OR ORANGE
RS PINK
RT RED
SW BLACK
VI VIOLET
WS WHITE

Air delivery circuit continued—7 Series

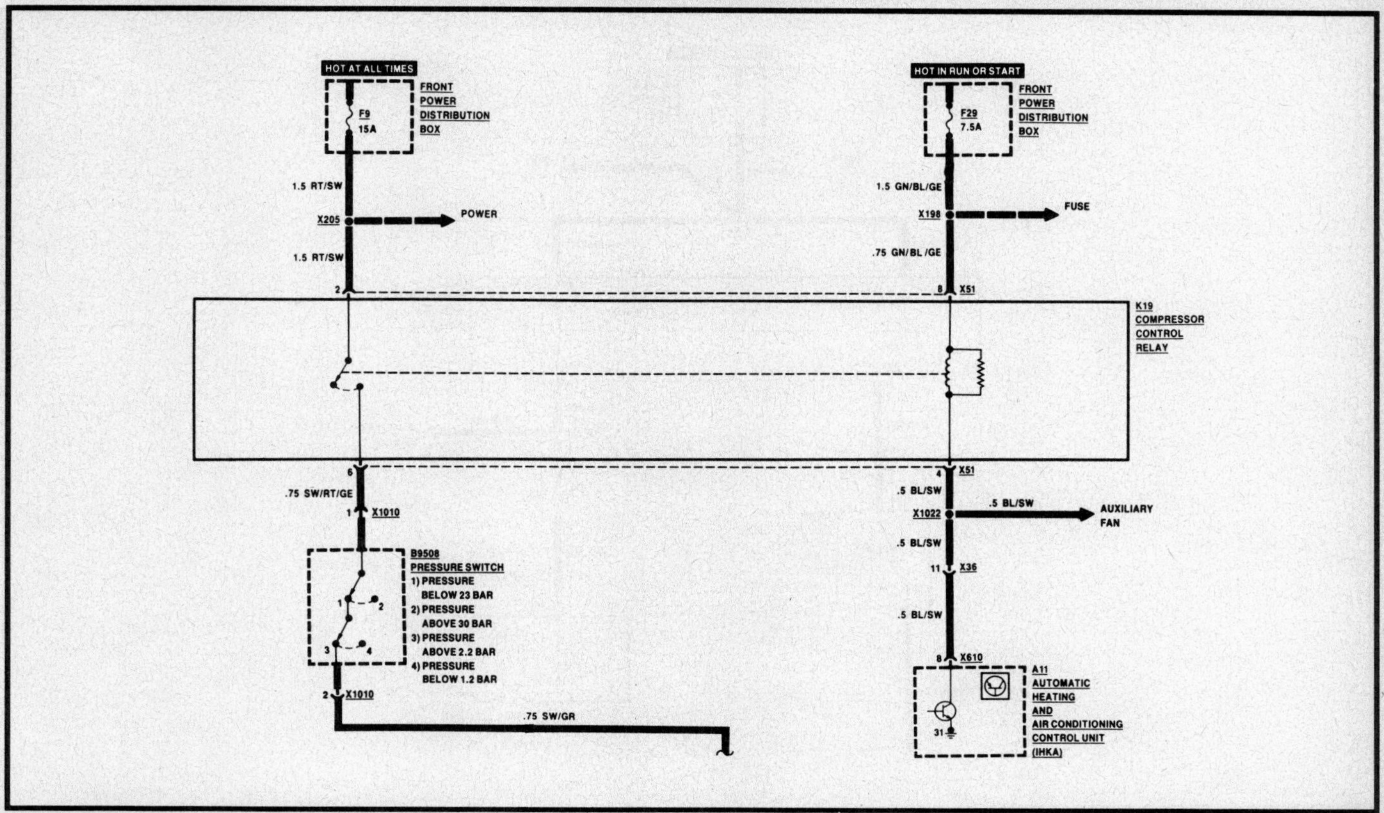
HOT AT ALL TIMES
F9
15A
FRONT POWER DISTRIBUTION BOX
1.5 RT/SW
X205
POWER
1.5 RT/SW
HOT IN RUN OR START
F29
7.5A
FRONT POWER DISTRIBUTION BOX
1.5 GN/BL/GE
X198
FUSE
.75 GN/BL/GE
X51
K19 COMPRESSOR CONTROL RELAY
.75 SW/RT/GE
X1010
B9508 PRESSURE SWITCH
1) PRESSURE BELOW 23 BAR
2) PRESSURE ABOVE 30 BAR
3) PRESSURE ABOVE 2.2 BAR
4) PRESSURE BELOW 1.2 BAR
.75 SW/GR
.5 BL/SW
X1022
.5 BL/SW
AUXILIARY FAN
X36
X610
A11 AUTOMATIC HEATING AND AIR CONDITIONING CONTROL UNIT (IHKA)

Compressor control circuit—7 Series

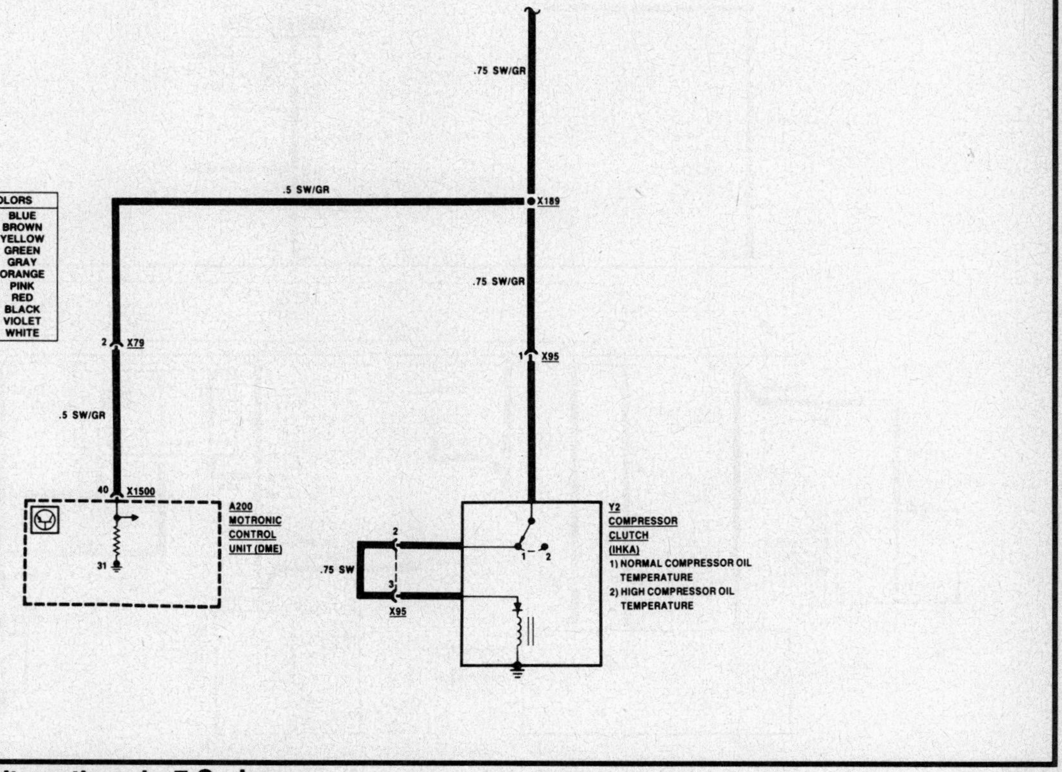
.75 SW/GR
.5 SW/GR
X189
X79
X95
X1500
A200 MOTRONIC CONTROL UNIT (DME)
.75 SW
Y2 COMPRESSOR CLUTCH (IHKA)
1) NORMAL COMPRESSOR OIL TEMPERATURE
2) HIGH COMPRESSOR OIL TEMPERATURE

WIRE COLORS	
BL	BLUE
BR	BROWN
GE	YELLOW
GN	GREEN
GR	GRAY
OR	ORANGE
RS	PINK
RT	RED
SW	BLACK
VI	VIOLET
WS	WHITE

Compressor control circuit continued—7 Series

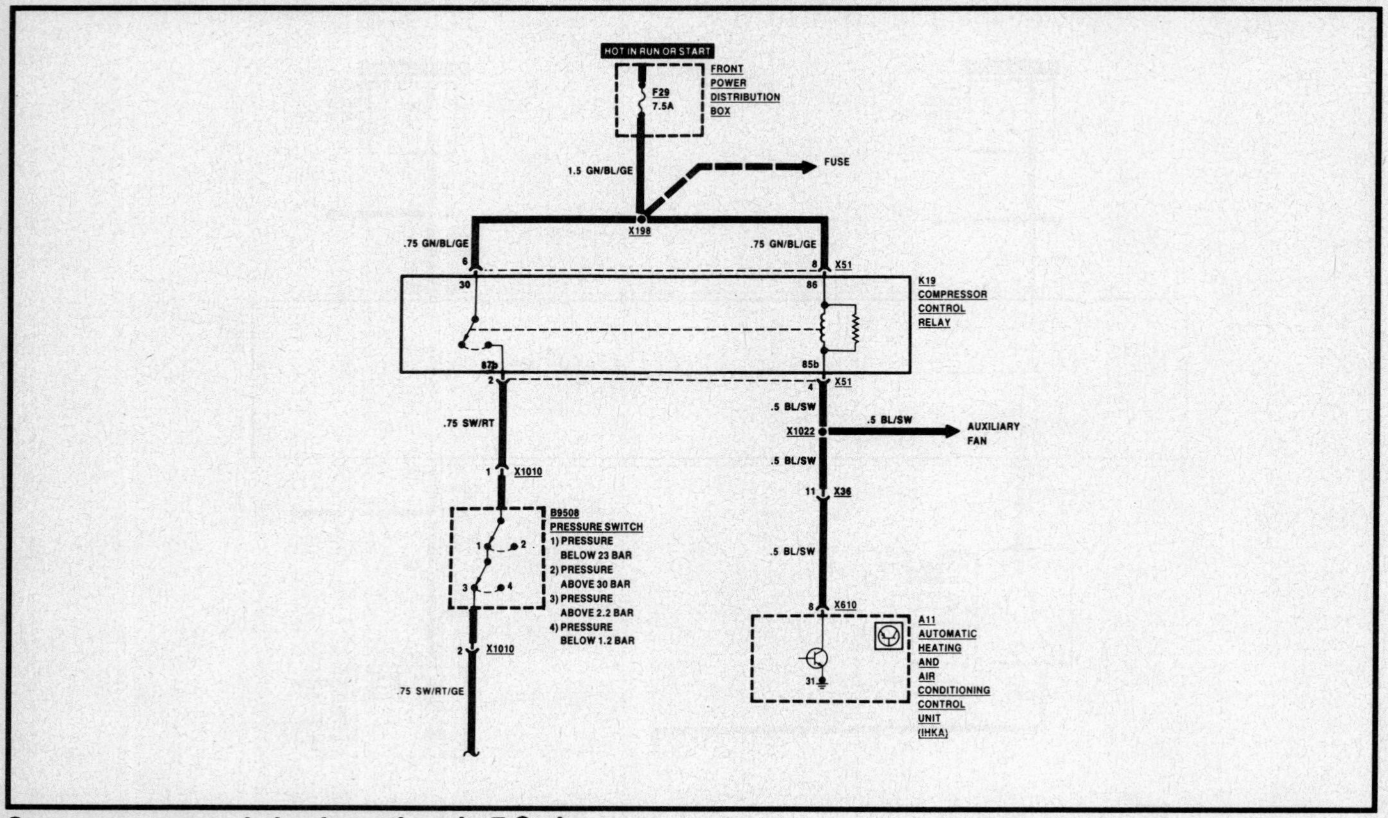
HOT IN RUN OR START
F29
7.5A
FRONT
POWER
DISTRIBUTION
BOX
1.5 GN/BL/GE
FUSE
X198
.75 GN/BL/GE
.75 GN/BL/GE
X51
K19
COMPRESSOR
CONTROL
RELAY
30
86
87b
85b
X51
.75 SW/RT
.5 BL/SW
.5 BL/SW
X1022
AUXILIARY
FAN
.5 BL/SW
X1010
X36
B9508
PRESSURE SWITCH
1) PRESSURE
BELOW 23 BAR
2) PRESSURE
ABOVE 30 BAR
3) PRESSURE
ABOVE 2.2 BAR
4) PRESSURE
BELOW 1.2 BAR
.5 BL/SW
X610
X1010
A11
AUTOMATIC
HEATING
AND
AIR
CONDITIONING
CONTROL
UNIT
(IHKA)
.75 SW/RT/GE

Compressor control circuit continued – 7 Series

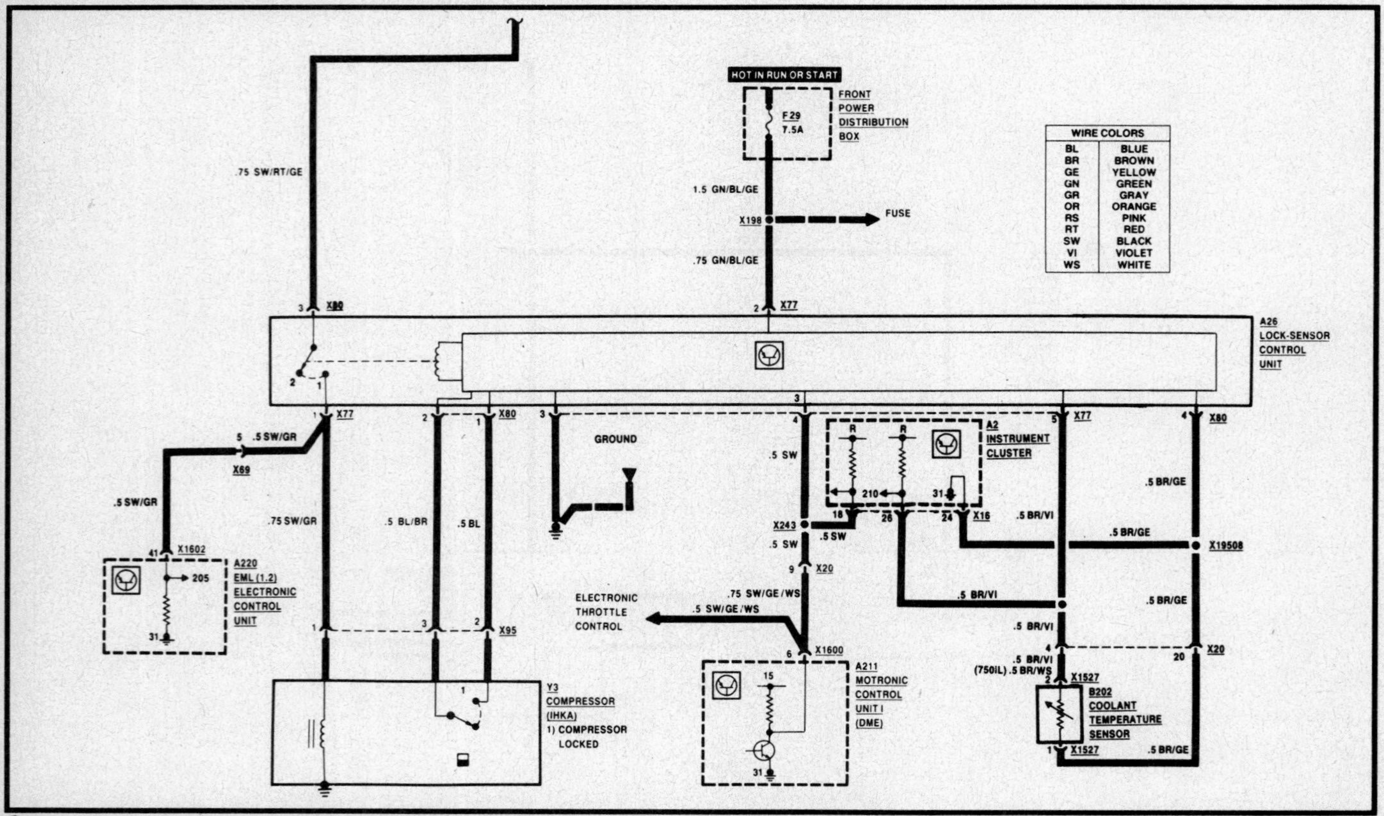
HOT IN RUN OR START
F29
7.5A
FRONT
POWER
DISTRIBUTION
BOX
.75 SW/RT/GE
1.5 GN/BL/GE
X198
FUSE
.75 GN/BL/GE
WIRE COLORS
BL BLUE
BR BROWN
GE YELLOW
GN GREEN
GR GRAY
OR ORANGE
RS PINK
RT RED
SW BLACK
VI VIOLET
WS WHITE
X80
X77
A26
LOCK-SENSOR
CONTROL
UNIT
X77
X80
X77
X80
5 .5 SW/GR
X69
GROUND
A2
INSTRUMENT
CLUSTER
.5 SW/GR
.75 SW/GR
.5 BL/BR
.5 BL
.5 SW
210
X16
.5 BR/VI
.5 BR/GE
X1602
X243
.5 SW
.5 SW
X20
.5 BR/GE
X19508
A220
EML (1.2)
ELECTRONIC
CONTROL
UNIT
205
ELECTRONIC
THROTTLE
CONTROL
.75 SW/GE/WS
.5 SW/GE/WS
.5 BR/VI
.5 BR/GE
X95
X1600
.5 BR/VI
X20
.5 BR/VI
(750iL) .5 BR/WS
X1527
Y3
COMPRESSOR
(IHKA)
1) COMPRESSOR
LOCKED
A211
MOTRONIC
CONTROL
UNIT I
(DME)
B202
COOLANT
TEMPERATURE
SENSOR
X1527
.5 BR/GE

Compressor control circuit continued – 7 Series

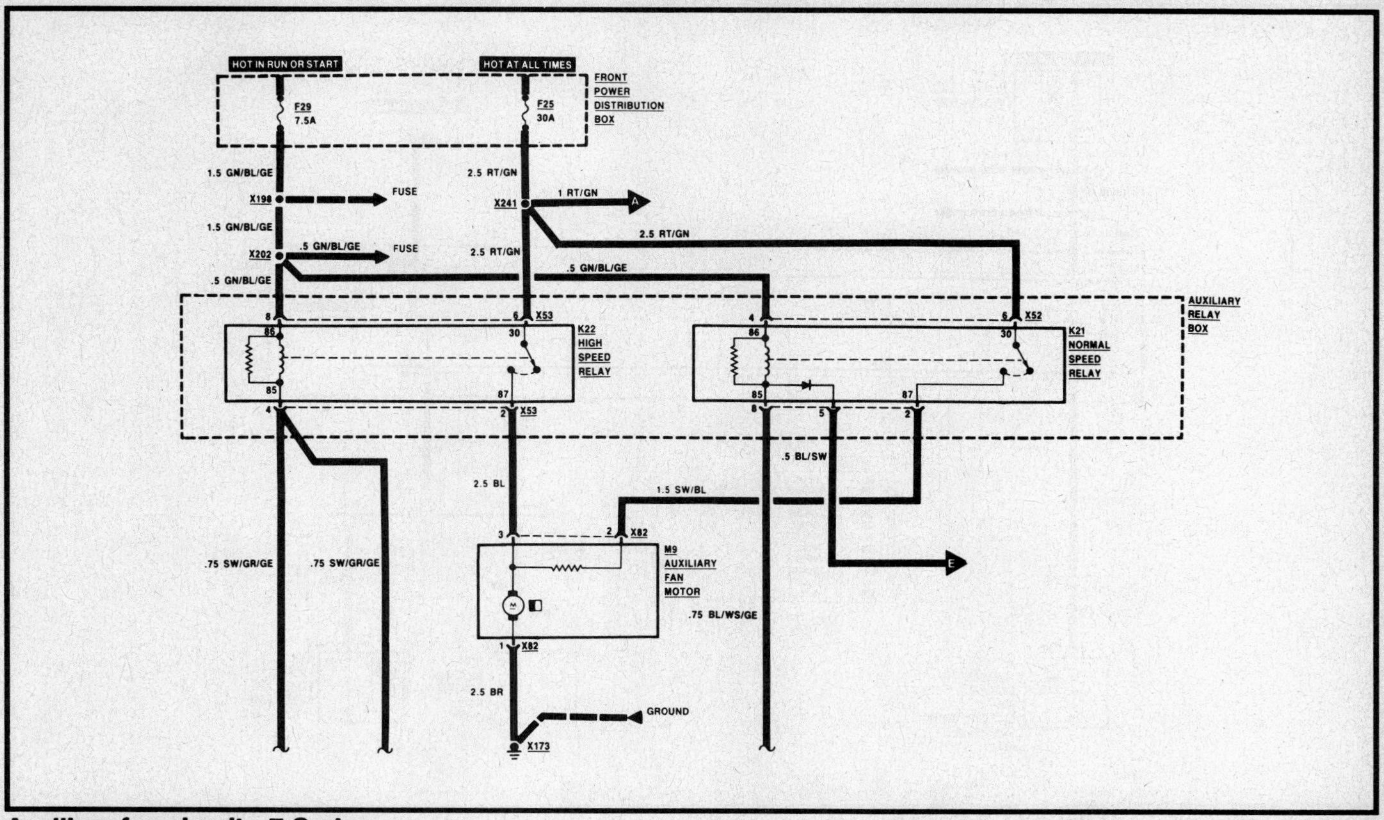
HOT IN RUN OR START
HOT AT ALL TIMES
F29
7.5A
F25
30A
FRONT
POWER
DISTRIBUTION
BOX
1.5 GN/BL/GE
X198
FUSE
1.5 GN/BL/GE
X202
.5 GN/BL/GE
FUSE
.5 GN/BL/GE
2.5 RT/GN
X241
1 RT/GN
A
2.5 RT/GN
2.5 RT/GN
.5 GN/BL/GE
X53
K22
HIGH
SPEED
RELAY
X52
K21
NORMAL
SPEED
RELAY
AUXILIARY
RELAY
BOX
X53
.5 BL/SW
2.5 BL
1.5 SW/BL
X82
M9
AUXILIARY
FAN
MOTOR
E
.75 SW/GR/GE
.75 SW/GR/GE
.75 BL/WS/GE
X82
2.5 BR
GROUND
X173
Auxiliary fan circuit—7 Series

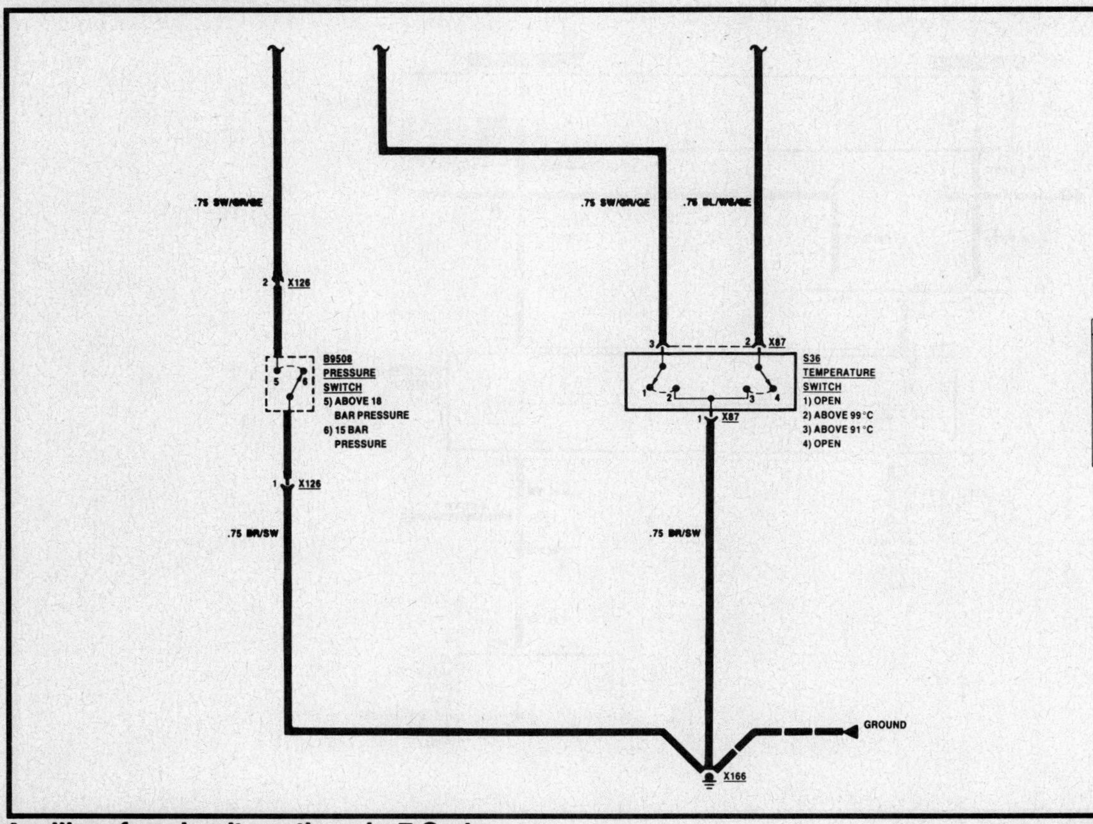
.75 SW/GR/GE
.75 SW/GR/GE
.75 BL/WS/GE
X126
B9508
PRESSURE
SWITCH
5) ABOVE 18
BAR PRESSURE
6) 15 BAR
PRESSURE
X126
X87
S36
TEMPERATURE
SWITCH
1) OPEN
2) ABOVE 99°C
3) ABOVE 91°C
4) OPEN
X87
.75 BR/SW
.75 BR/SW
GROUND
X166

WIRE COLORS	
BL	BLUE
BR	BROWN
GE	YELLOW
GN	GREEN
GR	GRAY
OR	ORANGE
RS	PINK
RT	RED
SW	BLACK
VI	VIOLET
WS	WHITE

Auxiliary fan circuit continued—7 Series

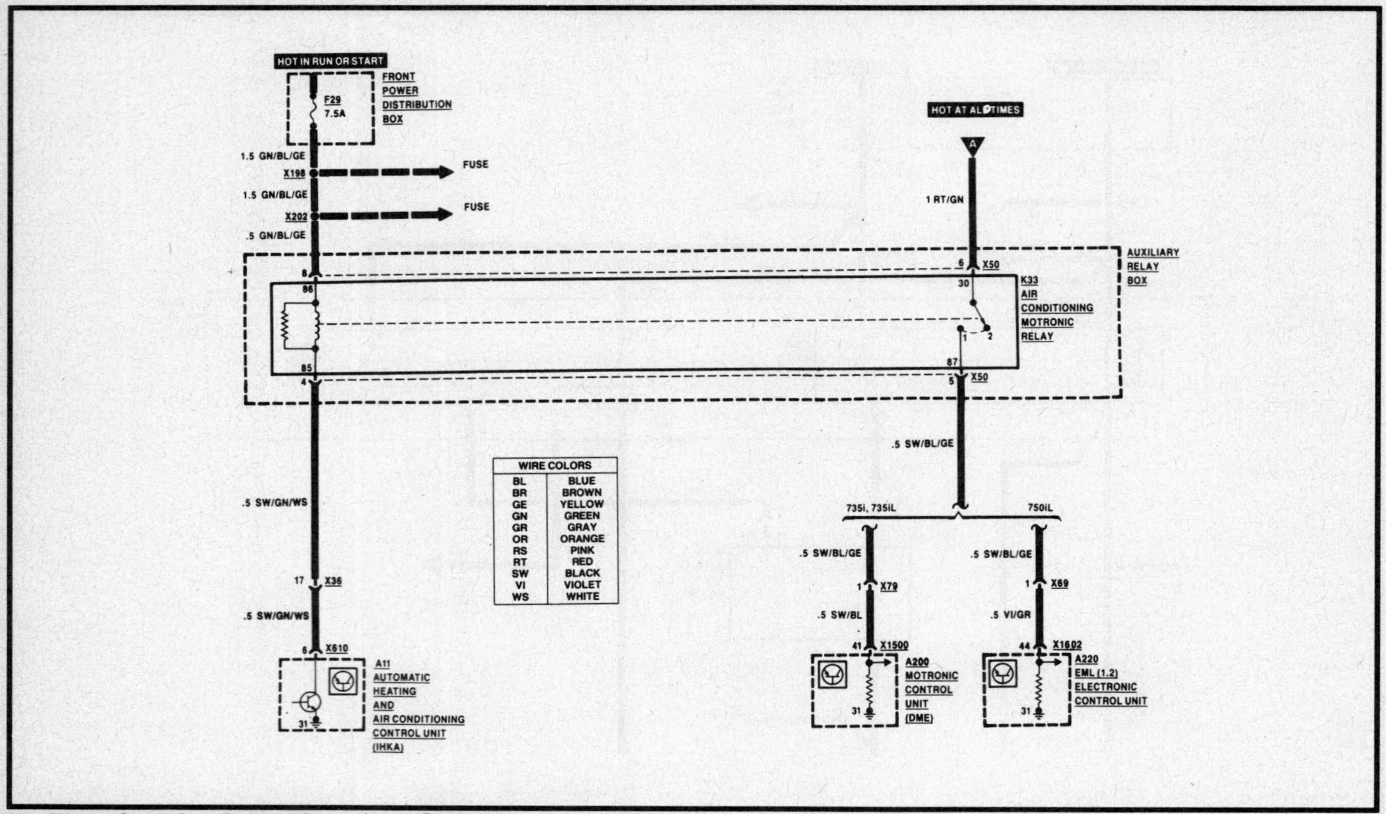
HOT IN RUN OR START
F29 7.5A
FRONT POWER DISTRIBUTION BOX
1.5 GN/BL/GE
X198
FUSE
1.5 GN/BL/GE
X202
FUSE
.5 GN/BL/GE
HOT AT ALL TIMES
A
1 RT/GN
X50
AUXILIARY RELAY BOX
K33 AIR CONDITIONING MOTRONIC RELAY
X50
.5 SW/BL/GE
.5 SW/GN/WS
WIRE COLORS
BL BLUE
BR BROWN
GE YELLOW
GN GREEN
GR GRAY
OR ORANGE
RS PINK
RT RED
SW BLACK
VI VIOLET
WS WHITE
735i, 735iL
750iL
.5 SW/BL/GE
X79
.5 SW/BL
X1500
A200 MOTRONIC CONTROL UNIT (DME)
.5 SW/BL/GE
X69
.5 VI/GR
X1602
A220 EML (1.2) ELECTRONIC CONTROL UNIT
X36
.5 SW/GN/WS
X610
A11 AUTOMATIC HEATING AND AIR CONDITIONING CONTROL UNIT (IHKA)

Auxiliary fan circuit continued – 7 Series

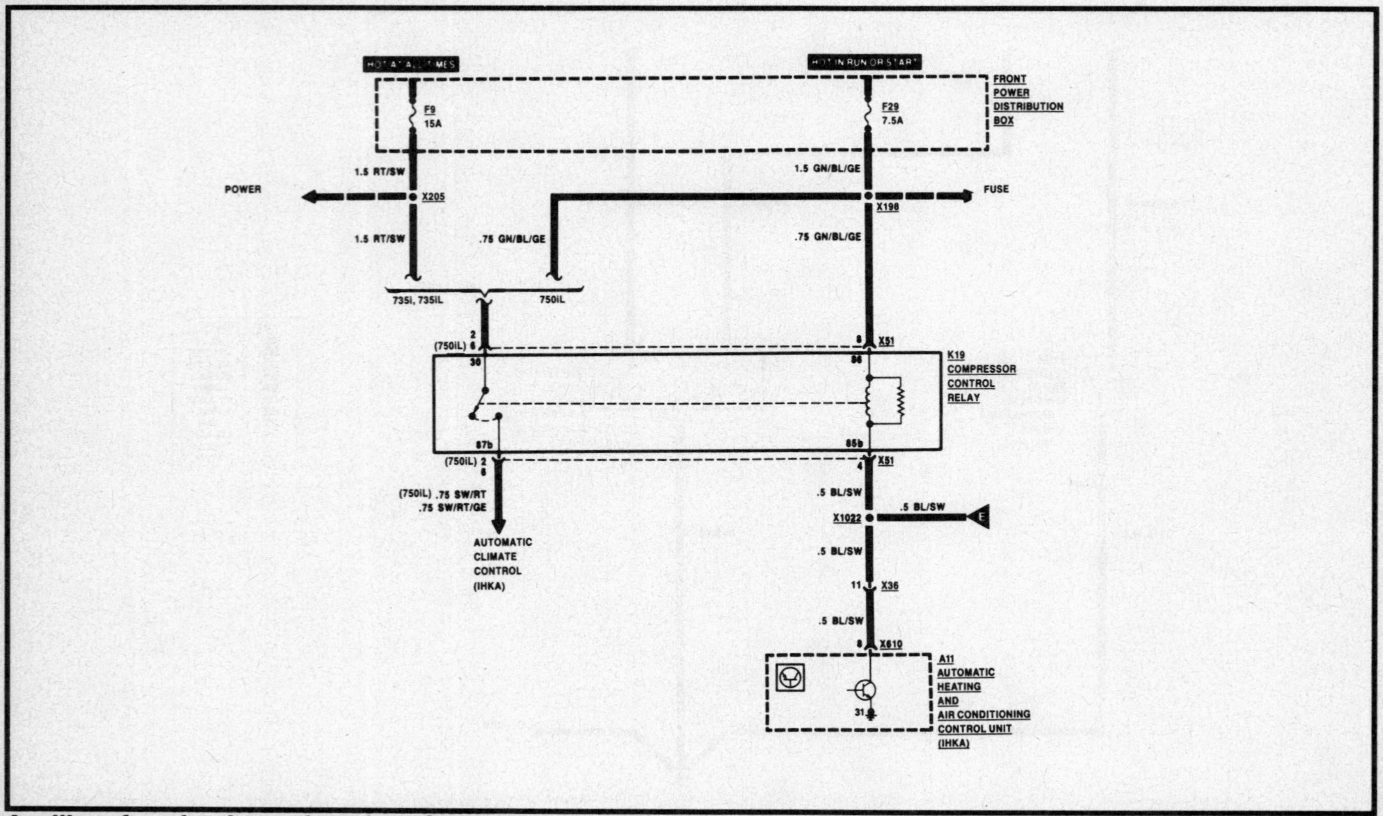
HOT AT ALL TIMES
HOT IN RUN OR START
F9 15A
F29 7.5A
FRONT POWER DISTRIBUTION BOX
1.5 RT/SW
POWER
X205
1.5 RT/SW
1.5 GN/BL/GE
FUSE
X198
.75 GN/BL/GE
.75 GN/BL/GE
735i, 735iL
750iL
X51
K19 COMPRESSOR CONTROL RELAY
X51
(750iL) .75 SW/RT
.75 SW/RT/GE
AUTOMATIC CLIMATE CONTROL (IHKA)
.5 BL/SW
X1022
.5 BL/SW
E
.5 BL/SW
X36
.5 BL/SW
X610
A11 AUTOMATIC HEATING AND AIR CONDITIONING CONTROL UNIT (IHKA)

Auxiliary fan circuit continued – 7 Series

14 CHRYSLER IMPORTS 14

COLT • COLT VISTA • CONQUEST

SPECIFICATIONS

ENGINE IDENTIFICATION

Year	Model	Engine Displacement cu. in. (liter)	Engine Series Identification (VIN)	No. of Cylinders	Engine Type
1989	Colt	90 (1468/1.5)	4G15	4	SOHC
	Colt	97 (1595/1.6)	4G51	4	DOHC
	Colt Wagon	107 (1755/1.8)	4G37	4	SOHC
	Colt Vista	122 (1997/2.0)	G63B	4	SOHC
	Conquest	156 (2555/2.6)	G64B	4	SOHC
1990	Colt	90 (1468/1.5)	4G15	4	SOHC
	Colt	97 (1595/1.6)	4G51	4	DOHC
	Colt Wagon	107 (1755/1.8)	4G37	4	SOHC
	Colt Vista	122 (1997/2.0)	G63B	4	SOHC
1991	Colt	90 (1468/1.5)	4G15	4	SOHC
	Colt Vista	122 (1997/2.0)	G63B	4	SOHC

REFRIGERANT CAPACITIES

Year	Model	Freon (oz.)	Oil	Type
1989	Colt	36	9.8 ①	R-12
	Colt Wagon	32	3 ②	R-12
	Colt Vista	32	3 ②	R-12
	Conquest	29	6 ②	R-12
1990	Colt	36	9.8 ①	R-12
	Colt Wagon	32	3 ②	R-12
	Colt Vista	32	3 ②	R-12
1991	Colt	36	9.8 ①	R-12
	Colt Vista	32	3 ②	R-12

① Cubic inches
② Fl. oz.

AIR CONDITIONING BELT TENSION CHART

Year	Model	Engine Displacement cu. in. (cc/liter)	Belt Type	Specification ① New	Specification ① Used
1989	Colt	90 (1468/1.5)	V-belt	0.23	0.25
	Colt	97 (1595/1.6)	V-belt	0.21	0.25
	Colt Wagon	107 (1755/1.8)	V-belt	0.16	0.24
	Colt Vista	122 (1997/2.0)	V-belt	0.35	0.43
	Conquest	156 (2555/2.6)	V-belt	0.50	0.75
1990	Colt	90 (1468/1.5)	V-belt	0.23	0.25
	Colt	97 (1595/1.6)	V-belt	0.21	0.25
	Colt Wagon	107 (1755/1.8)	V-belt	0.16	0.24
	Colt Vista	122 (1997/2.0)	V-belt	0.35	0.43
1991	Colt	90 (1468/1.5)	V-belt	0.23	0.25
	Colt Vista	122 (1997/2.0)	V-belt	0.35	0.43

① Inches of deflection using 22 lbs. force at the midpoint of the belt

SYSTEM DESCRIPTION

General Information

The heater unit is located in the center of the vehicle with the blower housing and blend-air system. In the blend-air system, hot air and cool air are controlled by blend-air damper to make a fine adjustment of the temperature. The heater system is also designed as a bi-level heater in which a separator directs warm air to the windshield or to the floor and cool air through the panel outlet.

The temperature inside the vehicle is controlled by means of the temperature control lever, the position of which determines the opening of the blend-air damper and the resulting mixing ratio of cool and hot air is used to control the outlet temperature.

The air conditioning compressor coil will be energized when all of the following conditions are met:

1. The air conditioner switch is depressed in either the **ECONO** or **A/C** position.
2. The blower motor switch is not off.
3. The evaporator outlet air temperature sensor is reading at least 39°F (4°C).
4. The evaporator inlet air temperature sensor is reading at least 39°F (4°C).
5. If equipped with a compressor refrigerant temperature sensor, the compressor discharge side refrigerant temperature must be less than 347°F (175°C).

Service Valve Location

Colt

The suction (low pressure) port is located on the compressor. The discharge (high pressure) port is located on the discharge line at the left front corner of the engine compartment.

Colt Vista

The suction (low pressure) port is located on the compressor. The discharge (high pressure) port is located on the discharge line near the compressor.

Conquest

Both service ports are located on the top of the compressor near the refrigerant line connections.

System Discharging

R-12 refrigerant is a chlorofluorocarbon which, when mishandled, can contribute to the depletion on the ozone layer in the upper atmosphere. Ozone filters out harmful radiation from the sun. In order to protect the ozone layer, an approved R-12 Recovery/Recycling machine that meets SAE standard J1991 should be employed when discharging the system. Follow the operating instructions provided with the approved equipment exactly to properly discharge the system.

System Evacuating

If the air conditioning system has been opened to the atmosphere, it should be air and moisture free before being recharged with refrigerant. Moisture and air mixed with refrigerant will raise the compressor head pressure, possibly damage the system's components and will reduce the performance of the system. Moisture will boil at normal room temperature when exposed to a vacuum. To evacuate the system, perform the following procedure:

1. Leak test the system and repair any leaks found.
2. Connect an approved charging station, Recovery/Recycling machine or manifold gauge set and vacuum pump to the discharge and suction ports. The red hose is normally connected to the discharge (high pressure) line and the blue hose is connected to the suction (low pressure) line.
3. Open the discharge and suction ports and start the vacuum pump. If the pump is not able to pull at least 26 in. Hg of vacuum, there is a leak that must be repaired before evacuation can occur.
4. Once the system has reached at least 26 in. Hg of vacuum, allow the system to evacuate for at least 10 minutes. The longer the system is evacuated, the more contaminants will be removed.
5. Close all valves and turn the pump off. If the system loses more than 2 in. Hg of vacuum after 15 minutes, there is a leak that should be repaired.

System Charging

1. Connect an approved charging station, Recovery/Recycling machine or manifold gauge set to the discharge and suction ports. The red hose is normally connected to the discharge (high pressure) line and the blue hose is connected to the suction (low pressure) line.
2. Follow the instructions provided with the equipment and charge the system with the specified amount of refrigerant.
3. Perform a leak test.

SYSTEM COMPONENTS

Radiator

REMOVAL AND INSTALLATION

1. Disconnect the negative battery cable.
2. Drain the cooling system. Remove necessary air intake ductwork.
3. Disconnect the overflow hose. If necessary, remove the overflow reservoir.
4. Disconnect the upper and lower radiator hoses.
5. Disconnect all electrical connectors to the electric cooling fan(s) and radiator sensors. Most of these connectors employ a waterproof connector. When disconnecting, make sure all parts of the connectors remain intact.
6. Remove the electric cooling fan(s).
7. Disconnect and plug the automatic transaxle or transmission cooler lines, if equipped.
8. Remove the upper radiator mounts and lift out the radiator assembly.

To install:

9. Carefully install the radiator, mounts and retaining bolts.
10. Connect the automatic transaxle or transmission cooler lines, if equipped.

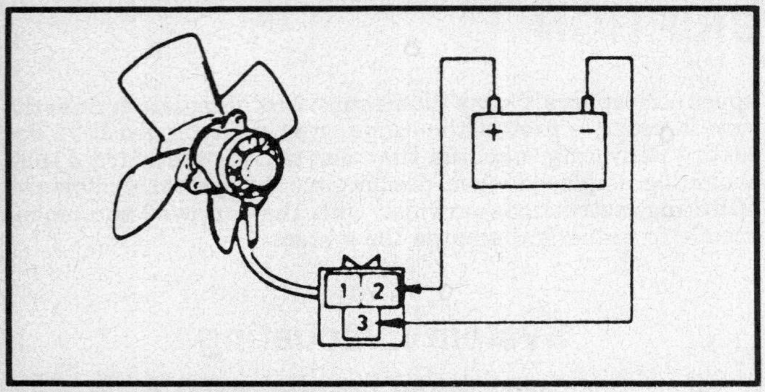
+
−
1
2
3

Radiator cooling fan check—Colt

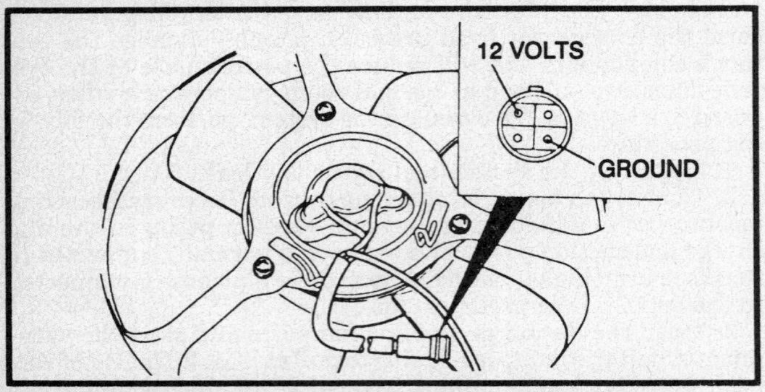
12 VOLTS
GROUND

Radiator and condenser cooling fans check—Conquest

11. Install the electric cooling fan(s).
12. Connect all previously disconnected connectors.
13. Install the radiator hoses.
14. Install the overflow reservoir and hose.
15. Install removed air intake ductwork.
16. Fill the radiator with coolant.
17. Connect the negative battery cable and check for leaks.

COOLING SYSTEM BLEEDING

All vehicles are equipped with a self-bleeding thermostat. Slowly fill the cooling system in the conventional manner; air will vent through the jiggle valve in the thermostat. Run the vehicle until the thermostat has opened and continue filling the radiator. Recheck the coolant level after the vehicle and cooled.

Electric Cooling Fan

TESTING

CAUTION

Make sure the key is in the OFF position when checking the electric cooling fan. If not, the fan could turn ON at any time, causing serious personal injury.

1. Disconnect the negative battery cable.
2. Disconnect the electrical plug from the fan motor harness.
3. Connect the appropriate terminals to the battery and make sure the fan runs smoothly, without abnormal noise or vibration.
4. Reconnect the negative battery cable.

REMOVAL AND INSTALLATION

Radiator Cooling Fan

1. Disconnect the negative battery cable.
2. Unplug the connector(s). Most of these connectors employ a waterproof connector. When disconnecting, make sure all parts of the connectors remain intact.
3. Remove the upper radiator hose if necessary.
4. Remove the mounting screws. The radiator and condenser cooling fans are separately removable.
5. Remove the fan assembly and disassemble as required.
6. The installation is the reverse of the removal procedure.
7. Check the coolant level and refill as required.
8. Connect the negative battery cable and check the fan for proper operation.

Condenser Cooling Fan

COLT

1. Disconnect the negative battery cable.
2. Unplug the connector(s). Most of these connectors employ a waterproof connector. When disconnecting, make sure all parts of the connectors remain intact.
3. Remove the upper radiator hose if necessary.
4. Remove the mounting screws. The radiator and condenser cooling fans are separately removable.
5. Remove the fan assembly and disassemble as required.
6. The installation is the reverse of the removal procedure.
7. Check the coolant level and refill as required.
8. Connect the negative battery cable and check the fan for proper operation.

COLT VISTA AND CONQUEST

The condenser fan is mounted between the condenser and grille, requiring grille and possibly bumper disassembly for removal. Remove the grille very carefully, since it is made of easily breakable plastic.

1. Disconnect the negative battery cable.
2. Remove the grille assembly. The grille is held in place with 1 or 2 screws and 5 or 6 clips that may require the use of a flat-tipped tool against the tab for release.
3. Unplug the connector. Most of these connectors employ a waterproof connector. When disconnecting, make sure all parts of the connectors remain intact.
4. Remove the mounting screws.
5. Remove the fan assembly through the grille opening.

To install:

6. Install the fan and secure with mounting screws.
7. Connect the connector. Connect the negative battery cable and check the fan for proper operation before assembling the remaining parts. Disconnect the negative battery cable before continuing.
8. Install the grille.
9. Connect the negative battery cable and recheck the system.

Condenser

REMOVAL AND INSTALLATION

Colt

1. Disconnect the negative battery cable.
2. Properly discharge the air conditioning system.
3. Remove the battery, battery tray and windshield washer reservoir.
4. Remove the upper radiator mounts to allow the radiator to be moved toward the engine. Remove the fans if they do not allow enough radiator movement.
5. Disconnect the refrigerant lines from the condenser. Cover the exposed ends of the lines to minimize contamination.
6. Remove the condenser mounting bolts.
7. Move the radiator toward the engine and lift the condenser from the vehicle. Inspect the lower rubber mounting insulators and replace, if necessary.

To install:

8. Lower the condenser into position and align the dowels with the lower mounting insulators. Install the bolts.
9. Replace the O-rings, lubricate and connect the refrigerant lines.
10. Install the radiator mounts and cooling fans.
11. Install remaining parts that were removed during the removal procedure.
12. Evacuate and recharge the air conditioning system. If the condenser was replaced, add 2 oz. of refrigerant oil during the recharge.
13. Connect the negative battery cable and check the entire climate control system for proper operation. Check the system for leaks.

Colt Vista and Conquest

1. Disconnect the negative battery cable.
2. Properly discharge the air conditioning system.
3. Remove the grille assembly. The grille is held in place with 1 or 2 screws and 5 or 6 clips that may require the use of a flat-tipped tool against the tab for release.
4. Unplug the fan connector. Most of these connectors employ a waterproof connector. When disconnecting, make sure all parts of the connectors remain intact.
5. Remove the mounting screws and remove the cooling fan assembly.
6. On Conquest, disconnect and plug the automatic transmission cooling lines and remove the transmission oil cooler, if equipped.
7. Disconnect the refrigerant lines from the condenser. Cover the exposed ends of the lines to minimize contamination.
8. Remove the condenser mounting bolts and remove the condenser.

To install:

9. Install the condenser and mounting bolts.
10. Replace the O-rings, lubricate and connect the refrigerant lines to the condenser.
11. Install automatic transmission oil cooling components, if removed.
12. Install the cooling fan and secure with mounting screws.
13. Connect the fan connector. Connect the negative battery cable and check the fan for proper operation before assembling the remaining parts. Disconnect the negative battery cable before continuing.
14. Install the grille.
15. Evacuate and recharge the air conditioning system. If the condenser was replaced, add 2 oz. of refrigerant oil during the recharge.
16. Connect the negative battery cable and check the entire climate control system for proper operation and leaks.

Compressor

REMOVAL AND INSTALLATION

Colt and Colt Vista

1. Disconnect the negative battery cable.
2. Properly discharge the air conditioning system.
3. Remove the distributor cap and wires so the compressor may be lifted from the engine compartment.
4. If equipped with 1.6L engine, remove the tensioner pulley assembly.
5. Remove the compressor drive belt. Disconnect the clutch coil connector.
6. Disconnect the refrigerant lines from the compressor and discard the O-rings. Cover the exposed ends of the lines to minimize contamination.
7. Remove the compressor mounting bolts and the compressor.

To install:

8. Install the compressor and torque the mounting bolts to 18 ft. lbs. (25 Nm). Connect the clutch coil connector.
9. Using new lubricated O-rings, connect the refrigerant lines to the compressor.
10. Install the belt and tensioner pulley, if removed. Adjust the belt to specifications.
11. Install the distributor cap and wires.
12. Evacuate and recharge the air conditioning system.
13. Connect the negative battery cable and check the entire climate control system for proper operation. Check the system for leaks.

Conquest

1. Disconnect the negative battery cable.
2. Properly discharge the air conditioning system.
3. Remove the ignition coil.
4. Loosen the tensioner adjustment bolt and remove the belt.
5. Disconnect the clutch coil connector.
6. Disconnect the refrigerant lines from the compressor. Cover the exposed ends of the lines to minimize contamination.
7. Remove the mounting bolts and remove the compressor from its mounting bracket.

To install:

8. Install the compressor to the bracket and install the mounting bolts.
9. Using new lubricated O-rings, connect the refrigerant lines.
10. Connect the clutch coil connector.
11. Install the belt and adjust to specification.
12. Install the ignition coil.
13. Evacuate and recharge the air conditioning system.
14. Connect the negative battery cable and check the entire climate control system for proper operation and leaks.

Receiver/Drier

REMOVAL AND INSTALLATION

Colt

1. Disconnect the negative battery cable.
2. Properly discharge the air conditioning system.
3. Disconnect the electrical connector from the switch on the receiver/drier, if equipped.
4. Disconnect the refrigerant lines from the receiver/drier assembly. Cover the exposed ends of the lines to minimize contamination.
5. Remove the mounting strap and the receiver/drier from its bracket. Remove the receiver/drier from the mounting strap.

To install:

6. Assemble the receiver/drier and mounting strap and install.
7. Using new lubricated O-rings. connect the refrigerant lines to the receiver/drier.
8. Connect the connector to the switch.
9. Evacuate and recharge the air conditioning system. Add 1 oz. of refrigerant oil during the recharge.
10. Connect the negative battery cable and check the entire climate control system for proper operation. Check the system for leaks.

Colt Vista and Conquest

1. Disconnect the negative battery cable.
2. Properly discharge the air conditioning system.
3. Remove the grille assembly.
4. Disconnect the refrigerant lines from the receiver/drier assembly. Cover the exposed ends of the lines to minimize contamination.

5. Remove the mounting strap and the receiver/drier from its bracket. Remove the receiver/drier from the mounting strap.

To install:

6. Assemble the receiver/drier and mounting strap and install.
7. Using new lubricated O-rings. connect the refrigerant lines to the receiver/drier.
8. Install the grille.
9. Evacuate and recharge the air conditioning system. Add 1 oz. of refrigerant oil during the recharge.
10. Connect the negative battery cable and check the entire climate control system for proper operation. Check the system for leaks.

Expansion Valve

REMOVAL AND INSTALLATION

1. Disconnect the negative battery cable.
2. Properly discharge the air conditioning system.
3. Remove the evaporator housing and separate the upper and lower cases.
4. Remove the expansion valve from the evaporator lines.
5. The installation is the reverse of the removal installation. Use new lubricated O-rings when assembling.
6. Evacuate and recharge the air conditioning system.
7. Connect the negative battery cable and check the entire climate control system for proper operation. Check the system for leaks.

Blower Motor

REMOVAL AND INSTALLATION

Colt

1. Disconnect the negative battery cable.
2. Remove the glove box assembly and pry off the speaker cover to the lower right of the glove box.
3. Remove the passenger side lower cowl side trim kick panel.
4. Remove the passenger side knee protector, which is the panel surrounding the glove box opening.
5. Remove the glove frame along the top of glove box opening.
6. Remove the lap heater duct. This is a small piece on vehicles without a rear heater and much larger on vehicles with a rear heater.
7. Disconnect the electrical connector from the blower motor.
8. Remove the cooling tube from the blower assembly.
9. Remove the MPI computer from the lower side of the cowl.
10. Remove the blower motor assembly and disassemble on a workbench.

To install:

11. Assemble the motor and fan. Install the blower motor assembly and connect the wiring and cooling tube.
12. Install the MPI computer.
13. Install the lap heater duct.
14. Install the glove box frame, interior trim pieces and glove box assembly.
15. Connect the negative battery cable and check the entire climate control system for proper operation.

Colt Vista and Conquest

1. Disconnect the negative battery cable.
2. Remove the instrument panel under cover and glove box assembly(s).
3. Disconnect the resistor and blower motor wire connectors, if necessary.
4. Remove the motor cooling tube. On Colt Vista, remove the absorber bracket.
5. Remove the attaching screws and remove the blower assembly from the blower case and disassemble.

To install:

6. Position the blower motor onto the blower case and install the attaching screws.
7. Install the absorber bracket, if removed. Install the cooling tube.
8. Connect the resistor and blower motor wire connector.
9. Install the glove box(s) and instrument panel under cover.
10. Connect the negative battery cable and check the blower for proper operation.

Blower Motor Resistor or Power Transistor

REMOVAL AND INSTALLATION

1. Disconnect the negative battery cable.
2. Remove the glove box assembly. The resistor or power transistor is accessible through the glove box opening and is mounted to the blower or evaporator case.
3. Disconnect the wire harness from the resistor.
4. Remove the mounting screws and remove the resistor.
5. The installation is the reverse of the removal procedure. Make sure the seal is intact when installing.
6. Connect the negative battery cable and check the entire climate control system for proper operation.

Heater Core

REMOVAL AND INSTALLATION

Colt

1. Disconnect the negative battery cable.
2. Drain the cooling system and disconnect the heater hoses.
3. Remove the front seats by removing the covers over the anchor bolts, the underseat tray, the seat belt guide ring, the seat mounting nuts and bolts and disconnect the seat belt switch wiring harness from under the seat. Then lift out the seats.
4. Remove the floor console by first taking out the coin holder and the console box tray. Remove the remote control mirror switch or cover. All of these items require only a plastic trim tool to carefully pry them out.
5. Remove the rear half of the console.
6. Remove the shift lever knob on manual transmission vehicles.
7. Remove the front console box assembly.
8. A number of the instrument panel pieces may be retained by pin type fasteners. They may be removed using the following procedure:
    a. This type of clip is removed by pressing down on the center pin with a suitable blunt pointed tool. Press down a little more than $\frac{1}{16}$ in. (2mm); this releases the clip. Pull the clip outward to remove it.
    b. Do not push the pin inward more than necessary because it may damage the grommet or the pin may fall in if pushed in too far. Once the clips are removed, use a plastic trim stick to pry the piece loose.
9. Remove both lower cowl trim panels (kick panels).
10. Remove the ashtray.
11. Remove the center panel around the radio.
12. Remove the sunglass pocket at the upper left side of panel and the side panel into which it mounts.
13. Remove the driver's side knee protector and the hood release handle.
14. Remove the steering column top and bottom covers.
15. Remove the radio.
16. Remove the glove box striker and box assembly.

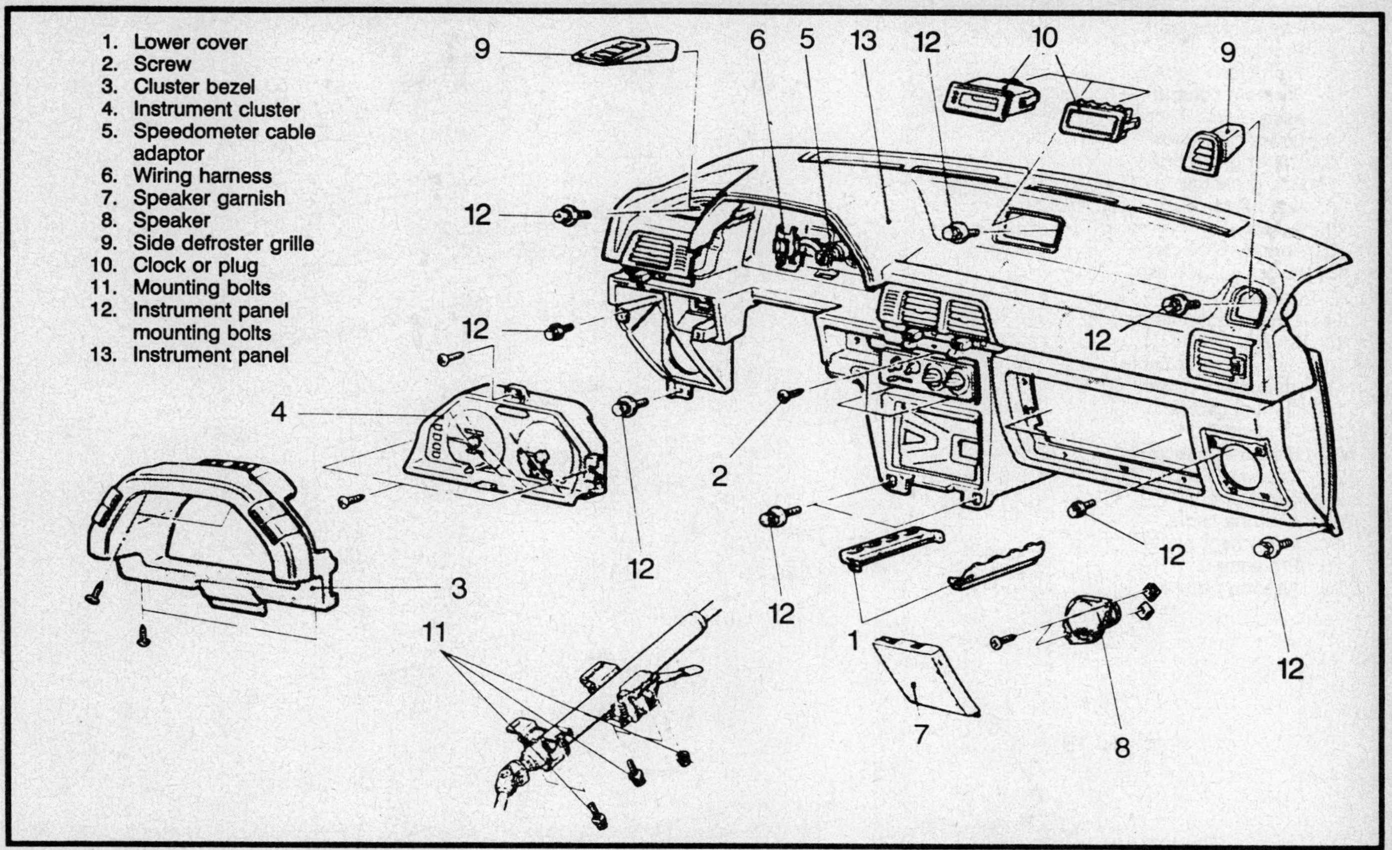
1. Lower cover
2. Screw
3. Cluster bezel
4. Instrument cluster
5. Speedometer cable adaptor
6. Wiring harness
7. Speaker garnish
8. Speaker
9. Side defroster grille
10. Clock or plug
11. Mounting bolts
12. Instrument panel mounting bolts
13. Instrument panel

Instrument panel and related components – Colt

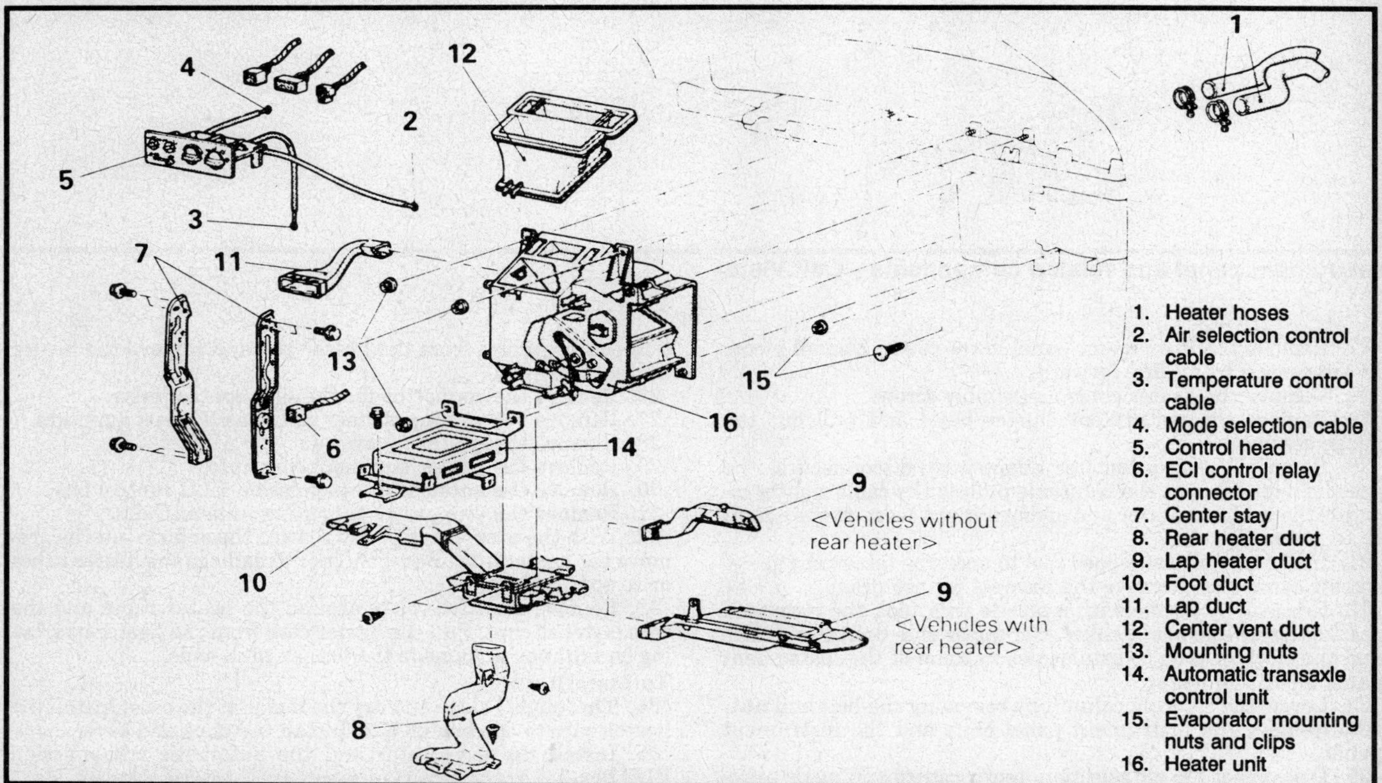
<Vehicles without rear heater>
<Vehicles with rear heater>
1. Heater hoses
2. Air selection control cable
3. Temperature control cable
4. Mode selection cable
5. Control head
6. ECI control relay connector
7. Center stay
8. Rear heater duct
9. Lap heater duct
10. Foot duct
11. Lap duct
12. Center vent duct
13. Mounting nuts
14. Automatic transaxle control unit
15. Evaporator mounting nuts and clips
16. Heater unit

Heater case and related components – Colt

1. Protector cover
2. Protector
3. Protector
4. Steering column assembly
5. Lower glove box
6. Upper glove box
7. Box protector
8. Lap heater duct
9. Ashtray
10. Ashtray protector
13. Hood lock release handle
14. Cluster hood cover
15. Cluster hood
16. Speedometer cable
17. Instrument cluster
18. Control cables
19. Air duct
20. Blower connector
21. Trim panel
22. Trim panel
23. Antenna cable
24. Instrument panel
25. Protector
26. Absorber bracket

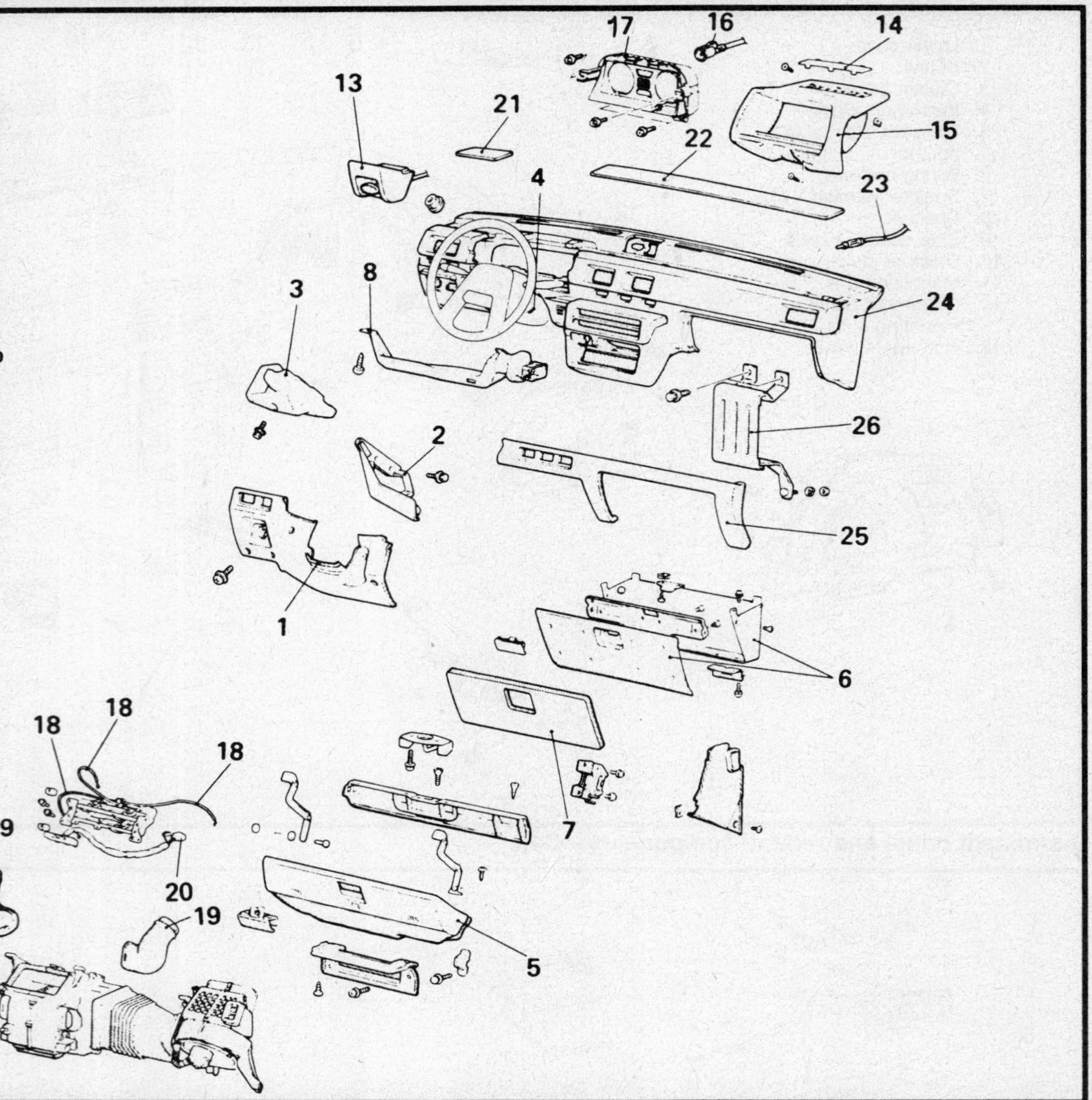
17
16
14
13
21
22
15
4
23
3
8
24
26
2
25
1
6
18
18
18
19
7
20
19
5

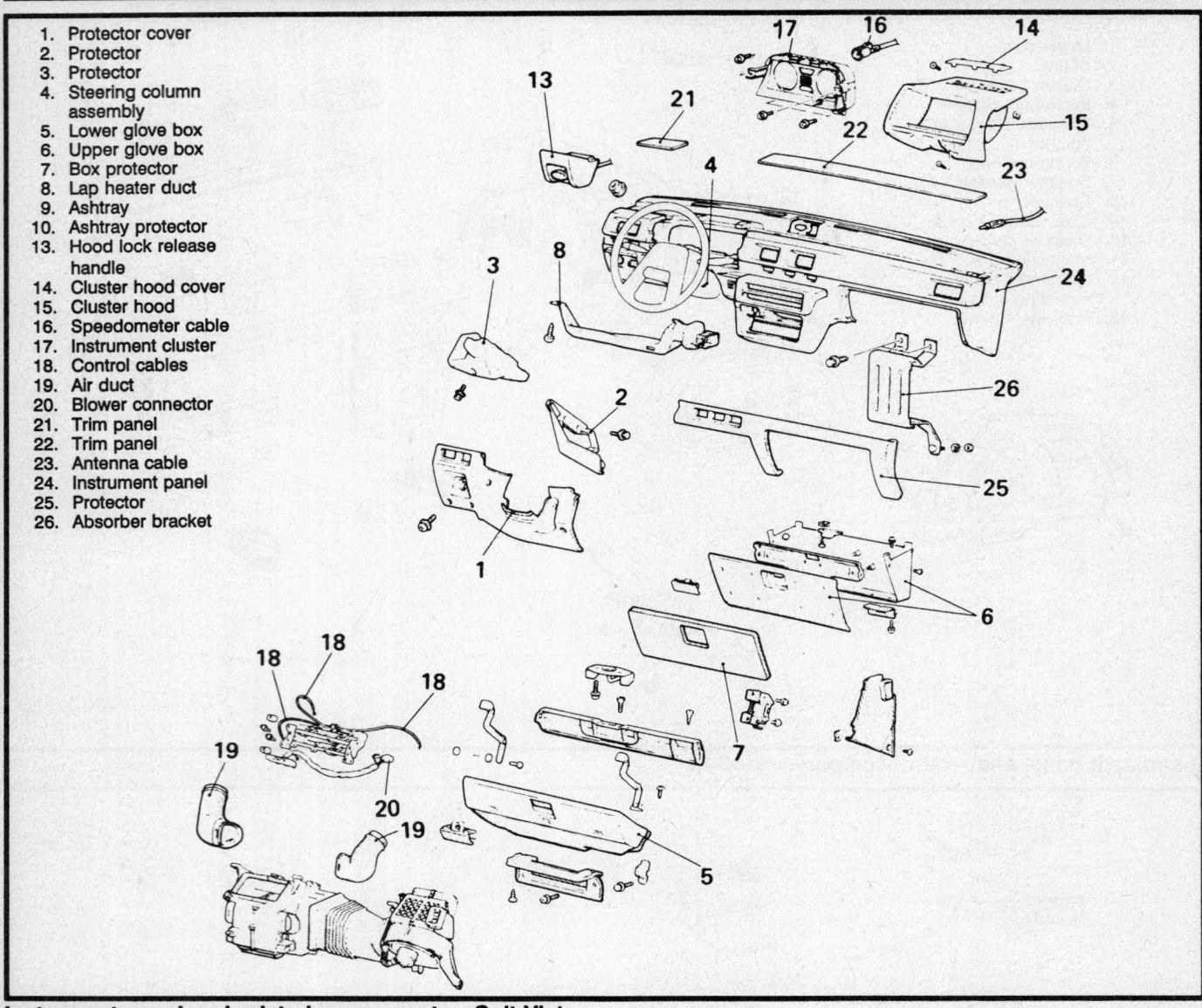

Instrument panel and related components—Colt Vista

17. Remove the instrument panel lower cover, 2 small pieces in the center, by pulling forward.
18. Remove the heater control assembly screw.
19. Remove the instrument cluster bezel and pull out the gauge assembly.
20. Remove the speedometer adapter by disconnecting the speedometer cable at the transaxle pulling the cable sightly towards the vehicle interior and giving a slight twist on the adapter to release it.
21. Insert a small flat-tipped tool to open the tab on the gauge cluster connector. Remove the harness connectors.
22. Remove, by prying with a plastic trim tool, the right side speaker cover and the speaker, the upper side defroster grilles and the clock or plug to gain access to some of the instrument panel mounting bolts.
23. Lower the steering column by removing the bolt and nut.
24. Remove the instrument panel bolts and the instrument panel.
25. Disconnect the air selection, temperature and mode selection control cables from the heater box and remove the heater control assembly.
26. Remove the connector for the ECI control relay.
27. Remove both stamped steel instrument panel supports.
28. Remove the heater ductwork.
29. Remove the heater box mounting nuts.
30. Remove the automatic transmission ELC control box.
31. Remove the evaporator mounting nuts and clips.
32. With the evaporator pulled toward the vehicle interior, remove the heater unit. Be careful not to damage the heater tubes or to spill coolant.
33. Remove the cover plate around the heater tubes and the core fastener clips. Pull the heater core from the heater box, being careful not to damage the fins or tank ends.

To install:

34. Thoroughly clean and dry the inside of the case. Install the heater core to the heater box. Install the clips and cover.
35. Install the evaporator and the automatic transmission ELC box.

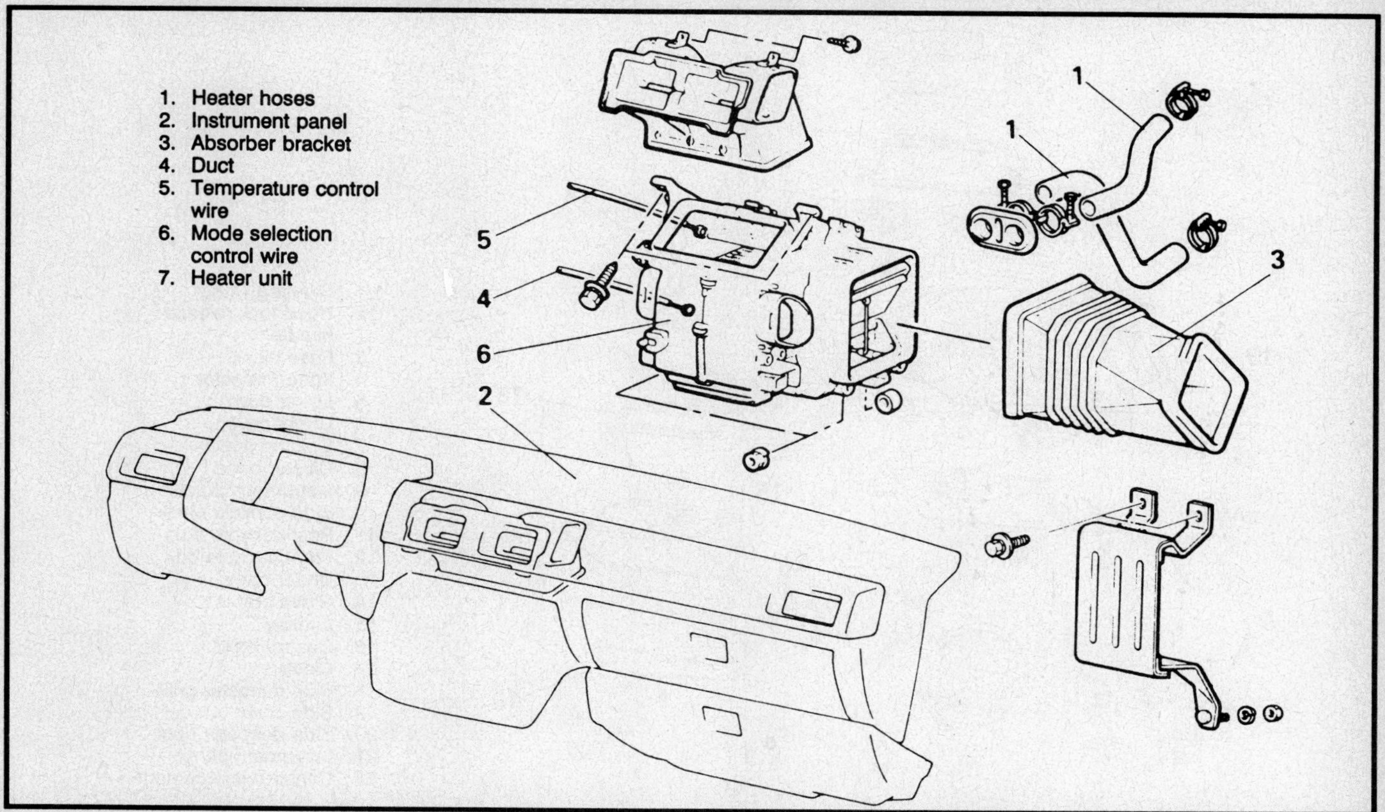
1. Heater hoses
2. Instrument panel
3. Absorber bracket
4. Duct
5. Temperature control wire
6. Mode selection control wire
7. Heater unit
1
1
2
3
4
5
6

Heater case and related components—Colt Vista

36. Install the heater box and connect the duct work.
37. Connect all wires and control cables.
38. Install the instrument panel assembly and the console by reversing their removal procedures.
39. Install the seats.
40. Refill the cooling system.
41. Evacuate and recharge the air conditioning system. Add 2 oz. of refrigerant oil during the recharge if the evaporator was replaced.
42. Connect the negative battery cable and check the entire climate control systm for proper operation. Check the system for leaks.

Colt Vista

1. Disconnect the negative battery cable.
2. Drain the coolant and disconnect the heater hoses from the core tubes.
3. Remove the steering column under coevers. Remove the steering column. This can be accomplished by removeing the pinch bolt at the U-joint below the instrument, disconnecting all connectors and pulling the column from the U-joint yoke.
4. Remove the entire glove box assemblies.
5. Remove the lap heater duct.
6. Remove the ashtray.
7. Remove the hood lock release cable from the instrument panel.
8. Remove the instrument cluster hood cover and hood. Pull the cluster out, disconnect the speedometer cable and remove the cluster.
9. Disconnect the control cables from the heater unit.
10. Remove the upper air ducts.
11. Disconnect the blower motor harness.
12. Remove the trim panels along the top of the instrument panel.
13. Disconnect the antenna feeder wire.
14. Remove the instrument panel retaining hardware and remove the assembly.
15. Remove the instrument panel absorber bracket, if equipped.
16. Remove the duct to the right of the heater unit.
17. Remove the mounting nuts and remove the heater unit from the vehicle.
18. To disassemble the heater unit, remove the water valve link, hose clamps and hoses. Remove the retaining screw and remove the heater core from the case.

To install:

19. Thoroughly clean and dry the inside of the case. Install the heater core to the case and assemble the unit.
20. Install the heater case to the vehicle and install the retaining nuts.
21. Install the duct on the right side of the unit.
22. Install the instrument panel absorber bracket, if equipped.
23. Install the instrument panel by reversing its removal procedure.
24. Install the hood lock release cable to the instrument panel.
25. Install the ashtray.
26. Install the lap heater duct.
27. Install the glove boxes.
28. Install the steering column and under covers.
29. Connect the heater hoses to the heater core tubes.
30. Fill the cooling system.
31. Connect the negative battery cable and check the entire climate control system for proper operation and leaks.

Conquest

1. With the engine cold, set the temperature control lever to the extreme right. If equipped with an automatic climate control system, start the engine and use the temperature change

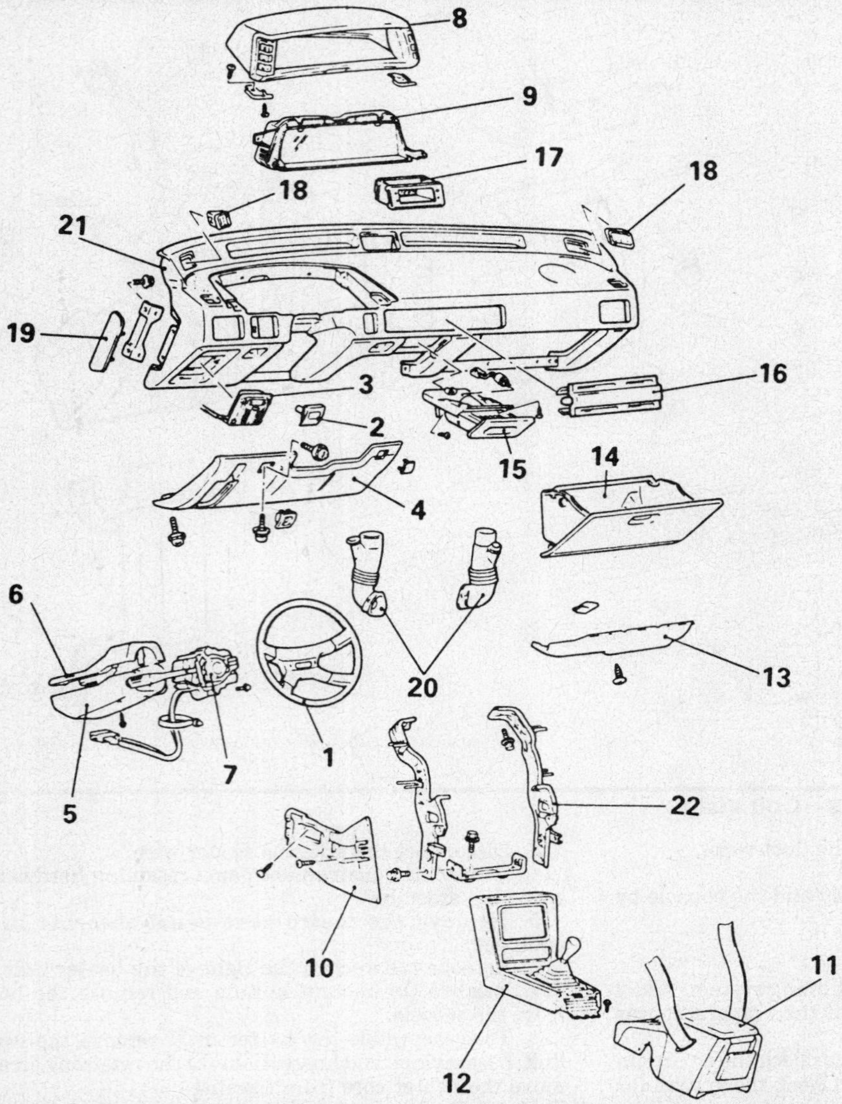

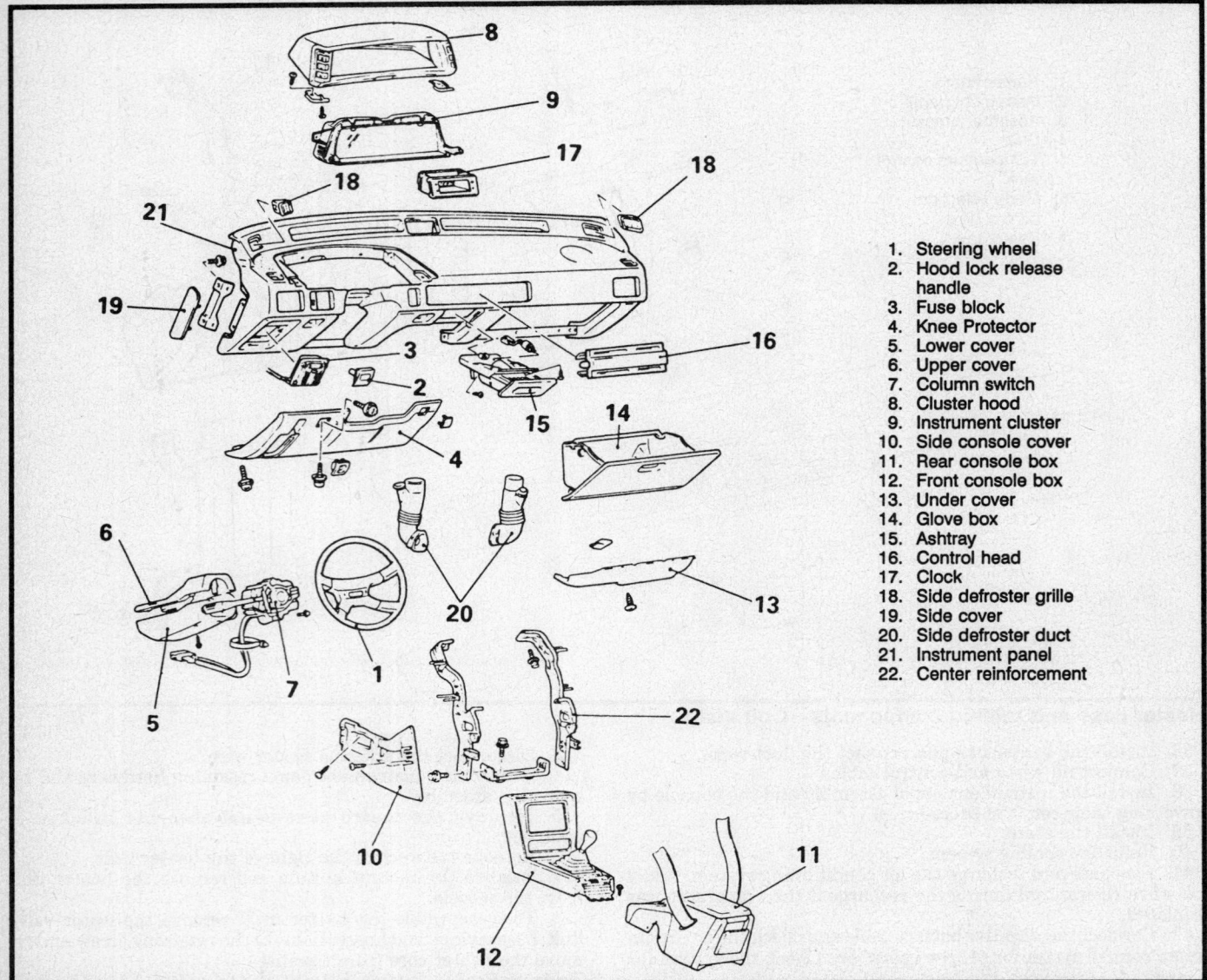

1. Steering wheel
2. Hood lock release handle
3. Fuse block
4. Knee Protector
5. Lower cover
6. Upper cover
7. Column switch
8. Cluster hood
9. Instrument cluster
10. Side console cover
11. Rear console box
12. Front console box
13. Under cover
14. Glove box
15. Ashtray
16. Control head
17. Clock
18. Side defroster grille
19. Side cover
20. Side defroster duct
21. Instrument panel
22. Center reinforcement

Instrument panel and related components – Conquest

switch to select the hottest temperature, then turn the engine **OFF**.

2. Disconnect the negative battery cable. Drain the engine coolant.
3. Disconnect the coolant hoses running to the heater pipes at the firewall.
4. Remove the floor console.
5. Remove the steering wheel.
6. Remove the screws holding the hood release handle to the instrument panel.
7. Unbolt the fuse box from the instrument panel.
8. Remove the knee protector on the left side. Some of the bolts are hidden behind covers.
9. Remove the screws from the bottom of the steering column cover. Remove both halves of the cover.
10. Remove the attaching screws for the combination switch on the steering column.
11. Disconnect the wiring harnesses and remove the switch.
12. Remove the instrument hood screws. Pull both edges of the bottom of the hood forward; hold it in this position and lift up and out.
13. Disconnect the harness connectors on both sides of the instrument hood.
14. Remove the screws on the bottom and the nuts on the top of the instrument cluster. Pull the bottom edge up and forward to remove. Disconnect the wiring and cables as it comes free.
15. Remove the console side cover mounting screws. Remove the cover downward while pushing slightly forward.
16. Remove the front and rear consoles.
17. Remove the passenger side under cover.
18. Remove the glove box and ashtray.
19. Carefully remove the heater control bezel.
20. Remove the clock. It may be removed with a gentle prying motion. Disconnect the harness when it is free.
21. Remove the grilles for the side defrosters by inserting a flat tool from the window side and prying forward and upward.
22. Use a non-marring tool to pry the side covers off the instrument panel.

23. Remove each mounting screw and bolt holding the instrument panel in place. As it comes loose, allow it to move into the interior. Disconnect the remaining wire harnesses.
24. The instrument panel may now be removed from the vehicle. Several components may still be attached.
25. Remove the center ventilator duct and lap heater duct.
26. Remove the 2 center reinforcement bars.
27. Remove the retaining nuts and bolts and remove the heater unit from the vehicle.
28. If equipped with automatic climate control, the servo motor should be removed before working with the case. With the heater unit removed, use a small pry bar to carefully disconnect the servo motor rod from the air blend damper.
29. Remove the screws holding the servo motor to the heater unit.
30. Carefully unlock the water valve lever clip and disconnect the link between the blend air damper and the water valve lever.
31. Remove the outer clamp from the 2 water tubes.
32. Loosen the clamps on the short joint hoses and disconnect the hoses. Remove the retaining screws holding the water valve in place and remove the water valve.
33. The heater core is held in place by a clip and retaining screw. Once removed, the core should come free of the housing. If the core is blocked by the blend air damper lever, remove the lever. Do not attempt to force the core past the lever.

To install:

34. Thoroughly clean and dry the inside of the case. Reassemble the heater unit, and secure the core with the retaining screw and clip. The valve and connecting hoses must be properly secured with new clamps.
35. Push the water valve lever all the way inward so the water valve is at the closed position. Move the blend damper lever counterclockwise so the blend air damper is fully closed.
36. Install the connecting link and secure the water valve lever clip.
37. Install the servo motor and connect the motor rod to the blend air damper.
38. Install the completely assembled heater unit into the vehicle. Tighten the retaining nuts and bolts evenly.
39. Reinstall the 2 center support brackets.
40. Install the lap heater duct and the center ventilation duct.
41. Make certain the reinforcement brackets are in place. Install the instrument panel assembly. The upper part of the heater unit has 2 guide bolts to which the instrument panel attaches. Reverse the removal procedure to complete the instrument panel installation.
42. Install the upper and lower steering column covers.
43. Install the fuse block to the instrument panel. Route the wire harnesses are properly.
44. Install the knee protector on the left side.
45. Attach the hood release handle to the instrument panel.
46. Install the steering wheel.
47. Reinstall the center console.
48. Connect the heater hoses to the heater pipes at the firewall.
49. Refill the cooling system.
50. Connect the negative battery cable and check the entire climate control system for proper operation and leaks.

Evaporator

REMOVAL AND INSTALLATION

Colt and Colt Vista

1. Disconnect the negative battery cable.
2. Properly discharge the air conditioning system.
3. Disconnect the refrigerant lines from the evaporator. Cover the exposed ends of the lines to minimize contamination.
4. Remove the condensation drain hose.
5. Remove the glove box assembly and lap heater duct work.
6. Remove the cowl side trim and speaker cover.
7. Remove the glove box bezel and frame.
8. Disconnect the electrical connector at the top of the evaporator housing.
9. Remove the mounting bolts and nuts and the housing.
10. Disassemble the housing and remove the expansion valve and evaporator.

To install:

11. Thoroughly clean and dry the inside of the case. Assemble the housing, evaporator and expansion valve, making sure the gaskets are in good condition.
12. Install the housing to the vehicle and connect the connector.
13. Install the glove box frame and bezel.
14. Install the speaker cover and side cowl trim.
15. Install the lap heater ductwork and glove box assembly.
16. Install the condensation drain hose.
17. Using new lubricated O-rings, connect the refrigerant lines to the evaporator.
18. Evacuate and recharge the air conditioning system. If the evaporator was replaced, add 2 oz. of refrigerant oil during the recharge.
19. Connect the negative battery cable and check the entire climate control system for proper operation. Check the system for leaks.

Conquest

1. Disconnect the negative battery cable.
2. Safely discharge the air conditioning system.
3. Disconnect the refrigerant lines. Cover the exposed ends of the lines to minimize contamination.
4. Remove the small nut from the firewall side.
5. Remove the grommet.
6. Remove the glove box.
7. Remove the under cover below the glove box.
8. Remove the lap heater duct and the side console duct.
9. Remove the lower frame of the glove box.
10. Remove the defroster duct.
11. Remove the duct joints between the evaporator and the adjoining components.
12. Disconnect the condensate drain hose.
13. Disconnect the electrical connectors and disconnect the vacuum hose.
14. Remove the retaining bolts and remove the evaporator case. Disassemble the housing and remove the expansion valve and evaporator.

To install:

15. Thoroughly clean and dry the inside of the case. Assemble the housing, evaporator and expansion valve, making sure the gaskets are in good condition. Install to the vehicle and install the retaining bolts.
16. Connect the electrical wiring and the vacuum hose.
17. Install the condensation drain hose.
18. Install the defroster duct and the joint ducts.
19. Install the lower glove box frame.
20. Replace the side console duct and the lap heater duct.
21. Install the under cover and the glove box.
22. Install the grommet and the vacuum hose at the firewall.
23. Install the nut.
24. Using new lubricated O-rings, connect the refrigerant lines to the evaporator.
25. Evacuate and recharge the air conditioning system. If the evaporator was replaced, add 2 oz. of refrigerant oil during the recharge.
26. Connect the negative battery cable and check the entire climate control system for proper operation and leaks.

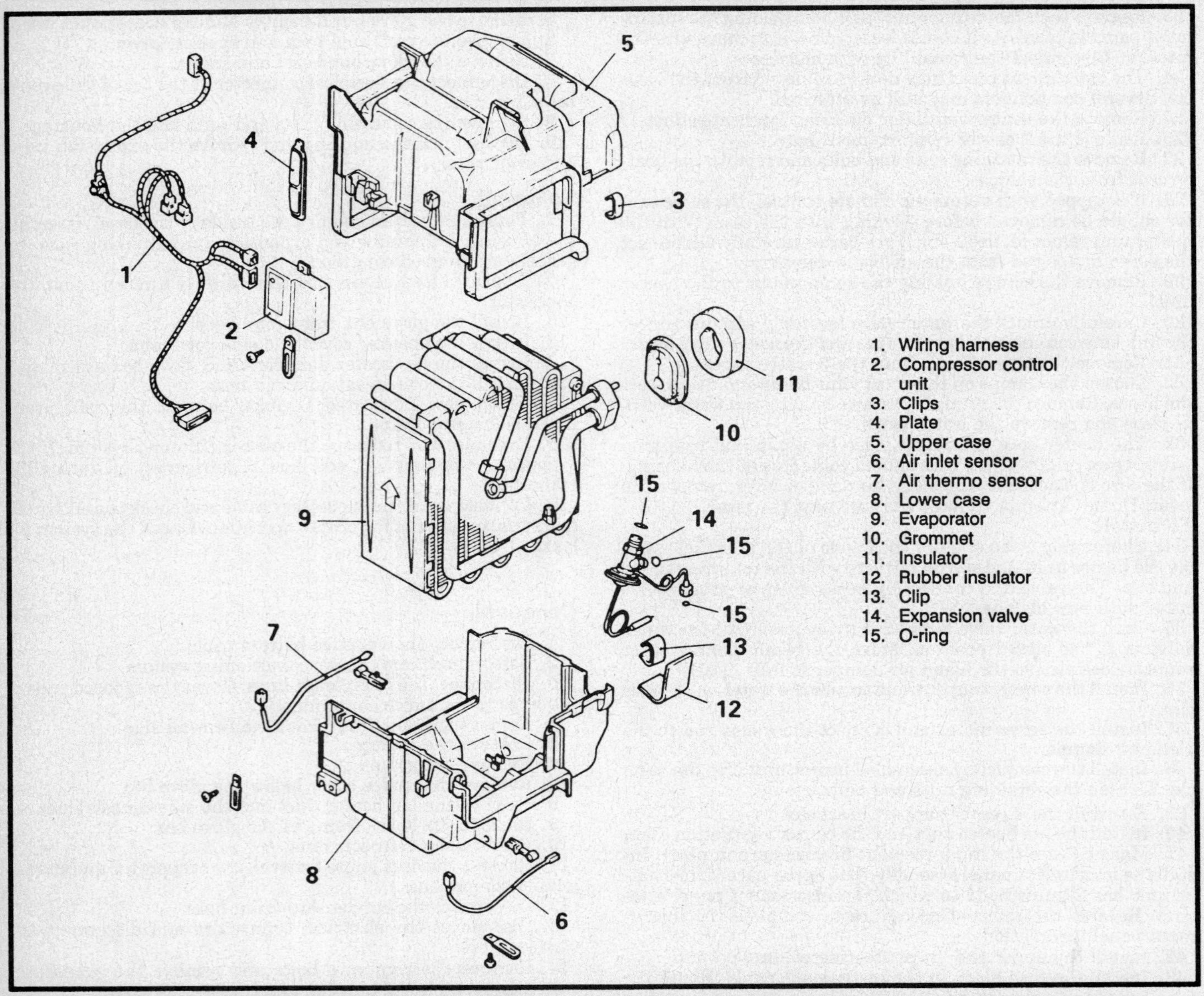
1
2
3
4
5
6
7
8
9
10
11
12
13
14
15
15
15
1. Wiring harness
2. Compressor control unit
3. Clips
4. Plate
5. Upper case
6. Air inlet sensor
7. Air thermo sensor
8. Lower case
9. Evaporator
10. Grommet
11. Insulator
12. Rubber insulator
13. Clip
14. Expansion valve
15. O-ring

Representative evaporator, expansion valve, case and related components. Assemblies may vary between vehicles

Refrigerant Lines

REMOVAL AND INSTALLATION

1. Disconnect the negative battery cable.
2. Properly discharge the air conditioning system.
3. Remove the nuts or bolts that attach the refrigerant lines sealing plates to the adjoining components. If the line is not equipped with a sealing plate, separate the flare connection. Always use a backup wrench when separating flare connections.
4. Remove the line and discard the O-rings.

To install:

5. Coat the new O-rings refrigerant oil and install. Connect the refrigerant lines to the adjoining components and tighten the nuts, bolts or flare connections.
6. Evacuate and recharge the air conditioning system.
7. Connect the negative battery cable and check the entire climate control system for proper operation. Check the system for leaks.

Manual Control Head

REMOVAL AND INSTALLATION

Colt

1. Disconnect the negative battery cable.
2. Remove the glove box and ashtray assembly.
3. Remove the heater control/radio bezel.
4. Remove the radio assembly.
5. Disconnect the air, temperature and mode selection control cables from the heater housing.
6. Remove the 3 control head mounting screws.
7. Separate the control head from the left side first, then press out the lower and upper mounting brackets from behind the instrument panel.
8. Pull the control head out and disconnect the 3 connectors. Remove the control head assembly.

To install:

9. Feed the control cable through the instrument panel, connect the connectors, install the control head assembly and secure with the screws.
10. Install the radio and bezel.
11. Move the mode selection lever to the **PANEL** position. Move the mode selection damper lever fully forward and connect the cable to the lever. Install the clip.
12. Move the temperature control lever to its coolest position. Move the blend air damper lever fully downward and connect the cable to the lever. Install the clip.
13. Move the air selection control lever to the **RECIRC** position. Move the air selection damper fully inward and connect the cable to the lever. Install the clip.
14. Connect the negative battery cable and check the entire climate control system for proper operation.
15. If everything is satisfactory, install the ashtray and glove box.

Colt Vista

1. Disconnect the negative battery cable.
2. Remove the lever knobs and remove the control head bezel.
3. Remove the glove box and the defroster duct.
4. Disconnect the control cables from the heater housing.
5. Remove the control head mounting screws and pull the unit out of the instrument panel. Disconnect the electrical connectors and remove the control head.
6. The installation is the reverse of the removal procedure.
7. Connect the negative battery cable and check the entire climate control system for proper operation and leaks.

Conquest

1. Disconnect the negative battery cable.
2. Remove the floor console.
3. Remove the steering wheel.
4. Remove the screws holding the hood release handle to the instrument panel.
5. Unbolt the fuse box from the instrument panel.
6. Remove the knee protector on the left side. Some of the bolts are hidden behind covers.
7. Remove the screws from the bottom of the steering column cover. Remove both halves of the cover.
8. Remove the attaching screws for the combination switch on the steering column.
9. Disconnect the wiring harnesses and remove the switch.
10. Remove the instrument hood screws. Pull both edges of the bottom of the hood forward; hold it in this position and lift up and out.
11. Disconnect the harness connectors on both sides of the instrument hood.
12. Remove the screws on the bottom and the nuts on the top of the instrument cluster. Pull the bottom edge up and forward to remove. Disconnect the wiring and cables as it comes free.
13. Remove the console side cover mounting screws. Remove the cover downward while pushing slightly forward.
14. Remove the front and rear consoles.
15. Remove the passenger side under cover.
16. Remove the glove box and ashtray.
17. Carefully remove the heater control knobs and bezel.
18. Remove the clock. It may be removed with a gentle prying motion. Disconnect the harness when it is free.
19. Remove the grilles for the side defrosters by inserting a flat tool from the window side and prying forward and upward.
20. Use a non-marring tool to pry the side covers off the instrument panel.
21. Remove each mounting screw and bolt holding the instrument panel in place. As it comes loose, allow it to move into the interior. Disconnect the remaining wire harnesses.
22. The instrument panel may now be removed from the vehicle. Several components may still be attached.
23. Disconnect the 3 control cables from the heater and blower cases.
24. Take careful note of the routing of the control cables. Remove the mounting screws and remove the control head from the instrument panel.

To install:

25. Feed the control cables through the instrument panel and route them in exactly the same position as before removal. Install the control head.
26. Install the instrument panel assembly. The upper part of the heater unit has 2 guide bolts to which the instrument panel attaches. Reverse the removal procedure to complete the instrument panel installation.
27. Install the upper and lower steering column covers.
28. Install the fuse block to the instrument panel. Route the wire harnesses are properly.
29. Install the knee protector on the left side.
30. Attach the hood release handle to the instrument panel.
31. Install the steering wheel.
32. Reinstall the center console.
33. Connect the negative battery cable and check the entire climate control system for proper operation.

Manual Control Cables

ADJUSTMENT

Alle control cables are self-adjusting. If any cable is not functioning properly, try to move the affected lever to either extreme position, observe what may be binding and reposition the connecting link if possible. Also, check for proper routing and lubricate all moving parts. These cables cannot be disassembled. Replace if faulty.

Electronic Control Head

REMOVAL AND INSTALLATION

Conquest

1. Disconnect the negative battery cable.
2. Remove the glove box.
3. Remove the control panel bezel if necessary.
4. Remove the mounting screws and pull the unit out of the instrument panel.
5. Disconnect all harnesses and remove the control head from the vehicle.
6. The installation is the reverse of the removal procedure.
7. Connect the negative battery cable and check the entire climate control system for proper operation.

SENSORS AND SWITCHES

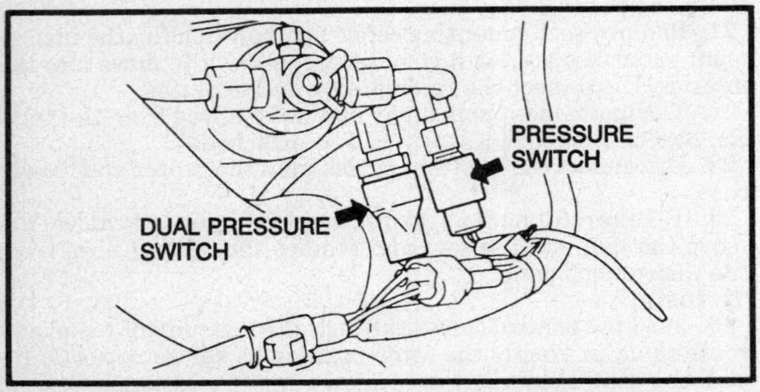
PRESSURE SWITCH
DUAL PRESSURE SWITCH

Air conditioning pressure switches – Conquest

Dual Pressure Switch

OPERATION

Colt and Conquest use a dual pressure switch, which is a combination of a low pressure cut off switch and high pressure cut off switch. These functions will stop operation of the compressor in the event of either high of low refrigerant charge, preventing damage to the system. The switch is located on the receiver drier on Colt and near the sight glass on the refrigerant line on Conquest.

The dual pressure switch is designed to cut off voltage to the compressor coil when the pressure either drops below 30 psi or rises above 384 psi.

TESTING

1. Check for continuity through the switch. Under all normal conditions, the switch should be continuous.
2. If the switch is open, check for insufficient refrigerant charge or excessive pressures.
3. If neither of the above conditions exist and the switch is open, replace the switch.

REMOVAL AND INSTALLATION

1. Disconnect the negative battery cable.
2. Properly discharge the air conditioning system.
3. Remove the switch from the refrigerant line or receiver/drier.
4. The installation is the reverse of the removal installation.
5. Evacuate and recharge the air conditioning system.
6. Connect the negative battery cable and check the entire climate control system for proper operation. Check the system for leaks.

Low Pressure Cut Off Switch

OPERATION

On Colt Vista, the low pressure cut off switch monitors the refrigerant gas pressure on the suction side of the system. The switch is connected in series with the compressor and will turn off voltage to the compressor clutch coil when the monitored pressure drops to levels that could damage the compressor. The switch is located on the receiver/drier and is a sealed unit that must be replaced if faulty.

TESTING

1. Start the engine and allow to idle. Turn the air conditioner **ON**.
2. Disconnect the switch connector and use a jumper wire to jump between terminals inside the connector boot.
3. If the compressor clutch does not engage, inspect the system for an open circuit.
4. If the clutch engages, connect an air conditioning manifold gauge to the system.
5. Read the low pressure gauge. The low pressure cut off switch should complete the circuit at pressures of at least 30 psi. Check the system for leaks if the pressures are too low.
6. If the pressures are nominal and the system works when the terminals are jumped, the cut off switch is faulty and should be replaced.

REMOVAL AND INSTALLATION

1. Disconnect the negative battery cable.
2. Properly discharge the air conditioning system.
3. Unplug the boot connector from the switch.
4. Using an oil pressure sending unit socket, remove the switch from the receiver/drier.

To install:

5. Seal the threads of the new switch with teflon tape.
6. Install the switch to the receiver/drier and connect the boot connector.
7. Evacuate and recharge the system. Check for leaks.
8. Check the switch for proper operation.

High Pressure Cut Off Switch

OPERATION

On Colt Vista, the high pressure cut off switch is located on the liquid line near the receiver/drier. The function of the switch is to disengage the compressor clutch by monitoring the discharge pressure when levels reach dangerously high levels, usually due to condenser restrictions. This switch is connected in series with the compressor clutch and is located on the liquid line near the reciever/drier.

TESTING

1. Start the engine and allow to idle. Turn the air conditioner **ON**.
2. Connect an air conditioning manifold gauge to the system. The system should operate at high gauge pressure below 300 psi.
3. Without allowing the engine to overheat, block the flow of air to the condenser with a cover. When the high pressure reaches the specified pressure, the clutch should disengage.
4. Remove the cover. When the gauge reading falls below about 230 psi, the clutch should cycle back on.
5. If faulty, replace the switch.

REMOVAL AND INSTALLATION

1. Disconnect the negative battery cable.
2. Properly discharge the air conditioning system.
3. Unplug the boot connector from the switch.
4. Remove the switch from the liquid line.

To install:

5. Seal the threads of the new switch with teflon tape.

6. Install the switch to the line and connect the boot connector.
7. Evacuate and recharge the system. Check for leaks.
8. Check the switch for proper operation.

Pressure Switch

OPERATION

The pressure switch, used on Colt with 1.6L engine and Conquest, is used to control the 2-speed condenser cooling fan. The switch is normally located on the high pressure line near the left front of the engine compartment.

TESTING

1. Install a manifold gauge set to the air conditioning system.
2. Check the continuity of the switch at different pressures. The switch should be open a pressures below 213 psi and closed at 256 psi or higher.
3. For the purpose of testing, the pressures can be lowered by using an auxiliary fan to cool the condenser and raised by placing a cover over the condenser to prevent air flow.
4. If faulty, replace the switch if faulty.

REMOVAL AND INSTALLATION

1. Disconnect the negative battery cable.
2. Properly discharge the air conditioning system.
3. Remove the switch from the refrigerant line.
4. The installation is the reverse of the removal procedure.
5. Evacuate and recharge the air conditioning system.
6. Connect the negative battery cable and check the entire climate control system for proper operation. Check the system for leaks.

Refrigerant Temperature Sensor

OPERATION

Located on the rear of the compressor on Colt, the refrigerant temperature sensor detects the temperature of the refrigerant delivered from the compressor during operation. The switch is designed to cut off the compressor when the temperature of the refrigerant exceeds 347°F (175°C), preventing overheating.

TESTING

1. Measure the resistance between the yellow-with-green-tracer wire and the black-with-yellow-tracer wire.
2. At 75–80°F, the resistance specification is about 80 kilo ohms.

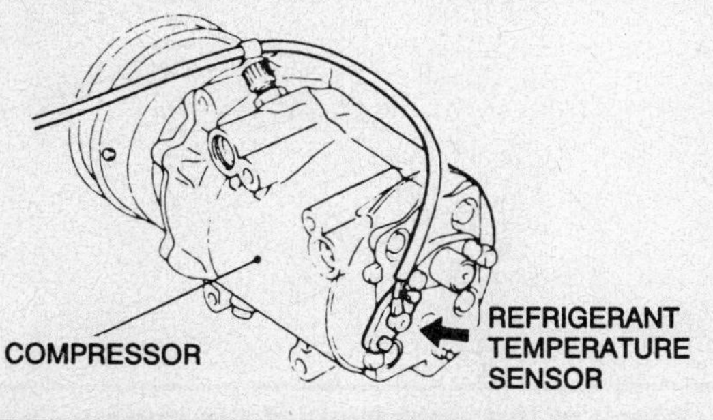
COMPRESSOR
REFRIGERANT
TEMPERATURE
SENSOR

Refrigerant temperature sensor—Colt

3. If the reading deviates greatly from the specification, replace the sensor.

REMOVAL AND INSTALLATION

1. Disconnect the negative battery cable.
2. Properly discharge the air conditioning system.
3. Disconnect the connector.
4. Remove the mounting screws and the sensor from the compressor.
5. The installation is the reverse of the removal installation. Use a new lubricated O-ring when installing.
6. Evacuate and recharge the air conditioning system.
7. Connect the negative battery cable and check the entire climate control system for proper operation. Check the system for leaks.

Engine Coolant Temperature Switch

OPERATION

The engine coolant temperature switch, located on or near the thermostat housing, is connected in series with the compressor clutch relay on all vehicles except Colt with 1.5L engine. The switch is designed to cut off the compressor when the engine coolant temperature rises above 239°F (115°C), preventing engine overheating when the supply of cooling air is not sufficient for both the radiator and condenser.

TESTING

1. If the switch is suspect, unplug and jump across the terminals in the connectors.
2. To test the switch, remove the switch from the engine. The switch should be closed at room temperature.
3. Place the switch in an oil bath and heat to at least 222°F (108°C).
4. The switch should open when it reaches the above temperature.

REMOVAL AND INSTALLATION

1. Disconnect the negative battery cable. Drain out some of the coolant.
2. Unplug the connector.
3. Unscrew the switch from the thermostat housing.
4. The installation is the reverse of the removal installation. Use sealant on the threads when installing.
5. Refill the cooling system.
6. Connect the negative battery cable and check the entire climate control system for proper operation.

Air Thermo and Air Inlet Sensors

OPERATION

These sensors function as cycling switches. Both sensors are located inside the evaporator housing. The air inlet sensor is normally on the right side of the housing and the air thermo sensor is normally on the left side.

The air thermo sensor detects the temperature of the air in the passenger compartment and the air inlet sensor detects the temperature of the air coming into the cooling unit. The information is input to the auto compressor control unit and the information is processed, causing the compressor clutch to cycle.

TESTING

1. Disconnect the sensor connector near the evaporator case.

2. Measure the resistance across the wires of the suspect sensor.
3. The resistance specifications for the air thermo sensor at different temperatures are:
32°F (0°C) – 11.4 kilo ohms
50°F (10°C) – 7.32 kilo ohms
68°F (20°C) – 4.86 kilo ohms
86°F (30°C) – 3.31 kilo ohms
104°F (40°C) – 2.32 kilo ohms
4. The resistance specifications for the air inlet sensor at different temperatures are:
32°F (0°C) – 3.31 kilo ohms
50°F (10°C) – 2.00 kilo ohms
68°F (20°C) – 1.25 kilo ohms
86°F (30°C) – 0.81 kilo ohms
104°F (40°C) – 0.53 kilo ohms
5. Replace the sensor if not within specifications.

REMOVAL AND INSTALLATION

1. Disconnect the negative battery cable.
2. Properly discharge the air conditioning system.
3. Remove the evaporator housing and the covers.
4. Unclip the sensor wires from the housing and remove the sensor(s).
5. The installation is the reverse of the removal installation.
6. Evacuate and recharge the air conditioning system.
7. Connect the negative battery cable and check the entire climate control system for proper operation. Check the system for leaks.

Photo Sensor

OPERATION

The Conquest has a photo sensor installed in the upper right side of the instrument panel when equipped with an automatic climate control system. The function of the photo sensor is to detect a great amount of sunlight and increase the speed of the blower motor. This will compensate for the increase in interior temperature due to the heat of the sunlight.

TESTING

With sunlight shining on the photo sensor, cover the sensor with hand. If the speed of the blower decreases, then increases when sensor is exposed again, it is functioning properly.

REMOVAL AND INSTALLATION

1. Disconnect the negative battery cable.
2. Open or remove the glove box, as required.
3. Disconnect the connector to the photo sensor.
4. Carefully pry the sensor from the instrument panel.
5. The installation is the reverse of the removal procedure.
6. Connect the negative battery cable and check the sensor for proper operation.

Temperature Sensor

OPERATION

The Conquest has a passenger compartment temperature sensor installed in the roof when equipped with an automatic climate control system. The function of this sensor is to detect a the temperature of the passenger compartment, change the information into resistance values and provide the information to the controller for processing. This information is used as input by the controller.

TESTING

1. Disconnect the sensor connector near the evaporator case.
2. Measure the resistance across the wires of the suspect sensor.
3. The resistance specifications for the passenger compartment sensor at different temperatures are:
32°F (0°C) – 11.4 kilo ohms
50°F (10°C) – 7.32 kilo ohms
68°F (20°C) – 4.86 kilo ohms
86°F (30°C) – 3.31 kilo ohms
104°F (40°C) – 2.32 kilo ohms
4. Replace the sensor if not within specifications.

REMOVAL AND INSTALLATION

1. Disconnect the negative battery cable.
2. Carefully pry the sensor from the headliner and disconnect the connector.
3. The installation is the reverse of the removal procedure.
4. Connect the negative battery cable and check the sensor for proper operation.

System Relays

OPERATION

Many of the systems within the air conditioning systems use relays to send current on its way and energize various components. The relays are positioned throughout the vehicles and many are interchangeable. All are conventional relays with internal contacts and a coil which pulls the contacts closed when energized.

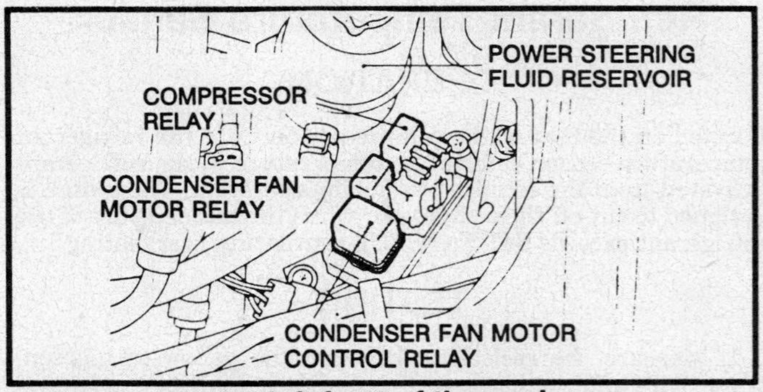
POWER STEERING
FLUID RESERVOIR
COMPRESSOR
RELAY
CONDENSER FAN
MOTOR RELAY
CONDENSER FAN MOTOR
CONTROL RELAY

Relay block at the left front of the engine compartment – Colt

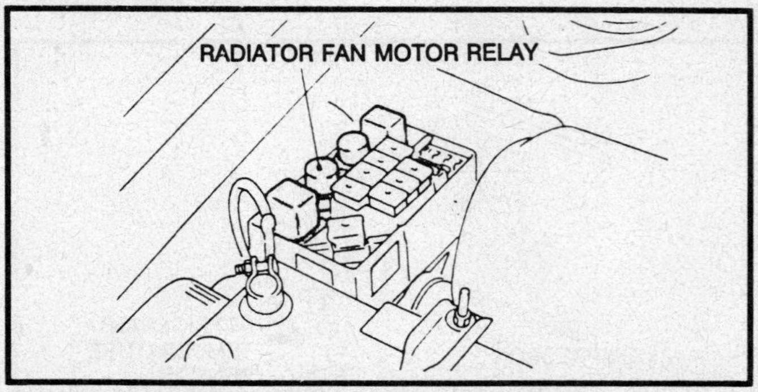
RADIATOR FAN MOTOR RELAY

Relay block at the right front of the engine compartment – Colt

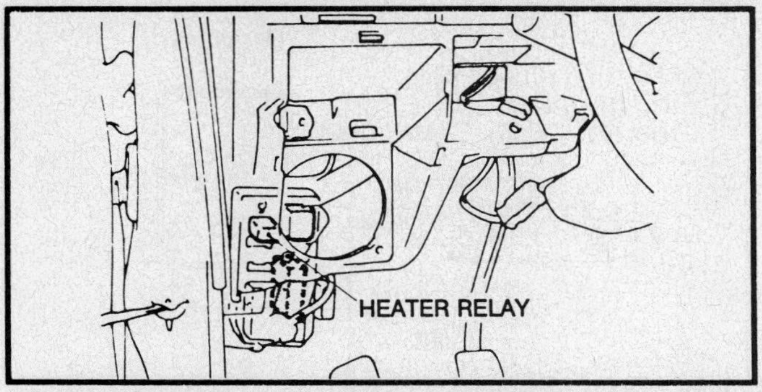
HEATER RELAY

Heater relay to the left of the steering column – Colt

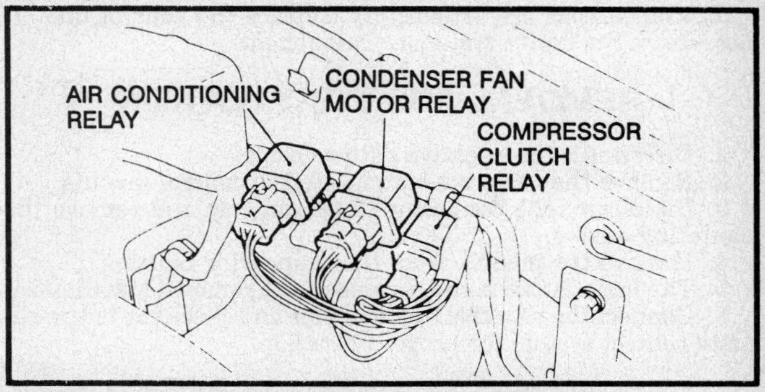
AIR CONDITIONING RELAY
CONDENSER FAN MOTOR RELAY
COMPRESSOR CLUTCH RELAY

Relay cluster near the hood prop – Colt Vista

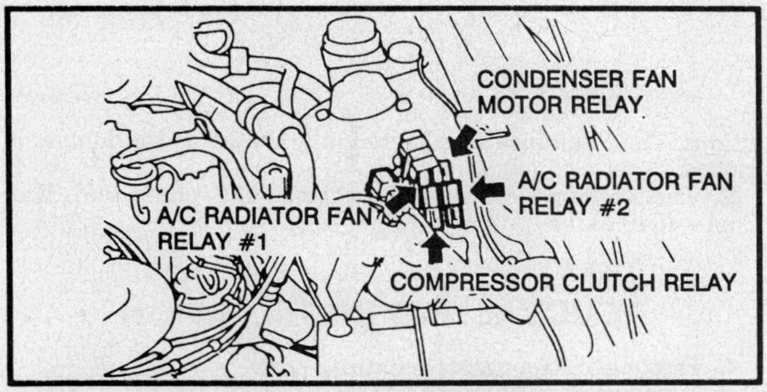
CONDENSER FAN MOTOR RELAY
A/C RADIATOR FAN RELAY #2
A/C RADIATOR FAN RELAY #1
COMPRESSOR CLUTCH RELAY

Relay cluster forward of the left front strut tower – Conquest

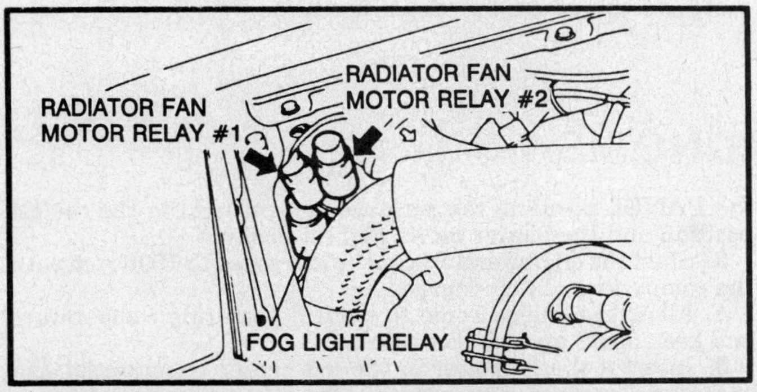
RADIATOR FAN MOTOR RELAY #2
RADIATOR FAN MOTOR RELAY #1
FOG LIGHT RELAY

Radiator fan relays at the right front of the engine compartment – Conquest

Air Conditioning Control Unit

OPERATION

The Colt uses an electronic control unit to process information received from various sensors and switches to control the air conditioning compressor. The unit is located behind the glove box on top or on the front side of the evaporator housing. The function of the control unit is to send current to the dual pressure switch when the following conditions are met:

1. The air conditioning switch is in either the **ECONO** or **A/C** mode.
2. The refrigerant temperature sensor, if equipped, is reading 347°F (175°C) or less.
3. The air thermo and air inlet sensors are both reading at least 39°F (4°C).

TESTING

1. Disconnect the control unit connector.
2. Turn the ignition switch **ON**.
3. Turn the air conditioning switch **ON**.
4. Turn the temperature control lever too its coolest position.
5. Turn the blower switch to its highest position.
6. Follow the chart and probe the various terminals of the control unit connector under the the specified conditions. This will rule out all possible faulty components in the system.

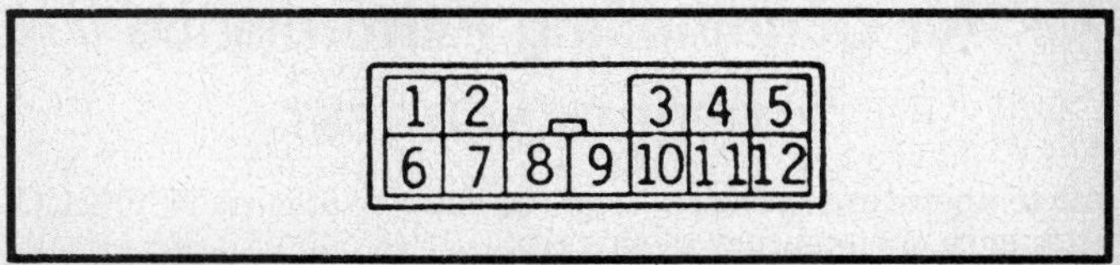
1 2 3 4 5
6 7 8 9 10 11 12

Air conditioning system electronic control unit connector terminals – Colt

AIR CONDITIONING CONTROL UNIT DIAGNOSTICS – COLT

Terminal No.	Signal	Conditions	Terminal voltage
1	Auto compressor control unit power supply	When ignition switch is ON	System voltage
5	Refrigerant temperature sensor ⊖	When air conditioner switch is OFF [Sensor temperature 25°C (77°F)]	0.15V
6	Air conditioner compressor relay	When all conditions for switch-ON of the compressor are satisfied	System voltage
8	Auto compressor control unit ground	At all times	0V
12	Refrigerant temperature sensor ⊕	At all times	5V

7. If all checks are satisfactory, replace the control unit. If not, check the faulty system or component.

REMOVAL AND INSTALLATION

1. Disconnect the negative battery cable.
2. Remove the glove box and locate the control module.
3. Disconnect the connector to the module and remove the mounting screws.
4. Remove the module from the evaporator housing.
5. The installation is the reverse of the removal installation.
6. Connect the negative battery cable and check the entire climate control system for proper operation.

Blend Air Damper Control Motor

OPERATION

The Conquest uses electric motors to control the positioning of the blend air damper electronically. Motor rotation is activated by signals sent by the air condtioning control unit, causing the damper to be move to the target position.

TESTING

Damper Motor

1. Apply battery voltage to the proper connector terminals. Make sure the motor turns smoothly and quietly and no binding occurs. Be sure to cut off voltage when the door has reached its stop or if the motor does not rotate.
2. Reverse the connections and make sure the motor turns in the opposite direction.

Blend Air Potentiometer

1. Connect an ohmmeter to the potentiometer terminals and measure the resistance at the hottest (MH) and coolest (MC) positions. The resistance should gradually change as the damper is moved.
2. The specifications are: Max Hot—180 ohms and Max Cool—4640 ohms

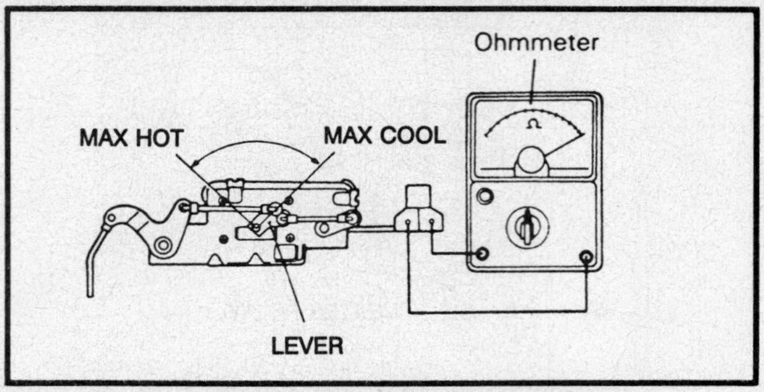
Ohmmeter
MAX HOT
MAX COOL
LEVER

Measure the resistance across the indicated terminals to check the blend air potentiometer—Conquest

REMOVAL AND INSTALLATION

1. Disconnect the negative battery cable.
2. If necessary, remove the heater unit.
3. Disconnect the actuating rod from the damper.
4. Remove the mounting bolts and remove the motor.
5. The installation is the reverse of the removal procedure.
6. Connect the negative battery cable and check the entire climate control system for proper operation.

SYSTEM DIAGNOSIS

Air Conditioning Performance

PERFORMANCE TEST

Air temperature in the testing area must be at least 70°F (21°C) to ensure the accuracy of this test.

1. Connect a manifold gauge set the the system.
2. Set the controls to **RECIRC** or **MAX**, the mode lever to the **PANEL** position, temperature control level to the coolest position and the blower on its highest position.
3. Start the engine and adjust the idle speed to 1000 rpm with the compressor clutch engaged.
4. Allow the engine come to normal operating temperature and keep doors and windows closed.
5. Insert a thermometer in the left center panel outlet and operate the engine for 10 minutes. The clutch may cycle depending on the ambient conditions.

AIR CONDITIONING PERFORMANCE CHART

Ambient Temperature °F (°C)	Air Temperature at Center Panel Vent °F (°C)	Compressor Discharge Pressure PSI (kPa)	Compressor Suction Pressure PSI (kPa)
70 (21)	34–45 (1–8)	130–190 (896–1295)	10–21 (70–145)
80 (27)	35–45 (2–8)	145–210 (1000–1450)	13–25 (90–175)
90 (32)	36–47 (2–9)	165–245 (1140–1690)	15–30 (103–110)
100 (38)	37–50 (3–10)	190–270 (1335–1860)	20–33 (140–230)
110 (43)	40–60 (4–16)	200–300 (1400–2110)	20-35 (140–245)

OPERATION CHECKS AND TROUBLESHOOTING—CONQUEST

No.	Action	Normal operation	Abnormal operation/ Probable cause
1	Start the engine. (Proceed to check after engine coolant is sufficiently warmed.)	• The AUTO switch light on control panel lights.	• AUTO switch light does not light and no beep sound is heard even if the switch is pressed. - Problem in switch
		• The display changes to preset temperature indication.	• No indication. - Problem in digital display
		• Air volume changes according to blower switch position.	• Blower motor does not operate even if the fan switch is set to ON. - Problem in fan controller
		• Compressor comes into operation.	• Compressor does not operate. - Problem in air conditioner
2	Change temperature setting to 32°C (90°F). (Set blower switch to AUTO position unless otherwise specified.)	• On depression of UP switch, beep sound is produced and the sound stops once 32°C (90°F) is reached.	• No beep sound. Temperature setting remains unchanged. - Problem in switch - Problem in wiring harness
		• Beep sound is heard while temperature setting is being changed.	
		• When 32°C (90°F) temperature is reached, the indication changes from "FACE" to "FACE/FOOT" and then to "FOOT", and also the air outlet accordingly.	• Air flow does not change to FOOT mode or air outlet does not correspond to mode indication. - Problem in air flow change vacuum solenoid or vacuum actuator
		• Outlet air reaches the warmest temperature.	• The warmest temperature cannot be attained or, conversely, temperature drops to the lowest. - Problem in blend air damper servo motor
		• Outside air is introduced.	• Interior air recirculates. - Problem in outside/inside air damper vacuum solenoid or actuator
		• Compressor stops.	• Compressor comes into operation. - Problem in wiring harness - Problem in control box
		• Blower speed becomes MH.	• Blower speed remains unchanged. - Problem in fan controller - Problem in wiring harness - Problem in control box

No.	Action	Normal operation	Abnormal operation/ Probable cause
3	Change temperature setting from 32 to 18°C (90 to 65°F.)	• Upon depression of DOWN switch, beep sound is produced and the sound stops once 18°C (65°F) temperature is reached.	• No beep sound. Temperature setting remains unchanged. - Problem in switch - Problem in wiring harness
		• Beep sound is heard while temperature setting is being changed.	• Temperature indication remains unchanged. - Problem in indicator - Problem in wiring harness
		• When 18°C (65°F) temperature is reached, the indication changes from "FOOT" to "FACE/FOOT" and then to "FACE", and also the air outlet accordingly. (Observe LED also.)	• Air flow does not change to FACE mode or air outlet does not correspond to the indicated mode. - Problem in air flow changeover vacuum solenoid or actuator
		• Outlet air temperature becomes the lowest (blend air damper is closed).	• Outlet air does not become cooler, much less the lowest temperature (blend air damper does not operate). - Problem in blend air damper servo motor
		• Compressor comes into operation.	• Compressor does not operate. - Problem in air conditioner
		• Air flow changes from introduction of outside air to recirculation of inside air.	• Outside air is introduced. - Problem in air selection damper actuator
		• Blower speed becomes "H" (H relay closes).	• Blower speed remains unchanged and H relay is inoperative. - Problem in power transistor - Problem in relay
4	Press air selection switch twice and then press AUTO switch. [Temperature setting is 25°C (77°F)]	• Every depression of air selection causes beep sound and switch light is kept lit in that while. Once AUTO switch is pressed, the air selection light goes off.	• Beep sound is produced but light does not light. - Blown light bulb • Neither beep sound is produced nor light lights. - Problem in switch
		• On depression of air selection switch, the damper position changes from recirculation position to outside air position and vice-versa.	• Damper position does not change (but air flow indication changes). - Problem in recirculation/outside air damper actuator
		• If AUTO switch is pressed, damper returns automatically to its original position and indication also returns to "AUTO".	

No.	Action	Normal operation	Abnormal operation/ Probable cause
5	Press ECONOMY switch three times and then press AUTO switch. [Temperature setting is 25°C (77°F)]	• Every depression of switch causes beep sound and switch light lights every other depression. • Second depression of switch causes compressor to stop and switch light and AUTO light to go off. • When AUTO switch is pressed, ECONOMY switch light goes off and air conditioner comes into operation continuously.	• No beep sound is produced (no response to switch action). - Problem in switch - Problem in wiring harness • Beep sound is produced but light does not light. - Blown light bulb (Switch does not operate.) • Compressor operates but condenser fan does not. - Problem in condenser motor - Problem in condenser motor relay
6	Push air flow mode switches one after another. ↓ ↓	• Beep sound is produced when respective switch is pushed; corresponding switch light and LED light. • AUTO light goes off when any of the switches is pushed. • Air comes out from the outlets corresponding to pushed switch. • Indication on air flow indicator changes according to depression of switch. * and modes cannot be selected simultaneously. If both are selected concurrently, will have priority over the other.	• No beep sound is produced (no response to switch action). - Problem in switch - Problem in wiring harness • Beep sound is produced but light does not light. - Blown switch light bulb • Air flow direction does not change. - Problem in damper actuator
7	Change blower switch position. OFF ↓ ↓	• Outlet air volume changes according to switch position. • If AUTO mode switch is activated, air volume changes automatically according to interior temperature. (For example, if the interior sensor is touched by hand when interior temperature is lower than bodily temperature, the air volume will increase.) • When engine is cold, if AUTO mode switch is activated, fan speed is fixed to low speed for some while after start of engine.	• No air volume change is caused by setting the switch to different positions (and). - Problem in switch - Problem in wiring harness • Fan motor does not operate in both and positions. - Problem in fan controller - Blown fuse - Broken harness • When AUTO mode switch is activated, fan turns at high speed even in cold season or stays turning at low speed even after the engine is warmed. - Problem in water temperature switch - Problem in water temperature switch wiring harness

No.	Action	Normal operation	Abnormal operation/ Probable cause
8	Check for AUTO mode function (interior temperature sensor operation). [Set AUTO mode switch to ON; temperature setting is 25°C (77°F)] * Touch interior temperature sensor heat sensing plate with hand to warm it to 30°C (86°F) or over. Then cool the plate down to 10°C (50°F) or below.	• When the interior temperature sensor is touched with hand, the air flow mode becomes to FACE, the blend air damper moves to the coolest position and blower speed changes to H level. The interior air recirculates under this condition. (If the system is in ECONOMY mode, the compressor comes into operation.) • When the interior temperature sensor is cooled down, the outside air is introduced, the blend air damper moves to the warmest position and the air flow mode becomes to FOOT. Also, the fan speed becomes MH level. (If the system is in ECONOMY mode, the compressor stops.)	• Neither touching the sensor with hand nor cooling it causes the results. - Problem in interior temperature sensor - Problem in wiring harness - Problem in controller
9	Check photo-sensor for function. [With the system in AUTO mode, set the blower switch to AUTO position temperature setting is 25°C (77°F)] Expose the photo-sensor to sunbeam for checking.	• When the sensor is exposed to sunbeam, the outlet air temperature lowers. (Blower speed increases in summer.) • When the sensor is covered by hand, the outlet air temperature rises. (Blower speed decreases in summer.)	• No change results from action on sensor. - Problem in photo-sensor - Broken wiring harness - Problem in controller (Clean the photo-sensor.)
10	Check engine coolant temperature switch for operation. (With the system in AUTO mode, set the blower switch to AUTO position; temperature setting.) * Cool the interior temperature sensor heat sensing plate down to 20°C (68°F) or lower.	• When engine coolant temperature is lower than 50°C (122°F), the blower speed is in L level and the air flow mode becomes DEF. • When engine coolant temperature rises to 50°C (122°F) or higher, the blower speed increases and air flow mode becomes FOOT, FACE/FOOT or FACE.	• Blower motor speed is not fixed to L level even when engine coolant temperature is lower than 50°C (122°F). - Problem in controller - Problem in wiring harness • Air flow remains in mode. - Problem in engine coolant temperature switch - Broken wiring harness - Problem in controller

TROUBLESHOOTING CHART—CONQUEST

	Check item / Symptom	Fuse	Harness	Light bulb	Damper control motor & link	Water valve	Magnetic clutch	Power relays	Sensor switches	Blower motor	Pusher fan motor	Control unit (diagnosis output)	Vacuum system (VSV, hose, check valve)
1	"AUTO" light does not illuminate when ignition switch is turned to "ON" position	①	④	③								②	
2	Inside temperature does not rise (no hot air)		⑤		③	④			②			①	
3	Inside temperature does not drop (no cool air)		⑤		③	④	⑦	⑥	②			①	
4	Blower does not run	①	⑥					⑤	④	③		②	
5	Blower does not stop		④					③	②			①	
6	Air inlet switching damper does not operate		④						③			①	②
7	Air outlet switching damper does not operate		④						③			①	②
8	Pusher fan does not operate when air conditioner is operating		④					①	②		③		
9	Temperature setting changes when ignition switch is turned to "OFF" position and then back to "ON" position		②									①	

NOTE
1. ○ indicates items requiring check (number in circle indicates check order).
2. Use self-diagnosis and measure terminal voltage for control unit check.

TROUBLESHOOTING BY SYMPTOM—CONQUEST

Symptom	Probable cause	Remedy
1. "AUTO" light does not illuminate when ignition switch is turned to "ON" position	Open No. 12 fuse	Replace fuse
	Faulty control unit	Check diagnosis output
	Faulty full auto air conditioner panel assembly	Replace full auto air conditioner panel assembly
	Burnt-out "AUTO" indicator bulb	Replace "AUTO" light bulb
	Open harness between full auto air conditioner panel assembly and control unit	Correct harness
2. Inside temperature does not rise (no hot air)	Faulty control unit	Check diagnosis output
	Faulty interior temperature sensor input circuit	
	Faulty foot area temperature sensor input circuit	
	Faulty thermistor input circuit	
	Faulty blend air damper potentiometer input circuit	
	Faulty blend air damper control motor	Replace blend air damper control motor
	Inadequate connection between blend air damper control motor lever and blend air damper	Correct connection
	Seized blend air damper	Correct blend air damper
	Water valve failure	Replace water valve
	Open harness between blend air damper control motor and control unit	Correct harness
3. Inside temperature does not drop (no cool air)	Faulty control unit	Check diagnosis output
	Faulty upper interior temperature sensor input circuit	
	Faulty lower interior temperature sensor input circuit	
	Faulty thermistor input circuit	
	Faulty blend air damper potentiometer input circuit	
	Faulty blend air damper control motor	Replace blend air damper control motor
	Inadequate connection between blend air damper control motor lever and blend air damper	Correct connection
	Seized blend air damper	Correct blend air damper

NOTE
When engine coolant temperature is below 50°C (122°F), blower speed is held at LOW.

Symptom	Probable cause	Remedy
3. Inside temperature does not drop (no cool air)	Water valve failure	Replace water valve
	Open harness between blend air damper control motor and control unit	Correct harness
	Faulty power relay (for compressor)	Replace power relay
	Faulty magnet clutch	Check or replace magnet clutch
	Refrigerant leaks	Replenish refrigerant
4. Blower does not run	Open fuse No. 5	Replace fuse
	Faulty control unit	Check diagnosis output
	Faulty blower motor	Replace blower motor
	Blown temperature fuse in power transistor or poor grounding	Replace temperature fuse or correct grounding
	Faulty power relay (for starter cut)	Replace power relay (for starter cut)
	Open harness between fuse and power relay (for starter cut)	Correct harness
	Open harness between power relay (for starter cut) and blower motor	
	Open harness between power transistor and control unit	
5. Blower does not stop	Faulty control unit	Check diagnosis output
	Faulty blower switch (OFF SW)	Replace full auto air conditioner panel assembly
	Faulty power relay (for high speed)	Replace power relay
	Shorted harness between blower switch and control unit	Correct harness
	Shorted harness between power relay (for high speed) and power transistor and control unit	
6. Air inlet switching damper does not operate	Faulty control unit	Check diagnosis output
	Defective vacuum solenoid valve	Replace vacuum solenoid valve
	Defective or disconnected vacuum hose	Check or replace vacuum hose
	Defective vacuum system including vacuum tank	Check or replace vacuum system
	Faulty full auto air conditioner switch (inside/outside air switching)	Replace full auto air conditioner panel assembly
	Faulty air inlet switching control vacuum actuator	Replace air inlet switching control vacuum actuator
	Air inlet switching damper failure	Correct air inlet switching damper

Symptom	Probable cause	Remedy
6. Air inlet switching damper does not operate	Open harness between full auto air conditioner panel assembly and control unit	Correct harness
	Open harness between air inlet switching vacuum solenoid valve and control unit	Correct harness
7. Air outlet switching damper does not operate	Faulty control unit	Check diagnosis output
	Defective vacuum solenoid valve	Replace vacuum solenoid valve
	Defective or disconnected vacuum hose	Check or replace vacuum hose
	Defective vacuum system including vacuum tank	Check or replace vacuum system
	Faulty full auto air conditioner switch (mode selection)	Replace full auto air conditioner panel assembly
	Faulty air outlet switching control vacuum actuator	Replace air outlet switching control vacuum actuator
	Inadequate engagement between cam and damper link or incorrect adjustment	Correct engagement or adjust
	FACE/DEF or FACE/FOOT damper failure	Correct FACE/DEF or FACE/FOOT damper
	Open harness between full auto air conditioner panel assembly and control unit	Correct harness
	Open harness between air outlet switching vacuum solenoid valve and control unit	
8. Pusher fan does not operate when air conditioner is operating	Faulty power relay (for pusher fan)	Replace power relay
	Faulty thermo sensor No. 2 (vehicles with an intercooler)	Check or replace thermo sensor
	Faulty pusher fan motor	Check or replace fan motor
	Faulty pressure switch (vehicles with an intercooler)	Check or replace pressure switch
9. Temperature setting changes when ignition switch is turned to "OFF" position and back to "ON" position	Faulty control unit	Check diagnosis output
	Insufficient battery charge or faulty battery	Recharge, adjust specific gravity or replace battery
	Open harness between ignition switch and control unit	Correct harness

6. With the clutch engaged, compare the discharge air temperature to the performance chart.
7. If the values do not meet specifications, check system components for proper operation.

Air Conditioning Compressor

COMPRESSOR NOISE

Noises that develop during air conditioning operation can be misleading. A noise that sounds like serious compressor damage may only be a loose belt, mounting bolt or clutch assembly. Improper belt tension can also emit a noise that can be mistaken for more serious problems. Check and adjust all possible causes of the noise, including oil level, before replacing the compressor.

COMPRESSOR CLUTCH INOPERATIVE

1. Verify refrigerant charge and charge, as required.
2. Check for 12 volts at the clutch coil connection. If voltage is detected, check the coil.
3. If voltage is not detected at the coil, check the fuse or fusible link. If the fuse is not blown, check for voltage at the clutch relay. If voltage is not detected there, continue working backwards through the system's switches, etc. until an open circuit is detected.
4. Inspect all suspect parts and replace as required.
5. When the repair is complete, perform a complete system performance test.

CLUTCH COIL TESTING

1. Disconnect the negative battery cable.
2. Disconnect the compressor clutch connector.
3. Apply 12 volts to the wire leading to the clutch coil. If the clutch is operating properly, an audible click will occur when the clutch is magnetically pulled into the coil. If no click is heard, inspect the coil.
4. Check the resistance across the coil lead wire and ground. The specification is 3.4–3.8 ohms at approximately 70°F (20°C).
5. If not within specifications, replace the clutch coil.

Full Automatic Air Conditioning System

SELF-DIAGNOSTICS

Conquest

OPERATION

The automatic system is equipped with self-diagnostic capabilities so the condition of the wire harnesses and components within the system can be analyzed. When the full automatic air conditioning system senses a malfunction, the fail-safe system is activated and a malfunction code is input to the electronic control unit. This information becomes output when the self-diagnostics connector is accessed. The connector is located behind the glove box.

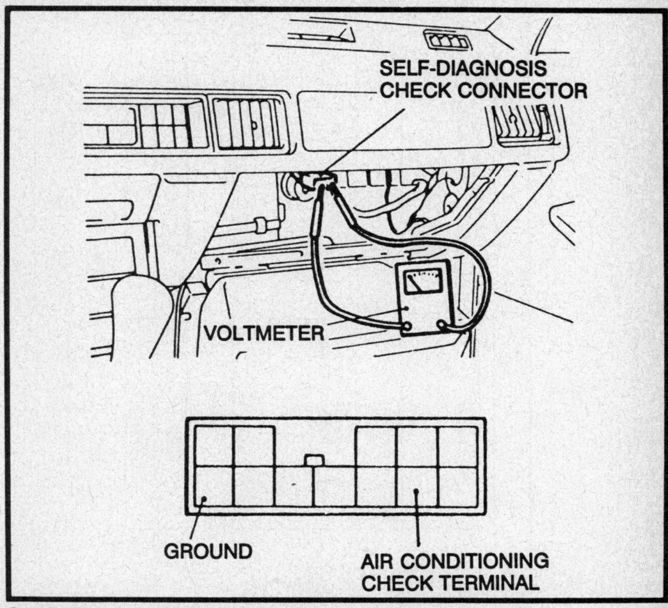
SELF-DIAGNOSIS
CHECK CONNECTOR
VOLTMETER
GROUND
AIR CONDITIONING
CHECK TERMINAL

Self-diagnostics using an anolog voltmeter—Conquest

USING MULTI-USE TESTER

Mitsubishi's Multi-Use Tester MB991269 or MB991341 in conjunction with the proper ROM pack can be used to check the system. To use the tester, connect the socket to the cigarette lighter and the connector to the vehicle's self-diagnosis check connector. Follow the manufacturer's instructions to set the tool and record the stored fault codes. Once the codes are recorded, check the faulty system(s) using the charts provided.

USING ANALOG VOLTMETER

Connect a voltmeter across the ground terminal and terminal designated for the full automatic air conditioning system on the check connector. The code number for the malfunction is determined by counting sweeps of the voltmeter needle. The long sweeps represent the tenths digit of the code and the shorter sweeps represent the single digits. For example, 1 long sweep followed by 5 short sweeps indicates Code 15.

DIAGNOSIS DISPLAY PATTERNS AND CODES CONQUEST

Code No.	Diagnosis display pattern	Malfunction (A/C condition)	Probable cause	Failsafe
0	12V 0V Continuous	Normal	–	–
2	12V 0V	Open or shorted interior temperature sensor circuit or faulty upper in-car sensor	• Disconnected interior temperature sensor connector • Open or shorted internal wiring of interior temperature sensor • Open or shorted harness in interior temperature sensor circuit or disconnected connector	Set interior temperature sensor input signal at 25°C (77°F)
3	12V 0V	Open or shorted foot area temperature sensor circuit or faulty foot area temperature sensor	• Disconnected foot area temperature sensor connector • Open or shorted internal wiring of foot area temperature sensor • Open or shorted harness in foot area temperature sensor circuit or disconnected connector	Set foot area temperature sensor input signal at 25°C (77°F)
4	12V 0V	Open or shorted wiring of thermistor circuit or faulty thermistor	• Disconnected thermistor connector • Open or shorted internal wiring of thermistor • Open or shorted harness in thermistor circuit or disconnected connector	Set thermistor input signal at 1°C (33.8°F) and turn off compressor
7	12V 0V	Open or shorted blend air damper potentiometer circuit or faulty blend air damper potentiometer	• Disconnected blend air damper potentiometer connector • Open or shorted internal wiring of blend air damper potentiometer • Open or shorted harness in blend air damper potentiometer circuit or disconnected connector	Set blend air damper at MAX HOT position
–	12V 0V Constantly 12V 12V 0V Constantly 0V	Internal failure of control unit	• Replace control unit	–

NOTE
1. Code Nos. 1, 5, 6 and 8 are intentionally omitted.
2. If two or more troubles are caused at the same time, one with the largest code No. is displayed.
3. The contents of troubles are stored until the ignition switch is turned off.

DIAGNOSIS OF DISPLAY PATTERN 2—CONQUEST

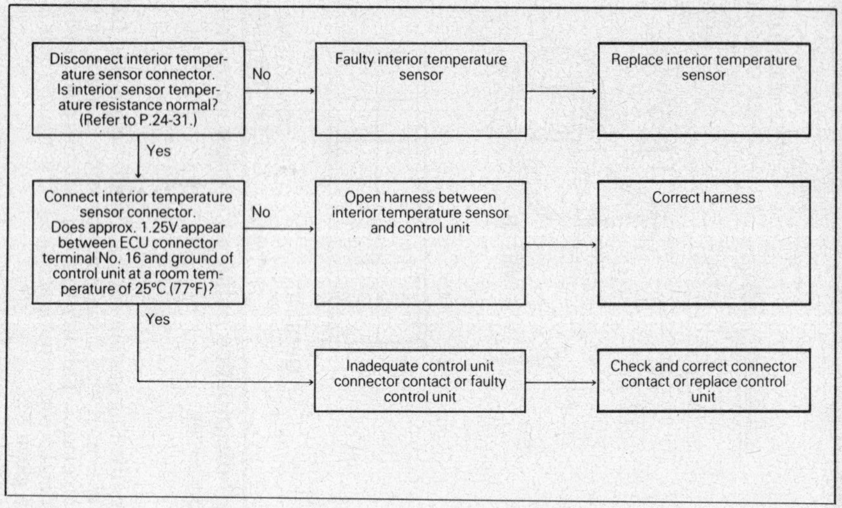
Disconnect interior temperature sensor connector. Is interior sensor temperature resistance normal? (Refer to P.24-31.)
No
Faulty interior temperature sensor
Replace interior temperature sensor
Yes
Connect interior temperature sensor connector. Does approx. 1.25V appear between ECU connector terminal No. 16 and ground of control unit at a room temperature of 25°C (77°F)?
No
Open harness between interior temperature sensor and control unit
Correct harness
Yes
Inadequate control unit connector contact or faulty control unit
Check and correct connector contact or replace control unit

DIAGNOSIS OF DISPLAY PATTERN 3—CONQUEST

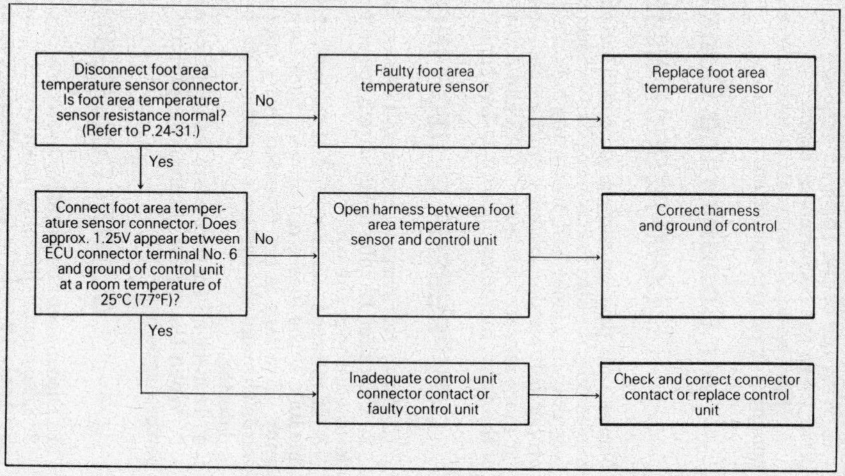
Disconnect foot area temperature sensor connector. Is foot area temperature sensor resistance normal? (Refer to P.24-31.)
No
Faulty foot area temperature sensor
Replace foot area temperature sensor
Yes
Connect foot area temperature sensor connector. Does approx. 1.25V appear between ECU connector terminal No. 6 and ground of control unit at a room temperature of 25°C (77°F)?
No
Open harness between foot area temperature sensor and control unit
Correct harness and ground of control
Yes
Inadequate control unit connector contact or faulty control unit
Check and correct connector contact or replace control unit

DIAGNOSIS OF DISPLAY PATTERN 4—CONQUEST

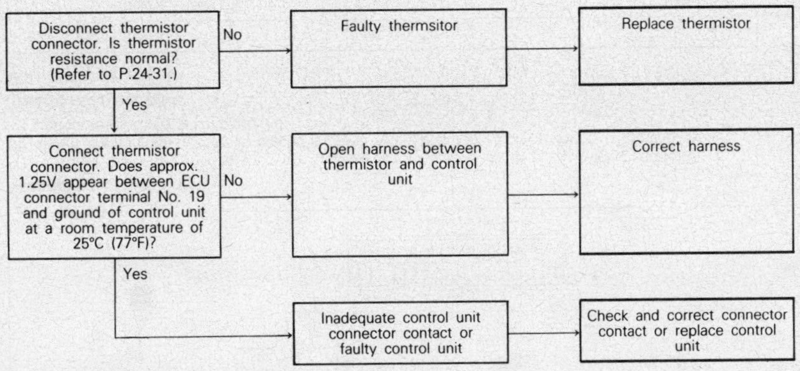
Disconnect thermistor connector. Is thermistor resistance normal? (Refer to P.24-31.)
No
Faulty thermsitor
Replace thermistor
Yes
Connect thermistor connector. Does approx. 1.25V appear between ECU connector terminal No. 19 and ground of control unit at a room temperature of 25°C (77°F)?
No
Open harness between thermistor and control unit
Correct harness
Yes
Inadequate control unit connector contact or faulty control unit
Check and correct connector contact or replace control unit

DIAGNOSIS OF DISPLAY PATTERN 7—CONQUEST

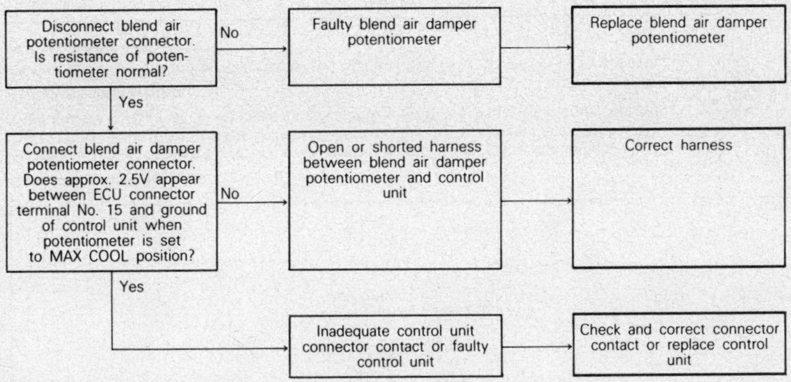
Disconnect blend air potentiometer connector. Is resistance of poten-tiometer normal?
No
Faulty blend air damper potentiometer
Replace blend air damper potentiometer
Yes
Connect blend air damper potentiometer connector. Does approx. 2.5V appear between ECU connector terminal No. 15 and ground of control unit when potentiometer is set to MAX COOL position?
No
Open or shorted harness between blend air damper potentiometer and control unit
Correct harness
Yes
Inadequate control unit connector contact or faulty control unit
Check and correct connector contact or replace control unit

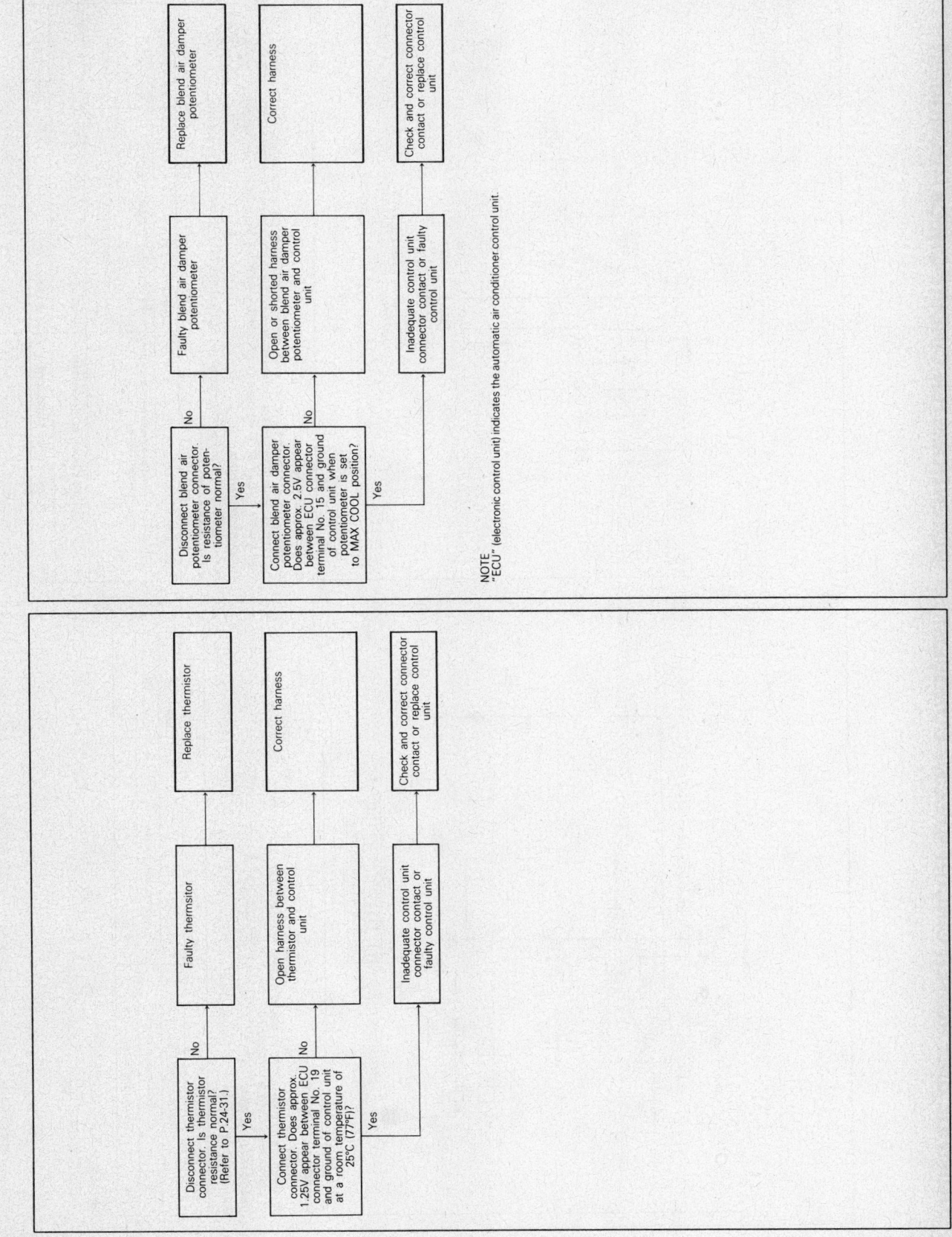

NOTE
"ECU" (electronic control unit) indicates the automatic air conditioner control unit.

CONTROL UNIT POWER CIRCUIT CHECK—CONQUEST

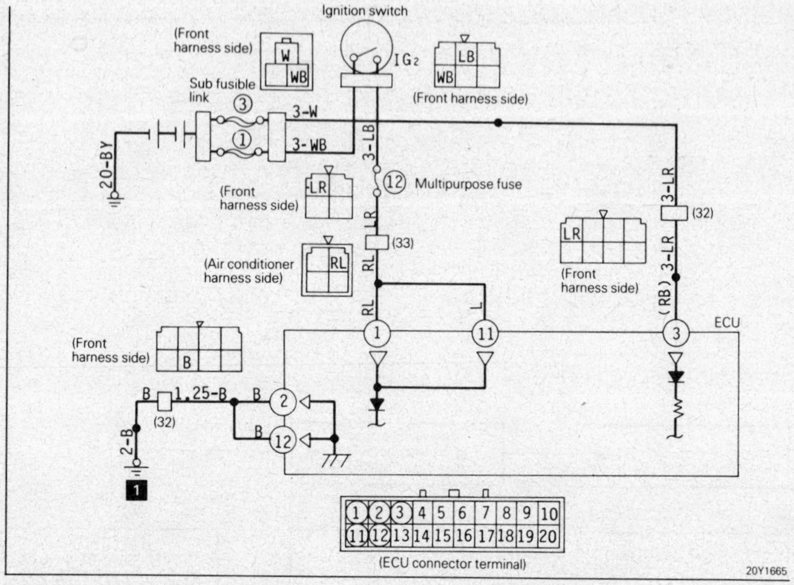
Ignition switch
(Front harness side)
W
WB
IG2
LB
WB
(Front harness side)
Sub fusible link
3
1
3-W
3-WB
3-LB
20-BY
(Front harness side)
LR
12 Multipurpose fuse
(33)
(Air conditioner harness side)
RL
LR
(Front harness side)
3-LR
(32)
RB
ECU
1
11
3
L
(Front harness side)
B
1.25-B
2-B
(32)
2
12
(ECU connector terminal)
20Y1665

Description of Operation

(1) Normally, current flows to the sub fusible link ③ to ECU to ground. (Backup current)
(2) When the ignition switch is placed in the "ON" position, current flows to ignition switch (IG_2) to multipurpose fuse to the ground.

Troubelshooting Hints

ECU terminal voltage

Terminal No.	Signal	Condition	Terminal voltage
3	Backup power supply signal	At all times	Approx. VB
1, 11	ECU power supply signal	When ignition switch is ON	Approx. VB
2, 12	ECU ground signal	At all times	0 V

NOTE
VB: Battery Voltage

POTENTIOMETER CIRCUIT CHECK—CONQUEST

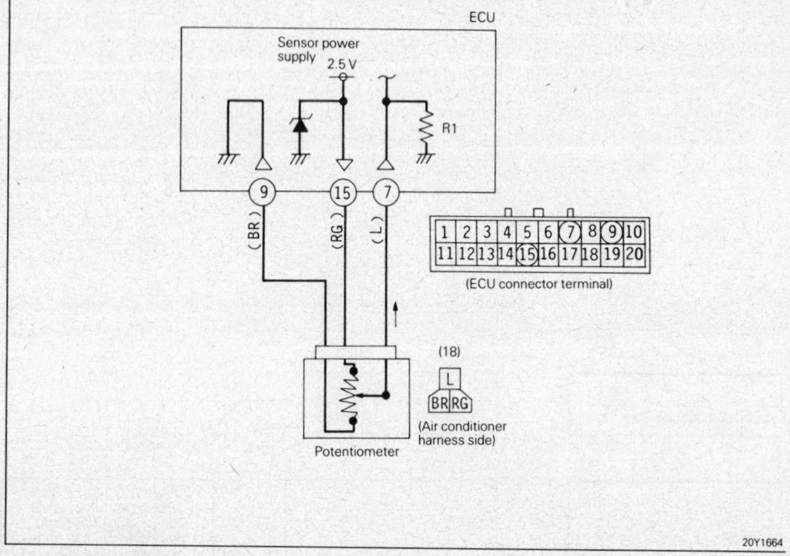
ECU
Sensor power supply 2.5 V
R1
9
15
7
(BR)
(RG)
(L)
(ECU connector terminal)
(18)
L
BR RG
(Air conditioner harness side)
Potentiometer
20Y1664

Description of Operation

Air conditioner control unit sensor power supply is applied to the potentiometer.
The terminal voltage of ⑦ is a voltage divided by the potentiometer and resistor R_1.
The terminal voltage of ⑦ changes proportionately with the blend air damper opening.

Troubleshooting Hints

Diagnosis – No. 7 blend air damper is set to the MAX HOT or MAX COOL position.

ECU terminal voltage

Terminal No.	Signal	Condition	Terminal voltage
7	Blend air damper potentiometer (output) signal	Blend air damper is in MAX COOL position	Approx. 0.2V
		Blend air damper is in MAX HOT position	Approx. 2.3V
9	Blend air damper potentiometer ⊖ signal	At all times	0 V
15	Sensor power supply signal	At all times	Approx. 2.5V

AIR CONDITIONING SENSORS CIRCUIT CHECK CONQUEST

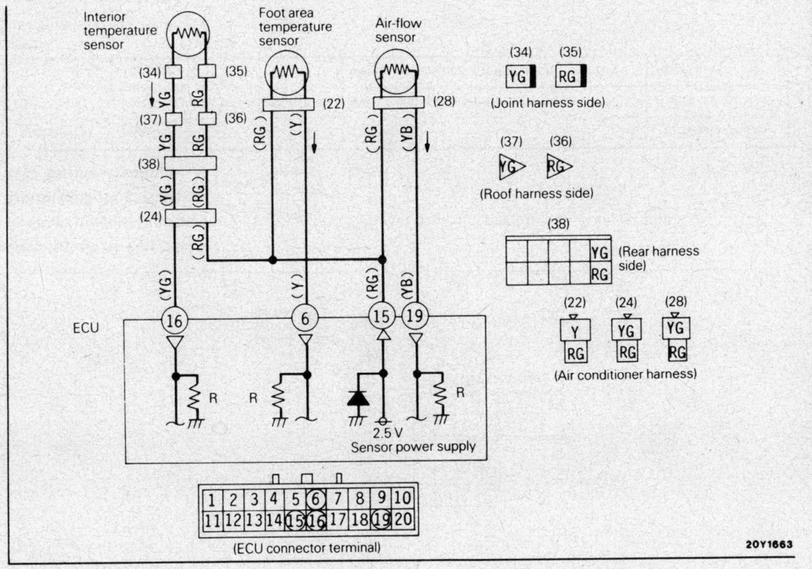
Interior temperature sensor
Foot area temperature sensor
Air-flow sensor
ECU
R
2.5 V
Sensor power supply
(ECU connector terminal)
(Joint harness side)
(Roof harness side)
(Rear harness side)
(Air conditioner harness)

20Y1663

Description of Operation

Each sensor uses negative characteristic thermistor to convert the ambient temperature into resistance. Air conditioner control unit sensor power supply (2.5 V) is applied to each sensor. Terminal voltage of ⑥, ⑯ or ⑲ is voltage devided by resistance of each sensor and resistor R.

Troubleshooting Hints

Diagnosis – No. 2 interior temperature sensor input signal is set to 25°C (77°F).
No. 3 foot area temperature sensor input signal is set to 25°C (77°F).
No. 4 air-flow sensor input signal is set to 1°C (33.8°F).

ECU terminal voltage

Terminal No.	Signal	Condition	Terminal voltage
6	Foot temperature sensor (4 kΩ) signal	Interior temperature is 25°C (77°F).	Approx. 1.25V
		Harness is broken.	0 V
15	Sensor power supply signal	At all times	Approx. 2.5V
16	Interior temperature sensor (4 kΩ) signal	Interior temperature is 25°C (77°F).	Approx. 1.25V
		Harness is broken.	0 V
19	Air-flow sensor (4 kΩ) signal	With air conditioner turned OFF, interior temperature is 25°C (77°F).	Approx. 1.25V
		Harness is broken.	0 V

PHOTO SENSOR CIRCUIT CHECK—CONQUEST

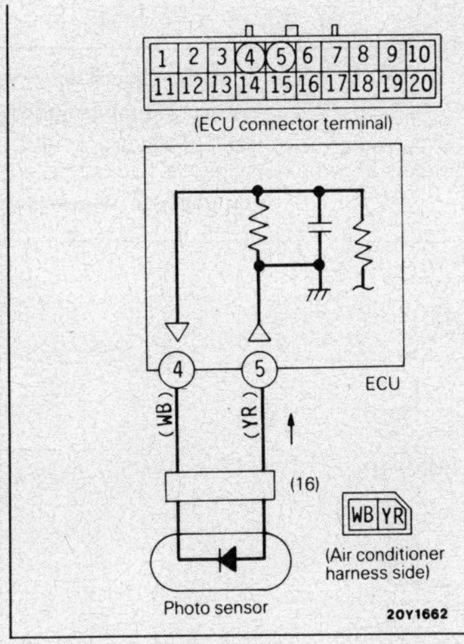
(ECU connector terminal)
ECU
Photo sensor
(Air conditioner harness side)

20Y1662

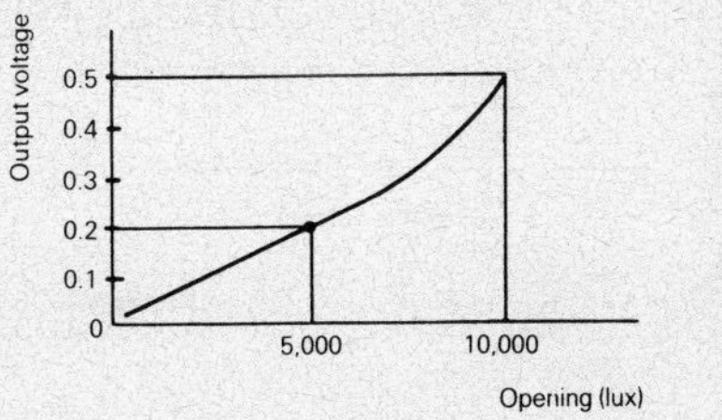
Output voltage
Opening (lux)
5,000
10,000

20Y1662

Description of Operation

The photo sensor is used to control increase of vehicle interior temperature with the amount of solar radiation. In combination with regulated resistance of ECU, it generates electromotive force corresponding to the amount of solar radiation received by the light receiving surface of photodiode. ECU terminal ⑤ (photo sensor ⊖) is grounded inside the unit. Therefore, negative voltage is generated at terminal ④.

Troubleshooting Hints

ECU terminal voltage

Terminal No.	Signal	Condition	Terminal voltage
5	Photo sensor ⊖	At all times	0 V
4	Photo sensor ⊕	Luminous intensity: 5,000 lux	Approx. –0.1 V
		Luminous intensity: 10,000 lux	Approx. –0.25 V

ENGINE COOLANT TEMPERATURE UNIT CIRCUIT CHECK—CONQUEST

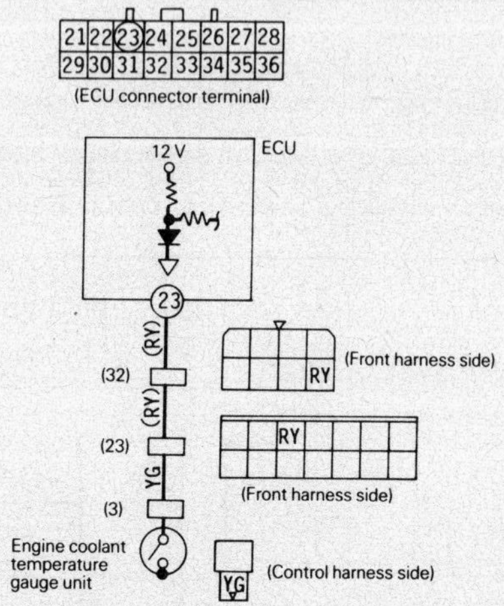
21 22 23 24 25 26 27 28
29 30 31 32 33 34 35 36
(ECU connector terminal)
ECU
12 V
23
(RY)
(32)
(RY)
(23)
YG
(3)
Engine coolant temperature gauge unit
RY
(Front harness side)
RY
(Front harness side)
YG
(Control harness side)

20Y1658

Description of Operation

The engine coolant temperature gauge unit is ON when engine coolant temperature is approx. 50°C (122°F).

Troubleshooting Hints

ECU terminal voltage

Terminal No.	Signal	Condition	Terminal voltage
23	Engine coolant temperature gauge unit	When engine coolant temperature is ON	Approx. 0.2 to 0.8V
		When engine coolant temperature is OFF	Approx. VB

NOTE
VB: Battery Voltage

BLEND AIR DAMPER MOTOR CIRCUIT CHECK CONQUEST

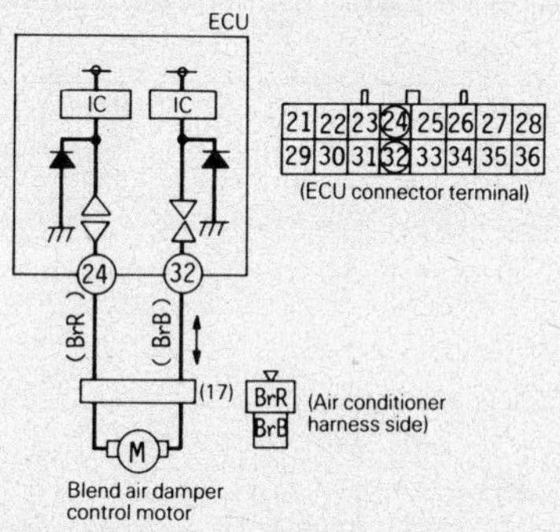
ECU
IC
IC
24
32
(BrR)
(BrB)
(17)
M
Blend air damper control motor
21 22 23 24 25 26 27 28
29 30 31 32 33 34 35 36
(ECU connector terminal)
BrR
BrB
(Air conditioner harness side)

20Y1660

Description of Operation

The DC motor is operated, reversed or stopped according to the signals from ECU to control the position of blend air damper in combination with the potentiometer.

Troubleshooting Hints

ECU terminal voltage

Terminal No.	Signal	Condition	Terminal voltage
24	Blend air damper control motor	When motor (reverse) is ON	Approx. VB
		When motor is OFF	0 V
32	Blend air damper control motor	When motor (forward) is ON	0 V
		When motor is OFF	Approx. VB

NOTE
VB: Battery Voltage

DAMPER MOTORS CIRCUIT CHECK—CONQUEST

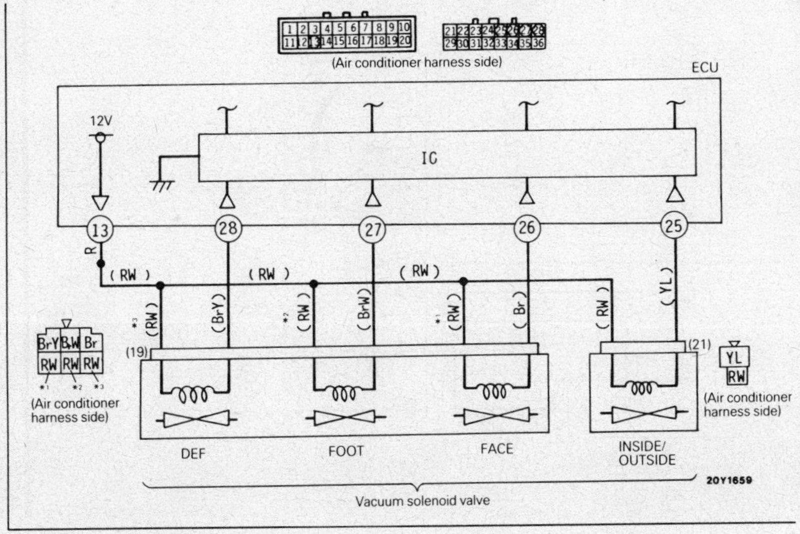
(Air conditioner harness side)
ECU
12V
IG
DEF
FOOT
FACE
INSIDE/
OUTSIDE
Vacuum solenoid valve
(Air conditioner harness side)
(Air conditioner harness side)
20Y1659

Description of Operation

Upon receipt of signals from ECU, the inside/outside air selection and air outlet mode selection are controlled by the vacuum actuator and link through the vacuum solenoid valve.

Troubleshooting Hints

ECU terminal voltage

Terminal No.	Signal	Condition	Terminal voltage
13	Vacuum solenoid valve power supply	–	Approx. VB
25	Inside/outside air switching vacuum solenoid valve	When ON (inside air)	Approx. 0.2 to 0.8V
		When OFF (outside air)	Approx. VB
26	Air outlet mode (FACE) selection vacuum solenoid valve	When ON (in FACE mode)	Approx. 0.2 to 0.8V
		When OFF (other than above)	Approx. VB
27	Air outlet mode (FOOT) selection vacuum solenoid valve	When ON (in FOOT or DEF mode)	Approx. 0.2 to 0.8V
		When OFF (other than above)	Approx. VB
28	Air outlet mode (DEF) selection vacuum solenoid valve	When ON (in DEF or DEF/FACE mode)	Approx. 0.2 to 0.8V
		When OFF (other than above)	Approx. VB

NOTE
VB: Battery Voltage

BLOWER MOTOR CIRCUIT CHECK—CONQUEST

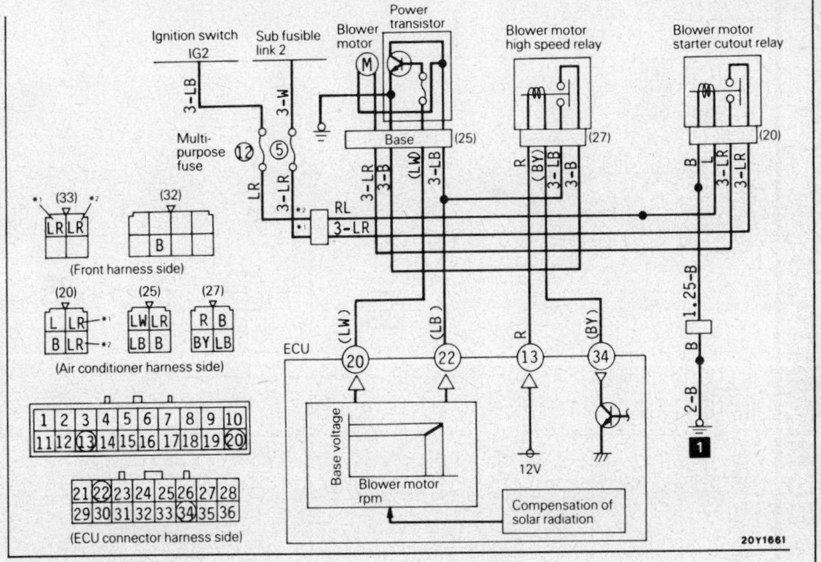
Ignition switch
IG2
Sub fusible link 2
Blower motor
Power transistor
Blower motor high speed relay
Blower motor starter cutout relay
Multi-purpose fuse
Base
(Front harness side)
(Air conditioner harness side)
(ECU connector harness side)
ECU
Base voltage
Blower motor rpm
12V
Compensation of solar radiation
20Y1661

Description of Operation

In accordance with the magnitude of the signal from ECU (voltage applied to the base terminal of the power transistor), this power transistor controls current flowing through the blower motor for control of blower moter operation.

For maximum operation (HI operation) in cooling, the signal to the power transistor is stopped and the blower motor HI relay is driven and battery voltage is applied directly to the blower motor to run the blower motor at the maximum speed (HI operation).

Troubleshooting Hints

ECU terminal voltage

Terminal No.	Signal	Condition	Terminal voltage
13	Blower motor high speed relay power supply	At all times	Approx. VB
20	Power transistor (base)	When blower is rotating	0 to 5 V
22	Blower motor	When switch HI is ON	Approx. 0 to 1 V
		When switch LO is ON	Approx. 6 V
		When switch is OFF	Approx. VB
34	Blower motor high speed relay	When blower speed is HI	Approx. 0.2 to 0.8V
		When blower speed is other than HI	Approx. VB

NOTE
VB: Battery Voltage

WIRING SCHEMATICS

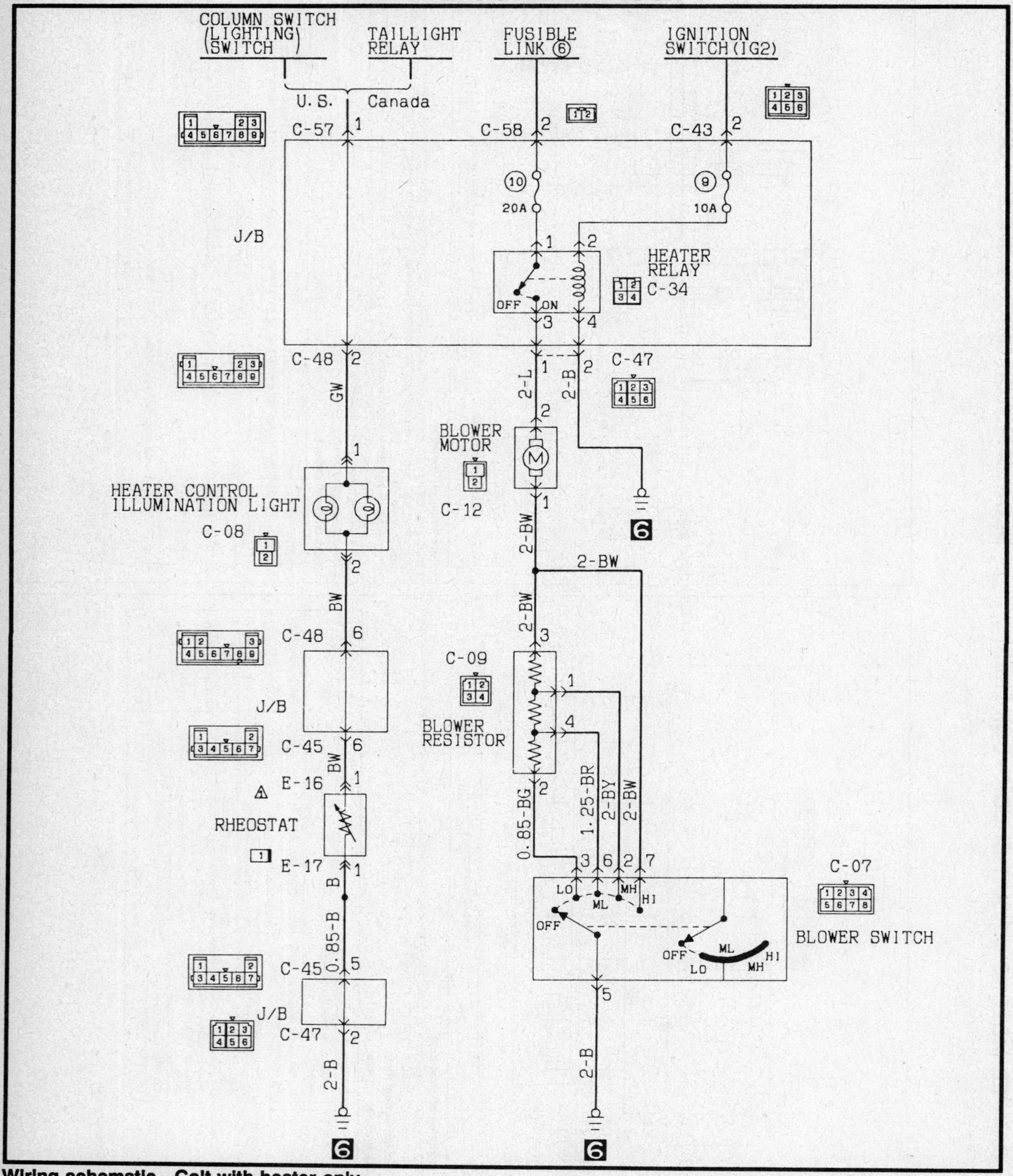
COLUMN SWITCH (LIGHTING SWITCH)
TAILLIGHT RELAY
FUSIBLE LINK ⑥
IGNITION SWITCH (IG2)
U.S.
Canada
C-57
C-58
C-43
J/B
20A
10A
HEATER RELAY
C-34
OFF
ON
C-48
C-47
GW
2-L
2-B
BLOWER MOTOR
C-12
HEATER CONTROL ILLUMINATION LIGHT
C-08
2-BW
BW
C-09
BLOWER RESISTOR
C-45
E-16
RHEOSTAT
E-17
B
0.85-B
0.85-BG
1.25-BR
2-BY
LO
ML
MH
HI
BLOWER SWITCH
C-07

Wiring schematic—Colt with heater only

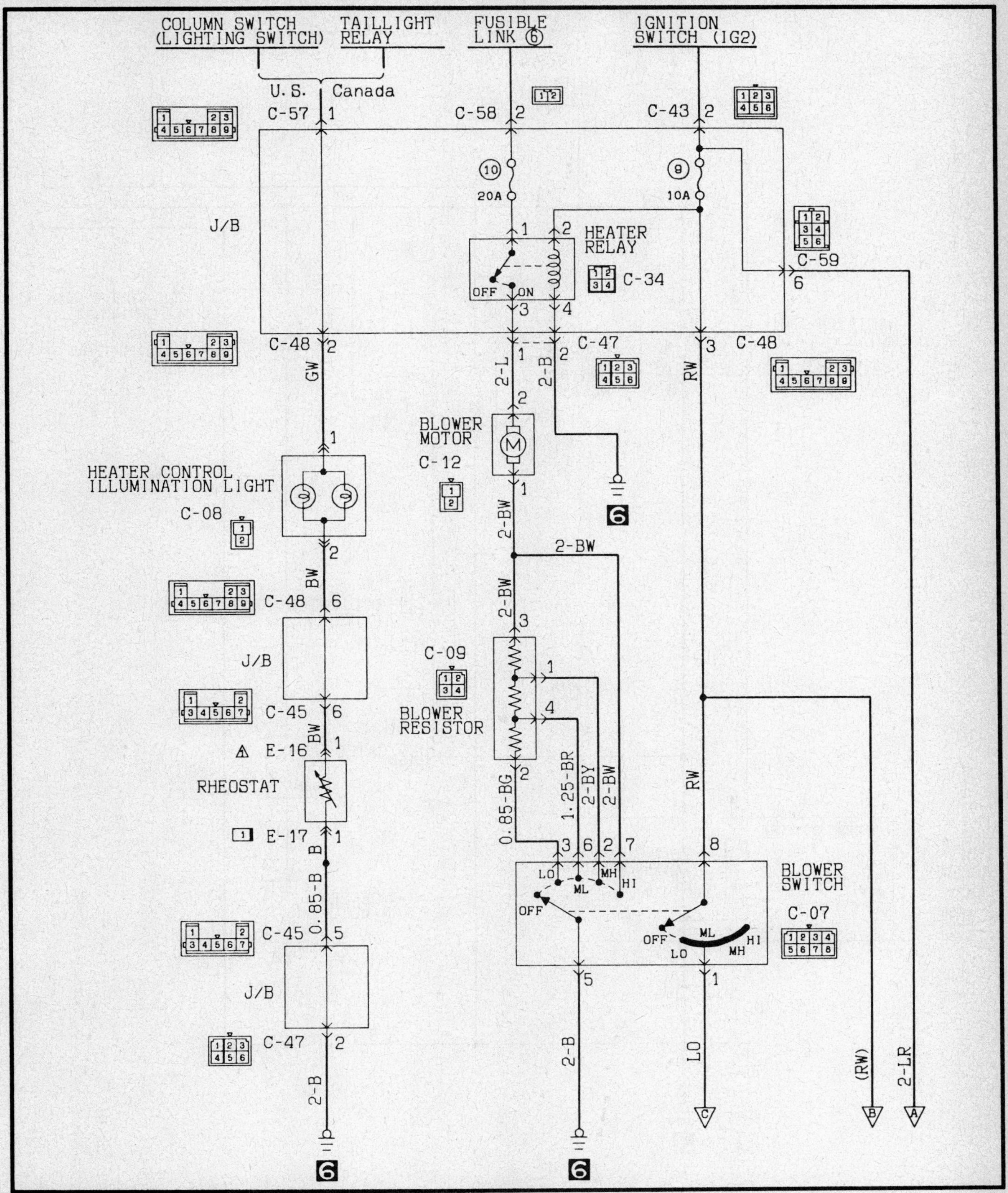
COLUMN SWITCH (LIGHTING SWITCH)
TAILLIGHT RELAY
FUSIBLE LINK ⑥
IGNITION SWITCH (IG2)
U.S.
Canada
C-57
C-58
C-43
J/B
20A
10A
HEATER RELAY
OFF
ON
C-34
C-59
C-48
C-47
GW
2-L
2-B
RW
BLOWER MOTOR
C-12
HEATER CONTROL ILLUMINATION LIGHT
C-08
2-BW
BW
C-09
BLOWER RESISTOR
C-45
E-16
RHEOSTAT
E-17
B
0.85-B
0.85-BG
1.25-BR
2-BY
LO
ML
MH
HI
BLOWER SWITCH
C-07
(RW)
2-LR

Wiring schematic—Colt with air conditioning—1.5L engine

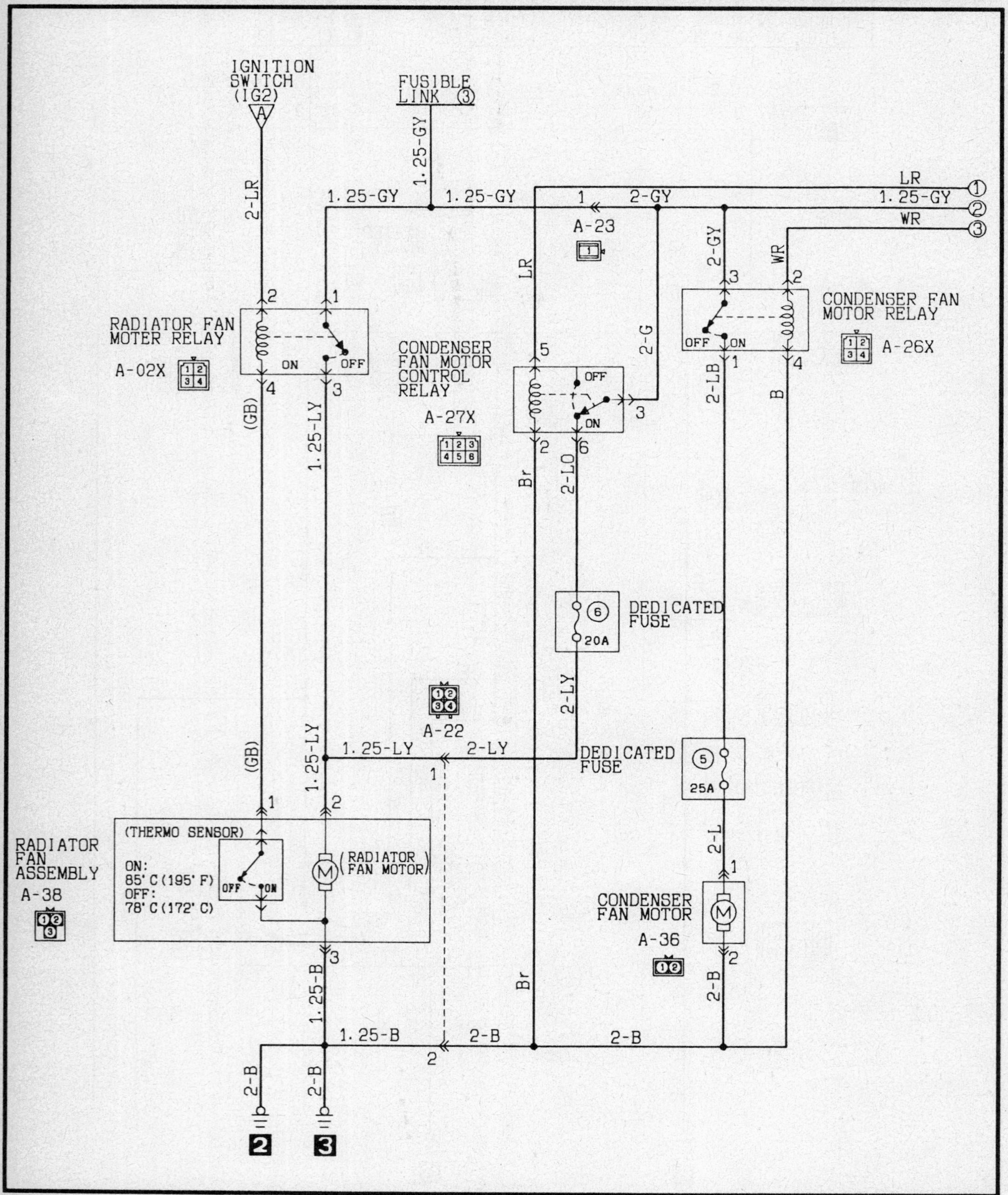
IGNITION SWITCH (IG2)
A
FUSIBLE LINK ③
2-LR
1.25-GY
1.25-GY
1.25-GY
1
2-GY
LR
1.25-GY
WR
①
②
③
A-23
LR
2-GY
WR
RADIATOR FAN MOTER RELAY
A-02X
ON
OFF
CONDENSER FAN MOTOR CONTROL RELAY
A-27X
CONDENSER FAN MOTOR RELAY
A-26X
OFF
ON
2-G
2-LB
B
(GB)
1.25-LY
Br
2-LO
DEDICATED FUSE
20A
2-LY
A-22
1.25-LY
2-LY
DEDICATED FUSE
25A
2-L
RADIATOR FAN ASSEMBLY
A-38
(THERMO SENSOR)
ON:
85°C (195°F)
OFF:
78°C (172°C)
(RADIATOR FAN MOTOR)
CONDENSER FAN MOTOR
A-36
1.25-B
1.25-B
2-B
2-B
2-B
2-B
2-B

Wiring schematic—Colt with air conditioning—1.5L engine

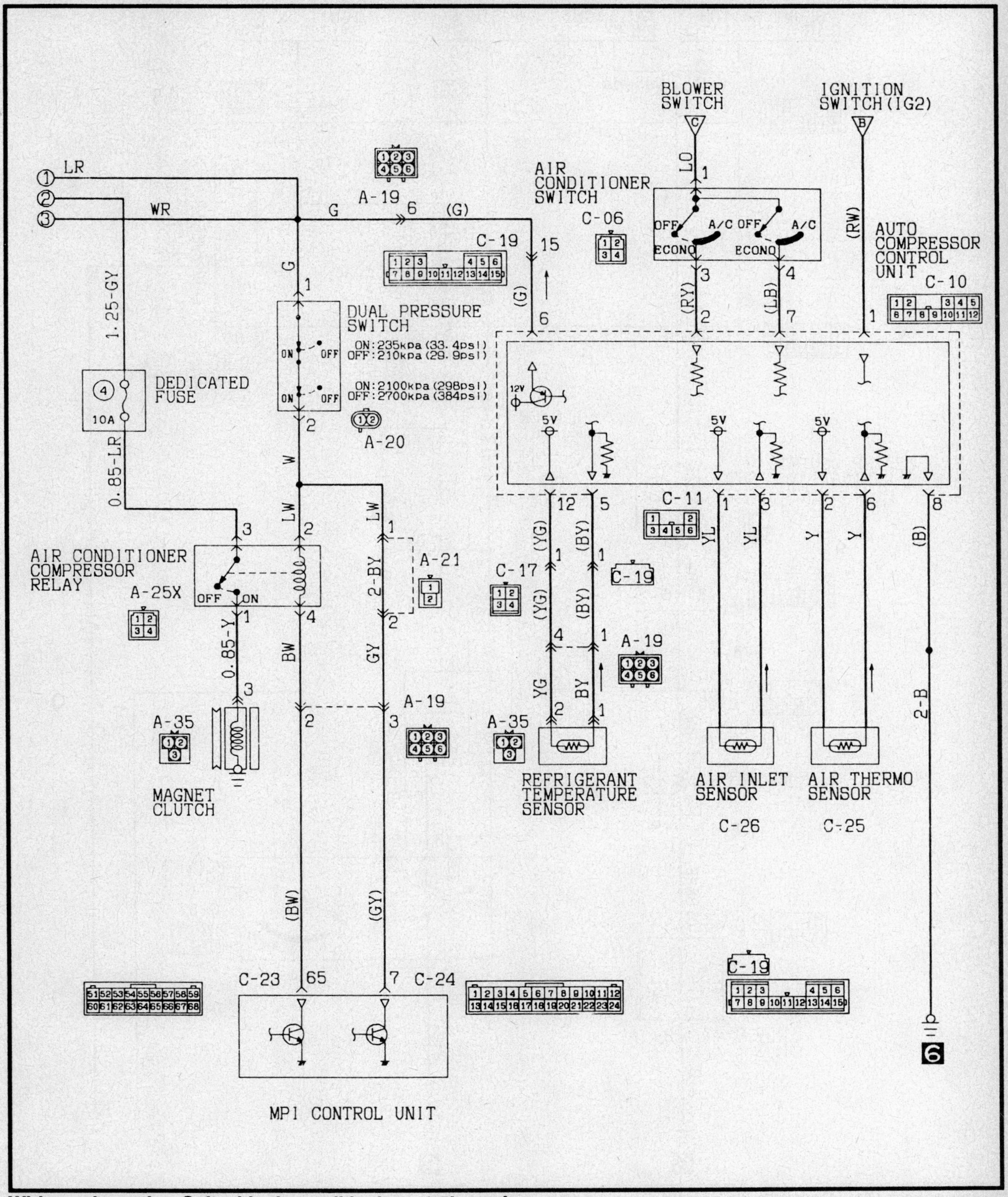
BLOWER SWITCH
IGNITION SWITCH (IG2)
AIR CONDITIONER SWITCH
AUTO COMPRESSOR CONTROL UNIT
DUAL PRESSURE SWITCH
ON:235kpa(33.4psi)
OFF:210kpa(29.9psi)
ON:2100kpa(298psi)
OFF:2700kpa(384psi)
DEDICATED FUSE
10A
AIR CONDITIONER COMPRESSOR RELAY
A-25X
MAGNET CLUTCH
REFRIGERANT TEMPERATURE SENSOR
AIR INLET SENSOR
C-26
AIR THERMO SENSOR
C-25
MPI CONTROL UNIT
C-23
C-24
A-19
A-20
A-21
A-35
C-06
C-10
C-11
C-17
C-19

Wiring schematic – Colt with air conditioning – 1.5L engine

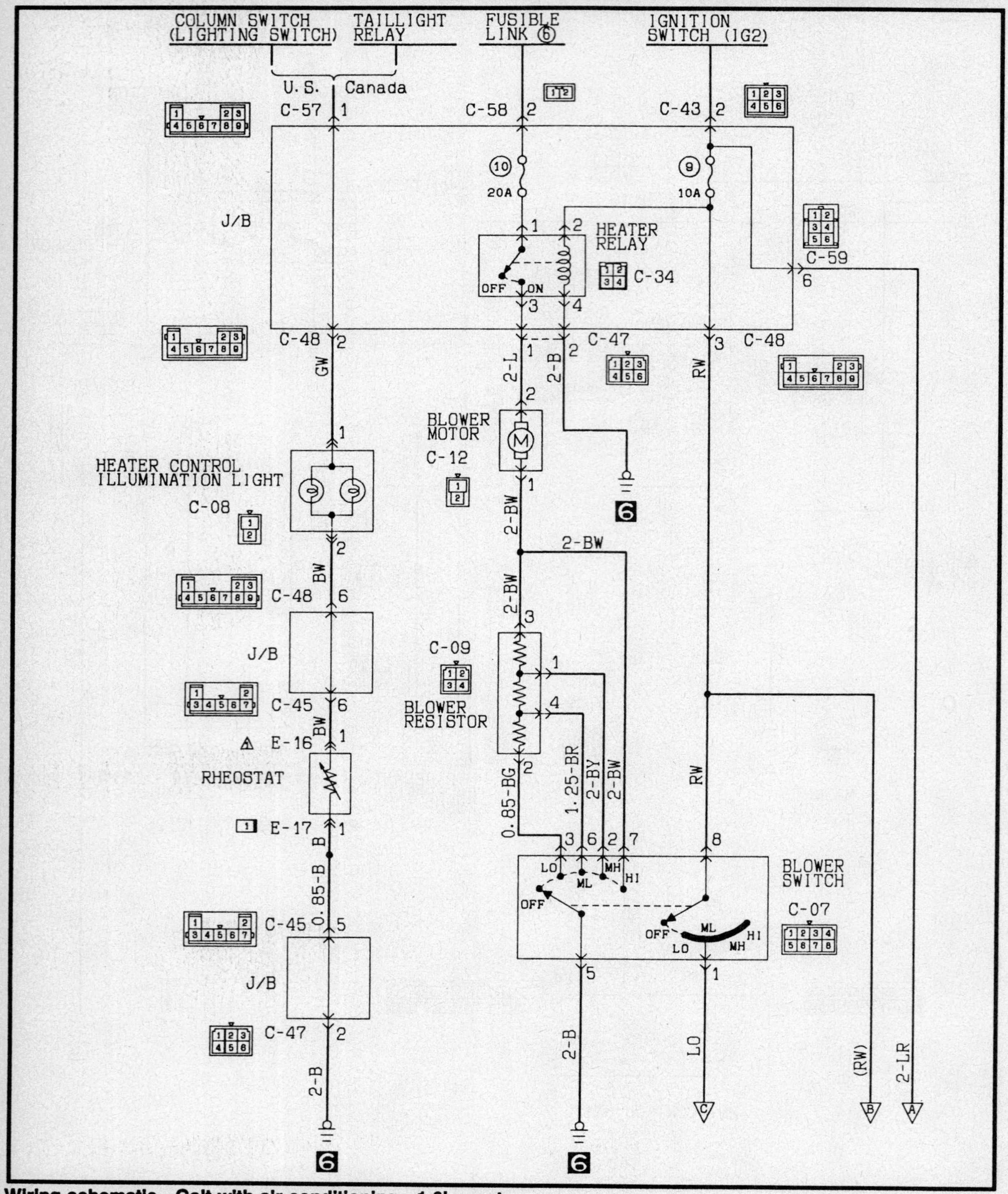
COLUMN SWITCH (LIGHTING SWITCH)
TAILLIGHT RELAY
FUSIBLE LINK ⑥
IGNITION SWITCH (IG2)
U.S.
Canada
C-57
C-58
C-43
J/B
20A
10A
HEATER RELAY
OFF
ON
C-34
C-59
C-48
C-47
GW
2-L
2-B
RW
BLOWER MOTOR
C-12
HEATER CONTROL ILLUMINATION LIGHT
C-08
2-BW
BW
C-09
BLOWER RESISTOR
C-45
E-16
RHEOSTAT
E-17
B
0.85-B
0.85-BG
1.25-BR
2-BY
LO
ML
MH
HI
BLOWER SWITCH
C-07
LO
(RW)
2-LR

Wiring schematic – Colt with air conditioning – 1.6L engine

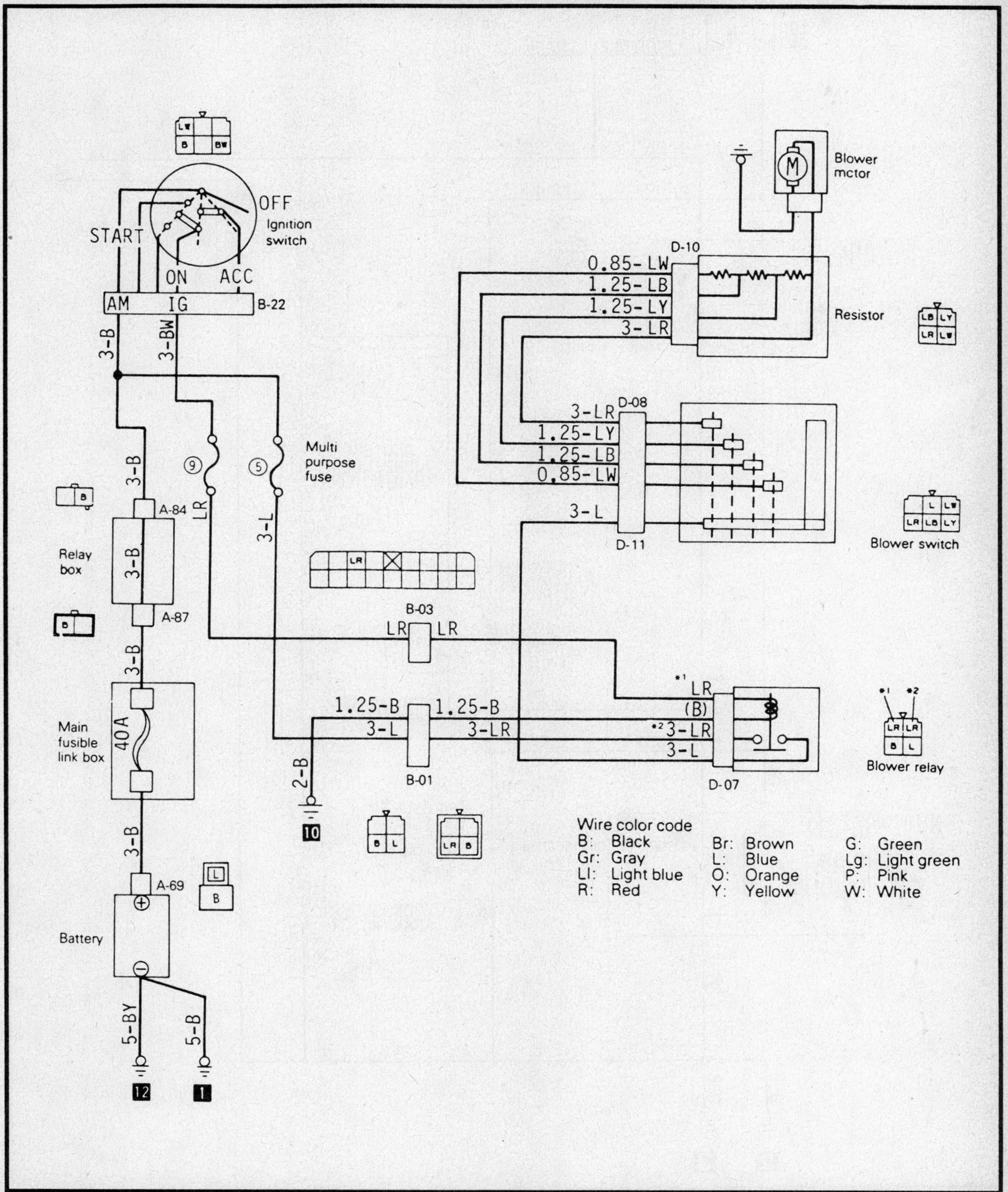
OFF
Ignition switch
START
ON
ACC
AM
IG
B-22
3-B
3-BW
Multi purpose fuse
9
5
LR
3-L
A-84
Relay box
A-87
Main fusible link box
40A
A-69
Battery
5-BY
5-B
12
1
2-B
10
Blower motor
M
D-10
0.85-LW
1.25-LB
1.25-LY
3-LR
Resistor
D-08
D-11
3-L
Blower switch
B-03
B-01
1.25-B
D-07
(B)
*1
*2
Blower relay
Wire color code
B: Black
Gr: Gray
LI: Light blue
R: Red
Br: Brown
L: Blue
O: Orange
Y: Yellow
G: Green
Lg: Light green
P: Pink
W: White

Wiring schematic—Colt Vista with heater only

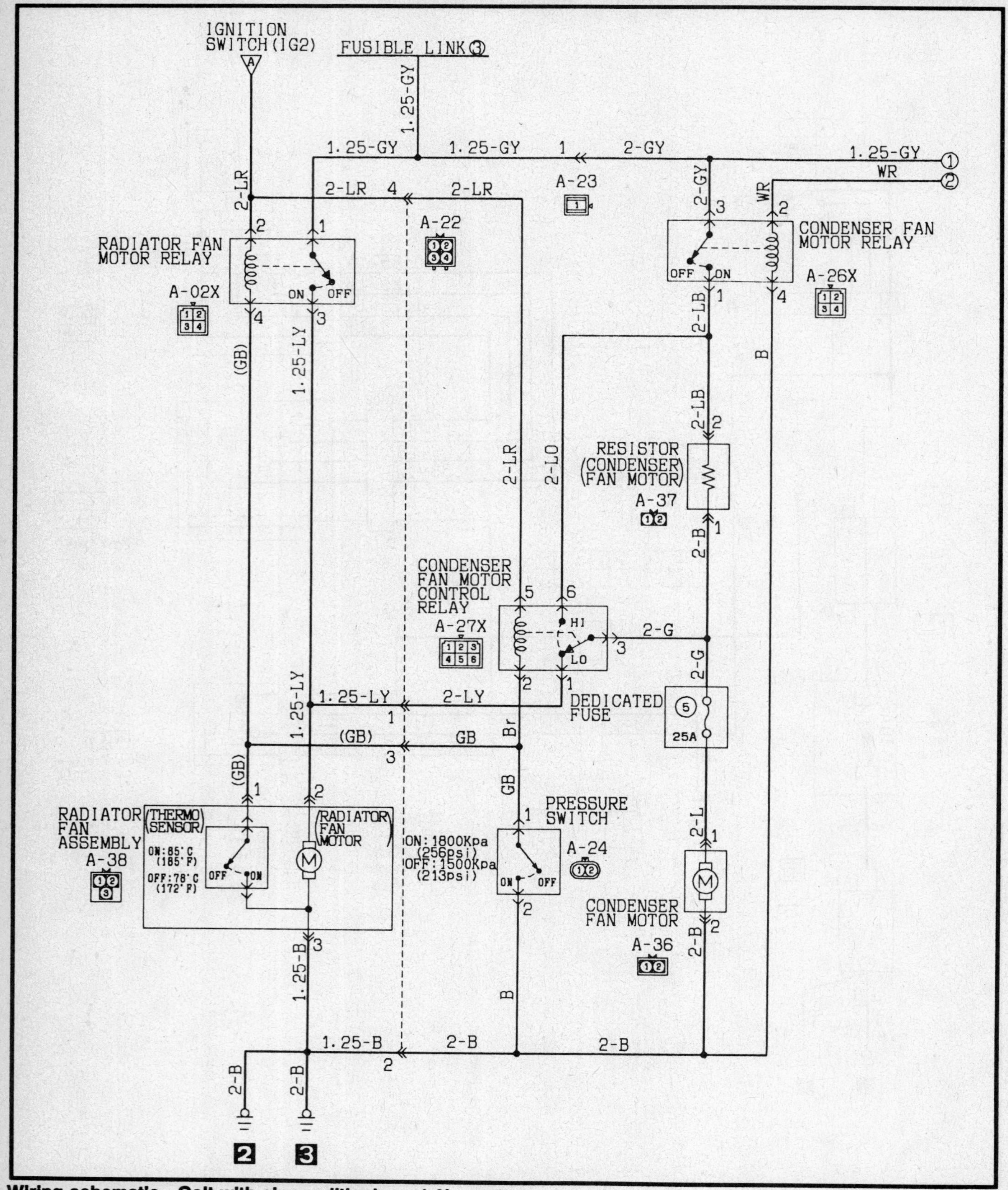
IGNITION SWITCH (IG2)
FUSIBLE LINK ③
1.25-GY
2-GY
2-LR
A-23
A-22
RADIATOR FAN MOTOR RELAY
A-02X
ON
OFF
CONDENSER FAN MOTOR RELAY
A-26X
WR
2-LB
(GB)
1.25-LY
B
RESISTOR (CONDENSER FAN MOTOR)
A-37
2-LO
2-B
CONDENSER FAN MOTOR CONTROL RELAY
A-27X
HI
LO
2-G
2-LY
DEDICATED FUSE
25A
GB
Br
PRESSURE SWITCH
A-24
ON:1800Kpa (256psi)
OFF:1500Kpa (213psi)
RADIATOR FAN ASSEMBLY
A-38
THERMO SENSOR
ON:85°C (185°F)
OFF:78°C (172°F)
RADIATOR FAN MOTOR
2-L
CONDENSER FAN MOTOR
A-36
1.25-B
2 3

Wiring schematic—Colt with air conditioning—1.6L engine

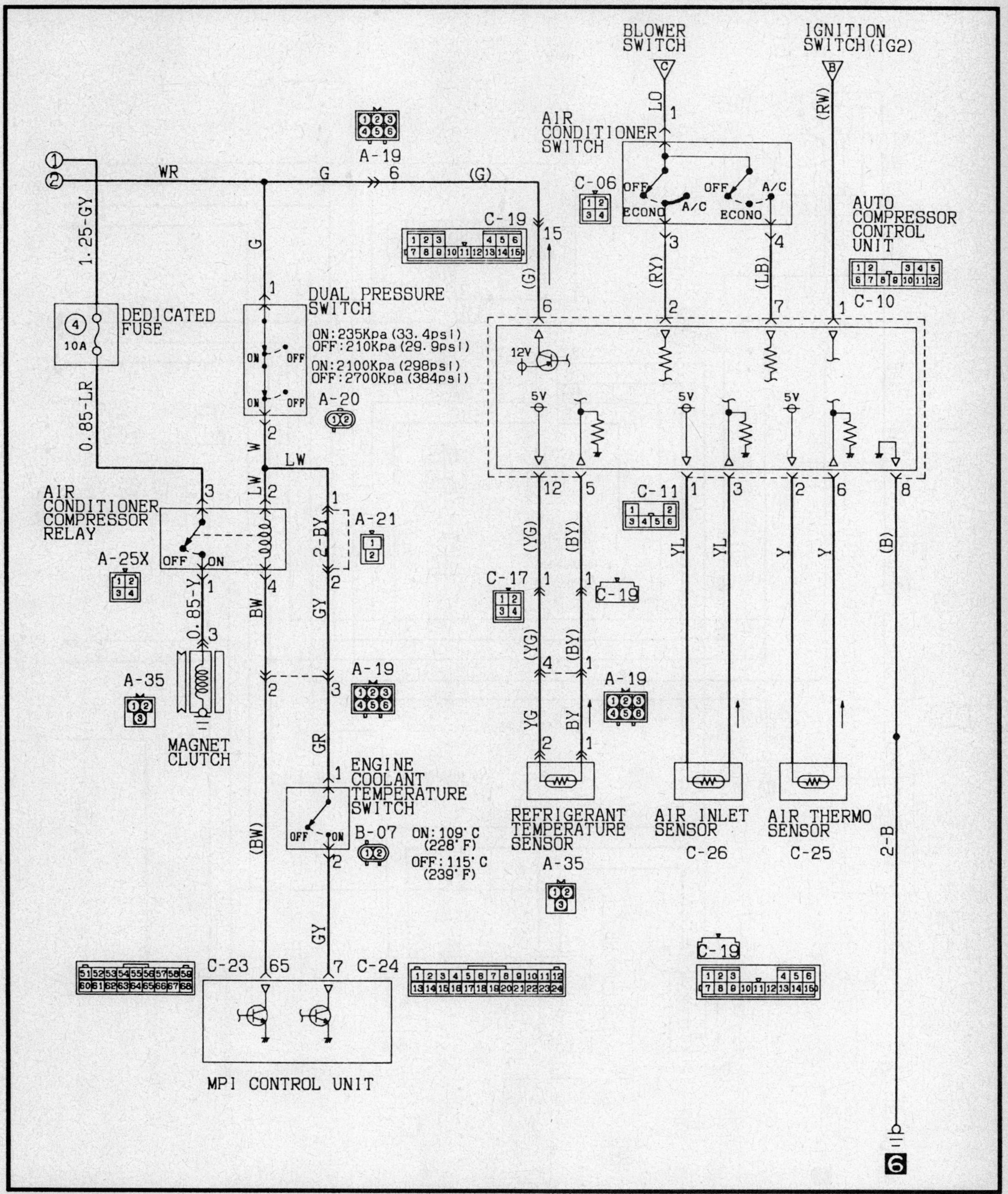
BLOWER SWITCH
IGNITION SWITCH (IG2)
AIR CONDITIONER SWITCH
A-19
C-06
C-19
AUTO COMPRESSOR CONTROL UNIT
C-10
DEDICATED FUSE
10A
DUAL PRESSURE SWITCH
ON:235Kpa (33.4psi)
OFF:210Kpa (29.9psi)
ON:2100Kpa (298psi)
OFF:2700Kpa (384psi)
A-20
AIR CONDITIONER COMPRESSOR RELAY
A-25X
A-21
C-11
C-17
A-35
MAGNET CLUTCH
ENGINE COOLANT TEMPERATURE SWITCH
B-07
ON:109°C (228°F)
OFF:115°C (239°F)
REFRIGERANT TEMPERATURE SENSOR
AIR INLET SENSOR
AIR THERMO SENSOR
C-26
C-25
C-23
C-24
MPI CONTROL UNIT

Wiring schematic – Colt with air conditioning – 1.6L engine

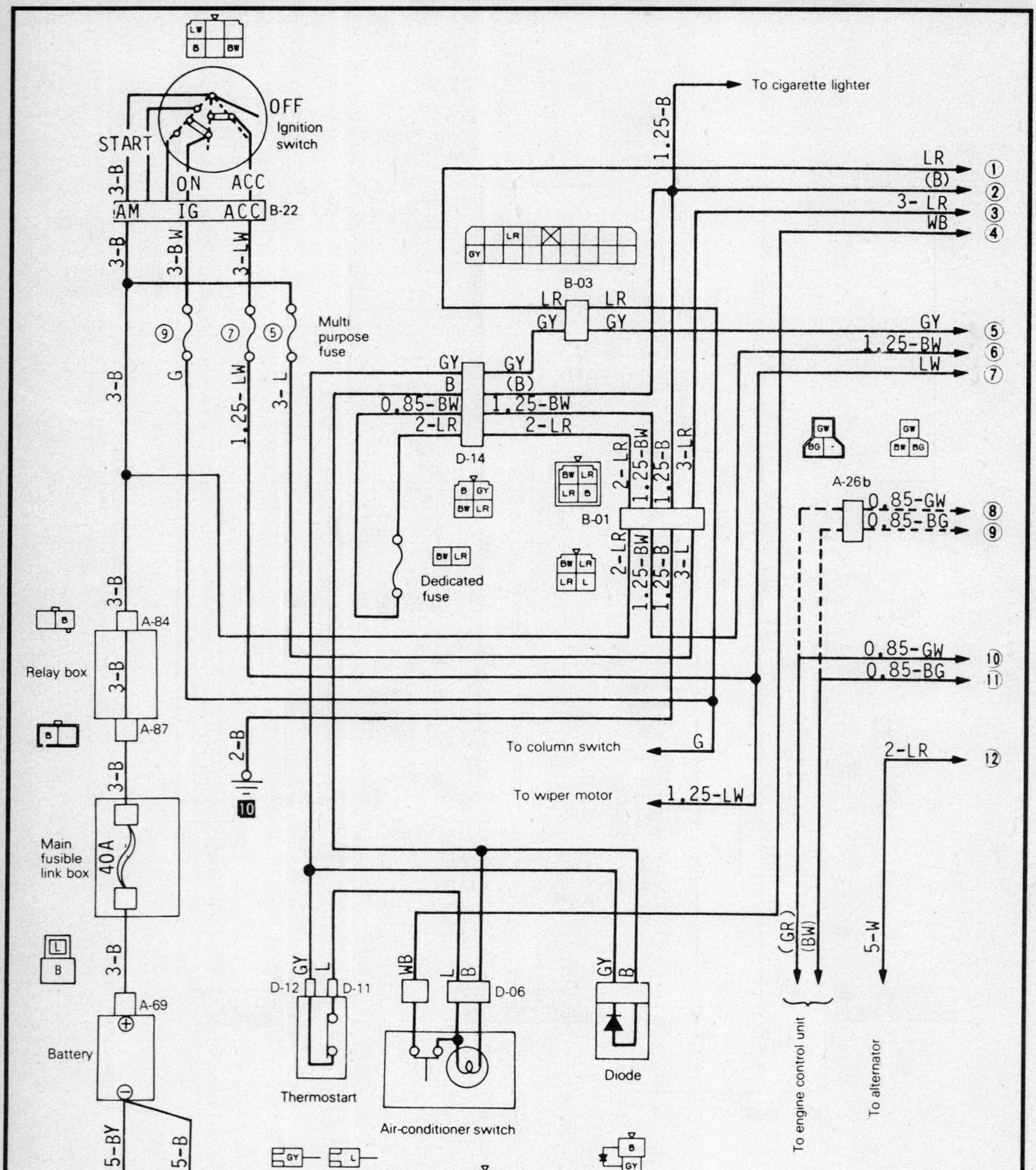
OFF
Ignition switch
START
ON
ACC
AM
IG
ACC
B-22
3-B
3-BW
3-LW
Multi purpose fuse
9
7
5
G
1.25-LW
3-L
To cigarette lighter
1.25-B
LR
(B)
3- LR
WB
1
2
3
4
B-03
GY
5
6
7
1.25-BW
LW
D-14
B
0.85-BW
2-LR
Dedicated fuse
B-01
2-LR
1.25-BW
1.25-B
3-LR
A-26b
0.85-GW
0.85-BG
8
9
10
11
12
A-84
Relay box
A-87
2-B
To column switch
To wiper motor
1.25-LW
2-LR
Main fusible link box
40A
A-69
Battery
5-BY
5-B
D-12
D-11
Thermostart
D-06
Air-conditioner switch
Diode
(GR)
(BW)
5-W
To engine control unit
To alternator
Wiring schematic—Colt Vista with air conditioning

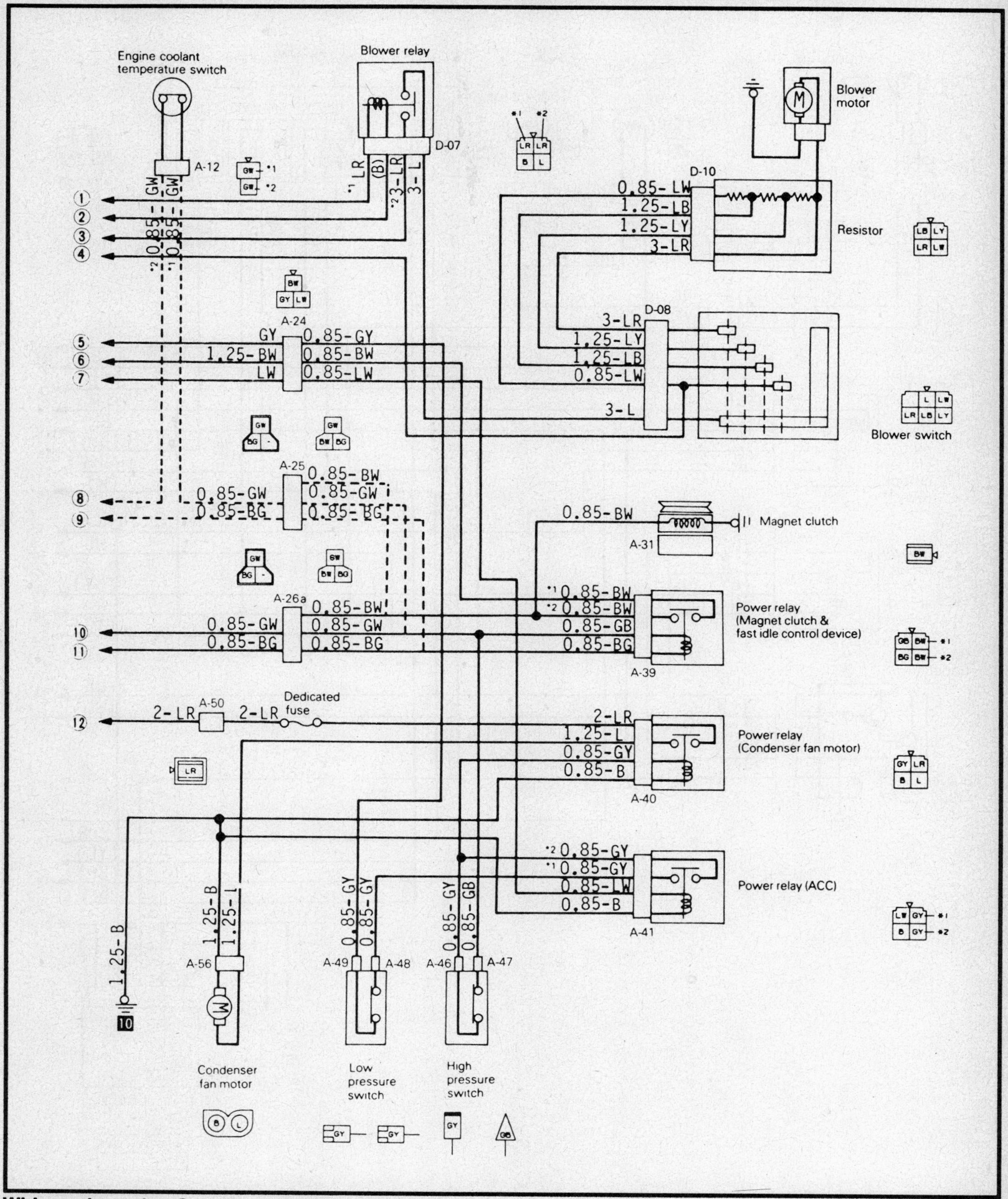
Engine coolant temperature switch
Blower relay
D-07
Blower motor
A-12
D-10
0.85-LW
1.25-LB
1.25-LY
3-LR
Resistor
D-08
Blower switch
A-24
A-25
A-26a
A-31
Magnet clutch
Power relay (Magnet clutch & fast idle control device)
A-39
A-50
Dedicated fuse
Power relay (Condenser fan motor)
A-40
Power relay (ACC)
A-41
A-56
A-49
A-48
A-46
A-47
Condenser fan motor
Low pressure switch
High pressure switch

Wiring schematic—Colt Vista with air conditioning

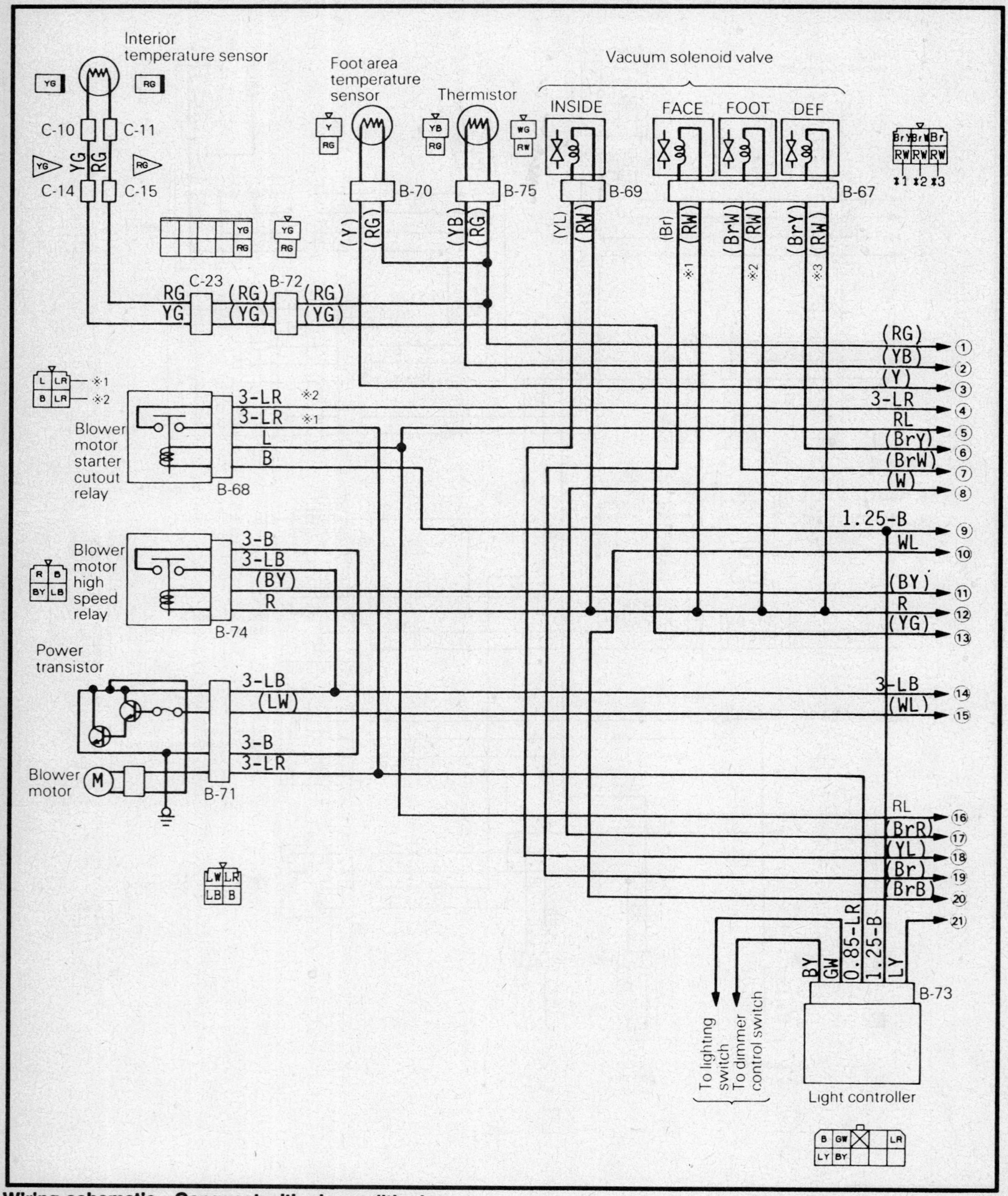
Interior temperature sensor
YG
RG
C-10
C-11
C-14
C-15
Foot area temperature sensor
Thermistor
Vacuum solenoid valve
INSIDE
FACE
FOOT
DEF
B-70
B-75
B-69
B-67
(Y)
(RG)
(YB)
(YL)
(RW)
(Br)
(BrW)
(BrY)
※1
※2
※3
C-23
B-72
(YG)
Blower motor starter cutout relay
B-68
3-LR
L
B
Blower motor high speed relay
B-74
3-B
3-LB
(BY)
R
Power transistor
(LW)
Blower motor
B-71
RL
(W)
1.25-B
WL
(WL)
(BrR)
(BrB)
BY
GW
0.85-LR
LY
B-73
To lighting switch
To dimmer control switch
Light controller

Wiring schematic—Conquest with air conditioning

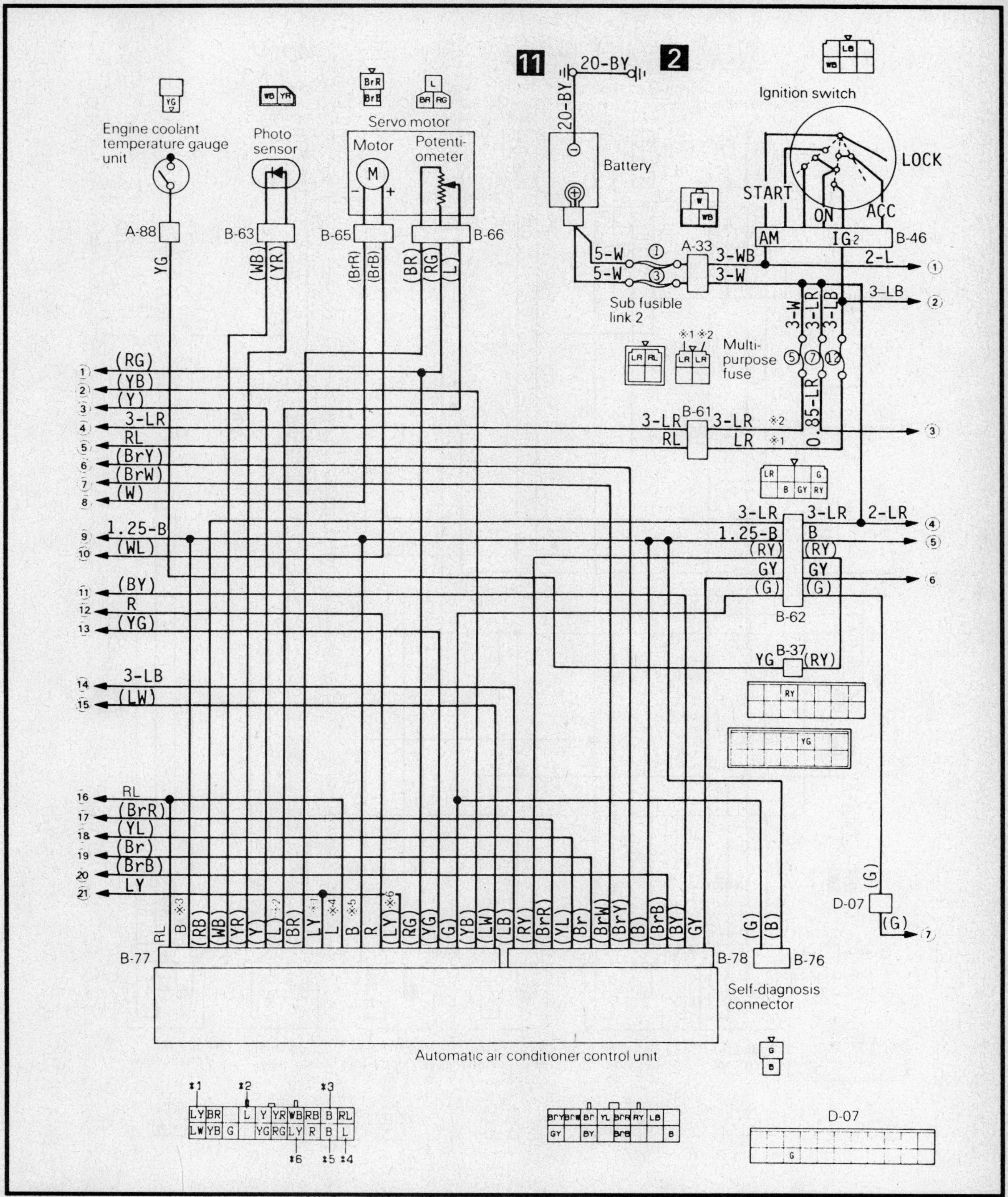
Engine coolant temperature gauge unit
Photo sensor
Servo motor
Motor
Potentiometer
Battery
Ignition switch
LOCK
START
ON
ACC
Sub fusible link 2
Multi-purpose fuse
Self-diagnosis connector
Automatic air conditioner control unit
A-88
B-63
B-65
B-66
A-33
B-46
B-61
B-62
B-37
B-77
B-78
B-76
D-07

Wiring schematic—Conquest with air conditioning

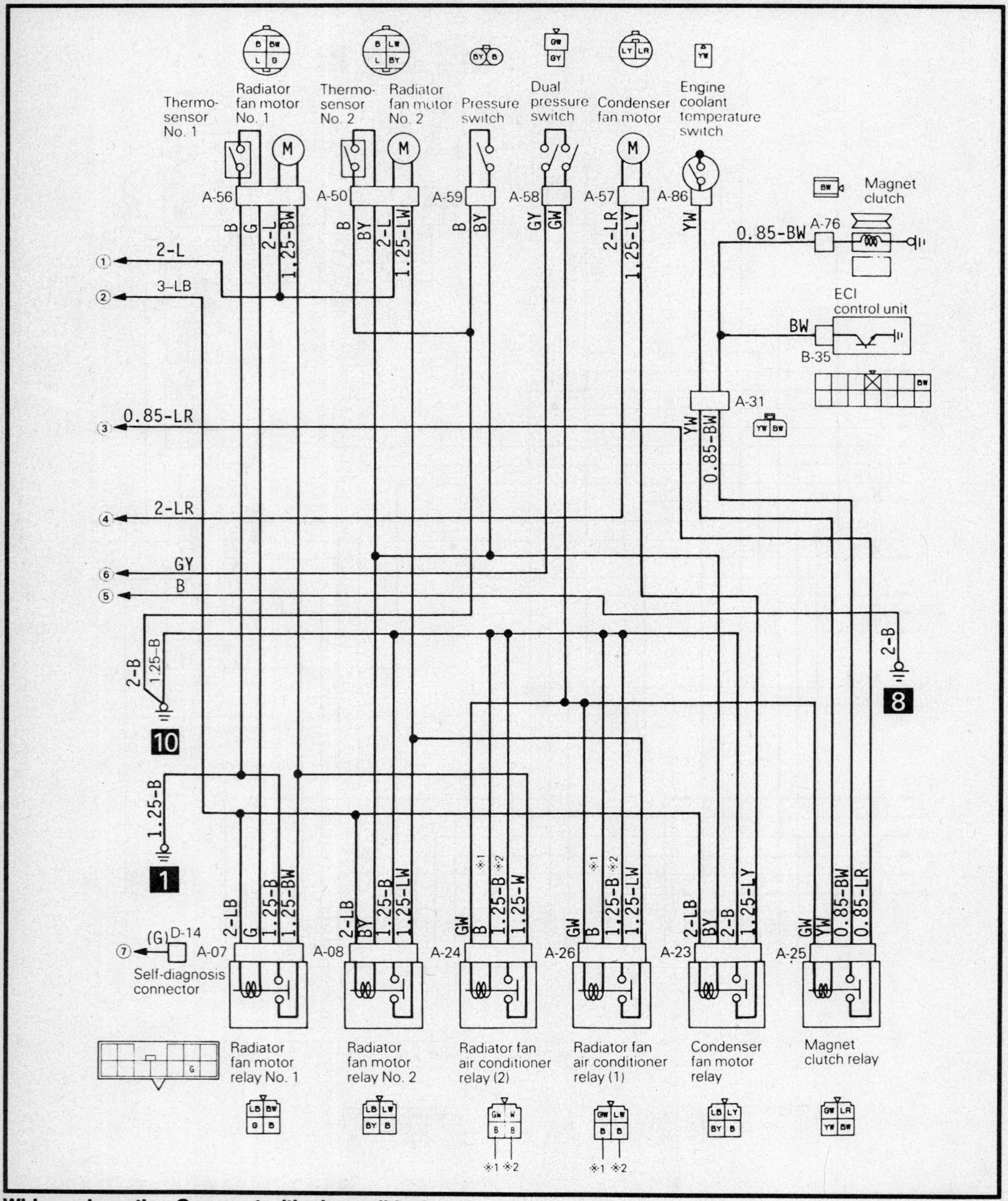
Thermo-sensor No. 1
Radiator fan motor No. 1
Thermo-sensor No. 2
Radiator fan motor No. 2
Pressure switch
Dual pressure switch
Condenser fan motor
Engine coolant temperature switch
Magnet clutch
ECI control unit
Self-diagnosis connector
Radiator fan motor relay No. 1
Radiator fan motor relay No. 2
Radiator fan air conditioner relay (2)
Radiator fan air conditioner relay (1)
Condenser fan motor relay
Magnet clutch relay
A-56
A-50
A-59
A-58
A-57
A-86
A-76
B-35
A-31
D-14
A-07
A-08
A-24
A-26
A-23
A-25
2-L
3-LB
0.85-LR
2-LR
GY
B
0.85-BW
BW
YW
2-B
1.25-B
10
8
1

Wiring schematic—Conquest with air conditioning

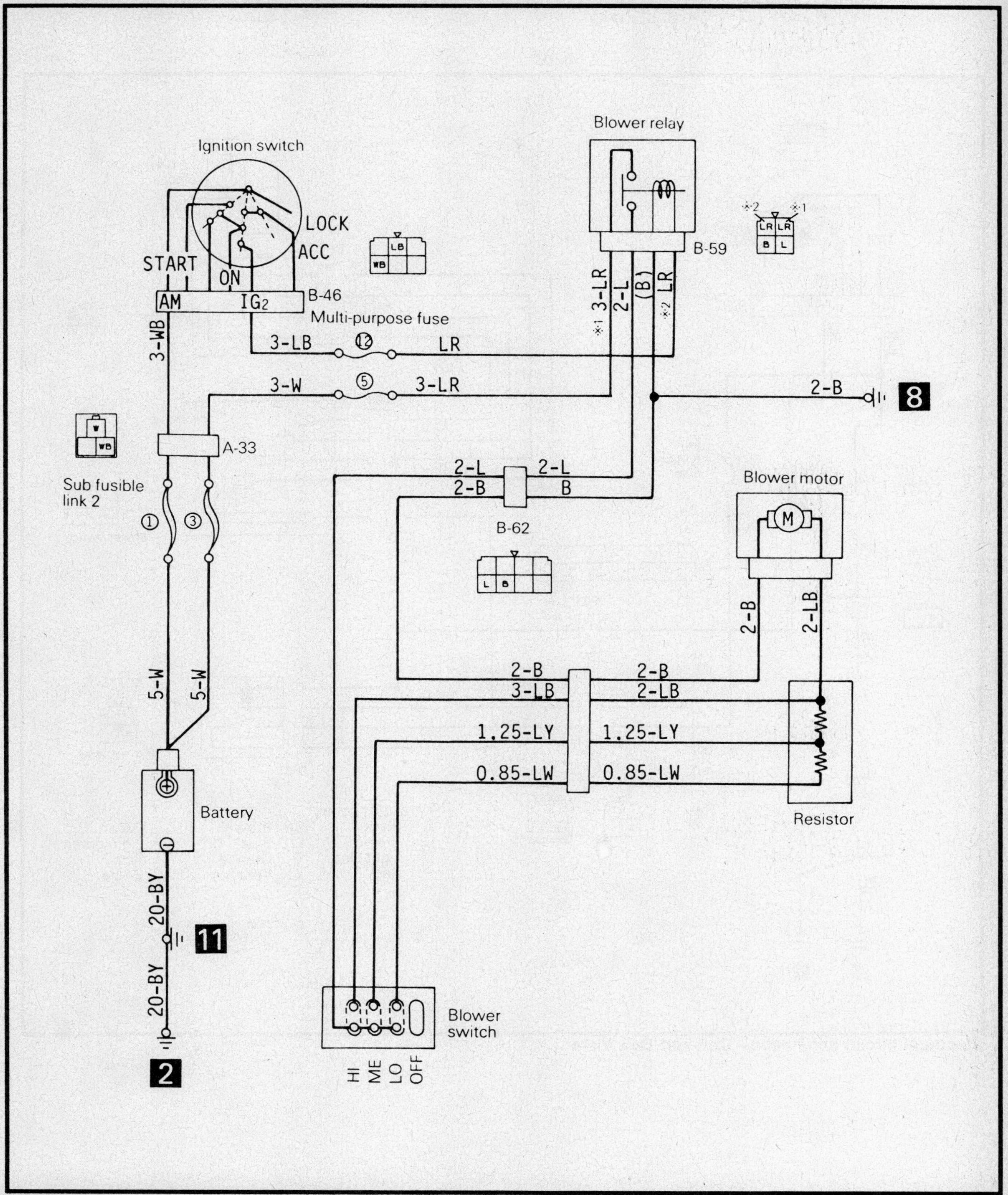
Blower relay
Ignition switch
LOCK
ACC
START
ON
AM
IG2
B-46
Multi-purpose fuse
B-59
3-LR
2-L
(B)
LR
3-WB
3-LB
LR
3-W
3-LR
2-B
8
A-33
Sub fusible link 2
2-L
2-B
2-L
B
B-62
Blower motor
2-B
2-LB
5-W
5-W
2-B
3-LB
2-B
2-LB
1.25-LY
1.25-LY
0.85-LW
0.85-LW
Battery
Resistor
20-BY
11
20-BY
2
Blower switch
HI
ME
LO
OFF

Wiring schematic—Conquest with heater only

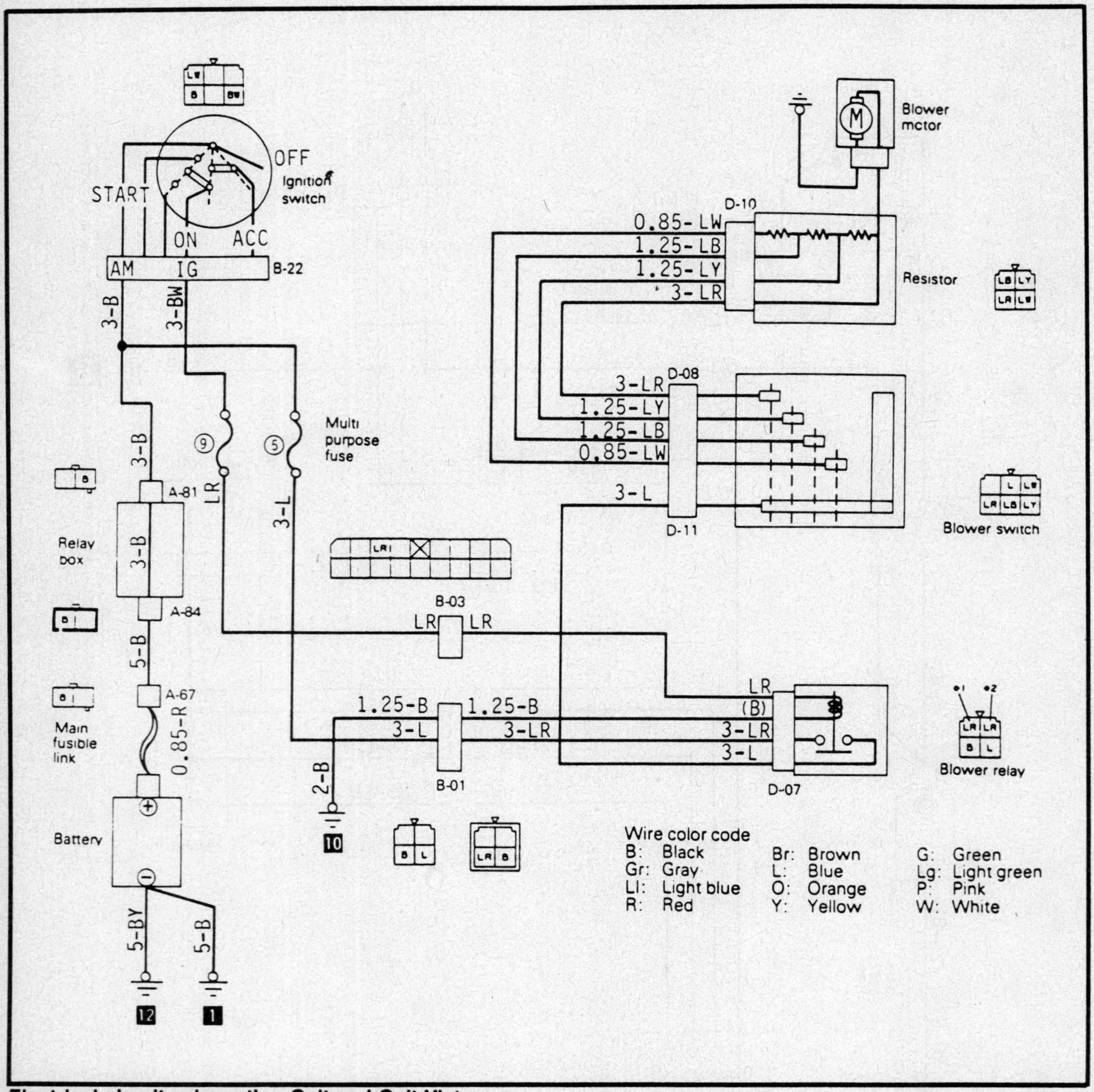
Ignition switch
OFF
START
ON
ACC
AM
IG
B-22
3-B
3-BW
Multi purpose fuse
9
5
LR
3-L
A-81
Relay box
A-84
5-B
A-67
Main fusible link
0.85-R
Battery
5-BY
5-B
12
1
B-03
B-01
1.25-B
3-LR
2-B
10
Blower motor
D-10
0.85-LW
1.25-LB
1.25-LY
Resistor
D-08
D-11
Blower switch
D-07
(B)
Blower relay
Wire color code
B: Black
Gr: Gray
Ll: Light blue
R: Red
Br: Brown
L: Blue
O: Orange
Y: Yellow
G: Green
Lg: Light green
P: Pink
W: White

Electrical circuit schematic – Colt and Colt Vista

15 GEO 15

METRO • PRIZM • SPECTRUM • STORM • TRACKER

SPECIFICATIONS

ENGINE IDENTIFICATION

Year	Model	Engine Displacement cu. in. (cc/liter)	Engine Series Identification	No. of Cylinders	Engine Type
1989	Tracker	97 (1590/1.6)	U	4	SOHC
	Metro	61 (1000/1.0)	5	3	SOHC
	Prizm	97 (1590/1.6)	6	4	SOHC
	Spectrum	90 (1475/1.5)	7	4	SOHC
1990	Tracker	97 (1590/1.6)	U	4	SOHC
	Metro	61 (1000/1.0)	5	3	SOHC
	Prizm	97 (1590/1.6)	6	4	SOHC
	Prizm	97 (1590/1.6)	5	4	DOHC
	Storm	97 (1590/1.6)	5	4	SOHC
	Storm	97 (1590/1.6)	6	4	DOHC
1991	Tracker	97 (1590/1.6)	U	4	SOHC
	Metro	61 (1000/1.0)	6	3	SOHC
	Prizm	97 (1590/1.6)	6	4	SOHC
	Prizm	97 (1590/1.6)	5	4	DOHC
	Storm	97 (1590/1.6)	5	4	SOHC
	Storm	97 (1590/1.6)	6	4	DOHC

SOHC—Single Overhead Cam
DOHC—Dual Overhead Cam

REFRIGERANT CAPACITIES

Year	Model	Freon (oz.)	Oil (fl. oz.)	Type ①
1989	Tracker	21.2	3.40	A-10
	Metro	17.6	3.40	A-10
	Prizm	21–27	3.35	Rotary
	Spectrum	28.23	3.35	DKS-13G
1990	Tracker	21.0	3.40	A-10
	Metro	17.6	3.40	A-10
	Prizm	21.0–27.0	3.35	Rotary
	Storm	21.0–27.0	7.10	KC-50
1991	Tracker	21.0	3.40	A-10
	Metro	17.6	3.40	A-10
	Prizm	21.0–27.0	3.35	Rotary
	Storm	21.0–27.0	7.10	KC-50

① Compressor

AIR CONDITIONING BELT TENSION CHART

Year	Model	Engine Displacement cu. in. (cc/liter)	Belt Type	New ①	Used ①
1989	Tracker	97 (1590/1.6)	V-belt	264	200
	Metro	61 (1000/1.0)	Serpentine	264	200
	Prizm	97 (1590/1.6)	Serpentine	160–185	100–120
	Spectrum	90 (1475/1.5)	V-belt	70-110	60–100

AIR CONDITIONING BELT TENSION CHART

Year	Model	Engine Displacement cu. in. (cc/liter)	Belt Type	New ①	Used ①
1990	Tracker	97 (1590/1.6)	V-belt	264	200
	Metro	61 (1000/1.0)	Serpentine	264	200
	Prizm	97 (1590/1.6)	Serpentine	160–185	100–120
	Storm	97 (1590/1.6)	Serpentine	130–160	100–140
1991	Tracker	97 (1590/1.6)	V-belt	264	200
	Metro	61 (1000/1.0)	Serpentine	264	200
	Prizm	97 (1590/1.6)	Serpentine	140–180	80–120
	Storm	97 (1590/1.6)	Serpentine	130–160	100–120

① Check the compressor drive belt using tool J-23600-B or an equivalent belt tension gauge. The measurements are in lbs.

SYSTEM DESCRIPTION

General Information

The compressor is driven by a drive belt from the engine crankshaft through an electromagnetic clutch. When voltage is applied to energize the clutch coil, a clutch plate and hub assembly are drawn rearward toward the pulley. As the compressor shaft turns, the compressor performs 2 functions. One is to compress the low pressure refrigerant vapor from the evaporator into a high pressure/temperature vapor. The other function is to pump refrigerant oil through the system to lubricate all components.

The condenser is mounted in front of the radiator and is comprised of small coils and cooling fins. When the high pressure/temperature vapor, from the compressor, enters the condenser, heat is transferred from the refrigerant to the air passing through the front of the vehicle. The refrigerant is cooled and condensed into a liquid.

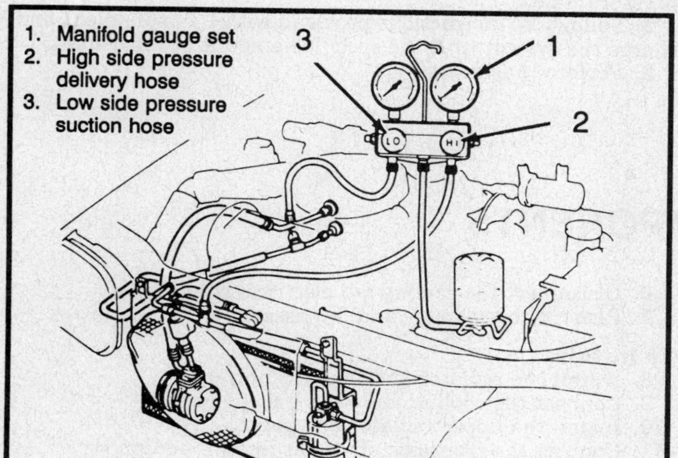
1. Manifold gauge set
2. High side pressure delivery hose
3. Low side pressure suction hose
3
1
2
LO
HI
Charging the air conditioning system

The receiver/drier is mounted on the fender and is connected to the condenser outlet and evaporator inlet. The receiver/drier is a temporary storage container for condensed liquid refrigerant, a filter which removes moisture and contaminants from the system and it incorporates a sight glass for checking the system's refrigerant charge.

The expansion valve regulates the flow of liquid refrigerant into the core of the evaporator. The condensed liquid is released through the expansion valve, the pressure is decreased and the temperature drops causing the cooling affect.

The evaporator is housed in the evaporator case, located behind the right side of the instrument panel. During the air conditioning operation, ambient air is directed through the fins of the evaporator and into the vehicle's passenger compartment.

Service Valve Location

The low side service valve is located in the suction hose (hose between the evaporator and compressor). The high side service valve is located in the hose between the condenser and receiver/drier.

System Discharging

1. Remove the caps from the high and low pressure charging valves in the high and low pressure lines.
2. Turn both manifold gauge set hand valves to the fully closed (clockwise) position.
3. Connect the manifold gauge set.
4. If the gauge set hoses do not have the gauge port actuating pins, install fitting adapters on the manifold gauge set hoses. If the vehicle does not have a service access gauge port valve, connect the gauge set low pressure hose to the evaporator service access gauge port valve. A special adapter may be required to attach the manifold gauge set to the high pressure service access gauge port valve.
5. Connect the center hose to the refrigerant recycling station.
6. Open the low pressure gauge valve slightly and allow the system pressure to bleed into the recycling station.
7. When the system is just about empty, open the high pressure valve very slowly to avoid losing an excessive amount of refrigerant oil. Allow any remaining refrigerant to escape.

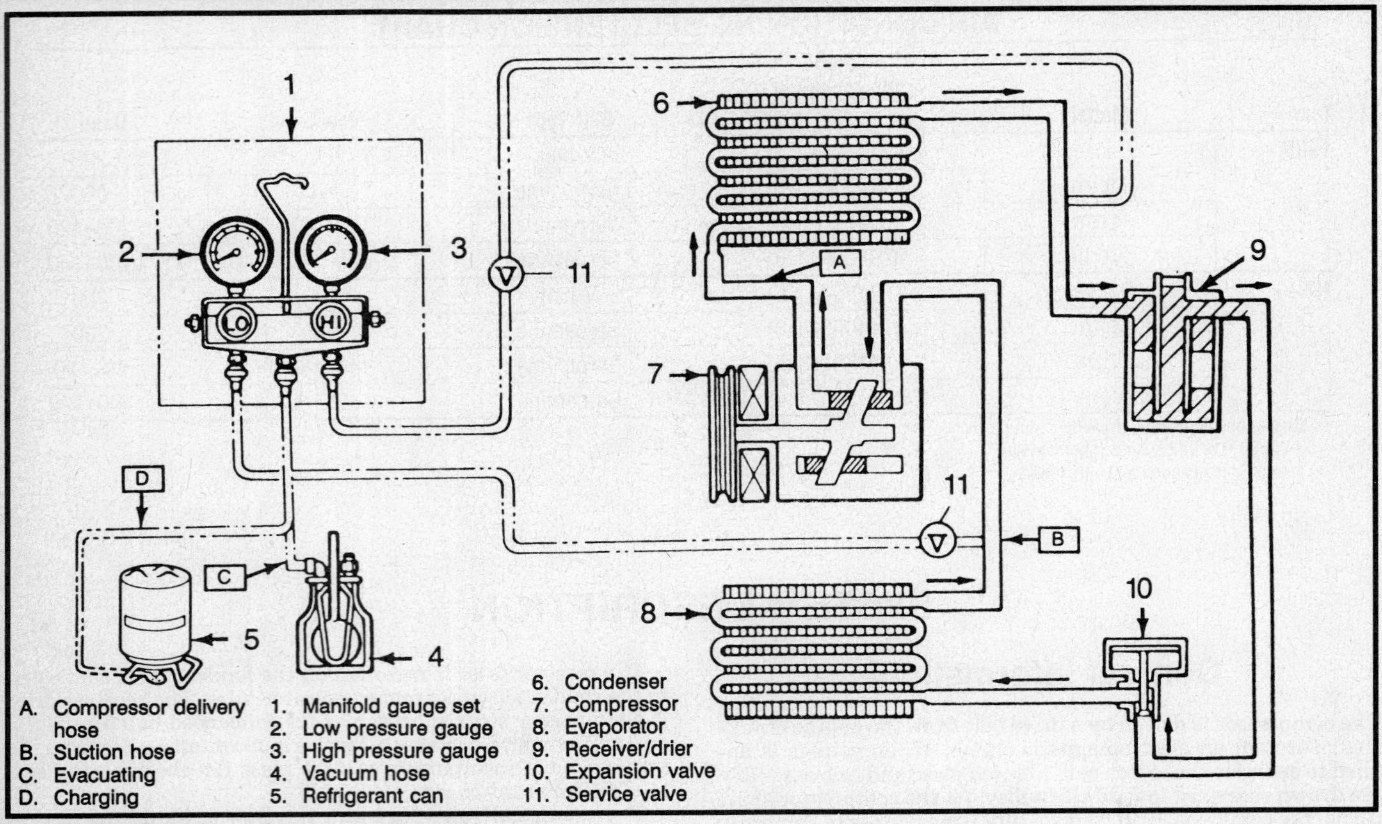
1
2
3
11
6
A
7
9
11
B
D
C
5
4
8
10
A. Compressor delivery hose
B. Suction hose
C. Evacuating
D. Charging
1. Manifold gauge set
2. Low pressure gauge
3. High pressure gauge
4. Vacuum hose
5. Refrigerant can
6. Condenser
7. Compressor
8. Evaporator
9. Receiver/drier
10. Expansion valve
11. Service valve

Air conditioning system and manifold gauges

System Evacuating

1. Connect the manifold gauge set.
2. Discharge the system into the refrigerant recycling station.
3. Connect the center hose to the recycling center or an air conditioning evacuator pump.
4. Turn both gauge set valves to the wide open position.
5. Start the pump and note the low side gauge reading.
6. Operate the pump until the low pressure gauge reads 25–30 in. Hg. vacuum. Continue running the vacuum pump for 10 minutes more. If components have been replaced in the system, run the pump for an additional 30 minutes.
7. To Leak test the system. Close both gauge set valves. Turn off the pump. The needle should remain stationary at the point at which the pump was turned off. If the needle drops to zero rapidly, there is a leak in the system which must be repaired.

System Charging

1. Connect an approved charging station, recovery/recycling machine or manifold gauge set to the discharge and suction ports. The red hose is normally connected to the discharge (high pressure) line, and the blue hose is connected to the suction (low pressure) line.
2. Follow the instructions provided with the equipment and charge the system with the specified amount of refrigerant.
3. Perform a leak test.

SYSTEM COMPONENTS

Radiator

REMOVAL AND INSTALLATION

1. Disconnect the negative battery cable.
2. Drain the cooling system. Remove the air intake duct, Spectrum only.
3. Remove the coolant reservoir, upper and lower radiator hoses.
4. Disconnect the transaxle oil cooler lines, if equipped.
5. Remove the upper radiator brackets.
6. Disconnect the cooling fan electrical connectors.
7. Remove the radiator and fan assembly.

To install:

8. Install the radiator and fan assembly.
9. Connect the cooling fan electrical connectors.
10. Install the upper radiator brackets.
11. Connect the transaxle oil cooler lines, if equipped.
12. Install the coolant reservoir, upper and lower radiator hoses.
13. Refill the cooling system.
14. Connect the negative battery cable.

COOLING SYSTEM BLEEDING

These vehicles are equipped with a self-bleeding thermostat. Fill the cooling system in the conventional manner; separate bleeding procedures are not necessary. Recheck the coolant level after the vehicle and cooled.

Cooling Fan

TESTING

1. Disconnect the cooling fan electrical connector.
2. Connect 12 volts to the fan connector and ground. The black/red is the positive wire for the Prizm. The black/blue is positive for the Storm, the black/red wire is positive for the Metro and the white/green is positive for the Spectrum.
3. If the fan runs, the motor is not defective; if it does not run, the motor or related components are defective. Make sure the unit is properly grounded.

REMOVAL AND INSTALLATION

Tracker

1. Disconnect the negative battery cable.
2. Discharge the air conditioning system, if equipped.
3. Remove the 4 fan mounting nuts, cooling fan and pump pulley. Do not allow the fan to come in contact with the radiator.
4. Remove the air conditioning line above the shroud.
5. Remove the shroud retaining bolts and remove the shroud and fan assembly together.
6. Installation is the reverse of removal. Torque the shroud bolts to 89 inch lbs. (10 Nm). Evacuate and recharge the air conditioning system.

Metro and Spectrum

1. Disconnect the negative battery cable.
2. Drain the cooling system.
3. Remove the coolant reservoir hose, upper and lower radiator hoses.
4. Disconnect the transaxle oil cooler lines, if equipped.
5. Remove the upper radiator brackets.
6. Disconnect the cooling fan electrical connectors.
7. Remove the radiator and cooling fan assembly.

To install:

8. Install the radiator and fan assembly.
9. Connect the cooling fan electrical connectors.
10. Install the upper radiator brackets.
11. Connect the transaxle oil cooler lines, if equipped.
12. Install the coolant reservoir, upper and lower radiator hoses.
13. Refill the cooling system.
14. Connect the negative battery cable.

Prizm

1. Disconnect the negative battery cable.
2. Disconnect the fan electrical connectors.
3. Remove the fan and shroud.
4. Separate the fan blade from the motor.
5. Installation is the reverse of removal. Torque the fan shroud nuts to 89 inch lbs. (10 Nm).

Storm

1. Disconnect the negative battery cable.
2. Drain the engine coolant.
3. Remove the upper radiator hose and disconnect the cooling fan electrical connectors.
4. Remove the cooling fan and motor assembly.
5. Installation is the reverse of removal.

Condenser

REMOVAL AND INSTALLATION

Spectrum

1. Disconnect the negative battery cable.
2. Discharge the air conditioning system.
3. Remove the radiator grille and emblem.
4. Remove the condenser discharge line, receiver/drier outlet line and electrical connector at the receiver. Plug the open lines to prevent contamination.
5. Remove the hood latch support.
6. Remove the retaining bolts and condenser.
7. Installation is the reverse of removal.

Tracker

1. Disconnect the negative battery cable.
2. Discharge the air conditioning system.
3. Remove the front grille.
4. Disconnect the compressor delivery and outlet hoses from the condenser fittings. Plug the open lines to prevent contamination.
5. Disconnect the condenser fan electrical connectors.
6. Remove the mounting bolts and condenser.

To install:

7. Install the condenser and bolts.
8. Connect the air conditioning hoses to the condenser and torque to 18 ft. lbs. (25 Nm).
9. Connect the electrical connections.
10. Install the front grille.
11. Evacuate, add 0.7–1.0 oz. of refrigerant oil and recharge the air conditioning system.

Metro and Storm

1. Disconnect the negative battery cable.
2. Discharge the air conditioning system.
3. Remove the compressor hose. Disconnect the inlet hose to the receiver/drier. Plug all open hoses to prevent contamination.
4. Remove the hood latch and lock assembly, Metro only.
5. Disconnect the condenser cooling fan connector.
6. Remove the condenser retaining bolts, condenser, cooling fan and receiver/drier.

To install:

7. Install the condenser and cooling fan assembly.
8. Add 0.7–1.0 oz. of refrigerant oil to the condenser before connecting hoses.
9. Connect the inlet and outlet hoses to the assembly.
10. Connect the electrical connectors.
11. Install the hood latch and lock, Metro only.
12. Evacuate and recharge the system.

Prizm

1. Disconnect the negative battery cable.
2. Discharge the air conditioning system.
3. Remove the front grille, hood latch and center radiator/condenser core support.
4. Drain the engine cooling system.
5. Remove the upper radiator hose and disconnect the condenser fan connector.
6. Remove the horn and condenser fan assembly.
7. Remove the receiver/drier and mounting bracket. Plug all open refrigerant hoses.
8. Remove the receiver-to-condenser pipe from the condenser.
9. Disconnect the compressor discharge pipe from the condenser.
10. Remove the upper condenser mounting brackets and slide the condenser to the left and remove the receiver/drier outlet

pipe hold-down bracket. Remove the condenser from the vehicle.

To install:

11. Install the condenser and upper condenser mounting brackets.
12. Connect the compressor discharge pipe to the condenser.
13. Install the receiver-to-condenser pipe to the condenser.
14. Install the receiver/drier and mounting bracket.
15. Install the horn and condenser fan assembly.
16. Install the upper radiator hose and connect the condenser fan connector.
17. Refill the engine cooling system.
18. Install the hood latch and front grille.
19. Evacuate and recharge the air conditioning system.
20. Connect the negative battery cable.

Compressor

REMOVAL AND INSTALLATION

Tracker

1. Disconnect the negative battery cable.
2. Discharge the air conditioning system.
3. Disconnect the suction, discharge hoses and electrical connector at the compressor. Plug all open hoses to prevent contamination.
4. Remove the upper compressor mounting bolts.
5. Raise and safely support the vehicle.
6. Remove the lower mounting bolt, disengage the drive belt and remove the compressor.

To install:

7. Install the compressor and install the lower mounting bolt.
8. Lower the vehicle.
9. Install the upper compressor mounting bolts.
10. Connect the suction, discharge hoses and electrical connector at the compressor.
11. Evacuate and recharge the air conditioning system.
12. Connect the negative battery cable.

Spectrum, Metro and Prizm

1. Disconnect the negative battery cable.
2. Discharge the air conditioning system.
3. Disconnect the suction, discharge hoses and electrical connector at the compressor. Plug all open hoses to prevent contamination.
4. Raise and safely support the vehicle.
5. Remove the right fender extension and oil filter. Loosen the compressor drive belt, Metro only. Remove the lower stone shield, Prizm.
6. Remove the compressor mounting bolts and compressor.

To install:

7. Install the compressor and mounting bolts.
8. Install the right fender extension and oil filter, Metro. Install the lower stone shield, Prizm. Adjust the compressor drive belt.
9. Lower the vehicle.
10. Connect the suction, discharge hoses and electrical connector at the compressor.
11. Evacuate and recharge the air conditioning system.
12. Connect the negative battery cable.

Storm

1. Disconnect the negative battery cable.
2. Discharge the air conditioning system.
3. Remove the power steering drive belt.
4. Disconnect the suction, discharge hoses and electrical connector at the compressor. Plug all open hoses to prevent contamination.
5. Raise and safely support the vehicle.
6. Remove the right undercover and 2 compressor mounting bolt.
7. Remove the compressor from the vehicle.

To install:

8. Install the compressor into the vehicle.
9. Install the compressor mounting bolts and right undercover.
10. Lower the vehicle.
11. Connect the suction, discharge hoses and electrical connector at the compressor.
12. Install the power steering drive belt.
13. Evacuate and recharge the air conditioning system.
14. Connect the negative battery cable.

Receiver/Drier

REMOVAL AND INSTALLATION

Except Storm

1. Disconnect the negative battery cable.
2. Discharge the air conditioning system.
3. Remove the the front grille and horn from the vehicle, Prizm and Spectrum only.
4. Disconnect the inlet and outlet to the receiver/drier. Plug the open pipes to prevent contamination.
5. Remove the assembly from the mounting bracket.
6. Installation is the reverse of removal. Add 0.3 oz. (10ml) of refrigerant oil to the inlet. Transfer electrical switch and use sealing tape on the threads.

Storm

1. Disconnect the negative battery cable.
2. Discharge the air conditioning system.
3. Remove the condenser support bracket and disconnect the discharge line from the condenser.
4. Remove the 2 condenser retaining bolts.
5. Disconnect the inlet, outlet pipes and electrical connectors from the receiver/drier. Plug open pipes to prevent contamination.
6. Remove the retaining bolts and receiver/drier.
7. Installation is the reverse of removal. Add 0.3 oz. (10ml) of refrigerant oil to the inlet. Torque the inlet and outlet pipe to 11 ft. lbs. (15 Nm).

Expansion Valve

REMOVAL AND INSTALLATION

Except Storm

1. Disconnect the negative battery cable.
2. Discharge the air conditioning system.
3. Remove the evaporator assembly from the vehicle.
4. Remove the clamps to separate the upper and lower halves.
5. Using backup wrenches, remove the expansion valve from the evaporator.
6. Installation is the reverse of removal. Torque the fittings to 18 ft. lbs. (25 Nm).

Storm

1. Disconnect the negative battery cable.
2. Discharge the air conditioning system.
3. Remove the clamps and 2 nuts attaching the refrigerant pipes to the expansion valve. Plug all open pipes to prevent contamination.
4. Remove the retaining clip and valve.
5. Installation is the reverse of removal. Torque the retaining nuts to 70 inch lbs. (8 Nm).

Blower Motor

REMOVAL AND INSTALLATION

Spectrum and Prizm

1. Disconnect the negative battery cable.
2. Remove the instrument panel trim panel, if equipped.
3. Disconnect the blower motor wiring and air hose.
4. Remove the retaining screws and motor assembly.
5. Remove the cage retaining clip and cage from the motor.

To install:

6. Install the cage onto the motor and install the clip.
7. Install the motor, retaining screws, wiring connector and air hose.
8. Connect the battery cable.

Tracker and Metro

1. Disconnect the negative battery cable.
2. Remove the glove compartment and disconnect the blower motor and resistor wiring connectors.
3. Disconnect the circ-fresh air control cable.
4. Loosen, but do not remove the blower housing retaining bolts, Tracker. Remove the blower case mounting bolts and case from the vehicle, Metro.
5. Remove the three motor retaining screws and blower motor. Disconnect the air hose, if equipped.
6. Installation is the reverse of removal.

Storm

1. Disconnect the negative battery cable.
2. Disconnect the blower motor connector.
3. Remove the 4 retaining screws and motor assembly.
4. Installation is the reverse of removal.

Blower Motor Resistor

REMOVAL AND INSTALLATION

Spectrum, Tracker and Prizm

1. Disconnect the negative battery cable.
2. Remove the glove compartment, Tracker and Prizm.
3. Disconnect the resistor connector.
4. Remove the retaining screws and resistor.
5. Installation is the reverse of removal.

Metro

1. Disconnect the negative battery cable.
2. Remove the heater case.
3. Disconnect the electrical connector and remove the resistor.
4. Installation is the reverse of removal.

Storm

1. Disconnect the negative battery cable.
2. Remove the duct between the blower assembly and heater unit.
3. Disconnect the harness connector and remove the resistor.
4. Installation is the reverse of removal.

Heater Core

REMOVAL AND INSTALLATION

Spectrum

1. Disconnect the negative battery cable.
2. Drain the engine coolant.
3. Disconnect the heater hoses from the core.
4. Remove the retaining clips, lower heater unit case and core assembly.
5. Installation is the reverse of removal.

Tracker and Metro

1. Disconnect the negative battery cable.
2. Drain the engine coolant.
3. Remove the steering column, Tracker only.
4. Remove the center console, Tracker only.
5. Remove the instrument panel and center supports.
6. Remove the heater control assembly from the support member, Metro only.
7. Disconnect all electrical connectors and cables from the heater case.
8. Disconnect the heater core hoses.
9. Remove the defrost duct and speedometer retaining bracket from the heater case.
10. Remove the fastening bolts, grommets and floor duct, if equipped, from the case and remove the case from the vehicle.
11. Separate the heater case and remove the heater core.

To install:

12. Install the core and assemble the heater case.
13. Install the fastening bolts, grommets and floor duct to the case after installation.
14. Install the defrost duct and speedometer retaining bracket to the heater case.
15. Connect the heater core hoses.
16. Connect all electrical connectors and cables to the heater case.
17. Install the center supports and instrument panel.
18. Install the center console, Tracker only.
19. Install the steering column, Tracker only.
20. Refill the engine coolant.
21. Connect the negative battery cable.

Prizm

1. Disconnect the negative battery cable.
2. Drain the engine coolant.
3. Remove the steering wheel.
4. Remove the trim bezel from the instrument panel.
5. Remove the cup holder from the console.
6. Remove the radio.
7. Remove the instrument cluster, panel, console and all console trim.
8. Remove the lower dash trim and side window air deflectors.
9. Disconnect all instrument panel wiring harnesses and cables.
10. Remove the 2 center console support braces.
11. Remove the 2 heater hoses from the core.
12. Remove all mounting bolts, nuts and clips from the heater and air distribution cases.
13. Remove the screws and clips from the case and separate.
14. Remove the heater core from the case.

To install:

15. Install the heater core to the case.
16. Install the screws and clips to the case.
17. Install all mounting bolts, nuts and clips to the heater and air distribution cases.
18. Install the 2 heater hoses to the core.
19. Install the 2 center console support braces.
20. Connect all instrument panel wiring harnesses and cables.
21. Install the lower dash trim and side window air deflectors.
22. Install the instrument panel, console and all console trim.
23. Install the radio.
24. Install the cup holder to the console.
25. Install the trim bezel to the instrument panel.
26. Install the steering wheel.
27. Refill the engine coolant.

28. Connect the negative battery cable.

Storm

1. Disconnect the negative battery cable.
2. Drain the engine coolant.
3. Disconnect the hoses at the heater core.
4. Remove the instrument panel.
5. Remove the evaporator assembly, air conditioning only.
6. Remove the duct between the blower assembly and heater unit.
7. Remove the center ventilation duct.
8. Remove the 4 heater unit retaining nuts and heater unit.
9. Remove the duct between the blower and heater unit.
10. Remove the 5 mode control case-to-heater core case retaining screws. Do not remove the link.
11. Separate the 2 halves and remove the core.

To install:

12. Assembly the 2 halves.
13. Install the five mode control case-to-heater core case retaining screws.
14. Install the duct between the blower and heater unit.
15. Install the heater unit and 4 heater unit retaining nuts.
16. Install the center ventilation duct.
17. Install the duct between the blower assembly and heater unit.
18. Install the evaporator assembly, air conditioning only.
19. Install the instrument panel.
20. Connect the hoses at the heater core.
21. Refill the engine coolant.
22. Connect the negative battery cable.

Evaporator

REMOVAL AND INSTALLATION

Spectrum

1. Disconnect the negative battery cable.
2. Discharge the air conditioning system.
3. Disconnect and plug the inlet and outlet pipe from the evaporator.
4. Remove the glove box and disconnect the thermo-switch wire.
5. Disconnect the defroster hose and remove the evaporator housing retaining nuts and bolts. Remove the evaporator assembly.
6. Remove the housing retaining clips and split the housing in half.
7. Using a backup and flarenut wrench, remove the expansion valve.
8. Remove the evaporator from the case.

To install:

9. Install the evaporator core into the case, making sure all seals are in place and good condition.
10. Install the expansion valve.
11. Install the housing halves and retaining clips.
12. Install the evaporator housing and connect the defroster hose.
13. Install the glove box and connect the thermo-switch wire.
14. Connect the inlet and outlet pipe to the evaporator.
15. Evacuate and recharge the air conditioning system.
16. Connect the negative battery cable.

Tracker

1. Disconnect the negative battery cable.
2. Discharge the air conditioning system.
3. Remove the glove compartment.
4. Remove the blower motor.
5. Remove the heater-to-evaporator duct.
6. Disconnect and plug the inlet and outlet pipes. Use a backup wrench.
7. Disconnect the evaporator case wiring.
8. Remove the mounting brackets and evaporator assembly.
9. Remove the housing retaining clips and split the housing in two.
10. Using a backup and flarenut wrench, remove the expansion valve.
11. Remove the evaporator from the case.

To install:

12. Install the evaporator to the case.
13. Install the expansion valve.
14. Assemble the housing.
15. Install the mounting brackets and evaporator assembly.
16. Connect the evaporator case wiring.
17. Connect the inlet and outlet pipes. Use a backup wrench.
18. Install the heater-to-evaporator duct.
19. Install the blower motor.
20. Install the glove compartment.
21. Evacuate and recharge the air conditioning system.
22. Connect the negative battery cable.

Metro

1. Disconnect the negative battery cable.
2. Discharge the air conditioning system.
3. Remove the 2 screws from the glove compartment striker and remove the striker. Remove the attaching screw from the rear of the glove compartment upper panel and remove panel.
4. Disconnect all electrical wiring and cables from the blower case.
5. Remove the blower case retaining bolts and case assembly.
6. Disconnect and plug the inlet and outlet lines to the evaporator.
7. Remove the upper and lower housing retaining bolts and remove the evaporator assembly from the vehicle.
8. Separate the case housing and remove the evaporator core.

To install:

9. Install the evaporator core and assemble the case housing.
10. Install the housing, upper and lower housing retaining bolts.
11. Connect the inlet and outlet lines to the evaporator.
12. Install the blower case and retaining bolts.
13. Connect all electrical wiring and cables to the blower case.
14. Install the striker and 2 glove compartment screws. Install the upper panel and attaching screw at the rear of the glove compartment upper panel.
15. Evacuate and recharge the air conditioning system.
16. Connect the negative battery cable.

Prizm

1. Disconnect the negative battery cable.
2. Discharge the air conditioning system.
3. Disconnect and plug the inlet and outlet pipe from the evaporator.
4. Remove the hold-down brackets for the evaporator pipes.
5. Remove the right lower instrument panel trim.
6. Disconnect all electrical wiring and cables from the housing.
7. Remove the air conditioning amplifier from the housing.
8. Remove the mounting bolts and evaporator assembly.
9. Separate the housing halves and remove the evaporator core.

To install:

10. Install the evaporator core and assemble the housing halves.
11. Install the housing and mounting bolts.
12. Install the air conditioning amplifier to the housing.
13. Connect all electrical wiring and cables to the housing.
14. Install the right lower instrument panel trim.
15. Connect the inlet and outlet pipe to the evaporator.

16. Install the hold-down brackets for the evaporator pipes.
17. Evacuate and recharge the air conditioning system.
18. Connect the negative battery cable.

Storm

1. Disconnect the negative battery cable.
2. Discharge the air conditioning system.
3. Disconnect and plug the pipes from the expansion valve.
4. Remove retaining clip and expansion valve from the evaporator.
5. Remove the glove compartment.
6. Remove the lower instrument panel reinforcement bracket.
7. Disconnect all electrical wiring and cables from the evaporator housing.
8. Remove the retaining clips and evaporator housing.
9. Separate the housing halves and remove the evaporator core.

To install:

10. Install the evaporator core and assemble the housing halves.
11. Install the housing and retaining clips.
12. Connect all electrical wiring and cables to the evaporator housing.
13. Install the lower instrument panel reinforcement bracket.
14. Install the glove compartment.
15. Connect the pipes to the expansion valve.
16. Install expansion valve and retaining clip to the evaporator.
17. Evacuate and recharge the air conditioning system.
18. Connect the negative battery cable.

Refrigerant Lines

REMOVAL AND INSTALLATION

1. Disconnect the negative battery cable.
2. Discharge the air conditioning system.
3. Remove the radiator grille if removing front refrigerant lines.
4. Loosen the connector at the compressor and attaching points. Use a backup wrench on pipes with flare nut fittings.
5. Remove the pipe retaining clips.
6. Installation is the reverse of removal. Install new replacement O-rings whenever a joint or fitting is disconnected. Lubricate with refrigerant oil during installation. Torque the ⅜ in. O.D. pipes to 11–18 ft. lbs. (15–25 Nm), ½ in. O.D. pipes to 15–22 ft. lbs. (20–30 Nm) and ⅝ in. O.D. pipes to 22–29 ft. lbs. (30–40 Nm).

Manual Control Head

REMOVAL AND INSTALLATION

1. Disconnect the negative battery cable.
2. Pull the control knobs from the levers.
3. Release the latches at the rear of the bezel. Remove the control assembly lens and disconnect the bulb.
4. Disconnect the control cables at the blower and heater assembly.
5. Remove the control assembly fasteners.
6. Pull the control assembly out and disconnect the electrical connections.
7. Disconnect the control cables from the levers.
8. Remove the blower, air conditioning and heater switch.

To install:

9. Install the blower, air conditioning and heater switch.
10. Connect the control cables to the levers.

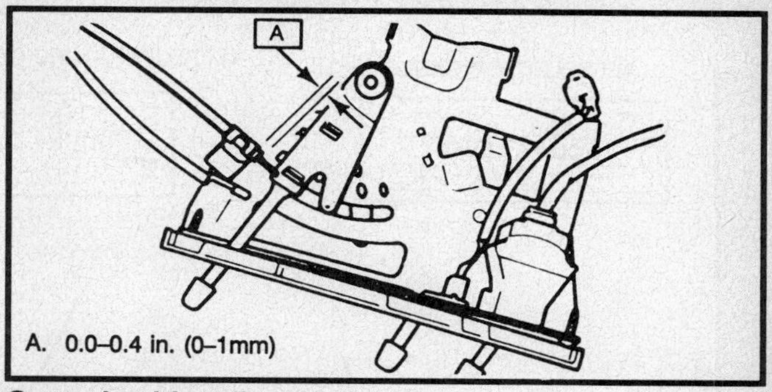
A
A. 0.0–0.4 in. (0–1mm)

Control cable adjustment

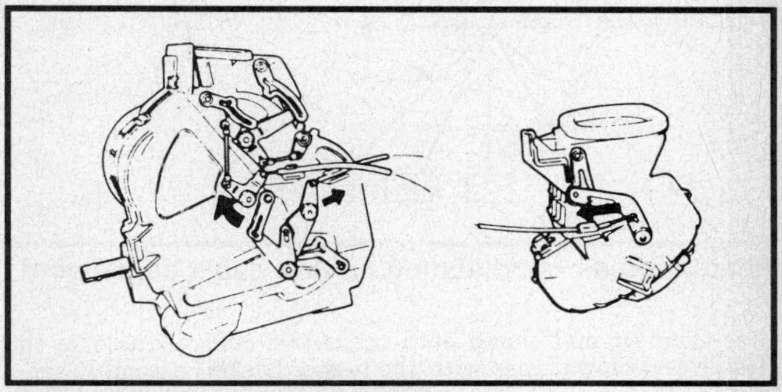

Heater control cable adjustment

11. Connect the electrical connections and install the control assembly.
12. Install the control assembly fasteners.
13. Connect the control cables at the blower and heater assembly.
14. Connect the bulb and install the control assembly lens.
15. Install the control knobs.
16. Adjust the control cables.
17. Connect the negative battery cable.

Manual Control Cables

ADJUSTMENT

Tracker

CONTROL CABLE

1. Move the control mode lever to vent.
2. Attach the control cable to control assembly with 0.000–0.039 in. (0–1mm) of cable projecting from the clamp.
3. At the heater case, push the door linkage fully in the direction of the arrow to affix the cable and rod into position.

TEMPERATURE CABLE

1. Move the temperature control lever to **COOL.**
2. At the heater case, push the door fully in the direction of the arrow to affix cable into position.

CIRC-FRESH CABLE

1. Move the circ-fresh lever to **FRESH**.
3. Adjust the cable at the heater case.

Metro

1. Set the temperature control lever to **HOT**.
2. Set the mode control lever to the **DEFROST** position.
3. Set the fresh/recirculate control lever to the **FRESH** position.

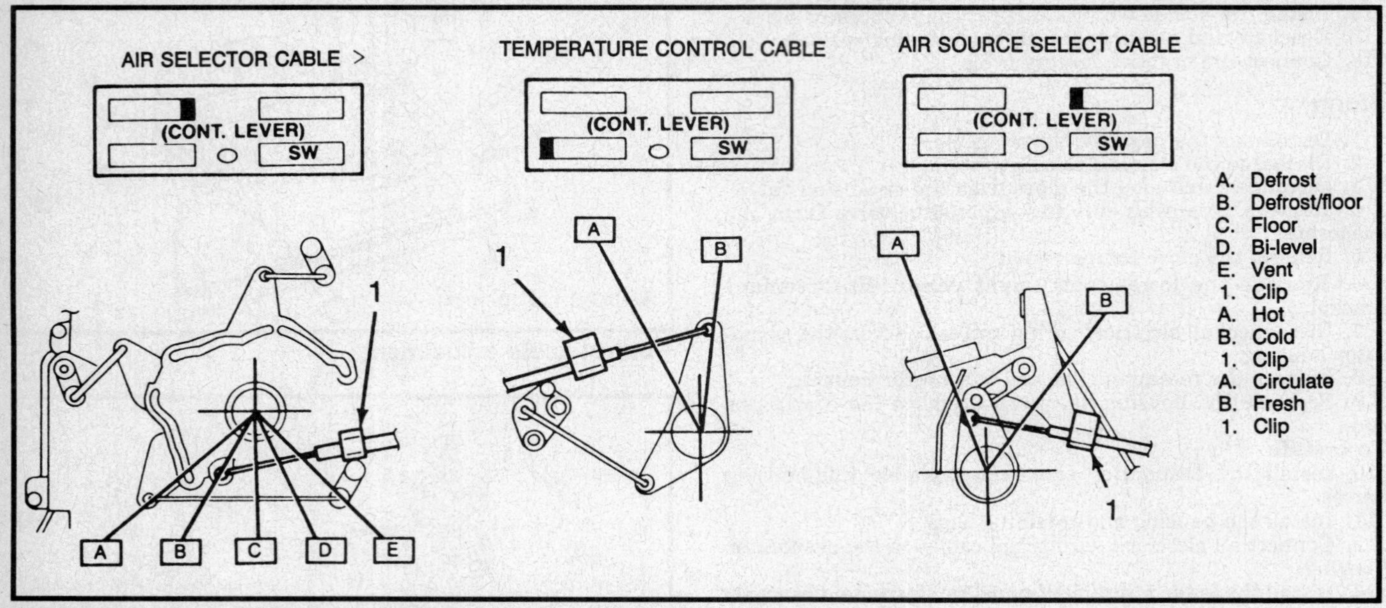
AIR SELECTOR CABLE
(CONT. LEVER)
SW
TEMPERATURE CONTROL CABLE
(CONT. LEVER)
SW
AIR SOURCE SELECT CABLE
(CONT. LEVER)
SW
1
A
B
C
D
E
A
B
1
A
B
1
A. Defrost
B. Defrost/floor
C. Floor
D. Bi-level
E. Vent
1. Clip
A. Hot
B. Cold
1. Clip
A. Circulate
B. Fresh
1. Clip

Heater and air conditioning control cable adjustment

4. Connect and clamp each respective control cable to the heater and blower case with the heater control assembly set.

Storm

AIR SOURCE CONTROL CABLE

1. Slide the select lever to the left.
2. Connect the control cable at the **CIRC** position and secure with the clip.

TEMPERATURE CONTROL CABLE

1. Slide the select lever to the left.
2. Connect the control cable at the **COLD** position and secure with the clip.

AIR SELECT CONTROL CABLE

1. Slide the select lever to the right.
2. Connect the control cable at the **DEFROST** position and secure with the clip.

REMOVAL AND INSTALLATION

1. Unlatch the cable from the retaining clip and slide the cable from the lever.
2. Route the cable through the vehicle.
3. Install the cable and adjust; do not overbend the cable.

SENSORS AND SWITCHES

Dual Pressure or Triple Switch

OPERATION

When the cycling refrigerant pressure drops due to leakage, a control switch stops further compressor rotation by turning off the compressor and condenser fan. The switch is located on top of the receiver/drier assembly. The switch opens when the pressure goes below 28 psi (196 kPa) and above 384 psi (2646 kPa) for the Spectrum. The switch opens when the pressure goes below 33 psi (206 kPa) and above 384 psi (2646 kPa) for the Tracker and Prizm.

TESTING

Spectrum

1. Disconnect air conditioning relay connector.
2. Connect a voltmeter between pin 4 (green/yellow) wire and ground.
3. Battery voltage is not present, check the dual pressure switch, evaporator temperature switch, fuse No. 16 and connecting wires for an open.

Storm

1. Back probe the triple switch connector with a test light from pin No. 3 (green/white) wire to ground.
2. If the lamp lights, repair the open in the green/white wire between the switch and the air conditioning thermo relay.
3. If the lamp does not light, back probe the switch connector from pin 4 (brown) wire to ground. If the lamp lights, replace the triple switch.

Prizm, Tracker and Metro

1. When the ignition key and air conditioning switch **ON**, disconnect the dual pressure switch connector and install a jumper wire between the 2 terminals.
2. If the compressor engages and the refrigerant pressures are normal, the switch is defective.

REMOVAL AND INSTALLATION

1. Disconnect the negative battery cable.
2. Disconnect the connector at the receiver/drier.
3. Discharge the air conditioning system.
4. Remove the switch from the receiver/drier.
5. Installation is the reverse of removal. Use thread sealing tape before installing the dual pressure or triple switch.

Compressor Relay

OPERATION

The location of the relay is the right front corner of the engine compartment on the Spectrum and Tracker. The relay has a 4 terminal connector. The relay is used to direct voltage to the compressor clutch through the ground circuit.

Sub-Relay

OPERATION

The sub-relay is located at the rear of the engine compartment, on the left side of the firewall for the Spectrum. It has a 4 terminal connector. The relay directs voltage to the compressor clutch from the compressor relay and power source.

Sub-Relay Condensor

OPERATION

The condensor is located at the lower right rear of the engine compartment, on the shock tower for the Spectrum.

Heater/Air Conditioning Relay

OPERATION

The relay is located under the left side of dash at the kick panel for the Spectrum. The relay has a 4 terminal connector. The relay receives voltage from the fuse box and applies voltage to the air conditioning controls.

Evaporator Temperature (Thermistor) Switch

OPERATION

The evaporator temperature switch is located behind the glove compartment, on the evaporator housing. The switch opens to cut voltage to the compressor when the evaporator temperature goes below 33°F (1.1°C). This switch prevents the evaporator from freezing. A frozen evaporator stops the flow of air to the passenger compartment.

TESTING

1. Use an ohmmeter to measure the resistance of the evaporator switch and use a thermometer to measure the room temperature.
2. Use the resistance temperature relationship chart to check whether the switch falls within the acceptable range.

REMOVAL AND INSTALLATION

1. Disconnect the negative battery cable.

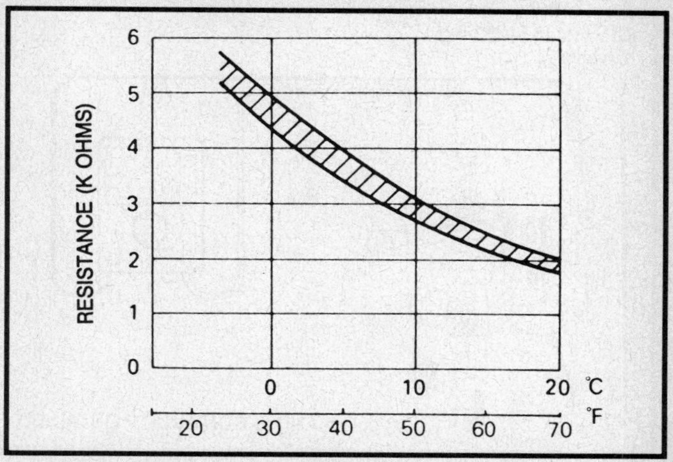
RESISTANCE (K OHMS)
6
5
4
3
2
1
0
0
10
20 °C
20
30
40
50
60
70 °F

Thermistor/evaporator temperature switch check

2. Remove the evaporator assembly. Separate the 2 halves to gain access to the capillary tube.
3. Remove the switch and capillary tube from the evaporator.
4. Installation is the reverse of removal.

Vacuum Switching Valve (VSV)

OPERATION

At low speeds, operating the air conditioning loads the engine. To prevent stalling, the vacuum switching valve utilizes intake manifold vacuum to increase the engine idle speed. The VSV is controlled by signals from the electronic control module and air conditioning amplifier.

The VSV is located at the bulkhead to the right of the ignition coil for the Metro. It is located on the right side of the engine compartment for the Prizm (base and LSi) and on the left side of the engine compartment for the Prizm (GSi model). The Spectrum's VSV is located top center of the engine.

TESTING

Metro

1. Check for proper vacuum continuity using a 12 volt supply to the VSV terminals.

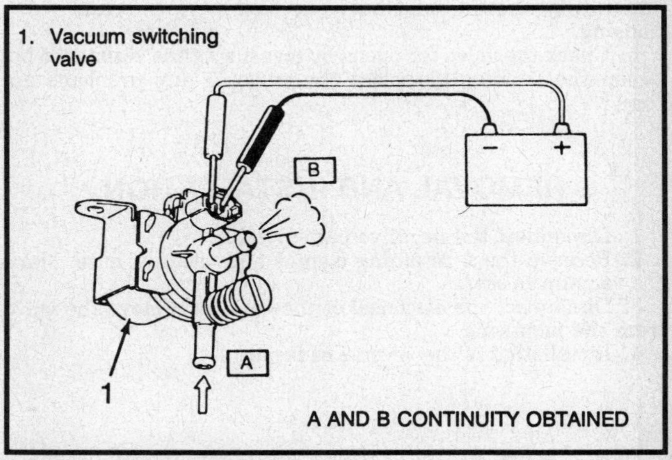
1. Vacuum switching valve
B
A
1
A AND B CONTINUITY OBTAINED

Vacuum Switching Valve (VSV) vacuum continuity check

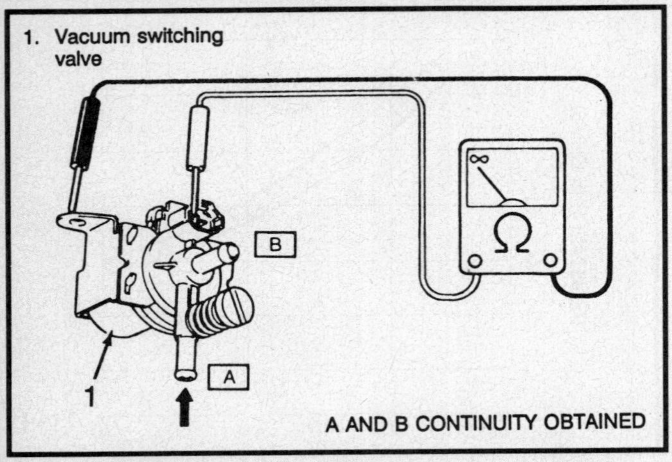
1. Vacuum switching valve
B
A
1
A AND B CONTINUITY OBTAINED

Vacuum Switching Valve (VSV) short circuit check

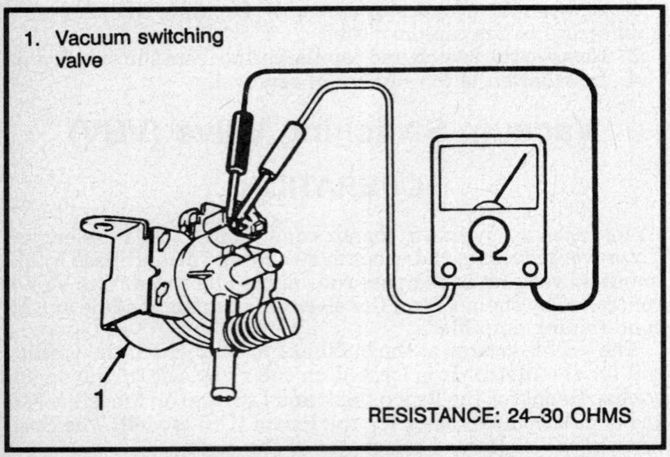
1. Vacuum switching valve
1
RESISTANCE: 24–30 OHMS

Vacuum Switching Valve (VSV) open circuit check

2. Check the VSV for a short circuit using an ohmmeter. No continuity should exist between each terminal and valve housing.
3. Check the valve for opens by measuring the resistance between the terminals; replace the valve, if any problems are found.

REMOVAL AND INSTALLATION

1. Disconnect the negative battery cable.
2. Remove the 2 retaining clamps and vacuum hose. Mark the vacuum hoses.
3. Disconnect the electrical connector and remove the valve from the mounting.
4. Installation is the reverse of removal.

Super Heat Switch and Control Unit

OPERATION

The switch is located behind the glove compartment and the control unit is under the left side of the dash, right of the steering column. The Spectrum (non-Turbo) is equipped with these components.

Timer Relay

OPERATION

The relay is located under the left side of the dash, right of the steering column. The timer relays voltage from the timer relay to the fast idle vacuum switching valve.

Air Conditioning Cut Control Unit

OPERATION

The control unit is located on top of the evaporator housing for the Storm with 4 speed automatic transaxle. The cut control unit senses engine coolant temperature and vehicle speed. At speeds of 20 mph (32 kph) the control unit signals the ECM to cycle the compressor off and on repeatedly should the engine coolant temperature rise above 230°F (110°C). If the engine temperature rises above 250°F (121°C), the control unit will signal the ECM to cycle the compressor regardless of vehicle speed.

Air Conditioning Coolant Temperature Sensor

OPERATION

The coolant temperature sensor is located on the right side of the engine compartment behind the radiator for the Tracker and Prizm. The sensor is located on the right side of the engine above the alternator on the Metro.

The sensor monitors engine temperature and signals the ECM to turn the compressor off is the temperature rises above normal.

Air Conditioning Amplifier/Controller

OPERATION

The amplifier/controller is located behind the right instrument panel above the evaporator case on the Prizm, Metro and Tracker. This unit is solid state and is performs many functions such as, controlling the vacuum switching valve, compressor clutch and condenser cooling fan motor based on signals received from various sensors and relays.

Revolution Detection Sensor

OPERATION

The sensor is located on the rear of the compressor for the Prizm (GSi). The sensor monitors compressor rpm. If excessive, the sensor sends a signal to the ECM to turn off the compressor.

SYSTEM DIAGNOSIS AND WIRING DIAGRAMS

AIR CONDITIONING SYSTEM DIAGNOSIS CHART—METRO AND TRACKER

CONDITION	POSSIBLE CAUSE	CORRECTION
No cooling or warm air.	Magnetic clutch does not engage properly.	
	• Fuse blown.	Replace fuse and check for short.
	• Magnetic clutch faulty.	Check clutch.
	• A/C switch faulty.	Check switch.
	• Temperature control switch faulty.	Check switch.
	• Low pressure switch faulty.	Check switch.
	Wiring or grounding faulty.	Check A/C circuit.
No refrigerant. Compressor is not rotating properly.	Drive belt loosened or broken.	Tighten or replace drive belt.
	Compressor faulty.	Check compressor.
	Blower inoperative.	Check heater.
	Expansion valve faulty.	Check expansion valve.
	Leak in system.	Check system for leaks.
	Receiver/dryer has blown fusible plug is clogged.	Check receiver/dryer.
Cool air comes out only intermittently.	Magnetic clutch slipping.	Check magnetic clutch.
	Wiring connection faulty.	Repair as necessary.
	Excessive mositure in system.	Evacuate and charge system.

AIR CONDITIONING SYSTEM DIAGNOSIS CHART—METRO AND TRACKER, CONT.

CONDITION	POSSIBLE CAUSE	CORRECTION
Cool air comes out only at high speeds.	Condenser clogged.	Check condenser.
	Drive belt slipping.	Check or replace drive belt.
	Compressor faulty.	Check compressor.
	Insufficient or excessive charge of refrigerant.	Check charge of refrigerant.
	Air in system.	Evacuate and charge system.
Insufficient cooling.	Condenser clogged.	Check condenser.
	Drive belt slipping.	Check or replace drive belt.
	Magnetic clutch faulty.	Check magnetic clutch.
	Compressor faulty.	Check compressor.
	Expansion valve faulty.	Check expansion valve.
	Temperature control switch faulty.	Check temperature control switch.
	Too little or too much charge of refrigerant.	Check charge of refrigerant.
	Air or excessive compressor oil in system.	Evacuate and charge system.
Insufficient velocity of cooled air.	Evaporator clogged or frosted.	Check evaporator.
	Air leaking from evaporator case or air duct.	Repair as necessary.
	Air inlet blocked.	Repair as necessary.
	Blower motor faulty.	Replace blower motor.

AIR CONDITIONING SYSTEM ELECTRICAL DIAGNOSIS CHART—TRACKER

AIR CONDITIONING: COMPRESSOR CONTROLS DIAGNOSTIC CHART A

	TEST	RESULT	ACTION
A1.	Start engine, turn A/C SWITCH to "ON" and BLOWER SWITCH to any position but "OFF."	A/C COMPRESSOR CLUTCH engages and blower motor operates at desired speed.	All systems diagnosed in this cell are functioning normally.
		A/C COMPRESSOR CLUTCH engages but blower motor does not operate.	Refer to blower motor and Heater System Diagnosis.
		Blower motor operates but A/C COMPRESSOR CLUTCH does not engage.	Shut off engine, turn ignition switch to "ON," and GO TO **A2**.
A2.	Backprobe A/C COMPRESSOR CLUTCH connector with a test lamp from connector cavity to chassis ground.	Test lamp lights.	Replace A/C COMPRESSOR CLUTCH.
		Test lamp does not light.	GO TO **A3**.
A3.	Backprobe A/C CLUTCH RELAY connector with a test lamp from connector cavity 4 to chassis ground.	Test lamp lights.	Repair open in BLK/WHT wire between A/C CLUTCH RELAY AND A/C COMPRESSOR CLUTCH.
		Test lamp does not light.	GO TO **A4**.
A4.	Backprobe A/C CLUTCH RELAY connector with a test lamp from connector cavity 2 to chassis ground.	Test lamp does not light	Repair open in RED wire between A/C CLUTCH RELAY and A/C FUSE HOLDER.
		Test lamp lights.	GO TO **A5**.
A5.	Backprobe DUAL PRESSURE SWITCH connector with a test lamp from cavity 1 to chassis ground.	Test lamp does not light.	Repair open in LT GRN wire between DUAL PRESSURE SWITCH and FUSE BLOCK.
		Test lamp lights.	GO TO **A6**.
A6.	Backprobe DUAL PRESSURE SWITCH connector with a test lamp from cavity 2 to chassis ground.	Test lamp does not light.	Replace DUAL PRESSURE SWITCH.
		Test lamp lights.	GO TO **A7**.
A7.	Backprobe A/C CLUTCH RELAY connector with a test lamp from terminal 1 to chassis ground.	Test lamp does not light.	Repair open in YEL wire between DUAL PRESSURE SWITCH and A/C CLUTCH RELAY.
		Test lamp lights.	GO TO **A8**.
A8.	Disconnect A/C CLUTCH RELAY connector. Connect a digital multimeter from connector cavity 3 to chassis ground. Measure resistance.	Less than 0.3 ohms.	Replace A/C CLUTCH RELAY.
		More than 0.3 ohms.	GO TO **A9**.
A9.	Disconnect A/C AMPLIFIER connector. Connect a digital multimeter from connector cavity 9 to chassis ground. Measure resistance.	More than 0.3 ohms.	Repair BLK ground wire between A/C AMPLIFIER and G200.
		Less than 0.3 ohms.	GO TO **A10**.
A10.	Backprobe BLOWER SPEED SELECTOR SWITCH connector with a test lamp from cavity 5 to chassis ground.	Test lamp does not light.	Repair open in LT GRN wire between BLOWER SPEED SELECTOR SWITCH and S209.
		Test lamp lights.	GO TO **A11**.
A11.	Backprobe BLOWER SPEED SELECTOR SWITCH connector with a test lamp from cavity 6 to chassis ground.	Test lamp does not light.	Replace BLOWER SPEED SELECTOR SWITCH.
		Test lamp lights.	GO TO **A12**.
A12.	Backprobe A/C SWITCH connector with a test lamp from cavity 1 to chassis ground.	Test lamp does not light.	Repair open in A/C SWITCH FUSE or PNK/BLK wire between BLOWER SPEED SELECTOR SWITCH and A/C SWITCH.
		Test lamp lights.	GO TO **A13**.
A13.	Backprobe A/C SWITCH connector with a test lamp from cavity 2 to chassis ground.	Test lamp does not light.	Replace A/C SWITCH.
		Test lamp lights.	GO TO **A14**.
A14.	With A/C AMPLIFIER connector disconnected, connect a test lamp from connector cavity 11 to chassis ground.	Test lamp does not light.	Repair open in BLU wire between A/C AMPLIFIER and A/C SWITCH.
		Test lamp lights.	GO TO **A15**.
A15.	Connect a digital multimeter from A/C AMPLIFIER connector cavity 12 to chassis ground. Measure resistance.	More than 0.3 ohms.	GO TO **A16**.
		Less than 0.3 ohms.	GO TO **A17**.
A16.	Backprobe A/C COOLANT TEMPERATURE SENSOR connector with a digital multimeter from connector cavity to chassis ground. Measure resistance.	More than 0.3 ohms.	Replace A/C COOLANT TEMPERATURE SENSOR.
		Less than 0.3 ohms.	Repair open in YEL/BLU wire.
A17.	Turn IGNITION SWITCH to "LOCK." Connect a test lamp from A/C AMPLIFIER connector cavity 2 to chassis ground.	Test lamp does not light.	GO TO **A22**.
		Test lamp lights.	GO TO **A18** with Automatic Transmission. GO TO **A20** with Manual Transmission.

AIR CONDITIONING SYSTEM ELECTRICAL DIAGNOSIS CHART—TRACKER, CONT.

AIR CONDITIONING: COMPRESSOR CONTROLS DIAGNOSTIC CHART A (CONT'D)

TEST	RESULT	ACTION
A18. Move gear selector to "P." Disconnect SHIFT SWITCH connector C1. Connect a test lamp from A/C AMPLIFIER connector cavity 2 to chassis ground.	Test lamp lights.	Repair short to voltage in BLK/YEL wire between SHIFT SWITCH and A/C AMPLIFIER.
	Test lamp does not light.	GO TO **A19**.
A19. Disconnect IGNITION SWITCH connector. Connect a test lamp from SHIFT SWITCH connector C1 cavity 1 to chassis ground.	Test lamp lights.	Repair short to voltage in BLK/RED wire between SHIFT SWITCH and IGNITION SWITCH.
	Test lamp does not light.	Replace IGNITION SWITCH.
A20. Disconnect CLUTCH START SWITCH. Connect a test lamp from A/C AMPLIFIER connector cavity 2 to chassis ground.	Test lamp lights.	Repair short to voltage in BLK/YEL wire between CLUTCH START SWITCH and A/C AMPLIFIER.
	Test lamp does not light.	GO TO **A21**.
A21. Disconnect IGNITION SWITCH connector. Connect a test lamp from CLUTCH START SWITCH connector cavity 2 to chassis ground.	Test lamp lights.	Repair short to voltage in BLK/RED wire between CLUTCH START SWITCH and IGNITION SWITCH.
	Test lamp does not light.	Replace IGNITION SWITCH.
A22. With A/C AMPLIFIER connector disconnected, connect a digital multimeter from connector cavity 10 to connector cavity 4. Measure resistance.	Less than 2000 ohms.	Replace A/C AMPLIFIER.
	More than 2000 ohms.	GO TO **A23**.
A23. Disconnect A/C THERMISTOR connector. Connect a digital multimeter from A/C THERMISTOR connector cavity 2 to A/C AMPLIFIER connector cavity 10. Measure resistance.	More than 0.3 ohms.	Repair open in YEL/GRN wire.
	Less than 0.3 ohms.	Repair open in WHT/BLU wire.

AIR CONDITIONING SYSTEM ELECTRICAL DIAGNOSIS CHART—TRACKER, CONT.

AIR CONDITIONING: COMPRESSOR CONTROLS DIAGNOSTIC CHART A

BASE AND LSi

TEST	RESULT	ACTION
A1. Start engine, turn A/C SWITCH to "ON" and BLOWER SWITCH to any position but "OFF."	A/C COMPRESSOR CLUTCH engages and BLOWER MOTOR operates at desired speed.	All systems diagnosed in this cell are functioning normally.
	A/C COMPRESSOR CLUTCH engages but BLOWER MOTOR does not operate.	Refer to BLOWER MOTOR and Heater System Diagnosis.
	BLOWER MOTOR operates but A/C COMPRESSOR CLUTCH does not engage.	GO TO **A2.**
	COMPRESSOR CLUTCH does not engage and BLOWER MOTOR does not operate.	Shut off engine, turn ignition switch to "ON," and GO TO **A24**.
A2. Backprobe A/C COMPRESSOR CLUTCH with a test lamp from connector to chassis ground.	Test lamp lights.	Replace A/C COMPRESSOR CLUTCH.
	Test lamp does not light.	GO TO **A3**.
A3. Unfasten JUNCTION BLOCK 5 from LH inner fender. Remove bottom cover. Backprobe JUNCTION BLOCK 5 with a test lamp from A/C Clutch Relay terminal 4 to chassis ground.	Test lamp lights.	Repair open in BLK/WHT wire between JUNCTION BLOCK 5 and A/C COMPRESSOR CLUTCH.
	Test lamp does not light.	GO TO **A4**.
A4. Backprobe JUNCTION BLOCK 5 with a test lamp from A/C Clutch Relay terminal 2 to chassis ground.	Test lamp does not light.	Repair open in BLK/YEL wire between FUSE BLOCK and JUNCTION BLOCK 5.
	Test lamp lights.	GO TO **A5**.
A5. Backprobe JUNCTION BLOCK 5 with a test lamp from A/C Clutch Relay terminal 1 to chassis ground.	Test lamp does not light.	GO TO **A6**.
	Test lamp lights.	GO TO **A7**.
A6. Remove A/C Fuse from JUNCTION BLOCK 4. Connect a test lamp from the BLK wire cavity to chassis ground.	Test lamp lights.	Repair open in BLU/RED wire between JUNCTION BLOCK 4 and JUNCTION BLOCK 5.
	Test lamp does not light.	Repair open in BLK wire between A/C Fuse and Heater Relay.

AIR CONDITIONING SYSTEM ELECTRICAL DIAGNOSIS CHART—TRACKER, CONT.

AIR CONDITIONING: COMPRESSOR CONTROLS — **DIAGNOSTIC CHART A (CONT'D)**

BASE AND LSi

TEST		RESULT	ACTION
A7.	Backprobe A/C SWITCH connector with a test lamp from cavity 5 to chassis ground.	Test lamp does not light.	Repair open in BLU/RED wire, YEL wire, or YEL/WHT wire between S206 and A/C SWITCH.
		Test lamp lights.	GO TO **A8**.
A8.	Backprobe A/C SWITCH connector with a test lamp from cavity 6 to chassis ground.	Test lamp does not light.	Replace A/C SWITCH.
		Test lamp lights	GO TO **A9**.
A9.	Backprobe A/C AMPLIFIER connector with a test lamp from cavity 4 to chassis ground.	Test lamp does not light.	Repair YEL or YEL/WHT wire between A/C SWITCH and A/C AMPLIFIER.
		Test lamp lights.	GO TO **A10**.
A10.	Turn ignition switch to "OFF" and disconnect A/C AMPLIFIER connector. Connect a digital multimeter from A/C AMPLIFIER connector cavity 10 to chassis ground. Measure resistance.	More than 0.3 ohms.	GO TO **A11**.
		Less than 0.3 ohms.	GO TO **A12**.
A11.	Backprobe JUNCTION BLOCK 4 connector with a digital multimeter from cavity 1 to chassis ground. Measure resistance.	Less than 0.3 ohms.	Repair open in WHT/BLK wire between A/C AMPLIFIER and JUNCTION BLOCK 4.
		More than 0.3 ohms.	Replace JUNCTION BLOCK 4.
A12.	Turn ignition switch to "ON." Backprobe JUNCTION BLOCK 5 with a test lamp from A/C Clutch Relay terminal 3 to chassis ground.	Test lamp does not light.	Replace A/C Clutch Relay.
		Test lamp lights.	GO TO **A13**.
A13.	Connect a test lamp from A/C AMPLIFIER connector cavity 2 to chassis ground.	Test lamp does not light.	Repair open in BLU/ORN wire, A/C DIODE, or LT GRN wire between JUNCTION BLOCK 5 and A/C AMPLIFIER.
		Test lamp lights.	GO TO **A14**.
A14.	Disconnect A/C COMPRESSOR CLUTCH connector. Connect a fused jumper from A/C AMPLIFIER connector cavity 2 to chassis ground. Connect a test lamp from A/C COMPRESSOR CLUTCH connector to chassis ground.	Test lamp does not light.	Replace A/C Clutch Relay.
		Test lamp lights.	GO TO **A15**.
A15.	Disconnect THERMISTOR connector. Connect a digital multimeter across terminals of THERMISTOR side of connector. Measure resistance at approximately 25° C (77° F).	More than 2.0k ohms.	Replace THERMISTOR.
		Less than 2.0k ohms.	GO TO **A16**.
A16.	Connect a digital multimeter from THERMISTOR connector cavity 2 (wiring harness side) to chassis ground. Measure resistance.	More than 0.3 ohms.	Repair open in WHT/BLK wire between THERMISTOR and S278.
		Less than 0.3 ohms.	GO TO **A17**.
A17.	Connect a digital multimeter from THERMISTOR connector cavity 1 (wiring harness side) to A/C AMPLIFIER connector cavity 12. Measure resistance.	More than 0.3 ohms.	Repair open in YEL/GRN wire between THERMISTOR and A/C AMPLIFIER.
		Less than 0.3 ohms.	GO TO **A18**.
A18.	Connect a digital multimeter across A/C AMPLIFIER connector cavities 6 and 12. Measure resistance.	More than 0.3 ohms.	Repair open in YEL/GRN wire between A/C AMPLIFIER connector cavity 6 and S287.
		Less than 0.3 ohms.	GO TO **A19**.
A19.	Connect a test lamp from A/C AMPLIFIER connector cavity 5 to chassis ground. Reinstall A/C Fuse.	Test lamp lights.	GO TO **A32**.
		Test lamp does not light.	GO TO **A20**.
A20.	Backprobe COOLANT TEMPERATURE A/C CUTOUT SWITCH with a test lamp from cavity 2 to chassis ground.	Test lamp lights.	Repair open in BLK/YEL wire between COOLANT TEMPERATURE A/C CUTOUT SWITCH and A/C AMPLIFIER.
		Test lamp does not light.	GO TO **A21**.
A21.	Backprobe COOLANT TEMPERATURE A/C CUTOUT SWITCH with a test lamp from cavity 1 to chassis ground.	Test lamp lights.	Replace COOLANT TEMPERATURE A/C CUTOUT SWITCH.
		Test lamp does not light.	GO TO **A22**.
A22.	Backprobe A/C DUAL PRESSURE SWITCH with a test lamp from cavity 2 to chassis ground.	Test lamp lights.	Repair open in PNK wire.
		Test lamp does not light.	GO TO **A23**.
A23.	Backprobe A/C DUAL PRESSURE SWITCH with a test lamp from cavity 1 to chassis ground.	Test lamp lights.	Replace A/C DUAL PRESSURE SWITCH.
		Test lamp does not light.	Repair open in BLU/RED wire between JUNCTION BLOCK 4 and A/C DUAL PRESSURE SWITCH.
A24.	Backprobe AUDO ALARM MODULE connector with a test lamp from cavity 9 to chassis ground.	Test lamp does not light.	Replace AUDIO ALARM MODULE.
		Test lamp lights.	GO TO **A25**.

AIR CONDITIONING SYSTEM ELECTRICAL DIAGNOSIS CHART—TRACKER, CONT.

AIR CONDITIONING: COMPRESSOR CONTROLS — DIAGNOSTIC CHART A (CONT'D)

BASE AND LSi

	TEST	RESULT	ACTION
A25.	Remove Heater Relay from JUNCTION BLOCK 4. Probe JUNCTION BLOCK 4 with a test lamp from Heater Relay cavity 3 to chassis ground.	Test lamp does not light.	Repair open in RED/BLU wire between AUDIO ALARM MODULE and JUNCTION BLOCK 4.
		Test lamp lights.	GO TO **A26**.
A26.	Probe JUNCTION BLOCK 4 with a test lamp from Heater Relay cavity 5 to chassis ground.	Test lamp does not light.	GO TO **A27**.
		Test lamp lights.	GO TO **A28**.
A27.	Remove Heater Circuit Breaker from JUNCTION BLOCK 4. Connect a digital multimeter from Heater Circuit Breaker cavity 2 to Heater Relay cavity 5. Measure resistance.	Less than 0.3 ohms.	Replace Heater Circuit Breaker.
		More than 0.3 ohms.	Repair open in BLU wire between Heater Circuit Breaker and Heater Relay.
A28.	Turn ignition switch to "OFF." Probe JUNCTION BLOCK 4 with a digital multimeter from Heater Relay cavity 1 to chassis ground. Measure resistance with BLOWER SWITCH in any position but "OFF."	Less than 0.3 ohms.	Replace HEATER RELAY.
		More than 0.3 ohms.	GO TO **A29**.
A29.	Backprobe BLOWER SWITCH connector with a digital multimeter from cavity 5 to chassis ground. Measure resistance with BLOWER SWITCH in any position but "OFF."	Less than 0.3 ohms.	Repair open in BLU/WHT wire between JUNCTION BLOCK 4 and BLOWER SWITCH.
		More than 0.3 ohms.	GO TO **A30**.
A30.	Backprobe BLOWER SWITCH connector with a digital multimeter from cavity 6 to chassis ground. Measure resistance.	Less than 0.3 ohms.	Replace BLOWER SWITCH.
		More than 0.3 ohms.	GO TO **A31**.
A31.	Backprobe JUNCTION BLOCK 4 connector with a digital multimeter from cavity 2 to chassis ground. Measure resistance.	More than 0.3 ohms.	Replace JUNCTION BLOCK 4.
		Less than 0.3 ohms.	Repair open in WHT/BLK wire between BLOWER SWITCH and JUNCTION BLOCK 4.
A32.	Turn ignition switch to "OFF". Disconnect ENGINE CONTROL MODULE connector C1. Connect a digital multimeter from A/C AMPLIFIER connector cavity 9 to chassis ground. Measure resistance.	Less than infinite.	Repair short to ground in RED/YEL wire between A/C AMPLIFIER and ENGINE CONTROL MODULE.
		Infinite.	GO TO **A33**.
A33.	Reconnect A/C AMPLIFIER and ENGINE CONTROL MODULE connectors. Start engine. Backprobe A/C AMPLIFIER connector with a digital multimeter from cavity 9 to chassis ground. Measure voltage.	Less than 12.0 volts.	An undesired A/C cutout signal is being sent to the A/C AMPLIFIER by the ENGINE CONTROL MODULE.
		More than 12.0 volts.	GO TO **A34**.
A34.	Backprobe A/C AMPLIFIER connector with a digital multimeter from cavity 14 to chassis ground. Measure voltage while increasing and decreasing engine speed.	Voltage varies slightly with changes in engine speed.	Replace A/C AMPLIFIER.
		Voltage does not vary with changes in engine speed.	Repair open in BLK wire between DISTRIBUTOR and A/C AMPLIFIER.

AIR CONDITIONING SYSTEM ELECTRICAL DIAGNOSIS CHART—TRACKER, CONT.

AIR CONDITIONING: COMPRESSOR CONTROLS — DIAGNOSTIC CHART B

GSi

	TEST	RESULT	ACTION
B1.	Start engine, turn A/C SWITCH to "ON" and BLOWER SWITCH to any position but "OFF."	A/C COMPRESSOR CLUTCH engages and BLOWER MOTOR operates at desired speed.	All systems diagnosed in this cell are functioning normally.
		A/C COMPRESSOR CLUTCH engages but BLOWER MOTOR does not operate.	Refer to Cell 60 for BLOWER MOTOR and Heater System Diagnosis.
		BLOWER MOTOR operates but A/C COMPRESSOR CLUTCH does not engage.	GO TO **B2**.
		COMPRESSOR CLUTCH does not engage and BLOWER MOTOR does not operate.	Shut off engine, turn ignition switch to "ON," and GO TO **B31**.
B2.	Backprobe A/C COMPRESSOR CLUTCH with a test lamp from connector to chassis ground.	Test lamp lights.	Replace A/C COMPRESSOR CLUTCH.
		Test lamp does not light.	GO TO **B3**.
B3.	Backprobe A/C COMPRESSOR TEMPERATURE SWITCH connector with a test lamp from cavity 1 to chassis ground.	Test lamp lights.	Repair open in BLK/WHT wire between A/C COMPRESSOR TEMPERATURE SWITCH and A/C COMPRESSOR CLUTCH.
		Test lamp does not light.	GO TO **B4**.

AIR CONDITIONING SYSTEM ELECTRICAL DIAGNOSIS CHART—TRACKER, CONT.

AIR CONDITIONING: COMPRESSOR CONTROLS — **DIAGNOSTIC CHART B (CONT'D)**

GSi

	TEST	RESULT	ACTION
B4.	Backprobe A/C COMPRESSOR TEMPERATURE SWITCH connector with a test lamp from cavity 2 to chassis ground.	Test lamp lights.	Replace A/C COMPRESSOR.
		Test lamp does not light.	GO TO **B5**.
B5.	Unfasten JUNCTION BLOCK 5 from LH inner fender. Remove bottom cover. Backprobe JUNCTION BLOCK 5 with a test lamp from A/C Clutch Relay terminal 4 to chassis ground.	Test lamp lights.	Repair open in BLK/WHT or BLK/BLU wire between JUNCTION BLOCK 5 and A/C COMPRESSOR TEMPERATURE SWITCH.
		Test lamp does not light.	GO TO **B6**.
B6.	Backprobe JUNCTION BLOCK 5 with a test lamp from A/C Clutch Relay terminal 2 to chassis ground.	Test lamp does not light.	Repair open in BLK/YEL wire between FUSE BLOCK and JUNCTION BLOCK 5.
		Test lamp lights.	GO TO **B7**.
B7.	Backprobe JUNCTION BLOCK 5 with a test lamp from A/C Clutch Relay terminal 1 to chassis ground.	Test lamp does not light.	GO TO **B8**.
		Test lamp lights.	GO TO **B9**.
B8.	Remove A/C Fuse from JUNCTION BLOCK 4. Connect a test lamp from the BLK wire terminal to chassis ground.	Test lamp lights.	Repair open in BLU/RED wire between JUNCTION BLOCK 4 and JUNCTION BLOCK 5.
		Test lamp does not light.	Repair open in BLK wire between Heater Relay and A/C Fuse.
B9.	Backprobe A/C SWITCH connector with a test lamp from cavity 5 to chassis ground.	Test lamp does not light.	Repair open in BLU/RED, YEL or YEL/WHT wire between S206 and A/C SWITCH.
		Test lamp lights.	GO TO **B10**.
B10.	Backprobe A/C SWITCH connector with a test lamp from cavity 6 to chassis ground.	Test lamp does not light.	Replace A/C SWITCH.
		Test lamp lights.	GO TO **B11**.
B11.	Backprobe A/C AMPLIFIER connector with a test lamp from cavity 1 to chassis ground.	Test lamp does not light.	Repair open in YEL/WHT wire between A/C SWITCH and A/C AMPLIFIER.
		Test lamp lights.	GO TO **B12**.
B12.	Turn ignition switch to "OFF" and disconnect A/C AMPLIFIER connector. Connect a digital multimeter from A/C AMPLIFIER connector cavity 13 to chassis ground. Measure resistance.	More than 0.3 ohms.	GO TO **B13**.
		Less than 0.3 ohms.	GO TO **B14**.
B13.	Backprobe JUNCTION BLOCK 4 with a digital multimeter from cavity 1 to chassis ground. Measure resistance.	Less than 0.3 ohms.	Repair open in WHT/BLK wire between A/C AMPLIFIER and JUNCTION BLOCK 4.
		More than 0.3 ohms.	Replace JUNCTION BLOCK 4.
B14.	Turn ignition switch to "ON." Backprobe JUNCTION BLOCK 5 with a test lamp from A/C Clutch Relay terminal 3 to chassis ground.	Test lamp does not light.	Replace A/C Clutch Relay.
		Test lamp lights.	GO TO **B15**.
B15.	Connect a test lamp from A/C AMPLIFIER connector cavity 4 to chassis ground.	Test lamp does not light.	Repair open in A/C DIODE or BLU/ORN wire between JUNCTION BLOCK 5 and A/C AMPLIFIER.
		Test lamp lights.	GO TO **B16**.
B16.	Disconnect A/C COMPRESSOR CLUTCH connector. Connect a fused jumper from A/C AMPLIFIER connector cavity 4 to chassis ground. Connect a test lamp from A/C COMPRESSOR CLUTCH connector to chassis ground.	Test lamp does not light.	Replace A/C Clutch Relay.
		Test lamp lights.	Leave jumper attached and GO TO **B17**.
B17.	Connect a test lamp from A/C AMPLIFIER connector cavity 8 to chassis ground.	Test lamp does not light.	Repair open in BLK/WHT, YEL/BLK or BLK/YEL wire between A/C COMPRESSOR CLUTCH and A/C AMPLIFIER.
		Test lamp lights.	GO TO **B18**.
B18.	Disconnect thermistor connector. Connect a digital multimeter across terminals of THERMISTOR side of connector. Measure resistance at approximately 25°C (77°F).	More than 2.0k ohms.	Replace THERMISTOR.
		Less than 2.0k ohms.	GO TO **B19**.
B19.	Connect a digital multimeter from THERMISTOR connector cavity 2 (wiring harness side) to A/C AMPLIFIER connector cavity 14. Measure resistance.	More than 0.3 ohms.	Repair open in BLK/RED wire between THERMISTOR and A/C AMPLIFIER.
		Less than 0.3 ohms.	GO TO **B20**.
B20.	Connect a digital multimeter from THERMISTOR connector cavity 1 (wiring harness side) to A/C AMPLIFIER connector cavity 2. Measure resistance.	More than 0.3 ohms.	Repair open in YEL/GRN wire between THERMISTOR and A/C AMPLIFIER.
		Less than 0.3 ohms.	GO TO **B21**.
B21.	Connect a digital multimeter across A/C AMPLIFIER connector cavities 2 and 9. Measure resistance.	More than 0.3 ohms.	Repair open in YEL/GRN wire between A/C AMPLIFIER connector cavity 9 and S287.
		Less than 0.3 ohms.	GO TO **B22**.
B22.	Connect a test lamp from A/C AMPLIFIER connector cavity 5 to chassis ground. Reinstall A/C Fuse.	Test lamp lights.	GO TO **B25**.
		Test lamp does not light.	GO TO **B23**.
B23.	Backprobe A/C DUAL PRESSURE SWITCH connector with a test lamp from cavity 2 to chassis ground.	Test lamp lights.	Repair open in BLK/YEL wire between A/C DUAL PRESSURE SWITCH and A/C AMPLIFIER.
		Test lamp does not light.	GO TO **B24**.

AIR CONDITIONING SYSTEM ELECTRICAL DIAGNOSIS CHART—TRACKER, CONT.

AIR CONDITIONING: COMPRESSOR CONTROLS — DIAGNOSTIC CHART B (CONT'D)

GSi

TEST	RESULT	ACTION
B24. Backprobe A/C DUAL PRESSURE SWITCH connector with a test lamp from cavity 1 to chassis ground.	Test lamp does not light.	Repair open in BLU/RED wire between JUNCTION BLOCK 5 and A/C AMPLIFIER.
	Test lamp lights.	Replace A/C DUAL PRESSURE SWITCH.
B25. Turn ignition switch to "OFF." Disconnect ENGINE CONTROL MODULE connector C1. Connect a digital multimeter from A/C AMPLIFIER connector cavity 11 to chassis ground. Measure resistance.	Less than infinite.	Repair short to ground in RED/YEL wire between ENGINE CONTROL MODULE and A/C AMPLIFIER.
	Infinite.	GO TO **B26**.
B26. Reconnect ENGINE CONTROL MODULE and A/C AMPLIFIER connectors. Start engine. Backprobe A/C AMPLIFIER connector with a digital multimeter from cavity 11 to chassis ground. Measure voltage.	Less than 12.0 volts.	An undesired A/C cutout signal is being sent to the A/C AMPLIFIER by the ENGINE CONTROL MODULE.
	More than 12.0 volts.	GO TO **B27**.
B27. Backprobe A/C AMPLIFIER connector with a digital multimeter from cavity 10 to chassis ground. Measure AC voltage while varying engine speed.	AC voltage is not present or does not vary with engine speed.	Repair open in BLK wire between A/C AMPLIFIER and IGNITER.
	AC voltage varies from approximately 0.5 to 5.0 millivolts from idle to 3000 rpm.	GO TO **B28**.
B28. Backprobe A/C AMPLIFIER connector with a digital multimeter from cavity 17 to chassis ground. Measure AC voltage while varying engine speed.	AC voltage varies from approximately 18.0 to 25.0 millivolts from idle to 3000 rpm.	Replace A/C AMPLIFIER.
	AC voltage is not present or does not vary with engine speed.	GO TO **B29**.
B29. Turn ignition switch to "OFF." Disconnect A/C AMPLIFIER connector. Disconnect connector C106. Connect a digital multimeter from A/C AMPLIFIER connector cavity 17 to connector C106 cavity 4. Measure resistance.	More than 0.3 ohms.	Repair open in WHT/RED wire between A/C AMPLIFIER and REVOLUTION DETECTING SENSOR.
	Less than 0.3 ohms.	GO TO **B30**.
B30. Connect a digital multimeter from A/C AMPLIFIER connector cavity 14 to connector C106 cavity 3. Measure resistance.	More than 0.3 ohms.	Repair open in BLK/RED or BRN wire between A/C AMPLIFIER and REVOLUTION DETECTING SENSOR.
	Less than 0.3 ohms.	Replace A/C COMPRESSOR
B31. Backprobe AUDIO ALARM MODULE connector with a test lamp from cavity 9 to chassis ground.	Test lamp does not light.	Replace AUDIO ALARM MODULE.
	Test lamp lights.	GO TO **B32**.
B32. Remove Heater Relay from JUNCTION BLOCK 4. Probe JUNCTION BLOCK 4 with a test lamp from Heater Relay cavity 3 to chassis ground.	Test lamp does not light.	Repair open in RED/BLU wire between AUDIO ALARM MODULE and JUNCTION BLOCK 4.
	Test lamp lights.	GO TO **B33**.
B33. Probe JUNCTION BLOCK 4 with a test lamp from Heater Relay cavity 5 to chassis ground.	Test lamp does not light.	GO TO **B34**.
	Test lamp lights.	GO TO **B35**.
B34. Remove Heater Circuit Breaker from JUNCTION BLOCK 4. Connect a digital multimeter from Heater Circuit Breaker cavity 2 to Heater Relay cavity 5. Measure resistance.	More than 0.3 ohms.	Repair open in BLU wire between Heater Circuit Breaker and Heater Relay.
	Less than 0.3 ohms.	Replace Heater Circuit Breaker.
B35. Turn ignition switch to "OFF." Probe JUNCTION BLOCK 4 with a digital multimeter from Heater Relay cavity 1 to chassis ground. Measure resistance with BLOWER SWITCH in any position but "OFF."	Less than 0.3 ohms.	Replace Heater Relay.
	More than 0.3 ohms.	GO TO **B36**.
B36. Backprobe BLOWER SWITCH connector with a digital multimeter from cavity 5 to chassis ground. Measure resistance with BLOWER SWITCH in any position but "OFF."	Less than 0.3 ohms.	Repair open in BLU/WHT wire between JUNCTION BLOCK 4 and BLOWER SWITCH.
	More than 0.3 ohms.	GO TO **B37**.
B37. Backprobe BLOWER SWITCH with a digital multimeter from cavity 6 to chassis ground. Measure resistance with BLOWER SWITCH in any position but "OFF."	Less than 0.3 ohms.	Replace BLOWER SWITCH.
	More than 0.3 ohms.	GO TO **B38**.
B38. Backprobe JUNCTION BLOCK 4 with a digital multimeter from cavity 2 to chassis ground. Measure resistance.	Less than 0.3 ohms.	Repair open in WHT/BLK wire between BLOWER SWITCH and JUNCTION BLOCK 4.
	More than 0.3 ohms.	Replace JUNCTION BLOCK 4.

CIRCUIT OPERATION

A/C Compressor Clutch

Whenever the ignition switch is in the "ON" position, battery voltage is applied through the GAUGE Fuse and AUDIO ALARM MODULE to the coil of the Heater Relay. With the BLOWER SWITCH in any position but "OFF," the Heater Relay coil is provided with a ground through the BLOWER SWITCH at JUNCTION BLOCK 4. With a ground provided, the Heater Relay is energized, the relay contacts close, and battery voltage is applied through the Heater Circuit Breaker, the closed Heater Relay contacts, and the A/C Fuse to the coil of the A/C Clutch Relay.

When the proper inputs are received, the A/C AMPLIFIER provides a ground for the coil of the A/C Clutch Relay. This set of inputs includes the following signals:

- Power input indicating that the A/C SWITCH has been turned to "ON."

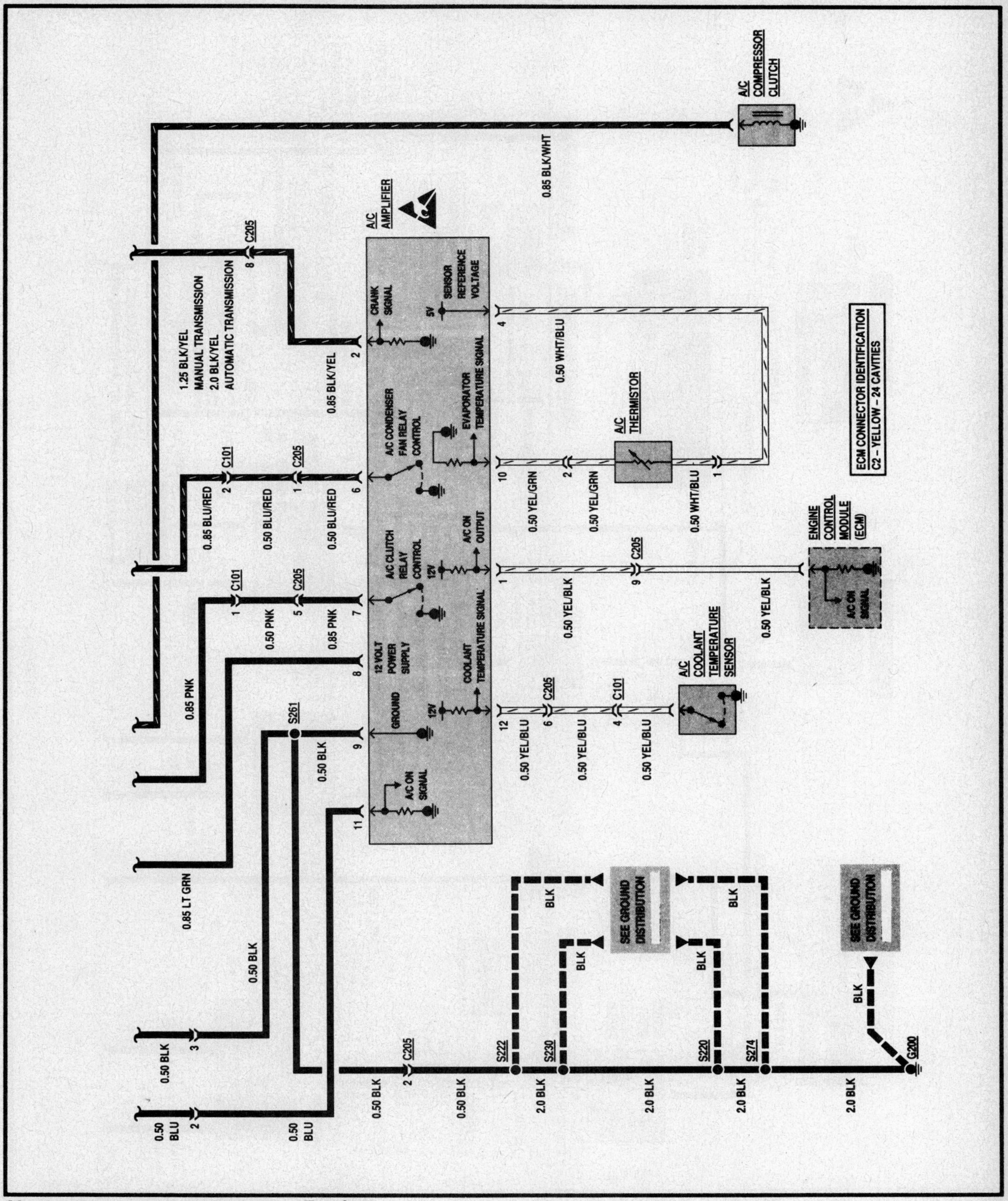
A/C COMPRESSOR CLUTCH
0.85 BLK/WHT
A/C AMPLIFIER
C205
8
1.25 BLK/YEL
MANUAL TRANSMISSION
2.0 BLK/YEL
AUTOMATIC TRANSMISSION
0.85 BLK/YEL
2
CRANK SIGNAL
5V
SENSOR REFERENCE VOLTAGE
4
0.50 WHT/BLU
ECM CONNECTOR IDENTIFICATION
C2 – YELLOW – 24 CAVITIES
C101
0.85 BLU/RED
0.50 BLU/RED
6
A/C CONDENSER FAN RELAY CONTROL
EVAPORATOR TEMPERATURE SIGNAL
10
0.50 YEL/GRN
A/C THERMISTOR
0.50 WHT/BLU
1
A/C CLUTCH RELAY CONTROL
12V
A/C ON OUTPUT
0.50 YEL/BLK
9
ENGINE CONTROL MODULE (ECM)
A/C ON SIGNAL
0.85 PNK
0.50 PNK
5
7
12 VOLT POWER SUPPLY
COOLANT TEMPERATURE SIGNAL
A/C COOLANT TEMPERATURE SENSOR
12
0.50 YEL/BLU
GROUND
S261
0.50 BLK
11
0.85 LT GRN
BLK
SEE GROUND DISTRIBUTION
S222
S230
S220
S274
G200
2.0 BLK
3
0.50 BLU

Air conditioning wiring diagram—Tracker

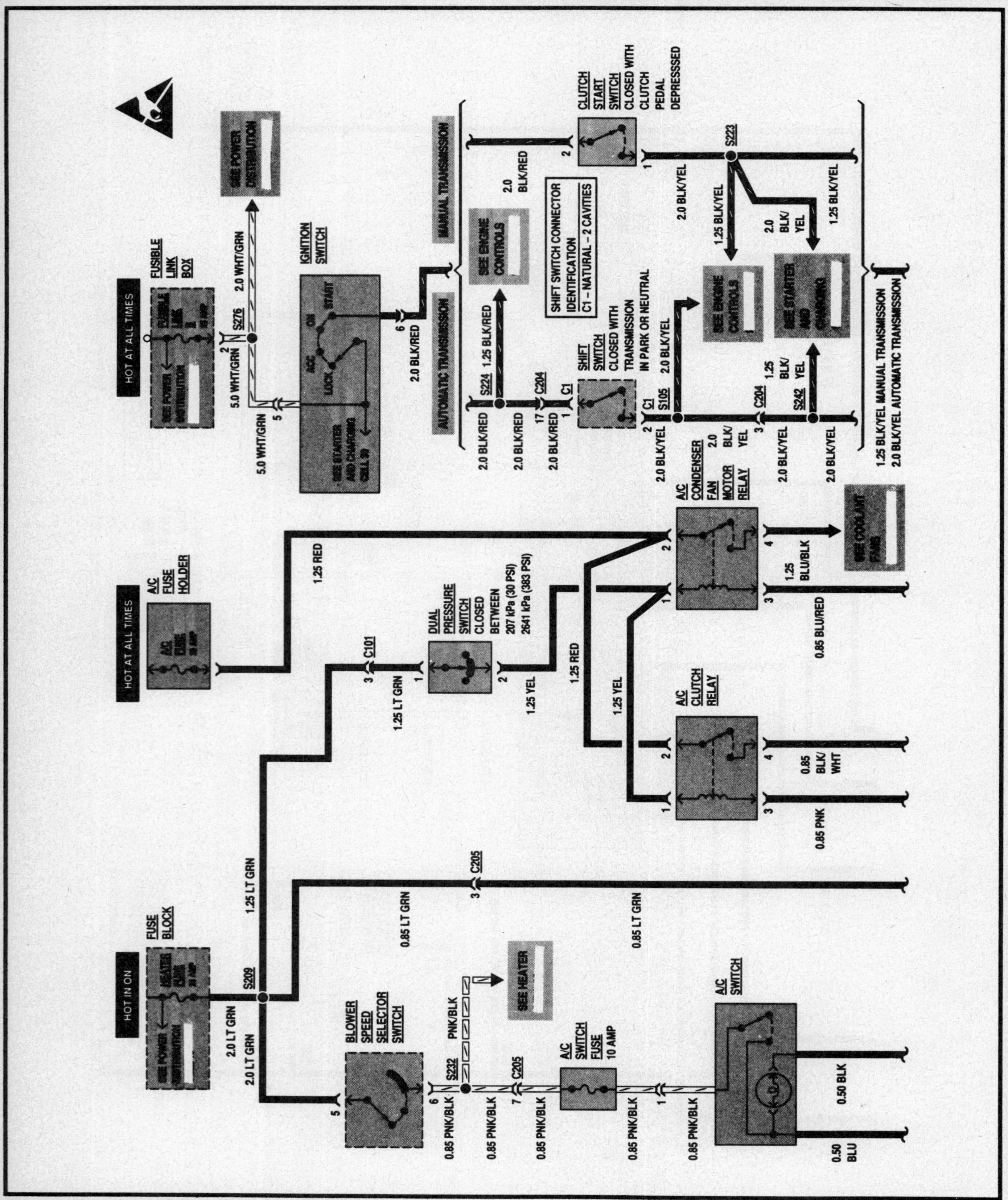
HOT AT ALL TIMES
FUSIBLE LINK BOX
SEE POWER DISTRIBUTION
S276
2.0 WHT/GRN
5.0 WHT/GRN
IGNITION SWITCH
ACC
LOCK
ON
START
SEE STARTER AND CHARGING
2.0 BLK/RED
MANUAL TRANSMISSION
AUTOMATIC TRANSMISSION
SEE ENGINE CONTROLS
1.25 BLK/RED
S224
C204
C1
CLUTCH START SWITCH CLOSED WITH CLUTCH PEDAL DEPRESSSED
SHIFT SWITCH CONNECTOR IDENTIFICATION
C1 – NATURAL – 2 CAVITIES
SHIFT SWITCH CLOSED WITH TRANSMISSION IN PARK OR NEUTRAL
S223
2.0 BLK/YEL
1.25 BLK/YEL
S105
S242
1.25 BLK/YEL MANUAL TRANSMISSION
2.0 BLK/YEL AUTOMATIC TRANSMISSION
A/C FUSE HOLDER
1.25 RED
A/C CONDENSER FAN MOTOR RELAY
SEE COOLANT FANS
1.25 BLU/BLK
0.85 BLU/RED
DUAL PRESSURE SWITCH CLOSED BETWEEN 207 kPa (30 PSI) 2641 kPa (383 PSI)
C101
1.25 LT GRN
1.25 YEL
A/C CLUTCH RELAY
0.85 BLK/WHT
0.85 PNK
HOT IN ON
FUSE BLOCK
S209
2.0 LT GRN
C205
0.85 LT GRN
BLOWER SPEED SELECTOR SWITCH
S232
PNK/BLK
SEE HEATER
0.85 PNK/BLK
A/C SWITCH FUSE 10 AMP
A/C SWITCH
0.50 BLK
0.50 BLU

Air conditioning wiring diagram—Tracker, cont.

AIR CONDITIONING SYSTEM ELECTRICAL DIAGNOSIS CHART—METRO

AIR CONDITIONING	DIAGNOSTIC CHART A		
	TEST	**RESULT**	**ACTION**
A1.	Start engine, press A/C SWITCH to "ON" and turn BLOWER SPEED SELECTOR SWITCH to any position but "OFF."	A/C COMPRESSOR CLUTCH engages and Blower Motor operates at desired speed.	All systems diagnosed in this cell are functioning normally.
		A/C COMPRESSOR CLUTCH engages but Blower Motor does not operate.	Refer to Blower Motor and Heater System Diagnosis.
		Blower Motor operates but A/C COMPRESSOR CLUTCH does not engage.	Shut off engine, turn IGNITION SWITCH to "ON" and GO TO **A2.**
A2.	Backprobe A/C COMPRESSOR CLUTCH connector with a test lamp from cavity 1 to chassis ground.	Test lamp lights.	Replace A/C COMPRESSOR CLUTCH.
		Test lamp does not light.	GO TO **A3**.
A3.	Backprobe A/C (Condenser Fan) Relay connector with a test lamp from cavity 1 to chassis ground.	Test lamp lights.	Repair open in BLK/WHT wire between A/C (Condenser Fan) Relay and A/C COMPRESSOR CLUTCH.
		Test lamp does not light.	GO TO **A4**.
A4.	Backprobe A/C (Clutch) Relay connector with a test lamp from cavity 4 to chassis ground.	Test lamp lights.	Repair open in BLK/WHT wire between A/C (Clutch) Relay and A/C (Condenser Fan) Relay.
		Test lamp does not light.	GO TO **A5**.
A5.	Backprobe A/C (Clutch) Relay connector with a test lamp from cavity 2 to chassis ground.	Test lamp does not light.	Repair open in RED wire between A/C (Clutch) Relay and FUSE AND RELAY BOX.
		Test lamp lights.	GO TO **A6**.
A6.	Backprobe A/C (Clutch) Relay connector with a test lamp from cavity 1 to chassis ground.	Test lamp lights.	GO TO **A7**.
		Test lamp does not light.	GO TO **A9**.
A7.	Disconnect A/C CONTROLLER connector. Connect a jumper from A/C CONTROLLER connector cavity 7 to chassis ground. Backprobe A/C (Clutch) Relay with a test lamp from cavity 4 to chassis ground.	Test lamp does not light.	GO TO **A8**.
		Test lamp lights.	GO TO **A12**.
A8.	Remove jumper. Disconnect A/C (Clutch) Relay connector. Connect a digital multimeter from A/C (Clutch) Relay connector cavity 3 to A/C CONTROLLER connector cavity 7. Measure resistance.	•More than 0.3 ohms.	Repair open in PNK wire between A/C (Clutch) Relay and A/C CONTROLLER.
		Less than 0.3 ohms.	Replace A/C (Clutch) Relay.
A9.	Backprobe DUAL PRESSURE SWITCH connector with a test lamp from cavity 1 to chassis ground.	Test lamp lights.	Repair open in YEL wire between DUAL PRESSURE SWITCH and A/C (Clutch) Relay.
		Test lamp does not light.	GO TO **A10**.
A10.	Backprobe DUAL PRESSURE SWITCH connector with a test lamp from cavity 2 to chassis ground.	Test lamp lights.	Replace DUAL PRESSURE SWITCH.
		Test lamp does not light.	GO TO **A11**.
A11.	Disconnect JUNCTION BLOCK connector C7, DUAL PRESSURE SWITCH connector, and A/C CONTROLLER connector. Connect a digital multimeter from JUNCTION BLOCK connector C7 cavity 1 to DUAL PRESSURE SWITCH connector cavity 2. Measure resistance.	More than 0.3 ohms.	Repair open in LT GRN or BLK/WHT wire between JUNCTION BLOCK and DUAL PRESSURE SWITCH.
		Less than 0.3 ohms.	Repair or replace JUNCTION BLOCK.
A12.	Connect a digital multimeter from A/C CONTROLLER connector cavity 12 to chassis ground. Measure resistance.	More than 0.3 ohms.	GO TO **A13**.
		Less than 0.3 ohms.	GO TO **A14**.

AIR CONDITIONING SYSTEM ELECTRICAL DIAGNOSIS CHART—METRO, CONT.

AIR CONDITIONING **DIAGNOSTIC CHART A (CONT'D)**

	TEST	RESULT	ACTION
A13.	Disconnect A/C COOLANT TEMPERATURE SWITCH connector. Connect a digital multimeter from A/C COOLANT TEMPERATURE SWITCH terminal to chassis ground. Measure resistance.	Less than 0.3 ohms.	Repair open in YEL/BLK wire between A/C CONTROLLER and A/C COOLANT TEMPERATURE SWITCH.
		More than 0.3 ohms.	Replace A/C COOLANT TEMPERATURE SWITCH.
A14.	Connect a test lamp from A/C CONTROLLER connector cavity 8 to chassis ground.	Test lamp does not light.	Repair open in LT GRN or BLK/WHT wire between A/C CONTROLLER and JUNCTION BLOCK.
		Test lamp lights.	GO TO **A15**.
A15.	Connect a digital multimeter from A/C CONTROLLER connector cavity 9 to chassis ground. Measure resistance.	More than 0.3 ohms.	Repair BLK ground wire between A/C CONTROLLER and G201.
		Less than 0.3 ohms.	GO TO **A16**.
A16.	Connect a test lamp from A/C CONTROLLER connector cavity 11 to chassis ground.	Test lamp does not light.	GO TO **A17**.
		Test lamp lights.	GO TO **A19**.
A17.	Backprobe A/C SWITCH connector with a test lamp from cavity 2 to chassis ground.	Test lamp lights.	Repair open in BLK/WHT wire between A/C SWITCH and A/C CONTROLLER.
		Test lamp does not light.	GO TO **A18**.
A18.	Backprobe A/C SWITCH connector with a test lamp from cavity 3 to chassis ground.	Test lamp does not light.	Repair open in PNK/BLK wire between A/C SWITCH and S234.
		Test lamp lights.	Replace A/C SWITCH.
A19.	Disconnect A/C THERMISTOR. Connect a digital multimeter across A/C THERMISTOR terminals 1 and 2. Measure resistance at room temperature.	More than 2000 ohms.	Replace A/C THERMISTOR.
		Less than 2000 ohms.	GO TO **A20**.
A20.	Reconnect A/C THERMISTOR. Connect a digital multimeter from A/C CONTROLLER connector cavity 10 to A/C CONTROLLER connector cavity 4. Measure resistance.	More than 2000 ohms.	Repair open in YEL/GRN or WHT/BLU wire between A/C THERMISTOR and A/C CONTROLLER.
		Less than 2000 ohms.	GO TO **A21** with manual transaxle GO TO **A23** with automatic transaxle.
A21.	Disconnect A/C ACCELERATOR CUTOFF SWITCH connector. Connect a digital multimeter from A/C CONTROLLER connector cavity 5 to chassis ground. Measure resistance.	Less than infinite.	Repair short to ground in BLK/WHT wire between A/C CONTROLLER and A/C ACCELERATOR CUTOFF SWITCH.
		Infinite.	GO TO **A22**.
A22.	Reconnect A/C CONTROLLER. Connect a test lamp from A/C COMPRESSOR CLUTCH connector cavity 1 to chassis ground.	Test lamp lights.	Replace A/C ACCELERATOR CUTOFF SWITCH.
		Test lamp does not light.	Replace A/C CONTROLLER.
A23.	Disconnect AUTOMATIC TRANSAXLE CONTROLLER connector C1. Connect a digital multimeter from A/C CONTROLLER connector cavity 5 to chassis ground. Measure resistance.	Less than infinite.	Repair short to ground in BLK/WHT or LT GRN/RED wire between A/C CONTROLLER and AUTOMATIC TRANSAXLE CONTROLLER.
		Infinite.	GO TO **A24**.
A24.	Reconnect A/C CONTROLLER. Connect a test lamp from A/C COMPRESSOR CLUTCH connector cavity 1 to chassis ground.	Test lamp lights.	Refer to AUTOMATIC TRANSAXLE GENERAL DESCRIPTION AND ON-VEHICLE SERVICE (SEC.7A) for system diagnosis procedures.
		Test lamp does not light.	Replace A/C CONTROLLER.

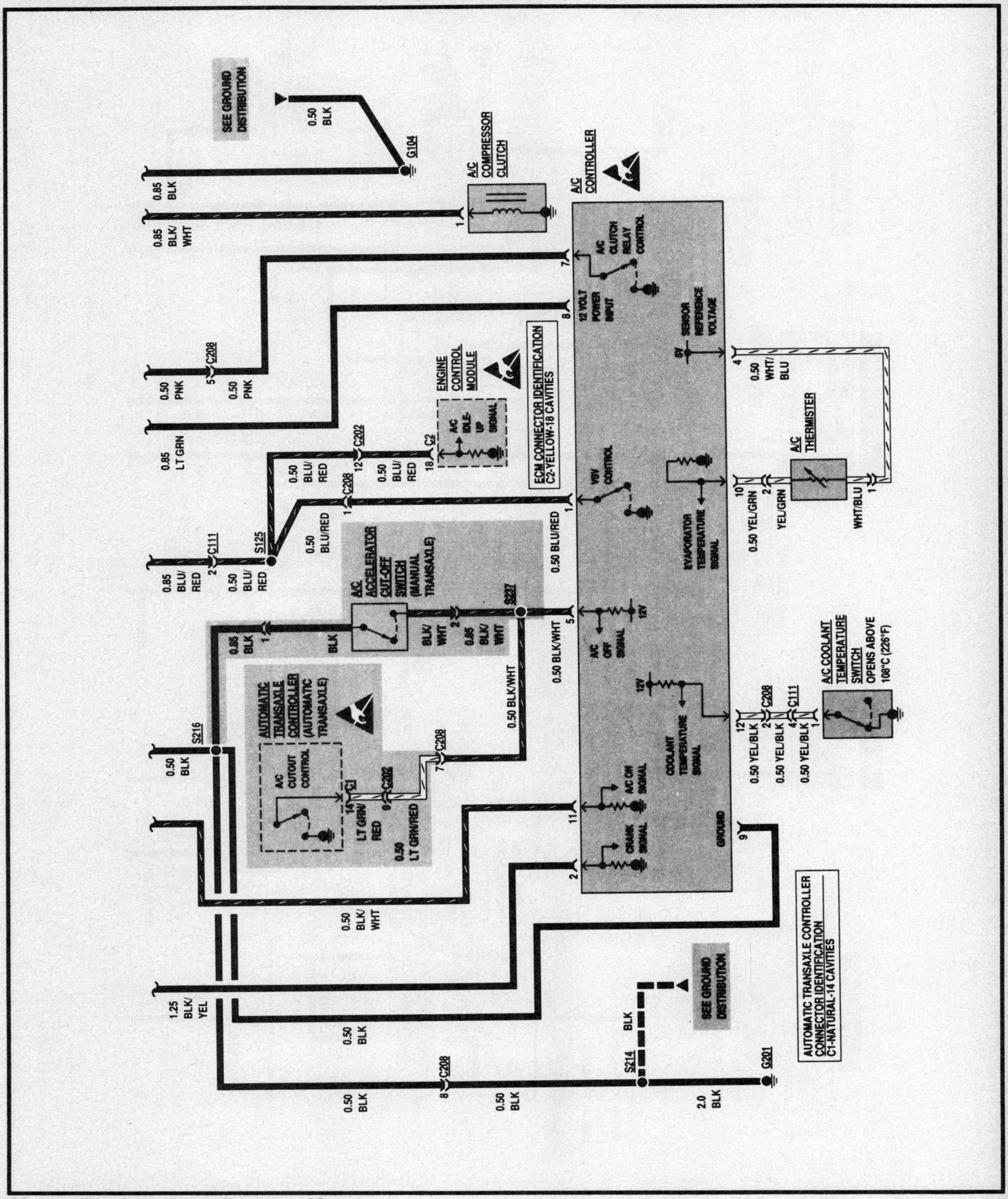
SEE GROUND DISTRIBUTION
G104
A/C COMPRESSOR CLUTCH
A/C CONTROLLER
A/C CLUTCH RELAY CONTROL
12 VOLT POWER INPUT
SENSOR REFERENCE VOLTAGE
ENGINE CONTROL MODULE
A/C IDLE-UP SIGNAL
ECM CONNECTOR IDENTIFICATION
C2-YELLOW-18 CAVITIES
VSV CONTROL
EVAPORATOR TEMPERATURE SIGNAL
A/C THERMISTER
A/C ACCELERATOR CUT-OFF SWITCH (MANUAL TRANSAXLE)
A/C OFF SIGNAL
AUTOMATIC TRANSAXLE CONTROLLER (AUTOMATIC TRANSAXLE)
A/C CUTOUT CONTROL
A/C ON SIGNAL
COOLANT TEMPERATURE SIGNAL
CRANK SIGNAL
GROUND
A/C COOLANT TEMPERATURE SWITCH
OPENS ABOVE 108°C (226°F)
AUTOMATIC TRANSAXLE CONTROLLER CONNECTOR IDENTIFICATION
C1-NATURAL-14 CAVITIES
S216
S125
S227
S214
G201

Air conditioning wiring diagram – Metro

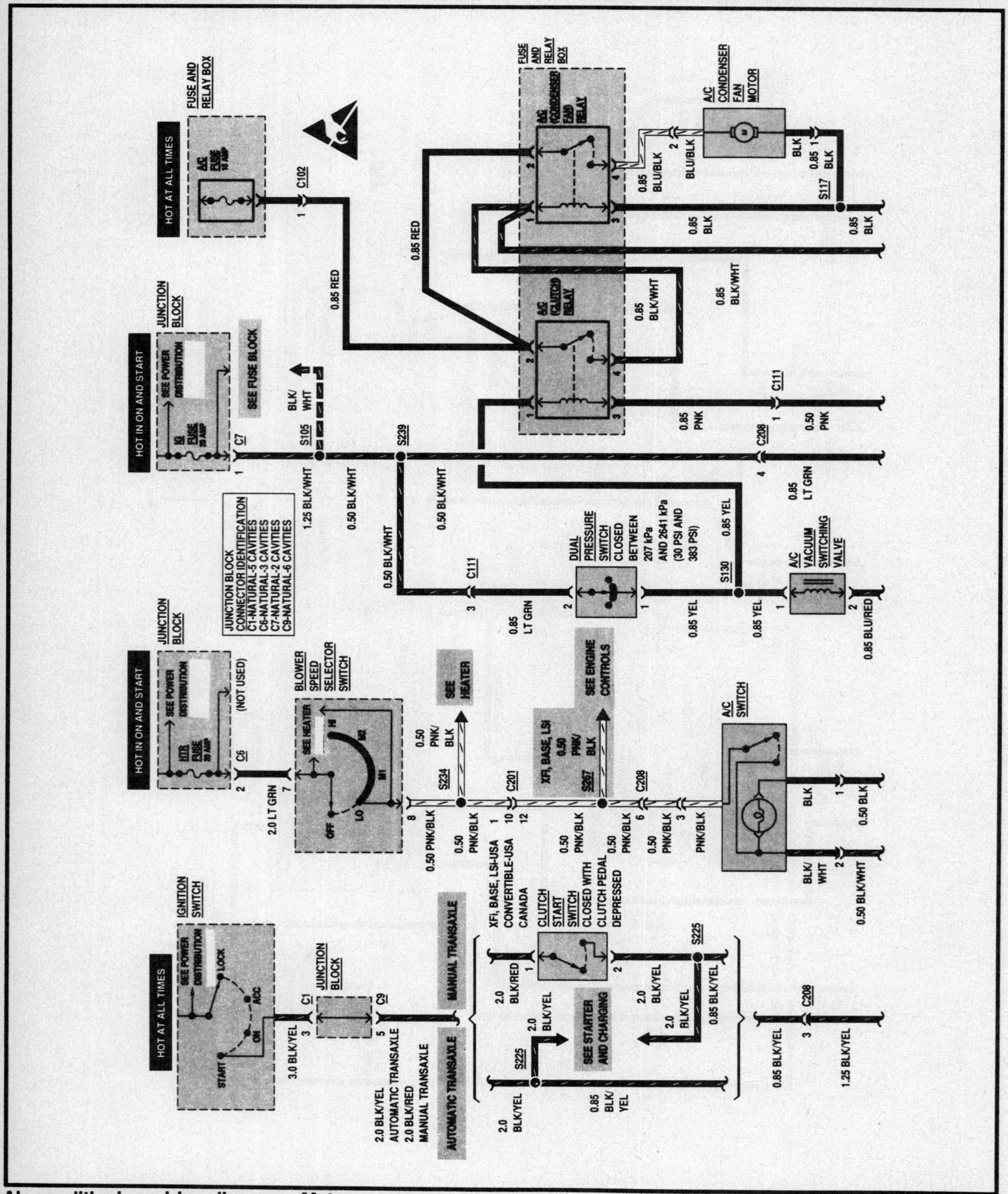
HOT AT ALL TIMES
FUSE AND RELAY BOX
A/C FUSE 15 AMP
C102
HOT IN ON AND START
JUNCTION BLOCK
SEE POWER DISTRIBUTION
IG FUSE 20 AMP
SEE FUSE BLOCK
C7
S105
BLK/WHT
S239
1.25 BLK/WHT
0.50 BLK/WHT
0.85 RED
FUSE AND RELAY BOX
A/C (CONDENSER FAN) RELAY
A/C (CLUTCH) RELAY
A/C CONDENSER FAN MOTOR
0.85 BLU/BLK
BLU/BLK
BLK
0.85 BLK
S117
0.85 BLK/WHT
C111
0.85 PNK
0.50 PNK
C208
0.85 LT GRN
JUNCTION BLOCK CONNECTOR IDENTIFICATION
C1-NATURAL-5 CAVITIES
C6-NATURAL-3 CAVITIES
C7-NATURAL-2 CAVITIES
C9-NATURAL-6 CAVITIES
DUAL PRESSURE SWITCH CLOSED BETWEEN 207 kPa AND 2641 kPa (30 PSI AND 383 PSI)
0.85 YEL
S130
A/C VACUUM SWITCHING VALVE
0.85 BLU/RED
HTR FUSE 20 AMP
(NOT USED)
C6
2.0 LT GRN
BLOWER SPEED SELECTOR SWITCH
SEE HEATER
OFF
LO
M1
M2
HI
0.50 PNK/BLK
S234
C201
SEE HEATER
XFI, BASE, LSI
SEE ENGINE CONTROLS
S267
A/C SWITCH
0.50 BLK
BLK/WHT
0.50 BLK/WHT
IGNITION SWITCH
LOCK
ACC
ON
START
C1
C9
3.0 BLK/YEL
2.0 BLK/YEL AUTOMATIC TRANSAXLE
2.0 BLK/RED MANUAL TRANSAXLE
MANUAL TRANSAXLE
AUTOMATIC TRANSAXLE
XFI, BASE, LSI-USA CONVERTIBLE-USA CANADA
CLUTCH START SWITCH CLOSED WITH CLUTCH PEDAL DEPRESSED
2.0 BLK/RED
S225
2.0 BLK/YEL
0.85 BLK/YEL
SEE STARTER AND CHARGING
0.85 BLK/YEL
1.25 BLK/YEL

Air conditioning wiring diagram—Metro, cont.

AIR CONDITIONING SYSTEM DIAGNOSIS CHART—SPECTRUM AND STORM

TROUBLE	POSSIBLE CAUSE	CORRECTION
No cooling, or warm air.	1. Magnetic clutch does not engage properly.	
	• Fuse blown.	Replace fuse and check for short.
	• Magnetic clutch.	Check clutch.
	• A/C switch faulty.	Check switch.
	• Temperature control switch faulty.	Check switch.
	• Dual pressure switch faulty.	Check switch.
	• Wiring or grounding.	Repair as necessary.
	• No refrigerant.	Check A/C circuit.
	2. Compressor is not rotating properly.	
	• Drive belt loosened or broken.	Tighten or replace drive belt.
	• Compressor faulty.	Check compressor.
	3. Blower inoperative.	Check heater.
	4. Expansion valve faulty.	Check expansion valve.
	5. Leak in system.	Check system for leaks.
	6. Accumulator/dehydrator has blown fusible plug or clogged screw.	Check receiver/dryer.
Cool air comes out only intermittently.	1. Magnetic clutch.	Check magnetic clutch.
	2. Expansion valve faulty.	Check expansion valve.
	3. Wiring connection faulty.	Repair as necessary.
	4. Excessive moisture in system.	Evacuate and charge system.
Cool air comes out only at high speeds.	1. Condenser clogged.	Check condenser.
	2. Drive belt slipping.	Check or replace drive belt.
	3. Compressor fualty.	Check compressor.
	4. Insufficient or excessive charge of refrigerant.	Check charge of refrigerant.
	5. Air in system.	Evacuate and charge system.

AIR CONDITIONING SYSTEM DIAGNOSIS CHART—SPECTRUM AND STORM, CONT.

TROUBLE	POSSIBLE CAUSE	CORRECTION
Insufficient cooling.	1. Condenser clogged.	Check condenser.
	2. Drive belt slipping.	Check or replace drive belt.
	3. Magnetic clutch faulty.	Check magnetic clutch.
	4. Compressor faulty.	Check compressor.
	5. Expansion valve faulty.	Check expansion valve.
	6. Temperature control switch faulty.	Check temperature control switch.
	7. Too little or too much charge of refrigerant.	Check charge of refrigerant.
	8. Air or excessive compressor oil in system.	Evacuate and charge system.
	9. Accumulator/dehydrator plugged.	Check accumulator/ dehydrator.
Insufficient velocity of cooled air	1. Evaporator clogged or frosted.	Check evaporator.
	2. Air leaking from cooling unit or air duct.	Repair as necessary.
	3. Air inlet blocked.	Repair as necessary.
	4. Blower motor faulty.	Replace blower motor.

AIR CONDITIONING SYSTEM DIAGNOSIS CHART—SPECTRUM

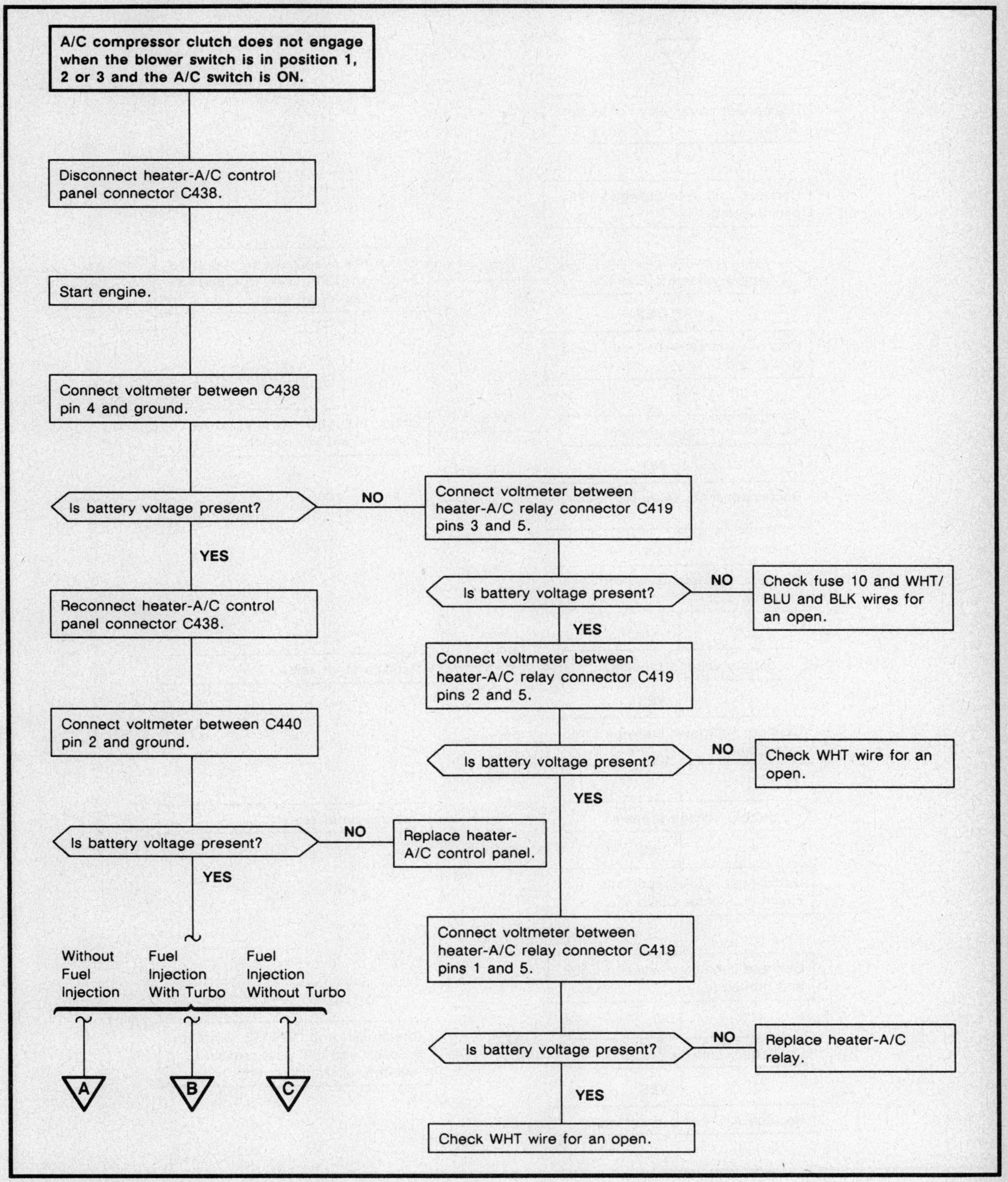
A/C compressor clutch does not engage when the blower switch is in position 1, 2 or 3 and the A/C switch is ON.
Disconnect heater-A/C control panel connector C438.
Start engine.
Connect voltmeter between C438 pin 4 and ground.
Is battery voltage present?
NO
Connect voltmeter between heater-A/C relay connector C419 pins 3 and 5.
Is battery voltage present?
NO
Check fuse 10 and WHT/BLU and BLK wires for an open.
YES
Connect voltmeter between heater-A/C relay connector C419 pins 2 and 5.
Is battery voltage present?
NO
Check WHT wire for an open.
YES
Connect voltmeter between heater-A/C relay connector C419 pins 1 and 5.
Is battery voltage present?
NO
Replace heater-A/C relay.
YES
Check WHT wire for an open.
YES
Reconnect heater-A/C control panel connector C438.
Connect voltmeter between C440 pin 2 and ground.
Is battery voltage present?
NO
Replace heater-A/C control panel.
YES
Without Fuel Injection
Fuel Injection With Turbo
Fuel Injection Without Turbo
A
B
C

AIR CONDITIONING SYSTEM DIAGNOSIS CHART—SPECTRUM, CONT.

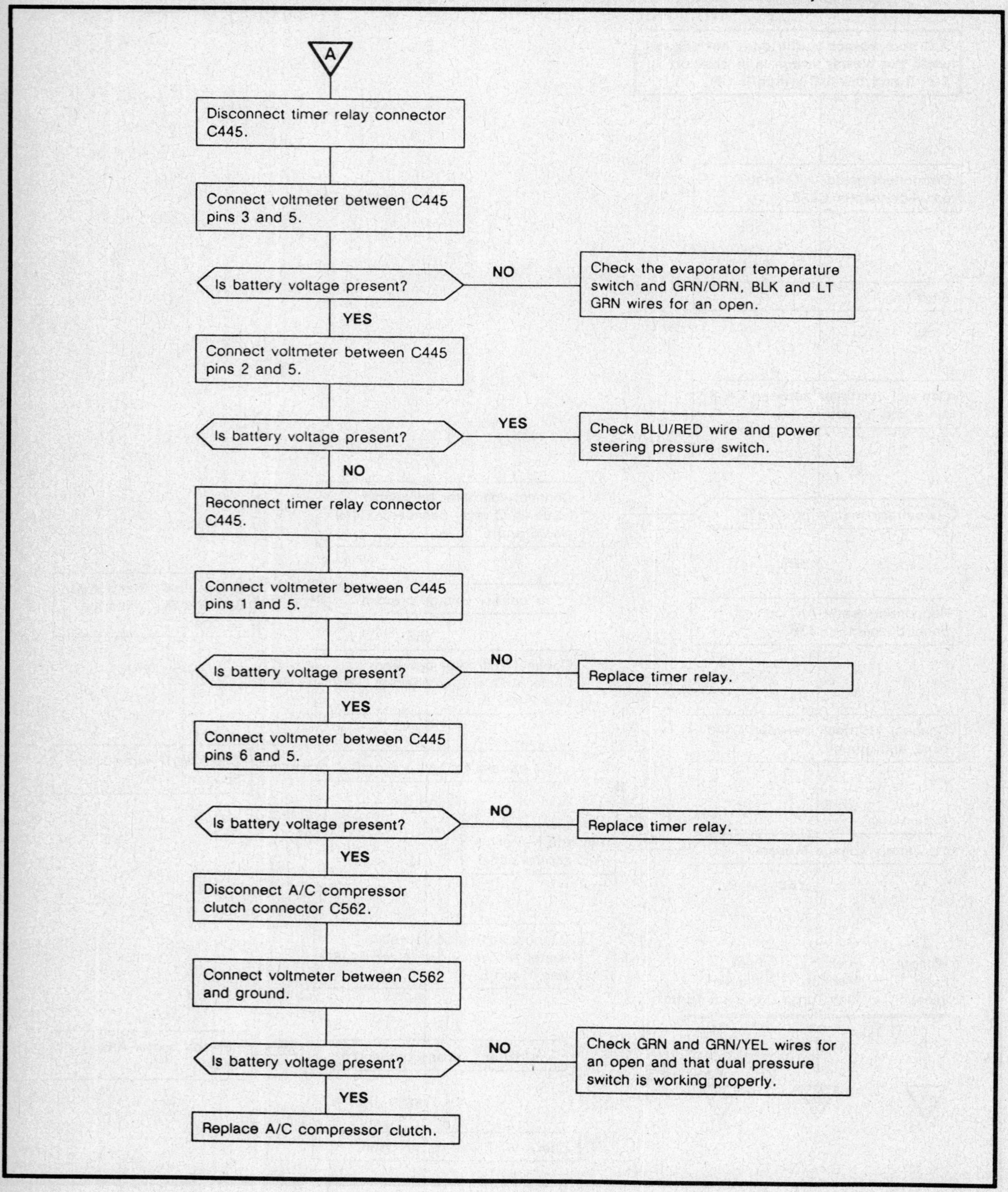
A
Disconnect timer relay connector C445.
Connect voltmeter between C445 pins 3 and 5.
Is battery voltage present?
NO
Check the evaporator temperature switch and GRN/ORN, BLK and LT GRN wires for an open.
YES
Connect voltmeter between C445 pins 2 and 5.
Is battery voltage present?
YES
Check BLU/RED wire and power steering pressure switch.
NO
Reconnect timer relay connector C445.
Connect voltmeter between C445 pins 1 and 5.
Is battery voltage present?
NO
Replace timer relay.
YES
Connect voltmeter between C445 pins 6 and 5.
Is battery voltage present?
NO
Replace timer relay.
YES
Disconnect A/C compressor clutch connector C562.
Connect voltmeter between C562 and ground.
Is battery voltage present?
NO
Check GRN and GRN/YEL wires for an open and that dual pressure switch is working properly.
YES
Replace A/C compressor clutch.

AIR CONDITIONING SYSTEM DIAGNOSIS CHART—SPECTRUM, CONT.

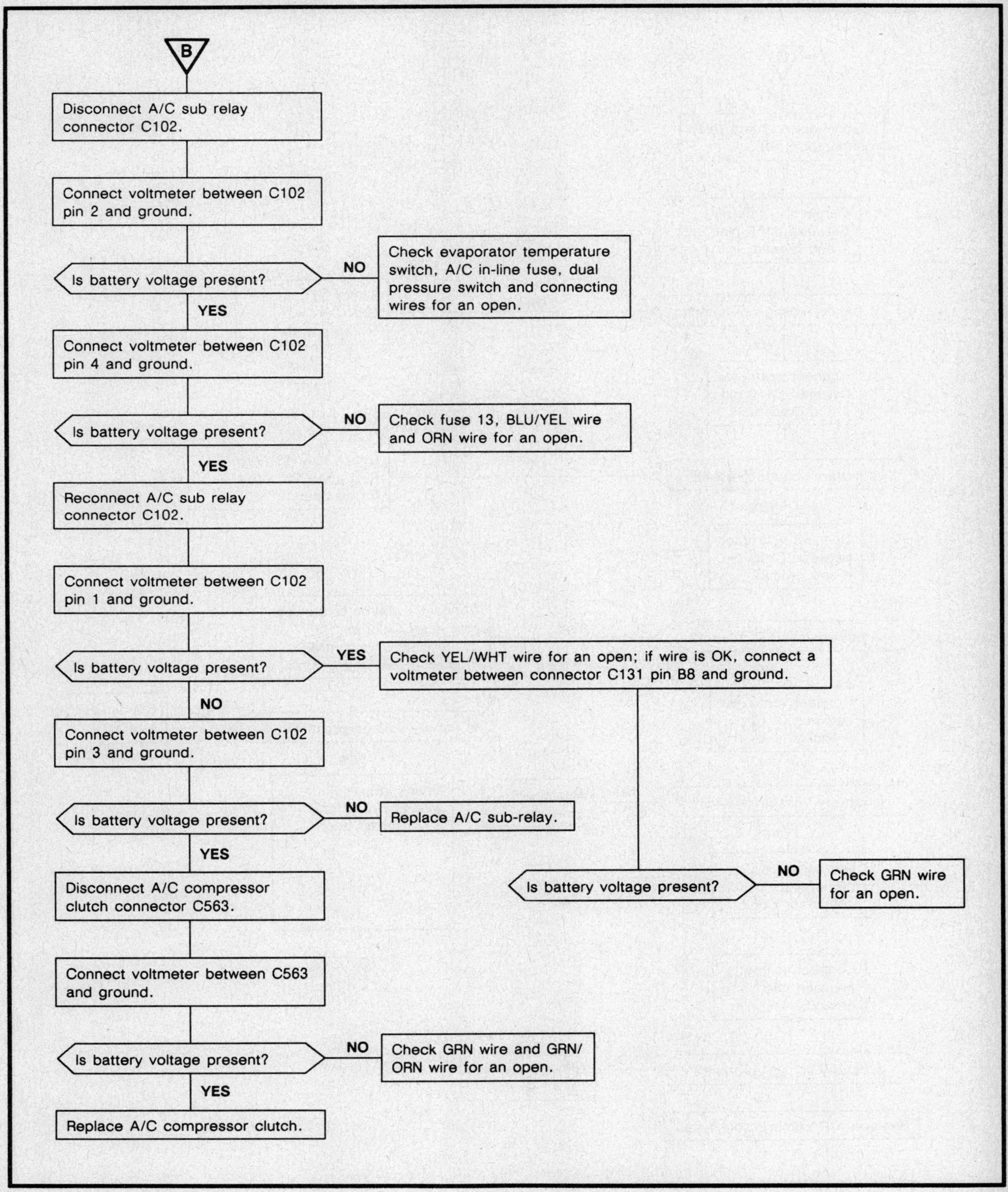
B
Disconnect A/C sub relay connector C102.
Connect voltmeter between C102 pin 2 and ground.
Is battery voltage present?
NO
Check evaporator temperature switch, A/C in-line fuse, dual pressure switch and connecting wires for an open.
YES
Connect voltmeter between C102 pin 4 and ground.
Is battery voltage present?
NO
Check fuse 13, BLU/YEL wire and ORN wire for an open.
YES
Reconnect A/C sub relay connector C102.
Connect voltmeter between C102 pin 1 and ground.
Is battery voltage present?
YES
Check YEL/WHT wire for an open; if wire is OK, connect a voltmeter between connector C131 pin B8 and ground.
Is battery voltage present?
NO
Check GRN wire for an open.
NO
Connect voltmeter between C102 pin 3 and ground.
Is battery voltage present?
NO
Replace A/C sub-relay.
YES
Disconnect A/C compressor clutch connector C563.
Connect voltmeter between C563 and ground.
Is battery voltage present?
NO
Check GRN wire and GRN/ORN wire for an open.
YES
Replace A/C compressor clutch.

AIR CONDITIONING SYSTEM DIAGNOSIS CHART—SPECTRUM, CONT.

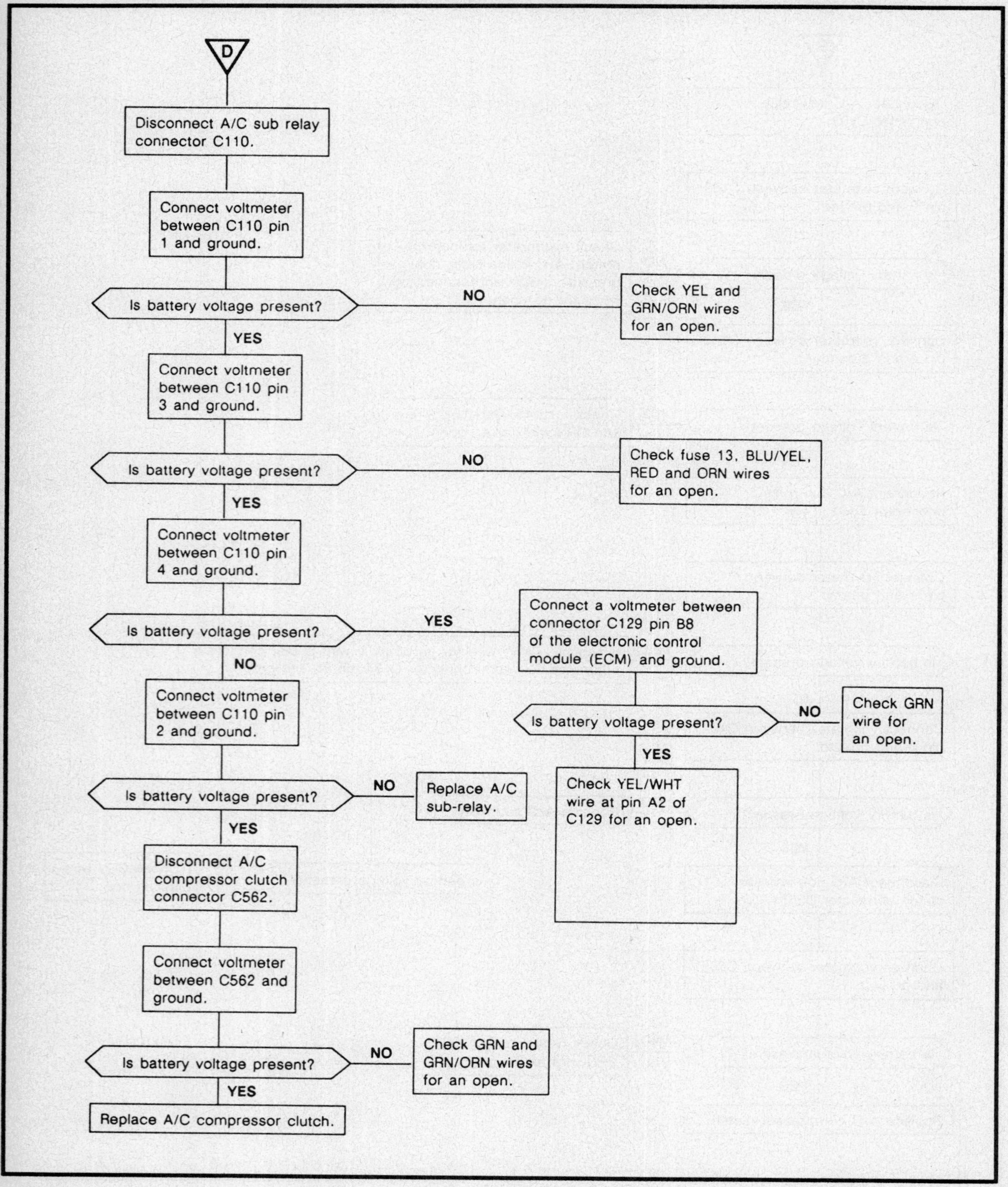
D
Disconnect A/C sub relay connector C110.
Connect voltmeter between C110 pin 1 and ground.
Is battery voltage present?
NO
Check YEL and GRN/ORN wires for an open.
YES
Connect voltmeter between C110 pin 3 and ground.
Is battery voltage present?
NO
Check fuse 13, BLU/YEL, RED and ORN wires for an open.
YES
Connect voltmeter between C110 pin 4 and ground.
Is battery voltage present?
YES
Connect a voltmeter between connector C129 pin B8 of the electronic control module (ECM) and ground.
Is battery voltage present?
NO
Check GRN wire for an open.
YES
Check YEL/WHT wire at pin A2 of C129 for an open.
NO
Connect voltmeter between C110 pin 2 and ground.
Is battery voltage present?
NO
Replace A/C sub-relay.
YES
Disconnect A/C compressor clutch connector C562.
Connect voltmeter between C562 and ground.
Is battery voltage present?
NO
Check GRN and GRN/ORN wires for an open.
YES
Replace A/C compressor clutch.

AIR CONDITIONING SYSTEM DIAGNOSIS CHART—SPECTRUM, CONT.

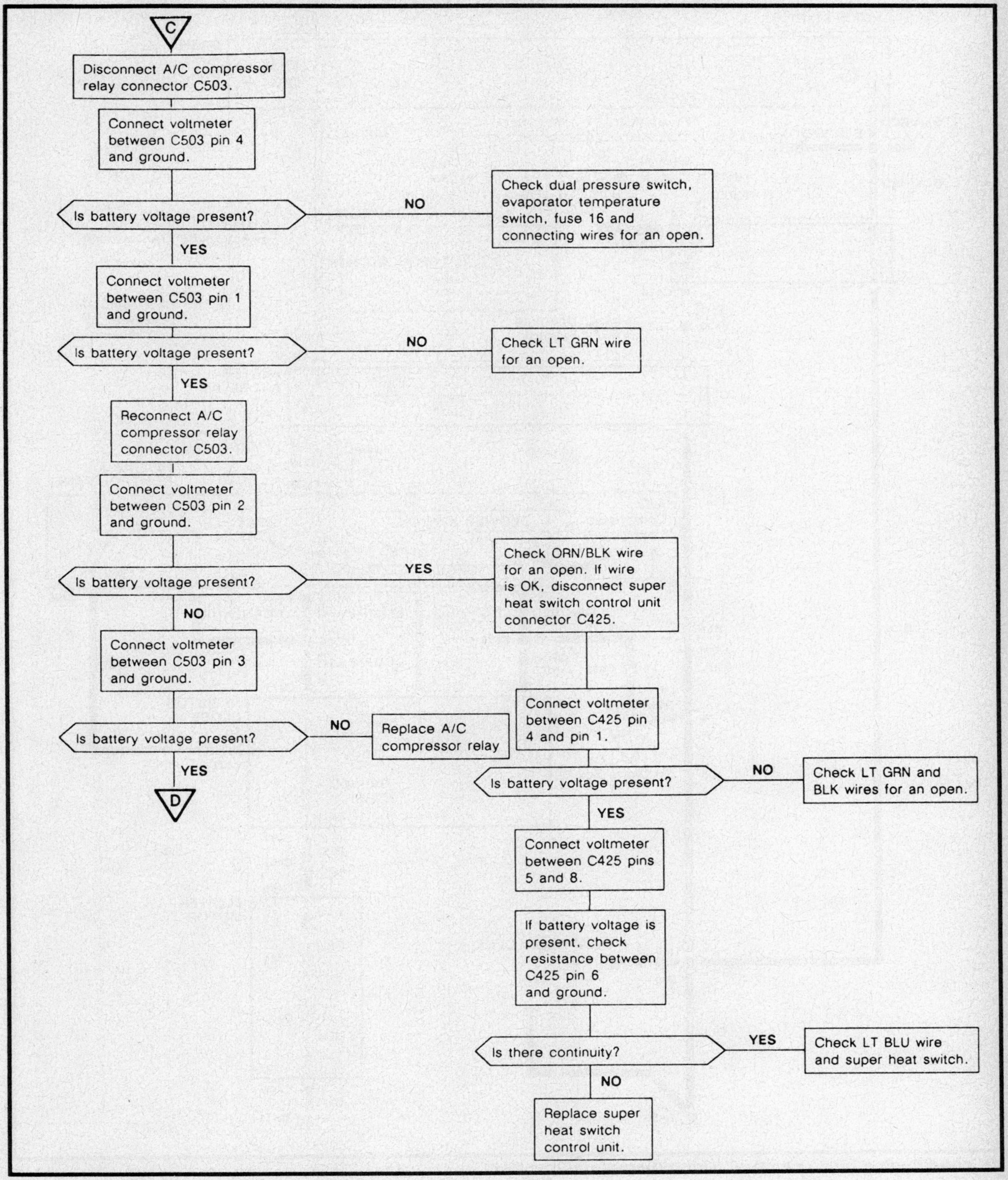
C
Disconnect A/C compressor relay connector C503.
Connect voltmeter between C503 pin 4 and ground.
Is battery voltage present?
NO
Check dual pressure switch, evaporator temperature switch, fuse 16 and connecting wires for an open.
YES
Connect voltmeter between C503 pin 1 and ground.
Is battery voltage present?
NO
Check LT GRN wire for an open.
YES
Reconnect A/C compressor relay connector C503.
Connect voltmeter between C503 pin 2 and ground.
Is battery voltage present?
YES
Check ORN/BLK wire for an open. If wire is OK, disconnect super heat switch control unit connector C425.
NO
Connect voltmeter between C503 pin 3 and ground.
Is battery voltage present?
NO
Replace A/C compressor relay
YES
D
Connect voltmeter between C425 pin 4 and pin 1.
Is battery voltage present?
NO
Check LT GRN and BLK wires for an open.
YES
Connect voltmeter between C425 pins 5 and 8.
If battery voltage is present, check resistance between C425 pin 6 and ground.
Is there continuity?
YES
Check LT BLU wire and super heat switch.
NO
Replace super heat switch control unit.

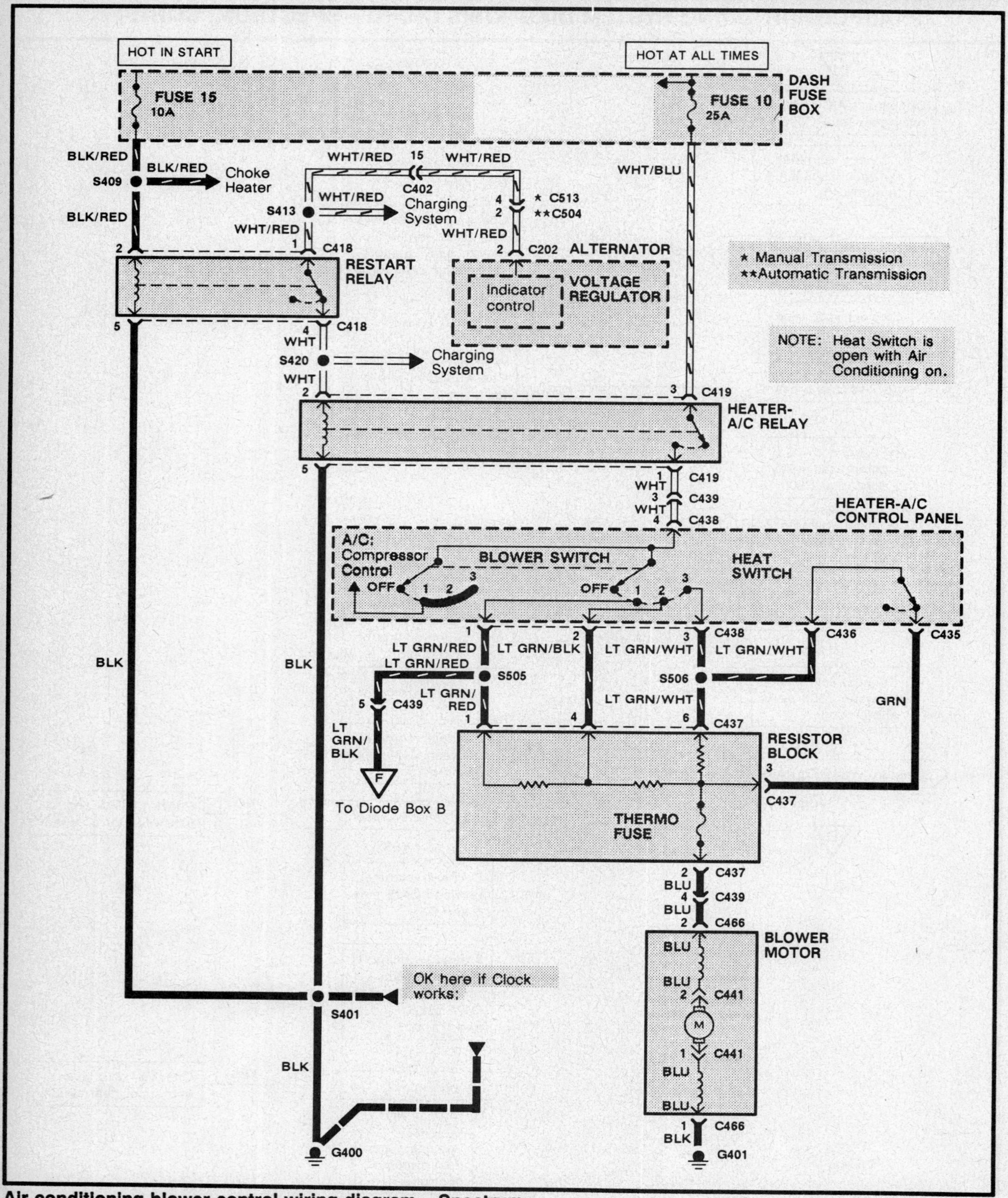
HOT IN START
HOT AT ALL TIMES
FUSE 15 10A
FUSE 10 25A
DASH FUSE BOX
BLK/RED
S409
Choke Heater
WHT/RED
C402
S413
Charging System
★ C513
★★C504
C418
C202
ALTERNATOR
RESTART RELAY
Indicator control
VOLTAGE REGULATOR
★ Manual Transmission
★★Automatic Transmission
NOTE: Heat Switch is open with Air Conditioning on.
WHT
S420
WHT/BLU
C419
HEATER-A/C RELAY
C439
C438
HEATER-A/C CONTROL PANEL
A/C: Compressor Control
BLOWER SWITCH
HEAT SWITCH
OFF
C436
C435
LT GRN/RED
LT GRN/BLK
LT GRN/WHT
S505
S506
GRN
LT GRN/BLK
To Diode Box B
C437
RESISTOR BLOCK
THERMO FUSE
BLU
C466
BLOWER MOTOR
C441
BLK
OK here if Clock works;
S401
G400
G401

Air conditioning blower control wiring diagram– Spectrum

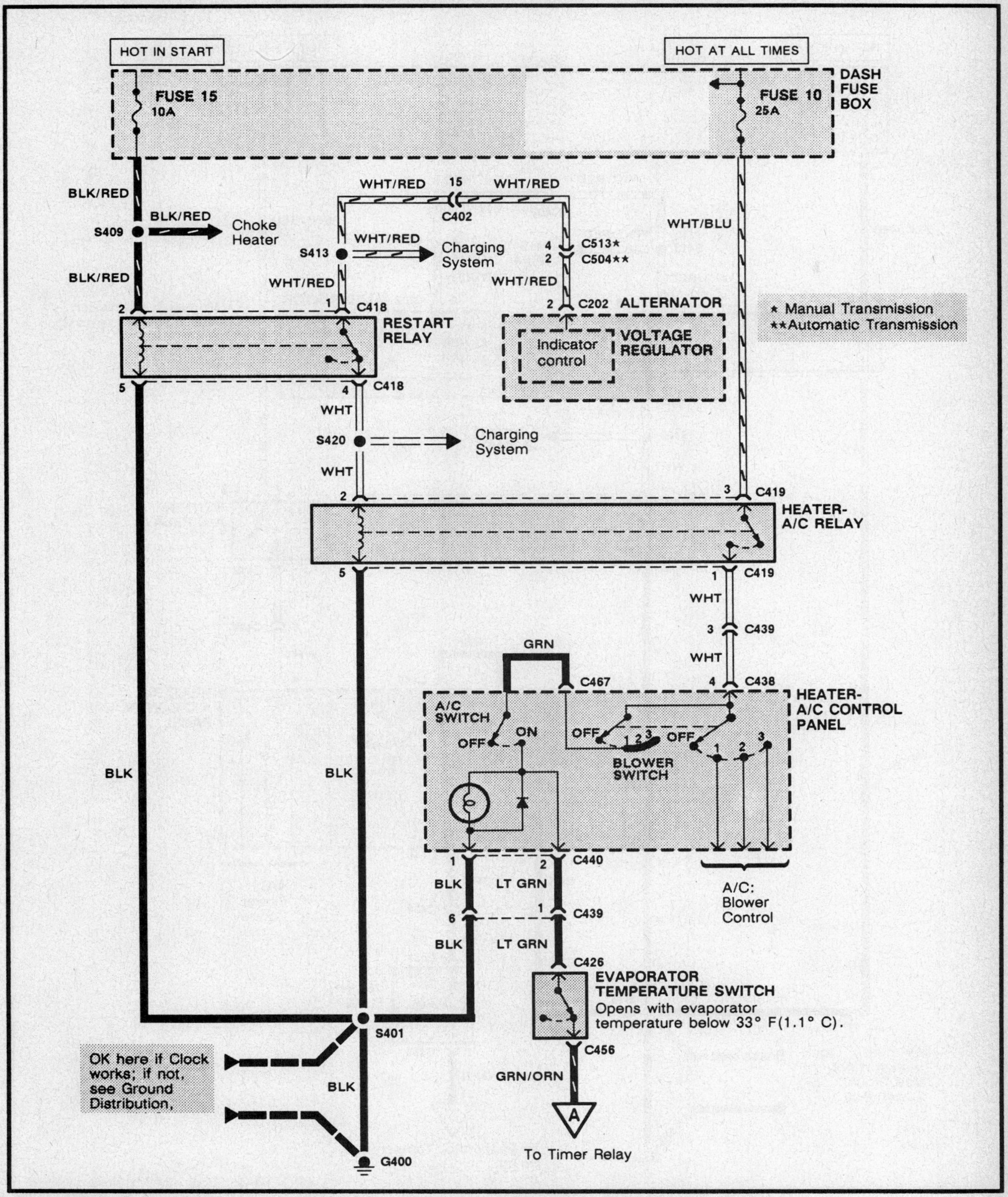
HOT IN START
HOT AT ALL TIMES
FUSE 15
10A
FUSE 10
25A
DASH FUSE BOX
BLK/RED
S409
BLK/RED
Choke Heater
BLK/RED
WHT/RED
15
WHT/RED
C402
S413
WHT/RED
Charging System
WHT/RED
4 C513★
2 C504★★
WHT/RED
WHT/BLU
2 C202 ALTERNATOR
Indicator control
VOLTAGE REGULATOR
★ Manual Transmission
★★Automatic Transmission
2
1
C418
RESTART RELAY
5
4
C418
WHT
S420
Charging System
WHT
2
3
C419
HEATER-A/C RELAY
5
1
C419
WHT
3
C439
WHT
GRN
C467
4
C438
HEATER-A/C CONTROL PANEL
A/C SWITCH
OFF
ON
OFF
1 2 3
OFF
1 2 3
BLOWER SWITCH
BLK
BLK
1
2
C440
BLK
LT GRN
6
1
C439
BLK
LT GRN
A/C: Blower Control
C426
EVAPORATOR TEMPERATURE SWITCH
Opens with evaporator temperature below 33° F(1.1° C).
C456
GRN/ORN
A
To Timer Relay
S401
OK here if Clock works; if not, see Ground Distribution,
BLK
G400

Air conditioning compressor control wiring diagram— Spectrum, without fuel injection

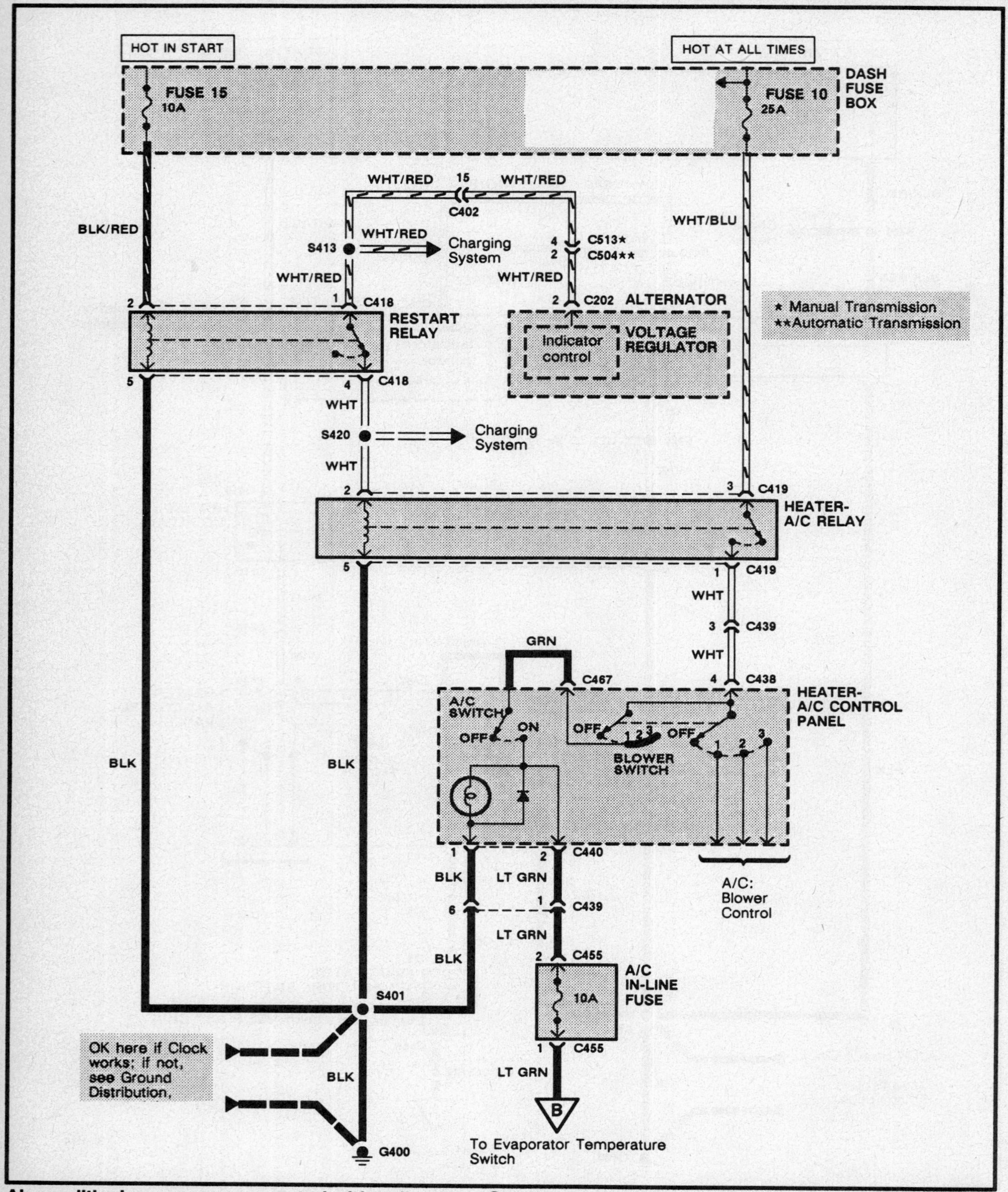
HOT IN START
HOT AT ALL TIMES
FUSE 15 10A
FUSE 10 25A
DASH FUSE BOX
BLK/RED
WHT/RED
15
C402
WHT/BLU
S413
Charging System
4 C513*
2 C504**
C418
RESTART RELAY
C202
ALTERNATOR
Indicator control
VOLTAGE REGULATOR
* Manual Transmission
**Automatic Transmission
WHT
S420
C419
HEATER-A/C RELAY
C439
GRN
C467
C438
A/C SWITCH
OFF
ON
BLOWER SWITCH
HEATER-A/C CONTROL PANEL
BLK
LT GRN
C440
A/C: Blower Control
C455
A/C IN-LINE FUSE
10A
S401
OK here if Clock works; if not, see Ground Distribution.
G400
B
To Evaporator Temperature Switch

Air conditioning compressor control wiring diagram– Spectrum, fuel injection with turbo

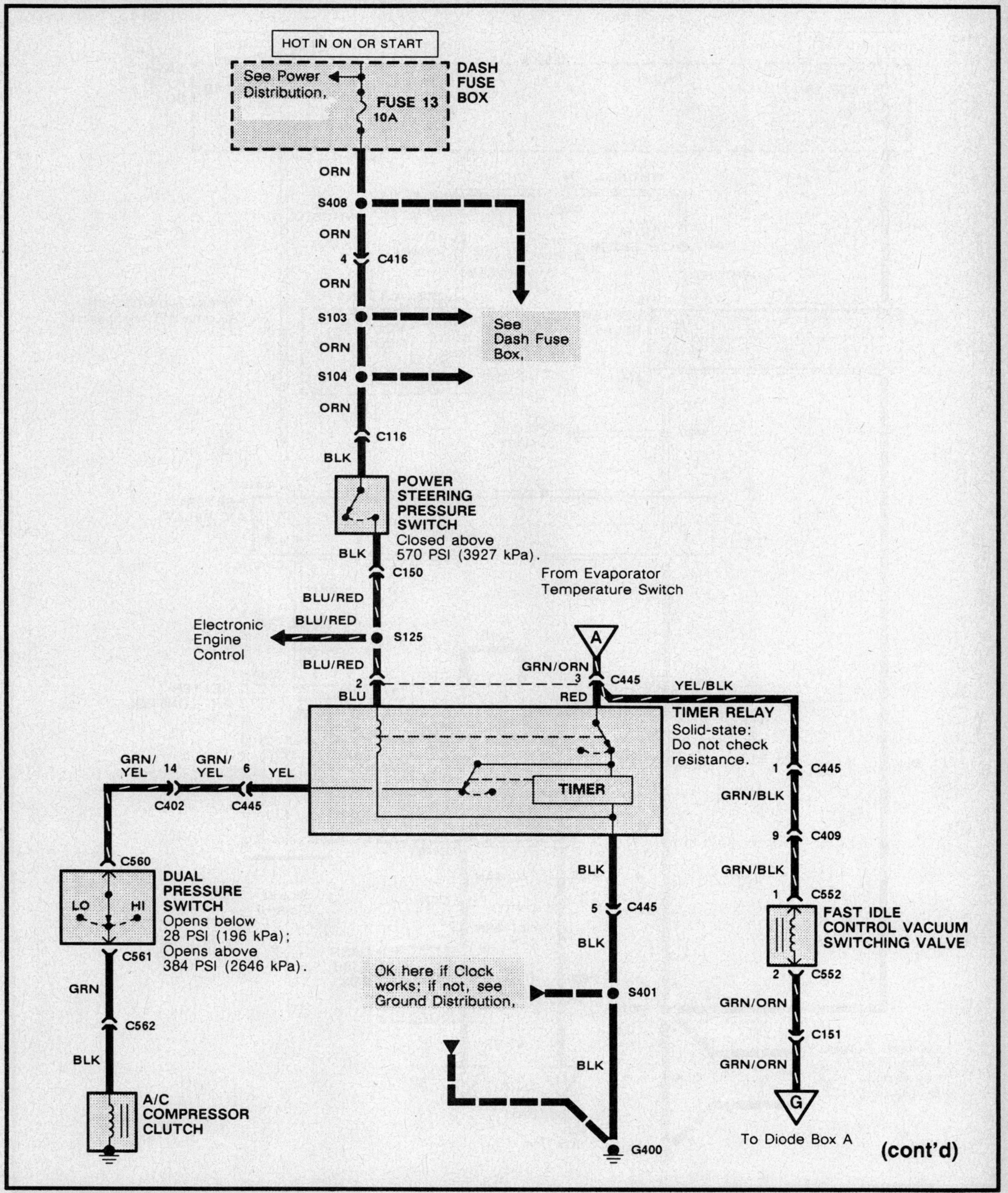
HOT IN ON OR START
See Power Distribution,
FUSE 13
10A
DASH FUSE BOX
ORN
S408
ORN
4
C416
ORN
S103
See Dash Fuse Box,
ORN
S104
ORN
C116
BLK
POWER STEERING PRESSURE SWITCH
Closed above 570 PSI (3927 kPa).
BLK
C150
BLU/RED
BLU/RED
Electronic Engine Control
S125
BLU/RED
From Evaporator Temperature Switch
A
GRN/ORN
3
C445
2
BLU
RED
YEL/BLK
TIMER RELAY
Solid-state: Do not check resistance.
TIMER
GRN/YEL
14
GRN/YEL
6
YEL
C402
C445
1
C445
GRN/BLK
9
C409
GRN/BLK
1
C552
FAST IDLE CONTROL VACUUM SWITCHING VALVE
2
C552
GRN/ORN
C151
GRN/ORN
G
To Diode Box A
C560
DUAL PRESSURE SWITCH
Opens below 28 PSI (196 kPa); Opens above 384 PSI (2646 kPa).
LO
HI
C561
GRN
C562
BLK
A/C COMPRESSOR CLUTCH
BLK
5
C445
BLK
OK here if Clock works; if not, see Ground Distribution,
S401
BLK
G400
(cont'd)

Air conditioning compressor control wiring diagram— Spectrum, fuel injection with turbo, cont.

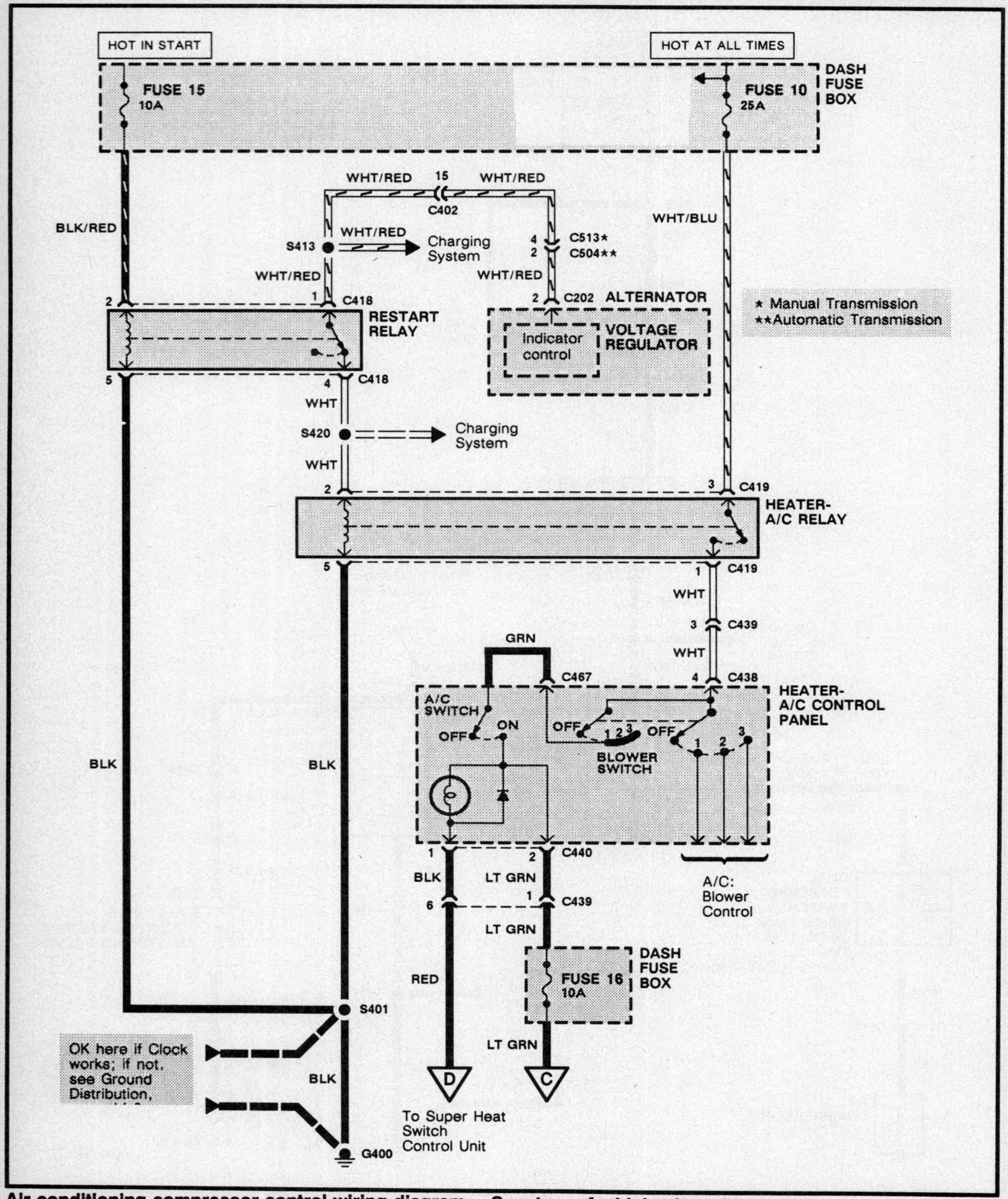
HOT IN START
HOT AT ALL TIMES
FUSE 15 10A
FUSE 10 25A
DASH FUSE BOX
BLK/RED
WHT/RED
15
C402
WHT/BLU
S413
Charging System
C513★
C504★★
C418
C202
ALTERNATOR
RESTART RELAY
Indicator control
VOLTAGE REGULATOR
★ Manual Transmission
★★Automatic Transmission
WHT
S420
C419
HEATER-A/C RELAY
C439
GRN
C467
C438
A/C SWITCH
OFF
ON
BLOWER SWITCH
HEATER-A/C CONTROL PANEL
BLK
LT GRN
C440
A/C: Blower Control
RED
FUSE 16 10A
S401
OK here if Clock works; if not, see Ground Distribution,
D
C
To Super Heat Switch Control Unit
G400

Air conditioning compressor control wiring diagram— Spectrum, fuel injection without turbo

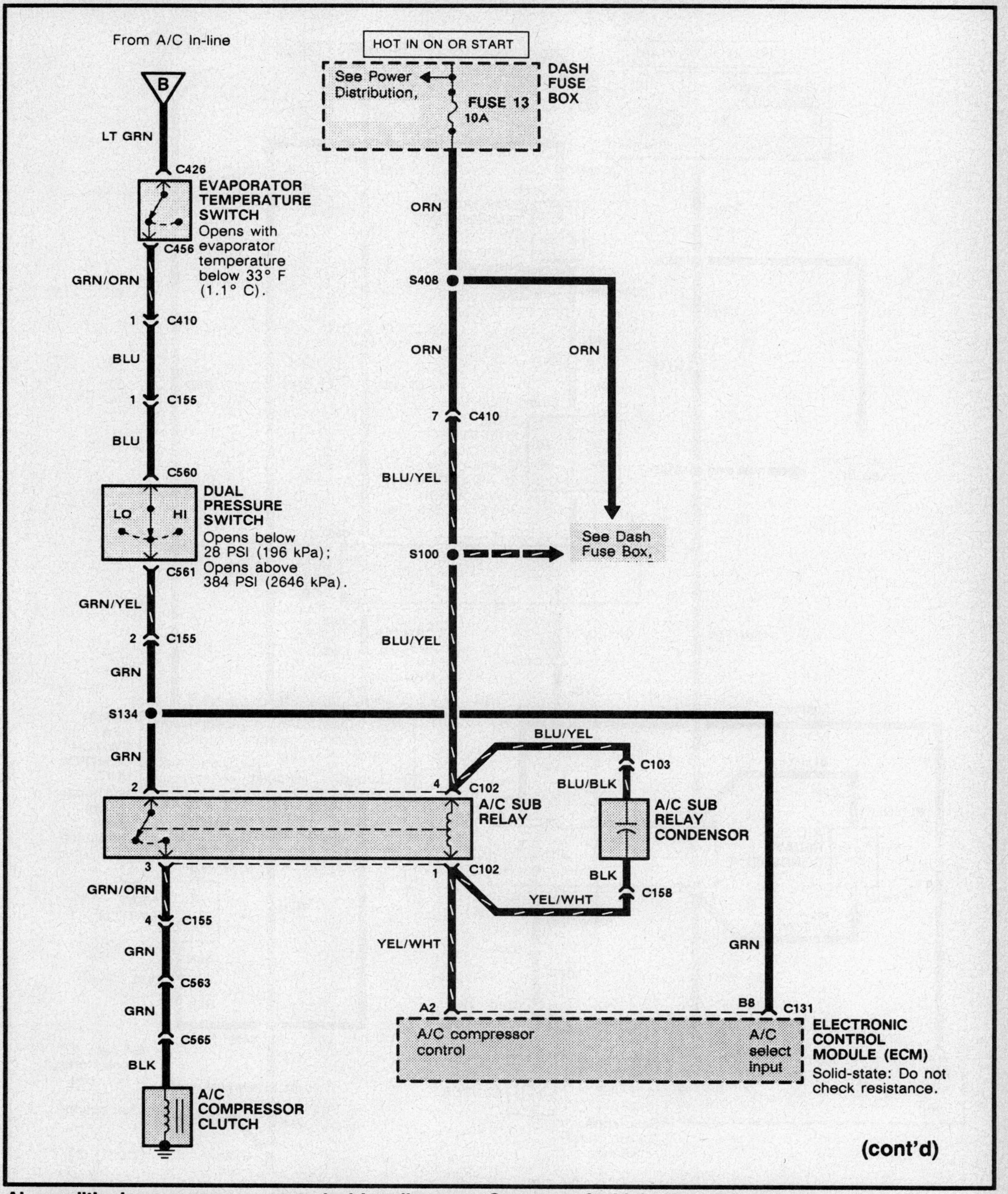
From A/C In-line
B
LT GRN
C426
EVAPORATOR TEMPERATURE SWITCH
Opens with evaporator temperature below 33° F (1.1° C).
C456
GRN/ORN
1 C410
BLU
1 C155
BLU
C560
DUAL PRESSURE SWITCH
LO HI
Opens below 28 PSI (196 kPa); Opens above 384 PSI (2646 kPa).
C561
GRN/YEL
2 C155
GRN
S134
GRN
2
A/C SUB RELAY
3
GRN/ORN
4 C155
GRN
C563
GRN
C565
BLK
A/C COMPRESSOR CLUTCH
HOT IN ON OR START
See Power Distribution,
FUSE 13 10A
DASH FUSE BOX
ORN
S408
ORN
ORN
7 C410
BLU/YEL
S100
See Dash Fuse Box,
BLU/YEL
BLU/YEL
4 C102
C103
BLU/BLK
A/C SUB RELAY CONDENSOR
1 C102
BLK
C158
YEL/WHT
YEL/WHT
GRN
A2
B8 C131
A/C compressor control
A/C select input
ELECTRONIC CONTROL MODULE (ECM)
Solid-state: Do not check resistance.
(cont'd)

Air conditioning compressor control wiring diagram – Spectrum, fuel injection without turbo, cont.

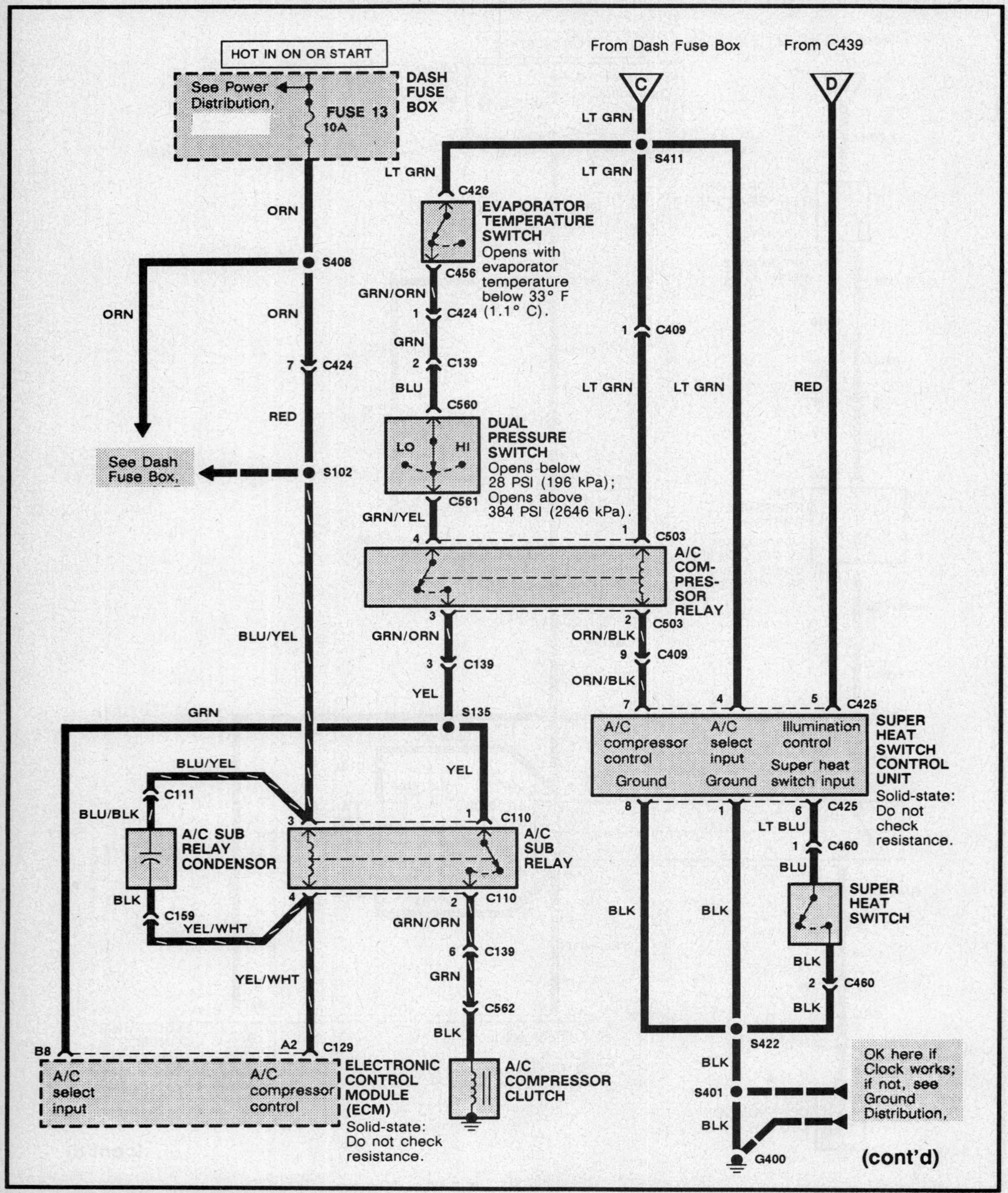
HOT IN ON OR START
See Power Distribution,
FUSE 13 10A
DASH FUSE BOX
From Dash Fuse Box
From C439
C
D
LT GRN
S411
LT GRN
LT GRN
C426
EVAPORATOR TEMPERATURE SWITCH
Opens with evaporator temperature below 33° F (1.1° C).
ORN
S408
C456
GRN/ORN
ORN
ORN
1 C424
1 C409
GRN
7 C424
2 C139
BLU
C560
LT GRN
LT GRN
RED
RED
DUAL PRESSURE SWITCH
LO
HI
Opens below 28 PSI (196 kPa); Opens above 384 PSI (2646 kPa).
See Dash Fuse Box,
S102
C561
GRN/YEL
4
1 C503
A/C COM-PRES-SOR RELAY
3
2 C503
BLU/YEL
GRN/ORN
ORN/BLK
9 C409
3 C139
ORN/BLK
YEL
7
4
5 C425
GRN
S135
A/C compressor control
A/C select input
Illumination control
Super heat switch input
Ground
Ground
SUPER HEAT SWITCH CONTROL UNIT
Solid-state: Do not check resistance.
BLU/YEL
YEL
C111
BLU/BLK
3
1 C110
8
1
6 C425
A/C SUB RELAY CONDENSOR
A/C SUB RELAY
LT BLU
1 C460
BLU
SUPER HEAT SWITCH
BLK
C159
YEL/WHT
4
2 C110
GRN/ORN
BLK
BLK
6 C139
BLK
GRN
2 C460
YEL/WHT
C562
BLK
BLK
S422
B8
A2 C129
A/C select input
A/C compressor control
ELECTRONIC CONTROL MODULE (ECM)
Solid-state: Do not check resistance.
A/C COMPRESSOR CLUTCH
BLK
S401
OK here if Clock works; if not, see Ground Distribution,
BLK
G400
(cont'd)

Air conditiongin compressor control wiring diagram— Spectrum, fuel injection without turbo, cont.

AIR CONDITIONING SYSTEM DIAGNOSIS CHART—PRIZM

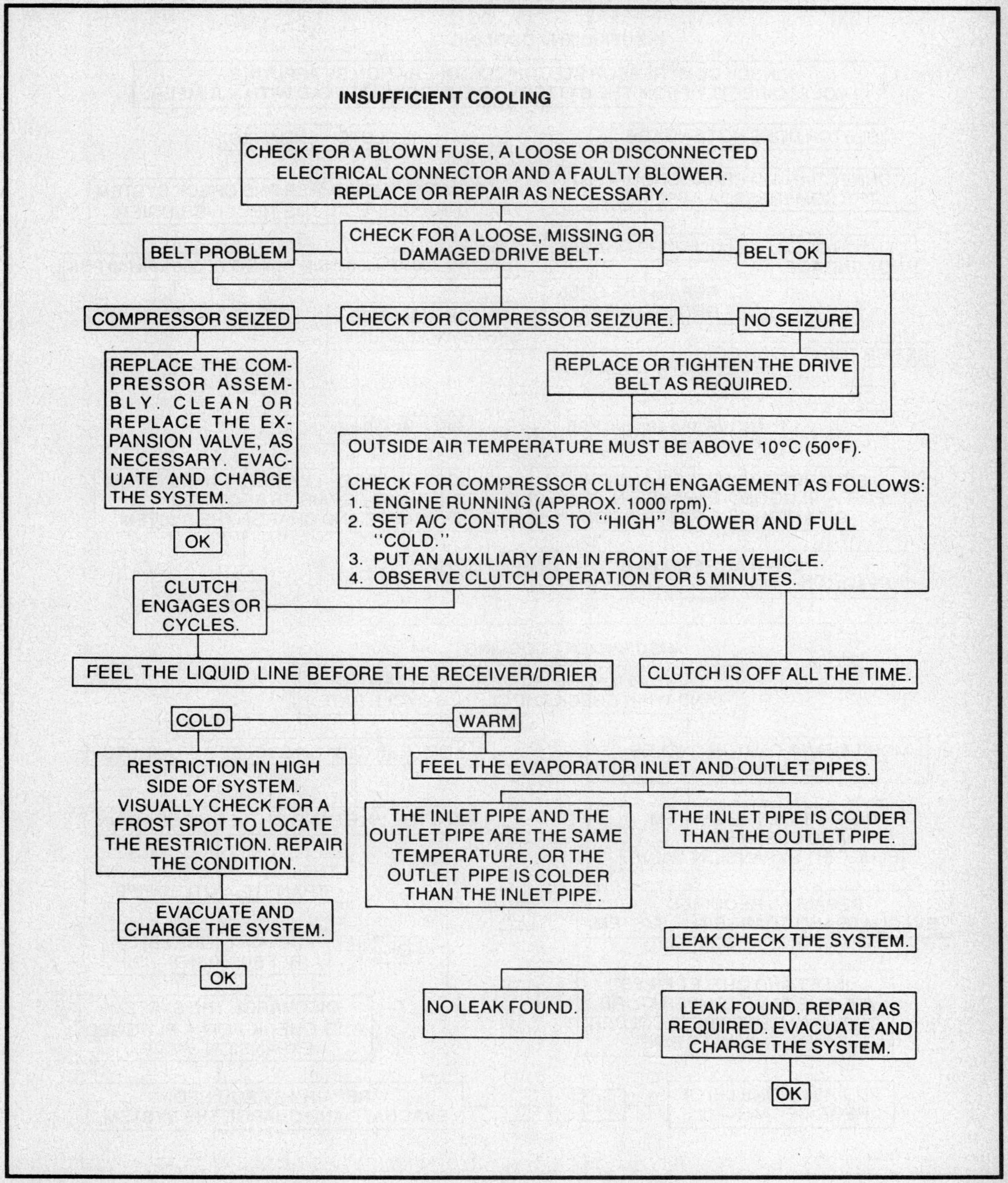
INSUFFICIENT COOLING
CHECK FOR A BLOWN FUSE, A LOOSE OR DISCONNECTED ELECTRICAL CONNECTOR AND A FAULTY BLOWER. REPLACE OR REPAIR AS NECESSARY.
CHECK FOR A LOOSE, MISSING OR DAMAGED DRIVE BELT.
BELT PROBLEM
BELT OK
CHECK FOR COMPRESSOR SEIZURE.
COMPRESSOR SEIZED
NO SEIZURE
REPLACE THE COMPRESSOR ASSEMBLY. CLEAN OR REPLACE THE EXPANSION VALVE, AS NECESSARY. EVACUATE AND CHARGE THE SYSTEM.
OK
REPLACE OR TIGHTEN THE DRIVE BELT AS REQUIRED.
OUTSIDE AIR TEMPERATURE MUST BE ABOVE 10°C (50°F).
CHECK FOR COMPRESSOR CLUTCH ENGAGEMENT AS FOLLOWS:
1. ENGINE RUNNING (APPROX. 1000 rpm).
2. SET A/C CONTROLS TO "HIGH" BLOWER AND FULL "COLD."
3. PUT AN AUXILIARY FAN IN FRONT OF THE VEHICLE.
4. OBSERVE CLUTCH OPERATION FOR 5 MINUTES.
CLUTCH ENGAGES OR CYCLES.
FEEL THE LIQUID LINE BEFORE THE RECEIVER/DRIER
CLUTCH IS OFF ALL THE TIME.
COLD
WARM
RESTRICTION IN HIGH SIDE OF SYSTEM. VISUALLY CHECK FOR A FROST SPOT TO LOCATE THE RESTRICTION. REPAIR THE CONDITION.
EVACUATE AND CHARGE THE SYSTEM.
OK
FEEL THE EVAPORATOR INLET AND OUTLET PIPES.
THE INLET PIPE AND THE OUTLET PIPE ARE THE SAME TEMPERATURE, OR THE OUTLET PIPE IS COLDER THAN THE INLET PIPE.
THE INLET PIPE IS COLDER THAN THE OUTLET PIPE.
LEAK CHECK THE SYSTEM.
NO LEAK FOUND.
LEAK FOUND. REPAIR AS REQUIRED. EVACUATE AND CHARGE THE SYSTEM.
OK

AIR CONDITIONING SYSTEM DIAGNOSIS CHART—PRIZM, CONT.

INSUFFICIENT COOLING

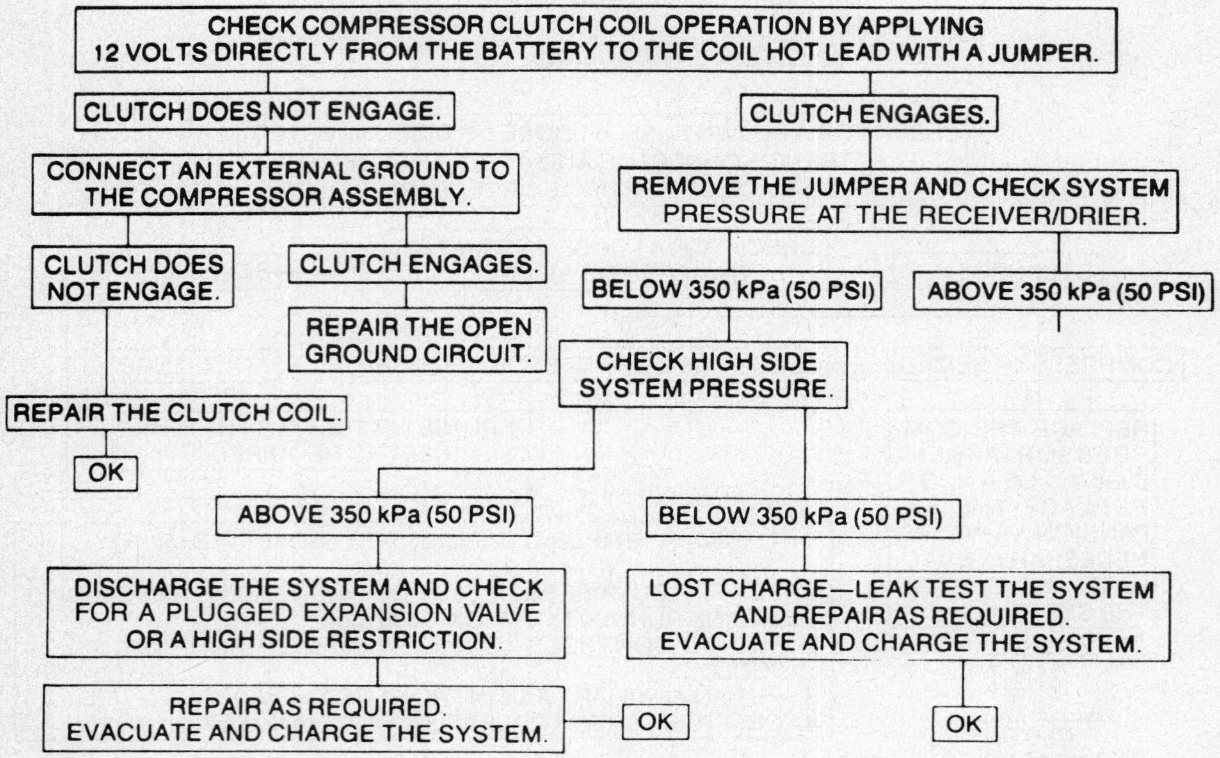
CHECK COMPRESSOR CLUTCH COIL OPERATION BY APPLYING 12 VOLTS DIRECTLY FROM THE BATTERY TO THE COIL HOT LEAD WITH A JUMPER.
CLUTCH DOES NOT ENGAGE.
CLUTCH ENGAGES.
CONNECT AN EXTERNAL GROUND TO THE COMPRESSOR ASSEMBLY.
REMOVE THE JUMPER AND CHECK SYSTEM PRESSURE AT THE RECEIVER/DRIER.
CLUTCH DOES NOT ENGAGE.
CLUTCH ENGAGES.
BELOW 350 kPa (50 PSI)
ABOVE 350 kPa (50 PSI)
REPAIR THE OPEN GROUND CIRCUIT.
CHECK HIGH SIDE SYSTEM PRESSURE.
REPAIR THE CLUTCH COIL.
OK
ABOVE 350 kPa (50 PSI)
BELOW 350 kPa (50 PSI)
DISCHARGE THE SYSTEM AND CHECK FOR A PLUGGED EXPANSION VALVE OR A HIGH SIDE RESTRICTION.
LOST CHARGE—LEAK TEST THE SYSTEM AND REPAIR AS REQUIRED. EVACUATE AND CHARGE THE SYSTEM.
REPAIR AS REQUIRED. EVACUATE AND CHARGE THE SYSTEM.
OK
OK

INSUFFICIENT COOLING

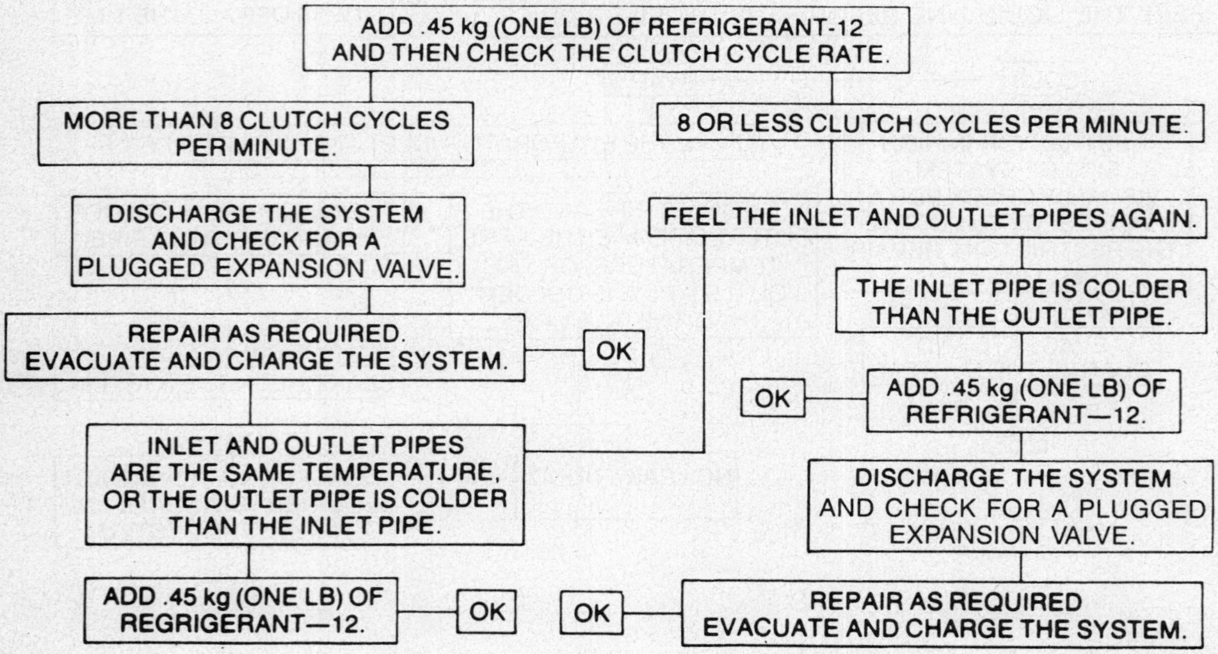
ADD .45 kg (ONE LB) OF REFRIGERANT-12 AND THEN CHECK THE CLUTCH CYCLE RATE.
MORE THAN 8 CLUTCH CYCLES PER MINUTE.
8 OR LESS CLUTCH CYCLES PER MINUTE.
DISCHARGE THE SYSTEM AND CHECK FOR A PLUGGED EXPANSION VALVE.
FEEL THE INLET AND OUTLET PIPES AGAIN.
THE INLET PIPE IS COLDER THAN THE OUTLET PIPE.
REPAIR AS REQUIRED. EVACUATE AND CHARGE THE SYSTEM.
OK
OK
ADD .45 kg (ONE LB) OF REFRIGERANT—12.
INLET AND OUTLET PIPES ARE THE SAME TEMPERATURE, OR THE OUTLET PIPE IS COLDER THAN THE INLET PIPE.
DISCHARGE THE SYSTEM AND CHECK FOR A PLUGGED EXPANSION VALVE.
ADD .45 kg (ONE LB) OF REGRIGERANT—12.
OK
OK
REPAIR AS REQUIRED EVACUATE AND CHARGE THE SYSTEM.

AIR CONDITIONING SYSTEM DIAGNOSIS CHART—PRIZM, CONT.

INSUFFICIENT COOLING

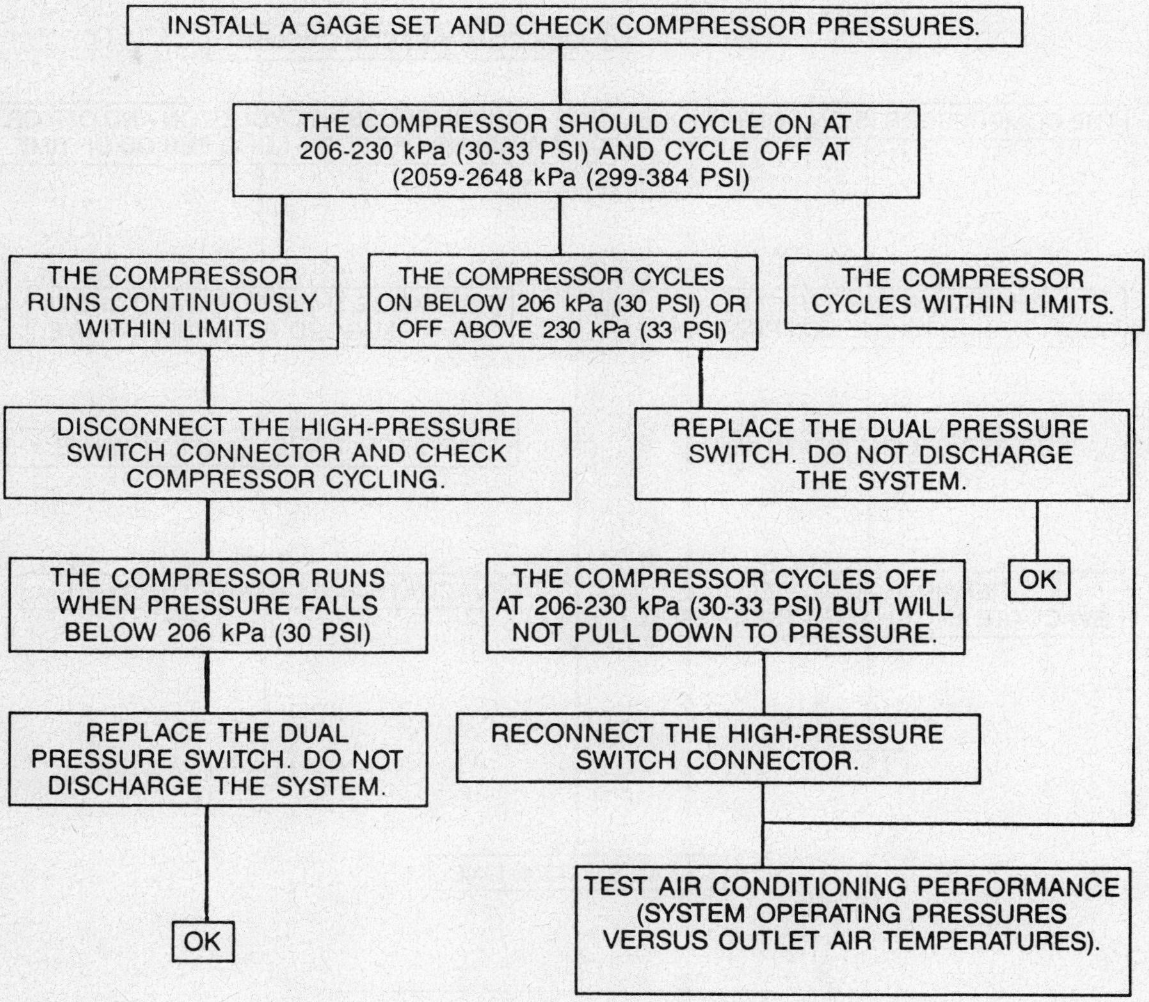
INSTALL A GAGE SET AND CHECK COMPRESSOR PRESSURES.
THE COMPRESSOR SHOULD CYCLE ON AT 206-230 kPa (30-33 PSI) AND CYCLE OFF AT (2059-2648 kPa (299-384 PSI)
THE COMPRESSOR RUNS CONTINUOUSLY WITHIN LIMITS
THE COMPRESSOR CYCLES ON BELOW 206 kPa (30 PSI) OR OFF ABOVE 230 kPa (33 PSI)
THE COMPRESSOR CYCLES WITHIN LIMITS.
DISCONNECT THE HIGH-PRESSURE SWITCH CONNECTOR AND CHECK COMPRESSOR CYCLING.
REPLACE THE DUAL PRESSURE SWITCH. DO NOT DISCHARGE THE SYSTEM.
OK
THE COMPRESSOR RUNS WHEN PRESSURE FALLS BELOW 206 kPa (30 PSI)
THE COMPRESSOR CYCLES OFF AT 206-230 kPa (30-33 PSI) BUT WILL NOT PULL DOWN TO PRESSURE.
REPLACE THE DUAL PRESSURE SWITCH. DO NOT DISCHARGE THE SYSTEM.
RECONNECT THE HIGH-PRESSURE SWITCH CONNECTOR.
OK
TEST AIR CONDITIONING PERFORMANCE (SYSTEM OPERATING PRESSURES VERSUS OUTLET AIR TEMPERATURES).

AIR CONDITIONING SYSTEM DIAGNOSIS CHART—PRIZM, CONT.

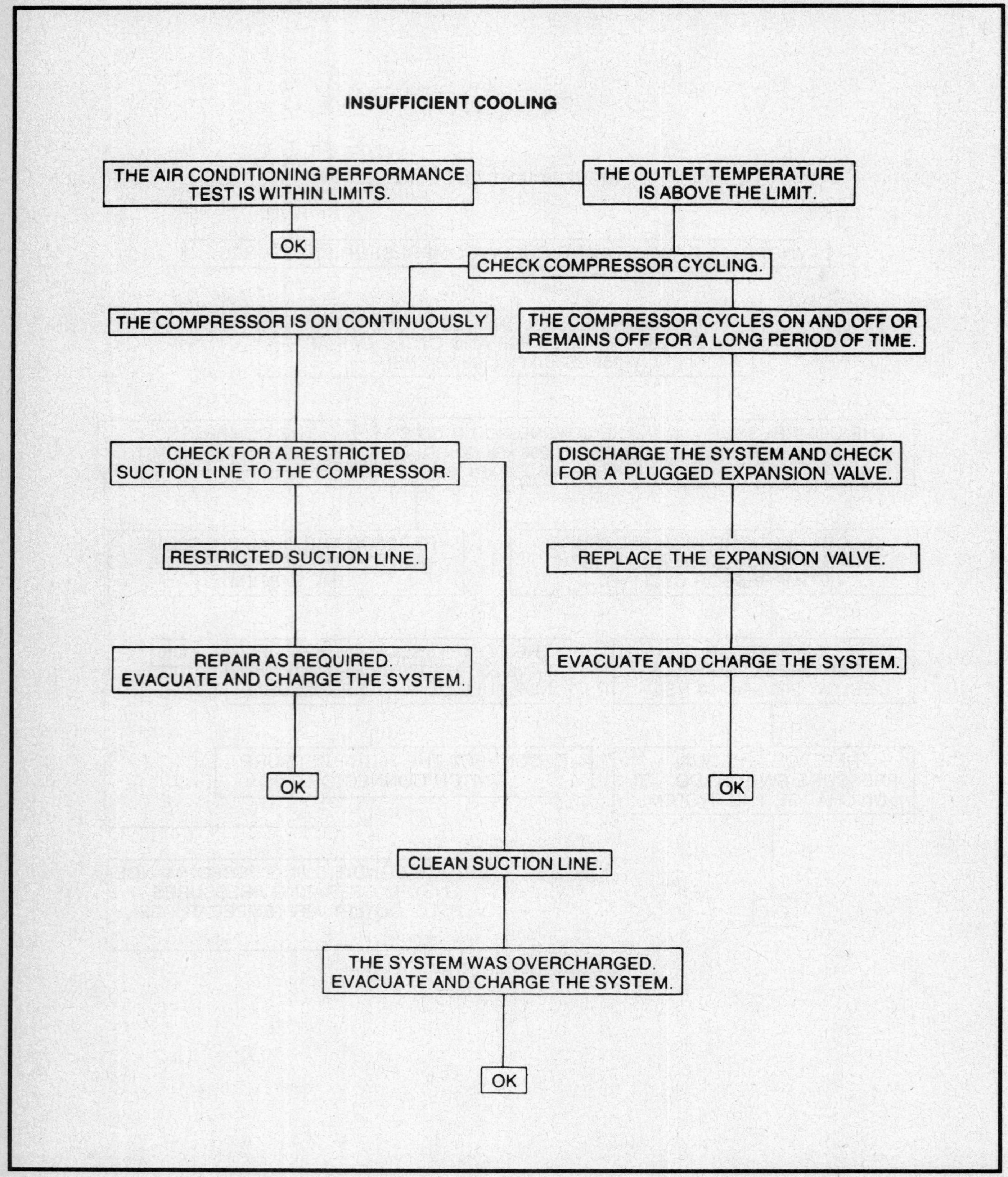
INSUFFICIENT COOLING
THE AIR CONDITIONING PERFORMANCE TEST IS WITHIN LIMITS.
OK
THE OUTLET TEMPERATURE IS ABOVE THE LIMIT.
CHECK COMPRESSOR CYCLING.
THE COMPRESSOR IS ON CONTINUOUSLY
THE COMPRESSOR CYCLES ON AND OFF OR REMAINS OFF FOR A LONG PERIOD OF TIME.
CHECK FOR A RESTRICTED SUCTION LINE TO THE COMPRESSOR.
DISCHARGE THE SYSTEM AND CHECK FOR A PLUGGED EXPANSION VALVE.
RESTRICTED SUCTION LINE.
REPLACE THE EXPANSION VALVE.
REPAIR AS REQUIRED. EVACUATE AND CHARGE THE SYSTEM.
EVACUATE AND CHARGE THE SYSTEM.
OK
OK
CLEAN SUCTION LINE.
THE SYSTEM WAS OVERCHARGED. EVACUATE AND CHARGE THE SYSTEM.
OK

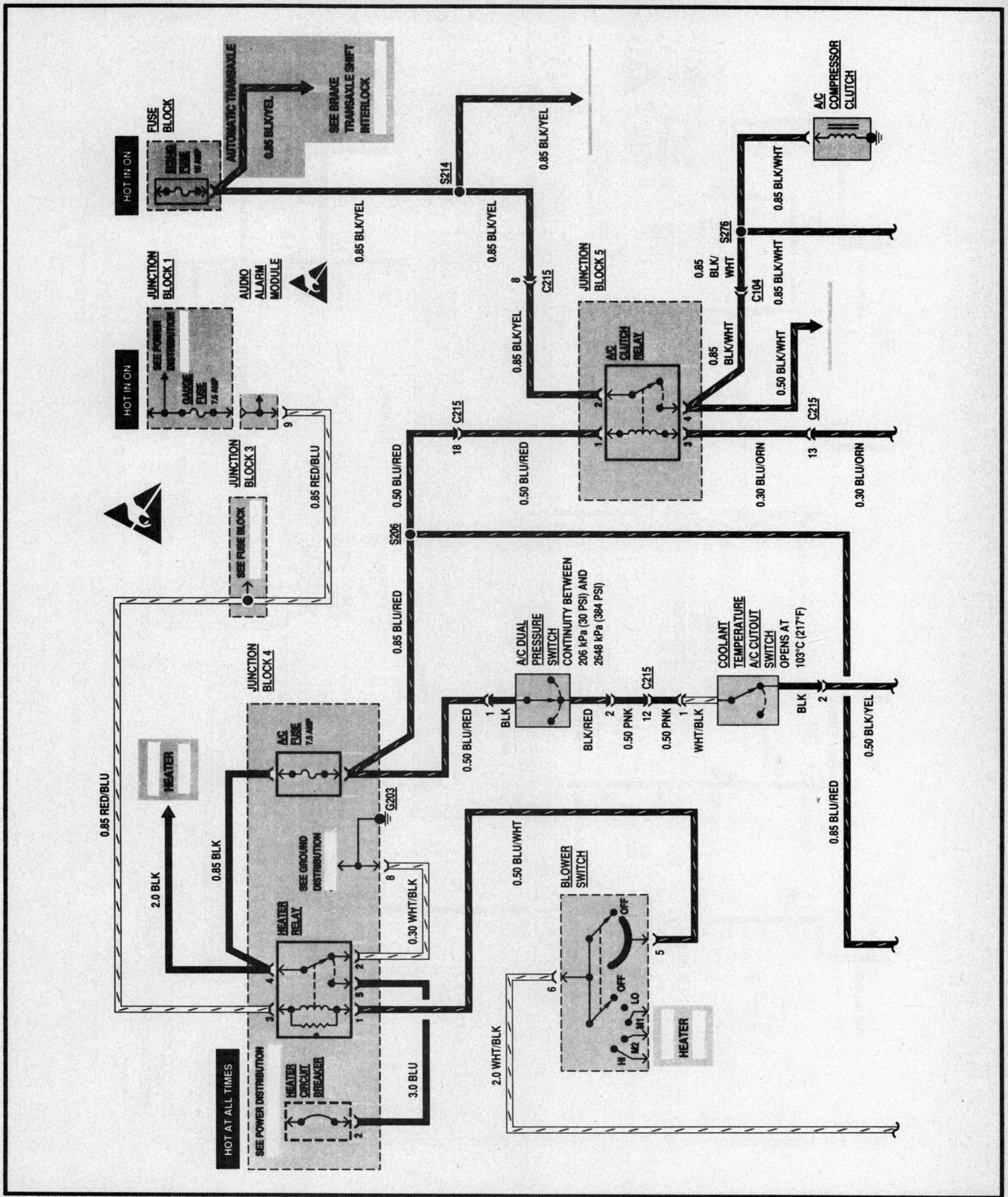
HOT IN ON
FUSE BLOCK
AUTOMATIC TRANSAXLE
0.85 BLK/YEL
SEE BRAKE TRANSAXLE SHIFT INTERLOCK
S214
0.85 BLK/YEL
A/C COMPRESSOR CLUTCH
0.85 BLK/WHT
S276
JUNCTION BLOCK 1
SEE POWER DISTRIBUTION
GAUGE FUSE 7.5 AMP
AUDIO ALARM MODULE
C215
JUNCTION BLOCK 5
A/C CLUTCH RELAY
C104
0.50 BLK/WHT
JUNCTION BLOCK 3
SEE FUSE BLOCK
0.85 RED/BLU
0.50 BLU/RED
0.30 BLU/ORN
S206
0.85 BLU/RED
A/C DUAL PRESSURE SWITCH
CONTINUITY BETWEEN 206 kPa (30 PSI) AND 2648 kPa (384 PSI)
COOLANT TEMPERATURE A/C CUTOUT SWITCH
OPENS AT 103°C (217°F)
JUNCTION BLOCK 4
A/C FUSE 7.5 AMP
BLK
BLK/RED
0.50 PNK
WHT/BLK
0.50 BLK/YEL
HEATER
G203
SEE GROUND DISTRIBUTION
2.0 BLK
0.85 BLK
HEATER RELAY
0.30 WHT/BLK
0.50 BLU/WHT
BLOWER SWITCH
OFF
LO
M1
M2
HI
HOT AT ALL TIMES
SEE POWER DISTRIBUTION
HEATER CIRCUIT BREAKER
3.0 BLU
2.0 WHT/BLK

Air conditioning wiring diagram—Prizm

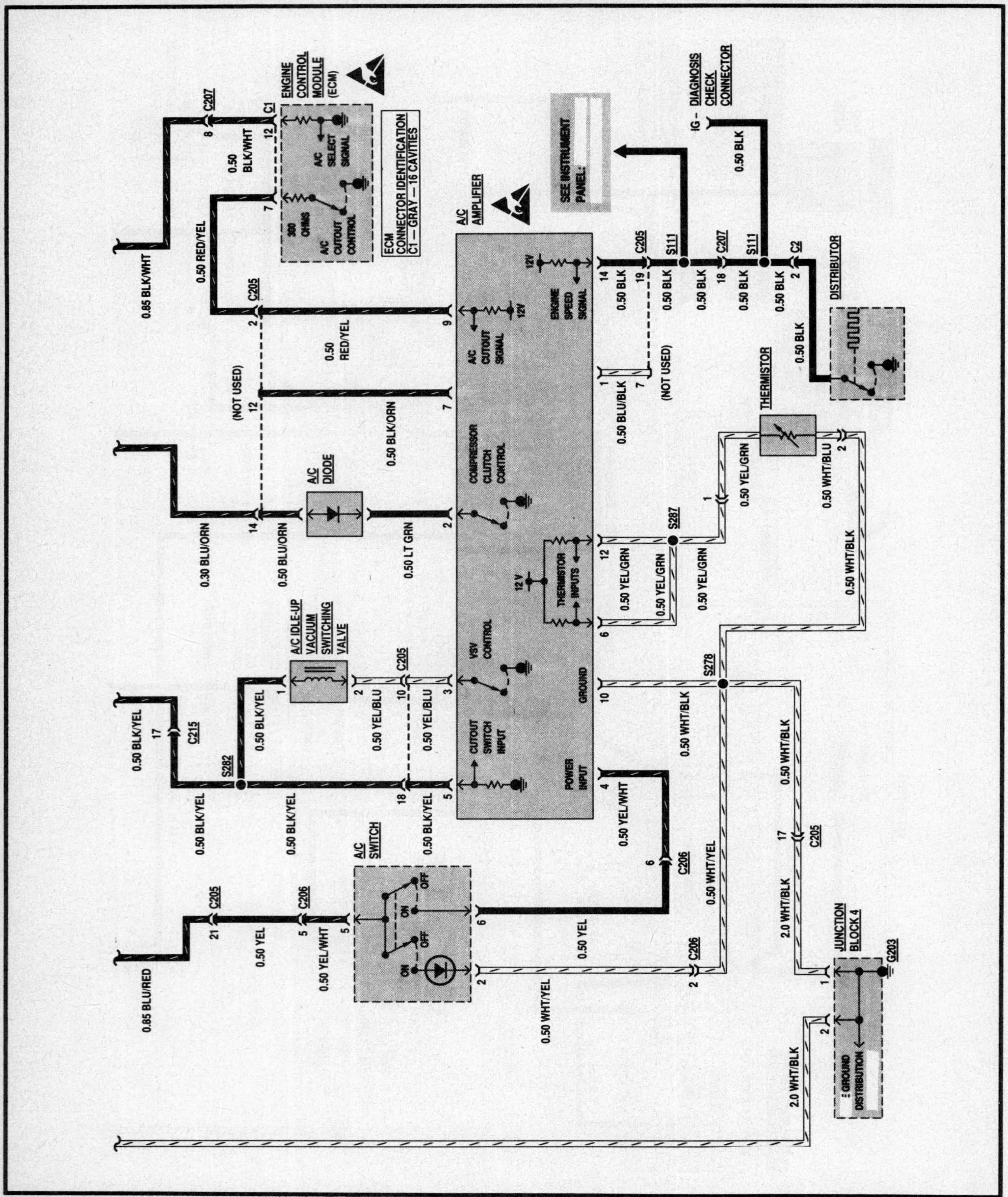
ENGINE CONTROL MODULE (ECM)
A/C SELECT SIGNAL
300 OHMS
A/C CUTOUT CONTROL
ECM CONNECTOR IDENTIFICATION C1 — GRAY — 16 CAVITIES
A/C AMPLIFIER
SEE INSTRUMENT PANEL
IG - DIAGNOSIS CHECK CONNECTOR
DISTRIBUTOR
THERMISTOR
A/C DIODE
A/C IDLE-UP VACUUM SWITCHING VALVE
A/C SWITCH
JUNCTION BLOCK 4
GROUND DISTRIBUTION
ENGINE SPEED SIGNAL
A/C CUTOUT SIGNAL
COMPRESSOR CLUTCH CONTROL
THERMISTOR INPUTS
VSV CONTROL
GROUND
CUTOUT SWITCH INPUT
POWER INPUT
(NOT USED)
0.85 BLK/WHT
0.50 BLK/WHT
0.50 RED/YEL
0.50 BLK/ORN
0.30 BLU/ORN
0.50 BLU/ORN
0.50 LT GRN
0.50 BLK/YEL
0.50 YEL/BLU
0.85 BLU/RED
0.50 YEL
0.50 YEL/WHT
0.50 WHT/YEL
0.50 BLK
0.50 BLU/BLK
0.50 YEL/GRN
0.50 WHT/BLU
0.50 WHT/BLK
2.0 WHT/BLK
C1
C2
C205
C206
C207
C215
S111
S278
S282
S287
G203

Air conditioning wiring diagram—Prizm, cont.

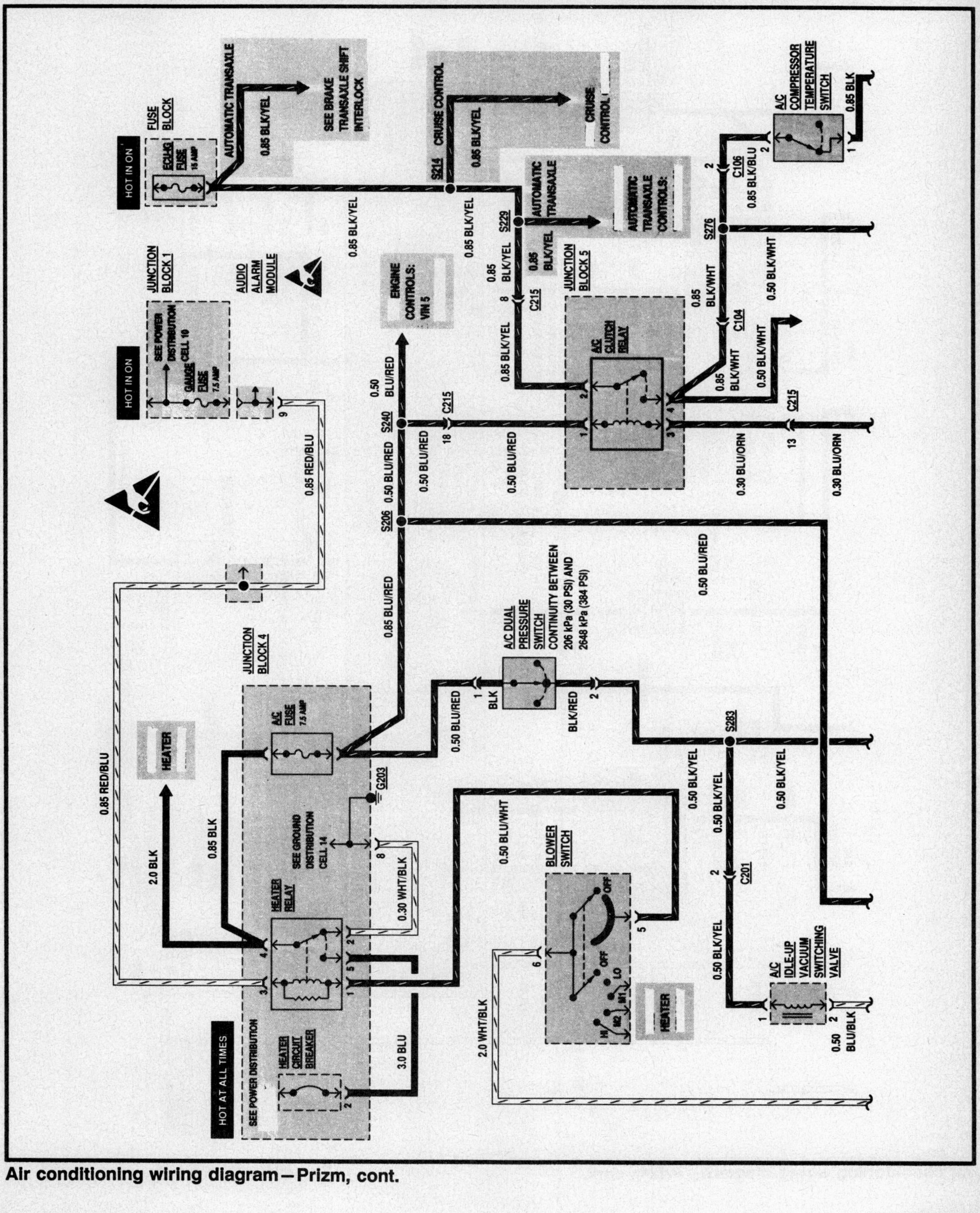
HOT IN ON
FUSE BLOCK
ECU-IG FUSE 15 AMP
AUTOMATIC TRANSAXLE
0.85 BLK/YEL
SEE BRAKE TRANSAXLE SHIFT INTERLOCK
S214
CRUISE CONTROL
S229
AUTOMATIC TRANSAXLE
AUTOMATIC TRANSAXLE CONTROLS:
JUNCTION BLOCK 1
SEE POWER DISTRIBUTION CELL 10
GAUGE FUSE 7.5 AMP
AUDIO ALARM MODULE
ENGINE CONTROLS: VIN 5
JUNCTION BLOCK 5
A/C CLUTCH RELAY
C215
C104
C106
S276
S240
S206
0.50 BLU/RED
0.85 BLK/WHT
0.50 BLK/WHT
0.30 BLU/ORN
0.85 RED/BLU
0.85 BLU/RED
A/C COMPRESSOR TEMPERATURE SWITCH
0.85 BLK
0.85 BLK/BLU
JUNCTION BLOCK 4
A/C FUSE 7.5 AMP
A/C DUAL PRESSURE SWITCH
CONTINUITY BETWEEN 206 kPa (30 PSI) AND 2648 kPa (384 PSI)
BLK/RED
S283
0.50 BLK/YEL
C201
HEATER
G203
SEE GROUND DISTRIBUTION CELL 14
HEATER RELAY
0.30 WHT/BLK
2.0 BLK
0.85 BLK
0.50 BLU/WHT
BLOWER SWITCH
OFF
LO
M1
M2
HI
A/C IDLE-UP VACUUM SWITCHING VALVE
0.50 BLU/BLK
2.0 WHT/BLK
3.0 BLU
HOT AT ALL TIMES
SEE POWER DISTRIBUTION
HEATER CIRCUIT BREAKER

Air conditioning wiring diagram—Prizm, cont.

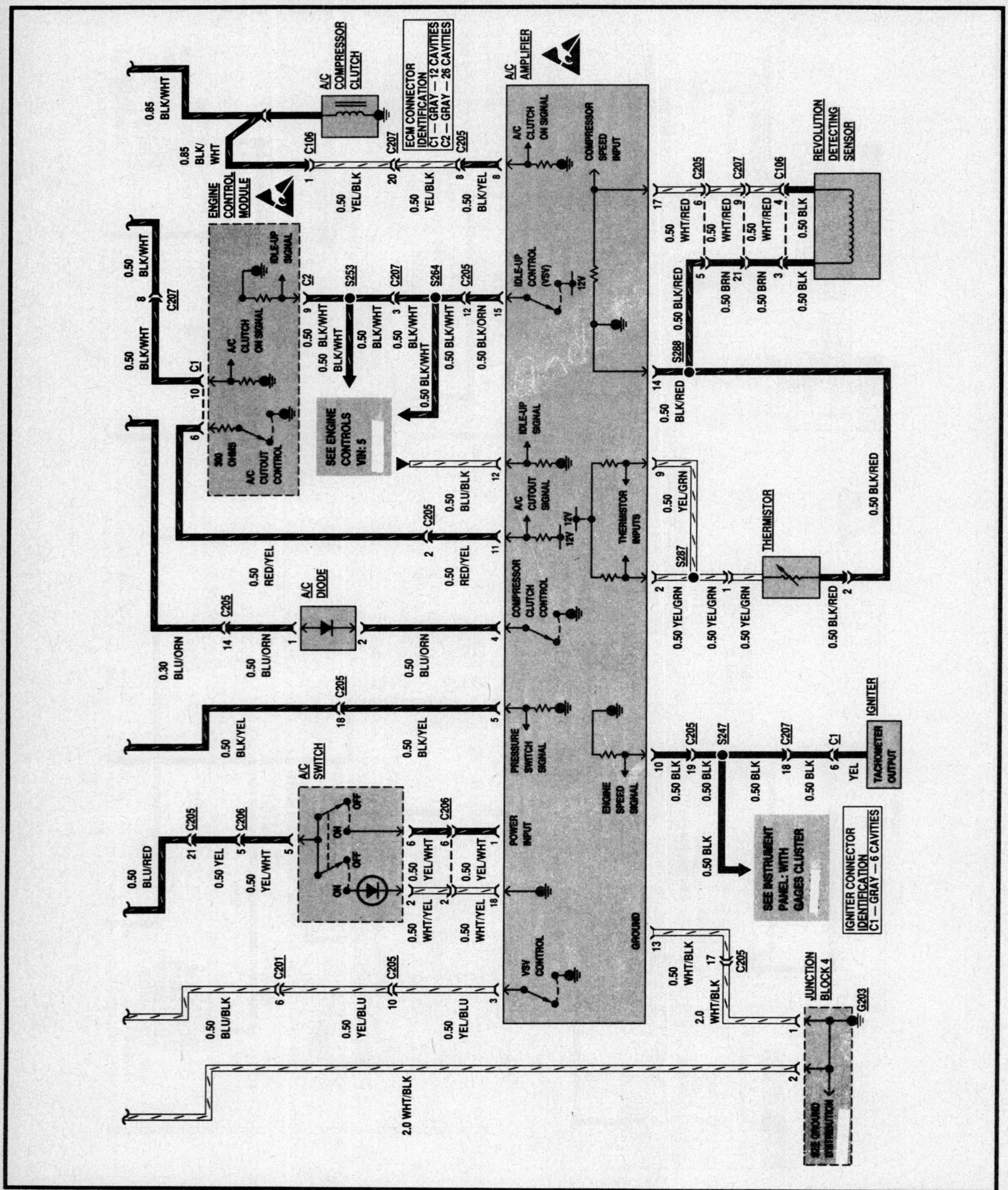
A/C COMPRESSOR CLUTCH
ECM CONNECTOR IDENTIFICATION
C1 — GRAY — 12 CAVITIES
C2 — GRAY — 26 CAVITIES
A/C AMPLIFIER
ENGINE CONTROL MODULE
REVOLUTION DETECTING SENSOR
A/C CLUTCH ON SIGNAL
COMPRESSOR SPEED INPUT
IDLE-UP SIGNAL
IDLE-UP CONTROL (VSV)
A/C CUTOUT CONTROL
330 OHMS
SEE ENGINE CONTROLS VIN: 5
A/C CUTOUT SIGNAL
THERMISTOR INPUTS
THERMISTOR
A/C DIODE
COMPRESSOR CLUTCH CONTROL
PRESSURE SWITCH SIGNAL
ENGINE SPEED SIGNAL
IGNITER
TACHOMETER OUTPUT
A/C SWITCH
POWER INPUT
SEE INSTRUMENT PANEL: WITH GAGES CLUSTER
IGNITER CONNECTOR IDENTIFICATION
C1 — GRAY — 6 CAVITIES
GROUND
VSV CONTROL
JUNCTION BLOCK 4
G203
SEE GROUND DISTRIBUTION
2.0 WHT/BLK

Air conditioning wiring diagram—Prizm, cont.

AIR CONDITIONING SYSTEM ELECTRICAL DIAGNOSIS CHART—STORM

AIR CONDITIONING **DIAGNOSTIC CHART A**

	TEST	RESULT	ACTION
A1.	Raise and suitably support vehicle. Start engine and operate drive wheels at 20 mph. Press AIR CONDITIONING SWITCH to "ON." Turn FAN SWITCH to "LOW."	AIR CONDITIONING COMPRESSOR CLUTCH engages.	All systems in this cell are functioning normally.
		AIR CONDITIONING COMPRESSOR CLUTCH does not engage.	GO TO **A2**.
A2.	Disconnect A/C COMPRESSOR CLUTCH connector. Connect a test lamp from cavity 1 to chassis ground.	Test lamp lights.	Replace AIR CONDITIONING COMPRESSOR CLUTCH.
		Test lamp does not light.	GO TO **A3**.
A3.	Backprobe A/C Compressor Relay connector with a test lamp from cavity 4 to chassis ground.	Test lamp lights.	Repair open in GRN wire between A/C Compressor Relay and AIR CONDITIONING COMPRESSOR CLUTCH.
		Test lamp does not light.	GO TO **A4**.
A4.	Backprobe A/C Compressor Relay connector with a test lamp from cavity 2 to chassis ground.	Test lamp lights.	GO TO **A5**.
		Test lamp does not light.	GO TO **A16**.
A5.	Backprobe A/C Compressor Relay connector with a test lamp from cavity 1 to chassis ground.	Test lamp lights.	GO TO **A6**.
		Test lamp does not light.	GO TO **A9**.
A6.	Backprobe A/C Compressor Relay connector with a digital multimeter from cavity 3 to chassis ground. Measure resistance.	Less than 0.3 ohms.	Replace A/C Compressor Relay.
		More than 0.3 ohms.	GO TO **A7**.
A7.	Backprobe ENGINE CONTROL MODULE connector C2 with a digital multimeter from cavity A2 to chassis ground. Measure resistance.	Less than 0.3 ohms.	Repair open in GRN/RED wire between A/C Compressor Relay and ENGINE CONTROL MODULE.
		More than 0.3 ohms.	GO TO **A8** with manual transaxle and 3-speed automatic transaxle. GO TO **A32** with 4-speed automatic transaxle.
A8.	Backprobe ENGINE CONTROL MODULE connector C1 with a test lamp from cavity B8 to chassis ground.	Test lamp does not light.	Repair open in GRN/ORN wire between ENGINE CONTROL MODULE and A/C Thermo Relay.
		Test lamp lights.	Replace ENGINE CONTROL MODULE.
A9.	Backprobe Heater and A/C Relay connector with a test lamp from cavity 4 to chassis ground.	Test lamp lights.	Repair open in BLU wire between Heater and A/C Relay and FUSE AND RELAY BOX, Fuse E-2, or BRN wire between FUSE AND RELAY BOX and A/C Compressor Relay.
		Test lamp does not light.	GO TO **A10**.
A10.	Backprobe Heater and A/C Relay connector with a test lamp from cavity 2 to chassis ground.	Test lamp does not light.	Repair open in WHT wire between Heater and A/C Relay and FUSE AND RELAY BOX.
		Test lamp lights.	GO TO **A11**.
A11.	Backprobe Heater and A/C Relay connector with a test lamp from cavity 1 to chassis ground.	Test lamp lights.	GO TO **A12**.
		Test lamp does not light.	GO TO **A13**.
A12.	Disconnect Heater and A/C Relay connector. Connect a digital multimeter from cavity 3 to chassis ground. Measure resistance.	More than 0.3 ohms.	Repair BLK ground wire between Heater and A/C Relay and G102.
		Less than 0.3 ohms.	Replace Heater and A/C Relay.
A13.	Backprobe Restart Relay connector with a test lamp from cavity 5 to chassis ground.	Test lamp lights.	Repair open in WHT/RED wire between Restart Relay and Heater and A/C Relay.
		Test lamp does not light.	GO TO **A14**.
A14.	Backprobe Restart Relay connector with a test lamp from cavity 4 to chassis ground.	Test lamp lights.	If starter is operating normally, replace Restart Relay.
		Test lamp does not light.	GO TO **A15**.
A15.	Backprobe GENERATOR connector with a test lamp from cavity 1 to chassis ground.	Test lamp lights.	Repair open in WHT/BLU wire between Restart Relay and GENERATOR.
		Test lamp does not light.	See STARTER AND CHARGING SYSTEM
A16.	Backprobe A/C Thermo Relay connector with a test lamp from cavity 4 to chassis ground.	Test lamp lights.	Repair open in GRN/ORN wire between A/C Thermo Relay and A/C Compressor Relay.
		Test lamp does not light.	GO TO **A17**.
A17.	Backprobe A/C Thermo Relay connector with a test lamp from cavity 2 to chassis ground.	Test lamp does not light.	GO TO **A18**.
		Test lamp lights.	GO TO **A21**.
A18.	Backprobe TRIPLE SWITCH connector with a test lamp from cavity 3 to chassis ground.	Test lamp lights	Repair open in GRN/WHT wire between TRIPLE SWITCH and A/C Thermo Relay.
		Test lamp does not light.	GO TO **A19**.
A19.	Backprobe TRIPLE SWITCH connector with a test lamp from cavity 4 to chassis ground.	Test lamp lights.	Replace TRIPLE SWITCH.
		Test lamp does not light.	GO TO **A20**.
A20.	Backprobe Heater and A/C Relay connector with a test lamp from cavity 4 to chassis ground.	Test lamp lights.	Repair open in BLU wire between Heater and A/C Relay and FUSE AND RELAY BOX, Fuse E-2, or BRN wire between FUSE AND RELAY BOX and TRIPLE SWITCH.
		Test lamp does not light.	GO TO **A9**.

AIR CONDITIONING SYSTEM ELECTRICAL DIAGNOSIS CHART—STORM, CONT.

AIR CONDITIONING — DIAGNOSTIC CHART A (CONT'D)

TEST	RESULT	ACTION
A21. Backprobe A/C Thermo Relay connector with a test lamp from cavity 1 to chassis ground.	Test lamp does not light.	GO TO **A22**.
	Test lamp lights.	GO TO **A25**.
A22. Backprobe AIR CONDITIONING SWITCH connector with a test lamp from cavity 2 to chassis ground.	Test lamp lights.	Repair open in LT GRN wire between AIR CONDITIONING SWITCH and A/C Thermo Relay.
	Test lamp does not light.	GO TO **A23**.
A23. Backprobe AIR CONDITIONING SWITCH connector with a test lamp from cavity 1 to chassis ground.	Test lamp lights.	Replace A/C SWITCH.
	Test lamp does not light.	GO TO **A24**.
A24. Backprobe Heater and A/C Relay connector with a test lamp from cavity 4 to chassis ground.	Test lamp lights.	Repair open in BRN wire between A/C SWITCH and S112.
	Test lamp does not light.	GO TO **A9**.
A25. Backprobe A/C Thermo Relay connector with a digital multimeter from cavity 3 to chassis ground. Measure resistance.	Less than 0.3 ohms.	Replace A/C Thermo Relay.
	More than 0.3 ohms.	GO TO **A26**.
A26. Backprobe ELECTRO THERMO SWITCH connector with a digital multimeter from cavity 1 to chassis ground. Measure Resistance.	Less than 0.3 ohms.	Repair open in PNK/GRN wire between ELECTRO THERMO SWITCH and A/C Thermo Relay.
	More than 0.3 ohms.	GO TO **A27**.
A27. Backprobe ELECTRO THERMO SWITCH connector with a test lamp from cavity 3 to chassis ground.	Test lamp does not light.	Repair open in LT GRN wire between ELECTRO THERMO SWITCH and AIR CONDITIONING SWITCH.
	Test lamp lights.	GO TO **A28**.
A28. Backprobe ELECTRO THERMO SWITCH connector with a digital multimeter from cavity 2 to chassis ground. Measure resistance.	Less than 0.3 ohms.	Replace ELECTRO THERMO SWITCH.
	More than 0.3 ohms.	GO TO **A29**.
A29. Backprobe FAN SWITCH connector with a digital multimeter from cavity 5 to chassis ground. Measure resistance.	Less than 0.3 ohms.	Repair open in GRN/YEL wire between FAN SWITCH and ELECTRO THERMO SWITCH.
	More than 0.3 ohms.	GO TO **A30**.
A30. Backprobe FAN SWITCH connector with a digital multimeter from cavity 6 to chassis ground. Measure resistance.	Less than 0.3 ohms.	Replace FAN SWITCH.
	More than 0.3 ohms.	GO TO **A31**.
A31. Backprobe FAN SWITCH connector with a digital multimeter from cavity 2 to chassis ground. Measure resistance.	Less than 0.3 ohms.	Repair BLK ground wire between FAN SWITCH cavity 2 and cavity 6.
	More than 0.3 ohms.	Repair BLK ground wire between FAN SWITCH cavity 2 and G202.
A32. Backprobe AIR CONDITIONING CUT CONTROL UNIT connector with a test lamp from cavity 2 to chassis ground.	Test lamp does not light.	Repair open in GRN/ORN wire between AIR CONDITIONING CUT CONTROL UNIT and S141.
	Test lamp lights.	GO TO **A33**.
A33. Backprobe AIR CONDITIONING CUT CONTROL UNIT connector with a test lamp from cavity 4 to chassis ground.	Test lamp lights.	GO TO **A34**.
	Test lamp does not light.	Replace A/C CUT CONTROL UNIT.
A34. Backprobe ENGINE CONTROL MODULE connector C1 with a test lamp from cavity B8 to chassis ground.	Test lamp does not light.	Repair open in ORN/BLU wire between AIR CONDITIONING CUT CONTROL UNIT and ENGINE CONTROL MODULE.
	Test lamp lights.	GO TO **A35**.
A35. Disconnect AIR CONDITIONING CUT CONTROL UNIT connector. Connect a digital multimeter from cavity 1 to chassis ground. Measure voltage.	Voltage does not vary.	Refer to VEHICLE SPEED SENSOR Cell 33.
	Voltage varies.	GO TO **A36**.
A36. Connect a digital multimeter from AIR CONDITIONING CUT CONTROL UNIT connector cavity 7 to chassis ground. Measure resistance.	More than 0.3 ohms.	Replace AIR CONDITIONING CUT CONTROL UNIT.
	Less than 0.3 ohms.	GO TO **A37**.
A37. Disconnect THERMO SWITCH connector. Connect a digital multimeter from switch terminal to chassis ground. Measure resistance.	More than 0.3 ohms.	Repair short to ground in LT GRN/YEL wire between A/C CUT CONTROL UNIT and THERMO SWITCH.
	Less than 0.3 ohms.	Replace THERMO SWITCH.

CIRCUIT OPERATION

Manual Transaxle/3-Speed Automatic Transaxle

With the engine running, the GENERATOR applies battery voltage through the closed contacts of the Restart Relay, to the Heater-A/C Relay. The Heater-A/C Relay energizes, and battery voltage from Fuse E-2 is applied to the closed contacts of the AIR CONDITIONING SWITCH, TRIPLE SWITCH, and the A/C Compressor Relay. With the AIR CONDITIONING SWITCH on and the FAN SWITCH on "L," "M1," "M2," or "H" the A/C Thermo Relay is energized, allowing voltage to pass through the closed contacts of the A/C Compressor Relay to the AIR CONDITIONING COMPRESSOR CLUTCH.

4-Speed Automatic Transaxle

With the engine running, the GENERATOR applies battery voltage through the closed contacts of the Restart Relay to the Heater-A/C Relay. The Heater-A/C Relay energizes, and battery voltage from Fuse E-2 is applied to the closed contacts of the AIR CONDITIONING SWITCH, TRIPLE SWITCH, and the A/C Compressor Relay. With the AIR CONDITIONING SWITCH on and the FAN SWITCH on "L," "M1," "M2," or "H" the A/C Thermo Relay is energized, passing an A/C signal through the closed contacts of the AIR CONDITIONING CUT CONTROL UNIT to the ENGINE CONTROL MODULE, thus grounding the ENGINE CONTROL MODULE. This allows voltage to pass through the closed contacts of the A/C Compressor Relay to the AIR CONDITIONING COMPRESSOR CLUTCH.

The AIR CONDITIONING CUT CONTROL UNIT receives a signal from the VEHICLE SPEED SENSOR. If the cooling system reaches a temperature of 110° C (230° F) the THERMO SWITCH moves to a closed position (THERMO SWITCH is closed to ground through a resistor) causing the AIR CONDITIONING CUT CONTROL UNIT to cycle the AIR CONDITIONING COMPRESSOR CLUTCH every 15 seconds when the vehicle is moving less than 20 mph. If the cooling system temperature reaches 120° C (248° F) the THERMO SWITCH closes completely disabling the AIR CONDITIONING COMPRESSOR CLUTCH completely. The Air Conditioning will not operate at all

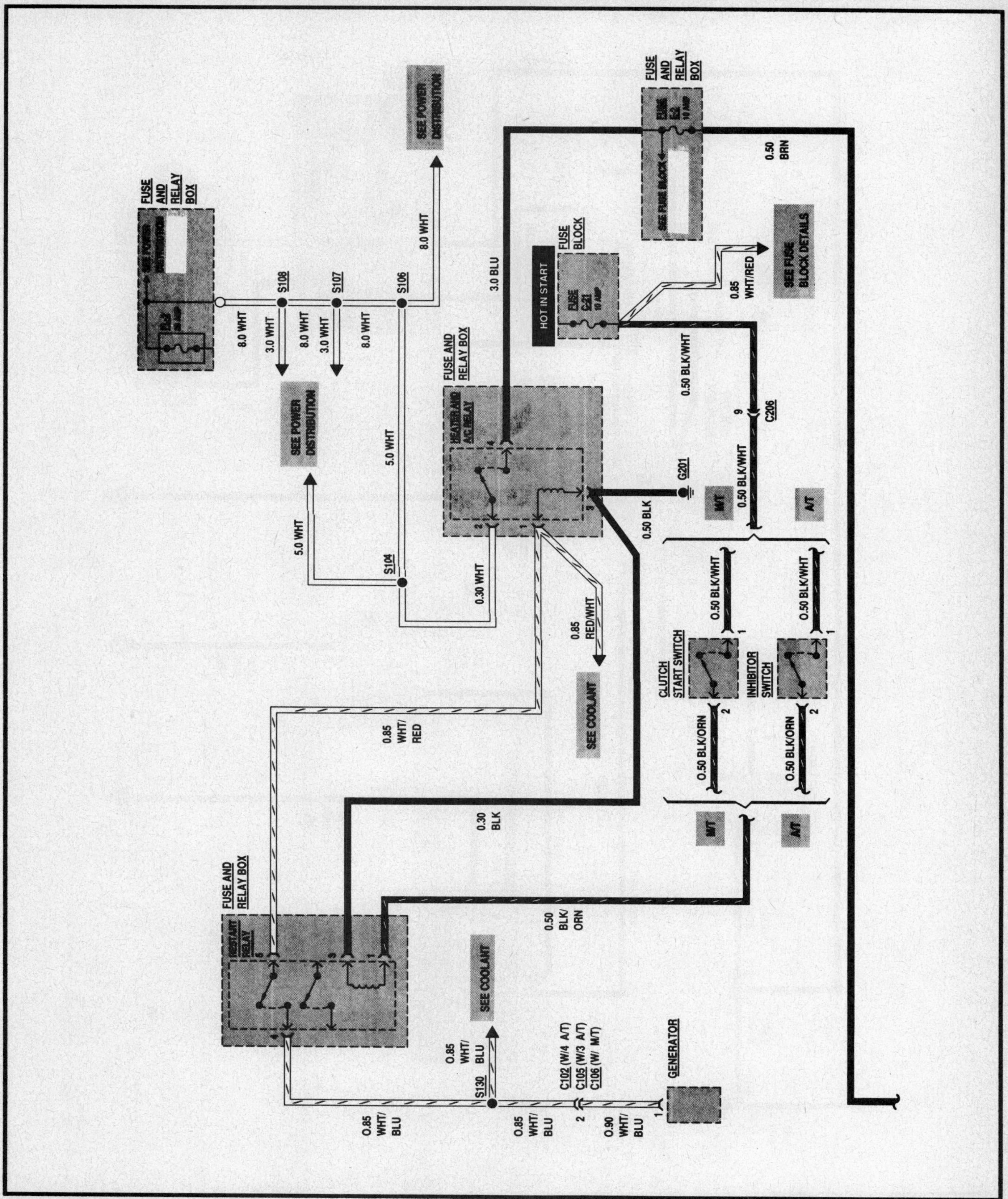
FUSE AND RELAY BOX
SEE POWER DISTRIBUTION
8.0 WHT
3.0 WHT
S108
S107
S106
5.0 WHT
S104
0.30 WHT
3.0 BLU
FUSE AND RELAY BOX
HEATER AND A/C RELAY
HOT IN START
FUSE BLOCK
FUSE C-21 10 AMP
0.85 WHT/RED
SEE FUSE BLOCK DETAILS
0.50 BRN
0.50 BLK/WHT
C206
G201
0.50 BLK
0.85 RED/WHT
SEE COOLANT
M/T
A/T
CLUTCH START SWITCH
INHIBITOR SWITCH
0.50 BLK/ORN
0.30 BLK
0.50 BLK/ORN
FUSE AND RELAY BOX
RESTART RELAY
0.85 WHT/BLU
S130
C102 (W/4 A/T)
C105 (W/3 A/T)
C106 (W/ M/T)
0.90 WHT/BLU
GENERATOR

Air conditioning wiring diagram—Storm

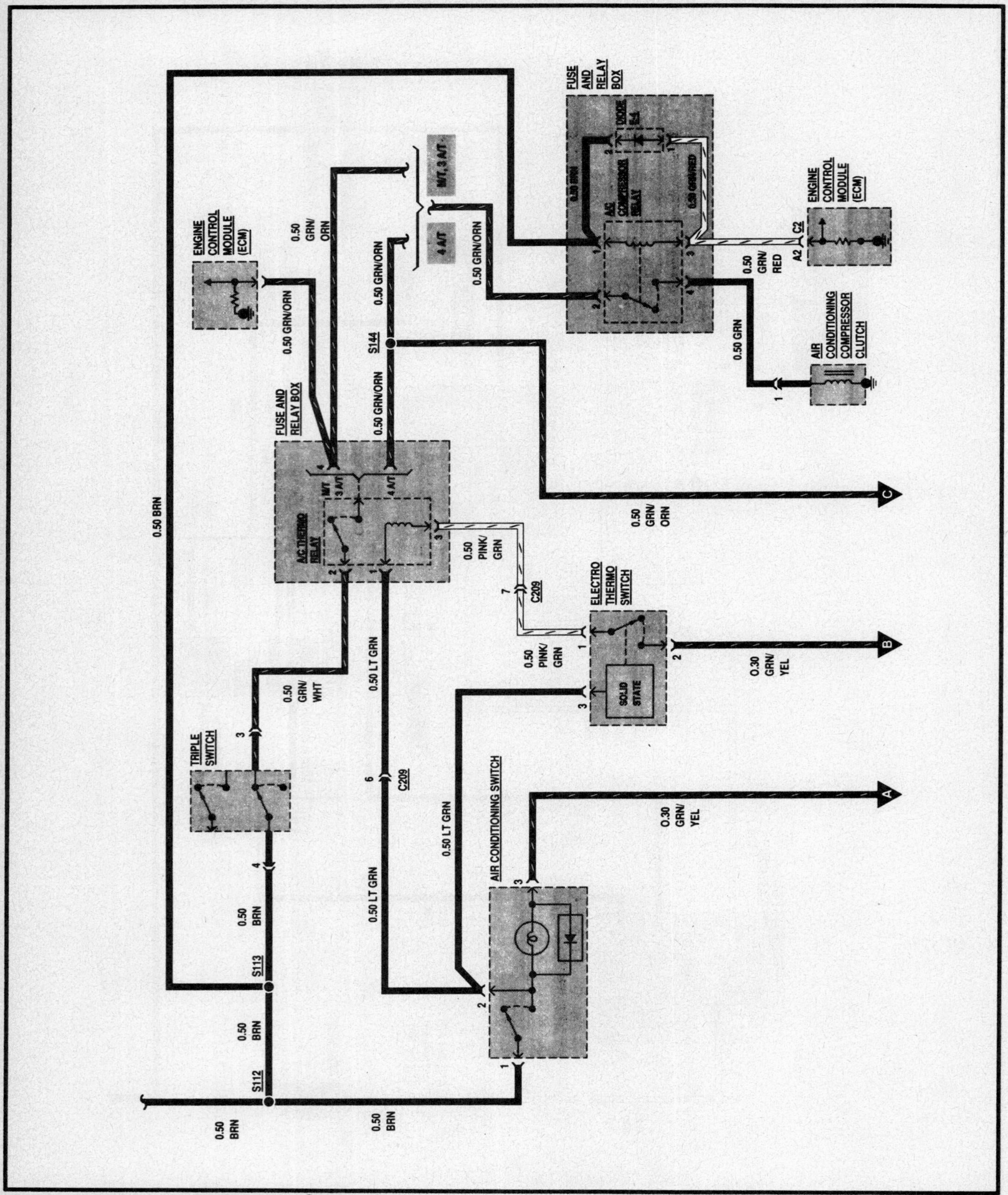
FUSE AND RELAY BOX
A/C COMPRESSOR RELAY
ENGINE CONTROL MODULE (ECM)
M/T, 3 A/T
4 A/T
0.50 GRN/ORN
0.50 BRN
S144
A/C THERMO RELAY
0.50 PINK/GRN
C209
ELECTRO THERMO SWITCH
SOLID STATE
0.30 GRN/YEL
TRIPLE SWITCH
0.50 GRN/WHT
0.50 LT GRN
AIR CONDITIONING SWITCH
S113
S112
AIR CONDITIONING COMPRESSOR CLUTCH
0.50 GRN/RED
0.50 GRN
C2
A2
A
B
C

Air conditioning wiring diagram—Storm, cont.

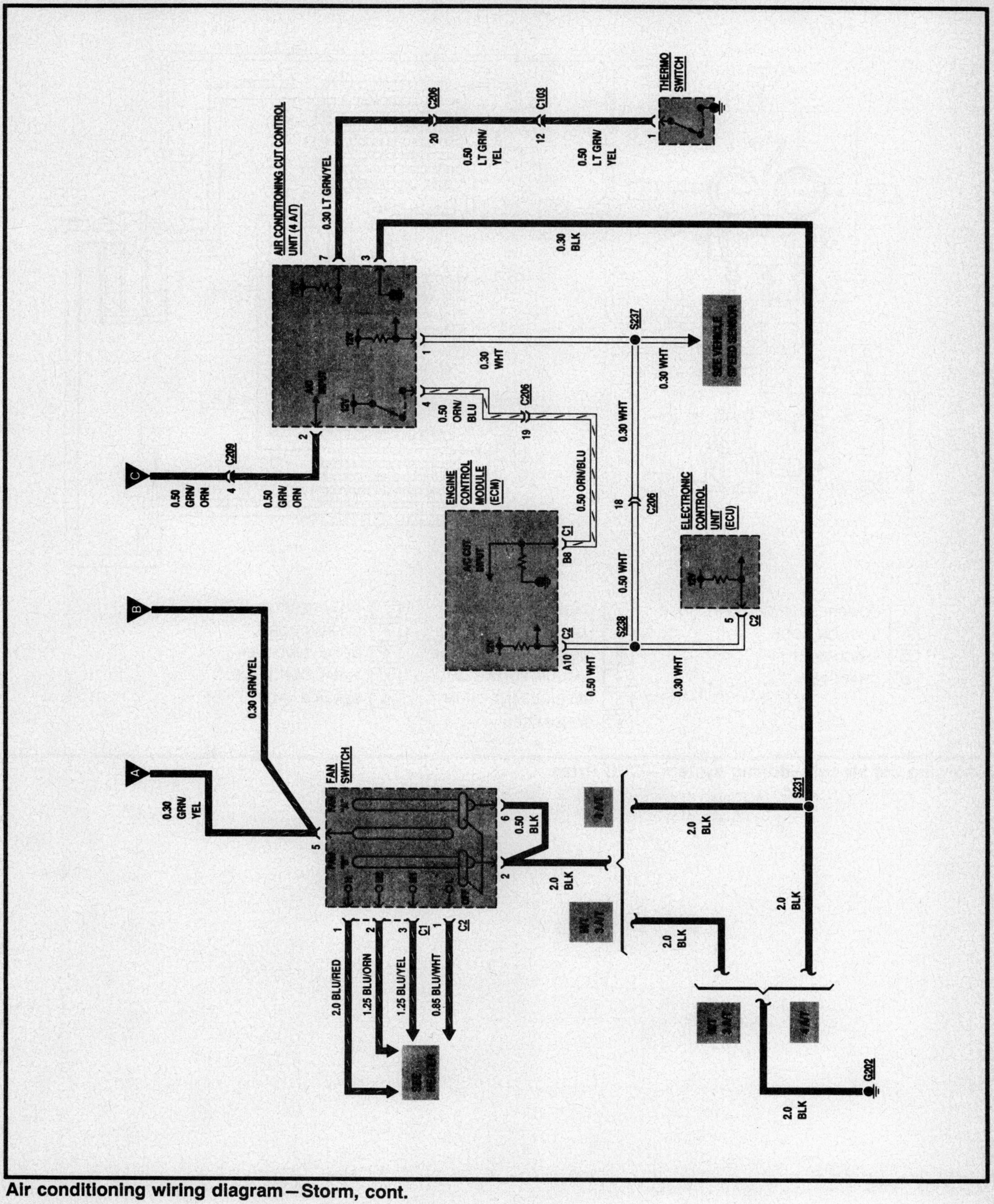
THERMO SWITCH
C206
C103
20
12
1
0.50 LT GRN/ YEL
0.50 LT GRN/ YEL
AIR CONDITIONING CUT CONTROL UNIT (4 A/T)
0.30 LT GRN/YEL
7
3
0.30 BLK
S237
SEE VEHICLE SPEED SENSOR
0.30 WHT
0.30 WHT
4
0.50 ORN/ BLU
C206
19
0.30 WHT
2
C209
C
4
0.50 GRN/ ORN
0.50 GRN/ ORN
ENGINE CONTROL MODULE (ECM)
0.50 ORN/BLU
18
C206
C1
B8
0.50 WHT
ELECTRONIC CONTROL UNIT (ECU)
B
S238
C2
A10
0.50 WHT
0.30 WHT
5
C2
0.30 GRN/YEL
A
0.30 GRN/ YEL
FAN SWITCH
5
6
0.50 BLK
2
2.0 BLK
S231
2.0 BLK
2.0 BLK
2.0 BLK
1
2
3
C1
1
C2
2.0 BLU/RED
1.25 BLU/ORN
1.25 BLU/YEL
0.85 BLU/WHT
G202
2.0 BLK

Air conditioning wiring diagram—Storm, cont.

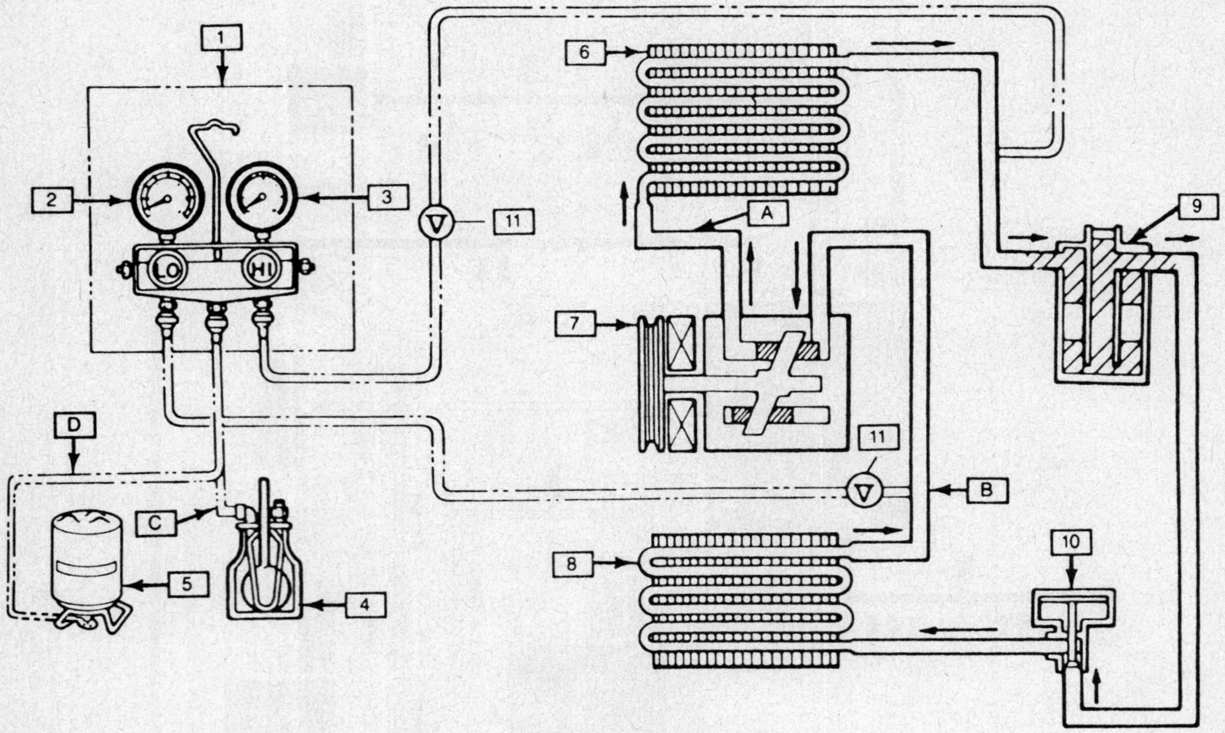
1
2
3
11
6
A
9
7
11
B
D
C
5
4
8
10
LO
HI

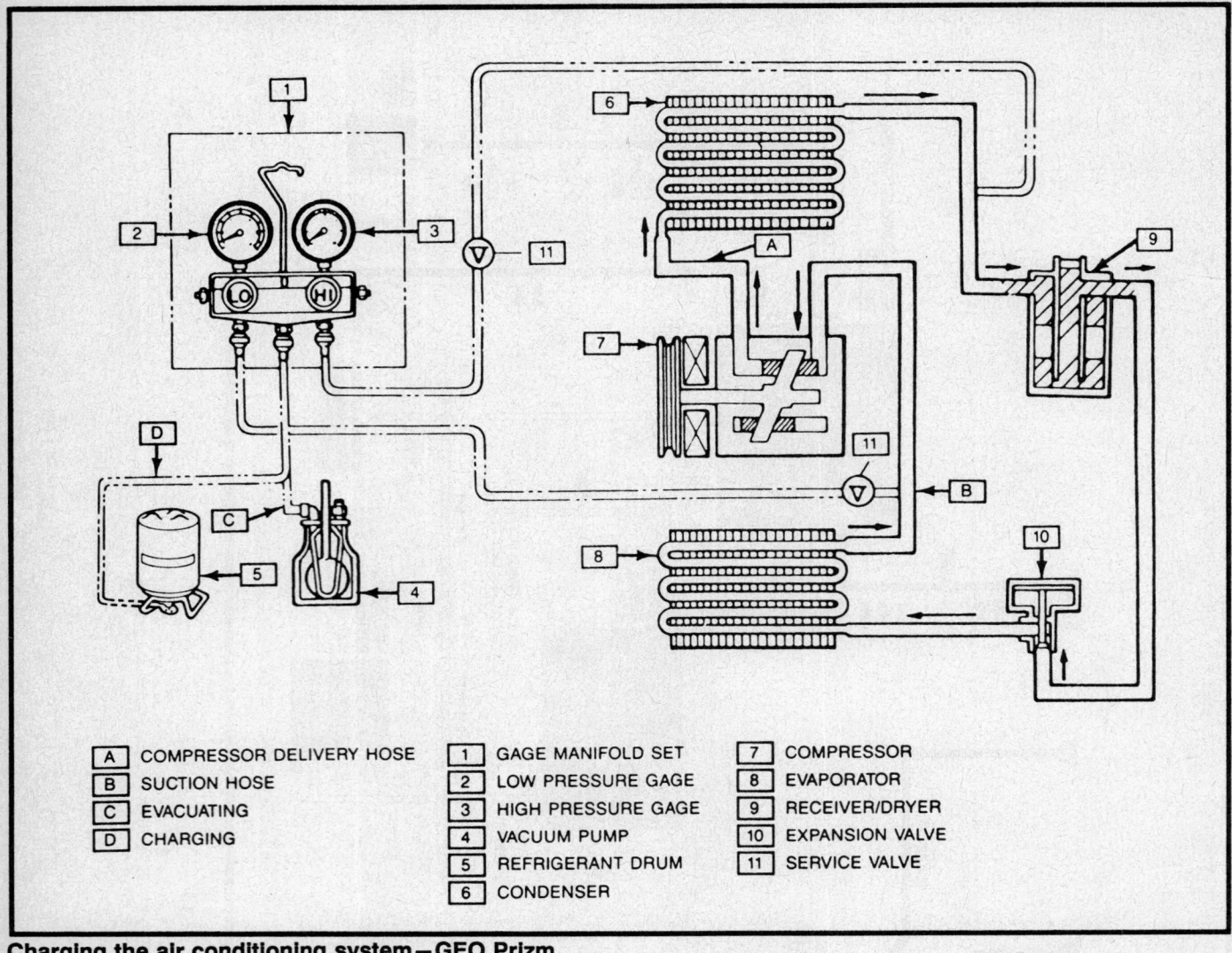

A	COMPRESSOR DELIVERY HOSE	1	GAGE MANIFOLD SET	7	COMPRESSOR
B	SUCTION HOSE	2	LOW PRESSURE GAGE	8	EVAPORATOR
C	EVACUATING	3	HIGH PRESSURE GAGE	9	RECEIVER/DRYER
D	CHARGING	4	VACUUM PUMP	10	EXPANSION VALVE
		5	REFRIGERANT DRUM	11	SERVICE VALVE
		6	CONDENSER		

Charging the air conditioning system – GEO Prizm

16 HONDA 16

CIVIC • CRX • ACCORD • PRELUDE

SPECIFICATIONS

ENGINE IDENTIFICATION

Year	Model	Engine Displacement cu. in. (cc/liter)	Engine Series Identification	No. of Cylinders	Engine Type
1989	Civic	91.0 (1493/1.5)	D15B1	4	SOHC-16V
	Civic/CRX	91.0 (1493/1.5)	D15B2	4	SOHC-16V
	Civic/CRX, HF	91.0 (1493/1.5)	D15B6	4	SOHC-8V
	Civic/CRX, Si	97.0 (1590/1.6)	D16A6	4	SOHC-16V
	Accord, DX/LX	119.0 (1955/2.0)	A20A1	4	SOHC-12V
	Accord, LX-i	119.0 (1955/2.0)	A20A3	4	SOHC-12V
	Prelude	119.0 (1955/2.0)	B20A3	4	SOHC-12V
	Prelude Si	119.0 (1955/2.0)	B20A5	4	DOHC-16V
1990	Civic	91.0 (1493/1.5)	D15B1	4	SOHC-16V
	Civic/CRX	91.0 (1493/1.5)	D15B2	4	SOHC-16V
	Civic/CRX, HF	91.0 (1493/1.5)	D15B6	4	SOHC-8V
	Civic/CRX, Si	97.0 (1590/1.6)	D16A6	4	SOHC-16V
	Accord, DX/LX	132.0 (2156/2.2)	F22A1	4	SOHC-16V
	Accord, EX	132.0 (2156/2.2)	F22A4	4	SOHC-16V
	Prelude 2.0 S	119.0 (1955/2.0)	B20A3	4	SOHC-12V
	Prelude 2.0 Si	119.0 (1955/2.0)	B20A5	4	DOHC-16V
	Prelude Si	125.0 (2056/2.1)	B21A1	4	DOHC-16V
1991	Civic	91.0 (1493/1.5)	D15B1	4	SOHC-16V
	Civic/CRX	91.0 (1493/1.5)	D15B2	4	SOHC-16V
	Civic/CRX, HF	91.0 (1493/1.5)	D15B6	4	SOHC-8V
	Civic/CRX, Si	97.0 (1590/1.6)	D16A6	4	SOHC-16V
	Accord, DX/LX	132.0 (2156/2.2)	F22A1	4	SOHC-16V
	Accord, EX	132.0 (2156/2.2)	F22A4	4	SOHC-16V
	Prelude 2.0 S	119.0 (1955/2.0)	B20A3	4	SOHC-12V
	Prelude 2.0 Si	119.0 (1955/2.0)	B20A5	4	DOHC-16V
	Prelude Si	125.0 (2056/2.1)	B21A1	4	DOHC-16V

REFRIGERANT CAPACITIES

Year	Model	Freon (oz.)	Oil (fl. oz.)	Type
1989	Civic	30.0–33.0	①	R-12
	Civic/CRX	30.0–33.0	①	R-12
	Civic/CRX, HF	30.0–33.0	①	R-12
	Civic/CRX, Si	30.0–33.0	①	R-12
	Accord, DX/LX	28.0–32.0	②	R-12
	Accord LXi	28.0–32.0	②	R-12
	Prelude	32.0–36.0	5.1	R-12
	Prelude Si	32.0–36.0	5.1	R-12
1990	Civic	30.0–33.0	①	R-12
	Civic/CRX	30.0–33.0	①	R-12
	Civic/CRX, HF	30.0–33.0	①	R-12
	Civic/CRX, Si	30.0–33.0	①	R-12
	Accord, DX/LX	32.0–34.0	3.0–4.1	R-12

REFRIGERANT CAPACITIES

Year	Model	Freon (oz.)	Oil (fl. oz.)	Type
	Accord, EX	32.0–34.0	3.0–4.1	R-12
	Prelude 2.0 S	32.0–34.0	①	R-12
	Prelude 2.0 Si	32.0–34.0	①	R-12
	Prelude Si	32.0–34.0	①	R-12
1991	Civic	30.0–33.0	①	R-12
	Civic/CRX	30.0–33.0	①	R-12
	Civic/CRX, HF	30.0–33.0	①	R-12
	Civic/CRX, Si	30.0–33.0	①	R-12
	Accord, DX/LX	32.0–34.0	3.0–4.1	R-12
	Accord, EX	32.0–34.0	3.0–4.1	R-12
	Prelude 2.0 S	32.0–34.0	①	R-12
	Prelude 2.0 Si	32.0–34.0	①	R-12
	Prelude Si	32.0–34.0	①	R-12

① Matsushita Compressor 4.4
Sanden Compressor 4.1

② Keihin Compressor 2.4
Nippodenso Compressor 2.7

AIR CONDITIONING BELT TENSION CHART

Year	Model	Engine Displacement cu. in. (cc/liter)	Belt Type	New ①	Used ①
1989	Civic	91.0 (1493/1.5)	Ribbed	0.28–0.35	0.35–0.43
	Civic/CRX	91.0 (1493/1.5)	Ribbed	0.28–0.35	0.35–0.43
	Civic/CRX, HF	91.0 (1493/1.5)	Ribbed	0.28–0.35	0.35–0.43
	Civic/CRX, Si	97.0 (1590/1.6)	Ribbed	0.28–0.35	0.35–0.43
	Accord, DX/LX	119.0 (1955/2.0)	Ribbed	0.33–0.43	0.39–0.47
	Accord LXi	119.0 (1955/2.0)	Ribbed	0.33–0.43	0.39–0.47
	Prelude	119.0 (1955/2.0)	Ribbed	0.24–0.32	0.39–0.49
	Prelude Si	119.0 (1955/2.0)	Ribbed	0.24–0.32	0.39–0.49
1990	Civic	91.0 (1493/1.5)	Ribbed	0.28–0.35	0.35–0.43
	Civic/CRX	91.0 (1493/1.5)	Ribbed	0.28–0.35	0.35–0.43
	Civic/CRX, HF	91.0 (1493/1.5)	Ribbed	0.28–0.35	0.35–0.43
	Civic/CRX, Si	97.0 (1590/1.6)	Ribbed	0.28–0.35	0.35–0.43
	Accord, DX/LX	132.0 (2156/2.2)	Ribbed	0.33–0.43	0.39–0.47
	Accord EX	132.0 (2156/2.2)	Ribbed	0.33–0.43	0.39–0.47
	Prelude 2.0 S	119.0 (1955/2.0)	Ribbed	0.24–0.32	0.39–0.49
	Prelude 2.0 Si	119.0 (1955/2.0)	Ribbed	0.24–0.32	0.39–0.49
	Prelude Si	125.0 (2056/2.1)	Ribbed	0.24–0.32	0.39–0.49
1991	Civic	91.0 (1493/1.5)	Ribbed	0.28–0.35	0.35–0.43
	Civic/CRX	91.0 (1493/1.5)	Ribbed	0.28–0.35	0.35–0.43
	Civic/CRX, HF	91.0 (1493/1.5)	Ribbed	0.28–0.35	0.35–0.43
	Civic/CRX, Si	97.0 (1590/1.6)	Ribbed	0.28–0.35	0.35–0.43
	Accord, DX/LX	132.0 (2156/2.2)	Ribbed	0.33–0.43	0.39–0.47
	Accord EX	132.0 (2156/2.2)	Ribbed	0.33–0.43	0.39–0.47
	Prelude 2.0 S	119.0 (1955/2.0)	Ribbed	0.24–0.32	0.39–0.49
	Prelude 2.0 Si	119.0 (1955/2.0)	Ribbed	0.24–0.32	0.39–0.49
	Prelude Si	125.0 (2056/2.1)	Ribbed	0.24–0.32	0.39–0.49

① Inches of deflection at midpoint of belt using 22 lbs. of force.

SYSTEM DESCRIPTION

General Information

The heater unit is located in the center of the vehicle along the firewall. The heater system is a bi-level system designed to direct warm air through the vents to either the windshield or the floor and cool air through the panel outlet. The air conditioning system is designed to be activated in combination with a separate air conditioning switch installed in the control assembly and the fan speed switch. The system incorporates a compressor, condenser, evaporator, receiver/drier, pressure switch, expansion valve, thermo-switch, refrigerant lines and some models are equipped with an electronic control head assembly versus the standard cable operated control head.

Service Valve Location

Charging valve locations will vary but most of the time the high or low pressure fitting will be located at the compressor, receiver/drier or along the refrigerant lines. Always discharge, evacuate and recharge at the low side service fitting.

System Discharging

R-12 refrigerant is a chlorofluorocarbon, which, when mishandled, can contribute to the depletion on the ozone layer in the upper atmosphere. The ozone filters out harmful radiation from the sun. In order to protect the ozone layer, an approved R-12 recovery/recycling machine that meets SAE standard J1991 should be employed when discharging the system. Follow the operating instructions provided with the approved equipment exactly to properly discharge the system.

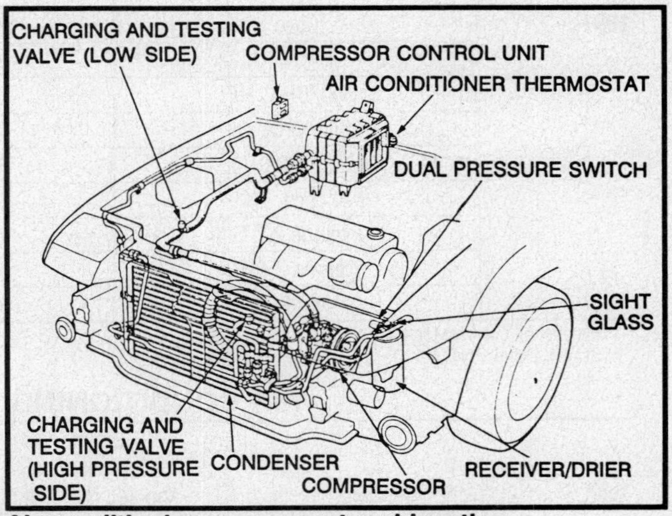
CHARGING AND TESTING VALVE (LOW SIDE)
COMPRESSOR CONTROL UNIT
AIR CONDITIONER THERMOSTAT
DUAL PRESSURE SWITCH
SIGHT GLASS
CHARGING AND TESTING VALVE (HIGH PRESSURE SIDE)
CONDENSER
COMPRESSOR
RECEIVER/DRIER

Air conditioning component and location

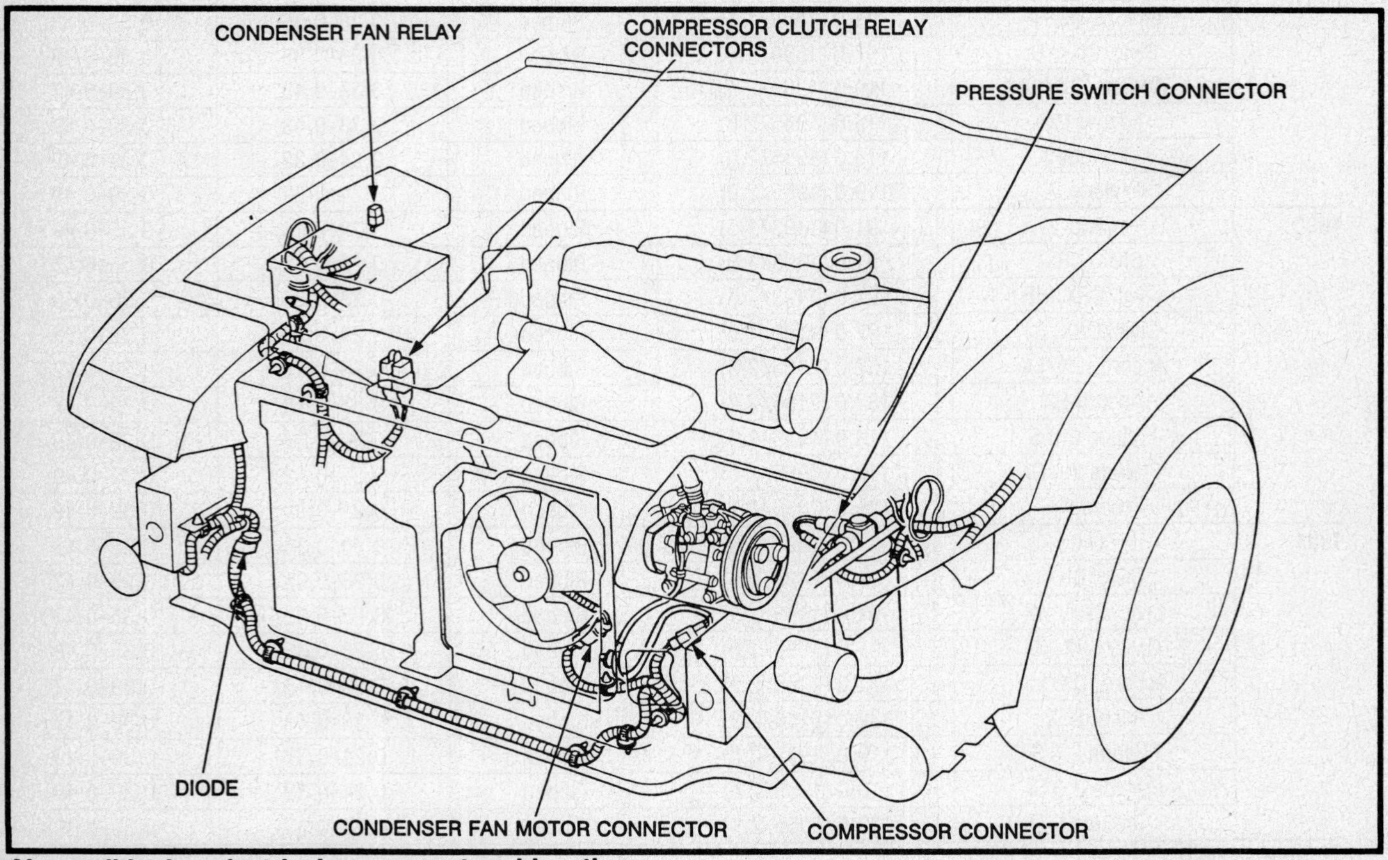
CONDENSER FAN RELAY
COMPRESSOR CLUTCH RELAY CONNECTORS
PRESSURE SWITCH CONNECTOR
DIODE
CONDENSER FAN MOTOR CONNECTOR
COMPRESSOR CONNECTOR

Air conditioning electrical component and location

System Evacuating

If the air conditioning system has been opened to the atmosphere, it should be air and moisture free before being recharged with refrigerant. Moisture and air mixed with refrigerant will raise the compressor head pressure, damage the system's components and will reduce the performance of the system. Moisture will boil at normal room temperature when exposed to a vacuum, the moisture then becomes a vapor and will be easily removed from the system by the vacuum pump.

To evacuate or rid the system of air and moisture:

1. Leak test the system and repair any leaks.
2. Connect an approved charging station, recovery/recycling machine or manifold gauge set and vacuum pump to the discharge and suction ports. The red hose is connected to the discharge (high pressure) line, and the blue hose is connected to the suction (low pressure) line.
3. Open the discharge and suction ports and start the vacuum pump. If the pump is not able to pull at least 26 in. Hg vacuum, there is a leak that must be repaired before evacuation can occur.
4. Once the system has reached at least 26 in. Hg vacuum, allow the system to evacuate for 20 minutes. The longer the system is evacuated, the more contaminants will be removed.
5. Close all valves and turn the pump off. If the system loses more than 2 in. Hg vacuum after 15 minutes, there is a leak that should be repaired.

System Charging

1. Connect an approved charging station, recovery/recycling machine or manifold gauge set to the discharge and suction ports. The red hose is connected to the discharge (high pressure) line, and the blue hose is connected to the suction (low pressure) line.
2. Follow the instructions provided with the equipment and charge the system with the specified amount of refrigerant.
3. Perform a leak test.

SYSTEM COMPONENTS

Radiator

REMOVAL AND INSTALLATION

1. Disconnect the negative battery cable.
2. Properly drain the cooling system.
3. Disconnect the fan motor and thermo-switch wire connector.
4. Disconnect the upper and lower radiator hoses.
5. Disconnect and plug the automatic transaxle cooling lines at the radiator, if equipped.
6. Disconnect the coolant reservoir overflow hose.
7. Remove the radiator attaching bolts and brackets.
8. Remove the radiator with the cooling fan attached.
9. Remove the cooling fan and shroud from the radiator.

To install:

10. Attach the cooling fan and shroud to the radiator and install the assembly.
11. Attach the radiator bolts and brackets.

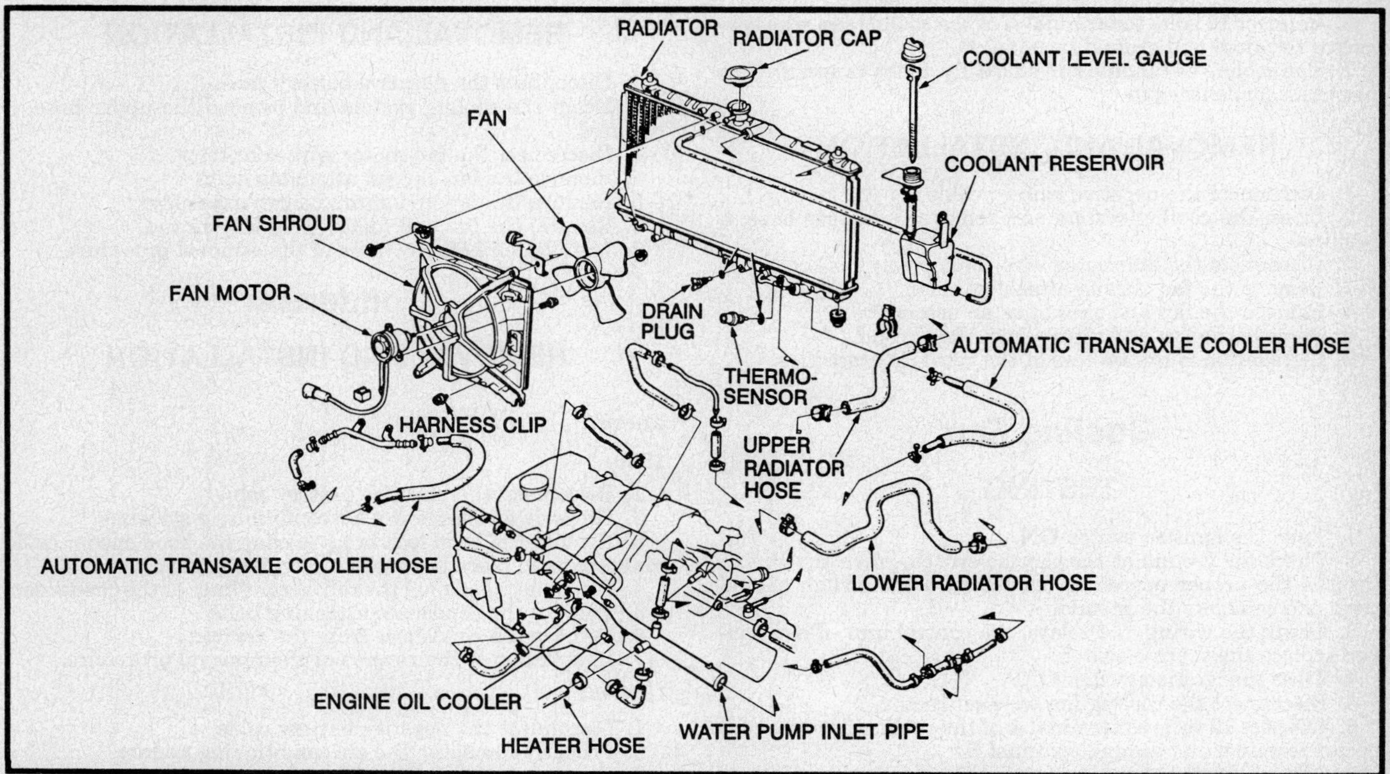
RADIATOR
RADIATOR CAP
COOLANT LEVEL GAUGE
FAN
COOLANT RESERVOIR
FAN SHROUD
FAN MOTOR
DRAIN PLUG
AUTOMATIC TRANSAXLE COOLER HOSE
THERMO-SENSOR
HARNESS CLIP
UPPER RADIATOR HOSE
AUTOMATIC TRANSAXLE COOLER HOSE
LOWER RADIATOR HOSE
ENGINE OIL COOLER
HEATER HOSE
WATER PUMP INLET PIPE

Exploded view of the radiator assembly

12. Connect the coolant reservoir overflow hose.
13. Connect the automatic transaxle cooling lines to the radiator, if equipped.
14. Connect the upper and lower radiator hoses.
15. Connect the fan motor and thermo-switch wire connector.
16. Refill the system with the proper type and quantity of coolant, check for leaks and bleed the cooling system.
17. Reconnect the negative battery cable.

COOLING SYSTEM BLEEDING

1. Loosen the air bleed bolt in the water outlet.
2. Fill the radiator to the bottom of the filler neck with the proper type and quantity of coolant.
3. Tighten the bleed bolt as soon as coolant flows out in a steady stream without bubbles.
4. With the radiator cap off, start and run the engine until the cooling fan cycles twice and the engine is warmed up.
5. Add coolant to bring the level up to the bottom of the radiator filler neck.
6. Install the radiator cap and check for cooling system leaks.

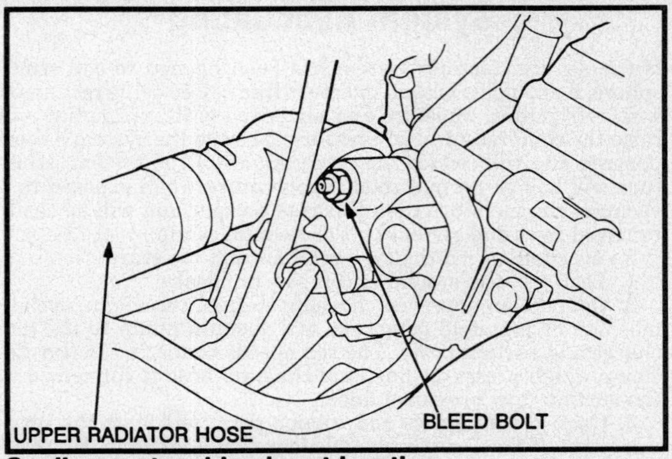
UPPER RADIATOR HOSE
BLEED BOLT
Cooling system bleed port location

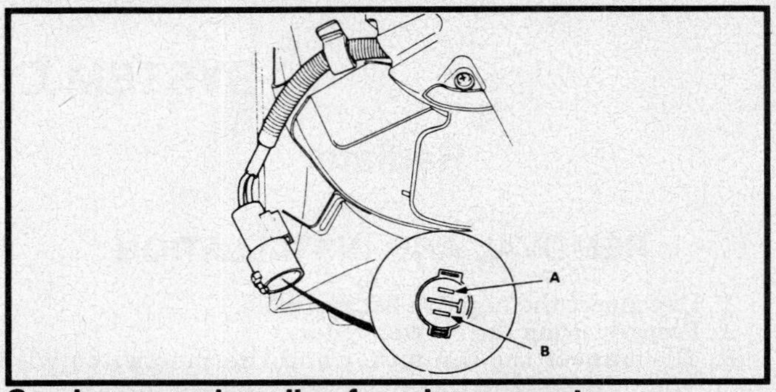
A
B
Condenser and cooling fan wire connector

Condenser Fan

TESTING

1. Turn the ignition, air conditioner and blower speed switch **ON**.
2. Check for voltage at the condenser fan motor using a voltmeter.
3. There should be approximately 12 volts, if not as specified check the fuses, relay, wiring and control unit.
4. Turn the ignition switch **OFF**.
5. Disconnect the condenser fan wire connector.
6. Connect 12 volts to terminal **A** of the cooling fan wire connector terminal and ground terminal **B**.
7. The cooling fan should run smoothly, if not as specified replace the condenser fan

REMOVAL AND INSTALLATION

1. Disconnect the negative battery cable.
2. Drain the cooling system and remove the upper hose, if required.
3. Disconnect the fan motor wire connector.
4. Remove the fan shroud attaching bolts.
5. Remove the fan and shroud as an assembly.
6. Remove the fan and motor from the shroud.
7. Installation is the reverse of the removal procedure.

Cooling Fan

TESTING

1. Turn the ignition switch **ON**.
2. Check for ground at the thermo-switch, when the engine reaches the proper operating temperature the switch should close and complete the ground.
3. Check the wiring, the relays, the control unit, if as specified replace the thermo-switch.
4. Turn the ignition switch **OFF**.
5. Disconnect the cooling fan wire connector.
6. Connect 12 volts to terminal **A** of the cooling fan wire connector terminal and ground terminal **B**.
7. The cooling fan should run smoothly, if not as specified replace the cooling fan

REMOVAL AND INSTALLATION

1. Disconnect the negative battery cable.
2. Drain the cooling system and remove the upper hose, if required.
3. Disconnect the fan motor wire connector.
4. Remove the fan shroud attaching bolts.
5. Remove the fan and shroud as an assembly.
6. Remove the fan and motor from the shroud.
7. Installation is the reverse of the removal procedure.

Condenser

REMOVAL AND INSTALLATION

Accord

1989

1. Disconnect the negative battery cable.
2. Properly discharge the air conditioning system.
3. Remove the hood lock brace leaving the hood opener cable connected and place the assembly on the engine.
4. Disconnect and plug the refrigerant lines at the condenser.
5. Remove the condenser attaching bolts.
6. Remove the condenser from the vehicle.
7. Installation is the reverse of the removal procedure.

1990–91

1. Disconnect the negative battery cable.
2. Properly discharge the air conditioning system.
3. Remove the reservoir tank, tube and bracket.
4. Remove the front grille.

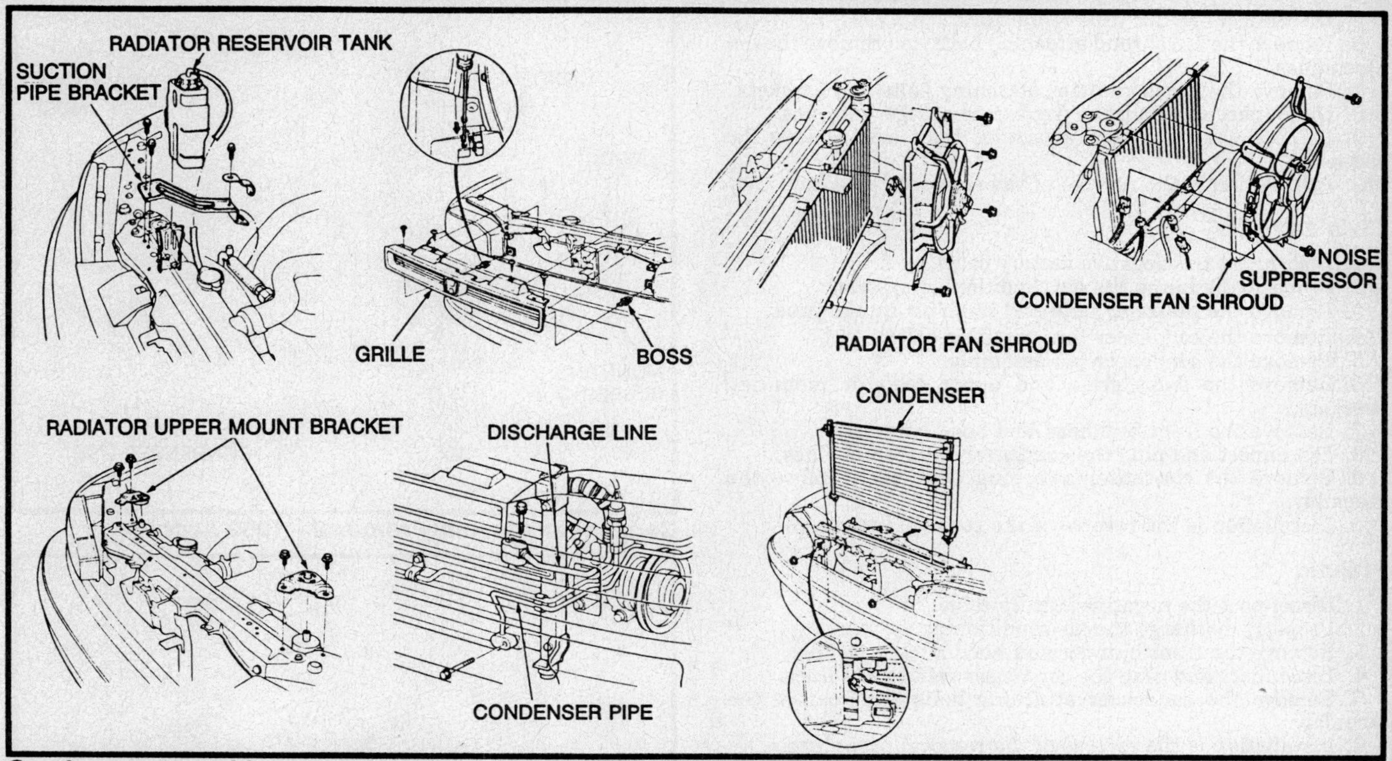
RADIATOR RESERVOIR TANK
SUCTION PIPE BRACKET
GRILLE
BOSS
NOISE SUPPRESSOR
CONDENSER FAN SHROUD
RADIATOR FAN SHROUD
CONDENSER
RADIATOR UPPER MOUNT BRACKET
DISCHARGE LINE
CONDENSER PIPE

Condenser assembly removal—1990–91 Accord

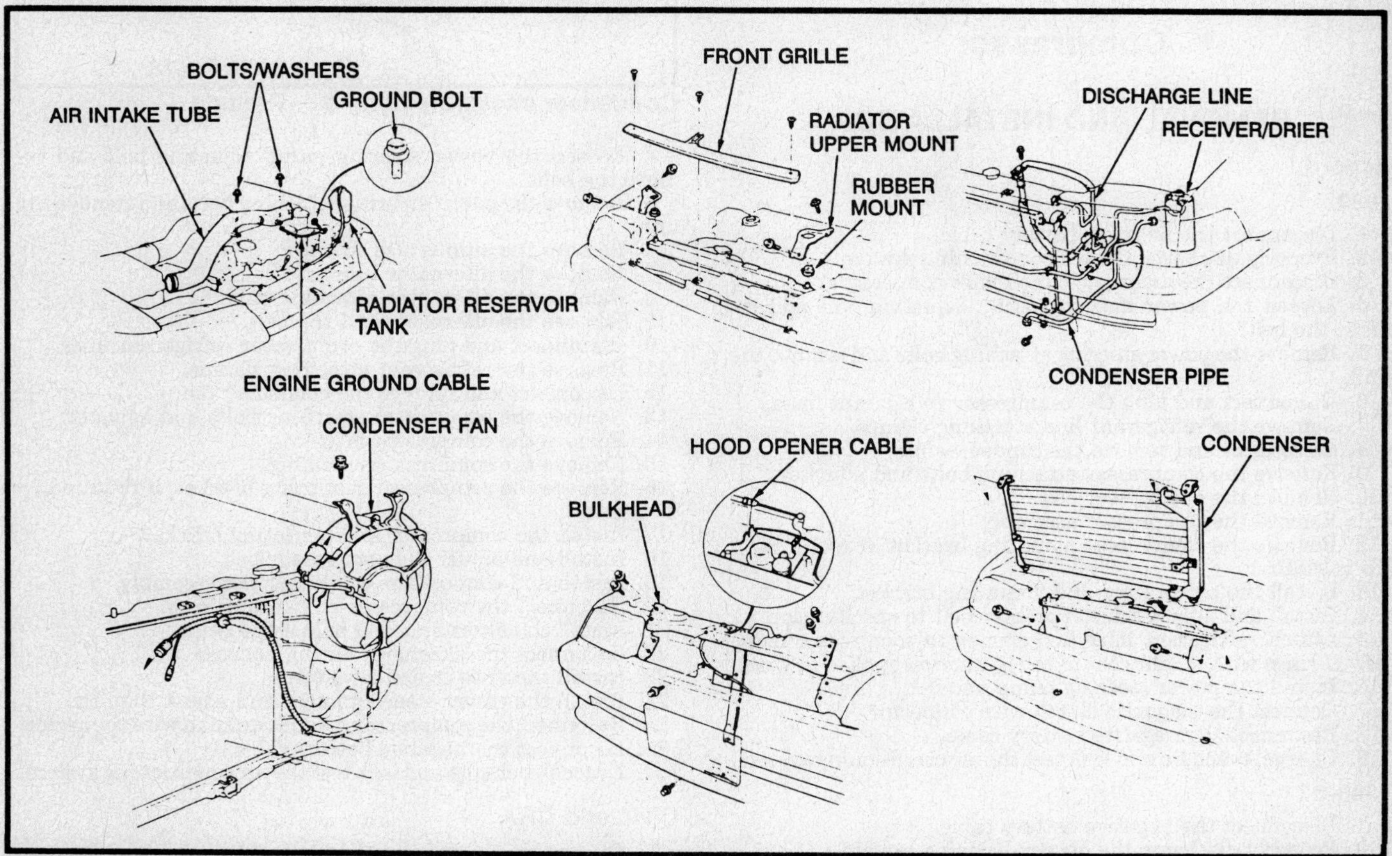
BOLTS/WASHERS
GROUND BOLT
AIR INTAKE TUBE
RADIATOR RESERVOIR TANK
ENGINE GROUND CABLE
FRONT GRILLE
RADIATOR UPPER MOUNT
RUBBER MOUNT
DISCHARGE LINE
RECEIVER/DRIER
CONDENSER PIPE
CONDENSER FAN
HOOD OPENER CABLE
BULKHEAD
CONDENSER

Condenser assembly removal—Civic and CRX

5. Disconnect the fan wire connectors.
6. Remove the fan shroud attaching bolts and remove the fan assemblies.
7. Remove the upper radiator attaching bolts and brackets.
8. Disconnect and plug the condenser refrigerant lines.
9. Remove the condenser attaching bolts and remove the assembly.
10. Installation is the reverse of the removal procedure.

Civic and CRX

1. Disconnect the negative battery cable.
2. Properly discharge the air conditioning system.
3. Remove the reservoir tank and fresh air intake tube.
4. Remove the condenser fan attaching bolts.
5. Remove the condenser fan assembly.
6. Remove the front grille and upper radiator mounting brackets.
7. Remove the front bulkhead and hood latch cable.
8. Disconnect and plug the condenser refrigerant lines.
9. Remove the condenser attaching bolts and remove the assembly.
10. Installation is the reverse of the removal procedure.

Prelude

1. Disconnect the negative battery cable.
2. Properly discharge the air conditioning system.
3. Remove the front bumper and hood latch assembly.
4. Disconnect and plug the condenser refrigerant lines.
5. Remove the condenser attaching bolts and remove the assembly.
6. Installation is the reverse of the removal procedure.

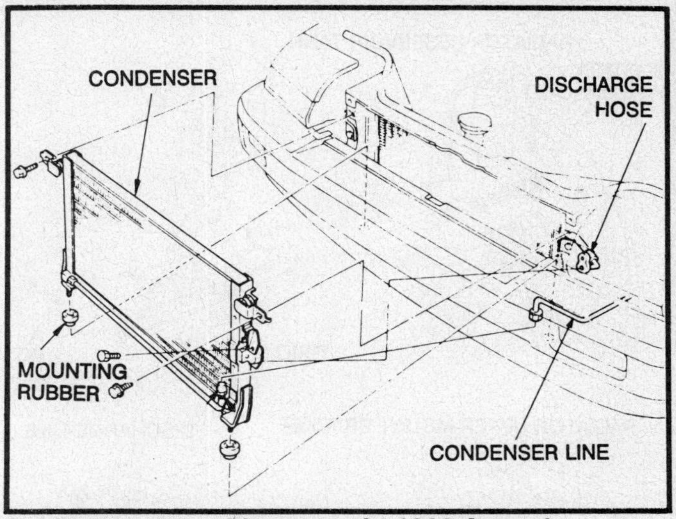
CONDENSER
DISCHARGE HOSE
MOUNTING RUBBER
CONDENSER LINE
Condenser assembly removal—1989 Accord

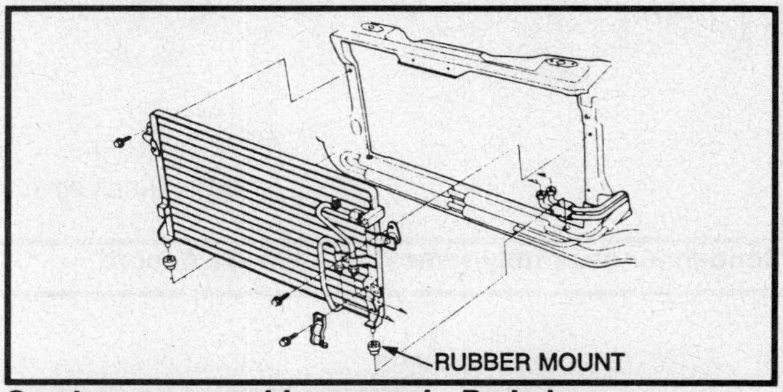
RUBBER MOUNT
Condenser assembly removal—Prelude

Compressor

REMOVAL AND INSTALLATION

Accord

1989

1. Disconnect the negative battery cable.
2. Properly discharge the air conditioning system.
3. Disconnect the magnetic clutch wire connector.
4. Loosen the power steering pump adjusting bolt and remove the belt.
5. Remove the power steering attaching bolts and remove the unit.
6. Disconnect and plug the compressor refrigerant lines.
7. Remove the refrigerant line attaching clamps.
8. Disconnect and remove the condenser fan.
9. Remove the compressor attaching bolts and adjuster.
10. Remove the compressor belt.
11. Remove the compressor assembly.
12. Remove the compressor mounting bracket, if required.

To install:

13. Install the compressor and mounting bracket.
14. Install and adjust the compressor belt to specification.
15. Attach refrigerant lines and clamps to compressor using new O-rings with a light coat of refrigerant oil applied to them.
16. Install the power steering pump and belt.
17. Connect the magnetic clutch wire connector.
18. Reconnect the negative battery cable.
19. Charge, evacuate and leak test the air conditioning system.

1990–91

1. Disconnect the negative battery cable.
2. Properly discharge the air conditioning system.
3. Disconnect the magnetic clutch wire connector.
4. Loosen the power steering pump adjusting bolt and remove the belt.
5. Remove the power steering attaching bolts and remove the unit.
6. Remove the auto cruise actuator.
7. Remove the alternator harness.
8. Remove the alternator attaching bolts.
9. Remove the alternator and the belt.
10. Disconnect and plug the compressor refrigerant lines.
11. Remove the refrigerant attaching clamps.
12. Disconnect and remove the condenser fan.
13. Remove the compressor attaching bolts and adjuster.
14. Remove the compressor belt.
15. Remove the compressor assembly.
16. Remove the compressor mounting bracket, if required.

To install:

17. Install the compressor and mounting bracket.
18. Install and adjust the compressor belt.
19. Install and connect the condenser fan assembly.
20. Reconnect the compressor refrigerant lines.
21. Install the alternator and adjust the belt.
22. Reconnect the alternator wiring harness.
23. Install the auto cruise actuator.
24. Install the power steering pump and adjust the belt.
25. Reconnect the compressor magnetic clutch wire connector.
26. Reconnect the negative battery cable.
27. Evacuate, charge and leak test the air conditioning system.

Civic and CRX

1. Disconnect the negative battery cable.
2. Properly discharge the air conditioning system.

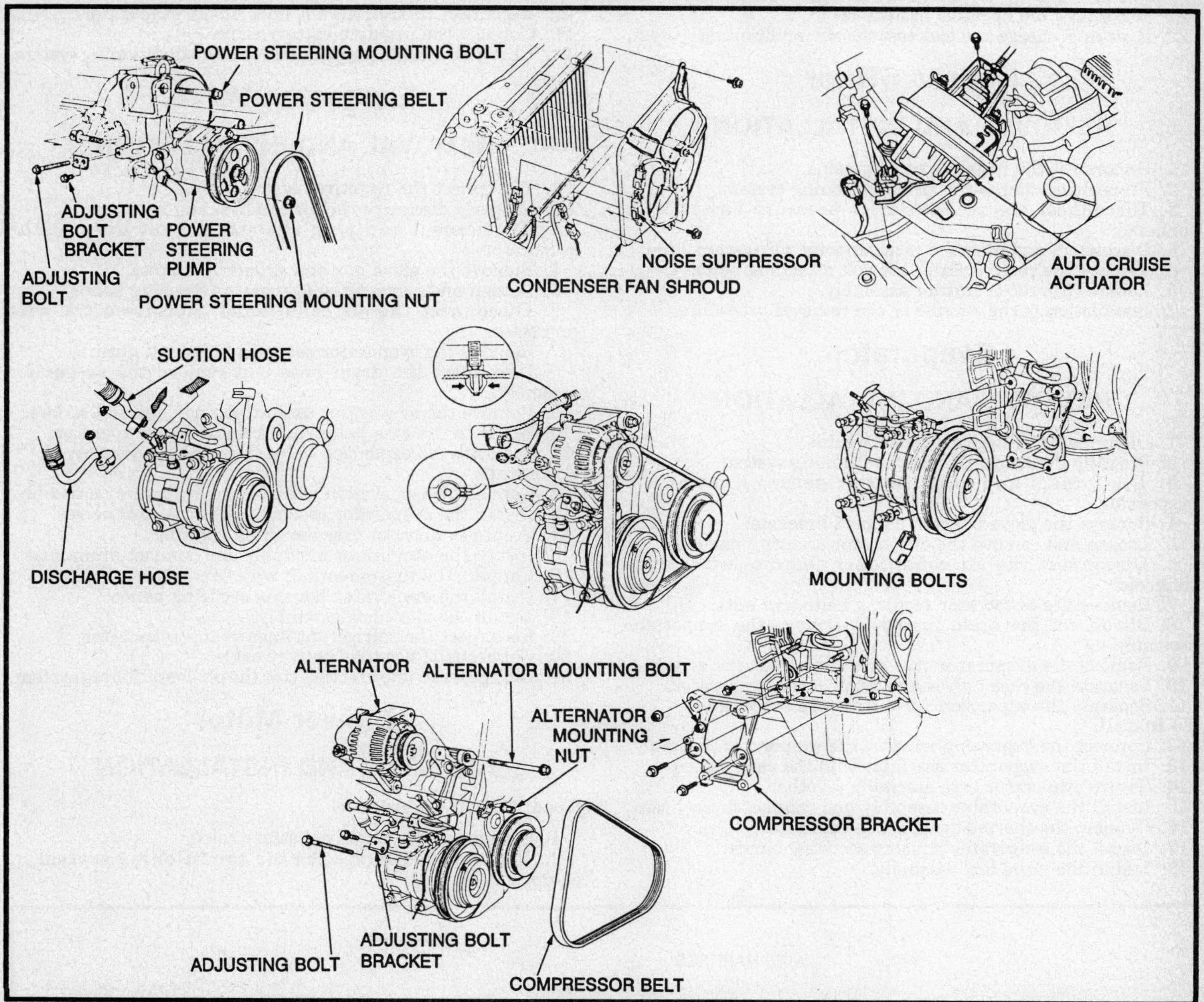
POWER STEERING MOUNTING BOLT
POWER STEERING BELT
ADJUSTING BOLT BRACKET
POWER STEERING PUMP
ADJUSTING BOLT
POWER STEERING MOUNTING NUT
NOISE SUPPRESSOR
CONDENSER FAN SHROUD
AUTO CRUISE ACTUATOR
SUCTION HOSE
DISCHARGE HOSE
MOUNTING BOLTS
ALTERNATOR
ALTERNATOR MOUNTING BOLT
ALTERNATOR MOUNTING NUT
COMPRESSOR BRACKET
ADJUSTING BOLT BRACKET
ADJUSTING BOLT
COMPRESSOR BELT

Compressor assembly removal

3. Disconnect the magnetic clutch wire connector.
4. Loosen the power steering pump adjusting bolt and remove the belt.
5. Remove the power steering attaching bolts and remove the unit.
6. Disconnect and plug the compressor refrigerant lines.
7. Loosen the compressor attaching bolts and adjuster.
8. Remove the compressor belt.
9. Remove the compressor attaching bolts and assembly.
10. Remove the compressor mounting bracket, if required.
11. Installation is the reverse of the removal procedure.

Prelude

1. Disconnect the negative battery cable.
2. Properly discharge the air conditioning system.
3. Disconnect the magnetic clutch wire connector.
4. Loosen the power steering pump idler pulley bolt and remove the belt.
5. Disconnect and plug the power steering pump inlet hose.
6. Remove the power steering attaching bolts and remove the unit.
7. Disconnect the alternator wiring harness.
8. Remove the alternator attaching bolts.
9. Remove the alternator and the belt.
10. Disconnect and plug the compressor refrigerant lines.
11. Remove the compressor attaching bolts.
12. Disconnect the compressor magnetic clutch wire connector.
13. Remove the compressor assembly.
14. Remove the compressor mounting bracket, if required.

To install:

15. Install the compressor and mounting bracket.
16. Reconnect the compressor refrigerant lines.
17. Install the alternator and adjust the belt.
18. Reconnect the alternator wiring harness.
19. Install the power steering pump and inlet hose and adjust the belt.
20. Reconnect the compressor magnetic clutch wire connector.

21. Reconnect the negative battery cable.
22. Evacuate, charge and leak test the air conditioning system.

Receiver/Drier

REMOVAL AND INSTALLATION

1. Disconnect the negative battery cable.
2. Properly discharge the air conditioning system.
3. Disconnect the receiver/drier pressure switch wire connector.
4. Disconnect and plug the receiver/drier refrigerant lines.
5. Remove the receiver/drier bracket attaching bolts.
6. Remove the receiver/drier assembly.
7. Installation is the reverse of the removal procedure.

Evaporator

REMOVAL AND INSTALLATION

1. Disconnect the negative battery cable.
2. Properly discharge the air conditioning system.
3. Disconnect and plug the refrigerant lines at the evaporator.
4. Remove the glove box and support brackets.
5. Loosen and remove the evaporator securing bands.
6. Disconnect the air conditioner thermo-switch wire connector.
7. Remove the evaporator securing bolts and nuts.
8. Disconnect the drain hose and remove the evaporator assembly.
9. Remove the evaporator case attaching clips and screws.
10. Separate the case halves and remove the evaporator.
11. Separate the expansion valve from the evaporator.

To install:

12. Connect the expansion valve to the evaporator assembly.
13. Install the evaporator assembly into the case halves.
14. Secure evaporator case assembly together.
15. Install the evaporator assembly and connect drain hose.
16. Connect the thermo-switch wire connector.
17. Install the evaporator housing securing bands.
18. Install the glove box assembly.
19. Reconnect the refrigerant lines at the evaporator.
20. Connect the negative battery cable.
21. Charge, evacuate and leak test the air conditioning system.

Expansion Valve

REMOVAL AND INSTALLATION

1. Disconnect the negative battery cable.
2. Properly discharge the air conditioning system.
3. Disconnect and plug the refrigerant lines at the evaporator.
4. Remove the glove box and support brackets.
5. Loosen and remove the evaporator securing bands.
6. Disconnect the air conditioner thermo-switch wire connector.
7. Remove the evaporator securing bolts and nuts.
8. Disconnect the drain hose and remove the evaporator assembly.
9. Remove the evaporator case attaching clips and screws.
10. Separate the case halves and remove the evaporator.
11. Separate the expansion valve from the evaporator.

To install:

12. Connect the expansion valve to the evaporator assembly.
13. Install the evaporator assembly into the case halves.
14. Secure evaporator case assembly together.
15. Install the evaporator assembly and connect drain hose.
16. Connect the thermo-switch wire connector.
17. Install the evaporator housing securing bands.
18. Install the glove box assembly.
19. Reconnect the refrigerant lines at the evaporator.
20. Connect the negative battery cable.
21. Charge, evacuate and leak test the air conditioning system.

Blower Motor

REMOVAL AND INSTALLATION

Except 1990–91 Accord

1. Disconnect the negative battery cable.
2. Properly discharge the air conditioning system, if equipped.

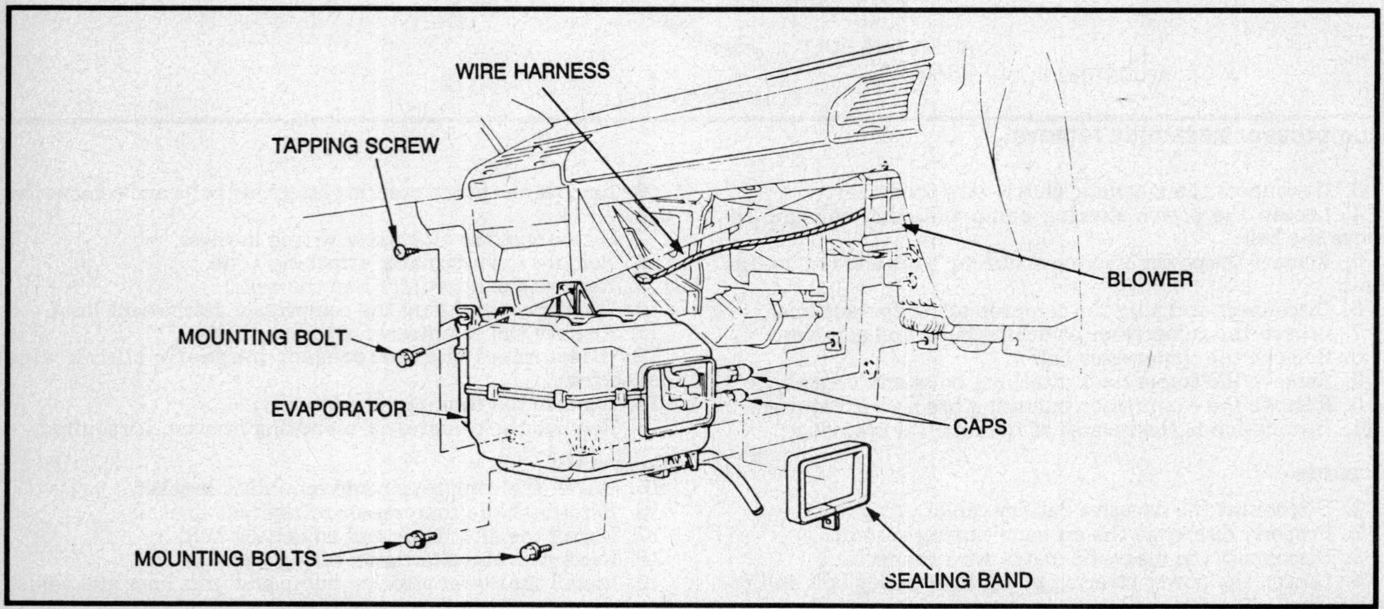
WIRE HARNESS
TAPPING SCREW
BLOWER
MOUNTING BOLT
EVAPORATOR
CAPS
MOUNTING BOLTS
SEALING BAND

Evaporator assembly removal

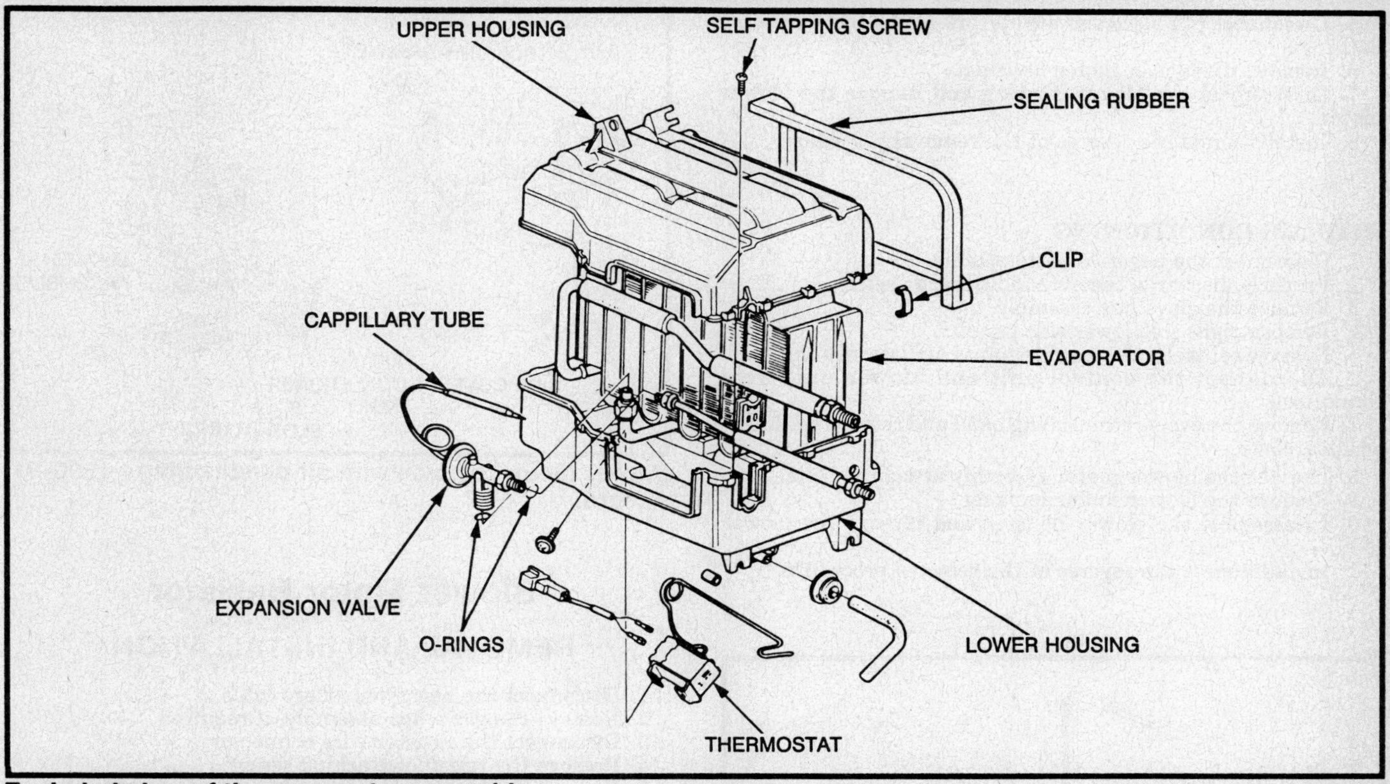
UPPER HOUSING
SELF TAPPING SCREW
SEALING RUBBER
CLIP
CAPPILLARY TUBE
EVAPORATOR
EXPANSION VALVE
O-RINGS
LOWER HOUSING
THERMOSTAT

Exploded view of the evaporator assembly

3. Remove the glove box assembly.
4. Remove the blower duct, if not equipped with air conditioning.
5. Remove the evaporator assembly, if equipped.
6. Disconnect the wire connectors at the blower motor assembly.
7. Remove the blower motor housing attaching bolts.
8. Disassemble the housing and remove the blower motor.
9. Installation is the reverse of the removal procedure.

1990–91 Accord

WITHOUT AIR CONDITIONING

1. Disconnect the negative battery cable.
2. Remove the glove box assembly.
3. Remove the blower duct assembly.
4. Remove the blower motor assembly attaching bolts.

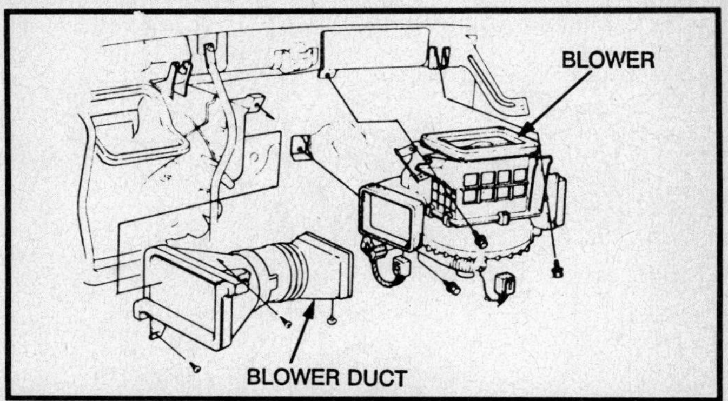
BLOWER
BLOWER DUCT

Blower motor removal without air conditioning—except 1990–91 Accord

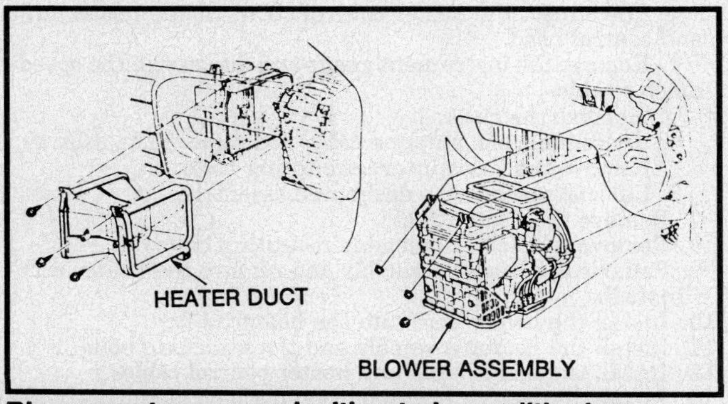
HEATER DUCT
BLOWER ASSEMBLY

Blower motor removal without air conditioning—1990–91 Accord

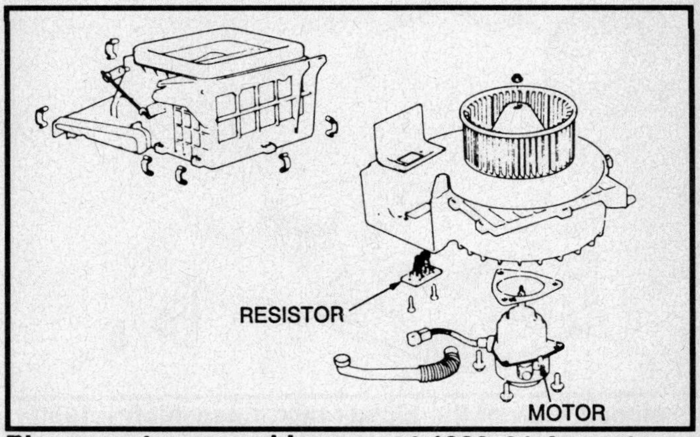
RESISTOR
MOTOR

Blower motor assembly—except 1990–91 Accord

5. Disconnect the electrical connectors at the blower motor housing.
6. Remove the blower motor housing.
7. Disassemble the blower housing and remove the blower motor.
8. Installation is the reverse of the removal procedure.

WITH AIR CONDITIONING

1. Disconnect the negative battery cable.
2. Properly discharge the air conditioning system.
3. Remove the glove box assembly.
4. Remove right side lower side panel.
5. Remove control unit attaching nuts and remove the unit.
6. Disconnect the control unit and blower unit wire connectors.
7. Remove the evaporator sealing band and remove the blower undercover.
8. Remove the blower motor assembly attaching bolts.
9. Remove the blower motor housing.
10. Disassemble the blower housing and remove the blower motor.
11. Installation is the reverse of the removal procedure.

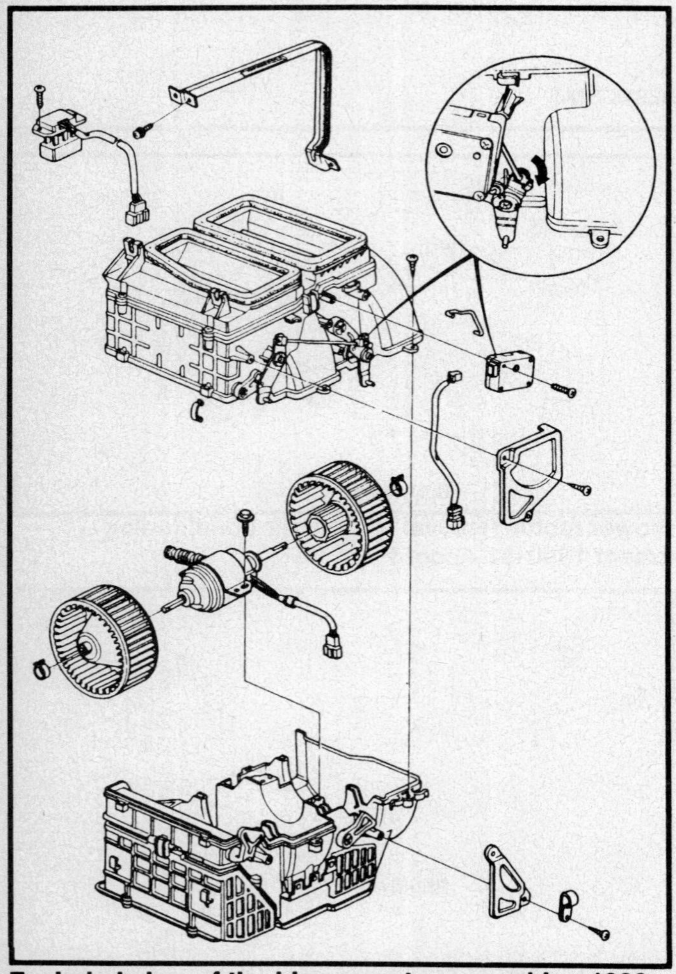

Exploded view of the blower motor assembly—1990–91 Accord

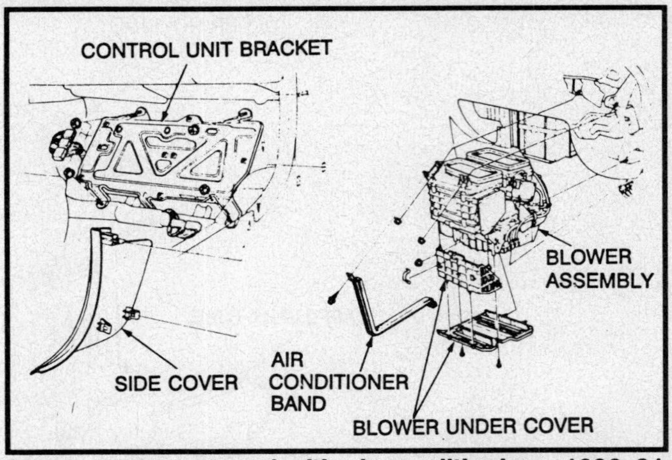
CONTROL UNIT BRACKET
BLOWER ASSEMBLY
SIDE COVER
AIR CONDITIONER BAND
BLOWER UNDER COVER

Blower motor removal with air conditioning—1990–91 Accord

Blower Motor Resistor

REMOVAL AND INSTALLATION

1. Disconnect the negative battery cable.
2. Remove the glove box assembly, if required.
3. Disconnect the resistor wire connector.
4. Remove the resistor attaching screws.
5. Remove the blower motor resistor.
6. Installation is the reverse of the removal procedure.

Heater Core

REMOVAL AND INSTALLATION

Accord

1989

1. Disconnect the negative battery cable.
2. Properly drain the cooling system.
3. Disconnect and plug the heater hoses at the firewall.
4. Disconnect the heater valve control cable.
5. Remove the heater unit attaching nuts on firewall.
6. Remove the dashboard as follows:
   a. Remove the hood release handle.
   b. Disconnect the wire connectors at the fuse box.
   c. Lower the steering column.
   d. Remove the heater control head and the radio.
   e. Disconnect the heater control cables at the heater unit and control head.
   f. Remove the instrument guage and disconnect the speedometer cable.
   g. Remove the clock.
   h. Disconnect the antenna cable and remove the ashtray.
   i. Remove the 7 dashboard mounting bolts.
   j. Lift and remove the dashboard assembly.
7. Remove the heater duct.
8. Remove the heater assembly mounting bolts.
9. Remove the heater assembly and remove the heater core.

To install:

10. Install the heater core into the heater unit.
11. Install the heater assembly and the attaching bolts.
12. Install the heater duct and heater control cables.
13. Install the dashboard assembly and attach mounting bolts.
14. Connect the antenna cable and install the ashtray.
15. Install the clock.

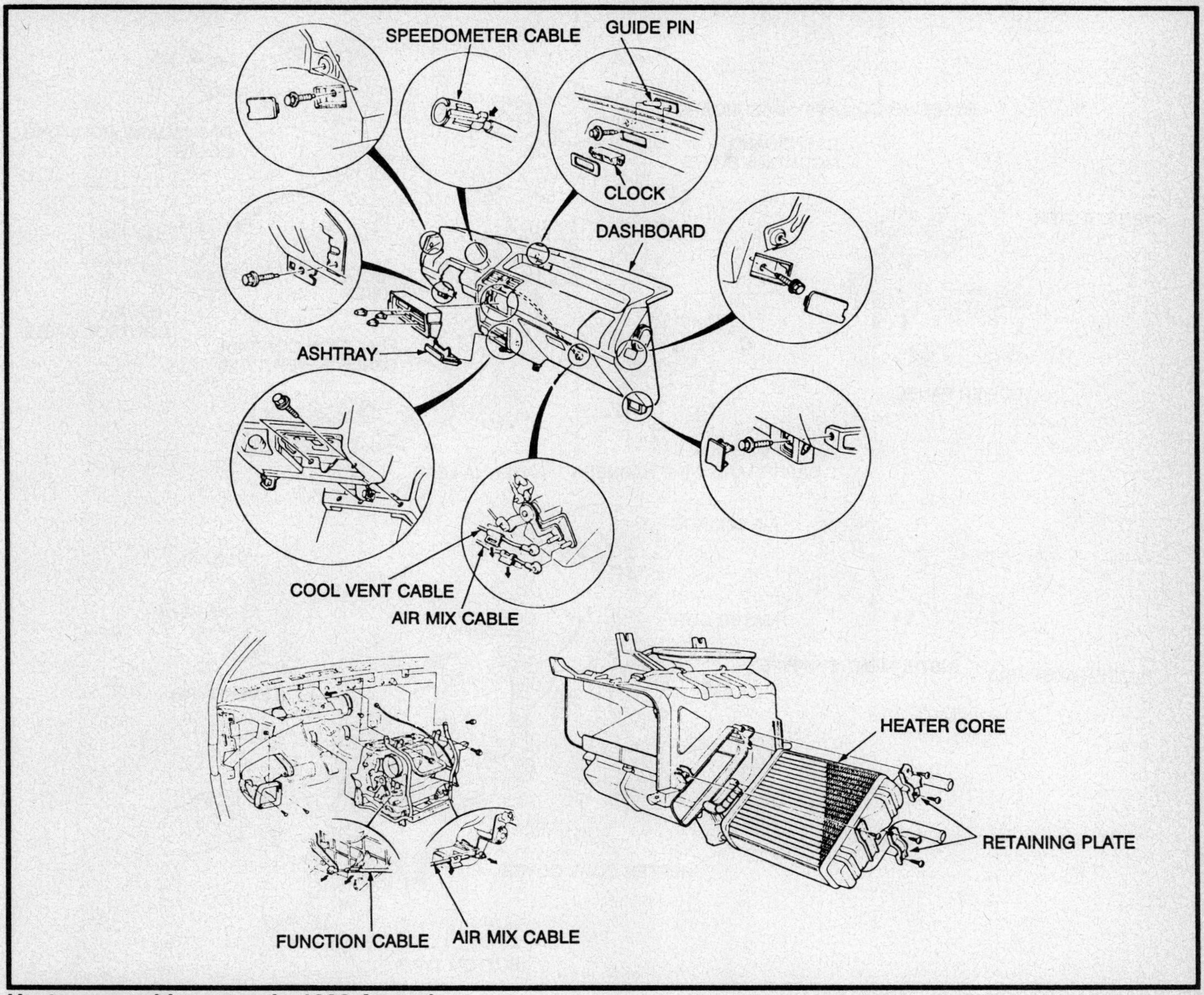
SPEEDOMETER CABLE
GUIDE PIN
CLOCK
DASHBOARD
ASHTRAY
COOL VENT CABLE
AIR MIX CABLE
HEATER CORE
RETAINING PLATE
FUNCTION CABLE
AIR MIX CABLE

Heater assembly removal—1989 Accord

16. Connect the speedometer cable and install the instrument gauge assembly.
17. Reconnect the control head cables and install the control head.
18. Install the radio assembly.
19. Reattach steering column mounting bolts.
20. Install hood release handle.
21. Connect wire connectors at fuse panel.
22. Install the heater unit attaching nuts on firewall.
23. Connect the heater valve control cable.
24. Connect the heater hoses at the firewall.
25. Fill, bleed and leak check the cooling system.
26. Connect the negative battery cable.

1990–91

1. Disconnect the negative battery cable.
2. Properly drain the cooling system.
3. Disconnect and plug the heater hoses at the firewall.
4. Disconnect the heater valve control cable.
5. Remove the dashboard as follows:
   a. Disconnect the wire connectors at the fuse box.
   b. Remove the center console assembly.
   c. Remove the knee bolster and lower panel.
   d. Remove the steering column.
   e. Remove the carpet clips and disconnect the antenna cable.
   f. Disconnect the heater control cables at the heater unit.
   g. Remove the dash attaching bolt caps on both sides and the clock.
   h. Remove the 7 dashboard mounting bolts.
   i. Lift and remove the dashboard assembly.
6. Remove the heater duct.
7. Remove the instrument panel sub-pipe.
8. Remove the heater assembly mounting bolts.
9. Remove the heater assembly and remove the heater core.

To install:

10. Install the heater core into the heater unit.
11. Install the heater assembly and the attaching bolts.
12. Install the heater duct and heater control cables.
13. Install the instrument sub-pipe.

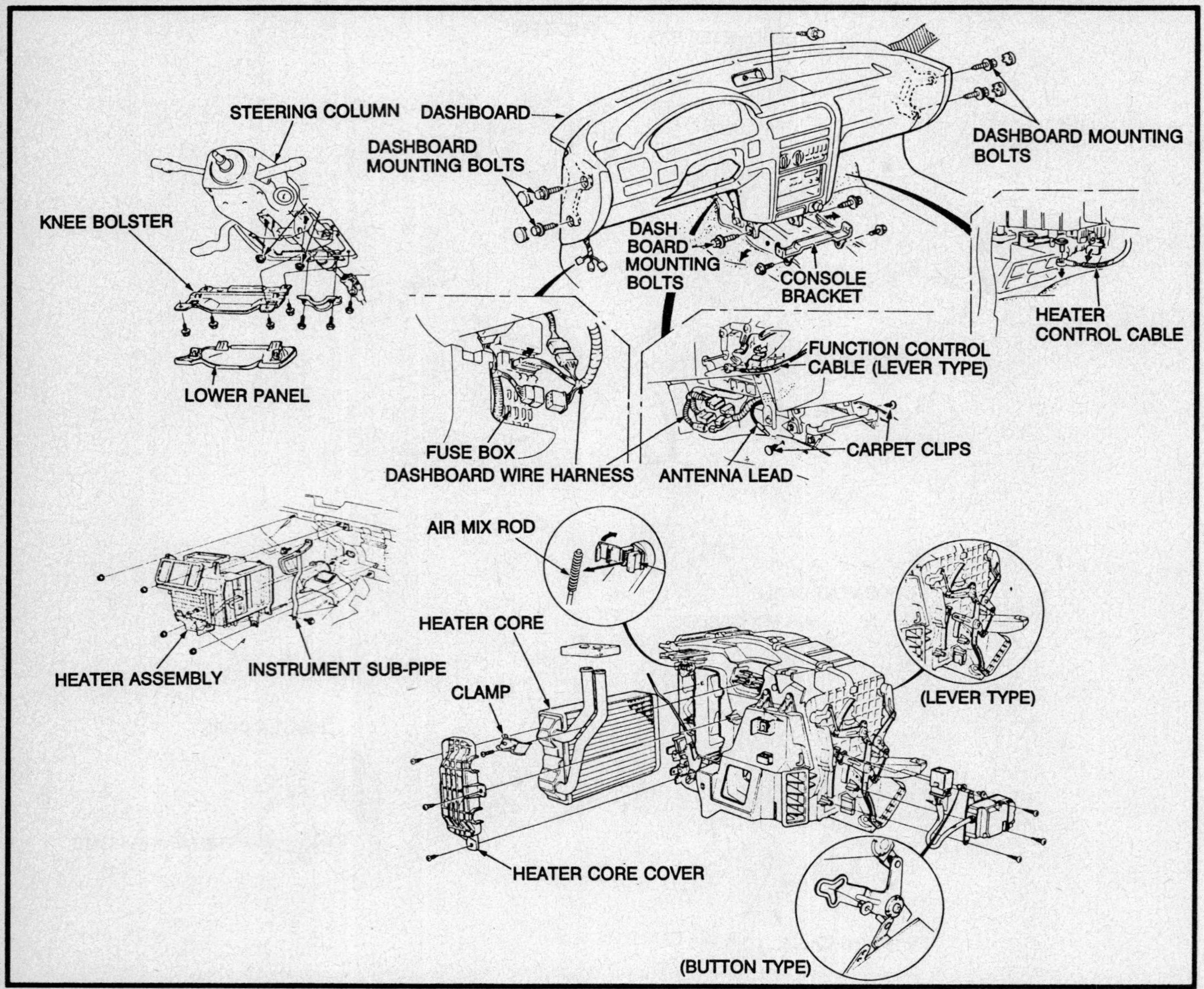
STEERING COLUMN
DASHBOARD
DASHBOARD MOUNTING BOLTS
DASHBOARD MOUNTING BOLTS
KNEE BOLSTER
DASH BOARD MOUNTING BOLTS
CONSOLE BRACKET
HEATER CONTROL CABLE
LOWER PANEL
FUNCTION CONTROL CABLE (LEVER TYPE)
CARPET CLIPS
FUSE BOX
DASHBOARD WIRE HARNESS
ANTENNA LEAD
AIR MIX ROD
HEATER CORE
HEATER ASSEMBLY
INSTRUMENT SUB-PIPE
CLAMP
(LEVER TYPE)
HEATER CORE COVER
(BUTTON TYPE)

Heater assembly removal—1990–91 Accord

14. Install the heater control cables.
15. Install the dashboard assembly and attach mounting bolts.
16. Connect the antenna cable and install the clock.
17. Install the carpet clips.
18. Reattach steering column and mounting bolts.
19. Install the knee bolster and lower panel.
20. Connect wire connectors at fuse panel.
21. Install the center console assembly.
22. Connect the heater valve control cable.
23. Connect the heater hoses at the firewall.
24. Fill, bleed and leak check the cooling system.
25. Connect the negative battery cable.

Civic and CRX

1. Disconnect the negative battery cable.
2. Properly drain the cooling system.
3. Disconnect and plug the heater hoses at the firewall.
4. Disconnect the heater valve control cable.
5. Remove the heater unit attaching nut on the firewall.
6. Remove the dashboard as follows:

a. Remove the center panel.
b. Disconnect the wire connectors at the fuse box.
c. Disconnect the sunroof switch connector, if equipped.
d. Disconnect the ground cable at the right of the steering column and the power mirror switch wire connector.
e. Remove the side air vent knob and face plate.
f. Remove the screws attaching the air vent control lever.
g. Remove the center panel, radio and heater control head.
h. Remove the gauge upper panel (4 door) or instrument panel (3 door).
i. Disconnect the speedometer cable.
j. Remove the center upper lid.
k. Remove the side defroster garnishes on both ends of the dash.
l. Lower the steering column.
m. Remove the dashboard mounting bolts.
n. Lift and remove the dashboard assembly.

7. Remove the heater duct.
8. Remove the steering column bracket and duct assembly.
9. Remove the heater assembly mounting bolts.

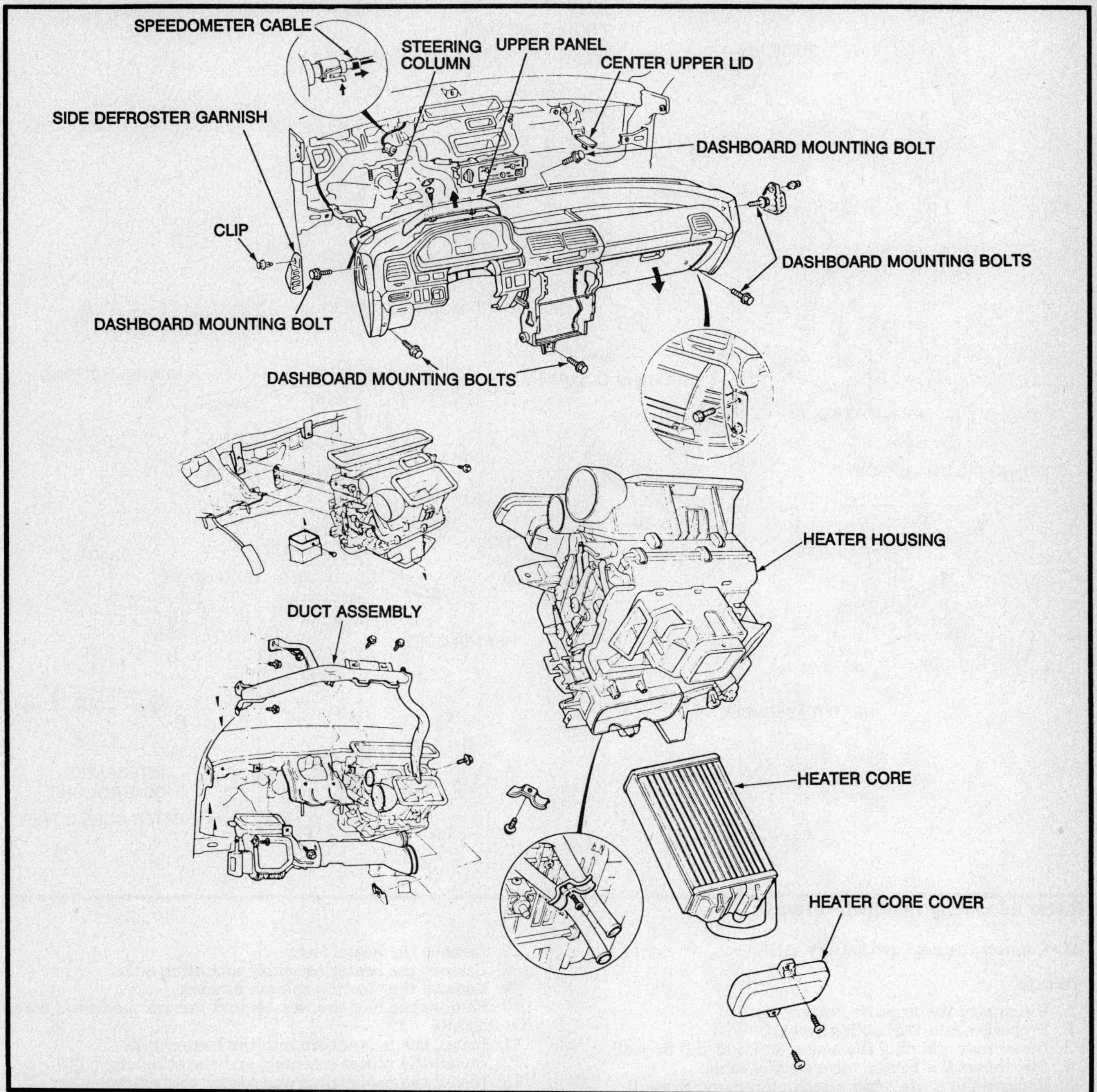
SPEEDOMETER CABLE
STEERING COLUMN
UPPER PANEL
CENTER UPPER LID
SIDE DEFROSTER GARNISH
DASHBOARD MOUNTING BOLT
CLIP
DASHBOARD MOUNTING BOLTS
DASHBOARD MOUNTING BOLT
DASHBOARD MOUNTING BOLTS
HEATER HOUSING
DUCT ASSEMBLY
HEATER CORE
HEATER CORE COVER

Heater assembly removal—Civic and CRX

10. Remove the heater assembly and remove the heater core.

To install:

11. Install the heater core into the heater unit.
12. Install the heater assembly and the attaching bolts.
13. Install the heater duct and steering column bracket.
14. Install the dashboard assembly and attach mounting bolts.
15. Raise and attach the steering column.
16. Install the center upper panel.
17. Connect the speedometer cable and install the instrument gauge assembly.
18. Install the control head, radio and center panel.
19. Install the side vent and face plate.
20. Connect the ground cable at the right of the steering column and the power mirror switch wire connector.
21. Connect the sunroof switch connector, if equipped.
22. Connect wire connectors at fuse panel.
23. Install the heater unit attaching nut on firewall.
24. Connect the heater valve control cable.
25. Connect the heater hoses at the firewall.
26. Fill, bleed and leak check the cooling system.

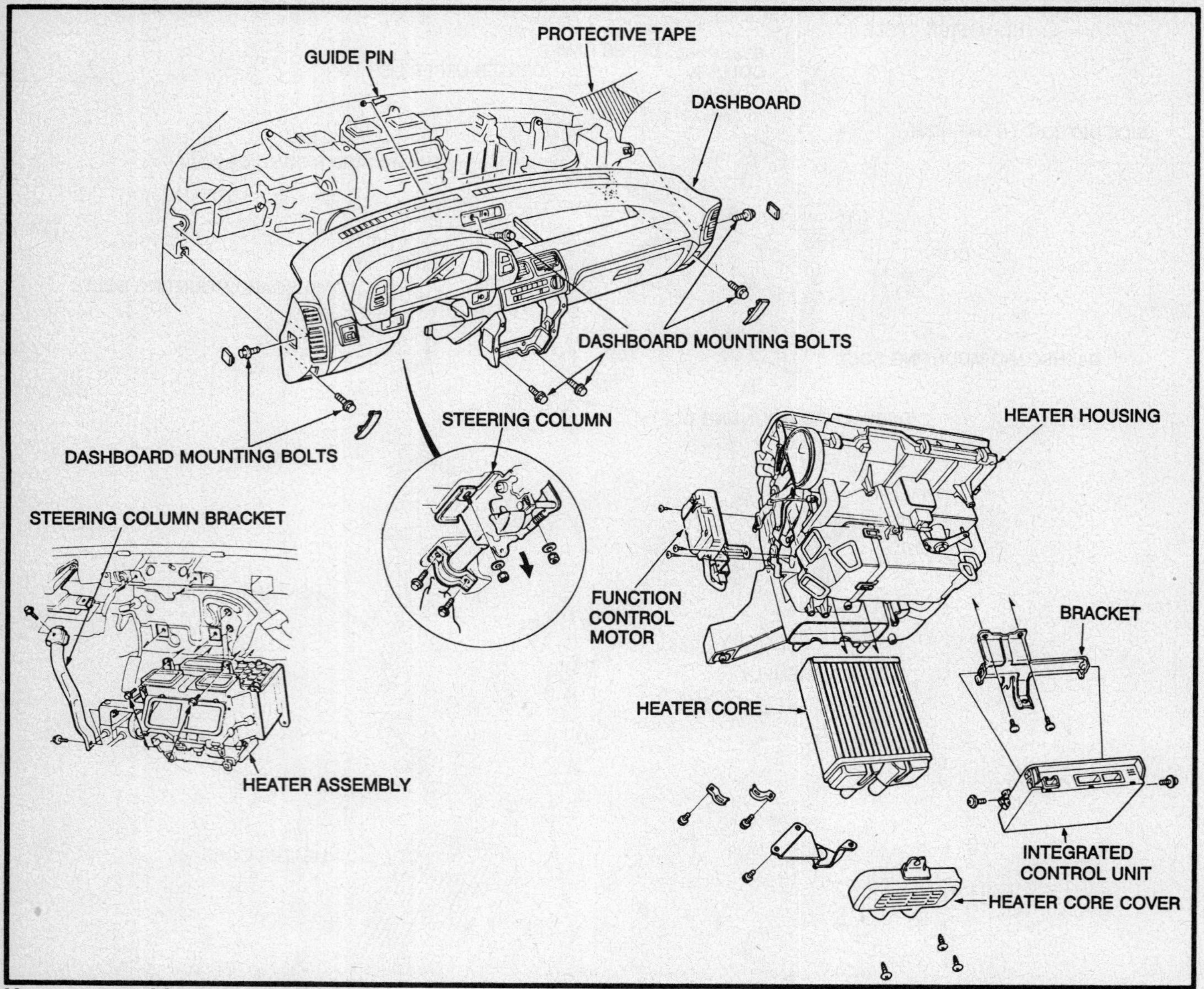
PROTECTIVE TAPE
GUIDE PIN
DASHBOARD
DASHBOARD MOUNTING BOLTS
STEERING COLUMN
DASHBOARD MOUNTING BOLTS
HEATER HOUSING
STEERING COLUMN BRACKET
FUNCTION CONTROL MOTOR
BRACKET
HEATER CORE
HEATER ASSEMBLY
INTEGRATED CONTROL UNIT
HEATER CORE COVER

Heater assembly removal—Prelude

27. Connect the negative battery cable.

Prelude

1. Disconnect the negative battery cable.
2. Properly drain the cooling system.
3. Disconnect and plug the heater hoses at the firewall.
4. Disconnect the heater valve control cable.
5. Remove the heater unit attaching nuts on firewall.
6. Remove the dashboard as follows:
   a. Remove the dashboard lower panel and center console assembly.
   b. Disconnect the wire harness connectors at the fuse box.
   c. Remove the radio panel, disconnect the wire connectors and antenna cable.
   d. Disconnect the heater control head cables and wire harness connectors.
   e. Remove the clock from the top of the dashboard.
   f. Lower the steering column.
   g. Remove the 7 dashboard mounting bolts.
   h. Lift and remove the dashboard assembly.
7. Remove the heater duct.
8. Remove the heater assembly mounting bolts.
9. Remove the steering column bracket.
10. Remove the heater assembly and remove the heater core.

To install:

11. Install the heater core into the heater unit.
12. Install the heater assembly and the attaching bolts.
13. Install the heater duct and heater control cables.
14. Install the steering column bracket.
15. Install the dashboard assembly and attach mounting bolts.
16. Install the clock.
17. Reattach steering column mounting bolts.
18. Connect the heater control head cables and wire harness connectors.
19. Connect the radio wire connectors, antenna cable and install the radio panel.
20. Connect the speedometer cable and install the instrument gauge assembly.
21. Reconnect the control head cables and install the control head.

22. Install the radio assembly.
23. Connect wire connectors at fuse panel.
24. Install the dashboard lower panel and center console assembly.
25. Install the heater unit attaching nuts on firewall.
26. Connect the heater valve control cable.
27. Connect the heater hoses at the firewall.
28. Fill, bleed and leak check the cooling system.
29. Connect the negative battery cable.

Refrigerant Lines

REMOVAL AND INSTALLATION

1. Disconnect the negative battery cable.
2. Properly discharge the air conditioning system.
3. Remove chassis, engine or body parts, if required.
4. Using a backup wrench loosen, disconnect and immediately plug the refrigerant line.
5. Disconnect pressure switch wire connectors, if required.
6. Remove all attaching brackets and bolts.
7. Remove the refrigerant lines.

To install:

8. Apply a light coat of refrigerant oil to new O-rings.
9. Route refrigerant lines in original locations.
10. Use original securing brackets and bolts.
11. Evacuate, charge and check system for leaks.

Manual Control Head

REMOVAL AND INSTALLATION

Accord

1989

1. Disconnect the negative battery cable.
2. Remove the heater control panel.
3. Remove the radio assembly.
4. Remove the heater control head attaching screws.
5. Disconnect the control cables from the heater assembly.
6. Disconnect the control head switch wires and remove the control head.
7. Installation is the reverse of the removal procedure.

1990–91

1. Disconnect the negative battery cable.
2. Remove the ashtray assembly and center console.
3. Remove the instrument panel switches, coin box and air vents.
4. Remove the radio and instrument housing assembly.
5. Disconnect the control cables at the heater assembly.
6. Remove the heater control head attaching screws and pull the unit out.
7. Disconnect the wire connectors and remove the heater control head.
8. Installation is the reverse of the removal procedure.

Civic

1. Disconnect the negative battery cable.
2. Remove the control head face panel attaching screws.
3. Disconnect the cigarette lighter connector and remove the face panel.
4. Remove the radio attaching screws and remove the assembly.
5. Disconnect the control cables at the heater unit.
6. Remove the attaching screws at the control head and pull assembly out.
7. Disconnect the control head wire connectors and remove the unit.
8. Installation is the reverse of the removal procedure.

Control Head Cables

ADJUSTMENT

1989 Accord

AIR MIX CABLE

1. Disconnect the negative battery cable.
2. Disconnect the heater valve cable.
3. Slide the air mix cable to the **COLD** position.
4. Close the air mix door linkage.
5. Connect the air mix cable.
6. Close the heater valve.
7. Reconnect the heater valve cable.
8. After adjustment, make sure the heater valve cable is adjusted properly.

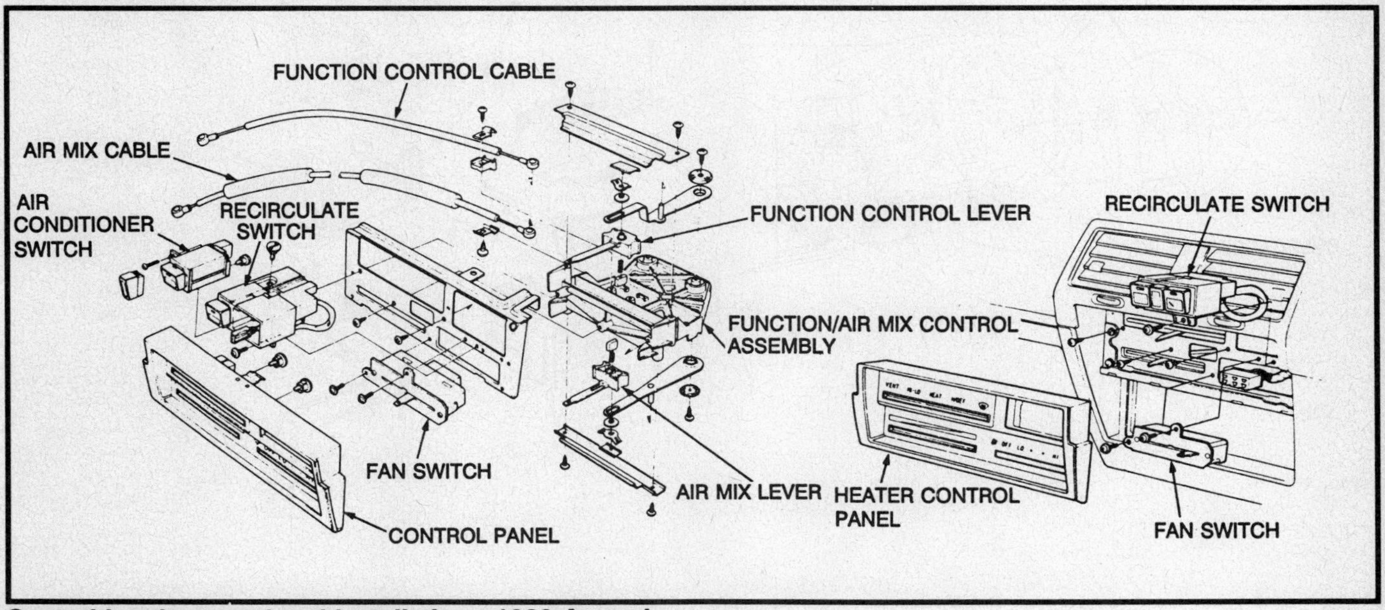
FUNCTION CONTROL CABLE
AIR MIX CABLE
AIR CONDITIONER SWITCH
RECIRCULATE SWITCH
FUNCTION CONTROL LEVER
RECIRCULATE SWITCH
FUNCTION/AIR MIX CONTROL ASSEMBLY
FAN SWITCH
AIR MIX LEVER
HEATER CONTROL PANEL
CONTROL PANEL
FAN SWITCH

Control head removal and installation—1989 Accord

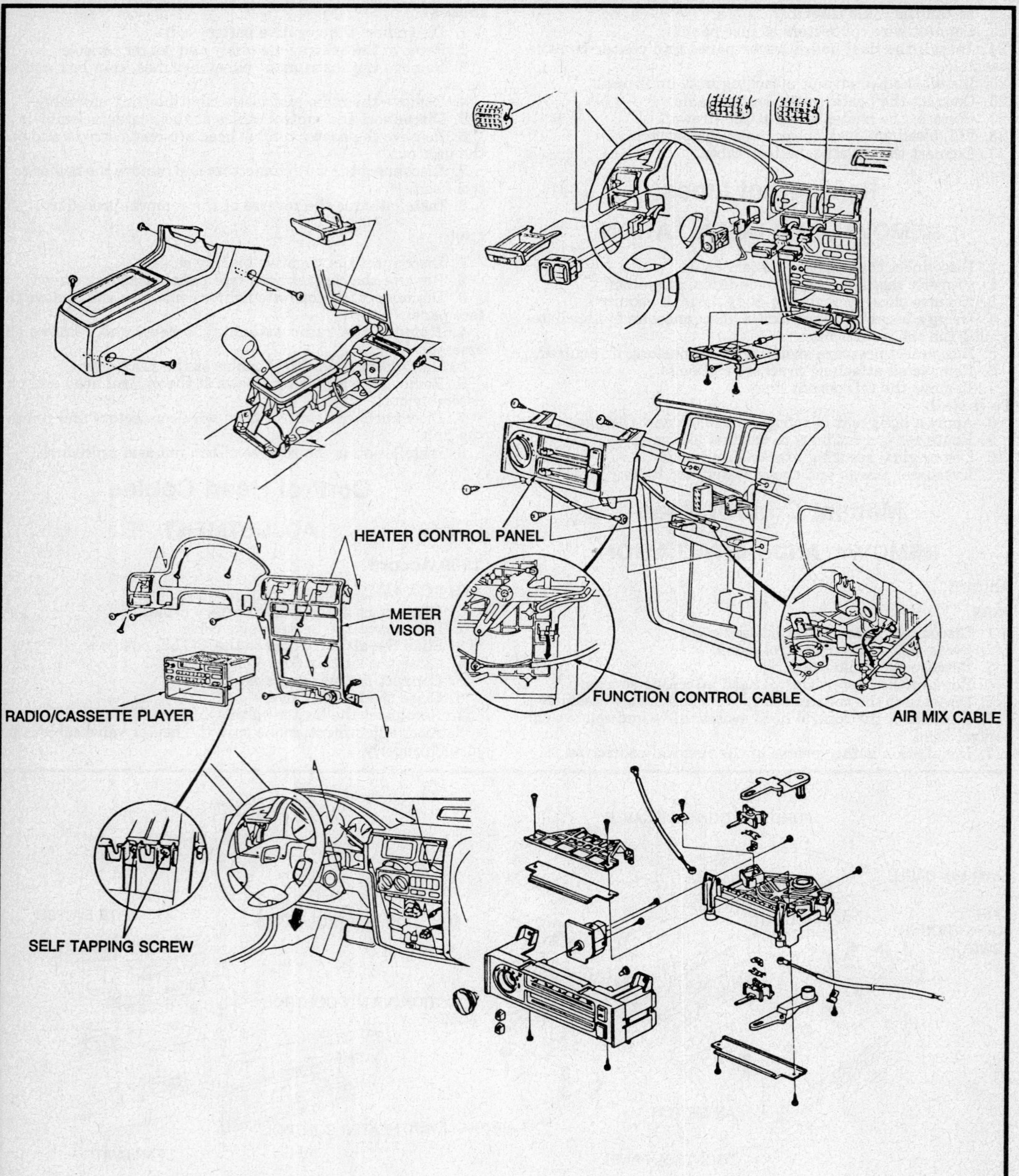
HEATER CONTROL PANEL
METER VISOR
RADIO/CASSETTE PLAYER
FUNCTION CONTROL CABLE
AIR MIX CABLE
SELF TAPPING SCREW

Control head removal and installation – 1990–91 Accord

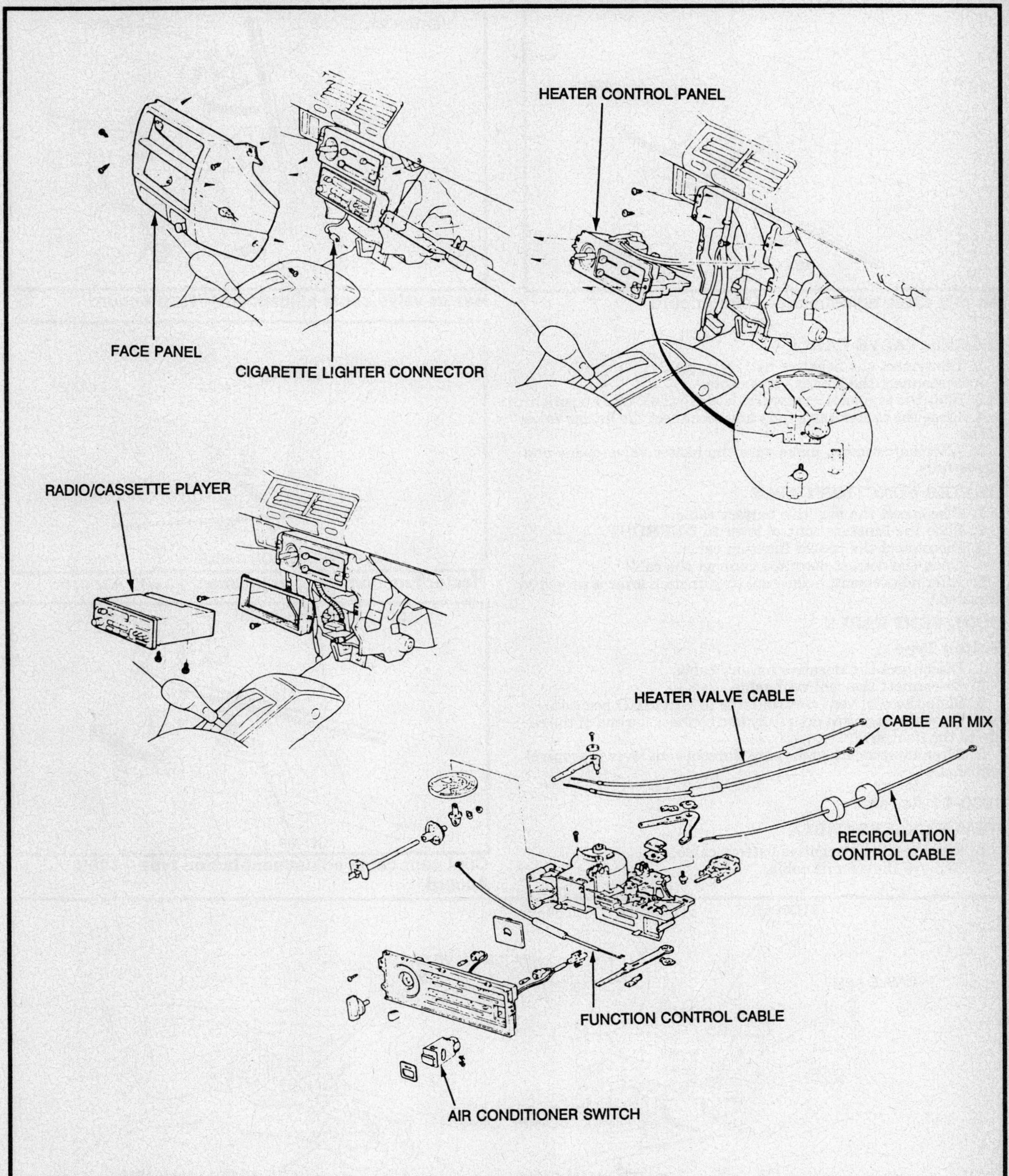
HEATER CONTROL PANEL
FACE PANEL
CIGARETTE LIGHTER CONNECTOR
RADIO/CASSETTE PLAYER
HEATER VALVE CABLE
CABLE AIR MIX
RECIRCULATION
CONTROL CABLE
FUNCTION CONTROL CABLE
AIR CONDITIONER SWITCH

Control head removal and installation—Civic and CRX

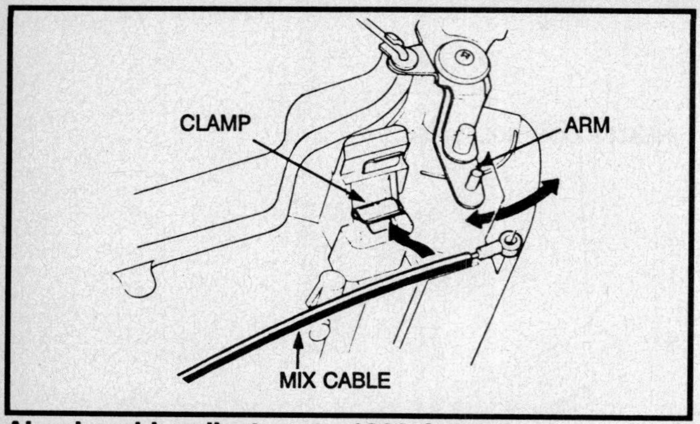
CLAMP
ARM
MIX CABLE

Air mix cable adjustment—1989 Accord

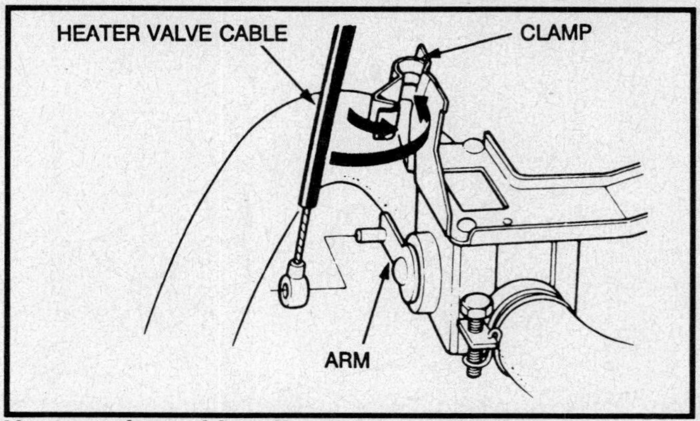
HEATER VALVE CABLE
CLAMP
ARM

Heater valve cable adjustment—1989 Accord

HEATER VALVE CABLE

1. Disconnect the negative battery cable.
2. Disconnect the heater valve cable.
3. Slide the temperature control lever to the **COLD** position.
4. Close the heater valve fully and reconnect the heater valve cable.
5. After adjustment, make sure the heater valve opens and closes fully.

HEATER FUNCTION CABLE

1. Disconnect the negative battery cable.
2. Slide the function control lever to **DEFROST**.
3. Disconnect the heater function cable.
4. Open the defrost door and connect the cable.
5. After adjustment, make sure the function lever is properly adjusted.

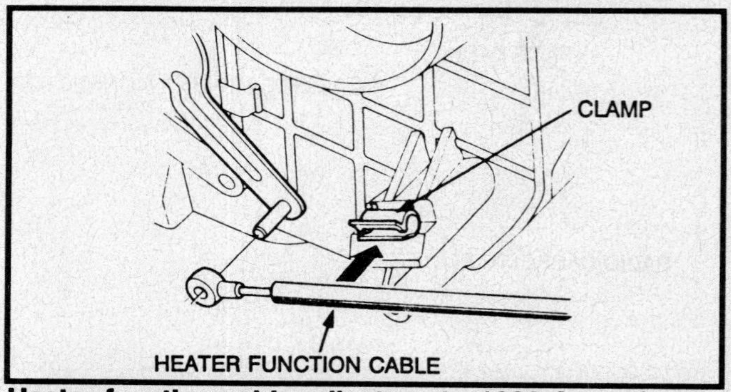
CLAMP
HEATER FUNCTION CABLE

Heater function cable adjustment—1989 Accord

COOL VENT CABLE

Button Type

1. Disconnect the negative battery cable.
2. Disconnect the cool vent cable.
3. Slide the cool vent control lever to **CLOSED** position.
4. Close the cool vent door fully and connect the end of the cable to the door arm.
5. After adjustment, make sure the cool vent lever is properly adjusted.

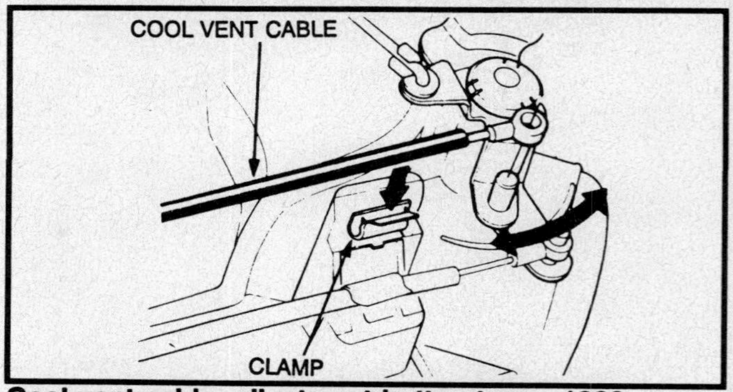
COOL VENT CABLE
CLAMP

Cool vent cable adjustment-button type—1989 Accord

1990–91 Accord

HEATER VALVE CABLE

1. Disconnect the negative battery cable.
2. Remove the air mix cable.

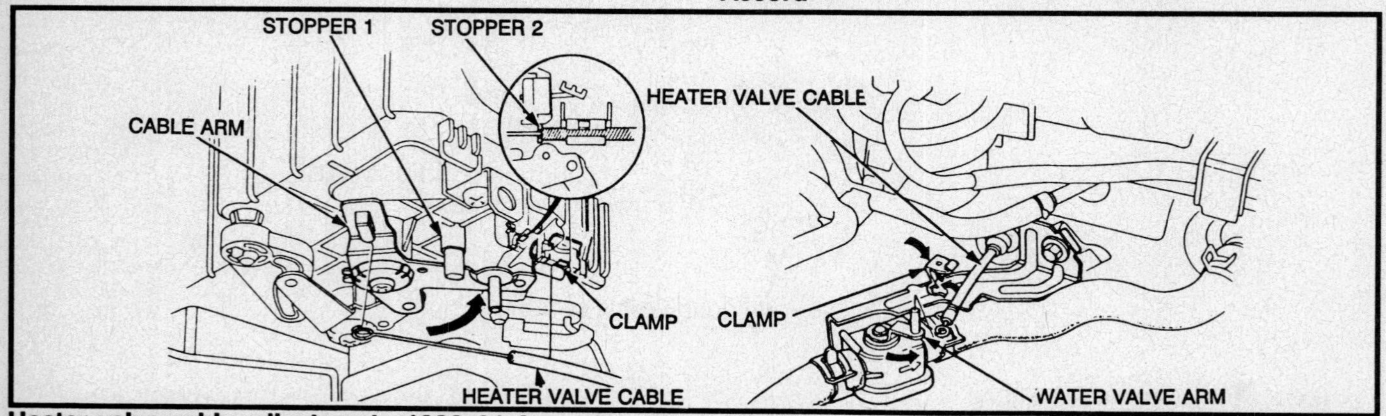
STOPPER 1
STOPPER 2
CABLE ARM
HEATER VALVE CABLE
CLAMP
CLAMP
HEATER VALVE CABLE
WATER VALVE ARM

Heater valve cable adjustment—1990–91 Accord

3. Turn the cable arm to stopper No. 1 and connect the end of the cable to the arm.
4. Gently slide the cable outer housing back from the end enough to take up slack in the cable but do not make the control lever move.
5. Snap the cable housing into the clamp.
6. Hold the end of the cable housing to stopper No. 2.
7. Turn the water valve arm to the shut position and connect the end of the cable to the arm.
8. Gently slide the cable outer housing back from the end enough to take up slack in the cable but do not make the control lever move.
9. After adjustment, make sure the function lever is properly adjusted.

AIR MIX ROD AND CABLE

1. Disconnect the negative battery cable.
2. Set the temperature lever to the **COOL** position.
3. Turn the rod arm to the engine compartment side and connect the rod to the clip.
4. Turn the cable arm to the stopper and connect the end of the cable to the arm.
5. Gently slide the cable outer housing back from the end enough to take up slack in the cable but do not make the control lever move.
6. Snap the cable into the clamp.
7. After adjustment, make sure the temperature lever is properly adjusted.

FUNCTION CONTROL CABLE

1. Disconnect the negative battery cable.
2. Slide the function control lever to the **DEFROST** position.
3. Disconnect the function control cable.
4. Turn the function control arm to the front and connect the end of the cable to the arm.
5. Gently slide the cable outer housing back from the end enough to take up slack in the cable but do not make the control lever move.
6. Connect the cable housing to the clamp.

Civic and CRX

AIR MIX CABLE

1. Disconnect the negative battery cable.
2. Slide the temperature control to the **HOT** position.
3. Turn the air mix door shaft arm to the left and connect the end of the cable to the arm.
4. Gently slide the cable outer housing back from the end enough to take up slack in the cable but do not make the control lever move.
5. Connect the cable housing to the clamp.

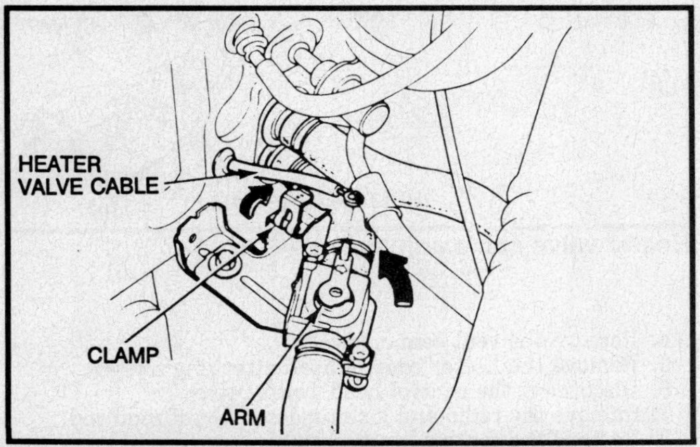
HEATER
VALVE CABLE
CLAMP
ARM

Heater valve cable adjustment—Civic and CRX

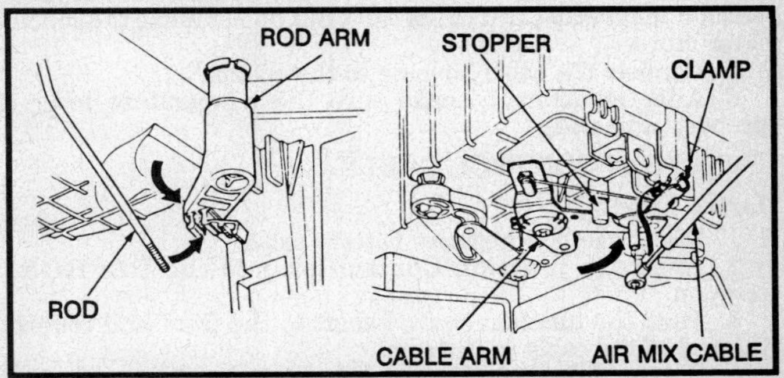
ROD ARM
STOPPER
CLAMP
ROD
CABLE ARM
AIR MIX CABLE

Air mix rod and cable adjustment—1990–91 Accord

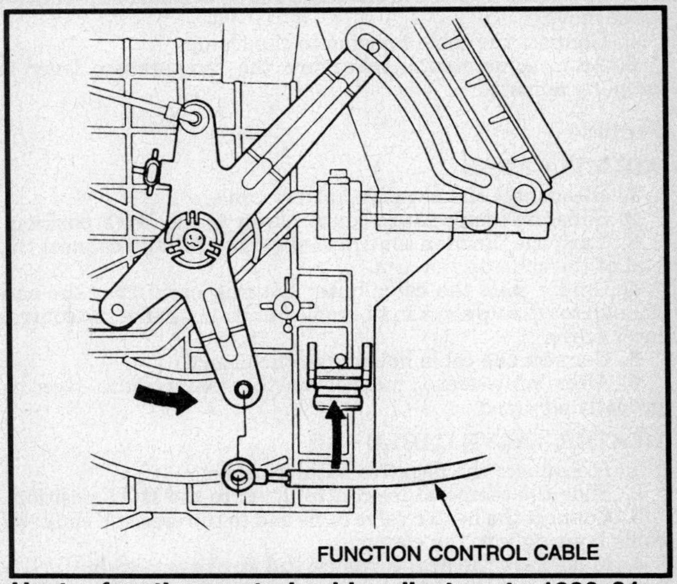
FUNCTION CONTROL CABLE

Heater function control cable adjustment—1990–91 Accord

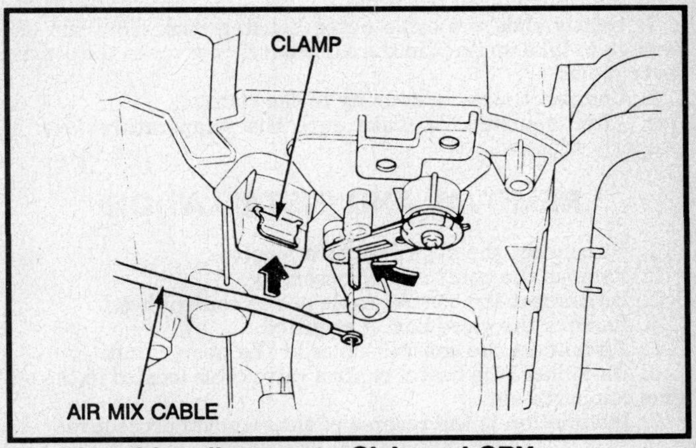
CLAMP
AIR MIX CABLE

Air mix cable adjustment—Civic and CRX

6. After adjustment, make sure the temperature lever is properly adjusted.

HEATER VALVE CABLE

1. Disconnect the negative battery cable.
2. Slide the temperature control lever to the **HOT** position.
3. Disconnect the heater control cable at the valve.
4. Gently slide the cable outer housing back from the end

enough to take up slack in the cable but do not make the control lever move.

5. Connect the cable housing to the clamp.
6. After adjustment, make sure the temperature lever is properly adjusted.

FUNCTION CONTROL CABLE

Lever Type

1. Disconnect the negative battery cable.
2. Slide the function Control lever to the **DEFROST** position.
3. Turn the function control shaft to the front and connect the end of the cable to the arm.
4. Gently slide the cable outer housing back from the end enough to take up slack in the cable but do not make the control lever move.
5. Connect the cable housing to the clamp.
6. After adjustment, make sure the temperature lever is properly adjusted.

Prelude

AIR MIX CABLE

1. Disconnect the negative battery cable.
2. Slide the temperature control lever to the **HOT** position.
3. Turn the function control shaft to the left and connect the end of the cable to the arm.
4. Gently slide the cable outer housing back from the end enough to take up slack in the cable but do not make the control lever move.
5. Connect the cable housing to the clamp.
6. After adjustment, make sure the temperature lever is properly adjusted.

HEATER VALVE CABLE

1. Disconnect the negative battery cable.
2. Slide the temperature control lever to the **HOT** position.
3. Connect the heater valve cable end to the arm and snap the cable housing into the clamp.
4. Make sure the arm turns its full stroke smoothly.
5. Slide the temperature control lever to the **COLD** position.
6. Turn the heater valve arm to the close position and connect the cable end to the arm.
7. Gently slide the cable outer housing back from the end enough to take up slack in the cable but do not make the control lever move.
8. Connect the cable housing to the clamp.
9. After adjustment, make sure the temperature lever is properly adjusted.

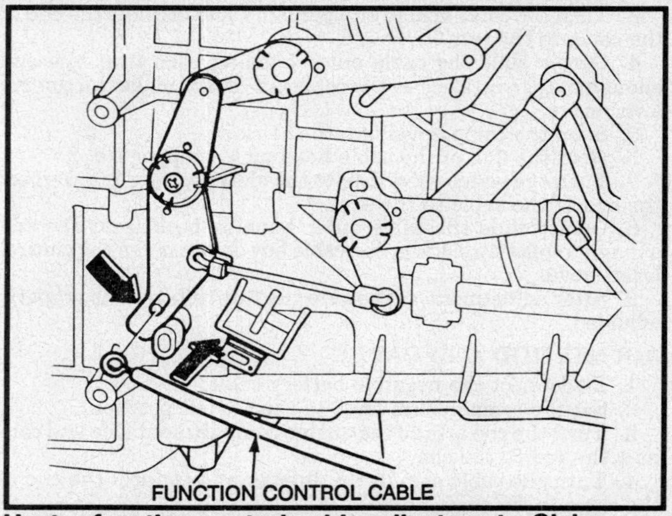
FUNCTION CONTROL CABLE
Heater function control cable adjustment—Civic

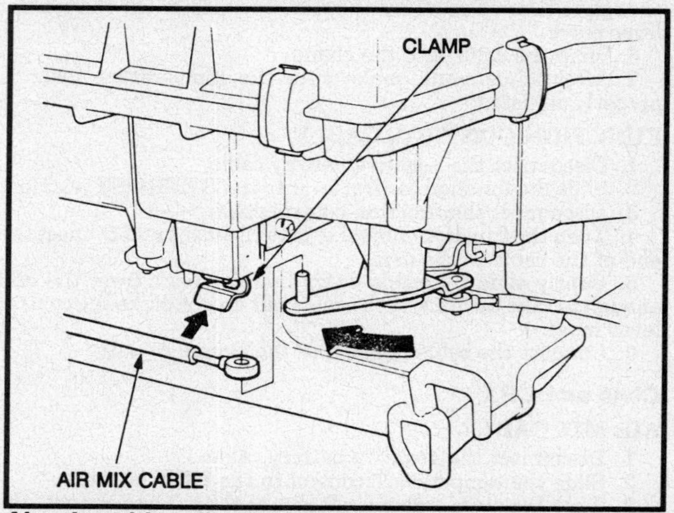
CLAMP
AIR MIX CABLE
Air mix cable adjustment—Prelude

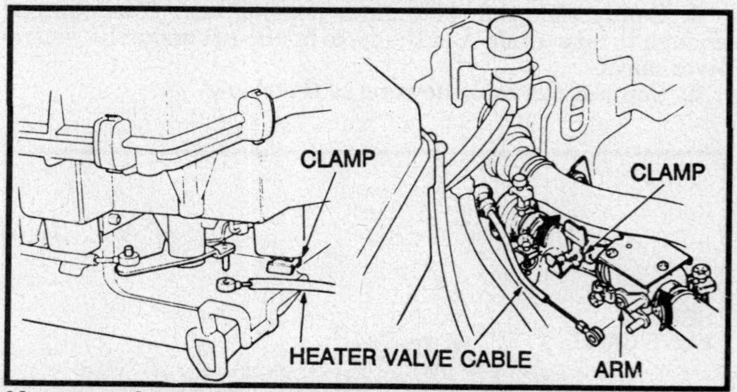
CLAMP
CLAMP
HEATER VALVE CABLE
ARM
Heater valve cable adjustment—Prelude

REMOVAL AND INSTALLATION

1. Disconnect the negative battery cable.
2. Remove the control head assembly.
3. Disconnect the control cable at the control head.
4. Remove the glove box, if required.
5. Disconnect the control cables at the heater unit.
6. Disconnect the heater control valve cable located in the engine compartment.
7. Installation is the reverse of the removal procedure.

Electronic Control Head

REMOVAL AND INSTALLATION

Accord

1989

1. Disconnect the negative battery cable.
2. Remove the heater control panel.
3. Remove the instrument gauge visor.
4. Remove the vent center outlet.
5. Remove the heater control head attaching screws.
6. Disconnect the control head switch wires.
7. Remove the radio and air mix assembly, if required.
8. Remove the control head assembly.
9. Installation is the reverse of the removal procedure.

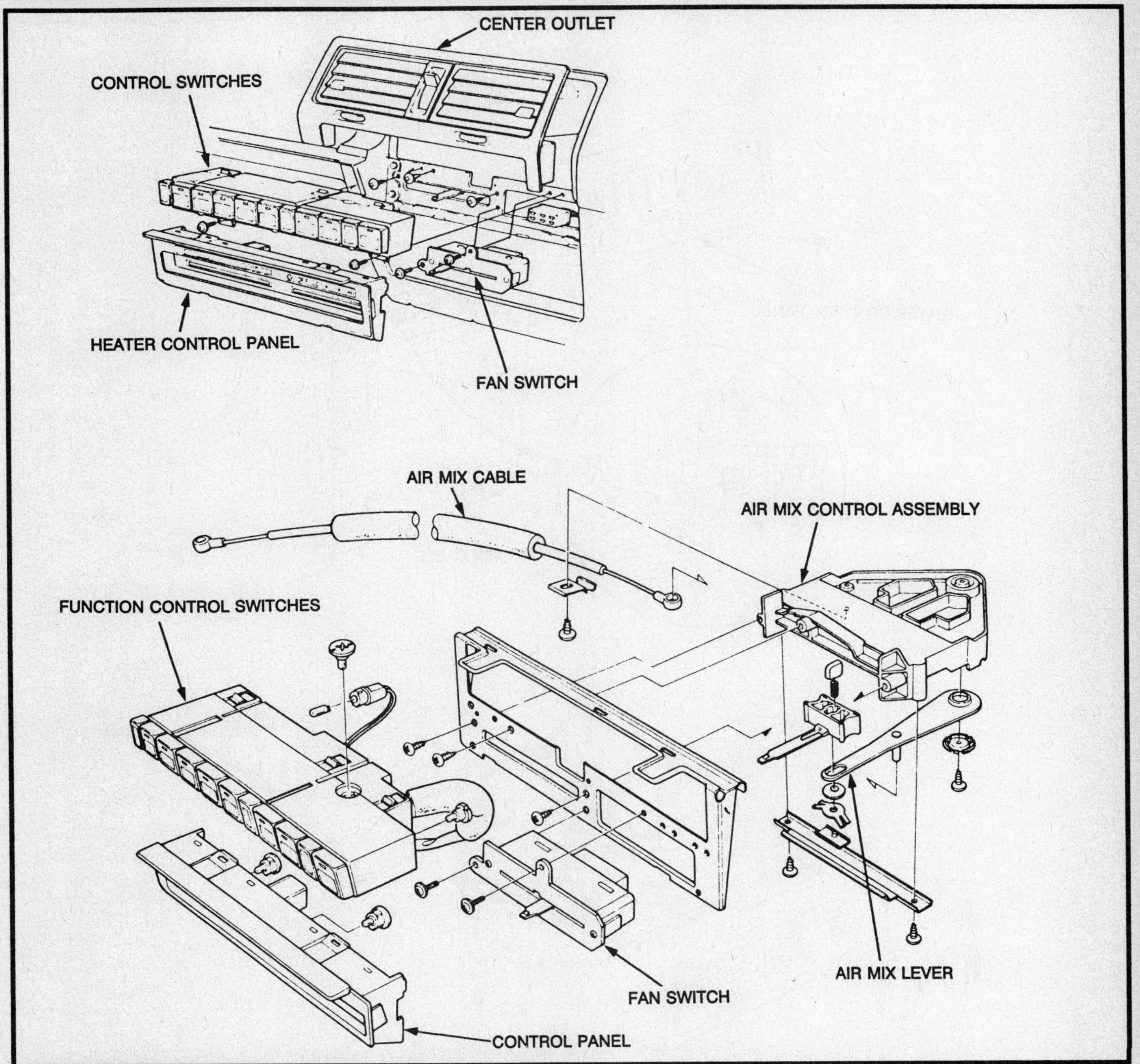
CENTER OUTLET
CONTROL SWITCHES
HEATER CONTROL PANEL
FAN SWITCH
AIR MIX CABLE
AIR MIX CONTROL ASSEMBLY
FUNCTION CONTROL SWITCHES
AIR MIX LEVER
FAN SWITCH
CONTROL PANEL

Electronic control head assembly—1989 Accord

1990–91

1. Disconnect the negative battery cable.
2. Remove the ashtray assembly and center console.
3. Remove the instrument panel switches, coin box and air vents.
4. Remove the radio and instrument housing assembly.
5. Remove the heater control head attaching screws and pull the unit out.
6. Disconnect the air mix control cable.
7. Disconnect the wire connectors and remove the heater control head.
8. Installation is the reverse of the removal procedure.

CRX

1. Disconnect the negative battery cable.
2. Remove the center console assembly.
3. Remove the radio attaching screws and remove the assembly.
4. Disconnect the air mix control cable at the heater unit.
5. Remove the attaching screws and setting plate at the control head.
6. Disconnect the control head cables and wire connectors and remove the unit.
7. Installation is the reverse of the removal procedure.

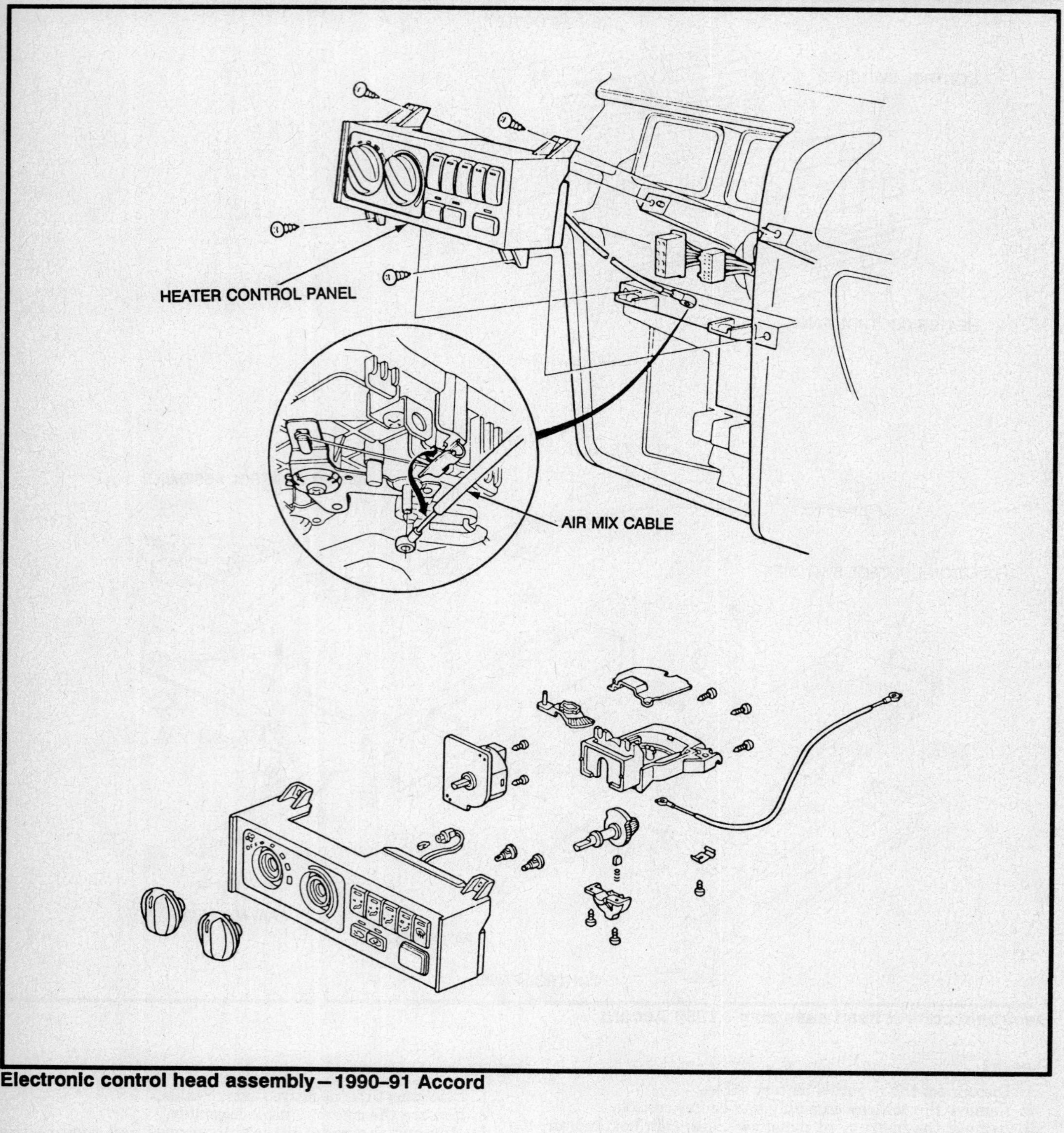
HEATER CONTROL PANEL
AIR MIX CABLE

Electronic control head assembly—1990–91 Accord

Prelude

1. Disconnect the negative battery cable.
2. Remove the center console assembly.
3. Remove the radio assembly.
4. Remove the center air vent outlet.
5. Remove the heater control head attaching screws.
6. Disconnect the control head switch wires.
7. Disconnect the air mix cable at the heater unit.
8. Remove the control head assembly.
9. Installation is the reverse of the removal procedure.

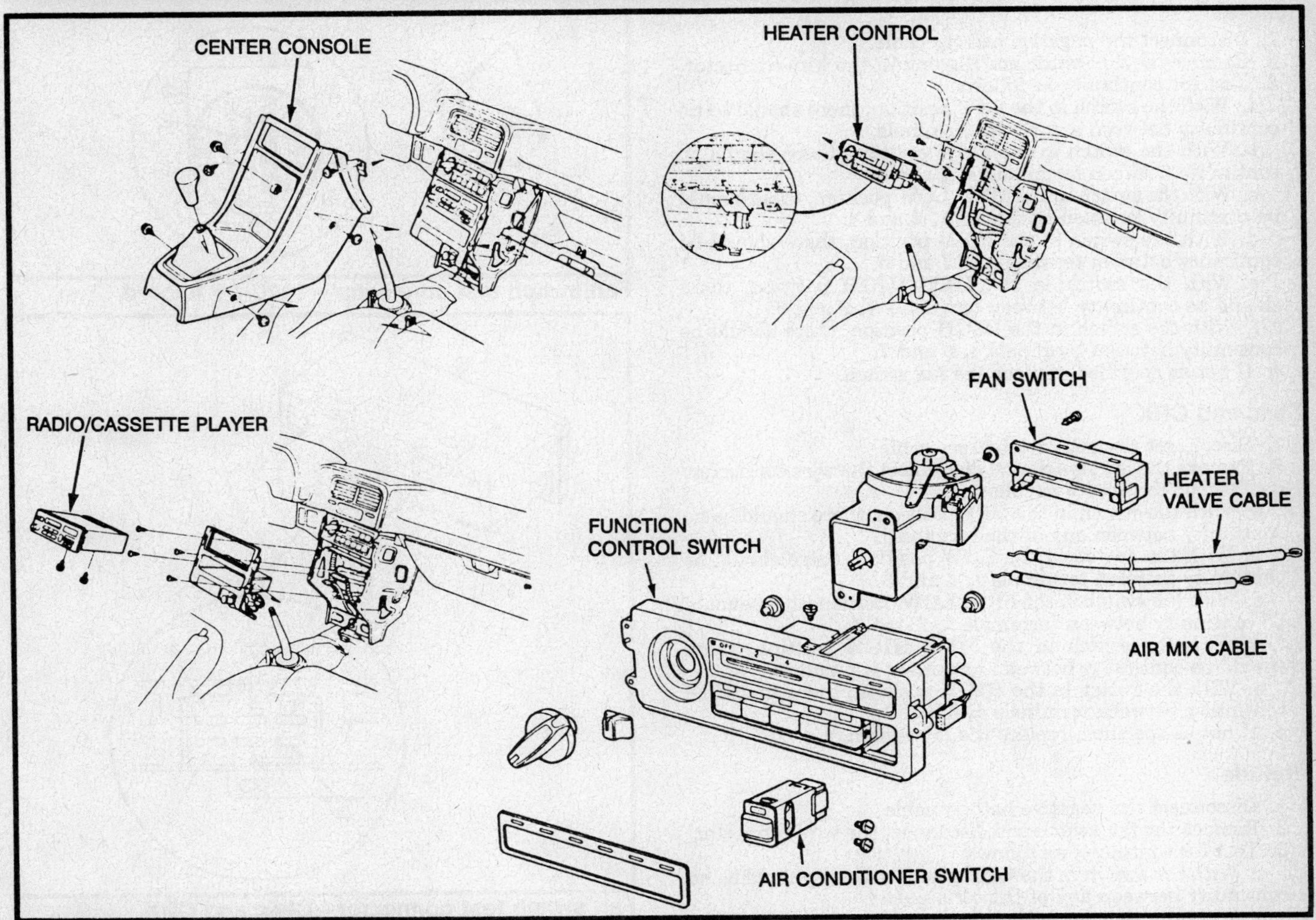
CENTER CONSOLE
HEATER CONTROL
FAN SWITCH
RADIO/CASSETTE PLAYER
HEATER VALVE CABLE
FUNCTION CONTROL SWITCH
AIR MIX CABLE
AIR CONDITIONER SWITCH

Electronic control head assembly—CRX

SENSORS AND SWITCHES

Fan Switch

OPERATION

The fan switch is located with the control head and has 5 or 6 speeds including the **OFF** position. The blower motor always has approximately 12 volts and the fan switch then completes the circuit by supplying a ground through a resistor, thus varying the fan speed.

TESTING

Accord

1989

1. Disconnect the negative battery cable.
2. Remove the fan switch and disconnect the wire connector.
3. Test for continuity as follows:
   a. With the switch in the **OFF** position, there should be no continuity between any of the terminals.
   b. With the switch in the **LOW** position, there should be continuity between terminals **A, B** and **C.**
   c. With the switch in the **MED LOW** position, there should be continuity between terminals **A, B** and **D.**
   d. With the switch in the **MED HIGH** position, there should be continuity between terminals **A, B** and **E.**
   e. With the switch in the **HIGH** position, there should be continuity between terminals **A, B** and **F.**
4. If not as specified, replace the fan switch.

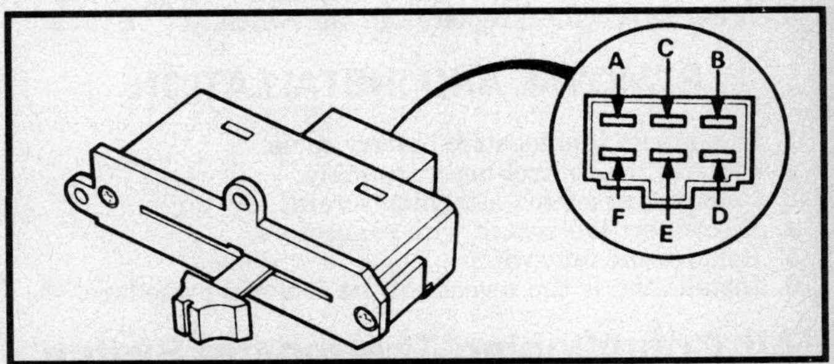
A
C
B
F
E
D

Fan switch test connector—1989 Accord

1990–91

1. Disconnect the negative battery cable.
2. Remove the fan switch and disconnect the wire connector.
3. Test for continuity as follows:
   a. With the switch in the **OFF** position, there should be no continuity between any of the terminals.
   b. With the switch in the **LOW** position, there should be continuity between terminals **1, 2** and **3**.
   c. With the switch in the **MED LOW** position, there should be continuity between terminals **1, 2** and **4**.
   d. With the switch in the **MED** position, there should be continuity between terminals **1, 2** and **5**.
   e. With the switch in the **MED HIGH** position, there should be continuity between terminals **1, 2** and **6**.
   f. With the switch in the **HIGH** position, there should be continuity between terminals **1, 2** and **7**.
4. If not as specified, replace the fan switch.

Civic and CRX

1. Disconnect the negative battery cable.
2. Remove the fan switch and disconnect the wire connector.
3. Test for continuity as follows:
   a. With the switch in the **OFF** position, there should be no continuity between any of the terminals.
   b. With the switch in the **LOW** position, there should be continuity between terminals **1, 4** and **6**.
   c. With the switch in the **MED LOW** position, there should be continuity between terminals **1, 2** and **6**.
   d. With the switch in the **MED HIGH** position, there should be continuity between terminals **1, 5** and **6**.
   e. With the switch in the **HIGH** position, there should be continuity between terminals **1, 3** and **6**.
4. If not as specified, replace the fan switch.

Prelude

1. Disconnect the negative battery cable.
2. Remove the fan switch and disconnect the wire connector.
3. Test for continuity as follows:
   a. With the switch in the **OFF** position, there should be no continuity between any of the terminals.
   b. With the switch in the **LOW** position, there should be continuity between terminals **1, 2** and **4**.
   c. With the switch in the **MED LOW** position, there should be continuity between terminals **1, 2** and **5**.
   d. With the switch in the **MED HIGH** position, there should be continuity between terminals **1, 2** and **6**.
   e. With the switch in the **HIGH** position, there should be continuity between terminals **1, 2** and **3**.
4. If not as specified, replace the fan switch.

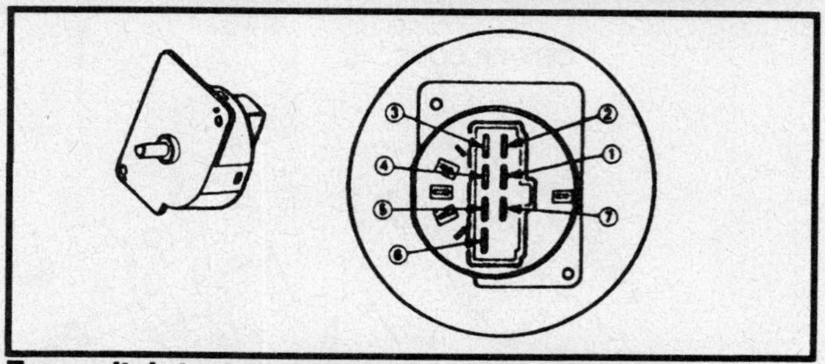
③
②
④
①
⑤
⑦
⑥

Fan switch test connector—1990–91 Accord

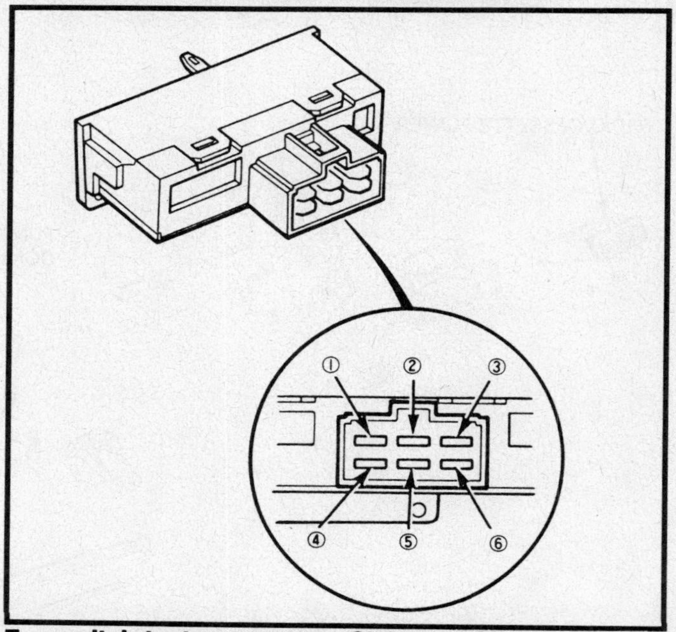
①
②
③
④
⑤
⑥

Fan switch test connector—Civic and CRX

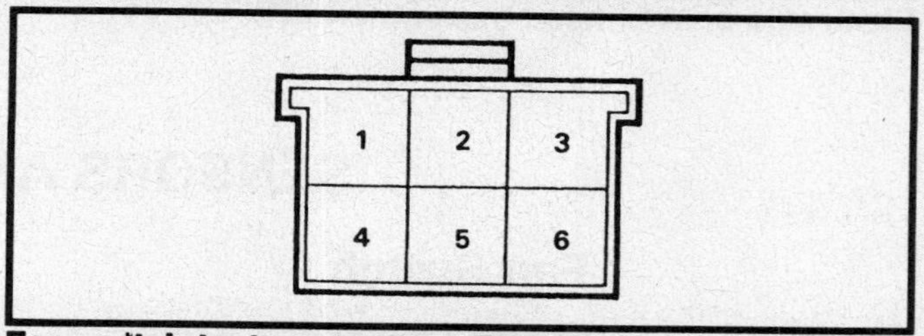
1
2
3
4
5
6

Fan switch test connector—Prelude

REMOVAL AND INSTALLATION

1. Disconnect the negative battery cable.
2. Remove the control head assembly.
3. Remove fan switch attaching screws.
4. Disconnect fan switch wire connectors.
5. Remove the fan switch.
6. Installation is the reverse of the removal procedure.

Air Conditioning Thermostat Switch

OPERATION

The thermostat switch is mounted at the evaporator core outlet and senses the temperature of the cool air coming through the evaporator. Temperature signals then determine whether the circuit is opened or closed, thus completing the ground. This information is then compared by the electronic control unit and the results are outputted to the air conditioner relay and turn the magnetic clutch ON and OFF.

TESTING

1. Disconnect the negative battery cable.
2. Disconnect and remove the thermostat.
3. Place the thermostat capillary tube in ice water.
4. Check that there is no continuity below 33–35°F (0.5–1.5°C).
5. Check that there is continuity above 37–41°F (2.5–5.0°C).
6. If not within specification, replace the thermostat.

REMOVAL AND INSTALLATION

1. Disconnect the negative battery cable.
2. Properly discharge the air conditioning system.

3. Remove the evaporator assembly.
4. Separate the assembly.
5. Remove the thermostat switch.
6. Installation is the reverse of the removal procedure.

Pressure Switches

OPERATION

There are 2 pressure switches used, the first style is used on the 1989 Accord and is a low pressure switch which interrupts current to the compressor clutch relay when high pressure drops below 28 psi, to prevent compressor damage. The second style is a dual pressure switch which turns the magnetic clutch ON or OFF as a result of irregularly high or low pressures of the refrigerant. The pressure switch is located at the receiver/drier or condenser.

TESTING

Accord

1989

1. Disconnect the pressure switch wire connector from the receiver/drier or from the high pressure line.
2. Start the vehicle and turn the air conditioner **ON**.
3. Hook up the air conditioner gauges or charging station.
4. Check for 12 volts at the pressure switch wire connector.
5. If there is no voltage at either terminal of wire connector, check the air conditioner relay.
6. Connect a jumper wire between the 2 terminals.
7. Check to see if compressor clutch engages.
8. If the compressor magnetic clutch fails to operate check the magnetic clutch and the wiring.
9. Check for continuity through the switch using an ohmmeter.
10. At system normal operating pressures and the pressure at the high side above 28 psi there should be continuity and/or voltage through the switch.

1990–91

1. Disconnect the pressure switch wire connector from the receiver/drier or from the high pressure line.
2. Start the vehicle and turn the air conditioner **ON**.
3. Hook up the air conditioner gauges or charging station.
4. Check for 12 volts at the pressure switch wire connector.
5. If there is no voltage at either terminal of wire connector, check the air conditioner relay.
6. Connect a jumper wire between the 2 terminals.
7. Check to see if compressor clutch engages.
8. If the compressor magnetic clutch fails to operate check the magnetic clutch and the wiring.
9. Check for continuity through the switch using an ohmmeter.
10. At system normal operating pressures and the pressure at the high side between 38–242 psi there should be continuity and/or voltage through the switch.

Civic, CRX and Prelude

1. Disconnect the pressure switch wire connector from the receiver/drier or from the high pressure line.
2. Start the vehicle and turn the air conditioner **ON**.
3. Hook up the air conditioner gauges or charging station.
4. Check for 12 volts at the pressure switch wire connector.
5. If there is no voltage at either terminal of wire connector, check the air conditioner relay.
6. Connect a jumper wire between the 2 terminals.
7. Check that the compressor clutch engages.
8. If the compressor magnetic clutch fails to operate check the magnetic clutch and the wiring.

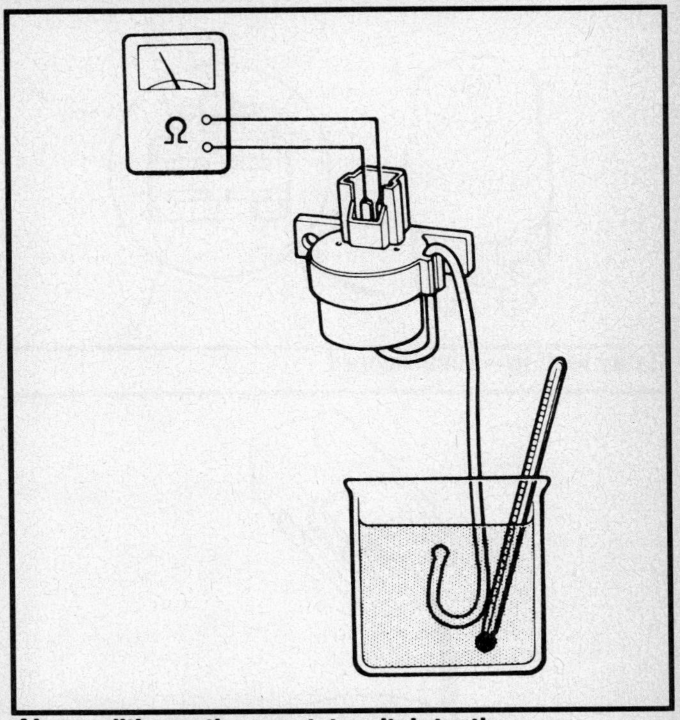
Ω
Air conditioner thermostat switch testing

9. Check for continuity through the switch using an ohmmeter.
10. At system normal operating pressures and the high side pressure between 33–340 psi there should be continuity and/or voltage through the switch.

REMOVAL AND INSTALLATION

1. Disconnect the negative battery cable.
2. Properly discharge the air conditioning system.
3. If required, remove radiator grille.
4. Using 2 wrenches, remove the pressure switch.
5. Installation is the reverse of removal procedure.

Relays

OPERATION

Battery and load location may require that a switch be placed some distance from either component. This means a longer wire and a higher voltage drop. The installation of a relay between the battery and the load reduces the voltage drop. Because the switch controls the relay, this means amperage through the switch can be reduced.

TESTING

1. Disconnect the negative battery cable.
2. Check that there is no continuity between terminals **3** and **4** or **A** and **B**.
3. Apply 12 volts between terminals **1** and **2** or **C** and **d**.
4. Check that there is continuity between terminals **3** and **4** or **A** and **B**.
5. If not as specified, replace the relay.

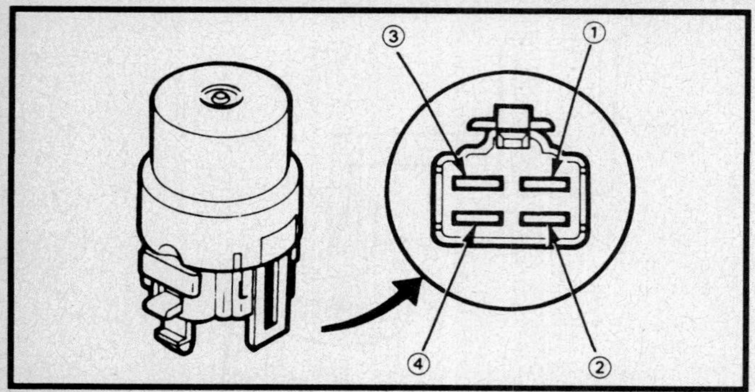
3
1
4
2
Relay testing—1989 Accord

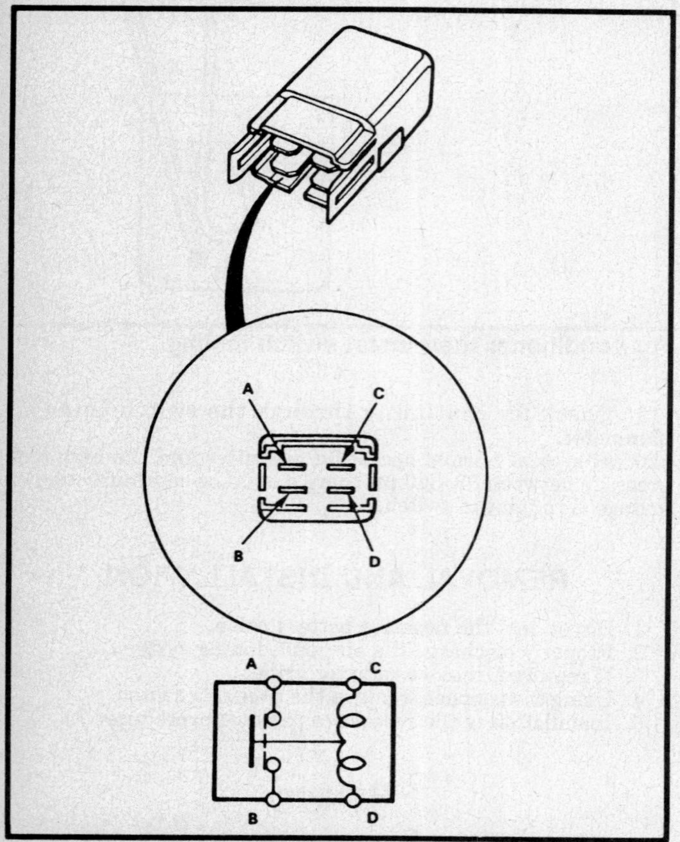
A
C
B
D
A
C
B
D
Relay testing—1990–91 Accord

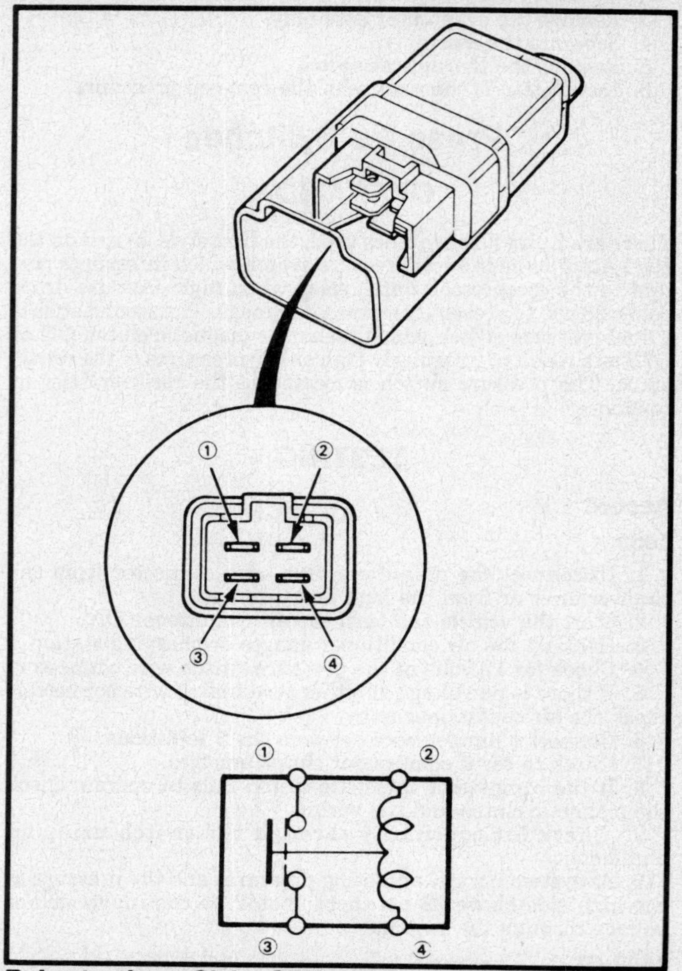
1
2
3
4
1
2
3
4
Relay testing—Civic, CRX and Prelude

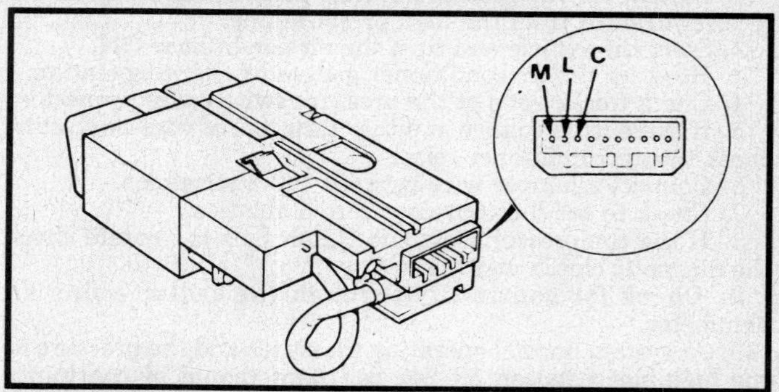
M
L
C
Recirculate/Fresh switch test-lever type—1989 Accord

REMOVAL AND INSTALLATION

1. Disconnect negative battery cable.
2. Locate relay and disconnect wire connector.
3. If required, remove attaching bolt and remove relay.
4. Installation is the reverse of the removal procedure.

Recirculate/Fresh Switch

OPERATION

The recirculate/fresh switch sends a voltage signal to the recirculation control motor which then opens the recirculate/fresh door to allow outside air to enter the vehicle or to recirculate the air that is already in the vehicle.

TESTING

1989 Accord

LEVER TYPE

1. Check that there is continuity at the switch between terminals **L** and **C** with the recirculate button depressed.
2. Check that there is continuity between terminals **M** and **C** with the recirculate button not depressed.
3. If not as specified, replace the switch.

BUTTON TYPE

1. Check that there is continuity at the switch between terminals **11** and **12** with the recirculate button depressed.
2. Check that there is continuity between terminals **11** and **10** with the recirculate button not depressed.
3. If not as specified, replace the control head assembly.

1990–91 Accord

LEVER TYPE

1. Check that there is continuity at the switch between terminals **A** and **C** with the recirculate button depressed in the activated position.
2. Check that there is continuity between terminals **A** and **B** with the recirculate button not depressed.
3. If not as specified, replace the switch.

BUTTON TYPE

1. Check that there is continuity at the switch between terminals **A** and **C** with the recirculate button depressed in the activated position.
2. Check that there is continuity between terminals **A** and **B** with the recirculate button not depressed.
3. If not as specified, replace the switch.

Prelude

BUTTON TYPE

1. Check that there is continuity at the switch between terminals **12** and **6** with the recirculate button depressed in the activated position.
2. Check that there is continuity between terminals **11** and **6** with the recirculate button not depressed.
3. If not as specified, replace the switch.

REMOVAL AND INSTALLATION

1. Disconnect the negative battery cable.
2. Remove the control head assembly.
3. Remove recirculate/fresh switch attaching screws.
4. Disconnect the switch wire connectors.
5. Remove the recirculate/fresh switch.
6. Installation is the reverse of the removal procedure.

Recirculation Control Motor

OPERATION

The recirculate/fresh switch sends a voltage signal to the recirculation control motor which then opens the recirculate/fresh door to allow outside air to enter the vehicle or to recirculate the air that is already in the vehicle.

TESTING

Accord

1989

1. Disconnect the negative battery cable.
2. Disconnect the control motor wire connector.
3. Connect a 12 volt positive lead to terminal **4** and the negative lead to terminal **1** of the control motor connector.
4. Using a jumper wire, connect terminal **1** to terminal **5** and the motor should turn to the **FRESH** position.
5. Next, connect terminal **1** to terminal **6** and the motor should turn to the **REC** position.
6. If not as specified, replace the recirculation control motor.

1990–91

1. Disconnect the negative battery cable.
2. Disconnect the control motor wire connector.

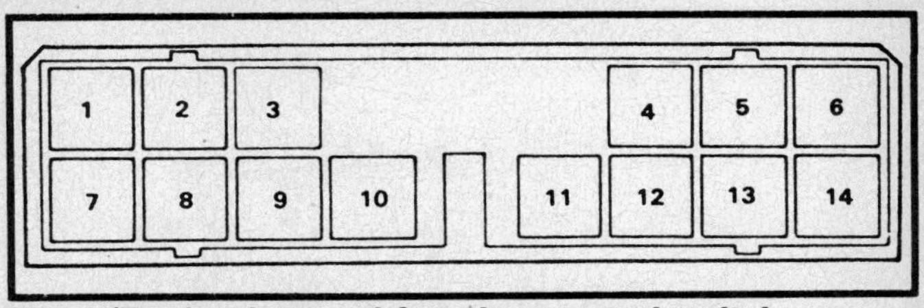
1
2
3
4
5
6
7
8
9
10
11
12
13
14

Fresh/Recirculate and function control switch connector-button type—1989 Accord

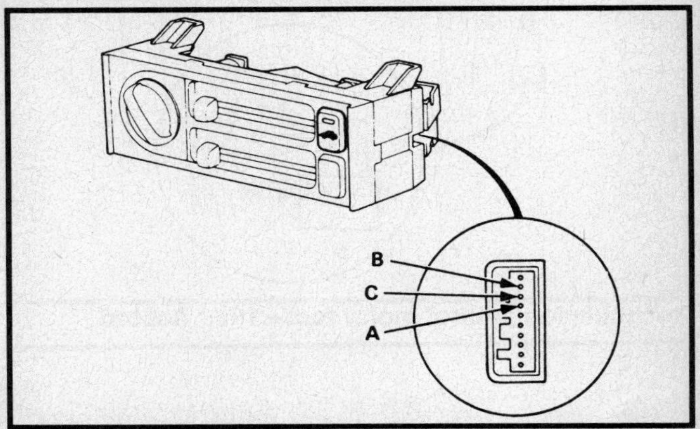
B
C
A

Recirculate/Fresh switch test-lever type—1990–91 Accord

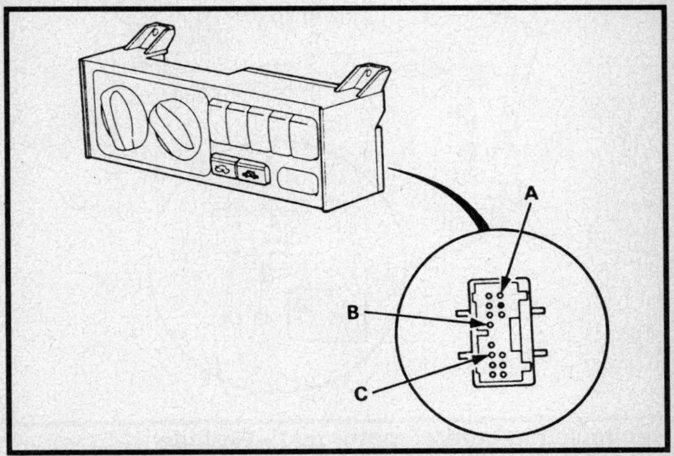
A
B
C

Recirculate/Fresh switch test-button type—1990–91 Accord

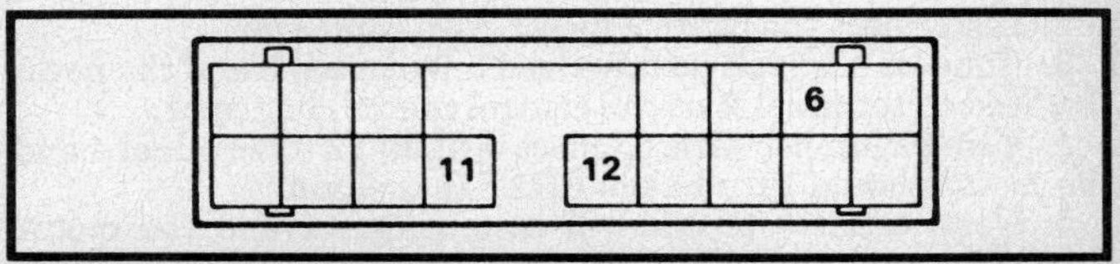
6
11
12

Recirculate/Fresh switch test-button type—Prelude

3. Connect a 12 volt positive lead to terminal **1** and the negative lead to terminals **2** and **3** of the control motor connector.
4. The control motor should rotate.
5. Next, disconnect the negative lead from terminals **2** or **3** and the motor should stop at the **REC** or **FRESH** position.
6. If not as specified, replace the recirculation control motor.

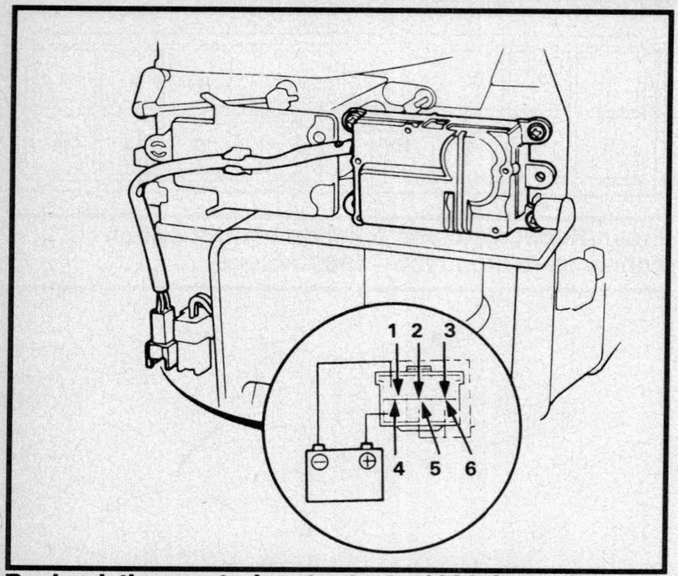
1 2 3
4 5 6
Recirculation control motor test—1989 Accord

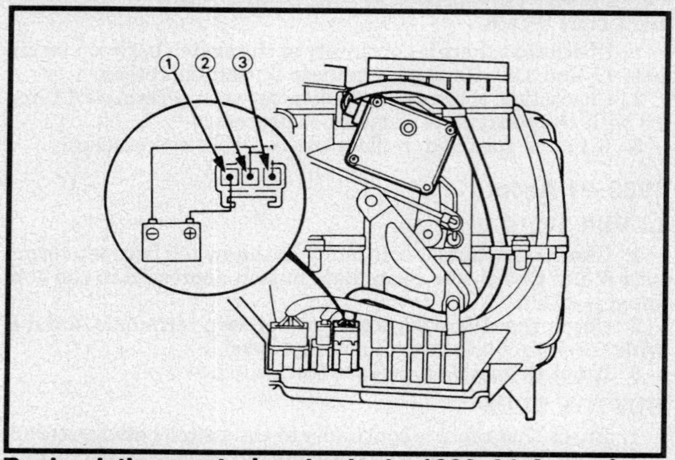
① ② ③
Recirculation control motor test—1990–91 Accord

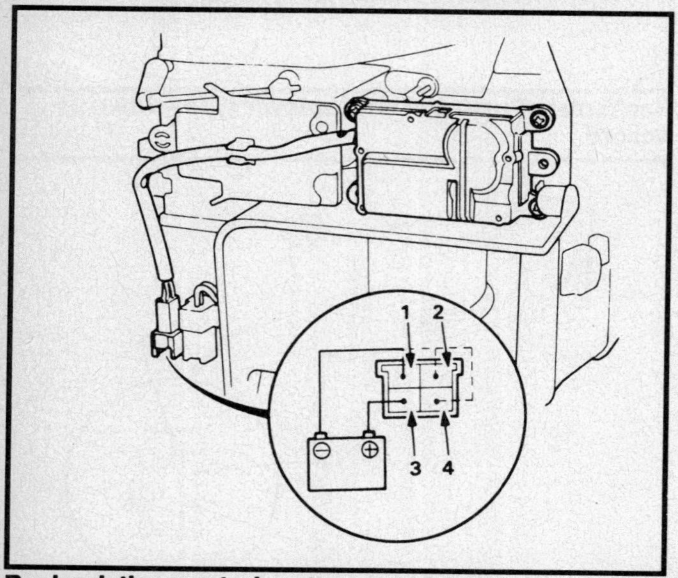
1 2
3 4
Recirculation control motor test—Prelude

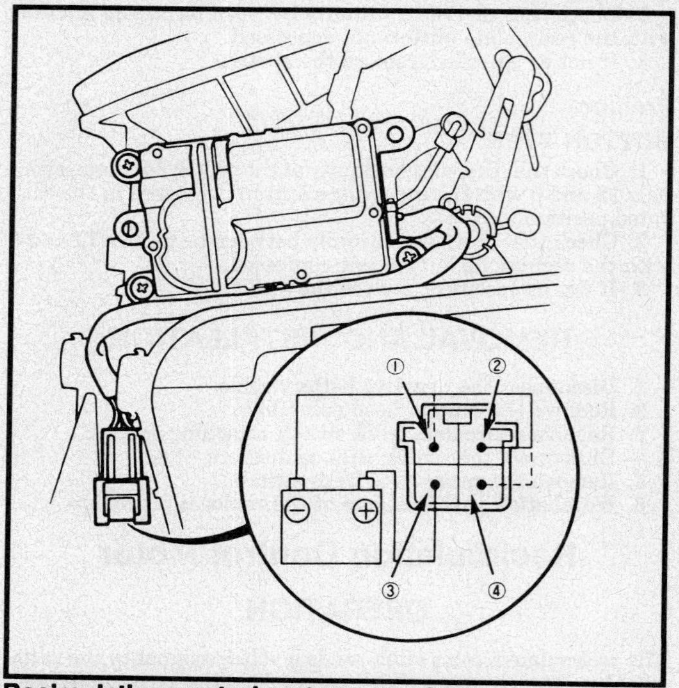
① ②
③ ④
Recirculation control motor test—CRX

CRX

1. Disconnect the negative battery cable.
2. Disconnect the control motor wire connector.
3. Connect a 12 volt positive lead to terminal **3** and the negative lead to terminal **2** of the control motor connector.
4. Using a jumper wire, connect terminal **2** to terminal **4** and the motor should turn to the **FRESH** position.
5. Next, connect terminal **2** to terminal **1** and the motor should turn to the **REC** position.
6. If not as specified, replace the recirculation control motor.

Prelude

1. Disconnect the negative battery cable.
2. Disconnect the control motor wire connector.
3. Connect a 12 volt positive lead to terminal **3** and the negative lead to terminal **1** of the control motor connector.
4. Using a jumper wire, connect terminal **1** to terminal **2** and the motor should turn to the **FRESH** position.
5. Next, connect terminal **1** to terminal **4** and the motor should turn to the **REC** position.
6. If not as specified, replace the recirculation control motor.

REMOVAL AND INSTALLATION

1. Disconnect the negative battery cable.
2. Remove the blower motor assembly.
3. Remove screws attaching recirculation control motor.
4. Remove wire connectors.
5. Disconnect all linkage.
6. Installation is the reverse of the removal procedure.

Function Control Switch

OPERATION

The function control switch is located at the electronic control head. The main purpose of the switch is to complete the ground circuit to the control motor, which then determines the specified air mix door to open or close.

TESTING

Accord

1989

1. Disconnect the function switch wire connector at the electronic control head.
2. Check that there is continuity at the switch between terminals **1** and **2** with the **VENT** button depressed.
3. Check that there is continuity at the switch between terminals **1** and **3** with the **HI-LO** button depressed.
4. Check that there is continuity at the switch between terminals **1** and **4** with the **HEAT** button depressed.
5. Check that there is continuity at the switch between terminals **1** and **5** with the **HEAT/DEFROST** button depressed.
6. Check that there is continuity at the switch between terminals **1** and **6** with the **DEFROST** button depressed.
7. If not as specified, replace the switch.

1990–91

1. Disconnect the function switch wire connector at the electronic control head.
2. Check that there is continuity at the switch between terminals **1** and **6** with the **VENT** button depressed.
3. Check that there is continuity at the switch between terminals **2** and **6** with the **HI-LO** button depressed.
4. Check that there is continuity at the switch between terminals **3** and **6** with the **HEAT** button depressed.
5. Check that there is continuity at the switch between terminals **4** and **6** with the **HEAT/DEFROST** button depressed.
6. Check that there is continuity at the switch between terminals **5** and **6** with the **DEFROST** button depressed.
7. If not as specified, replace the switch.

CRX

1. Disconnect the function switch wire connector at the electronic control head.
2. Check that there is continuity at the switch between terminals **8** and **12** or **13** with the **VENT** button depressed.
3. Check that there is continuity at the switch between terminals **3** and **12** or **13** with the **HI-LO** button depressed.
4. Check that there is continuity at the switch between terminals **9** and **12** or **13** with the **HEAT** button depressed.
5. Check that there is continuity at the switch between terminals **10** and **12** or **13** with the **HEAT/DEFROST** button depressed.
6. Check that there is continuity at the switch between terminals **4** and **12** or **13** with the **DEFROST** button depressed.
7. If not as specified, replace the switch.

Prelude

1. Disconnect the function switch wire connector at the electronic control head.
2. Check that there is continuity at the switch between terminals **14** and **1** with the **VENT** button depressed.
3. Check that there is continuity at the switch between terminals **14** and **2** with the **HI-LO** button depressed.
4. Check that there is continuity at the switch between terminals **14** and **10** with the **HEAT** button depressed.
5. Check that there is continuity at the switch between terminals **14** and **13** with the **HEAT/DEFROST** button depressed.
6. Check that there is continuity at the switch between terminals **14** and **15** with the **DEFROST** button depressed.
7. If not as specified, replace the switch.

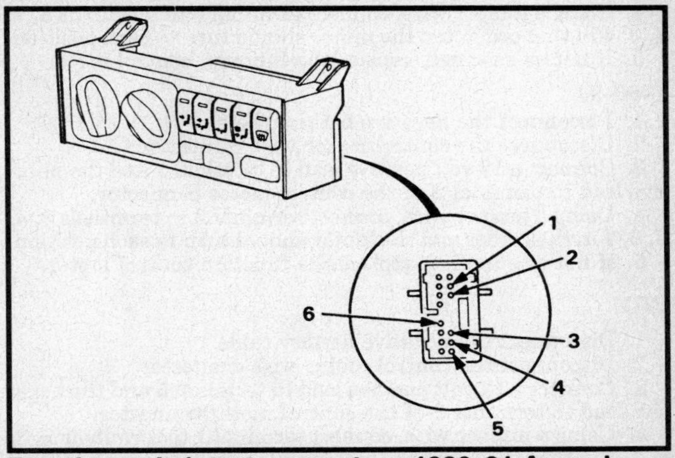
1
2
3
4
5
6
Function switch test connector – 1990–91 Accord

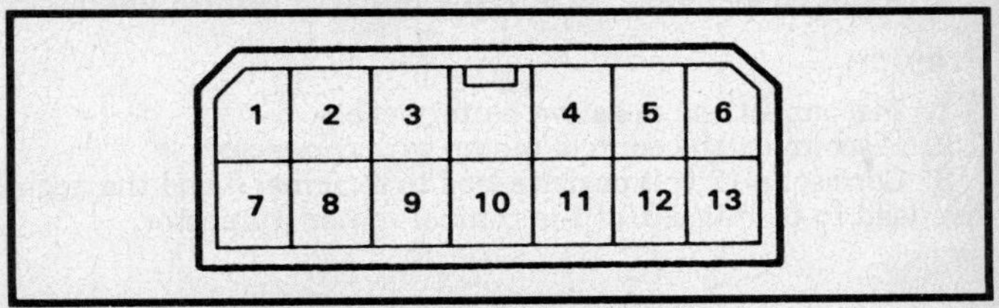
1 2 3 4 5 6
7 8 9 10 11 12 13
Function switch test connector – CRX

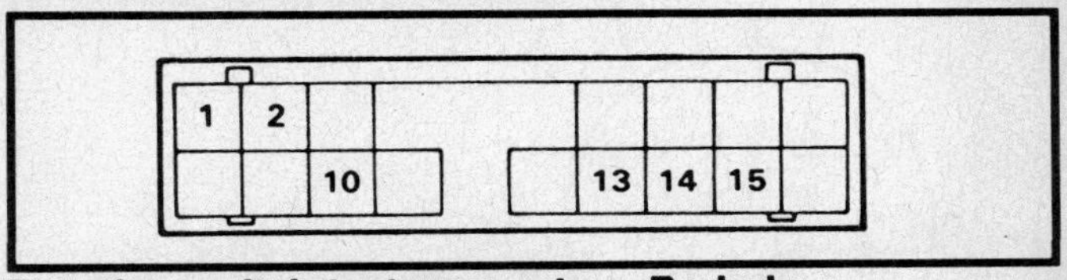
1 2
10 13 14 15
Function switch test connector – Prelude

REMOVAL AND INSTALLATION

1. Disconnect the negative battery cable.
2. Remove the electronic control head.
3. Disconnect the wire harness connectors.
4. Installation is the reverse of the removal procedure.

Function Control Motor

OPERATION

The function control motor receives a voltage signal from the control head when each individual switch is pushed, then the control motor rotates to a predetermined position and changes the air passage ways to defrost, combination defrost and feet, feet only, face and feet or face only position.

TESTING

Accord

1989

1. Disconnect the negative battery cable.
2. Disconnect the control motor wire connector.
3. Connect a 12 volt positive lead to terminal **5** and the negative lead to terminal **1** of the control motor connector.

4. Using a jumper wire, connect terminal **6** to terminals **8, 7, 2, 3, 4** in that order and the motor should turn to each position.
5. If not as specified, replace the function control motor.

1990–91

1. Disconnect the negative battery cable.
2. Disconnect the control motor wire connector.
3. Connect a 12 volt positive lead to terminal **1** and the negative lead to terminal **2** of the control motor connector.
4. Using a jumper wire, connect terminal **2** to terminals **3, 4, 5, 6, 7** in that order and the motor should turn to each position.
5. If not as specified, replace the function control motor.

CRX

1. Disconnect the negative battery cable.
2. Disconnect the control motor wire connector.
3. Connect a 12 volt positive lead to terminal **5** and the negative lead to terminal **1** of the control motor connector.
4. Using a jumper wire, connect terminal **1** to terminals **2, 3, 4, 7, 8** in that order and the motor should turn to each position.
5. If not as specified, replace the function control motor.

Prelude

1. Disconnect the negative battery cable.
2. Disconnect the control motor wire connector.
3. Connect a 12 volt positive lead to terminal **5** and the negative lead to terminal **1** of the control motor connector.

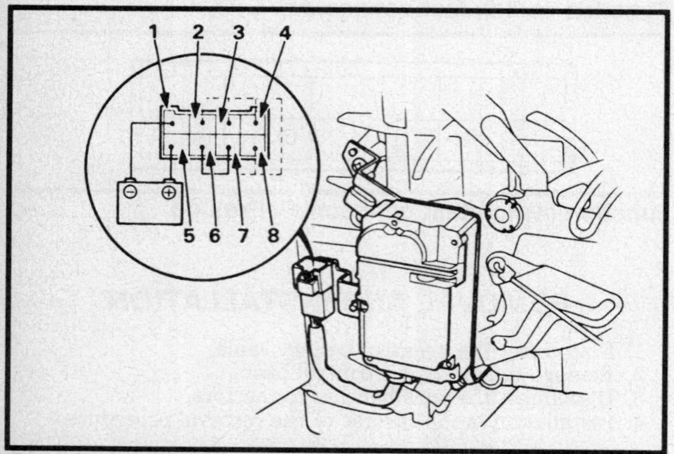
1
2
3
4
5
6
7
8
Function control motor testing—1989 Accord

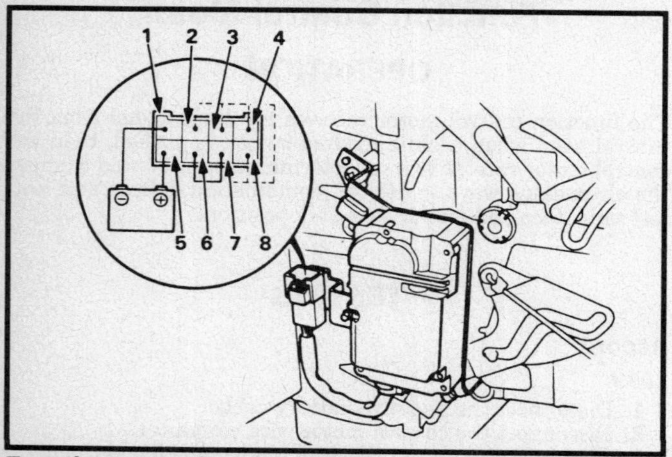
1
2
3
4
5
6
7
8
Function control motor testing connector—Prelude

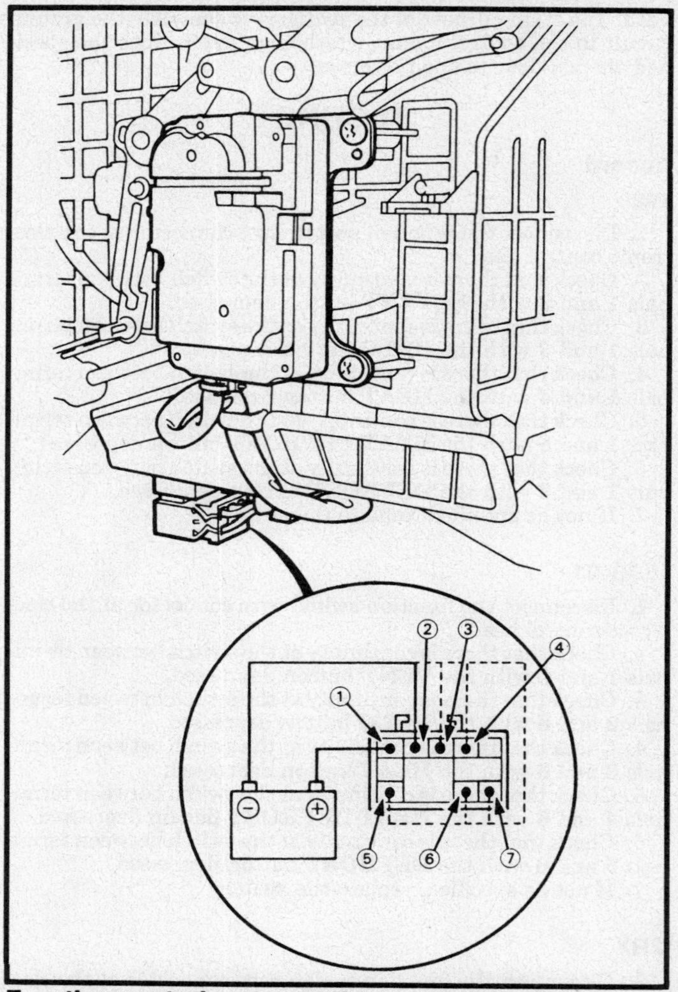
1
2
3
4
5
6
7
Function control motor testing connector—1990–91 Accord

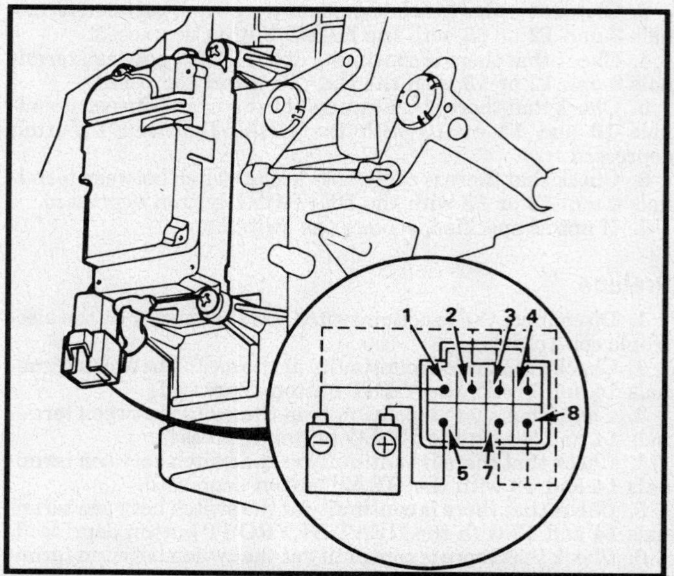
1
2
3
4
8
5
7
Function control motor testing connector—CRX

4. Using a jumper wire, connect terminal **6** to terminals **7, 8, 4, 3, 2** in that order and the motor should turn to each position.
5. If not as specified, replace the function control motor.

REMOVAL AND INSTALLATION

1. Disconnect the negative battery cable.
2. Remove the heater unit, if required.
3. Remove control motor wire connectors.
4. Remove the control motor attaching screws.
5. Disconnect the linkage.
6. Remove the control motor.
7. Installation is the reverse of the removal.

Cooling Fan Timer Unit

OPERATION

The cooling fan timer unit operates the radiator and condenser fan by monitoring the coolant temperature and or the air conditioning switch, thus keeping the engine from overheating.

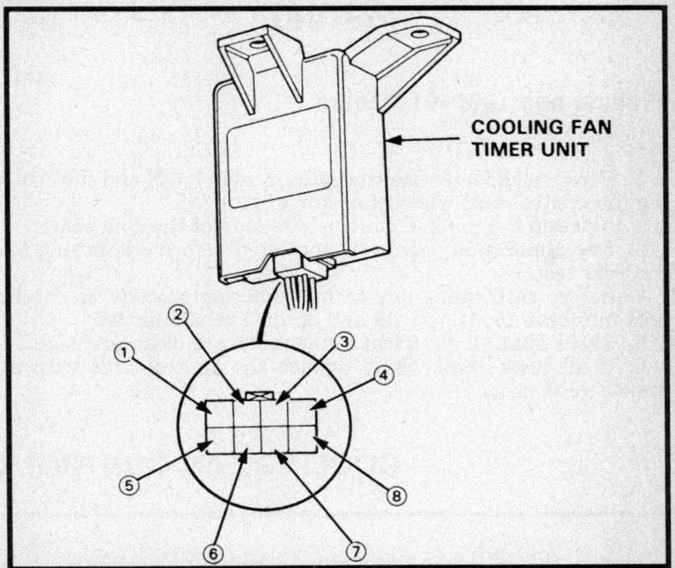
COOLING FAN TIMER UNIT
①
②
③
④
⑤
⑥
⑦
⑧

Cooling fan timer control unit test connector—1990–91 Accord

COOLING FAN TIMER UNIT DIAGNOSTIC CHART

WIRE POSITION	TEST CONDITION	DESIRED RESULTS	CORRECTIVE ACTION IF DESIRED RESULTS ARE NOT OBTAINED
④ BLK	Check for continuity to body ground.	Should have continuity.	Repair open to body ground.
⑥ WHT	Check for battery voltage.	Should have battery voltage.	Check No. 29 fuse, if OK repair open in WHT wire.
⑦ BLK/YEL	Check for battery voltage (Ignition switch—ON)		Check No. 2 fuse, if OK repair open in BLK/YEL wire.
② YEL/BLK	Check for battery voltage (Ignition switch—ON)		Check No. 8 fuse, if OK repair open in YEL/BLK wire.
① YEL/WHT	Check for battery voltage.		Replace cooling fan timer unit.
③ YEL	Check for battery voltage.		Replace cooling fan timer unit.
⑧ BLU	Connect to body ground.	Condenser fan and cooling fan should come on.	Check for open in BLU between cooling fan timer and condenser fan relay or cooling fan relay. If OK, check for open YEL/WHT between cooling fan timer and condenser fan relay or YEL between cooling fan timer and cooling fan relay. If OK, test condenser fan relay or cooling fan relay.
⑤ WHT/GRN	Check for voltage.	Approx 11 V (water temperature below 108°C)	Faulty water temp switch, short to body ground or faulty cooling fan timer unit.

TESTING

Prelude and 1990–91 Accord

1. Perform all tests with the ignition switch **ON** and the cooling fan control unit wire connector unplugged.
2. All tests are made from the wire side of the connector.
3. Any abnormality must be corrected before continuing to the next test.
4. Before performing any troubleshooting procedures check fuse numbers 17, 12, 36, 39 and 35 on Prelude model.
5. Check that all electrical connections are clean and tight.
6. If all tests check okay, replace the control unit with a known good unit.

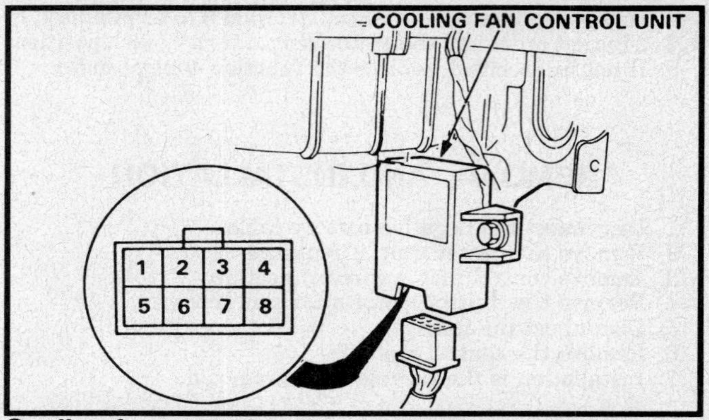
COOLING FAN CONTROL UNIT
C
1 2 3 4
5 6 7 8

Cooling fan control unit test connector—Prelude

COOLING FAN CONTROL UNIT DIAGNOSTIC CHART

WIRE COLOR	TEST CONDITION	IF DESIRED RESULTS ARE NOT OBTAINED:
YEL/BLK	Connect to WHT/YEL using a jumper wire. Condenser fan should come on.	Repair open in YEL/BLK between cooling fan control unit and underhood relay box.
BLK/YEL[2]	Check for battery voltage.	Repair open in BLK/YEL[2] between fuse No. 17 and cooling fan control unit.
RED/GRN	Connect to WHT/YEL using a jumper wire. Radiator fan should come on.	Repair open in RED/GRN between cooling fan control unit and underhood relay box.
BLK	Check for continuity to ground.	Repair open circuit to body ground.
WHT/YEL	Check for battery voltage.	Repair open between fuse No. 35 and cooling fan control unit.
BLK/YEL[1]	Check for battery voltage.	Repair open in BLK/YEL[1] between fuse No. 12 and cooling fan control unit.

Air Conditioner Compressor Control Unit

OPERATION

The air conditioner compressor control unit has a system designed to protect the compressor belt in the event of a seizure, thereby allowing the alternator to continue operating. This is done by comparing the engine rpm and the compressor pulley rpm. When there is a difference in rpm that continues for more than 3 seconds, the compressor relays are turned off and the warning light comes on. To reset, push the the air conditioner switch off and on again. If the switch is pushed more than twice, it will be necessary to turn the ignition off to reset.

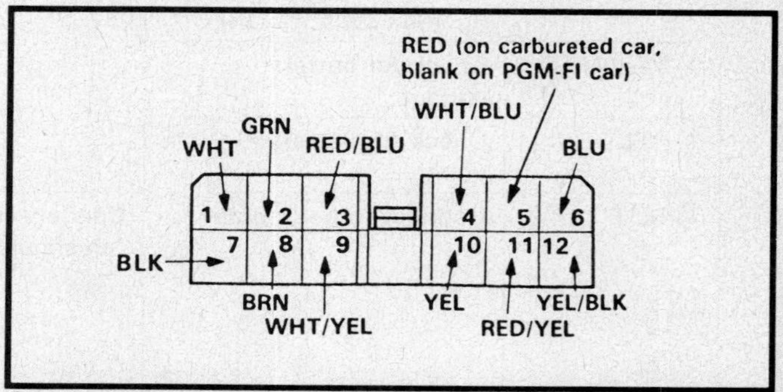
RED (on carbureted car, blank on PGM-FI car)
WHT/BLU
GRN
WHT
RED/BLU
BLU
1 2 3 4 5 6
7 8 9 10 11 12
BLK
BRN
WHT/YEL
YEL
RED/YEL
YEL/BLK

Compressor control unit input test connector—Prelude

TESTING

Prelude

1. Make sure all connections are clean and tight.
2. Make all tests from the wire side of the connector with a digital multimeter.
3. Any abnormality found during these tests must be corrected before continuing.
4. If all tests produce the desired results, substitute a known good control unit and retest.

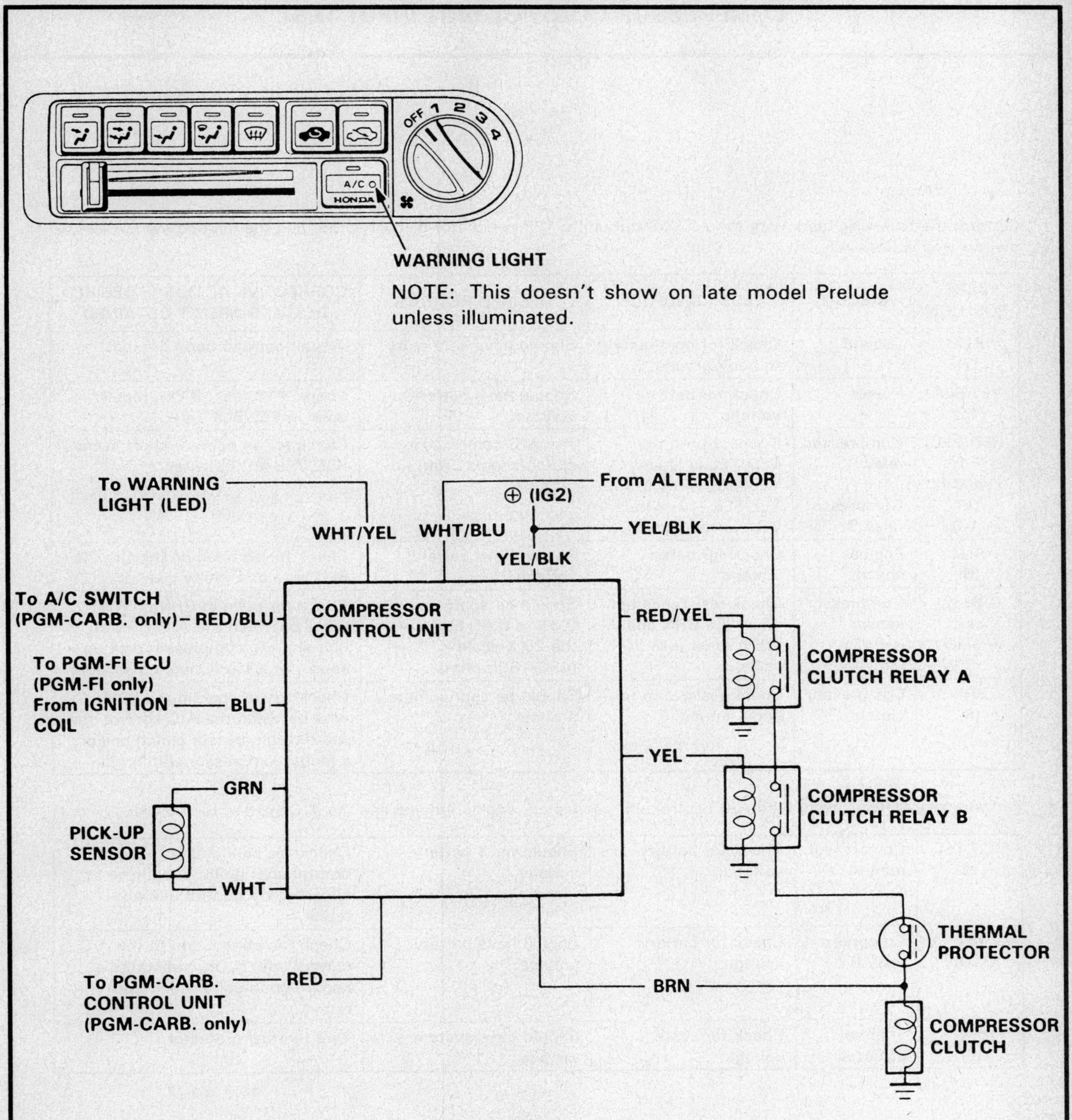
OFF
1
2
3
4
A/C
HONDA
WARNING LIGHT
NOTE: This doesn't show on late model Prelude unless illuminated.
To WARNING LIGHT (LED)
WHT/YEL
WHT/BLU
From ALTERNATOR
⊕ (IG2)
YEL/BLK
YEL/BLK
To A/C SWITCH (PGM-CARB. only)
RED/BLU
COMPRESSOR CONTROL UNIT
RED/YEL
COMPRESSOR CLUTCH RELAY A
To PGM-FI ECU (PGM-FI only) From IGNITION COIL
BLU
YEL
COMPRESSOR CLUTCH RELAY B
GRN
PICK-UP SENSOR
WHT
THERMAL PROTECTOR
To PGM-CARB. CONTROL UNIT (PGM-CARB. only)
RED
BRN
COMPRESSOR CLUTCH

Compressor control system—Prelude

COMPRESSOR CONTROL UNIT INPUT TEST

Perform the following tests with the A/C control unit's 12P connector disconnected, and the ignition switch, blower switch, and A/C switch ON.

WIRE POSITION	CIRCUIT	TEST CONDITION	DESIRED RESULTS	CORRECTIVE ACTION IF DESIRED RESULTS AREN'T OBTAINED
BLK (7)	Ground	Check for continuity to body ground.	Should have continuity.	Repair open to body ground.
YEL/BLK (12)	Power	Check for battery voltage.	Should have battery voltage.	Check #18 fuse; if OK, repair open in YEL/BLK wire.
RED/YEL (11) and YEL (10)	Compressor relay A Compressor relay B	Connect both the RED/YEL (11) and YEL (10) wires to the YEL/BLK (12) wire with jumper wires.	The A/C compressor clutch should click.	Check for an open or short in the RED/YEL or YEL wires.
BLU (6)	Engine speed	Check for battery voltage.	Should have battery voltage.	Check for an open or short in the BLU wire or a faulty coil.
GRN (2) and WHT (1)	Compressor sensor	Check resistance between the GRN and WHT wires (use 20 K scale).	Should be approximately 0.45 to 0.60 ohms on the 20 K scale (450–600 ohms).	Check for open in GRN or WHT wires between the A/C control unit and the compressor pick-up sensor or a faulty pick-up sensor.
BRN (8)	Compressor clutch	Check resistance to body ground.	Should be approximately 4 ohms.	Check for an open in the BRN wire between the A/C control unit and the compressor clutch coil or a faulty compressor clutch.

Perform the following tests with A/C control unit connected, engine running and the A/C system turned ON.

RED/YEL (11)	Compressor relay A	Check for battery voltage.	Should have battery voltage.	Check the connection to the A/C control unit; if OK, substitute a known-good control unit and retest.
YEL (10)	Compressor relay B	Check for battery voltage	Should have battery voltage.	Check the connection to the A/C control unit; if OK, substitute a known-good control unit and retest.
BRN (8)	Thermal protector	Check for system voltage.	Should have system voltage.	Test thermal protector.

SYSTEM DIAGNOSIS

AIR CONDITIONER COMPRESSOR DIAGNOSTIC CHART

TEST RESULTS	RELATED SYMPTOMS	PROBABLE CAUSE	REMEDY
Discharge (high) pressure abnormally high	After stopping compressor, pressure drops to about 196 kPa (28 psi) quickly, and then falls gradually	Air in system	Evacuate system; then recharge
	No bubbles in sight glass when condenser is cooled by water	Excessive refrigerant in system	Discharge refrigerant as required
	Reduced or no air flow through condenser.	• Clogged condenser or radiator fins • Condenser or radiator fan not working properly.	• Clean • Check voltage and fan rpm
	Line to condenser is excessively hot	Restricted flow of refrigerant in system	Expansion valve
Discharge pressure abnomally low	Excessive bubbles in sight glass; condenser is not hot	Insufficient refrigerant	• Charge system • Check for leak
	High and low pressures are balanced soon after stopping compressor	• Faulty compressor discharge or inlet valve • Faulty compressor seal	Replace compressor Repair
	Outlet of expansion valve is not frosted, low pressure gauge indicates vacuum	• Faulty expansion valve	Repair or Replace
Suction (low) pressure abnormally low	Excessive bubbles in sight glass; condenser is not hot Expansion valve is not frosted and low pressure line is not cold. Low pressure gauge indicates vacuum.	Insufficient refrigerant • Frozen expansion valve • Faulty expansion valve	Check for leaks. Charge as required. Replace expansion valve
	Discharge temperature is low and the air flow from vents is restricted	Frozen evaporator	Run the fan with compressor off then check the thermostat and capillary tube.
	Expansion valve frosted	Clogged expansion valve	Clean or Replace
	Receiver dryer is cool (should be warm during operation)	Clogged receiver dryer	Replace
Suction pressure abnormally high	Low pressure hose and check joint are cooler than around evaporator	• Expansion valve open too long • Loose expansion valve	Repair or Replace
	Suction pressure is lowered when condenser is cooled by water	Excessive refrigerant in system	Discharge refrigerant as necessary
	High and low pressure are balanced too equalized as soon as the compressor is stopped	• Faulty gasket • Faulty high pressure valve • Foreign particle stuck in high pressure valve	Replace compressor
Suction and discharge pressures abnormally high	Reduced air flow through condenser	• Clogged condenser or radiator fins • Condenser or radiator fan not working properly	• Clean condenser and radiator • Check voltage and fan rpm
	No bubbles in sight glass when condenser is cooled by water	Excessive refrigerant in system	Discharge refrigerant as necessary.
Suction and discharge pressure abnormally low	Low pressure hose and metal end areas are cooler than evaporator	Clogged or kinked low pressure hose parts	Repair or Replace
	Temperature around expansion valve is too low compared with that around receiver-driver.	Clogged high pressure line	Repair or Replace
Refrigerant leaks	Compressor clutch is dirty	Compressor shaft seal leaking	Replace compressor shaft seal
	Compressor bolt(s) are dirty	Leaking around bolt(s)	Replace compressor
	Compressor gasket is wet with oil	Gasket leaking	Repalce compressor

WIRING SCHEMATICS

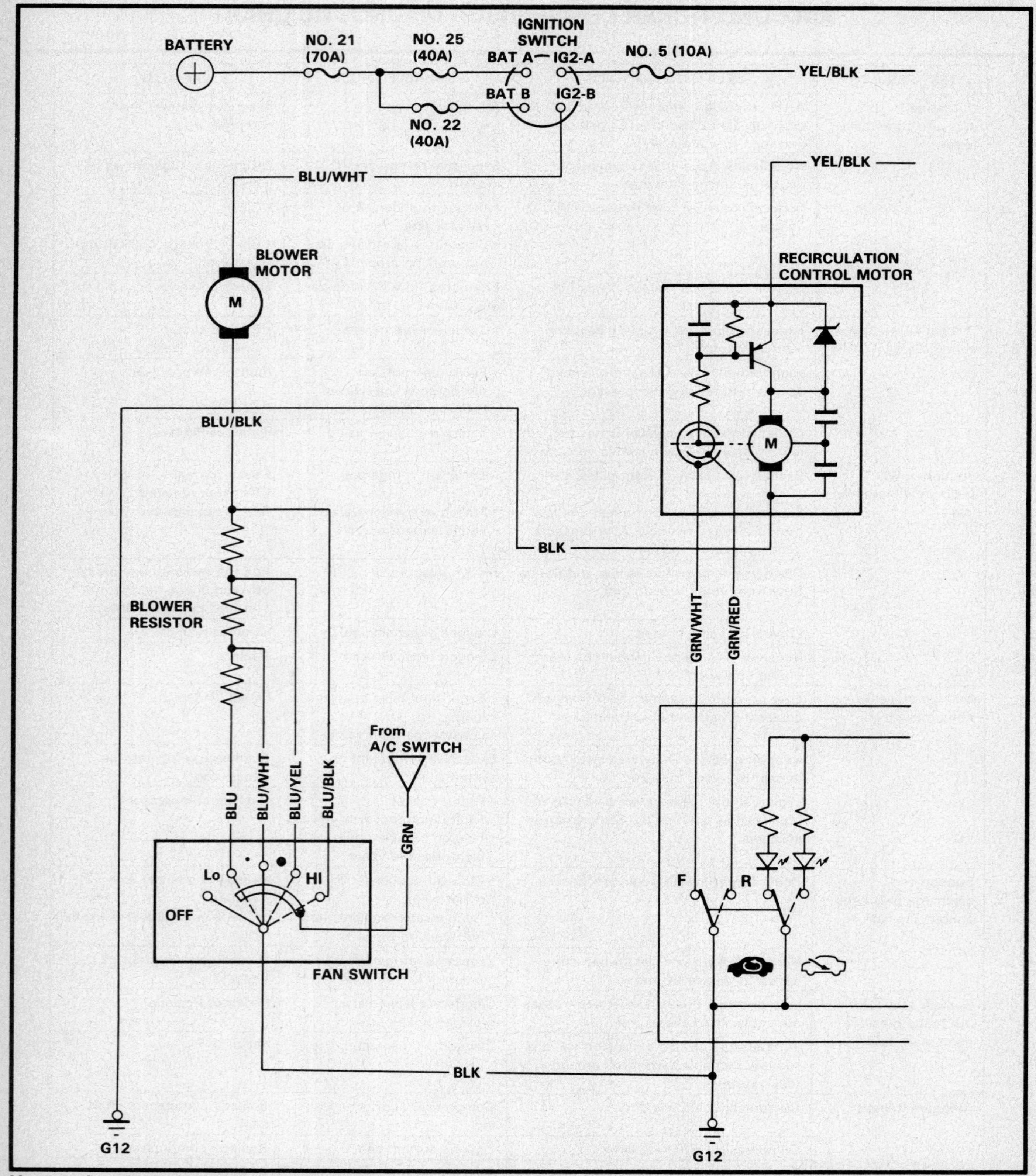
BATTERY
NO. 21 (70A)
NO. 25 (40A)
IGNITION SWITCH
BAT A
IG2-A
BAT B
IG2-B
NO. 22 (40A)
NO. 5 (10A)
YEL/BLK
BLU/WHT
YEL/BLK
BLOWER MOTOR
M
RECIRCULATION CONTROL MOTOR
M
BLU/BLK
BLK
BLOWER RESISTOR
GRN/WHT
GRN/RED
From A/C SWITCH
BLU
BLU/WHT
BLU/YEL
BLU/BLK
GRN
Lo
HI
OFF
FAN SWITCH
F
R
BLK
G12
G12

Heater electrical schematic—1989 Accord

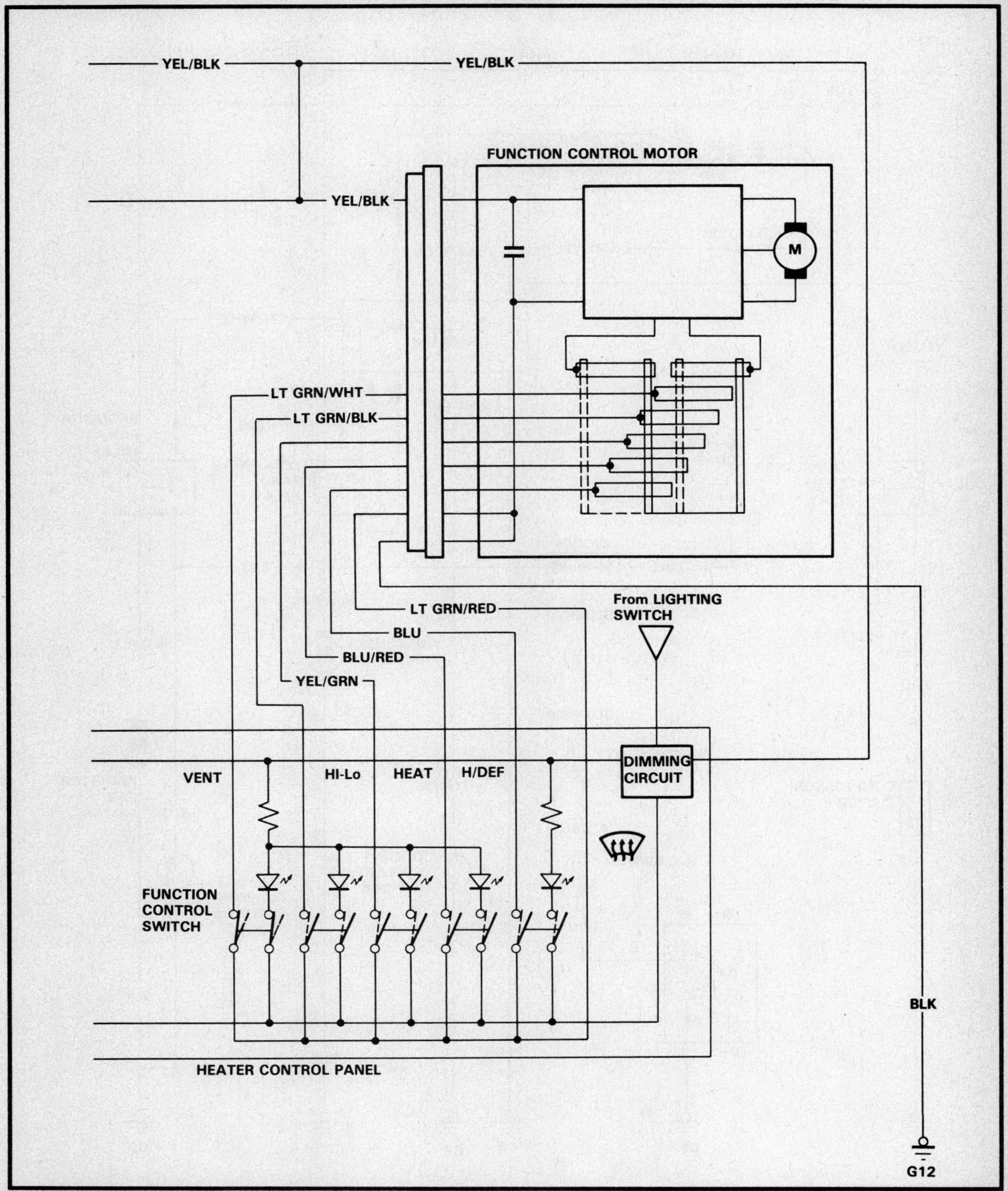
YEL/BLK
YEL/BLK
FUNCTION CONTROL MOTOR
YEL/BLK
M
LT GRN/WHT
LT GRN/BLK
LT GRN/RED
From LIGHTING SWITCH
BLU
BLU/RED
YEL/GRN
VENT
HI-Lo
HEAT
H/DEF
DIMMING CIRCUIT
FUNCTION CONTROL SWITCH
BLK
HEATER CONTROL PANEL
G12

Heater electrical schematic—1989 Accord, continued

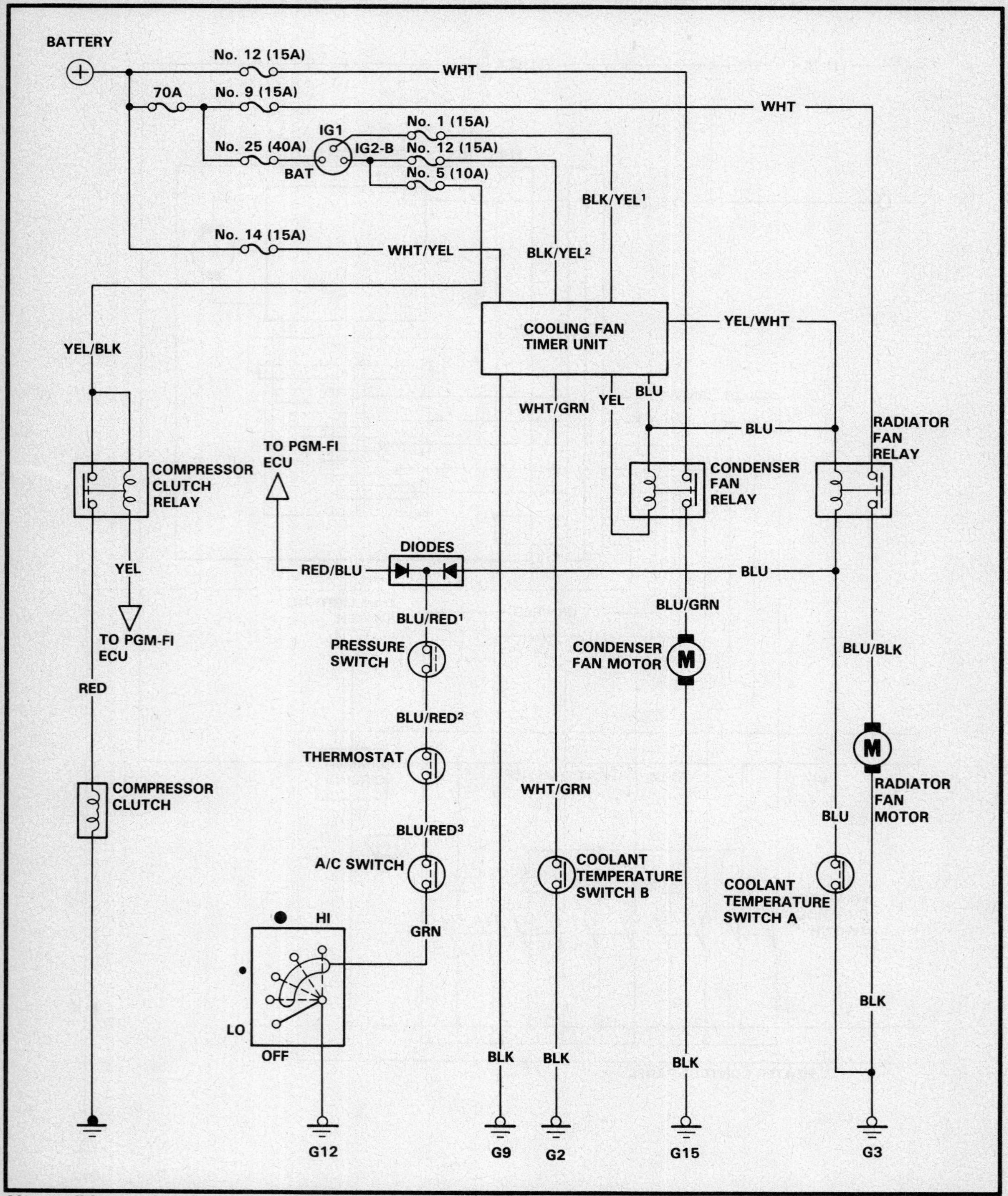
BATTERY
No. 12 (15A)
WHT
70A
No. 9 (15A)
WHT
IG1
No. 1 (15A)
No. 25 (40A)
IG2-B
No. 12 (15A)
BAT
No. 5 (10A)
BLK/YEL1
No. 14 (15A)
WHT/YEL
BLK/YEL2
COOLING FAN TIMER UNIT
YEL/WHT
YEL/BLK
WHT/GRN
YEL
BLU
BLU
RADIATOR FAN RELAY
TO PGM-FI ECU
COMPRESSOR CLUTCH RELAY
CONDENSER FAN RELAY
DIODES
YEL
RED/BLU
BLU
BLU/GRN
BLU/RED1
TO PGM-FI ECU
PRESSURE SWITCH
CONDENSER FAN MOTOR
BLU/BLK
RED
BLU/RED2
THERMOSTAT
WHT/GRN
RADIATOR FAN MOTOR
COMPRESSOR CLUTCH
BLU/RED3
BLU
A/C SWITCH
COOLANT TEMPERATURE SWITCH B
COOLANT TEMPERATURE SWITCH A
HI
GRN
BLK
LO
OFF
BLK
BLK
BLK
G12
G9
G2
G15
G3

Air conditioner electrical schematic—1989 Accord with fuel injected engine

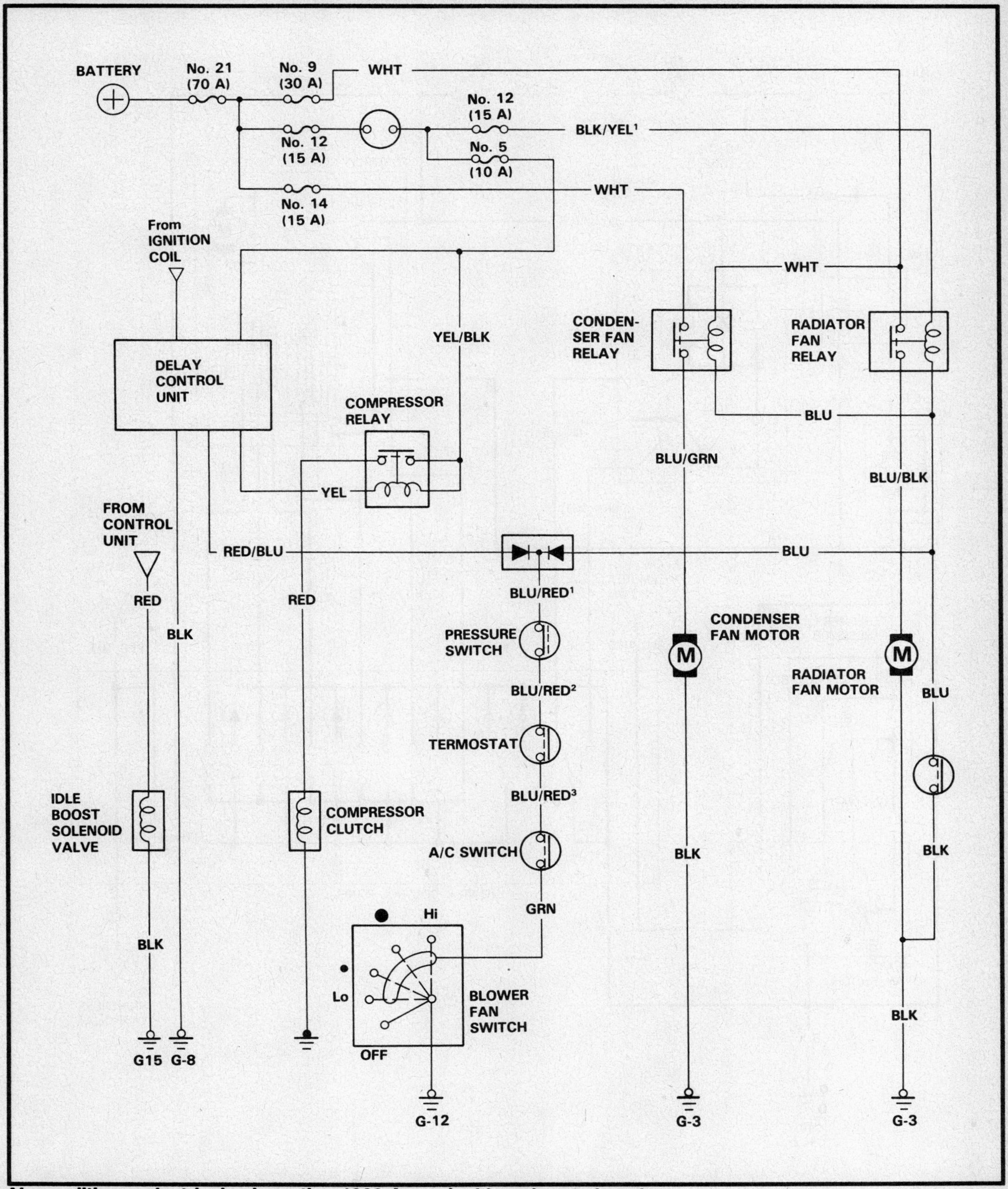
BATTERY
No. 21
(70 A)
No. 9
(30 A)
WHT
No. 12
(15 A)
BLK/YEL¹
No. 12
(15 A)
No. 5
(10 A)
WHT
No. 14
(15 A)
From
IGNITION
COIL
WHT
CONDEN-
SER FAN
RELAY
RADIATOR
FAN
RELAY
YEL/BLK
DELAY
CONTROL
UNIT
COMPRESSOR
RELAY
BLU
BLU/GRN
BLU/BLK
YEL
FROM
CONTROL
UNIT
RED/BLU
BLU
RED
RED
BLK
BLU/RED¹
PRESSURE
SWITCH
CONDENSER
FAN MOTOR
M
M
RADIATOR
FAN MOTOR
BLU/RED²
BLU
TERMOSTAT
BLU/RED³
IDLE
BOOST
SOLENOID
VALVE
COMPRESSOR
CLUTCH
A/C SWITCH
BLK
BLK
GRN
Hi
BLK
Lo
BLOWER
FAN
SWITCH
BLK
OFF
G15
G-8
G-12
G-3
G-3

Air conditioner electrical schematic—1989 Accord with carbureted engine

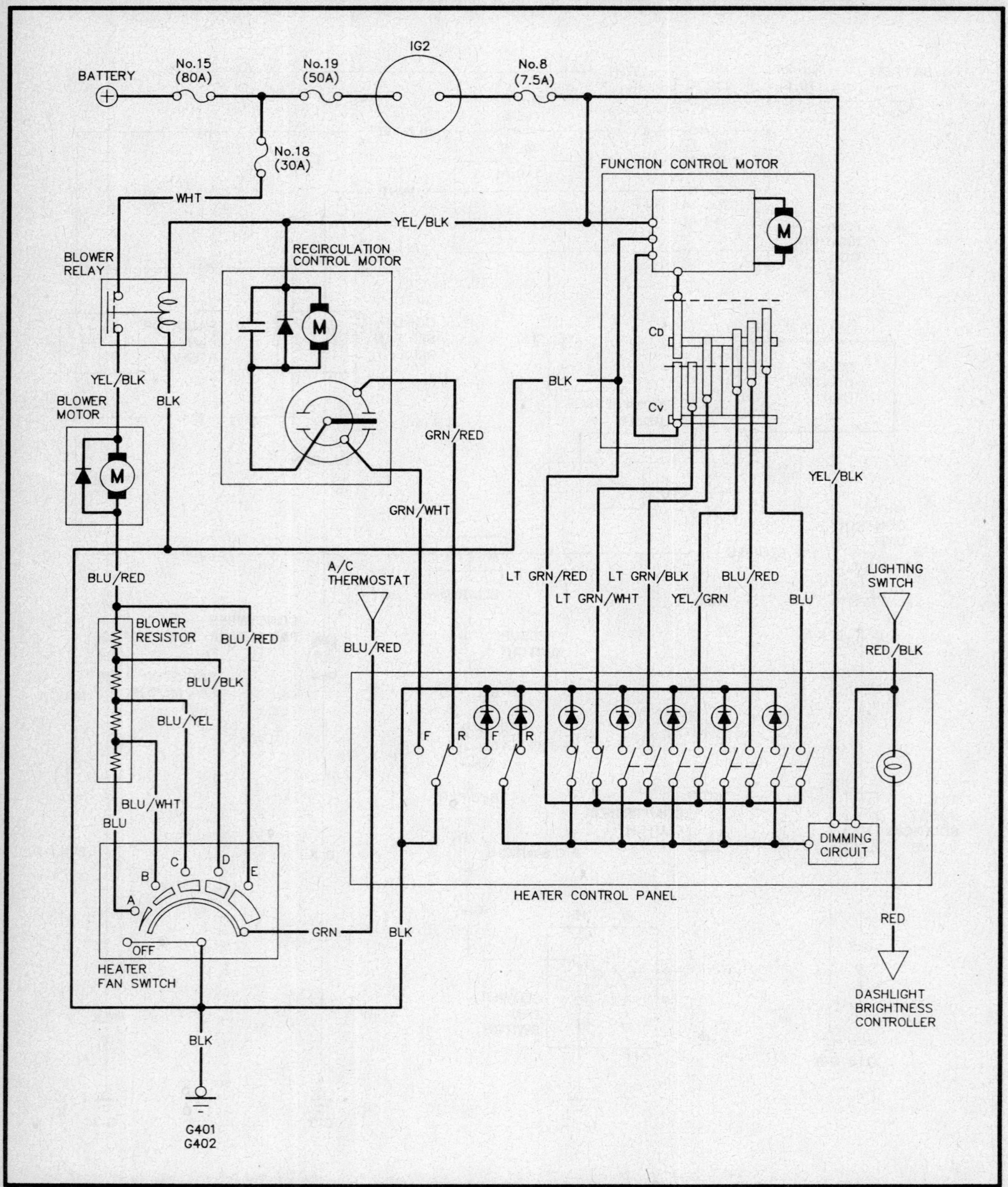
BATTERY
No.15 (80A)
No.19 (50A)
IG2
No.8 (7.5A)
No.18 (30A)
WHT
YEL/BLK
FUNCTION CONTROL MOTOR
M
BLOWER RELAY
RECIRCULATION CONTROL MOTOR
M
CD
CV
YEL/BLK
BLK
BLOWER MOTOR
BLK
GRN/RED
M
YEL/BLK
GRN/WHT
BLU/RED
A/C THERMOSTAT
LT GRN/RED
LT GRN/BLK
BLU/RED
LIGHTING SWITCH
LT GRN/WHT
YEL/GRN
BLU
BLOWER RESISTOR
BLU/RED
BLU/RED
RED/BLK
BLU/BLK
F
R
F
R
BLU/YEL
BLU/WHT
BLU
DIMMING CIRCUIT
A
B
C
D
E
HEATER CONTROL PANEL
GRN
BLK
RED
OFF
HEATER FAN SWITCH
DASHLIGHT BRIGHTNESS CONTROLLER
BLK
G401
G402

Heater electrical schematic—1990–91 Accord with button type control head

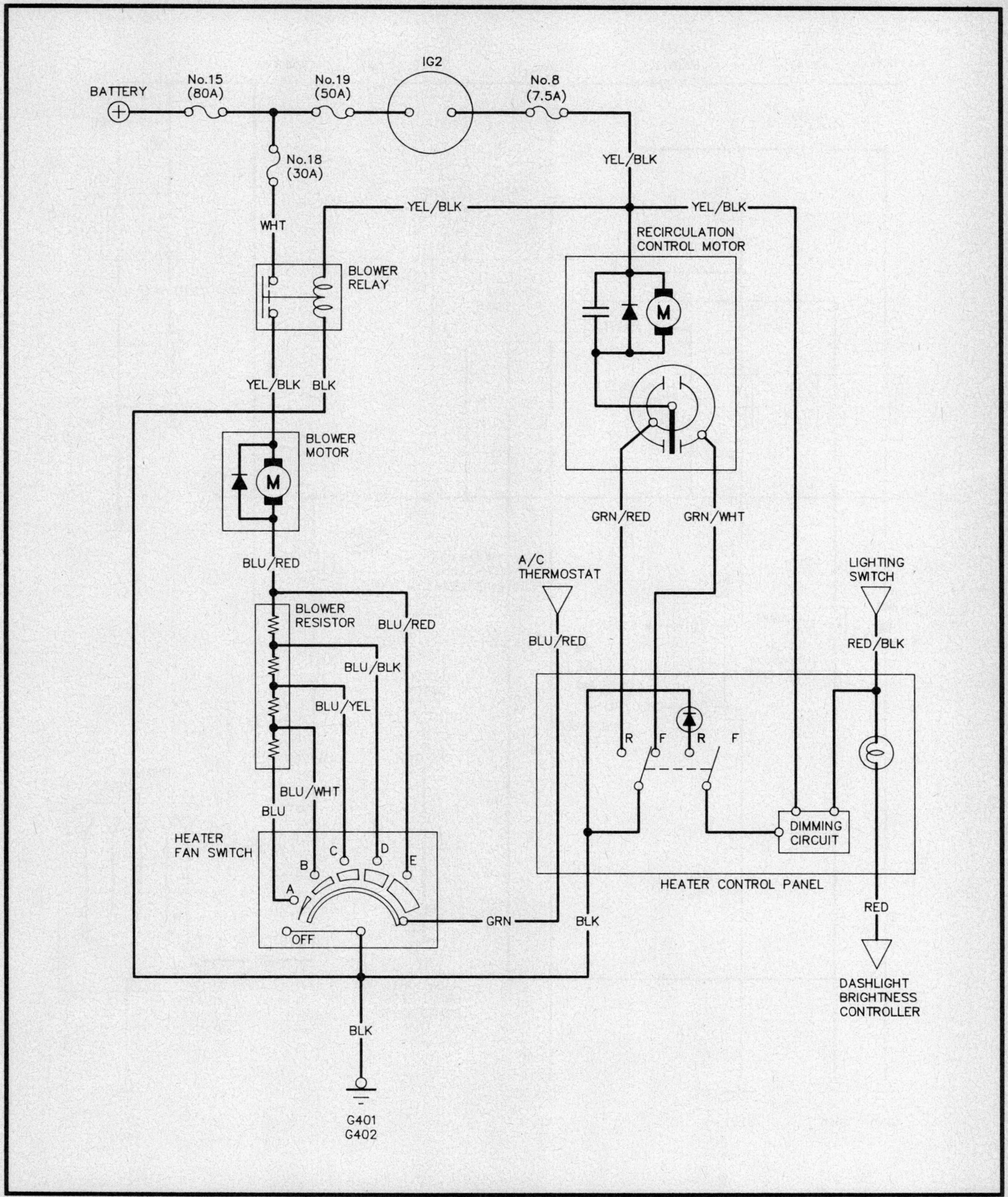
BATTERY
No.15 (80A)
No.19 (50A)
IG2
No.8 (7.5A)
No.18 (30A)
WHT
YEL/BLK
YEL/BLK
YEL/BLK
RECIRCULATION CONTROL MOTOR
BLOWER RELAY
YEL/BLK
BLK
BLOWER MOTOR
GRN/RED
GRN/WHT
BLU/RED
A/C THERMOSTAT
LIGHTING SWITCH
BLOWER RESISTOR
BLU/RED
BLU/BLK
BLU/RED
RED/BLK
BLU/YEL
R
F
R
F
BLU/WHT
BLU
DIMMING CIRCUIT
HEATER FAN SWITCH
HEATER CONTROL PANEL
GRN
BLK
RED
OFF
DASHLIGHT BRIGHTNESS CONTROLLER
BLK
G401
G402

Heater electrical schematic—1990–91 Accord with lever type control head

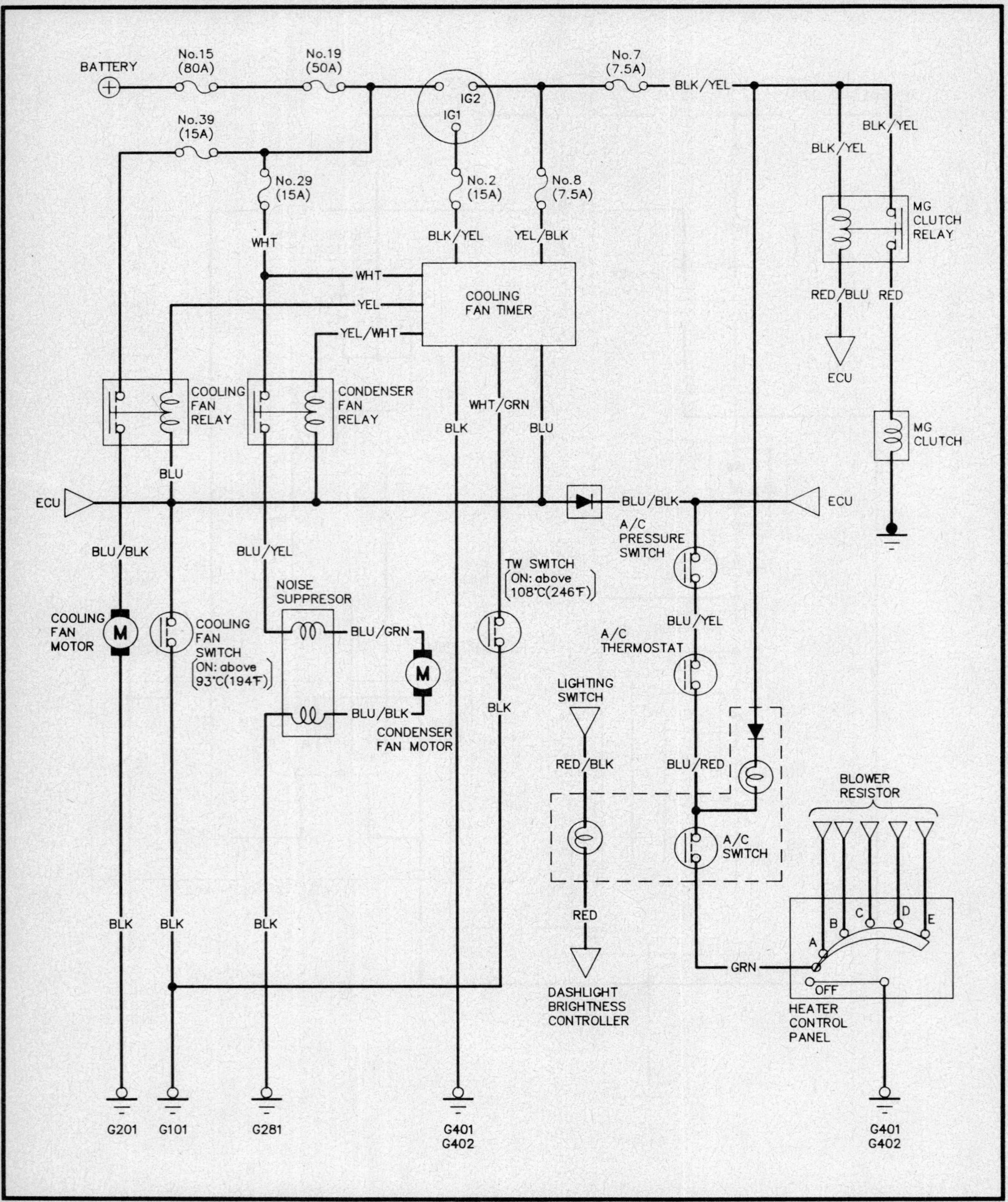
BATTERY
No.15 (80A)
No.19 (50A)
No.39 (15A)
No.29 (15A)
IG1
IG2
No.2 (15A)
No.8 (7.5A)
No.7 (7.5A)
BLK/YEL
WHT
YEL/BLK
YEL
YEL/WHT
COOLING FAN TIMER
MG CLUTCH RELAY
RED/BLU
RED
ECU
MG CLUTCH
COOLING FAN RELAY
CONDENSER FAN RELAY
WHT/GRN
BLK
BLU
BLU/BLK
BLU/YEL
A/C PRESSURE SWITCH
TW SWITCH (ON: above 108°C(246°F))
NOISE SUPPRESOR
COOLING FAN MOTOR
COOLING FAN SWITCH (ON: above 93°C(194°F))
BLU/GRN
CONDENSER FAN MOTOR
A/C THERMOSTAT
LIGHTING SWITCH
RED/BLK
BLU/RED
A/C SWITCH
BLOWER RESISTOR
A B C D E
OFF
GRN
DASHLIGHT BRIGHTNESS CONTROLLER
HEATER CONTROL PANEL
G201
G101
G281
G401
G402

Air conditioner electrical schematic—1990–91 Accord

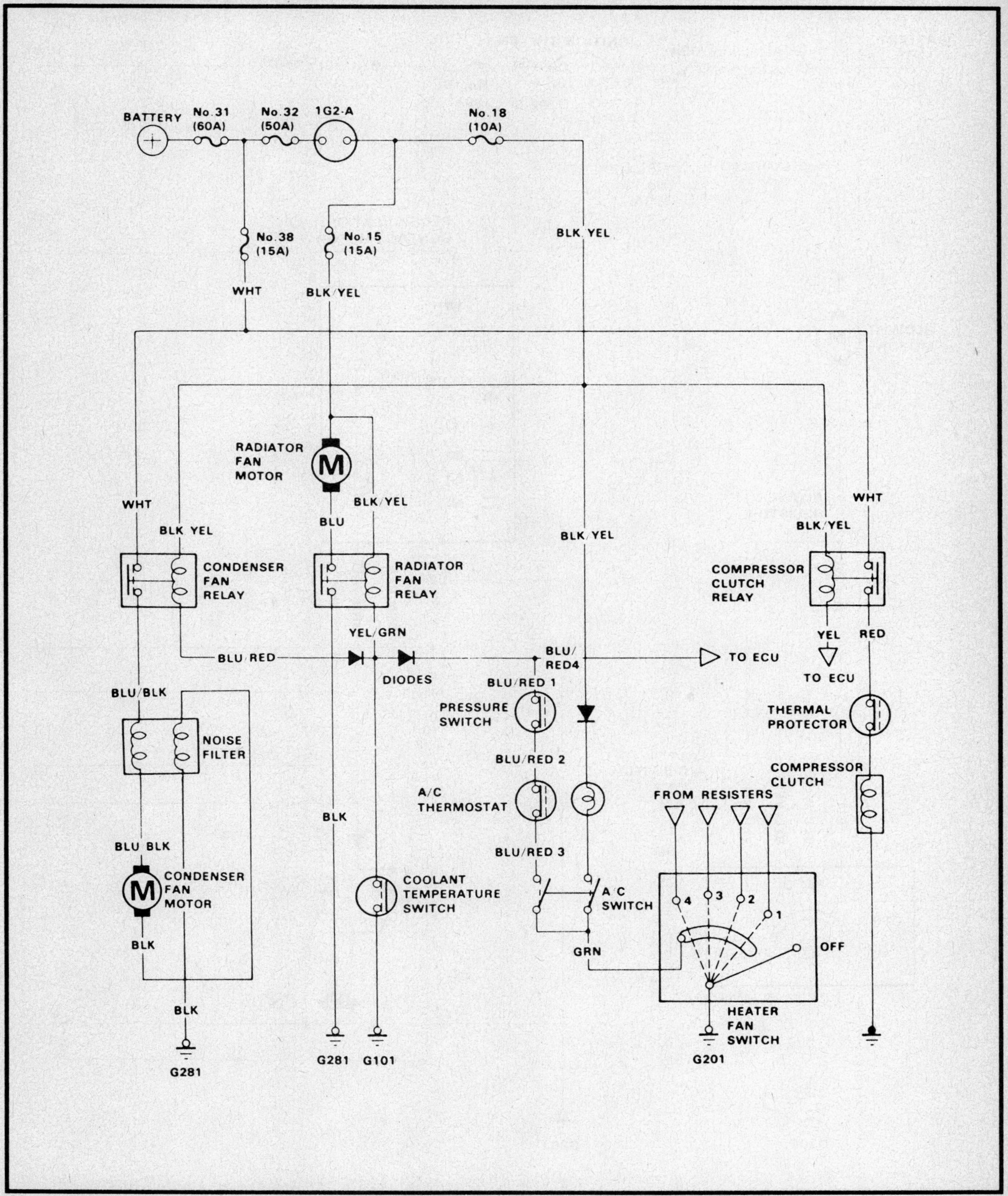
BATTERY
No.31 (60A)
No.32 (50A)
1G2-A
No.18 (10A)
No.38 (15A)
No.15 (15A)
BLK/YEL
WHT
BLK/YEL
RADIATOR FAN MOTOR
BLK/YEL
WHT
BLK/YEL
BLU
BLK/YEL
WHT
BLK/YEL
CONDENSER FAN RELAY
RADIATOR FAN RELAY
COMPRESSOR CLUTCH RELAY
YEL/GRN
BLU/RED
DIODES
BLU/RED4
TO ECU
YEL
RED
TO ECU
BLU/BLK
BLU/RED 1
PRESSURE SWITCH
THERMAL PROTECTOR
NOISE FILTER
BLU/RED 2
COMPRESSOR CLUTCH
A/C THERMOSTAT
FROM RESISTERS
BLK
BLU/BLK
BLU/RED 3
CONDENSER FAN MOTOR
COOLANT TEMPERATURE SWITCH
A/C SWITCH
4
3
2
1
OFF
BLK
GRN
BLK
HEATER FAN SWITCH
G281
G281
G101
G201

Air conditioner electrical schematic—Civic and CRX

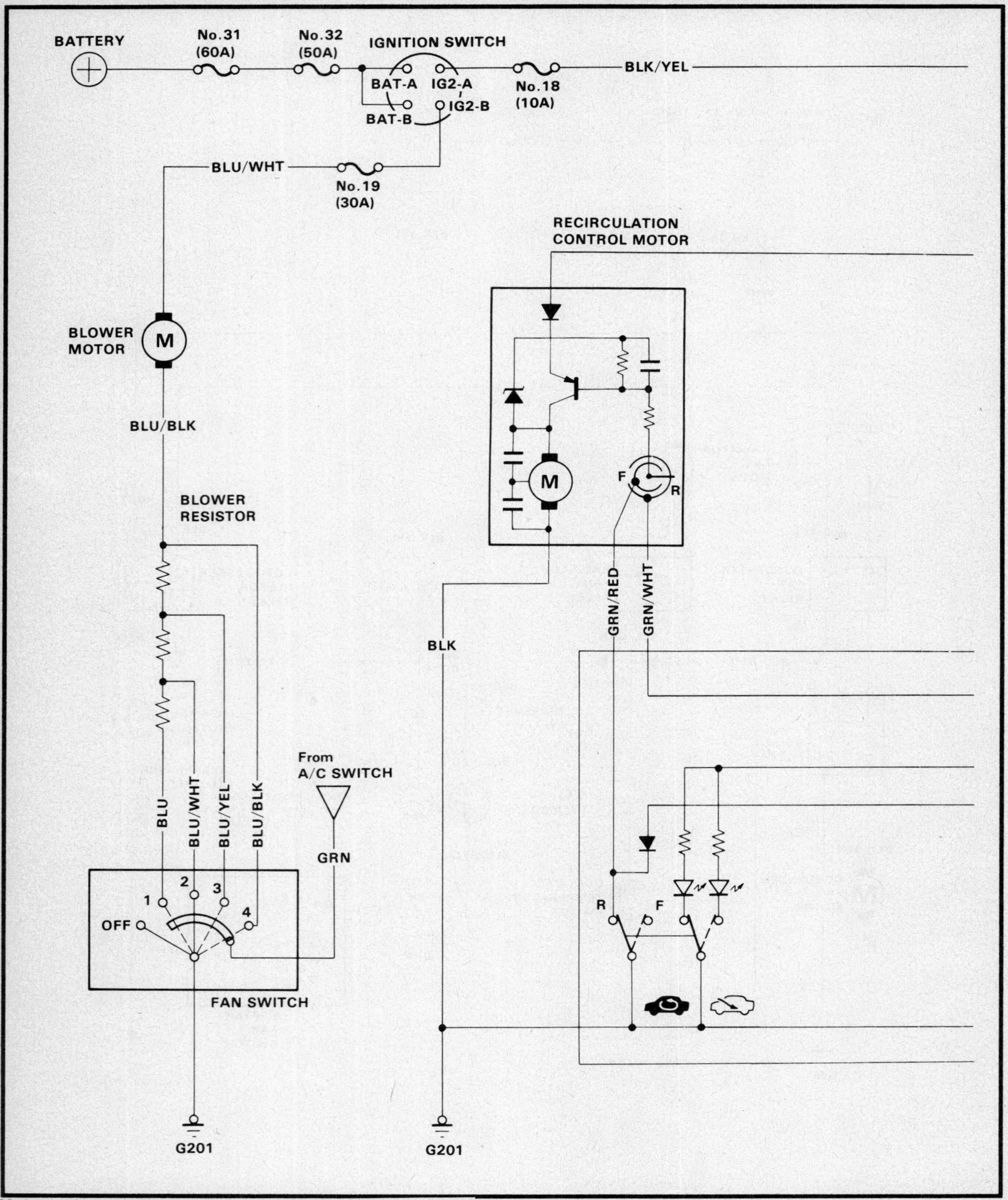
BATTERY
No.31
(60A)
No.32
(50A)
IGNITION SWITCH
BAT-A
IG2-A
BAT-B
IG2-B
No.18
(10A)
BLK/YEL
BLU/WHT
No.19
(30A)
RECIRCULATION
CONTROL MOTOR
BLOWER
MOTOR
M
BLU/BLK
F
R
BLOWER
RESISTOR
GRN/RED
GRN/WHT
BLK
From
A/C SWITCH
BLU
BLU/WHT
BLU/YEL
BLU/BLK
GRN
1
2
3
4
OFF
R
F
FAN SWITCH
G201
G201

Heater electrical schematic—Civic and CRX

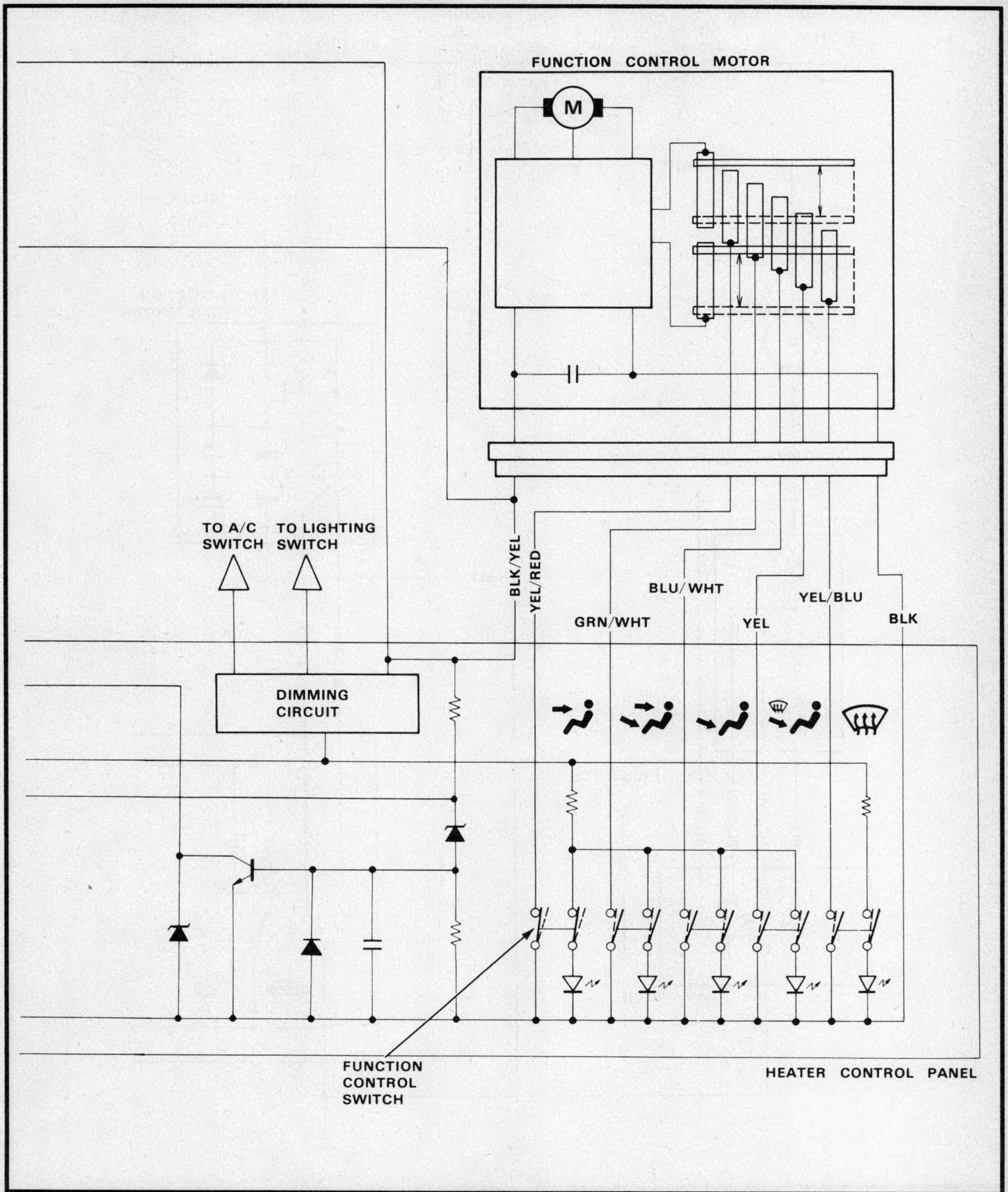
FUNCTION CONTROL MOTOR
M
TO A/C SWITCH
TO LIGHTING SWITCH
BLK/YEL
YEL/RED
BLU/WHT
YEL/BLU
GRN/WHT
YEL
BLK
DIMMING CIRCUIT
FUNCTION CONTROL SWITCH
HEATER CONTROL PANEL

Heater electrical schematic—Civic and CRX, continued

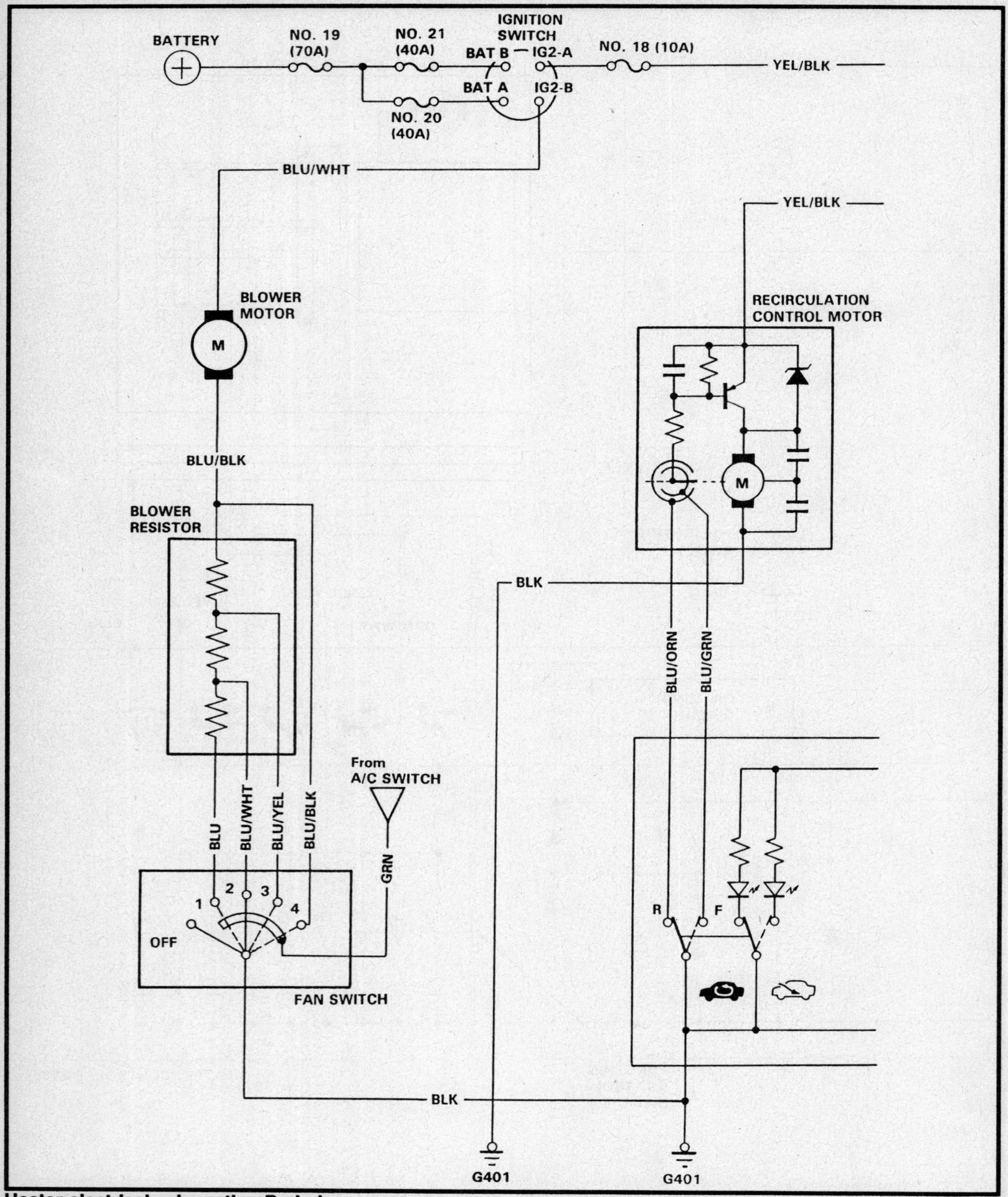
BATTERY
NO. 19 (70A)
NO. 21 (40A)
IGNITION SWITCH
BAT B
IG2-A
NO. 18 (10A)
YEL/BLK
BAT A
IG2-B
NO. 20 (40A)
BLU/WHT
YEL/BLK
BLOWER MOTOR
M
RECIRCULATION CONTROL MOTOR
M
BLU/BLK
BLOWER RESISTOR
BLK
BLU/ORN
BLU/GRN
From A/C SWITCH
BLU
BLU/WHT
BLU/YEL
BLU/BLK
GRN
1
2
3
4
OFF
FAN SWITCH
R
F
BLK
G401
G401

Heater electrical schematic—Prelude

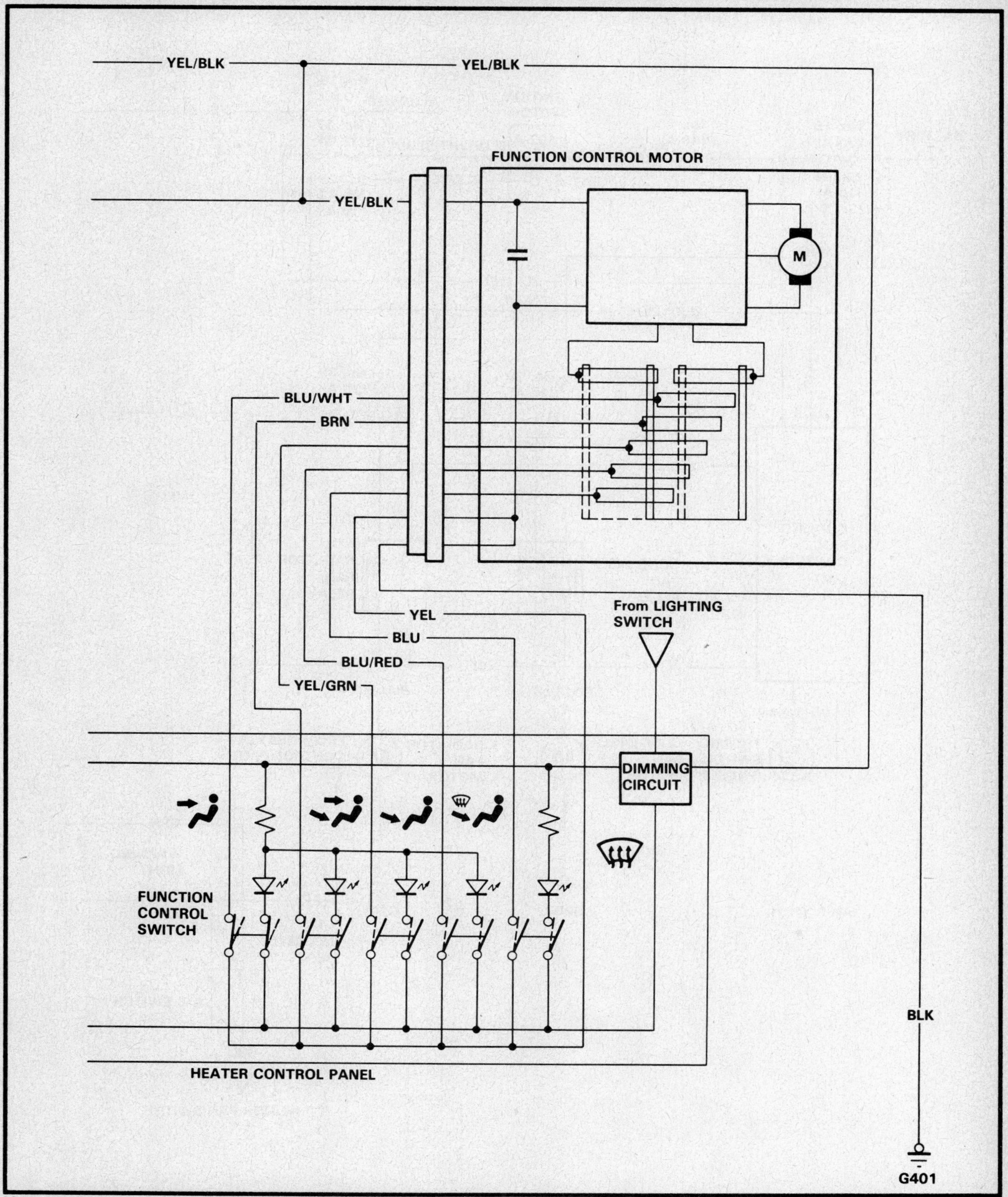
YEL/BLK
YEL/BLK
FUNCTION CONTROL MOTOR
YEL/BLK
M
BLU/WHT
BRN
YEL
BLU
BLU/RED
YEL/GRN
From LIGHTING SWITCH
DIMMING CIRCUIT
FUNCTION CONTROL SWITCH
BLK
HEATER CONTROL PANEL
G401

Heater electrical schematic—Prelude, continued

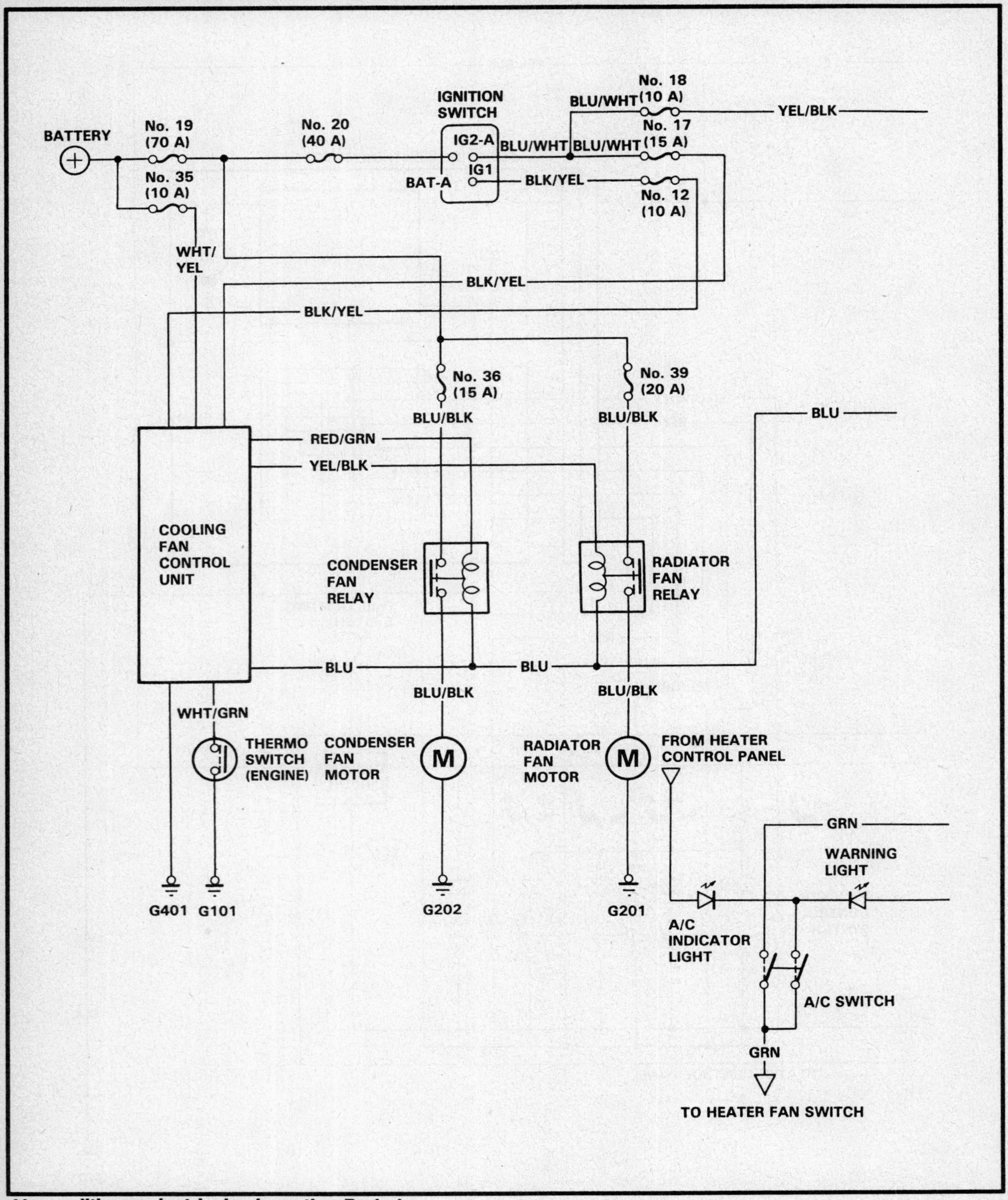
BATTERY
No. 19
(70 A)
No. 35
(10 A)
No. 20
(40 A)
IGNITION
SWITCH
IG2-A
IG1
BAT-A
BLU/WHT
No. 18
(10 A)
YEL/BLK
No. 17
(15 A)
BLK/YEL
No. 12
(10 A)
WHT/
YEL
BLK/YEL
BLK/YEL
No. 36
(15 A)
No. 39
(20 A)
BLU/BLK
BLU/BLK
BLU
RED/GRN
YEL/BLK
COOLING
FAN
CONTROL
UNIT
CONDENSER
FAN
RELAY
RADIATOR
FAN
RELAY
BLU
BLU
BLU/BLK
BLU/BLK
WHT/GRN
THERMO
SWITCH
(ENGINE)
CONDENSER
FAN
MOTOR
M
RADIATOR
FAN
MOTOR
M
FROM HEATER
CONTROL PANEL
GRN
WARNING
LIGHT
G401
G101
G202
G201
A/C
INDICATOR
LIGHT
A/C SWITCH
GRN
TO HEATER FAN SWITCH

Air conditioner electrical schematic—Prelude

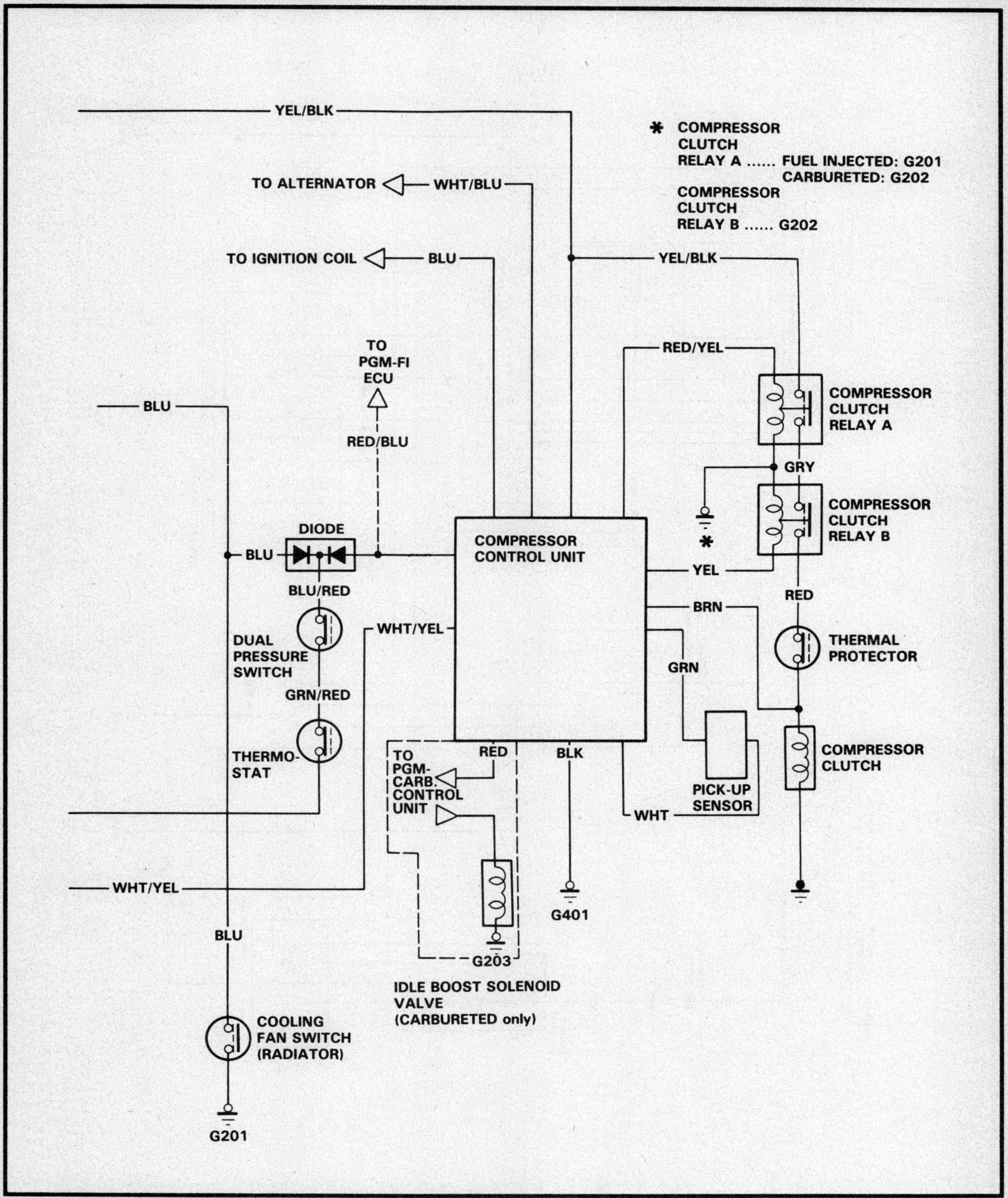
YEL/BLK
TO ALTERNATOR
WHT/BLU
TO IGNITION COIL
BLU
✱ COMPRESSOR CLUTCH RELAY A ...... FUEL INJECTED: G201
CARBURETED: G202
COMPRESSOR CLUTCH RELAY B G202
YEL/BLK
TO PGM-FI ECU
RED/BLU
RED/YEL
COMPRESSOR CLUTCH RELAY A
GRY
COMPRESSOR CLUTCH RELAY B
BLU
DIODE
BLU
COMPRESSOR CONTROL UNIT
YEL
BLU/RED
RED
BRN
DUAL PRESSURE SWITCH
WHT/YEL
THERMAL PROTECTOR
GRN
GRN/RED
THERMOSTAT
TO PGM-CARB. CONTROL UNIT
RED
BLK
COMPRESSOR CLUTCH
PICK-UP SENSOR
WHT
WHT/YEL
G401
BLU
G203
IDLE BOOST SOLENOID VALVE (CARBURETED only)
COOLING FAN SWITCH (RADIATOR)
G201

Air conditioner electrical schematic—Prelude, continued

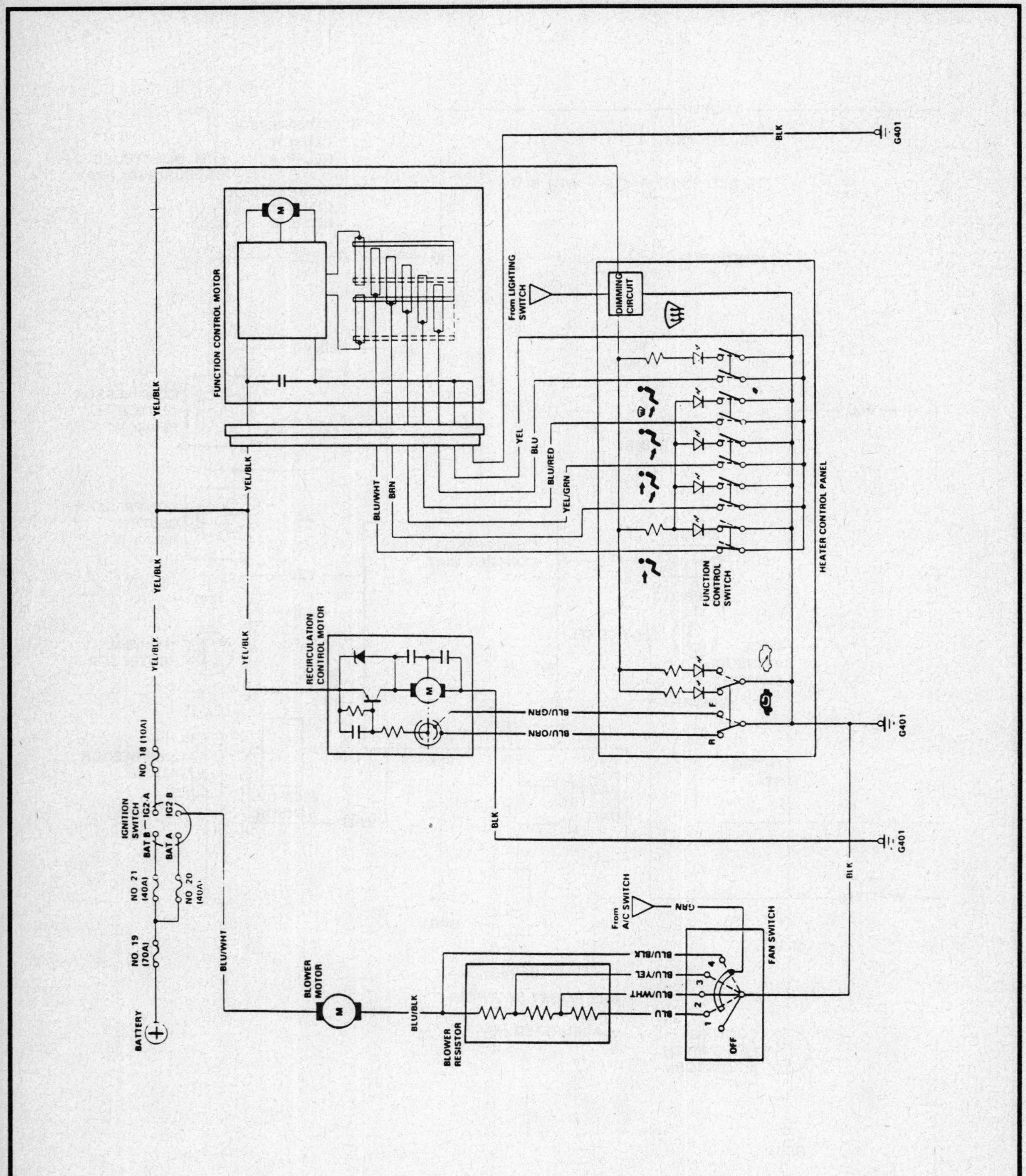
BLK
G401
FUNCTION CONTROL MOTOR
From LIGHTING SWITCH
DIMMING CIRCUIT
YEL/BLK
YEL
BLU
BLU/RED
YEL/GRN
BLU/WHT
BRN
HEATER CONTROL PANEL
FUNCTION CONTROL SWITCH
RECIRCULATION CONTROL MOTOR
BLU/GRN
BLU/ORN
F
R
NO. 18 (10A)
IGNITION SWITCH
BAT B
IG2 A
IG2 B
BAT A
NO. 21 (40A)
NO. 20 (40A)
NO. 19 (70A)
BATTERY
BLOWER MOTOR
BLU/BLK
BLOWER RESISTOR
From A/C SWITCH
GRN
FAN SWITCH
BLU/YEL
OFF
1
2
3
4

Heater system wiring diagram—Prelude

17 HYUNDAI 17

EXCEL • SCOUPE • SONATA

SPECIFICATIONS

ENGINE IDENTIFICATION

Year	Model	Engine Displacement cu. in. (cc/liter)	Engine Series Identification	No. of Cylinders	Engine Type
1989	Excel	89.6 (1468/1.5)	—	4	OHC
	Sonata	143.5 (2351/2.4)	—	4	OHC
	Sonata	181.4 (2972/3.0)	—	6	OHC
1990	Excel	89.6 (1468/1.5)	—	4	OHC
	Sonata	143.5 (2351/2.4)	—	4	OHC
1991	Excel	89.6 (1468/1.5)	—	4	OHC
	Scoupe	89.6 (1468/1.5)	—	4	OHC
	Sonata	143.5 (2351/2.4)	—	4	OHC
	Sonata	181.4 (2972/3.0)	—	6	OHC

REFRIGERANT CAPACITIES

Year	Model	Freon (oz.)	Oil (fl. oz.)	Type
1989	Excel	30–35	5.1	R-12
	Sonata	30–32	7.6	R-12
1990	Excel	28–30	8.1	R-12
	Sonata	30–32	7.6	R-12
1991	Excel	30–32	8.1	R-12
	Scoupe	30–32	8.1	R-12
	Sonata	30–32	7.6	R-12

AIR CONDITIONING BELT TENSION CHART

Year	Model	Engine Displacement cu. in. (cc/liter)	Belt Type	New ①	Used
1989	Excel	89.6 (1468/1.5)	Serpentine	0.32–0.40	0.31
	Sonata	143.5 (2351/2.4)	Serpentine	0.35–0.43	0.45
	Sonata	181.4 (2932/3.0)	Serpentine	0.18–0.22	0.45
1990	Excel	89.6 (1468/1.5)	Serpentine	0.18–0.22	0.24
	Sonata	89.6 (1468/1.5)	Serpentine	0.35–0.43	0.45
1991	Excel	89.6 (1468/1.5)	Serpentine	0.32–0.34	0.36
	Scoupe	89.6 (1468/1.5)	Serpentine	0.32–0.34	0.36
	Scoupe	143.5 (2351/2.4)	Serpentine	0.35–0.43	0.45
	Sonata	181.4 (2932/3.0)	Serpentine	0.18–0.22	0.24

① Inches of deflection at the midpoint of the belt, using 22 lbs. force.

SYSTEM DESCRIPTION

General Information

The air distribution system is centrally located in the dash. The blower motor assembly is positioned on the passengers side and is connected by a series of air ducts.

The air distribution system directs fresh air from the outside or inside recirculated air, by the use of air mixture dampers. These dampers are located within the air mixture chamber and control the amount of air passing through the heating and air conditioning systems. The air is then mix accordingly and conducted to the various outlets. The air damper doors are opened and closed by manual control cables or vacuum actuated devices. The system operates as follows:

Door D1 is used to select either fresh air from the outside or to distribute recirculated air through the passenger compartment. If the Recirc/Fresh control lever is moved to the **FRESH** position, air from the outside will be allowed to enter the passenger compartment. If the control lever is moved to the **RECIRC** position, inside air will be allowed to recirculate.

Door D2 is always open and functions to admit recirculated air regardless of the position of door D1.

Outlet air flow is controlled by doors D4, D5 and D6. The mode control lever opens and shuts the doors to establish the desired air flow. If the mode control lever is moved to the **VENT** position, air flows from the ventilator outlets. If the mode control lever is moved to the **BI-LEVEL** position, air flows to the ventilator, floor and defroster outlets. By moving the lever to the **HEAT** position, air flows to the floor and defroster outlets. If the the **DEF** position is selected, air flows to the defroster outlets.

Cooling or heating temperature is controlled by door D3. This door is connected to the temperature control lever by a cable. The water valve is also connected to the temperature control lever by a cable.

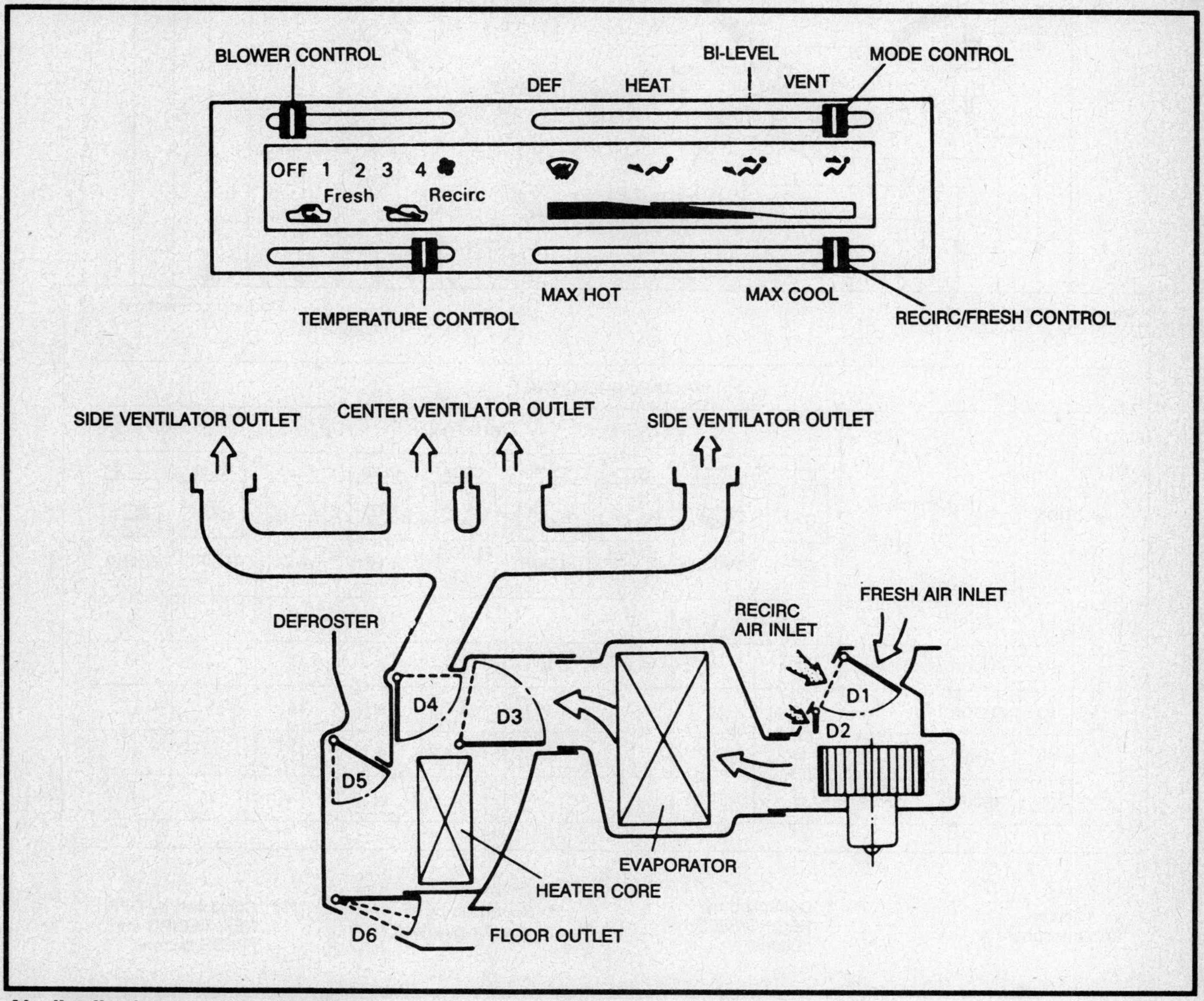
BLOWER CONTROL
BI-LEVEL
MODE CONTROL
DEF
HEAT
VENT
OFF 1 2 3 4
Fresh
Recirc
MAX HOT
MAX COOL
TEMPERATURE CONTROL
RECIRC/FRESH CONTROL
SIDE VENTILATOR OUTLET
CENTER VENTILATOR OUTLET
SIDE VENTILATOR OUTLET
DEFROSTER
FRESH AIR INLET
RECIRC AIR INLET
D1
D2
D3
D4
D5
D6
EVAPORATOR
HEATER CORE
FLOOR OUTLET

Air distribution system–1989 Excel

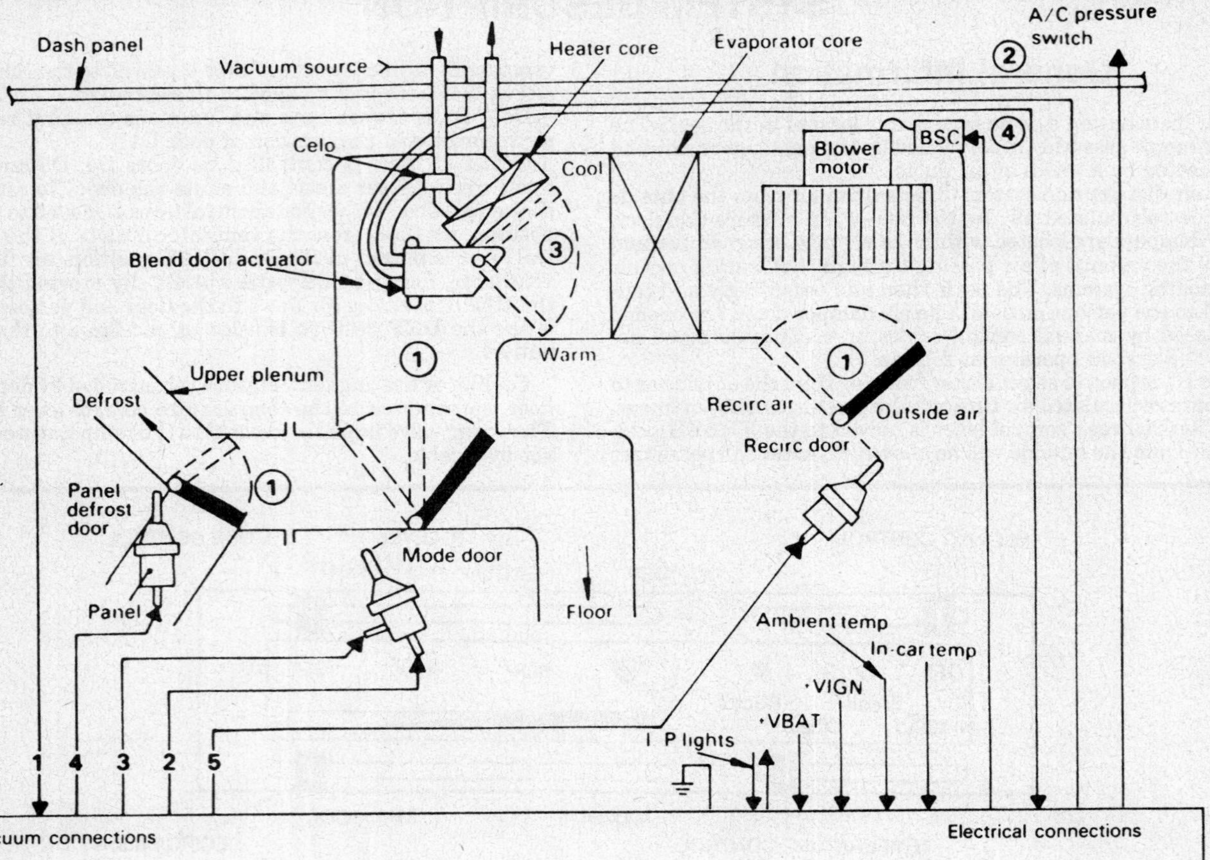
Dash panel
Vacuum source
Heater core
Evaporator core
A/C pressure switch
2
Celo
Cool
Blower motor
BSC
4
Blend door actuator
3
1
Warm
Upper plenum
Defrost
Panel defrost door
1
Panel
Mode door
Floor
Recirc air
Outside air
Recirc door
Ambient temp
In-car temp
VIGN
VBAT
I. P lights
1
4
3
2
5
Vacuum connections
Electrical connections

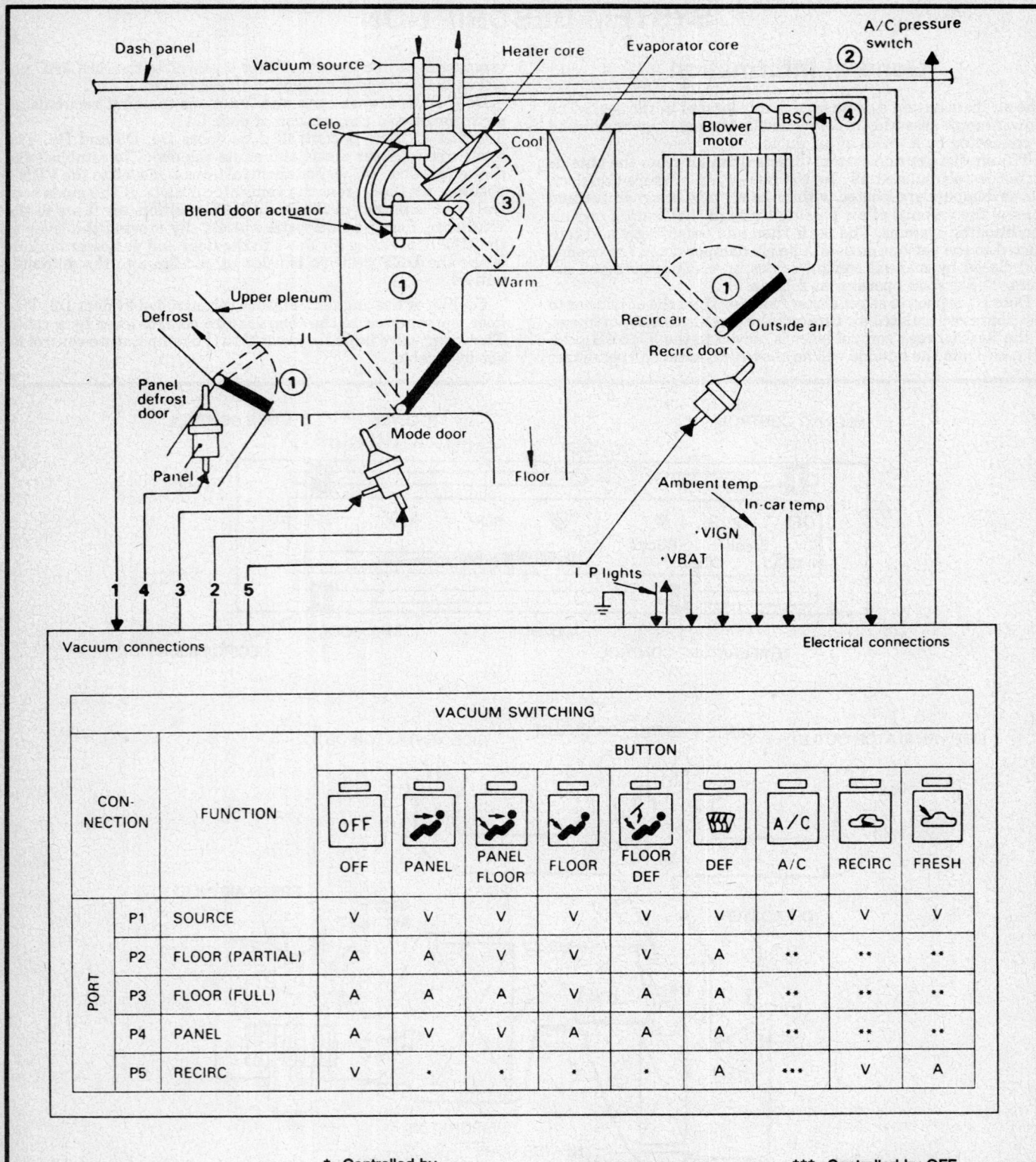

VACUUM SWITCHING

CONNECTION		FUNCTION	OFF	PANEL	PANEL FLOOR	FLOOR	FLOOR DEF	DEF	A/C	RECIRC	FRESH
PORT	P1	SOURCE	V	V	V	V	V	V	V	V	V
	P2	FLOOR (PARTIAL)	A	A	V	V	V	A	**	**	**
	P3	FLOOR (FULL)	A	A	A	V	A	A	**	**	**
	P4	PANEL	A	V	V	A	A	A	**	**	**
	P5	RECIRC	V	*	*	*	*	A	***	V	A

V: Vacuum
A: Atmosphere

* Controlled by RECIRC/FRESH buttons

** Controlled by all selector positions

*** Controlled by OFF, DEF, RECIRC and FRESH buttons

Air distribution system–1989–90 Sonata, Canadian series

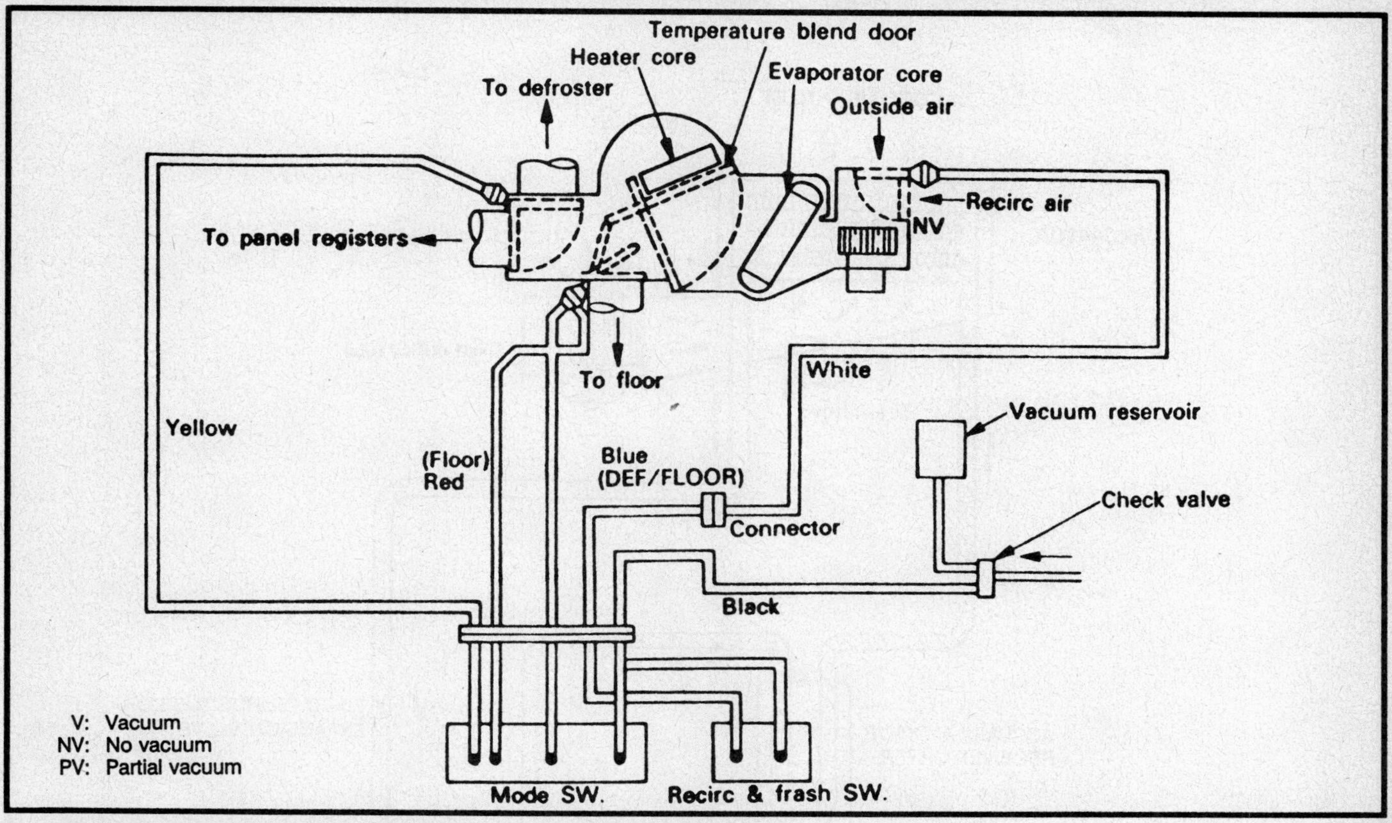
Temperature blend door
Heater core
To defroster
Evaporator core
Outside air
Recirc air
NV
To panel registers
To floor
White
Vacuum reservoir
Yellow
(Floor) Red
Blue (DEF/FLOOR)
Check valve
Connector
Black
V: Vacuum
NV: No vacuum
PV: Partial vacuum
Mode SW.
Recirc & frash SW.

Air distribution system–1990–91 Excel, Scoupe and 1991 Sonata

When the air conditioning switch is set to the **ON** position, it energizes the magnetic clutch on the compressor and the following components are used to control the air conditioning compressor operation by de-energizing the magnetic clutch when required:

1. The thermostat prevents ice build up on the evaporator fins.
2. The low pressure switch protects the compressor in excessive low freon charge condition.
3. The water temperature switch keeps the engine from overheating by sensing higher than normal engine operating temperatures.
4. An idle control system is used to maintain engine idle speed when the compressor magnetic clutch is energized.

Service Valve Location

Both high and low service valve ports are located directly at the rear of the compressor unit.

System Discharging

CAUTION

The pressurized refrigerant inside the system must be discharged prior to the replacement or repair of any air conditioning system components. When discharging the system always wear protective eye wear.

1. Attach the low and high gauge hose of the manifold gauge set to the low side and high side service fittings on the compressor or refrigerant lines.
2. Place the free end of the center hose in a shop towel or suitable container.

NOTE: Do not allow the refrigerant to rush out, as the compressor oil will be discharged along with the refrigerant.

3. Slowly open the compressor discharge and suction line pressure valves and allow the refrigerant to escape into the shop towel or container.
4. Periodically check the shop towel or container to make certain that no oil is being discharged from the system.
5. When the high pressure gauge reading drops below 50 psi, slowly open the low pressure manifold to obtain a maximum discharge of refrigerant without the loss of oil.
6. As the system pressure drops, slowly open both manifold gauges until the pressure drops to 0.
7. Disconnect the manifold gauge set and cap the service fittings to prevent the entry of moisture.

System Evacuating

Whenever the system has been opened to the atmosphere, it is absolutely necessary that the system be evacuated to remove the air and moisture from the system. Air in the refrigerant system will cause a loss in the systems performance, a high compressor discharge pressure and oxidation of the compressor oil into gum or varnish. Moisture in the system will cause the expansion valve to malfunction.

After a new component is installed, the system should be evacuated for a minimum of 15 minutes. If an in-service component was opened for repair, evacuate the system for 30 minutes.

1. Connect the manifold gauge set to the compressor or refrigerant lines and a long test hose from the gauge set manifold center connection to a vacuum pump. This should be done with the engine not running.

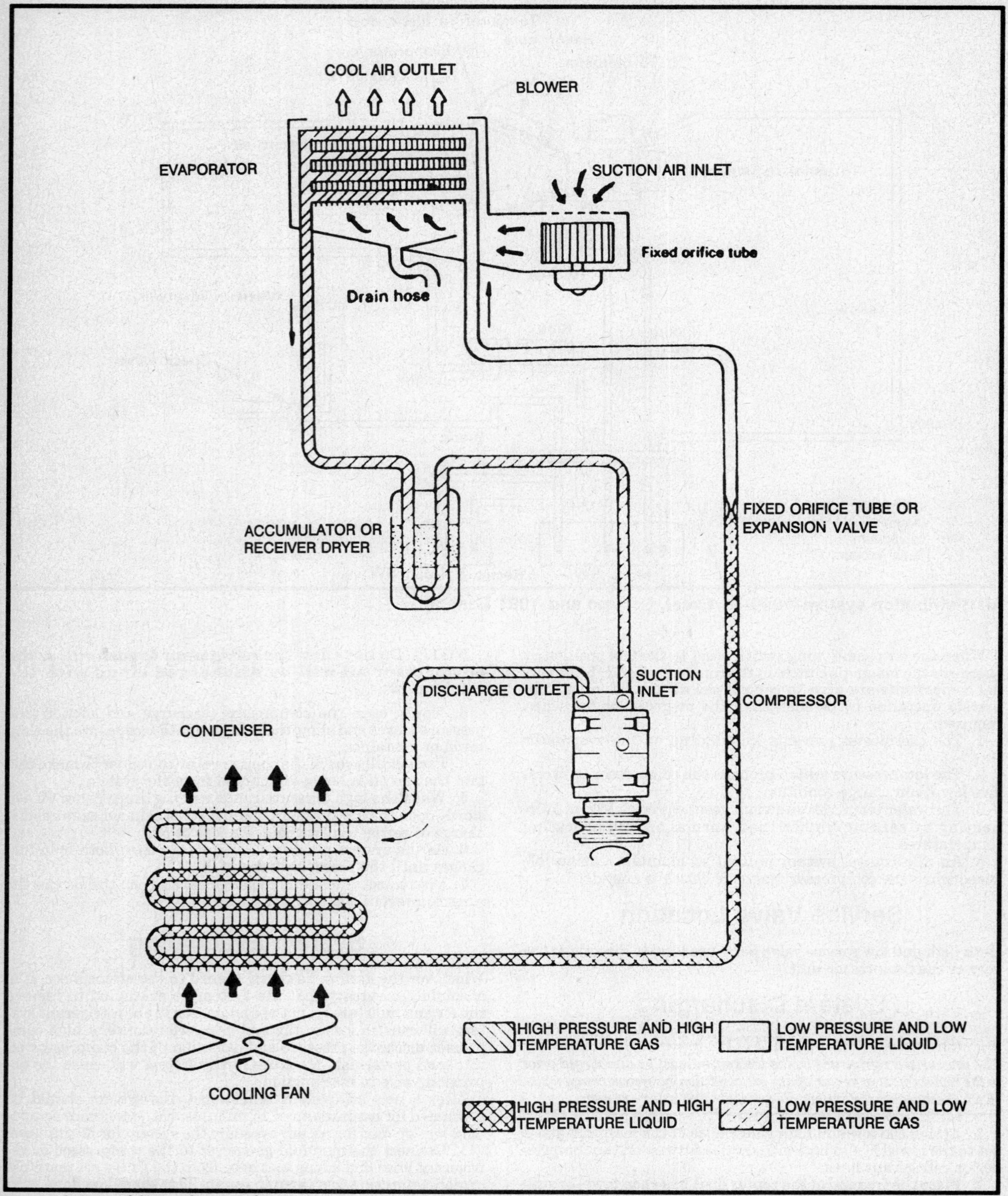
COOL AIR OUTLET
BLOWER
EVAPORATOR
SUCTION AIR INLET
Fixed orifice tube
Drain hose
ACCUMULATOR OR
RECEIVER DRYER
FIXED ORIFICE TUBE OR
EXPANSION VALVE
SUCTION
INLET
DISCHARGE OUTLET
COMPRESSOR
CONDENSER
COOLING FAN
HIGH PRESSURE AND HIGH
TEMPERATURE GAS
LOW PRESSURE AND LOW
TEMPERATURE LIQUID
HIGH PRESSURE AND HIGH
TEMPERATURE LIQUID
LOW PRESSURE AND LOW
TEMPERATURE GAS

View of the refrigeration cycle

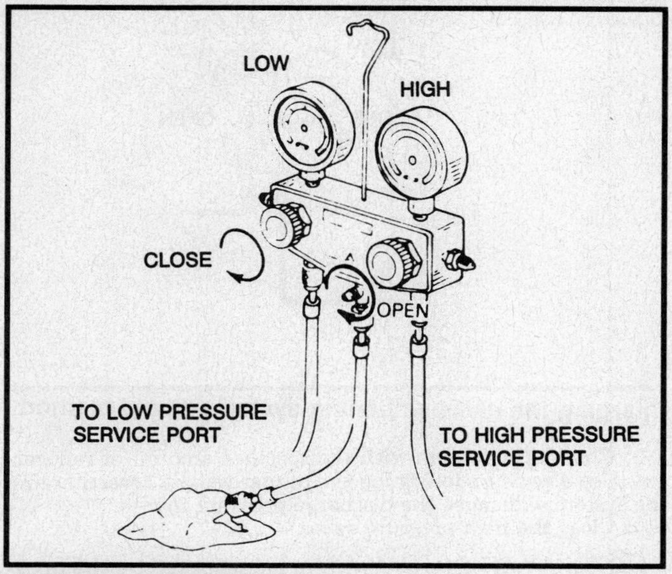
LOW
HIGH
CLOSE
OPEN
TO LOW PRESSURE SERVICE PORT
TO HIGH PRESSURE SERVICE PORT

Discharging the system

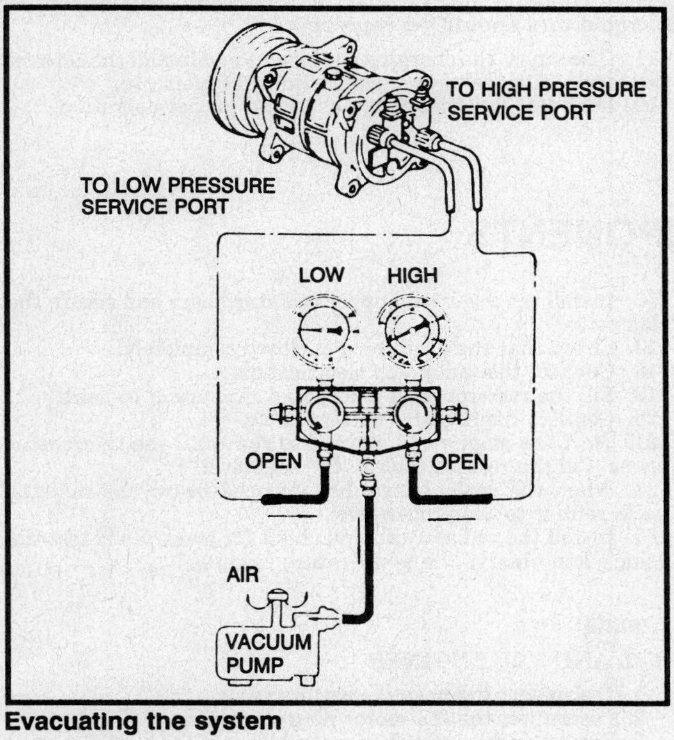
TO HIGH PRESSURE SERVICE PORT
TO LOW PRESSURE SERVICE PORT
LOW
HIGH
OPEN
OPEN
AIR
VACUUM PUMP

Evacuating the system

2. Close both manifold gauge set valves.
3. Start the vacuum pump and then open the high and low manifold pressure valves.
4. After 10 minutes, check that the low pressure gauge reads more than 37.7 in. Hg of vacuum. If the pressure rises or a vacuum cannot be obtained, there is a leak in the system. If a leak is suspected, stop the pump, charge the system with a 1 lb. can of refrigerant and check for leaks with a suitable leak dectector. Repair any leaks in the system and discharge and evacuate the system.
5. If no leaks are found, continue operation of the vacuum pump.
6. Open both manifold valves to obtain as close to a vacuum of 37.7 in. Hg as possible. After the low pressure gauge reads approximately 37.7 in. Hg, continue evacuating the system for 15 min., 30 for in-service repairs.
7. After the system has been evacuated for 15 or 30 minutes, close both manifold gauge valves and stop the vacuum pump.
8. Disconnect the hose from the vacuum pump and charge the system.

System Charging

VAPOR CHARGE

NOTE: Use this procedure to charge air conditioning systems that are either empty or are known to have partial charges. With the vapor charge, the system is charged through the low pressure side with refrigerant in a vapor state by placing the refrigerant canister right side up.

1. Before installing the tap valve on the refrigerant container, turn the valve handle counterclockwise until the valve needle is fully retracted.
2. Turn the tap valve disc counterclockwise until it is at its highest position and screw down the valve onto the refrigerant container.
3. Connect the center hose to the valve fitting and tighten the disc fully.
4. Turn tap handle fully counterclockwise to fill the center hose with gas. Do not open the high and low pressure valves.
5. Slightly loosen the flare nut at the gauge manifold to expel air and refrigerant from the charging hose. Tighten the flare nut immediately after the expelling air.
6. Open the low pressure valve. Adjust the valve so the low pressure gauge reading is not higher than 60 psi.
7. Place the refrigerant container in a pan of warm water, no more than 104°F, to keep the vapor pressure in the container slightly higher that the system pressure.
8. Run the engine at fast idle and operate the air conditioning system.
9. Hold the service can upright and loosen the low-pressure valve of the gauge manifold so the gaseous refrigerant will be drawn into the equipment.

NOTE: Keep the refrigerant container upright to prevent liquid refrigerant from being charged into the system (liquid floodback) through the suction side and damaging the compressor.

10. Charge the system with the specified amount of refrigerant, then close the low pressure valve. No bubbles in the receiver sight glass indicates a fully charged system.

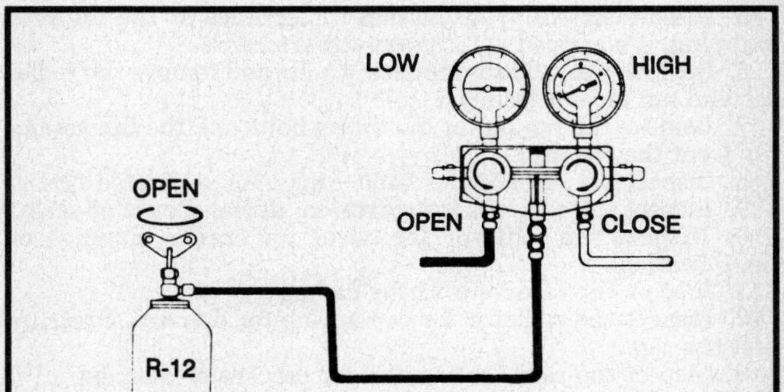
LOW
HIGH
OPEN
OPEN
CLOSE
R-12

Charging the air conditioning system—vapor method

LIQUID CHARGE

NOTE: Use this procedure to charge air conditioning systems that are empty. With the liquid charge, the system is charged through the high pressure side with refrigerant in a liquid state by holding the refrigerant canister upside down.

CAUTION

Never run the engine when charging the system through the high pressure side. Do not open the low pressure valve when charging the system with liquid refrigerant. This could admit high pressure into the low pressure side and cause the low pressure line or gauge to rupture, thus resulting in the possiblity of personal injury.

1. Evacuate the air conditioning system.
2. Close the high and low pressure manifold gauge valves.
3. Turn the tap valve handle counterclockwise until the valve needle is fully retracted.
4. Turn the tap valve disc counterclockwise until it is at its highest position and screw down the valve onto the refrigerant container.
5. Connect the center hose to the valve fitting and tighten the disc fully.
6. Turn tap handle fully counterclockwise to fill the center hose with gas. Do not open the high and low pressure valves.
7. Slightly loosen the flare nut at the gauge manifold to expel air, from inside the charging hose, with the refrigerant and tighten the flare nut immediately after the expelling air.
8. Fully open the high pressure valve and turn the refrigerant can upside down.

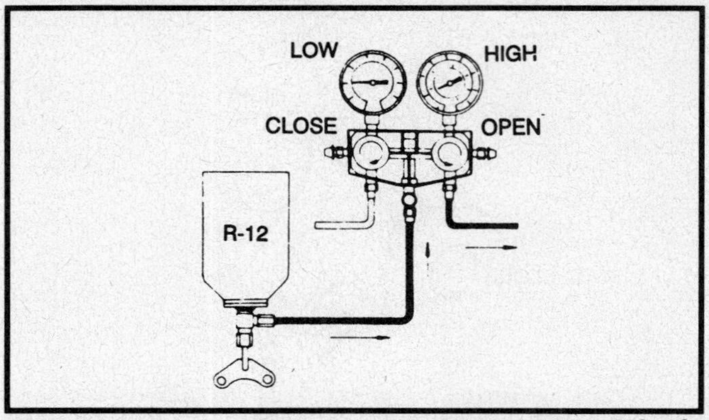
LOW
HIGH
CLOSE
OPEN
R-12

Charging the air conditioning system—liquid method

9. Charge the system with the specified amount of refrigerant. Use a scale to determine the proper weight. Overcharging the system will cause the discharge pressure to rise.
10. Close the high pressure valve.

NOTE: A fully charged system is indicated by the presence of bubbles in the receiver sight glass. If the low pressure gauge does not show a reading, the system is clogged and should be repaired.

11. Disconnect the charging equipment and install the caps on the service fittings to prevent the entry of moisture.
12. Leak test the system and check for proper operation.

SYSTEM COMPONENTS

Radiator

REMOVAL AND INSTALLATION

Excel and Scoupe

1.5L ENGINE

1. Disconnect the negative battery cable.
2. Disconnect the fan motor plug connection.
3. Set the warm water flow control lever of the heater control to the **HOT** position.
4. Remove the radiator drain plug and drain the radiator coolant.
5. Disconnect the transmission cooler lines at the radiator and plug, if equipped with automatic transaxle.
6. Remove the radiator mounting bolts and remove the radiator and fan as an assembly.
7. Remove the fan motor mounting bolts and the fan assembly from the radiator.
8. Inspect the radiator for bent, broken or restricted fins.
9. Inspect the radiator for corrosion, damage, rust or scale.
10. Inspect the radiator for hoses for cracks, damage or deterioration.
11. Inspect the reserve tank for damage.
12. Inspect the radiator for cap spring for damage. Pressure test the cap.
13. Inspect the radiator cap seal for crackes or damage.

To install:

14. Assemble the radiator fan assembly to the radiator.
15. Carefully install the radiator and fan assembly in place, to the radiator support. Install the mounting bolts.
16. Install the lower and upper radiator hoses and secure the clamps.
17. Check that the drain plug is closed completely.
18. Connect the fan motor electrical plug.
19. Fill the radiator with a approved mixture of coolant.
20. Connect the negative battery cable.
21. Start the engine and allow it to run until the thermostat opens. Fill the reserve tank to the cold level.
22. When the coolant level has dropped below the radiator neck, refill it to the proper level.
23. Install the radiator cap and check for leaks. Road test the vehicle and observe the temperature reading.

Sonata

2.4L AND 3.0L ENGINES

1. Disconnect the negative battery cable.
2. Disconnect the fan motor plug connection.
3. Set the warm water flow control lever of the heater control to the hot position.
4. Remove the radiator drain plug and drain the radiator coolant.
5. Disconnect the transmission cooler lines at the radiator and plug, if equipped with automatic transaxle.
6. Remove the radiator mounting bolts and remove the radiator and fan as an assembly.
7. Remove the fan motor mounting bolts and the fan assembly from the radiator.
8. Inspect the radiator for bent, broken or restricted fins.
9. Inspect the radiator for corrosion, damage, rust or scale.
10. Inspect the radiator for hoses for cracks, damage or deterioration.

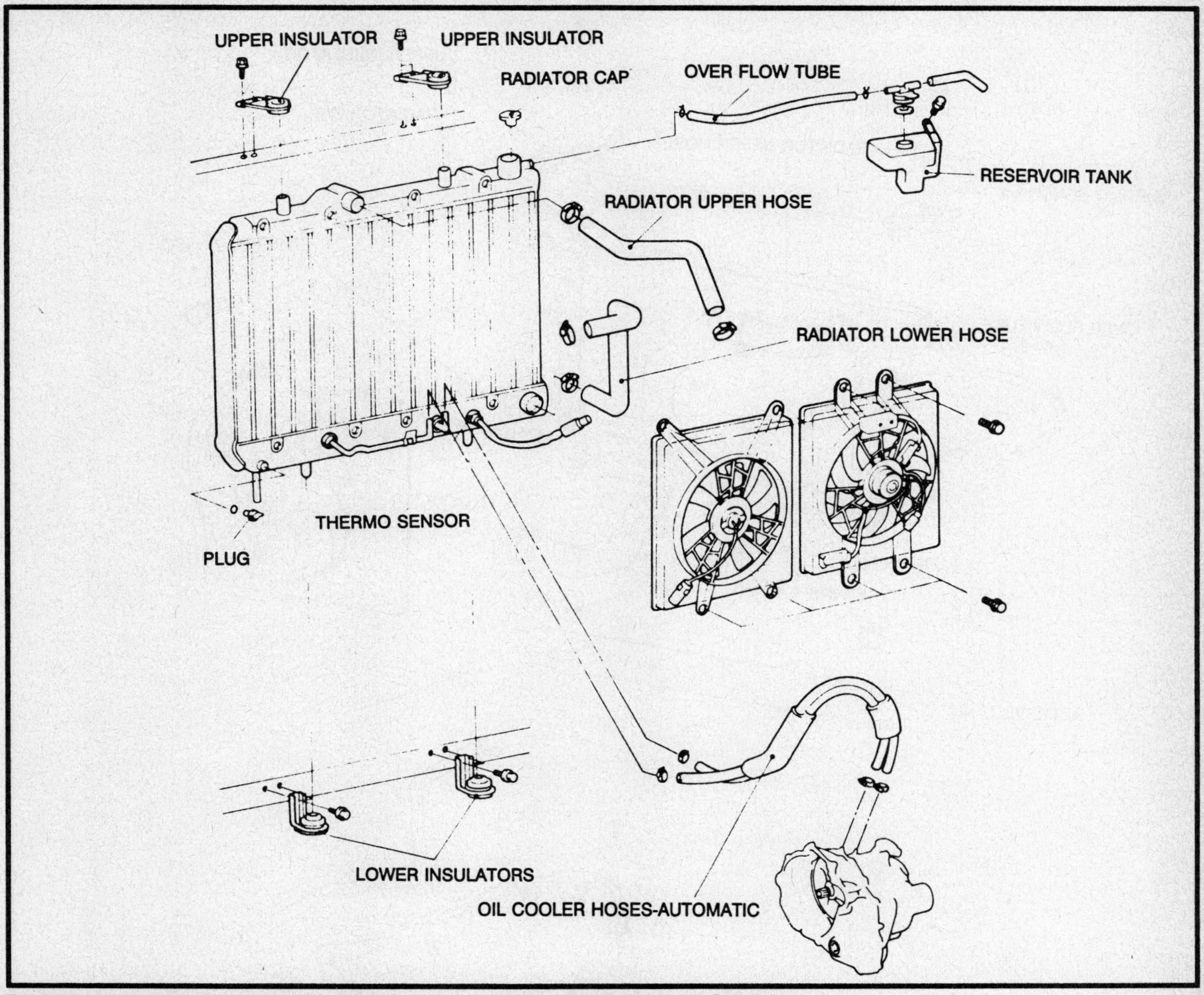
UPPER INSULATOR
UPPER INSULATOR
RADIATOR CAP
OVER FLOW TUBE
RESERVOIR TANK
RADIATOR UPPER HOSE
RADIATOR LOWER HOSE
THERMO SENSOR
PLUG
LOWER INSULATORS
OIL COOLER HOSES-AUTOMATIC

Exploded view of the radiator and related components–Excel and Scoupe

11. Inspect the reserve tank for damage.
12. Inspect the radiator for cap spring for damage. Pressure test the cap.
13. Inspect the radiator cap seal for cracks or damage.

To install:

14. Assemble the radiator fan assembly to the radiator.
15. Carefully install the radiator and fan assembly in place, to the radiator support. Install the mounting bolts.
16. Install the lower and upper radiator hoses and secure the clamps.
17. Check that the drain plug is closed completely.
18. Connect the fan motor electrical plug.
19. Fill the radiator with a approved mixture of coolant.
20. Connect the negative battery cable.
21. Start the engine and allow it to run until the thermostat opens. Fill the reserve tank to the cold level.
22. When the coolant level has dropped below the radiator neck, refill it to the proper level.
23. Install the radiator cap and check for leaks. Road test the vehicle and observe the temperature reading.

Cooling Fan

TESTING

1. Disconnect the negative battery cable.
2. Disconnect the cooling fan electrical connector.
3. Apply and 12 volt source between the positive an negative terminals of the fan motor connector. The fan should operate.

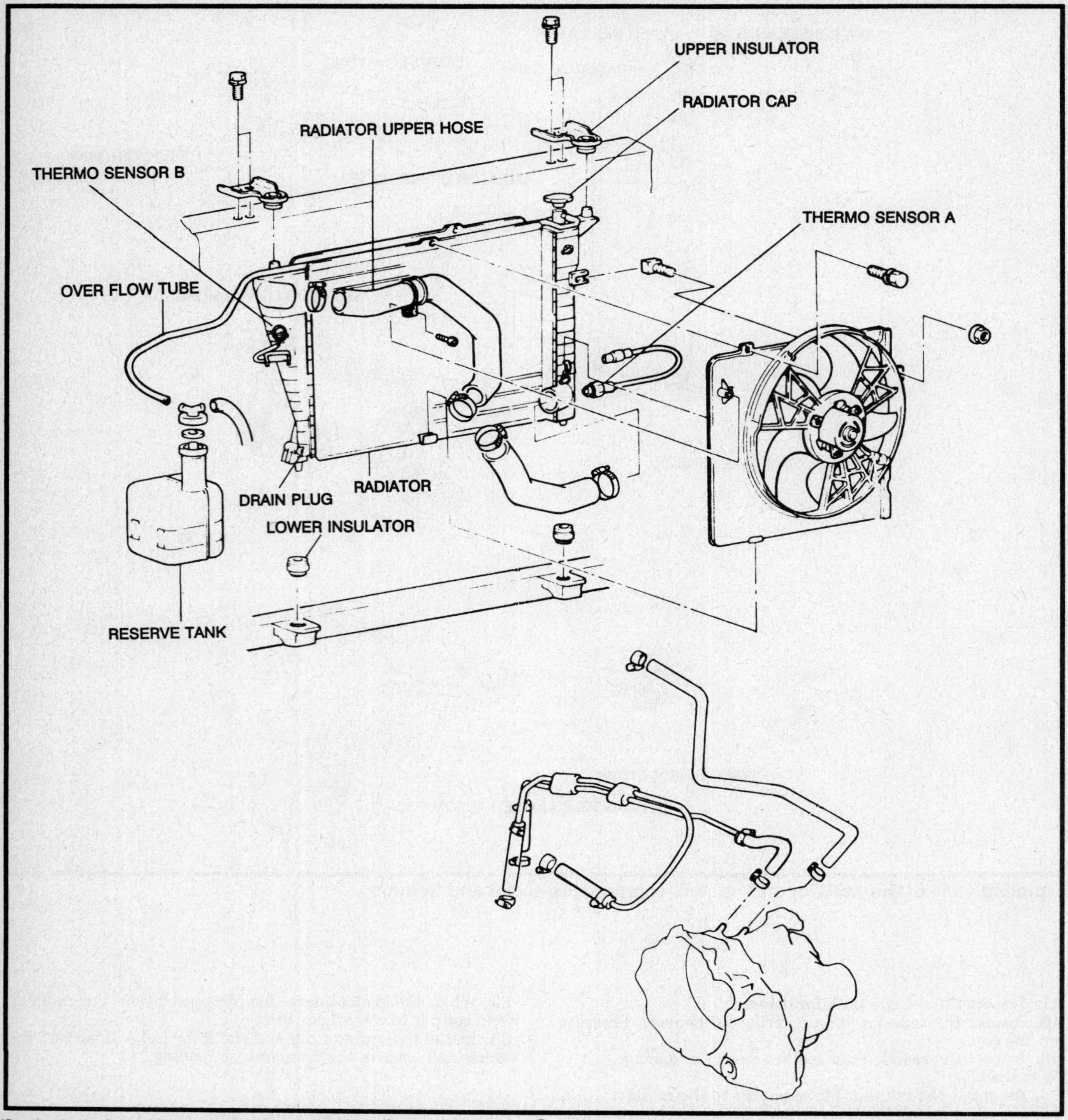
UPPER INSULATOR
RADIATOR CAP
RADIATOR UPPER HOSE
THERMO SENSOR B
THERMO SENSOR A
OVER FLOW TUBE
DRAIN PLUG
RADIATOR
LOWER INSULATOR
RESERVE TANK

Exploded view of the radiator and related components—Sonata

4. While the fan is in operation, take notice to any abnormal noises, vibrations or fan-to-shroud interference.
5. If the fan motor is inoperative, inspect the connector and harness leading from the fan motor, for damage.
6. If the fan motor checks good, test the thermo sensor.
7. Connect the negative battery cable.

REMOVAL AND INSTALLATION

1. Disconnect the negative battery cable.
2. Disconnect the connectors from the fan motor and remove the harness from the shroud.

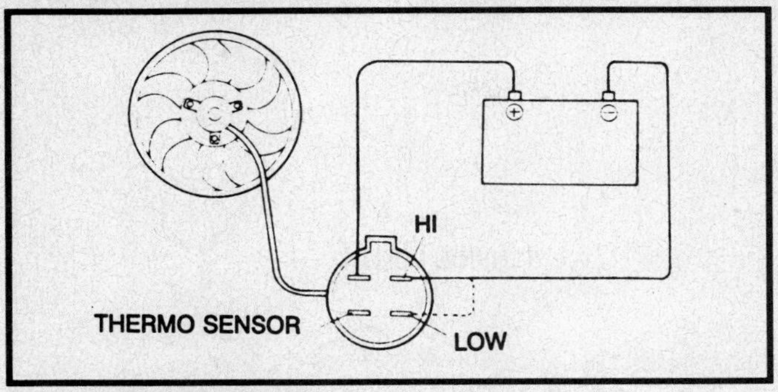
HI
THERMO SENSOR
LOW

Testing the cooling fan

3. Remove the shroud-to-radiator bolts and remove the shroud and fan motor as an assembly.
4. Remove the fan motor-to-shroud bolts and remove the detach the fan motor from the shroud.
5. Remove the fan-to-motor retaining clip and detach the fan from the motor.

To install:

6. Assemble the fan and motor together and secure with the retaining clip.
7. Assemble the fan motor assembly the shroud and secure in place with the retaining nuts.
8. Position the fan assembly in place to the radiator and install the mounting bolts.
9. Connect the fan motor connectors and secure the harness in place to the shroud.
10. Make sure the cooling fan does not come in contact with the shroud when it is installed.
11. Connect the negative battery cable and test the fan motor operation.

Condenser

REMOVAL AND INSTALLATION

1. Disconnect the negative battery cable.
2. Discharge the air conditioning system.
3. Drain the radiator coolant and remove the radiator and hoses.
4. Disconnect the discharge hose from the condenser inlet fitting.
5. Disconnect the liquid line from the pipe from the receiver/drier.
6. Remove the upper mounting bracket bolts and remove the condenser with the mounts.
7. Cap all fittings to prevent the entry of moisture. Remove the condenser from the vehicle.

To install:

8. Position the condenser and mounts onto the support member and install the mounting bracket bolts.
9. Connect the liquid line to the receiver/drier.
10. Connect the discharge hose to the condenser inlet fitting.
11. Install the radiator and hoses. Fill the cooling system.
12. If a new condenser was installed, add 1.6–1.8 oz. of clean compressor oil to the compressor.
13. Connect the negative battery cable.
14. Start the engine and recheck the radiator coolant level, top the level off, as required.
15. Evacuate, charge and test the air conditioning system.

COMPRESSOR

Removal and Installation

1. Disconect the negative battery cable and discharge the air conditioning system.

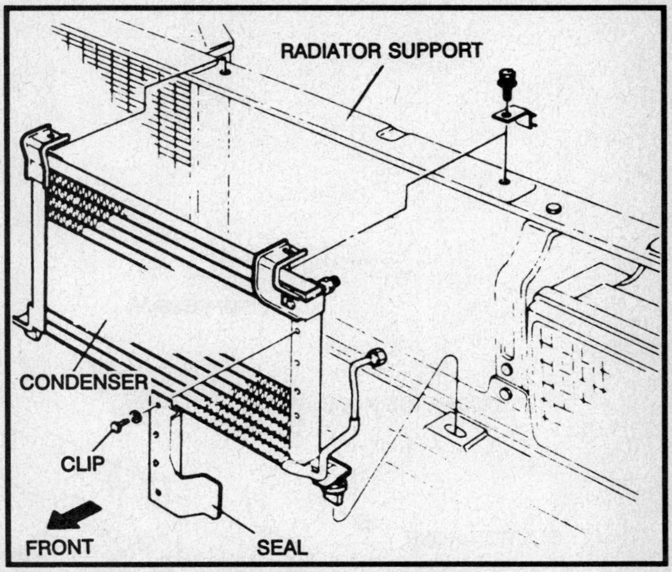
RADIATOR SUPPORT
CONDENSER
CLIP
FRONT
SEAL

Removal and installation of the condenser

2. Detach the high tension cable from the ignition coil and remove the distributor cap, air cleaner and air hose.
3. Loosen the tension pulley and remove the drive belt.
4. Remove the tension pulley from the bracket and disconnect the electrical harness from the magnetic clutch.
5. Remove the high and low pressure refrigerant lines.
6. Raise and support vehicle safely. From under the vehicle, remove the compressor with the magnetic clutch in the upright position. It may be necessary to loosen the engine mounting bracket bolts and raise the engine to remove the compressor.

To install:

7. A new compressor is filled with 5.1 oz. of oil and a charge of nitrogen gas. When mounting a new compressor, perform the following:
   a. Loosen the cap and carefully release the nitrogen gas from the discharge side of the compressor. Do not allow the oil to escape.
   b. Turn the compressor several times by hand to distribute the oil which has settled in the cylinder.
   c. When installing the compressor on a used system, adjust the oil level before installation.

NOTE: When attaching the compressor to the mounting bracket, make sure there is no clearance. Use adjusting shims as necessary to take up the clearance. Shims are available in sizes ranging from 0.008–0.012 in.

8. Position the compressor and magnetic clutch onto the engine mounting bracket and install the mounting bolts. Check that there is no clearance and adjust, as necessary.
9. Lower the vehicle.
10. Connect the high and low pressure refrigerant lines.
11. Connect the harness to the magnetic clutch and install the tension pulley.
12. Install the drive belt and adjust pulley tension.
13. Install the air cleaner, air cleaner hose, distributor cap and coil cable.
14. Evacuate, charge and leak test the system. Conect the negative battery cable.

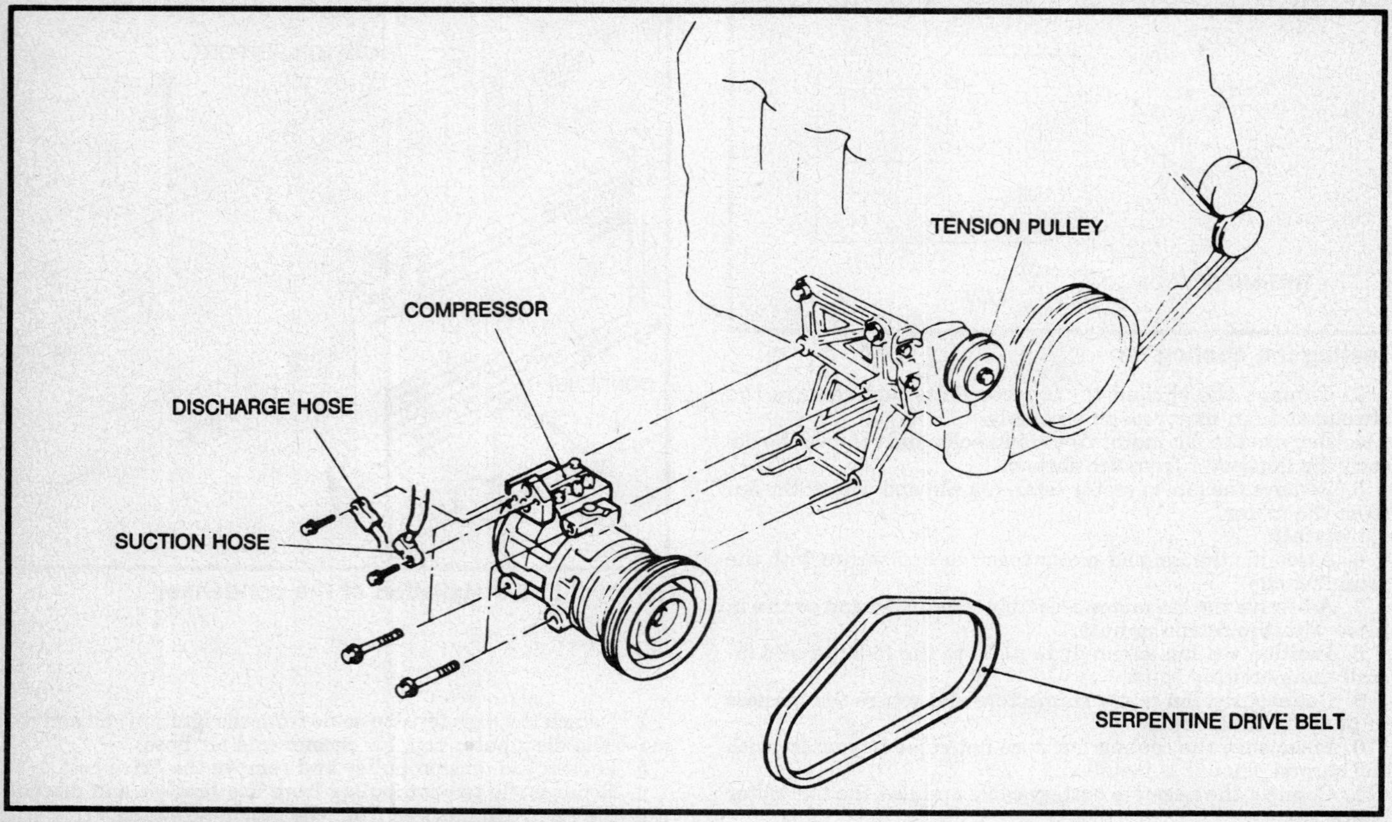
TENSION PULLEY
COMPRESSOR
DISCHARGE HOSE
SUCTION HOSE
SERPENTINE DRIVE BELT

Removal and installation of the compressor—typical

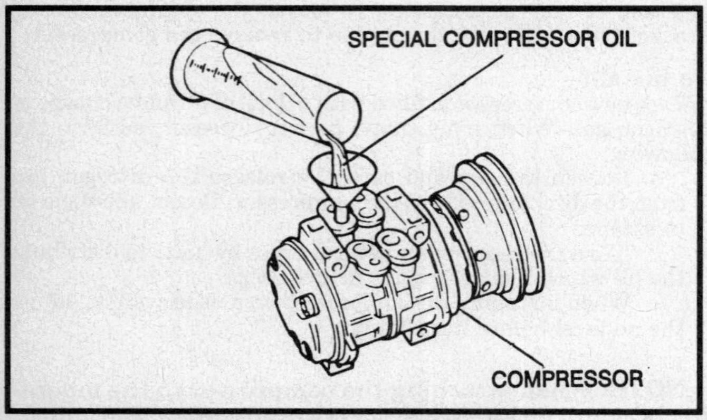
SPECIAL COMPRESSOR OIL
COMPRESSOR

Adding refrigerant oil to the compressor

Receiver/Drier

REMOVAL AND INSTALLATION

1989 Excel

1. Disconnect the negative battery cable.
2. Disconnect the pressure switch lead wire from the air conditioning harness.
3. Discharge the air conditioning system.
4. Disconnect the 2 liquid line tubes from the receiver/drier.

NOTE: Cap the open fittings to keep moisture out of the air conditioning system.

5. Loosen the bracket bolt and lift the receiver/drier from the mounting bracket.

To install:

6. Install the receiver/drier into the mounting bracket and tighten the bolt.
7. Connect the 2 liquid lines.
8. If the receiver/drier was replaced, add 1.8 oz. of refrigerant oil to the compressor.
9. Evacuate, charge and leak test the system.
10. Connect the negative battery cable.

Accumulator

REMOVAL AND INSTALLATION

1. Disconnect the negative battery cable.
2. Disconnect the pressure switch connector from the accumulator.
3. Discharge the air conditioning system.
4. Disconnect the 2 liquid line tubes from the accumulator.

NOTE: Cap the open fittings to keep moisture out of the air conditioning system.

5. Loosen the bracket bolt and lift the accumulator from the mounting bracket.

To install:

6. Install the accumulator into the mounting bracket and tighten the bolt.
7. Connect the 2 liquid lines.

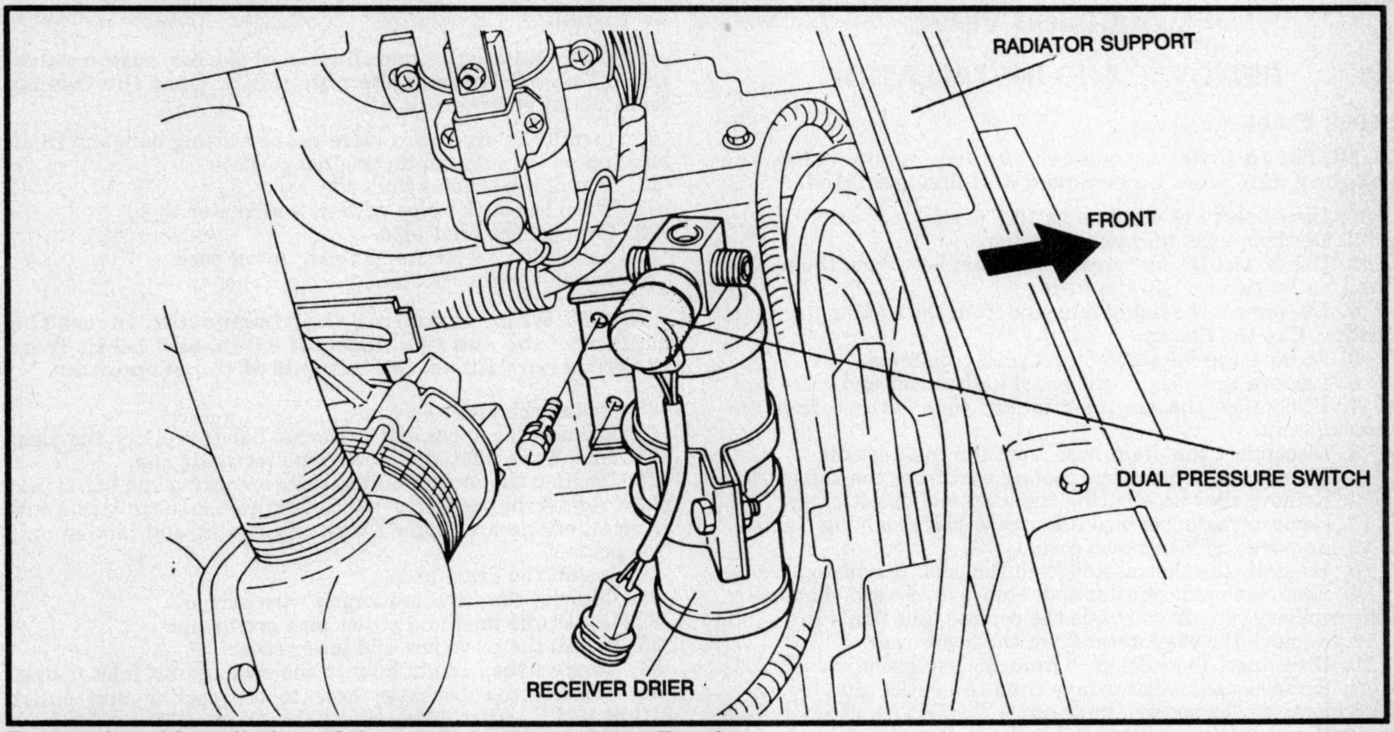
RADIATOR SUPPORT
FRONT
DUAL PRESSURE SWITCH
RECEIVER DRIER

Removal and installation of the receiver drier—1989 Excel

8. If the accumulator was replaced, add 1.8 oz. of refrigerant oil to the compressor.
9. Evacuate, charge and leak test the system.
10. Connect the negative battery cable.

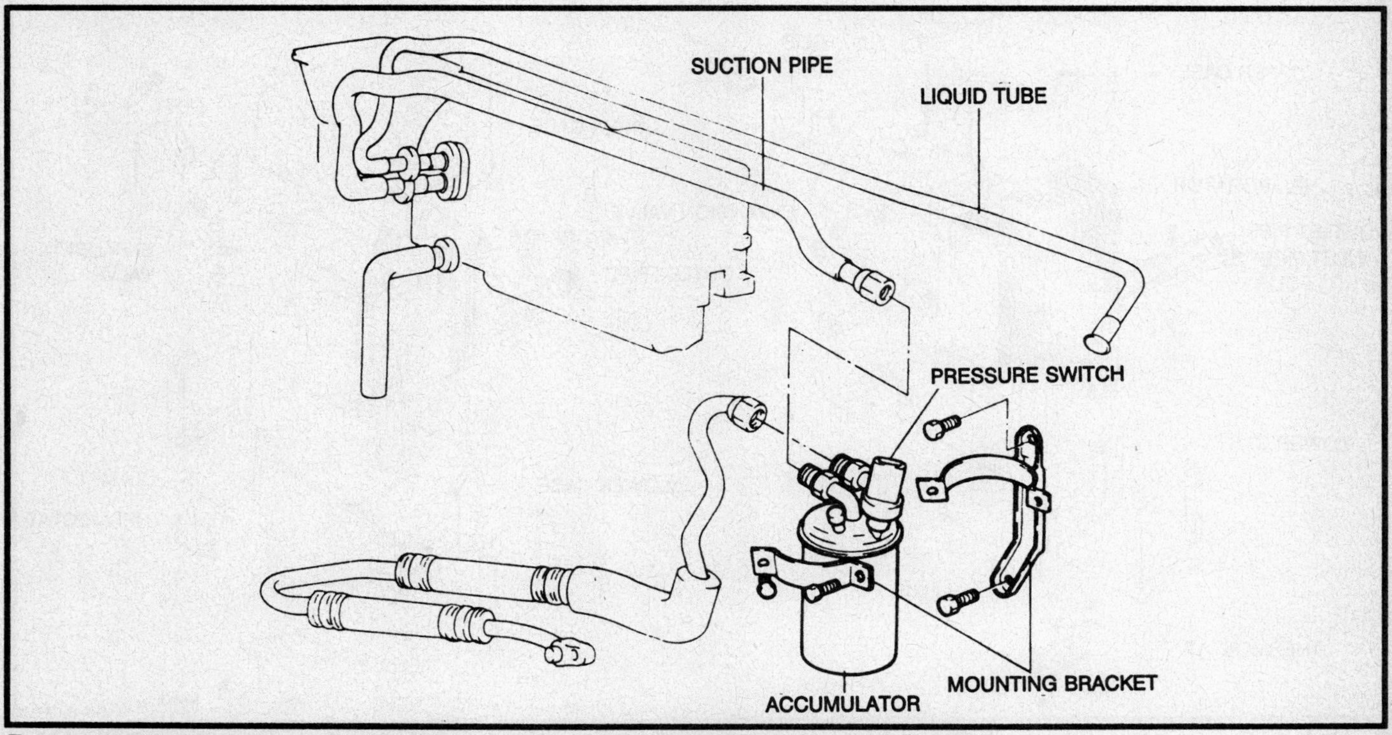
SUCTION PIPE
LIQUID TUBE
PRESSURE SWITCH
MOUNTING BRACKET
ACCUMULATOR

Removal and installation of the receiver/drier—1990 Excel, Scoupe and Sonata

Expansion Valve

REMOVAL AND INSTALLATION

1989 Excel

NOTE: In order to remove the expansion valve, the cooling unit must be removed and disassembled.

1. Disconnect the negative battery cable.
2. Discharge the refrigerant system.
3. Disconnect the low pressure suction hose from the cooling unit outlet fitting. Cap the fitting.
4. Disconnect the liquid line pipe from the cooling unit inlet fitting. Cap the fitting.
5. Remove the inlet and outlet pipe grommets.
6. Remove the instrument panel undercover and glove box.
7. Disconnect the air conditioning wire harness from the cooling unit.
8. Disconnect the drain hose from the cooling unit.
9. Unbolt and remove the cooling unit from the vehicle.
10. Remove the clip securing the inlet and outlet pipes.
11. Remove the upper and lower case half retaining clamps.
12. Remove the lower case cover.
13. Unscrew the thermostat from the cooling housing.
14. Remove the thermostat and remove the screws that secure the capillary tube from inside the cooling unit fins.
15. Remove the evaporator from the lower case.
16. Disconnect the inlet pipe from the expansion valve.
17. Remove the insulator tape from the outlet pipe.
18. Remove the sensing bulb clip.
19. Note how the capillary and bulb are routed and remove the expansion valve.

To install:

NOTE: During the installation of the expansion valve, use all new O-rings at the pipe joints. Coat the O-rings with clean refrigerant oil.

20. Install the expansion valve so the sensing bulb and capillary tubing is routed in its original position.
21. Install the sensing bulb clip.
22. Wrap the outlet pipe with new insulator tape.
23. Connect the inlet pipe.
24. Install the evaporator into the lower case.
25. Install the thermostat.

NOTE: When installing the thermostat, insert the capillary tube end to a depth of 2.0 in. and 1.6 in. from the third core fin on the left side of the evaporator.

26. Install the lower case cover.
27. Connect the upper and lower case halves and lock the clips.
28. Install the inlet and outlet pipe retaining clip.
29. Position the cooling unit onto its mounting and bolt it into place. Adjust the position of the cooling unit so the inlet and outlet connections are aligned with the heater and blower unit connections.
30. Install the drain hose.
31. Connect the air conditioning wire harness.
32. Install the inlet and outlet pipe grommets.
33. Install the glove box and lower cover.
34. Connect the suction hose to the cooling unit inlet fitting.
35. Connect the discharge hose to the cooling unit outlet fitting.
36. If a new evaporator was installed, add 1.6 oz. of clean compressor oil to the compressor.

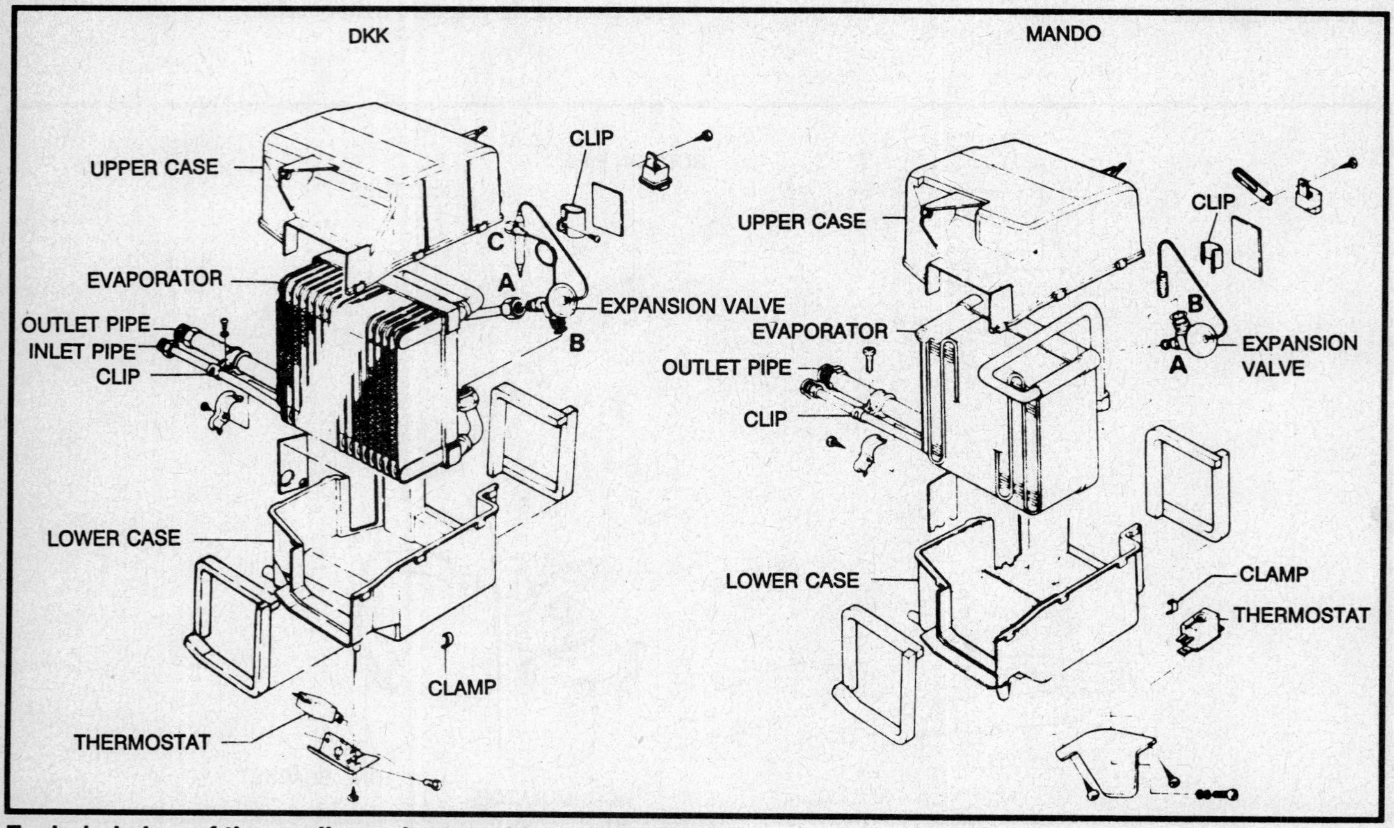
DKK
MANDO
UPPER CASE
CLIP
C
EVAPORATOR
A
EXPANSION VALVE
OUTLET PIPE
INLET PIPE
B
CLIP
LOWER CASE
CLAMP
THERMOSTAT
UPPER CASE
CLIP
B
EVAPORATOR
EXPANSION VALVE
A
OUTLET PIPE
CLIP
LOWER CASE
CLAMP
THERMOSTAT

Exploded view of the cooling unit assemblys—1989 Excel

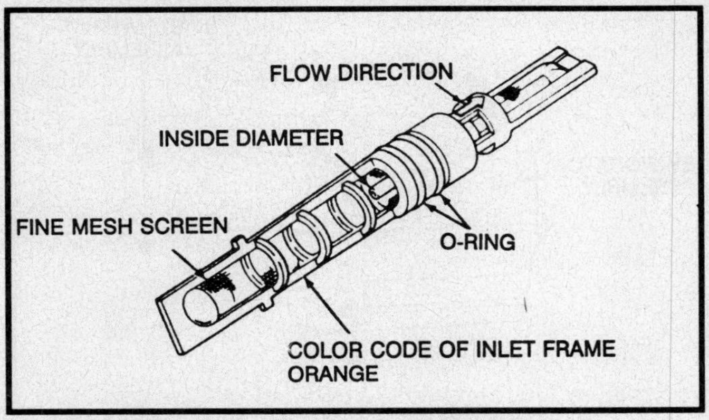
FLOW DIRECTION
INSIDE DIAMETER
FINE MESH SCREEN
O-RING
COLOR CODE OF INLET FRAME
ORANGE

Cross-sectional view of the fixed orifice tube

37. Connect the negative battery cable.
38. Evacuate, charge and test the system.

Fixed Orifice Tube

REMOVAL AND INSTALLATION

NOTE: The fixed orifice tube in a non-adjustable, non-servicable part. The orfice tube is located within the liquid line near the evaporator and can not be removed from the line. If the orifice tube is defective, the complete liquid line must be replaced. The fixed orifice tube should also be replaced whenever a compressor is replaced.

1. Disconnect the negative battery cable.
2. Discharge the refrigerant from the the air conditioning system.
3. Disconnect the liquid line from the evaporator and at the condenser.
4. Remove the brackets retaining the liquid line in place and remove the line.

To install:

5. Coat the O-rings with compressor oil and install the liquid line to the evaporator and condenser.
6. Secure the liquid line in place the with the retaining brackets.
7. Connect the negative battery cable. Evacuate, charge and test the system.

Blower Motor

REMOVAL AND INSTALLATION

1. Disconect the negative battery cable.
2. Remove the instrument under cover and the glove box.
3. Disconnect the resistor and blower motor wire connector.
4. Pull the blower unit out and disconnect the RECIRC/FRESH vacuum connector.
5. Remove the attaching screws and remove the blower assembly from the blower case.

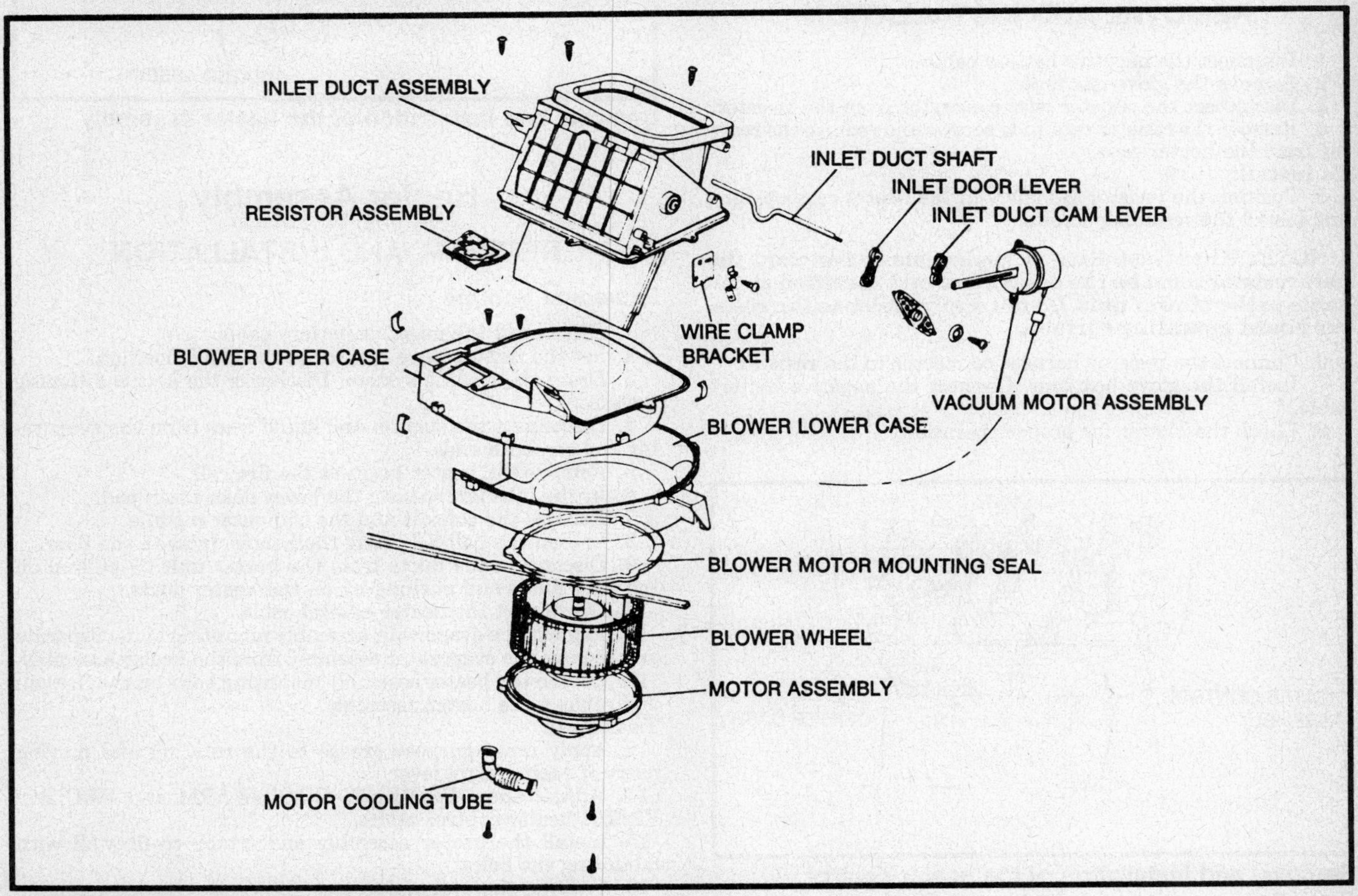
INLET DUCT ASSEMBLY
RESISTOR ASSEMBLY
INLET DUCT SHAFT
INLET DOOR LEVER
INLET DUCT CAM LEVER
WIRE CLAMP
BRACKET
BLOWER UPPER CASE
VACUUM MOTOR ASSEMBLY
BLOWER LOWER CASE
BLOWER MOTOR MOUNTING SEAL
BLOWER WHEEL
MOTOR ASSEMBLY
MOTOR COOLING TUBE

Exploded view of the blower motor assembly

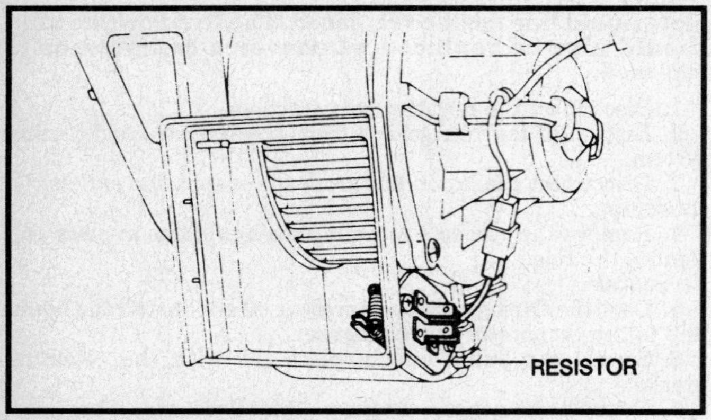
RESISTOR

Removal and installation of the resistor

To install:

6. Position the blower motor onto the blower case and install the attaching screws.
7. Connect the RECIRC/FRESH vacuum connector.
8. Connect the resistor and blower motor wire connector.
9. Install the glove box and instrument panel undercover.
10. Conect the negative battery cable.
11. Check the blower for proper operation.

Blower Motor Resistor

REMOVAL AND INSTALLATION

1. Disconect the negative battery cable.
2. Remove the glove box unit.
3. Disconnect the resistor wire connector from the resistor.
4. Remove the resistor retaining screws and remove the resistor from the heater case.

To install:

5. Position the resistor assembly in the heater case opening and install the retaining screws.

NOTE: When installing a replacement resistor, the new resistor must be the equivalent and specified applicable to the blower unit. Do not apply sealer to the resistor board mounting surface.

6. Connect the resistor harness connector to the resistor.
7. Install the glove box unit. Connect the negative battery cable.
9. Check the blower for proper operation.

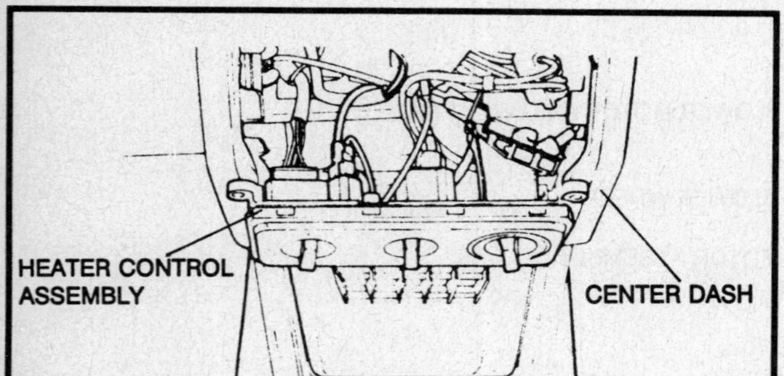
HEATER CONTROL
ASSEMBLY
CENTER DASH

Removal and installation of the heater control assembly

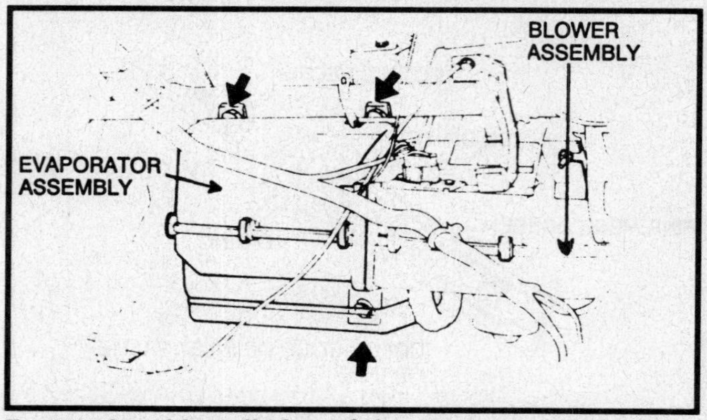
BLOWER
ASSEMBLY
EVAPORATOR
ASSEMBLY

Removal and installation of the evaporator assembly

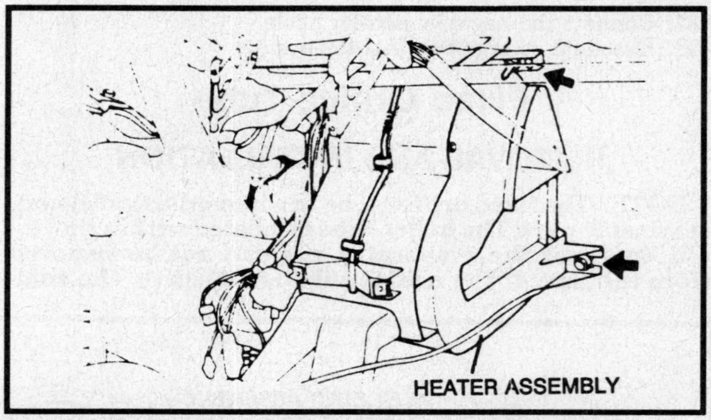
HEATER ASSEMBLY

Removal and installation of the heater assembly

Heater Assembly

REMOVAL AND INSTALLATION

Excel and Scoupe

1. Disconnect the negative battery cable.
2. Set the temperature control to the **HOT** position.
3. Drain the cooling system. Discharge the air conditioning system.
4. Disconnect the suction and liquid lines from the evaporator and cap both ends.
5. Remove the heater hoses at the firewall.
6. In the interior, remove the lower dash crash pad.
7. Remove the console and the computer module.
8. Loosen the bolt retaining the heater ducts to the floor.
9. Disconnect the ducts from the heater unit by pulling on the floor ducts and pushing up on the heater ducts.
10. Disconnect the heater control cable.
11. Remove the evaporator assembly mounting bolts. Separate and remove the evaporator assembly from the heater assembly.
12. Loosen the heater assembly mounting bolts on the firewall and remove the heater assembly.

To install:

13. Apply multi-purpose grease to the rotating and moving parts of each control lever.
14. Adjust the DEF-VENT, COOL-WARM and RECIRC/FRESH heater control cables.
15. Install the heater assembly and attach to firewall with mounting the bolts.
16. Position the evaporator assembly to the heater assembly and install the mounting bolts.

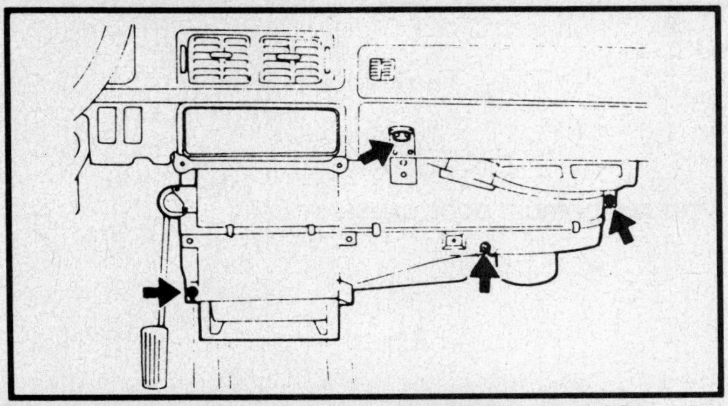

Removal and installation of the heater assembly—Sonata

17. Connect the heater control cable. Connect the ducts to the heater unit.
18. Install and tighten the heater duct retaining screw.
19. Install the computer module and supplement console.
20. Install the lower crash pad.
21. Connect the heater hoses.
22. Apply compressor oil to the O-rings and connect the suction and liquid lines to the evaporator.
23. Fill the cooling system and connect the negative battery cable.
24. Evacuate, charge and test the system. Check the system for proper operation.
25. Recheck and top off the radiator coolant level, as required.

Sonata

1. Disconnect the negative battery cable.
2. Drain the cooling system.
3. Remove the heater hoses and the evaporator drain hose.
4. Remove the evaporator suction and liquid tubes.
5. Remove the front and rear console assembly and remove both side covers.
6. Remove the the glove box, center pad cover, the center crash pad and the cassette assembly.
7. Remove the lower crash pad. Remove the console mounting bracket and the center support bracket.
8. Disconnect the ducts from the heater unit by pulling on the floor ducts and pushing up on the heater ducts.
9. Remove the control assembly.
10. Remove the heater assembly mounting bolts on the firewall and remove the heater assembly as a complete unit.

To install:

11. Install the heater assembly and attach to firewall with mounting the bolts.
12. Install the heater control assembly.
13. Connect the ducts to the heater unit.
14. Install the console mounting bracket and the center support bracket.
15. Install the lower crash pad and both side covers.
16. Install lthe front and rear console assembly.
17. Connect the evaporator tubes, heater hoses and drain hose.
18. Fill the cooling system and connect the negative battery cable.
19. Check the system for proper operation.

Heater Core

REMOVAL AND INSTALLATION

Excel and Scoupe

1. Disconnect the negative battery cable.
2. Drain the cooling system.
3. Remove the heater hoses and the evaporator drain hose.
4. Remove the evaporator suction and liquid tubes.
5. Remove the heater assembly.
6. Remove the heater cover and disconnect the water control valve links.
7. Remove the hose, pipe clamps and the heater valve.
8. Detach the heater core from the heater assembly and remove it.

To install:

9. Install the heater core into the heater assembly.
10. Install the heater valve and connect the hoses with pipe clamps.
11. Connect the water control valve links and install the heater cover.
12. Install the heater assembly. Connect the heater hoses and fill the cooling system.
13. Connect the negative battery cable. Evacuate, charge and test the air conditioning system.
14. When the the engine is completely warmed up, check and top off the radiator coolant level.
15. Check the heating system for proper operation.

Sonata

1. Disconnect the negative battery cable. Drain the cooling system.
2. Discharge the air conditioning system.
3. Remove the heater hoses and the evaporator drain hose.
4. Remove the evaporator suction and liquid tubes.
5. Remove the heater assembly.
6. With the heater asssembly removed from the vehicle, detach the heater core from the heater assembly and remove it.

To install:

7. Install the heater core into the heater assembly. Install the heater assembly into the vehicle.
8. Fill the cooling system. Connect the negative battery cable.
9. Evacuate, charge and test the air conditioning system.
10. When the the engine is completely warmed up, check and top off the radiator coolant level.
11. Check the heating system for proper operation.

Evaporator

REMOVAL AND INSTALLATION

Excel and Scoupe

1. Disconnect the negative battery cable.
2. Discharge the refrigerant from the the air conditioning system.
3. Disconnect the low pressure suction line from the cooling unit outlet fitting. Cap the fitting.
4. Disconnect the liquid line pipe from the cooling unit inlet fitting. Cap the fitting.
5. Remove the inlet and outlet pipe grommets.
6. Remove the console assembly. Remove the glove box assembly.
7. Remove the lower dash crash pad and the lower crash pad center panel.
8. Remove the blower motor assembly mounting bolts and remove the blower assembly.
9. Remove the evaporator assembly mounting bolts. Separate and remove the evaporator assembly from the heater assembly.

To install:

10. Position the evaporator assembly in place to the heater assembly and install the mounting bolts.
11. Position the blower assembly in place and install the blower assembly mounting bolts.
12. Install the lower dash crash pad and the lower crash pad center panel.

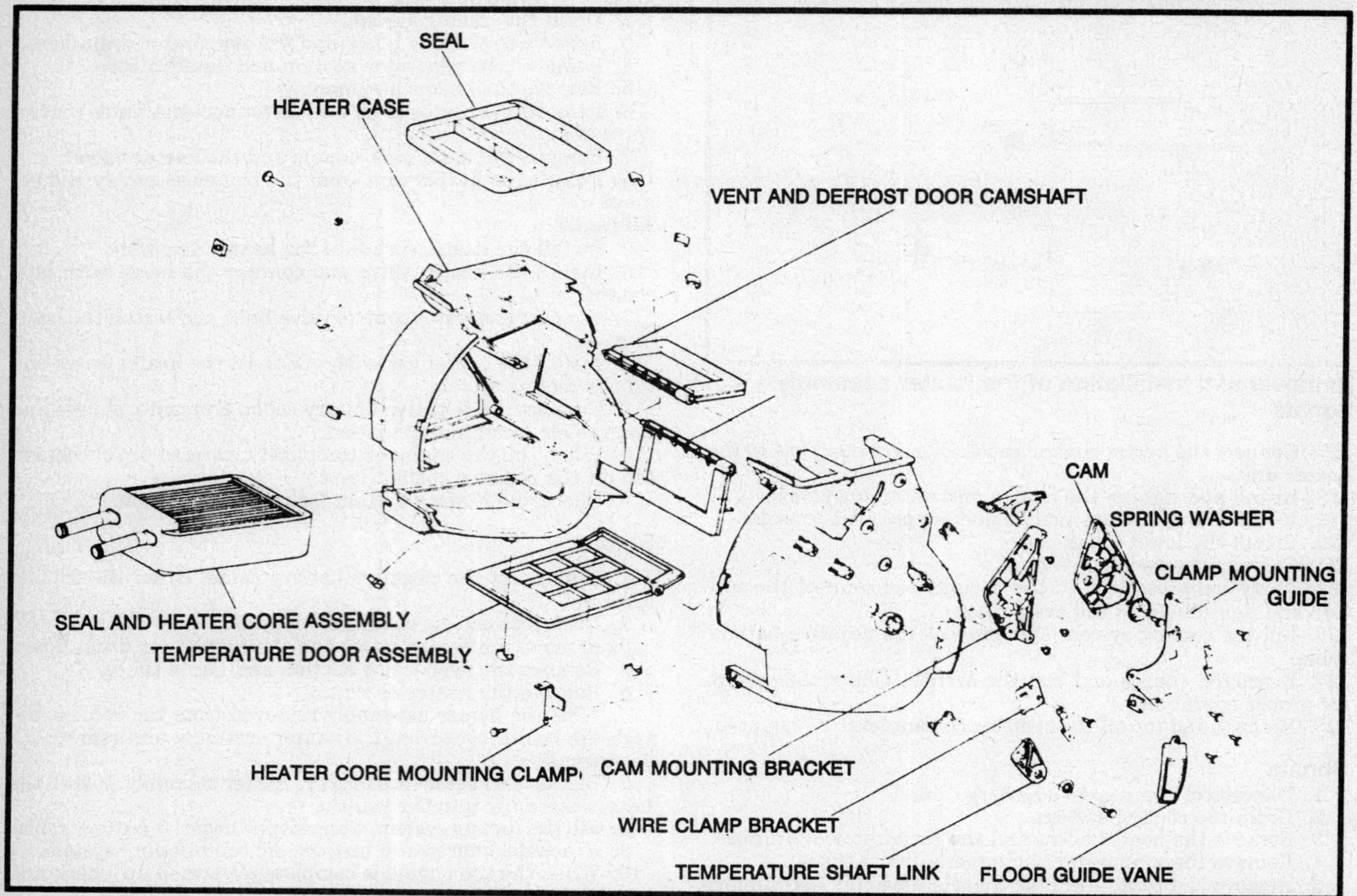
SEAL
HEATER CASE
VENT AND DEFROST DOOR CAMSHAFT
CAM
SPRING WASHER
CLAMP MOUNTING GUIDE
SEAL AND HEATER CORE ASSEMBLY
TEMPERATURE DOOR ASSEMBLY
HEATER CORE MOUNTING CLAMP
CAM MOUNTING BRACKET
WIRE CLAMP BRACKET
TEMPERATURE SHAFT LINK
FLOOR GUIDE VANE

Exploded view of the heater core and related components—Excel and Scoupe

13. Install the console assembly. Install the glove box assembly.
14. Coat the O-rings with compressor oil, install the grommet over the evaporator lines and connect the lines to the evaporator.
15. If a new evaporator was installed, add 1.6 oz. of clean compressor oil to the compressor.
16. Evacuate, charge and test the system. Connect the negative battery cable.

Sonata

1. Disconnect the negative battery cable and discharge the air conditioning system.
2. Disconnect the low pressure suction hose from the cooling unit outlet fitting. Cap the fitting.
3. Disconnect the liquid line pipe from the cooling unit inlet fitting. Cap the fitting.
4. Remove the inlet and outlet pipe grommets.
5. Remove the instrument panel undercover and glove box.
6. Remove the connector to the control switch, connector to the power supply and the connector to the magnetic clutch of the compressor.
7. Remove the drain hose and disconnect the piping in the engine compartment.
8. Disconnect the electrical harness from the cooling unit housing.
9. Remove the lower bolt and 2 upper bracket nuts and remove the cooling unit from the vehicle.
10. Remove the clip securing the inlet and outlet pipes.
11. Remove the upper and lower case half retaining clamps.
12. Remove the lower case cover.
13. Remove the 2 screws that hold the thermostat to the cooling housing.
14. Remove the thermostat and remove the screws that secure the capillary tube from inside the cooling unit fins.
15. Lift the evaporator coil (cooling unit) assembly from the lower cooling unit case to remove it. Be sure to hold the lower cooling unit case firmly when removing the evaporator coil (cooling unit) assembly.

To install:

16. Install the evaporator into the lower case.
17. Install the thermostat.

NOTE: When installing the thermostat, insert the capillary tube end to a depth of 2.0 in. and 1.6 in. from the third core fin on the left side of the the evaporator.

18. Install the lower case cover.
19. Connect the upper and lower case halves and lock the clips.
20. Install the inlet and outlet pipe retaining clip.
21. Postion the cooling unit onto its mounting with the lower bolt and 2 upper nuts. Adjust the position of the cooling unit so the inlet and outlet connections are aligned with the heater and blower unit connections.
22. Install the drain hose.

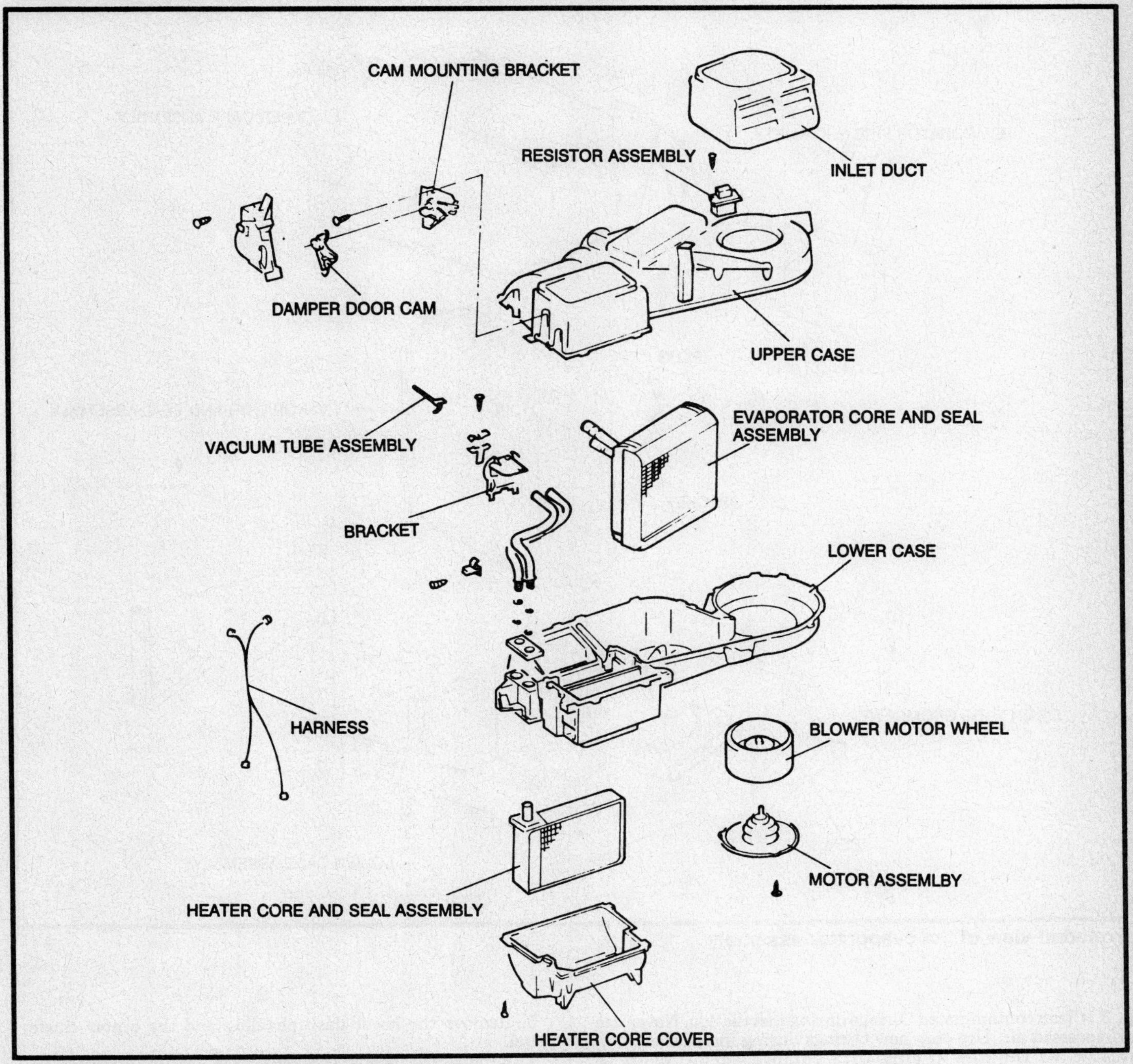
CAM MOUNTING BRACKET
RESISTOR ASSEMBLY
INLET DUCT
DAMPER DOOR CAM
UPPER CASE
VACUUM TUBE ASSEMBLY
EVAPORATOR CORE AND SEAL ASSEMBLY
BRACKET
LOWER CASE
HARNESS
BLOWER MOTOR WHEEL
MOTOR ASSEMLBY
HEATER CORE AND SEAL ASSEMBLY
HEATER CORE COVER

Exploded view of the heater assembly—Sonata

23. Connect the air conditioning wire harness.
24. Install the inlet and outlet pipe grommets.
25. Install the glove box and lower cover.
26. Connect the suction hose to the cooling unit inlet fitting.
27. Connect the discharge hose to the cooling unit outlet fitting.
28. If a new evaporator was installed, add 1.6 oz. of clean compressor oil to the compressor.
29. Evacuate, charge and test the system. Connect the negative battery cable.

Refrigerant Lines

REMOVAL AND INSTALLATION

1. When disconnecting or connecting refrigerant lines, always use 2 wrenches.
2. Use protective plugs and plug each open line, to prevent contamination and moisture from entering the lines and related components.

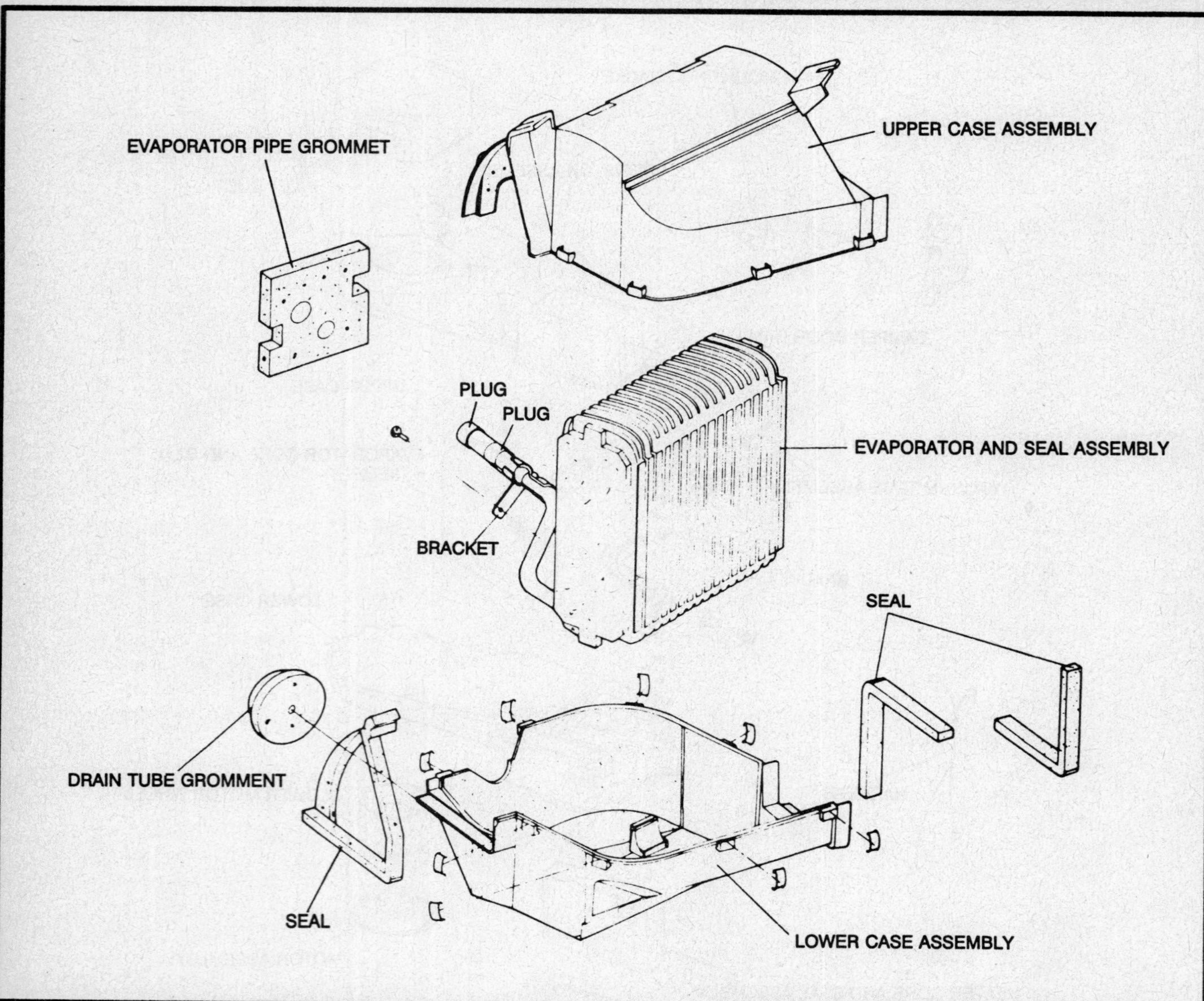
UPPER CASE ASSEMBLY
EVAPORATOR PIPE GROMMET
PLUG
PLUG
EVAPORATOR AND SEAL ASSEMBLY
BRACKET
SEAL
DRAIN TUBE GROMMENT
SEAL
LOWER CASE ASSEMBLY

Exploded view of the evaporator assembly

3. Clean contaminated O-rings during installation. Never use compressed air. Use only new O-rings during installation.
4. Coat the new O-ring with compressor oil prior to installation.
5. Install the O-ring against the shoulder to ensure proper seating.
6. When connecting 2 lines together, insert the tube section into the union and tighten the retaining nut by hand. Then, tighten the nut to 29–33 ft. lbs. (39–44 Nm).

Manual Control Head

REMOVAL AND INSTALLATION

1989 Excel

1. Disconnect the negative battery cable.
2. Set the temperature control to the **HOT** position.
3. Remove the lower dash paneling and the center cluster panel.
4. Remove the heater control switch retaining screws and pull the control switch away from the dash.
5. Disconnect the electrical and vacuum connections at the switch.
6. Disconnect the heater control cables and remove the control switch.

To install:

7. Insert the control switch into the dash cavity. Connect the control cables to the control levers.
8. Plug the electrical and vacuum connectors in to the control switch.
9. Secure the control switch to the dash with the retaining screws and adjust the cables accordingly.
10. Install the center and lower crash panels. Connect the negative battery cable and test the switch operation.

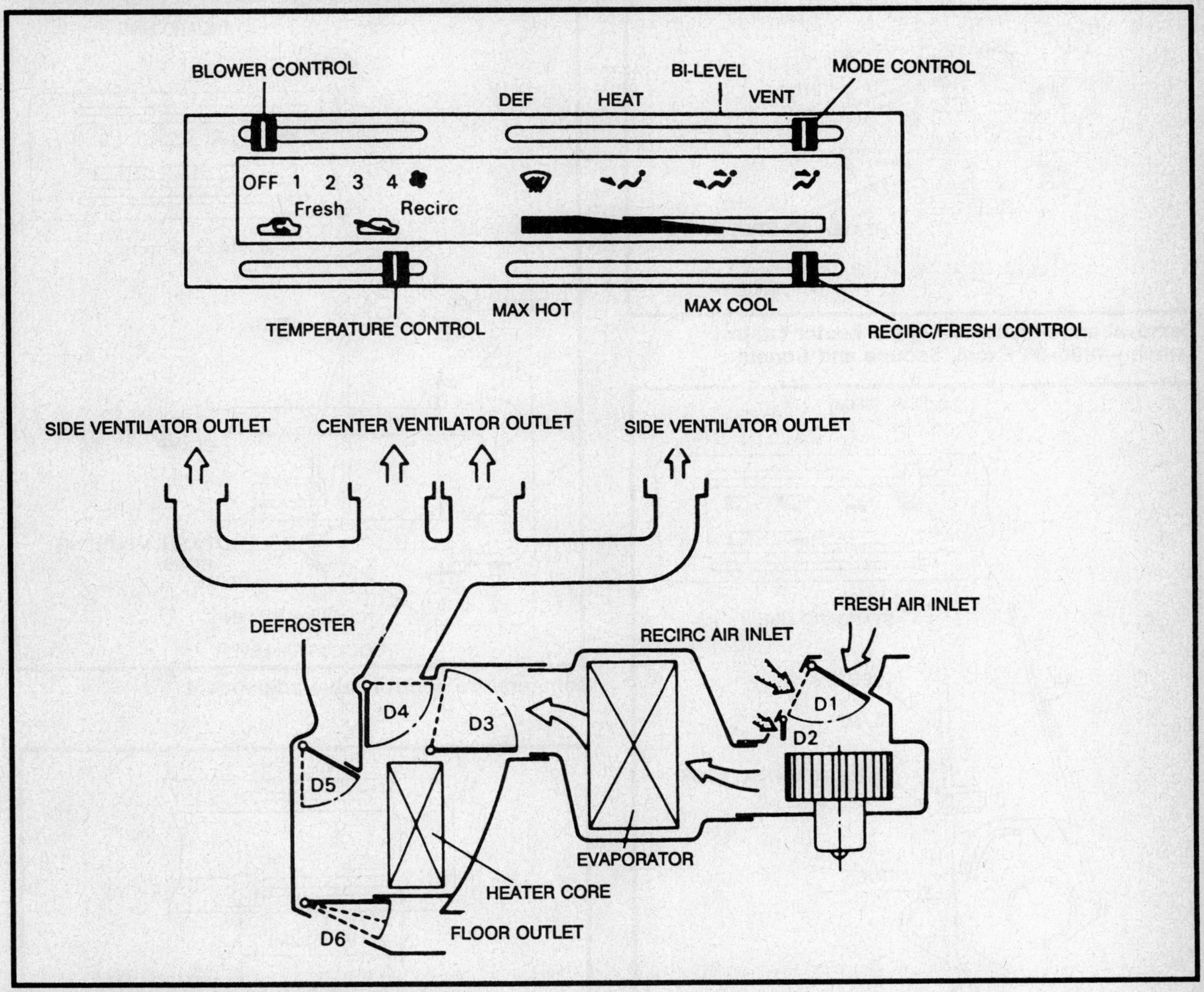
BLOWER CONTROL
BI-LEVEL
MODE CONTROL
DEF
HEAT
VENT
OFF 1 2 3 4
Fresh
Recirc
MAX HOT
MAX COOL
TEMPERATURE CONTROL
RECIRC/FRESH CONTROL
SIDE VENTILATOR OUTLET
CENTER VENTILATOR OUTLET
SIDE VENTILATOR OUTLET
FRESH AIR INLET
DEFROSTER
RECIRC AIR INLET
D1
D2
D3
D4
D5
D6
EVAPORATOR
HEATER CORE
FLOOR OUTLET

View of the heater control switch–1989 Excel

Except 1989 Excel

1. Disconnect the negative battery cable.
2. Remove ash tray and the center dash cluster.
3. Disconnect the vacuum and electrical connectors at the switch and disconnect the cigarette lighter connector.
4. Remove the heater control switch retaining screws.
5. Pull the heater control switch from the dash and disconnect the blower motor switch connector, the vacuum connection and the temperature control cable. Remove the control switch from the dash.

To install:

6. Position the control switch to the dash cavity and connect the blower motor switch connector, the vacuum connection and the temperature control cable.
7. Secure the control switch to the dash with the retaining screws.
8. Connect the vacuum and electrical connectors at the switch and cigarette lighter connector.

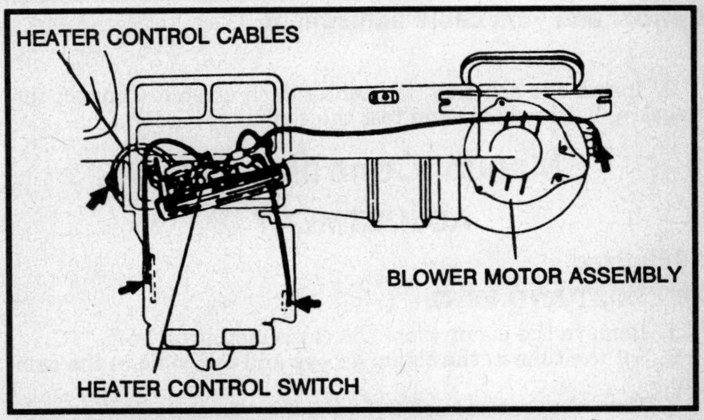
HEATER CONTROL CABLES
BLOWER MOTOR ASSEMBLY
HEATER CONTROL SWITCH

Removal and Installation of the heater control switch–1989 Excel

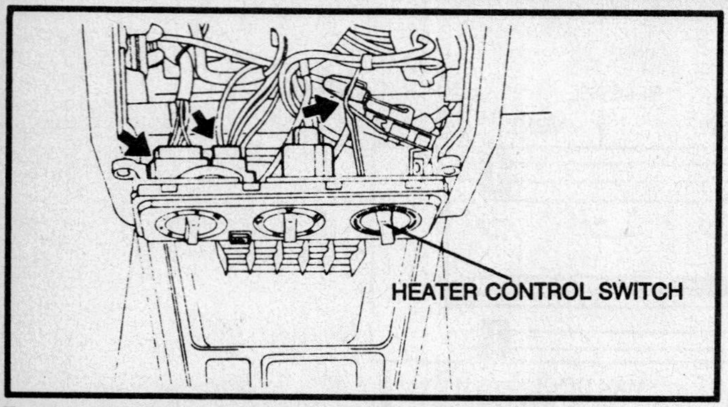
HEATER CONTROL SWITCH

Removal and installation of the heater control switch—1990–91 Excel, Scoupe and Sonata

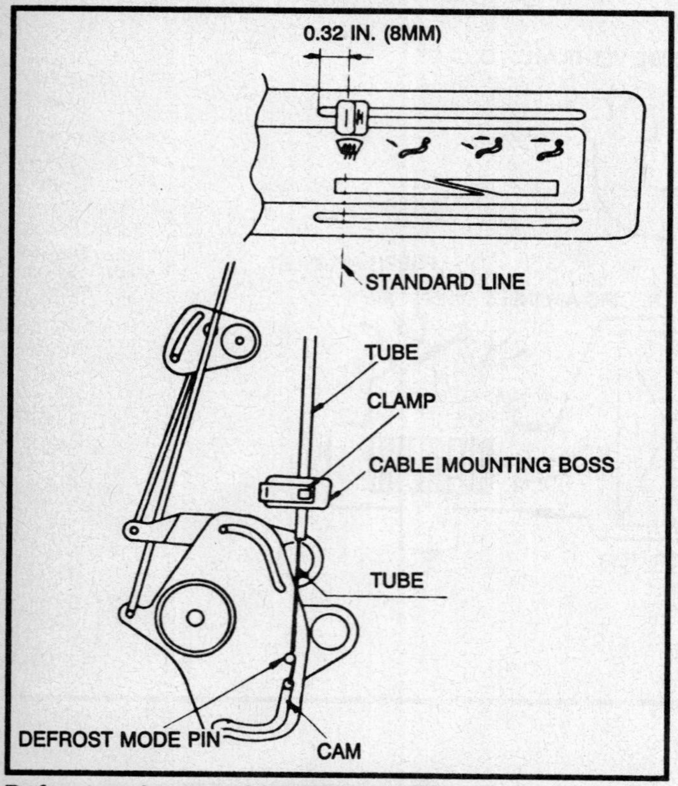
0.32 IN. (8MM)
STANDARD LINE
TUBE
CLAMP
CABLE MOUNTING BOSS
TUBE
DEFROST MODE PIN
CAM

Defrost and vent cable adjustment

9. Install the ash tray, the center dash cluster. Connect the negative battery cable and test the switch operation.

Manual Control Cables

ADJUSTMENT

1989 Excel

DEFROST AND VENT

1. Remove the clamp from the cable mounting boss.
2. Set the tube in the clamp groove and the cable in the cam pin.
3. Move the control knob to fix the cam pin at the lowest position, then set the control lever to the **DEFROST** position.
4. Secure the cable clamp.

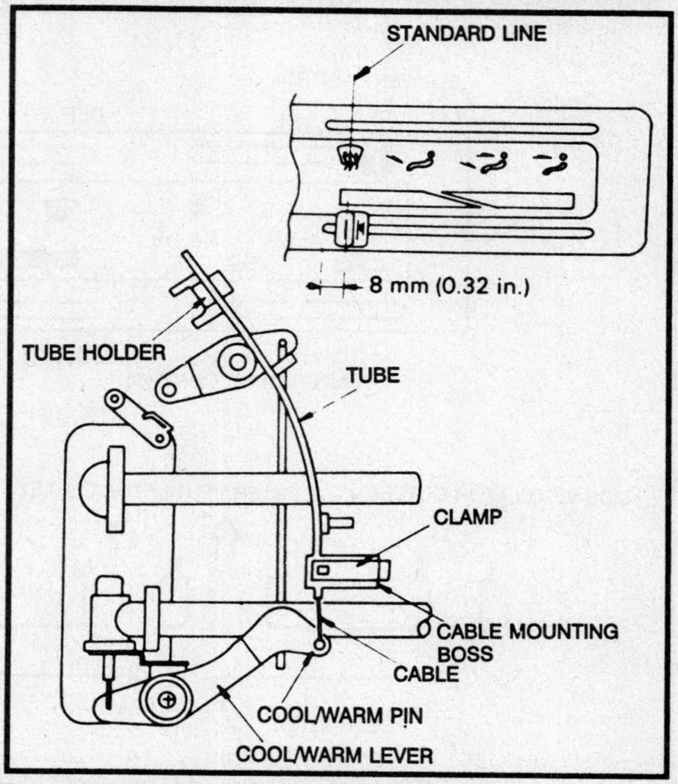
STANDARD LINE
8 mm (0.32 in.)
TUBE HOLDER
TUBE
CLAMP
CABLE MOUNTING BOSS
CABLE
COOL/WARM PIN
COOL/WARM LEVER

Temperature control cable adjustment

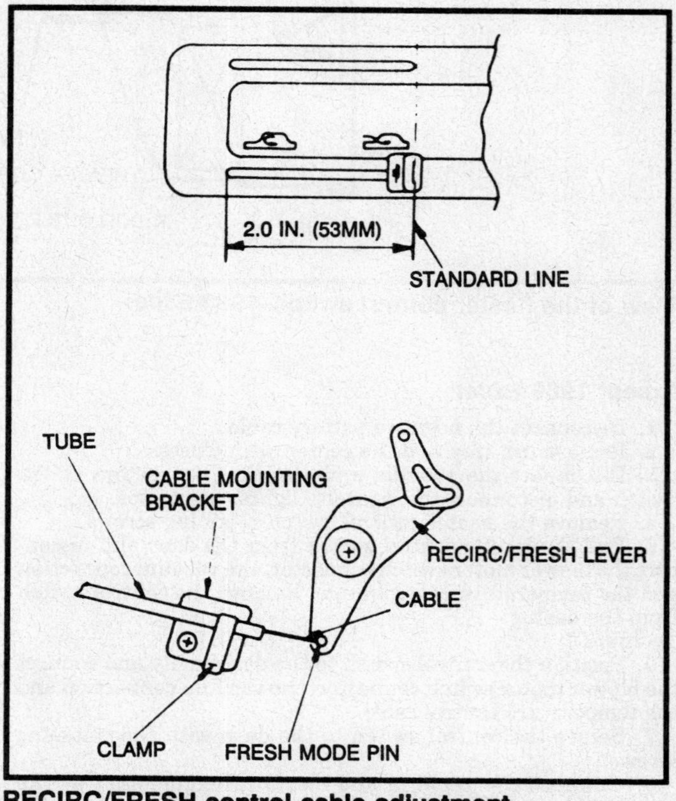
2.0 IN. (53MM)
STANDARD LINE
TUBE
CABLE MOUNTING BRACKET
RECIRC/FRESH LEVER
CABLE
CLAMP
FRESH MODE PIN

RECIRC/FRESH control cable adjustment

TEMPERATURE CONTROL

1. Remove the clamp from the cable mounting boss.
2. Set the tube in the clamp.
3. Insert the cable into the cool-warm lever pin.
4. Move the control knob to position the cool warm lever pin at the highest position (**WARM** mode), then set the control knob to the **DEFROST** position.
5. Secure the cable clamp.

FRESH/RECIRC

1. Remove the clamp from the cable mounting boss.
2. Move the tube to the fresh-recirc lever pin and put the tube inside the clamp.
3. Move the lever fully backward, and then secure the control knob to the **RECIRC** position.

SENSORS AND SWITCHES

Fast Idle Control Device

OPERATION

The Fast Idle Control Device (FICD) is apart of the engines vacuum system. It is designed to raise the idle speed during air conditioning operation, to ensure efficient cooling when the vehicle is stationary.

When the air conditioning system is turned **ON**, current flows from the air conditioning relay, through the pressure switch and to an electric vacuum operated solenoid. When the solenoid is energized, vacuum is applied the Fast Idle Control Device (FICD) actuator diaphram.

Vacuum acts on the diaphram plunger, forcing the plunger against the accelerator adjustment screw. This in turn raises the idle rpm to 850–900 rpm.

TESTING

1. Start the engine and allow it to warm up sufficiently.
2. Check the curb idle speed with the air conditioning **OFF** and adjust, as required.
3. Turn the air conditioning **ON**. The engine idle should raise between 850–900 rpm.
4. If the there is no rpm increase, check to see if there is vacuum present at the Fast Idle Control Device (FICD).
5. If vacuum is present and the device is inoperative, replace it. If actuator is working properly, adjust the idle to specification.
6. Set the engine speed by adjusting the adjustment screw until 850–900 rpm is attained.
7. If vacuum was not present at the actuator, check the air conditioning soleniod and connecting vacuum tubing.
8. Depress and release the accellerator pedal several times and make sure the engine speed returns to the specified rpm.

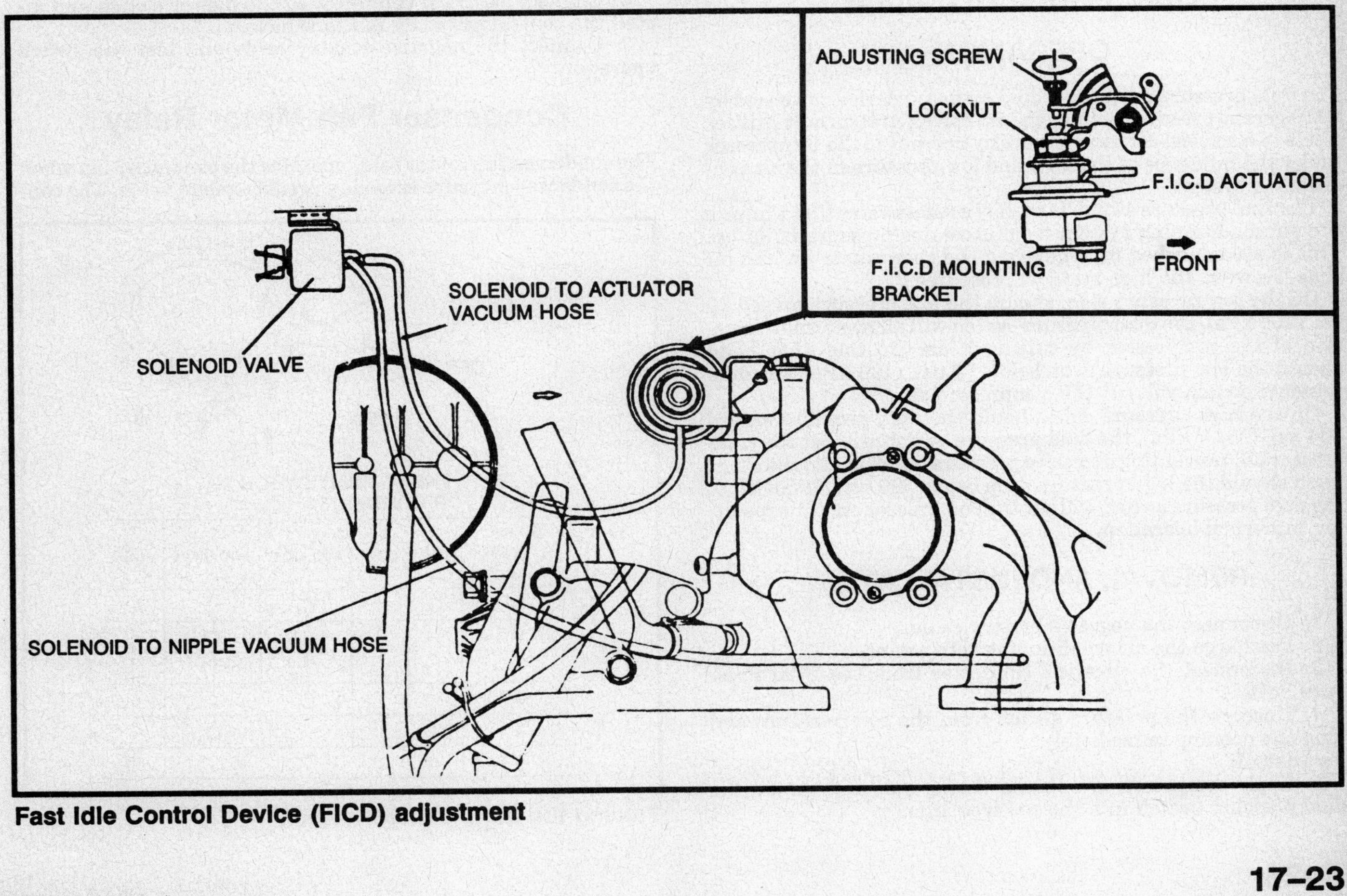
ADJUSTING SCREW
LOCKNUT
F.I.C.D ACTUATOR
F.I.C.D MOUNTING BRACKET
FRONT
SOLENOID TO ACTUATOR VACUUM HOSE
SOLENOID VALVE
SOLENOID TO NIPPLE VACUUM HOSE

Fast Idle Control Device (FICD) adjustment

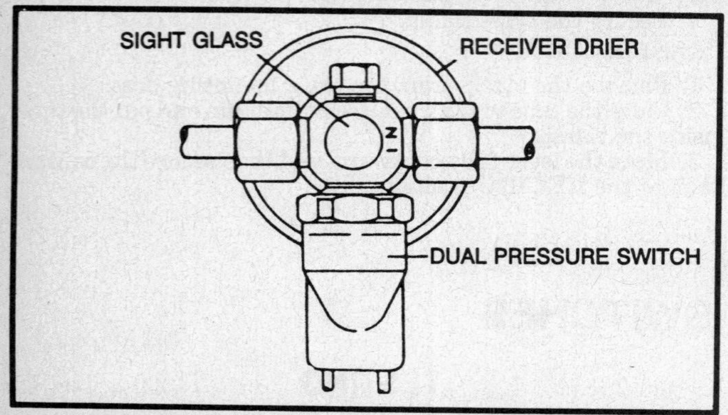
SIGHT GLASS
RECEIVER DRIER
DUAL PRESSURE SWITCH

View of the Dual Pressure switch and receiver/drier

REMOVAL AND INSTALLATION

1. Disconnect the negative battery cable.
2. Remove the air cleaner assembly.
3. Disconnect the vacuum hose from the Fast Idle Device (FICD).
4. Remove the nut attaching the Fast Idle Device (FICD) to the mounting bracket and remove it.
5. Position the Fast Idle Device (FICD), to the mounting bracket and install the retaining nut.
6. Connect the vacuum hose to the Fast Idle Device (FICD). Connect the negative battery cable.
7. Start the engine and test operation. Adjust, as required.
8. Install the air cleaner assembly.

Dual Pressure Switch

OPERATION

The dual pressure switch is a dual actuated device, governed by refriegerant pressure acting against spring pressure. It utilizes 2 sets of electrical contacts that relay current to the compressor under the influence of the high and low pressure in the air conditioning system.

The dual pressure switch is merely a safety valve that protects the air conditioning system from excessive pressure build up. This is accomplished by regulating the compressor on and off time, between the high and low pressures.

On the low pressure side, should the low pressure exceed 30 psi. (206 kPa), the dual pressure switch will allow normal operation of the compressor by cutting it on. On the other hand should the low pressure drop below 28 psi. (196 kPa), the dual pressure switch will cut the compressor off.

On the high pressure side, should the high pressure exceed 384 psi. (264.7 kPa), the dual pressure switch will cut the compressor off, preventing excessive pressure build up. On the other hand should the high pressure drop below 300 psi. (205.9 kPa), the dual pressure switch will cut the compressor on, thus resulting in normal operation.

REMOVAL AND INSTALLATION

1. Disconnect the negative battery cable.
2. Discharge the air conditioning refrigerant.
3. Disconnect the electrical connector from the Dual Pressure Switch.
4. Unscrew the pressure switch from the receiver/drier and plug the opening immediately.

To install:

5. Apply compressor oil on the O-ring seal and thread the dual pressure switch into the receiver/drier.
6. Connect the electrical connector. Connect the negative battery cable.
7. Evacuate, charge and test the system.

Blower Switch

OPERATION

The blower switch selects what speed the blower motor will operate. This is accomplished by joining a series of the contacts incorporated internally of the blower switch.

Approximately 12 volts is applied to the blower switch, in turn, the switch relays the current to the blower motor resistor. There, the 12 volt source is utilizeed a full voltage requirement or is reduced accordingly. This is determined by 4 speed settings, on the blower switch.

TESTING

Operate the blower switch and check for continuity. The switch is good when there is continuity between the **O-O** positions as the switch is being operated.

REMOVAL AND INSTALLATION

1. Disconnect the negative battery cable.
2. Remove the manual control head assembly.
3. Disconnect the blower switch electrical connector.
4. Remove the switch-to-control assembly retaining screws and remove the blower switch.

To install:

5. Assemble the blower switch to the control assembly and install the retaining screws.
6. Connect electrical connector to the blower switch and install the control assembly in the vehicle.
7. Connect the negative battery cable and test the switch operation.

Condenser Fan Motor Relay

The condenser fan motor relay operates the condenser fan when the condenser pressure exceeds a predetermend value. The con-

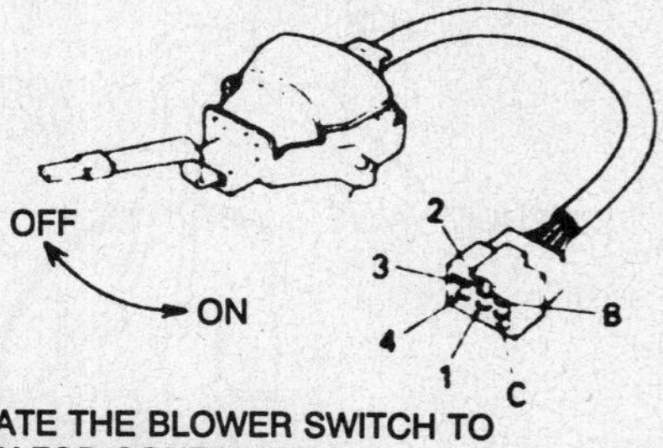
OFF
ON
2
3
4
1
B
C

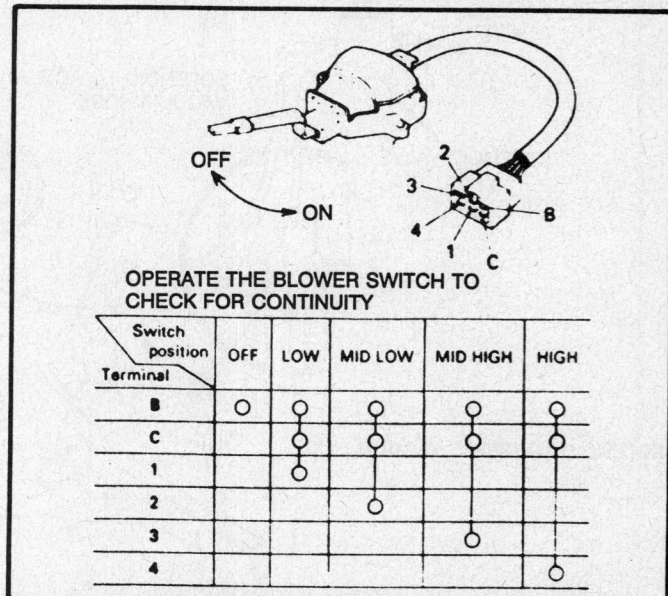

OPERATE THE BLOWER SWITCH TO CHECK FOR CONTINUITY

Terminal \ Switch position	OFF	LOW	MID LOW	MID HIGH	HIGH
B	O	O	O	O	O
C		O	O	O	O
1		O			
2			O		
3				O	
4					O

Testing the blower motor switch

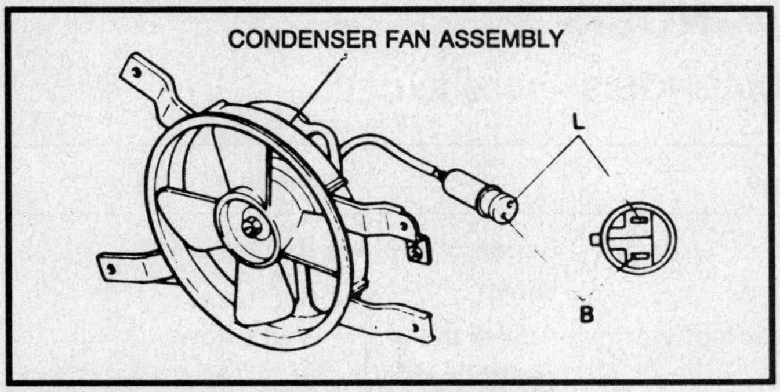
CONDENSER FAN ASSEMBLY
L
B

Testing the condenser fan motor relay

denser fan relay is located in the relay box, in engine compartment, near the right shock tower.

TESTING

1. Check that there is no continuity between terminals 3 and 4.
2. Apply 12 volts across terminals 1 and 2, then check for continuity between terminals 3 and 4.
3. If continuity does not exist, replace the relay.

REMOVAL AND INSTALLATION

1. Remove the relay box cover. Remove the relay by pulling straight up.
2. Install the relay by aligning the relay contacts and pushing it firmly into the relay box.

Air Conditioning Relay

The air condioning relay, relays current to the dual pressure switch and in turn to the compressor.

TESTING

1. Check that there is no continuity between terminals 3 and 4.
2. Apply 12 volts across terminals 1 and 2, then check for continuity between terminals 3 and 4.
3. If continuity does not exist, replace the relay.

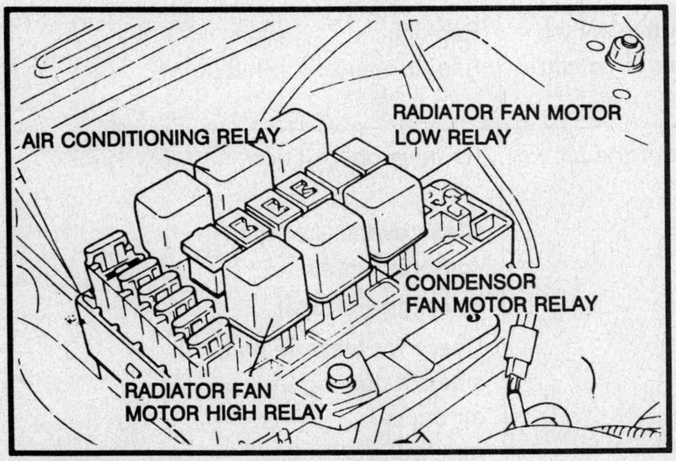
AIR CONDITIONING RELAY
RADIATOR FAN MOTOR
LOW RELAY
CONDENSOR
FAN MOTOR RELAY
RADIATOR FAN
MOTOR HIGH RELAY

Location of the relay box—Sonata

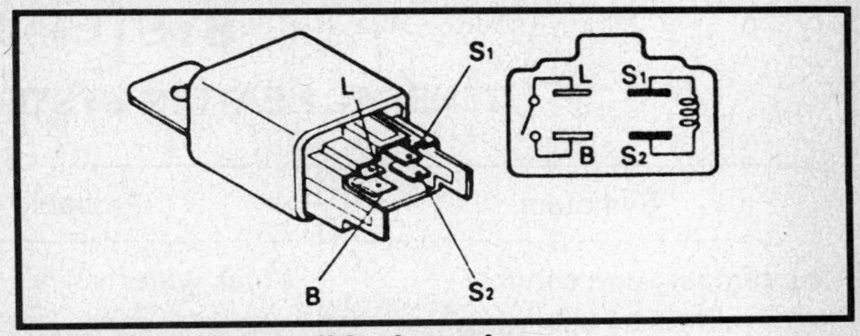
S1
L
L
S1
B
S2
B
S2

Testing the air conditioning relay

REMOVAL AND INSTALLATION

The air conditioning relay is located in engine compartment. On the Excel and Scoupe, it located on the left inner fender apron, near the battery. On the Sonata, it is located in the relay box, near the right shock tower.

1. Disconnect the negative battery cable.
2. On the Excel, remove the relay bracket retaining screw.
3. Disconnect the electrical connector and remove the relay.
4. On Sonata, remove the relay box cover. Remove the relay by pulling straight up.

To install:

5. On the Excel and Scoupe, plug the electrical harness connector into the relay. Position the relay to the fender apron and install the retaining screw.
6. On the Sonata, install the relay by aligning the relay contacts and pushing it firmly into the relay box. Install the relay box cover.
7. Connect the negative battery cable.

Blower Motor Resistor

TESTING

1. Check that there is no continuity between terminals 1 and 5.
2. If continuity does not exist, replace the resister.

REMOVAL AND INSTALLATION

1. Disconnect the negative battery cable.
2. Remove the glove box assembly.
3. Disconnect the wiring harness connector from the resistor assembly.
4. Remove the resitor-to-heater case retaining screws and remove the resistor from the case.

To install:

5. Attach the wiring harness connector to the resistor. Install the glove box assembly.
6. Connect the negative battery cable and test the resistor operation.

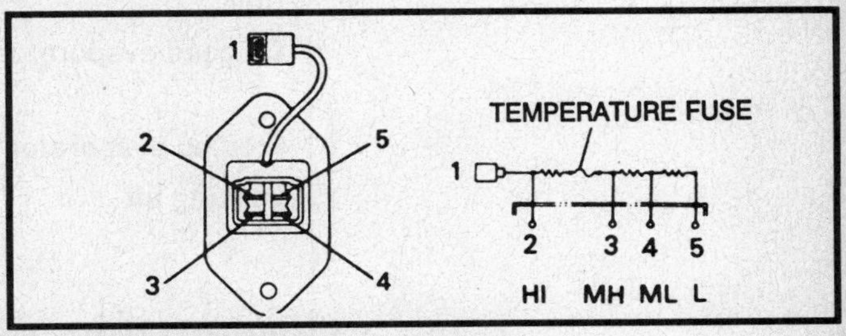
1
2
5
3
4
TEMPERATURE FUSE
1
2
3
4
5
HI
MH
ML
L

Testing the blower motor resistor

SYSTEM DIAGNOSIS

GENERAL HEATING SYSTEM DIAGNOSIS—1989 EXCEL

Symptom	Probable cause	Remedy
The temperature cannot be regulated by operating the temperature control lever on the panel	Stuck water valve	Repair or replace the water valve
	Incorrect adjust installation of warm water flow control cable	Adjust the warm water flow control cable
	Incorrect adjustment of water valve link	Adjust the mode control cable
No ventilation even when the mode control lever is operated	Incorrect adjustment of change over dampers	Adjust the mode control cable
	Loose duct connection	Connect the duct securely or replace the packing
Abnormal sound from blower motor	Foreign material inside blower	Remove foreign material
	Incorrect balance of blower motor or fan	Replace the blower motor or fan
	Damaged blower	Replace
Duct enters passenger compartment	Ventilator duct connection malfunction	Connect the duct securely or replace the packing
	Incorrect adjustment of inside/outside air changeover damper	Adjust the inside/outside fresh air changeover cable

GENERAL AIR CONDITIONING DIAGNOSIS—1989 EXCEL

Symptom	Probable cause	Remedy
No blower operation	Blown "BLOWER" fuse	Replace
	Malfunction blower motor	Replace
	Faulty resistor	Replace
	Malfunction blower control switch	Replace
	Open or loose connection in electric circuit	Repair open-circuited point
Insufficient air	Obstruction in the inlet of the blower unit	Remove obstruction
	Clogged evaporator	Clean evaporator with compressed air
	Frosted evaporator	Check thermostat
	Leaking air	Check for leakage on both sides of cooling unit and air ducts
	Blown "COMP." Fuse	Replace

GENERAL AIR CONDITIONING DIAGNOSIS—1989 EXCEL

Symptom	Probable cause	Remedy
Compressor does not run, or runs poorly	Malfunctioning A/C relay	Check operation
	Malfunctioning dual pressure switch	Check operation
	Malfunctioning thermostat	Check operation
	Malfunctioning A/C switch	Check operation
	Malfunctioning blower switch	Check operation
	Blown "A/C" fuse and/or "BLOWER" fuse	Replace
	Loose compressor drive belt	Readjust
	Battery voltage too low	Recharge battery
	Internal malfunction of compressor	Repair or replace compressor
	Short circuit in the magnet coil	Replace
	Oil on clutch face	Clean or replace clutch
	Gap between drive plate and pulley too large	Adjust gap
	Open circuit in the magnet coil	Replace
	Open or loose connection in electric circuit	Repair open-circuited point
Refrigerant pressure is abnormal	Normal pressure are: High pressure ..... 1,470-1,760 kPa (213-256 psi, 15-18 kg/cm^2) Low pressure .... 190-290 kPa (28-42 psi, 1.9-2.9 kg/cm^2) When, ambient temperature .... 35°C (95°F) Engine speed .... 1,500 rpm	
Low pressure is too high	Internal malfunction of compressor	Repair or replace compressor
	Faulty contact at sensing bulb of the expansion valve	Repair
	Faulty insulation at sensing bulb of the expansion valve	Repair
	Expansion valve opening is too large	Repair
Low pressure is too low	Insufficient refrigerant	Charge refrigerant
	Receiver-drier clogged	Replace
	Expansion valve clogged	Replace
	Faulty thermostat	Check operation
	Frosted piping	Clean or replace piping
High pressure is too high	Insufficient cooling of the condenser	Check and clean condenser
	Too much refrigerant	Discharge refrigerant
	Air in system	Evacuate and charge system
	Malfunctioning condenser fan motor	Check operation
High pressure is too low	Insufficient refrigerant	Charge refrigerant
	Internal malfunction of compressor	Repair or replace compressor

GENERAL AIR CONDITIONING DIAGNOSIS—1989 EXCEL
REFRIGERANT LEVEL TEST

Check item / Amount of refrigerant	Almost no refrigerant	Insufficient	Suitable	Too much refrigerant
Temperature of high pressure and low pressure lines	Almost no difference between high pressure and low pressure side temperature	High pressure side is warm and low pressure side is fairly cold	High pressure side is hot and low pressure side is cold	High pressure side is abnormally hot
State in sight glass	Bubbles flow continuously. **Bubbles will disappear and something like mist will flow when refrigerant is nearly gone** 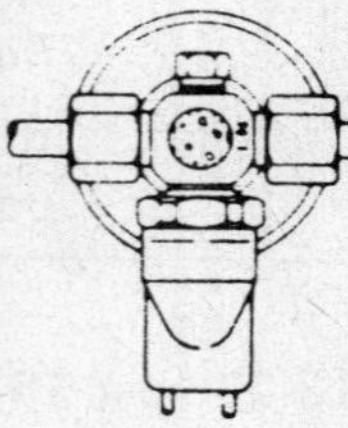	The bubbles are seen at intervals of 1-2 seconds 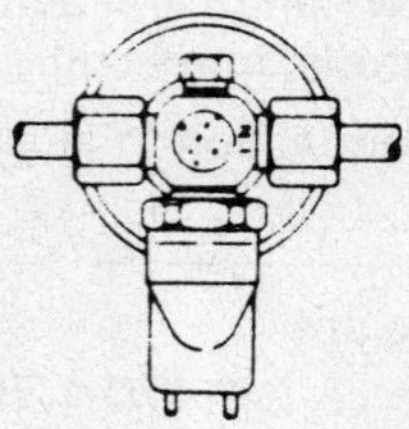	Almost transparent. Bubbles may appear when engine speed is raised and lowered **No clear difference exists between these two conditions** 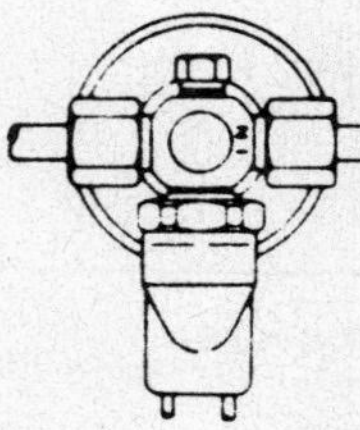	No bubbles can be seen
Pressure of system	High pressure side is abnormally low	Both pressure on high and low pressure sides are slightly low	Both pressure on high and low pressure sides are normal	Both pressure on high and low pressure sides are abnormally high
Repair	**Stop compressor** and conduct an overall check	Check for gas leakage, repair as required, replenish and charge system		Discharge refrigerant from service valve of low pressure side

GENERAL AIR CONDITIONING DIAGNOSIS—1989 EXCEL
PERFORMANCE TEST

PERFORMANCE TEST

1. Install the manifold gauge set.
2. Run the engine at 2,000 rpm and set the controls for maximum cooling and high blower speed.
3. Keep all windows and doors open.
4. Place a dry-bulb thermometer in the cool air outlet.
5. Place a psychrometer close to the inlet of the cooling unit.
6. Check that the reading on the high pressure gauge is 1,373-1,575 kPa (14-16 kg/cm², 199-228 psi).
   If the reading is too high, pour water on the condenser.
   If the reading to too low, cover the front of the condenser.
7. Check that the reading on the dry-bulb thermometer at the air inlet at 25-35°C (77-95°F).
8. Calculate the relative humidity from the psychrometric graph by comparing the wet-and dry-bulb reading of the psychrometer at the air inlet.

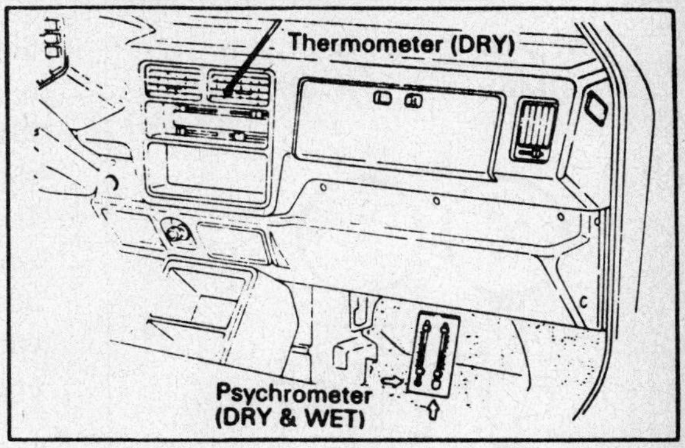
Thermometer (DRY)
Psychrometer
(DRY & WET)

HOW TO READ THE GRAPH:
After measuring the temperatures of the wet and dry-bulb thermometers at the evaporator air inlet, relative humidity (%) can be obtained
Example: Supposing dry-and wet-bulb temperatures at the evaporator air inlet are 25°C (77°F) and 19.5°C (67°F) respectively, the pint of intersection of the dotted lines in the graph is 60%.

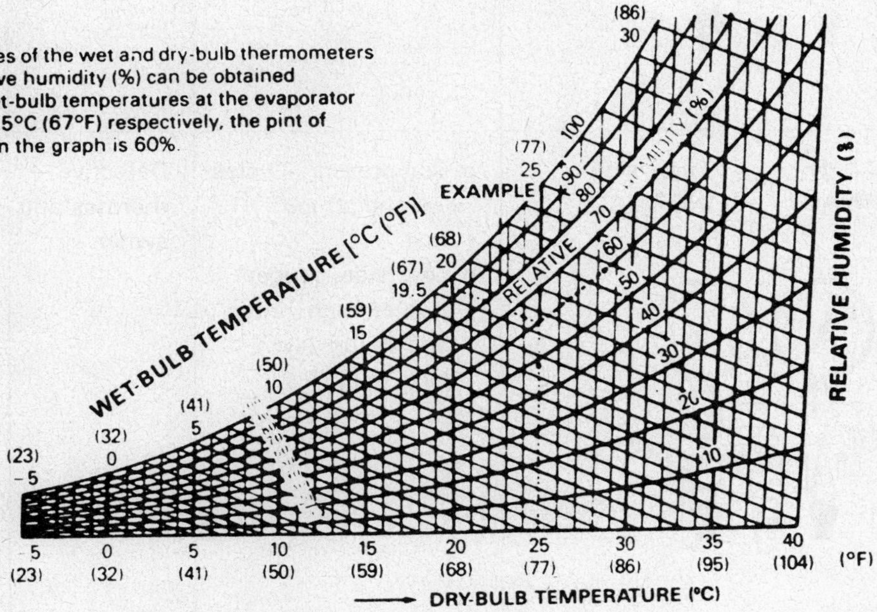
WET-BULB TEMPERATURE [°C (°F)]
EXAMPLE
RELATIVE HUMIDITY (%)
RELATIVE HUMIDITY (%)
DRY-BULB TEMPERATURE (°C)
(°F)
-5 (23)
0 (32)
5 (41)
10 (50)
15 (59)
19.5 (67)
20 (68)
25 (77)
30 (86)
35 (95)
40 (104)
100
90
80
70
60
50
40
30
20
10

GENERAL AIR CONDITIONING DIAGNOSIS—1989 EXCEL PERFORMANCE TEST

GAUGE READINGS	OTHER SYMPTOMS	DIAGNOSIS	CORRECTION
Low side NORMAL High side NORMAL 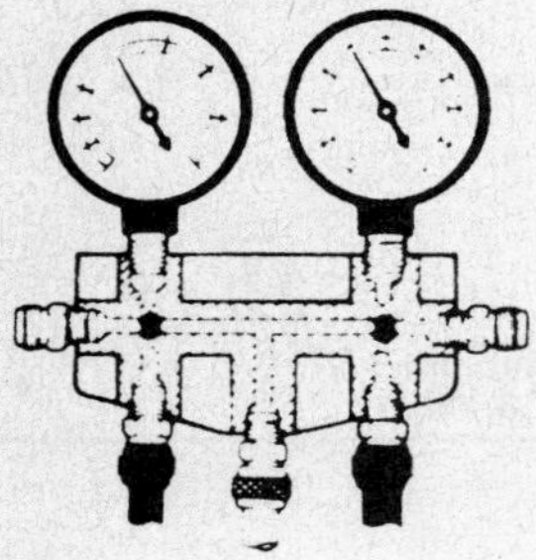	o Sight glass: clear or few bubbles. o Discharge air: slightly cool. o Thermostatic switch: Low side gauge dosen't fluctuate with switch "ON" and "OFF" cycle.	Some air and moisture in system.	1. Leak test system. 2. Discharge refrigerant from system. 3. Repair leaks as located. 4. Replace receiver-drier The drier is probably saturated with moisture. 5. Evacuate the system for at least 30 minutes. 6. Charge system with R-12. 7. Operate system and check performance.
Low side NORMAL High side NORMAL 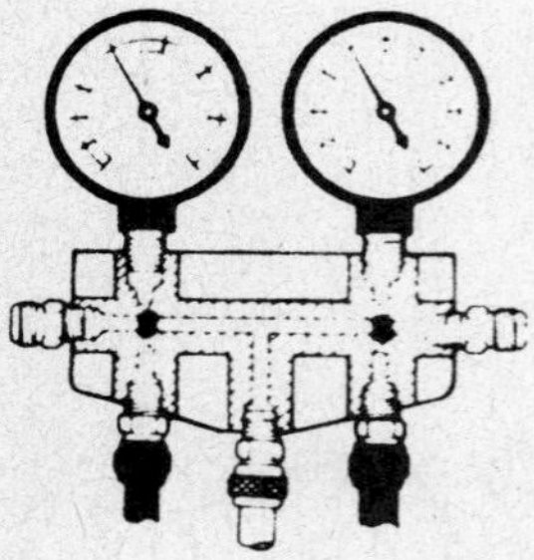	o Sight glass: Tiny bubbles. o Discharge air: Becomes warm as low side cycles into vacuum. o Discharge air: Becomes warm all the time during hot part of day.	Excessive moisture in system	1. Discharge refrigerant 2. Replace receiver-drier 3. Evacuate system with a vacuum pump. 4. Recharge system to proper capacity. 5. Operate system and check performance.
Low side NORMAL High side NORMAL 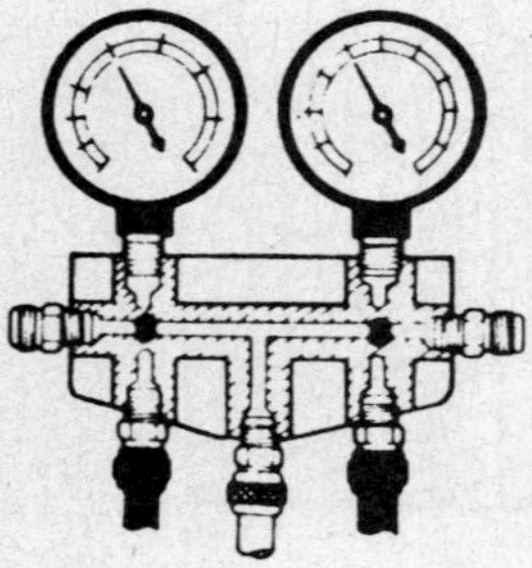	o Compressor: Cycles on and off too fast. o Low side gauge: Not enough range shown on low side gauge.	Defective thermostatic switch	1. Stop engine and turn air conditioner "OFF" 2. Replace thermostatic switch when installing new thermostic switch, make sure that capillary tube is installed in the same position and to the same depth in evaporator core as old switch tube. 3. Operate system and check performance.

GENERAL AIR CONDITIONING DIAGNOSIS—1989 EXCEL
PERFORMANCE TEST

GAUGE READINGS	OTHER SYMPTOMS	DIAGNOSIS	CORRECTION
Low side NORMAL to HIGH; High side NORMAL 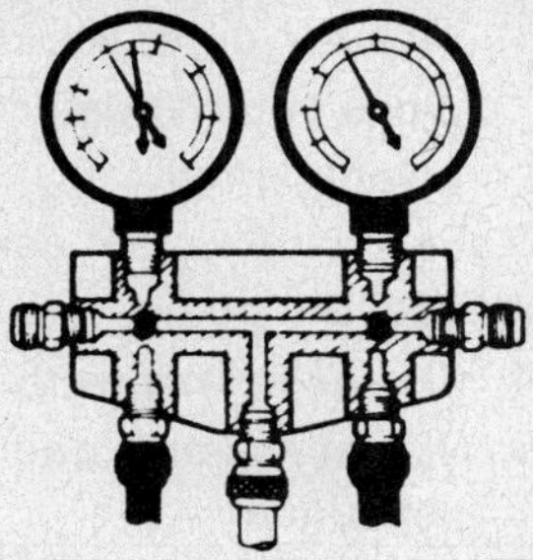	o Compressor: low side pressure builds too high before compressor turns on (cycle "ON" point too high)	Faulty thermostatic switch	1. Stop engine and turn air conditioner "OFF" 2. Repair or replace thermostatic switch (make sure that all wiring is positioned so that no short circuiting can occurred. 3. Operate system and check performance.
Low side LOW; High side LOW 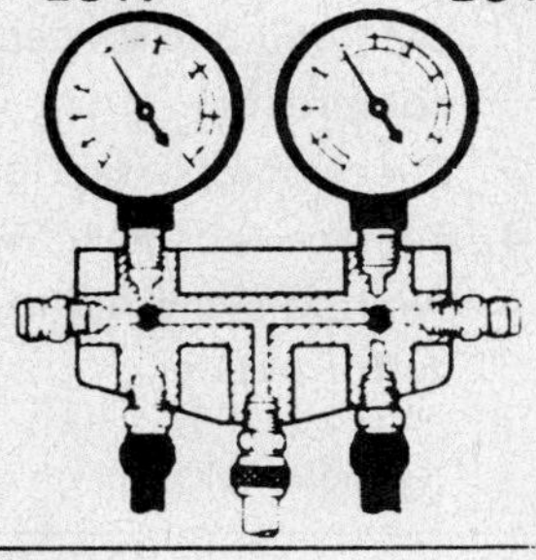	o Discharge air: Slightly cool. o Sight glass: Some bubbles.	o System slightly low on R-12	1. Check leaks. 2. Discharge refrigerant. 3. Repair leaks. 4. Check compressor oil level. 5. Evacuate system using a vacuum pump. 6. Charge system with R-12 7. Operate system and check performance.
Low side LOW; High side LOW 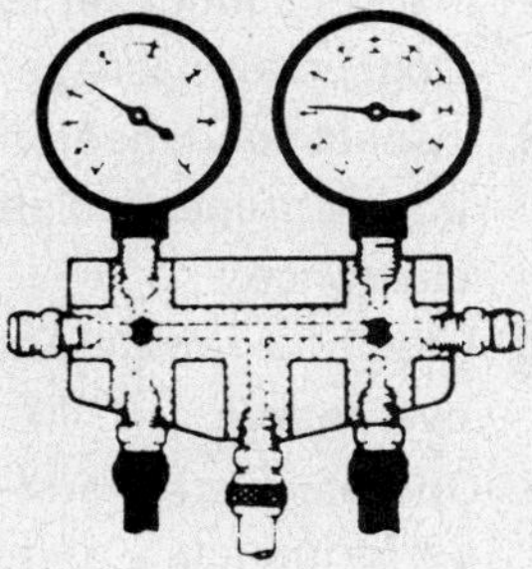	o Discharge air: Warm o Sight glass: Clear	o System very low on R-12 o Possible leak in system.	1. Check leaks. 2. Leak test compressor seal area very carefully. 3. Discharge refrigerant. 4. Check compressor oil level. 5. Evaporate system using a vacuum pump. 6. Charge system with R-12. 7. Operate system and check performance.
Low side LOW; High side LOW 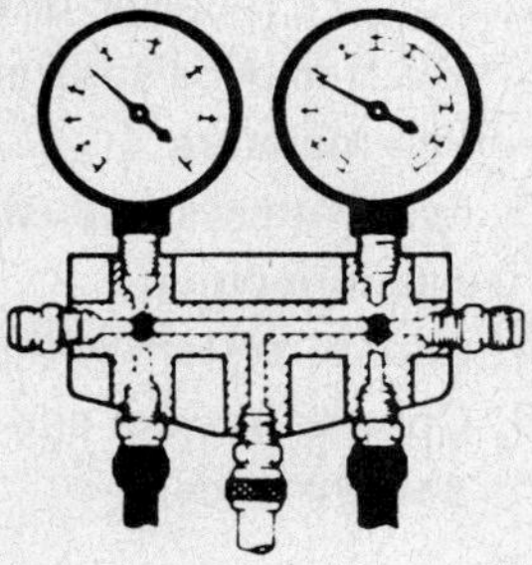	o Discharge air: Slightly cool. o Expansion valve: Sweating or frost build up.	o Expansion valve stuck closed. o Screen plugged. o Sensing bulb malfunction.	1. Discharge system. 2. Disconnect inlet line at expansion valve and remove and inspect screen. 3. Clean and replace screen and reconnect inlet line. 4. Evacuate system using a vacuum pump. 5. Charge system with R-12.

GENERAL AIR CONDITIONING DIAGNOSIS—1989 EXCEL PERFORMANCE TEST

GAUGE READINGS	OTHER SYMPTOMS	DIAGNOSIS	CORRECTION
Low side LOW High side LOW 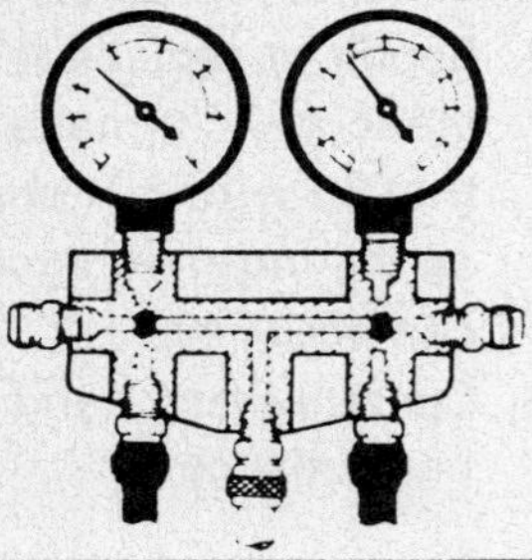	o Discharge air: slightly cool. o High side pipe: Cool and also shows sweating or frost.	o Restriction in high side of system	1. Discharge system. 2. Remove and replace receiver-drier, liquid pipes or other defective components. 3. Evacuate system using a vacuum pump. 4. Charge system with R-12 5. Operate system and check performance.
Low side HIGH High side LOW 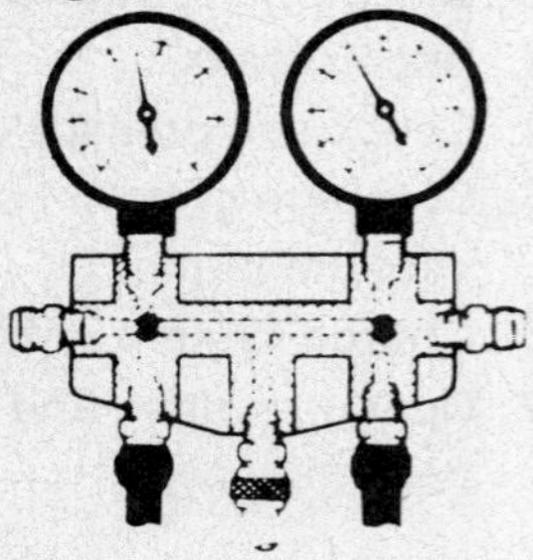	o Compressor: Noisy	o Compressor malfunction	1. Isolate compressor. 2. Remove compressor cylinder head and inspect compressor. 3. Check compressor oil level. 4. Replace receiver-drier. 5. Operate system and check performance.
Low side HIGH High side HIGH 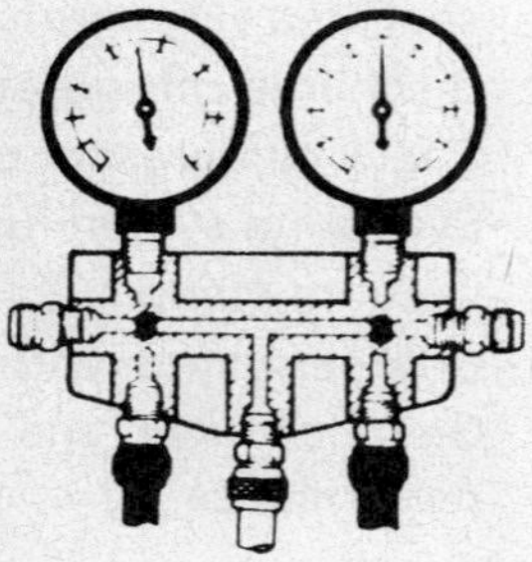	o Discharge air: Warm. o Sight glass: Bubbles. o High side pipe: Very hot	o Malfunctioning condenser overcharge.	1. Check for loose or worn fan belt. 2. Inspect condenser for clogged air passage. 3. Inspect condenser mounting for proper radiator clearance. 4. Check for refrigerant overcharge. 5. Operate system and check performance.
Low side HIGH High side HIGH 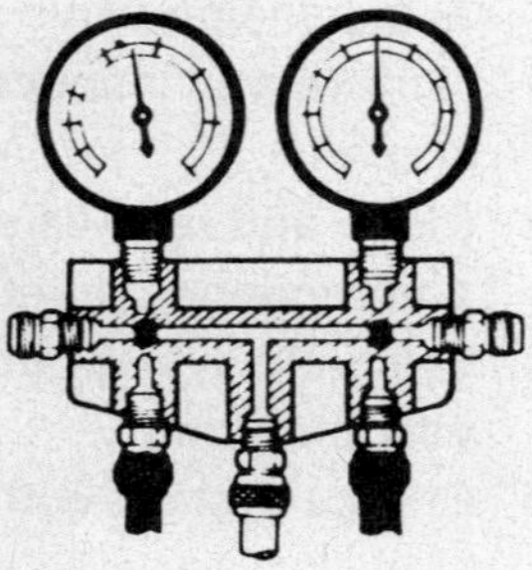	o Sight glass: Occasional bubbles o Discharge air: Slightly cool.	o Large amount of air and moisture	1. Discharge refrigerant from system. 2. Replace receiver-drier which may be saturated with moisture. 3. Evacuate system using vacuum pump. 4. Charge system with R-12. 5. Operate system and check performance.

GENERAL HEATING SYSTEM DIAGNOSIS—1990–91 EXCEL VACUUM SYSTEM TEST

Symptom	Probable cause
On "FLOOR" position. All air through defroster or DEF/FLOOR.	o Blue and/or red vacuum hose pinched or disconnected at vacuum motor. o Black source hose pinched or disconnected at the connector. o Engine compartment A/C source hose pinched or disconnected at the vacuum manifold. o Defective vacuum motor.
On "DEF/FLOOR" position. All air through defroster.	o Blue hose pinched or disconnected at vacuum motor. o Blue vacuum hoses installed improperly (reversed). o Black source hose pinched or disconnected at the connector. o Engine compartment A/C source hose pinched or disconnected at the vacuum manifold. o Defective vacuum motor.
On "PANEL VENTS" position. All air through defroster.	o Yellow vacuum hose pinched or disconnected at vacuum motor. o Black source hose pinched or disconnected at the connector. o Engine compartment A/C source hose pinched or disconnected at the vacuum manifold. o Defective vacuum motor.
On "PANEL/FLOOR" position. All air through defroster or panel	o Yellow vacuum hose pinched or disconnected at vacuum motor. o Blue hose pinched or disconnected at vacuum motor. o Black source hose pinched or disconnected at the connector. o Engine compartment A/C source hose pinched or disconnected at the vacuum manifold. o Defective vacuum motor.
On "DEF" position. (No vacuum) On "RECIRC" position. All air through fresh.	o White vacuum hose disconnected at the connector or recirc duct vacuum motor. o Black source hose pinched or disconnected at the connector. o Engine compartment A/C source hose pinched or disconnected at the vacuum manifold. o Defective vacuum motor.

GENERAL AIR CONDITIONING DIAGNOSIS—1990–91 EXCEL PERFORMANCE TEST

REFRIGERANT SYSTEM PERFORMANCE EVALUATION

The best way to diagnose a problem in the refrigerant system is to note the system pressures (shown by the manifold gauges) and the clutch cycle rate and times. Then, compare the findings with the charts

The system pressures are low (compressor suction) and high (compressor discharge).

Clutch cycle times are the lengths of time (in seconds) that the clutch is ON and OFF.

The following procedure is recommended for achieving accurate diagnosis results in the least amount of time.

1. Connect a manifold gauge set.

NOTE:

The test conditions, specified at the top of each chart, must be met to obtain accurate test results.

2. As soon as the system is stabilized, record the high and low-pressures as shown by the manifold gauges.
3. Determine the clutch cycle time.
4. Record clutch off time in seconds.
5. Record clutch on time in seconds.
6. Record center register discharge temperature.
7. Determine and record ambient temperatures.
8. Compare test readings with the applicable chart.

Plot a vertical line for recorded ambient temperature from scale at bottom of each chart to top of each chart.

Plot a horizontal line for each of the other test readings from scale at LH side of appropriate chart.

If the point where the two lines cross or each of the charts falls within the band of acceptable limits, the system is operating normally. If the lines cross outside the band on one or more of the charts, there is a problem and the specific cause must be determined. this is easily done by using the Refrigerant System and Clutch Cycle Timing Evaluation chart

Refer to the following five system operating conditions indicated by where the lines cross on the charts.

System high (discharge) pressure is high, low, or normal.

System low (suction) pressure is high, low, or normal.

Clutch cycle rate is fast, slow, or the clutch runs continuously.

IMPORTANT TEST REQUIREMENTS

The following test conditions must be established to obtain accurate clutch cycle rate and cycle time readings.

- o Run engine at 1500 rpm for 10 minutes.
- o Operate A/C system on max A/C (recirculating air)
- o Run blower at max speed.
- o Stabilize in temperature 70°F to 80°F (21°C to 22°C)

NORMAL CENTER REGISTER DISCHARGE TEMPERATURES

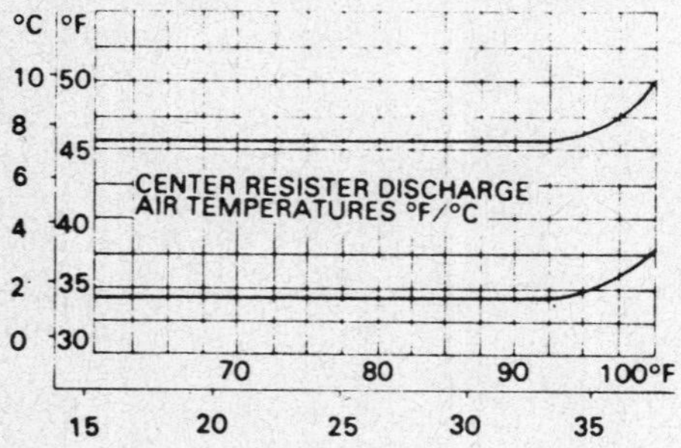
°C
°F
10
8
6
4
2
0
50
45
40
35
30
CENTER RESISTER DISCHARGE AIR TEMPERATURES °F/°C
70
80
90
100°F
15
20
25
30
35

AMBIENT TEMPERATURES

NORMAL FIXED ORIFICE TUBE CYCLING CLUTCH REFRIGERANT SYSTEM PRESSURES

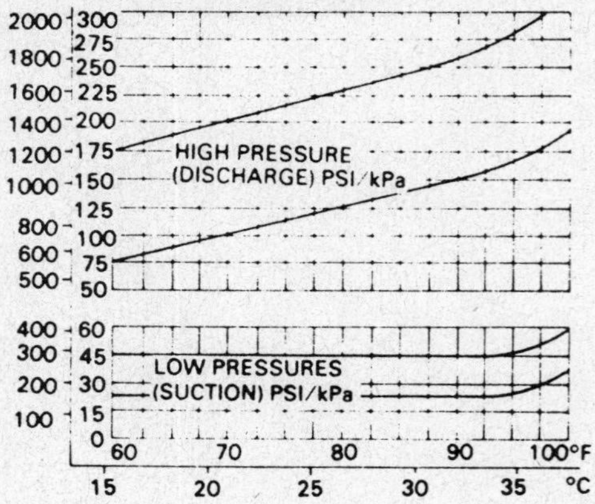
2000
1800
1600
1400
1200
1000
800
600
500
300
275
250
225
200
175
150
125
100
75
50
HIGH PRESSURE (DISCHARGE) PSI/kPa
400
300
200
100
60
45
30
15
0
LOW PRESSURES (SUCTION) PSI/kPa
60
70
80
90
100°F
15
20
25
30
35
°C

AMBIENT TEMPERATURES

GENERAL AIR CONDITIONING DIAGNOSIS—1990–91 EXCEL
INSUFFICIENT OR NO COOLING—FIXED ORIFICE TUBE CYCLING CLUTCH SYSTEM

TEST STEP		RESULT	ACTION TO TAKE
A1	VERIFY THE CONDITION		
	Check system operation	System cooling properly	INSTRUCT vehicle owner on proper use of the system
		System not cooling Properly	GO to A2
A2	CHECK A/C COMPRESSOR CLUTCH		
	Does the A/C compressor clutch engage?	Yes	GO to A3
		No	REFER to clutch circuit diagnosis in this section
A3	CHECK OPERATION OF COOLING FAN		
	Check that the cooling fan runs when the A/C compressor clutch is engaged	Yes	GO to A4
		No	Check for cooling fan electric circuit
A4	COMPONENT CHECK		
	o Under-hood check of the following: Loose, missing or damaged compressor drive belt. Loose or disconnected A/C clutch or clutch cycling pressure switch connectors. Disconnected resistor assembly. Loose vacuum lines or misadjusted control cables o Inside vehicle check for: Blown fuse or improper blower motor operation. Vacuum motors/temperature door movement-full travel. Electrical and vacuum connections.	OK but still not cooling	GO to A6
		Not OK	REPAIR AND GO to A5
A5	CHECK SYSTEM		
	Check system operation	OK	Condition Corrected GO to A1
		Not OK	GO to A6

GENERAL AIR CONDITIONING DIAGNOSIS—1990–91 EXCEL
INSUFFICIENT OR NO COOLING—FIXED ORIFICE TUBE CYCLING CLUTCH SYSTEM

TEST STEP		RESULT	ACTION TO TAKE
A1	VERIFY THE CONDITION		
	Check system operation	System cooling properly	INSTRUCT vehicle owner on proper use of the system
		System not cooling Properly	GO to A2
A2	CHECK A/C COMPRESSOR CLUTCH		
	Does the A/C compressor clutch engage?	Yes	GO to A3
		No	
A3	CHECK OPERATION OF COOLING FAN		
	Check that the cooling fan runs when the A/C compressor clutch is engaged	Yes	GO to A4
		No	Check for cooling fan electric circuit
A4	COMPONENT CHECK		
	o Under-hood check of the following: Loose, missing or damaged compressor drive belt. Loose or disconnected A/C clutch or clutch cycling pressure switch connectors. Disconnected resistor assembly. Loose vacuum lines or misadjusted control cables o Inside vehicle check for: Blown fuse or improper blower motor operation. Vacuum motors/temperature door movement-full travel. Electrical and vacuum connections.	OK but still not cooling	GO to A6
		Not OK	REPAIR AND GO to A5
A5	CHECK SYSTEM		
	Check system operation	OK	Condition Corrected GO to A1
		Not OK	GO to A6

GENERAL AIR CONDITIONING DIAGNOSIS—1990–91 EXCEL
INSUFFICIENT OR NO COOLING—FIXED ORIFICE TUBE CYCLING CLUTCH SYSTEM

TEST STEP	RESULT	ACTION TO TAKE
A1 VERIFY THE CONDITION		
Check system operation	System cooling properly	INSTRUCT vehicle owner on proper use of the system
	System not cooling Properly	GO to A2
A2 CHECK A/C COMPRESSOR CLUTCH		
Does the A/C compressor clutch engage?	Yes	GO to A3
	No	
A3 CHECK OPERATION OF COOLING FAN		
Check that the cooling fan runs when the A/C compressor clutch is engaged	Yes	GO to A4
	No	Check for cooling fan electric circuit
A4 COMPONENT CHECK		
o Under-hood check of the following: Loose, missing or damaged compressor drive belt. Loose or disconnected A/C clutch or clutch cycling pressure switch connectors. Disconnected resistor assembly. Loose vacuum lines or misadjusted control cables o Inside vehicle check for: Blown fuse or improper blower motor operation. Vacuum motors/temperature door movement-full travel. Electrical and vacuum connections.	OK but still not cooling	GO to A6
	Not OK	REPAIR AND GO to A5
A5 CHECK SYSTEM		
Check system operation	OK	Condition Corrected GO to A1
	Not OK	GO to A6

GENERAL AIR CONDITIONING DIAGNOSIS—1990-91 EXCEL
INSUFFICIENT OR NO COOLING—FIXED ORIFICE TUBE CYCLING CLUTCH SYSTEM

TEST STEP		RESULT	ACTION TO TAKE
A8	CHECK SYSTEM PRESSURES		
	Compare readings with normal system pressure ranges.	Clutch cycles within limits. System pressure within limits	System OK GO to A1
		Compressor runs continuously (normal operation in ambient temperature above 27°C (80°F.) depending on humidity conditions).	GO to A11
		Compressor cycles high or low ON above 359 kPa (52 psi) OFF below 144 kPa (21 psi).	REPLACE clutch cycling pressure switch. Do not discharge system Switch timing has Schrader valve CHECK system OK.GO to A1 NOT OK.GO to A9
A9	CHECK SYSTEM		
	Check system for leaks	Leak found	REPAIR, discharge, evacuate and charge system. System OK GO to A1
		No Leak found	Low refrigerant charge or moisture in system. Discharge, evacuate and charge system. System OK
A10	CHECK CLUTCH CYCLING		
	Disconnect blower motor wire and check for clutch cycling off at 144 kPa (21 psi) (suction pressure)	Clutch cycles OFF at 144—179 kPa (21—26 psi)	Connect blower motor wire. System OK GO to A1
		Pressure falls below 144 kPa (21 psi)	REPLACE clutch cycling pressure switch. Do not discharge system. Switch fitting has Schrader valve. System OK.GO to A1

GENERAL AIR CONDITIONING DIAGNOSIS—1990–91 EXCEL
INSUFFICIENT OR NO COOLING—FIXED ORIFICE TUBE CYCLING CLUTCH SYSTEM

TEST STEP		RESULT	ACTION TO TAKE
A8	CHECK SYSTEM PRESSURES		
	Compare readings with normal system pressure ranges.	Clutch cycles within limits. System pressure within limits	System OK GO to A1
		Compressor runs continuously (normal operation in ambient temperature above 27°C (80°F.) depending on humidity conditions).	GO to A11
		Compressor cycles high or low ON above 359 kPa (52 psi) OFF below 144 kPa (21 psi).	REPLACE clutch cycling pressure switch. Do not discharge system Switch timing has Schrader valve CHECK system OK.GO to A1 NOT OK.GO to A9
A9	CHECK SYSTEM		
	Check system for leaks	Leak found	REPAIR, discharge, evacuate and charge system. System OK GO to A1
		No Leak found	Low refrigerant charge or moisture in system. Discharge, evacuate and charge system. System OK
A10	CHECK CLUTCH CYCLING		
	Disconnect blower motor wire and check for clutch cycling off at 144 kPa (21 psi) (suction pressure)	Clutch cycles OFF at 144—179 kPa (21—26 psi)	Connect blower motor wire. System OK GO to A1
		Pressure falls below 144 kPa (21 psi)	REPLACE clutch cycling pressure switch. Do not discharge system. Switch fitting has Schrader valve. System OK.GO to A1

SEMI-AUTOMATIC TEMPERATURE CONTROL SYSTEM (SATC)
CHART 1—GENERAL DIAGNOSTIC PROCEDURE

REFRIGERANT SYSTEM PERFORMANCE EVALUATION

The best way to diagnose a problem in the refrigerant system is to note the system pressures (shown by the manifold gauges) and the clutch cycle rate and times. Then, compare the findings with the charts

- o The system pressures are low (compressor suction) and high (compressor discharge).
- o Clutch cycle times are the lengths of time (in seconds) that the clutch is ON and OFF.

The following procedure is recommended for achieving accurate diagnosis results in the least amount of time.

1. Connect a manifold gauge set.

   NOTE:
   The test conditions, specified at the top of each chart, must be met to obtain accurate test results.

2. As soon as the system is stabilized, record the high and low-pressures as shown by the manifold gauges.
3. Determine the clutch cycle time.
4. Record clutch off time in seconds.
5. Record clutch on time in seconds.
6. Record center register discharge temperature.
7. Determine and record ambient temperatures.
8. Compare test readings with the applicable chart.

- o Plot a vertical line for recorded ambient temperature from scale at bottom of each chart to top of each chart.
- o Plot a horizontal line for each of the other test readings from scale at LH side of appropriate chart.

If the point where the two lines cross or each of the charts falls within the band of acceptable limits, the system is operating normally. If the lines cross outside the band on one or more of the charts, there is a problem and the specific cause must be determined. this is easily done by using the Refrigerant System and Clutch Cycle Timing Evaluation chart

Refer to the following five system operating conditions indicated by where the lines cross on the charts.

- o System high (discharge) pressure is high, low, or normal.
- o System low (suction) pressure is high, low, or normal.
- o Clutch cycle rate is fast, slow, or the clutch runs continuously.

IMPORTANT TEST REQUIREMENTS

The following test conditions must be established to obtain accurate clutch cycle rate and cycle time readings.

- o Run engine at 1500 rpm for 10 minutes.
- o Operate A/C system on max A/C (recirculating air)
- o Run blower at max speed.
- o Stabilize in temperature 70°F to 80°F (21°C to 22°C)

NORMAL CENTER REGISTER DISCHARGE TEMPERATURES

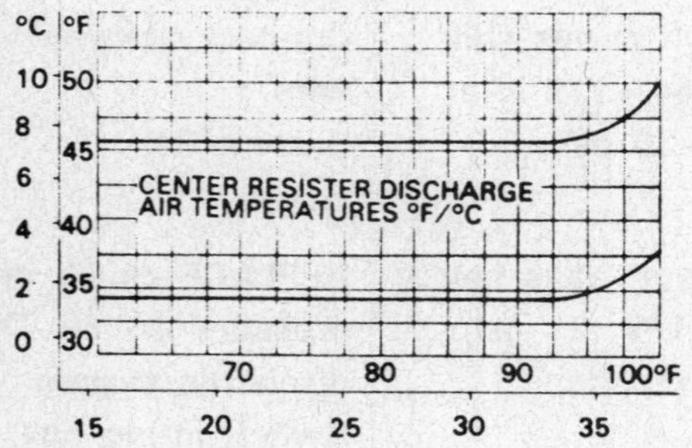
°C
°F
10
8
6
4
2
0
50
45
40
35
30
CENTER RESISTER DISCHARGE
AIR TEMPERATURES °F/°C
70
80
90
100°F
15
20
25
30
35

AMBIENT TEMPERATURES

NORMAL FIXED ORIFICE TUBE CYCLING CLUTCH REFRIGERANT SYSTEM PRESSURES

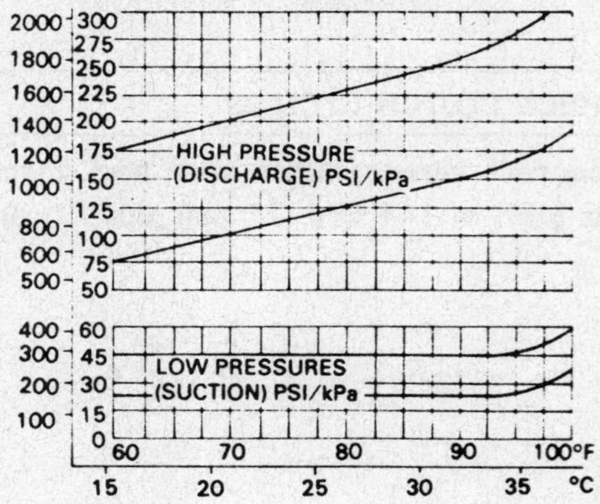
2000
1800
1600
1400
1200
1000
800
600
500
300
275
250
225
200
175
150
125
100
75
50
HIGH PRESSURE
(DISCHARGE) PSI/kPa
400
300
200
100
60
45
30
15
0
LOW PRESSURES
(SUCTION) PSI/kPa
60
70
80
90
100°F
15
20
25
30
35
°C

AMBIENT TEMPERATURES

SEMI-AUTOMATIC TEMPERATURE CONTROL SYSTEM (SATC)
CHART 1 – GENERAL DIAGNOSTIC PROCEDURE

TROUBLESHOOTING

Chart 1. GENERAL DIAGNOSTIC PROCEDURES

The *SATC unit provides a self diagnostic feature. This diagnostic feature provides error codes for system components with suspected failures.
The use of this diagnostic feature is outlined under General Diagnostic Procedures.

The general diagnostic procedures should be followed in the order presented.

1. Self Diagnostic - Record all error codes displayed during the test.
   Follow the troubleshooting/repair procedures listed for each error code.
2. If a malfunction exists but no error code was displayed during the test, then follow the functional check and then the system diagnosis procedures if required.

Self Test

The SATC unit self test feature will detect electrical malfunctions and provide error codes for system components with suspected failures.
The self test diagnostic mode procedures are outlined below.

TO ENTER DIAGNOSTIC MODE

1. Ignition switch must be on.
2. Engine coolant must be warm.
3. Temperature lever in "full" A/C position.
4. Blower lever in "auto" position.
5. OFF button latched.
6. The A/C and FLOOR buttons should now be pressed simultaneously within 2 seconds after pressing the OFF button. If the time limit is exceeded repeat step 5. The OFF button must be pressed from any on position.
   (i.e. PNL. PNL/FLR. FLR. FLR/DEF. or DEF)

The diagnostic LED will come on indicating that the control is in the diagnostic mode.
After 30 seconds has expired, the LED will go off.
If any errors were detected, their codes will begin flashing immediately.
If no codes were detected, the LED will remain off. An error code is read by counting the number of times the LED flashes.
When the code is finished flashing there will be a pause of about 7 to 14 seconds and then the next code will again begin to flash. This sequence will repeat until the diagnostics mode is terminated.

*SATC = Semi Automatic Temperature Control

To terminate the diagnostics mode turn the ignition off or press the SATC OFF button.
Diagnostic mode will also be terminated if no codes were detected during the test.
The system does continue to operate normally while in the diagnostic mode (except for the blend door during the first 30 seconds)

If the diagnostic LED stays on continuously, consult the System Diagnosis chart.

If a malfunction exists but no error code is displayed, refer to SATC Functional Check.

The diagnostic feature will only detect codes during the initial 30 seconds of the diagnostic test time.
If you suspect a new failure has occurred or need to verify a service repair, the diagnostic mode must be terminated and then re-entered to run the initial 30 second portion of the test again. Follow the steps outlined in the service procedures prior to the diagnostic test if any SATC components have been disconnected or replaced. (i.e. replacement of the ambient temperature sensor requires specific procedures, otherwise, an error code could be displayed when no defect exists).

ERROR DESCRIPTION	NUMBER OFF LASHES	TROUBLE SHOOTING
NO ERROR FOUND	0	
IN-CAR SENSOR OPEN OR SHORTED	8	Check the IN-CAR Sensor
AMBIENT SENSOR OPEN OR SHORTED	7	Check the AMBIENT Sensor
BLEND DOOR FEED BACK OUT OF RANGE	6	Check the BLEND DOOR ACTUATOR

SEMI-AUTOMATIC TEMPERATURE CONTROL SYSTEM (SATC) CHART 2—FUNCTIONAL CHECK

This test is used to determine system failures which the SATC self-test mode cannot detect.

To perform this test;

1. Make sure the engine is cold.
2. The in-vehicle and ambient temperature must be warner than 55°F (18°C).
3. Set the control to full heat (RED), Auto Blower, Floor, Outside and A/C off.

INSTRUCTIONS	RESULT	ACTION
A		
o Turn the ignition switch on o Turn the instrument panel illumination lights on.	o Instrument panel illumination light on. o Control doesn't light.	o GO TO B
B		
o Verify that the blower does not come on-CELO TEST. (Test must be performed within the first minute).	o Blower off o Blower on	o GO TO C o Refer to Chart 6.
C		
o Make sure that engine temperature is warm. -CELO TEST- (APPROX. 5 min or less, coolant temp. 120°F)	o Blower on o Blower off	o GO TO D o Refer to Chart 5.
D		
o Verify that air is discharged from the FLOOR duct. -FLOOR mode function test-	o Air is being discharged from FLOOR duct. o Otherwise	o GO TO E o Refer to Chart 7.
E		
o Blower lever set to LO	o Blower goes to low o Blower does not go to low	o GO TO F o Refer to Chart 5.
F		
o Blower lever set to HI	o Blower goes to high o Blower does not go to high	o GO TO G o Refer to Chart 5.
G		
o Depress the DEFROST button.	o Air is being discharged from the defroster nozzle with a small bleed out the side window demisters. o Otherwise o A/C is on. o A/C is off.	o GO TO H o Refer to Chart 7. o GO TO H o Refer to Chart 4.

SEMI-AUTOMATIC TEMPERATURE CONTROL SYSTEM (SATC)
CHART 2—FUNCTIONAL CHECK

INSTRUCTIONS	RESULT	ACTION
H		
o Depress the OFF button	o Blower stops and the system inlet door is in the recirc position.	o GO TO I
	o Blower on.	o Refer to Chart 5.
	o Inlet door is in the outside position	o Refer to Chart 7.
	o A/C operation is off	o GO TO I
	o A/C operation is on	o Refer to Chart 4.
I		
o Depress the (PANEL, PANEL/FLOOR FLOOR/DEFROST, RECIRC & OUTSIDE) buttons one after the other	O Air is being discharged from the proper duct when each button is pressed.	o GO TO J
	o Air is not being discharged from the proper locations.	o Refer to Chart 4.
J		
o Depress the A/C button with the system in the panel mode.	o A/C is operating	o GO TO Chart 3.
	o A/C is not operating	o Refer to Chart 4.

SEMI-AUTOMATIC TEMPERATURE CONTROL SYSTEM (SATC)
CHART 3—SYSTEM DIAGNOSIS

The purpose of this section is to provide possible cause and repair procedures for several control and system related failure symptoms.
To ensure proper test conditions, the checks outlined under this section should be performed directly after the section functional check.

SYMPTOM	POSSIBLE CAUSE	TEST/REPAIR PROCEDURE
Cool discharge air when the temperature lever is set to the full heat position	o Heater system malfunction o Blend door not in the full heat position	o Refer to appropriate service procedure o Check the position of the blend door o Check the blend door shaft attachment o Refer to Chart 6.
Cool discharge air at 85°F (29°C) max heat at full heat (RED)	o Sensor shorted or open	o Refer to Chart 8.
Warm discharge air when the temperature lever is set to the full cool position (blue).	o Clutch circuit malfunction. o Refrigerant system malfunction	o Refer to Chart 4.

SEMI-AUTOMATIC TEMPERATURE CONTROL SYSTEM (SATC)
CHART 3–SYSTEM DIAGNOSIS

SYMPTOM	POSSIBLE CAUSE	TEST/REPAIR PROCEDURE
Warm discharge air when the temperature lever is set to the full cool position (blue).	o Blend door not in the full cool position.	o Check the blend door position o Check the blend door shaft attachment o Refer to Chart 6.
Warm discharge air when the temperature lever is set to the full cool position (blue).	o System inlet door not in the recirc position (Recirc position required for max cooling)	o The outboard panel registers should be closed for max cooling-hot ambient ram air will increase the outboard panel register discharge air temperature
o No blower	o Faulty CELO switch/wiring o Faulty blower speed controller o Faulty blower motor o Faulty wiring o Faulty control head	o Refer to Blower Speed Controller Test
o High blower only	o Faulty control head o Faulty blower speed controller o Faulty wiring	o Refer to Chart 5.
o Clutch is "on" in OFF Mode	o Faulty control head o Faulty wiring o Faulty A/C compressor control circuit	o Refer to Chart 4.
o Control lighting does not work	o Fuse blown o Illumination circuit open o Faulty control	o Replace fuse. o Verify that pin 9 provides a variable voltage based on the dimmer position o Replace control if no failures were detected in the above test.
o Control diagnostic LED does not light	o Faulty CELO switch o Control head malfunction	o Refer to Chart 6. o Replace control head if CELO switch test proves control malfunction.
o Control diagnostic LED stays on	o Control head malfunction	o Replace control head.
o Cold air is discharged during heating (FOOR, AUTO BLOWER) when the engine is cold	o Damaged wiring o LOW coolant level	o Refer to Chart 6. o Reference radiator coolant level service.
o Control does not function	o Fuse blown on battery voltage line o Wiring short or open on battery voltage to SATC module	o Replace fuse. o Verify by checking pin #16 of SATC unit connector C197.

SEMI-AUTOMATIC TEMPERATURE CONTROL SYSTEM (SATC)
CHART 4—COMPRESSOR CONTROL CIRCUIT TEST

1. No clutch operation
   - o Ignition key "ON"
   - o Engine running
   - o Ambient temperature greater than 50°F
   - o A/C or DEFROST button depressed

INSTRUCTION	RESULT	ACTION
A		
o With connector C197 disconnected from the SATC unit jump pin 2 and pin 1. (Refer to Diagram)	o Clutch engages o Clutch does not engage	o Perform test per B. o Troubleshoot according to the appropriate service manual for blown fuse, faulty clutch, faulty wiring, faulty relays, faulty pressure switch, or faulty engine control unit (ECU).
B		
o Turn ignition switch to the OFF position. o With connector C190 disconnected from the ambient sensor jump pin 1 and pin 2 of C190, then connect C197 to the SATC unit, then turn the ignition switch to the "ON" run position.	o Clutch does not engage o Clutch engages	o Replace the control. o Ambient sensor could be defective. o Refer to Chart 8.

2. Clutch does not disengage
   - o When in the OFF mode.
   - o A/C button OFF except with the DEFROST button depressed.

INSTRUCTIONS	RESULT	ACTION
A		
o Disconnect C197 from the SATC unit.	o Clutch disengages o Clutch stays on	o Change the control. o Troubleshoot according to the appropriate service manual for the faulty clutch, faulty wiring, faulty relays, or faulty engine control unit. (ECU)

SEMI-AUTOMATIC TEMPERATURE CONTROL SYSTEM (SATC)
CHART 5—BLOWER SPEED CONTROL TEST

1. No blower
   - o Ignition switch "ON"
   - o Engine warm
   - o Blower & Auto setting
   - o Full heat (RED) temperature setting.

TEST INSTRUCTIONS (CELO TEST)	RESULT	CAUSE/ACTION
A —CELO TEST— o Change temperature to full cool.	o Blower comes on o No blower	o GO TO Chart 6. o GO TO B
B —Fuse & Wiring test BSC power— o Using a voltmeter measure the voltage between pin #3 and pin #4 of the BSC connector C181. (Refer to V Diagram)	o 0 volt o More than 10 volts	o Check ignition circuit fuse and wire continuity (i.e. between fuse panel and pin #3 and between pin #4 and ground) o GO TO C
C —BSC input signal test— o Using a voltmeter measure the voltage between pin #2 and pin #4 of the BSC connector C181.	o More than 3 volts o Less than 3 volts	o GO TO E o GO TO D
D —BSC/Blower motor feed test— o Measure the Voltage between pin #3 and pin #4 of the SATC unit connector C197.	o Less than 1 volt o More than 1 volt	o Check the blower motor feed. (Fuse, Wiring, Relay, etc) o Replace the VBC.
E —SATC unit BSC signal/wirings continuity test— o Measure the Voltage between pin #13 and pin #4 of the SATC unit connector C197.	o More than 3 volts o Less than 3 volts	o Replace the SATC module. o Check the circuit continuity (i.e. between pin #13 of C197 and pin #2 of C181, pin #4 of C197 is a good ground)

SEMI-AUTOMATIC TEMPERATURE CONTROL SYSTEM (SATC)
CHART 5—BLOWER SPEED CONTROL TEST

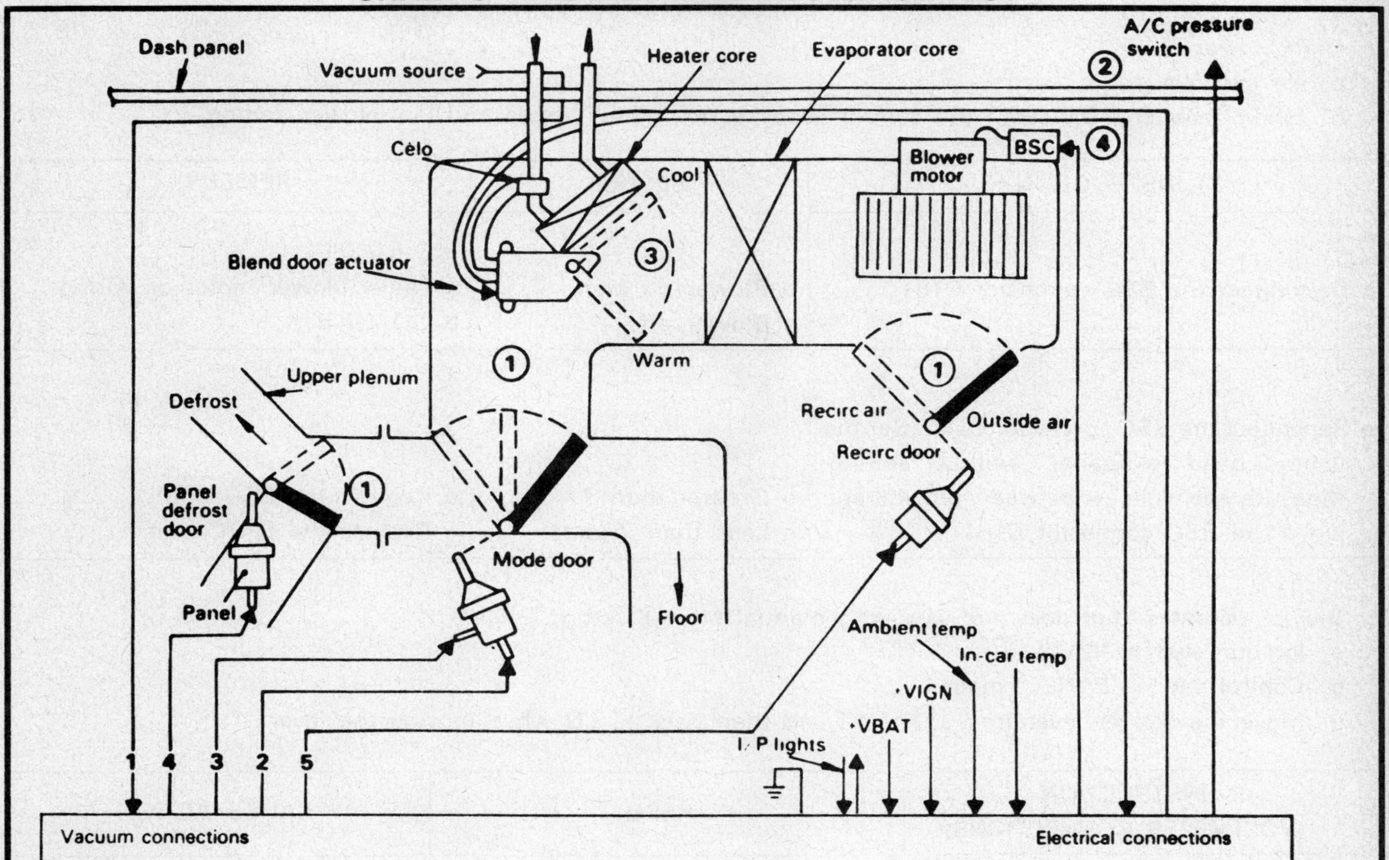
Dash panel
Vacuum source
Heater core
Evaporator core
A/C pressure switch
②
Célo
Cool
Blower motor
BSC
④
Blend door actuator
③
①
Warm
Upper plenum
Defrost
Panel defrost door
Recirc air
Outside air
Recirc door
Mode door
Panel
Floor
Ambient temp
In-car temp
•VIGN
•VBAT
I/P lights
1 4 3 2 5
Vacuum connections
Electrical connections

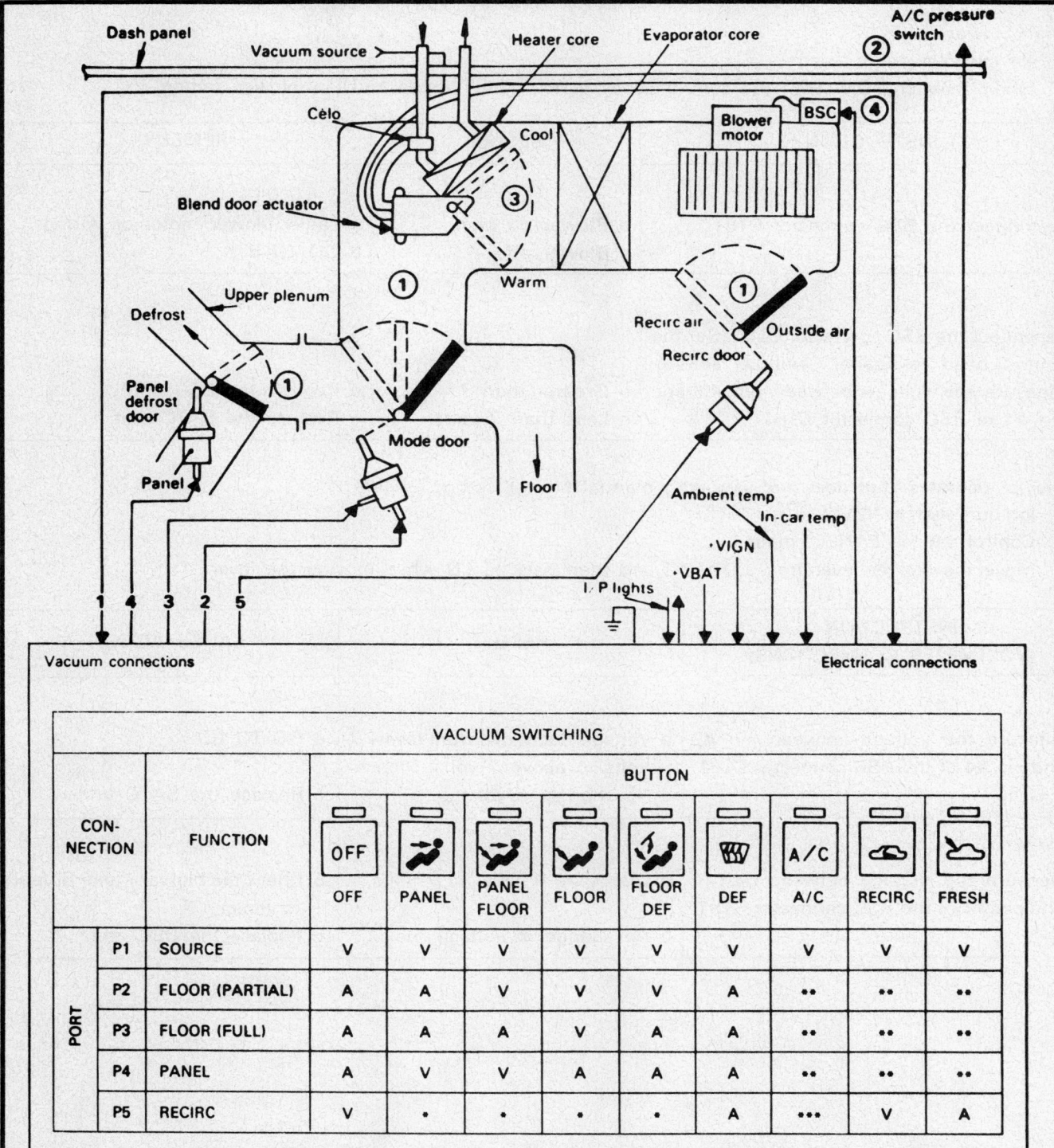

CONNECTION		FUNCTION	OFF	PANEL	PANEL FLOOR	FLOOR	FLOOR DEF	DEF	A/C	RECIRC	FRESH
PORT	P1	SOURCE	V	V	V	V	V	V	V	V	V
PORT	P2	FLOOR (PARTIAL)	A	A	V	V	V	A	••	••	••
PORT	P3	FLOOR (FULL)	A	A	A	V	A	A	••	••	••
PORT	P4	PANEL	A	V	V	A	A	A	••	••	••
PORT	P5	RECIRC	V	•	•	•	•	A	•••	V	A

(VACUUM SWITCHING — BUTTON)

V = Vacuum A = Atmosphere
• = Controlled by "RECIRC" and "FRESH" buttons.
•• = Controlled by "OFF" "PANEL" "PANEL/FLOOR" "FLOOR" "FLOOR/DEF and "DEF" buttons.
••• = Controlled by "OFF" "DEF" "RECIRC" and "FRESH" buttons.

SEMI-AUTOMATIC TEMPERATURE CONTROL SYSTEM (SATC)
CHART 5—BLOWER SPEED CONTROL TEST

2. High blower only
   - o No low blower
   - o Ignition switch "ON" with the control head set to "panel" mode and low blower setting.

INSTRUCTION	RESULT	REMEDY
A		
o Disconnect the BSC connector C181.	o Blower on high o Blower off	o Faulty blower motor or wiring. o GO TO B
B		
o Reconnect the BSC connector C181. Set the control head to "panel" and LO setting. Measure the voltage between pin #2 and pin #4 of BSC connector C181.	o Greater than 7 volts o Less than 7 volts	o Replace the BSC unit. o Replace the SATC unit.

3. Blower operates—but does not vary with manual blower setting LO—HI
   - o Ignition switch "ON"
   - o Control set to "PANEL" mode
   - o Move the blower lever from LO to HI and then back to LO while moving the lever.

INSTRUCTION (VOLTMETER CONNECTIONS)	RESULT	CAUSE/ACTION
A		
o Measure the Voltage between pin #2 and pin #4 of the BSC connector C181.	o Voltage fluctuates from below 7 volts to above 7 volts, then to o No change in voltage	o GO TO B o Replace the SATC unit
B		
o Measure the Voltage between pin #1 and pin #4 of the BSC connector C181.	o Less than 1 volts to 7 volts o No change in voltage	o Check the blower motor or feed to motor. o Replace the BSC unit.

SEMI-AUTOMATIC TEMPERATURE CONTROL SYSTEM (SATC)
CHART 6—BLEND DOOR ACTUATOR AND CELO TEST

1. Actuator test

INSTRUCTION	RESULT	ACTION
A		
o With connector C197 disconnected from the SATC unit, drive the actuator in the CW and then CCW direction. Make sure the ignition is on. CW jump pin #5 and pin #4; CCW jump pin #12 and pin #4	o Actuator drives in both directions o Actuator does not drive in both directions	o GO TO B o GO TO C

*CW: Clockwise
CCW: Counterclockwise

INSTRUCTIONS	RESULT	ACTION
B		
o With connector C197 disconnected from the SATC unit measure the resistance for the following pin combinations. 1) pin 7 to pin 5 = 5000—7000Ω 2) pin 10 to pin 7 = 300—7500Ω 3) pin 10 to pin 5 = 300—7300Ω	o All resistances match o Resistances do not match	o GO TO G o GO TO C
C		
o With connectors C197 & C201 disconnected from the SATC unit and blend door actuator respectively, check the vehicle wiring and connector continuity as shown below. Connect C197-to-connector C201 pin 4 — pin 11 pin 2 — pin 12 pin 1 — pin 5 pin 8 — pin 3 pin 7 — pin 10 pin 6 — pin 7	o The continuity is good. o The continuity is bad.	o GO TO E o GO TO D
D		
o Fix or replace the wiring harness or connector as required. Connect and test according to Chart 2 "Functional check".	o Test successful o Test fails	o Done o GO TO A
E		
o Verify actuator ground and ignition power on connector C201. Place Voltmeter across pin 3 and pin 5.	o Battery voltage is available o Battery voltage is not available	o Proceed to F o Fuse replacement
F		
o Replace blend door actuator and test according to Chart 2 Functional check.	o Test successful o Test fails	o Done o GO TO A

SEMI-AUTOMATIC TEMPERATURE CONTROL SYSTEM (SATC)
CHART 6—BLEND DOOR ACTUATOR AND CELO TEST

2. Celo test

INSTRUCTIONS	RESULT	ACTION
A		
o CELO inoperative, blower turns on immediately. o Engine cold, FLOOR mode, AUTO Blower, Full Heat (RED)	o Blower on o Blower off	o GO TO B. o Blower switch is working properly
B		
o Disconnect the blend actuator/CELO connector C201.	o Blower turns on o Blower turns off	o GO TO C. o The following items could be the problem. 1) Low coolant level. 2) CELO switch is not attached to the heater core inlet tube. 3) Faulty CELO switch. o If item 1 or 2 are not the problem replace the blend actuator/CELO assembly.
C		
o Disconnect the SATC unit C197. o Using an Ohm meter check for a short to ground on pin #11 of C197.	o Circuit on pin #11 is shorted o Circuit on pin #11 is not shorted	o Repair and test according to Chart 2 "Functional check". o Replace the SATC unit.

3. No blower
   o FLOOR mode, AUTO Blower, Full Heat (RED) Engine Warm

INSTRUCTIONS	RESULT	ACTION
A		
o Disconnect blend actuator/CELO connector C201.	o Blower turns on	o CELO switch faulty. Replace blend actuator/CELO assembly.
B		
o Disconnect the SATC unit connector C201. o Ohm meter check for a short to ground on pin #11 of C197.	o Circuit on pin #11 is shorted. o Circuit on pin #11 is not shorted.	o Repair and test according to Chart 2 "Function check". o Replace the SATC unit.

SEMI-AUTOMATIC TEMPERATURE CONTROL SYSTEM (SATC)
CHART 7—VACUUM SYSTEM TEST

- o Reference Appendix B for vacuum system schematic.
- o Figure #1 outlines the vacuum system connections referenced in this test procedure.
- o The vacuum tester used to diagnose vacuum system problem is shown in figure #2.
- o Figure #3 provides a brief description of how the vacuum motor operates.

1. Vacuum supply test

INSTRUCTIONS	RESULT	ACTION
A		
o Connect vacuum tester (figure #2) to system side of check valve. (Figure #1, Connection #3) o Start engine.	o Approximately quote mmHg also Hg (380 mmHg) of vacuum. o Less than quote mmHg also Hg (380 mmHg) vacuum	o GO TO E. o Perform leak check per B through D.
B		
o Connect vacuum tester to check valve side of vacuum source tube. (Connection #1)	o Approximately quote mmHg also Hg (380 mmHg) of vacuum. o Less than quote mmHg also Hg (380 mmHg) vacuum	o GO TO C. o Repair vacuum source tube.
C		
o With the check valve connected to the source line (Connection #1) and the system side of the check valve plugged, (Connection #3) connect the vacuum tester to the vacuum tank side of the check valve (Connection #2)	o Approximately quote mmHg also Hg (380 mmHg) vacuum o Less than quote mmHg also Hg (380 mmHg) vacuum	o Replace the check valve. o Replace the check valve.
D		
o With connections specified per C except connect vacuum tank hose to vacuum tank side of the check valve (Connection #2) and vacuum tester to vacuum tank hose at connection #4.	o Approximately quote mmHg also Hg (380 mmHg) vacuum o Less than quote mmHg also Hg (380 mmHg) vacuum	o Replace the vacuum tank. o Replace the vacuum tank hose.
E		
o Turn off engine and observe gauge.	o Vacuum holds o Vacuum fails	o Supply OK. o Replace the check valve, vacuum tank, vacuum source tube, or vacuum tank tube based on tests outlined per B through D.

WIRING SCHEMATICS

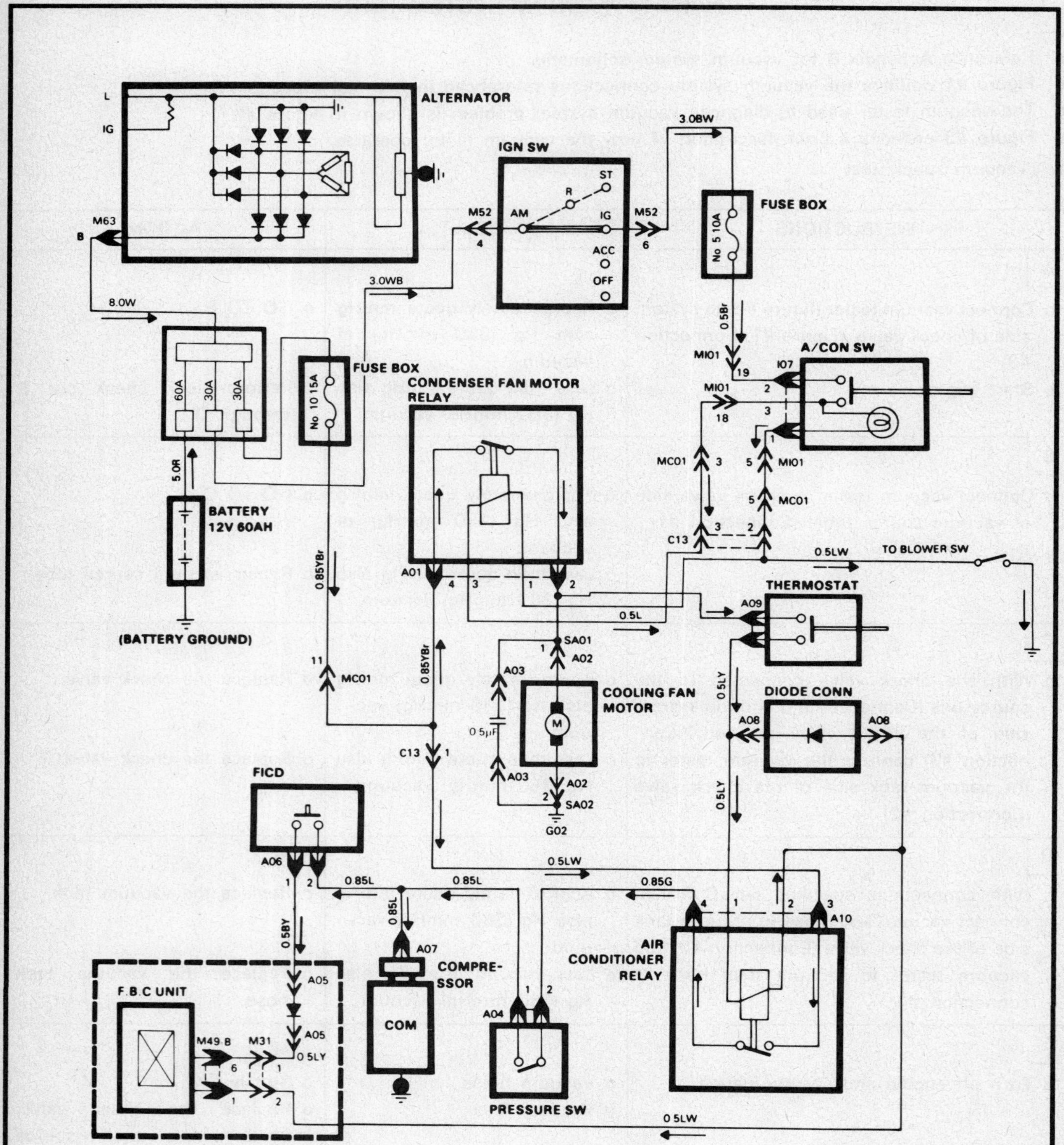
ALTERNATOR
L
IG
M63
B
8.0W
IGN SW
ST
R
AM
IG
ACC
OFF
M52
4
M52
6
3.0BW
3.0WB
FUSE BOX
No 5 10A
0.5Br
60A
30A
30A
FUSE BOX
No 10 15A
5.0R
BATTERY
12V 60AH
(BATTERY GROUND)
CONDENSER FAN MOTOR
RELAY
A/CON SW
MI01
19
I07
2
MI01
18
3
1
MC01
3
5
MI01
5
MC01
C13
3
2
0.5LW
TO BLOWER SW
0.85YBr
A01
4
3
1
2
THERMOSTAT
A09
0.5L
SA01
A02
A03
COOLING FAN
MOTOR
0.5μF
A03
A02
SA02
G02
11
MC01
0.85YBr
C13
1
0.5LY
DIODE CONN
A08
A08
0.5LY
FICD
A06
1
2
0.85L
0.85L
0.5LW
0.85G
0.85L
A07
COMPRE-
SSOR
COM
4
1
2
3
A10
AIR
CONDITIONER
RELAY
0.5BY
A05
F.B.C UNIT
M49.B
M31
A05
0.5LY
6
1
1
2
A04
1
2
PRESSURE SW
0.5LW

Air conditioning wiring schematic—1989 Excel

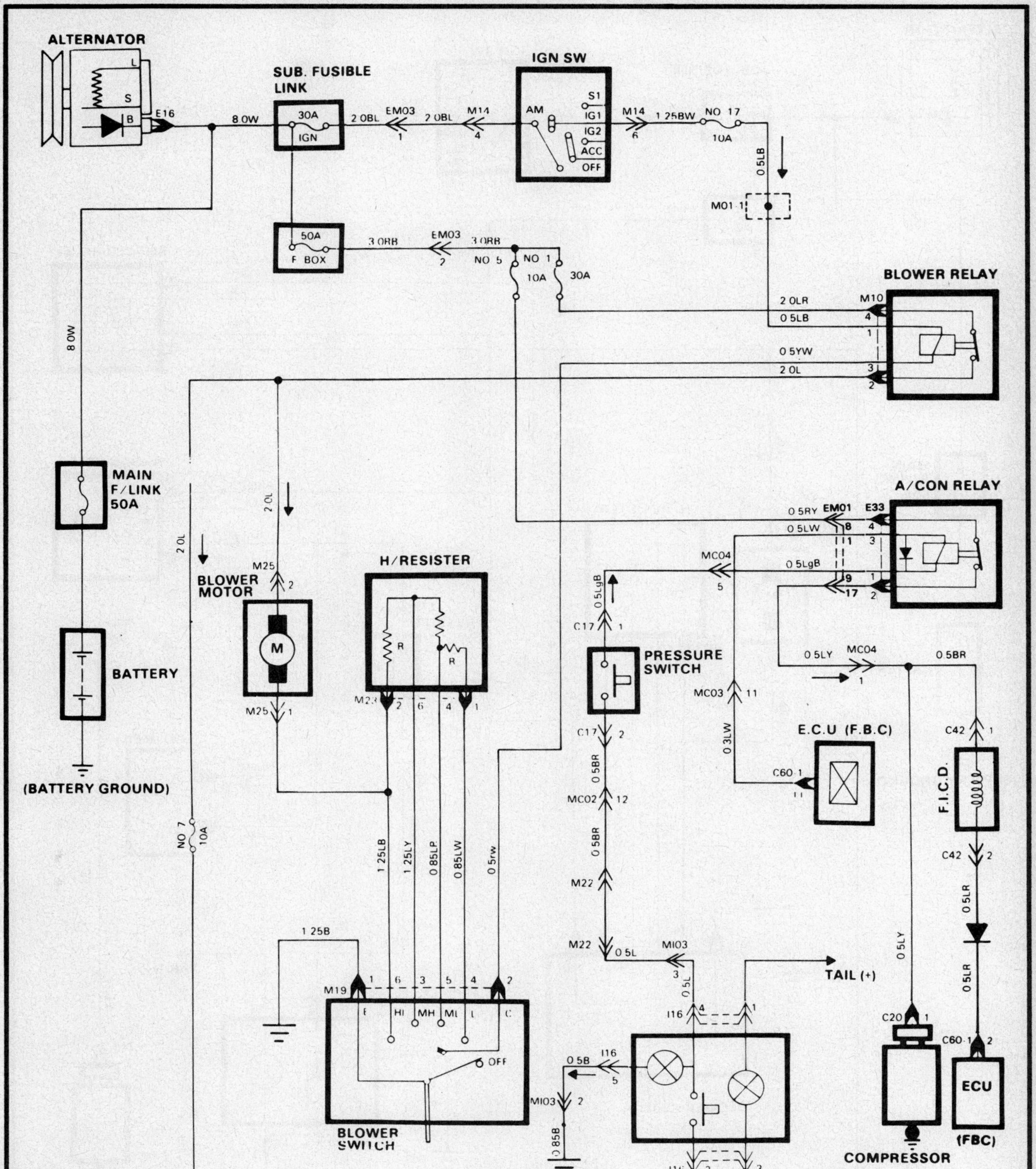
ALTERNATOR
SUB. FUSIBLE LINK
IGN SW
BLOWER RELAY
MAIN F/LINK 50A
A/CON RELAY
H/RESISTER
BLOWER MOTOR
BATTERY
(BATTERY GROUND)
PRESSURE SWITCH
E.C.U (F.B.C)
F.I.C.D.
BLOWER SWITCH
TAIL (+)
COMPRESSOR
ECU
(FBC)
RHEOSTAT (–)

Air conditioning and heating system wiring schematic—1990–91 Excel, with FBC System

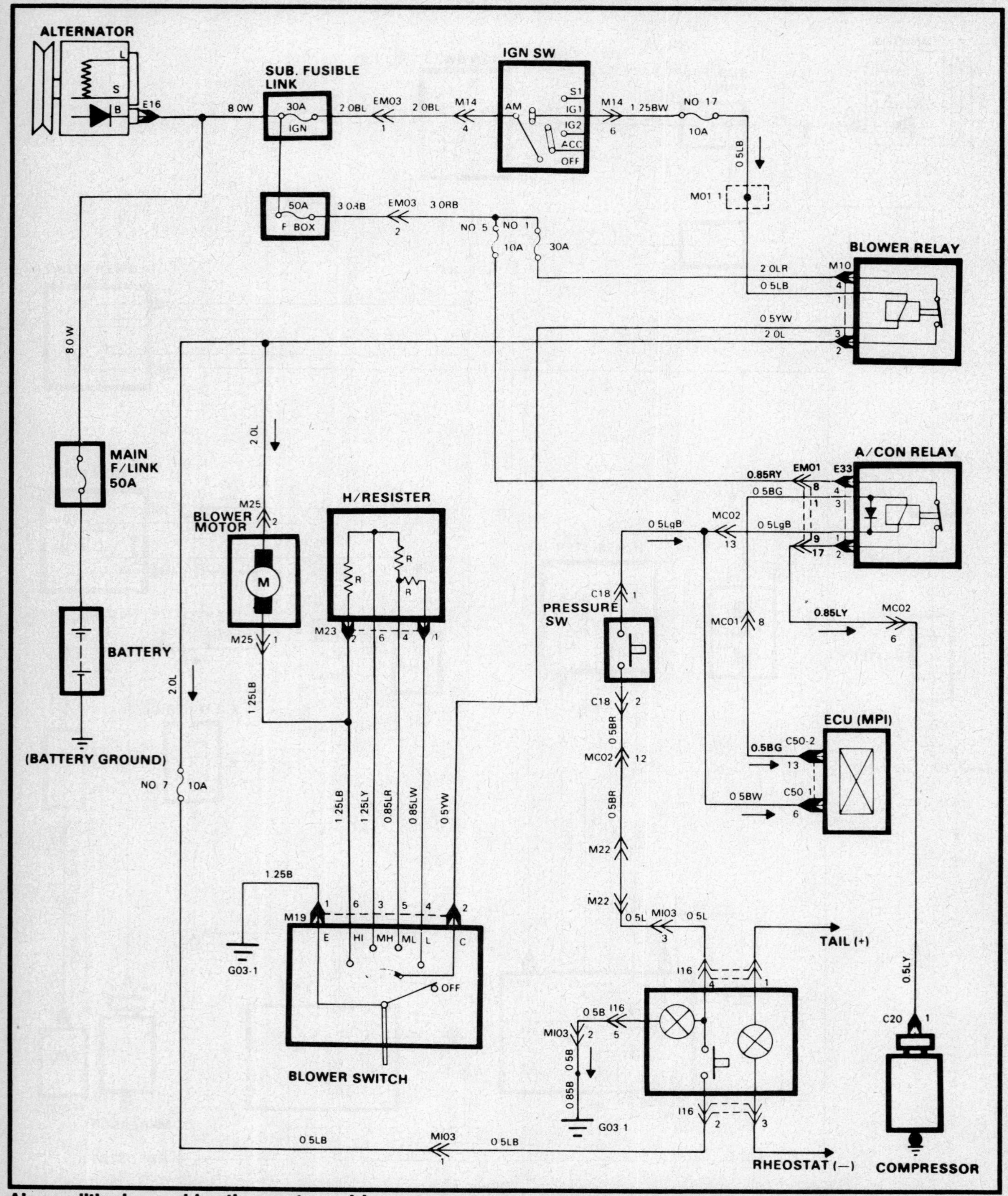
ALTERNATOR
L
S
B
E16
8 0W
SUB. FUSIBLE LINK
30A
IGN
2 0BL
EM03
1
2 0BL
M14
4
IGN SW
AM
S1
IG1
IG2
ACC
OFF
M14
6
1 25BW
NO 17
10A
0 5LB
M01 1
50A
F BOX
3 0RB
EM03
2
3 0RB
NO 5
10A
NO 1
30A
BLOWER RELAY
2 0LR
M10
0 5LB
4
1
0 5YW
2 0L
3
2
8 0W
MAIN F/LINK 50A
BATTERY
(BATTERY GROUND)
2 0L
M25
BLOWER MOTOR
M
M25
1 25LB
H/RESISTER
R
M23
2 0L
NO 7
10A
A/CON RELAY
0.85RY
EM01
E33
0 5BG
0 5LgB
MC02
13
0 5LgB
9
17
C18
PRESSURE SW
C18
0 5BR
MC02
12
0 5BR
M22
M22
MC01
8
0.85LY
MC02
6
ECU (MPI)
0.5BG
C50-2
13
0 5BW
C50-1
6
1 25LB
1 25LY
0 85LR
0 85LW
0 5YW
1.25B
M19
E
HI
MH
ML
L
C
OFF
G03-1
BLOWER SWITCH
0 5L
MI03
3
0 5L
TAIL (+)
I16
4
1
0 5B
I16
5
MI03
2
0 5B
0 85B
G03 1
I16
2
3
0 5LB
MI03
1
0 5LB
RHEOSTAT (—)
0 5LY
C20
1
COMPRESSOR

Air conditioning and heating system wiring schematic—1990–91 Excel and Scoupe, with MPI System

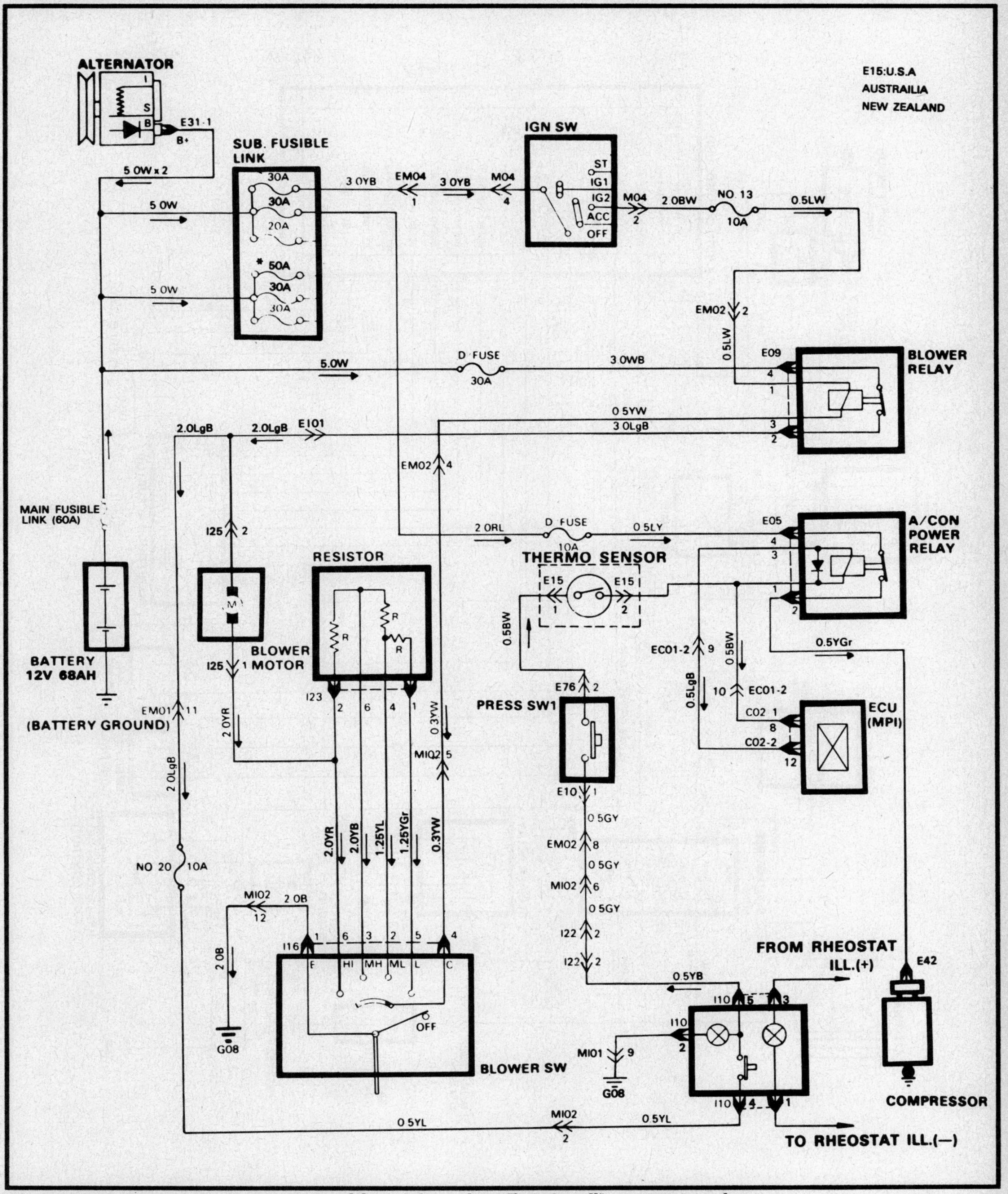
ALTERNATOR
E31-1
B+
SUB. FUSIBLE LINK
5.0W x 2
5.0W
30A
30A
20A
* 50A
30A
30A
IGN SW
ST
IG1
IG2
ACC
OFF
3.0YB
EM04
3.0YB
M04
M04
2.0BW
NO. 13
10A
0.5LW
E15:U.S.A
AUSTRAILIA
NEW ZEALAND
EM02
BLOWER RELAY
E09
D FUSE
30A
3.0WB
5.0W
0.5YW
3.0LgB
2.0LgB
E101
EM02
MAIN FUSIBLE LINK (60A)
A/CON POWER RELAY
E05
2.0RL
D FUSE
10A
0.5LY
THERMO SENSOR
E15
BATTERY 12V 68AH
BLOWER MOTOR
RESISTOR
I25
I23
0.3YW
0.5BW
E76
PRESS SW1
EC01-2
0.5LgB
0.5YGr
ECU (MPI)
C02
C02-2
(BATTERY GROUND)
EM01
2.0YR
MI02
2.0LgB
E10
0.5GY
EM02
MI02
2.0YR
2.0YB
1.25YL
1.25YGr
0.3YW
NO 20
10A
2.0B
I16
I22
FROM RHEOSTAT ILL.(+)
E42
0.5YB
I10
E
HI
MH
ML
L
C
OFF
2.0B
G08
BLOWER SW
MI01
COMPRESSOR
0.5YL
TO RHEOSTAT ILL.(—)

Air conditioning and heating system wiring schematic—Sonata with, manual system

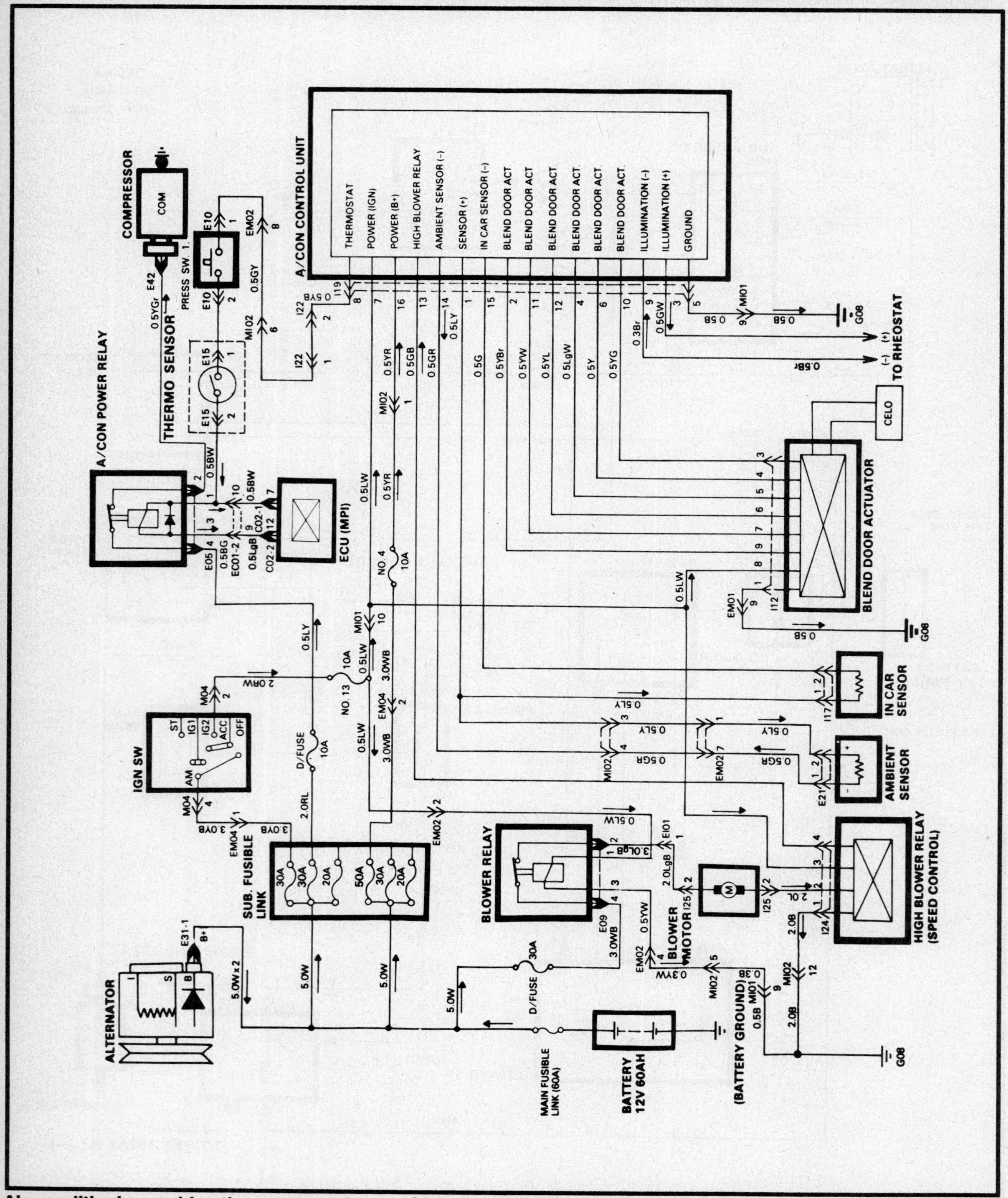
A/CON CONTROL UNIT
THERMOSTAT
POWER (IGN)
POWER (B+)
HIGH BLOWER RELAY
AMBIENT SENSOR (-)
SENSOR (+)
IN CAR SENSOR (-)
BLEND DOOR ACT
ILLUMINATION (-)
ILLUMINATION (+)
GROUND
COMPRESSOR
COM
PRESS SW. 1
THERMO SENSOR
A/CON POWER RELAY
ECU (MPI)
TO RHEOSTAT
CELO
BLEND DOOR ACTUATOR
IN CAR SENSOR
AMBIENT SENSOR
HIGH BLOWER RELAY (SPEED CONTROL)
IGN SW
SUB. FUSIBLE LINK
BLOWER RELAY
BLOWER MOTOR
ALTERNATOR
MAIN FUSIBLE LINK (60A)
BATTERY 12V 60AH
(BATTERY GROUND)
D/FUSE

Air conditioning and heating system wiring schematic—Sonata, with SATC system

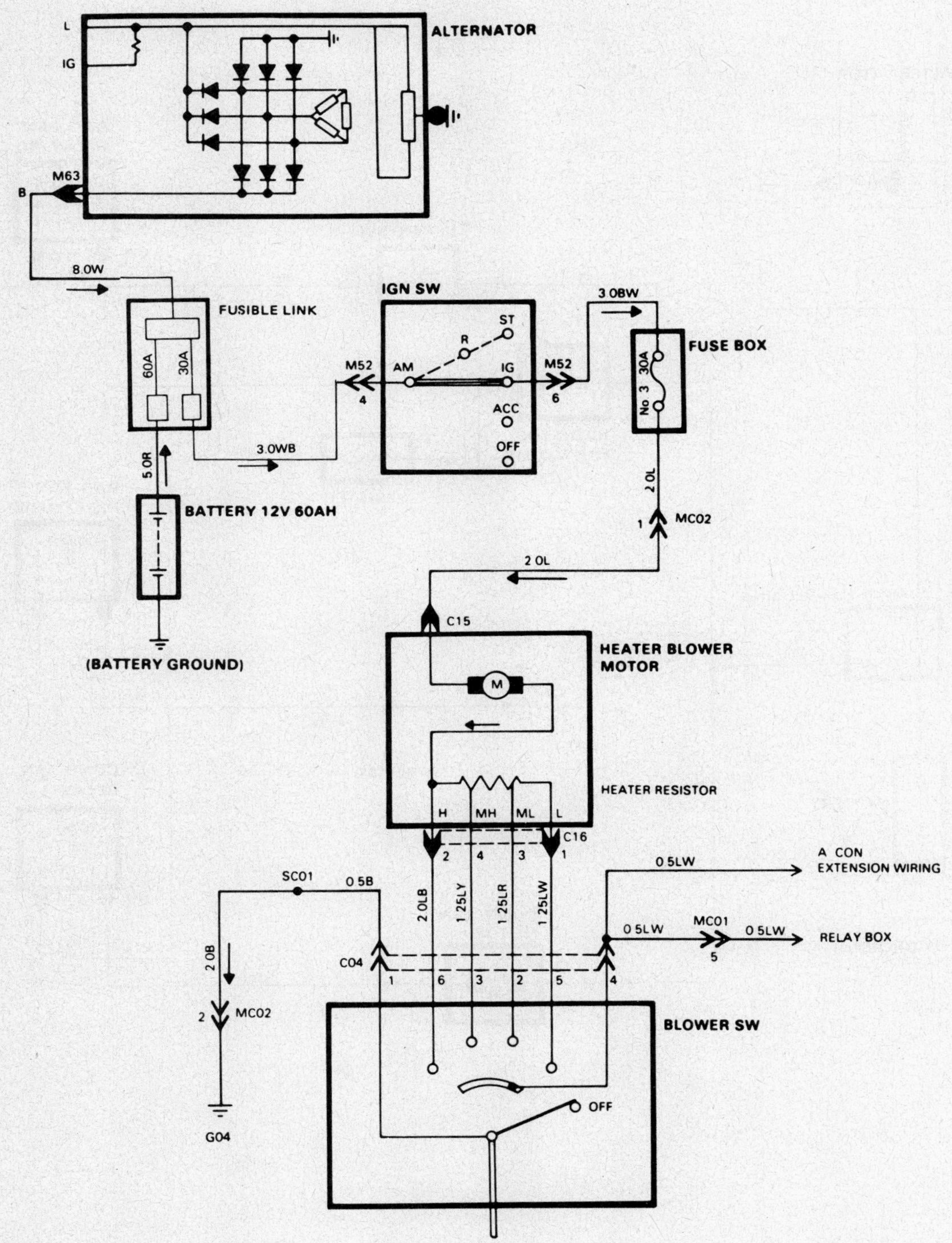
ALTERNATOR
L
IG
M63
B
8.0W
FUSIBLE LINK
60A
30A
5.0R
BATTERY 12V 60AH
(BATTERY GROUND)
3.0WB
IGN SW
ST
R
AM
IG
ACC
OFF
M52
4
M52
6
3.0BW
FUSE BOX
No 3 30A
2.0L
1
MC02
2.0L
C15
HEATER BLOWER MOTOR
M
HEATER RESISTOR
H
MH
ML
L
C16
2
4
3
1
SC01
0.5B
2.0B
2
MC02
G04
2.0LB
1.25LY
1.25LR
1.25LW
0.5LW
A CON EXTENSION WIRING
0.5LW
MC01
0.5LW
RELAY BOX
5
C04
1
6
3
2
5
4
BLOWER SW
OFF

Heating system wiring schematic—1989 Excel

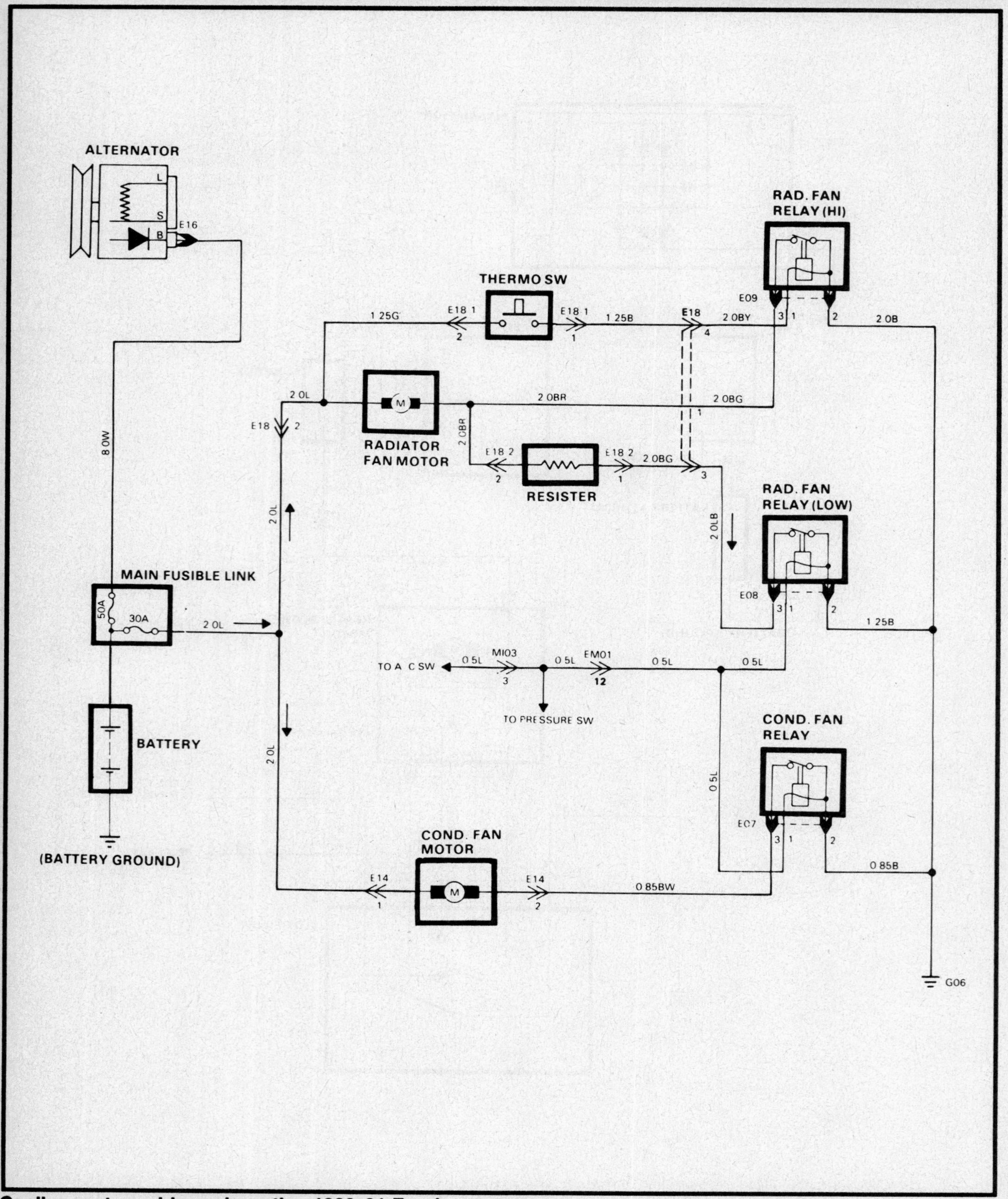
ALTERNATOR
L
S
B
E16
8 0W
MAIN FUSIBLE LINK
50A
30A
2 0L
BATTERY
(BATTERY GROUND)
THERMO SW
1 25G
E18 1
2
E18 1
1 25B
1
E18
2 0BY
4
RAD. FAN
RELAY (HI)
E09
3
1
2
2 0B
2 0L
E18
2
RADIATOR
FAN MOTOR
2 0BR
2 0BG
1
2 0BR
E18 2
RESISTER
E18 2
1
2 0BG
3
RAD. FAN
RELAY (LOW)
2 0LB
E08
1 25B
TO A C SW
0 5L
MI03
3
0 5L
EM01
12
0 5L
0 5L
TO PRESSURE SW
COND. FAN
RELAY
0 5L
E07
0 85B
COND. FAN
MOTOR
E14
1
E14
2
0 85BW
G06

Cooling system wiring schematic—1990–91 Excel and Scoupe

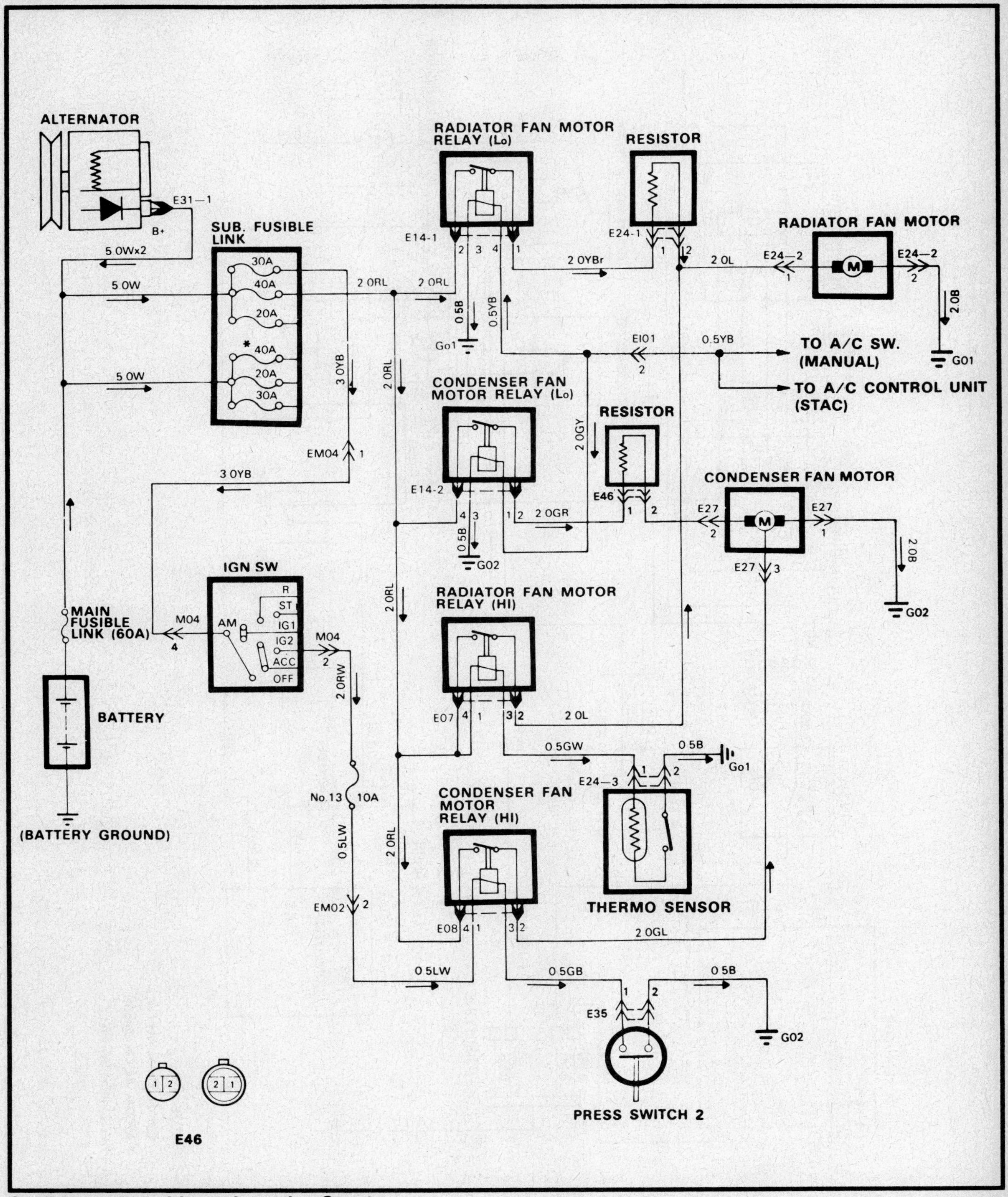
ALTERNATOR
E31—1
B+
SUB. FUSIBLE LINK
5.0Wx2
5.0W
5.0W
30A
40A
20A
*40A
20A
30A
RADIATOR FAN MOTOR RELAY (Lo)
E14-1
RESISTOR
E24-1
RADIATOR FAN MOTOR
E24—2
E24—2
2.0ORL
2.0ORL
0.5B
0.5YB
Go1
2.0YBr
2.0L
2.0B
G01
E101
0.5YB
TO A/C SW. (MANUAL)
TO A/C CONTROL UNIT (STAC)
3.0YB
2.0RL
CONDENSER FAN MOTOR RELAY (Lo)
RESISTOR
2.0GY
EM04
3.0YB
E14-2
E46
CONDENSER FAN MOTOR
E27
E27
2.0GR
0.5B
G02
2.0B
G02
E27
IGN SW
R
ST
IG1
IG2
ACC
OFF
AM
M04
M04
2.0RL
RADIATOR FAN MOTOR RELAY (HI)
MAIN FUSIBLE LINK (60A)
BATTERY
2.0RW
E07
2.0L
0.5GW
0.5B
Go1
E24—3
No.13
10A
(BATTERY GROUND)
0.5LW
2.0RL
CONDENSER FAN MOTOR RELAY (HI)
THERMO SENSOR
EM02
E08
2.0GL
0.5LW
0.5GB
0.5B
E35
G02
PRESS SWITCH 2
E46

Cooling system wiring schematic—Sonata

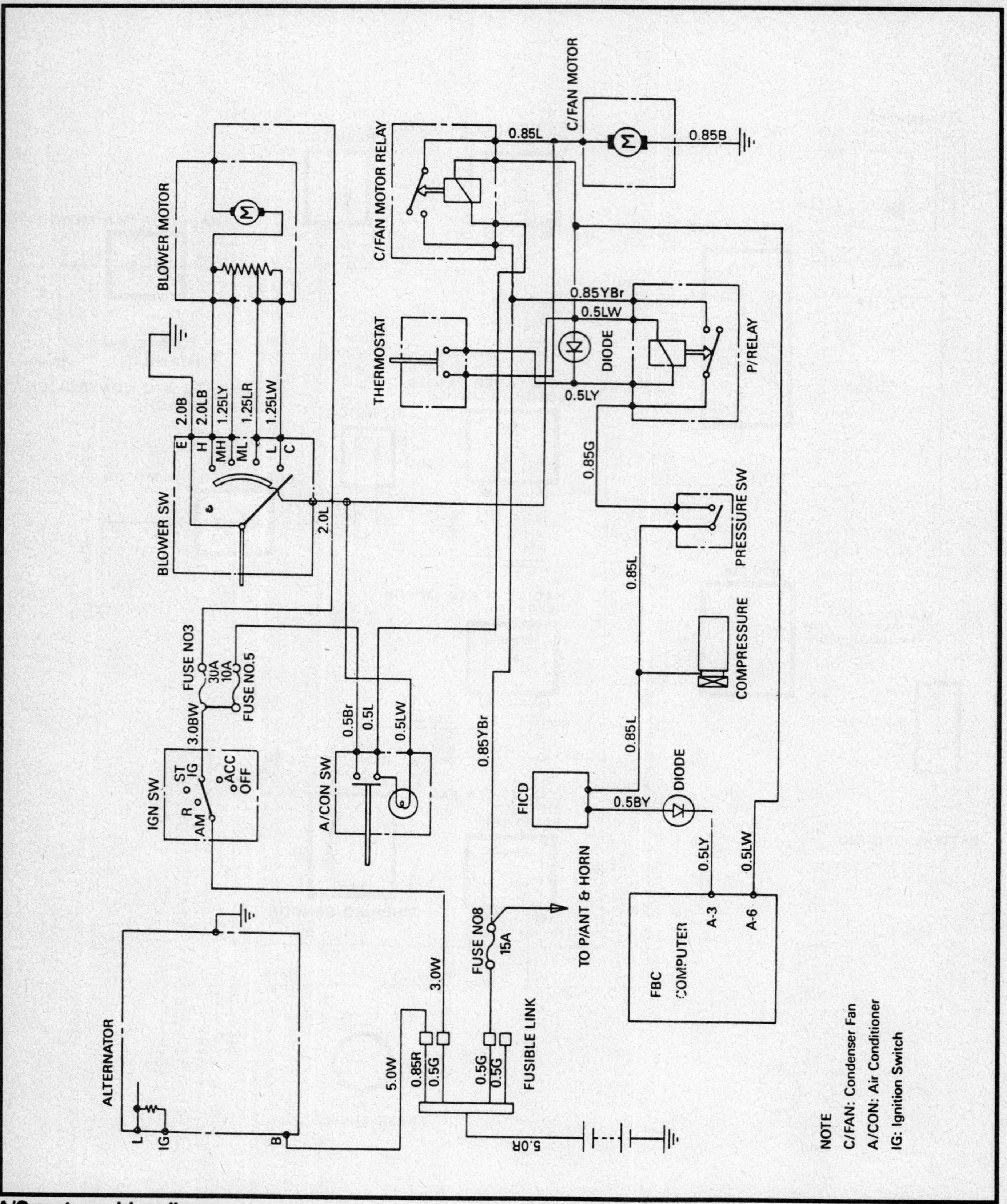
BLOWER MOTOR
BLOWER SW
E
H
MH
ML
L
C
2.0B
2.0LB
1.25LY
1.25LR
1.25LW
2.0L
C/FAN MOTOR RELAY
C/FAN MOTOR
0.85L
0.85B
THERMOSTAT
0.85YBr
0.5LW
DIODE
0.5LY
P/RELAY
0.85G
PRESSURE SW
0.85L
COMPRESSURE
0.85L
FICD
0.5BY
DIODE
0.5LY
0.5LW
A-3
A-6
FBC
COMPUTER
IGN SW
R
AM
ST
IG
ACC
OFF
3.0BW
FUSE NO3
30A
10A
FUSE NO.5
A/CON SW
0.5Br
0.5L
0.5LW
0.85YBr
TO P/ANT & HORN
FUSE NO8
15A
FUSIBLE LINK
3.0W
5.0W
0.85R
0.5G
0.5G
0.5G
5.0R
ALTERNATOR
L
IG
B
NOTE
C/FAN: Condenser Fan
A/CON: Air Conditioner
IG: Ignition Switch

A/C system wiring diagram

18 INFINITI 18

G20 • M30 • Q45

SPECIFICATIONS

ENGINE IDENTIFICATION

Year	Model	Engine Displacement cu. in. (cc/liter)	Engine Series Identification	No. of Cylinders	Engine Type
1990	M30	181 (2960/3.0)	VG30E	6	OHC
	Q45	274 (4494/4.5)	VH45DE	8	DOHC
1991	G20	121 (1998/2.0)	SR20DE	4	DOHC
	M30	181 (2960/3.0)	VG30E	6	OHC
	Q45	274 (4494/4.5)	VH45DE	8	DOHC

OHC—Overhead cam
DOHC—Dual overhead cam

REFRIGERANT CAPACITIES

Year	Model	Freon (oz.)	Oil (fl. oz.)	Type
1990	M30	28.8–32.0	6.8	R-12
	Q45	40.6–44.1	8.0	R-12
1991	G20	24.6–28.1	6.8	R-12
	M30	28.8–32.0	6.8	R-12
	Q45	38.4–41.6	8.0	R-12

AIR CONDITIONING BELT TENSION CHART

Year	Model	Engine Displacement cu. in. (cc/liter)	Belt Type	New	Used
1990	M30	181 (2960/3.0)	Poly V	0.31–0.35 ②	0.35–0.55 ②
	Q45	274 (4494/4.5)	Poly V	0.29–0.33 ③	0.33–0.47 ③
1991	G20	121 (1998/2.0)	Poly V	0.25–0.29 ①	0.28–0.49 ①
	M30	181 (2960/3.0)	Poly V	0.31–0.35 ②	0.35–0.55 ②
	Q45	274 (4494/4.5)	Poly V	0.29–0.33 ③	0.33–0.47 ③

① Inches of deflection mid-way between crankshaft and alternator pulleys
② Inches of deflection mid-way between idler and compressor pulleys
③ Inches of deflection between crankshaft and compressor pulleys

SYSTEM DESCRIPTION

General Information

The heater in all vehicles is a standard type, circulating engine coolant through a radiator core inside the vehicle. Temperature is controlled by moving a door in the air distribution system with a cable connected to the temperature control lever or by a door motor. Movement of the door also operates the water valve on the heater core.

A standard configuration air conditioning system, charged with R-12, is used in all vehicles. The system consists of a compressor pumping the refrigerant to a condenser, a reciever/drier with a dual (high and low) pressure switch, an evaporator in the vehicle, then back to the compressor. The evaporator housing also contains the expansion valve. On M30 automatic system, a suction throttle valve prevents evaporator coil freezing. The Q45 uses a variable displacement compressor to control evaporator coil temperature. On each vehicle, high and low pressure service valves are mounted directly on the lines and an over-pressure relief valve is mounted in the high pressure line or on the compressor. There is also be a fusible plug on the receiver/

drier, which melts above about 220°F (105°C) and allows the system to vent if overheated. On G20 the compressor has a thermal protector, which is have an over–temperature switch that will disengage the clutch to prevent damage from overheating.

The air distribution system inside the vehicle uses doors to direct the air flow. The air mix door is the master control for temperature and is either adjusted manually with a lever and cable or controlled with an electric motor. Air enters the system from outside or inside the vehicle and passes over the evaporator first, then on to the heater core and/or out through various vents. This allows use of the air conditioner to dry the air for defogging the windshield when the temperature control is set for heat. All systems include an electric clutch on the compressor, a fan to move air through the condenser and a blower fan to move air through the distribution system. On manual systems, a thermo control amplifier senses the evaporator coil temperature and cycles the compressor on and off to prevent ice fromation.

Automatic Temperature Control (ATC) systems have a microcomputer, called an auto amplifier, to control the blower fan speed, door motors and compressor duty cycle. When the ignition is switched off, the auto amplifier stores all information reguarding the last temperature setting. The information available to the amplifier is; outside and inside air temperatures, blower fan speed, air mix door position, sun load, and on Q45, engine coolant temperature in the heater core. To aid in trouble shooting, this amplifier has a self diagnostic program accessed through the user controls.

On all vehicles, the air conditioner switch does not directly turn on the compressor clutch but feeds the demand signal to the engine control computer. The engine computer looks at engine load via the throttle position sensor and will turn the clutch on if the throttle is below a certain percentage of full throttle. On the automatic system, when the compressor is switched on it runs continuously rather than cycling on and off. The M30 has a suction throttle valve in the evaporator housing to modulate the pressure in the evaporator to prevent ice formation on the coils. This valve is in addition to the expansion valve used on all systems, which controls the amount of refrigerant flowing through the evaporator.

Service Valve Location

G20

The high pressure valve is on the discharge line near the brake booster. The low pressure valve is on the suction line close to where it passes through the firewall.

M30

The high pressure valve is on the discharge line next to the condenser. The low pressure valve is on the suction line near the compressor.

Q45

The high pressure valve is on the discharge line just above the receiver/drier. The low pressure valve is on the suction line near where it passes through the firewall.

Special Precautions

1. All refrigerant service work must be done with the proper recycling equipment. Carefully follow the manufacturer's instructions for use of that equipment. Do not allow the freon to discharge to the air.
2. Any amount of water will make the system less effective. When any part of the system has been removed, plug or cap the lines to prevent moisture from the air entering the system. When installing a new component, do not uncap the fittings until ready to attach the lines.
3. When assembling a fitting, always use a new O-ring and lightly lubricate the fitting with compressor oil.
4. When a compressor is removed, do not leave it on its side or upside down for more than 10 minutes. The oil may leak into a pumping chamber.
5. The proper amount of oil must be maintained in the system to prevent compressor damage and to maintain system efficiency. Be sure to measure and adjust the amount of oil removed or added to the system, especially when replacing the compressor.

System Performance Testing

1. Vehicle must be in a well ventilated area where the engine can be safely run at 1500 rpm, preferably not in direct sunlight. Open the hood to help engine cooling.
2. With windows open, operate the system in **AUTO** set for full cooling, blower fan on high speed. On manual systems, set the mode control to **VENT**.
3. Set the system to recirculate the air.
4. Operate the system for more than 10 minutes, then use a thermometer to measure the air outlet temperature at the center dash vent.
5. With a relative humidity of 60–80 percent, the outlet air temperature should be about 25–30°F cooler than the outside air. The Q45 will have slightly better performance. The effectiveness of any system will decrease as the humidity increases.
6. The following chart assumes a relative humidity of 50–70 percent. The compressor discharge and suction pressures will increase with higher outside air temperature and humidity.

TEMPERATURE/PRESSURE CHART

Vehicle	Outside Temperature (°F)	High Side Pressure (psi)	Low Side Pressure (psi)
G20	68	100–148	9–18
	77	128–178	11–21
	86	162-210	14–26
	95	199–252	18–33
	104	240–293	28–46
M30	68	159–199	13–17
	77	176–216	14–20
	86	193–236	16–21
	95	210–259	18–23
	104	228–279	20–27

TEMPERATURE/PRESSURE CHART

Vehicle	Outside Temperature (°F)	High Side Pressure (psi)	Low Side Pressure (psi)
Q45	68	95–118	27–33
	77	118–146	27–33
	86	142–173	27–33
	95	166-202	27–33
	104	189–230	28–34

System Discharging

1. Install adapter valves to the vehicle service valves and/or connect the refrigerant recycling equipment according to the manufacturer's instructions.
2. Open both the adapter or manifold valves slowly to prevent excess oil loss. Allow the freon to stop flowing before going on to the next step.

System Evacuating

1. Open both the high and low pressure valves and run the vacuum pump for more than 5 minutes. The gauges should stabilize at 29.13–29.92 in. (740–760mm) Hg vacuum.
2. Close the valves and turn the pump off. Check to see that the vacuum gauges remain stable. If the gauge on the low pressure side moves 3.94 in. (100mm) Hg vacuum in about 10 minutes, the system will discharge itself in about one month.
3. If the system will not hold vacuum, first check that the service equipment is properly connected and in good working order. If any connections in the vehicle system have been disturbed, make sure they have been properly reconnected. Be sure to use new lightly oiled O-rings and that the fitting is not over torqued.
4. If the system holds vacuum, open the valves and run the pump for more than 20 minutes. Close the valves and turn the pump off.

System Charging

1. If using recycle equipment, the equipment in use will determine the charging procedure. Carefully, follow the manufacturer's instructions and add the correct amount of freon as noted in the specifications chart. Never add freon through the high pressure service valve.
2. If charging directly from the R-12 container, add freon gas, not liquid, to the low pressure side until it slows or stops flowing. Start the engine, set the controls to maximum cooling and, with the R-12 can upright, continue to flow freon gas into the low pressure side until the specified amount has been added.
3. With the system fully charged and with the correct oil level in the compressor, run the air conditioner at the full cold setting for more than 5 minutes.
4. Stop the engine and immediately check the system for leaks using a suitable leak detector. Be sure to check at every line fitting, the service valves, the pressure switch at the receiver/drier, at the compressor shaft seals, bolt holes and clutch, and the pressure and temperature relief valves.
5. To check the evaporator and valves inside the vehicle, insert the leak detector probe into the water drain hose for more than 10 minutes. Leaking freon is heavier than air and will seek the lower exit, so always look for leaks at the lowest point.

Compressor Oil Service

The compressor is lubricated with a special oil that circulates with the freon when the system is operating and drops out of the freon when the system is stopped. Insufficient oil will cause damage to the compressor but too much oil will inhibit the system's cooling ability. When installing new parts of the system or a new compressor, the oil quantity must be adjusted.

1. If a new compressor is being installed, drain the oil out of the old unit and measure it.
2. Refer to the specification chart to determine how much oil the system should have.
3. Adjust the quantity of oil in the new compressor as needed. New compressors usually come with the full amount of oil, so it will probably be necessary to remove oil. The amount to be removed is the difference between the system specification and the amount drained from the old unit.
4. If installing another major system component, add oil according the the following table:
   The evaporator holds about 30 percent of the total amount.
   The condenser holds about 20 percent of the total amount.
   The reciever/drier holds about 10 percent of the total amount.
5. If a large oil leak is indicated, make the necessary repairs and run the system at idle speed set for full cooling for about 10 minutes. Stop the engine and drain the oil from the compressor to measure how much oil to add.

SYSTEM COMPONENTS

CAUTION

M30 and Q45 vehicles are equipped with air bag supplimental restraint systems. The system is still active for about 10 minutes after disconnecting the battery. Wait for more than 10 minutes before starting electrical work and do not use a memory saver. If power is required for diagnostic work, the air bag module can be disconnected inside the panel on the back of the steering wheel after the system is inactive. Reconnect the module before reconnecting the battery, then make sure no one is in the vehicle when reconnecting the battery.

NOTE: When removing any component of the refrigerant system, properly discharge the freon into recovery equipment. Do not vent the freon into the air.

Radiator

REMOVAL AND INSTALLATION

1. Disconnect the negative battery cable. On vehicles with an

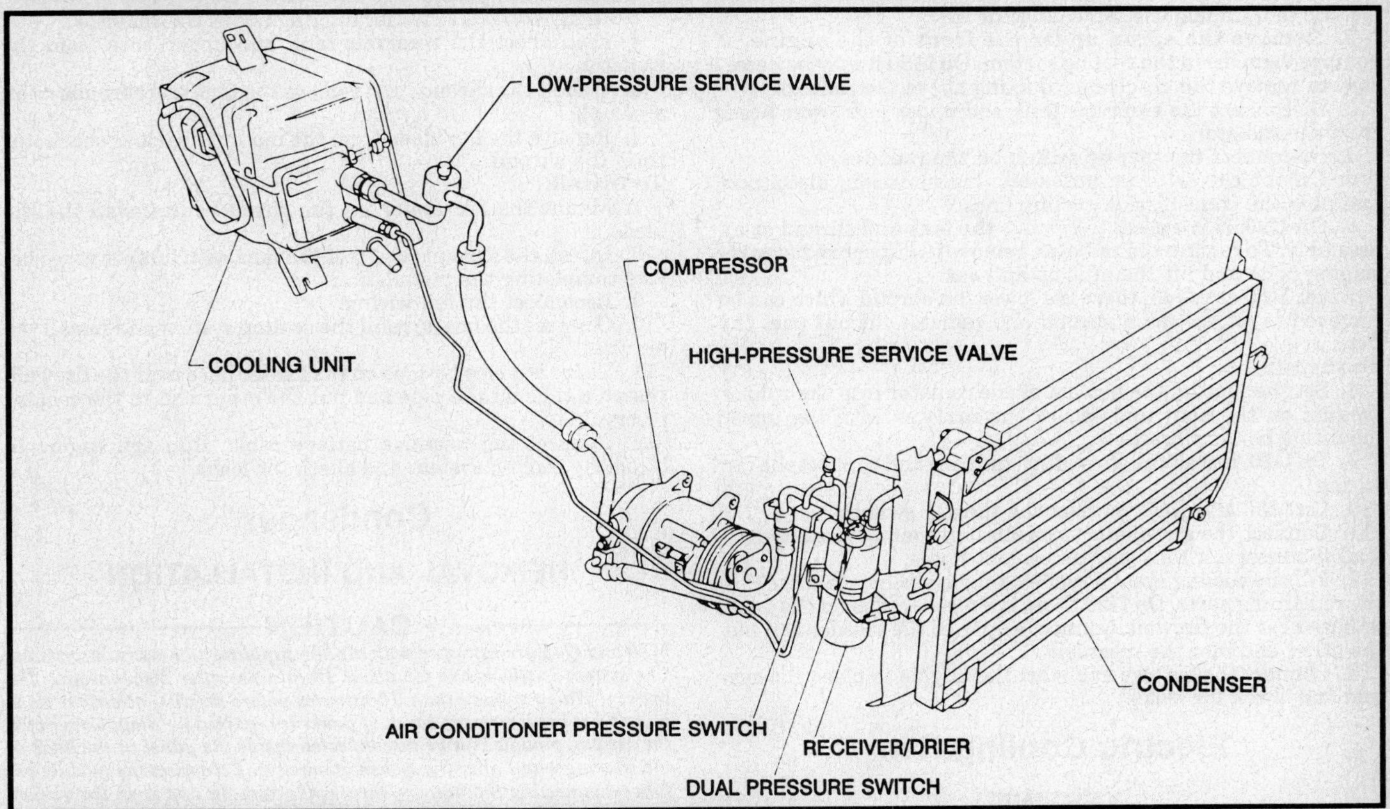
LOW-PRESSURE SERVICE VALVE
COMPRESSOR
COOLING UNIT
HIGH-PRESSURE SERVICE VALVE
CONDENSER
AIR CONDITIONER PRESSURE SWITCH
RECEIVER/DRIER
DUAL PRESSURE SWITCH

Typical Infiniti refrigerant system components, Q45 shown

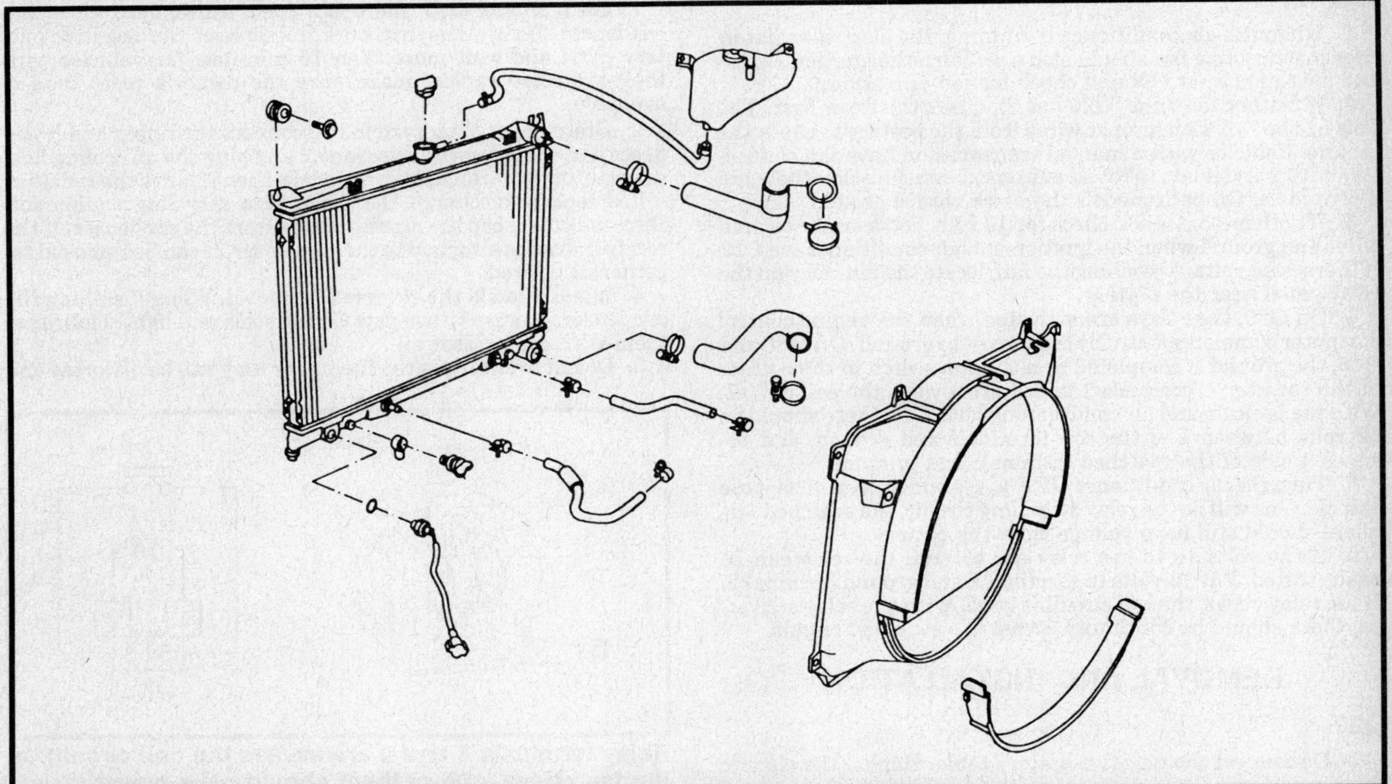

Remove the lower fan shroud to lift the radiator and shroud out past the fan, M30 shown

electric fan, unplug the fan connector first.

2. Remove the apron under the front of the engine, if equipped and drain the cooling system. On M30 it may be necessary to remove the air cleaner ducting above the radiator.

3. Disconnect the reservoir tank and upper and lower hoses from the radiator.

4. Disconnect the thermo switch on the radiator.

5. On vehicles with an automatic transmission, disconnect and plug the transmission cooling lines.

6. On G20, it is easiest to remove the fans and shroud as an assembly. To remove the radiator, remove the upper radiator retaining bolts and lift the unit up and out.

7. On M30 and Q45, there is a lower fan shroud which can be removed to let the main shroud and radiator lift out past the fan.

To install:

8. Set the lugs on the bottom of the radiator into the rubber mounts on the body and secure the radiator with the upper mounting bolts or brackets.

9. On G20, install the shrouding and fans and connect the fan wiring.

10. On M30 and Q45, connect the thermo switch.

11. Connect the automatic transmission cooling lines and install the reservoir tank and all coolant hoses.

12. Fill the cooling system and look for leaks before installing the remaining parts. On G20 there is a bleeder pipe on the heater hose near the firewall. Connect a tube to the bleeder and put the other end into the reservoir.

13. Connect the battery and start the engine to bleed the system and check for leaks.

Electric Cooling Fan

TESTING

G20

1. When the air conditioner is running, the electric radiator/condenser cooling fan should also run. Turn the ignition switch and air conditioner **ON** and check for fan operation.

2. If neither fan runs (G20 has 2), check the fuses first. The fans can be run with jumper wires from the battery to check the motors. Vehicles with a manual transmission have fan connectors with 2 terminals. With an automatic transmission there are 4 terminals. On both models the black wire is ground.

3. If both motors work, check for 12 volts between the colored wires and ground when the ignition and air conditioner are **ON**. If there is no voltage reaching the fan, locate the fan relay on the relay panel near the battery.

4. On G20, the relays are activated when the engine control computer completes the relay coil circuit to ground. On M30 and Q45, the ground is completed by a thermo switch in the bottom of the radiator. Terminals 1 and 2 are always the coil circuit. With the ignition and air conditioning both **ON**, there should be 12 volts between 1 of the coil terminals and ground, and between 1 side of the switched terminals and ground.

5. Turn the air conditioner **OFF** to see which terminals loose voltage. One will be the relay switching circuit, the switched terminal should still have voltage from the battery.

6. If the voltages to the relay are correct, the relay can be bench tested. Put 12 volts to terminal 1 and ground terminal 2. If the relay clicks, the coil circuit is good. With the relay activated, there should be continuity across the switched circuit.

REMOVAL AND INSTALLATION

G20

1. Disconnect the negative battery cable. Unplug the electric fan connectors.

2. Drain about 2 quarts of coolant from the radiator.

3. Remove the air cleaner ducting above the radiator.

4. Disconnect the reservoir tank and upper hose from the radiator.

5. Unbolt the shrouds and remove the fans and shrouds as an assembly.

6. Remove the fan blade from the motor to remove the motor from the shroud.

To install:

7. Mount the fan motor on the shroud and install the the blade.

8. Install the shrouds and test the fans with jumper wires before completing the installation.

9. Reconnect the fan wiring.

10. Connect the hoses, refill the cooling system and install the air duct.

11. There is a bleeder pipe on the heater hose near the firewall. Install a tube on the pipe and put the other end in the coolant reservoir.

12. Connect the negative battery cable. Run the engine to bleed the cooling system and check for leaks.

Condenser

REMOVAL AND INSTALLATION

CAUTION

M30 and Q45 are equipped with air bag supplimental restraint systems. The system is still active for about 10 minutes after disconnecting the battery. Wait for more than 10 minutes before starting electrical work and do not use a memory saver. If power is required for diagnostic work, the air bag module can be disconnected inside the panel in the back of the steering wheel after the system is inactive. Reconnect the module before reconnecting the battery, then make sure on one is in the vehicle when connecting the battery.

1. On M30 and Q45, there is a crash sensor in front of the condenser. Before starting work, disconnect the negative battery cable and wait more than 10 minutes. On vehicles with theft-protected radios, make sure the owner's reset code is available.

2. Drain the cooling system. Disconnect the upper and lower hoses and the reservoir. Disconnect and plug the oil cooling hoses on automatic transmission models, then remove the radiator.

3. Properly discharge the freon into recycling equipment. Disconnect and cap the pressure lines from the condenser. If the receiver/drier is attached to the condenser, it can be removed together, if desired.

4. Installation is the reverse of removal. When installing the condenser, be sure to use new O-ring seals and lightly lubricate them with compressor oil.

5. Do not over torque the fittings or they will be distorted and

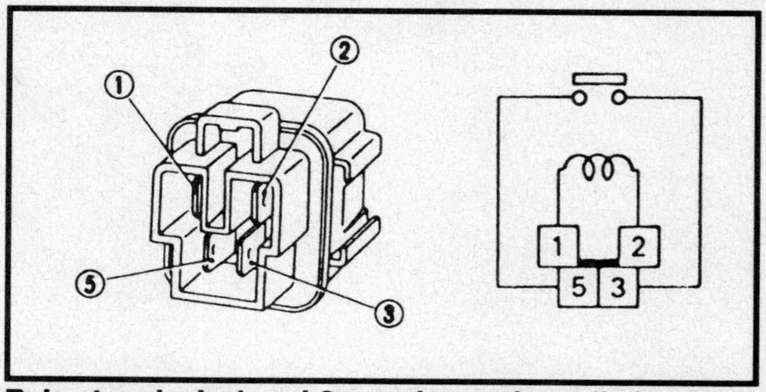
1
2
5
3
1
2
5
3

Relay terminals 1 and 2 are always the coil circuit; on the fan relays, one of them should have power whenever the ignition is on

leak. On M30 and Q45, condenser fittings secured with bolts are torqued to 5–8 ft. lbs. (8–11 Nm). The line fittings are torqued to 7–14 ft. lbs. (10–20 Nm). The receiver/drier fitting bolts are torqued to 2.5–3 ft. lbs. (3–4 Nm).

6. On G20, torque the condenser inlet fitting to 10–13 ft. lbs. (13–18 Nm). Torque the outlet fitting at the receiver/drier to 2.5–3 ft. lbs. (3–4 Nm).

7. Recharge the system and use a leak detector to check for leaks.

Compressor

REMOVAL AND INSTALLATION

1. Properly discharge the system using freon recovery equipment.
2. On rear wheel drive vehicles, the compressor is more easily removed from under the vehicle. Raise and safely support the vehicle.
3. Disconnect the pressure lines and plug them. Disconnect the wiring.
4. Loosen the drive belt and remove the compressor.
5. Installation is the reverse of removal. Be sure to tighten the belt to specification, do not over tighten or bearing damage will result.
6. On G20, torque the line fitting bolts to 10–13 ft. lbs. (13–18 Nm).
7. On M30 and Q45, torque the line fitting bolts to 5–8 ft. lbs. (8–11 Nm).
8. Recharge the system and use a leak detector to check for leaks.

Receiver/Drier

REMOVAL AND INSTALLATION

1. On G20 and Q45, the receiver/drier is on the condenser. Properly discharge the system into freon recovery equipment.
2. Disconnect the pressure switch.
3. Disconnect the freon lines and cap them to prevent moisture from entering the system.
4. Loosen the clamp and remove the receiver/drier.
5. Installation is the reverse of removal. Be sure to use new O-rings and properly torque the fittings to 3 ft. lbs. (4 Nm).
6. Recharge the system and use a leak detector to check for leaks.

Expansion Valve

REMOVAL AND INSTALLATION

1. The expansion valve, on all models, is in the same housing with the evaporator inside the vehicle. The evaporator, which is between the blower and the heater, can be removed without removing the heater core. Properly discharge the system using freon recovery equipment.
2. Disconnect and plug the evaporator line fittings at the firewall.
3. It may be necessary to remove the blower motor and its housing first. Removing the glove compartment makes this easier.
4. With the evaporator housing removed, split the housing to gain access to the expansion valve.
5. Installation is the reverse of removal. Make sure the seals between the housings are in good condition, replace as necessary. Always use new O-rings and torque the fittings to 14 ft. lbs. (20 Nm).
6. Recharge the system and use a leak detector to check for leaks.

Blower Motor

REMOVAL AND INSTALLATION

1. The blower can be removed without removing the housing. Remove the glove compartment to gain access. On some vehicles, it is possible to squeeze the sides of the door to let it fall open beyond the normal stops.
2. On vehicles with Automatic Temperature Control (ATC), disconnect the wiring at the fan control amplifier on the evaporator housing. On G20, the fan resistor is clipped to the blower housing.
3. Remove the mounting bolts to lower the motor out.
4. Installation is the reverse of removal.

Heater Core

REMOVAL AND INSTALLATION

G20

1. It should be possible to remove the heating unit without removing the dash board. Disconnect the negative battery cable.
2. With the **TEMP** lever set to the **HOT** position, drain the cooling system.
3. Disconnect the heater hoses at the driver's side of the heater unit.
4. Remove the glove compartment and the front panel from the center console.
5. Remove the radio and heater/air conditioner controls to remove the lower portion of the center console.
6. Disconnect the outlet vent ducts and remover the heater unit.
7. Disassemble the housing to remove the core.

To install:

8. Install the heater core and assemble the heater unit housing. Use new gaskets and seals, as required, and check for smooth movement of the doors and linkage.
9. Install the heater unit and attach the ducts. Be careful not to damage the gasket between the heater and cooling units.
10. Install the lower center console and the radio and heater controls. Before completing the assembly, connect the battery and adjust the door motor linkage.
11. Install the glove compartment and console panel.
12. Connect the heater hoses and refill the cooling system with the temperature control set for full heat.

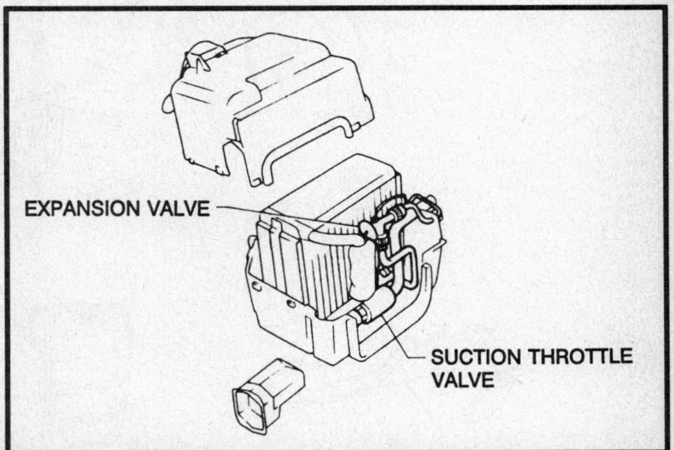
EXPANSION VALVE
SUCTION THROTTLE VALVE

The expansion valve is in the evaporator housing, M30 with suction throttle valve for Automatic Temperature Control shown

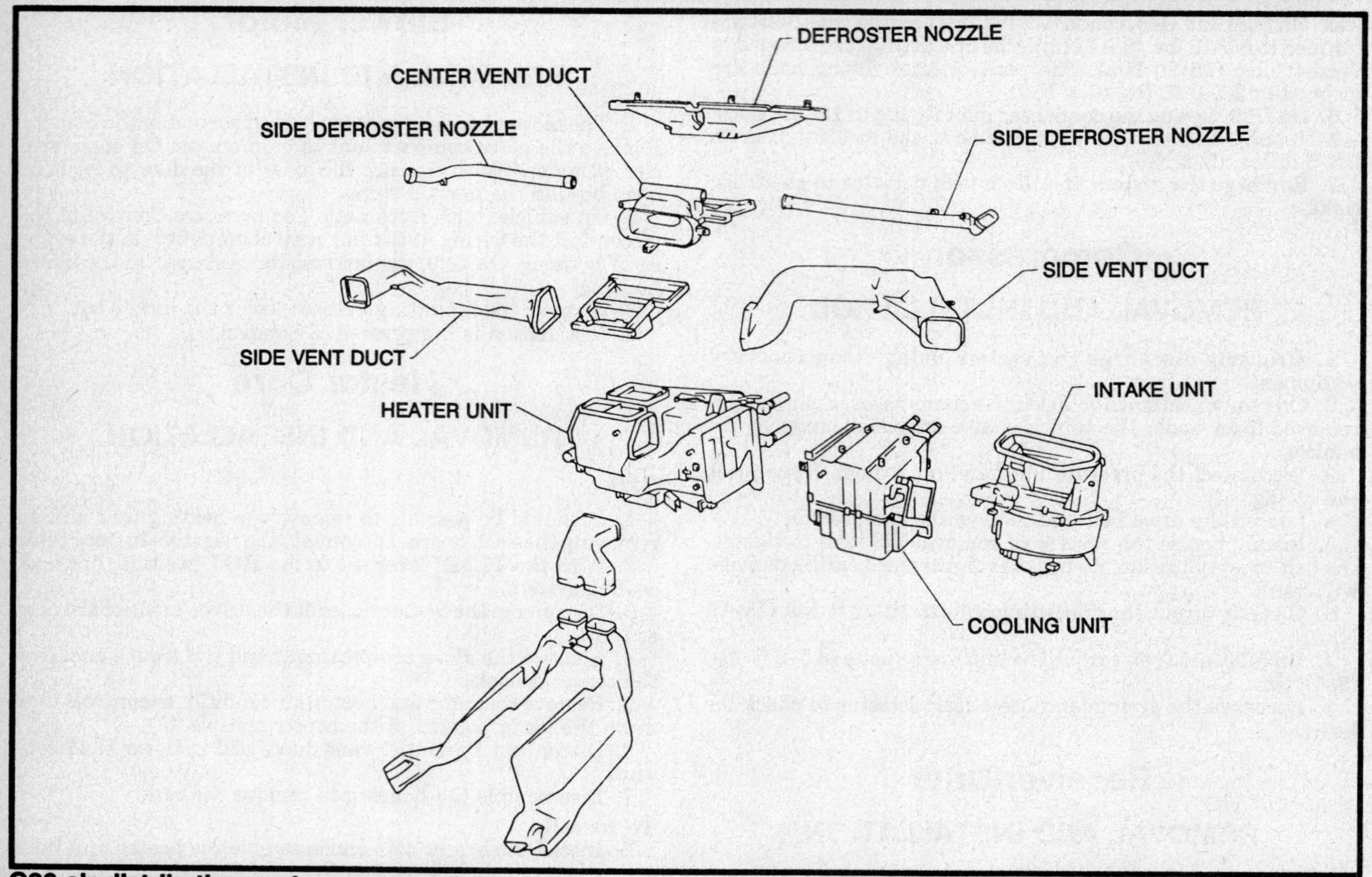
DEFROSTER NOZZLE
CENTER VENT DUCT
SIDE DEFROSTER NOZZLE
SIDE DEFROSTER NOZZLE
SIDE VENT DUCT
SIDE VENT DUCT
INTAKE UNIT
HEATER UNIT
COOLING UNIT

G20 air distribution system components

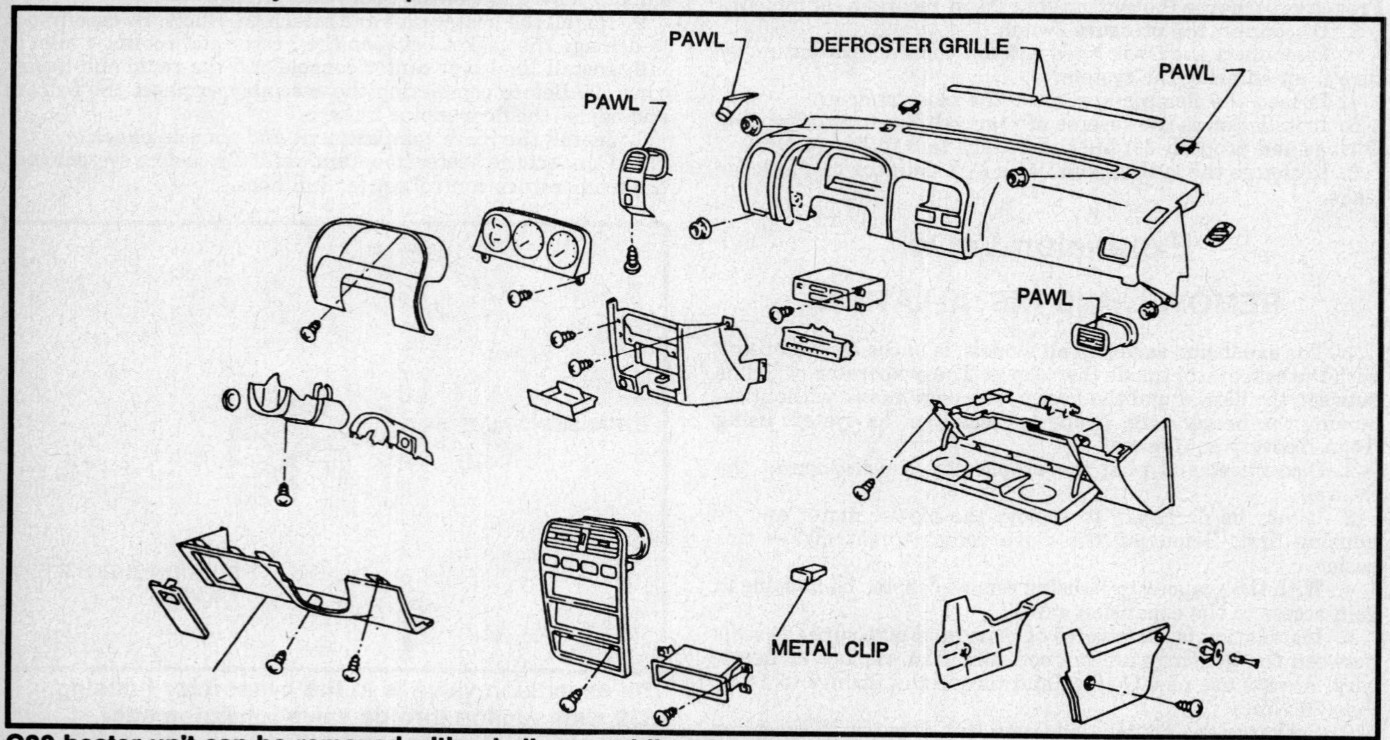
PAWL
DEFROSTER GRILLE
PAWL
PAWL
PAWL
METAL CLIP

G20 heater unit can be removed without disassembling the dash board

13. Run the engine to bleed the system. Connect a tube to the bleeder pipe near the heater hose connection and put the other end into the coolant reservoir.

M30

CAUTION

The vehicle is equipped with an air bag supplimental restraint system. The system is still active for about 10 minutes after disconnecting the battery. Wait for more than 10 minutes before starting electrical work and do not use a memory saver. If power is required for diagnostic work, the air bag module can be disconnected inside the panel in the back of the steering wheel after the system is inactive. Reconnect the module before reconnecting the battery and make sure no one is in the vehicle when connecting the battery.

1. With the ignition switch **ON**, set the temperature and air mix controls for full heat.
2. Turn the ignition **OFF**, drain the cooling system and disconnect the heater hoses.
3. The entire instrument panel must be removed to remove the heater unit. Disconnect the battery and wait more than 10 minutes.
4. Open the panel on the back of the steering wheel and disconnect the air bag module. Remove the T50H torx head bolts from the sides of the steering wheel to remove the horn pad with the air bag module. Store it in a safe place with the pad side facing up.
5. Make sure the front wheels are pointed straight ahead and remove the steering wheel. Remove the covers on the steering column, the spiral spring for the air bag and the combinatation switch.
6. Remove the A-pillar trim.
7. Remove the instrument cluster cover and carefully remove the instruments.
8. Remove the upper ash tray to access the screw to remove the dash center console panel. The bottom is held by plastic pawls.
9. Remove the radio and heater/air conditioner controls.
10. Remove the glove compartment assembly. There is a total of 10 screws.
11. Remove the lower ash tray to access the screw holding the shifter cover. Remove the floor center console.
12. Remove the defroster grille and sun load sensor.
13. Remove the hood latch cable and disconnect the rear seat heater ducts.
14. Remove the fuse block and disconnect the plugs.
15. Remove the 4 bolts, 2 nuts and 2 screws to remove the dash board.
16. Remove the heater unit and disassemble the case to remove the heater core.

To install:

17. When reassembling the heater unit, be careful to install the mode doors properly. Make sure the linkage operates smoothly.
18. Install the heater unit using a new gasket between the housings. Install the door motor but do not connect the linkage yet.
19. Install the dash board and fuse block. Reconnect the wiring.
20. Install the defroster grille and sun load sensor.
21. Install the hood latch.
22. Install the floor center console and shifter cover.
23. Install the heater controls, instrument panel and combination switch. When installing the spiral spring, make sure the arrow on the housing points to the alignment mark on the left. Install the steering wheel but do not install the air bag module yet. Carefully check all the wiring to make sure it is correctly connected.

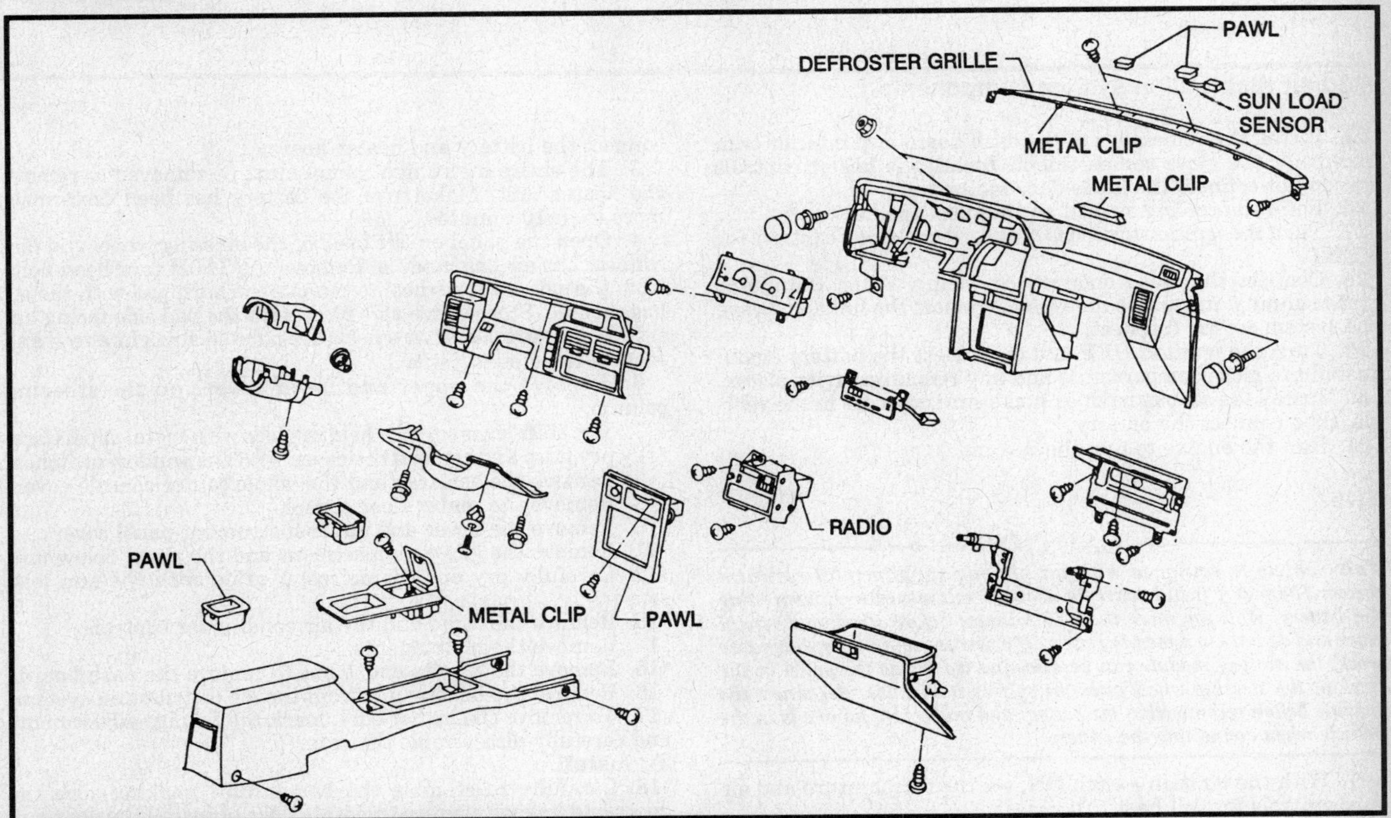
PAWL
DEFROSTER GRILLE
SUN LOAD SENSOR
METAL CLIP
METAL CLIP
RADIO
PAWL
METAL CLIP
PAWL

M30 dash board must be removed to remove the heater core.

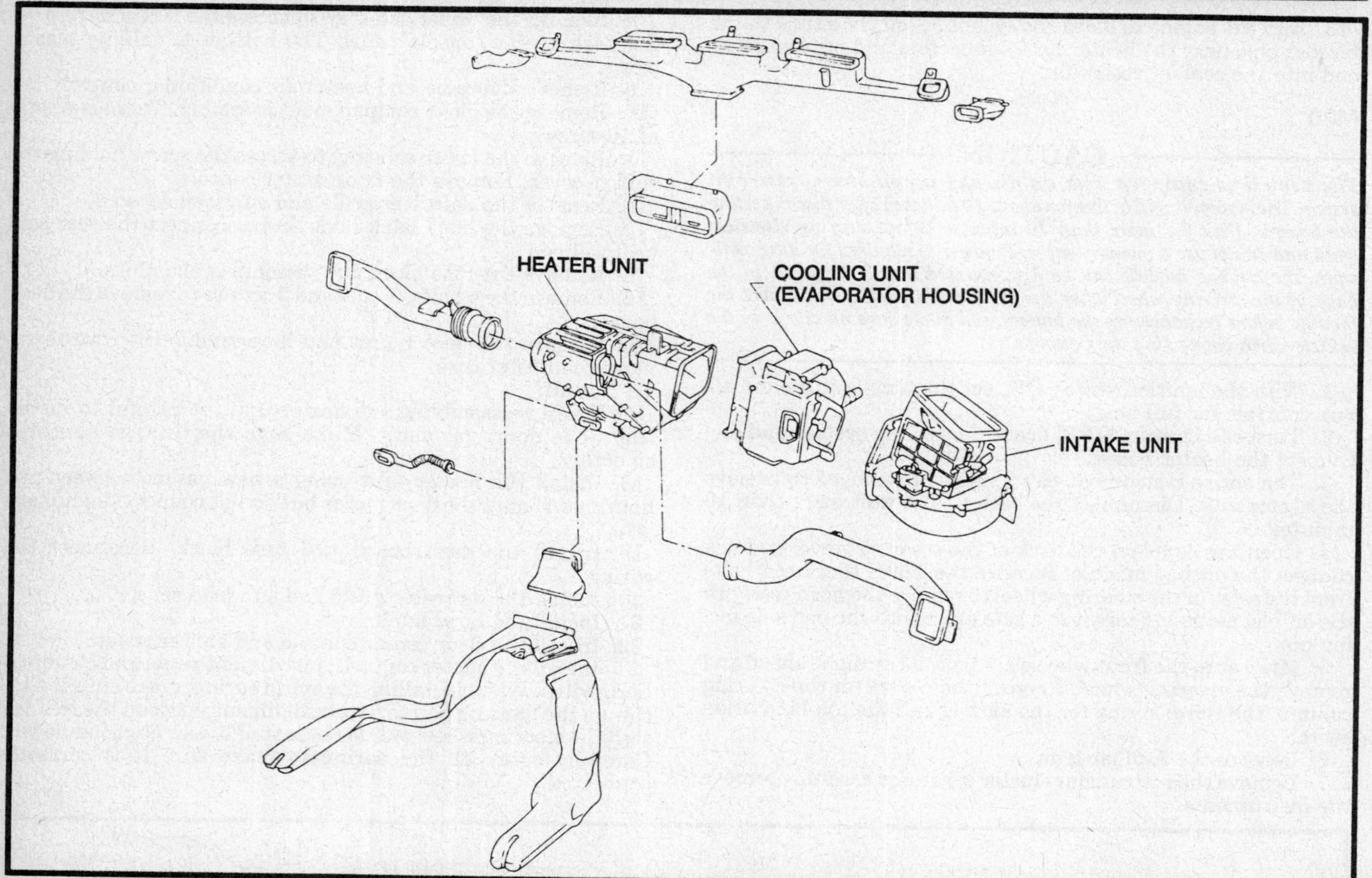
HEATER UNIT
COOLING UNIT
(EVAPORATOR HOUSING)
INTAKE UNIT

M30 air distribution system components

24. Install the remainder of the dash board and interior trim except for the glove compartment. Install the heater controls but do not connect the mode door motor yet.
25. Refill the cooling system and connect the battery.
27. Turn the ignition switch **ON** and set the mode controls for **VENT**.
28. Connect the mode door motor wiring. When the motor stops running, install the motor and connect the linkage. Leave the system set for full heat.
29. Turn the ignition **OFF** and disconnect the battery again. Install the glove compartment and any remaining trim pieces.
30. Install the air bag module, make sure no one is in the vehicle, then connect the battery.
31. Run the engine to test the system.

Q45

CAUTION

This vehicle is equipped with an air bag supplimental restraint system. The system is still active for about 10 minutes after disconnecting the battery. Wait for more than 10 minutes before starting electrical work and do not use a memory saver. If power is required for diagnostic work, the air bag module can be disconnected inside the panel in the back of the steering wheel after the system is inactive. Reconnect the module before reconnecting the battery and make sure no one is in the vehicle when connecting the battery.

1. With the ignition switch **ON**, set the temperature and air mix controls for full heat.
2. Turn the ignition **OFF**, drain the cooling system and disconnect the battery and heater hoses.
3. The entire instrument panel must be removed to remove the heater unit. Make sure the battery has been disconnect more than 10 minutes.
4. Open the panel on the back of the steering wheel and disconnect the air bag module. Remove the T50H torx head bolts from the sides of the wheel to remove the horn pad with the air bag module. Store it in a safe place with the pad side facing up.
5. Make sure the front wheels are pointed straight ahead and remove the steering wheel.
6. Remove the upper and lower covers on the steering column.
7. The shift lever cover is held in place with metal clips. Carefully pry it up and remove the cover with the window switches.
8. Remove the ash tray and the whole center console cover.
9. Remove the center floor console.
10. Remove the lower and upper instrument panel covers.
11. Remove the glove compartment and the panel below it.
12. Carefully pry out the defroster grille with the sun load sensor.
13. Remove the radio and the air conditioner controls.
14. Remove the instruments.
15. Remove the 3 bolts and 1 nut to remove the dash board.
16. Remove the heater unit from the air distribution system.
17. To remove the heater core, mark the linkage adjustments and carefully disassemble the case.

To install:

18. Carefully reassemble the heater unit, making sure the doors and linkage operate smoothly. Do not install the door motor yet.

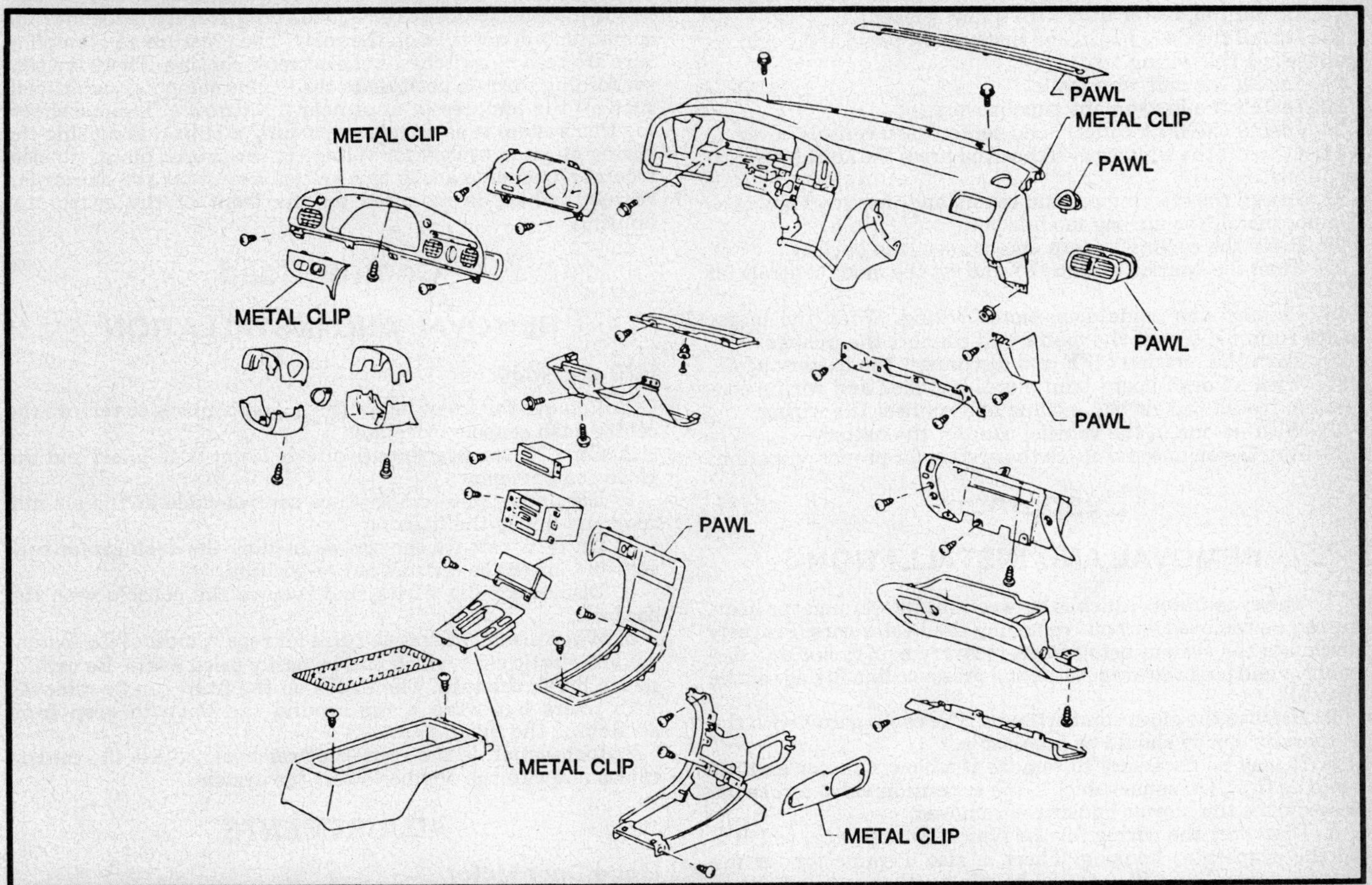
METAL CLIP
METAL CLIP
PAWL
METAL CLIP
PAWL
PAWL
PAWL
PAWL
METAL CLIP
METAL CLIP

Q45 dash board must be removed to remove the heater unit

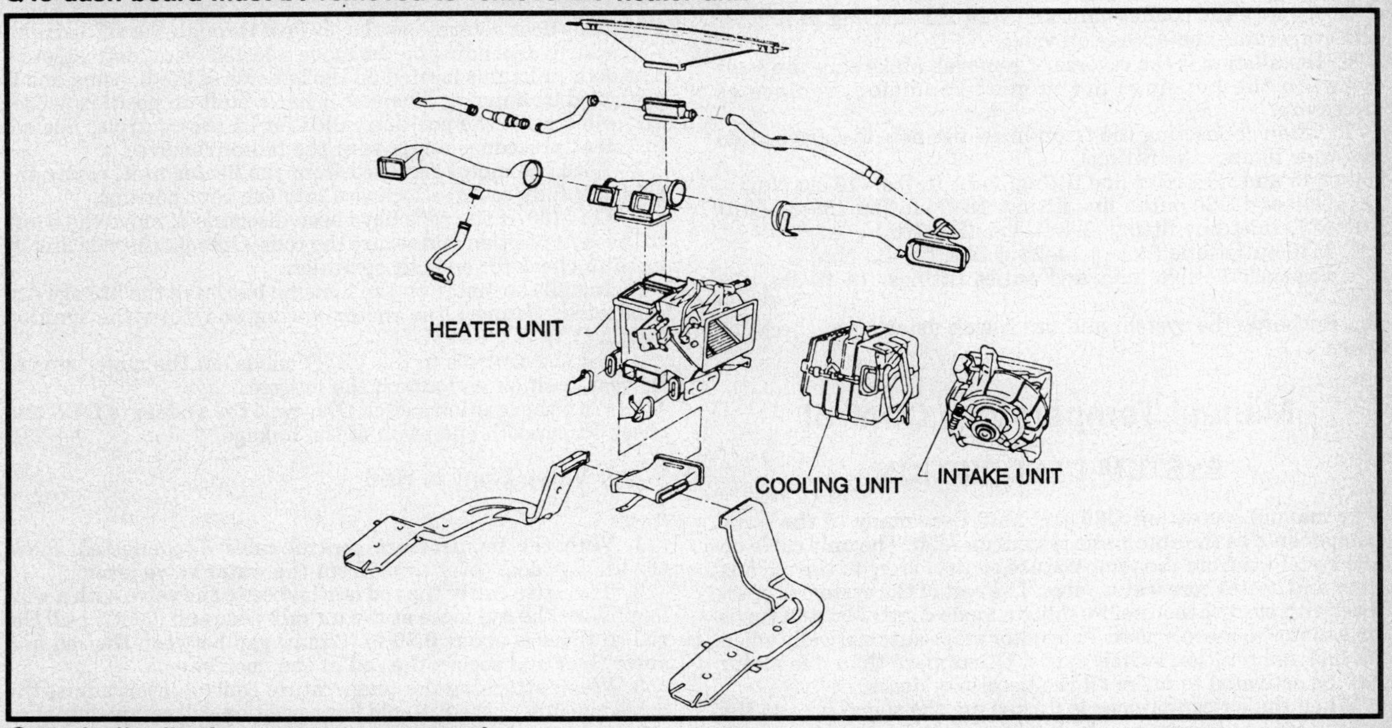
HEATER UNIT
COOLING UNIT
INTAKE UNIT

Q45 air distribution system components

19. Install the heater unit with a new gasket.
20. Install the dash board and instrument panel and begin reconnecting the wiring.
21. Install the defroster grille.
22. Install the instrument panel covers.
23. Install the floor console and center dash console cover.
24. Connect the window switches and press the shift lever cover in place.
25. Install the steering column covers and the steering wheel. Do not install the air bag module yet.
26. Refill the cooling system and connect the battery.
27. Turn the ignition switch **ON** and set the mode controls for **VENT**.
28. Connect the mode door motor wiring. When the motor stops running, install the motor and connect the linkage.
29. Turn the ignition **OFF** and disconnect the battery again.
30. With all dash board trim pieces installed and wiring connected, install the air bag module and connect the wiring.
31. With no one in the vehicle, connect the battery.
32. Run the engine and check the system for proper operation.

Evaporator

REMOVAL AND INSTALLATION

1. The evaporator, which is between the blower and the heater, can be removed without removing the heater core. Properly discharge the system using freon recovery equipment and disconnect and plug the evaporator and pressure line fittings at the firewall.
2. Remove the glove compartment. The cooling unit with the evaporator inside should be accessable.
3. It may be necessary to remove the blower motor and its' housing first. On some vehicles, the expansion valve can be accessed once the blower housing is removed.
4. Disconect the wiring for the blower fan resistor, which is on the evaporator housing. There is also a connector for the thermo control amplifier on the housing, either on the front or the top right.
5. Remove the cooling unit and split the housing to remove the evaporator and expansion valve.
6. Installation is the reverse of removal. Make sure the seals between the housings are in good condition, replace as necessary.
7. When connecting the freon lines, use new O-rings and do not over tighten the fittings.
   Q45 and G20 inlet line fitting: 7–14 ft. lbs. (10–20 Nm)
   Q45 and G20 outlet line fitting: 18–24 ft. lbs. (25–35 Nm)
   M30 inlet line fitting: 2–3 ft. lbs. (3–4 Nm)
   M30 outlet line fitting: 14–22 ft. lbs. (20–29 Nm)
   Expansion valve inlet and outlet fittings: 14 ft. lbs. (20 Nm)
8. Recharge the system and use a leak detector to check for leaks.

Manual Temperature Control

SYSTEM DESCRIPTION

The manual system on G20 and M30 uses many of the same components as the automatic system on M30. The only cable on the system is from the temperature control lever to the air mix door and heater core water valve. The rest of the system is operated with electric motors. Pushing a mode control button turns on a motor to move a door. The motor stops automatically when an internal position switch opens. Often more than one motor will be activated to move all the necessary doors.

When the air conditioner is turned on, the signal goes to the engine control computer, which will operate the compressor relay. If the freon pressure or outside temperature is too low, the computer will not turn on the relay. The pressure and temperature are read by switches, not electronic sensors. There is a sensor feeding throttle position to the engine computer, which will turn off the compressor at or near full throttle. Trouble shooting this system is as simple as pushing a button and using the wiring diagram to look for voltage in the proper place. No electronic components are in this system except for the blower fan resistor, which is mounted on the front of the evaporator housing.

Control Head

REMOVAL AND INSTALLATION

G20 and M30

1. Remove the screw below the heater controls to remove the center dash console faceplate.
2. On G20, remove the driver side lower dash panel and the glove compartment.
3. Disconnect the temperature control cable at the air mix door and unclip the housing.
4. On G20, remove the screws holding the dash center console and lower the console out of position.
5. Disconnect the wiring and remove the console with the controls.
6. When disassembling the unit for repair, most of the fasteners are plastic clips which can be easily pried apart. Be careful not to break the tabs. The knobs on the front can be removed with pliers but wrap a rag around the knob to keep from scratching the finish.
7. Installation is the reverse of removal. Adjust the control cables and run the engine to test the system.

ADJUSTMENTS

Mode Door Motor

G20 AND M30

The mode door determines the air flow through the air distribution system depending on the mode selected (vent, defrost, etc.). The door linkage is located on the left side of the housing and is controled by a motor. The motor has a built–in position sensor and will stop at the position called for by the controls. The adjustment procedure starts with the motor removed.

1. With the motor removed from the heater unit, rotate the side link fully counterclockwise into the vent position.
2. On M30, if the rods have been disconnect, move the doors to the vent position and secure the rods. Operate the side link by hand to check for smooth operation.
3. Install the motor on the housing but leave the linkage disconnected. Connect the motor wiring and turn the ignition switch **ON**.
4. Set the controls to the **VENT** mode, let the motor stop at its vent position and attach the linkage.
5. With the ignition switch **ON**, cycle the system to **DEF** and check for smooth operation of the linkage.

Water Valve Control Rod

M30

1. With the temperature control cable disconnected, move the air mix door lever away from the water valve lever.
2. The valve end of the rod is attached to the valve with a wire loop. With the rod loose at the air mix door end, gently pull the rod so there is about 0.80 in. (2mm) gap between the rod and valve lever and secure the rod at the door lever.
3. When attaching the temperature control lever, adjust the cable housing so the full cold lever position will completely shut off the heat.

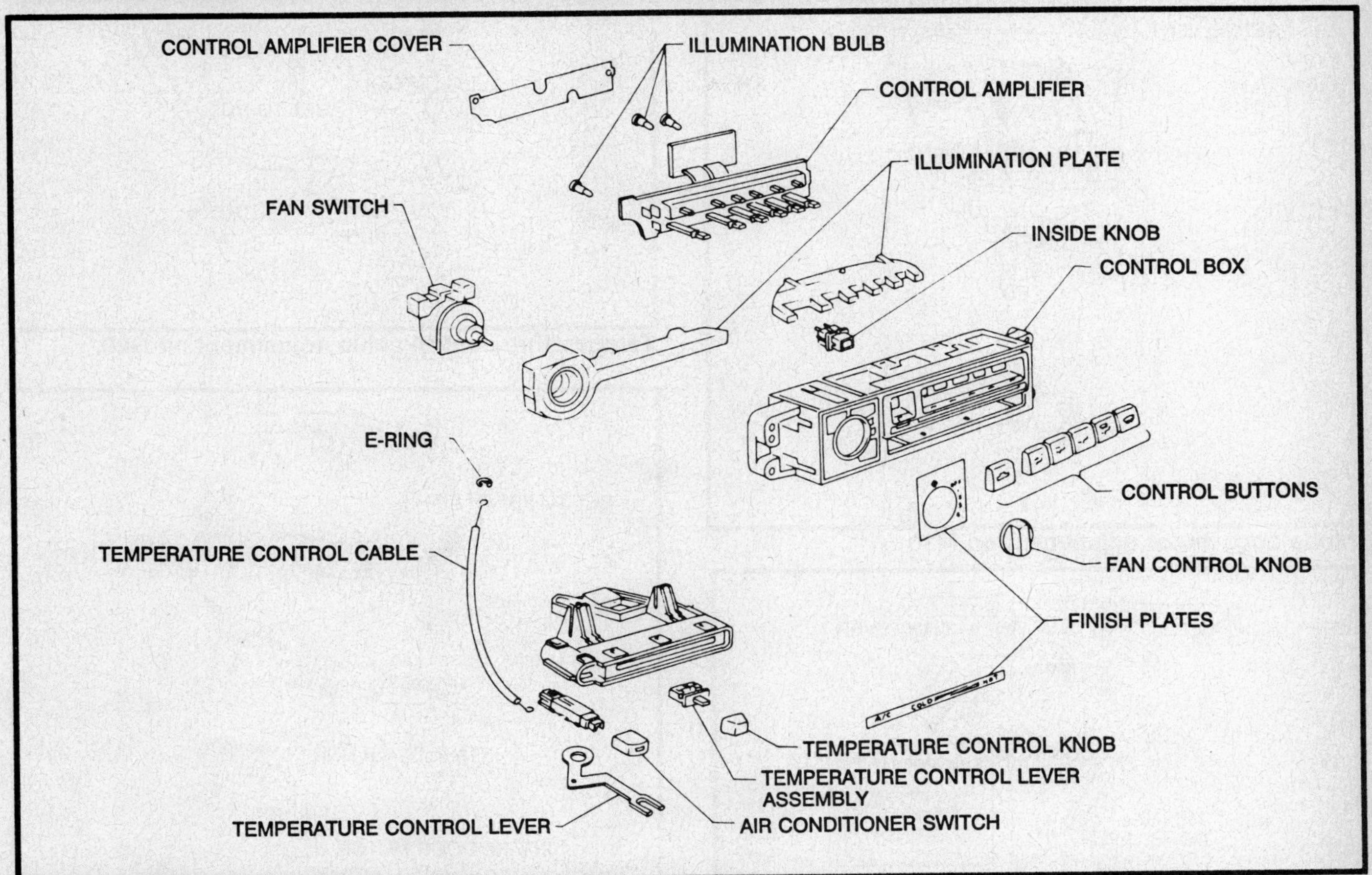
CONTROL AMPLIFIER COVER
ILLUMINATION BULB
CONTROL AMPLIFIER
ILLUMINATION PLATE
FAN SWITCH
INSIDE KNOB
CONTROL BOX
E-RING
CONTROL BUTTONS
TEMPERATURE CONTROL CABLE
FAN CONTROL KNOB
FINISH PLATES
TEMPERATURE CONTROL KNOB
TEMPERATURE CONTROL LEVER ASSEMBLY
TEMPERATURE CONTROL LEVER
AIR CONDITIONER SWITCH

Heater/air conditioner control assembly on G20

Temperature Control Cable

G20 AND M30

1. On G20, with the cable disconnected from the heater, move the temperature control lever to the full hot position.
2. On M30, with the cable disconnected from the heater, move the temperature control lever to the full cold position.
3. Attach the cable to the air mix door lever. Take up the slack in the housing away from the lever and secure the housing.
4. Operate the temperature control lever and check for smooth operation.

Air Intake Door

G20

1. With the door motor removed but wiring connected, turn the ignition switch **ON** and make sure the recirculate button is **OFF**. The motor will stop at the correct position.
2. Hold the door in the fresh air position, install the motor and connect the control rod.
3. Switch the recirculate button **ON** and **OFF** to check for smooth operation of the door.

M30

1. With the door motor removed but wiring connected, turn the ignition switch **ON** and make sure the recirculate button is **ON**. The motor will stop at the correct position.
2. Hold the door in the recirculated air position, install the

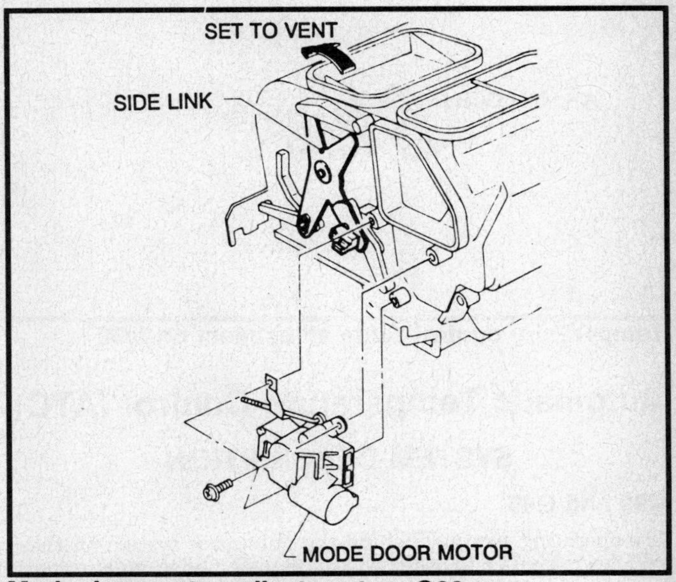
SET TO VENT
SIDE LINK
MODE DOOR MOTOR

Mode door motor adjustment on G20

motor and connect the control rod.
3. Switch the recirculate button **ON** and **OFF** to check for smooth operation of the door.

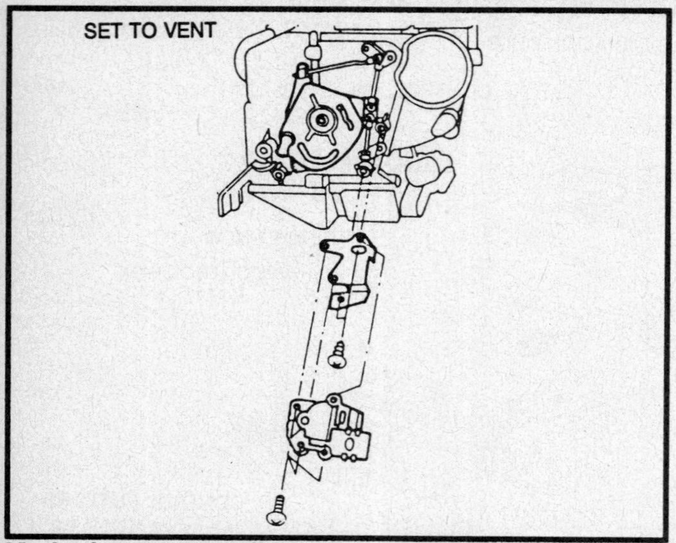
SET TO VENT
Mode door motor adjustment on M30

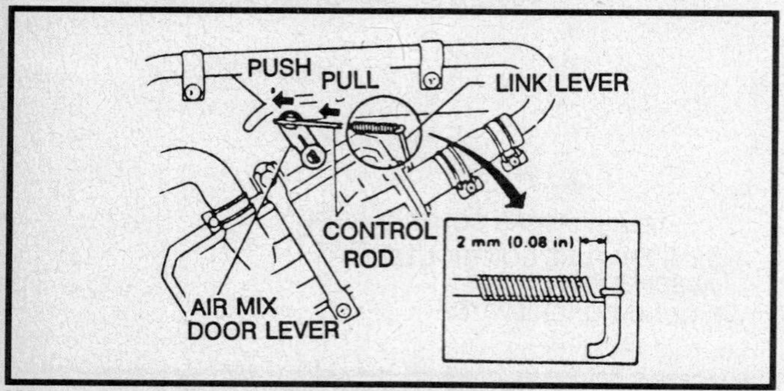
PUSH
PULL
LINK LEVER
CONTROL
ROD
AIR MIX
DOOR LEVER
2 mm (0.08 in)
Water valve rod adjustment on M30

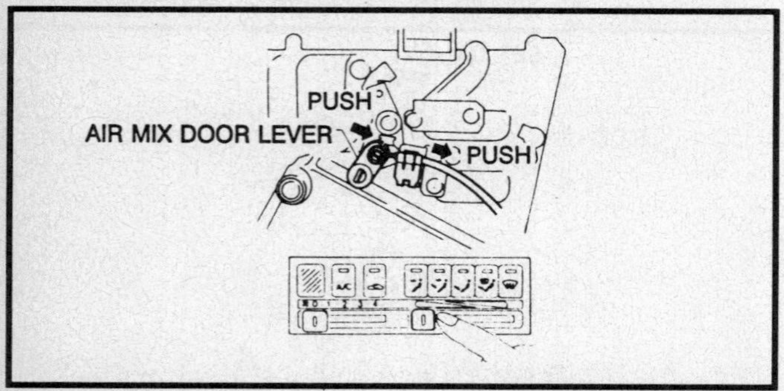
PUSH
AIR MIX DOOR LEVER
PUSH
Temperature control cable adjustment on M30

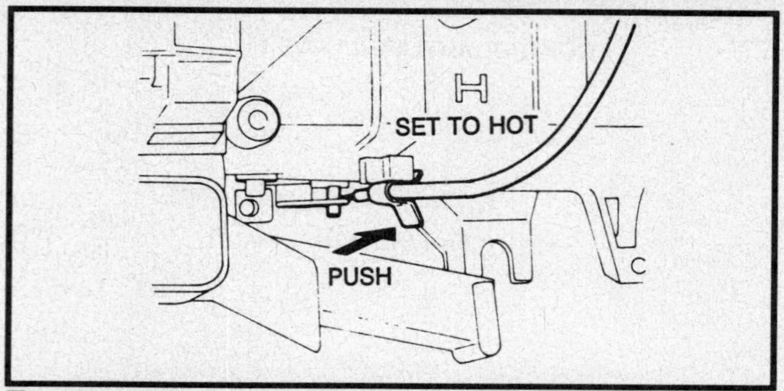
SET TO HOT
PUSH
Temperature control cable adjustment on G20

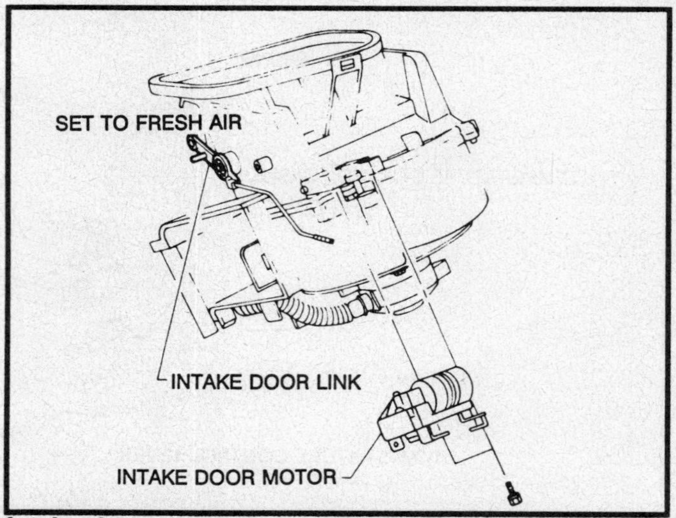
SET TO FRESH AIR
INTAKE DOOR LINK
INTAKE DOOR MOTOR
Intake door adjustment on G20

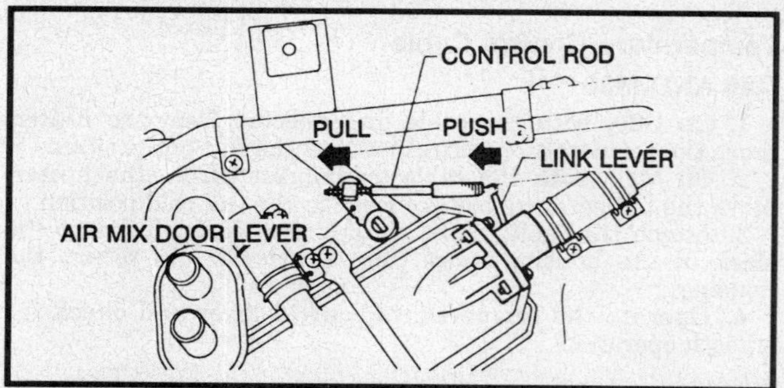
CONTROL ROD
PULL
PUSH
LINK LEVER
AIR MIX DOOR LEVER
Intake door adjustment on M30

Automatic Temperature Control (ATC)

SYSTEM DESCRIPTION

M30 and Q45

The operating stratagy behind the automatic system on these vehicles is similar to other Nissan models. When an automatic temperature setting is selected, the auto amplifier in the control head determines door positions, blower fan speed and compressor operation to maintain that target temperature inside the vehicle. Control is biased to admit as much fresh air as possible while maintaining the target temperature. Blower fan speed and air inlet and outlet modes can be operated manually or the entire system can be turned off at any time. If full air recirculation is selected, it will operate this way for 10 minutes, then return to fresh air mix mode.

The information fed to the auto amplifier comes from temperature sensors in the intake duct, behind the front grille and inside the vehicle. The auto amplifier also reads sun load, mode door position and, on Q45, water temperature in the heater core. Output signals are sent to the blower fan amplifier, door motors and the engine control computer. The engine computer operates the compressor and a fast idle control solenoid. It will also turn the compressor off if the engine is under full throttle. The auto amplifier program includes the ability to average the input from the sun load sensor, so sudden changes like driving in and out of shady areas will not cause sudden oscillations in air conditioner output. On Q45, when the engine is started in cold weather, the auto amplifier will run the blower fan at low speed until the heater core temperature is at least 120°F (50°C).

Auto Amplifier/Control Head

REMOVAL AND INSTALLATION

Q45

1. Using a thin prying tool and a rag to protect the finish, carefully pry up on the rear of the shift lever plate, which also houses the window swithces.
2. Remove the ash tray assembly.
3. Remove the screws holding the center dash panel and lift it off from the rear.
4. The screws for the auto amplifier are now accessable. Slide the unit out far enough to disconnect the plugs on the back.
5. Installation is the reverse of removal.

M30

1. Remove the screws at the top of the center dash panel.
2. Tilt the top of the panel out, disconnect the lighter wires and remove the panel.
3. The screws for the auto amplifier are now accessable. Slide the unit out far enough to disconnect the plugs on the back.
4. Installation is the reverse of removal.

ADJUSTMENTS

Each door motor has a position switch built-in which reports door position to the auto amplifier. The air mix door motor has a Potentiometer Balance Resistor (PRB) built into the air mix door motor. A voltage is supplied to terminal No. 28 on the motor and a variable resistor returns a portion of the voltage to the amplifier from terminals 16 and 27. The amplifier interprets the return voltage as a door position. The position switches or PBR can be tested but not repaired. The motor must be replaced if it does not stop at the position commanded by the auto amplifier. To adjust the motors and rods, the system must be operated in Test 4 of the self diagnostic function. Install all the motors and connect the wiring but do not attach the control rods yet. Turn the ignition switch **ON** and within 10 seconds, press the **OFF** button for more than 5 seconds. The system should enter Teat 1, the light check function. Press the temperature increase button 3 times to skip to Test 4, the actuator test. Remember the position sensor for the controller is in the motor itself.

Mode Door Motor

1. With the system in Test 4 of the self diagnostic function, make sure the code in the display reads number 41. If it does not, press the defrost button until it does. This will drive the system into **VENT** mode.
2. Rotate the side link on the heater housing full counterclockwise to put the doors into the vent position.
3. Attach the control rod and press the defrost button to cycle the system through all 6 modes. Check for smooth operation and correct air outlet.

Air Mix Door Motor

1. With the motor installed but the linkage disconnected, press the defrost button to set up code number 46 in the display.
2. Move the air mix door lever to the full hot position and attach the rod.
3. Cycle the system through all 6 modes to check for smooth operation.

Intake Door Motor

1. With the motor installed but the linkage disconnected, press the defrost button to set up code number 41 in the display.

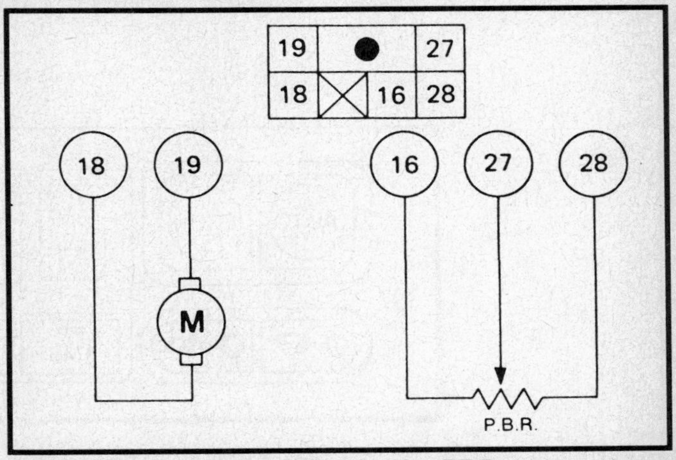
19
27
18
16
28
18
19
16
27
28
M
P.B.R.

Air Mix Door motor schematic, the PBR reports door position to the auto amplifier

2. Rotate the door linkage to set the doors in the recirculate position.
3. Attach the rod and cycle the system by pressing the defrost button to check for smooth operation.

SYSTEM DIAGNOSTICS

The micro computer in the auto amplifier has a self diagnostic function which stores trouble codes. This function can be accessed through the system controls or through Nissan's Consult hand held module. The Consult is menu driven, meaning the procedure for its use is shown step by step on the unit's own read out screen. The procedures described here are for the onboard self diagnostic system only. The first step in diagnostic work is to operate the system with the engine running to find which functions do not work properly.

Function Test

1. With the vehicle in a well ventilated area above 32°F, start the engine and warm it up. Operate the mode control manually and feel for air exiting the correct vents. With the blower fan at full speed, it should be easy to hear changes in air flow, especially when the system is switched from fresh air to recuiculated air.
2. When the **AUTO** button is pressed, the display will show the most receiently selected temperature the system will attempt to maintain. Press the temperature increase and decrease buttons to see that the display changes.
3. When the **AMB** button is pressed, the ambient temperature measured at the sensor behind the grille will be displayed for 5 seconds. When the **DEF** button is pressed, the recirculation function is canceled.
4. When the **ECON** button is pressed, all other modes will be canceled and the system will default to automatic temperature control for heat only. Make sure the compressor stops.
5. When ambient and engine coolant temperatures are low, the blower fan automatically will not operate for up to 150 seconds after the engine is started. As coolant temperature rises, blower fan gradually increases to the objective speed.
6. Press the **OFF** button and turn the engine off. Wait about 15 seconds and start the engine, then press the **AUTO** button. The system should return the the same temperature setting.

Self-Diagnostics

The self-diagnostic function is divided into 5 tests: light check, sensor circuit check, mode door position, actuator test and temperature sensor read-out. A 5th Step is also available for correct-

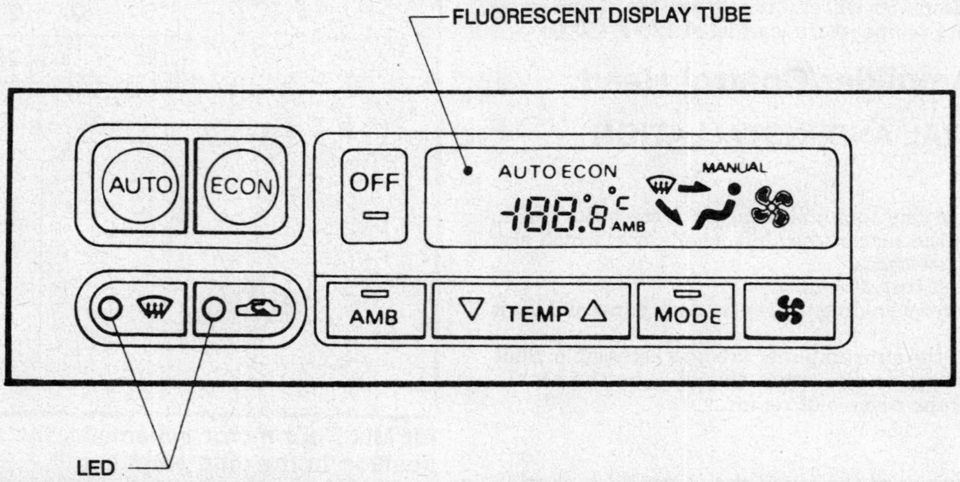
FLUORESCENT DISPLAY TUBE
AUTO
ECON
OFF
AUTO ECON
MANUAL
188.8 °C AMB
AMB
TEMP
MODE
LED

Test 1 on M30 and Q45 ATC self diagnostics is a light check; if any segments do not light, the remaining tests will not be accurate

SENSOR CIRCUIT FAULT CODES

Code No.	Sensor	Open circuit	Short circuit
21	Ambient sensor	Less than -41.9°C (-43°F)	Greater than 100°C (212°F)
22	In-vehicle sensor	Less than -41.9°C (-43°F)	Greater than 100°C (212°F)
23	Water temperature sensor	Less than -25.6°C (-14°F)	Greater than 150°C (302°F)
24	Intake sensor	Less than -41.9°C (-43°F)	Greater than 100°C (212°F)
25	Sunload sensor*2	Less than 0.0319 mA	Greater than 1.147 mA
26	P.B.R.*1	Greater than 50%	Less than 30%

ing temperature off-set. To access the self diagnostic function, start the engine or turn the ignition switch **ON** and, within 10 seconds, press the **OFF** button for more than 5 seconds. Pressing the temperature increase or decrease buttons moves up or down the test menu. Pressing the **AUTO** button or turning the ignition switch **OFF** will exit the self-diagnostic function.

LIGHT CHECK

With the system in Test 1 of the self diagnostic mode, the LEDs in the defrost and recirculate buttons will light. All segments in the fluorescent display tube should also illuminate. If any segment is missing from the tube display, it will be impossible to complete the self diagnostics accurately. If the system will not enter the diagnostic mode, the **OFF** button may be faulty or the auto amplifier itself is faulty.

SENSOR CIRCUIT TEST

1. Press the temperature increase button to leave the light check and move into the sensor circuit test. The system will take about 4 seconds to check all circuits.
2. If all circuits are good, the number 20 will appear in the display indicating test 2 with 0 faults. If any number from 21–26 appears, it will blink on and off indicating a circuit is faulty. If more than one circuit is faulty, each circuit number will blink twice. A minus (−) sign in front the the number indicates a short circuit.
3. Circuits 21–24 are temperature sensors. Number 25 is the sun load sensor circuit. Circuit 26 is the Potentiometer Balance Resistor (PBR), which is a position feed-back device used to tell the control amplifier what percentage of full stroke the air mix door has reached. 100 percent stroke is full heat.
4. If a faulty circuit is indicated, complete the rest of the diagnostics before starting repairs.

MODE DOOR POSITION TEST

1. Press the temperature increase button once to leave the

M30 AND Q45 ACTUATOR TEST

Actuator \ Code No.	41	42	43	44	45	46
Mode door	VENT	B/L 1	B/L 2	F/D 1	F/D 2	DEF
Intake door	REC	REC	20% FRE	FRE	FRE	FRE
Air mix door	Full Cold	Full Cold	Full Hot	Full Hot	Full Hot	Full Hot
Blower motor	4 - 5 V	9 -11 V	7 - 9 V	7 - 9 V	7 - 9 V	10 - 12 V
Compressor	ON	ON	ON	OFF	OFF	ON

circuit test and enter the door position test. The system will take about 16 seconds to cycle the door motors and test the position switches or sensor.

2. If all doors work correctly, the number 30 will appear in the display indicating Test 3 and 0 faults.

3. If any number from 31–36 appears, it will blink on and off indicating a door is not working properly. If more than one fault exists, each number will blink twice.

4. If a fault is indicated, complete the rest of the diagnostics before starting adjustment or repairs.

Code 31 – vent door position
Code 32 – floor and vent doors bi-level position 1
Code 33 – floor and vent doors bi-level position 2
Code 34 – floor and defrost doors position 1
Code 35 – floor and defrost doors position 2
Code 36 – defrost door position

ACTUATOR MOTOR TEST

1. Press the temperature increase button once to leave the door position test and enter the actuator test. The number 41 will appear in the display, indicating Test 4 and the first test position.

2. To advance to the next test position, press the defrost button. The number 42 will appear in the display. There are 6 positions all together and when the button is pressed with number 46 in the display, it returns to number 41.

3. In this Test, each actuator will receive a specific command from the auto amplifier. This will allow the technician to physically check that each actuator goes to the position specified.

4. Advance the system to each position and feel for the change in air flow, to check blower motor voltage and compressor operation. This test is also used to manually drive the system to a known state for adjusting control rods and door positions when installing door motors.

TEMPERATURE SENSOR TEST

1. Press the temperature increase button once to leave the actuator test and enter the sensor test. The number 5 will appear in the display, indicating Test 5.

2. Press the defrost button once to display read the ambient sensor reading.

3. Press the defrost button a 2nd time to display the inside sensor reading.

4. Press the defrost button a 3rd time to display the intake air sensor reading.

5. Pressing the button a 4th time will return to the display to the number 5 and the sequence starts again. On Q45, the heater core sensor reading is not displayed in any test.

6. If Test 1 indicated a good sensor circuit, but the reading in Test 5 varries greatly from the actual temperature at that sensor location, remove the sensor for individual testing. See the sensor resistance charts.

7. If Test 1 indicated a bad sensor circuit, the reading in Test 5 should be about the same. Check and repair the circuit continuity and repeat both tests.

TEMPERATURE TRIMMER

1. This procedure is to compensate for the actual cabin temperature that the system maintains being different from the temperature selected on the ATC. The total range of adjustment is ± 6°F (± 3°C). While still in Test 5 with the number 5 on the display, press the fan button once. The display will change to read 0°F on U.S. models or 0°C on Canadian models.

2. Press the temperature increase or decrease button to change the offset number in the display. Press the blower fan button to exit this procedure.

3. When the auto amplifier or battery is disconnected, this trimmer function will default to 0 degrees.

SENSORS, SWITCHES AND RELAYS

Fan and Compressor Relays

OPERATION

M30

1. The main air conditioner relay is on the relay panel near the battery, the 2nd one from the rear. The relay is activated by the engine computer to turn on the compressor clutch and fast idle control device. Terminals 1 and 2 are the relay coil.
2. The condenser fan relay is on the same panel, the 4th from the rear. The relay coil gets power from the ignition switch but is turned on by the thermo switch threaded into the bottom of the radiator. Terminals 1 and 2 are the relay coil.
3. The blower fan high speed relay is in the center dash console, behind the ash tray. Removing the console cover should provide access. Power for the relay coil is available any time the ignition switch is **ON**. Ground for the coil is through the auto amplifier, which will bypass the fan control amplifier to run the blower at full speed. Terminals 1 and 2 are the relay coil.

Q45

1. The main air conditioner relay is on the relay panel near the battery, the closest one to the rear panel mount. This relay has power to the coil any time the ignition switch is **ON**. The ground for the coil is provided by the engine computer, through the dual pressure switch on the receiver/drier. Terminals 1 and 2 are the relay coil.
2. The condenser fan relay is on the same row as the main air conditioner relay, the second from the front. The coil receives power from the main relay through a joint connector. The ground for the coil is provided by the thermo switch threaded into the bottom of the radiator or by the air conditioner pressure switch at the receiver/drier. Terminals 1 and 2 are the relay coil.
3. The blower fan high speed relay is mounted on the housing just below the blower fan. Power for the relay coil is available any time the ignition switch is **ON**. Ground for the coil is through the auto amplifier, which will bypass the fan control amplifier to run the blower at full speed. Terminals 1 and 2 are the relay coil.

TESTING

1. Locate the relay on the wiring diagram and determine when the coil should have power. Operate the necessary switches while touching the relay. It should be possible to feel the relay click on and off.
2. If the relay does not click, remove it from the socket and use a volt meter to determine is the coil terminals are getting power and a good ground.
3. The relay can be bench tested by putting voltage to the correct terminals and checking for continuity across the switched terminals. Relays cannot be repaired.

Dual Pressure Switch

OPERATION

The switch is mounted in the top of the reciever/drier. Its function is to turn the compressor clutch off if the freon pressure in the high side is too high or too low. It can only be properly tested when gauges are connected to the service valves. Replacing the switch requires discharging the freon from the system into recovery equipment.

TESTING

1. There should be voltage to 1 terminal of the switch whenever the main air conditioner relay is activated.
2. When pressure is decreasing, the switch should open (compressor off) when high side pressure is 26–31 psi. or close (compressor on) when pressure gets down to 270–327 psi.

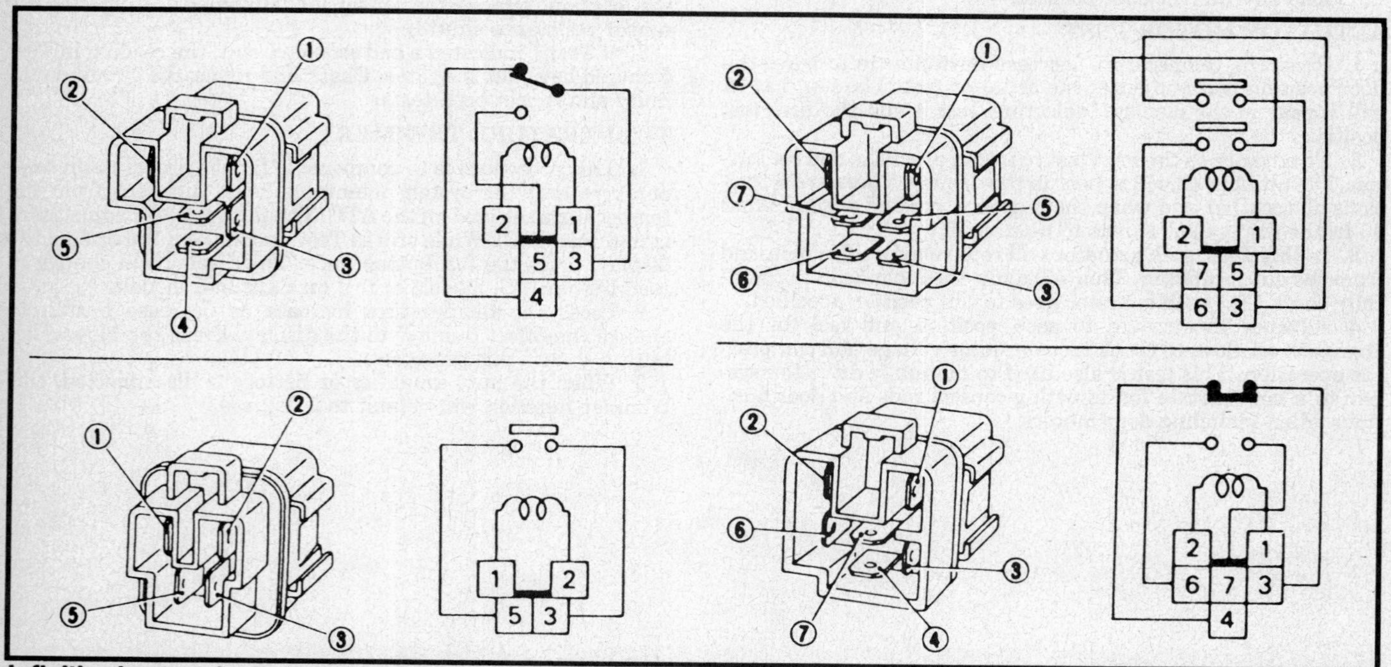

Infiniti relay terminals 1 and 2 are always for the coil

3. When pressure is increasing, the switch should close (compressor on) when high side pressure is 26–34 psi. or open (compressor off) when pressure is 356–412 psi.

4. If all other tests indicate a faulty dual pressure switch, disconnect the wiring and jumper the terminals to simulate a closed switch. If the compressor clutch operates, make sure the freon pressures are correct before replacing the switch.

REMOVAL AND INSTALLATION

1. Properly discharge the system into freon recovery equipment.
2. Locate the switch on top of the receiver/drier and disconnect the wiring.
3 Remove the switch and quickly cap the hole to prevent moisture in the system.
4. When installing the switch, use a new gasket and torque to 7–9 ft. lbs. (10–12 Nm).

Air Conditioning Pressure Switch

Q45

This switch is used to provide a ground for the condenser fan relay, independent of the thermo switch in the cooling system. The compressor in this vehicle is a variable displacement type, which means it can be run continuously without cycling on and off. The low side freon pressure in the system is maintained at a steady 27–33 psi., but the high side pressure varries according to demand. The air conditioning pressure switch operates on the high side pressure to turn the condenser fan on reguardless of the coolant temperature. This allows use of the air conditioning system to dehumidify the air in the vehicle even when heat demanded.

TESTING

1. Locate the switch in the pressure line at the receiver/drier.
2. With the engine and air conditioner running, disconnect the wiring and check for continuity across the terminals. If there is no continuity, attach gauges to the service valves.
3. The switch closes to complete a ground circuit when system pressure is above 206 psi.
4. The switch opens when system pressure is less than 178–192 psi.

REMOVAL AND INSTALLATION

1. Properly discharge the system into freon recovery equipment.
2. Locate the switch in the high pressure line near of the receiver/drier and disconnect the wiring.
3 Remove the switch and quickly cap the hole to prevent moisture in the system.
4. When installing the switch, use a new gasket and torque to 7–9 ft. lbs. (10–12 Nm).

Thermo Switch

OPERATION

The thermo switch is activated by engine coolant temperature, and will close to complete a circuit to ground for the condenser fan relay coil. Since it is threaded into the bottom of the radiator, it is only exposed to the temperature in the radiator, not in the engine. It must be removed for complete testing.

TESTING

1. With the ignition switch **ON** and the air conditioner **OFF**, disconnect the thermo switch and jumper the terminals on the wiring harness. The fan should run, so stay away from the blades.
2. If the fan did not run, check the fan relay and circuits. If the fan runs when the terminals are shorted together but not when the engine is at normal operating temperature, drain the cooling system and remove the switch.
3. Connect the switch to an ohmmeter and put it in water. Heat the water and measure the temperature with a thermometer. The switch should close at 194°F (90°C).

Ambient Air Sensor

OPERATION

This sensor converts temperature into an electrical resistance which the auto amplifier can read. It operates in a much different range than the in-vehicle sensor and they are not interchangable. On M30, the sensor is mounted in front of the

M30 AMBIENT AIR TEMPERATURE SENSOR RESISTANCE

Temperature °C (°F)	Resistance kΩ
-15 (5)	12.73
-10 (14)	9.92
-5 (23)	7.80
0 (32)	6.19
5 (41)	4.95
10 (50)	3.99
15 (59)	3.24
20 (68)	2.65
25 (77)	2.19
30 (86)	1.81
35 (95)	1.51

Q45 AMBIENT AIR TEMPERATURE SENSOR RESISTANCE

Temperature °C (°F)	Resistance kΩ
-15 (5)	12.73
-10 (14)	9.92
-5 (23)	7.80
0 (32)	6.19
5 (41)	4.95
10 (50)	3.99
15 (59)	3.24
20 (68)	2.65
25 (77)	2.19
30 (86)	1.81
35 (95)	1.51

radiator, near the secondary hood latch. On Q45, it is between the hood latch and the left head light.

TESTING

1. Disconnect the sensor and connect an ohmmeter set on the 10,000 ohm scale.
2. Measure the resistance and the temperature, using a thermometer.
3. If the reading is greatly different from the specification, test the sensor at other temperatures before deciding to replace it. Use a cold drink container or a drop light to change the temperature but do not immerse the sensor.
4. If the sensor appears to work correctly, check the voltage supply to the sensor. With the ignition switch **ON**, there should be 5 volts between one of the terminals and ground.
5. If there is no voltage, check for continuity of the wires between the sensor and auto amplifier and for power output at the amplifier. If there is not 5 volts at the amplifier itself, chances are that other sensors are also not working.

In-vehicle Temperature Sensor

OPERATION

The sensor converts the cabin temperature into a resistance which the auto amplifier can read. On M30, it is in the right side of the heater control panel, behind the small grille. On Q45, it is behind the small grille next to the rear window defogger switch. The sensor can be accessed by removing the air conditioner controls.

TESTING

1. With the controls/auto amplifier removed, locate the sensor and its connector. Touch the probes of an ohmmeter to the terminals, with the meter on the 10,000 ohm scale.
2. Measure the resistance and the temperature, using a thermometer.
3. If the reading is greatly different from the specification, remove the sensor and test it at other temperatures before deciding to replace it. Use a cold drink container or a drop light to change the temperature but do not immerse the sensor.
4. If the sensor appears to work correctly, check the voltage supply to the sensor. With the auto amplifier connected and the ignition switch **ON**, there should be 5 volts between one of the terminals and ground.
5. If there is no voltage, check for continuity of the wires between the sensor and auto amplifier and for power output at the amplifier. If there is not 5 volts at the amplifier itself, chances are that other sensors are also not working.

Aspirator Motor

OPERATION

On M30, there is a small fan mounted on the front of the heater unit which runs whenever the ignition is on. This fan draws inside air past the in-vehicle temperature sensor through a duct leading up to the sensor. It can be replaced separately.

On Q45, this same function is accomplished without a motor by an aspirator tube mounted to the heating unit near the side link on the left. This tube is a venturi which gets its suction from the air flowing in the air distribution system. It can be tested the same way as in the M30, but only disassembly, blockage or damage to the tube can cause malfunction.

TESTING

1. Before removing or disconnecting anything, turn the ignition switch (and on Q45, the blower fan) **ON** and hold a lighted cigarette or other source of smoke up to the small grille in front of the in-vehicle sensor. The smoke should be drawn into the grille.
2. On M30, if the smoke does not flow into the sensor grille, locate the connector for the motor behind the radio. Unplug the connector and check for voltage.
3. If there is voltage to the motor, remove it for bench testing or replacement. If there is no voltage, use the wiring diagram to trace the fault.
4. On Q45, if smoke does not flow into the grille, trace the duct to the aspirator. Make sure it is installed correctly and not blocked.

M30 IN-VEHICLE TEMPERATURE SENSOR RESISTANCE

Temperature °C (°F)	Resistance kΩ
−15 (5)	13.01
−10 (14)	10.20
−5 (23)	8.08
0 (32)	6.47
5 (41)	5.23
10 (50)	4.27
15 (59)	3.52
20 (68)	2.93
25 (77)	2.47
30 (86)	2.09
35 (95)	1.79

Q45 IN-VEHICLE TEMPERATURE SENSOR RESISTANCE

Temperature °C (°F)	Resistance kΩ
−15 (5)	12.95
−10 (14)	10.14
−5 (23)	8.02
0 (32)	6.41
5 (41)	5.17
10 (50)	4.21
15 (59)	3.46
20 (68)	2.87
25 (77)	2.41
30 (86)	2.03
35 (95)	1.73

Intake Sensor

OPERATION

On M30, this sensor is mounted on the top of the evaporator housing, with the connector to the right. On Q45 it is on the front of the housing. It reads the air temperature after the evaporator converts it into a resistance which the auto amplifier can read. This information is used to control the air mix door and the evaporator temperature to prevent freezing at the coils.

TESTING

1. With the glove compartment removed, locate the sensor and its connector. Touch the probes of an ohmmeter to the terminals, with the meter on the 10,000 ohm scale.
2. Measure the resistance and the temperature, using a thermometer.
3. If the reading is greatly different from the specification, remove the sensor and test it at other temperatures before deciding to replace it. Use a cold drink container or a drop light to change the temperature but do not immerse the sensor.
4. If the sensor appears to work correctly, check the voltage supply to the sensor. With the ignition switch **ON**, there should be 5 volts between one of the terminals and ground.
5. If there is no voltage, check for continuity of the wires between the sensor and auto amplifier and for power output at the amplifier. If there is not 5 volts at the amplifier itself, chances are that other sensors are also not working.

Water Temperature Sensor

OPERATION

This sensor in only used on the Q45 and is mounted to the heater line near the water control valve. It converts engine coolant temperature into an electrical resistance which the auto amplifier can read. It is dedicated to this system and not connected to any other system.

Q45 WATER TEMPERATURE SENSOR RESISTANCE

Temperature °C (°F)	Resistance kΩ
0 (32)	3.99
5 (41)	3.17
10 (50)	2.54
15 (59)	2.05
20 (68)	1.67
25 (77)	1.36
30 (86)	1.12
35 (95)	0.93
40 (104)	0.78
45 (113)	0.65
50 (122)	0.55
55 (131)	0.47
60 (140)	0.40
65 (149)	0.34
70 (158)	0.29
75 (167)	0.25
80 (176)	0.22

M30 INTAKE AIR TEMPERATURE SENSOR RESISTANCE

Temperature °C (°F)	Resistance kΩ
-15 (5)	12.73
-10 (14)	9.92
-5 (23)	7.80
0 (32)	6.19
5 (41)	4.95
10 (50)	3.99
15 (59)	3.24
20 (68)	2.65
25 (77)	2.19
30 (86)	1.81
35 (95)	1.51

Q45 INTAKE AIR TEMPERATURE SENSOR RESISTANCE

Temperature °C (°F)	Resistance kΩ
-15 (5)	12.73
-10 (14)	9.92
-5 (23)	7.80
0 (32)	6.19
5 (41)	4.95
10 (50)	3.99
15 (59)	3.24
20 (68)	2.65
25 (77)	2.19
30 (86)	1.81
35 (95)	1.51

TESTING

1. Disconnect the sensor and connect an ohmmeter set on the 10,000 ohm scale.
2. Measure the resistance and the temperature, using a thermometer.
3. If the reading is greatly different from the specification, remove the sensor and test it at other temperatures before deciding to replace it. Use a cold drink container or a drop light to change the temperature but do not immerse the sensor.
4. If the sensor appears to work correctly, check the voltage supply to the sensor. With the ignition switch **ON**, there should be 5 volts between one of the terminals and ground.

5. If there is no voltage, check for continuity of the wires between the sensor and the auto amplifier and for power output from the amplifier. If there is not 5 volts at the amplifier itself, chances are that other sensors are also not working.

Sun Load Sensor

OPERATION

The sensor is a photo diode which converts light to a current that is fed to the auto amplifier. There the current is processed for use by the control amplifier. The sun load sensor is mounted in the defroster outlet vent, held by plastic spring clips on the sensor body. On M30, the connector is accessed at the defroster grille. On Q45, the connector is behind the glove compartment, above the evaporator housing.

TESTING

1. To test the sensor, remove the air conditioner controls and locate terminals 16 and 35 on the connector on the right side.
2. With all connectors plugged in and the ignition **ON**, measure the voltage between terminals 16 and 35.
3. Changing the light that strikes the sun load sensor should change the voltage and the current it puts out. A drop light may be enough to make a change in sensor output.
4. If the sensor appears to work correctly, check the voltage supply to the sensor. With the control amplifier connected and the ignition switch **ON**, there should be 5 volts between one of the terminals at the sensor end of the wire and ground.
5. If there is no voltage, check for continuity of the wires between the sensor and auto amplifier, and for power output at the amplifier itself. If there is not 5 volts at the amplifier itself, chances are that other sensors are also not working.

SUN LOAD SENSOR CURRENT AND VOLTAGE

Input current mA	Output voltage V
0	5.0
0.1	4.1
0.2	3.1
0.3	2.2
0.4	1.3
0.5	0.4

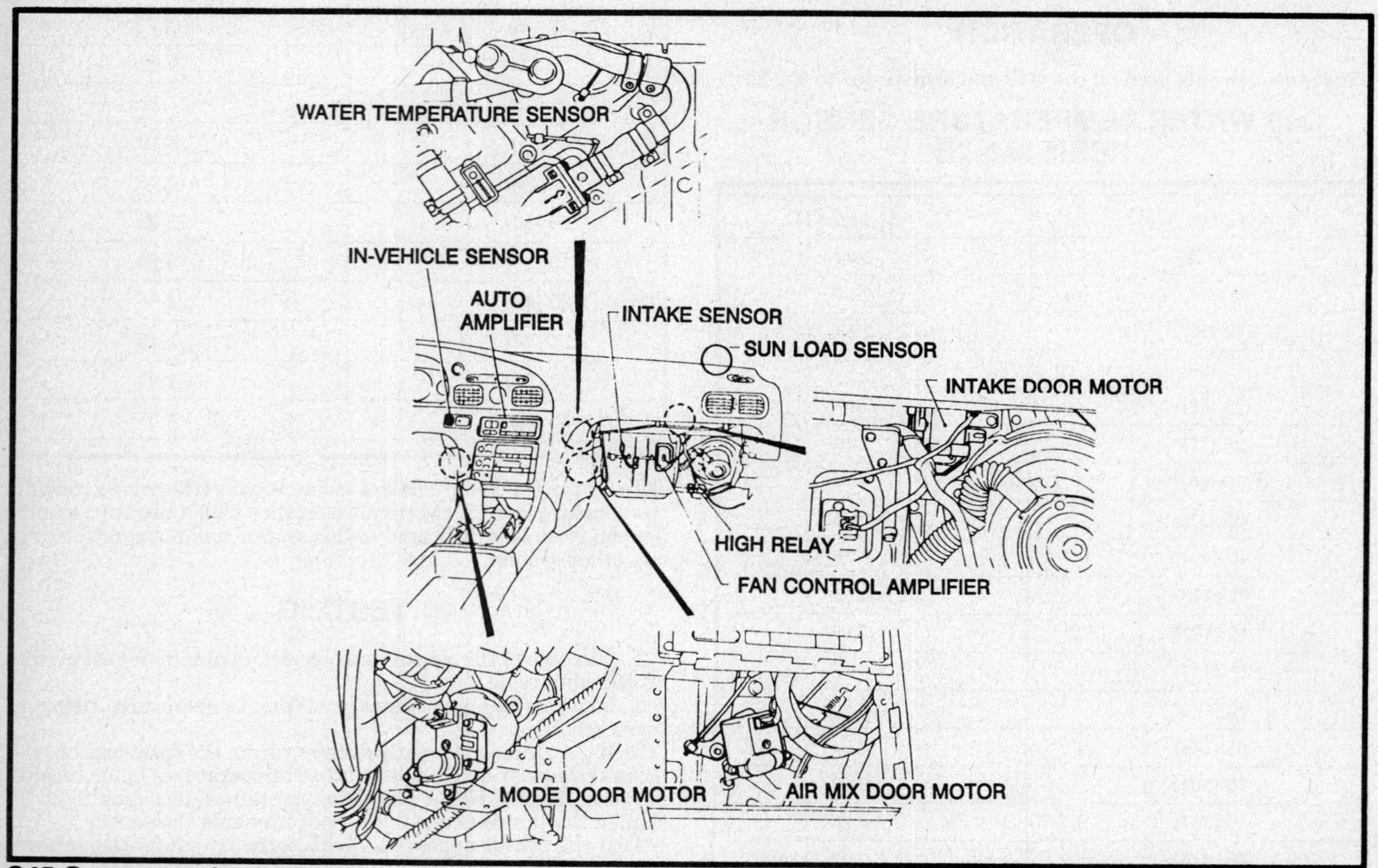
WATER TEMPERATURE SENSOR
IN-VEHICLE SENSOR
AUTO AMPLIFIER
INTAKE SENSOR
SUN LOAD SENSOR
INTAKE DOOR MOTOR
HIGH RELAY
FAN CONTROL AMPLIFIER
MODE DOOR MOTOR
AIR MIX DOOR MOTOR

Q45 Component lcations

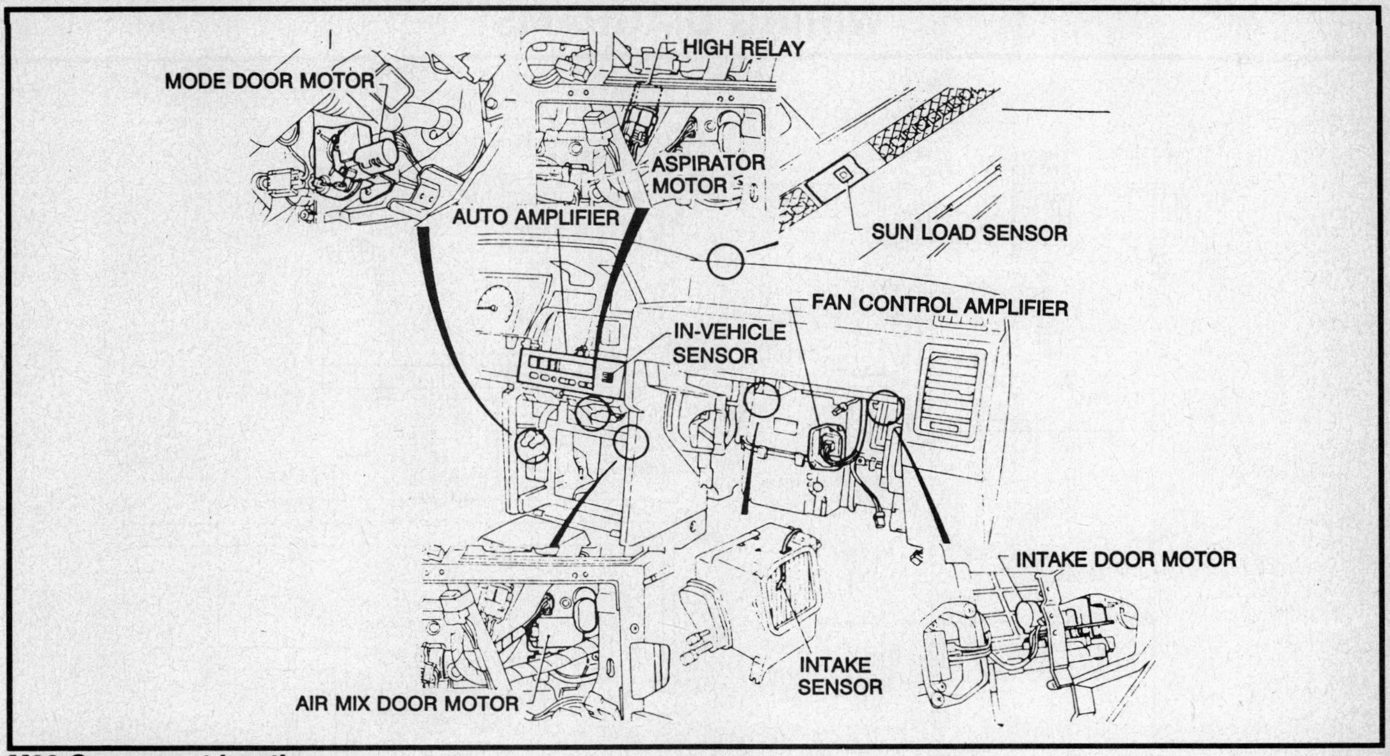
HIGH RELAY
MODE DOOR MOTOR
ASPIRATOR
MOTOR
AUTO AMPLIFIER
SUN LOAD SENSOR
FAN CONTROL AMPLIFIER
IN-VEHICLE
SENSOR
INTAKE DOOR MOTOR
INTAKE
SENSOR
AIR MIX DOOR MOTOR

M30 Component locations

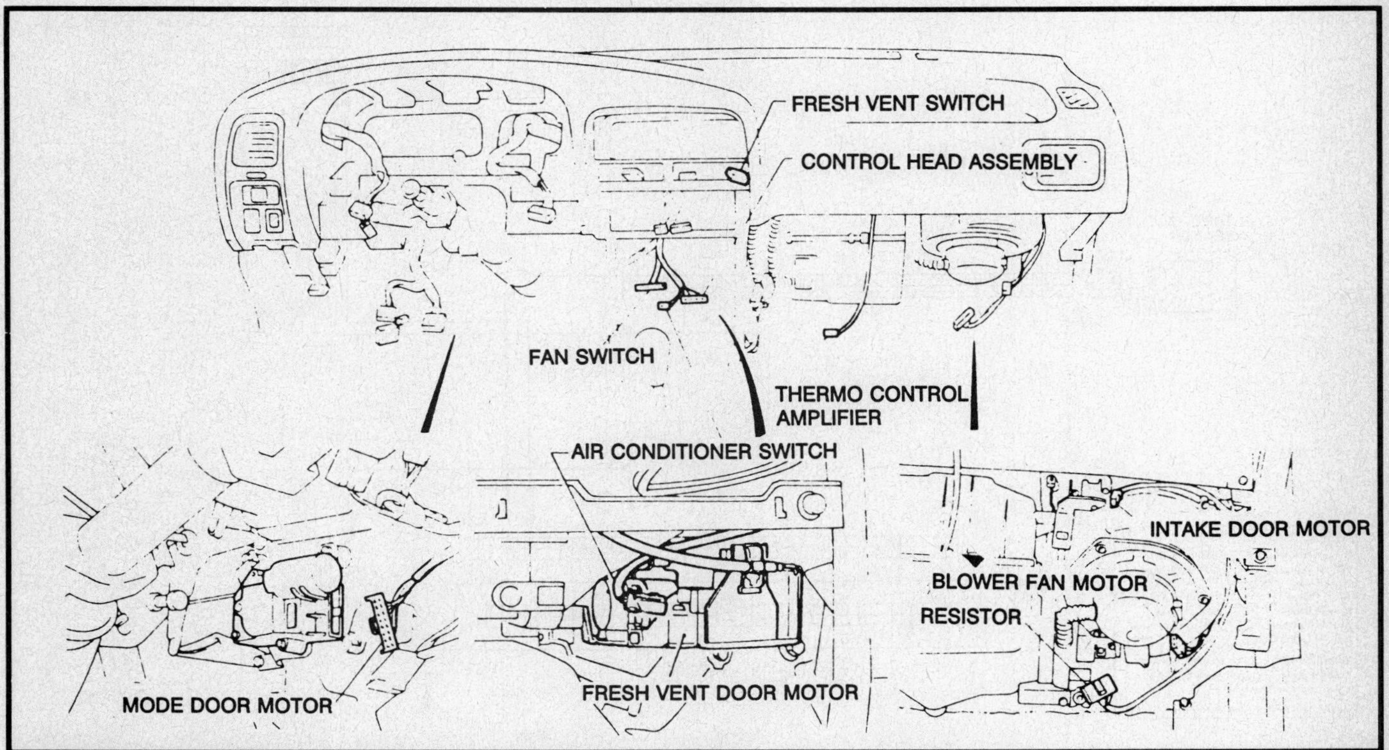
FRESH VENT SWITCH
CONTROL HEAD ASSEMBLY
FAN SWITCH
THERMO CONTROL
AMPLIFIER
AIR CONDITIONER SWITCH
INTAKE DOOR MOTOR
BLOWER FAN MOTOR
RESISTOR
MODE DOOR MOTOR
FRESH VENT DOOR MOTOR

G20 Component locations

WIRING DIAGRAMS

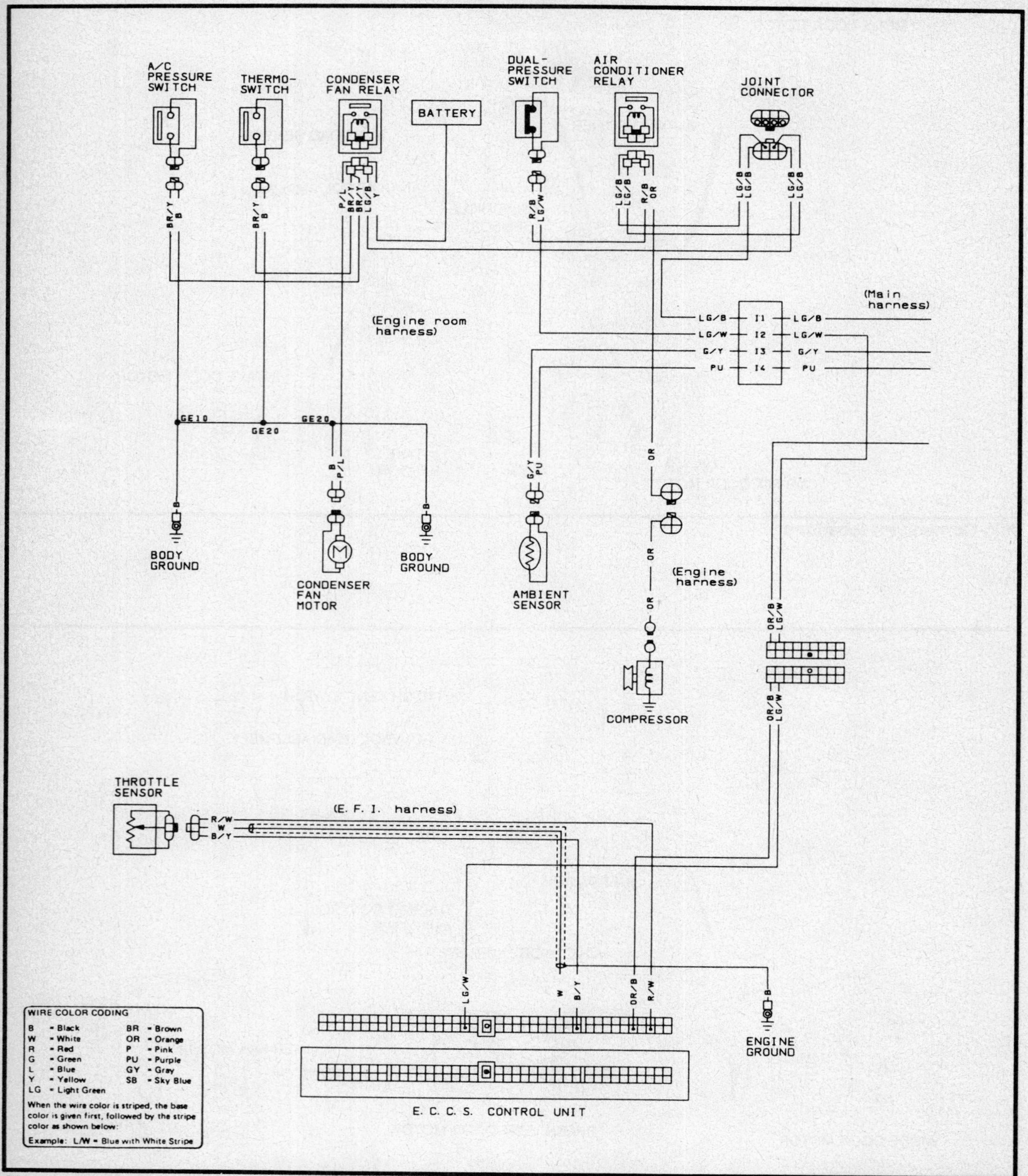
A/C PRESSURE SWITCH
THERMO-SWITCH
CONDENSER FAN RELAY
BATTERY
DUAL-PRESSURE SWITCH
AIR CONDITIONER RELAY
JOINT CONNECTOR
(Engine room harness)
(Main harness)
LG/B I1 LG/B
LG/W I2 LG/W
G/Y I3 G/Y
PU I4 PU
GE10
GE20
BODY GROUND
CONDENSER FAN MOTOR
BODY GROUND
AMBIENT SENSOR
(Engine harness)
COMPRESSOR
THROTTLE SENSOR
(E. F. I. harness)
ENGINE GROUND
E. C. C. S. CONTROL UNIT
WIRE COLOR CODING
B = Black
W = White
R = Red
G = Green
L = Blue
Y = Yellow
LG = Light Green
BR = Brown
OR = Orange
P = Pink
PU = Purple
GY = Gray
SB = Sky Blue
When the wire color is striped, the base color is given first, followed by the stripe color as shown below:
Example: L/W = Blue with White Stripe

Air conditioning electrical schematic—Q45

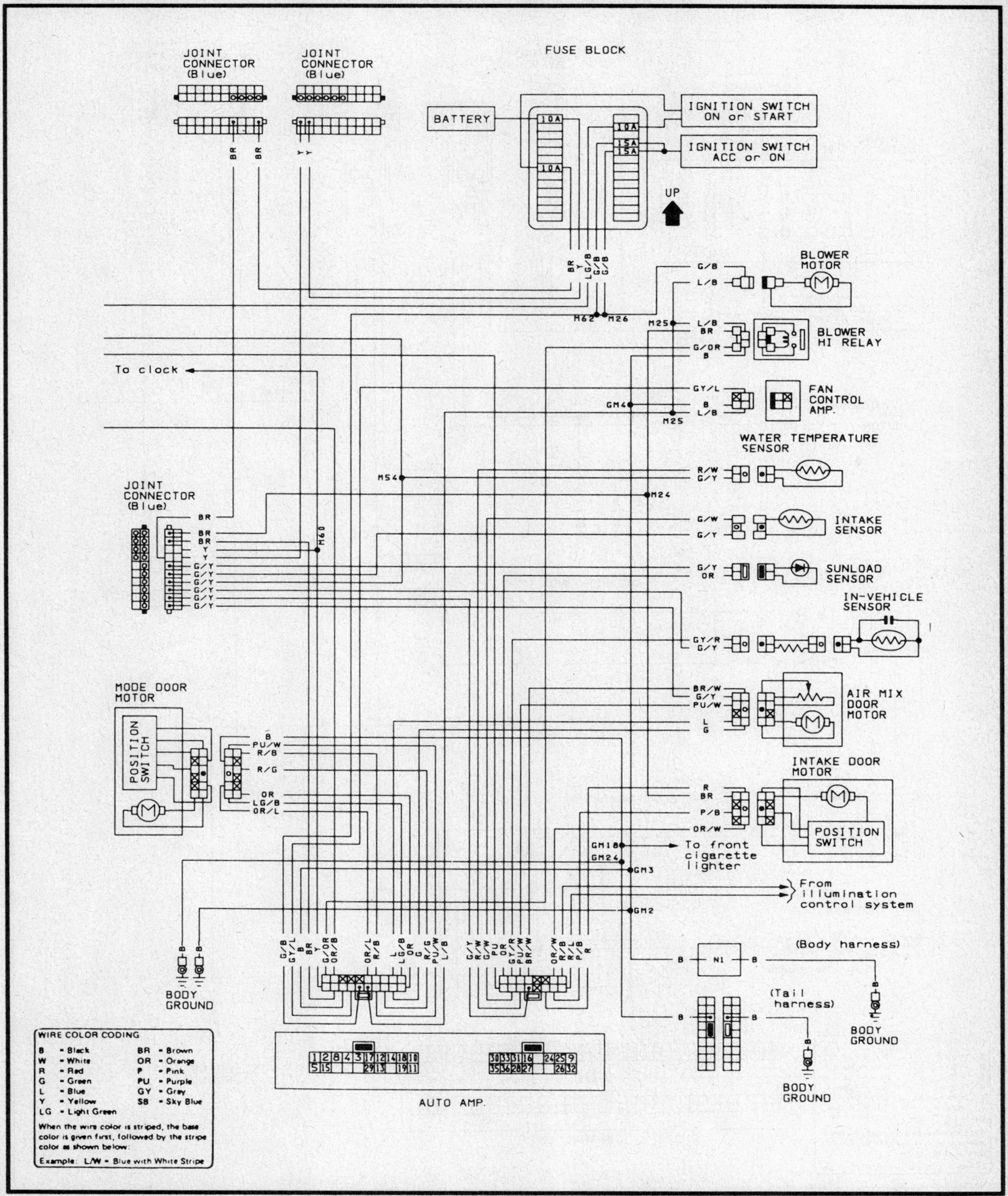
JOINT CONNECTOR (Blue)
JOINT CONNECTOR (Blue)
FUSE BLOCK
BATTERY
10A
10A
10A
15A
15A
IGNITION SWITCH ON or START
IGNITION SWITCH ACC or ON
UP
BLOWER MOTOR
BLOWER HI RELAY
FAN CONTROL AMP.
To clock
WATER TEMPERATURE SENSOR
JOINT CONNECTOR (Blue)
INTAKE SENSOR
SUNLOAD SENSOR
IN-VEHICLE SENSOR
MODE DOOR MOTOR
POSITION SWITCH
AIR MIX DOOR MOTOR
INTAKE DOOR MOTOR
POSITION SWITCH
To front cigarette lighter
From illumination control system
(Body harness)
(Tail harness)
BODY GROUND
BODY GROUND
BODY GROUND
AUTO AMP.
WIRE COLOR CODING
B = Black
W = White
R = Red
G = Green
L = Blue
Y = Yellow
LG = Light Green
BR = Brown
OR = Orange
P = Pink
PU = Purple
GY = Gray
SB = Sky Blue
When the wire color is striped, the base color is given first, followed by the stripe color as shown below:
Example: L/W = Blue with White Stripe

Air conditioning electrical schematic—Q45 cont.

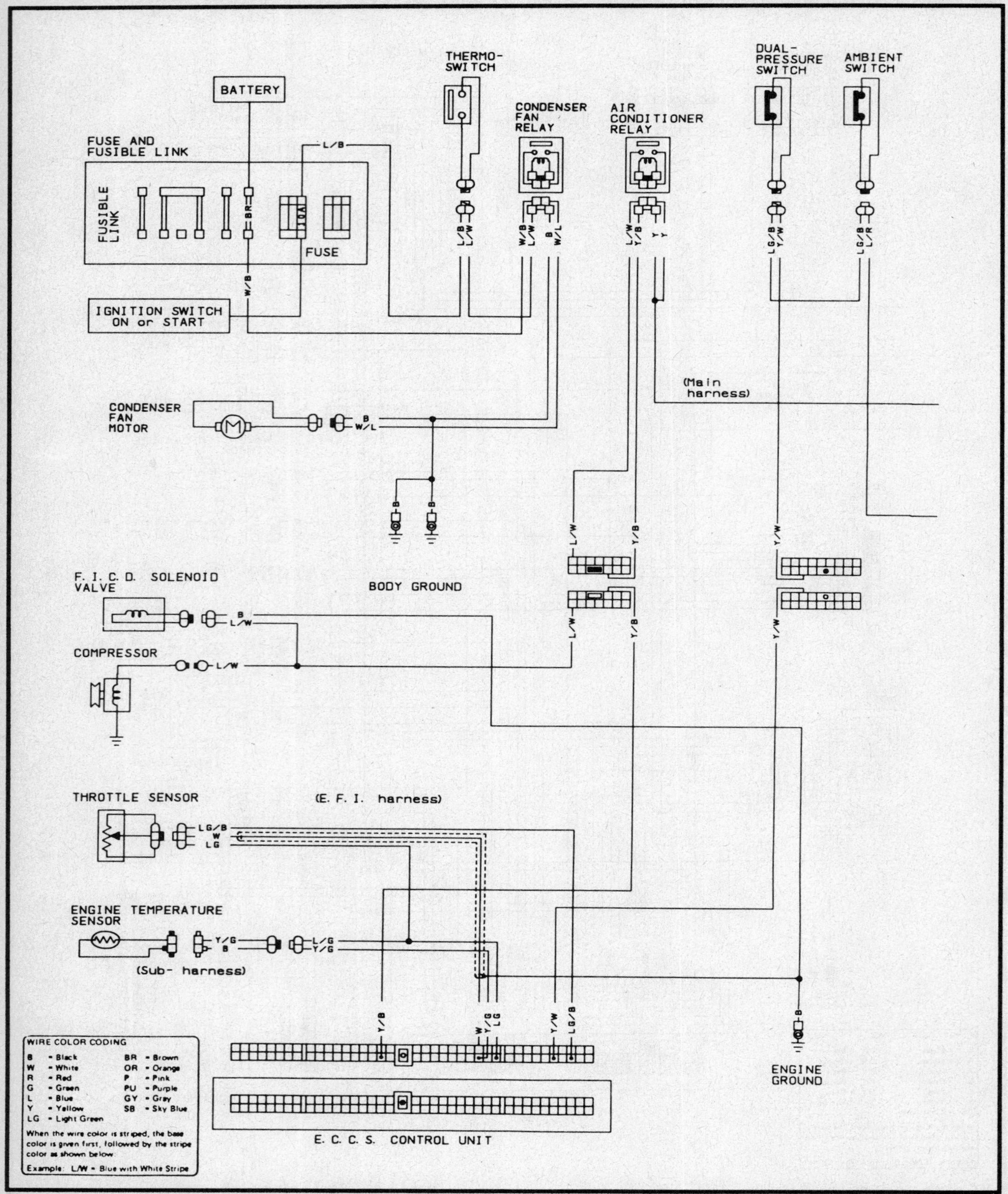
THERMO-SWITCH
DUAL-PRESSURE SWITCH
AMBIENT SWITCH
BATTERY
CONDENSER FAN RELAY
AIR CONDITIONER RELAY
FUSE AND FUSIBLE LINK
FUSIBLE LINK
10A
FUSE
IGNITION SWITCH ON or START
(Main harness)
CONDENSER FAN MOTOR
BODY GROUND
F. I. C. D. SOLENOID VALVE
COMPRESSOR
THROTTLE SENSOR
(E. F. I. harness)
ENGINE TEMPERATURE SENSOR
(Sub- harness)
ENGINE GROUND
E. C. C. S. CONTROL UNIT
WIRE COLOR CODING
B = Black
W = White
R = Red
G = Green
L = Blue
Y = Yellow
LG = Light Green
BR = Brown
OR = Orange
P = Pink
PU = Purple
GY = Gray
SB = Sky Blue
When the wire color is striped, the base color is given first, followed by the stripe color as shown below:
Example: L/W = Blue with White Stripe

Manual air conditioning electrical schematic – M30

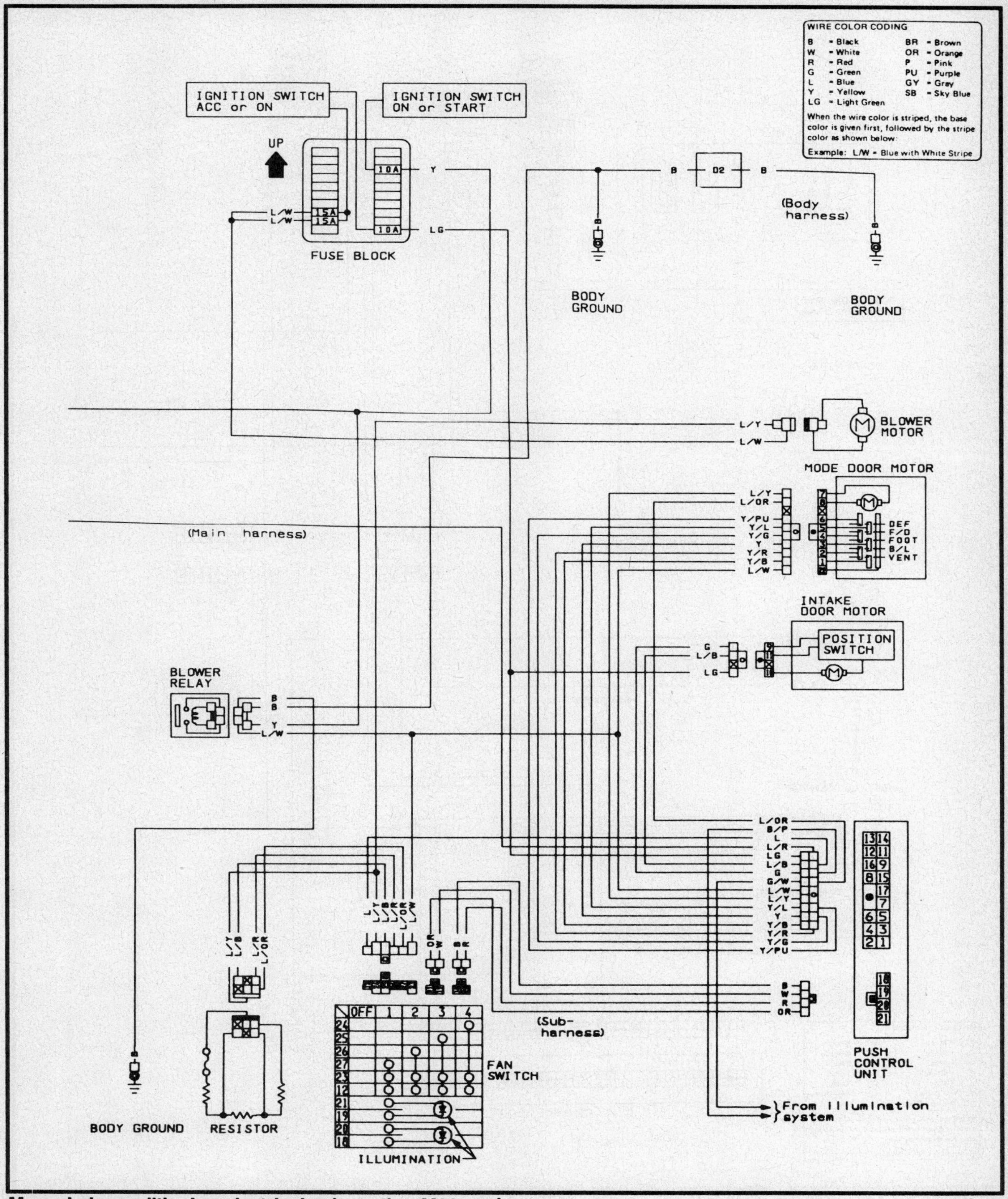
WIRE COLOR CODING
B = Black
W = White
R = Red
G = Green
L = Blue
Y = Yellow
LG = Light Green
BR = Brown
OR = Orange
P = Pink
PU = Purple
GY = Gray
SB = Sky Blue
When the wire color is striped, the base color is given first, followed by the stripe color as shown below:
Example: L/W = Blue with White Stripe
IGNITION SWITCH ACC or ON
IGNITION SWITCH ON or START
UP
10A
15A
15A
10A
FUSE BLOCK
D2
(Body harness)
BODY GROUND
BODY GROUND
BLOWER MOTOR
MODE DOOR MOTOR
DEF
F/D
FOOT
B/L
VENT
(Main harness)
INTAKE DOOR MOTOR
POSITION SWITCH
BLOWER RELAY
PUSH CONTROL UNIT
(Sub-harness)
FAN SWITCH
OFF
ILLUMINATION
BODY GROUND
RESISTOR
From illumination system

Manual air conditioning electrical schematic – M30 cont.

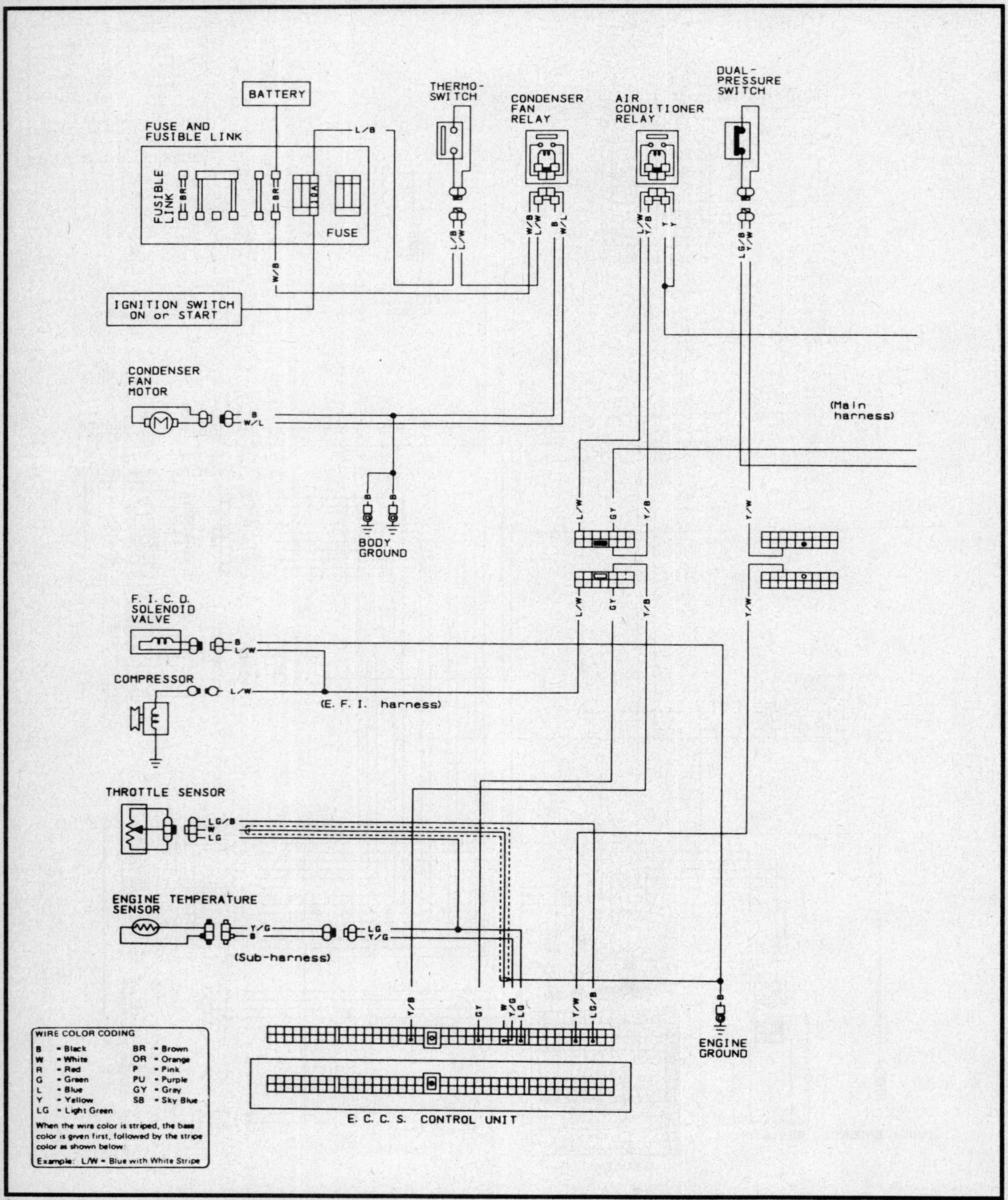
BATTERY
FUSE AND FUSIBLE LINK
FUSIBLE LINK
BR
BR
10A
FUSE
L/B
W/B
IGNITION SWITCH ON or START
THERMO-SWITCH
L/B
L/W
CONDENSER FAN RELAY
W/B
L/W
B
W/L
AIR CONDITIONER RELAY
L/W
Y/B
Y
Y
DUAL-PRESSURE SWITCH
LG/B
Y/W
CONDENSER FAN MOTOR
B
W/L
B
B
BODY GROUND
(Main harness)
L/W
GY
Y/B
Y/W
F. I. C. D. SOLENOID VALVE
B
L/W
COMPRESSOR
L/W
(E. F. I. harness)
THROTTLE SENSOR
LG/B
W
LG
G
ENGINE TEMPERATURE SENSOR
Y/G
B
LG
Y/G
(Sub-harness)
Y/B
GY
W
Y/G
LG
Y/W
LG/B
B
ENGINE GROUND
E. C. C. S. CONTROL UNIT
WIRE COLOR CODING
B = Black
W = White
R = Red
G = Green
L = Blue
Y = Yellow
LG = Light Green
BR = Brown
OR = Orange
P = Pink
PU = Purple
GY = Gray
SB = Sky Blue
When the wire color is striped, the base color is given first, followed by the stripe color as shown below:
Example: L/W = Blue with White Stripe

Automatic air conditioning electrical schematic—M30

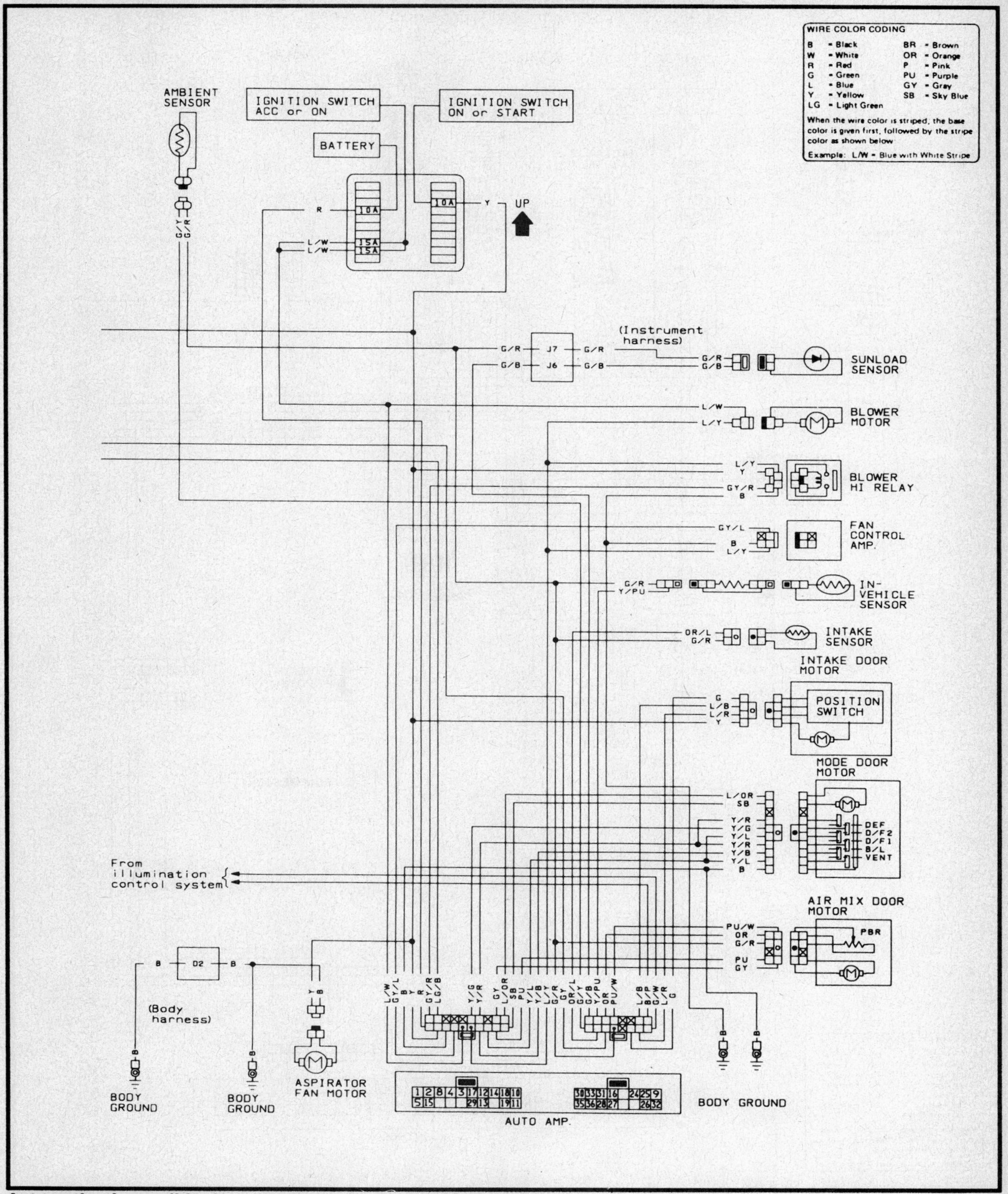
WIRE COLOR CODING
B = Black
W = White
R = Red
G = Green
L = Blue
Y = Yellow
LG = Light Green
BR = Brown
OR = Orange
P = Pink
PU = Purple
GY = Gray
SB = Sky Blue
When the wire color is striped, the base color is given first, followed by the stripe color as shown below:
Example: L/W = Blue with White Stripe
AMBIENT SENSOR
IGNITION SWITCH ACC or ON
IGNITION SWITCH ON or START
BATTERY
10A
15A
UP
(Instrument harness)
J7
J6
SUNLOAD SENSOR
BLOWER MOTOR
BLOWER HI RELAY
FAN CONTROL AMP.
IN-VEHICLE SENSOR
INTAKE SENSOR
INTAKE DOOR MOTOR
POSITION SWITCH
MODE DOOR MOTOR
DEF
D/F2
D/F1
B/L
VENT
AIR MIX DOOR MOTOR
PBR
From illumination control system
D2
(Body harness)
BODY GROUND
BODY GROUND
ASPIRATOR FAN MOTOR
AUTO AMP.
BODY GROUND

Automatic air conditioning electrical schematic—M30 cont.

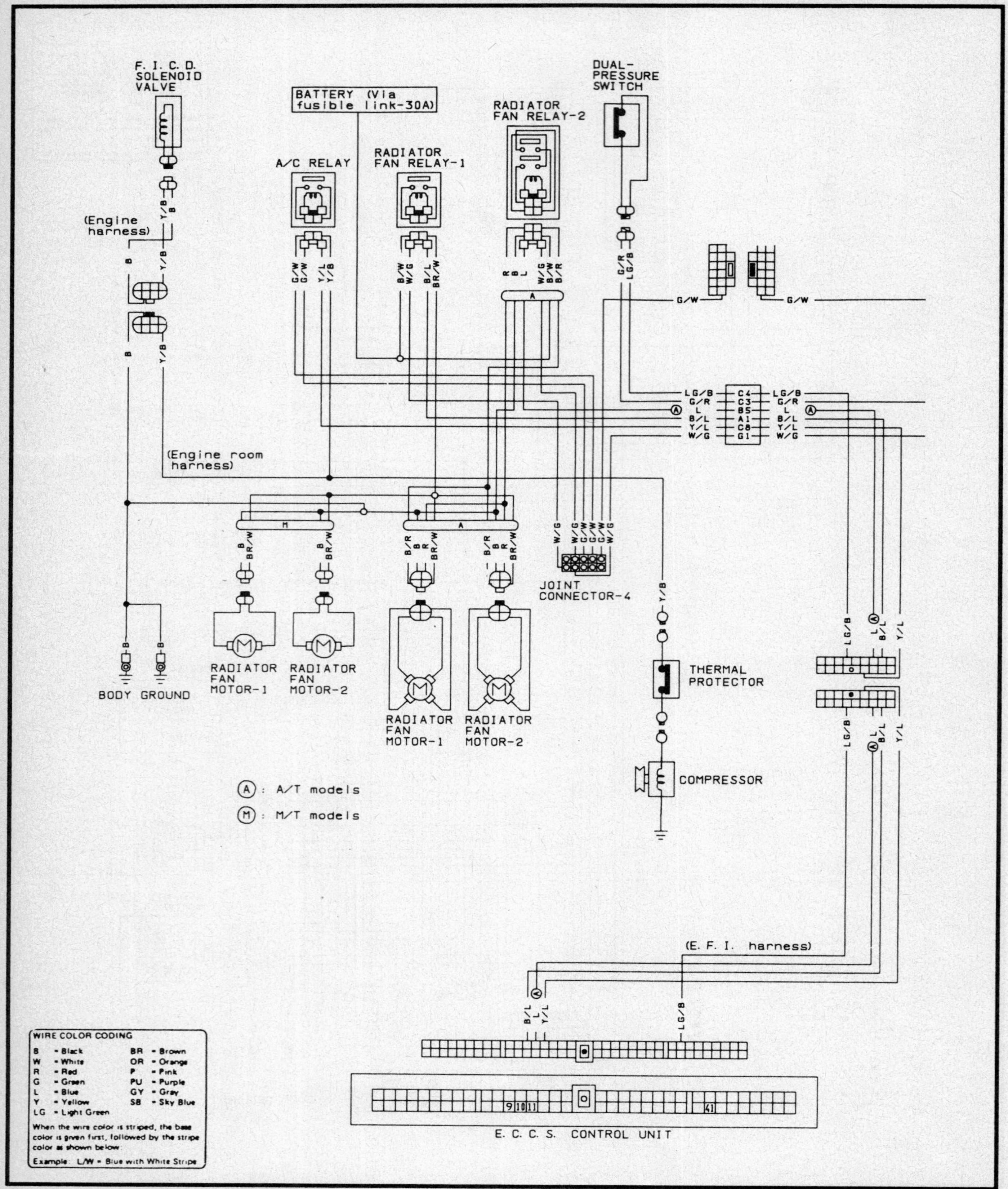
F. I. C. D. SOLENOID VALVE
BATTERY (Via fusible link-30A)
A/C RELAY
RADIATOR FAN RELAY-1
RADIATOR FAN RELAY-2
DUAL-PRESSURE SWITCH
(Engine harness)
(Engine room harness)
JOINT CONNECTOR-4
BODY GROUND
RADIATOR FAN MOTOR-1
RADIATOR FAN MOTOR-2
THERMAL PROTECTOR
COMPRESSOR
Ⓐ : A/T models
Ⓜ : M/T models
(E. F. I. harness)
E. C. C. S. CONTROL UNIT
WIRE COLOR CODING
B = Black
W = White
R = Red
G = Green
L = Blue
Y = Yellow
LG = Light Green
BR = Brown
OR = Orange
P = Pink
PU = Purple
GY = Gray
SB = Sky Blue
When the wire color is striped, the base color is given first, followed by the stripe color as shown below:
Example: L/W = Blue with White Stripe

Air conditioning electrical schematic—G20

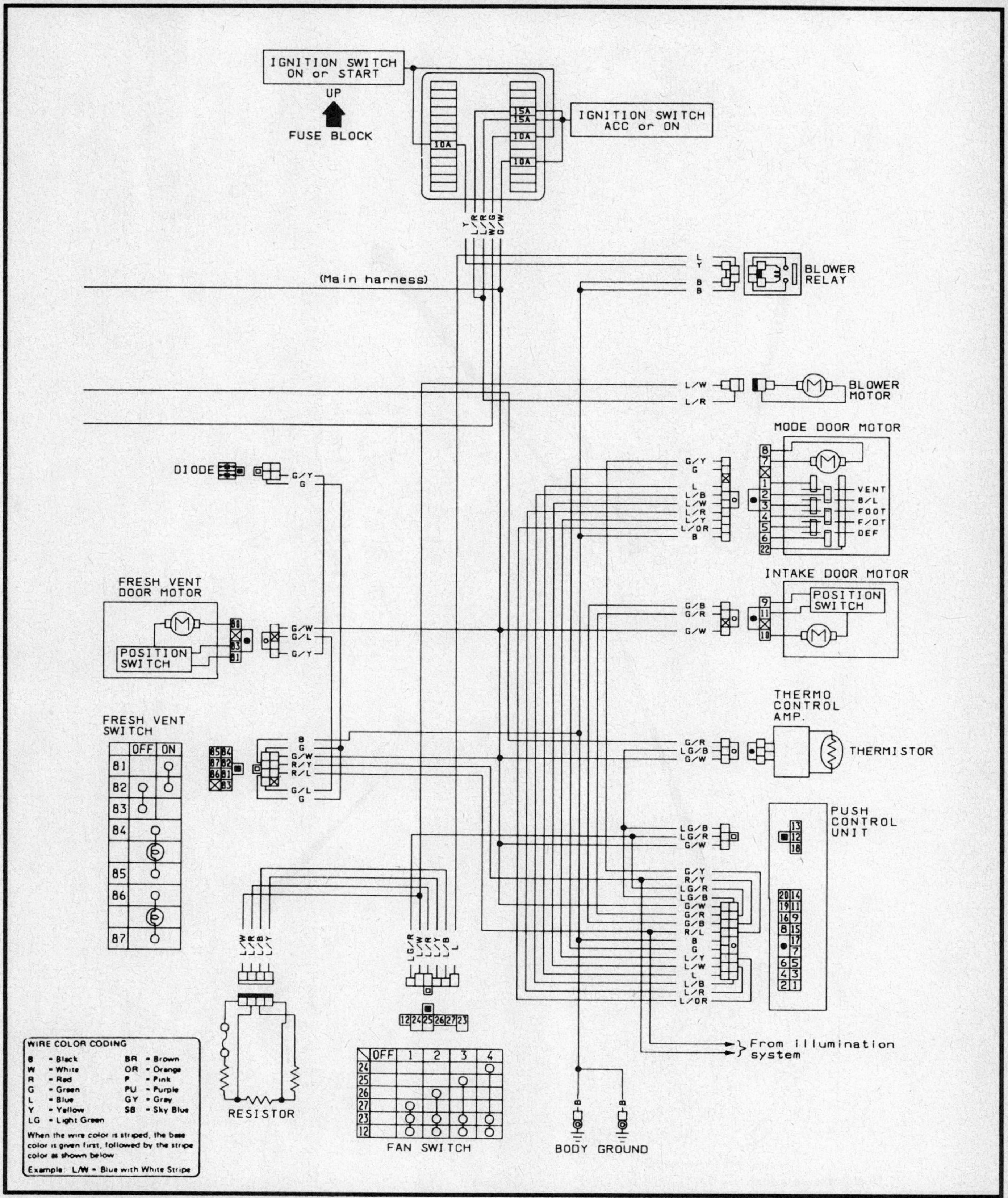
IGNITION SWITCH ON or START
UP
FUSE BLOCK
IGNITION SWITCH ACC or ON
10A
15A
15A
10A
10A
(Main harness)
BLOWER RELAY
BLOWER MOTOR
MODE DOOR MOTOR
VENT
B/L
FOOT
F/DT
DEF
DIODE
FRESH VENT DOOR MOTOR
POSITION SWITCH
INTAKE DOOR MOTOR
POSITION SWITCH
FRESH VENT SWITCH
OFF
ON
THERMO CONTROL AMP.
THERMISTOR
PUSH CONTROL UNIT
From illumination system
RESISTOR
FAN SWITCH
BODY GROUND
WIRE COLOR CODING
B - Black
W - White
R - Red
G - Green
L - Blue
Y - Yellow
LG - Light Green
BR - Brown
OR - Orange
P - Pink
PU - Purple
GY - Gray
SB - Sky Blue
When the wire color is striped, the base color is given first, followed by the stripe color as shown below
Example: L/W = Blue with White Stripe

Air conditioning electrical schematic – G20 cont.

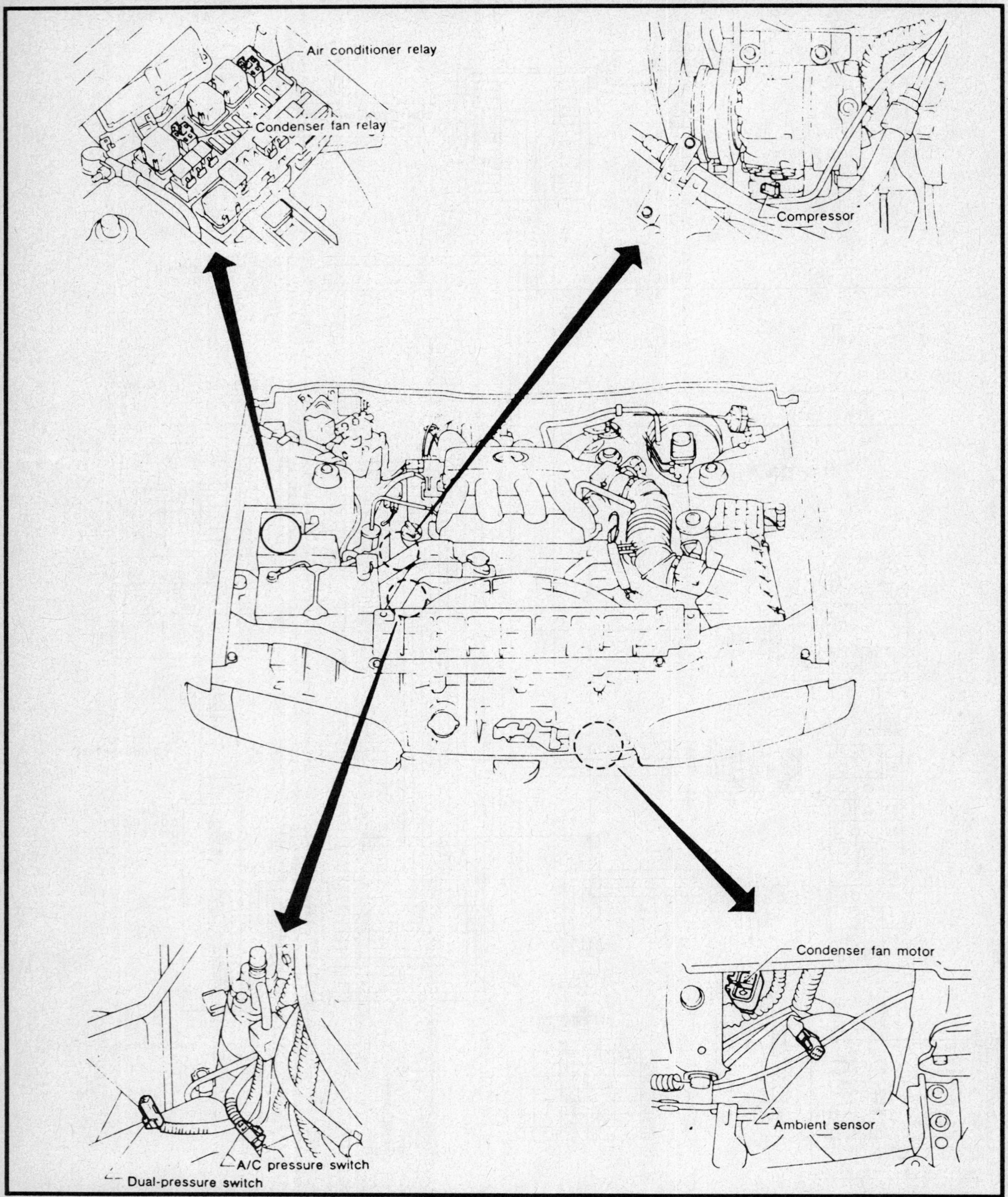
Air conditioner relay
Condenser fan relay
Compressor
Condenser fan motor
Ambient sensor
A/C pressure switch
Dual-pressure switch

Major air conditioning component locations–Q45

19 ISUZU 19

I-MARK • IMPULSE • STYLUS

SPECIFICATIONS

ENGINE IDENTIFICATION

Year	Model	Engine Displacement cu. in. (cc/liter)	Engine Series Identification	No. of Cylinders	Engine Type
1989	I-Mark	90 (1471/1.5)	4XC1-U	4	OHC
	I-Mark (Turbo)	90 (1471/1.5)	4XC-T	4	Turbo OHC
	I-Mark (DOHC)	92 (1588/1.6)	4XE1	4	DOHC
	Impulse (Turbo)	121.7 (1994/2.0)	4ZC1-T	4	Turbo OHC
	Impulse	138 (2254/2.3)	4ZD1	4	OHC
1990	Impulse	92 (1588/1.6)	4XE1	4	DOHC
1991	Impulse	92 (1588/1.6)	4XE1	4	DOHC
	Stylus	92 (1588/1.6)	4XE1	4	DOHC

REFRIGERANT CAPACITIES

Year	Model	Freon (oz.)	Oil (fl. oz.)	Type
1989	I-Mark	28.3	3.35	R-12
	Impulse	35.2	3.35	R-12
1990	Impulse	27.2	6.70	R-12
1991	Impulse	26.6	6.76	R-12
	Stylus	26.6	6.76	R-12

AIR CONDITIONING BELT TENSION CHART

Year	Model	Engine Displacement cu. in. (cc/liter)	Belt Type	New	Used
1989	I-Mark ② ④	90 (1471/1.5)	V-Belt	70–110	60–100
	I-Mark ③	92 (1588/1.6)	V-Belt	130–160	120–150
	Impulse	121.7 (1994/2.0)	V-Belt	13/32 ① ⑤	—
	Impulse	138 (2254/2.3)	V-Belt	13/32 ① ⑤	—
1990	Impulse	92 (1588/1.6)	Serpentine	130–160	120–150
1991	Impulse ④	92 (1588/1.6)	Serpentine	130–160	120–150
	Stylus ② ③	92 (1588/1.6)	Serpentine	130–160	120–150

① Inches of deflection at the midpoint of the belt using 22 lbs. of force
② SOHC
③ DOHC
④ Including Turbocharged engine
⑤ Metric measurement 10 mm

SYSTEM DESCRIPTION

General Information

The heater unit is located in the center of the vehicle along the firewall. The heater system is a bi-level system designed to direct warm air through the vents to either the windshield or the floor and cool air through the panel outlet. The air conditioning system is designed to be activated in combination with a separate air conditioning switch installed in the control assembly and the fan speed switch. The system incorporates a compressor, condenser, evaporator, receiver/dryer, pressure switch, expansion valve, thermo switch, refrigerant lines and some models are equipped with a air conditioning cut control unit.

Service Valve Location

Charging valve locations will vary, but most of the time the high or low pressure fitting will be located at the compressor, receiver/drier or along the refrigerant lines. Always discharge, evacuate and recharge at the low side service fitting.

System Discharging

R-12 refrigerant is a chloroflourocarbon which, when mishandled, can contribute to the depletion on the ozone layer in the upper atmosphere. Ozone filters out harmful radiation from the sun. In order to protect the ozone layer, an approved R-12 Recovery/Recycling machine that meets SAE standard J1991 should be employed when discharging the system. Follow the operating instructions provided with the approved equipment exactly to properly discharge the system.

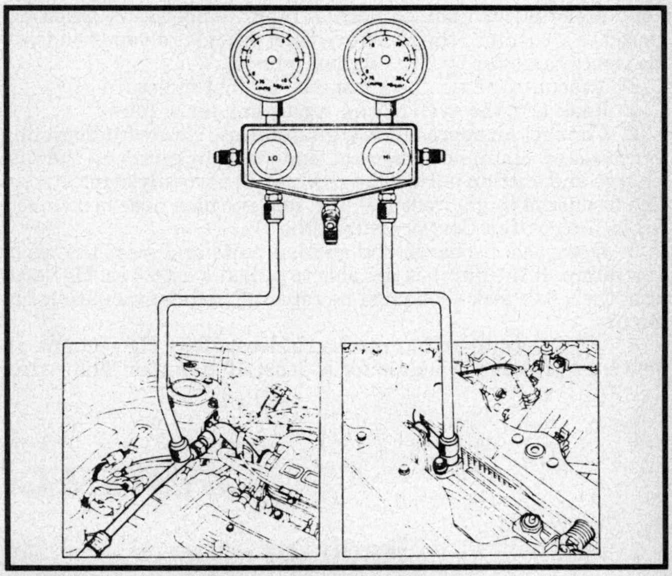
LO
HI
Typical air conditioner gauge hook up

System Evacuating

If the air conditioning system has been opened to the atmosphere, it should be air and moisture free before being recharged

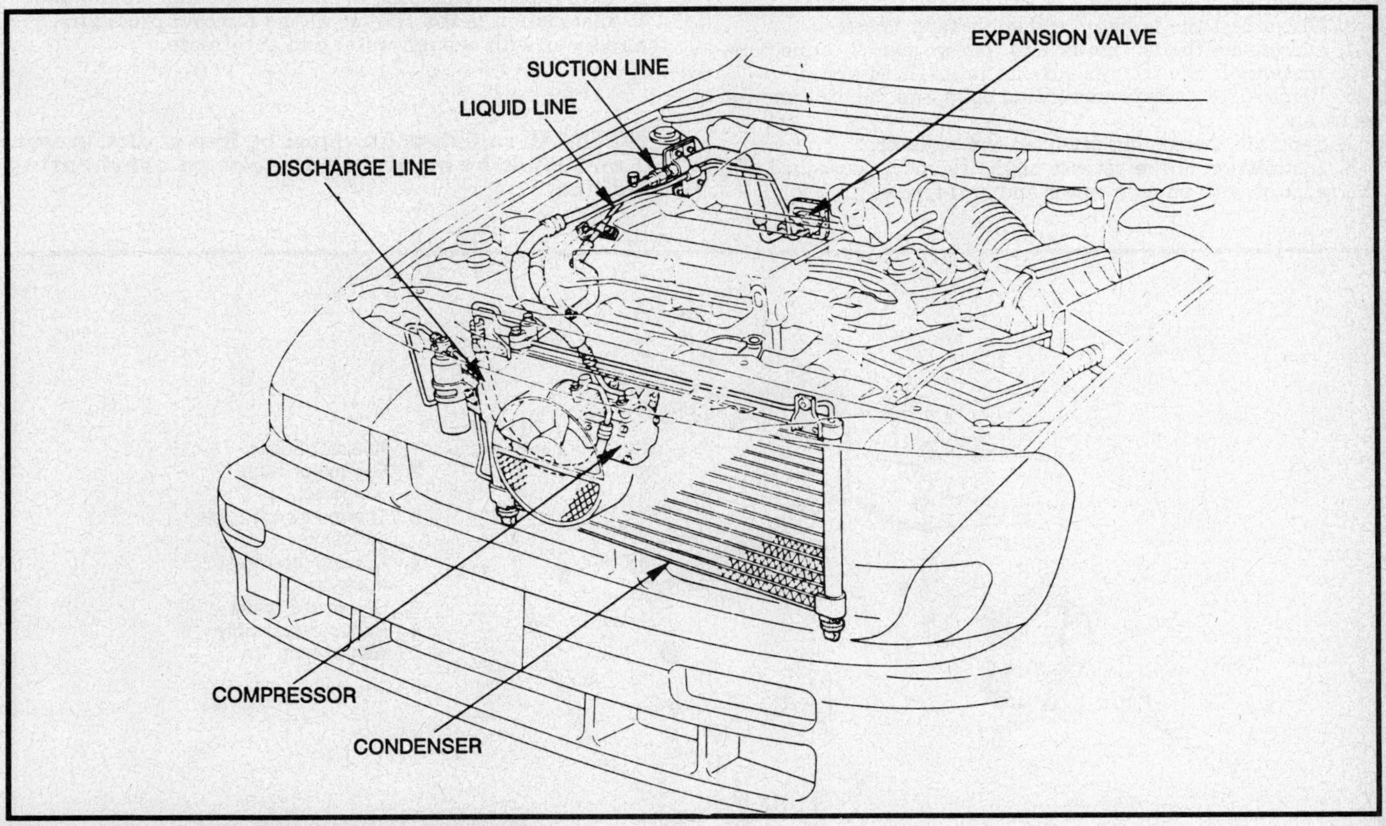
EXPANSION VALVE
SUCTION LINE
LIQUID LINE
DISCHARGE LINE
COMPRESSOR
CONDENSER
Typical air conditioning component locations

with refrigerant. Moisture and air mixed with refrigerant will raise the compressor head pressure, possibly damage the system's components and will reduce the performance of the system. Moisture will boil at normal room temperature when exposed to a vacuum, the moisture then becomes a vapor and will be easily removed by the vacuum pump.

To evacuate, or rid the system of air and moisture:

1. Leak test the system and repair any leaks found.
2. Connect an approved charging station, Recovery/Recycling machine or manifold gauge set and vacuum pump to the discharge and suction ports. The red hose is normally connected to the discharge (high pressure) line, and the blue hose is connected to the suction (low pressure) line.
3. Open the discharge and suction ports and start the vacuum pump. If the pump is not able to pull at least 26 in. Hg vacuum, there is a leak that must be repaired before evacuation can occur.
4. Once the system has reached at least 26 in. Hg vacuum, allow the system to evacuate for at least 10 minutes. The longer the system is evacuated, the more contaminants will be removed.
5. Close all valves and turn the pump off. If the system loses more than 2 in. Hg vacuum after 15 minutes, there is a leak that should be repaired.

System Charging

1. Connect an approved charging station, Recovery/Recycling machine or manifold gauge set to the discharge and suction ports. The red hose is normally connected to the discharge (high pressure) line, and the blue hose is connected to the suction (low pressure) line.
2. Follow the instructions provided with the equipment and charge the system with the specified amount of refrigerant.
3. Perform a leak test.

SYSTEM COMPONENTS

Radiator

REMOVAL AND INSTALLATION

Except 1989 Impulse

1. Disconnect the negative battery cable.
2. Remove the radiator cap and loosen the drain plug to drain the coolant from the system.
3. Disconnect the radiator and surge tank hoses.
4. Disconnect the fan motor and thermo switch connectors.
5. Disconnect the transaxle cooler hoses, if equipped.
6. Remove the radiator mounting bolts, the radiator and fan assembly.
7. Separate the cooling fan from the radiator.
8. Installation is the reverse of the removal procedure. Fill the radiator with enough water and anti-freeze.

1989 Impulse

1. Disconnect the negative battery cable.
2. Remove the radiator cap and loosen the drain plug to drain the coolant from the system.
3. Disconnect the radiator and surge tank hoses from the radiator. Disconnect the turbocharger water hose, if equipped.
4. Remove the fan shroud and the radiator support brackets.
5. Remove the remaining mounting bolts and the radiator.
6. Installation is the reverse of the removal procedure. Fill the radiator with enough water and anti-freeze.

NOTE: All radiators fins must be free of dirt, grease, oil and must be straight to avoid an overheating condition.

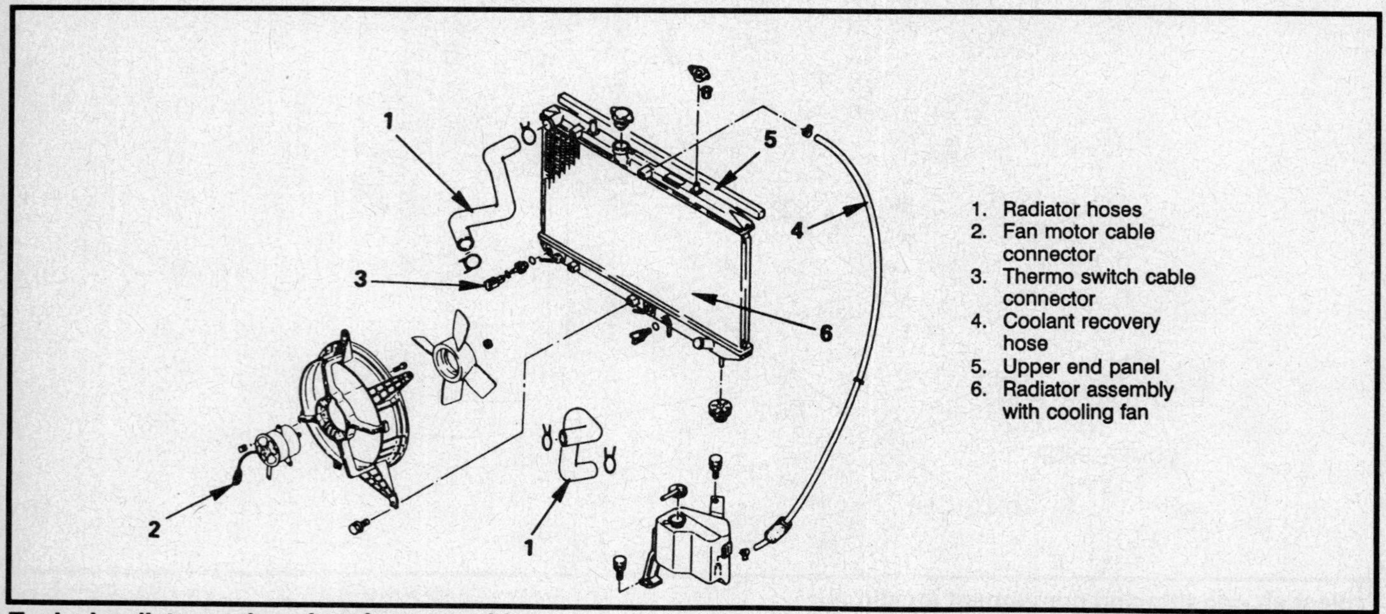
1
2
3
4
5
6
1
1. Radiator hoses
2. Fan motor cable connector
3. Thermo switch cable connector
4. Coolant recovery hose
5. Upper end panel
6. Radiator assembly with cooling fan

Typical radiator and coolant fan assembly

Cooling Fan

TESTING

Except 1989 Impulse

1. Disconnect the negative battery cable.
2. Disconnect the electrical connector at the cooling fan motor.
3. Connect one end of a jumper wire to one of the terminals of the cooling fan motor connector and the other end to the positive terminal of the battery.
4. Connect one end of a jumper wire to the other terminal of the connector and the other end of the wire to the negative battery cable.
5. The cooling fan motor should run smoothly. If not, the cooling fan motor must be replaced.

1989 Impulse

The clutch fan can be checked visually for damage, leaks, or other abnormal conditions, next check the fan by running the engine until the normal operating temperature is reached, then turn OFF the engine and disconnect the negative battery terminal. Using a rag to protect the hand, attempt to turn the the fan. Considerable effort should be required. If the fan turns easily, replace the fan clutch.

REMOVAL AND INSTALLATION

Except 1989 Impulse

1. Disconnect the negative battery cable.
2. Disconnect the electrical connector at the cooling fan motor.
3. Drain the coolant from the radiator and disconnect the upper radiator hose.
4. Remove the cooling fan mounting bolts and the cooling fan.
5. Installation is the reverse of the removal procedure.

1989 Impulse

1. Disconnect the negative battery terminal.
2. Drain cooling system.
3. Remove upper radiator hose.
4. Remove the fan shroud, if required.
5. Remove nuts from fan clutch to water pump.
6. Remove fan clutch.
7. Installation is the reverse of the removal procedure.

Condenser

REMOVAL AND INSTALLATION

1989 I-Mark

1. Disconnect the negative battery cable.
2. Properly discharge the air conditioning system.
3. Remove the radiator grille and attaching bracket.
4. Disconnect the pressure switch wire connector.
5. Disconnect the dual pressure switch wire connector.
6. Disconnect the high pressure hose and pipe.

NOTE: Always use 2 wrenches when removing or installing refrigerant lines.

7. Remove the condenser attaching bolts and the condenser.
8. When reinstalling the condenser all procedures are reverse. Use new O-rings and apply a light coat of oil to them.

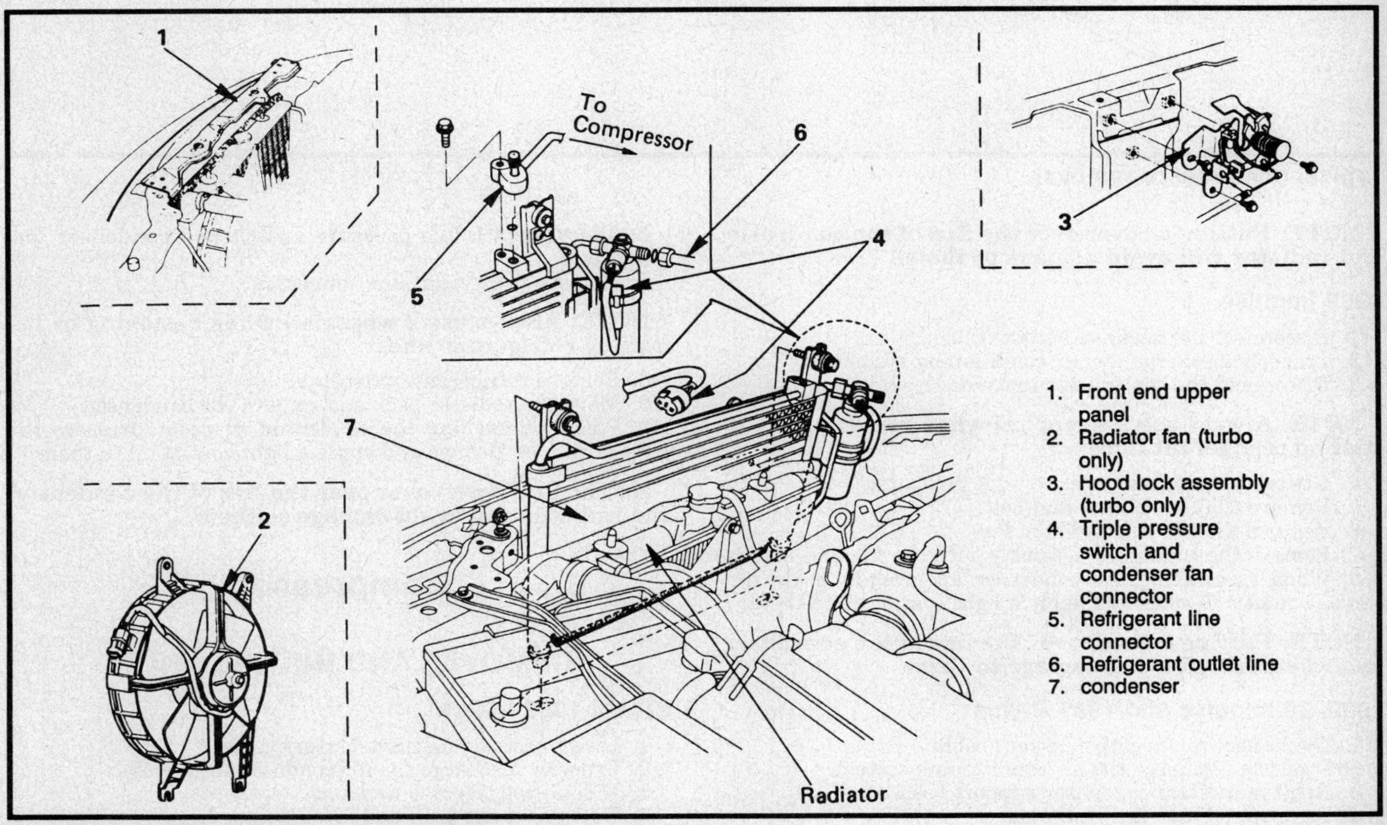
1
To Compressor
6
4
5
3
7
2
Radiator
1. Front end upper panel
2. Radiator fan (turbo only)
3. Hood lock assembly (turbo only)
4. Triple pressure switch and condenser fan connector
5. Refrigerant line connector
6. Refrigerant outlet line
7. condenser

Typical condenser and receiver-drier assembly

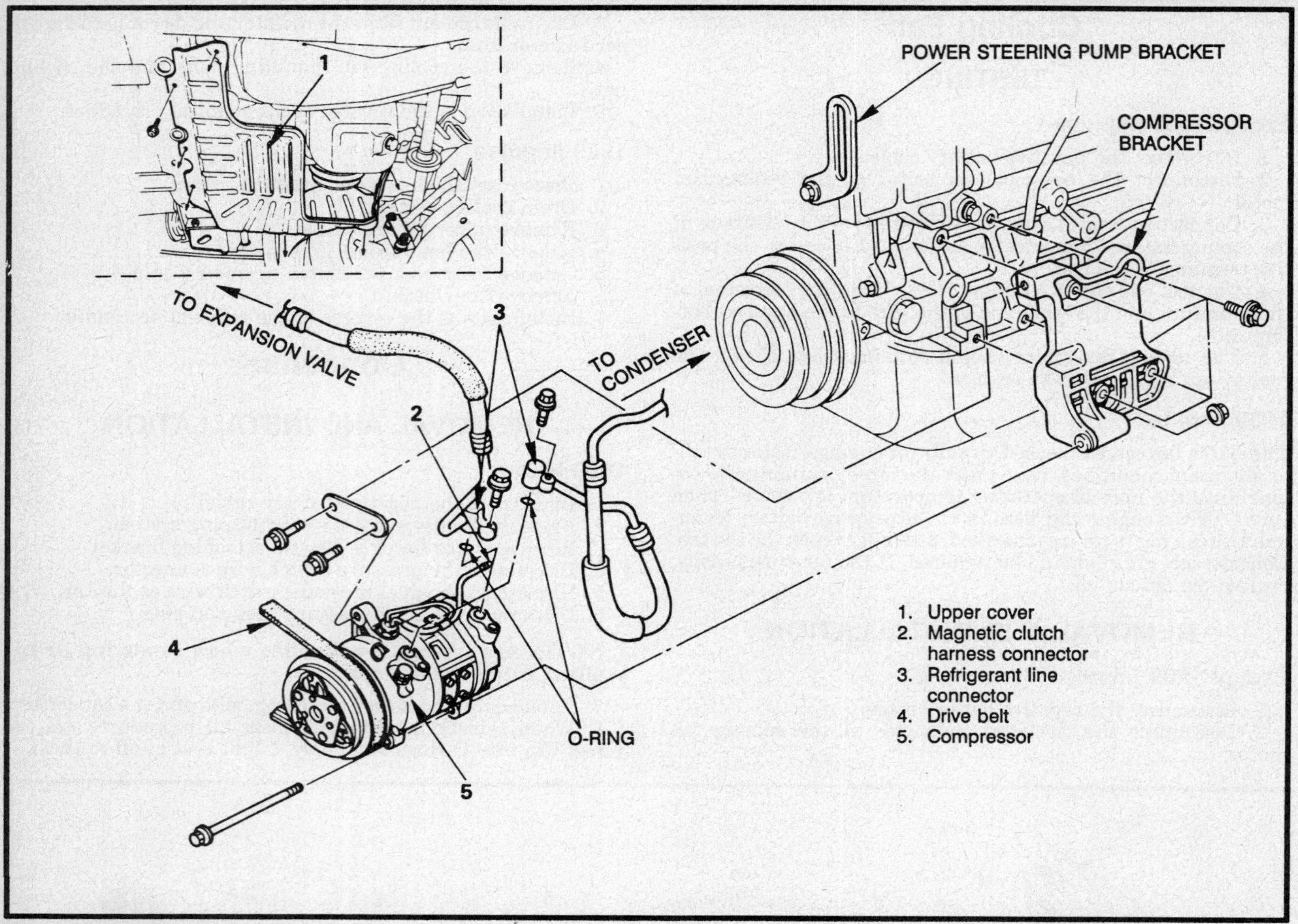
POWER STEERING PUMP BRACKET
COMPRESSOR BRACKET
TO EXPANSION VALVE
TO CONDENSER
O-RING
1
2
3
4
5
1. Upper cover
2. Magnetic clutch harness connector
3. Refrigerant line connector
4. Drive belt
5. Compressor

Typical compressor removal

NOTE: Putting a cover over the fins of the condenser and radiator will avoid damage to them.

1989 Impulse

1. Disconnect the negative battery cable.
2. Properly discharge the air conditioning system.
3. Disconnect the compressor to condenser hose joint.

NOTE: Always use 2 wrenches when removing or installing refrigerant lines.

4. Disconnect the condenser to tank pipe joint.
5. Remove the flange nuts and bolt.
6. Remove the left side radiator stay.
7. Remove the condenser assembly with the fan and motor.
8. When reinstalling the condenser all procedures are reverse. Use new O-rings and apply a light coat of oil to them.

NOTE: Putting a cover over the fins of the condenser and radiator will avoid damage to them.

1990–91 Impulse and 1991 Stylus

1. Disconnect the negative battery cable.
2. Properly discharge the air conditioning system.
3. Remove radiator/condenser support bracket.
4. Remove radiator fan (turbo only).
5. Remove hood lock assembly (turbo only).
6. Disconnect triple pressure switch and condenser fan connectors.
7. Remove refrigerant line connector.

NOTE: Always use 2 wrenches when removing or installing refrigerant lines.

8. Remove refrigerant outlet line.
9. Move the radiator back and remove the condenser.
10. When reinstalling the condenser all procedures are reverse. Use new O-rings and apply a light coat of oil to them.

NOTE: Putting a cover over the fins of the condenser and radiator will avoid damage to them.

Compressor

REMOVAL AND INSTALLATION

Except 1989 I-Mark

1. Disconnect the negative battery cable.
2. Properly discharge the air conditioning system.
3. If equipped, remove undercarriage cover.
4. Disconnect the high and low pressure lines from the back of the compressor.

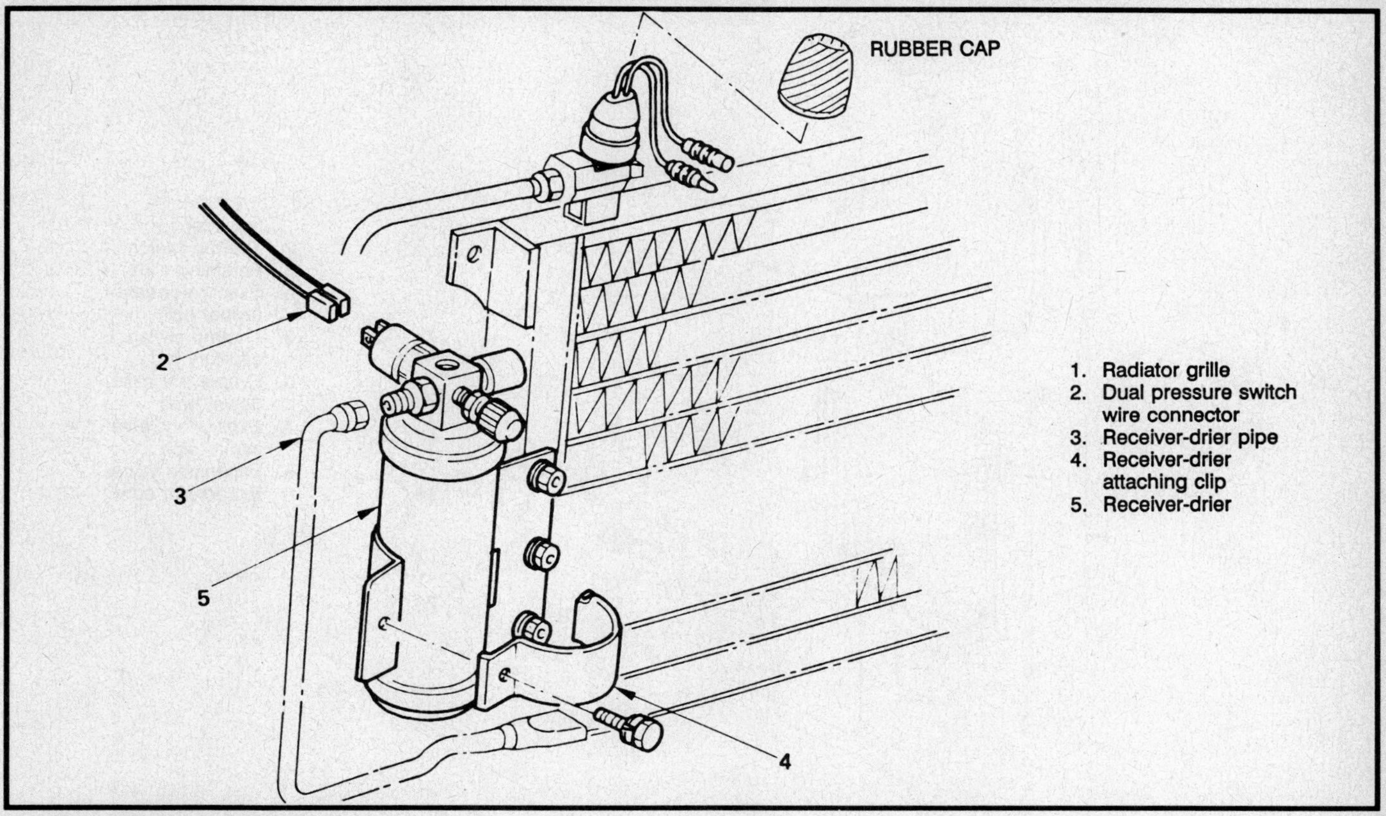
RUBBER CAP
2
3
5
4
1. Radiator grille
2. Dual pressure switch wire connector
3. Receiver-drier pipe
4. Receiver-drier attaching clip
5. Receiver-drier

Typical receiver-drier removal

5. If equipped, remove the power steering drive belt.
6. Remove the compressor mounting bolts and belt.
7. Disconnect the magnetic clutch wire connector.
8. Remove the compressor assembly.
9. Installation is the reverse of removal procedure.
10. Use new O-rings applying a thin coat of oil on them.
11. Tighten the compressor mounting bolts to 40–47 ft. lbs. (54–64 Nm).

1989 I-Mark

1. Disconnect the negative battery cable.
2. Properly discharge the air conditioning system.
3. Disconnect the magnetic clutch wire connector.
4. Remove the compressor drive belt.
5. Remove the compressor attaching bolts and the compressor.
6. Installation is the reverse of removal procedure.
7. Use new O-rings applying a thin coat of oil on them.

Receiver/Drier

REMOVAL AND INSTALLATION

1. Disconnect the negative battery cable.
2. Properly discharge the air conditioning system.
3. If required, remove radiator grille and attaching bracket.
4. If required, remove condenser/radiator support bracket.
5. If equipped, disconnect the condenser pressure switch wire connector.
6. Disconnect the receiver/drier tank lines.
7. Remove the receiver/drier mounting bolt.
8. Remove the receiver/drier tank.
9. Installation is the reverse of removal procedure.

Expansion Valve

REMOVAL AND INSTALLATION

1989 I-Mark

1. Disconnect the negative battery cable.
2. Properly discharge the air conditioning system.
3. Disconnect the high and low pressure evaporator lines in the engine compartment.
4. Remove the glove box.
5. Disconnect the thermo switch connecter.
6. Remove the defroster hose.
7. Remove the nuts, bolts and washers from the evaporator housing.
8. Remove the evaporator assembly.
9. Disassemble the evaporator case to remove the expansion valve.
10. Installation is the reverse of removal procedure.

1989 Impulse

1. Disconnect the negative battery cable.
2. Properly discharge the air conditioning system.
3. Drain engine coolant and remove heater core hoses.
4. Disconnect the high and low pressure evaporator lines in the engine compartment.

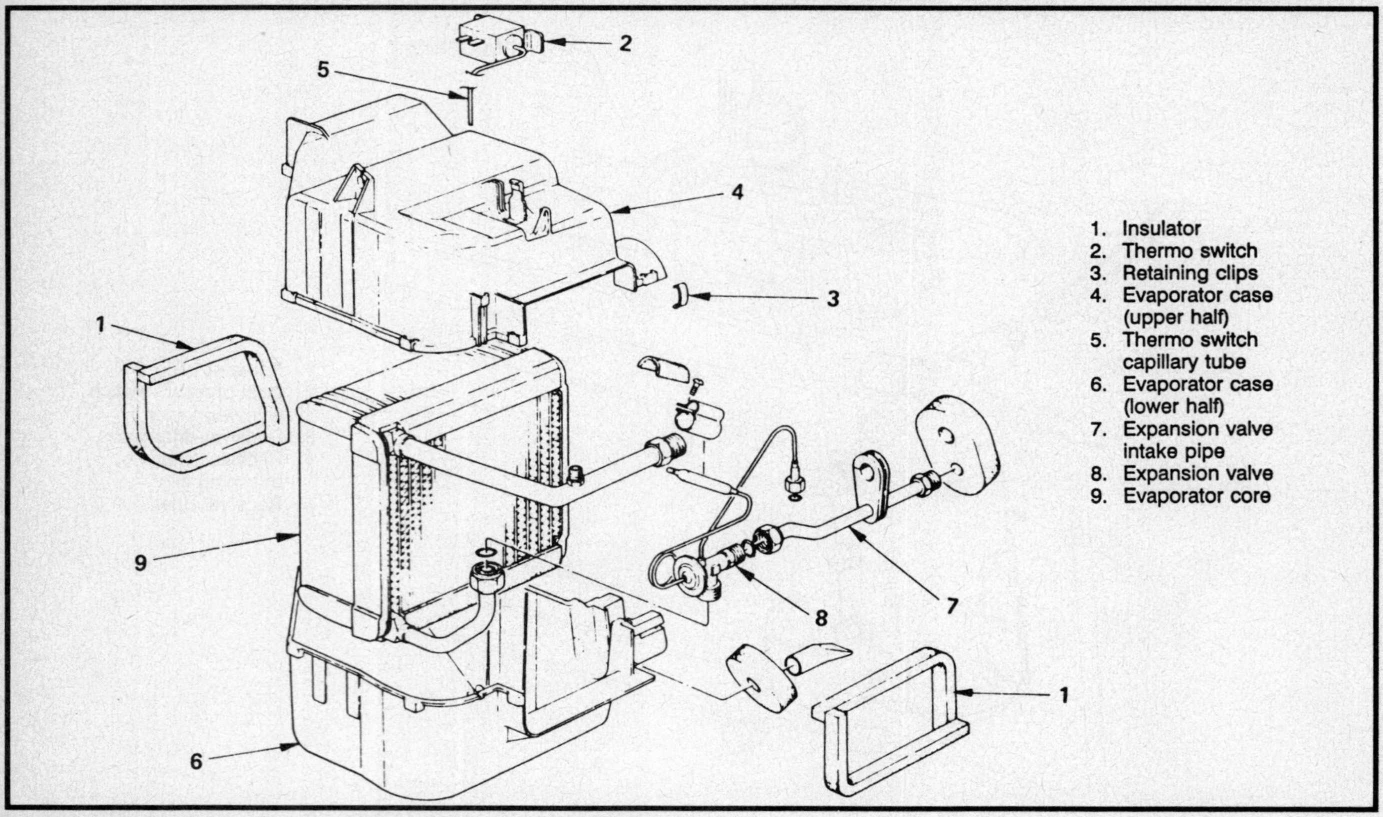
1. Insulator
2. Thermo switch
3. Retaining clips
4. Evaporator case (upper half)
5. Thermo switch capillary tube
6. Evaporator case (lower half)
7. Expansion valve intake pipe
8. Expansion valve
9. Evaporator core

Typical evaporator core and expansion valve assembly

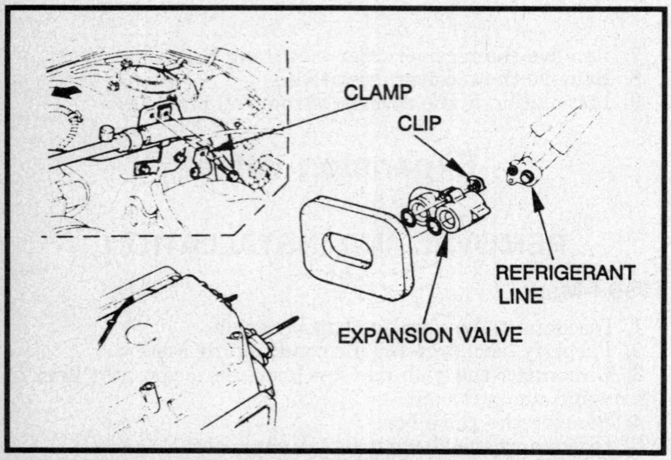
CLAMP
CLIP
REFRIGERANT LINE
EXPANSION VALVE

1990–91 Impulse and 1991 Stylus expansion valve removal

5. Remove the instrument panel and glove box assembly.
6. Remove the foot duct.
7. Remove nuts and bolts securing evaporator assembly.
8. Remove the evaporator assembly.
9. Disassemble the evaporator case to remove the expansionvalve.
10. Installation is the reverse of removal procedure.

1990–91 Impulse and 1991 Stylus

1. Disconnect the negative battery cable.
2. Properly discharge the air conditioning system.
3. Remove low pressure hose bracket attached to right side fender well.
4. Remove pressure line attaching nuts at expansion valve.
5. Remove clip at expansion valve.
6. Remove expansion valve.
8. Installation is the reverse of removal procedure.
9. Use new O-rings applying a thin coat of refrigerant oil.

Blower Motor

REMOVAL AND INSTALLATION

1989 I-Mark and Impulse

1. Disconnect the negative battery cable.
2. Disconnect the blower motor wire connector.
3. Remove the blower motor vent hose.
4. Remove the retaining clip and mounting screws.
5. Remove the blower motor.
6. Installation is the reverse of removal procedure.

1990–91 Impulse and 1991 Stylus

1. Disconnect the negative battery cable.
2. If required, remove glove box and lower reinforcing panel.
3. Remove blower motor wire connector.
4. Remove blower motor attaching screws.
5. Remove blower motor.
6. Installation is the reverse of removal procedure.

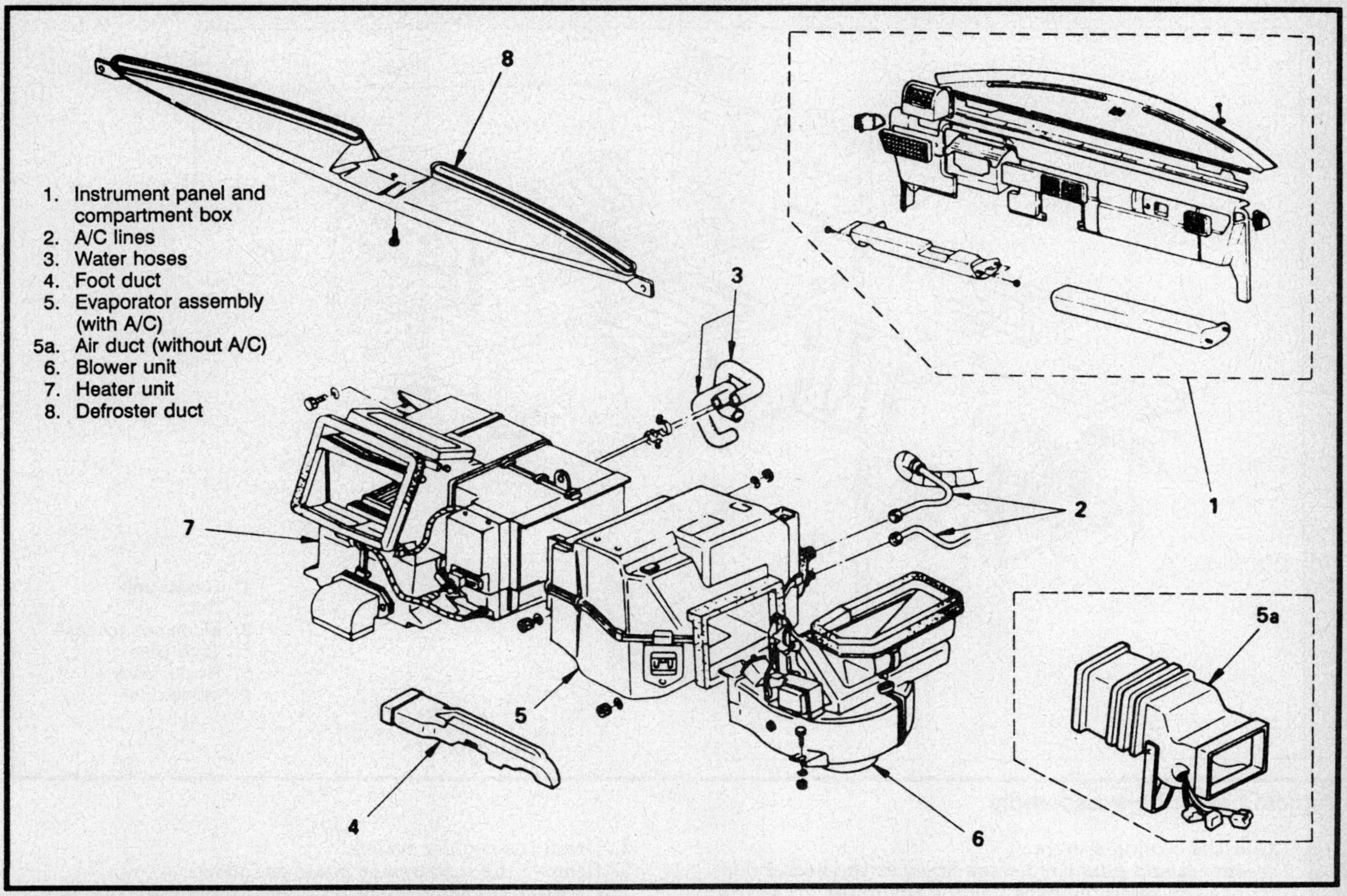
1. Instrument panel and compartment box
2. A/C lines
3. Water hoses
4. Foot duct
5. Evaporator assembly (with A/C)
5a. Air duct (without A/C)
6. Blower unit
7. Heater unit
8. Defroster duct
8
3
7
2
1
5a
5
4
6

Typical heater, blower and evaporator assembly

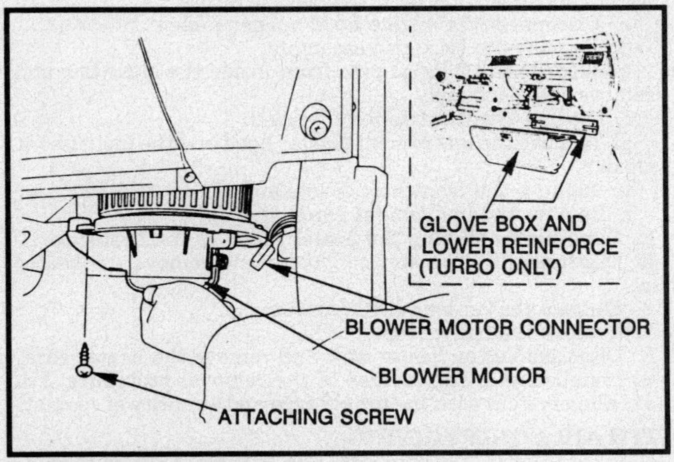
GLOVE BOX AND LOWER REINFORCE (TURBO ONLY)
BLOWER MOTOR CONNECTOR
BLOWER MOTOR
ATTACHING SCREW

Typical blower motor removal

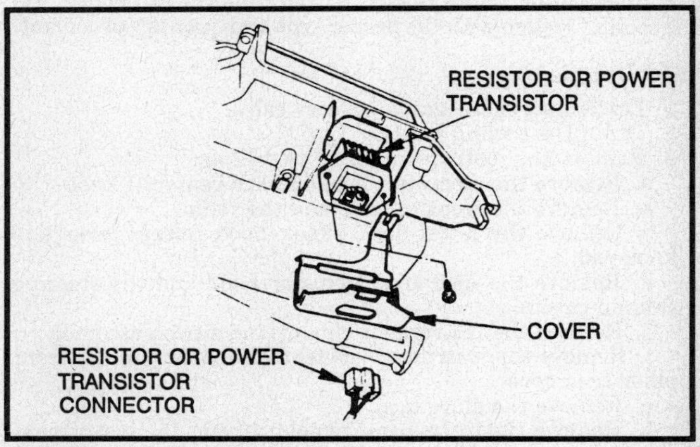
RESISTOR OR POWER TRANSISTOR
COVER
RESISTOR OR POWER TRANSISTOR CONNECTOR

Typical resistor assembly

Blower Motor Resistor

The blower motor resistor will usually be located under the dash attached to the heater or evaporator housing, it can be removed by disconnecting the battery negative terminal, the wire resistor connector and the mounting screw.

Heater Core

REMOVAL AND INSTALLATION

WITHOUT AIR CONDITIONING

1989 I-Mark

1. Disconnect the negative battery cable.

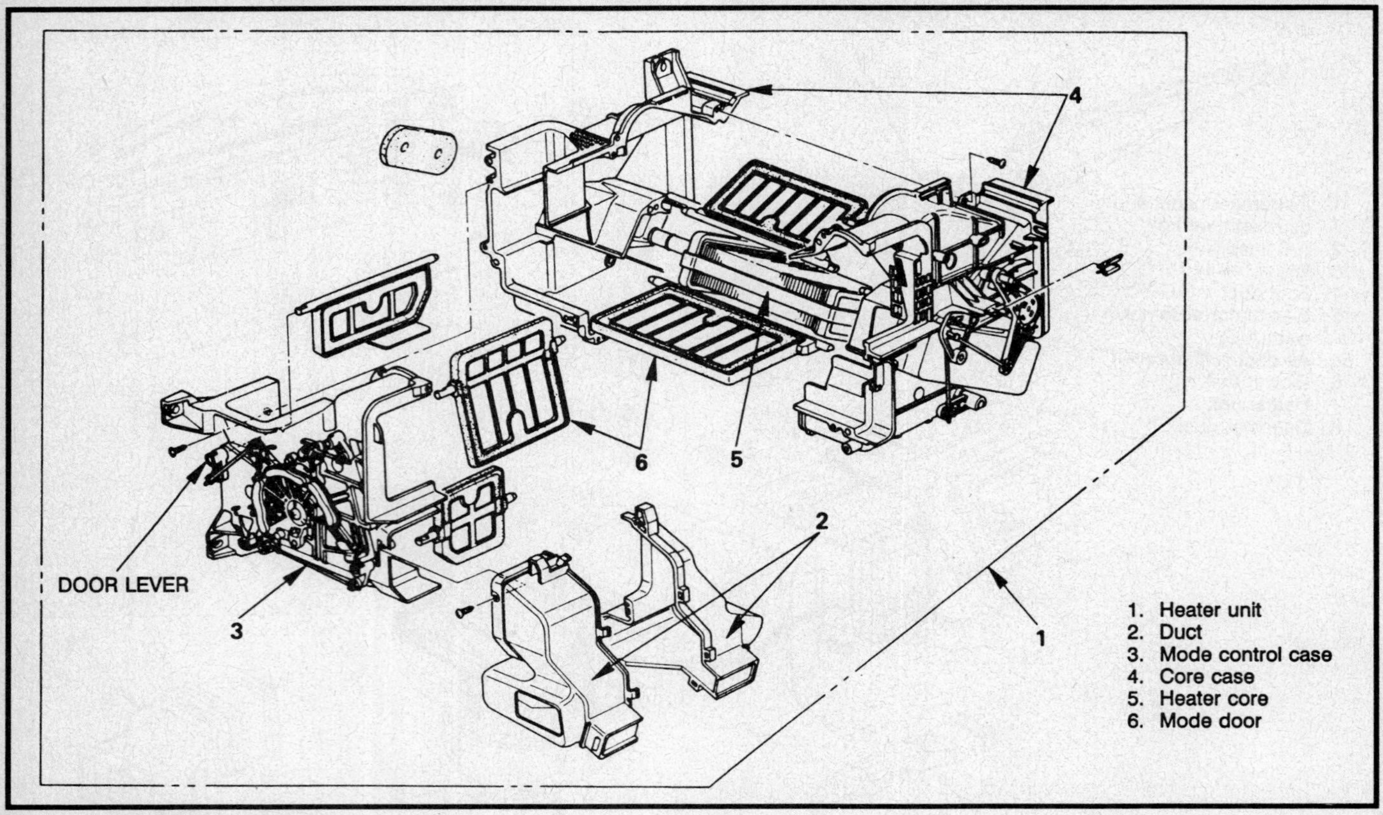
DOOR LEVER
1
2
3
4
5
6
1. Heater unit
2. Duct
3. Mode control case
4. Core case
5. Heater core
6. Mode door

Typical heater core assembly

2. Drain the cooling system.
3. Disconnect and plug the heater hoses at the heater core.
4. Remove the retaining clips holding the lower heater unit case and remove the lower case.
5. Remove the heater core assembly.
6. Installation is the reverse of the removal procedure. Fill the cooling system with the proper type and quantity of coolant.

1989 Impulse

1. Disconnect the negative battery cable.
2. Drain the cooling system.
3. Remove the instrument panel as follows:
   a. Remove the steering wheel and the gearshift knob.
   b. Remove the front console and the radio.
   c. Remove the lower dash panel, hood release lever and knee pad.
   d. Remove the instrument cluster hood and the steering column covers.
   e. Remove the instrument cluster and switch assembly.
   f. Remove the instrument panel front cover and the front pillar trim cover.
   g. Remove the glove box.
   h. Remove the instrument panel grill and the instrument panel cover assembly.
4. Disconnect and plug the heater hoses at the heater core and disconnect the electrical connectors from the heater unit.
5. Remove the heater unit mounting bolts and the heater unit.
6. Disassemble the heater unit and remove the heater core.
7. Installation is the reverse of the removal procedure. Fill the cooling system with the proper type and quantity of coolant.

1990–91 Impulse and 1991 Stylus

1. Disconnect the negative battery cable.
2. Drain the cooling system.
3. Remove the instrument panel as follows:
   a. Pull the switch bezel out and disconnect the switch connectors.
   b. Pull the cigarette lighter bezel out and disconnect the electrical connectors, then remove the bezel.
   c. Disconnect the engine hood opener cable.
   d. Remove the knee pad assembly.
   e. Remove the 2 hinge pins from inside the glove box and remove the glove box.
   f. Remove the front console bracket.
   g. Remove the instrument cluster hood and the instrument cluster.
   h. Remove the front hole covers and the front cover.
   i. Remove the instrument panel assembly.
4. Disconnect and plug the heater hoses at the heater core.
5. Disconnect the resistor connector and remove the heater duct.
6. Remove the center ventilator duct.
7. Remove the heater unit.
8. Disassemble the heater unit and remove the heater core.
9. Installation is the reverse of the removal procedure. Fill the cooling system with the proper type and quantity of coolant.

WITH AIR CONDITIONING

1989 I-Mark

1. Disconnect the negative battery cable.
2. Drain the cooling system.
3. Disconnect and plug the heater hoses at the heater core.
4. Remove the retaining clips holding the lower heater unit case and remove the lower case.
5. Remove the heater core assembly.
6. Installation is the reverse of the removal procedure. Fill the cooling system with the proper type and quantity of coolant.

1989 Impulse

1. Disconnect the negative battery cable.
2. Drain the cooling system and properly discharge the air conditioning system.
3. Remove the instrument panel as follows:
 a. Remove the steering wheel and the gearshift knob.
 b. Remove the front console and the radio.
 c. Remove the lower dash panel, hood release lever and knee pad.
 d. Remove the instrument cluster hood and the steering column covers.
 e. Remove the instrument cluster and switch assembly.
 f. Remove the instrument panel front cover and the front pillar trim cover.
 g. Remove the glove box.
 h. Remove the instrument panel grille and the instrument panel cover assembly.
4. Disconnect and plug the heater hoses at the heater core and disconnect the electrical connectors from the heater unit.
5. Disconnect and plug the air conditioning lines and disconnect the electrical connectors at the evaporator.
6. Remove the foot air duct, if equipped.
7. Remove the evaporator mounting nuts and the evaporator.
8. Remove the heater unit mounting bolts and the heater unit.
9. Disassemble the heater unit and remove the heater core.
10. Installation is the reverse of the removal procedure. Fill the cooling system with the proper type and quantity of coolant. Evacuate and charge the air conditioning system.

1990–91 Impulse and 1991 Stylus

1. Disconnect the negative battery cable.
2. Drain the cooling system and properly discharge the air conditioning system.
3. Remove the instrument panel as follows:
 a. Pull the switch bezel out and disconnect the switch connectors.
 b. Pull the cigarette lighter bezel out and disconnect the electrical connectors, then remove the bezel.
 c. Disconnect the engine hood opener cable.
 d. Remove the knee pad assembly.
 e. Remove the 2 hinge pins from inside the glove box and remove the glove box.
 f. Remove the front console bracket.
 g. Remove the instrument cluster hood and the instrument cluster.
 h. Remove the front hole covers and the front cover.
 i. Remove the instrument panel assembly.
4. Disconnect and plug the heater hoses at the heater core.
5. Disconnect the resistor connector.
6. Disconnect and plug the air conditioning lines at the evaporator.
7. Disconnect the hose and the electrical connectors at the evaporator.
8. Remove the 3 mounting nuts and the evaporator.
9. Remove the center ventilator duct.
10. Remove the heater unit.
11. Disassemble the heater unit and remove the heater core.
12. Installation is the reverse of the removal procedure. Fill the cooling system with the proper type and quantity of coolant. Evacuate and charge the air conditioning system.

Evaporator

REMOVAL AND INSTALLATION

1989 I-Mark

1. Disconnect the negative battery cable.

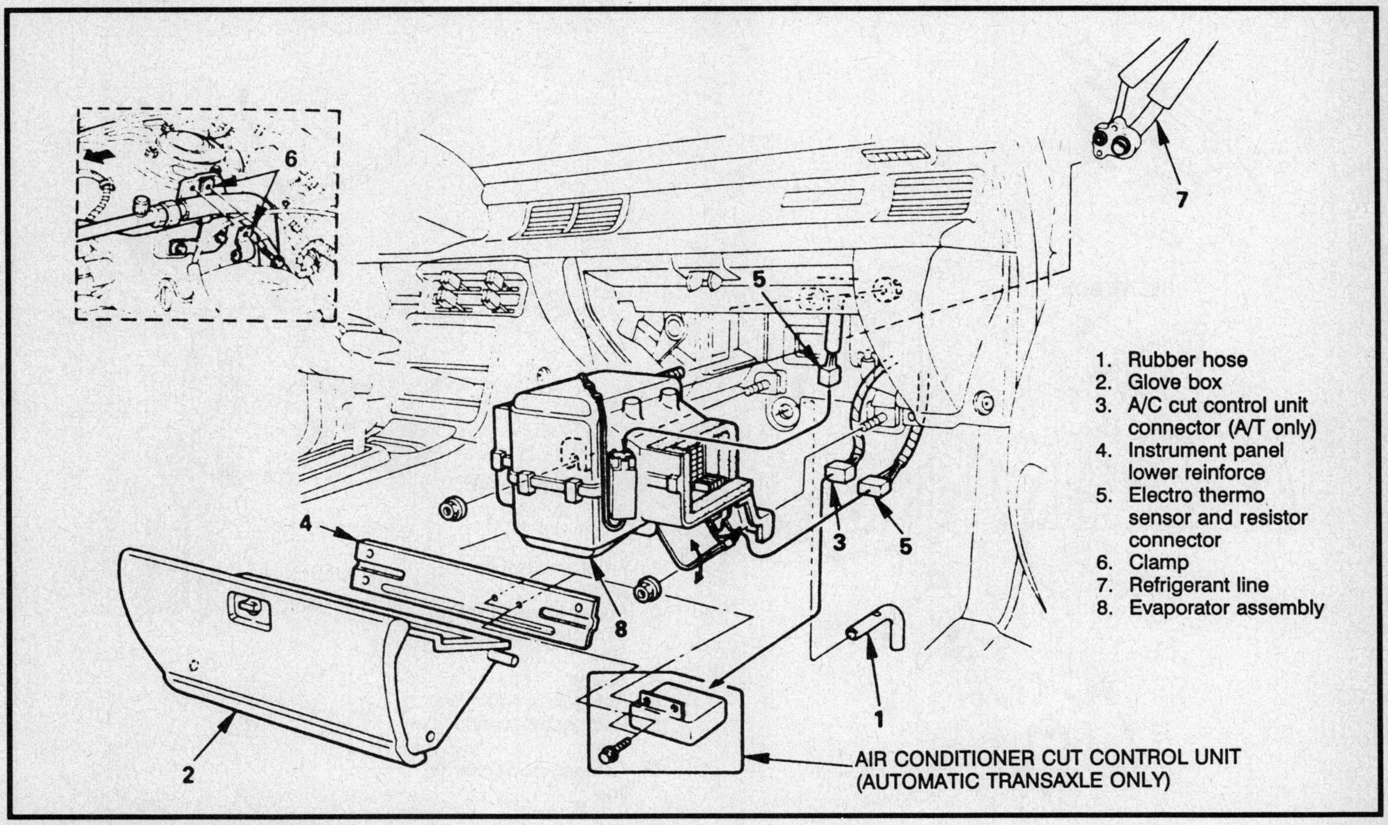
6
7
5
4
3
5
8
1
2
1. Rubber hose
2. Glove box
3. A/C cut control unit connector (A/T only)
4. Instrument panel lower reinforce
5. Electro thermo sensor and resistor connector
6. Clamp
7. Refrigerant line
8. Evaporator assembly
AIR CONDITIONER CUT CONTROL UNIT (AUTOMATIC TRANSAXLE ONLY)

Typical evaporator removal

2. Properly discharge the air conditioning system.
3. Disconnect the high and low pressure evaporator lines in the engine compartment.
4. Remove the glove box.
5. Disconnect the thermo switch connecter.
6. Remove the defroster hose.
7. Remove the nuts, bolts and washers from the evaporator housing.
8. Remove the evaporator assembly.
9. Remove the retaining clips from evaporator housing and separate the upper and lower cases.
10. Carefully pull the thermo-switch capillary tube from the evaporator core.
11. Remove the expansion valve.
12. Installation is the reverse of removal procedure.

1989 Impulse

1. Disconnect the negative battery cable.
2. Properly discharge the air conditioning system.
3. Drain engine coolant and remove heater core hoses.
4. Disconnect the high and low pressure evaporator lines in the engine compartment.
5. Remove the instrument panel and glove box assembly.
6. Remove the foot duct.
7. Remove nuts and bolts securing evaporator assembly.
8. Remove the evaporator assembly.
9. Remove the retaining clips from evaporator housing and separate the upper and lower cases.
10. Remove the expansion valve.
11. Installation is the reverse of removal procedure.

1990–91 Impulse and 1991 Stylus

1. Disconnect the negative battery cable.
2. Properly discharge the air conditioning system.
3. Remove low pressure hose bracket attached to right side fender well.
4. Remove pressure line attaching nuts and clip at expansion valve.
5. Inside vehicle, remove the evaporator drain hose.
6. Remove the glove box and lower panel reinforcement.
7. Remove the air conditioner cut control unit wire connector on vehicles with automatic transmission.
8. Remove the thermo sensor and the resistor wire connector.
9. Remove the 3 attaching nuts: one on the engine room side, and the two remaining on the blower assembly and the heater unit.
10. Remove the evaporator assembly.
11. Remove the 4 clips and 4 screws from the evaporator and split the cases.
12. Pull the evaporator core from the lower case.
13. Installation is the reverse of removal procedure.
14. Use new O-rings applying a thin coat of refrigerant oil.

Refrigerant Lines

REMOVAL AND INSTALLATION

1. Disconnect the negative battery cable.
2. Properly discharge the air conditioning system.
3. Disconnect the refrigerant lines using two wrenches where required.
4. Remove all attaching brackets.
5. Remove tanks as required.

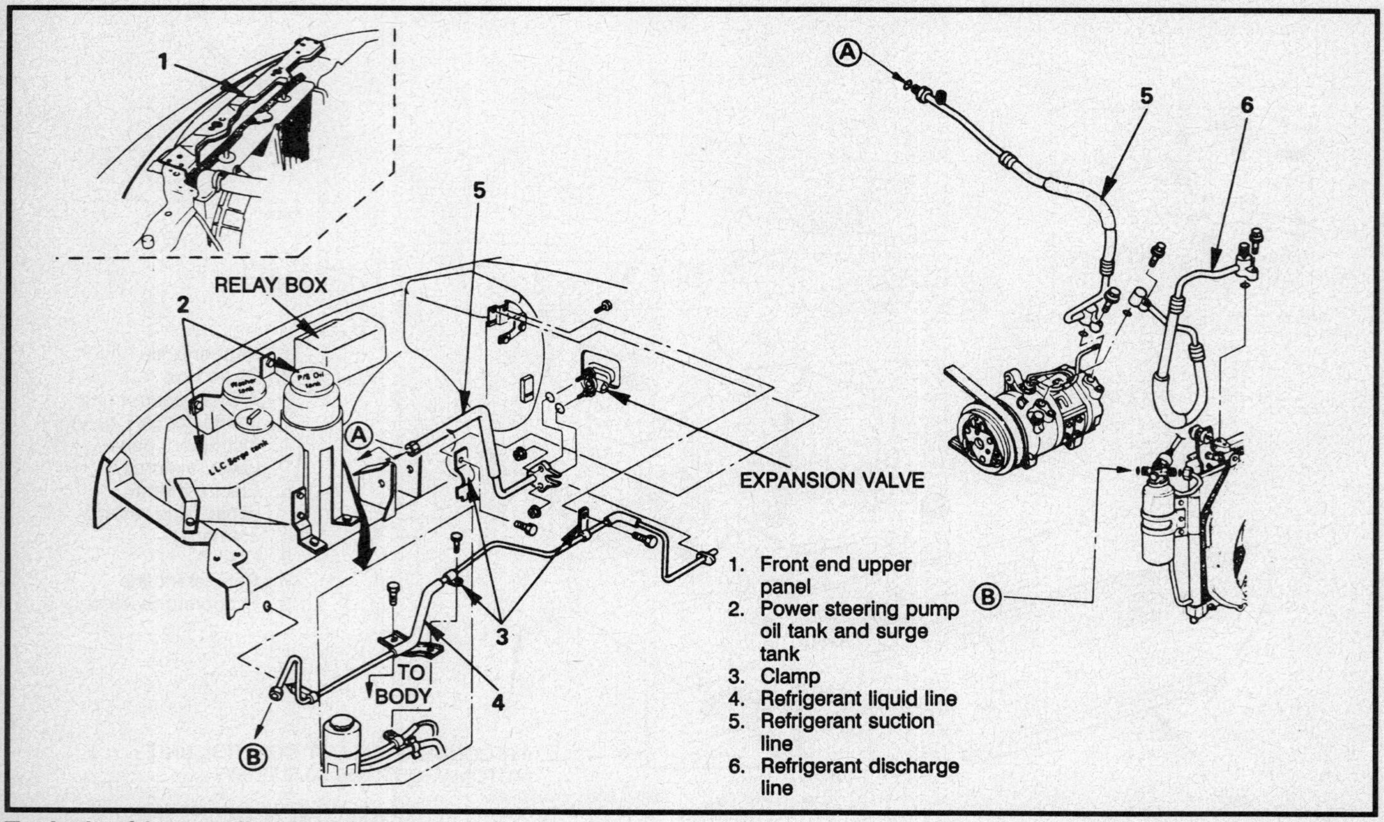
1
5
RELAY BOX
2
A
EXPANSION VALVE
3
TO
BODY
4
B
A
5
6
B
1. Front end upper panel
2. Power steering pump oil tank and surge tank
3. Clamp
4. Refrigerant liquid line
5. Refrigerant suction line
6. Refrigerant discharge line

Typical refrigerant line locations

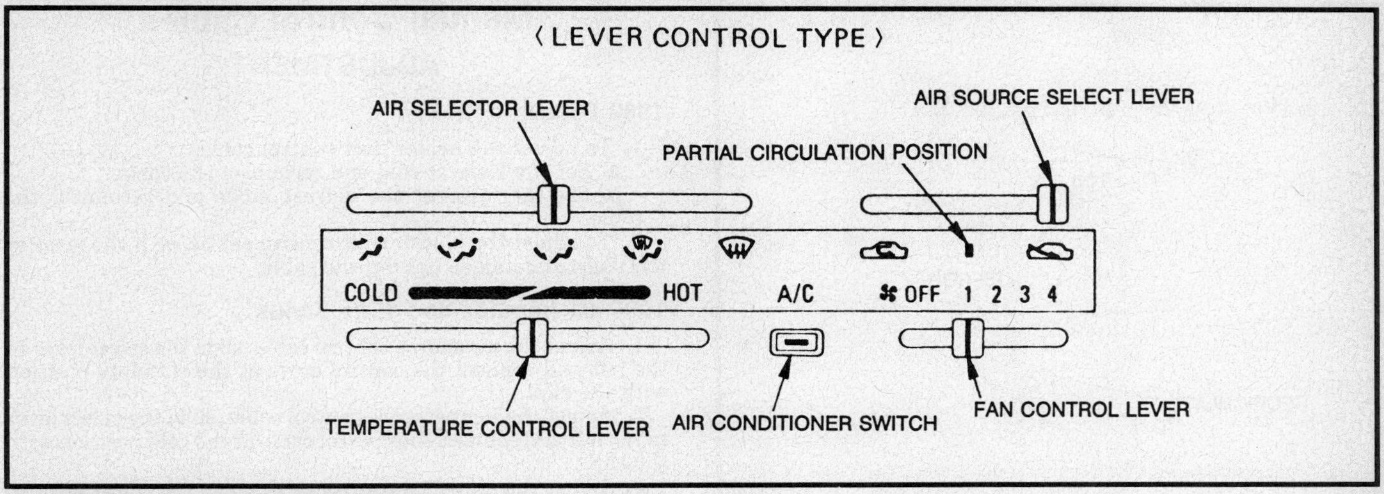
⟨ LEVER CONTROL TYPE ⟩
AIR SELECTOR LEVER
AIR SOURCE SELECT LEVER
PARTIAL CIRCULATION POSITION
COLD
HOT
A/C
OFF 1 2 3 4
TEMPERATURE CONTROL LEVER
AIR CONDITIONER SWITCH
FAN CONTROL LEVER

Typical lever control assembly type

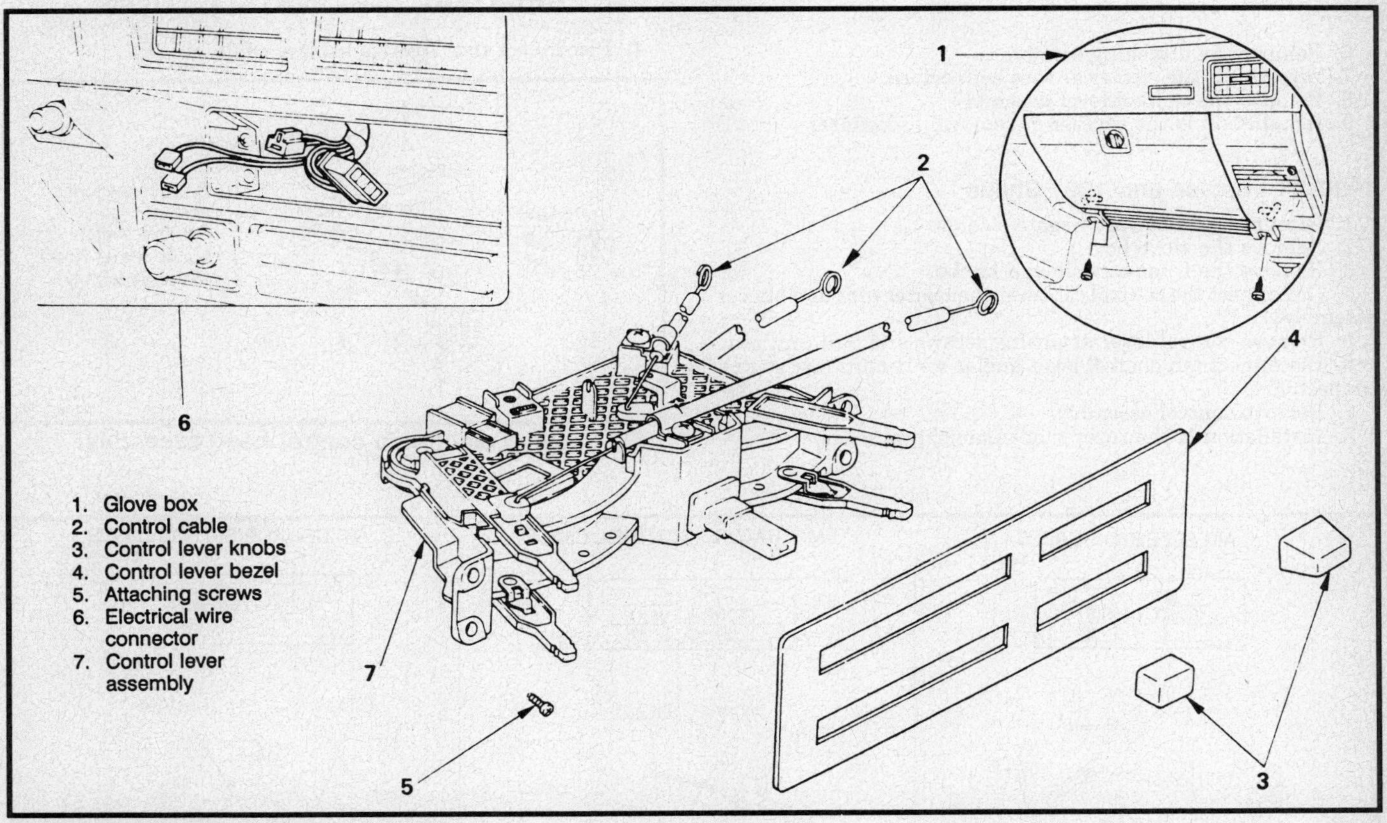
1. Glove box
2. Control cable
3. Control lever knobs
4. Control lever bezel
5. Attaching screws
6. Electrical wire connector
7. Control lever assembly

Control lever assembly removal

6. Remove the refrigerant line.
7. Installation is the reverse of removal procedure.
8. Evacuate, recharge and leak check the system.

NOTE: Always reroute hoses in original location and use new o-rings with a thin coat of refrigerant oil.

Manual Control Head

REMOVAL AND INSTALLATION

1989 I-Mark

1. Diconnect the battery negative cable.

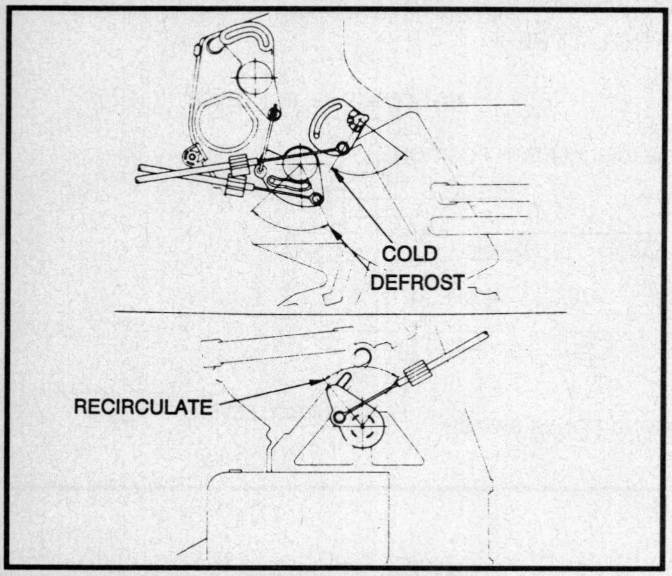
COLD
DEFROST
RECIRCULATE

1989 I-Mark control cable adjustments

6. Remove the attaching screws.
7. Disconnect the electrical wire connectors.
8. Remove the control lever assembly.
9. Installation is the reverse of removal procedure.

1990–91 Impulse and 1991 Stylus

1. Diconnect the battery negative cable.
2. Remove the glove box.
3. Remove the front console and knobs.
4. Disconnect the control cables at the heater unit and blower assembly.
5. Remove control lever attaching screws and pull unit out.
6. Disconnect fan control lever and/or air conditioner switch connector.
7. Remove control assembly.
8. Installation is the reverse of removal procedure.

Manual Control Cables

ADJUSTMENT

1989 I-Mark

1. To adjust the heater unit control cables.
   a. Set the lever at cold and reconnect the cable.
   b. Set the lever at the defrost mode and reconnect the cable.
2. To adjust the blower unit control cables with the lever at the recirculate mode tighten the cable.

1990–91 Impulse and 1991 Stylus

1. Adjust the air source control cable, slide the select lever to the left and connect the control cable at the circulate position with the clip.
2. Adjust the temperature control cable, slide the select lever to the left and connect the control cable at the cold position with the clip.
3. Adjust the air select control cable, slide the select lever to the right and connect the control cable at the defrost position with the clip.
4. Check operation of unit.

REMOVAL AND INSTALLATION

1. Disconnect the negative battery cable.

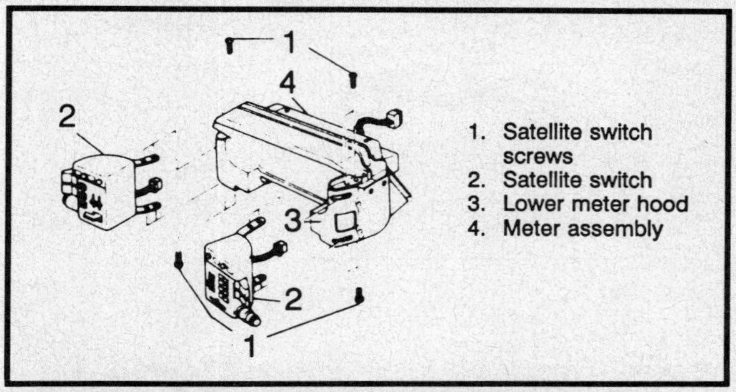
1
4
2
3
2
1
1. Satellite switch screws
2. Satellite switch
3. Lower meter hood
4. Meter assembly

1989 Impulse electronic control head assembly

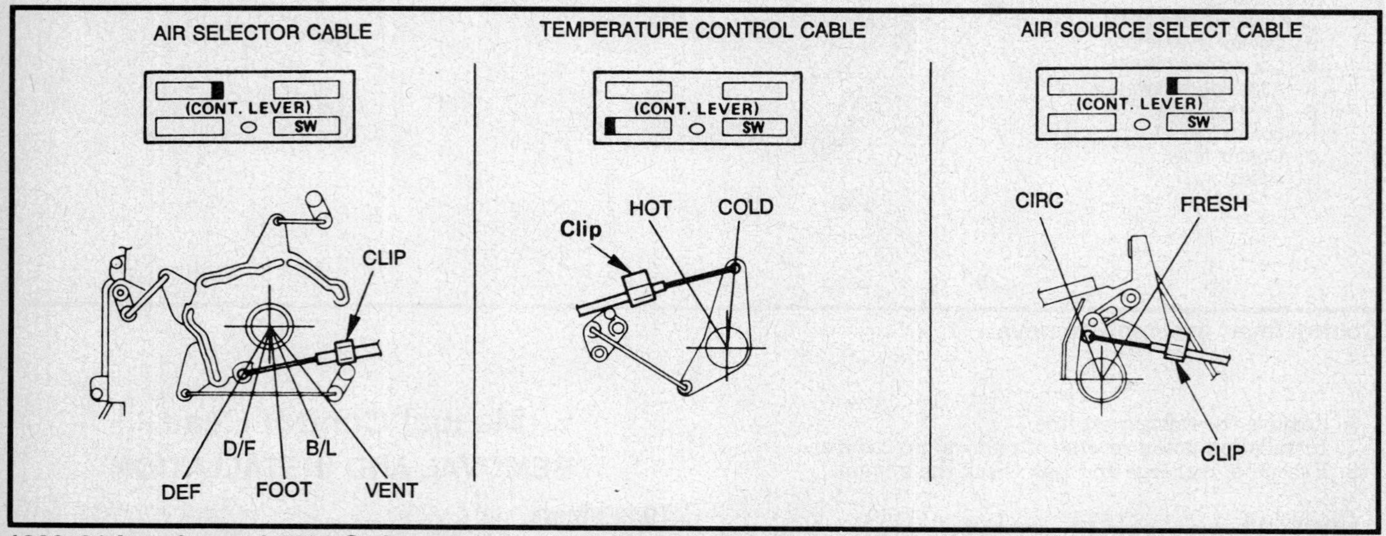
AIR SELECTOR CABLE
(CONT. LEVER)
SW
CLIP
D/F
B/L
DEF
FOOT
VENT
TEMPERATURE CONTROL CABLE
(CONT. LEVER)
SW
HOT
COLD
Clip
AIR SOURCE SELECT CABLE
(CONT. LEVER)
SW
CIRC
FRESH
CLIP

1990–91 Impulse and 1991 Stylus control cable adjustment

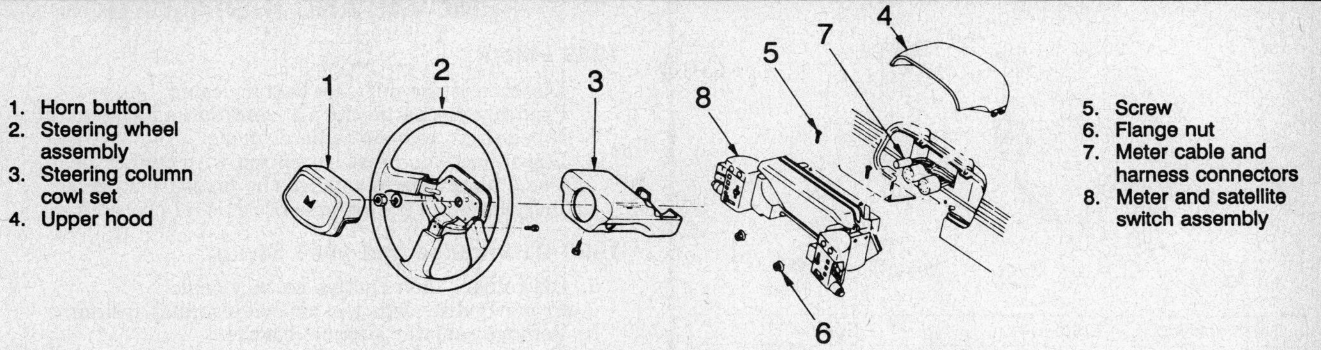
1. Horn button
2. Steering wheel assembly
3. Steering column cowl set
4. Upper hood
5. Screw
6. Flange nut
7. Meter cable and harness connectors
8. Meter and satellite switch assembly

1989 Impulse electronic control head assembly removal

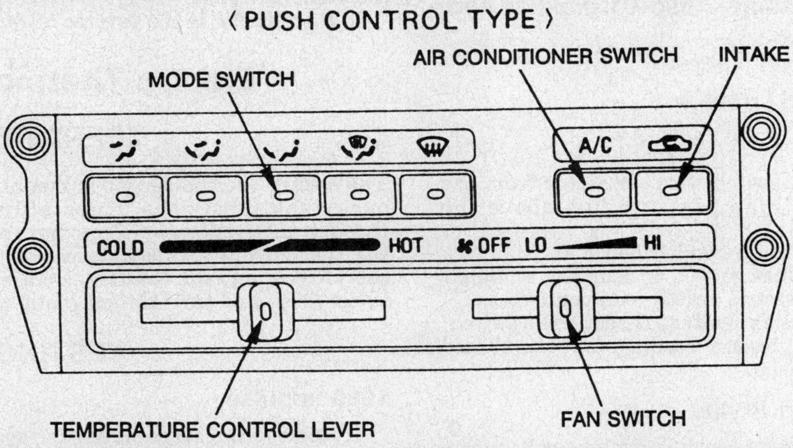
⟨PUSH CONTROL TYPE⟩
MODE SWITCH
AIR CONDITIONER SWITCH
INTAKE SWITCH
A/C
COLD
HOT
OFF
LO
HI
TEMPERATURE CONTROL LEVER
FAN SWITCH

Electronic control head—1991 Impulse

2. Remove glove box assembly.
3. Disconnect control cables at heater unit.
4. Remove control lever assembly.
5. Remove control assembly cables.
6. Installation is the reverse of removal procedure.

Electronic Control Head

REMOVAL AND INSTALLATION

1989 Impulse

1. Disconnect the negative battery cable.
2. Remove the horn button assembly.
3. Remove the steering wheel assembly.
4. Remove steering column housing.
5. Remove the instrument housing top cover.
6. Remove the instrument bezel screws and flange nuts.
7. Remove instrument wire connectors and cable.
8. Remove the instrument assembly.
9. Remove the 2 screws on the control head.
10. Remove the 6 screws on the lower cover.
11. Remove the switch harness clip on the lower back of the meter assembly.
12. Remove the control head assembly.
13. Installation is the reverse of removal procedure.

1990–91 Impulse

1. Disconnect the negative battery cable.
2. Remove the ashtray.
3. Remove the front console panel.
4. Remove the 4 attaching screws from the control assembly and remove the control head.
5. Installation is the reverse of removal procedure.

SENSORS AND SWITCHES

Pressure Switches

OPERATION

There are 2 styles of pressure switches being used, a dual pressure switch which switches the magnetic clutch ON or OFF as a result of irregularly high or low pressures of the refrigerant. The other switch is a triple pressure switch which utilizes the first design and incorporates a medium pressure switch to cycle ON and OFF the condenser fan according to system pressure on the high side, some systems use a separate switch for the condenser fan.

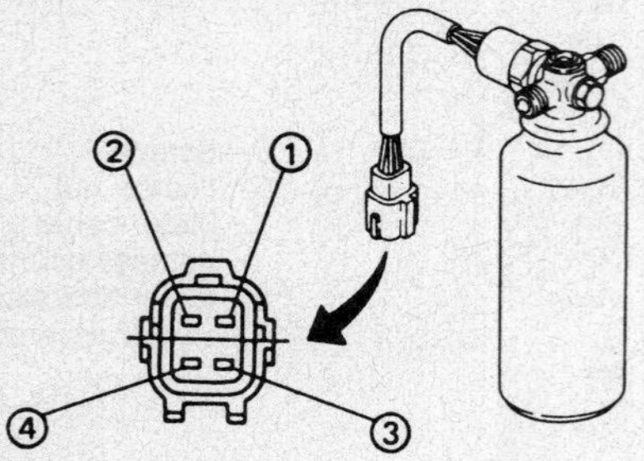

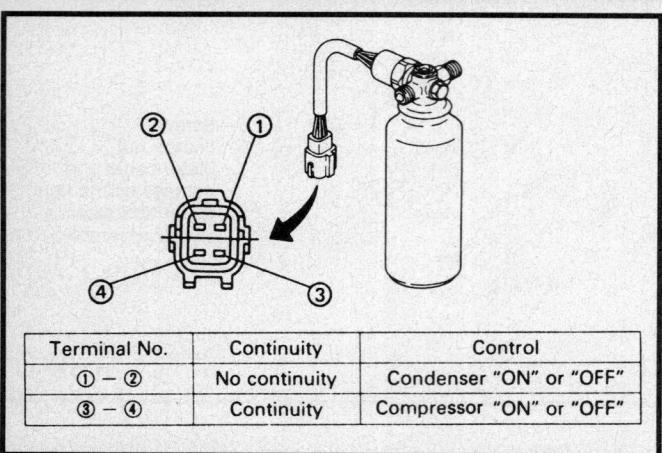

Terminal No.	Continuity	Control
① – ②	No continuity	Condenser "ON" or "OFF"
③ – ④	Continuity	Compressor "ON" or "OFF"

Triple pressure switch testing – 1990–91 Impulse and 1991 Stylus

TESTING

1989 I-Mark

1. Disconnect the pressure switch wire connector from the receiver/dryer or from the high pressure line above the condenser.
2. Start vehicle and turn the air conditioner ON.
3. Hook up the air conditioner gauges or charging station.
4. Check for 12 volts at pressure switch wire connector.
5. Reconnect wire and check for voltage through the switch.
6. At normal high and low pressure readings 12 volts should flow through the switch.

1990–91 Impulse and 1991 Stylus

1. Disconnect the triple pressure switch connector from the receiver/dryer.
2. Check for continuity between the terminals of the triple pressure switch side connector.

NOTE: Whether the condenser fan is turned ON or OFF is determined by continuity across terminals 1 and 2. Continuity is established when the air conditioner is turned on and the refrigerant pressure reaches 213 ± 14.2 psi.

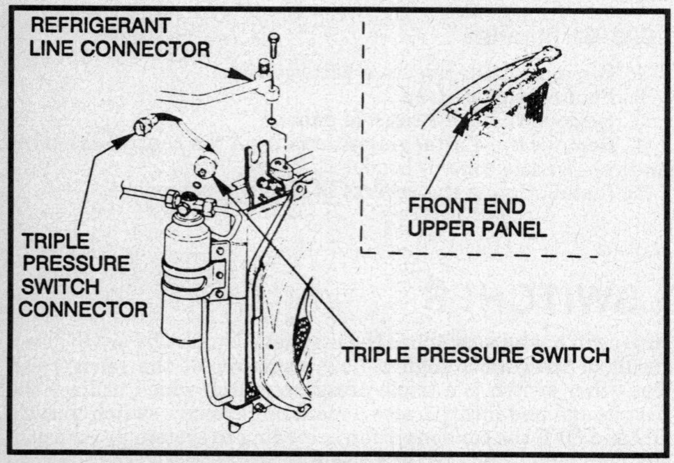
REFRIGERANT
LINE CONNECTOR
FRONT END
UPPER PANEL
TRIPLE
PRESSURE
SWITCH
CONNECTOR
TRIPLE PRESSURE SWITCH

Typical pressure switch assembly

REMOVAL AND INSTALLATION

1989 I-Mark

1. Disconnect the negative battery cable.
2. Properly discharge the air conditioning system.
3. If required, remove radiator grille.
4. Disconnect the pressure switch wire connector.
5. Use 2 wrenches to remove the pressure switch.
6. Installation is the reverse of removal procedure.

1990–91 Impulse and 1991 Stylus

1. Disconnect the negative battery cable.
2. Properly discharge the air conditioning system.
3. Remove radiator support bracket.
4. Remove refrigerant high pressure connection above condenser.
5. Disconnect pressure switch wire connector.
6. Using 2 wrenches, turn the triple pressure switch counterclockwise and remove.
7. Installation is the reverse of removal procedure.

Electro Thermo Sensor

OPERATION

The electro thermo sensor is mounted at the evaporator core outlet and senses the temperature of the cool air coming through the evaporator. Temperature signals are then input to the thermo unit. This information is then compared by the thermo unit and the results are output to operate the air conditioner relay and turn the magnetic clutch ON and OFF.

TESTING

1989 Impulse

1. Remove the sensor from the evaporator housing.
2. Put the sensor in ice water.
3. Apply voltage to terminals No. 1 and 4.
4. Check for continuity between terminals No. 2 and 4.

1990–91 Impulse and 1991 Stylus

1. Remove the electro thermo sensor from the evaporator.
2. Disconnect the compressor relay from the relay box.
3. Turn the ignition switch ON.
4. Turn the air conditioner and fan switch ON.

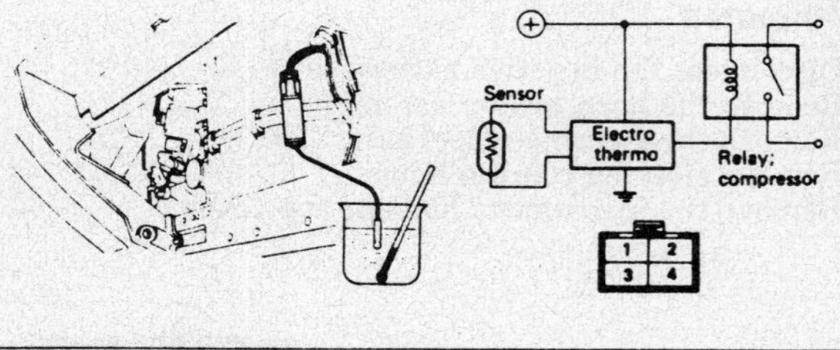
Sensor
Electro thermo
Relay; compressor
1 2
3 4

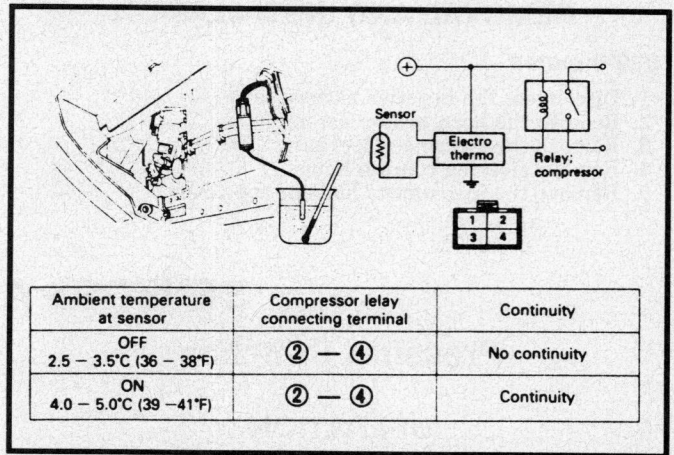

Ambient temperature at sensor	Compressor lelay connecting terminal	Continuity
OFF 2.5 – 3.5°C (36 – 38°F)	② — ④	No continuity
ON 4.0 – 5.0°C (39 – 41°F)	② — ④	Continuity

Thermo sensor testing

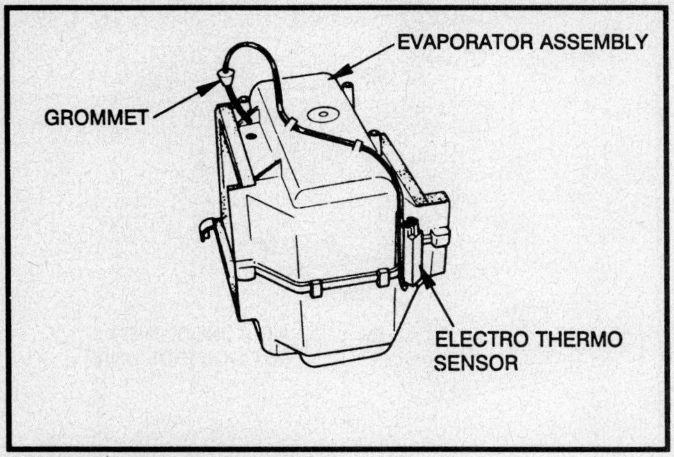
EVAPORATOR ASSEMBLY
GROMMET
ELECTRO THERMO
SENSOR

Thermo sensor assembly

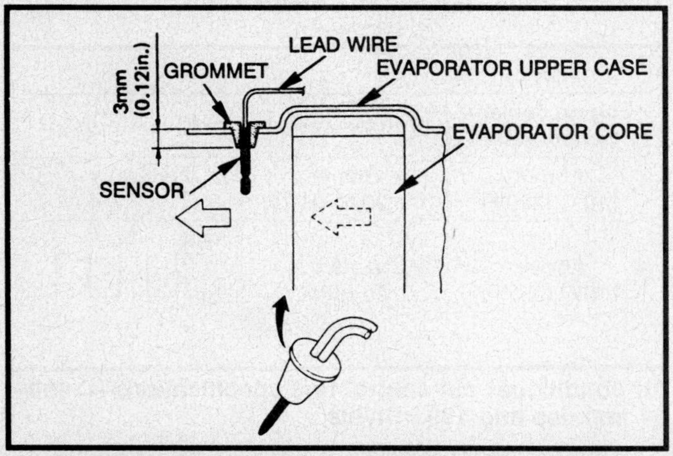
3mm
(0.12in.)
LEAD WIRE
GROMMET
EVAPORATOR UPPER CASE
EVAPORATOR CORE
SENSOR

Thermo sensor installation—1990–91 Impulse and 1991 Stylus

5. Put the electro thermo sensor into ice water.
6. Check for continuity between chassis side terminals of compressor relay.

REMOVAL AND INSTALLATION

1. Disconnect the negative battery cable.
2. Properly discharge the air conditioning system.
3. Remove the evaporator assembly, if required.
4. Remove the grommet in evaporator case around sensor wire, if required.
5. Remove the electro thermo sensor.
6. Installation is the reverse of removal procedure.
7. When installing, the sensor must be 3mm below the grommet.

Relays

OPERATION

Battery and load location may require that a switch be placed some distance from either component. This means a longer wire and a higher voltage drop. The installation of a relay between the battery and the load reduces the voltage drop. Because the switch controls the relay, this means amperage through the switch can be reduced.

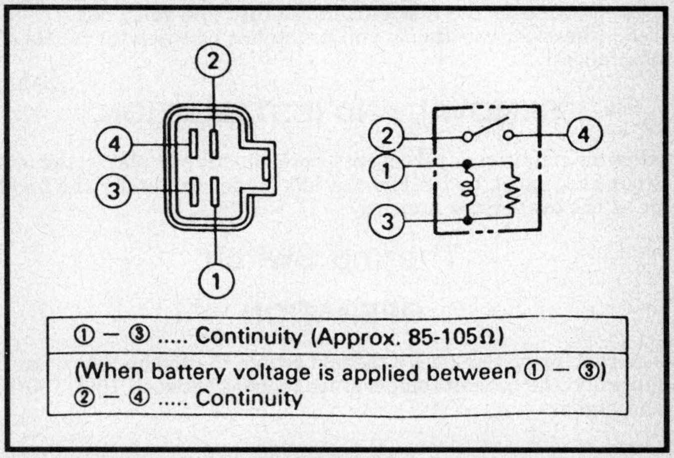
① – ③ ..... Continuity (Approx. 85-105Ω)
(When battery voltage is applied between ① – ③)
② – ④ ..... Continuity

Heater and air conditioning relay testing—1990–91 Impulse and 1991 Stylus

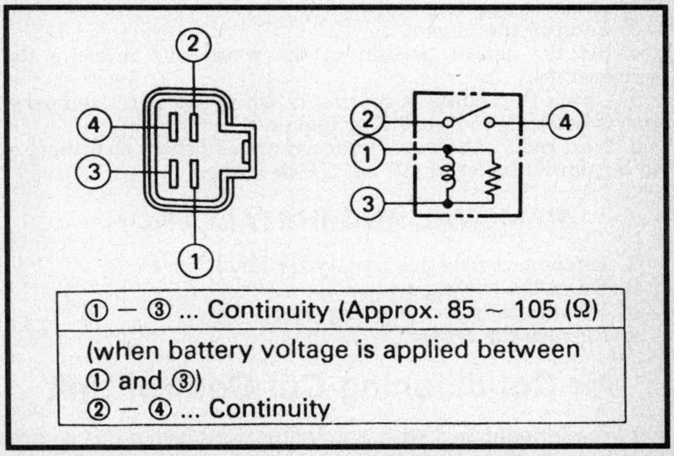
① – ③ ... Continuity (Approx. 85 ~ 105 (Ω)
(when battery voltage is applied between
① and ③)
② – ④ ... Continuity

Condenser, compressor and thermo switch relay testing—1990–91 Impulse and 1991 Stylus

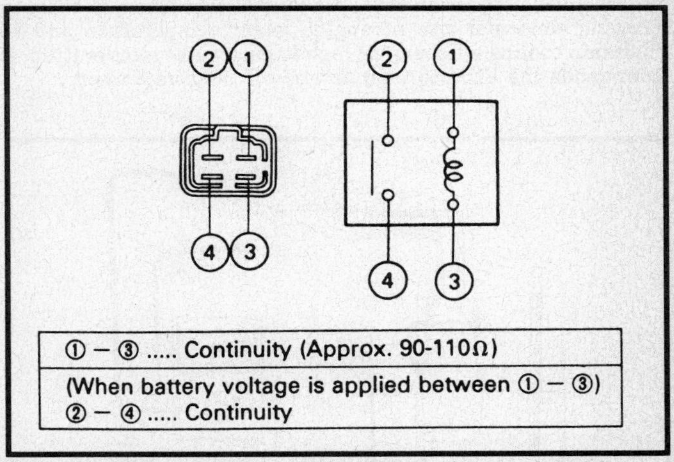
① – ③ ..... Continuity (Approx. 90-110Ω)
(When battery voltage is applied between ① – ③)
② – ④ ..... Continuity

Max HI relay testing—1990–91 Impulse and 1991 Stylus

TESTING

1. Disconnect the battery negative terminal

2. Disconnect the relays from the fuse and relay box.
3. Check for continuity and resistance between terminals of the relay.

REMOVAL AND INSTALLATION

Most air conditioner relays are located in one of 4 places; the left front kick panel, by the right or left fenderwell under the hood or at the evaporator housing.

Thermo Switch

OPERATION

The coolant system uses a thermo switch to turn on the coolant fan when the coolant temperature reaches between 180°–190°F and higher.

TESTING

1. Disconnect negative battery terminal.
2. Drain the cooling system.
3. Remove the sensor.
4. Set the sensor portion in the water and increase the temperature.
5. Check that there is continuity when the water temperature is between 180°–190°F or higher.
6. Next reduce the water temperature and check that there is no continuity between 167°–178°F or lower.

REMOVAL AND INSTALLATION

1. Disconnect negative battery terminal.
2. Drain the cooling system.
3. Remove sensor connecting wire.
4. Remove the sensor.

Air Conditioning Cut Control Unit

On vehicles equipped with automatic transaxle ,a cut control unit is used. The unit is located on the instrument panel lower reinforcement behind the glove box. The control unit senses the engine water temperature and the signal of the meter reed switch during operation of the air conditioner. Then, in order to prevent abnormal rise of engine water temperature and to maintain cooling efficiency at high engine water temperature, it commands the ECM to turn on and off the compressor.

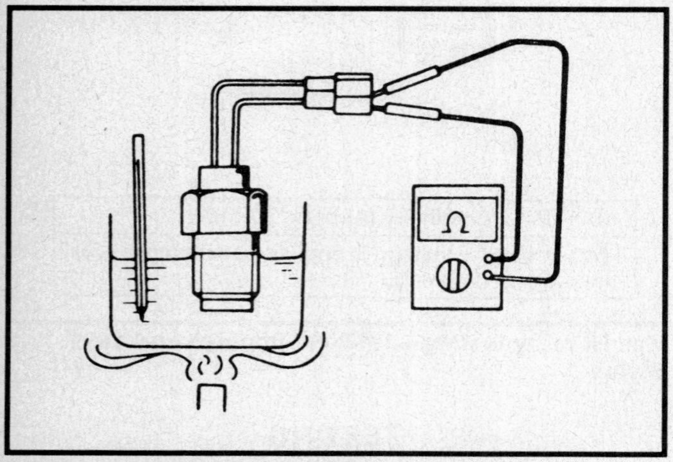

Radiator thermo switch testing

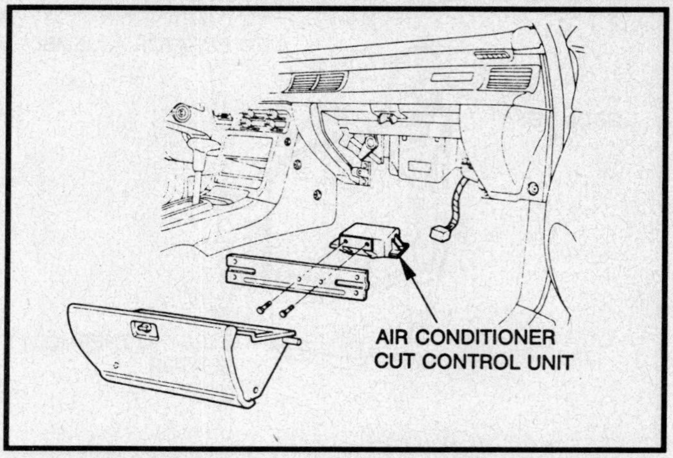
AIR CONDITIONER
CUT CONTROL UNIT

Air conditioner cut control location and removal—1990–91 Impulse and 1991 Stylus

Engine coolant temperature	Vehicle speed	A/C compressor
Above 110°C (230°F)	Below 20 MPH	ON
Above 110°C (230°F)	Above 20 MPH	ON, OFF, T, T=15Sec.

Air conditioner cut control test specifications—1990–91 Impulse and 1991 Stylus

TESTING

When the engine coolant temperature is above 230°F and the vehicle speed below 20 mph the air conditioner compressor will be on. When the temperature is above 230°F and the vehicle speed is above 20 mph the compressor will cycle in 15 second intervalls.

REMOVAL AND INSTALLATION

1990–91 Impulse and 1991 Stylus

1. Disconnect the negative battery
2. Remove the glove box assembly.
3. Remove the instrument panel lower reinforcement.
4. Remove the control unit wire connector.
5. Unbolt and remove the control unit.
6. Installation is the reverse of the removal.

Actuators

When the mode switch on the control head panel is depressed, an output signal corresponding to the depressed switch is issued to the mode actuator. The mode actuator, which then shifts to the selected position, performs opening and closing of the mode door and stops in the specified position.

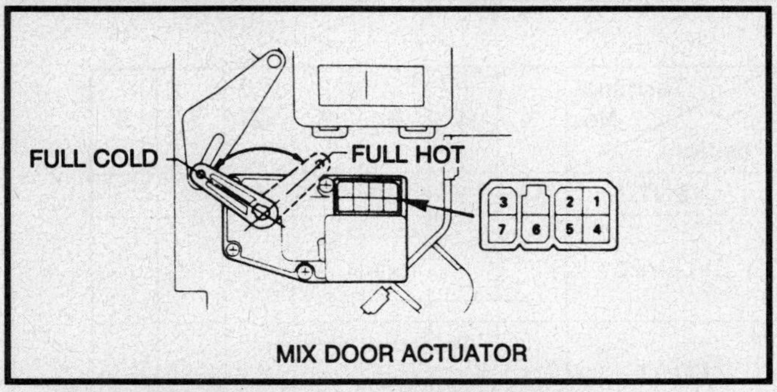
FULL COLD
FULL HOT
MIX DOOR ACTUATOR

Mix door actuator testing—1989 Impulse

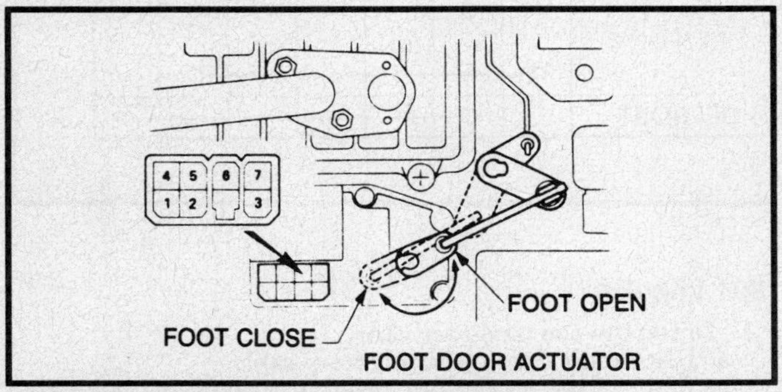
FOOT OPEN
FOOT CLOSE
FOOT DOOR ACTUATOR

Foot door actuator testing—1989 Impulse

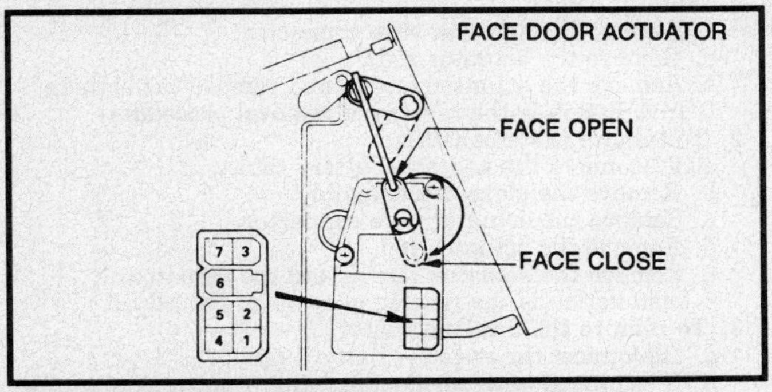
FACE DOOR ACTUATOR
FACE OPEN
FACE CLOSE

Face door actuator testing—1989 Impulse

TESTING

1989 Impulse

1. Check that the actuator lever moves smoothly and stops at the specified position when battery voltage is applied between the actuator terminals as follows.
2. Check the mix door actuator by connecting a ground to terminal 4, and 12 volts positive to terminal 6, the actuator should be in the full hot position. Now reverse the connection and the actuator should be in the full cold position.
3. Check the foot door actuator by connecting a ground to terminal 4, and 12 volts positive to terminal 6, the actuator should be in the foot open position. Next move the positive lead from terminal 6 to terminal 3, the actuator should be in the foot close position.
4. Check the face door by connecting a ground to terminal 4, and 12 volts positive to terminal 6, the actuator should be in the face open position. Next move the positive lead from terminal 6 to terminal 3, the actuator should now be in the face close position.

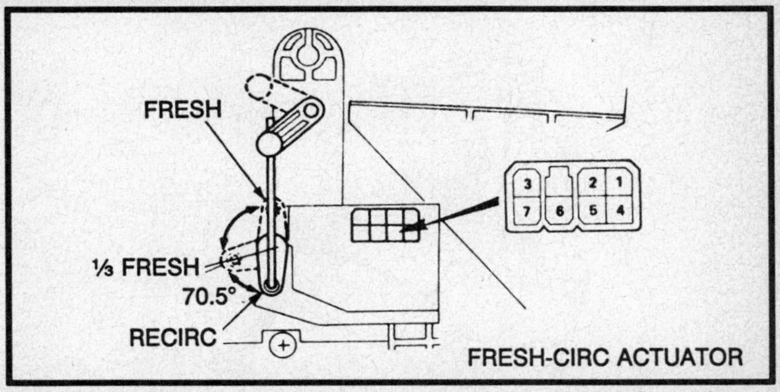
FRESH
⅓ FRESH
70.5°
RECIRC
FRESH-CIRC ACTUATOR

Fresh-circulate door actuator testing—1989 Impulse

5. Check the fresh-circ door actuator by connecting a ground to terminal 4, then take the 12 volts positive lead and connect it to the number 3 terminal, the actuator should move to the fresh position. Next move the positive terminal to terminal 7, the actuator should now be in the ⅓ fresh position. Next move the positive lead to terminal 6, the actuator should now be in the recirculate position.

1991 Impulse

1. To test the mode actuator.
   a. Disconnect the 9-pin connector from the heater unit.
   b. Check for continuity between the terminals of the mode actuator.
2. To test the mix actuator.
   a. Move the temperature control lever to the FULL COLD or HOT position.
   b. Disconnect the 8-pin connector from the heater unit.
   c. Connect a 12 volt positive test lead to terminal 4 and the negative test lead to terminal 2, the actuator should move from the FULL COLD to the FULL HOT position.
   d. Next reverse the connections so the positive lead is on terminal 2 and the negative lead is on terminal 4, the actuator should now move from the FULL HOT to the FULL COLD position.
3. To test the intake actuator.
   a. Turn the ignition switch ON and press the intake switch to the circulate or fresh position.
   b. Disconnect the 7-pin connector from the blower assembly.
   c. Check for continuity between terminal 4 and 6 for the circulate position and terminal 3 and 4 for the fresh position of the intake actuator.

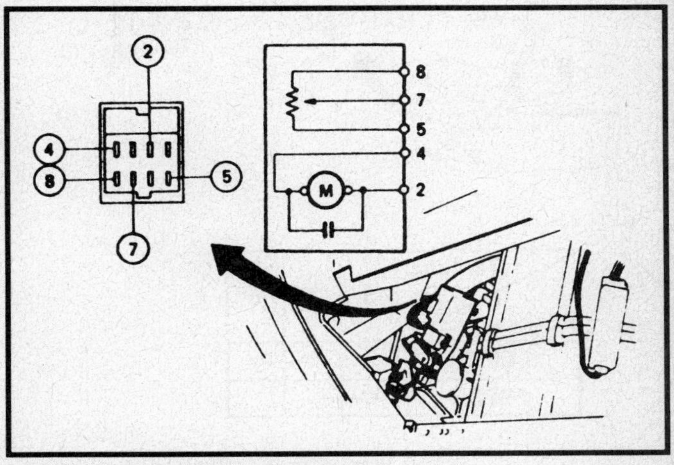
2
4
8
5
7
M

Mix actuator testing—1991 Impulse

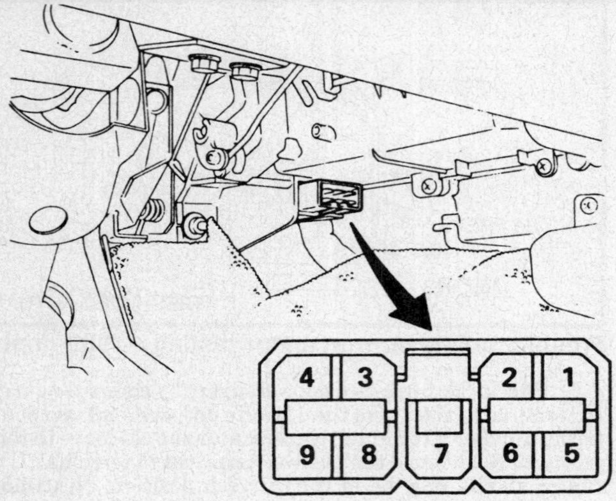
4
3
2
1
9
8
7
6
5

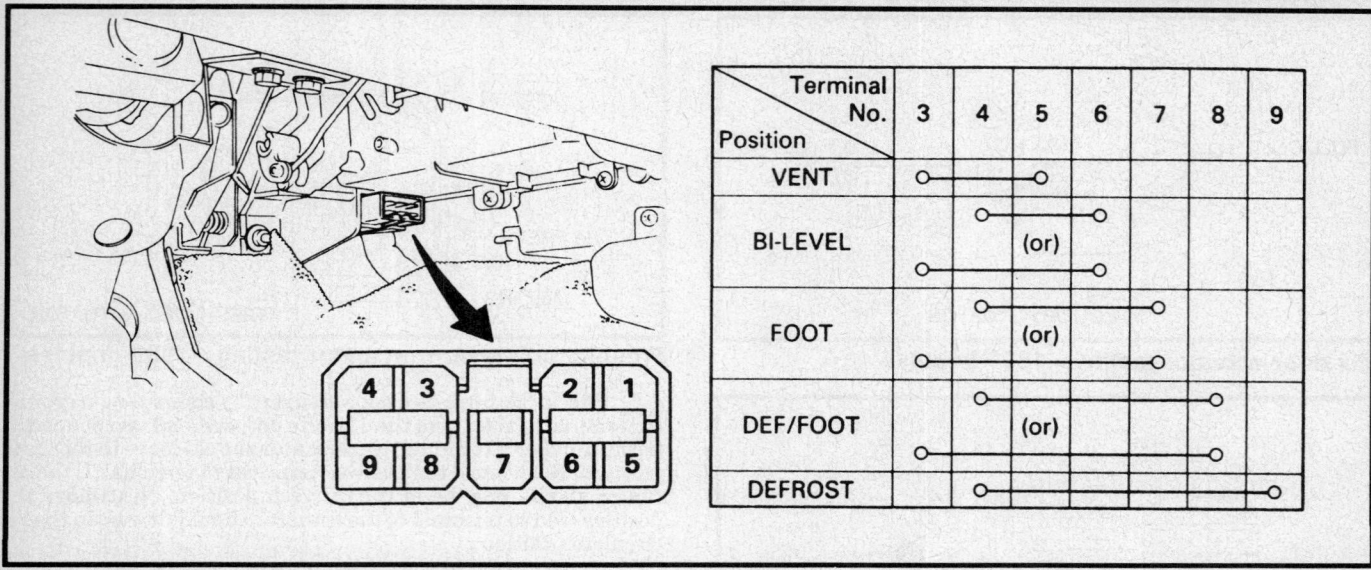

Terminal No. / Position	3	4	5	6	7	8	9
VENT	o		o				
BI-LEVEL		o		o			
(or)	o			o			
FOOT		o			o		
(or)	o				o		
DEF/FOOT		o				o	
(or)	o					o	
DEFROST		o					o

Mode actuator testing—1991 Impulse

REMOVAL AND INSTALLATION

1989 Impulse

There are 3 actuators which are located in the middle and one on each side of the heater unit.

1. Disconnect the negative battery cable.
2. If required, remove the instrument panel and glove compartment box.
3. If required, properly discharge the air conditioning system.
4. If required, remove the evaporator assembly.
5. Disconnect the wire connector at the actuator.
6. Disconnect the actuator control rod.
7. Remove the actuator screws and remove the actuator.
8. Installation is the reverse of removal procedure.

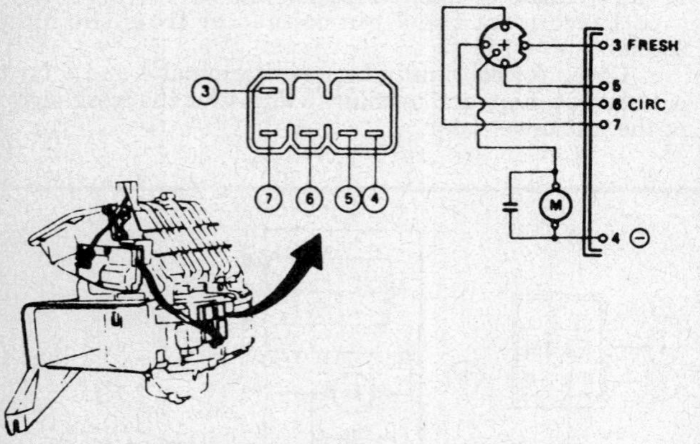
3
7
6
5
4
3 FRESH
5
6 CIRC
7
4 ⊖
M

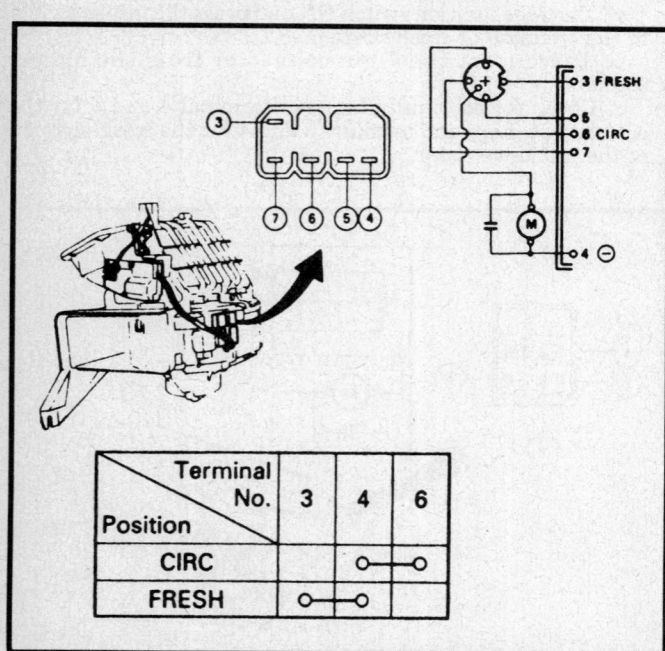

Terminal No. / Position	3	4	6
CIRC		o	o
FRESH	o	o	

Intake actuator testing—1991 Impulse

1991 Impulse

1. To remove the mode actuator.
   a. Disconnect the negative battery cable.
   b. Remove the accelerator pedal bracket fixing bolts and the accelerator pedal with bracket without disconnecting the accelerator cable.
   c. Remove the actuator wire connector.
   d. Remove the actuator rod.
   e. Remove the actuator screws and remove the actuator.
   f. Installation is the reverse of removal procedure.
2. To remove the mix actuator.
   a. Disconnect the negative battery cable.
   b. Remove the glove box assembly.
   c. Remove the actuator wire connector.
   d. Remove the actuator rod.
   e. Remove the actuator screws and the actuator.
   f. Installation is the reverse of removal procedure.
3. To remove the intake actuator.
   a. Disconnect the negative battery cable.
   b. If equipped with air conditioning, remove the duct or evaporator assembly.
   c. Remove the actuator rod.
   d. Remove the actuator wire connector.
   e. Remove the actuator screws and the actuator.
   f. Installation is the reverse of removal procedure.

Power Steering Pressure Switch

OPERATION

When parking, making a full turn or with the air conditioner ON and the engine idling the working pressure of the power steering will tend to overload the small, efficient engine. This problem is avoided by using a pressure switch. When the pressure at the switch reaches 569 ± 71 psi the switch will close. The ECM will activate the mixture bypass solenoid valve and raise the engine rpm. When the vehicle is equipped with air conditioning, the compressor clutch circuit will also be opened. The pressure switch will reopen when the pressure at the switch drops back to 433 ± 78.2 psi.

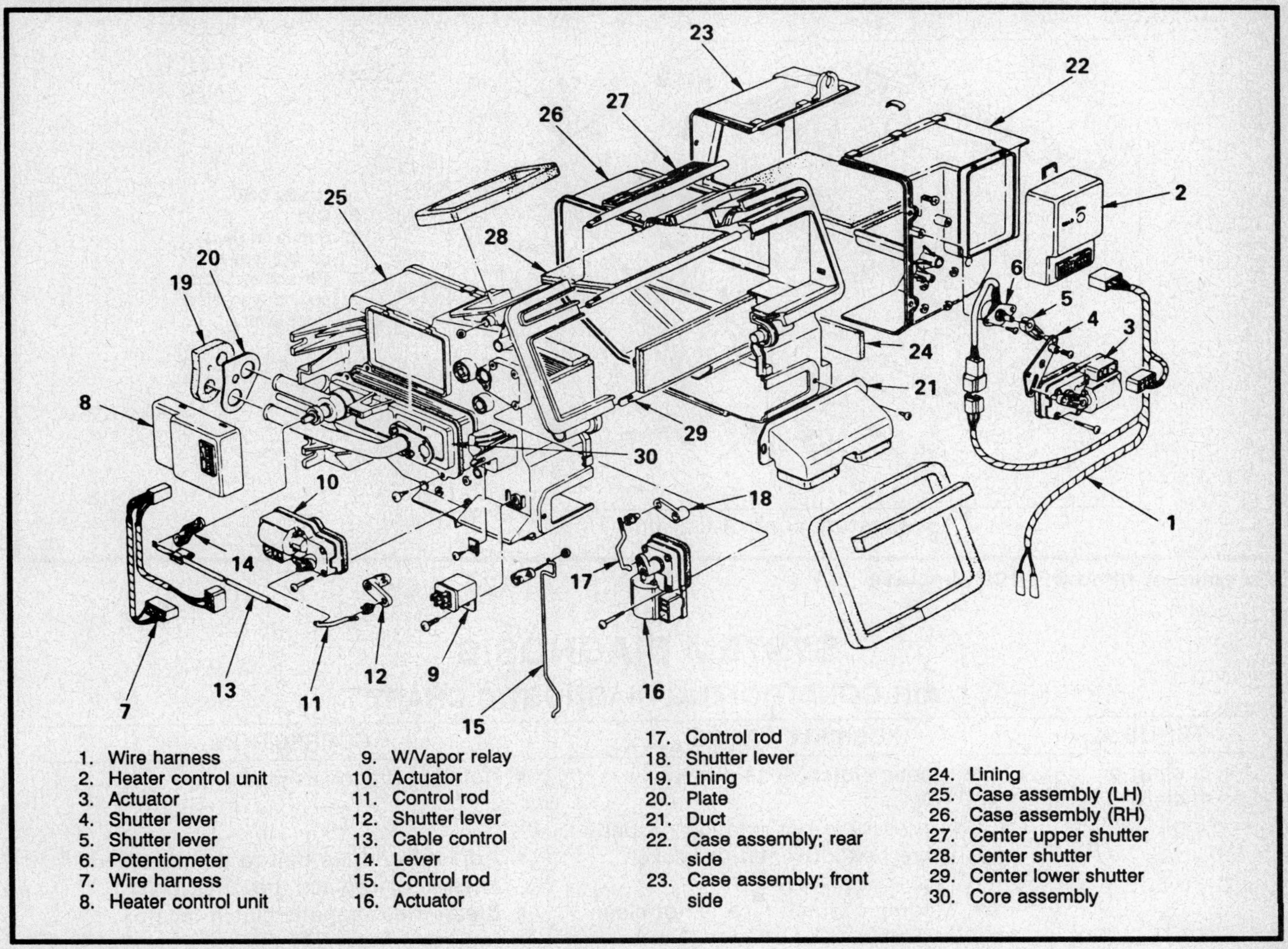
1. Wire harness
2. Heater control unit
3. Actuator
4. Shutter lever
5. Shutter lever
6. Potentiometer
7. Wire harness
8. Heater control unit
9. W/Vapor relay
10. Actuator
11. Control rod
12. Shutter lever
13. Cable control
14. Lever
15. Control rod
16. Actuator
17. Control rod
18. Shutter lever
19. Lining
20. Plate
21. Duct
22. Case assembly; rear side
23. Case assembly; front side
24. Lining
25. Case assembly (LH)
26. Case assembly (RH)
27. Center upper shutter
28. Center shutter
29. Center lower shutter
30. Core assembly

Actuator removal—1989 Impulse

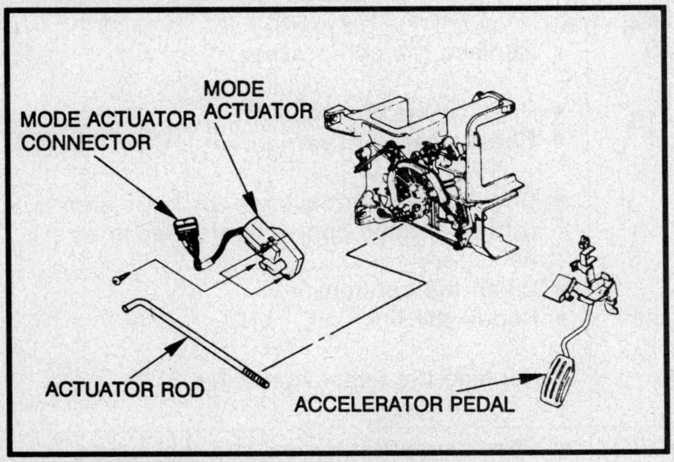
MODE ACTUATOR CONNECTOR
MODE ACTUATOR
ACTUATOR ROD
ACCELERATOR PEDAL

Mode actuator removal—1991 Impulse

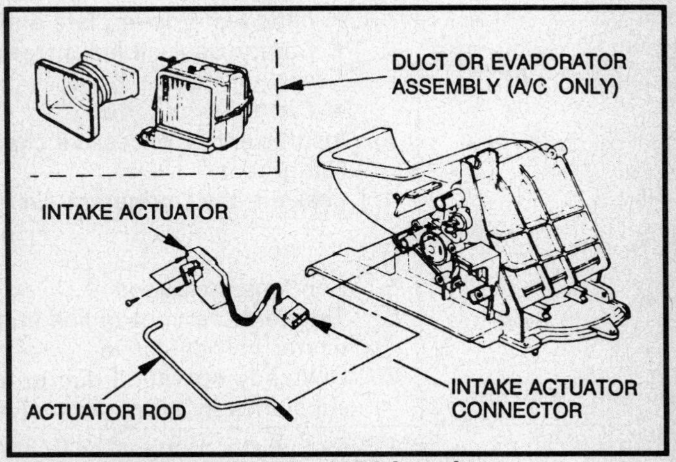
DUCT OR EVAPORATOR ASSEMBLY (A/C ONLY)
INTAKE ACTUATOR
ACTUATOR ROD
INTAKE ACTUATOR CONNECTOR

Intake actuator removal—1991 Impulse

TESTING

1. With the engine idling in **P** for automatic transaxle, neutral for manual transaxle and the air conditioner ON, turn the steering wheel fully to the left; the compressor clutch should disengage and engine rpm should increase.

2. If the system fails to operate properly, disconnect the connector at the pressure switch and repeat system check while testing continuity across the disconnected switch connector.

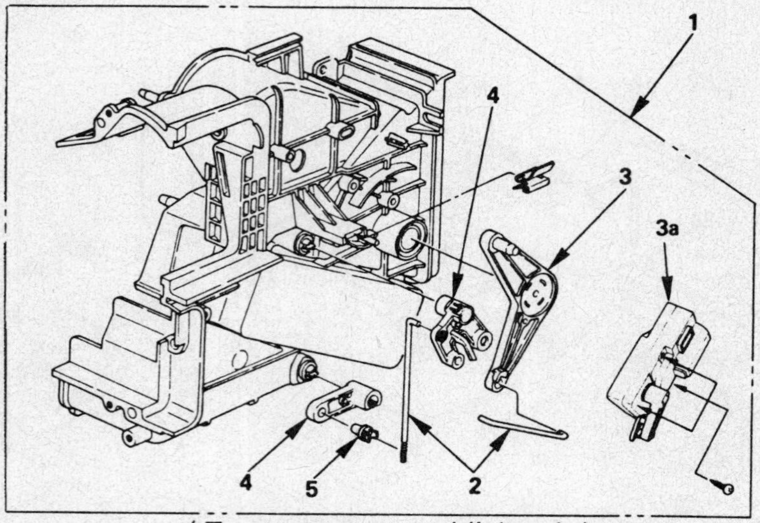
1
4
3
3a
4
5
2
〈 Temparature control link unit 〉
1. Heater unit
2. Rod
3. Sub-lever (lever control type only)
3a. Mix actuator (push control type only)
4. Door lever
5. Clip

Mix actuator removal—1991 Impulse

SYSTEM DIAGNOSIS

AIR CONDITIONING DIAGNOSTIC CHART

TROUBLE	POSSIBLE CAUSE	CORRECTION
No cooling or insufficient cooling	1. Magnetic clutch does not run	• Refer to diagnosis chart
	2. Compressor is not rotating properly	
	• Drive belt loosened or broken	• Adjust the drive belt to the specified tension or replace the drive belt
	• Magnetic clutch face is not clean and slips.	• Clean the magnetic clutch face or replace
	• Incorrect clearance between magnetic plate drive plate and pulley.	• Adjust the clearance
	• Compressor oil leaks from shaft seal or shell	• Replace the compressor
	• Compressor seized	• Replace the compressor
	3. Insufficient or excessive charge of refrigerant	• Check charge of refrigerant
	4. Leaks in the refrigerant system	• Check refrigerant system for leaks and refrigerant line connection or repair as necessary
	5. Condenser clogged	• Clean the condenser
	6. Temperature control link unit of the heater unit defective	• Repair the link unit
	7. Unsteady operation due to foreign substance in expansion valve	• Replace the expansion valve
Insufficient velocity of cooling air	1. Evaporator clogged or frosted	• Check evaporator core and replace or clean the core
	2. Air leaking from cooling unit or air duct	• Check evaporator and duct connection, then repair as necessary
	3. Blower motor does not rotate properly	• Refer to Section for blower motor

AIR CONDITIONING DIAGNOSTIC CHART—CONTINUED

RESULT	SYMPTOM	TROUBLE CAUSE	CORRECTION
Discharge (High) pressure gauge abnormally high	Reduced or no air flow through the condenser	• Condenser clogged or dirty • Condenser or radiator motor does not operate properly	• Clean • Check voltage and motor • Refer to diagnosis chart of condenser fan
	No bubbles in sight glass when condenser is cooled by water	• Excessive refrigerant in system	• Discharge refrigerant as required
	Refrigerant line to the condenser is excessive hot	• Restricted flow of refrigerant in system	• Check expansion valve
	After stopping air conditioner, pressure drops approx. 196 kPa (28 psi.) quickly	• Air in system	• Evacuate and charge refrigerant system
Discharge (High) pressure gauge abnormal low	Insufficient cooling and excessive bubbles in the sight glass	• Insufficient refrigerant in system	• Check for leaks and charge refrigerant as required
	Frost or dew seen on refrigerant line before and after receiver/dehydrator or expansion valve and low-pressure gauge indicates vacuum	• Unsatisfactory valve operation because of clogged expansion or defective temperature sensor of expansion valve • Refrigerant restricted by moisture or dirt in refrigerant freezing	• Evacuate and charge the refrigerant • Clean or replace the expansion valve • Replace the receiver/dehydrator
	When stopping air conditioner, high and low pressure gauge balanced quickly	• Compressor seal defective • Poor compression due to defective gasket of compressor	• Replace compressor
Suction (Low) pressure gauge abnormal high	Low pressure gauge is lowered after condenser is cooled by water	• Excessive refrigerant in system	• Discharge refrigerant as necessary
	Low pressure hose of around the compressor refrigerant line connector is lower than around evaporator	• Unsatisfactory operation of valve due to defective temperature sensor of expansion valve • Expansion valve opens too long • Compressor suction strainer defective	• Clean or replace expansion valve • Replace compressor
	When stopping air conditioner, high and low pressure gauge is balanced soon	• Compressor gasket is defective	• Replace compressor

AIR CONDITIONING DIAGNOSTIC CHART—CONTINUED

RESULT	SYMPTOM	TROUBLE CAUSE	CORRECTION
Suction (Low) pressure abnormal low	Air conditioner turns off before the room temperature is sufficiently cool	• Electro thermo sensor defective	• Check the electro thermo sensor and replace as necessary
	Condenser is not hot and excessive bubble in sight glass	• Insufficient refrigerant	• Charge refrigerant as required
	Frost on the expansion valve inlet line	• Expansion valve clogged	• Clean or replace the expansion valve
	A distinct difference in temperature develops between the inlet and outlet refrigerant lines of the receiver/dehydrator is frosted.	• Receiver/dehydrator clogged	• Replace the receiver/dehydrator
	Expansion valve outlet refrigerant line is not cold and low-pressure gauge indicates vacuum	• The temperature sensor of the expansion valve is defective, and the valve cannot regulate the correct flow of the refrigerant	• Replace the expansion valve
Suction (Low) and Discharge (High) pressure abnormal high	No bubbles in sight glass after condenser is cooled by water	• Excessive refrigerant in system	• Discharge refrigerant as required
	Reduce air flow through condenser	• Condenser clogged • Condenser or radiator motor does not rotate properly	• Clean • Check voltage and motor
	Suction (Low) pressure hose is not cold	• Air in system	• Evacuate and charge refrigerant
Suction (Low) and Discharge (High) pressure abnormal low	Excessive bubbles in the sight glass	• Insufficient refrigerant in system	• Check for leaks and repair • Charge refrigerant as required

WIRING SCHEMATICS

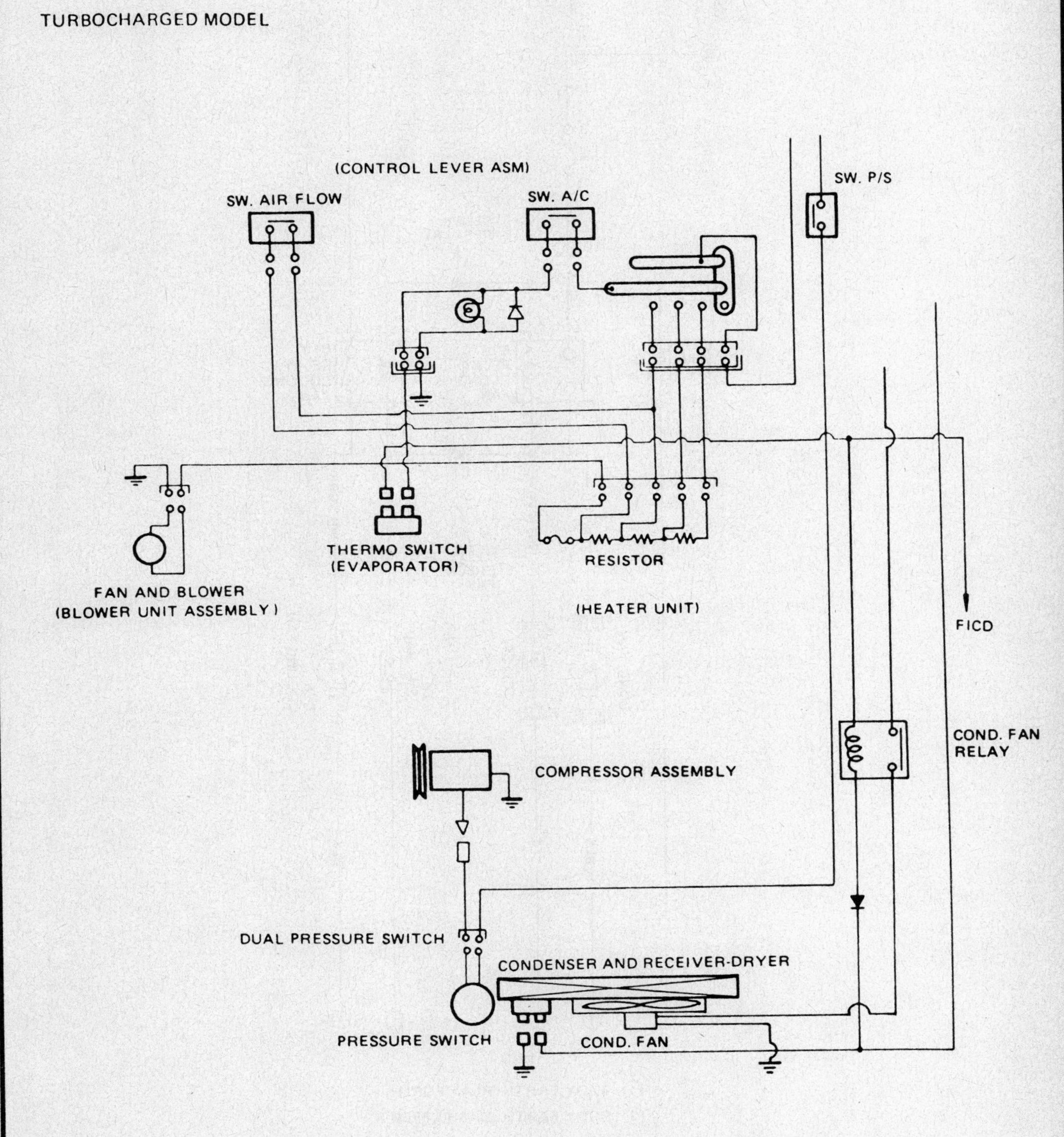
TURBOCHARGED MODEL
(CONTROL LEVER ASM)
SW. AIR FLOW
SW. A/C
SW. P/S
FAN AND BLOWER
(BLOWER UNIT ASSEMBLY)
THERMO SWITCH
(EVAPORATOR)
RESISTOR
(HEATER UNIT)
FICD
COND. FAN
RELAY
COMPRESSOR ASSEMBLY
DUAL PRESSURE SWITCH
CONDENSER AND RECEIVER-DRYER
PRESSURE SWITCH
COND. FAN

1989 I-Mark SOHC Turbo wiring schematic

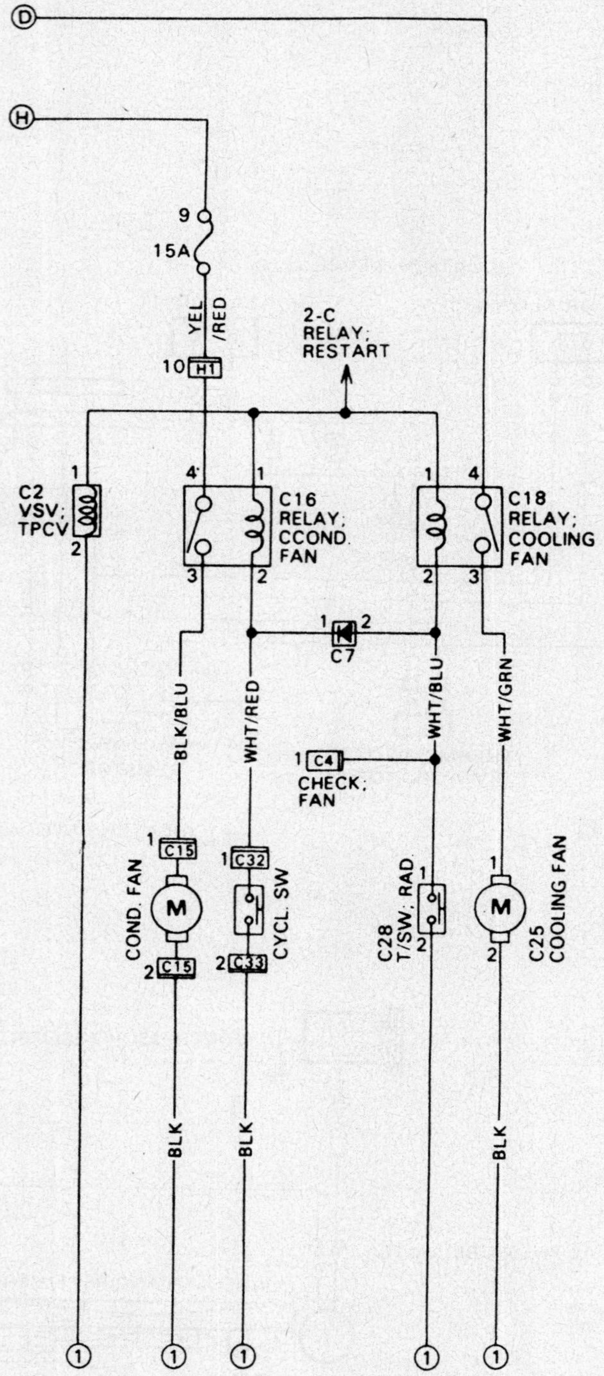
D
H
9
15A
YEL /RED
10 H1
2-C RELAY; RESTART
C2 VSV; TPCV
C16 RELAY; CCOND. FAN
C18 RELAY; COOLING FAN
C7
BLK/BLU
WHT/RED
WHT/BLU
WHT/GRN
C4 CHECK; FAN
C15
COND. FAN
C32
C33
CYCL. SW
C28 T/SW; RAD.
C25 COOLING FAN
BLK
BLK
BLK

① BODY EARTH: PLAT FORM
② BODY EARTH: DASH UPPER
③ BODY EARTH: RR END

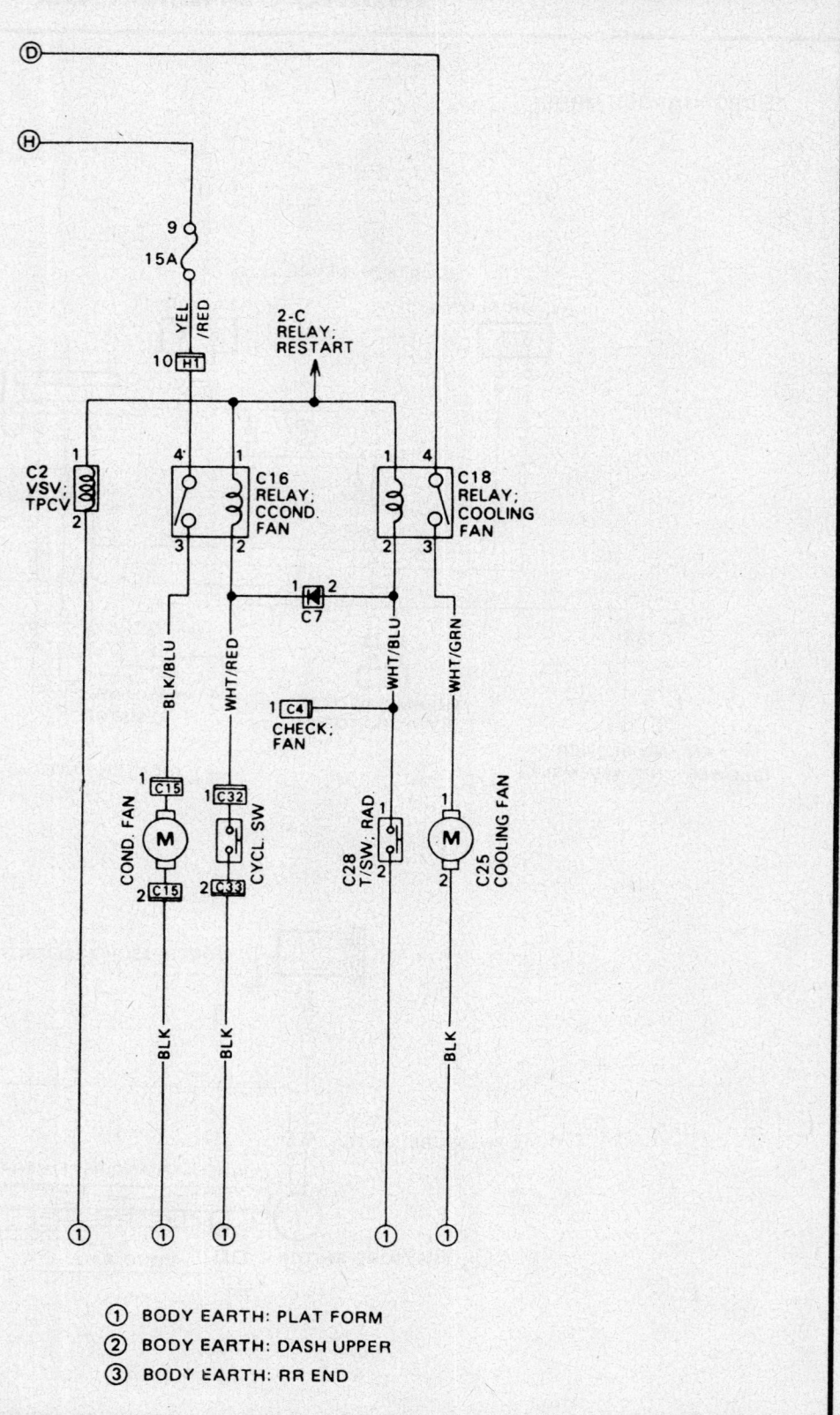

1989 I-Mark SOHC Turbo cooling fan wiring schematic—continued

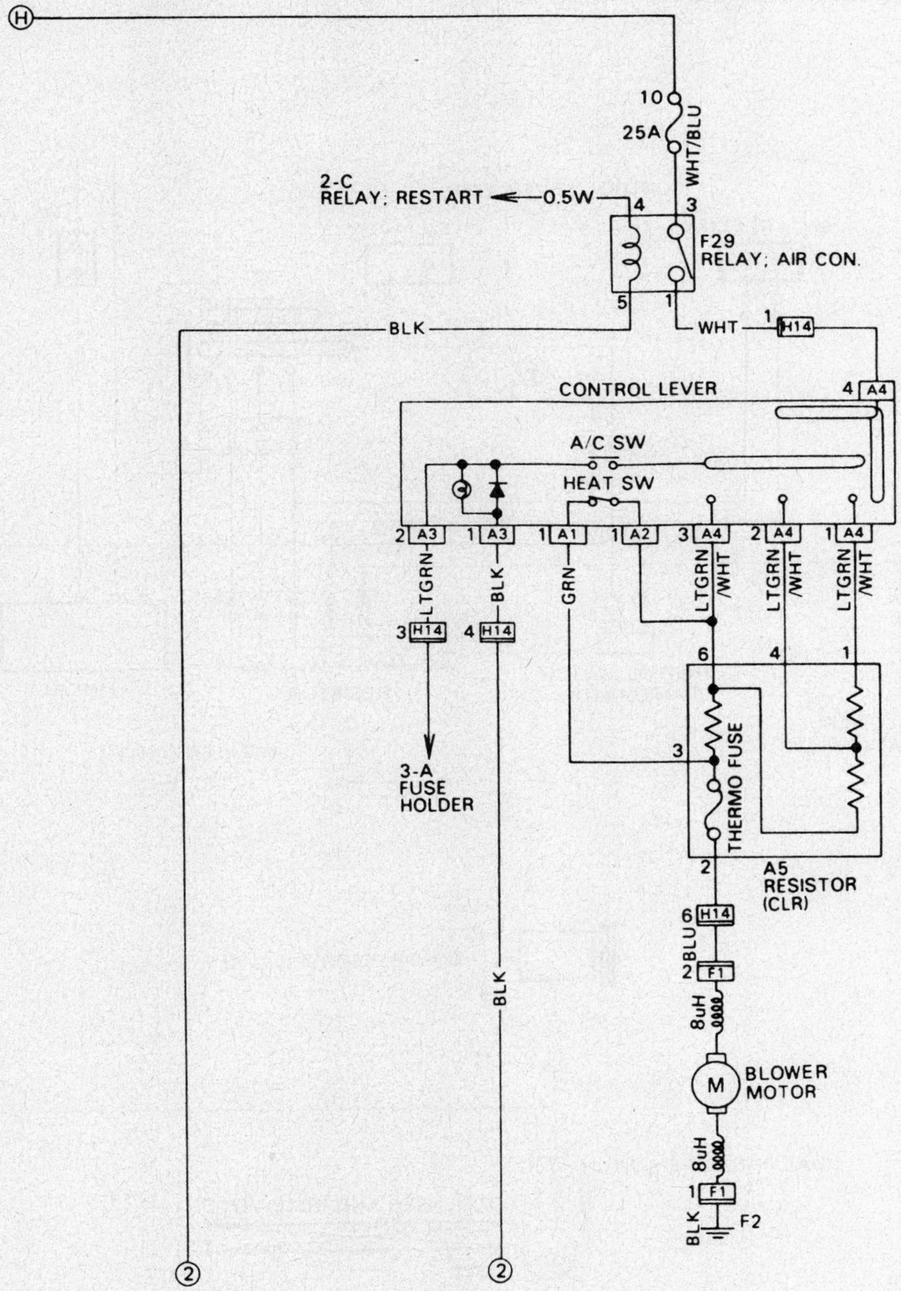
H
10
25A
WHT/BLU
2-C
RELAY; RESTART
0.5W
4
3
F29
RELAY; AIR CON.
5
1
BLK
WHT
H14
CONTROL LEVER
A4
A/C SW
HEAT SW
A3
A1
A2
LTGRN
BLK
GRN
LTGRN /WHT
3-A
FUSE
HOLDER
6
THERMO FUSE
A5
RESISTOR
(CLR)
BLU
F1
8uH
M
BLOWER
MOTOR
F2
2

① BODY EARTH: PLAT FORM
② BODY EARTH: DASH UPPER
③ BODY EARTH: RR END

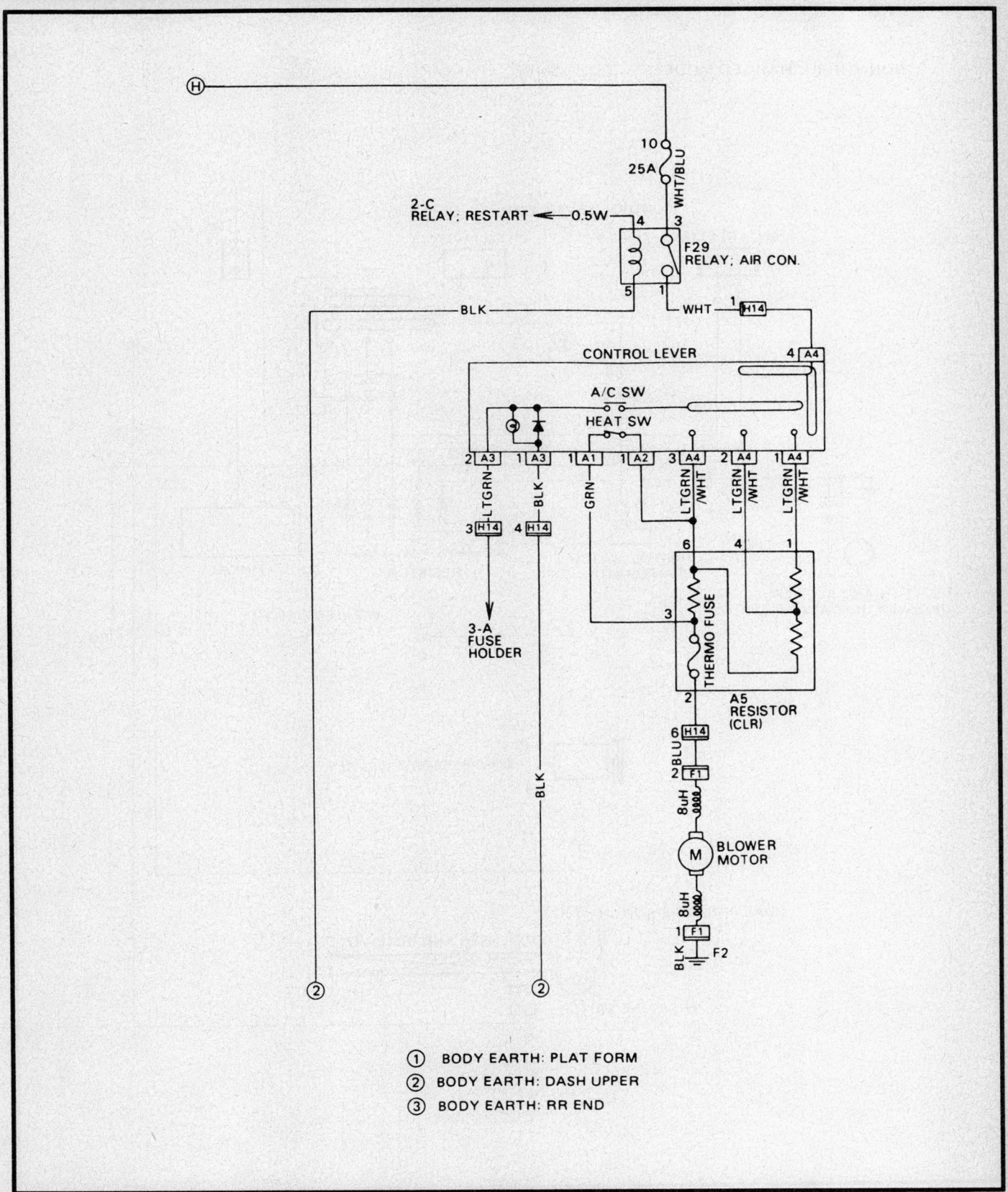

1989 I-Mark SOHC Turbo control switch wiring schematic—continued

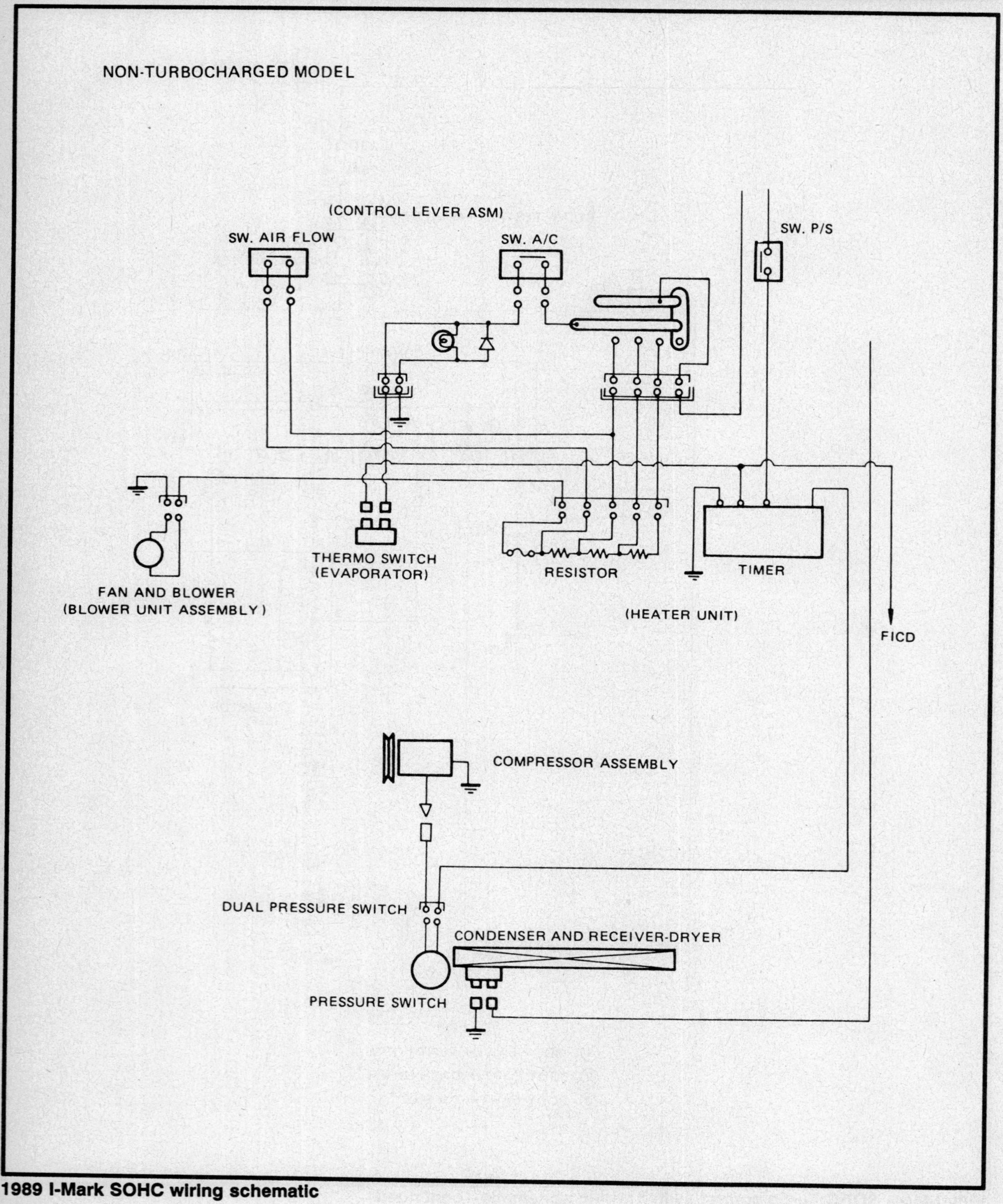
NON-TURBOCHARGED MODEL
(CONTROL LEVER ASM)
SW. AIR FLOW
SW. A/C
SW. P/S
THERMO SWITCH
(EVAPORATOR)
FAN AND BLOWER
(BLOWER UNIT ASSEMBLY)
RESISTOR
TIMER
(HEATER UNIT)
FICD
COMPRESSOR ASSEMBLY
DUAL PRESSURE SWITCH
CONDENSER AND RECEIVER-DRYER
PRESSURE SWITCH

1989 I-Mark SOHC wiring schematic

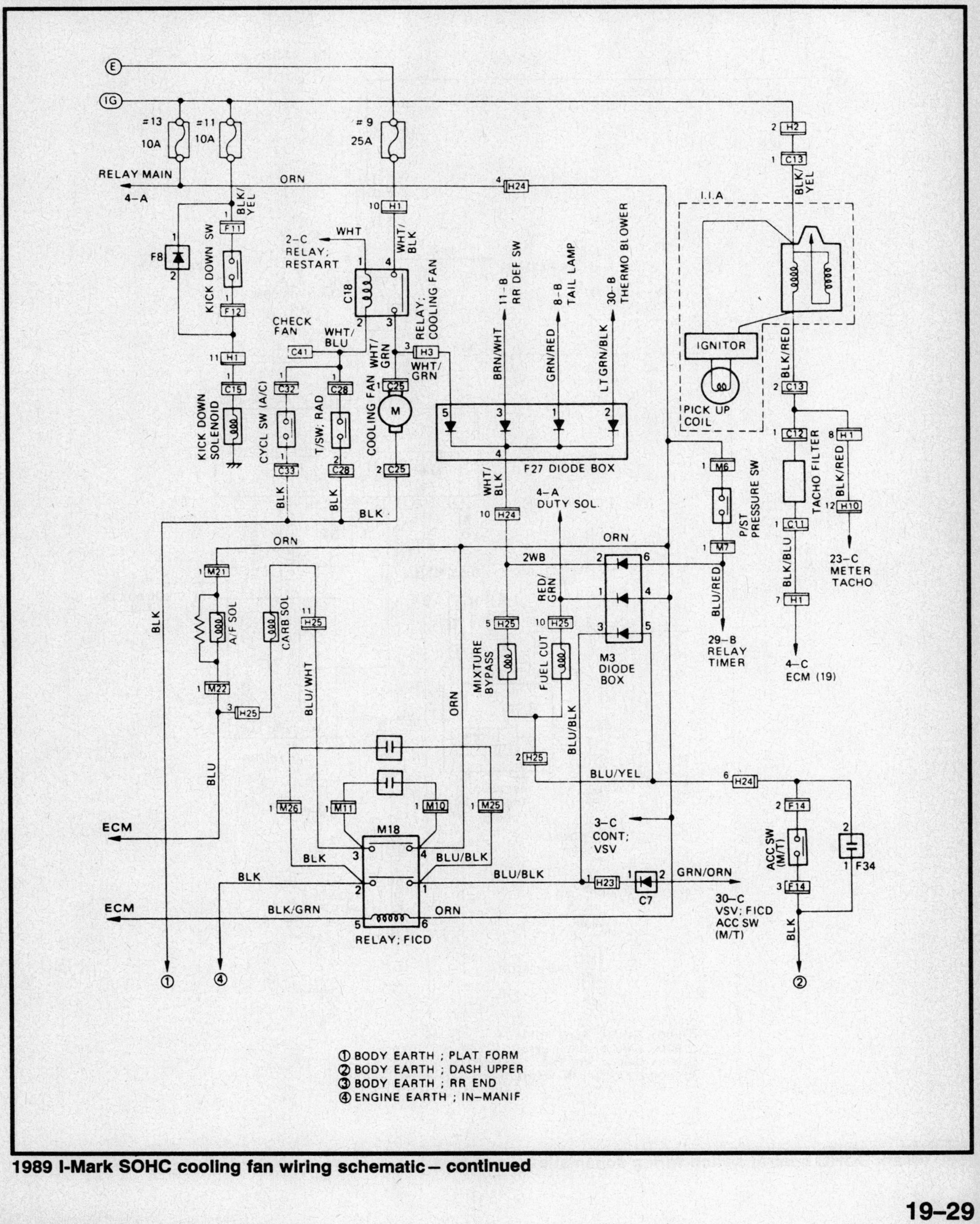
E
IG
#13
10A
#11
10A
#9
25A
RELAY MAIN
4–A
ORN
H24
H1
BLK/YEL
F11
F8
KICK DOWN SW
F12
2–C
RELAY; RESTART
WHT
WHT/BLK
C18
RELAY; COOLING FAN
CHECK FAN
WHT/BLU
C41
H3
WHT/GRN
C15
KICK DOWN SOLENOID
C32
CYCL SW (A/C)
C33
C28
T/SW; RAD
C25
COOLING FAN
M
11–B
RR DEF SW
8–B
TAIL LAMP
30–B
THERMO BLOWER
BRN/WHT
GRN/RED
LT GRN/BLK
F27 DIODE BOX
BLK
WHT/BLK
4–A
DUTY SOL.
2WB
RED/GRN
M3
DIODE BOX
MIXTURE BYPASS
FUEL CUT
H25
BLU/BLK
BLU/YEL
M21
A/F SOL
CARB SOL
M22
BLU/WHT
BLU
ECM
M26
M11
M10
M25
M18
BLK/GRN
RELAY; FICD
H23
C7
GRN/ORN
3–C
CONT; VSV
30–C
VSV; FICD
ACC SW
(M/T)
I.I.A
H2
C13
IGNITOR
PICK UP COIL
BLK/RED
C12
TACHO FILTER
C11
BLK/BLU
H10
23–C
METER TACHO
M6
P/ST PRESSURE SW
M7
BLU/RED
29–B
RELAY TIMER
4–C
ECM (19)
F14
ACC SW (M/T)
F34
① BODY EARTH ; PLAT FORM
② BODY EARTH ; DASH UPPER
③ BODY EARTH ; RR END
④ ENGINE EARTH ; IN–MANIF

1989 I-Mark SOHC cooling fan wiring schematic—continued

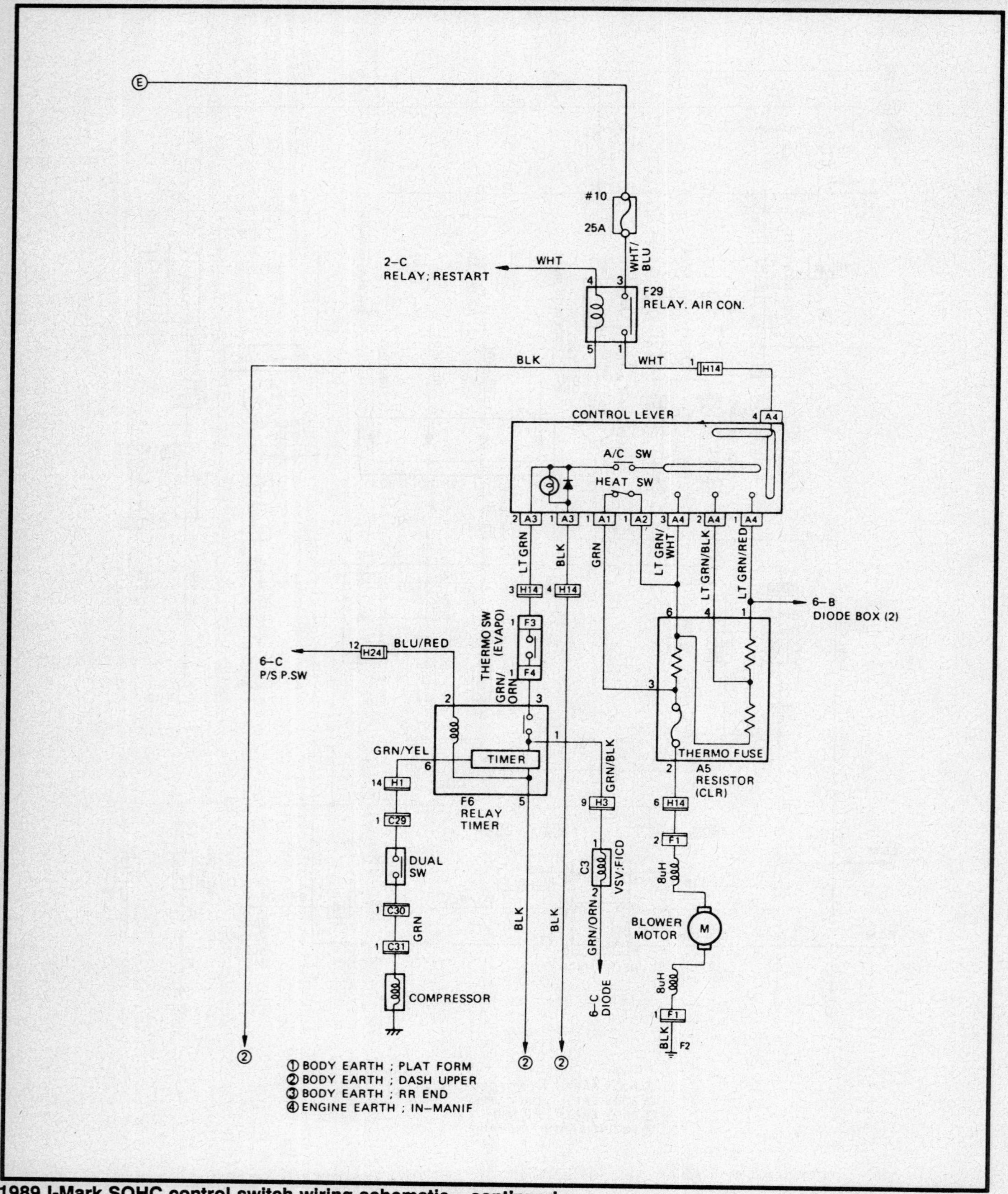
#10
25A
WHT/BLU
2–C
RELAY; RESTART
WHT
4
3
F29
RELAY. AIR CON.
5
1
BLK
WHT
H14
CONTROL LEVER
A4
A/C SW
HEAT SW
A3
A3
A1
A2
A4
A4
A4
LT GRN
BLK
GRN
LT GRN/WHT
LT GRN/BLK
LT GRN/RED
6–B
DIODE BOX (2)
H14
H14
THERMO SW (EVAPO)
F3
F4
GRN/ORN
6–C
P/S P.SW
H24
BLU/RED
TIMER
GRN/YEL
F6
RELAY
TIMER
GRN/BLK
THERMO FUSE
A5
RESISTOR
(CLR)
H1
C29
DUAL SW
C30
GRN
C31
COMPRESSOR
H3
C3
VSV;FICD
GRN/ORN
6–C
DIODE
F1
8uH
BLOWER MOTOR
M
F2
BLK
① BODY EARTH ; PLAT FORM
② BODY EARTH ; DASH UPPER
③ BODY EARTH ; RR END
④ ENGINE EARTH ; IN–MANIF

1989 I-Mark SOHC control switch wiring schematic – continued

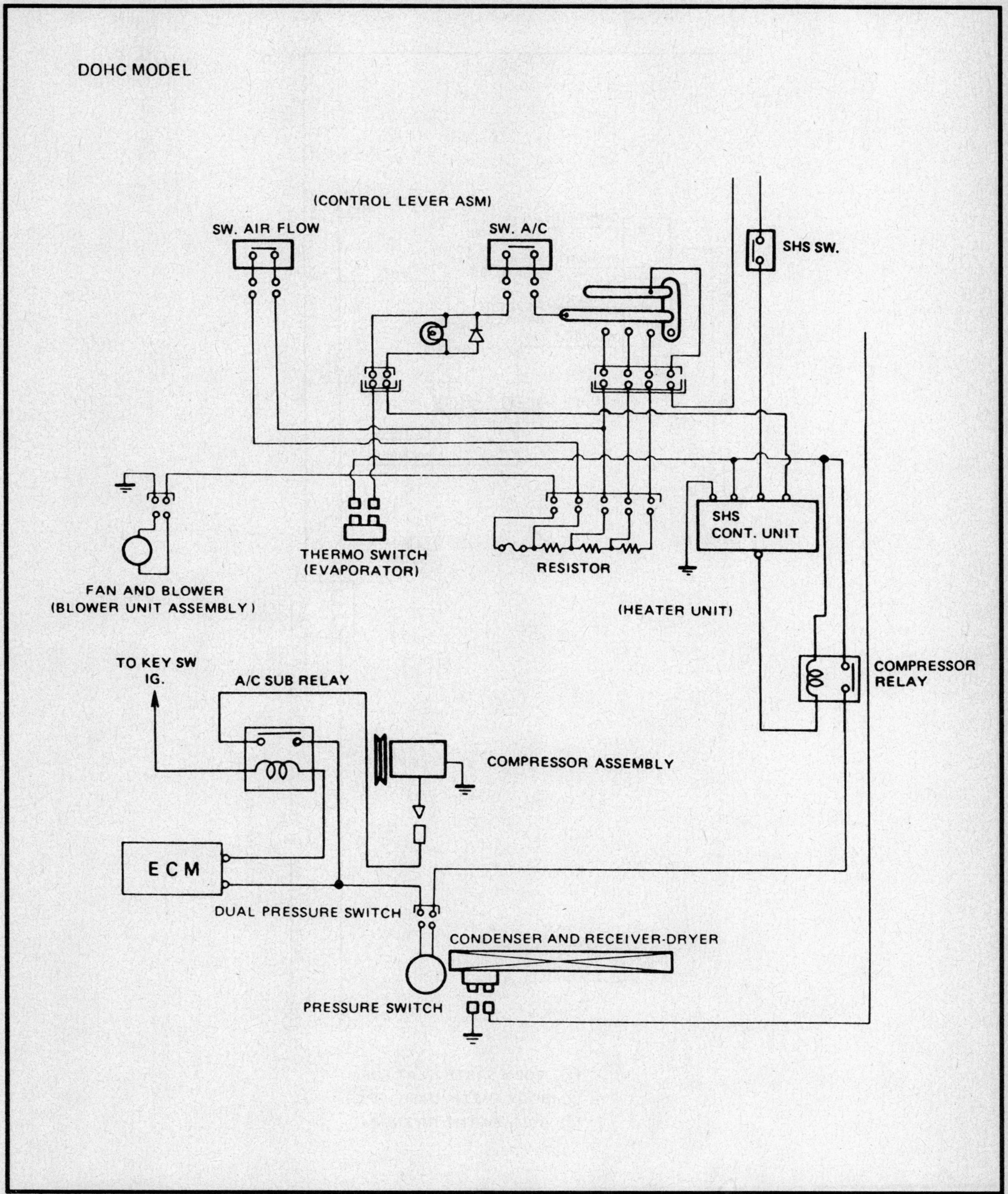
DOHC MODEL
(CONTROL LEVER ASM)
SW. AIR FLOW
SW. A/C
SHS SW.
THERMO SWITCH
(EVAPORATOR)
RESISTOR
FAN AND BLOWER
(BLOWER UNIT ASSEMBLY)
SHS
CONT. UNIT
(HEATER UNIT)
COMPRESSOR
RELAY
TO KEY SW
IG.
A/C SUB RELAY
COMPRESSOR ASSEMBLY
ECM
DUAL PRESSURE SWITCH
CONDENSER AND RECEIVER-DRYER
PRESSURE SWITCH

1989 I-Mark DOHC wiring schematic

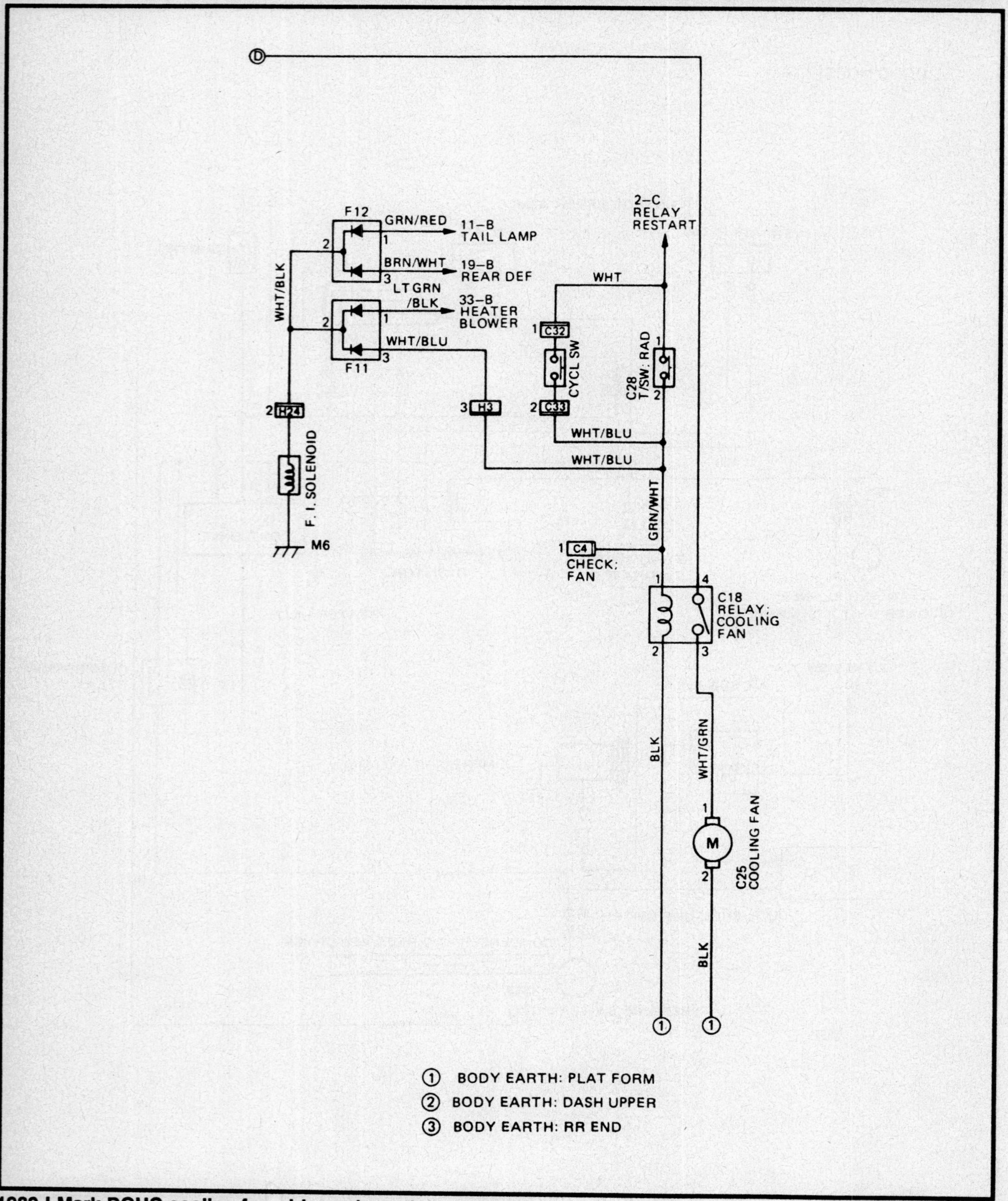
D
F12
GRN/RED
11–B
TAIL LAMP
BRN/WHT
19–B
REAR DEF
LTGRN
/BLK
33–B
HEATER
BLOWER
WHT/BLU
F11
WHT/BLK
H24
F. I. SOLENOID
M6
H3
2–C
RELAY
RESTART
WHT
C32
CYCL SW
C33
C28
T/SW: RAD
WHT/BLU
WHT/BLU
GRN/WHT
C4
CHECK:
FAN
C18
RELAY:
COOLING
FAN
BLK
WHT/GRN
M
C25
COOLING FAN
BLK
① BODY EARTH: PLAT FORM
② BODY EARTH: DASH UPPER
③ BODY EARTH: RR END

1989 I-Mark DOHC cooling fan wiring schematic— continued

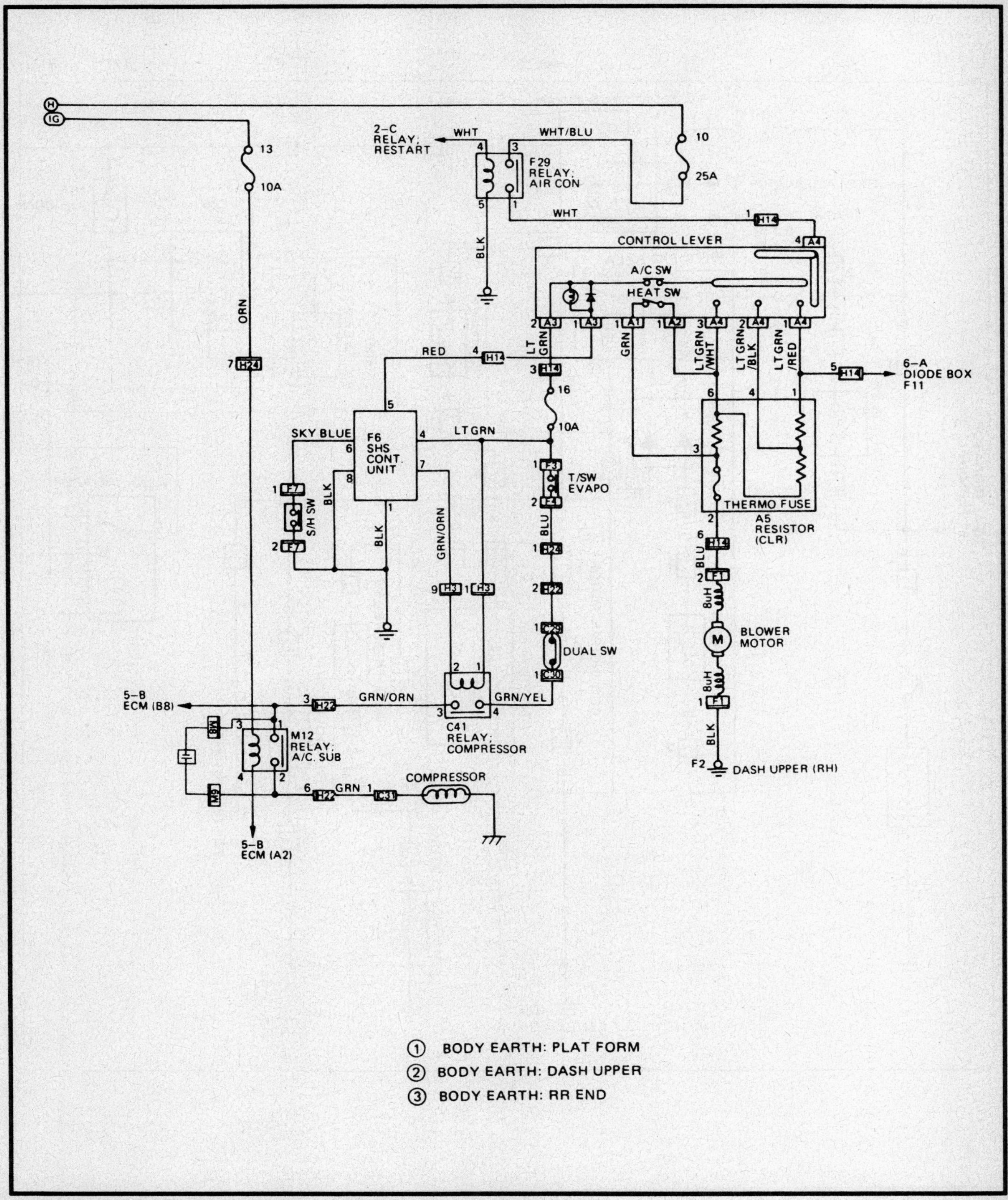
2-C
RELAY;
RESTART
WHT
WHT/BLU
F29
RELAY;
AIR CON
10
25A
13
10A
BLK
ORN
WHT
H14
CONTROL LEVER
A4
A/C SW
HEAT SW
A3
A1
A2
LT GRN
GRN
LTGRN /WHT
LT GRN /BLK
LT GRN /RED
RED
H14
6-A
DIODE BOX
F11
H24
16
10A
F6
SHS
CONT.
UNIT
SKY BLUE
LT GRN
THERMO FUSE
A5
RESISTOR
(CLR)
F7
S/H SW
T/SW
EVAPO
F3
F4
BLU
H24
H3
H22
C29
C30
DUAL SW
GRN/ORN
BLOWER
MOTOR
8uH
F1
5-B
ECM (B8)
GRN/ORN
GRN/YEL
C41
RELAY;
COMPRESSOR
M12
RELAY;
A/C. SUB
F2
DASH UPPER (RH)
COMPRESSOR
GRN
C31
M9
5-B
ECM (A2)
① BODY EARTH: PLAT FORM
② BODY EARTH: DASH UPPER
③ BODY EARTH: RR END

1989 I-Mark DOHC control switch wiring schematic— continued

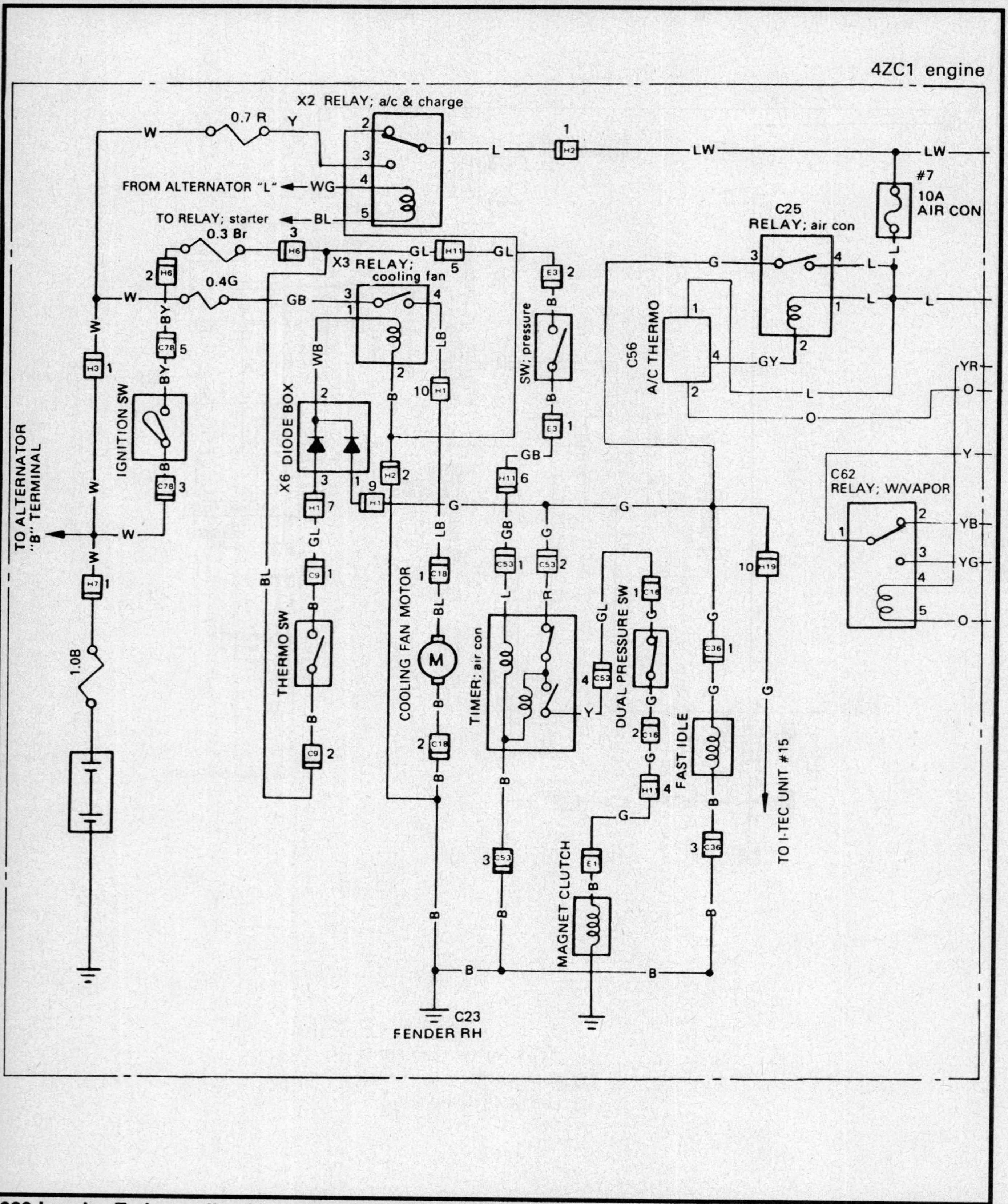
4ZC1 engine
X2 RELAY; a/c & charge
0.7 R
FROM ALTERNATOR "L"
TO RELAY; starter
0.3 Br
X3 RELAY; cooling fan
0.4G
#7
10A
AIR CON
C25
RELAY; air con
C56
A/C THERMO
SW; pressure
IGNITION SW
X6 DIODE BOX
TO ALTERNATOR "B" TERMINAL
C62
RELAY; W/VAPOR
THERMO SW
COOLING FAN MOTOR
TIMER; air con
DUAL PRESSURE SW
FAST IDLE
TO I-TEC UNIT #15
1.0B
MAGNET CLUTCH
C23
FENDER RH

1989 Impulse Turbo cooling fan and air conditioning wiring schematic

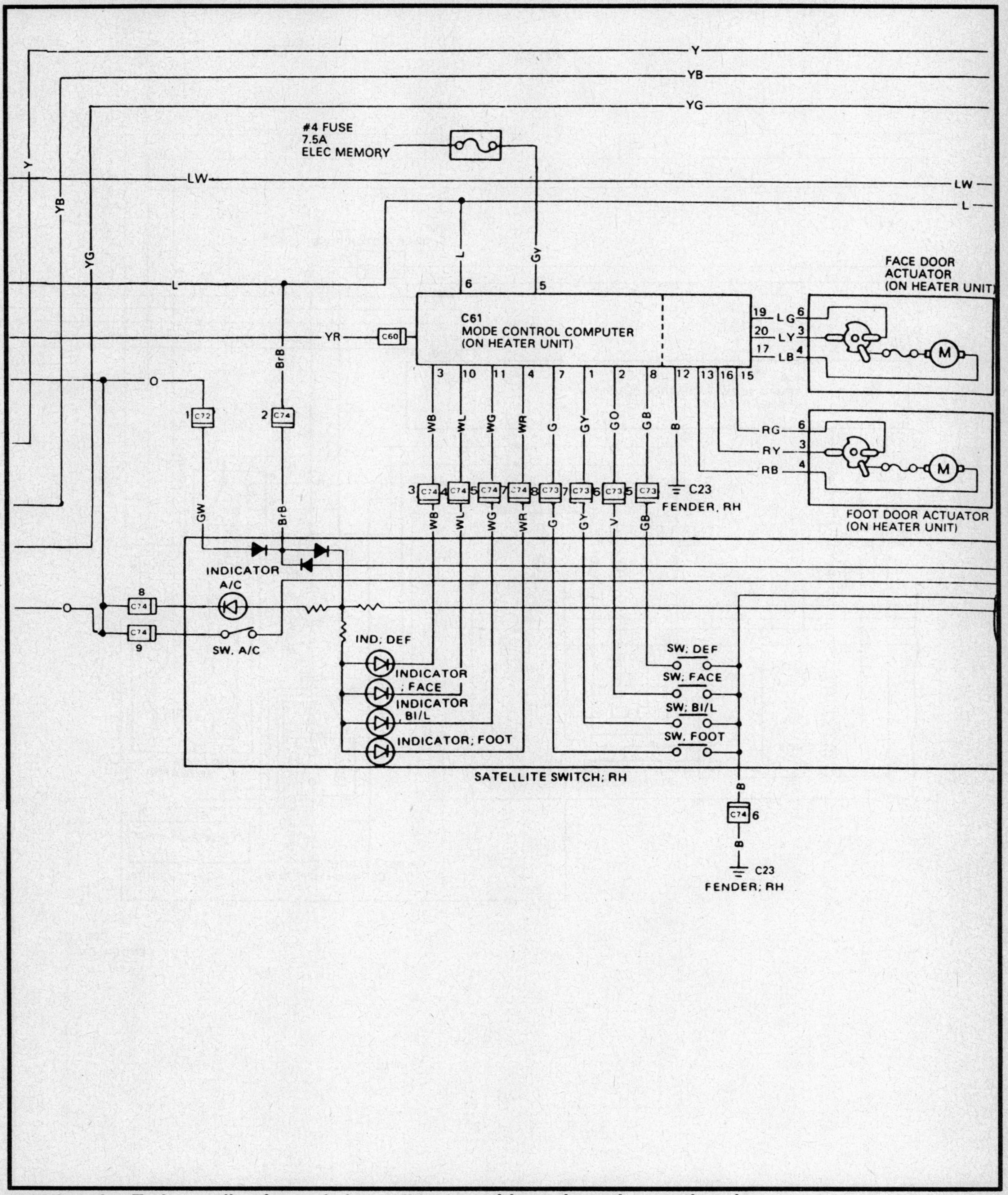
Y
YB
YG
#4 FUSE
7.5A
ELEC MEMORY
LW
L
Gy
C61
MODE CONTROL COMPUTER
(ON HEATER UNIT)
YR
C60
FACE DOOR
ACTUATOR
(ON HEATER UNIT)
LG
LY
LB
RG
RY
RB
FOOT DOOR ACTUATOR
(ON HEATER UNIT)
C72
C74
C73
C23
FENDER, RH
O
GW
BrB
WB
WL
WG
WR
G
GY
GO
GB
B
V
INDICATOR
A/C
SW, A/C
IND; DEF
INDICATOR
; FACE
INDICATOR
BI/L
INDICATOR; FOOT
SW; DEF
SW; FACE
SW; BI/L
SW, FOOT
SATELLITE SWITCH; RH
C23
FENDER; RH

1989 Impulse Turbo cooling fan and air conditioning wiring schematic—continued

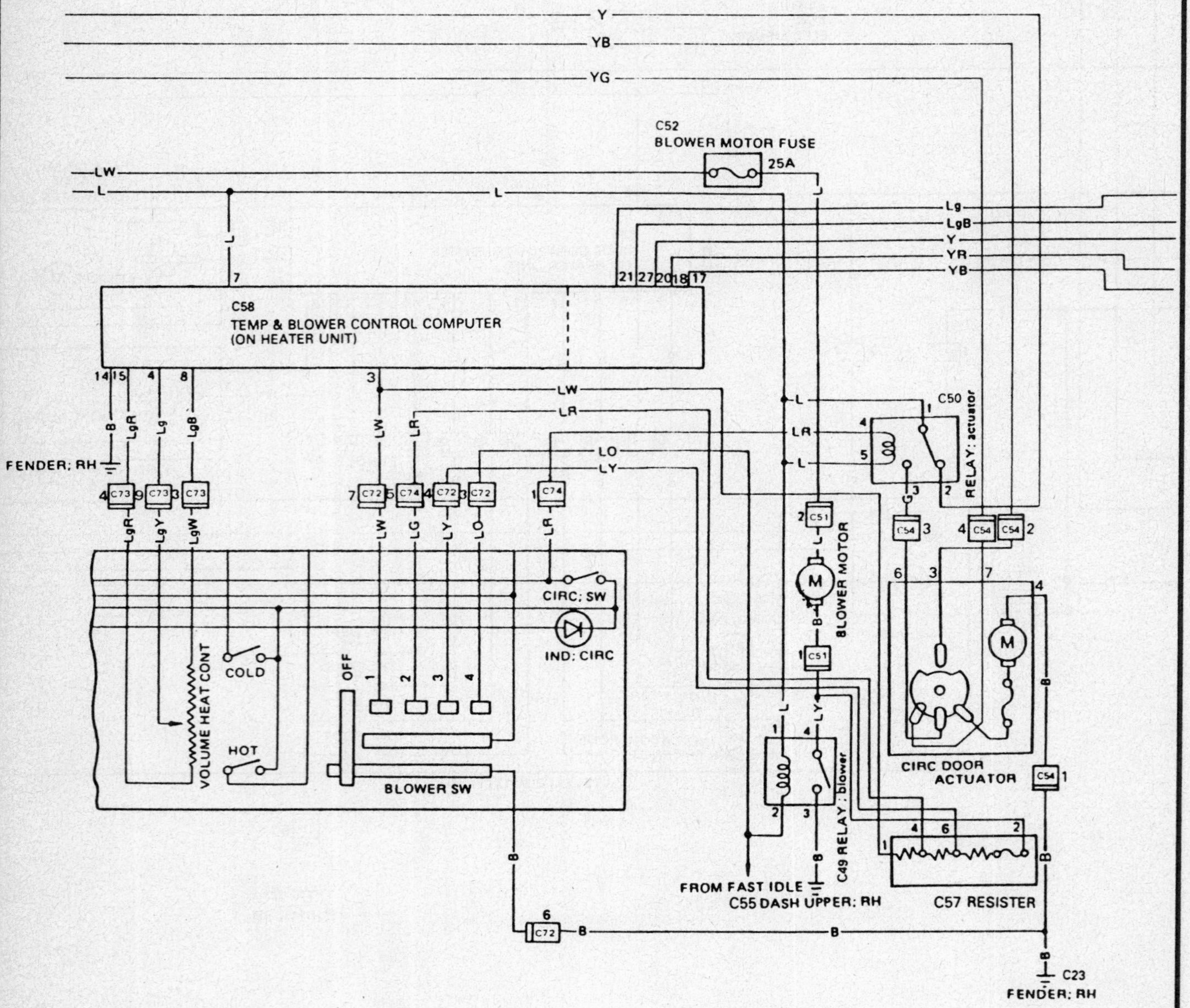
Y
YB
YG
C52
BLOWER MOTOR FUSE
25A
LW
L
Lg
LgB
Y
YR
YB
21 27 20 18 17
7
C58
TEMP & BLOWER CONTROL COMPUTER
(ON HEATER UNIT)
14 15 4 8 3
B
LgR
Lg
LgB
FENDER; RH
LW
LR
LO
LY
C73
C72
C74
LgR
LgY
LgW
LG
C50
RELAY; actuator
C51
BLOWER MOTOR
M
C54
CIRC; SW
IND; CIRC
VOLUME HEAT CONT
COLD
HOT
OFF
1 2 3 4
BLOWER SW
CIRC DOOR ACTUATOR
C49 RELAY; blower
FROM FAST IDLE
C55 DASH UPPER; RH
C57 RESISTER
C23
FENDER; RH

1989 Impulse Turbo cooling fan and air conditioning wiring schematic—continued

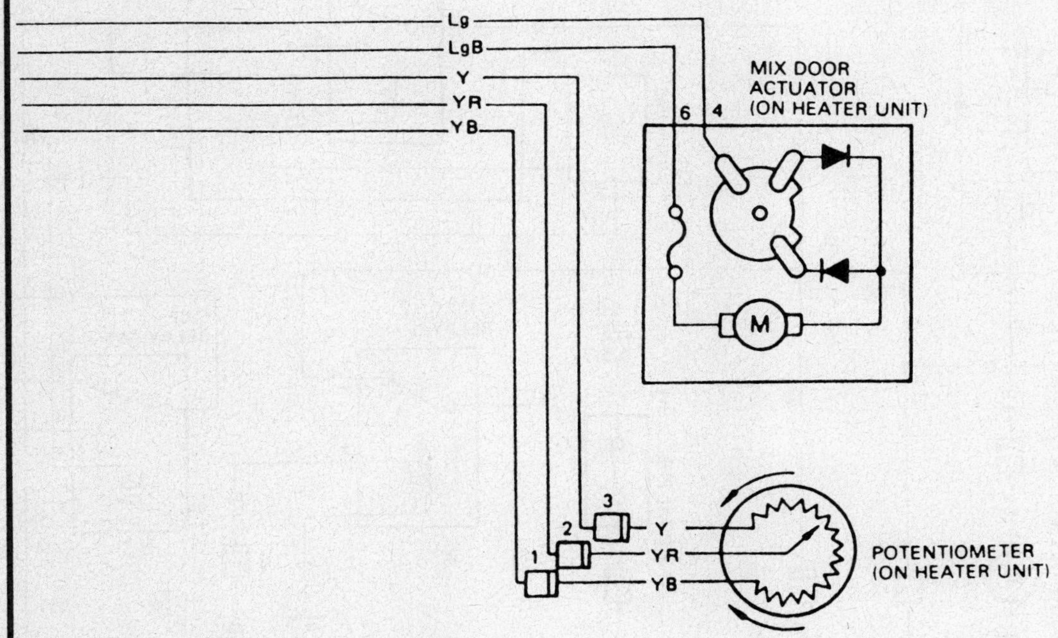
Lg
LgB
Y
YR
YB
MIX DOOR
ACTUATOR
(ON HEATER UNIT)
6
4
M
3
2
1
Y
YR
YB
POTENTIOMETER
(ON HEATER UNIT)

1989 Impulse Turbo cooling fan and air conditioning wiring schematic—continued

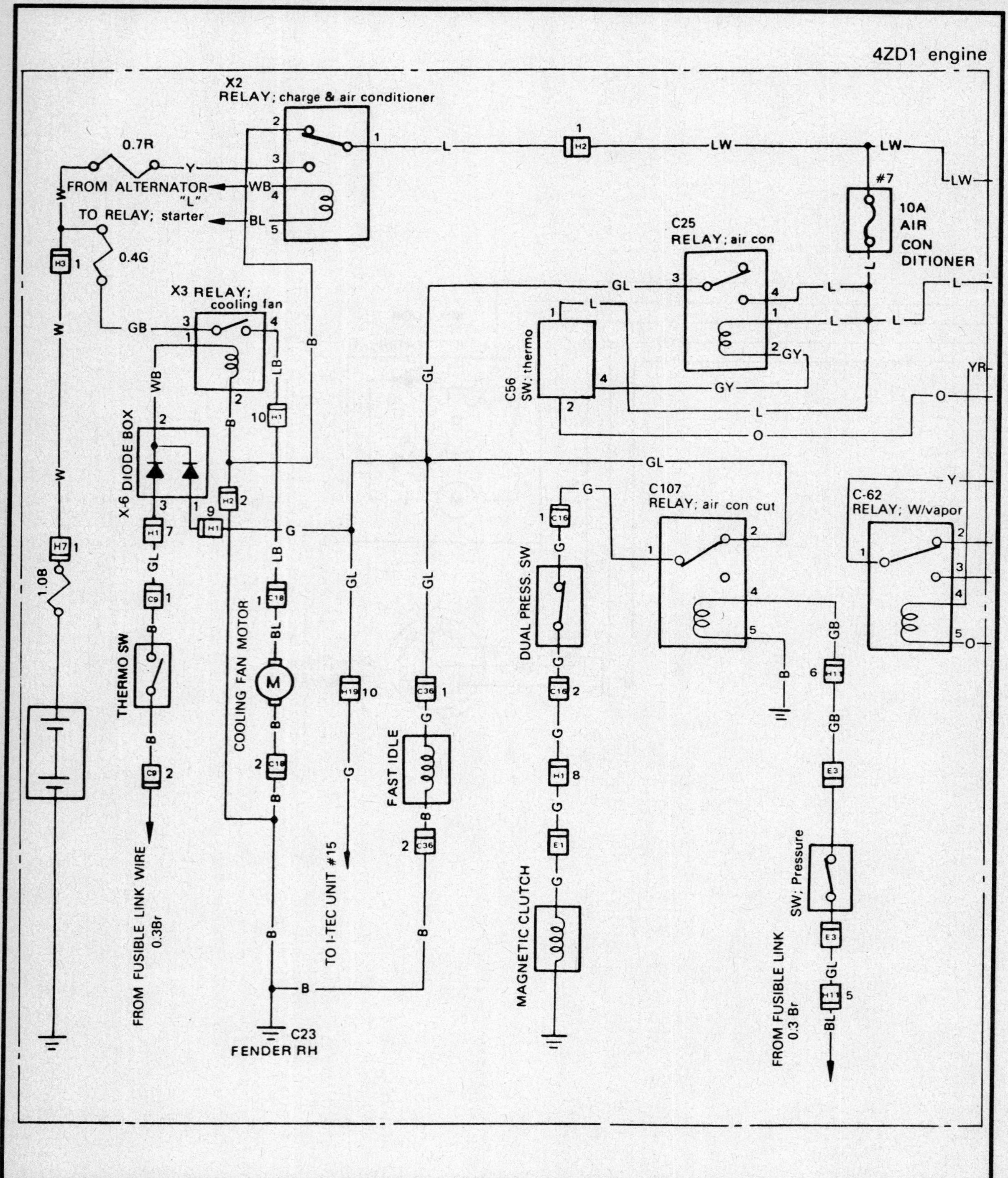
4ZD1 engine
X2
RELAY; charge & air conditioner
0.7R
FROM ALTERNATOR "L"
TO RELAY; starter
0.4G
X3 RELAY; cooling fan
X-6 DIODE BOX
THERMO SW
FROM FUSIBLE LINK WIRE 0.3Br
1.0B
COOLING FAN MOTOR
C23 FENDER RH
TO I-TEC UNIT #15
FAST IDLE
DUAL PRESS. SW
MAGNETIC CLUTCH
C56 SW; thermo
C25 RELAY; air con
C107 RELAY; air con cut
C-62 RELAY; W/vapor
#7 10A AIR CON DITIONER
SW; Pressure
FROM FUSIBLE LINK 0.3 Br

1989 Impulse Non-Turbo cooling fan and air conditioning wiring schematic

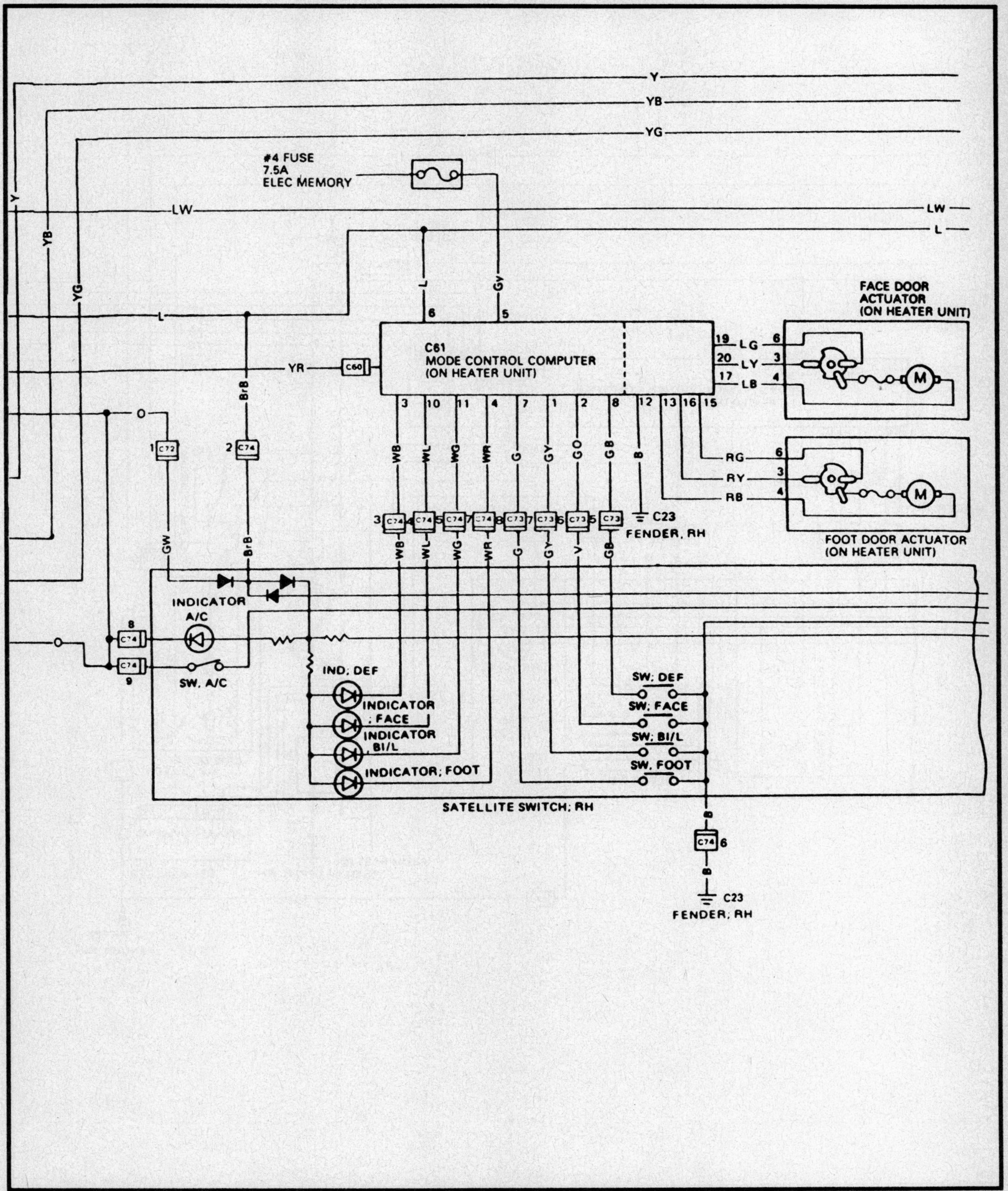
Y
YB
YG
#4 FUSE
7.5A
ELEC MEMORY
LW
L
Gy
6
5
FACE DOOR
ACTUATOR
(ON HEATER UNIT)
C61
MODE CONTROL COMPUTER
(ON HEATER UNIT)
YR
C60
19 LG 6
20 LY 3
17 LB 4
M
3 10 11 4 7 1 2 8 12 13 16 15
O
BrB
C72
C74
WB
WL
WG
WR
G
GY
GO
GB
B
RG 6
RY 3
RB 4
C73
C23
FENDER, RH
FOOT DOOR ACTUATOR
(ON HEATER UNIT)
GW
V
INDICATOR
A/C
8
9
SW, A/C
IND; DEF
INDICATOR
; FACE
INDICATOR
; BI/L
INDICATOR; FOOT
SW; DEF
SW; FACE
SW; BI/L
SW; FOOT
SATELLITE SWITCH; RH
6
C23
FENDER; RH

1989 Impulse Non-Turbo cooling fan and air conditioning wiring schematic—continued

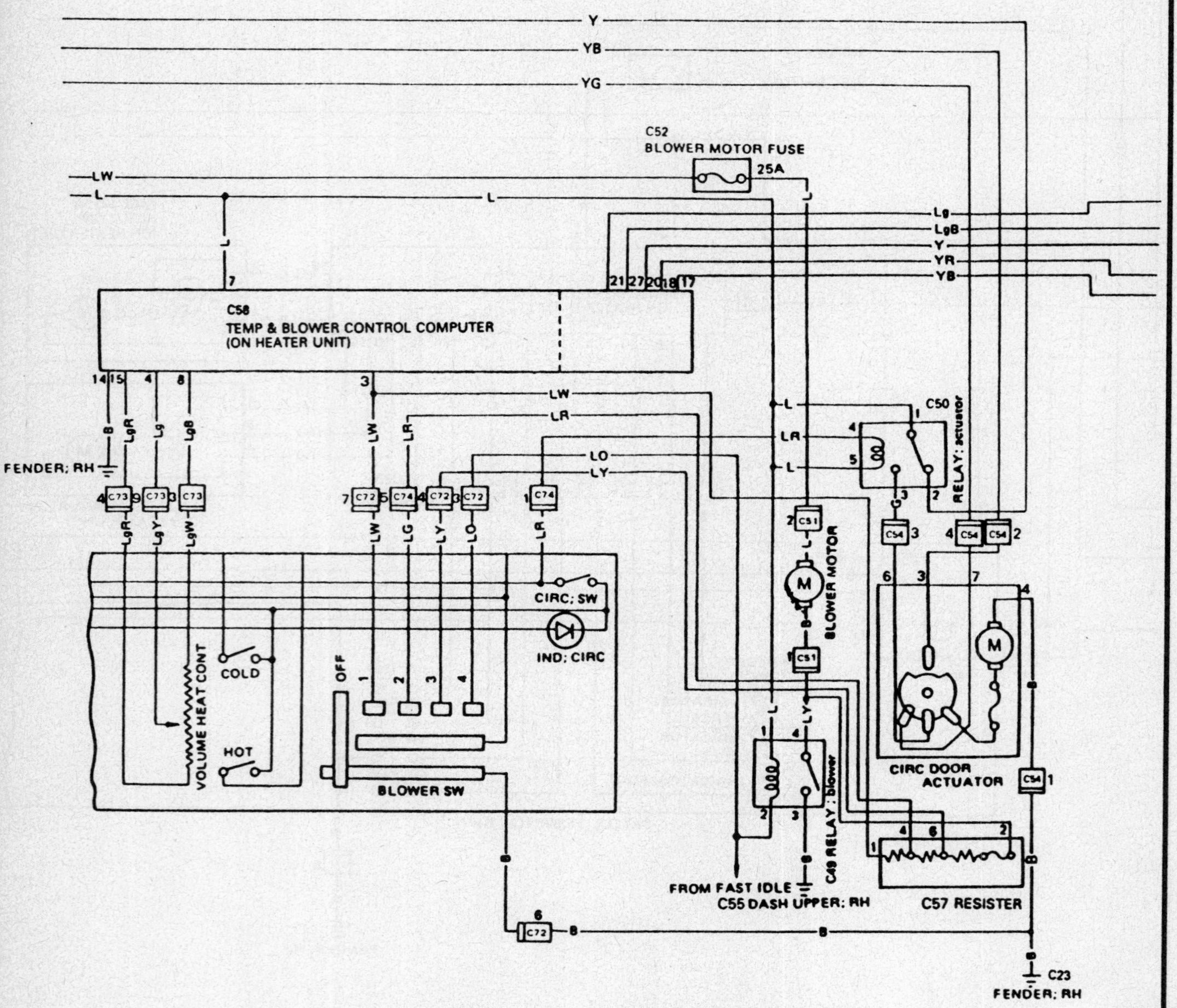
Y
YB
YG
C52
BLOWER MOTOR FUSE
25A
LW
L
Lg
LgB
Y
YR
YB
C58
TEMP & BLOWER CONTROL COMPUTER
(ON HEATER UNIT)
FENDER; RH
C73
C72
C74
LW
LR
LO
LY
C50
RELAY; actuator
C51
BLOWER MOTOR
C54
CIRC; SW
IND; CIRC
COLD
HOT
VOLUME HEAT CONT
OFF
BLOWER SW
CIRC DOOR ACTUATOR
C49 RELAY; blower
FROM FAST IDLE
C55 DASH UPPER; RH
C57 RESISTER
C23
FENDER; RH

1989 Impulse Non-Turbo cooling fan and air conditioning wiring schematic—continued

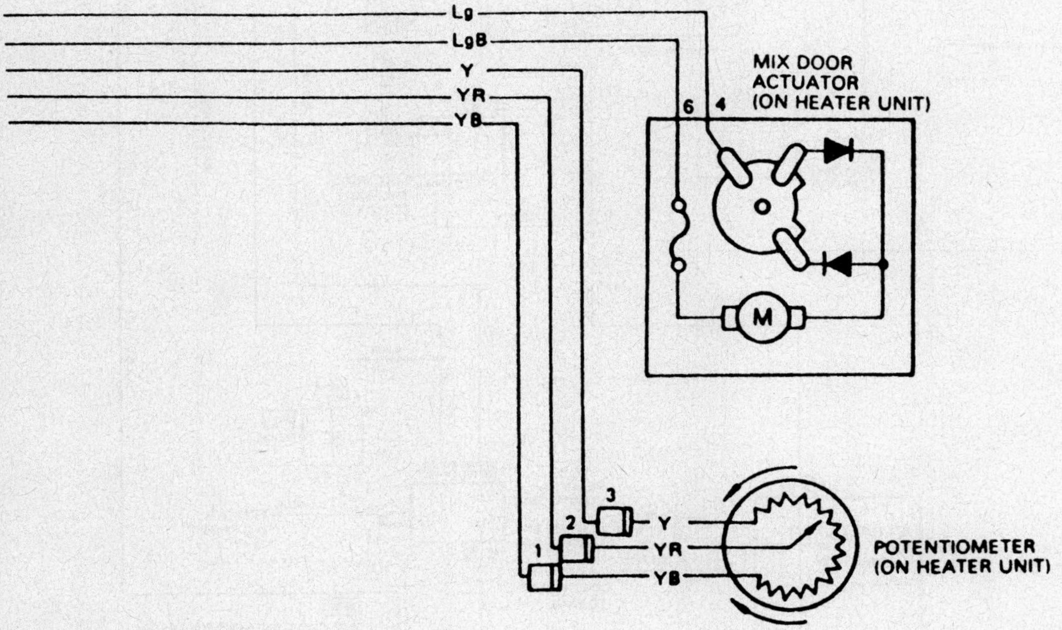
Lg
LgB
Y
YR
YB
MIX DOOR
ACTUATOR
(ON HEATER UNIT)
6
4
M
3
2
1
Y
YR
YB
POTENTIOMETER
(ON HEATER UNIT)

1989 Impulse Non-Turbo cooling fan and air conditioning wiring schematic—continued

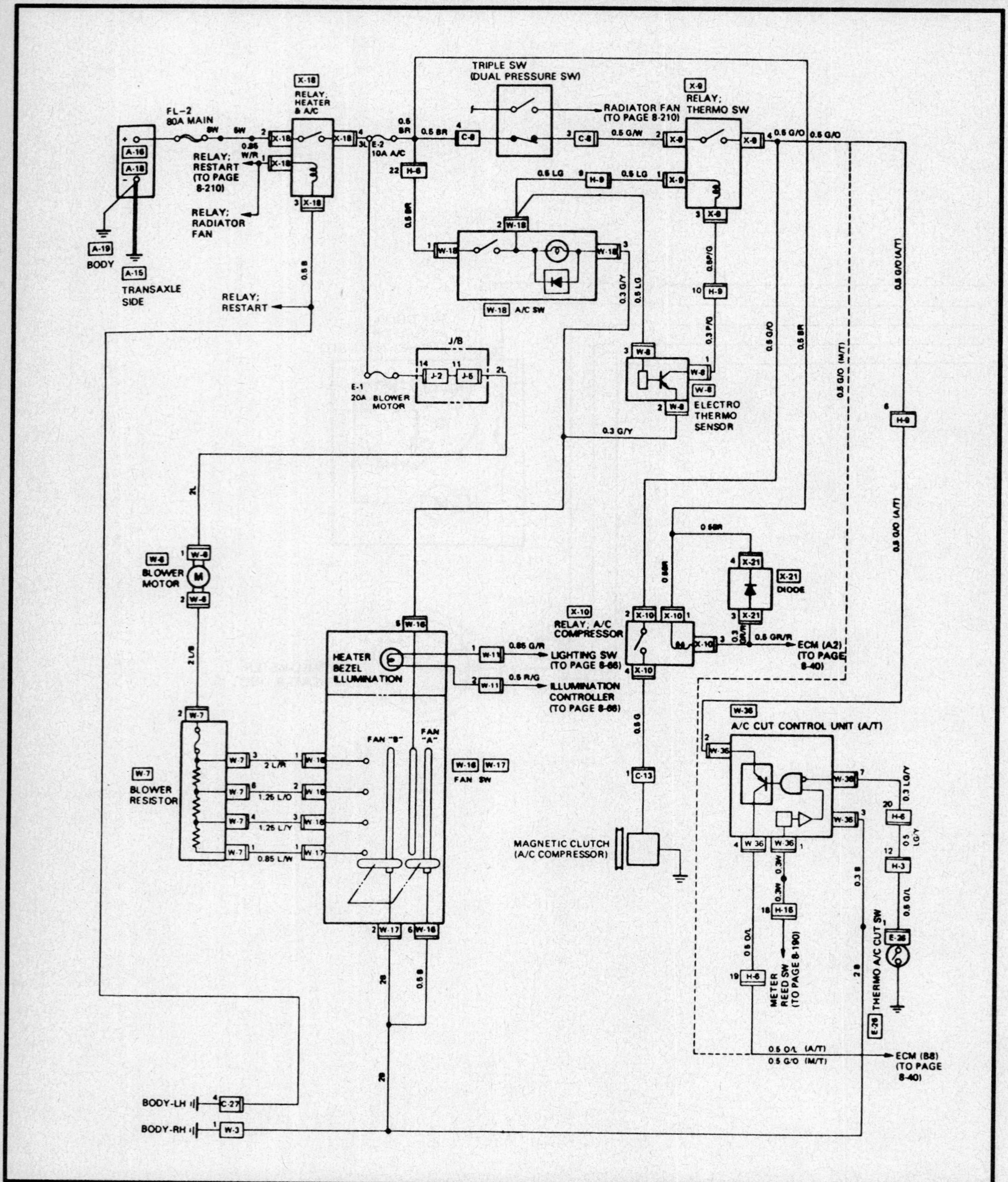
TRIPLE SW
(DUAL PRESSURE SW)
RADIATOR FAN
(TO PAGE 8-210)
RELAY; THERMO SW
RELAY; HEATER & A/C
FL-2
80A MAIN
BODY
TRANSAXLE SIDE
RELAY; RESTART (TO PAGE 8-210)
RELAY; RADIATOR FAN
RELAY; RESTART
E-2
10A A/C
A/C SW
J/B
E-1
20A BLOWER MOTOR
ELECTRO THERMO SENSOR
DIODE
BLOWER MOTOR
RELAY; A/C COMPRESSOR
ECM (A2)
(TO PAGE 8-40)
HEATER BEZEL ILLUMINATION
LIGHTING SW
(TO PAGE 8-66)
ILLUMINATION CONTROLLER
(TO PAGE 8-66)
A/C CUT CONTROL UNIT (A/T)
BLOWER RESISTOR
FAN "B"
FAN "A"
FAN SW
MAGNETIC CLUTCH
(A/C COMPRESSOR)
METER REED SW
(TO PAGE 8-190)
THERMO A/C CUT SW
ECM (B8)
(TO PAGE 8-40)
BODY-LH
BODY-RH

1990–91 Impulse and 1991 Stylus wiring schematic— lever control head type 1990

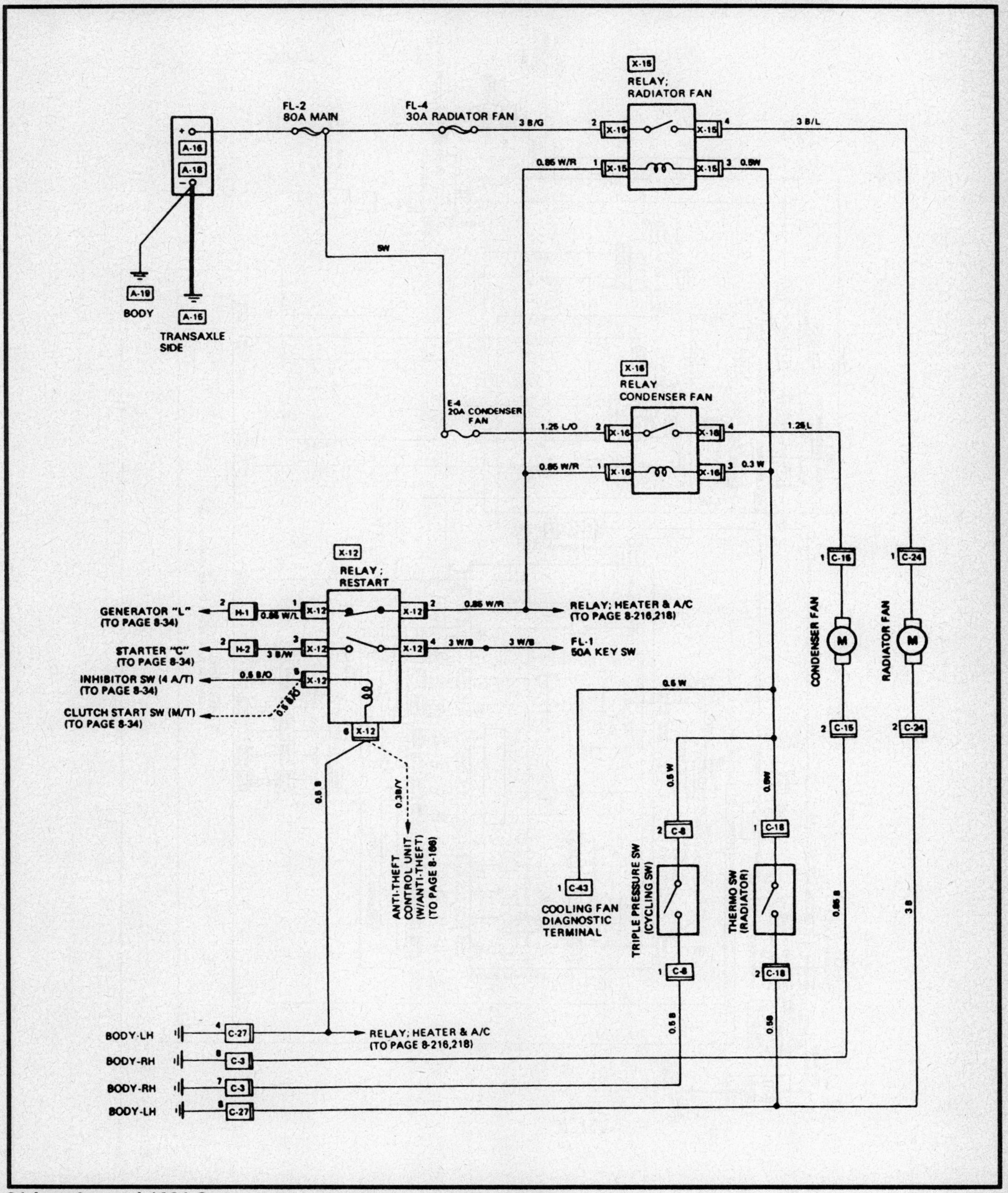
X-15
RELAY;
RADIATOR FAN
FL-2
80A MAIN
FL-4
30A RADIATOR FAN
3 B/G
3 B/L
0.85 W/R
0.5W
A-16
A-18
SW
A-19
BODY
A-15
TRANSAXLE
SIDE
X-16
RELAY
CONDENSER FAN
E-4
20A CONDENSER
FAN
1.25 L/O
1.25 L
0.85 W/R
0.3 W
X-12
RELAY;
RESTART
GENERATOR "L"
(TO PAGE 8-34)
0.85 W/L
0.85 W/R
RELAY; HEATER & A/C
(TO PAGE 8-216,218)
STARTER "C"
(TO PAGE 8-34)
3 B/W
3 W/B
3 W/B
FL-1
50A KEY SW
INHIBITOR SW (4 A/T)
(TO PAGE 8-34)
0.5 B/O
CLUTCH START SW (M/T)
(TO PAGE 8-34)
0.5 W
C-15
C-24
CONDENSER FAN
RADIATOR FAN
0.5 B
0.3B/Y
ANTI-THEFT
CONTROL UNIT
(W/ANTI-THEFT)
(TO PAGE 8-186)
0.5 W
0.5W
C-8
C-18
C-43
COOLING FAN
DIAGNOSTIC
TERMINAL
TRIPLE PRESSURE SW
(CYCLING SW)
THERMO SW
(RADIATOR)
0.85 B
3 B
0.5 B
0.5B
BODY-LH
C-27
RELAY; HEATER & A/C
(TO PAGE 8-216,218)
BODY-RH
C-3
BODY-RH
BODY-LH

91 Impulse and 1991 Stylus wiring schematic— cooling system

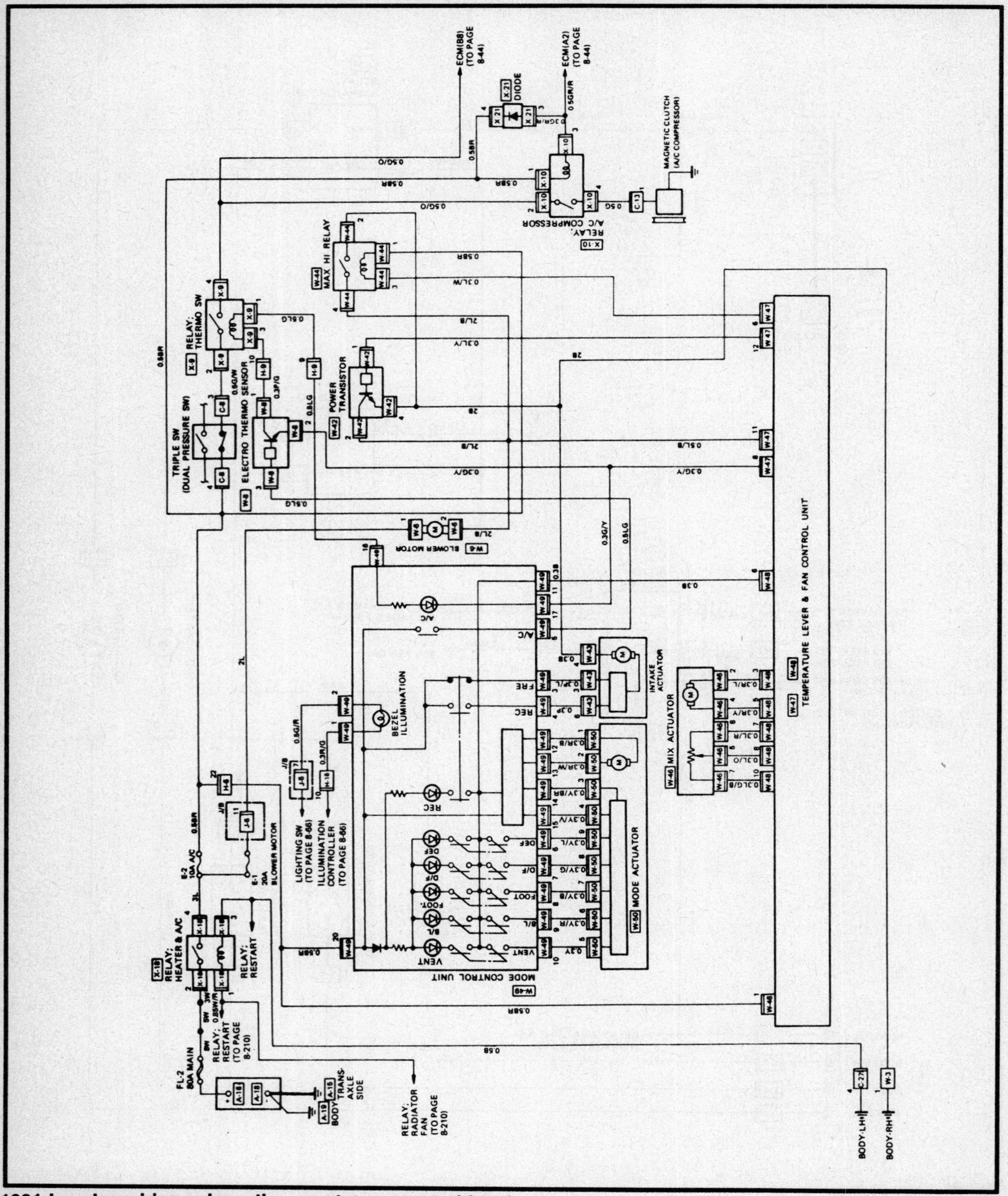
TEMPERATURE LEVER & FAN CONTROL UNIT
MODE CONTROL UNIT
MODE ACTUATOR
MIX ACTUATOR
INTAKE ACTUATOR
BLOWER MOTOR
POWER TRANSISTOR
MAX HI RELAY
ELECTRO THERMO SENSOR
TRIPLE SW (DUAL PRESSURE SW)
RELAY; THERMO SW
RELAY; A/C COMPRESSOR
MAGNETIC CLUTCH (A/C COMPRESSOR)
DIODE
ECM(B8) (TO PAGE 8-44)
ECM(A2) (TO PAGE 8-44)
BEZEL ILLUMINATION
LIGHTING SW (TO PAGE 8-66)
ILLUMINATION CONTROLLER (TO PAGE 8-66)
RELAY; HEATER & A/C
RELAY; RESTART
RELAY; RESTART (TO PAGE 8-210)
RELAY; RADIATOR FAN (TO PAGE 8-210)
FL-2 80A MAIN
BODY
TRANS-AXLE SIDE
BODY-LH
BODY-RH

1991 Impulse wiring schematic— push type control head

20 LEXUS 20

ES250 • LS400

SPECIFICATIONS

ENGINE IDENTIFICATION

Year	Model	Engine Displacement cu. in. (liter)	Engine Series Identification (VIN)	No. of Cylinders	Engine Type
1990	ES250	153 (2508/2.5)	2VZ-FE	6	DOHC
	LS400	242 (3969/4.0)	1UZ-FE	8	DOHC
1991	ES250	153 (2508/2.5)	2VZ-FE	6	DOHC
	LS400	242 (3969/4.0)	1UZ-FE	8	DOHC

DOHC—Dual overhead cam

REFRIGERANT CAPACITIES

Year	Model	Freon (oz.)	Oil (fl. oz.)	Type ①
1990	ES250	20.8–27.2	6.8–7.4	Nippondenso
	LS400	36.8	6.8–7.4	Nippondenso
1991	ES250	20.8–27.2	6.8–7.4	Nippondenso
	LS400	36.8	6.8–7.4	Nippondenso

① Compressor

AIR CONDITIONING BELT TENSION CHART

Year	Model	Engine (L)	Belt Type	Specification ① New	Used
1990	ES250	2.5	V-Ribbed	170–180	95–135
	LS400	4.0	V-Ribbed	②	②
1991	ES250	2.5	V-Ribbed	170–180	95–135
	LS400	4.0	V-Ribbed	②	②

① Lbs. using a belt tension gauge
② Automatic belt tensioner

SYSTEM DESCRIPTION

General Information

The climate control system on Lexus vehicles uses R-12 refrigerant in both a liquid and gaseous state to cool the inside of the vehicle. The components used to manipulate the refrigerant consist of the compressor, condenser, receiver/drier, expansion valve, evaporator and the necessary refrigerant lines and hoses. In order to warm the inside of the vehicle, the climate control system utilizes engine coolant heated by the internal friction of the engine. The components used in the heating function consist of the heater core, radiator, water pump and the necessary coolant hoses. There are also valves, sensors and switches which are used to regulate both cooling and heating functions.

To control the temperature and airflow inside the vehicle, a control assembly operated by the driver controls the blower motor and the doors that direct the airflow through the various ducts leading to the floor, dash registers and defroster nozzles. In addition, LS 400 vehicles are equipped with automatic temperature control. The driver sets the preferred temperature and the climate control system automatically regulates the mixture of cool and warm air, as well as blower speed, to maintain the desired temperature.

The refrigerant cycle of the climate control system operates as follows:

The compressor draws off gaseous refrigerant from the evaporator and compresses it. This causes the refrigerant gas temperature and pressure to rise rapidly. The high temperature and high pressure refrigerant, containing the heat absorbed from the evaporator plus the heat created by the compressor, is discharged into the condenser.

In the condenser, the heated refrigerant gas releases heat to the engine cooling air blowing across the fins and tubes. The refrigerant gas cools off in the condenser and condenses into a liquid state, then flows into the receiver/drier which stores and filters the liquid refrigerant until it is required in the evaporator.

The expansion valve meters the liquid refrigerant into the evaporator core, causing a drop in pressure and a consequent drop in temperature. In the evaporator core, the refrigerant expands and flows through the evaporator tubes. There it removes heat from the air blowing across the fins and tubes, the air consequently cooling the vehicle interior. The heat removed from the air and transferred to the liquid refrigerant causes the refrigerant to evaporate back into a gaseous state. It is then drawn into the compressor and the cycle repeats.

Service Valve Location

The high pressure service valve is located in the liquid line between the condenser and the evaporator. The low pressure service valve is located in the suction line between the evaporator and the compressor.

System Discharging

NOTE: R-12 refrigerant is a chlorofluorocarbon (CFC), which is believed to cause harm by depleting the

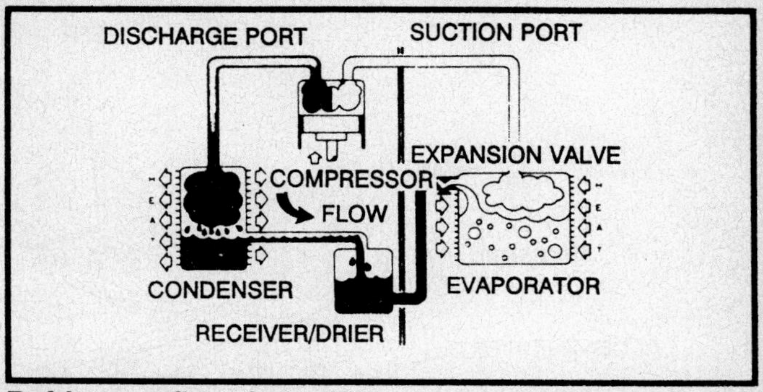
DISCHARGE PORT
SUCTION PORT
EXPANSION VALVE
COMPRESSOR
FLOW
CONDENSER
EVAPORATOR
RECEIVER/DRIER

Refrigerant flow through the air conditioning system

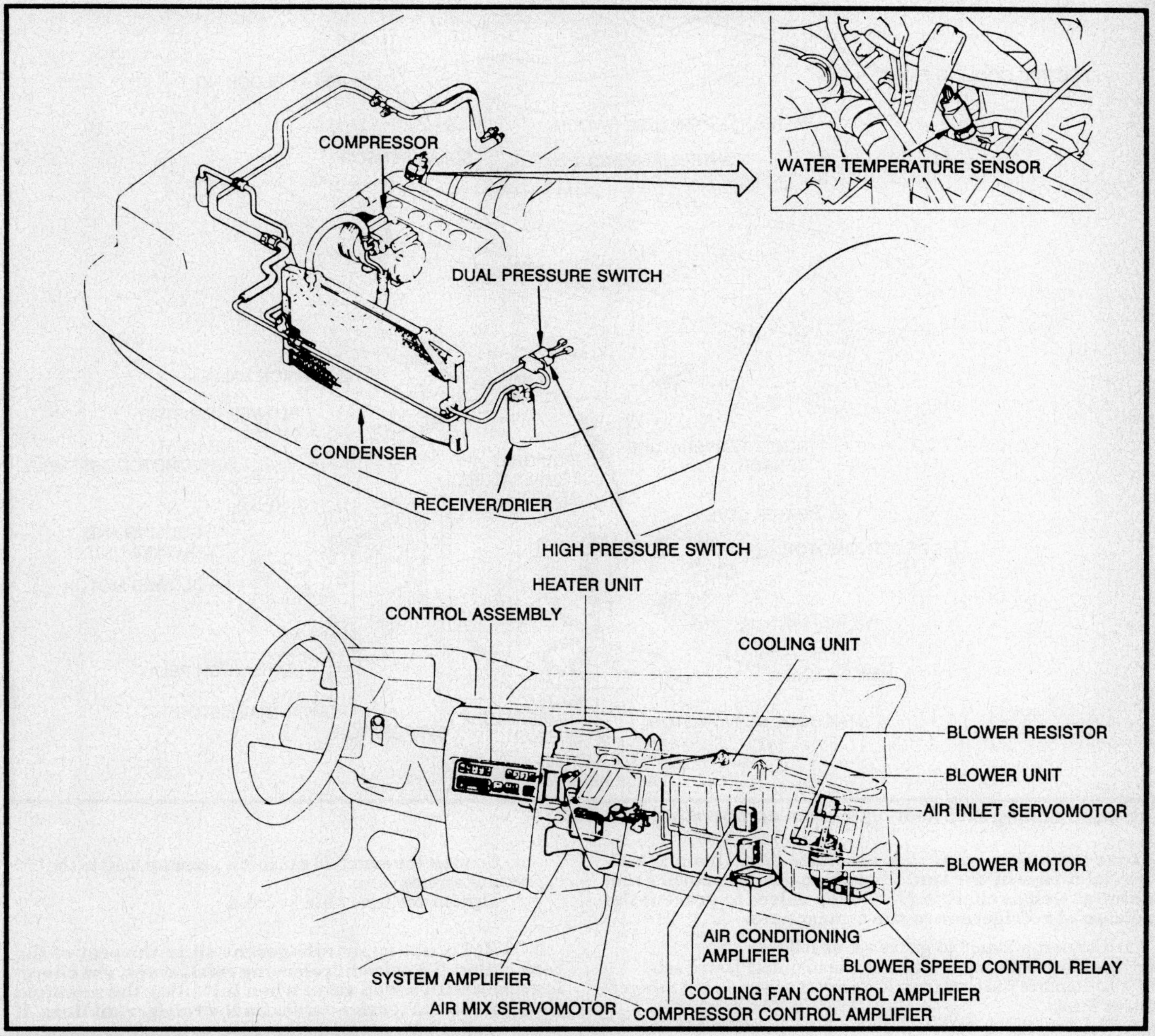
COMPRESSOR
WATER TEMPERATURE SENSOR
DUAL PRESSURE SWITCH
CONDENSER
RECEIVER/DRIER
HIGH PRESSURE SWITCH
HEATER UNIT
CONTROL ASSEMBLY
COOLING UNIT
BLOWER RESISTOR
BLOWER UNIT
AIR INLET SERVOMOTOR
BLOWER MOTOR
AIR CONDITIONING AMPLIFIER
BLOWER SPEED CONTROL RELAY
SYSTEM AMPLIFIER
COOLING FAN CONTROL AMPLIFIER
AIR MIX SERVOMOTOR
COMPRESSOR CONTROL AMPLIFIER

Air conditioning and heating system components— ES 250

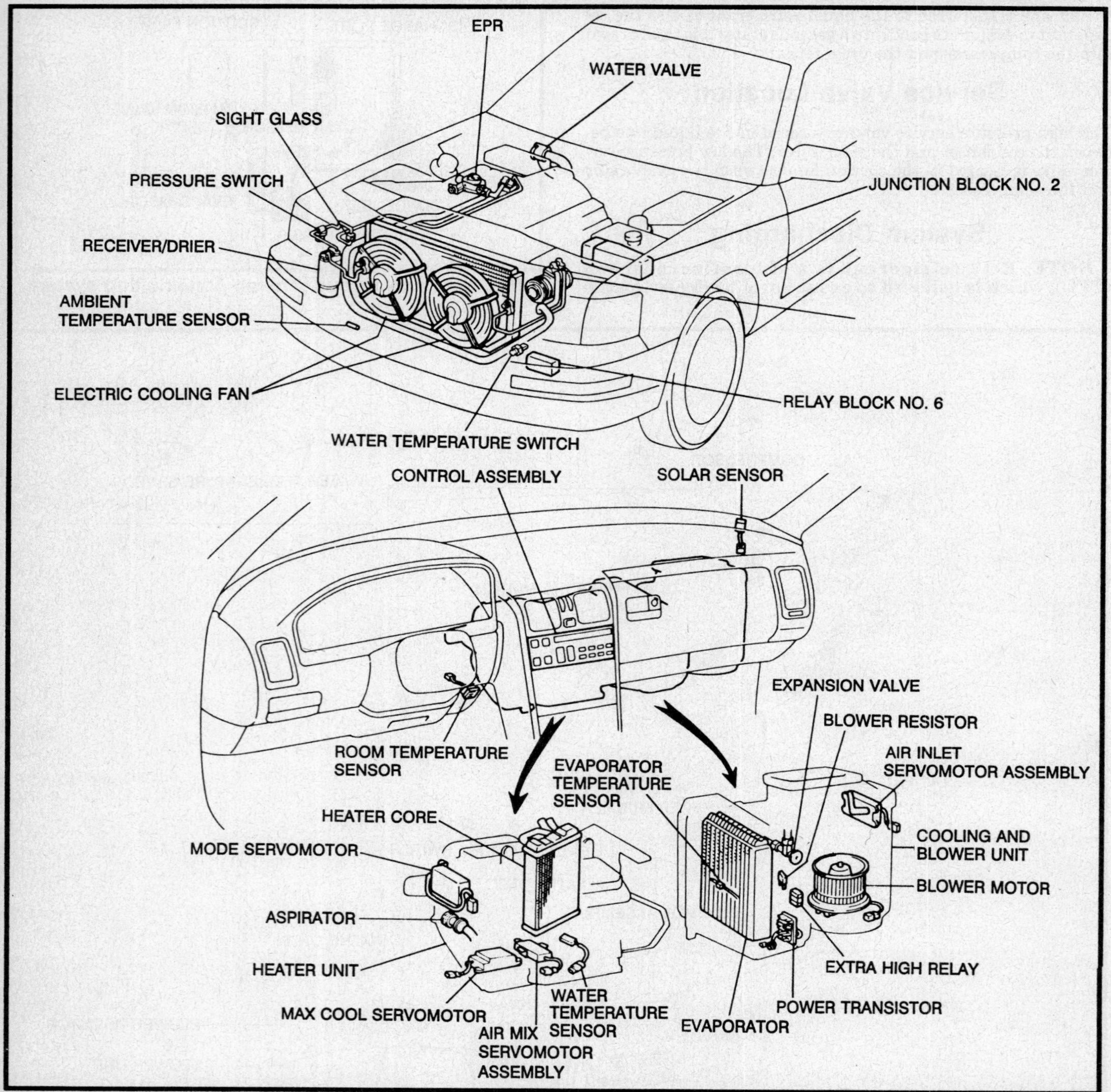
EPR
WATER VALVE
SIGHT GLASS
PRESSURE SWITCH
JUNCTION BLOCK NO. 2
RECEIVER/DRIER
AMBIENT TEMPERATURE SENSOR
ELECTRIC COOLING FAN
RELAY BLOCK NO. 6
WATER TEMPERATURE SWITCH
CONTROL ASSEMBLY
SOLAR SENSOR
EXPANSION VALVE
BLOWER RESISTOR
ROOM TEMPERATURE SENSOR
AIR INLET SERVOMOTOR ASSEMBLY
EVAPORATOR TEMPERATURE SENSOR
HEATER CORE
COOLING AND BLOWER UNIT
MODE SERVOMOTOR
BLOWER MOTOR
ASPIRATOR
HEATER UNIT
EXTRA HIGH RELAY
WATER TEMPERATURE SENSOR
POWER TRANSISTOR
MAX COOL SERVOMOTOR
EVAPORATOR
AIR MIX SERVOMOTOR ASSEMBLY

Air conditioning and heating system components—LS 400

ozone layer that helps to protect the earth from the ultraviolet rays of the sun. Therefore, use a recovery machine as well as charging hose stop valves to prevent the release of refrigerant to the atmosphere.

1. Connect a manifold gauge set as follows:
   a. Close both hand valves of the manifold gauge set.
   b. Remove the caps from the service valves on the refrigerant lines.
   c. Connect the manifold gauge high pressure hose to the high pressure service valve.
   d. Connect the manifold gauge low pressure hose to the low pressure service valve.
   e. Tighten the hose nuts by hand.

NOTE: Do not apply refrigerant oil to the seat of the connection. To prevent releasing refrigerant, use charging hoses with a stop valve when installing the manifold gauge set to the service valves on the refrigerant lines. If using a stop valve, close the valve prior to connecting the hoses to the service valves.

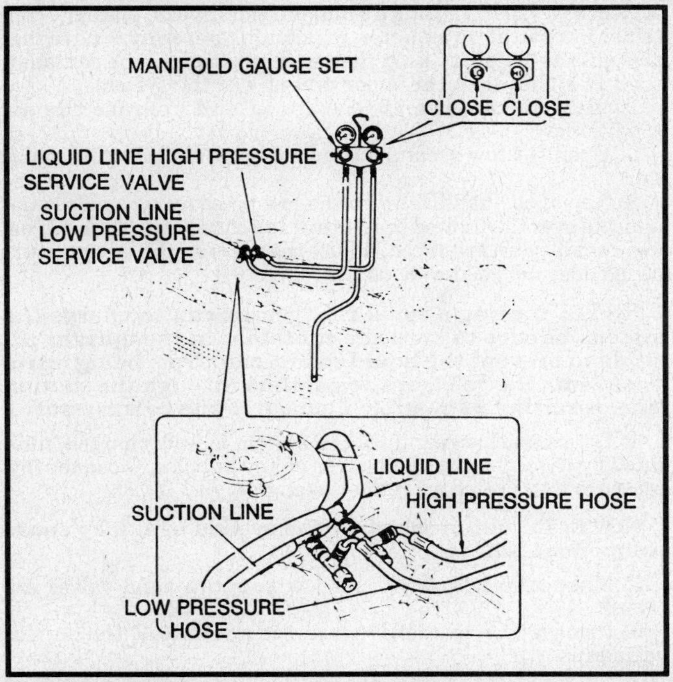
MANIFOLD GAUGE SET
CLOSE CLOSE
LIQUID LINE HIGH PRESSURE SERVICE VALVE
SUCTION LINE LOW PRESSURE SERVICE VALVE
LIQUID LINE
HIGH PRESSURE HOSE
SUCTION LINE
LOW PRESSURE HOSE

Manifold gauge set to service valve connections—ES 250

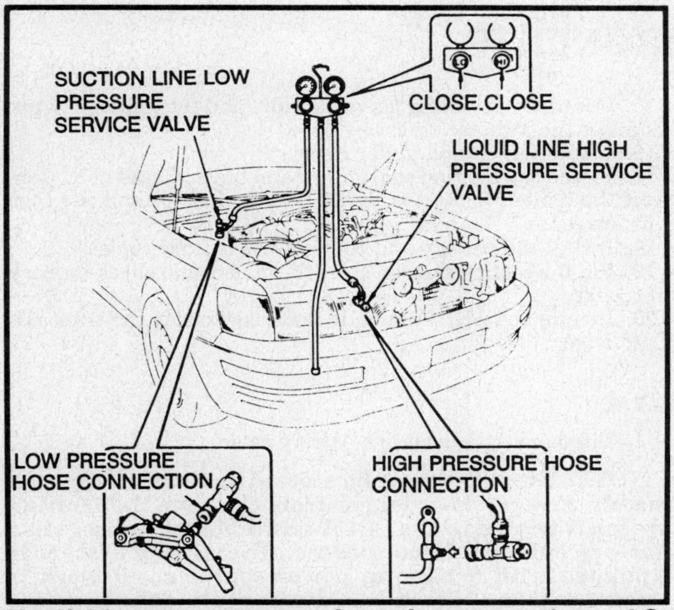
SUCTION LINE LOW PRESSURE SERVICE VALVE
CLOSE.CLOSE
LIQUID LINE HIGH PRESSURE SERVICE VALVE
LOW PRESSURE HOSE CONNECTION
HIGH PRESSURE HOSE CONNECTION

Manifold gauge set to service valve connections—LS 400

2. Connect the center manifold gauge hose to a recovery machine.
3. Operate the recovery machine.
4. Open both high and low pressure hand valves of the manifold gauge set.

NOTE: When operating the recovery machine, always follow the directions given in the instruction manual for the machine. After recovery, the amount of refrigerant oil removed must be measured and the same amount added into the system when recharging.

5. Stop the recovery machine when discharging has been completed.
6. Remove the manifold gauge set and replace the service valve caps.

System Evacuating

NOTE: Before charging the system with refrigerant, be sure to completely evacuate the system.

1. Properly connect a manifold gauge set to the service valves.
2. Discharge the refrigerant from the system according to the proper procedure but leave the high and low pressure manifold gauge hoses connected to the service valves.
3. Connect the center hose of the manifold gauge set to a vacuum pump.
4. Open both the high and low pressure hand valves and run the vacuum pump.

NOTE: If opening the low pressure hand valve pulls the high pressure gauge into the vacuum range, there is no blockage in the system.

5. After 10 minutes or more, check that the low pressure gauge indicates 29.53 in. Hg or more of vacuum.

NOTE: If the reading is not 29.53 in. Hg or more of vacuum, close both the high and low hand valves of the manifold gauge set and stop the vacuum pump. Then, check the system for leaks and repair, as necessary.

6. Close both the high and low hand valves and stop the vacuum pump.
7. Leave the system in this condition for 5 minutes or longer and check that there is no change in the gauge indicator.

System Charging

1. Properly connect a manifold gauge set to the service valves.
2. Discharge and evacuate the system according to the proper procedure.
3. With the high and low pressure hand valves closed, disconnect the center hose of the manifold gauge set from the vacuum pump.
4. With the high and low pressure hand valves closed, connect the center hose of the manifold gauge set to a refrigerant charging cylinder or a small can refrigerant dispensing valve tool. If a charging station is used, follow the instructions of the manufacturer. If a small can dispensing valve is used, install the small can(s) on the dispensing valve.

NOTE: Use only a safety type dispensing valve.

5. Loosen the center hose at the manifold gauge set and open the refrigerant charging cylinder valve or small can dispensing valve. Allow the refrigerant to escape to purge air and moisture from the center hose. Then, tighten the center hose connection at the manifold gauge set.

NOTE: If there is a schrader valve on the side of the manifold gauge set, press on the Schrader valve until refrigerant comes out, to expel the air from inside the center hose.

6. Open the high pressure hand valve to charge the system with refrigerant. If using a small refrigerant can, make sure the can is right side up so the refrigerant will enter the system as vapor.
7. When the low pressure gauge indicates 14 psi, close the high pressure hand valve.
8. Using a suitable leak detector, check the system for leakage. If a leak is found, repair the faulty component or connection.

CHARGE EMPTY REFRIGERATION SYSTEM WITH LIQUID REFRIGERANT

This procedure is used to charge an empty system through the high pressure side with refrigerant in a liquid state.

NOTE: Never run the engine when charging the system through the high pressure side with liquid refrigerant. Do not open the low pressure hand valve when the system is being charged with liquid refrigerant.

1. Open the high pressure hand valve fully. If using a small refrigerant can, keep the container upside down.
2. Charge the system with the proper amount of refrigerant, then close the high pressure hand valve.
3. A fully charged system is indicated by the receiver/drier sight glass being free of any bubbles.

NOTE: If the low pressure gauge does not show a reading, the system is clogged and must be repaired.

CHARGE PARTIALLY CHARGED SYSTEM WITH REFRIGERANT VAPOR

This procedure is used to charge the system through the low pressure side with the refrigerant in a vapor state. If using a small refrigerant can to charge the system, make sure the container is placed right side up, so the refrigerant will enter the system as a vapor. If using a small refrigerant can, place the container in a pan of warm water, maximum temperature no higher than 104°F (40°C), to keep the vapor pressure in the container slightly higher than the vapor pressure in the system.

1. Run the engine at idle speed and operate the air conditioner.
2. Open the low pressure hand valve on the manifold gauge set.
3. Adjust the hand valve so the low pressure gauge does not indicate over the limited pressure of the charging cylinder. If using a small refrigerant can, adjust the valve so the low pressure gauge does not read over 60 psi.

NOTE: If using a small refrigerant can to charge the system, be sure to keep the container in the upright position to prevent the liquid refrigerant from being introduced into the refrigeration system through the suction side, resulting in possible damage to the compressor.

4. Continue charging until the system is fully charged, indicated by the sight glass being free of any bubbles. Close the low pressure hand valve and stop the engine.

NOTE: Do not overcharge the system as it may cause component failure.

5. Make sure both high and low pressure hand valves are closed.
6. Remove the manifold gauge set and install the service valve caps.

SYSTEM COMPONENTS

Radiator

REMOVAL AND INSTALLATION

ES 250

1. Disconnect the battery cables and remove the battery.

NOTE: Work must not be started until after approximately 20 seconds or longer from the time the ignition switch is turned to the LOCK position and the negative battery cable is disconnected. The airbag system is equipped with a back-up power source so, if work is started within 20 seconds of disconnecting the negative battery cable, the airbag may be deployed.

2. Drain the engine coolant into a suitable container.
3. Disconnect the igniter connector, noise filter connector and the high tension cable.
4. Remove the ignition coil, igniter and bracket assembly.
5. Disconnect the radiator reservoir hose.
6. Remove the engine under cover.
7. Disconnect the radiator hoses.
8. Disconnect the cooling fan connectors.
9. If equipped with automatic transaxle, disconnect the oil cooler hoses.
10. Remove the 2 bolts and the radiator supports, then remove the radiator and electric cooling fans.
11. Remove the electric cooling fans from the radiator.

To install:

12. Install the electric cooling fans to the radiator.
13. Place the radiator in position and install the 2 supports and mounting bolts. After installation, check that the rubber cushions of the supports are not depressed.
14. If equipped with automatic transaxle, connect the oil cooler hoses.
15. Connect the cooling fan connectors and the radiator hoses. Connect the radiator reservoir hose.
16. Install the engine under cover.
17. Install the ignition coil, igniter and bracket assembly. Connect the igniter connector, noise filter connector and the high tension cable.
18. Install the battery and connect the battery cables.
19. Fill the cooling system, start the engine and check for coolant leaks.
20. If equipped with automatic transaxle, check the transaxle fluid level.

LS 400

1. Disconnect the negative battery cable.

NOTE: Work must not be started until after approximately 20 seconds or longer from the time the ignition switch is turned to the LOCK position and the negative battery cable is disconnected. The airbag system is equipped with a back-up power source so, if work is started within 20 seconds of disconnecting the negative battery cable, the airbag may be deployed.

2. Drain the engine coolant into a suitable container.
3. Remove the air intake duct.
4. Disconnect the automatic transmission oil cooler hoses. Plug the hoses to prevent leakage.
5. Disconnect the cooling fan motor connector and the water hose from the coolant reservoir tank.
6. Disconnect the 2 radiator hoses.
7. Remove the 2 radiator supports and the radiator.
8. Remove the fan shrouds.

To install:

9. Install the fan shrouds.
10. Place the radiator in position and install the 2 supports

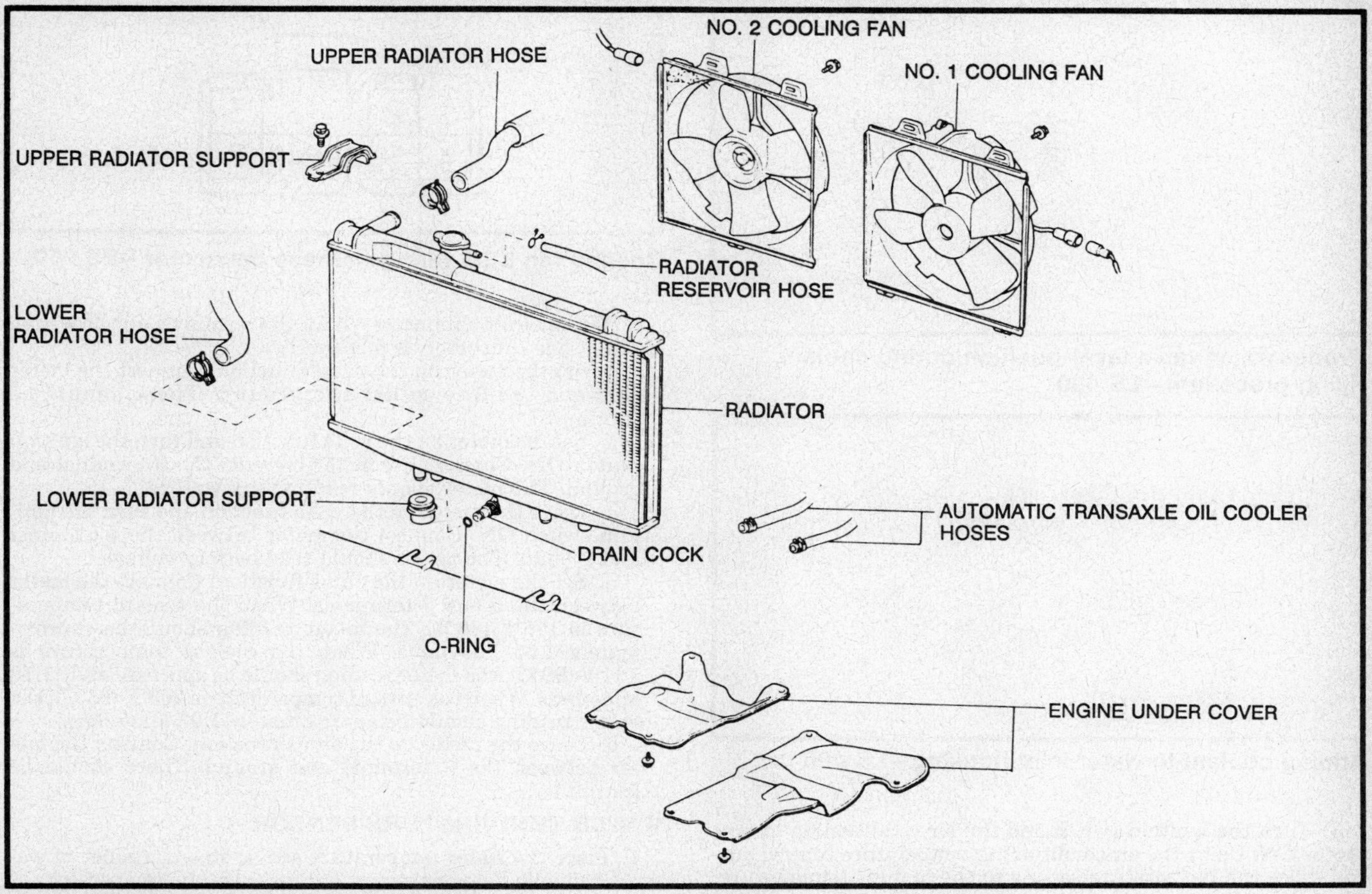
NO. 2 COOLING FAN
UPPER RADIATOR HOSE
NO. 1 COOLING FAN
UPPER RADIATOR SUPPORT
RADIATOR
RESERVOIR HOSE
LOWER
RADIATOR HOSE
RADIATOR
LOWER RADIATOR SUPPORT
AUTOMATIC TRANSAXLE OIL COOLER
HOSES
DRAIN COCK
O-RING
ENGINE UNDER COVER

Radiator and cooling fan assembly—ES 250

with the mounting bolts. After installation, check that the rubber cushions of the supports are not depressed.

11. Connect the water hose to the coolant reservoir tank, the cooling fan motor connector and the 2 automatic transmission fluid cooler hoses.
12. Install the air intake duct.
13. Connect the negative battery cable and refill the cooling system.
14. Check the automatic transmission fluid level.

COOLING SYSTEM BLEEDING

The following procedures should be used to ensure a complete refill after the cooling system has been completely drained.

ES 250

1. Make sure the drain cocks on the engine and radiator are closed. The engine drain cocks should be tightened to 22 ft. lbs. (29 Nm).
2. To release air that could be trapped in the system, loosen the union bolt of the water outlet 5 revolutions.
3. Slowly fill the system with coolant. Use an ethylene-glycol and water mixture containing more than 50 percent but less than 70 percent ethylene-glycol. The total cooling system capacity is 10 quarts, if equipped with a manual transaxle, and 9.9 quarts, if equipped with an automatic transaxle.
4. After all air has been expelled, tighten the union bolt to 13 ft. lbs. (18 Nm).

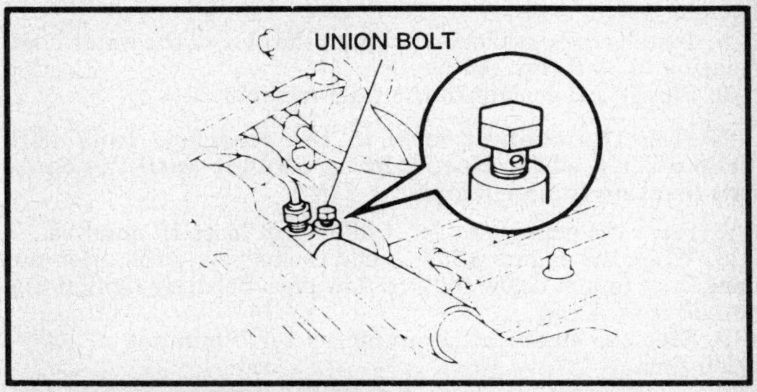
UNION BOLT

Union bolt location—ES 250

5. Install the radiator cap, warm up the engine and check for leaks.
6. Recheck the coolant level and refill, as necessary.

LS 400

1. Remove the reservoir tank cap and the filler plug from the water inlet housing.
2. Make sure the drain cocks on the engine and radiator are both closed. The engine drain cocks should be tightened to 18 ft. lbs. (25 Nm).

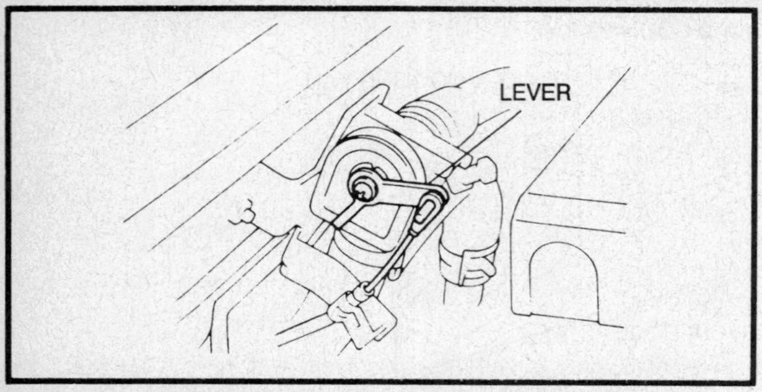
LEVER

Proper water valve lever position during coolant filling procedure—LS 400

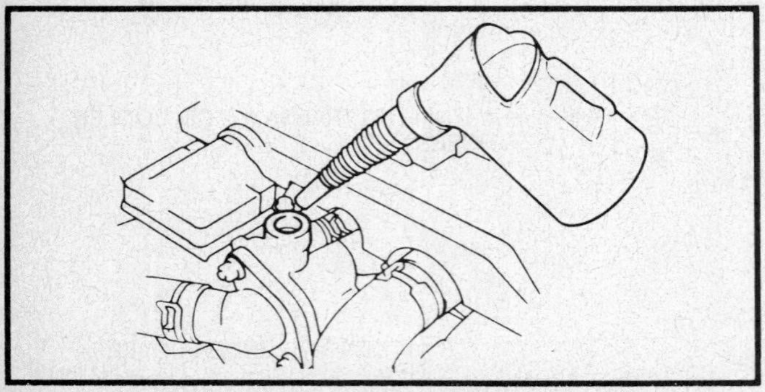

Adding coolant to water inlet housing—LS 400

3. Turn the ignition switch and the air conditioning blower motor **ON**. Using the air conditioning temperature control button, raise the temperature setting to the highest temperature. Make sure the lever of the water valve is in the proper position.
4. Slowly add coolant to the water inlet housing until it is full. Use an ethylene-glycol and water mixture containing more than 50 percent but less than 70 percent ethylene-glycol. The total cooling system capacity is 11.2 quarts.
5. Install a new gasket and tighten the plug of the water inlet housing to 33 ft. lbs. (44 Nm).
6. Slowly add coolant to the reservoir tank.

NOTE: The coolant level in the reservoir tank will drop after a while. Keep adding coolant until the coolant level no longer drops.

7. Start the engine and let it idle for at least 10 minutes.
8. While the engine is idling, add coolant up to the reservoir tank inlet to just below the overflow pipe. Securely tighten the reservoir tank cap.
9. Stop the engine after running it for 5 minutes at 2000–3000 rpm.
10. After the coolant drops, remove the reservoir tank cap and add coolant up to the reservoir tank inlet to just below the overflow pipe. Securely tighten the reservoir tank cap.
11. Check for leaks.

Cooling Fan

TESTING

ES 250

COOLING FAN ECU CIRCUIT

1. Disconnect the cooling fan ECU.

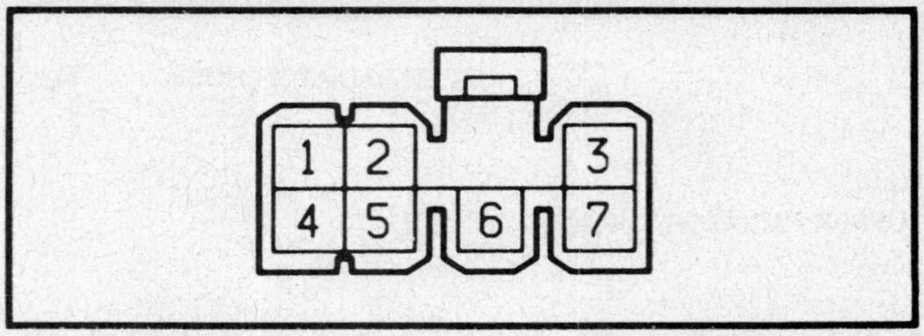
1
2
3
4
5
6
7

Cooling fan ECU wiring harness connector—ES 250

2. Using a volt/ohmmeter, check the terminals on the wiring harness side connector as follows:
   a. Set the meter on the ohms function. Connect the meter between the **2** terminal and ground. There should be continuity.
   b. Set the meter on the volts function and turn the ignition switch **ON**. Connect the meter between the **3** terminal and ground. The meter should read battery voltage.
   c. Leave the meter on the volts function and turn the ignition switch **ON**. Connect the meter between the **4** terminal and ground. The meter should read battery voltage.
   d. Set the meter on the ohms function. Connect the meter between the **5** and **7** terminals. When the coolant temperature is 176°F (80°C), the meter reading should be approximately 1.53 kilo-ohms. When the coolant temperature is 194°F (90°C), the meter reading should be approximately 1.18 kilo-ohms. When the coolant temperature is 203°F (95°C), the meter reading should be approximately 1.03 kilo-ohms.
   e. Leave the meter on the ohms function. Connect the meter between the **6** terminal and ground. There should be continuity.

WATER TEMPERATURE SENSOR

1. Place the water temperature sensor in a container of water. Gradually heat the water and measure the temperature.
2. Connect an ohmmeter between the terminals of the water temperature sensor.
3. When the water temperature reaches 176°F (80°C), the resistance should be approximately 1.53 kilo-ohms. When the water temperature reaches 194°F (90°C), the resistance should be approximately 1.18 kilo-ohms. When the water temperature reaches 203°F (95°C), the resistance should be approximately 1.03 kilo-ohms.
4. If the resistance is not as specified, replace the sensor.

ENGINE MAIN RELAY

1. Check the relay continuity as follows:
   a. Using an ohmmeter, check that there is continuity between terminals **1** and **3**.
   b. Check that there is continuity between the terminals **2** and **4**.

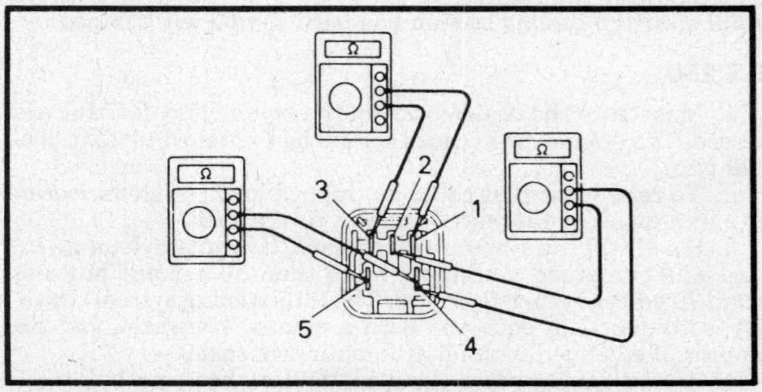
Ω
Ω
Ω
1
2
3
4
5

Engine main relay terminal location—ES 250

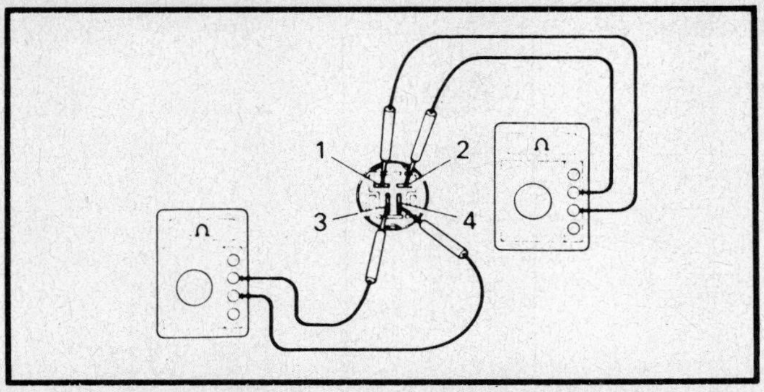
1
2
3
4

No. 1 cooling fan relay terminal locations—ES 250

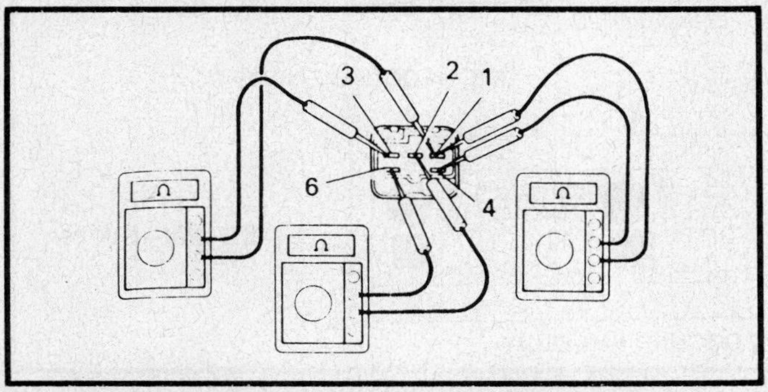
3
2
1
6
4

No. 2 cooling fan relay terminal locations—ES 250

c. Check that there is no continuity between terminals **4** and **5**.
2. If continuity is not as specified, replace the relay.
3. Inspect the relay operation as follows:
a. Apply battery voltage across terminals **1** and **3**.
b. Using an ohmmeter, check that there is continuity between terminals **4** and **5**.
c. Check that there is no continuity between terminals **2** and **4**.
4. If operation is not as specified, replace the relay.

NO. 1 COOLING FAN RELAY

1. Inspect relay continuity as follows:
a. Using an ohmmeter, check that there is continuity between terminals **1** and **2**.
b. Check that there is continuity between the terminals **3** and **4**.
2. If continuity is not as specified, replace the relay..
3. Check relay operation as follows:
a. Apply battery voltage across terminals **1** and **2**.
b. Using an ohmmeter, check that there is no continuity between terminals **3** and **4**.
4. If operation is not as specified, replace the relay.

NO. 2 COOLING FAN RELAY

1. Inspect relay continuity as follows:
a. Using an ohmmeter, check that there is continuity between terminals **2** and **6**.
b. Check that there is continuity between the terminals **1** and **3**.
c. Check that there is no continuity between terminals **1** and **4**.
2. If continuity is not as specified, replace the relay.
3. Inspect relay operation as follows:
a. Apply battery voltage across terminals **2** and **6**.
b. Using an ohmmeter, check that there is no continuity between terminals **1** and **3**.
c. Check that there is continuity between the terminals **1** and **4**.
4. If operation is not as specified, replace the relay.

NO. 3 COOLING FAN RELAY

1. Inspect relay continuity as follows:
a. Using an ohmmeter, check that there is continuity between terminals **1** and **3**.
b. Check that there is no continuity between terminals **2** and **4**.
2. If continuity is not as specified, replace the relay.
3. Inspect relay operation as follows:
a. Apply battery voltage across terminals **1** and **3**.
b. Using an ohmmeter, check that there is continuity between terminals **2** and **4**.
4. If operation is not as specified, replace the relay.

COOLING FAN MOTORS

1. Connect a battery and ammeter to the cooling fan connector.
2. Check that the cooling fan rotates smoothly and check the reading on the ammeter.
3. The standard amperage should be 12.1–15.1 amps on the No. 1 fan motor and 6.0–7.4 amps on the No. 2 fan motor.

LS 400

TEMPERATURE SWITCH

1. Place the temperature switch in a container of water. Heat the water and measure the water temperature.
2. Connect an ohmmeter to the terminals of the switch.
3. Check that there is no continuity when the coolant temperature is above 199°F (93°C).
4. Check that there is continuity when the coolant temperature is below 181°F (83°C).
5. If continuity is not as specified, replace the switch.

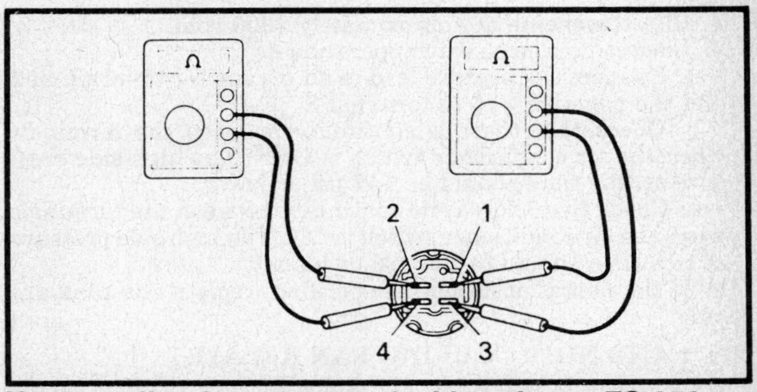
2
1
4
3

No. 3 cooling fan relay terminal locations—ES 250

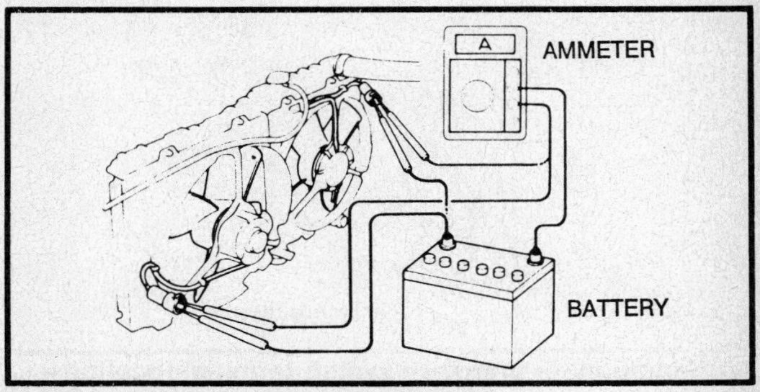
AMMETER
BATTERY

Cooling fan motor testing—ES 250

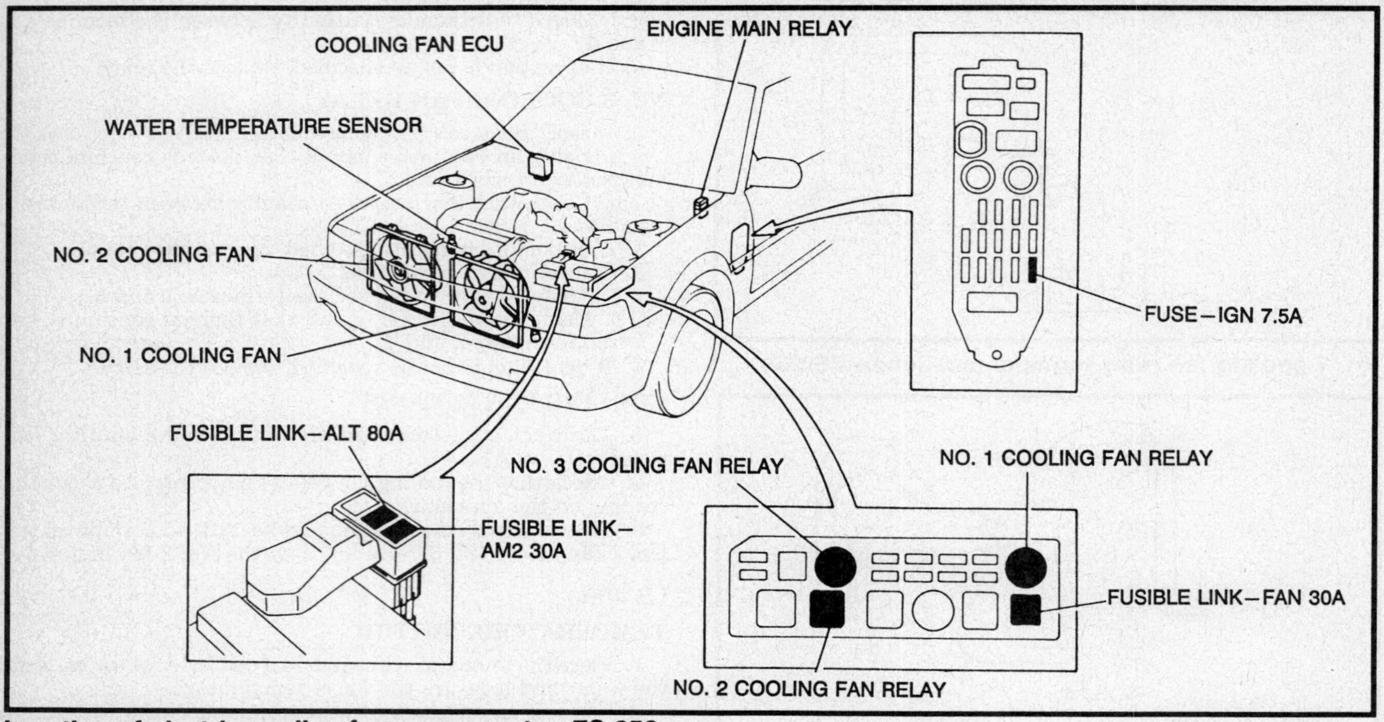
ENGINE MAIN RELAY
COOLING FAN ECU
WATER TEMPERATURE SENSOR
NO. 2 COOLING FAN
NO. 1 COOLING FAN
FUSE–IGN 7.5A
FUSIBLE LINK–ALT 80A
NO. 3 COOLING FAN RELAY
NO. 1 COOLING FAN RELAY
FUSIBLE LINK–AM2 30A
FUSIBLE LINK–FAN 30A
NO. 2 COOLING FAN RELAY

Location of electric cooling fan components–ES 250

AIR CONDITIONING HIGH PRESSURE SWITCH

1. Remove the headlight from the right side of the vehicle.
2. Disconnect the connector from the pressure switch.
3. Install a manifold gauge set according to the proper procedure.
4. Run the engine at approximately 2000 rpm.
5. Inspect pressure switch operation as follows:
   a. Connect the positive lead of an ohmmeter to terminal **2** and the negative lead to terminal **3**.
   b. Check that there is continuity between the terminals when the air conditioner switch is **OFF**. The high side pressure at this time should be 142 psi or lower.
   c. Check that there is no continuity between the terminals when the air conditioner switch is **ON**. The high side pressure at this time should be 192 psi or higher.
6. If the operation is not as specified, replace the pressure switch.

NO. 1 AND NO. 2 COOLING FAN RELAYS

1. Inspect relay continuity as follows:
   a. Using an ohmmeter, check that there is continuity between terminals **1** and **2**.
   b. Check that there is continuity between the terminals **3** and **4**.
2. If continuity is not as specified, replace the relay.
3. Inspect relay operation as follows:
   a. Apply battery voltage across terminals **1** and **2**.
   b. Check that there is no continuity between terminals **3** and **4**.
4. If the operation is not as specified, replace the relay.

NO. 3 COOLING FAN AND ENGINE MAIN RELAY

1. Inspect relay continuity as follows:
   a. Using an ohmmeter, check that there is continuity between terminals **1** and **3**.
   b. Check that there is continuity between the terminals **2** and **4**.
   c. Check that there is no continuity between terminals **4** and **5**.
2. If continuity is not as specified, replace the relay.

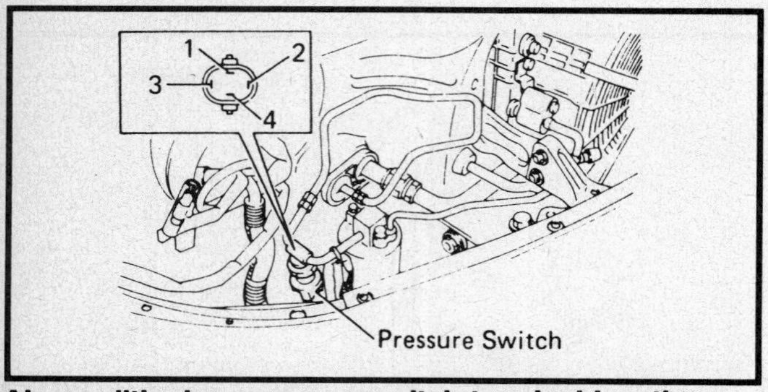
1
2
3
4
Pressure Switch

Air conditioning pressure switch terminal location–LS 400

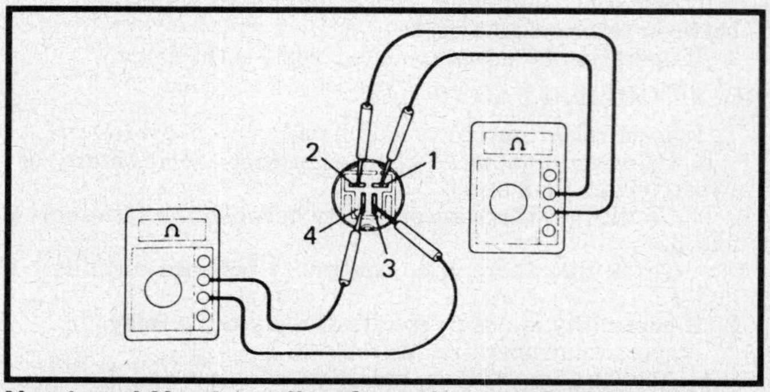
2
1
4
3

No. 1 and No. 2 cooling fan relay terminal locations–LS 400

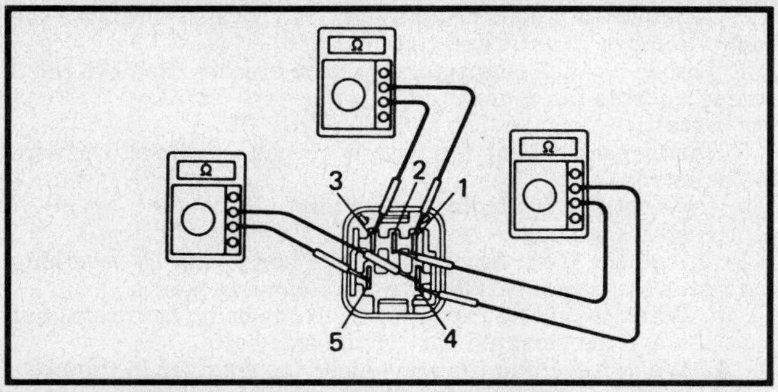
3
2
1
5
4

No. 3 cooling fan and engine main relay terminal locations—LS 400

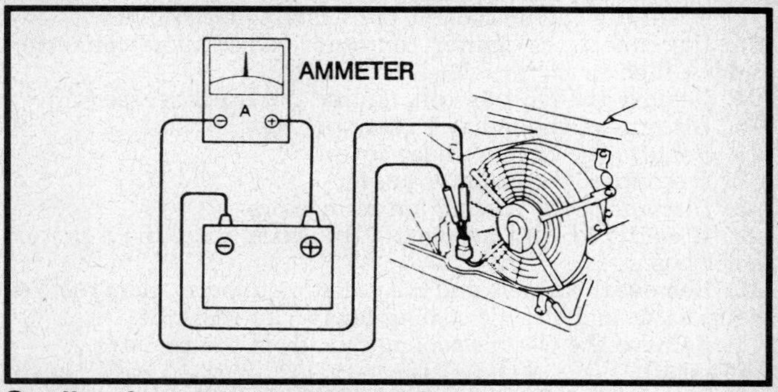
AMMETER

Cooling fan motor testing—LS 400

3. Inspect relay operation as follows:
   a. Apply battery voltage across terminals **1** and **3**.
   b. Using an ohmmeter, check that there is continuity between terminals **4** and **5**.
   c. Check that there is no continuity between terminals **2** and **4**.
4. If operation is not as specified, replace the relay.

NO. 1 AND NO. 2 COOLING FAN MOTORS

1. Connect the battery and ammeter to the fan motor connector.
2. Check to see that the motor rotates smoothly and the current is 4.2–4.4 amps.

REMOVAL AND INSTALLATION

ES 250

1. Disconnect the battery cables and remove the battery.

NOTE: Work must not be started until after approximately 20 seconds or longer from the time the ignition switch is turned to the LOCK position and the negative battery cable is disconnected. The airbag system is equipped with a back-up power source so, if work is started within 20 seconds of disconnecting the negative battery cable, the airbag may be deployed.

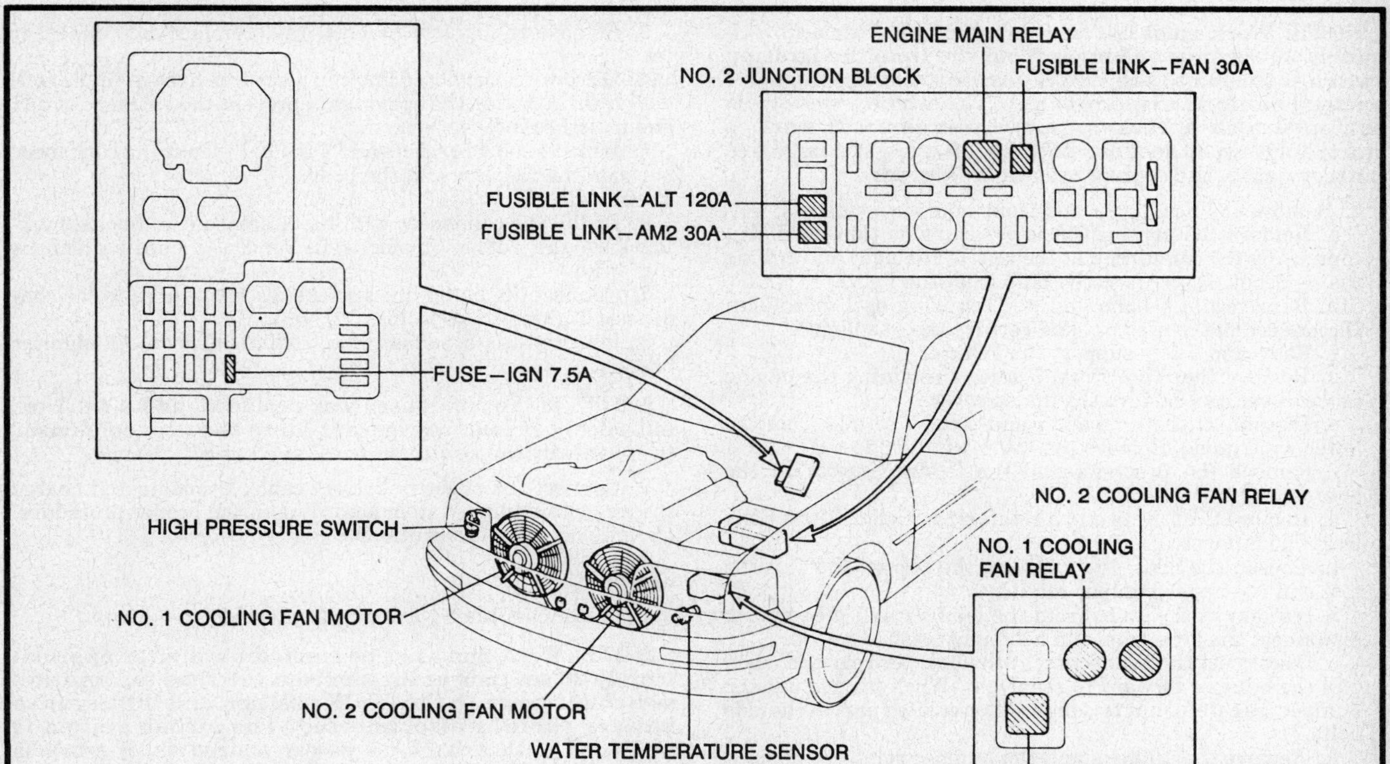
ENGINE MAIN RELAY
NO. 2 JUNCTION BLOCK
FUSIBLE LINK—FAN 30A
FUSIBLE LINK—ALT 120A
FUSIBLE LINK—AM2 30A
FUSE—IGN 7.5A
NO. 2 COOLING FAN RELAY
HIGH PRESSURE SWITCH
NO. 1 COOLING FAN RELAY
NO. 1 COOLING FAN MOTOR
NO. 2 COOLING FAN MOTOR
WATER TEMPERATURE SENSOR
NO. 3 COOLING FAN RELAY
NO. 6 RELAY BLOCK

Location of electric cooling fan components—LS 400

2. Drain the engine coolant into a suitable container.
3. Disconnect the igniter connector, noise filter connector and the high tension cable.
4. Remove the ignition coil, igniter and bracket assembly.
5. Disconnect the radiator reservoir hose.
6. Remove the engine under cover.
7. Disconnect the radiator hoses.
8. Disconnect the cooling fan connectors.
9. If equipped with automatic transaxle, disconnect the oil cooler hoses.
10. Remove the 2 bolts and the radiator supports, then remove the radiator and electric cooling fans as an assembly.
11. Remove the electric cooling fans from the radiator.

To install:

12. Install the electric cooling fans to the radiator.
13. Place the radiator in position and install the 2 supports and mounting bolts. After installation, check that the rubber cusshions of the supports are not depressed.
14. If equipped with automatic transaxle, connect the oil cooler hoses.
15. Connect the cooling fan connectors and the radiator hoses. Connect the radiator reservoir hose.
16. Install the engine under cover.
17. Install the ignition coil, igniter and bracket assembly. Connect the igniter connector, noise filter connector and the high tension cable.
18. Install the battery and connect the battery cables.
19. Fill the cooling system, start the engine and check for coolant leaks.
20. If equipped with automatic transaxle, check the transaxle fluid level.

LS 400

1. Disconnect the negative battery cable.

NOTE: Work must not be started until after approximately 20 seconds or longer from the time the ignition switch is turned to the LOCK position and the negative battery cable is disconnected. The airbag system is equipped with a back-up power source so, if work is started within 20 seconds of disconnecting the negative battery cable, the airbag may be deployed.

2. Remove the headlights and front bumper as follows:
   a. Remove the parking lights by removing the screw, disconnecting the connection at the rear of the light and pulling the light out. Disconnect the bulb from the light.
   b. Remove the 3 bolts and nut retaining each headlight. Disconnect the connectors and remove the headlights.
   c. Raise and safely support the vehicle.
   d. Remove the 8 bolts and 5 screws retaining the engine under cover and remove the under cover.
   e. Disconnect the tube and remove the 7 screws from the lower wind guide. Remove the lower wind guide.
   f. Remove the 6 screws and the fender liner from the bumper.
   g. Remove the 2 nuts and a retainer, as well as the 2 bolts from the bumper.
   h. Loosen the clips, then remove the clip with a suitable tool and the upper bumper retainer.
   i. Disconnect the bulbs from the bumper and if equipped, disconnect the hose from the headlight washer nozzle.
   j. Disconnect the connection at the bumper rear end, then pull the bumper forward to remove it. When pulling out the bumper, be careful not to damage the serrated part of the side bolts.
   k. Remove the 10 bolts and the bumper reinforcement.
3. Remove the horns.
4. Disconnect the fan motor connectors.
5. Disconnect the wire from the brackets, remove each set of 3 bolts and the cooling fans.
6. Remove the 4 bolts retaining the fan cover and remove the cover. Remove the nut and the fan.
7. Disconnect the connector from the bracket. Remove the 3 screws and the fan motor.

To install:

8. Install each cooling fan with it's 3 bolts. Connect the wire to the brackets.
9. Connect the fan motor connectors.
10. Install the horns.
11. Install the front bumper and the headlights by reversing the removal procedure. Observe the following points:
    a. When installing the bumper on the body, be careful not to damage the serrated part of the side bolts.
    b. When installing the stay, place the retainer in the hole, then push in the head of the clip and install it.
    c. After installing the headlight, adjust the light aiming.
12. Connect the negative battery cable.

Condenser

REMOVAL AND INSTALLATION

ES 250

1. Disconnect the battery cables and remove the battery.

NOTE: Work must not be started until after approximately 20 seconds or longer from the time the ignition switch is turned to the LOCK position and the negative battery cable is disconnected. The airbag system is equipped with a back-up power source so, if work is started within 20 seconds of disconnecting the negative battery cable, the airbag may be deployed.

2. Discharge the refrigerant from the air conditioning system according to the proper procedure.
3. Remove the igniter bracket, radiator fan and condenser fan.
4. Disconnect the liquid line and discharge hose from the condenser fittings. Cap the openings to prevent the entrance of dirt and moisture into the system.
5. Remove the 4 brackets and 4 bolts. Pull out the condenser between the radiator and the body.

To install:

6. Install the condenser with the 4 brackets and bolts, making sure the rubber cushions fit on the mounting flanges correctly.
7. Connect the liquid line and the discharge hose to the condenser. Tighten to 13 ft. lbs. (18 Nm).
8. Reinstall the condenser fan, radiator fan and the igniter bracket.

NOTE: If the condenser was replaced, add 1.4–1.7 oz. (40–50cc) of clean refrigerant oil to the new condenser to maintain the required total system oil charge.

9. Connect the negative battery cable. Evacuate and charge the air conditioning system according to the proper procedure. Observe all safety precautions.

LS 400

1. Disconnect the negative battery cable.

NOTE: Work must not be started until after approximately 20 seconds or longer from the time the ignition switch is turned to the LOCK position and the negative battery cable is disconnected. The airbag system is equipped with a back-up power source so, if work is started within 20 seconds of disconnecting the negative battery cable, the airbag may be deployed.

2. Remove the front bumper as follows:
   a. Remove the parking lights by removing the screw, dis-

connecting the connection at the rear of the light and pulling the light out. Disconnect the bulb from the light.

b. Remove the 3 bolts and nut retaining each headlight. Disconnect the connectors and remove the headlights.

c. Raise and safely support the vehicle.

d. Remove the 8 bolts and 5 screws retaining the engine under cover and remove the under cover.

e. Disconnect the tube and remove the 7 screws from the lower wind guide. Remove the lower wind guide.

f. Remove the 6 screws and the fender liner from the bumper.

g. Remove the 2 nuts and a retainer, as well as the 2 bolts from the bumper.

h. Loosen the clips, then remove the clip with a suitable tool and the upper bumper retainer.

i. Disconnect the bulbs from the bumper and if equipped, disconnect the hose from the headlight washer nozzle.

j. Disconnect the connection at the bumper rear end, then pull the bumper forward to remove it. When pulling out the bumper, be careful not to damage the serrated part of the side bolts.

k. Remove the 10 bolts and the bumper reinforcement.

3. Remove the 2 electric fans.
4. Remove the center brace and the 2 horns.
5. Discharge the refrigerant from the air conditioning system according to the proper procedure.
6. Disconnect the refrigerant lines from the condenser. To prevent the entrance of moisture or dirt, caps should be placed on the openings immediately.
7. Remove the 2 nuts and the condenser.

To install:

8. Install the condenser with the 2 nuts.
9. Connect the refrigerant lines. Tighten the suction line to 24 ft. lbs. (32 Nm) and the discharge and liquid lines to 7 ft. lbs. (10 Nm). Do not remove the caps until the lines are installed.

NOTE: If the condenser was replaced, add 1.4–1.7 oz. (40–50cc) of clean refrigerant oil to the new condenser to maintain the required total system oil charge.

10. Connect the negative battery cable. Evacuate and charge the air conditioning system according to the proper procedure. Observe all safety precautions.
11. Using a leak tester, check for refrigerant leaks.
12. Disconnect the negative battery cable.

NOTE: Work must not be started until after approximately 20 seconds or longer from the time the ignition switch is turned to the LOCK position and the negative battery cable is disconnected. The airbag system is equipped with a back-up power source so, if work is started within 20 seconds of disconnecting the negative battery cable, the airbag may be deployed.

13. Install the 2 horns and the center brace.
14. Install the 2 electric fans.
15. Install the front bumper. by reversing the removal procedure. Observe the following points:

a. When installing the bumper on the body, be careful not to damage the serrated part of the side bolts.

b. When installing the stay, place the retainer in the hole, then push in the head of the clip and install it.

c. After installing the headlight, adjust the light aiming.

Compressor

REMOVAL AND INSTALLATION

ES 250

1. Run the engine at idle speed with the air conditioning ON for 10 minutes.
2. Stop the engine.
3. Disconnect the battery cables and remove the battery.

NOTE: Work must not be started until after approximately 20 seconds or longer from the time the ignition switch is turned to the LOCK position and the negative battery cable is disconnected. The airbag system is equipped with a back-up power source so, if work is started within 20 seconds of disconnecting the negative battery cable, the airbag may be deployed.

4. Remove the igniter bracket, radiator fan and condenser fan.
5. Disconnect the connector from the magnetic clutch, temperature switch and revolution detecting sensor.
6. Discharge the refrigerant from the air conditioning system according to the proper procedure.
7. Disconnect the 2 hoses from the compressor service valves. Cap the open fittings immediately to keep moisture and dust out of the system.
8. Loosen the drive belt, remove the compressor mounting bolts and remove the compressor.

To install:

NOTE: If the compressor is being replaced, drain the refrigerant oil from the removed compressor into a calibrated container. Then drain the refrigerant oil from the replacement compressor into a clean calibrated container. Pour the same amount of clean refrigerant oil into the replacement compressor, as was drained from the removed compressor.

9. Install the compressor with the 4 mounting bolts. Tighten the bolts to 18 ft. lbs. (25 Nm).
10. Install the drive belt.
11. Connect the 2 hoses to the compressor service valves. Tighten to 18 ft. lbs. (25 Nm).
12. Connect the clutch lead wire to the wiring harness.
13. Install the condenser fan, radiator fan and igniter bracket.
14. Install the battery and connect the battery cables.
15. Evacuate and charge the air conditioning system according to the proper procedure. Observe all safety precautions.
16. Using a leak tester, check for refrigerant leaks.

LS 400

1. Run the engine at idle speed with the air conditioning ON for approximately 10 minutes.
2. Stop the engine.
3. Disconnect the battery cables and remove the battery.

NOTE: Work must not be started until after approximately 20 seconds or longer from the time the ignition switch is turned to the LOCK position and the negative battery cable is disconnected. The airbag system is equipped with a back-up power source so, if work is started within 20 seconds of disconnecting the negative battery cable, the airbag may be deployed.

4. Discharge the refrigerant from the air conditioning system according to the proper procedure.
5. Disconnect the electrical connector to the magnetic clutch.
6. Remove the 2 nuts and remove the discharge and suction hoses from the compressor. Cap the open fittings immediately to keep dirt and moisture out of the system.
7. Remove the drive belt.
8. Remove the ground wire harness set bolt. Remove the nut, 3 bolts, mounting bracket and the compressor.

To install:

NOTE: If the compressor is being replaced, drain the refrigerant oil from the removed compressor into a calibrated container. Then drain the refrigerant oil from the replacement compressor into a clean calibrated con-

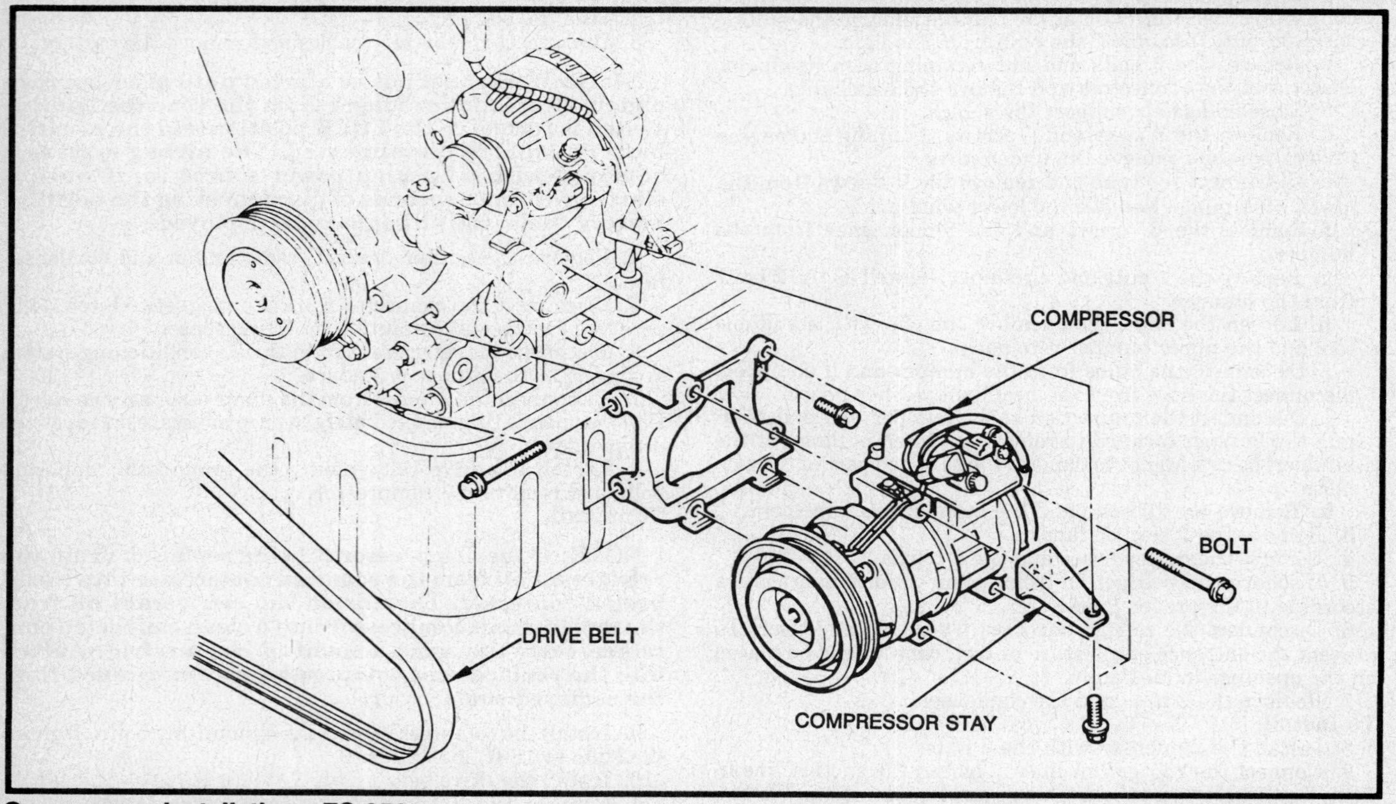
COMPRESSOR
BOLT
DRIVE BELT
COMPRESSOR STAY

Compressor installation – ES 250

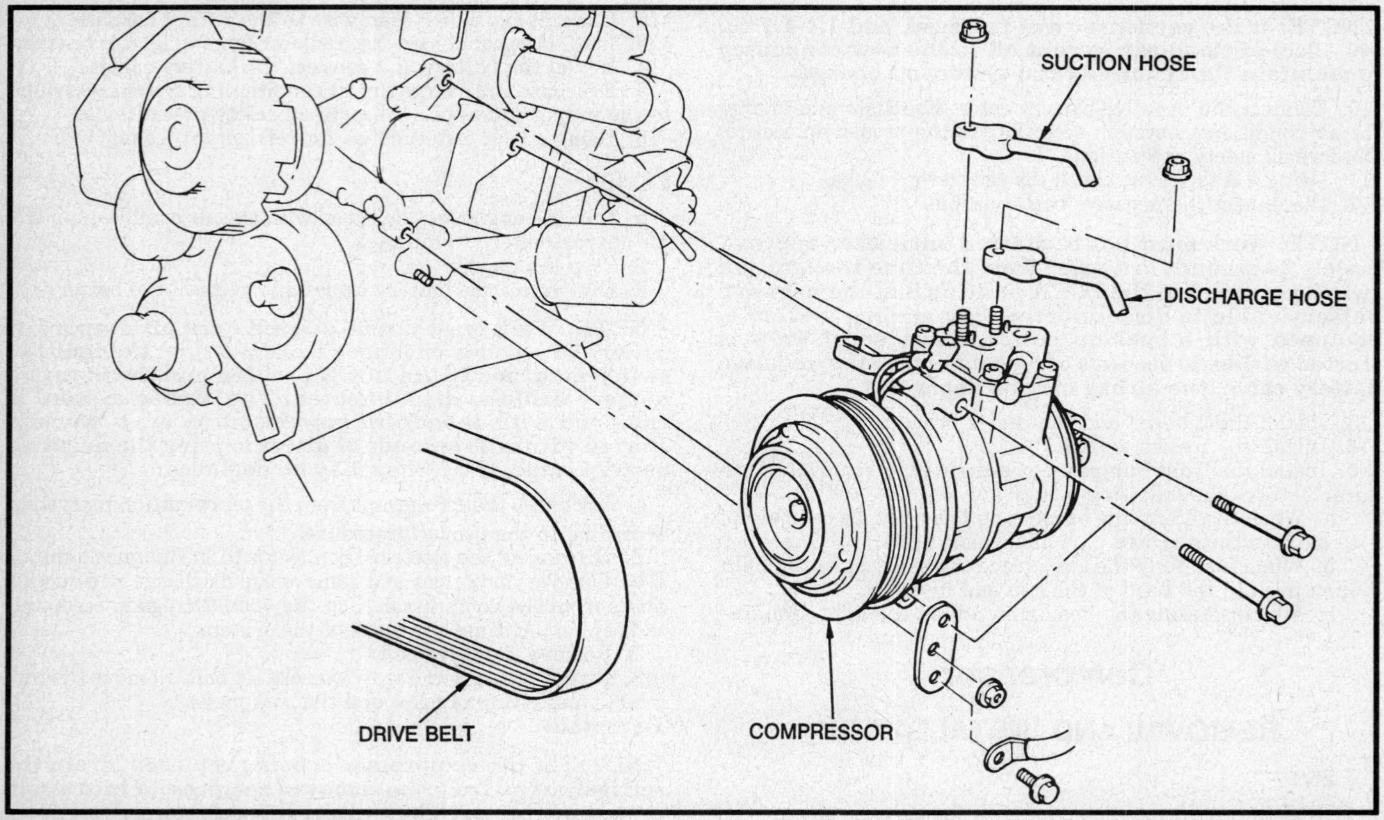
SUCTION HOSE
DISCHARGE HOSE
DRIVE BELT
COMPRESSOR

Compressor installation – LS 400

tainer. Pour the same amount of clean refrigerant oil into the replacement compressor, as was drained from the removed compressor.

9. Install the compressor with the bracket, nut and the 3 bolts. Tighten the bolts to 36 ft. lbs. (49 Nm) and the nut to 22 ft. lbs. (29 Nm). Install the ground wire harness with the bolts.
10. Install the drive belt.
11. Connect the discharge hose and the suction hose to the compressor. Tighten to 18 ft. lbs. (25 Nm). The hoses should be connected immediately after the caps have been removed.
12. Connect the connector to the magnetic clutch.
13. Install the battery and connect the battery cables.
14. Evacuate and charge the air conditioning system according to the proper procedure. Observe all safety precautions.
15. Using a leak tester, inspect the system for refrigerant leaks.

Receiver/Drier

REMOVAL AND INSTALLATION

1. Disconnect the negative battery cable.

NOTE: Work must not be started until after approximately 20 seconds or longer from the time the ignition switch is turned to the LOCK position and the negative battery cable is disconnected. The airbag system is equipped with a back-up power source so, if work is started within 20 seconds of disconnecting the negative battery cable, the airbag may be deployed.

2. On LS 400, remove the headlight from the right side of the vehicle.
3. Discharge the refrigerant from the air conditioning system according to the proper procedure.
4. On ES 250, remove the battery, reserve tank and igniter bracket.
5. Disconnect the 2 liquid lines from the receiver/drier. Cap the open fittings immediately to keep dirt and moisture out of the system.
6. Remove the receiver/drier from the holder.

To install:

7. Install the receiver/drier in the holder.

NOTE: If the receiver/drier was replaced, add 0.7 oz. (20cc) of clean refrigerant oil to the system to maintain total system oil requirements.

8. Connect the 2 liquid lines to the receiver/drier. Tighten to 48 inch lbs. (5.4 Nm). Do not remove the caps until the lines are connected.
9. On ES 250, reinstall the igniter bracket, reserve tank and battery.

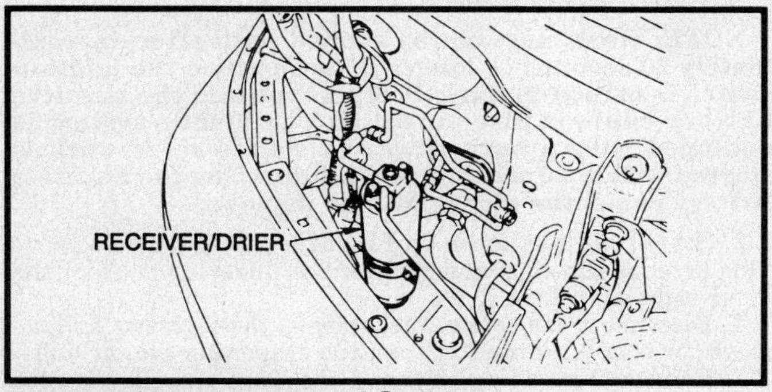
RECEIVER/DRIER

Receiver/drier location—LS 400

10. Connect the negative battery cable. Evacuate and charge the air conditioning system according to the proper procedure. Observe all safety precautions.
11. Use a leak tester to check for refrigerant leaks.
12. On LS 400, install the headlight on the right side of the vehicle.

Expansion Valve

REMOVAL AND INSTALLATION

ES 250

1. Disconnect the negative battery cable.

NOTE: Work must not be started until after approximately 20 seconds or longer from the time the ignition switch is turned to the LOCK position and the negative battery cable is disconnected. The airbag system is equipped with a back-up power source so, if work is started within 20 seconds of disconnecting the negative battery cable, the airbag may be deployed.

2. Discharge the refrigerant from the air conditioning system according to the proper procedure.
3. Disconnect the suction and liquid lines from the evaporator housing. Cap the open fittings immediately to keep dirt and moisture out of the system.
4. Remove the grommets from the inlet and outlet fittings.
5. Remove the glove box and disconnect the electrical connectors.
6. Remove the 3 nuts and 4 bolts and remove the evaporator housing.
7. Disassemble the evaporator housing as follows:
   a. Disconnect the connectors and remove the wire harness.
   b. Remove the 4 clips and the 5 screws.
   c. Remove the condenser fan control amplifier and the condenser control amplifier.
   d. Remove the upper case.
   e. Remove the thermistor with the thermistor holder.
   f. Remove the lower case.
8. Disconnect the liquid line from the inlet fitting of the expansion valve.
9. Remove the packing and heat sensing tube from the suction line of the evaporator.
10. Remove the expansion valve.

To install:

11. Connect the expansion valve to the inlet fitting of the evaporator. Tighten the nut to 17 ft. lbs. (23 Nm). Make sure the O-ring is positioned on the line fitting.
12. Install the heat sensing tube to the suction line with the holder.
13. Connect the liquid line to the inlet fitting of the expansion valve. Tighten the nut to 10 ft. lbs. (14 Nm).
14. Assemble the evaporator housing as follows:
   a. Install the lower case and the thermistor to the evaporator.
   b. Install the upper case and the screws and clips.
   c. Install the wire harness.
   d. Install the condenser fan control amplifier and the compressor control amplifier.
   e. Connect the connectors.
15. Install the evaporator housing with the 3 nuts and 4 bolts.
16. Connect the electrical connectors.
17. Install the glove box.
18. Install the grommets on the inlet and outlet fitting.
19. Connect the liquid line to the inlet fitting. Tighten the nut to 10 ft. lbs. (14 Nm). Connect the suction line to the outlet fitting. Tighten the nut to 24 ft. lbs. (32 Nm).
20. Connect the negative battery cable. Evacuate and charge the system according to the proper procedure. Observe all safety precautions.

21. Check the system for refrigerant leaks and for proper operation.

LS 400

1. Disconnect the negative battery cable.

NOTE: Work must not be started until after approximately 20 seconds or longer from the time the ignition switch is turned to the LOCK position and the negative battery cable is disconnected. The airbag system is equipped with a back-up power source so, if work is started within 20 seconds of disconnecting the negative battery cable, the airbag may be deployed.

2. Discharge the refrigerant from the air conditioning system according to the proper procedure.
3. Remove the cruise control actuator.
4. Remove the bolt and remove both tubes from the evaporator pressure regulator.
5. Remove the 2 bolts and both the liquid and suction lines.
6. Remove the 2 nuts and the cover plate.

NOTE: Cap all open fittings immediately to keep dirt and moisture out of the system.

7. Remove the drain hose clamp from the front side member.
8. Working inside the vehicle, remove the clips and remove the under cover from the lower right corner of the dash.
9. Remove the glove compartment as follows:
   a. Remove the glove compartment panel.
   b. Disconnect the left side check arm from the door.
   c. Using a suitable tool, push in the top of the clip and remove the 5 clips.
   d. Insert a suitable plate between the upper side of the compartment and the safety pad, to protect the pad. Pry against the plate to pry out the compartment and remove it.
   e. Disconnect the electrical connector.
10. Remove the 5 bolts and remove the lower pad from below the glove compartment opening. Disconnect the connectors from the pad.
11. Remove the bolt, 4 screws and the glove compartment door.
12. Remove the bolt and nut and remove the anti-lock brake ECU. Disconnect the connectors.
13. Remove the screw and pull out the heater ducts.
14. Remove the mirror control ECU.
15. Remove the 2 bolts and the bracket from the evaporator-blower unit. Disconnect the connectors.
16. Disconnect the vehicle side wire harness from the evaporator-blower unit.
17. Remove the 4 nuts and 2 screws, then remove the evaporator-blower unit.
18. Disassemble the evaporator-cooling unit as follows:
   a. Remove the screw and cover and disconnect the connector for the air inlet servomotor assembly. Remove the 3 screws and remove the servomotor assembly.
   b. Remove the screw and remove the power transistor. Remove the screw and remove the plate. Disconnect the connector.
   c. Remove the screw and the extra high relay. Disconnect the connector.
   d. Disconnect the connector, remove the 2 screws and the blower resistor.
   e. Remove the air conditioning wire harness. Remove the 8 screws and separate the upper and lower case.
19. Pull out the evaporator sensor from the evaporator fins. Remove the 2 bolts and separate the evaporator and the expansion valve.

To install:

20. Install the expansion valve to the evaporator and tighten the bolts to 48 inch lbs. (5.4 Nm). Position the evaporator sensor.
21. Assemble the evaporator-blower unit as follows:
   a. Install the evaporator in the lower case and install the upper case. Install the screws.
   b. Attach the air conditioning wire harness.
   c. Install the blower resistor, extra high relay, power transistor and the air inlet servomotor assembly. Connect the electrical connectors.
22. Install the evaporator-blower unit and secure with the nuts and screws.
23. Connect the vehicle side wire harness to the evaporator-blower unit. Install the connector bracket.
24. Install the mirror control ECU and connect the electrical connector.
25. Install the heater-to-register ducts.
26. Install the anti-lock brake ECU and connect the electrical connector.
27. Install the glove compartment door and the right lower pad.
28. Install the glove compartment.
29. Install the drain hose clamp to the front side member and install the cover plate.
30. Connect the liquid and suction lines. Tighten the bolts to 7 ft. lbs. (10 Nm).
31. Connect the equalizer tube to the evaporator pressure regulator. Tighten the bolt to 7 ft. lbs. (10 Nm).
32. Install the cruise control actuator.
33. Connect the negative battery cable. Evacuate and charge the system according to the proper procedure. Observe all safety precautions.
34. Check for refrigeant leaks and for proper system operation.

Blower Motor

REMOVAL AND INSTALLATION

ES 250

1. Disconnect the negative battery cable.

NOTE: Work must not be started until after approximately 20 seconds or longer from the time the ignition switch is turned to the LOCK position and the negative battery cable is disconnected. The airbag system is equipped with a back-up power source so, if work is started within 20 seconds of disconnecting the negative battery cable, the airbag may be deployed.

2. Remove the under cover from the right lower side of the dash.
3. Remove the blower motor mounting screws and remove the blower motor. Disconnect the electrical connector.
4. Installation is the reverse of the removal procedure.

LS 400

1. Disconnect the negative battery cable.

NOTE: Work must not be started until after approximately 20 seconds or longer from the time the ignition switch is turned to the LOCK position and the negative battery cable is disconnected. The airbag system is equipped with a back-up power source so, if work is started within 20 seconds of disconnecting the negative battery cable, the airbag may be deployed.

2. Set the air inlet mode on **FRESH**.
3. Remove the clips and remove the under cover from the lower right side of the dash.
4. Disconnect the connectors, remove the 2 screws and remove the connector bracket from the evaporator-blower unit.
5. Remove 9 retaining clips and the front passenger's door scuff plate.

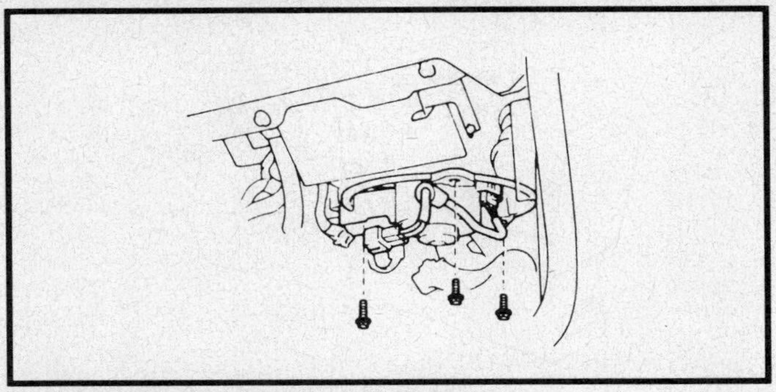

Blower motor removal—LS 400

6. Pull back the cowl side portion of the floor carpet.
7. Disconnect the shaft from the control lever, remove the 2 screws and remove the blower lower case.
8. Disconnect the electrical connector, remove the 3 screws and the blower motor.

To install:

9. Install the blower motor with the 3 screws and connect the electrical connector.
10. Install the blower lower case with the 2 screws. Install the blower lower case control lever on the shaft by turning it counterclockwise.
11. Reposition the carpet and install the front passenger's door scuff plate.
12. Install the connector bracket to the evaporator-blower unit with the 2 screws. Connect the connectors.
13. Install the instrument panel under cover.
14. Connect the negative battery cable.

Blower Motor Resistor

REMOVAL AND INSTALLATION

ES 250

1. Disconnect the negative battery cable.

NOTE: Work must not be started until after approximately 20 seconds or longer from the time the ignition switch is turned to the LOCK position and the negative battery cable is disconnected. The airbag system is equipped with a back-up power source so, if work is started within 20 seconds of disconnecting the negative battery cable, the airbag may be deployed.

2. Disconnect the electrical connector from the resistor.
3. Remove the resistor mounting screws and remove the resistor.
4. Installation is the reverse of the removal procedure.

LS 400

1. Disconnect the negative battery cable.

NOTE: Work must not be started until after approximately 20 seconds or longer from the time the ignition switch is turned to the LOCK position and the negative battery cable is disconnected. The airbag system is equipped with a back-up power source so, if work is started within 20 seconds of disconnecting the negative battery cable, the airbag may be deployed.

2. Remove the clips and remove the under cover from the lower right side of the dash.
3. Disconnect the connectors, remove the 2 screws and remove the connector bracket from the evaporator-blower unit.

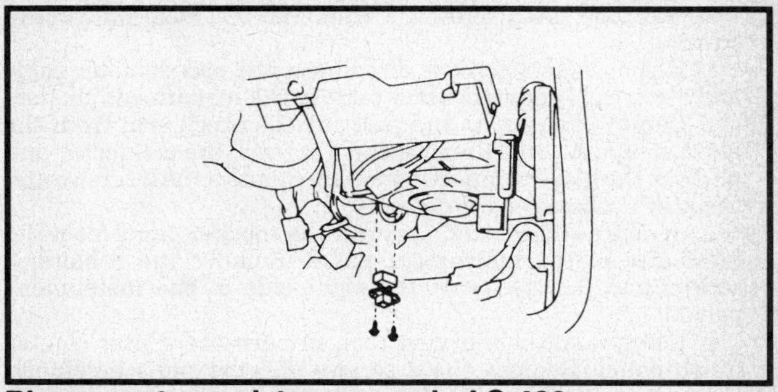

Blower motor resistor removal—LS 400

4. Disconnect the connector, remove the 2 screws and remove the resistor from the evaporator-blower unit.
5. Installation is the reverse of the removal procedure.

Heater Core

REMOVAL AND INSTALLATION

ES 250

1. Disconnect the negative battery cable.

NOTE: Work must not be started until after approximately 20 seconds or longer from the time the ignition switch is turned to the LOCK position and the negative battery cable is disconnected. The airbag system is equipped with a back-up power source so, if work is started within 20 seconds of disconnecting the negative battery cable, the airbag may be deployed.

2. Drain the cooling system into a suitable container.
3. Discharge the refrigerant from the air conditioning system according to the proper procedure.
4. Remove the water valve.
5. Remove the evaporator assembly.
6. Disconnect the heater hoses.
7. Remove the instrument panel as follows:
   a. Place the front wheels facing straight ahead and loosen the 4 Torx® head screws, 2 on either side of the steering wheel. Loosen the screws until the groove along the screw circumference catches on the screw case.
   b. Pull the wheel pad out from the steering wheel and disconnect the airbag connector.

NOTE: When removing the wheel pad, be careful not to pull the airbag wire harness.

CAUTION

When storing the wheel pad, keep the upper surface of the pad facing upward. Storing the pad with it's metallic surface up may lead to a serious accident and personal injury if the airbag inflates for some reason.

   c. Disconnect the electrical connector, remove the nut and using a suitable puller, remove the steering wheel.
   d. Pry out the clips and pull the front pillar garnish upward to remove it by hand.
   e. Remove the cover panels from under both sides of the instrument panel.
   f. Remove the 2 screws and the engine hood release lever. Using a suitable tool, pry out the switch bases and the speaker panel to the left of the steering column. Disconnect the connectors, remove the 7 bolts and remove the lower finish panel from under the steering column.
   g. Remove the 5 screws and the instrument cluster finish panel. Disconnect the connectors.

h. Remove the 5 screws, 2 bolts and the steering column cover.

i. Remove the 4 screws, disconnect the speedometer cable and electrical connectors and remove the instrument cluster.

j. Remove the screw and pull out the check arm from the glove compartment. Remove the 4 screws, the connector and pull out the glove compartment box. Remove the 2 screws and the glove compartment door.

k. Using a suitable tool, pry out the speaker panel from the right side of the instrument panel. Remove the 5 bolts, 3 screws and 2 nuts, from the right side of the instrument panel.

l. Using a suitable prying tool, remove the center cluster finish panel. Remove the 4 screws and the radio assembly. Disconnect the connectors and the antenna cable.

m. Remove the 4 screws and the heater control. Remove the 2 screws and pull out the center instrument panel register.

n. Remove the 9 screws from the center lower panel and the 4 bolts from the lower console box. Pull out the panel.

o. Use a suitable prying tool to remove the side defroster nozzle.

p. Remove the nut connecting the center bracket and the instrument panel.

q. Remove the speaker and the 2 screws and junction block from the left side of the instrument panel.

r. Push on the pawls of the speedometer cable bracket and pull it from the instrument panel. Remove the 2 bolts at each end of the instrument panel, the 2 screws from the center and the 2 nuts from the instrument cluster opening. Remove the instrument panel.

NOTE: The instrument panel has a boss on the reverse side for clamping onto the clip on the body side. Therefore, when removing, pull upward at an angle.

s. Remove the clips and disconnect the wire harness from the instrument panel.

8. Remove the necessary ducts to gain access to the heater unit.

9. Remove the mounting nuts and remove the heater unit.

10. Remove the heater core from the heater unit.

To install:

11. Install the heater core in the heater unit.

12. Install the heater unit with the mounting nuts.

12. Install the ducts.

13. Install the instrument panel by reversing the removal procedure. Note the following points:

a. Before installing the steering wheel, center the spiral cable by turning the cable counterclockwise by hand until it becomes harder to turn the cable. Then rotate the spiral cable clockwise about 2½ turns to align the red mark.

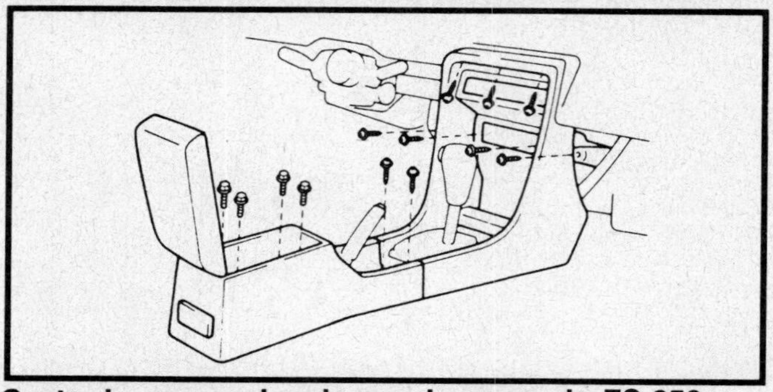

Center lower panel and console removal – ES 250

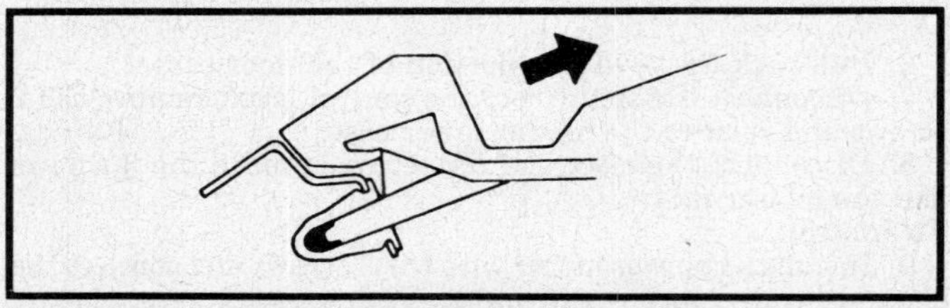

Instrument panel clip cross-section.

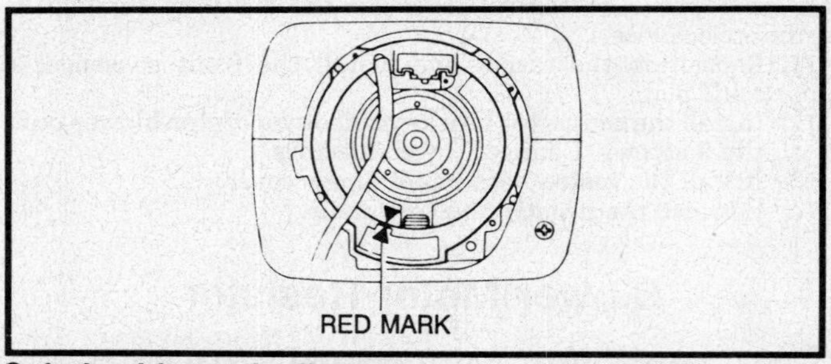
RED MARK

Spiral cable mark alignment

NOTE: The spiral cable will rotate about 2½ turns to either left or right of center.

b. Align the matchmarks on the steering wheel and main shaft and install the steering wheel. Tighten the nut to 26 ft. lbs. (35 Nm). Connect the connector.

c. Connect the airbag connector. Install the wheel pad after confirming that the circumference groove of the Torx® screws is caught on the screw case. Tighten the Torx® screws to 65 inch lbs. (7.4 Nm).

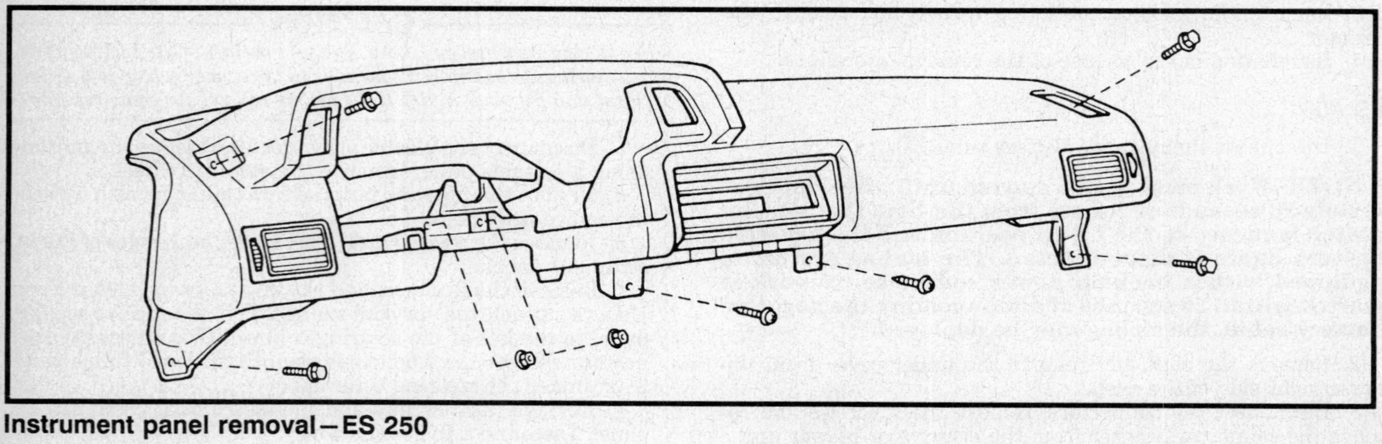

Instrument panel removal – ES 250

14. Connect the heater hoses to the heater core.
15. Install the evaporator housing.
16. Install the water valve.
17. Connect the negative battery cable.
18. Fill the cooling system to the proper level.
19. Evacuate and charge the air conditioning system according to the proper procedure. Observe all safety precautions.
20. Check for coolant and refrigerant leaks. Check the system for proper operation.

LS 400

1. Disconnect the negative battery cable.

NOTE: Work must not be started until after approximately 20 seconds or longer from the time the ignition switch is turned to the LOCK position and the negative battery cable is disconnected. The airbag system is equipped with a back-up power source so, if work is started within 20 seconds of disconnecting the negative battery cable, the airbag may be deployed.

2. Drain the cooling system into a suitable container.
3. Discharge the refrigerant from the air conditioning system according to the proper procedure.
4. Remove the water valve.
5. Remove the evaporator-blower assembly.
6. Disconnect the heater hose and remove the insulator retainer.
7. Remove the instrument panel as follows:
   a. Tilt down and pull out the steering wheel.
   b. Remove the right and left front pillar garnish by removing the 2 screws and the assist grip and removing the front seat belt anchor bolt. Disconnect the upper side of the roof side inner garnish. Using a suitable tool, remove the 7 clips and pull the garnish upper side.
   c. Place the front wheels facing straight ahead and loosen the 4 Torx® head screws, 2 on either side of the steering wheel. Loosen the screws until the groove along the screw circumference catches on the screw case.
   d. Pull the wheel pad out from the steering wheel and disconnect the airbag connector.

NOTE: When removing the wheel pad, be careful not to pull the airbag wire harness.

CAUTION

When storing the wheel pad, keep the upper surface of the pad facing upward. Storing the pad with it's metallic surface up may lead to a serious accident and personal injury if the airbag inflates for some reason.

   e. Disconnect the electrical connector, remove the nut and using a suitable puller, remove the steering wheel.
   f. Remove the 3 screws and the steering column cover.
   g. Using a suitable tool, pry out the rear side of the upper console panel. Pull the panel backwards to remove it. Remove the front ash tray and disconnect the connector.
   h. Pry out the front side of the lower console cover, slide the cover forward and remove it. Remove the rear console box garnish, remove the 4 screws and pry out the lower console box.
   i. Remove the 4 screws and the cup holder. Pry out the rear end panel of the console box, disconnect the connector, remove the 4 screws and remove the console box.
   j. Remove the 3 screws and remove the cover from under the lower left of the instrument panel. Disconnect the valve from the cover. Remove the 2 screws and the hood release lever. Disconnect the release cable from the lever.
   k. Remove the key cylinder pad.
   l. Remove the 6 bolts and the pad from under the steering column. Disconnect the connectors and hose from the pad. Remove the 3 bolts and the parking brake lever.
   m. Remove the 2 screws and pry out the outer mirror switch assembly. Disconnect the connectors.
   n. Remove the 3 screws at the top and pry out the clips at the bottom of the instrument cluster finish panel. Pry out the upper side of the panel and remove it. Disconnect the connectors from the panel. Remove the 4 screws and the instrument cluster. Disconnect the connectors from the cluster.
   o. Pry out and remove the center panel register. Remove the 4 screws and the radio with the air conditioning control assembly.
   p. Using a suitable tool, remove the clips from the cover under the right side of the instrument panel. Remove the cover.
   q. Remove the glove compartment panel and disconnect the left side check arm from the door. Using a suitable tool, push in the top of the clip and remove the 5 clips. Insert a protective plate between the upper side of the compartment and the instrument panel and pry against the plate to remove the compartment. Disconnect the connector from the glove compartment.
   r. Remove the 5 bolts and remove the pad from under the glove compartment opening. Disconnect the connectors from the pad.
   s. Remove the bolt, 4 screws and the glove compartment door. Remove the bolt and nut and remove the anti-lock brake ECU. Disconnect the connectors.
   t. Remove the heater-to-register ducts.
   u. On the driver's side, loosen the lock bolt and disconnect the junction block. Using a suitable tool, disconnect the 3 clips at the floor carpet. Remove the 4 screws and the combination switch from the steering column.
   v. On the passenger's side, disconnect the connectors and separate the wire harness from the retainer. Using a suitable tool, disconnect the 3 clips at the floor carpet.
   w. Remove the 9 bolts and 1 nut and remove the instrument panel.
8. Remove the necessary heater ducts.
9. Remove the 4 nuts and the heater unit.
10. Disconnect the connector, remove the 4 screws and remove the servomotor from the heater unit.
11. Remove the screw and remove the aspirator.
12. Remove the packing and the plate from around the heater core tubes. Remove the 2 screws and the clamp.
13. Remove the heater core from the heater unit.

To install:

14. Install the heater core in the heater unit.
15. Install the clamp and the 2 retaining screws. Install the plate and the packing around the heater core tubes.
16. Install the aspirator and the servomotor. Connect the connector.
17. Install the heater unit in the vehicle with the 4 mounting nuts.
18. Install the heater ducts.
19. Install the instrument panel by reversing the removal procedure. Note the following points:
   a. Before installing the steering wheel, center the spiral cable by turning the cable counterclockwise by hand until it becomes harder to turn the cable. Then rotate the spiral cable clockwise about 2½ turns to align the red mark.

NOTE: The spiral cable will rotate about 2½ turns to either left or right of center.

   b. Align the matchmarks on the steering wheel and main shaft and install the steering wheel. Tighten the nut to 26 ft. lbs. (35 Nm). Connect the connector.
   c. Connect the airbag connector. Install the wheel pad after confirming that the circumference groove of the Torx® screws is caught on the screw case. Tighten the Torx® screws to 65 inch lbs. (7.4 Nm).
20. Install the insulator retainer and attach the heater hose.
21. Install the evaporator-blower assembly.

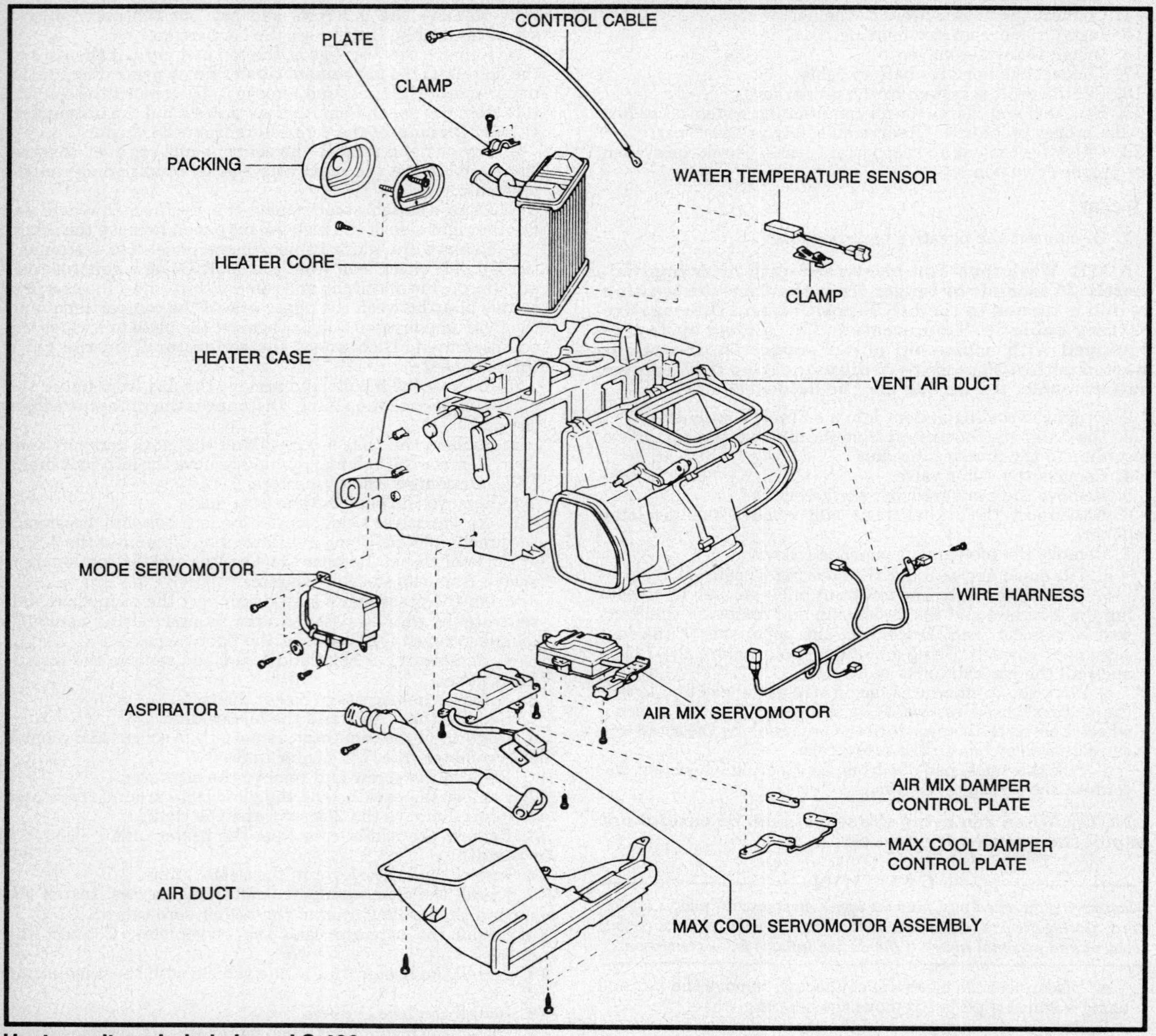
CONTROL CABLE
PLATE
CLAMP
PACKING
WATER TEMPERATURE SENSOR
HEATER CORE
CLAMP
HEATER CASE
VENT AIR DUCT
MODE SERVOMOTOR
WIRE HARNESS
ASPIRATOR
AIR MIX SERVOMOTOR
AIR MIX DAMPER
CONTROL PLATE
MAX COOL DAMPER
CONTROL PLATE
AIR DUCT
MAX COOL SERVOMOTOR ASSEMBLY

Heater unit exploded view—LS 400

22. Install the water valve.
23. Connect the negative battery cable.
24. Fill the cooling system to the proper level.
25. Evacuate and charge the system according to the proper procedure. Observe all safety precautions.
26. Check for coolant and refrigerant leaks. Check the system for proper operation.

Evaporator

REMOVAL AND INSTALLATION

ES 250

1. Disconnect the negative battery cable.

NOTE: Work must not be started until after approximately 20 seconds or longer from the time the ignition switch is turned to the LOCK position and the negative battery cable is disconnected. The airbag system is equipped with a back-up power source so, if work is started within 20 seconds of disconnecting the negative battery cable, the airbag may be deployed.

2. Discharge the refrigerant from the air conditioning system according to the proper procedure.
3. Disconnect the suction and liquid lines from the evaporator housing. Cap the open fittings immediately to keep dirt and moisture out of the system.
4. Remove the grommets from the inlet and outlet fittings.

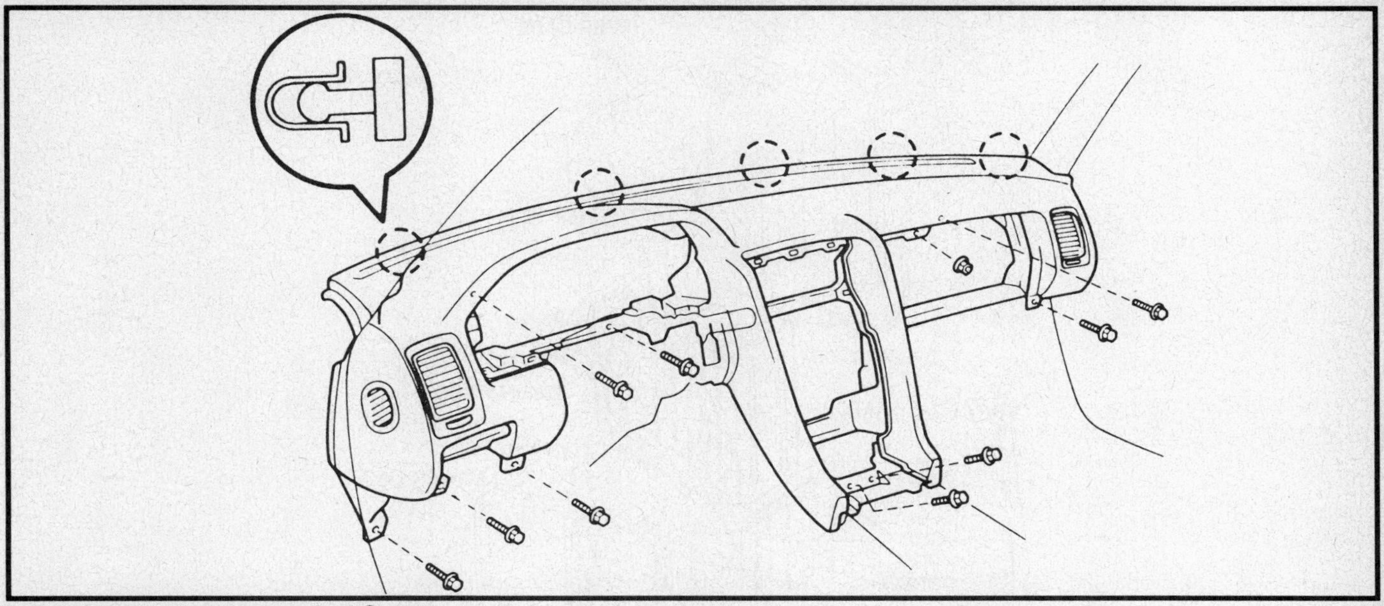

Instrument panel removal—LS 400

5. Remove the glove box and disconnect the electrical connectors.
6. Remove the 3 nuts and 4 bolts and remove the evaporator housing.
7. Disassemble the evaporator housing as follows:
   a. Disconnect the connectors and remove the wire harness.
   b. Remove the 4 clips and the 5 screws.
   c. Remove the condenser fan control amplifier and the condenser control amplifier.
   d. Remove the upper case.
   e. Remove the thermistor with the thermistor holder.
   f. Remove the lower case.
8. Disconnect the liquid line from the inlet fitting of the expansion valve.
9. Remove the packing and heat sensing tube from the suction line of the evaporator.
10. Remove the expansion valve from the evaporator core.

To install:

11. Connect the expansion valve to the inlet fitting of the evaporator core. Tighten the nut to 17 ft. lbs. (23 Nm). Make sure the O-ring is positioned on the line fitting.
12. Install the heat sensing tube to the suction line with the holder.
13. Connect the liquid line to the inlet fitting of the expansion valve. Tighten the nut to 10 ft. lbs. (14 Nm).
14. Assemble the evaporator housing as follows:
   a. Install the lower case and the thermistor to the evaporator.
   b. Install the upper case and the screws and clips.
   c. Install the wire harness.
   d. Install the condenser fan control amplifier and the compressor control amplifier.
   e. Connect the connectors.

NOTE: If the evaporator core was replaced, add 1.4–1.7 oz. of clean refrigerant oil to the system to maintain the total system oil requirements.

15. Install the evaporator housing with the 3 nuts and 4 bolts.
16. Connect the electrical connectors.
17. Install the glove box.
18. Install the grommets on the inlet and outlet fitting.
19. Connect the liquid line to the inlet fitting. Tighten the nut to 10 ft. lbs. (14 Nm). Connect the suction line to the outlet fitting. Tighten the nut to 24 ft. lbs. (32 Nm).
20. Connect the negative battery cable. Evacuate and charge the system according to the proper procedure. Observe all safety precautions.
21. Check the system for refrigerant leaks and for proper operation.

LS 400

1. Disconnect the negative battery cable.

NOTE: Work must not be started until after approximately 20 seconds or longer from the time the ignition switch is turned to the LOCK position and the negative battery cable is disconnected. The airbag system is equipped with a back-up power source so, if work is started within 20 seconds of disconnecting the negative battery cable, the airbag may be deployed.

2. Discharge the refrigerant from the air conditioning system according to the proper procedure.
3. Remove the cruise control actuator.
4. Remove the bolt and remove both tubes from the evaporator pressure regulator.
5. Remove the 2 bolts and both the liquid and suction lines.
6. Remove the 2 nuts and the cover plate.

NOTE: Cap all open fittings immediately to keep dirt and moisture out of the system.

7. Remove the drain hose clamp from the front side member.
8. Working inside the vehicle, remove the clips and remove the under cover from the lower right corner of the dash.
9. Remove the glove compartment as follows:
   a. Remove the glove compartment panel.
   b. Disconnect the left side check arm from the door.
   c. Using a suitable tool, push in the top of the clip and remove the 5 clips.
   d. Insert a suitable plate between the upper side of the compartment and the safety pad, to protect the pad. Pry against the plate to pry out the compartment and remove it.

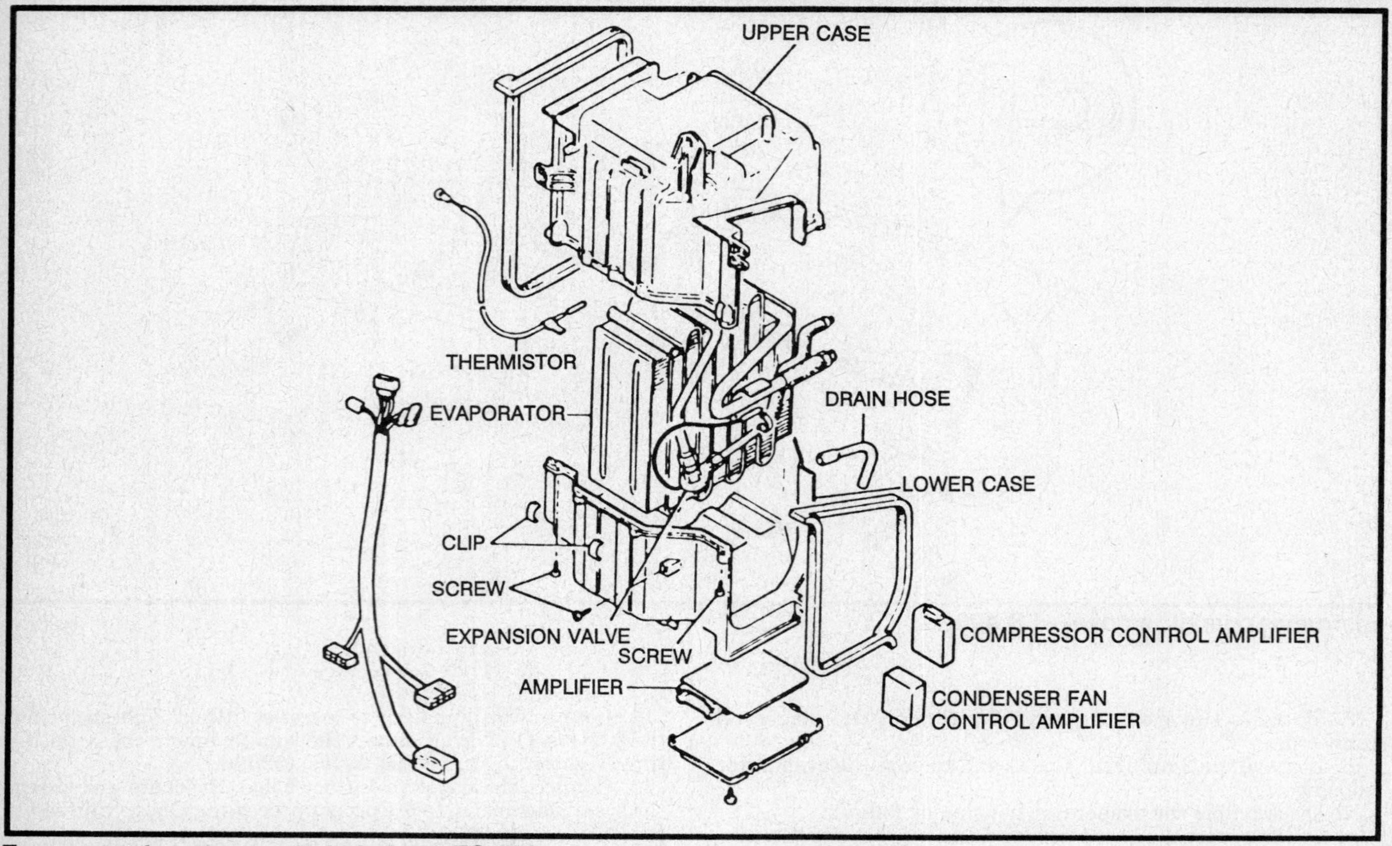
UPPER CASE
THERMISTOR
EVAPORATOR
DRAIN HOSE
LOWER CASE
CLIP
SCREW
EXPANSION VALVE
SCREW
COMPRESSOR CONTROL AMPLIFIER
AMPLIFIER
CONDENSER FAN
CONTROL AMPLIFIER

Evaporator housing exploded view—ES 250

e. Disconnect the electrical connector.

10. Remove the 5 bolts and remove the lower pad from below the glove compartment opening. Disconnect the connectors from the pad.

11. Remove the bolt, 4 screws and the glove compartment door.

12. Remove the bolt and nut and remove the anti-lock brake ECU. Disconnect the connectors.

13. Remove the screw and pull out the heater ducts.

14. Remove the mirror control ECU.

15. Remove the 2 bolts and the bracket from the evaporator-blower unit. Disconnect the connectors.

16. Disconnect the vehicle side wire harness from the evaporator-blower unit.

17. Remove the 4 nuts and 2 screws, then remove the evaporator-blower unit.

18. Disassemble the evaporator-blower unit as follows:

a. Remove the screw and cover and disconnect the connector for the air inlet servomotor assembly. Remove the 3 screws and remove the servomotor assembly.

b. Remove the screw and remove the power transistor. Remove the screw and remove the plate. Disconnect the connector.

c. Remove the screw and the extra high relay. Disconnect the connector.

d. Disconnect the connector, remove the 2 screws and the blower resistor.

e. Remove the air conditioning wire harness. Remove the 8 screws and separate the upper and lower case.

19. Pull out the evaporator sensor from the evaporator fins. Remove the 2 bolts and separate the evaporator and the expansion valve.

To install:

20. Install the expansion valve to the evaporator and tighten the bolts to 48 inch lbs. (5.4 Nm). Position the evaporator sensor.

21. Assemble the evaporator-blower unit as follows:

a. Install the evaporator in the lower case and install the upper case. Install the screws.

b. Attach the air conditioning wire harness.

c. Install the blower resistor, extra high relay, power transistor and the air inlet servomotor assembly. Connect the electrical connectors.

NOTE: If the evaporator core was replaced, add 1.4–1.7 oz. of clean refrigerant oil to the system to maintain the total system oil requirements.

22. Install the evaporator-blower unit and secure with the nuts and screws.

23. Connect the vehicle side wire harness to the evaporator-blower unit. Install the connector bracket.

24. Install the mirror control ECU and connect the electrical connector.

25. Install the heater-to-register ducts.

26. Install the anti-lock brake ECU and connect the electrical connector.

27. Install the glove compartment door and the right lower pad.

28. Install the glove compartment.

29. Install the drain hose clamp to the front side member and install the cover plate.

30. Connect the liquid and suction lines. Tighten the bolts to 7 ft. lbs. (10 Nm).

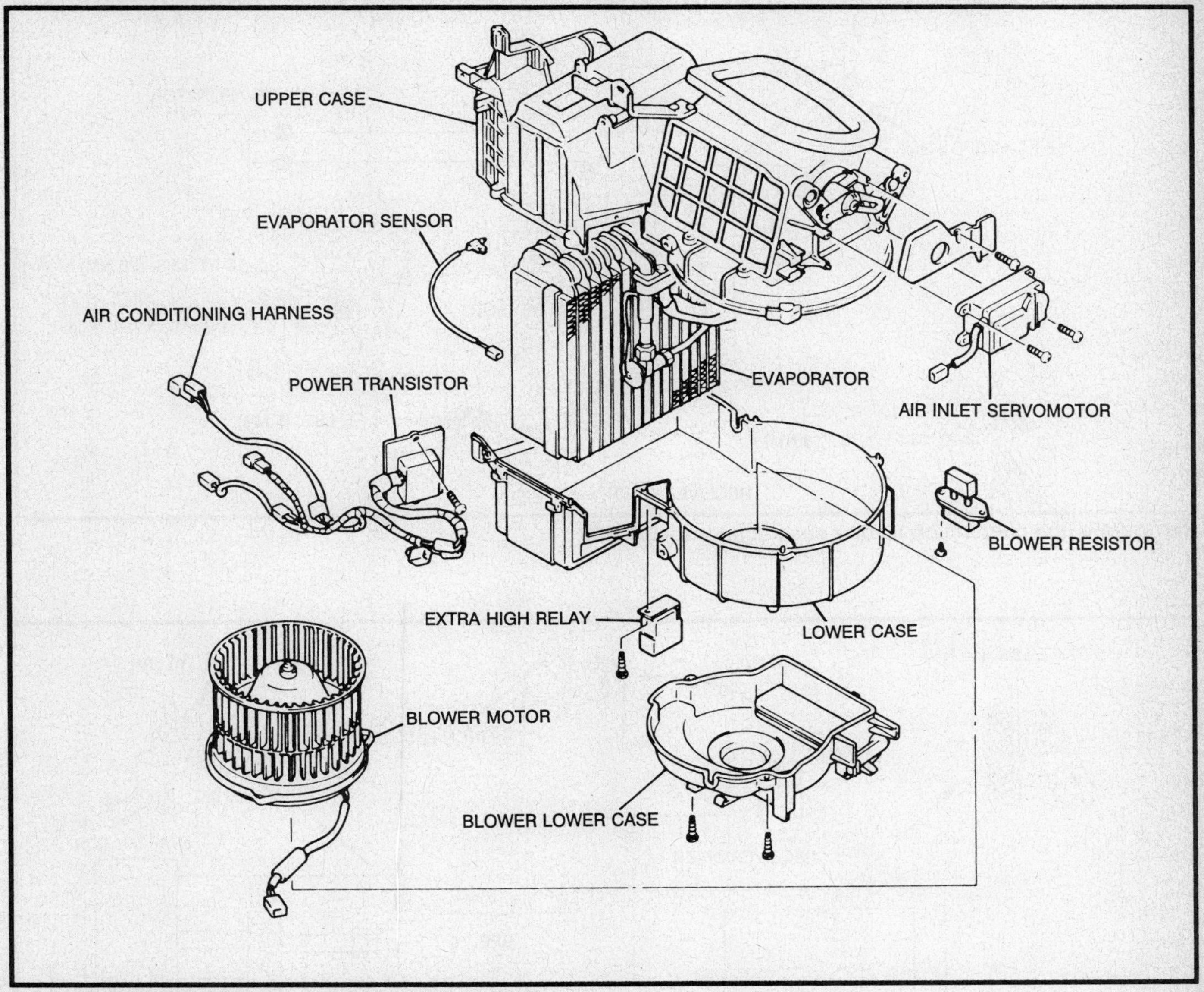
UPPER CASE
EVAPORATOR SENSOR
AIR CONDITIONING HARNESS
POWER TRANSISTOR
EVAPORATOR
AIR INLET SERVOMOTOR
BLOWER RESISTOR
EXTRA HIGH RELAY
LOWER CASE
BLOWER MOTOR
BLOWER LOWER CASE

Evaporator-blower housing exploded view—LS 400

31. Connect the equalizer tube to the evaporator pressure regulator. Tighten the bolt to 7 ft. lbs. (10 Nm).
32. Install the cruise control actuator.
33. Connect the negative battery cable. Evacuate and charge the system according to the proper procedure. Observe all safety precautions.
34. Check for refrigeant leaks and for proper system operation.

Refrigerant Lines

REMOVAL AND INSTALLATION

1. Disconnect the negative battery cable.

NOTE: Work must not be started until after approximately 20 seconds or longer from the time the ignition switch is turned to the LOCK position and the negative battery cable is disconnected. The airbag system is equipped with a back-up power source so, if work is started within 20 seconds of disconnecting the negative battery cable, the airbag may be deployed.

2. Discharge the refrigerant from the air conditioning system according to the proper procedure.
3. Disconnect the refrigerant line to be replaced at the connection fittings. Cap the open connections on the vehicle to prevent the entrance of dirt and moisture.
4. Remove the refrigerant line.

To install:

5. Route the new refrigerant line into place with the protective end caps installed.
6. Remove the protective caps and connect the line to the connection fittings. Tighten to the proper torque specification.
7. Connect the negative battery cable. Evacuate and charge the system according to the proper procedure. Observe all safety precautions.

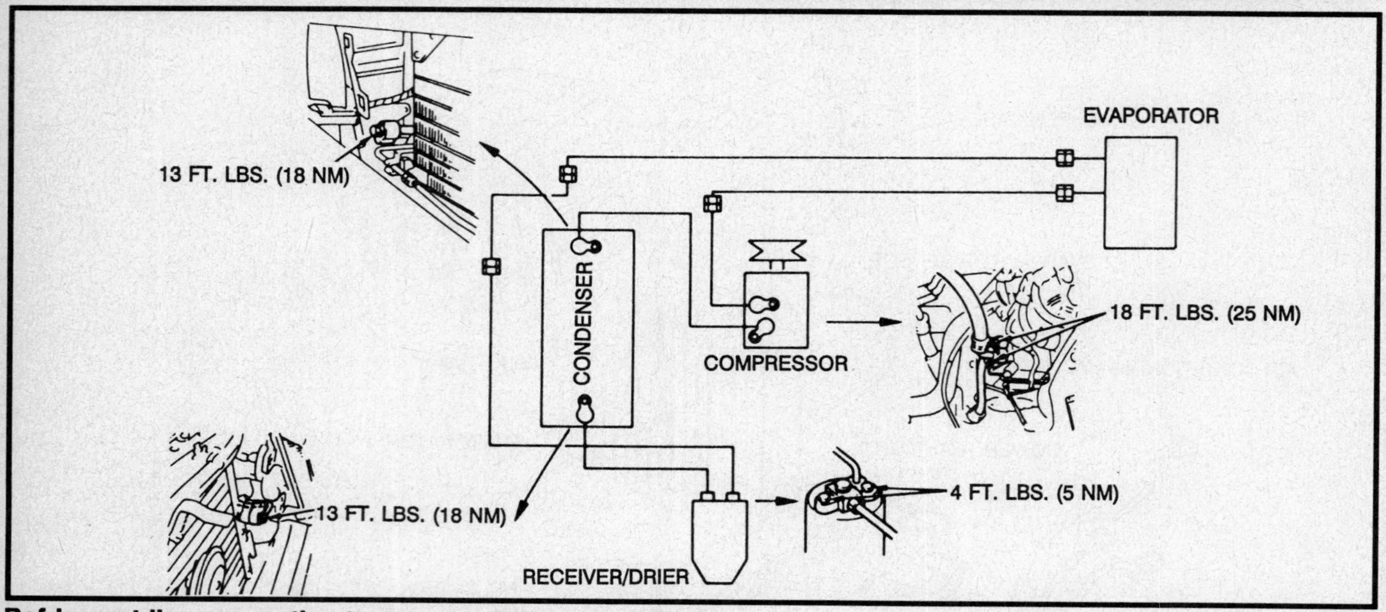
EVAPORATOR
13 FT. LBS. (18 NM)
CONDENSER
COMPRESSOR
18 FT. LBS. (25 NM)
4 FT. LBS. (5 NM)
13 FT. LBS. (18 NM)
RECEIVER/DRIER

Refrigerant line connection torque specifications – ES 250

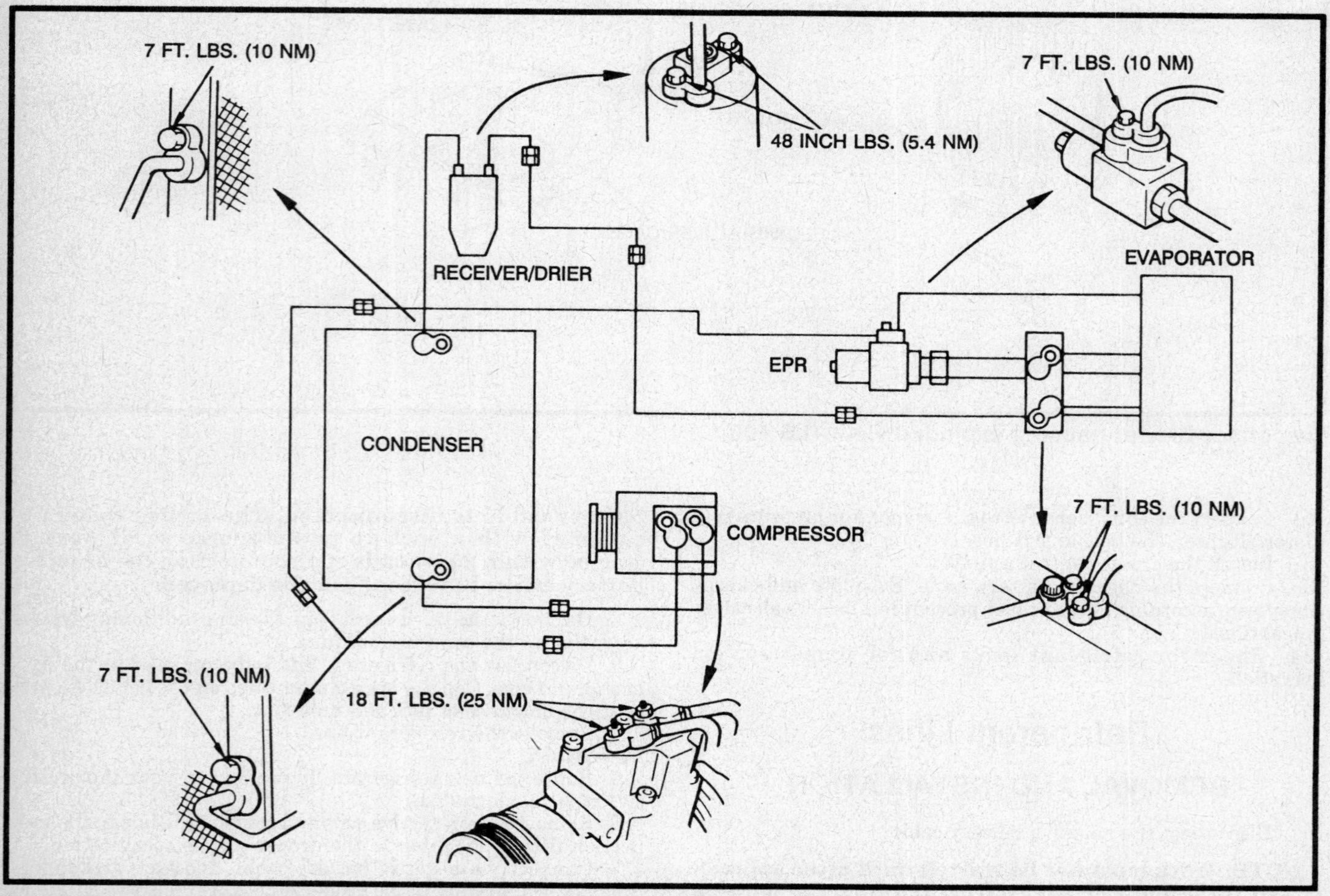
7 FT. LBS. (10 NM)
48 INCH LBS. (5.4 NM)
7 FT. LBS. (10 NM)
RECEIVER/DRIER
EVAPORATOR
EPR
CONDENSER
COMPRESSOR
7 FT. LBS. (10 NM)
7 FT. LBS. (10 NM)
18 FT. LBS. (25 NM)

Refrigerant line connection torque specifications – LS 400

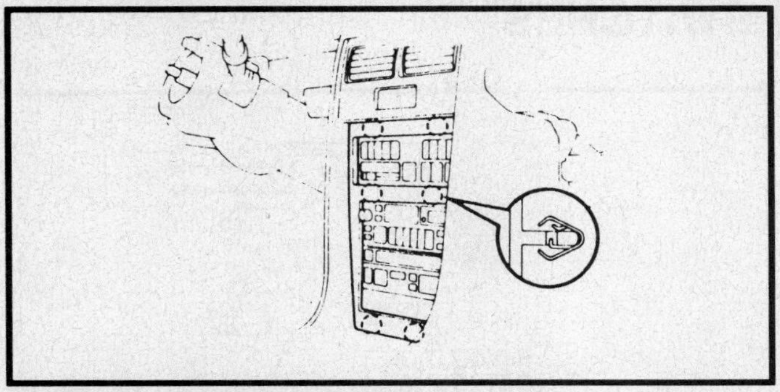

Cluster finish panel—ES 250

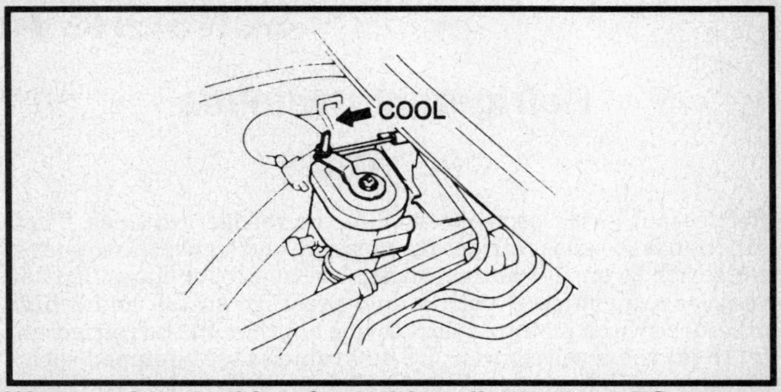
COOL

Water valve position for cable adjustment—ES 250

8. Inspect for refrigerant leaks and for proper system operation.

Manual Control Head

REMOVAL AND INSTALLATION

ES 250

1. Disconnect the negative battery cable.

NOTE: Work must not be started until after approximately 20 seconds or longer from the time the ignition switch is turned to the LOCK position and the negative battery cable is disconnected. The airbag system is equipped with a back-up power source so, if work is started within 20 seconds of disconnecting the negative battery cable, the airbag may be deployed.

2. Using a suitable prying tool, remove the center cluster finish panel.
3. Remove the 4 screws and remove the control assembly.
4. Disconnect the electrical connectors and remove the control assembly from the vehicle.
5. Installation is the reverse of the removal procedure.

Manual Control Cable

ADJUSTMENT

ES 250 and LS 400

The manual control cable connects the air mix servomotor and the water valve.

1. Disconnect the control cable from the water valve.
2. Turn the ignition switch **ON**.
3. Turn the blower switch **ON**.
4. Set the temperature control switch on the **COOL** position on ES 250 or the **MAX COOL** position on LS 400.
5. Set the water valve lever on the **COOL** position, install the control cable and lock the clamp.

REMOVAL AND INSTALLATION

ES 250

1. Disconnect the negative battery cable.

NOTE: Work must not be started until after approximately 20 seconds or longer from the time the ignition switch is turned to the LOCK position and the negative battery cable is disconnected. The airbag system is equipped with a back-up power source so, if work is started within 20 seconds of disconnecting the negative battery cable, the airbag may be deployed.

2. Disconnect the control cable from the water valve.
3. Disconnect the control cable from the servomotor.

NOTE: It may be necessary to remove the heater unit in order to disconnect the cable from the servomotor.

4. Remove the control cable.
5. Installation is the reverse of the removal procedure.

Electronic Control Head

REMOVAL AND INSTALLATION

LS 400

1. Disconnect the negative battery cable.

NOTE: Work must not be started until after approximately 20 seconds or longer from the time the ignition switch is turned to the LOCK position and the negative battery cable is disconnected. The airbag system is equipped with a back-up power source so, if work is started within 20 seconds of disconnecting the negative battery cable, the airbag may be deployed.

2. Using a suitable prying tool, pry out the rear side of the upper console panel. Pull the panel backwards to remove it.
3. With the ash tray fully closed, use a suitable pry tool to remove the front ash tray. Disconnect the connector.
4. Use a suitable prying tool to remove the center instrument panel register.
5. Remove the 4 mounting screws and remove the radio with the control assembly. Disconnect the connectors.
6. Remove the 4 screws, open the brackets on the outside, release the connection of the claws and remove the control assembly from the radio.
7. Installation is the reverse of the removal procedure.

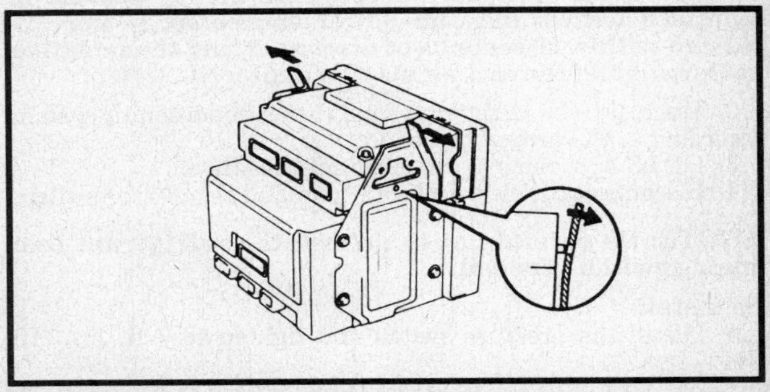

Removing the control assembly from the radio—LS 400

SENSORS AND SWITCHES

Refrigerant Switches

OPERATION

Refrigerant switches are located in the refrigerant lines. Their function is to sense refrigerant pressure and signal the compressor clutch to engage and disengage at the proper times. ES 250 vehicles are equipped with a dual pressure switch and a high pressure switch mounted next to one another on the refrigerant line near the receiver/drier. LS 400 vehicles are equipped with a pressure switch mounted on a refrigerant line close to the receiver/drier.

TESTING

Dual Pressure Switch

ES 250

1. Disconnect the connector from the dual pressure switch.
2. Install a manifold gauge set according to the proper procedure.
3. Use an ohmmeter to check that there is continuity between the terminals of the switch. The indication for the manifold gauge high pressure side should be 30–384 psi.
4. Remove the manifold gauge set and connect the connector to the dual pressure switch.

High Pressure Switch

ES 250

1. Disconnect the connector from the high pressure switch.
2. Install a manifold gauge set according to the proper procedure.
3. Run the engine at approximately 2000 rpm.
4. When the air conditioning switch is **OFF**, use an ohmmeter to check that there is continuity between the terminals and that the high side pressure is 178 psi or lower.
5. When the air conditioning switch and blower switches are **ON**, check that there is no continuity between terminals and the high pressure is 220 psi or higher.

REMOVAL AND INSTALLATION

ES 250 and LS 400

1. Disconnect the negative battery cable.

NOTE: Work must not be started until after approximately 20 seconds or longer from the time the ignition switch is turned to the LOCK position and the negative battery cable is disconnected. The airbag system is equipped with a back-up power source so, if work is started within 20 seconds of disconnecting the negative battery cable, the airbag may be deployed.

2. Discharge the refrigerant from the air conditioning system according to the proper procedure.
3. On LS 400, remove the right side headlight.
4. Disconnect the electrical connector and remove the switch.

NOTE: Be careful not to deform the refrigerant line during switch removal.

To install:

5. Install the pressure switch and tighten to 7 ft. lbs. (10 Nm).

NOTE: Be careful not to deform the refrigerant line during switch installation.

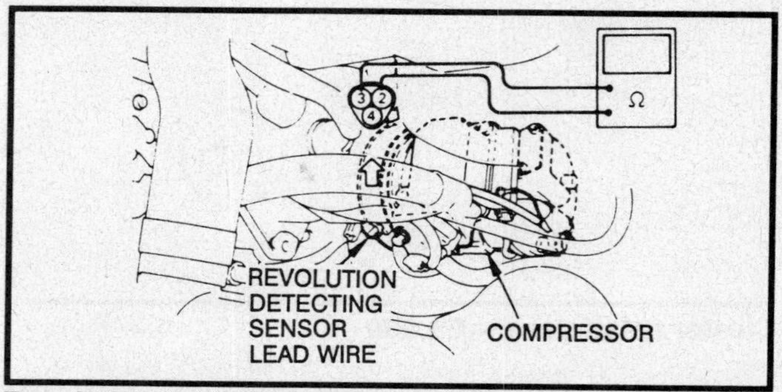
Ω
3
2
4
REVOLUTION DETECTING SENSOR LEAD WIRE
COMPRESSOR

Revolution detecting sensor testing—ES 250

6. Connect the connector.
7. Install the headlight.
8. Evacuate and charge the system according to the proper procedure. Observe all safety precautions.
9. Check for refrigerant leaks and proper system operation.

Sensors

OPERATION

Sensors are used in the air conditioning system mostly to provide temperature information. The sensors are especially important in supplying input to the automatic temperature control system on LS 400 vehicles.

TESTING

Revolution Detecting Sensor

ES 250

1. Using an ohmmeter, measure the resistance between terminals 2 and 3 of the sensor.
2. The resistance should be 100–130 ohms at 68°F (20°C).
3. If the resistance is not as specified, replace the revolution detecting sensor.

Evaporator Temperature Sensor

ES 250

1. Remove the sensor.
2. Using an ohmmeter, measure the resistance between the terminals at 77°F (25°C). The resistance should be 1500 ohms.
3. Place the thermistor in cold water. While varying the temperature of the water, measure the resistance at the connector

EVAPORATOR TEMPERATURE SENSOR RESISTANCE

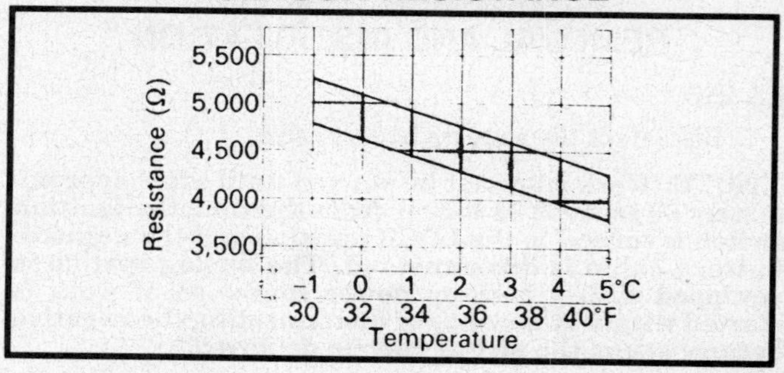
5,500
5,000
4,500
4,000
3,500
Resistance (Ω)
-1 0 1 2 3 4 5°C
30 32 34 36 38 40°F
Temperature

and at the same time, measure the temperature of the water with a thermometer.

4. Compare the 2 readings on the chart. If the resistance is not as specified, replace the sensor.

REMOVAL AND INSTALLATION

Revolution Detecting Sensor

ES 250

1. Disconnect the negative battery cable.

NOTE: Work must not be started until after approximately 20 seconds or longer from the time the ignition switch is turned to the LOCK position and the negative battery cable is disconnected. The airbag system is equipped with a back-up power source so, if work is started within 20 seconds of disconnecting the negative battery cable, the airbag may be deployed.

2. Discharge the refrigerant from the air conditioning system according to the proper procedure.
3. Disconnect the connector and remove the sensor from the compressor.
4. Installation is the reverse of the removal procedure. Evacuate and charge the system according to the proper procedure. Observe all safety precautions.

Evaporator Temperature Sensor

ES 250 and LS 400

1. Disconnect the negative battery cable.

NOTE: Work must not be started until after approximately 20 seconds or longer from the time the ignition switch is turned to the LOCK position and the negative battery cable is disconnected. The airbag system is equipped with a back-up power source so, if work is started within 20 seconds of disconnecting the negative battery cable, the airbag may be deployed.

2. Discharge the refrigerant from the air conditioning system according to the proper procedure.
3. Remove the evaporator assembly from the vehicle.
4. Remove the evaporator temperature sensor.
5. Installation is the reverse of the removal procedure. Evacuate and charge the system according to the proper procedure. Observe all safety precautions.

Room Temperature Sensor

LS 400

1. Disconnect the negative battery cable.

NOTE: Work must not be started until after approximately 20 seconds or longer from the time the ignition switch is turned to the LOCK position and the negative battery cable is disconnected. The airbag system is equipped with a back-up power source so, if work is started within 20 seconds of disconnecting the negative battery cable, the airbag may be deployed.

2. Working inside the vehicle, remove the 3 screws from the cover under the lower left side of the instrument panel. Use a suitable prying tool to remove the cover. Disconnect the valve from the cover.
3. Remove the 2 screws and the hood release lever. Disconnect the release cable from the lever.
4. Using a suitable prying tool, remove the key cylinder pad.
5. Remove the 6 bolts and the lower pad from under the steering column. Remove the sensor from the lower pad.
6. Installation is the reverse of the removal procedure.

Ambient Temperature Sensor

LS 400

1. Disconnect the negative battery cable.

NOTE: Work must not be started until after approximately 20 seconds or longer from the time the ignition switch is turned to the LOCK position and the negative battery cable is disconnected. The airbag system is equipped with a back-up power source so, if work is started within 20 seconds of disconnecting the negative battery cable, the airbag may be deployed.

2. Remove the clip and the sensor from the bumper reinforcement. Disconnect the connector.
3. Installation is the reverse of the removal procedure.

Solar Sensor

LS 400

1. Disconnect the negative battery cable.

NOTE: Work must not be started until after approximately 20 seconds or longer from the time the ignition switch is turned to the LOCK position and the negative battery cable is disconnected. The airbag system is equipped with a back-up power source so, if work is started within 20 seconds of disconnecting the negative battery cable, the airbag may be deployed.

2. Use a suitable tool to pry loose the clips and remove the passenger's side defroster nozzle garnish.
3. Remove the solar sensor and disconnect the connector.
4. Installation is the reverse of the removal procedure.

Heater Unit Water Temperature Sensor

LS 400

1. Disconnect the negative battery cable.

NOTE: Work must not be started until after approximately 20 seconds or longer from the time the ignition switch is turned to the LOCK position and the negative battery cable is disconnected. The airbag system is equipped with a back-up power source so, if work is started within 20 seconds of disconnecting the negative battery cable, the airbag may be deployed.

2. Discharge the refrigerant from the air conditioning system according to the proper procedure.
3. Drain the cooling system into a suitable container.
4. Remove the heater unit.
5. Remove the water temperature sensor from the heater unit by taking off the clamp and disconnect the connector.
6. Installation is the reverse of the removal procedure. Fill the cooling system to the proper level and evacuate and charge the refrigerant system according to the proper procedure.

Servomotors

OPERATION

Servomotors are electric motors that operate the air doors in the heater and evaporator units. The air doors control airflow as follows: mixing hot and cool air to attain the desired temperature, mixing outside and recirculated air and controlling the direction of air flow, directing airflow to the instrument panel registers, floor ducts or defroster nozzles.

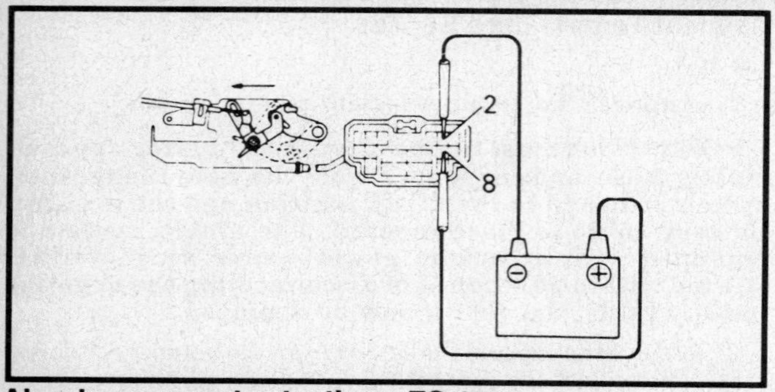
2
8

Air mix servomotor testing—ES 250

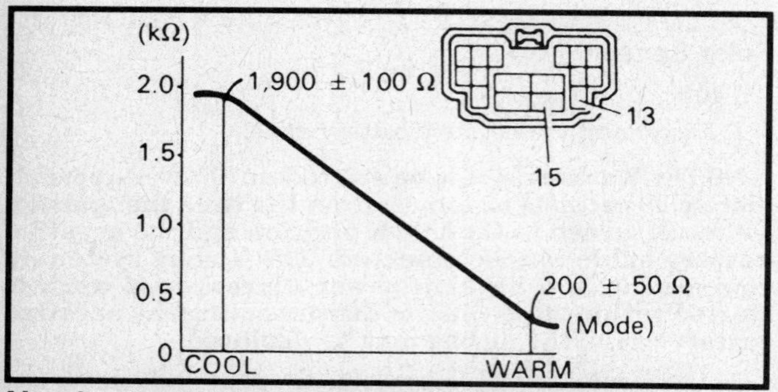
(kΩ)
2.0
1.5
1.0
0.5
0
1,900 ± 100 Ω
13
15
200 ± 50 Ω
(Mode)
COOL
WARM

Air mix servomotor resistance values—ES 250

TESTING

Air Mix Servomotor

ES 250

1. Connect a positive lead from a battery to terminal **8** and a negative lead to terminal **2**. Check that the lever moves smoothly to the **COOL** position.
2. Reverse the polarity, then check that the lever moves smoothly to the **WARM** position.
3. While operating the servomotor, use an ohmmeter to measure the resistance values at terminals **13** and **15**.
4. In the **COOL** position, the resistance should be 1800–2000 ohms. In the **WARM** position, the resistance should be 150–250 ohms. The resistance values should successively decrease from cool to warm.
5. If the servomotor does not operate as specified, replace the servomotor.

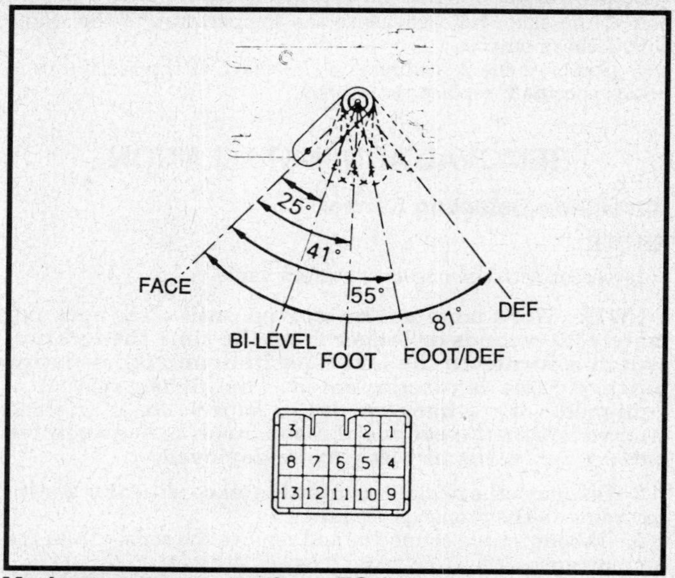
25°
41°
55°
81°
FACE
BI-LEVEL
FOOT
FOOT/DEF
DEF
3
2
1
8
7
6
5
4
13
12
11
10
9

Mode servomotor testing—ES 250

MODE SERVOMOTOR CONTINUITY

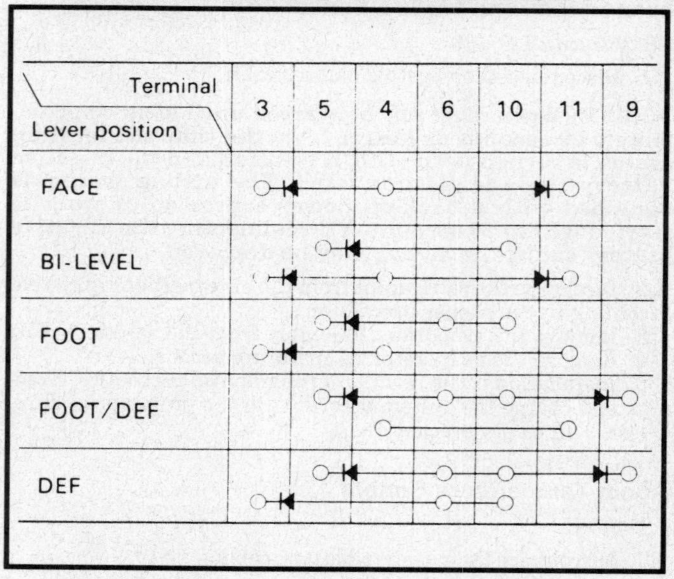
Terminal
Lever position
3
5
4
6
10
11
9
FACE
BI-LEVEL
FOOT
FOOT/DEF
DEF

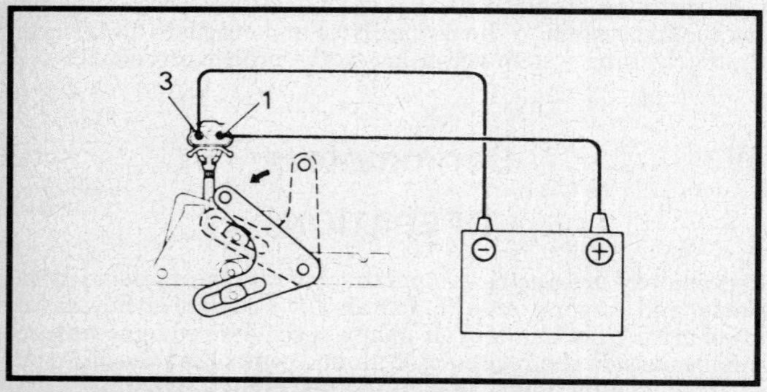
3
1

Air inlet servomotor testing—ES 250

Air Inlet Servomotor

ES 250

1. Connect a positive lead from a battery to terminal **1** and the negative lead to terminal **2**, then check that the lever moves smoothly to the **RECIRC** position.
2. Connect the positive lead to terminal **1** and the negative lead to terminal **3**, then check that the lever moves smoothly to the **FRESH** position.
3. If the operation is not as specified, replace the servomotor.

Mode Servomotor

ES 250

1. Connect a positive lead from a battery to terminal **2** and a negative lead to terminal **1**, then check that the lever moves smoothly to the **FACE** position.

2. Reverse the polarity, then check that the lever moves smoothly to the **DEF** position.
3. Check for continuity between the terminals. If the operation is not as specified, replace the servomotor.

REMOVAL AND INSTALLATION

Air Mix Servomotor

ES 250 AND LS 400

1. Disconnect the negative battery cable.

NOTE: Work must not be started until after approximately 20 seconds or longer from the time the ignition switch is turned to the LOCK position and the negative battery cable is disconnected. The airbag system is equipped with a back-up power source so, if work is started within 20 seconds of disconnecting the negative battery cable, the airbag may be deployed.

2. Drain the cooling system into a suitable container.
3. Discharge the refrigerant from the air conditioning system according to the proper procedure.
4. Remove the heater unit.
5. Remove the air mix servomotor from the heater unit.
6. Installation is the reverse of the removal procedure. Fill the cooling system to the proper level. Evacuate and charge the system according to the proper procedure. Observe all safety precautions.

Air Inlet Servomotor

ES 250 AND LS 400

1. Disconnect the negative battery cable.

NOTE: Work must not be started until after approximately 20 seconds or longer from the time the ignition switch is turned to the LOCK position and the negative battery cable is disconnected. The airbag system is equipped with a back-up power source so, if work is started within 20 seconds of disconnecting the negative battery cable, the airbag may be deployed.

2. Discharge the refrigerant from the air conditioning system according to the proper procedure.
3. Remove the evaporator unit.
4. Remove the air inlet servomotor.
5. Installation is the reverse of the removal procedure. Evacuate and charge the system according to the proper procedure. Observe all safety precautions.

Mode Servomotor

ES 250 AND LS 400

1. Disconnect the negative battery cable.

NOTE: Work must not be started until after approximately 20 seconds or longer from the time the ignition switch is turned to the LOCK position and the negative battery cable is disconnected. The airbag system is equipped with a back-up power source so, if work is started within 20 seconds of disconnecting the negative battery cable, the airbag may be deployed.

2. Drain the cooling system into a suitable container.
3. Discharge the refrigerant from the air conditioning system according to the proper procedure.
4. Remove the heater unit.
5. Remove the mode servomotor from the heater unit.
6. Installation is the reverse of the removal procedure. Fill the cooling system to the proper level. Evacuate and charge the system according to the proper procedure. Observe all safety precautions.

Max Cool Servomotor

LS 400

1. Disconnect the negative battery cable.

NOTE: Work must not be started until after approximately 20 seconds or longer from the time the ignition switch is turned to the LOCK position and the negative battery cable is disconnected. The airbag system is equipped with a back-up power source so, if work is started within 20 seconds of disconnecting the negative battery cable, the airbag may be deployed.

2. Drain the cooling system into a suitable container.
3. Discharge the refrigerant from the air conditioning system according to the proper procedure.
4. Remove the heater unit.
5. Remove the air duct from the heater unit.
6. Using a suitable tool, pry loose the 2 clips and pull out the max cool damper control plates. Remove the screw and disconnect the connector. Remove the 2 screws and the servomotor.
7. Installation is the reverse of the removal procedure. Fill the cooling system to the proper level. Evacuate and charge the refrigerant system according to the proper procedure. Observe all safety precautions.

System Relays

OPERATION

Many of the systems within the air conditioning systems use relays to send current on its way and energize various components. All are conventional relays with internal contacts and a coil which pulls the contacts closed when energized. Both ES 250 and LS 400 vehicles use a main relay, a heater relay and a magnetic clutch relay as well as several cooling fan relays. ES 250 vehicles are equipped with a blower control relay. LS 400 vehicles are equipped with an extra high relay in the blower motor circuit.

On ES 250, the engine main relay, magnetic clutch relay and cooling fan relays are located in a junction block in the driver's side of the engine compartment. The heater relay is located on the relay block under the passenger's side of the instrument panel. The blower control relay is located under the passenger's side of the instrument panel near the blower motor.

On LS 400, all relays except the extra high relay are located in junction blocks in the driver's side of the engine compartment. The extra high relay is located in the evaporator-blower assembly.

REMOVAL AND INSTALLATION

Extra High Relay

LS 400

1. Disconnect the negative battery cable.

NOTE: Work must not be started until after approximately 20 seconds or longer from the time the ignition switch is turned to the LOCK position and the negative battery cable is disconnected. The airbag system is equipped with a back-up power source so, if work is started within 20 seconds of disconnecting the negative battery cable, the airbag may be deployed.

2. Using a suitable tool, remove the clips and remove the lower cover panel from the passenger's side of the instrument panel.

MAGNETIC CLUTCH RELAY CONTINUITY TEST—ES 250

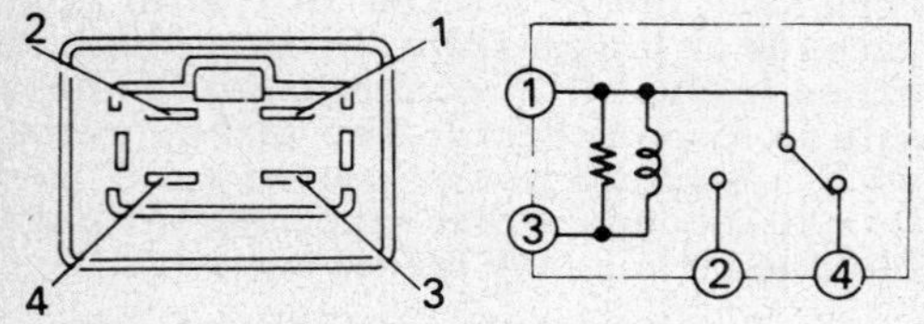
2
1
4
3
1
3
2
4

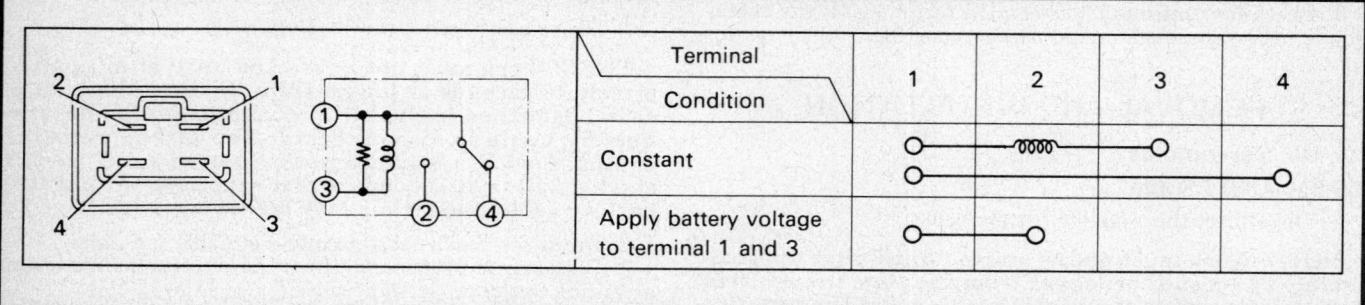

Terminal / Condition	1	2	3	4
Constant	○	—ꝏ—	○	
	○	—	—	○
Apply battery voltage to terminal 1 and 3	○	○		

HEATER RELAY CONTINUITY TEST—ES 250

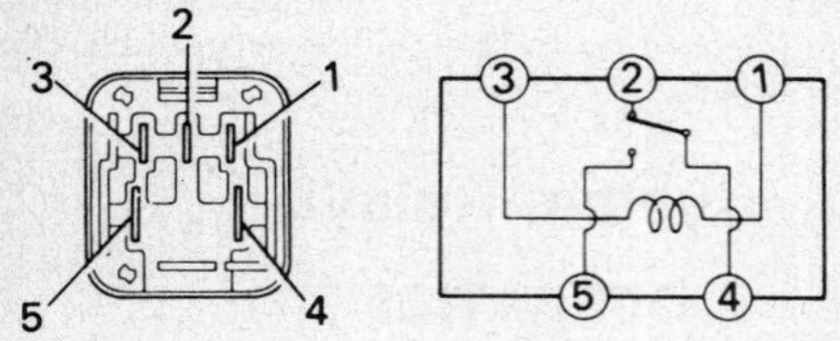
2
3
1
5
4
3
2
1
5
4

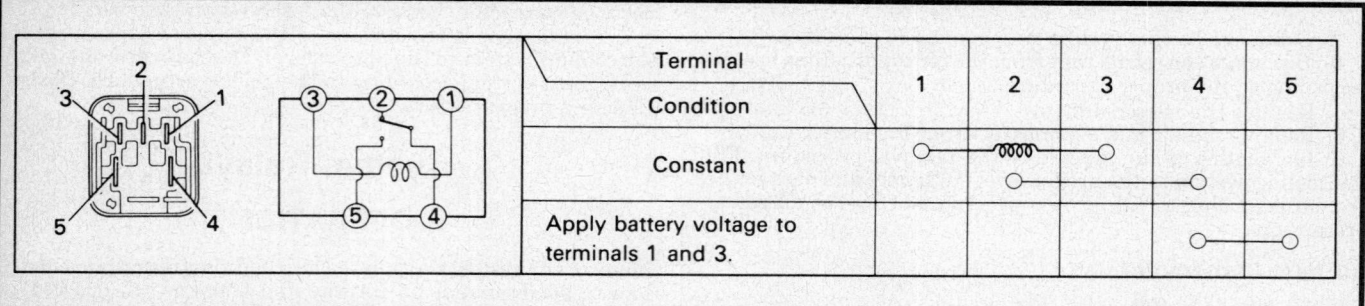

Terminal / Condition	1	2	3	4	5
Constant	○	—ꝏ—	○		
		○	—	○	
Apply battery voltage to terminals 1 and 3.				○	○

BLOWER SPEED CONTROL RELAY CONTINUITY TEST—ES 250

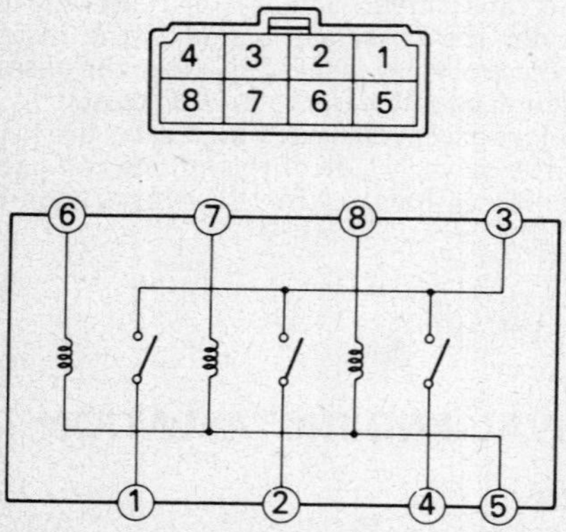
4
3
2
1
8
7
6
5
6
7
8
3
1
2
4
5

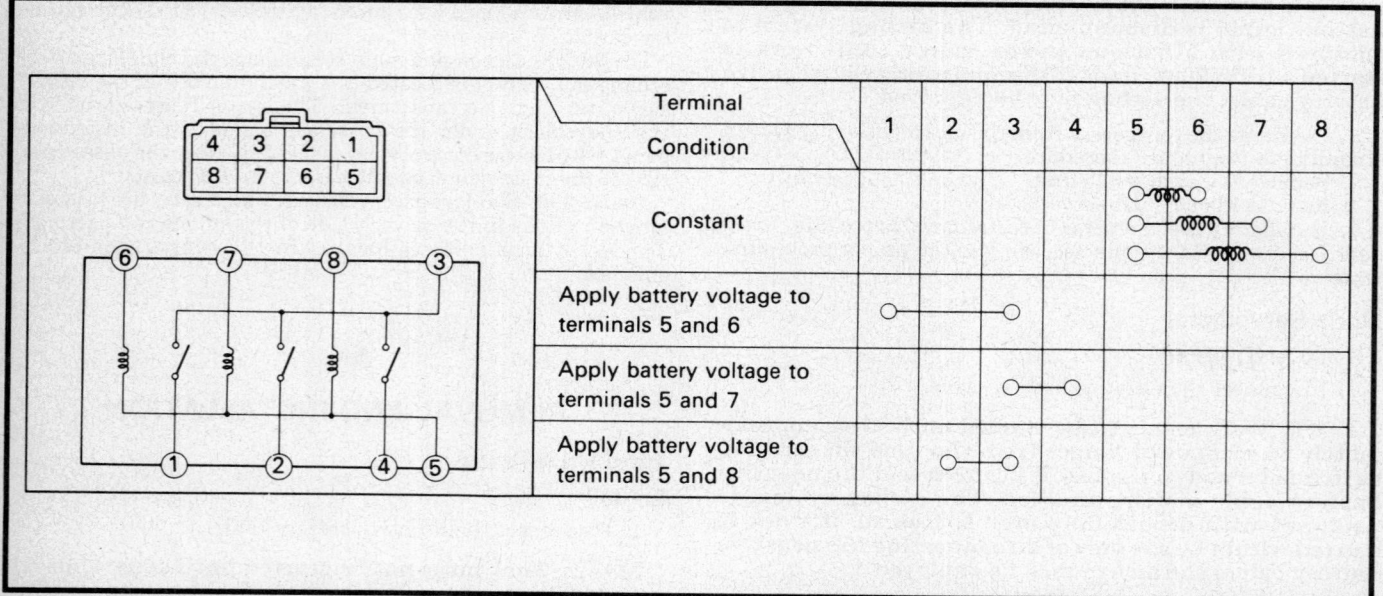

Terminal / Condition	1	2	3	4	5	6	7	8
Constant					○ꝏ	○		
					○	ꝏ	○	
					○	—	ꝏ	○
Apply battery voltage to terminals 5 and 6	○	—	○					
Apply battery voltage to terminals 5 and 7			○	○				
Apply battery voltage to terminals 5 and 8		○	○					

3. Disconnect the connectors, remove the 2 screws and remove the connector bracket from the evaporator-blower unit.
4. Remove the mounting screw and remove the extra high relay from the evaporator-blower unit. Disconnect the electrical connector.
5. Installation is the reverse of the removal procedure.

SYSTEM DIAGNOSIS

Refrigerant System

The following conditions must be met before checking the refrigerant system for volume and checking for cooling using a manifold gauge set:

REFRIGERANT VOLUME

1. Run the engine at approximately 2000 rpm.
2. Operate the air conditioning at maximum cooling for a few minutes.
3. Inspect the amount of refrigerant by observing the sight glass on the receiver/drier.

CHECKING WITH A MANIFOLD GAUGE SET

1. The temperature at the air inlet with the switch set at **RECIRC** is 86°–95°F (30°–35°C).
2. Run the engine at 2000 rpm.
3. Set the blower fan speed switch at high speed.
4. Set the temperature control switch at **MAX COOL**.

NOTE: Manifold gauge indications may vary slightly due to ambient temperature conditions.

REFRIGERANT VOLUME DIAGNOSIS

Item	Symptom	Amount of refrigerant	Remedy
1	Bubbles present in sight glass	Insufficient*	(1) Check for gas leakage with gas leak tester and repair if necessary (2) Add refrigerant until bubbles disappear
2	No bubbles present in sight glass	None, sufficient or too much	Refer to items 3 and 4
3	No temperature difference between compressor inlet and outlet	Empty or nearly empty	(1) Check for gas leakage with gas leak tester and repair if necessary (2) Add refrigerant until bubbles disappear
4	Temperature between compressor inlet and outlet is noticeably different	Proper or too much	Refer to items 5 and 6
5	Immediately after air conditioner is turned off, refrigerant in sight glass stays clear	Too much	(1) Recover refrigerant (2) Evacuate air and charge proper amount of purified refrigerant
6	When air conditioner is turned off, refrigerant foams and then stay clear	Proper	—

REFRIGERANT SYSTEM DIAGNOSIS USING A MANIFOLD GAUGE SET

No	Gauge reading kg/cm^2 (psi, kPa)	Condition	Probable cause	Remedy
1	LO: 1.5 – 2.0 (21 – 28, 147 – 196) HI: 14.5 – 15.0 (206 – 213, 1,422 – 1,471) 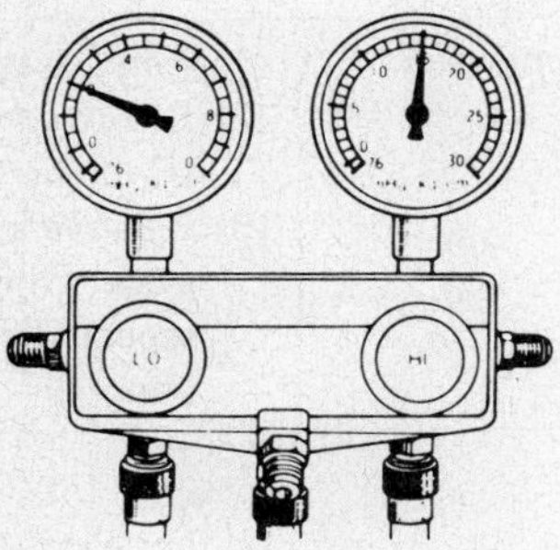	Normal cooling	Normally functioning system	

REFRIGERANT SYSTEM DIAGNOSIS USING A MANIFOLD GAUGE SET CONT.

No	Gauge reading kg/cm² (psi, kPa)	Condition	Probable cause	Remedy
2	During operation, pressure at low pressure side sometimes becomes a vacuum and sometimes normal 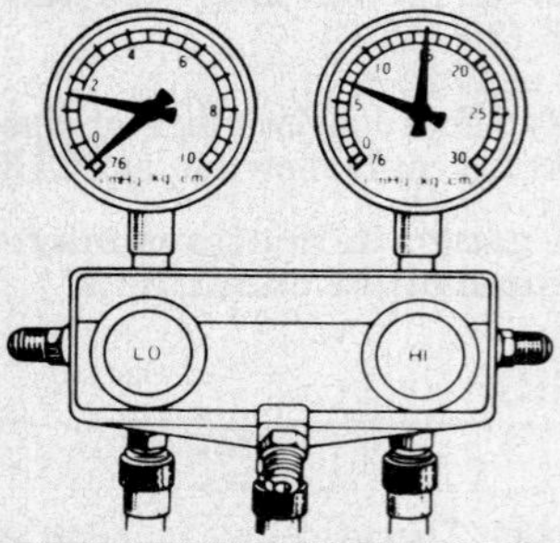LO HI	Periodically cools and then fails to cool	Moisture present in refrigeration system	(1) Replace receiver (2) Remove moisture in system through repeatedly evacuating air
3	Pressure low at both low and high pressure sides 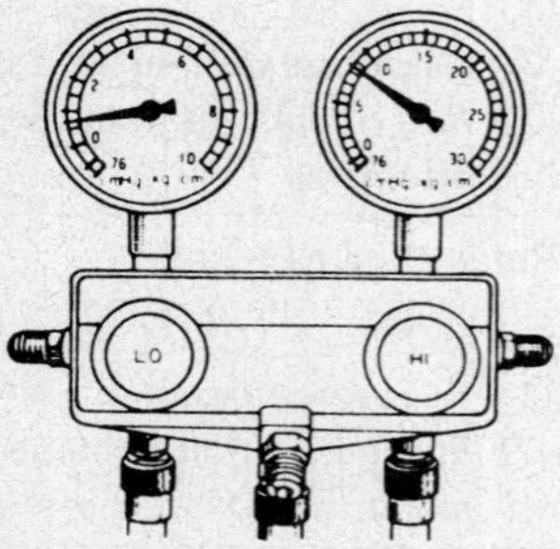LO HI	• Insufficient cooling • Bubbles seen in sight glass	Insufficient refrigerant	(1) Check for gas leakage with gas leak tester and repair if necessary (2) Add refrigerant until bubbles disappear
		• Insufficient cooling • Frost on tubes from receiver to unit	Refrigerant flow obstructed by dirt in receiver	Replace receiver
4	Pressure too high at both low and high pressure sides 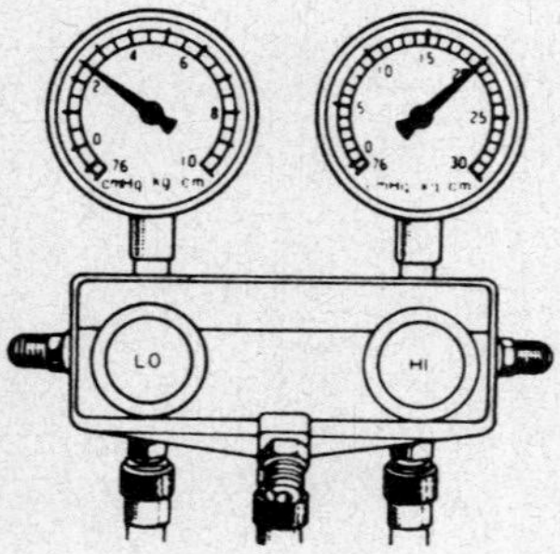LO HI	Insufficient cooling	Insufficient cooling of condenser	(1) Clean condenser (2) Check fan motor operation
5			Refrigerant overcharged	(1) Check amount of refrigerant If refrigerant is overcharged (2) Recover refrigerant (3) Evacuate air and charge proper amount of purified refrigerant
6			Air present in system	(1) Replace receiver (2) Check compressor oil to see if dirty (3) Remove air in system through repeatedly evacuating air

REFRIGERANT SYSTEM DIAGNOSIS USING A MANIFOLD GAUGE SET CONT.

No.	Gauge reading kg/cm² (psi, kPa)	Condition	Probable cause	Remedy
7		● Insufficient cooling ● Frost or Large amount of dew on piping at low pressure side	Expansion valve improperly mounted, heat sensing tube defective (Opens too wide)	(1) Check heat sensing tube installation condition If (1) is normal (2) Check expansion valve and replace If defective
3	Pressure low at both low and high pressure sides 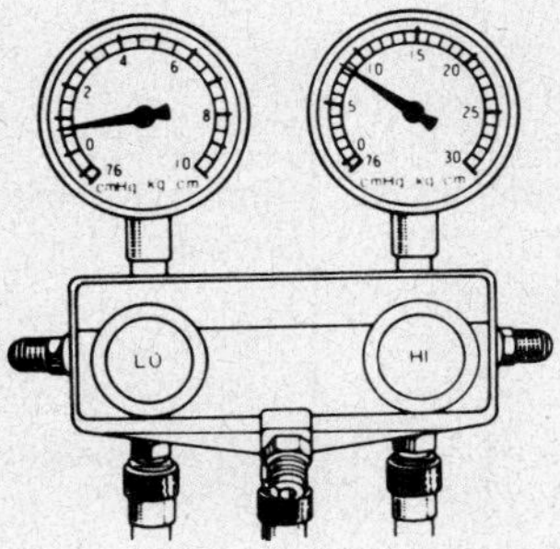 AC0069	• Insufficient cooling • Bubbles seen in sight glass	Insufficient refrigerant	(1) Check for gas leakage with gas leak tester and repair if necessary (2) Add refrigerant until bubbles disappear
		• Insufficient cooling • Frost on tubes from receiver to unit	Refrigerant flow obstructed by dirt in receiver	Replace receiver
4	Pressure too high at both low and high pressure sides	Insufficient cooling	Insufficient cooling of condenser	(1) Clean condenser (2) Check fan motor operation
5	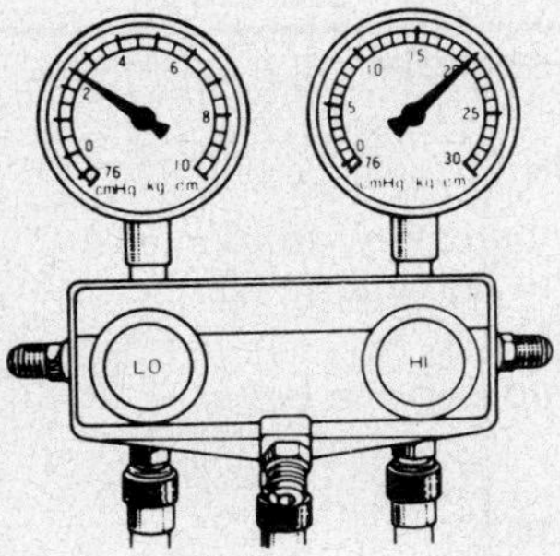		Refrigerant overcharged	(1) Check amount of refrigerant If refrigerant is overcharged (2) Recover refrigerant (3) Evacuate air and charge proper amount of purified refrigerant
6			Air present in system	(1) Replace receiver (2) Check compressor oil to see if dirty (3) Remove air in system through repeatedly evacuating air
7	AC0070	• Insufficient cooling • Frost or Large amount of dew on piping at low pressure side	Expansion valve improperly mounted, heat sensing tube defective (Opens too wide)	(1) Check heat sensing tube installation condition If (1) is normal (2) Check expansion valve and replace if defective

REFRIGERANT SYSTEM DIAGNOSIS USING A MANIFOLD GAUGE SET CONT.

No.	Gauge reading kg/cm² (psi, kPa)	Condition	Probable cause	Remedy
8	Vacuum indicated at low pressure side, very low pressure indicated at high pressure 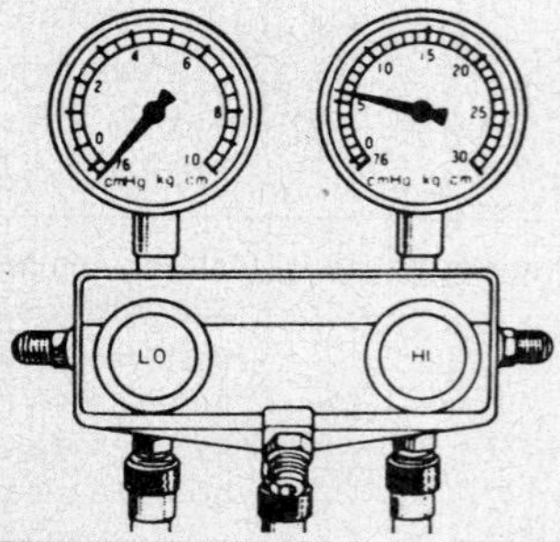 LO HI	• Does not cool(Cools from time to time in some cases) • Frost or dew seen on piping before and after receiver or expansion valve	Refrigerant does not circulate	(1)Check heat sensing tube for gas leakage and replace expansion valve if defective If (1) is normal (2) Clean out dirt in expansion valve by blowing with air If not able to remove dirt, replace expansion valve (3) replace receiver
	Pressure too high at low pressure side, pressure too low at high pressure side 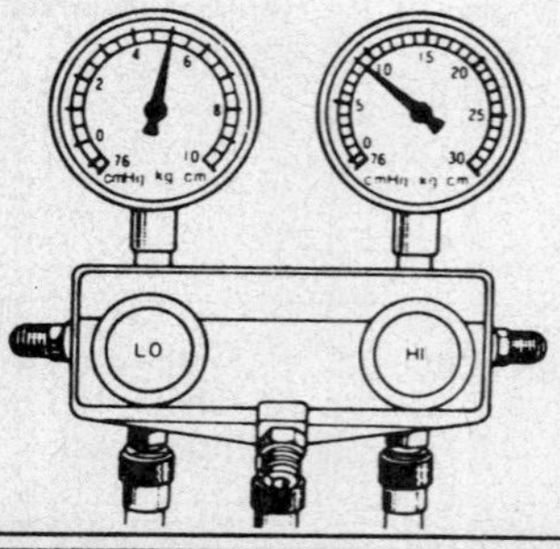 LO HI	Does not cool	Insufficient compression	Repair or replace compressor

AIR CONDITIONING CONTROL ASSEMBLY TESTING – ES 250

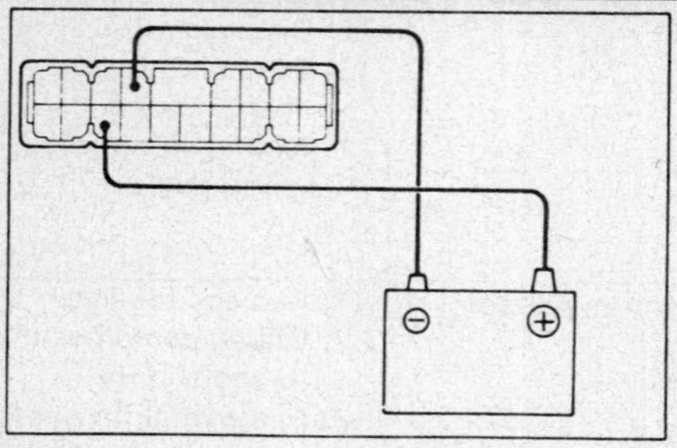

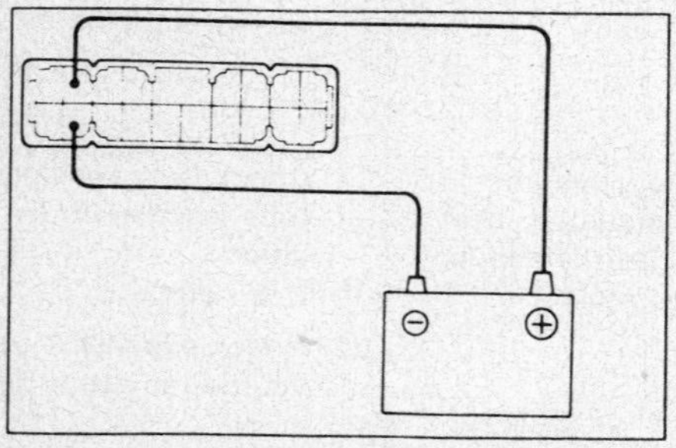

If operation is not as specified, replace the A/C control assembly.

Inspection of A/C Control Assembly (Illumination)

INSPECT ILLUMINATION OPERATION

Connect positive (+) lead from the battery to terminal 16/18 and the negative (–) lead to terminal 5/18, then check that the illumination lights up.

If the illumination does not light up, test the bulbs.

(Indicators)

INSPECT INDICATOR LIGHT OPERATION

(a) Connect the positive (+) lead from the battery to terminal 7/18 and the negative (–) lead to terminal 17/18.

(b) With the blower button pushed in, check that the indicator light lights up. (The indicator light will not light up when the blower button is in the OFF position.)

(c) With the RECIRC button pushed in, check that the indicator light lights up.

(d) Next, push the FRESH button in, and check that the indicator light lights up and that the RECIRC indicator light goes off.

(e) Press each of the mode buttons in and check that their indicator light lights up.

AIR CONDITIONING CONTROL ASSEMBLY TESTING—ES 250 CONT.

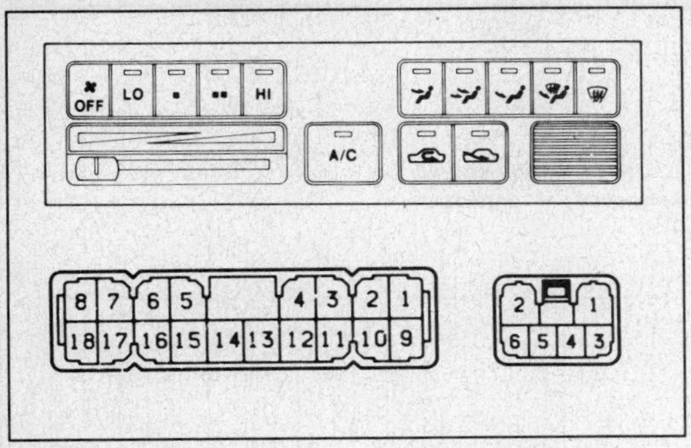
OFF
LO
HI
A/C
8 7 6 5 4 3 2 1
18 17 16 15 14 13 12 11 10 9
2 1
6 5 4 3

(A/C Switch)

INSPECT A/C SWITCH CONTINUITY

Terminal / Switch position	6/18	14/18
OFF		
ON	O	O

If the continuity is not as specified, replace the A/C control assembly.

(Temperature Control Switch)

INSPECT TEMPERATURE CONTROL SWITCH RESISTANCE

Measure the resistance between terminals 1/18 and 9/18 for each switch position.

Level position	Resistance (kΩ)
Max. Cool	∞
Middle	Approx. 1.5
Max. Warm	0

If the resistance value is not as specified, replace the A/C control assembly.

(Air Inlet Control Switch)

INSPECT AIR INLET CONTROL SWITCH CONTINUITY

Terminal / Switch position	2/18	10/18	17/18
RECIRC	O		O
FRESH		O	O

If the continuity is not as specified, replace the A/C control assembly.

(Air Flow Mode Control Switch)

INSPECT AIR FLOW MODE CONTROL SWITCH

Terminal / Switch position	3/18	4/18	11/18	12/18	15/18	17/18
FACE		O				O
BI-LEVEL				O		O
FOOT	O					O
FOOT/DEF					O	O
DEF			O			O

If the continuity is not as specified, replace the A/C control assembly.

(Blower Fan Speed Control Switch)

INSPECT BLOWER FAN SPEED CONTROL SWITCH CONTINUITY

Terminal / Switch position	17/18	3/6	4/6	5/6	6/6
OFF					
LO	O	O			
I	O	O	O		
II	O	O		O	
HI	O	O			O

If the continuity is not as specified, replace the A/C control assembly.

AIR CONDITIONING TROUBLESHOOTING—ES 250

NOTE: Across each row in the chart, the systems that could be sources of a system are ranked in the order they should be inspected, starting with ①. Find the symptom in the left column, read across to the most likey source, If inspection shows the system is OK, try the next system ②, etc.

Trouble \ Parts Name	Inspect Volume of Refrigerant	Inspect Refrigeration System with Manifold Gauge Set	Inspect Drive Belt Tension	Fusible Link (ALT)	Circuit Breaker (HEATER)	Fuse (A/C)	Dual Pressure Switch	High Pressure Switch	Evaporator Temp. Sensor	Water Temp. Sensor	Revolution Detecting Sensor	Blower Speed Control Relay	Heater Main Relay	Magnetic Clutch Relay	Engine Main Relay and No. 1, 2, 3 Cooling Fan Relays
No blower operation				1	2							5	3		
No blower control												2			
No air flow mode control															
No air inlet control															
Insufficient flow of cool air													1		
Insufficient flow of warm air													1		
No cool air comes out	3	4	5			1	6		15		9			2	
Cool air comes out intermittently	1	2	3						7		4				
Cool air comes out only at high engine speed	2	3	1												
Insufficient cooling	1	2	3					7	17	8					6
No warm air comes out															
Air temp. control not functioning															
No engine idle up when A/C switch on															

AIR CONDITIONING TROUBLESHOOTING—ES 250 CONT.

Blower Resistor	Air Inlet Servomotor	Air Mix Servomotor	Mode Servomotor	Blower Motor	Cooling Fan Motor	A/C Control Assembly	A/C Amplifier	Compressor Control Amplifier	Condenser Fan Control Amplifier	System Amplifier	Compressor	Condenser	Evaporator	Expansion Valve (Replace)	Magnetic Clutch	Receiver	Water Valve (Adjustment)	Radiator (in Heater Unit)	Wiring or Wiring Connection
7				6		4													8
						1													3
			2			1				3									4
	2					1													3
3				2									4						5
3				2														4	5
		11				12	14	13			8				7		10		16
							6	5						8					9
											5	4							
		11			9		16	15	14		13	4	18	19	12	5	10		
		3				2											1	4	5
		3				2											1		4
							1												2

SYSTEM AMPLIFIER TESTING—ES 250

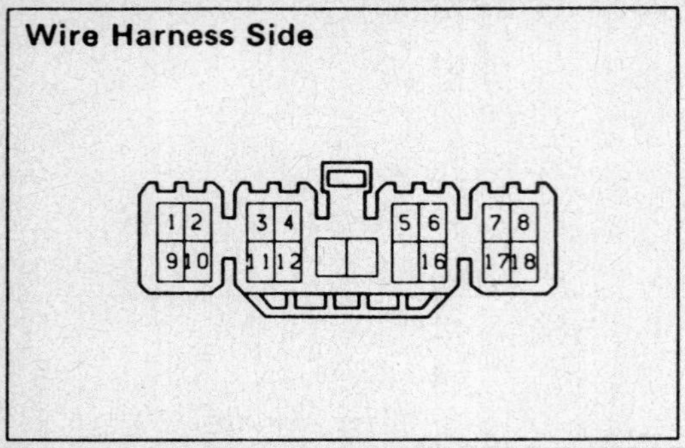
Wire Harness Side
1 2 3 4 5 6 7 8
9 10 11 12 16 17 18

SYSTEM AMPLIFIER

Inspection of System Amplifier

(Power Source)

INSPECT POWER SOURCE CIRCUIT

Remove the amplifier and inspect the connector on the wire harness side as shown in the chart.

If the circuit is normal, check each of the function.

Check for	Tester connection	Condition	Specified value
Continuity	16/18 – Ground	Constant	Continuity
Voltage	17/18 – Ground	Turn ignition switch on.	Battery voltage
		Turn ignition switch to LOCK or ACC	No voltage

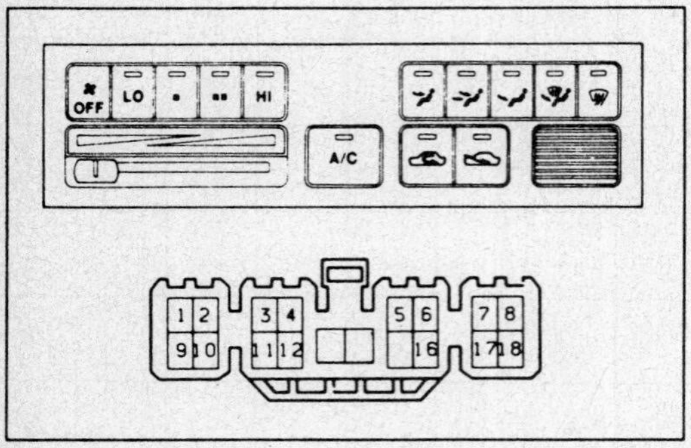
OFF
LO
HI
A/C
1 2 3 4 5 6 7 8
9 10 11 12 16 17 18

(Air Mix Control Function)

1. **INSPECT TEMERATURE CONTROL SWITCH CIRCUIT**

   Gradually move the switch knob from the COOL to the HOT position, then check that the resistance between terminals 8/18 and 10/18 on the wire harness side connector change from ∞ to 0 Ω.

   If the circuit is as specified, inspect the air mix servomotor circuit.

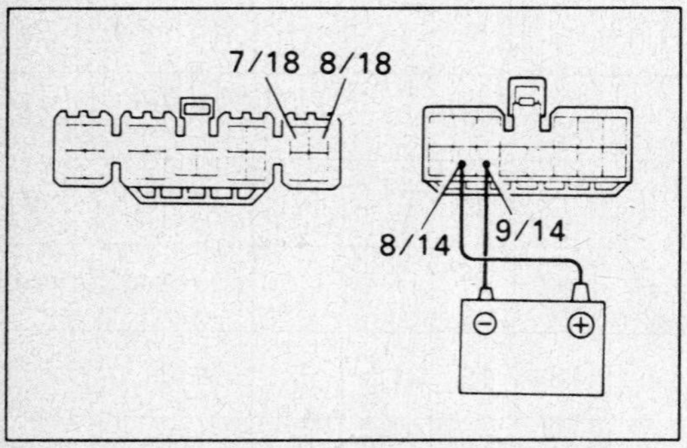
7/18
8/18
8/14
9/14

2. **INSPECT AIR MIX SERVOMOTOR CIRCUIT**

   (a) Connect the positive (+) lead from the battery to terminal 8/14 and the negative (–) lead to terminal 9/14 on the wire harness side connector.

   (b) Check that the resistance between terminals 7/18 and 8/18 change to approx. 1,900 Ω.

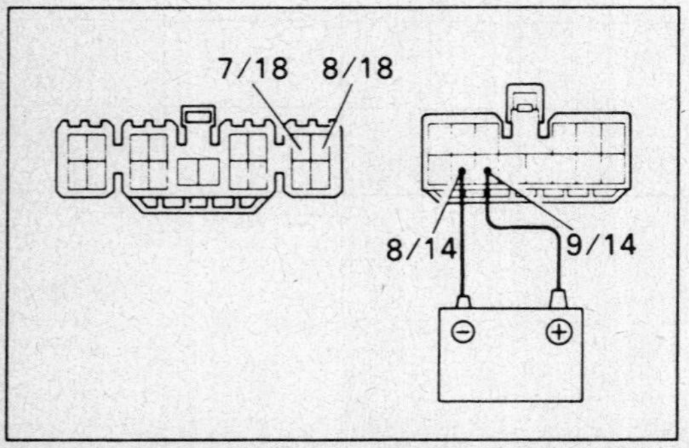
7/18
8/18
8/14
9/14

   (c) Reverse the polarity, then check that the resistance between terminals 7/18 and 8/18 changes from approx. 1,900 to 200 Ω.

   If the circuit is as specified, replace the amplifier.

SYSTEM AMPLIFIER TESTING—ES 250 CONT.

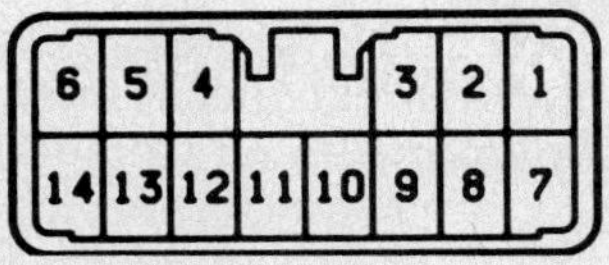
6 5 4 3 2 1
14 13 12 11 10 9 8 7

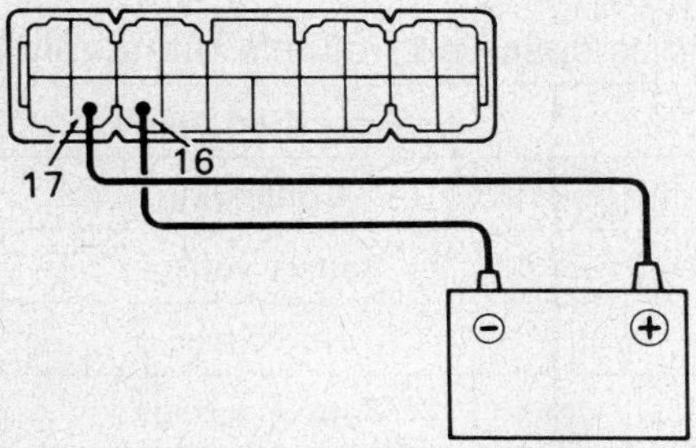
17
16

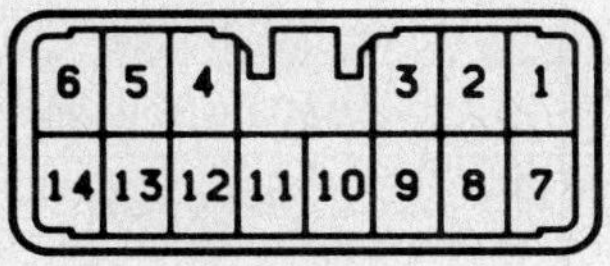
6 5 4 3 2 1
14 13 12 11 10 9 8 7

(Air Flow Control Function)

1. **INSPECT AMPLIFIER CONTINUITY**
   (a) Remove the amplifier.
   (b) Check that there is continuity between terminals 1/14 and 2/14.

   If there is no continuity, replace the amplifier.

2. **INSPECT AMPLIFIER OPERATION**
   (a) Connect the positive (+) lead from the battery to terminal 17/18 and the negative (–) lead to terminal 16/18.
   (b) Check that the voltage between terminal 4/14 and the battery's negative (–) terminal, and between terminal 5/14 and the battery's negative (–) terminal fluctuates in accordance with the condition of terminals 10/14 and 11/14.

	10/14	11/14	Voltage	
			4/14 – Ground	5/14 – Ground
Condition 1	Open	Open	No voltage	No voltage
Condition 2	Ground	Open	Battery voltage	No voltage
Condition 3	Open	Ground	No voltage	Battery voltage
Condition 4	Ground	Ground	No voltage	No voltage

If operation is not as specified, replace the amplifier.

COMPRESSOR CONTROL AMPLIFIER TESTING—ES 250

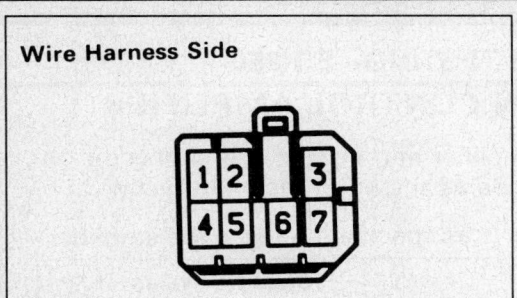

Wire Harness Side

1 2 3
4 5 6 7

COMPRESSOR CONTROL AMPLIFIER

Inspection of Compressor Control Amplifier

INSPECT COMPRESSOR CONTROL AMPLIFIER

Disconnect the amplifier and inspect the connector on the wire harness side as shown in the chart below.

Check for	Tester connection	Condition		Specified value
Continuity	6 – Ground	Constant		Continuity
	2 – Ground	Turn ignition switch on.	A/C switch on	Battery voltage
			A/C switch off	No voltage
Voltage	3 – Ground	Turn ignition switch on.		Battery voltage
		Turn ignition switch off.		No voltage
Resistance	5 – 7	Constant		Approx. 4.4 kΩ 25°C (77°F)

If the circuit is as specified, replace the amplifier.

AIR CONDITIONING AMPLIFIER TESTING—ES 250

Wire Harness Side

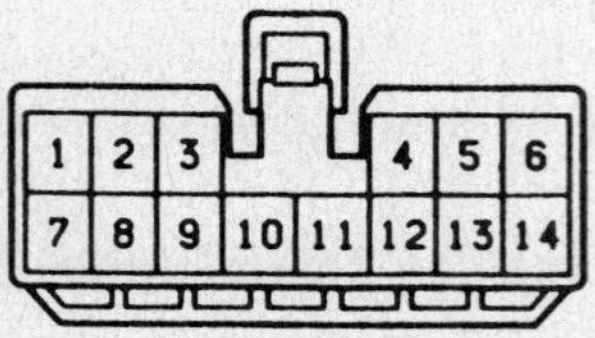
1
2
3
4
5
6
7
8
9
10
11
12
13
14

A/C AMPLIFIER
Parts Inspection

INSPECT A/C AMPLIFIER CIRCUIT

Disconnect the amplifier and inspect the connector on the wire harness side as shown in the chart below.

Test conditions:
(1) Temperature control lever: MAX.COOL
(2) Blower switch: HI

If the circuit is as specified, replace the amplifier.

Check for	Tester connection	Condition	Specified value
Continuity	3 – Ground	Constant	Continuity
Voltage	14 – Ground	Turn ignition switch on.	Battery voltage
		Turn ignition switch off.	No voltage
	11 – Ground	Turn ignition switch on.	Battery voltage
		Turn ignition switch off.	No voltage
	2 – Ground	Turn A/C switch on.	Battery voltage
		Turn A/C switch off.	No voltage
	10 – Ground	Turn A/C switch on.	Battery voltage
		Turn A/C switch off.	No voltage
	7 – Ground	Start engine.	Approx. 10 to 14 V
		Stop engine	No voltage
Resistance	5 – 9	Constant	Approx. 1.5kΩ at 27°C (77°F)
	8 – 9	Constant	Approx. 250Ω

CONDENSER FAN CONTROL AMPLIFIER TESTING—ES 250

Wire Harness Side

1
2
3
4
5
6
7

CONDENSER FAN CONTROL AMPLIFIER

Disconnect the amplifier and inspect the connector on the wire harness side as shown in the chart below.

If circuit is as specified, replace the amplifier.

Check for	Tester connection	Condition	Specified value
Continuity	1 – Ground	Constant	Continuity
	2 – Ground	Constant	Continuity
	5 – Ground	Constant	Continuity
	6 – Ground	Constant	Continuity
Voltage	3 – 6	Turn ignition switch on.	Battery voltage
		Turn ignition switch off.	No voltage
	4 – 6	Turn ignition switch on.	Battery voltage
		Turn ignition switch off.	No voltage

Automatic Temperature Control—LS 400

AUTOMATIC TEMPERATURE CONTROL TROUBLESHOOTING PROCEDURE—LS 400

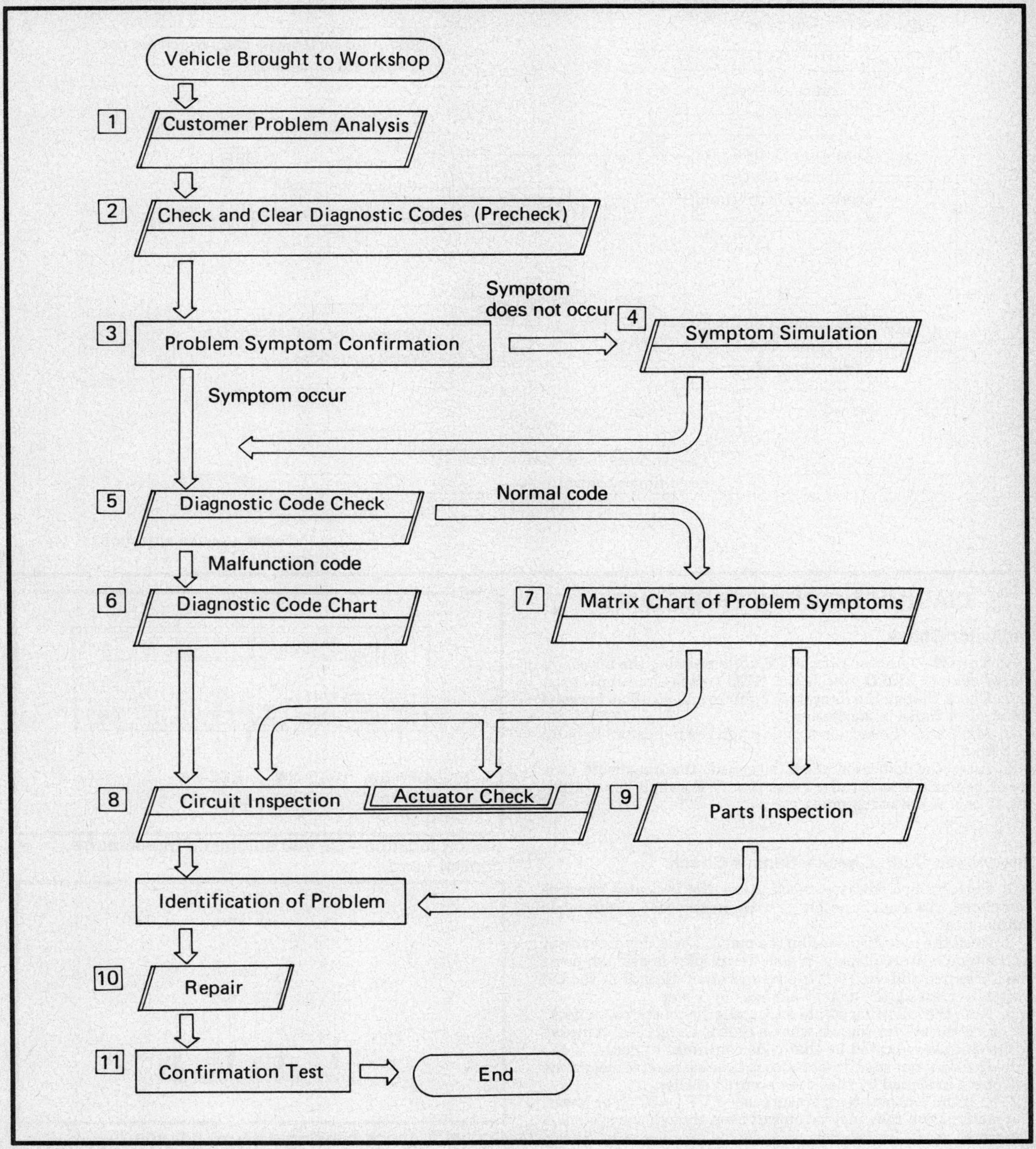
Vehicle Brought to Workshop
1
Customer Problem Analysis
2
Check and Clear Diagnostic Codes (Precheck)
3
Problem Symptom Confirmation
Symptom does not occur
4
Symptom Simulation
Symptom occur
5
Diagnostic Code Check
Normal code
Malfunction code
6
Diagnostic Code Chart
7
Matrix Chart of Problem Symptoms
8
Circuit Inspection
Actuator Check
9
Parts Inspection
Identification of Problem
10
Repair
11
Confirmation Test
End

DIAGNOSTIC CHECK PROCEDURE—LS 400

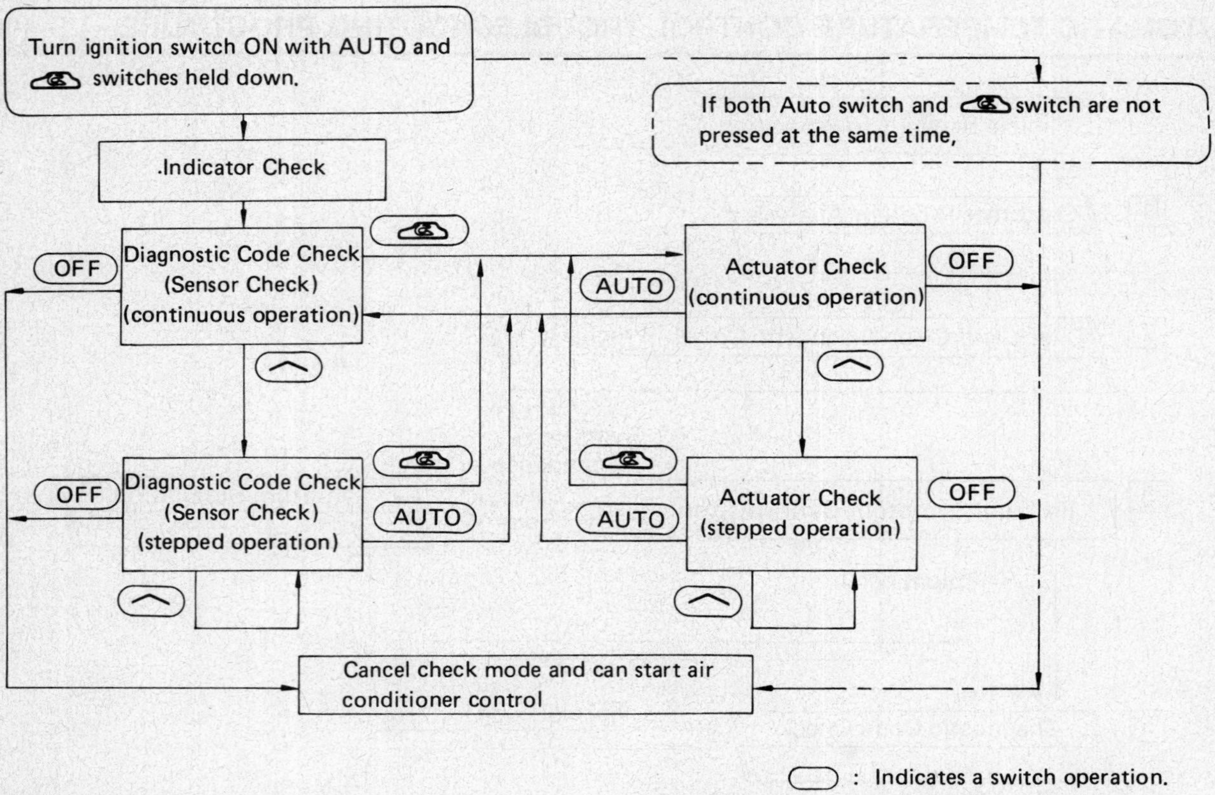
Turn ignition switch ON with AUTO and switches held down.
If both Auto switch and switch are not pressed at the same time,
.Indicator Check
Diagnostic Code Check (Sensor Check) (continuous operation)
Actuator Check (continuous operation)
Diagnostic Code Check (Sensor Check) (stepped operation)
Actuator Check (stepped operation)
OFF
AUTO
Cancel check mode and can start air conditioner control
: Indicates a switch operation.

DIAGNOSTIC CODE PROCEDURE

Indicator Check

1. Turn the ignition switch **ON** while pressing the air conditioner control **AUTO** switch and **REC** switch simultaneously.
2. Check that all the indicators light up and go off at 1 second intervals 4 times in succession.
3. Make sure the buzzer sounds when the indicators light up in Step 2.
4. After the indicator check is ended, the diagnostic code check begins automatically. Press the **OFF** switch when desiring to cancel the check mode.

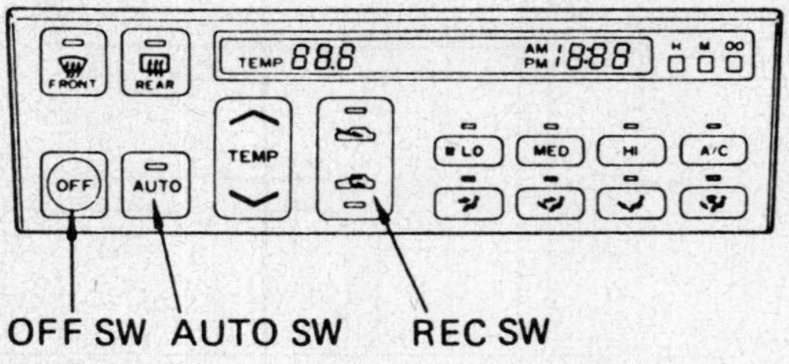
TEMP
AUTO
OFF
OFF SW
AUTO SW
REC SW

Switch location—LS 400 automatic temperature control head

Diagnostic Code Check—Sensor Check

1. Perform an indicator check. After the indicator check is completed, the system enters the diagnostic code check mode automatically.
2. Read the code displayed on the panel. The codes are output at the temperature display. If a slower display is desired, press the UP switch and change it to step operation. Each time the UP switch is pressed, the display changes by 1 step.
3. Note the following points during the diagnostic code check:
   a. If the buzzer sounds when a code is being read, it means the trouble indicated by that code continues to occur. If the buzzer does not sound when a code is being read, it means the trouble indicated by that code occured earlier.
   b. If the ambient temperature is −22°F (−30°C) or lower, a malfunction code may be output even though the system is normal.

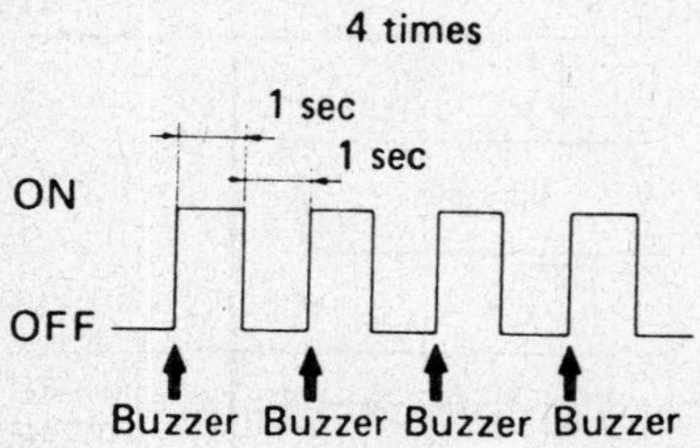
4 times
1 sec
1 sec
ON
OFF
Buzzer Buzzer Buzzer Buzzer

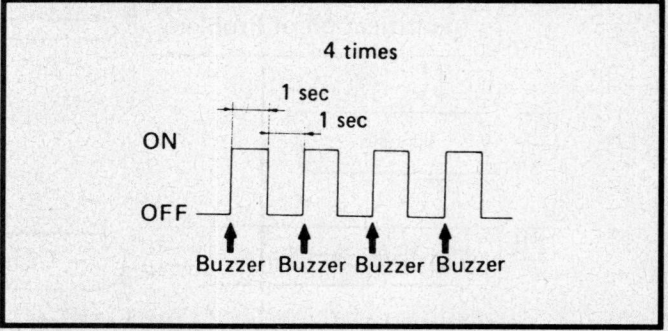

Indicator check blinking pattern—LS 400

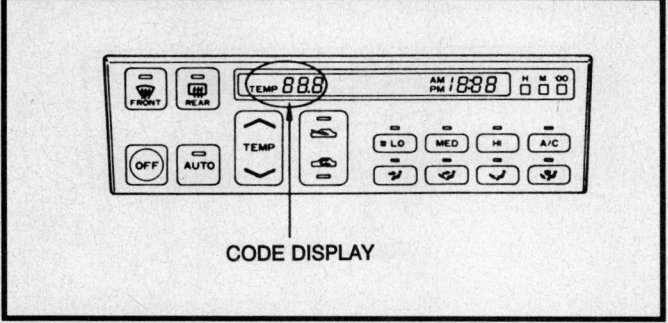

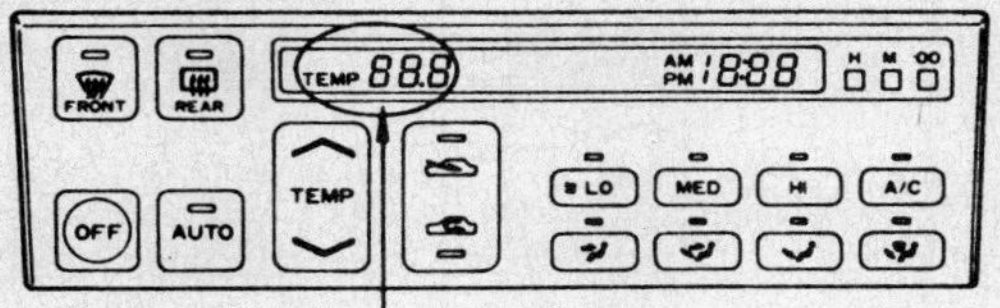
CODE DISPLAY
Diagnostic code display—LS 400

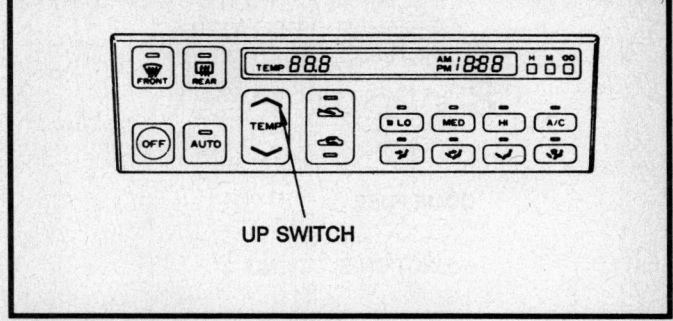

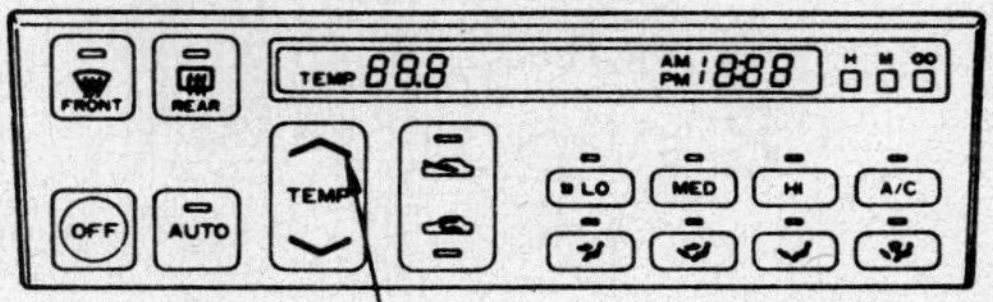
UP SWITCH
UP switch location—LS 400

AUTOMATIC TEMPERATURE CONTROL DIAGNOSTIC CODES—LS 400

Code No.	Diagnosis
00	Normal
11	Open or short in room temperature sensor circuit.
12	Open or short in ambient temperature sensor circuit.
13	Open or short in evaporator temperature sensor circuit.
14	Open or short in water temperature sensor circuit.
21*	Open or short in solar sensor circuit.
22*	• Compressor motor locked. • Open or short in compressor lock sensor circuit.
31	Open or short in air mix damper position sensor circuit.
32	Open or short in air inlet damper position sensor circuit.
33	• Open in air mix damper position sensor circuit. • Open or short in air mix servomotor circuit. • Air mix servomotor locked.
34	• Open in air inlet damper position sensor circuit. • Open or short in air inlet servomotor circuit. • Air inlet servomotor locked.

* Open circuit in the solar sensor and locking of the compressor are detected only when they are current troubles. Other codes detect both current trouble (buzzer sound) are past trouble (no buzzer sound).

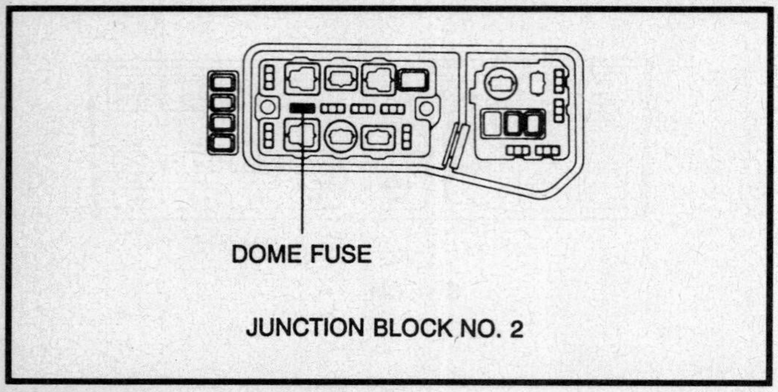
DOME FUSE
JUNCTION BLOCK NO. 2

DOME fuse location—LS 400

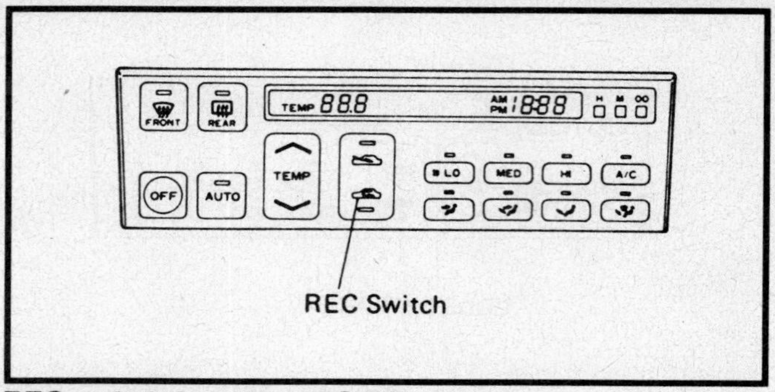
REC Switch

REC switch location—LS 400

c. Codes are displayed in order from the smallest code numbers to the largest.

d. If the diagnostic code check is being performed in a dark place, Code 21, solar sensor circuit abnormal, could be displayed. In this case, perform the diagnostic code check again while shining a light on the solar sensor. If Code 21 is still displayed, there could be trouble in the solar sensor circuit.

Clearing Diagnostic Codes

1. Pull out the DOME fuse in junction block no. 2, located in the engine compartment on the driver's side, for 10 seconds or longer to clear the memory of diagnostic codes.
2. After reinserting the fuse, check that the normal code is output.

Actuator Check

1. After entering the sensor check mode, press the REC switch.
2. Since each damper, motor and relay automatically operates at 1 second intervals beginning in order from 20 in the temperature display, check the temperature and air flow visually and by hand.
3. If a slower display is desired, press the UP switch and change it to step operation. Each time the UP switch is pressed, the display changes by 1 step.
4. Note the following points during the actuator check:
   a. The buzzer sounds when the display code changes.
   b. Codes are displayed in order from the smaller to the larger numbers.
   c. To cancel the check mode, press the **OFF** switch.

ACTUATOR CHECK CODES—LS 400

Step No.	Display code	Conditions							
		Heater relay	Ex-Hi. relay	Blower motor	Air flow vent	Max cool damper	Air inlet damper	Magnet clutch	Air mix damper
1	20	OFF	OFF	OFF	(FACE)	100% open	(FRESH)	OFF	Cool side (0% open)
2	21	ON	↑	LO	↑	↑	↑	↑	↑
3	22	↑	↑	MED	↑	50% open	(F/R)	ON	↑
4	23	↑	↑	↑	↑	0% open	(RECIRC)	↑	↑
5	24	↑	↑	↑	(BI-LEVEL)	↑	(FRESH)	↑	Cool/Hot (50% open)
6	25	↑	↑	↑	↑	↑	↑	↑	↑
7	26	↑	↑	↑	(FOOT)	↑	↑	↑	↑
8	27	↑	↑	↑	↑	↑	↑	↑	Hot side (100% open)
9	28	↑	↑	↑	(FOOT/DEF)	↑	↑	↑	↑
10	29	↑	ON	HI	(DEF)	↑	↑	↑	↑

AUTOMATIC TEMPERATURE CONTROL TROUBLESHOOTING MATRIX CHART—LS 400

Symptom \ Suspect Area		Volume of refrigerant	Drive belt tension	Inspect refrigeration system with manifold gauge set	Backup power source circuit	IG power source circuit	Acc power source circuit	Heater main relay circuit	Blower motor circuit	Power transistor circuit	Ex-Hi relay circuit	Air mix damper position sensor circuit	Air inlet damper position sensor circuit	Air mix servomotor circuit	Air inlet servomotor circuit	Mode servomotor circuit	Max. cool servomotor circuit	Room temp. sensor circuit
Air Flow Control	No blower operation					1	2	3	4									
	No blower control					1		4	5	2	3							
	Insufficient air flow								1									
Temperature Control	No cool air comes out	1	2	3								7		8				9
	No warm air comes out											2		3				4
	Output air is warmer or colder than the set temperature or response is slow	1	2	3								11	13	12	14			7
	No temperature control (only Max. cool or Max. warm)											3		4				1
No air inlet control													1		2			
No air flow mode control																1	2	
Engine idle up does not occur, or is continuous																		
Diagnostic code not recorded. Set mode is cleared when IG switch is turned off.					1													

Symptom \ Suspect Area		Ambient temp. sensor circuit	Evaporator temp. sensor circuit	Water temp. sensor circuit	Solar sensor circuit	Compressor lock sensor circuit	Compressor circuit	Pressure switch circuit	Igniter circuit	ECU (A/C control assy)	Cooling fan system	Water valve	Condenser	Receiver	Evaporator	Radiator (in heater unit)	Expansion valve
Air Flow Control	No blower operation			5						6							
	No blower control			6						7							
	Insufficient air flow																
Temperature Control	No cool air comes out	10				6	4	5	11	12							
	No warm air comes out	5	6							7		1					
	Output air is warmer or colder than the set temperature or response is slow	8	9	10	6					20	4	5	15	16	17	18	19
	No temperature control (only Max. cool or Max. warm)	2								5							
No air inlet control										3							
No air flow mode control										3							
Engine idle up does not occur, or is continuous							1			2							
Diagnostic code not recorded. Set mode is cleared when IG switch is turned off.										2							

BACKUP POWER SOURCE CIRCUIT DIAGNOSIS AND TESTING—LS 400

Backup Power Source Circuit

CIRCUIT DESCRIPTION

This is the backup power source for the air conditioner control assembly. Power is supplied even when the ignition switch is off and is used for diagnostic code memory, etc.

DIAGNOSTIC CHART

1. Check voltage between terminal B of air conditioner control assembly connector and body ground.
   - OK → Proceed to next circuit inspection shown on matrix chart
   - NG → go to 2
2. Check DOME fuse.
   - NG → Check for short in all the harness and components connected to the DOME fuse
   - OK → Check and repair harness and connector between air conditioner control assembly and battery.

WIRING DIAGRAM

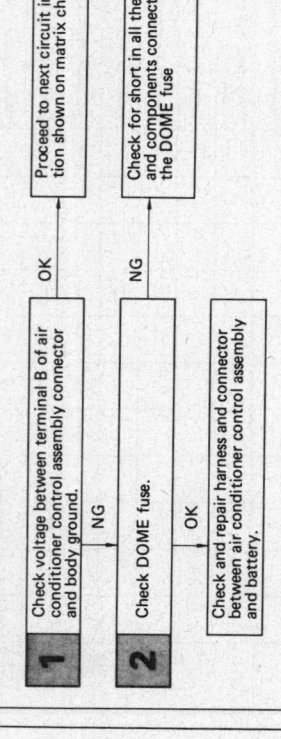

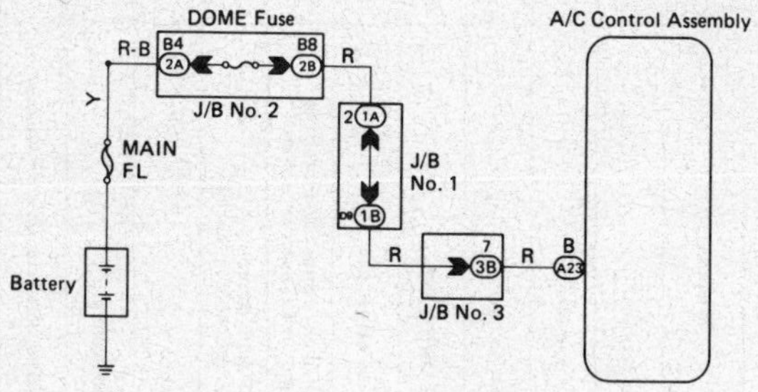
DOME Fuse
R-B
B4
2A
B8
2B
R
J/B No. 2
Y
MAIN
FL
Battery
2
1A
1B
J/B
No. 1
R
7
3B
R
J/B No. 3
B
A23
A/C Control Assembly

BACKUP POWER SOURCE CIRCUIT WIRING ROUTING LS 400

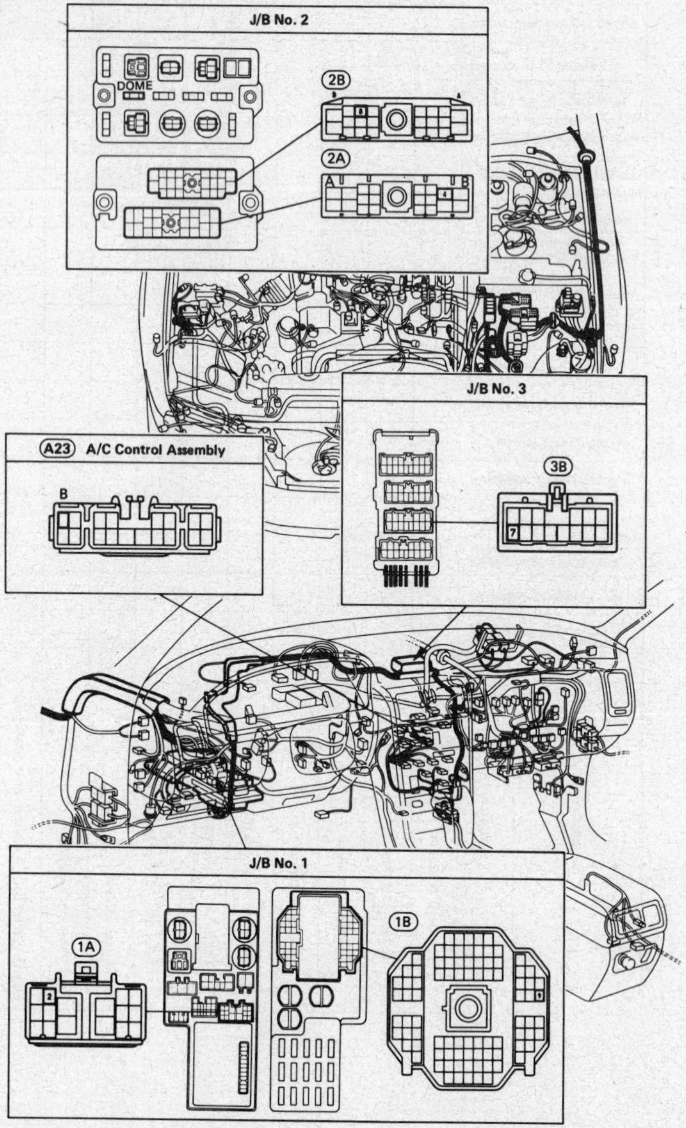
J/B No. 2
DOME
2B
2A
J/B No. 3
3B
7
A23 A/C Control Assembly
B
J/B No. 1
1A
1B

BACKUP POWER SOURCE CIRCUIT INSPECTION PROCEDURE—LS 400

1 Check voltage between terminal B of air conditioner control assembly connector and body ground.

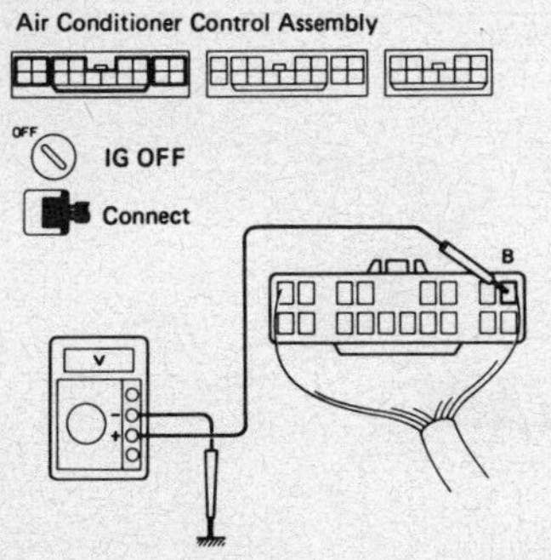
Air Conditioner Control Assembly
OFF
IG OFF
Connect
B
V

P Remove the air conditioner control assembly with connector still connected.

C Measure voltage between terminal B of air conditioner control assembly connector and body ground.

OK **Voltage: Battery voltage**

OK → **Proceed to next circuit inspection shown on matrix chart**

NG ↓

2 Check DOME fuse.

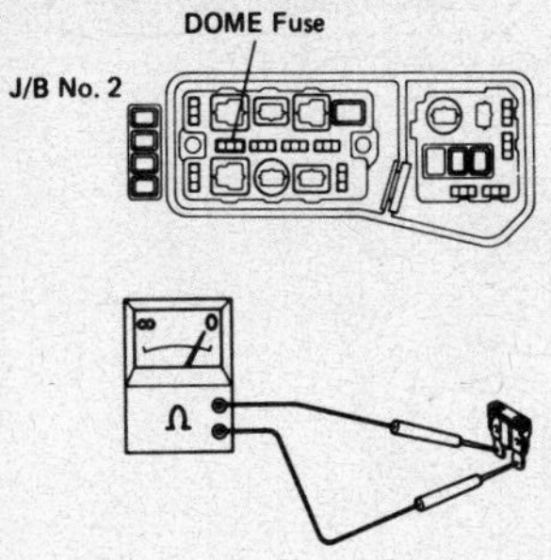
DOME Fuse
J/B No. 2

P Remove DOME fuse from J/B No. 2.

C Check continuity of DOME fuse.

OK **Continuity**

NG → **Check for short in all the harness and components connected to the DOME fuse**

OK ↓

Check and repair harness and connector between air conditioner control assembly and battery.

IG POWER SOURCE CIRCUIT DIAGNOSIS AND TESTING—LS 400

IG Power Source Circuit

CIRCUIT DESCRIPTION

This is the power source for the air conditioner control assembly (contains the ECU) and servo motors, etc.

DIAGNOSTIC CHART

1. Check voltage between terminals IG and GND of air conditioner control assembly connector. — OK → Proceed to next circuit inspection shown on matrix chart
   - NG ↓
2. Check continuity between terminal GND of air conditioner control assembly and body ground. — NG → Repair or replace harness or connector.
   - OK ↓
3. Check HEATER fuse. — NG → Check for short in all the harness and components connected to the HEATER fuse
   - OK ↓

Check and repair harness and connector between air conditioner control assembly and battery.

WIRING DIAGRAM

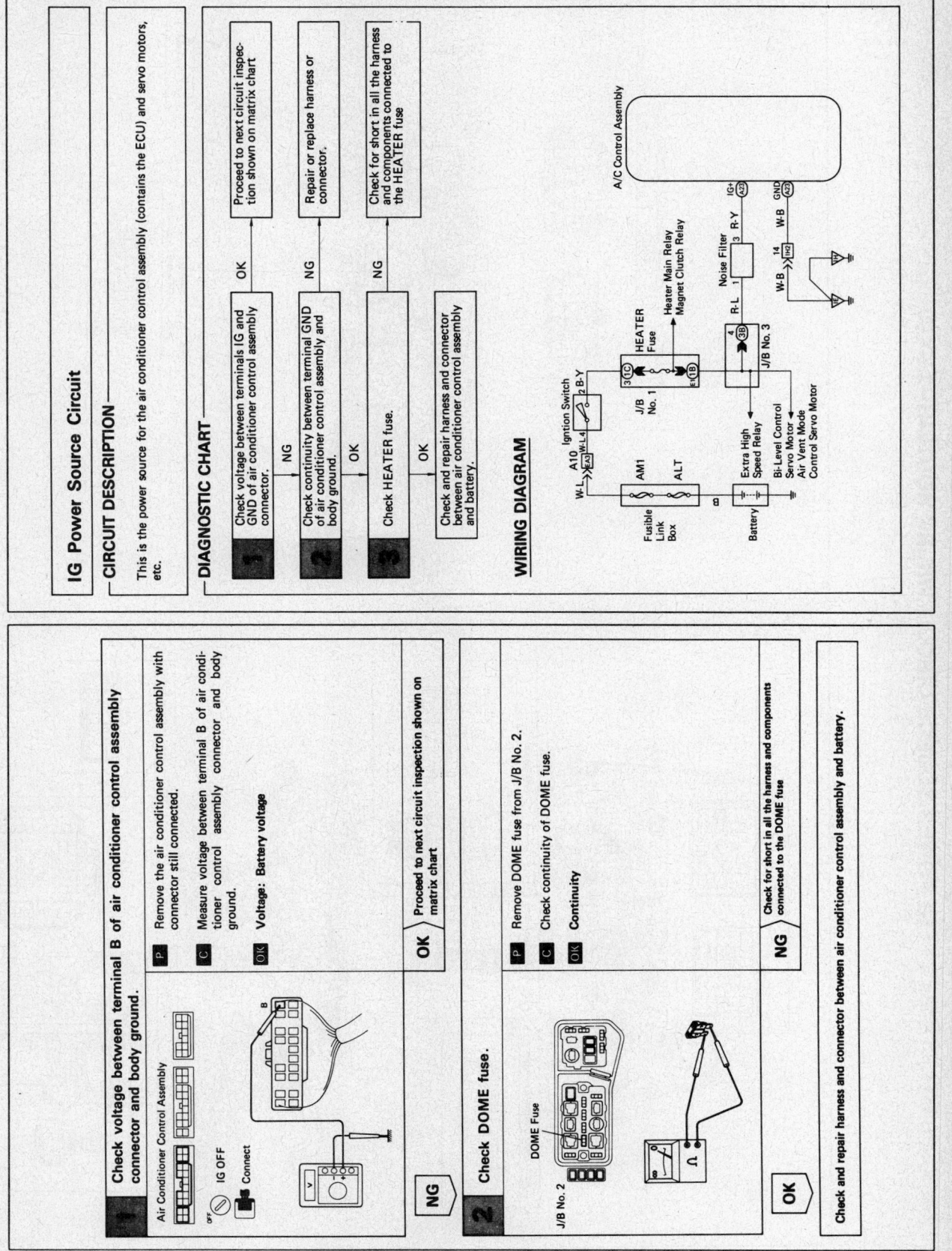

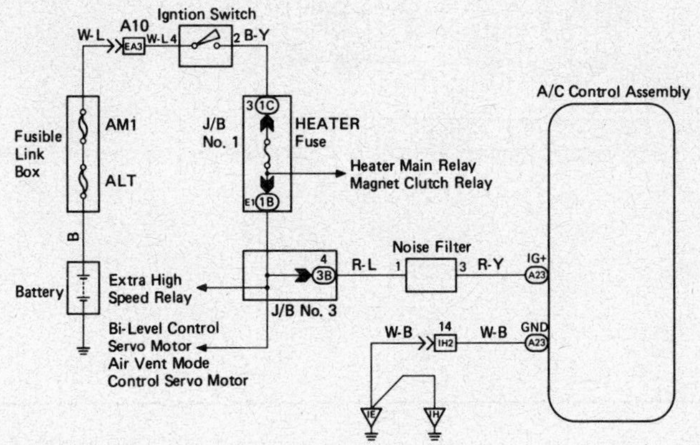
Igntion Switch
A10
W-L
W-L 4
EA3
2 B-Y
Fusible
Link
Box
AM1
ALT
J/B
No. 1
3 1C
HEATER
Fuse
E1 1B
Heater Main Relay
Magnet Clutch Relay
A/C Control Assembly
B
Battery
Extra High
Speed Relay
4
3B
J/B No. 3
R-L
Noise Filter
1
3
R-Y
IG+
A23
Bi-Level Control
Servo Motor
Air Vent Mode
Control Servo Motor
W-B
14
IH2
W-B
GND
A23
IE
IH

IG POWER SOURCE CIRCUIT WIRING ROUTING—LS 400

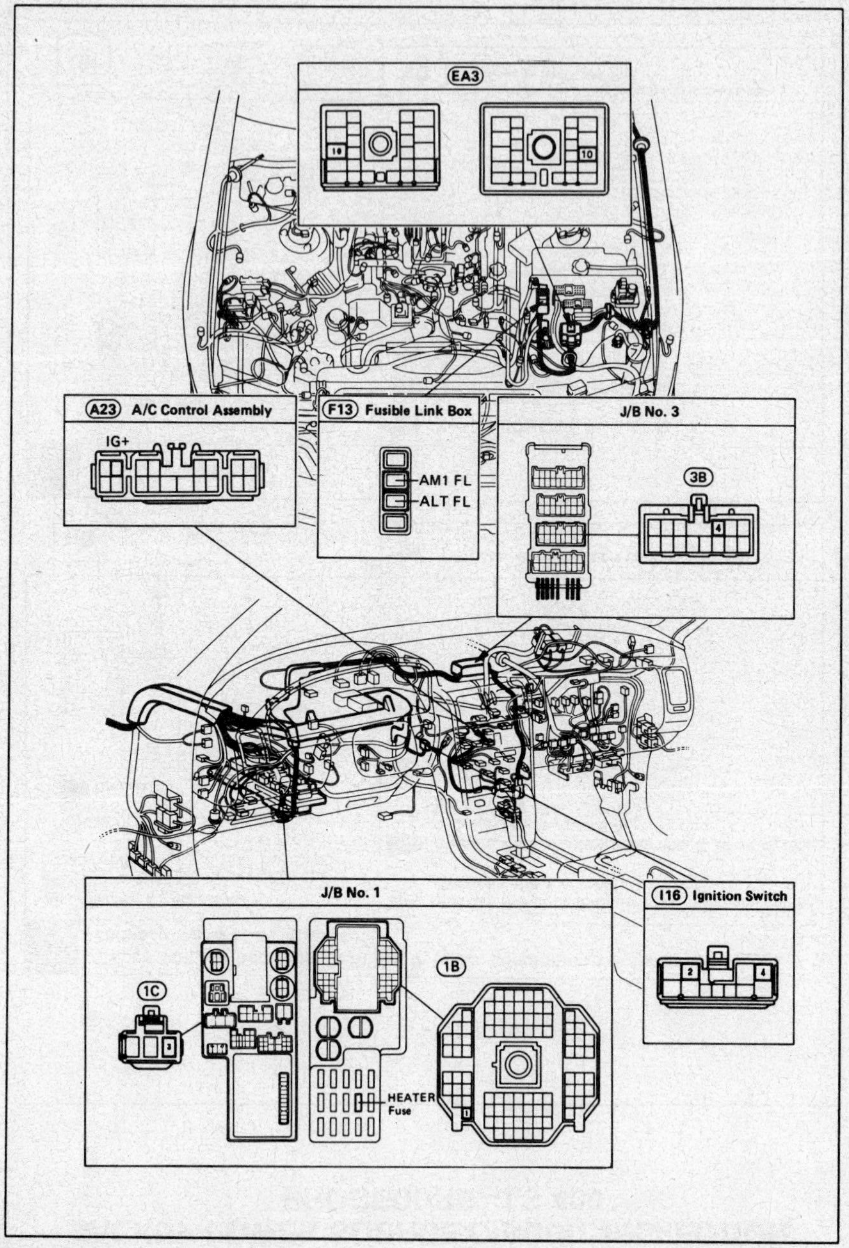
EA3
10
10
A23 A/C Control Assembly
IG+
F13 Fusible Link Box
AM1 FL
ALT FL
J/B No. 3
3B
4
J/B No. 1
1C
3
1B
HEATER
Fuse
I16 Ignition Switch
2
4

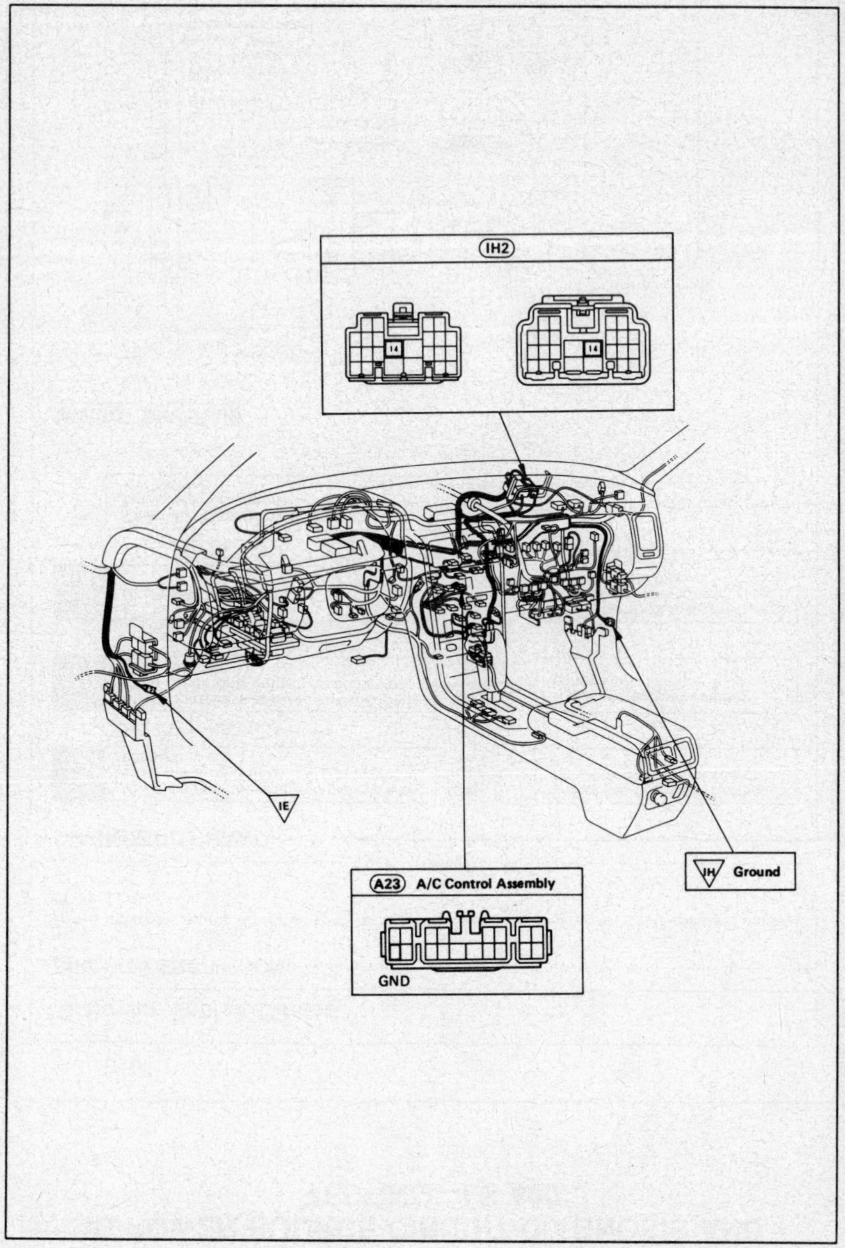
IH2
14
14
IE
A23 A/C Control Assembly
GND
IH
Ground

IG POWER SOURCE CIRCUIT INSPECTION PROCEDURE—LS 400

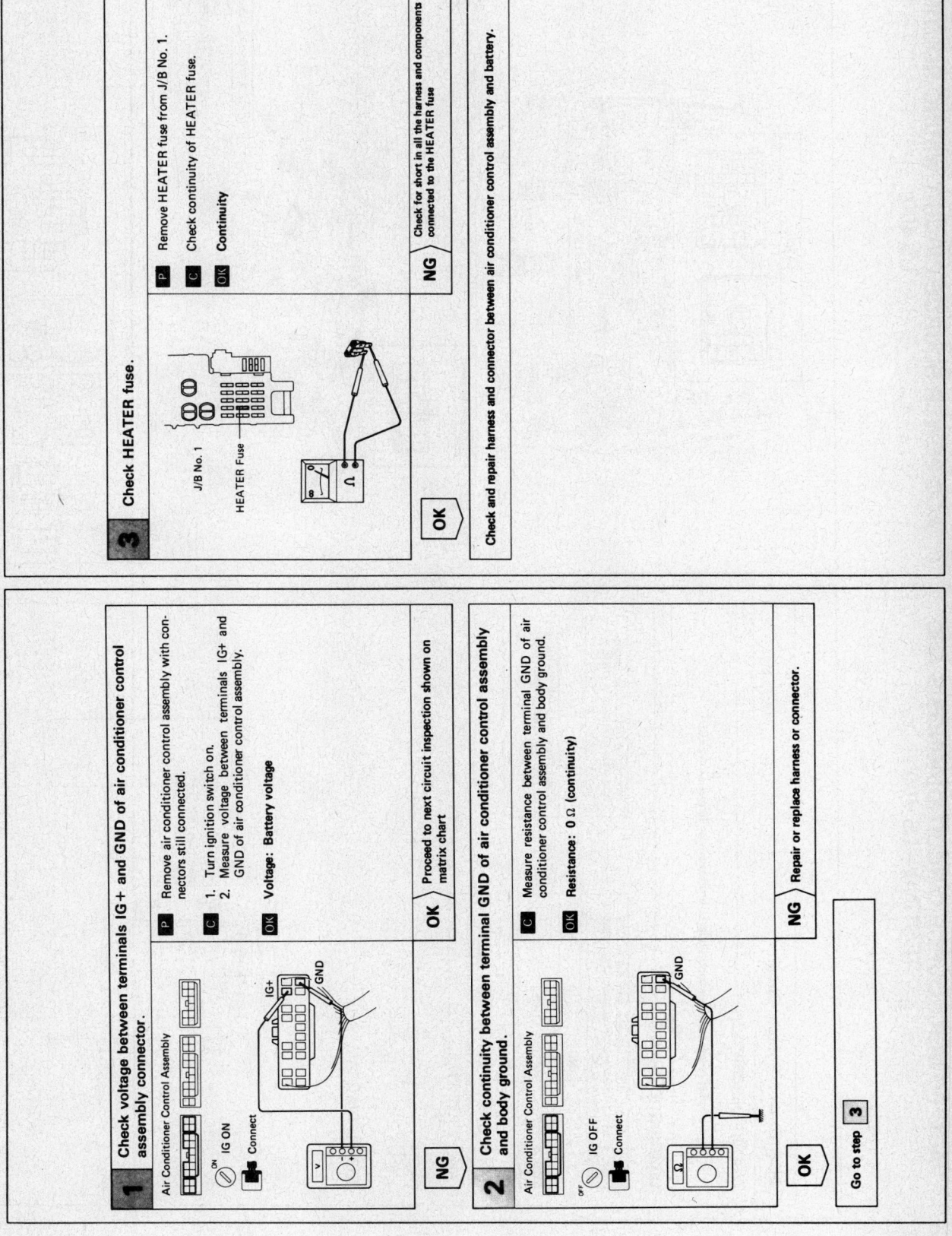

1 Check voltage between terminals IG+ and GND of air conditioner control assembly connector.

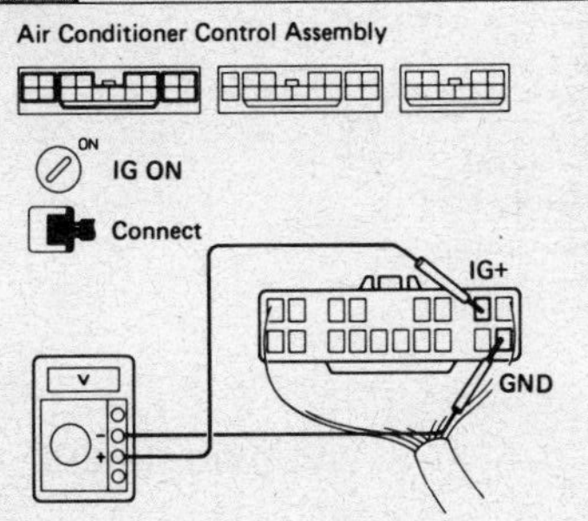
Air Conditioner Control Assembly
ON
IG ON
Connect
IG+
GND
V

P Remove air conditioner control assembly with connectors still connected.

C
1. Turn ignition switch on.
2. Measure voltage between terminals IG+ and GND of air conditioner control assembly.

OK **Voltage: Battery voltage**

OK → Proceed to next circuit inspection shown on matrix chart

NG ↓

2 Check continuity between terminal GND of air conditioner control assembly and body ground.

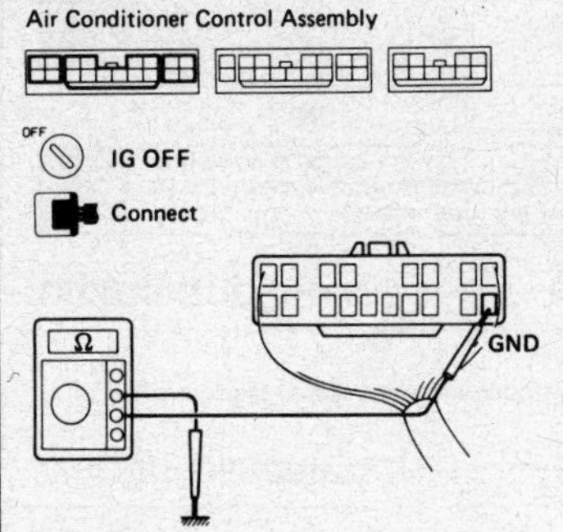
Air Conditioner Control Assembly
OFF
IG OFF
Connect
GND
Ω

C Measure resistance between terminal GND of air conditioner control assembly and body ground.

OK **Resistance: 0 Ω (continuity)**

NG → Repair or replace harness or connector.

OK ↓

Go to step 3

3 Check HEATER fuse.

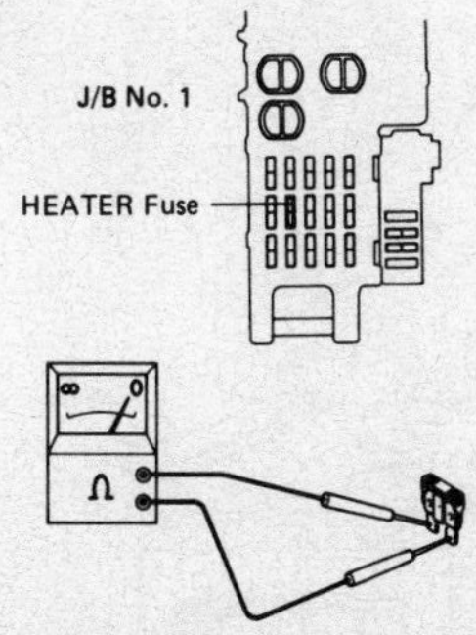
J/B No. 1
HEATER Fuse
Ω

P Remove HEATER fuse from J/B No. 1.

C Check continuity of HEATER fuse.

OK **Continuity**

NG → Check for short in all the harness and components connected to the HEATER fuse

OK ↓

Check and repair harness and connector between air conditioner control assembly and battery.

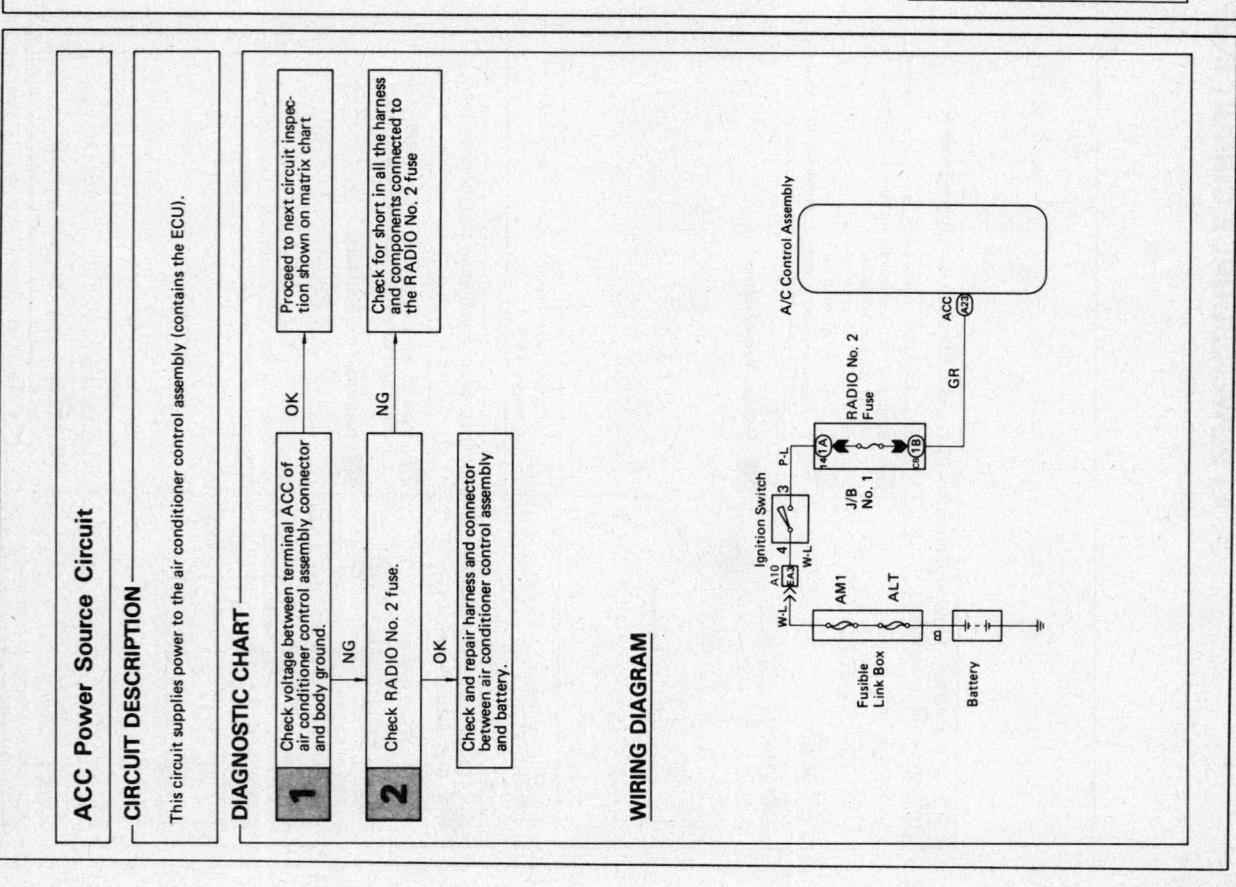

ACC POWER SOURCE CIRCUIT DIAGNOSIS AND TESTING—LS 400

ACC Power Source Circuit

CIRCUIT DESCRIPTION

This circuit supplies power to the air conditioner control assembly (contains the ECU).

DIAGNOSTIC CHART

Step	Check	Result	Action
1	Check voltage between terminal ACC of air conditioner control assembly connector and body ground.	OK	Proceed to next circuit inspection shown on matrix chart
		NG	Go to step 2
2	Check RADIO No. 2 fuse.	NG	Check for short in all the harness and components connected to the RADIO No. 2 fuse
		OK	Check and repair harness and connector between air conditioner control assembly and battery.

WIRING DIAGRAM

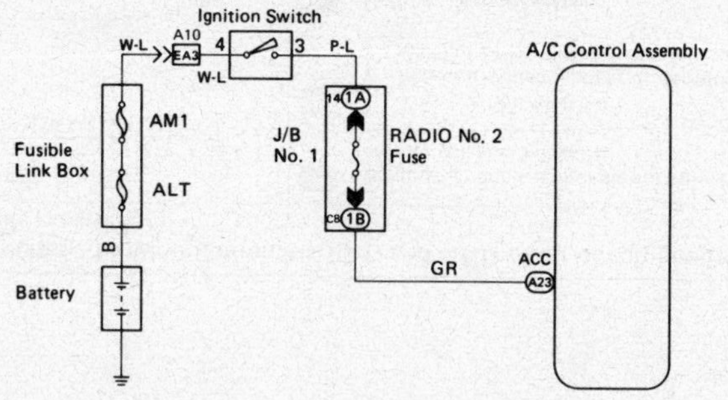
Ignition Switch
W-L
A10
EA3
4
3
W-L
P-L
A/C Control Assembly
AM1
Fusible Link Box
ALT
B
Battery
J/B No. 1
14 1A
RADIO No. 2 Fuse
C8 1B
GR
ACC
A23

ACC POWER SOURCE CIRCUIT WIRING ROUTING LS 400

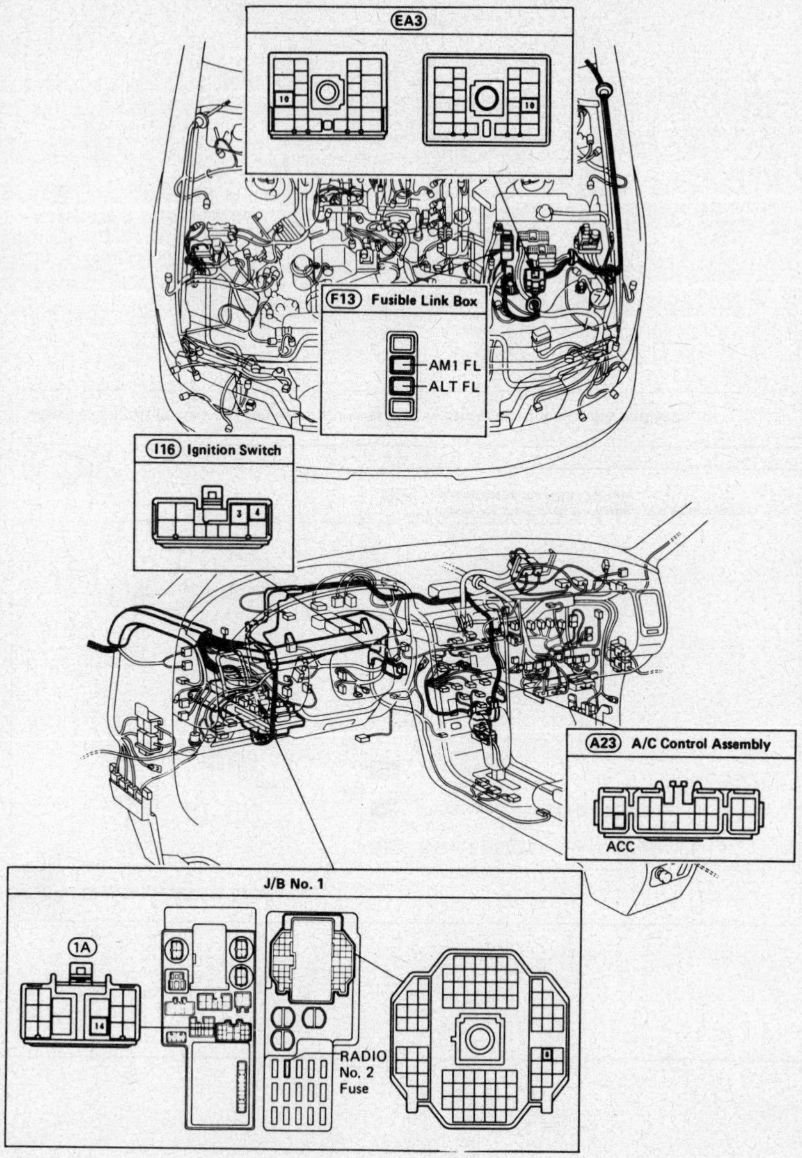
EA3
F13 Fusible Link Box
AM1 FL
ALT FL
I16 Ignition Switch
A23 A/C Control Assembly
ACC
J/B No. 1
1A
RADIO No. 2 Fuse

ACC POWER SOURCE CIRCUIT INSPECTION PROCEDURE–LS 400

1 **Check voltage between terminal ACC of air conditioner control assembly connector and body ground.**

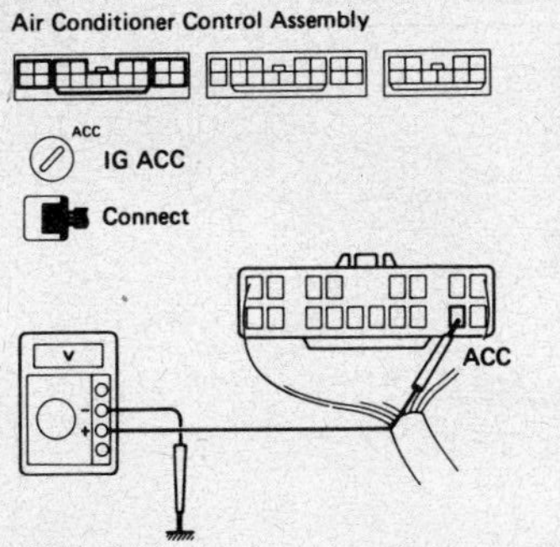
Air Conditioner Control Assembly
ACC
IG ACC
Connect
ACC
V

P Remove air conditioner control assembly with connector still connected.

C
1. Turn ignition switch ACC.
2. Measure voltage between terminal ACC of air conditioner control assembly connector and body ground.

OK **Voltage: Battery voltage**

OK → **Proceed to next circuit inspection shown on matrix chart**

NG ↓

2 **Check RADIO No. 2 fuse.**

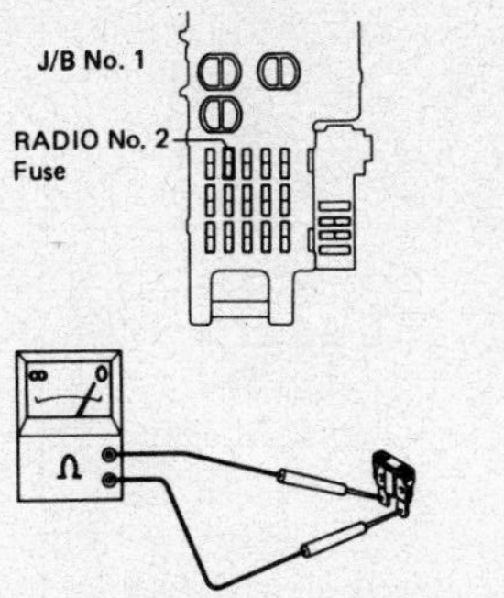
J/B No. 1
RADIO No. 2
Fuse
Ω

P Remove RADIO No. 2 fuse from J/B No. 1.

C Check continuity of RADIO No. 2 fuse.

OK **Continuity**

NG → **Check for short in all the harness and components connected to the RADIO No. 2 fuse**

OK ↓

Check and repair harness and connector between air conditioner control assembly and battery.

HEATER MAIN RELAY CIRCUIT DIAGNOSIS AND TESTING–LS 400

Heater Main Relay Circuit

CIRCUIT DESCRIPTION

The heater main relay is switched on by signals from the air conditioner control assembly.
It supplies power to the blower motor.

DIAGNOSTIC CHART

1 Check voltage between terminal HR of air conditioner control assembly connector and body ground. — OK → Proceed to next circuit inspection shown on matrix chart

NG ↓

2 Check heater main relay. — NG → Replace heater main relay.

OK ↓

3 Check HEATER fuse. — NG → Check for short in all the harness and components connected to the HEATER fuse

OK ↓

Check and repair harness and connector between air conditioner control assembly and battery.

WIRING DIAGRAM

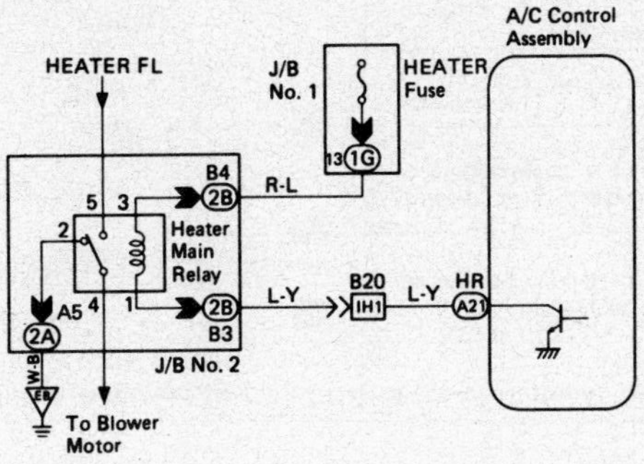
HEATER FL
J/B
No. 1
HEATER
Fuse
A/C Control
Assembly
13
1G
B4
2B
R-L
5
3
2
Heater
Main
Relay
A5
4
1
2A
2B
B3
L-Y
B20
IH1
L-Y
HR
A21
J/B No. 2
W-B
EB
To Blower
Motor

HEATER MAIN RELAY CIRCUIT WIRING ROUTING LS 400

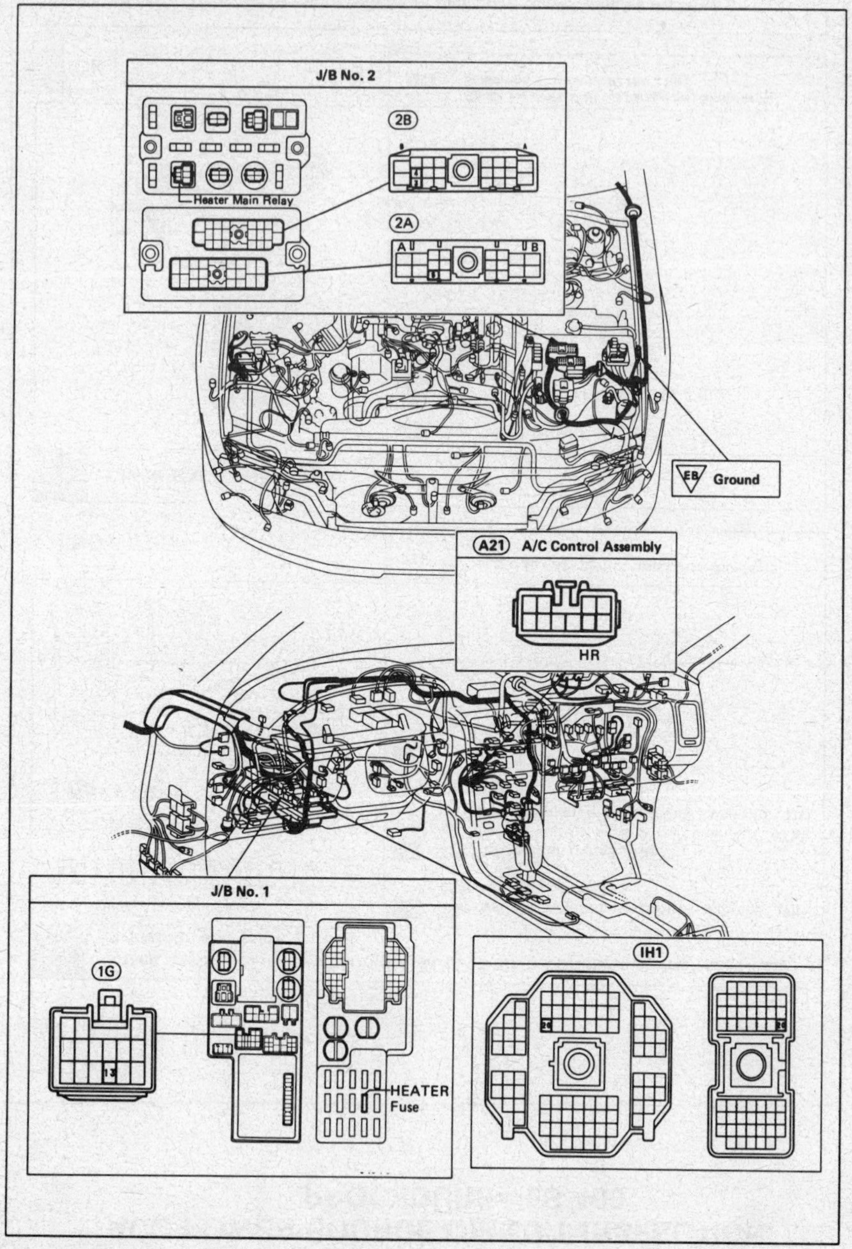
J/B No. 2
2B
2A
A
B
Heater Main Relay
Ground
A21 A/C Control Assembly
HR
J/B No. 1
1G
HEATER Fuse
IH1

HEATER MAIN RELAY CIRCUIT INSPECTION PROCEDURE – LS 400

1 Check voltage between terminal HR of air conditioner control assembly connector and body ground.

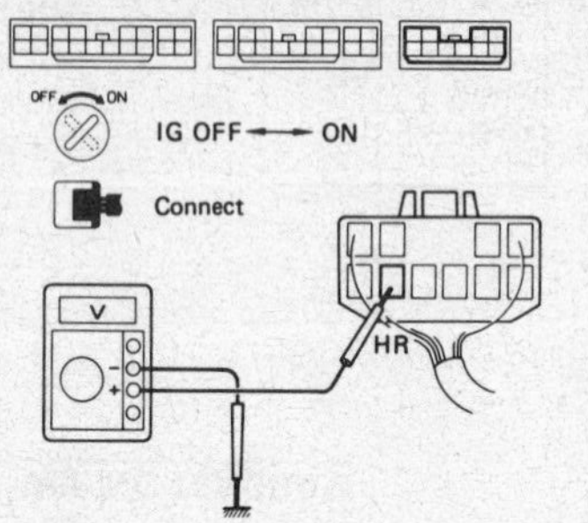
Air Conditioner Control Assembly
OFF ON
IG OFF ←→ ON
Connect
V
HR

P Remove air conditioner control assembly with connectors still connected.

C Measure voltage between terminal HR of air conditioner control assembly and body ground when ignition switch is on and off.

OK

Ignition Switch	Voltage	
OFF	0 V	
ON	Blower ON	0 V
	Blower OFF	Battery voltage

NG ↓

OK → Proceed to next circuit inspection shown on matrix chart

2 Check heater main relay.

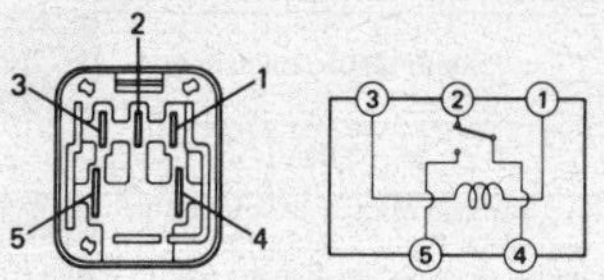
1
2
3
4
5

C Check continuity between each pair of terminals of heater main relay shown below.

OK

Terminals 4 and 5	Open
Terminals 1 and 3 Terminals 2 and 4	Continuity

P
1. Apply battery voltage between terminals 1 and 3.
2. Check continuity between each pair of terminal shown below.

OK

Terminals 2 and 4	Open
Terminals 4 and 5	Continuity

OK ↓

NG → Replace heater main relay.

3 Check HEATER fuse.

NG → Check for short in all the harness and components connected to the HEATER fuse

OK ↓

Check and repair harness and connector between air conditioner control assembly and battery.

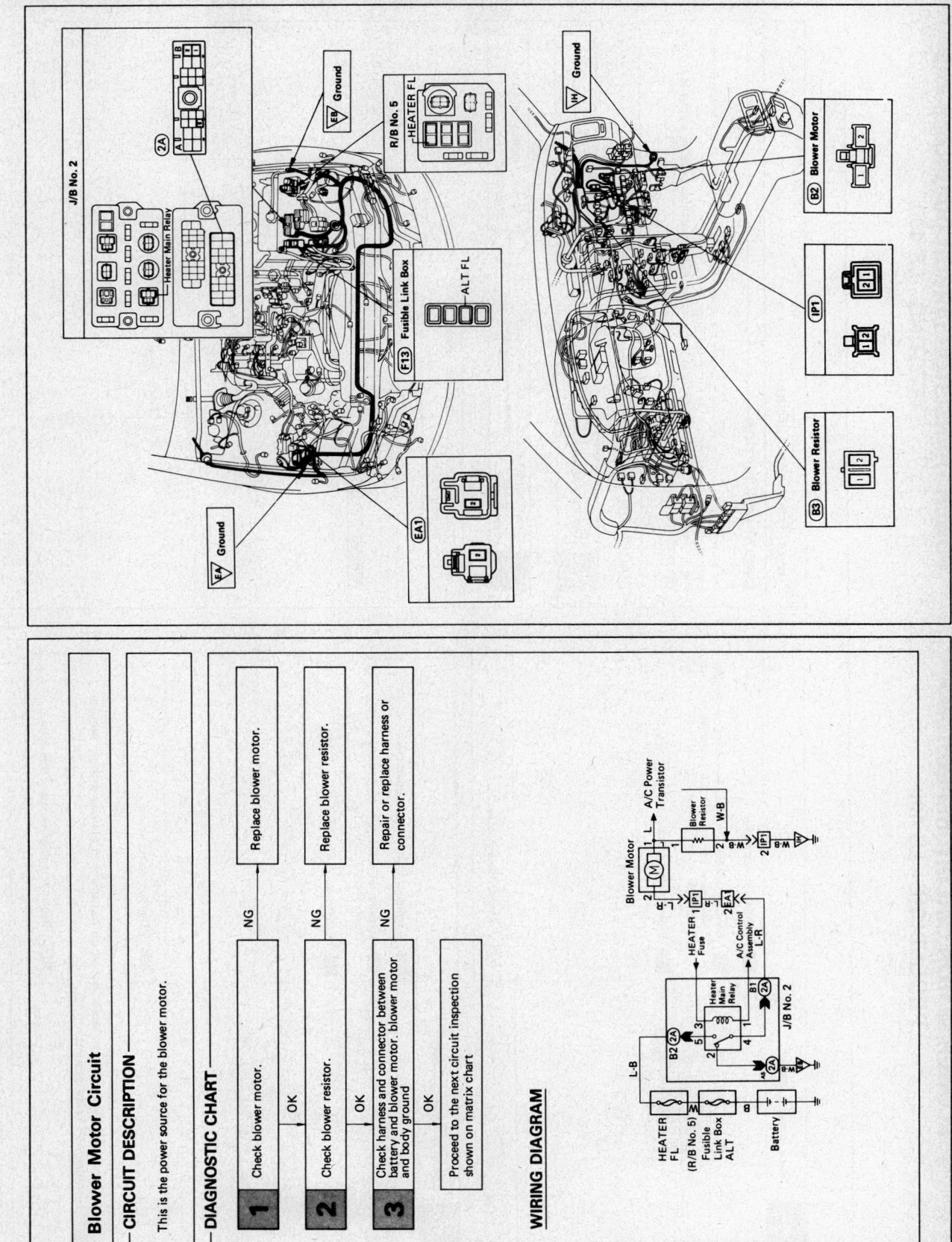

BLOWER MOTOR CIRCUIT DIAGNOSIS AND TESTING—LS 400

Blower Motor Circuit

CIRCUIT DESCRIPTION

This is the power source for the blower motor.

DIAGNOSTIC CHART

1. Check blower motor. — NG → Replace blower motor.
   - OK ↓
2. Check blower resistor. — NG → Replace blower resistor.
   - OK ↓
3. Check harness and connector between battery and blower motor. blower motor and body ground — NG → Repair or replace harness or connector.
   - OK ↓

Proceed to the next circuit inspection shown on matrix chart

WIRING DIAGRAM

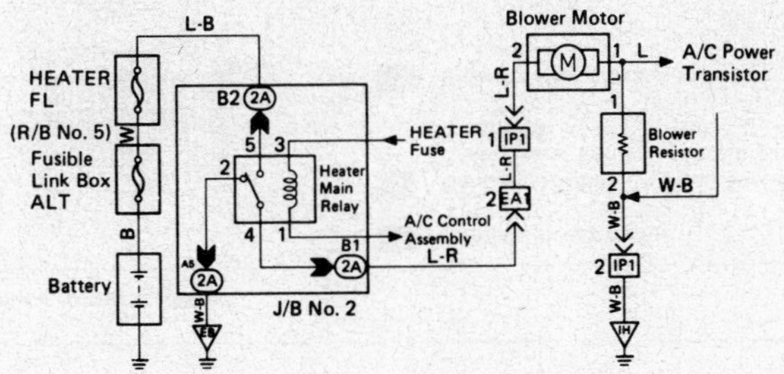
HEATER FL
(R/B No. 5)
Fusible Link Box ALT
Battery
L-B
W
B
B2 2A
5 3
2
4 1
Heater Main Relay
HEATER Fuse
A/C Control Assembly
L-R
B1 2A
A5 2A
W-B
EB
J/B No. 2
Blower Motor
M
L-R
1 IP1
2 EA1
L
A/C Power Transistor
Blower Resistor
W-B
2 IP1
IH

BLOWER MOTOR CIRCUIT WIRING ROUTING—LS 400

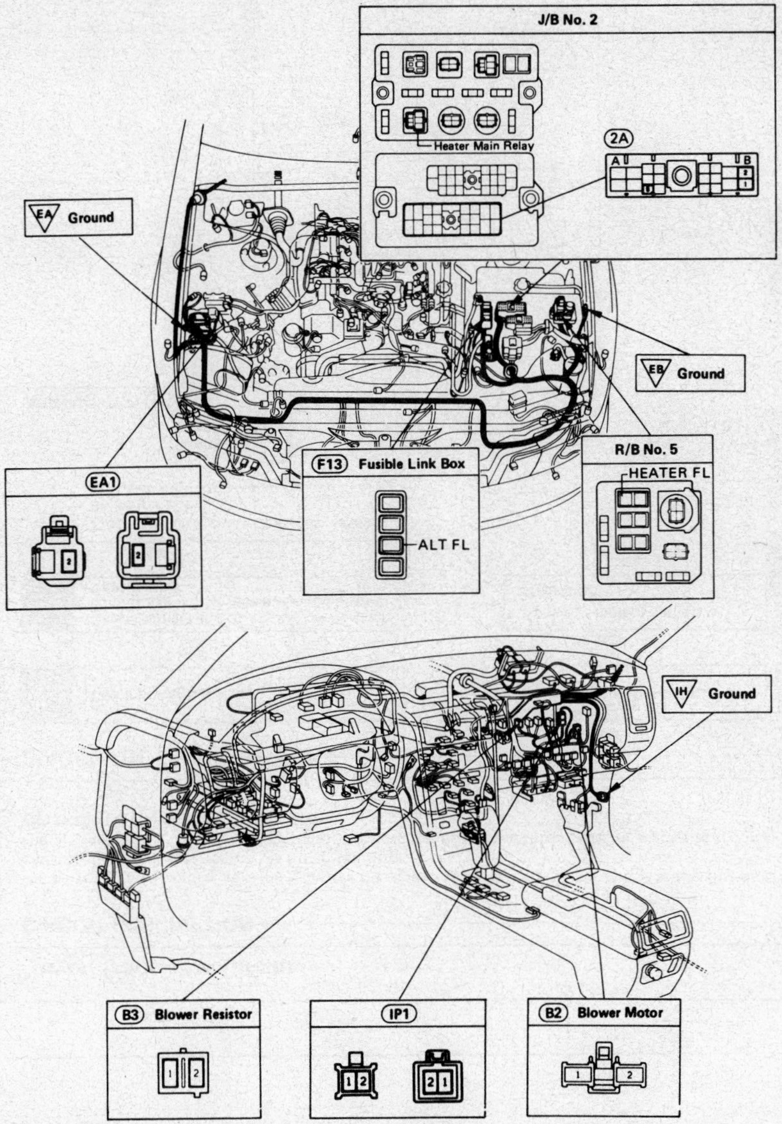
J/B No. 2
Heater Main Relay
2A
EA Ground
EB Ground
R/B No. 5
HEATER FL
F13 Fusible Link Box
ALT FL
EA1
IH Ground
B3 Blower Resistor
IP1
B2 Blower Motor

BLOWER MOTOR CIRCUIT INSPECTION PROCEDURE—LS 400

1 Check blower motor.

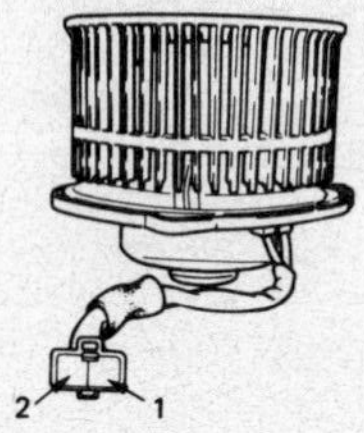
2
1

P Remove blower motor

C Connect positive ⊕ lead connected to terminal 2 of blower motor connector, negative ⊖ lead to terminal 1.

OK **Blower motor operates smoothly.**

OK

NG **Replace blower motor.**

2 Check blower resistor.

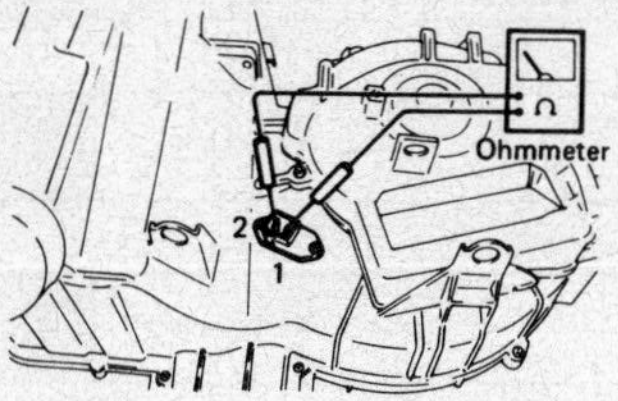
Ohmmeter
Ω
2
1

P Disconnect blower resistor connector.

C Measure resistance between terminals 1 and 2 of blower resistor connector.

OK Resistance: 1.8 – 2.2 Ω

OK

NG **Replace blower resister.**

3 Check harness and connector between battery and blower motor, blower motor and body ground

OK

NG **Repair or replace harness or connector.**

Proceed to next circuit inspection shown on matrix chart

POWER TRANSISTOR CIRCUIT DIAGNOSIS AND TESTING—LS 400

Power Transistor Circuit

CIRCUIT DESCRIPTION

The air conditioner control assembly controls the blower speed by varying the voltage at terminal BLW which applies the base current to the power transistor.
The air conditioner control assembly also monitors the power transistor collector voltage at terminal VM, to control blower air volume precisely.

DIAGNOSTIC CHART

1 Check power transistor. — NG → Replace power transistor.

OK ↓

2 Check harness and connector between air conditioner control assembly and power transistor — NG → Repair or replace harness or connector.

OK ↓

Proceed to next circuit inspection shown on matrix chart

WIRING DIAGRAM

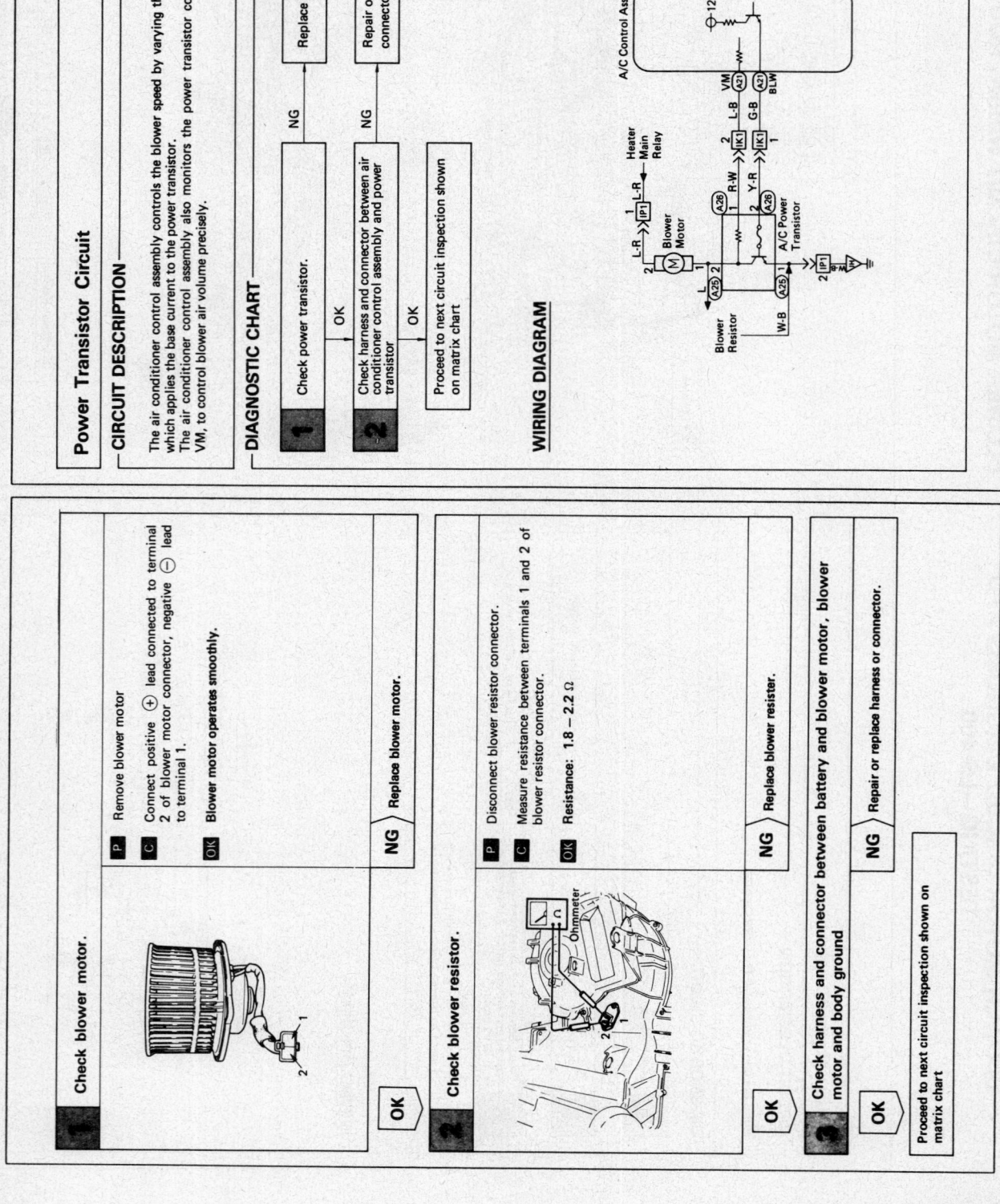

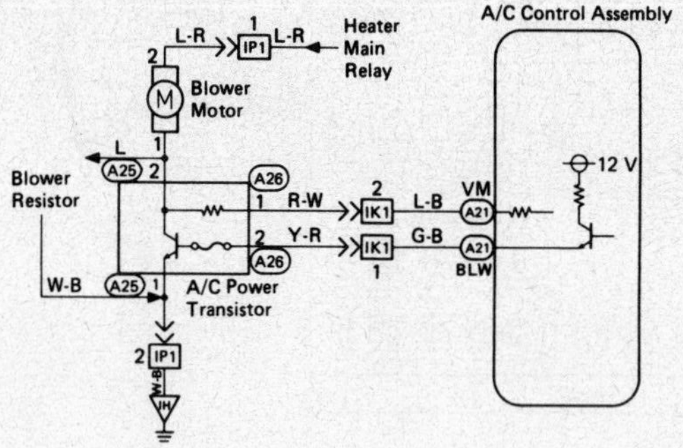
A/C Control Assembly
Heater
Main
Relay
L-R
IP1
1
2
Blower
Motor
M
L
A25
Blower
Resistor
A26
R-W
Y-R
IK1
L-B
G-B
VM
A21
BLW
12 V
W-B
A/C Power
Transistor
IH

POWER TRANSISTOR CIRCUIT WIRING ROUTING LS 400

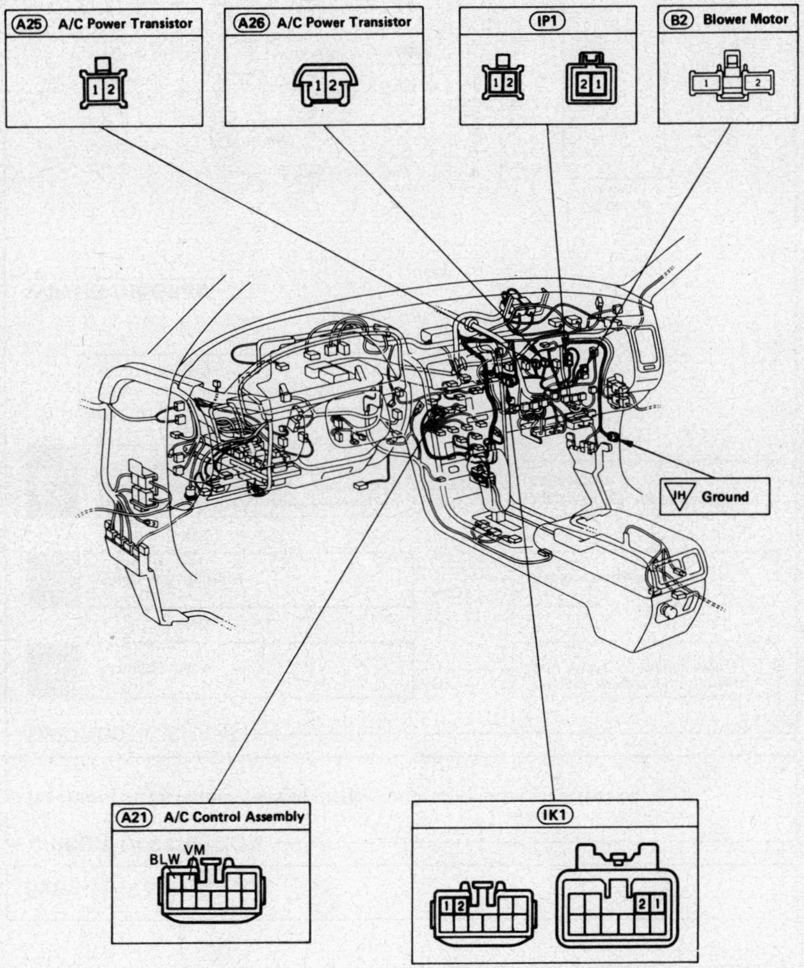
A25 A/C Power Transistor
1 2
A26 A/C Power Transistor
1 2
IP1
1 2
2 1
B2 Blower Motor
1
2
IH Ground
A21 A/C Control Assembly
BLW
VM
IK1
1 2
2 1

POWER TRANSISTOR CIRCUIT INSPECTION PROCEDURE—LS 400

1 Check power transistor.

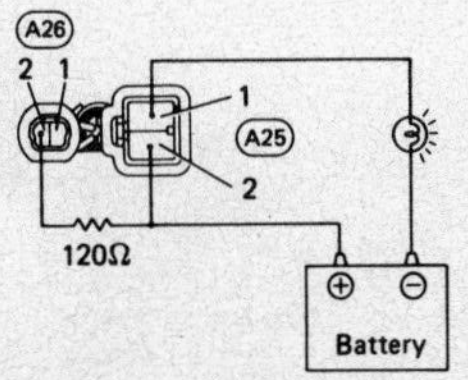
A26
2 1
1
A25
2
120Ω
Battery

P
1. Remove cooling unit
2. Disconnect power transistor connector.

C Connect positive ⊕ lead to terminals (A25) 2 and (A26) 2 of power transistor connectors and negative ⊖ lead to terminal (A25) 1 through a 12 V – 3.4 W test bulb.

OK **The bulb lights up.**

NG → **Replace power transistor.**

OK ↓

2 Check harness and connector between air conditioner control assembly and power transistor

NG → **Repair or replace harness or connector.**

OK ↓

Proceed to next circuit inspection shown on matrix chart

EXTRA-HI RELAY CIRCUIT DIAGNOSIS AND TESTING—LS 400

Extra-Hi Relay Circuit

CIRCUIT DESCRIPTION

The extra-Hi relay is switched on by signals from the air conditioner control assembly.

DIAGNOSTIC CHART

Step	Result	Action
Actuator check.	OK	Proceed to next circuit inspection shown on matrix chart
	NG	Check extra-hi relay.
Check extra-hi relay.	NG	Replace extra-hi relay.
	OK	Check harness and connector between air conditioner control assembly and extra-hi relay, extra-hi relay and battery (See
Check harness and connector between air conditioner control assembly and extra-hi relay, extra-hi relay and battery (See	NG	Repair or replace harness or connector.
	OK	Check and replace air conditioner control assembly.

WIRING DIAGRAM

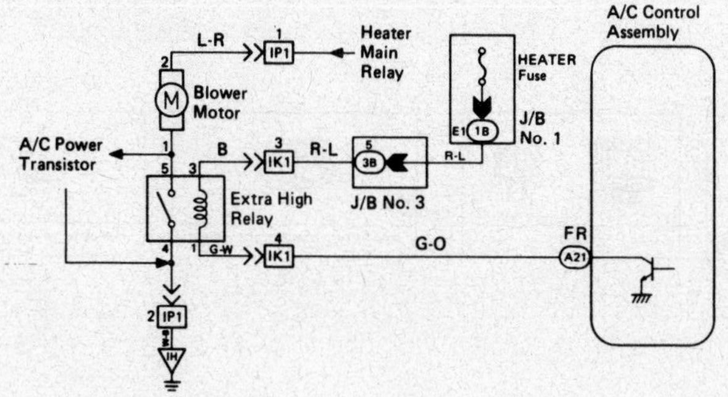

L-R
IP1
Heater Main Relay
Blower Motor
HEATER Fuse
J/B No. 1
1B
A/C Control Assembly
A/C Power Transistor
B
IK1
R-L
3B
J/B No. 3
Extra High Relay
G-W
G-O
FR
A21
IP1
IH

EXTRA-HI RELAY CIRCUIT WIRING ROUTING—LS 400

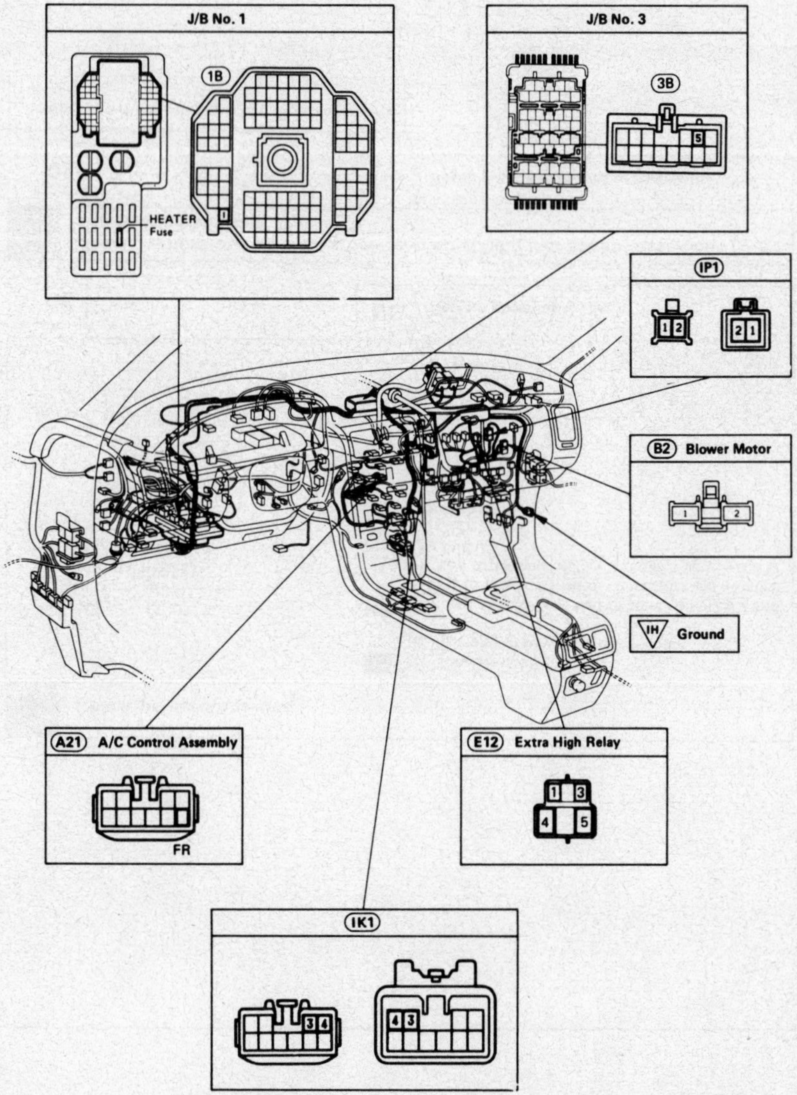

J/B No. 1
1B
HEATER Fuse
J/B No. 3
3B
IP1
B2 Blower Motor
IH Ground
A21 A/C Control Assembly
FR
E12 Extra High Relay
IK1

EXTRA-HI RELAY CIRCUIT INSPECTION PROCEDURE—LS 400

1 Actuator check.

Display Code	Blower
21 ~ 28	Med
29	Hi

P 1. Set to the actuator check mode
2. Press the up switch and change it to step operation.

C Press the up switch in order and check the condition of the blower.

OK **Blower speed changes from Med to Hi as shown in the table when the display code is changed from 28 to 29.**

OK — **Proceed to next circuit inspection shown on matrix chart**

NG ↓

2 Check extra-hi relay.

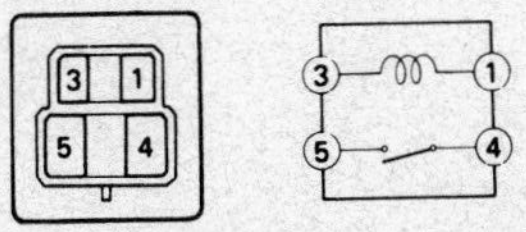

3
1
5
4
3
1
5
4

P Remove extra-hi relay.

C Check continuity between each pair of terminal shown below of extra-hi relay.

OK

Terminals 1 and 3	Continuity
Terminals 4 and 5	Open

P 1. Apply battery voltage between terminals 1 and 3.
2. Check continuity between terminals 4 and 5.

OK

Terminals 4 and 5	Continuity

NG — **Replace extra-hi relay.**

OK ↓

3 Check harness and connector between air conditioner control assembly and extra-hi relay, extra-hi relay and battery

NG — **Repair or replace harness or connector.**

OK ↓

Check and replace air conditioner control assembly.

AIR MIX DAMPER POSITION SENSOR CIRCUIT DIAGNOSIS AND TESTING—LS 400

Diag. Code	31, 33	Air Mix Damper Position Sensor Circuit

CIRCUIT DESCRIPTION

This sensor detects the position of the air mix damper and sends the appropriate signals to the air conditioner control assembly.
The position sensor is built into the air mix servo-motor assembly.

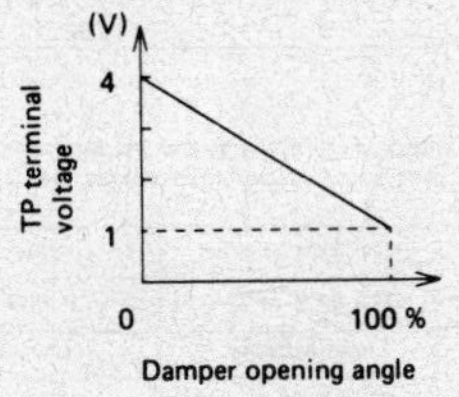

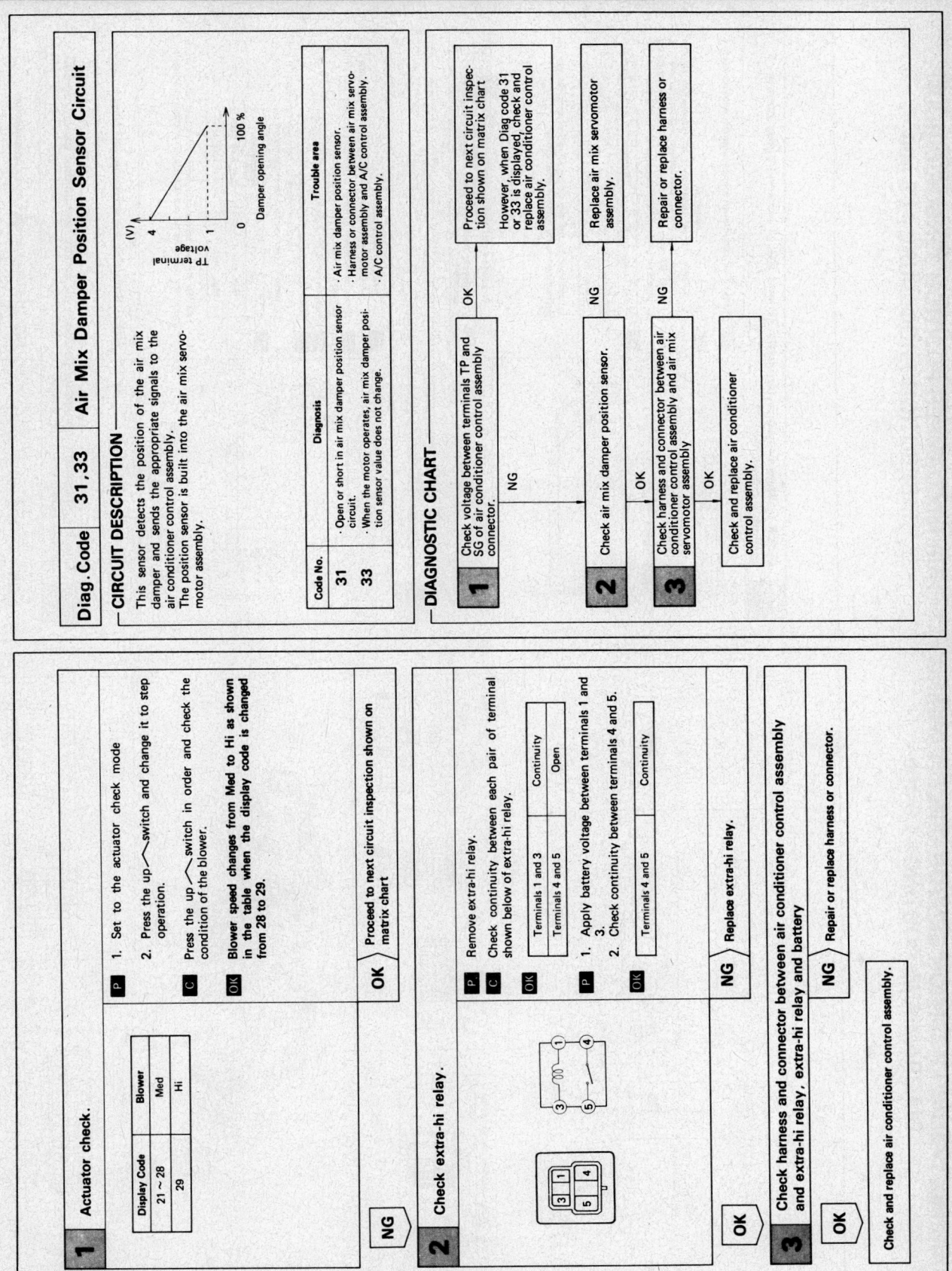

(V)
4
1
TP terminal voltage
0
100 %
Damper opening angle

Code No.	Diagnosis	Trouble area
31 33	· Open or short in air mix damper position sensor circuit. · When the motor operates, air mix damper position sensor value does not change.	· Air mix damper position sensor. · Harness or connector between air mix servo-motor assembly and A/C control assembly. · A/C control assembly.

DIAGNOSTIC CHART

1 Check voltage between terminals TP and SG of air conditioner control assembly connector.
- OK → Proceed to next circuit inspection shown on matrix chart. However, when Diag code 31 or 33 is displayed, check and replace air conditioner control assembly.
- NG ↓

2 Check air mix damper position sensor.
- NG → Replace air mix servomotor assembly.
- OK ↓

3 Check harness and connector between air conditioner control assembly and air mix servomotor assembly
- NG → Repair or replace harness or connector.
- OK ↓

Check and replace air conditioner control assembly.

AIR MIX DAMPER POSITION SENSOR CIRCUIT WIRING DIAGRAM AND ROUTING—LS 400

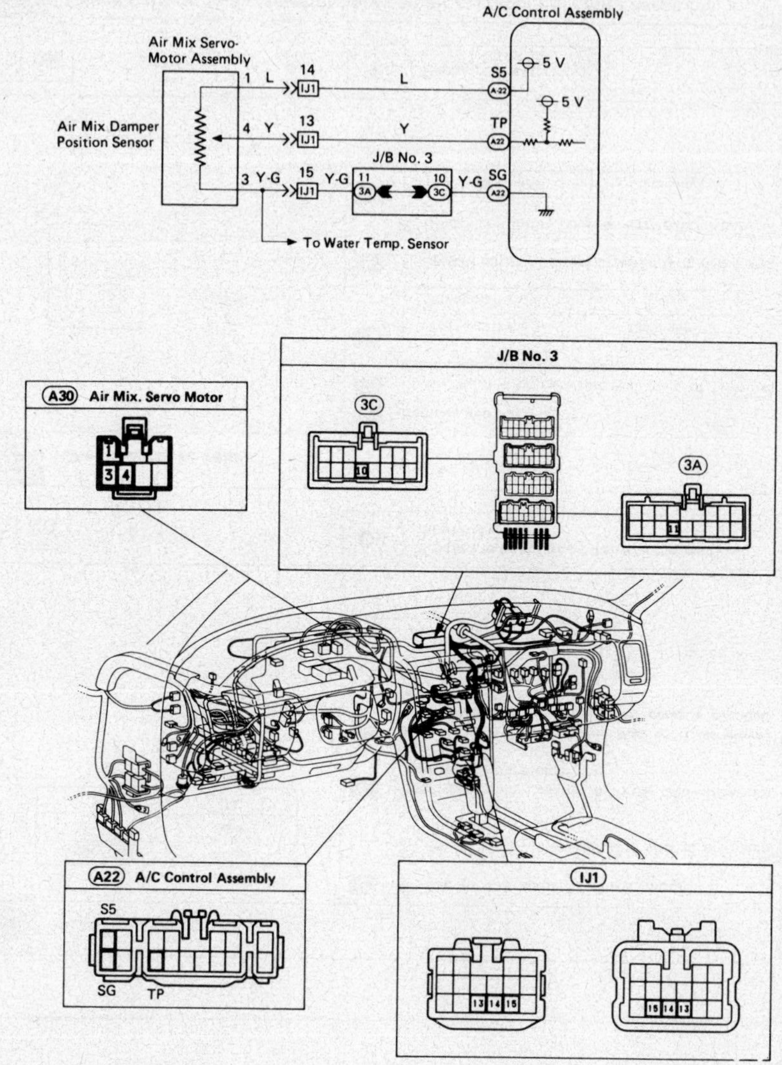
A/C Control Assembly
Air Mix Servo-Motor Assembly
Air Mix Damper Position Sensor
5 V
5 V
S5
TP
SG
L
Y
Y-G
J/B No. 3
IJ1
To Water Temp. Sensor
A30 Air Mix. Servo Motor
J/B No. 3
3C
3A
A22 A/C Control Assembly
S5
SG
TP
IJ1

AIR MIX DAMPER POSITION SENSOR CIRCUIT INSPECTION PROCEDURE—LS 400

1 Check voltage between terminals TP and SG of air conditioner control assembly connector.

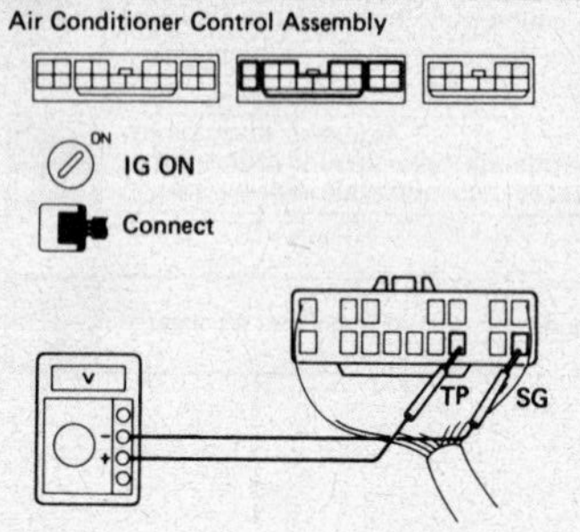
Air Conditioner Control Assembly
IG ON
Connect
V
TP
SG

P Remove air conditioner control assembly with connectors still connected.

C
1. Turn ignition switch on.
2. Change the set temperature to activate the air mix damper, and measure the voltage between terminals TP and SG of air conditioner control assembly connector each time when the set temperature is changed.

OK

Set Temperature	Voltage
Max. cool	3.70 – 4.27 V
Max. hot	0.88 – 1.16 V

In addition, as the set temperature increases the voltage decreases gradually without interruption.

OK — **Proceed to next circuit inspection shown on matrix chart However, when Diag. code 31 or 33 is displayed, check and replace air conditioner control assembly.**

NG ↓

2 Check air mix damper position sensor.

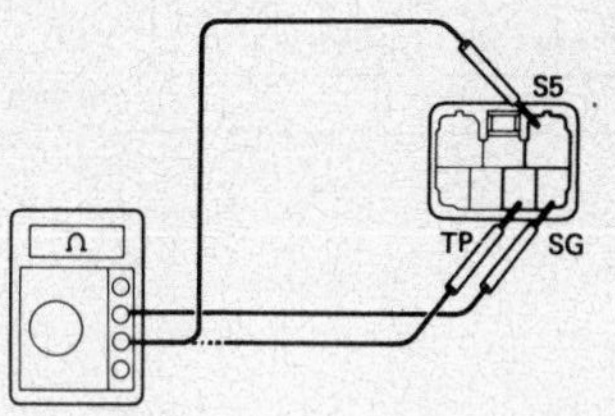
S5
TP
SG

P
1. Remove heater unit.
2. Disconnect air mix servomotor assembly connector.

C Measure resistance between terminals S5 and SG of air mix servomotor assembly connector.

OK **Resistance: 4.7 ~ 7.2 kΩ**

C While operating air mix servomotor measure resistance between terminals TP and SG of air mix servomotor assembly connector.

OK

Position	Resistance
Max. cool	3.76 ~ 5.76 kΩ
Max. warm	0.94 ~ 1.44 kΩ

As the air mix servomotor moves from cool side to warm side, the resistance decreases gradually without interruption.

NG — **Replace air mix servomotor assembly.**

OK ↓

3 Check harness and connector between air conditioner control assembly and air mix servomotor assembly

NG — **Repair or replace harness or connector.**

OK ↓

Check and replace air conditioner control assembly.

AIR MIX DAMPER POSITION SENSOR CIRCUIT DIAGNOSIS AND TESTING—LS 400

Diag. Code	32,34	Air Inlet Damper Position Sensor Circuit

CIRCUIT DESCRIPTION

This sensor detects the position of the air inlet damper and sends the appropriate signals to the air conditioner control assembly.
The position sensor is built into the air mix servo-motor assembly.

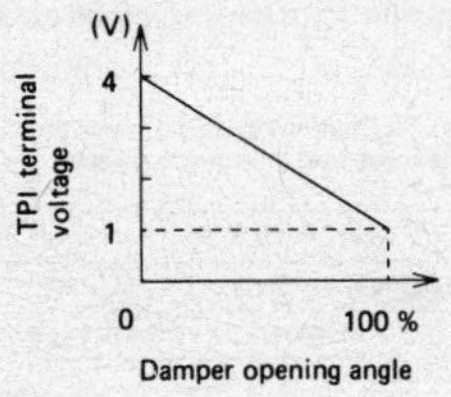
(V)
4
1
TPI terminal voltage
0
100 %
Damper opening angle

Code No.	Diagnosis	Trouble area
32 34	· Open or short in air inlet damper position sensor circuit. · When the motor operates, air inlet damper position sensor value does not change.	· Air inlet damper position sensor. · Harness or connector between air inlet servo-motor assembly and A/C control assembly. · A/C control assembly.

DIAGNOSTIC CHART

1 Check voltage between terminals TPI and SG of air conditioner control assembly connector.
- OK → Proceed to next circuit inspection shown on matrix chart. However, when Diag. code 32 or 34 is displayed, check and replace air conditioner control assembly.
- NG ↓

2 Check air inlet damper position sensor.
- NG → Replace air inlet servomotor assembly.
- OK ↓

3 Check harness and connectors between air conditioner control assembly and air inlet servomotor assembly
- NG → Repair or replace harness or connector.
- OK ↓

Check and replace air conditioner control assembly.

AIR MIX DAMPER POSITION SENSOR CIRCUIT WIRING DIAGRAM AND ROUTING—LS 400

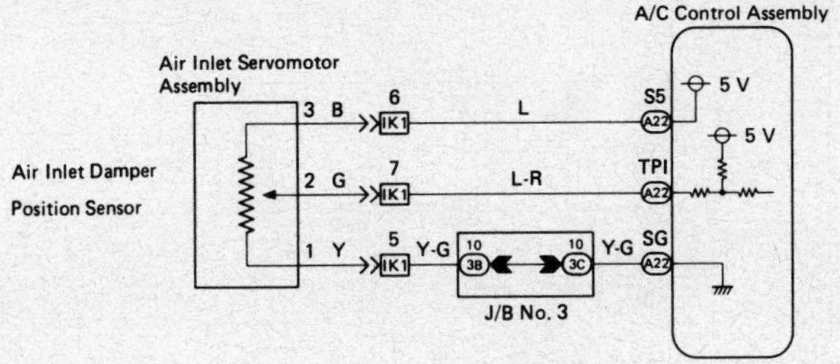
A/C Control Assembly
Air Inlet Servomotor Assembly
Air Inlet Damper Position Sensor
3 B
2 G
1 Y
6
7
5
IK1
L
L-R
Y-G
10
3B
3C
J/B No. 3
S5
TPI
SG
A22
5 V

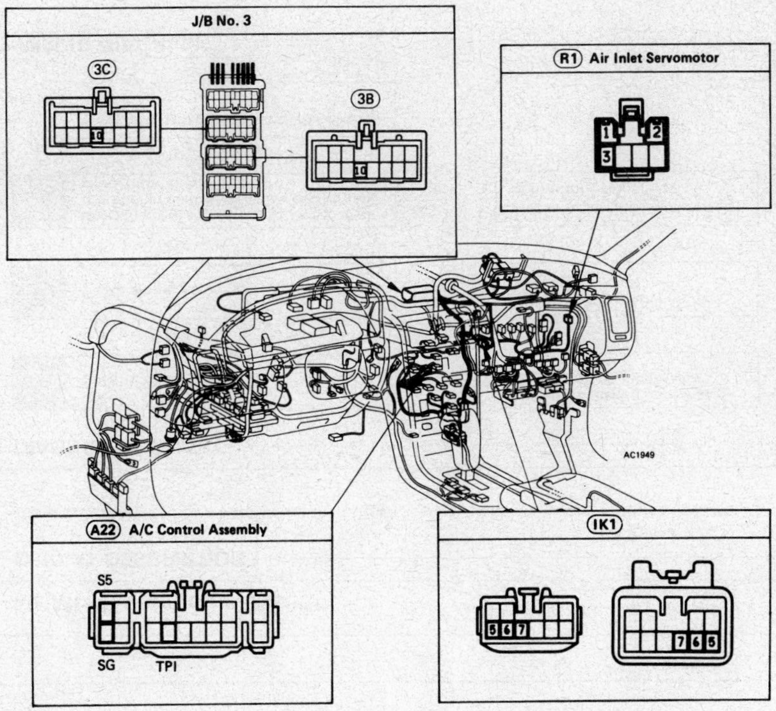
J/B No. 3
3C
3B
R1 Air Inlet Servomotor
A22 A/C Control Assembly
S5
SG
TPI
IK1
AC1949

AIR MIX DAMPER POSITION SENSOR CIRCUIT INSPECTION PROCEDURE—LS 400

1 Check voltage between terminals TPI and SG of air conditioner control assembly connector.

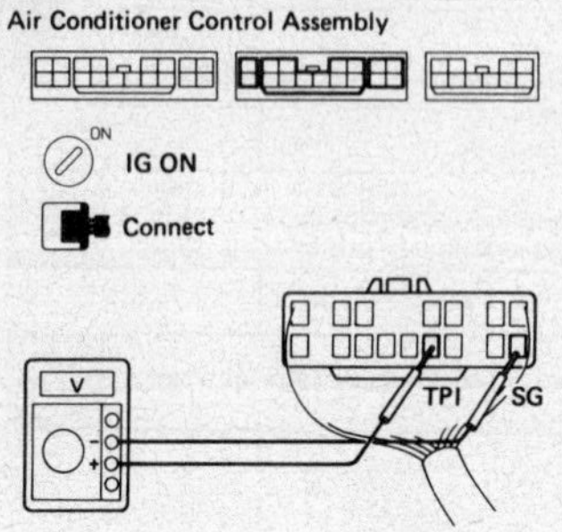
Air Conditioner Control Assembly
ON
IG ON
Connect
V
TPI
SG

P Remove air conditioner control assembly with connectors still connected.

C
1. Turn ignition switch on.
2. Press REC/FRS switch to change air inlet between fresh and recirculation air, and measure voltage between terminals TPI and SG of air conditioner control assembly when the air inlet servomotor operates.

OK

FRS-REC Switch	Voltage
REC	3.70 ~ 4.27 V
FRS	0.88 ~ 1.16 V

In addition, as the air inlet servomotor is moved from REC side to FRS side, the voltage decreases gradually without interruption.

OK — **Proceed to next circuit inspection shown on matrix chart However, when Diag. code 32 or 34 is displayed, check and replace air conditioner control assembly.**

NG

2 Check air inlet damper position sensor.

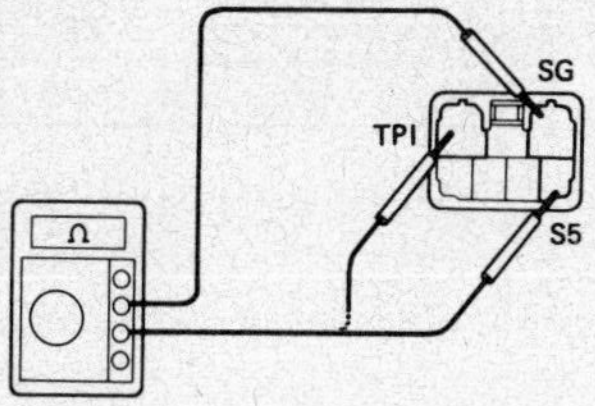
Ω
TPI
SG
S5

P
1. Remove heater unit.
2. Disconnect air inlet servomotor assembly connector.

C Measure resistance between terminals S5 and SG of air inlet servomotor assembly connector.

OK **Resistance: 4.7 ~ 7.2 kΩ**

C While operating air inlet servomotor measure resistance between terminals TPI and SG of air inlet servomotor assembly connector.

OK **Resistance**

Damper Position	Resistance
REC side	3.76 ~ 5.76 kΩ
FRS side	0.94 ~ 1.44 kΩ

As the air inlet servomotor moves from REC side to FRS side, the resistance decreases gradually without interruption.

NG — **Replace air inlet servomotor assembly.**

OK

3 Check harness and connectors between air conditioner control assembly and air inlet servomotor assembly

NG — **Repair or replace harness or connector.**

OK

Check and replace air conditioner control assembly.

AIR MIX SERVOMOTOR CIRCUIT DIAGNOSIS AND TESTING—LS 400

Air Mix Servomotor Circuit

CIRCUIT DESCRIPTION

The air mix servomotor is controlled by the ECU and moves the air mix damper to the desired position.

DIAGNOSTIC CHART

1 Actuator check. — OK → Proceed to next circuit inspection shown on matrix chart

NG ↓

2 Check air mix servomotor. — NG → Replace air mix servomotor assembly.

OK ↓

3 Check harness and connector between air conditioner control assembly and air mix servomotor assembly. — NG → Repair or replace harness or connector.

OK ↓

Check and replace air conditioner control assembly.

WIRING DIAGRAM

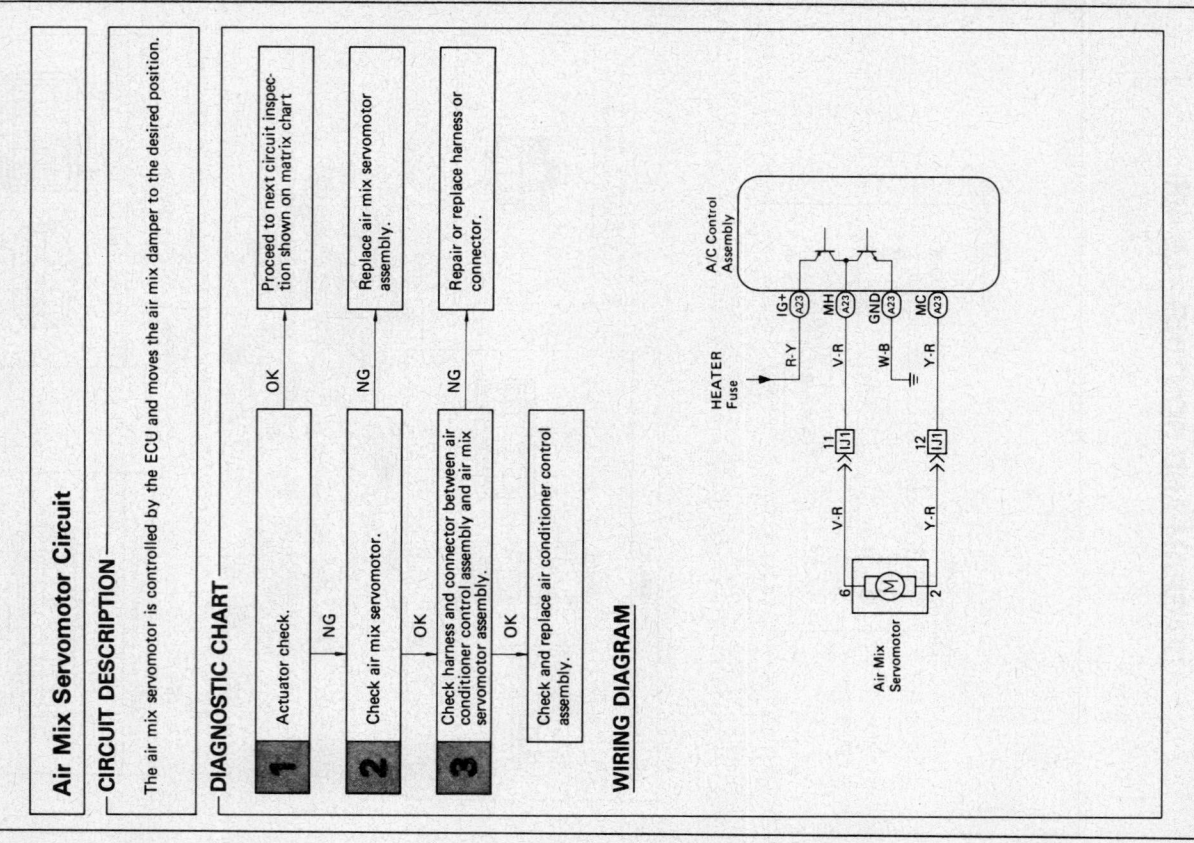

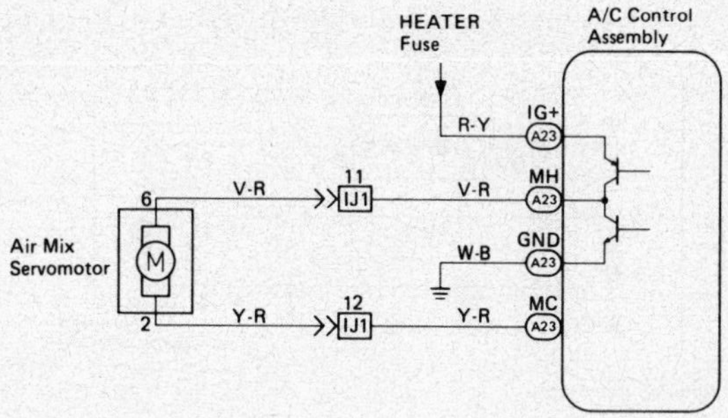
HEATER
Fuse
A/C Control
Assembly
R-Y
IG+
A23
Air Mix
Servomotor
6
V-R
11
IJ1
V-R
MH
A23
W-B
GND
A23
2
Y-R
12
IJ1
Y-R
MC
A23
M

AIR MIX SERVOMOTOR CIRCUIT WIRING ROUTING—LS 400

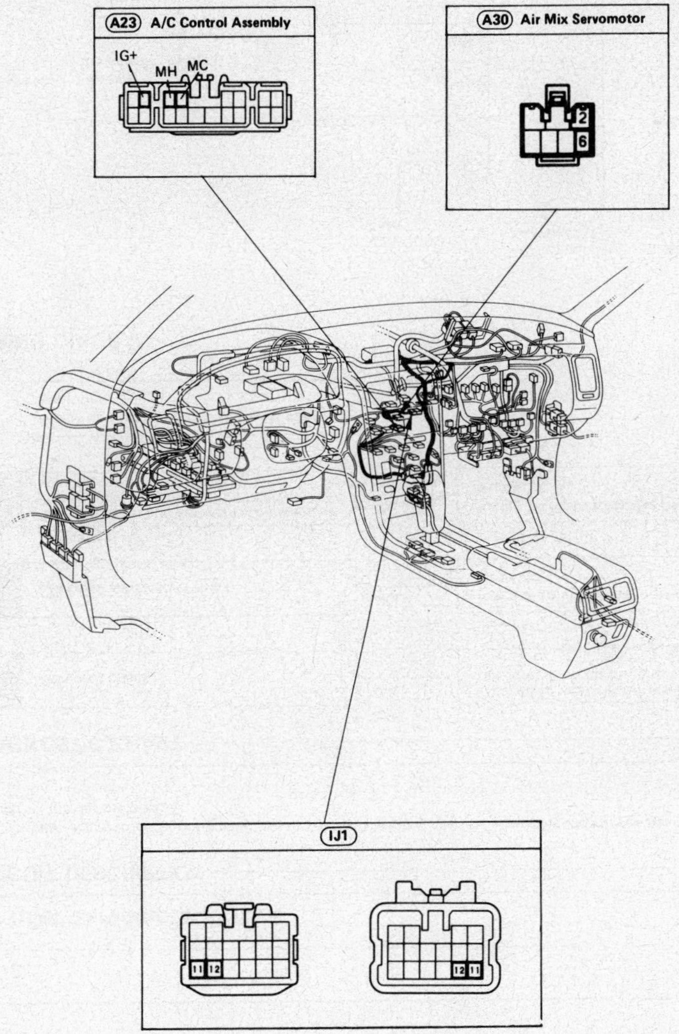
A23 A/C Control Assembly
IG+
MH
MC
A30 Air Mix Servomotor
2
6
IJ1
11
12
12
11

AIR MIX SERVOMOTOR CIRCUIT INSPECTION PROCEDURE—LS 400

1 Actuator check.

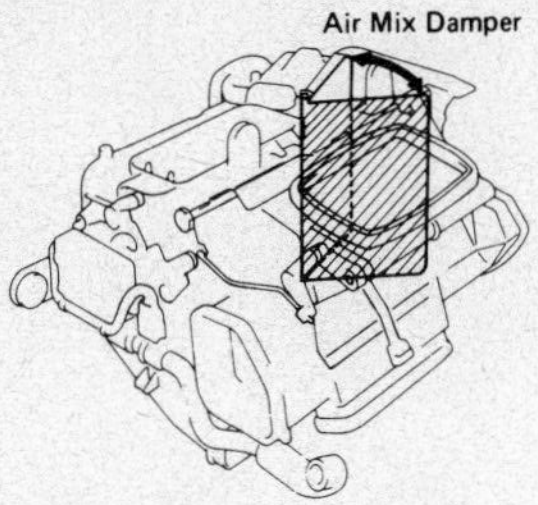
Air Mix Damper

P
1. Warm up the engine.
2. Set to the actuator check mode
3. Press the up ⌒ switch and change it to step operation.

C Press the up ⌒ temperature control switch and check the operation of the air mix damper and the condition of the blower.

OK

Display Code	Air Mix Damper	Condition
20 ~ 23	0%(Fully closed)	Cool air comes out
24 ~ 26	50%	
27 ~ 29	100%(Fully opened)	Warm air comes out

OK → Proceed to next circuit inspection shown on matrix chart

NG ↓

2 Check air mix servomotor.

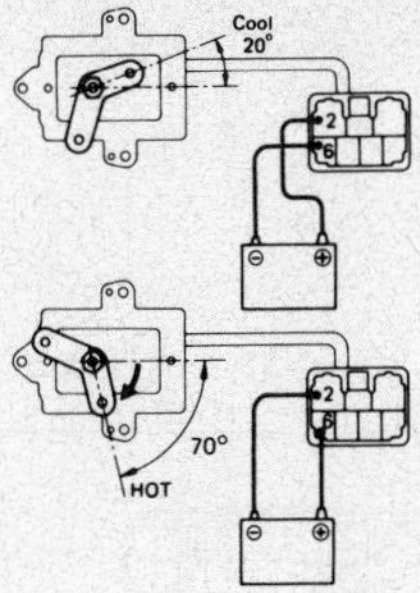
Cool
20°
2
6
70°
HOT
2
6

P Remove heater unit.

C Connect positive ⊕ lead to terminal 2 and negative ⊖ lead to terminal 6.

OK **The lever turns smoothly to cool side.**

C Connect negative ⊖ lead to terminal 2 and positive ⊕ lead to terminal 6.

OK **The lever turns smoothly to warm side.**

NG → **Replace air mix servomotor assembly.**

OK ↓

3 Check harness and connector between air conditioner control assembly and air mix servomotor assembly

NG → **Repair or replace harness or connector.**

OK ↓

Check and replace air conditioner control assembly.

AIR INLET SERVOMOTOR CIRCUIT DIAGNOSIS AND TESTING—LS 400

Air Inlet Servomotor Circuit

CIRCUIT DESCRIPTION

The air inlet servomotor is controlled by the air conditioner control assembly and moves the air inlet damper to the desired position.

DIAGNOSTIC CHART

Step	Check	Result	Action
1	Actuator check.	OK	Proceed to next circuit inspection shown on matrix chart
		NG	Go to 2
2	Check air inlet servomotor.	NG	Replace air inlet servomotor assembly.
		OK	Go to 3
3	Check harness and connector between air conditioner control assembly and air inlet servomotor	NG	Repair or replace harness or connector.
		OK	Check and replace air conditioner control assembly.

WIRING DIAGRAM

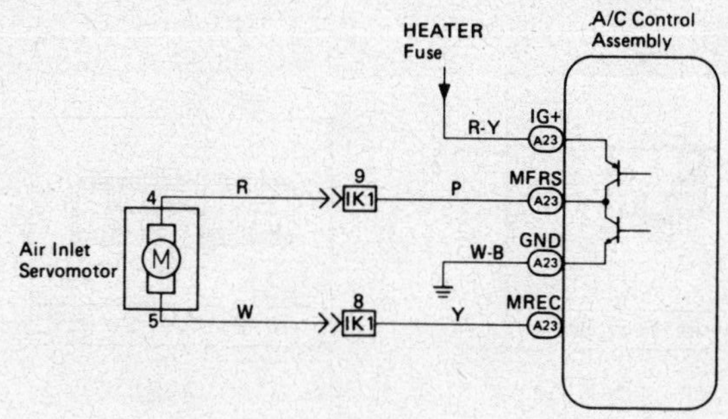
HEATER Fuse
A/C Control Assembly
R-Y
IG+ A23
R
9 IK1
P
MFRS A23
W-B
GND A23
Air Inlet Servomotor
4
5
M
W
8 IK1
Y
MREC A23

AIR INLET SERVOMOTOR CIRCUIT WIRING ROUTING LS 400

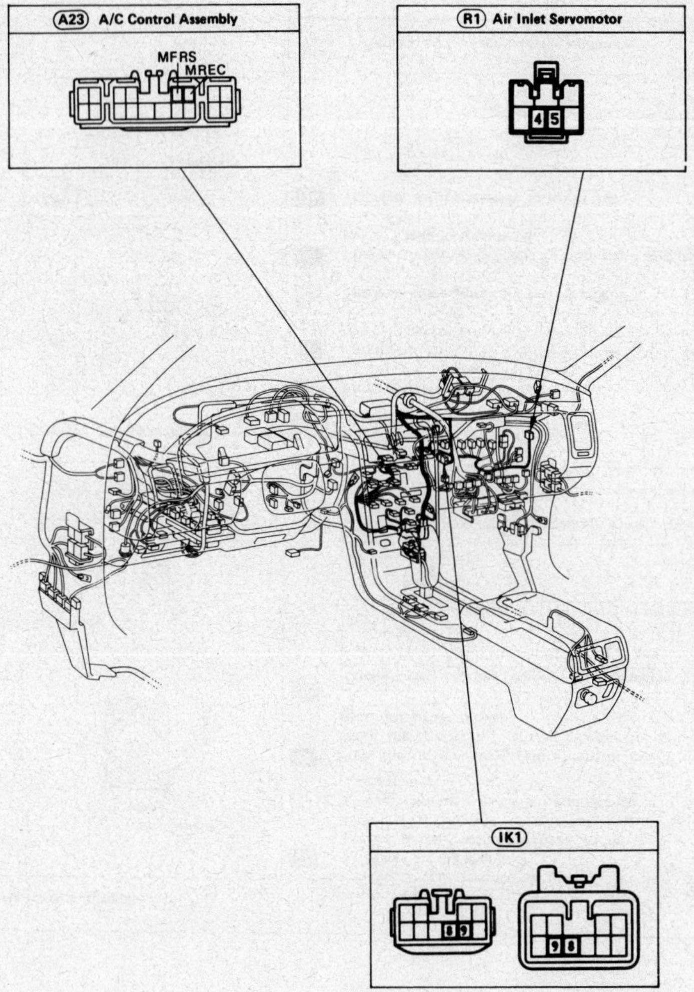
A23 A/C Control Assembly
MFRS
MREC
R1 Air Inlet Servomotor
4 5
IK1
8 9
9 8

AIR INLET SERVOMOTOR CIRCUIT INSPECTION PROCEDURE—LS 400

1 Actuator check.

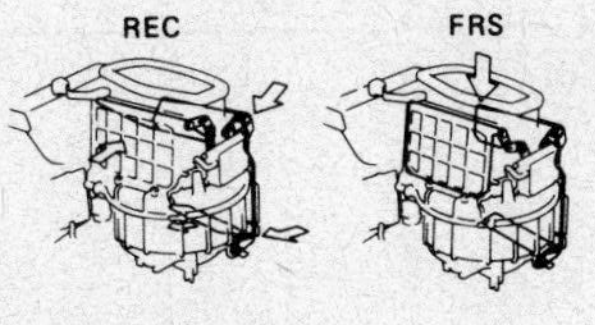
REC
FRS

P
1. Remove glove box to see and check the air inlet damper operation.
2. Set to the actuator check mode
3. Press the up switch and change it to step operation.

C Press the up switch in order and check the operation of air inlet damper.

OK

Display Code	Air Inlet Damper
20 ~ 21	FRS
22	F/R
23	REC
24 ~ 29	FRS

OK Proceed to next circuit inspection shown on matrix chart

NG

2 Check air inlet servomotor.

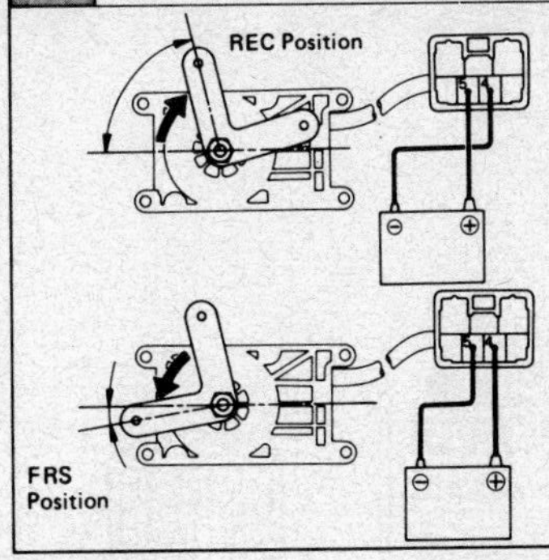
REC Position
FRS Position

P Remove cooling unit.

C Connect positive (+) lead to terminal 5 and negative (−) lead to terminal 4.

OK **The lever moves smoothly to REC position.**

C Connect negative (−) lead to terminal 5 and positive (+) lead to terminal 4.

OK **The lever moves smoothly to FRS position.**

NG Replace air inlet servomotor assembly.

OK

3 Check harness and connector between air conditioner control assembly and air inlet servomotor

NG Repair or replace harness or connector.

OK

Check and replace air conditioner control assembly.

MODE SERVOMOTOR CIRCUIT DIAGNOSIS AND TESTING—LS 400

Mode Servomotor Circuit

CIRCUIT DESCRIPTION

This circuit turns the servomotor and changes each mode damper position by the signals from the ECU. When the AUTO switch is on, the ECU changes the mode automatically between (FACE), (BI-LEVEL) and (FOOT) according to the temperature setting.

DIAGNOSTIC CHART

1. Actuator check. — OK → Proceed to next circuit inspection shown on matrix chart
   - NG ↓
2. Check mode servomotor. — NG → Replace mode servomotor.
   - OK ↓
3. Check harness and connector between air conditioner control assembly and mode servomotor, mode servomotor and battery, mode servomotor and body ground. — NG → Repair or replace harness or connector.
   - OK ↓

Check and replace air conditioner control assembly.

WIRING DIAGRAM

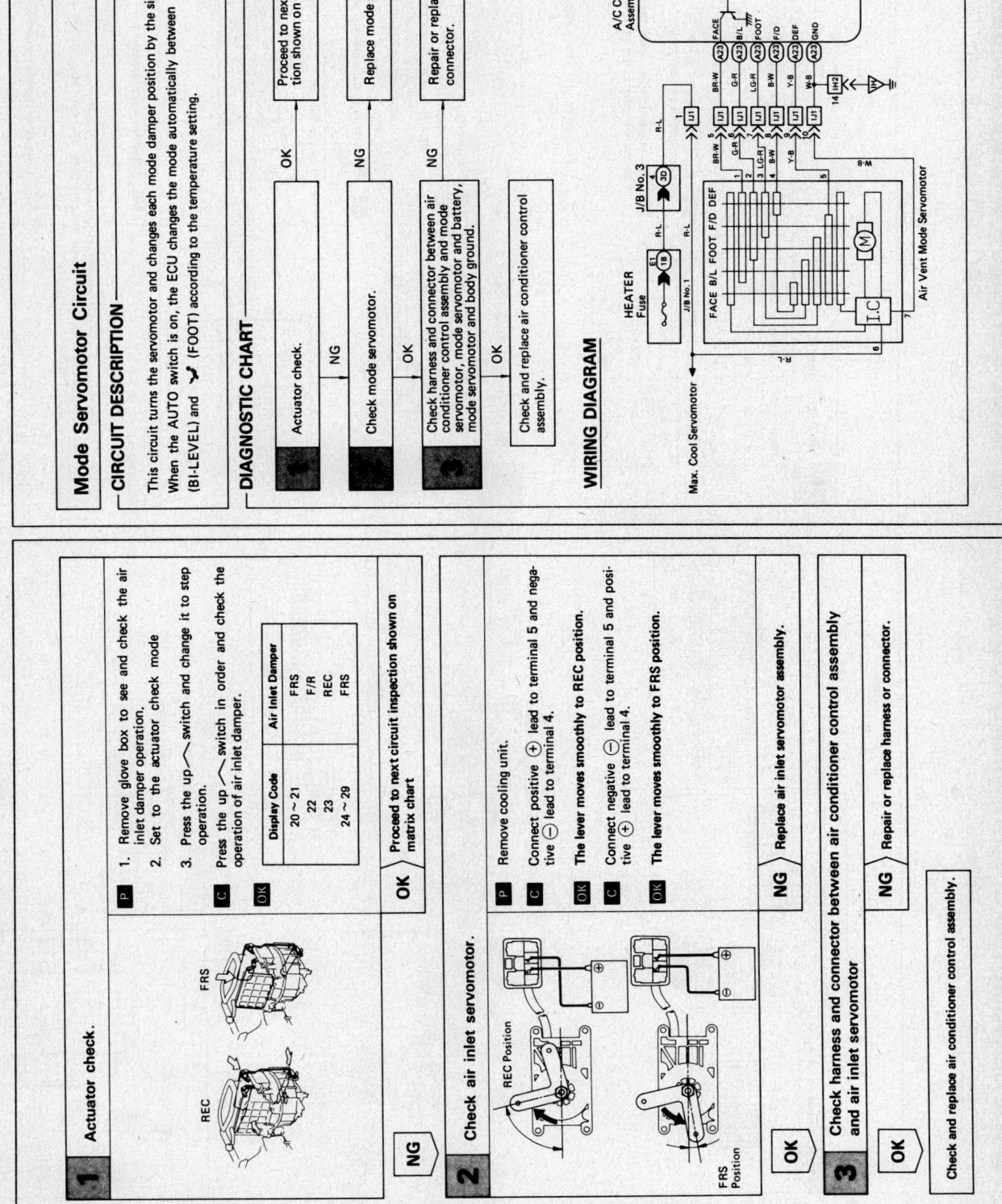

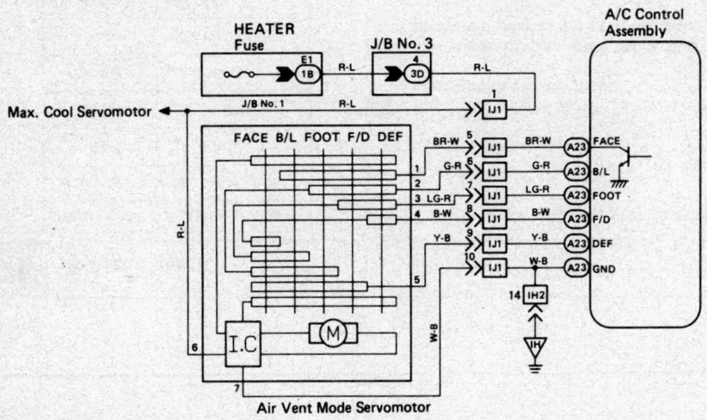
HEATER Fuse
J/B No. 3
A/C Control Assembly
Max. Cool Servomotor
J/B No. 1
R-L
FACE B/L FOOT F/D DEF
BR-W
G-R
LG-R
B-W
Y-B
W-B
IJ1
A23
FACE
B/L
FOOT
F/D
DEF
GND
IH2
IH
I.C
M
Air Vent Mode Servomotor

MODE SERVOMOTOR CIRCUIT WIRING ROUTING LS 400

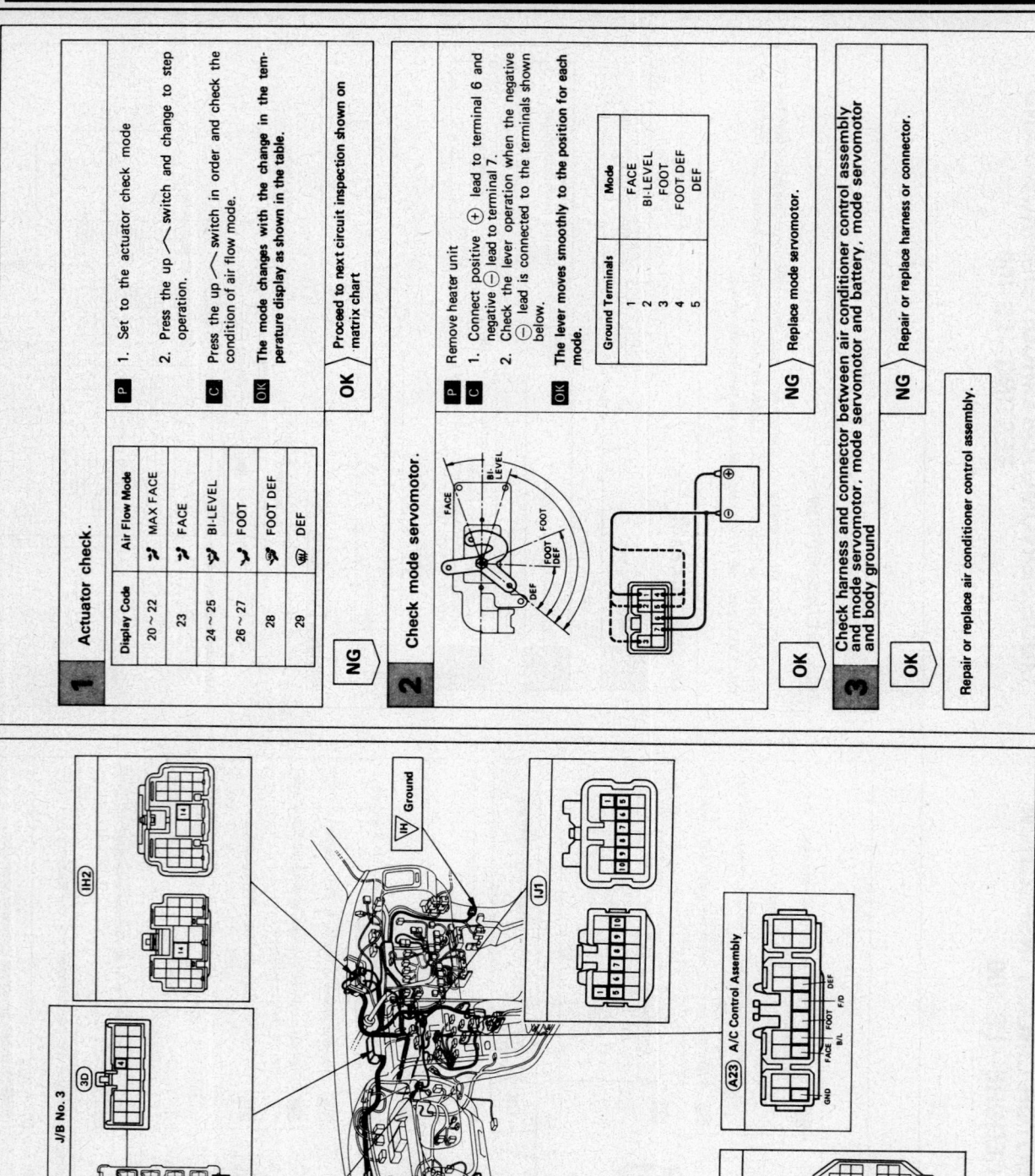

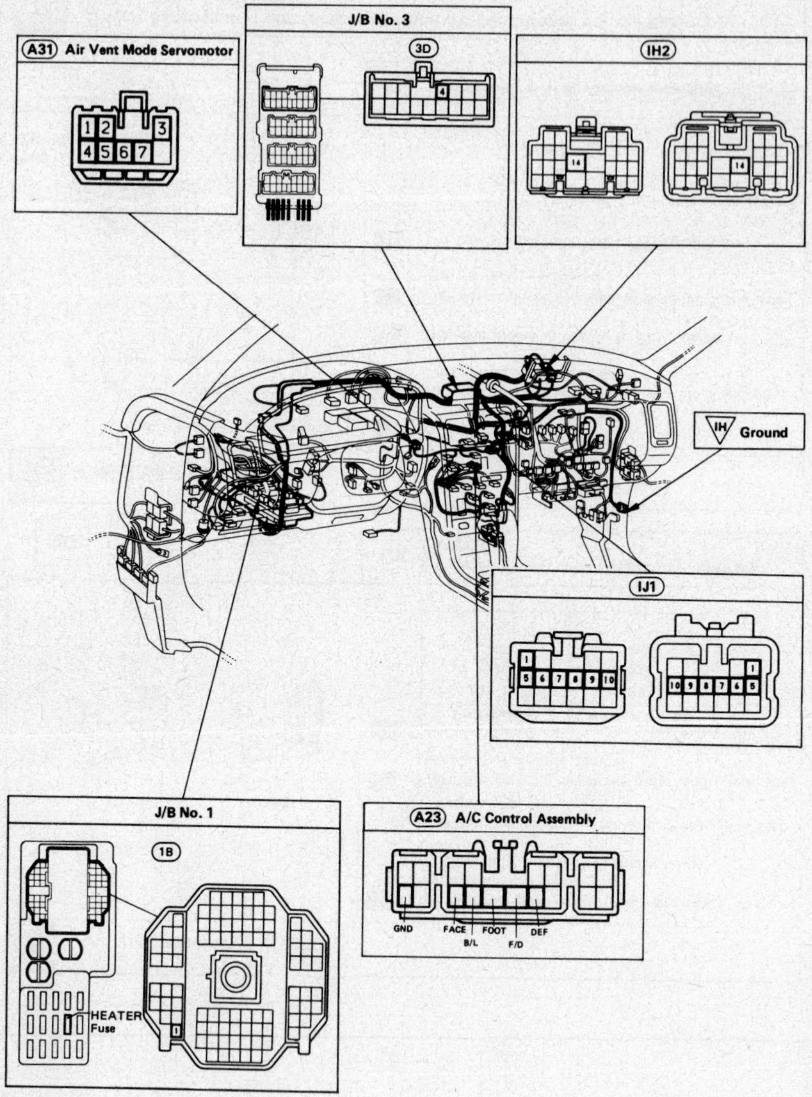
A31 Air Vent Mode Servomotor
1 2 3
4 5 6 7
J/B No. 3
3D
4
IH2
14
14
IH Ground
IJ1
1
5 6 7 8 9 10
10 9 8 7 6 5
J/B No. 1
1B
HEATER
Fuse
A23 A/C Control Assembly
GND
FACE
B/L
FOOT
F/D
DEF

MODE SERVOMOTOR CIRCUIT INSPECTION PROCEDURE—LS 400

1 Actuator check.

Display Code	Air Flow Mode
20 ~ 22	MAX FACE
23	FACE
24 ~ 25	BI-LEVEL
26 ~ 27	FOOT
28	FOOT DEF
29	DEF

P 1. Set to the actuator check mode

2. Press the up ︿ switch and change to step operation.

C Press the up ︿ switch in order and check the condition of air flow mode.

OK **The mode changes with the change in the temperature display as shown in the table.**

NG

OK — **Proceed to next circuit inspection shown on matrix chart**

2 Check mode servomotor.

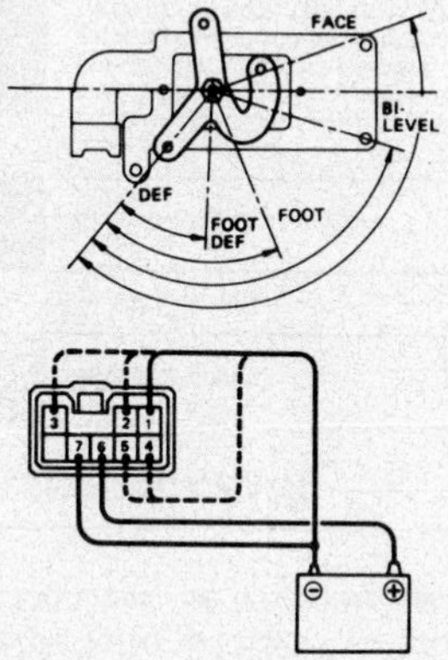
FACE
BI-LEVEL
FOOT
FOOT DEF
DEF
3
2 1
7 6 5 4

P Remove heater unit

C 1. Connect positive ⊕ lead to terminal 6 and negative ⊖ lead to terminal 7.
2. Check the lever operation when the negative ⊖ lead is connected to the terminals shown below.

OK **The lever moves smoothly to the position for each mode.**

Ground Terminals	Mode
1	FACE
2	BI-LEVEL
3	FOOT
4	FOOT DEF
5	DEF

OK

NG — **Replace mode servomotor.**

3 Check harness and connector between air conditioner control assembly and mode servomotor, mode servomotor and battery, mode servomotor and body ground

OK

NG — **Repair or replace harness or connector.**

Repair or replace air conditioner control assembly.

MAX COOL SERVOMOTOR CIRCUIT DIAGNOSIS AND TESTING—LS 400

Max. Cool Servomotor Circuit

CIRCUIT DESCRIPTION

The max. cool servomotor changes the positions of the max. cool damper in 3 positions by the signals from the ECU. When the AUTO switch is on, and the vent is in (FACE) position, the air conditioner control assembly controls the damper to open, half open and closed positions. The damper is kept closed at all times while in the (FOOT) or (BI-LEVEL) position.

DIAGNOSTIC CHART

1. Actuator check. — OK → Proceed to next circuit inspection shown on matrix chart. NG ↓
2. Check max. cool servomotor. — NG → Replace max. cool servomotor. OK ↓
3. Check harness and connector between air conditioner control assembly and max. cool servomotor, max. cool servomotor and battery — NG → Repair or replace harness or connector. OK ↓

Check and replace air conditioner control assembly.

WIRING DIAGRAM

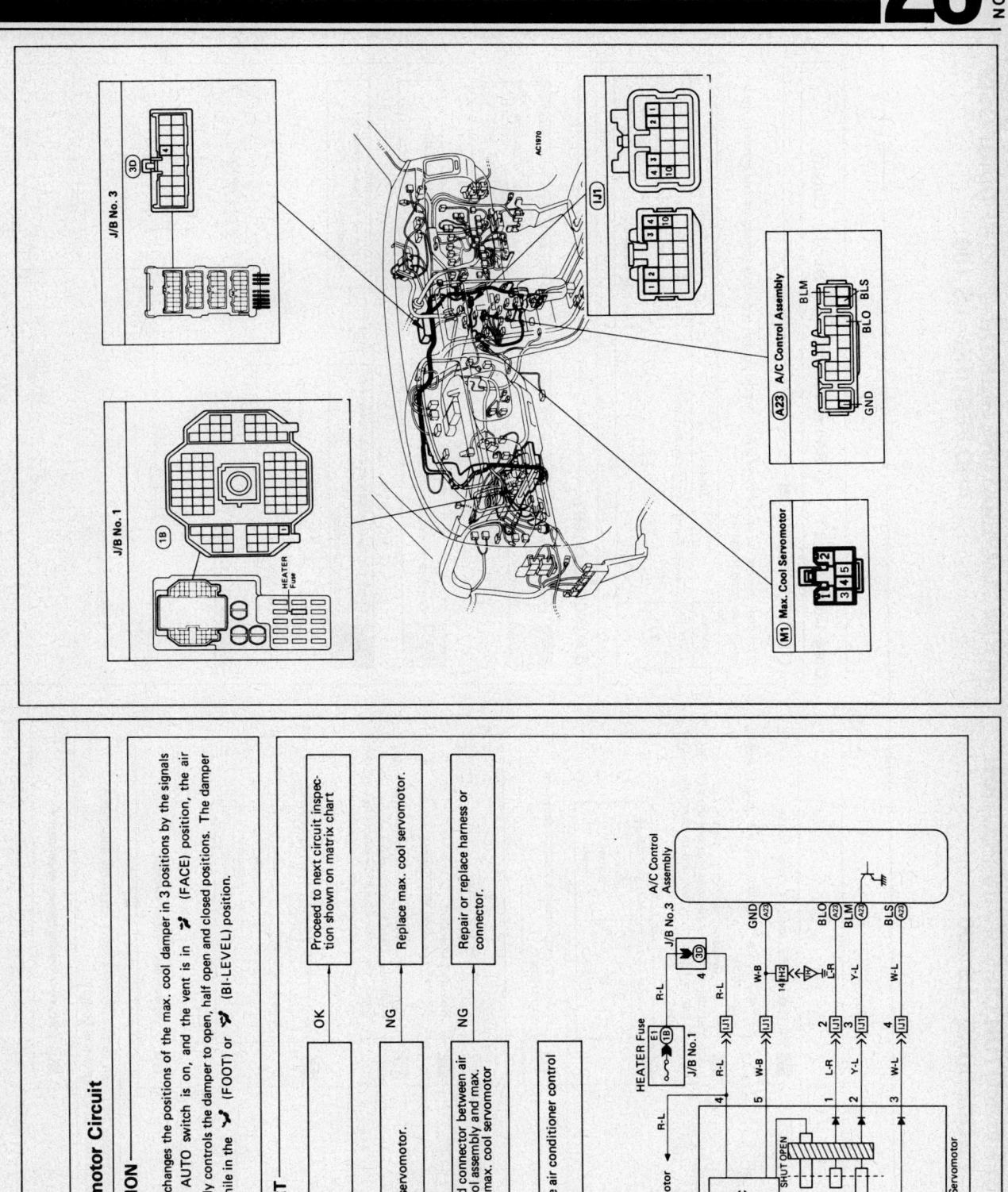

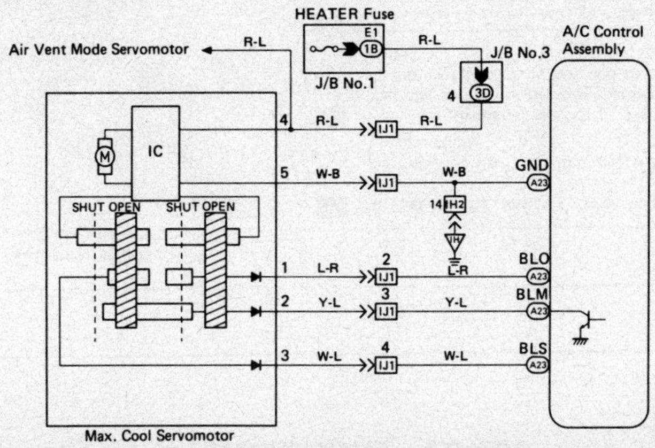
HEATER Fuse
E1
1B
J/B No.1
R-L
J/B No.3
3D
A/C Control Assembly
Air Vent Mode Servomotor
IC
M
SHUT OPEN
SHUT OPEN
W-B
L-R
Y-L
W-L
IJ1
GND
BLO
BLM
BLS
A23
14 IH2
Max. Cool Servomotor

MAX COOL SERVOMOTOR CIRCUIT WIRING ROUTING LS 400

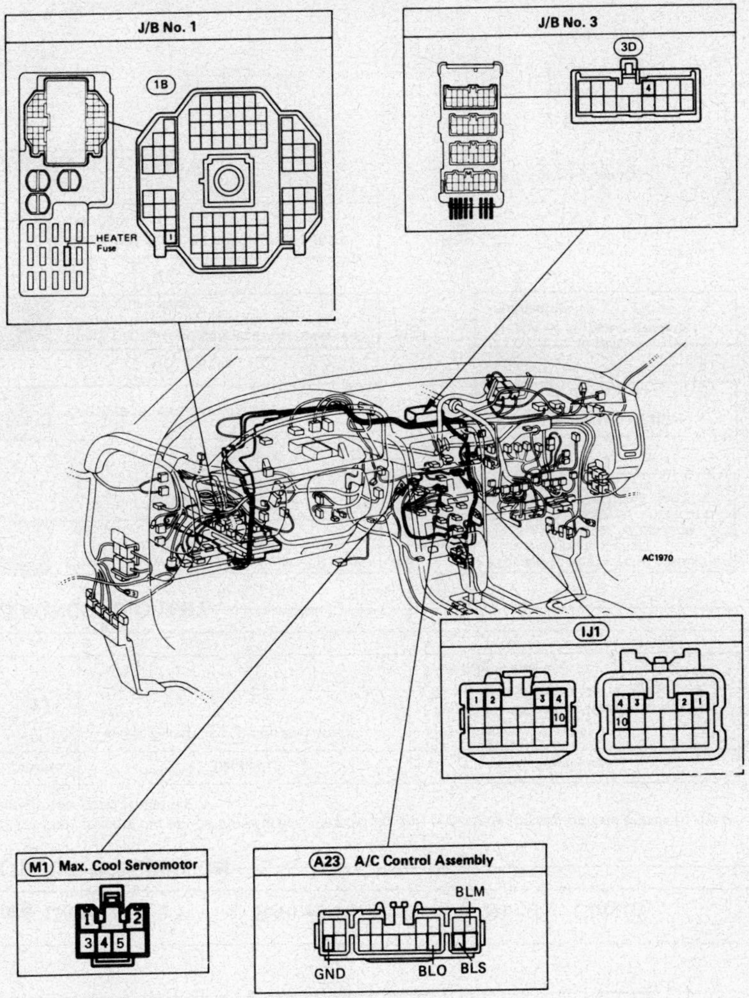
J/B No. 1
1B
HEATER Fuse
J/B No. 3
3D
AC1970
IJ1
M1 Max. Cool Servomotor
A23 A/C Control Assembly
BLM
GND
BLO
BLS

MAX COOL SERVOMOTOR CIRCUIT INSPECTION PROCEDURE – LS 400

1 Actuator check.

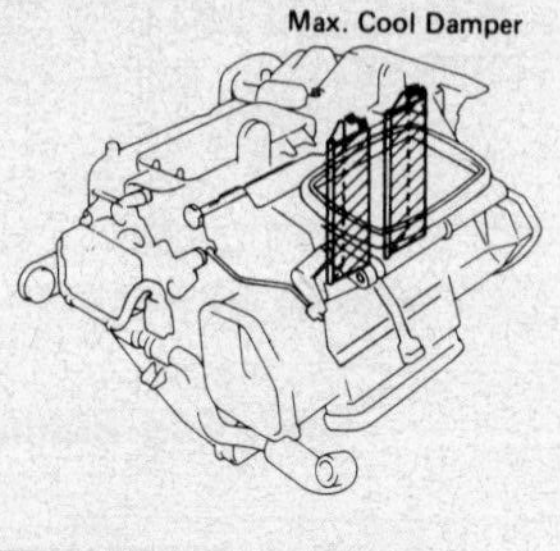
Max. Cool Damper

P 1. Set to the actuator check mode

2. Press the up switch and change it to step operation.

C Push the temperature control switch and check that the max. cool damper operates with changes in the vent blower output and damper operation noise.

OK

Display Code	Max. Cool Damper
20 ~ 21	Opened
22	Medium
23 ~ 29	Closed

OK → Proceed to next circuit inspection shown on matrix chart

NG ↓

2 Check max. cool servomotor.

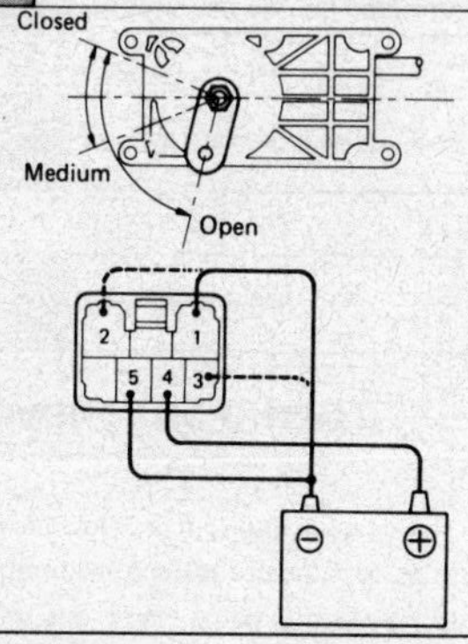
Closed
Medium
Open
2
1
5
4
3

P 1. Remove heater unit.
2. Remove max. cool servomotor.

C 1. Connect positive ⊕ lead to terminal 4 and negative ⊖ lead to terminal 5.
2. Check the lever operation when the negative ⊖ lead is connected to the terminals shown below.

OK The lever moves smoothly to each position.

Ground Terminals	Position
1	Open
2	Medium
3	Closed

NG → Replace max. cool servomotor.

OK ↓

3 Check harness and connector between air conditioner control assembly and max. cool servomotor, max. cool servomotor and battery

NG → Repair or replace harness or connector.

OK ↓

Check and replace air conditioner control assembly.

ROOM TEMPERATURE SENSOR CIRCUIT DIAGNOSIS AND TESTING – LS 400

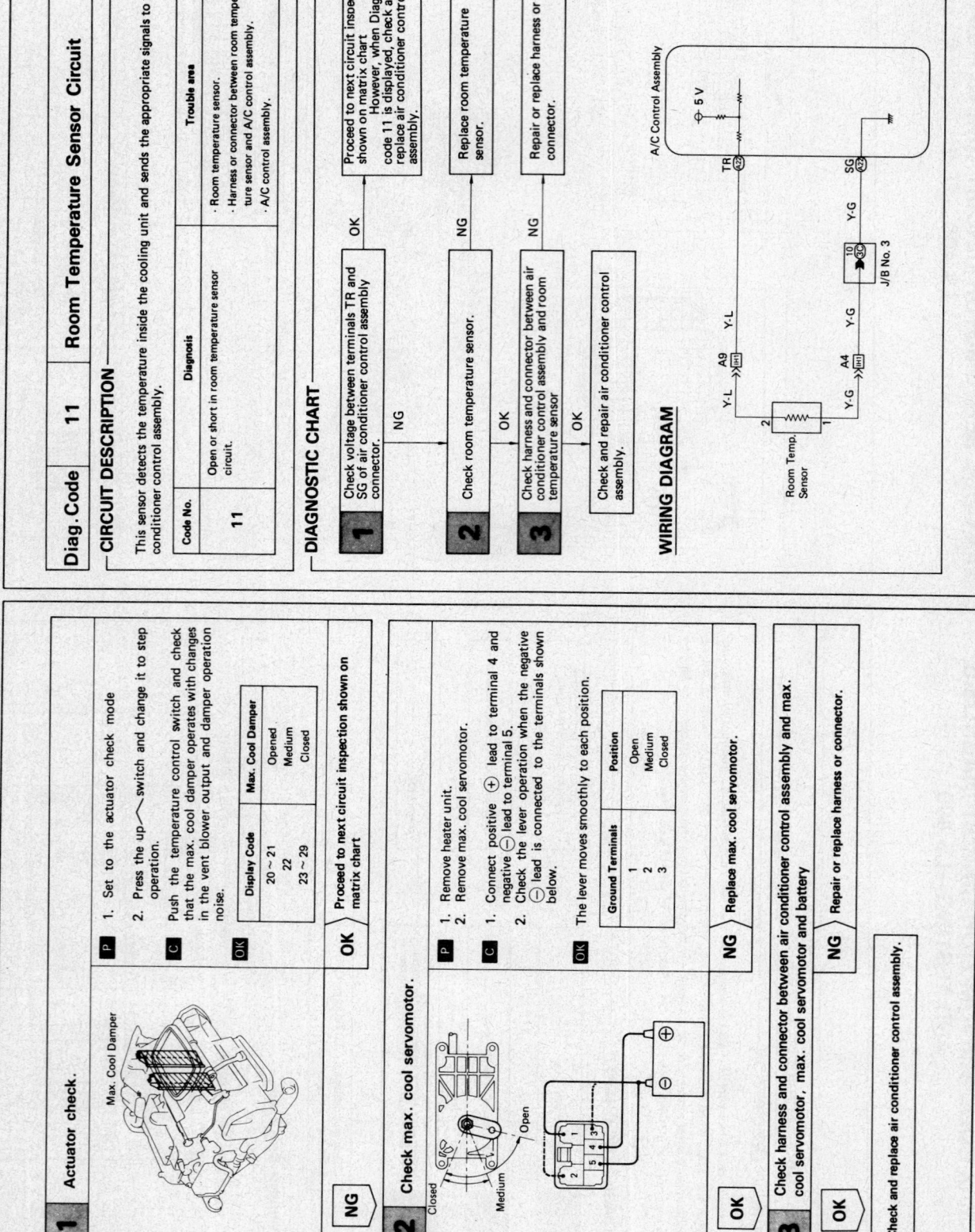

Diag. Code	11	Room Temperature Sensor Circuit

CIRCUIT DESCRIPTION

This sensor detects the temperature inside the cooling unit and sends the appropriate signals to the air conditioner control assembly.

Code No.	Diagnosis	Trouble area
11	Open or short in room temperature sensor circuit.	· Room temperature sensor. · Harness or connector between room temperature sensor and A/C control assembly. · A/C control assembly.

DIAGNOSTIC CHART

1 Check voltage between terminals TR and SG of air conditioner control assembly connector.

OK → Proceed to next circuit inspection shown on matrix chart
However, when Diag. code 11 is displayed, check and replace air conditioner control assembly.

NG ↓

2 Check room temperature sensor.

NG → Replace room temperature sensor.

OK ↓

3 Check harness and connector between air conditioner control assembly and room temperature sensor

NG → Repair or replace harness or connector.

OK ↓

Check and repair air conditioner control assembly.

WIRING DIAGRAM

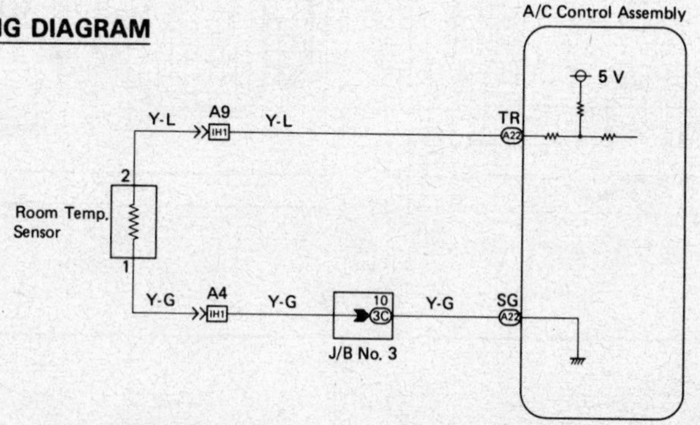
A/C Control Assembly
5 V
Y-L
A9
Y-L
TR
A22
2
Room Temp. Sensor
1
Y-G
A4
Y-G
10
3C
Y-G
SG
A22
J/B No. 3

ROOM TEMPERATURE SENSOR CIRCUIT WIRING ROUTING—LS 400

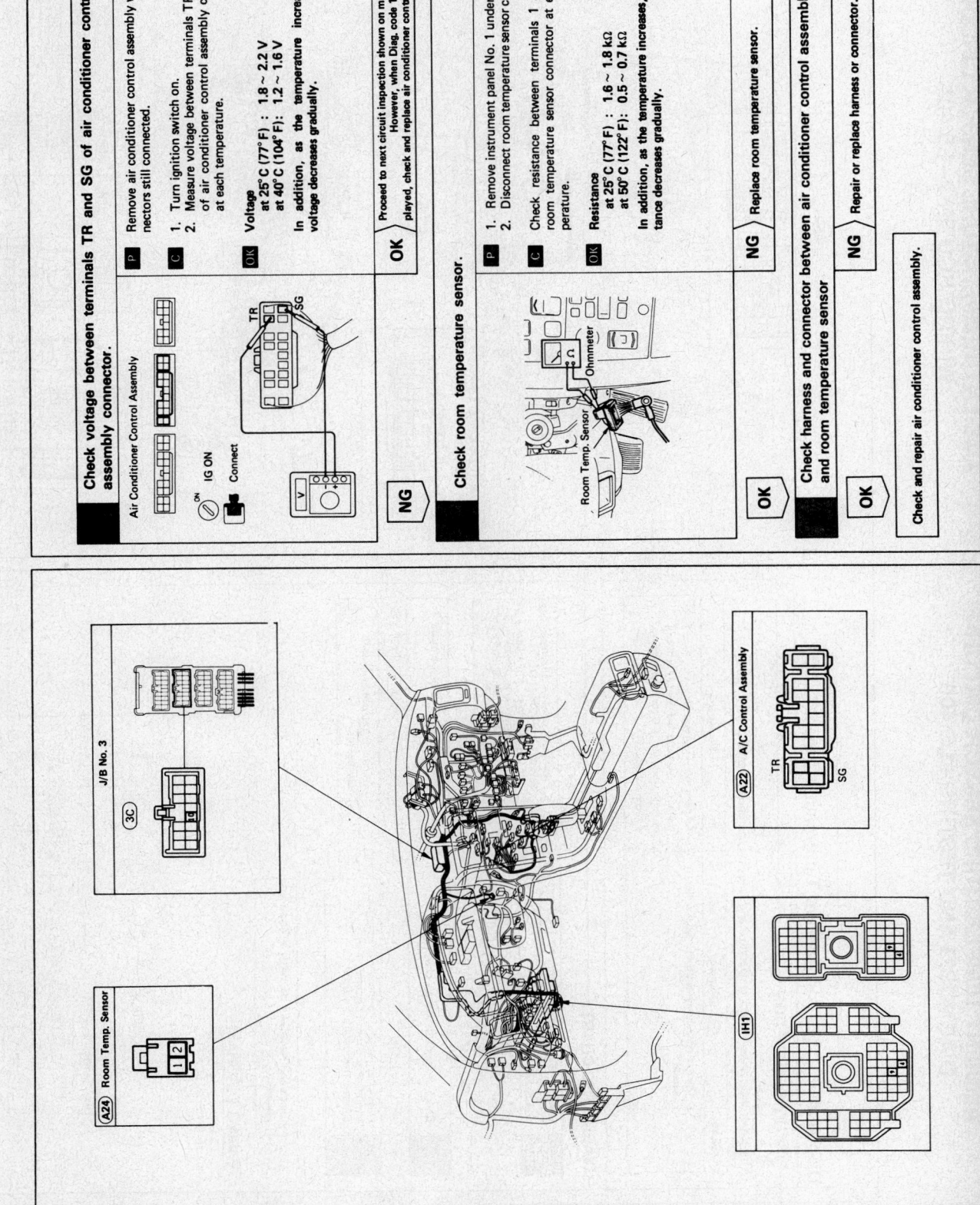

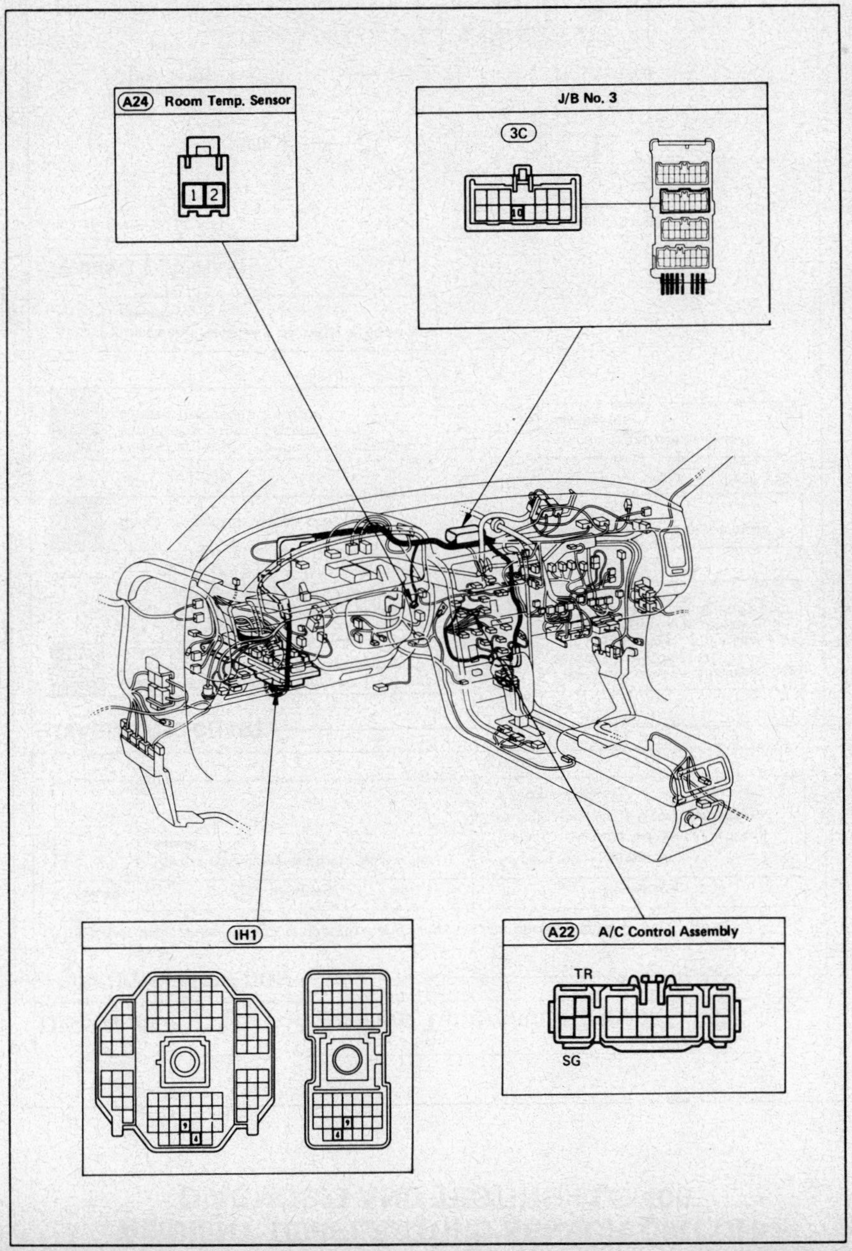
A24 Room Temp. Sensor
1 2
J/B No. 3
3C
10
IH1
9
4
A22 A/C Control Assembly
TR
SG

ROOM TEMPERATURE SENSOR CIRCUIT INSPECTION PROCEDURE—LS 400

Check voltage between terminals TR and SG of air conditioner control assembly connector.

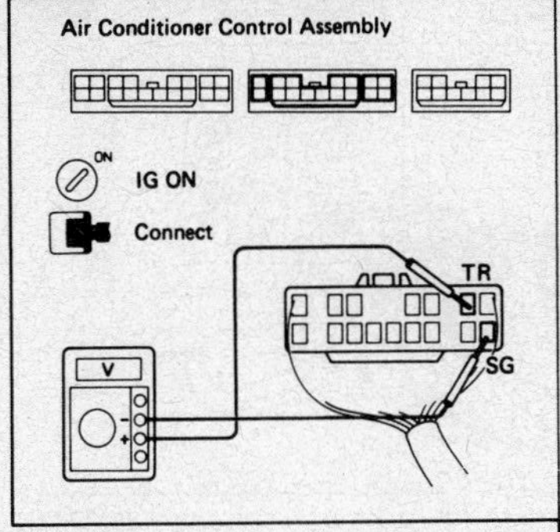
Air Conditioner Control Assembly
ON
IG ON
Connect
TR
SG
V

P Remove air conditioner control assembly with connectors still connected.

C
1. Turn ignition switch on.
2. Measure voltage between terminals TR and SG of air conditioner control assembly connector at each temperature.

OK **Voltage**
at 25°C (77°F) : 1.8 ~ 2.2 V
at 40°C (104°F): 1.2 ~ 1.6 V

In addition, as the temperature increases, the voltage decreases gradually.

OK — Proceed to next circuit inspection shown on matrix chart. However, when Diag. code 11 is displayed, check and replace air conditioner control assembly.

NG

Check room temperature sensor.

Room Temp. Sensor
Ohmmeter

P
1. Remove instrument panel No. 1 under cover.
2. Disconnect room temperature sensor connector.

C Check resistance between terminals 1 and 2 of room temperature sensor connector at each temperature.

OK **Resistance**
at 25°C (77°F) : 1.6 ~ 1.8 kΩ
at 50°C (122°F): 0.5 ~ 0.7 kΩ

In addition, as the temperature increases, the resistance decreases gradually.

NG — Replace room temperature sensor.

OK

Check harness and connector between air conditioner control assembly and room temperature sensor

NG — Repair or replace harness or connector.

OK

Check and repair air conditioner control assembly.

AMBIENT TEMPERATURE SENSOR CIRCUIT DIAGNOSIS AND TESTING—LS 400

Diag. Code	12	Ambient Temperature Sensor Circuit

CIRCUIT DESCRIPTION

This sensor detects the ambient temperature and sends the appropriate signals to the ECU.

Code No.	Diagnosis	Trouble area
12	Open or short in ambient temperature sensor circuit.	· Ambient temperature sensor. · Harness or connector between ambient temperature sensor and A/C control assembly. · A/C control assembly.

DIAGNOSTIC CHART

1. Check voltage between terminals TAM and SG of air conditioner control assembly connector.
   - OK → Proceed to next circuit inspection shown on matrix chart. However, when Diag. code 12 is displayed, check and replace air-conditioner control assembly.
   - NG ↓
2. Check ambient temperature sensor.
   - NG → Replace ambient temperature sensor.
   - OK ↓
3. Check harness and connector between air conditioner control assembly and ambient temperature sensor
   - NG → Repair or replace harness or connector.
   - OK ↓

Check and replace air conditioner control assembly.

WIRING DIAGRAM

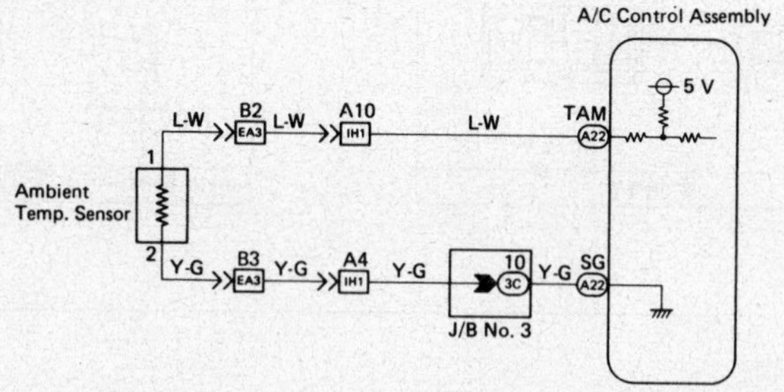
A/C Control Assembly
5 V
TAM
A22
SG
L-W
B2
EA3
A10
IH1
Ambient Temp. Sensor
1
2
Y-G
B3
A4
10
3C
J/B No. 3

AMBIENT TEMPERATURE SENSOR CIRCUIT WIRING ROUTING—LS 400

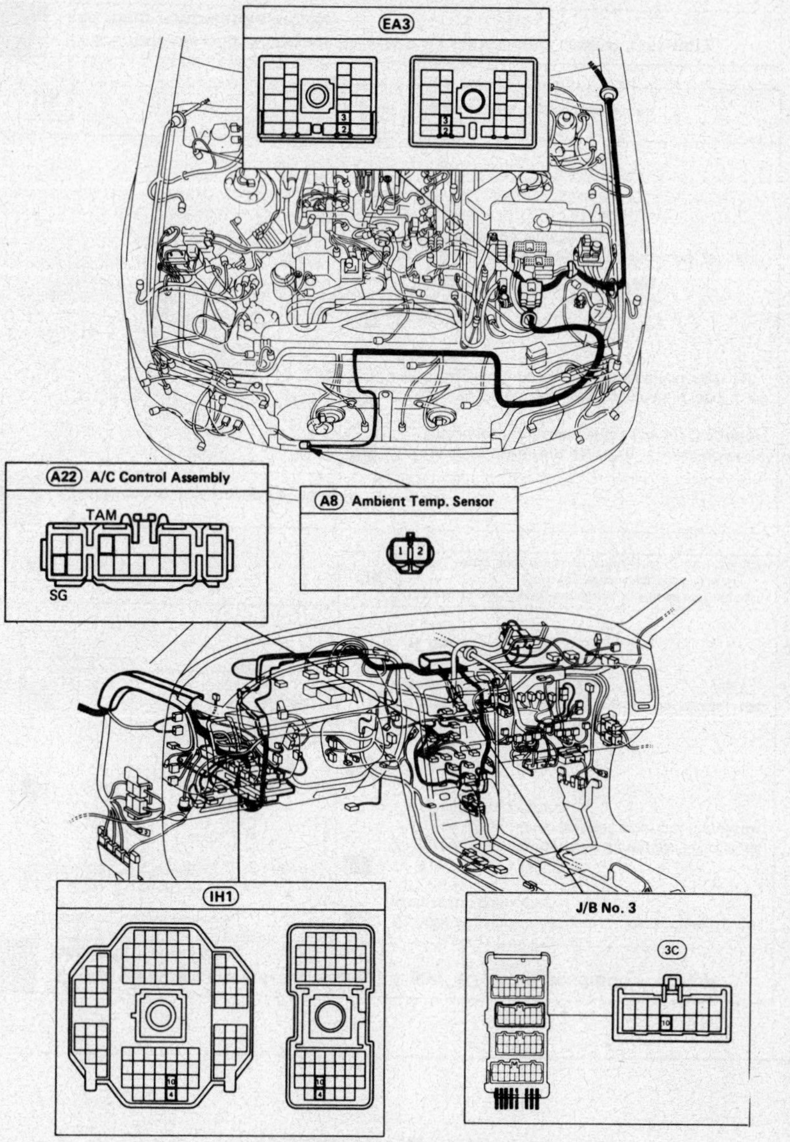
EA3
A22 A/C Control Assembly
TAM
SG
A8 Ambient Temp. Sensor
IH1
J/B No. 3
3C

AMBIENT TEMPERATURE SENSOR CIRCUIT INSPECTION PROCEDURE – LS 400

1 Check voltage between terminals TAM and SG of air conditioner control assembly connector.

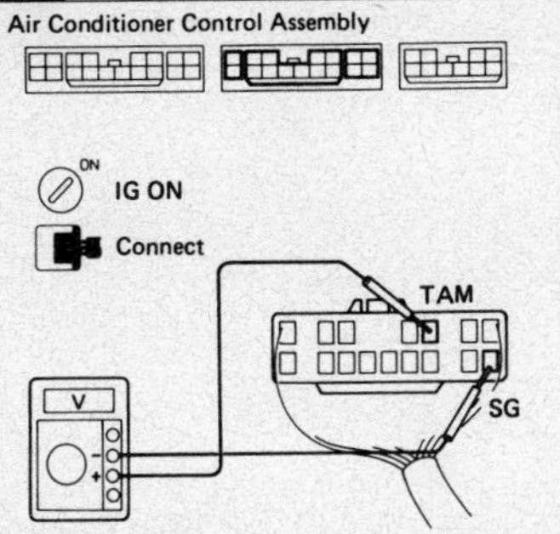

Air Conditioner Control Assembly
IG ON
Connect
TAM
SG
V

P: Remove air conditioner control assembly with connectors still connected.

C:
1. Turn ignition switch on.
2. Check voltage between terminals TAM and SG of air conditioner control assembly connector at each temperature.

OK: **Voltage**
at 25°C (77°F) : 1.35 ~ 1.75 V
at 40°C (104°F): 0.85 ~ 1.25 V

In addition, as the temperature increases, the voltage decreases gradually.

OK → **Proceed to next circuit inspection shown on matrix chart. However, when Diag. code 12 is displayed, check and replace air conditioner control assembly.**

NG ↓

2 Check ambient temperature sensor.

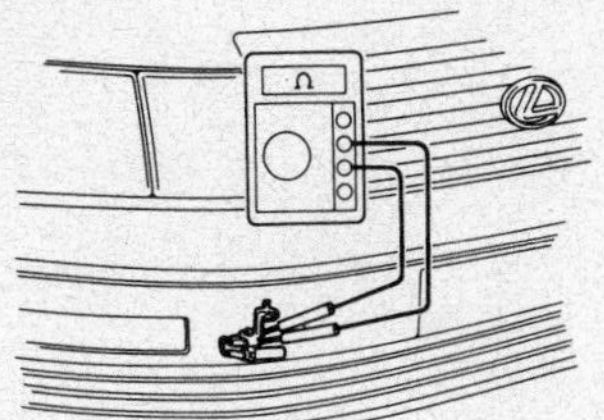

Ω

P:
1. Remove front radiator grille.
2. Disconnect ambient temperature sensor connector.

C:
1. Check resistance between terminals 1 and 2 of ambient temperature sensor connector at each temperature.

OK: **Resistance**
at 25°C (77°F) : 1.6 ~ 1.8 kΩ
at 50°C (122°F): 0.5 ~ 0.7 kΩ

In addition, as the temperature increases, the resistance decreases gradually.

NG → **Replace ambient temperature sensor.**

OK ↓

3 Check harness and connector between air conditioner control assembly and ambient temperature sensor

NG → **Repair or replace harness or connector.**

OK ↓

Check and replace air conditioner control assembly.

EVAPORATOR TEMPERATURE SENSOR CIRCUIT DIAGNOSIS AND TESTING – LS 400

Diag. Code	13	Evaporator Temperature Sensor Circuit

CIRCUIT DESCRIPTION

This sensor detects the temperature inside the cooling unit and sends the appropriate signals to the air conditioner control assembly.

Code No.	Diagnosis	Trouble area
13	Open or short in evaporator temperature sensor circuit.	· Evaporator temperature sensor. · Harness or connector between evaporator temperature sensor and A/C control assembly. · A/C control assembly.

DIAGNOSTIC CHART

1 Check voltage between terminals TE and SG of air conditioner control assembly connector.
- OK → Proceed to next circuit inspection shown on matrix chart. However, when Diag. code 13 is displayed check and replace air conditioner control assembly.
- NG ↓

2 Check evaporator temperature sensor.
- NG → Replace evaporator temperature sensor.
- OK ↓

3 Check harness and connector between air-conditioner control assembly and evaporator temperature sensor
- NG → Repair or replace harness or connector.
- OK ↓

Check and replace air conditioner control assembly.

WIRING DIAGRAM

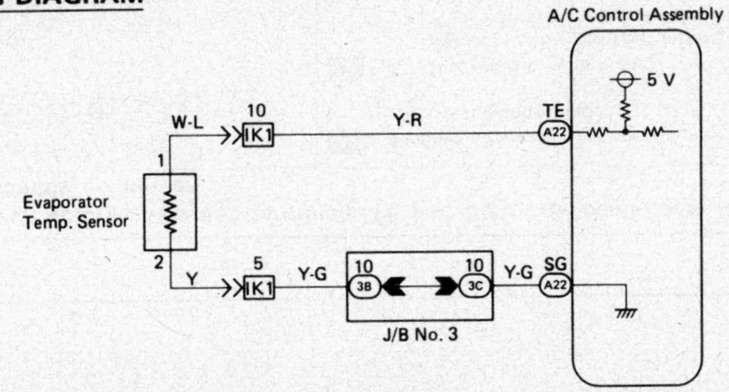

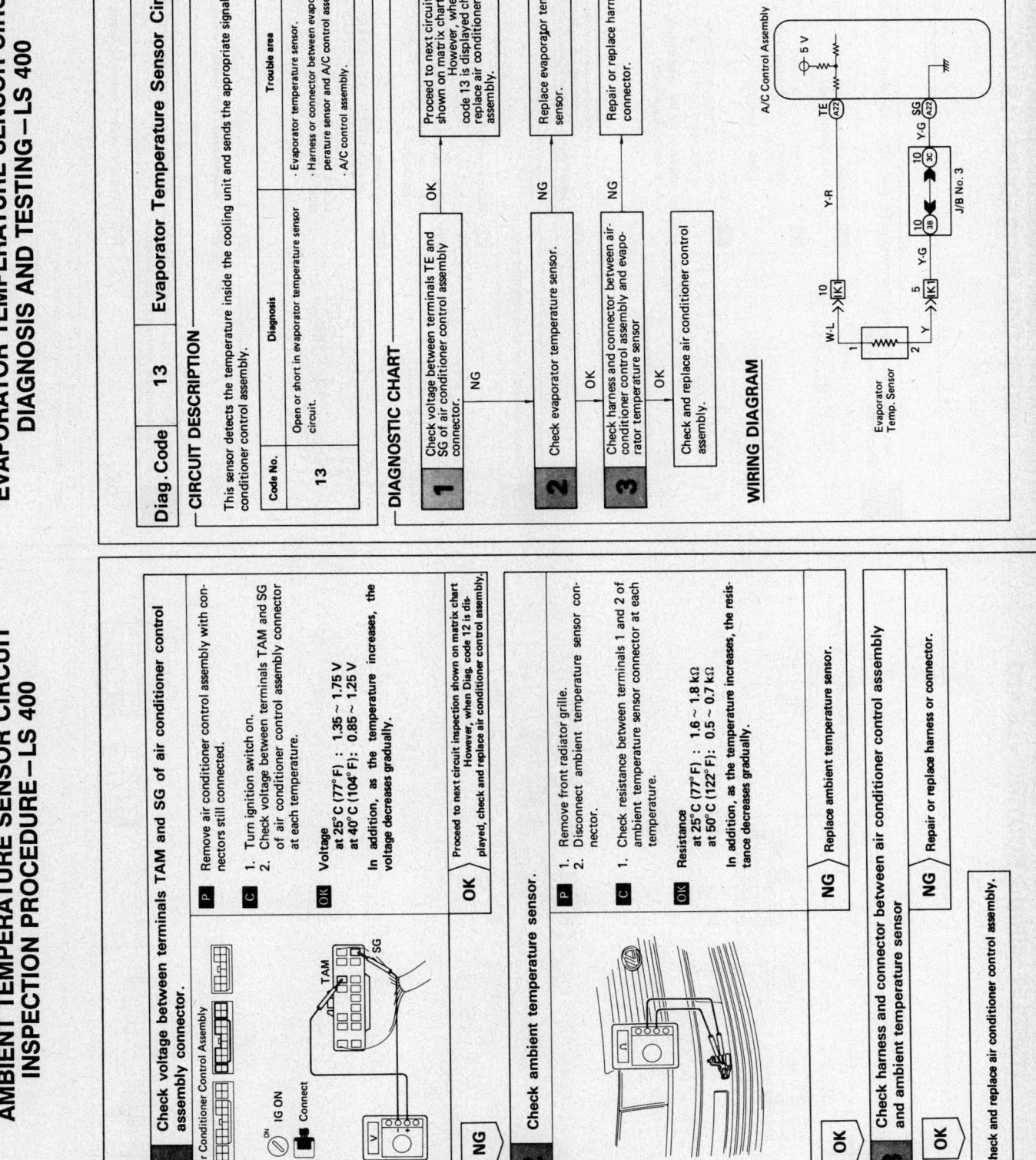

A/C Control Assembly
5 V
TE
A22
SG
A22
W-L
10
IK1
Y-R
1
2
Evaporator
Temp. Sensor
Y
5
IK1
Y-G
10
3B
10
3C
Y-G
J/B No. 3

EVAPORATOR TEMPERATURE SENSOR CIRCUIT WIRING ROUTING—LS 400

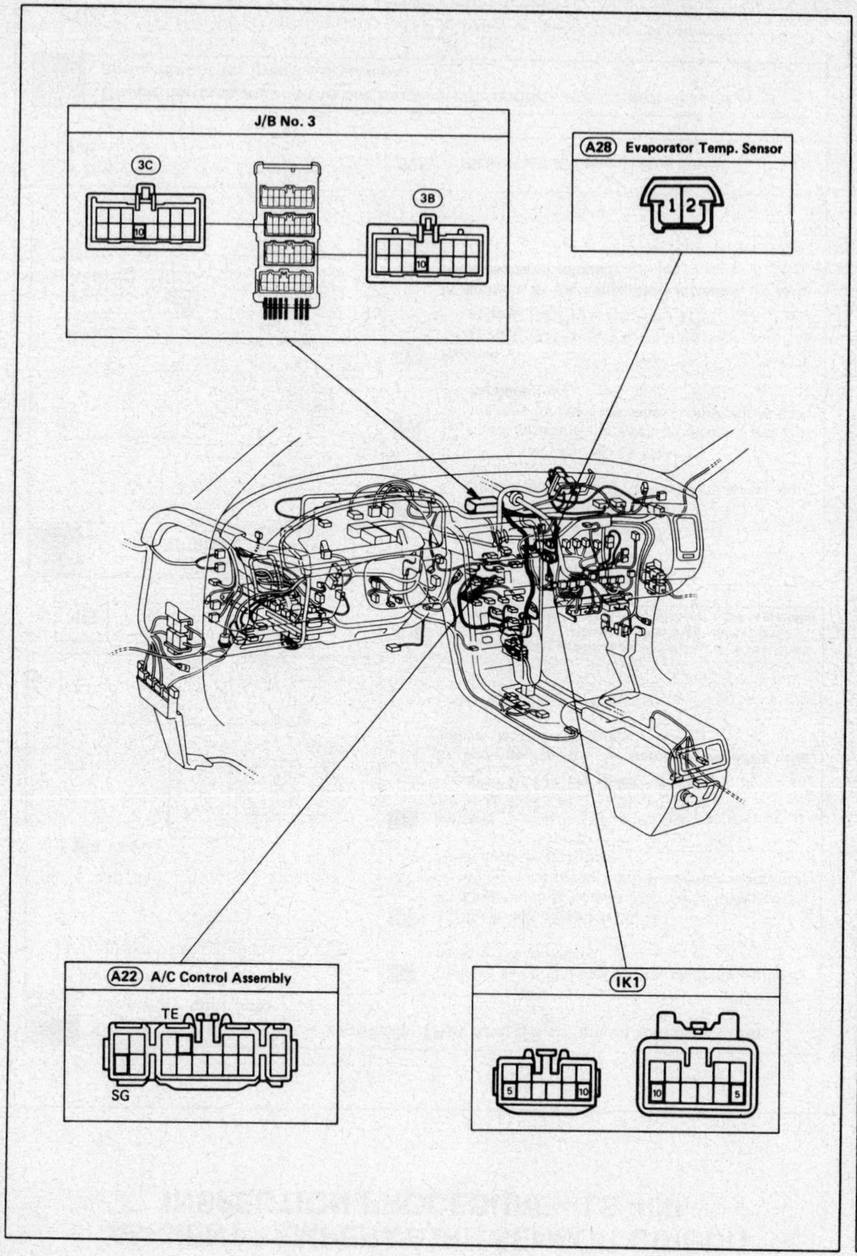
J/B No. 3
3C
3B
10
A28 Evaporator Temp. Sensor
1
2
A22 A/C Control Assembly
TE
SG
IK1
5
10

EVAPORATOR TEMPERATURE SENSOR CIRCUIT INSPECTION PROCEDURE—LS 400

1 Check voltage between terminals TE and SG of air conditioner control assembly connector.

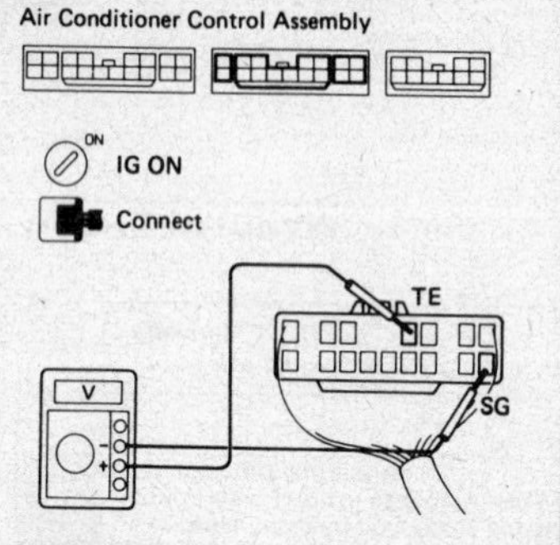
Air Conditioner Control Assembly
ON
IG ON
Connect
TE
SG
V

P Remove air conditioner control assembly with connectors still connected.

C
1. Turn ignition switch on.
2. Measure voltage between terminals TE and SG of air conditioner control assembly connector at each temperature.

OK **Voltage**
at 0°C (32°F): 2.0 ~ 2.4 V
at 15°C (59°F): 1.4 ~ 1.8 V

In addition, as the temperature increases, the voltage decreases gradually.

OK → **Proceed to next circuit inspection shown on matrix chart However, when Diag. code 13 is displayed, check and replace air conditioner control assembly.**

NG ↓

2 Check evaporator temperature sensor.

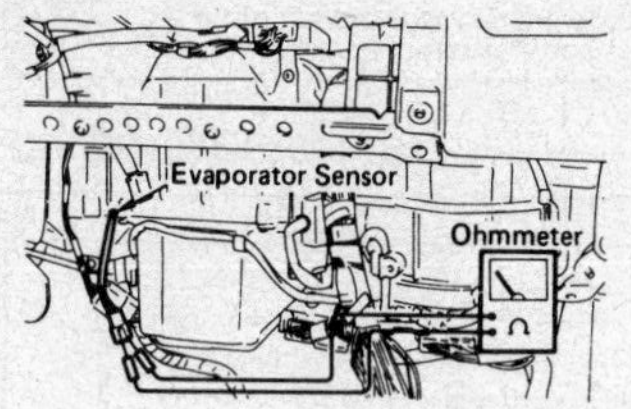
Evaporator Sensor
Ohmmeter

P Remove evaporator temperature sensor

C Check resistance between terminals 1 and 2 of evaporator temperature sensor connector at each temperature.

OK **Resistance**
at 0°C (32°F): 4.5 ~ 5.2 kΩ
at 15°C (59°F): 2.0 ~ 2.7 kΩ

In addition, as the temperature increases, the resistance decreases gradually.

NG → **Replace evaporator temperature sensor.**

OK ↓

3 Check harness and connector between air conditioner control assembly and evaporator temperature sensor

NG → **Repair or replace harness or connector.**

OK ↓

Check and replace air conditioner control assembly.

WATER TEMPERATURE SENSOR CIRCUIT DIAGNOSIS AND TESTING—LS 400

Diag. Code	14	Water Temperature Sensor Circuit

CIRCUIT DESCRIPTION

This sensor detects the coolant temperature and sends the appropriate signals to the air conditioner control assembly. These signals are used for warm up control when the engine is cold.

Code No.	Diagnosis	Trouble area
14	Open or short in water temperature sensor circuit.	· Water temperature sensor. · Harness or connector between water temperature sensor and A/C control assembly. · A/C control assembly.

DIAGNOSTIC CHART

1 Check voltage between terminals TW and SG of air conditioner control assembly connector.
- OK → Proceed to next circuit inspection shown on matrix chart. However, when Diag. code 14 is displayed, check and replace air conditioner control assembly.
- NG ↓

2 Check water temperature sensor.
- NG → Replace water temperature sensor.
- OK ↓

3 Check harness and connector between air conditioner control assembly and water temperature sensor
- NG → Repair or replace harness or connector.
- OK ↓

Check and replace air conditioner control assembly.

WIRING DIAGRAM

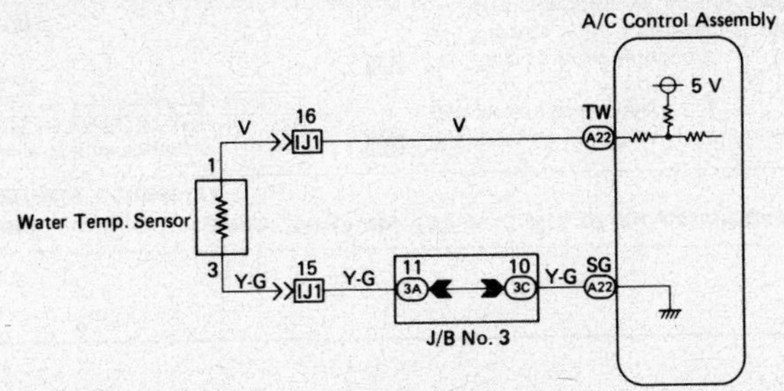
A/C Control Assembly
5 V
V
16
IJ1
V
TW
A22
1
Water Temp. Sensor
3
Y-G
15
IJ1
Y-G
11
3A
10
3C
Y-G
SG
A22
J/B No. 3

WATER TEMPERATURE SENSOR CIRCUIT WIRING ROUTING—LS 400

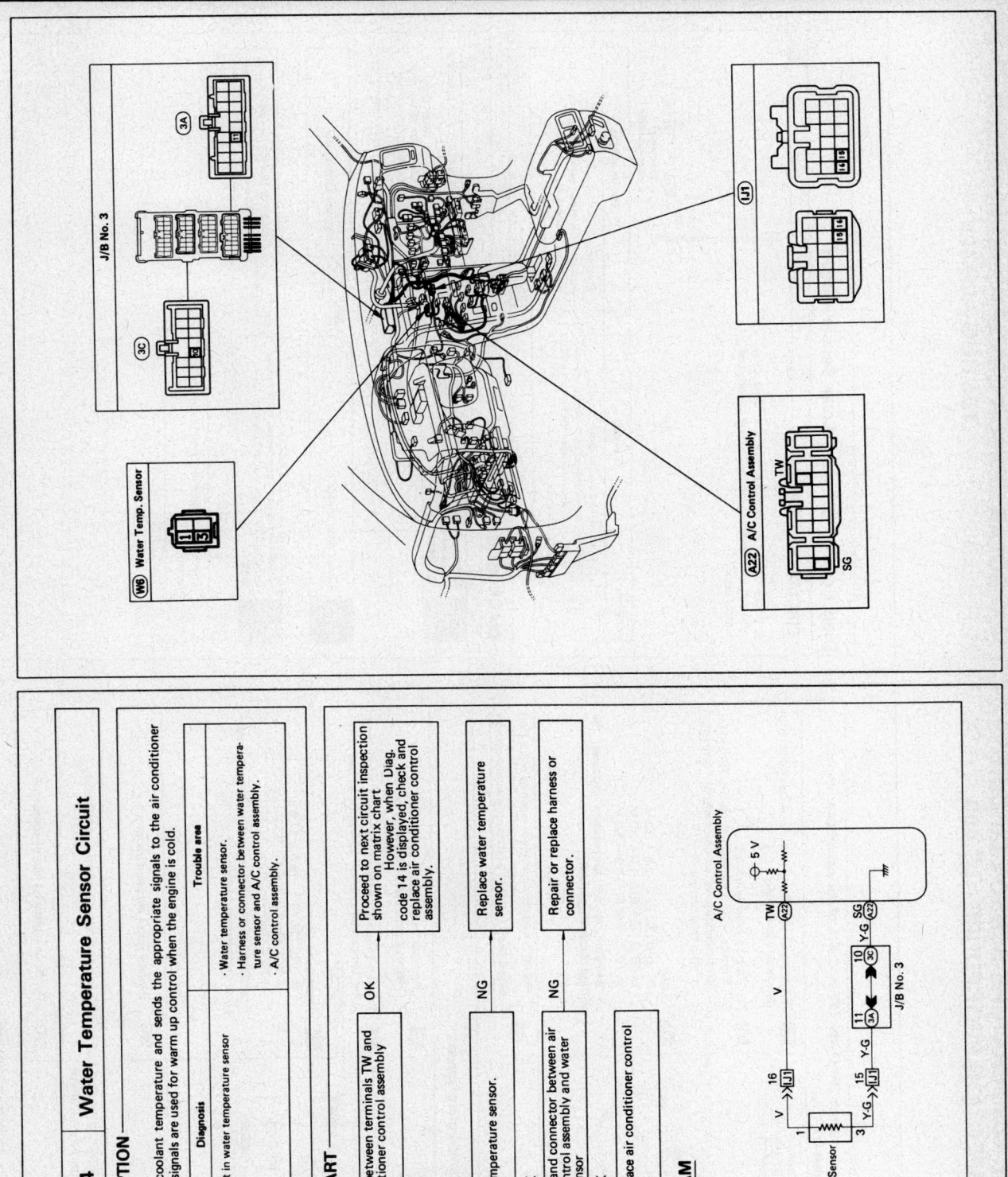

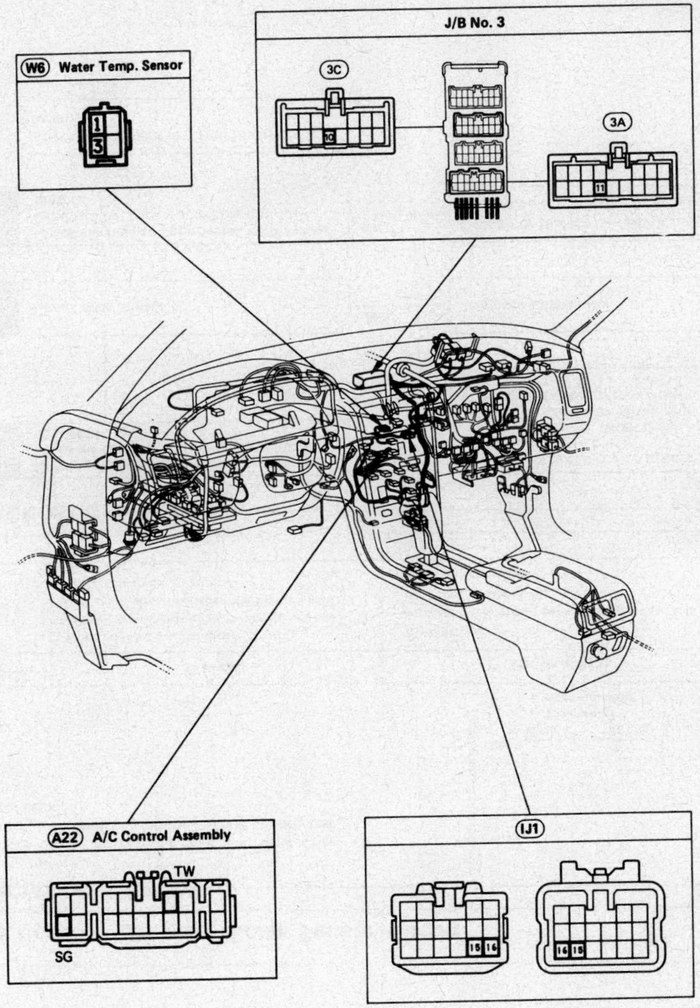
W6 Water Temp. Sensor
1
3
J/B No. 3
3C
10
3A
11
A22 A/C Control Assembly
TW
SG
IJ1
15 16
16 15

WATER TEMPERATURE SENSOR CIRCUIT INSPECTION PROCEDURE—LS 400

Check voltage between terminals TW and SG of air conditioner control assembly connector.

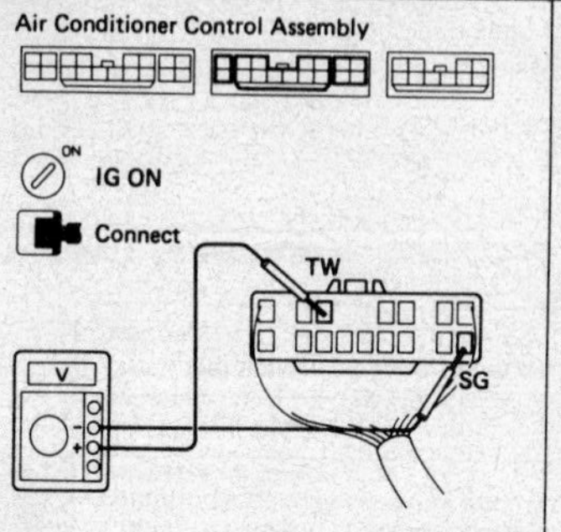
Air Conditioner Control Assembly
ON
IG ON
Connect
TW
SG
V

P Remove air conditioner control assembly with connectors still connected.

C 1. Turn ignition switch on.
2. Measure voltage between terminals TW and SG of air conditioner control assembly connector at each temperature.

OK Voltage
at 0°C (32°F) : 2.8 ~ 3.2 V
at 40°C (104°F): 1.8 ~ 2.2 V
at 70°C (158°F): 0.9 ~ 1.3 V

In addition, as the temperature increases, the voltage decreases gradually.

OK — Proceed to next circuit inspection shown on matrix chart. However, when Diag. code 14 is displayed, check and repair air conditioner control assembly.

NG

Check water temperature sensor.

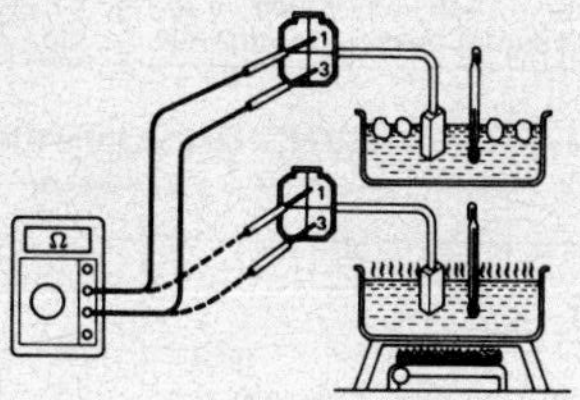
Ω

P 1. Remove heater unit.
2. Remove water temperature sensor.

C Measure resistance between terminals 7 and 3 of water temperature sensor connector at each temperature.

OK Resistance
at 0°C (32°F) : 16.5 ~ 17.5 kΩ
at 40°C (104°F): 2.4 ~ 2.8 kΩ
at 70°C (158°F): 0.7 ~ 1.0 kΩ

In addition, as the temperature increases, the resistance decreases gradually.

NG — Replace water temperature sensor.

OK

Check harness and connector between air conditioner control assembly and water temperature sensor

NG — Repair or replace harness or connector.

OK

Check and replace air conditioner control assembly.

SOLAR SENSOR CIRCUIT DIAGNOSIS AND TESTING—LS 400

Diag. Code	21	Solar Sensor Circuit

CIRCUIT DESCRIPTION

A photo diode in the solar sensor detects solar radiation and sends signals to the air conditioner control assembly.

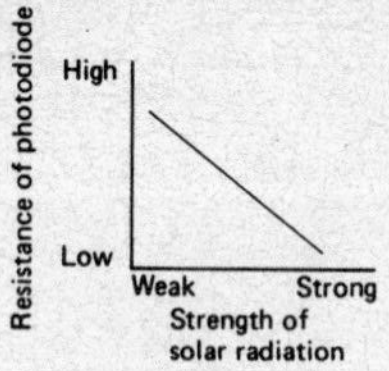
Resistance of photodiode
High
Low
Weak
Strong
Strength of solar radiation

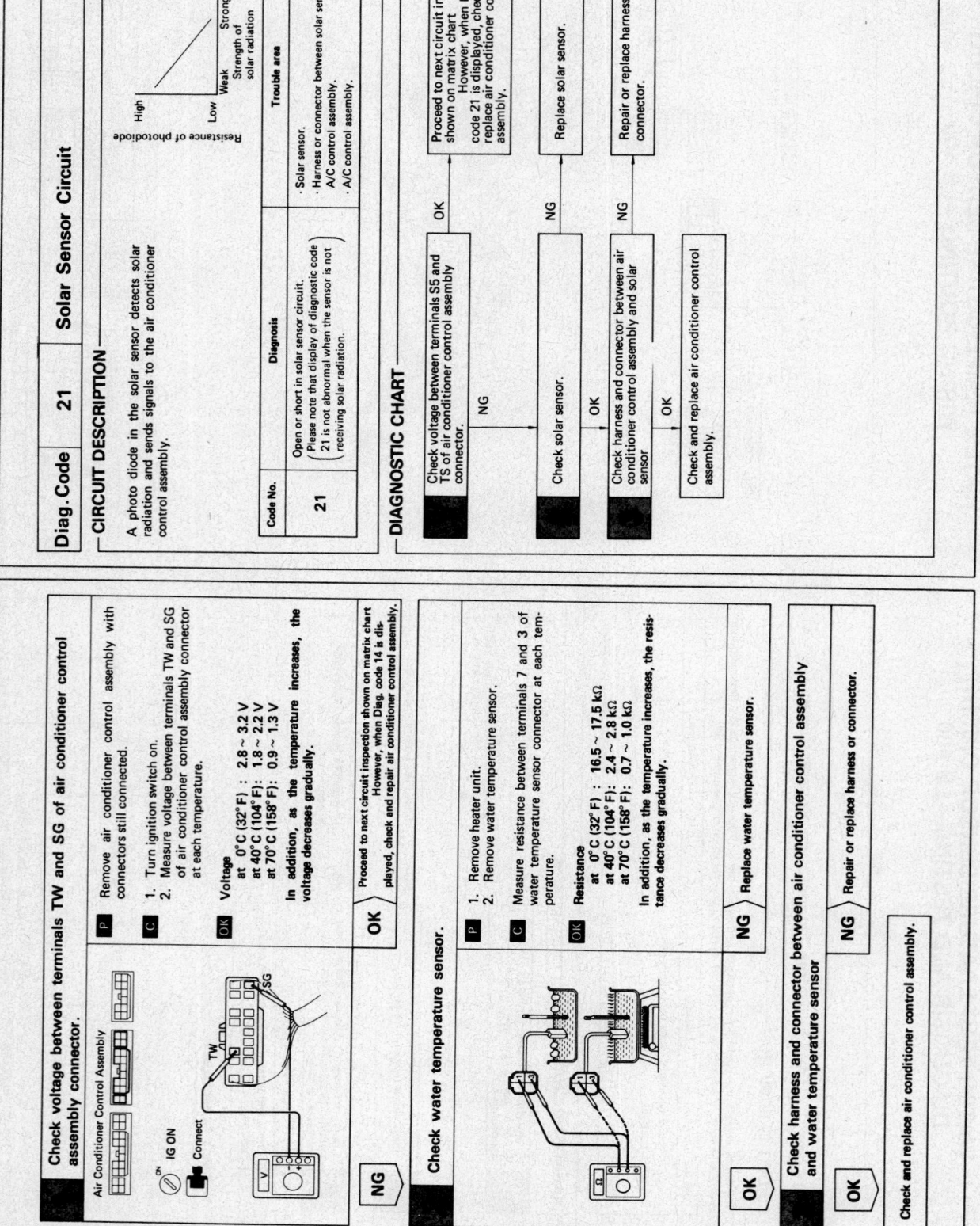

Code No.	Diagnosis	Trouble area
21	Open or short in solar sensor circuit. (Please note that display of diagnostic code 21 is not abnormal when the sensor is not receiving solar radiation.)	· Solar sensor. · Harness or connector between solar sensor and A/C control assembly. · A/C control assembly.

DIAGNOSTIC CHART

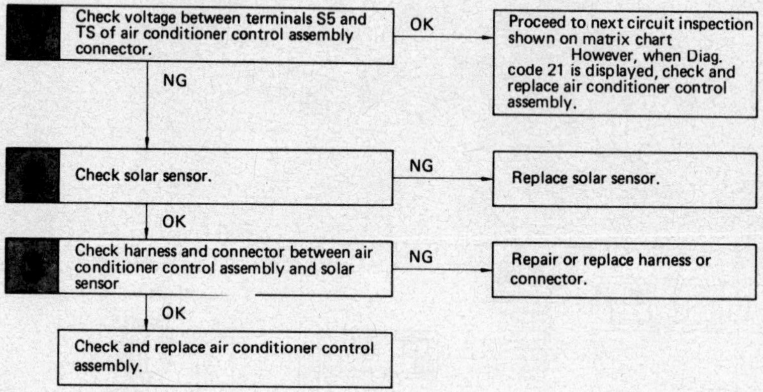
Check voltage between terminals S5 and TS of air conditioner control assembly connector.
OK
Proceed to next circuit inspection shown on matrix chart However, when Diag. code 21 is displayed, check and replace air conditioner control assembly.
NG
Check solar sensor.
NG
Replace solar sensor.
OK
Check harness and connector between air conditioner control assembly and solar sensor
NG
Repair or replace harness or connector.
OK
Check and replace air conditioner control assembly.

SOLAR SENSOR CIRCUIT WIRING DIAGRAM AND ROUTING–LS 400

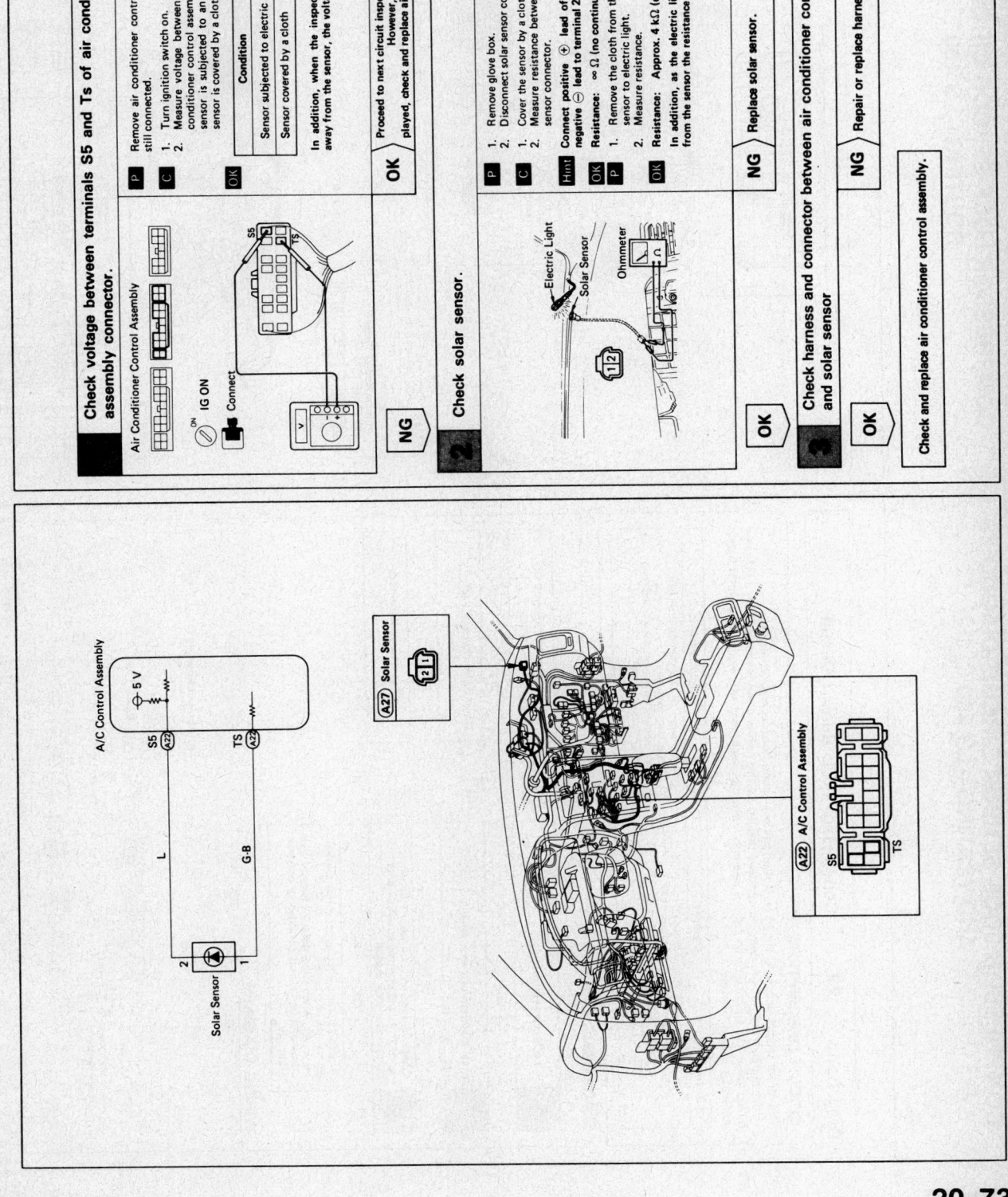

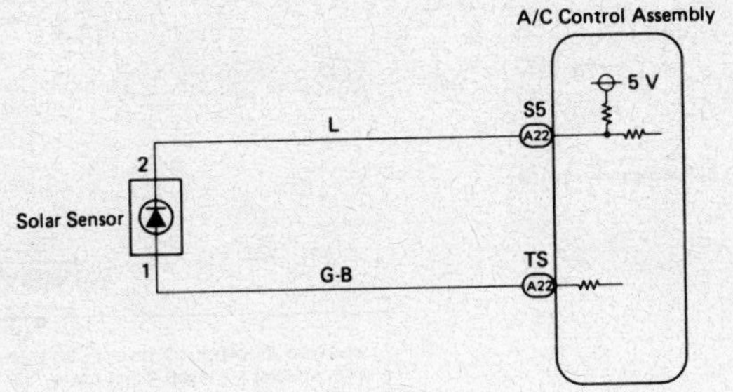
A/C Control Assembly
5 V
S5
A22
L
2
Solar Sensor
1
G-B
TS
A22

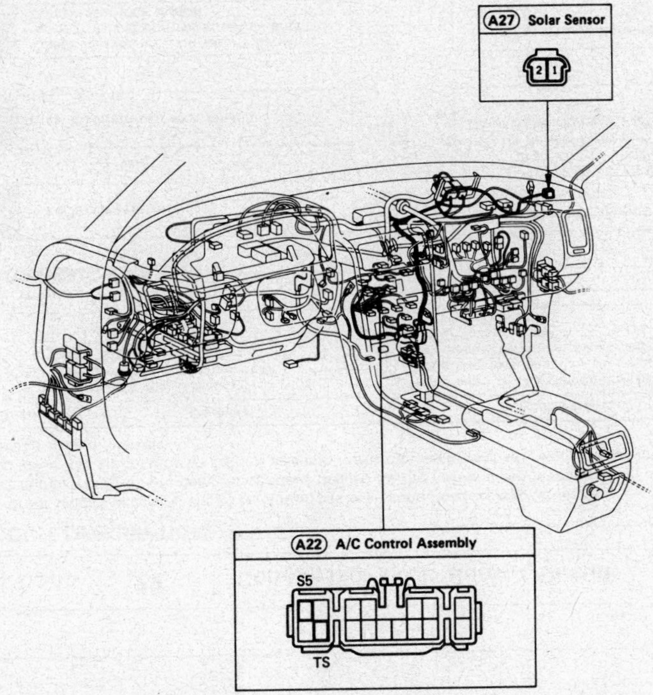
A27 Solar Sensor
2 1
A22 A/C Control Assembly
S5
TS

SOLAR SENSOR CIRCUIT INSPECTION PROCEDURE LS 400

1 Check voltage between terminals S5 and Ts of air conditioner control assembly connector.

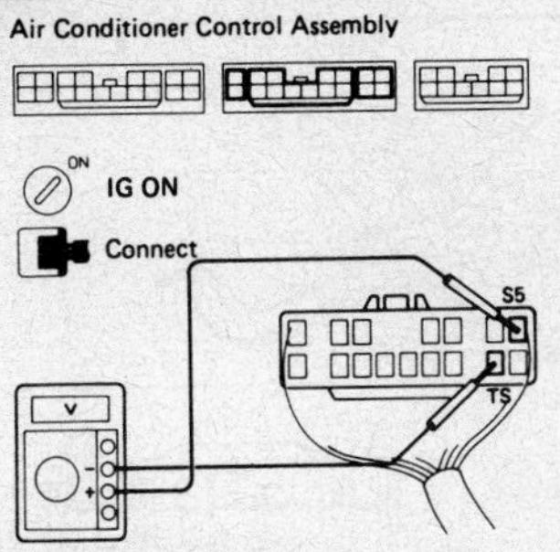
Air Conditioner Control Assembly
ON
IG ON
Connect
S5
TS
V

P Remove air conditioner control assembly with connectors still connected.

C
1. Turn ignition switch on.
2. Measure voltage between terminals S5 and Ts of air conditioner control assembly connector when the solar sensor is subjected to an electric light, and when the sensor is covered by a cloth.

OK

Condition	Voltage
Sensor subjected to electric light	below 4 V
Sensor covered by a cloth	4 ~ 4.5 V

In addition, when the inspection light is gradually moved away from the sensor, the voltage increases.

OK → **Proceed to next circuit inspection shown on matrix chart However, when Diag. code 21 is displayed, check and replace air conditioner control assembly.**

NG ↓

2 Check solar sensor.

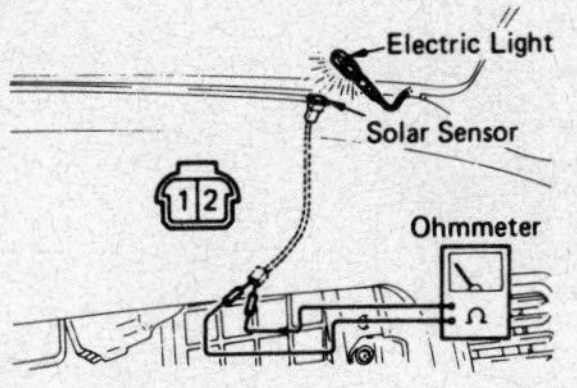
Electric Light
Solar Sensor
1 2
Ohmmeter

P
1. Remove glove box.
2. Disconnect solar sensor connector.

C
1. Cover the sensor by a cloth.
2. Measure resistance between terminals 1 and 2 of solar sensor connector.

Hint **Connect positive ⊕ lead of ohmmeter to terminal 1 and negative ⊖ lead to terminal 2 of the solar sensor.**

OK **Resistance: ∞ Ω (no continuity)**

P
1. Remove the cloth from the solar sensor and subject the sensor to electric light.
2. Measure resistance.

OK **Resistance: Approx. 4 kΩ (continuity)**

In addition, as the electric light is moved gradually away from the sensor the resistance increases.

NG → **Replace solar sensor.**

OK ↓

3 Check harness and connector between air conditioner control assembly and solar sensor

NG → **Repair or replace harness or connector.**

OK ↓

Check and replace air conditioner control assembly.

COMPRESSOR LOCK SENSOR CIRCUIT DIAGNOSIS AND TESTING – LS 400

Diag. Code	22	Compressor Lock Sensor Circuit

CIRCUIT DESCRIPTION

This sensor sends 4 pulses per engine revolution to the air conditioner control assembly.
If the number ratio of the compressor speed divided by the engine speed is smaller than a predetermined value, the air conditioner control assembly turns the compressor off. And, the indicator flashes at about 1 second intervals.

Code No.	Diagnosis	Trouble area
22	· Compressor lock is detected. · Open or short in compressor lock sensor circuit.	· Compressor · Compressor drive belt. · Compressor lock sensor. · Harness and connector between compressor and A/C control assembly. · A/C control assembly.

DIAGNOSTIC CHART

1 Check compressor. — NG → Adjust drive belt tension or repair compressor.

OK ↓

2 Check compressor lock sensor. — NG → Replace compressor lock sensor.

OK ↓

3 Check harness and connectors between air conditioner control assembly and compressor lock sensor — NG → Repair or replace harness or connector.

OK ↓

Proceed to next circuit inspection shown on matrix chart
However, when Diag. code 22 is displayed, check and replace air conditioner control assembly.

WIRING DIAGRAM

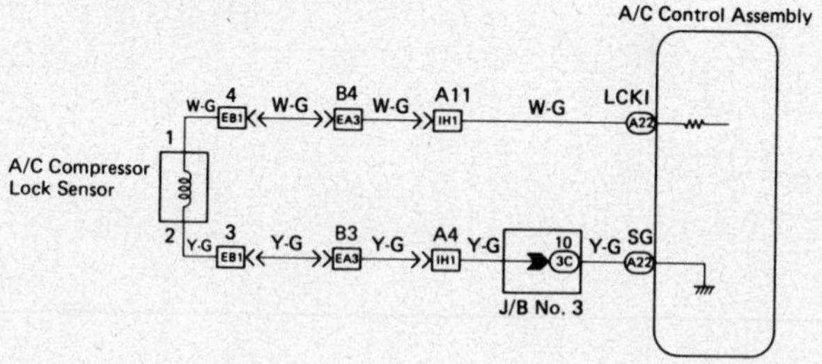
A/C Control Assembly
A/C Compressor Lock Sensor
W-G
4
EB1
W-G
B4
EA3
W-G
A11
IH1
W-G
LCKI
A22
1
2
Y-G
3
EB1
Y-G
B3
EA3
Y-G
A4
IH1
Y-G
10
3C
Y-G
SG
A22
J/B No. 3

COMPRESSOR LOCK SENSOR CIRCUIT WIRING ROUTING – LS 400

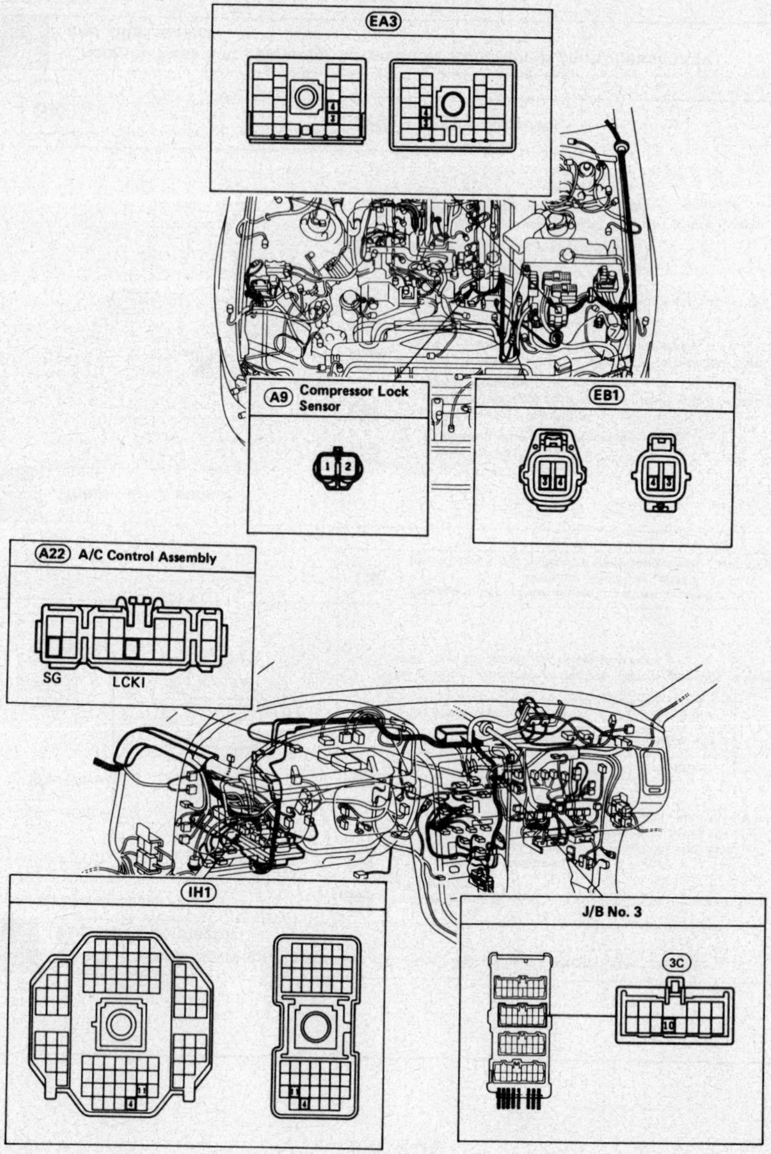
EA3
A9 Compressor Lock Sensor
EB1
A22 A/C Control Assembly
SG
LCKI
IH1
J/B No. 3
3C

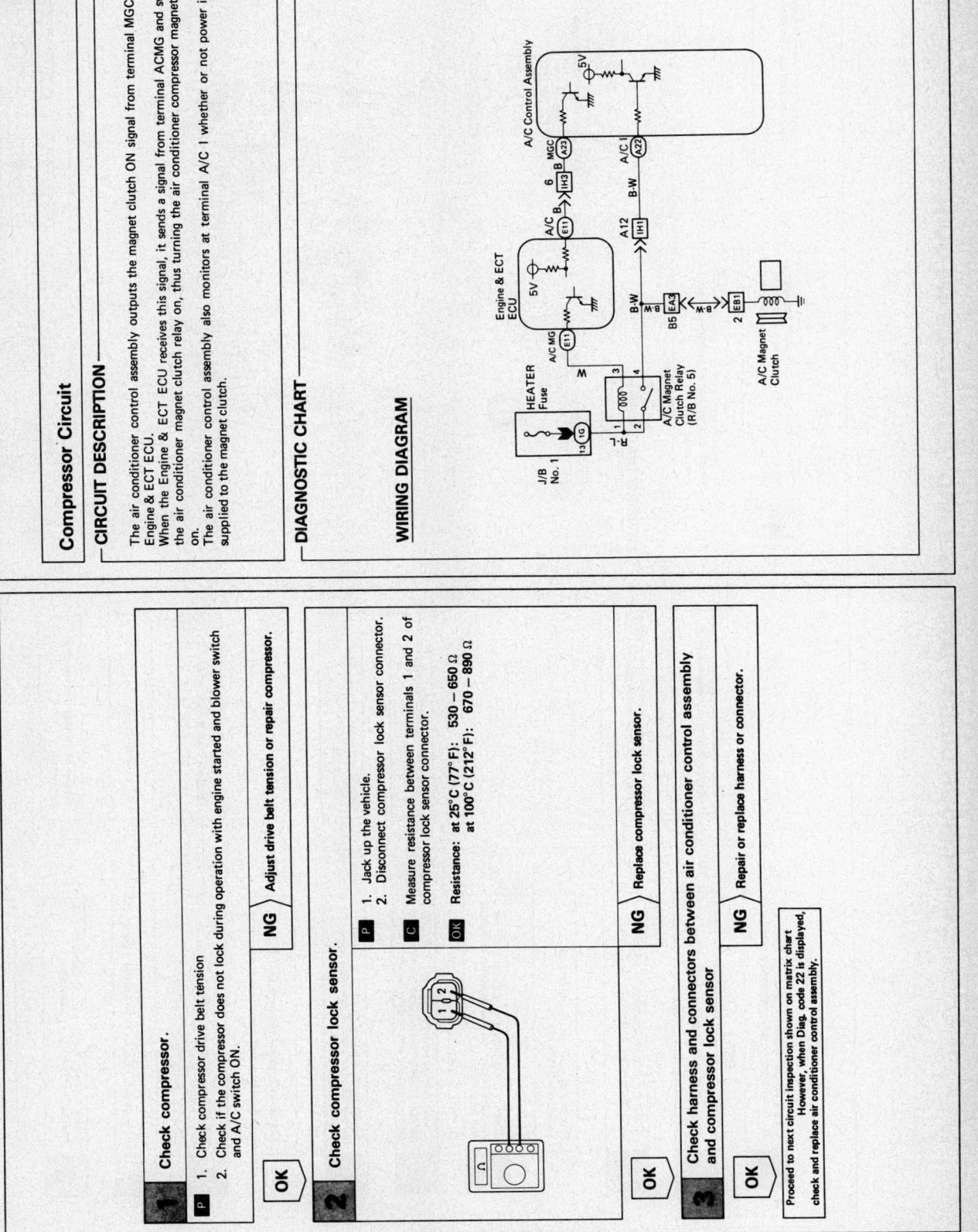

COMPRESSOR LOCK SENSOR CIRCUIT INSPECTION PROCEDURE—LS 400

1 Check compressor.

P
1. Check compressor drive belt tension
2. Check if the compressor does not lock during operation with engine started and blower switch and A/C switch ON.

OK

NG **Adjust drive belt tension or repair compressor.**

2 Check compressor lock sensor.

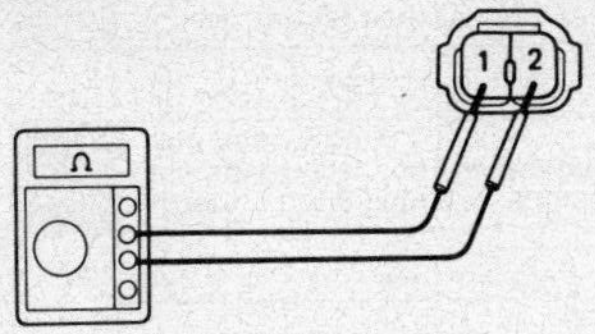
Ω
1 2

P
1. Jack up the vehicle.
2. Disconnect compressor lock sensor connector.

C Measure resistance between terminals 1 and 2 of compressor lock sensor connector.

OK Resistance: at 25°C (77°F): 530 – 650 Ω
at 100°C (212°F): 670 – 890 Ω

OK

NG **Replace compressor lock sensor.**

3 Check harness and connectors between air conditioner control assembly and compressor lock sensor

OK

NG **Repair or replace harness or connector.**

Proceed to next circuit inspection shown on matrix chart
However, when Diag. code 22 is displayed, check and replace air conditioner control assembly.

COMPRESSOR CIRCUIT DIAGNOSIS AND TESTING LS 400

Compressor Circuit

CIRCUIT DESCRIPTION

The air conditioner control assembly outputs the magnet clutch ON signal from terminal MGC to the Engine & ECT ECU.
When the Engine & ECT ECU receives this signal, it sends a signal from terminal ACMG and switches the air conditioner magnet clutch relay on, thus turning the air conditioner compressor magnet clutch on.
The air conditioner control assembly also monitors at terminal A/C I whether or not power is being supplied to the magnet clutch.

DIAGNOSTIC CHART

WIRING DIAGRAM

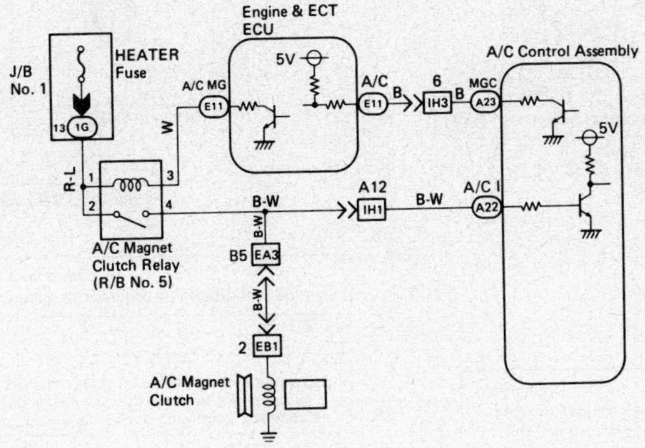
J/B
No. 1
HEATER
Fuse
13
1G
R-L
W
1
2
3
4
A/C Magnet
Clutch Relay
(R/B No. 5)
Engine & ECT
ECU
5V
A/C MG
E11
A/C
E11
B
6
IH3
B
MGC
A23
A/C Control Assembly
5V
B-W
A12
IH1
B-W
A/C I
A22
B5
EA3
2
EB1
A/C Magnet
Clutch

COMPRESSOR CIRCUIT DIAGNOSIS AND TESTING—LS 400 CONT.

1 Check voltage between terminal A/C I of air conditioner control assembly connector and body ground.
- NG → Go to step 4.
- OK ↓

2 Check A/C compressor magnet clutch.
- NG → Repair A/C compressor magnet clutch.
- OK ↓

3 Check harness and connector between A/C compressor and compressor relay
- NG → Repair or replace harness or connector.
- OK → Proceed to next circuit inspection shown on matrix chart

4 Check voltage between terminal MGC of air conditioner control assembly connector and body ground.
- OK → Go to step 7.
- NG ↓

5 Check voltage between terminal MGC of air conditioner control assembly harness side connector and body ground.
- OK → Check and replace air conditioner control assembly.
- NG ↓

6 Check harness and connector between air conditioner control assembly and engine & ECT ECU
- NG → Repair or replace harness or connector.
- OK → Check and replace engine & ECT ECU.

7 Check magnet clutch relay.
- NG → Replace compressor relay.
- OK ↓

8 Check voltage between terminal A/C MG of engine & ECT ECU and body ground.
- OK → Go to Step **10**.
- NG ↓

9 Check harness and connector between engine & ECT ECU and battery
- NG → Repair or replace harness or connector.
- OK → Check and replace engine & ECT ECU.

10 Check harness and connector between air conditioner control assembly and compressor relay, compressor relay and battery
- NG → Repair or replace harness or connector.
- OK → Check and replace air conditioner control assembly.

WIRING DIAGRAM

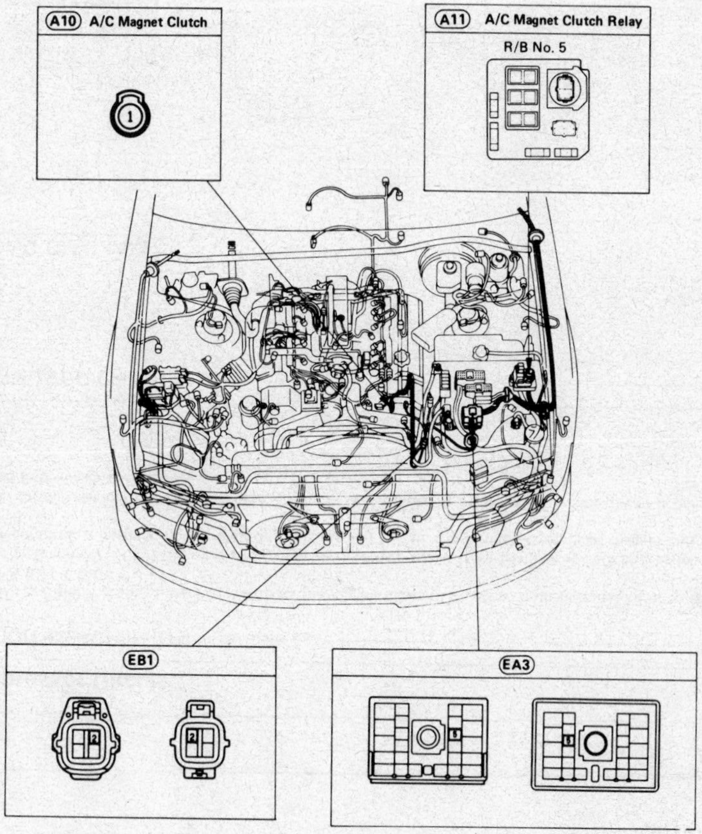
A10 A/C Magnet Clutch
1
A11 A/C Magnet Clutch Relay
R/B No. 5
EB1
EA3

COMPRESSOR CIRCUIT WIRING ROUTING – LS 400

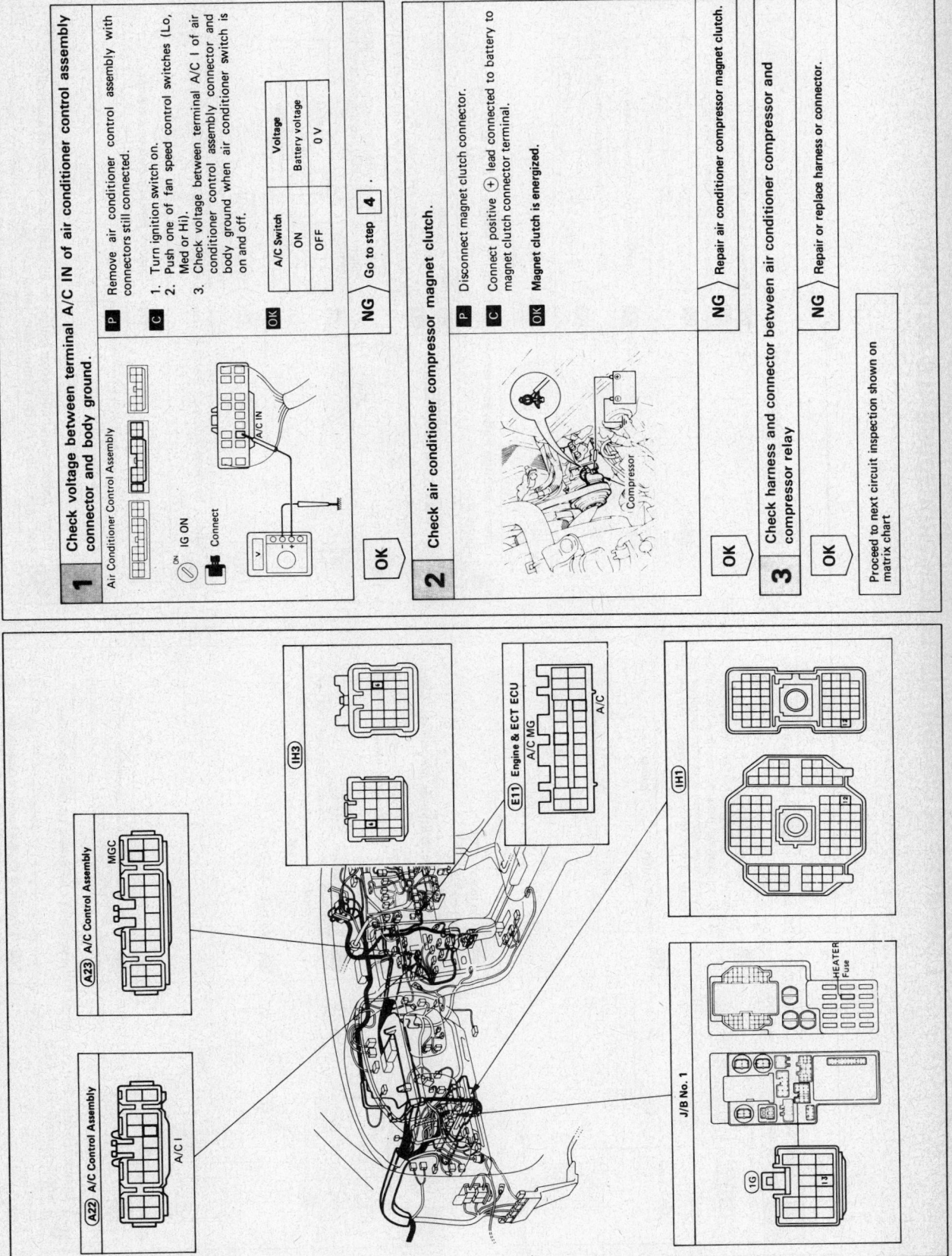

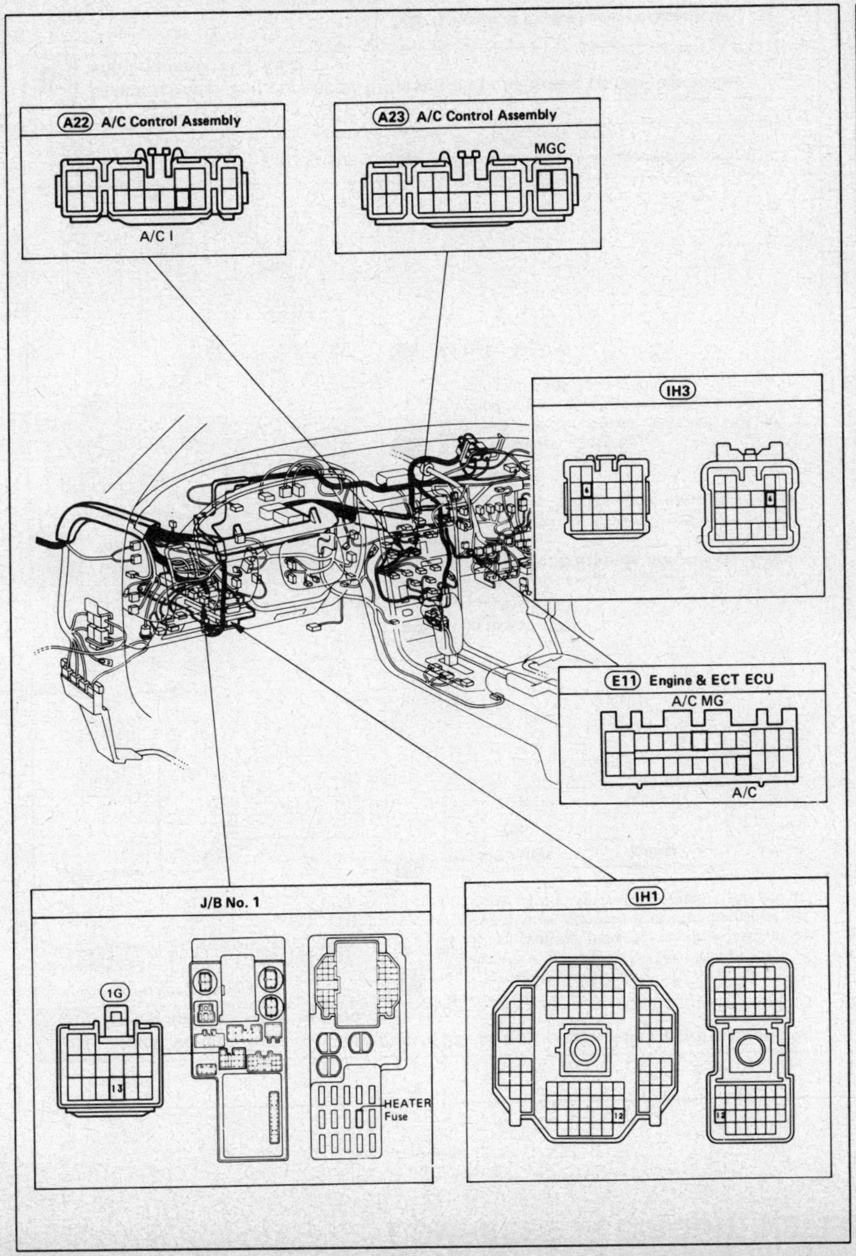
A22 A/C Control Assembly
A/C I
A23 A/C Control Assembly
MGC
IH3
E11 Engine & ECT ECU
A/C MG
A/C
J/B No. 1
1G
13
HEATER
Fuse
IH1
12

COMPRESSOR CIRCUIT INSPECTION PROCEDURE LS 400

1 Check voltage between terminal A/C IN of air conditioner control assembly connector and body ground.

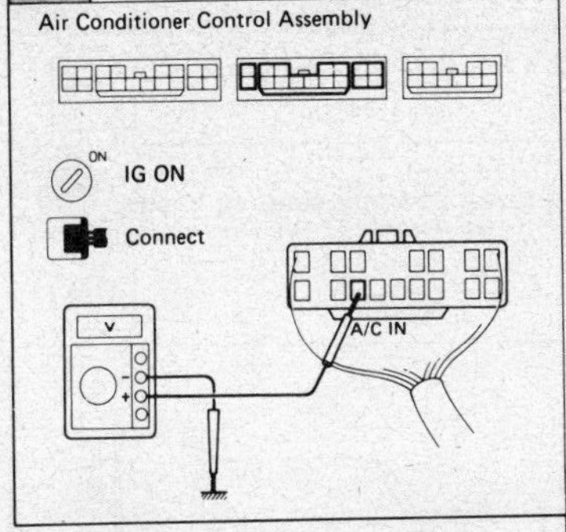
Air Conditioner Control Assembly
ON
IG ON
Connect
V
A/C IN

P Remove air conditioner control assembly with connectors still connected.

C
1. Turn ignition switch on.
2. Push one of fan speed control switches (Lo, Med or Hi).
3. Check voltage between terminal A/C I of air conditioner control assembly connector and body ground when air conditioner switch is on and off.

OK

A/C Switch	Voltage
ON	Battery voltage
OFF	0 V

NG Go to step 4.

OK

2 Check air conditioner compressor magnet clutch.

Compressor

P Disconnect magnet clutch connector.

C Connect positive ⊕ lead connected to battery to magnet clutch connector terminal.

OK **Magnet clutch is energized.**

NG **Repair air conditioner compressor magnet clutch.**

OK

3 Check harness and connector between air conditioner compressor and compressor relay

NG **Repair or replace harness or connector.**

OK

Proceed to next circuit inspection shown on matrix chart

COMPRESSOR CIRCUIT INSPECTION PROCEDURE – LS 400 CONT.

4 Check voltage between terminal MGC of air conditioner control assembly connector and body ground.

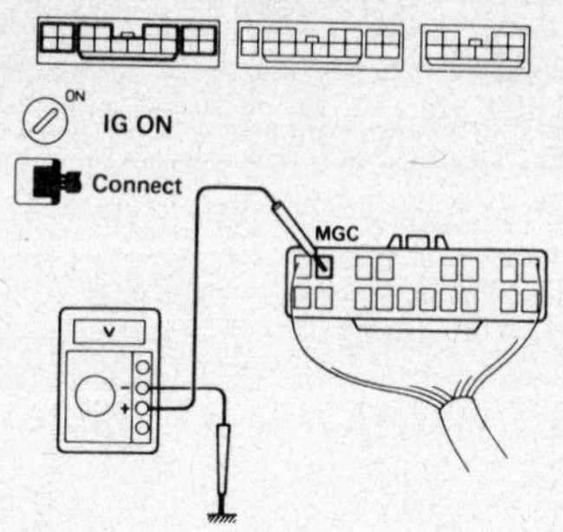

Air Conditioner Control Assembly
ON
IG ON
Connect
MGC
V

C
1. Turn ignition switch on.
2. Push one of the switches (Lo, Med or Hi).
3. Check voltage between terminal MGC of air conditioner control assembly connector and body ground when A/C switch is on and off.

OK

A/C Switch	Voltage
ON	0 V
OFF	4 – 6 V

NG ⟩

OK ⟩ Go to step **7**.

5 Check voltage between terminals MGC of air conditioner control assembly harness side connector and body ground.

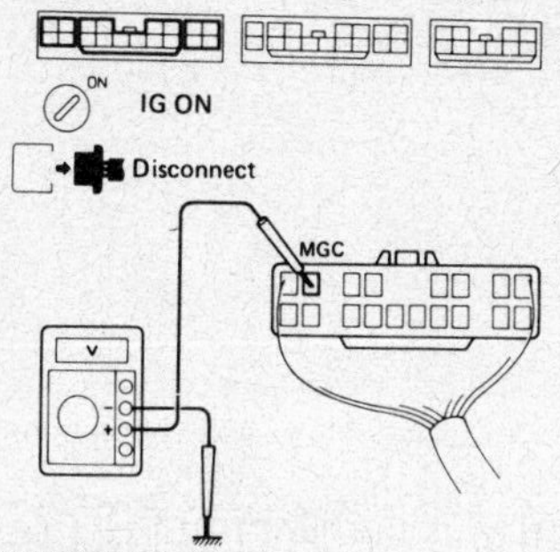

Air Conditioner Control Assembly
ON
IG ON
Disconnect
MGC
V

P Disconnect air conditioner control assembly connector.

C
1. Turn ignition switch on.
2. Check voltage between terminal MGC of air conditioner control assembly harness side connector and body ground.

OK Voltage: 4 – 6 V

NG ⟩

OK ⟩ Check and replace air conditioner control assembly.

6 Check harness and connector between air conditioner control assembly and engine & ECT ECU

OK ⟩

NG ⟩ Repair or replace harness or connector.

Check and replace engine & ECT ECU.

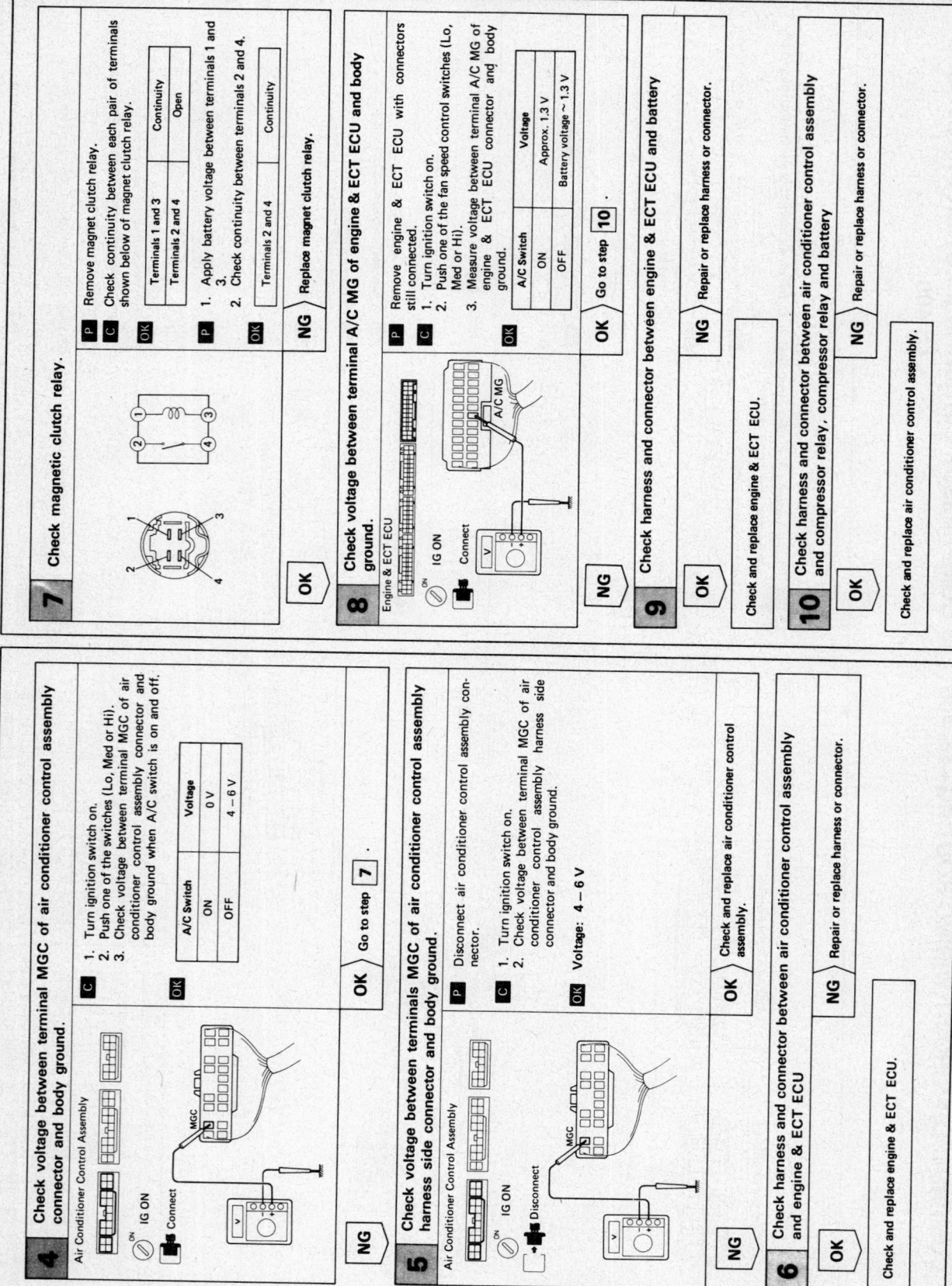

7 Check magnetic clutch relay.

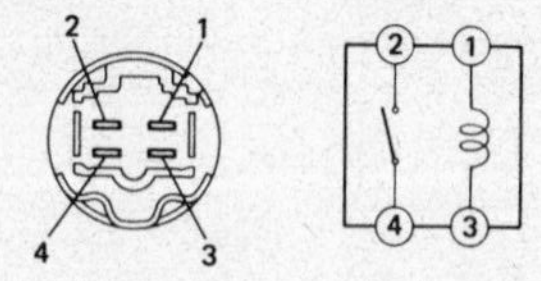

2
1
4
3

P Remove magnet clutch relay.

C Check continuity between each pair of terminals shown below of magnet clutch relay.

OK

Terminals	Continuity
Terminals 1 and 3	Continuity
Terminals 2 and 4	Open

P
1. Apply battery voltage between terminals 1 and 3.
2. Check continuity between terminals 2 and 4.

OK

Terminals 2 and 4	Continuity

OK ⟩

NG ⟩ Replace magnet clutch relay.

8 Check voltage between terminal A/C MG of engine & ECT ECU and body ground.

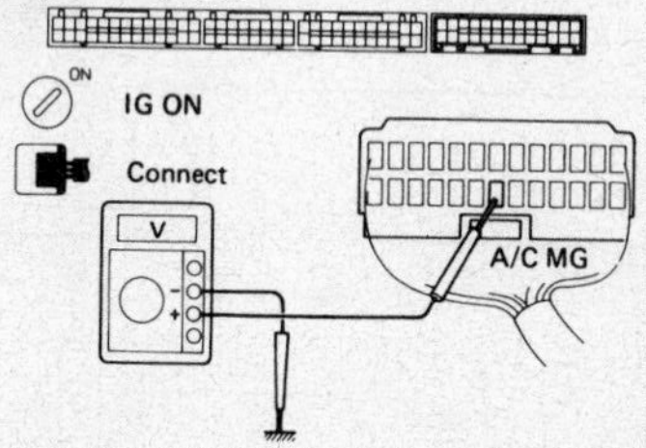

Engine & ECT ECU
ON
IG ON
Connect
V
A/C MG

P Remove engine & ECT ECU with connectors still connected.

C
1. Turn ignition switch on.
2. Push one of the fan speed control switches (Lo, Med or Hi).
3. Measure voltage between terminal A/C MG of engine & ECT ECU connector and body ground.

OK

A/C Switch	Voltage
ON	Approx. 1.3 V
OFF	Battery voltage ~ 1.3 V

NG ⟩

OK ⟩ Go to step **10**.

9 Check harness and connector between engine & ECT ECU and battery

OK ⟩

NG ⟩ Repair or replace harness or connector.

Check and replace engine & ECT ECU.

10 Check harness and connector between air conditioner control assembly and compressor relay, compressor relay and battery

OK ⟩

NG ⟩ Repair or replace harness or connector.

Check and replace air conditioner control assembly.

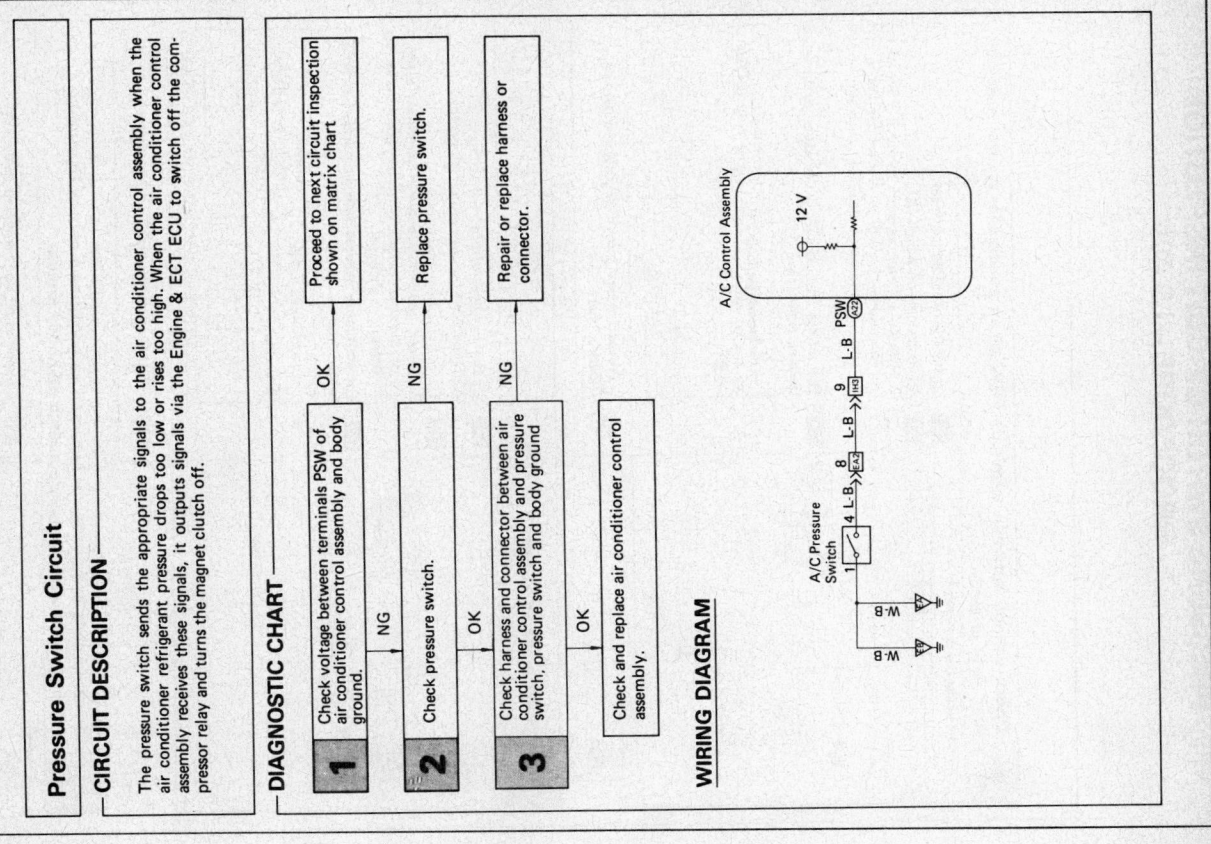

PRESSURE SWITCH CIRCUIT DIAGNOSIS AND TESTING—LS 400

Pressure Switch Circuit

CIRCUIT DESCRIPTION

The pressure switch sends the appropriate signals to the air conditioner control assembly when the air conditioner refrigerant pressure drops too low or rises too high. When the air conditioner control assembly receives these signals, it outputs signals via the Engine & ECT ECU to switch off the compressor relay and turns the magnet clutch off.

DIAGNOSTIC CHART

Step	Check	Result	Action
1	Check voltage between terminals PSW of air conditioner control assembly and body ground.	OK	Proceed to next circuit inspection shown on matrix chart
		NG	Go to step 2
2	Check pressure switch.	NG	Replace pressure switch.
		OK	Go to step 3
3	Check harness and connector between air conditioner control assembly and pressure switch, pressure switch and body ground	NG	Repair or replace harness or connector.
		OK	Check and replace air conditioner control assembly.

WIRING DIAGRAM

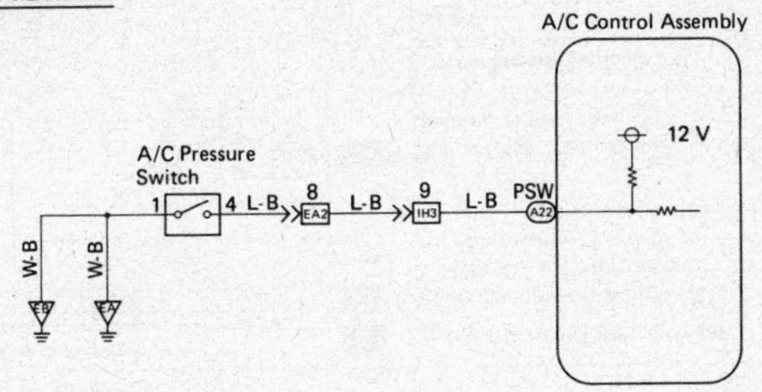
A/C Control Assembly
12 V
A/C Pressure Switch
1
4 L-B
8
EA2
L-B
9
IH3
L-B
PSW
A22
W-B
W-B
EB
EA

PRESSURE SWITCH CIRCUIT WIRING ROUTING LS 400

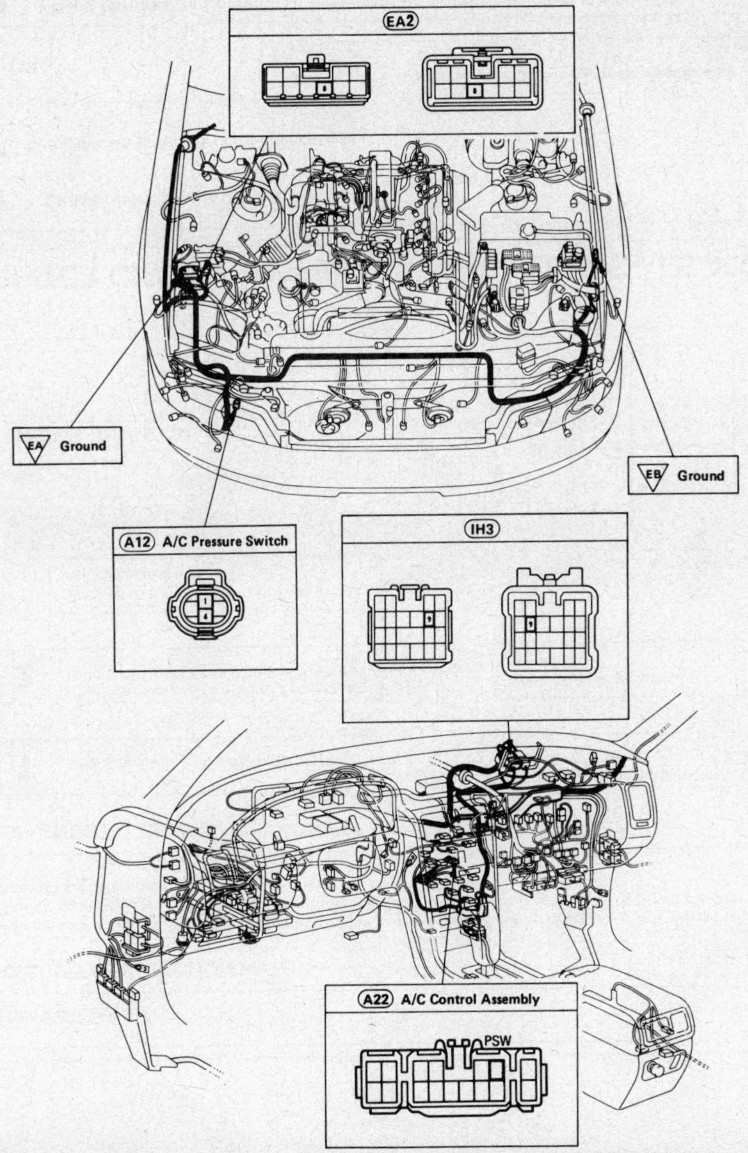
EA2
EA Ground
EB Ground
A12 A/C Pressure Switch
IH3
A22 A/C Control Assembly
PSW

PRESSURE SWITCH CIRCUIT INSPECTION PROCEDURE—LS 400

1 **Check voltage between terminals PSW of air conditioner control assembly and body ground.**

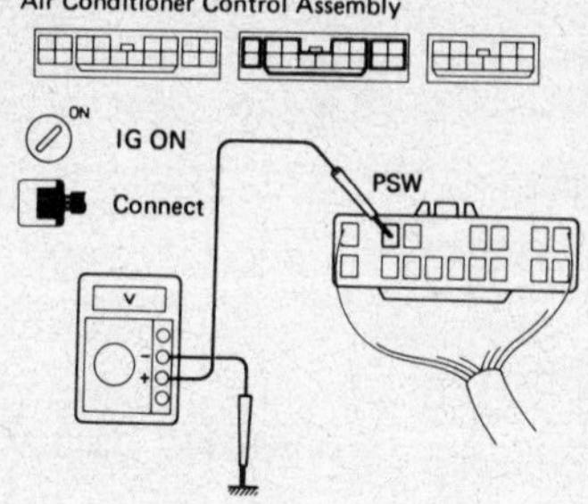
Air Conditioner Control Assembly
ON
IG ON
Connect
V
PSW

P Install the manifold gauge set.

C
1. Turn ignition switch ON.
2. Check voltage between terminal PSW of air conditioner control assembly connector and body ground when air conditioner gas pressure is changed.

OK **The voltage changes with gas pressure, as shown in the diagram below.**

Low Pressure Cut Side	<Reference> High Pressure Cut Side
ON (0 V) / OFF (12 V) — 2 kgf/cm²	ON (0 V) / OFF (12 V) — 27 kgf/cm²

NG — OK **Proceed to next circuit inspection shown on matrix chart**

2 **Check pressure switch.**

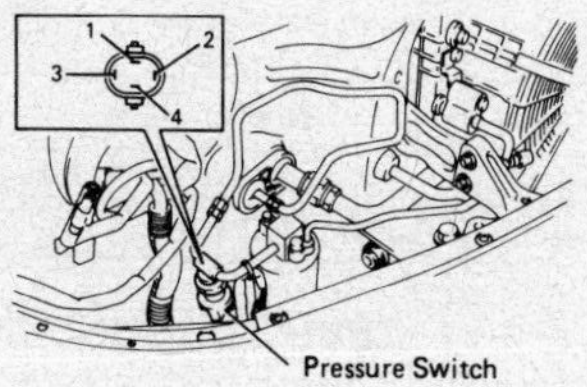
1
2
3
4
Pressure Switch

P
1. Remove headlight (on right side).
2. Disconnect pressure switch connector.

C
1. Turn ignition switch on.
2. Check continuity between terminals 1 and 4 of pressure switch when air conditioner gas pressure is changed.

OK **The continuity changes with gas pressure as shown below.**

Low Pressure Cut Side	<Reference> High Pressure Cut Side
ON (continuity) / OFF (no continuity) — 2 kgf/cm²	ON (continuity) / OFF (no continuity) — 27 kgf/cm²

OK — NG **Repair or replace harness or connector.**

3 **Check harness and connector between air conditioner control assembly and pressure switch, pressure switch and body ground**

OK — NG **Repair or replace harness or connector.**

Check and replace air conditioner control assembly.

IGNITER CIRCUIT DIAGNOSIS AND TESTING—LS 400

Igniter Circuit

CIRCUIT DESCRIPTION

The air conditioner control assembly monitors the engine speed through signals sent from the igniter. The air conditioner control assembly uses these signals and compressor speed signals to detect the compressor lock condition.

DIAGNOSTIC CHART

1 Check operation of tachometer. — NG → Proceed to combination meter troubleshooting

OK ↓

2 Check harness and connector between air conditioner control assembly and igniter — NG → Repair or replace harness or connector.

OK ↓

Proceed to next circuit inspection shown on matrix chart

WIRING DIAGRAM

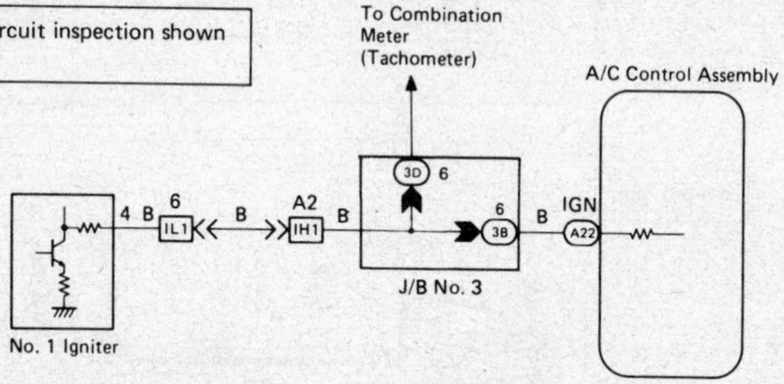
To Combination Meter (Tachometer)
A/C Control Assembly
4 B
6
IL1
B
A2
IH1
B
3D 6
6
3B
B
IGN
A22
J/B No. 3
No. 1 Igniter

IGNITER CIRCUIT INSPECTION PROCEDURE—LS 400

1 **Check operation of tachometer.**

P Check that the tachometer operates normally.

OK — NG **Proceed to combination meter troubleshooting**

2 **Check harness and connector between air conditioner control assembly and igniter**

OK — NG **Repair or replace harness or connector.**

Proceed to next circuit inspection shown on matrix chart

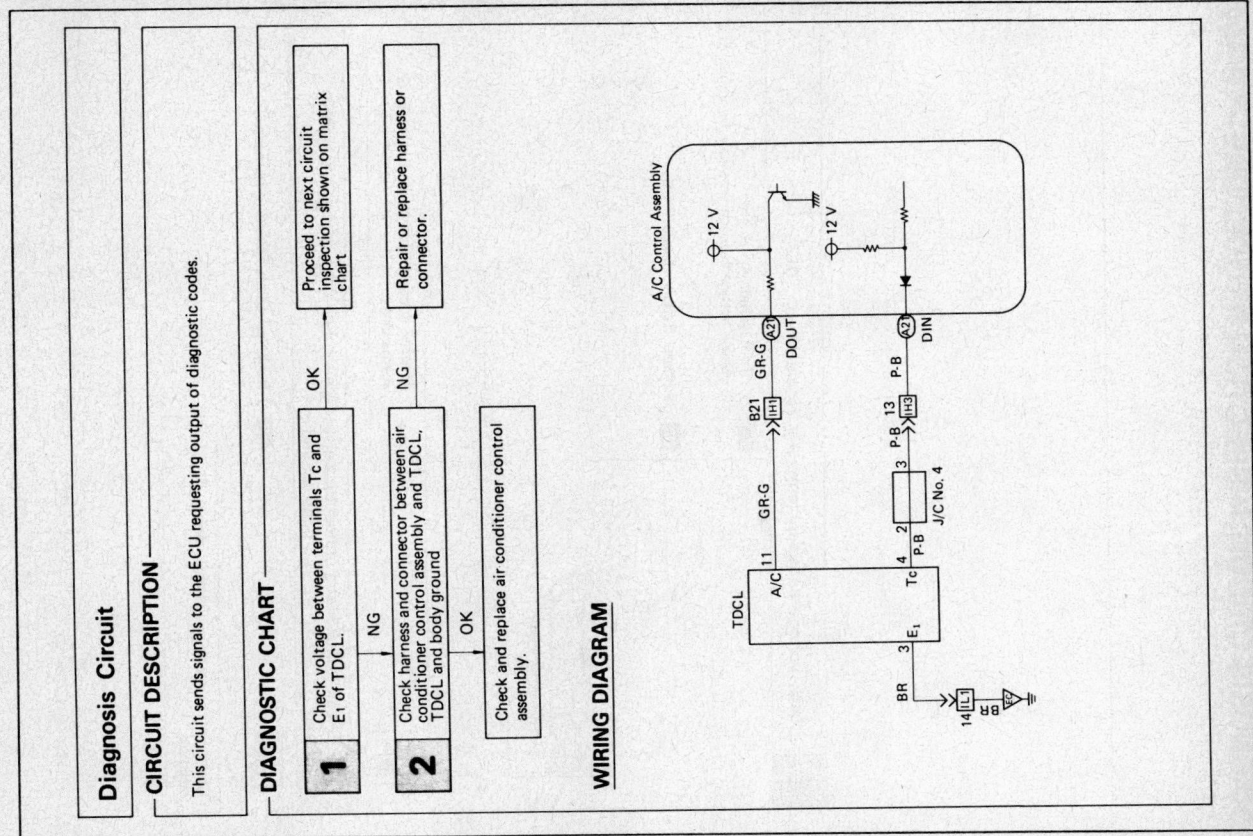

IGNITER CIRCUIT WIRING ROUTING—LS 400

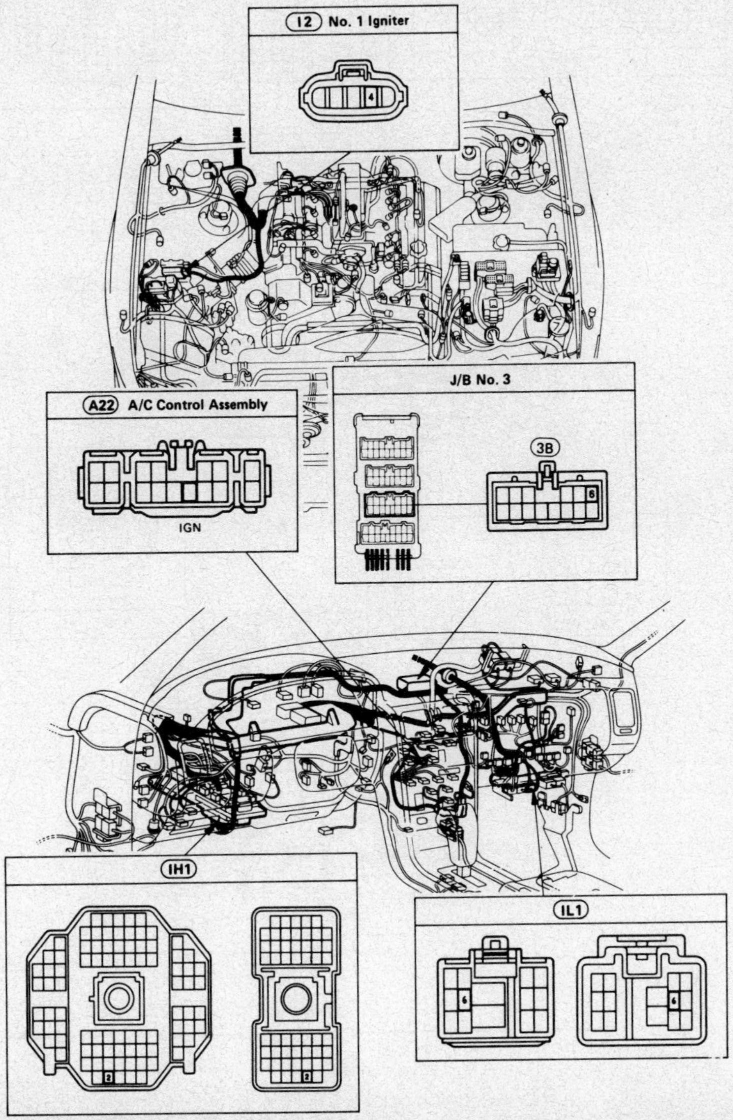
12 No. 1 Igniter
A22 A/C Control Assembly
IGN
J/B No. 3
3B
IH1
IL1

DIAGNOSIS CIRCUIT DIAGNOSIS AND TESTING—LS 400

Diagnosis Circuit

CIRCUIT DESCRIPTION

This circuit sends signals to the ECU requesting output of diagnostic codes.

DIAGNOSTIC CHART

Step	Check	Result	Action
1	Check voltage between terminals Tc and E_1 of TDCL.	OK	Proceed to next circuit inspection shown on matrix chart
		NG	Go to 2
2	Check harness and connector between air conditioner control assembly and TDCL, TDCL and body ground	NG	Repair or replace harness or connector.
		OK	Check and replace air conditioner control assembly.

WIRING DIAGRAM

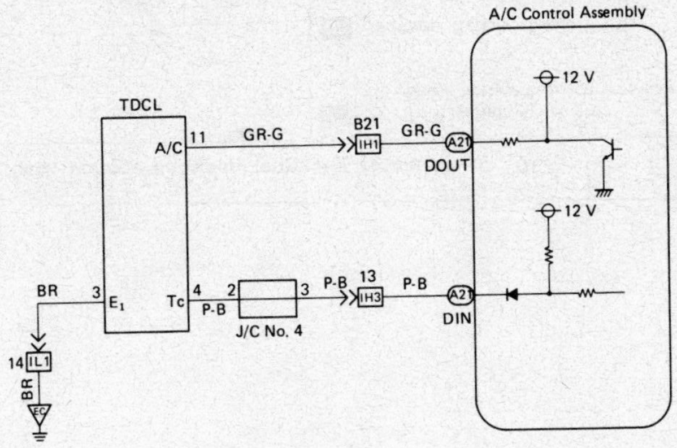
A/C Control Assembly
12 V
12 V
TDCL
A/C
11
GR-G
B21
IH1
GR-G
A21
DOUT
BR
3
E1
Tc
4
2
P-B
3
P-B
13
IH3
P-B
A21
DIN
J/C No. 4
14
IL1
BR
EC

DIAGNOSIS CIRCUIT WIRING ROUTING—LS 400

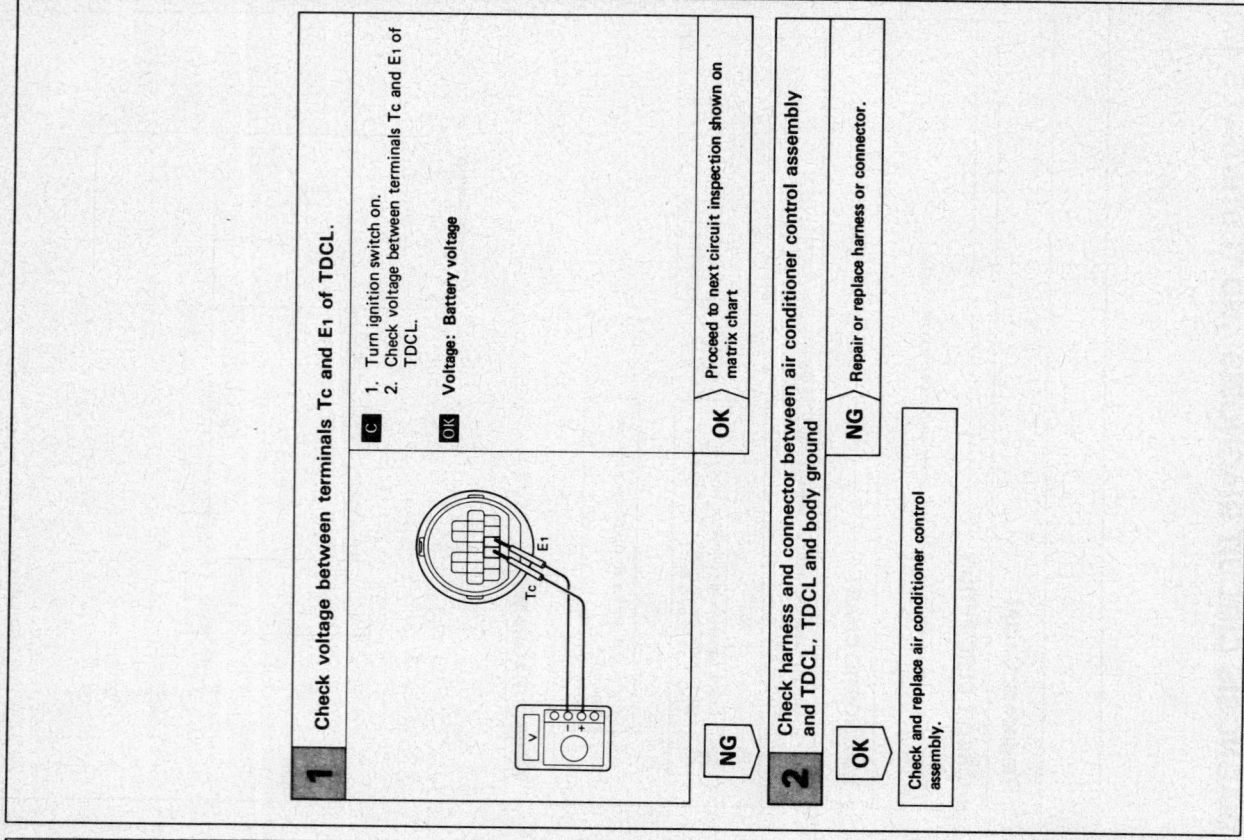

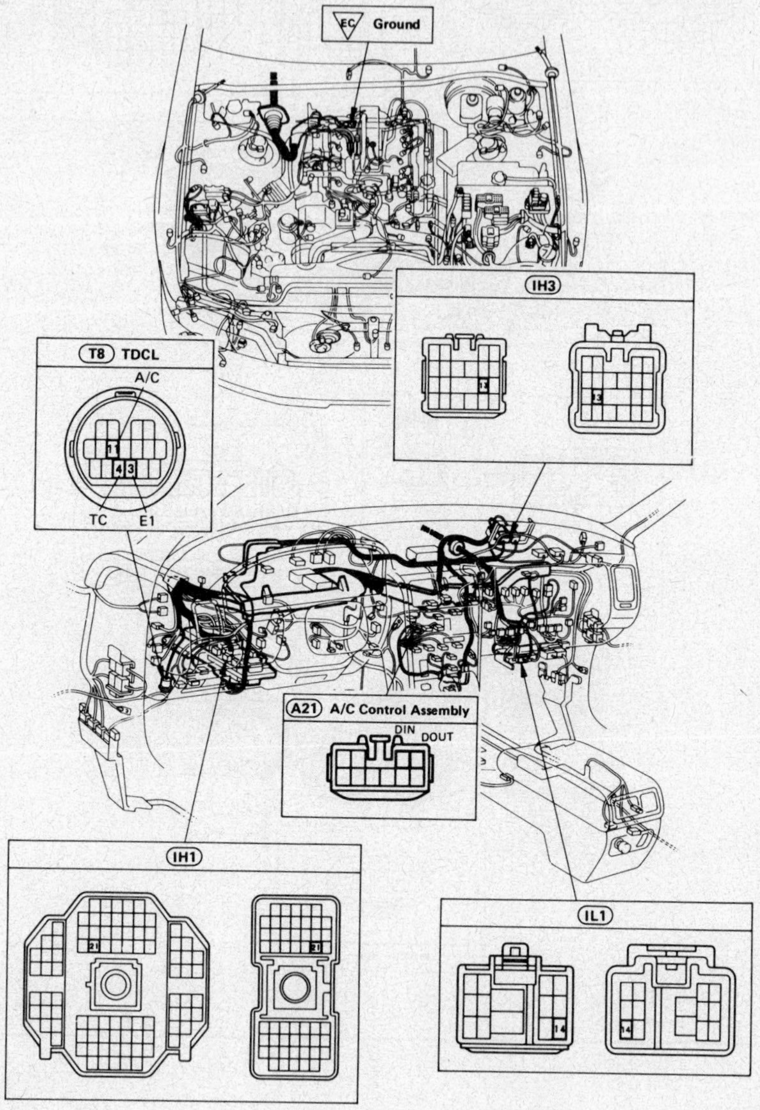
EC Ground
T8 TDCL
A/C
TC
E1
IH3
A21 A/C Control Assembly
DIN
DOUT
IH1
IL1

DIAGNOSIS CIRCUIT INSPECTION PROCEDURE—LS 400

1 **Check voltage between terminals Tc and E₁ of TDCL.**

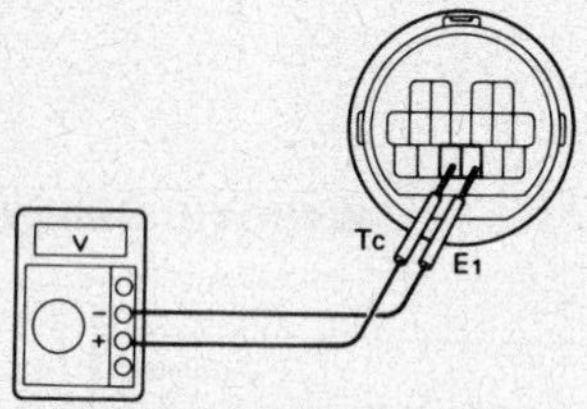
V
Tc
E1

C
1. Turn ignition switch on.
2. Check voltage between terminals Tc and E₁ of TDCL.

OK Voltage: Battery voltage

OK → Proceed to next circuit inspection shown on matrix chart

NG ↓

2 **Check harness and connector between air conditioner control assembly and TDCL, TDCL and body ground**

NG → Repair or replace harness or connector.

OK ↓

Check and replace air conditioner control assembly.

21 MAZDA 21

323 • 626 • 929 • MIATA • MX-6 • PROTEGE • RX-7

SPECIFICATIONS

ENGINE IDENTIFICATION

Year	Model	Engine Displacement cu. in. (cc/liter)	Engine Series Identification	No. of Cylinders	Engine Type
1989	323	97.4 (1597/1.6)	B6	4	SOHC
	323	97.4 (1597/1.6)	B6	4	DOHC
	626	133.2 (2184/2.1)	FZ	4	SOHC
	626	133.2 (2184/2.1)	F2	4	Turbo
	929	180.2 (2954/3.0)	JE	6	OHC
	MX-6	133.2 (2184/2.1)	F2	4	SOHC
	MX-6	133.2 (2184/2.1)	F2	4	SOHC
	RX7	80 (1380/1.3)	13B	—	Rotary
	RX7	80 (1380/1.3)	13B	—	Rotary-Turbo
1990	323	97.4 (1597/1.6)	B6	4	SOHC
	323/Protege	97.4 (1597/1.6)	BP	4	SOHC-16 valve
	323/Protege	112.2 (1839/1.8)	BP	4	DOHC
	626	133.2 (2184/2.1)	F2	4	SOHC
	626	133.2 (2184/2.1)	F2	4	Turbo
	929	180.2 (2954/3.0)	JE	6	OHC
	929	180.2 (2954/3.0)	JE	6	DOHC
	Miata	97.4 (1597/1.6)	B6	4	DOHC
	MX-6	133.2 (2184/2.1)	F2	4	SOHC
	MX-6	133.2 (2184/2.1)	F2	4	Turbo
	RX7	80 (1380/1.3)	13B	—	Rotary
	RX7	80 (1380/1.3)	13B	—	Rotary-Turbo
1991	323	97.4 (1597/1.6)	B6	4	SOHC
	323/Protege	97.4 (1597/1.6)	BP	4	SOHC-16 valve
	323/Protege	112.2 (1839/1.8)	BP	4	DOHC
	626	133.2 (2184/2.1)	F2	4	SOHC
	626	133.2 (2184/2.1)	F2	4	Turbo
	929	180.2 (2954/3.0)	JE	6	OHC
	929	180.2 (2954/3.0)	JE	6	DOHC
	Miata	97.4 (1597/1.6)	B6	4	DOHC
	MX6	133.2 (2184/2.1)	F2	4	SOHC
	MX6	133.2 (2184/2.1)	F2	4	Turbo
	RX7	80 (1380/1.3)	13B	—	Rotary
	RX7	80 (1380/1.3)	13B	—	Rotary-Turbo

REFRIGERANT CAPACITIES

Year	Model	Freon (oz.)	Oil (fl. oz.)	Type
1989	323	28.0	3.3–4.0	R-12
	626	33.5–37.1	3.3–4.0	R-12
	929	37.1–40.1	3.3–4.0	R-12
	MX6	33.5–37.1	3.3–4.0	R-12
	RX7	28.0	2.0–3.3	R-12/Nippon
	RX7	28.0	4.5	R-12/Sanden

REFRIGERANT CAPACITIES

Year	Model	Freon (oz.)	Oil (fl. oz.)	Type
1990	323/Protege	28.0	3.3–4.0	R-12
	626	33.5–37.1	3.3–4.0	R-12
	929	37.1–40.1	3.3–4.0	R-12
	Miata	28.0	2.7–3.3	R-12
	MX6	33.5–37.1	3.3–4.0	R-12
	RX7	28.0	2.0–3.3	R-12/Nippon
	RX7	28.0	4.5	R-12/Sanden
1991	323/Protege	28.0	3.3–4.0	R-12
	626	33.5–37.1	3.3–4.0	R-12
	929	37.1–40.1	3.3–4.0	R-12
	Miata	28.0	2.7–3.3	R-12
	MX6	33.5–37.1	3.3–4.0	R-12
	RX7	28.0	2.0–3.3	R-12/Nippon
	RX7	28.0	4.5	R-12/Sanden

AIR CONDITIONING BELT TENSION CHART

Year	Model	Engine Displacement cu. in. (cc/liter)	Belt Type	New ①	Used ①
1989	323	97.4 (1597/1.6)	V-Belt	0.31–0.35	0.35–0.39
	323	97.4 (1597/1.6)	V-Belt	0.31–0.35	0.35–0.39
	626	133.2 (2184/2.1)	V-Belt	0.27–0.35	0.31–0.39
	626	133.2 (2184/2.1)	V-Belt	0.27–0.35	0.31–0.39
	929	180.2 (2954/3.0)	V-Belt	0.28–0.35	0.35–0.43
	MX6	133.2 (2184/2.1)	V-Belt	0.27–0.35	0.31–0.39
	MX6	133.2 (2184/2.1)	V-Belt	0.27–0.35	0.31–0.39
	RX7	80 (1380/1.3)	V-Belt	0.24–0.31	0.31–0.39
	RX7	80 (1380/1.3)	V-Belt	0.24–0.31	0.31–0.39
1990	323	97.4 (1597/1.6)	V-Belt	0.31–0.35	0.35–0.39
	323/Protege	97.4 (1597/1.6)	V-Belt	0.31–0.35	0.35–0.39
	323/Protege	112.2 (1839/1.8)	V-Belt	0.31–0.35	0.35–0.39
	626	133.2 (2184/2.1)	V-Belt	0.27–0.35	0.31–0.39
	626	133.2 (2184/2.1)	V-Belt	0.27–0.35	0.31–0.39
	929	180.2 (2954/3.0)	V-Belt	0.28–0.35	0.35–0.43
	929	180.2 (2954/3.0)	V-Belt	0.28–0.35	0.35–0.43
	Miata	97.4 (1597/1.6)	V-Belt	0.31–0.35	0.35–0.39
	MX6	133.2 (2184/2.1)	V-Belt	0.27–0.35	0.31–0.39
	MX6	133.2 (2184/2.1)	V-Belt	0.27–0.35	0.31–0.39
	RX7	80 (1380/1.3)	V-Belt	0.24–0.31	0.31–0.35
	RX7	80 (1380/1.3)	V-Belt	0.24–0.31	0.31–0.35
1991	323	97.4 (1597/1.6)	V-Belt	0.31–0.35	0.35–0.39
	323/Protege	97.4 (1597/1.6)	V-Belt	0.31–0.35	0.35–0.39
	323/Protege	112.2 (1839/1.8)	V-Belt	0.31–0.35	0.35–0.39
	626	133.2 (2184/2.1)	V-Belt	0.27–0.35	0.31–0.39
	626	133.2 (2184/2.1)	V-Belt	0.27–0.35	0.31–0.39

AIR CONDITIONING BELT TENSION CHART

Year	Model	Engine Displacement cu. in. (cc/liter)	Belt Type	New ①	Used ①
1991	929	180.2 (2954/3.0)	V-Belt	0.28–0.35	0.35–0.43
	929	180.2 (2954/3.0)	V-Belt	0.28–0.35	0.35–0.43
	Miata	97.4 (1597/1.6)	V-Belt	0.31–0.35	0.35–0.39
	MX6	133.2 (2184/2.1)	V-Belt	0.27–0.35	0.31–0.39
	MX6	133.2 (2184/2.1)	V-Belt	0.27–0.35	0.31–0.39
	RX7	80 (1380/1.3)	V-Belt	0.24–0.31	0.31–0.35
	RX7	80 (1380/1.3)	V-Belt	0.24–0.31	0.31–0.35

① Inches of deflection at midpoint of belt using 22 lbs. of force.

SYSTEM DESCRIPTION

General Information

The heater unit is located in the center of the vehicle along the firewall. The heater system is a bi-level system designed to direct warm air through the vents to either the windshield or the floor and cool air through the panel outlet. The air conditioning system is designed to be activated in combination with a separate air conditioning switch installed in the control assembly and the fan speed switch. The system incorporates a compressor, condenser, evaporator, receiver/drier, pressure switch, expansion valve, thermo-switch, refrigerant lines and some models are equipped with an electronic control head assembly versus the standard cable operated control head. The 929 model utilizes a self diagnostic program built into the control head assembly.

Service Valve Location

Charging valve locations will vary, but most of the time the high or low pressure fitting will be located at the compressor, receiver/drier or along the refrigerant lines. Always discharge, evacuate and recharge at the low side service fitting.

System Discharging

R-12 refrigerant is a chloroflourocarbon which, when mishandled, can contribute to the depletion on the ozone layer in the upper atmosphere. Ozone filters out harmful radiation from the sun. In order to protect the ozone layer, an approved R-12 Recovery/Recycling machine that meets SAE standard J1991 should be employed when discharging the system. Follow the

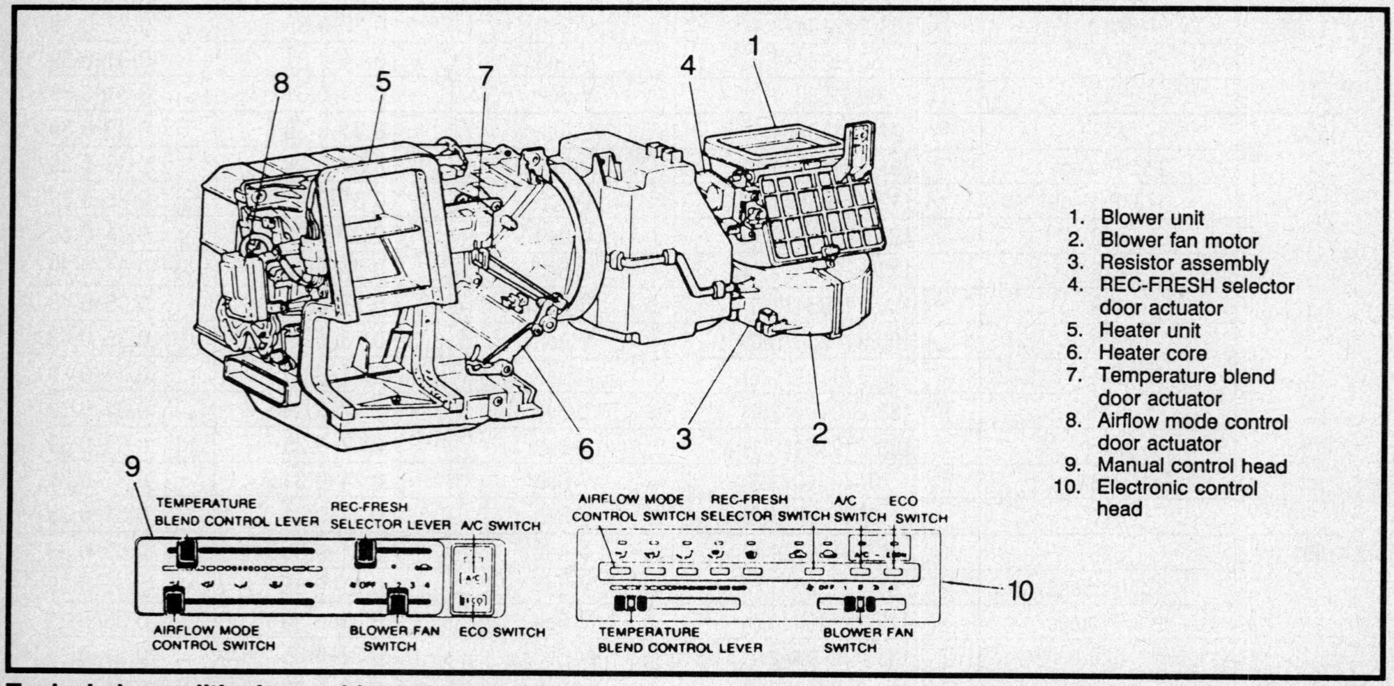
1
2
3
4
5
6
7
8
9
10
TEMPERATURE BLEND CONTROL LEVER
REC-FRESH SELECTOR LEVER
A/C SWITCH
AIRFLOW MODE CONTROL SWITCH
BLOWER FAN SWITCH
ECO SWITCH
AIRFLOW MODE CONTROL SWITCH
REC-FRESH SELECTOR SWITCH
A/C SWITCH
ECO SWITCH
TEMPERATURE BLEND CONTROL LEVER
BLOWER FAN SWITCH
1. Blower unit
2. Blower fan motor
3. Resistor assembly
4. REC-FRESH selector door actuator
5. Heater unit
6. Heater core
7. Temperature blend door actuator
8. Airflow mode control door actuator
9. Manual control head
10. Electronic control head

Typical air conditioning and heater assembly

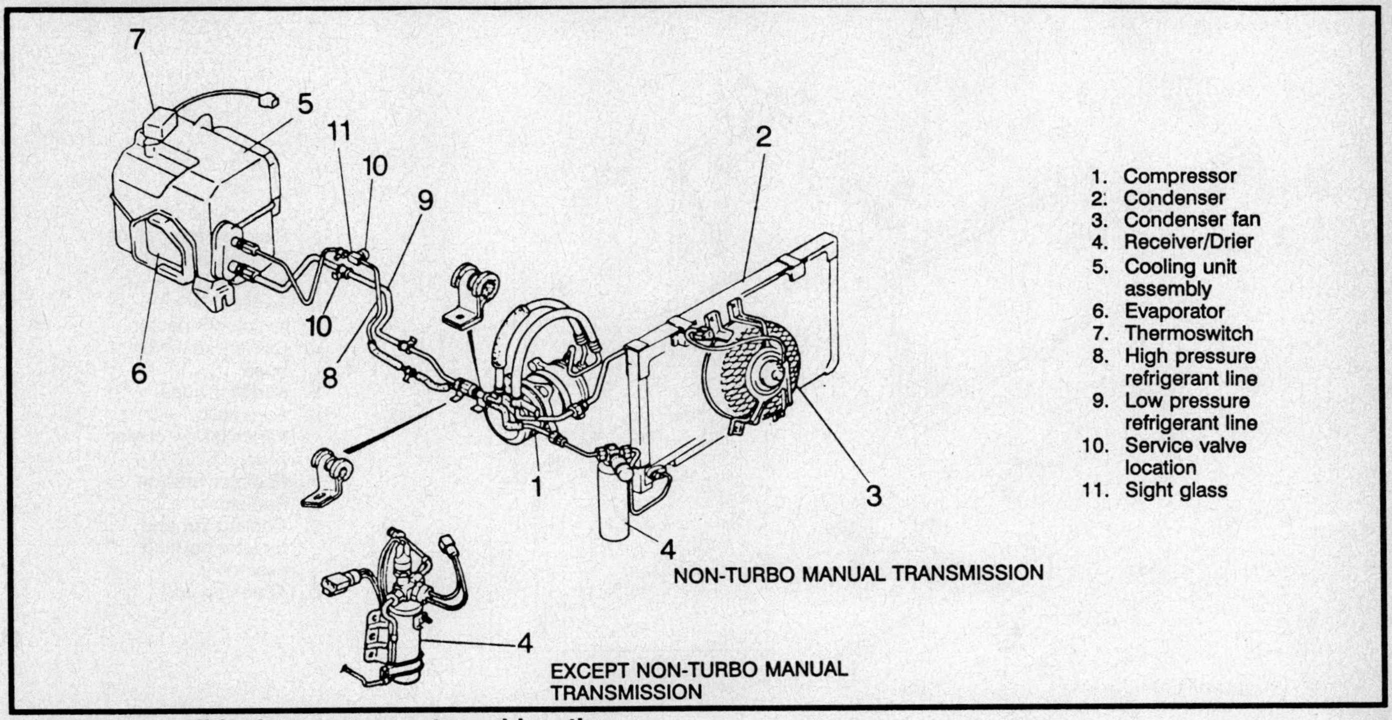
7
5
11
10
9
2
10
6
8
1
3
4
NON-TURBO MANUAL TRANSMISSION
4
EXCEPT NON-TURBO MANUAL TRANSMISSION
1. Compressor
2. Condenser
3. Condenser fan
4. Receiver/Drier
5. Cooling unit assembly
6. Evaporator
7. Thermoswitch
8. High pressure refrigerant line
9. Low pressure refrigerant line
10. Service valve location
11. Sight glass

Typical air conditioning components and location

operating instructions provided with the approved equipment exactly to properly discharge the system.

System Evacuating

If the air conditioning system has been opened to the atmosphere, it should be air and moisture free before being recharged with refrigerant. Moisture and air mixed with refrigerant will raise the compressor head pressure, possibly damage the system's components and will reduce the performance of the system. Moisture will boil at normal room temperature when exposed to a vacuum, the moisture then becomes a vapor and will be easily removed by the vacuum pump.

To evacuate, or rid the system of air and moisture:

1. Leak test the system and repair any leaks found.
2. Connect an approved charging station, Recovery/Recycling machine or manifold gauge set and vacuum pump to the discharge and suction ports. The red hose is normally connected to the discharge (high pressure) line, and the blue hose is connected to the suction (low pressure) line.
3. Open the discharge and suction ports and start the vacuum pump. If the pump is not able to pull at least 26 in. Hg vacuum, there is a leak that must be repaired before evacuation can occur.
4. Once the system has reached at least 26 in. Hg vacuum, allow the system to evacuate for at least 10 minutes. The longer the system is evacuated, the more contaminants will be removed.
5. Close all valves and turn the pump off. If the system loses more than 2 in. Hg vacuum after 15 minutes, there is a leak that should be repaired.

System Charging

1. Connect an approved charging station, Recovery/Recycling machine or manifold gauge set to the discharge and suction ports. The red hose is normally connected to the discharge (high pressure) line, and the blue hose is connected to the suction (low pressure) line.
2. Follow the instructions provided with the equipment and charge the system with the specified amount of refrigerant.
3. Perform a leak test.

SYSTEM COMPONENTS

CAUTION

Some vehicles are equipped with the Supplemental Inflatable Restraint or air bag system. The air bag system must be disabled by disconnecting the battery negative terminal and the orange–blue connector located near steering wheel before performing service on or around the air bag, instrument panel components, wiring and sensors. Failure to follow safety and disabling procedures could result in accidental air bag deployment, possible personal injury and unnecessary air bag system repairs.

Radiator

REMOVAL AND INSTALLATION

Except RX-7

1. Disconnect the negative terminal at the battery.
2. Drain the cooling system.
3. Disconnect the coolant reservoir hose.
4. Remove the fresh air duct, if equipped.
5. Remove the upper and lower radiator hoses.

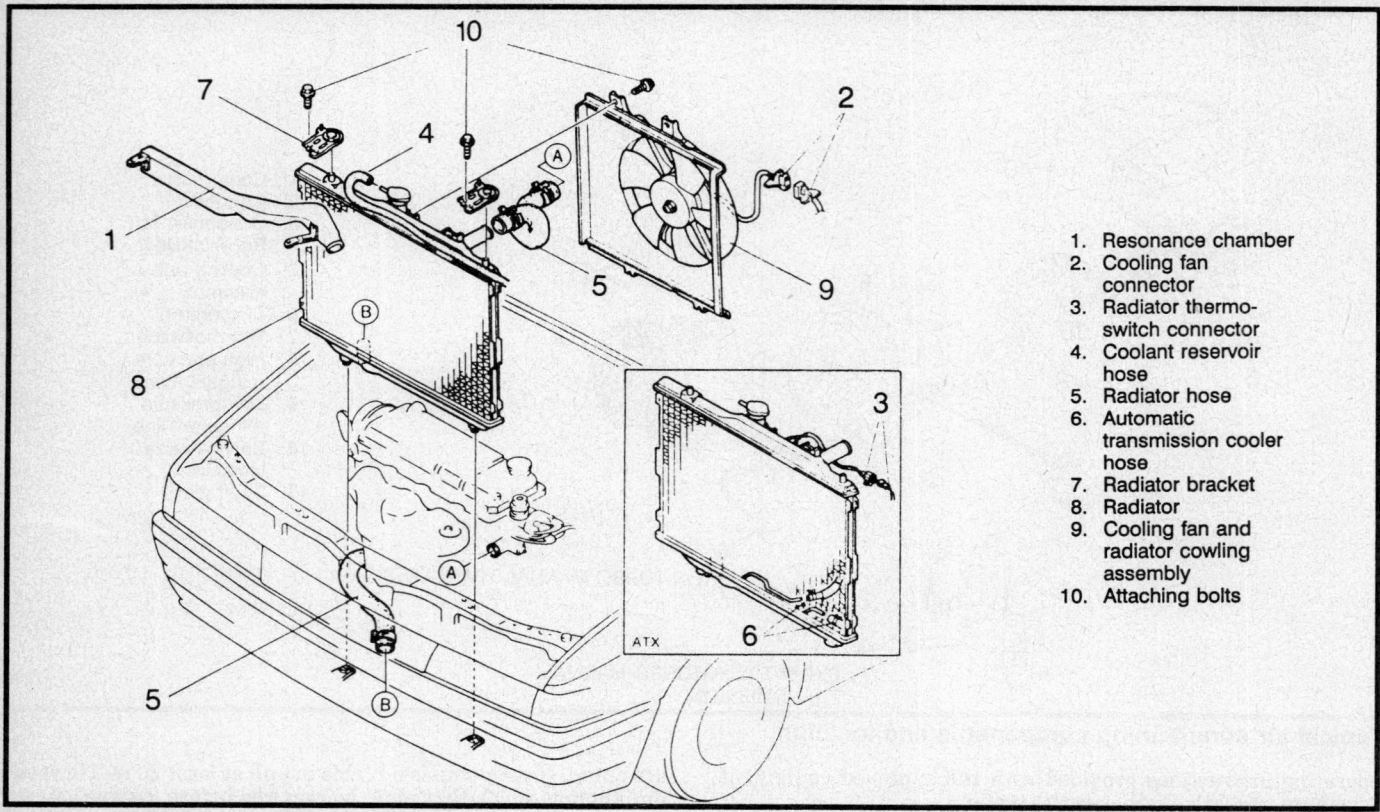

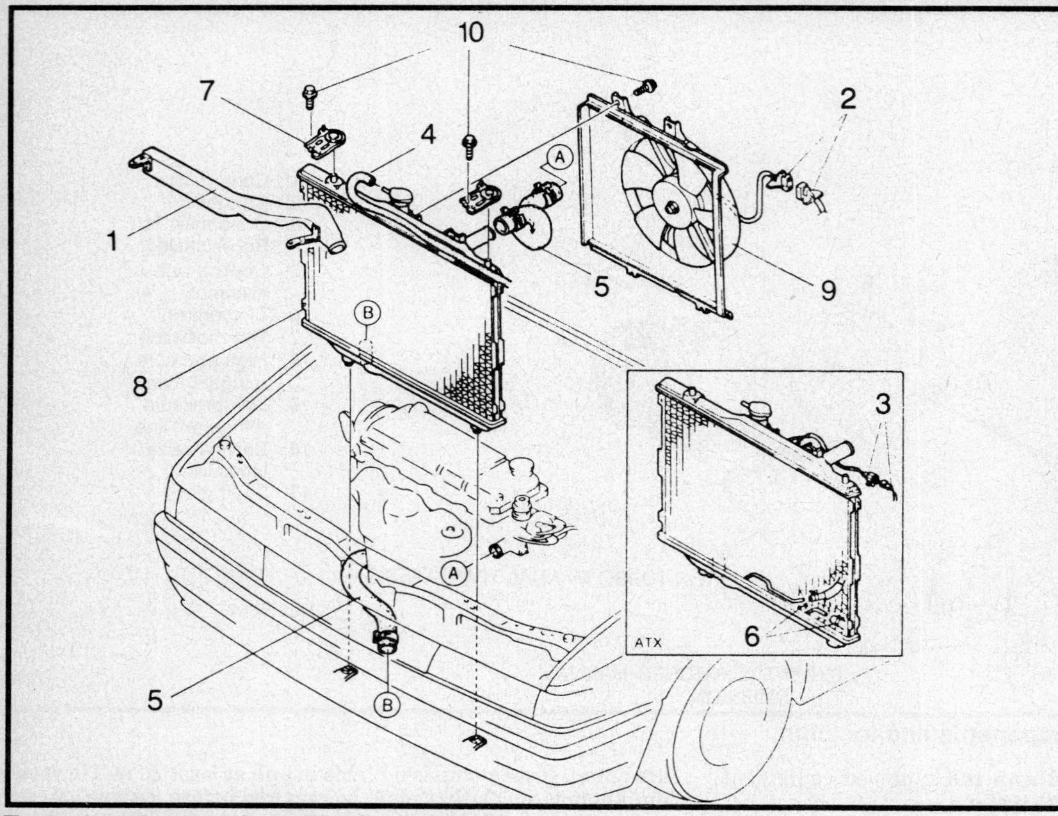
10
7
4
2
1
5
9
8
3
ATX
6
5
A
B
1. Resonance chamber
2. Cooling fan connector
3. Radiator thermo-switch connector
4. Coolant reservoir hose
5. Radiator hose
6. Automatic transmission cooler hose
7. Radiator bracket
8. Radiator
9. Cooling fan and radiator cowling assembly
10. Attaching bolts

Typical radiator and cooling fan assembly

6. Disconnect electric fan and thermoswitch wire connector, if equipped.
7. Remove electric fan or clutch fan and cowling assembly.
8. Disconnect and plug automatic transmission cooler lines, if equipped.
9. Remove radiator mounting brackets and bolts.
10. Remove radiator assembly.

To install

11. Install the radiator assembly.
12. Install the radiator mounting brackets and bolts.
13. Connect and automatic transmission cooler lines, if equipped.
14. Install the electric or clutch fan and cowling assembly.
15. Install the upper and lower radiator hoses.
16. Install the fresh air duct, if equipped.
17. Connect the coolant reservoir hose.
18. Refill radiator with specified type and quantity of coolant.
13. Check the automatic transmission fluid level, if equipped.
14. Check cooling system for leaks.
15. Reconnect the negative battery terminal.

RX-7

1. Disconnect the battery terminals and remove the battery.
2. Remove battery support bracket and tray.
3. Drain the cooling system.
4. Remove fresh air intake duct.
5. Remove upper, lower and heater hose at radiator.
6. Disconnect level sensor connector on radiator.
7. Disconnect and plug automatic transmission lines, if equipped.
8. Remove the clutch fan assembly.
9. Remove the radiator fan cowling.
10. Remove the radiator filler neck.
11. Unbolt and remove the radiator assembly.

To install

11. Install the radiator assembly.
12. Install the clutch fan assembly.
13. Connect and plug automatic transmission lines, if equipped.
14. Install the upper, lower and heater hose at radiator.
15. Refill the radiator with specified type and quantity of coolant.
16. Check the automatic transmission fluid level, if equipped.
17. Check the cooling system for leaks.
18. Install the fresh air intake duct.
19. Install the battery support bracket and tray.
20. Install the battery and connect the battery terminals.
21. Refill the radiator with the specified type and quantity of coolant.
22. Check the cooling system for leaks.

Cooling Fan

TESTING

323 and Miata

SINGLE SPEED FAN

1. Attach a jumper wire across the fan test (TFA) terminal and the ground (GND) terminal of the diagnosis connector.
2. Turn the ignition switch **ON** and verify that the fan operates; if the fan does not operate, inspect the cooling fan system components and the wiring harness.

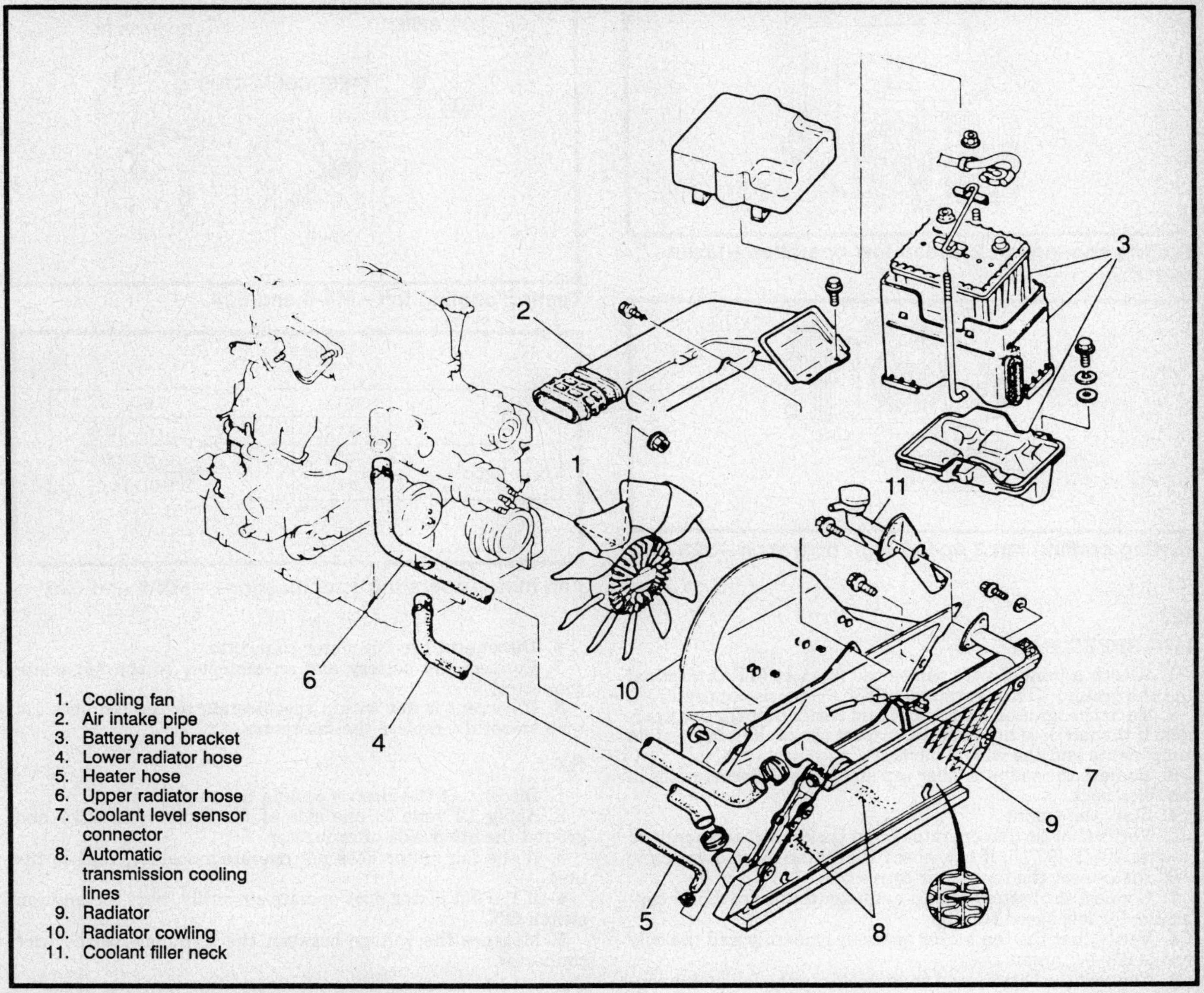
1. Cooling fan
2. Air intake pipe
3. Battery and bracket
4. Lower radiator hose
5. Heater hose
6. Upper radiator hose
7. Coolant level sensor connector
8. Automatic transmission cooling lines
9. Radiator
10. Radiator cowling
11. Coolant filler neck

Radiator and cooling fan removal—RX-7

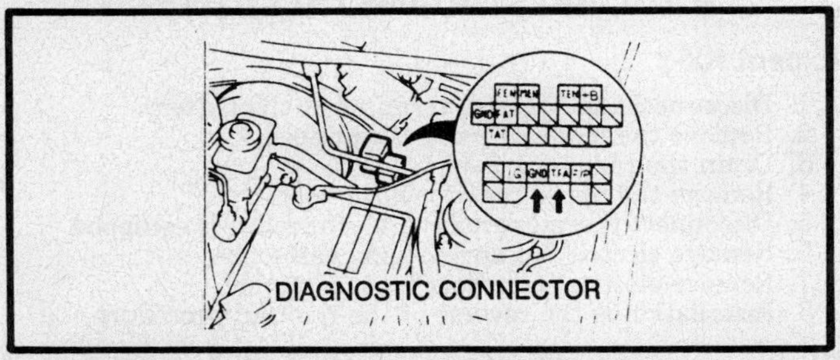
DIAGNOSTIC CONNECTOR

Cooling fan test terminal—323, 626 and MX-6

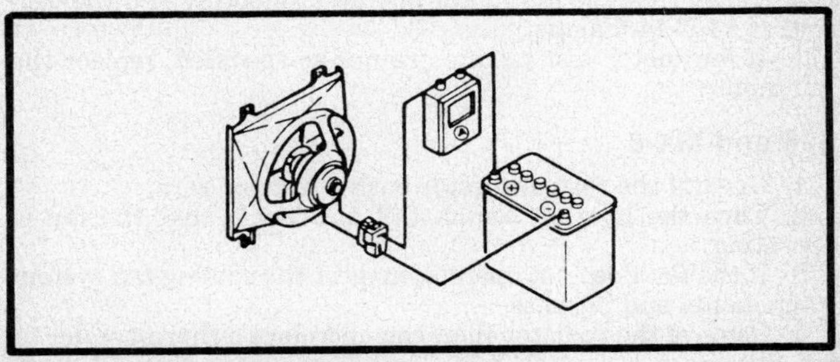

Typical radiator testing procedure

3. Remove the radiator filler cap and place a thermometer in the filler neck.
4. Start the engine.
5. Verify that the fan operates when the coolant temperature reaches 207°F (97°C), if not, check the water thermo-switch.
6. Disconnect the fan motor connector.
7. Connect the battery and an ammeter to the fan motor connector.
8. Verify that current is 5.3–6.5 amps.
9. If current is not within specification or the fan does not turn smoothly, replace the fan motor.

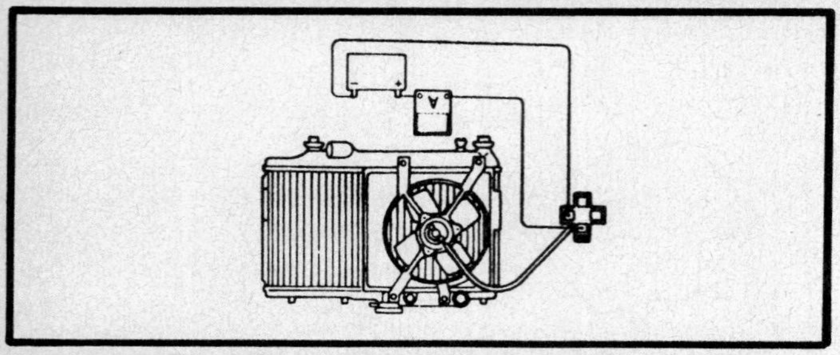

Testing cooling fan 2 speed low operation—Miata and 323

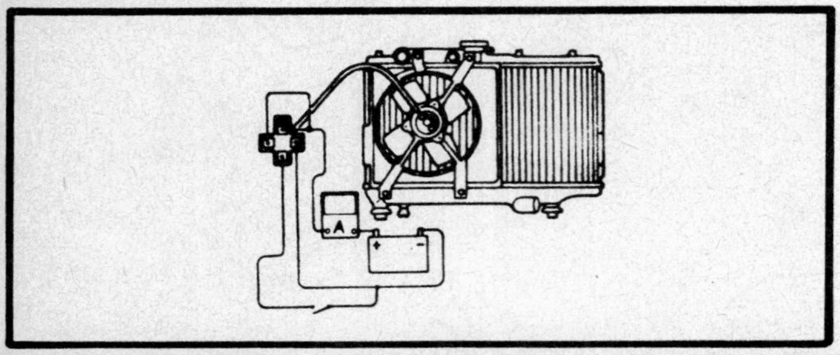

Testing cooling fan 2 speed high operation—323 only

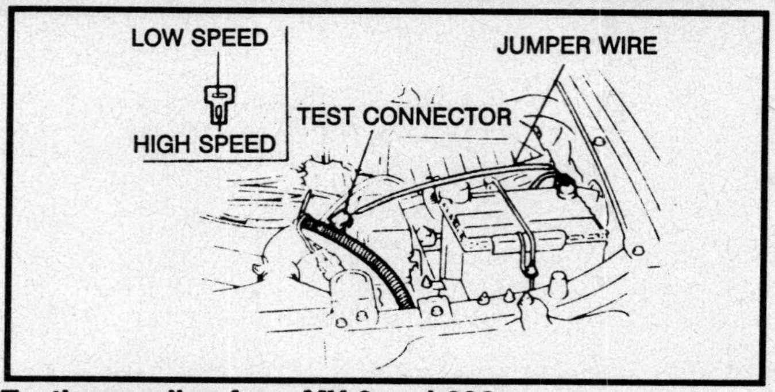
LOW SPEED
HIGH SPEED
TEST CONNECTOR
JUMPER WIRE

Testing cooling fan—MX-6 and 626

Turbo	MTX	5.6—7.6
	ATX	10.6—16.6
Non-Turbo	MTX	5.6—7.6
	ATX	8.0—11.0

Fan motor operating specifications—MX-6 and 626

323

TWO SPEED FAN

1. Attach a jumper wire across the fan test (TFA) terminal and the ground (GND) terminal of the diagnosis connector.
2. Turn the ignition switch **ON** and verify that the fan operates; if the fan does not operate, inspect the cooling fan system components and the wiring harness.
3. Remove the radiator filler cap and place a thermometer in the filler neck.
4. Start the engine.
5. Verify that the fan operates when the coolant temperature reaches 207°F (97°C), if not, check the water thermo-switch.
6. Disconnect the fan motor connector.
7. Connect the battery and an ammeter to the fan motor connectors for low speed testing.
8. Verify that the fan motor operates smoothly and the current is 8.8–9.7 amps.
9. Connect the battery and an ammeter to the fan motor connection for high speed testing.
10. Verify that the fan motor operates smoothly and the current is 13.3–14.6 amps.
11. If fan motor test results are not as specified, replace the fan motor.

626 and MX-6

1. Ground the test connector with a jumper wire.
2. Turn the ignition switch **ON** and verify that the fan is operating.
3. If the fan does not operate, inspect the cooling fan system components and harness.
4. Remove the radiator filler cap and place a thermometer in the filler neck.
4. Start the engine.
5. Verify that the fan operates when the coolant temperature reaches 207°F (97°C), if not, check the water thermoswitch.

NOTE: If equipped with automatic transmission, the above procedure cannot be used to test the high speed fan operation. The high speed operation requires 226°F (108°C) or above.

6. Disconnect the fan motor connector.
7. Connect the battery and an ammeter to the fan motor connector.
8. If current is not within specification or the fan does not turn smoothly, replace the fan motor.

RX-7

1. Disconnect the electric cooling fan connector.
2. Apply 12 volts to one side of fan motor connector and ground the other side of connector.
3. If the fan motor does not operate smoothly, replace the unit.
4. If the fan motor does operate smoothly, turn the ignition switch **ON**.
5. Measure the voltage between the terminals of the wire connector.

REMOVAL AND INSTALLATION

Except RX-7

1. Disconnect the negative terminal at the battery.
2. Remove the fresh air duct, if equipped.
3. Drain the radiator coolant.
4. Remove the upper radiator hose.
5. Disconnect thermoswitch wire connector, if equipped.
6. Remove electric fan and cowling assembly.
7. Remove electric fan motor from assembly.
8. Installation is the reverse of the removal procedure.

RX-7

1. Disconnect the negative battery terminal.
2. Properly discharge the air conditioning system.
3. Remove the coolant reservoir tank.
4. Remove the plastic clips and the upper duct covers.
5. Remove the hood lock assembly.
6. Remove the electric cooling fan.
7. Installation is the reverse of the removal procedure.

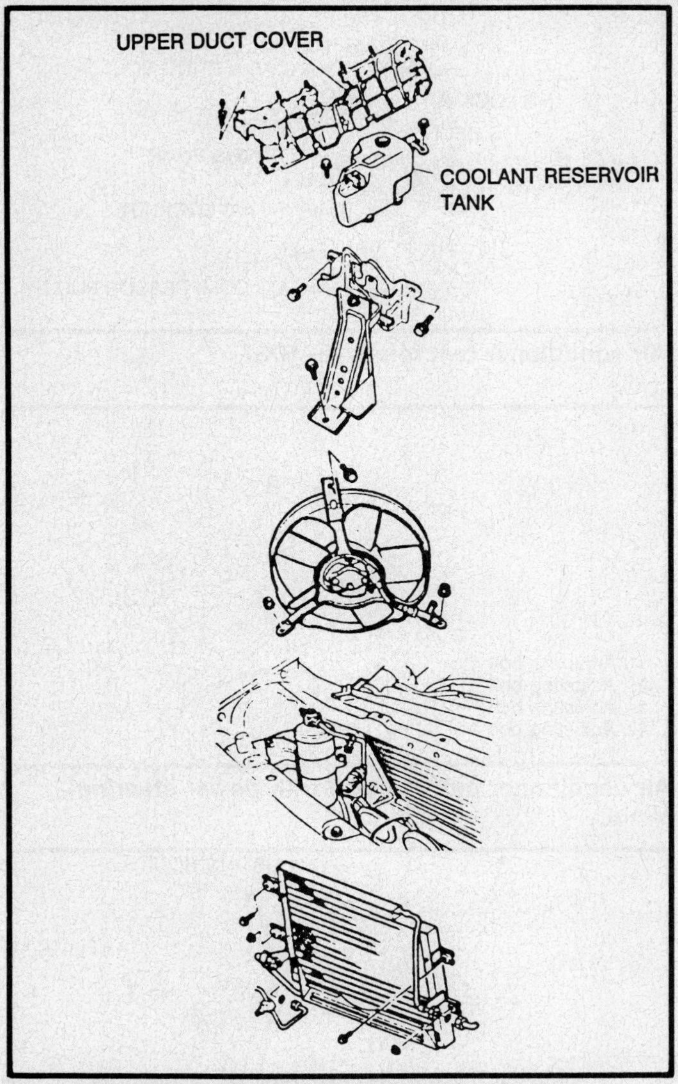
UPPER DUCT COVER
COOLANT RESERVOIR TANK

Fan, condenser and receiver/drier removal – RX-7

Condenser

REMOVAL AND INSTALLATION

Except Miata and RX-7

1. Disconnect the negative battery terminal.
2. Properly discharge the air conditioning system.
3. Remove the radiator grille.
4. Remove the air seal cover, if equipped.
5. Disconnect the refrigerant lines at condenser.
6. Remove the receiver/drier, if required.
7. Remove the radiator support brackets.
8. Cover radiator fins to avoid damage.
9. Lift radiator and push toward front of engine, if required.
10. Remove condenser mounting bolts.
11. Remove the condenser.
12. Installation is the reverse of removal.

Miata

1. Disconnect the negative battery terminal.
2. Properly discharge the air conditioning system.
3. Raise and support the vehicle safely.
4. Remove the splash shield and air guide.
5. Disconnect and plug the refrigerant lines at receiver/drier and condenser.
6. Unbolt condenser assembly.
7. Remove receiver/drier and condenser as an assembly.
8. Unbolt receiver/drier and remove from condenser.
9. Installation is the reverse of the removal procedure.

RX-7

1. Disconnect the negative battery terminal.
2. Properly discharge the air conditioning system.
3. Remove the coolant reservoir tank.
4. Remove the plastic clips and the upper duct covers.
5. Remove the hood lock assembly.
6. Remove the electric cooling fan.
7. Disconnect the refrigerant lines.
8. Remove the receiver/drier.
9. Remove condenser mounting bolts.
10. Remove the condenser.
11. Installation is the reverse of the removal procedure.

Compressor

REMOVAL AND INSTALLATION

Except 323 and Miata

1. Disconnect the negative battery terminal.
2. Properly discharge the air conditioning system.
3. On RX-7, remove the battery and battery box.
4. Disconnect the magnetic clutch wire connector.
5. Loosen the locknut and adjusting bolts and remove the compressor belt.
6. Disconnect and plug refrigerant lines at the compressor.
7. Remove compressor mounting bolts and remove compressor.
8. Installation is the reverse of the removal procedure.

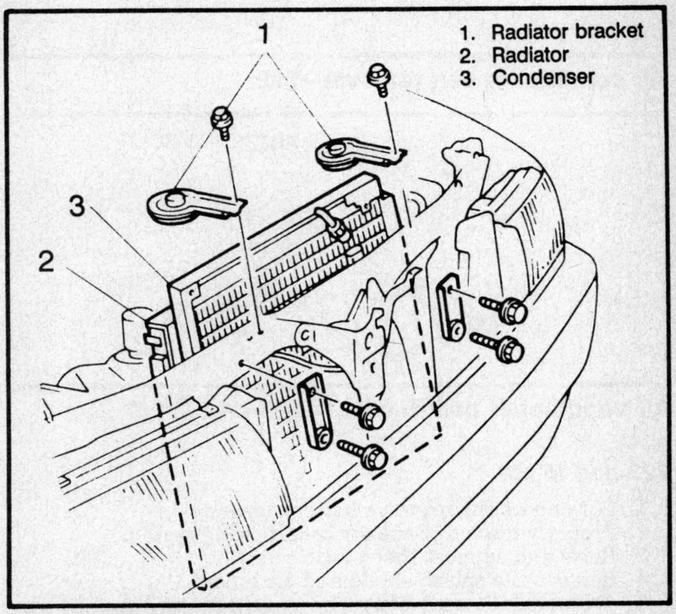
1
2
3
1. Radiator bracket
2. Radiator
3. Condenser

Typical condenser removal

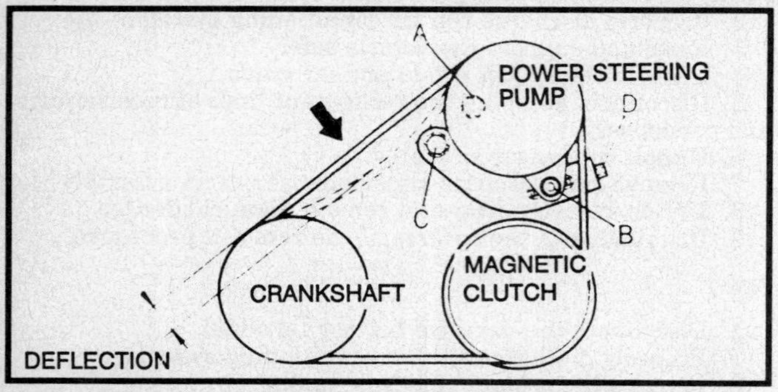
A
POWER STEERING PUMP
D
C
B
MAGNETIC CLUTCH
CRANKSHAFT
DEFLECTION

Air conditioner belt removal with power steering—323

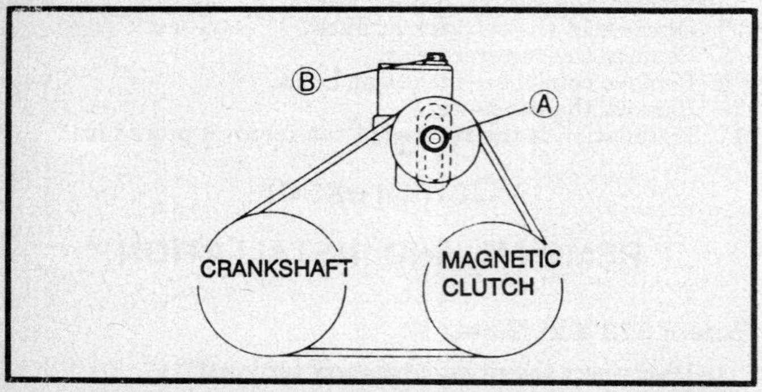
B
A
CRANKSHAFT
MAGNETIC CLUTCH

Air conditioner belt removal without power steering—323

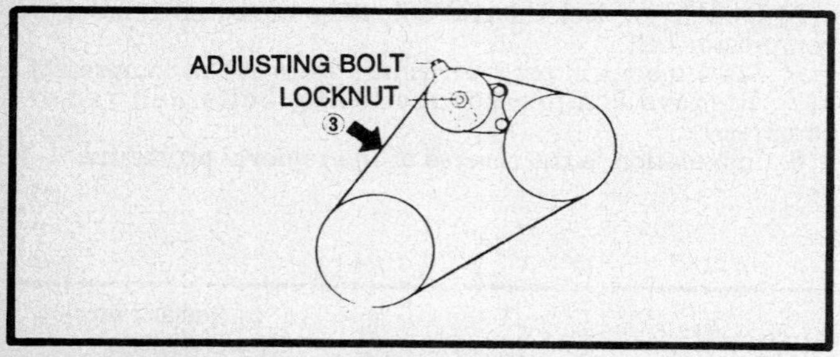
ADJUSTING BOLT
LOCKNUT
3

Air conditioner belt removal—929

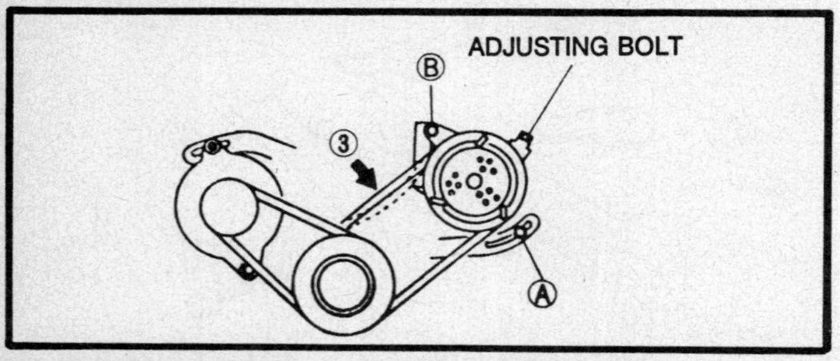
ADJUSTING BOLT
B
3
A

Air conditioner belt removal—626 and MX-6

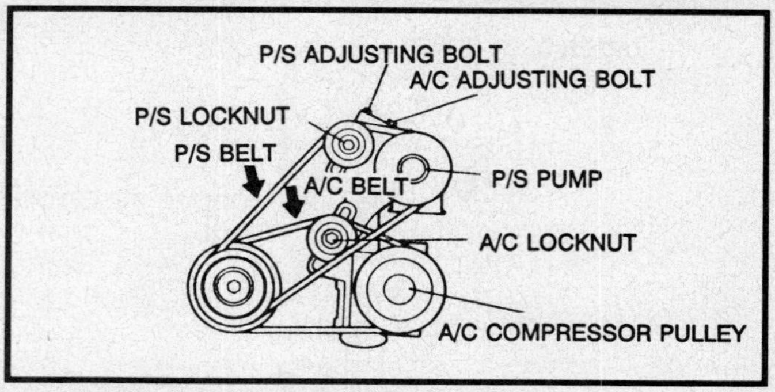
P/S ADJUSTING BOLT
A/C ADJUSTING BOLT
P/S LOCKNUT
P/S BELT
A/C BELT
P/S PUMP
A/C LOCKNUT
A/C COMPRESSOR PULLEY

Air conditioner belt removal—RX-7

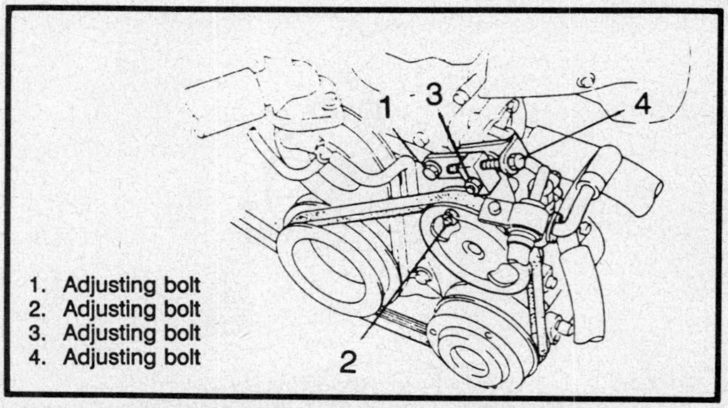
1
3
4
2
1. Adjusting bolt
2. Adjusting bolt
3. Adjusting bolt
4. Adjusting bolt

Air conditioner belt removal with power steering—Miata

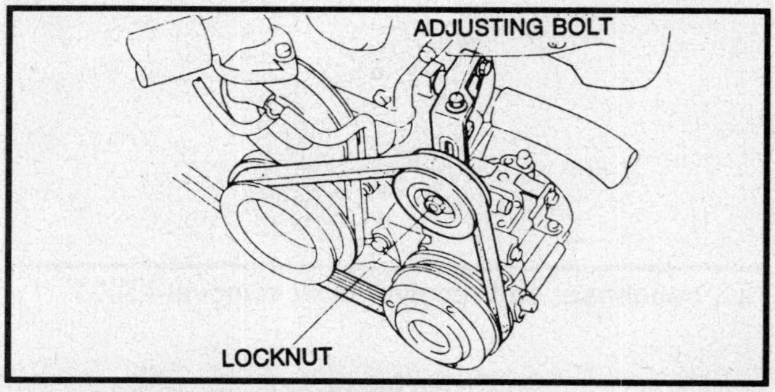
ADJUSTING BOLT
LOCKNUT

Air conditioner belt removal—Miata

323 and Miata

1. Disconnect the negative battery terminal.
2. Properly discharge the air conditioning system.
3. Raise and support the vehicle safely.
4. Remove the splash shield and air guide.
5. Disconnect and plug the refrigerant lines at the compressor.
6. Disconnect the magnetic clutch wire connector.
7. Remove compressor belt.
8. Unbolt and remove the air conditioning compressor.
9. Installation is the reverse of the removal procedure.

Receiver/Drier

REMOVAL AND INSTALLATION

Except Miata and RX-7

1. Disconnect the negative battery terminal.
2. Properly discharge the air conditioning system.
3. Remove the radiator grille.
4. Disconnect the refrigerant lines at the receiver/drier.
5. Disconnect the pressure switch wire connector, if equipped.

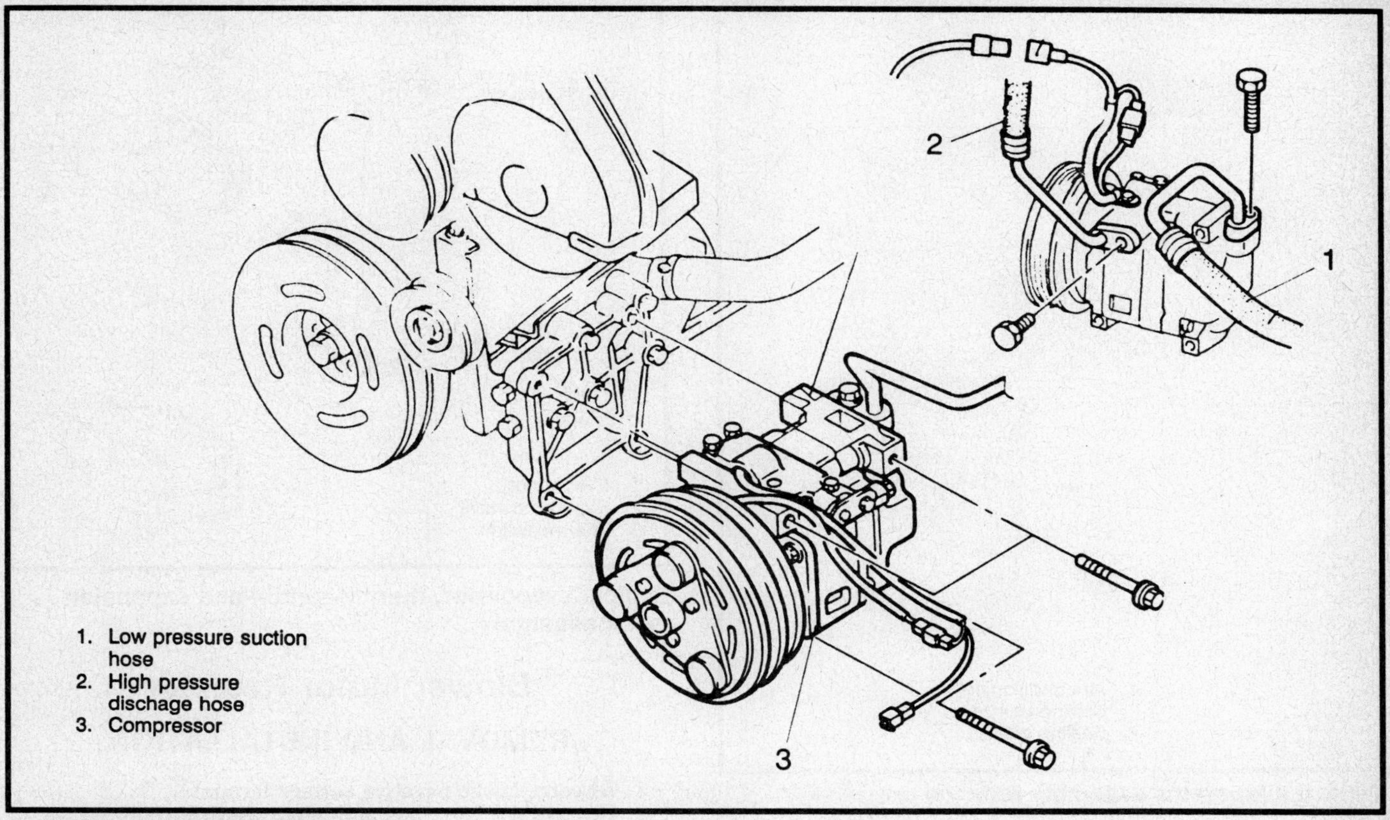
1. Low pressure suction hose
2. High pressure dischage hose
3. Compressor
1
2
3

Typical compressor removal

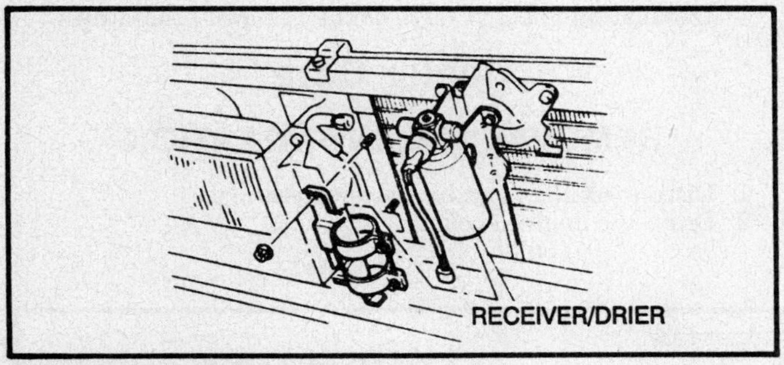
RECEIVER/DRIER

Typical receiver/drier removal

6. Remove attaching bolts at receiver/drier.
7. Remove the receiver/drier.
8. Installation is the reverse of removal.

Miata

1. Disconnect the negative battery terminal.
2. Properly discharge the air conditioning system.
3. Raise and support the vehicle safely.
4. Remove the splash shield and air guide.
5. Disconnect and plug the refrigerant lines at receiver/drier and condenser.
6. Unbolt condenser assembly.
7. Remove receiver/drier and condenser as an assembly.
8. Unbolt receiver/drier and remove from condenser.
9. Installation is the reverse of the removal procedure.

RX-7

1. Disconnect the negative battery terminal.
2. Properly discharge the air conditioning system.
3. Remove the coolant reservoir tank.
4. Remove the plastic clips and the upper duct covers.
5. Disconnect the refrigerant lines.
6. Remove the receiver/drier.
7. Installation is the reverse of the removal procedure.

Evaporator

REMOVAL AND INSTALLATION

1. Disconnect the negative battery terminal.
2. Properly discharge the air conditioning system.
3. Disconnect and plug the refrigerant lines at the evaporator.
4. Remove the grommets at the expansion valve, if equipped.
5. Remove the glove box and lower panel.
6. Remove the air flow ducts.
7. Remove the evaporator unit drain hose.
8. Remove the seal plates from both sides of the evaporator unit.
9. Disconnect the air conditioning wiring harness at the evaporator.
10. Remove the attaching bolts at the evaporator and remove the unit.
11. Installation is the reverse of the removal procedure.

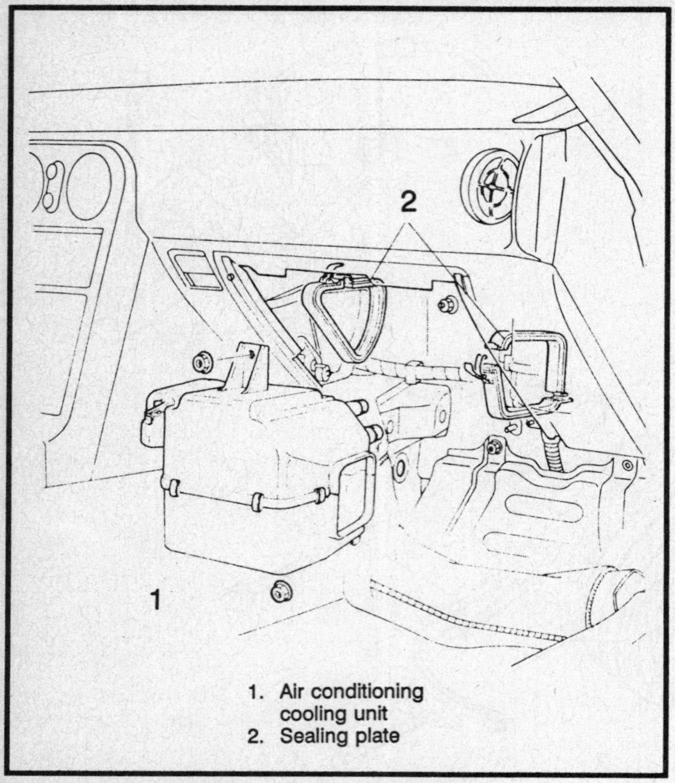
2
1
1. Air conditioning cooling unit
2. Sealing plate

Typical evaporator assembly removal

Expansion Valve

REMOVAL AND INSTALLATION

1. Disconnect the negative battery terminal.
2. Properly discharge the air conditioning system.
3. Disconnect and plug the refrigerant lines at the evaporator.
4. Remove the grommets at the expansion valve, if equipped.
5. Remove the glove box and lower panel.
6. Remove the air flow ducts.
7. Remove the evaporator unit.
8. Remove evaporator clamps.
9. Disassemble the unit.
10. Remove the thermo-switch.
11. Remove the capillary tube from the outlet pipe.
12. Remove the expansion valve.
13. Installation is the reverse of the removal procedure.

Blower Motor

REMOVAL AND INSTALLATION

1. Disconnect the negative battery terminal.
2. Remove the glove box and lower panel, if required.
2. Disconnect the blower motor wire connector.
3. Remove the 3 attaching screws and remove the blower motor.
4. Installation is the reverse of the removal procedure.

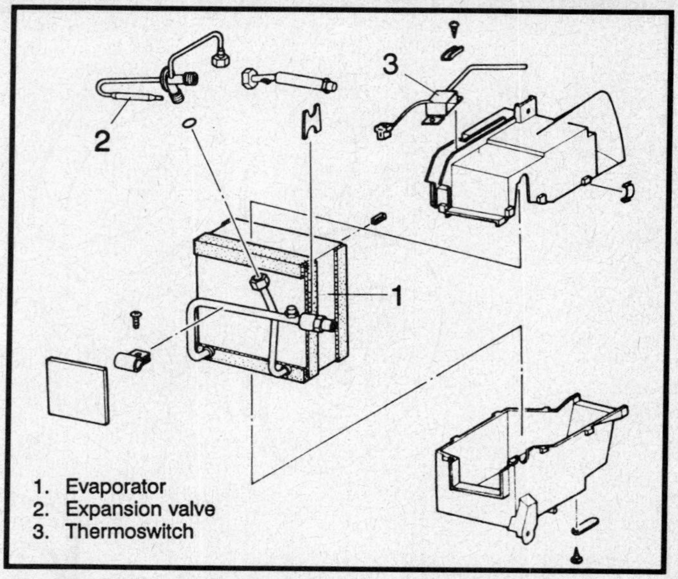
3
2
1
1. Evaporator
2. Expansion valve
3. Thermoswitch

Typical evaporator, thermo-switch and expansion valve assembly

Blower Motor Resistor

REMOVAL AND INSTALLATION

1. Disconnect the negative battery terminal.
2. Remove the glove box and lower panel, if required.
2. Disconnect the blower motor resistor wire connector.
3. Remove the attaching screw and remove the resistor.
4. Installation is the reverse of the removal procedure.

Heater Core

REMOVAL AND INSTALLATION

1. Disconnect the negative battery terminal.
2. Drain the engine coolant.

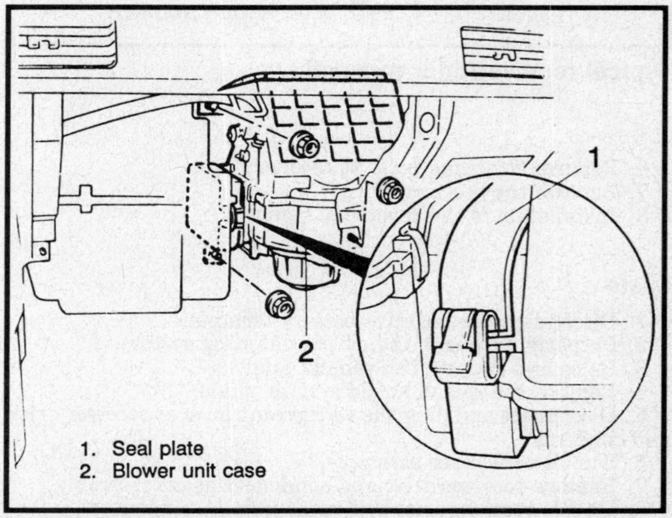
1
2
1. Seal plate
2. Blower unit case

Typical blower unit removal

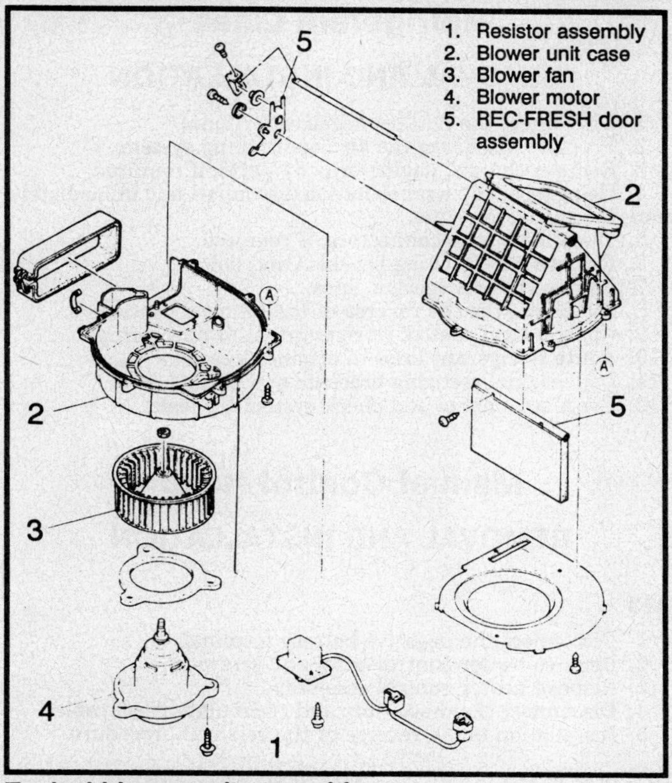
1. Resistor assembly
2. Blower unit case
3. Blower fan
4. Blower motor
5. REC-FRESH door assembly
1
2
3
4
5
A

Typical blower unit assembly

3. Disconnect heater core hoses.
4. Remove transmission selector lever or knob. Remove center console.
5. Remove the steering wheel. Remove the upper and lower steering column covers.
6. Remove the instrument meter hood. Remove the instrument cluster assembly.
7. Disconnect the speedometer cable.
8. Remove the heater ducts. Remove the instrument hosing lower panels. Remove the glove box assembly.
9. Remove the heater control switch and cables. Remove header and side trim, if required. Remove the center cap, the side covers and the center bracket bolts on the instrument panel.
10. Remove the steering shaft bolts. Disconnect any necessary wire harness connectors. Remove the instrument panel.
11. Remove the seal plate.
12. Remove the attaching nuts.
13. Remove the heater unit.
14. Remove the attaching clips on heater unit and separate assembly.
15. Remove heater core.

To install

16. Install heater core.
17. Reattach heater case halves with clips.
18. Install the heater unit. Install the seal plates.
19. Install the instrument panel. Connect wire harness connectors.
20. Install the steering shaft bolts. Install the center cap, the side covers and the center bracket bolts on the instrument panel.
21. Install header and side trim, if removed. Install the heater control switch and cables.

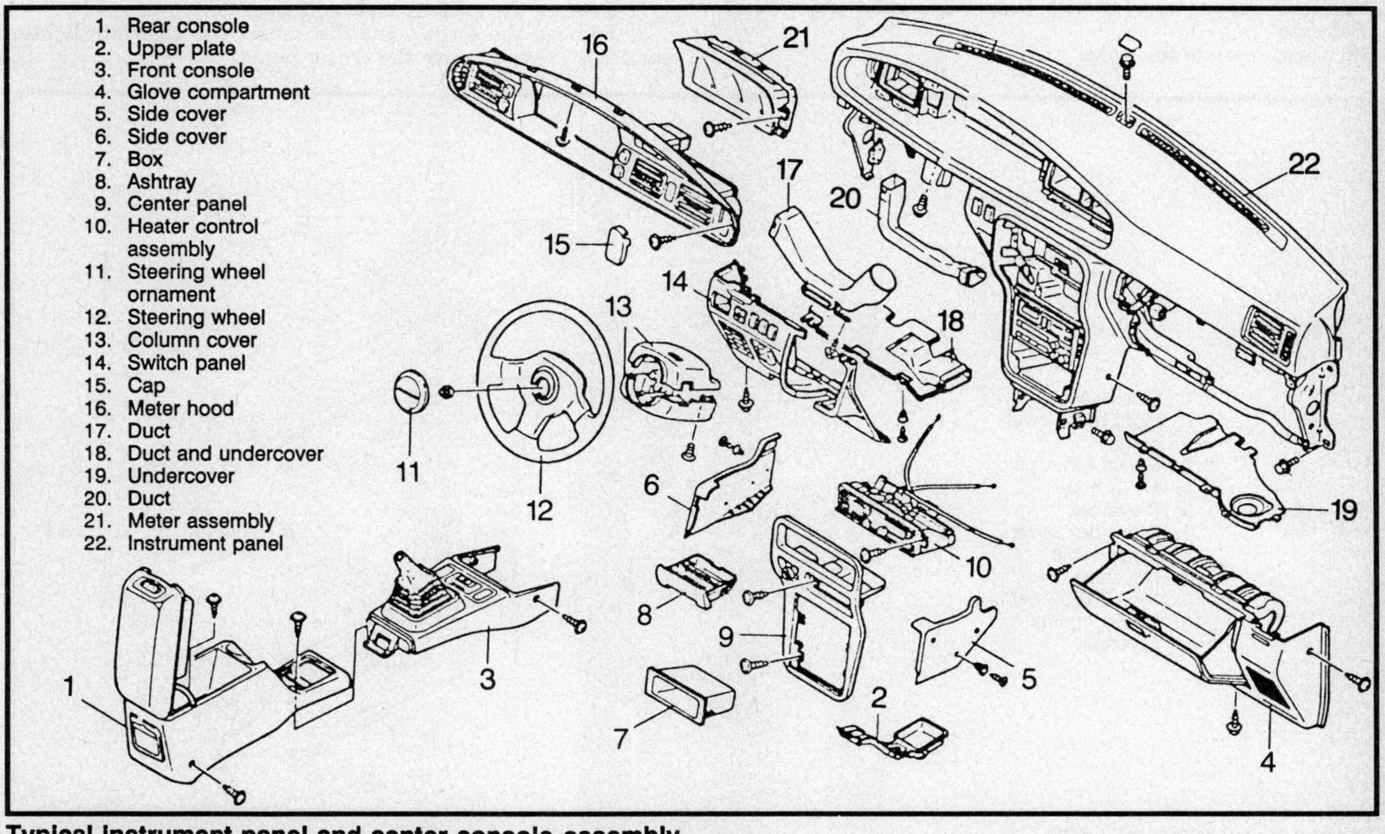
1. Rear console
2. Upper plate
3. Front console
4. Glove compartment
5. Side cover
6. Side cover
7. Box
8. Ashtray
9. Center panel
10. Heater control assembly
11. Steering wheel ornament
12. Steering wheel
13. Column cover
14. Switch panel
15. Cap
16. Meter hood
17. Duct
18. Duct and undercover
19. Undercover
20. Duct
21. Meter assembly
22. Instrument panel

Typical instrument panel and center console assembly

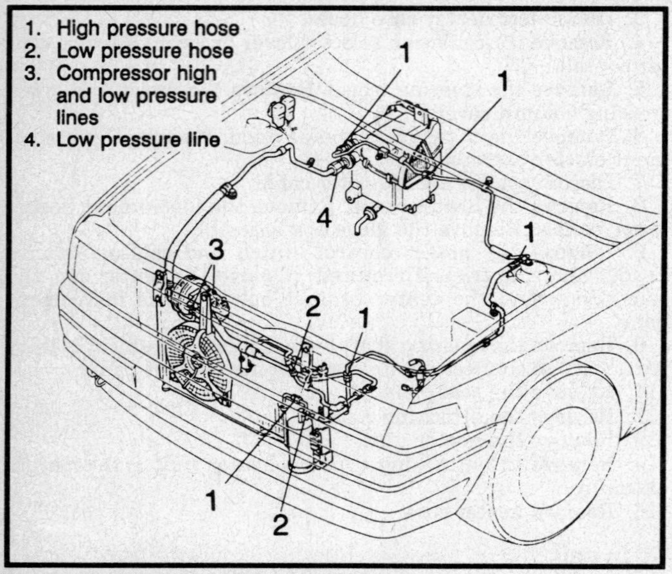
1. High pressure hose
2. Low pressure hose
3. Compressor high and low pressure lines
4. Low pressure line
1
1
4
1
3
2
1
1
2

Typical refrigerant line location

22. Install the glove box assembly. Install the instrument hosing lower panels. Install the heater ducts.
23. Reconnect speedometer cable. Install the instrument cluster and meter hood assembly.
24. Install the upper and lower steering column covers. Install the steering wheel.
25. Install the center console and the shift lever or knob.
26. Reconnect heater core hoses.
27. Reconnect the negative battery terminal.
28. Refill cooling system with proper quantity and type of antifreeze.
29. Check system for leaks.

Refrigerant Lines

REMOVAL AND INSTALLATION

1. Disconnect the battery negative terminal.
2. Properly discharge the air conditioning system.
3. Remove chassis, engine or body parts, if required.
4. Using a backup wrench loosen disconnect and immediately plug the refrigerant line.
5. Disconnect wire connectors, if required.
6. Remove all attaching brackets and bolts.
7. Remove the refrigerant lines.
8. Installation is the reverse of the removal procedure.
9. Apply a light coat of refrigerant oil to new o-rings.
10. Route refrigerant lines in original locations.
11. Use original securing brackets and bolts.
12. Evacuate, charge and check system for leaks.

Manual Control Head

REMOVAL AND INSTALLATION

323

1. Disconnect the negative battery terminal.
2. Remove heater control bezel and screws.
3. Remove heater control assembly.
4. Disconnect the mode, mix and recirculate-fresh cable.
5. Installation is the reverse of the removal procedure.

626 and MX-6

1. Disconnect the negative battery terminal.
2. Remove the ashtray and radio box.
3. Remove the screws and disconnect the cigarette lighter connector, then remove the center panel.

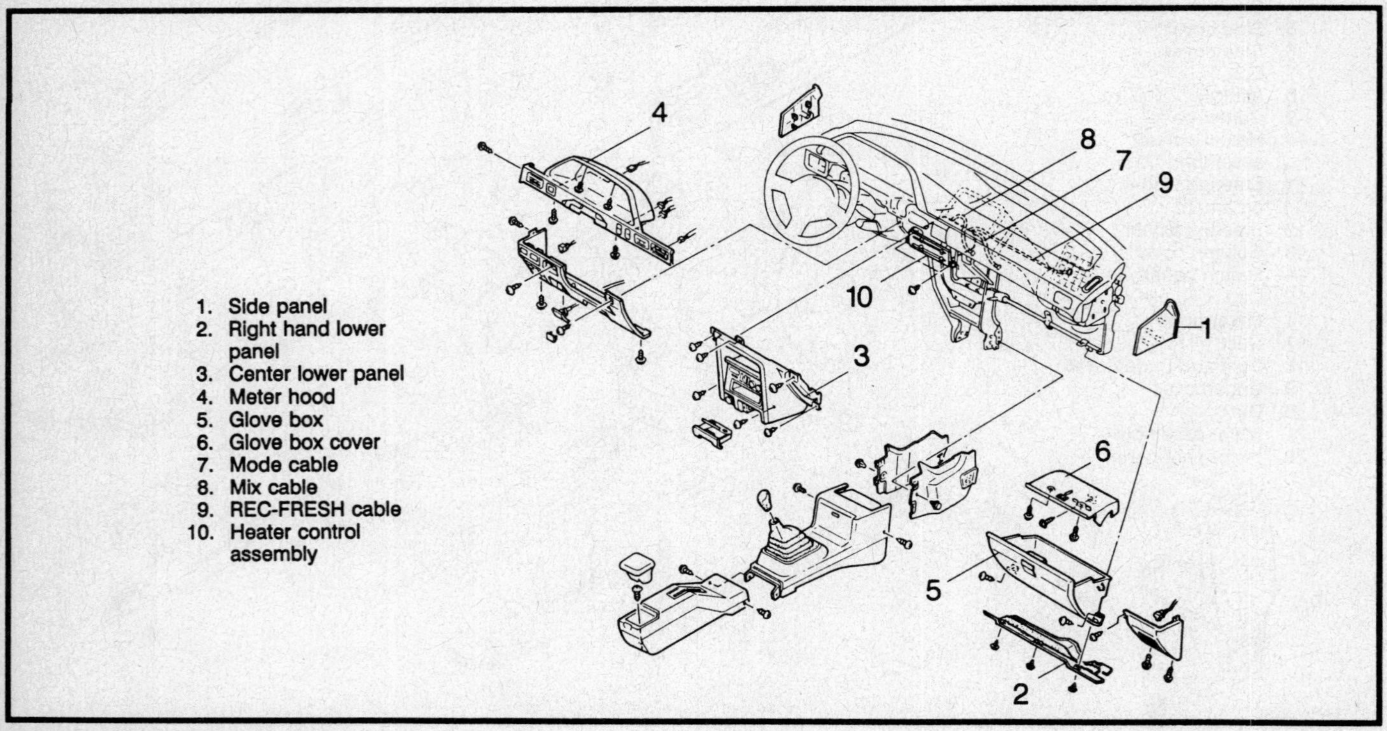
1. Side panel
2. Right hand lower panel
3. Center lower panel
4. Meter hood
5. Glove box
6. Glove box cover
7. Mode cable
8. Mix cable
9. REC-FRESH cable
10. Heater control assembly
4
8
7
9
10
1
3
6
5
2

Control head removal—323

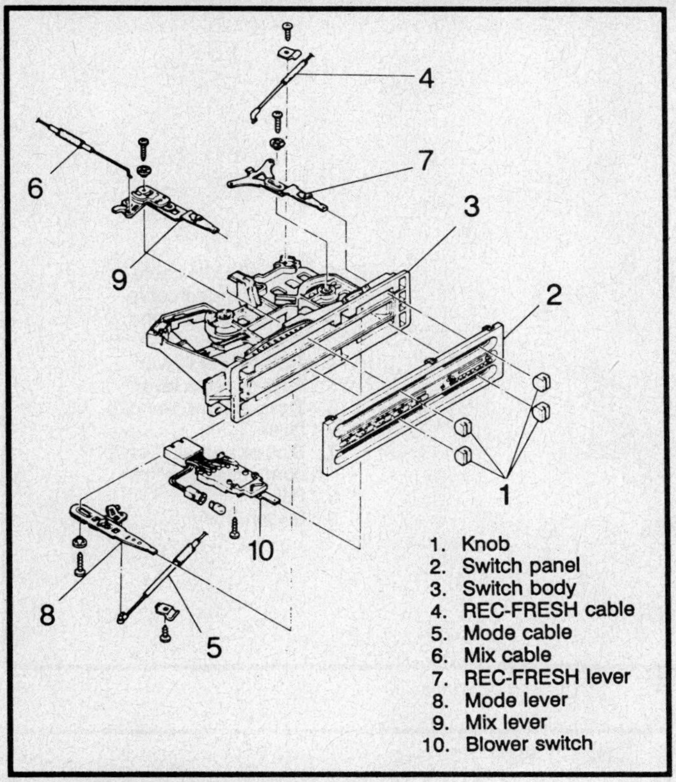
1. Knob
2. Switch panel
3. Switch body
4. REC-FRESH cable
5. Mode cable
6. Mix cable
7. REC-FRESH lever
8. Mode lever
9. Mix lever
10. Blower switch

Control head assembly—323

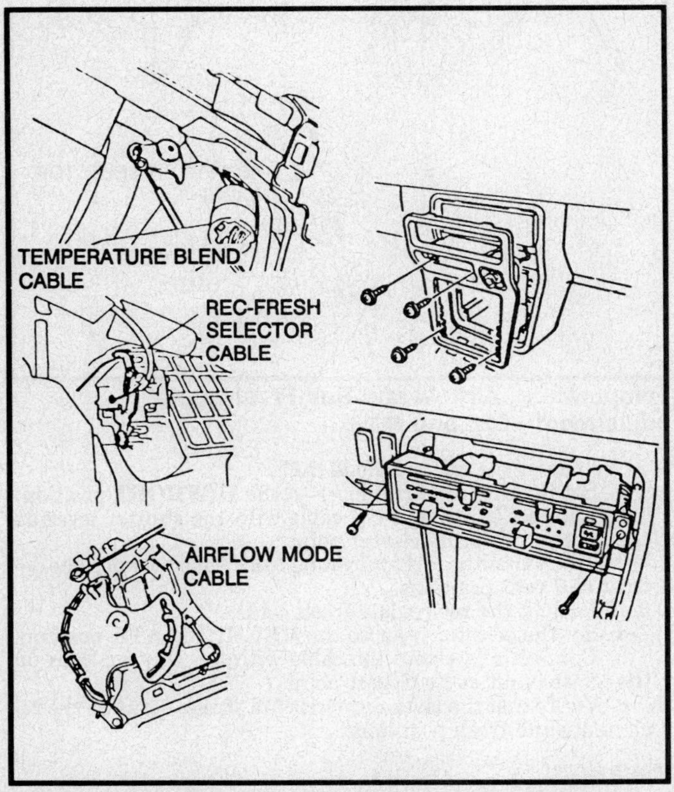
TEMPERATURE BLEND CABLE
REC-FRESH SELECTOR CABLE
AIRFLOW MODE CABLE

Control head assembly removal—626 and MX-6

4. Disconnect the temperature, airflow and recirculate-fresh mode unit cable.
5. Remove the control unit screws and remove assembly.
6. Installation is the reverse of the removal procedure.

Miata

1. Disconnect the negative battery terminal.
2. Remove shift lever knob and center console.
3. Remove outlet vents.
4. Remove switch panel attaching screws and remove assembly.
5. Remove heater switch attaching screws.
6. Remove switch assembly and disconnect heater control cables.
7. Installation is the reverse of the removal procedure.

Manual Control Cables

ADJUSTMENT

323

1. To adjust recirculate-fresh cable:
   a. Disconnect negative battery terminal.
   b. Set the recirculate-fresh lever to the **FRESH** position.
   c. Connect the recirculate-fresh cable to the recirculate-fresh door.
   d. Set the door to the fresh position and clamp the cable into place.
   e. Verify that the recirculate-fresh lever moves its full stroke.
2. To adjust the mode cable:
   a. Disconnect the negative battery terminal.
   b. Set the mode lever to the **DEFROST** position.
   c. Connect the mode cable to the mode door.
   d. Set the door to the defrost position and clamp the cable into place.
   e. Verify that the mode lever moves its full stroke.
3. To adjust the mix cable:
   a. Disconnect the negative battery terminal.
   b. Set the mix lever to the **COLD** position.
   c. Connect the mix cable to the mix door.

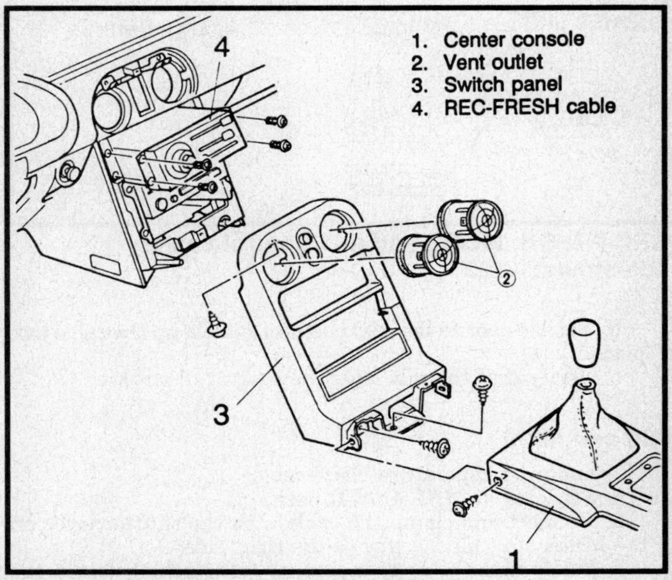
1. Center console
2. Vent outlet
3. Switch panel
4. REC-FRESH cable

Manual control head removal—Miata

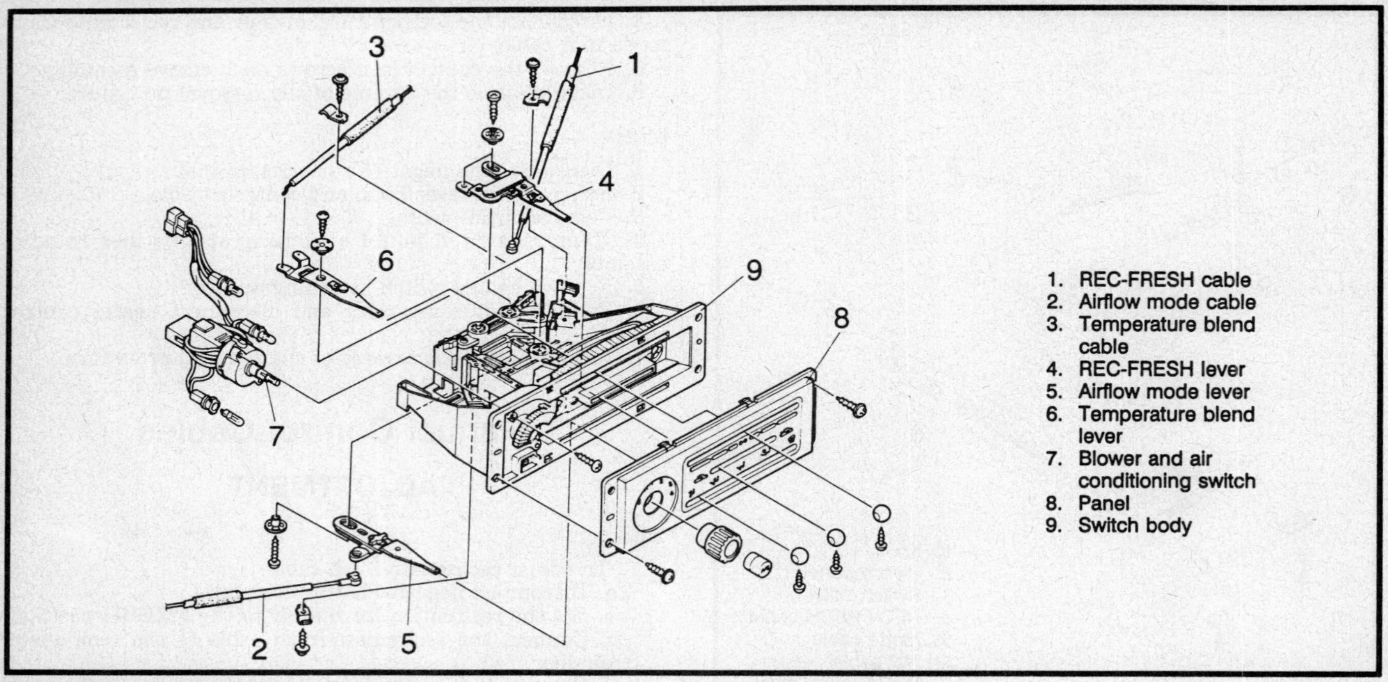
1
2
3
4
5
6
7
8
9
1. REC-FRESH cable
2. Airflow mode cable
3. Temperature blend cable
4. REC-FRESH lever
5. Airflow mode lever
6. Temperature blend lever
7. Blower and air conditioning switch
8. Panel
9. Switch body

Control head assembly—Miata

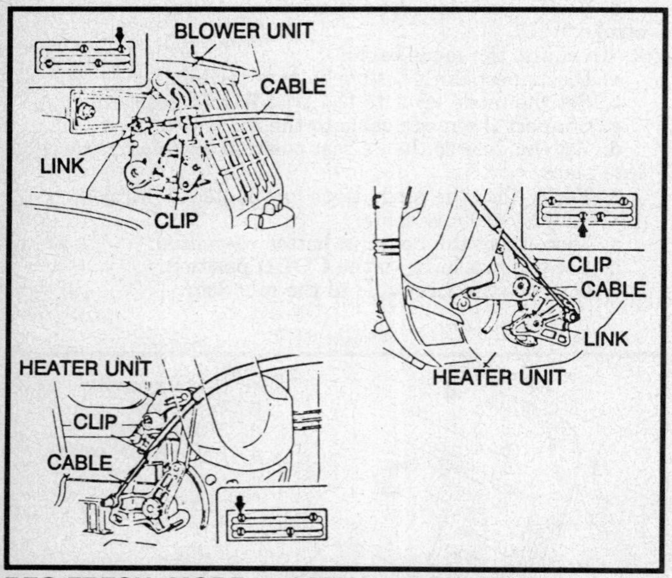
BLOWER UNIT
CABLE
LINK
CLIP
CLIP
CABLE
LINK
HEATER UNIT
HEATER UNIT
CLIP
CABLE

REC-FRESH, MODE and MIX control cable adjustment—323

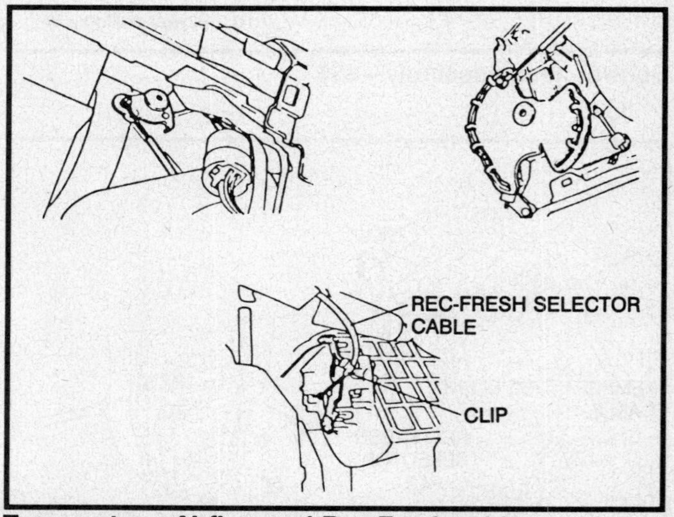
REC-FRESH SELECTOR CABLE
CLIP

Temperature, Airflow and Rec-Fresh cable adjustment—626 and MX-6

d. Set the door to the cold position and clamp the cable into place.

e. Verify that the mix lever moves its full stroke.

626 and MX-6

1. To adjust temperature blend cable:

a. Set lever at **MAX-COLD** position.

b. Connect and clamp the cable with the shutter lever on the heater unit all the way to the right side.

c. Verify that the lever moves its full stroke between the hot and cold positions.

2. To adjust the airflow mode cable:

a. Set the mode control lever to the **DEFROST** position.

b. Connect and clamp the cable with the shutter lever on the heater unit at its closest point.

c. Verify that the lever moves its full stroke between the defrost and vent positions.

3. To adjust the recirculate-fresh cable:

a. Set the selector lever to the **RECIRCULATE** position.

b. Connect and clamp the cable with the shutter lever on the blower unit at its closest point.

c. Verify that the lever moves its full stroke between the recirculate and fresh positions.

Miata

1. To adjust temperature blend cable:

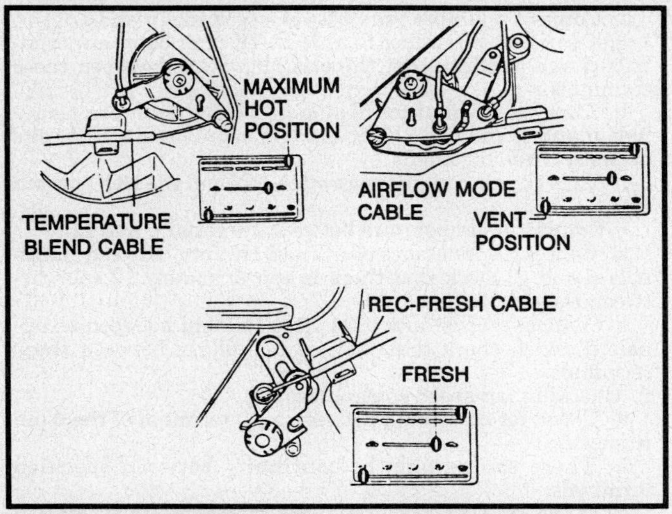
MAXIMUM
HOT
POSITION
TEMPERATURE
BLEND CABLE
AIRFLOW MODE
CABLE
VENT
POSITION
REC-FRESH CABLE
FRESH

Temperature, Airflow and Rec-Fresh blend cable adjustment—Miata

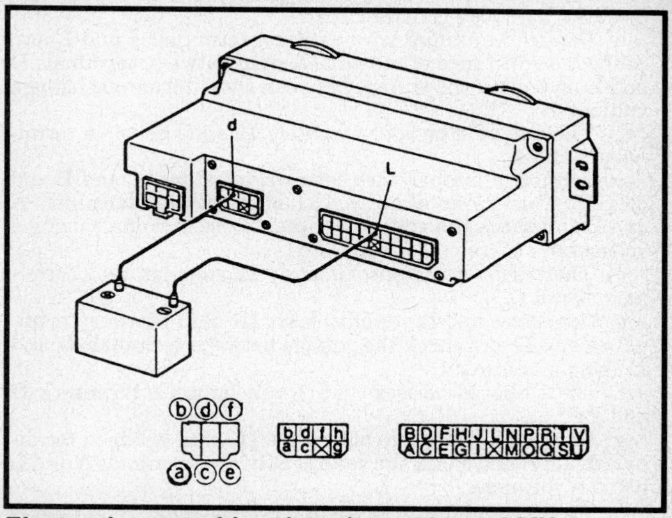
d
L

Electronic control head testing—626 and MX-6

a. Set lever at **MAX-HOT** position.
b. Connect and clamp the cable with the shutter lever on the heater unit all the way to the right side.
c. Verify that the lever moves its full stroke between the hot and cold positions.
2. To adjust the airflow mode cable:
a. Set the mode control lever to the **VENT** position.
b. Connect and clamp the cable with the shutter lever on the heater unit at its closest point.
c. Verify that the lever moves its full stroke between the defrost and vent positions.
3. To adjust the recirculate-fresh cable.
a. Set the selector lever to the **FRESH** position.
b. Connect and clamp the cable with the shutter lever on the blower unit at its closest point.
c. Verify that the lever moves its full stroke between the recirculate and fresh positions.

REMOVAL AND INSTALLATION

323

1. Disconnect the negative battery terminal.
2. Remove the instrument housing side and lower panels.
3. Remove the instrument panel meter hood.
4. Remove the glove box assembly.
5. Disconnect the mode, mix and recirculate-fresh cable.
6. Remove heater control bezel and screws.
7. Remove heater control assembly.
8. Remove cable attaching screws and cables.
9. Installation is the reverse of the removal procedure.

626 and MX-6

1. Disconnect the negative battery terminal.
2. Remove the glove box and undercover assembly.
3. Disconnect the temperature and recirculate-fresh heater unit cable.
4. Remove the duct and undercover on driver's side.
5. Disconnect the airflow mode cable.
6. Remove the ashtray and radio box.
7. Remove the screws and disconnect the cigarette lighter connector, the remove the center panel.
8. Remove the temperature control screws and remove assembly.
9. Disconnect the control cables and remove the cables.
10. Installation is the reverse of the removal procedure.

Miata

1. Disconnect the negative battery terminal.
2. Remove shift lever knob and center console.
3. Remove outlet vents.
4. Remove switch panel attaching screws and remove assembly.
5. Remove heater switch attaching screws.
6. Remove switch assembly and disconnect heater control cables.
7. Remove glove box assembly to gain access to heater unit control cables.
8. Disconnect and remove control cables.
9. Installation is the reverse of the removal procedure.

Electronic Control Head

TESTING

626 and MX-6

1. Disconnect the negative battery terminal.
2. Remove the control head assembly.
3. Supply 12 volts to terminal **d** and ground terminal **l**.
4. Check each circuit as follows.
5. Checking REC-FRESH air selector circuit:
a. Connect a jumper wire between terminal **M** and terminal **L**, connect a resistance of at least 1K ohm between terminal **B** and terminal **O** and check the voltage between these terminals using a voltmeter.
b. There should be 12 volts between terminals **B** and **O**.
c. Connect a resistance of at least 1K ohm between terminals **d** and **B** and check the voltage between terminals **B** and **O** using a voltmeter.
d. There should be less than 1 volt between terminals **B** and **O**.
e. Check for continuity between terminals **n** and **l** with the REC-FRESH switch in the **FRESH** position using an ohmmeter.
f. Check for continuity between terminals **P** and **L** with the REC-FRESH air selector switch in the **RECIRCULATE** position using an ohmmeter.

6. Checking mode control circuit:
a. Connect a jumper wire between terminals **I** and **L** and connect a resistance of at least 1K ohm between terminals **D** and **L** and check the voltage between these terminals using a voltmeter.
b. There should be approximately 12 volts between terminals **D** and **L**.
c. Connect a jumper wire between terminals **C** and **L** and connect a resistance of at least 1k ohm between terminals **A** and **L** and check the voltage between these terminals using a voltmeter.
d. There should be approximately 12 volts between terminals **A** and **L**.
e. Connect a resistance of at least 1K ohm between terminals **d** and **D** and check the voltage between terminals **D** and **L** using a voltmeter.
f. There should be less than 1 volt between terminals **D** and **L**.
g. Connect a resistance of at least 1K ohm between terminals **d** and **A** and check the voltage between terminals **A** and **L** using a voltmeter.
h. There should be less than 1 volt between terminals **A** and **L**.
i. Push the **VENT** switch in and check that there is continuity between terminals **J** and **L**.
j. Push the **BI-LEVEL** switch in and check that there is continuity between terminals **G** and **L**.
k. Push the **HEAT** switch in and check that there is continuity between terminals **H** and **L**.
l. Push the **HEAT-DEF** switch in and check that there is continuity between terminals **E** and **L**.
m. Push the **DEF** switch in and check that there is continuity between terminals **F** and **L**.
7. Checking the air mix control circuit:
a. Connect a resistance of at least 1K ohm between terminals **Q** and **T**.
b. Set the temperature lever in the midpoint between **MAX-HOT** and **MAX-COLD**.
c. Connect a jumper wire between terminals **V** and **U**.
d. Check voltage between terminals **T** and **L**, there should be approximately 12 volts.
e. Check voltage between terminals Q and L, there should be less than 1 volt.
f. Connect a resistance of at least 1K ohm between terminals **Q** and **T**.
g. Set the temperature lever in the midpoint between **MAX-HOT** and **MAX-COLD**.
h. Connect a jumper wire between terminals **V** and **S**.
i Check voltage between terminals **Q** and **L**, there should be approximately 12 volts.
j. Check voltage between terminals **T** and **L**, there should be less than 1 volt.
k. Connect a resistance of at least 1K ohm between terminals **Q** and **T**.
l. Set the temperature lever to **MAX-HOT**, and check that **Q** terminal voltage is higher than **T** terminal voltage.
m. Connect a resistance of at least 1K ohm between terminals **Q** and **T**.
n. Set the temperature lever to **MAX-COLD**, and check that **T** terminal voltage is higher than **Q** terminal voltage.
8. Checking air conditioning switch and ECO switch circuit:
a. Turn the air conditioning switch **OFF**.
b. Connect a jumper wire between terminal **c** and **L**.
c. Connect a resistance of at least 1K ohm between terminals **d** and **g**, check that there is no voltage between these terminals.
d. Connect a resistance of at least 1K ohm between terminals **d** and **f**, check that there is no voltage between these terminals.
e. Turn the air conditioner switch **ON** and the **ECO** switch **OFF**.
f. Connect a jumper wire between terminal **c** and **L**.
g. Connect a resistance of at least 1K ohm between terminals **d** and **g**, check that there is no voltage between these terminals.
h. Connect a resistance of at least 1K ohm between terminals **d** and **f**, and check that there is approximately 12 volts between these terminals.
i. Turn the air conditioner switch **ON** and the **ECO** switch **ON**.
j. Connect a jumper wire between terminal **c** and **L**.
k. Connect a resistance of at least 1K ohm between terminals **d** and **g**, check that there is approximately 12 volts between these terminals.
l. Connect a resistance of at least 1K ohm between terminals **d** and **f**, check that there is no voltage between these terminals.
9. Checking fan speed control lever:
a. Check for continuity between each terminal of the 6 pin connector.
b. There should only be continuity between specified terminals.
c. In the fan **OFF** position, there is no continuity between any terminals.
d. In the fan No. 1 position there should only be continuity between terminals **d** and **f**.
e. In the fan No. 2 position there should only be continuity between terminals **c** and **e**
f. In the fan No. 3 position there should only be continuity between terminals **b**, **e** and **f**.
g. In the fan No. 4 position there should only be continuity between terminals **a**, **e** and **f**.
10. Checking the dim indicator circuit:
a. Connect a jumper wire between terminals **c** and **L**.
b. Check for illumination at air conditioner switch indicator with air conditioner switch **ON**.
c. Check for illumination at ECO switch indicator with **ECO** switch **ON**.
d. Check that the mode conrol switch and RECIRC-FRESH select switch indicators illuminate when the respective switches are **ON**.
e. Apply 12 volts to terminal **a** and check that the indicators are dim.
11. Checking the illumination circuit:
a. Connect a jumper wire between terminals **b** and terminal **L**.
b. Apply 12 volts to terminal **a** and check that the indicators are dim.

RX-7

1. Disconnect the negative battery terminal.
2. Remove the control head assembly.
3. Supply 12 volts to terminal **l** and ground terminal **h**, except during continuity tests.
4. Checking temperature control circuit.
a. Set the temperature control lever to the midway position.
b. Connect a jumper wire between terminals **D** and **E**.
c. Check that there is 12 volts between terminals **F** and **G**.
d. If not as specified, replace the control assembly.
e. Disconnect the jumper wire.
f. Connect a jumper wire between terminals **C** and **D**.
g. Check that there is 12 volts between terminals **G** and **F**.
h. If not as specified, replace the control assembly.
5. Continuity tests:
a. Check for continuity between terminal **h** and **N** with the **VENT** switch pushed **ON**.
b. Check for continuity between terminal **h** and **M** with the **B/L** switch pushed **ON**
c. Check for continuity between terminal **h** and **L** with the

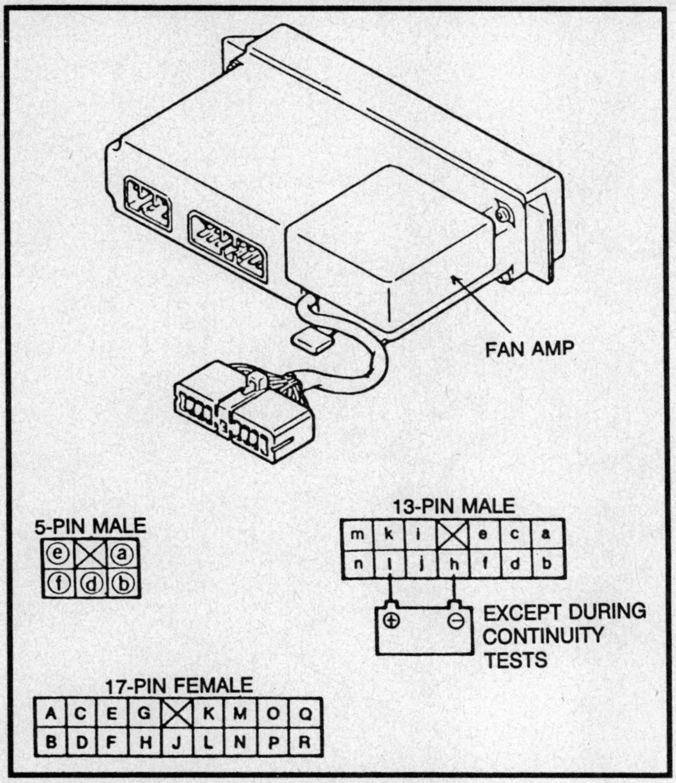
FAN AMP
5-PIN MALE
e a
f d b
13-PIN MALE
m k i e c a
n l j h f d b
EXCEPT DURING
CONTINUITY
TESTS
17-PIN FEMALE
A C E G K M O Q
B D F H J L N P R

Electronic control head testing—RX-7

HEAT switch pushed **ON**.

d. Check for continuity between terminal **h** and **K** with the **H/D** switch pushed **ON**.

e. Check for continuity between terminal **h** and **J** with the **DEF** switch pushed **ON**.

f. If any terminals do not have continuity, replace the control head assembly.

6. Checking indicator lamps:

a. Check for illumination of the indicator lamp as each switch is pushed.

b. If any lamp fails to illuminate, replace the control head assembly.

c. Connect a jumper wire between terminals **l** and **j**, and verify that the indicator lamps dim.

d. If they do not, replace the control head assembly.

7. Checking mode control circuit:

a. Connect a jumper wire between terminals **h** and **O**.

b. Measure the voltage between terminals **P** and **Q**.

c. There should be approximately 12 volts between terminals **P** and **Q**.

d. If not as specified, replace the control head assembly.

e. Disconnect the jumper wire.

f. Connect a jumper wire between terminals **h** and **H**.

g. Measure the voltage between terminals **Q** and **P**.

h. There should be approximately 12 volts between terminals **Q** and **P**.

i. If not as specified, replace the control head assembly.

8. Checking unit illumination lamp:

a. Connect a jumper wire between terminals **b** and **l**.

b. Check for illumination of the unit illumination lamps.

c. If there is no illumination of either lamp, replace the control head assembly.

9. Checking heater relay output:

a. Connect a test light between terminal **l** and the 5 pin connector terminal **d**.

b. Turn the blower switch **ON**.

c. If the test light does not light, check the fan amp.

d. If the fan amp is good, replace the control head assembly.

10. Checking the air conditioner indicator lamp:

a. Connect a test light between terminals **l** and **f**.

b. Turn the blower switch **ON**.

c. If the test light does not light, check the fan amp.

d. If the fan amp is good, replace the control head assembly.

11. Checking the EX-HI relay output:

a. Connect a test light between terminals **l** and terminal **b** of the 5 pin connector.

b. Set the blower switch to maximum.

c. If the test light does not light, check the fan amp.

d. If the fan amp is good, replace the control head assembly.

12. Checking power transistor output:

a. Measure the voltage at terminal **a** while turning the blower switch.

b. Verify that the voltage with the the switch at maximum position is more than the voltage at off position.

c. If not, check the fan amp.

d. If the fan amp is good, replace the control head assembly.

13. Checking REC/FRESH select switch:

a. Check for continuity between terminals **h** and **i** with the **FRESH** switch depressed.

b. Check for continuity between terminals **h** and **k** with the **REC** switch depressed.

c. Both tests should have continuity, if not as specified replace the control head assembly.

14. Checking REC/FRESH indicator lamp:

a. Depress the **FRESH** switch, indicator lamp should be OFF.

b. Depress **REC** switch, indicator lamp should be ON.

c. If not as specified, replace the control head assembly.

15. Checking REC/FRESH motor circuit

a. Connect a jumper wire between terminals **c** and **h**.

b. Measure the voltage between terminals **h** and **d**.

c. There should be approximately 12 volts between terminals **h** and **d**.

d. If not as specified, replace the control head assembly.

16. Checking the air conditioner switch:

a. Check for continuity between terminal **e** and the 5 pin connector terminal **e**.

b. With the air conditioner switch **ON** there should be continuity.

c. With the air conditioner switch **OFF** there should be no continuity.

d. If not as specified, replace the control head assembly.

17. Checking air conditioner indicator lamp:

a. Connect a jumper wire between terminals **h** and **e**.

b. Check that the indicator lamp is **ON** when the air conditioner switch is **ON**.

c. Check that the indicator lamp is **OFF** when the air conditioner switch is **OFF**.

d. If not as specified, replace the control head assembly.

REMOVAL AND INSTALLATION

626 and MX-6

1. Disconnect the negative battery terminal.
2. Remove the ashtray and radio box.
3. Remove the screws and disconnect the cigarette lighter connector, then remove the center panel.
4. Remove the control unit screws and remove assembly.
5. Disconnect the control unit wire harness.
6. Installation is the reverse of the removal procedure.

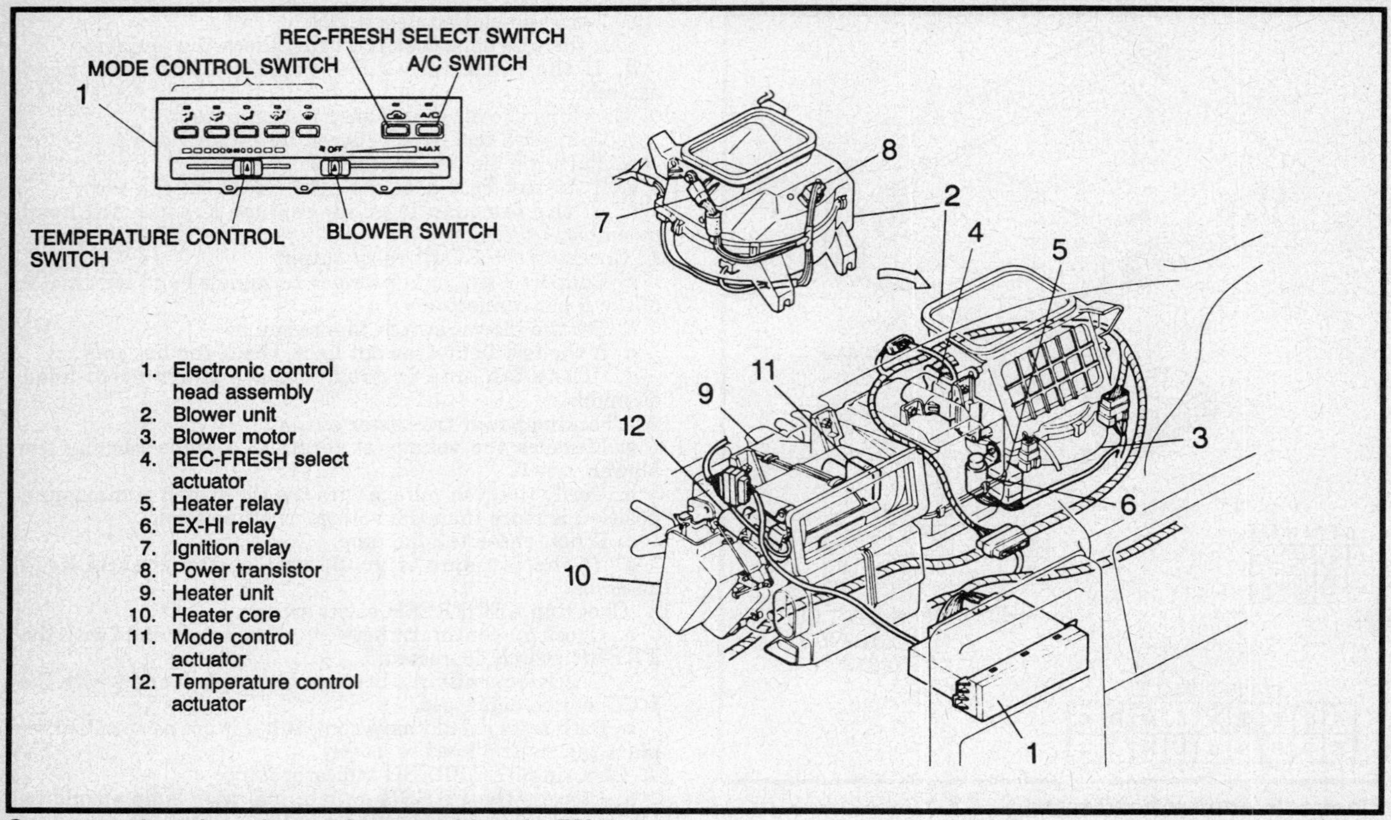
REC-FRESH SELECT SWITCH
MODE CONTROL SWITCH
A/C SWITCH
TEMPERATURE CONTROL SWITCH
BLOWER SWITCH
1. Electronic control head assembly
2. Blower unit
3. Blower motor
4. REC-FRESH select actuator
5. Heater relay
6. EX-HI relay
7. Ignition relay
8. Power transistor
9. Heater unit
10. Heater core
11. Mode control actuator
12. Temperature control actuator

Compnent location electronic control head—RX-7

929

1. Disconnect the negative battery terminal.
2. Remove the steering wheel and column covers.
3. Remove the instrument panel screws and pull the switch panel outward.
4. Disconnect the instrument panel wire connectors.
5. Remove the instrument panel.
6. Remove the heater control head panel screws and pull switch assembly outward.
7. Disconnect control head wire harness and remove assembly.
8. Installation is the reverse of the removal procedure.

RX-7

1. Disconnect the negative battery terminal.
2. Remove the center louver and ashtray.
3. Remove the center panel attaching screws.
4. Disconnect the cigarette lighter connector.
5. Remove the center panel.
6. Remove the heater control attaching screws.
7. Remove the dash panel center cap and bolt.
8. Turn the dash panel 30 degrees toward the front of vehicle and remove the dash panel.
9. Disconnect the control head assembly connector and remove it from the clip.
10. Tie a string to the harness connector so the harness can be pulled through the dash during installation.
11. Disconnect the control head connector and remove the assembly.
12. Installation is the reverse of the removal procedure.

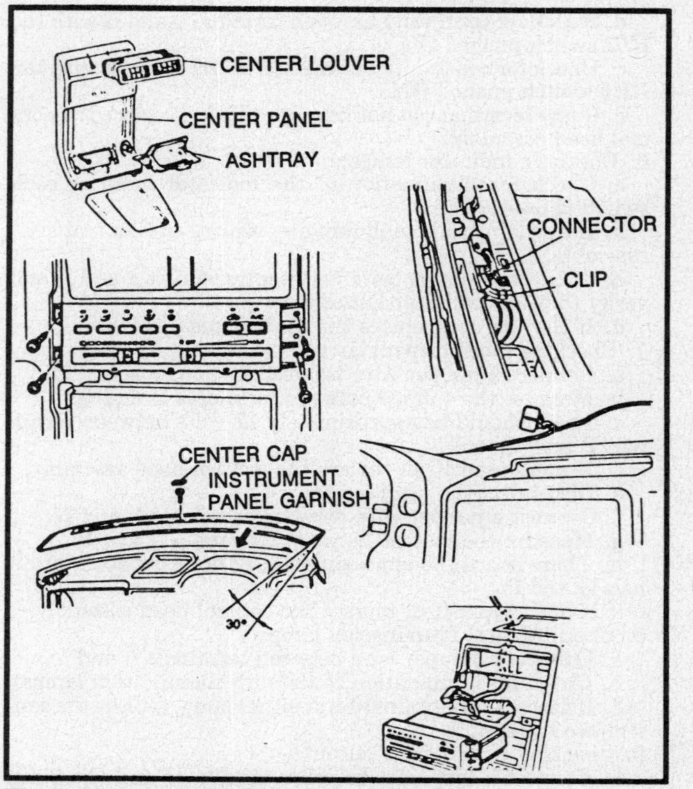
CENTER LOUVER
CENTER PANEL
ASHTRAY
CONNECTOR
CLIP
CENTER CAP
INSTRUMENT PANEL GARNISH
30°

Electronic control head removal—RX-7

SENSORS AND SWITCHES

Pressure Switches

OPERATION

There are 2 styles of pressure switches being used, the first pressure switch, which switches the magnetic clutch ON or OFF as a result of irregularly high or low pressures of the refrigerant. The second pressure switch is used on vehicles with automatic transmission to cycle ON and OFF the condenser fan according to system pressure. Both pressure switches are located on the high side.

1. Disconnect the pressure switch wire connector from the receiver/drier or from the high pressure line.
2. Start vehicle and turn the air conditioner ON.
3. Hook up the air conditioner gauges or charging station.
4. Check for 12 volts at pressure switch wire connector.
5. If there is no voltage at either terminal of wire connector, check air conditioner relay.
6. Connect a jumper wire between the 2 terminals.
7. Check to see if compressor clutch engages or if condenser fan operates, on vehicles with automatic transmission.
8. If condenser fan and compressor magnetic clutch fail to operate check the unit and the wiring to the unit.
9. Check for continuity through the switch, at normal operating pressures there will be continuity through the switch.

REMOVAL AND INSTALLATION

Except RX-7

1. Disconnect the negative battery cable.
2. Properly discharge the air conditioning system.
3. If required, remove radiator grille.
4. Disconnect the pressure switch wire connector.
5. Using 2 wrenches, remove the pressure switch.
6. Installation is the reverse of removal procedure.

RX-7

1. Disconnect the negative battery cable.
2. Properly discharge the air conditioning system.
3. Remove the coolant reservoir tank and upper duct cover.
4. Disconnect the pressure switch wire connector.
5. Using 2 wrenches, remove the pressure switch.
6. Installation is the reverse of removal procedure.

Thermo-Switch

OPERATION

The electro thermo-sensor is mounted at the evaporator core outlet and senses the temperature of the cool air coming through the evaporator. Temperature signals are then input to the thermo unit. This information is then compared by the thermo unit and the results are output to operate the air conditioner relay and turn the magnetic clutch ON and OFF.

TESTING

323 and Miata

1. Disconnect negative battery terminal.
2. Remove the thermoswitch.
3. Place thermoswitch in ice water.
4. Check continuity through the switch.
5. There should be no continuity through the switch when it reaches 32°F (0°C).

626, 929 and MX-6

1. Remove the glove box and the undercover.
2. Start the vehicle and run the engine at idle.
3. Set the air conditioning switch**ON** at **MAX-COOLING**.
4. Press the **ECONOMY** switch **ON**.
5. Block the air inlet of the blower unit to hasten the evaporator cooling.
6. The compressor magnetic clutch should disengage when the evaporator temperature reaches 44.6°F (7°C).
7. Press the **ECONOMY** switch **OFF** and check that the compressor magnetic clutch operates.
8. The compressor magnetic clutch should disengage when the evaporator temperature becomes 33.8°F (1°C).

RX-7

1. Disconnect negative battery terminal.
2. Remove the thermoswitch.
3. Place thermoswitch in ice water.
4. Check continuity through the switch.
5. There should be no continuity through the switch when it reaches 32.9–36.5°F (0.5–2.5°C), if equipped with a Nippon Denso compressor or 32–35.6°F (0–3°C), if equipped with a Sanden compressor.

REMOVAL AND INSTALLATION

1. Disconnect the negative battery terminal.
2. Remove the glove box and undercover.
3. Remove the cooling unit.
4. Disassemble the cooling unit.
5. Remove the thermoswitch.
6. Installation is the reverse of the removal procedure.

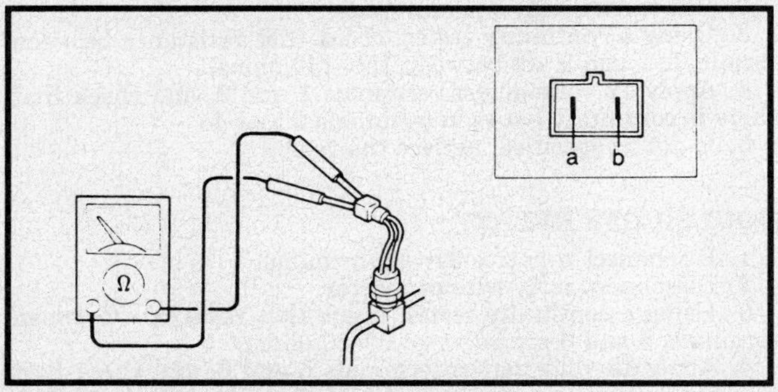
a
b

Typical pressure switch testing

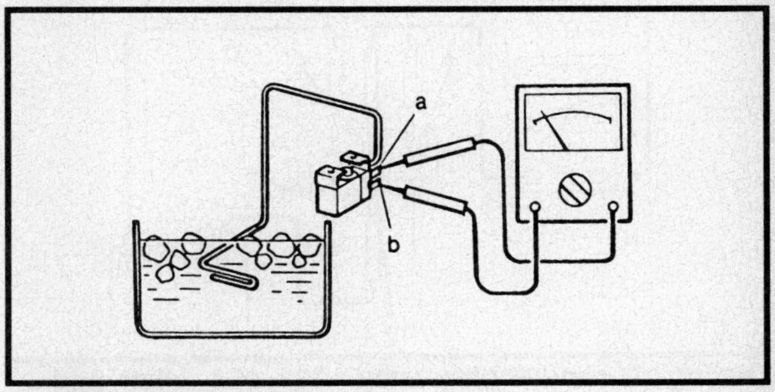
a
b

Thermo-Switch testing

Relays

OPERATION

Battery and load location may require that a switch be placed some distance from either component. This means a longer wire and a higher voltage drop. The installation of a relay between the battery and the load reduces the voltage drop. Because the switch controls the relay, this means amperage through the switch can be reduced.

TESTING

323, 626, Miata and MX-6

AIR CONDITIONING RELAY

1. Disconnect the negative battery terminal.
2. Disconnect the relay wire connector.
3. Check for continuity between the terminals of the relay.
4. If not as specified, replace the relay.
5. Apply 12 volts to terminal **d** and ground terminal **a**.
6. Check for continuity between terminals **c** and **e**.
7. If not as specified, replace the relay.

CONDENSER FAN RELAY

1. Disconnect the negative battery terminal.
2. Disconnect the relay wire connector.
3. Check for continuity between the terminals of the relay.
4. If not as specified, replace the relay.
5. Apply 12 volts to terminal **a** and ground terminal **b**.
6. Check for continuity between terminals **c** and **d**.
7. If not as specified, replace the relay.

929

AIR CONDITIONER AND MAX-HI RELAY

1. Disconnect negative battery terminal.

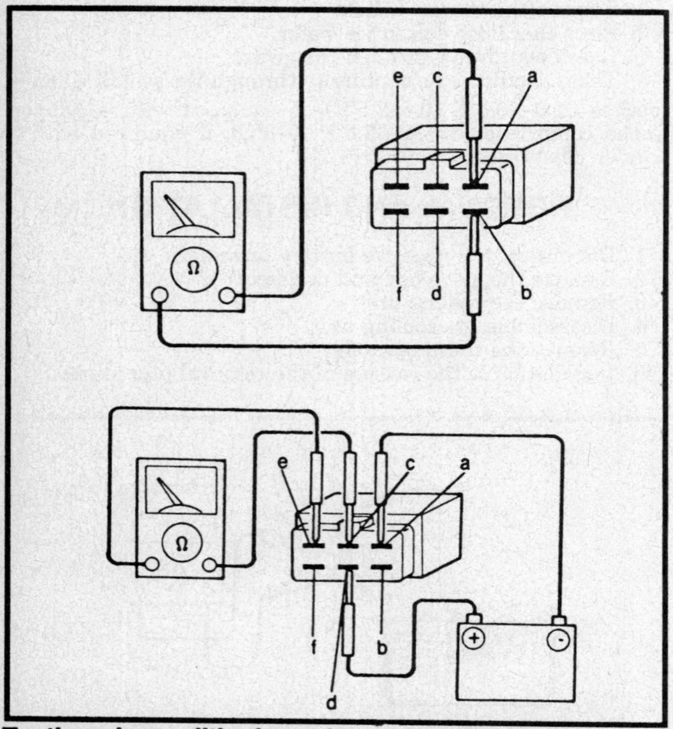
e
c
a
f
d
b
e
c
a
f
b
d
Testing air conditioning relay—323, 626, Miata and MX-6

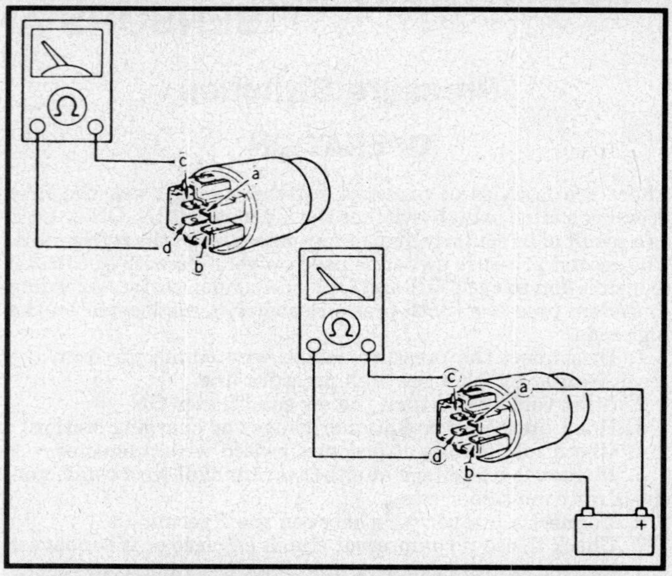
c
a
d
b
c
a
d
b
Testing condenser fan relay—323, 626, Miata and MX-6

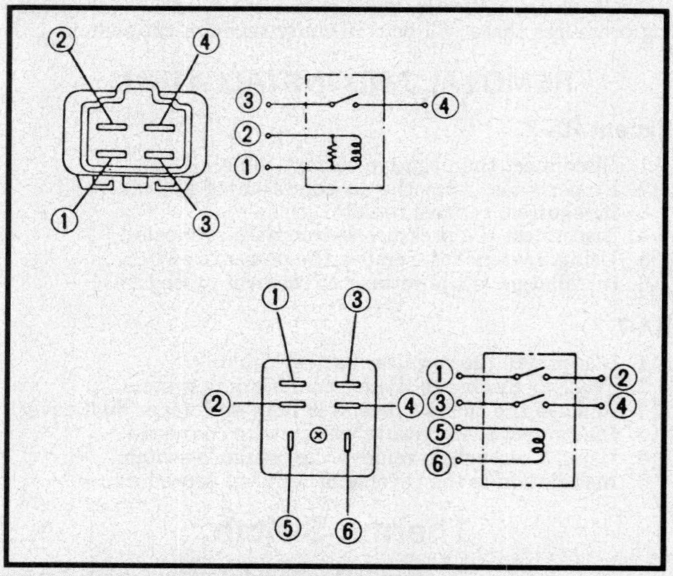
2
4
3
4
2
1
1
3
1
3
1
2
2
4
3
4
5
6
5
6
Testing air conditioning relay—929

2. Disconnect relay wire connector.
3. Using a continuity tester, check that resistance between terminals 1 and 2 are between 120–140 ohms.
4. Apply 12 volts across terminals **1** and **2**, and check that there is continuity between terminals **3** and **4**.
5. If not as specified, replace the relay.

COOLER OFF RELAY

1. Disconnect negative battery terminal.
2. Disconnect relay wire connector.
3. Using a continuity tester, check that resistance between terminals **5** and **6** are between 60–80 ohms.
4. Apply 12 volts across terminals **5** and **6**, and check that there is continuity between terminals **3** and **4**, and **1** and **2**.
5. If not as specified, replace the relay.

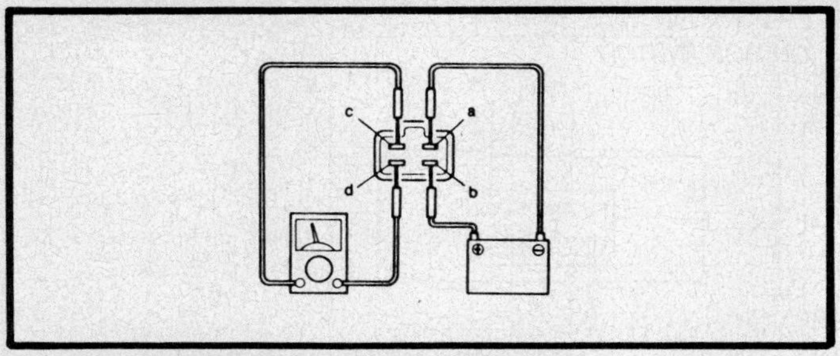
c
a
d
b

Testing air conditioning relay—RX-7

RX-7

AIR CONDITIONING MAIN RELAY

1. Disconnect the negative battery terminal.
2. Disconnect the relay wire connector.
3. Check for continuity between the terminals of the relay.
4. If not as specified, replace the relay.
5. Apply 12 volts to terminal **b** and ground terminal **a**.
6. Check for continuity between terminals **c** and **d**.
7. If not as specified, replace the relay.

REMOVAL AND INSTALLATION

1. Disconnect negative battery terminal.
2. Locate relay and disconnect wire connector.
3. If required, remove attaching bolt and remove relay.
4. Installation is the reverse of the removal procedure.

Thermo-Switch

OPERATION

There are 2 styles of thermo-switches being used, the first is used to turn on the coolant fan when the coolant temperature reaches 207°F (97°C) and higher. The second style is used in the heater unit to send a signal to the electronic control unit when the heater core is at a specified temperature to permit the blower fan to operate, on the 929 model.

TESTING

1. Disconnect the negative battery terminal.
2. Remove the water thermo-switch.
3. Place the thermo-switch and thermometer in water.
4. Heat the water gradually while checking the switch for continuity.
5. When temperature reaches 207°F (97°C) or higher, there should be continuity through switch.
6. If equipped with a 2nd thermo-switch, the No. 2 switch should have continuity at 226°F (108°C).
7. The 929's thermo-switch will have continuity at approximately 41°F (5°C).

REMOVAL AND INSTALLATION

1. Disconnect negative battery terminal.
2. Drain cooling system.
3. Remove alternator belt and alternator, if required.
4. Disconnect thermo-switch wire connector.
5. Remove thermo-switch
6. Installation is the reverse of the removal procedure.

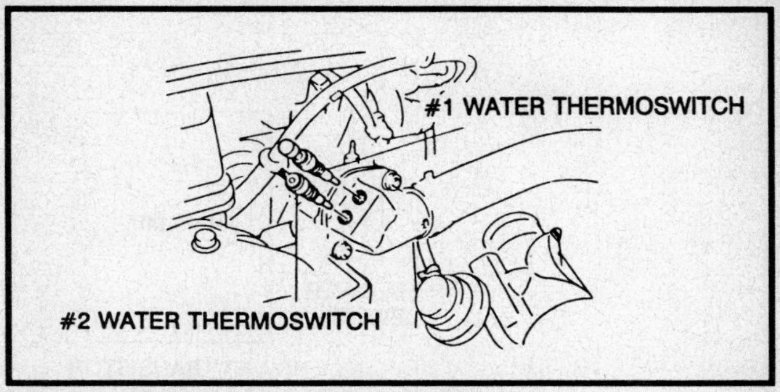
#1 WATER THERMOSWITCH
#2 WATER THERMOSWITCH

Dual thermo-switch—626 and MX-6

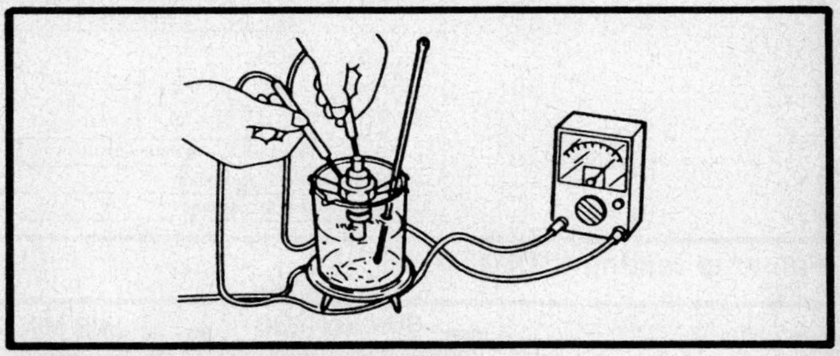

Typical thermo-switch testing

Blower Motor Fan Amp (Control Module)

OPERATION

The blower motor fan amp or control module is located on the electronic control head assembly. The main function of the fan amp is to electronically regulate voltage signals to the blower motor.

TESTING

RX-7

1. Checking the fan amp
   a. Turn the ignition switch **ON**.
   b. Turn the air conditioner switch **ON**.
   c. Measure the voltage at the terminal wires of the fan amp.
   d. If not as specified, replace the fan amp

Sensors

OPERATION

The 929 incorporates a passenger compartment, ambient air, duct and sun sensor into the electronic temperature control system. The temperature sensitive conductor inputs a signal to the air conditioner control unit which in turn adjusts the vehicle inside comfort zone. The sensors are located on the dash, at the ducts and at the receiver/drier.

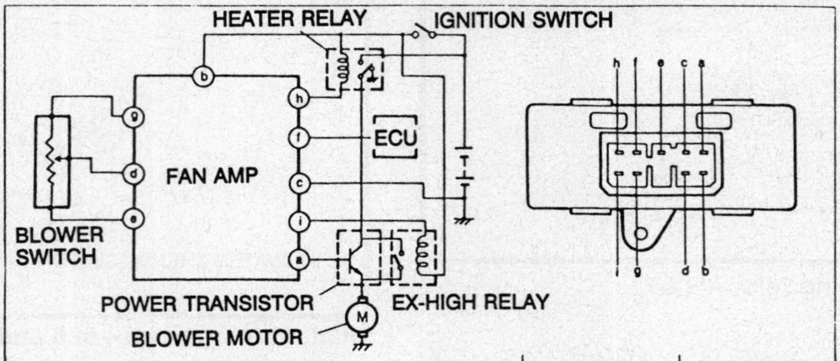
HEATER RELAY
IGNITION SWITCH
ECU
FAN AMP
BLOWER SWITCH
POWER TRANSISTOR
EX-HIGH RELAY
BLOWER MOTOR

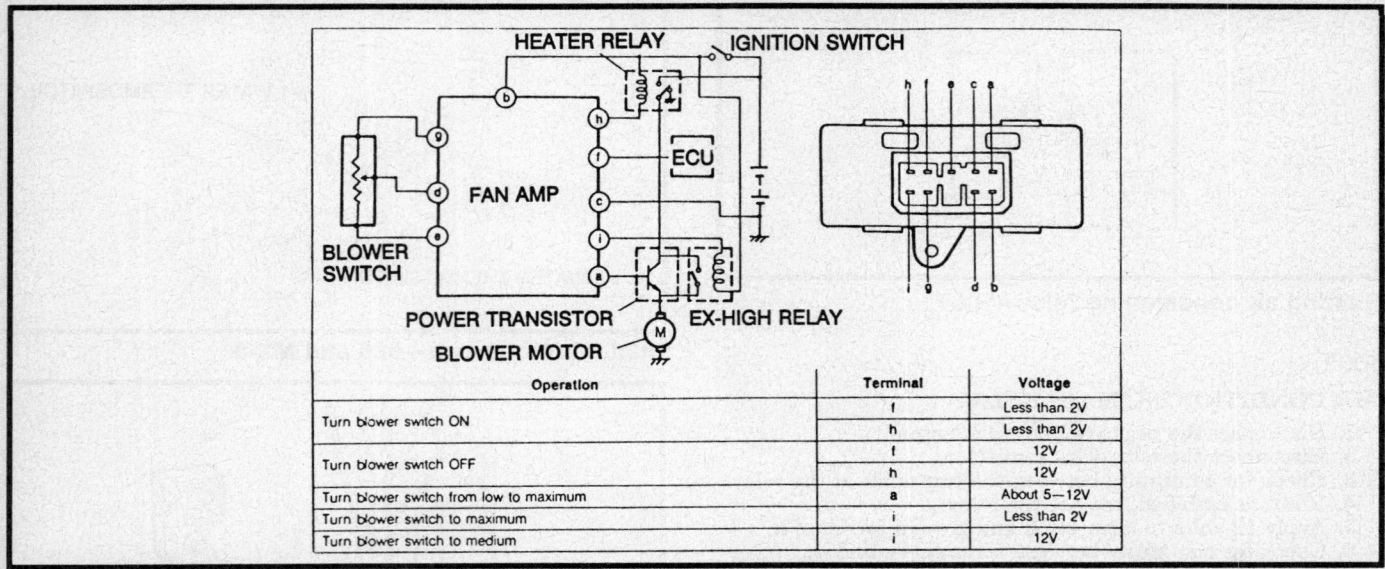

Operation	Terminal	Voltage
Turn blower switch ON	f	Less than 2V
	h	Less than 2V
Turn blower switch OFF	f	12V
	h	12V
Turn blower switch from low to maximum	a	About 5–12V
Turn blower switch to maximum	i	Less than 2V
Turn blower switch to medium	i	12V

Fan amp testing—RX-7

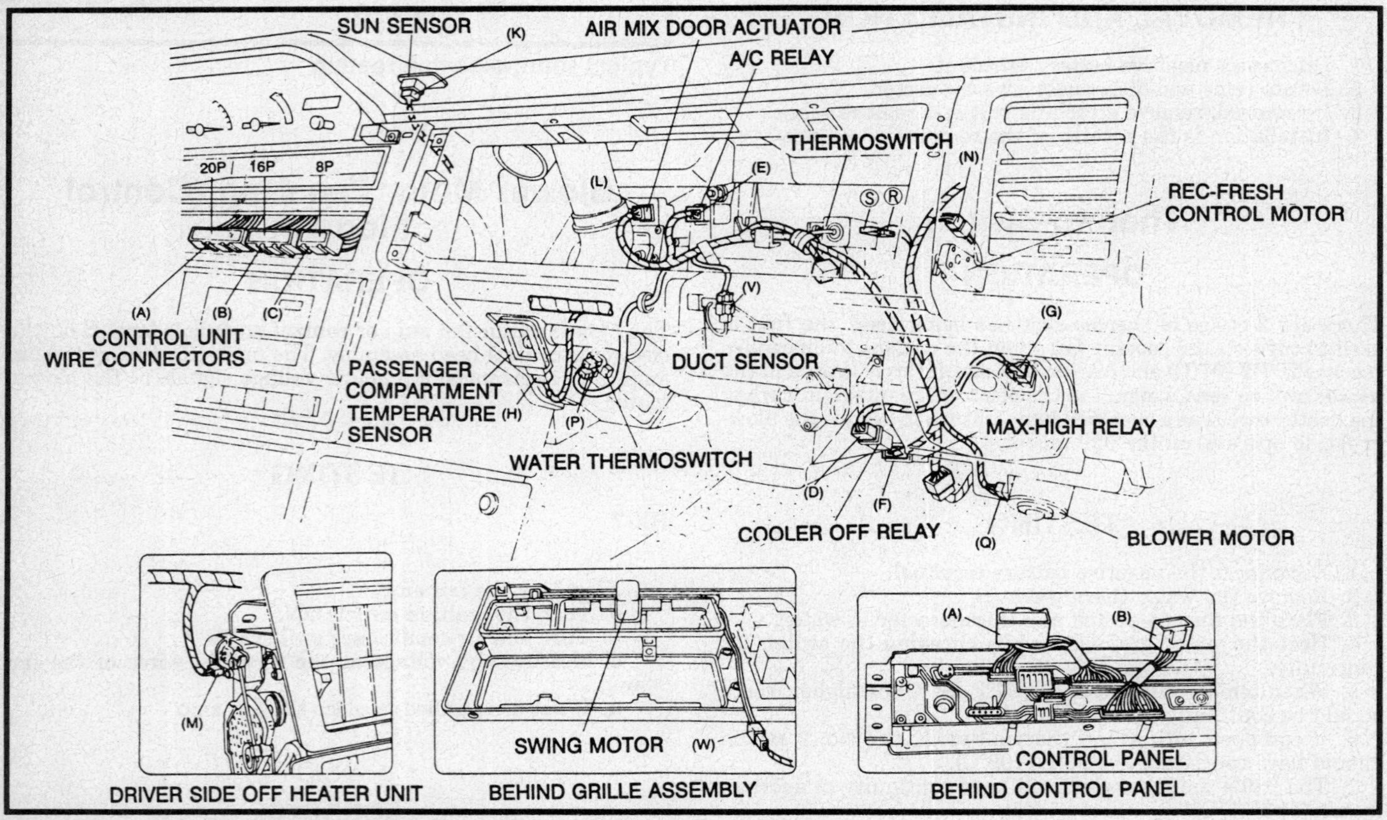
SUN SENSOR
(K)
AIR MIX DOOR ACTUATOR
A/C RELAY
THERMOSWITCH
(N)
REC-FRESH
CONTROL MOTOR
20P
16P
8P
(L)
(E)
(A)
(B)
(C)
CONTROL UNIT
WIRE CONNECTORS
(V)
(G)
PASSENGER
COMPARTMENT
TEMPERATURE
SENSOR
(H)
(P)
DUCT SENSOR
MAX-HIGH RELAY
WATER THERMOSWITCH
(D)
(F)
COOLER OFF RELAY
(Q)
BLOWER MOTOR
(M)
DRIVER SIDE OFF HEATER UNIT
SWING MOTOR
(W)
BEHIND GRILLE ASSEMBLY
CONTROL PANEL
BEHIND CONTROL PANEL

Electronic control head component and wire harness location—929

TESTING

929

PASSENGER COMPARTMENT SENSOR, AMBIENT AIR SENSOR AND DUCT SENSOR

1. Disconnect the negative battery terminal.
2. Disconnect the sensor wire connector.
3. Measure the resistance between the 2 terminals.
4. If the sensors resistance is not 2.9–3.1K ohms at 77°F (25°C), replace the sensor.

SUN SENSOR

1. Disconnect the negative battery terminal.

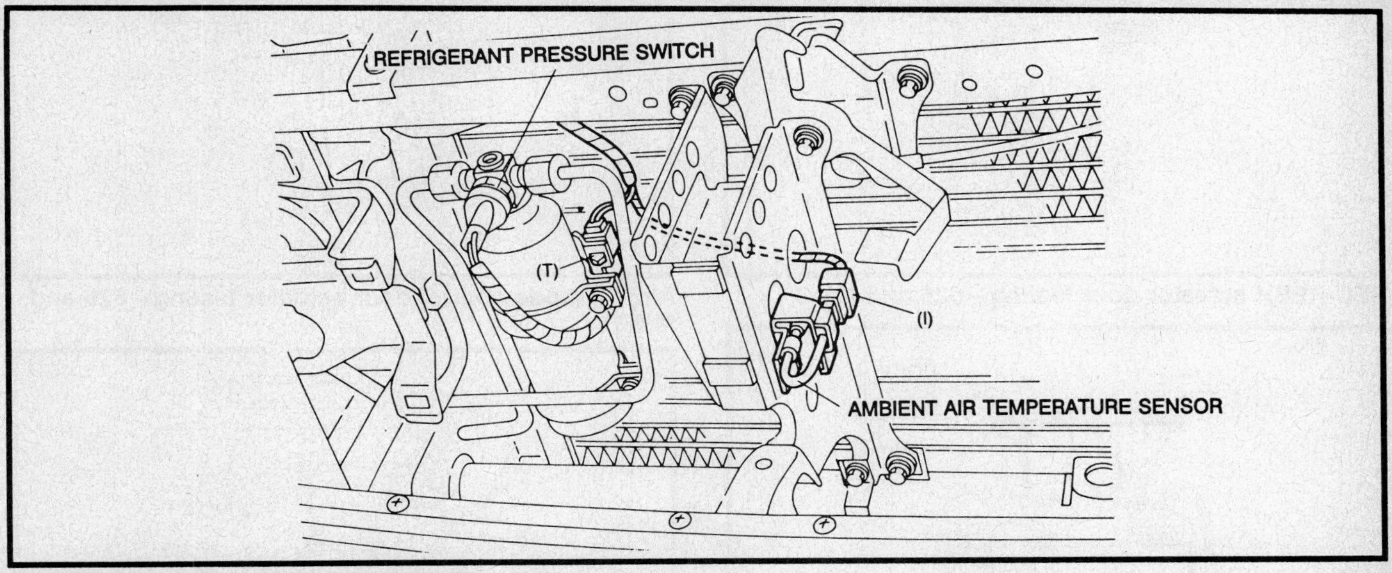
REFRIGERANT PRESSURE SWITCH
(T)
(I)
AMBIENT AIR TEMPERATURE SENSOR

Ambient air temperature sensor location—929

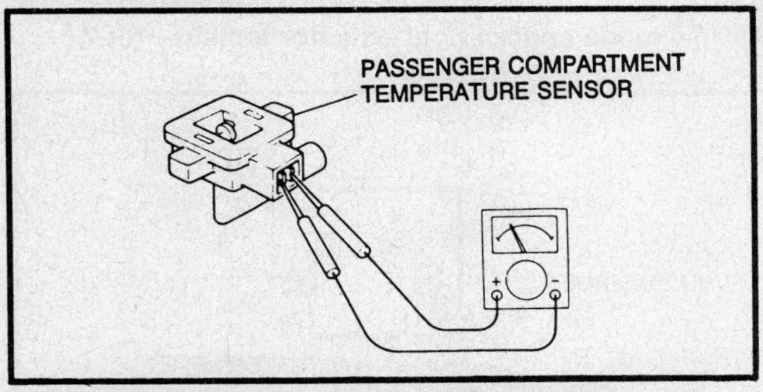
PASSENGER COMPARTMENT
TEMPERATURE SENSOR

Passenger compartment temperature sensor testing—929

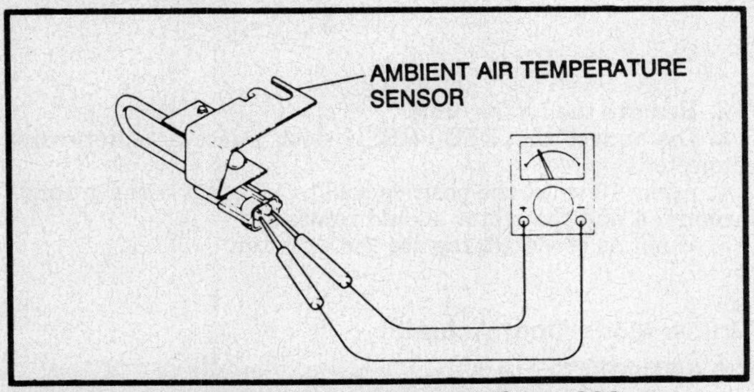
AMBIENT AIR TEMPERATURE
SENSOR

Ambient air temperature sensor testing—929

2. Disconnect the sensors wire connector.
3. Measure the resistance between the terminals, with the positive lead on terminal **1** and ground on terminal **2** there should be 10K ohms–infinity .
4. Measure the resistance between the terminals, with the positive lead on terminal **2** and ground on terminal **1** there should be 0–199 ohms.
5. Set the tester at the 3 milli-amp range.
6. Hold an incandescent lamp of 60w, 5.9 inches from the sensor.

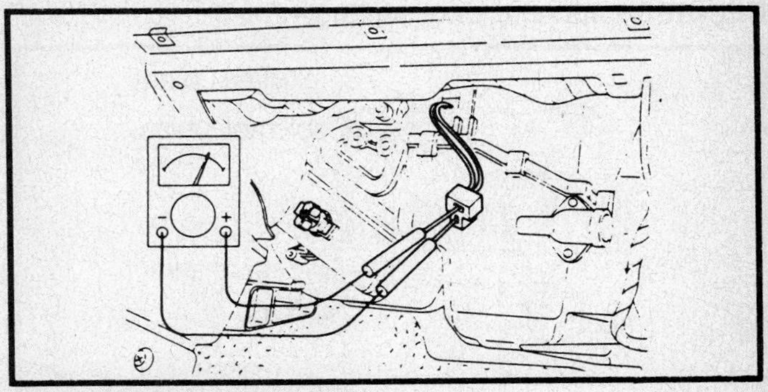

Duct sensor testing—929

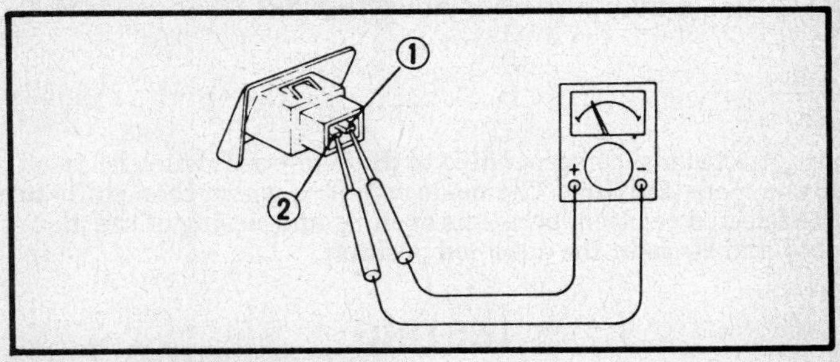
①
②

Sun sensor testing—929

7. Measure the current.
8. If less than 0.2 milli-amp, replace the sensor.

REMOVAL AND INSTALLATION

1. Disconnect negative battery terminal.
2. Locate sensor and disconnect wire connector.
3. Remove attaching bolt and remove sensor.
4. Installation is the reverse of the removal procedure.

Actuators

OPERATION

When the mode switch on the control head panel is depressed,

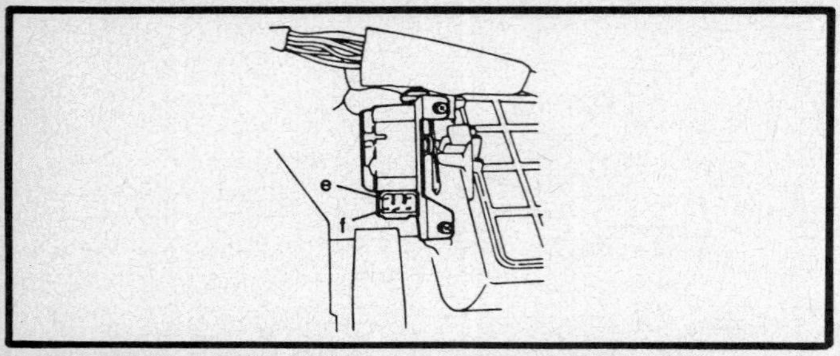
e
f

REC-RESH actuator door testing—626 and MX-6

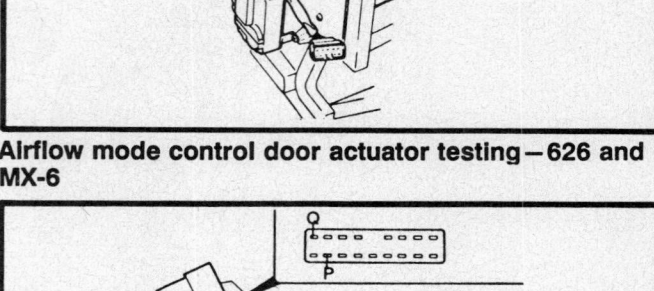

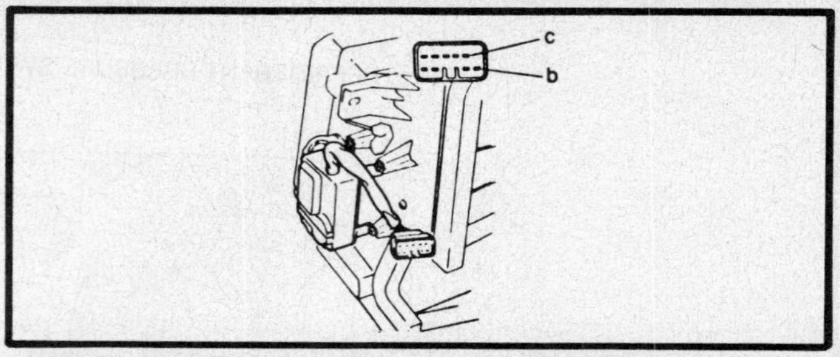
c
b

Airflow mode control door actuator testing—626 and MX-6

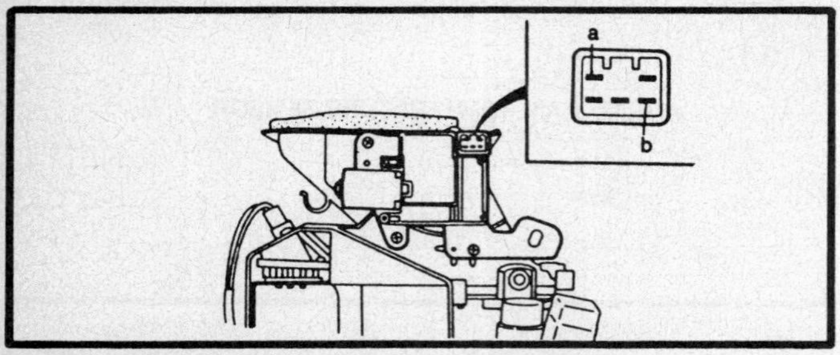
a
b

REC-RESH actuator door testing—RX-7

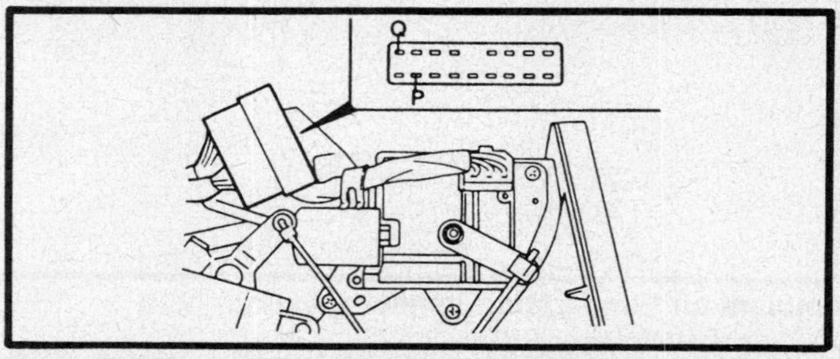
Q
P

Airflow mode control door actuator testing—RX-7

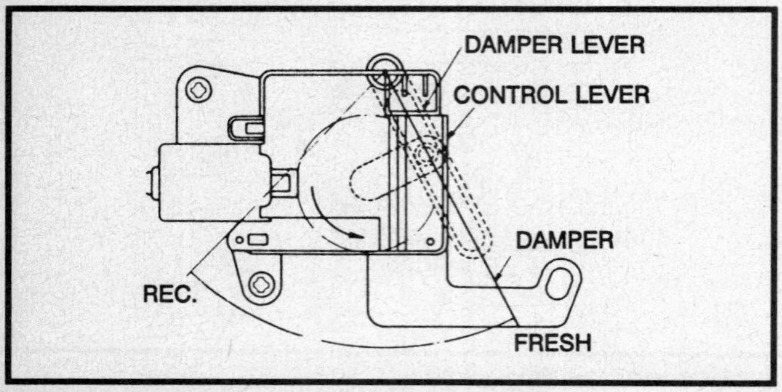
DAMPER LEVER
CONTROL LEVER
DAMPER
REC.
FRESH

REC-RESH actuator door action—RX-7

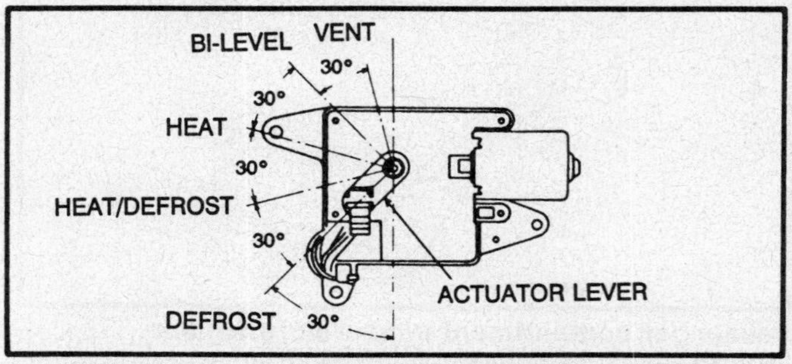
BI-LEVEL
VENT
30°
30°
HEAT
30°
HEAT/DEFROST
30°
ACTUATOR LEVER
DEFROST
30°

Airflow mode control door actuator action—RX-7

an output signal corresponding to the depressed switch is issued to the mode actuator. The mode actuator, which then shifts to the selected position, performs opening and closing of the mode door and stops in the specified position.

TESTING

Rec-Fresh Selector Door Actuator

626 AND MX-6

1. Disconnect the negative battery terminal.
2. Remove the glove box and the undercover.
3. Disconnect the REC-FRESH selector door actuator wire connector.
4. Apply 12 volts, the positive lead to terminal **e** and ground terminal **f** and the motor should rotate to the REC position.
5. Apply 12 volts, the positive lead to terminal **f** and ground terminal **e** and the motor should rotate to the FRESH position.
6. If not as specified, replace the actuator.

RX-7

1. Disconnect the negative battery terminal.
2. Remove the blower unit.
3. Disconnect the REC-FRESH door select actuator wire connector.
4. Apply 12 volts, the positive lead to terminal **b** and ground terminal **a** and the motor should rotate.
5. If not as specified, replace the actuator.

Airflow Mode Door Actuator

626 AND MX-6

1. Disconnect the negative battery terminal.
2. Remove the instrument panel.
3. Disconnect the actuator wire connector.
4. Apply 12 volts, the positive lead to terminal **c** and ground terminal **b** and the motor should rotate to the VENT position.
5. Apply 12 volts, the positive lead to terminal **b** and ground terminal **c** and the motor should rotate to the HEAT position.
6. If not as specified, replace the actuator.

RX-7

1. Disconnect the negative battery terminal.
2. Remove the instrument panel.

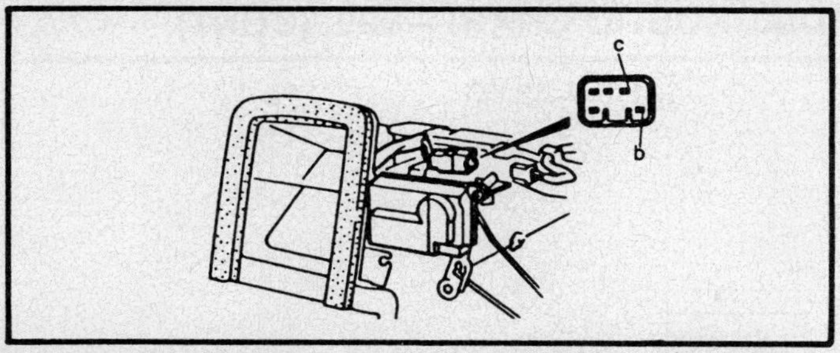
c
b

Temperature blend door actuator testing – 626 and MX-6

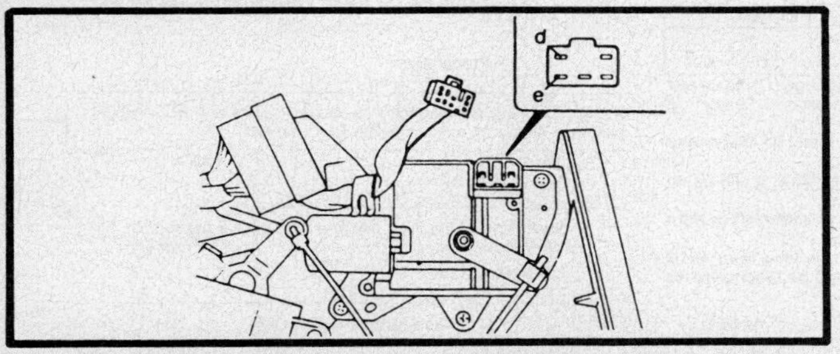
d
e

Temperature blend door actuator testing – RX-7

3. Disconnect the actuator wire connector.
4. Apply 12 volts, the positive lead to terminal **P** and ground terminal **Q** and the motor should rotate to the DEF position.
5. Apply 12 volts, the positive lead to terminal **Q** and ground terminal **P** and the motor should rotate to the VENT position.
6. If not as specified, replace the actuator.

Temperature Control Door Actuator

626 AND MX-6

1. Disconnect the negative battery terminal.
2. Remove the instrument panel.
3. Disconnect the actuator wire connector.
4. Apply 12 volts, the positive lead to terminal **b** and ground terminal **c** and the motor should rotate to the VENT position.
5. Apply 12 volts, the positive lead to terminal **c** and ground terminal **b** and the motor should rotate to the HEAT position.
6. If not as specified, replace the actuator.

RX-7

1. Disconnect the negative battery terminal.
2. Remove the instrument panel.
3. Disconnect the actuator wire connector.
4. Apply 12 volts, the positive lead to terminal **d** and ground terminal **e** and the motor should rotate to the HOT position.
5. Apply 12 volts, the positive lead to terminal **e** and ground terminal **d** and the motor should rotate to the COLD position.
6. If not as specified, replace the actuator.

REMOVAL AND INSTALLATION

1. Disconnect negative battery terminal.
2. Locate the actuator.
3. Remove the instrument panel or glove box, if required.
4. Remove heater unit, if required.
5. Disconnect the actuator wire connector.
6. Remove actuator attaching screws.
7. Remove the actuator.
8. Installation is the reverse of the removal procedure.

SYSTEM DIAGNOSIS

ELECTRONIC CONTROL HEAD SELF DIAGNOSTIC CHART – 929

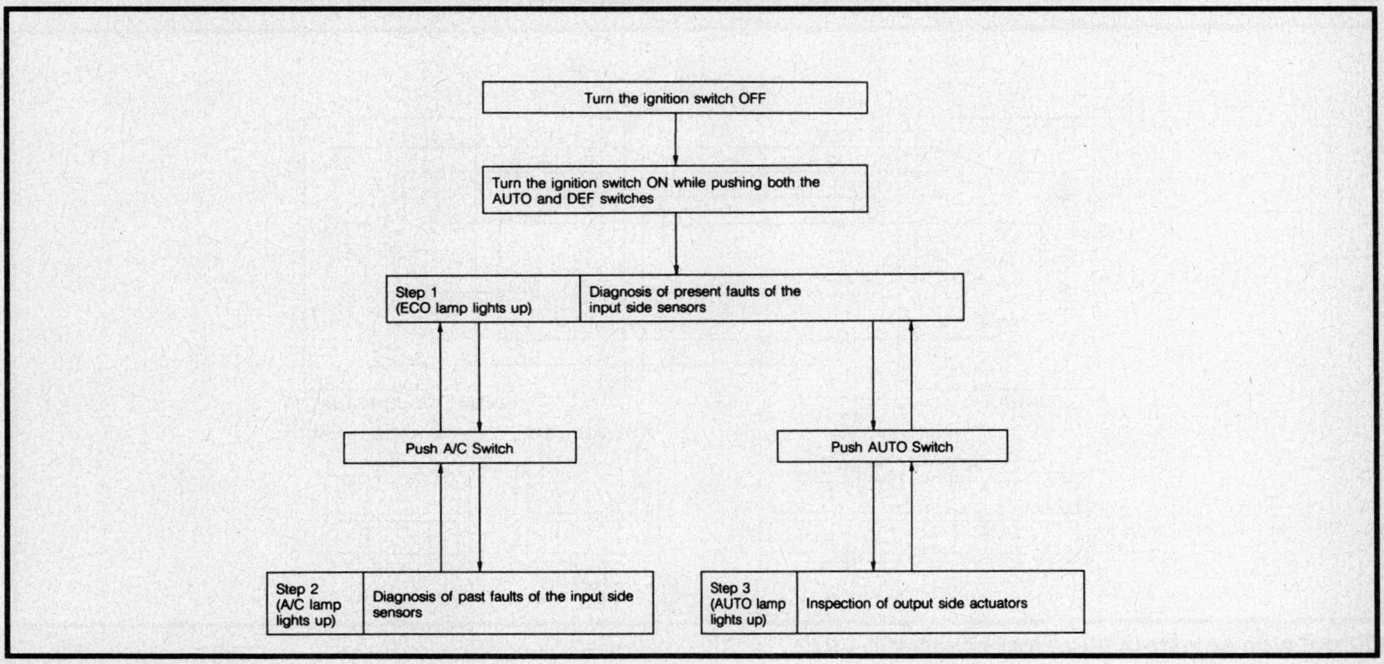
Turn the ignition switch OFF
Turn the ignition switch ON while pushing both the AUTO and DEF switches
Step 1 (ECO lamp lights up)
Diagnosis of present faults of the input side sensors
Push A/C Switch
Push AUTO Switch
Step 2 (A/C lamp lights up)
Diagnosis of past faults of the input side sensors
Step 3 (AUTO lamp lights up)
Inspection of output side actuators

ELECTRONIC CONTROL HEAD SELF DIAGNOSTIC CHART—929, (CONT).

Operation Sequence

Preparation:
Warm up engine
Turn ignition switch OFF
Set blower switch to AUTO
Set T/L at 75
Set 60W bulb 15 cm (6 in) from solar radiation sensor

Starting:
Turn ignition switch ON while pushing both AUTO and DEF switches

Step 1 (Diagnosis of present faults of input side sensors):
Are VENT and FRESH LED's lit? — NO → Sensor or Harness Faults

YES → Push A/C switch

Sensor or Harness Faults

LED (flashes ON and OFF)	Corresponding sensor
VENT	*PCT Sensor
BI-LEVEL	Ambient Air Sensor
HEAT	Duct Sensor
HEAT/DEF	Sun Sensor
DEFROST	Potentiometer
FRESH	Water thermosensor
RECIRC	Fan Switch
SWING	Temperature control lever

*PCT Sensor = Passenger Compartment Temperature Sensor

Note
- **If no light strikes the sun sensor, it will be diagnosed as faulty.**
- **If the blower switch is set at OFF or MAX, it will be diagnosed as faulty.**
- **If the temperature control lever is set at the left or right side, it will be diagnosed as faulty.**
- **If the engine coolant temperature is less than 40°C (104°F), the water thermoswitch will be diagnosed as faulty.**

Step 2 (Diagnosis of past faults of input side sensors):
Are VENT and FRESH LED's lit? — NO → Inspection for faulty sensor or harness connections

Inspection for faulty sensor or harness connections

LED (flashes ON and OFF)	Corresponding sensor
VENT	PCT Sensor
BI-LEVEL	Ambient Air Sensor
HEAT	Duct Sensor
DEFROST	Potentiometer

YES → Return to step 1 by pushing A/C Switch

Push AUTO switch

Step 3 (Inspection of actuators):
Are output side components operating normally (actuator, blower, magnetic clutch)? — NO → Faulty actuator or harness / Faulty blower motor or harness / Faulty magnetic clutch or harness

YES → Turn ignition switch OFF

Erasure of Past Faults from MEMORY

Preparation

While performing self-diagnosis, push both AUTO and REC/FRESH switches. Then turn ignition switch OFF and ON

Does AUTO LED flash ON and OFF for 4.5 seconds? — NO → (return to previous step)

YES → Turn ignition switch OFF

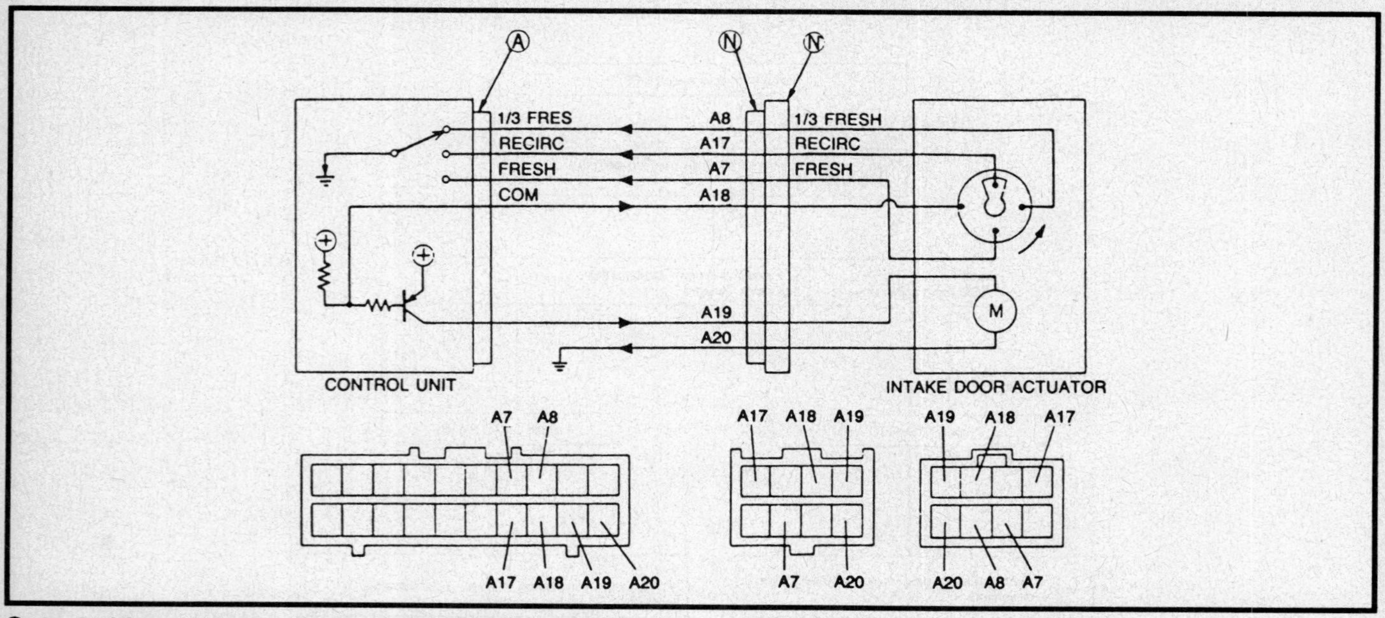
A
N
N'
1/3 FRES
RECIRC
FRESH
COM
A8
A17
A7
A18
A19
A20
1/3 FRESH
RECIRC
FRESH
M
CONTROL UNIT
INTAKE DOOR ACTUATOR
A7 A8
A17 A18 A19 A20
A17 A18 A19
A7 A20
A19 A18 A17
A20 A8 A7

Output side actuators electrical schematic—929

INTAKE DOOR ACTUATOR DIAGNOSTIC CHART—929

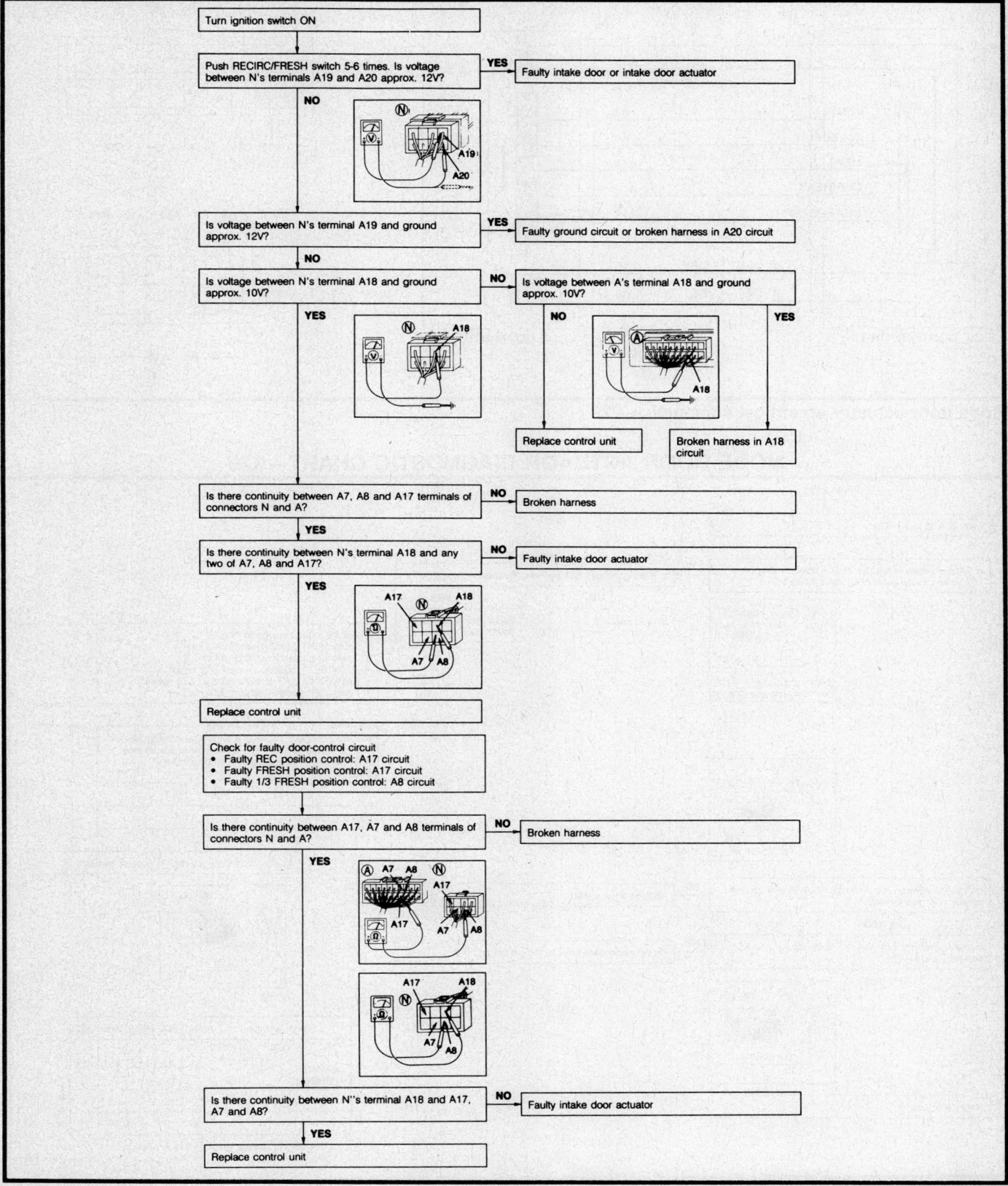

Turn ignition switch ON

↓

Push RECIRC/FRESH switch 5-6 times. Is voltage between N's terminals A19 and A20 approx. 12V?
- YES → Faulty intake door or intake door actuator
- NO ↓

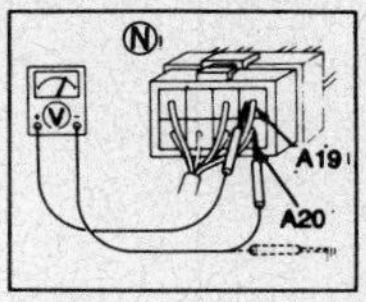
N
V
A19
A20

Is voltage between N's terminal A19 and ground approx. 12V?
- YES → Faulty ground circuit or broken harness in A20 circuit
- NO ↓

Is voltage between N's terminal A18 and ground approx. 10V?
- NO → Is voltage between A's terminal A18 and ground approx. 10V?
  - NO → Replace control unit
  - YES → Broken harness in A18 circuit
- YES ↓

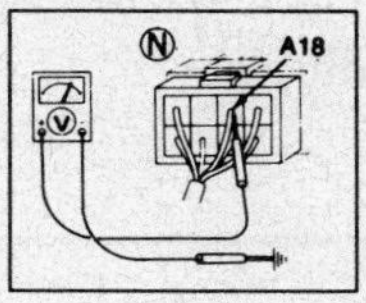
N
A18
V

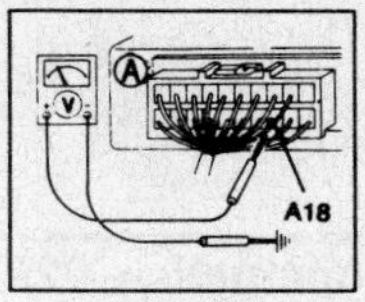
A
V
A18

Is there continuity between A7, A8 and A17 terminals of connectors N and A?
- NO → Broken harness
- YES ↓

Is there continuity between N's terminal A18 and any two of A7, A8 and A17?
- NO → Faulty intake door actuator
- YES ↓

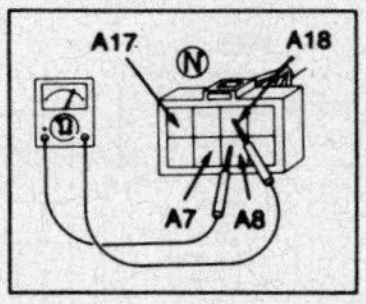
A17
N
A18
Ω
A7
A8

Replace control unit

Check for faulty door-control circuit
- Faulty REC position control: A17 circuit
- Faulty FRESH position control: A17 circuit
- Faulty 1/3 FRESH position control: A8 circuit

↓

Is there continuity between A17, A7 and A8 terminals of connectors N and A?
- NO → Broken harness
- YES ↓

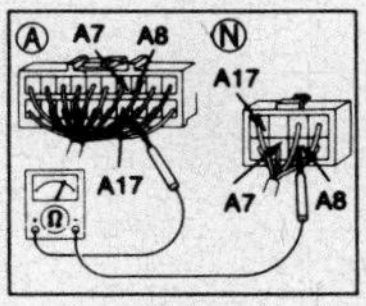
A
A7
A8
N
A17
Ω
A17
A7
A8

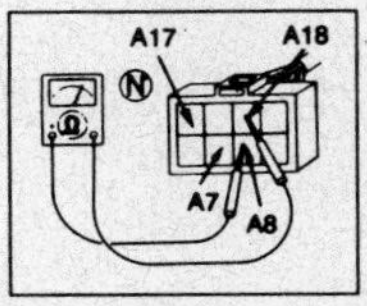
A17
A18
N
Ω
A7
A8

Is there continuity between N''s terminal A18 and A17, A7 and A8?
- NO → Faulty intake door actuator
- YES ↓

Replace control unit

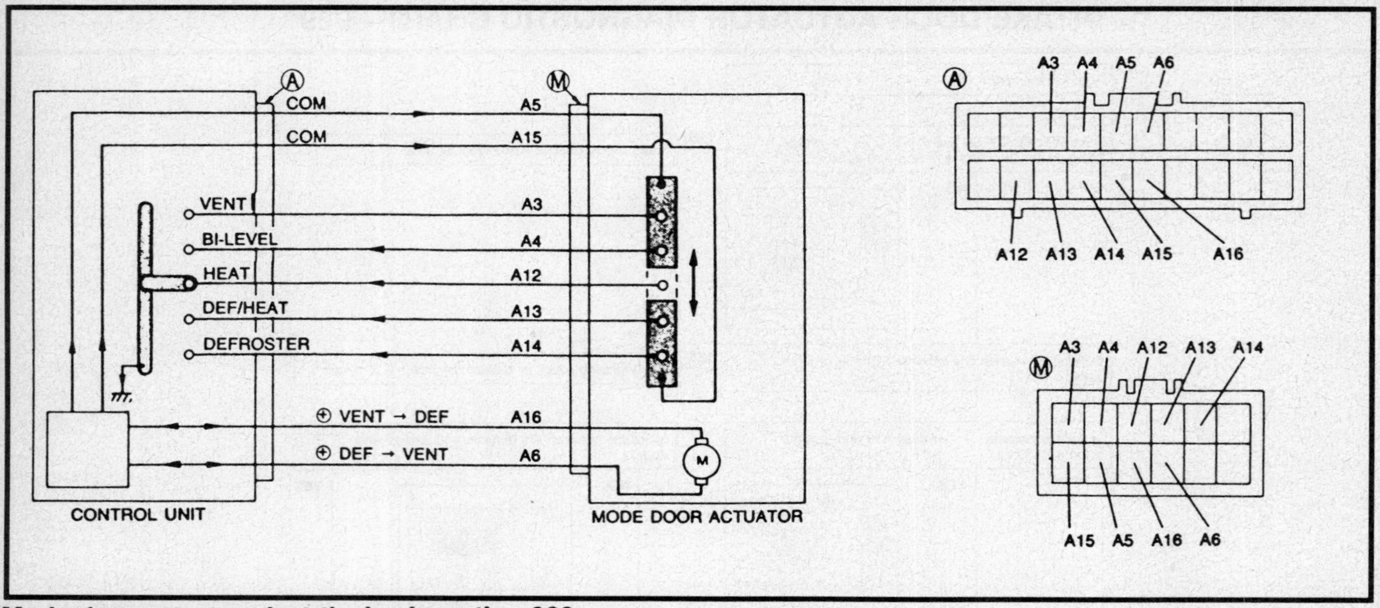
Ⓐ
COM
COM
VENT
BI-LEVEL
HEAT
DEF/HEAT
DEFROSTER
⊕ VENT → DEF
⊕ DEF → VENT
CONTROL UNIT
Ⓜ
A5
A15
A3
A4
A12
A13
A14
A16
A6
M
MODE DOOR ACTUATOR
Ⓐ
A3 A4 A5 A6
A12 A13 A14 A15 A16
Ⓜ
A3 A4 A12 A13 A14
A15 A5 A16 A6

Mode door actuator electrtical schematic—929

MODE DOOR ACTUAOR DIAGNOSTIC CHART—929

Turn ignition switch ON

Is voltage between A's terminals A16 and A6 approx. 10V while changing between each mode?

- YES → Is there continuity between A's terminals A6 and A16?
  - NO → Broken harness
  - YES → Faulty mode door(s) or mode door actuator
- NO ↓

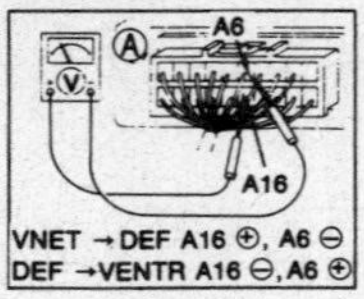
Ⓐ
A6
A16
VNET → DEF A16 ⊕, A6 ⊖
DEF → VENTR A16 ⊖, A6 ⊕

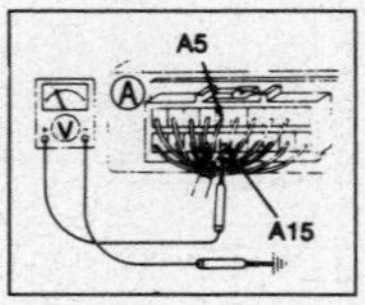
A5
Ⓐ
A15

Is voltage between A's terminals A5, A15 and ground approx. 10V respectively?

- NO → Replace control unit
- YES ↓

Is there continuity between A's terminals A5 and A3, and A15 and A14?

- NO → Faulty mode door actuator or broken harness
- YES ↓

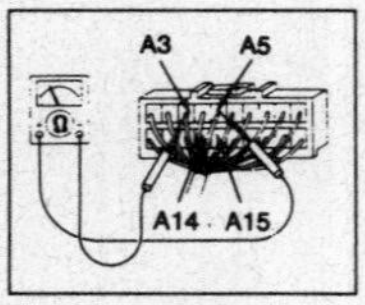
A3 A5
A14 A15

Replace control unit

Check for faulty door-control circuit
- Faulty VENT position control: A3 circuit
- Faulty BI-L position control: A4 circuit
- Faulty HEAT position control: A12 circuit
- Faulty DEF/HEAT position control: A13 circuit
- Faulty DEF position control: A14 circuit

Is there continuity between A's terminal A5 and A3, A4, A12, and A13 respectively, and between A's terminal A15 and A4, A12, A13, and A14 respectively? Refer to *1

- YES → Replace control unit
- NO → Faulty mode door actuator or broken harness

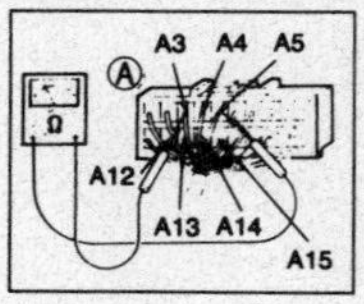
A3 A4 A5
Ⓐ
A12
A13 A14
A15

Switch position	VENT	BI-L	HEAT	DEF/HEAT	DEF
MODE POSITION TERMINAL / COMMON TERMINAL	A3	A4	A12	A13	A14
A5	O	O	O	O	X
A15	X	O	O	O	O

O: CONTINUITY except when in switch position
X : NO CONTINUITY

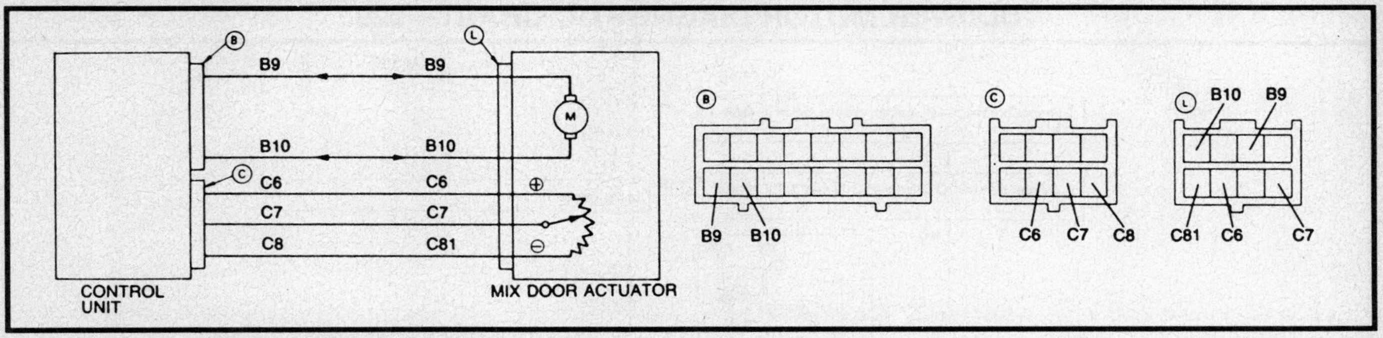
B9
B9
B10
B10
C6
C6
C7
C7
C8
C81
CONTROL UNIT
MIX DOOR ACTUATOR
B9
B10
C6
C7
C8
B10
B9
C81
C6
C7

Air mix door actuator electrical schematic—929

AIR MIX DOOR ACTUATOR DIAGNOSTIC CHART—929

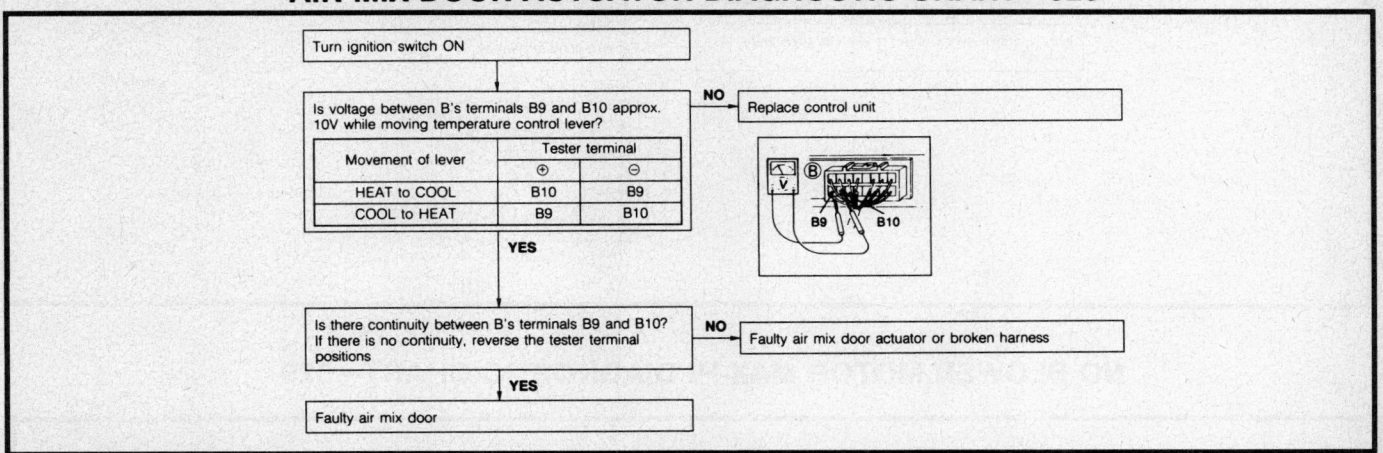

Turn ignition switch ON

Is voltage between B's terminals B9 and B10 approx. 10V while moving temperature control lever?

Movement of lever	Tester terminal	
	⊕	⊖
HEAT to COOL	B10	B9
COOL to HEAT	B9	B10

NO → Replace control unit

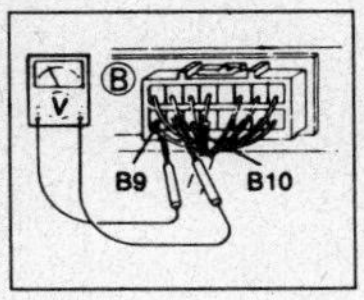
V
B
B9
B10

YES ↓

Is there continuity between B's terminals B9 and B10? If there is no continuity, reverse the tester terminal positions

NO → Faulty air mix door actuator or broken harness

YES ↓

Faulty air mix door

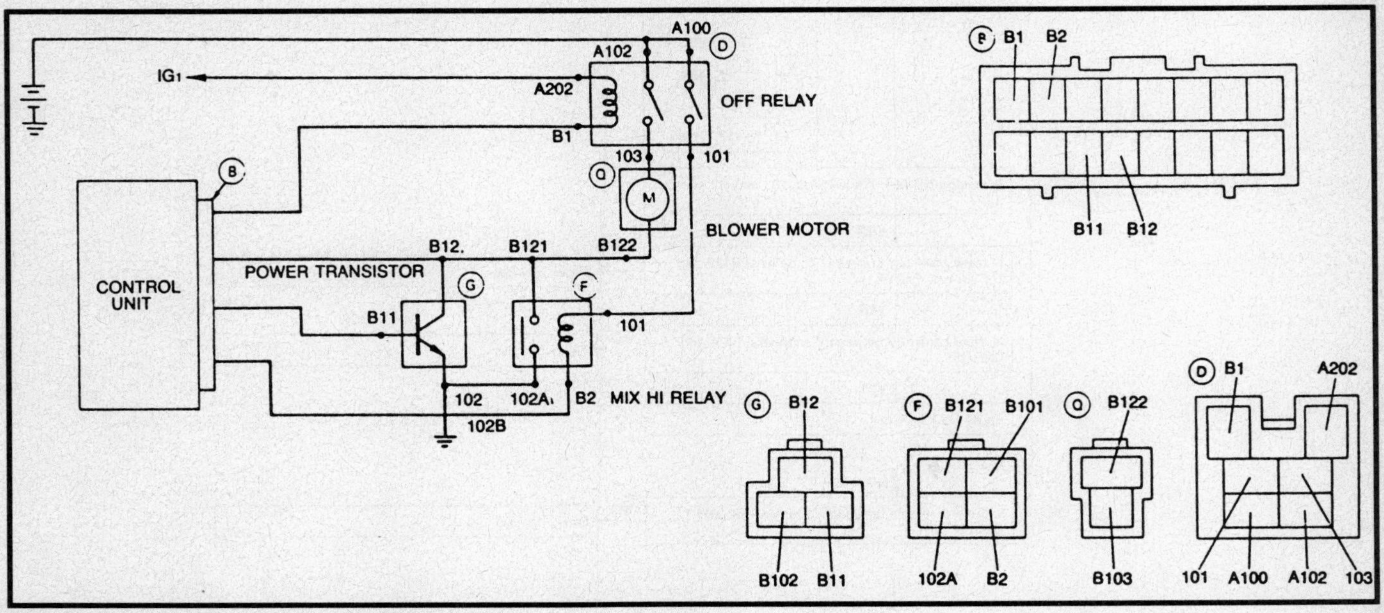
A100
A102
IG1
A202
OFF RELAY
B1
103
101
BLOWER MOTOR
CONTROL UNIT
B12.
B121
B122
POWER TRANSISTOR
B11
101
102
102A
B2
MIX HI RELAY
102B
B1
B2
B11
B12
B1
A202
B12
B121
B101
B122
B102
B11
102A
B2
B103
101
A100
A102
103

Blower motor electrical schematic—929

BLOWER MOTOR DIAGNOSTIC CHART—929

Turn ignition switch ON and set blower switch at MAX position

↓

Is voltage between Q's terminals 103 and B122 approx. 12V?
- YES → Faulty blower motor
- NO ↓

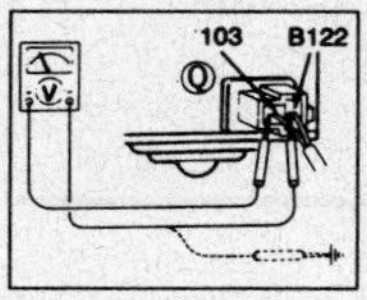
103
B122
Q
V

Is there continuity between Q's terminal 103 and ground?
- NO → Go to inspection
- YES ↓

Is there continuity between F's terminal 102A and ground?
- NO → Faulty ground or harness

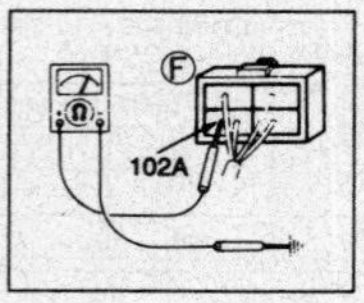
F
102A
Ω

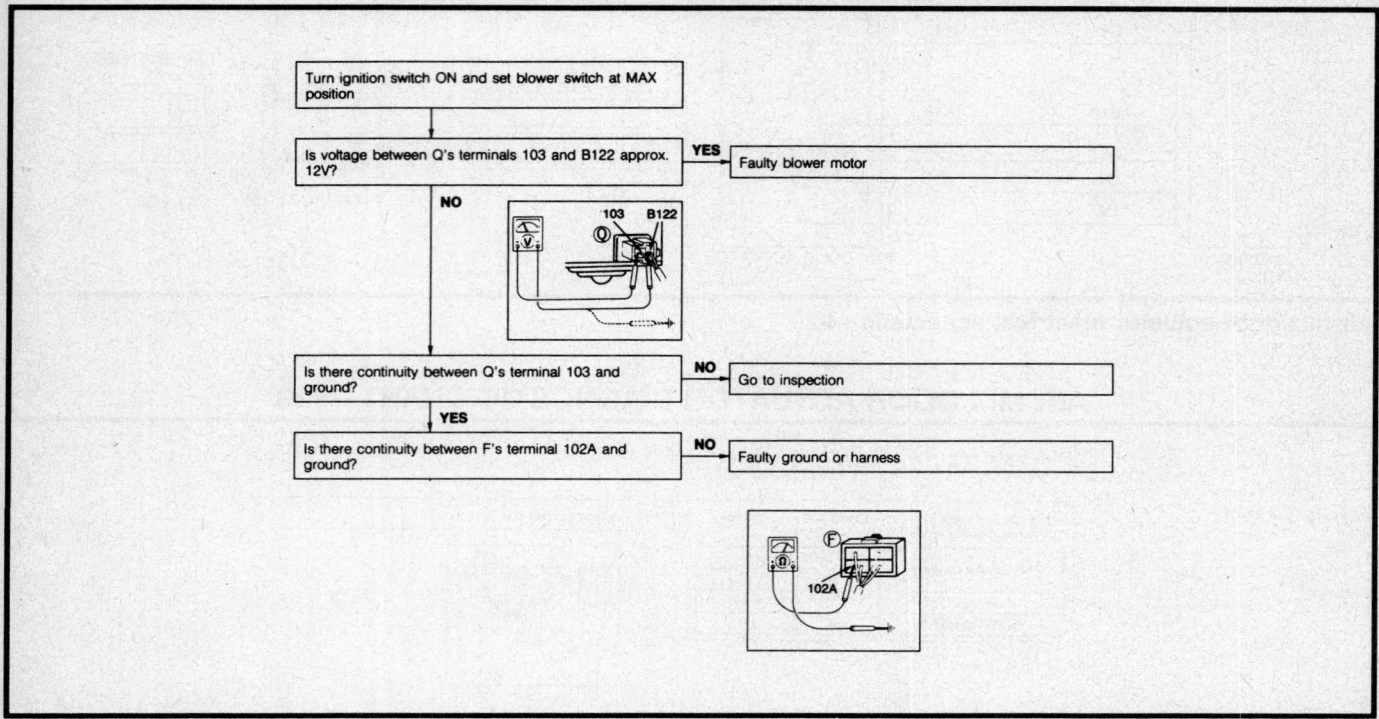

NO BLOWER MOTOR MAX-HI DIAGNOSTIC CHART—929

Turn ignition switch ON and set blower switch at MAX

↓

Is voltage between F's terminal 101 and ground approx. 12V?
- NO → Go to inspection
- YES ↓

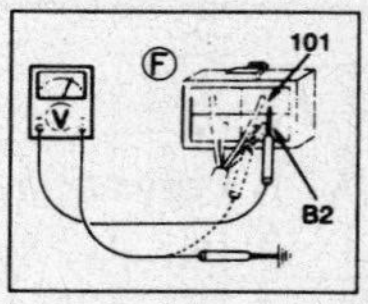
F
101
B2
V

Is voltage between F's terminals 101 and B2 approx. 12V?
- YES ↓

Is there continuity between Q's terminal B122 and F's terminal B121?
- NO → Faulty harness
- YES ↓

Is there continuity between F's terminal 102A and ground?
- NO → Faulty harness
- YES ↓

Faulty MAX HI relay

NO ↓

Is there continuity between F's terminal B2 and B's terminal B2?
- NO → Faulty harness

BLOWER MOTOR MAX-HI ONLY DIAGNOSTIC CHART—929

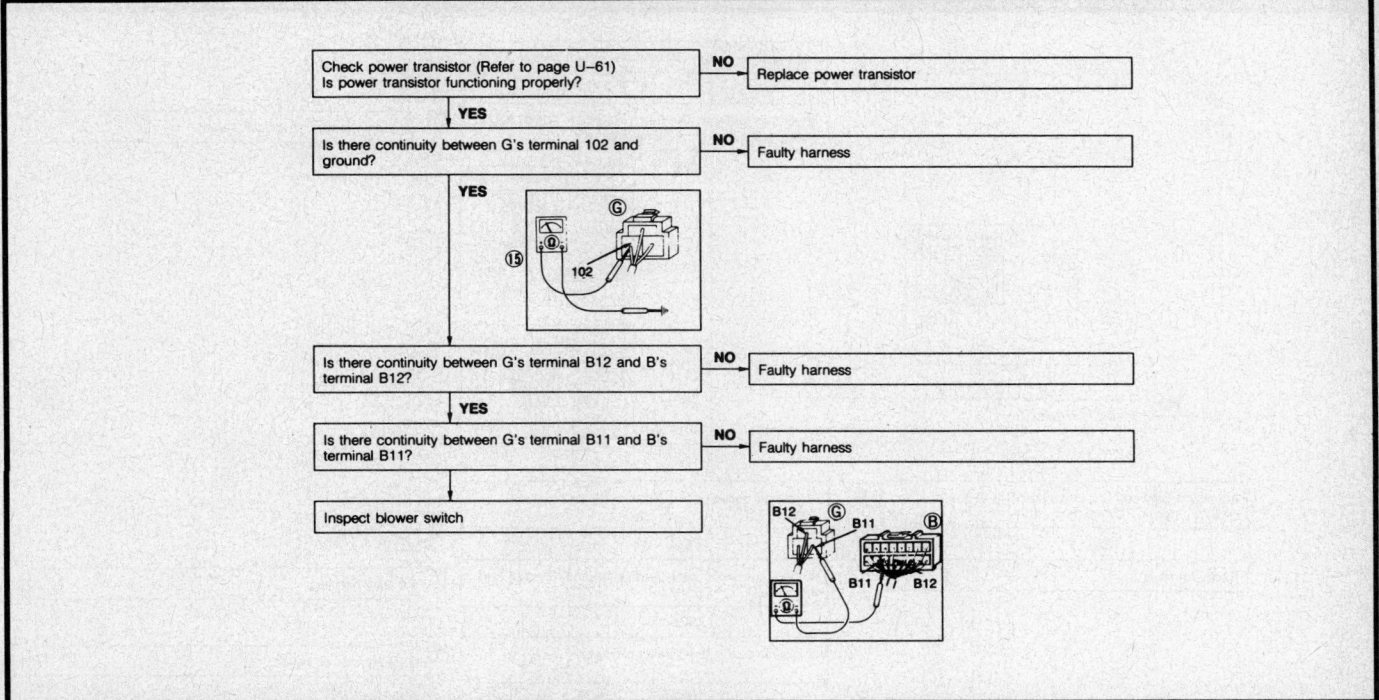

Check power transistor (Refer to page U–61)
Is power transistor functioning properly?
- NO → Replace power transistor
- YES ↓

Is there continuity between G's terminal 102 and ground?
- NO → Faulty harness
- YES ↓

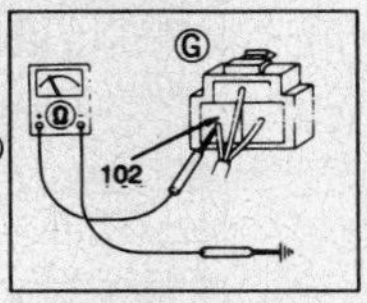
G
15
102

Is there continuity between G's terminal B12 and B's terminal B12?
- NO → Faulty harness
- YES ↓

Is there continuity between G's terminal B11 and B's terminal B11?
- NO → Faulty harness
- ↓

Inspect blower switch

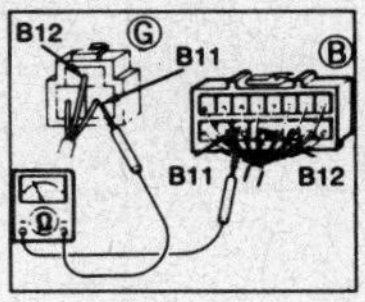
B12
G
B11
B
B11
B12

BLOWER MOTOR DIAGNOSTIC CHART—929

Turn ignition switch ON and set blower switch at OFF
↓

Is voltage between D's terminals A202 and B1 approx. 12V?
- NO → Replace OFF relay
- YES ↓

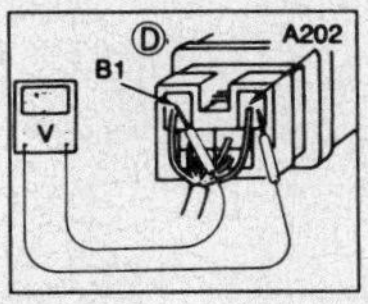
D
A202
B1
V

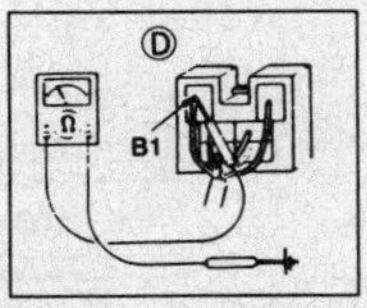
D
B1

Is there continuity between D's terminal B1 and ground?
- YES → Short circuit in harness
- NO ↓

Is blower switch functioning properly?
- NO → Faulty blower switch
- YES ↓

Replace control unit

OFF RELAY DIAGNOSTIC CHART – 929

Turn ignition switch ON and set blower switch at ON

Is voltage between D's terminals A102, A100, A202 and ground approx. 12V respectively?
- NO → Faulty harness or ignition switch
- YES ↓

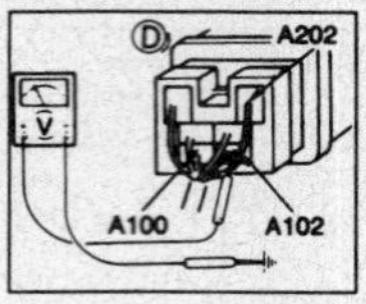
D
A202
A100
A102

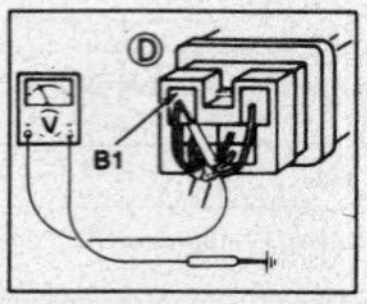
D
B1

Is voltage between D's terminal B1 and ground approx. 12V?
- NO → Is voltage between D's terminals 101, 103 and ground approx. 12V respectively?

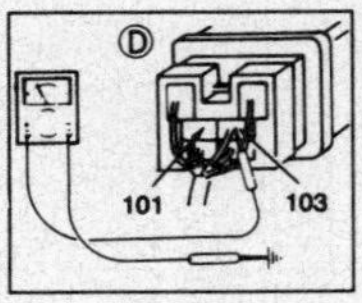
D
101
103

  - NO → Faulty OFF relay
  - YES → Faulty harness
- YES ↓

Is there continuity between D's terminal B1 and B's terminal B1?
- NO → Faulty harness
- YES ↓

Is blower switch functioning properly?
- NO → Faulty blower switch
- YES → Replace control unit

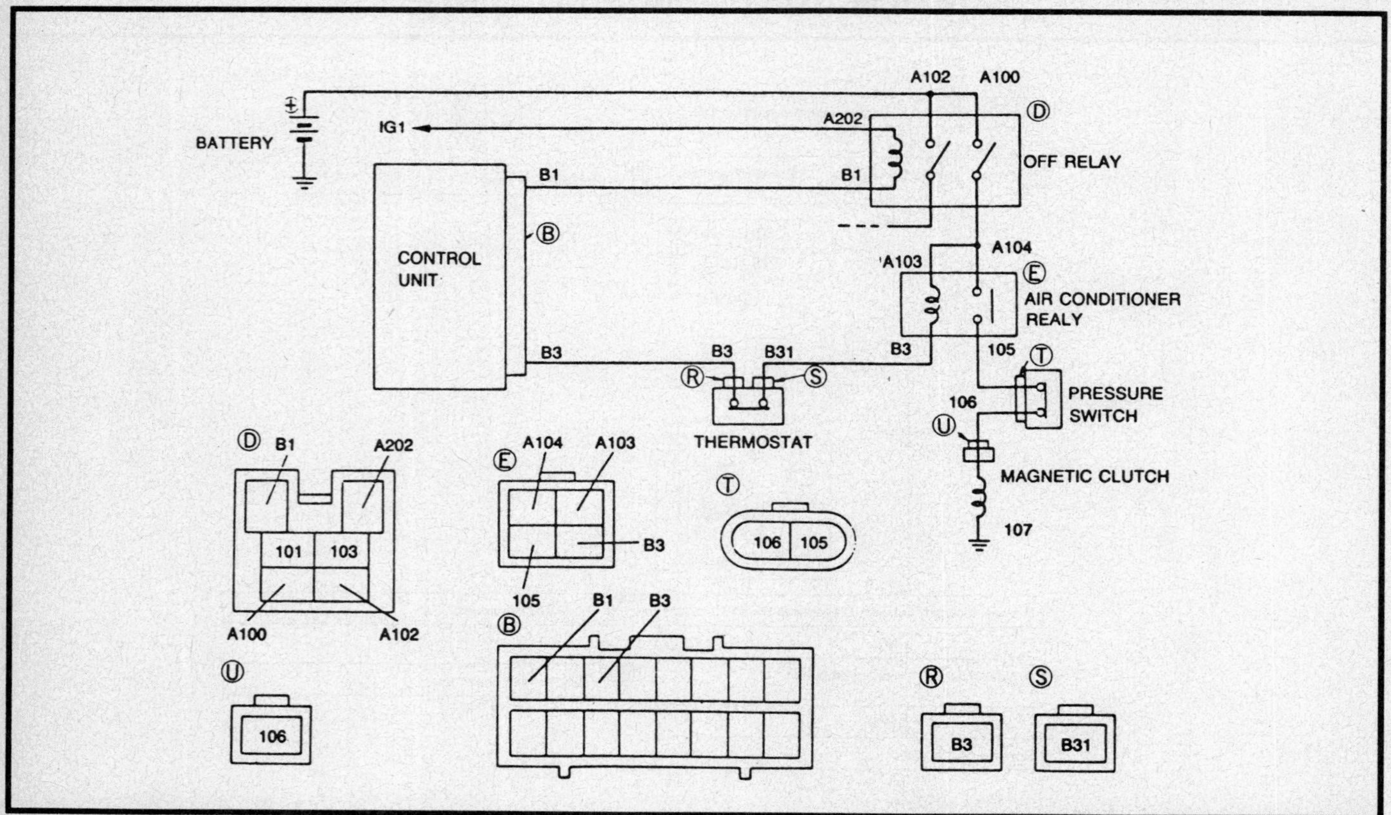
BATTERY
IG1
A202
A102
A100
D
OFF RELAY
B1
B1
CONTROL UNIT
B
A103
A104
E
AIR CONDITIONER REALY
B3
B3
B31
B3
R
S
THERMOSTAT
105
T
PRESSURE SWITCH
106
U
MAGNETIC CLUTCH
107
D B1 A202
101 103
A100 A102
E A104 A103
B3
105
T
106 105
B B1 B3
U
106
R
B3
S
B31

Compressor electrical schematic – 929

MAGNETIC CLUTCH DIAGNOSTIC CHART – 929

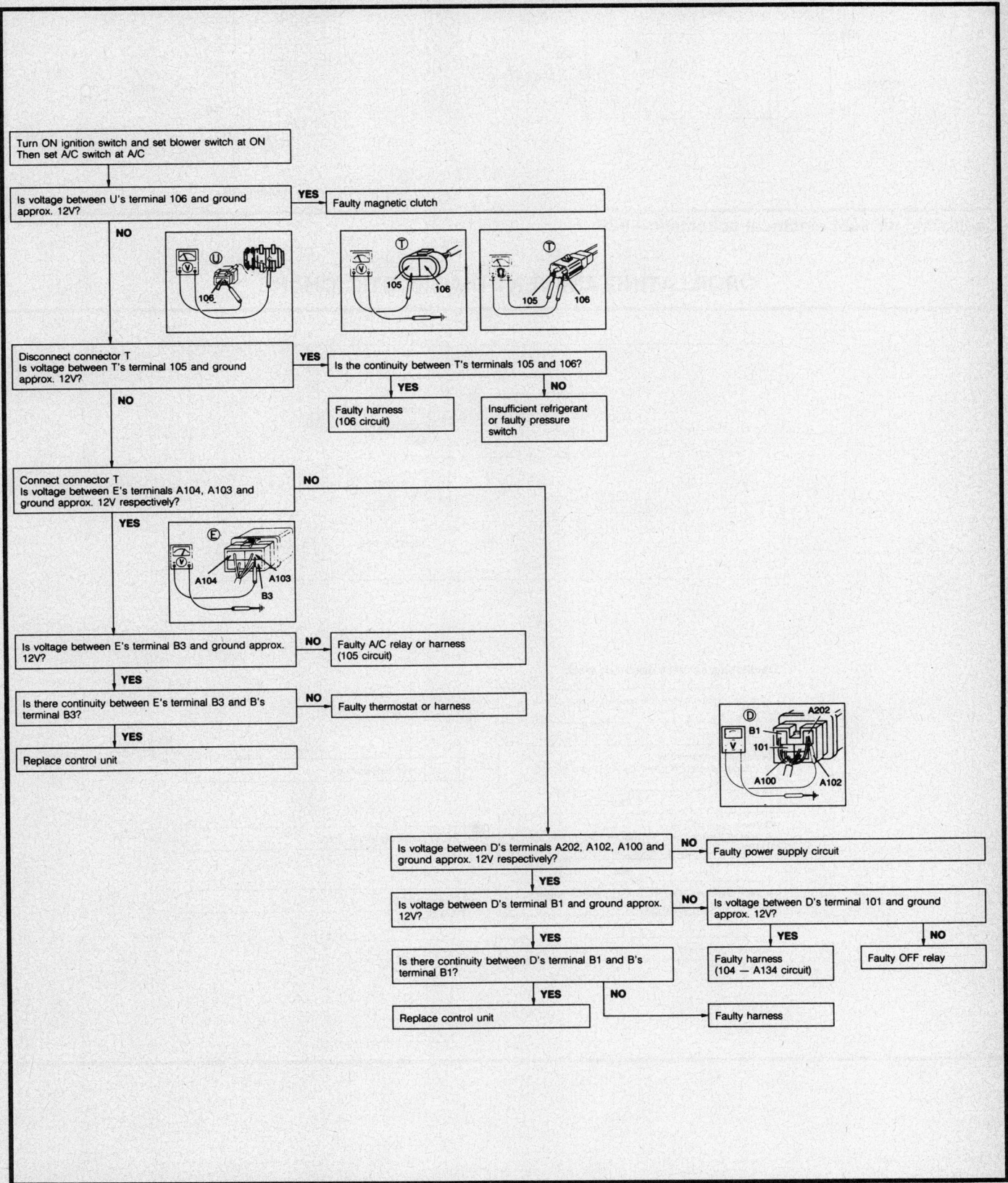

Turn ON ignition switch and set blower switch at ON
Then set A/C switch at A/C

Is voltage between U's terminal 106 and ground approx. 12V?
- YES → Faulty magnetic clutch
- NO → next step

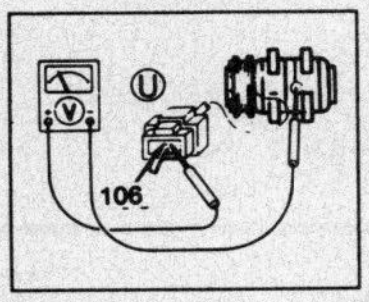
U
106

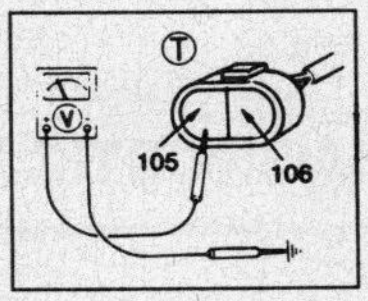
T
105
106

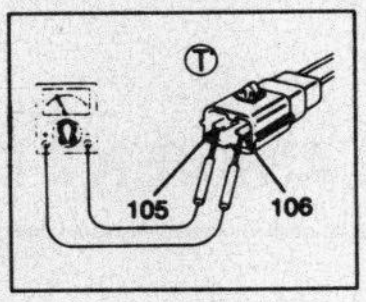
T
105
106

Disconnect connector T
Is voltage between T's terminal 105 and ground approx. 12V?
- YES → Is the continuity between T's terminals 105 and 106?
  - YES → Faulty harness (106 circuit)
  - NO → Insufficient refrigerant or faulty pressure switch
- NO → next step

Connect connector T
Is voltage between E's terminals A104, A103 and ground approx. 12V respectively?
- NO → Is voltage between D's terminals A202, A102, A100 and ground approx. 12V respectively?
- YES → next step

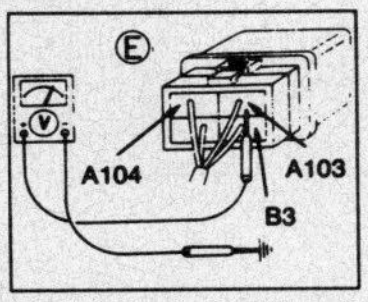
E
A104
A103
B3

Is voltage between E's terminal B3 and ground approx. 12V?
- NO → Faulty A/C relay or harness (105 circuit)
- YES → next step

Is there continuity between E's terminal B3 and B's terminal B3?
- NO → Faulty thermostat or harness
- YES → Replace control unit

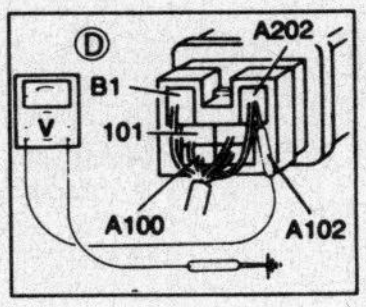
D
A202
B1
101
A100
A102

Is voltage between D's terminals A202, A102, A100 and ground approx. 12V respectively?
- NO → Faulty power supply circuit
- YES → next step

Is voltage between D's terminal B1 and ground approx. 12V?
- NO → Is voltage between D's terminal 101 and ground approx. 12V?
  - YES → Faulty harness (104 — A134 circuit)
  - NO → Faulty OFF relay
- YES → next step

Is there continuity between D's terminal B1 and B's terminal B1?
- YES → Replace control unit
- NO → Faulty harness

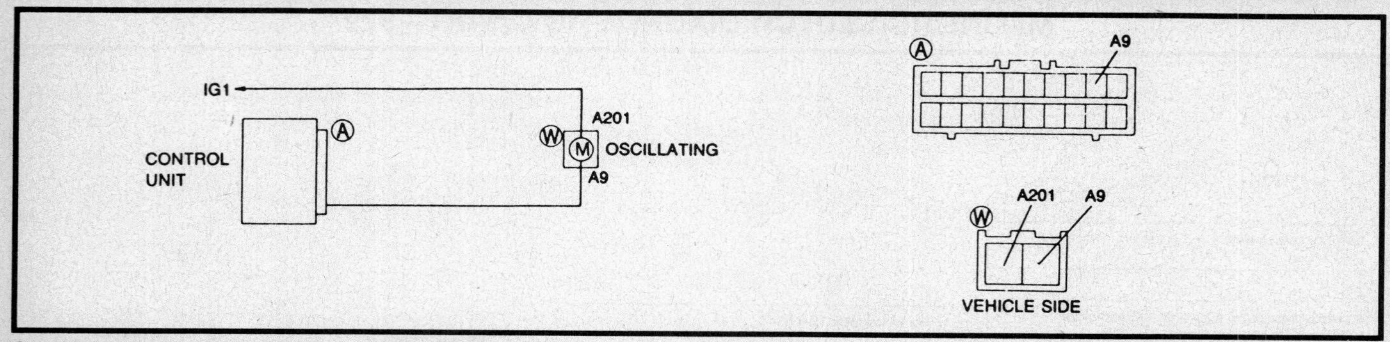
IG1
CONTROL UNIT
A
W
M
A201
OSCILLATING
A9
A
A9
A201
A9
W
VEHICLE SIDE

Oscillating air vent electrical schematic—929

OSCILLATING AIR VENT DIAGNOSTIC CHART

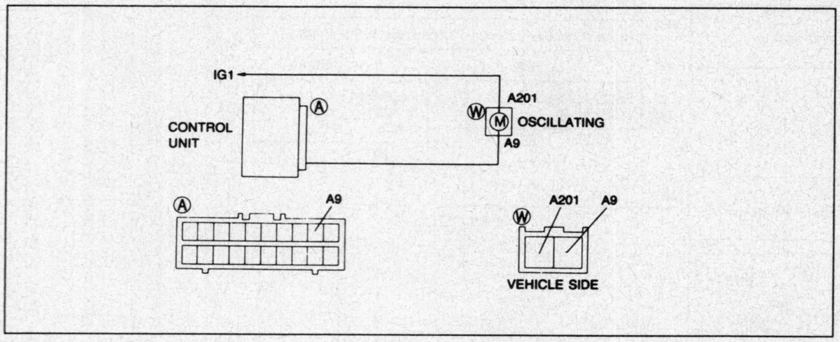
IG1
CONTROL UNIT
A
W
M
A201
OSCILLATING
A9
A
A9
W
A201
A9
VEHICLE SIDE

Oscillating air vent does not work

Turn ON ignition switch, blower switch, and oscillating switch

↓

Disconnect connector W
Is voltage between W's terminal A201 and ground approx. 12V?
- **NO** → Faulty power supply circuit
- **YES** ↓

Connect connector W
Is voltage between W's terminal A9 and ground approx. 0.5V?
- **YES** → Faulty oscillating louver motor
- **NO** ↓

Is there continuity between W's terminal A9 and A's terminal A9?
- **NO** → Broken harness
- **YES** ↓

Replace control unit

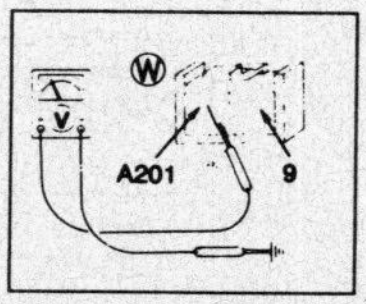
W
V
A201
9

WIRING SCHEMATICS

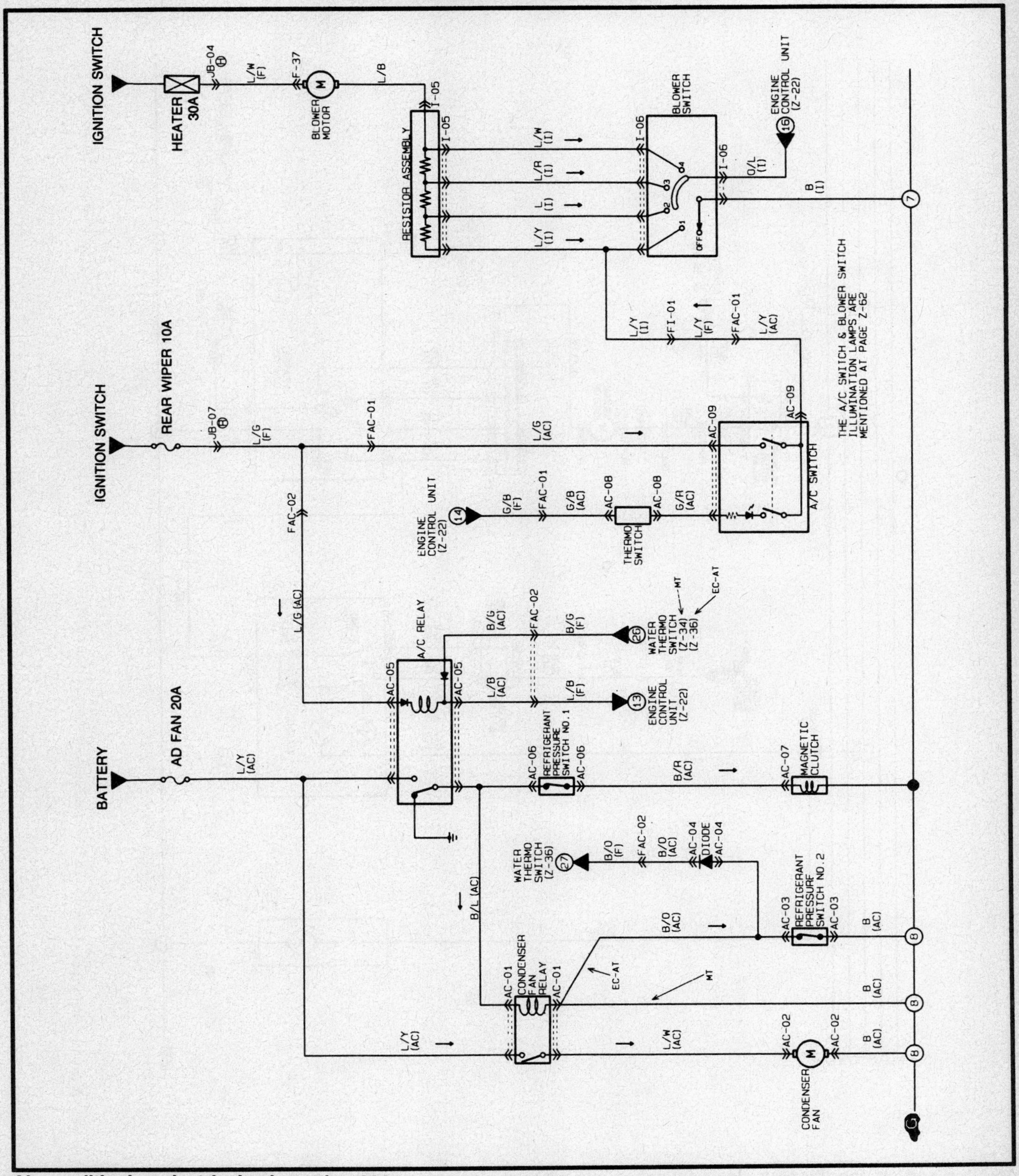
IGNITION SWITCH
HEATER 30A
JB-04
L/W (F)
F-37
BLOWER MOTOR
L/B
I-05
RESISTOR ASSEMBLY
L/W (I)
L/R (I)
L (I)
L/Y (I)
I-06
BLOWER SWITCH
OFF
O/L (I)
B (I)
ENGINE CONTROL UNIT (Z-22)
IGNITION SWITCH
REAR WIPER 10A
JB-07
L/G (F)
FAC-01
L/G (AC)
AC-09
A/C SWITCH
L/Y (I)
FI-01
L/Y (F)
L/Y (AC)
THE A/C SWITCH & BLOWER SWITCH ILLUMINATION LAMPS ARE MENTIONED AT PAGE Z-62
FAC-02
ENGINE CONTROL UNIT (Z-22)
G/B (F)
G/B (AC)
AC-08
THERMO SWITCH
G/B (AC)
L/G (AC)
A/C RELAY
AC-05
B/G (AC)
B/G (F)
WATER THERMO SWITCH (Z-34) (Z-36)
MT
EC-AT
L/B (AC)
L/B (F)
ENGINE CONTROL UNIT (Z-22)
BATTERY
AD FAN 20A
L/Y (AC)
AC-06
REFRIGERANT PRESSURE SWITCH NO.1
B/R (AC)
AC-07
MAGNETIC CLUTCH
WATER THERMO SWITCH (Z-36)
B/O (F)
B/O (AC)
AC-04
DIODE
B/L (AC)
B/O (AC)
AC-03
REFRIGERANT PRESSURE SWITCH NO.2
B (AC)
AC-01
CONDENSER FAN RELAY
EC-AT
MT
L/Y (AC)
L/W (AC)
AC-02
CONDENSER FAN

Air conditioning electrical schematic—323

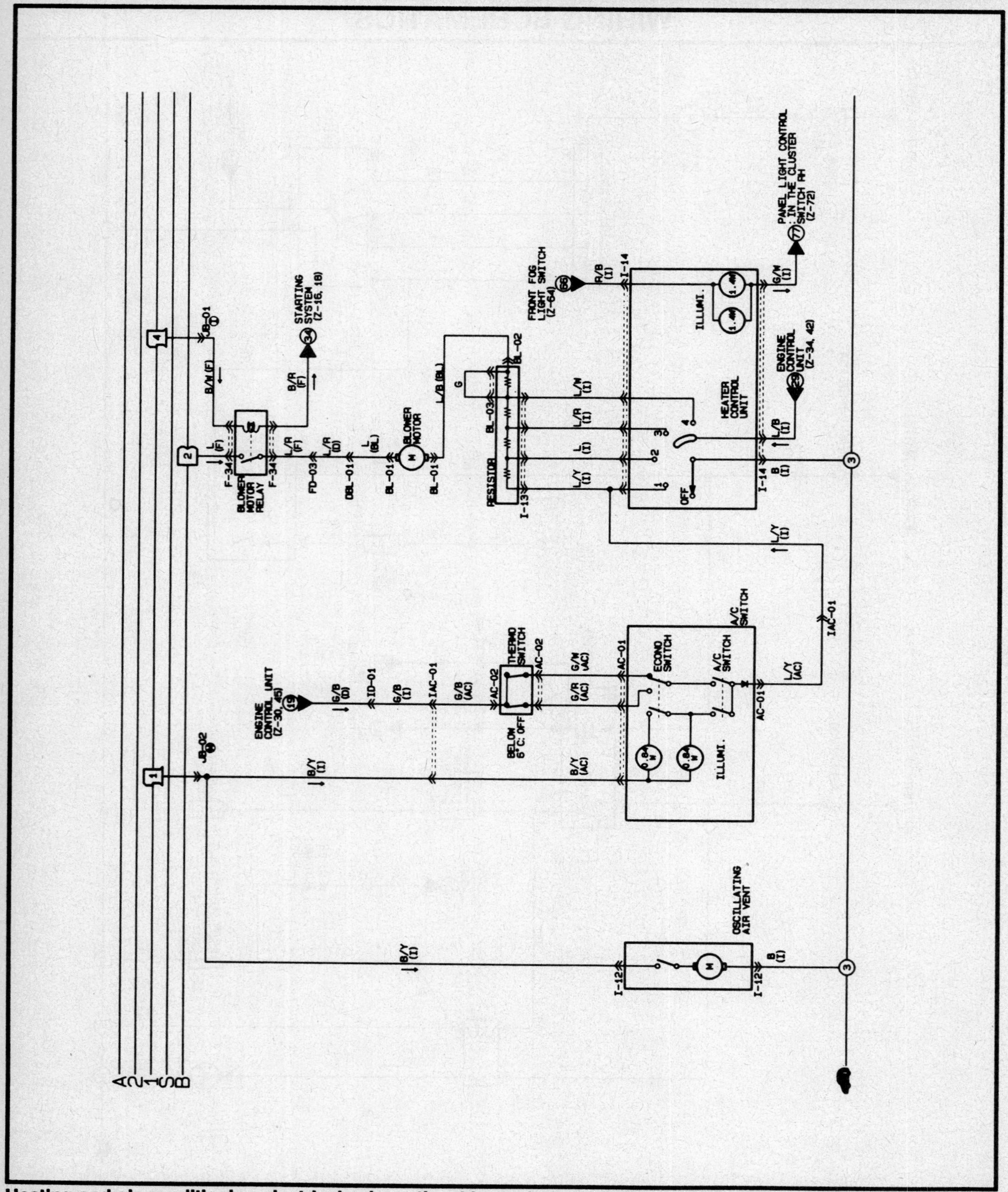
BLOWER MOTOR RELAY
STARTING SYSTEM (Z-16, 18)
BLOWER MOTOR
RESISTOR
FRONT FOG LIGHT SWITCH (Z-64)
PANEL LIGHT CONTROL IN THE CLUSTER SWITCH RH (Z-72)
ILLUMI.
HEATER CONTROL UNIT
ENGINE CONTROL UNIT (Z-34, 42)
OFF
ENGINE CONTROL UNIT (Z-30, 45)
THERMO SWITCH
BELOW 6°C: OFF
ECONO SWITCH
A/C SWITCH
ILLUMI.
OSCILLATING AIR VENT

Heating and air conditioning electrical schematic without electronic control head—626 and MX-6

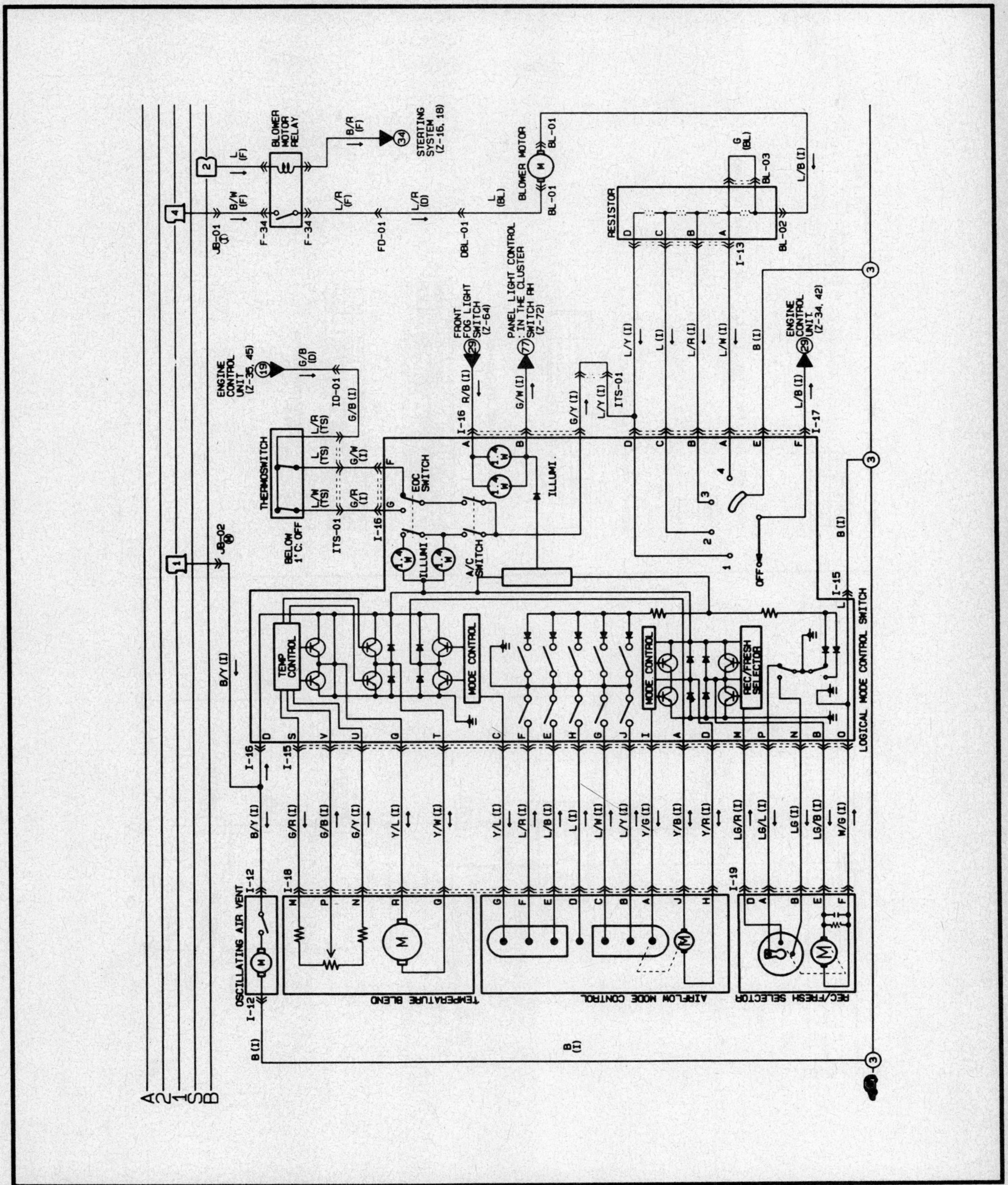
BLOWER MOTOR RELAY
STERTING SYSTEM (Z-16, 18)
BLOWER MOTOR
RESISTOR
ENGINE CONTROL UNIT (Z-35, 45)
THERMOSWITCH
BELOW 1°C: OFF
EOC SWITCH
FRONT FOG LIGHT SWITCH (Z-64)
PANEL LIGHT CONTROL : IN THE CLUSTER SWITCH RH (Z-72)
ENGINE CONTROL UNIT (Z-34, 42)
A/C SWITCH
ILLUMI.
TEMP CONTROL
MODE CONTROL
REC/FRESH SELECTOR
LOGICAL MODE CONTROL SWITCH
OSCILLATING AIR VENT
TEMPERATURE BLEND
AIRFLOW MODE CONTROL
REC/FRESH SELECTOR

Heating and air conditioning electrical schematic with electronic control head—626 and MX-6

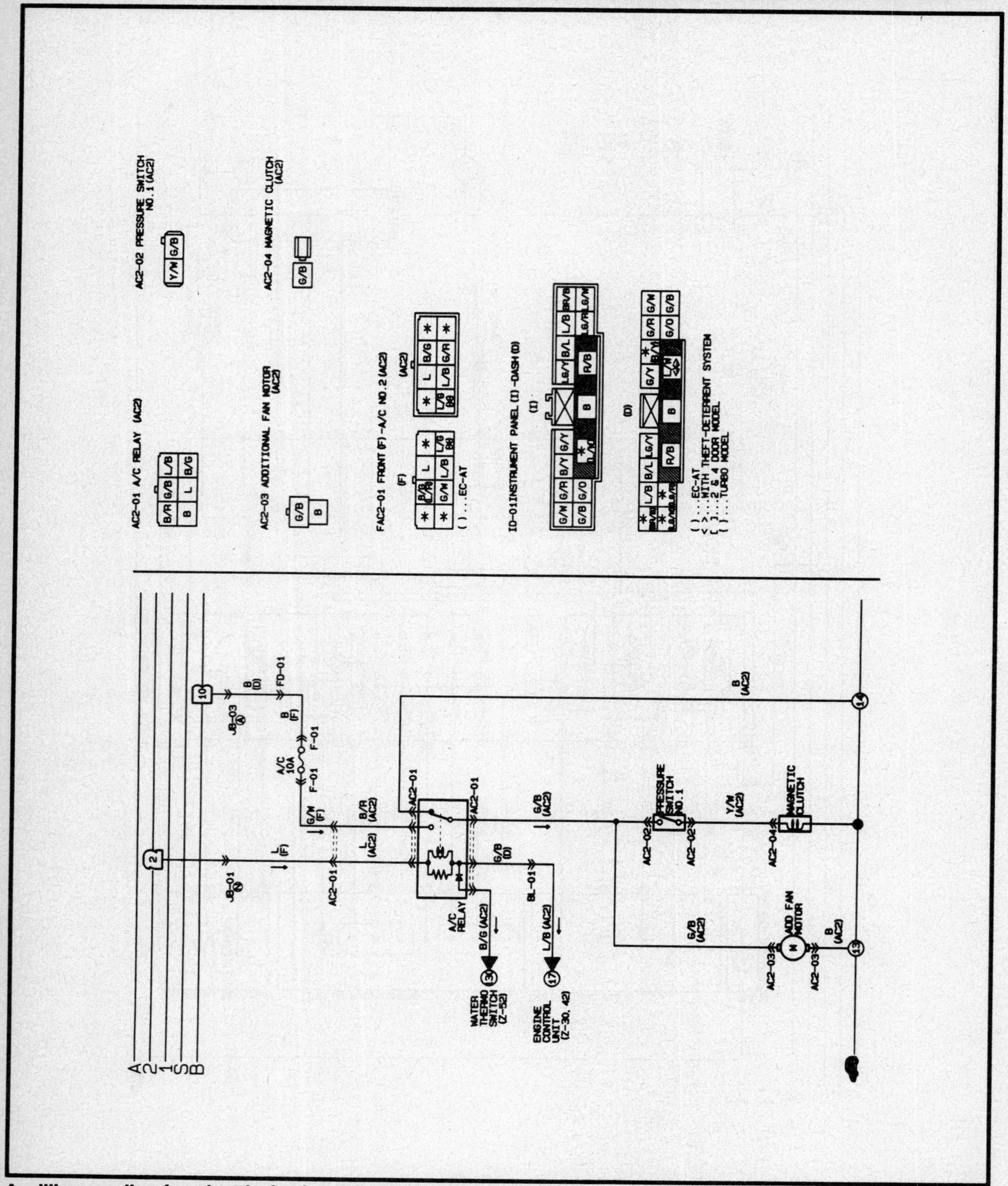
AC2-01 A/C RELAY (AC2)
AC2-02 PRESSURE SWITCH NO.1 (AC2)
AC2-03 ADDITIONAL FAN MOTOR (AC2)
AC2-04 MAGNETIC CLUTCH (AC2)
FAC2-01 FRONT (F)-A/C NO.2 (AC2)
ID-01 INSTRUMENT PANEL (I)-DASH (D)
( )...EC-AT
< >...WITH THEFT-DETERRENT SYSTEM
[ ]...2 & 4 DOOR MODEL
{ }...TURBO MODEL
A/C 10A
A/C RELAY
PRESSURE SWITCH NO.1
MAGNETIC CLUTCH
ADD FAN MOTOR
WATER THERMO SWITCH (Z-52)
ENGINE CONTROL UNIT (Z-30, 42)

Auxiliary cooling fan electrical schematic without electronic control head

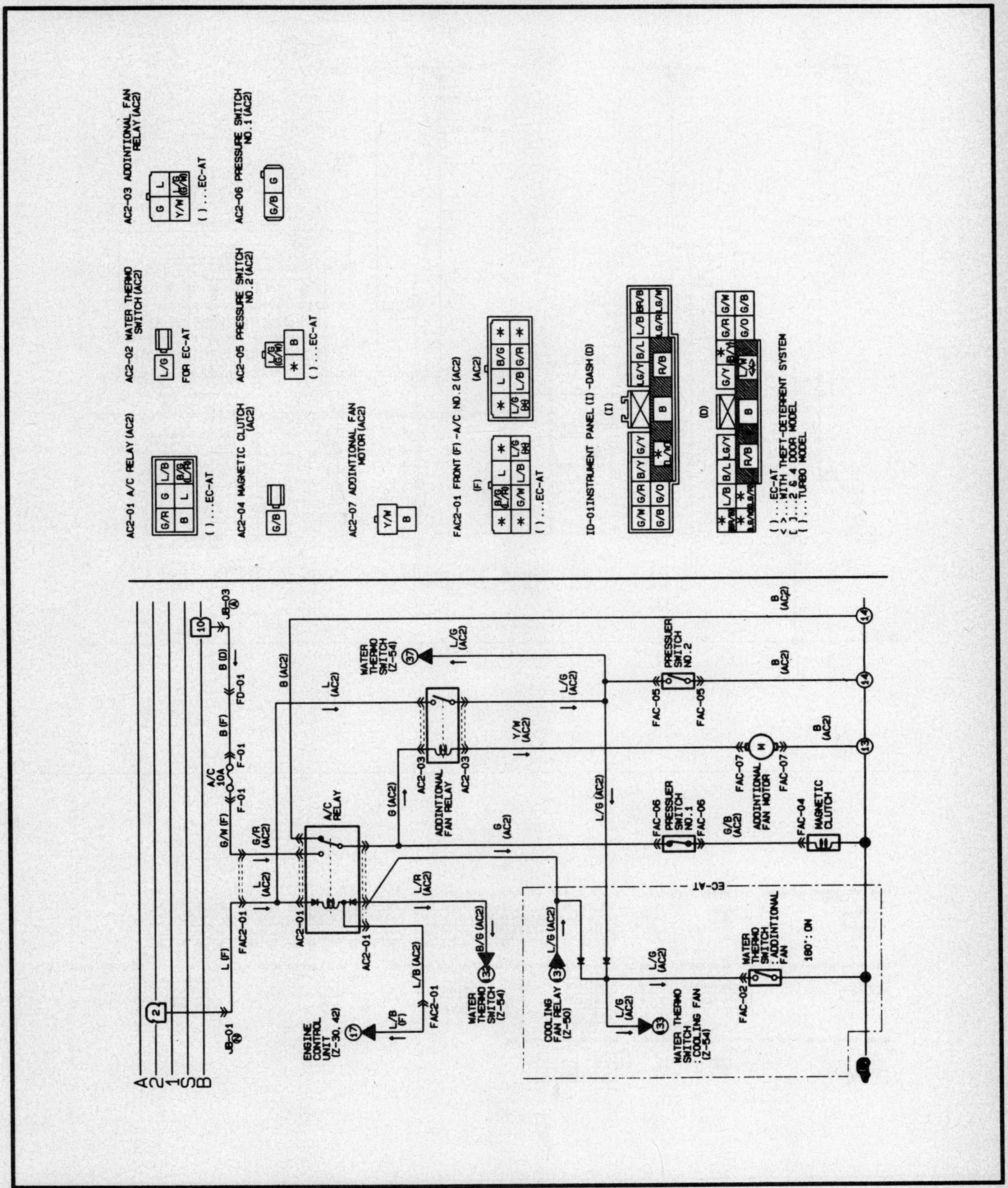
AC2-01 A/C RELAY (AC2)
AC2-02 WATER THERMO SWITCH (AC2)
AC2-03 ADDINTIONAL FAN RELAY (AC2)
AC2-04 MAGNETIC CLUTCH (AC2)
AC2-05 PRESSURE SWITCH NO.2 (AC2)
AC2-06 PRESSURE SWITCH NO.1 (AC2)
AC2-07 ADDINTIONAL FAN MOTOR (AC2)
FAC2-01 FRONT (F) -A/C NO.2 (AC2)
ID-01 INSTRUMENT PANEL (I) -DASH (D)
( )...EC-AT
FOR EC-AT
WITH THEFT-DETERRENT SYSTEM
2 & 4 DOOR MODEL
TURBO MODEL
A/C RELAY
ADDINTIONAL FAN RELAY
ADDINTIONAL FAN MOTOR
MAGNETIC CLUTCH
ENGINE CONTROL UNIT (Z-30, 42)
COOLING FAN RELAY (Z-50)
180°: ON

Auxiliary cooling fan electrical schematic with electronic control head

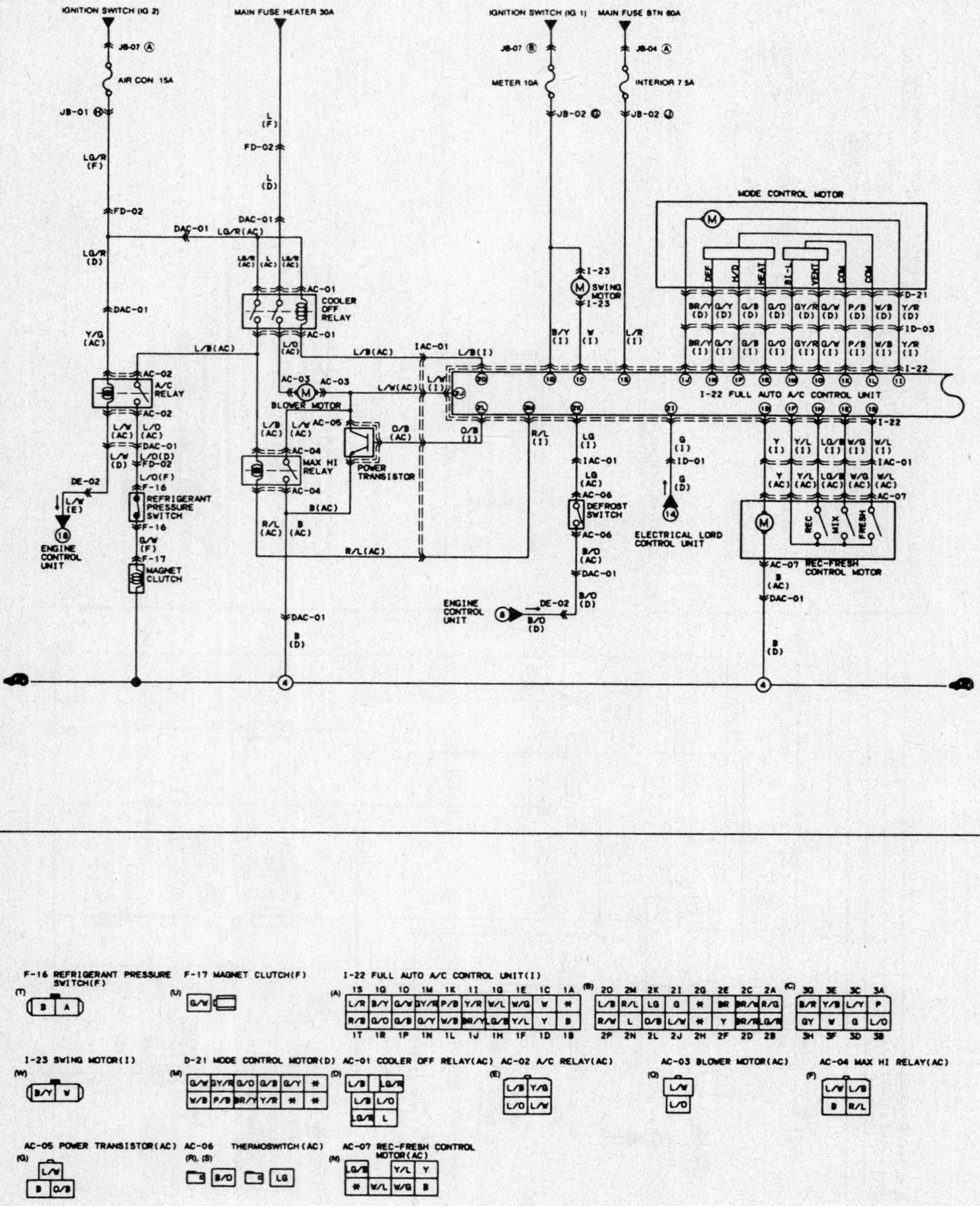
IGNITION SWITCH (IG 2)
MAIN FUSE HEATER 30A
IGNITION SWITCH (IG 1)
MAIN FUSE BTN 60A
AIR CON 15A
METER 10A
INTERIOR 7.5A
MODE CONTROL MOTOR
DEF
H/D
HEAT
BI-L
VENT
COM
COM
SWING MOTOR
COOLER OFF RELAY
A/C RELAY
BLOWER MOTOR
MAX HI RELAY
POWER TRANSISTOR
I-22 FULL AUTO A/C CONTROL UNIT
REFRIGERANT PRESSURE SWITCH
MAGNET CLUTCH
ENGINE CONTROL UNIT
DEFROST SWITCH
ELECTRICAL LORD CONTROL UNIT
REC
MIX
FRESH
REC-FRESH CONTROL MOTOR
F-16 REFRIGERANT PRESSURE SWITCH(F)
F-17 MAGNET CLUTCH(F)
I-22 FULL AUTO A/C CONTROL UNIT(I)
I-23 SWING MOTOR(I)
D-21 MODE CONTROL MOTOR(D)
AC-01 COOLER OFF RELAY(AC)
AC-02 A/C RELAY(AC)
AC-03 BLOWER MOTOR(AC)
AC-04 MAX HI RELAY(AC)
AC-05 POWER TRANSISTOR(AC)
AC-06 THERMOSWITCH(AC)
AC-07 REC-FRESH CONTROL MOTOR(AC)

Air conditioning electrical schematic—929

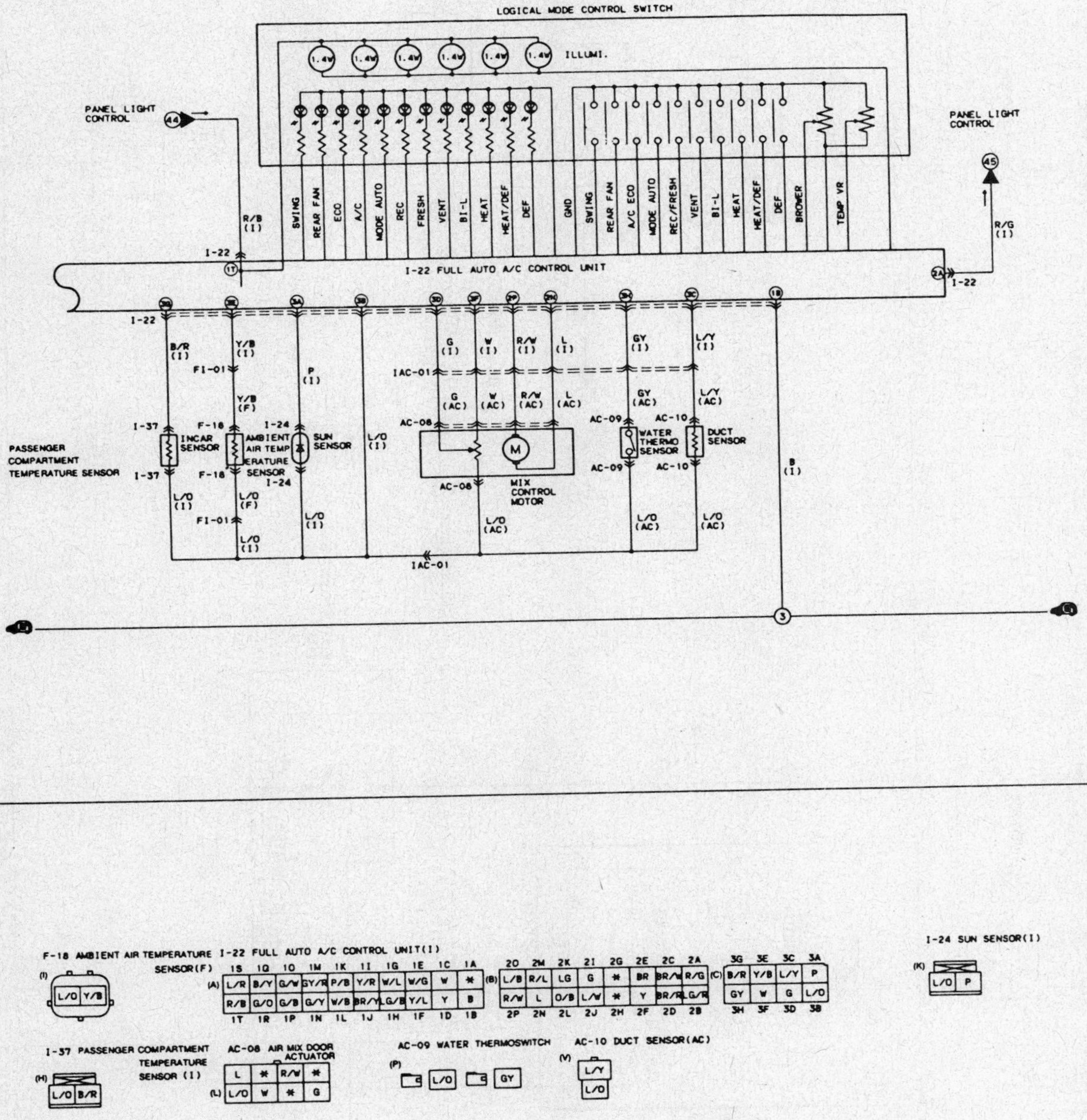
LOGICAL MODE CONTROL SWITCH
ILLUMI.
PANEL LIGHT CONTROL
SWING
REAR FAN
ECO
A/C
MODE AUTO
REC
FRESH
VENT
BI-L
HEAT
HEAT/DEF
DEF
GND
A/C ECO
REC/FRESH
BROWER
TEMP VR
I-22 FULL AUTO A/C CONTROL UNIT
PASSENGER COMPARTMENT TEMPERATURE SENSOR
INCAR SENSOR
AMBIENT AIR TEMPERATURE SENSOR
SUN SENSOR
MIX CONTROL MOTOR
WATER THERMO SENSOR
DUCT SENSOR
F-18 AMBIENT AIR TEMPERATURE SENSOR(F)
I-22 FULL AUTO A/C CONTROL UNIT(I)
I-24 SUN SENSOR(I)
I-37 PASSENGER COMPARTMENT TEMPERATURE SENSOR (I)
AC-08 AIR MIX DOOR ACTUATOR
AC-09 WATER THERMOSWITCH
AC-10 DUCT SENSOR(AC)

Electronic control head and sensors electrical schematic—929

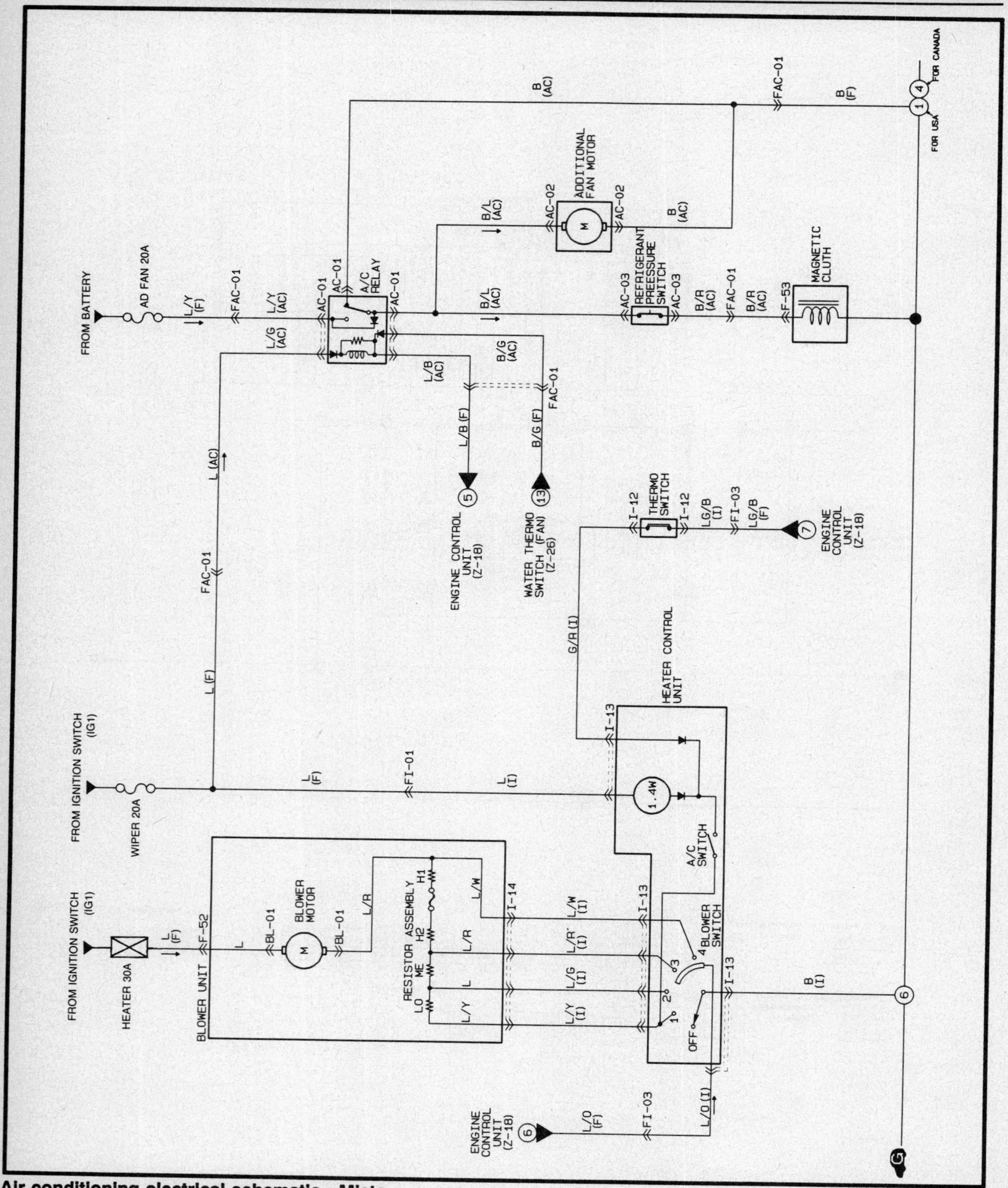
FROM BATTERY
AD FAN 20A
A/C RELAY
ADDITIONAL FAN MOTOR
REFRIGERANT PREESSURE SWITCH
MAGNETIC CLUTH
FOR USA
FOR CANADA
ENGINE CONTROL UNIT (Z-18)
WATER THERMO SWITCH (FAN) (Z-26)
THERMO SWITCH
HEATER CONTROL UNIT
FROM IGNITION SWITCH (IG1)
WIPER 20A
HEATER 30A
BLOWER UNIT
BLOWER MOTOR
RESISTOR ASSEMBLY
A/C SWITCH
BLOWER SWITCH
OFF

Air conditioning electrical schematic—Miata

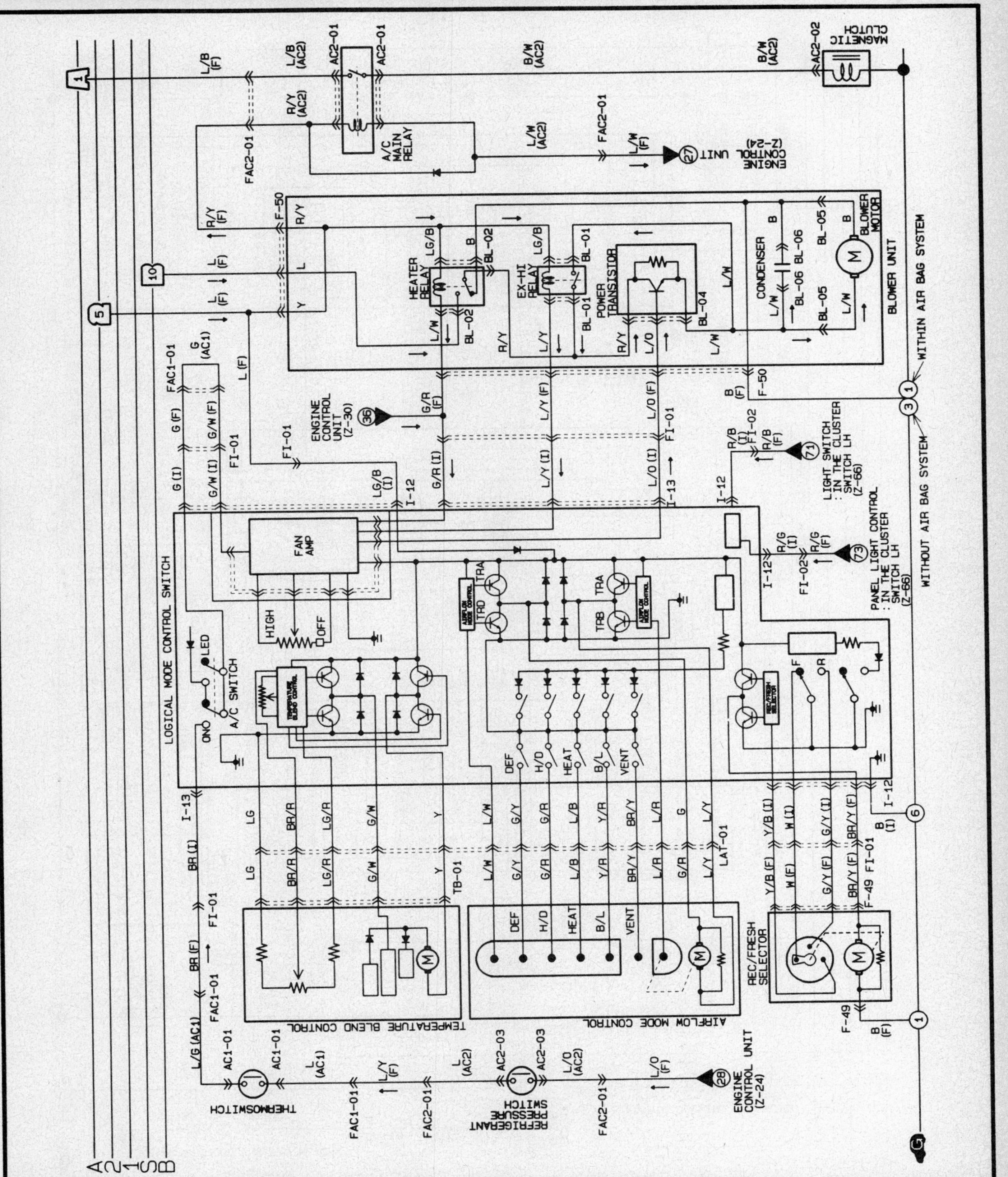
A/C MAIN RELAY
ENGINE CONTROL UNIT (Z-24)
MAGNETIC CLUTCH
HEATER RELAY
EX-HI RELAY
POWER TRANSISTOR
CONDENSER
BLOWER MOTOR
BLOWER UNIT
WITHIN AIR BAG SYSTEM
WITHOUT AIR BAG SYSTEM
ENGINE CONTROL UNIT (Z-30)
LIGHT SWITCH : IN THE CLUSTER SWITCH LH (Z-66)
PANEL LIGHT CONTROL : IN THE CLUSTER SWITCH LH (Z-66)
FAN AMP
LOGICAL MODE CONTROL SWITCH
A/C SWITCH
LED
HIGH
OFF
DEF
H/D
HEAT
B/L
VENT
TEMPERATURE BLEND CONTROL
AIRFLOW MODE CONTROL
REC/FRESH SELECTOR
THERMOSWITCH
REFRIGERANT PRESSURE SWITCH
ENGINE CONTROL UNIT (Z-24)

Heating and air conditioning electrical schematic — RX-7 with manual transmission non-turbocharged

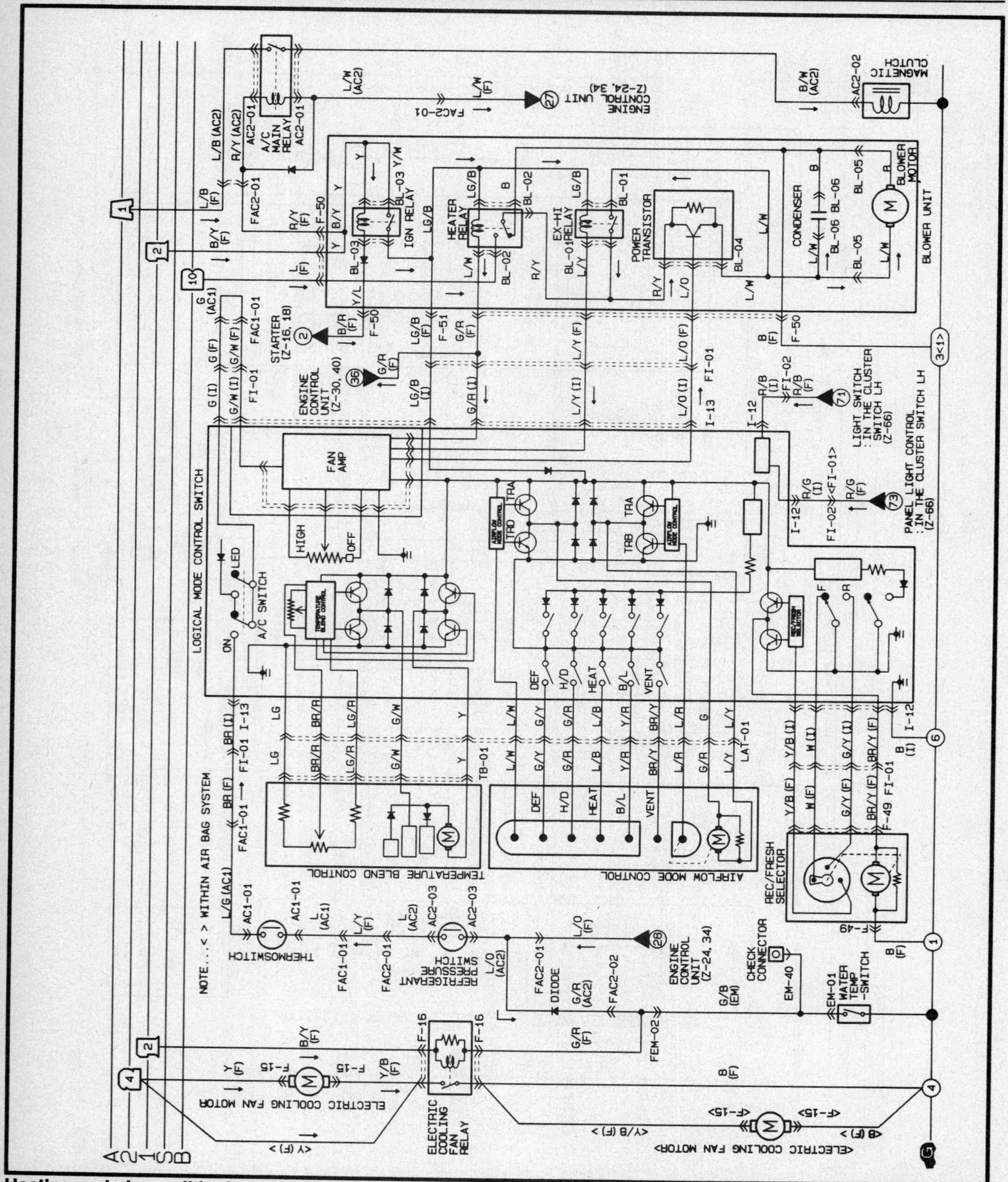
A/C MAIN RELAY
ENGINE CONTROL UNIT (Z-24, 34)
MAGNETIC CLUTCH
IGN RELAY
HEATER RELAY
EX-HI RELAY
POWER TRANSISTOR
CONDENSER
BLOWER MOTOR
BLOWER UNIT
STARTER (Z-16, 18)
ENGINE CONTROL UNIT (Z-30, 40)
FAN AMP
LIGHT SWITCH : IN THE CLUSTER SWITCH LH (Z-66)
PANEL LIGHT CONTROL : IN THE CLUSTER SWITCH LH (Z-66)
LOGICAL MODE CONTROL SWITCH
A/C SWITCH
TEMPERATURE BLEND CONTROL
AIRFLOW MODE CONTROL
REC/FRESH SELECTOR
NOTE...< > WITHIN AIR BAG SYSTEM
THERMOSWITCH
REFRIGERANT PRESSURE SWITCH
DIODE
CHECK CONNECTOR
WATER TEMP -SWITCH
ELECTRIC COOLING FAN MOTOR
ELECTRIC COOLING FAN RELAY
<ELECTRIC COOLING FAN MOTOR>

Heating and air conditioning electrical schematic – RX-7 with automatic transmission turbocharged or non-turbocharged

AIR DISTRIBUTION DIAGNOSTIC CHART

Problem	Possible cause	Remedy
Insufficient air	• Obstruction in inlet of blower unit • Clogged evaporator • Air leakage	Remove obstruction Clean evaporator Check for leakage at both sides of cooling unit
Outlet air mode cannot be changed	• Mode control wire is loose (wire control) • Open or loose connection (logic control)	Readjust wires Repair or reconnect
Temperature control cannot be done	• Temperature control wire is loose (wire control) • Open or loose connection (logic control) • Trouble in refrigeration system	Readjust wires Repair or reconnect Refer to below items
Blower does not operate	• Open or loose connection in circuit • Main fuse (40 A) is burned out • Defective blower motor relay or IG relay • Defective blower switch in switch panel • Open circuit in blower motor • Open circuit in resistor assembly	Repair or reconnect Check if short circuit is made, then replace fuse Replace Replace Replace Replace

AIR CONDITIONING CONDENSER FAN DIAGNOSTIC CHART

Problem	Possible cause	Remedy
Additional cooling fan does not run	• Open or loose connection in system • Open circuit in condenser fan motor • Defective condenser fan relays • Defective water thermoswitch	Repair Replace Replace Replace
Condenser fan remains ON	• Defective condenser fan relay	Replace

AIR CONDITIONING DIAGNOSTIC CHART

Problem	Possible cause	Remedy
Compressor runs inconsistantly	• Compressor drive belt loose • Clutch face dirty with oil • Excessive gap between the drive plate and pulley	Readjust Clean or replace clutch Readjust gap
Compressor does not run	• Open or loose connection in circuit • Defective A/C relay • Open or short circuit in magnetic clutch • Excessive gap between drive plate and pulley • Defective thermoswitch • Defective refrigerant pressure switch • Defective engine control devices	Repair or reconnect Replace Replace Readjust gap Replace Replace Replace
Insufficient cooling	• Internal malfunction of compressor • Faulty contact of sensing bulb of expansion valve • Faulty insulation of sensing bulb of expansion valve • Expansion valve stuck open • Insufficient refrigerant • Receiver-drier clogged • Expansion valve clogged • Frosted piping • Poor cooling of condenser • Defective condenser fan control circuit • Too much refrigerant • Air in the system	Repair or replace Repair or replace Repair or replace Replace Charge refrigerant Replace Replace Clean or replace Check and clean Refer to above item (Condenser fan does not run) Discharge excess refrigerant Evacuate and charge system

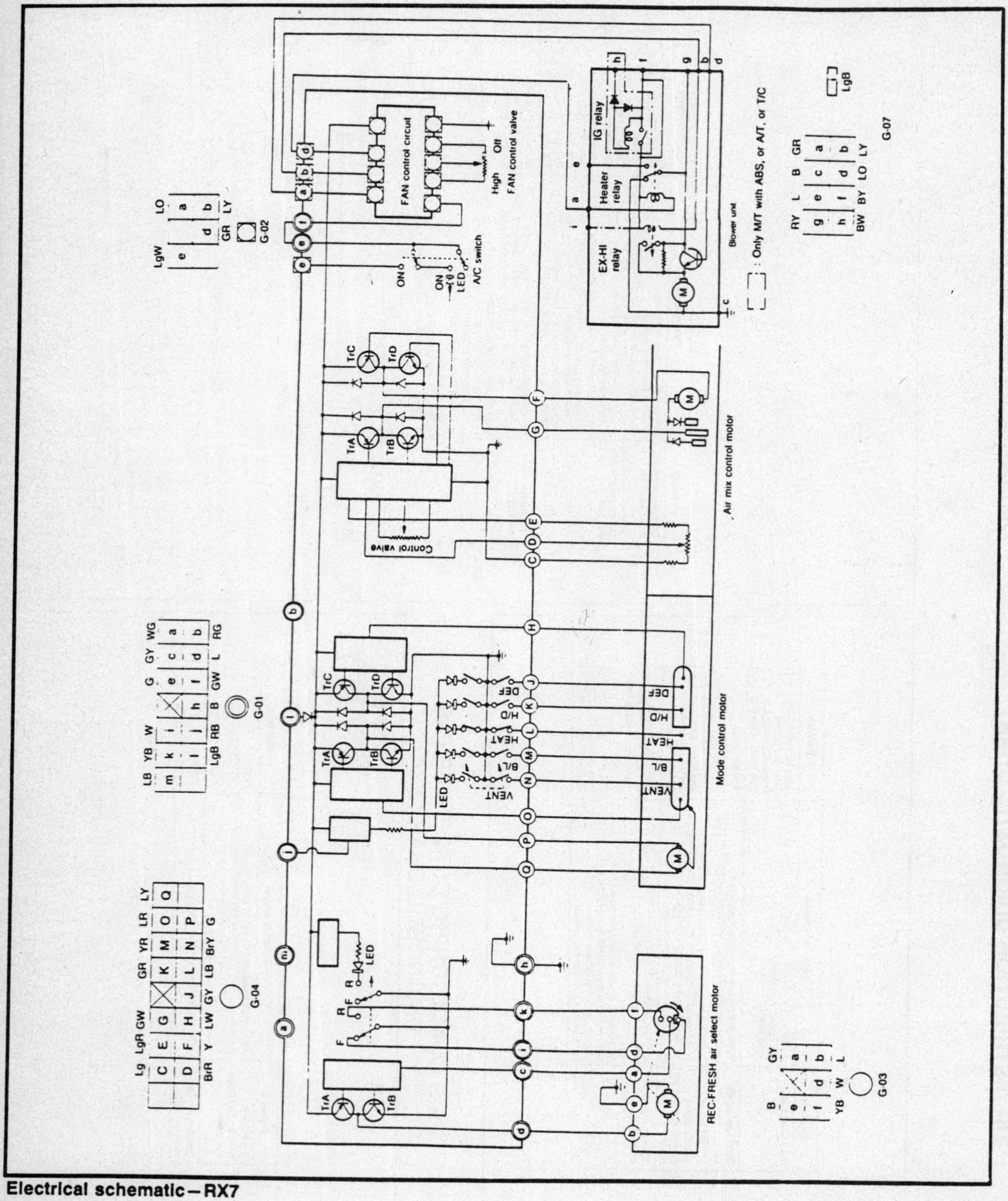
FAN control circuit
High
Off
FAN control valve
A/C switch
IG relay
Heater relay
EX-HI relay
Blower unit
: Only M/T with ABS, or A/T, or T/C
G-02
G-07
Control valve
Air mix control motor
G-01
DEF
H/D
HEAT
B/L
VENT
Mode control motor
G-04
REC-FRESH air select motor
G-03

Electrical schematic—RX7

22 MERCEDES—BENZ 22

190 • 260 • 300 • 420 • 500 • 560

SPECIFICATIONS

ENGINE IDENTIFICATION

Year	Model	Engine Displacement cu. in. (cc/liter)	Engine Series Identification	No. of Cylinders	Engine Type
1989	190E	159 (2599/2.6)	M103	6	103.942
	190D	152 (2497/2.5)	OM602	5	602.911
	260E	159 (2599/2.6)	M103	6	103.940
	300E	181 (2962/3.0)	M103	6	103.983
	300CE	181 (2962/3.0)	M103	6	103.983
	300TE	181 (2962/3.0)	M103	6	103.983
	300SE	181 (2962/3.0)	M103	6	103.981
	300SEL	181 (2962/3.0)	M103	6	103.981
	420SEL	256 (4196/4.2)	M116	8	116.965
	560SEL	338 (5547/5.6)	M117	8	117.967
	560SEC	338 (5547/5.6)	M117	8	117.968
	560SL	338 (5547/5.6)	M117	8	117.968
1990	190E	159 (2599/2.6)	M103	6	103.942
	300E	181 (2962/3.0)	M103	6	103.983
	300CE	181 (2962/3.0)	M103	6	104.980
	300SE	181 (2962/3.0)	M103	6	103.981
	300SL	181 (2962/3.0)	M104	6	104.981
	300TE	181 (2962/3.0)	M103	6	103.983
	300SEL	181 (2962/3.0)	M103	6	103.981
	420SEL	256 (4196/4.2)	M116	8	116.965
	500SL	304 (4973/5.0)	M119	8	119.960
	560SEC	338 (5547/5.6)	M117	8	117.968
	560SEL	338 (5547/5.6)	M117	8	117.968
1991	190E	159 (2599/2.6)	M103	6	103.942
	300E	181 (2962/3.0)	M103	6	103.983
	300CE	181 (2962/3.0)	M103	6	104.980
	300SE	181 (2962/3.0)	M103	6	103.981
	300SL	181 (2962/3.0)	M104	6	104.981
	300TE	181 (2962/3.0)	M103	6	103.983
	300SEL	181 (2962/3.0)	M103	6	103.981
	420SEL	256 (4196/4.2)	M116	8	116.965
	500SL	304 (4973/5.0)	M119	8	119.960
	560SEC	338 (5547/5.6)	M117	8	117.968
	560SEL	338 (5547/5.6)	M117	8	117.968

REFRIGERANT CAPACITIES

Year	Model	Freon (oz.)	Oil (fl. oz.)	Type
1989	190E	38.4	NA	R-12
	190D	38.4	NA	R-12
	260E	38.4	NA	R-12
	300E	38.4	NA	R-12
	300CE	38.4	NA	R-12

REFRIGERANT CAPACITIES

Year	Model	Freon (oz.)	Oil (fl. oz.)	Type
1989	300TE	38.4	NA	R-12
	300SE	35.2	NA	R-12
	300SEL	35.2	NA	R-12
	420SEL	35.2	NA	R-12
	560SEL	35.2	NA	R-12
	560SEC	35.2	NA	R-12
	560SL	35.2	NA	R-12
1990	190E	38.4	NA	R-12
	300E	38.4	NA	R-12
	300CE	38.4	NA	R-12
	300SE	35.2	NA	R-12
	30SL	35.2	NA	R-12
	300TE	38.4	NA	R-12
	300SEL	35.2	NA	R-12
	420SEL	35.2	NA	R-12
	500SL	35.2	NA	R-12
	560SEC	35.2	NA	R-12
	560SEL	35.2	NA	R-12
1991	190E	38.4	NA	R-12
	300E	38.4	NA	R-12
	300CE	38.4	NA	R-12
	300SE	35.2	NA	R-12
	300SL	35.2	NA	R-12
	300TE	38.4	NA	R-12
	300SEL	35.2	NA	R-12
	420SEL	35.2	NA	R-12
	500SL	35.2	NA	R-12
	560SEC	35.2	NA	R-12
	560SEL	35.2	NA	R-12

NA—Not available

AIR CONDITIONING BELT TENSION CHART

Year	Model	Engine Displacement cu. in. (cc/liter)	Belt Type	New	Used
1989	190E	159 (2599/2.6)	Serpentine	①	①
	190D	152 (2497/2.5)	Serpentine	①	①
	260E	159 (2599/2.6)	Serpentine	①	①
	300E	181 (2962/3.0)	Serpentine	①	①
	300CE	181 (2962/3.0)	Serpentine	①	①
	300TE	181 (2962/3.0)	Serpentine	①	①
	300SE	181 (2962/3.0)	V-Belt	②	②
	300SEL	181 (2962/3.0)	V-Belt	②	②
	420SEL	256 (4196/4.2)	V-Belt	②	②
	560SEL	338 (5547/5.6)	V-Belt	②	②
	560SEC	338 (5547/5.6)	V-Belt	②	②
	560SL	338 (5547/5.6)	Serpentine	①	①

AIR CONDITIONING BELT TENSION CHART

Year	Model	Engine Displacement cu. in. (cc/liter)	Belt Type	New	Used
1990	190E	159 (2599/2.6)	Serpentine	①	①
	300E	181 (2962/3.0)	Serpentine	①	①
	300CE	181 (2962/3.0)	Serpentine	①	①
	300SE	181 (2962/3.0)	V-Belt	②	②
	300SL	181 (2962/3.0)	Serpentine	①	①
	300TE	181 (2962/3.0)	V-Belt	②	②
	300SEL	181 (2962/3.0))	V-Belt	②	②
	420SEL	256 (4196/4.2)	V-Belt	②	②
	500SL	304 (4973/5.0)	Serpentine	①	①
	560SEC	338 (5547/5.6)	V-Belt	②	②
	560SEL	338 (5547/5.6)	V-Belt	②	②
1991	190E	159 (2599/2.6)	Serpentine	①	①
	300E	181 (2962/3.0)	Serpentine	①	①
	300CE	181 (2962/3.0)	Serpentine	①	①
	300SE	181 (2962/3.0)	V-Belt	②	②
	300SL	181 (2962/3.0)	Serpentine	①	①
	300TE	181 (2962/3.0)	Serpentine	①	①
	300SEL	181 (2962/3.0)	V-Belt	②	②
	420SEL	256 (4196/4.2)	V-Belt	②	②
	500SL	304 (4973/5.0)	Serpentine	①	①
	560SEC	338 (5547/5.6)	V-Belt	②	②
	560SEL	338 (5547/5.6)	V-Belt	②	②

① Self adjusting
② Use Mercedes Benz belt tension gauge

SYSTEM DESCRIPTION

General Information

Automatic Climate Control

The 260E, 300E, 300CE and 300TE models are equipped with an Automatic Climate Control (ACC) system which controls the cooling capacity electronically.

The system operates on the same principle as the system used on the 190D, 190E, 300SE, 300SEL, 420SEL, 560SEL and 560SEC, except it is equipped with a control unit which utilizes various switches, sensors and vacuum motors.

Service Valve Location

260E, 300E, 300CE and 300TE

The service valve is located in the air conditioning pipe near the compressor.

System Discharging

R-12 refrigerant is a chlorofluorocarbon which, when released into the atmosphere, can contribute to the depletion on the ozone layer in the upper atmosphere. Ozone filters out harmful radiation from the sun. In order to protect the ozone layer, an approved R-12 Recovery/Recycling machine that meets SAE standards should be employed when discharging the system. Follow the operating instructions provided with the approved equipment exactly to properly discharge the system.

System Evacuating

If the air conditioning system has been opened to the atmosphere, it should be air and moisture free before being recharged with refrigerant. Moisture and air mixed with refrigerant will raise the compressor head pressure, possibly damage the system's components and will reduce the performance of the system. In addition, air and moisture in the system can lead to internal corrosion of the system components. Moisture will boil at normal room temperature when exposed to a vacuum. To evacuate or rid the system of air and moisture:

1. Leak test the system and repair any leaks found.
2. Connect an approved charging station, Recovery/Recycling machine or manifold gauge set and vacuum pump to the discharge and suction ports. The red hose is normally connected to the discharge (high pressure) line. The blue hose is connected to the suction (low pressure) line. If using a manifold gauge set, the center (usually yellow) hose is connected to the charging station or Recovery/Recycling machine.

3. Open the discharge and suction ports and start the vacuum pump. If the pump is not able to pull at least 26 in. Hg of vacuum there is a leak that must be repaired before evacuation can occur.

4. Once the system has reached at least 26 in. Hg of vacuum, allow the system to evacuate for at least 10 minutes. The longer the system is evacuated, the more moisture will be removed.

5. Close all valves and turn the pump off. If the system loses more than 2 in. Hg of vacuum after 15 minutes, there is a leak that should be repaired.

System Charging

1. Connect an approved charging station, Recovery/Recycling machine or manifold gauge set to the discharge and suction ports. The red hose is normally connected to the discharge (high pressure) line, and the blue hose is connected to the suction (low pressure) line. If using a manifold gauge set, the center (usually yellow) hose is connected to the charging station or Recovery/Recycling machine.
2. Follow the instructions provided with the equipment and charge the system with the specified amount of refrigerant.
3. Perform a leak test.

SYSTEM COMPONENTS

Radiator

REMOVAL AND INSTALLATION

190D

1. Disconnect the negative battery cable. If equipped with an automatic transmission, pinch oil lines from or to transmission with special tool 000 589 40 37 00 or equivalent, displacing coil spring slightly laterally and removing from radiator for this purpose.
2. Disconnect coolant hoses on radiator.
3. Pull out flat contour springs for fan cover, slightly lift fan cover and place over fan.
4. On some models, pull off holding clamps at right and left below.
5. Pull out flat contour springs for radiator and lift out radiator.

To install:

6. Reverse the removal procedure. Take note that the fastening mounts of the radiator are correctly introduced into rubber grommets of lower holders and the holders of the fan cover into holding lugs on radiator.
7. Fill with coolant, pressure test cooling system with tester and check for leaks.

Except 190D

1. Disconnect the negative battery cable. Remove the radiator cap.
2. Unscrew the radiator drain plug and drain the coolant from the radiator. If all of the coolant in the system is to be drained, move the heater controls to **WARM** and open the drain cocks on the engine block.
3. If equipped with an oil cooler, drain the oil from the cooler.
4. If equipped, loosen the radiator shell.
5. Loosen the hose clips on the top and bottom radiator hoses and remove the hoses from the connections on the radiator.
6. Unscrew and plug the bottom line on the oil cooler.
7. If equipped with an automatic transmission, unscrew and plug the lines on the transmission cooler.
8. Disconnect the right and left side rubber loops and pull the radiator up and from the body.

To install:

9. Inspect and replace any hoses which have become hardened or spongy.
10. Install the radiator shell and radiator, if the shell was removed, from the top and connect the top and bottom hoes to the radiator.
11. Bolt the shell to the radiator.
12. Attach the rubber loops or position the retaining spring, as applicable.
13. Position the hose clips on the top and bottom hoses.
14. Attach the lines to the oil cooler.
15. If equipped with an automatic transmission, connect the lines to the transmission cooler.
16. Move the heater levers to the **WARM** position and slowly add coolant, allowing air to escape.
17. Check the oil level and fill if necessary. Run the engine for about 1 minute at idle with the filler neck open.
18. Add coolant to the specified level. Install the radiator cap and turn it until it seats in the 2nd notch. Run the engine and check for leaks.

COOLING SYSTEM BLEEDING

Procedure on bleeding the cooling system as required by the manufacturer.

Cooling Fan

TESTING

260E, 300E, 300CE and 300TE

1. Using a jumper wire, connect it to the 2 terminals of the pressure switch, located near the left inner fender well.
2. Turn the ignition switch **ON**; the fan should operate.
3. Check the fan's rotation, it should be clockwise; if the rotation is counterclockwise, reverse the 2-pole plug connector, located near the pressure switch.

REMOVAL AND INSTALLATION

190D and 190E

The vehicles are equipped with 2 fans: left and right.

1. Disconnect the negative battery cable.
2. Disconnect the fan(s) electrical connector(s). Remove the clamp the secures the wiring.
3. Disconnect the horns electrical and remove the horn assembly-to-radiator strut.
4. Remove the radiator and condenser clips from the radiator support. Pull the radiator and condenser from the lower holder and move them as far as possible toward the engine; do not disconnect the radiator hoses or disconnect the air conditioning lines.
5. Loosen both cable straps from the condenser.
6. Remove the auxiliary fan-to-radiator support screws.
7. Move the auxiliary fan to the right and then in the forward direction. Remove the fan assembly from the vehicle.
8. If necessary, unclip the protective grille and remove the lower holder from the fan.

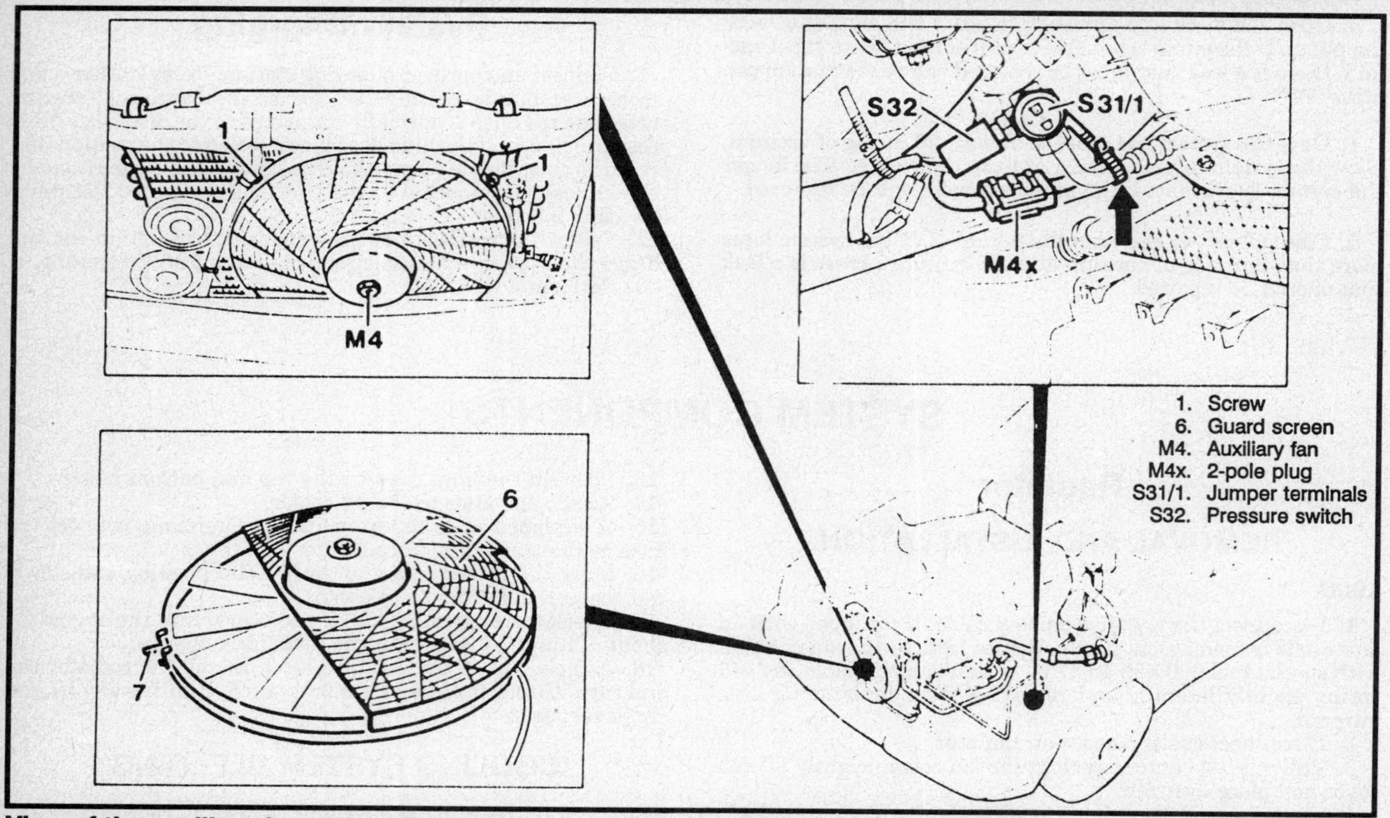
1
1
M4
6
7
S32
S31/1
M4x
1. Screw
6. Guard screen
M4. Auxiliary fan
M4x. 2-pole plug
S31/1. Jumper terminals
S32. Pressure switch

View of the auxiliary fan and related components— 260E, 300E, 300CE and 300TE

To install:

9. Pull the rubber mount from the lower holder of the auxiliary fan and wind approximately 5 layers of insulating tape around the bolt; then, slip the rubber mount on the holder.

NOTE: The insulating tape makes sure the rubber mount will not fall off when installing the auxiliary fan.

10. Insert the auxiliary fan and slip the rubber mount into the holder on the crossmember.
11. Install the auxiliary fan-to-radiator support screws.
12. Secure both cable straps to the condenser.
13. Reposition the condenser and radiator and secure with the clips.
14. Install the horn assembly to the radiator strut and connect the electrical connectors.
15. Secure the fan wiring with the clamp and connect the fan(s) electrical connector(s).
16. Connect the negative battery cable. Connect the fan(s) electrical connector(s) and check the fan(s) operation.

260E, 300E, 300CE and 300TE

1. Disconnect the negative battery cable.
2. At the left inner fender well, near the pressure switch, disconnect the fan's 2-pole electrical connector and loosen the cable clamp.
3. At the front of the vehicle, remove the fan to support screws and move the fan assembly forward to remove it.
4. If necessary, disconnect the guard screen and the mount from the fan assembly.

To install:

5. If removed, connect the guard screen and the mount to the fan assembly.
6. Position the fan assembly into the vehicle and secure it with the 2 screws.
7. At the left inner fender well, near the pressure switch, connect the fan's 2-pole electrical connector and tighten the cable clamp.
8. Connect the negative battery cable.

300SE, 300SEL, 420SEL, 560SEC and 560SEL

1. Disconnect the negative battery cable.
2. From the front left side of the vehicle, at the radiator supporting frame, disconnect the 2-pole electrical connector.
3. Disconnect the cable strap and expose the harness up to the auxiliary fan.
4. Remove the radiator support and crossmember screws.
5. Remove the stiffening strut-to-radiator support frame screw and the auxiliary fan from the vehicle.
6. Remove the auxiliary fan holder and protective grille.

To install:

7. Install the auxiliary fan holder and protective grille to the auxiliary fan.
8. Install the auxiliary fan to the vehicle and secure with the stiffening strut and radiator support frame screw.
9. Install the radiator support and crossmember screws.
10. Connect the cable strap and reposition the harness up to the auxiliary fan.
11. At the front left side of the vehicle, at the radiator supporting frame, connect the 2-pole electrical connector.
12. Connect the negative battery cable and check the fan operation.

Condenser

REMOVAL AND INSTALLATION

190D, 190E, 260E, 300E, 300CE and 300TE

1. Disconnect the negative battery cable.

2. Drain the cooling system. Discharge the air conditioning system according to the proper procedure.
3. Remove the radiator.
4. Loosen the lower air conditioning pipe-to-condenser clamp nut and separate the pipe from the condenser.
5. Loosen the upper air conditioning pipe-to-condenser fitting and separate the pipe from the condenser.
6. Remove the condensor-to-chassis clamp, 2 clips and lift the condenser from the vehicle.

To install:

NOTE: If the condenser is not reinstalled immediately, blow it out with nitrogen and plug the connections. When replacing the condenser, fill it with ⅔ oz. of refrigerant oil.

7. Position the condenser into the vehicle and install the condenser-to-chassis clamp and clips.
8. Install both air conditioning pipes to the condenser by lubricating the fitting with refrigerant oil. Torque the air conditioning pipe-to-condenser fitting to 11–13 ft. lbs. (15–18 Nm) and the air conditioning pipe-to-condenser clamp nut to 22–27 ft. lbs. (29–37 Nm).
9. Install the radiator.
10. Refill the cooling system. Connect the negative battery cable.
11. Evacuate, recharge, check for proper function and leakage; allow the engine to run at idle speed only for the 1st 4 minutes.

300SE, 300SEL, 420SEL, 560SEC and 560SEL

1. Disconnect the negative battery cable.
2. Drain the cooling system. Discharge the air conditioning system according to the proper procedure.
3. Remove the radiator.
4. On the 300SE and 300SEL, remove the air conditioning pipe from the right side of the condenser and the air conditioning line from the left side of the condenser.
5. On the 420SEL and 560SEL, remove the air conditioning pipes from the left side of the condenser.
6. On the 560SEC, perform the following procedures:
   a. Loosen the lower air conditioning pipe-to-condenser clamp nut and separate the pipe from the condenser.
   b. Loosen the upper air conditioning pipe-to-condenser fitting and separate the pipe from the condenser.
7. Remove the condensor-to-chassis clamp, 2 clips and lift the condenser from the vehicle.

To install:

NOTE: If the condenser is not reinstalled immediately, blow it out with nitrogen and plug the connections. When replacing the condenser, fill it with ⅔ oz. of refrigerant oil.

8. Position the condenser into the vehicle and install the condenser-to-chassis clamp and clips.
9. Using refrigerant oil, lubricate the O-rings and fitting threads.
10. Install both air conditioning pipes to the condenser by lubricating the fitting with refrigerant oil. Torque the air conditioning pipe-to-condenser fitting to 25 ± 2 ft. lbs. (33 ± 4 Nm), the air conditioning line-to-condenser to 11–13 ft. lbs. (15–18 Nm) and the air conditioning pipe-to-condenser clamp nut to 22–27 ft. lbs. (29–37 Nm).
11. Install the radiator.
12. Refill the cooling system. Connect the negative battery cable.
13. Evacuate, recharge, check for proper function and leakage; allow the engine to run at idle speed only for the 1st 4 minutes.

Compressor

REMOVAL AND INSTALLATION

190D and 190E

1. Disconnect the negative battery cable.
2. Discharge the air conditioning system according to the proper procedure.
3. Raise and safely support the vehicle. Remove the lower engine compartment panel.
4. Loosen and remove the V-belt from the compressor.
5. Disconnect the 3-pole electrical connector from the compressor.
6. Remove the air conditioning pipes-to-compressor screw and separate the connector from the compressor; discard the O-rings. Using dummy plugs, plug the pipes and the compressor.
7. At the front of the compressor, remove the 2 compressor-to-bracket bolts. At the left side of the compressor, remove the compressor-to-engine bolts and lower the compressor from the vehicle.

To install:

8. If installing a new compressor, fill it with 4 oz. of refrigerant oil.

NOTE: If replacing the compressor because of internal damage, be sure to replace the piping at the compressor and the expansion valve.

9. Install the compressor and torque the left side of the compressor-to-engine bolts to 17 ± 1.7 ft. lbs. (23 ± 2.3 Nm). and the front bracket-to-compressor bolts to 17 ± 1.7 ft. lbs. (23 ± 2.3 Nm).
10. Using new O-rings lubricated with refrigerant oil, install them on the compressor and torque the air conditioning pipes connector-to-compressor bolt to 17 ± 1.7 ft. lbs. (23 ± 2.3 Nm).
11. Connect the 3-pole electrical connector to the compressor.
12. Install the V-belt and adjust the belt tension. Install the lower engine compartment panel.
13. Lower the vehicle and connect the negative battery cable.
14. Evacuate, recharge, check for proper function and leakage; allow the engine to run at idle speed only for the 1st 4 minutes.

260E, 300E, 300CE and 300TE

1. Disconnect the negative battery cable.
2. Discharge the air conditioning system according to the proper procedure.
3. Raise and safely support the vehicle. Remove the lower engine compartment panel.
4. Loosen and remove the V-belt from the compressor.
5. Disconnect the 3-pole electrical connector from the compressor.
6. Remove the air conditioning pipes-to-compressor screw and separate the connector from the compressor; discard the O-rings. Using dummy plugs, plug the pipes and the compressor.
7. Remove the compressor-to-engine bolts and lower the compressor from the vehicle.

To install:

8. If installing a new compressor, fill it with 4 oz. of refrigerant oil.

NOTE: If replacing the compressor because of internal damage, be sure to replace the piping at the compressor and the expansion valve.

9. Install the compressor and torque the compressor-to-engine bolts to 17 ± 1.7 ft. lbs. (23 ± 2.3 Nm).
10. Using new O-rings lubricated with refrigerant oil, install them on the compressor and torque the air conditioning pipes connector-to-compressor bolt to 17 ± 1.7 ft. lbs. (23 ± 2.3 Nm).
11. Connect the 3-pole electrical connector to the compressor.
12. Install the V-belt and adjust the belt tension. Install the

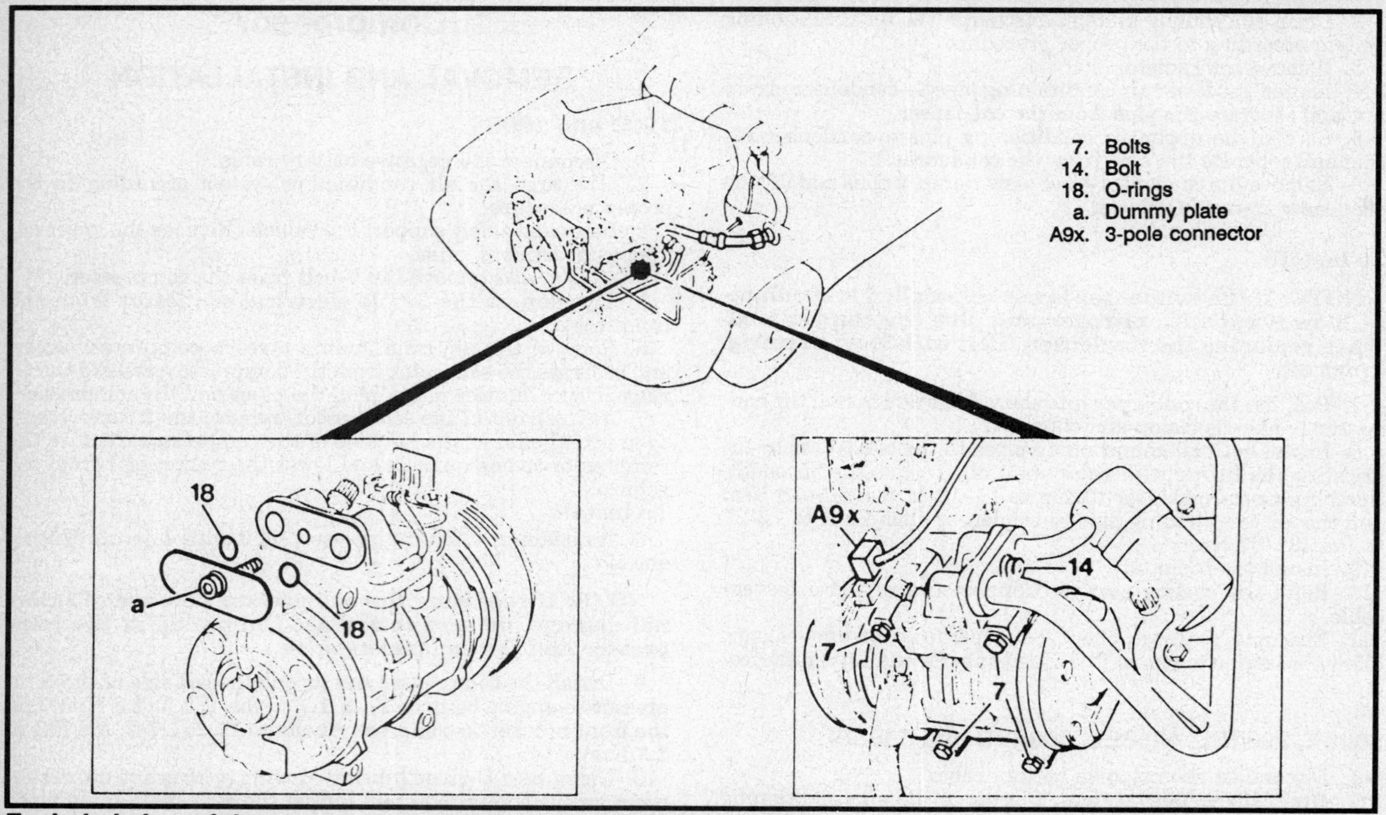
7. Bolts
14. Bolt
18. O-rings
a. Dummy plate
A9x. 3-pole connector
18
a
18
A9x
14
7
7
Exploded view of the compressor—260E, 300E, 300CE and 300TE

lower engine compartment panel.

13. Lower the vehicle and connect the negative battery cable.
14. Evacuate, recharge, check for proper function and leakage; allow the engine to run at idle speed only for the 1st 4 minutes.

300SE, 300SEL, 420SEL, 560SEC and 560SEL

1. Disconnect the negative battery cable.
2. Loosen the V-belt tensioner pulley bolt.
3. Slacken the V-belt tensioner pulley adjusting bolt, located behind the pulley, and remove the tensioner pulley.
4. Remove the V-belt from the compressor.
5. Properly, discharge the air conditioning system. Disconnect the refrigerant pipes from the compressor; be sure to plug and cap the connectors.
6. Disconnect the electrical connector from the compressor.
7. Remove the compressor-to-engine bolts and remove the compressor. Drain the oil from the compressor.

NOTE: New compressors are filled with refrigerant oil. Slowly, drain the oil from the suction end.

To install:

8. Using the 4.5 oz. of refrigerant oil, install it into the compressor at the suction end.
9. Install the compressor to the compressor mount and torque the bolts to 15 ± 1.8 ft. lbs. (20 ± 2.5 Nm).
10. Connect the electrical connector to the compressor.
11. Install the V-belt onto the compressor and the tensioner pulley. Install the tensioner pulley adjusting screw and adjust the belt to the correct tension.
12. Install the tensioner pulley bolt and torque to 31 ± 1.5 ft. lbs. (42 ± 2 Nm).
13. If the fluid reservoir has been replaced with a new one, add ⅓ oz. refrigerant oil into the compresssor.
14. Using new O-rings, lubricate them with refrigerant oil, and install them onto the refrigerant pipes. Torque the refrigerant pipes-to-compressor to 31 ± 1.5 ft. lbs. (42 ± 2 Nm).
15. Evacuate the air conditioning system and recharge.
16. Check the air conditioning system for operation.

Fluid Reservoir

The fluid reservoir is attached to the left fender well, near the pressure switches.

REMOVAL AND INSTALLATION

260E, 300E, 300CE and 300TE

1. Disconnect the negative battery cable.
2. Properly discharge the air conditioning system.
3. Disconnect the electrical connectors from pressure switches.
4. Remove both pressure switches from the fluid reservoir.
5. Disconnect the air conditioning pipes from the fluid reservoir.
6. Remove the fluid reservoir-to-chassis screws and the reservoir.

To install:

NOTE: If the fluid reservoir is replaced, add approx. ⅓ oz. of refrigerant oil to the new reservoir.

7. Install the fluid reservoir and secure with the screws.
8. Using refrigerant oil, lubricated the air conditioning pipe threads and install the pipes to the fluid reservoir; torque the pipes to 11–13 ft. lbs. (15–18 Nm).
9. Install both pressure switches to the fluid reservoir.
10. Connect the electrical connectors to pressure switches.
11. Using the proper procedure, evacuate and recharge the air

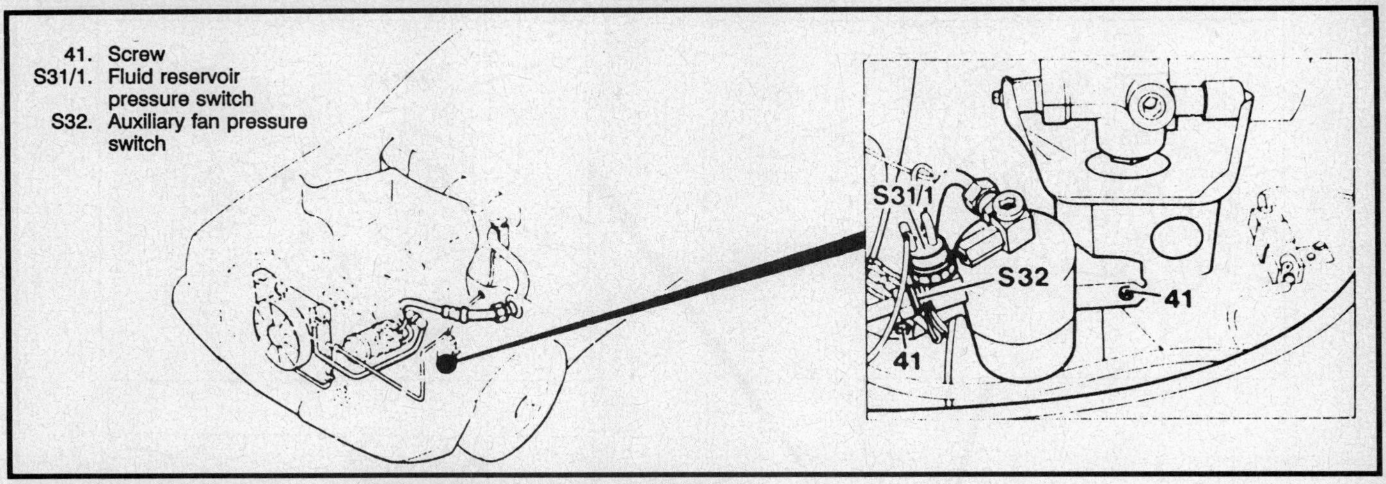
41. Screw
S31/1. Fluid reservoir pressure switch
S32. Auxiliary fan pressure switch
S31/1
S32
41
41

View of the fluid reservoir—260E, 300E, 300CE and 300TE

conditioning system.

12. Connect the negative battery cable.
13. Start the engine and allow it to run at idle for the 1st 4 minutes and check for leaks.

Receiver/Drier

The receiver/drier is attached to the left fender well, near the pressure switches.

REMOVAL AND INSTALLATION

190D, 190E, 300SE, 300SEL, 420SEL, 560SEC and 560SEL

1. Disconnect the negative battery cable.
2. Properly, discharge the air conditioning system.
3. At the receiver/drier, disconnect the electrical connectors from the temperature switch and the pressure switch.
4. Remove both switches from the receiver/drier.
5. Disconnect the air conditioning pipes from the receiver/drier.
6. Remove the receiver/drier-to-chassis screws and the receiver/drier; be sure to plug the connector openings.

To install:

NOTE: If the receiver/drier is replaced, add approx. ⅓ oz. of refrigerant oil to the new unit.

7. Install the receiver/drier and secure with the screws.
8. Using refrigerant oil, lubricated the air conditioning pipe threads and install the pipes to the receiver/drier; torque the pipes to 11–13 ft. lbs. (15–18 Nm).
9. Install both switches to the receiver/drier.
10. Connect the electrical connectors to the temperature switch and pressure switch.
11. Using the proper procedure, evacuate and recharge the air conditioning system.
12. Connect the negative battery cable.
13. Start the engine and allow it to run at idle for the 1st 4 minutes and check for leaks.

Expansion Valve

REMOVAL AND INSTALLATION

190D and 190E

1. Disconnect the negative battery cable.
2. Properly discharge the air conditioning system.
3. Remove the air inlet cover.
4. Remove the refrigerant pipes-to-expansion valve screw and pull the assembly from the expansion valve.
5. Remove the expansion valve-to-evaporator screws and the expansion valve.
6. Plug the opening of the expansion valve.

To install:

7. Using refrigerant oil, lubricate the O-rings on the evaporator pipes.
8. Install the expansion valve to the evaporator and torque the screws to 5–7 ft. lbs. (6–10 Nm).
9. Install the refrigerant pipes to the expansion valve and torque the screw to 5–9 ft. lbs. (7–13 Nm).
10. Connect the negative battery cable.
11. Evacuate and recharge the air conditioning system. To test for proper function and leakage; operate the engine, at idle, for the 1st 4 minutes.
12. Install the air inlet cover.

260E, 300E, 300CE and 300TE

1. Disconnect the negative battery cable.
2. Discharge the air conditioning system according to the proper procedure.
3. In front of the brake master cylinder, loosen the clamp located on the air conditioning pipe.
4. At the cowl, above the power brake booster, remove the mount for the check valves.
5. At the cowl, remove the air conditioning pipes-to-expansion valve screw and separate the pipe connector from the expansion valve. Remove and discard both O-rings.
6. Remove the expansion valve screws and pull off the valve; be sure to plug the evaporator pipes and fittings with dummy plugs.

To install:

7. Using new seals, install the expansion valve and torque the bolts to 6 ± 1.5 ft. lbs. (8 ± 2 Nm).
8. Using new O-rings at the cowl, attach the pipe connector to the expansion valve and install the air conditioning pipes-to-expansion valve screw; torque the screw to 7 ± 2 ft. lbs. (10 ± 3 Nm).
9. At the cowl, above the power brake booster, install the mount for the check valves.
10. In front of the brake master cylinder, tighten the clamp located on the air conditioning pipe.
11. Connect the negative battery cable.
12. Evacuate and recharge the air conditioning system. To test for proper function and leakage; operate the engine, at idle, for

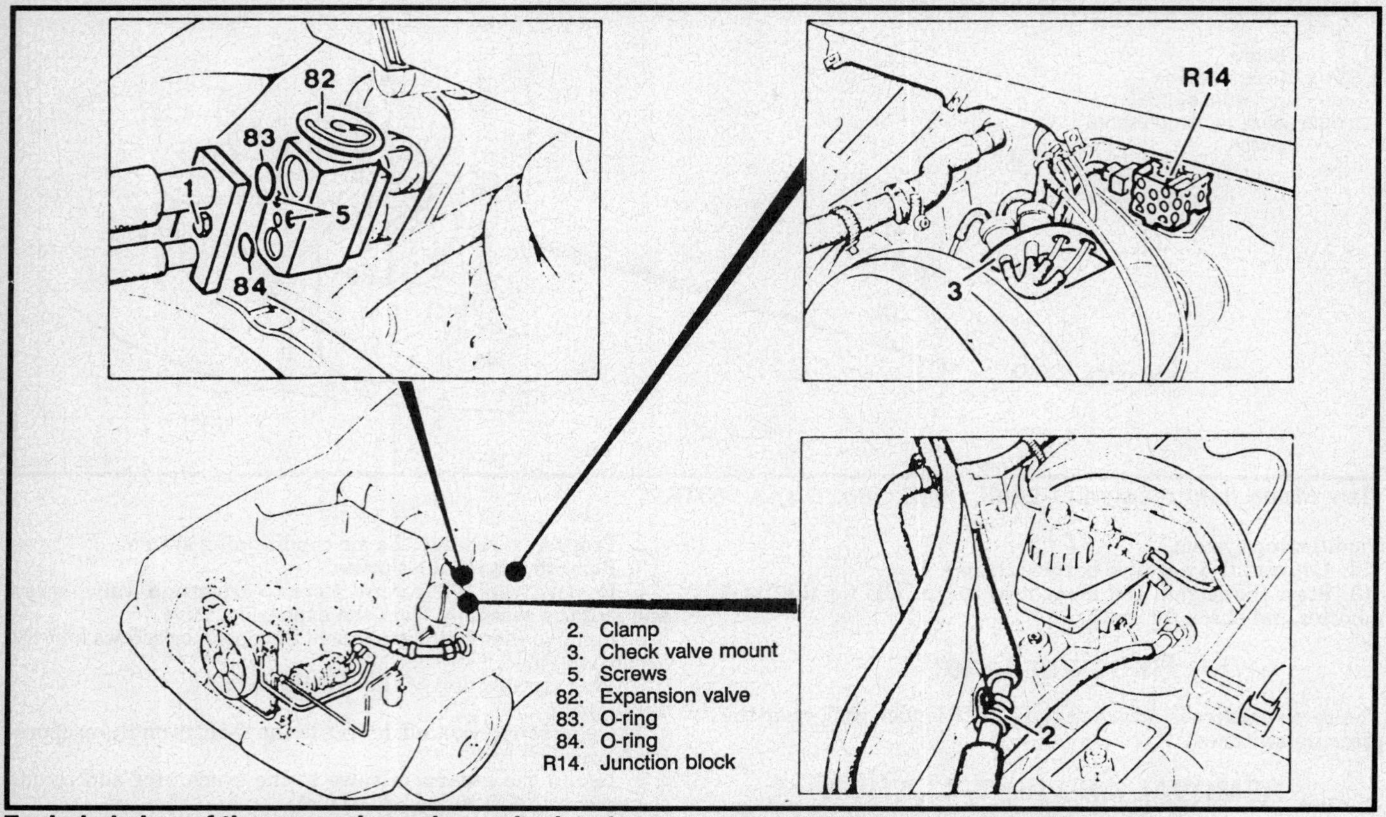
82
83
1
5
84
R14
3
2
2. Clamp
3. Check valve mount
5. Screws
82. Expansion valve
83. O-ring
84. O-ring
R14. Junction block

Exploded view of the expansion valve and related components—260E, 300E, 300CE and 300TE

the 1st 4 minutes.

300SE, 300SEL, 420SEL, 560SEC and 560SEL

1. Disconnect the negative battery cable.
2. Discharge the air conditioning system according to the proper procedure.
3. Front under the left side of the instrument panel, remove the cover.
4. Open the expansion valve housing halfway.
5. Using a box wrench, loosen and remove the air conditioning hoses and pipes from the expansion valve.
6. Remove the expansion valve and plug the openings.

To install:

7. Using refrigerant oil, lubricate the expansion valve threads. Check the O-rings and replace, if necessary.
8. Connect and tighten the pressure hose-to-expansion valve to 11–13 ft. lbs. (15–18 Nm) and the suction hose-to-expansion valve to 22–27 ft. lbs. (29–37 Nm).
9. Connect the negative battery cable.
10. Evacuate and recharge the air conditioning system. To test for proper function and leakage; operate the engine, at idle, for the 1st 4 minutes.
11. Fasten the expansion valve to the housing.
12. Install the undercover to the instrument panel.

Blower Motor

REMOVAL AND INSTALLATION

190D and 190E

1. Disconnect the negative battery cable.
2. Remove the air intake cover.
3. Remove the bulkhead screws from both sides and move the bulkhead toward the engine as far as possible.
4. Remove the wiper arm.
5. Remove the wiper arm linkage screws and move the wiper linkage, with the wiper motor, aside.
6. Unclip the blower motor housing straps and lift the housing from the heater/air conditioning box.
7. Using a pointed tool, unclip the blower motor from the housing.
8. Pull off the flat plug and lift the blower motor from the housing.

To install:

9. Install the blower motor into the housing so the connections are pointing in the driving direction and the motor housing is held in the motor holder.
10. Refit the flat plug and clip the blower motor into the housing.
11. Install the upper heater/air conditioning box housing and secure with the straps.
12. Install the wiper linkage with the wiper motor.
13. Install the wiper arm.
14. Reposition the bulkhead and secure with the screws.
15. Install the air inlet cover.
16. Connect the negative battery cable. Test the blower motor for proper operation.

260E, 300E, 300CE and 300TE

1. Disconnect the negative battery cable.
2. Remove the windshield wiper system.
3. Pull out the air temperature sensor from the upper heater/air conditioning box cover.
4. Remove the upper heater/air conditioning box cover clips and the cover.
5. Unclip the blower motor-to-heater/air conditioning box mounting strap.

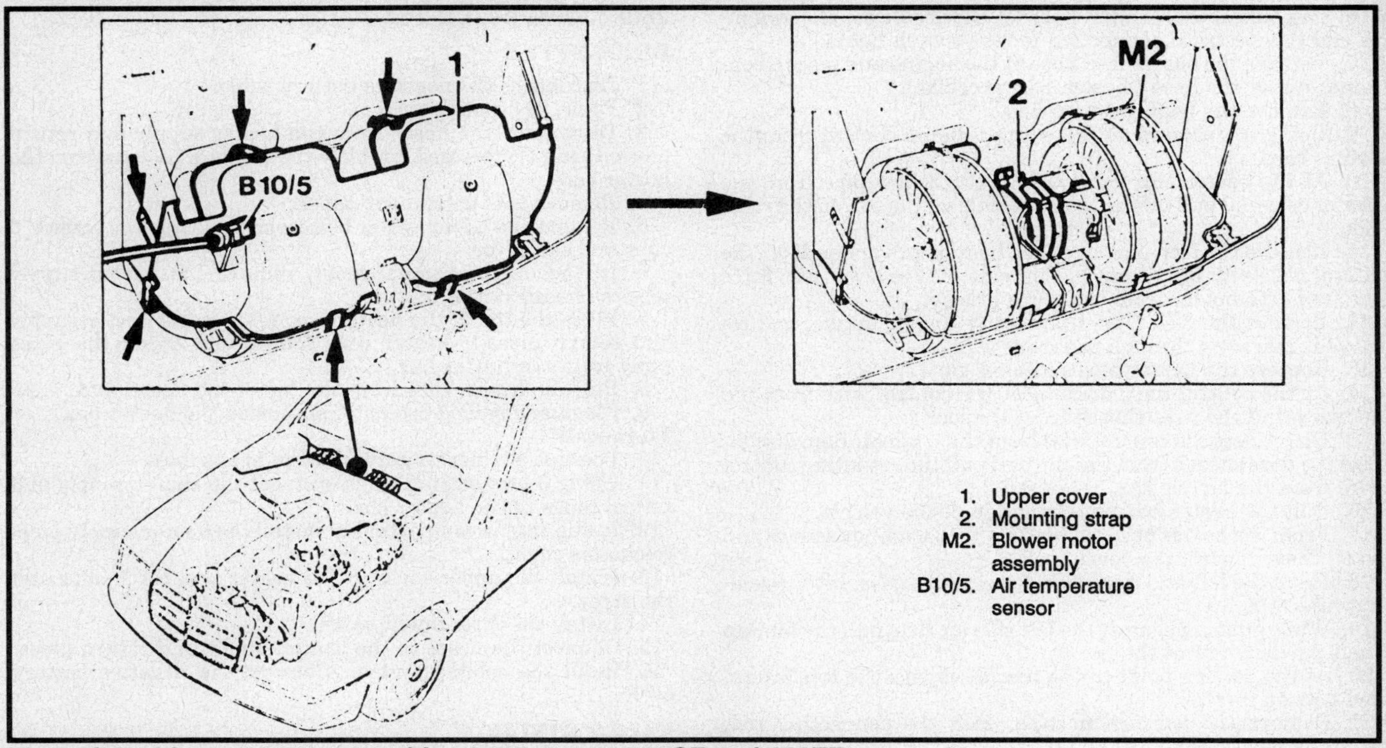
1
B10/5
M2
2
1. Upper cover
2. Mounting strap
M2. Blower motor assembly
B10/5. Air temperature sensor

View of the blower motor assembly—260E, 300E, 300CE and 300TE

6. Pull the blower motor from the heater/air conditioning box.

To install:

7. Install the blower motor into the heater/air conditioning box and secure with the mounting strap.
8. Install the upper cover to the heater/air conditioning box and secure with the clips.
9. Install the air temperature sensor into the upper heater/air conditioning box cover.
10. Install the windshield wiper system. Connect the negative battery cable.

300SE and 300SEL

1. Disconnect the negative battery cable. Remove the cover from under the right side of the instrument panel.
2. Disconnect the plug from the blower motor.
3. Unscrew the contact plate screw, lift the contact plate and disconnect both wires to the series resistor.
4. Loosen the blower motor flange screws and lift out the blower motor.
5. Installation is in the reverse order or removal.

560SL

1. Disconnect the negative battery cable. Working in the engine compartment, unscrew the 8 mounting screws and remove the panel which covers the blower motor.
2. Disconnect the plug from the series resistor at the firewall.
3. Remove the mounting bolts and remove the series resistor.
4. Unscrew the 4 blower motor retaining nuts and lift out the motor.
5. Installation is in the reverse order of removal. Be sure the rubber sealing strip is not damaged.

420SEL, 560SEC and 560SEL

1. Disconnect the negative battery cable. Remove the cover from under the right side of the instrument panel.
2. Remove the cover for the blower motor and disconnect the 2-prong plug.
3. Remove the blower motor flange bolts and the blower motor.
4. Installation is in the reverse order of removal.

190D and 190E

1. Disconnect the negative battery cable. Open the hood to a 90 degree position and remove the wiper arms.
2. Disconnect the retaining clips for the air intake cover at the firewall.
3. Remove the rubber sealing strip from the cover and remove the retaining screw. Slide the cover from the lower windshield trim strip and remove it.
4. Disconnect the vacuum line from the heater valve.
5. Remove the heater cover retaining screws.
6. Pull up the rubber sealing strip from the engine side of the defroster plenum (firewall), unscrew the retaining screws and pull up and out on the blower motor cover.
7. Loosen the cable straps on the connecting cable and disconnect the plug.
8. Unscrew the mounting bolts and remove the blower motor.
9. Installation is in the reverse order of removal.

Heater Core

REMOVAL AND INSTALLATION

190D and 190E

1. Disconnect the negative battery cable.
2. Drain the cooling system.
3. Remove the air intake cover.
4. Open the cable strap on the left side of the heater box and unscrew the cable connector screw.
5. Disconnect the blower switch electrical connector.

6. Disconnect the vacuum lines for the heater control switches and the electrical connectors for the switch lights.
7. Remove the heater feed hose at the engine and place a container under the hose to catch excess coolant.
8. Remove the heater return hose.
9. Using compressed air, blow the residual coolant from the heater core.
10. At the heater box, remove the return flow pipe from the heater core and pull off the lateral nozzle air duct from the right side.
11. Remove the feed pipe from the heater core and pull off the lateral nozzle air duct from the left side. At the lower left, force the feed pipe holder from the angle bracket.
12. Remove the feed pipe, from below the air intake, and remove it rearward through the front wall.
13. Remove the heater box-to-chassis nuts.
14. At the control unit, disconnect the control wire from the actuator and the wire sheath from the lock.
15. Disconnect the control wire from the main air flap, disconnect the wire sheath from the clip and pull the actuating control wire from the heater box.
16. Pull the heater box out of the top of the vehicle.
17. From the heater box, remove the 3 cover-to-box screws and rivet; then, remove the cover.
18. From the left and right side defroster nozzles, lift the sealing rubber ½ way.
19. While pushing against the left side air flap, pull the air flap shaft partially out of the nozzle.
20. At the parting point of the box, disengage the top, lateral and bottom clamps.
21. Remove the legroom nozzles, with the connecting rod, from the heater box.
22. Separate the heater boxes at the parting line.
23. Remove the heater core-to-holding frame screws and remove the frame.
24. Remove the heater core from the heater box.

To install:

25. Insert the heater core into the heater box. Install the frame and secure with the screws.
26. Reassemble the heater box halves, install the legroom nozzles with the connecting rod and secure the box halves with the clips.
27. Install the air flap shaft into the defroster nozzle; make sure the flap bearings are correctly seated on the housing and the shaft lug engages the nozzle flap.
28. Reposition the defroster nozzle sealing rubber.
29. Install the heater box screws and rivet.
30. Install the heater box assembly into the vehicle.
31. Connect the control wire to the main air flap control and actuator.
32. Install the heater box-to-chassis nuts.
33. Install the feed pipe through the front wall and position it below the air intake.
34. At the lower left, force the feed pipe holder into the angle bracket. Install the lateral nozzle air duct to the left side and connect the feed pipe to the heater core.
35. Install the lateral nozzle air duct to the right side and connect the return flow pipe to the heater core, at the heater box.
36. Install the heater return hose and the heater feed hose.
37. Connect the vacuum lines for the heater control switches and the electrical connectors for the switch lights.
38. Connect the blower switch electrical connector.
39. Install the cable connector screw and secure the cable strap on the left side of the heater box.
40. Install the air intake cover.
41. Refill the cooling system. Connect the negative battery cable.
42. Start the engine, allow it to reach normal operating temperatures and check for leaks.

260E, 300E, 300CE and 300TE

BEHR STYLE

1. Disconnect the negative battery cable.
2. Drain the cooling system.
3. Disconnect the hoses from the heater supply and return pipes. Using compressed air, blow the residual coolant from the heater core.
4. Remove the instrument panel.
5. Remove the upper heater box cover-to-heater box screws, 6 clips and the cover.
6. In the engine compartment, remove the heater supply pipe-to-chassis clamp.
7. From the top of the heater box, remove the heater supply and return pipes-to-heater core screws and swing the pipes away from the heater box.
8. Pull the heater core from the top of the heater box.
9. Clean any spilled coolant from inside the heater box.

To install:

10. Position the heater core into the heater box.
11. Using 3 new sealing rings, connect the heater supply and return pipes to the heater box.
12. In the engine compartment, install the heater supply pipe-to-chassis clamp.
13. Install the upper cover to the heater box, the 6 clips and the screws.
14. Install the instrument panel.
15. Connect the hoses to the heater supply and return pipes.
16. Refill the cooling system. Connect the negative battery cable.

VALEO STYLE

1. Disconnect the negative battery cable.
2. Drain the cooling system.
3. Disconnect the hoses from the heater supply and return pipes. Using compressed air, blow the residual coolant from the heater core.
4. Remove the instrument panel and the center console.
5. From the lower front of the heater box, pull off the temperature sensor heat exchanger, left and right 2-pole couplings.
6. Pull the air ducts from the bottom of the heater box.
7. From the front of the heater box, remove the crossmember and strut. From under the heater box, remove the bracket.
8. Loosen the ignition switch housing-to-steering column bolt. Turn the ignition key to position **1**, press the ignition switch housing locking button and pull the steering lock from the steering column.
9. Pull the air ducts from both sides of the heater box.
10. Remove the heater box-to-chassis nuts and pull the heater box from the firewall.
11. Disconnect the electrical connectors and clip from the blower motor. Disconnect the main air flap control cable from the heater box.
12. Remove the heater box retaining clips and pull the front case from the rear case. Remove the heater core from the heater case.
13. Remove the heater supply and return pipes-to-heater core screws and the pipes from the heater core.
14. Clean any spilled coolant from inside the heater box.

To install:

15. Using 3 new sealing rings, connect the heater supply and return pipes to the heater box.
16. Position the heater core into the heater box; make sure the rubber pipe grommets are seated properly.
17. Position the front case onto the heater box secure with the clips.
18. Connect the main air flap control cable to the heater box. Connect the electrical connectors and clip to the blower motor.
19. Using a new seal, position the heater box against the firewall and install the heater box-to-chassis nuts. Install the air ducts to both sides of the heater box.

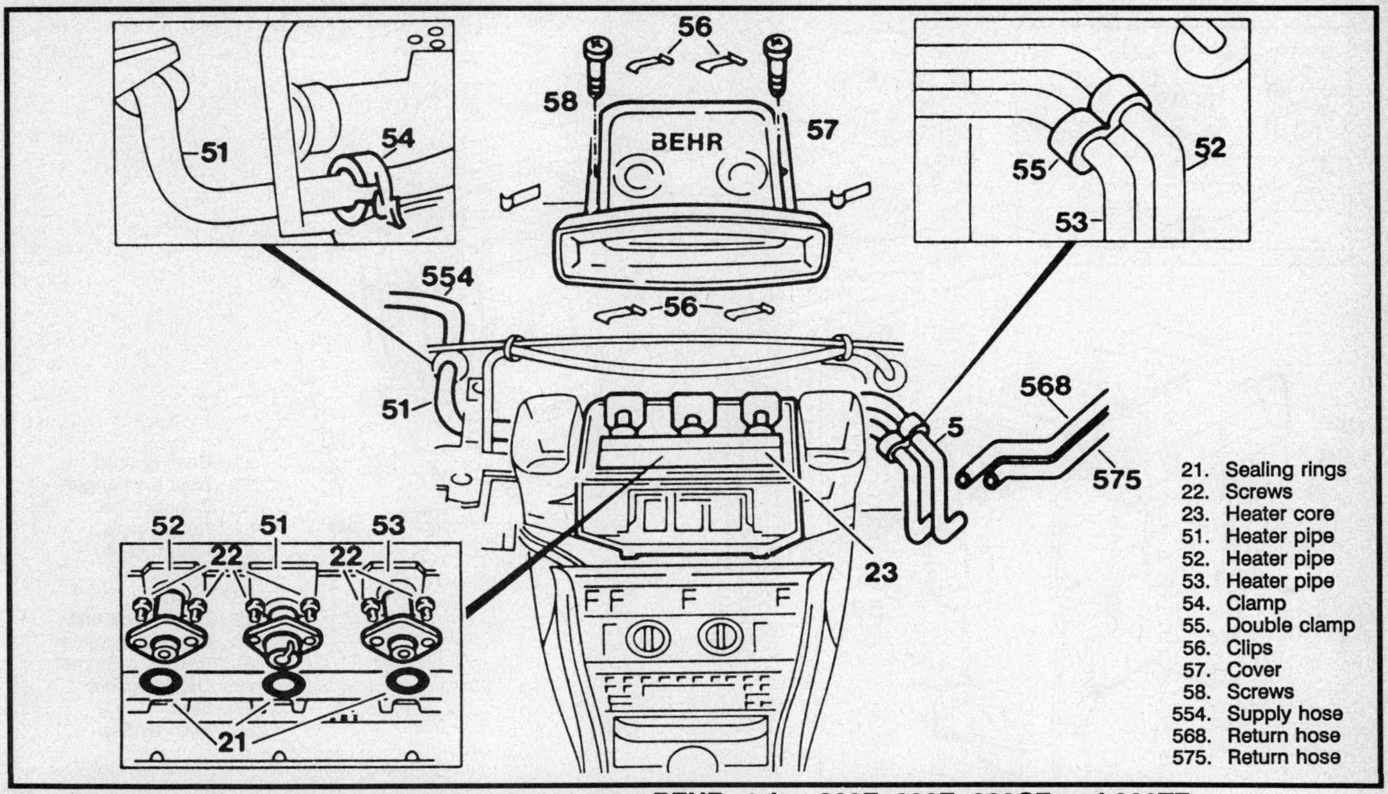
BEHR
21. Sealing rings
22. Screws
23. Heater core
51. Heater pipe
52. Heater pipe
53. Heater pipe
54. Clamp
55. Double clamp
56. Clips
57. Cover
58. Screws
554. Supply hose
568. Return hose
575. Return hose

Exploded view of the heater box and components—BEHR style—260E, 300E, 300CE and 300TE

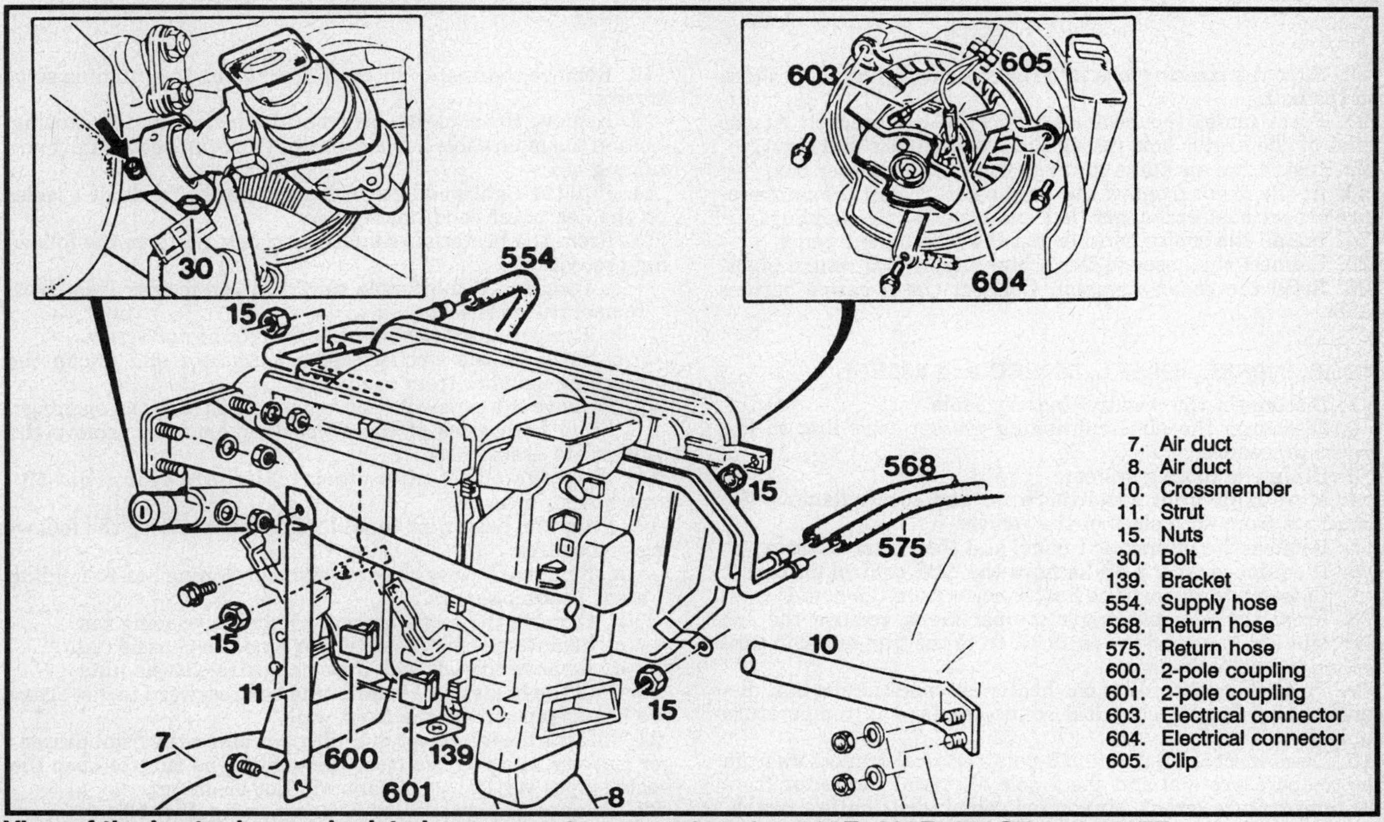
7. Air duct
8. Air duct
10. Crossmember
11. Strut
15. Nuts
30. Bolt
139. Bracket
554. Supply hose
568. Return hose
575. Return hose
600. 2-pole coupling
601. 2-pole coupling
603. Electrical connector
604. Electrical connector
605. Clip

View of the heater box and related components—VALEO style—260E, 300E, 300CE and 300TE

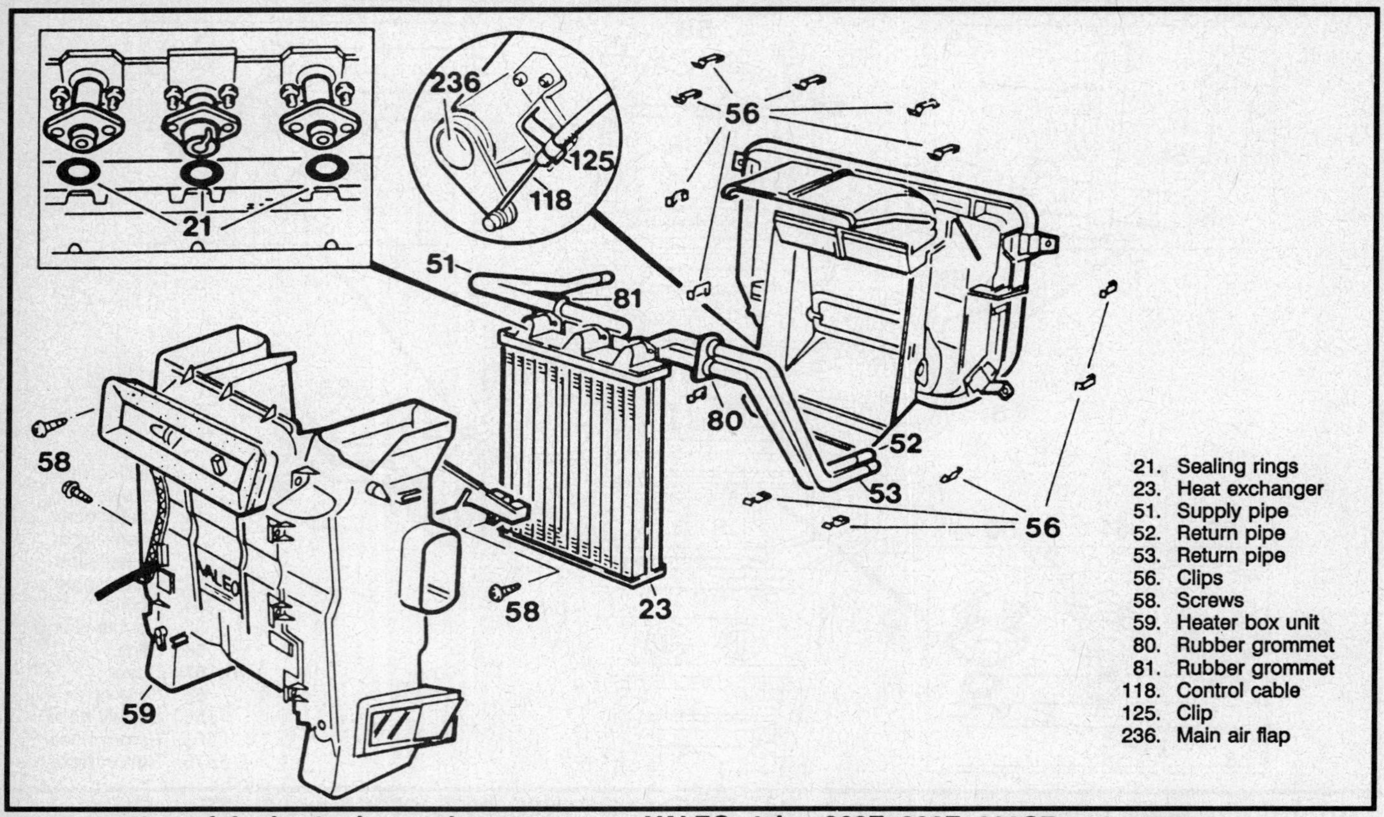
236
125
118
21
56
51
81
80
52
53
56
58
58
23
59
21. Sealing rings
23. Heat exchanger
51. Supply pipe
52. Return pipe
53. Return pipe
56. Clips
58. Screws
59. Heater box unit
80. Rubber grommet
81. Rubber grommet
118. Control cable
125. Clip
236. Main air flap

Exploded view of the heater box and components — VALEO style — 260E, 300E, 300CE and 300TE

20. Slide the steering lock into the steering column and tighten the bolt.
21. From under the heater box, install the bracket. At the front of the heater box, install the crossmember and strut.
22. Install the air ducts to the bottom of the heater box.
23. At the lower front of the heater box, install the temperature sensor heat exchanger, left and right 2-pole couplings.
24. Install the center console and the instrument panel.
25. Connect the hoses to the heater supply and return pipes.
26. Refill the cooling system. Connect the negative battery cable.

300SE, 300SEL, 420SEL, 560SEC and 560SEL

1. Disconnect the negative battery cable.
2. Discharge the air conditioning system according to the proper procedure.
3. Drain the cooling system.
4. Move both front seats rearward and cover. Remove the floormats from both sides of the vehicle.
5. Remove the instrument panel and the center console.
6. If equipped with ABS, remove the ABS control unit.
7. Loosen and remove the heater hoses from the heater core.
8. From the rear passenger compartment, remove the left and right air ducts and the air ducts from the transmission tunnel, on the driver's floor.
9. From the right side of the heater/air conditioning box, disconnect the 12-pole electrical connector for the temperature control.
10. Disconnect the 5-pole and 6-pole electrical connectors from the temperature dial and the 2-pole electrical connector from the temperature sensor, air volume and air distributing switch.
11. Disconnect the vacuum lines from the air volume switch.
12. Remove the heater/air conditioning box-to-stiffening strut screws.
13. Remove the cable straps from the blower motor housing. Loosen the main cable harness straps from the heater/air conditioning box.
14. Pull the right and left air ducts from the fresh air nozzles on the heater/air conditioning box.
15. From the heater/air conditioning box, perform the following procedures:
    a. Disconnect the 2-pole electrical connectors from both temperature sensors.
    b. Remove the electric lines cable connector screw.
    c. Separate the electrical plug connector and unclip the coupling member from the holder.
16. Remove the expansion valve; be sure to plug the openings.
17. From both sides of the evaporator housing, remove the condensate drain hoses.
18. Remove the 2-pole electrical connector from the switchover valve.
19. From the heater/air conditioning box, perform the following procedures:
    a. Remove the lower heater/air conditioning box-to-holding angle bracket screws.
    b. Remove the angle bracket-to-blower housing nut.
    c. Remove the right side upper angle-to-chassis nut.
    d. Remove the left side upper angle-to-chassis nut.
20. Pull the heater/air conditioning box rearward to disengage the heater pipes from the front wall.
21. Lift the heater/air conditioning box above the front passenger legroom and remove from the vehicle; be sure to keep the heater pipes vertical so coolant will not drain out.
22. Remove the evaporator housing and pull the heater core from the heater/air conditioning box.

To install:

NOTE: When assembling the cases, be sure to seal them especially well along the horizontal separating joint. Pay particular attention to the areas behind the expansion valve and temperature or blower control.

23. Install the heater core and the evaporator housing onto the heater/air conditioning box.
24. Install the heater/air conditioning box against the front wall and position the heater pipes through the front wall.
25. Connect the heater/air conditioning box to the left side upper angle bracket and screw.
26. Connect the heater/air conditioning box to the right side upper angle bracket and nuts.
27. Install the lower angle bracket with screws.
28. Connect the 2-pole electrical connector to the switchover valve.
29. Install the condensate drain hoses to the heater/air conditioning box.
30. Using refrigerant oil, lubricate the O-rings and threads; then, connect the refrigerant lines to the expansion valve.
31. Connect the electric lines on the cable connector.
32. Connect the 2-pole electrical connectors to the temperature sensors.
33. Install both fresh air duct nozzles onto the heater/air conditioning box.
34. Install the main cable harness onto the heater/air conditioning box and secure with the cable straps.
35. Install the electric lines onto the blower housing and secure with the cable straps.
36. Mount the stiffening strut and screws.
37. Connect the vacuum lines to the air volume switch.
38. Connect the 2-pole, 5-pole and 6-pole electrical connectors onto the temperature dials. Connect the 2-pole connector onto the flow sensor switch and the air distributing switch.
39. Connect the 12-pole connector onto the electronic switchgear.
40. Install both heater air ducts for the rear passenger compartment. Install the heater boxes.
41. If equipped with ABS, install the ABS control unit.
42. Fill the cooling system and check for leaks.
43. Install the center console and the instrument panel.
44. Install the both foot mats into the legroom.
45. Connect the negative battery cable.
46. Evacuate and recharge the air conditioning system. To test for proper function and leakage; operate the engine, at idle, for the 1st 4 minutes.

Evaporator

REMOVAL AND INSTALLATION

190D and 190E

1. Disconnect the negative battery cable.
2. Properly discharge the air conditioning system.
3. Remove the air intake cover.
4. Remove the bulkhead screws from both sides and move the bulkhead toward the engine as far as possible.
5. Remove the expansion valve.
6. Remove the blower motor.
7. Remove the lower blower motor housing screws and lift out the lower part of the housing.
8. Pull the temperature sensor from the guide tube.
9. Laterally, from left to right, remove the flange frame-to-evaporator housing clips and remove the flange frame.
10. Lift the evaporator, with the pan and drain hoses, from the evaporator housing.

To install:

11. Clean the evaporator and make sure the drain hoses are open.
12. Insert the evaporator into the pan. Insert the evaporator assembly, with the pan, into the evaporator housing.
13. Install the flange frame to the evaporator housing and secure with the clips.
14. Insert the temperature sensor into the guide tube up to the stop.
15. Install the lower part of the blower housing and secure with the screws.
16. Install the blower motor.
17. Unplug the refrigerant lines and connect them to the evaporator.
18. Install the expansion valve.
19. Reposition the bulkhead and secure with the screws.
20. Install the air inlet cover.
21. Connect the negative battery cable.
22. Evacuate and recharge the air conditioning system. To test for proper function and leakage; operate the engine, at idle, for the 1st 4 minutes.

260E, 300E, 300CE and 300TE

1. Disconnect the negative battery cable.
2. Drain the cooling system. Discharge the air conditioning system according to the proper procedure.
3. Disconnect the heater hoses from the heater core.
4. In front of the brake master cylinder, loosen the clamp located on the air conditioning pipe.
5. At the cowl, above the power brake booster, remove the mount for the check valves.
6. At the cowl, remove the air conditioning pipes-to-expansion valve screw and separate the pipe connector from the expansion valve. Remove and discard both O-rings.
7. At the cowl, above the power brake booster, disconnect and pull out the fan motor lead from the junction block.
8. Remove the instrument panel and the center console.
9. Loosen and pull off both floor air ducts from the heater/air conditioning box.
10. From in front of the heater/air conditioning box, remove the crossmember and brace. From under the heater/air conditioning box, remove the box-to-chassis mount.
11. Loosen the ignition switch housing-to-steering column bolt. Turn the ignition key to position **1**, press the ignition switch housing locking button and pull the steering lock from the steering column.
12. Pull the air ducts from both sides of the heater box.
13. From the lower front of the heater/air conditioning box, disconnect the heat exchanger temperature sensors, left and right 2-pole couplings, and the evaporator temperature sensor.
14. From the lower right of the heater/air conditioning box, disconnect the vacuum lines and the 2-pole connector from the switch-over valve and remove the valve.
15. Pull the left and right side air ducts from the nozzles of the heater/air conditioning box.
16. Remove the heater/air conditioning box-to-chassis nuts. Pull the outside air temperature sensor from the holder. Move the heater/air conditioning box down and outward.
17. Remove the heater/air conditioning box clips. At the top, remove the 4 cover-to-box screws and remove the cover.
18. At both sides of the box, remove the heater pipe clamps.
19. At the rear side of the box, disconnect the connecting rod from the fresh air recirculated air flap.
20. Remove both vacuum cylinders-to-chassis screws and the vacuum cylinder elements from the heater/air conditioning box.
21. Pull the heater core upward and out of the box.
22. Remove the 2 screws from the left and the right side parts. Pull the right side part out sightly and unclip the leg room flap joint. Remove both side parts.
23. Remove the upper 3 clips, from both sides of the heater/air conditioning box, and remove the upper section of the housing.
24. Remove the upper 3 clips, from both sides of the heater/air conditioning box, and the 1 from the center of the blower motor

housing. On the left side of the box, near the evaporator air conditioning pipes, press the clip from the housing.
25. Pry the evaporator from the heater/air conditioning box.

To install:

26. Clean the inside of the evaporator housing.
27. If using a new evaporator, remove the screen from the old evaporator and glue it to the new one. If using a new evaporator, unscrew the expansion valve from the old evaporator; then, install new O-rings and the expansion valve onto the new evaporator.
28. Check and replace the bulkhead gasket, if necessary; add sealant to the sealing surface.
29. Position the evaporator into the heater/air conditioning box.
30. On the left side of the box, near the evaporator air conditioning pipes, press the clip into the housing. Install the upper 3 clips, onto both sides of the heater/air conditioning box, and the 1 from the center of the blower motor housing.
31. Install the upper section of the housing and press the upper 3 clips, onto both sides of the heater/air conditioning box.
32. Position both side parts onto the heater/air conditioning box and secure with the screws.

NOTE: When installing the right side part, reclip the leg room flap joint.

33. Reposition the heater core into the box.
34. Reposition the vacuum cylinder elements into the heater/air conditioning box and install both vacuum cylinders-to-chassis screws.
35. At the rear side of the box, connect the connecting rod to the fresh air recirculated air flap.
36. At both sides of the box, install the heater pipe clamps.
37. Install the upper cover and the 4 screws. Reclip the heater/air conditioning box clips.
38. Reposition the heater/air conditioning box, install the outside air temperature sensor into the holder and install the heater/air conditioning box-to-chassis nuts.
39. Install the left and right side air ducts onto the nozzles of the heater/air conditioning box.
40. Install the switch-over valve to the lower right of the heater/air conditioning box. Reconnect the vacuum lines and the 2-pole connector to the valve.
41. At the lower front of the heater/air conditioning box, connect the heat exchanger temperature sensors, left and right 2-pole couplings, and the evaporator temperature sensor.
42. Press the air ducts onto both sides of the heater box.
43. Slide the steering lock into the steering column and tighten the bolt.
44. From under the heater/air conditioning box, install the bracket. At the front of the heater box, install the crossmember and strut.
45. Install the air ducts to the bottom of the heater box.
46. Install the center console and the instrument panel.
47. At the cowl, above the power brake booster, connect the fan motor lead to the junction block.
48. Using new O-rings at the cowl, attach the pipe connector to the expansion valve and install the air conditioning pipes-to-expansion valve screw.
49. At the cowl, above the power brake booster, install the mount for the check valves.
50. In front of the brake master cylinder, tighten the clamp located on the air conditioning pipe.
51. Connect the heater hoses from the heater core.
52. Refill the cooling system. Connect the negative battery cable.
53. Evacuate and recharge the air conditioning system. To test for proper function and leakage; operate the engine, at idle, for the 1st 4 minutes.

300SE, 300SEL, 420SEL, 560SEC and 560SEL

1. Disconnect the negative battery cable.
2. Discharge the air conditioning system according to the proper procedure.
3. Drain the cooling system.
4. Move both front seats rearward and cover. Remove the floormats from both sides of the vehicle.
5. Remove the instrument panel and the center console.
6. If equipped with ABS, remove the ABS control unit.
7. Loosen and remove the heater hoses from the heater core.
8. From the rear passenger compartment, remove the left and right air ducts and the air ducts from the transmission tunnel, on the driver's floor.
9. From the right side of the heater/air conditioning box, disconnect the 12-pole electrical connector for the temperature control.
10. Disconnect the 5-pole and 6-pole electrical connectors from the temperature dial and the 2-pole electrical connector from the temperature sensor, air volume and air distributing switch.
11. Disconnect the vacuum lines from the air volume switch.
12. Remove the heater/air conditioning box-to-stiffening strut screws.
13. Remove the cable straps from the blower motor housing. Loosen the main cable harness straps from the heater/air conditioning box.
14. Pull the right and left air ducts from the fresh air nozzles on the heater/air conditioning box.
15. From the heater/air conditioning box, perform the following procedures:
   a. Disconnect the 2-pole electrical connectors from both temperature sensors.
   b. Remove the electric lines cable connector screw.
   c. Separate the electrical plug connector and unclip the coupling member from the holder.
16. Remove the expansion valve; be sure to plug the openings.
17. From both sides of the evaporator housing, remove the condensate drain hoses.
18. Remove the 2-pole electrical connector from the switchover valve.
19. From the heater/air conditioning box, perform the following procedures:
   a. Remove the lower heater/air conditioning box-to-holding angle bracket screws.
   b. Remove the angle bracket-to-blower housing nut.
   c. Remove the right side upper angle-to-chassis nut.
   d. Remove the left side upper angle-to-chassis nut.
20. Pull the heater/air conditioning box rearward to disengage the heater pipes from the front wall.
21. Lift the heater/air conditioning box above the front passenger legroom and remove from the vehicle; be sure to keep the heater pipes vertical so coolant will not drain out.
22. From the heater/air conditioning box, perform the following procedures:
   a. Remove the evaporator housing and pull the heater core from the heater/air conditioning box.
   b. Remove the main air flap housing screws and clamps; then, lift the housing from the box.
   c. Disconnect the bowden wires and remove the clamps for the legroom and defroster nozzle flaps.
   d. Remove the evaporator housing cover clamps and the housing.
   e. Pull the vacuum lines from the switch over valve and remove the screw.
   f. Using a small prybar, at the right side of the box, lift of the bowden wire clamp for not heatable fresh air bearing shaft and pull out the shaft.
   g. At the right side, remove the side member clamps and lift off the side member.
   h. Using a small prybar, at the left side of the box, lift of the bowden wire clamp for not heatable fresh air bearing shaft and pull out the shaft. Remove the fastening screw.
   i. At the left side, remove the side member clamps and lift off the side member.

j. Lift the heater box top from the evaporator housing bottom.

k. Pull the temperature sensor from the evaporator or capillary of the ETR switch out of the guide tube and remove the evaporator from the housing's lower half.

To install:

23. Clean the evaporator housing and pay special attention to the condensate drain connection.

NOTE: When assembling the cases, be sure to seal them especially well along the horizontal separating joint. Pay particular attention to the areas behind the expansion valve and temperature or blower control.

24. To assemble the heater/air conditioning box, perform the following procedures:

a. Position the evaporator into the evaporator housing.

b. Carefully, insert the temperature sensor between the evaporator plates and make sure the sensor is correctly seated or slip the capillary up to the red mark in the guide tube of the ETR switch.

c. Position the heater box top onto the evaporator housing bottom.

d. Install the both side members and secure with clamps and screws.

e. Slip both not heatable fresh air flap bearing shafts into the heater box, check the operation; then, secure the bowden wires to the shafts with the clamps.

f. Connect the vacuum lines to the switchover valve.

g. Place the blower housing onto the evaporator housing and secure with the clamps.

h. Connect the bowden wires for the legroom and defroster nozzle flaps and secure with the clamps.

i. Position the main air flap housing onto the blower housing and secure with the claps and screws.

j. Using refrigerant oil, lubricate the O-rings and threads; then, connect the expansion valve onto the evaporator pipes.

k. Attach the electronic switching unit.

l. Install the heater core and the evaporator housing.

25. Install the heater/air conditioning box against the front wall and position the heater pipes through the front wall.
26. Connect the heater/air conditioning box to the left side upper angle bracket and screw.
27. Connect the heater/air conditioning box to the right side upper angle bracket and nuts.
28. Install the lower angle bracket with screws.
29. Connect the 2-pole electrical connector to the switchover valve.
30. Install the condensate drain hoses to the heater/air conditioning box.
31. Using refrigerant oil, lubricate the O-rings and threads; then, connect the refrigerant lines to the expansion valve.
32. Connect the electric lines on the cable connector.
33. Connect the 2-pole electrical connectors to the temperature sensors.
34. Install both fresh air duct nozzles onto the heater/air conditioning box.
35. Install the main cable harness onto the heater/air conditioning box and secure with the cable straps.
36. Install the electric lines onto the blower housing and secure with the cable straps.
37. Mount the stiffening strut and screws.
38. Connect the vacuum lines to the air volume switch.
39. Connect the 2-pole, 5-pole and 6-pole electrical connectors onto the temperature dials. Connect the 2-pole connector onto the flow sensor switch and the air distributing switch.
40. Connect the 12-pole connector onto the electronic switchgear.
41. Install both heater air ducts for the rear passenger compartment. Install the heater boxes.
42. If equipped with ABS, install the ABS control unit.
43. Fill the cooling system and check for leaks.
44. Install the center console and the instrument panel.
45. Install the both foot mats into the legroom.
46. Connect the negative battery cable.
47. Evacuate and recharge the air conditioning system. To test for proper function and leakage; operate the engine, at idle, for the 1st 4 minutes.

Refrigerant Lines

REMOVAL AND INSTALLATION

1. Disconnect the negative battery cable.
2. Discharge the air conditioning system according to the proper procedure.
3. At the cowl, remove the air conditioning pipes-to-expansion valve screw and separate the pipe connector from the expansion valve. Remove and discard both O-rings.
4. Remove the air conditioning pipes-to-compressor screw and separate the connector from the compressor; discard the O-rings. Using dummy plugs, plug the pipes and the compressor.
5. At the condenser, loosen the lower air conditioning pipe clamp nut and separate the pipe from the condenser.
6. Loosen the upper air conditioning pipe-to-condenser fitting and separate the pipe from the condenser.
7. Remove the air conditioning pipes from the vehicle.

To install:

8. Position the air conditioning pipes into the vehicle.
9. Using new O-rings at the cowl, attach the pipe connector to the expansion valve and install the air conditioning pipes-to-expansion valve screw; torque the screw to 7 ± 2 ft. lbs. (10 ± 3 Nm).
10. In front of the brake master cylinder, tighten the clamp located on the air conditioning pipe.
11. Using new O-rings lubricated with refrigerant oil, install them on the compressor and torque the air conditioning pipes connector-to-compressor bolt to 17 ± 1.7 ft. lbs. (23 ± 2.3 Nm).
12. Install both air conditioning pipes to the condensor by lubricating the fitting with refrigerant oil. Torque the air conditioning pipe-to-condenser fitting to 11–13 ft. lbs. (15–18 Nm) and the air conditioning pipe-to-condenser clamp nut to 22–27 ft. lbs. (29–37 Nm).
13. Connect the negative battery cable.
14. Evacuate and recharge the air conditioning system. To test for proper function and leakage; operate the engine, at idle, for the 1st 4 minutes.

Manual Control Head

REMOVAL AND INSTALLATION

260E, 300E, 300CE and 300TE

1. Disconnect the negative battery cable.
2. Pull the control knobs from the manual control unit.
3. Remove the control switches-to-control unit nuts.
4. Remove the faceplate-to-control unit screws and the faceplate.
5. Remove the control unit-to-dash screws. If equipped, remove the control unit bulb(s).
6. Pull the control unit forward and disconnect the electrical connector from the unit.
7. Remove the control unit from the vehicle.

To install:

8. Install the control unit and connect the electrical connector to it.
9. If equipped with bulbs, install them.
10. Install the control unit to the dash and secure with the screws.

11. Position the faceplate and install the faceplate-to-control unit screws.
12. Install the control switches-to-control unit nuts.
13. Refit the control knobs. Connect the negative battery cable and check the control switches operation.

Electronic Control Head

REMOVAL AND INSTALLATION

190D and 190E

1. Disconnect the negative battery cable.
2. Pull outlets from the center of the instrument panel.
3. Remove the upper instrument panel-to-center console screws and push the console slightly downward.
4. Pull off the blower switch knob and pull the blower switch molding from the center console.
5. Disconnect the fresh air/recirculating air switch.
6. Using a pointed tool, lift clamp from both upper sides of the control head and pull the control head forward.
7. Disconnect both 12-pole electrical connectors from the control head and remove the control head.
8. To install, reverse the removal procedures. Connect the negative battery cable.

SENSORS AND SWITCHES

Circulating Pump

REMOVAL AND INSTALLATION

260E, 300E, 300CE and 300TE

1. Disconnect the negative battery cable.
2. Drain the cooling system to a level below the circulationg pump.
3. Remove the coolant hose clamp and disconnect the hoses from the circulating pump.
4. Disconnect the 2-pole electrical connector from the circulating pump.
5. Remove the circulating pump bracket bolt and pull the pump from the vehicle.

To install:

6. Install the circulating pump and secure with the bolt.
7. Install the coolant hoses and tighten the clamps.
8. Connect the electrical connector to the circulating pump.
9. Refill the cooling system. Connect the negative battery cable.

Duo Valve

REMOVAL AND INSTALLATION

260E, 300E, 300CE and 300TE

1. Disconnect the negative battery cable.
2. Release the pressure in the cooling system by loosening the radiator cap.
3. Disconnect the electrical connector from the duo valve.
4. Remove the heater hose clamps and pull the 3 hoses from the duo valve.
5. Press the rubber buffers from the duo valve brackets.
6. Remove the duo valve from the vehicle.

To install:

7. Install the duo valve and press the rubber buffers into the valve brackets.
8. Install the heater hoses and secure with the clamps.
9. Connect the electrical connector to the duo valve.
10. If necessary, top of the radiator and install the cap.
11. Connect the negative battery cable.

Air Flow Jet

The air flow jet is installed on vehicles without a sliding roof.

TESTING

260E, 300E, 300CE and 300TE

1. Turn the ignition switch **ON**.
2. Set the blower switch to **III** and the air distribution **DOWNWARD**.
3. Place a 1cm sq. piece of paper on the temperature sensor interior air grid. If the paper adheres to the grid, the jet is functioning; if not, replace the jet.

REMOVAL AND INSTALLATION

260E, 300E, 300CE and 300TE

1. Disconnect the negative battery cable.
2. Position a cover under the heater box on the passenger's side to protect the interior.
3. Remove the insturment panel.
4. Pull the hoses from the air flow jet.
5. Loosen the air flow jet screw and pull the jet from it's mount.

To install:

6. Position the air flow jet onto it's mount and tighten the screw.
7. Push the hoses onto the air flow jet.
8. Install the instrument panel.
9. Connect the negative battery cable.

Interior Air Temperature Sensor

TESTING

1. Remove the temperature sensor from the dome light.
2. Place the sensor into an enviormental oven and connect voltmeter to the electrical connectors.
3. Use the chart to determine if the resistance is acceptable to the temperature ranges.
4. If the sensor does not meet specifications, replace the sensor.

REMOVAL AND INSTALLATION

260E, 300E, 300CE and 300TE

1. Disconnect the negative battery cable.
2. Pull the dome light from the ceiling.
3. Disconnect the 2-pole electrical connector from the temperature sensor.
4. Disconnect the hose from the temperature sensor and remove the sensor from the vehicle.

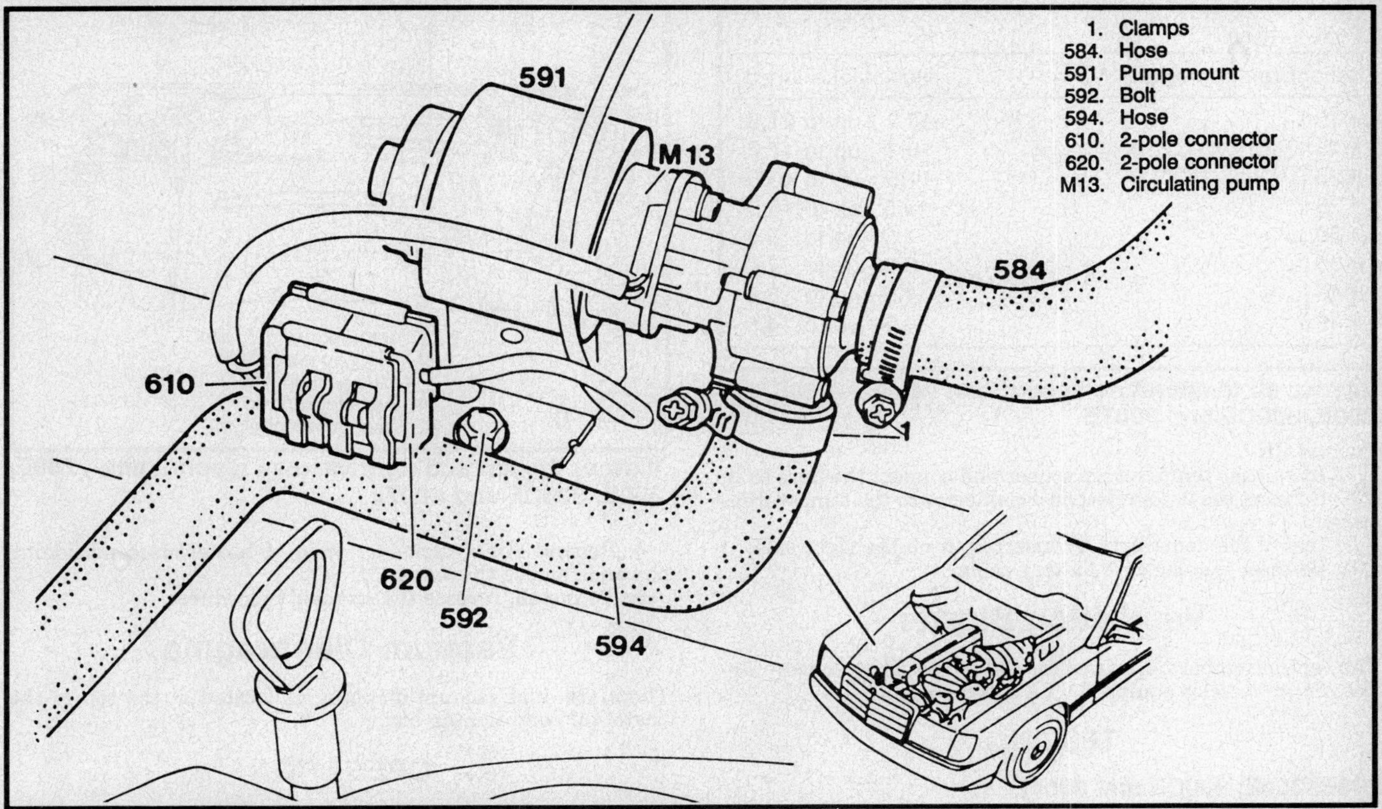
1. Clamps
584. Hose
591. Pump mount
592. Bolt
594. Hose
610. 2-pole connector
620. 2-pole connector
M13. Circulating pump
591
M13
584
610
1
620
592
594

View of the circulating pump—260E, 300E, 300CE and 300TE

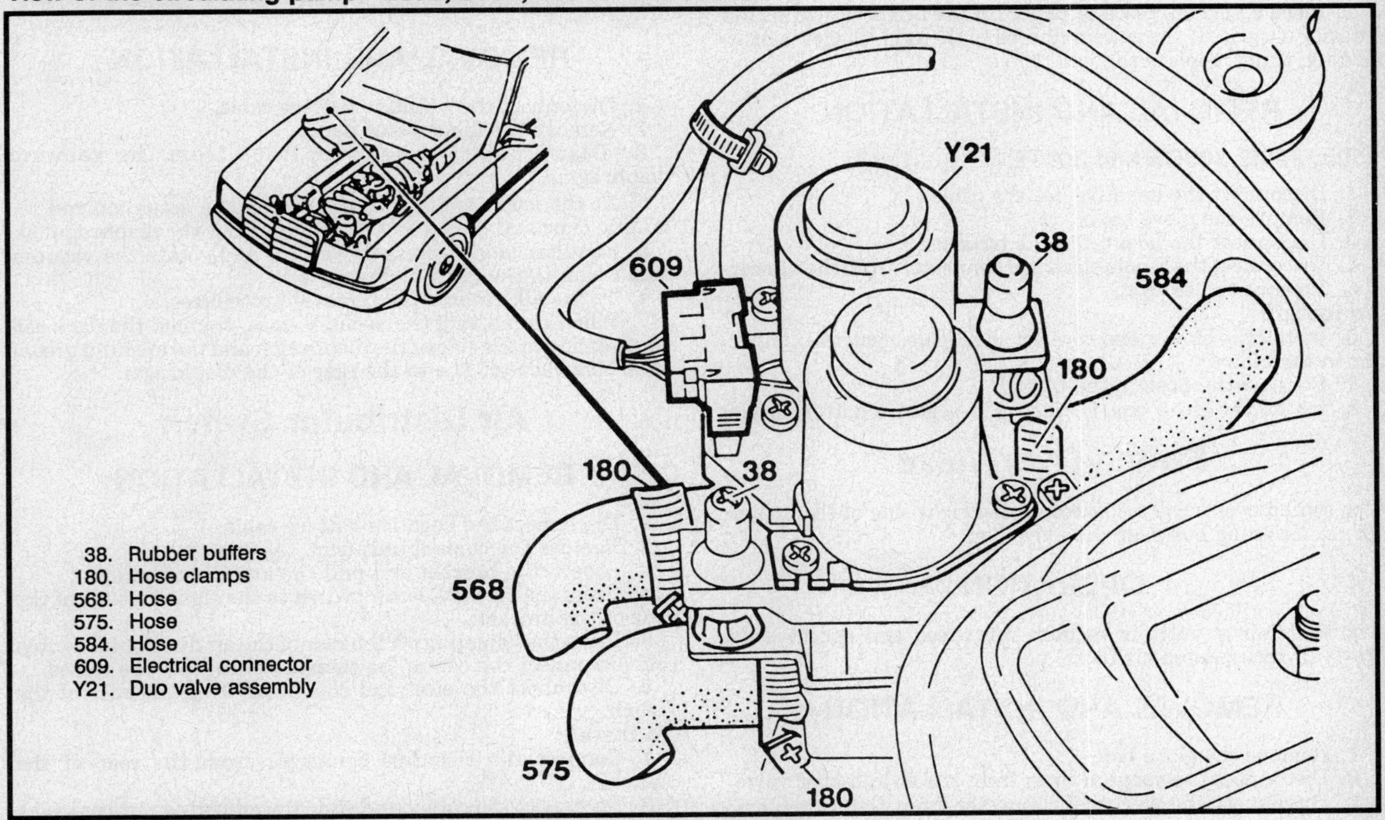
Y21
38
609
584
180
180
38
568
575
180
38. Rubber buffers
180. Hose clamps
568. Hose
575. Hose
584. Hose
609. Electrical connector
Y21. Duo valve assembly

View of the duo valve assembly—260E, 300E, 300CE and 300TE

Test values	
Sensor temperature in °C	Resistance in kΩ
+10	18.2 up to 21.5
+15	15.3 up to 17.2
+20	11.5 up to 13.5
+25	9.5 up to 10.5
+30	7.5 up to 8.5
+35	6.0 up to 7.0
+40	4.5 up to 5.5
+45	3.5 up to 4.5

Interior air temperature sensor test values—260E, 300E, 300CE and 300TE

To install:

5. Install the temperature sensor and connect the hose to it.
6. Connect the 2-pole electrical connector to the temperature sensor.
7. Install the dome light by inserting it on the right side.
8. Connect the negative battery cable.

Ventilation Blower

The ventilation blower is used for the temperature sensor interior air on vehicles equipped with a sliding roof.

TESTING

260E, 300E, 300CE and 300TE

1. Turn the ignition switch **ON**.
2. Place a 1cm sq. piece of paper on the temperature sensor interior air grid. If the paper adheres to the grid, the jet is functioning; if not, replace the jet.

REMOVAL AND INSTALLATION

260E, 300E, 300CE and 300TE

1. Disconnect the negative battery cable.
2. Remove the glove box.
3. Disconnect the hose from the blower.
4. Disconnect the 2-pole electrical connector from the blower.
5. Remove the blower.

To install:

6. Install the blower and connect the 2-pole electrical connector to the blower.
7. Connect the hose to the blower.
8. Install the glove box. Connect the negative battery cable.

Switch-Over Valve

The switch-over valve is located on the right side of the heater/air conditioning box near the glove box.

OPERATION

The switch-over valve is vacuum controlled and operates the fresh air/recirculated air flap.

REMOVAL AND INSTALLATION

1. Remove the glove box.
2. Disconnect the vacuum lines from the switch-over valve.
3. Disconnect the electrical connector from the switch-over valve

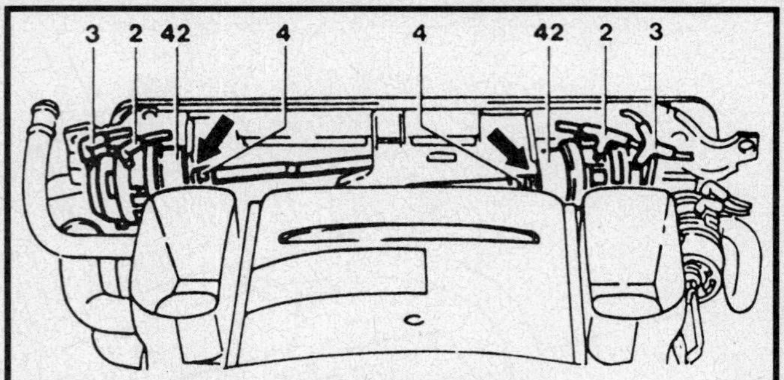
3
2
42
4
4
42
2
3

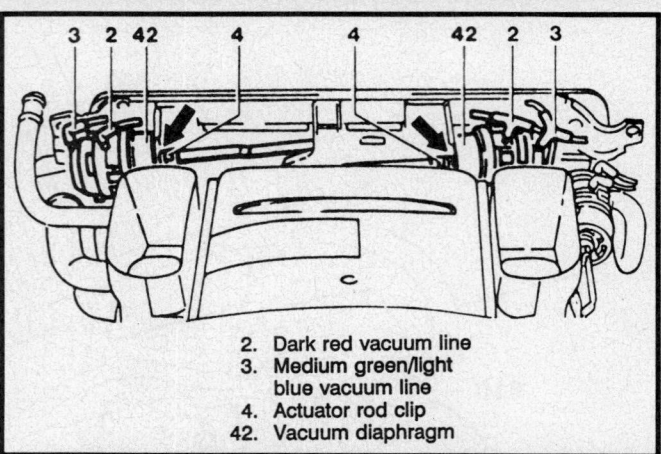

2. Dark red vacuum line
3. Medium green/light blue vacuum line
4. Actuator rod clip
42. Vacuum diaphragm

View of the left and right vacuum diaphragms—260E, 300E, 300CE and 300TE

4. Remove the switch-over valve-to-heater/air conditioning box and remove the valve.
5. To install, reverse the removal procedures.

Vacuum Diaphragms

There are dual vacuum diaphragms located at the top of the heater/air conditioning box.

OPERATION

The vacuum diaphragms control air flaps to change the air flow between fresh or recirculated.

REMOVAL AND INSTALLATION

1. Disconnect the negative battery cable.
2. Remove the instrument panel.
3. Disconnect the vacuum lines from the vacuum diaphragms.
4. At the vacuum diaphragm(s), open the actuation rod retaining clips and disconnect the rod(s) from the diaphragm(s).
5. Simultaneously, press downward and rotate the vacuum diaphragm to the right and remove it.
6. To install, reverse the removal procedures.
7. When connecting the vacuum lines, connect the dark red vacuum line to the side of the diaphragm and the medium green/light blue vacuum line to the rear of the diaphragm.

Air Distributor Switch

REMOVAL AND INSTALLATION

1. Disconnect the negative battery cable.
2. Remove the control unit from the console.
3. Loosen the bracket and pull the assembly forward.
4. Press the air distributor switch to the right and out of the rear of the bracket.
5. Press the adjusting off the rear of the air distributor switch and disconnect the cables; be careful not to kink the cables.
6. Disconnect the electrical connector from the rear of the switch.

To install:

7. Connect the electrical connector from the rear of the switch.
8. Reconnect the cables and slide the adjusting nuts onto the air distributor switch.

9. Press the air distributor switch into the bracket and to the right.
10. Install the bracket and tighten the screw.
11. Install the control unit onto the console. Connect the negative battery cable.

Air Distributor Switch Control Cables

REMOVAL AND INSTALLATION

260E, 300E, 300CE and 300TE

1. Disconnect the negative battery cable. Remove the air distributor switch.
2. Remove the lower cover at the front of the passenger's side.
3. Remove the instrument panel and the glove box.
4. Disconnect the control cable from the footwell air flap control lever.
5. Disconnect the control cable from the defroster nozzle control lever.

To install:

6. Connect the control cable to the defroster nozzle control lever.
7. Connect the control cable to the footwell air flap control lever.
8. Adjust the control cables, by turning the adjusting nuts, so the footwell air flaps and the defroster nozzles are fully closed with the air distributor switch in the **9 O'CLOCK** position.
9. Install the glove box and the instrument panel.
10. Install the lower cover at the front of the passenger's side.
11. Install the air distributor switch. Connect the negative battery cable.

Heat Exchanger Temperature Sensor

TESTING

1. Remove the temperature sensor(s) from the console.
2. Place the sensor into an enviormental oven and connect voltmeter to the electrical connectors.
3. Use the chart to determine if the resistance is acceptable to the temperature ranges.
4. If the sensor does not meet specifications, replace the sensor.

REMOVAL AND INSTALLATION

1. Disconnect the negative battery cable.
2. Remove the control unit. Unclip the bracket.
3. Disconnect both 2-pole electrical connectors from the temperature sensors.

Test values

Sensor temperature in°C	Resistance in kΩ
+ 10	18.2 up to 21.5
+ 15	15.3 up to 17.2
+ 20	11.5 up to 13.5
+ 25	9.5 up to 10.5
+ 30	7.5 up to 8.5
+ 35	6.0 up to 7.0
+ 40	4.5 up to 5.5
+ 45	3.5 up to 4.5

Heat exchanger temperature sensor test values—260E, 300E, 300CE and 300TE

4. Remove both temperature sensors from the dash.

To install:

5. Push both temperature sensors into the dash.
6. Connect both 2-pole electrical connectors to the temperature sensors.
7. Clip in the bracket. Install the control unit.
8. Connect the negative battery cable.

Pressure Switch

TESTING

260E, 300E, 300CE and 300TE

FLUID RESERVOIR SWITCH

1. Turn the ignition switch **ON** and the air conditioning **ON**.
2. Using a voltmeter, check the pressure switch terminals for ground and battery voltage.

NOTE: If ground is present at only 1 terminal, the air conditioner is either not fully charged or the pressure switch is defective. If ground is present at both terminals and the compressor does not switch ON, check the compressor shut-off switch.

3. To check the refrigerant level, perform the following procedures:
   a. Operate the engine at idle.
   b. Using a jumper wire, connect it to both pressure switch terminals.
   c. Assure that the refrigerant flows without bubbles after the compressor switches ON.
   d. If necessary recharge the air conditioning system.

AUXILIARY FAN SWITCH

1. Turn the ignition switch **ON**.
2. Using a jumper wire, jump the terminals of the auxiliary fan switch.
3. Connect a high pressure gauge to the refrigerant line near the compressor.
4. Turn the air conditioning switch **ON** and the fan switch to speed **4**.
5. Operate the engine at idle until the pressure on the gauge reaches apporx. 22.18 ± 0.5 bars (this corresponds to pressure of approx. 20.16 ± 0.5 bars on the pressure switch), slowly increase engine speed, if necessary. If the auxiliary fan does not turn ON at speed **1**, the pressure switch is defective.
6. Operate the engine at idle until the gauge pressure reaches approx. 17.14 ± 0.5 bars (this corresponds to pressure of approx. 15.12 ± 0.5 bars on the pressure switch), disconnect 1 plug from the pressure switch, if necessary. If the auxiliary fan does not switch OFF, the pressure switch is defective.

300SE, 300SEL, 420SEL, 560SEC and 560SEL

CUT-IN PRESSURE

1. Operate the engine and turn the air conditioning system **ON**; turn **ON** the blower motor and temperature dial.
2. If the compressor's electromagnetic clutch is not attracting, use a voltmeter to check for voltage at both terminals of the pressure switch; do not disconnect the electrical connectors.
3. If both terminals of the pressure switch are carrying voltage, check for:
   a. A fault in the wire between the pressue switch and the electromagnetic clutch coil.
   b. A defective electromagnetic clutch coil.
4. If only 1 terminal of the pressure switch are carrying voltage, check for:
   a. Insufficiently charged air conditioning system.
   b. Defective pressure switch.

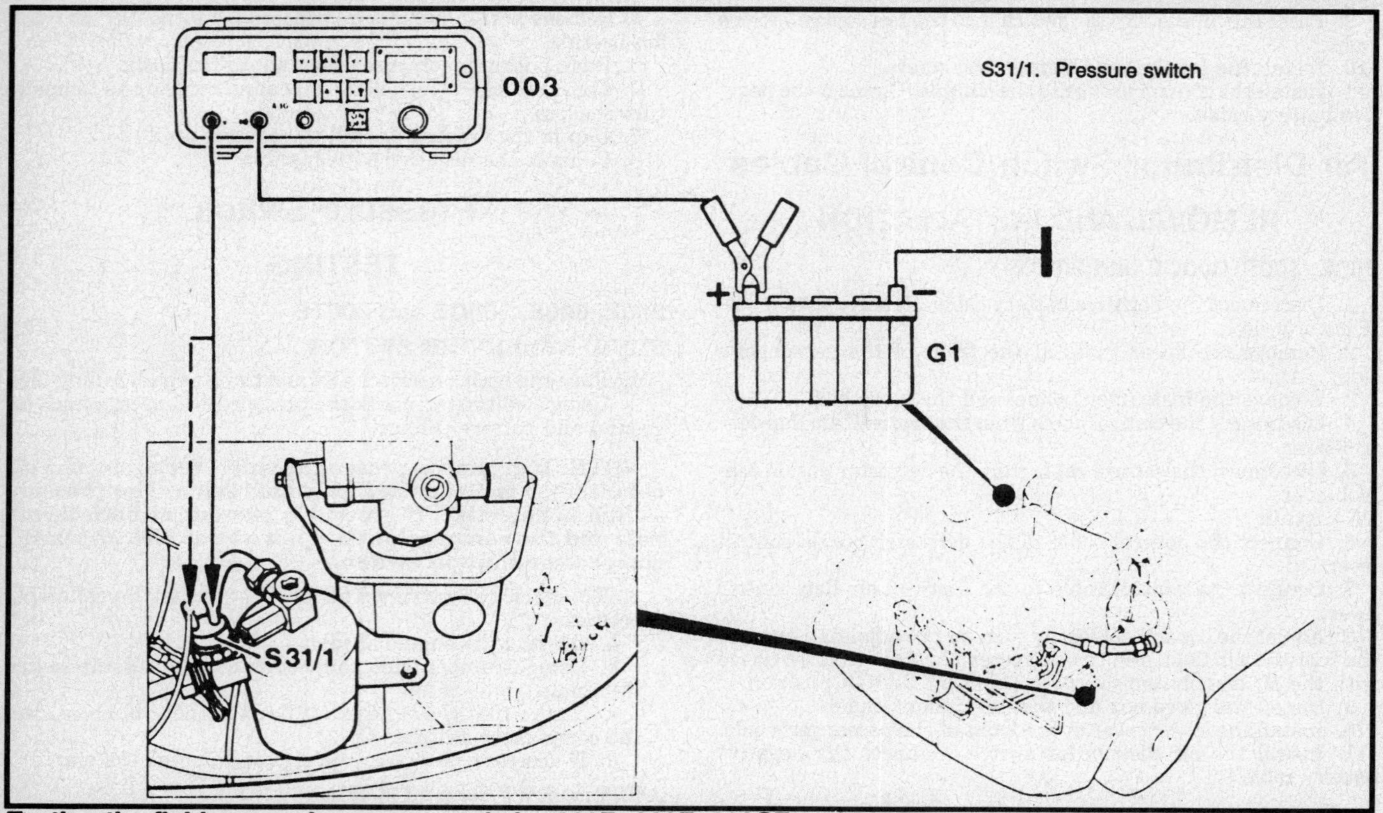
003
S31/1. Pressure switch
G1
+
–
S31/1
Testing the fluid reservoir pressure switch—260E, 300E, 300CE and 300TE

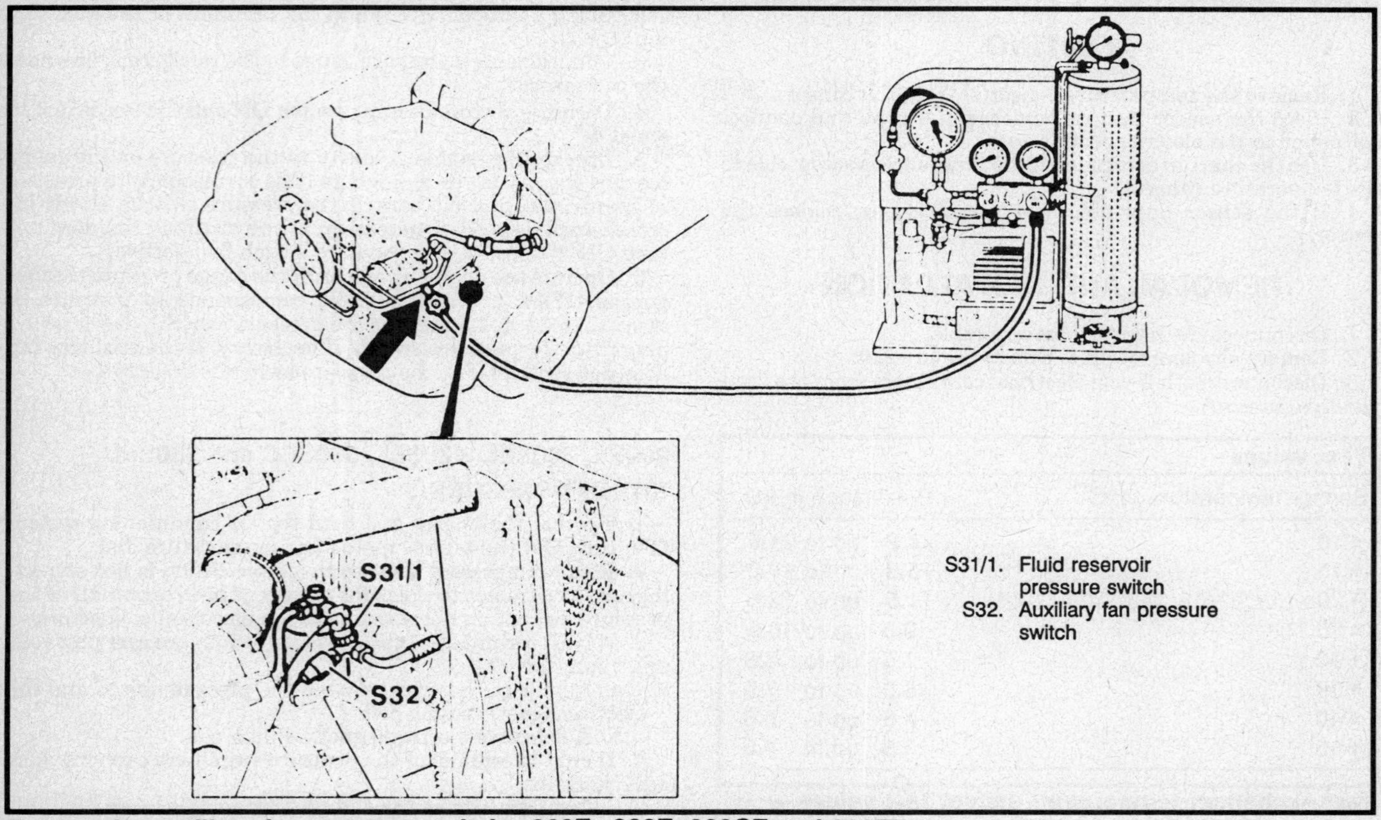
S31/1
S32
S31/1. Fluid reservoir pressure switch
S32. Auxiliary fan pressure switch
Testing the auxiliary fan pressure switch—260E, 300E, 300CE and 300TE

5. To check the refrigerant level, perform the following procedures:

a. Pull the electrical connectors from the pressure switch and connect a jumper wire between them.

b. Operate the air conditioning system for 2–3 minutes.

c. With the electromagnetic clutch in operation, assure that the refrigerant flows without bubbles, past the sight glass.

d. If necessary, recharge the air conditioning system.

6. If the refrigerant level is adequate, the pressure switch is defective.

CUT-OUT PRESSURE

1. After the cut-in pressure test has passed, connect an air conditioning pressure gauge to the pressure end of the service valve.
2. Disconnect both electrical connectors from the pressure switch and connect an ohmmeter to the pressure switch terminals.
3. Properly, discharge the air conditioning system by about 2 ± 0.2 bars; at this point, the ohmmeter should register infinity.

REMOVAL AND INSTALLATION

260E, 300E, 300CE and 300TE

FLUID RESERVOIR SWITCH

1. Disconnect the negative battery cable.
2. Properly, discharge the air conditioning system.
3. Disconnect the electrical connectors from both pressure switch.
4. Remove the pressure switch by screwing it from the fluid reservoir; be sure to plug the reservoir.

To install:

5. Using refrigerant oil, lubricate the pressure switch threads and install the switch to the fluid reservoir; torque the switch to 20 ± 4 Nm.
6. Connect both electrical connectors to pressure switch.
7. Using the proper procedure, evacuate and charge the air conditioning system.
8. Connect the negative battery cable.
9. Start the engine and allow it to run at idle for the 1st 4 minutes and check for leaks.

AUXILIARY FAN SWITCH

1. Disconnect the negative battery cable.
2. Properly discharge the air conditioning system.
3. Disconnect the electrical connectors from both pressure switch.
4. Remove the pressure switch by screwing it from the fluid reservoir; be sure to plug the reservoir.

To install:

5. Using refrigerant oil, lubricate the O-ring and install the switch to the fluid reservoir; torque the swicth to 7 ± 1.5 ft. lbs. (10 ± 2 Nm).
6. Connect both electrical connectors to pressure switch.
7. Using the proper procedure, evacuate and charge the air conditioning system.
8. Connect the negative battery cable.
9. Start the engine and allow it to run at idle for the 1st 4 minutes and check for leaks.

300SE, 300SEL, 420SEL, 560SEC and 560SEL

1. Disconnect the negative battery cable.
2. Properly, discharge the air conditioning system.
3. Disconnect the electrical connectors from the pressure switch.
4. Remove the pressure switch by screwing it from the reciever/drier; be sure to plug the reservoir.

To install:

5. Using refrigerant oil, lubricate the pressure switch threads and install the switch to the reciever/drier; torque the switch to 20 ± 4 Nm.
6. Connect both electrical connectors to pressure switch.
7. Using the proper procedure, evacuate and charge the air conditioning system.
8. Connect the negative battery cable.
9. Start the engine and allow it to run at idle for the 1st 4 minutes and check for leaks.

Pre-Resistor Group

REMOVAL AND INSTALLATION

260E, 300E, 300CE and 300TE

1. Position the hood vertically. Disconnect the negative battery cable.
2. On the left side, lift the hood-to-chassis seal.
3. Press the trim moulding from the vehicle. Pull out the clip.
4. Remove the water drain-to-chassis screws and remove the water drain.
5. Disconnect the 2-pole and the 6-pole electrical connectors from the pre-resistor group.
6. Below the instrument panel on the driver's side, remove the cover.
7. From inside the vehicle, remove the pre-resistor group-to-chassis nuts.
8. Remove the pre-resistor group from the outside of the vehicle.

To install:

9. Position the pre-resistor group and secure with the nuts.
10. Below the instrument panel on the driver's side, install the cover.
11. Connect the 2-pole and the 6-pole electrical connectors to the pre-resistor group.
12. Insert the water drain into the drain pipe and secure with the screws.
13. Install the clip and press the trim moulding onto the vehicle.
14. Refit the hood-to-chassis seal. Connect the negative battery cable.

Outside Air Temperature Sensor

The outside air temperature sensor is attached to the upper heater/air conditioning box and is located under the windshield wiper assembly on top of the cowl.

TESTING

1. Remove the outside air temperature sensor from the heater/air conditioning box.
2. Place the sensor into an enviormental oven and connect voltmeter to the electrical connectors.
3. Use the chart to determine if the resistance is acceptable to the temperature ranges.
4. If the sensor does not meet specifications, replace the sensor.

REMOVAL AND INSTALLATION

260E, 300E, 300CE and 300TE

1. Disconnect the negative battery cable.
2. Remove the air inlet cover from the top of the cowl.
3. Remove the glove box.
4. Disconnect the 2-pole electrical connector from behind the glove box.

5. Pull the air temperature sensor from the heater/air conditioning box and pull the electrical cable through the cowl.

To install:

6. To install, reverse the removal procedures.
7. Connect the negative battery cable.

Evaporator Temperature Sensor

The evaporator temperature sensor is attached to the left side of the heater/air conditioning box.

TESTING

1. Remove the temperature sensor from the dome light.
2. Place the sensor into an enviormental oven and connect voltmeter to the electrical connectors.
3. Use the chart to determine if the resistance is acceptable to the temperature ranges.
4. If the sensor does not meet specifications, replace the sensor.

Sensor temperature in °C	Resistance in kΩ
+ 10	5.0 up to 6.0
+ 15	4.0 up to 4.6
+ 20	3.1 up to 3.9
+ 25	2.4 up to 3.0
+ 30	1.9 up to 2.3
+ 35	1.6 up to 2.0
+ 40	1.4 up to 1.6
+ 45	1.1 up to 1.3

Outside air temperature sensor test values—260E, 300E, 300CE and 300TE

Sensor temperature in °C	Resistance in kΩ
+ 10	18.2 up to 21.5
+ 15	15.3 up to 17.2
+ 20	11.5 up to 13.5
+ 25	9.5 up to 10.5
+ 30	7.5 up to 8.5
+ 35	6.0 up to 7.0
+ 40	4.5 up to 5.5
+ 45	3.5 up to 4.5

Evaporator temperature sensor test values—260E, 300E, 300CE and 300TE

REMOVAL AND INSTALLATION

260E, 300E, 300CE and 300TE

1. Disconnect the negative battery cable.
2. Remove the lower instrument panel cover from the left side.
3. Disconnect the cable strap.
4. Disconnect the 2-pole electrical connector from the evaporator temperature sensor.
5. Pull the temperature sensor from the heater/air conditioning box.
6. To install, reverse the removal procedures.
7. Connect the negative battery cable.

Coolant Temperature Switch

OPERATION

The temperature switch sends a resistance value corresponding to the coolant temperature to the control unit. The control unit processes the value and switches the compressor OFF in 2 stages.

TESTING

260E, 300E, 300CE and 300TE

At the coolant temperature of 242°F (117°C) for a gasoline engine or 251°F (122°C) for a diesel engine, the switch ON period is reduced by 50 percent. The compressor is switched ON and OFF, in cycles: approx. 20 seconds ON and 20 seconds OFF. If the coolant temperature drops to 237°F (114°C) for a gasoline engine or to 251°F (122°C) for a diesel engine, the compressor is switched ON permanently.

At the coolant temperature of 248°F (120°C) for a gasoline engine or 262°F (128°C) for a diesel engine, the compressor is switched OFF completely. When the coolant temperature drops to 242°F (117°C) for a gasoline engine or 251°F (122°C) for a diesel engine, the compressor is switched on in cyclic operation.

Air Capacity Switch

REMOVAL AND INSTALLATION

260E, 300E, 300CE and 300TE

1. Disconnect the negative battery cable.
2. Remove heater/air conditioning control unit from the center console.
3. At the air capacity switch, unclip the lateral straps or remove the bracket bolts.
4. From the driver's side, remove the cover below the instrument panel.
5. At the opposite end of the control cable, disconnect the cable from the cable bracket clip.
6. Disconnect the cable from the lever.
7. Slide the air capacity switch bracket to the right and remove it from the console with the control cable; guide the control cable through the heater box.
8. Disconnect the 8-pole electrical connector from the air capacity switch.

To install:

9. Connect the 8-pole electrical connector to the air capacity switch.
10. Guide the control cable through the heater box. Slide the air capacity switch bracket to the left and install it into the console.
11. Connect the cable to the lever.
12. At the opposite end of the control cable, connect the cable to the cable bracket clip.
13. At the driver's side, install the cover under the instrument panel.
14. At the air capacity switch, reclip the lateral straps or install the bracket bolts.
15. Install heater/air conditioning control unit into the center console.
16. Connect the negative battery cable.

SYSTEM DIAGNOSIS

Air Conditioning System Repairs

The following diagnosis and repair procedures pertain to the air conditioning/automatic temperature control for models 260E, 300E, 300CE and 300TE

Refrigerant compressor does not switch ON

1ST CAUSE

System not charged with sufficient quantity of refrigerant (R-12)—possible leak or pressure switch defective.

REMEDY

1. Allow engine to run at idle.
2. Switch **ON** the function switch.
3. Disconnect both electrical connectors from the pressure switch, located on the fluid reservoir. Connect the electrical connectors to a new pressure switch.
4. If the compressor runs, check fluid level in air conditioner, elimate leakage, if required.
5. If the fluid level is O.K., replace pressure switch.
6. If the compressor does not run, see cause 2.

2ND CAUSE

Malfunction in actuation from control unit or control panel to compressor shut-off control unit.

REMEDY

Check electrical components in air-conditioner automatic temperature control.

3RD CAUSE

Compressor shut-off not functioning.

REMEDY

Check compressor shut-off.

Imprecise customer complaint

TESTS

Check control quality and heating capacity.

In the event of deviations from the nominal functions, check electrical components in air conditioner automatic temperature control.

Air Outlet Temperature Too Low When Maximum Heating State Required

1ST CAUSE

Circulation pump not running.

REMEDY

Check activation and current consumption (max. 0.8 amps) of circulation pump, replace circulation pump, if required.

2ND CAUSE

Duo valve defective

REMEDY

Check duo valve, replace, if required.

3RD CAUSE

Heat exchanger duty or defective.

REMEDY

Flush cooling system. Replace heat exhanger, if required.

Heater Does Not Heat Up Passenger Compartment To Temperature of Approx. 72°F (22°C) at Head Level With Adjustment Wheel Set to 72°F (22°C) and at Outside Temperature Below 0°C

1ST CAUSE

Electrical malfunction in system.

REMEDY

Check electrical components in air conditioner automatic temperature control and replace defective component, if required.

2ND CAUSE

Heat exhanger dirty or defective.

REMEDY

Flush heating system. Flush cooling system, if required, and replace heat exchanger, if required.

Heater Does Not Heat Up to Comfortable Temperature. Air Outlet Temperature Increases and Decreases Slowly at Regular Intervals

CAUSE

Ventilation of interior air temperature sensor not functioning properly.

REMEDY

Check ventilation fan for interior air temperature sensor. For this purpose switch **ON** ignition and position a small piece of paper approx. 1cm^2 on grate for interior temperature sensor. The paper should remain in place. If not, remove glove box, check ventilation fan and replace it, if required.

Heater Only Heats Occasionally or Heats Continuously at Maximum Capacity.

1ST CAUSE

Discontinuity in one of the temperature sensors or leads.

REMEDY

Check electrical components in air-conditioner automatic temperature control and replace defective component, if required.

2ND CAUSE

Poor contact due to widened sockets.

REMEDY

Check all sockets from cable harness on control unit or control panel on temperature sensors (interior air, heat exhanges, outside air) and on duo valve individually and bend, as required.

Poor Refreigeration Capacity

1ST CAUSE

Coolant quantity in system too low.

REMEDY

Check system for leakage, replace fluid reservoir and refill system.

2ND CAUSE

Expansion valve sticks, is dirty or defective; therefore, vacuum too low or too high.

REMEDY

Replace expansion valve and fluid reservoir.

3RD CAUSE

Evaporator temperature sensor defective, therefore refrigerant compressor switches off too early.

REMEDY

Replace evaporator temperature sensor.

Refrigeration capacity decreases after longer period. Moreover air quantity from center and side nozzles decreases. Ice vapor comes out of center nozzles.

1ST CAUSE

Short circuit in evaporator temperature sensor.

REMEDY

Replace evaporator temperature sensor.

2ND CAUSE

Expansion valve defective.

REMEDY

Replace expansion valve.

Screeching noise from area of evaporator at idle immediately after refrigerant compressor switches on.

CAUSE

Expansion valve defective.

REMEDY

Replace expansion valve

23 MITSUBISHI 23

ECLIPSE • GALANT • MIRAGE
PRECIS • STARION • SIGMA • 3000 GT

SPECIFICATIONS

ENGINE IDENTIFICATION

Year	Model	Engine Displacement cu. in. (cc/liter)	Engine Series Identification	No. of Cylinders	Engine Type
1989	Precis	90 (1468/1.5)	4G15	4	SOHC
	Mirage	90 (1468/1.5)	4G15	4	SOHC
	Mirage	97 (1565/1.6)	4G51	4	DOHC
	Starion	156 (2555/2.6)	G64B	4	SOHC
	Galant	122 (1997/2.0)	4G63	4	SOHC & DOHC
	Sigma	181 (2972/3.0)	6G72	6	SOHC
1990	Precis	90 (1468/1.5)	4G15	4	SOHC
	Mirage	90 (1468/1.5)	4G15	4	SOHC
	Mirage	97 (1565/1.6)	4G51	4	DOHC
	Eclipse	107 (1755/1.8)	4G37	4	SOHC
	Eclipse	122 (1997/2.0)	4G63	4	DOHC
	Galant	122 (1997/2.0)	4G63	4	SOHC & DOHC
	Sigma	181 (2972/3.0)	6G72	6	SOHC
1991	Precis	90 (1468/1.5)	4G15	4	SOHC
	Mirage	90 (1468/1.5)	4G15	4	SOHC
	Mirage	97 (1565/1.6)	4G51	4	DOHC
	Eclipse	107 (1755/1.8)	4G37	4	SOHC
	Eclipse	122 (1997/2.0)	G63B	4	DOHC
	Galant	122 (1997/2.0)	4G63	4	SOHC & DOHC
	3000 GT	181 (2972/3.0)	6G72	6	DOHC

SOHC—Single Overhead Cam
DOHC—Dual Overhead Cam

REFRIGERANT CAPACITIES

Year	Model	Freon (oz.)	Oil	Type
1989	Precis	32	8 ①	R-12
	Mirage	36	9.8 ②	R-12
	Starion	29	6 ①	R-12
	Galant	33	10 ②	R-12
	Sigma	32	3 ①	R-12
1990	Precis	32	8 ①	R-12
	Mirage	36	9.8 ②	R-12
	Eclipse	32	6 ②	R-12
	Galant	33	10 ②	R-12
	Sigma	32	3 ①	R-12
1991	Precis	32	8 ①	R-12
	Mirage	36	9.8 ②	R-12
	Eclipse	32	6 ②	R-12
	Galant	33	10 ②	R-12
	3000 GT	34	9.8 ②	R-12

① Fl. oz.
② Cubic inches

AIR CONDITIONING BELT TENSION CHART

Year	Model	Engine Displacement cu. in. (cc/liter)	Belt Type	New ①	Used ①
1989	Precis	90 (1468/1.5)	V-belt	0.32	0.40
	Mirage	90 (1468/1.5)	V-belt	0.23	0.25
	Mirage	97 (1565/1.6)	V-belt	0.21	0.25
	Starion	156 (2555/2.6)	V-belt	0.50	0.75
	Galant	122 (1997/2.0)	V-belt	0.21	0.25
	Sigma	181 (2972/3.0)	V-belt	0.16	0.19
1990	Precis	90 (1468/1.5)	V-belt	0.32	0.40
	Mirage	90 (1468/1.5)	V-belt	0.23	0.25
	Mirage	97 (1565/1.6)	V-belt	0.21	0.25
	Eclipse	107 (1755/1.8)	V-belt	0.20	0.23
	Eclipse	122 (1997/2.0)	V-belt	0.20	0.23
	Galant	122 (1997/2.0)	V-belt	0.21	0.25
	Sigma	181 (2972/3.0)	V-belt	0.16	0.19
1991	Precis	90 (1468/1.5)	V-belt	0.32	0.40
	Mirage	90 (1468/1.5)	V-belt	0.23	0.25
	Mirage	97 (1565/1.6)	V-belt	0.21	0.25
	Eclipse	107 (1755/1.8)	V-belt	0.20	0.23
	Eclipse	122 (1997/2.0)	V-belt	0.20	0.23
	Galant	122 (1997/2.0)	V-belt	0.21	0.25
	3000-GT	181 (2972/3.0)	Poly-V	0.15	0.19

① Inches of deflection using 22 lbs. force at the midpoint of the belt.

SYSTEM DESCRIPTION

General Information

Except Precis

The heater unit is located in the center of the vehicle with the blower housing and blend-air system. In the blend-air system, hot air and cool air are controlled by blend-air damper to make a fine adjustment of the temperature. The heater system is also designed as a bi-level heater in which a separator directs warm air to the windshield or to the floor and cool air through the panel outlet.

The temperature inside the vehicle is controlled by means of the temperature control lever, the position of which determines the opening of the blend-air damper and the resulting mixing ratio of cool and hot air is used to control the outlet temperature.

The air conditioning compressor coil will be energized when all of the following conditions are met:

1. The air conditioner switch is depressed in either the **ECONO** or **A/C** position.
2. The blower motor switch is not off.
3. The evaporator outlet air temperature sensor is reading at least 39°F (4°C).
4. The evaporator inlet air temperature sensor is reading at least 39°F (4°C).
5. If equipped with a compressor refrigerant temperature sensor, the compressor discharge side refrigerant temperature must be less than 347°F (175°C).

The Starion, Sigma and 3000GT are equipped with versions of an automatic climate control system. In these systems, the signals from the various sensors are processed and controlled by the air conditioning control unit according to the set temperature. Thereafter, the system automatically controls the temperature of the air flow, the amount of air flow, the direction of air outflow and the selection and direction of flow of either outside air or interior recirculated air.

Precis

The air distribution system is located behind the center of the instrument panel. The blower motor assembly is positioned on the passenger side and is connected by a series of air ducts.

The air distribution system directs fresh air from the outside or inside recirculated air, by the use of air mixture dampers. These dampers are located within the air mixture chamber and control the amount of air passing through the heating and air conditioning systems. The air is then mix accordingly and directed to the various outlets. The air damper doors are opened and closed by manual control cables or vacuum actuated devices.

When the air conditioning switch is set to the **ON** position, it energizes the magnetic clutch on the compressor and the following components are used to control the air conditioning compressor operation by de-energizing the magnetic clutch when required:

1. The thermostat prevents ice from building up on the evaporator fins.

2. The low pressure switch protects the compressor in a low refrigerant condition.
3. The water temperature switch keeps the engine from overheating by sensing high engine operating temperatures.
4. An idle control system is used to maintain engine idle speed when the compressor magnetic clutch is energized.

Service Valve Location

Precis

The suction (low pressure) port is located either on the accumulator or on the rear of the compressor. The discharge (high pressure) port is located either on the discharge line near the compressor or on the rear of the compressor.

Mirage, Eclipse and Galant

The suction (low pressure) port is located on the compressor. The discharge (high pressure) port is located on the discharge line at the left front corner of the engine compartment.

Sigma and 3000GT

The suction (low pressure) port is located on the compressor. The discharge (high pressure) port is located on the discharge line near the compressor.

Starion

Both service ports are located on the top of the compressor near the refrigerant line connections.

System Discharging

R-12 refrigerant is a chlorofluorocarbon which, when mishandled, can contribute to the depletion on the ozone layer in the upper atmosphere. Ozone filters out harmful radiation from the sun. In order to protect the ozone layer, an approved R-12 Recovery/Recycling machine that meets SAE standard J1991 should be employed when discharging the system. Follow the operating instructions provided with the approved equipment exactly to properly discharge the system.

System Evacuating

If the air conditioning system has been opened to the atmosphere, it should be air and moisture free before being recharged with refrigerant. Moisture and air mixed with refrigerant will raise the compressor head pressure, possibly damage the system's components and will reduce the performance of the system. Moisture will boil at normal room temperature when exposed to a vacuum. To evacuate the system, perform the following procedure:

1. Leak test the system and repair any leaks found.
2. Connect an approved charging station, Recovery/Recycling machine or manifold gauge set and vacuum pump to the discharge and suction ports. The red hose is normally connected to the discharge (high pressure) line and the blue hose is connected to the suction (low pressure) line.
3. Open the discharge and suction ports and start the vacuum pump. If the pump is not able to pull at least 26 in. Hg of vacuum, there is a leak that must be repaired before evacuation can occur.
4. Once the system has reached at least 26 in. Hg of vacuum, allow the system to evacuate for at least 10 minutes. The longer the system is evacuated, the more contaminants will be removed.
5. Close all valves and turn the pump off. If the system loses more than 2 in. Hg of vacuum after 15 minutes, there is a leak that should be repaired.

System Charging

1. Connect an approved charging station, Recovery/Recycling machine or manifold gauge set to the discharge and suction ports. The red hose is normally connected to the discharge (high pressure) line and the blue hose is connected to the suction (low pressure) line.
2. Follow the instructions provided with the equipment and charge the system with the specified amount of refrigerant.
3. Perform a leak test.

SYSTEM COMPONENTS

Radiator

REMOVAL AND INSTALLATION

1. Disconnect the negative battery cable.
2. Drain the cooling system. Remove necessary air intake ductwork.
3. Disconnect the overflow hose. If necessary, remove the overflow reservoir.
4. Disconnect the upper and lower radiator hoses.
5. Disconnect all electrical connectors to the electric cooling fan(s) and radiator sensors. Most of these connectors employ a waterproof connector. When disconnecting, make sure all parts of the connectors remain intact.
6. Remove the electric cooling fan(s).
7. Disconnect and plug the automatic transaxle or transmission cooler lines, if equipped.
8. Remove the upper radiator mounts and lift out the radiator assembly.

To install:

9. Carefully install the radiator, mounts and retaining bolts.
10. Connect the automatic transaxle or transmission cooler lines, if equipped.
11. Install the electric cooling fan(s).
12. Connect all previously disconnected connectors.
13. Install the radiator hoses.
14. Install the overflow reservoir and hose.
15. Install removed air intake ductwork.
16. Fill the radiator with coolant.
17. Connect the negative battery cable and check for leaks.

COOLING SYSTEM BLEEDING

All vehicles are equipped with a self-bleeding thermostat. Slowly fill the cooling system in the conventional manner; air will vent through the jiggle valve in the thermostat. Run the vehicle until the thermostat has opened and continue filling the radiator. Recheck the coolant level after the vehicle and cooled.

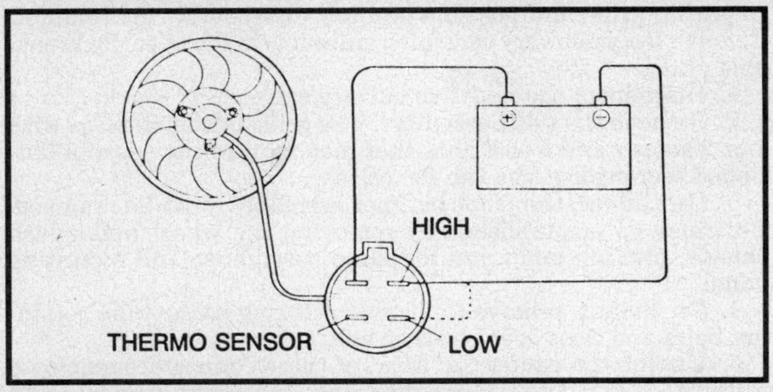
HIGH
THERMO SENSOR
LOW

Radiator cooling fan check—Precis

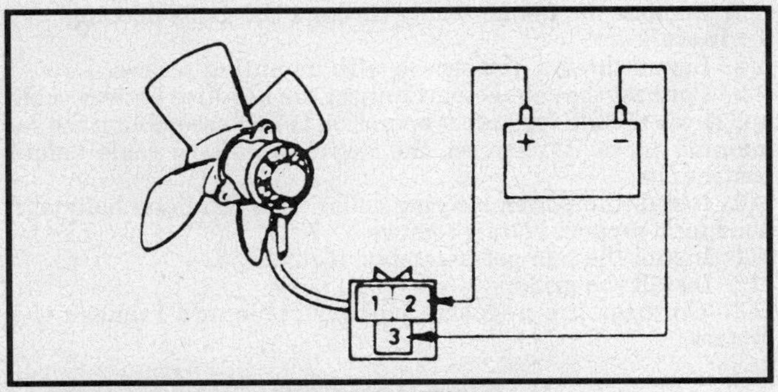

Radiator cooling fan check—Mirage

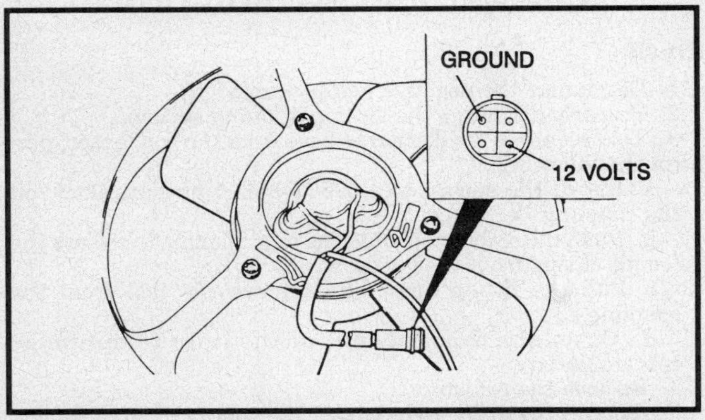
GROUND
12 VOLTS

Radiator and condenser cooling fans check—Starion

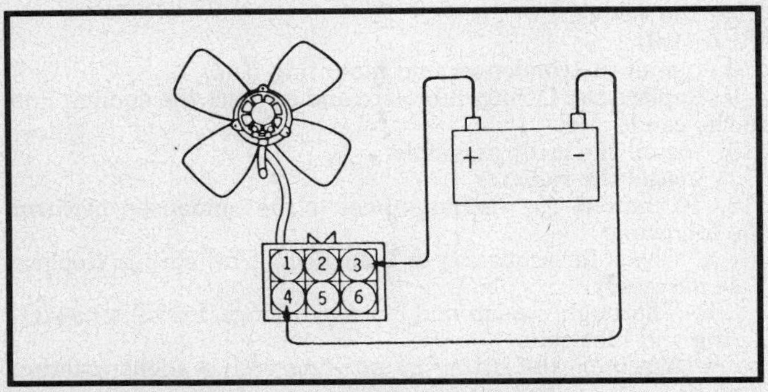

Radiator cooling fan check—Galant with turbocharged engine and non-turbo engine with AWD and automatic transaxle

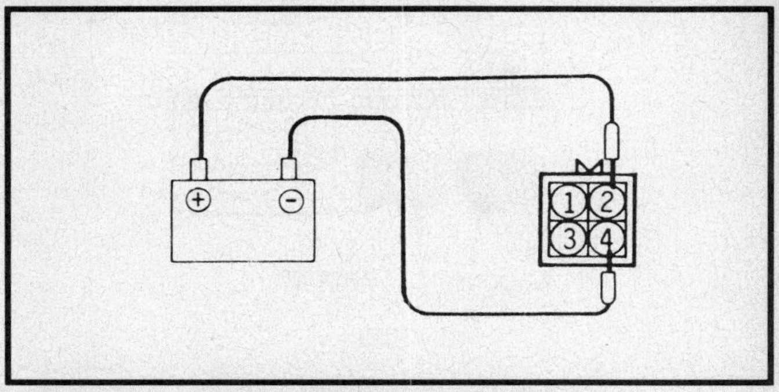

Radiator fan check—FWD Galant without turbocharger, AWD with manual transaxle, and Eclipse. The same connector is used for the condenser cooling fan in Galant

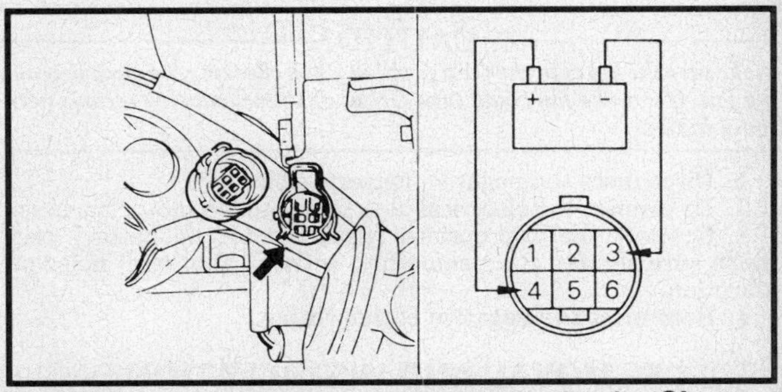

Radiator and condenser cooling fans check—Sigma

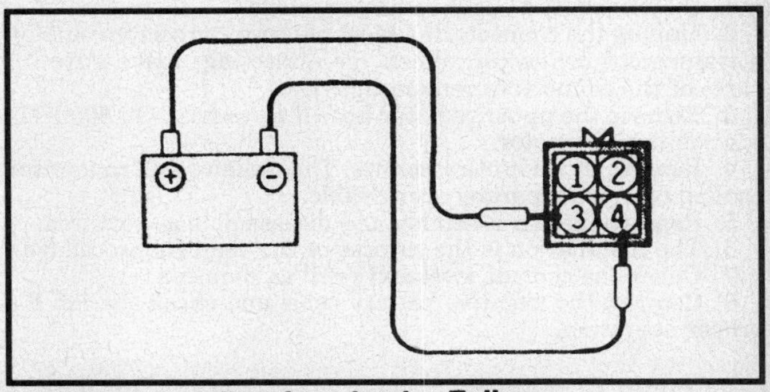

Condenser cooling fan check—Eclipse

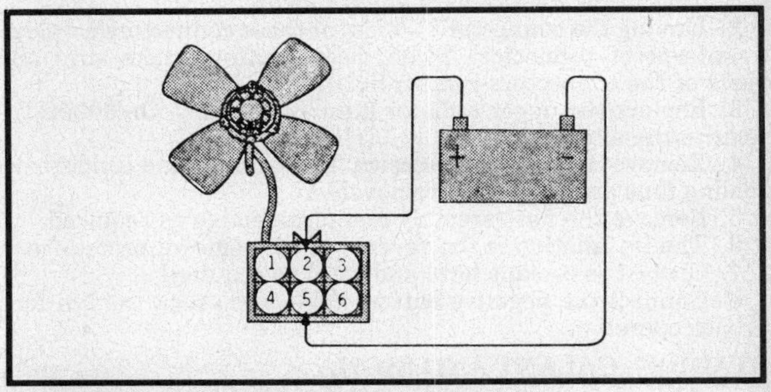

Radiator cooling fan check—3000GT

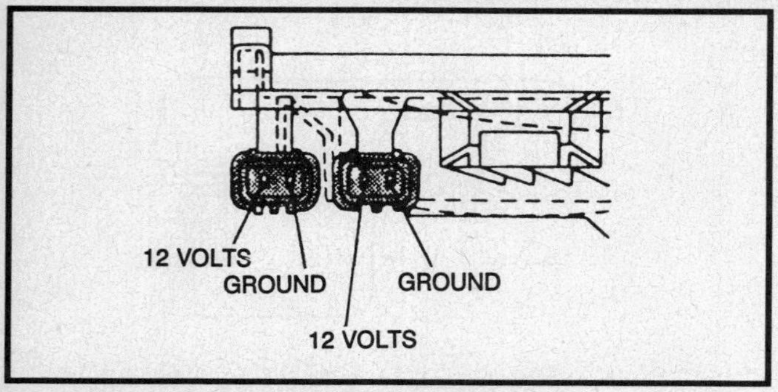
12 VOLTS
GROUND
GROUND
12 VOLTS

Condenser cooling fan check—3000GT

Electric Cooling Fan

TESTING

CAUTION

Make sure the key is in the OFF position when checking the electric cooling fan. If not, the fan could turn ON at any time, causing serious personal injury.

1. Disconnect the negative battery cable.
2. Disconnect the electrical plug from the fan motor harness.
3. Connect the appropriate terminals to the battery and make sure the fan runs smoothly, without abnormal noise or vibration.
4. Reconnect the negative battery cable.

REMOVAL AND INSTALLATION

Radiator Cooling Fan

1. Disconnect the negative battery cable.
2. Unplug the connector(s). Most of these connectors employ a waterproof connector. When disconnecting, make sure all parts of the connectors remain intact.
3. Remove the upper radiator hose if necessary. On 3000GT, remove the alternator.
4. Remove the mounting screws. The radiator and condenser cooling fans are separately removable.
5. Remove the fan assembly and disassemble as required.
6. The installation is the reverse of the removal procedure.
7. Check the coolant level and refill as required.
8. Connect the negative battery cable and check the fan for proper operation.

Condenser Cooling Fan

EXCEPT STARION, GALANT AND SIGMA

1. Disconnect the negative battery cable.
2. Unplug the connector(s). Most of these connectors employ a waterproof connector. When disconnecting, make sure all parts of the connectors remain intact.
3. Remove the upper radiator hose if necessary. On 3000GT, remove the alternator.
4. Remove the mounting screws. The radiator and condenser cooling fans are separately removable.
5. Remove the fan assembly and disassemble as required.
6. The installation is the reverse of the removal procedure.
7. Check the coolant level and refill as required.
8. Connect the negative battery cable and check the fan for proper operation.

STARION, GALANT AND SIGMA

Thecondenser fan is mounted between the condenser and grille, requiring grille and possibly bumper disassembly for removal. Remove the grille very carefully, since it is made of easily breakable plastic.

1. Disconnect the negative battery cable.
2. Remove the grille assembly. The grille is held in place with 1 or 2 screws and 5 or 6 clips that may require the use of a flat-tipped tool against the tab for release.
3. On Galant, the front bumper assembly must be removed. This may be accomplished by removing the wheel well splash shields, parking lamp and fog lamp assemblies and mounting bolts.
4. On Galant, remove the power steering collar tube retaining bolts and hood lock support bolt.
5. Unplug the connector. Most of these connectors employ a waterproof connector. When disconnecting, make sure all parts of the connectors remain intact.
6. Remove the mounting screws.
7. Remove the fan assembly through the grille opening.

To install:

8. Install the fan and secure with mounting screws.
9. Connect the connector. Connect the negative battery cable and check the fan for proper operation before assembling the remaining parts. Disconnect the negative battery cable before continuing.
10. Install the power steering collar tube retaining bolts and hood lock support bolt, if removed.
11. Install the bumper assembly, if removed.
12. Install the grille.
13. Connect the negative battery cable and recheck the system.

Condenser

REMOVAL AND INSTALLATION

Precis

1. Disconnect the negative battery cable.
2. Properly discharge the air conditioning system.
3. To disconnect the discharge hose from the condenser, perform the following:
   a. Install the special tool 09977-33600 or equivalent, on the coupling.
   b. Push the special tool onto the cage opening to release the female fitting from the garter spring.
   c. Pull the fitting apart and remove the tool from the coupling.
   d. Cover the exposed ends of the lines to minimize contamination.
4. Remove the radiator.
5. Remove the grille assembly.
6. Disconnect the suction line from the condenser.
7. Remove the mounting bolts and remove the condenser from the vehicle.

To install:

8. Install the condenser and mounting bolts.
9. Replace the O-ring, lubricate and connect the suction line to the condenser.
10. Install the grille assembly.
11. Install the radiator.
12. To connect the discharge hose to the condenser, perform the following:
    a. Check for a missing or damaged garter spring. Replace as necessary.
    b. Thoroughly clean and dry the fittings, install a new O-ring and lubricate.
    c. Assemble the fitting by pushing with a slight twisting motion.
    d. To visually verify positive engagement, make sure the garter spring is over the flared end of the female fitting.
13. Fill the cooling system.

14. Evacuate and recharge the air conditioning system. If the condenser was replaced, add 2 oz. of refrigerant oil during the recharge.
15. Connect the negative battery cable and check the entire climate control system for proper operation and leaks.

Mirage, Eclipse, Galant and 3000GT

1. Disconnect the negative battery cable.
2. Properly discharge the air conditioning system.
3. On Mirage, remove the battery, battery tray and windshield washer reservoir.
4. On Galant, remove all necessary air intake ductwork.
5. On 3000GT, remove the alternator.
6. Remove the upper radiator mounts to allow the radiator to be moved toward the engine. Remove the fans if they do not allow enough radiator movement.
7. Disconnect the refrigerant lines from the condenser. Cover the exposed ends of the lines to minimize contamination.
8. On Galant, remove the brace in front of the condenser. Remove the condenser mounting bolts.
9. Move the radiator toward the engine and lift the condenser from the vehicle. Inspect the lower rubber mounting insulators and replace, if necessary.

To install:

10. Lower the condenser into position and align the dowels with the lower mounting insulators. Install the bolts. Install the brace, if removed.
11. Replace the O-rings, lubricate and connect the refrigerant lines.
12. Install the radiator mounts and cooling fans.
13. Install remaining parts that were removed during the removal procedure.
14. Evacuate and recharge the air conditioning system. If the condenser was replaced, add 2 oz. of refrigerant oil during the recharge.
15. Connect the negative battery cable and check the entire climate control system for proper operation. Check the system for leaks.

Starion and Sigma

1. Disconnect the negative battery cable.
2. Properly discharge the air conditioning system.
3. Remove the grille assembly. The grille is held in place with 1 or 2 screws and 5 or 6 clips that may require the use of a flat-tipped tool against the tab for release.
4. Unplug the fan connector. Most of these connectors employ a waterproof connector. When disconnecting, make sure all parts of the connectors remain intact.
5. Remove the mounting screws and remove the cooling fan assembly.
6. On Starion, disconnect and plug the automatic transmission cooling lines and remove the transmission oil cooler, if equipped.
7. Disconnect the refrigerant lines from the condenser. Cover the exposed ends of the lines to minimize contamination.
8. Remove the condenser mounting bolts and remove the condenser.

To install:

9. Install the condenser and mounting bolts.
10. Replace the O-rings, lubricate and connect the refrigerant lines to the condenser.
11. Install automatic transmission oil cooling components, if removed.
12. Install the cooling fan and secure with mounting screws.
13. Connect the fan connector. Connect the negative battery cable and check the fan for proper operation before assembling the remaining parts. Disconnect the negative battery cable before continuing.
14. Install the grille.
15. Evacuate and recharge the air conditioning system. If the condenser was replaced, add 2 oz. of refrigerant oil during the recharge.
16. Connect the negative battery cable and check the entire climate control system for proper operation and leaks.

Compressor

REMOVAL AND INSTALLATION

Precis and Mirage

1. Disconnect the negative battery cable.
2. Properly discharge the air conditioning system.
3. Remove the distributor cap and wires so the compressor may be lifted from the engine compartment.
4. If equipped with 1.6L engine, remove the tensioner pulley assembly.
5. Remove the compressor drive belt. Disconnect the clutch coil connector.
6. Disconnect the refrigerant lines from the compressor and discard the O-rings. Cover the exposed ends of the lines to minimize contamination.
7. Remove the compressor mounting bolts and the compressor.

To install:

8. Install the compressor and torque the mounting bolts to 18 ft. lbs. (25 Nm). Connect the clutch coil connector.
9. Using new lubricated O-rings, connect the refrigerant lines to the compressor.
10. Install the belt and tensioner pulley, if removed. Adjust the belt to specifications.
11. Install the distributor cap and wires.
12. Evacuate and recharge the air conditioning system.
13. Connect the negative battery cable and check the entire climate control system for proper operation. Check the system for leaks.

Starion

1. Disconnect the negative battery cable.
2. Properly discharge the air conditioning system.
3. Remove the ignition coil.
4. Loosen the tensioner adjustment bolt and remove the belt.
5. Disconnect the clutch coil connector.
6. Disconnect the refrigerant lines from the compressor. Cover the exposed ends of the lines to minimize contamination.
7. Remove the mounting bolts and remove the compressor from its mounting bracket.

To install:

8. Install the compressor to the bracket and install the mounting bolts.
9. Using new lubricated O-rings, connect the refrigerant lines.
10. Connect the clutch coil connector.
11. Install the belt and adjust to specification.
12. Install the ignition coil.
13. Evacuate and recharge the air conditioning system.
14. Connect the negative battery cable and check the entire climate control system for proper operation and leaks.

Eclipse and Galant

1. Disconnect the negative battery cable.
2. Properly discharge the air conditioning system.
3. On Eclipse, remove the distributor cap and wires so the compressor may be lifted from the engine compartment.
4. On Eclipse with turbocharged engine, remove the VSV bracket on the cowl top.
5. If equipped with AWD, remove the center bearing bracket mounting bolts.
6. Remove the tensioner pulley assembly.

7. Remove the compressor drive belt.
8. Disconnect the clutch coil connector.
9. Disconnect the refrigerant lines from the compressor.
10. Cover the exposed ends of the lines to minimize contamination.
11. Remove the compressor mounting bolts and remove the compressor.

To install:

12. Install the compressor and torque the mounting bolts to 18 ft. lbs. (25 Nm). Connect the clutch coil connector.
13. Using new lubricated O-rings, connect the refrigerant lines to the compressor.
14. Install the belt and tensioner pulley. Adjust the belt to specifications.
15. Install the center bearing bracket mounting bolts and VSV bracket, if removed. Torque the center bearing bracket mounting bolts to 30 ft. lbs. (41 Nm).
16. Install the distributor cap and wires, if removed.
17. Evacuate and recharge the air conditioning system.
18. Connect the negative battery cable and check the entire climate control system for proper operation. Check the system for leaks.

Sigma and 3000GT

1. Disconnect the negative battery cable.
2. Properly discharge the air conditioning system.
3. On Sigma, remove the air cleaner assembly.
4. On 3000GT, remove the alternator and condenser cooling fan.
5. Loosen the tensioner adjustment bolt and remove the belt. Disconnect the clutch coil connector.
6. Disconnect the refrigerant lines from the compressor. Cover the exposed ends of the lines to minimize contamination.
7. Remove the mounting bolts and remove the compressor from its mounting bracket.

To install:

8. Install the compressor to the bracket and install the mounting bolts.
9. Using new lubricated O-rings, connect the refrigerant lines.
10. Connect the clutch coil connector.
11. Install the belt and adjust to specification.
12. Install the fan, alternator or air cleaner.
13. Evacuate and recharge the air conditioning system.
14. Connect the negative battery cable and check the entire climate control system for proper operation and leaks.

Accumulator

REMOVAL AND INSTALLATION

1990–91 Precis

1. Disconnect the negative battery cable.
2. Properly discharge the air conditioning system.
3. Disconnect the refrigerant lines from the accumulator. Cover the exposed ends of the lines to minimize contamination.
4. Disconnect the wiring to the cycling switch.
5. Remove the accumulator from its mounting bracket.
6. Remove the cycling switch from the accumulator.

To install:

7. If installing a new accumulator, add 1 oz. of refrigerant oil to the accumulator prior to installation.
8. Install the cycling switch to the accumulator.
9. Install the accumulator to the bracket and conect the wiring.
10. Using new lubricated O-rings, connect the refrigerant lines to the accumulator.
11. Evacuate and recharge the air conditioning system.
12. Connect the negative battery cable and check the entire climate control system for proper operation and leaks.

Receiver/Drier

REMOVAL AND INSTALLATION

Mirage, Eclipse, Galant, 3000GT and 1989 Precis

1. Disconnect the negative battery cable. On Eclipse, remove the battery.
2. Properly discharge the air conditioning system.
3. On Eclipse and Galant, remove the coolant reserve tank.
4. On Galant, remove the receiver/drier cover.
5. Disconnect the electrical connector from the switch on the receiver/drier, if equipped.
6. Disconnect the refrigerant lines from the receiver/drier assembly. Cover the exposed ends of the lines to minimize contamination.
7. Remove the mounting strap and the receiver/drier from its bracket. Remove the receiver/drier from the mounting strap.

To install:

8. Assemble the receiver/drier and mounting strap and install.
9. Using new lubricated O-rings. connect the refrigerant lines to the receiver/drier.
10. Connect the connector to the switch.
11. Install the receiver cover, if equipped.
12. Install the coolant reserve tank, if removed.
13. Evacuate and recharge the air conditioning system. Add 1 oz. of refrigerant oil during the recharge.
14. Connect the negative battery cable and check the entire climate control system for proper operation. Check the system for leaks.

Starion and Sigma

1. Disconnect the negative battery cable.
2. Properly discharge the air conditioning system.
3. Remove the grille assembly.
4. On Sigma without anti-lock brakes, remove the receiver/drier cover.
5. Disconnect the refrigerant lines from the receiver/drier assembly. Cover the exposed ends of the lines to minimize contamination.
6. Remove the mounting strap and the receiver/drier from its bracket. Remove the receiver/drier from the mounting strap.

To install:

7. Assemble the receiver/drier and mounting strap and install.
8. Using new lubricated O-rings. connect the refrigerant lines to the receiver/drier.
9. Install the receiver cover, if equipped.
10. Install the grille.
11. Evacuate and recharge the air conditioning system. Add 1 oz. of refrigerant oil during the recharge.
12. Connect the negative battery cable and check the entire climate control system for proper operation. Check the system for leaks.

Expansion Valve

REMOVAL AND INSTALLATION

Except 1990–91 Precis

1. Disconnect the negative battery cable.

NOTE: If equipped with an air bag, wait for 1 minute to elapse before working inside the vehicle. The air bag system is set to deploy for a short period of time after the battery is disconnected.

2. Properly discharge the air conditioning system.

3. Remove the evaporator housing and separate the upper and lower cases.
4. Remove the expansion valve from the evaporator lines.
5. The installation is the reverse of the removal installation. Use new lubricated O-rings when assembling.
6. Evacuate and recharge the air conditioning system.
7. Connect the negative battery cable and check the entire climate control system for proper operation. Check the system for leaks.

Fixed Orifice Tube

REMOVAL AND INSTALLATION

1990–91 Precis

NOTE: The fixed orifice tube in a non-serviceable part. The orifice tube is located within the liquid line near the evaporator and cannot be removed from the line. If the orifice tube is defective, the liquid line assembly must be replaced. The fixed orifice tube should also be replaced whenever the compressor is replaced.

1. Disconnect the negative battery cable.
2. Properly discharge the air conditioning system.
3. Disconnect the liquid line from the evaporator and condenser.
4. Remove the brackets retaining the liquid line in place and remove the line.

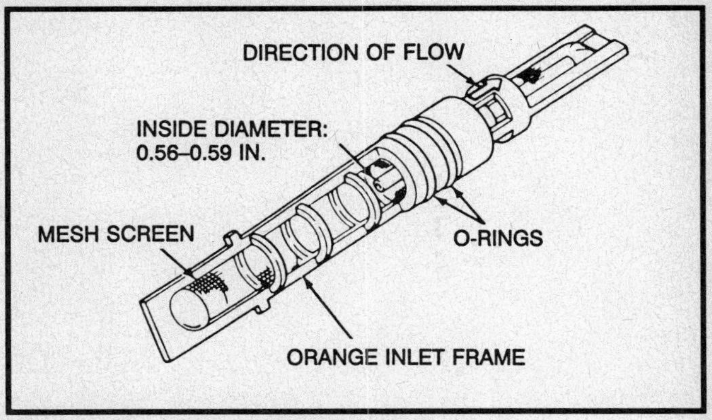
DIRECTION OF FLOW
INSIDE DIAMETER:
0.56–0.59 IN.
MESH SCREEN
O-RINGS
ORANGE INLET FRAME

Fixed orifice tube—1990–91 Precis

To install:

5. Using new lubricated O-rings, install the liquid line to the evaporator and condenser.
6. Secure the liquid line in place the with the retaining brackets.
7. Evacuate and recharge the air conditioning system.
8. Connect the negative battery cable and check the entire climate control system for proper operation and leaks.

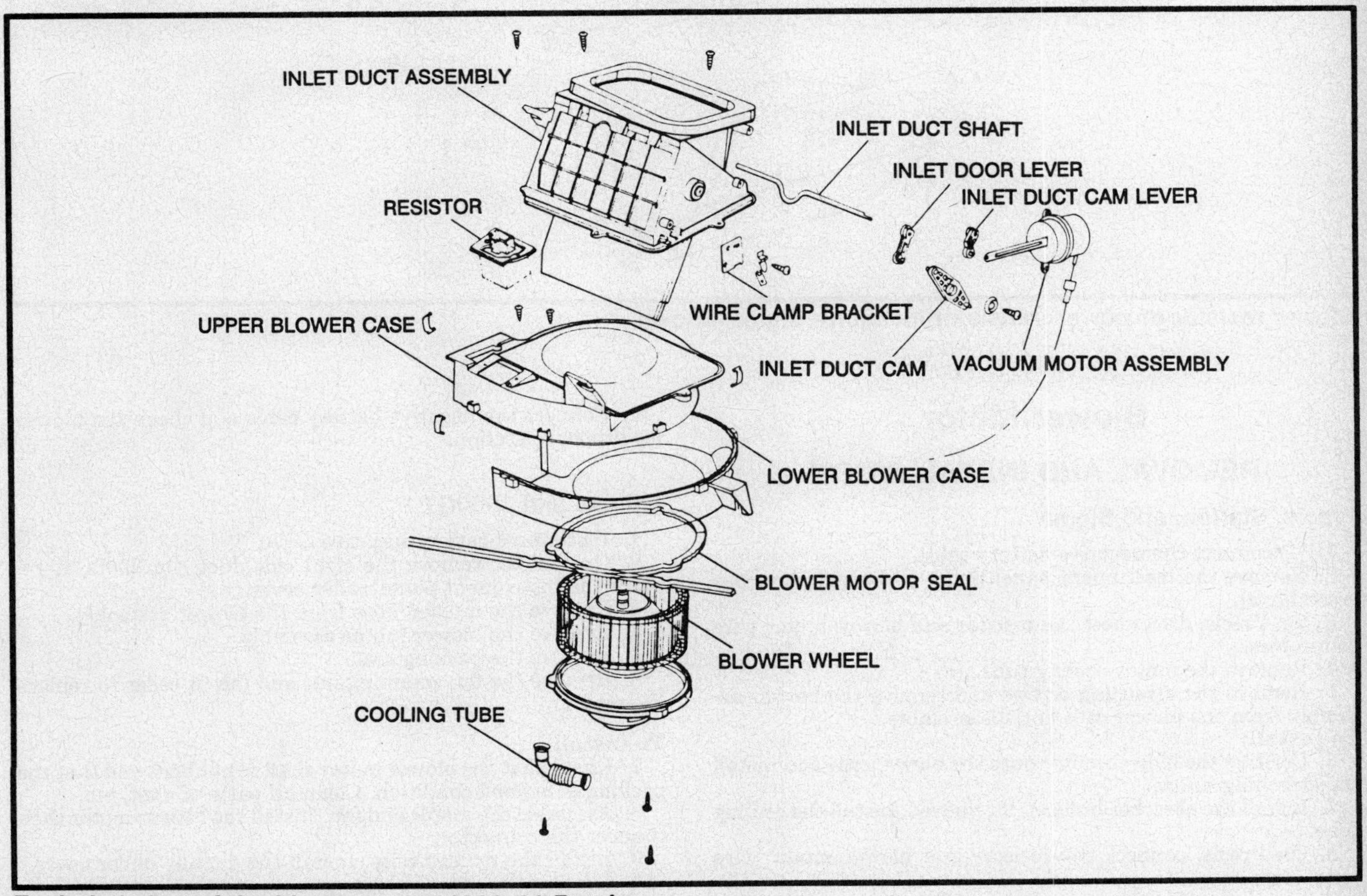
INLET DUCT ASSEMBLY
INLET DUCT SHAFT
INLET DOOR LEVER
INLET DUCT CAM LEVER
RESISTOR
WIRE CLAMP BRACKET
UPPER BLOWER CASE
INLET DUCT CAM
VACUUM MOTOR ASSEMBLY
LOWER BLOWER CASE
BLOWER MOTOR SEAL
BLOWER WHEEL
COOLING TUBE

Exploded view of the blower case—1990–91 Precis

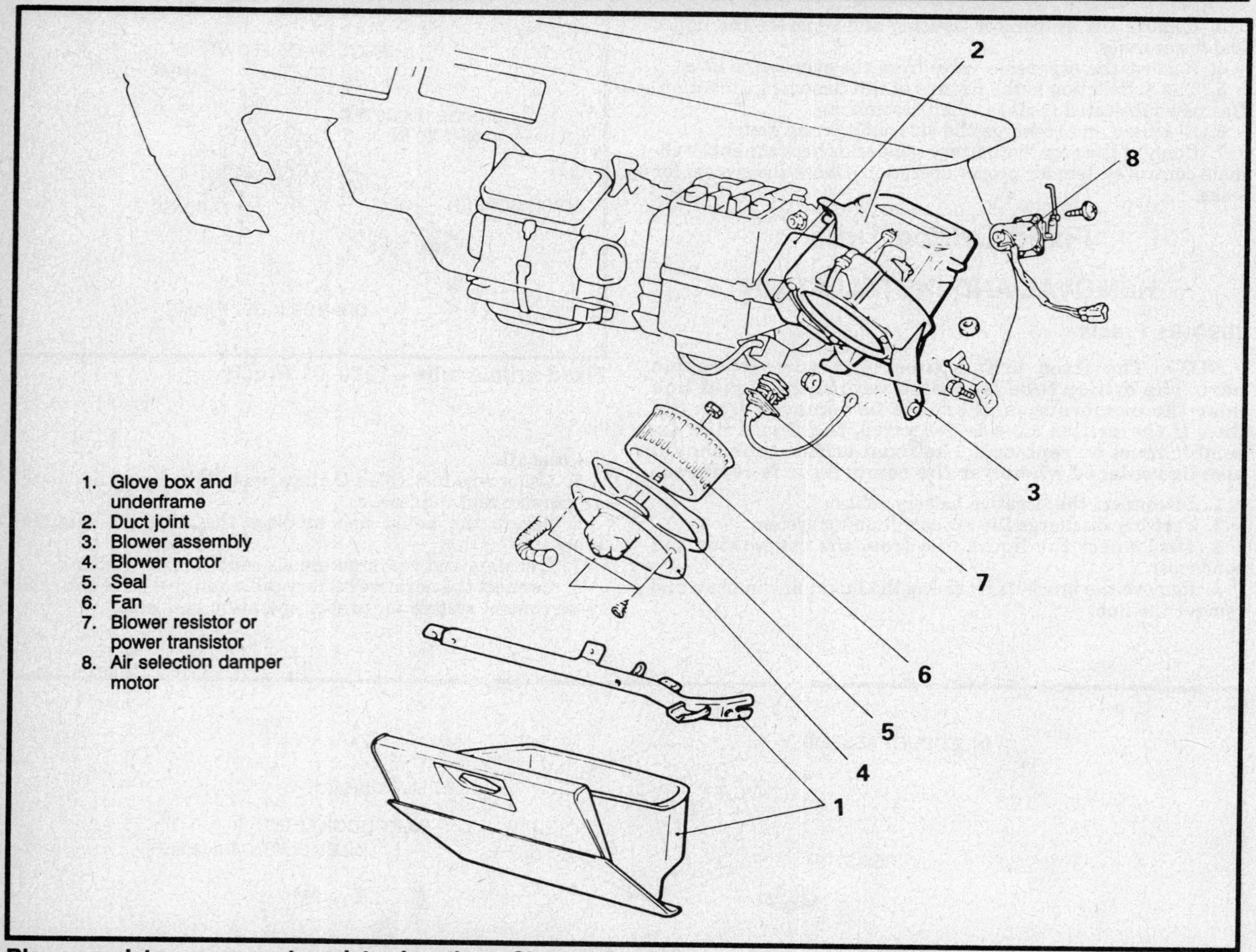
1. Glove box and underframe
2. Duct joint
3. Blower assembly
4. Blower motor
5. Seal
6. Fan
7. Blower resistor or power transistor
8. Air selection damper motor
1
2
3
4
5
6
7
8

Blower resistor or power transistor location—Sigma shown

Blower Motor

REMOVAL AND INSTALLATION

Precis, Starion, and Sigma

1. Disconnect the negative battery cable.
2. Remove the instrument panel under cover and glove box assembly(s).
3. On Precis, disconnect the resistor and blower motor wire connectors.
4. Remove the motor cooling tube.
5. Remove the attaching screws and remove the blower assembly from the blower case and disassemble.

To install:

6. Position the blower motor onto the blower case and install the attaching screws.
7. Install the absorber bracket, if removed. Install the cooling tube.
8. On Precis, connect the resistor and blower motor wire connector.
9. Install the glove box(s) and instrument panel under cover.
10. Connect the negative battery cable and check the blower for proper operation.

Eclipse and 3000GT

1. Disconnect battery negative cable.
2. On Eclipse, remove the right side duct. On 3000GT, remove the instrument panel under cover.
3. Remove the molded hose from the blower assembly.
4. Remove the blower motor assembly.
5. Remove the packing seal.
6. Remove the fan retaining nut and fan in order to replace the motor.

To install:

7. Check that the blower motor shaft is not bent and that the packing is in good condition. Clean all parts of dust, etc.
8. Assemble the motor and fan. Install the blower motor then connect the connector.
9. Install the molded hose. Install the duct or under cover.
10. Connect the negative battery cable and check the entire climate control system for proper operation.

Mirage

1. Disconnect the negative battery cable.
2. Remove the glove box assembly and pry off the speaker cover to the lower right of the glove box.
3. Remove the passenger side lower cowl side trim kick panel.
4. Remove the passenger side knee protector, which is the panel surrounding the glove box opening.
5. Remove the glove frame along the top of glove box opening.
6. Remove the lap heater duct. This is a small piece on vehicles without a rear heater and much larger on vehicles with a rear heater.
7. Disconnect the electrical connector from the blower motor.
8. Remove the cooling tube from the blower assembly.
9. Remove the MPI computer from the lower side of the cowl.
10. Remove the blower motor assembly and disassemble on a workbench.

To install:

11. Assemble the motor and fan. Install the blower motor assembly and connect the wiring and cooling tube.
12. Install the MPI computer.
13. Install the lap heater duct.
14. Install the glove box frame, interior trim pieces and glove box assembly.
15. Connect the negative battery cable and check the entire climate control system for proper operation.

Galant

1. Disconnect the negative battery cable.
2. Remove the glove box assembly and under cover.
3. Remove the foot heater duct.
4. Disconnect the MPI relay and glove box switch.
5. Remove the glove box frame.
6. Remove the cowl side trim.
7. Remove the motor cooling tube and disconnect the motor connector.
8. Remove the screws and remove the blower assembly from the blower case. Disassemble on a workbench.

To install:

9. Assemble the unit and install the blower assembly to the case.
10. Install the cooling tube and connect the connector.
11. Install the cowl side trim and glove box frame.
12. Connect the MPI relay and glove box switch.
13. Install the foot heater duct.
14. Install the glove box assembly and under cover.
15. Connect the negative battery cable and check the entire climate control system for proper operation and leaks.

Blower Motor Resistor or Power Transistor

REMOVAL AND INSTALLATION

1. Disconnect the negative battery cable.

NOTE: If equipped with an air bag, wait for 1 minute to elapse before working inside the vehicle. The air bag system is set to deploy for a short period of time after the battery is disconnected.

2. Remove the glove box assembly. The resistor or power transistor is accessible through the glove box opening and is mounted to the blower or evaporator case.
3. Disconnect the wire harness from the resistor.
4. Remove the mounting screws and remove the resistor.
5. The installation is the reverse of the removal procedure. Make sure the seal is intact when installing.
6. Connect the negative battery cable and check the entire climate control system for proper operation.

Heater Core

REMOVAL AND INSTALLATION

Precis

1. Disconnect the negative battery cable.
2. Set the temperature control lever to its hottest position and drain the cooling system.
3. Disconnect the heater hoses.
4. Remove the lower instrument panel pad.
5. Remove the center console.
6. Remove the screw holding the 2 heating ducts. The heating ducts may be removed by pulling out at the bottom while pushing inward at the top.
7. Disconnect the control cables.
8. If equipped with air conditioning, remove the evaporator case.
9. Loosen the heater unit retaining bolts and remove the heater unit.
10. With the case removed, the heater core may be changed after the water valve is removed. Remove the plastic cover, remove the clamps and hose and remove the water valve.

To install:

11. Install the core and the water valve, using new hoses and/or clamps as necessary.
12. Install the heater unit and tighten the mounting bolts.
13. Install the evaporator case, if removed.
14. Connect the heater control cables and retaining clip. Check the operation of each control through its full range of motion.
15. Install the lower ductwork. Install or tighten the bolt holding the ducts together.
16. Install the center console.
17. Install the lower instrument panel pad.
18. Connect the heater hoses. Fill the cooling system.
19. If equipped with air conditioning, evacuate and recharge the air conditioning system.
20. Connect the negative battery cable and check the entire climate control system for proper operation and leaks.

Mirage

1. Disconnect the negative battery cable.
2. Drain the cooling system and disconnect the heater hoses.
3. Remove the front seats by removing the covers over the anchor bolts, the underseat tray, the seat belt guide ring, the seat mounting nuts and bolts and disconnect the seat belt switch wiring harness from under the seat. Then lift out the seats.
4. Remove the floor console by first taking out the coin holder and the console box tray. Remove the remote control mirror switch or cover. All of these items require only a plastic trim tool to carefully pry them out.
5. Remove the rear half of the console.
6. Remove the shift lever knob on manual transmission vehicles.
7. Remove the front console box assembly.
8. A number of the instrument panel pieces may be retained by pin type fasteners. They may be removed using the following procedure:
   a. This type of clip is removed by pressing down on the center pin with a suitable blunt pointed tool. Press down a little more than $\frac{1}{16}$ in. (2mm); this releases the clip. Pull the clip outward to remove it.
   b. Do not push the pin inward more than necessary because it may damage the grommet or the pin may fall in if pushed in too far. Once the clips are removed, use a plastic trim stick to pry the piece loose.
9. Remove both lower cowl trim panels (kick panels).
10. Remove the ashtray.
11. Remove the center panel around the radio.

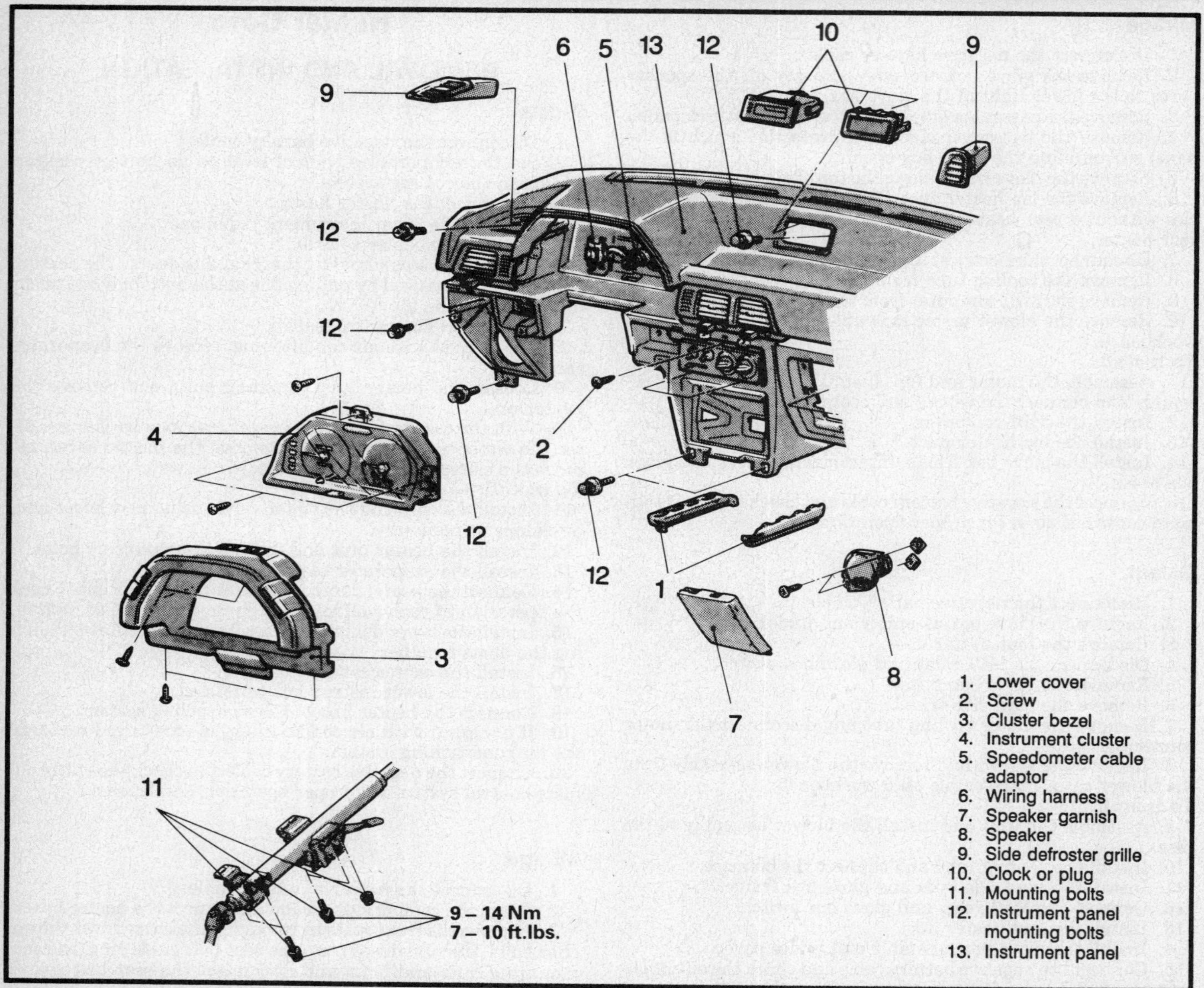
1
2
3
4
5
6
7
8
9
10
11
12
13
9 – 14 Nm
7 – 10 ft.lbs.
1. Lower cover
2. Screw
3. Cluster bezel
4. Instrument cluster
5. Speedometer cable adaptor
6. Wiring harness
7. Speaker garnish
8. Speaker
9. Side defroster grille
10. Clock or plug
11. Mounting bolts
12. Instrument panel mounting bolts
13. Instrument panel

Instrument panel and related components – Mirage

12. Remove the sunglass pocket at the upper left side of panel and the side panel into which it mounts.
13. Remove the driver's side knee protector and the hood release handle.
14. Remove the steering column top and bottom covers.
15. Remove the radio.
16. Remove the glove box striker and box assembly.
17. Remove the instrument panel lower cover, 2 small pieces in the center, by pulling forward.
18. Remove the heater control assembly screw.
19. Remove the instrument cluster bezel and pull out the gauge assembly.
20. Remove the speedometer adapter by disconnecting the speedometer cable at the transaxle pulling the cable sightly towards the vehicle interior and giving a slight twist on the adapter to release it.
21. Insert a small flat-tipped tool to open the tab on the gauge cluster connector. Remove the harness connectors.
22. Remove, by prying with a plastic trim tool, the right side speaker cover and the speaker, the upper side defroster grilles and the clock or plug to gain access to some of the instrument panel mounting bolts.
23. Lower the steering column by removing the bolt and nut.
24. Remove the instrument panel bolts and the instrument panel.
25. Disconnect the air selection, temperature and mode selection control cables from the heater box and remove the heater control assembly.
26. Remove the connector for the ECI control relay.
27. Remove both stamped steel instrument panel supports.
28. Remove the heater ductwork.
29. Remove the heater box mounting nuts.
30. Remove the automatic transmission ELC control box.
31. Remove the evaporator mounting nuts and clips.
32. With the evaporator pulled toward the vehicle interior, remove the heater unit. Be careful not to damage the heater tubes or to spill coolant.

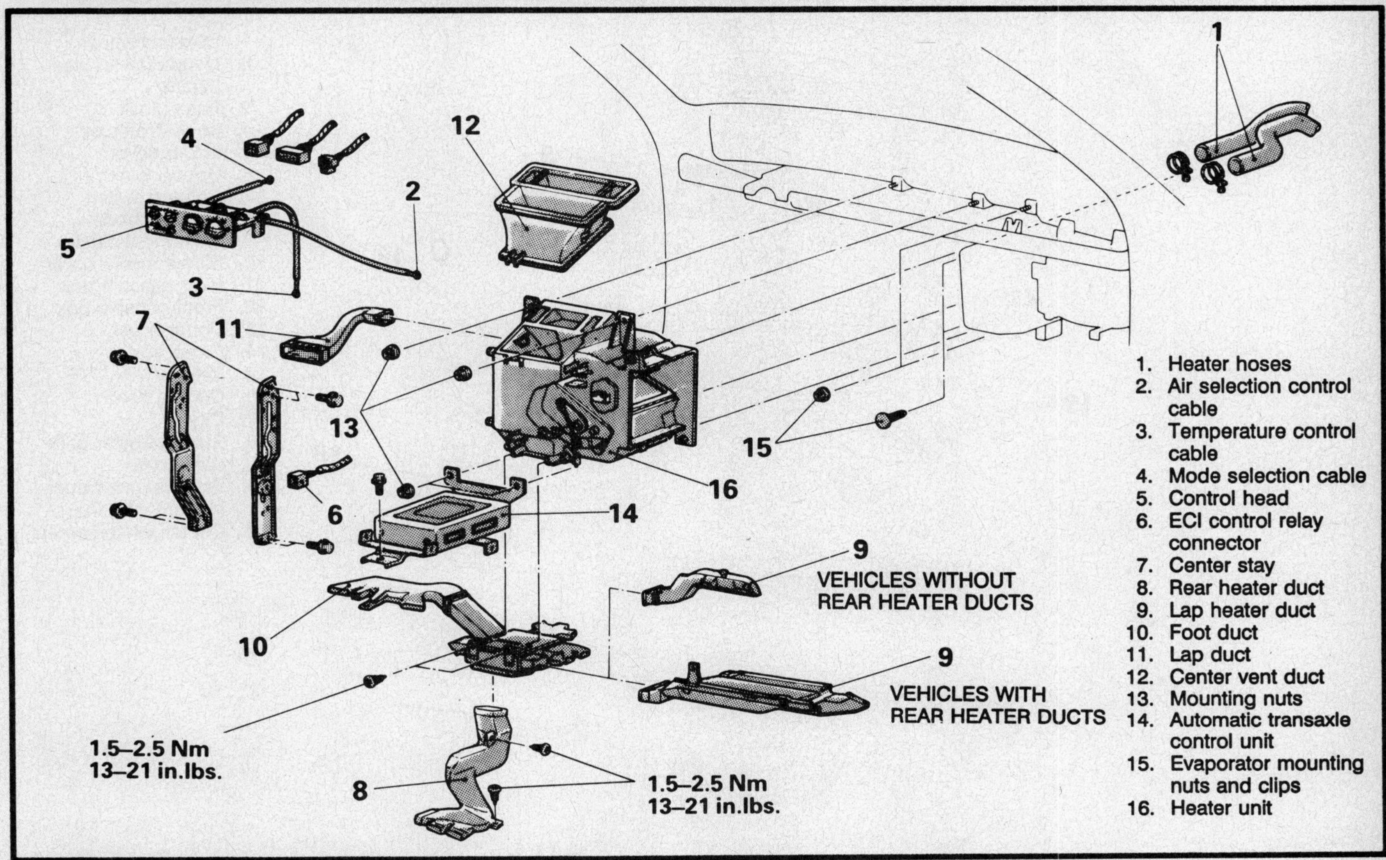
1
12
4
2
5
3
7
11
13
15
16
6
14
9
VEHICLES WITHOUT
REAR HEATER DUCTS
10
9
VEHICLES WITH
REAR HEATER DUCTS
1.5–2.5 Nm
13–21 in.lbs.
8
1.5–2.5 Nm
13–21 in.lbs.
1. Heater hoses
2. Air selection control cable
3. Temperature control cable
4. Mode selection cable
5. Control head
6. ECI control relay connector
7. Center stay
8. Rear heater duct
9. Lap heater duct
10. Foot duct
11. Lap duct
12. Center vent duct
13. Mounting nuts
14. Automatic transaxle control unit
15. Evaporator mounting nuts and clips
16. Heater unit

Heater case and related components – Mirage

33. Remove the cover plate around the heater tubes and the core fastener clips. Pull the heater core from the heater box, being careful not to damage the fins or tank ends.

To install:

34. Thoroughly clean and dry the inside of the case. Install the heater core to the heater box. Install the clips and cover.
35. Install the evaporator and the automatic transmission ELC box.
36. Install the heater box and connect the duct work.
37. Connect all wires and control cables.
38. Install the instrument panel assembly and the console by reversing their removal procedures.
39. Install the seats.
40. Refill the cooling system.
41. Evacuate and recharge the air conditioning system. Add 2 oz. of refrigerant oil during the recharge if the evaporator was replaced.
42. Connect the negative battery cable and check the entire climate control systm for proper operation. Check the system for leaks.

Starion

1. With the engine cold, set the temperature control lever to the extreme right. If equipped with an automatic climate control system, start the engine and use the temperature change switch to select the hottest temperature, then turn the engine **OFF**.
2. Disconnect the negative battery cable. Drain the engine coolant.
3. Disconnect the coolant hoses running to the heater pipes at the firewall.
4. Remove the floor console.
5. Remove the steering wheel.
6. Remove the screws holding the hood release handle to the instrument panel.
7. Unbolt the fuse box from the instrument panel.
8. Remove the knee protector on the left side. Some of the bolts are hidden behind covers.
9. Remove the screws from the bottom of the steering column cover. Remove both halves of the cover.
10. Remove the attaching screws for the combination switch on the steering column.
11. Disconnect the wiring harnesses and remove the switch.
12. Remove the instrument hood screws. Pull both edges of the bottom of the hood forward; hold it in this position and lift up and out.
13. Disconnect the harness connectors on both sides of the instrument hood.
14. Remove the screws on the bottom and the nuts on the top of the instrument cluster. Pull the bottom edge up and forward to remove. Disconnect the wiring and cables as it comes free.
15. Remove the console side cover mounting screws. Remove the cover downward while pushing slightly forward.
16. Remove the front and rear consoles.
17. Remove the passenger side under cover.
18. Remove the glove box and ashtray.
19. Carefully remove the heater control bezel.
20. Remove the clock. It may be removed with a gentle prying motion. Disconnect the harness when it is free.

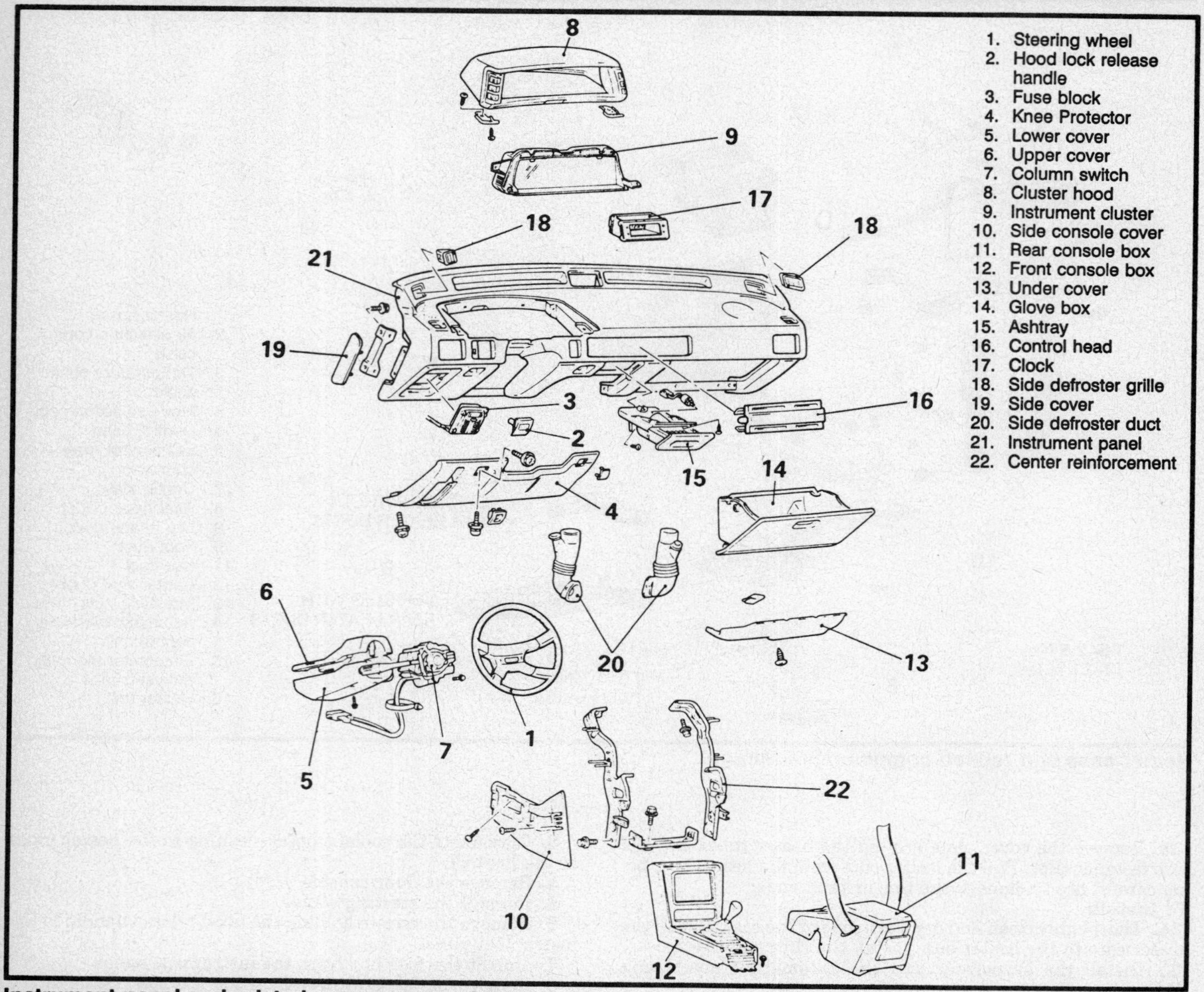
1. Steering wheel
2. Hood lock release handle
3. Fuse block
4. Knee Protector
5. Lower cover
6. Upper cover
7. Column switch
8. Cluster hood
9. Instrument cluster
10. Side console cover
11. Rear console box
12. Front console box
13. Under cover
14. Glove box
15. Ashtray
16. Control head
17. Clock
18. Side defroster grille
19. Side cover
20. Side defroster duct
21. Instrument panel
22. Center reinforcement

Instrument panel and related components—Starion

21. Remove the grilles for the side defrosters by inserting a flat tool from the window side and prying forward and upward.
22. Use a non-marring tool to pry the side covers off the instrument panel.
23. Remove each mounting screw and bolt holding the instrument panel in place. As it comes loose, allow it to move into the interior. Disconnect the remaining wire harnesses.
24. The instrument panel may now be removed from the vehicle. Several components may still be attached.
25. Remove the center ventilator duct and lap heater duct.
26. Remove the 2 center reinforcement bars.
27. Remove the retaining nuts and bolts and remove the heater unit from the vehicle.
28. If equipped with automatic climate control, the servo motor should be removed before working with the case. With the heater unit removed, use a small pry bar to carefully disconnect the servo motor rod from the air blend damper.
29. Remove the screws holding the servo motor to the heater unit.
30. Carefully unlock the water valve lever clip and disconnect the link between the blend air damper and the water valve lever.
31. Remove the outer clamp from the 2 water tubes.
32. Loosen the clamps on the short joint hoses and disconnect the hoses. Remove the retaining screws holding the water valve in place and remove the water valve.
33. The heater core is held in place by a clip and retaining screw. Once removed, the core should come free of the housing. If the core is blocked by the blend air damper lever, remove the lever. Do not attempt to force the core past the lever.

To install:

34. Thoroughly clean and dry the inside of the case. Reassemble the heater unit, and secure the core with the retaining screw and clip. The valve and connecting hoses must be properly secured with new clamps.
35. Push the water valve lever all the way inward so the water valve is at the closed position. Move the blend damper lever counterclockwise so the blend air damper is fully closed.

36. Install the connecting link and secure the water valve lever clip.
37. Install the servo motor and connect the motor rod to the blend air damper.
38. Install the completely assembled heater unit into the vehicle. Tighten the retaining nuts and bolts evenly.
39. Reinstall the 2 center support brackets.
40. Install the lap heater duct and the center ventilation duct.
41. Make certain the reinforcement brackets are in place. Install the instrument panel assembly. The upper part of the heater unit has 2 guide bolts to which the instrument panel attaches. Reverse the removal procedure to complete the instrument panel installation.
42. Install the upper and lower steering column covers.
43. Install the fuse block to the instrument panel. Route the wire harnesses are properly.
44. Install the knee protector on the left side.
45. Attach the hood release handle to the instrument panel.
46. Install the steering wheel.
47. Reinstall the center console.
48. Connect the heater hoses to the heater pipes at the firewall.
49. Refill the cooling system.
50. Connect the negative battery cable and check the entire climate control system for proper operation and leaks.

Galant and Sigma

1. Disconnect the negative battery cable.

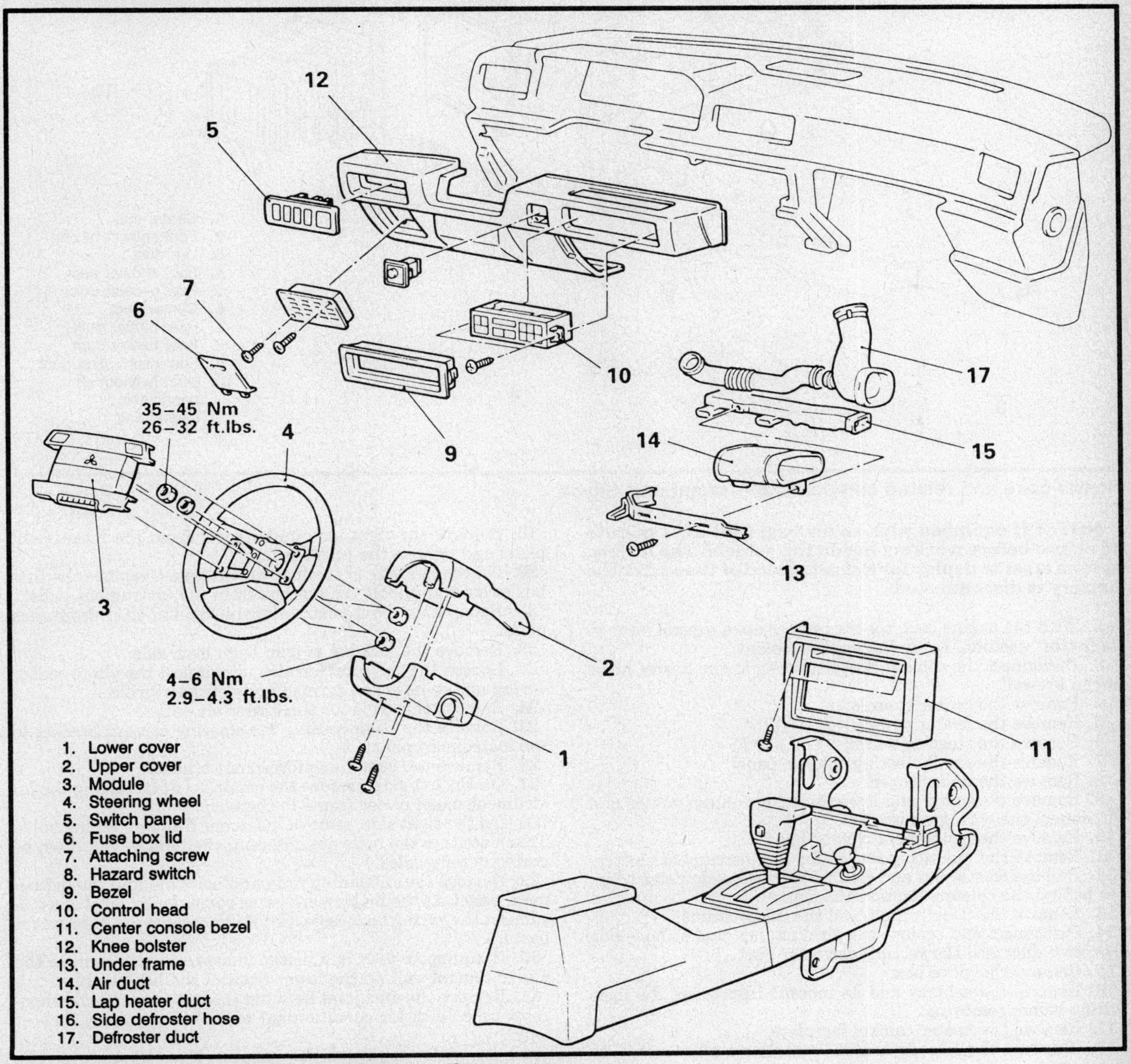
12
5
7
6
10
17
35–45 Nm
26–32 ft.lbs.
4
9
14
15
13
3
2
4–6 Nm
2.9–4.3 ft.lbs.
1
11
1. Lower cover
2. Upper cover
3. Module
4. Steering wheel
5. Switch panel
6. Fuse box lid
7. Attaching screw
8. Hazard switch
9. Bezel
10. Control head
11. Center console bezel
12. Knee bolster
13. Under frame
14. Air duct
15. Lap heater duct
16. Side defroster hose
17. Defroster duct

Instrument panel and related components—Sigma shown

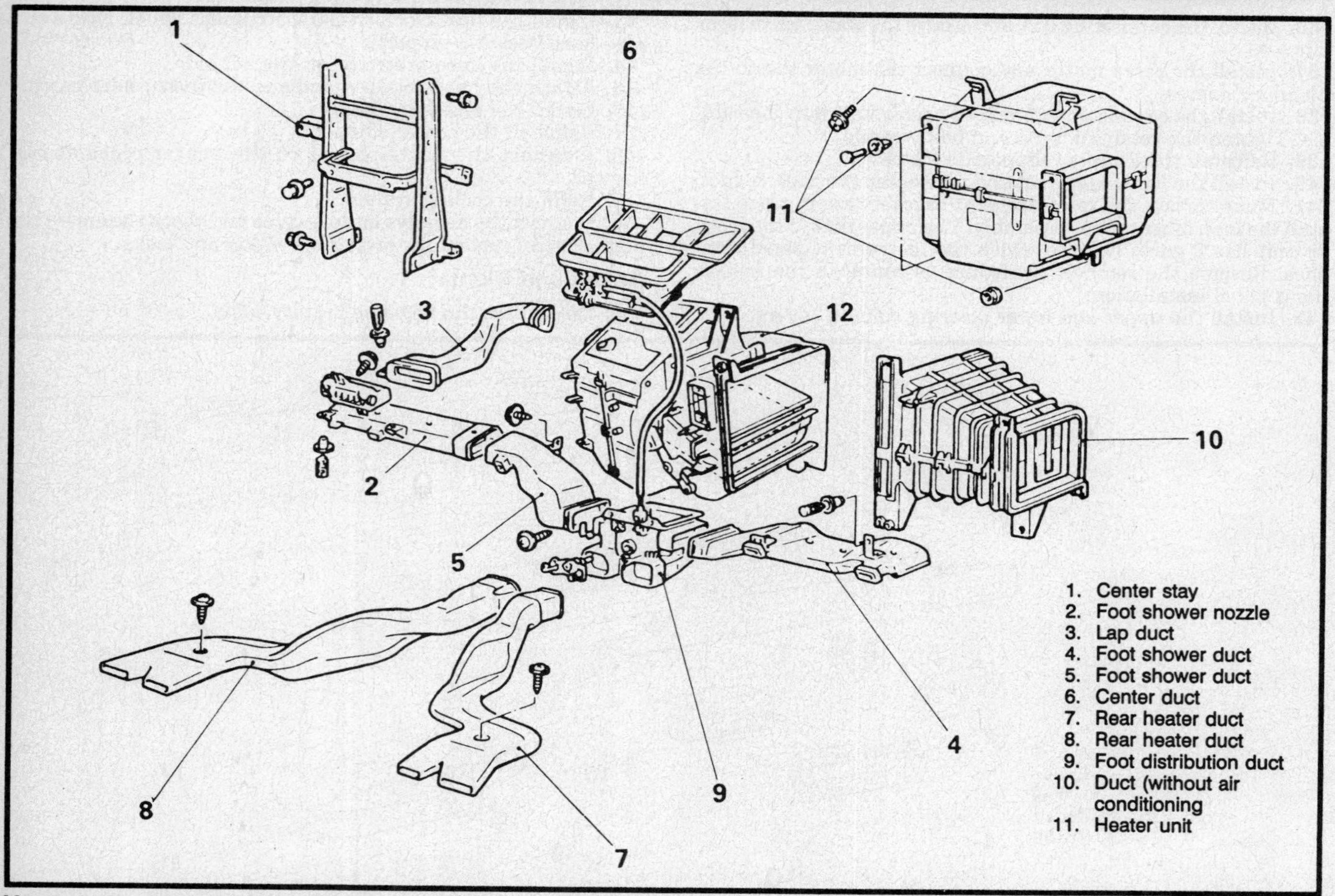
1
2
3
4
5
6
7
8
9
10
11
12
1. Center stay
2. Foot shower nozzle
3. Lap duct
4. Foot shower duct
5. Foot shower duct
6. Center duct
7. Rear heater duct
8. Rear heater duct
9. Foot distribution duct
10. Duct (without air conditioning
11. Heater unit

Heater case and related components—Galant and Sigma

NOTE: If equipped with an air bag, wait for 1 minute to elapse before working inside the vehicle. The air bag system is set to deploy for a short period of time after the battery is disconnected.

2. With the engine cold, set the temperature control lever to its hottest position. Drain the engine coolant.
3. Disconnect the coolant hoses running to the heater pipes at the firewall.
4. Remove the center console.
5. Remove the heater cover.
6. Remove the steering wheel.
7. Remove the small steering column panel.
8. Remove the under cover.
9. Remove the upper and lower steering column covers and disconnect the wiring connectors.
10. Remove the instrument cluster hood.
11. Remove the mounting screws for the instrument cluster.
12. Pull the cluster out and disconnect the speedometer adaptor behind the cluster. Remove the cluster.
13. Remove the floor console and the under frame.
14. Disconnect and remove the air duct, lap heater duct, side defroster duct and the vertical defroster duct.
15. Remove the glove box.
16. Remove the ashtray and its mount. Disconnect the light wiring before removing.
17. Remove the heater control faceplate.
18. Remove the heater control panel and disconnect its harness.
19. Remove the right side under cover from the instrument panel and remove the under frame.
20. On the left side of the instrument panel, remove the fuse box cover and unbolt the fusebox from the instrument panel.
21. Remove the front pillar (windshield pillar trim) from each pillar.
22. Remove the kick panel trim from each side.
23. Loosen the defroster garnish, disconnect the photo sensor wiring and remove the garnish and defroster grille.
24. Remove the grille for the center air outlet.
25. Remove the bolts holding the steering column bracket to the instrument panel.
26. Remove the center reinforcement bracket.
27. On the left side, remove the retaining nuts holding the instrument panel under frame to the body.
28. On the right side, remove the under frame retaining bolts. Take note that the bolts are different; the flanged bolt must be correctly reinstalled.
29. Remove the remaining nuts and bolts holding the instrument panel. As the instrument panel comes loose, label and disconnect the wiring harnesses. Carefully remove the instrument panel.
30. If equipped with automatic climate control, remove the power control unit on the lower front of the heater unit.
31. Remove the duct joint between the heater unit and evaporator case (with air conditioning) or blower assembly (heater only).
32. Carefully separate the vacuum hose harness at the connector.

33. Remove the heater unit from the vehicle.
34. To remove the heater core, first remove the cover from the water valve. Disconnect the links and remove the vacuum actuator.
35. Remove the clamps and slide the heater core out of the case. Remove the water valve after the core is removed.
36. With the case removed, the heater core may be changed after the water valve is removed. Remove the plastic cover, remove the clamps and hose and remove the water valve.

To install:

37. Thoroughly clean and dry the inside of the case. Install the core and the water valve, using new hose or clamps.
38. Install the vacuum actuator and the connecting link. Put the cover on the water valve.
39. Install the heater unit and tighten the mounting bolts.
40. Carefully attach the vacuum hose connector to the vacuum harness. Make certain the hoses mate firmly and securely.
41. Install the heater cover, then install the center console.
42. Install the duct joint between heater and evaporator or blower.
43. Install the power control unit and carefully connect the links and rods.
44. Install the heater hoses under the hood.
45. Install the instrument panel by reversing its removal procedure.
46. Install the center console.
47. Install the upper and lower steering column covers.
48. Install the center panel under cover.
49. Install the small column panel.
50. Install the steering wheel.
51. Fill the cooling system.
52. Connect the negative battery cable and check the entire climate control system for proper operation and leaks.

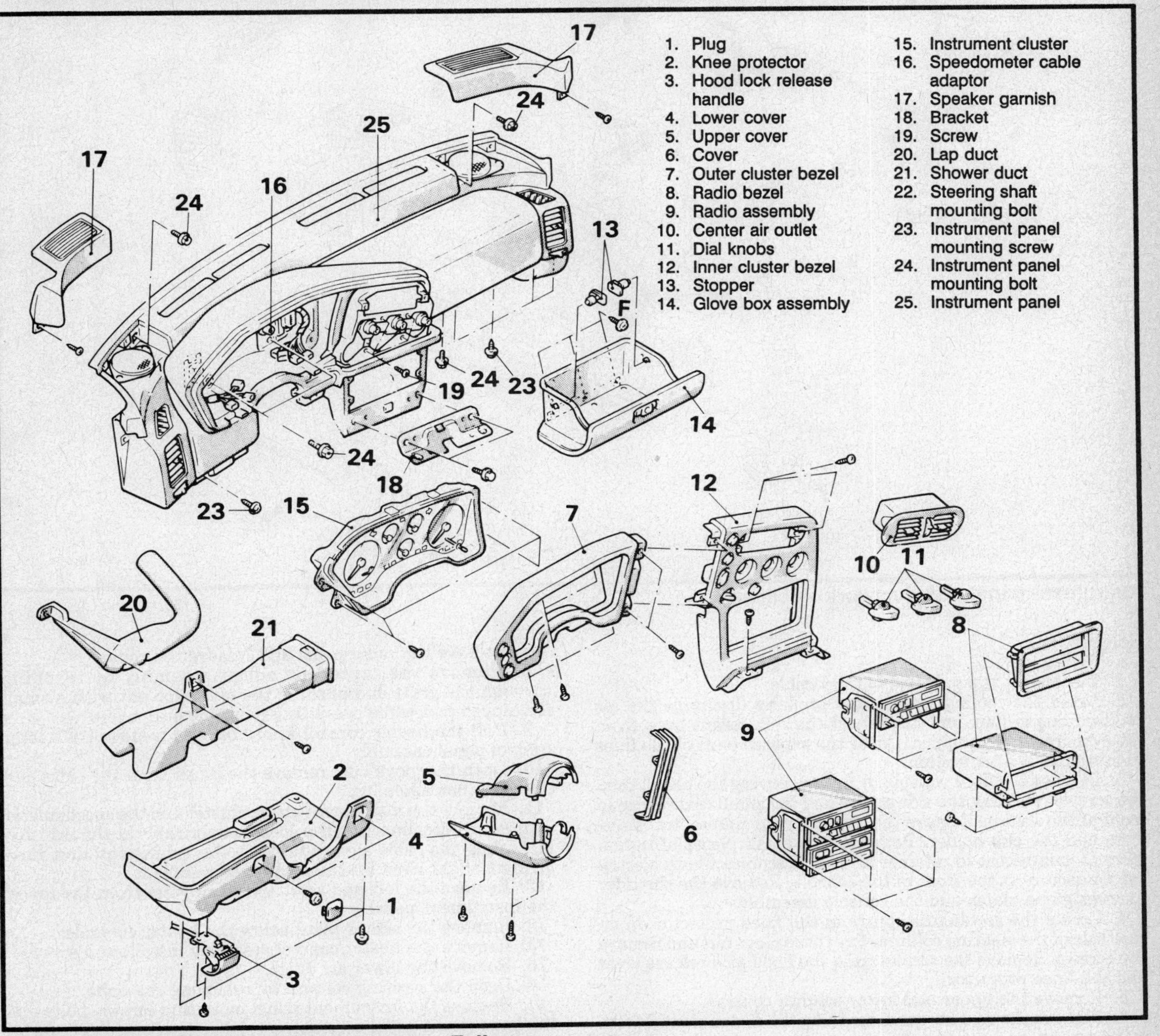
1. Plug
2. Knee protector
3. Hood lock release handle
4. Lower cover
5. Upper cover
6. Cover
7. Outer cluster bezel
8. Radio bezel
9. Radio assembly
10. Center air outlet
11. Dial knobs
12. Inner cluster bezel
13. Stopper
14. Glove box assembly
15. Instrument cluster
16. Speedometer cable adaptor
17. Speaker garnish
18. Bracket
19. Screw
20. Lap duct
21. Shower duct
22. Steering shaft mounting bolt
23. Instrument panel mounting screw
24. Instrument panel mounting bolt
25. Instrument panel
F

Instrument panel and related components – Eclipse

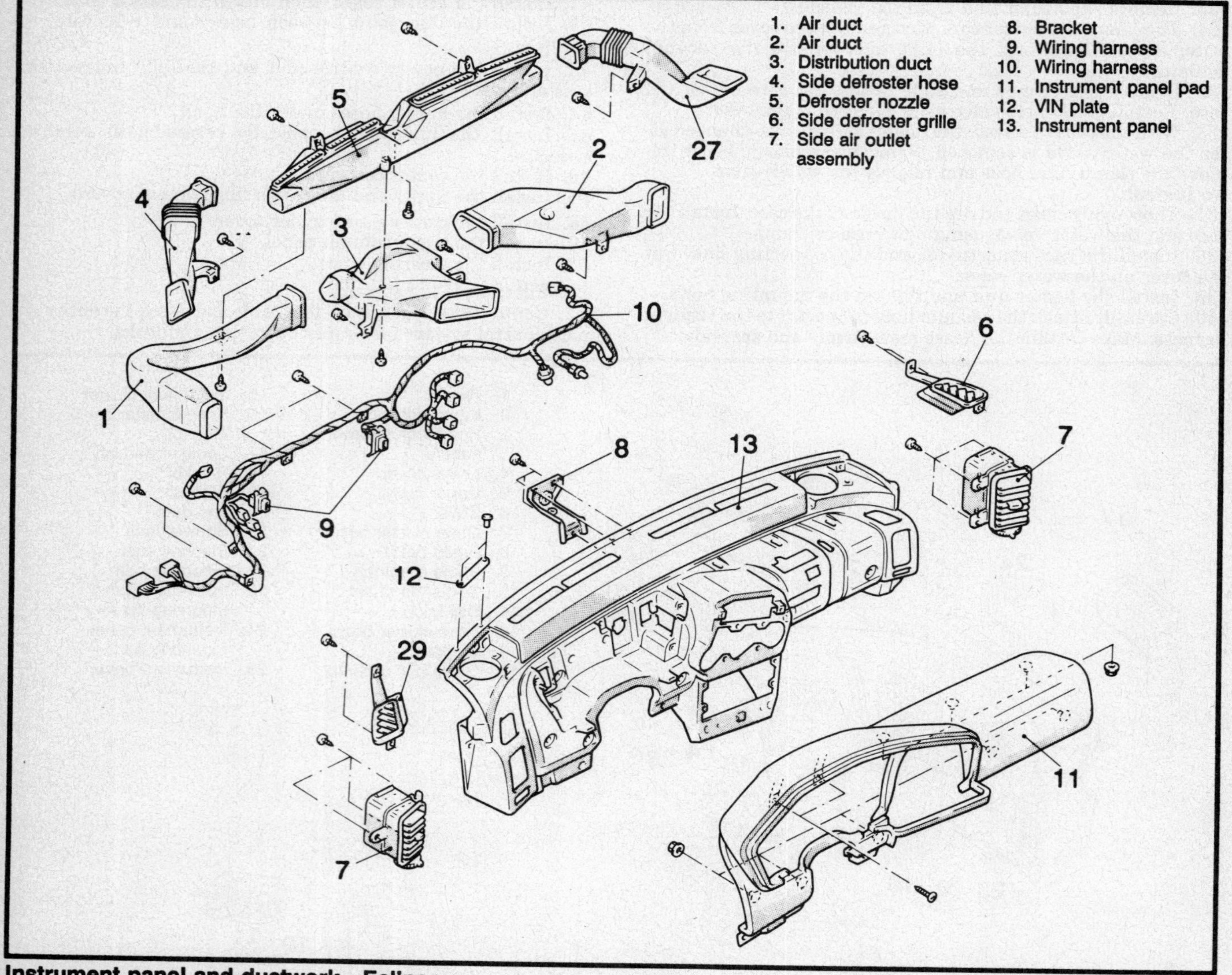
1. Air duct
2. Air duct
3. Distribution duct
4. Side defroster hose
5. Defroster nozzle
6. Side defroster grille
7. Side air outlet assembly
8. Bracket
9. Wiring harness
10. Wiring harness
11. Instrument panel pad
12. VIN plate
13. Instrument panel
27
29

Instrument panel and ductwork – Eclipse

Eclipse

1. Disconnect the negative battery cable.
2. Drain the cooling system and properly discharge the air conditioning system and disconnect the refrigerant lines from the evaporator, if equipped. Cover the exposed ends of the lines to minimize contamination.
3. Remove the floor console by first removing the plugs, then the screws retaining the side covers and the small cover piece in front of the shifter. Remove the shifter knob, manual transmission, and the cup holder. Remove both small pieces of upholstery to gain access to retainer screws. Disconnect both electrical connectors at the front of the console. Remove the shoulder harness guide plates and the console assembly.
4. Locate the rectangular plugs in the knee protector on either side of the steering column. Pry these plugs out and remove the screws. Remove the screws from the hood lock release lever and the knee protector.
5. Remove the upper and lower column covers.
6. Remove the narrow panel covering the instrument cluster cover screws, and remove the cover.
7. Remove the radio panel and remove the radio.
8. Remove the center air outlet assembly by reaching through the grille and pushing the side clips out with a small flat-tipped tool while carefully prying the outlet free.
9. Pull the heater control knobs off and remove the heater control panel assembly.
10. Open the glove box, remove the plugs from the sides and the glove box assembly.
11. Remove the instrument gauge cluster and the speedometer adapter by disconnecting the speedometer cable at the transaxle, pulling the cable sightly towards the vehicle interior, then giving a slight twist on the adapter to release it.
12. Remove the left and right speaker covers from the top of the instrument panel.
13. Remove the center plate below the heater controls.
14. Remove the heater control assembly installation screws.
15. Remove the lower air ducts.
16. Drop the steering column by removing the bolts.
17. Remove the instrument panel mounting screws, bolts and the instrument panel assembly.
18. Remove both stamped steel reinforcement pieces.

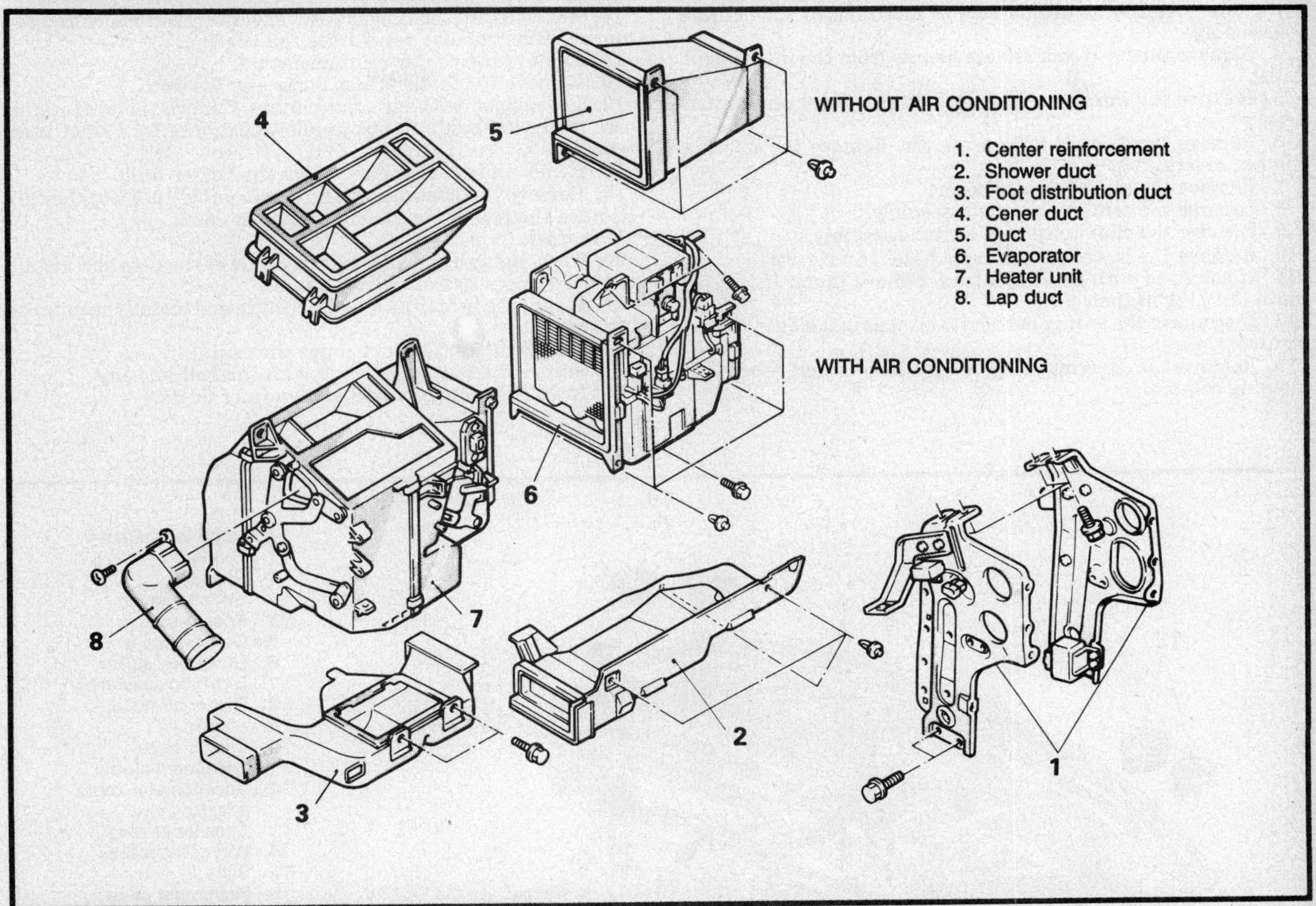
WITHOUT AIR CONDITIONING
1. Center reinforcement
2. Shower duct
3. Foot distribution duct
4. Cener duct
5. Duct
6. Evaporator
7. Heater unit
8. Lap duct
WITH AIR CONDITIONING
1
2
3
4
5
6
7
8

Heater case and related components—Eclipse

19. Remove the lower ductwork from the heater box.
20. Remove the upper center duct.
21. Vehicles without air conditioning will have a square duct in place of the evaporator; remove this duct if present. If equipped with air conditioning, remove the evaporator assembly:
    a. Remove the wiring harness connectors and the electronic control unit.
    b. Remove the drain hose and lift out the evaporator unit.
    c. If servicing the assembly, disassemble the housing and remove the expansion valve and evaporator.
22. With the evaporator removed, remove the heater unit. To prevent bolts from falling inside the blower assembly, set the inside/outside air-selection damper to the position that permits outside air introduction.
23. Remove the cover plate around the heater tubes and remove the core fastener clips. Pull the heater core from the heater box, being careful not to damage the fins or tank ends.

To install:

24. Thoroughly clean and dry the inside of the case. Install the heater core to the heater box. Install the clips and cover.
25. Install the heater box and connect the duct work.
26. Assemble the housing, evaporator and expansion valve, making sure the gaskets are in good condition. Install the evaporator housing.
27. Using new lubricated O-rings, connect the refrigerant lines to the evaporator.
28. Install the electronic transmission ELC box. Connect all wires and control cables.
29. Install the instrument panel assembly and the console by reversing their removal procedures.
30. Evacuate and recharge the air conditioning system. If the evaporator was replaced, add 2 oz. of refrigerant oil during the recharge.
31. Connect the negative battery cable and check the entire climate control system for proper operation. Check the system for leaks.

3000GT

1. Disconnect the negative battery cable.

NOTE: Wait for 1 minute to elapse before working inside the vehicle. The air bag system is set to deploy for a short period of time after the battery is disconnected.

2. Drain the coolant and disconnect the heater hoses from the core tubes.
3. To remove the console, perform the following:
    a. Remove the cup holder and console plug.
    b. Remove the rear console.
    c. Remove the radio bezels and radio.
    d. Remove the switch bezel.
    e. Remove the side covers and front console garnish.
    f. If equipped with a manual transaxle, remove the shifter knob.

g. Remove the mounting screws and remove the console assembly.
4. Remove the hood lock release handle from the instrument panel.
5. Remove the interior and dash lights rheostat and switch bezel to its right.
6. Remove the driver's knee protector. Remove the steering column covers.
7. Remove the glove box and cover.
8. Remove the center air outlet assembly.
9. Remove the climate control switch assembly.
10. Remove the instrument cluster bezel and cluster.
11. If equipped with front speakers, remove them. If not, remove the plug in their place.
12. Disconnect the wiring harnesses on the right side of the instrument panel.
13. Remove the steering shaft support bolts and lower the steering column.
14. Remove the instrument panel mounting hardware and remove the instrument panel from the vehicle.
15. Remove the center reinforcement.
16. Remove the foot warmer ducts and lap duct.
17. If equipped with air conditioning, remove the evaporator case mounting bolt and nut to allow clearance for heater unit removal.
18. Remove the center duct above the heater unit.
19. Remove the heater unit and disassemble on a workbench. Remove the heater core from the heater case.

To install:

20. Thoroughly clean and dry the inside of the case and install the heater core and all related parts.
21. Install the heater unit to the vehicle and install the mounting screws.
22. Install the center duct above the unit.
23. Secure the evaporator case with the bolt and nut.
24. Install the lap duct and foot warmer ducts.

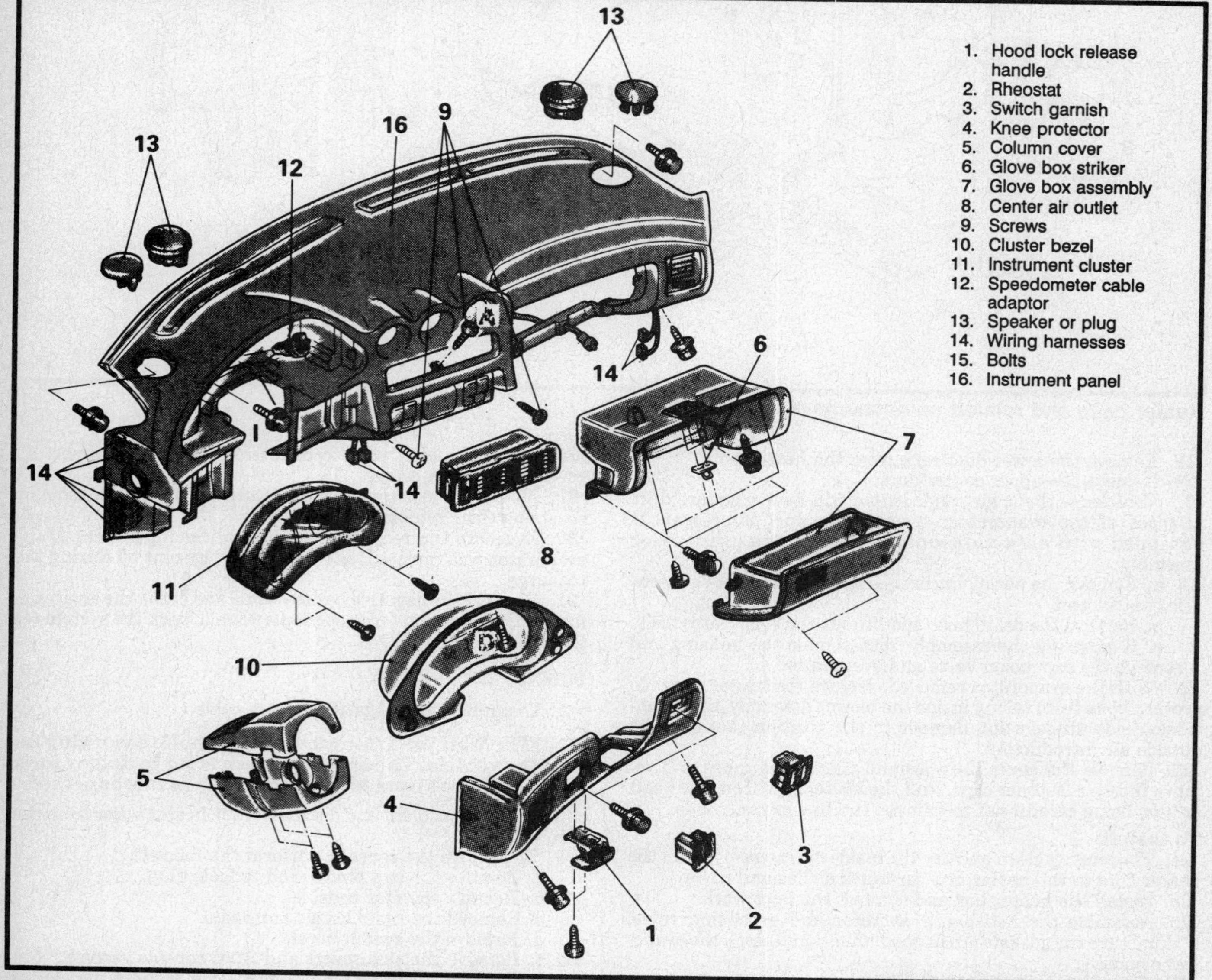
1. Hood lock release handle
2. Rheostat
3. Switch garnish
4. Knee protector
5. Column cover
6. Glove box striker
7. Glove box assembly
8. Center air outlet
9. Screws
10. Cluster bezel
11. Instrument cluster
12. Speedometer cable adaptor
13. Speaker or plug
14. Wiring harnesses
15. Bolts
16. Instrument panel

Instrument panel and related components—3000GT

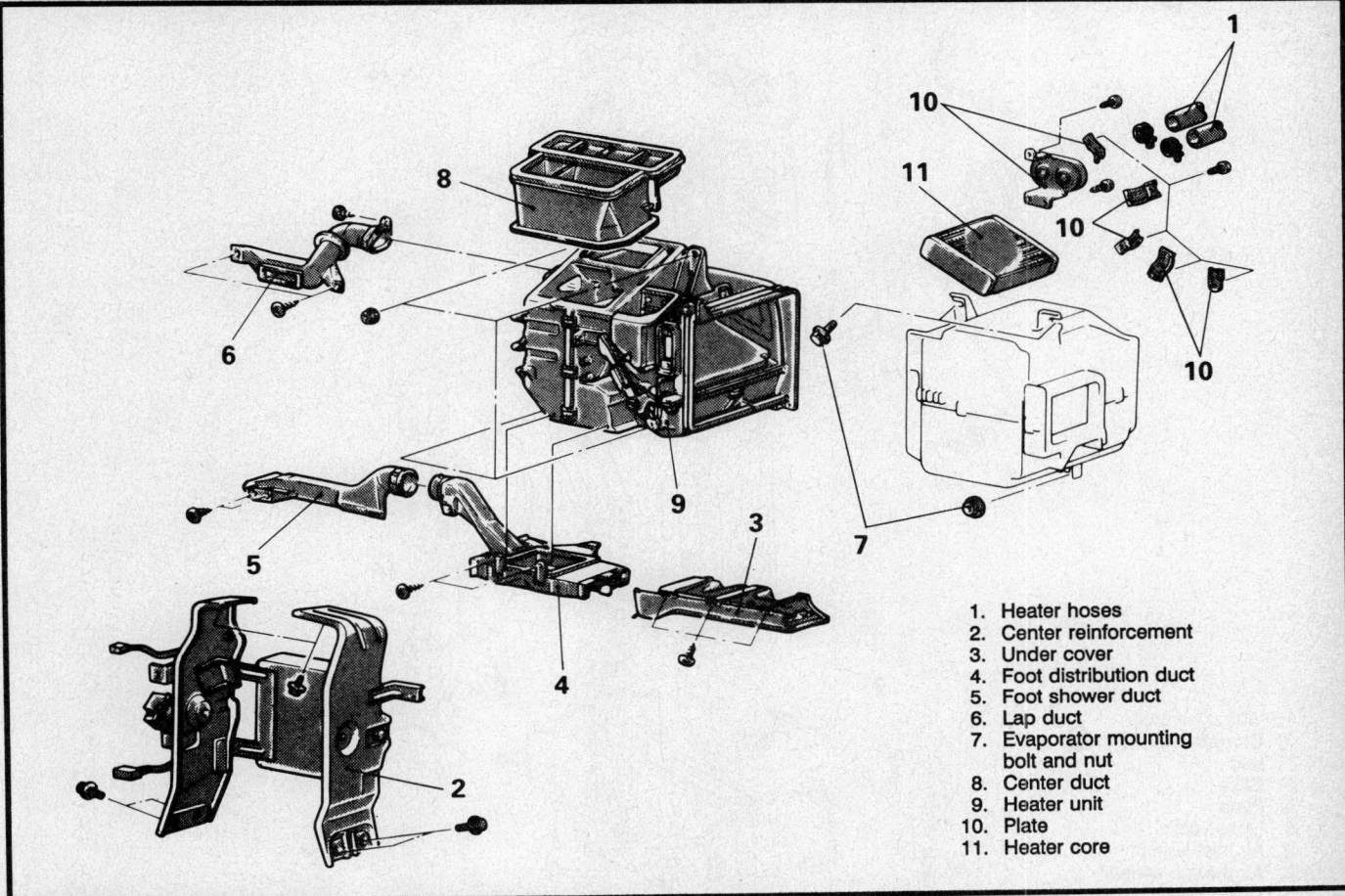

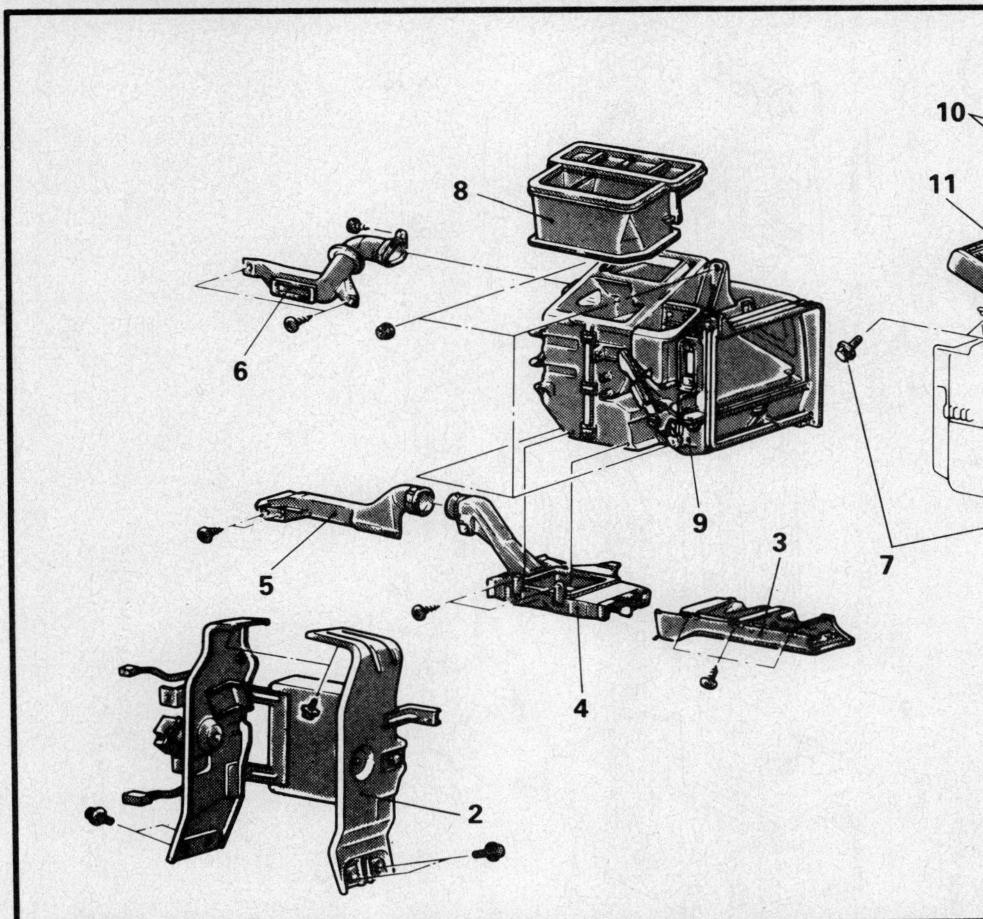
1
10
11
10
8
6
10
9
3
7
5
4
2
1. Heater hoses
2. Center reinforcement
3. Under cover
4. Foot distribution duct
5. Foot shower duct
6. Lap duct
7. Evaporator mounting bolt and nut
8. Center duct
9. Heater unit
10. Plate
11. Heater core

Heater case and related components—3000GT

25. Install the center reinforcement.
26. Install the instrument panel by reversing its removal procedure.
27. Install the hood lock release cable handle.
28. Install the console.
29. Fill the cooling system.
30. Connect the negative battery cable and check the entire climate control system for proper operation and leaks.

Evaporator

REMOVAL AND INSTALLATION

Precis

1. Disconnect the negative battery cable.
2. Properly discharge the air conditioning system.
3. Disconnect the low pressure suction line from the cooling unit outlet fitting.
4. Disconnect the liquid line pipe from the cooling unit inlet fitting. Cover the exposed ends of the lines to minimize contamination.
5. Remove the inlet and outlet pipe grommets.
6. Remove the console assembly. Remove the glove box assembly.
7. Remove the lower instrument panel crash pad and the lower crash pad center panel.
8. Remove the blower motor assembly mounting bolts and remove the blower assembly.
9. Remove the evaporator assembly mounting bolts. Separate and remove the evaporator assembly from the heater assembly. Disassemble the unit on a workbench.

To install:

10. Thoroughly clean and dry the inside of the case and assemble. Position the evaporator assembly in place to the heater assembly and install the mounting bolts.
11. Position the blower assembly in place and install the blower assembly mounting bolts.
12. Install the lower instrument panel crash pad and the lower crash pad center panel.
13. Install the console assembly. Install the glove box assembly.
14. Coat the O-rings with compressor oil, install the grommet over the evaporator lines and connect the lines to the evaporator.
15. Evacuate and recharge the air conditioning system. If the evaporator was replaced, add 1.5 oz. of refrigerant oil during the recharge.
16. Connect the negative battery cable and check the entire climate control system for proper operation and leaks.

Mirage, Eclipse and 3000GT

1. Disconnect the negative battery cable.

NOTE: If equipped with an air bag, wait for 1 minute to elapse before working inside the vehicle. The air bag system is set to deploy for a short period of time after the battery is disconnected.

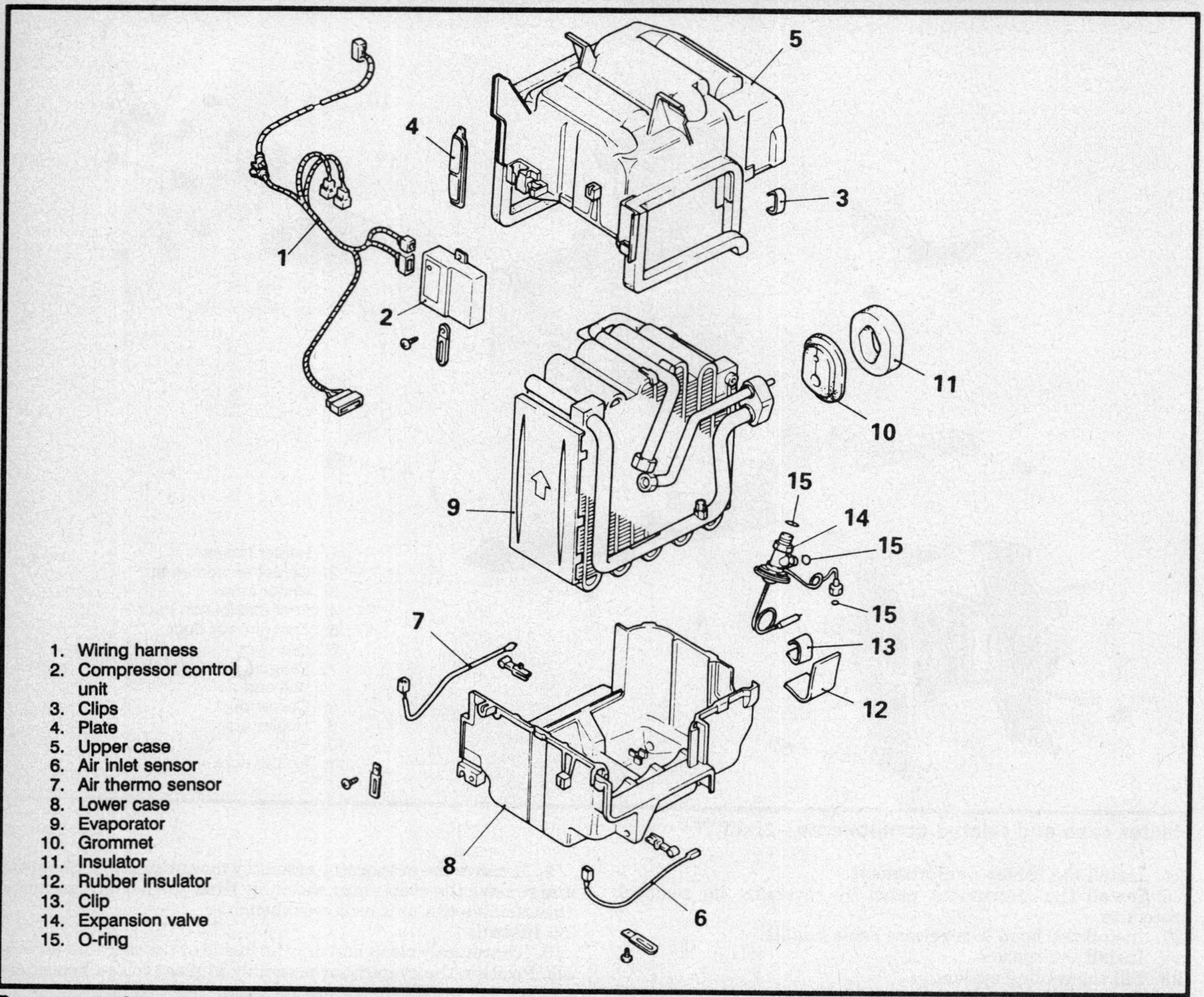
1
2
3
4
5
6
7
8
9
10
11
12
13
14
15
15
15
15
1. Wiring harness
2. Compressor control unit
3. Clips
4. Plate
5. Upper case
6. Air inlet sensor
7. Air thermo sensor
8. Lower case
9. Evaporator
10. Grommet
11. Insulator
12. Rubber insulator
13. Clip
14. Expansion valve
15. O-ring

Representative evaporator, expansion valve, case and related components. Assemblies may vary between vehicles

2. Properly discharge the air conditioning system.
3. Disconnect the refrigerant lines from the evaporator. Cover the exposed ends of the lines to minimize contamination.
4. Remove the condensation drain hose.
5. Remove the glove box assembly and lap heater duct work.
6. Remove the cowl side trim and speaker cover.
7. Remove the glove box bezel and frame.
8. Disconnect the electrical connector at the top of the evaporator housing.
9. Remove the mounting bolts and nuts and the housing.
10. Disassemble the housing and remove the expansion valve and evaporator.

To install:

11. Thoroughly clean and dry the inside of the case. Assemble the housing, evaporator and expansion valve, making sure the gaskets are in good condition.
12. Install the housing to the vehicle and connect the connector.
13. Install the glove box frame and bezel.
14. Install the speaker cover and side cowl trim.
15. Install the lap heater ductwork and glove box assembly.
16. Install the condensation drain hose.
17. Using new lubricated O-rings, connect the refrigerant lines to the evaporator.
18. Evacuate and recharge the air conditioning system. If the evaporator was replaced, add 2 oz. of refrigerant oil during the recharge.
19. Connect the negative battery cable and check the entire climate control system for proper operation. Check the system for leaks.

Starion

1. Disconnect the negative battery cable.
2. Safely discharge the air conditioning system.
3. Disconnect the refrigerant lines. Cover the exposed ends of

the lines to minimize contamination.
4. Remove the small nut from the firewall side.
5. Remove the grommet.
6. Remove the glove box.
7. Remove the under cover below the glove box.
8. Remove the lap heater duct and the side console duct.
9. Remove the lower frame of the glove box.
10. Remove the defroster duct.
11. Remove the duct joints between the evaporator and the adjoining components.
12. Disconnect the condensate drain hose.
13. Disconnect the electrical connectors and disconnect the vacuum hose.
14. Remove the retaining bolts and remove the evaporator case. Disassemble the housing and remove the expansion valve and evaporator.

To install:

15. Thoroughly clean and dry the inside of the case. Assemble the housing, evaporator and expansion valve, making sure the gaskets are in good condition. Install to the vehicle and install the retaining bolts.
16. Connect the electrical wiring and the vacuum hose.
17. Install the condensation drain hose.
18. Install the defroster duct and the joint ducts.
19. Install the lower glove box frame.
20. Replace the side console duct and the lap heater duct.
21. Install the under cover and the glove box.
22. Install the grommet and the vacuum hose at the firewall.
23. Install the nut.
24. Using new lubricated O-rings, connect the refrigerant lines to the evaporator.
25. Evacuate and recharge the air conditioning system. If the evaporator was replaced, add 2 oz. of refrigerant oil during the recharge.
26. Connect the negative battery cable and check the entire climate control system for proper operation and leaks.

Galant

1. Disconnect the negative battery cable.
2. Properly discharge the air conditioning system. Remove the condensation drain hose.
3. Disconnect the refrigerant lines from the evaporator. Cover the exposed ends of the lines to minimize contamination.
4. Remove the instrument panel side cover.
5. Remove the instrument panel under cover.
6. Remove the shower duct.
7. Remove the glove box stopper, the glove box and the glove box frame.
8. Disconnect the wiring connectors behind the glove box frame.
9. Remove the ashtray.
10. Remove the knobs from the heater control levers but don't remove the round dial controls.
11. Remove the heater control faceplate.
12. Disconnect the air conditioning switch connector at the control panel.
13. At the bottom of the evaporator case, disconnect the wiring harness.
14. Remove the plate from the evaporator, then remove the screws retaining the evaporator. Support the unit in position.
15. After the plate is removed, carefully work the notched part of the evaporator clear of the instrument panel.
16. Disassemble the housing and remove the expansion valve and evaporator.

To install:

17. Thoroughly clean and dry the inside of the case. Assemble the housing, evaporator and expansion valve, making sure the gaskets are in good condition. Install the case through the instrument panel and install the retaining nuts and bolts. Install the plate.
18. Connect the wiring harness to the bottom of the evaporator case.
19. Connect the wiring at the control panel and install the faceplate.
20. Install the knobs on the control levers. Install the ashtray.
21. Install the glove box frame and connect the wiring harnesses.
22. Install the glove box and stopper.
23. Install the shower duct and the under cover.
24. Install the side cover on the instrument panel.
25. Using new lubricated O-rings, connect the refrigerant lines to the evaporator.
26. Install the condensation drain tube.
27. Evacuate and recharge the air conditioning system. If the evaporator was replaced, add 2 oz. of refrigerant oil during the recharge.
28. Connect the negative battery cable and check the entire climate control system for proper operation and leaks.

Sigma

1. Disconnect the negative battery cable.

NOTE: If equipped with an air bag, wait for 1 minute to elapse before working inside the vehicle. The air bag system is set to deploy for a short period of time after the battery is disconnected.

2. Properly discharge the air conditioning system.
3. Disconnect the refrigerant lines from the evaporator. Cover the exposed ends of the lines to minimize contamination. Remove the small nut at the firewall.
4. Remove the glove box and under frame.
5. Remove the defroster duct from the right side of the heater case.
6. Disconnect the electrical connectors for the fan and air conditioner.
7. Remove the duct joints between the evaporator and the component on either side (fan and heater units).
8. Remove the condensation drain hose from the evaporator case.
9. Remove the retaining bolts and carefully lift out the evaporator case.
10. Disassemble the housing and remove the expansion valve and evaporator.

To install:

11. Thoroughly clean and dry the inside of the case. Assemble the housing, evaporator and expansion valve, making sure the gaskets are in good condition. Reinstall the evaporator unit and secure with the retaining bolts.
12. Connect the electrical connectors.
13. Connect the drain hose.
14. Install the duct joints, making sure each is properly seated. Once both are in place, adjust the clearance between the evaporator and the duct seal to about 2.5mm on each side.
15. Install the defroster duct.
16. Install the glove box and under frame.
17. Using new lubricated O-rings, connect the refrigerant lines to the evaporator.
18. Evacuate and recharge the air conditioning system. If the evaporator was replaced, add 2 oz. of refrigerant oil during the recharge.
19. Connect the negative battery cable and check the entire climate control system for proper operation and leaks.

Refrigerant Lines

REMOVAL AND INSTALLATION

Except Precis with Spring Lock Coupling

1. Disconnect the negative battery cable.

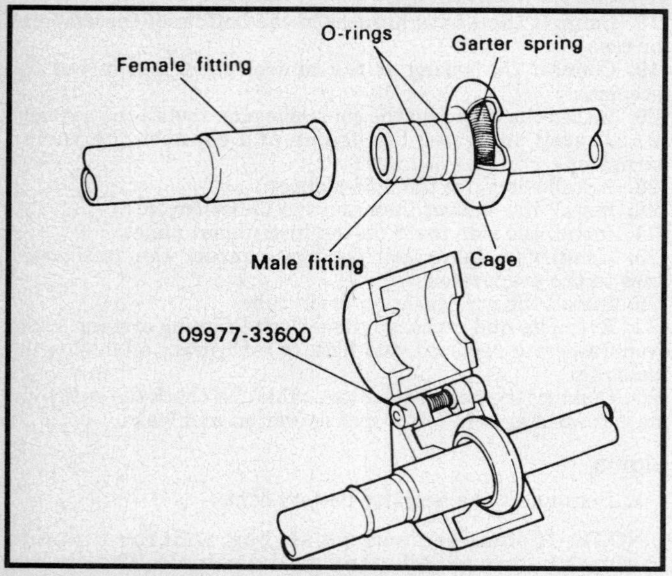
O-rings
Garter spring
Female fitting
Male fitting
Cage
09977-33600

Spring lock coupling service—Precis

2. Properly discharge the air conditioning system.
3. Remove the nuts or bolts that attach the refrigerant lines sealing plates to the adjoining components. If the line is not equipped with a sealing plate, separate the flare connection. Always use a backup wrench when separating flare connections.
4. Remove the line and discard the O-rings.

To install:

5. Coat the new O-rings refrigerant oil and install. Connect the refrigerant lines to the adjoining components and tighten the nuts, bolts or flare connections.
6. Evacuate and recharge the air conditioning system.
7. Connect the negative battery cable and check the entire climate control system for proper operation. Check the system for leaks.

Precis with Spring Lock Coupling

1. Install the special tool 09977-33600 or equivalent, on the coupling.
2. Push the special tool onto the cage opening to release the female fitting from the garter spring.
3. Pull the fitting apart and remove the tool from the coupling.
4. Cover the exposed ends of the lines to minimize contamination.

To install:

5. Check for a missing or damaged garter spring. Replace as necessary.
6. Thoroughly clean and dry the fittings, install a new O-ring and lubricate.
7. Assemble the fitting by pushing with a slight twisting motion.
8. To visually verify positive engagement, make sure the garter spring is over the flared end of the female fitting.

Manual Control Head

REMOVAL AND INSTALLATION

Precis

1. Disconnect the negative battery cable.
2. Remove the glove box. Remove the ashtray and remove the revealed screw.
3. Pull out the control assembly and disconnect the connectors.
4. Remove the control head mounting screws and pull the unit out of the instrument panel. Disconnect the electrical and vacuum connectors and the temperature control cable and remove the control head.
5. The installation is the reverse of the removal procedure.
6. Connect the negative battery cable and check the entire climate control system for proper operation and leaks.

Mirage

1. Disconnect the negative battery cable.
2. Remove the glove box and ashtray assembly.
3. Remove the heater control/radio bezel.
4. Remove the radio assembly.
5. Disconnect the air, temperature and mode selection control cables from the heater housing.
6. Remove the 3 control head mounting screws.
7. Separate the control head from the left side first, then press out the lower and upper mounting brackets from behind the instrument panel.
8. Pull the control head out and disconnect the 3 connectors. Remove the control head assembly.

To install:

9. Feed the control cable through the instrument panel, connect the connectors, install the control head assembly and secure with the screws.
10. Install the radio and bezel.
11. Move the mode selection lever to the **PANEL** position. Move the mode selection damper lever fully forward and connect the cable to the lever. Install the clip.
12. Move the temperature control lever to its coolest position. Move the blend air damper lever fully downward and connect the cable to the lever. Install the clip.
13. Move the air selection control lever to the **RECIRC** position. Move the air selection damper fully inward and connect the cable to the lever. Install the clip.
14. Connect the negative battery cable and check the entire climate control system for proper operation.
15. If everything is satisfactory, install the ashtray and glove box.

Starion

1. Disconnect the negative battery cable.
2. Remove the floor console.
3. Remove the steering wheel.
4. Remove the screws holding the hood release handle to the instrument panel.
5. Unbolt the fuse box from the instrument panel.
6. Remove the knee protector on the left side. Some of the bolts are hidden behind covers.
7. Remove the screws from the bottom of the steering column cover. Remove both halves of the cover.
8. Remove the attaching screws for the combination switch on the steering column.
9. Disconnect the wiring harnesses and remove the switch.
10. Remove the instrument hood screws. Pull both edges of the bottom of the hood forward; hold it in this position and lift up and out.
11. Disconnect the harness connectors on both sides of the instrument hood.
12. Remove the screws on the bottom and the nuts on the top of the instrument cluster. Pull the bottom edge up and forward to remove. Disconnect the wiring and cables as it comes free.
13. Remove the console side cover mounting screws. Remove the cover downward while pushing slightly forward.
14. Remove the front and rear consoles.
15. Remove the passenger side under cover.
16. Remove the glove box and ashtray.
17. Carefully remove the heater control knobs and bezel.

18. Remove the clock. It may be removed with a gentle prying motion. Disconnect the harness when it is free.
19. Remove the grilles for the side defrosters by inserting a flat tool from the window side and prying forward and upward.
20. Use a non-marring tool to pry the side covers off the instrument panel.
21. Remove each mounting screw and bolt holding the instrument panel in place. As it comes loose, allow it to move into the interior. Disconnect the remaining wire harnesses.
22. The instrument panel may now be removed from the vehicle. Several components may still be attached.
23. Disconnect the 3 control cables from the heater and blower cases.
24. Take careful note of the routing of the control cables. Remove the mounting screws and remove the control head from the instrument panel.

To install:

25. Feed the control cables through the instrument panel and route them in exactly the same position as before removal. Install the control head.
26. Install the instrument panel assembly. The upper part of the heater unit has 2 guide bolts to which the instrument panel attaches. Reverse the removal procedure to complete the instrument panel installation.
27. Install the upper and lower steering column covers.
28. Install the fuse block to the instrument panel. Route the wire harnesses are properly.
29. Install the knee protector on the left side.
30. Attach the hood release handle to the instrument panel.
31. Install the steering wheel.
32. Reinstall the center console.
33. Connect the negative battery cable and check the entire climate control system for proper operation.

Galant

1. Disconnect the negative battery cable.
2. Release or remove the stopper for the glove box and remove the glove box. Remove the ashtray.
3. Disconnect the air selection control cable and the temperature control cable.
4. Remove the knobs from the levers (not the round dials) by pulling them off with moderate force.
5. Remove the heater control faceplate. The retaining screws are concealed; make sure all are removed before removing the faceplate.
6. Remove the foot heater ducts and nozzle from the left side.
7. Disconnect the mode selection control cable.
8. Remove the radio trim panel and the radio.
9. Disconnect the left/right air volume control cable at the left side of the distribution duct lever.
10. Remove the retaining screws and remove the heater control assembly. Note that once removed, the lever assembly may be separated from the dial controls for inspection or replacement.

To install:

11. When reinstalling, make certain the lever assembly is connected to the dial panel before inserting the unit into the dash. Route the control cables to the heater case and install the retaining screws.
12. Move the selector lever for the left/right air volume to the **L** position. Move the foot distribution duct lever in a clockwise direction (right side low/left side high) and connect the cable. Secure the outer cable in the spring clip.
13. Install the radio and the radio faceplate.
14. Move the mode selection lever to the **DEFROST** position. Move the mode selection damper lever fully inward (counterclockwise) and connect the control cable to the damper lever. Secure the outer cable in the spring clip.
15. Install the foot nozzle and ductwork.
16. Install the heater control trim plate.
17. Install the knobs on the control levers and install the ashtray.
18. Move the temperature control lever to the extreme left. Move the blend air damper lever inward (downward) and connect the control cable to the lever. Secure the outer cable in the spring clip.
19. Move the air selection control lever to the **RECIRCULATE** position. Press the air selection damper lever inward (towards the interior of the car or clockwise) and connect the control cable. Secure the outer cable in the spring clip.
20. Install the glove box and ashtray.
21. Connect the negative battery cable and check the entire climate control system for proper operation.

Eclipse

1. Disconnect the negative battery cable.
2. Remove the glove box assembly.
3. Remove the dial control knobs from the control head.
4. Remove the center air outlet by disengaging the tabs with a flat blade tool and carefully prying out.
5. Remove the instrument cluster bezel and radio bezel.
6. Remove the knee protector and lower the hood lock release handle.
7. Remove the left side lower duct work.
8. Disconnect the air, temperature and mode selection control cables from the heater housing.
9. Remove the mounting screws and the control head from the instrument panel.

To install:

10. Feed the control cable through the instrument panel, connect the connectors, install the control head assembly and secure with the screws.
11. Move the mode selection lever to the **DEFROST** position. Move the mode selection damper lever fully inward and connect the cable to the lever. Install the clip.
12. Move the temperature control lever to its hottest position. Move the blend air damper lever fully downward and connect the cable to the lever. Install the clip.
13. Move the air selection control lever to the **RECIRC** position. Move the air selection damper fully inward and connect the cable to the lever. Install the clip.
14. Connect the negative battery cable and check the entire climate control system for proper operation.
15. If everything is satisfactory, install the remaining interior pieces.

3000GT

1. Disconnect the negative battery cable.

NOTE: If equipped with an air bag, wait for 1 minute to elapse before working inside the vehicle. The air bag system is set to deploy for a short period of time after the battery is disconnected.

2. Remove the glove box and outer case assembly.
3. Disconnect the air selection control wire, revealed behind the glove box opening.
4. Remove the hood lock release handle screws.
5. Remove the interior lights rheostat and rear wiper and washer switch.
6. Remove the passenger's knee protector and air duct.
7. Disconnect the 2 remaining control cables.
8. Remove the center air outlet assembly.
9. Remove the mounting screws and remove the control head. Note the routing of the control cables as they are removed.

To install:

10. Feed the control cables through the instrument panel and route them in exactly the same position as before removal. Install the control head.
11. Install the center air outlet assembly.
12. Connect the control cables.

13. Install air duct and passenger's knee protector.
14. Install the interior lights rheostat and rear wiper and washer switch.
15. Install the hood lock release handle.
16. Install the glove box assembly.
17. Connect the negative battery cable and check the entire climate control system for proper operation.

Manual Control Cables

ADJUSTMENT

All control cables are self-adjusting. If any cable is not functioning properly, try to move the affected lever to either extreme position, observe what may be binding and reposition the connecting link if possible. Also, check for proper routing and lubricate all moving parts. These cables cannot be disassembled. Replace if faulty.

Electronic Control Head

REMOVAL AND INSTALLATION

Starion, Sigma and 3000GT

1. Disconnect the negative battery cable.

NOTE: If equipped with an air bag, wait for 1 minute to elapse before working inside the vehicle. The air bag system is set to deploy for a short period of time after the battery is disconnected.

2. On Starion, remove the glove box. On 3000GT, remove the center air outlet.
3. Remove the control panel bezel if necessary.
4. Remove the mounting screws and pull the unit out of the instrument panel.
5. Disconnect all harnesses and remove the control head from the vehicle.
6. The installation is the reverse of the removal procedure.
7. Connect the negative battery cable and check the entire climate control system for proper operation.

SENSORS AND SWITCHES

Fast Idle Control Device

OPERATION

On 1989–90 Precis, the fast idle control device is designed to raise the idle speed during air conditioning operation, to ensure efficient cooling when the vehicle is stationary and prevent poor idle quality while the compressor is running. The device is mounted to the carburetor.

While the air conditioning system is on, current flows from the air conditioning relay, through the pressure switch and to an electronic vacuum-operated solenoid. When the solenoid is energized, vacuum is applied the fast idle control device actuator diaphragm, forcing the plunger against the accelerator adjustment screw. The raised rpm specification is 850–900 rpm.

TESTING

1. Start the engine and allow it to warm up sufficiently.
2. Adjust the curb idle speed to specification with the air conditioning off.
3. Operate the air conditioning. The idle speed should raise to 850–900 rpm each time the compressor cycles on.
4. If the there is no rpm increase, check to see if there is vacuum present at the fast idle control device.

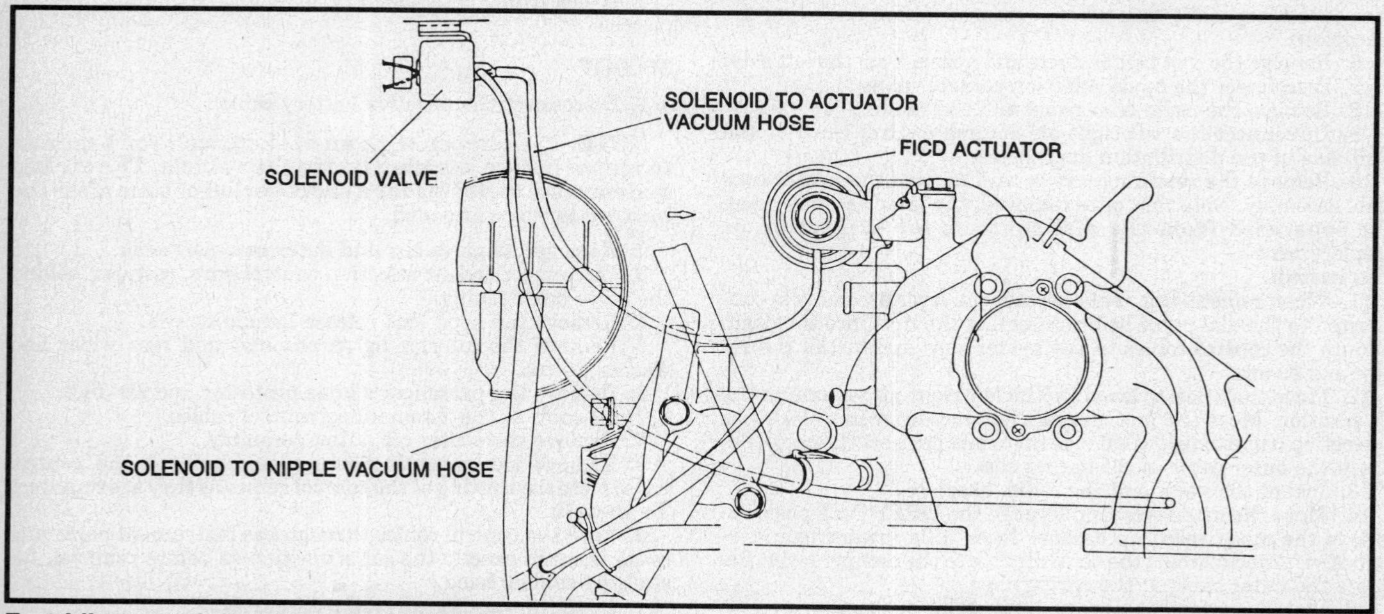
SOLENOID TO ACTUATOR
VACUUM HOSE
FICD ACTUATOR
SOLENOID VALVE
SOLENOID TO NIPPLE VACUUM HOSE

Fast idle control device system—1989 Precis

5. If vacuum is present and the device is inoperative, replace it. If the actuator is working properly, adjust the idle to specification.
6. Set the engine speed by adjusting the adjustment screw until 850–900 rpm is attained.
7. If vacuum was not present at the actuator, check the air conditioning solenoid and connecting vacuum tubing.
8. Depress and release the accelerator pedal several times and make sure the engine speed returns to the specified rpm.

REMOVAL AND INSTALLATION

1. Disconnect the negative battery cable.
2. Remove the air cleaner assembly.
3. Disconnect the vacuum hose from the fast idle control device.
4. Remove the nut attaching the fast idle control device to the mounting bracket and remove the unit.

To install:

5. Position the fast idle control device to the mounting bracket and install the retaining nut.
6. Connect the vacuum hose to the fast idle control device.
7. Connect the negative battery cable.
8. Start the engine and test operation.
9. Install the air cleaner assembly.

Dual Pressure Switch

OPERATION

All vehicles use a dual pressure switch, which is a combination of a low pressure cut off switch and high pressure cut off switch. These functions will stop operation of the compressor in the event of either high of low refrigerant charge, preventing damage to the system. The switch is located near the sight glass on the refrigerant line on Starion and Eclipse, on the accumulator on 1990–91 Precis and on the receiver/drier on all other vehicles.

The dual pressure switch is designed to cut off voltage to the compressor coil when the pressure either drops below 30 psi or rises above 384 psi.

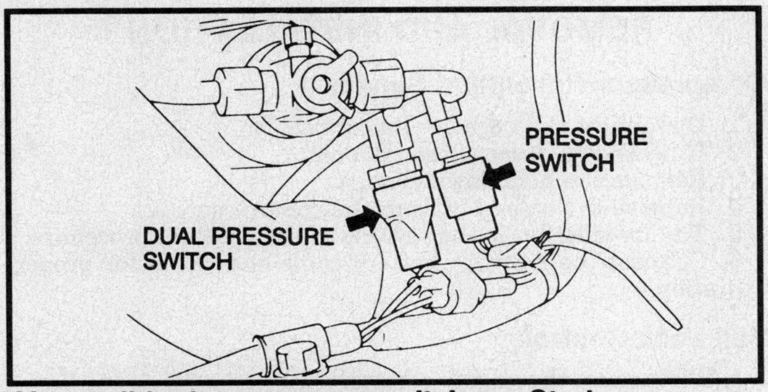
PRESSURE SWITCH
DUAL PRESSURE SWITCH

Air conditioning pressure switches – Starion

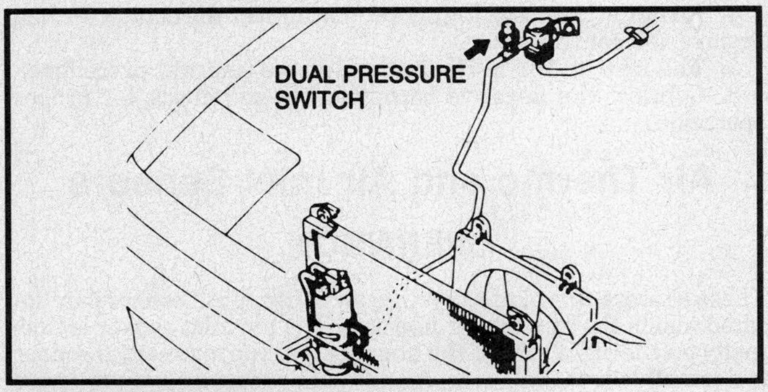
DUAL PRESSURE SWITCH

Dual pressure switch – Eclipse

TESTING

1. Check for continuity through the switch. Under all normal conditions, the switch should be continuous.
2. If the switch is open, check for insufficient refrigerant charge or excessive pressures.
3. If neither of the above conditions exist and the switch is open, replace the switch.

REMOVAL AND INSTALLATION

1. Disconnect the negative battery cable.
2. Properly discharge the air conditioning system.
3. Remove the switch from the refrigerant line or receiver/drier.
4. The installation is the reverse of the removal installation.
5. Evacuate and recharge the air conditioning system.
6. Connect the negative battery cable and check the entire climate control system for proper operation. Check the system for leaks.

Pressure Switch

OPERATION

The pressure switch, used on all vehicles except Precis, Mirage with 1.5L engine and 3000GT, is used to control the 2-speed condenser cooling fan. The switch is normally located on the high pressure line near the left front of the engine compartment.

TESTING

1. Install a manifold gauge set to the air conditioning system.
2. Check the continuity of the switch at different pressures. The switch should be open a pressures below 213 psi and closed at 256 psi or higher.
3. For the purpose of testing, the pressures can be lowered by using an auxiliary fan to cool the condenser and raised by placing a cover over the condenser to prevent air flow.
4. If faulty, replace the switch if faulty.

REMOVAL AND INSTALLATION

1. Disconnect the negative battery cable.
2. Properly discharge the air conditioning system.
3. Remove the switch from the refrigerant line.
4. The installation is the reverse of the removal procedure.
5. Evacuate and recharge the air conditioning system.
6. Connect the negative battery cable and check the entire climate control system for proper operation. Check the system for leaks.

Refrigerant Temperature Sensor

OPERATION

Located on the rear of the compressor on Mirage and Galant, the refrigerant temperature sensor detects the temperature of the refrigerant delivered from the compressor during operation. The switch is designed to cut off the compressor when the temperature of the refrigerant exceeds 347°F (175°C), preventing overheating.

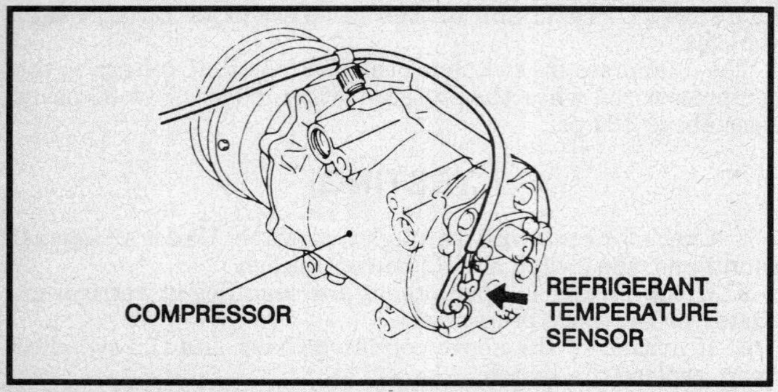
COMPRESSOR
REFRIGERANT
TEMPERATURE
SENSOR

Refrigerant temperature sensor—Mirage and Galant

TESTING

1. Measure the resistance between the yellow-with-green-tracer wire and the black-with-yellow-tracer wire.
2. At 75–80°F, the resistance specification is about 80 kilo ohms.
3. If the reading deviates greatly from the specification, replace the sensor.

REMOVAL AND INSTALLATION

1. Disconnect the negative battery cable.
2. Properly discharge the air conditioning system.
3. Disconnect the connector.
4. Remove the mounting screws and the sensor from the compressor.
5. The installation is the reverse of the removal installation. Use a new lubricated O-ring when installing.
6. Evacuate and recharge the air conditioning system.
7. Connect the negative battery cable and check the entire climate control system for proper operation. Check the system for leaks.

Engine Coolant Temperature Switch

OPERATION

The engine coolant temperature switch, located on or near the thermostat housing, is connected in series with the compressor clutch relay on all vehicles except Precis and Mirage with 1.5L engine, Eclipse with 1.8L engine. The switch is designed to cut off the compressor when the engine coolant temperature rises above 239°F (115°C), preventing engine overheating when the supply of cooling air is not sufficient for both the radiator and condenser.

TESTING

1. If the switch is suspect, unplug and jump across the terminals in the connectors.
2. To test the switch, remove the switch from the engine. The switch should be closed at room temperature.
3. Place the switch in an oil bath and heat to at least 222°F (108°C).
4. The switch should open when it reaches the above temperature.

REMOVAL AND INSTALLATION

1. Disconnect the negative battery cable. Drain out some of the coolant.
2. Unplug the connector.
3. Unscrew the switch from the thermostat housing.
4. The installation is the reverse of the removal installation. Use sealant on the threads when installing.
5. Refill the cooling system.
6. Connect the negative battery cable and check the entire climate control system for proper operation.

Compressor Revolution Sensor and Belt Lock Controller

OPERATION

On 3000GT, an additional compressor cut off switch has been incorporated into the automatic climate control system. The belt lock controller, located behind the glove box, is equipped with circuitry to detect belt slippage according to signals received from the compressor revolution sensor, mounted on the compressor. If it is determined that for 3 seconds the compressor is turning at 70 percent of its expected speed according to engine speed, the controller will cut off current to the compressor coil. This system is designed to prevent alternator slippage if the belt condition cannot handle the additional strain of the compressor.

If the belt is audibly slipping or visually loose and the air conditioning will not work, try adjusting the belt tension to rule out that portion of this system's operation.

TESTING

1. Disconnect the negative battery cable.
2. Disconnect the compressor revolution sensor.
3. Measure the resistance between the yellow-with-green-tracer wire and yellow-with-red wire.
4. The resistance specification is 370–440 ohms at 68°F (20°C).
5. Replace the sensor if not within specification.

REMOVAL AND INSTALLATION

Compressor Revolution Sensor

1. Disconnect the negative battery cable.
2. If necessary, remove the alternator.
3. Remove the hold-down clamps.
4. Remove the assembly from the compressor.
5. The installation is the reverse of the removal procedure.
6. Connect the negative battery cable and check for proper operation.

Belt Lock Controller

1. Disconnect the negative battery cable.
2. Open the glove box and remove its outer case.
3. Remove the under cover.
4. Remove the mounting screw, disconnect the connector and remove the controller.
5. The installation is the reverse of the removal procedure.
6. Connect the negative battery cable and check for proper operation.

Air Thermo and Air Inlet Sensors

OPERATION

These sensors function as cycling switches. Both sensors are located inside the evaporator housing. The air inlet sensor is normally on the right side of the housing and the air thermo sensor is normally on the left side. All vehicles except Precis use these sensors.

The air thermo sensor detects the temperature of the air in the passenger compartment and the air inlet sensor detects the temperature of the air coming into the cooling unit. The information is input to the auto compressor control unit and the information is processed, causing the compressor clutch to cycle.

TESTING

1. Disconnect the sensor connector near the evaporator case.
2. Measure the resistance across the wires of the suspect sensor.
3. The resistance specifications for the air thermo sensor at different temperatures are:
   32°F (0°C) – 11.4 kilo ohms
   50°F (10°C) – 7.32 kilo ohms
   68°F (20°C) – 4.86 kilo ohms
   86°F (30°C) – 3.31 kilo ohms
   104°F (40°C) – 2.32 kilo ohms
4. The resistance specifications for the air inlet sensor at different temperatures are:
   32°F (0°C) – 3.31 kilo ohms
   50°F (10°C) – 2.00 kilo ohms
   68°F (20°C) – 1.25 kilo ohms
   86°F (30°C) – 0.81 kilo ohms
   104°F (40°C) – 0.53 kilo ohms
5. Replace the sensor if not within specifications.

REMOVAL AND INSTALLATION

1. Disconnect the negative battery cable.
2. Properly discharge the air conditioning system.
3. Remove the evaporator housing and the covers.
4. Unclip the sensor wires from the housing and remove the sensor(s).
5. The installation is the reverse of the removal installation.
6. Evacuate and recharge the air conditioning system.
7. Connect the negative battery cable and check the entire climate control system for proper operation. Check the system for leaks.

Photo Sensor

OPERATION

The Starion, Sigma and 3000GT have a photo sensor installed in the upper right side of the instrument panel when equipped with an automatic climate control system. The function of the photo sensor is to detect a great amount of sunlight and increase the speed of the blower motor. This will compensate for the increase in interior temperature due to the heat of the sunlight.

TESTING

With sunlight shining on the photo sensor, cover the sensor with hand. If the speed of the blower decreases, then increases when sensor is exposed again, it is functioning properly.

REMOVAL AND INSTALLATION

1. Disconnect the negative battery cable.
2. Open or remove the glove box, as required.
3. Disconnect the connector to the photo sensor.
4. Carefully pry the sensor from the instrument panel.
5. The installation is the reverse of the removal procedure.
6. Connect the negative battery cable and check the sensor for proper operation.

Passenger Compartment Temperature Sensor

OPERATION

The Starion, Sigma and 3000GT have a passenger compartment temperature sensor installed in the roof when equipped with an automatic climate control system. The function of this sensor is to detect a the temperature of the passenger compartment, change the information into resistance values and provide the information to the controller for processing. This information is used as input by the controller.

TESTING

1. Disconnect the sensor connector near the evaporator case.
2. Measure the resistance across the wires of the suspect sensor.
3. The resistance specifications for the passenger compartment sensor at different temperatures are:
   32°F (0°C) – 11.4 kilo ohms
   50°F (10°C) – 7.32 kilo ohms
   68°F (20°C) – 4.86 kilo ohms
   86°F (30°C) – 3.31 kilo ohms
   104°F (40°C) – 2.32 kilo ohms
4. Replace the sensor if not within specifications.

REMOVAL AND INSTALLATION

1. Disconnect the negative battery cable.
2. Carefully pry the sensor from the headliner and disconnect the connector.
3. The installation is the reverse of the removal procedure.
4. Connect the negative battery cable and check the sensor for proper operation.

System Relays

OPERATION

Many of the systems within the air conditioning systems use relays to send current on its way and energize various components. The relays are positioned throughout the vehicles and many are interchangeable. All are conventional relays with internal contacts and a coil which pulls the contacts closed when energized.

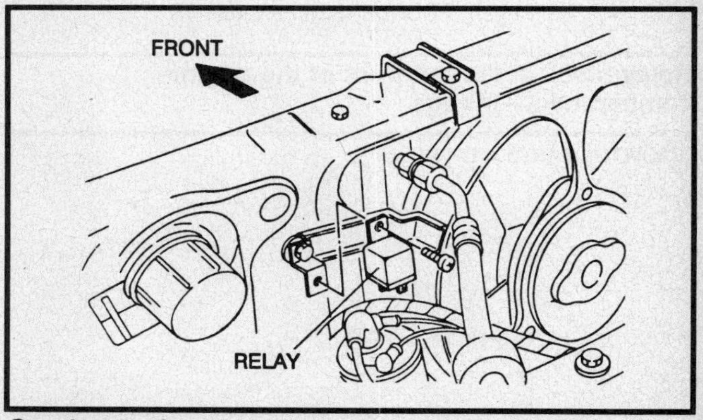
FRONT
RELAY

Condenser fan motor relay on the radiator support—1989 Precis

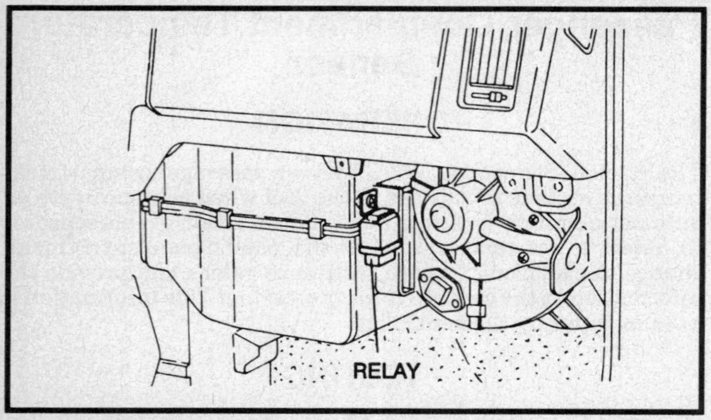
RELAY

Air conditioning relay on the heater unit—1989 Precis

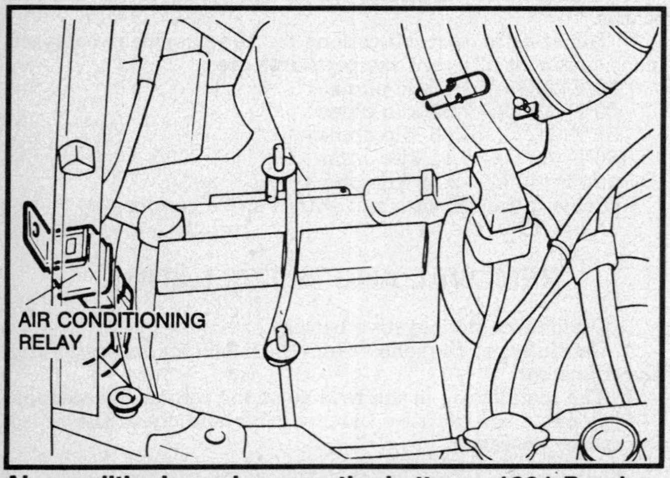
AIR CONDITIONING
RELAY

Air conditioning relay near the battery—1991 Precis

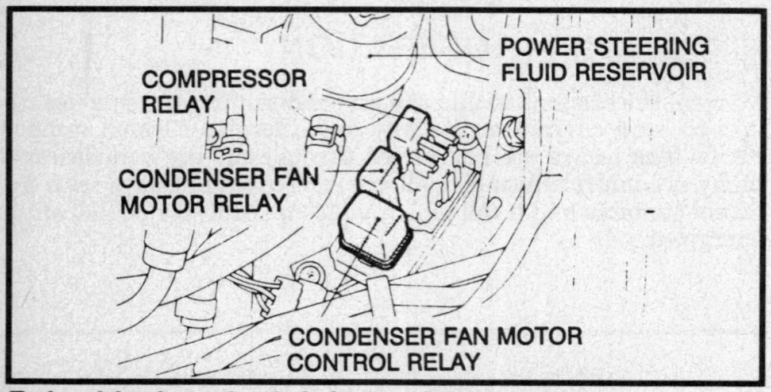
POWER STEERING
FLUID RESERVOIR
COMPRESSOR
RELAY
CONDENSER FAN
MOTOR RELAY
CONDENSER FAN MOTOR
CONTROL RELAY

Relay block at the left front of the engine compartment—Mirage

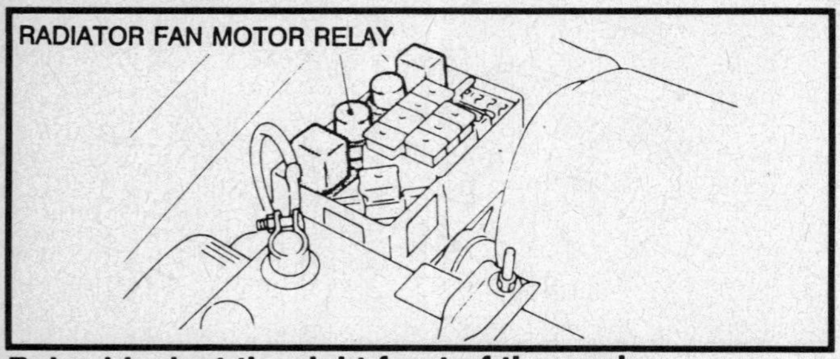
RADIATOR FAN MOTOR RELAY

Relay block at the right front of the engine compartment—Mirage

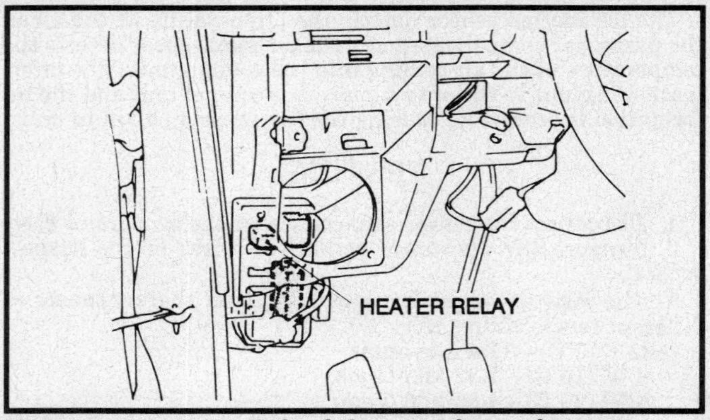
HEATER RELAY

Heater relay to the left of the steering column—Mirage

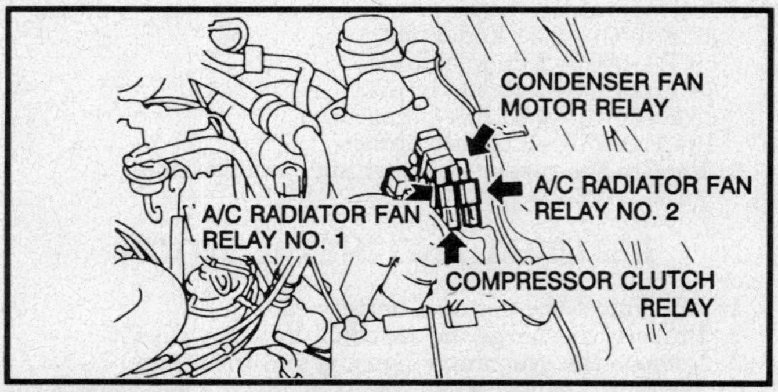
CONDENSER FAN
MOTOR RELAY
A/C RADIATOR FAN
RELAY NO. 2
A/C RADIATOR FAN
RELAY NO. 1
COMPRESSOR CLUTCH
RELAY

Relay cluster forward of the left front strut tower—Starion

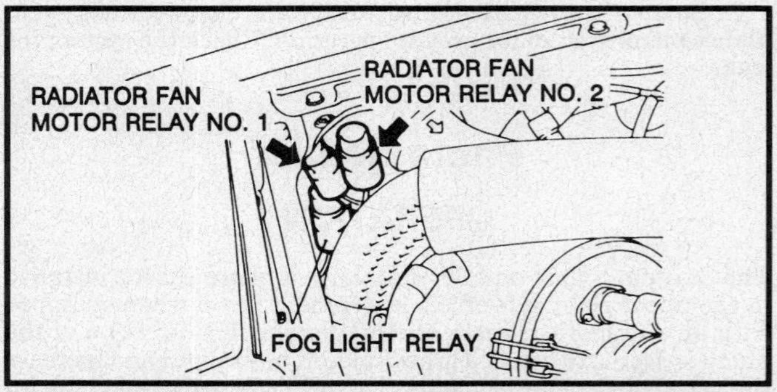
RADIATOR FAN
MOTOR RELAY NO. 1
RADIATOR FAN
MOTOR RELAY NO. 2
FOG LIGHT RELAY

Radiator fan relays at the right front of the engine compartment—Starion

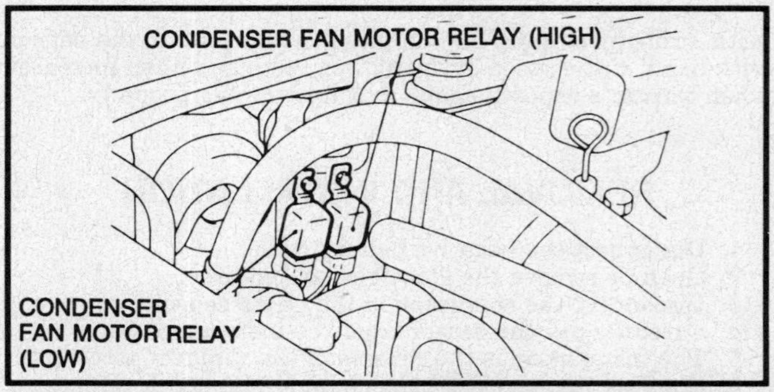
CONDENSER FAN MOTOR RELAY (HIGH)
CONDENSER
FAN MOTOR RELAY
(LOW)

Condenser fan relays on the radiator support—Galant

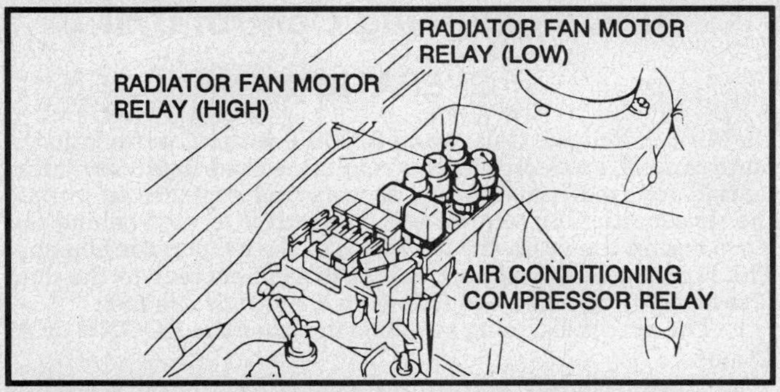
RADIATOR FAN MOTOR
RELAY (LOW)
RADIATOR FAN MOTOR
RELAY (HIGH)
AIR CONDITIONING
COMPRESSOR RELAY

Relay block forward of the right front strut tower—Galant

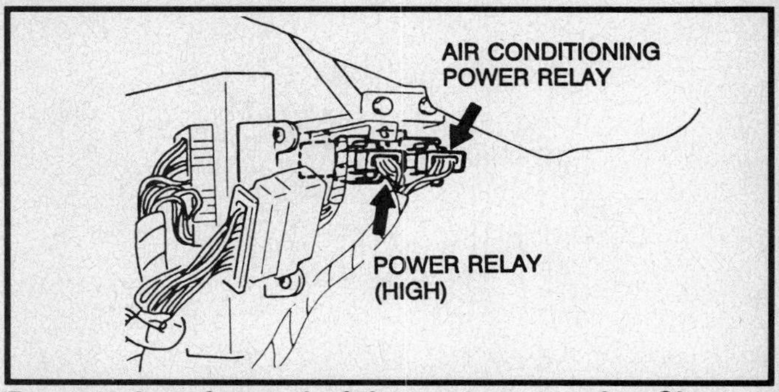
AIR CONDITIONING
POWER RELAY
POWER RELAY
(HIGH)

Power relays forward of the center console—Sigma

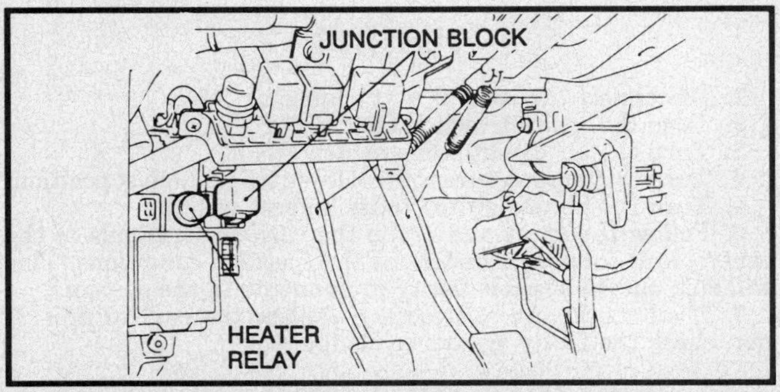
JUNCTION BLOCK
HEATER
RELAY

Relay block to the left of the steering column—Galant

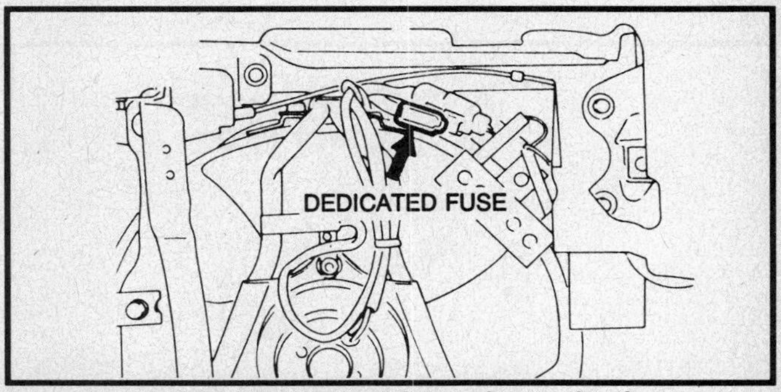
DEDICATED FUSE

Air conditioning dedicated fuse above the fan—Sigma

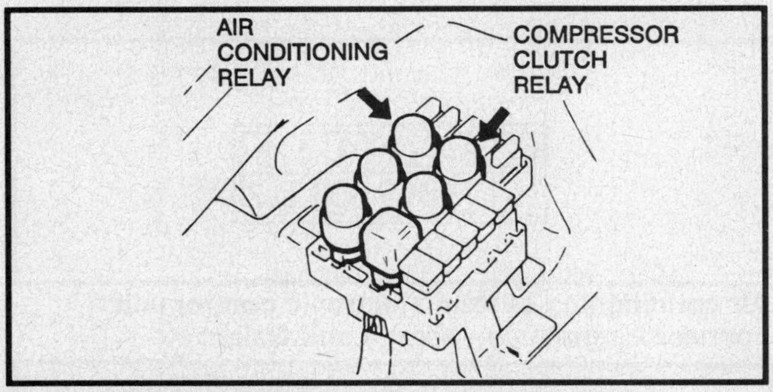
AIR
CONDITIONING
RELAY
COMPRESSOR
CLUTCH
RELAY

Relay block on the right side of the engine compartment—Sigma

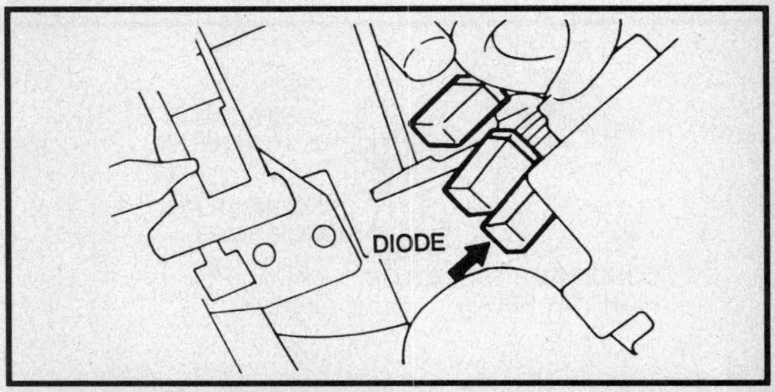
DIODE

Air conditioning system diode under the left side of the instrument panel—Sigma

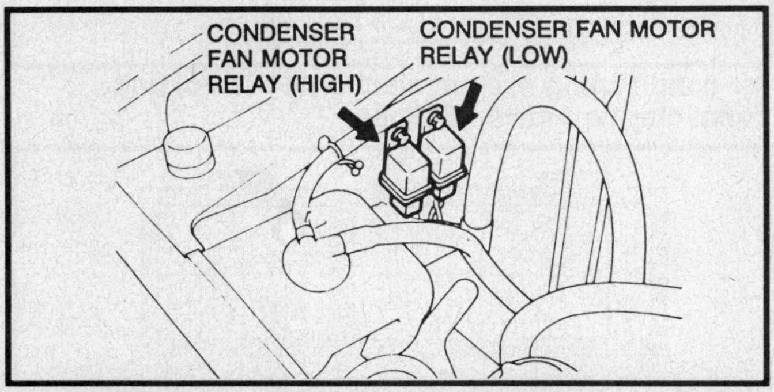
CONDENSER
FAN MOTOR
RELAY (HIGH)
CONDENSER FAN MOTOR
RELAY (LOW)

Condenser fan motor relays on the radiator suppor—Sigm

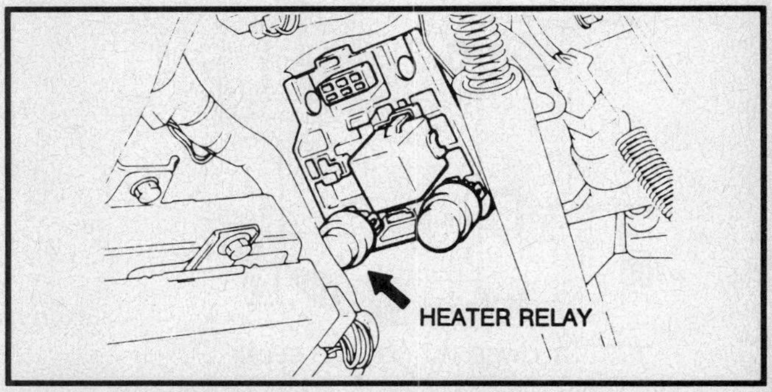
HEATER RELAY

Heater relay to the left of the steering column—Sigma

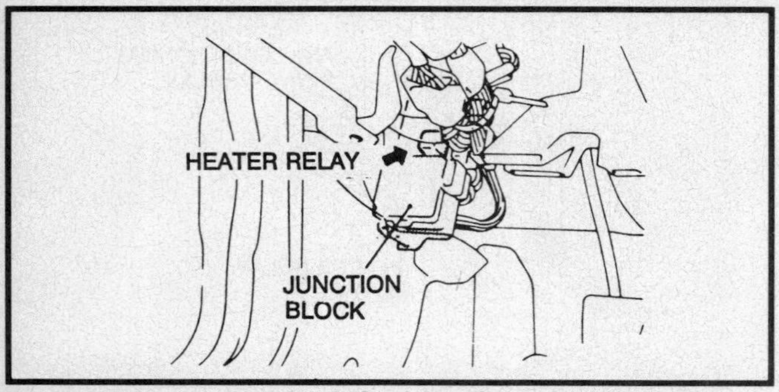
HEATER RELAY
JUNCTION
BLOCK

Heater relay under the left side of the instrument panel–Eclipse

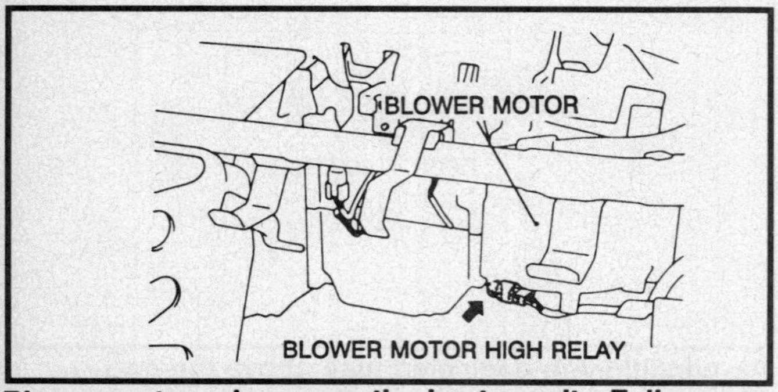
BLOWER MOTOR
BLOWER MOTOR HIGH RELAY

Blower motor relays near the heater unit–Eclipse

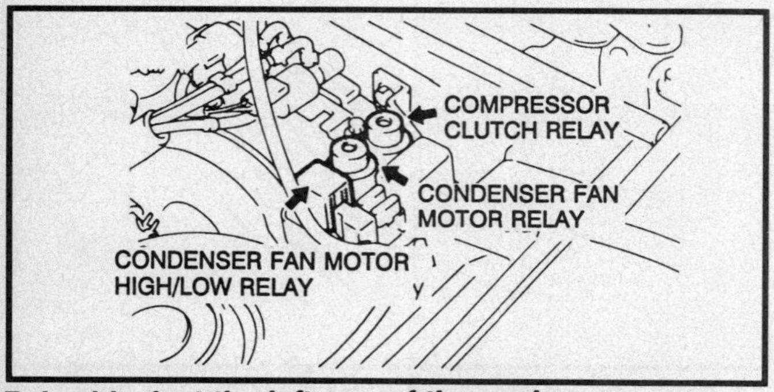
COMPRESSOR
CLUTCH RELAY
CONDENSER FAN
MOTOR RELAY
CONDENSER FAN MOTOR
HIGH/LOW RELAY

Relay block at the left rear of the engine compartment–Eclipse

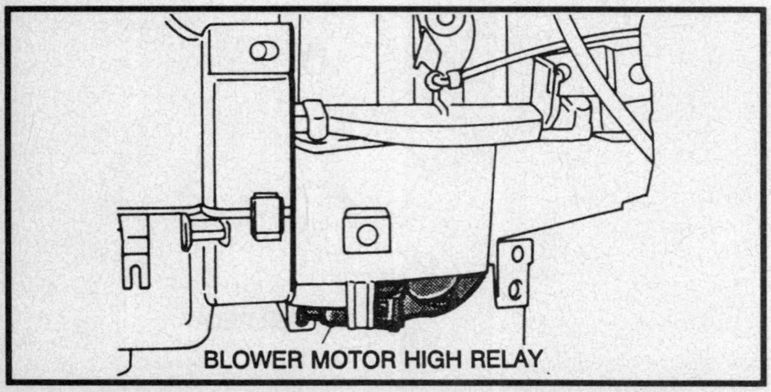
BLOWER MOTOR HIGH RELAY

Blower motor high relay near the heater unit–3000GT

Air Conditioning Control Unit

OPERATION

On Mirage, Eclipse, Galant and 3000GT without automatic climate control, an electronic control unit is used to process information received from various sensors and switches to control the air conditioning compressor. The unit is located behind the glove box on top or on the front side of the evaporator housing. The function of the control unit is to send current to the dual pressure switch when the following conditions are met:

1. The air conditioning switch is in either the **ECONO** or **A/C** mode.
2. The refrigerant temperature sensor, if equipped, is reading 347°F (175°C) or less.
3. The air thermo and air inlet sensors are both reading at least 39°F (4°C).

TESTING

1. Disconnect the control unit connector.
2. Turn the ignition switch **ON**.
3. Turn the air conditioning switch **ON**.
4. Turn the temperature control lever too its coolest position.
5. Turn the blower switch to its highest position.
6. Follow the chart and probe the various terminals of the control unit connector under the the specified conditions. This will rule out all possible faulty components in the system.
7. If all checks are satisfactory, replace the control unit. If not, check the faulty system or component.

REMOVAL AND INSTALLATION

1. Disconnect the negative battery cable.

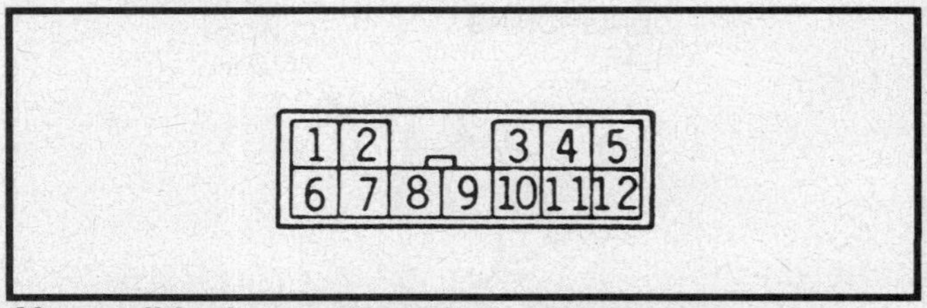
1 2 3 4 5
6 7 8 9 10 11 12

Air conditioning system electronic control unit connector terminals–Mirage and Galant

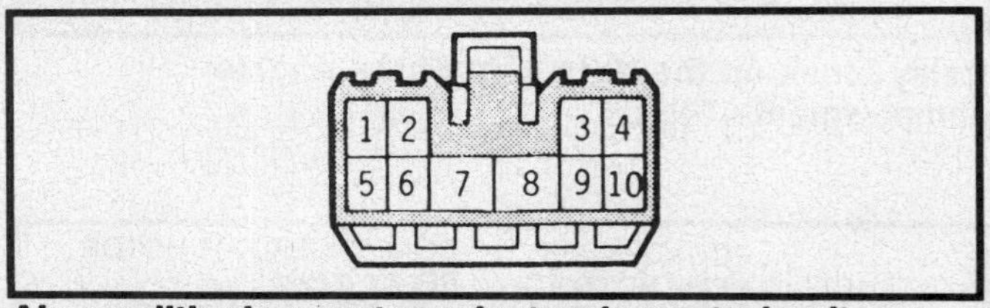
1 2 3 4
5 6 7 8 9 10

Air conditioning system electronic control unit connector terminals–Eclipse

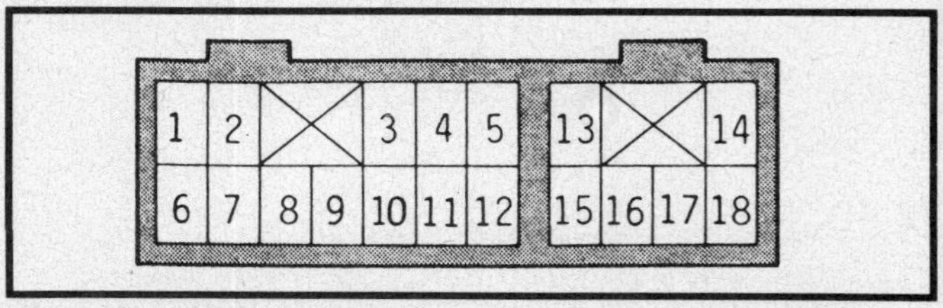
1 2 3 4 5 13 14
6 7 8 9 10 11 12 15 16 17 18

Air conditioning system electronic control unit connector terminals–3000GT

AIR CONDITIONING CONTROL UNIT DIAGNOSTICS—MIRAGE AND GALANT

Terminal No.	Signal	Conditions	Terminal voltage
8/9	Auto compressor control unit ground	At all times	0V
1	Auto compressor control unit power supply	When ignition switch is ON	System voltage
5	Refrigerant-temperature sensor ⊖	When air conditioner switch is OFF [Sensor temperature 25°C (58°F)]	Approx. 0.15V
6	Air conditioner compressor relay	When all conditions for switch-ON of the compressor are satisfied	System voltage
12	Refrigerant-temperature sensor ⊕	At all times	5V

AIR CONDITIONING CONTROL UNIT DIAGNOSTICS—ECLIPSE

Terminal	Measurement item	Tester connection	Conditions		Specified value
1	Resistance	1–6	—		1,500±150 Ω at 25°C (77°F)
2	Voltage	2–3 2–8	Air conditioner switch	ON	System voltage
				OFF	0 V
3	Continuity	3-Ground	—		Continuity
4	Continuity	4-Ground	—		Continuity
5	Resistance	5–7	—		1,500±150 Ω at 25°C (77°F)
8	Continuity	8-Ground	—		Continuity
9	Voltage	9–3 9–8	Thermo sensor	OFF 78°C (172°F)	System voltage
				ON 85°C (185°F)	0 V
10	Voltage	10–3 10–8	ECONO switch	ON	System voltage
				OFF	0 V

AIR CONDITIONING CONTROL UNIT DIAGNOSTICS—3000GT

Terminal No.	Signal	Conditions	Terminal voltage
8	Auto compressor control unit ground	At all times	0V
1	Auto compressor control unit power supply	When ignition switch is ON	Battery voltage
6	Air conditioner compressor relay	When all conditions for switch-ON of the compressor are satisfied	Battery voltage
7	Air conditioner switch: A/C	When air conditioner switch pressed in to second step	Battery voltage
2	Air conditioner switch: ECONO	When air conditioner switch pressed in to first step	Battery voltage
13	Fin-thermo sensor ⊕	Ignition switch, blower switch and air conditioner switch: ON	Approx. 2.5V
14	Air-inlet sensor ⊕	Ignition switch, blower switch and air conditioner switch: ON	Approx. 1V
15	Fin-thermo sensor ⊖	Ignition switch, blower switch and air conditioner switch: ON Ambient temperature: 4°C (39°F)	0V
18	Air-inlet sensor ⊖	Ignition switch, blower switch and air conditioner switch: ON Ambient temperature: 4°C (39°F)	0V

2. Remove the glove box and locate the control module.
3. Disconnect the connector to the module and remove the mounting screws.
4. Remove the module from the evaporator housing.
5. The installation is the reverse of the removal installation.
6. Connect the negative battery cable and check the entire climate control system for proper operation.

Damper Control Motors

OPERATION

The Starion, Sigma and 3000GT with full automatic air conditioning use electric motors to control the positioning of certain dampers. On Starion, the blend air damper is controlled electronically. On Sigma, the blend air and mode select dampers are controlled electronically. On 3000GT, the inside/ouside air select, blend air and mode select dampers are all controlled electronically. Motor rotation is activated by signals sent by the air condtioning control unit, causing the damper to be move to the target position.

TESTING

Damper Motors

1. Apply battery voltage to the proper connector terminals. Make sure the motor turns smoothly and quietly and no binding occurs. Be sure to cut off voltage when the door has reached its stop or if the motor does not rotate.
2. Reverse the connections and make sure the motor turns in the opposite direction.

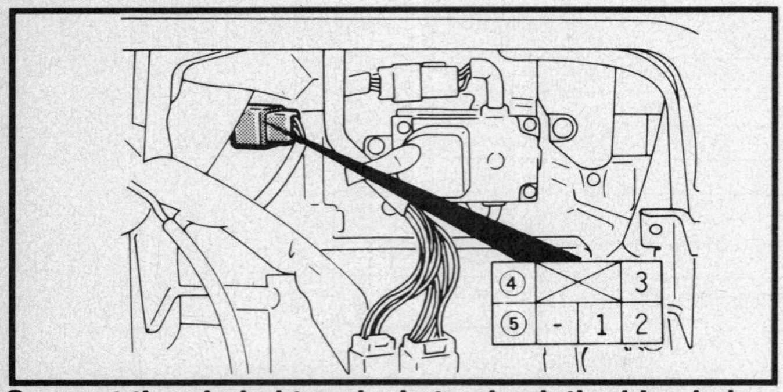
④
3
⑤
-
1
2

Connect the circled terminals to check the blend air damper motor—3000GT

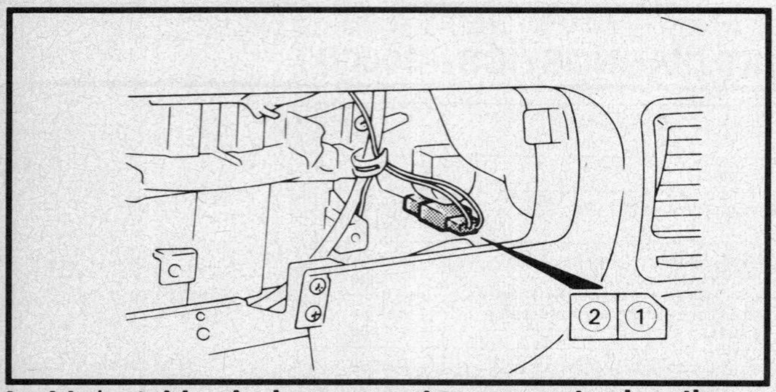
②
①

Inside/outside air damper motor connector location—3000GT

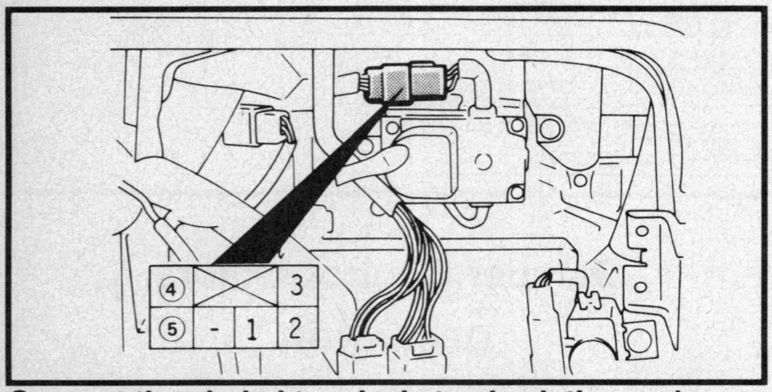
④
3
⑤
-
1
2

Connect the circled terminals to check the mode select damper motor—3000GT

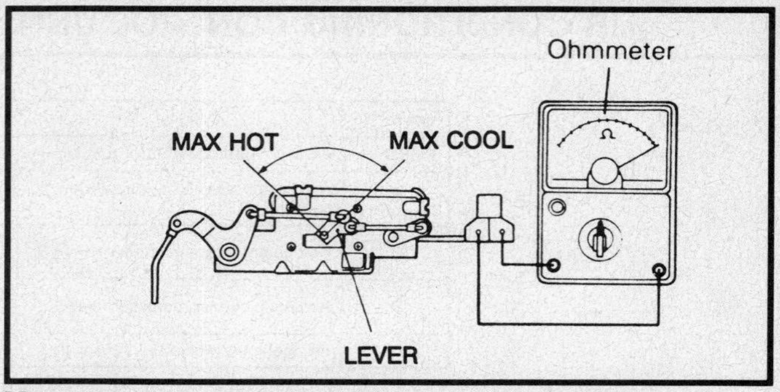
Ohmmeter
MAX HOT
MAX COOL
LEVER

Measure the resistance across the indicated terminals to check the blend air potentiometer—Starion

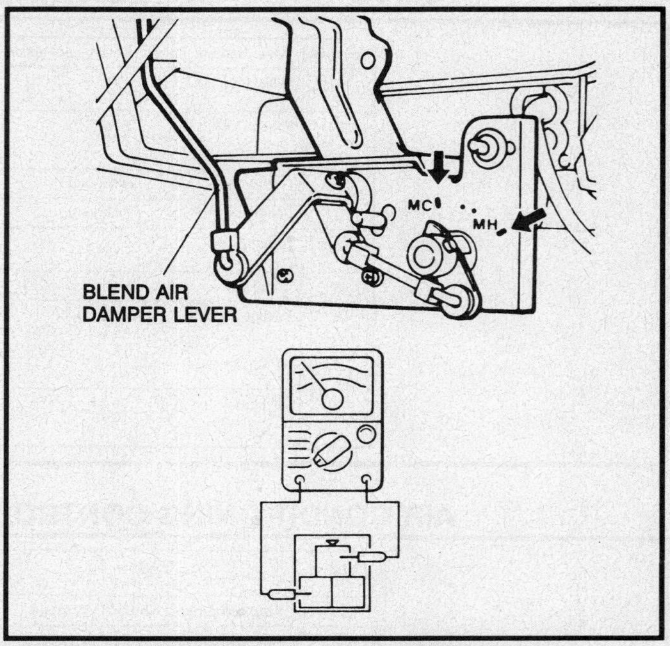
MC
MH
BLEND AIR
DAMPER LEVER

Measure the resistance across the indicated terminals to check the blend air potentiometer—Sigma

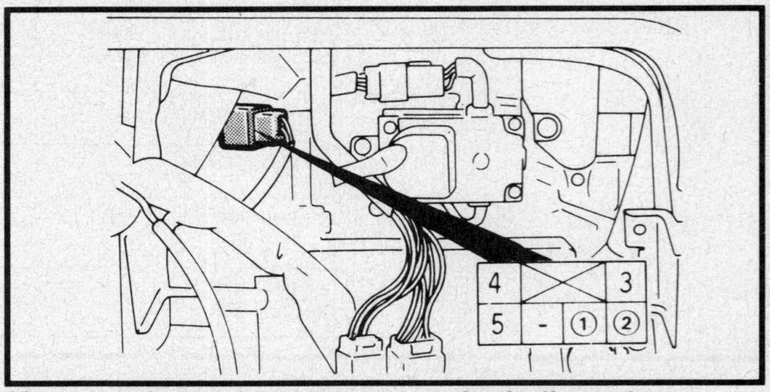
4
3
5
-
①
②

Measure the resistance across the indicated terminals to check the blend air damper potentiometer—3000GT

Blend Air Potentiometer

1. Connect an ohmmeter to the potentiometer terminals and measure the resistance at the hottest (MH) and coolest (MC) po-

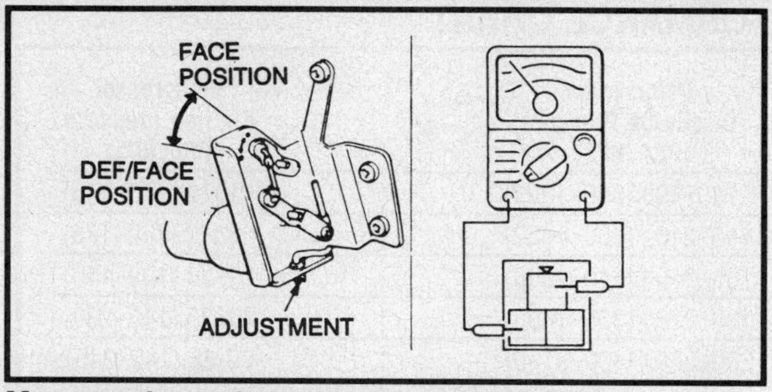
FACE POSITION
DEF/FACE POSITION
ADJUSTMENT

Measure the resistance across the indicated terminals to check the mode select damper potentiometer—Sigma

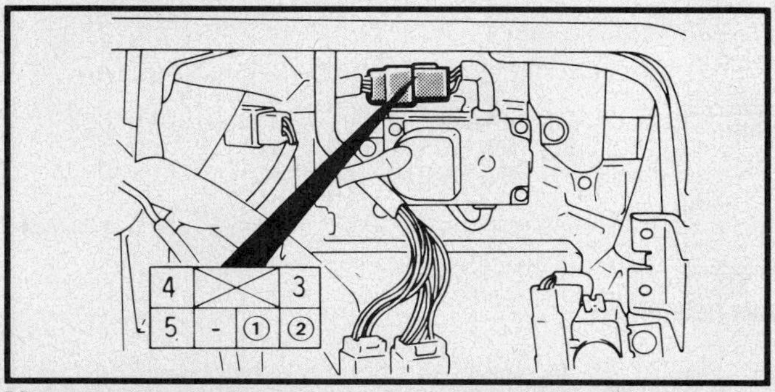
4
3
5
-
①
②

Measure the resistance across the indicated terminals to check the mode select damper potentiometer—3000GT

sitions. The resistance should gradually change as the damper is moved.

2. The specifications are:
Starion: Max Hot—180 ohms and Max Cool—4640 ohms
Sigma: Max Hot—400 ohms and Max Cool—2000 ohms
3000GT: Max Hot—200 ohms and Max Cool—4900 ohms

Mode Select Damper Potentiometer

SIGMA AND 3000GT

1. Connect an ohmmeter to the potentiometer terminals and measure the resistance at the FACE and FACE/DEF positions. The resistance should gradually change as the damper is moved.
2. The specifications are:
Sigma: FACE position—430 ohms and DEF/FACE position—5000 ohms
3000GT: FACE position—4300 ohms and DEF position—2000 ohms
3. If not within specifications, the mode select potentiometer on Sigma is adjustable.

REMOVAL AND INSTALLATION

Starion and Sigma

1. Disconnect the negative battery cable.
2. If necessary, remove the heater unit.
3. Disconnect the actuating rod from the damper.
4. Remove the mounting bolts and remove the motor.
5. The installation is the reverse of the removal procedure.
6. Connect the negative battery cable and check the entire climate control system for proper operation.

3000GT

1. Disconnect the negative battery cable.
2. To gain access to the inside/outside air select damper motor, remove the glove box stopper and outer glove box case. Disconnect the connector, remove the screws and remove the motor.
3. To gain access to the blend air damper motor:
   a. Remove the floor console.
   b. Remove the air conditioner control unit.
   c. Remove the center air outlet.
   d. Remove the air conditioning control head.
   e. Remove the mounting screws and remove the motor.
4. To gain access to the mode select damper motor:
   a. Remove the driver's side knee protector.
   b. Remove the side console cover.
   c. Remove the ductwork.
   d. Remove the mounting screws and remove the motor.
5. The installation is the reverse of the removal procedure.
6. Connect the negative battery cable and check the entire climate control system for proper operation.

SYSTEM DIAGNOSIS

Air Conditioning Performance

PERFORMANCE TEST

Air temperature in the testing area must be at least 70°F (21°C) to ensure the accuracy of this test.

1. Connect a manifold gauge set the the system.
2. Set the controls to **RECIRC** or **MAX**, the mode lever to the **PANEL** position, temperature control level to the coolest position and the blower on its highest position.
3. Start the engine and adjust the idle speed to 1000 rpm with the compressor clutch engaged.
4. Allow the engine come to normal operating temperature and keep doors and windows closed.
5. Insert a thermometer in the left center panel outlet and operate the engine for 10 minutes. The clutch may cycle depending on the ambient conditions.
6. With the clutch engaged, compare the discharge air temperature to the performance chart.
7. If the values do not meet specifications, check system components for proper operation.

Air Conditioning Compressor

COMPRESSOR NOISE

Noises that develop during air conditioning operation can be misleading. A noise that sounds like serious compressor damage

AIR CONDITIONING PERFORMANCE CHART

Ambient Temperature °F (°C)	Air Temperature at Center Panel Vent °F (°C)	Compressor Discharge Pressure PSI (kPa)	Compressor Suction Pressure PSI (kPa)
70 (21)	34–45 (1–8)	130–190 (896–1295)	10–21 (70–145)
80 (27)	35–45 (2–8)	145–210 (1000–1450)	13–25 (90–175)
90 (32)	36–47 (2–9)	165–245 (1140–1690)	15–30 (103–110)
100 (38)	37–50 (3–10)	190–270 (1335–1860)	20–33 (140–230)
110 (43)	40–60 (4–16)	200–300 (1400–2110)	20-35 (140–245)

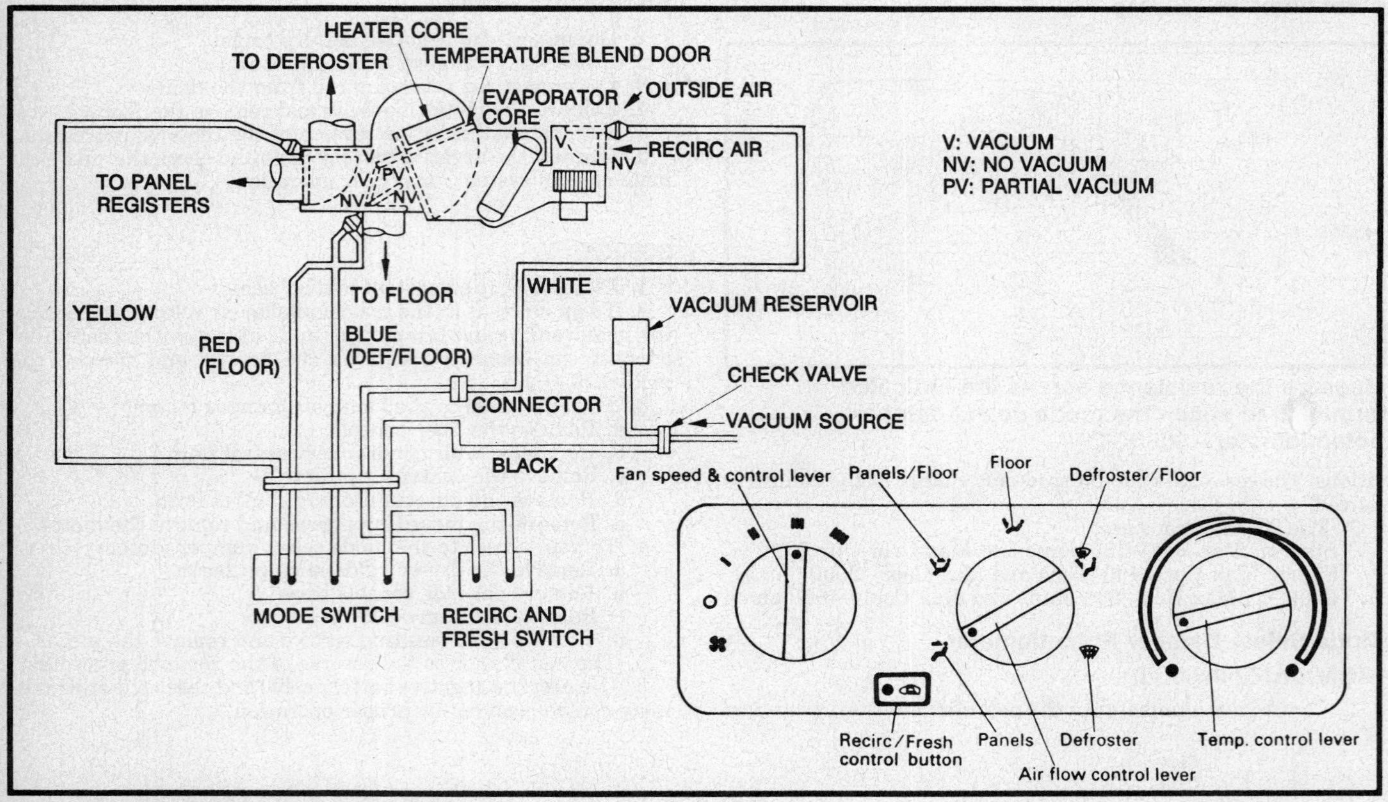
HEATER CORE
TO DEFROSTER
TEMPERATURE BLEND DOOR
EVAPORATOR CORE
OUTSIDE AIR
RECIRC AIR
V: VACUUM
NV: NO VACUUM
PV: PARTIAL VACUUM
TO PANEL REGISTERS
TO FLOOR
WHITE
VACUUM RESERVOIR
YELLOW
RED (FLOOR)
BLUE (DEF/FLOOR)
CHECK VALVE
CONNECTOR
VACUUM SOURCE
BLACK
MODE SWITCH
RECIRC AND FRESH SWITCH
Fan speed & control lever
Panels/Floor
Floor
Defroster/Floor
Recirc/Fresh control button
Panels
Defroster
Temp. control lever
Air flow control lever

Vacuum schematic—1990–91 Precis

may only be a loose belt, mounting bolt or clutch assembly. Improper belt tension can also emit a noise that can be mistaken for more serious problems. Check and adjust all possible causes of the noise, including oil level, before replacing the compressor.

COMPRESSOR CLUTCH INOPERATIVE

1. Verify refrigerant charge and charge, as required.
2. Check for 12 volts at the clutch coil connection. If voltage is detected, check the coil.
3. If voltage is not detected at the coil, check the fuse or fusible link. If the fuse is not blown, check for voltage at the clutch relay. If voltage is not detected there, continue working backwards through the system's switches, etc. until an open circuit is detected.
4. Inspect all suspect parts and replace as required.
5. When the repair is complete, perform a complete system performance test.

CLUTCH COIL TESTING

1. Disconnect the negative battery cable.
2. Disconnect the compressor clutch connector.
3. Apply 12 volts to the wire leading to the clutch coil. If the clutch is operating properly, an audible click will occur when the clutch is magnetically pulled into the coil. If no click is heard, inspect the coil.
4. Check the resistance across the coil lead wire and ground. The specification is 3.4–3.8 ohms at approximately 70°F (20°C).
5. If not within specifications, replace the clutch coil.

Vacuum Actuating System

INSPECTION

1990–91 Precis

Check the system for proper operation. Air should come from

the appropriate vents when the corresponding mode is selected under all driving conditions. If a problem is detected, check the flow of vacuum.

1. Check the engine for sufficient vacuum and the main supplier hose for leaks or kinks.
3. Check the check valve for proper operation. It should not hold vacuum when vacuum is applied from the engine side but should when applied from the system side.
4. Check all interior vacuum lines, especially the connections behind the instrument panel for leaks or kinks.
5. Check the control head for leaky ports or damaged parts.
6. Check all actuators for ability to hold vacuum.

Full Automatic Air Conditioning System

SELF-DIAGNOSTICS

Starion, Sigma and 3000GT

OPERATION

The automatic system is equipped with self-diagnostic capabilities so the condition of the wire harnesses and components within the system can be analyzed. When the full automatic air conditioning system senses a malfunction, the fail-safe system is activated and a malfunction code is input to the electronic control unit. This information becomes output when the self-diagnostics connector is accessed. The connector is located behind the glove box on Starion and Sigma or under the instrument panel to the left of the steering column on 3000GT.

USING MULTI-USE TESTER

Mitsubishi's Multi-Use Tester MB991269 or MB991341 in conjunction with the proper ROM pack can be used to check the system. To use the tester, connect the socket to the cigarette lighter and the connector to the vehicle's self-diagnosis check connector. Follow the manufacturer's instructions to set the tool and record the stored fault codes. Once the codes are recorded, check the faulty system(s) using the charts provided.

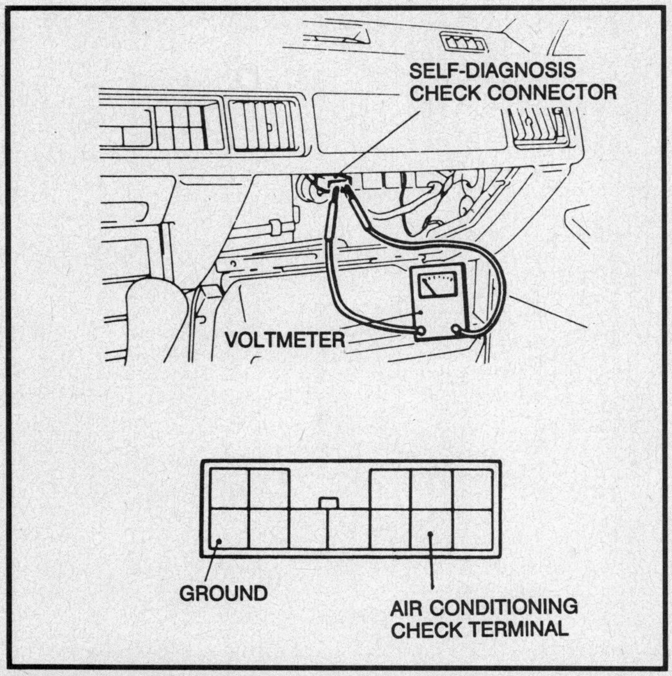
SELF-DIAGNOSIS
CHECK CONNECTOR
VOLTMETER
GROUND
AIR CONDITIONING
CHECK TERMINAL

Self-diagnostics using an anolog voltmeter—Starion

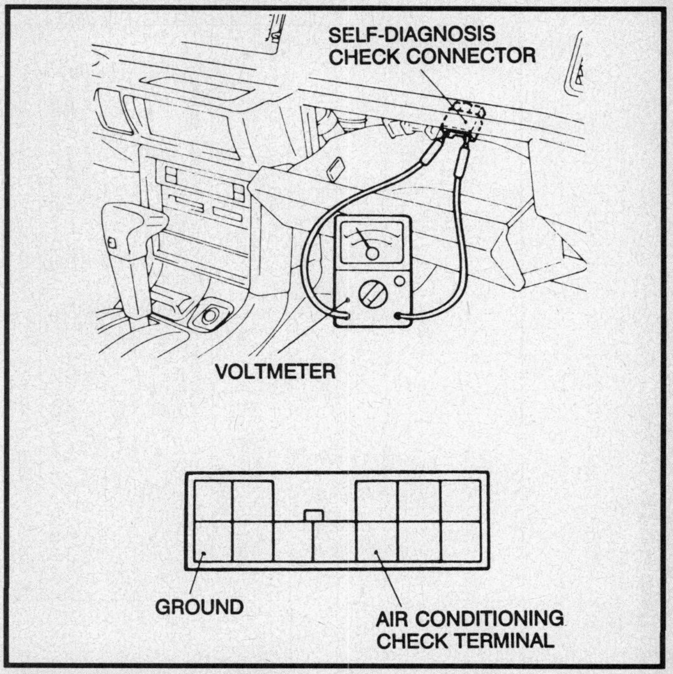
SELF-DIAGNOSIS
CHECK CONNECTOR
VOLTMETER
GROUND
AIR CONDITIONING
CHECK TERMINAL

Self-diagnostics using an anolog voltmeter—Sigma

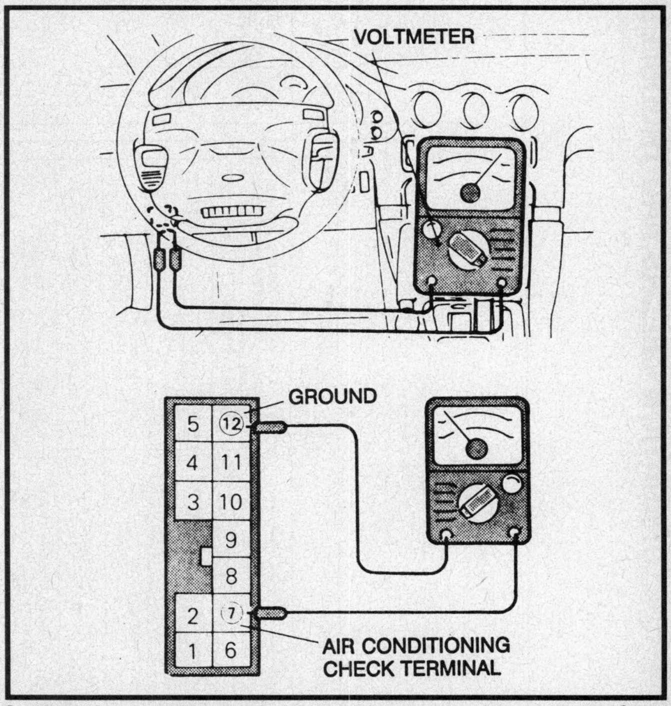
VOLTMETER
GROUND
5
12
4
11
3
10
9
8
2
7
1
6
AIR CONDITIONING
CHECK TERMINAL

Self-diagnostics using an anolog voltmeter—3000GT

USING ANALOG VOLTMETER

Connect a voltmeter across the ground terminal and terminal designated for the full automatic air conditioning system on the check connector. The code number for the malfunction is determined by counting sweeps of the voltmeter needle. The long sweeps represent the tenths digit of the code and the shorter sweeps represent the single digits. For example, 1 long sweep followed by 5 short sweeps indicates Code 15.

OPERATION CHECKS AND TROUBLESHOOTING—STARION

No.	Action	Normal operation	Abnormal operation/ Probable cause
1	Start the engine. (Proceed to check after engine coolant is sufficiently warmed.)	• The AUTO switch light on control panel lights.	• AUTO switch light does not light and no beep sound is heard even if the switch is pressed. - Problem in switch
		• The display changes to preset temperature indication.	• No indication. - Problem in digital display
		• Air volume changes according to blower switch position.	• Blower motor does not operate even if the fan switch is set to ON. - Problem in fan controller
		• Compressor comes into operation.	• Compressor does not operate. - Problem in air conditioner
2	Change temperature setting to 32°C (90°F) (Set blower switch to AUTO position unless otherwise specified.)	• On depression of UP switch, beep sound is produced and the sound stops once 32°C (90°F) is reached.	• No beep sound. Temperature setting remains unchanged. - Problem in switch - Problem in wiring harness
		• Beep sound is heard while temperature setting is being changed.	
		• When 32°C (90°F) temperature is reached, the indication changes from "FACE" to "FACE/FOOT" and then to "FOOT", and also the air outlet accordingly.	• Air flow does not change to FOOT mode or air outlet does not correspond to mode indication. - Problem in air flow change vacuum solenoid or vacuum actuator
		• Outlet air reaches the warmest temperature.	• The warmest temperature cannot be attained or, conversely, temperature drops to the lowest. - Problem in blend air damper servo motor
		• Outside air is introduced.	• Interior air recirculates. - Problem in outside/inside air damper vacuum solenoid or actuator
		• Compressor stops.	• Compressor comes into operation. - Problem in wiring harness - Problem in control box
		• Blower speed becomes MH.	• Blower speed remains unchanged. - Problem in fan controller - Problem in wiring harness - Problem in control box
3	Change temperature setting from 32 to 18°C (90 to 65°F.)	• Upon depression of DOWN switch, beep sound is produced and the sound stops once 18°C (65°F) temperature is reached.	• No beep sound. Temperature setting remains unchanged. - Problem in switch - Problem in wiring harness
		• Beep sound is heard while temperature setting is being changed.	• Temperature indication remains unchanged. - Problem in indicator - Problem in wiring harness
		• When 18°C (65°F) temperature is reached, the indication changes from "FOOT" to "FACE/FOOT" and then to "FACE", and also the air outlet accordingly. (Observe LED also.)	• Air flow does not change to FACE mode or air outlet does not correspond to the indicated mode. - Problem in air flow changeover vacuum solenoid or actuator
		• Outlet air temperature becomes the lowest (blend air damper is closed).	• Outlet air does not become cooler, much less the lowest temperature (blend air damper does not operate). - Problem in blend air damper servo motor
		• Compressor comes into operation.	• Compressor does not operate. - Problem in air conditioner
		• Air flow changes from introduction of outside air to recirculation of inside air.	• Outside air is introduced. - Problem in air selection damper actuator
		• Blower speed becomes "H" (H relay closes).	• Blower speed remains unchanged and H relay is inoperative. - Problem in power transistor - Problem in relay
4	Press air selection switch twice and then press AUTO switch. [Temperature setting is 25°C (77°F)]	• Every depression of air selection causes beep sound and switch light is kept lit in that while. Once AUTO switch is pressed, the air selection light goes off.	• Beep sound is produced but light does not light. - Blown light bulb • Neither beep sound is produced nor light lights. - Problem in switch
		• On depression of air selection switch, the damper position changes from recirculation position to outside air position and vice-versa.	• Damper position does not change (but air flow indication changes). - Problem in recirculation/outside air damper actuator
		• If AUTO switch is pressed, damper returns automatically to its original position and indication also returns to "AUTO".	

OPERATION CHECKS AND TROUBLESHOOTING—STARION

No.	Action	Normal operation	Abnormal operation/ Probable cause
5	Press ECONOMY switch three times and then press AUTO switch. [Temperature setting is 25°C (77°F.)]	• Every depression of switch causes beep sound and switch light lights every other depression. • Second depression of switch causes compressor to stop and switch light and AUTO light to go off. • When AUTO switch is pressed, ECONOMY switch light goes off and air conditioner comes into operation continuously.	• No beep sound is produced (no response to switch action). - Problem in switch - Problem in wiring harness • Beep sound is produced but light does not light. - Blown light bulb (Switch does not operate.) • Compressor operates but condenser fan does not. - Problem in condenser motor - Problem in condenser motor relay
6	Push air flow mode switches one after another. ↓ ↓	• Beep sound is produced when respective switch is pushed; corresponding switch light and LED light. • AUTO light goes off when any of the switches is pushed. • Air comes out from the outlets corresponding to pushed switch. • Indication on air flow indicator changes according to depression of switch. * and modes cannot be selected simultaneously. If both are selected concurrently, will have priority over the other.	• No beep sound is produced (no response to switch action). - Problem in switch - Problem in wiring harness • Beep sound is produced but light does not light. - Blown switch light bulb • Air flow direction does not change. - Problem in damper actuator
7	Change blower switch position. OFF ↓ ↓	• Outlet air volume changes according to switch position. • If AUTO mode switch is activated, air volume changes automatically according to interior temperature. (For example, if the interior sensor is touched by hand when interior temperature is lower than bodily temperature, the air volume will increase.) • When engine is cold, if AUTO mode switch is activated, fan speed is fixed to low speed for some while after start of engine.	• No air volume change is caused by setting the switch to different positions (and). - Problem in switch - Problem in wiring harness • Fan motor does not operate in both and positions. - Problem in fan controller - Blown fuse - Broken harness • When AUTO mode switch is activated, fan turns at high speed even in cold season or stays turning at low speed even after the engine is warmed. - Problem in water temperature switch - Problem in water temperature switch wiring harness
8	Check for AUTO mode function (interior temperature sensor operation). [Set AUTO mode switch to ON; temperature setting is 25°C (77°F.)] * Touch interior temperature sensor heat sensing plate with hand to warm it to 30°C (86°F) or over. Then cool the plate down to 10°C (50°F) or below.	• When the interior temperature sensor is touched with hand, the air flow mode becomes to FACE, the blend air damper moves to the coolest position and blower speed changes to H level. The interior air recirculates under this condition. (If the system is in ECONOMY mode, the compressor comes into operation.) • When the interior temperature sensor is cooled down, the outside air is introduced, the blend air damper moves to the warmest position and the air flow mode becomes to FOOT. Also, the fan speed becomes MH level. (If the system is in ECONOMY mode, the compressor stops.)	• Neither touching the sensor with hand nor cooling it causes the results. - Problem in interior temperature sensor - Problem in wiring harness - Problem in controller
9	Check photo-sensor for function. [With the system in AUTO mode, set the blower switch to AUTO position temperature setting is 25°C (77°F.)] Expose the photo-sensor to sunbeam for checking.	• When the sensor is exposed to sunbeam, the outlet air temperature lowers. (Blower speed increases in summer.) • When the sensor is covered by hand, the outlet air temperature rises. (Blower speed decreases in summer.)	• No change results from action on sensor. - Problem in photo-sensor - Broken wiring harness - Problem in controller (Clean the photo-sensor.)
10	Check engine coolant temperature switch for operation. (With the system in AUTO mode, set the blower switch to AUTO position; temperature setting.) * Cool the interior temperature sensor heat sensing plate down to 20°C (68°F) or lower.	• When engine coolant temperature is lower than 50°C (122°F), the blower speed is in L level and the air flow mode becomes DEF. • When engine coolant temperature rises to 50°C (122°F) or higher, the blower speed increases and air flow mode becomes FOOT, FACE/FOOT or FACE.	• Blower motor speed is not fixed to L level even when engine coolant temperature is lower than 50°C (122°F). - Problem in controller - Problem in wiring harness • Air flow remains in mode. - Problem in engine coolant temperature switch - Broken wiring harness - Problem in controller

TROUBLESHOOTING CHART—STARION

	Check item \ Symptom	Fuse	Harness	Light bulb	Damper control motor & link	Water valve	Magnetic clutch	Power relays	Sensor switches	Blower motor	Pusher fan motor	Control unit (diagnosis output)	Vacuum system (VSV, hose, check valve)
1	"AUTO" light does not illuminate when ignition switch is turned to "ON" position	①	④	③								②	
2	Inside temperature does not rise (no hot air)		⑤		③	④			②			①	
3	Inside temperature does not drop (no cool air)		⑤		③	④	⑦	⑥	②			①	
4	Blower does not run	①	⑥					⑤	④	③		②	
5	Blower does not stop		④					③	②			①	
6	Air inlet switching damper does not operate		④						③			①	②
7	Air outlet switching damper does not operate		④						③			①	②
8	Pusher fan does not operate when air conditioner is operating		④					①	②		③		
9	Temperature setting changes when ignition switch is turned to "OFF" position and then back to "ON" position		②									①	

NOTE
1. ○ indicates items requiring check (number in circle indicates check order).
2. Use self-diagnosis and measure terminal voltage for control unit check.

TROUBLESHOOTING BY SYMPTOM—STARION

Symptom	Probable cause	Remedy
1. "AUTO" light does not illuminate when ignition switch is turned to "ON" position	Open No. 12 fuse	Replace fuse
	Faulty control unit	Check diagnosis output
	Faulty full auto air conditioner panel assembly	Replace full auto air conditioner panel assembly
	Burnt-out "AUTO" indicator bulb	Replace "AUTO" light bulb
	Open harness between full auto air conditioner panel assembly and control unit	Correct harness
2. Inside temperature does not rise (no hot air)	Faulty control unit	Check diagnosis output
	Faulty interior temperature sensor input circuit	
	Faulty foot area temperature sensor input circuit	
	Faulty thermistor input circuit	
	Faulty blend air damper potentiometer input circuit	
	Faulty blend air damper control motor	Replace blend air damper control motor
	Inadequate connection between blend air damper control motor lever and blend air damper	Correct connection
	Seized blend air damper	Correct blend air dampér
	Water valve failure	Replace water valve
	Open harness between blend air damper control motor and control unit	Correct harness
3. Inside temperature does not drop (no cool air)	Faulty control unit	Check diagnosis output
	Faulty upper interior temperature sensor input circuit	
	Faulty lower interior temperature sensor input circuit	
	Faulty thermistor input circuit	
	Faulty blend air damper potentiometer input circuit	
	Faulty blend air damper control motor	Replace blend air damper control motor
	Inadequate connection between blend air damper control motor lever and blend air damper	Correct connection
	Seized blend air damper	Correct blend air damper

NOTE
When engine coolant temperature is below 50°C (122°F), blower speed is held at LOW.

TROUBLESHOOTING BY SYMPTOM—STARION

Symptom	Probable cause	Remedy
3. Inside temperature does not drop (no cool air)	Water valve failure	Replace water valve
	Open harness between blend air damper control motor and control unit	Correct harness
	Faulty power relay (for compressor)	Replace power relay
	Faulty magnet clutch	Check or replace magnet clutch
	Refrigerant leaks	Replenish refrigerant
4. Blower does not run	Open fuse No. 5	Replace fuse
	Faulty control unit	Check diagnosis output
	Faulty blower motor	Replace blower motor
	Blown temperature fuse in power transistor or poor grounding	Replace temperature fuse or correct grounding
	Faulty power relay (for starter cut)	Replace power relay (for starter cut)
	Open harness between fuse and power relay (for starter cut)	Correct harness
	Open harness between power relay (for starter cut) and blower motor	
	Open harness between power transistor and control unit	
5. Blower does not stop	Faulty control unit	Check diagnosis output
	Faulty blower switch (OFF SW)	Replace full auto air conditioner panel assembly
	Faulty power relay (for high speed)	Replace power relay
	Shorted harness between blower switch and control unit	Correct harness
	Shorted harness between power relay (for high speed) and power transistor and control unit	
6. Air inlet switching damper does not operate	Faulty control unit	Check diagnosis output
	Defective vacuum solenoid valve	Replace vacuum solenoid valve
	Defective or disconnected vacuum hose	Check or replace vacuum hose
	Defective vacuum system including vacuum tank	Check or replace vacuum system
	Faulty full auto air conditioner switch (inside/outside air switching)	Replace full auto air conditioner panel assembly
	Faulty air inlet switching control vacuum actuator	Replace air inlet switching control vacuum actuator
	Air inlet switching damper failure	Correct air inlet switching damper

Symptom	Probable cause	Remedy
6. Air inlet switching damper does not operate	Open harness between full auto air conditioner panel assembly and control unit	Correct harness
	Open harness between air inlet switching vacuum solenoid valve and control unit	Correct harness
7. Air outlet switching damper does not operate	Faulty control unit	Check diagnosis output
	Defective vacuum solenoid valve	Replace vacuum solenoid valve
	Defective or disconnected vacuum hose	Check or replace vacuum hose
	Defective vacuum system including vacuum tank	Check or replace vacuum system
	Faulty full auto air conditioner switch (mode selection)	Replace full auto air conditioner panel assembly
	Faulty air outlet switching control vacuum actuator	Replace air outlet switching control vacuum actuator
	Inadequate engagement between cam and damper link or incorrect adjustment	Correct engagement or adjust
	FACE/DEF or FACE/FOOT damper failure	Correct FACE/DEF or FACE/FOOT damper
	Open harness between full auto air conditioner panel assembly and control unit	Correct harness
	Open harness between air outlet switching vacuum solenoid valve and control unit	
8. Pusher fan does not operate when air conditioner is operating	Faulty power relay (for pusher fan)	Replace power relay
	Faulty thermo sensor No. 2 (vehicles with an intercooler)	Check or replace thermo sensor
	Faulty pusher fan motor	Check or replace fan motor
	Faulty pressure switch (vehicles with an intercooler)	Check or replace pressure switch
9. Temperature setting changes when ignition switch is turned to "OFF" position and back to "ON" position	Faulty control unit	Check diagnosis output
	Insufficient battery charge or faulty battery	Recharge, adjust specific gravity or replace battery
	Open harness between ignition switch and control unit	Correct harness

OPERATION CHECKS AND TROUBLESHOOTING—SIGMA

Operation step	Normal operation	Abnormal operation	Probable cause(s)
Start the engine. Operate the switches after the coolant has warmed up. (about 5 minutes after starting)	The switch light illuminates when the AUTO switch is pressed.	The switch light does not illuminate when the AUTO switch is pressed.	Malfunction of the AUTO switch.
	The temperature setting digital indicator displays 31°C (88°F) for two seconds and then displays the set temperature.	The temperature setting digital indicator does not display 31°C (88°F), or displays nothing.	Malfunction of the temperature setting digital indicator.
	The blower motor operates at the speed corresponding to the blower switch setting.	The blower motor doesn't operate when the blower switch is switched ON.	Malfunction of the blower controller.
		The blower motor continues to operate when the blower switch is switched OFF.	Malfunction of the blower switch and harness.
	The compressor operates when the outside air temperature is high.	The compressor doesn't operate although the outside air temperature is high.	Malfunction of the air conditioner.
Press the TEMP switch to select a higher temperature [32°C (90°F)].	An electronic sound is produced when the switch is pressed. As the set temperature becomes higher and reaches 32°C (90°F), it stops.	No electronic sound when the switch is pressed. There is no change of the set temperature.	Malfunction of the TEMP switch. Malfunction of the wiring harness.
	When the set temperature reaches 32°C (90°F), the air outlets being used change from FACE to FACE/FOOT to FOOT.	The air outlets used don't change to the FOOT outlets.	Malfunction of the mode-selection damper control motor.
	The temperature of the air flow becomes that of maximum heating.	The temperature of the air flow doesn't become that of maximum heating. The temperature of the air flow becomes that of maximum cooling.	Malfunction of the blend air damper control motor.
	Outside air is introduced.	Inside air is introduced.	Malfunction of the air-selection damper control motor.
	The compressor doesn't operate.	The compressor operates.	Malfunction of the wiring harness. Malfunction of the air conditioner control unit.
	The air-flow amount becomes maximum.	The air-flow amount doesn't change.	Malfunction of the blower controller. Malfunction of the wiring harness. Malfunction of the air conditioner control unit.

Operation step	Normal operation	Abnormal operation	Probable cause(s)
Press the TEMP switch to select a lower [32°C–16°C (90°F–60°F)] set temperature.	An electronic sound is produced when the switch is pressed. A temperature of 16°C (60°F) or below is not displayed.	No electronic sound when the switch is pressed. There is no change of the set temperature when the switch is pressed.	Malfunction of the TEMP switch.
	When 16°C (60°F) is reached, the air outlets being used change from FOOT to FACE/FOOT to FACE.	There is no change of which air outlets are used when the temperature reaches 16°C (60°F).	Malfunction of the mode-selection damper control motor.
	The temperature of the air flow becomes that of maximum cooling.	The temperature of the air flow doesn't become that of maximum cooling.	Malfunction of the blend air damper control motor.
	The compressor operates.	The compressor doesn't operate.	Malfunction of the air conditioner.
	Inside air is introduced.	Outside air is introduced.	Malfunction of the air-selection damper control motor.
	The blower speed changes to HI.	The blower speed doesn't change. The power relay doesn't function.	Malfunction of the power transistor. Malfunction of the power relay.
Press the inside/outside air-select switch to switch to inside air or outside air. Press the AUTO switch.	An electronic sound is heard each time the switch is pressed, and the switch light remains ON. The switch light is switched OFF when the AUTO switch is pressed.	An electronic sound is heard each time the switch is pressed, but the switch light doesn't switch ON.	Malfunction of the switch light.
		No electronic sound is heard when the switch is pressed, and the switch light doesn't switch ON.	Malfunction of the switch.
	The air-selection damper functions when the switch is pressed, and there is a change to inside air (or outside air). The air-selection damper return to the original status when the AUTO switch is pressed.	When the switch is pressed, the air-selection damper doesn't operate.	Malfunction of the air-selection damper control motor.
Set the temperature setting to 23°C (74°F), and repeatedly switch the ECONO switch ON and OFF. Press the AUTO switch.	An electronic sound is heard each time the switch is pressed, and the switch light is alternately switched ON and OFF.	No electronic sound is heard when the switch is pressed.	Malfunction of the ECONO switch. Malfunction of the wiring harness.
		An electronic sound is heard when the switch is pressed, but the switch light doesn't switch ON.	Malfunction of the switch light.
	When the switch is pressed two times, the compressor stops, and the switch light and the AUTO light are switched OFF.	When the switch is pressed, the switch light is switched ON, but the compressor doesn't operate.	A problem with the refrigerant. Malfunction of the pressure switch. Malfunction of the wiring harness or compressor clutch.
		When the switch is pressed, the compressor operates, but the condenser fan does not.	Malfunction of the condenser motor. Malfunction of the condenser motor relay.

OPERATION CHECKS AND TROUBLESHOOTING – SIGMA

Operation step	Normal operation	Abnormal operation	Probable cause(s)
Press each mode-selection switch.	An electronic sound is heard each time the switch is pressed, and the switch light is switched ON. The AUTO light switches OFF at the same time.	No electronic sound is heard when the switch is pressed.	Malfunction of the mode-selection switch. Malfunction of the wiring harness.
		An electronic sound is heard each time the switch is pressed, but the switch light doesn't switch ON.	Malfunction of the switch light.
	Air flows from the air-outer corresponding to the mode-selection switch setting.	The direction of the air flow doesn't change when the switch is pressed.	Malfunction of the mode-selection damper control motor.
		There is no air flow from the air outlet corresponding to the mode-selection switch.	Malfunction of the mode-selection damper control motor potentiometer. Malfunction of the wiring harness.
Operate the blower switch. (from OFF to LO to HI)	Outlet air volume changes according to switch position.	No air volume change is caused by setting the switch to different positions (LO and HI).	Malfunction of the blower switch. Malfunction of the wiring harness.
	If AUTO mode switch is activated, air volume changes automatically according to passenger compartment temperature. (For example, if the passenger compartment temperature sensor is touched by hand when passenger compartment temperature is lower than bodily temperature, the air volume will increase.)	Fan motor does not operate in both LO and HI positions.	Malfunction of the blower control. Malfunction of the wiring harness.
	When engine is cold, if AUTO mode switch is activated, fan speed is fixed to low speed for some while after start of engine.	When AUTO mode switch is activated, fan turns at high speed even in cold season or stays turning at low speed even after the engine is warmed.	Malfunction of the thermo switch. Malfunction of the wiring harness.
Follow the procedures described below to check the operation of the passenger compartment temperature sensor. 1. Press the AUTO switch. 2. Set the temperature setting to 23°C (74°F). 3. Touch the passenger compartment temperature sensor until a temperature of 30°C (86°F) or higher is obtained. Then, cool to 1°C (34°F) or lower.	The following operations are activated when the passenger compartment temperature sensor is touched [30°C (86°F) or higher]: • The compressor operates. • The temperature of the outflow air becomes that of maximum cooling. • The air-flow outlets form which air is flowing are the FACE outlets. Interior air is recirculated under the above conditions for about ten minutes.	The conditions described at the left are not activated when the passenger compartment temperature sensor is touched [30°C (86°F) or higher] or is cooled [1°C (34°F) or lower].	Malfunction of the passenger compartment temperature sensor. Malfunction of the wiring harness. Malfunction of the air conditioner control unit.
	The following conditions are activated when the passenger compartment temperature sensor is cooled [1°C (34°F) or lower]: • The compressor stops. • The temperature of the outflow air becomes that of maximum heating. • The blower speed becomes M or HI speed. • The air-flow outlets from which air is flowing are the FOOT outlets.		

Operation step	Normal operation	Abnormal operation	Probable cause(s)
Follow the procedures described below to check the operation of the photo sensor. 1. Press the AUTO switch. 2. Set the temperature setting to 23°C (74°F). 3. Touch the passenger compartment temperature sensor to change to the cooling operation. 4. Expose the photo sensor to light.	The blower speed increases when the photo sensor is exposed to light.	The blower speed does not change when the photo sensor is exposed to light or shielded from light.	Malfunction of the photo sensor. Damaged or disconnected wiring of the wiring harness. Malfunction of the air conditioner control unit.
	The blower speed decreases when the photo sensor is covered by hand (to shield it from light).		
Follow the procedures described below to check the operation of the engine coolant temperature switch. 1. Press the AUTO switch. 2. Set the temperature setting to 23°C (74°F). 3. Cool the passenger compartment temperature sensor to 20°C (68°F) or lower. 4. After starting the engine, disconnect and reconnect the connector of the engine coolant temperature switch.	The blower speed changes to low speed, and the air-flow outlets from which air is flowing are the DEF outlets, when the connector of the engine coolant temperature switch is disconnected.	There is no change when the connector of the engine coolant temperature switch is disconnected.	Malfunction of the air conditioner control unit. Malfunction of the wiring harness.
	The blower speed increases, and the air-flow outlets from which air is flowing are the FOOT, FACE/FOOT or FACE outlets, when the connector of the engine coolant temperature switch is connected.	The air-flow outlets from which air is flowing remain the DEF outlets when the connector of the engine coolant temperature switch is connected.	Malfunction of the engine coolant temperature switch. Damaged or disconnected wiring of the wiring harness. Malfunction of the air conditioner control unit.

TROUBLESHOOTING BY SYMPTOM—3000GT

No.	Symptom	Probable cause	Remedy
1	Air conditioner does not operate when the ignition switch in the ON position.	Open-circuited power circuit harness	Correct harness.
		Defective control panel	Replace control panel.
		Defective air conditioner control unit	Check diagnosis output.
2	Interior temperature does not raise (No warm air coming out).	Defective room-temperature sensor input circuit	Check diagnosis output. Replace defective parts.
		Defective air mix damper potentiometer input circuit	
		Defective air mix damper drive motor	Replace air mix damper drive motor.
		Incorrect engagement of air mix damper drive motor lever and air mix damper	Engage correctly.
		Sticking air mix damper	Correct air mix damper.
		Open-circuited harness between air mix damper drive motor and air conditioner control unit	Correct harness.
		Defective control panel	Replace control panel.
		Defective air conditioner control unit	Replace air conditioner control unit.
3	Interior temperature does not lower (No cold air coming out).	Defective room-temperature sensor input circuit	Check diagnosis output. Replace defective parts.
		Defective outside-air-temperature sensor input circuit	
		Defective air thermo sensor input circuit	
		Defective refrigerant-temperature sensor input circuit	
		Defective air mix damper potentiometer input circuit	
		Defective photo sensor	Replace photo sensor.
		Defective air mix damper drive motor	Replace air mix damper drive motor.
		Incorrect engagement of air mix damper drive motor lever and air mix damper	Engage correctly.
		Sticking air mix damper	Correct air mix damper.
		Open-circuited harness between air mix damper drive motor and air conditioner control unit	Correct harness.
		Open-circuited harness between photo sensor and air conditioner control unit	Correct harness.
		Defective air-conditioner compressor relay in the relay box	Replace.
3	Interior temperature does not lower (No cold air coming out)	Defective water-temperature sensor	Replace water-temperature sensor.
		Refrigerant leak	Charge refrigerant, correct leak.
		Defective air inlet sensor	Replace air inlet sensor.
		Defective magnetic clutch	Replace.
		Defective belt lock controller	Replace belt lock controller.
		Defective control panel	Replace control panel.
		Defective air conditioner control unit	Replace air conditioner control unit.
4	Blower motor does not rotate.	Defective blower motor	Replace blower motor.
		Blown thermal fuse inside power transistor	Replace power transistor.
		Defective heater relay	Replace heater relay.
		Open-circuited harness between fuse and heater relay	Correct harness.
		Open-circuited harness between heater relay and blower motor	
		Open-circuited harness between power transistor and air conditioner control unit	Correct harness.
		Defective control panel	Replace control panel.
		Defective air conditioner control unit	Replace air conditioner control unit.
5	Blower motor does not stop rotating.	Defective blower motor relay	Replace power relay.
		Short-circuited harness between blower motor relay and power transistor air conditioner control unit	Correct harness.
		Defective control panel	Replace control panel.
		Defective air conditioner control unit	Replace air conditioner control unit.
6	Inside/outside-air selector damper does not operate.	Defective inside/outside-air selector drive motor	Replace inside/outside-air selector drive motor.
		Incorrect engagement of inside/outside-air selector drive motor and inside/outside-air selector damper	Engage correctly.
		Malfunctioning inside/outside-air selector damper	Correct inside/outside-air selector damper.
		Open-circuited harness between inside/outside-air selector motor and air conditioner control unit	Correct harness.

TROUBLESHOOTING BY SYMPTOM—3000GT

No.	Symptom	Probable cause	Remedy
6	Inside/outside-air selector damper does not operate.	Defective control panel	Replace control panel.
		Defective air conditioner control unit	Replace air conditioner control unit.
7	Outlet selector damper does not operate.	Defective outlet selector damper potentiometer input circuit	Check diagnosis output. Replace defective parts.
		Defective outlet selector drive motor	Replace outlet selector drive motor.
		Incorrect engagement of outlet selector drive motor and outlet selector damper	Engage correctly.
		Malfunctioning DEF., FACE, and FOOT damper	Correct DEF., FACE, and FOOT damper.
		Open-circuited harness between outlet selector motor and control unit	Correct harness.
		Defective control panel	Replace control panel.
		Defective air conditiner control unit	Replace air conditioner control unit.
8	Condenser fan does not operate when the air conditioner is activated.	Defective condenser fan motor relay	Replace power relay.
		Defective water temperature switch	Replace water temperature switch.
		Defective condenser fan motor	Replace condenser fan motor.
9	Air-conditioner graphic display does not function correctly	Open-circuited harness between control panel and air conditioner control unit	Correct harness.
		Defective control panel	Replace control panel.
		Defective air conditioner control unit	Replace air conditioner control unit.
10	Set temperature returns to 25°C (112°F) when the ignition switch is turned ON and OFF.	Open-circuited power circuit harness	Correct harness.
		Defective air conditioner control unit	Replace air conditioner control unit.

DIAGNOSIS DISPLAY PATTERNS AND CODES—STARION

Code No.	Diagnosis display pattern	Malfunction (A/C condition)	Probable cause	Failsafe
0	 12V 0V Continuous	Normal	–	–
2	 12V 0V	Open or shorted interior temperature sensor circuit or faulty upper in-car sensor	• Disconnected interior temperature sensor connector • Open or shorted internal wiring of interior temperature sensor • Open or shorted harness in interior temperature sensor circuit or disconnected connector	Set interior temperature sensor input signal at 25°C (77°F)
3	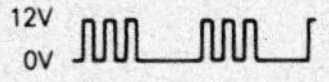 12V 0V	Open or shorted foot area temperature sensor circuit or faulty foot area temperature sensor	• Disconnected foot area temperature sensor connector • Open or shorted internal wiring of foot area temperature sensor • Open or shorted harness in foot area temperature sensor circuit or disconnected connector	Set foot area temperature sensor input signal at 25°C (77°F)
4	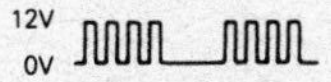 12V 0V	Open or shorted wiring of thermistor circuit or faulty thermistor	• Disconnected thermistor connector • Open or shorted internal wiring of thermistor • Open or shorted harness in thermistor circuit or disconnected connector	Set thermistor input signal at 1°C (33.8°F) and turn off compressor
7	 12V 0V	Open or shorted blend air damper potentiometer circuit or faulty blend air damper potentiometer	• Disconnected blend air damper potentiometer connector • Open or shorted internal wiring of blend air damper potentiometer • Open or shorted harness in blend air damper potentiometer circuit or disconnected connector	Set blend air damper at MAX HOT position
–	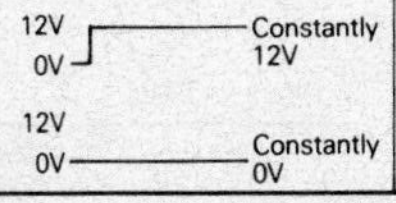 12V 0V Constantly 12V 12V 0V Constantly 0V	Internal failure of control unit	• Replace control unit	–

NOTE
1. Code Nos. 1, 5, 6 and 8 are intentionally omitted.
2. If two or more troubles are caused at the same time, one with the largest code No. is displayed.
3. The contents of troubles are stored until the ignition switch is turned off.

DIAGNOSIS OF DISPLAY PATTERN 2—STARION

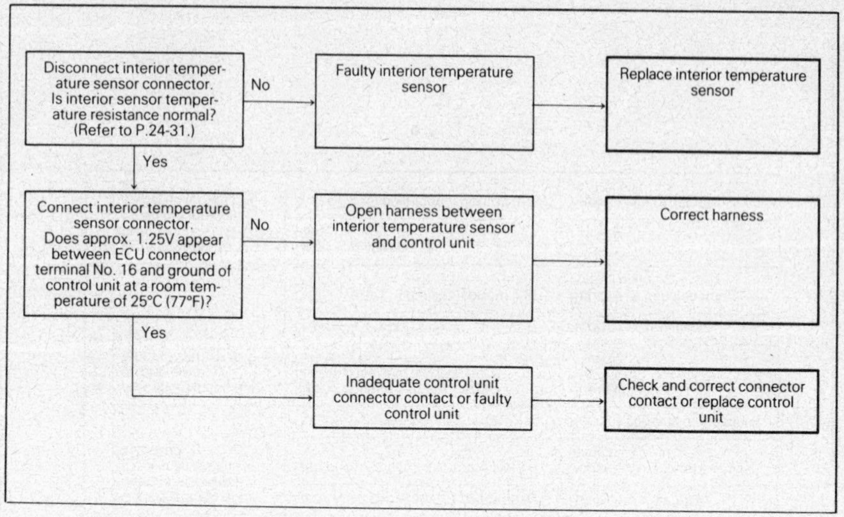
Disconnect interior temperature sensor connector. Is interior sensor temperature resistance normal? (Refer to P.24-31.)
No
Faulty interior temperature sensor
Replace interior temperature sensor
Yes
Connect interior temperature sensor connector. Does approx. 1.25V appear between ECU connector terminal No. 16 and ground of control unit at a room temperature of 25°C (77°F)?
No
Open harness between interior temperature sensor and control unit
Correct harness
Yes
Inadequate control unit connector contact or faulty control unit
Check and correct connector contact or replace control unit

DIAGNOSIS OF DISPLAY PATTERN 4—STARION

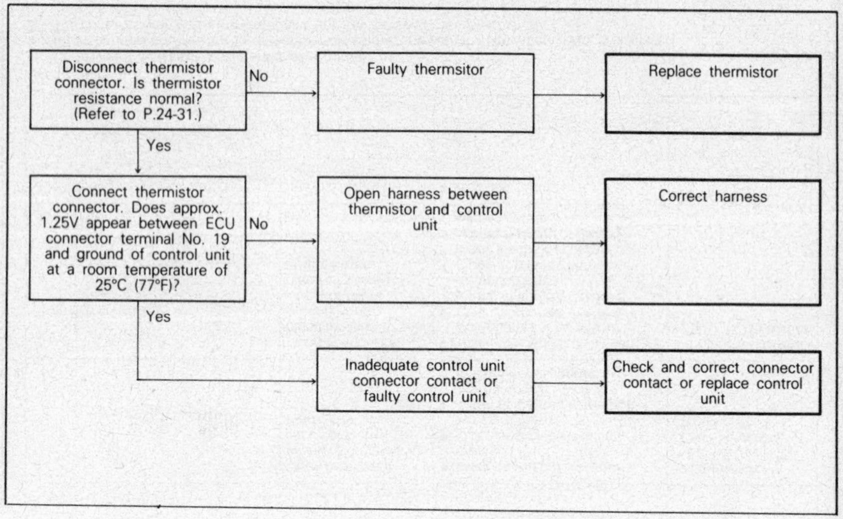
Disconnect thermistor connector. Is thermistor resistance normal? (Refer to P.24-31.)
No
Faulty thermsitor
Replace thermistor
Yes
Connect thermistor connector. Does approx. 1.25V appear between ECU connector terminal No. 19 and ground of control unit at a room temperature of 25°C (77°F)?
No
Open harness between thermistor and control unit
Correct harness
Yes
Inadequate control unit connector contact or faulty control unit
Check and correct connector contact or replace control unit

DIAGNOSIS OF DISPLAY PATTERN 3—STARION

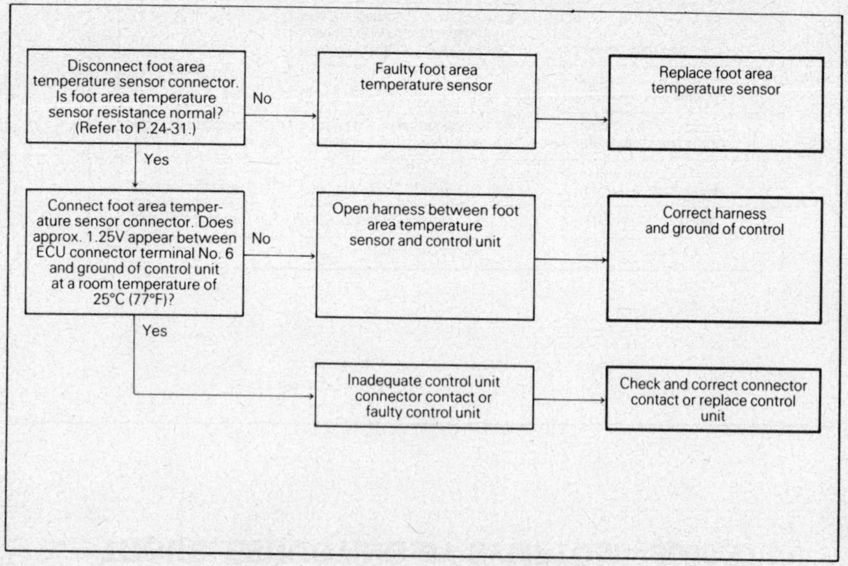
Disconnect foot area temperature sensor connector. Is foot area temperature sensor resistance normal? (Refer to P.24-31.)
No
Faulty foot area temperature sensor
Replace foot area temperature sensor
Yes
Connect foot area temperature sensor connector. Does approx. 1.25V appear between ECU connector terminal No. 6 and ground of control unit at a room temperature of 25°C (77°F)?
No
Open harness between foot area temperature sensor and control unit
Correct harness and ground of control
Yes
Inadequate control unit connector contact or faulty control unit
Check and correct connector contact or replace control unit

DIAGNOSIS OF DISPLAY PATTERN 7—STARION

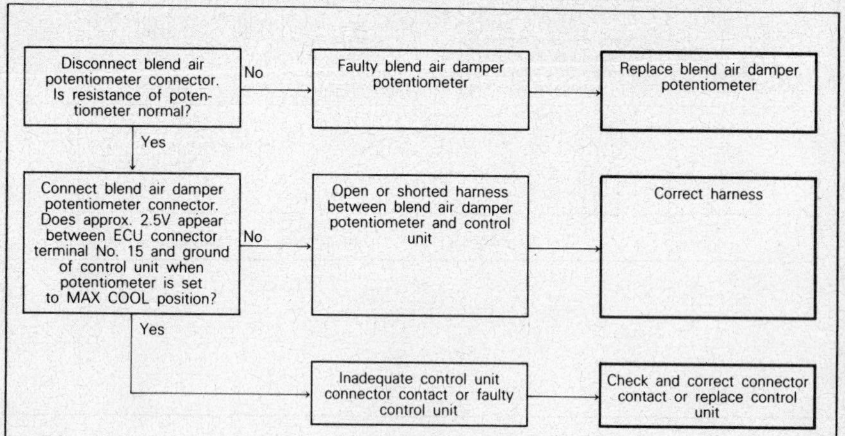
Disconnect blend air potentiometer connector. Is resistance of potentiometer normal?
No
Faulty blend air damper potentiometer
Replace blend air damper potentiometer
Yes
Connect blend air damper potentiometer connector. Does approx. 2.5V appear between ECU connector terminal No. 15 and ground of control unit when potentiometer is set to MAX COOL position?
No
Open or shorted harness between blend air damper potentiometer and control unit
Correct harness
Yes
Inadequate control unit connector contact or faulty control unit
Check and correct connector contact or replace control unit

NOTE
"ECU" (electronic control unit) indicates the automatic air conditioner control unit.

CONTROL UNIT POWER CIRCUIT CHECK—STARION

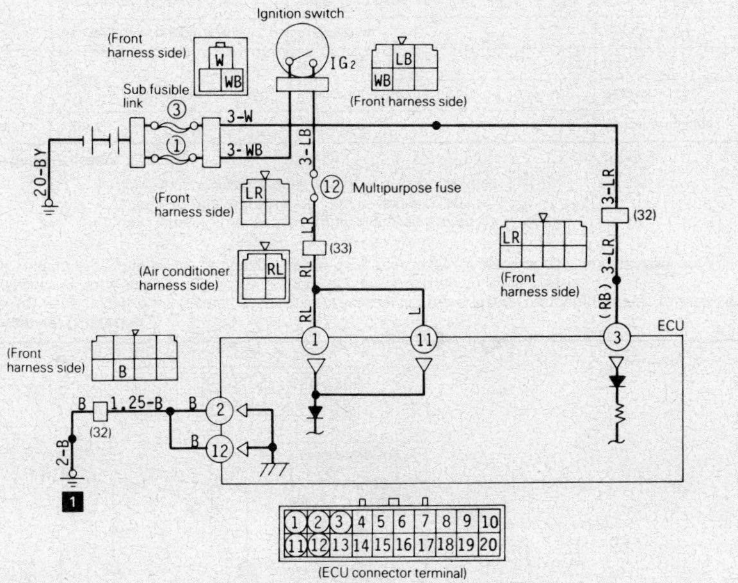
Ignition switch
IG2
(Front harness side)
W
WB
LB
WB
(Front harness side)
Sub fusible link
3
1
3-W
3-WB
3-LB
20-BY
12
Multipurpose fuse
(Front harness side)
LR
LR
(33)
RL
(Air conditioner harness side)
RL
RL
L
3-LR
(32)
3-LR
(RB)
LR
(Front harness side)
ECU
1
11
3
(Front harness side)
B
B
1.25-B
B
(32)
2
12
B
2-B
1
1 2 3 4 5 6 7 8 9 10
11 12 13 14 15 16 17 18 19 20
(ECU connector terminal)

Description of Operation

(1) Normally, current flows to the sub fusible link ③ to ECU to ground. (Backup current)
(2) When the ignition switch is placed in the "ON" position, current flows to ignition switch (IG_2) to multipurpose fuse to the ground.

ECU terminal voltage

Terminal No.	Signal	Condition	Terminal voltage
3	Backup power supply signal	At all times	Approx. VB
1, 11	ECU power supply signal	When ignition switch is ON	Approx. VB
2, 12	ECU ground signal	At all times	0 V

NOTE
VB: Battery Voltage

POTENTIOMETER CIRCUIT CHECK—STARION

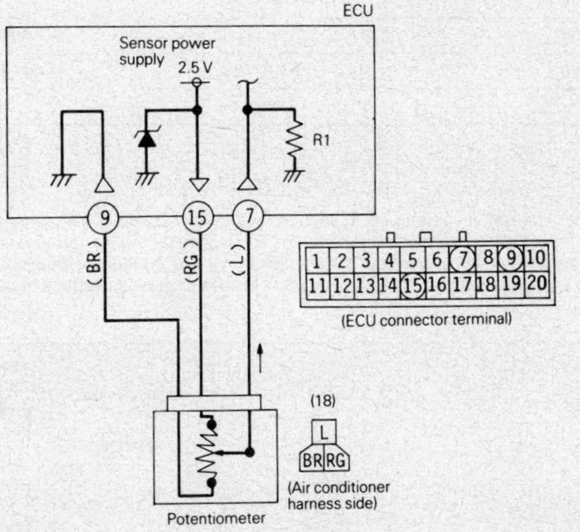
ECU
Sensor power supply
2.5 V
R1
9
15
7
(BR)
(RG)
(L)
1 2 3 4 5 6 7 8 9 10
11 12 13 14 15 16 17 18 19 20
(ECU connector terminal)
(18)
L
BR RG
(Air conditioner harness side)
Potentiometer

Description of Operation

Air conditioner control unit sensor power supply is applied to the potentiometer.
The terminal voltage of ⑦ is a voltage divided by the potentiometer and resistor R_1.
The terminal voltage of ⑦ changes proportionately with the blend air damper opening.

Diagnosis – No. 7 blend air damper is set to the MAX HOT or MAX COOL position.

ECU terminal voltage

Terminal No.	Signal	Condition	Terminal voltage
7	Blend air damper potentiometer (output) signal	Blend air damper is in MAX COOL position	Approx. 0.2V
		Blend air damper is in MAX HOT position	Approx. 2.3V
9	Blend air damper potentiometer ⊖ signal	At all times	0 V
15	Sensor power supply signal	At all times	Approx. 2.5V

AIR CONDITIONING SENSORS CIRCUIT CHECK STARION

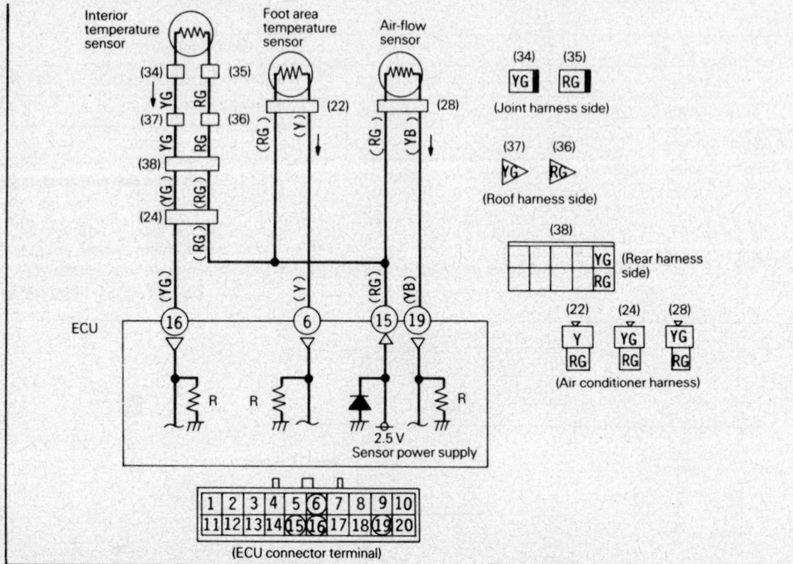
Interior temperature sensor
Foot area temperature sensor
Air-flow sensor
(34)
(35)
(37)
(36)
(38)
(24)
(22)
(28)
ECU
R
2.5 V
Sensor power supply
(Joint harness side)
(Roof harness side)
(Rear harness side)
(Air conditioner harness)
(ECU connector terminal)

Description of Operation
Each sensor uses negative characteristic thermistor to convert the ambient temperature into resistance. Air conditioner control unit sensor power supply (2.5 V) is applied to each sensor.
Terminal voltage of ⑥, ⑯ or ⑲ is voltage devided by resistance of each sensor and resistor R.

Diagnosis – No. 2 interior temperature sensor input signal is set to 25°C (77°F).
No. 3 foot area temperature sensor input signal is set to 25°C (77°F).
No. 4 air-flow sensor input signal is set to 1°C (33.8°F).

ECU terminal voltage

Terminal No.	Signal	Condition	Terminal voltage
6	Foot temperature sensor (4 kΩ) signal	Interior temperature is 25°C (77°F).	Approx. 1.25V
		Harness is broken.	0 V
15	Sensor power supply signal	At all times	Approx. 2.5V
16	Interior temperature sensor (4 kΩ) signal	Interior temperature is 25°C (77°F).	Approx. 1.25V
		Harness is broken.	0 V
19	Air-flow sensor (4 kΩ) signal	With air conditioner turned OFF, interior temperature is 25°C (77°F).	Approx. 1.25V
		Harness is broken.	0 V

PHOTO SENSOR CIRCUIT CHECK—STARION

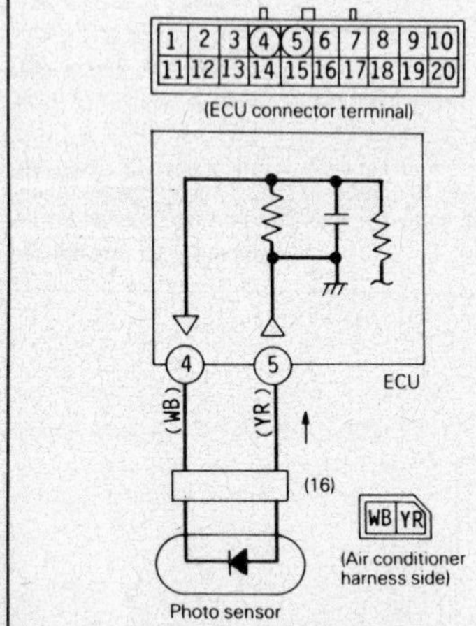
(ECU connector terminal)
ECU
(WB)
(YR)
(16)
Photo sensor
(Air conditioner harness side)

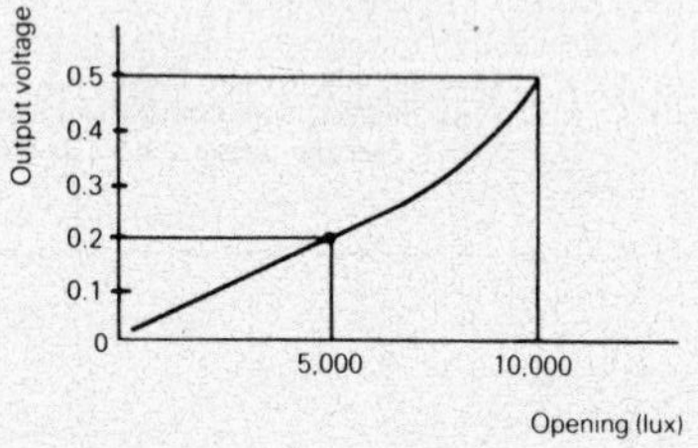
Output voltage
0.5
0.4
0.3
0.2
0.1
0
5,000
10,000
Opening (lux)

Description of Operation
The photo sensor is used to control increase of vehicle interior temperature with the amount of solar radiation. In combination with regulated resistance of ECU, it generates electromotive force corresponding to the amount of solar radiation received by the light receiving surface of photodiode. ECU terminal ⑤ (photo sensor ⊖) is grounded inside the unit. Therefore, negative voltage is generated at terminal ④.

ECU terminal voltage

Terminal No.	Signal	Condition	Terminal voltage
5	Photo sensor ⊖	At all times	0 V
4	Photo sensor ⊕	Luminous intensity: 5,000 lux	Approx. -0.1 V
		Luminous intensity: 10,000 lux	Approx. -0.25 V

ENGINE COOLANT TEMPERATURE UNIT CIRCUIT CHECK—STARION

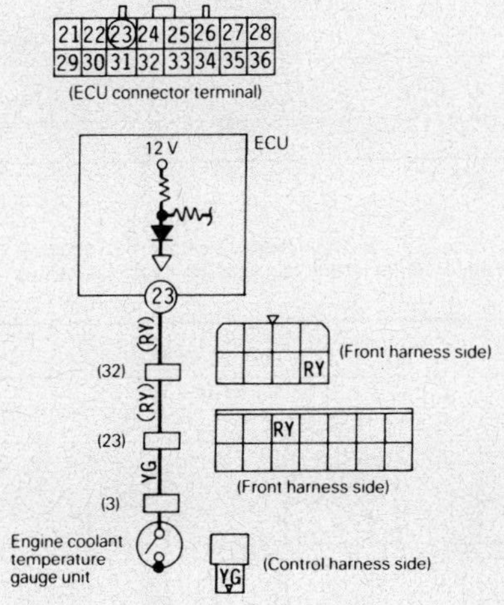
21 22 23 24 25 26 27 28
29 30 31 32 33 34 35 36
(ECU connector terminal)
ECU
12 V
23
(RY)
(32)
(RY)
(23)
YG
(3)
Engine coolant temperature gauge unit
RY
(Front harness side)
RY
(Front harness side)
YG
(Control harness side)

Description of Operation

The engine coolant temperature gauge unit is ON when engine coolant temperature is approx. 50°C (122°F).

ECU terminal voltage

Terminal No.	Signal	Condition	Terminal voltage
23	Engine coolant temperature gauge unit	When engine coolant temperature is ON	Approx. 0.2 to 0.8V
		When engine coolant temperature is OFF	Approx. VB

NOTE
VB: Battery Voltage

BLEND AIR DAMPER MOTOR CIRCUIT CHECK STARION

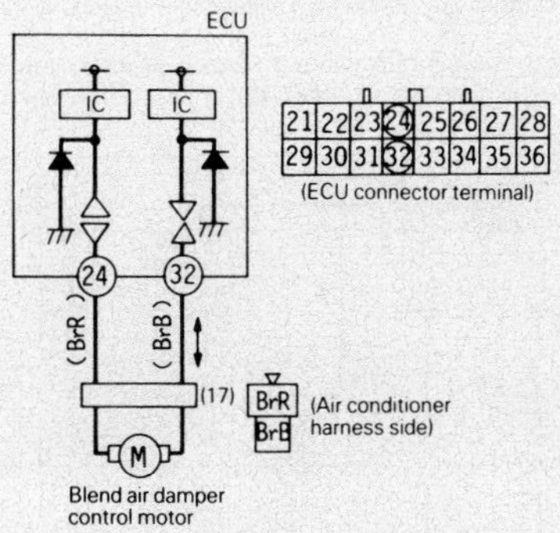
ECU
IC
IC
24
32
(BrR)
(BrB)
(17)
BrR
BrB
(Air conditioner harness side)
Blend air damper control motor
21 22 23 24 25 26 27 28
29 30 31 32 33 34 35 36
(ECU connector terminal)

Description of Operation

The DC motor is operated, reversed or stopped according to the signals from ECU to control the position of blend air damper in combination with the potentiometer.

ECU terminal voltage

Terminal No.	Signal	Condition	Terminal voltage
24	Blend air damper control motor	When motor (reverse) is ON	Approx. VB
		When motor is OFF	0 V
32	Blend air damper control motor	When motor (forward) is ON	0 V
		When motor is OFF	Approx. VB

NOTE
VB: Battery Voltage

DAMPER MOTORS CIRCUIT CHECK—STARION

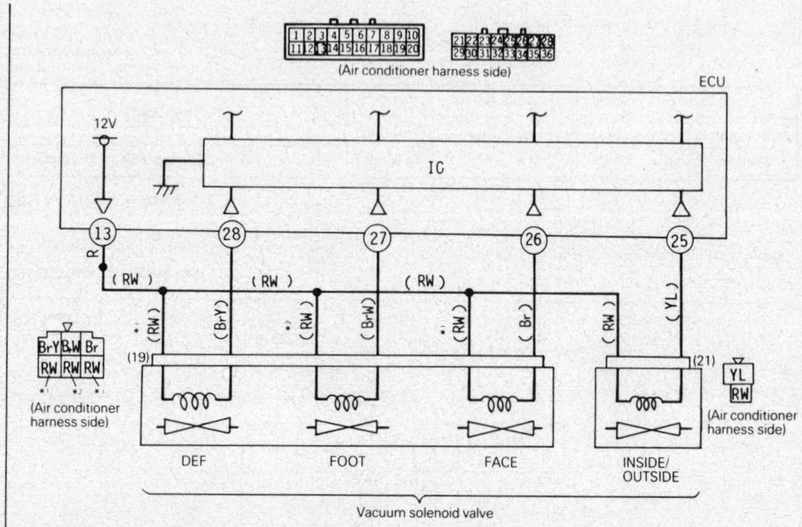
(Air conditioner harness side)
ECU
12V
IC
(Air conditioner harness side)
DEF
FOOT
FACE
INSIDE/OUTSIDE
Vacuum solenoid valve

Description of Operation

Upon receipt of signals from ECU, the inside/outside air selection and air outlet mode selection are controlled by the vacuum actuator and link through the vacuum solenoid valve.

ECU terminal voltage

Terminal No.	Signal	Condition	Terminal voltage
13	Vacuum solenoid valve power supply	–	Approx. VB
25	Inside/outside air switching vacuum solenoid valve	When ON (inside air)	Approx. 0.2 to 0.8V
		When OFF (outside air)	Approx. VB
26	Air outlet mode (FACE) selection vacuum solenoid valve	When ON (in FACE mode)	Approx. 0.2 to 0.8V
		When OFF (other than above)	Approx. VB
27	Air outlet mode (FOOT) selection vacuum solenoid valve	When ON (in FOOT or DEF mode)	Approx. 0.2 to 0.8V
		When OFF (other than above)	Approx. VB
28	Air outlet mode (DEF) selection vacuum solenoid valve	When ON (in DEF or DEF/FACE mode)	Approx. 0.2 to 0.8V
		When OFF (other than above)	Approx. VB

NOTE
VB: Battery Voltage

BLOWER MOTOR CIRCUIT CHECK—STARION

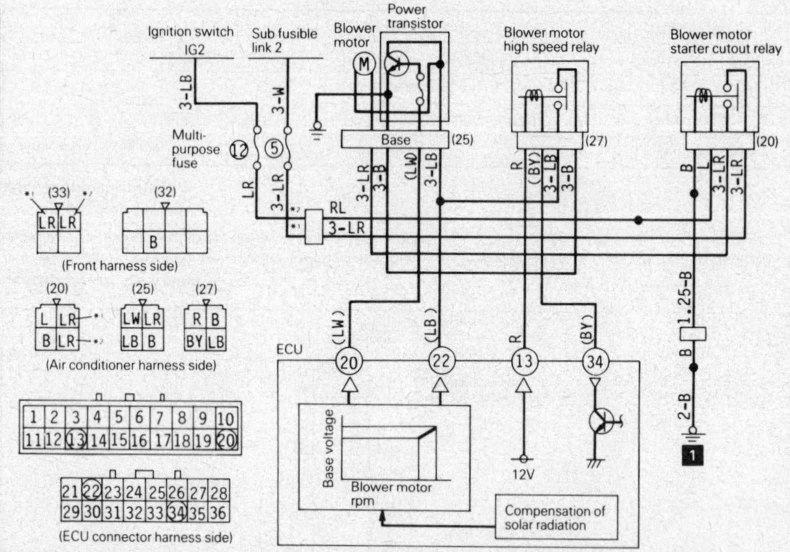
Ignition switch IG2
Sub fusible link 2
Blower motor
Power transistor
Blower motor high speed relay
Blower motor starter cutout relay
Multi-purpose fuse
Base
(Front harness side)
(Air conditioner harness side)
ECU
Base voltage
Blower motor rpm
12V
Compensation of solar radiation
(ECU connector harness side)

Description of Operation

In accordance with the magnitude of the signal from ECU (voltage applied to the base terminal of the power transistor), this power transistor controls current flowing through the blower motor for control of blower moter operation.

For maximum operation (HI operation) in cooling, the signal to the power transistor is stopped and the blower motor HI relay is driven and battery voltage is applied directly to the blower motor to run the blower motor at the maximum speed (HI operation).

ECU terminal voltage

Terminal No.	Signal	Condition	Terminal voltage
13	Blower motor high speed relay power supply	At all times	Approx. VB
20	Power transistor (base)	When blower is rotating	0 to 5 V
22	Blower motor	When switch HI is ON	Approx. 0 to 1 V
		When switch LO is ON	Approx. 6 V
		When switch is OFF	Approx. VB
34	Blower motor high speed relay	When blower speed is HI	Approx. 0.2 to 0.8V
		When blower speed is other than HI	Approx. VB

NOTE
VB: Battery Voltage

DIAGNOSIS DISPLAY PATTERNS AND CODES—SIGMA

Code	Display patterns (output codes) (use with voltmeter)	Nature of the malfunction (Condition of air conditioner)	Probable cause(s)	Fail safe
NOR-MAL!!	ON / OFF Continuous	normal	—	—
02	ON / OFF	Damaged or disconnected wiring, or short-circuit, of the passenger compartment temperature sensor circuit, or malfunction of the passenger compartment temperature sensor.	• Positional deviation of the passenger compartment temperature sensor connector. • Damaged or disconnected wiring, or short-circuit, within the passenger compartment temperature sensor. • Damaged or disconnected wiring, or short-circuit, or positional deviation, of the passenger compartment temperature sensor circuit's wiring harness, or disconnection of the connector.	Passenger compartment temperature sensor input signal setting to 25°C (77°F).
03	ON / OFF	Damaged or disconnected wiring, or short-circuit, of the outside-air-temperature sensor circuit, or malfunction of the outside-air-temperature sensor.	• Disconnection of the outside-air-temperature sensor connector. • Internal damaged or disconnected wiring, or short-circuit, of the outside-air-temperature sensor. • Damaged or disconnected wiring, or short-circuit, of the outside-air-temperature sensor circuit wiring harness, or disconnection of the connector.	Outside-air-temperature sensor input signal setting to 25°C (77°F).
04	ON / OFF	Damaged or disconnected wiring, or short-circuit, of the air-flow sensor, or malfunction of the air-flow sensor.	• Disconnection of the air-flow sensor connector. • Damaged or disconnected wiring, or short-circuit, of the air-flow sensor circuit wiring harness, or disconnection of the connector.	Air-flow sensor input signal setting to 1°C (34°F); compressor switch OFF.
06	ON / OFF	Damaged or disconnected wiring, or short-circuit, of the blend-air damper potentiometer, or malfunction of the blend-air damper potentiometer.	• Disconnection of the blend-air damper potentiometer connector. • Internal damaged or disconnected wiring, or short-circuit, of the blend-air damper potentiometer. • Damaged or disconnected wiring, or short-circuit, of the blend-air damper potentiometer circuit wiring harness, or disconnection of the connector.	Blend-air damper setting to the MAX-HOT position. Setting to the MAX-COOL position at a setting temperature of 17°C (63°F).
07	ON / OFF	Damaged or disconnected wiring, or short-circuit, of the mode-selection damper potentiometer circuit, or malfunction of the mode-selection damper potentiometer.	• Disconnection of the mode-selection damper potentiometer connector. • Internal damaged or disconnected wiring, or short-circuit, of the mode-selection damper potentiometer. • Damaged or disconnected wiring, or short-circuit, of the mode-selection damper potentiometer circuit wiring harness, or disconnection of the connector.	Mode-selection damper setting to the DEF/FACE position. Setting to the FACE position at a setting temperature of 17°C (63°F).
08	ON / OFF	Damaged or disconnected wiring, or short-circuit, of the blower switch circuit, or malfunction of the blower switch.	• Disconnection of the blower switch connector. • Malfunction of the blower switch. • Damaged or disconnected wiring, or short-circuit, of the blower switch circuit wiring harness, or disconnection of the connector.	Setting of the air-flow control to the AUTO mode.
—	ON / OFF Always illuminated. ON / OFF Always not illuminated.	Internal malfunction of the air conditioner control unit.	• Malfunction of the air conditioner control unit.	—

NOTE: (1) If two or more abnormal conditions occur at the same time, the code numbers are alternately displayed, in order, repeatedly.
(2) The nature of the malfunction is entered and stored in the memory from the time the malfunction occurs until the ignition switch is next turned to OFF.

CONTROL UNIT POWER CIRCUIT CHECK—SIGMA

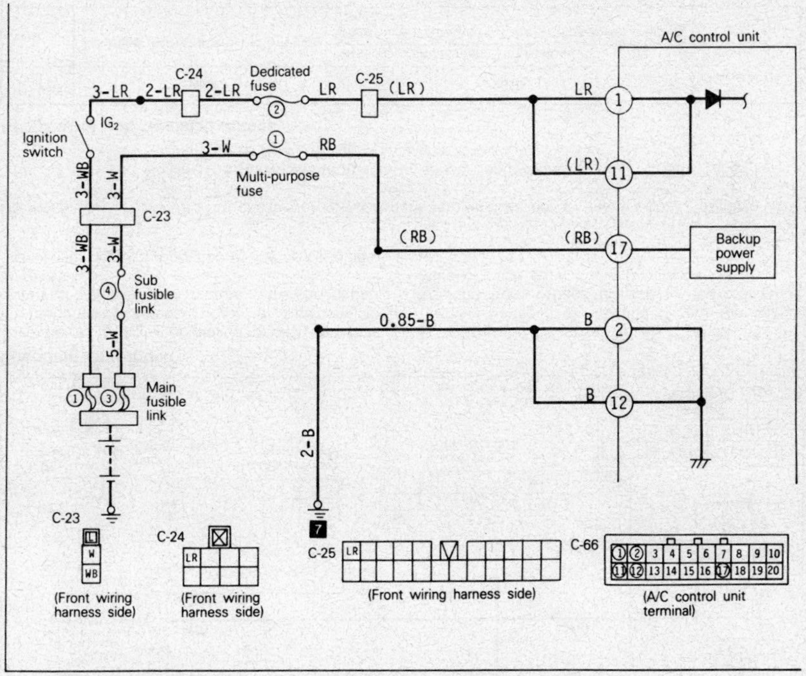
A/C control unit
Ignition switch
IG2
3-LR
2-LR
C-24
Dedicated fuse
LR
C-25
(LR)
3-W
Multi-purpose fuse
RB
3-WB
C-23
Sub fusible link
5-W
Main fusible link
(RB)
Backup power supply
0.85-B
B
2-B
(Front wiring harness side)
C-66
(A/C control unit terminal)

Operation description

(1) Current always flows to the sub-fusible link ④, the multi-purpose fuse ①, the air conditioner control unit, and to ground. (back-up power source)

(2) When the ignition switch is switched ON, current flows to the ignition switch (IG_2), the dedicated fuse ②, the air conditioner control unit, and to ground.

A/C control unit terminal voltage

Terminal No.	Signal	Condition	Terminal voltage (V)
1	IG_2 power supply	Ignition key: ON position	Over 10
		Ignition key: other than ON position	0
2	Ground	—	0
11	IG_2 power supply	Ignition key: ON position	Over 10
		Ignition key: other than ON position	0
12	Ground	—	0
17	Battery power supply	When battery is connected	Over 10
		When battery is not connected	0

POTENTIOMETER CIRCUIT CHECK—SIGMA

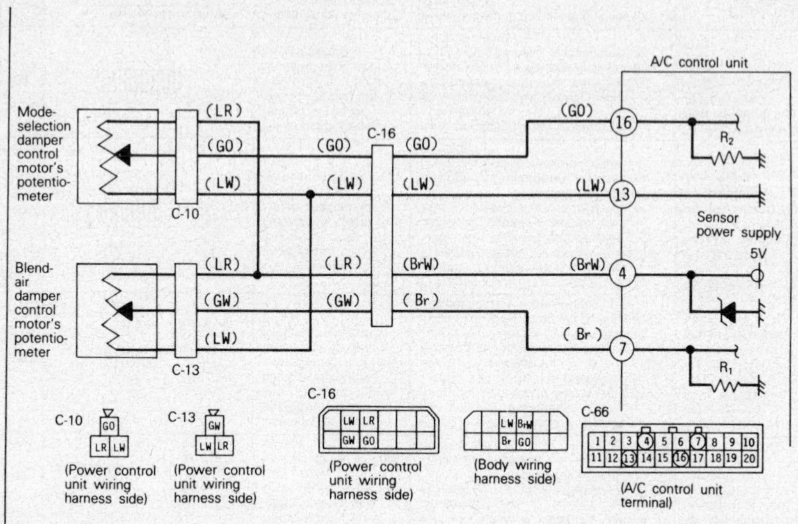
A/C control unit
Mode-selection damper control motor's potentiometer
Blend-air damper control motor's potentiometer
Sensor power supply
5V
C-10
C-13
C-16
C-66
(Power control unit wiring harness side)
(Body wiring harness side)
(A/C control unit terminal)

Operation description

The sensor power supply (5V) of the air conditioner control unit is applied to each potentiometer.

Blend-air damper control motor's potentiometer
Terminal voltage ⑦ is the value resulting from voltage division by the resistance value of potentiometer and resistance R_1.
Terminal voltage ⑦ changes proportionally to the degree of opening of the blend-air damper.

Mode-selector damper control motor's potentiometer
Terminal voltage ⑯ is the value resulting from voltage division by the resistance value of potentiometer and resistance R_2.

Diagnosis No.06 (The blend-air damper is held at the MAX HOT or MAX COOL position.)
No.07 (The mode-selector damper at the FACE or DEF/FACE position.)

A/C control unit terminal voltage

Terminal No.	Signal	Condition	Terminal voltage (V)
7	Blend-air damper control motor's potentiometer	MAX. HOT position	approx. 5
16	Mode-selector damper control motor's potentiometer	FACE position	approx. 5
		When there is damaged or disconnected wiring of wiring harness	0
13	Potentiometer and blower switch ground	—	0
4	Air-flow sensor and passenger compartment temperature sensor power supply	—	approx. 5

AIR CONDITIONING SENSORS CIRCUIT CHECK SIGMA

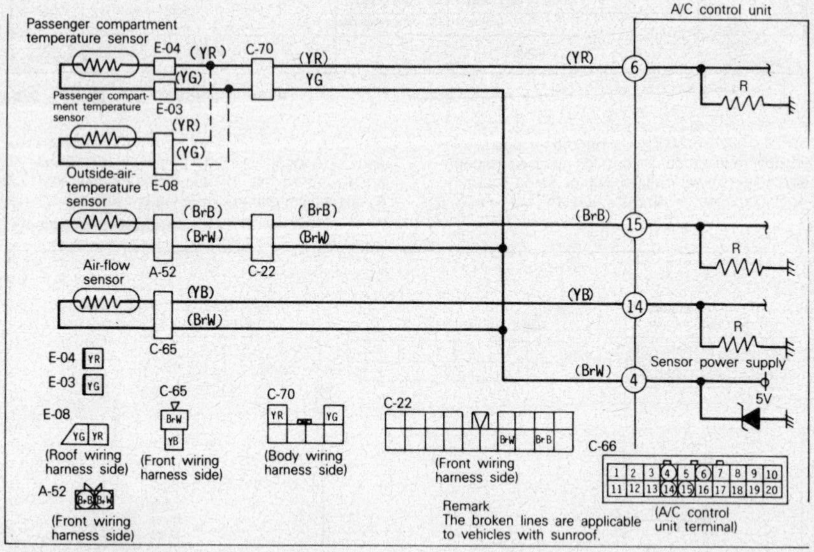
A/C control unit
Passenger compartment temperature sensor
Passenger compartment temperature sensor
Outside-air-temperature sensor
Air-flow sensor
Sensor power supply
5V
E-04
E-03
E-08
A-52
C-65
C-70
C-22
C-66
(Roof wiring harness side)
(Front wiring harness side)
(Body wiring harness side)
(A/C control unit terminal)
Remark
The broken lines are applicable to vehicles with sunroof.

Operation description

The type of thermistor employed for each sensor is the negative-characteristic type; it functions to convert the ambient temperature of the sensor part to resistance.
The sensor power supply (5V) of the air conditioner control unit is applied to each sensor.
Terminal voltages ⑮, ⑭ and ⑥ are the values resulting from voltage division by the resistance value of each sensor and resistance R.

Diagnosis No.02 [The passenger compartment temperature sensor input signal is held to 25°C (77°F).]
No.03 [The outside-air-temperature sensor input signal is held to 25°C (77°F).]
No.04 [The air-flow sensor input signal is held to 1°C (34°F).]

A/C control unit terminal voltage

Terminal No.	Signal	Condition	Terminal voltage (V)
6	Passenger compartment temperature sensor	Passenger compartment temperature 25°C (77°F)	approx. 2.5
		When there is damaged or disconnected wiring of wiring harness	0
15	Outside-air-temperature sensor	Passenger compartment temperature 25°C (77°F)	approx. 2.5
		When there is damaged or disconnected wiring of wiring harness	0
14	Air-flow sensor	Passenger compartment temperature 25°C (77°F)	approx. 2.5
		When there is damaged or disconnected wiring of wiring harness	0
4	Air-flow sensor and passenger compartment temperature sensor power supply	—	approx. 5

PHOTO SENSOR CIRCUIT CHECK—SIGMA

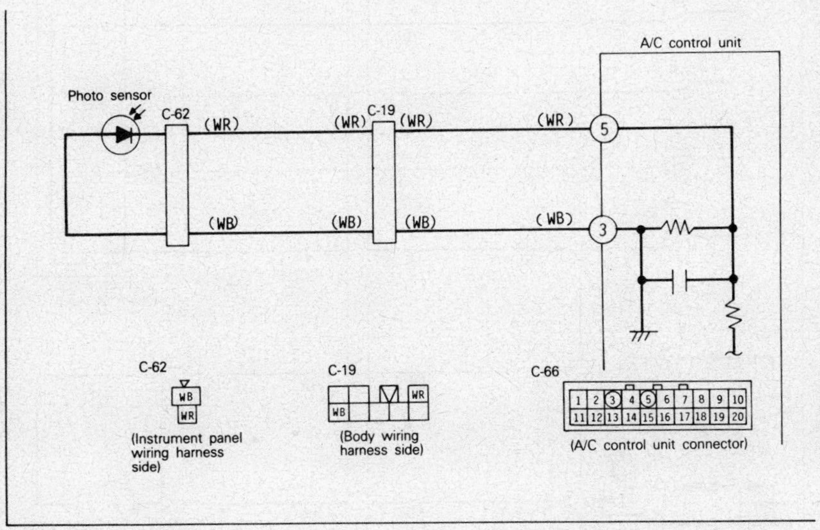
A/C control unit
Photo sensor
C-62
(WR)
(WB)
C-19
(WR)
(WB)
5
3
C-62
WB
WR
(Instrument panel wiring harness side)
C-19
WB
WR
(Body wiring harness side)
C-66
1 2 3 4 5 6 7 8 9 10
11 12 13 14 15 16 17 18 19 20
(A/C control unit connector)

Operation description

The photo sensor is a sensor that functions to regulate so that an increase of the temperature within the passenger compartment (resulting from an increase in the amount of solar radiation) is suppressed.
By a combination with the adjustment resistance of the air conditioner control unit, electromotive force is generated in accordance with the amount of solar radiation received at the light-receptor surface of the photo diode.
Because the air conditioner control unit terminal ③ (solar-radiation sensor negative ⊖ terminal) is grounded within the unit, a negative voltage is generated at terminal ⑤.

A/C control unit terminal voltage

Terminal No.	Signal	Condition	Terminal voltage (V)
5	Photo sensor	Light intensity: 5,000 lux	approx. −0.1
		Light intensity: 10,000 lux	approx. −0.25
		When there is damaged or disconnected wiring of wiring harness	0
3	Photo sensor ground	—	0

COOLANT TEMPERATURE THERMO SWITCH CIRCUIT CHECK—SIGMA

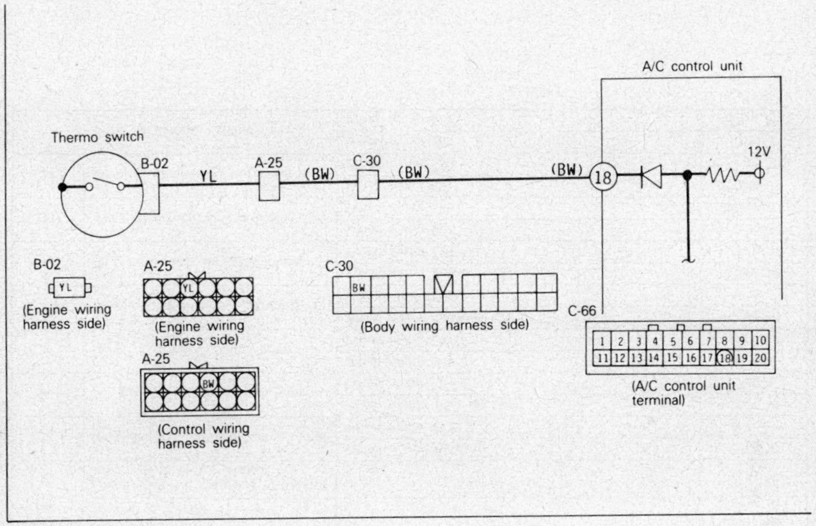
A/C control unit
Thermo switch
B-02
YL
A-25
(BW)
C-30
(BW)
(BW)
18
12V
B-02
YL
(Engine wiring harness side)
A-25
YL
(Engine wiring harness side)
A-25
BW
(Control wiring harness side)
C-30
BW
(Body wiring harness side)
C-66
1 2 3 4 5 6 7 8 9 10
11 12 13 14 15 16 17 18 19 20
(A/C control unit terminal)

Operation description

The thermo switch is switched ON when the engine coolant temperature becomes 50°C (122°F).

A/C control unit terminal voltage

Terminal No.	Signal	Condition	Terminal voltage (V)
18	Engine coolant temperature switch	When switch ON	0 to 1
		When switch OFF	Over 10

DAMPER MOTORS CIRCUIT CHECK—SIGMA

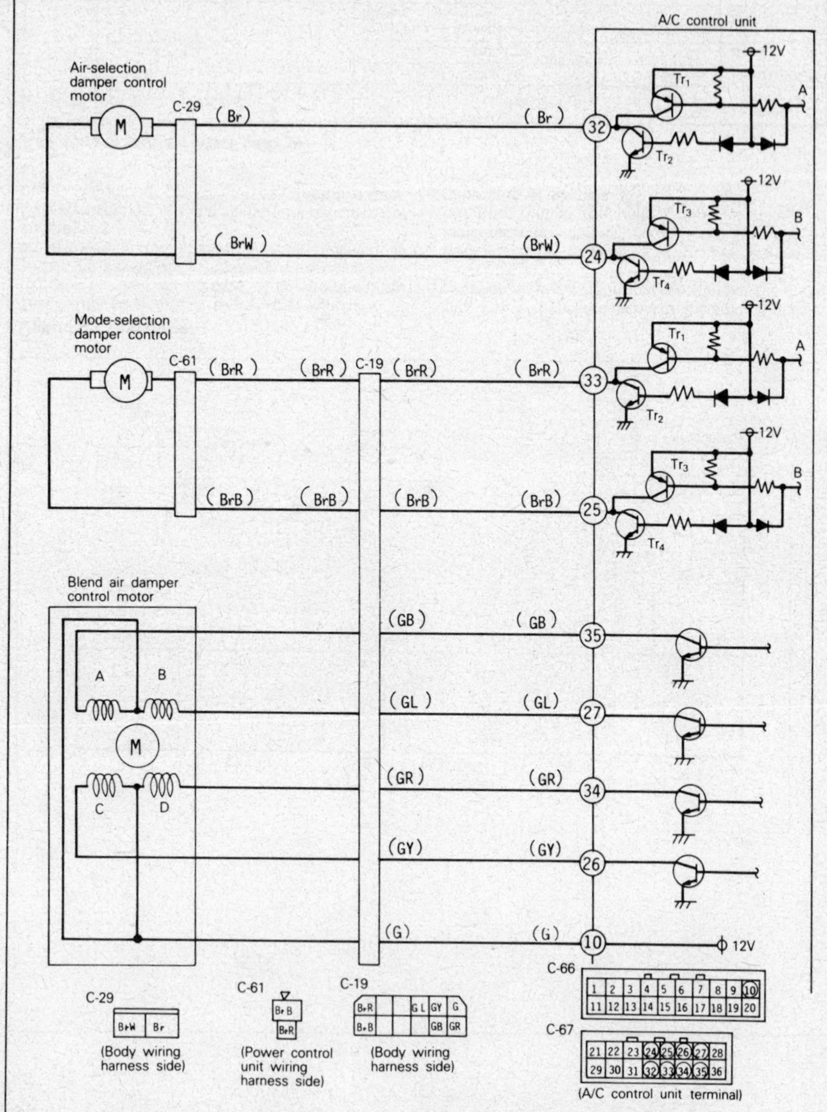
A/C control unit
Air-selection damper control motor
Mode-selection damper control motor
Blend air damper control motor
C-29
C-61
C-19
C-66
C-67
(Br)
(BrW)
(BrR)
(BrB)
(GB)
(GL)
(GR)
(GY)
(G)
12V
Tr1
Tr2
Tr3
Tr4
A
B
C
D
M
(Body wiring harness side)
(Power control unit wiring harness side)
(Body wiring harness side)
(A/C control unit terminal)

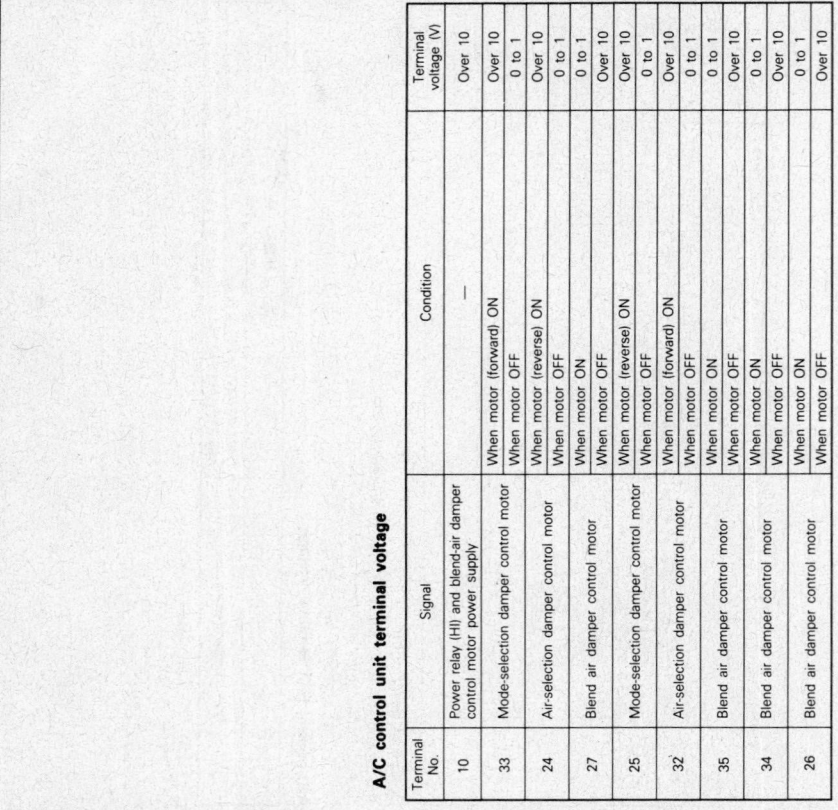

A/C control unit terminal voltage

Terminal No.	Signal	Condition	Terminal voltage (V)
10	Power relay (HI) and blend-air damper control motor power supply	—	Over 10
33	Mode-selection damper control motor	When motor (forward) ON	Over 10
		When motor OFF	0 to 1
24	Air-selection damper control motor	When motor (reverse) ON	Over 10
		When motor OFF	0 to 1
27	Blend air damper control motor	When motor ON	0 to 1
		When motor OFF	Over 10
25	Mode-selection damper control motor	When motor (reverse) ON	Over 10
		When motor OFF	0 to 1
32	Air-selection damper control motor	When motor (forward) ON	Over 10
		When motor OFF	0 to 1
35	Blend air damper control motor	When motor ON	0 to 1
		When motor OFF	Over 10
34	Blend air damper control motor	When motor ON	0 to 1
		When motor OFF	Over 10
26	Blend air damper control motor	When motor ON	0 to 1
		When motor OFF	Over 10

BLOWER MOTOR CIRCUIT CHECK—SIGMA

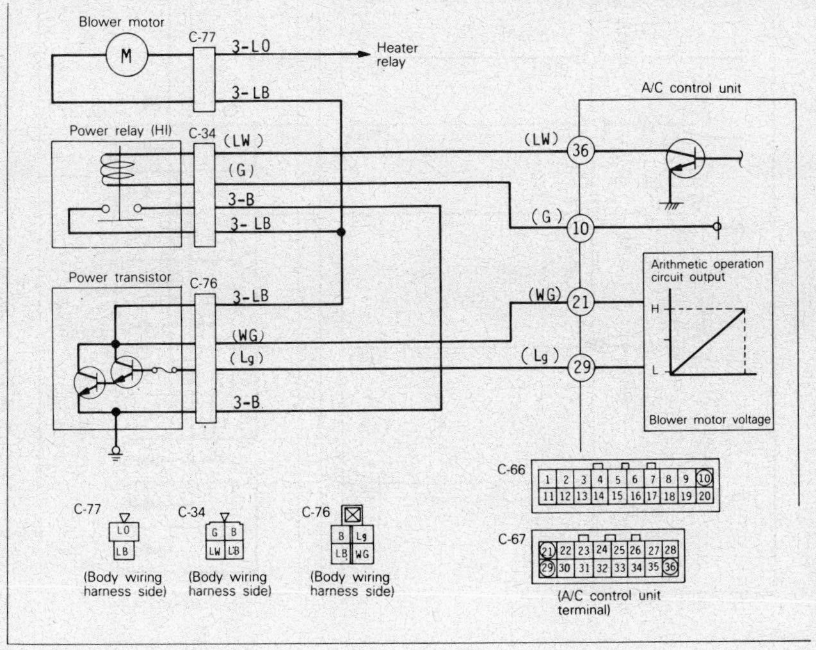
Blower motor
M
C-77
3-LO
Heater relay
3-LB
Power relay (HI)
C-34
(LW)
(G)
3-B
3-LB
Power transistor
C-76
3-LB
(WG)
(Lg)
3-B
A/C control unit
(LW) 36
(G) 10
(WG) 21
(Lg) 29
Arithmetic operation circuit output
H
L
Blower motor voltage
C-66
C-67
(A/C control unit terminal)
C-77
LO
LB
(Body wiring harness side)
C-34
G B
LW LB
(Body wiring harness side)
C-76
B Lg
LB WG
(Body wiring harness side)

A/C control unit terminal voltage

Terminal No.	Signal	Condition	Terminal voltage (V)
10	Power relay (HI) and blend-air damper control motor power supply	—	Over 10
21	Blower motor	When switch HI ON	0
		When switch LO ON	approx. 6
		When switch OFF	Over 10
36	Power relay (HI)	When power relay ON	0 to 1
		When power relay OFF	Over 10
29	Power transistor	When blower is operating	0 to 5

AIR CONDITIONING SWITCH CIRCUIT CHECK—SIGMA

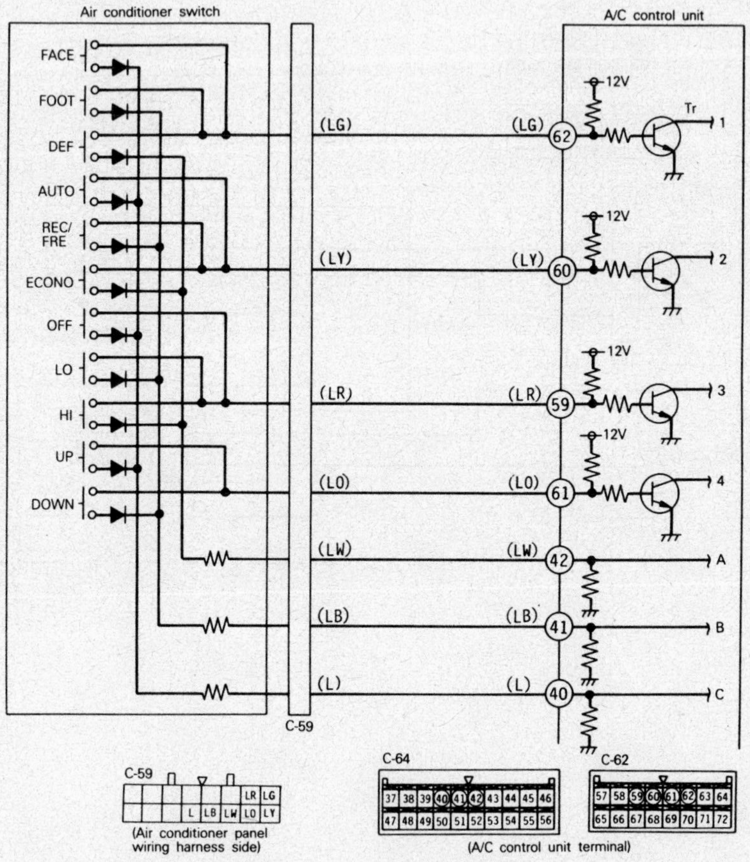
Air conditioner switch
FACE
FOOT
DEF
AUTO
REC/FRE
ECONO
OFF
LO
HI
UP
DOWN
C-59
(LG)
(LY)
(LR)
(LO)
(LW)
(LB)
(L)
A/C control unit
12V
Tr
62
60
59
61
42
41
40
1
2
3
4
A
B
C
C-59
LR LG
L LB LW LO LY
(Air conditioner panel wiring harness side)
C-64
37 38 39 40 41 42 43 44 45 46
47 48 49 50 51 52 53 54 55 56
C-62
57 58 59 60 61 62 63 64
65 66 67 68 69 70 71 72
(A/C control unit terminal)

A/C control unit terminal voltage

Terminal No.	Signal	Condition	Terminal voltage (V)
40	Air conditioner switch	When FACE, AUTO, OFF or UP switch is ON	3 to 4.5
		When FACE, AUTO, OFF and UP switches are all OFF	0
41	Air conditioner switch	When FOOT, REC/FRE, LO or DOWN switch is ON	3 to 4.5
		When FOOT, REC/FRE, LO and DOWN switches are all OFF	0
42	Air conditioner switch	When DEF, ECONO or HI switch is ON	3 to 4.5
		When DEF, ECONO and HI switches are all OFF	0
62	Air conditioner switch (FACE, FOOT or DEF switch)	When switch ON	3 to 4.5
		When switch OFF	Over 10
60	Air conditioner switch (AUTO, REC/FRE or ECONO switch)	When switch ON	3 to 4.5
		When switch OFF	Over 10
59	Air conditioner switch (OFF, LO or HI switch)	When switch ON	3 to 4.5
		When switch OFF	Over 10
61	Air conditioner switch (TEMP switch)	When switch ON	3 to 4.5
		When switch OFF	Over 10

A/C SWITCH INDICATOR LIGHT CIRCUIT CHECK—SIGMA

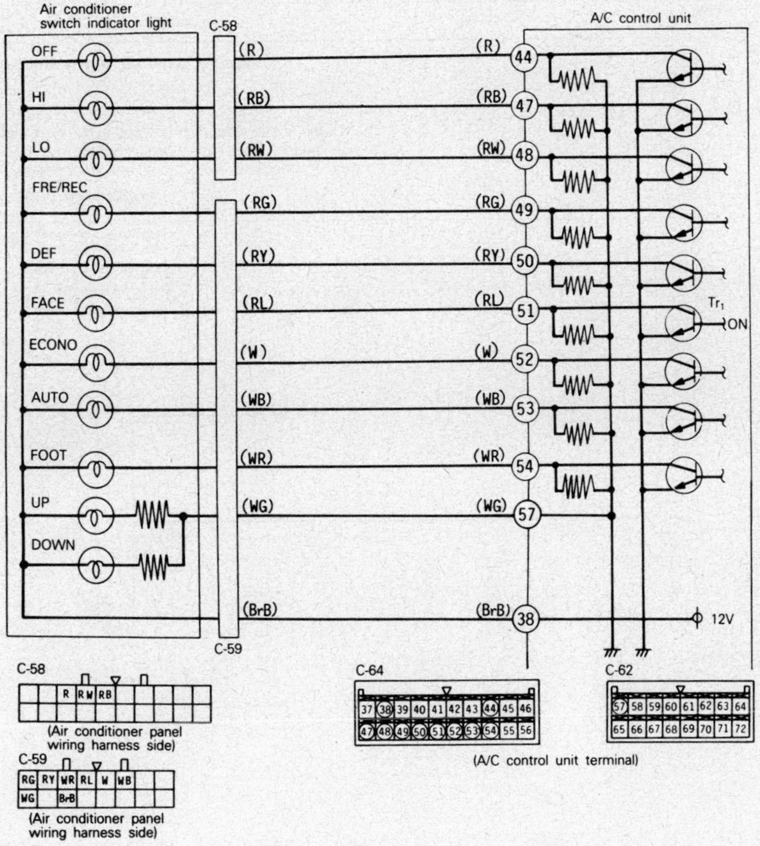
Air conditioner switch indicator light
OFF
HI
LO
FRE/REC
DEF
FACE
ECONO
AUTO
FOOT
UP
DOWN
C-58
C-59
A/C control unit
(R)
(RB)
(RW)
(RG)
(RY)
(RL)
(W)
(WB)
(WR)
(WG)
(BrB)
44
47
48
49
50
51
52
53
54
57
38
Tr1
ON
12V
C-64
C-62
(Air conditioner panel wiring harness side)
(A/C control unit terminal)

A/C control unit terminal voltage

Terminal No.	Signal	Condition	Terminal voltage (V)
44	Air conditioner switch indicator light	When OFF indicator light is illuminated	0 to 1
		When OFF indicator light is not illuminated	approx. 10
47	Air conditioner switch indicator light	When HI indicator light is illuminated	0 to 1
		When HI indicator light is not illuminated	approx. 10
48	Air conditioner switch indicator light	When LO indicator light is illuminated	0 to 1
		When LO indicator light is not illuminated	approx. 10
49	Air conditioner switch indicator light	When REC/FRE indicator light is illuminated	0 to 1
		When REC/FRE indicator light is not illuminated	approx. 10
50	Air conditioner switch indicator light	When DEF indicator light is illuminated	0 to 1
		When DEF indicator light is not illuminated	approx. 10
51	Air conditioner switch indicator light	When FACE indicator light is illuminated	0 to 1
		When FACE indicator light is not illuminated	approx. 10
52	Air conditioner switch indicator light	When ECONO indicator light is illuminated	0 to 1
		When ECONO indicator light is not illuminated	approx. 10
53	Air conditioner switch indicator light	When AUTO indicator light is illuminated	0 to 1
		When AUTO indicator light is not illuminated	approx. 10
54	Air conditioner switch indicator light	When FOOT indicator light is illuminated	0 to 1
		When FOOT indicator light is not illuminated	approx. 10
57	Air conditioner switch indicator light	When UP and DOWN indicator light is illuminated	0 to 1
		When UP and DOWN indicator light is not illuminated	approx. 10
38	Air conditioner switch indicator light power supply	—	Over 10

SELF DIAGNOSIS CIRCUIT CHECK—SIGMA

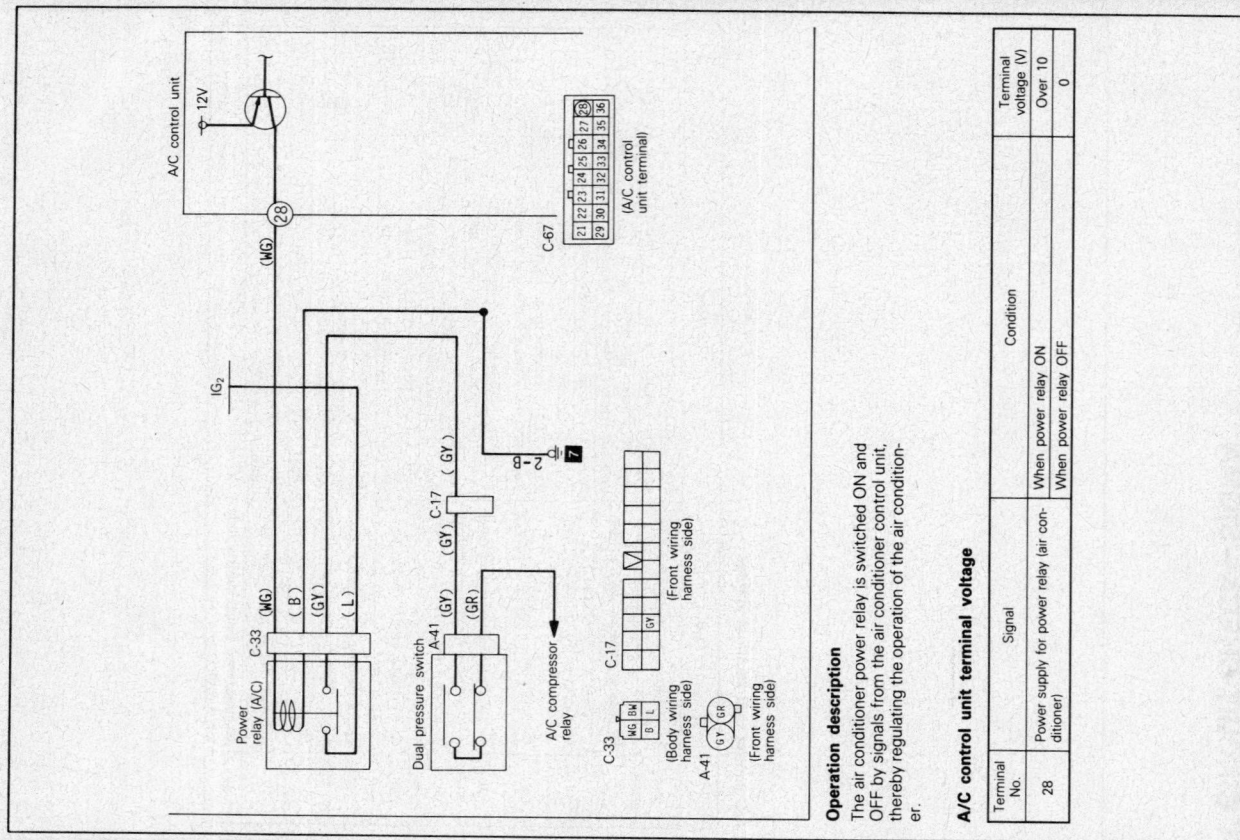

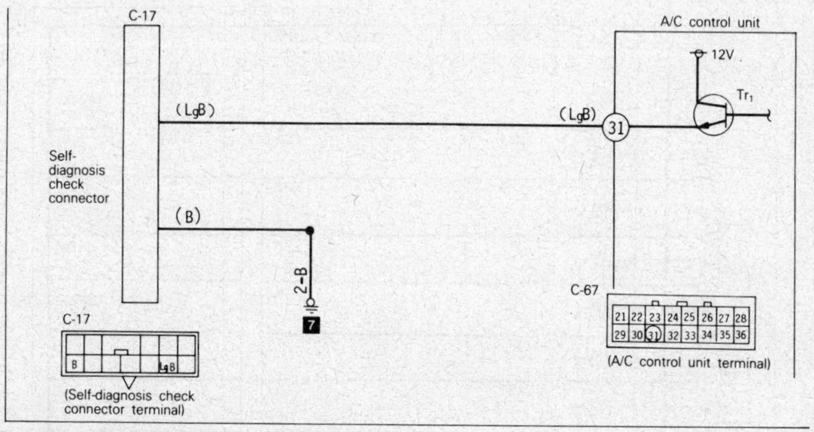
C-17
(LgB)
Self-diagnosis check connector
(B)
2-B
7
A/C control unit
12V
Tr₁
31
C-67
21 22 23 24 25 26 27 28
29 30 31 32 33 34 35 36
(A/C control unit terminal)
B
LgB
(Self-diagnosis check connector terminal)

Operation description

For the diagnosis indication, Tr_1 is switched ON and OFF by the diagnosis signal (flashing signal), and signals are sent to the self-diagnosis check connector.

A/C control unit terminal voltage

Terminal No.	Signal	Condition	Terminal voltage (V)
31	Diagnosis output	During diagnosis signal output	Over 10
		When no diagnosis signal is output	0

AIR CONDITIONING POWER RELAY CIRCUIT CHECK—SIGMA

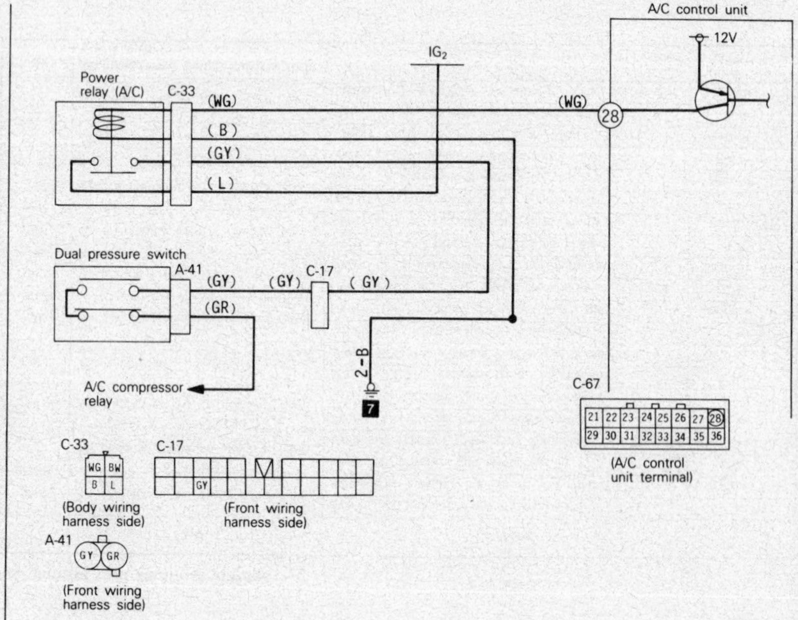
Power relay (A/C)
C-33
(WG)
(B)
(GY)
(L)
IG₂
A/C control unit
12V
28
Dual pressure switch
A-41
(GY)
(GR)
C-17
2-B
7
A/C compressor relay
C-67
21 22 23 24 25 26 27 28
29 30 31 32 33 34 35 36
(A/C control unit terminal)
WG BW
B L
(Body wiring harness side)
GY
(Front wiring harness side)
GY GR
(Front wiring harness side)

Operation description

The air conditioner power relay is switched ON and OFF by signals from the air conditioner control unit, thereby regulating the operation of the air conditioner.

A/C control unit terminal voltage

Terminal No.	Signal	Condition	Terminal voltage (V)
28	Power supply for power relay (air conditioner)	When power relay ON	Over 10
		When power relay OFF	0

BUZZER CIRCUIT CHECK—SIGMA

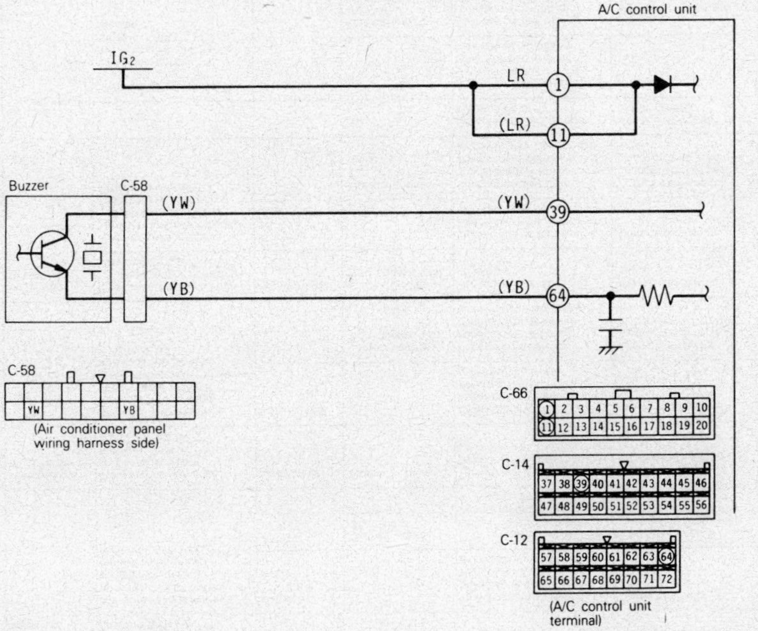
A/C control unit
IG_2
LR
(LR)
1
11
Buzzer
C-58
(YW)
(YW)
39
(YB)
(YB)
64
C-58
YW
YB
(Air conditioner panel wiring harness side)
C-66
C-14
C-12
(A/C control unit terminal)

Operation description

Signals are sent from the air conditioner control unit in accordance with the operation of the air conditioner switch, and the buzzer then sounds.

A/C control unit terminal voltage

Terminal No.	Signal	Condition	Terminal voltage (V)
39	Buzzer power supply	Ignition key: ON position	Over 10
		Ignition key: other than ON position	0
64	Electronic sound	When electronic sound is produced	0 to 1
		When electronic sound is not produced	Over 10

DIAGNOSIS DISPLAY PATTERNS AND CODES—3000GT

Code	Display pattern (output codes) (use with voltmeter)	Cause	Fail safe
0	ON OFF Continuous	Normal	–
11		Open-circuited room-temperature sensor	Condition in which 25°C (77°F) is detected
12		Short-circuited room-temperature sensor	
13		Open-circuited outside-air sensor	Condition in which 20°C (68°F) is detected
14		Short-circuited outside-air sensor	
21		Open-circuited air thermo sensor	Condition in which −2°C (−35.6°F) is detected
22		Short-circuited air thermo sensor	
31		Short-circuited and open-circuited air mix damper potentiometer	MAX. HOT (or MAX. COOL when it is at MAX. COOL)
32		Short-circuited and open-circuited mode selector damper potentiometer	DEF. (or FACE when it is at FACE)
41		Defective air mix damper motor	–
42		Defective mode selector damper motor	–

NOTE: (1) If two or more abnormal conditions occur at the same time, the code numbers are alternately displayed, in order, repeatedly.
(2) The nature of the malfunction is entered and stored in the memory from the time the malfunction occurs until the ignition switch is next turned to OFF.

TROUBLESHOOTING BY CODE—3000GT

Item no.	Inspection point	Method	Criteria: Normal	Criteria: Abnormal	Probable cause	Remedy
11	Room-temperature sensor	Measure resistance of sensor when room temperature is 25°C (77°F).	Approx. 4 kΩ	Largely deviates from approx. 4 kΩ	Defective room-temperature sensor	Replace room-temperature sensor.
		Measure voltage across terminal (16) of air conditioner control unit and ground when room temperature is 25°C (77°F).	In approx. 2.3 – 2.9 V range	–	Open-circuited harness between room-temperature sensor and air conditioner control unit	Correct harness.
			–	Outside approx. 2.3 – 2.9 V range	Poor connection of air conditioner control unit connector or defective air conditioner control unit	Correct connector connection or replace air conditioner control unit.
13	Outside-air-temperature sensor	Measure resistance of sensor when ambient temperature is 25°C (77°F).	Approx. 4 kΩ	Largely deviates from approx. 4 kΩ	Defective outside-air sensor	Replace outside-air-temperature sensor.
		Measure voltage across terminal (5) of air control conditioner unit and ground when ambient temperature is 25°C (77°F).	In approx. 2.2 – 2.8 V range	–	Open-circuited harness between outside-air-temperature sensor and air conditioner control unit	Correct harness.
			–	Outside approx. 2.2 – 2.8 V range	Poor connection of air-conditioner control unit connector or defective air conditioner control unit	Correct connector connection or replace air conditioner control unit.
15	Water-temperature sensor	Measure resistance of sensor when water temperature is 22.5 to 30.5°C (57.6 to 86.9°F).	Conductive	Nonconductive	Defective water-temperature sensor	Replace water-temperature sensor.
		Measure voltage across terminal (8) of air conditioner control unit and ground when water temperature is 22.5 to 30.5°C (57.6 to 86.9°F).	Approx. 12 V	–	Open-circuited harness between water-temperature sensor and air conditioner control unit	Correct harness.
			–	Largely deviates from approx. 12 V	Poor connection of air conditioner control unit connector or defective air conditioner control unit	Correct connector connection or replace air conditioner control unit.
21	Air thermo sensor	Measure resistance of sensor when sensor's sensing temperature is 25°C (77°F).	Approx. 4 kΩ	Largely deviates from approx. 4 kΩ	Defective air thermo sensor	Replace air thermo sensor.
		Measure voltage across terminal (17) of air conditioner control unit and ground when sensor's sensing temperature is 25°C (77°F).	In approx. 2.3 – 2.9 V range	–	Open-circuited harness between air thermo sensor and air conditioner control unit	Correct harness.
			–	Outside approx. 2.3 – 2.9 V range	Poor connection of air conditioner control unit connector or defective air conditioner control unit	Correct connector connection or replace air conditioner control unit.
31	Air mix damper potentiometer				Defective air mix damper potentiometer	Replace air mix damper potentiometer.
		Measure voltage across terminal (8) of air conditioner control unit and ground when potentiometer is in MAX. COOL position.	In approx. 0.1 – 0.3 V range	–	Open-circuited harness between air mix damper potentiometer and air conditioner control unit	Correct harness.
			–	Outside approx. 0.1 – 0.3 V range	Poor connection of air conditioner control unit connector or defective air conditioner control unit	Correct connector connection or replace air conditioner control unit.
33	Outlet selector damper potentiometer				Defective outlet selector damper potentiometer	Replace outlet selector damper potentiometer.
		Measure voltage across terminal (8) of air conditioner control unit and ground when potentiometer is in FACE position.	In approx. 0.1 – 0.3 V range	–	Open-circuited harness between outlet selector damper potentiometer and air conditioner control	Correct harness.
			–	Outside approx. 0.1 – 0.3 V range	Poor connection of air conditioner control unit connector or defective air conditioner control unit	Correct connector connection or replace air conditioner control unit.

CONTROL UNIT POWER CIRCUIT CHECK—3000GT

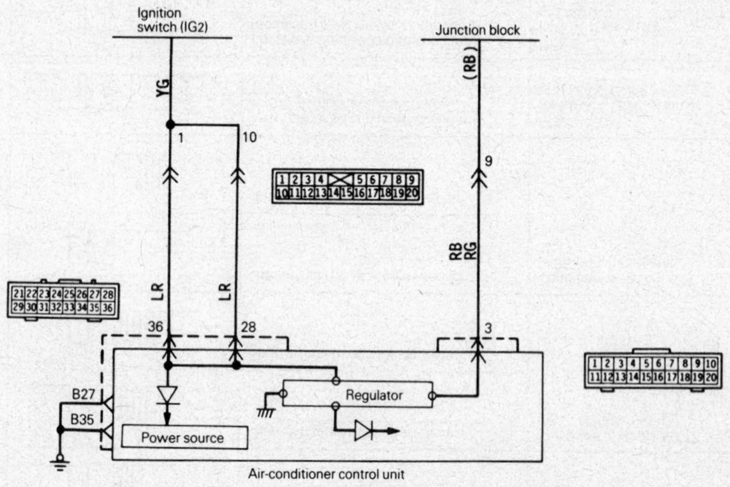
Ignition switch (IG2)
Junction block
YG
(RB)
1
10
9
LR
LR
RB
RG
36
28
3
B27
B35
Regulator
Power source
Air-conditioner control unit

• Air conditioner control unit terminal voltage

Terminal No.	Signal name	Condition	Terminal voltage
3	Backup power source	Normally	Battery voltage
28, 36	Air conditioner control unit power source	Ignition switch ON	Battery voltage
27, 35	Air conditioner control unit ground	Normally	0 V

POTENTIOMETER CIRCUIT CHECK—3000GT

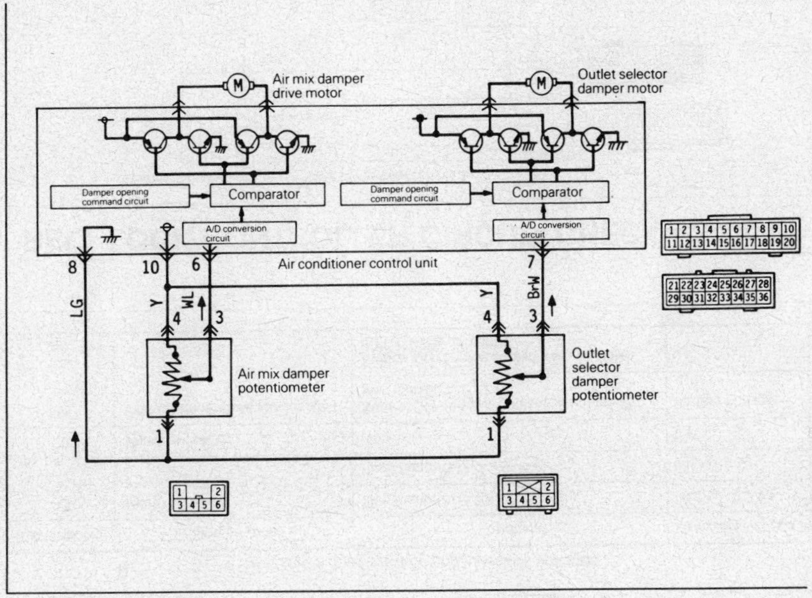
Air mix damper drive motor
Outlet selector damper motor
Damper opening command circuit
Comparator
A/D conversion circuit
Air conditioner control unit
Air mix damper potentiometer
Outlet selector damper potentiometer
LG
Y
WL
B-W

- Diagnosis
  No. 31 (Fix air mix damper at MAX. HOT position, or at MAX. COOL position when it is at MAX. COOL position.)
  No. 32 (Fix outlet selector damper at FACE position, or at FACE position when it is at FACE position.)
- Air conditioner control unit terminal voltages

Terminal No.	Signal name	Condition	Terminal voltage
6	Air mix damper potentiometer (input)	Air mix damper at MAX. COOL position	0.1 – 0.3 V
		Air mix damper at MAX. HOT position	4.7 – 5.0 V
7	Outlet selector damper potentiometer (input)	Outlet selector damper at FACE position	0.1 – 0.3 V
		Outlet selector damper at DEF. position	4.7 – 5.0 V
8	Air mix damper and outlet selector damper potentiometer ⊖	Normally	0 V
10	Sensor power source	Normally	4.8 – 5.2 V

AIR CONDITIONING SENSORS CIRCUIT CHECK 3000GT

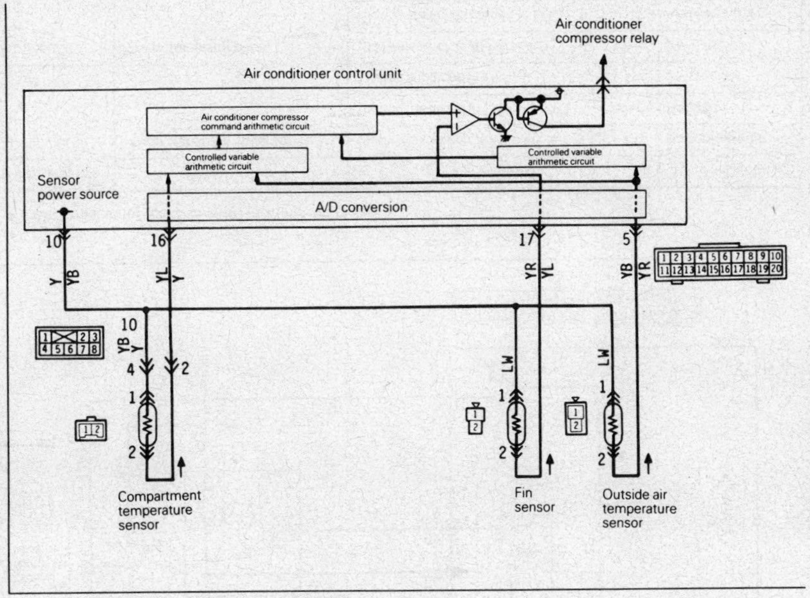
Air conditioner compressor relay
Air conditioner control unit
Air conditioner compressor command arithmetic circuit
Controlled variable arithmetic circuit
Sensor power source
A/D conversion
Compartment temperature sensor
Fin sensor
Outside air temperature sensor
YB
YL
YR
LW

- Diagnosis
  No. 11, 12 [Fix compartment temperature sensor input signal at 25°C (77°F).]
  No. 13, 14 [Fix outside-air-temperature sensor input signal at 15°C (59°F).]
  No. 21, 22 [Fix fin thermo sensor input signal at −2°C (−35.6°F).]
- Air conditioner control unit terminal voltages

Terminal No.	Signal name	Condition	Terminal voltage
5	Outside-air-temperature sensor	Temperature at sensor 25°C (77°F) (4 kΩ)	2.2 – 2.8 V
10	Sensor power source	Normally	4.8 – 5.2 V
16	Compartment temperature sensor	Temperature at sensor 25°C (77°F) (4 kΩ)	2.3 – 2.9 V
17	Fin thermo sensor	Temperature at sensor 25°C (77°F) (4 kΩ) when air conditioner is OFF	2.3 – 2.9 V

WATER TEMPERATURE AND PHOTO SENSOR CIRCUIT CHECK—3000GT

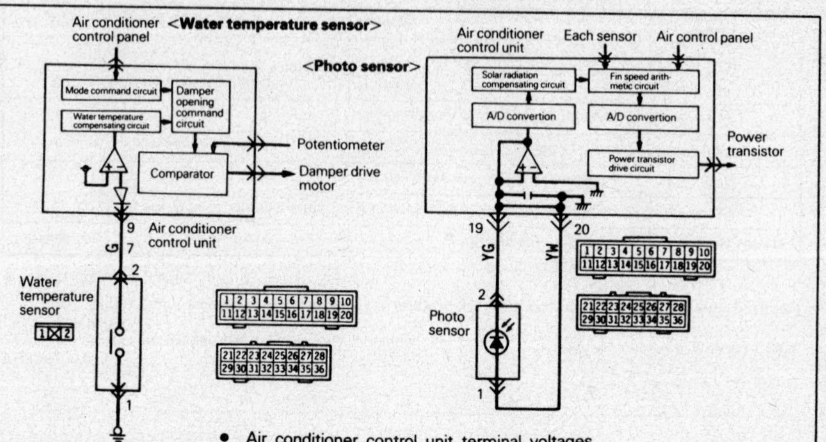
Air conditioner control panel
<Water temperature sensor>
Mode command circuit
Damper opening command circuit
Water temperature compensating circuit
Comparator
Potentiometer
Damper drive motor
Air conditioner control unit
Water temperature sensor
<Photo sensor>
Air conditioner control unit
Each sensor
Air control panel
Solar radiation compensating circuit
Fin speed arithmetic circuit
A/D convertion
Power transistor drive circuit
Power transistor
Photo sensor

• Air conditioner control unit terminal voltages

Terminal No.	Signal name	Condition	Terminal voltage
19	Photo sensor ⊖	Illuminance 100,000 lux or more	–0.1 to –0.2 V
		Illuminance less than 0 lux	0 V
20	Photo sensor ⊕	Normally	0 V
9	Water-temperature sensor ⊕	Switch OFF [Engine coolant temperature less than 50°C (122°F)]	Battery voltage
		Switch ON [Engine coolant temperature 50°C (122°F) or higher]	0 V

BLOWER MOTOR CIRCUIT CHECK—3000GT

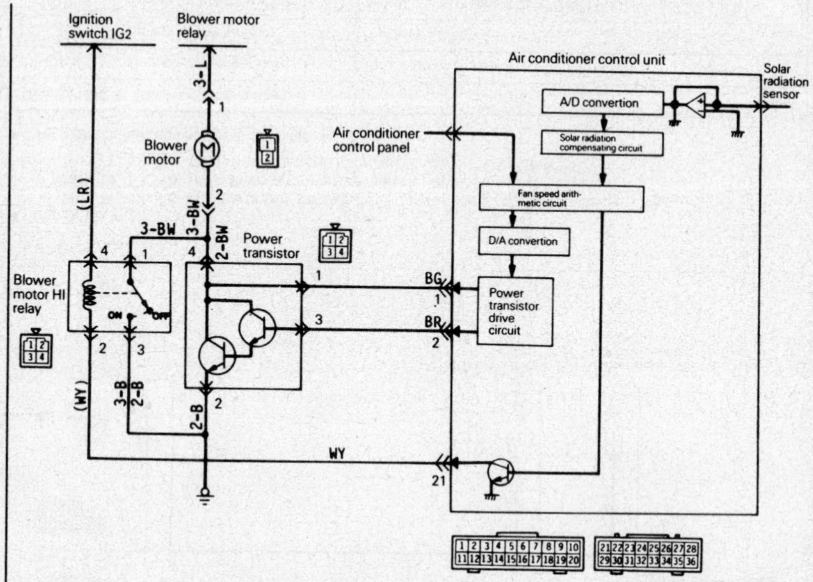
Ignition switch IG2
Blower motor relay
Blower motor
Blower motor HI relay
Power transistor
Air conditioner control unit
Air conditioner control panel
Solar radiation sensor
A/D convertion
Solar radiation compensating circuit
Fan speed arithmetic circuit
D/A convertion
Power transistor drive circuit

• Air conditioner control unit terminal voltages

Terminal No.	Signal name	Condition	Terminal voltage
1	Power transistor collector	Switch is turned OFF.	Battery voltage
		Switch is placed in LO.	Approx. 7 V
		Switch is placed in HI.	0 V
2	Power transistor base	Blower switch is turned OFF.	0 V
		Blower switch is placed in LO.	Approx. 1.3 V
		Blower switch is placed in HI.	Approx. 1.2 V
21	Blower motor HI relay	Fan switch HI is ON.	1.5 V or less
		Fan switch in ME, LO, or OFF.	Battery voltage

BELT LOCK CONTROLLER CIRCUIT CHECK—3000GT

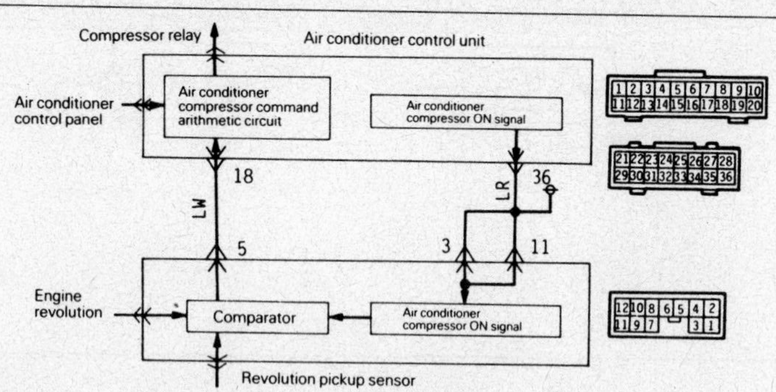
Compressor relay
Air conditioner control unit
Air conditioner control panel
Air conditioner compressor command arithmetic circuit
Air conditioner compressor ON signal
Engine revolution
Comparator
Revolution pickup sensor

• Air conditioner control unit terminal voltages

Terminal No.	Signal name	Condition	Terminal voltage
11	Air conditioner output	Compressor ON	10 V to battery voltage

DAMPER MOTORS CIRCUIT CHECK—3000GT

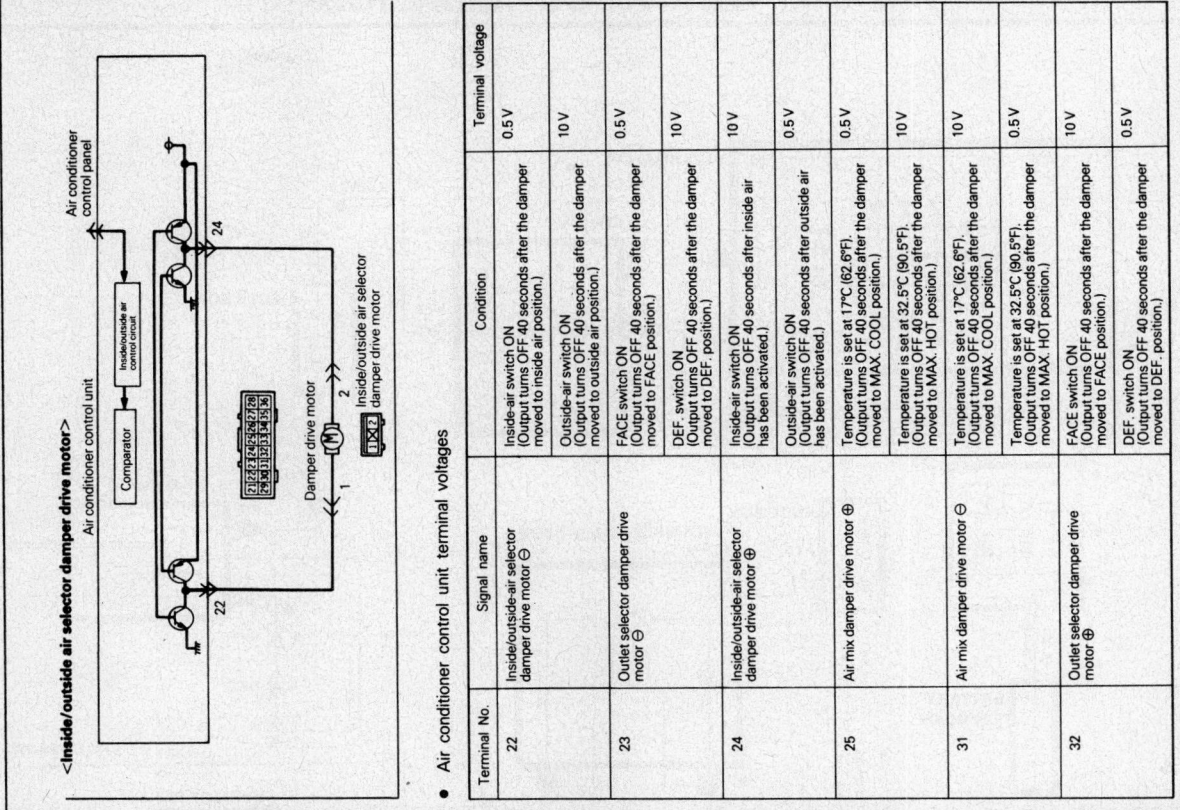

<**Air mix damper drive motor**>

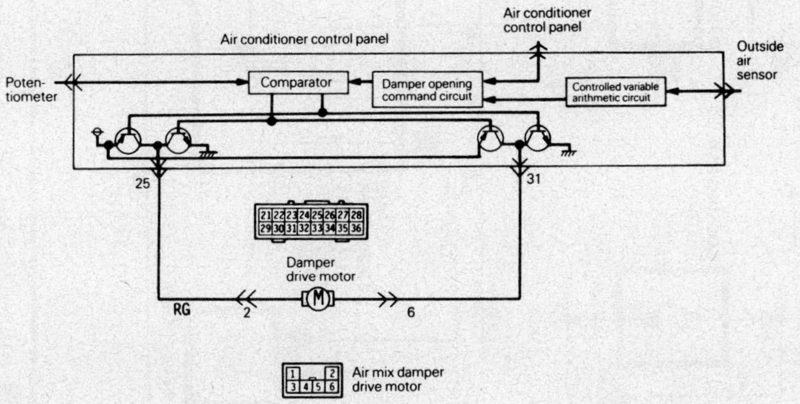
Air conditioner control panel
Air conditioner control panel
Outside air sensor
Poten- tiometer
Comparator
Damper opening command circuit
Controlled variable arithmetic circuit
25
31
21 22 23 24 25 26 27 28
29 30 31 32 33 34 35 36
Damper drive motor
RG
2
6
1 2
3 4 5 6
Air mix damper drive motor

<**Outlet selector damper drive motor**>

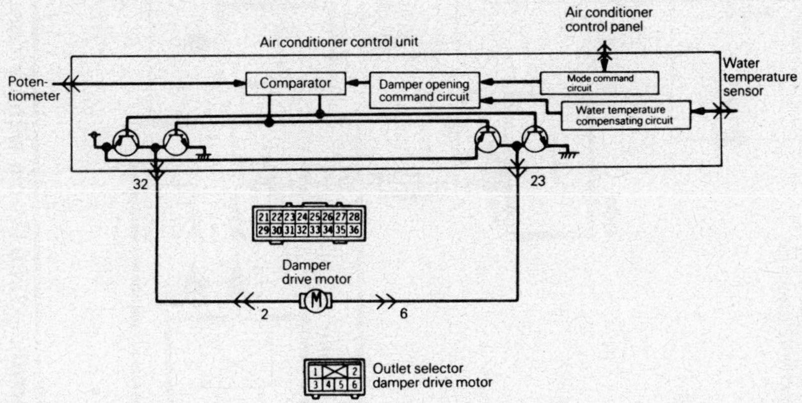
Air conditioner control panel
Air conditioner control unit
Water temperature sensor
Poten- tiometer
Comparator
Damper opening command circuit
Mode command circuit
Water temperature compensating circuit
32
23
21 22 23 24 25 26 27 28
29 30 31 32 33 34 35 36
Damper drive motor
2
6
1 2
3 4 5 6
Outlet selector damper drive motor

<**Inside/outside air selector damper drive motor**>

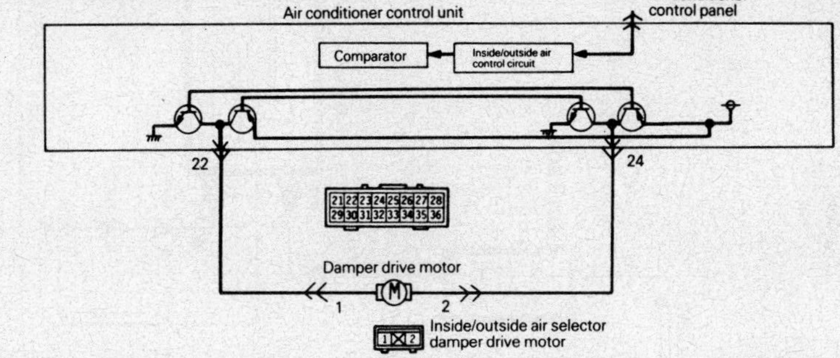
Air conditioner control unit
Air conditioner control panel
Comparator
Inside/outside air control circuit
22
24
21 22 23 24 25 26 27 28
29 30 31 32 33 34 35 36
Damper drive motor
1
2
Inside/outside air selector damper drive motor

- Air conditioner control unit terminal voltages

Terminal No.	Signal name	Condition	Terminal voltage
22	Inside/outside-air selector damper drive motor ⊖	Inside-air switch ON (Output turns OFF 40 seconds after the damper moved to inside air position.)	0.5 V
		Outside-air switch ON (Output turns OFF 40 seconds after the damper moved to outside air position.)	10 V
23	Outlet selector damper drive motor ⊖	FACE switch ON (Output turns OFF 40 seconds after the damper moved to FACE position.)	0.5 V
		DEF. switch ON (Output turns OFF 40 seconds after the damper moved to DEF. position.)	10 V
24	Inside/outside-air selector damper drive motor ⊕	Inside-air switch ON (Output turns OFF 40 seconds after inside air has been activated.)	10 V
		Outside-air switch ON (Output turns OFF 40 seconds after outside air has been activated.)	0.5 V
25	Air mix damper drive motor ⊕	Temperature is set at 17°C (62.6°F). (Output turns OFF 40 seconds after the damper moved to MAX. COOL position.)	0.5 V
		Temperature is set at 32.5°C (90.5°F). (Output turns OFF 40 seconds after the damper moved to MAX. HOT position.)	10 V
31	Air mix damper drive motor ⊖	Temperature is set at 17°C (62.6°F). (Output turns OFF 40 seconds after the damper moved to MAX. COOL position.)	10 V
		Temperature is set at 32.5°C (90.5°F). (Output turns OFF 40 seconds after the damper moved to MAX. HOT position.)	0.5 V
32	Outlet selector damper drive motor ⊕	FACE switch ON (Output turns OFF 40 seconds after the damper moved to FACE position.)	10 V
		DEF. switch ON (Output turns OFF 40 seconds after the damper moved to DEF. position.)	0.5 V

WIRING SCHEMATICS

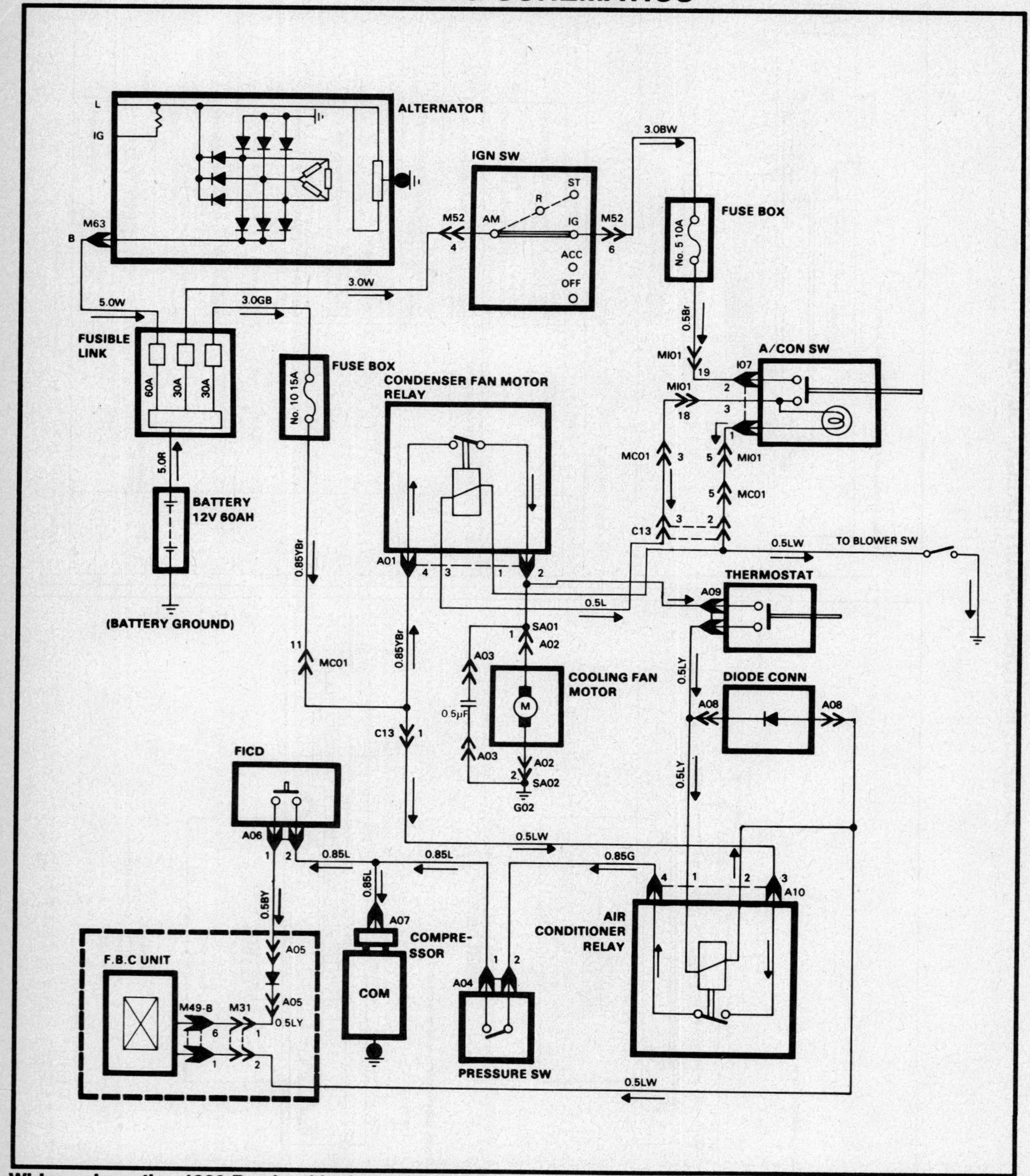
ALTERNATOR
L
IG
M63
B
IGN SW
ST
R
AM
IG
ACC
OFF
M52
4
M52
6
3.0BW
FUSE BOX
No. 5 10A
5.0W
3.0W
3.0GB
FUSIBLE LINK
60A
30A
30A
5.0R
BATTERY 12V 60AH
(BATTERY GROUND)
FUSE BOX
No. 10 15A
0.85YBr
CONDENSER FAN MOTOR RELAY
0.5Br
MI01
19
I07
A/CON SW
2
MI01
18
3
1
MC01
3
5
MI01
5
MC01
C13
3
2
0.5LW
TO BLOWER SW
A01
4
3
1
2
THERMOSTAT
0.5L
A09
SA01
1
A02
A03
COOLING FAN MOTOR
0.5μF
M
A03
A02
2
SA02
G02
11
MC01
0.85YBr
C13
1
0.5LY
DIODE CONN
A08
A08
0.5LY
FICD
A06
1
2
0.85L
0.85L
0.5LW
0.85G
4
1
2
3
A10
0.58Y
0.85L
A07
COMPRE-SSOR
COM
AIR CONDITIONER RELAY
1
2
A04
PRESSURE SW
F.B.C UNIT
A05
A05
M49-B
M31
6
1
0.5LY
1
2
0.5LW

Wiring schematic—1989 Precis with air conditioning

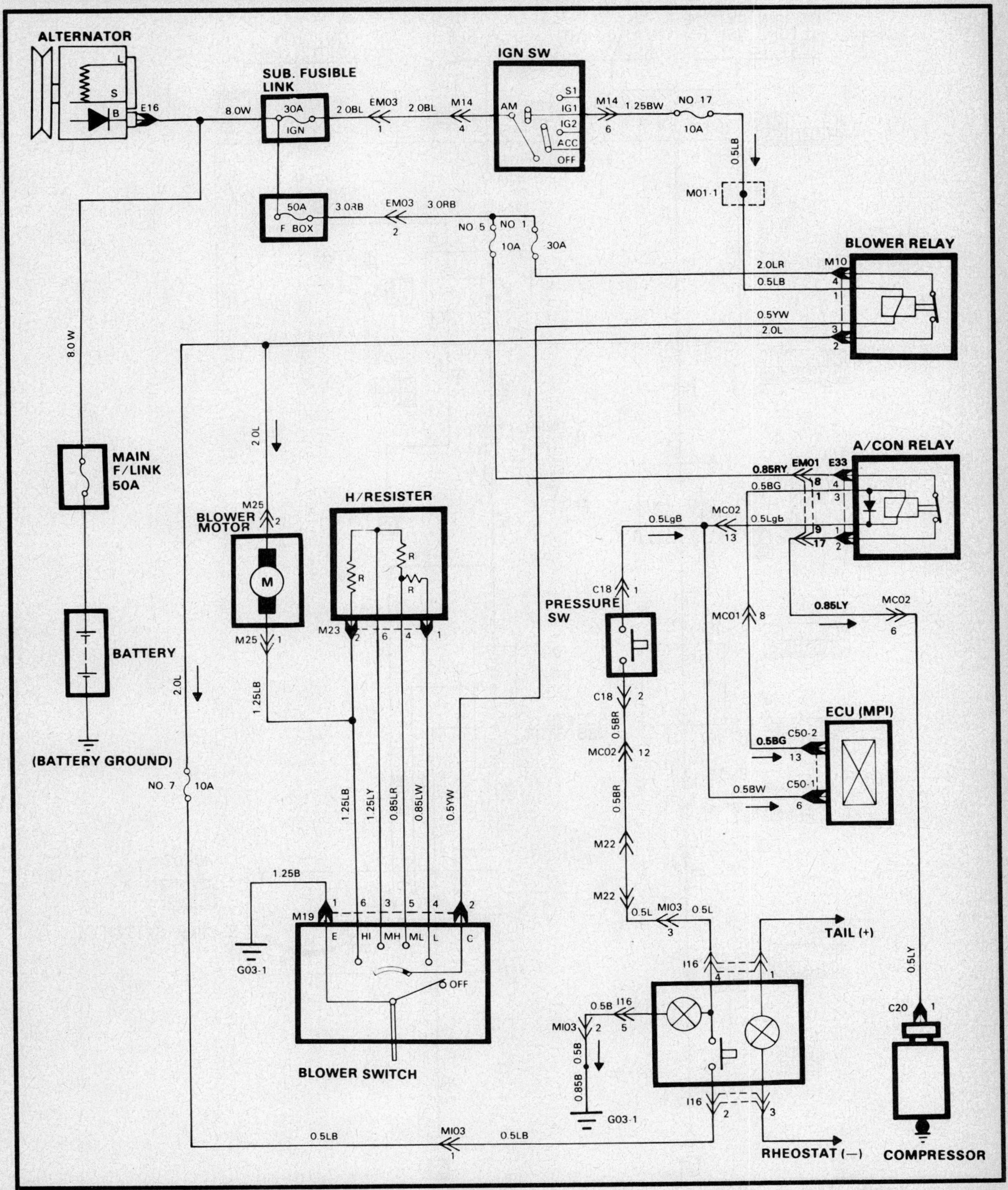
ALTERNATOR
L
S
B
E16
8.0W
SUB. FUSIBLE LINK
30A
IGN
2.0BL
EM03
1
2.0BL
M14
4
IGN SW
AM
S1
IG1
IG2
ACC
OFF
M14
6
1.25BW
NO. 17
10A
0.5LB
M01-1
50A
F BOX
3.0RB
EM03
2
3.0RB
NO. 5
NO. 1
10A
30A
BLOWER RELAY
2.0LR
M10
0.5LB
4
1
0.5YW
3
2.0L
2
8.0W
MAIN F/LINK 50A
BATTERY
(BATTERY GROUND)
2.0L
M25
2
BLOWER MOTOR
M
M25
1
H/RESISTER
R
R
R
M23
2
6
4
1
1.25LB
2.0L
NO. 7
10A
1.25LB
1.25LY
0.85LR
0.85LW
0.5YW
1.25B
M19
1
6
3
5
4
2
E
HI
MH
ML
L
C
OFF
G03-1
BLOWER SWITCH
A/CON RELAY
0.85RY
EM01
E33
0.5BG
8
4
1
3
0.5LgB
MC02
0.5Lgb
13
9
1
17
2
C18
1
PRESSURE SW
C18
2
0.5BR
MC02
12
0.5BR
M22
M22
0.5L
MI03
0.5L
3
TAIL (+)
I16
4
1
0.5B
I16
5
MI03
2
0.5B
0.85B
G03-1
I16
2
3
0.5LB
MI03
1
0.5LB
RHEOSTAT (—)
MC01
8
0.85LY
MC02
6
ECU (MPI)
0.5BG
C50-2
13
0.5BW
C50-1
6
0.5LY
C20
1
COMPRESSOR

Wiring schematic—1990–91 Precis with air conditioning

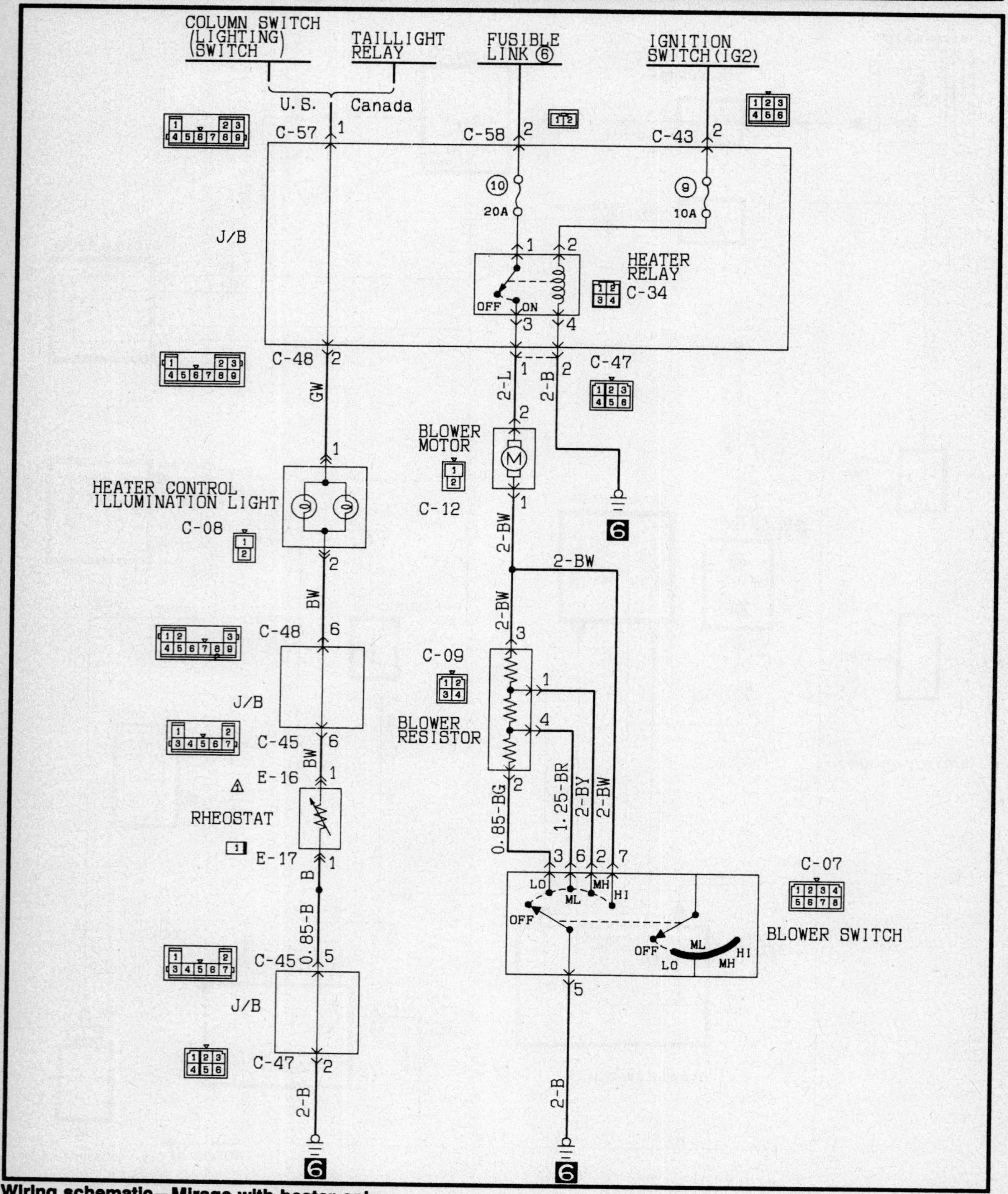
COLUMN SWITCH (LIGHTING) (SWITCH)
TAILLIGHT RELAY
FUSIBLE LINK ⑥
IGNITION SWITCH (IG2)
U.S.
Canada
C-57
C-58
C-43
J/B
20A
10A
HEATER RELAY
C-34
OFF
ON
C-48
C-47
GW
2-L
2-B
BLOWER MOTOR
C-12
HEATER CONTROL ILLUMINATION LIGHT
C-08
2-BW
BW
C-09
BLOWER RESISTOR
C-45
E-16
RHEOSTAT
E-17
B
0.85-B
0.85-BG
1.25-BR
2-BY
C-07
LO
ML
MH
HI
BLOWER SWITCH
2-B
6

Wiring schematic—Mirage with heater only

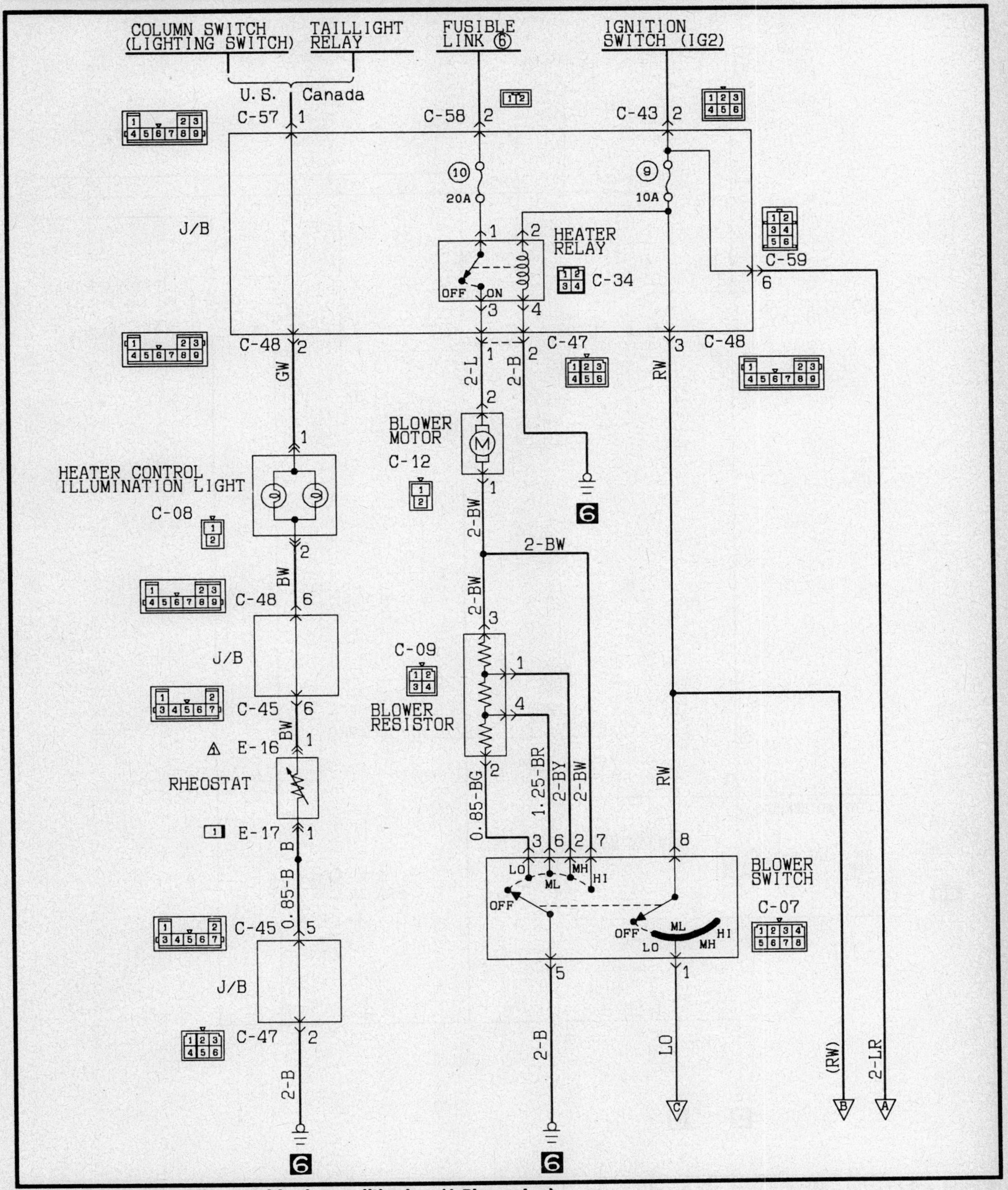
COLUMN SWITCH (LIGHTING SWITCH)
TAILLIGHT RELAY
FUSIBLE LINK ⑥
IGNITION SWITCH (IG2)
U.S.
Canada
C-57
C-58
C-43
J/B
20A
10A
HEATER RELAY
OFF
ON
C-34
C-59
C-48
C-47
GW
2-L
2-B
RW
BLOWER MOTOR
C-12
HEATER CONTROL ILLUMINATION LIGHT
C-08
2-BW
BW
C-09
BLOWER RESISTOR
C-45
E-16
RHEOSTAT
E-17
B
0.85-B
0.85-BG
1.25-BR
2-BY
LO
ML
MH
HI
BLOWER SWITCH
C-07
(RW)
2-LR

Wiring schematic—Mirage with air conditioning (1.5L engine)

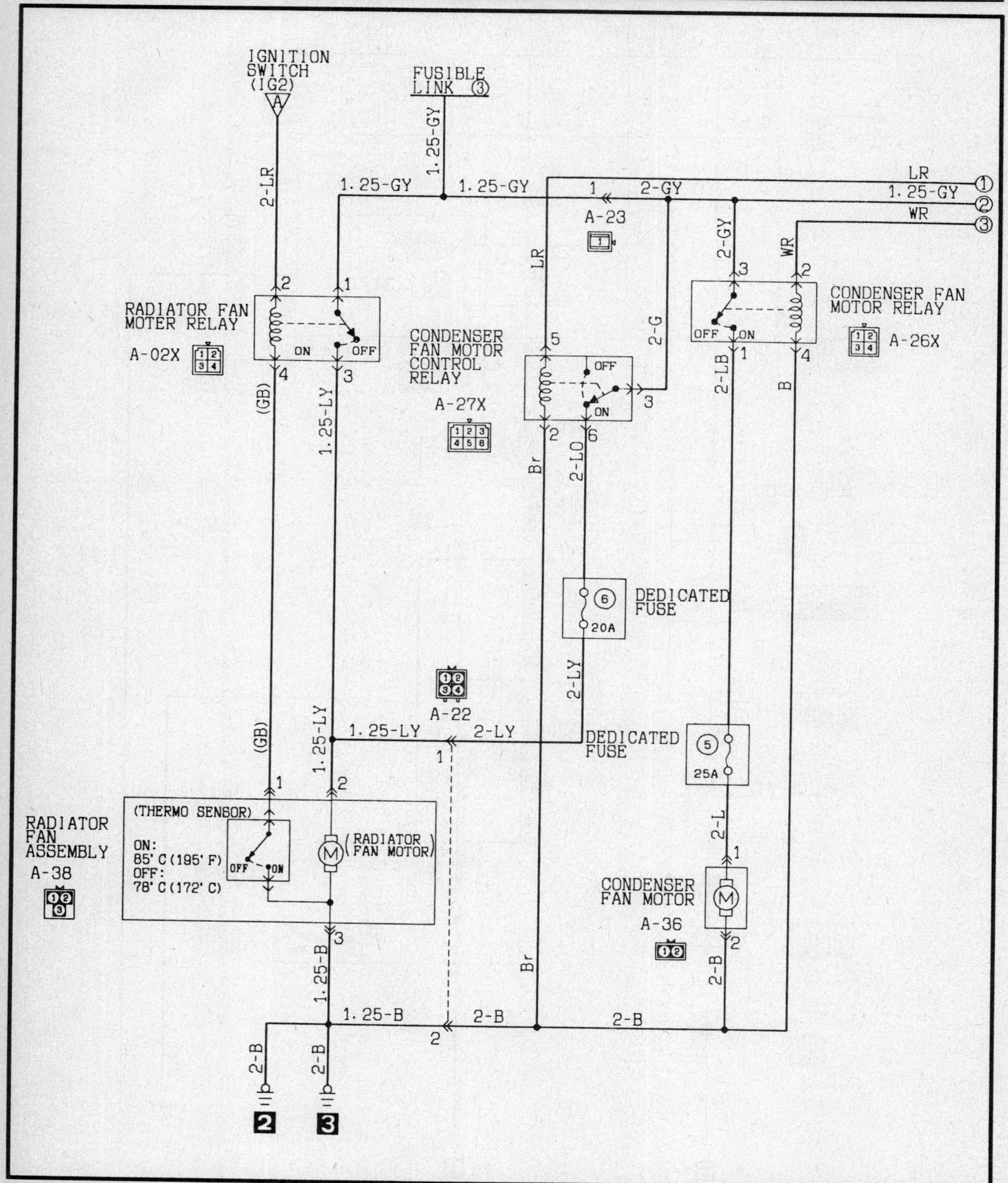
IGNITION SWITCH (IG2)
FUSIBLE LINK ③
RADIATOR FAN MOTER RELAY
A-02X
CONDENSER FAN MOTOR CONTROL RELAY
A-27X
A-23
CONDENSER FAN MOTOR RELAY
A-26X
DEDICATED FUSE ⑥ 20A
DEDICATED FUSE ⑤ 25A
A-22
RADIATOR FAN ASSEMBLY
A-38
(THERMO SENSOR)
ON: 85° C (195° F)
OFF: 78° C (172° C)
RADIATOR FAN MOTOR
CONDENSER FAN MOTOR
A-36
1.25-GY
2-LR
2-GY
LR
WR
1.25-LY
2-LY
2-LO
2-LB
2-L
2-G
Br
B
1.25-B
2-B
(GB)

Wiring schematic—Mirage with air conditioning (1.5L engine)

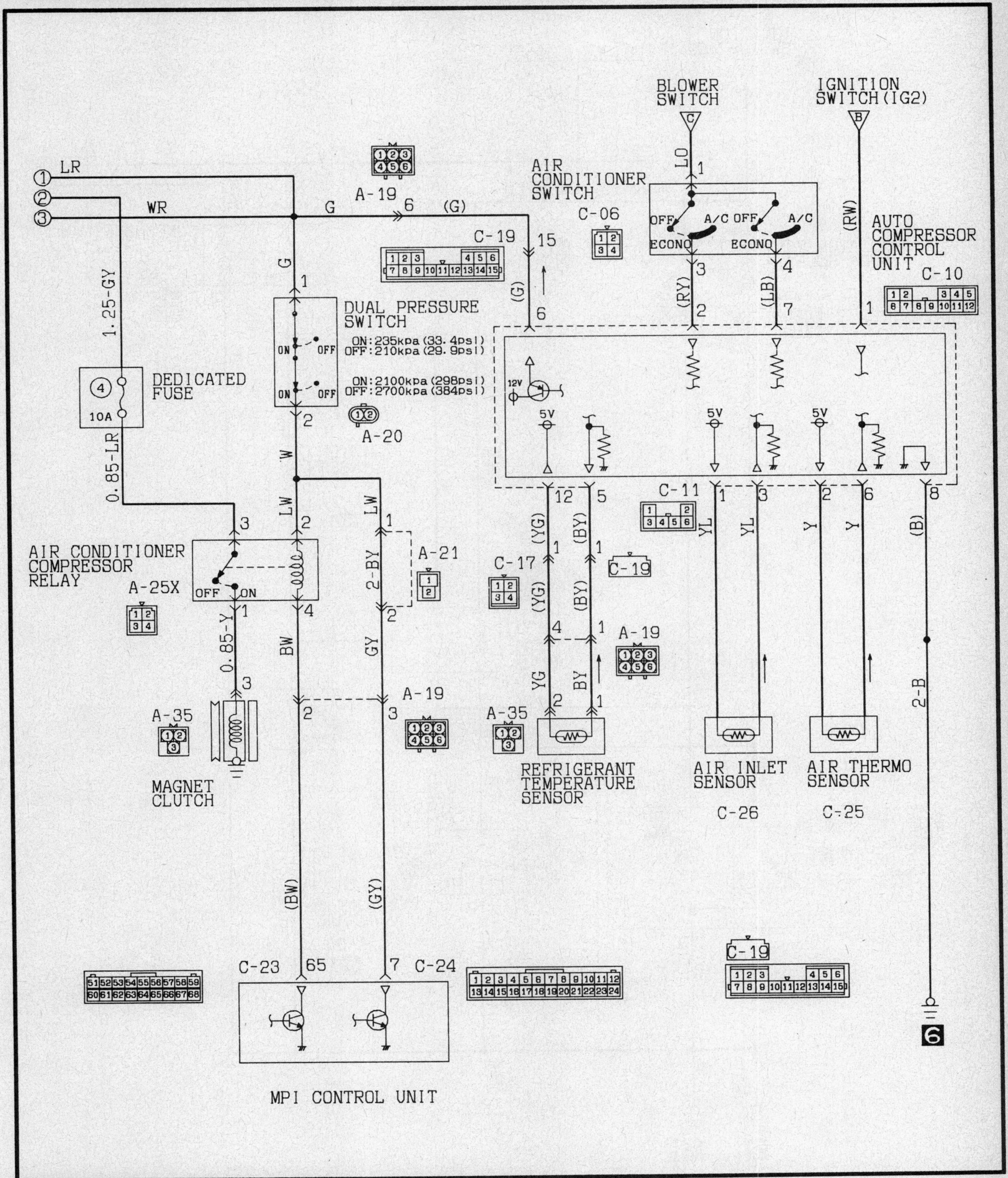
BLOWER SWITCH
IGNITION SWITCH (IG2)
AIR CONDITIONER SWITCH
C-06
OFF
A/C
ECONO
LO
(RW)
AUTO COMPRESSOR CONTROL UNIT
C-10
LR
WR
G
A-19
(G)
C-19
1.25-GY
DUAL PRESSURE SWITCH
ON:235kpa (33.4psi)
OFF:210kpa (29.9psi)
ON:2100kpa (298psi)
OFF:2700kpa (384psi)
A-20
DEDICATED FUSE
10A
0.85-LR
(RY)
(LB)
12V
5V
C-11
YL
Y
(B)
LW
W
AIR CONDITIONER COMPRESSOR RELAY
A-25X
OFF
ON
A-21
2-BY
C-17
(YG)
(BY)
0.85-Y
BW
GY
YG
BY
2-B
A-35
MAGNET CLUTCH
REFRIGERANT TEMPERATURE SENSOR
AIR INLET SENSOR
C-26
AIR THERMO SENSOR
C-25
(BW)
(GY)
C-23
C-24
MPI CONTROL UNIT

Wiring schematic—Mirage with air conditioning (1.5L engine)

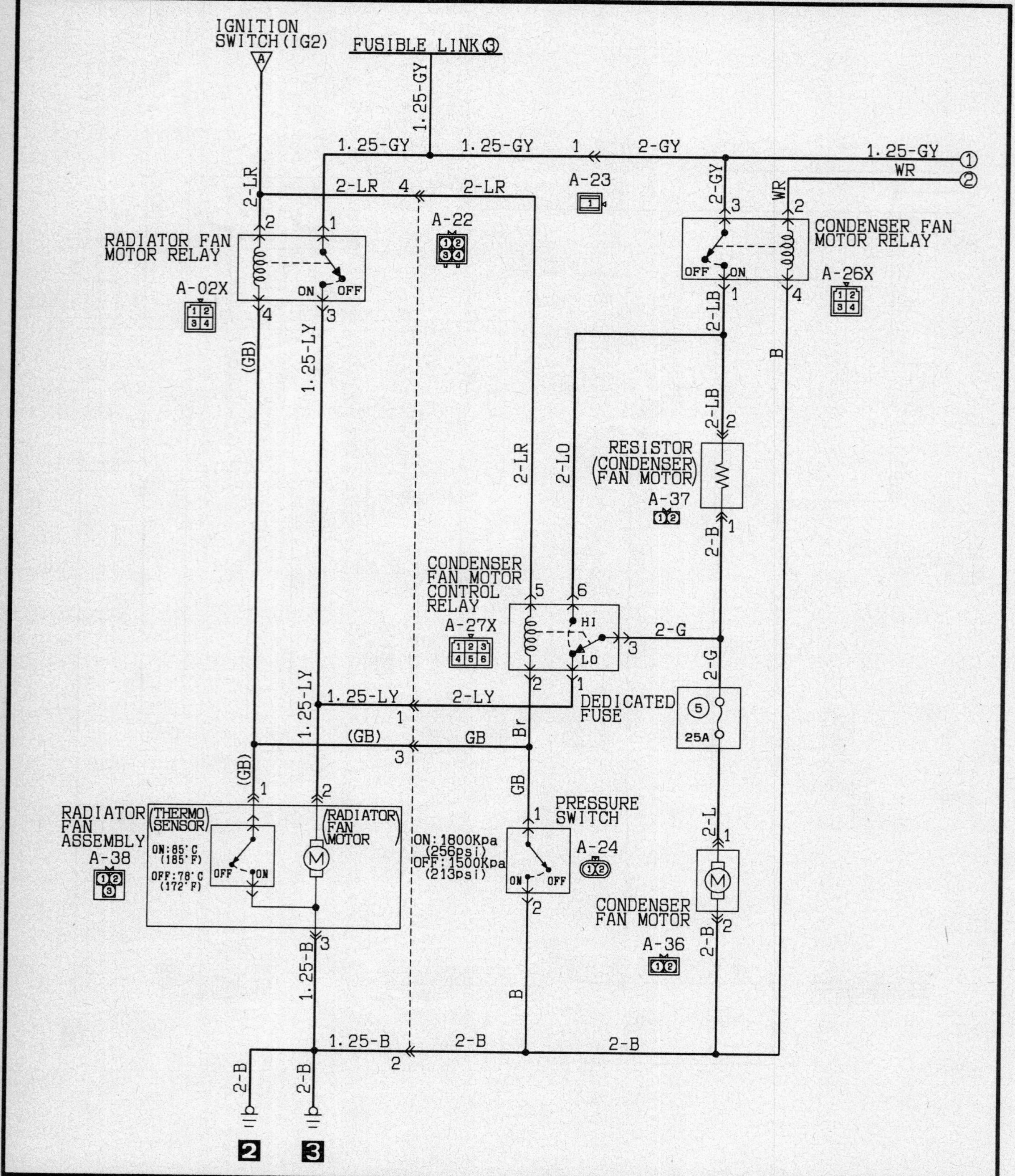
IGNITION SWITCH (IG2)
FUSIBLE LINK ③
1.25-GY
2-GY
WR
2-LR
A-23
A-22
RADIATOR FAN MOTOR RELAY
A-02X
ON
OFF
CONDENSER FAN MOTOR RELAY
A-26X
(GB)
1.25-LY
2-LB
B
RESISTOR (CONDENSER FAN MOTOR)
A-37
2-LO
2-B
CONDENSER FAN MOTOR CONTROL RELAY
A-27X
HI
LO
2-G
1.25-LY
2-LY
DEDICATED FUSE
25A
GB
Br
RADIATOR FAN ASSEMBLY
A-38
(THERMO SENSOR)
ON: 85°C (185°F)
OFF: 78°C (172°F)
(RADIATOR FAN MOTOR)
PRESSURE SWITCH
A-24
ON: 1800Kpa (256psi)
OFF: 1500Kpa (213psi)
2-L
CONDENSER FAN MOTOR
A-36
1.25-B
2-B

Wiring schematic—Mirage with air conditioning (1.6L engine)

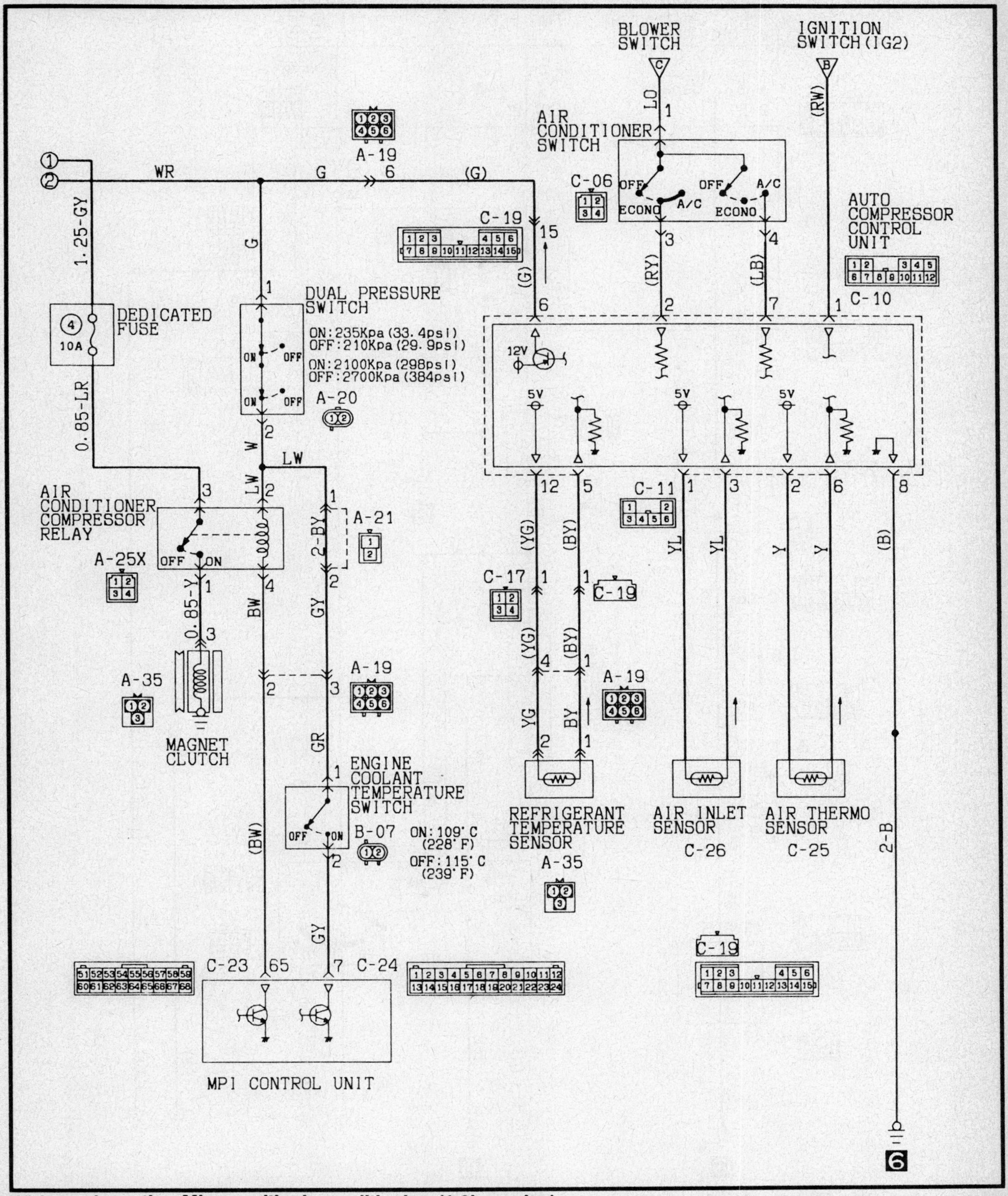
BLOWER SWITCH
IGNITION SWITCH (IG2)
AIR CONDITIONER SWITCH
C-06
OFF
ECONO
A/C
AUTO COMPRESSOR CONTROL UNIT
C-10
A-19
WR
G
(G)
C-19
1.25-GY
DEDICATED FUSE
10A
DUAL PRESSURE SWITCH
ON:235Kpa (33.4psi)
OFF:210Kpa (29.9psi)
ON:2100Kpa (298psi)
OFF:2700Kpa (384psi)
A-20
0.85-LR
LW
AIR CONDITIONER COMPRESSOR RELAY
A-25X
A-21
2-BY
0.85-Y
BW
GY
A-35
MAGNET CLUTCH
GR
ENGINE COOLANT TEMPERATURE SWITCH
B-07
ON: 109°C (228°F)
OFF: 115°C (239°F)
(BW)
C-11
C-17
(YG)
(BY)
YG
BY
YL
Y
(B)
(RY)
(LB)
(RW)
LO
12V
5V
REFRIGERANT TEMPERATURE SENSOR
AIR INLET SENSOR
AIR THERMO SENSOR
C-26
C-25
2-B
C-23
C-24
MPI CONTROL UNIT

Wiring schematic—Mirage with air conditioning (1.6L engine)

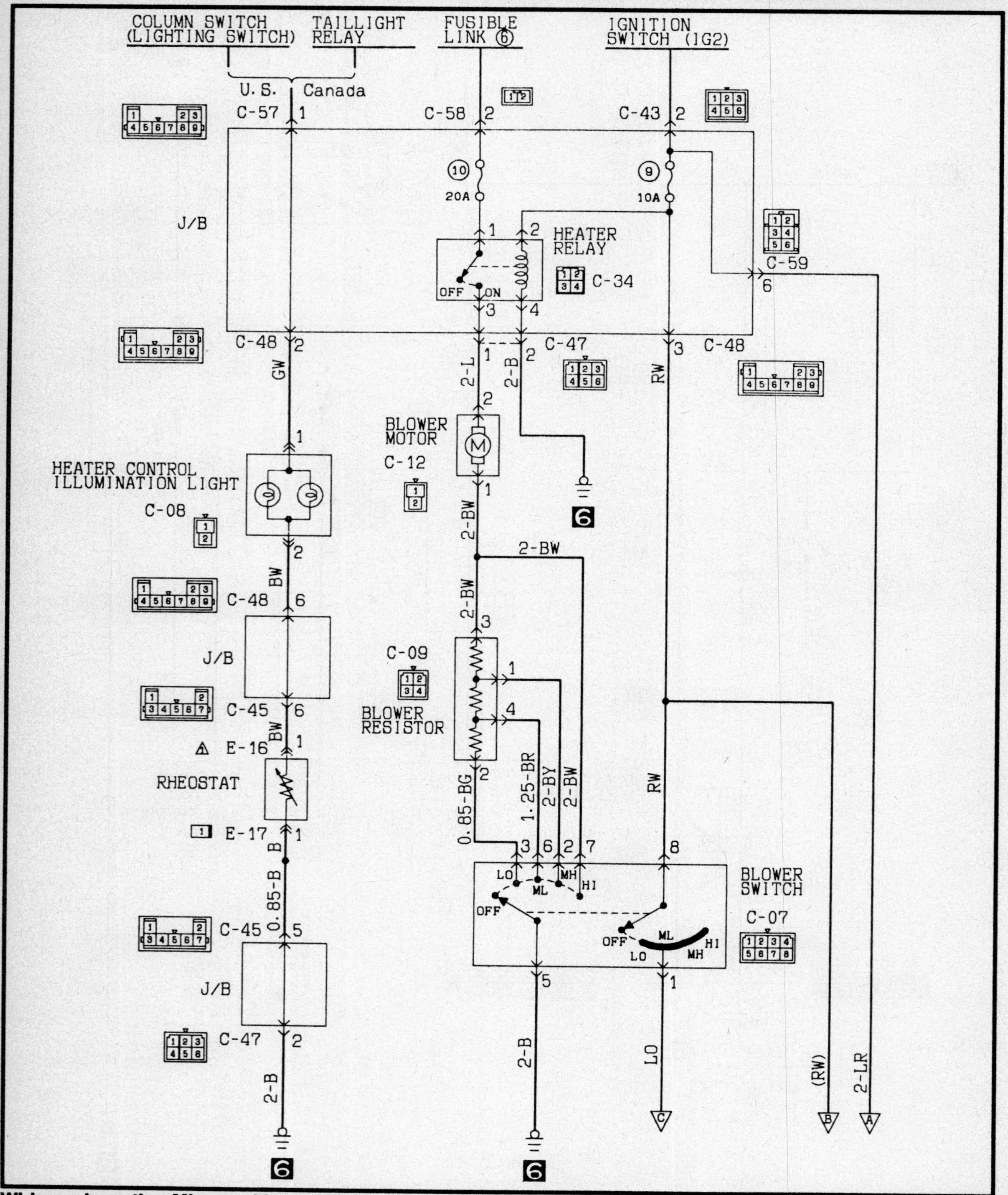
COLUMN SWITCH (LIGHTING SWITCH)
TAILLIGHT RELAY
FUSIBLE LINK ⑥
IGNITION SWITCH (IG2)
U.S.
Canada
C-57
C-58
C-43
J/B
20A
10A
HEATER RELAY
C-34
C-59
OFF
ON
C-48
C-47
GW
2-L
2-B
RW
BLOWER MOTOR
C-12
HEATER CONTROL ILLUMINATION LIGHT
C-08
2-BW
BW
C-09
BLOWER RESISTOR
C-45
E-16
RHEOSTAT
E-17
B
0.85-B
0.85-BG
1.25-BR
2-BY
LO
ML
MH
HI
BLOWER SWITCH
C-07
(RW)
2-LR
6

Wiring schematic—Mirage with air conditioning (1.6L engine)

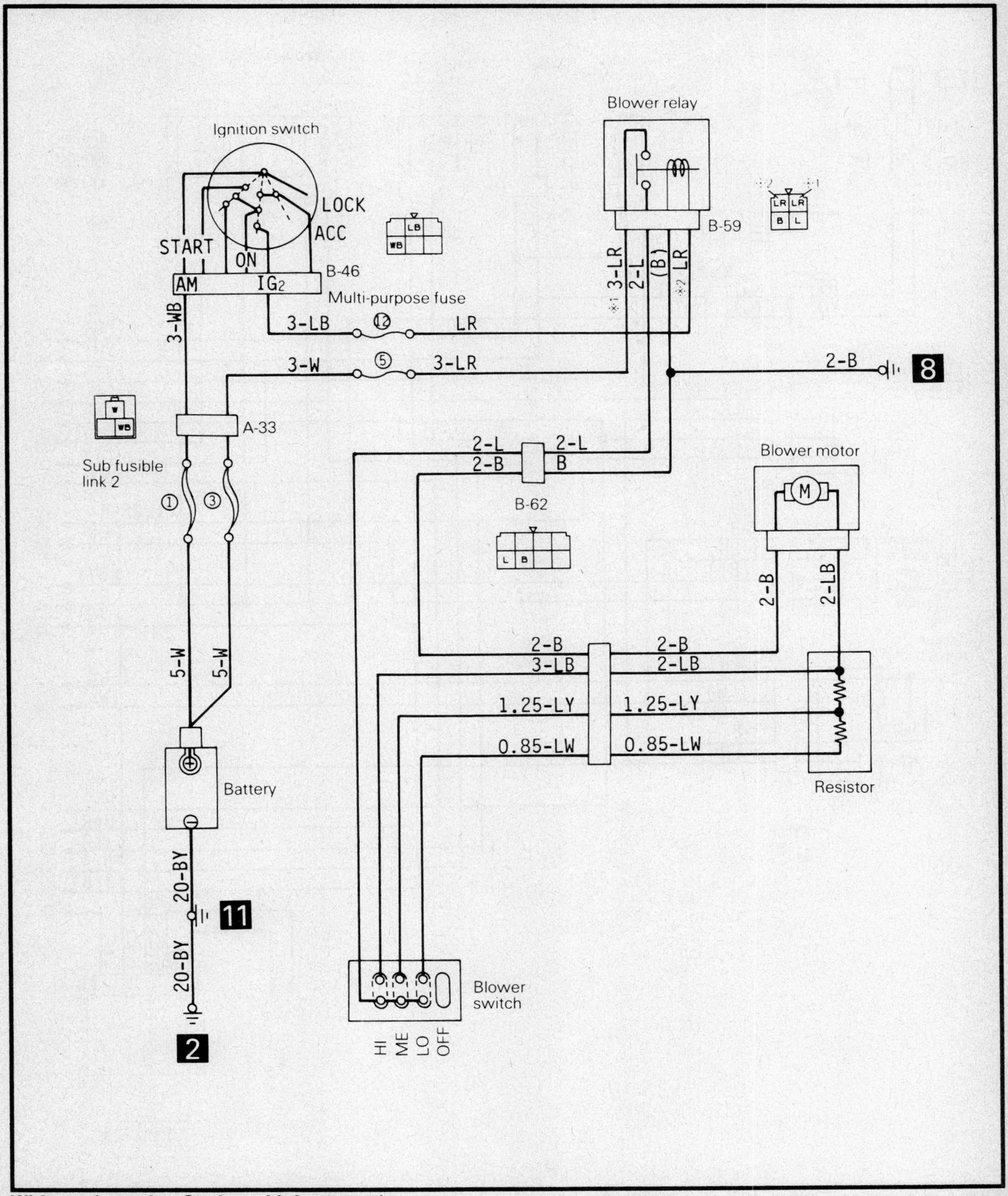
Blower relay
Ignition switch
LOCK
ACC
START
ON
AM
IG2
B-46
B-59
Multi-purpose fuse
3-WB
3-LB
LR
3-W
3-LR
2-L
(B)
2-B
8
A-33
Sub fusible link 2
2-L
2-B
B
B-62
Blower motor
2-LB
3-LB
1.25-LY
0.85-LW
5-W
Battery
Resistor
20-BY
11
2
Blower switch
HI
ME
LO
OFF

Wiring schematic—Starion with heater only

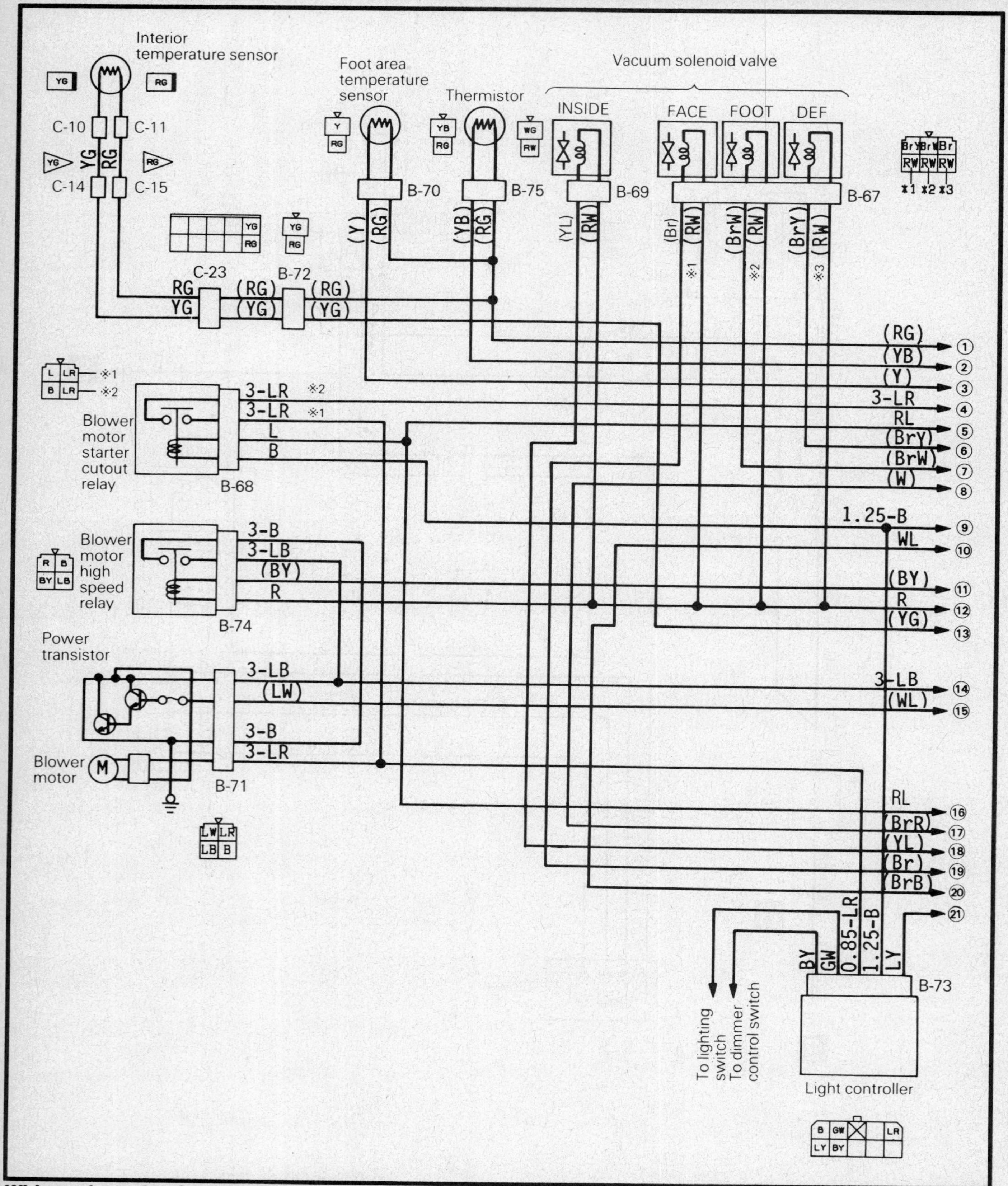
Interior temperature sensor
Foot area temperature sensor
Thermistor
Vacuum solenoid valve
INSIDE
FACE
FOOT
DEF
C-10
C-11
C-14
C-15
C-23
B-72
B-70
B-75
B-69
B-67
Blower motor starter cutout relay
B-68
Blower motor high speed relay
B-74
Power transistor
Blower motor
B-71
To lighting switch
To dimmer control switch
B-73
Light controller

Wiring schematic—Starion with air conditioning

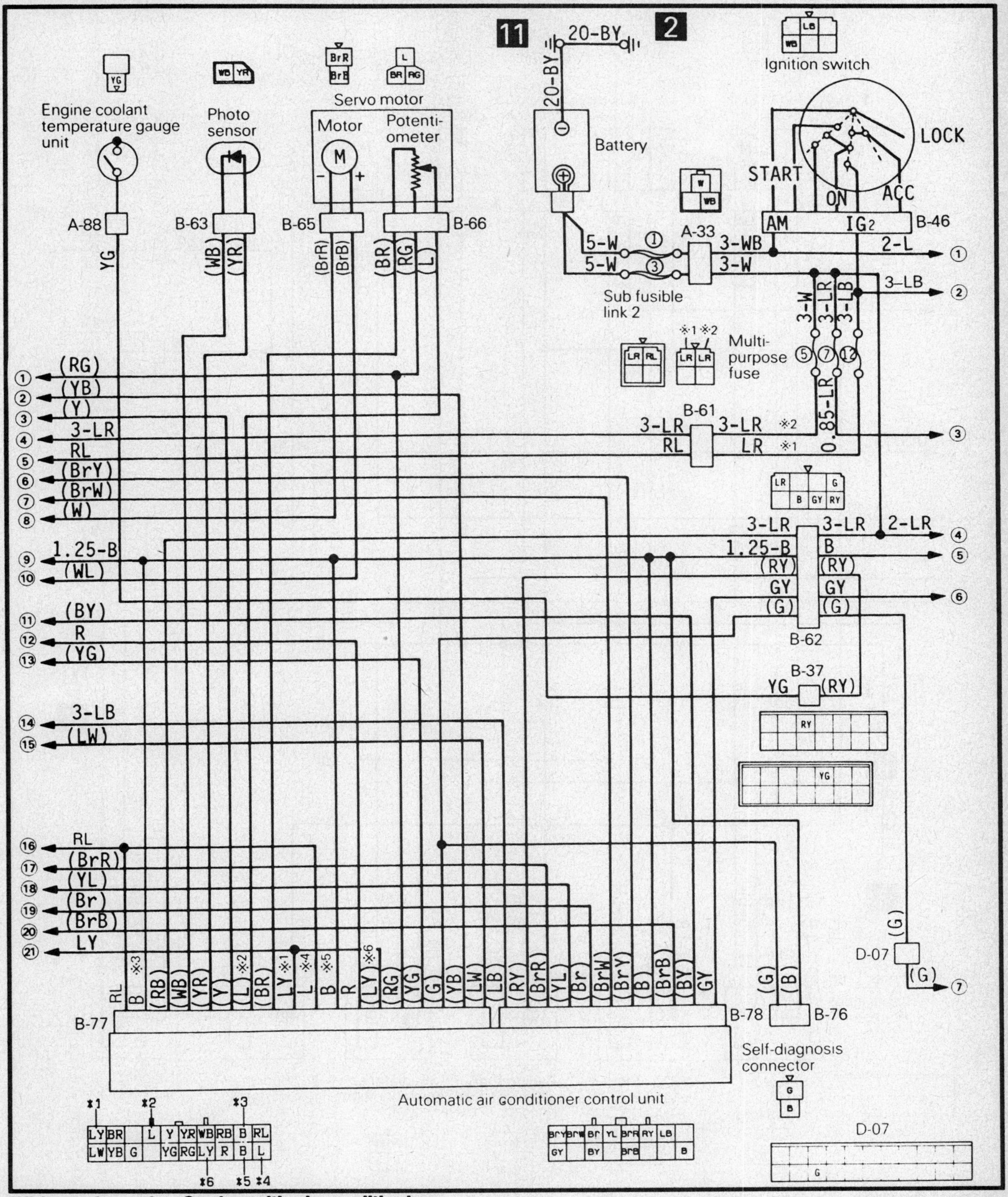
Engine coolant temperature gauge unit
Photo sensor
Servo motor
Motor
Potentiometer
Battery
Ignition switch
LOCK
START
ON
ACC
Sub fusible link 2
Multi-purpose fuse
Self-diagnosis connector
Automatic air conditioner control unit
A-88
B-63
B-65
B-66
A-33
B-46
B-61
B-62
B-37
B-77
B-78
B-76
D-07

Wiring schematic—Starion with air conditioning

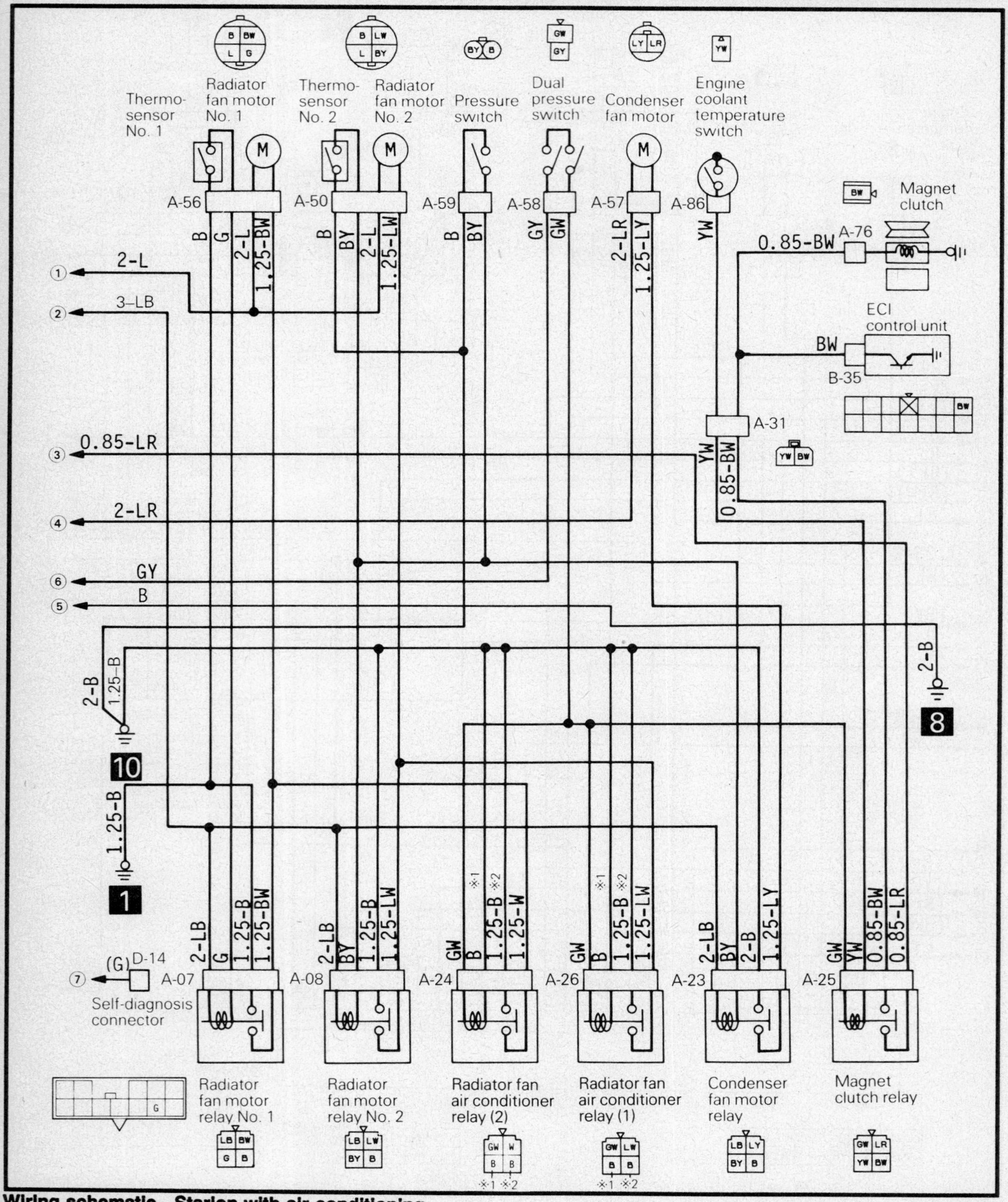
Thermo-sensor No. 1
Radiator fan motor No. 1
Thermo-sensor No. 2
Radiator fan motor No. 2
Pressure switch
Dual pressure switch
Condenser fan motor
Engine coolant temperature switch
Magnet clutch
ECI control unit
A-56
A-50
A-59
A-58
A-57
A-86
A-76
B-35
A-31
0.85-BW
BW
2-L
3-LB
0.85-LR
2-LR
GY
B
2-B
1.25-B
10
8
1
(G) D-14
A-07
A-08
A-24
A-26
A-23
A-25
Self-diagnosis connector
Radiator fan motor relay No. 1
Radiator fan motor relay No. 2
Radiator fan air conditioner relay (2)
Radiator fan air conditioner relay (1)
Condenser fan motor relay
Magnet clutch relay

Wiring schematic—Starion with air conditioning

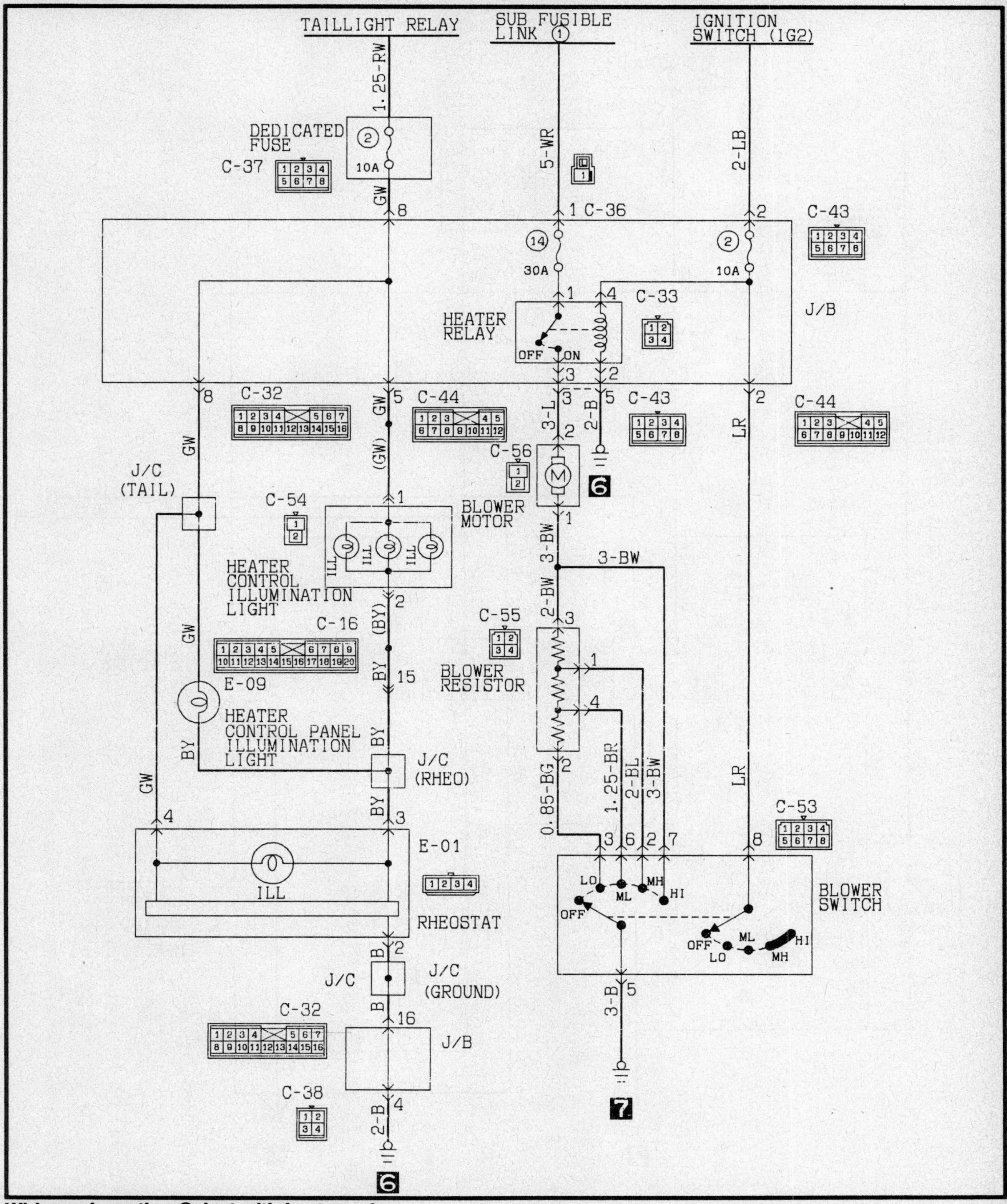
TAILLIGHT RELAY
SUB FUSIBLE LINK ①
IGNITION SWITCH (IG2)
1.25-RW
5-WR
2-LB
DEDICATED FUSE
C-37
10A
GW
C-36
C-43
30A
HEATER RELAY
OFF
ON
C-33
J/B
C-32
C-44
3-L
2-B
LR
C-56
BLOWER MOTOR
J/C (TAIL)
C-54
(GW)
HEATER CONTROL ILLUMINATION LIGHT
ILL
3-BW
2-BW
C-55
BLOWER RESISTOR
C-16
(BY)
BY
E-09
HEATER CONTROL PANEL ILLUMINATION LIGHT
J/C (RHEO)
0.85-BG
1.25-BR
2-BL
C-53
E-01
RHEOSTAT
BLOWER SWITCH
LO
ML
MH
HI
B
J/C
J/C (GROUND)
3-B
C-38
2-B

Wiring schematic—Galant with heater only

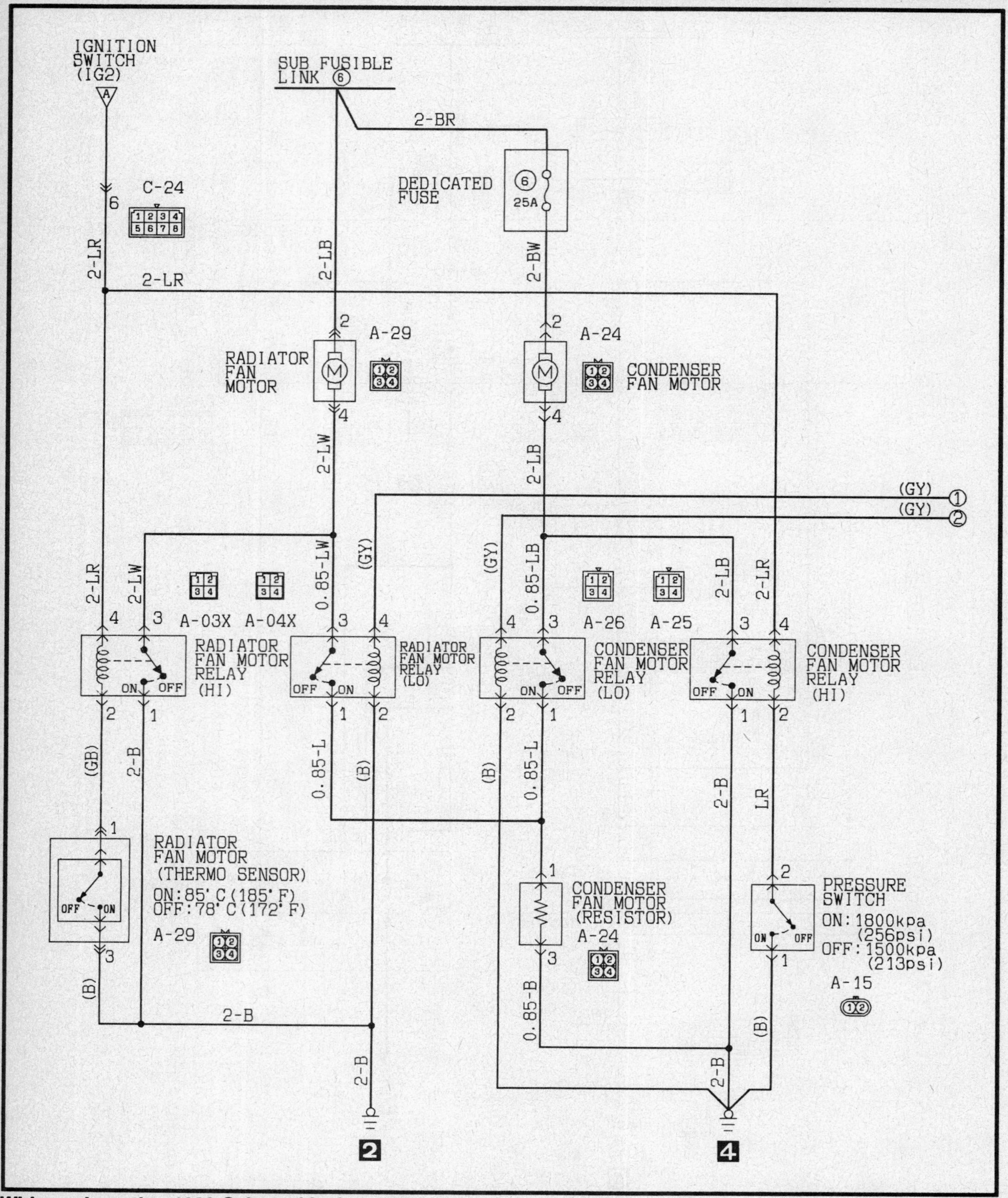
IGNITION SWITCH (IG2)
SUB FUSIBLE LINK ⑥
2-BR
DEDICATED FUSE
⑥ 25A
C-24
2-LR
2-LB
2-BW
A-29
RADIATOR FAN MOTOR
A-24
CONDENSER FAN MOTOR
2-LW
2-LB
(GY)
A-03X A-04X
0.85-LW
0.85-LB
A-26 A-25
RADIATOR FAN MOTOR RELAY (HI)
RADIATOR FAN MOTOR RELAY (LO)
CONDENSER FAN MOTOR RELAY (LO)
CONDENSER FAN MOTOR RELAY (HI)
ON OFF
(GB)
2-B
0.85-L
(B)
LR
RADIATOR FAN MOTOR (THERMO SENSOR)
ON:85° C (185° F)
OFF:78° C (172° F)
A-29
CONDENSER FAN MOTOR (RESISTOR)
A-24
PRESSURE SWITCH
ON:1800kpa (256psi)
OFF:1500kpa (213psi)
A-15
0.85-B
2
4

Wiring schematic—1989 Galant with air conditioning

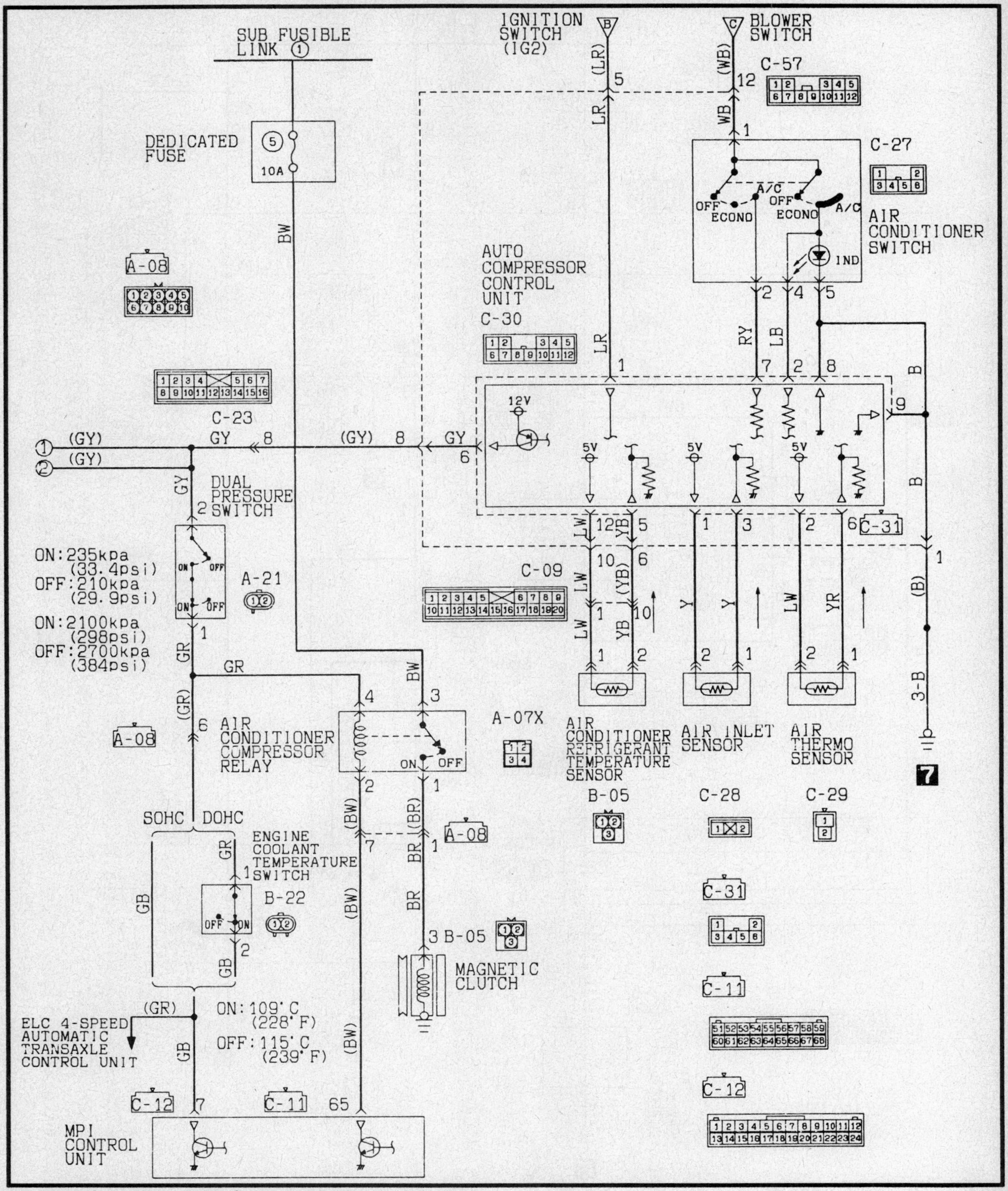
SUB FUSIBLE LINK ①
DEDICATED FUSE
⑤ 10A
BW
IGNITION SWITCH (IG2)
B
(LR)
5
LR
BLOWER SWITCH
C
(WB)
12
WB
1
C-57
C-27
OFF
ECONO
A/C
AIR CONDITIONER SWITCH
IND
2
4
5
RY
LB
B
AUTO COMPRESSOR CONTROL UNIT
C-30
A-08
C-23
(GY)
GY
8
6
7
12V
5V
9
DUAL PRESSURE SWITCH
ON:235kpa (33.4psi)
OFF:210kpa (29.9psi)
ON:2100kpa (298psi)
OFF:2700kpa (384psi)
ON
OFF
A-21
GR
C-09
LW
YB
(YB)
10
Y
YR
C-31
(B)
3-B
AIR CONDITIONER COMPRESSOR RELAY
A-07X
AIR CONDITIONER REFRIGERANT TEMPERATURE SENSOR
AIR INLET SENSOR
AIR THERMO SENSOR
B-05
C-28
C-29
(GR)
SOHC
DOHC
ENGINE COOLANT TEMPERATURE SWITCH
B-22
GB
(BW)
(BR)
BR
MAGNETIC CLUTCH
ON: 109°C (228°F)
OFF: 115°C (239°F)
ELC 4-SPEED AUTOMATIC TRANSAXLE CONTROL UNIT
C-11
C-12
65
MPI CONTROL UNIT
7

Wiring schematic—1989 Galant with air conditioning

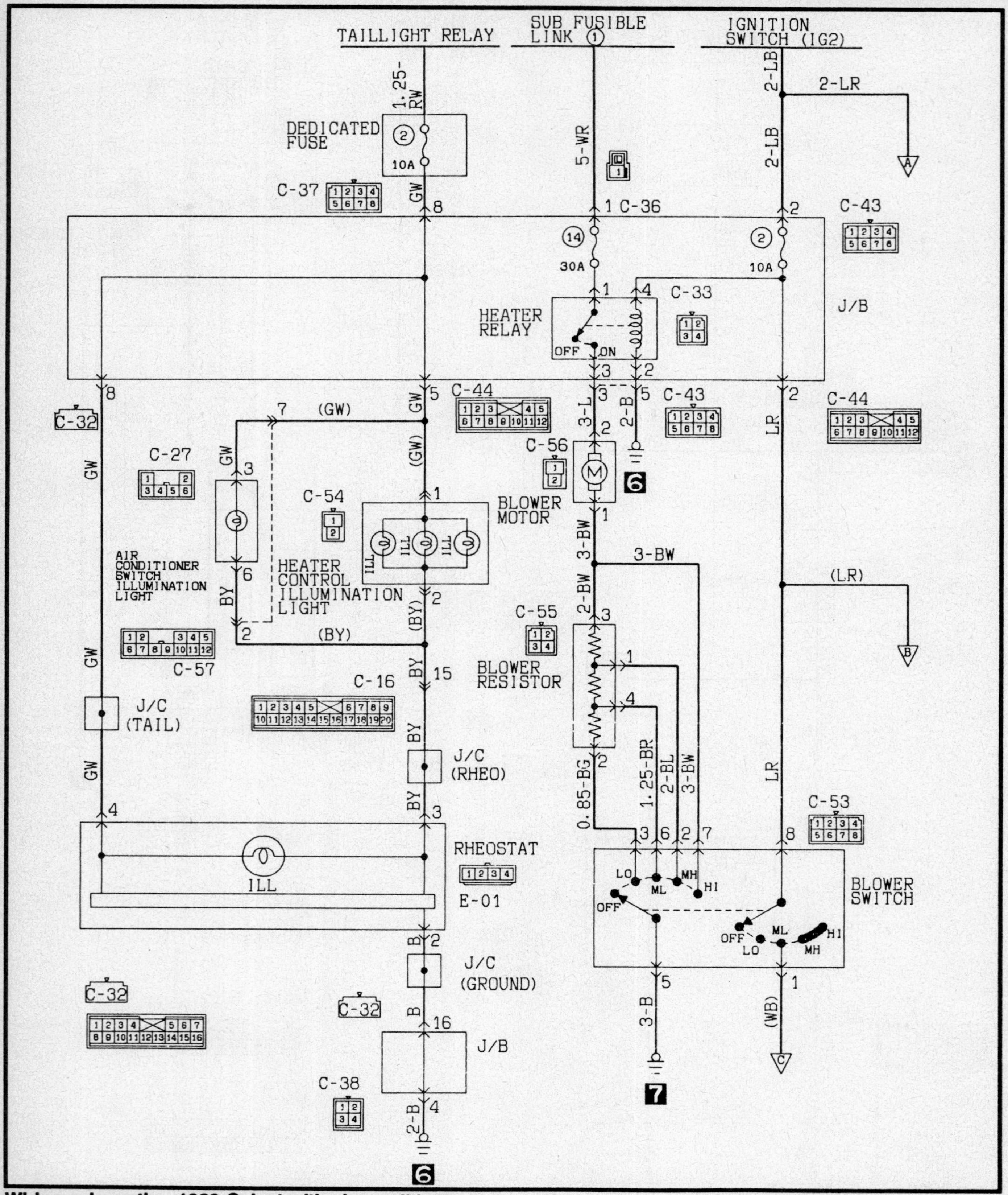
TAILLIGHT RELAY
SUB FUSIBLE LINK 1
IGNITION SWITCH (IG2)
DEDICATED FUSE
10A
C-37
C-36
C-43
C-33
HEATER RELAY
OFF
ON
J/B
C-44
C-32
C-27
C-54
C-56
BLOWER MOTOR
AIR CONDITIONER SWITCH ILLUMINATION LIGHT
HEATER CONTROL ILLUMINATION LIGHT
ILL
C-55
BLOWER RESISTOR
C-57
C-16
J/C (TAIL)
J/C (RHEO)
C-53
RHEOSTAT
E-01
BLOWER SWITCH
LO
ML
MH
HI
J/C (GROUND)
C-38
30A
5-WR
2-LB
2-LR
3-BW
2-BW
0.85-BG
1.25-BR
2-BL
3-B
2-B
GW
BY
LR
(WB)
B

Wiring schematic—1989 Galant with air conditioning

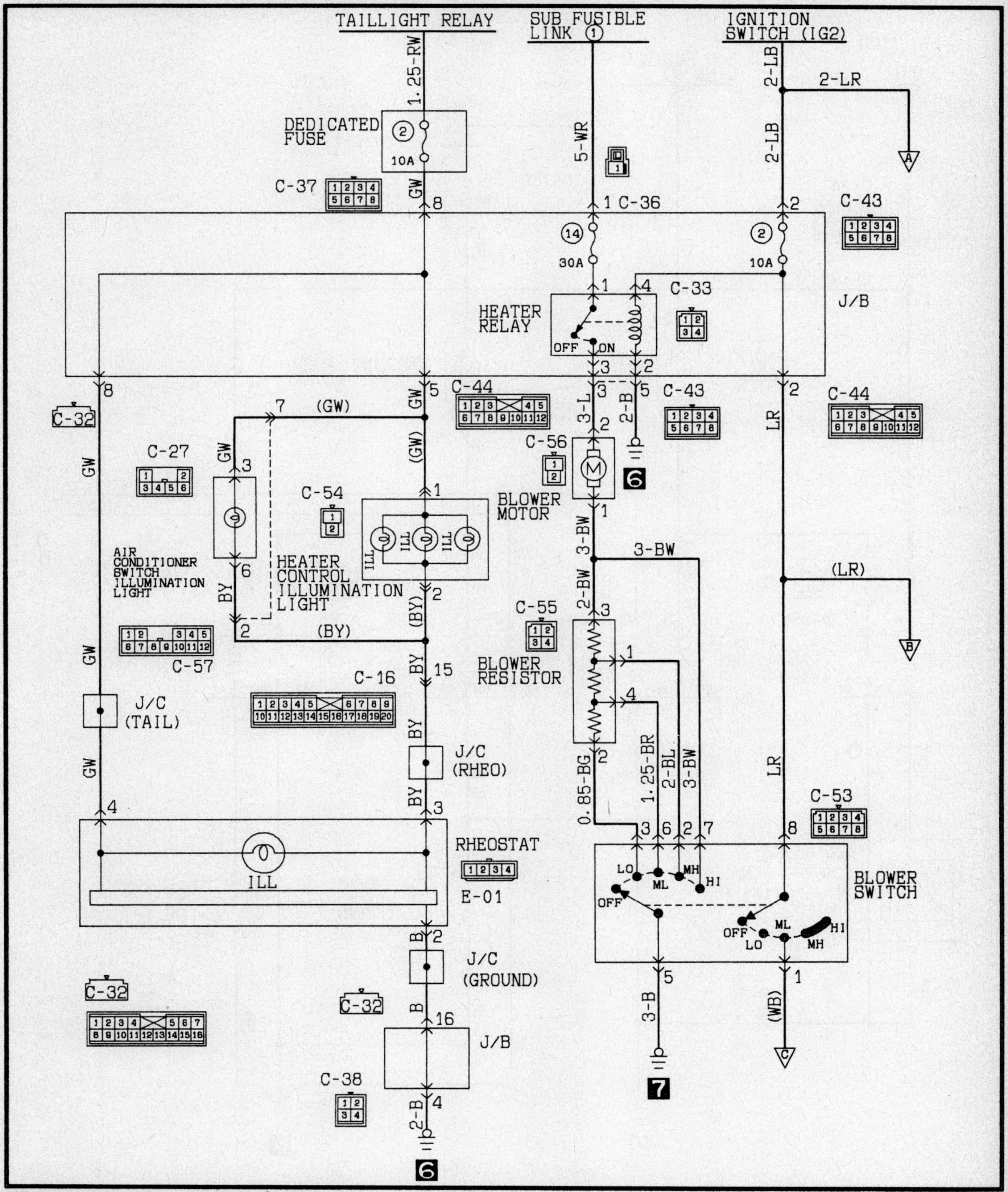
TAILLIGHT RELAY
SUB FUSIBLE LINK ①
IGNITION SWITCH (IG2)
1.25-RW
5-WR
2-LB
2-LR
DEDICATED FUSE
10A
C-37
GW
8
1 C-36
2
C-43
30A
10A
HEATER RELAY
OFF
ON
C-33
J/B
C-32
C-44
7
(GW)
3-L
2-B
LR
C-27
C-56
6
C-54
BLOWER MOTOR
AIR CONDITIONER SWITCH ILLUMINATION LIGHT
HEATER CONTROL ILLUMINATION LIGHT
ILL
3-BW
2-BW
(LR)
BY
(BY)
C-55
C-57
BLOWER RESISTOR
C-16
15
J/C (TAIL)
J/C (RHEO)
0.85-BG
1.25-BR
2-BL
C-53
RHEOSTAT
E-01
LO
ML
MH
HI
OFF
BLOWER SWITCH
J/C (GROUND)
B
16
3-B
(WB)
C-38
2-B
7
A
B
C

Wiring schematic—1990–91 Galant with air conditioning

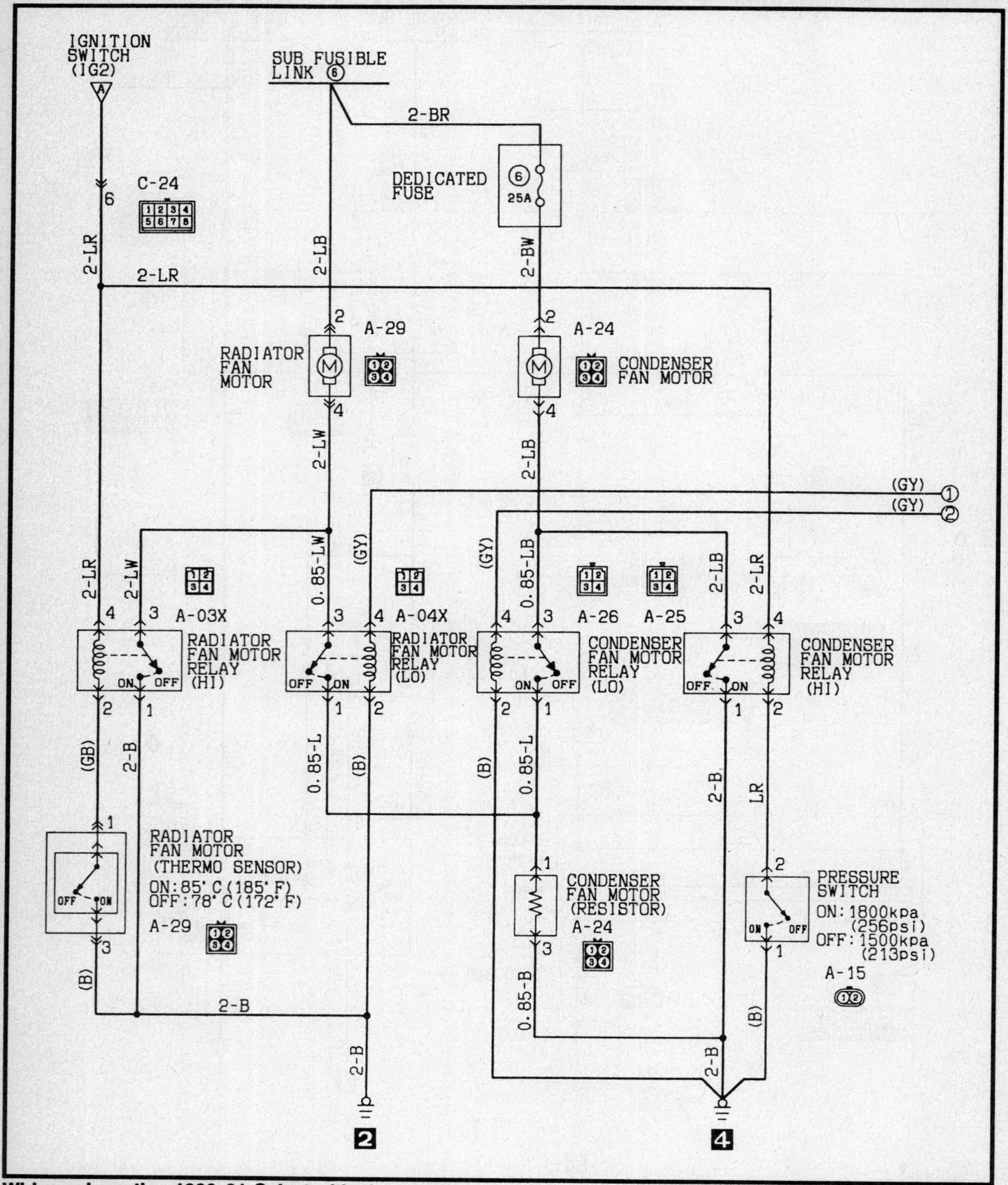
IGNITION SWITCH (IG2)
SUB FUSIBLE LINK ⑥
2-BR
DEDICATED FUSE
25A
C-24
2-LR
2-LB
2-BW
RADIATOR FAN MOTOR
A-29
A-24
CONDENSER FAN MOTOR
2-LW
(GY)
0.85-LW
0.85-LB
A-03X
A-04X
A-26
A-25
RADIATOR FAN MOTOR RELAY (HI)
RADIATOR FAN MOTOR RELAY (LO)
CONDENSER FAN MOTOR RELAY (LO)
CONDENSER FAN MOTOR RELAY (HI)
ON
OFF
(GB)
2-B
0.85-L
(B)
LR
RADIATOR FAN MOTOR (THERMO SENSOR)
ON: 85° C (185° F)
OFF: 78° C (172° F)
CONDENSER FAN MOTOR (RESISTOR)
PRESSURE SWITCH
ON: 1800kpa (256psi)
OFF: 1500kpa (213psi)
A-15
0.85-B

Wiring schematic—1990–91 Galant with air conditioning

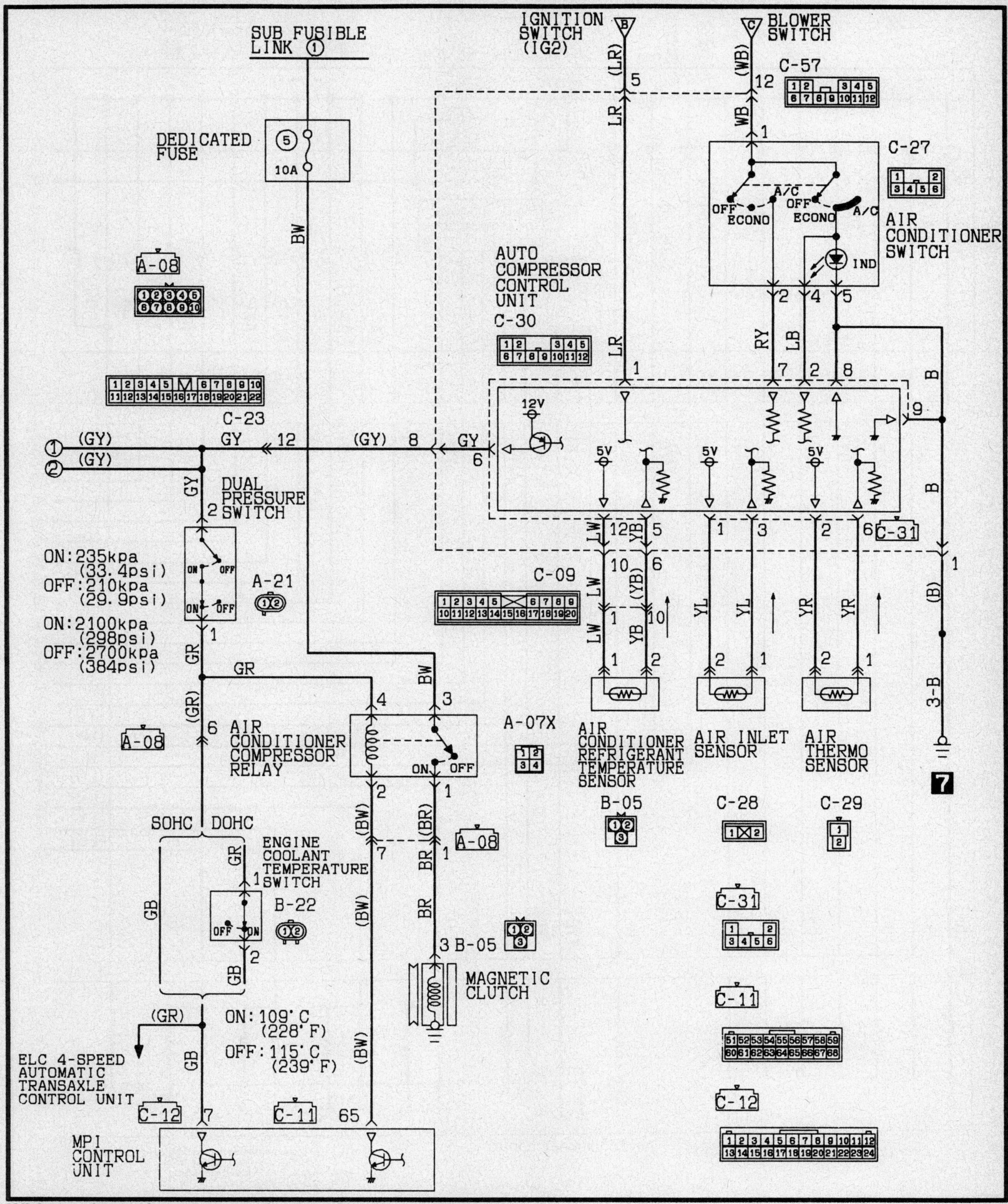
SUB FUSIBLE LINK ①
DEDICATED FUSE
10A
IGNITION SWITCH (IG2)
BLOWER SWITCH
C-57
C-27
AIR CONDITIONER SWITCH
OFF
ECONO
A/C
IND
AUTO COMPRESSOR CONTROL UNIT
C-30
A-08
C-23
DUAL PRESSURE SWITCH
ON:235kpa (33.4psi)
OFF:210kpa (29.9psi)
ON:2100kpa (298psi)
OFF:2700kpa (384psi)
A-21
C-09
C-31
AIR CONDITIONER COMPRESSOR RELAY
A-07X
AIR CONDITIONER REFRIGERANT TEMPERATURE SENSOR
AIR INLET SENSOR
AIR THERMO SENSOR
B-05
C-28
C-29
SOHC
DOHC
ENGINE COOLANT TEMPERATURE SWITCH
B-22
MAGNETIC CLUTCH
ON: 109°C (228°F)
OFF: 115°C (239°F)
ELC 4-SPEED AUTOMATIC TRANSAXLE CONTROL UNIT
C-12
C-11
MPI CONTROL UNIT

Wiring schematic—1990–91 Galant with air conditioning

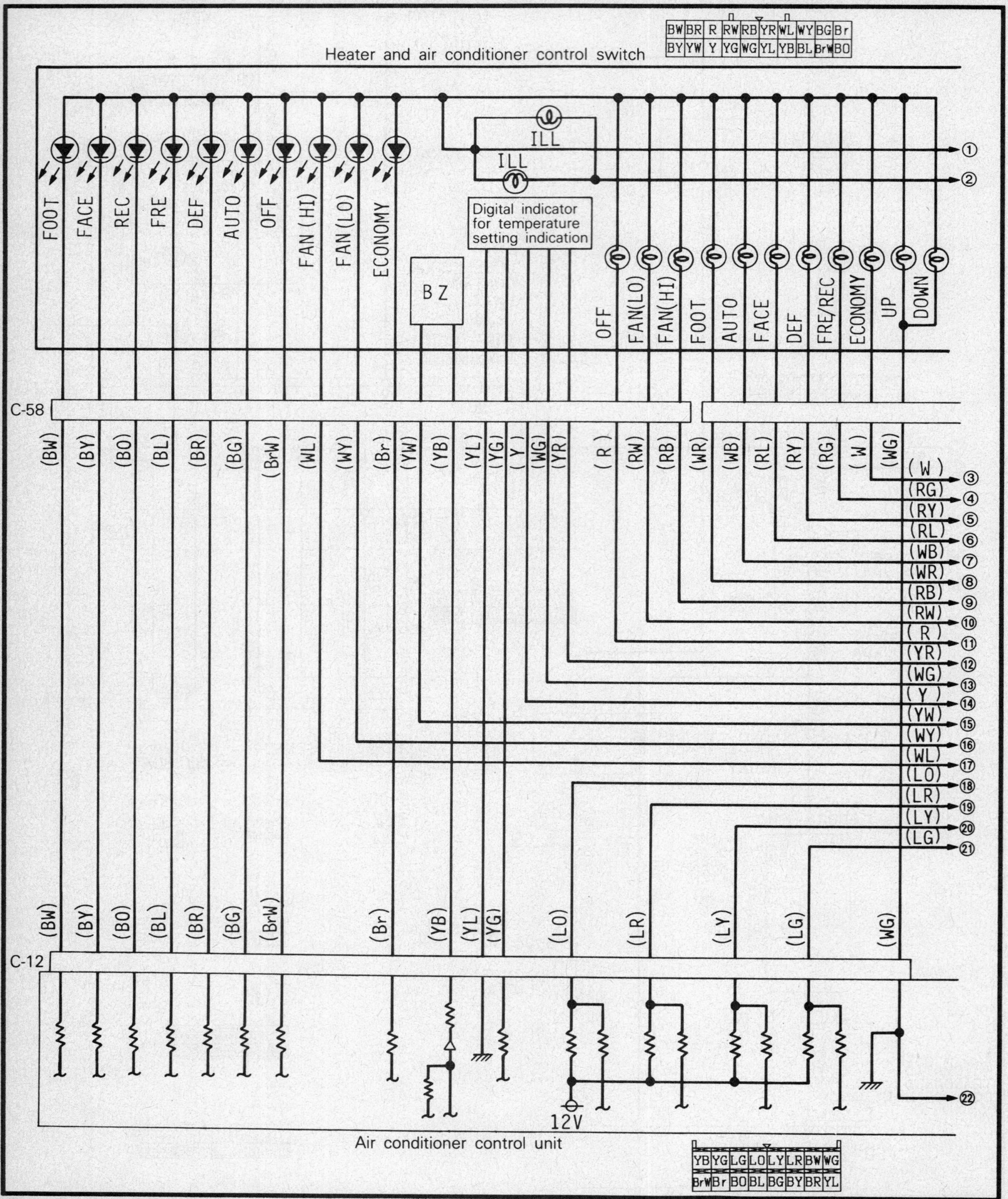
Heater and air conditioner control switch
ILL
ILL
FOOT
FACE
REC
FRE
DEF
AUTO
OFF
FAN (HI)
FAN (LO)
ECONOMY
BZ
Digital indicator for temperature setting indication
OFF
FAN(LO)
FAN(HI)
FOOT
AUTO
FACE
DEF
FRE/REC
ECONOMY
UP
DOWN
C-58
C-12
12V
Air conditioner control unit

Wiring schematic—Sigma with automatic climate control

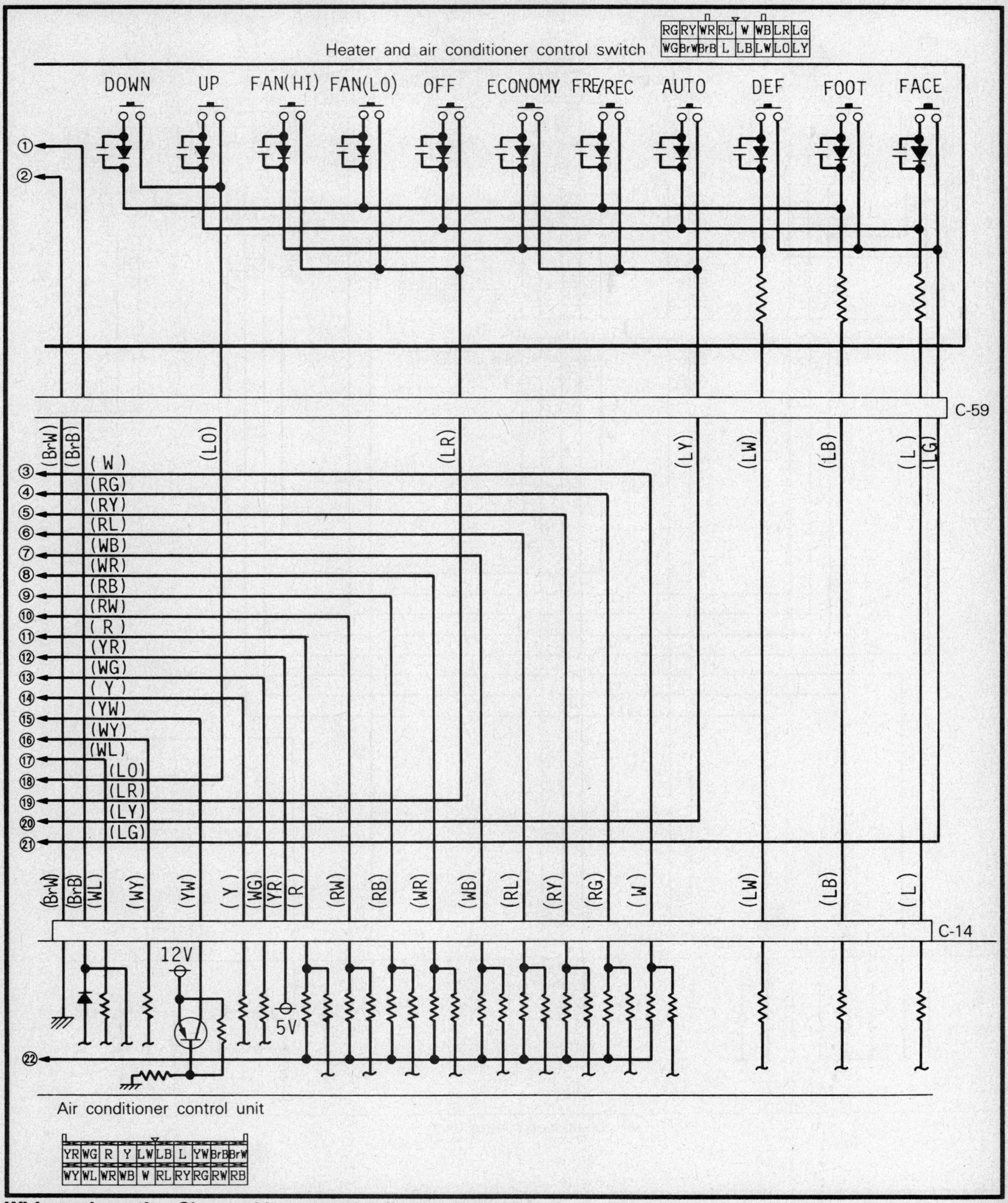
Heater and air conditioner control switch
RG RY WR RL W WB LR LG
WG BrW BrB L LB LW LO LY
DOWN
UP
FAN(HI)
FAN(LO)
OFF
ECONOMY
FRE/REC
AUTO
DEF
FOOT
FACE
C-59
(BrW) (BrB) (LO) (LR) (LY) (LW) (LB) (L) (LG)
(W) (RG) (RY) (RL) (WB) (WR) (RB) (RW) (R) (YR) (WG) (Y) (YW) (WY) (WL) (LO) (LR) (LY) (LG)
(BrW) (BrB) (WL) (WY) (YW) (Y) (WG) (YR) (R) (RW) (RB) (WR) (WB) (RL) (RY) (RG) (W) (LW) (LB) (L)
C-14
12V
5V
Air conditioner control unit
YR WG R Y LW LB L YW BrB BrW
WY WL WR WB W RL RY RG RW RB

Wiring schematic—Sigma with automatic climate control

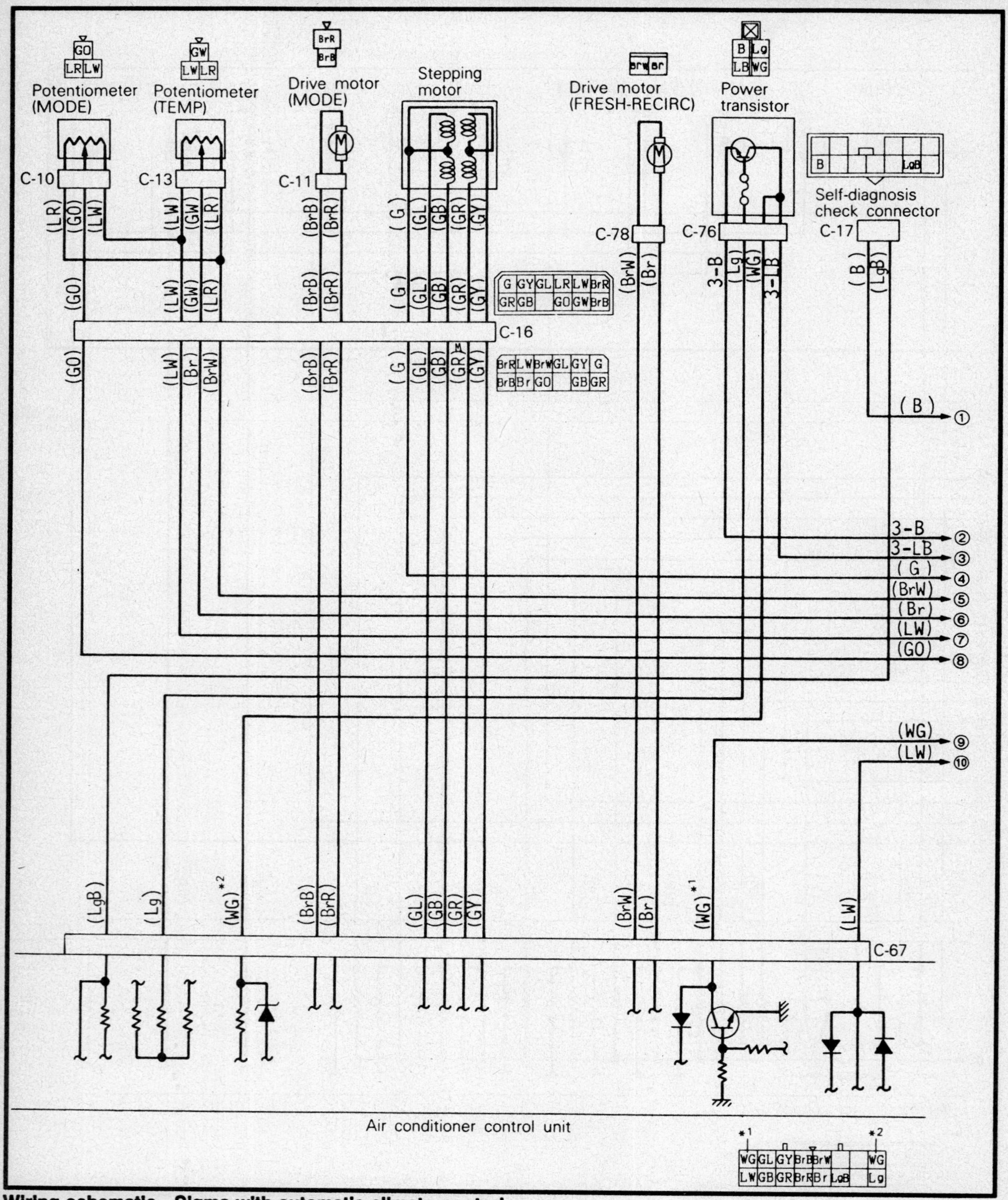
Potentiometer (MODE)
Potentiometer (TEMP)
Drive motor (MODE)
Stepping motor
Drive motor (FRESH-RECIRC)
Power transistor
Self-diagnosis check connector
C-10
C-13
C-11
C-78
C-76
C-17
C-16
C-67
Air conditioner control unit

Wiring schematic—Sigma with automatic climate control

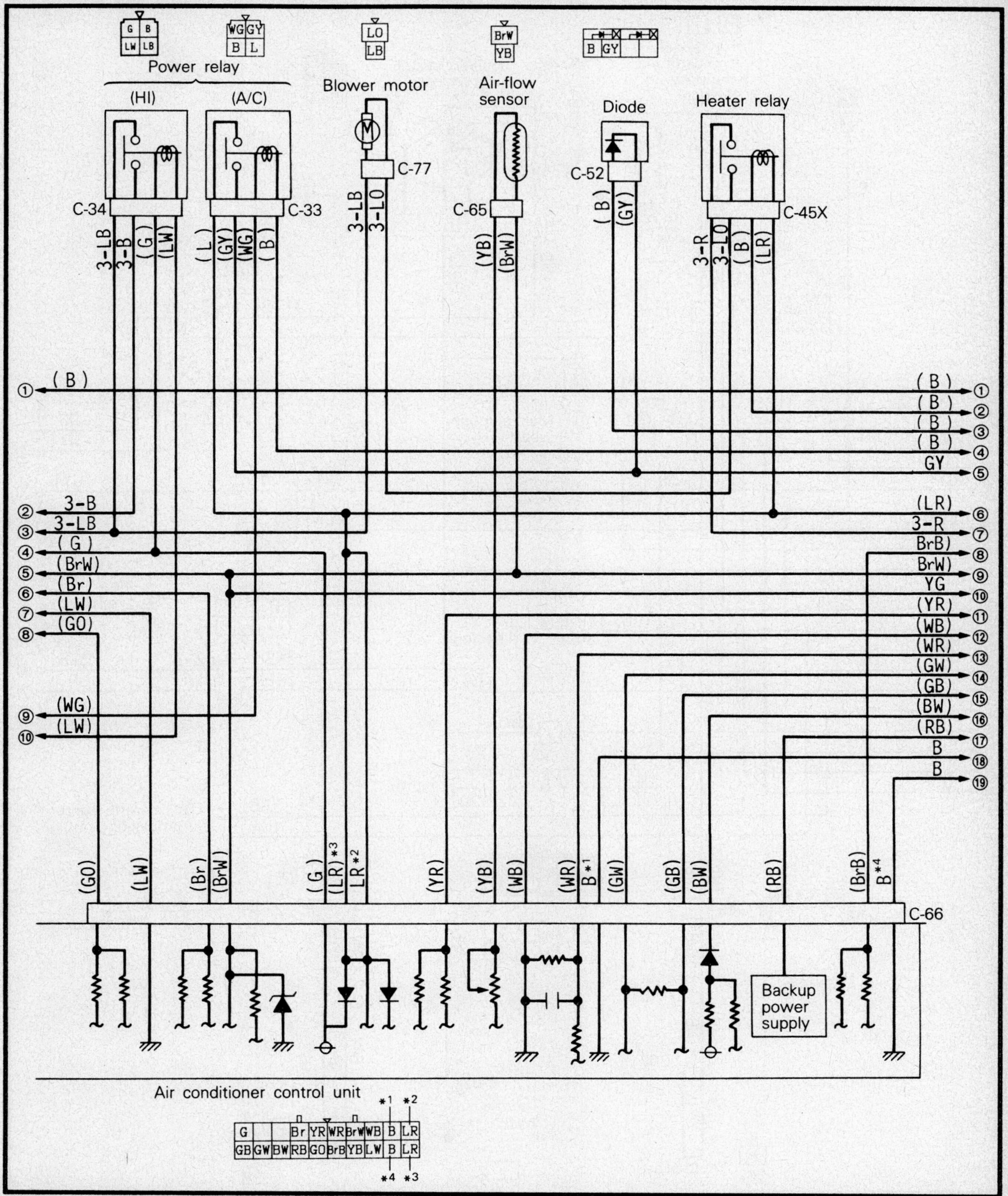
G B LW LB
WG GY B L
LO LB
BrW YB
B GY
Power relay
(HI)
(A/C)
Blower motor
Air-flow sensor
Diode
Heater relay
C-34
C-33
C-77
C-65
C-52
C-45X
3-LB 3-B (G) (LW)
(L) (GY) (WG) (B)
3-LB 3-LO
(YB) (BrW)
(B) (GY)
3-R 3-LO (B) (LR)
① (B)
② 3-B
③ 3-LB
④ (G)
⑤ (BrW)
⑥ (Br)
⑦ (LW)
⑧ (GO)
⑨ (WG)
⑩ (LW)
(B) ①
(B) ②
(B) ③
(B) ④
GY ⑤
(LR) ⑥
3-R ⑦
BrB) ⑧
BrW) ⑨
YG ⑩
(YR) ⑪
(WB) ⑫
(WR) ⑬
(GW) ⑭
(GB) ⑮
(BW) ⑯
(RB) ⑰
B ⑱
B ⑲
(GO) (LW) (Br) (BrW) (G) (LR)*3 LR*2 (YR) (YB) (WB) (WR) B*1 (GW) (GB) (BW) (RB) (BrB) B*4
C-66
Backup power supply
Air conditioner control unit
*1 *2
G Br YR WR BrW WB B LR
GB GW BW RB GO BrB YB LW B LR
*4 *3

Wiring schematic—Sigma with automatic climate control

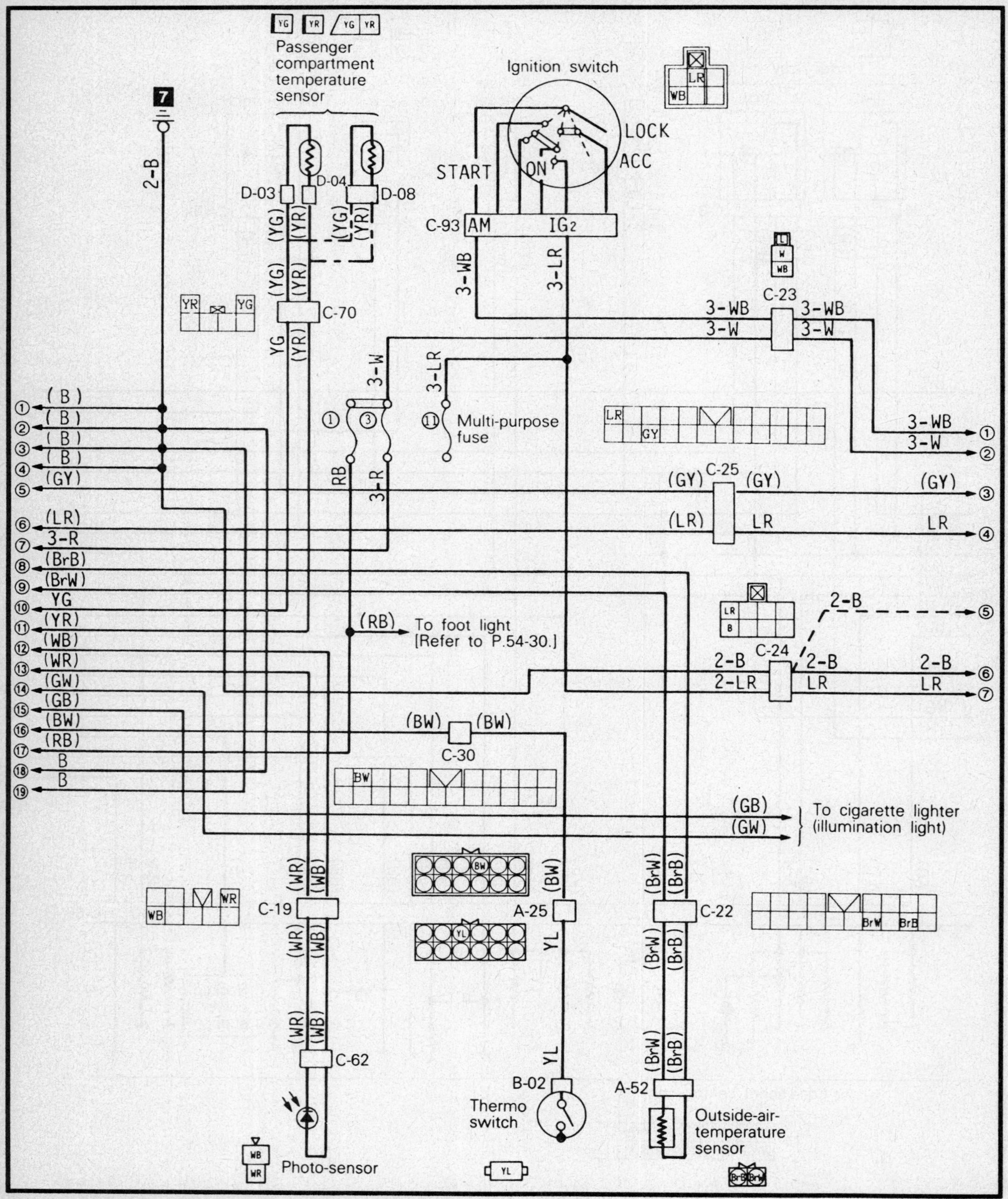
Passenger compartment temperature sensor
Ignition switch
LOCK
ACC
START
ON
C-93 AM IG2
D-03
D-04
D-08
(YG) (YR)
C-70
YG (YR)
2-B
3-WB
3-LR
3-W
C-23
3-WB 3-W
Multi-purpose fuse
RB
3-R
(RB)
To foot light [Refer to P.54-30.]
(B)
(GY)
(LR)
3-R
(BrB)
(BrW)
YG
(YR)
(WB)
(WR)
(GW)
(GB)
(BW)
(RB)
B
C-25
(GY)
LR
C-24
2-B
2-LR
C-30
(BW)
(GB)
(GW)
To cigarette lighter (illumination light)
C-19
A-25
C-22
(BrW) (BrB)
YL
C-62
B-02
Thermo switch
A-52
Outside-air-temperature sensor
Photo-sensor

Wiring schematic—Sigma with automatic climate control

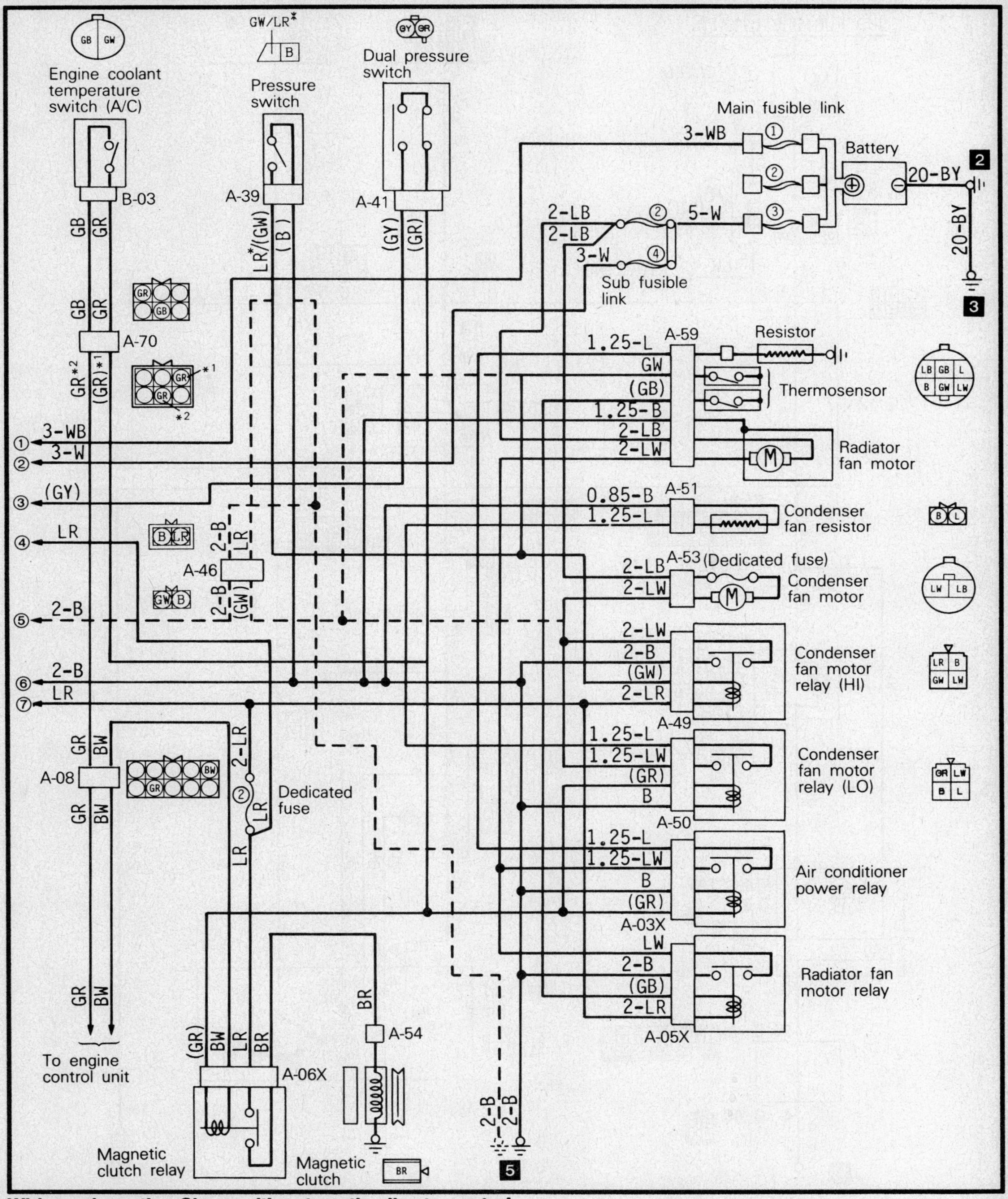
Engine coolant temperature switch (A/C)
GB GW
B-03
GB GR
A-70
GR*2 (GR)*1
*1
*2
GW/LR*
B
Pressure switch
A-39
LR*/(GW) (B)
Dual pressure switch
GY GR
A-41
(GY) (GR)
Main fusible link
3-WB
Battery
20-BY
2
3
2-LB
2-LB
5-W
3-W
Sub fusible link
1.25-L
A-59
Resistor
GW
(GB)
Thermosensor
1.25-B
2-LB
2-LW
Radiator fan motor
LB GB L
B GW LW
0.85-B
A-51
1.25-L
Condenser fan resistor
B L
2-LB
A-53 (Dedicated fuse)
2-LW
Condenser fan motor
LW LB
2-LW
2-B
(GW)
2-LR
A-49
Condenser fan motor relay (HI)
LR B
GW LW
1.25-L
1.25-LW
(GR)
B
A-50
Condenser fan motor relay (LO)
GR LW
B L
1.25-L
1.25-LW
B
(GR)
A-03X
Air conditioner power relay
LW
2-B
(GB)
2-LR
A-05X
Radiator fan motor relay
3-WB
3-W
(GY)
LR
2-B
2-B
LR
2-B LR
A-46
2-B (GW)
B LR
GW B
GR BW
A-08
2-LR
Dedicated fuse
LR
To engine control unit
(GR) BW LR BR
A-06X
Magnetic clutch relay
BR
A-54
Magnetic clutch
BR
2-B 2-B
5

Wiring schematic—Sigma with automatic climate control

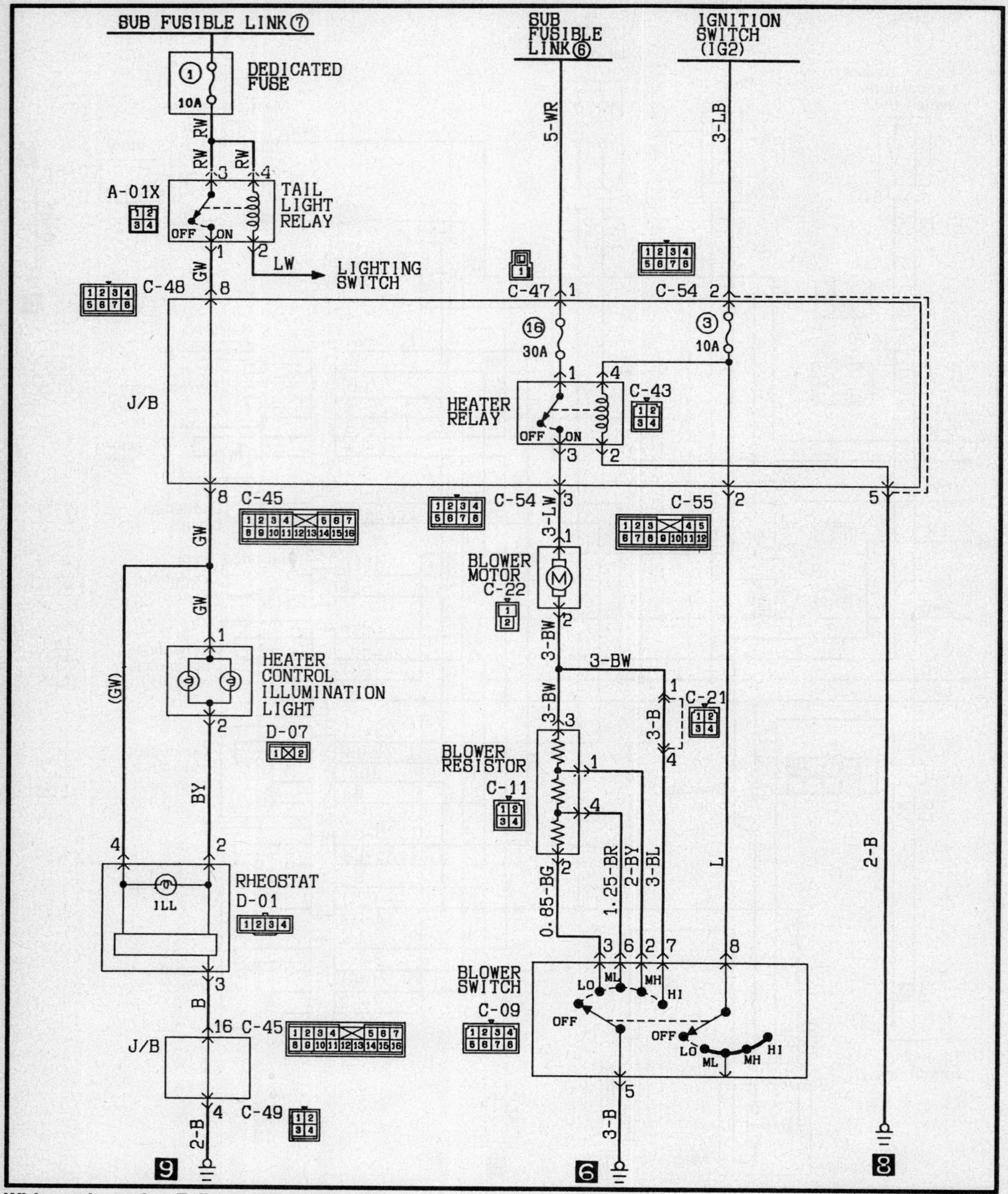
SUB FUSIBLE LINK ⑦
DEDICATED FUSE
10A
A-01X
TAIL LIGHT RELAY
OFF
ON
LW
LIGHTING SWITCH
C-48
J/B
SUB FUSIBLE LINK ⑥
5-WR
IGNITION SWITCH (IG2)
3-LB
C-47
C-54
30A
10A
HEATER RELAY
C-43
C-45
C-54
3-LW
C-55
BLOWER MOTOR
C-22
3-BW
C-21
3-B
HEATER CONTROL ILLUMINATION LIGHT
D-07
(GW)
GW
BY
BLOWER RESISTOR
C-11
0.85-BG
1.25-BR
2-BY
3-BL
L
2-B
RHEOSTAT
D-01
ILL
B
BLOWER SWITCH
C-09
LO
ML
MH
HI
OFF
C-45
J/B
C-49
2-B
3-B
9
6
8

Wiring schematic—Eclipse with heater only

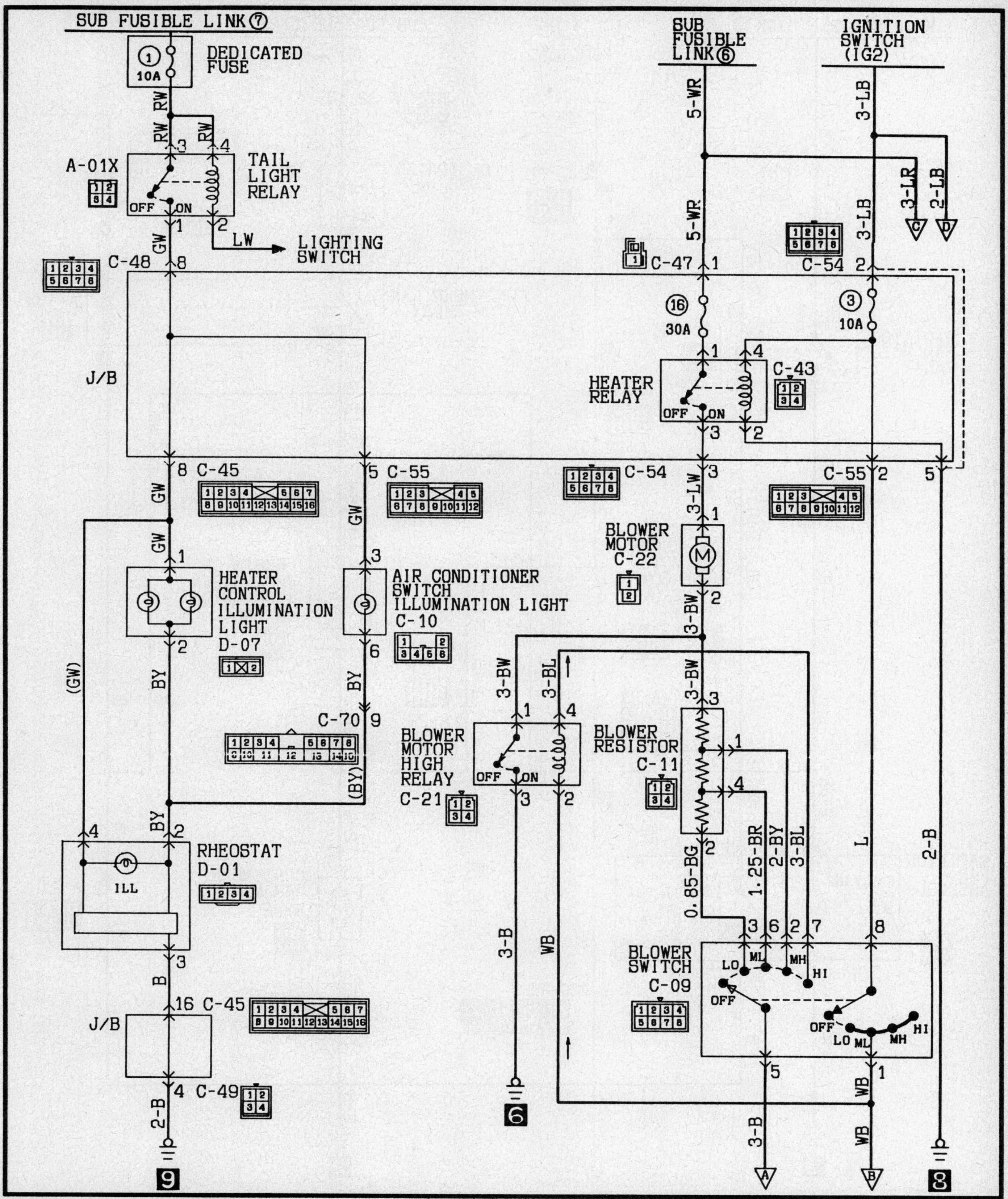
SUB FUSIBLE LINK ⑦
DEDICATED FUSE
10A
A-01X
TAIL LIGHT RELAY
LIGHTING SWITCH
C-48
J/B
C-45
C-55
HEATER CONTROL ILLUMINATION LIGHT D-07
AIR CONDITIONER SWITCH ILLUMINATION LIGHT C-10
C-70
RHEOSTAT D-01
ILL
C-49
SUB FUSIBLE LINK ⑥
IGNITION SWITCH (IG2)
C-47
C-54
30A
HEATER RELAY
C-43
BLOWER MOTOR C-22
BLOWER MOTOR HIGH RELAY C-21
BLOWER RESISTOR C-11
BLOWER SWITCH C-09
OFF
LO
ML
MH
HI

Wiring schematic—Eclipse with air conditioning

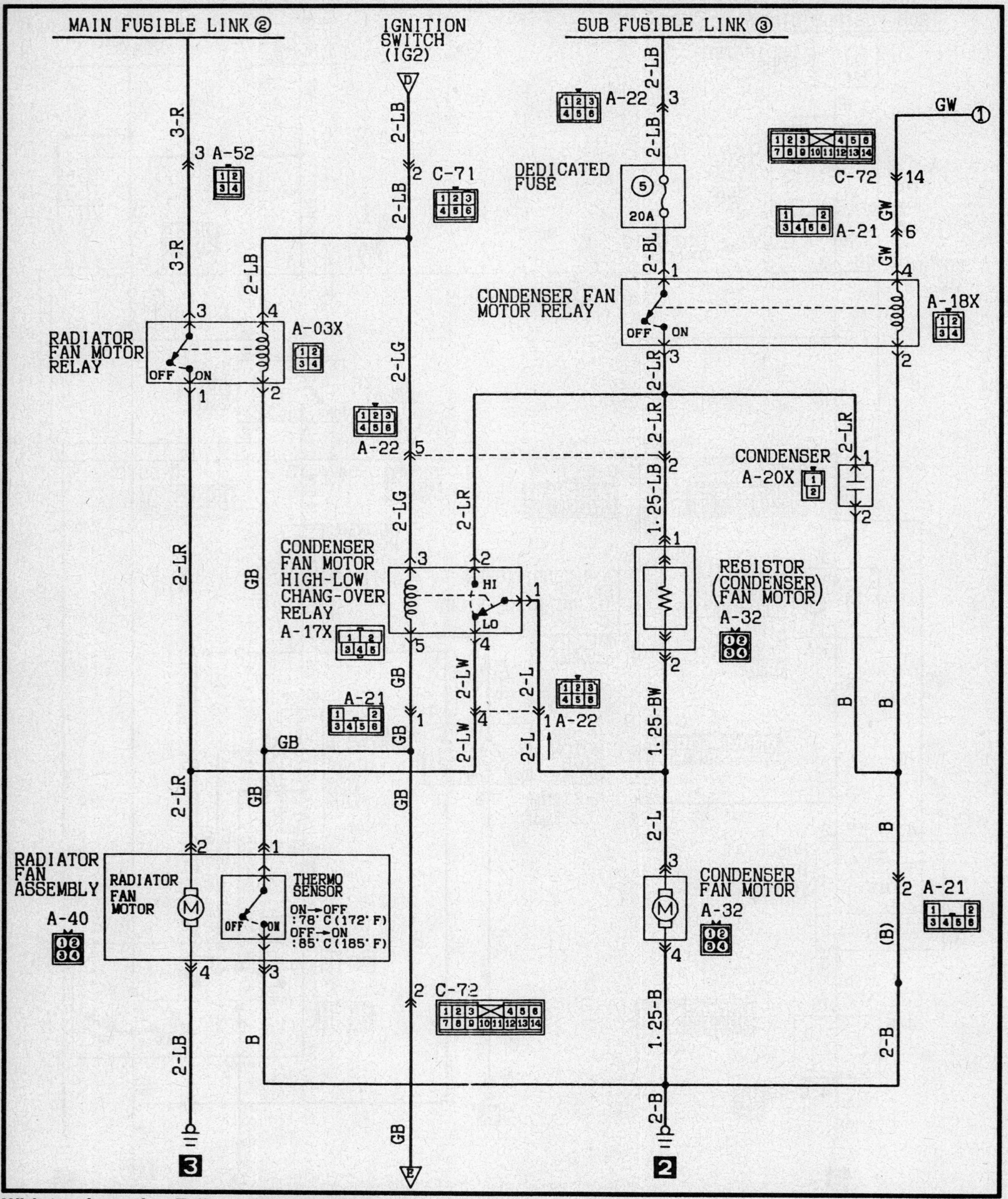
MAIN FUSIBLE LINK ②
IGNITION SWITCH (IG2)
SUB FUSIBLE LINK ③
DEDICATED FUSE
20A
CONDENSER FAN MOTOR RELAY
OFF
ON
RADIATOR FAN MOTOR RELAY
A-03X
A-22
A-52
C-71
C-72
A-21
A-18X
GW
CONDENSER
A-20X
CONDENSER FAN MOTOR HIGH-LOW CHANG-OVER RELAY
A-17X
HI
LO
RESISTOR (CONDENSER FAN MOTOR)
A-32
RADIATOR FAN ASSEMBLY
A-40
RADIATOR FAN MOTOR
THERMO SENSOR
ON→OFF :78°C (172°F)
OFF→ON :85°C (185°F)
CONDENSER FAN MOTOR
3-R
2-LB
2-LG
2-BL
2-LR
1.25-LB
1.25-BW
2-L
1.25-B
2-B
GB
B
(B)
2-LW
3
2
Wiring schematic—Eclipse with air conditioning

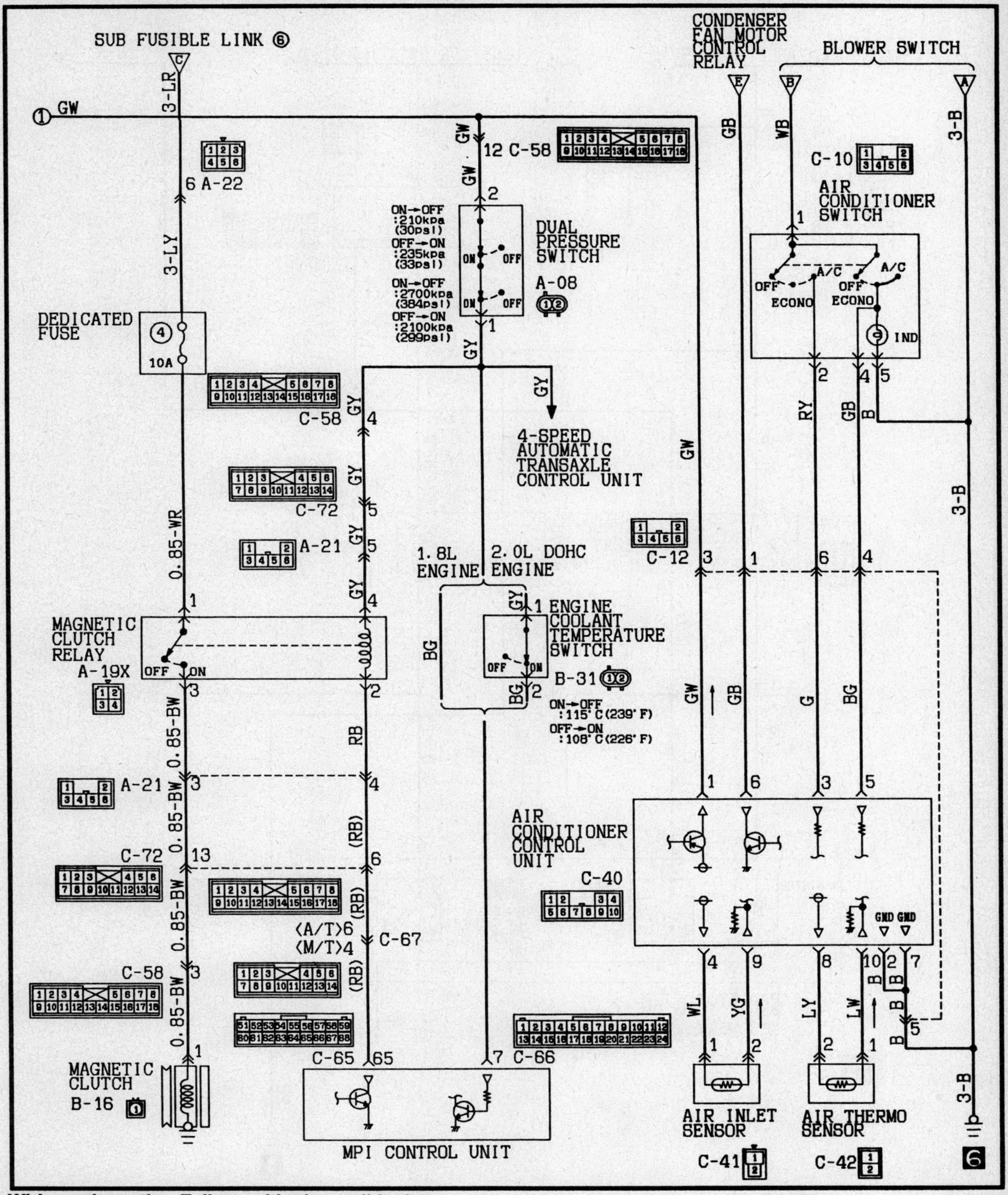
SUB FUSIBLE LINK ⑥
CONDENSER FAN MOTOR CONTROL RELAY
BLOWER SWITCH
GW
3-LR
6 A-22
12 C-58
DUAL PRESSURE SWITCH
A-08
ON→OFF :210kpa (30psi)
OFF→ON :235kpa (33psi)
ON→OFF :2700kpa (384psi)
OFF→ON :2100kpa (299psi)
C-10
AIR CONDITIONER SWITCH
A/C
OFF
ECONO
IND
3-LY
DEDICATED FUSE
10A
GY
C-58
4-SPEED AUTOMATIC TRANSAXLE CONTROL UNIT
RY
GB
WB
3-B
C-72
A-21
1.8L ENGINE
2.0L DOHC ENGINE
C-12
0.85-WR
MAGNETIC CLUTCH RELAY
A-19X
OFF
ON
ENGINE COOLANT TEMPERATURE SWITCH
B-31
ON→OFF :115°C(239°F)
OFF→ON :108°C(226°F)
BG
RB
0.85-BW
AIR CONDITIONER CONTROL UNIT
C-40
(RB)
<A/T>6
<M/T>4
C-67
GND GND
WL
YG
LY
LW
MAGNETIC CLUTCH
B-16
C-65
C-66
MPI CONTROL UNIT
AIR INLET SENSOR
AIR THERMO SENSOR
C-41
C-42
6

Wiring schematic—Eclipse with air conditioning

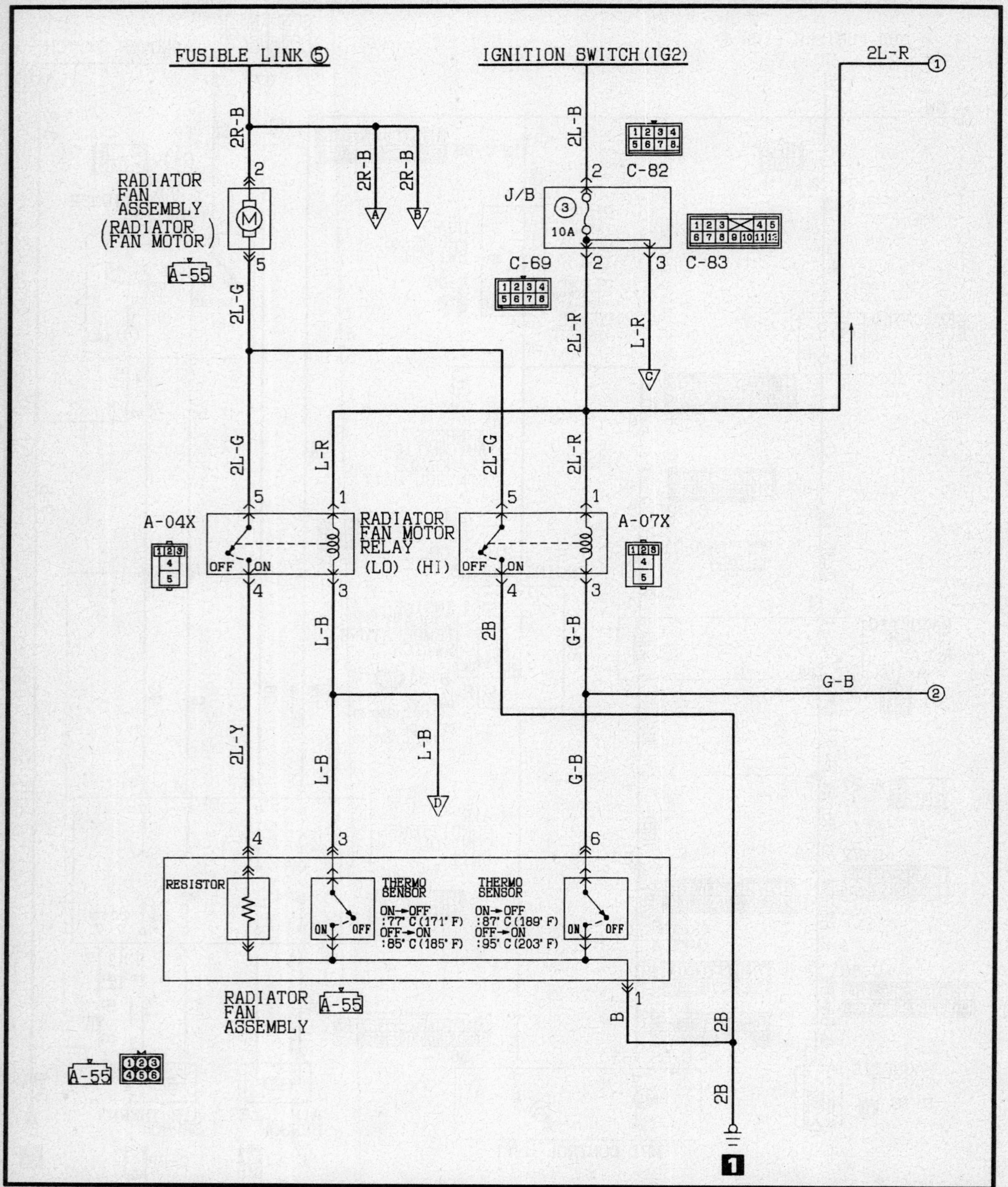
FUSIBLE LINK ⑤
IGNITION SWITCH (IG2)
2L-R
2R-B
RADIATOR FAN ASSEMBLY (RADIATOR FAN MOTOR)
A-55
2L-G
J/B
10A
C-82
C-69
C-83
2L-R
L-R
A-04X
A-07X
RADIATOR FAN MOTOR RELAY
(LO) (HI)
OFF ON
L-B
2B
G-B
2L-Y
RESISTOR
THERMO SENSOR
ON→OFF :77° C (171° F)
OFF→ON :85° C (185° F)
THERMO SENSOR
ON→OFF :87° C (189° F)
OFF→ON :95° C (203° F)
RADIATOR FAN ASSEMBLY
B

Wiring schematic—3000GT with manual air conditioning

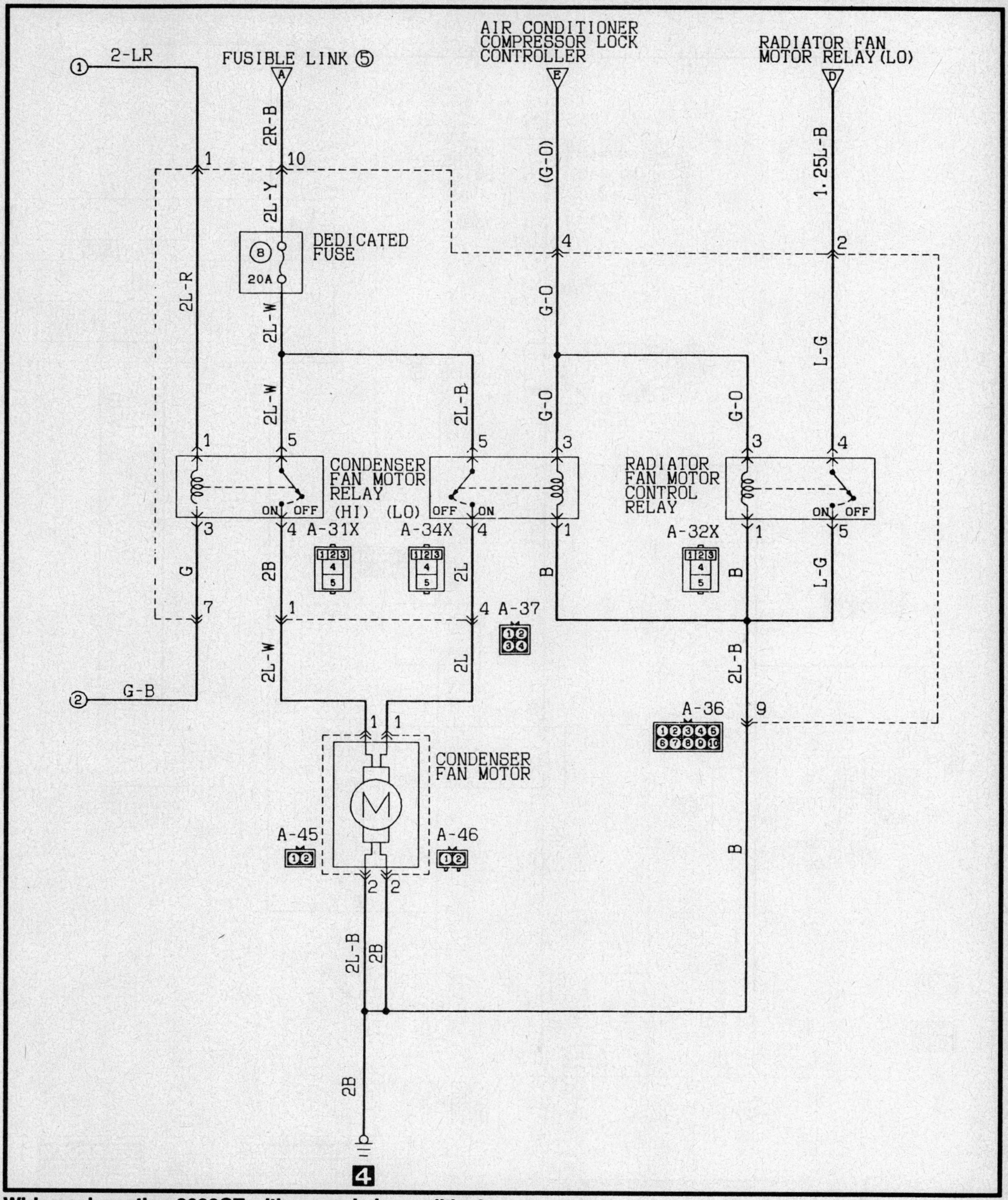
2-LR
FUSIBLE LINK ⑤
AIR CONDITIONER COMPRESSOR LOCK CONTROLLER
RADIATOR FAN MOTOR RELAY (LO)
2R-B
(G-O)
1.25L-B
2L-Y
DEDICATED FUSE
20A
2L-R
2L-W
G-O
L-G
2L-B
CONDENSER FAN MOTOR RELAY
(HI)
(LO)
ON
OFF
A-31X
A-34X
RADIATOR FAN MOTOR CONTROL RELAY
A-32X
G
2B
2L
B
A-37
G-B
2L-B
A-36
CONDENSER FAN MOTOR
M
A-45
A-46
2B
4

Wiring schematic—3000GT with manual air conditioning

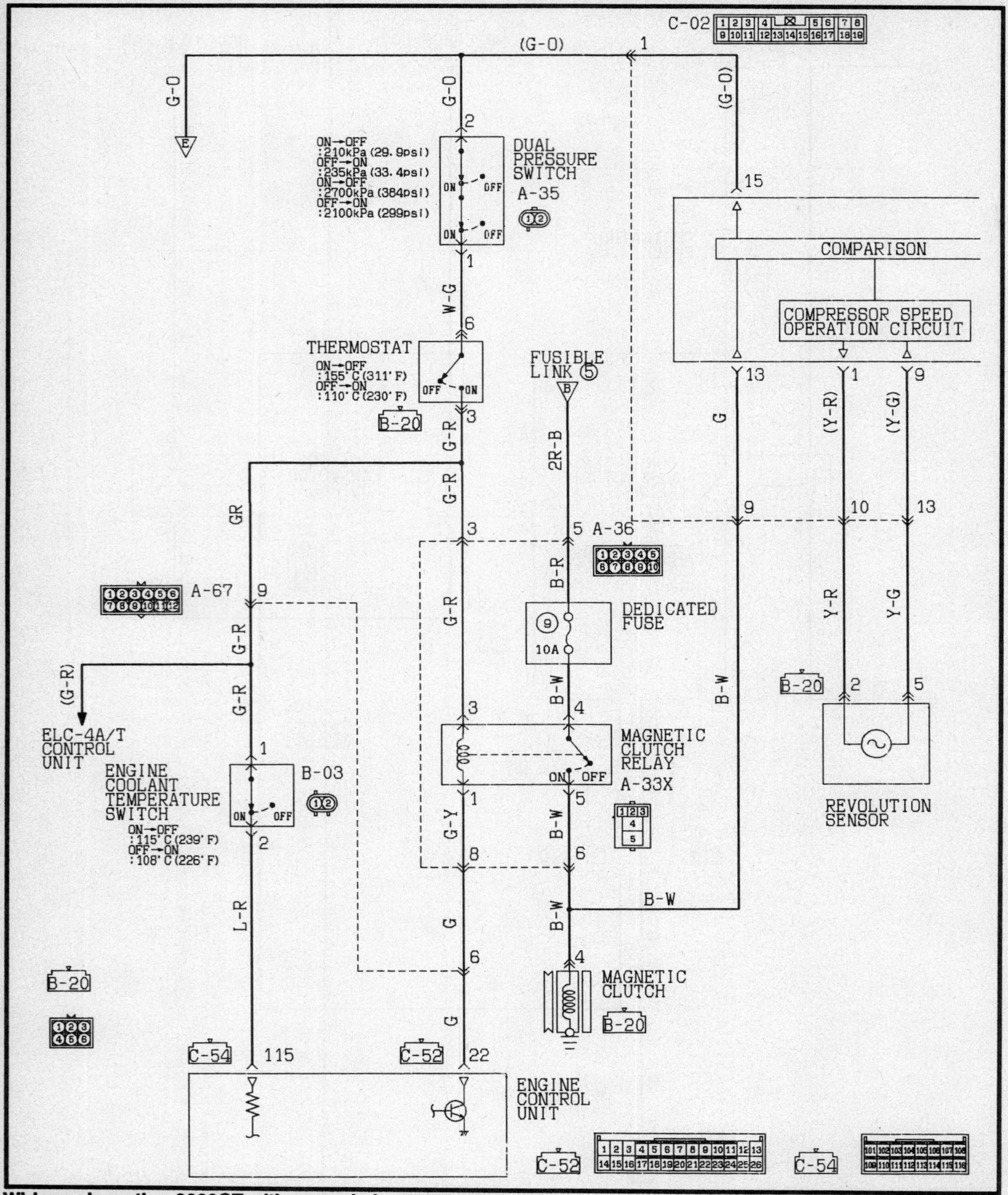
C-02
(G-O)
G-O
DUAL PRESSURE SWITCH
A-35
ON→OFF :210kPa (29.9psi)
OFF→ON :235kPa (33.4psi)
ON→OFF :2700kPa (384psi)
OFF→ON :2100kPa (299psi)
W-G
THERMOSTAT
ON→OFF :155°C (311°F)
OFF→ON :110°C (230°F)
B-20
FUSIBLE LINK 5
2R-B
G-R
GR
A-36
B-R
DEDICATED FUSE
10A
B-W
MAGNETIC CLUTCH RELAY
A-33X
MAGNETIC CLUTCH
COMPARISON
COMPRESSOR SPEED OPERATION CIRCUIT
(Y-R)
(Y-G)
Y-R
Y-G
REVOLUTION SENSOR
A-67
(G-R)
ELC-4A/T CONTROL UNIT
ENGINE COOLANT TEMPERATURE SWITCH
B-03
ON→OFF :115°C (239°F)
OFF→ON :108°C (226°F)
L-R
G-Y
G
C-54
C-52
ENGINE CONTROL UNIT
Wiring schematic—3000GT with manual air conditioning

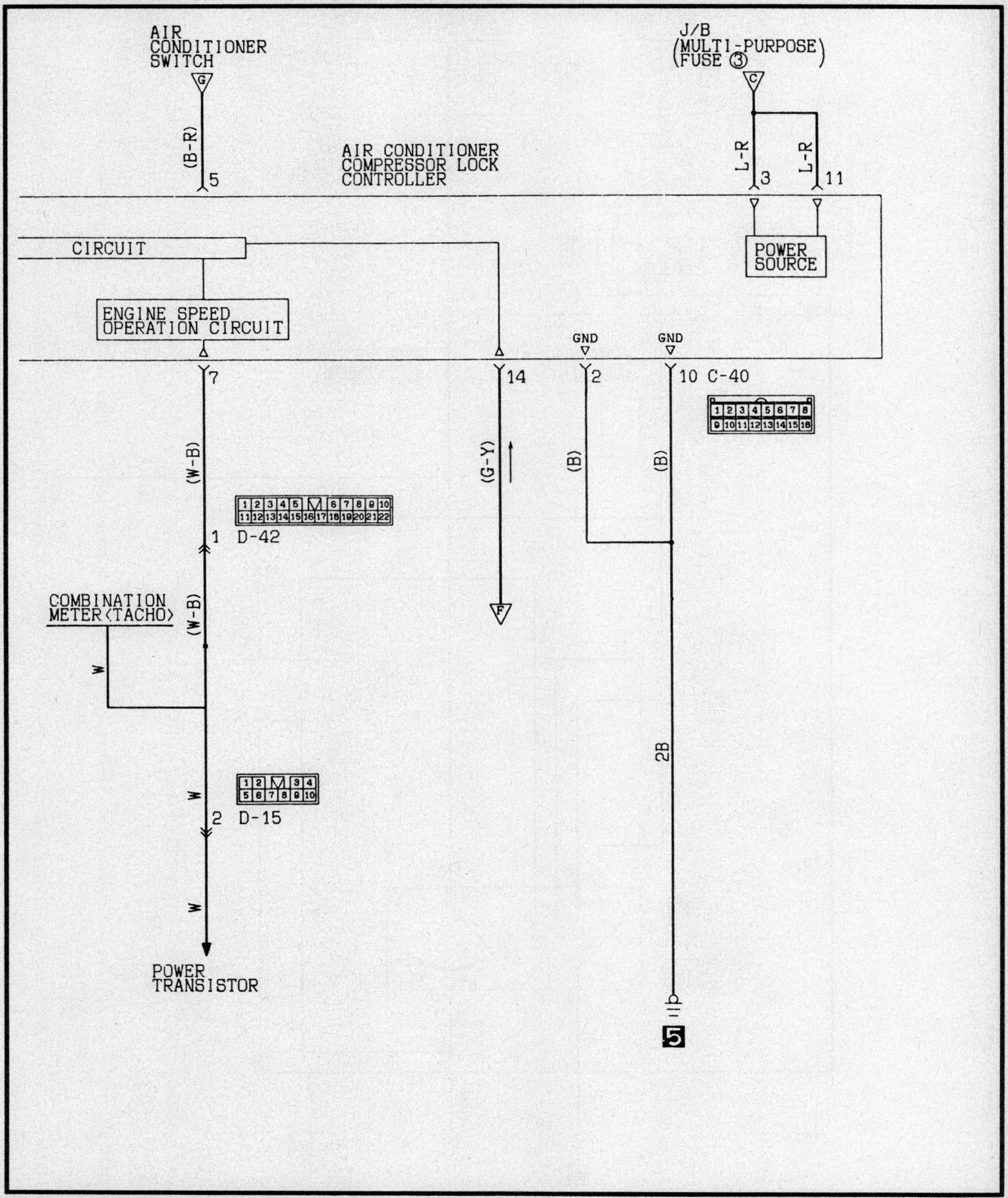
AIR CONDITIONER SWITCH
J/B (MULTI-PURPOSE FUSE ③)
(B-R)
5
AIR CONDITIONER COMPRESSOR LOCK CONTROLLER
L-R
3
L-R
11
CIRCUIT
POWER SOURCE
ENGINE SPEED OPERATION CIRCUIT
GND
GND
7
14
2
10 C-40
(W-B)
(G-Y)
(B)
(B)
1 D-42
COMBINATION METER ‹TACHO›
(W-B)
W
2B
W
2 D-15
W
POWER TRANSISTOR
5

Wiring schematic—3000GT with manual air conditioning

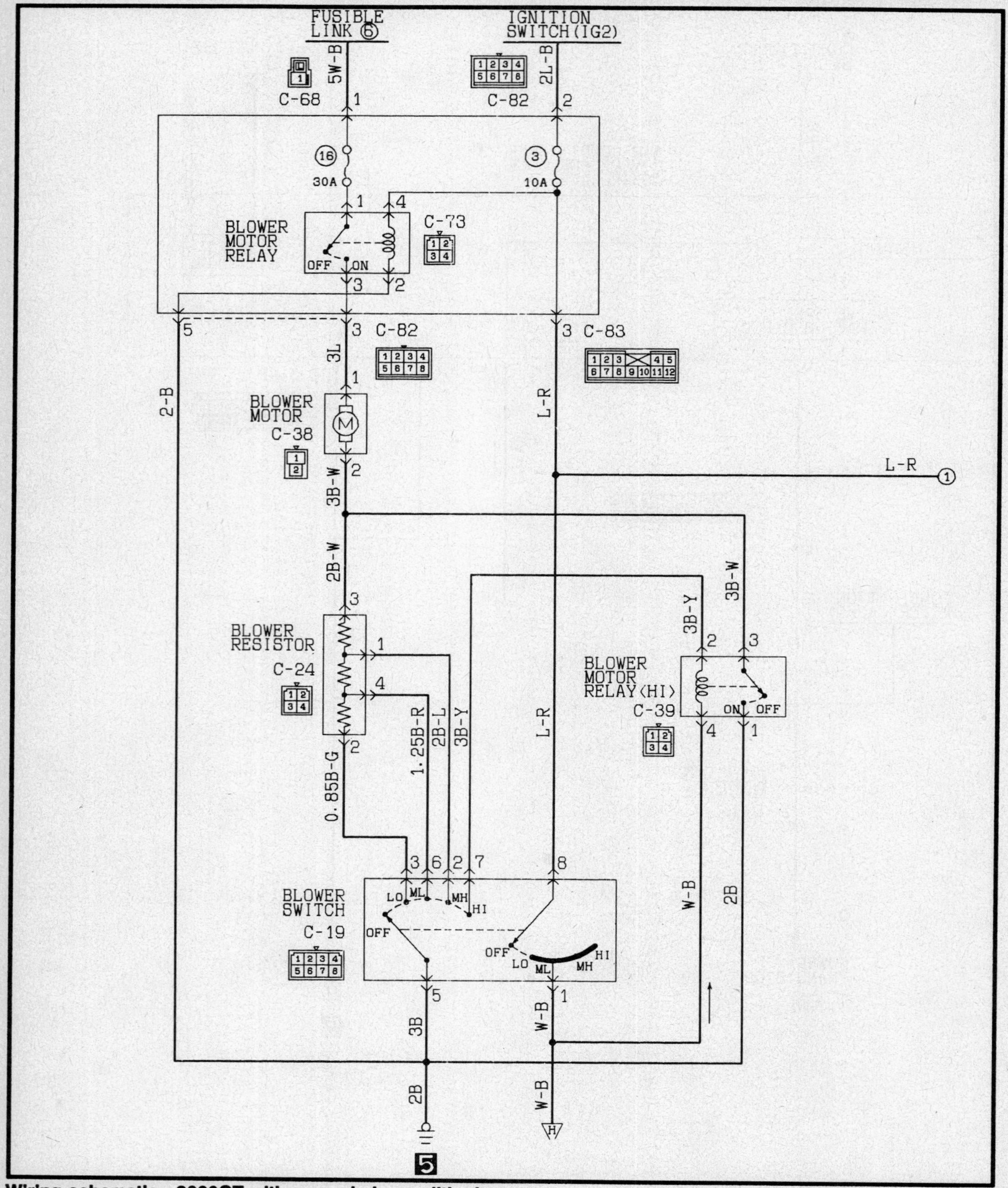
FUSIBLE LINK 6
IGNITION SWITCH (IG2)
5W-B
2L-B
C-68
C-82
16
30A
3
10A
BLOWER MOTOR RELAY
C-73
OFF
ON
C-82
C-83
3L
2-B
L-R
BLOWER MOTOR
C-38
3B-W
L-R
1
2B-W
BLOWER RESISTOR
C-24
3B-Y
3B-W
BLOWER MOTOR RELAY (HI)
C-39
0.85B-G
1.25B-R
2B-L
3B-Y
L-R
W-B
2B
BLOWER SWITCH
C-19
LO
ML
MH
HI
OFF
3B
W-B
2B
W-B
5

Wiring schematic—3000GT with manual air conditioning

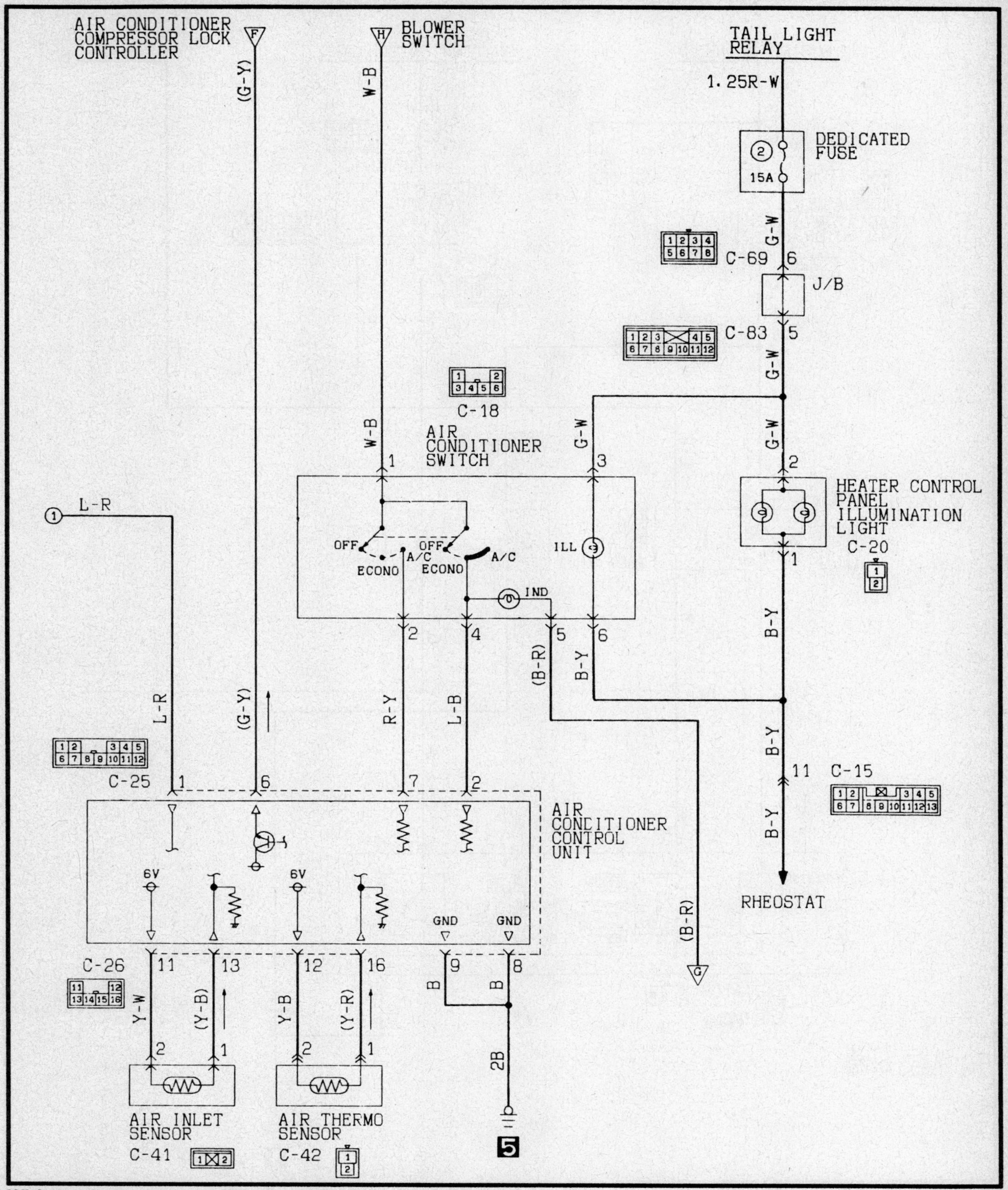
AIR CONDITIONER COMPRESSOR LOCK CONTROLLER
F
(G-Y)
H
BLOWER SWITCH
W-B
TAIL LIGHT RELAY
1.25R-W
DEDICATED FUSE
2
15A
G-W
C-69
6
J/B
C-83
5
C-18
AIR CONDITIONER SWITCH
1
3
OFF
A/C
ECONO
ILL
IND
2
4
5
6
HEATER CONTROL PANEL ILLUMINATION LIGHT
C-20
1
B-Y
L-R
R-Y
L-B
(B-R)
C-25
7
11
C-15
AIR CONDITIONER CONTROL UNIT
6V
GND
RHEOSTAT
C-26
13
12
16
9
8
Y-W
(Y-B)
Y-B
(Y-R)
B
2B
G
AIR INLET SENSOR
C-41
AIR THERMO SENSOR
C-42
5

Wiring schematic—3000GT with manual air conditioning

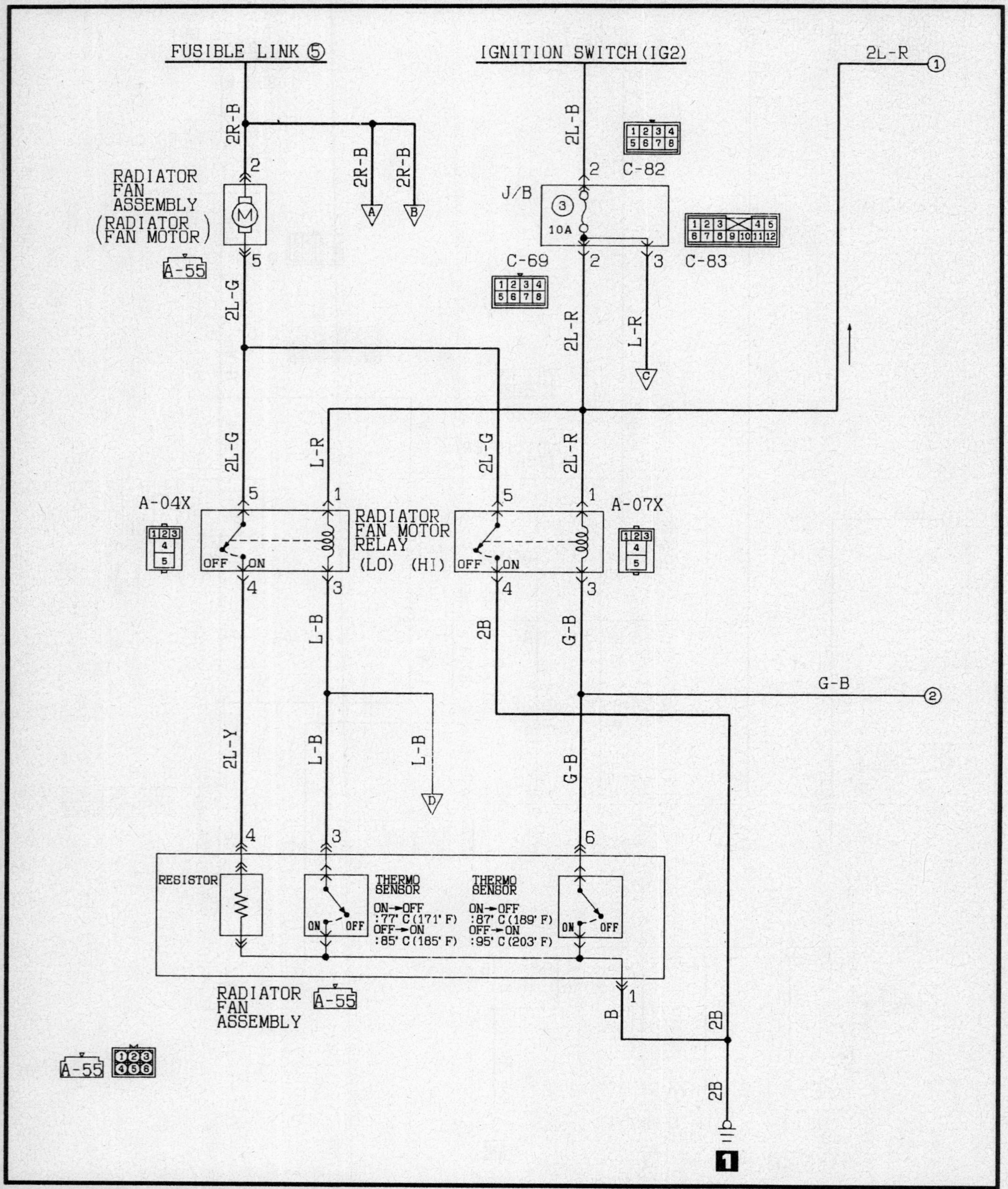
FUSIBLE LINK ⑤
IGNITION SWITCH (IG2)
2L-R
2R-B
RADIATOR FAN ASSEMBLY (RADIATOR FAN MOTOR)
A-55
2L-G
J/B
10A
C-82
C-69
C-83
2L-B
2L-R
L-R
A-04X
A-07X
RADIATOR FAN MOTOR RELAY
(LO) (HI)
OFF ON
L-B
2B
G-B
2L-Y
RESISTOR
THERMO SENSOR
ON→OFF :77° C (171° F)
OFF→ON :85° C (185° F)
THERMO SENSOR
ON→OFF :87° C (189° F)
OFF→ON :95° C (203° F)
RADIATOR FAN ASSEMBLY
B

Wiring schematic—3000GT with full auto air conditioning

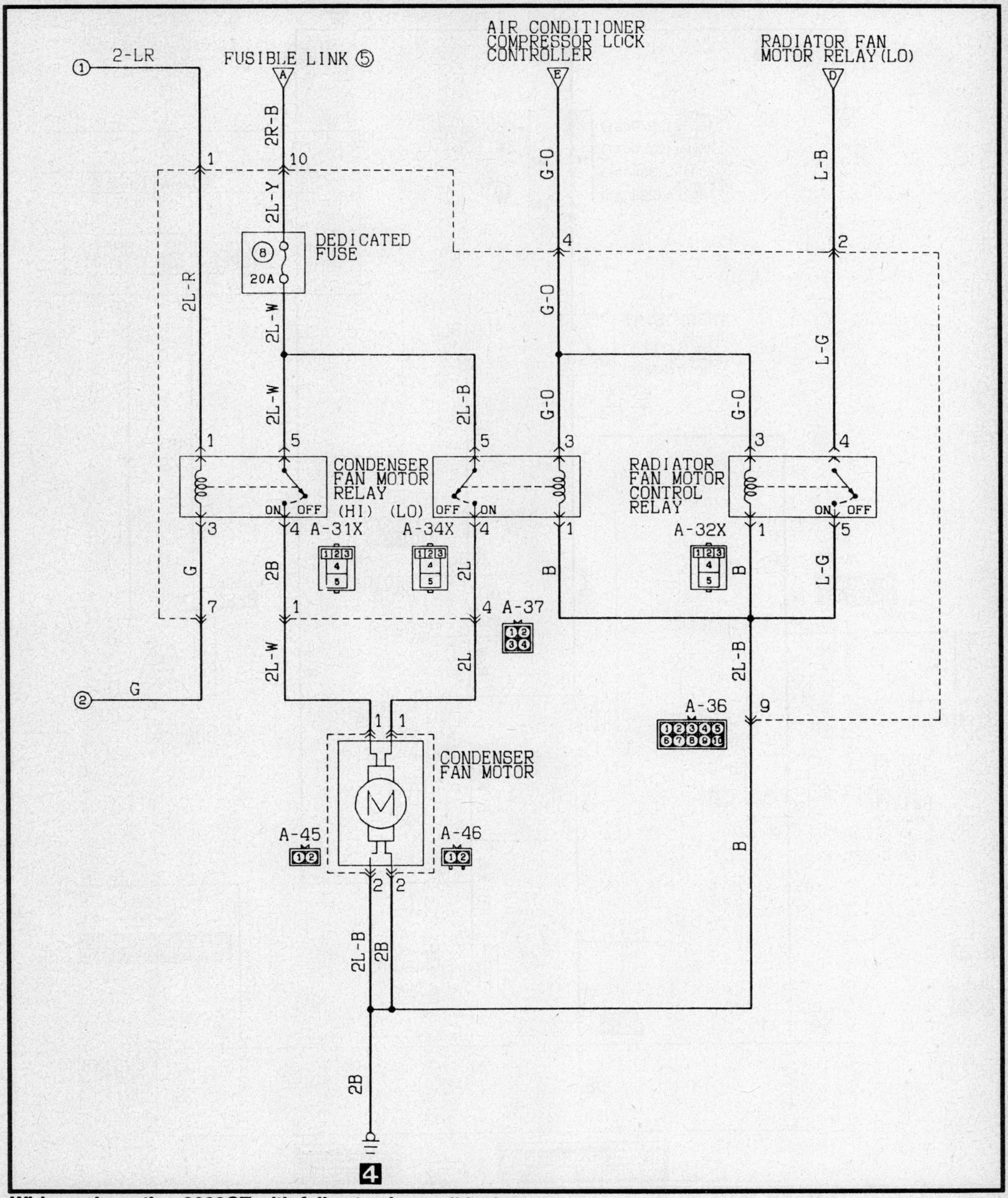
2-LR
FUSIBLE LINK ⑤
AIR CONDITIONER COMPRESSOR LOCK CONTROLLER
RADIATOR FAN MOTOR RELAY (LO)
2R-B
2L-Y
G-O
L-B
DEDICATED FUSE
20A
2L-R
2L-W
2L-B
L-G
CONDENSER FAN MOTOR RELAY
(HI)
(LO)
RADIATOR FAN MOTOR CONTROL RELAY
ON
OFF
A-31X
A-34X
A-32X
A-37
A-36
G
2B
2L
B
2L-B
CONDENSER FAN MOTOR
A-45
A-46
M
2L-B
2B
4

Wiring schematic—3000GT with full auto air conditioning

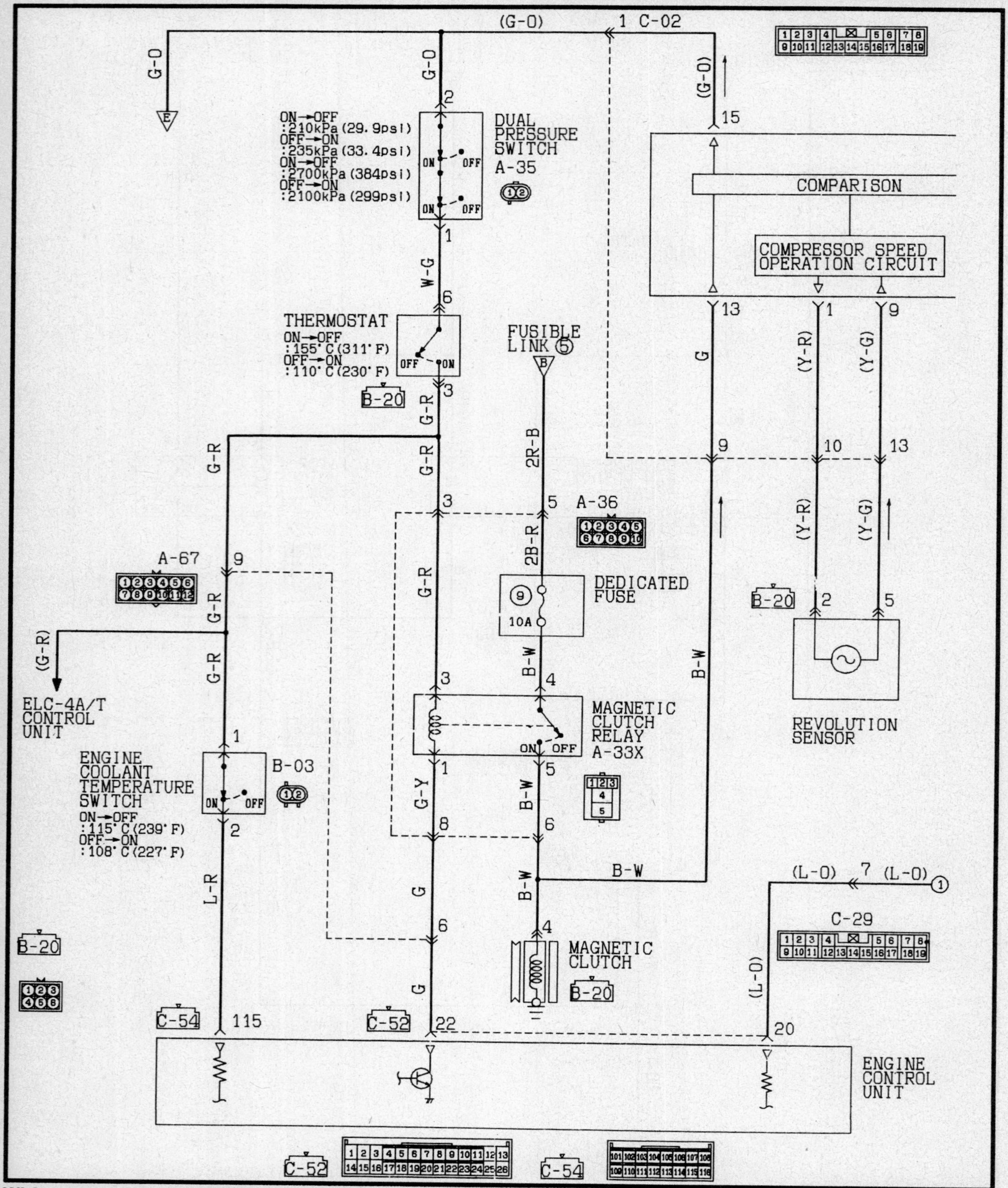
(G-O)
1 C-02
G-O
DUAL PRESSURE SWITCH
A-35
ON→OFF :210kPa (29.9psi)
OFF→ON :235kPa (33.4psi)
ON→OFF :2700kPa (384psi)
OFF→ON :2100kPa (299psi)
ON
OFF
W-G
THERMOSTAT
ON→OFF :155°C (311°F)
OFF→ON :110°C (230°F)
B-20
G-R
FUSIBLE LINK ⑤
2R-B
A-36
2B-R
DEDICATED FUSE
10A
B-W
MAGNETIC CLUTCH RELAY
A-33X
G-Y
MAGNETIC CLUTCH
A-67
(G-R)
ELC-4A/T CONTROL UNIT
ENGINE COOLANT TEMPERATURE SWITCH
B-03
ON→OFF :115°C (239°F)
OFF→ON :108°C (227°F)
L-R
G
C-54
C-52
115
22
20
ENGINE CONTROL UNIT
COMPARISON
COMPRESSOR SPEED OPERATION CIRCUIT
(Y-R)
(Y-G)
REVOLUTION SENSOR
(L-O)
C-29

Wiring schematic—3000GT with full auto air conditioning

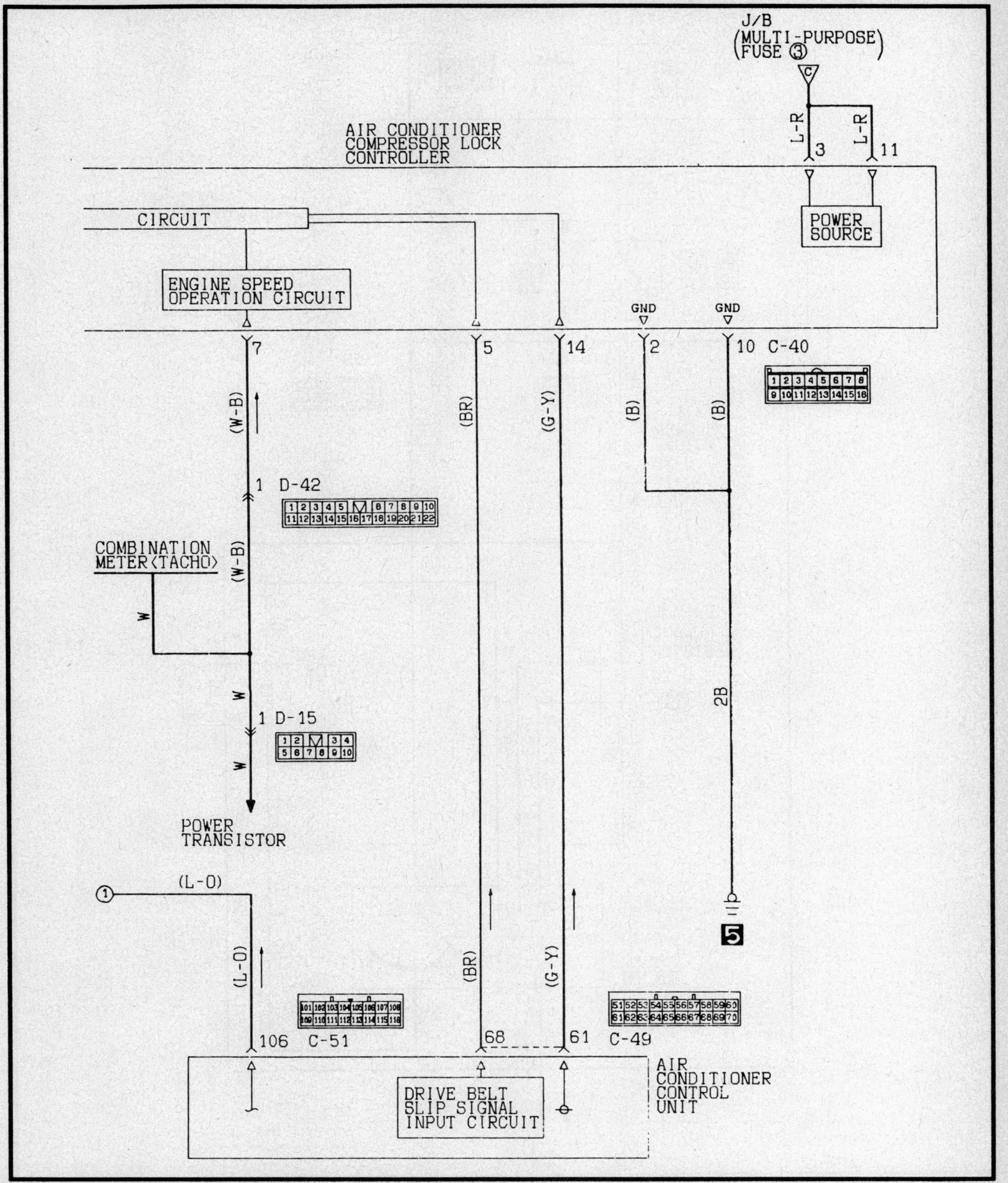
J/B
(MULTI-PURPOSE FUSE ③)
C
L-R
L-R
3
11
AIR CONDITIONER
COMPRESSOR LOCK
CONTROLLER
POWER
SOURCE
CIRCUIT
ENGINE SPEED
OPERATION CIRCUIT
GND
GND
7
5
14
2
10 C-40
(W-B)
(BR)
(G-Y)
(B)
(B)
1 D-42
COMBINATION
METER〈TACHO〉
(W-B)
W
W
1 D-15
W
2B
POWER
TRANSISTOR
(L-O)
(L-O)
(BR)
(G-Y)
5
106 C-51
68
61 C-49
AIR
CONDITIONER
CONTROL
UNIT
DRIVE BELT
SLIP SIGNAL
INPUT CIRCUIT

Wiring schematic—3000GT with full auto air conditioning

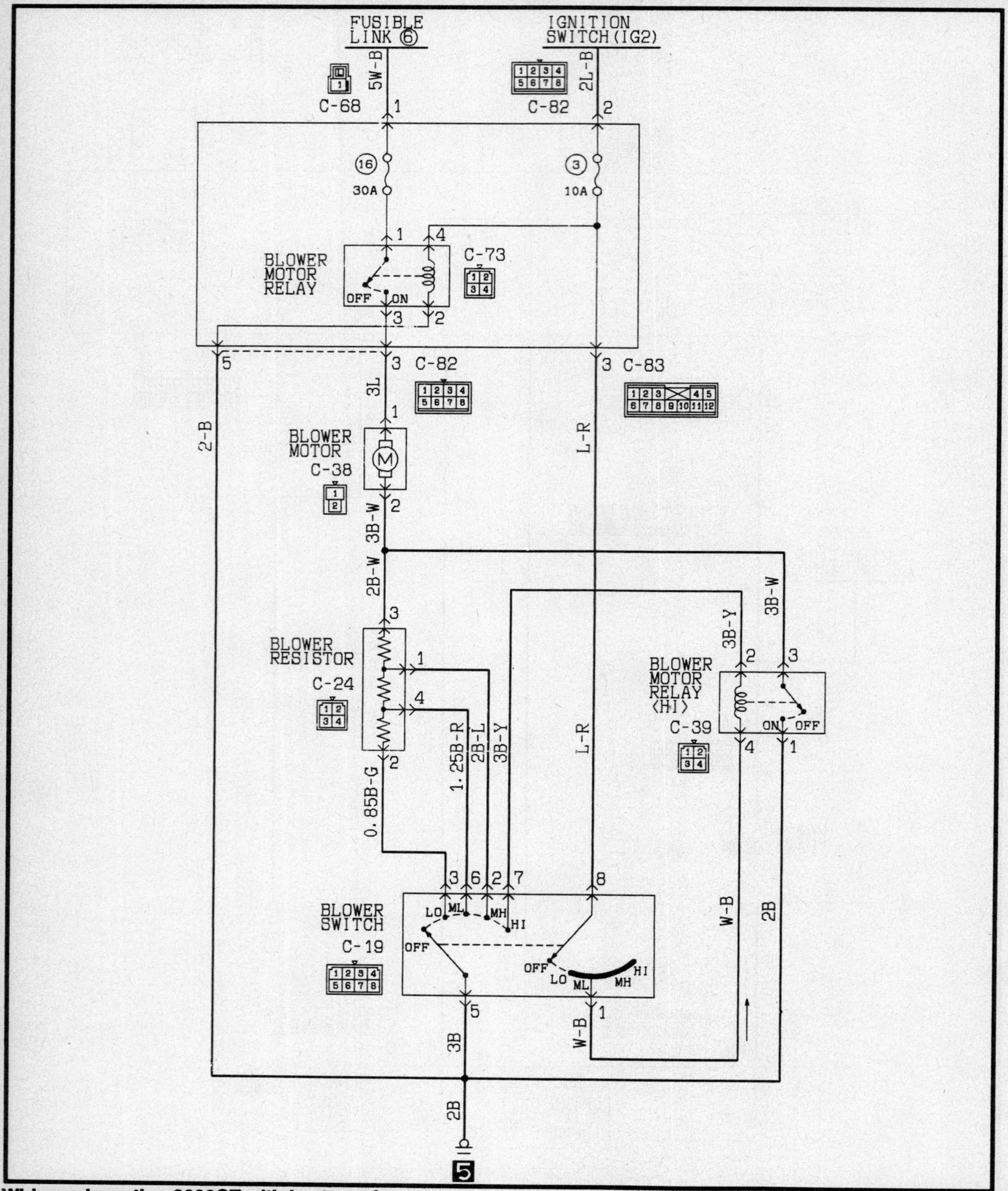
FUSIBLE LINK ⑥
IGNITION SWITCH (IG2)
5W-B
2L-B
C-68
C-82
16
30A
3
10A
BLOWER MOTOR RELAY
C-73
OFF
ON
5
3 C-82
3 C-83
3L
2-B
L-R
BLOWER MOTOR
C-38
3B-W
2B-W
BLOWER RESISTOR
C-24
3B-Y
BLOWER MOTOR RELAY (HI)
C-39
0.85B-G
1.25B-R
2B-L
BLOWER SWITCH
C-19
LO
ML
MH
HI
W-B
2B
3B

Wiring schematic—3000GT with heater only

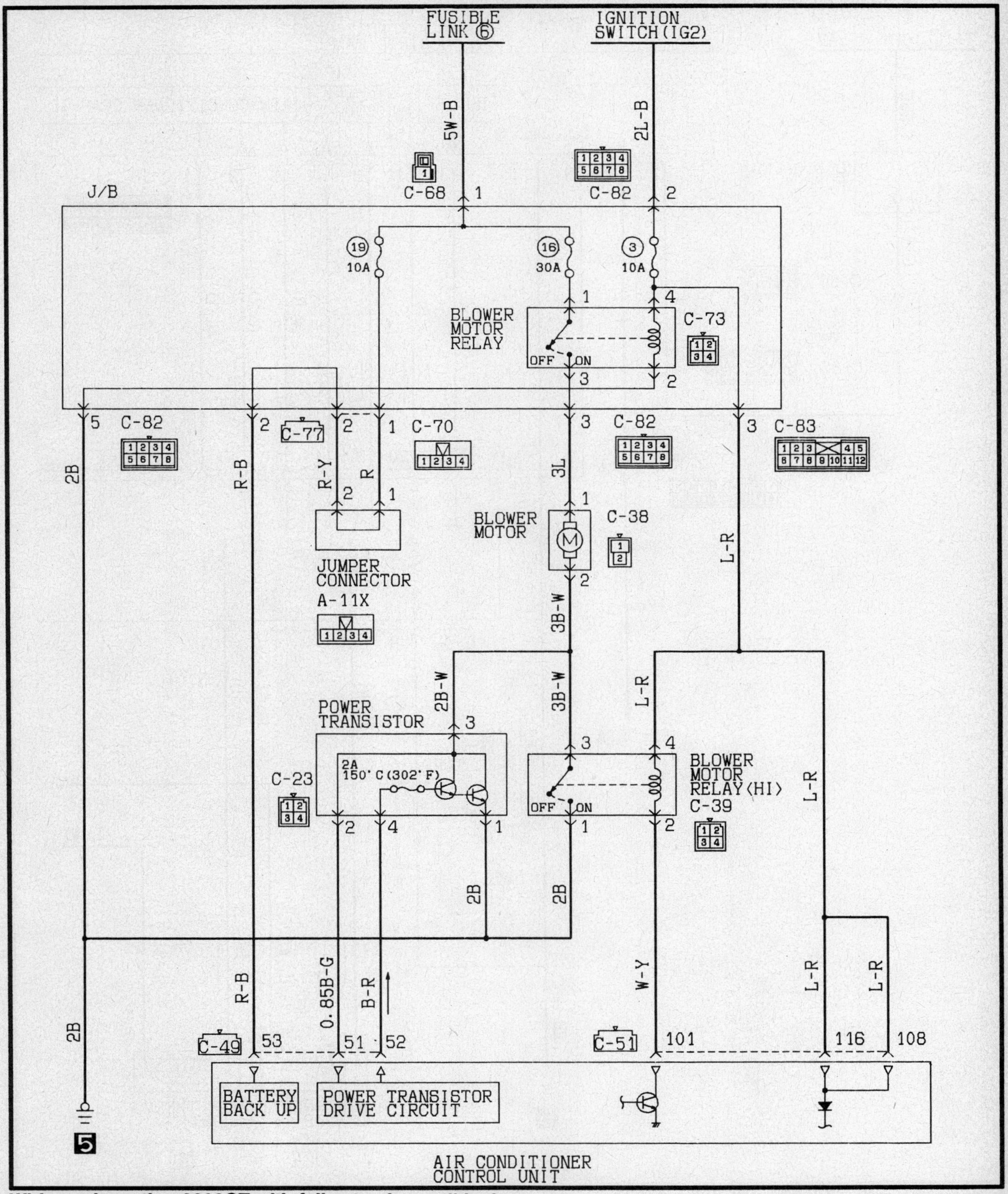
FUSIBLE LINK ⑥
IGNITION SWITCH (IG2)
5W-B
2L-B
J/B
C-68
C-82
19 10A
16 30A
3 10A
BLOWER MOTOR RELAY
OFF
ON
C-73
C-77
C-70
C-83
R-B
R-Y
R
3L
2B
L-R
BLOWER MOTOR
C-38
JUMPER CONNECTOR
A-11X
3B-W
2B-W
POWER TRANSISTOR
2A 150° C (302° F)
C-23
BLOWER MOTOR RELAY (HI)
C-39
0.85B-G
B-R
W-Y
C-49
C-51
53
51
52
101
116
108
BATTERY BACK UP
POWER TRANSISTOR DRIVE CIRCUIT
AIR CONDITIONER CONTROL UNIT
5

Wiring schematic—3000GT with full auto air conditioning

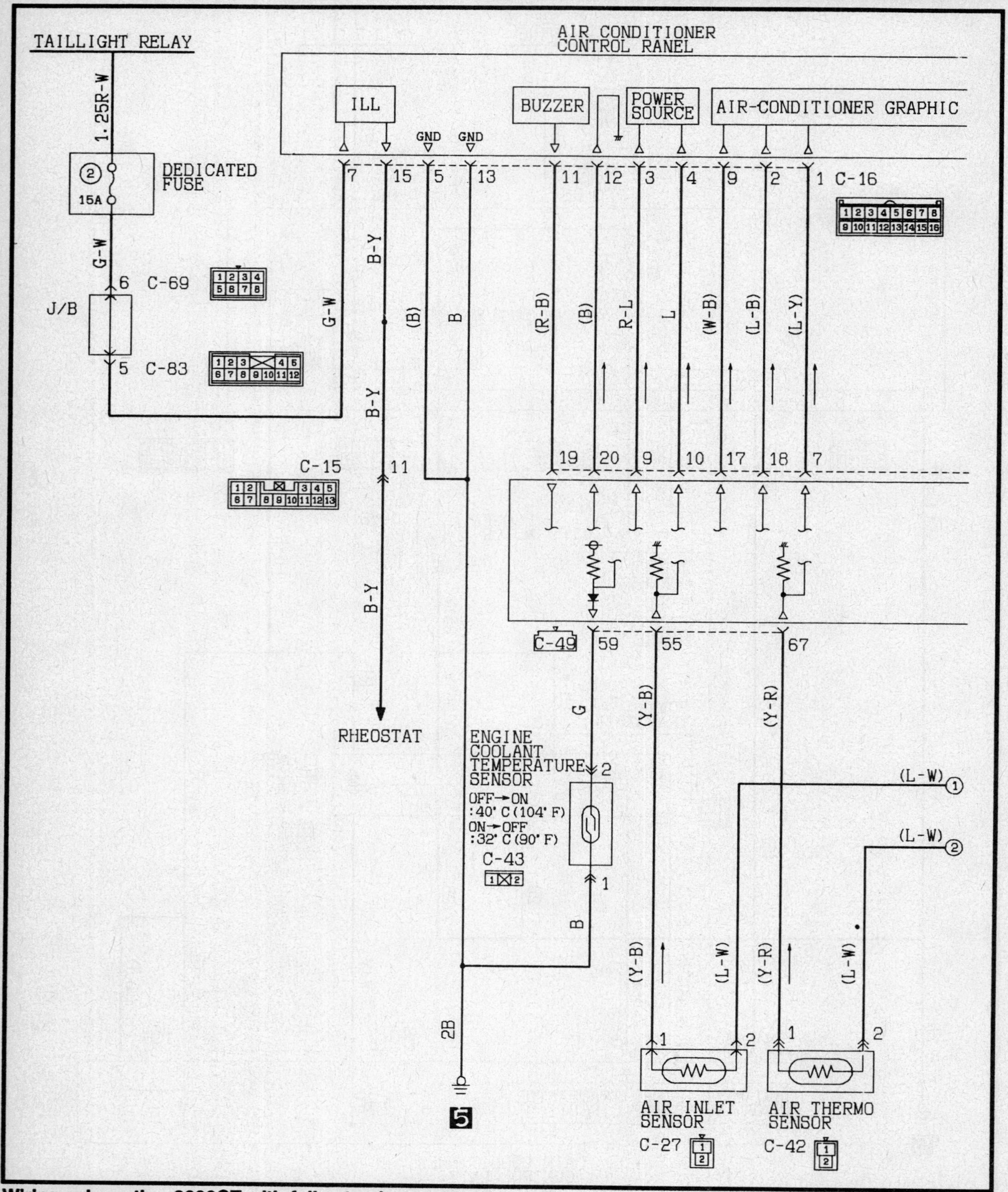
TAILLIGHT RELAY
1.25R-W
DEDICATED FUSE
15A
G-W
J/B
C-69
C-83
AIR CONDITIONER CONTROL RANEL
ILL
GND
GND
BUZZER
POWER SOURCE
AIR-CONDITIONER GRAPHIC
C-16
B-Y
(B)
B
(R-B)
(B)
R-L
L
(W-B)
(L-B)
(L-Y)
C-15
C-49
G
(Y-B)
(Y-R)
RHEOSTAT
ENGINE COOLANT TEMPERATURE SENSOR
OFF→ON :40° C (104° F)
ON→OFF :32° C (90° F)
C-43
(L-W)
2B
AIR INLET SENSOR
C-27
AIR THERMO SENSOR
C-42

Wiring schematic—3000GT with full auto air conditioning

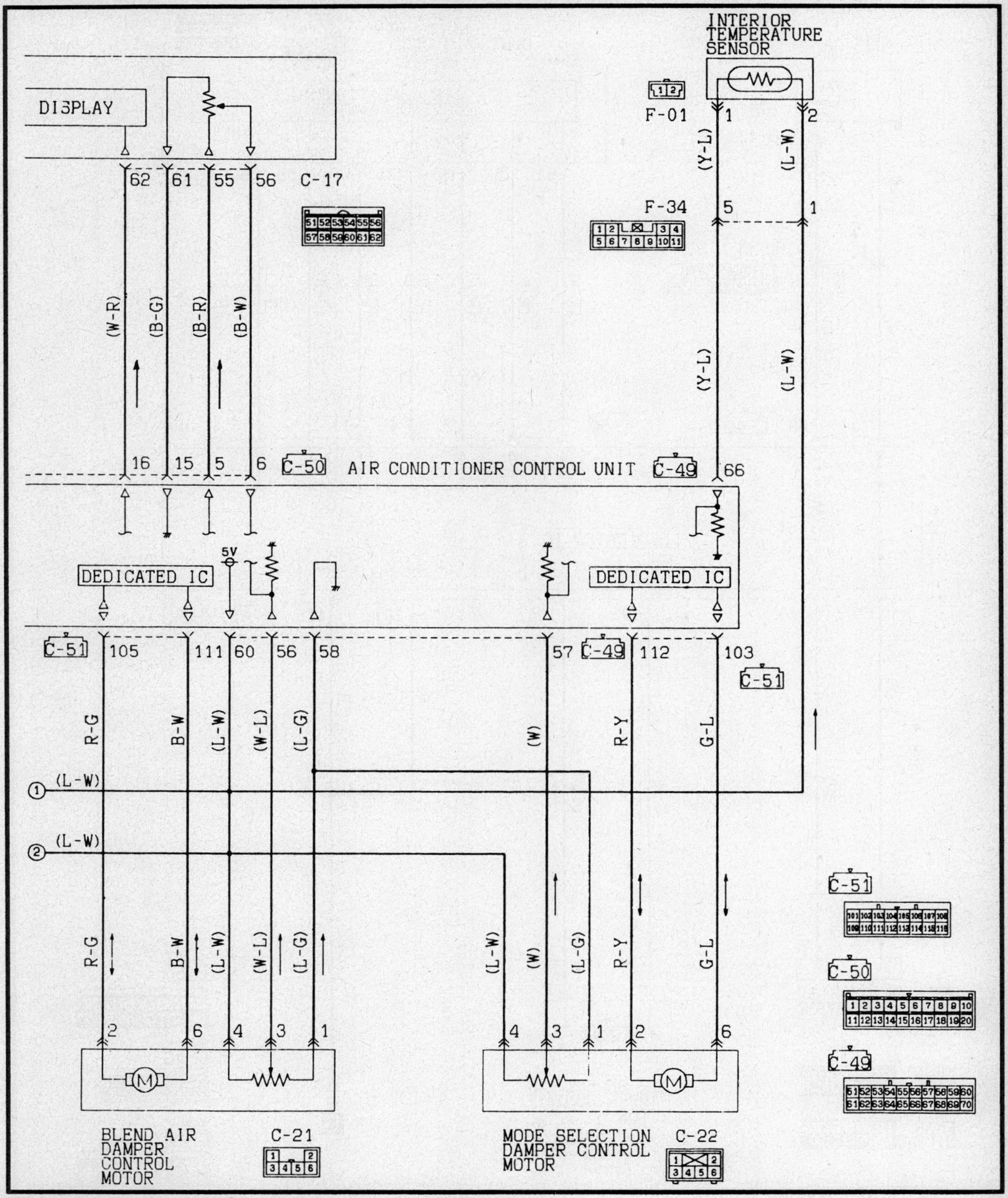
INTERIOR TEMPERATURE SENSOR
DISPLAY
F-01
C-17
F-34
AIR CONDITIONER CONTROL UNIT
C-50
C-49
C-51
DEDICATED IC
DEDICATED IC
5V
BLEND AIR DAMPER CONTROL MOTOR
C-21
MODE SELECTION DAMPER CONTROL MOTOR
C-22

Wiring schematic—3000GT with full auto air conditioning

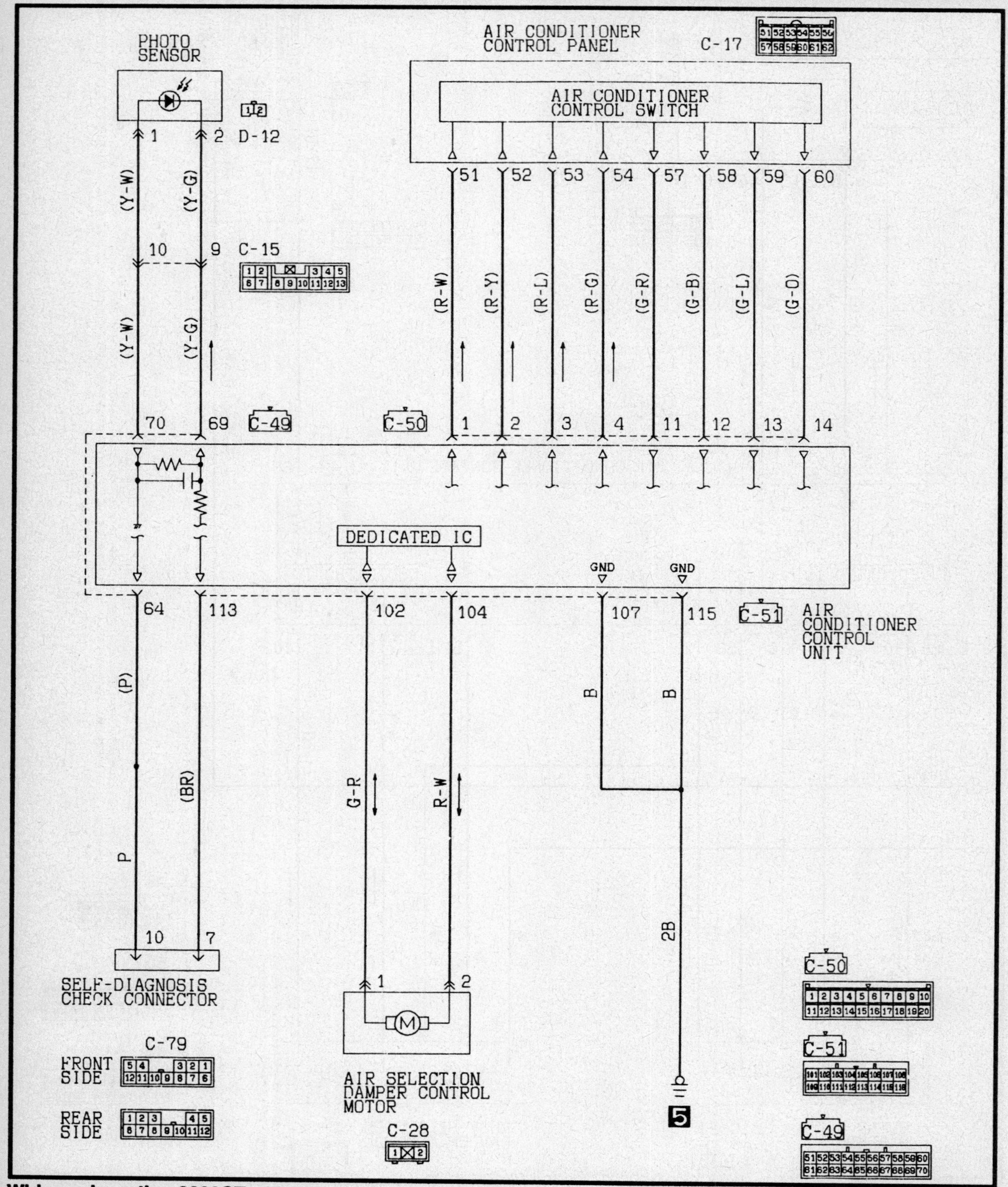
PHOTO SENSOR
D-12
AIR CONDITIONER CONTROL PANEL
C-17
AIR CONDITIONER CONTROL SWITCH
C-15
(Y-W)
(Y-G)
(R-W)
(R-Y)
(R-L)
(R-G)
(G-R)
(G-B)
(G-L)
(G-O)
C-49
C-50
DEDICATED IC
GND
C-51
AIR CONDITIONER CONTROL UNIT
(P)
(BR)
G-R
R-W
B
2B
SELF-DIAGNOSIS CHECK CONNECTOR
C-79
FRONT SIDE
REAR SIDE
AIR SELECTION DAMPER CONTROL MOTOR
C-28

Wiring schematic—3000GT with full auto air conditioning

NISSAN

240SX • 300ZX • MAXIMA • PULSAR • SENTRA • STANZA

SPECIFICATIONS

ENGINE IDENTIFICATION

Year	Model	Engine Displacement cu. in. (cc/liter)	Engine Series Identification	No. of Cylinders	Engine Type
1989	240SX	145.8 (2389/2.4)	KA24E	4	SOHC
	300ZX	180.6 (2960/3.0)	VG30E	6	SOHC
		180.6 (2960/3.0)	VG30ET (Turbo)	6	SOHC
	Maxima	180.6 (2960/3.0)	VG30E	6	SOHC
	Pulsar	97.5 (1597/1.6)	GA16i	4	SOHC
		110.3 (1809/1.8)	CA18DE	4	DOHC
	Sentra	97.5 (1597/1.6)	GA16i	4	SOHC
	Stanza	120.4 (1974/2.0)	CA20E	4	SOHC
1990	240SX	145.8 (2389/2.4)	KA24E	4	SOHC
	300ZX	180.6 (2960/3.0)	VG30DE	6	DOHC
		180.6 (2960/3.0)	VC30DETT (Twin Turbo)	6	SOHC
	Maxima	180.6 (2960/3.0)	VG30E	6	SOHC
	Pulsar	97.5 (1597/1.6)	GA16i	4	SOHC
	Sentra	97.5 (1597/1.6)	GA16i	4	SOHC
	Stanza	145.8 (2389/2.4)	KA24E	4	SOHC
1991	240SX	145.8 (2389/2.4)	KA24E	4	SOHC
	300ZX	180.6 (2960/3.0)	VG30DE	6	DOHC
		180.6 (2960/3.0)	VC30DETT (Twin Turbo)	6	SOHC
	Maxima	180.6 (2960/3.0)	VG30E	6	SOHC
	Pulsar	97.5 (1597/1.6)	GA16i	4	SOHC
	Sentra	97.5 (1597/1.6)	GA16i	4	SOHC
	Stanza	145.8 (2389/2.4)	KA24E	4	SOHC

SOHC—Single overhead camshaft
DOHC—Double overhead camshaft

REFRIGERANT CAPACITIES

Year	Model	Freon (oz.)	Oil (fl. oz.)	Type
1989	240SX	32.0–35.5	6.8 ①	R12
	300ZX	32.0–38.4	6.8 ①	R12
	Maxima	32.0–35.5	6.8 ①	R12
	Pulsar N/X	30.0–33.4	6.8 ①	R12
	Sentra	30.0–33.4	6.8 ①	R12
	Stanza	32.0–38.4	6.8 ①	R12
1990	240SX	32.0–35.5	6.8 ①	R12
	300ZX	30.0–33.4	6.8 ①	R12
	Maxima	32.0–35.5	6.8 ①	R12
	Pulsar N/X	30.0–33.4	6.8 ①	R12
	Sentra	30.0–33.4	6.8 ①	R12
	Stanza	29.0–32.0	6.8 ①	R12

REFRIGERANT CAPACITIES

Year	Model	Freon (oz.)	Oil (fl. oz.)	Type
1991	240SX	29.0–32.0	8.0 ①	R12
	300ZX	26.5–30.0	6.8 ①	R12
	Maxima	30.0–33.4	6.8 ①	R12
	Sentra	23.0–26.5	6.8 ①	R12
	Stanza	26.5–30.0	6.8 ①	R12

① Total system capacity

AIR CONDITIONING BELT TENSION CHART

Year	Model	Engine Displacement cu. in. (cc/liter)	Belt Type	New	Used
1989	240SX	146 (2400/2.4)	Poly V	0.24–0.28 ①	0.47 ①
	300ZX	183 (3000/3.0)	Poly V	0.31–0.35 ①	0.43 ①
	300ZX Turbo	183 (3000/3.0)	Poly V	0.31–0.35 ①	0.43 ①
	Maxima	183 (3000/3.0)	Poly V	0.16–0.24 ①	0.39 ①
	Pulsar	97 (1600/1.6)	Poly V	0.12–0.20 ②	0.30 ②
	Pulsar	110 (1800/1.8)	Poly V	0.12–0.16 ①	0.24 ①
	Sentra	97 (1600/1.6)	Poly V	0.12–0.20 ②	0.30 ②
	Stanza	122 (2000/2.0)	Poly V	0.12–0.16 ②	0.24 ②
1990	240SX	146 (2400/2.4)	Poly V	0.28–0.31 ①	0.47 ①
	300ZX	183 (3000/3.0)	Poly V	0.31–0.35 ①	0.50 ①
	300ZX Turbo	183 (3000/3.0)	Poly V	0.31–0.35 ①	0.50 ①
	Maxima	183 (3000/3.0)	Poly V	0.20–0.28 ①	0.39 ①
	Pulsar	97 (1600/1.6)	Poly V	0.16–0.24 ②	0.30 ②
	Sentra	97 (1600/1.6)	Poly V	0.16–0.24 ②	0.30 ②
	Stanza	146 (2400/2.4)	Poly V	0.20–0.24 ②	0.31 ②
1991	240SX	146 (2400/2.4)	Poly V	0.29–0.33 ①	0.47 ①
	300ZX	183 (3000/3.0)	Poly V	0.31–0.35 ①	0.49 ①
	300ZX Turbo	183 (3000/3.0)	Poly V	0.31–0.35 ①	0.49 ①
	Maxima	183 (3000/3.0)	Poly V	0.20–0.28 ①	0.39 ①
	Sentra	97 (1600/1.6)	Poly V	0.16–0.24 ②	0.30 ②
	Stanza	146 (2400/2.4)	Poly V	0.20–0.24 ②	0.31 ②

① Inches of deflection at the upper mid-point of belt, using 22 lbs. (10 kg) force.
② Inches of deflection at the lower mid-point of belt, using 22 lbs. (10 kg) force.

SYSTEM DESCRIPTION

General Information

The heater in all vehicles is a standard type, circulating engine coolant through a radiator core inside the vehicle. Temperature is controlled with a door in the air distribution system, operated with a cable from the temperature control lever, which also operates a valve on the heater core. Some automatic systems use an electrically controled vacuum operated valve to regulate the coolant flow through the core.

A standard configuration air conditioning system, charged with R-12, is used in all vehicles. The system consists of a compressor pumping the refrigerant to a condenser, a reciever/drier with a pressure switch, an evaporator in the vehicle, then back to the compressor. The evaporator incorporates the expansion valve or on automatic systems, a suction throttle valve. High and low pressure service valves are mounted directly on the lines and a pressure relief valve is mounted in the high pressure line near the compressor. There may also be a fusable plug, which melts above about 220°F (105°C) and allows the system to vent if overheated. Some vehicles have an over–temperature switch in the compressor which will disengage the clutch to prevent damage from overheating.

The air distribution system inside the vehicle uses doors to direct the air flow. These doors are either adjusted manually with levers and cables or controlled automatically with electric motors. In both systems the air enters the system from outside or inside the vehicle and passes over the evaporator first, then on to the heater core and/or out through various vents. This allows use of the air conditioner to dry the air for defogging the windshield even if the temperature control is set for heat. All systems include an electric clutch on the compressor, an electric fan to move air through the condenser and a blower fan to move air through the distribution system. On manual systems, a thermo control amplifier senses the evaporator coil temperature and cycles the compressor on and off to prevent ice fromation.

Automatic Temperature Control (ATC) systems also have a micro-computer, called an auto amplifier, to control the blower fan speed, inside-outside air mix, heater core valve and compressor duty cycle. When the ignition is switched off, the auto amplifier stores all information reguarding the last temperature setting. The information available to the amplifier is; outside and inside air temperatures, blower fan speed, air mix door position, engine coolant temperature and sun load. To aid in trouble shooting, this amplifier has a self diagnostic program accessed through the user controls.

On vehicles with Automatic Temperature Control (ATC), the ATC computer does not directly turn on the compressor clutch but feeds the demand signal to the engine control computer. The engine computer looks at the throttle position sensor or manifold vacuum and will turn the clutch on if the throttle is below a certain percentage of full throttle. When the compressor is switched on, it runs continuously rather than cycling on and off. A suction throttle valve in the evaporator housing modulates the pressure in the evaporator to prevent ice formation on the coils. This valve is in addition to the expansion valve, which controls the amount of refrigerant flowing through the evaporator on all types of systems.

Service Valve Location

Pulsar and Sentra:

The low pressure valve is near the firewall, the high pressure valve is near the condenser.

Stanza:

The low pressure valve is near the condenser or the firewall, the high pressure valve is at the condenser.

Maxima:

The low pressure valve is at the compressor, the high pressure valve is at the condenser.

240SX:

Both valves are near the compressor or the high pressure valve is near the condenser.

300ZX:

Both valves are at the compressor, near the firewall or on the right fender. Models with the high side valve on the fender also have the sight glass near the valve.

Special Precautions

1. All refrigerant service work must be done with the proper recycling equipment. Carefully follow the manufacturer's instructions for use of that equipment. Do not allow the freon to discharge to the air.
2. Any amount of water will make the system less effective. When any part of the system has been removed, plug or cap the lines to prevent moisture from the air entering the system. When installing a new component, do not uncap the fittings until ready to attach the lines.
3. When assembling a fitting, always use a new O-ring and lightly lubricate the fitting with compressor oil.
4. When a compressor is removed, do not leave it on its side or upside down for more than 10 minutes. The oil may leak into the low pressure chamber.
5. The proper amount of oil must be maintained in the system to prevent compressor damage and to maintain system efficiency. Be sure to measure and adjust the amount of oil removed or added to the system, especially when replacing the

System Performance Testing

1. Vehicle must be in a well ventilated area where the engine can be safely run at 1500 rpm, preferably not in direct sunlight. Open the hood to help engine cooling.
2. With windows open, operate the system set for full cooling of recirculated air, blower fan on high speed. On manual systems, set the mode control to **VENT**.
3. Operate the system for more than 10 minutes, then use a thermometer to measure the air outlet temperature at the center dash vent.
4. With a relative humidity of 50–60 percent, the outlet air temperature should be about 30–35°F (18–23°C) cooler than the outside air. The system effectiveness will decrease as the humidity increases.
5. The following chart assumes a relative humidity of 50–70 percent. The compressor discharge and suction pressures will increase with higher outside air temperature and humidity.

TEMPERATURE/PRESSURE CHART

Outside Air Temperature	High Side Pressure (PSI)	Low Side Pressure (PSI)
68°F (20°C)	149–182	14.5–20.6
77°F (25°C)	173–213	17.8–24.9
86°F (30°C)	203–247	23.5–30.6
95°F (35°C)	233–286	29.9–37.7
104°F (40°C)	267–327	37.7–46.2

System Discharging

1. Install adapter valves to the vehicle service valves and/or connect the refrigerant recycling equipment according to the manufacturer's instructions.
2. Open both the adapter or manifold valves slowly to prevent excess oil loss. Allow the freon to stop flowing before going on to the next step.

System Evacuating

1. Open both the high and low pressure valves and run the vacuum pump for more than 5 minutes. The gauges should stabilize at 29.13–29.92 in. (740–760mm) Hg vacuum.
2. Close the valves and turn the pump off. Check to see that the vacuum gauges remain stable. If the gauge on the low pressure side moves 3.94 in. (100mm) Hg in about 10 minutes, the system will discharge itself in about one month.
3. If the system will not hold vacuum, first check that the service equipment is properly connected and in good working order. If any connections in the vehicle system have been disturbed, make sure they have been properly reconnected. Be sure to use new lightly oiled O-rings and that the fitting is not over torqued.
4. If the system holds vacuum, open the valves and run the pump for more than 20 minutes. Close the valves, then turn the pump off.

System Charging

1. If using recycle equipment, the equipment in use will determine the charging procedure. Carefully follow the manufacturer's instructions and add the correct amount of freon as noted in the specifications chart. Never add freon through the high pressure service valve.
2. If charging directly from the R-12 container, add freon to the low pressure side until it slows or stops flowing. Start the engine, set the controls to maximum cooling and, with the R-12 can upright, continue to flow freon into the low pressure side until the specified amount has been added.
3. With the system fully charged and with the correct oil level in the compressor, run the air conditioner at the full cold setting for more than 5 minutes.
4. Stop the engine and immediately check the system for leaks using a suitable leak detector. Be sure to check at every line fitting, the service valves, the pressure switch at the receiver/drier, at the compressor shaft seals, bolt holes and clutch, and the pressure and temperature relief valves.

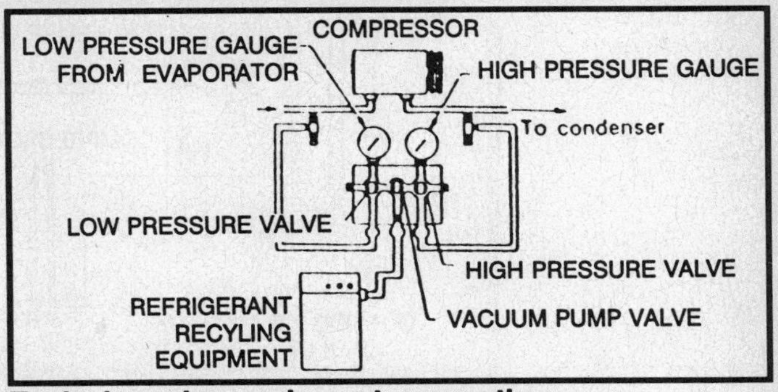
COMPRESSOR
LOW PRESSURE GAUGE
FROM EVAPORATOR
HIGH PRESSURE GAUGE
To condenser
LOW PRESSURE VALVE
HIGH PRESSURE VALVE
REFRIGERANT
RECYLING
EQUIPMENT
VACUUM PUMP VALVE

Typical service equipment connections

5. To check the evaporator and valves inside the vehicle, insert the leak detector probe into the water drain hose for more than 10 minutes. Leaking freon is heavier than air and will seek the lower exit, so always look for leaks at the lowest point.

Compressor Oil Service

The compressor is lubricated with a special oil that circulates with the freon when the system is operating and drops out of the freon when the system is stopped. Insufficient oil will cause damage to the compressor but too much oil will inhibit the system's cooling ability. When installing new parts of the system or a new compressor, the oil quantity must be adjusted.

1. If a new compressor is being installed, drain the oil out of the old unit and measure it.
2. Refer to the specification chart to determine how much oil the system should have.
3. Adjust the quantity of oil in the new compressor as needed. New compressors usually come with the full amount of oil, so it will probably be necessary to remove oil. The amount to be removed is the difference between the system specification and the amount drained from the old unit.
4. If installing another major system component, add oil according the the following table:

   The evaporator holds about 30 percent of the total amount.
   The condenser holds about 20 percent of the total amount.
   The reciever/drier holds about 10 percent of the total amount.
5. If a large oil leak is indicated, make the necessary repairs and run the system at idle speed set for full cooling for about 10 minutes. Stop the engine and drain the oil from the compressor to measure how much oil to add.

SYSTEM COMPOMNENTS

CAUTION

Some vehicles are equipped with air bag supplimental restraint systems. The system is still active for about 10 minutes after disconnecting the battery. Wait for more than 10 minutes before starting electrical work and do not use a memory saver. If power is required for diagnostic work, the air bag module can be disconnected inside the panel in the bottom of the steering wheel after the system is inactive. Reconnect the module before reconnecting the battery.

NOTE: When removing any component of the refrigerant system, properly discharge the freon into recovery equipment. Do not vent the freon into the air.

Radiator and Cooling Fan

REMOVAL AND INSTALLATION

1. Disconnect the negative battery cable. On vehicles with theft-protected radios, make sure the owner's reset code is available.
2. Remove the apron under the front of the engine, if equipped and drain the cooling system. On some vehicles it will be necessary to remove the air cleaner ducting above the radiator.
3. Disconnect the reservoir tank and upper and lower hosesfrom the radiator.
4. Disconnect the temperature switch and electric fan connectors.

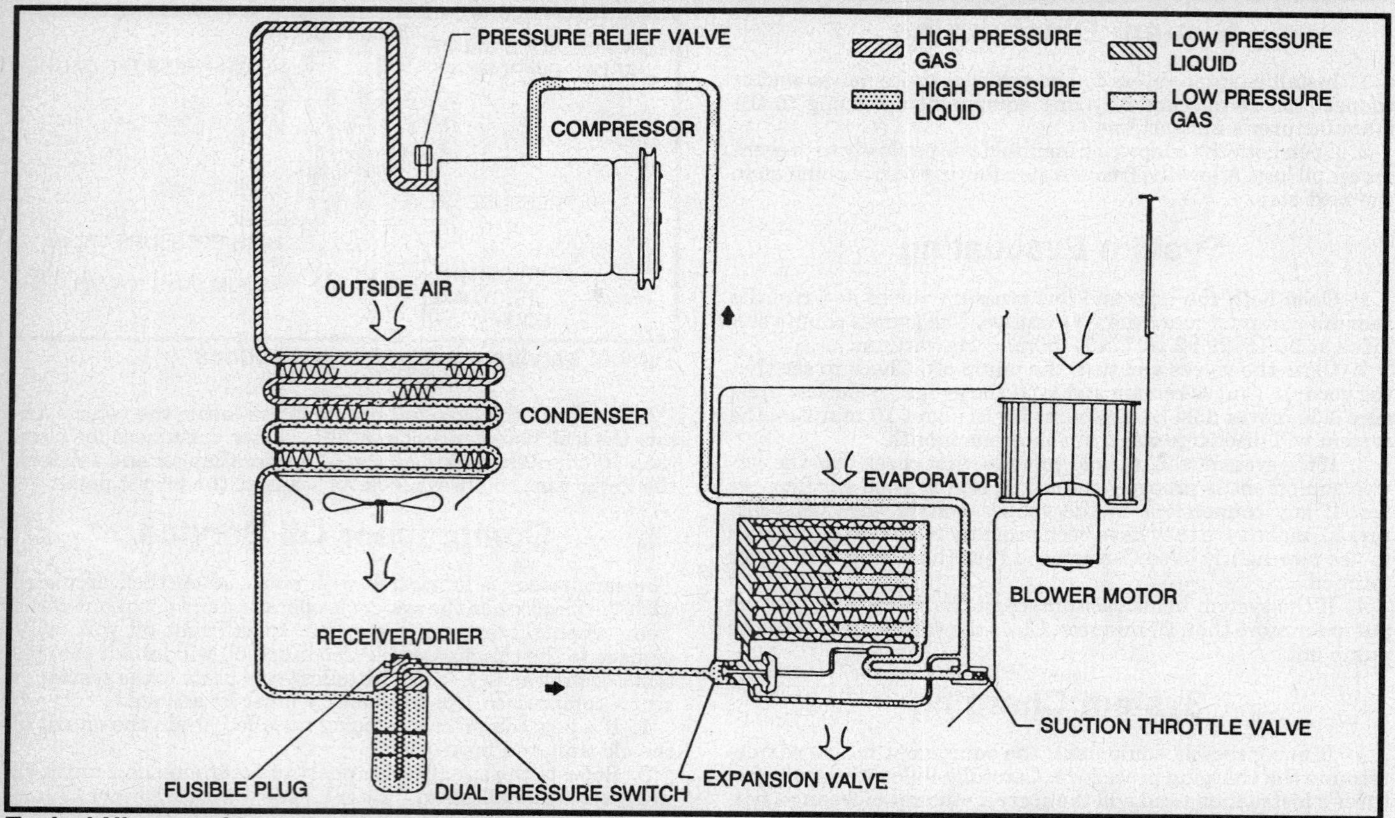
PRESSURE RELIEF VALVE
HIGH PRESSURE GAS
LOW PRESSURE LIQUID
HIGH PRESSURE LIQUID
LOW PRESSURE GAS
COMPRESSOR
OUTSIDE AIR
CONDENSER
EVAPORATOR
BLOWER MOTOR
RECEIVER/DRIER
SUCTION THROTTLE VALVE
EXPANSION VALVE
FUSIBLE PLUG
DUAL PRESSURE SWITCH

Typical Nissan refrigerant system components on automatic air conditioning. Manual systems do not have the suction throttle valve

5. On 1989 300ZX, remove the front bumper.
6. On vehicles with automatic transmissions, disconnect and plug the transmission cooling lines.
7. On rear wheel drive vehicles with electric fans, it should be possible to remove the fans and shroud as an assembly. To remove the radiator, remove the upper radiator retaining bolts and lift the unit up and out.
8. On rear drive vehicles with the fan on the water pump, remove the fan from the coupling and lay it in the shroud. Remove the shroud retaining screws and lift the fan and shroud out together.
9. On some front wheel drive vehicles, the air conditioner condenser and/or the receiver/drier must be removed with the fan to gain access to the radiator. Be sure to properly discharge the system using freon recovery equipment. Do not discharge freon into the air. Remove the upper radiator rataining bolts and lift the radiator out.

To install:

10. Set the lugs on the bottom of the radiator into the rubber mounts on the body and secure the unit with the upper mounting bolts.
11. Install the shrouding and fans. If any air conditioner components were removed, reconnect the lines and add freon to check for leaks.
12. Connect the automatic transmission cooling lines and the reservoir tank with all coolant hoses.
13. Fill the cooling system and look for leaks before installing the remaining parts.
14. On 1989 300ZX, install the front bumper.
15. Plug in all the electrical connectors for the fan(s) and temperature switches.
16. Connect the battery and start the engine to bleed the cooling system and check for leaks.

Cooling Fan

TESTING

1. When the air conditioner is running, the electric radiator/condenser cooling fan should also run. Turn the ignition switch and air conditioner **ON** and check for fan operation.
2. If the fan does not run, disconnect the plug to the fan and check for 12 volts between one of the terminals and ground. If voltage is present, test the fan with jumper wires from the battery.
3. If there is no voltage reaching the fan, locate the fan relay on the under-hood relay panel. With the ignition and air conditioning both **ON**, there should be 12 volts between 2 of the terminals and ground.
4. Turn the air conditioner **OFF** to see which terminal looses voltage. That one will be the relay switching circuit, which may be controlled by the engine control computer. The other terminal should still have voltage from the battery.
5. If the voltages to the relay are correct, the relay is faulty. If there is no battery voltage to the relay, check the wiring from the thermo–switch in the cooling system.
6. On some vehicles, the engine computer activates the fan relay. If no battery voltage is present at the relay with the air conditioner **ON**, check the wiring from the engine computer. Also check the temperature sensor and the thermo–switch in the cooling system.

REMOVAL AND INSTALLATION

1. Disconnect the negative battery cable. On vehicles with

theft-protected radios, make sure the owner's reset code is available.

2. Remove the apron under the front of the engine, if equipped, and drain about 2 quarts from the cooling system. On some vehicles, it will be necessary to remove the air cleaner ducting above the radiator.

3. Disconnect the reservoir tank and upper hose from the radiator.

4. Disconnect the temperature switch and electric fan connectors, if equipped.

5. On vehicles with electric fans, it should be possible to remove the fans and shroud as an assembly.

6. On rear drive vehicles with the fan on the water pump, remove the fan from the coupling and lay it in the shroud. Remove the shroud retaining screws and lift the fan and shroud out together.

To install:

7. On rear drive vehicles with the fan on the water pump, hold the fan inside the shroud and slip the shroud in place. Bolt the shroud in place and bolt the fan to the coupling.

8. On vehicles with electric fans, mount the fan on the shroud and install the shroud.

9. Reconnect the switch and fan wiring.

10. Connect the hoses and refill the cooling system.

11. Install any ducting or covers that were removed and start the engine to check for coolant leaks and proper fan operation.

Condenser

REMOVAL AND INSTALLATION

1. Disconnect the negative battery cable. On vehicles with theft-protected radios, make sure the owner's reset code is available.

2. On some front wheel drive vehicles, the radiator can be pushed towards the rear far enough to remove the condenser without disconnecting the engine coolant hoses. Unbolt the upper radiator mounts and tilt the top of the radiator back.

3. If the radiator must be removed, remove the apron under the front of the engine, if equipped, and drain the cooling system. Disconnect and plug the oil cooling hoses on automatic transmission models, then remove the radiator.

4. Properly discharge the freon and disconnect and cap the pressure lines from the condenser. If the receiver/drier is bolted to the condenser, unbolt it before lifting the condenser out.

5. Installation is the reverse of removal. When installing the condenser, be sure to use new O-ring seals and lightly lubricate them with compressor oil.

6. Do not over torque the fittings or they will be distorted and leak. Those secured with bolts are torqued to 5–8 ft. lbs. (8–11 Nm.).

Compressor

REMOVAL AND INSTALLATION

1. Properly discharge the system using freon recovery equipment.

2. On some models, the compressor is more easily removed from under the vehicle. On the 1990–91 300ZX, the front stabilizer bar bushings must be removed so the bar can be swung down out of the way. When installing the bushings, torque the bolts to 29–36 ft. lbs. (39–49 Nm.).

3. Disconnect the pressure lines and plug them.

4. Loosen the drive belt and remove the compressor.

5. Installation is the reverse of removal. Be sure to tighten the belt to specification, do not over tighten or bearing damage will result.

6. Torque the pressure line fitting–to–compressor bolts:

1989 300ZX – 19–26 ft. lbs. (25–35 Nm)
1990–91 300ZX – 11–14 ft. lbs. (20–29 Nm)
1989 240SX – 9–12 ft. lbs. (13–16 Nm)
All others – 5–8 ft. lbs. (8–11 Nm)

Receiver/Drier

REMOVAL AND INSTALLATION

1. On all models, the receiver/drier is on or near the condenser. Properly discharge the system into freon recovery equipment.

2. Disconnect the pressure switch.

3. Disconnect the freon lines and cap them to prevent moisture from entering the system.

4. Unbolt and remove the receiver/drier.

5. Installation is the reverse of removal. Be sure to use new O-rings and gaskets.

Expansion Valve

REMOVAL AND INSTALLATION

1. The expansion valve on all models is in the same housing with the evaporator inside the vehicle. The evaporator, which is between the blower and the heater, can be removed without removing the heater core. Properly discharge the system using freon recovery equipment and disconnect and plug the evaporator line fittings at the firewall.

2. The blower motor and its' housing must be removed first. Removing the glove compartment makes this easier. On some vehicles, the expansion valve can be accessed once the blower housing is removed.

3. On 1989 Sentra and Pulsar with factory installed air conditioning, it is necessary to cut a section from the dash board behind the glove compartment to remove the evaporator. This piece cannot be reinstalled.

4. Installation is the reverse of removal. Make sure the seals between the housings are in good condition, replace as necessary. Always use new O-rings on the freon line fittings.

Blower Motor

REMOVAL AND INSTALLATION

1. The blower can be removed without removing the housing. Disconnect the negative battery cable first.

2. If necessary, remove the glove compartment to gain access. On most vehicles, it is possible to squeeze the sides of the door to let it fall open beyond the normal stops.

3. Disconnect the wiring and remove the mounting bolts to lower the motor out.

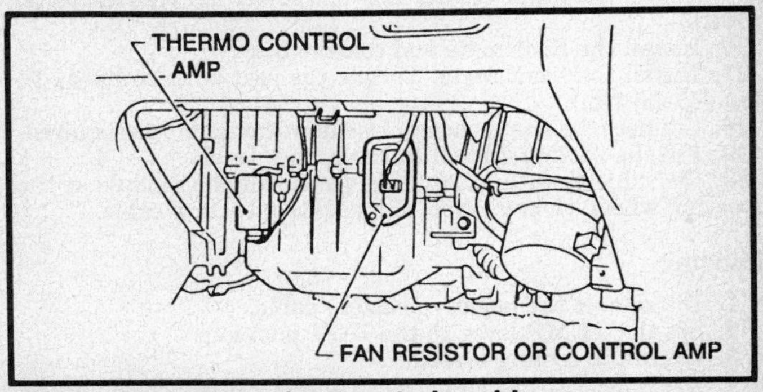
THERMO CONTROL AMP
FAN RESISTOR OR CONTROL AMP

Blower fan resistor is mounted on blower or evaporator housing, 1991

4. Installation is the reverse of removal. The resistor or speed control amplifier is mounted on the evaporator housing and is accessable without removing the blower.

Heater Core

REMOVAL AND INSTALLATION

240SX and 300ZX

1. Disconnect the negative battery cable.
2. With the **TEMP** lever set to the **HOT** position, drain the cooling system.
3. Disconnect the heater hoses from the driver's side of the heater unit.
4. Remove the console box and the floor mats.
5. Remove the instrument panel lower covers from both the driver's and passenger's sides of the vehicle. Remove the lower cluster lids.
6. Remove the left side ventilator duct. On 240SX, detach the defroster duct from the upper center heater unit opening.
7. On vehicles with air bag systems, disconnect the negative battery cable and wait more than 10 minutes for the system capicitor to drain down. Do not use a memory saver.
8. Remove the panel from the back side of the steering wheel and disconnect the air bag connector. Remove the radio, equalizer and stereo cassette deck, as required.
9. Remove the instrument panel-to-transmission tunnel stay.
10. Remove the rear heater duct from the floor of the vehicle.
11. Remove the center ventilator duct.
12. Remove the left and right side ventilator ducts from the lower heater outlets.
13. Disconnect and label the wiring harness connections.
14. Separate the heating unit. Remove the 2 screws at the bottom sides of the heater unit and the 1 screw at the top of the unit and remove the unit together with the heater control assembly.
15. Separate the heater case halves and slide the core from the case.

To install:

16. Install the heater core and assemble the heater case halves. Use new gaskets and seals, as required.
17. Mount the heater unit/control assembly and install the upper and lower attaching screws.
18. Plug in the wiring harness connectors.
19. Connect the left and right side ducts to the lower heater outlets.
20. Connect the center ventilator duct.
21. Connect the rear heater duct.
22. Attach the instrument panel-to-transmission stay.
23. Install the cassette deck, equalizer and radio.
24. On 240SX, connect the upper defroster duct to the upper center heater opening. Connect the left side ventilator duct.
25. Install the lower cluster lids and lower instrument panel covers.
26. Install the floor mats and console box.
27. Install the front seats. Torque the seat bolts to 32–41 ft. lbs. (43–55 Nm).
28. Connect the heater hoses. Use new grommets as required.
29. Fill the cooling system to the proper level.
30. On vehicles with an air bag, reconnect the module at the steering wheel, then connect the negative battery cable.

Maxima

1. Disconnect the negative battery cable.
2. Set the **TEMP** lever to the **HOT** position.
3. Drain the cooling system.
4. Disconnect the heater hoses from the driver's side of the heater unit.
5. Remove the front floor mats.
6. Remove the instrument panel lower covers from both the driver's and passenger's sides of the vehicle.
7. Remove the left side ventilator duct.
8. Remove the instrument panel.
9. Remove the rear heater duct from the floor of the vehicle.
10. Disconnect the wiring harness connectors.
11. Separate the heating unit from the cooling unit. Remove the 2 screws at the bottom sides of the heater unit and the 1 screw from the top of the unit. Lift out the heater together with the heater control assembly.
12. Remove the center vent cover and heater control assembly, loosening the clips and screws.
13. Remove the screws securing the door shafts.
14. Remove the clips from the case and split the case. Remove the core.
15. Separate the heater case halves and slide the core from the case.

To install:

16. Install the heater core and assemble the heater case halves. Use new gaskets and seals, as required.
17. Install the door shaft retaining screws.
18. Install the heater control assembly and center vent cover.
19. Mount the heater unit/control assembly and install the upper and lower attaching screws.
20. Plug in the wiring harness connectors.
21. Install the rear heater duct.
22. Install the instrument panel.
23. Install the left side ventilator duct.
24. Install the instrument panel lower covers.
25. Install the floor mats.
26. Connect the heater hoses. Use new grommets, as required.
27. Fill the cooling system to the proper level.
28. Connect the negative battery cable.

Pulsar and Sentra

1. Disconnect the negative battery cable.
2. Set the **TEMP** lever to the maximum **HOT** position and drain the engine coolant.
3. Disconnect the heater hoses at the engine compartment.
4. Remove the instrument panel assembly.
5. Remove the heater control assembly.
6. If equipped with air conditioning, separate the heating unit from the cooling unit.
7. Remove the heater unit assembly.
8. Remove the case clips and split the case. Remove the core.

To install:

9. Install the heater core and assemble the heater case halves. Use new gaskets and seals as required. Always check the operation of the air mix door when re-attaching the heater case halves.
10. Mount the heater unit and connect it the cooling unit, if equipped.
11. Install the heater control assembly.
12. Install the instrument panel.
13. Connect the heater hoses. Use new grommets, as required.
14. Fill and bleed the cooling system.
15. Connect the negative battery cable.

Stanza

1. Disconnect the negative battery cable.
2. Set the **TEMP** lever to the maximum **HOT** position and drain the engine coolant.
3. Disconnect the heater hoses at the engine compartment.
4. Remove the instrument panel assembly.
5. Remove the heater control assembly.
6. Remove pedal bracket mounting bolts, steering column mounting bolts, brake and clutch pedal cotter pins.
7. Move the pedal bracket and steering column to the left.
8. Disconnect the air mix door control cable and heater valve control lever, then remove the control lever.

9. Remove the core cover and remove the core.

To install:

10. Install the core and cover. Use new seals and gaskets, as required.
11. Install the control and heater valve levers. Connect the air mix door control cable.
12. Move the steering column and brake pedal bracket to the right. Install the clutch and brake pedal cotter pins and steering column and brake pedal bolts.
13. Install the heater control assembly.
14. Install the instrument panel.
15. Connect the heater hoses to the core. Use new grommets, as required.
16. Fill and bleed the cooling system.
17. Connect the negative battery cable.

Evaporator

REMOVAL AND INSTALLATION

1. The evaporator, which is between the blower and the heater, can be removed without removing the heater core. Properly discharge the system using freon recovery equipment and disconnect and plug the evaporator and pressure line fittings at the firewall.
2. The blower motor and its' housing must be removed first. Removing the glove compartment makes this easier. On some vehicles, the expansion valve can be accessed once the blower housing is removed.
3. On some models it may be necessary to remove the center console. On vehicles with an air bag, some of the wiring for that system is in the console. Disconnect the negative battery cable and wait more than 10 minutes for the system capacitor to drain down. Do not use a memory saver.
4. Remove the panel from the back side of the steering wheel and disconnect the air bag connector.
5. On 1989 Sentra and Pulsar with factory installed air conditioning, it is necessary to cut a section from the dash board behind the glove compartment to remove the evaporator. This piece cannot be reinstalled.
6. Installation is the reverse of removal. Make sure the seals between the housings are in good condition, replace as necessary.

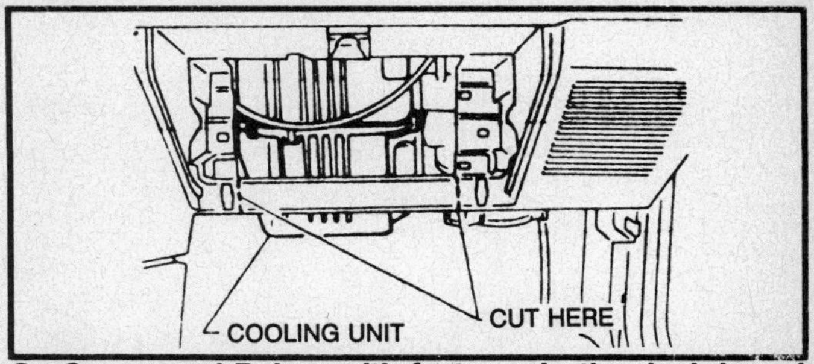
COOLING UNIT
CUT HERE
On Sentra and Pulsar with factory air, the dash board must be cut to remove the evaporator

7. On vehicles with an air bag, reconnect the module at the steering wheel, then connect the negative battery cable.

Manual Control Head

REMOVAL AND INSTALLATION

240SX

1. Disconnect the negative battery cable. If the vehicle has a theft protected radio, obtain the owner's security code.
2. To remove the center console bezel, remove the ash tray and reach in with one finger to push up on the right rear corner of the shifter opening.
3. Remove the screws and lift the control unit out far enough to disconnect the cables and wiring.
4. When disassembling the unit for repair, all fasteners are plastic clips which can be easily pried apart. Be careful to not break the tabs. The knobs on the front can be removed with pliers but wrap a rag around the knob to keep from scratching the finish.

300ZX

1989

1. Disconnect the negative battery cable. If the vehicle has a theft protected radio, obtain the owner's security code.

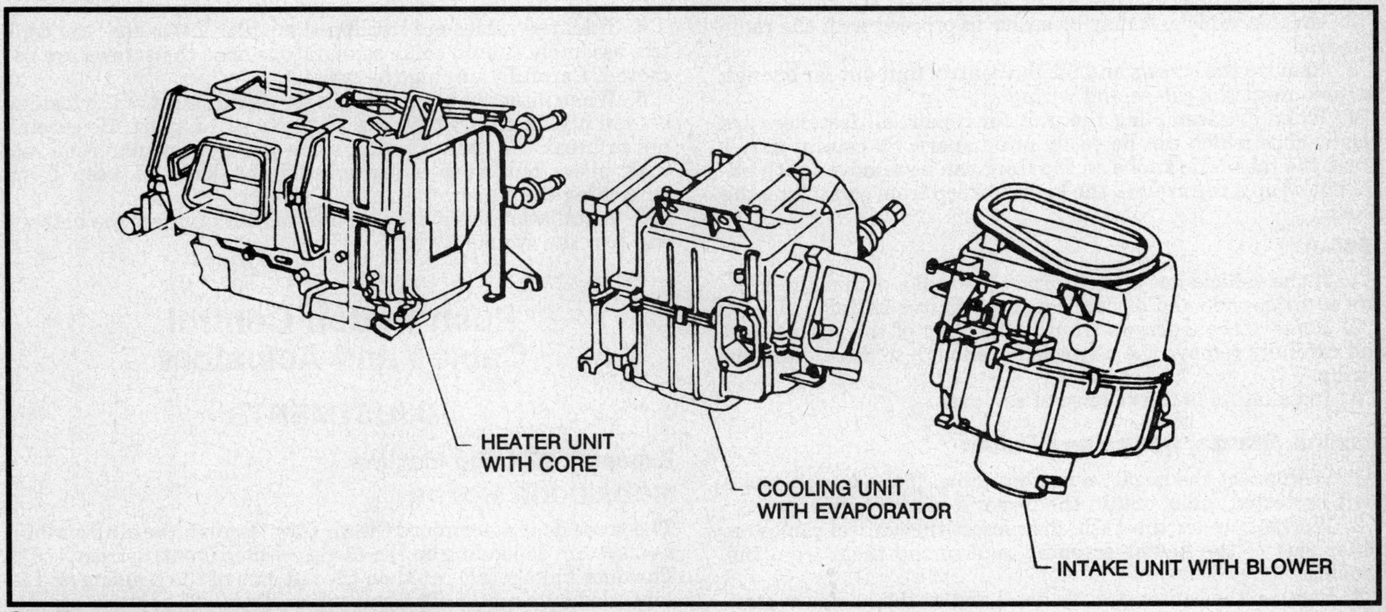
HEATER UNIT
WITH CORE
COOLING UNIT
WITH EVAPORATOR
INTAKE UNIT WITH BLOWER
Cooling unit assembly and related components

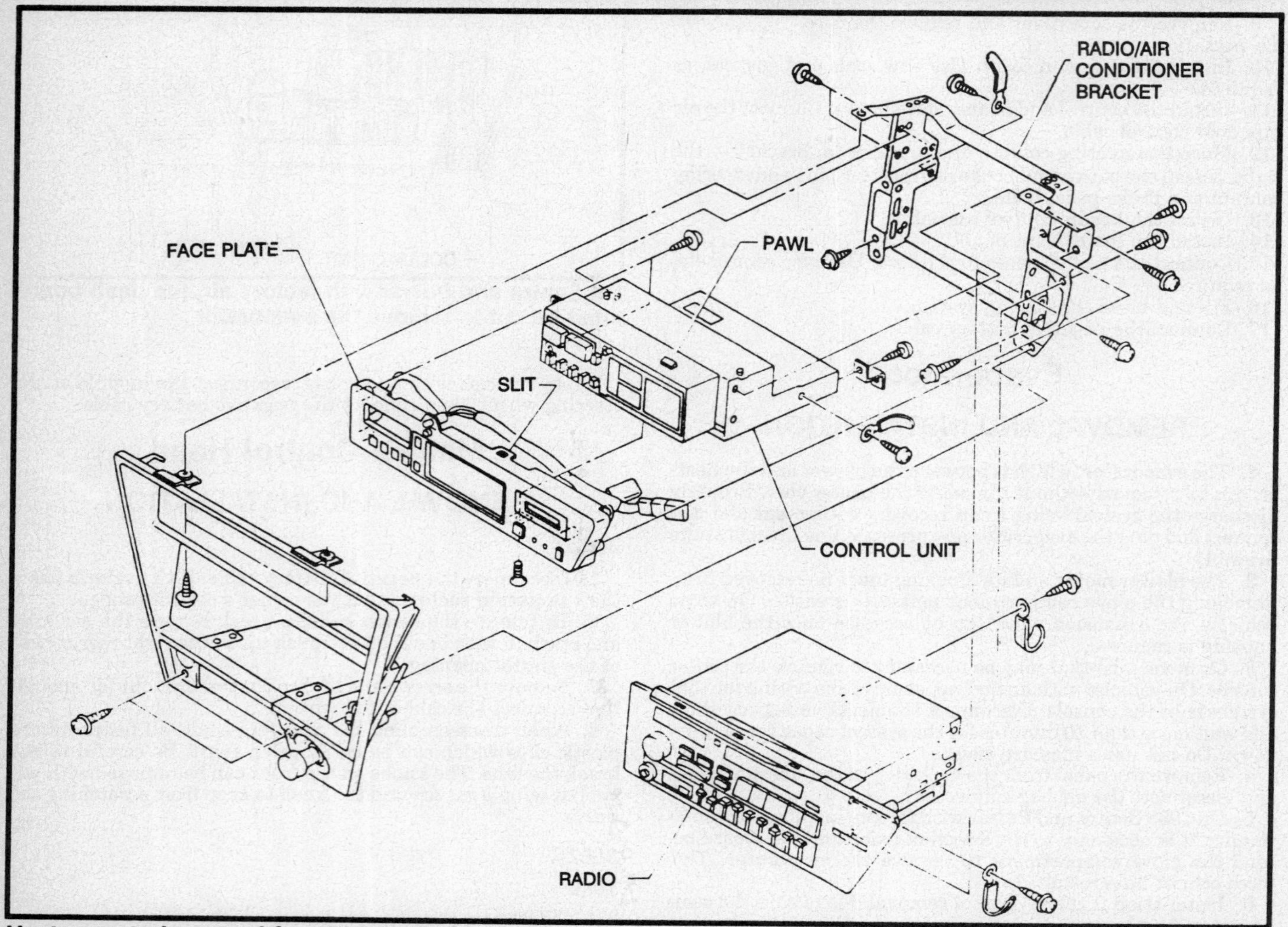
RADIO/AIR
CONDITIONER
BRACKET
FACE PLATE
PAWL
SLIT
CONTROL UNIT
RADIO

Heater control removal for 1989 300ZX

2. On this vehicle, it may be easier to proceed with the radio removed.

3. Remove the screws and lift the control unit out far enough to disconnect the cables and wiring.

4. When disassembling the unit for repair, all fasteners are plastic clips which can be easily pried apart. Be careful to not break the tabs. The knobs on the front can be removed with pliers but wrap a rag around the knob to keep from scratching the finish.

1990–91

1. If the vehicle has a theft protected radio, obtain the owner's security code and disconnect the negaitve battery cable.
2. Remove the 2 screws from the bottom of the control pod and carefully remove the controls far enough to disconnect the wiring.
3. Installation is the reverse of removal.

Maxima, Stanza, Sentra and Pulsar

1. Disconnect the negative battery cable. If the vehicle has a theft protected radio, obtain the owner's security code.
2. Working under the dash, disconnect the control cables on either side of the heater assembly and unclip them from the housing.
3. Remove the center console bezel and/or the heater control bezel as required.
4. If all the cables are unclipped at their lower end, the control assembly should come straight out once the screws are removed. Carefully unplug the wires.
5. When disassembling the unit for repair, most of the fasteners are plastic clips which can be easily pried apart. Be careful not to break the tabs. The knobs on the front can be removed with pliers but wrap a rag around the knob to keep from scratching the finish.
6. Installation is the reverse of removal. Connect the battery and test the system.

Push Button Control Cables and Actuators

ADJUSTMENTS

Except 300ZX and Maxima

MODE DOOR MOTOR

The mode door determines the air flow through the air distribution system depending on the mode selected (vent, defrost, etc.). The door linkage is located on the left side of the housing and is controled by a motor. The motor has a built–in position sensor and will stop at the position called for by the controls. The adjustment procedure starts with the motor removed from the housing.

1. With the motor removed from the housing, connect the motor wiring and set the controls to the **VENT** mode.
2. Turn the ignition switch **ON**, let the motor go to its vent position, then turn the ignition **OFF**.
3. Manually move the linkage on the housing to the vent position, install the motor and attach the linkage.
4. With the ignition switch **ON**, cycle the system through all the modes and check the operation of the linkage.

AIR INTAKE DOOR

1. With the door motor removed but wiring connected, turn the ignition switch **ON** and set the controls to recirculate by pushing the **REC** button.
2. Install the motor onto the blower housing.
3. Hold the door in the recirculate position and attach the linkage. Turn the **REC** button **ON** and **OFF** to check operation of the door.

TEMPERATURE CONTROL CABLE

This cable operates the air mix door inside the air distribution system. A control rod connects the air mix door lever and the water valve link lever on the heater core. The control rod should be adjusted first.

1. To adjust the control rod, disconnect the temperature control cable from the door lever.
2. The valve end of the rod is attached to the valve with a wire loop. With the rod loose at the air mix door end, move the air mix door lever and the valve lever all the way in the direction that would pull the rod away from the valve lever.
3. Gently pull the rod so there is about 0.80 in. (2mm) gap between the rod and valve lever and secure the rod at the door lever.
4. When attaching the temperature control lever, adjust the cable housing so the full cold lever position will completely shut off the heat.

Slide Lever Control Cables and Actuators

ADJUSTMENT

If the linkage has been disassembled, it should be adjusted as an assembly rather than trying to adjust only one part. First adjust the rods and levers, then connect and adjust the cables to the linkage.

Ventilator Door Conrtol Rod

1. Viewed from the driver's side, rotate the side link fully clockwise.
2. With the upper and lower door levers pushed down, connect the lower rod first, then the upper rod.

Defroster Door Control Rod

1. Rotate the side link fully counterclockwise.
2. Push the defroster door lever towards the firewall and connect the rod.

Air Control Cable

1. Rotate the side link fully clockwise.
2. With the control lever in the **DEFROST** position, hook the cable to the side link.
3. Take up the slack in the cable housing by pushing it gently away from the firewall and secure the housing.

Water Valve Control Rod

1. To adjust the control rod, disconnect the temperature control cable from the door lever.
2. The valve end of the rod is attached to the valve with a wire loop. With the rod loose at the air mix door end, move the air mix door lever and the valve link lever all the way in the direction that would pull the rod away from the valve lever.
3. Gently pull the rod so there is about 0.080 in. (2mm) gap between the rod and valve lever and secure the rod at the door lever.

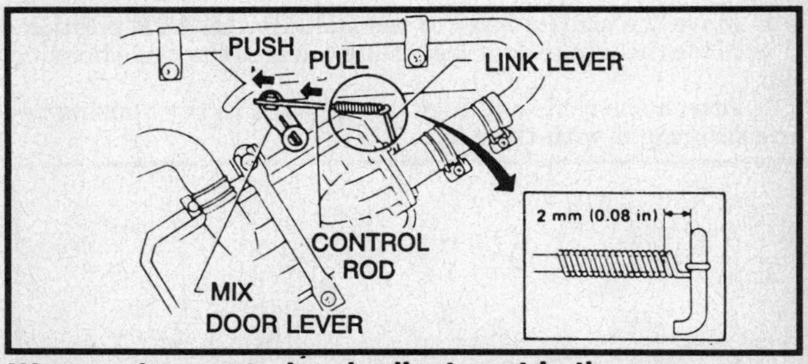
PUSH
PULL
LINK LEVER
2 mm (0.08 in)
CONTROL ROD
MIX DOOR LEVER

Water valve control rod adjustment is the same on both systems

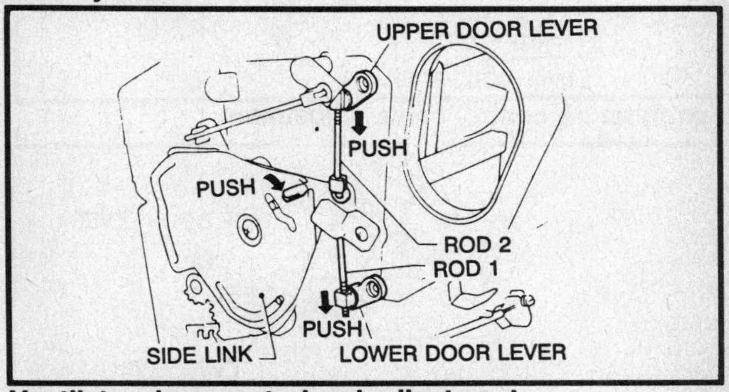
UPPER DOOR LEVER
PUSH
PUSH
ROD 2
ROD 1
PUSH
SIDE LINK
LOWER DOOR LEVER

Ventilator door control rod adjustment

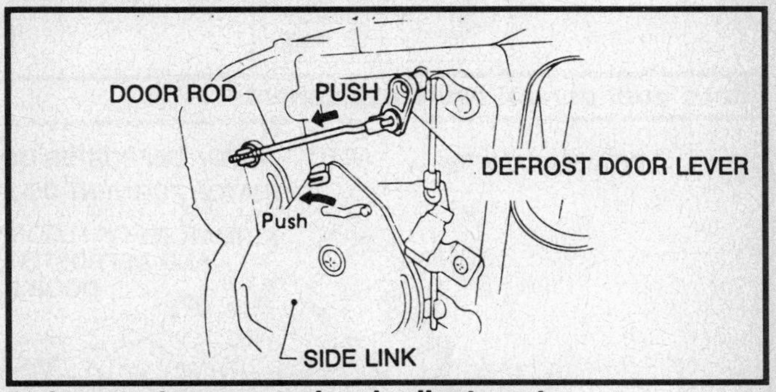
DOOR ROD
PUSH
DEFROST DOOR LEVER
Push
SIDE LINK

Defroster door control rod adjustment

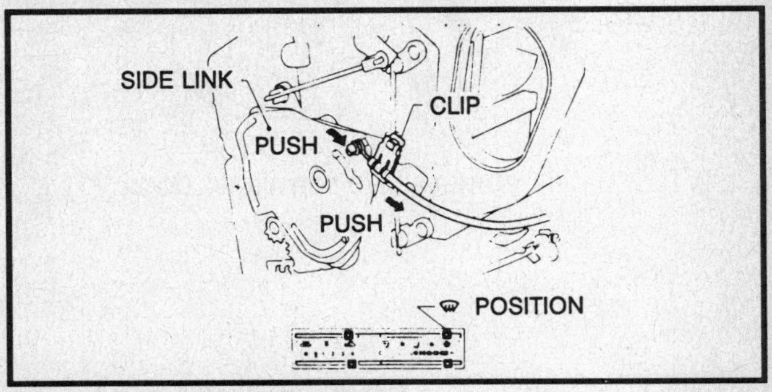
SIDE LINK
CLIP
PUSH
PUSH
POSITION

Air control cable adjustment

Temperature Control Cable

1. Move the control levers to the full **COLD** position.
2. Rotate the air mix door linkage towards the full cold position.
3. Attach the cable and take up the slack in the cable housing before securing it with the clip.

Intake Door Control Cable

1. Move the control lever to the **RECIRCULATE** position.
2. Move the intake door lever fully towards the cable housing clip.
3. Attach the cable and take up the slack in the housing before securing it with the clip.

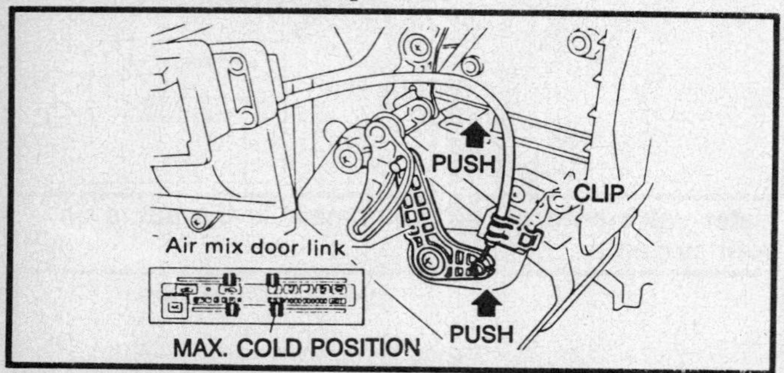
PUSH
CLIP
Air mix door link
MAX. COLD POSITION
PUSH

Temperature control cable adjustment

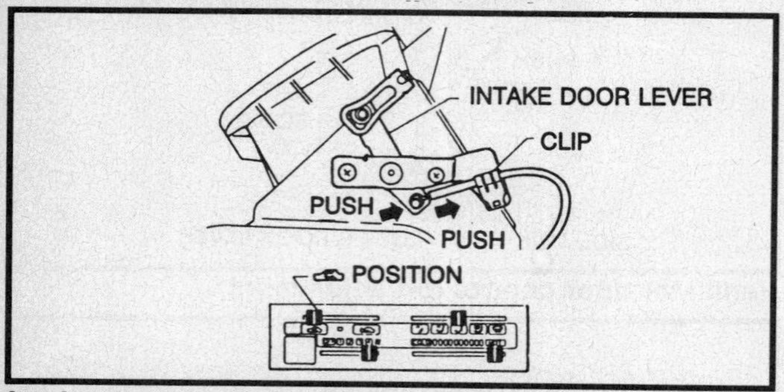
INTAKE DOOR LEVER
CLIP
PUSH
PUSH
POSITION

Intake door control cable adjustment

1989 300ZX

MANUAL CONTROL SYSTEM

System Description

VACUUM ACTUATORS

The air flow doors and water valve are operated with solenoid controlled vacuum actuators. A vacuum storage tank is near the right head light door motor. Turbocharged models have a motor driven vacuum pump mounted just to the left of the right head light. On these vehicles, as the vacuum in the tank moves closer to atmospheric, a pressure switch in the tank closes at about 13.75 in. Hg (350mm) vacuum to turn on the pump. There is no adjustment on this switch, the actuators or the solenoids; they either work on they don't. Actuators can be tested with a hand vacuum pump and solenoids can be individually tested with a 12 volt power source.

In the vacuum system diagram, position **a** is the door position when the solenoid is not activated, position **b** is the activated

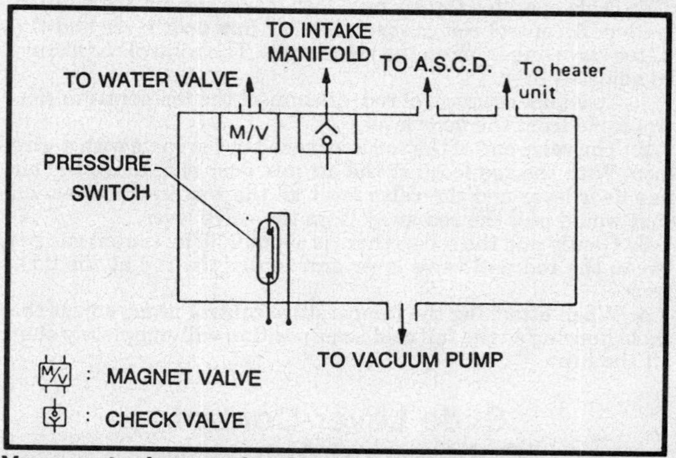
TO INTAKE MANIFOLD
TO A.S.C.D.
To heater unit
TO WATER VALVE
M/V
PRESSURE SWITCH
TO VACUUM PUMP
M/V : MAGNET VALVE
: CHECK VALVE

Vacuum tank on turbocharged vehicle has a switch to turn on the pump. A.S.C.D. is the automatic speed control device

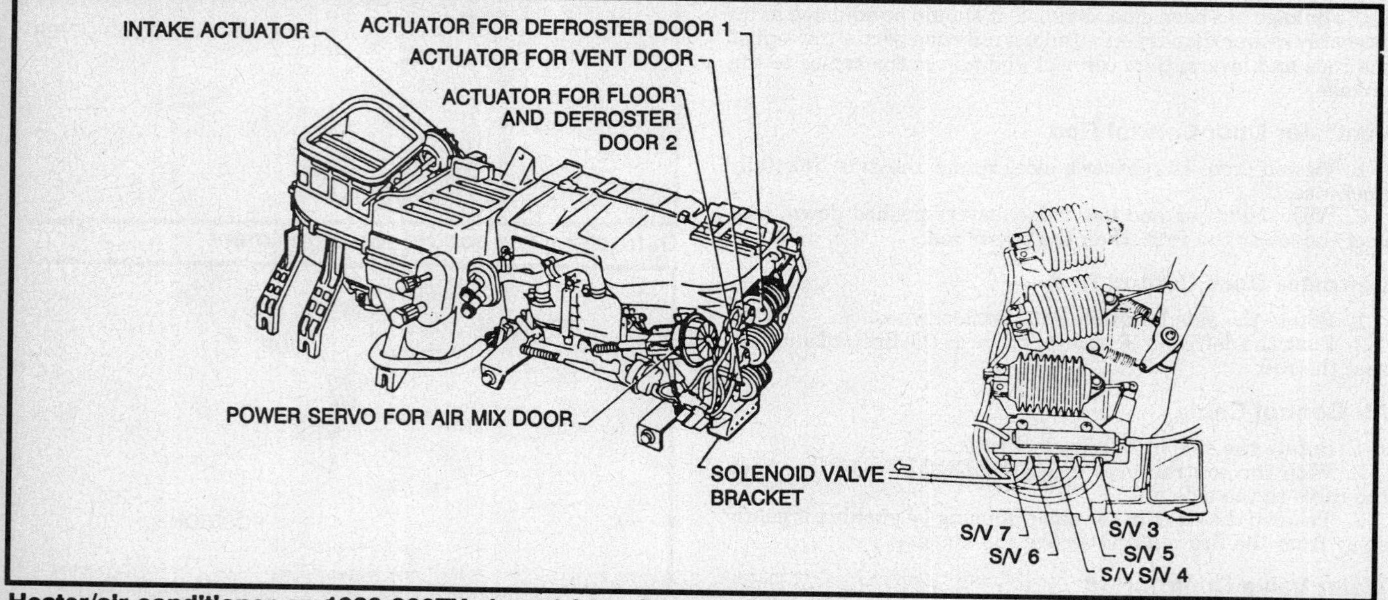
INTAKE ACTUATOR
ACTUATOR FOR DEFROSTER DOOR 1
ACTUATOR FOR VENT DOOR
ACTUATOR FOR FLOOR AND DEFROSTER DOOR 2
POWER SERVO FOR AIR MIX DOOR
SOLENOID VALVE BRACKET
S/V 7
S/V 6
S/V 3
S/V 5
S/V S/V 4

Heater/air conditioner on 1989 300ZX viewed from firewall side

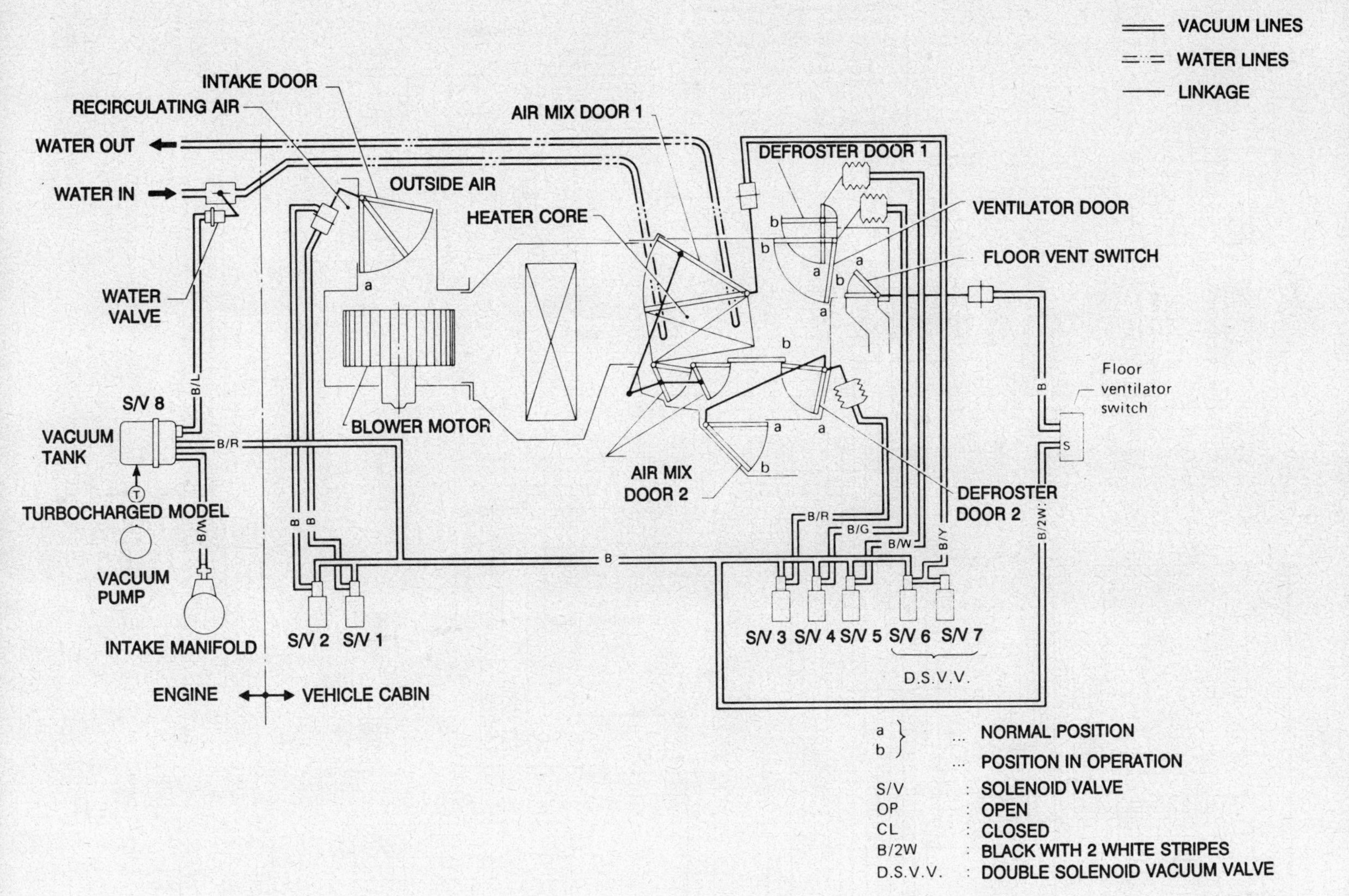
VACUUM LINES
WATER LINES
LINKAGE
INTAKE DOOR
RECIRCULATING AIR
AIR MIX DOOR 1
WATER OUT
DEFROSTER DOOR 1
WATER IN
OUTSIDE AIR
HEATER CORE
VENTILATOR DOOR
FLOOR VENT SWITCH
WATER VALVE
Floor ventilator switch
S/V 8
VACUUM TANK
BLOWER MOTOR
B/L
B/R
B/W
B
B/G
B/Y
B/2W
S
TURBOCHARGED MODEL
AIR MIX DOOR 2
DEFROSTER DOOR 2
VACUUM PUMP
INTAKE MANIFOLD
S/V 2 S/V 1
S/V 3 S/V 4 S/V 5 S/V 6 S/V 7
D.S.V.V.
ENGINE
VEHICLE CABIN
a ... NORMAL POSITION
b ... POSITION IN OPERATION
S/V : SOLENOID VALVE
OP : OPEN
CL : CLOSED
B/2W : BLACK WITH 2 WHITE STRIPES
D.S.V.V. : DOUBLE SOLENOID VACUUM VALVE

OUTLET CONTROL

MODE		FACE	B/L	FOOT	DEMIST	DEF
DOOR POSITION	DEF. DOOR 1	b	b	b	a	a
	VENT. DOOR	b	b	a	a	a
	FLOOR. DOOR	a	b	b	b	a
	DEF. DOOR 2	a	b	b	b	a
OPERATION OF SOLENOID VALVE	S/V 3	CL.	OP.	OP.	OP.	CL.
	S/V 4	OP.	OP.	CL.	CL.	CL.
	S/V 5	OP.	OP.	OP.	CL.	CL.

AIR MIX DOOR CONTROL

			HOT side	HOLD	COLD side
Air mix door 1, 2	OPERATION OF SOLENOID VALVE	S/V 6	CL.	CL.	OP
		S/V 7	OP	CL.	CL

INTAKE CONTROL

		RECIRC	REC/ OUTSIDE	OUTSIDE
INTAKE DOOR		c	b	a
OPERATION OF SOLENOID VALVE	S/V 1	OP.	OP.	CL.
	S/V 2	OP.	CL.	CL.

FLOOR VENTILATOR SWITCH

DOOR \ SWITCH	PULL UP	PRESS DOWN
FLOOR VENT DOOR	a	b

WATER COCK CONTROL

		OPEN	CLOSE
OPERATION OF SOLENOID VALVE	S/V 8	CL	OP

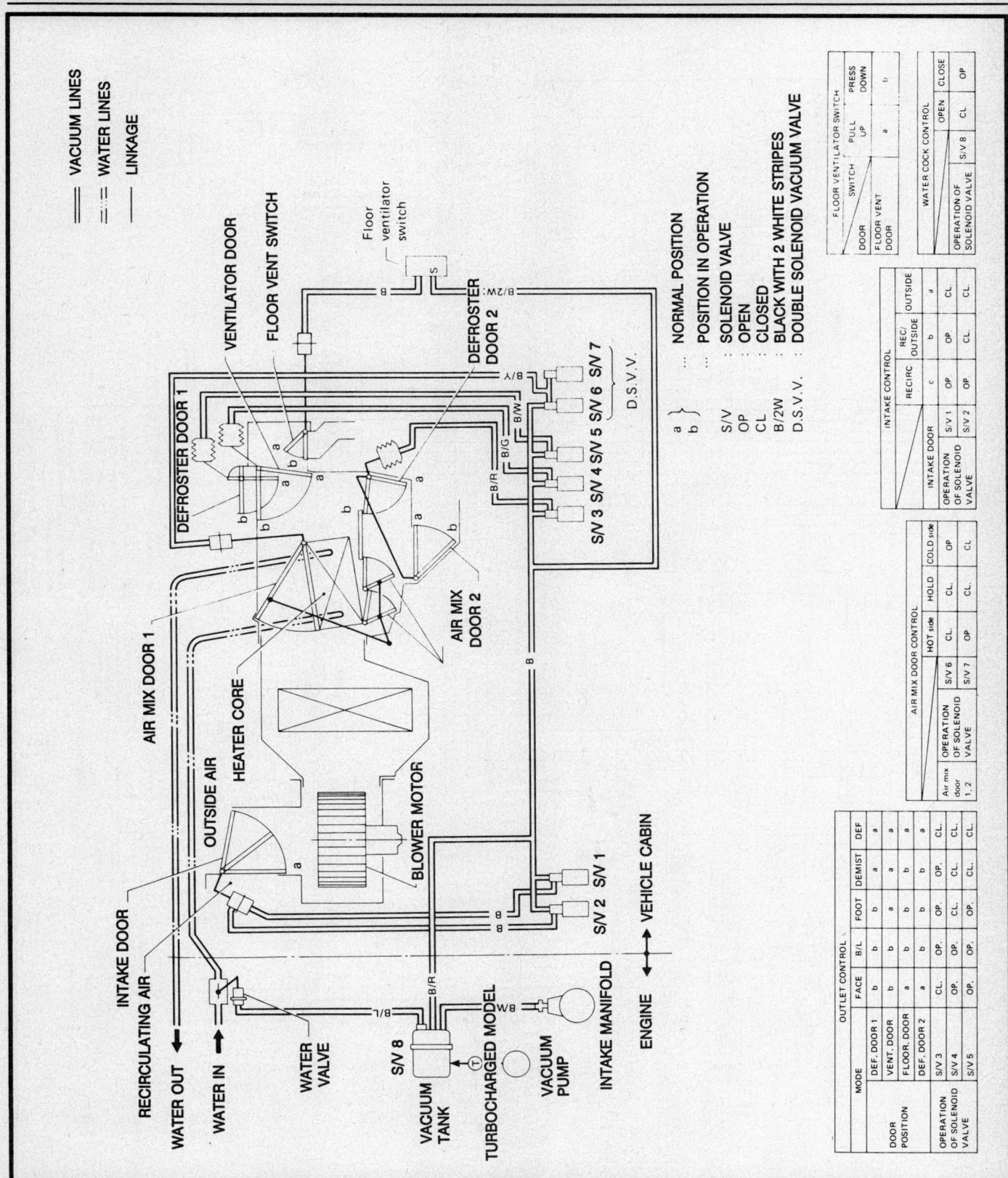

Vacuum system and solenoid valve diagram on 1989 300ZX with manual controls. Turbocharged vehicles have an electric vacuum pump

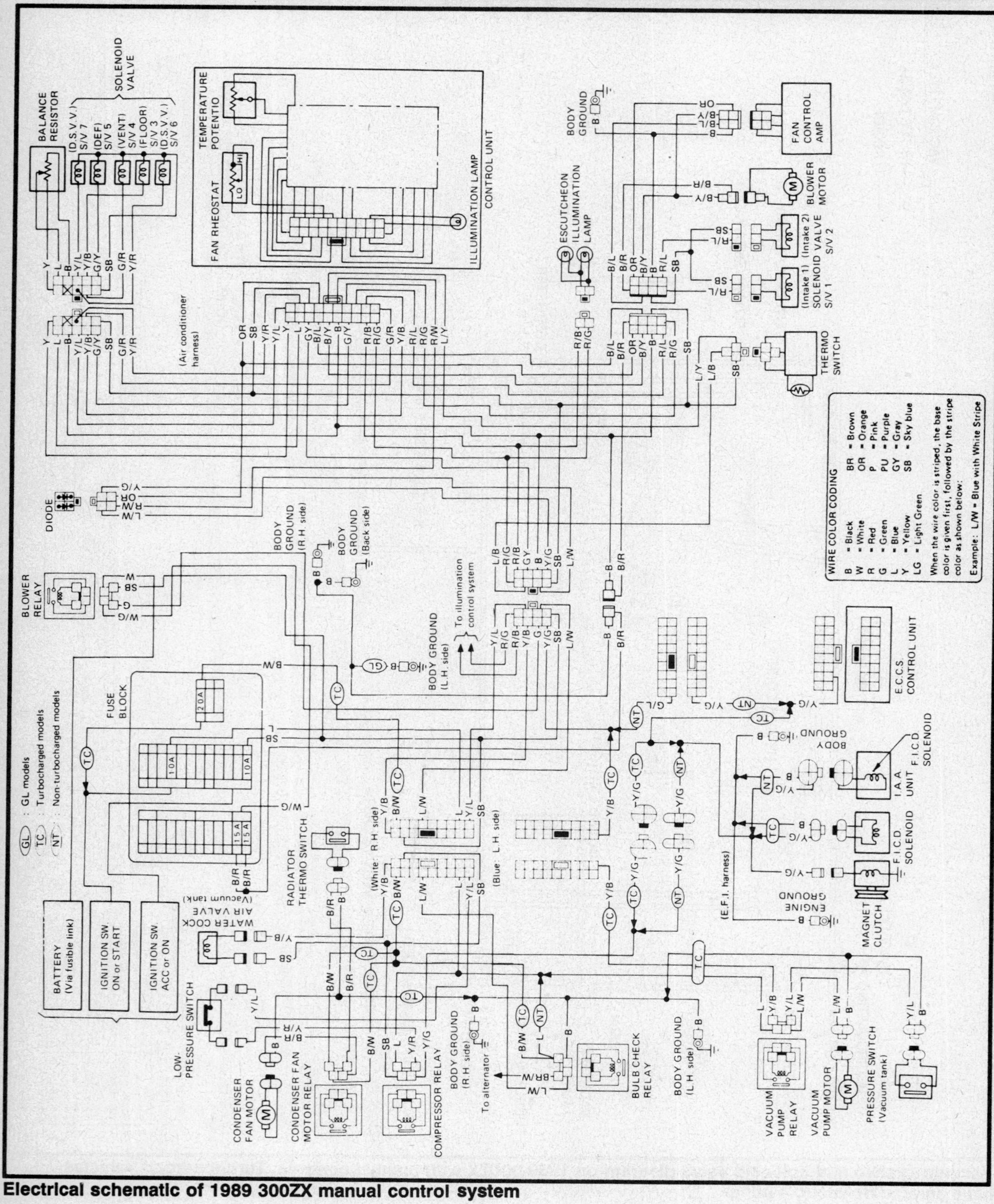
BALANCE RESISTOR
SOLENOID VALVE
TEMPERATURE POTENTIO
FAN RHEOSTAT
ILLUMINATION LAMP
CONTROL UNIT
BODY GROUND
FAN CONTROL AMP
BLOWER MOTOR
ESCUTCHEON ILLUMINATION LAMP
SOLENOID VALVE S/V 2
SOLENOID VALVE S/V 1
THERMO SWITCH
(Air conditioner harness)
DIODE
BLOWER RELAY
To illumination control system
FUSE BLOCK
GL : GL models
TC : Turbocharged models
NT : Non-turbocharged models
E.C.C.S. CONTROL UNIT
BODY GROUND
I.A.A. UNIT
F.I.C.D. SOLENOID
ENGINE GROUND
(E.F.I. harness)
MAGNET CLUTCH
BATTERY (Via fusible link)
IGNITION SW. ON or START
IGNITION SW. ACC or ON
WATER COCK AIR VALVE (Vacuum tank)
RADIATOR THERMO SWITCH
LOW-PRESSURE SWITCH
CONDENSER FAN MOTOR
CONDENSER FAN MOTOR RELAY
COMPRESSOR RELAY
To alternator
BULB CHECK RELAY
VACUUM PUMP RELAY
VACUUM PUMP MOTOR
PRESSURE SWITCH (Vacuum tank)
WIRE COLOR CODING
B = Black
W = White
R = Red
G = Green
L = Blue
Y = Yellow
LG = Light Green
BR = Brown
OR = Orange
P = Pink
PU = Purple
GY = Gray
SB = Sky blue
When the wire color is striped, the base color is given first, followed by the stripe color as shown below:
Example: L/W = Blue with White Stripe

Electrical schematic of 1989 300ZX manual control system

door. The table below the diagram indicates which solenoid valve **S/V** operates each door actuator. The driver's floor ventilator switch is not an electric switch but is directly connected to the vacuum system.

CONTROLS

On manually controled heating and air conditioning systems, the user can select outside or recirculated air, heated or cooled air, which vents the air exits and blower fan speed.

The blower fan rheostat operates the blower through a fan control amplifier. This amplifier is mounted in the air flow for cooling, on the blower fan housing near the motor. The amplifier has been found to collect water from the inlet air. Sometimes drying the amplifier will restore correct blower operation. When installing an amplifier, use a sealant around the power transistor cover and terminals to keep water out.

The temperature is controlled through a potentiometer in the control unit and a balancing resistor mounted on the air mix door power servo. When air conditioning is selected, a ground circuit is completed. The signal first goes to the thermo–switch mounted on the evaporator housing, which senses the blower inlet air temperature. If that temperature is above about 60°F, the signal then goes to the low pressure switch on the receiver/drier. If the freon pressure is above about 28 psi, the compressor relay is activated. The thermo–switch in the evaporator housing will cycle the compressor on and off. The compressor clutch and a fast idle control device are both activated at the same time. In non-turbocharged vehicles, the fast idle is adjustable at the auxiliary air control valve mounted to the right of the intake manifold. In turbocharged vehicles the fast idle device is controlled by the engine computer.

When heat is selected, a voltage is sent to the solenoid on the vacuum tank. Vacuum is then sent to the water valve mounted near the battery under the hood. The solenoid valve is modulated to allow more or less vacuum to the water valve actuator, which allows more or less water to flow through the heater core.

Since everything in the control system is electric or electronic, there are no adjustments.

AUTOMATIC CONTROL SYSTEM

System Description

This system is truly automatic. When the engine is first started in cold weather, the system turns on and runs in defrost mode but without the compressor. As the engine coolant temperature rises, the outlet doors change from defrost to foot well heat and automatic temperature control begins. When the engine is started in warm weather, the air conditioning compressor will not run and the blower stays on low until the engine coolant warms up. At that point the systems goes to automatic temperature control. At any time fan speed can be manually over-ridden or the system can be turned off.

Inside, temperature sensors are placed in the foot well area and in the overhead center console. Each of these 2 sensors has a tiny aspirator fan to draw air across it. A temperature differential can be selected for the upper and lower vents by turning the **SET TEMPERATURE ADJUSTER** in the top center of the control panel. Turning it towards the (–) sign will increase the output temperature of the lower vents and decrease the temperature at the upper vents. Turning towards the (+) sign reverses the bias. The small vertical graph shows which way the warmer air is biased.

A sun load sensor is mounted at the base of the windshield in the defroster grille. Other sensors detect defroster duct, vent duct, floor duct and outside air temperatures and door positions. The amplfier reads all of these inputs and adjusts the inside-outside air mix, various door positions, compressor operation, water valve operation and blower fan speed. It acts quickly enough to hold upper and lower temperature settings to within about ± 3.5°F. Automatic fan speed control can be over-ridden or at any time the system can be turned off.

System Self-Diagnostics

The micro computer in the amplifier has a built-in self diagnostic function which can be accessed through the user buttons on the front. Diagnostics is split into 2 sections, input and output systems. To access the diagnostic program, locate the (unused) test connector near the right footwell outlet duct and short the terminals as shown. Always test the input system first, then the output system.

INPUT SECTION TEST

1. Jumper the test connector to access the system input section.
2. Turn the ignition switch to **ACC** and press the **ECON A/C** button once.
3. The upper **Set** window displays the sensor being tested. It should read "0" at this time. The lower **Amb** window displays the sensor read-out. Temperature sensor readings will be indicated as degrees C or degrees F.
4. Use the **SET TEMP** buttons to choose the sensor number being checked. Steps 0 through 4 are temperature sensors, Step 5 is the water temperature switch.
5. Step 6 is the sun load sensor. A bright light, such as a drop light shined at the sensor, should be enough to change the read out.
6. Step 7 tests the **Set Temperature Adjuster** at the top center of the control panel.
7. Steps 8 and 9 test the potentiometer balance resistors on the air mix doors. These are position sensors mounted to the door servos, reporting door position to the computer.

OUTPUT SECTION TEST

1. Turn the ignition switch **OFF** and jumper the test connector terminals as shown to access the output section.
2. Start the engine and press the **ECON A/C** button once.
3. Push the **SET TEMP** buttons as before to select the items to be tested. The item number will appear in the upper window.
4. Push the **OFF** button to select the Step in each item test. Each push of the **OFF** button advances to the next Step. The 4th push will return to test Step 1 of that item.
5. Using the test sequence in the chart, the door actuators can be checked 3 different ways:
   a. The position sensor read out in the lower window will change as the door moves.
   b. The air flow indicator lights on the panel will change.
   c. The change in air flow can be felt at the outlet vents.

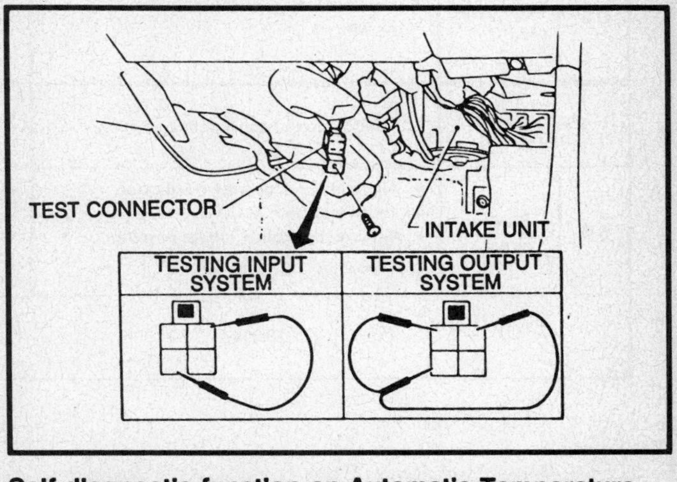
TEST CONNECTOR
INTAKE UNIT
TESTING INPUT SYSTEM
TESTING OUTPUT SYSTEM

Self diagnostic function on Automatic Temperature Control system is accessed by shorting the appropriate terminals on the test connector. Always test input system first.

OUTPUT SECTION DIAGNOSTIC TABLE: 1989 300ZX AUTOMATIC SYSTEM

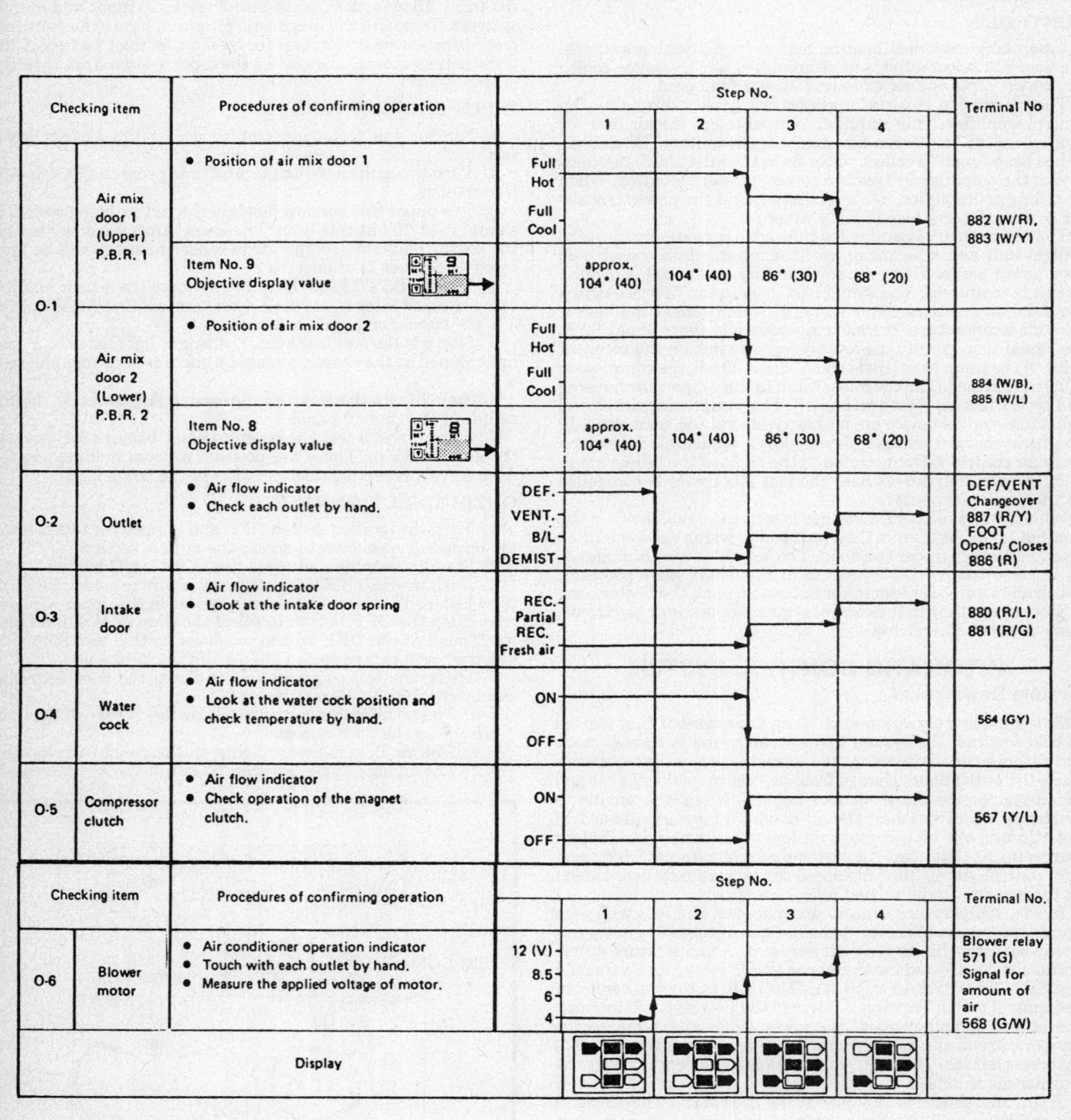

Checking item		Procedures of confirming operation		Step No. 1	2	3	4	Terminal No
O-1	Air mix door 1 (Upper) P.B.R. 1	• Position of air mix door 1	Full Hot Full Cool					882 (W/R), 883 (W/Y)
		Item No. 9 Objective display value 		approx. 104° (40)	104° (40)	86° (30)	68° (20)	
	Air mix door 2 (Lower) P.B.R. 2	• Position of air mix door 2	Full Hot Full Cool					884 (W/B), 885 (W/L)
		Item No. 8 Objective display value 		approx. 104° (40)	104° (40)	86° (30)	68° (20)	
O-2	Outlet	• Air flow indicator • Check each outlet by hand.	DEF. VENT. B/L DEMIST					DEF/VENT Changeover 887 (R/Y) FOOT Opens/ Closes 886 (R)
O-3	Intake door	• Air flow indicator • Look at the intake door spring	REC. Partial REC. Fresh air					880 (R/L), 881 (R/G)
O-4	Water cock	• Air flow indicator • Look at the water cock position and check temperature by hand.	ON OFF					564 (GY)
O-5	Compressor clutch	• Air flow indicator • Check operation of the magnet clutch.	ON OFF					567 (Y/L)

Checking item		Procedures of confirming operation		Step No. 1	2	3	4	Terminal No.
O-6	Blower motor	• Air conditioner operation indicator • Touch with each outlet by hand. • Measure the applied voltage of motor.	12 (V) 8.5 6 4					Blower relay 571 (G) Signal for amount of air 568 (G/W)
Display								

INPUT SECTION DIAGNOSTIC TABLE: 1989 300ZX AUTOMATIC SYSTEM

Step No.	Unit to be checked	"Set"	Results (Ambient section)	
			Correct	Incorrect
0	In-vehicle sensor (foot level) (TL)	0	Indicates the approximate temperature at the location of the sensor.	All other figures: −17 (2) indicates open circuit. 83 (181) indicates short circuit.
1	In-vehicle sensor (head level) (Tu)	1		
2	Floor duct sensor (Tdl)	2		
3	Vent duct sensor (Tdu)	3		
4	Defrost duct sensor (Tdd)	4		
5	Water temperature switch (Tu)	5	Water temp. under 40°C (104°F) = −17 (2) Water temp. over 40°C (104°F) = 83 (181)	All others
6	Sunload sensor (Tc)	6	0 (32) no sunload 40 (104) high sunload	No change
7	Objective temperature adjusting switch	7	Set temperature adjuster setting equal to approx. temp. difference	Varies from actual temp. difference.
8	Potentio balance resistor (Air mix door No. 2)	8	Varies in the range of approx. 40 to approx. 20 (approx. 104 to approx. 68). (Must perform output system diagnosis to read variation)	No variation Improper variation
9	Potentio balance resistor (Air mix door No. 1)	9		

System Component Location

1. The vacuum tank is in front of the relays on the right front fender. On turbocharged vehicles, follow the vacuum line from the tank to the vacuum pump, mounted just in-board of the right headlight.

2. The compressor relay is the second from the front, closest to the fender. The vacuum pump relay for turbocharged vehicles is to the rear of the compressor relay.

3. The water temperature switch is next to the water valve on the heater hose. This switch can be tested for open when cold and closed when hot but should not be removed from the valve assembly.

4. The ambient temperature sensor is under the front bumper, just in-board of the left fog light.

5. The blower fan relay is above the fuse block behind the driver's kick panel, the second one from the front.

6. The low pressure switch for the air conditioner compressor is on the receiver/drier.

7. The head level temperature sensor and aspirator fan assembly is in the panel just behind the over head interior light. The foot well temperature sensor with aspirator fan is on the right side, near the blower fan.

Fault Codes

TEMPERATURE SENSOR FAULT

1. If the input system test indicates a faulty temperature sensor in Steps 0–5, locate the sensor inside the air duct and disconnect it. The read out should be about 2°F (−17°C).

2. Check for 5 volts between one of the terminals on the amplifier side of the connector and ground. With the voltage side grounded, the read out should be 181°F (83°C).

3. If Steps 1 and 2 produce the noted read outs, the amplifier and wiring are good. The fault is most likely in the temperature sensor.

4. If there is no voltage, check for continuity in the wiring between the sensor and the amplifier. If the wiring harness is good but no voltage reaches the sensor, the amplifier is faulty.

SUNLOAD SENSOR FAULT

This sensor is a light detecting diode which converts light into electrical current at an unspecified voltage. The current is in the very low milliamp (mA) range. If the sunload sensor test at Step 6 shows no change in read out with different light levels on the sensor, unplug the sensor and check the current comming directly from the sensor. Under bright light, the sensor will put out 0.05–2.0 mA and will drop to 0 mA when covered.

DOOR POSITION FAULT

1. If a sensor read out indicates no air mix door movement, there are 4 possible reasons:
   a. Door not moving
   b. No voltage to sensor
   c. No signal returned from the sensor
   d. Sensor loose or mis-adjusted

2. If the door cannot be moved by hand, look for mechanical problems in the servo linkage or obstruction of the door itself.

3. If the door can be moved by hand, check that the servo and solenoid are working. Use the diagram to find the correct vacuum line and solenoid valve.

4. Make sure the ignition is **OFF**, connect the vacuum line to a hand vacuum pump and draw a vacuum on the servo. When 12 volts is applied to the correct solenoid, the door should operate. Keep pumping the hand pump to determine if the servo reaches full travel.

5. If the door does move when operated with a hand pump, locate the white 14 pin harness connector near the top of the evaporator housing. With the ignition switch in the **ACC** position, check for 12 volts between the black/white wire and ground.

6. If there is no voltage, turn the ignition switch **OFF** and slide the control unit out of the dash without disconnecting it. Turn the ignition switch to **ACC** and check for voltage at the black/white wire, pin no. 19 on the largest connector.

7. If the control unit is supplying 12 volts, turn ignition

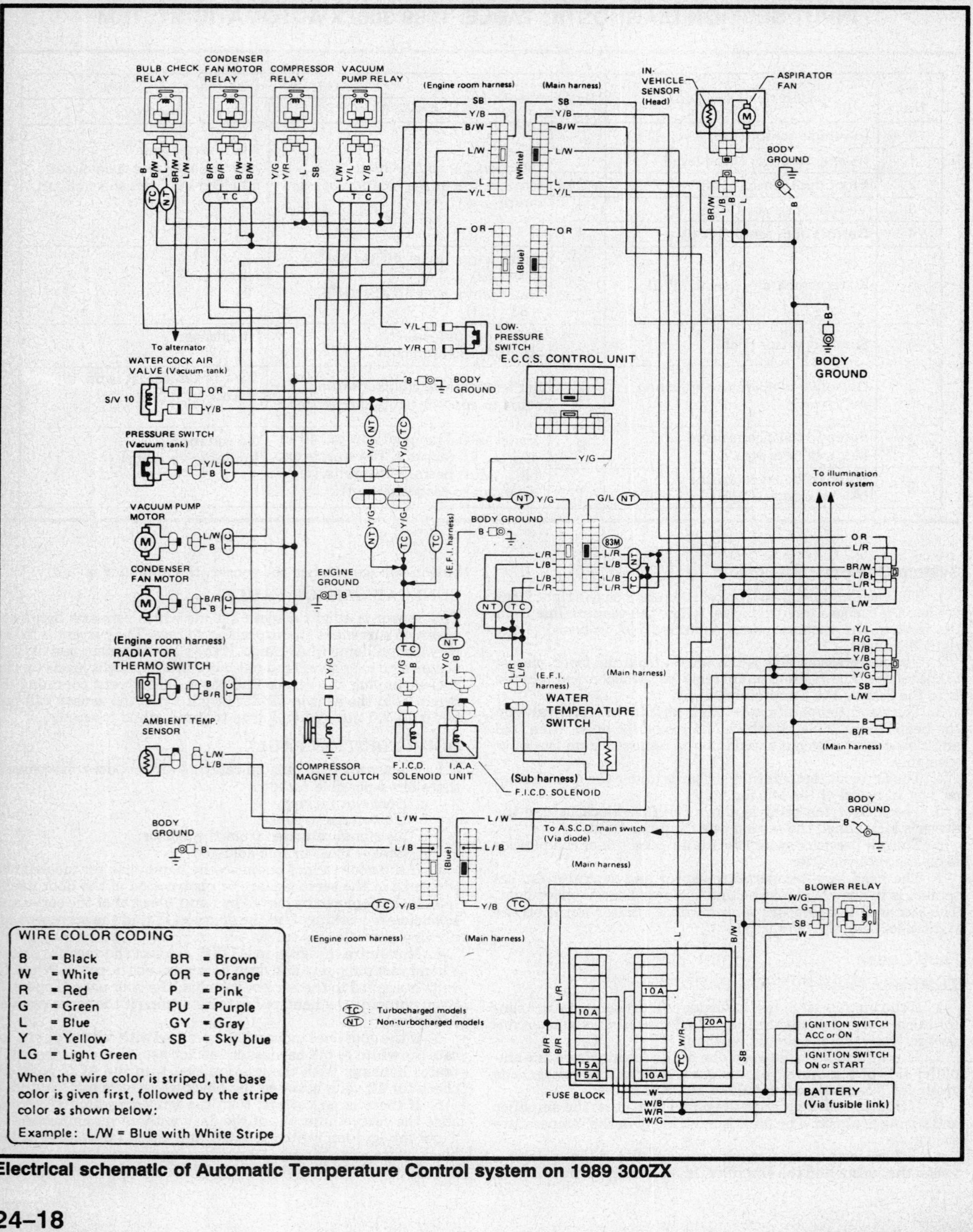
BULB CHECK RELAY
CONDENSER FAN MOTOR RELAY
COMPRESSOR RELAY
VACUUM PUMP RELAY
(Engine room harness)
(Main harness)
IN-VEHICLE SENSOR (Head)
ASPIRATOR FAN
BODY GROUND
(White)
(Blue)
To alternator
WATER COCK AIR VALVE (Vacuum tank)
S/V 10
LOW-PRESSURE SWITCH
E.C.C.S. CONTROL UNIT
PRESSURE SWITCH (Vacuum tank)
VACUUM PUMP MOTOR
CONDENSER FAN MOTOR
ENGINE GROUND
(E.F.I. harness)
To illumination control system
(Engine room harness)
RADIATOR THERMO SWITCH
AMBIENT TEMP. SENSOR
COMPRESSOR MAGNET CLUTCH
F.I.C.D. SOLENOID
I.A.A. UNIT
WATER TEMPERATURE SWITCH
(Sub harness)
F.I.C.D. SOLENOID
To A.S.C.D. main switch (Via diode)
BLOWER RELAY
FUSE BLOCK
IGNITION SWITCH ACC or ON
IGNITION SWITCH ON or START
BATTERY (Via fusible link)
TC : Turbocharged models
NT : Non-turbocharged models
WIRE COLOR CODING
B = Black
W = White
R = Red
G = Green
L = Blue
Y = Yellow
LG = Light Green
BR = Brown
OR = Orange
P = Pink
PU = Purple
GY = Gray
SB = Sky blue
When the wire color is striped, the base color is given first, followed by the stripe color as shown below:
Example: L/W = Blue with White Stripe

Electrical schematic of Automatic Temperature Control system on 1989 300ZX

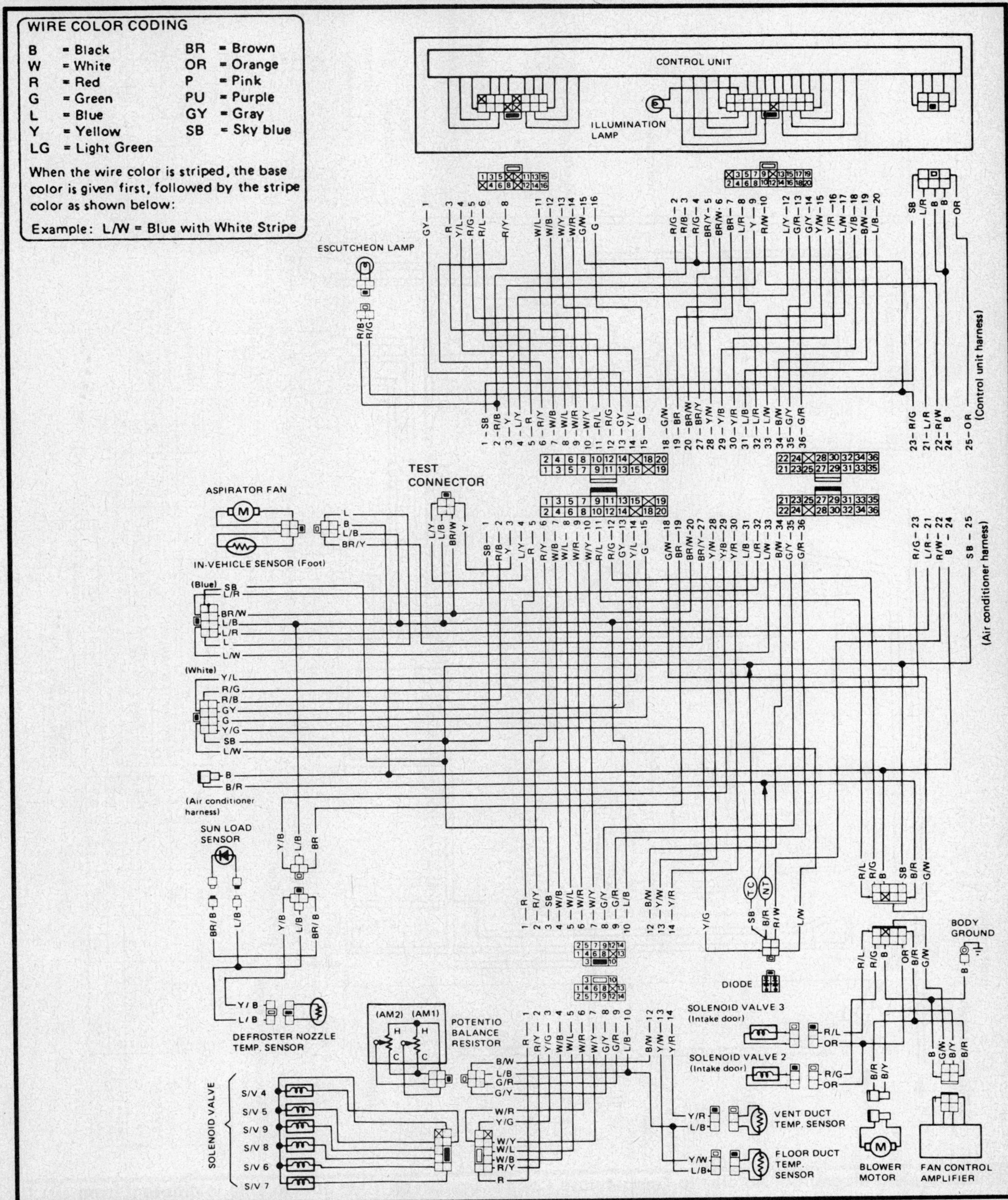
WIRE COLOR CODING
B = Black
W = White
R = Red
G = Green
L = Blue
Y = Yellow
LG = Light Green
BR = Brown
OR = Orange
P = Pink
PU = Purple
GY = Gray
SB = Sky blue
When the wire color is striped, the base color is given first, followed by the stripe color as shown below:
Example: L/W = Blue with White Stripe
CONTROL UNIT
ILLUMINATION LAMP
ESCUTCHEON LAMP
(Control unit harness)
TEST CONNECTOR
ASPIRATOR FAN
IN-VEHICLE SENSOR (Foot)
(Blue)
(White)
(Air conditioner harness)
SUN LOAD SENSOR
DEFROSTER NOZZLE TEMP. SENSOR
POTENTIO BALANCE RESISTOR
SOLENOID VALVE
S/V 4
S/V 5
S/V 9
S/V 8
S/V 6
S/V 7
DIODE
SOLENOID VALVE 3 (Intake door)
SOLENOID VALVE 2 (Intake door)
VENT DUCT TEMP. SENSOR
FLOOR DUCT TEMP. SENSOR
BODY GROUND
BLOWER MOTOR
FAN CONTROL AMPLIFIER

Electrical schematic of Automatic Temperature Control system on 1989 300ZX

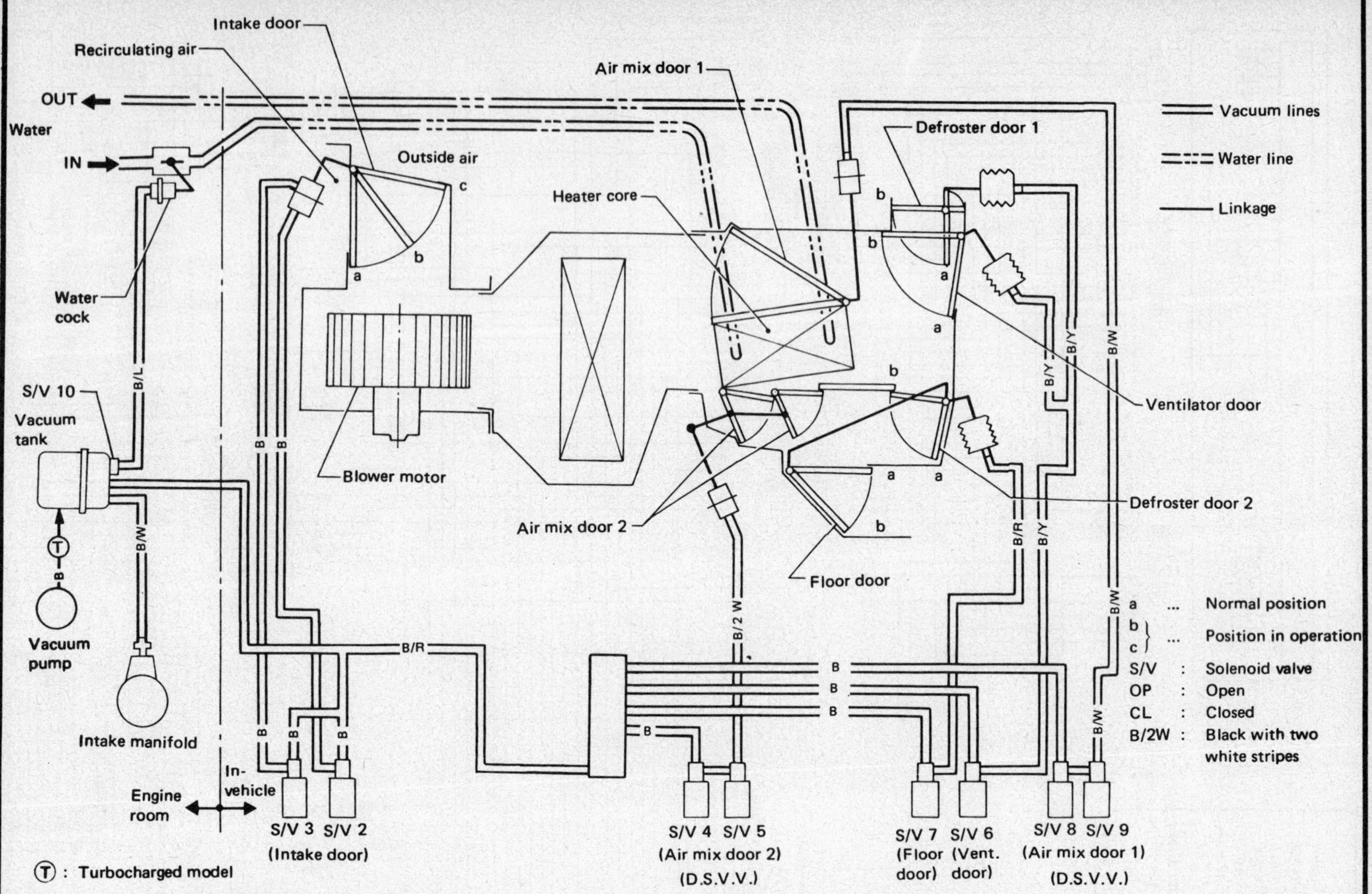
Intake door
Recirculating air
Air mix door 1
OUT
Water
IN
Defroster door 1
Vacuum lines
Water line
Linkage
Outside air
Heater core
Water cock
S/V 10
Vacuum tank
Blower motor
Ventilator door
Air mix door 2
Defroster door 2
Floor door
Vacuum pump
Intake manifold
B/L
B/W
B/R
B/Y
B/2 W
In-vehicle
Engine room
a ... Normal position
b, c ... Position in operation
S/V : Solenoid valve
OP : Open
CL : Closed
B/2W : Black with two white stripes
S/V 3 S/V 2
(Intake door)
S/V 4 S/V 5
(Air mix door 2)
(D.S.V.V.)
S/V 7 S/V 6
(Floor door) (Vent. door)
S/V 8 S/V 9
(Air mix door 1)
(D.S.V.V.)
T : Turbocharged model

OUTLET CONTROL

MODE		VENT	B/L	HEAT/DEMIST	DEF
DOOR POSITION	DEF, DOOR 1	b	b	a	a
	VENT, DOOR	b	b	a	a
	FLOOR, DOOR	a	b	b	a
	DEF, DOOR 2	a	b	b	a
OPERATION OF SOLENOID VALVE	S/V6	OP	OP	CL	CL
	S/V7	CL	OP	OP	CL

AIR MIX DOOR CONTROL

			HOT side	HOLD	COLD side
Air mix door 1	OPERATION OF SOLENOID VALVE	S/V8	CL	CL	OP
		S/V9	OP	CL	CL
Air mix door 2		S/V4	CL	CL	OP
		S/V5	OP	CL	OP

WATER COCK CONTROL

		OPEN	CLOSED
OPERATION OF SOLENOID VALVE	S/V10	CL	OP

INTAKE CONTROL

INTAKE AIR		RECIRC	PARTIAL OUTSIDE	OUTSIDE
INTAKE DOOR POSITION		c	b	a
OPERATION OF SOLENOID VALVE	S/V2	OP	CL	CL
	S/V3	OP	OP	CL

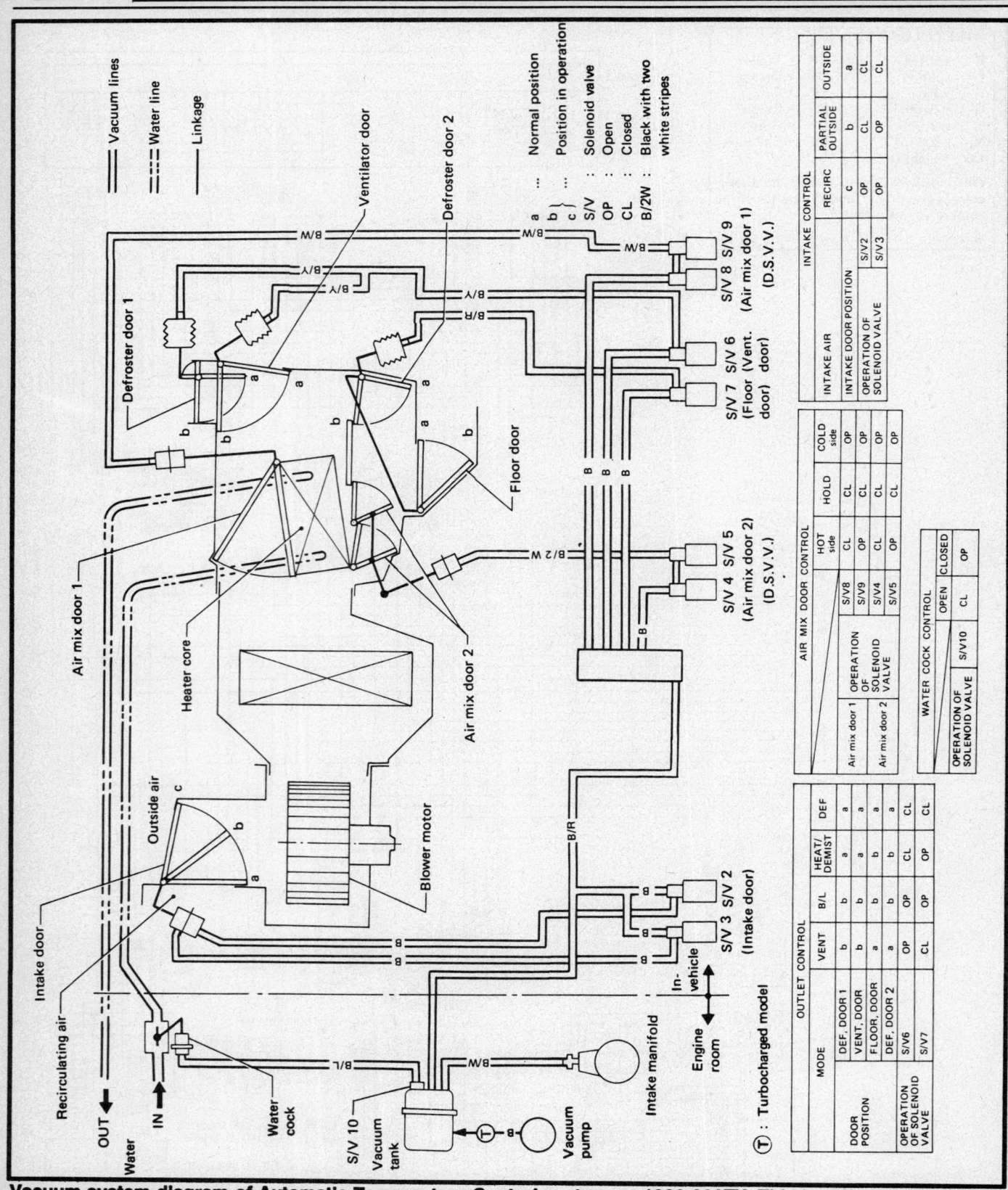

Vacuum system diagram of Automatic Temperature Control system on 1989 300ZX. This is different from the manual system

switch **OFF** and check for continuity from the control unit to the position sensor.

8. If voltage is reaching the sensor, check for the return signal at the green/yellow wire for door 1 or the green/red wire for door 2. If the door moves but the return signal does not change, the sensor it self is faulty or not properly adjusted or secured to the linkage.

9. To change or adjust the sensor, the entire system should be removed from the vehicle as an assembly. With the doors in the full heat position, the resistance between the black/white and the green/yellow wires should be 2.8k ohms. The resistance between the black/white and the green/red wires should be 3.0k ohm.

BLOWER FAN FAULT

1. If the fan does not run, first check for mechanical interference or a seized motor. Other possibilities are the wiring, fuses or relay, the fan control amplifier or the main control amplifier. With the ignition switch in the **ACC** position, there should be 12 volts at the black/red wire to the fan. This voltage comes from the relay above the fuse block, second one from the front, then to the fuse and out to the motor.

2. At the fan control amplifier, the black wire is ground. The green/white wire is the signal coming from the main control amplifier and should cycle in steps from 0–4 volts when the self diagnostic test is run.

3. The black/yellow wire is the signal from the fan control amplifier and should cycle in steps from 0–12 volts when the self diagnostic test is run.

4. If either test shows a fault, check continuities, connectors, fuses and relays before replacing an amplifier.

CONTROL AMPLIFIER FAULT

1. If the amplifier does not operate at all, first check for power supply. Turn the ignition switch to **ACC**. On the smallest connector on the right side of the amplifier, there should be more than 9 volts at the 2 blue wires and the orange wire. The 2 black wires should have continuity to ground.

2. The amplifier is made up of 2 sub-assemblies, the control unit and the switch panel. If power is avaliable but none of the LCD's glow, the bulbs in the display panel may be out. These can be replaced separately.

3. If the bulbs work but no numbers show in the read out windows or if none of the indicator lights near the buttons work, the switch panel assembly can be replaced separately.

4. If the panel lights and numbers work but the system will not operate at all in **AUTO** or **DEF** mode, the control sub-assembly is faulty and can be replaced separately.

5. The buzzer in the control sub-assembly can be tested or replaced separately. If the buzzer sounds when the switches are operated but the air flow does not change, the problem is most likely in the control assembly. If the buzzer works when tested but not when switches are operated, the problem is most likely in the switch assembly.

1990–91 300ZX

MANUAL AND AUTOMATIC CONTROL SYSTEMS

System Description

The manual system is almost identical to the automatic system except for the temperature sensors and control amplifier. All door positions and heating and cooling functions are operated with the same equipment. Except for the onboard diagnostic function of the automatic system, the service procedures will be the same on both systems, although only the automatic system is discussed.

The operating strategy behind this system is similar to previous models but the vacuum actuators and solenoids have been replaced with electric motors. When an automatic temperature setting is selected, the control amplifier decides what the upper and lower cabin temperatures should be, based on internal programming. This differential is dependent on the temperature selected and outside conditions; it is computed and updated every 5 seconds. The control amplifier then determines door positions, blower speed and compressor or water valve operation to maintain upper and lower target temperatures inside the vehicle. Control is biased to admit as much fresh air as possible while maintaining the target temperatures. The system can be operated manually or turned off at any time.

The information fed to the control amplifier comes from temperature sensors in the ducts, under the front bumper and an upper and a lower ambient sensor with aspirator fan to draw air across it. The amplifier also reads engine coolant temperature and sun load. The control amplifier sends output signals to the blower fan amplifier, door motors and the engine control computer. The engine computer operates the compressor, condenser fan and a fast idle control solenoid. The water valve for the heater core is moved by a rod attached to the air mix door actuator and is operated with those doors.

System Diagnostics

The micro computer in the control amplifier has a self diagnostic function which stores trouble codes. This function can be accessed through the system controls or through Nissan's Consult hand held module. The Consult is menu driven, meaning the procedure for its use is shown step by step on the unit's own read out screen. The procedures described here are for the onboard self diagnostic system only. The first step in diagnostic work is to operate the system with the engine running to find which function does not work properly.

Function Test

1. With the vehicle in a well ventilated area above 32°F, start the engine and warm it up. On 1990 models, the display will show the selected temperature and the ambient temperature measured at the sensor under the front bumper. Press the blower fan button 1 time to increase fan speed. On 1991 models, the **ECON** button and one blade on the fan indicator should light. Each time the button is pushed, another blade will light indicating each of the 4 fan speeds. Leave the fan on high speed for the next step.

2. On 1990 models, mode control is fully automatic except for the **REC** function. On 1991 models, the button above the fan button is the mode control, changing which vents the air is discharged from. Push the button 1 time and the face vent indicator should light up. Push the button again to switch to bi-level, then foot vents, then defrost vents. Listen and feel for the change in air discharge. Leave the system in defrost mode for the next step.

3. Pressing the **REC** button will close the intake air door to recirculate the cabin air for maximum cooling. Operate this button and listen for the change in blower sound. This function automatically cancels after about 10 minutes and the system goes to automatic mode.

4. Press the **DEF** button; all the other lights and modes should be cancled. The air should be comming only from the defrost vents and the compressor should be running.

5. When the **ECON** button is pressed, the defrost mode will be cancled and the system will default to an automatic control mode without the compressor. Make sure the compressor stops.

6. Press the **AUTO** button and, if the ambient temperature is above 32°F, the compressor should start again. Use the **SET TEMP** control to set minimum, then maximum temperatures and listen for changes in compressor operation, blower fan speed and mode doors opening and closing. Leave the temperature on full high or low for the next test.

7. Press the **OFF** button and turn the engine off. Wait about

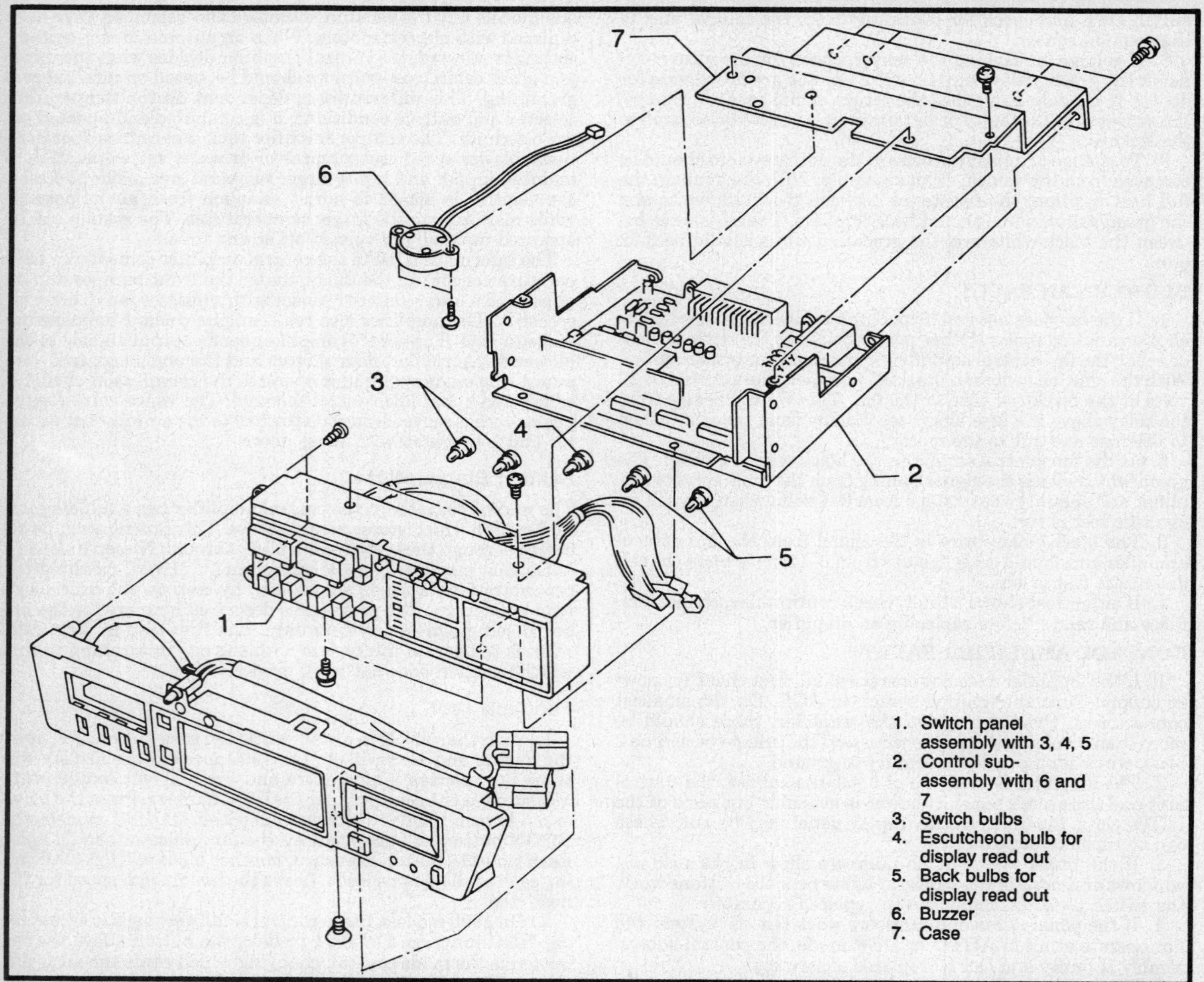
1
2
3
4
5
6
7
1. Switch panel assembly with 3, 4, 5
2. Control sub-assembly with 6 and 7
3. Switch bulbs
4. Escutcheon bulb for display read out
5. Back bulbs for display read out
6. Buzzer
7. Case

Control amplifier assembly on 1989 300ZX

15 seconds and start the engine, then press the **AUTO** button. The system should return the the same setting.

Self Diagnostics on 1990 300ZX

The self-diagnostic function is divided into 4 Steps: sensor monitor, actuator test, target temperature differential and stored trouble codes. To access this function, start the engine or turn the ignition switch to **ON** and press the **AUTO** and **OFF** buttons together for more than 5 seconds. Pressing the **OFF** button or turning the ignition switch **OFF** will exit the self diagnostic function.

SENSOR MONITOR

1. Enter self-diagnostic function. The display should show 00 in the **SET** display, which is a sensor number. The **AMB** display, will show the temperature detected by that sensor. Use a thermometer and compare the sensor reading with an independent reading to pin-point a bad sensor.
2. Press the temperature increase or decrease buttons to call up each sensor number. Any sensor out of the listed range is faulty and if the sunload sensor reads greater than 1.047, it is shorted. If a sensor fault is encountered, check the wiring between the sensor and the amplifier first, then the sensor itself.

00.......Ambient sensor: −30–45°C (−22–113°F)
01.......Upper cabin sensor: 18–30°C (64–86°F)
02.......Lower cabin sensor: 20–35°C (68–95°F)
03.......Defroster duct sensor: 5–70°C (41–158°F)
04.......Face duct sensor: 5–40°C (41–104°F)
05.......Floor duct sensor: 20–70°C (68–158°F)
06.......Sunload sensor: 0–1.047kW
07.......Engine coolant sensor: 20° or 80°C (68° or 176°F)
08.......Mode door voltage: 0–5 volts
09–16....Internal program data

ACTUATOR TEST

1. Press the **AUTO** button once to move from the sensor test to the actuator test. The number 30 will appear in the **SET** display, indicating that this is the actuator test. This number will not change in this test.
2. The first digit in the **AMB** display is the actuator number,

which will range from 3 to 6. The second digit is the blower fan voltage code, which will also change from 3 through 6.

3. When the temperature increase button is pressed once, the first code digit advances to the next actuator. When the temperature decrease button is pressed once, the second code digit advances. By working these buttons, each mode can be manually called up to check that the actuator has moved the doors correctly. The water valve for the heater moves with the air mix doors.

4. Operate each mode and check for air comming out of the correct ducts, compressor operation and blower fan speed changes. If necessary, this test can be used to read blower fan voltage from the blower amplifier in each mode.

TARGET TEMPERATURE DIFFERENTIAL

1. This Step allows checking and setting the difference between the upper and lower target temperatures. Press the **AUTO** button once to change from the previous test. The number 40 will appear in the **SET** display.

2. The number in the **AMB** display will be the difference between the upper and lower cabin temperatures the system will try to maintain. At the factory it is set at 0, meaning the system will adjust to maintain the same temperature at both levels.

3. Pressing the temperature increase button will increase the number in the **AMB** display. The number in the **SET** display may also change but ignore it, the system is still in the same Step. Pressing the temperature decrease button will decrease the number in the **AMB** display.

4. The total range of difference is ± 2°C or ± 3.6°F. The display will show a total change of ± 20 or ± 36. A positive difference will make the foot well target temperature warmer.

5. The setting will be maintained until it is changed again or until the battery is disconnected. The default setting is 0 degrees differential.

TROUBLE CODE READ-OUT

1. Press the **AUTO** button once to move from Step 3 to Step 4. The number 50 will appear in the **SET** display, indicating a sensor number. The number in the **AMB** display will indicate the trouble data. This function reads only the temperature and sun load sensors.

2. Pressing the tempareture increase and decrease buttons will change the sensor number in the **SET** display, from 50 through 56. If the number 50 appears in the **AMB** display, the sensor is good. If the number 0 appears, the sensor is faulty. If any other number appears, the sensor is or was malfunctioning but may be working now.

3. If the number in the **AMB** display is not 50 or 0, that number indicates how many times the ignition switch has been turned on since the fault was first detected. A verticle bar to the left of the number indicates the sensor circuit is open, a horizontal bar indicates a short circuit.

Sensor 50—outside ambient
Sensor 51—cabin upper
Sensor 52—cabin lower
Sensor 53—defroster duct
Sensor 54—face vent duct
Sensor 55—floor duct
Sensor 56—sun load

Self Diagnostics on 1991 300ZX

The self-diagnostic function is divided into 4 tests: sensor monitor, actuator test, target temperature differential and stored trouble codes. To access this function, start the engine or turn the ignition switch to **ON** and press the **AUTO** and **OFF** buttons together for more than 5 seconds. Pressing the **OFF** button or turning the ignition switch **OFF** will exit the self diagnostic function.

ACTUATOR TEST CODES: 1990 300ZX

Actuator \ First code No.	3	4	5	6
Mode door	DEF	HEAT	B/L	VENT
Intake door	FRE	FRE	50% FRE	REC
Air mix door	Full Hot	Full Hot	30°C (86°F)	Full Cold
Compressor	OFF	OFF	ON	ON
Blower motor \ Second code No.	**3**	**4**	**5**	**6**
Voltage	4V	6V	9V	12V

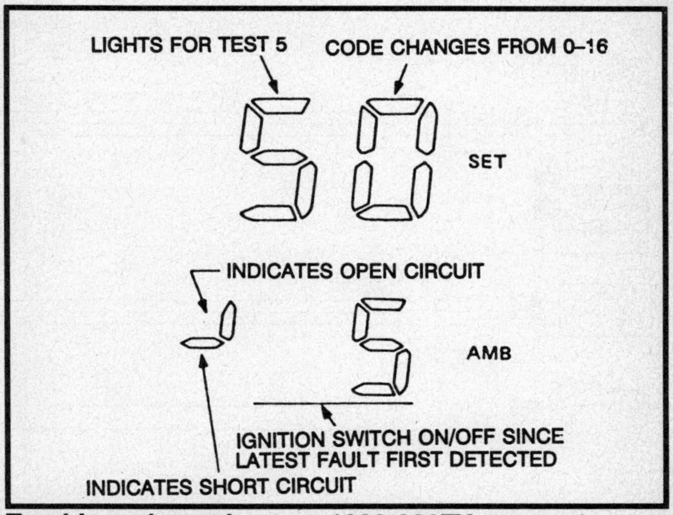
LIGHTS FOR TEST 5
CODE CHANGES FROM 0–16
SET
INDICATES OPEN CIRCUIT
AMB
IGNITION SWITCH ON/OFF SINCE LATEST FAULT FIRST DETECTED
INDICATES SHORT CIRCUIT

Trouble code read-out on 1990 300ZX automatic temperature control system

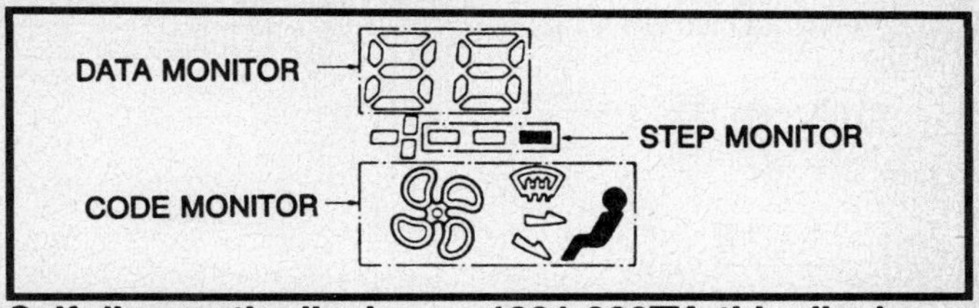
DATA MONITOR
STEP MONITOR
CODE MONITOR

Self diagnostic display on 1991 300ZX: this display indicates the sensor monitor test

SENSOR MONITOR

1. With the diagnostic function activated, a bar display on the Step monitor will show the bar on the right lit, indicating that this is the sensor monitor test.

2. The number in the data monitor is a sensor or voltage reading. The code monitor has a variety of symbols to light up

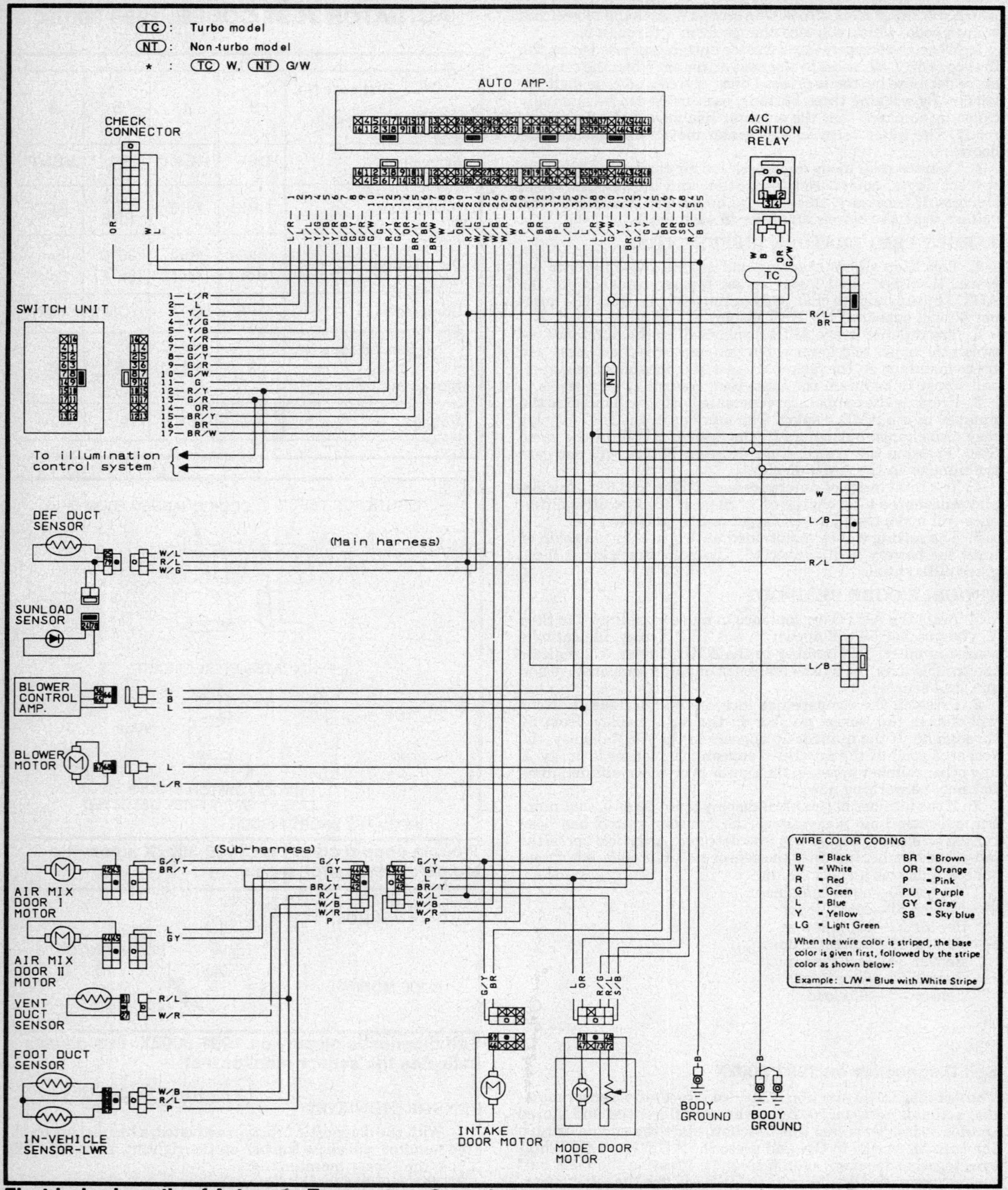
TC : Turbo model
NT : Non-turbo model
* : TC W, NT G/W
AUTO AMP.
CHECK CONNECTOR
A/C IGNITION RELAY
SWITCH UNIT
To illumination control system
DEF DUCT SENSOR
(Main harness)
SUNLOAD SENSOR
BLOWER CONTROL AMP.
BLOWER MOTOR
(Sub-harness)
AIR MIX DOOR I MOTOR
AIR MIX DOOR II MOTOR
VENT DUCT SENSOR
FOOT DUCT SENSOR
IN-VEHICLE SENSOR-LWR
INTAKE DOOR MOTOR
MODE DOOR MOTOR
BODY GROUND
BODY GROUND
WIRE COLOR CODING
B = Black
W = White
R = Red
G = Green
L = Blue
Y = Yellow
LG = Light Green
BR = Brown
OR = Orange
P = Pink
PU = Purple
GY = Gray
SB = Sky blue
When the wire color is striped, the base color is given first, followed by the stripe color as shown below:
Example: L/W = Blue with White Stripe

Electrical schematic of Automatic Temperature Control system on 1990 300ZX

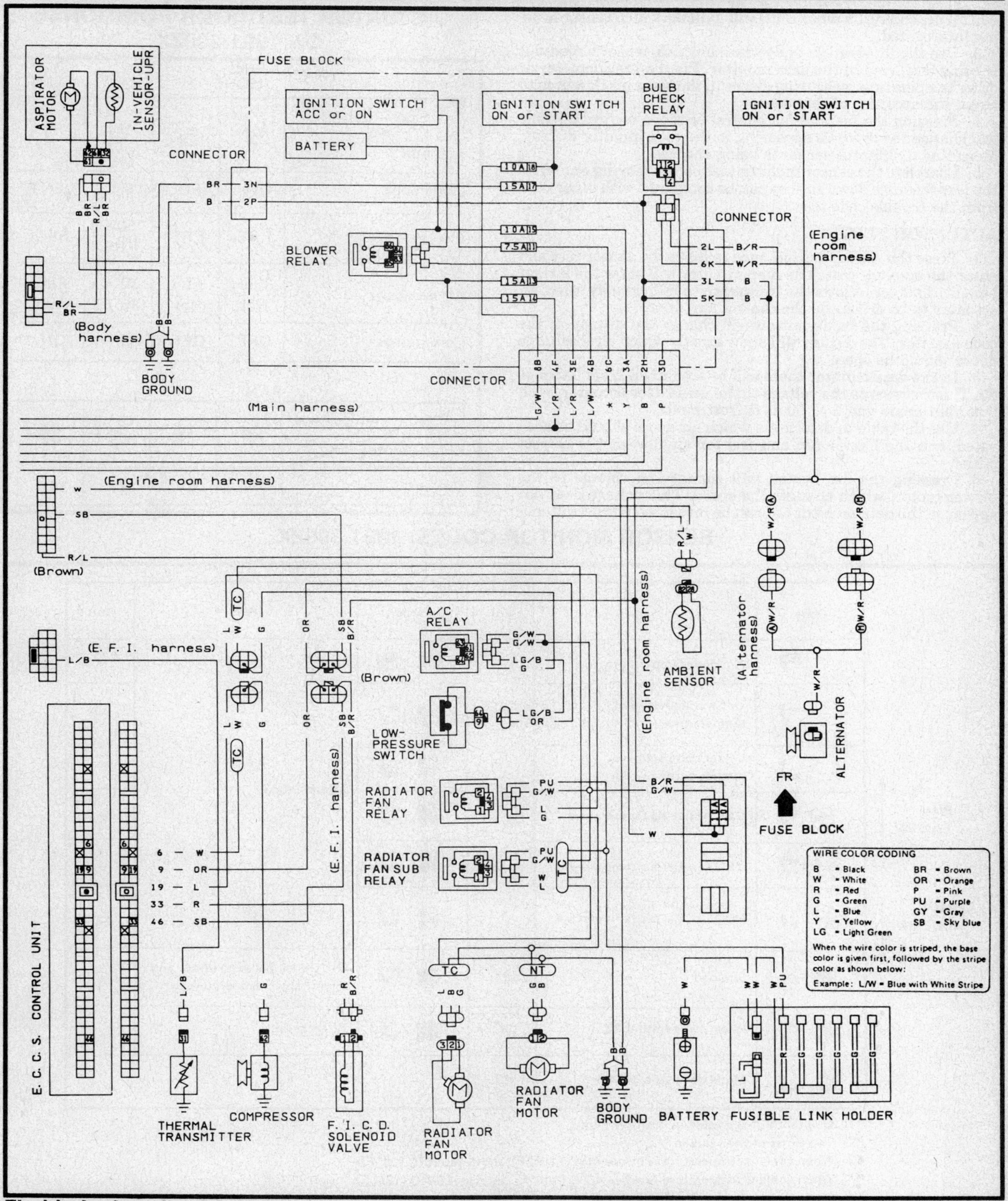
ASPIRATOR MOTOR
IN-VEHICLE SENSOR-UPR
FUSE BLOCK
IGNITION SWITCH ACC or ON
IGNITION SWITCH ON or START
BULB CHECK RELAY
IGNITION SWITCH ON or START
BATTERY
CONNECTOR
BLOWER RELAY
CONNECTOR
(Engine room harness)
(Body harness)
BODY GROUND
CONNECTOR
(Main harness)
(Engine room harness)
(Brown)
(E. F. I. harness)
A/C RELAY
(Brown)
LOW-PRESSURE SWITCH
AMBIENT SENSOR
(Engine room harness)
(Alternator harness)
ALTERNATOR
RADIATOR FAN RELAY
RADIATOR FAN SUB RELAY
(E. F. I. harness)
FR
FUSE BLOCK
E. C. C. S. CONTROL UNIT
THERMAL TRANSMITTER
COMPRESSOR
F. I. C. D. SOLENOID VALVE
RADIATOR FAN MOTOR
RADIATOR FAN MOTOR
BODY GROUND
BATTERY
FUSIBLE LINK HOLDER
WIRE COLOR CODING
B = Black
W = White
R = Red
G = Green
L = Blue
Y = Yellow
LG = Light Green
BR = Brown
OR = Orange
P = Pink
PU = Purple
GY = Gray
SB = Sky blue
When the wire color is striped, the base color is given first, followed by the stripe color as shown below:
Example: L/W = Blue with White Stripe

Electrical schematic of Automatic Temperature Control system on 1990 300ZX

which, depending on what is lit, will indicate which sensor is being interogated.

3. Use the illustration to determine which sensor's read-out is being displayed in the data monitor. Place a thermometer or other temperature measuring device in the same air flow area to check the accuracy of that sensor.

4. Pressing the manual fan control or mode control buttons will change the symbols appearing in the code monitor display, indicating a different sensor is being checked.

5. Complete the sensor monitor test before moving on. Write the test readings down so they can be compared with other data from the trouble code test.

ACTUATOR TEST

1. Press the **AUTO** button once to leave the sensor test and enter the actuator test. The Step monitor will show the 2 right bars lit. This test allows the technician to individually select an actuator to be driven by the control amplifier.

2. Pressing the mode button will change the display in the code monitor. The display will show exactly which air discharge doors should be open.

3. In the data monitor there will be a number, from 0 to 5 or 50. This represents the voltage to the mode door actuator, with 0 as vent mode and 5 or 50 as defrost mode.

4. Use the table to determine which air doors should be activated, run the blower fan and feel for air flow at the correct outlet.

5. Pressing the fan button will change the voltage to the blower motor, which changes the speed. This voltage does not appear in the data monitor but can be measured with a volt me-

ACTUATOR TEST DOOR POSITIONS ON 1991 300ZX

Press MODE ⟶

Actuator \ Display				
Mode door	DEF	D/FOOT	B/L	VENT
Intake door	FRE	FRE	50% FRE	REC
Air mix door	Full Hot	Full Hot	30°C (86°F)	Full Cold
Compressor	OFF	OFF	ON	ON

Press FAN ⟶

Blower motor \ Display				
Voltage	4V	6V	9V	12V

SENSOR MONITOR CODES: 1991 300ZX

Press FAN SW. ↑
Press MODE SW. ↓

Code	Item	Unit	Code	Item	Unit
	Ambient temperature	°C (°F)		Internal data	–
	Upper compartment temperature	°C (°F)		Internal data	–
	Lower compartment temperature	°C (°F)		Internal data	–
	DEF outlet air temperature	°C (°F)		Internal data	–
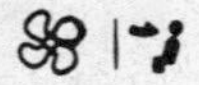	VENT outlet air temperature	°C (°F)		Internal data	–
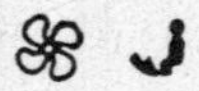	FOOT outlet air temperature	°C (°F)		Internal data	–
	Sunload	*1		Difference between upper and lower target temperatures	°C (°F)
	Water temperature *3	°C (°F)		Internal data	–
	Mode door voltage*4	*2			

*1: One tenth of the value in kcal/h·m² unit
*2: Ten times of the value in V
*3: When coolant temperature is below 40°C (104°F), indicates 20°C (68°F)
When coolant temperature is avove 40°C (104°F), indicates 80°C (176°F)
*4: Mode door voltage: 0 = VENT, 5 = DEF

ter. Remember this voltage does not come directly from the main control amplifier but from the blower control amplifier.

TARGET TEMPERATURE DIFFERENTIAL

1. Press the **AUTO** button once to leave the actuator test and enter the differential check. The Step monitor will show 3 bars lit.

2. The number in the data monitor will be the difference between the upper and lower cabin temperatures the system will try to maintain. At the factory it is set at 0, meaning the system will adjust to maintain the same temperature at both levels.

3. Pressing the mode button will increase the number in the data monitor, pressing the fan button will decrease the number. The total range of difference is ± 2°C or ± 3.6°F. There is no decimal point in the display, so the display will show a total change of ± 20 or ± 36. A positive difference will make the foot well target temperature warmer.

4. The setting will be maintained until it is changed again or until the battery is disconnected. The default setting is 0 degrees differential.

TROUBLE CODE READ-OUT

1. Press the **AUTO** button once to leave the temperature differential section and enter the trouble code read-out. The Step monitor will show the 2 end bars lit, the middle one off.

2. Pressing the fan or mode buttons will change the display in the code monitor, changing which sensor is being checked. This test is different from test 1 in that the sensor condition is being displayed.

3. If a third bar appears to the left of the Step monitor bars, a sensor fault is indicated. A verticle bar indicates an open sensor circuit, a horizontal bar indicates a short circuit.

4. If a sensor is faulty, the number in the data monitor shows how many times the ignition switch has been turned on since the fault was first detected.

5. Use the table to determine which sensor is being checked. If a sensor fault is reported, check the sensor reading obtained in the first test to confirm that there is a fault. Check the wiring between the sensor and control amplifier before replacing the sensor.

System Component Location

1. The control amplifier is behind and to the right of the instrument panel. Removing the lower panel in front of the driver's knees may provide enough access. The user controls can be removed by removing the screws from under the front of the pod and pivot the controls out.

2. The main relay for the blower fan is on the inside relay panel behind the fuse block. When the panel is turned to access the relays, the blower relay is at the bottom towards front of the vehicle. The blower control amplifier is mounted to the evaporator housing next to the blower. Removing the glove compartment may ease access.

3. The compressor relay is on the relay panel under the hood, just above the fuses. The radiator fan relay is to the left of the compressor relay. The low pressure switch is on top of the receiver drier.

4. The thermal transmitter that feeds coolant temperature signals to the control amplifier is on the upper radiator hose. It is the smaller connector towards the left side of the vehicle.

5. The lower cabin temperature sensor is on the driver's side, mounted to the floor duct. The upper sensor with its aspirator fan is in the same panel as the interior spot lights. The defroster duct and sun load sensors are both mounted to the center defroster duct. They can be accessed by removing the center console panel and radio.

6. The ambient temperature sensor is behind and under the front bumper. It should be accessable from under the vehicle.

7. The air mix door motors are reached from the passenger side floor. The mode door motor is near the control amplifier deep in the dash. It may be easier to remove the radio to access this motor. The intake door motor is above the blower motor and can be accessed by removing the glove compartment.

Door Motor and Control Rod Adjustments

This procedure should be necessary only when a door motor has been removed. The mode door operates the side link, which operates all the air outlet doors. The intake door motor operates a door to select fresh or recirculated air. The 2 air mix doors each have a motor and control rod to be adjusted. Each door motor has a position sensor or switch that reports to the control amplifier. To complete the mode and intake door adjustments on vehicles with ATC, the system must be operated in the manual control mode described in the actuator test of the Self Diagnostic procedure.

MODE AND INTAKE DOORS

1. With the system completely assembled except for the mode door motor, rotate the side link fully counter-clockwise to put the system into **VENT** mode. For the intake door adjustment, set the door to full recirculate position,

TROUBLE CODE TABLE FOR 1991 300ZX

Code	Sensor	Open circuit	Short circuit
	Ambient sensor	Less than −70°C (−94°F)	Greater than 141°C (286°F)
	Room upper sensor	Less than −38°C (−36°F)	Greater than 141°C (286°F)
	Room lower sensor	Less than −38°C (−36°F)	Greater than 141°C (286°F)
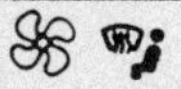	DEF duct sensor	Less than −38°C (−36°F)	Greater than 141°C (286°F)
	VENT duct sensor	Less than −38°C (−36°F)	Greater than 141°C (286°F)
	Floor duct sensor	Less than −38°C (−36°F)	Greater than 141°C (286°F)
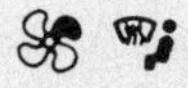	Sunloaded sensor	Open circuit can not be detected by self-diagnosis.	Greater than 1.784 kW (1,534 kcal/h, 6,087 BTU/h)/m^2 [19.19 kW (16,506 kcal/h, 65,502 BTU/h)/sq ft]

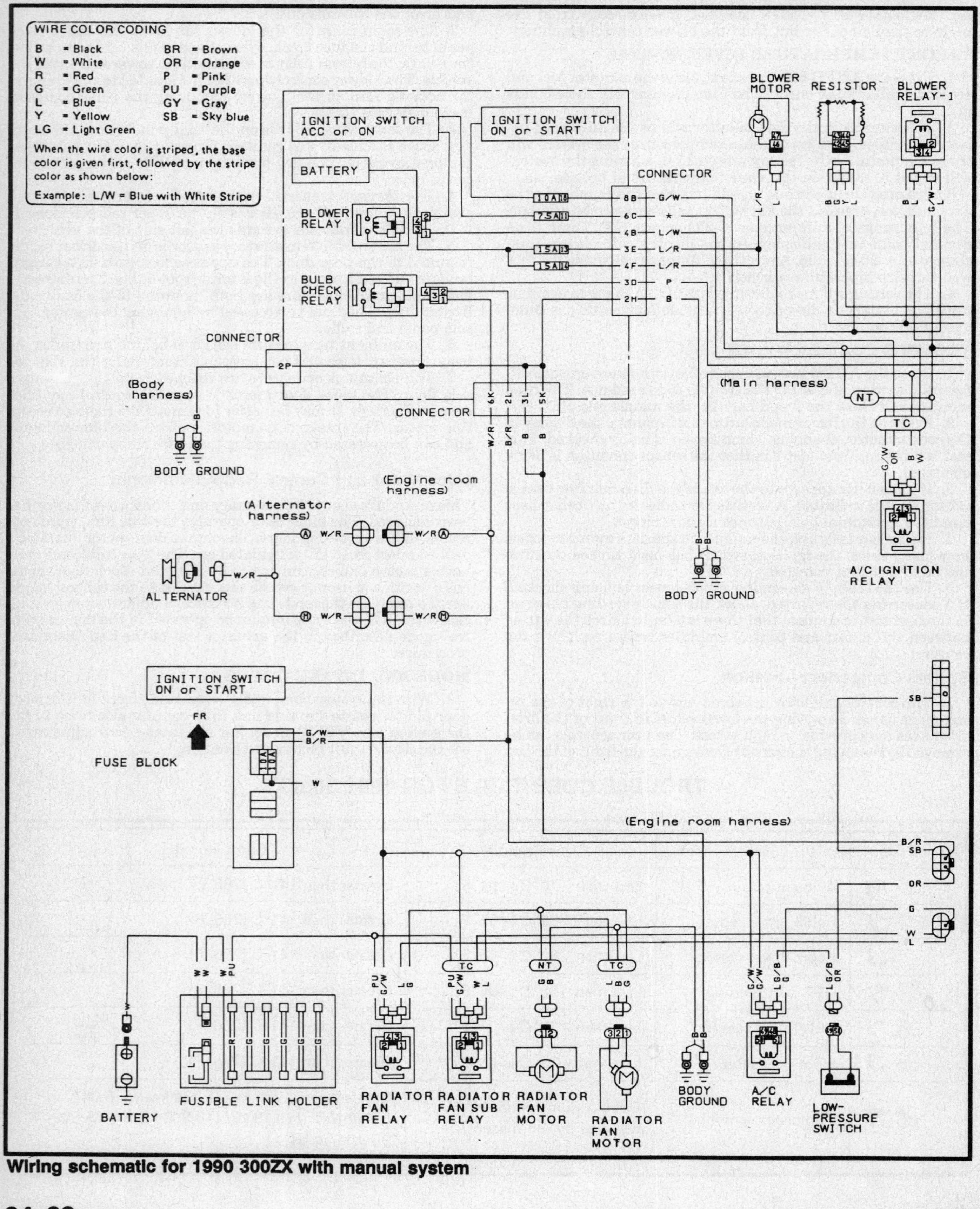
WIRE COLOR CODING
B = Black
W = White
R = Red
G = Green
L = Blue
Y = Yellow
LG = Light Green
BR = Brown
OR = Orange
P = Pink
PU = Purple
GY = Gray
SB = Sky blue
When the wire color is striped, the base color is given first, followed by the stripe color as shown below:
Example: L/W = Blue with White Stripe
IGNITION SWITCH ACC or ON
IGNITION SWITCH ON or START
BATTERY
BLOWER RELAY
BULB CHECK RELAY
CONNECTOR
BLOWER MOTOR
RESISTOR
BLOWER RELAY-1
(Body harness)
BODY GROUND
(Main harness)
(Engine room harness)
(Alternator harness)
ALTERNATOR
A/C IGNITION RELAY
IGNITION SWITCH ON or START
FR
FUSE BLOCK
BATTERY
FUSIBLE LINK HOLDER
RADIATOR FAN RELAY
RADIATOR FAN SUB RELAY
RADIATOR FAN MOTOR
RADIATOR FAN MOTOR
BODY GROUND
A/C RELAY
LOW-PRESSURE SWITCH

Wiring schematic for 1990 300ZX with manual system

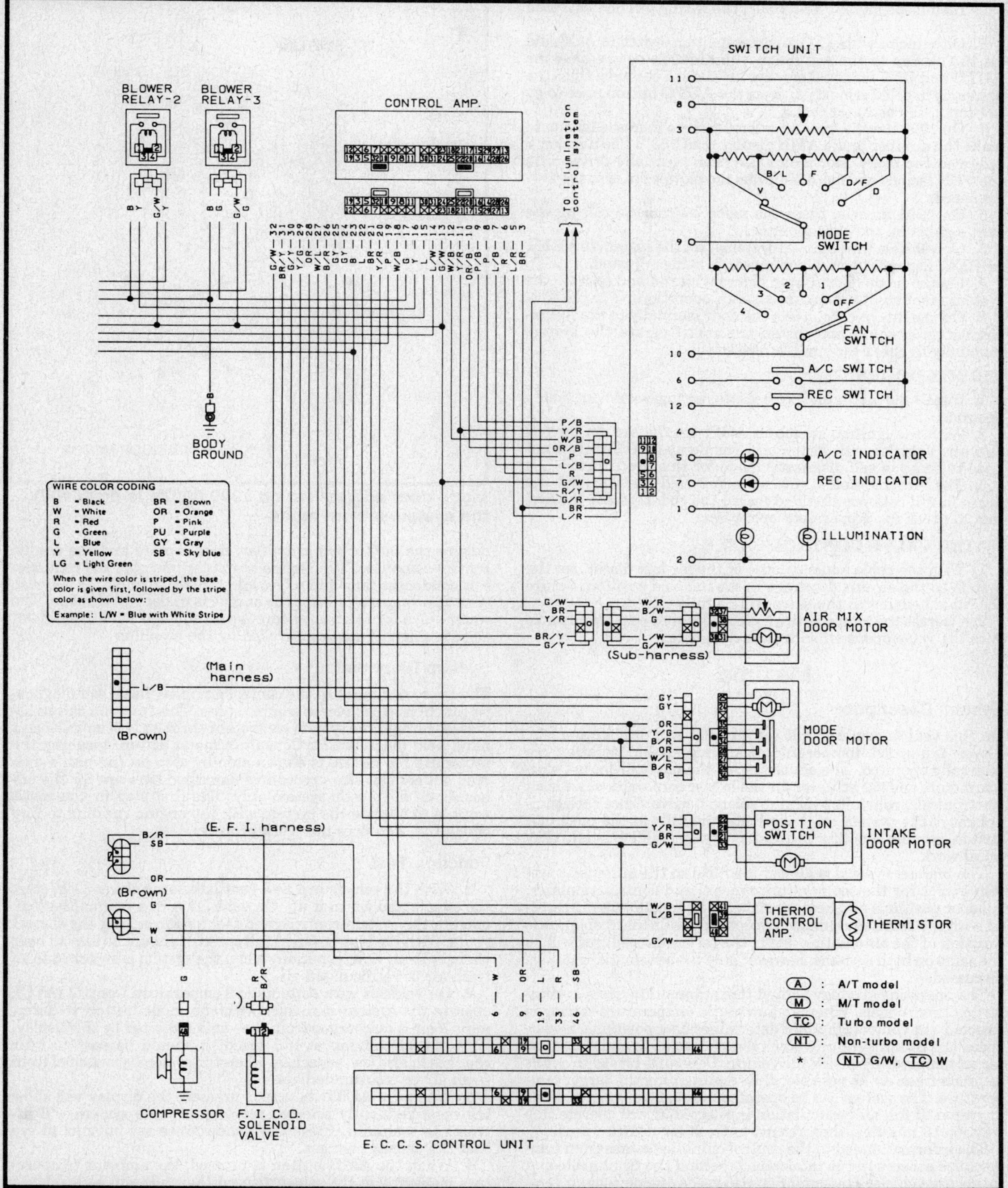
SWITCH UNIT
BLOWER RELAY-2
BLOWER RELAY-3
CONTROL AMP.
TO illumination control system
MODE SWITCH
FAN SWITCH
A/C SWITCH
REC SWITCH
A/C INDICATOR
REC INDICATOR
ILLUMINATION
BODY GROUND
WIRE COLOR CODING
B = Black
W = White
R = Red
G = Green
L = Blue
Y = Yellow
LG = Light Green
BR = Brown
OR = Orange
P = Pink
PU = Purple
GY = Gray
SB = Sky blue
When the wire color is striped, the base color is given first, followed by the stripe color as shown below:
Example: L/W = Blue with White Stripe
AIR MIX DOOR MOTOR
(Sub-harness)
(Main harness)
(Brown)
MODE DOOR MOTOR
(E. F. I. harness)
POSITION SWITCH
INTAKE DOOR MOTOR
THERMO CONTROL AMP.
THERMISTOR
A : A/T model
M : M/T model
TC : Turbo model
NT : Non-turbo model
* : NT G/W, TC W
COMPRESSOR
F. I. C. D. SOLENOID VALVE
E. C. C. S. CONTROL UNIT

Wiring schematic for 1990 300ZX with manual system

2. Install the motor and connect the wiring but do not fasten the rod(s).

3. On vehicles with ATC turn the ignition switch to **ACC** and set the system to the self diagnostic function by pressing the **AUTO** and **OFF** buttons together for about 5 seconds. Once the system is in self diagnostics, press the **AUTO** button once to go to Step 2, the actuator test.

4. On 1990 models, press the temperature increase button to make the number in the **AMB** display read "63". The number 6 indicates the mode door motor has been manually driven into the **VENT** mode and the 3 indicates the blower fan is at the lowest speed.

5. On 1991 models, press the mode button the call up the vent symbol on the code monitor.

6. On vehicles with manual systems, set the system to **VENT** or **REC**, depending on which motor is being adjusted.

7. On the mode door, fasten the control rod and operate the system manually to check for smooth operation.

8. On the intake door, move the door manually to the full recirculation position and fasten the rod. Operate the system manually to check for smooth operation.

AIR MIX DOORS

1. Install the motor and connect the wiring but do not fasten the rod.

2. With the ignition switch in **ACC**, set the system for full cold air. Vehicles with Automatic Temperature Control do not need to be be in self diagnostic mode for this procedure.

3. The motors should now be in full cold position. Set the doors in full cold position and fasten the rod. Operate the system to check for proper door operation.

WATER VALVE CONTROL CABLE

1. With the cable housing loose at the air mix motor, set the system so the air mix doors are in the full cold position. Secure the cable housing so the valve will be fully closed.

2. Operate the temperature increase lever or buttons to make sure the valve opens when heat is demanded.

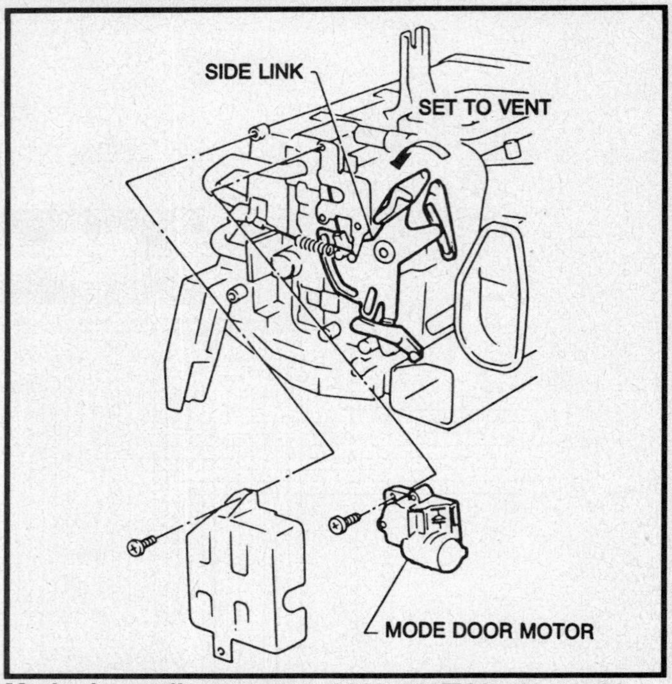
SIDE LINK
SET TO VENT
MODE DOOR MOTOR

Mode door adjustment on 1990 300ZX is done with the system in vent mode

Maxima

System Description

On this vehicle, the controls for air inlet and discharge mode, blower fan speed, temperature and compressor operation are manually operated. The actuators for the mode doors are electric motors and the actuator for the heater core water valve is an electronically conrtolled vacuum solenoid valve. Since each component of the system can be operated literally at the push of a button, trouble shooting the control system will be mostly electrical work.

The manual system is almost identical to the automatic system except for the temperature sensors and control amplifier. All door positions and heating and cooling functions are operated with the same equipment. Except for the onboard diagnostic function of the automatic system, the service procedures will be the same on both systems, however only the automatic system is discussed.

The operating stratagy behind this automatic system is similar to other models. When an automatic temperature setting is selected, the control amplifier determines door positions, blower speed and compressor or water valve operation to maintain that target temperature inside the vehicle. Control is biased to admit as much fresh air as possible while maintaining the target temperature. The system can be operated manually or turned off at any time. If full air recirculation is selected, it will operate this way for 10 minutes, then return to fresh air mixture mode.

The information fed to the control amplifier comes from temperature sensors in the intake duct, behind the front grille and inside the vehicle. The amplifier also reads engine coolant temperature and sun load. The control amplifier sends output signals to the blower fan amplifier, door motors and the engine control computer. The engine computer operates the compressor, condenser fans and a fast idle control solenoid. It will also turn the compressor off if the engine is under full throttle. The water valve for the heater core is vacuum operated through an electric solenoid valve controlled by the amplifier.

System Diagnostics

The micro computer in the control amplifier has a self diagnostic function which stores trouble codes. This function can be accessed through the system controls or through Nissan's Consult hand held module. The Consult is menu driven, meaning the procedure for its use is shown step by step on the unit's own read out screen. The procedures described here are for the onboard self diagnostic system only. The first step in diagnostic work is to operate the system with the engine running to find which function does not work properly.

Function Test

1. With the vehicle in a well ventilated area above 32°F, start the engine and warm it up. On vehicles with a manual system, operate the system controls and feel for air exiting the correct vents. With the blower fan at full speed, it should be easy to hear changes in air flow, especially when the system is switched from fresh air to recuiculated air.

2. On vehicles with Automatic Temperature Control (ATC), operate the system manually with the mode button to determine if air is discharged from the vents indicated by the display. With the blower fan at full speed, it should be easy to hear changes in air flow, especially when the system is switched from fresh air to recuiculated air.

3. When the **AUTO** button is pressed, the display will show the most receiently selected temperature the system will attempt to maintain. Press the temperature set buttons to see that the display changes.

4. When the **AMB** button is pressed, the ambient temperature measured at the sensor behind the grille will be displayed for 5 seconds. When the **DEF** button is pressed, the recircula-

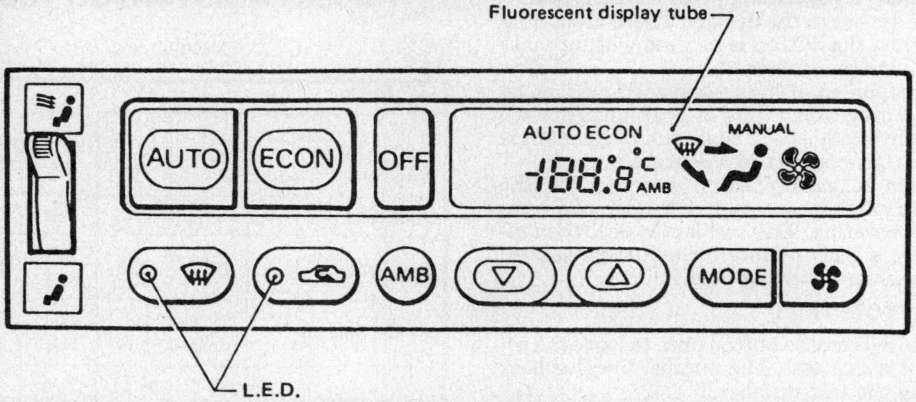
Fluorescent display tube
AUTO ECON
MANUAL
AUTO
ECON
OFF
AMB
MODE
L.E.D.

Step 1 on Maxima automatic system self diagnostics is a light check; if any segments do not light, the remaining tests will not be accurate

tion function is canceled.

5. When the **ECON** button is pressed, all other modes will be canceled and the system will default to an automatic control mode without the compressor. Make sure the compressor stops.

6. When engine coolant and ambient temperatures are low, the system automatically will not operate for about 150 seconds after the engine is started.

7. Press the **OFF** button and turn the engine off. Wait about 15 seconds and start the engine, then press the **AUTO** button. The system should return the the same temperature setting.

Self-Diagnostics

The self-diagnostic function is divided into 5 Steps: light check, sensor circuit check, mode door position, actuator test and temperature sensor read-out. A sixth Step is also available for correcting temperature off-set. Before starting these tests, make sure the manual fresh air vent to the left of the control panel is closed. To access the self diagnostic function, start the engine or turn the ignition switch to **ON** and, within 10 seconds, press the **OFF** button for more than 5 seconds. Pressing the **AUTO** button or turning the ignition switch **OFF** will exit the self-diagnostic function.

LIGHT CHECK

With the system in Step 1 of the self diagnostic mode, the LEDs in the defrost and recirculate buttons will light. All segments in the fluorescent display tube should also illuminate. If any segment is missing from the tube display, it will be impossible to complete the self diagnostics accurately. If the system will not enter the diagnostic mode, the **OFF** button may be faulty or the control amplifier itself is faulty.

SENSOR CIRCUIT TEST

1. Press the temperature increase button to leave the light check and move into the sensor circuit test. The system will take about 4 seconds to check all circuits.

2. If all circuits are good, the number 20 will appear in the display indicating test 2 with 0 faults. If any number from 21–26 appears, it will blink on and off indicating a circuit is faulty. If more than one circuit is faulty, each circuit number will blink twice. A minus (–) sign in front the the number indicates a short circuit.

3. Circuits 21–24 are temperature sensors. Number 25 is the sun load sensor circuit, which can be tested with a drop light. Circuit 26 is the Potentiometer Balance Resistor (P.B.R.), which is a position feed-back device used to tell the control amplifier what percentage of full stroke the air mix door has reached.

4. If a faulty circuit is indicated, complete the rest of the diagnostics before starting repairs.

MODE DOOR POSITION TEST

1. Press the temperature increase button once to leave the circuit test and enter the door position test. The system will take about 16 seconds to cycle the door motors and test the position switches or sensor.

2. If all positions are correct, the number 30 will appear in the display indicating test 3 and 0 faults. If any number from 31–36 appears, it will blink on and off indicating a door is not correctly positioned or a circuit is faulty. If more than one fault exists, each number will blink twice.

3. If a fault is indicated, complete the rest of the diagnostics before starting adjustment or repairs.

Code 31 – vent door position
Code 32 – floor and vent doors bi-level position 1
Code 33 – floor and vent doors bi-level position 2
Code 34 – floor and defrost doors position 1
Code 35 – floor and defrost doors position 2
Code 36 – defrost door position

ACTUATOR TEST

1. Press the temperature increase button once to leave the door position test and enter the actuator test. The number 41 will appear in the display, indicating test 4 and the first test position.

MAXIMA SENSOR FAULT CODES AND SENSOR RANGES

Code No.	Sensor	Open circuit	Short circuit
21	Ambient sensor	Less than –41.9°C (–43°F)	Greater than 100°C (212°F)
22	In-vehicle sensor	Less than –41.9°C (–43°F)	Greater than 100°C (212°F)
24	Intake sensor	Less than –41.9°C (–43°F)	Greater than 100°C (212°F)
25	Sunload sensor	Less than 0.0319 mA	Greater than 1.147 mA
26	P.R.B.	Greater than 50%	Less than 30%

2. To advance to the next test position, press the defrost button. The number 42 will appear in the display. There are 6 positions all together and when the button is pressed with number 46 in the display, it returns to number 41.

3. In this test, each component of the system will be driven by the control amplifier to a programed state or position. This will allow the technician to physically check that each component is working as specified for that position in the chart.

4. Advance the system to each position and feel for the change in air flow and to check blower motor voltage and compressor and water valve operation. This test is also used to manually drive the system to a known state for adjusting control rods and door positions when installing door motors.

TEMPERATURE SENSOR TEST

1. Press the temperature increase button once to leave the actuator test and enter the sensor test. The number 5 will appear in the display, indicating the test number.

2. Press the defrost button once to read the sensor output. The number in the display will be the temperature reported to the control amplifier by the ambient sensor.

3. Pressing the defrost button again will advance to the inside sensor and then the intake air sensor. Pressing the button a 4th time will return to the number 5 and the sequence starts again.

4. If the sensor reading varries greatly from the actual temperature, check the resistance across the sensor connector terminals and compare it to the chart. If the resistance is correct at 3 or 4 different temperatures, check the circuit between the sensor and the control amplifier.

TEMPERATURE TRIMMER

1. This procedure is to compensate for the actual cabin temperature that is maintained being different from the temperature selected on the automatic control system. The total range of adjustment is ± 3°C (± 6°F). While still in test 5 with the number 5 on the display, press the fan button once. The display will change to read 0°C on Canadian models or 0°F on U.S. models.

2. Press the temperature increase or decrease button to change the offset number in the display. Press the blower fan button to exit this procedure.

3. When the control amplifier or battery is disconnected, this trimmer function will default to 0 degrees.

WATER VALVE TESTING

When heat is selected, a voltage is sent to the solenoid on the water valve mounted at the firewall under the hood. The solenoid valve is modulated to allow more or less vacuum to the water valve actuator, which allows more or less water to flow through the heater core.

1. To test the valve, disconnect the vacuum line from the solenoid valve to the water valve. Use a hand vacuum pump to draw a vacuum on the water valve actuator to see if it moves.

2. If the valve moves, reconnect the vacuum line and draw a vacuum at the solenoid valve vacuum port which connects to the intake manifold.

3. Apply 12 volts to the upper terminal and ground the lower one. The soleniod should activate and let the vacuum open the valve.

4. If the valve, actuator and solenoid all work properly, look for a vacuum leak to the solenoid or a lack of voltage at the soleniod connector. On manual systems, there is a full cold switch on the temperature slide control to open the circuit to the solenoid.

System Component Location

1. The sun load sensor is mounted in the defroster outlet, which can be removed be carefully prying the vent out of the dash. The inside temperature sensor is in the center console to the left of the radio. This sensor is mounted on the end of an aspirator tube which pulls air through the sensor. Be careful not

MAXIMA ACTUATOR TEST CODES

Actuator \ Code No.	41	42	43	44	45	46
Mode door	VENT	B/L	B/L	F/D 1	F/D 2	DEF
Intake door	REC	REC	20% FRE	FRE	FRE	FRE
Air mix door	Full Cold	Full Cold	Full Hot	Full Hot	Full Hot	Full Hot
Blower motor	4 - 5 V	9 - 11 V	7 - 9 V	7 - 9 V	7 - 9 V	10 - 12 V
Compressor	ON	ON	ON	OFF	OFF	ON

MAXIMA TEMPERATURE SENSOR RESISTANCE

Temperature °C (°F)	Resistance kΩ
−35 (−31)	38.35
−30 (−22)	28.62
−25 (−13)	21.61
−20 (−4)	16.50
−15 (5)	12.73
−10 (14)	9.92
−5 (23)	7.80
0 (32)	6.19
5 (41)	4.95
10 (50)	3.99
15 (59)	3.24
20 (68)	2.65
25 (77)	2.19
30 (86)	1.81
35 (95)	1.51
40 (104)	1.27
45 (113)	1.07
50 (122)	0.91
55 (131)	0.77
60 (140)	0.66
65 (149)	0.57

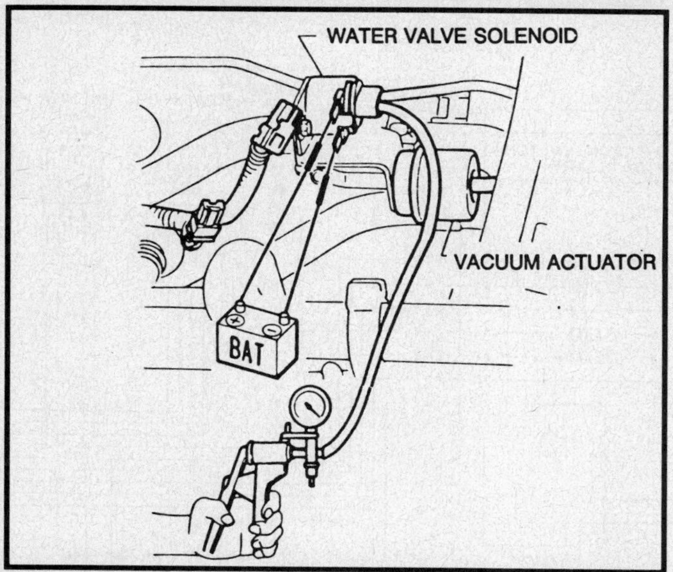
WATER VALVE SOLENOID
VACUUM ACTUATOR
BAT

Checking the heater valve actuator and solenoid on Maxima

to damage or disconnect the tube. The intake air sensor is mounted to the evaporator housing between the evaporator and heater. The ambient sensor is mounted behind the grille, between the horns.

2. The blower fan control amplifier is mounted to the evaporator housing. The fan is operated at full speed by a relay mounted behind the passengers side kick panel.

3. The air mix door is manually controlled but the full cold mode is motor controlled. That motor is behind the right side of the center console, the mode door motor is behind the left side. It may be easier to remove the radio to gain access to these motors. The intake door motor is to the left of and above the blower fan motor. Removing the glove compartment will ease access.

4. On the relay panel in front of the battery, the air conditioner relay is in the front row, second from the left. In the back row, the 3 relays on the right are for the radiator fans. The dual pressure switch for the compressor is on the receiver/drier.

5. The coolant temperature sensor is in the top of the water inlet housing, between the heads. The water valve for the heater is near the center of the firewall.

Control Rod and Cable Adjustments

MANUAL SYSTEMS

This procedure should be necessary only when a door motor, rod or cable has been removed. The mode door operates the side link, which operates all the air outlet doors. The intake door motor operates a door to select fresh or recirculated air. The air mix door has a motor and control rod to be adjusted. Each door motor has a position sensor or switch that reports to the controller.

Mode Door Motor

1. With the system completely assembled except for the mode door motor, rotate the side link fully counter-clockwise to put the system into **VENT** mode.

2. Install the motor and connect the wiring but do not fasten the rod.

3. Turn the ignition switch **ON**. Set the system controls to **VENT**.

4. On the mode door, fasten the control rod and operate the system to **DEF** to check for smooth operation.

Intake Door Motor

1. With the system assembled, rotate the link clockwise to set the door in the recirculation position.

2. Connect the wiring to the motor, turn the ignition switch to **ON** and push the recirculate button. Be sure it is lit.

3. Install the motor and attach the rod. Operate the system to check for proper operation.

Air Mix Door and Temperature Cable

1. Connect the wiring but do not install the motor or fasten the rod yet.

2. With the ignition switch in **ACC**, set the system for **DEF**, with the temperature control lever at the full hot position.

3. Install the motor and fasten the rod. Operate the system between **VENT** and **DEF** to check for proper door operation.

4. Attach the temperature control cable, then take up the slack in the cable housing towards the end of the cable. Secure the clamp and move the control to check for proper operation.

Fresh Air Vent Cable

1. With the vent control lever on the left side of the control panel in the closed position, attach the cable to the vent shaft.

2. Make sure the vent is closed. Take up the slack in the cable housing away from the shaft and secure the housing.

Full Cold Door

1. Connect the wiring to the motor and turn the ignition switch **ON**.

2. Set the controls to **DEF**, full hot and install the motor.

3. Attach the rod and operate the system to check for proper operation.

AUTOMATIC SYSTEMS

To adjust the motors and rods, the system must be operated in test 4 of the self diagnostic function. Install all the motors and connect the wiring but do not attach the control rods yet. Turn the ignition switch **ON** and within 10 seconds, press the **OFF** button for more than 5 seconds. The system should enter the light check function. Press the temperature increase button 3 times to skip to test 4, the actuator test. Remember the position sensor for the controller is in the motor itself.

Mode Door Motor

1. With the system in test 4 of the self diagnostic function, make sure the code in the display reads number 41. If it does not, press the defrost button until it does. This will drive the system into **VENT** mode.

2. Rotate the side link on the heater housing full counter-clockwise to put the doors into the vent position.

3. Attach the control rod and press the defrost button to cycle the system through all 6 modes. Check for smooth operation and correct air outlet.

Air Mix and Full Cold Door Motors

1. With the wiring connected and the motor installed, press the defrost button to set up code number 46 in the display.

2. Move the air mix door lever to the full hot position and attach the rod.

3. Move the full cold door rod holder toward the driver's side to close the door.

4. With the door closed, attach the rod so as not to stress the motor or linkage. Cycle the system by pressing the defrost button and check for smooth operation.

Intake Door Motor

1. With the wiring connected and the motor installed, press the defrost button to set up code number 41 in the display.

2. Rotate the door linkage clockwise to set the doors in the recirculate position.

3. Attach the rod and cycle the system by pressing the defrost button to check for smooth operation.

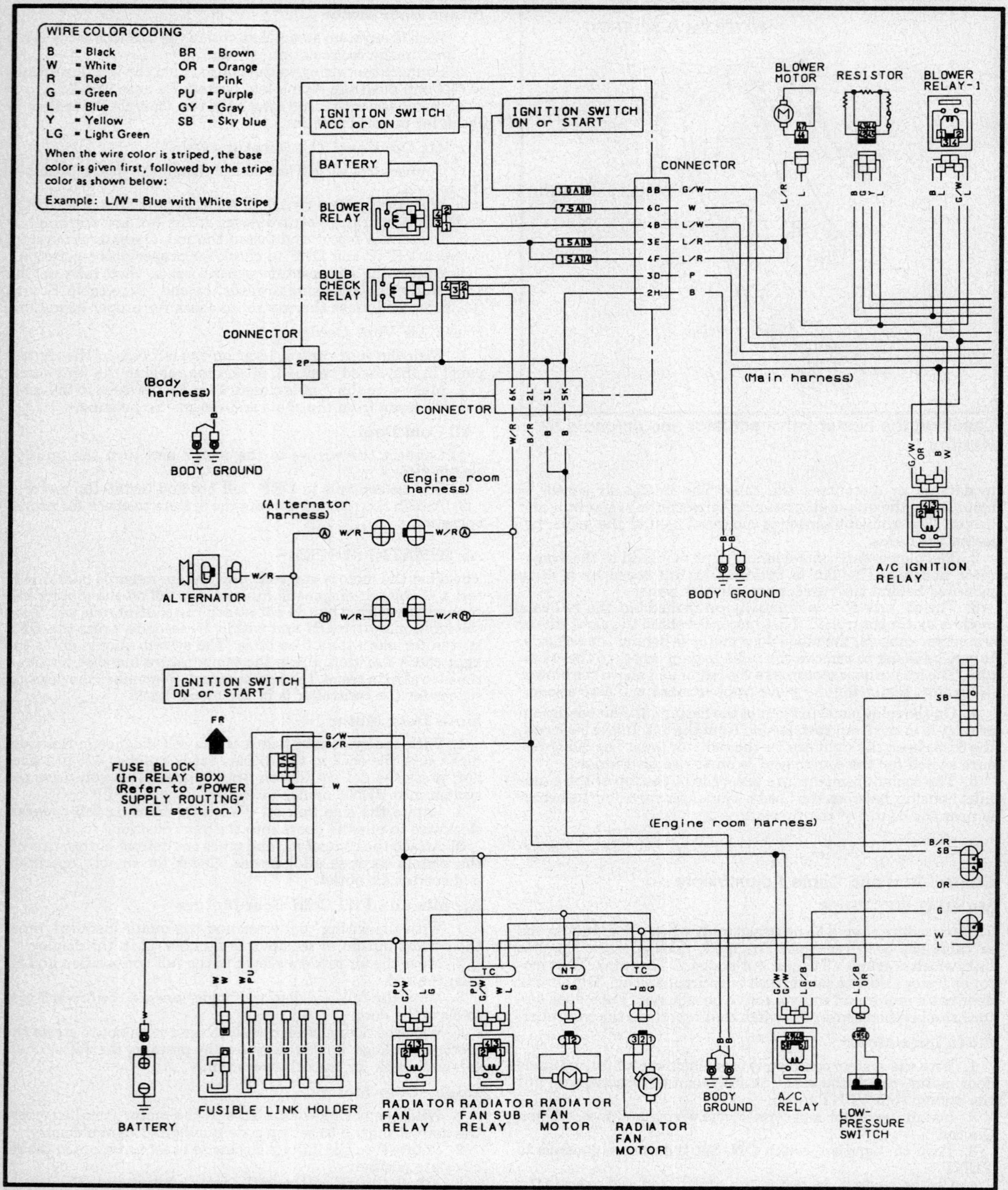
WIRE COLOR CODING
B = Black
W = White
R = Red
G = Green
L = Blue
Y = Yellow
LG = Light Green
BR = Brown
OR = Orange
P = Pink
PU = Purple
GY = Gray
SB = Sky blue
When the wire color is striped, the base color is given first, followed by the stripe color as shown below:
Example: L/W = Blue with White Stripe
IGNITION SWITCH ACC or ON
IGNITION SWITCH ON or START
BATTERY
BLOWER RELAY
BULB CHECK RELAY
CONNECTOR
(Body harness)
BODY GROUND
BLOWER MOTOR
RESISTOR
BLOWER RELAY-1
10A
7.5A
15A
15A
(Main harness)
(Engine room harness)
(Alternator harness)
ALTERNATOR
A/C IGNITION RELAY
IGNITION SWITCH ON or START
FR
FUSE BLOCK (In RELAY BOX) (Refer to "POWER SUPPLY ROUTING" in EL section.)
BATTERY
FUSIBLE LINK HOLDER
RADIATOR FAN RELAY
RADIATOR FAN SUB RELAY
RADIATOR FAN MOTOR
RADIATOR FAN MOTOR
BODY GROUND
A/C RELAY
LOW-PRESSURE SWITCH

Electrical schematic for Maxima manual air conditioning system

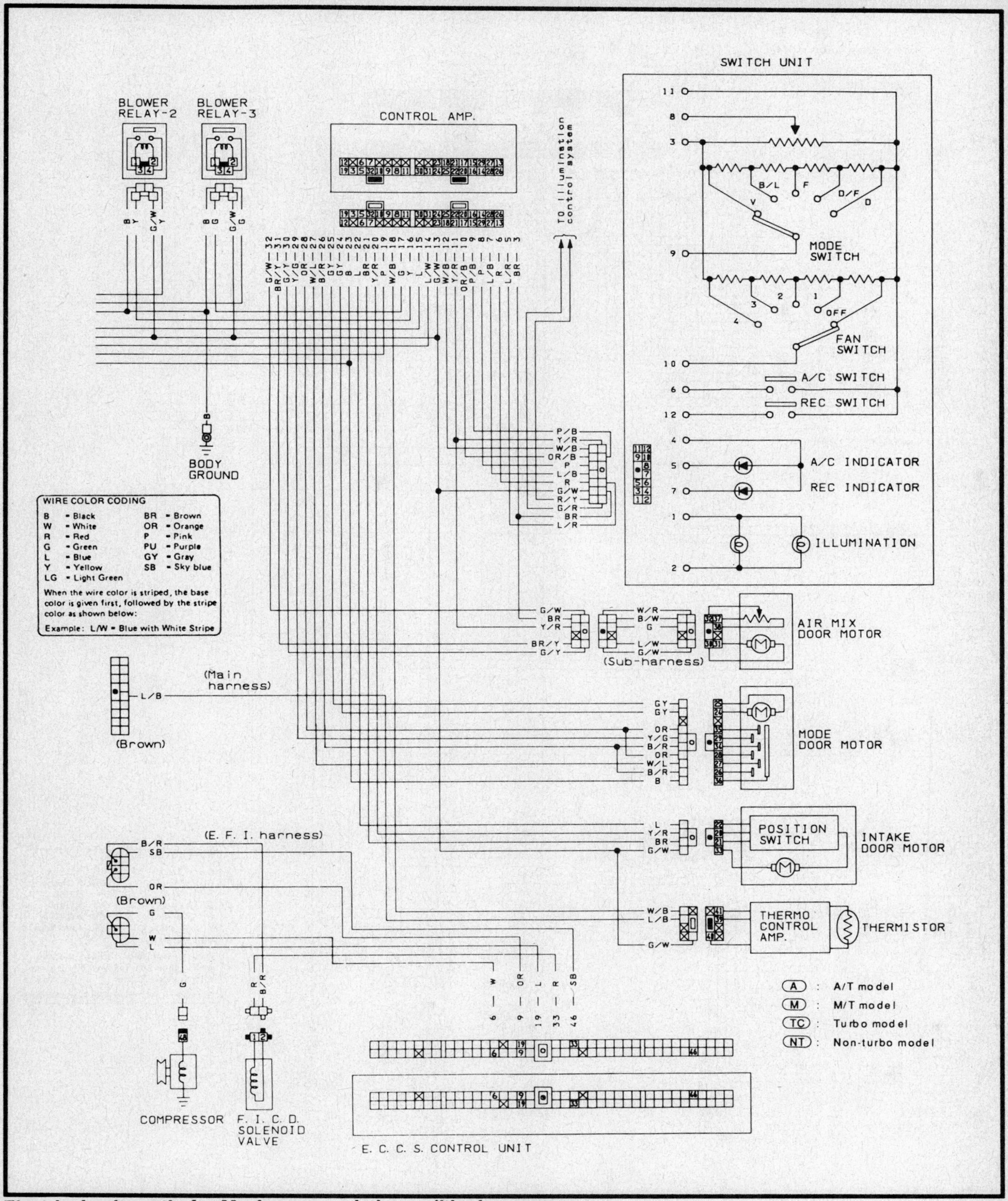
SWITCH UNIT
BLOWER RELAY-2
BLOWER RELAY-3
CONTROL AMP.
TO illumination control system
MODE SWITCH
FAN SWITCH
A/C SWITCH
REC SWITCH
A/C INDICATOR
REC INDICATOR
ILLUMINATION
BODY GROUND
WIRE COLOR CODING
B = Black
W = White
R = Red
G = Green
L = Blue
Y = Yellow
LG = Light Green
BR = Brown
OR = Orange
P = Pink
PU = Purple
GY = Gray
SB = Sky blue
When the wire color is striped, the base color is given first, followed by the stripe color as shown below:
Example: L/W = Blue with White Stripe
AIR MIX DOOR MOTOR
(Sub-harness)
(Main harness)
(Brown)
MODE DOOR MOTOR
POSITION SWITCH
INTAKE DOOR MOTOR
(E. F. I. harness)
THERMO CONTROL AMP.
THERMISTOR
A : A/T model
M : M/T model
TC : Turbo model
NT : Non-turbo model
COMPRESSOR
F. I. C. D. SOLENOID VALVE
E. C. C. S. CONTROL UNIT

Electrical schematic for Maxima manual air conditioning system

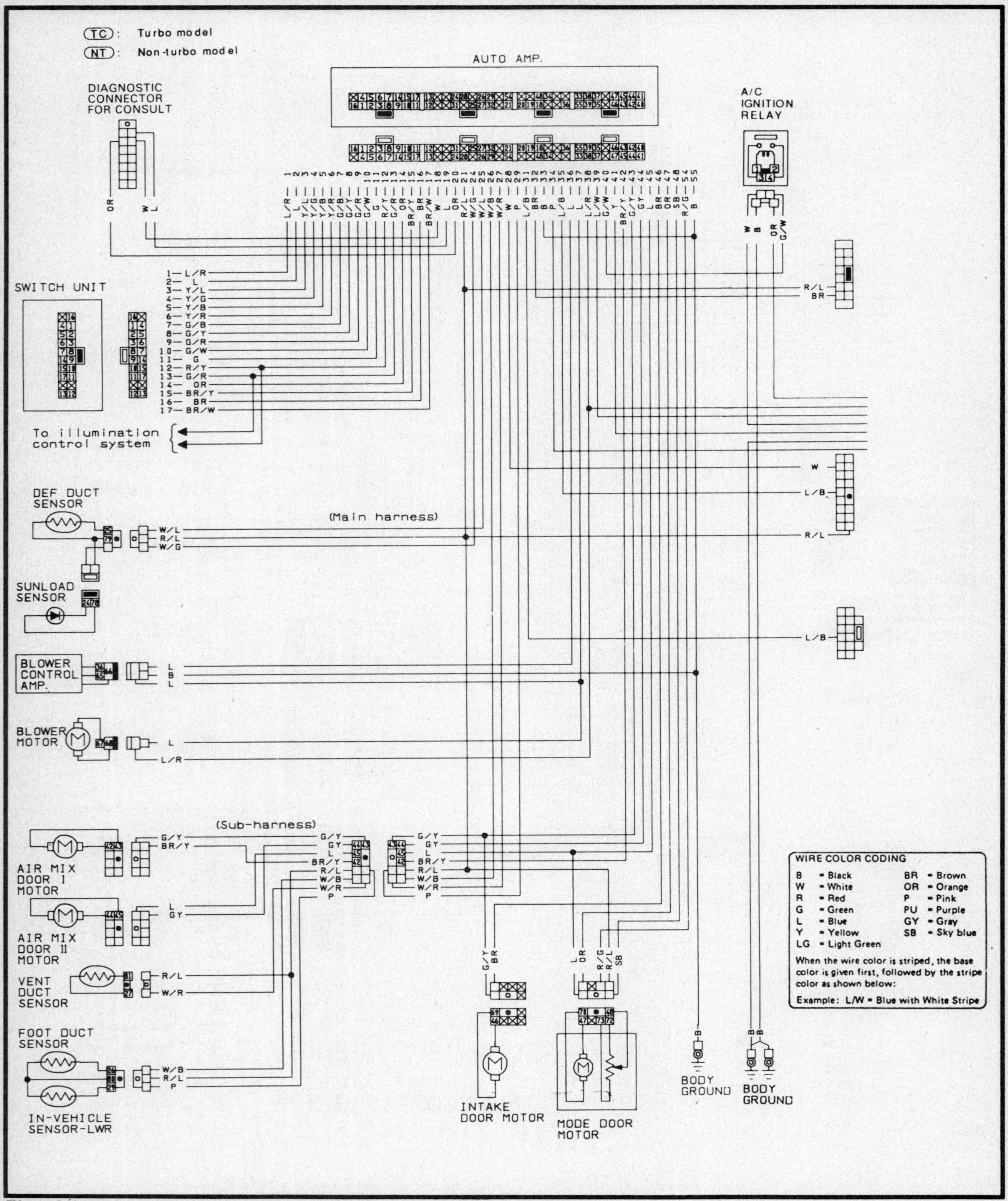
(TC): Turbo model
(NT): Non-turbo model
AUTO AMP.
DIAGNOSTIC CONNECTOR FOR CONSULT
A/C IGNITION RELAY
SWITCH UNIT
To illumination control system
DEF DUCT SENSOR
(Main harness)
SUNLOAD SENSOR
BLOWER CONTROL AMP.
BLOWER MOTOR
(Sub-harness)
AIR MIX DOOR I MOTOR
AIR MIX DOOR II MOTOR
VENT DUCT SENSOR
FOOT DUCT SENSOR
IN-VEHICLE SENSOR-LWR
INTAKE DOOR MOTOR
MODE DOOR MOTOR
BODY GROUND
BODY GROUND
WIRE COLOR CODING
B = Black
W = White
R = Red
G = Green
L = Blue
Y = Yellow
LG = Light Green
BR = Brown
OR = Orange
P = Pink
PU = Purple
GY = Gray
SB = Sky blue
When the wire color is striped, the base color is given first, followed by the stripe color as shown below:
Example: L/W = Blue with White Stripe

Electrical schematic for Maxima automatic air conditioning system

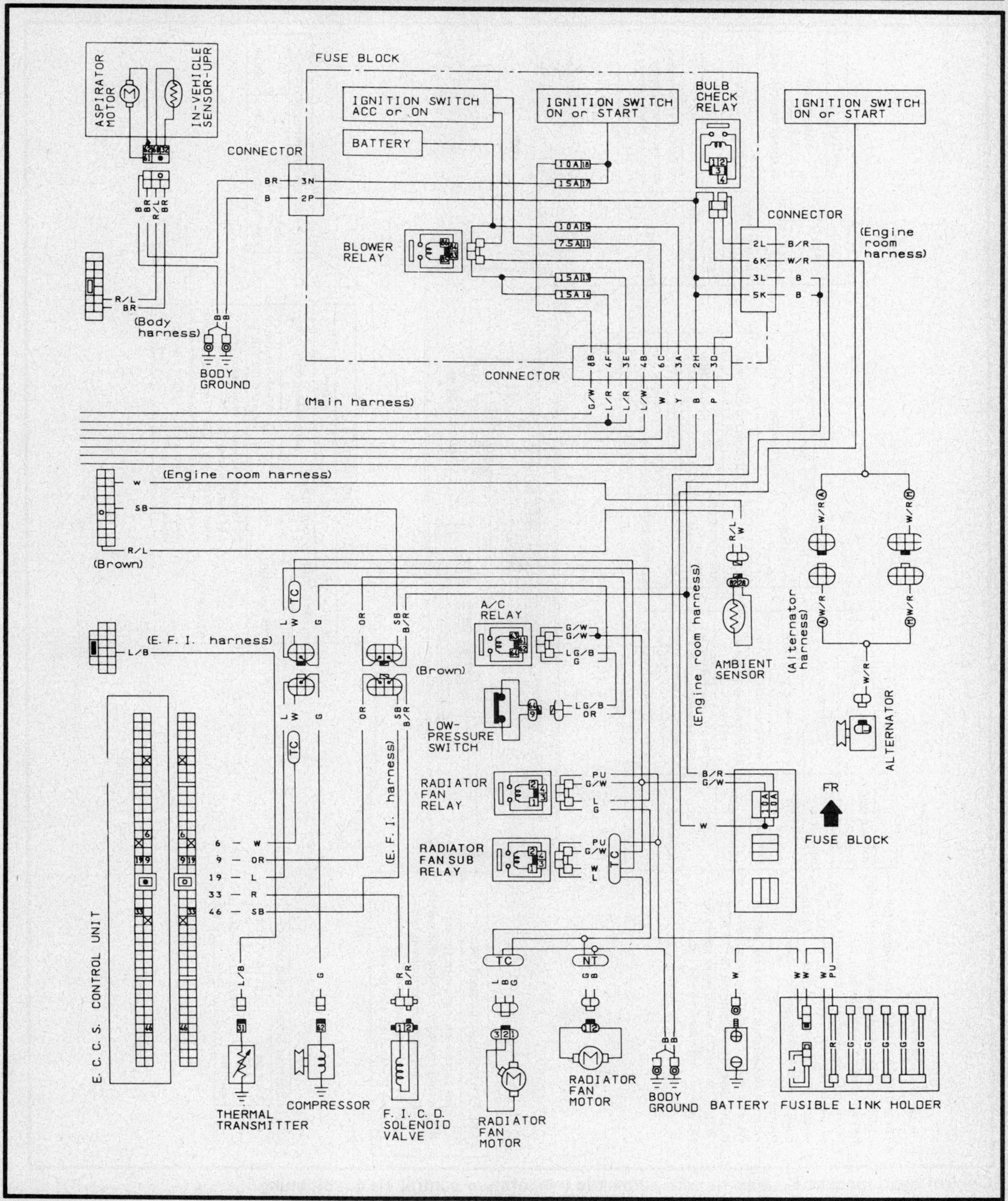
FUSE BLOCK
ASPIRATOR MOTOR
IN-VEHICLE SENSOR-UPR
IGNITION SWITCH ACC or ON
IGNITION SWITCH ON or START
BULB CHECK RELAY
IGNITION SWITCH ON or START
BATTERY
CONNECTOR
BLOWER RELAY
CONNECTOR
(Engine room harness)
(Body harness)
BODY GROUND
CONNECTOR
(Main harness)
(Engine room harness)
(Brown)
(E. F. I. harness)
A/C RELAY
(Brown)
LOW-PRESSURE SWITCH
AMBIENT SENSOR
(Engine room harness)
(Alternator harness)
ALTERNATOR
RADIATOR FAN RELAY
FR
FUSE BLOCK
RADIATOR FAN SUB RELAY
(E. F. I. harness)
E. C. C. S. CONTROL UNIT
THERMAL TRANSMITTER
COMPRESSOR
F. I. C. D. SOLENOID VALVE
RADIATOR FAN MOTOR
RADIATOR FAN MOTOR
BODY GROUND
BATTERY
FUSIBLE LINK HOLDER

Electrical schematic for Maxima automatic air conditioning system

- There are push ON switches except for ECON switch. And push on switch cannot be canceled by pushing again.
- When ignition switch is turned off, all the systems stop their action. At the time of restart, they begin to operate in the same condition as before ignition switch is turned off.
- When auto switch is pushed on, all the systems are controlled automatically. In this case, discharging mode ("FACE", "B/L", "FOOT") and blower speed (LO, Hi) are not indicated on the indicator.

DEF SWITCH	
INTAKE DOOR position	OUTSIDE AIR
OUTLET DOOR position	DEFROSTER
AIR MIX DOOR position	AUTOMATIC CONTROL
FAN SPEED	AUTOMATIC CONTROL
COMPRESSOR	ON [Outside air temperature above 0°C (32°F)]
REMARKS	• When HI switch is ON, fan rotates with fan speed at HI. • When ECON switch is ON, compressor turns ON, and ECON indicator remains illuminated.

AUTO SWITCH	
INTAKE DOOR position	AUTOMATIC CONTROL
OUTLET DOOR position	AUTOMATIC CONTROL
AIR MIX DOOR position	AUTOMATIC CONTROL
FAN SPEED	AUTOMATIC CONTROL
COMPRESSOR	ON-OFF of compressor is controlled by ECON switch.

OFF SWITCH	
INTAKE DOOR position	OUTSIDE AIR
OUTLET DOOR position	AUTOMATIC CONTROL
AIR MIX DOOR position	AUTOMATIC CONTROL
FAN SPEED	OFF
COMPRESSOR	OFF
REMARKS	For ON-OFF of compressor, auto amp. memorizes the condition prior to depressing the OFF switch.

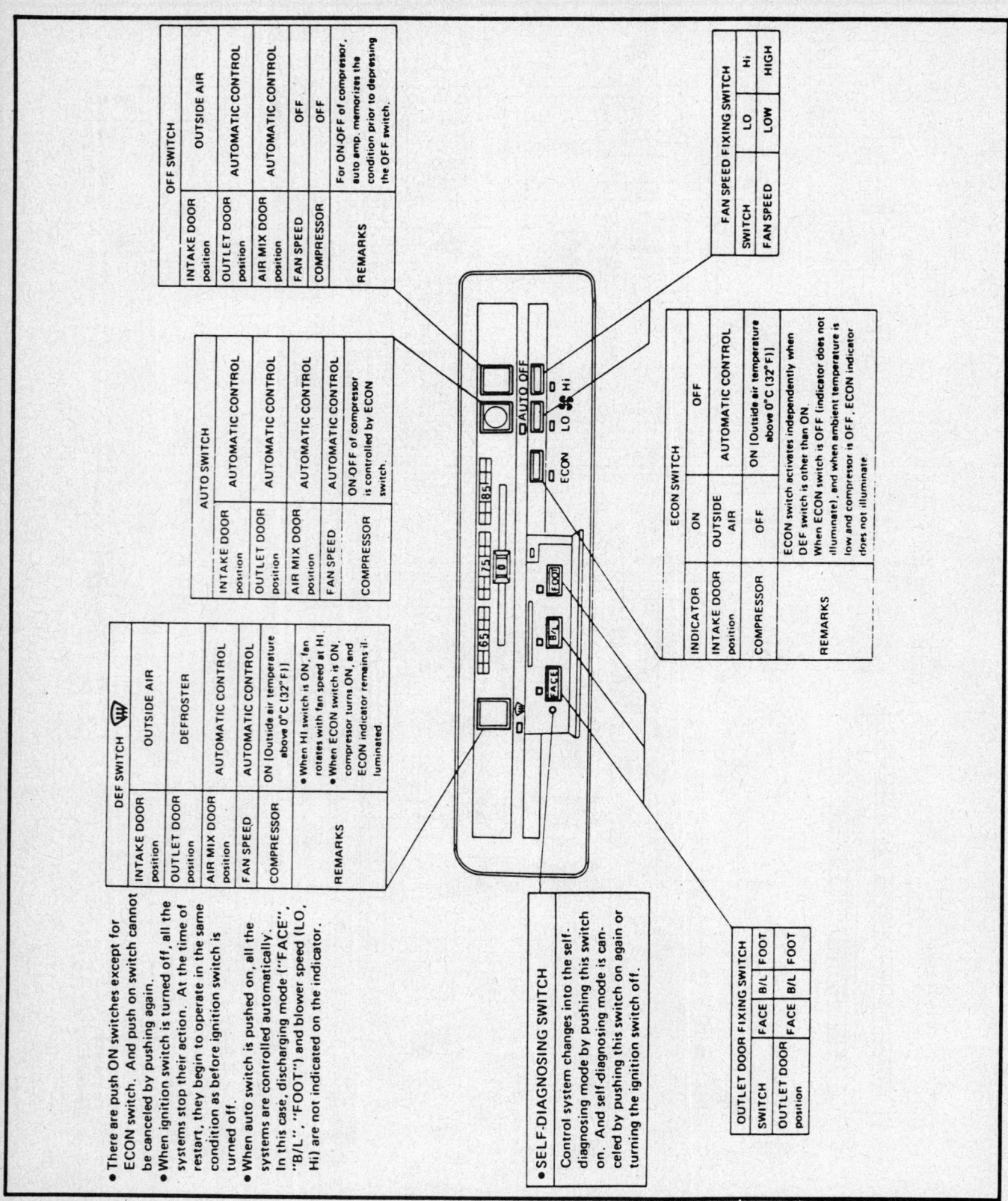

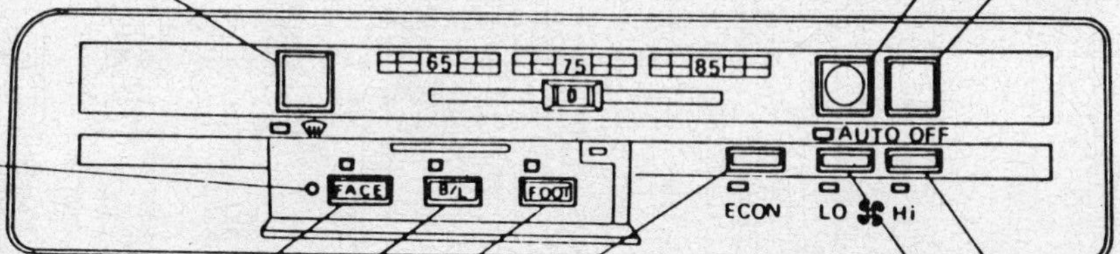
65
75
85
AUTO
OFF
FACE
B/L
FOOT
ECON
LO
Hi

• SELF-DIAGNOSING SWITCH

Control system changes into the self-diagnosing mode by pushing this switch on. And self-diagnosing mode is canceled by pushing this switch on again or turning the ignition switch off.

OUTLET DOOR FIXING SWITCH			
SWITCH	FACE	B/L	FOOT
OUTLET DOOR position	FACE	B/L	FOOT

ECON SWITCH		
INDICATOR	ON	OFF
INTAKE DOOR position	OUTSIDE AIR	AUTOMATIC CONTROL
COMPRESSOR	OFF	ON [Outside air temperature above 0°C (32°F)]
REMARKS	ECON switch activates independently when DEF switch is other than ON. When ECON switch is OFF (indicator does not illuminate), and when ambient temperature is low and compressor is OFF, ECON indicator does not illuminate.	

FAN SPEED FIXING SWITCH		
SWITCH	LO	Hi
FAN SPEED	LOW	HIGH

Control head functions – Maxima with automatic temperature control air conditioning

25 SUBARU 25

LEGACY • LOYALE • XT COUPE • SEDAN • STATION WAGON

SPECIFICATIONS

ENGINE IDENTIFICATION

Year	Model	Engine Displacement cu. in. (cc/liter)	Engine Series Identification	No. of Cylinders	Engine Type
1989	Hatchback	109 (1800/1.8)	4	4	OHC
	Sedan	109 (1800/1.8)	4 ①	4	OHC
	RX Coupe	109 (1800/1.8)	5	4	OHC
	XT Coupe	109 (1800/1.8)	4 ②	4	OHC
1990	Loyale	109 (1800/1.8)	4	4	OHC
	XT Coupe	109 (1800/1.8)	4 ②	4	OHC
	Legacy	135 (2200/2.2)	6	4	OHC
1991	Loyale	109 (1800/1.8)	4	4	OHC
	XT Coupe	109 (1800/1.8)	4 ②	4	OHC
	Legacy	135 (2200/2.2)	6	4	OHC

NOTE: Sedan Covers—4 Door Sedan
Station Wagon
Touring Wagon

① 4WD vehicles—5
② 4WD vehicles
(with air suspension)—7

REFRIGERANT CAPACITIES

Year	Model	Freon (oz.)	Oil (oz.) ①	Type
1989	Hatchback	28	2.4	R-12
	Sedan	28	2.4	R-12
	RX Coupe	28	2.4	R-12
	XT Coupe	28	2.4	R-12
1990	Loyale	①	2.4	R-12
	XT Coupe	28	2.4	R-12
	Legacy	32	②	R-12
1991	Loyale	①	2.4	R-12
	XT Coupe	28	2.4	R-12
	Legacy	32	②	R-12

① Hitachi—28
Panasonic—30
② Diesel kiki—2.4
Calsonic—2.9

AIR CONDITIONING BELT TENSION CHART

Year	Model	Engine Displacement cu. in. (cc/liter)	Belt Type	New	Used
1989	Hatchback	109 (1800/1.8)	V Belt	0.29 ①	0.34 ①
	Sedan	109 (1800/1.8)	V Belt	0.29 ①	0.34 ①
	RX Coupe	109 (1800/1.8)	V Belt	0.29 ①	0.34 ①
	XT Coupe	109 (1800/1.8)	Serpentine	0.29 ①	0.29 ①

AIR CONDITIONING BELT TENSION CHART

Year	Model	Engine Displacement cu. in. (cc/liter)	Belt Type	New	Used
1990	Loyale	109 (1800/1.8)	V Belt	0.29 ①	0.34 ①
	XT Coupe	109 (1800/1.8)	Serpentine	0.25 ①	0.29 ①
	Legacy	135 (2200/2.2)	Serpentine	0.29 ①	0.34 ①
1991	Loyale	109 (1800/1.8)	V Belt	0.29 ①	0.34 ①
	XT Coupe	109 (1800/1.8)	Serpentine	0.25 ①	0.29 ①
	Legacy	135 (2200/2.2)	Serpentine	0.29 ①	0.34 ①

① Inches of deflection at the midpoint of the belt, using 22 lbs. force

SYSTEM DESCRIPTION

General Information

HEATING SYSTEM

The heating and ventilating systems consist of a control unit, heater unit, blower assembly, connecting heater ducts and heater hoses. Fresh air from the outside is introduced into the passenger compartment through the center and side ventilator grilles when the ventilator fan is operated.

Fresh outside air can also be introduced through the side vents on the driver side and passenger side, by ram pressure produced while the vehicle is in motion. A high performance heating system is adopted. All vehicles are equipped with a front side window defroster and some vehicles are further equipped with the rear heater duct.

AIR CONDITONING SYSTEM

When the mode control switch is set at **A/C-MAX, A/C-LO** or **DEF** positions the air conditioner microswitch will be turned on. In this condition, when the blower switch is turned **ON**, USA vehicles, or when the blower motor and air conditioner switch are turned **ON**, Canadian vehicles the blower relay and air conditioner relay will activate. This in turn causes the blower motor, Fast Idle Control Device (FICD) and compressor clutch to activate. This in turn activates the pressure switch main fan control or the thermo switch, causing the main fan to activate.

When either the high-low pressure switch or the thermostat activates, all air conditioning circuits, except the blower motor, will deactivate. In this condition, when the temperature of the coolant in the radiator is high enough and the thermo switch turns on, the radiator main fan will activate. When refrigerant pressure exceeds the specified value with the air conditioning switch to **ON**, the main fan will activate to help cool the condenser.

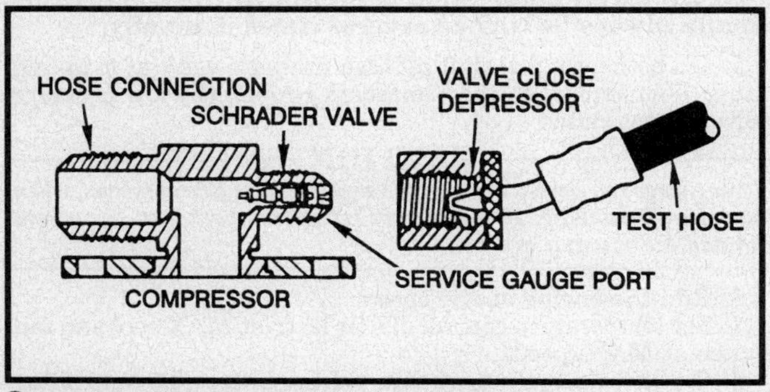
HOSE CONNECTION
SCHRADER VALVE
VALVE CLOSE DEPRESSOR
TEST HOSE
SERVICE GAUGE PORT
COMPRESSOR

Cross section view of the service valve

Service Valve Location

The low pressure service port is located at the center of the compressor, on the suction hose connection.

The high pressure service port is located at the rear of the compressor, on the metal portion of the flexible hose.

System Discharging

The pressurized refrigerant inside the system must be discharged to a pressure approaching atmospheric pressure prior to evacuating refrigerant inside system. This operation should be made to permit safe removal when replacing system components.

1. Disconnect the negative battery cable.
2. Connect a set of manifold gauges to the high and low service valves.

NOTE: Prior to connecting the manifold lines to the service valves, close the high and low pressure valves of

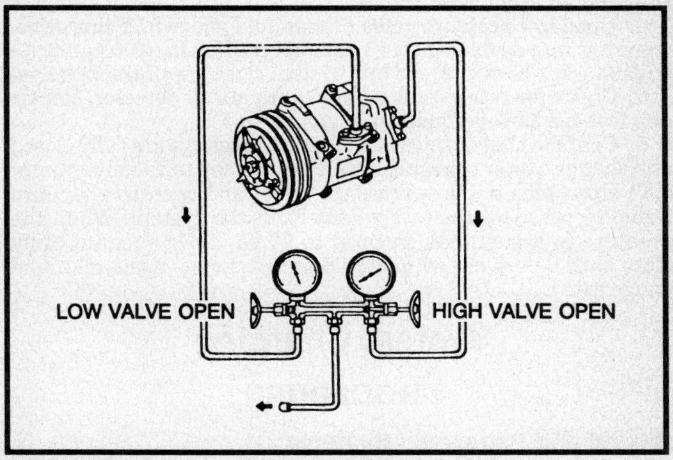
LOW VALVE OPEN
HIGH VALVE OPEN

Discharging the air conditioning system

manifold gauge, to their respective service valve. This will prevent an unexpected surge of freon from the manifold center charging line.

3. Open both manifold gauge valves slightly and slowly discharge refrigerant from system.

NOTE: Do not allow refrigerant to rush out; otherwise, compressor oil will be discharged along with refrigerant.

System Evacuating

PROCEDURE

1. Disconnect the negative battery cable.
2. Discharge the refrigerant from system.
3. When refrigerant has been discharged to a pressure approaching atmospheric pressure, connect center charging hose to a vacuum pump.
4. Close both valves of manifold gauge fully. Start vacuum pump.
5. Open low pressure valve of the manifold gauge and evacuate the old refrigerant from system.
6. When the low pressure gauge reading has reached to approximately 19.69 in. Hg vacuum, slowly open high pressure valve.
7. When pressure inside system has dropped to 27.95 in. Hg vacuum, fully close both of valves of manifold gauge and stop vacuum pump. Allow the system to remain in this state for 5–10 minutes and confirm that the reading does not rise.

NOTE: The low pressure gauge reads lower by 0.98 in. Hg vacuum per a 1000 ft. elevation. Perform evacuation according to the following observation: The rate of ascension of the low pressure gauge, should be less than 0.98 in. Hg vacuum within 5 minutes. If system leakage is suspected, perform a leak test.

LEAK TEST

If the pressure rises or the specified negative pressure can not be obtained, there is a leak in the system. In this case, immediately charge system with refrigerant and repair the leak described in the following.

1. Confirm that both valves of manifold gauge are fully closed and then disconnect center charging hose from vacuum pump.
2. Connect center hose to can tap in place of vacuum pump. Attach refrigerant can top and pass refrigerant to manifold gauge.
3. Loosen the connection of center fitting of manifold gauge to purge air from center hose.
4. Open low pressure valve of manifold gauge and charge refrigerant into system. After 1 can, about 0.09 lb. (0.4 kg) of refrigerant has been charged into system close low pressure valve.
5. Check for refrigerant leakage with a leak detector. Repair any leakage as it is found.
6. Confirm that both valves of manifold gauge are fully closed and change center charging hose from can tap to vacuum pump.
7. Open high and low pressure valves and operate a vacuum pump to evacuate the refrigerant from the system. When the pressure in system has dropped to 27.95 in Hg vacuum, fully close both valves of the manifold gauge. Remove the manifold gauge set.

System Charging

PROCEDURE

Hitachi and Panasonic Systems

1. Install manifold gauge to system.

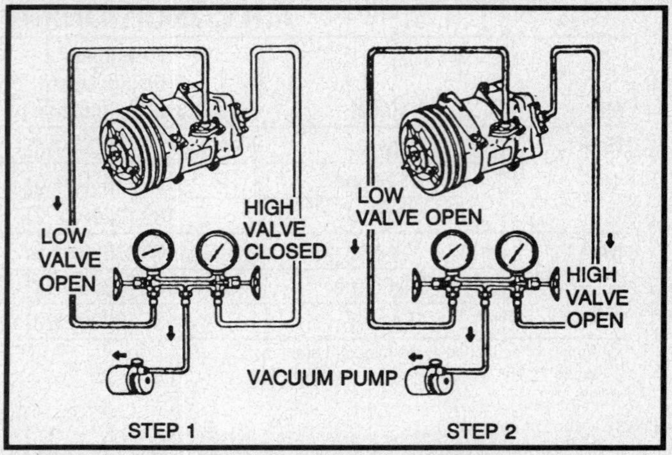
LOW
VALVE
OPEN
HIGH
VALVE
CLOSED
LOW
VALVE OPEN
HIGH
VALVE
OPEN
VACUUM PUMP
STEP 1
STEP 2

Evacuating the refrigerant from the system

NOTE: Be sure to purge air from the high and low pressure charging hoses. If air is mixed with refrigerant in system, evacuation of system should be performed.

2. Attach center charging hose of manifold gauge to refrigerant can through can tap. Break seal of refrigerant can to allow refrigerant to enter manifold gauge. Loosen charging hose at the center fitting of manifold gauge and purge air from inside charging hose.
3. On Hitachi system, open high and low pressure valves of manifold gauge and charge refrigerant into system. On Panasonic system, open only the high pressure valve of the manifold gauge.

NOTE: When refrigerant charging speed is slow, immerse refrigerant can in water heated to a temperature of about 104°F (40°C). However, note that this is dangerous when water is hot.

CAUTION

Under any circumstances the refrigerant can must not be warmed in water heated to a temperature of over 126°F (52°C). A blow torch or stove must never be used to warm the can.

NOTE: When charging liquid refrigerant into the system, with the can turned upside down to reduce charging time, charge it only through high pressure valve, but not through low pressure valve.

4. On Hitachi system only, if refrigerant charging speed slows down, charge it while running the compressor for ease of charging. After performing Steps 1–3 above, proceed with charging system in the following order.

NOTE: After completion of charging, the compressor should always be turned several times manually.

5. On both systems, shut off high pressure valve of manifold gauge. Remember, on the Panasonic system, the low pressure valve is kept closed.

CAUTION

Never charge refrigerant through the high pressure side of system, when the engine is running. This will force refrigerant back into refrigerant can and the can may explode.

6. Run the engine at idle speed.
7. Set temperature control dial or lever at **MAX** cool and fan switch at **MAX** speed.
8. On Hitachi system, charge refrigerant while controlling low pressure gauge reading a 40 psi or less by turning in or out

low pressure valve of manifold gauge. On the Panasonic system, charge refrigerant into the system through the low pressure valve after difference of pressure between low and high pressure gauge appears. Repeat from Step 7 when difference of pressure between low and high pressure gauges does not appear after 1 minute of operation. It is not possible to charge refrigerant without pressure difference between low and high pressure gauges.

9. When refrigerant can is empty, fully close both valves of manifold gauge and replace refrigerant can with a new one. Before opening the manifold gauge valve to charge refrigerant from the new can, be sure to purge air from inside charging hose.

10. Charge the specified amount of refrigerant into system by weighing charged refrigerant with scale. Overcharging will cause discharge pressure to rise.

NOTE: Measure the amount of charged refrigerant with a scale. Make a note of the amount charged for can. The presence of bubbles in sight glass of receiver/drier is an unsuitable method of checking the amount of refrigerant charged in system. The state of the bubbles in sight glass should only be used for checking whether the amount of charged refrigerant is small or not. The amount of charged refrigerant can be correctly judged by means of discharge pressure.

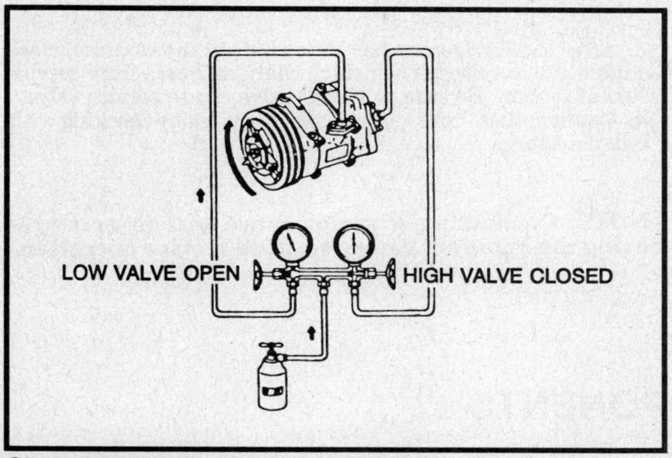
LOW VALVE OPEN
HIGH VALVE CLOSED

Charging the air conditioning system on the low pressure side

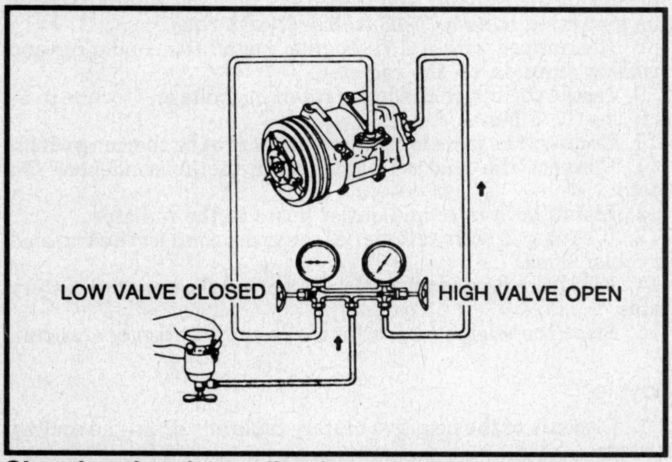
LOW VALVE CLOSED
HIGH VALVE OPEN

Charging the air conditoning system on the high pressure side

11. After the specified amount of refrigerant has been charged into system, close manifold gauge valves. Detach the charging hoses from the service valves of system. Be sure to install valve cap on service valve.

12. Confirm that there are no leaks in system by checking with a leak detector.

NOTE: Conducting a performance test prior to removing the manifold gauge is a good service operation.

Diesel Kiki System

1. Install manifold gauge to system.

NOTE: Be sure to purge air from the high and low pressure charging hoses. If air is mixed with refrigerant in system, evacuation of system should be performed.

2. Attach center charging hose of manifold gauge to refrigerant can through can tap. Break seal of refrigerant can to allow refrigerant to enter manifold gauge. Loosen the charging hose at the center fitting of manifold gauge and purge air from inside charging hose.

3. Open only the low pressure valve of the manifold gauge to charge the refrigerant into the system.

NOTE: When refrigerant charging speed is slow, immerse refrigerant can in water heated to a temperature of about 104°F (40°C). However, note that this is dangerous when water is hot.

CAUTION

Under any circumstances, the refrigerant can must not be warmed in water heated to a temperature of over 126°F (52°C). A blow torch or stove must never be used to warm up the can.

4. Should the refrigerant charging speed slow down, charge it with the engine running and the compressor engaged.

5. After having completed Steps 1–3, proceed with the charging in the following manner:

6. Run the engine at idling speed.

7. Set temperature control dial or lever at **MAX** cool and fan switch at **MAX** speed. Charge refrigerant into the system.

8. When refrigerant can is empty, fully close both valves of manifold gauge and replace refrigerant can with a new one. Before opening manifold gauge valve to charge refrigerant from anew can, be sure to purge air from inside charging hose.

9. Charge a maximum 2.0 lbs. (0.9 kg) of refrigerant into system. Weigh the charged refrigerant with scale. Overcharging will cause discharge pressure to rise.

NOTE: Measure the amount of charged refrigerant with a scale. Make a note of the amount charged from the can. The presence of bubbles in sight glass of receiver/drier is an unsuitable method of checking the amount of refrigerant charged in system. The state of the bubbles in sight glass should only be used for checking whether the amount of charged refrigerant is small or not. The amount of charged refrigerant can be correctly judged by means of discharge pressure.

10. After the refrigerant has been charged into system, close manifold gauge valves. The detach charging hoses from service valves of system. Be sure on install valve cap to service valve.

11. Confirm that there are no leaks in system by checking with a leak detector.

NOTE: Conducting a performance test prior to removing the manifold gauge is a good service operation.

Calsonic System

1. Install manifold gauge to system.

NOTE: Be sure to purge air from the high and low pressure charging hoses. If air is mixed with refrigerant in system, evacuation of system should be performed.

2. Attach center charging hose of manifold gauge to refrigerant can through can tap. Break seal of refrigerant can to allow refrigerant to enter manifold gauge. Loosen the charging hose at the center fitting of manifold gauge and purge air from inside charging hose.
3. Open only the high pressure valve of the manifold gauge to charge the refrigerant into the system.

NOTE: If charging liquid refrigerant into the system with the can turned upside down to reduce charging time, charge it only through the high pressure service valve only. After charging, the compressor should always be turned several times manually.

4. When the low pressure gauge reading reaches 14 psi, approximately 1.0 lb. (98 kPa) of refrigerant has been charged into the system. Compeletely close the high pressure valve of the manifold gauge and stop the charging.
5. If charging the system through the low pressure side, proceed as follows:
6. With the engine off, open the lower pressure valve of the manifold gauge and charge the refrigerant through the system.
7. When the refrigerant charging speed slows down, close the high pressure valve of the manifold gauge and open the low pressure.
8. Start the engine, set temperature control dial or lever at **MAX** cool and fan switch at **MAX** speed. Charge refrigerant into the system.
9. Charge the system until the bubbles in the sight glass is clear.

NOTE: Keep in mine, air conditioning systems that utilize a recylcing clutch, produce bubbles in the sight glass when the clutch engages. Allow 5 seconds after the clutch engages to determine if bubbles continue. If so, add refrigerant to clear the sight glass.

CAUTION

Never charge refrigerant through the high pressure side of the system. This will force refrigerant back into the refrigerant can and may cause the can to explode.

10. Charge the refrigerant while controlling the low pressure gauge reading at 40 psi. (275 kPa) or less by turning the low pressure valve at the manifold gauge.
11. When the refrigerant can is empty, fully close both valves of manifold gauge and replace refrigerant can with a new one. Before opening manifold gauge valve to charge refrigerant from a new can, be sure to purge air from inside charging hose.
12. Charge a maximum 2.0 lbs. (0.9 kg) of refrigerant into system. Weigh the charged refrigerant with scale. Overcharging will cause discharge pressure to rise.

NOTE: Measure the amount of charged refrigerant with a scale. Make a note of the amount charged for can. The presence of bubbles in sight glass of receiver/drier is an unsuitable method of checking the amount of refrigerant charged in system. The state of the bubbles in sight glass should only be used for checking whether the amount of charged refrigerant is small or not. The amount of charged refrigerant can be correctly judged by means of discharge pressure.

13. After the refrigerant has been charged into system, close manifold gauge valves. The detach charging hoses from service valves of system. Be sure to install valve cap to service valve.
14. Confirm that there are no leaks in system by checking with a leak detector.

NOTE: Conducting a performance test prior to removing the manifold gauge is a good service operation.

SYSTEM COMPONENTS

Radiator

REMOVAL AND INSTALLATION

Except Loyale

1. Disconnect the negative battery cable and drain the cooling system.
2. Disconnect the inlet and outlet radiator hoses.
3. If equipped with automatic transmission, disconnect the inlet and outlet oil cooler lines from the radiator.
4. Disconnect the following wires:
   a. The thermo-switch connector.
   b. The radiator ground wire.
   c. The fan motor wire connector.
5. If equipped with 2.7L engine:
   a. Disconnect the lead wire connector from the condenser fan motor.
   b. Remove the upper and lower bolts securing the condenser and radiator fans to the radiator.
   c. Remove condenser and radiator fan shrouds with the motor assemblies.
6. Remove the radiator mounting bolts and lift the radiator upward from the vehicle.

To install:

7. Attach the raditor mounting cushions to the lower pins, on the side of the radiator and install the mounting bolts. Torque the mounting bolts to 7–13 ft. lbs. (10–18 Nm).
8. If equipped with a 2.7L engine, install the condenser and radiator shrouds, on the radiator.
9. Install the upper and lower retaining bolts and torque to 5–6 ft. lbs. (7–8 Nm).
10. Connect the main harness connector to the thermo-switch.
11. Connect the lead wire connector to the condenser fan motor.
12. Install both inlet and outlet hoses to the radiator.
13. If equipped with automatic transaxle, connect the transaxle cooler lines.
14. Fill the radiator with coolant. Connect the negative battery cable.
15. Start the engine, check for leaks and test fan operation.

Loyale

1. Disconnect the negative battery cable and drain the cooling system.
2. Disconnect the inlet and outlet hoses from the engine side. Disconnect the overflow hose from the radiator.

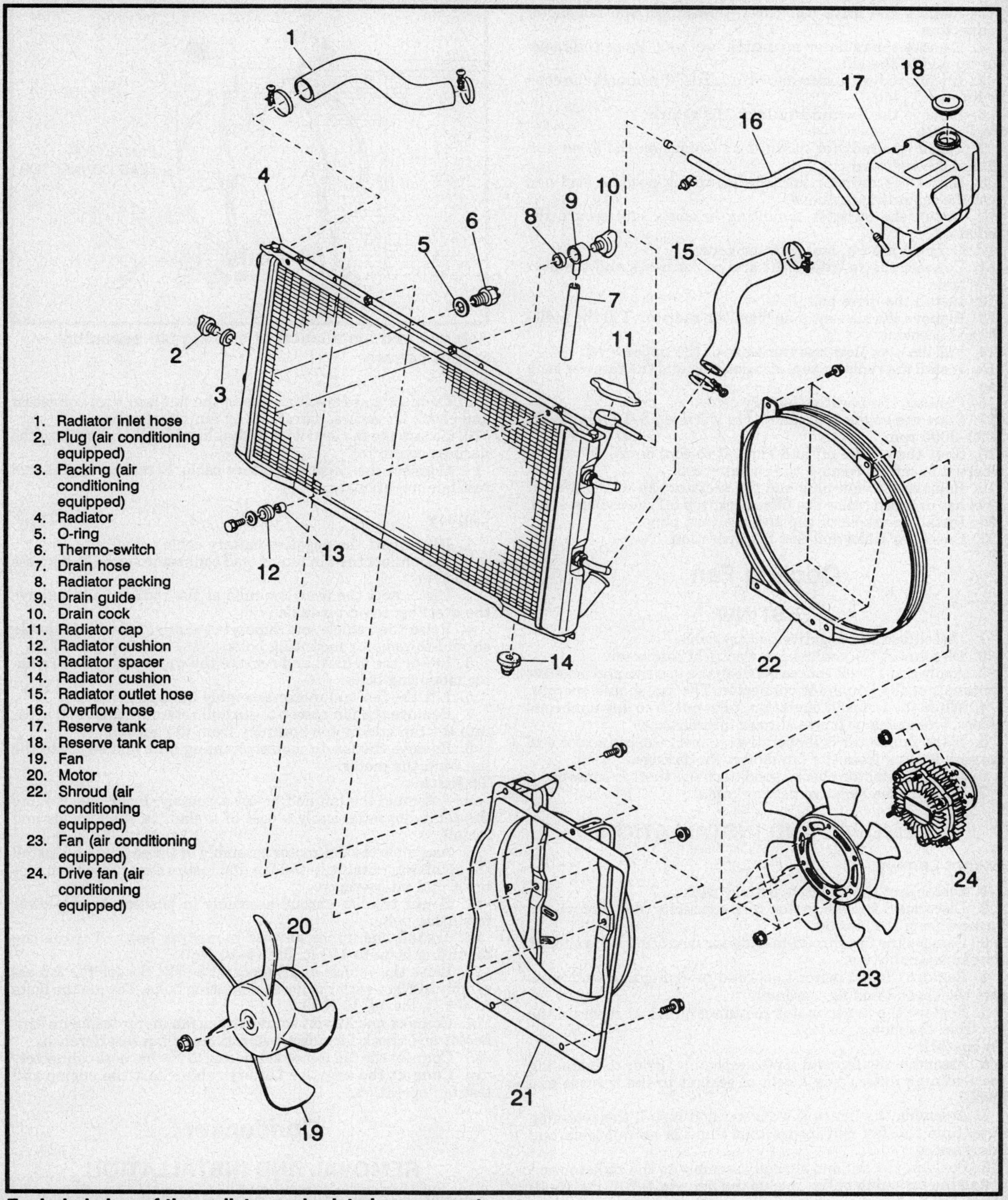
1
2
3
4
5
6
7
8
9
10
11
12
13
14
15
16
17
18
19
20
21
22
23
24
1. Radiator inlet hose
2. Plug (air conditioning equipped)
3. Packing (air conditioning equipped)
4. Radiator
5. O-ring
6. Thermo-switch
7. Drain hose
8. Radiator packing
9. Drain guide
10. Drain cock
11. Radiator cap
12. Radiator cushion
13. Radiator spacer
14. Radiator cushion
15. Radiator outlet hose
16. Overflow hose
17. Reserve tank
18. Reserve tank cap
19. Fan
20. Motor
22. Shroud (air conditioning equipped)
23. Fan (air conditioning equipped)
24. Drive fan (air conditioning equipped)

Exploded view of the radiator and related components

3. Remove the drive belt cover. Disconnect the fan motor connectors.
4. Remove the radiator mounting brackets. Raise the radiator up and to the left.
5. If equipped with automatic transaxle, disconnect the cooler lines and plug.
6. Remove the the radiator from the vehicle.

To install:

7. Attach the radiator mounting cushions on the lower section of the radiator.
8. Lower the radiator into the mounting position and and seat the mounting cushions.
9. Install the radiator mounting brackets and secure the radiator.
10. Connect the fan motor connectors.
11. Connect the radiator inlet and outlet hoses and the over flow hose.
12. Install the drive belt.
13. Remove the air vent plug from the radiator. Fill the radiator with coolant.
14. Fill the over flow resevior tank to the upper level.
15. Install the radiator cap, air vent plug and the resevior tank cap.
16. Connect the negative battery cable.
17. Start the engine and allow it to warm up 5–10 minutes at 2000–3000 rpm.
18. Shut the engine off and allow it to cool down, enough to where it is safe to remove the radiator cap.
19. Remove the vent plug and the radiator cap. If the coolant level has dropped below the filler neck, top off the coolant level.
20. Install the radiator cap and the vent plug.
21. Check for leaks and test fan operation.

Cooling Fan

TESTING

1. Disconnect the negative battery cable.
2. Disconnect the cooling fan electrical connector.
3. Apply and 12 volt source between the positive and negative terminals of the fan motor connector. The fan should operate.
4. While the fan is in operation, take notice to any abnormal noises, vibrations or fan-to-shroud interference.
5. If the fan motor is inoperative, inspect the connector and harness leading from the fan motor, for damage.
6. If the fan motor checks good, test the thermo-sensor.
7. Connect the negative battery cable.

REMOVAL AND INSTALLATION

Except Legacy

1. Disconnect the negative battery cable.
2. Disconnect the fan motor wire connector and remove the harness from the shroud.
3. Remove the fan shroud-to-radiator mounting bolts and lift the fan assembly out.
4. Remove the fan motor-to-shroud retaining nuts and separate the shroud and fan assembly.
5. Remove the fan-to-motor retaining nuts and separate the fan from the motor.

To install:

6. Assemble the fan and motor assembly. Prior to installing the retaining nuts, apply a coat of sealant to the threads and install.
7. Assemble the fan to the shroud and install the retaining nuts. Spin the fan and insure that there is no fan-to-shroud interference.
8. Position the fan and shroud assembly to the radiator and install the retaining bolts. Torque the bolts to 4–7 ft. lbs. (4–10 Nm).

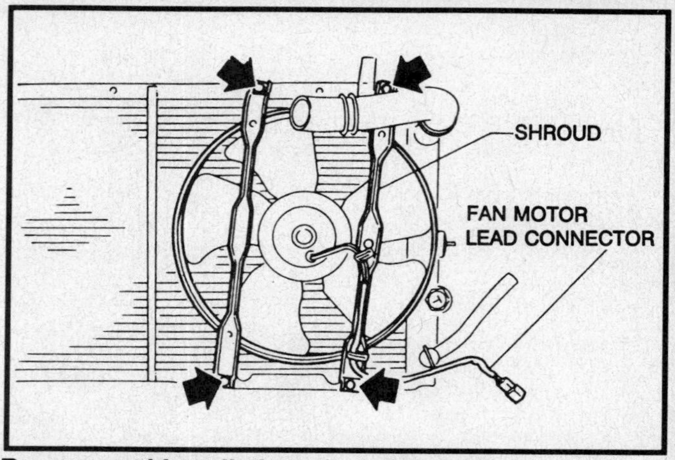
SHROUD
FAN MOTOR
LEAD CONNECTOR

Remove and installation of cooling fan assembly—except Legacy

9. Connect and 12 volt source to the fan lead wire connector and check for noises, vibrations or fan interference.
10. Secure the fan lead wire to the shroud and connect it to the harness connector.
11. Connect the negative battery cable. Start the engine and test fan operation.

Legacy

1. Disconnect the negative battery cable.
2. Disconnect the fan motor lead connector from the harness connector.
3. Disconnect the overflow tube at the radiator and remove the overflow reservoir tank.
4. Raise the vehicle and support it safely. Loosen the lower shroud-to-radiator mounting bolts.
5. Lower the vehicle and remove the upper shroud-to-radiator mounting bolts.
6. Lift the fan and motor assembly out and remove.
7. Remove the fan motor-to-shroud retaining nuts and separate the fan and motor assembly from the shroud.
8. Remove the fan-to-motor retaining nuts and separate the fan from the motor.

To install:

9. Assemble the fan and motor assembly. Prior to installing the retaining nuts, apply a coat of sealant to the threads and install.
10. Assemble the fan/motor assembly to the shroud and install the retaining nuts. Spin the fan and insure that there is no fan-to-shroud interference.
11. Lower the fan shroud assembly in position to the lower mounting bolts.
12. Install the upper shroud mounting bolts. Torque the mounting bolts to 4–7 ft. lbs. (4–10 Nm).
13. Raise the vehicle and support it safely. Secure the fan assembly in place with the lower mounting bolts. Torque the bolts to 4–7 ft. lbs. (4–10 Nm).
14. Connect and 12 volt source to the fan motor lead wire connector and check for noises, vibrations or fan interference.
15. Connect the fan motor connector to the harness connector.
16. Connect the negative battery cable. Start the engine and test fan operation.

Condenser

REMOVAL AND INSTALLATION

1. Disconnect the negative battery cable.

1. Information label
2. High pressure liquid line
3. Receiver/drier
4. Bracket
5. Trinary switch
6. Grommet
7. Clamp
8. High pressure liquid line
9. Condenser
10. Discharge line—high pressure
11. Clamp
12. High pressure vapor line (discharge)
13. Low pressure vapor line (suction)
14. Main relay (fan control)
15. Air conditioning relay
16. Bracket
17. Air conditioning fuse

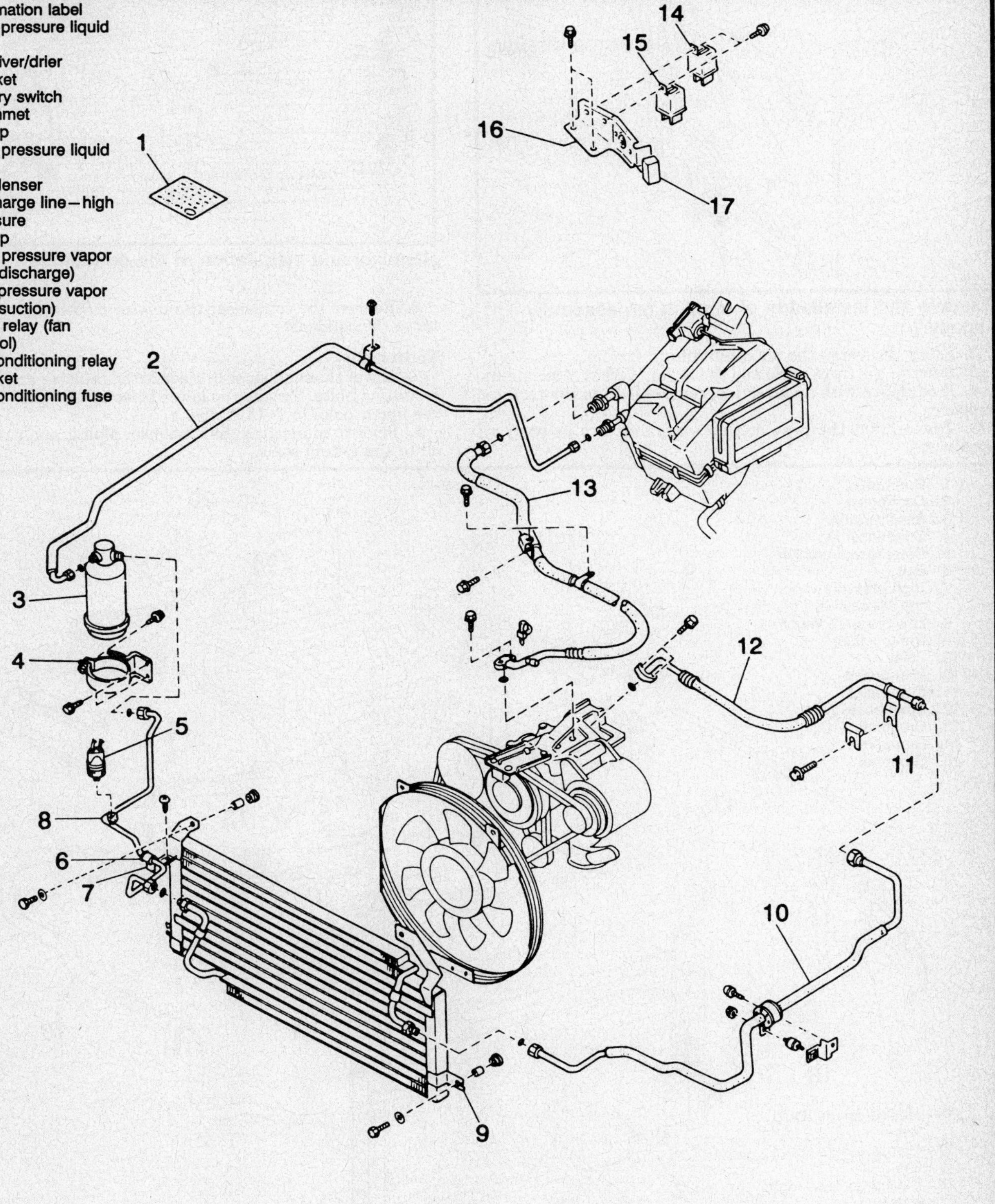
1
2
3
4
5
6
7
8
9
10
11
12
13
14
15
16
17

Exploded view of the air conditioning system— Hitachi

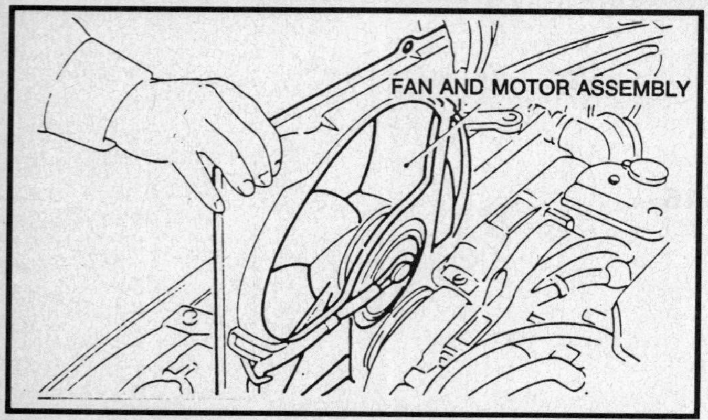
FAN AND MOTOR ASSEMBLY

Remove and installation of cooling fan assembly—Legacy

2. Safely discharge the air conditioning system.
3. Remove the front grille and the lower bracket attachment.
4. If equipped with an air guide, remove it from the radiator support.
5. Disconnect the pipe connections and cap or plug all openings.

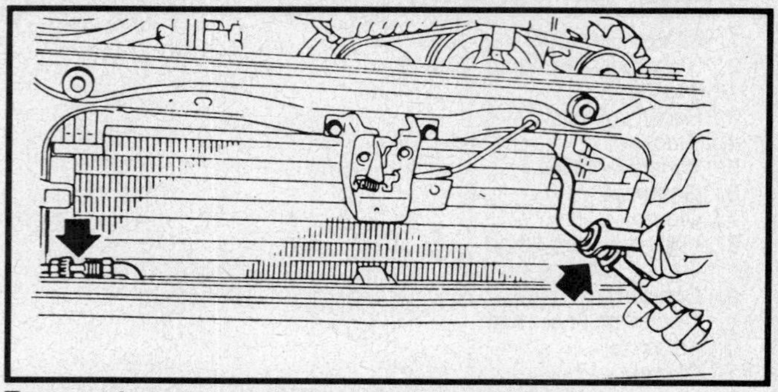

Removal and installation of the condenser

6. Remove the condenser-to-radiator mounting bolts and remove the condenser.

To install:

7. Lower the condensor in place to the radiator and install the mounting bolts. Torque the lower bolts to 7 ft. lbs. (4 Nm) and the upper bolts to 7–13 ft. lbs.
8. Prior to connecting the condenser piping, apply refrigerant oil to the O-ring seals.

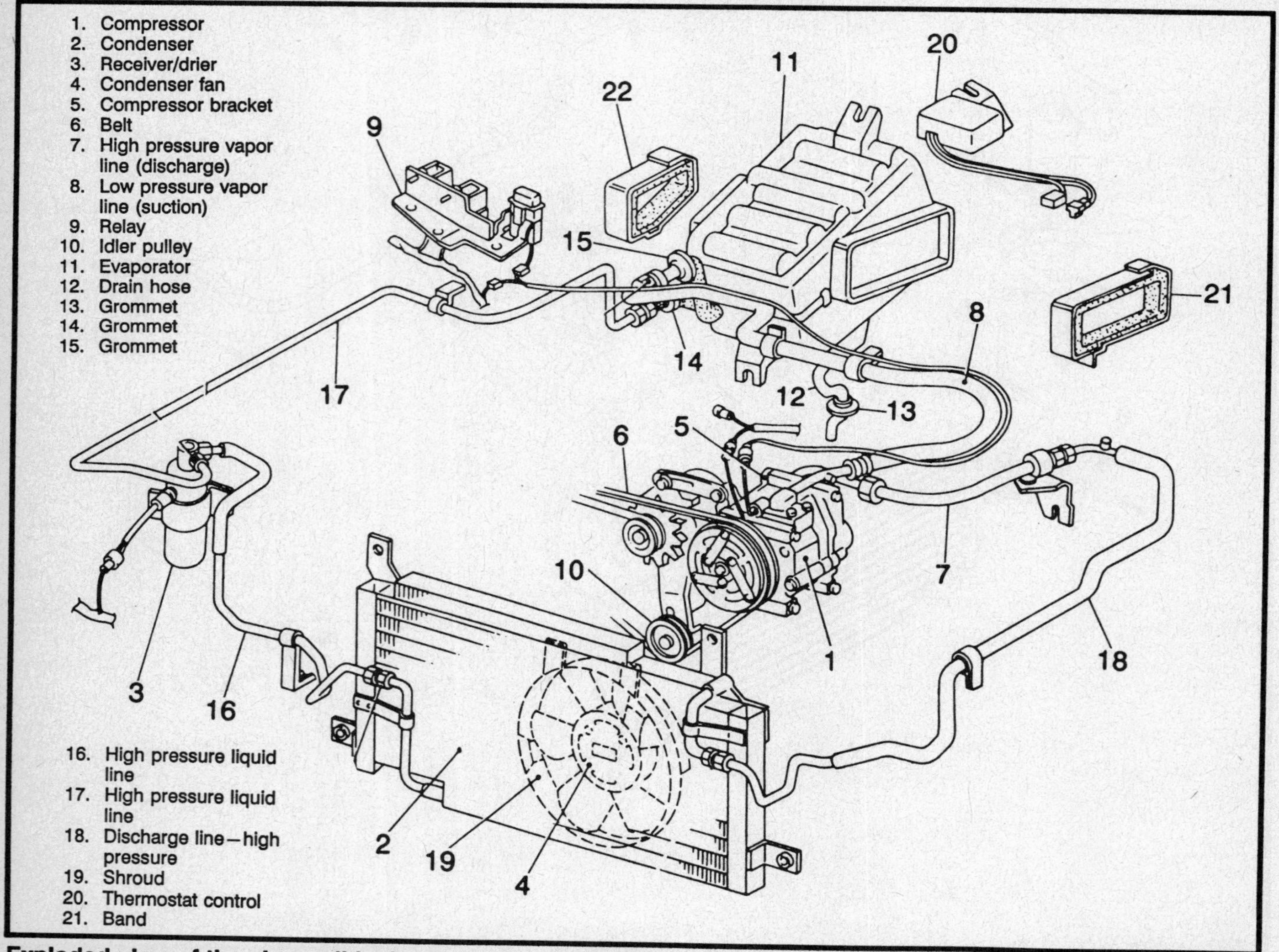
1. Compressor
2. Condenser
3. Receiver/drier
4. Condenser fan
5. Compressor bracket
6. Belt
7. High pressure vapor line (discharge)
8. Low pressure vapor line (suction)
9. Relay
10. Idler pulley
11. Evaporator
12. Drain hose
13. Grommet
14. Grommet
15. Grommet
16. High pressure liquid line
17. High pressure liquid line
18. Discharge line—high pressure
19. Shroud
20. Thermostat control
21. Band
1
2
3
4
5
6
7
8
9
10
11
12
13
14
15
16
17
18
19
20
21
22

Exploded view of the air conditioning system— Panasonic

1. Compressor
2. Condenser
3. Receiver/drier
4. Evaporator
5. High pressure liquid line
6. High pressure liquid line
7. High pressure liquid line
8. High pressure vapor line (discharge)
9. Low pressure vapor line (suction)
10. Clip
11. Clip
12. Relay (main fan, sub fan, fan control and air conditioning)
13. Air conditioning control relay
14. Fuses (sub fan and accessory)
15. Information label

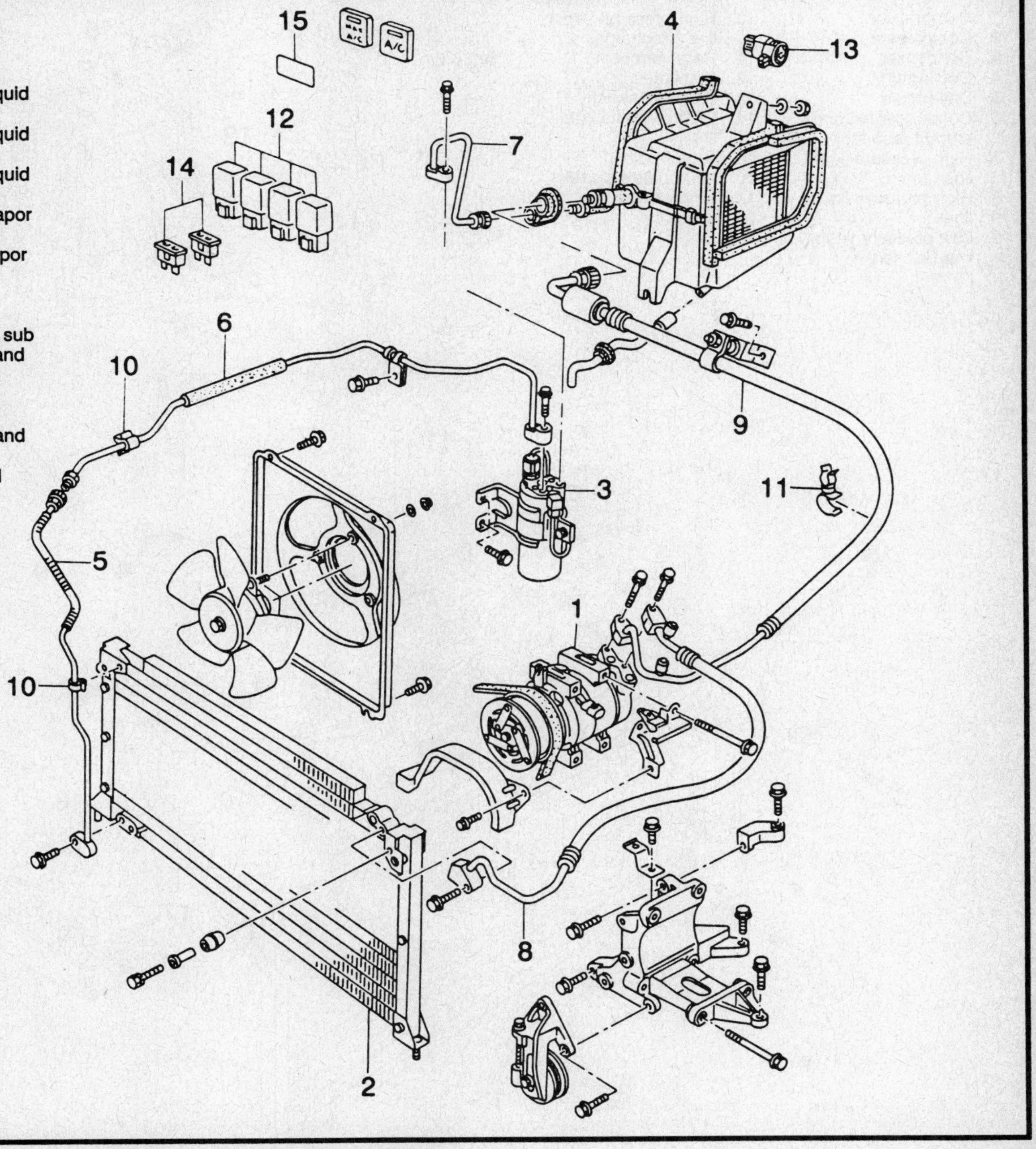
15
12
14
4
13
7
6
10
9
3
11
5
1
10
8
2

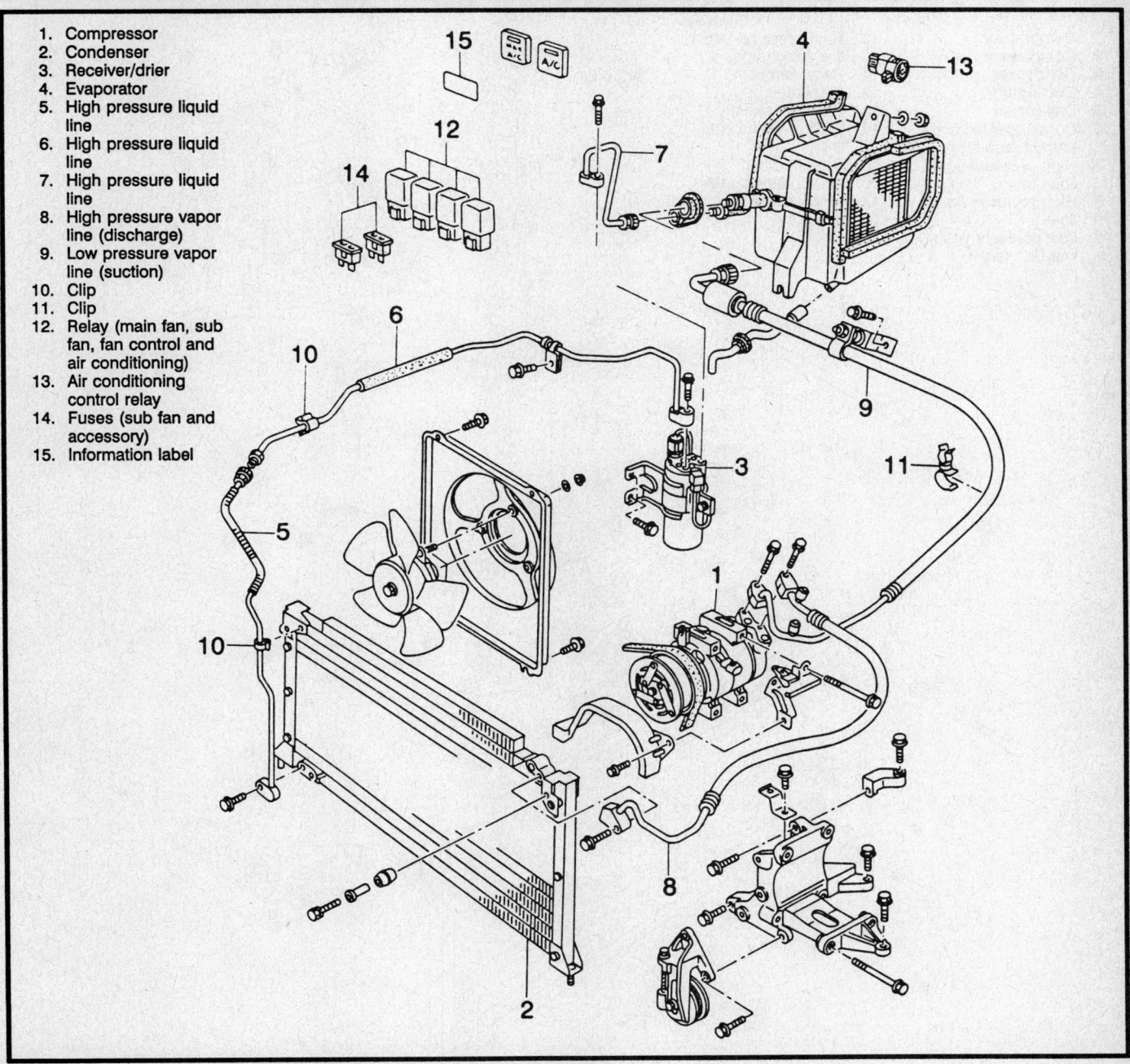

Exploded view of the air conditioning system—Diesel Kiki

9. Connect the condenser piping to the condenser. Torque the right side nut to 7–14 ft. lbs. (10–20 Nm) and the left side nut to 11–18 ft. lbs. (15–25 Nm).
10. If equipped with an air guide, install it to the radiator support.
11. Install the front grille and the lower bracket attachment.
12. Evacuate, leak test and recharge the air conditioning system.
13. Connect the negative battery cable. Start the engine and test air conditioning system.

Compressor

REMOVAL AND INSTALLATION

Loyale, XT Coupe and Sedan

HATACHI

1. Disconnect the negative battery cable.
2. Remove the spare tire.
4. Remove the pulser from the compressor.

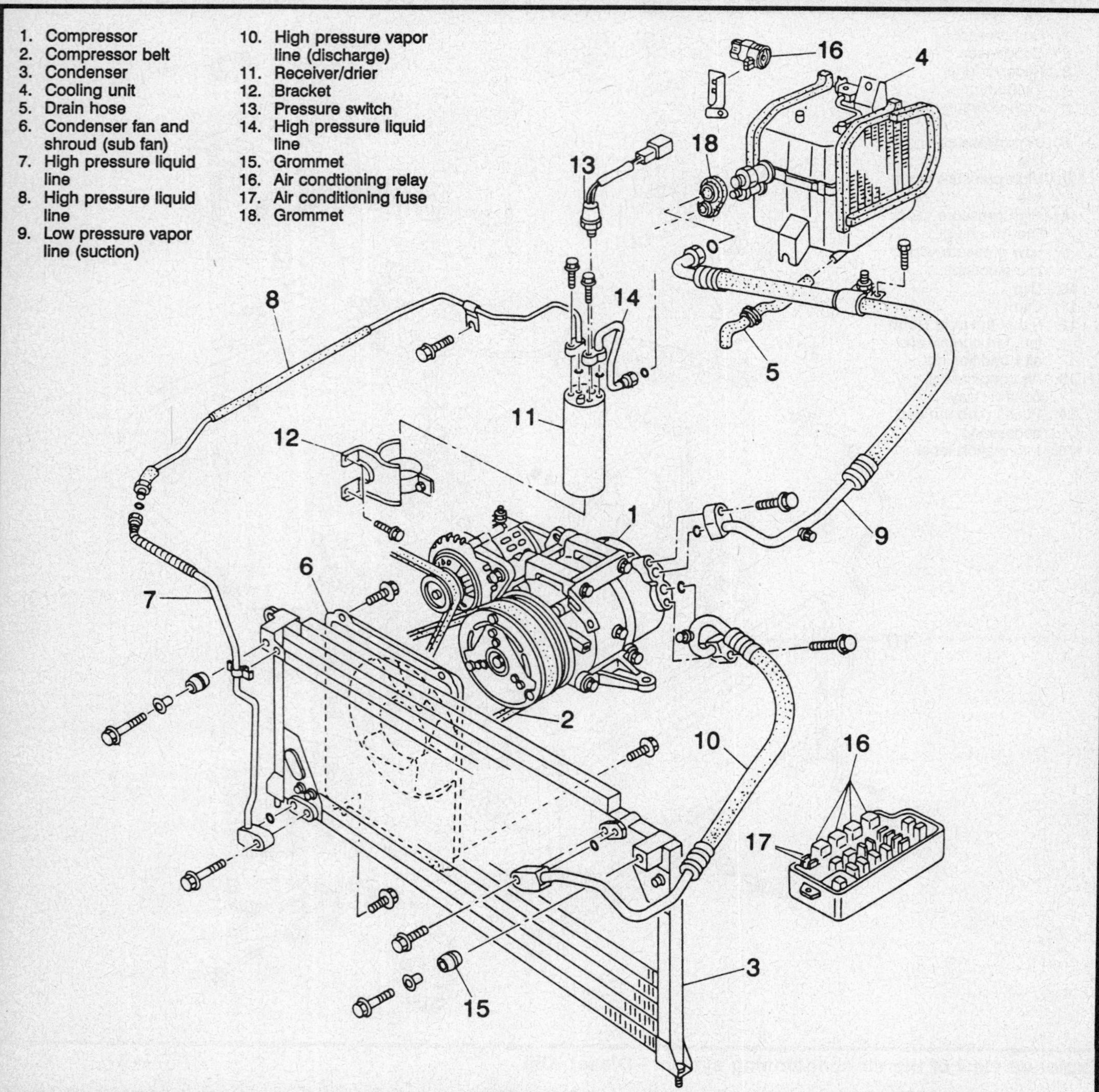
1. Compressor
2. Compressor belt
3. Condenser
4. Cooling unit
5. Drain hose
6. Condenser fan and shroud (sub fan)
7. High pressure liquid line
8. High pressure liquid line
9. Low pressure vapor line (suction)
10. High pressure vapor line (discharge)
11. Receiver/drier
12. Bracket
13. Pressure switch
14. High pressure liquid line
15. Grommet
16. Air condtioning relay
17. Air conditioning fuse
18. Grommet

Exploded view of the air conditioning system— Calsonic

5. Remove the fan shroud.
6. Discharge the refrigerant using an air conditioning manifold gauge set.
7. Remove the low pressure hose then the high pressure hose and plug the openings on both. Take care not to loose the O-ring when removing the hose connections.
8. Remove the alternator drive belt, the drive belt and upper compressor bracket.
9. Remove the condenser fan assembly from the water pump.
10. Loosen the idler pulley and remove the drive belt. Remove idler pulley retaining bolt and remove the idler pulley assembly.
11. Remove the compressor and compressor lower bracket as an assembly. Separate the assembly with the unit removed from the vehicle.

To install:

12. Install the lower compressor bracket on the compressor and temporarily install to the engine. Align the lower bracket

and spacer. Torque the retaining bolts to 18–26 ft. lbs. (25–35 Nm).

13. Temporarily install the upper compressor bracket onto the compressor and secure the lower compressor bracket and upper bracket in this order. Torque the retaining bolts: large bolts to 18–26 ft. lbs. (25–35 Nm) and the smaller bolts to 4–7 ft. lbs. (5–9 Nm).

14. Temporarily install the idler pulley assembly on the lower compressor bracket.

15. Place the rear belt on the crankshaft, power steering, oil pump, compressor, idler and water pump pulleys.

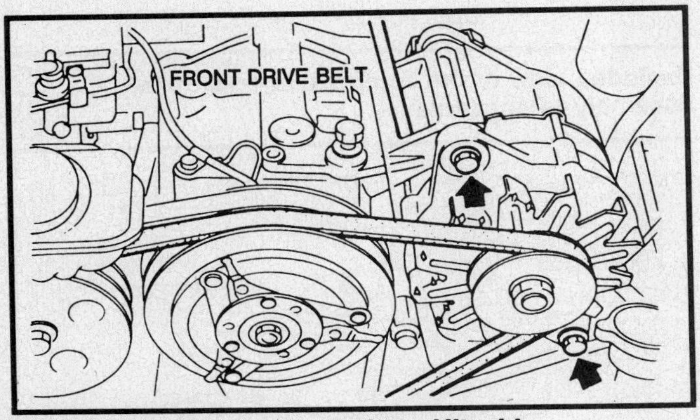
FRONT DRIVE BELT

Adjusting the front belt tension—Hitachi

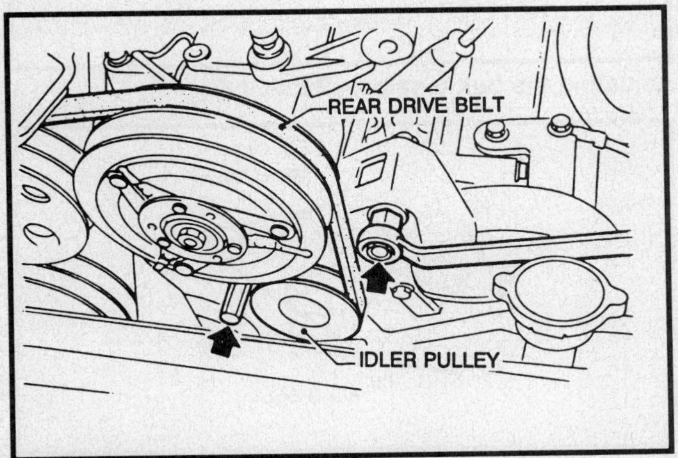
REAR DRIVE BELT
IDLER PULLEY

Adjusting the rear drive belt tension—Hitachi

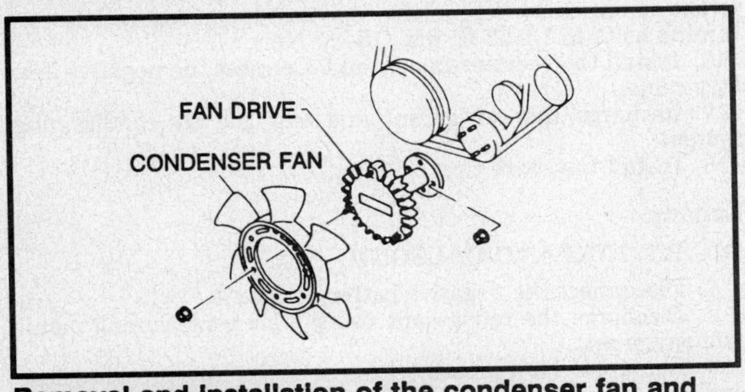
FAN DRIVE
CONDENSER FAN

Removal and installation of the condenser fan and drive assembly—Hatachi and Panasonic

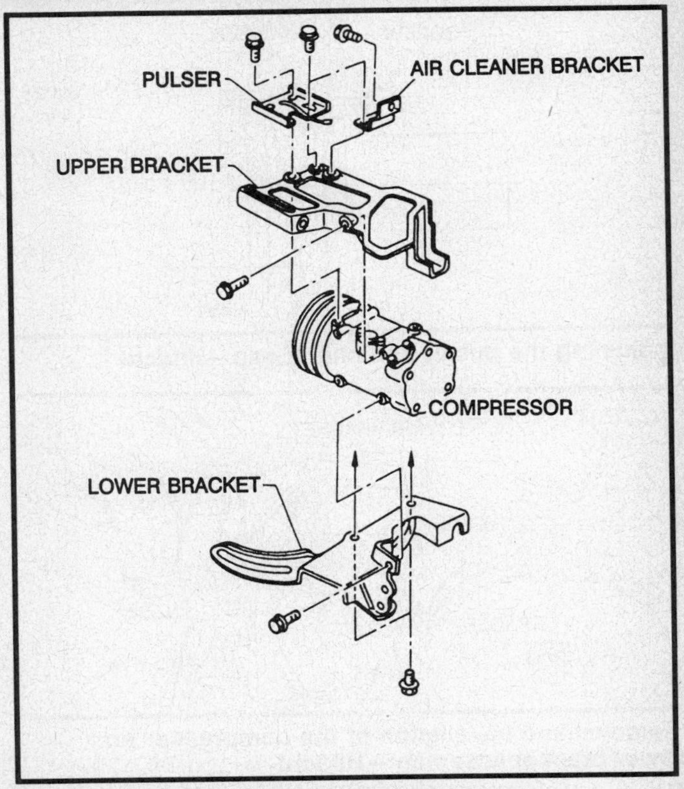
PULSER
AIR CLEANER BRACKET
UPPER BRACKET
COMPRESSOR
LOWER BRACKET

Exploded view of the compressor-to-bracket assembly—Hitachi

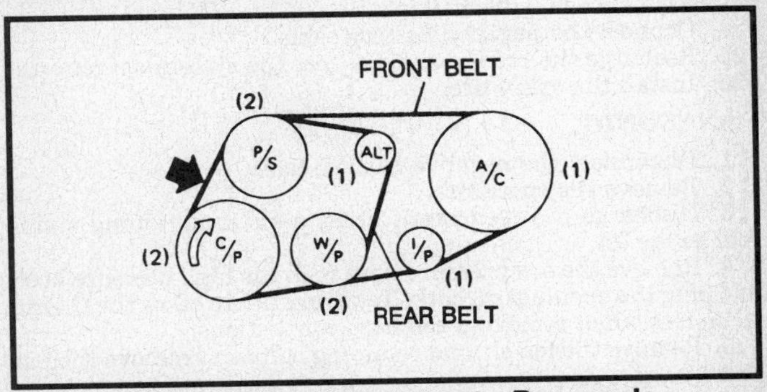
FRONT BELT
(2)
P/S
ALT
(1)
A/C
(1)
(2)
C/P
W/P
I/P
(1)
(2)
REAR BELT

Drive belt and pulley arrangement—Panasonic

16. Adjust the belt tension by changing the idler pulley position.

17. Tempoarily install the alternator on the compressor bracket then place the front belt on the crankshaft, power steering, oil pump, compressor pulley, alternator and water pump pulleys.

18. Adjust the belt tension by changing the alternator position.

19. Connect the compressor wire connector to the harness connector.

20. Assemble the condenser fan and fan drive and install the assembly to the water pump.

21. Apply compressor oil to the outside edges of the O-rings and connect the high pressure hose, then the low pressure hose to the compressor. Torque the high and low pressure hose retaining bolts to 13–23 ft. lbs. (18–31 Nm).

22. Install the radiator fan shroud to the radiator. Install the retaining bolts and torque to 6–9 ft. lbs. (5–9 Nm).

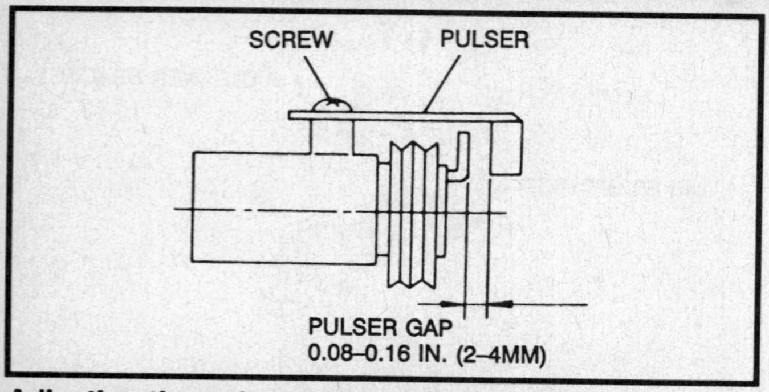
SCREW
PULSER
PULSER GAP
0.08–0.16 IN. (2–4MM)
Adjusting the pulser and clutch gap—Hitachi

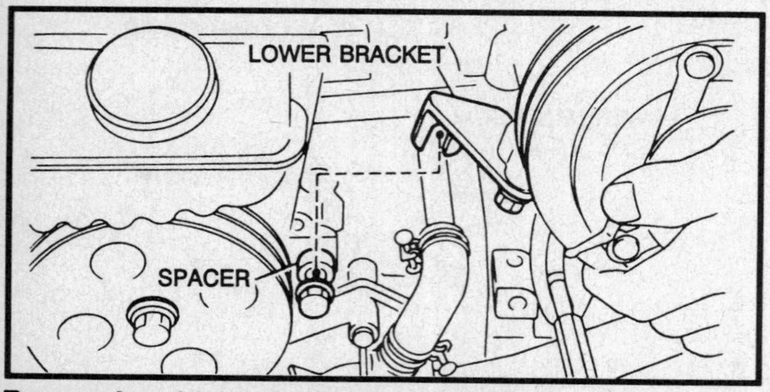
LOWER BRACKET
SPACER
Removal and installation of the compressor and lower bracket assembly—Hitachi

23. Install the pulser on the compressor. Make sure the clearance between the pulser's sending portion and compressor clutch is between 0.08–0.16 in.
24. Connect the negative battery cable.
25. Recharge the refrigerant and test the system operation.
26. Install the spare tire.

PANASONIC

1. Disconnect the negative battery cable.
2. Remove the spare tire.
3. Discharge the refrigerant using a air conditioning manifold gauge set.
4. Remove the low pressure hose then the high pressure hose and plug the openings on both. Take care not to allow the O-ring to be loss when removing the hose connections.
5. Remove the fan shroud retaining bolts and remove the fan shroud.
6. Remove the condenser fan assembly.
7. Loosen the idler pulley locknut.
8. Loosen the compressor bolts, move the compressor forward and remove the compressor drive belt.
9. Disconnect the compressor connector from the harness connector, then remove the compressor from the engine.

To install:

10. Install the compressor on the compressor bracket and install the mounting bolts. Torque the mounting bolts to 14–20 ft. lbs. (20–30 Nm).
11. Place the drive belt over the crankshaft, power steering, oil pump, water pump, idler and compressor pulleys.
12. Adjust the drive belt tension by changing the idler pulley position.
13. Connect the compressor wire connector to the harness connector.
14. Assemble the condenser fan to the fan drive and install the assembly to the water pump.
15. Apply compressor oil to the outside edges of the O-rings and connect the high pressure hose, then the low pressure hose to the compressor. Torque the high and low pressure hose retaining bolts to 13–23 ft. lbs. (18–31 Nm).
16. Install the radiator fan shroud. Connect the negative battery cable.
17. Recharge the refrigerant and test the air conditioning system.
18. Install the spare tire.

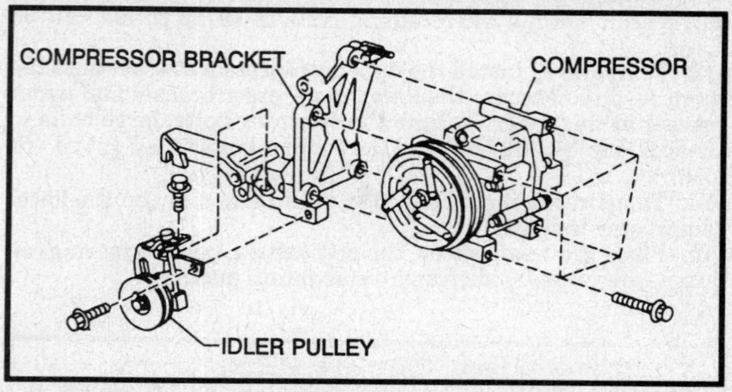
COMPRESSOR BRACKET
COMPRESSOR
IDLER PULLEY
Exploded view of the compressor-to-bracket assembly—Panasonic

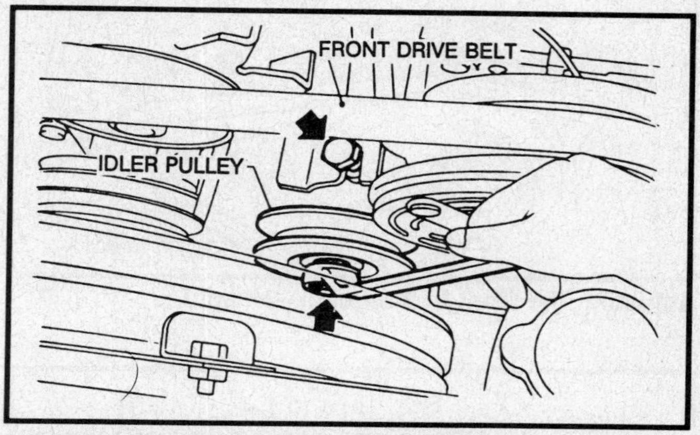
FRONT DRIVE BELT
IDLER PULLEY
Adjusting the belt tension—Panasonic

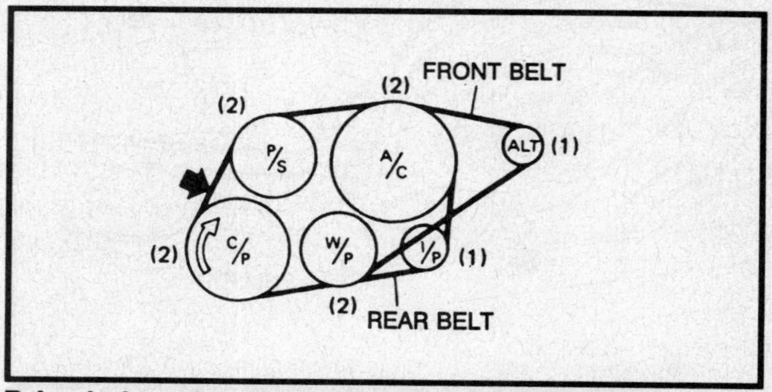
FRONT BELT
(2)
(2)
P/S
A/C
ALT (1)
(2)
C/P
W/P
I/P (1)
(2)
REAR BELT
Drive belt and pulley arrangement—Panasonic

Legacy

DIESEL KIKI AND CALSONIC

1. Disconnect the negative battery cable.
2. Discharge the refrigerant using a air conditioning manifold gauge set.
3. Remove the low pressure hose, then the high pressure hose and plug the openings on both. Take care not to allow the O-ring to be loss when removing the hose connections.

Loosen

Removing the drive belt cover—Calsonic and Diesel Kiki

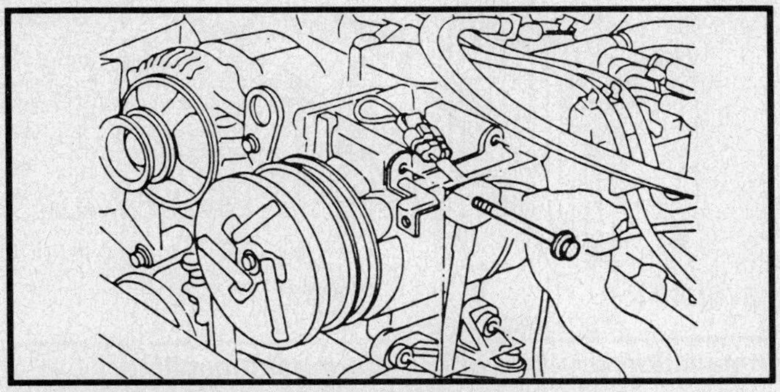

Removal and installation of the compressor

4. Remove the retaining bolts from the alternator and compressor belt cover and remove the belt cover.
5. Loosen the lock bolt on the alternator bracket, turn the adjustment bolt and remove the alternator drive belt.
6. Loosen the lock bolt on the idler pulley, turn the adjustment bolt and remove the compressor drive belt.
7. Disconnect the alterator harness connector from the alternator.
8. Disconnect the compressor wire connector from the harness connector.
9. On the Calsonic system, remove the compressor-to-lower bracket mounting bolts and remove the lower bracket. Remove the compressor-to-upper bracket mounting bolts and remove the compressor from the engine.
10. On Diesel Kiki system, remove the compressor-to-bracket mounting bolts and remove the compressor from the engine.

To install:

11. On the Diesel Kiki system, position the compressor to the mounting bracket and install the retaining bolts. Torque the retaining bolts to 17–31 ft. lbs. (23–42 Nm).
12. On the Calsonic system, position the compressor to the upper bracket and install the retaining bolts. Install the lower bracket to the compressor and install the retaining bolts. Torque the retaining bolts to 17–31 ft. lbs. (23–42 Nm).
13. Connect the compressor wire connector to the harness connector.
14. Plug the alternator connector to the alternator.
15. Install the compressor drive belt and adjust the belt tension. Tighten the pulley lock bolt to 17–31 ft. lbs. (23–42 Nm).
16. Install the alternator drive belt and adjust the belt tension. Tighten the pulley lock bolt to 17–31 ft. lbs. (23–42 Nm).
17. Apply compressor oil to the outside edges of the O-rings and connect the high pressure hose and low pressure hoses to the compressor. Torque the retaining bolts to: 10–18 ft. lbs. (14–25 Nm) for Diesel Kiki system and 7–14 ft. lbs. (10–20 Nm) for Calsonic system.

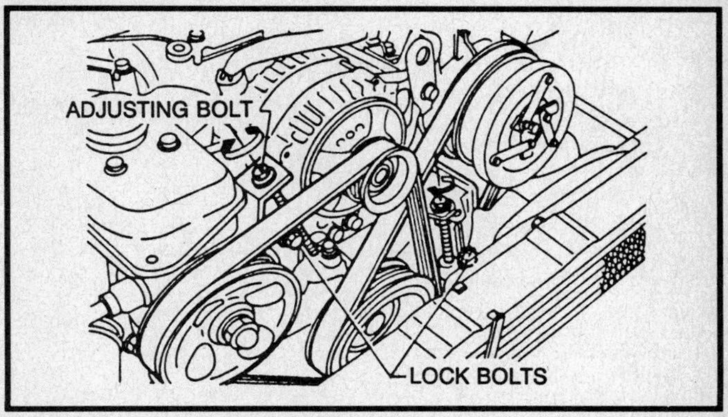
ADJUSTING BOLT
LOCK BOLTS

Adjusting the alternator and compressor drive belt tension—Calsonic and Diesel Kiki

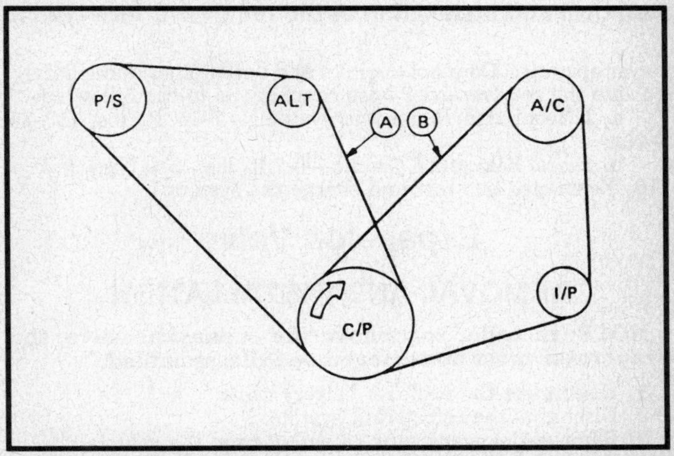
P/S
ALT
A
B
A/C
I/P
C/P

Drive belt and pulley arrangement—Calsonic and Diesel Kiki

18. Install the drive belt cover over the alternator and compressor pulleys.
19. Connect the negative battery cable.
20. Recharge the refrigerant and test the system operation.

Receiver/Drier

REMOVAL AND INSTALLATION

1. Disconnect the negative battery cable.
2. Discharge the air conditioning system.
4. Disconnect the harness connector from the pressure switch.
5. Disconnect the receiver/drier inlet and outlet pipes. Cap or plug the openings immediately.
6. Plug the openings at the receiver/drier immediately.

NOTE: Keep in mind, the receiver/drier incorporates a desiccant filter. If the moisture is allowed to inner the drier, it must be replaced. The openings must be plugged immediately.

7. Remove the mounting bolts and remove the receiver/drier.

To install:

8. Position the receiver/drier into mounting bracket and install the retaining bolts. Torque the bolts to 4–7 ft. lbs. (5–4 Nm).
9 Remove the caps from the receiver hoses and from the re-

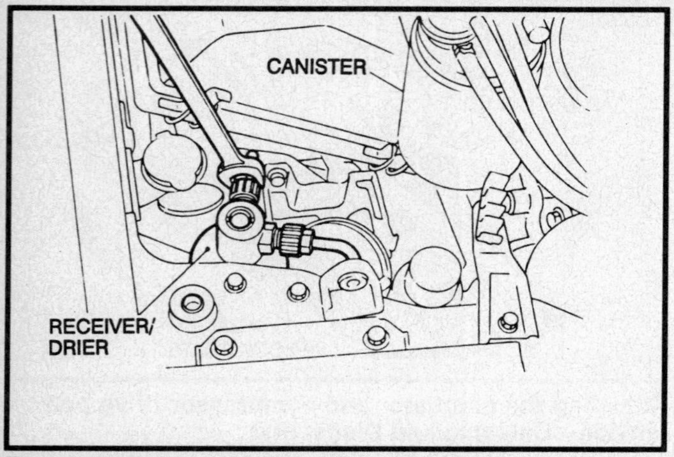
CANISTER
RECEIVER/
DRIER
Removal and installation of the receiver/drier—typical

ceiver openings. Connect the inlet and outlet pipes immediately. Torque the receiver/drier hose connections to the following:

a. Hitachi and Panasonic systems—7–14 ft. lbs. (10–20 Nm).

b. Diesel Kiki and Calsonic—4–7 ft. lbs. (5–9 Nm).

10. Evacuate, leak test and charge the system.

Expansion Valve

REMOVAL AND INSTALLATION

NOTE: In order to remove the expansion valve, the evaporator must be removed and disassembled.

1. Disconnect the negative battery cable.
2. Discharge the refrigerant system.
3. Remove the evaporator assembly from the vehicle.
4. Remove the the evaporator upper and lower case half retaining clamps. Separate the upper and lower case halfs from the evaporator.

NOTE: The thermostat capillary is inserted into evaporator fin, at a specified position. Take note to this location prior to removing it.

5. Remove the thermostat retaining screws. While holding the thermostat, carefully remove the capillary from the evaporator fins and remove the thermostat.
6. Remove the insulation from the evaporator discharge pipe wraping the expansion valve capillary tube.
7. Remove the clamp securing the capillary tube on the side of the discharge pipe.
8. Disconnect the inlet pipe from the expansion valve.
9. Disconnect the expansion valve from the evaporator fitting and remove the expansion valve.

To install:

NOTE: During the installation of the expansion valve, use all new O-rings at the pipe joints. Coat the O-rings with clean refrigerant oil.

10. Install the expansion valve to the evaporator fitting; do not tighten the fitting at this time.
11. Install the expansion valve so the capillary tubing is routed in its original position.
12. Install the expansion valve capillary tube, on the discharge pipe and secure it in place with the retaining clamp.
13. Wrap the capillary tube and discharge pipe with new insulator tape.
14. Connect the inlet pipe to the expansion valve. Torque the following:

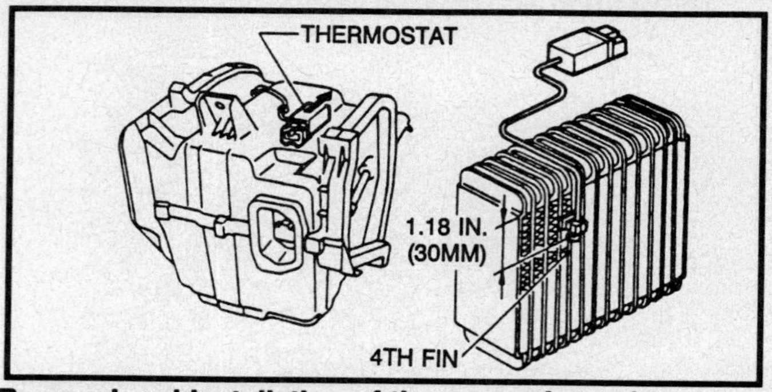
THERMOSTAT
1.18 IN.
(30MM)
4TH FIN
Removal and installation of the expansion valve

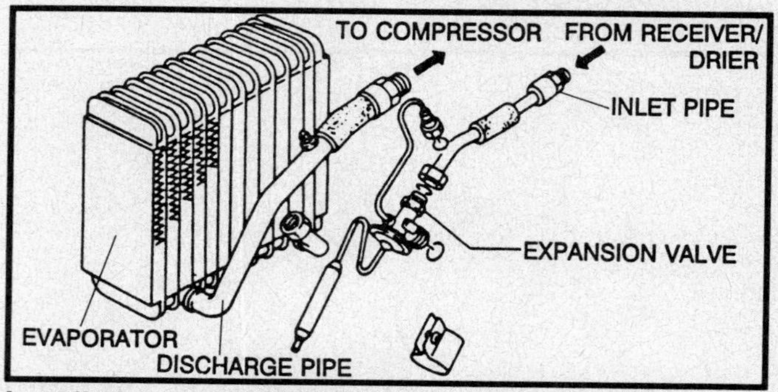
TO COMPRESSOR
FROM RECEIVER/
DRIER
INLET PIPE
EXPANSION VALVE
EVAPORATOR
DISCHARGE PIPE
Installation position of the thermostat capillary

Inlet fitting-to-expansion valve 7–14 ft. lbs. (1–2 Nm).

Evaporator-to-expansion valve 7–14 ft. lbs. (10–20 Nm).

Expansion valve sensing tube-to-discharge pipe 5–9 ft.lbs. (7–13 Nm).

15. Place the evaporator into the lower case half.
16. Install the thermostat to the upper case and insert the capillary into the evaporator fins.

NOTE: When installing the thermostat, insert the capillary tube end into the 4th core fin and to a depth of 1.2 in., on the left side of the evaporator.

17. Install the upper case half and secure with the retaining clips.
18. Install the evaporator assembly into the vehicle.
19. Connect the negative battery cable.
20. Evacuate, charge and test the system.

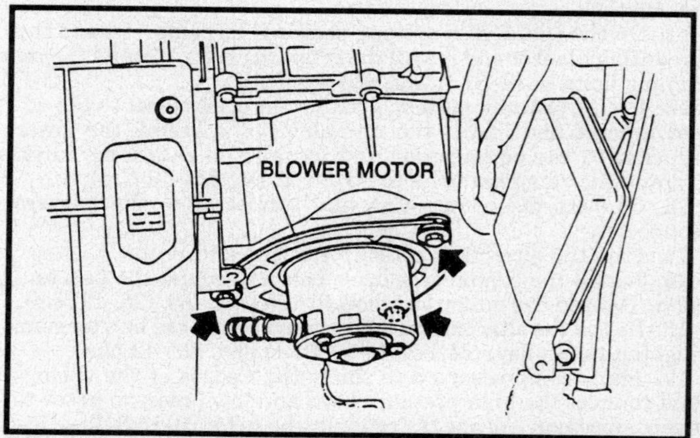
BLOWER MOTOR
Removal and installation of the blower motor assembly

Blower Motor

REMOVAL AND INSTALLATION

1. Disconnect the negative battery cable.
2. Remove the lower right trim panel retaining screws and remove the trim panel.
3. Remove the glove box.
4. Vehicles without air conditioning, remove the heater duct.
5. If equipped with air conditioning, separate the blower assembly from the evaporator unit.
6. Disconnect the blower vacuum hose from the instrument panel vacuum hose.
7. Disconnect the motor harness and resistor harness.
8. Remove the blower motor mounting bolts and nuts.
9. Remove the ventilation duct bracket and remove the blower motor from the vehicle.

To install:

10. Install the blower motor assembly and ventilation duct bracket under the dash. Install the retaining nuts and bolts. Torque the bolts and nuts to 4–7 ft. lbs. (5–9 Nm).
11. Connect the blower motor harness and resistor harness.
12. Connect the vacuum hose to instrument panel vacuum hose.

NOTE: The vacuum hose fitting must be a greater length than, 0.31 in. (8mm).

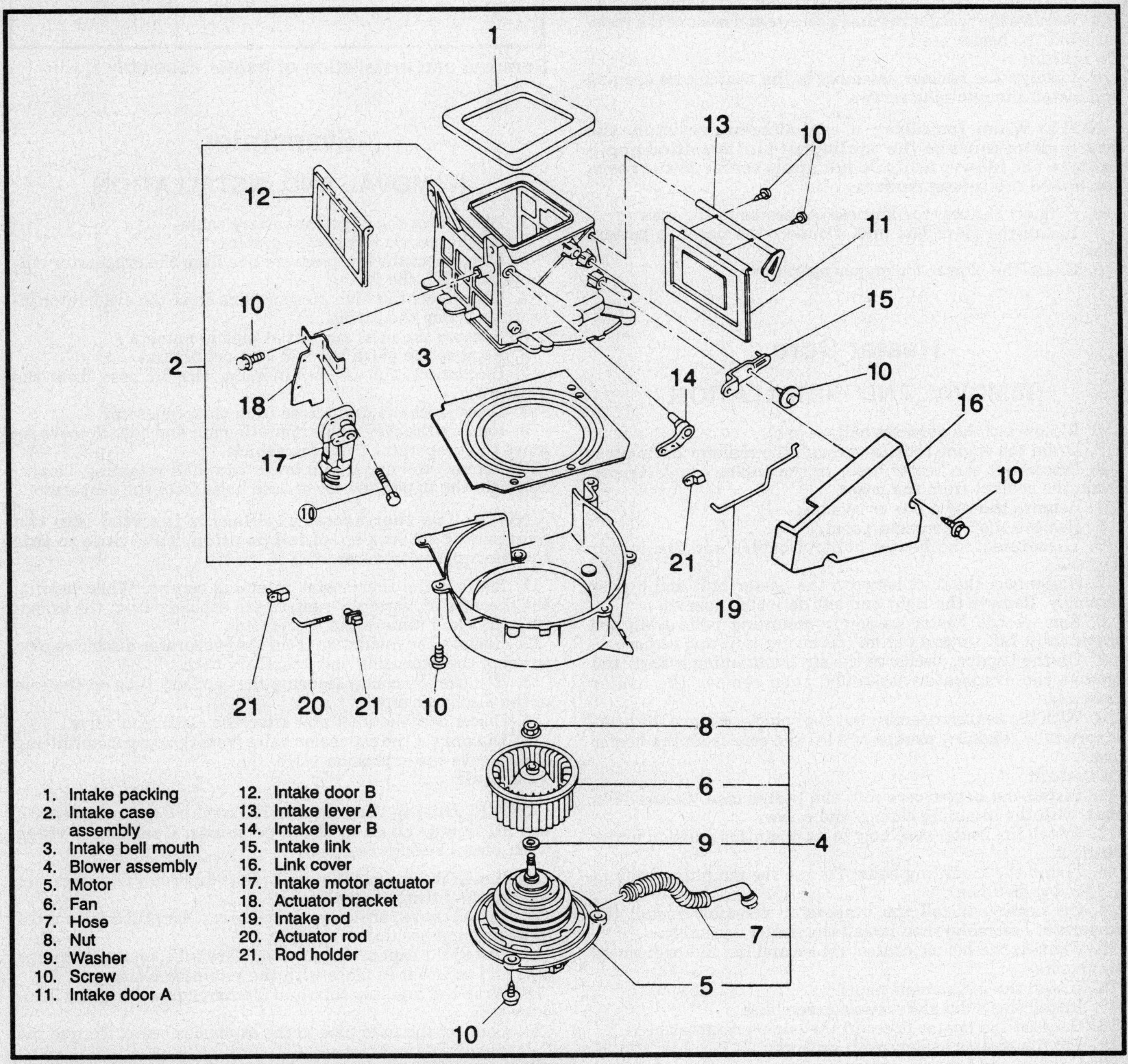
1
13
10
12
11
10
15
2
3
18
14
10
16
17
10
10
21
19
21
20
21
10
8
6
9
4
7
5
10
1. Intake packing
2. Intake case assembly
3. Intake bell mouth
4. Blower assembly
5. Motor
6. Fan
7. Hose
8. Nut
9. Washer
10. Screw
11. Intake door A
12. Intake door B
13. Intake lever A
14. Intake lever B
15. Intake link
16. Link cover
17. Intake motor actuator
18. Actuator bracket
19. Intake rod
20. Actuator rod
21. Rod holder

Exploded view of blower motor and ventilator assembly

13. Vehicles without air conditioning, install the heater duct.
14. Install the glove box, trim panel and retaining screws.
15. Connect the negative battery cable. Test the blower motor operation.

Blower Motor Resistor

REMOVAL AND INSTALLATION

1. Disconect the negative battery cable.
2. Remove the glove box unit.
3. Disconnect the resistor wire connector from the resistor.
4. Remove the resistor retaining screws and remove the resistor from the heater case.

To install:

5. Position the resistor assembly in the heater case opening and install the retaining screws.

NOTE: When installing a replacement resistor, the new resistor must be the equivalent and specified applicable to the blower unit. Do not apply sealer to the resistor board mounting surface.

6. Connect the resistor harness connector to the resistor.
7. Install the glove box unit. Connect the negative battery cable.
9. Check the blower for proper operation.

Heater Core

REMOVAL AND INSTALLATION

1. Disconnect the negative battery cable.
2. Drain the engine coolant through the radiator drain plug.
3. Disconnect the heater hoses in the engine compartment. Drain the coolant from the hoses.
4. Remove the radio box or console.
5. Remove the instrument panel.
6. Disconnect the heater control cables and fan motor harness.
7. Disconnect the duct between the heater unit and blower assembly. Remove the right and left defroster nozzles.
8. Remove the heater assembly mounting bolts from the heater unit. Lift up and out on the heater unit and remove.
9. On the Legacy, discharge the air conditioning system and remove the evaporator assembly, then remove the heater assembly.
10. With the heater assembly out the vehicle, remove the heater core tube retaining clamps and lift the core from the heater case.

To install:

11. Install the heater core into the heater case. Secure it in place with the retaining clamps and screws.
12. Install the heater assembly to its mounting position under the dash.
13. Install the mounting bolts. Torque the mounting bolts to 4–7 ft. lbs. (5–9 Nm).
14. On Legacy, install the evaporator assembly install the evaporator assembly, then install the heater assembly.
15. Connect the heater control cables and fan motor harness connectors.
16. Install the instrument panel.
17. Install the radio and console assemblies.
18. Connect the heater hoses in the engine compartment.
19. Fill the cooling system with coolant.
20. Connect the negative battery cable.

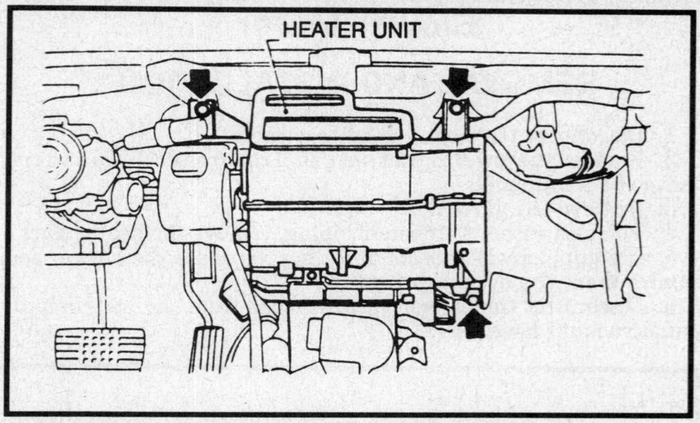
HEATER UNIT
Removal and installation of heater assembly

Evaporator

REMOVAL AND INSTALLATION

1. Disconnect the negative battery cable.
2. Discharge the refrigerant system.
3. Disconnect the low pressure line from the evaporator outlet fitting. Cap the fitting.
4. Disconnect the high pressure line from the evaporator inlet fitting. Cap the fitting.
5. Remove the inlet and outlet pipe grommets.
6. Remove the glove box and support bracket.
7. Disconnect the air conditioning wire harness from the evaporator.
8. Disconnect the drain hose from the evaporator.
9. Remove the evaporator mounting nut and bolt. Remove remove the evaporator from the vehicle.
10. Remove the upper and lower case half retaining clamps. Separate the upper and lower case halfs from the evaporator.

NOTE: The thermostat capillary is inserted into the evaporator fin at a specified position. Take note to this location prior to removing it.

11. Remove the thermostat retaining screws. While holding the thermostat, carefully remove the capillary from the evaporator fins and remove the thermostat.
12. Remove the insulation from the evaporator discharge pipe wraping the expansion valve capillary tube.
13. Remove the clamp securing the capillary tube on the side of the discharge pipe.
14. Disconnect the inlet pipe from the expansion valve.
15. Disconnect the expansion valve from the evaporator fitting and remove the expansion valve.

To install:

NOTE: During the installation of the expansion valve, use all new O-rings at the pipe joints. Coat the O-rings with clean refrigerant oil.

16. Install the expansion valve to the evaporator fitting; do not tighten the fitting at this time.
17. Install the expansion valve so the capillary tubing is routed in its original position.
18. Install the expansion valve capillary tube, on the discharge pipe and secure it in place with the retaining clamp.
19. Wrap the capillary tube and discharge pipe with new insulator tape.
20. Connect the inlet pipe to the expansion valve. Torque the following:

Inlet fitting-to-expansion valve 7–14 ft. lbs. (1–2 Nm).

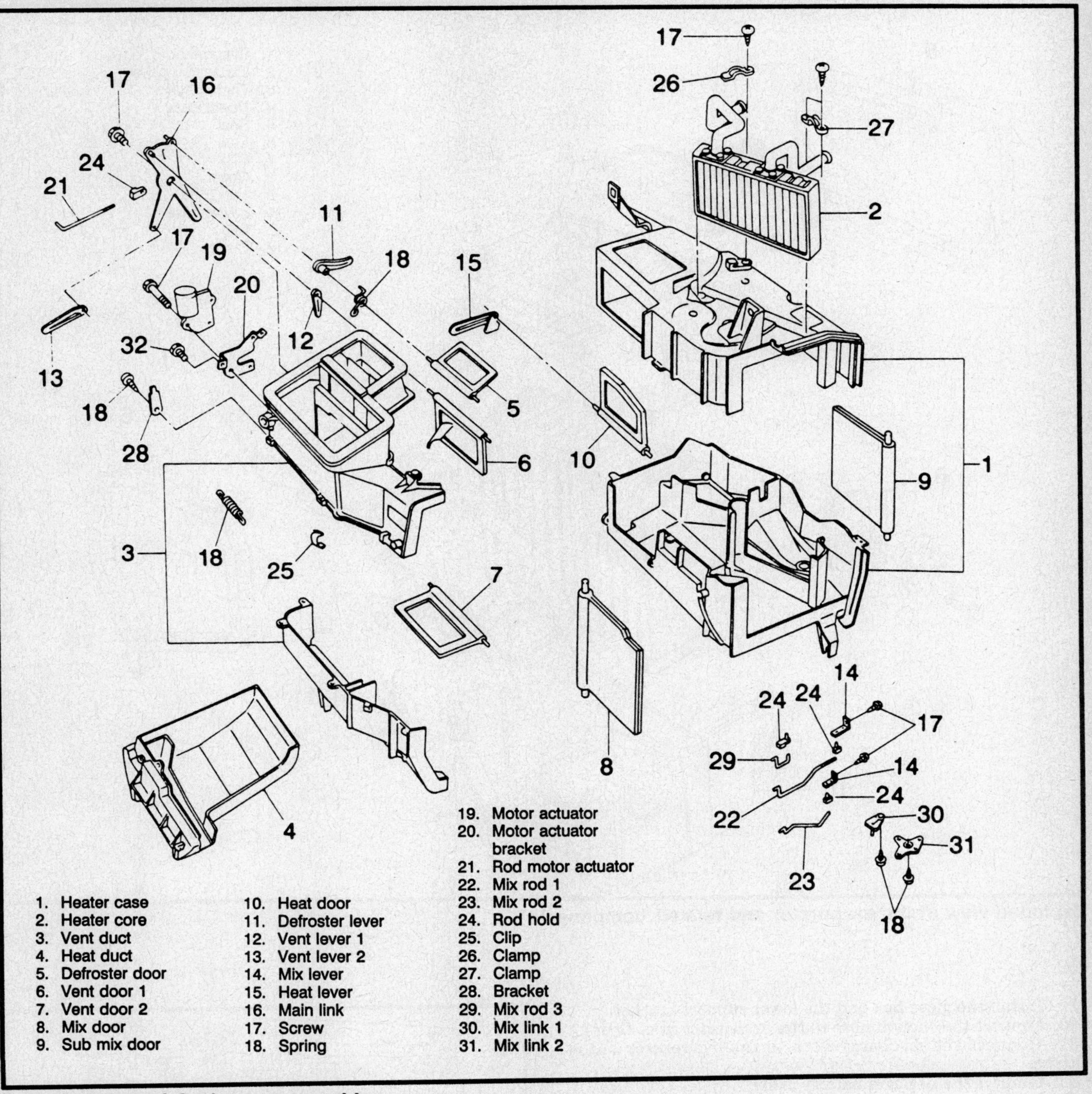
1. Heater case
2. Heater core
3. Vent duct
4. Heat duct
5. Defroster door
6. Vent door 1
7. Vent door 2
8. Mix door
9. Sub mix door
10. Heat door
11. Defroster lever
12. Vent lever 1
13. Vent lever 2
14. Mix lever
15. Heat lever
16. Main link
17. Screw
18. Spring
19. Motor actuator
20. Motor actuator bracket
21. Rod motor actuator
22. Mix rod 1
23. Mix rod 2
24. Rod hold
25. Clip
26. Clamp
27. Clamp
28. Bracket
29. Mix rod 3
30. Mix link 1
31. Mix link 2

Exploded view of the heater assembly

Evaporator-to-expansion valve 7–14 ft. lbs. (10–20 Nm).

Expansion valve sensing tube-to-discharge pipe 5–9 ft. lbs. (7–13 Nm).

21. Place the evaporator into the lower case half.
22. Install the thermostat to the upper case and insert the thermister into the evaporator fins.

NOTE: When installing the thermostat, insert the capillary tube end into the 4th core fin and to a depth of 1.2 in., on the left side of the evaporator.

23. Install the upper case half and secure with the retaining clips.
24. Install the evaporator assembly under the dash and into the mounting position. Install the retaining nut and and bolt.
25. Adjust the position of the evaporator assembly so the inlet and outlet connections are aligned with the heater and blower unit connections.
26. Install the drain hose.
27. Connect the air conditioning wire harness.
28. Install the inlet and outlet pipe grommets.

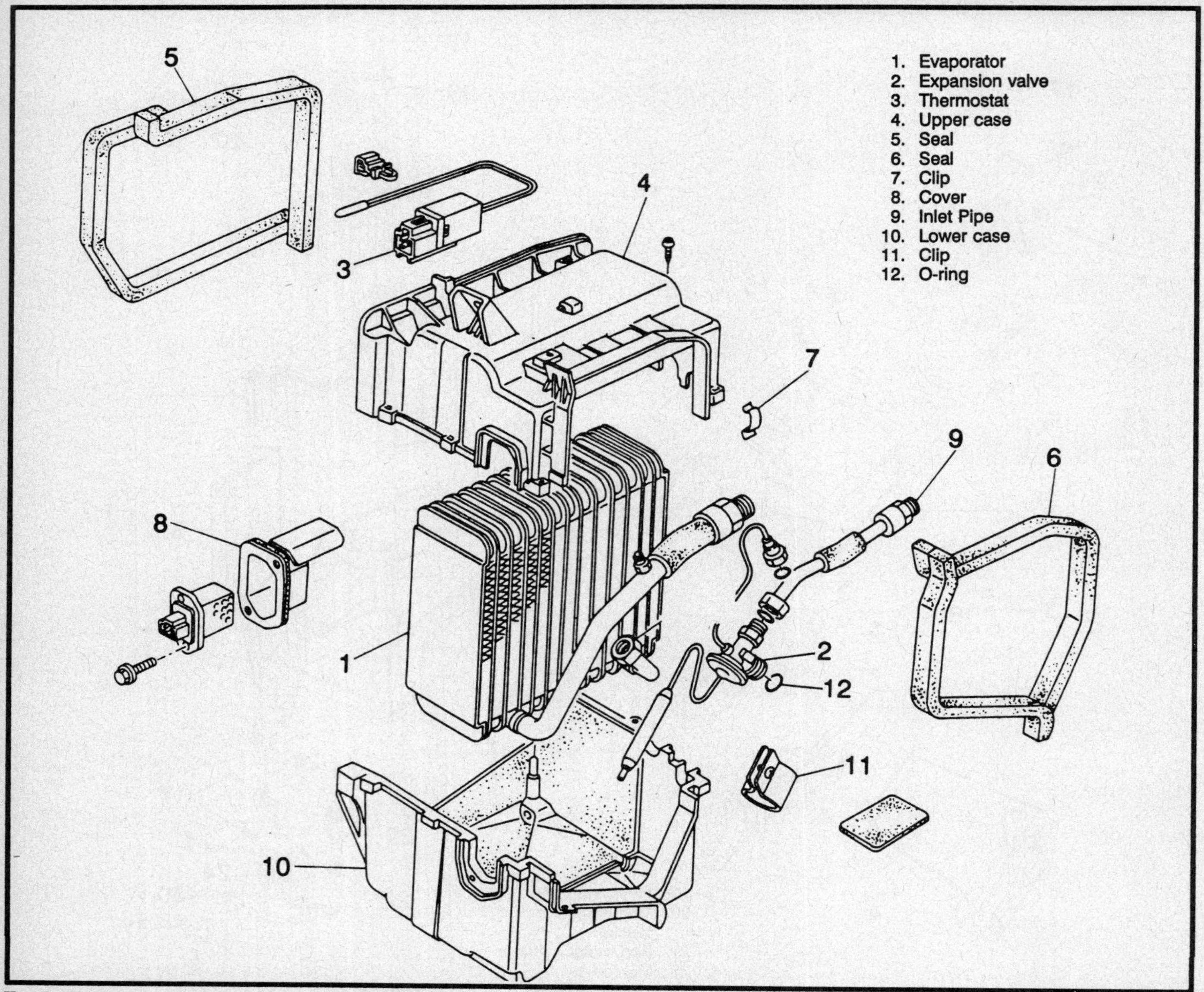
1. Evaporator
2. Expansion valve
3. Thermostat
4. Upper case
5. Seal
6. Seal
7. Clip
8. Cover
9. Inlet Pipe
10. Lower case
11. Clip
12. O-ring

Exploded view of the evaporator and related components

29. Install the glove box and the lower support bracket.
30. Connect the suction hose to the evaporator inlet fitting.
31. Connect the discharge hose to the evaporator outlet fitting.
32. Connect the negative battery cable.
33. Evacuate, charge and test the system.

Refrigerant Lines

REMOVAL AND INSTALLATION

1. When disconnecting or connecting refrigerant lines, always use 2 wrenches.
2. Use protective plugs and plug each open line, to prevent contamination and moisture from entering the lines and related components.

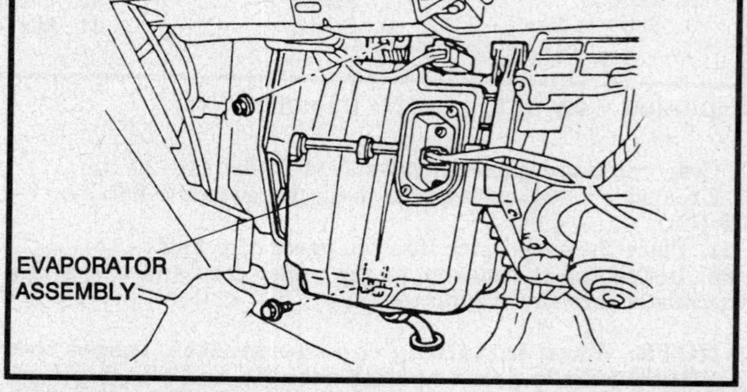
EVAPORATOR
ASSEMBLY

Removal and installation of the evaporator assembly

3. Clean contaminated O-rings during installation. Never use compressed air. Use only new O-rings during installation.
4. Coat the new O-ring with compressor oil prior to installation.
5. Install the O-ring against the shoulder to ensure proper seating.
6. When connecting 2 lines together, insert the tube section into the union and tighten the retaining nut by hand. Then, tighten the nut to 29–33 ft. lbs. (39–44 Nm).

Manual Control Head

REMOVAL AND INSTALLATION

XT Coupe

1. Disconnect the negative battery cable.
2. Remove the lower instrument panel cover retaining screws and remove the cover.
3. Remove the screws retaining the steering column cover and remove the cover.
4. Remove the screws which hold the combination switch to the control wing bracket.
5. Remove the harness retaining clips from the lower section of the meter.
6. Remove the retaining band which holds the harness to the steering column.
7. Remove the control wing retaining bolts and remove the control wing.

To install:

8. Install the control wing to the column and install the retaining bolts.
9. Secure the harness to the steering column with the retaining band and install the retaining clips.
10. Place the combination switch on the control wing bracket and install it at the lower section of the meter.
11. Install the steering column cover and retaining screws.
12. Install the lower instrument panel cover and retaining screws.
13. Connect the negative battery cable. Test the control switch operation.

Loyale and Sedan

1. Disconnect the negative battery cable.
2. Remove the temperature cable from the heater unit.
3. Remove the control knobs DEF, OFF, TEMP, from the mode and panel assembly.
4. Remove the visor from the instrument panel.
5. Remove the heater control from the visor by removing the retaining screws.

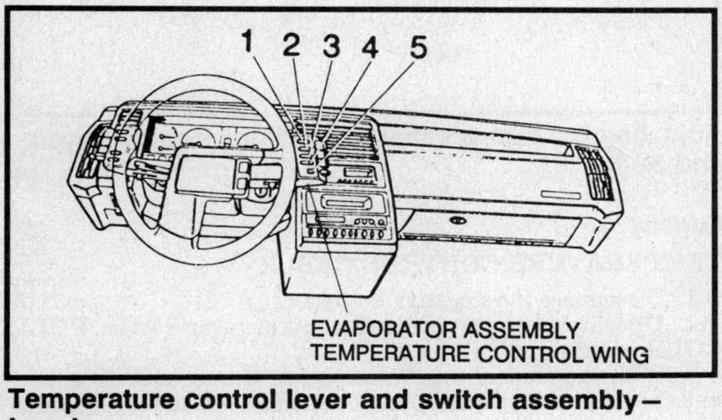
1
2
3
4
5
EVAPORATOR ASSEMBLY
TEMPERATURE CONTROL WING

Temperature control lever and switch assembly—Loyale

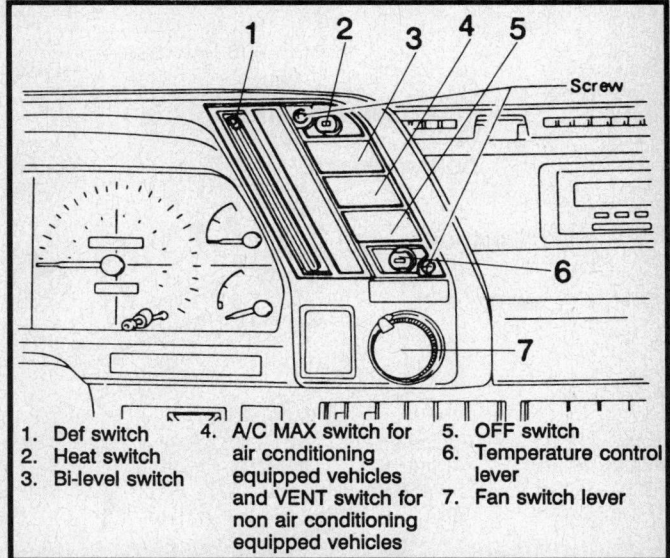

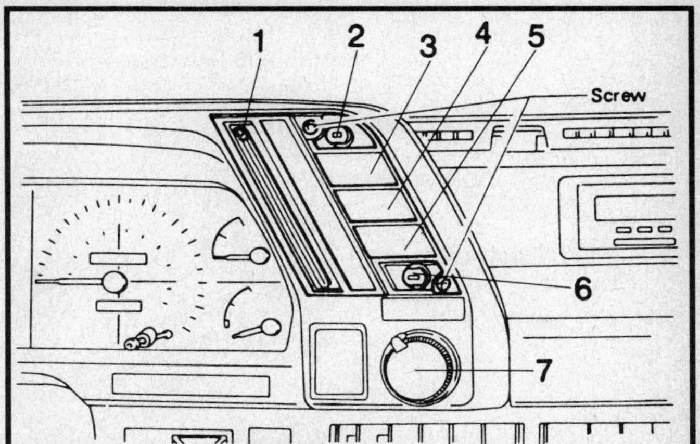
1
2
3
4
5
Screw
6
7
1. Def switch
2. Heat switch
3. Bi-level switch
4. A/C MAX switch for air conditioning equipped vehicles and VENT switch for non air conditioning equipped vehicles
5. OFF switch
6. Temperature control lever
7. Fan switch lever

Removal and installation of the temperature control unit—Legacy

6. Remove the vacuum hose from the mode pad panel assembly.
7. Separate the temperature control assembly from the mode and panel assembly by loosening the screws.
8. Remove the screws from the mode and panel assembly.
9. Remove the mode and panel assembly and the and the temperature control assembly.

To install:

10. Install the temperature control assembly to the dash.
11. Install the mode and panel assembly to the dash. Install the bulbs into the assembly.
12. Install the retaining screws and secure the mode and panel assembly in place.
13. Install the vacuum hose to the mode pad panel assembly.
14. Install the heater control to the visor and secure it in place with the retaining screws.
15. Install the visor to the instrument panel.
16. Install controls knobs to the panel assembly.
17. Connect the temperature cable to the heater unit.
18. Connect the negative battery cable. Test the control switch operation.

Legacy

1. Disconnect the negative battery cable.
2. Remove the temperature cable from the heater unit.
3. Remove the visor from the instrument panel.
4. Disconnect the temperature control unit harness connectors.
5. Remove the temperature control unit retaining screws and remove the control unit from the dash.

To install:

6. Install the temperature control unit to the dash and secure it in place with the retaining screws.
7. Connect the temperature control unit harness connectors.
8. Install the visor to the instrument panel.
9. Connect the temperature control cable to the heater unit.
10. Connect the negative battery cable. Test the control switch operation.

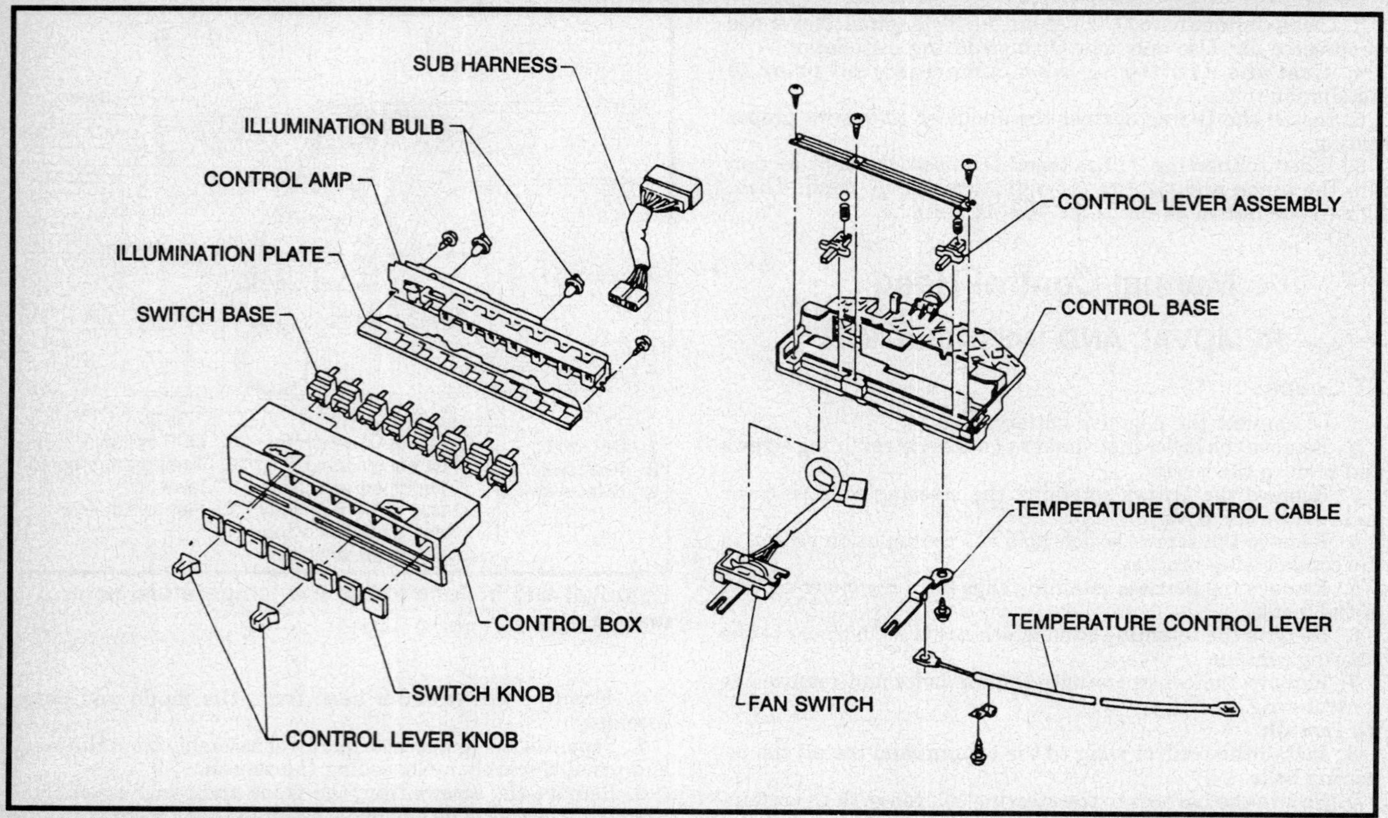
SUB HARNESS
ILLUMINATION BULB
CONTROL AMP
ILLUMINATION PLATE
SWITCH BASE
CONTROL BOX
SWITCH KNOB
CONTROL LEVER KNOB
CONTROL LEVER ASSEMBLY
CONTROL BASE
TEMPERATURE CONTROL CABLE
TEMPERATURE CONTROL LEVER
FAN SWITCH

Exploded view of the temperature control unit– Legacy

Manual Control Cables

ADJUSTMENT

XT Coupe

The manual control cable is preset at the factory; do not remove it at the base. If the cable is out of adjustment, the cable and fan lever switch are replaced as a unit.

Loyale and Sedan

RAM PRESSURE VENTILATION CABLE

1. Disconnect the negative battery cable.
2. Remove the lower trim panel retaining screws and remove the panel from the instrument panel lower section.
3. Remove the fuse box retaining screws and remove the fuse box.
4. Remove the ram pressure ventilation cable from the retaining clip.
5. Set the ventilation lever to **A/C** for USA vehicles and to **VENT** for Canadian vehicles.
6. Set the inner cable end to the **FULL UP** position and apply pressure to the lever in this position.
7. Pull the outer cable down.
8. While holding the 2 cables in this position, set the locking clip in place.
9. Run the vehicle and check for air leakage.
10. Install the fuse box and retaining screws.
11. Install the lower trim panel to the instrument panel and install the retaining screws.
12. Connect the negative battery cable.

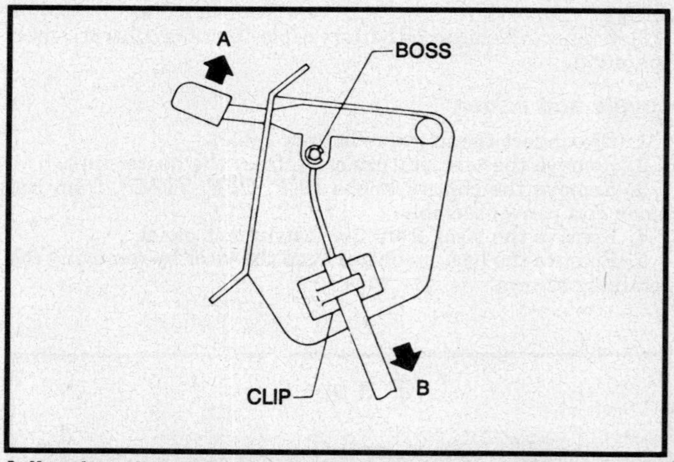
A
BOSS
CLIP
B

Adjusting the ram pressure ventilation cable–Loyale and Sedan

Legacy

TEMPERATURE CONTROL CABLE

1. Disconnect the negative battery cable.
2. Operate the temperature control lever to the **FULL COLD** position.
3. With the control cable attached to the air mix door link, pull the outer cable out and push the inner cable in the opposite direction.

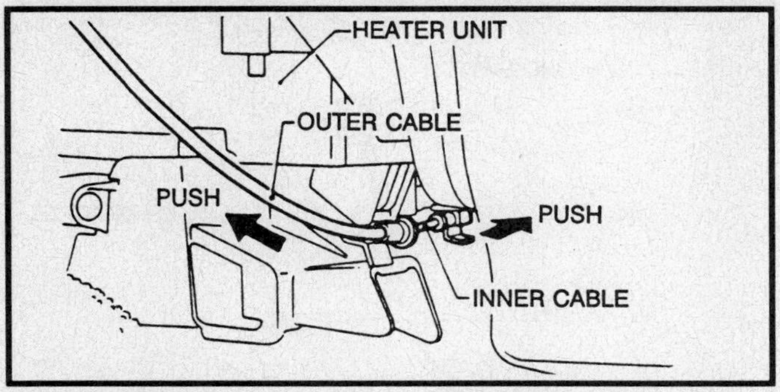
HEATER UNIT
OUTER CABLE
PUSH
PUSH
INNER CABLE

Adjusting the temperature control cable—Legacy

4. Secure the cable in this position with the retaining clamp.
5. Operate the temperature control lever and check freedom of movement at full stroke range.
6. Connect the negative battery cable.

REMOVAL AND INSTALLATION

1. Disconnect the negative battery cable.
2. Remove the instrument panel visor retaining screws and remove the visor from the dash.
3. Disconnect the clip securing the control cable to the control lever and lift the cable from the lever.
4. From the heater unit, remove the temperature cable retaining clamp and disconnect the cable from the mix door link.
6. Remove the cable from under the dash.

To install:

7. Install the new cable under the dash and route it up to the temperature control unit.
8. Connect the cable to the control lever. Adjust as required and install the retaining clip.
9. Install the instrument visor and the retaining screws.
10. Connect the opposite end of the control cable to the mix door link at the heater unit. Adjust, as required.
11. Connect the negative battery cable.

SENSORS AND SWITCHES

Fast Idle Control Device (FICD)

OPERATION

The fast idle control device is of the solenoid valve type and is incorporated in the throttle body of the SPFI and MPFI fuel injection system. This system operates when the air conditioner is turned on. The idle speed need not be adjusted. It will automatically adjust its self to a 850 rpm, ± 50 rpm.

The fast idle control device is controlled by the Electronic Control Unit (ECU), activated through the air conditioning compressor circuit.

TESTING

1. Start the engine and allow it to warm up.
2. Connect a tachometer to the engine and observe the engine idle rpm. The idle should be between 700–800 rpm when the air conditioning system is off.
3. Energize the air condtioning system. The idle should automatically adjust its self to a 850 rpm, ± 50 rpm.
4. If the idle does not change, connect a test light and check for current at the fast idle control device. If current is evident, disconnect the electrical connector at the fast idle control device. If the fast idle control device is operating, the engine rpm will drop when the compressor is engaged.
5. If there was no change in rpm, the fast idle control device may be at fault. To confirm this, turn the engine **OFF**. Connect a 12 volt source directly to it intermitently. A noticeable clicking from the device will be heard if the device is working. If there is no response, the device is defective.

REMOVAL AND INSTALLATION

1. Disconnect the negative battery cable.
2. Disconnect the electrical connector at the fast idle control device.
3. Unscrew the device from the throttle body.

To install:

4. Screw the fast idle control device to the throttle body.
5. Connect the electrical connector to the device.
6. Connect the negative battery cable and test the device.

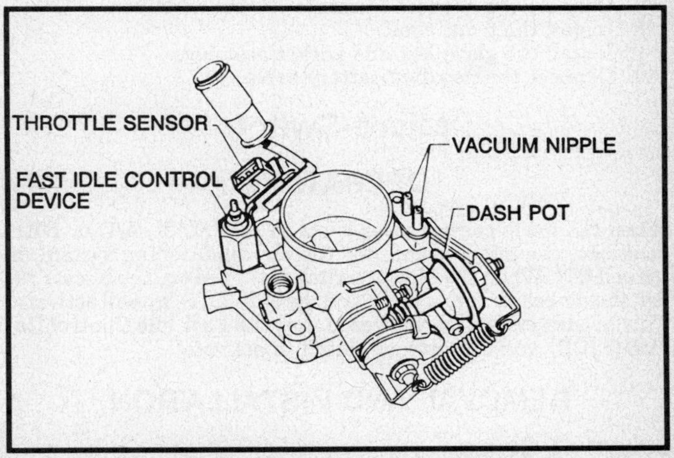
THROTTLE SENSOR
VACUUM NIPPLE
FAST IDLE CONTROL DEVICE
DASH POT

Location of the Fast Idle Control Device (FICD)

Pulser Amplifier

OPERATION

Whenever the compressor rpm drops below a specific value, the belt protection system quickly turns off the magnetic clutch of the compressor. This allows the operation to the alternator, water pump and power steering units to operate normally and also prevents breakage or damage to the compressor belt.

To control the belt protection system, the ratio of the compressor rpm to the engine rpm is monitored by a pulse amplifier. When the compressor rpm drops more than 20–25 percent below the normal rpm, the systems determines if the compressor is locked and turns off the magnetic clutch of the compressor.

When the systems detected a locked compressor and turned the air conditioning system off, the magnetic clutch will remain off until the air conditioning switch is turned offand turned on again.

TESTING

1. Start the engine. Turn the air conditioning switch, blower switch and high/low switch, to the **ON** positions.
2. Disconnect the 2 pin pole connector from the pulser amplifier.
3. Observe the compressor magnetic clutch reaction, it should turn off.
4. If not, perform a continuity test of the wiring circuit from the amplifier to the negative side of the ignition coil.
5. If continuity does not exist, the wiring circuit is faulty.
6. If continuity exits, disconnect the wire at the air conditioning relay exicting coil, leading to the amplifier. If the magnetic clutch turns off the amplifier is at fault.
7. If the magnetic clutch remains on, the relay is at fault.

REMOVAL AND INSTALLATION

1. Disconnect the negative battery cable.
2. Remove the glove box and pocket assembly.
3. Remove the front shelf.
4. Disconnect the harness connector at the pulser amplifier.
5. Remove the amplifier-to-evaporator retaining bolt and remove the amplifier.

To install:

6. Install the pulser amplifier to the evaporator and install the retaining bolt.
7. Connect the harness connector to the amplifier.
8. Install the front shelf.
9. Install the glove box and pocket assmbly.
10. Connect the negative battery cable.

Micro-Switch

OPERATION

When the mode control lever is set to **A/C MAX, A/C** or **DEF** positions, the micro-switch for the air conditioning system, is turned **ON**. When the blower switch is turned on, the blower relay, the air conditioning relay and the sub-fan relay will activate. This in turn causes the blower motor, the Fast Idle Control Device (FICD) and compressor clutch to activate.

REMOVAL AND INSTALLATION

Except XT Coupe

1. Disconnect the negative battery cable.
2. The micro-switch is located on the left side of the heater/evaporator unit.

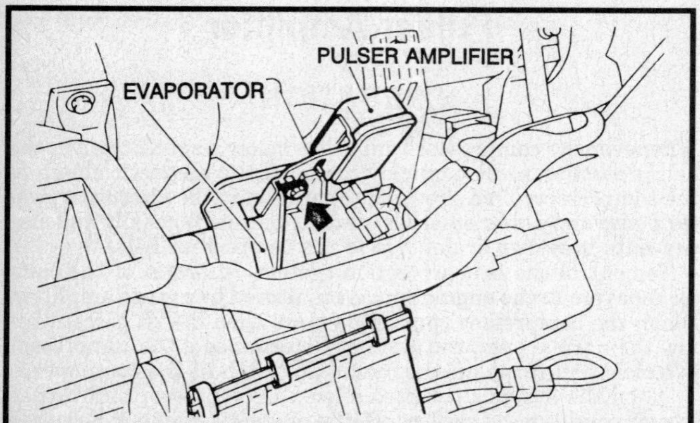
PULSER AMPLIFIER
EVAPORATOR
Removal and installation of the pulser amplifier

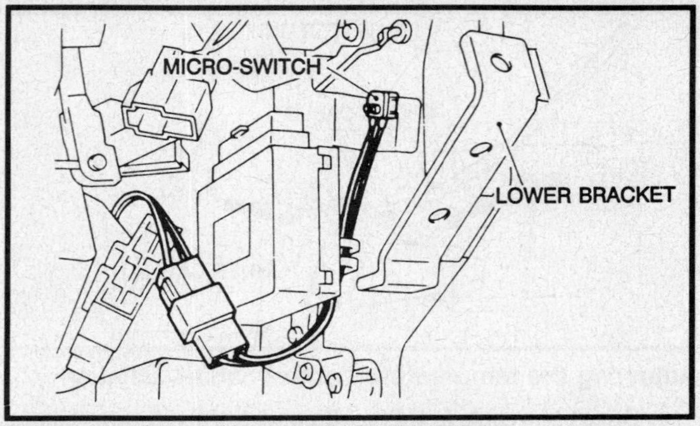
MICRO-SWITCH
LOWER BRACKET
Location of the mircroswitch – Loyale

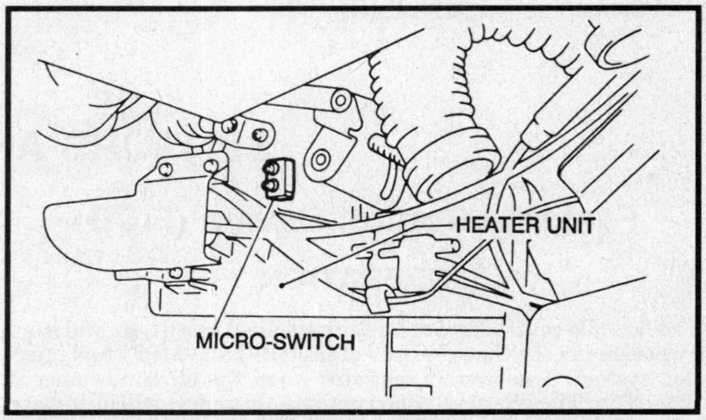
HEATER UNIT
MICRO-SWITCH
Location of the mircroswitch – except XT Coupe

3. Remove the lower left instrument trim panel retaining screws. Remove the trim panel.
4. Remove the micro-switch bracket retaining screws and remove the micro-switch and bracket, as an assembly.

To install:

5. Install the micro-switch in mounting position to the heater/evaporator unit. Secure it in place with the retaining screws.
6. Install the lower trim panel and install the retaining screws.
7. Connect the negative battery cable.

XT Coupe

1. Disconnect the negative battery cable.
2. Select the **HEAT** mode on the control wing.
3. Lift up on the steering wheel.
4. Remove the left lower instrument panel cover.
5. Remove the left side ventilation duct.
6. Disconnect the harness connector from the micro-switch.
7. Push the harness up out of the way that comes from the meter assembly.
8. Remove the bracket retaining screws. Remove the micro-switch and bracket as an assembly.

To install:

9. Install the micro-switch in position and secure it in place with the retaining screws.
10. Connect the harness connector to the micro-switch.
11. Install the left side ventilation duct.
12. Install the lower trim panel and install the retaining screws.
13. Connect the negative battery cable.

Pressure Switch

REMOVAL AND INSTALLATION

The pressure switch is located on either the receiver/drier or on the refrigerant line between the receiver/drier and evaporator.

1. Disconnect the negative battery cable.
2. Discharge the refrigerant from the air conditioning system.
3. If the pressure switch is located on the refrigerant line, remove the charcoal canister and place it on the engine.
4. Disconnect the pressure switch and harness connections.
5. Unscrew the pressure switch from the refrigerant line and remove.
6. If the pressure switch located on the receiver/drier, disconnect the harness connector and unclip the harness from its mounting point.
7. Unscrew the pressure switch from the receiver/drier and remove.

To install:

8. If the pressure switch located on the receiver/drier; thread the pressure switch into the receiver/drier.
9. Connect the harness connector and secure the harness in place, to the reciever/drier.
10. If the pressure switch located on the refrigerant line; thread the pressure switch into refrigerant line.
11. Connect the harness and pressure switch connections.
12. Place the charcoal canister in the mounting bracket a secure it in place.
13. Connect the negative battery cable.
14. Evacuate and recharge the refrigerant in the system.

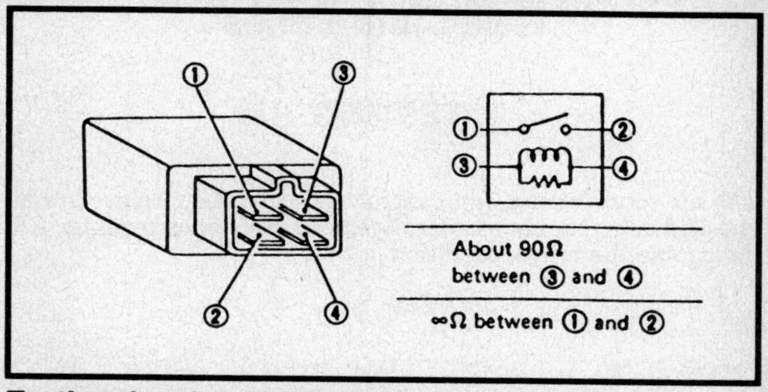
About 90Ω
between ③ and ④
∞Ω between ① and ②
Testing the air conditioning or fan control relay—Panasonic

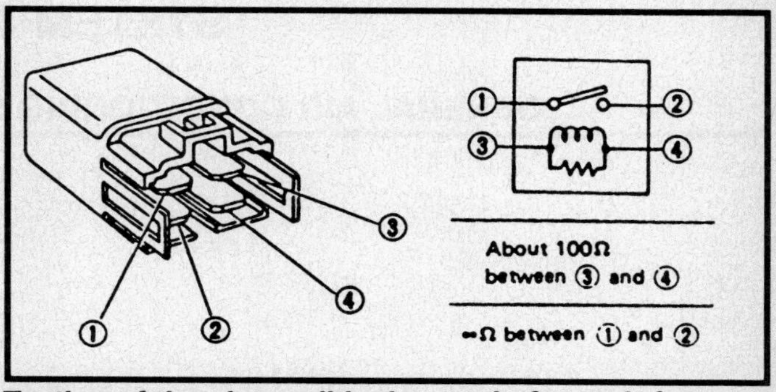
About 100Ω
between ③ and ④
∞Ω between ① and ②
Testing of the air conditioning, main fan, sub fan or fan control relay—Diesel Kiki and Calsonic

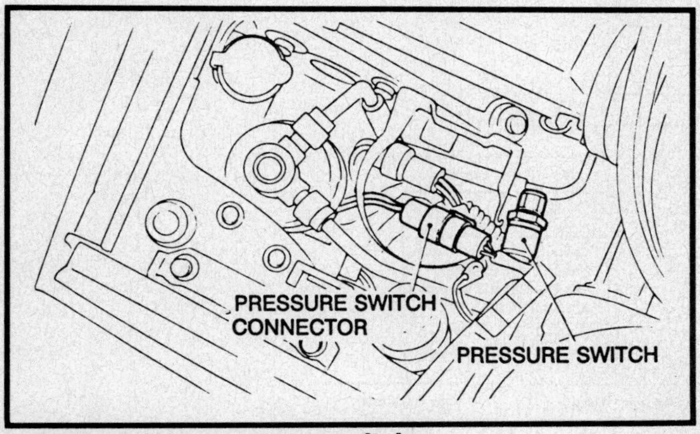
PRESSURE SWITCH
CONNECTOR
PRESSURE SWITCH
Location of the pressure switch

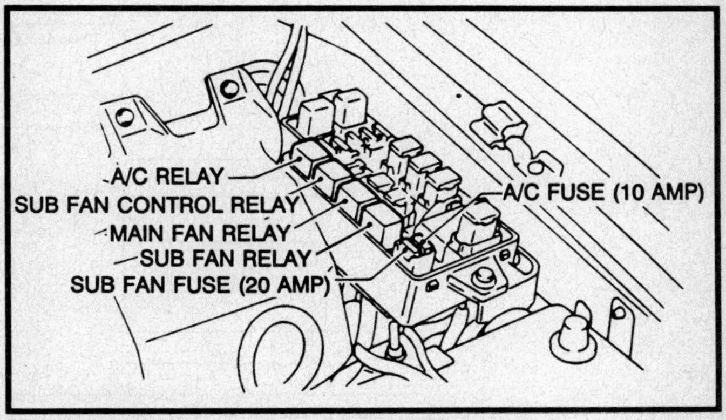
A/C RELAY
SUB FAN CONTROL RELAY
MAIN FAN RELAY
SUB FAN RELAY
SUB FAN FUSE (20 AMP)
A/C FUSE (10 AMP)
Location of the relays and fuses—Legacy

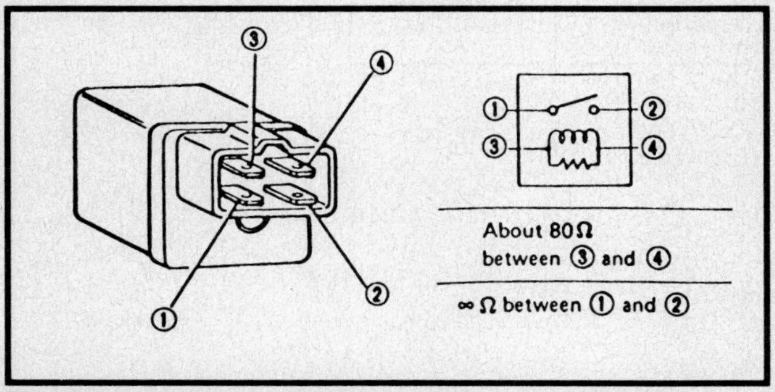
About 80Ω
between ③ and ④
∞Ω between ① and ②
Testing the air conditioning or fan control relay—Hatachi

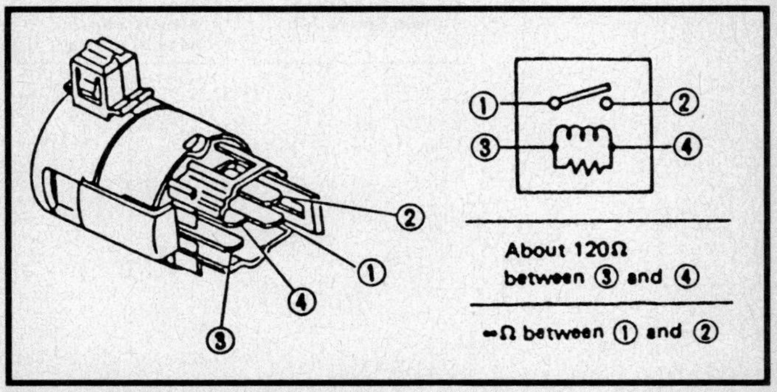
About 120Ω
between ③ and ④
∞Ω between ① and ②
Testing the air conditioning cut out relay—Diesel Kiki and Calsonic

Relay and Fuses

TESTING

The air conditioning, fan control and condenser relays are all checked using an ohm meter. Specified resistance readings will determine the relays condition.

REMOVAL AND INSTALLATION

The air conditioning relay, the main fan control relay and air conditioner fuse are located in the engine compartment.

1. Disconnect the negative battery cable.
2. Disconnect the harness connector from the relay.
3. Remove the retaining bolts securing the relay to the side of the fender apron.
4. Remove the relay.
5. Installation is the reverse of the removal procedure.

SYSTEM DIAGNOSIS

GENERAL AIR CONDITIONING SYSTEM DIAGNOSIS—XT COUPE

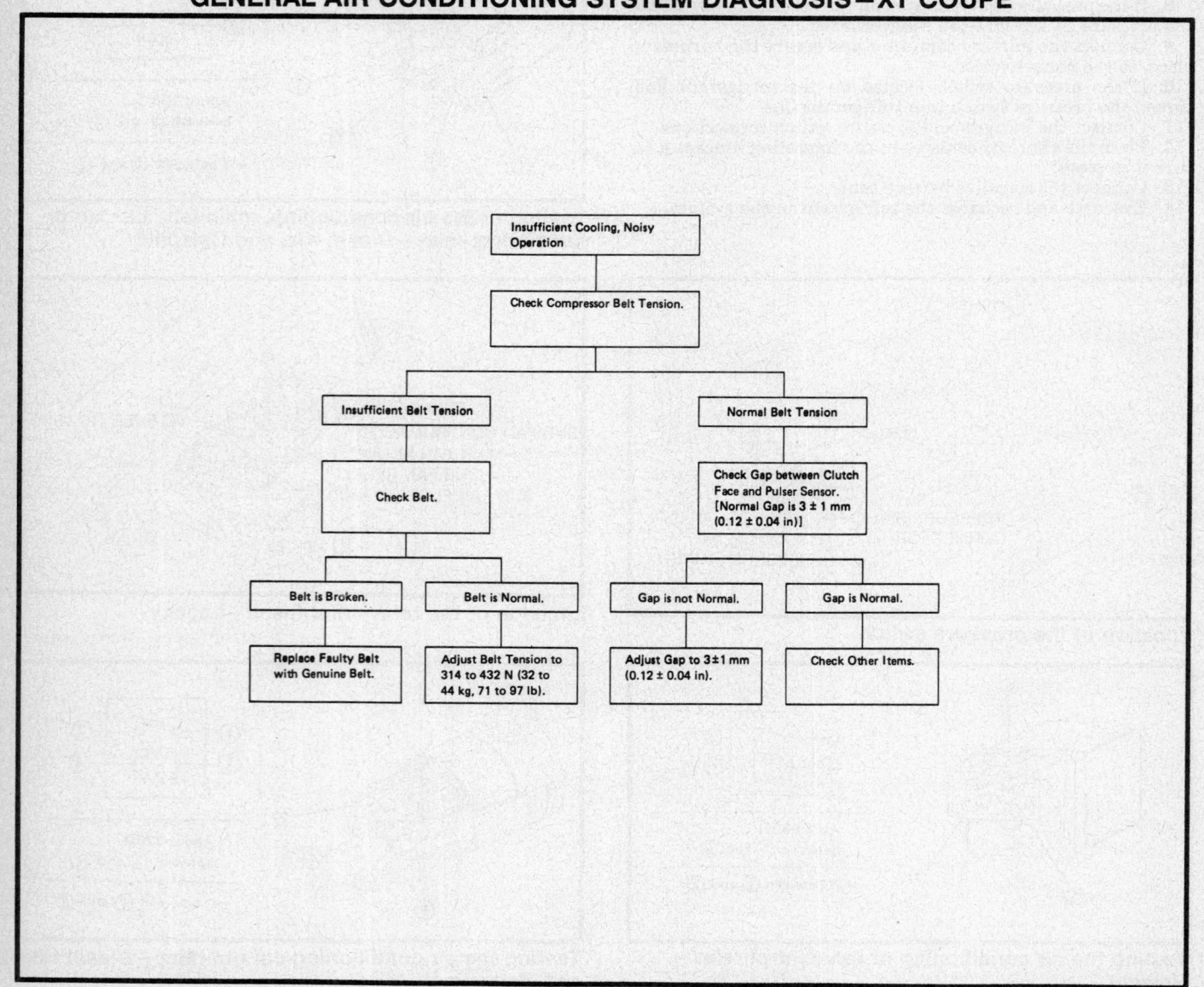

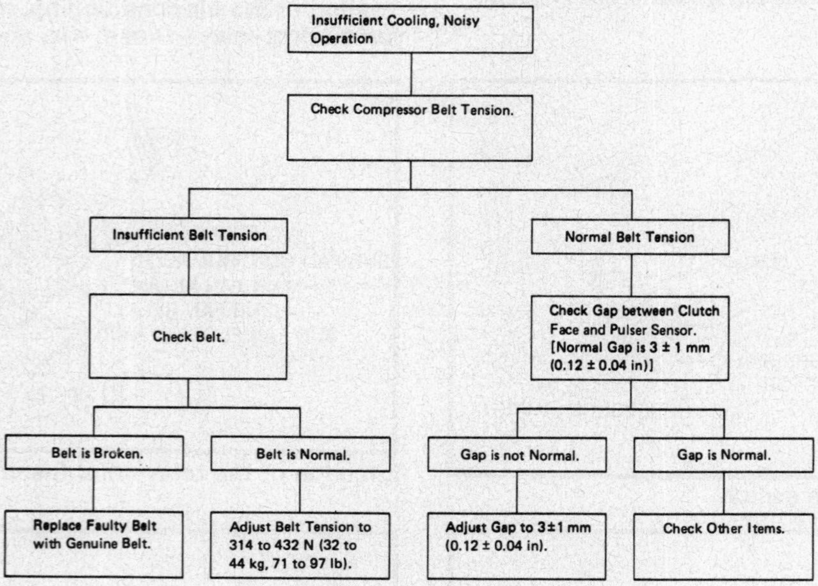
Insufficient Cooling, Noisy Operation
Check Compressor Belt Tension.
Insufficient Belt Tension
Normal Belt Tension
Check Belt.
Check Gap between Clutch Face and Pulser Sensor. [Normal Gap is 3 ± 1 mm (0.12 ± 0.04 in)]
Belt is Broken.
Belt is Normal.
Gap is not Normal.
Gap is Normal.
Replace Faulty Belt with Genuine Belt.
Adjust Belt Tension to 314 to 432 N (32 to 44 kg, 71 to 97 lb).
Adjust Gap to 3±1 mm (0.12 ± 0.04 in).
Check Other Items.

GENERAL AIR CONDITIONING SYSTEM DIAGNOSIS—XT COUPE

- **Noisy**
  - **Compressor OFF**
    - Blower makes noise. Repair or replace blower.
    - Bearings of compressor clutch or idler pulley make noise. Repair.
  - **Compressor ON**
    - Compressor itself makes noise. Repair or replace compressor.
    - Belt is loose. Adjust belt.
    - When engine rpm is changed, there are resonant sounds. Retighten compressor bracket bolts. Piping is resonating. Add cramp.
- **Insufficient cooling**
  - **Bubbles in sight glass**
    - Check refrigeration line for gas leaks, and repair leaks if any. Charge refrigerant to correct level. In case of too many leaks, stop compressor, discharge the system, evacuate and recharge the system. As necessary, replace receiver drier.
      Air in system may cause bubbles in sight glass.
  - **No bubbles in sight glass**
    - With manifold gauge, check system pressures. Measure temperature of discharge air. Refer to "Performance Test".

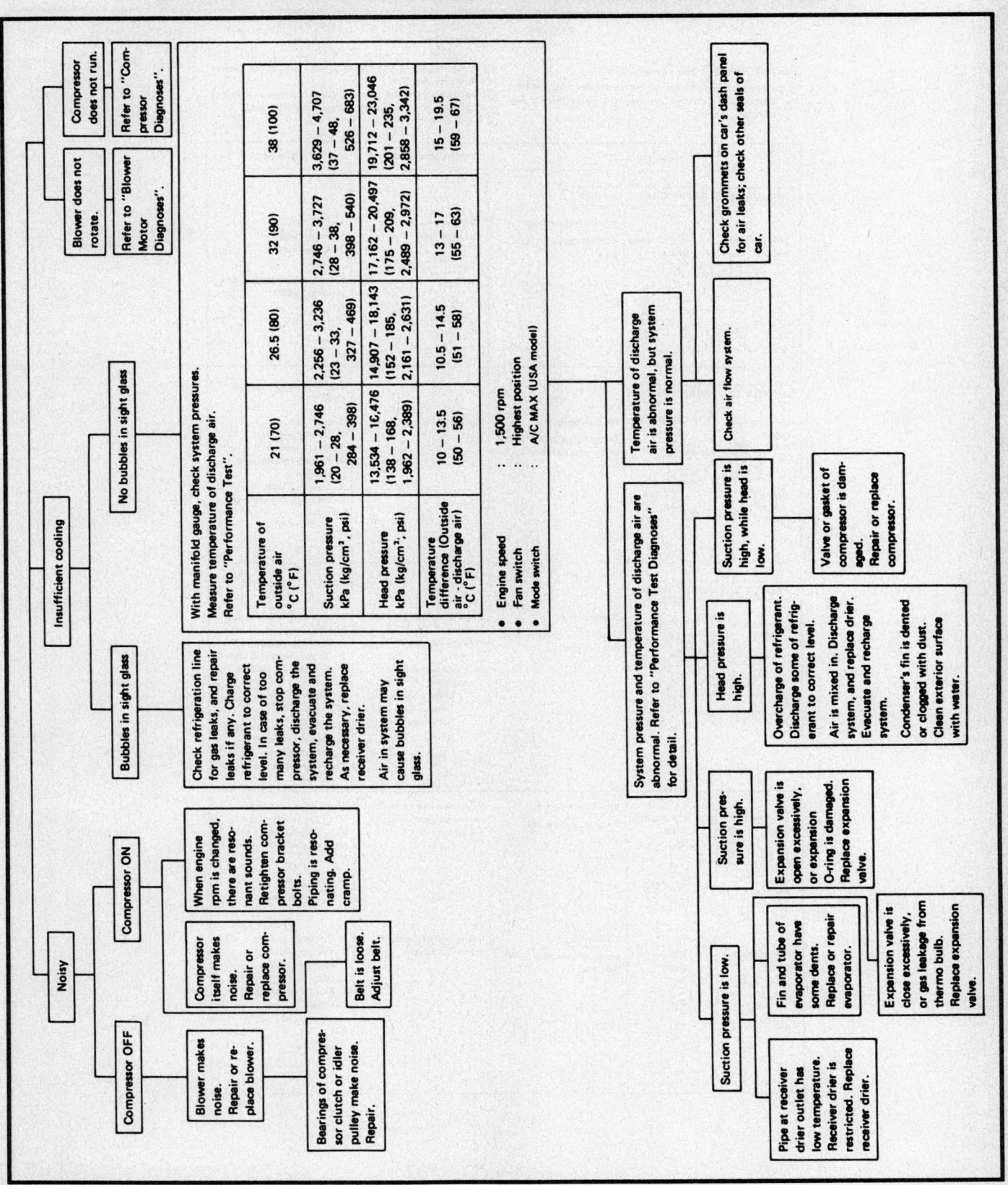

Temperature of outside air °C (°F)	21 (70)	26.5 (80)	32 (90)	38 (100)
Suction pressure kPa (kg/cm², psi)	1,961 – 2,746 (20 – 28, 284 – 398)	2,256 – 3,236 (23 – 33, 327 – 469)	2,746 – 3,727 (28 – 38, 398 – 540)	3,629 – 4,707 (37 – 48, 526 – 683)
Head pressure kPa (kg/cm²; psi)	13,534 – 16,476 (138 – 168, 1,962 – 2,389)	14,907 – 18,143 (152 – 185, 2,161 – 2,631)	17,162 – 20,497 (175 – 209, 2,489 – 2,972)	19,712 – 23,046 (201 – 235, 2,858 – 3,342)
Temperature difference (Outside air - discharge air) °C (°F)	10 – 13.5 (50 – 56)	10.5 – 14.5 (51 – 58)	13 – 17 (55 – 63)	15 – 19.5 (59 – 67)

      - Engine speed : 1,500 rpm
      - Fan switch : Highest position
      - Mode switch : A/C MAX (USA model)

    - **System pressure and temperature of discharge air are abnormal. Refer to "Performance Test Diagnoses" for detail.**
      - **Suction pressure is low.**
        - Pipe at receiver drier outlet has low temperature. Receiver drier is restricted. Replace receiver drier.
        - Fin and tube of evaporator have some dents. Replace or repair evaporator.
        - Expansion valve is close excessively, or gas leakage from thermo bulb. Replace expansion valve.
      - **Suction pressure is high.**
        - Expansion valve is open excessively, or expansion O-ring is damaged. Replace expansion valve.
      - **Head pressure is high.**
        - Overcharge of refrigerant. Discharge some of refrigerant to correct level.
          Air is mixed in. Discharge system, and replace drier. Evacuate and recharge system.
          Condenser's fin is dented or clogged with dust. Clean exterior surface with water.
      - **Suction pressure is high, while head is low.**
        - Valve or gasket of compressor is damaged. Repair or replace compressor.
    - **Temperature of discharge air is abnormal, but system pressure is normal.**
      - Check air flow system.
      - Check grommets on car's dash panel for air leaks; check other seals of car.
- **Blower does not rotate.**
  - Refer to "Blower Motor Diagnoses".
- **Compressor does not run.**
  - Refer to "Compressor Diagnoses".

PERFORMANCE TEST DIAGNOSIS—XT COUPE

Performance Test Diagnoses

Of various conditions caused to the air conditioning system, the characteristics revealed on manifold gauge reading are shown in the following.

As to the method of a performance test, refer to the item of "Performance Test".

Each shaded area on the following tables indicates a reading of the normal system when the temperature of outside air is 32.5°C (91°F).

Condition		Probable cause	Corrective action
INSUFFICIENT REFRIGERANT CHARGE			
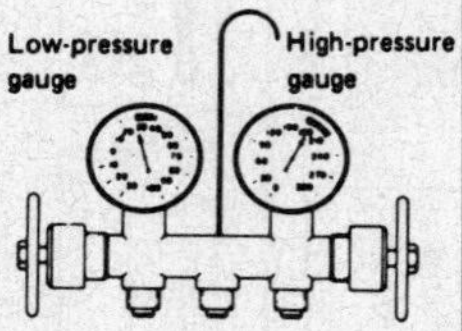 Low-pressure gauge High-pressure gauge	Insufficient cooling. Bubbles appear in sight glass.	Refrigerant is small, or leaking a little.	1. Leak test. 2. Repair leak. 3. Charge system. **Evacuate, as necessary, and recharge system.**
ALMOST NO REFRIGERANT			**Stop compressor immediately.**
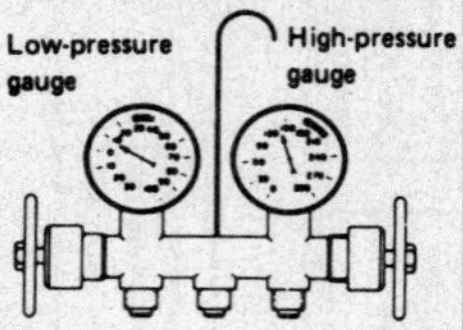 Low-pressure gauge High-pressure gauge	No cooling action. In sight glass appear a lot of bubbles or something like mist.	Serious refrigerant leak.	1. Leak test. 2. Discharge system. 3. Repair leak(s). 4. Replace receiver drier if necessary. 5. Check oil level. 6. Evacuate and recharge system.
FAULTY EXPANSION VALVE			
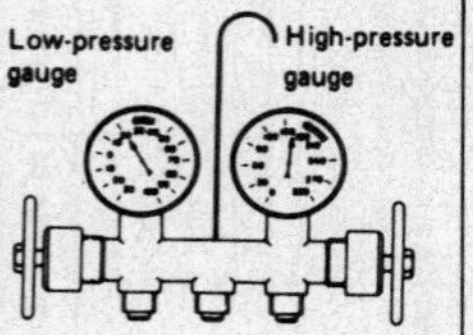 Low-pressure gauge High-pressure gauge	Slight cooling. Sweating or frosted expansion valve inlet.	Expansion valve restricts refrigerant flow. • Expansion valve is clogged. • Expansion valve is inoperative. Valve stuck closed. Thermal bulb has lost charge.	If valve inlet reveals sweat or frost: 1. Discharge system. 2. Remove valve and clean it. Replace it if necessary. 3. Evacuate system. 4. Charge system. If valve does not operate: 1. Discharge system. 2. Replace valve. 3. Evacuate and charge system.
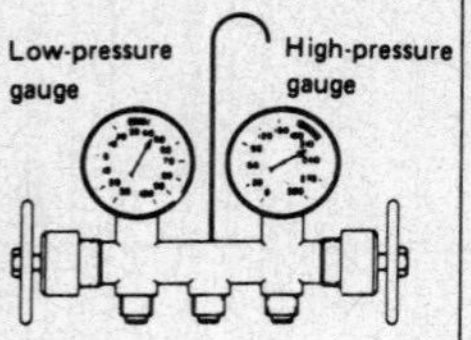 Low-pressure gauge High-pressure gauge	Insufficient cooling. Sweated suction line.	Expansion valve allows too much refrigerant through evaporator.	Check valve for operation. If suction side does not show a pressure decrease, replace valve.
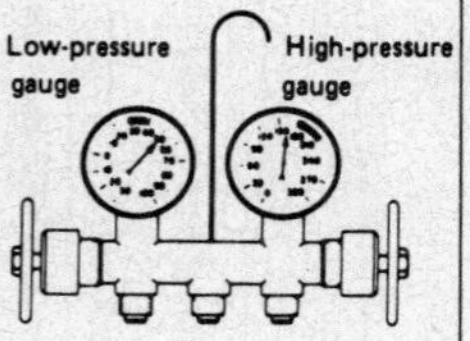 Low-pressure gauge High-pressure gauge	No cooling. Sweating or frosted suction line.	Faulty seal of O-ring in expansion valve.	1. Discharge system. 2. Remove expansion valve and replace O-ring. 3. Evacuate and replace system.

PERFORMANCE TEST DIAGNOSIS—XT COUPE

Condition		Probable cause	Corrective action
AIR IN SYSTEM 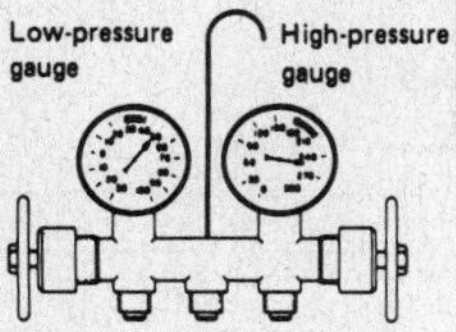Low-pressure gauge High-pressure gauge	Insufficient cooling. Sight glass shows occasional bubbles.	Air mixed with refrigerant in system.	1. Discharge system. 2. Replace receiver drier. 3. Evacuate and charge system.
MOISTURE IN SYSTEM 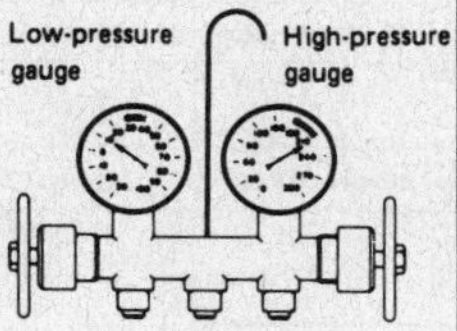Low-pressure gauge High-pressure gauge	After operation for a while, pressure on suction side may show vacuum pressure reading. During this condition, discharge air will be warm. As warning of this, reading shows 39 kPa (0.4 kg/cm^2, 6 psi) vibration.	Drier is saturated with moisture. Moisture has frozen at expansion valve. Refrigerant flow is restricted.	1. Discharge system. 2. Replace receiver drier (twice if necessary). 3. Evacuate system completely. (Repeat 30-minute evacuating three times.) 4. Recharge system.
FAULTY CONDENSER 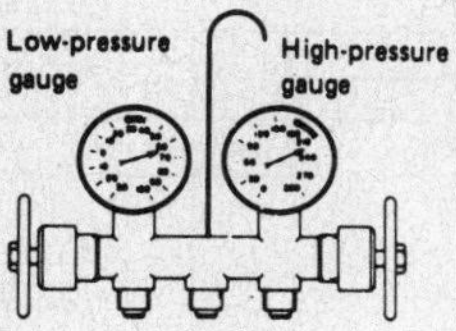Low-pressure gauge High-pressure gauge	No cooling action: engine may overheat. Bubbles appear in sight glass of drier. Suction line is very hot.	Condenser is often found not functioning well.	• Check condenser cooling fan. • Check condenser for dirt accumulation. • Check engine cooling system for overheat. • Check for refrigerant overcharge. **If pressure remains high in spite of all above actions taken, remove and inspect the condenser for possible oil clogging.**
HIGH PRESSURE LINE BLOCKED 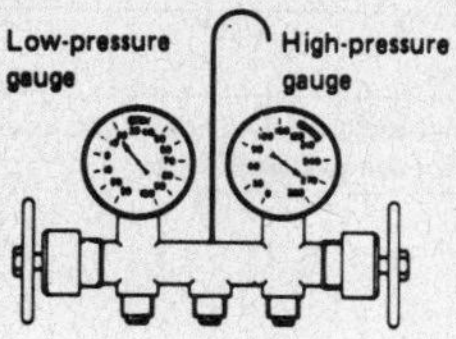Low-pressure gauge High-pressure gauge	Insufficient cooling. Frosted high pressure liquid line.	Drier clogged, or restriction in high pressure line.	1. Discharge system. 2. Remove receiver drier or strainer and replace it. 3. Evacuate and charge system.
FAULTY COMPRESSOR 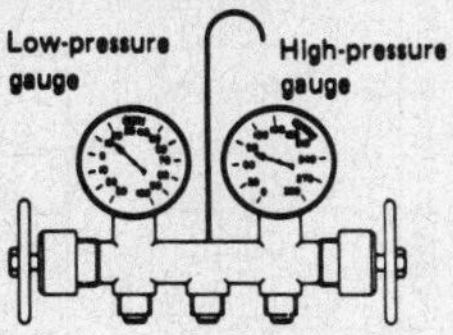Low-pressure gauge High-pressure gauge	Insufficient cooling.	Internal problem in compressor, or damaged gasket and valve.	1. Discharge system. 2. Remove and check compressor. 3. Repair or replace compressor. 4. Check oil level. 5. Replace receiver drier. 6. Evacuate and charge system.

BLOWER MOTOR DIAGNOSIS—XT COUPE

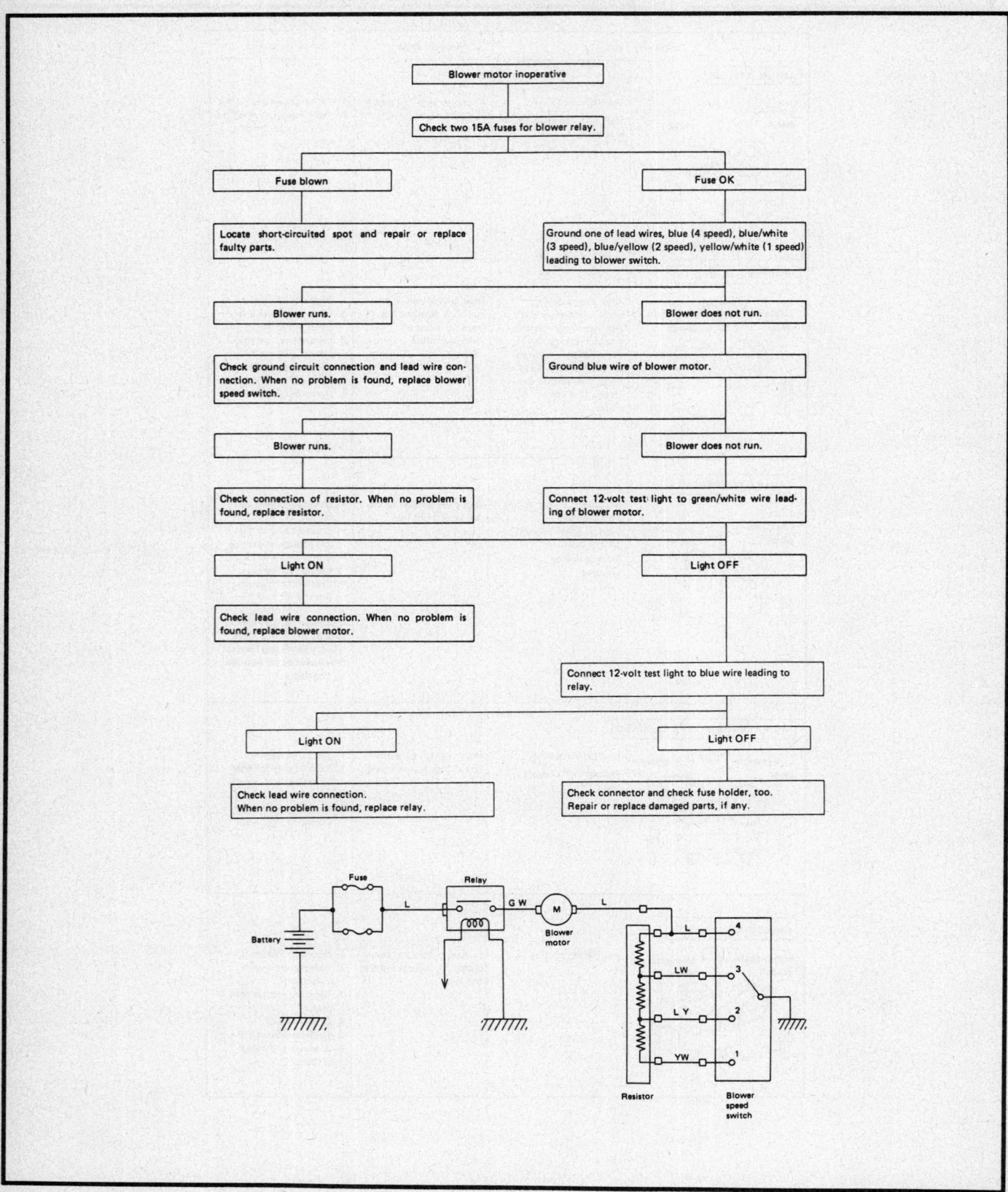

Blower motor inoperative

Check two 15A fuses for blower relay.

- **Fuse blown**
  - Locate short-circuited spot and repair or replace faulty parts.
- **Fuse OK**
  - Ground one of lead wires, blue (4 speed), blue/white (3 speed), blue/yellow (2 speed), yellow/white (1 speed) leading to blower switch.
    - **Blower runs.**
      - Check ground circuit connection and lead wire connection. When no problem is found, replace blower speed switch.
    - **Blower does not run.**
      - Ground blue wire of blower motor.
        - **Blower runs.**
          - Check connection of resistor. When no problem is found, replace resistor.
        - **Blower does not run.**
          - Connect 12-volt test light to green/white wire leading of blower motor.
            - **Light ON**
              - Check lead wire connection. When no problem is found, replace blower motor.
            - **Light OFF**
              - Connect 12-volt test light to blue wire leading to relay.
                - **Light ON**
                  - Check lead wire connection. When no problem is found, replace relay.
                - **Light OFF**
                  - Check connector and check fuse holder, too. Repair or replace damaged parts, if any.

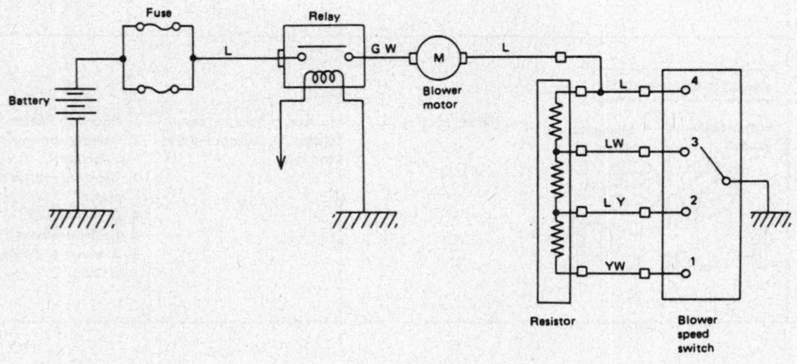
Fuse
Relay
L
G W
M
L
Battery
Blower motor
L
4
LW
3
L Y
2
YW
1
Resistor
Blower speed switch

COMPRESSOR DIAGNOSIS—XT COUPE

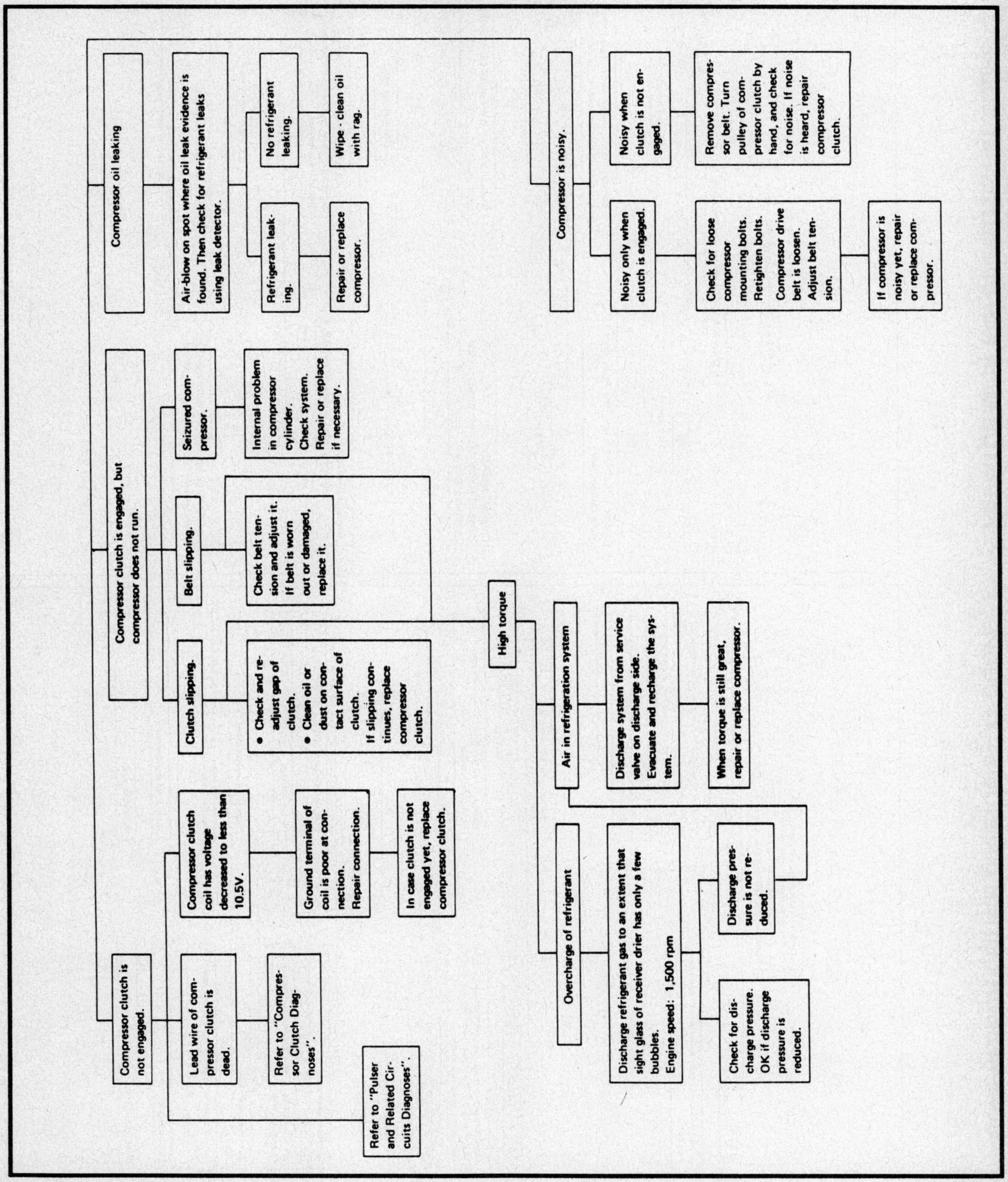
Compressor oil leaking
Air-blow on spot where oil leak evidence is found. Then check for refrigerant leaks using leak detector.
No refrigerant leaking.
Wipe - clean oil with rag.
Refrigerant leaking.
Repair or replace compressor.
Compressor is noisy.
Noisy when clutch is not engaged.
Remove compressor belt. Turn pulley of compressor clutch by hand, and check for noise. If noise is heard, repair compressor clutch.
Noisy only when clutch is engaged.
Check for loose compressor mounting bolts. Retighten bolts. Compressor drive belt is loosen. Adjust belt tension.
If compressor is noisy yet, repair or replace compressor.
Compressor clutch is engaged, but compressor does not run.
Seizured compressor.
Internal problem in compressor cylinder. Check system. Repair or replace if necessary.
Belt slipping.
Check belt tension and adjust it. If belt is worn out or damaged, replace it.
Clutch slipping.
• Check and readjust gap of clutch.
• Clean oil or dust on contact surface of clutch.
If slipping continues, replace compressor clutch.
High torque
Air in refrigeration system
Discharge system from service valve on discharge side. Evacuate and recharge the system.
When torque is still great, repair or replace compressor.
Overcharge of refrigerant
Discharge refrigerant gas to an extent that sight glass of receiver drier has only a few bubbles. Engine speed: 1,500 rpm
Discharge pressure is not reduced.
Check for discharge pressure. OK if discharge pressure is reduced.
Compressor clutch is not engaged.
Lead wire of compressor clutch is dead.
Refer to "Compressor Clutch Diagnoses".
Compressor clutch coil has voltage decreased to less than 10.5V.
Ground terminal of coil is poor at connection. Repair connection.
In case clutch is not engaged yet, replace compressor clutch.
Refer to "Pulser and Related Circuits Diagnoses".

COMPRESSOR CLUTCH DIAGNOSIS—XT COUPE

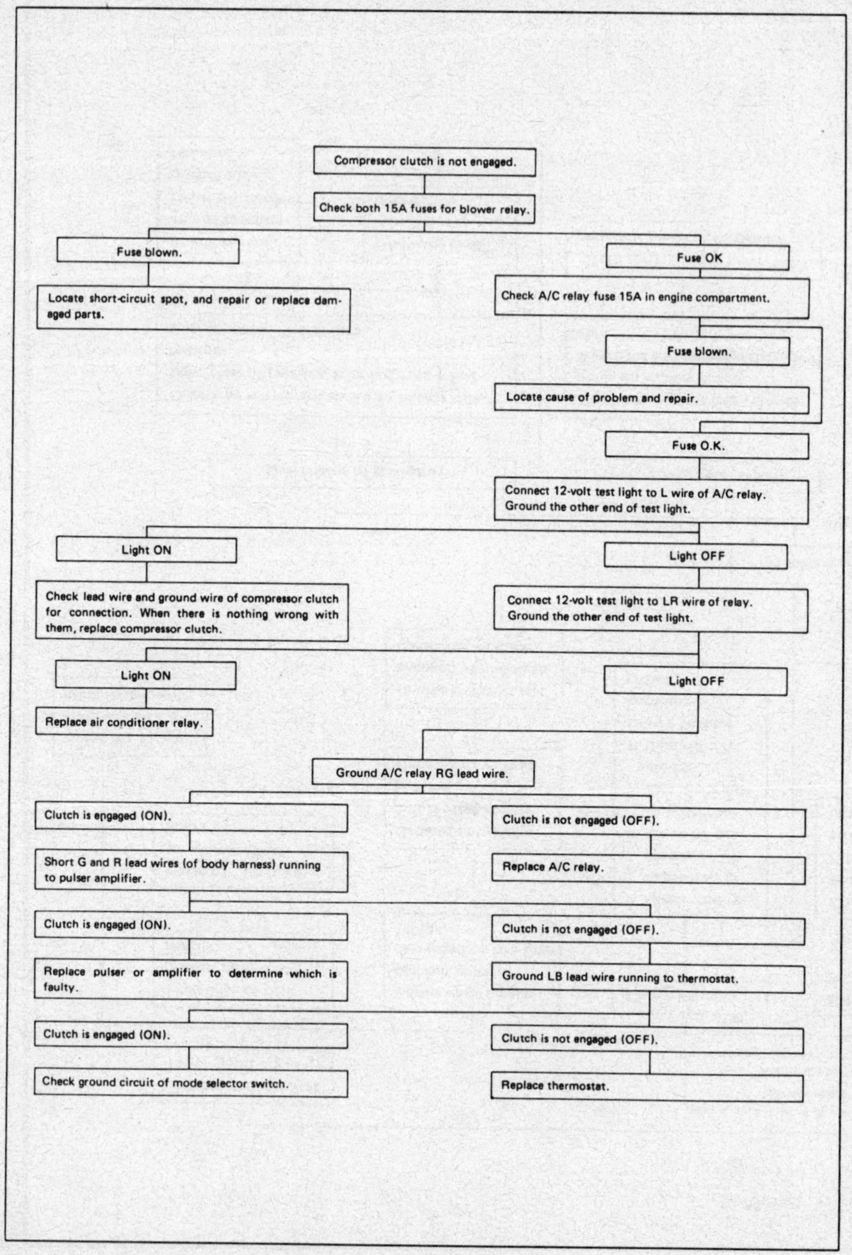
Compressor clutch is not engaged.
Check both 15A fuses for blower relay.
Fuse blown.
Locate short-circuit spot, and repair or replace damaged parts.
Fuse OK
Check A/C relay fuse 15A in engine compartment.
Fuse blown.
Locate cause of problem and repair.
Fuse O.K.
Connect 12-volt test light to L wire of A/C relay. Ground the other end of test light.
Light ON
Check lead wire and ground wire of compressor clutch for connection. When there is nothing wrong with them, replace compressor clutch.
Light OFF
Connect 12-volt test light to LR wire of relay. Ground the other end of test light.
Light ON
Replace air conditioner relay.
Light OFF
Ground A/C relay RG lead wire.
Clutch is engaged (ON).
Short G and R lead wires (of body harness) running to pulser amplifier.
Clutch is not engaged (OFF).
Replace A/C relay.
Clutch is engaged (ON).
Replace pulser or amplifier to determine which is faulty.
Clutch is not engaged (OFF).
Ground LB lead wire running to thermostat.
Clutch is engaged (ON).
Check ground circuit of mode selector switch.
Clutch is not engaged (OFF).
Replace thermostat.

RADIATOR MAIN FAN DIAGNOSIS—XT COUPE

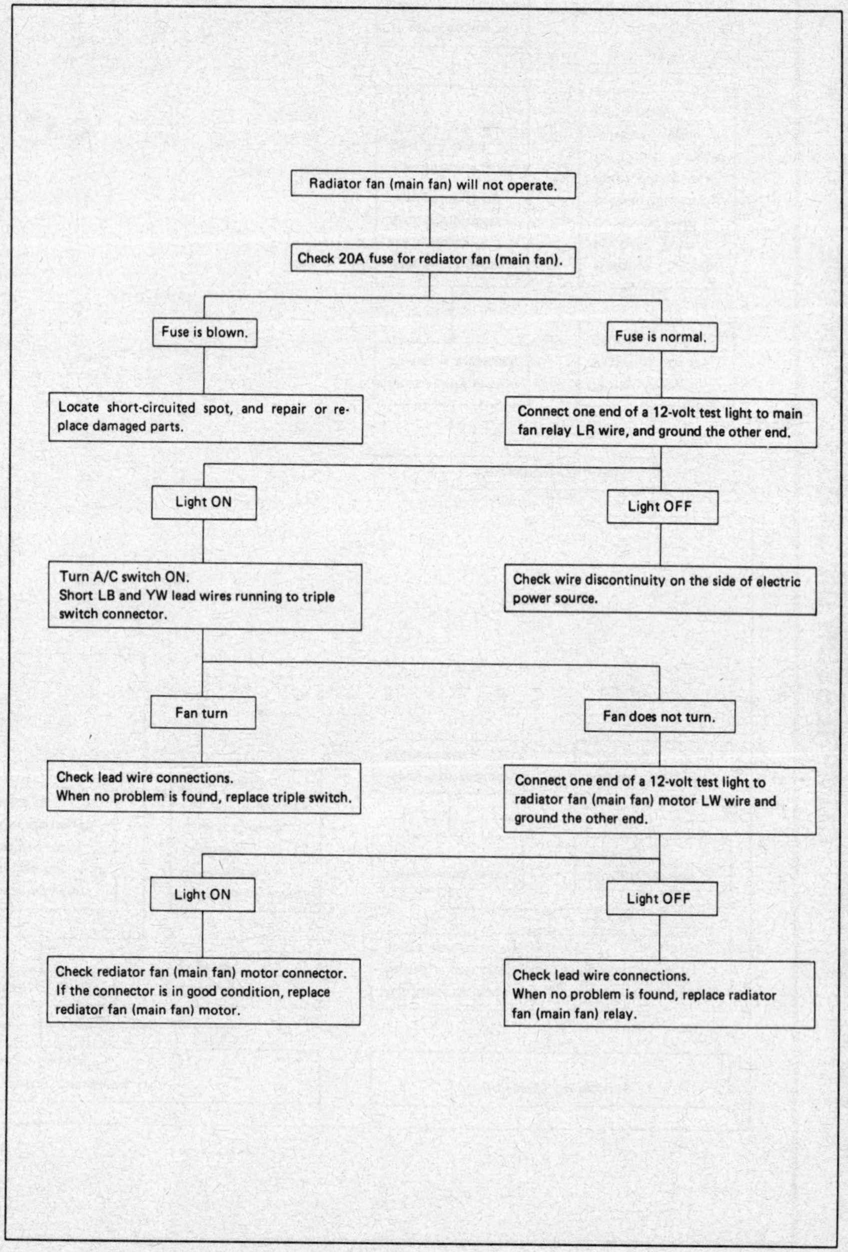
Radiator fan (main fan) will not operate.
Check 20A fuse for rediator fan (main fan).
Fuse is blown.
Locate short-circuited spot, and repair or replace damaged parts.
Fuse is normal.
Connect one end of a 12-volt test light to main fan relay LR wire, and ground the other end.
Light ON
Turn A/C switch ON.
Short LB and YW lead wires running to triple switch connector.
Light OFF
Check wire discontinuity on the side of electric power source.
Fan turn
Check lead wire connections.
When no problem is found, replace triple switch.
Fan does not turn.
Connect one end of a 12-volt test light to radiator fan (main fan) motor LW wire and ground the other end.
Light ON
Check rediator fan (main fan) motor connector.
If the connector is in good condition, replace rediator fan (main fan) motor.
Light OFF
Check lead wire connections.
When no problem is found, replace radiator fan (main fan) relay.

CONDENSER SUB FAN DIAGNOSIS—XT COUPE

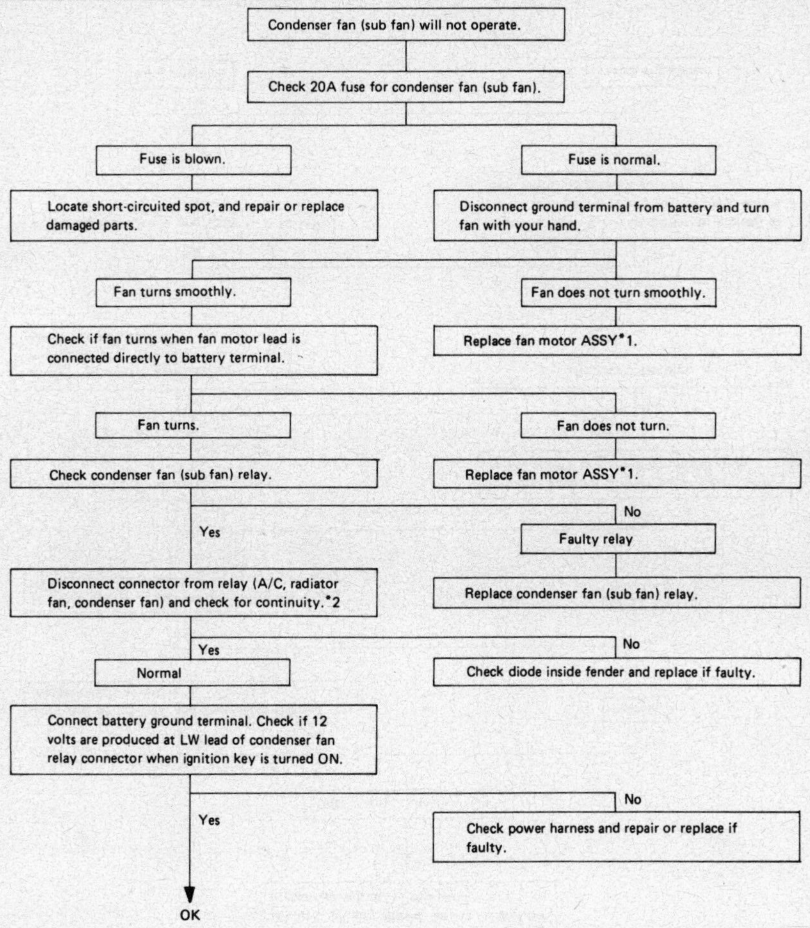
Condenser fan (sub fan) will not operate.
Check 20A fuse for condenser fan (sub fan).
Fuse is blown.
Locate short-circuited spot, and repair or replace damaged parts.
Fuse is normal.
Disconnect ground terminal from battery and turn fan with your hand.
Fan turns smoothly.
Check if fan turns when fan motor lead is connected directly to battery terminal.
Fan does not turn smoothly.
Replace fan motor ASSY*1.
Fan turns.
Check condenser fan (sub fan) relay.
Fan does not turn.
Replace fan motor ASSY*1.
Yes
Disconnect connector from relay (A/C, radiator fan, condenser fan) and check for continuity.*2
No
Faulty relay
Replace condenser fan (sub fan) relay.
Yes
Normal
Connect battery ground terminal. Check if 12 volts are produced at LW lead of condenser fan relay connector when ignition key is turned ON.
No
Check diode inside fender and replace if faulty.
Yes
OK
No
Check power harness and repair or replace if faulty.

*1: Replace fan and fan motor as a unit because they are balanced.
*2: Connect tester leads to LR leads of condenser fan relay connector, YW lead of radiator fan relay connector and L lead of A/C relay connector. Check for continuity, as shown in Table below.

	Tester lead	
	Positive (+)	Negative (−)
No continuity	LR LR	L YW
Continuity	L YW	LR LR

PULSER AND RELATED CIRCUIT DIAGNOSIS XT COUPE

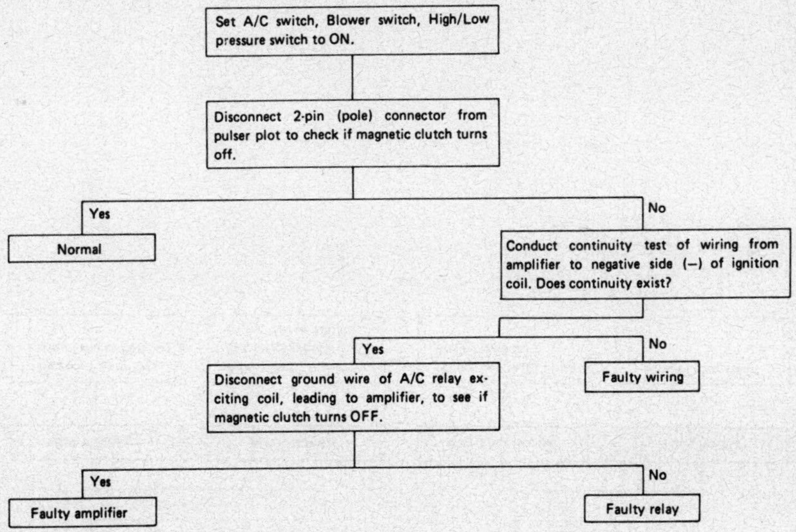
Set A/C switch, Blower switch, High/Low pressure switch to ON.
Disconnect 2-pin (pole) connector from pulser plot to check if magnetic clutch turns off.
Yes
Normal
No
Conduct continuity test of wiring from amplifier to negative side (−) of ignition coil. Does continuity exist?
Yes
Disconnect ground wire of A/C relay exciting coil, leading to amplifier, to see if magnetic clutch turns OFF.
No
Faulty wiring
Yes
Faulty amplifier
No
Faulty relay

PULSER AND RELATED CIRCUIT DIAGNOSIS XT COUPE

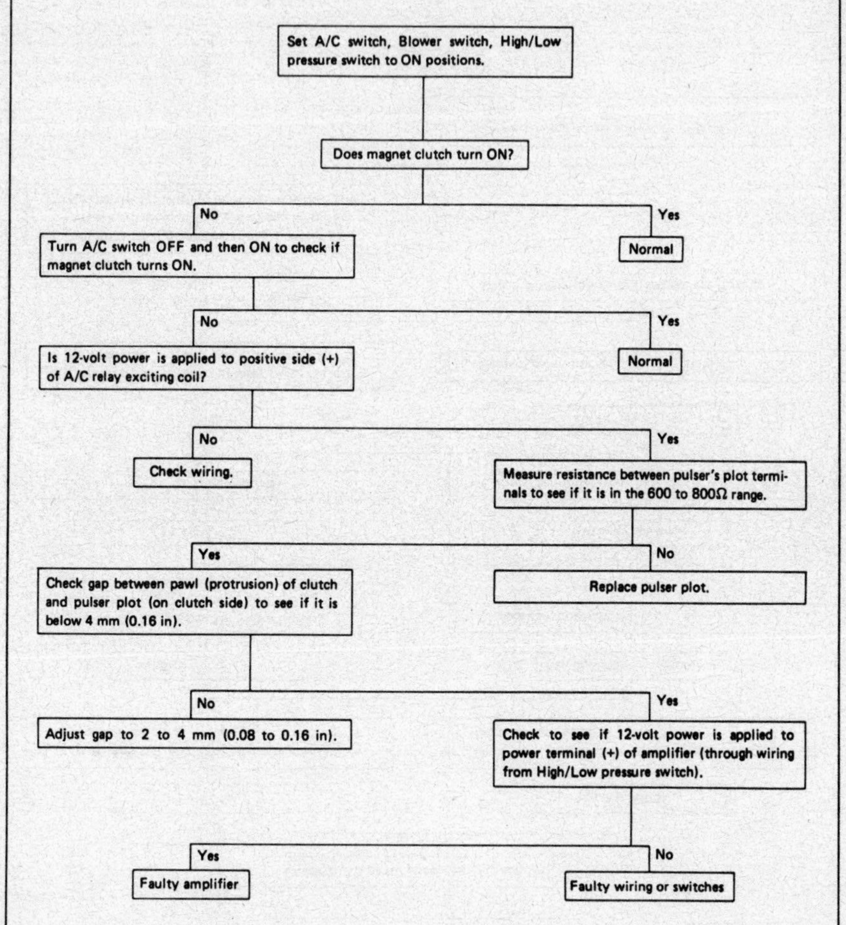
Set A/C switch, Blower switch, High/Low pressure switch to ON positions.
Does magnet clutch turn ON?
No
Yes
Normal
Turn A/C switch OFF and then ON to check if magnet clutch turns ON.
No
Yes
Normal
Is 12-volt power is applied to positive side (+) of A/C relay exciting coil?
No
Check wiring.
Yes
Measure resistance between pulser's plot terminals to see if it is in the 600 to 800Ω range.
Yes
Check gap between pawl (protrusion) of clutch and pulser plot (on clutch side) to see if it is below 4 mm (0.16 in).
No
Replace pulser plot.
No
Adjust gap to 2 to 4 mm (0.08 to 0.16 in).
Yes
Check to see if 12-volt power is applied to power terminal (+) of amplifier (through wiring from High/Low pressure switch).
Yes
Faulty amplifier
No
Faulty wiring or switches

GENERAL AIR CONDITIONING SYSTEM DIAGNOSIS LOYALE AND SEDAN

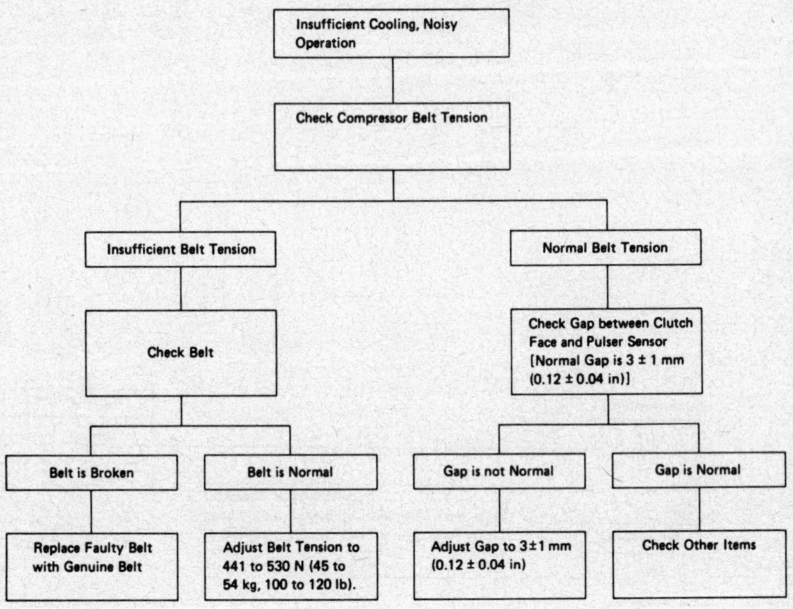
Insufficient Cooling, Noisy Operation
Check Compressor Belt Tension
Insufficient Belt Tension
Normal Belt Tension
Check Belt
Check Gap between Clutch Face and Pulser Sensor [Normal Gap is 3 ± 1 mm (0.12 ± 0.04 in)]
Belt is Broken
Belt is Normal
Gap is not Normal
Gap is Normal
Replace Faulty Belt with Genuine Belt
Adjust Belt Tension to 441 to 530 N (45 to 54 kg, 100 to 120 lb).
Adjust Gap to 3±1 mm (0.12 ± 0.04 in)
Check Other Items

GENERAL AIR CONDITIONING SYSTEM DIAGNOSIS—LOYALE AND SEDAN

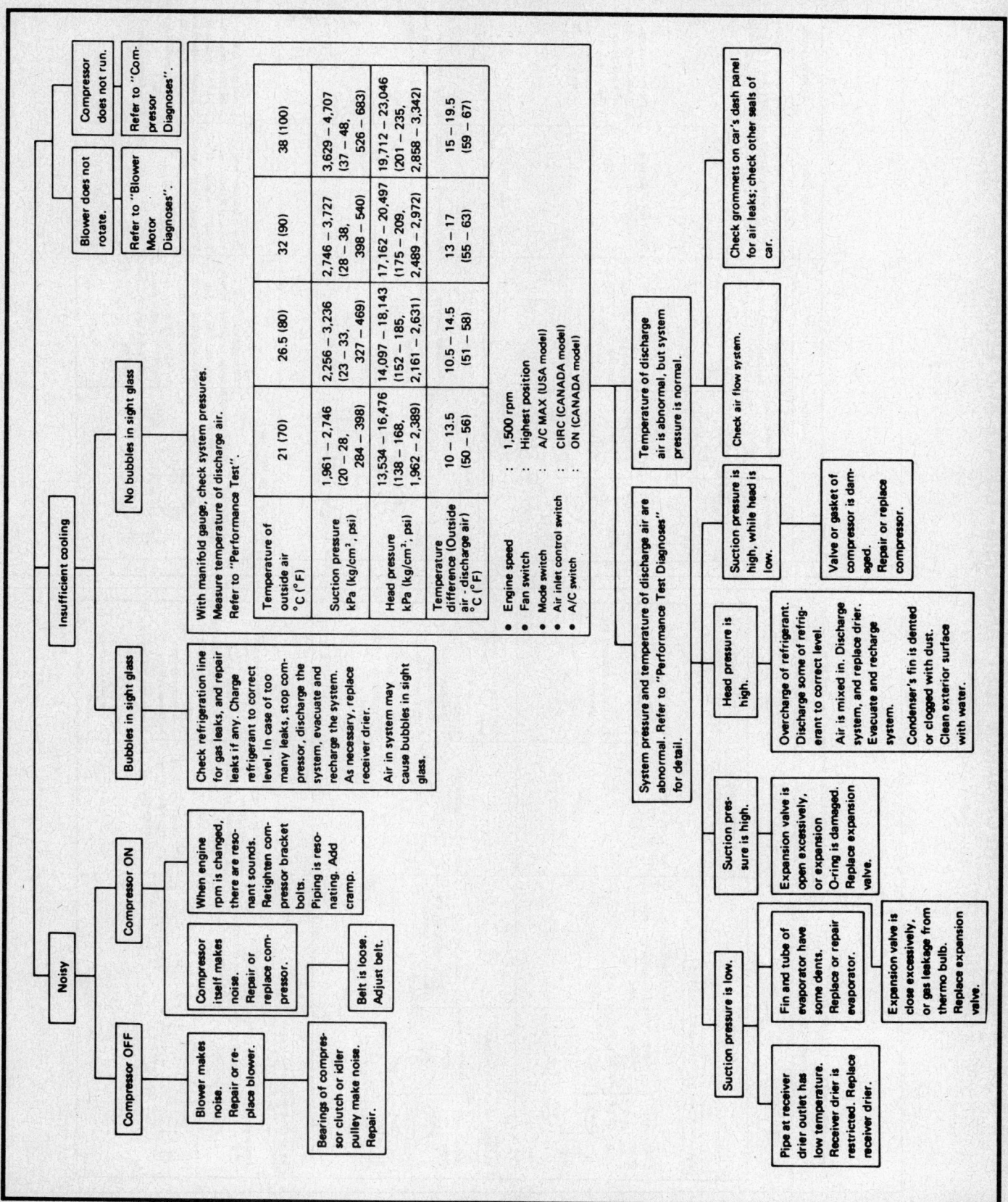

- **Noisy**
  - **Compressor OFF**
    - Blower makes noise. Repair or replace blower.
    - Bearings of compressor clutch or idler pulley make noise. Repair.
  - **Compressor ON**
    - Compressor itself makes noise. Repair or replace compressor.
    - Belt is loose. Adjust belt.
    - When engine rpm is changed, there are resonant sounds. Retighten compressor bracket bolts. Piping is resonating. Add cramp.
- **Insufficient cooling**
  - **Bubbles in sight glass**
    - Check refrigeration line for gas leaks, and repair leaks if any. Charge refrigerant to correct level. In case of too many leaks, stop compressor, discharge the system, evacuate and recharge the system. As necessary, replace receiver drier.

      Air in system may cause bubbles in sight glass.
  - **No bubbles in sight glass**
    - With manifold gauge, check system pressures. Measure temperature of discharge air. Refer to "Performance Test".

Temperature of outside air °C (°F)	21 (70)	26.5 (80)	32 (90)	38 (100)
Suction pressure kPa (kg/cm², psi)	1,961 – 2,746 (20 – 28, 284 – 398)	2,256 – 3,236 (23 – 33, 327 – 469)	2,746 – 3,727 (28 – 38, 398 – 540)	3,629 – 4,707 (37 – 48, 526 – 683)
Head pressure kPa (kg/cm², psi)	13,534 – 16,476 (138 – 168, 1,962 – 2,389)	14,097 – 18,143 (152 – 185, 2,161 – 2,631)	17,162 – 20,497 (175 – 209, 2,489 – 2,972)	19,712 – 23,046 (201 – 235, 2,858 – 3,342)
Temperature difference (Outside air - discharge air) °C (°F)	10 – 13.5 (50 – 56)	10.5 – 14.5 (51 – 58)	13 – 17 (55 – 63)	15 – 19.5 (59 – 67)

- Engine speed : 1,500 rpm
- Fan switch : Highest position
- Mode switch : A/C MAX (USA model)
- Air inlet control switch : CIRC (CANADA model)
- A/C switch : ON (CANADA model)

    - **System pressure and temperature of discharge air are abnormal. Refer to "Performance Test Diagnoses" for detail.**
      - Suction pressure is low.
        - Pipe at receiver drier outlet has low temperature. Receiver drier is restricted. Replace receiver drier.
        - Fin and tube of evaporator have some dents. Replace or repair evaporator.
        - Expansion valve is close excessively, or gas leakage from thermo bulb. Replace expansion valve.
      - Suction pressure is high.
        - Expansion valve is open excessively, or expansion O-ring is damaged. Replace expansion valve.
      - Head pressure is high.
        - Overcharge of refrigerant. Discharge some of refrigerant to correct level.

          Air is mixed in. Discharge system, and replace drier. Evacuate and recharge system.

          Condenser's fin is dented or clogged with dust. Clean exterior surface with water.
      - Suction pressure is high, while head is low.
        - Valve or gasket of compressor is damaged. Repair or replace compressor.
    - **Temperature of discharge air is abnormal, but system pressure is normal.**
      - Check air flow system.
      - Check grommets on car's dash panel for air leaks; check other seals of car.
- **Blower does not rotate.**
  - Refer to "Blower Motor Diagnoses".
- **Compressor does not run.**
  - Refer to "Compressor Diagnoses".

PERFORMANCE TEST DIAGNOSIS—LOYALE AND SEDAN

Performance Test Diagnoses

Of various conditions caused to the air conditioning system, the characteristics revealed on manifold gauge reading are shown in the following.

As to the method of a performance test, refer to the item of "Performance Test".

Each shaded area on the following tables indicates a reading of the normal system when the temperature of outside air is 32.5°C (91°F).

Condition		Probable cause	Corrective action
INSUFFICIENT REFRIGERANT CHARGE 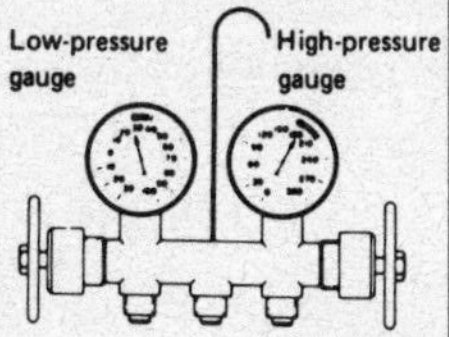 Low-pressure gauge High-pressure gauge	Insufficient cooling. Bubbles appear in sight glass.	Refrigerant is small, or leaking a little.	1. Leak test. 2. Repair leak. 3. Charge system. **Evacuate, as necessary, and recharge system.**
ALMOST NO REFRIGERANT 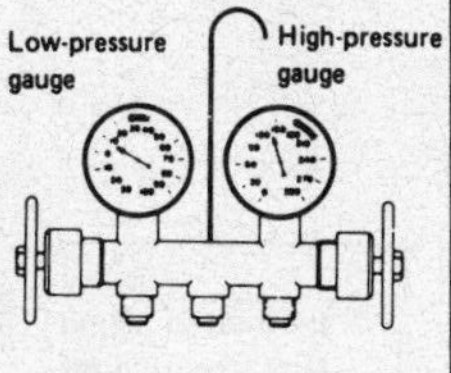 Low-pressure gauge High-pressure gauge	No cooling action. In sight glass appear a lot of bubbles or something like mist.	Serious refrigerant leak.	**Stop compressor immediately.** 1. Leak test. 2. Discharge system. 3. Repair leak(s). 4. Replace receiver drier if necessary. 5. Check oil level. 6. Evacuate and recharge system.
FAULTY EXPANSION VALVE 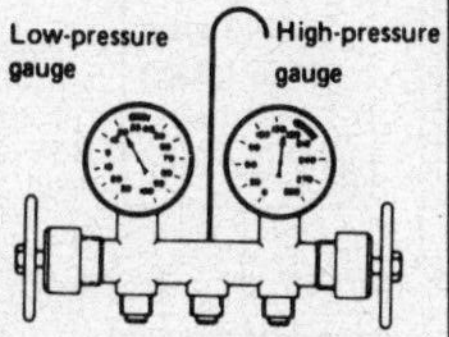 Low-pressure gauge High-pressure gauge	Slight cooling. Sweating or frosted expansion valve inlet.	Expansion valve restricts refrigerant flow. • Expansion valve is clogged. • Expansion valve is inoperative. Valve stuck closed. Thermal bulb has lost charge.	If valve inlet reveals sweat or frost: 1. Discharge system. 2. Remove valve and clean it. Replace it if necessary. 3. Evacuate system. 4. Charge system. If valve does not operate: 1. Discharge system. 2. Replace valve. 3. Evacuate and charge system.

Condition		Probable cause	Corrective action
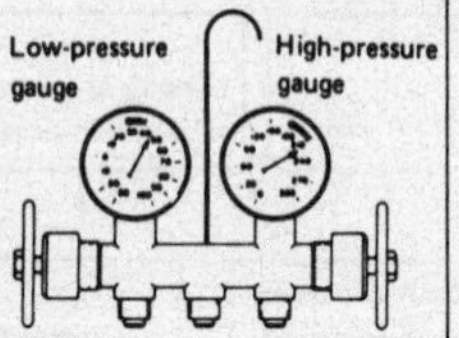 Low-pressure gauge High-pressure gauge	Insufficient cooling. Sweated suction line.	Expansion valve allows too much refrigerant through evaporator.	Check valve for operation. If suction side does not show a pressure decrease, replace valve.
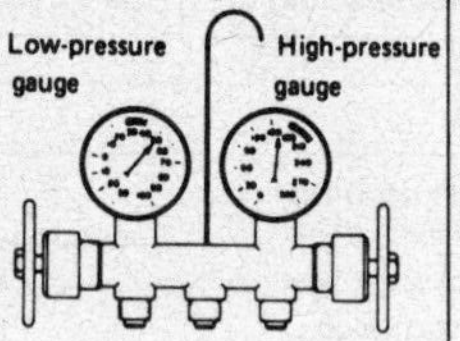 Low-pressure gauge High-pressure gauge	No cooling. Sweating or frosted suction line.	Faulty seal of O-ring in expansion valve.	1. Discharge system. 2. Remove expansion valve and replace O-ring. 3. Evacuate and replace system.
AIR IN SYSTEM 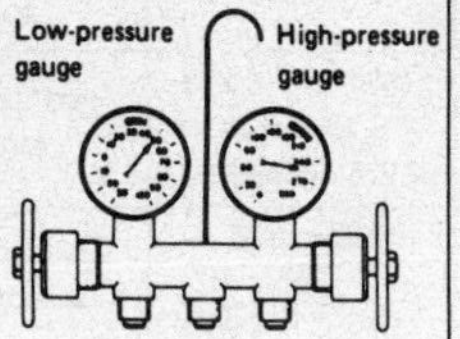 Low-pressure gauge High-pressure gauge	Insufficient cooling. Sight glass shows occasional bubbles.	Air mixed with refrigerant in system.	1. Discharge system. 2. Replace receiver drier. 3. Evacuate and charge system.
MOISTURE IN SYSTEM 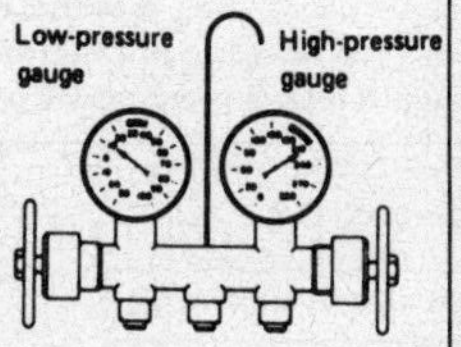 Low-pressure gauge High-pressure gauge	After operation for a while, pressure on suction side may show vacuum pressure reading. During this condition, discharge air will be warm. As warning of this, reading shows 39 kPa (0.4 kg/cm², 6 psi) vibration.	Drier is saturated with moisture. Moisture has frozen at expansion valve. Refrigerant flow is restricted.	1. Discharge system. 2. Replace receiver drier (twice if necessary). 3. Evacuate system completely. (Repeat 30-minute evacuating three times.) 4. Recharge system.

PERFORMANCE TEST DIAGNOSIS—LOYALE AND SEDAN

Condition		Probable cause	Corrective action
FAULTY CONDENSER 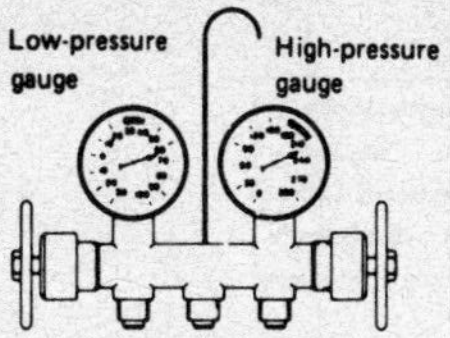	No cooling action: engine may overheat. Bubbles appear in sight glass of drier. Suction line is very hot.	Condenser is often found not functioning well.	• Check condenser cooling fan. • Check condenser for dirt accumulation. • Check engine cooling system for overheat. • Check for refrigerant overcharge. **If pressure remains high in spite of all above actions taken, remove and inspect the condenser for possible oil clogging.**
HIGH PRESSURE LINE BLOCKED 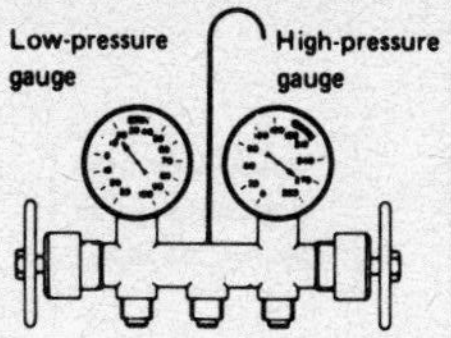	Insufficient cooling. Frosted high pressure liquid line.	Drier clogged, or restriction in high pressure line.	1. Discharge system. 2. Remove receiver drier or strainer and replace it. 3. Evacuate and charge system.
FAULTY COMPRESSOR 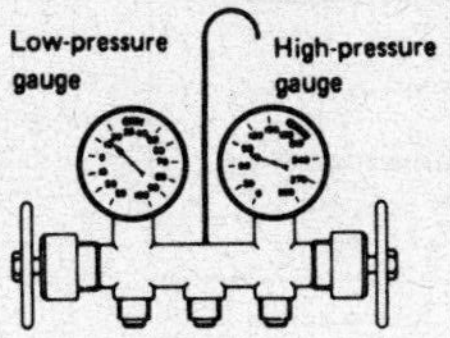	Insufficient cooling.	Internal problem in compressor, or damaged gasket and valve.	1. Discharge system. 2. Remove and check compressor. 3. Repair or replace compressor. 4. Check oil level. 5. Replace receiver drier. 6. Evacuate and charge system.

BLOWER MOTOR DIAGNOSIS—LOYALE AND SEDAN

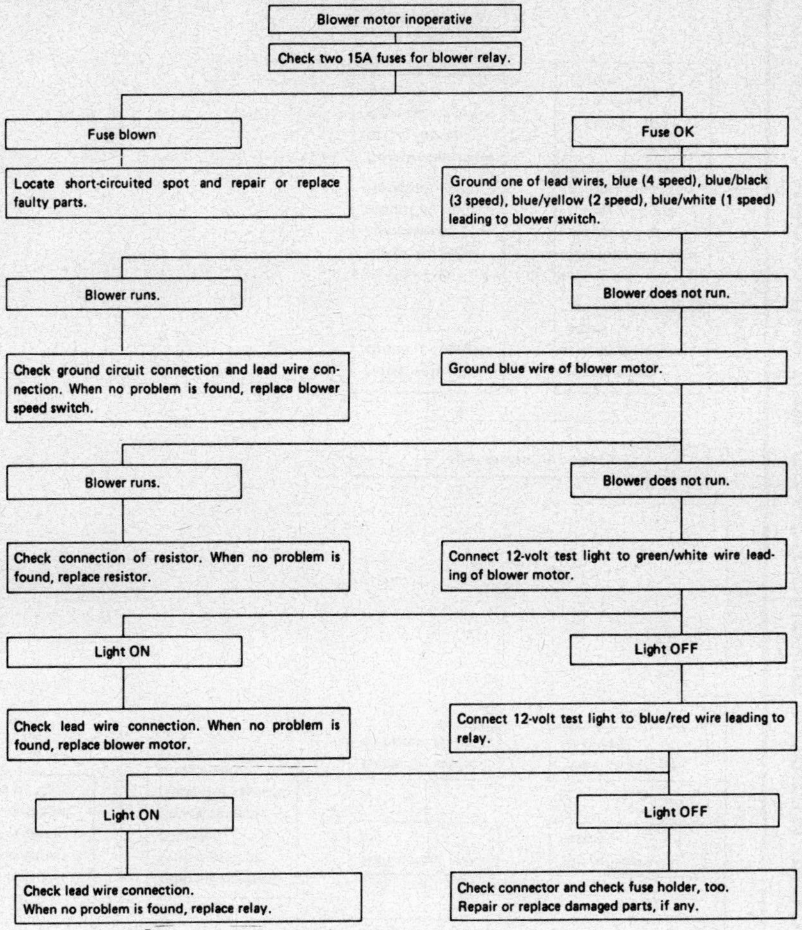

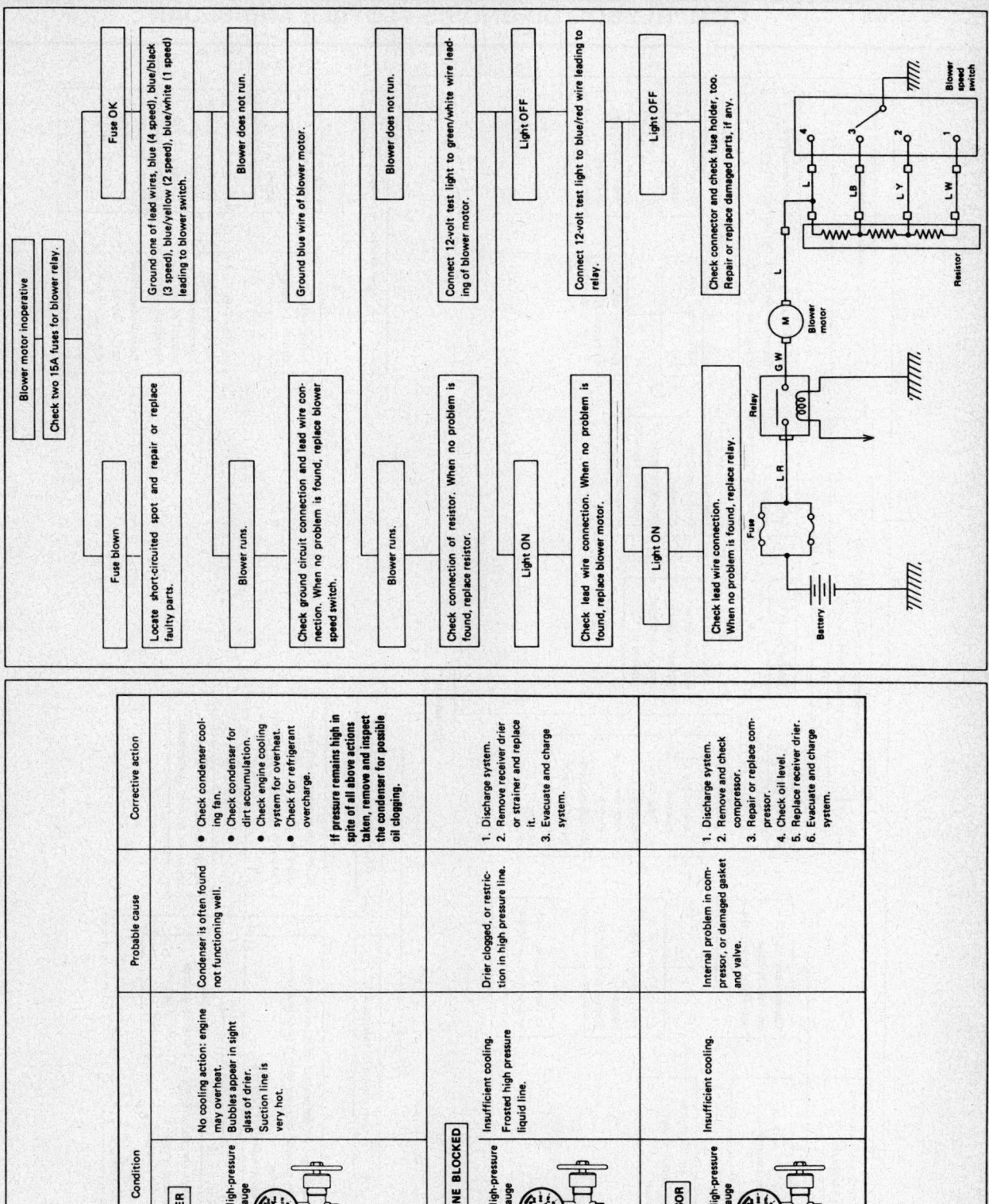

- Blower motor inoperative
- Check two 15A fuses for blower relay.
  - Fuse blown → Locate short-circuited spot and repair or replace faulty parts.
  - Fuse OK → Ground one of lead wires, blue (4 speed), blue/black (3 speed), blue/yellow (2 speed), blue/white (1 speed) leading to blower switch.
    - Blower runs. → Check ground circuit connection and lead wire connection. When no problem is found, replace blower speed switch.
    - Blower does not run. → Ground blue wire of blower motor.
      - Blower runs. → Check connection of resistor. When no problem is found, replace resistor.
      - Blower does not run. → Connect 12-volt test light to green/white wire leading of blower motor.
        - Light ON → Check lead wire connection. When no problem is found, replace blower motor.
        - Light OFF → Connect 12-volt test light to blue/red wire leading to relay.
          - Light ON → Check lead wire connection. When no problem is found, replace relay.
          - Light OFF → Check connector and check fuse holder, too. Repair or replace damaged parts, if any.

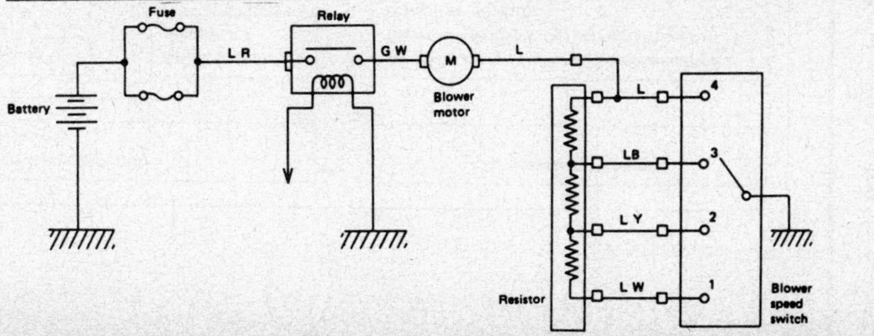
Fuse
Relay
L R
G W
M
L
Battery
Blower motor
L
LB
L Y
L W
4
3
2
1
Resistor
Blower speed switch

COMPRESSOR DIAGNOSIS—LOYALE AND SEDAN

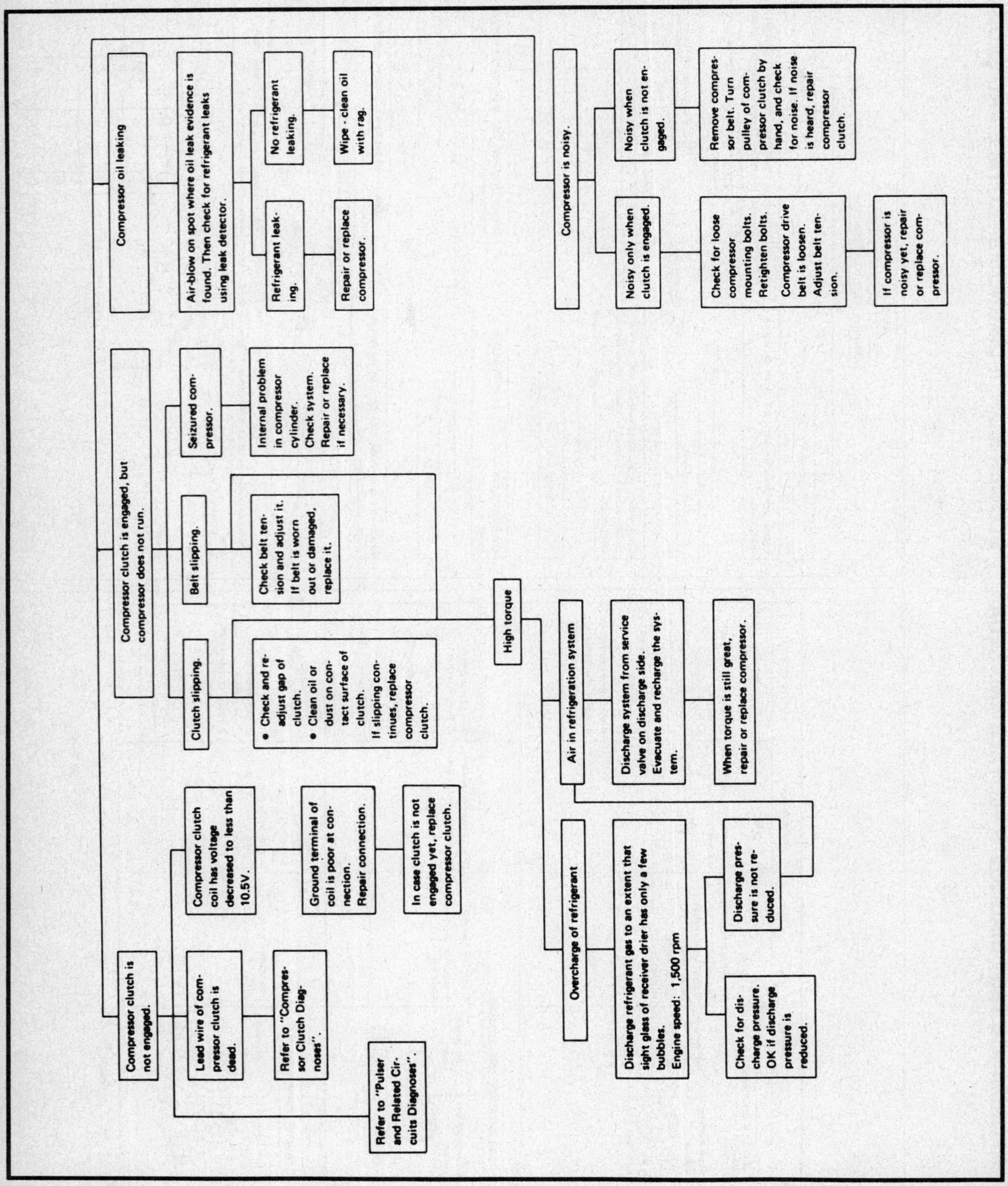
Compressor oil leaking
Air-blow on spot where oil leak evidence is found. Then check for refrigerant leaks using leak detector.
No refrigerant leaking.
Wipe - clean oil with rag.
Refrigerant leaking.
Repair or replace compressor.
Compressor is noisy.
Noisy when clutch is not engaged.
Remove compressor belt. Turn pulley of compressor clutch by hand, and check for noise. If noise is heard, repair compressor clutch.
Noisy only when clutch is engaged.
Check for loose compressor mounting bolts. Retighten bolts. Compressor drive belt is loosen. Adjust belt tension.
If compressor is noisy yet, repair or replace compressor.
Compressor clutch is engaged, but compressor does not run.
Seizured compressor.
Internal problem in compressor cylinder. Check system. Repair or replace if necessary.
Belt slipping.
Check belt tension and adjust it. If belt is worn out or damaged, replace it.
Clutch slipping.
• Check and re-adjust gap of clutch.
• Clean oil or dust on contact surface of clutch.
If slipping continues, replace compressor clutch.
High torque
Air in refrigeration system
Discharge system from service valve on discharge side. Evacuate and recharge the system.
When torque is still great, repair or replace compressor.
Compressor clutch is not engaged.
Lead wire of compressor clutch is dead.
Refer to "Compressor Clutch Diagnoses".
Compressor clutch coil has voltage decreased to less than 10.5V.
Ground terminal of coil is poor at connection. Repair connection.
In case clutch is not engaged yet, replace compressor clutch.
Refer to "Pulser and Related Circuits Diagnoses".
Overcharge of refrigerant
Discharge refrigerant gas to an extent that sight glass of receiver drier has only a few bubbles. Engine speed: 1,500 rpm
Discharge pressure is not reduced.
Check for discharge pressure. OK if discharge pressure is reduced.

COMPRESSOR CLUTCH DIAGNOSIS LOYALE AND SEDAN WITH HITACHI SYSTEM

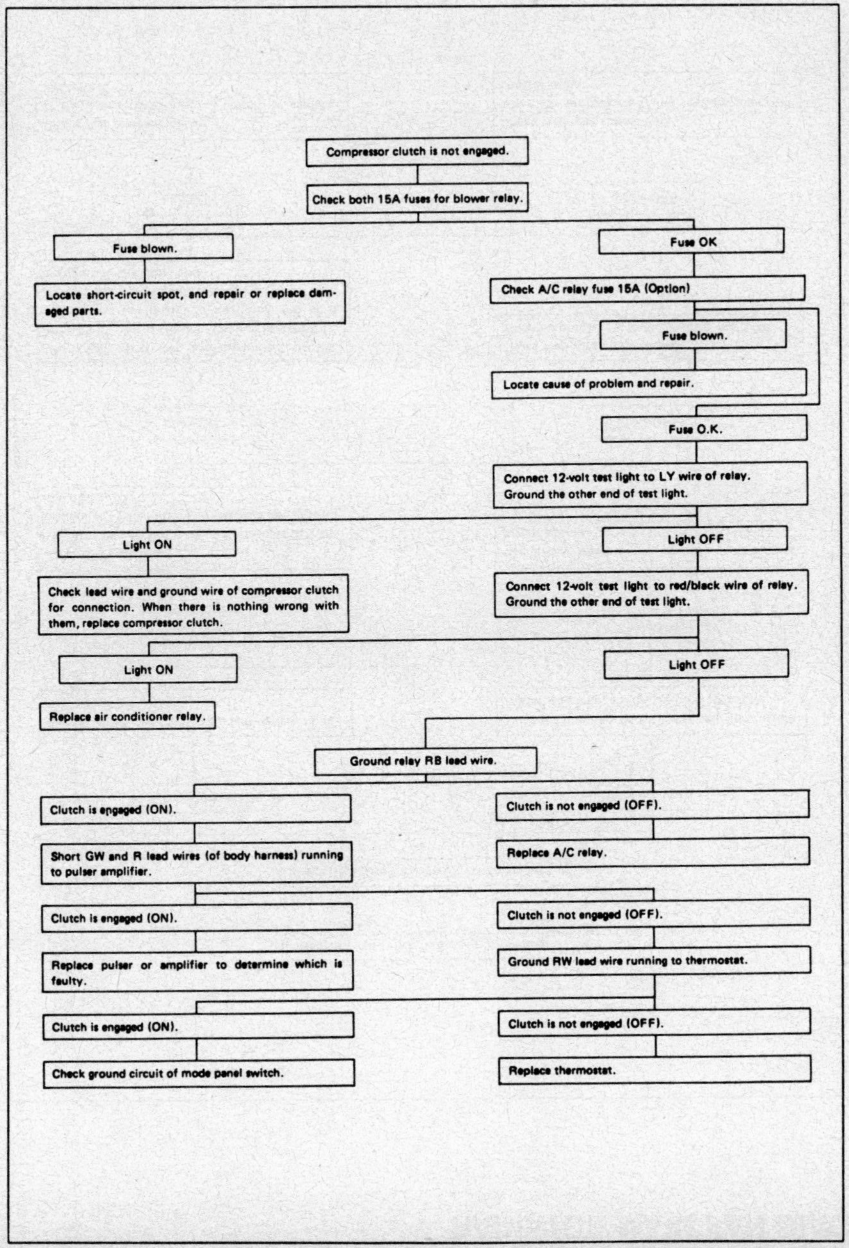
Compressor clutch is not engaged.
Check both 15A fuses for blower relay.
Fuse blown.
Locate short-circuit spot, and repair or replace damaged parts.
Fuse OK
Check A/C relay fuse 15A (Option)
Fuse blown.
Locate cause of problem and repair.
Fuse O.K.
Connect 12-volt test light to LY wire of relay. Ground the other end of test light.
Light ON
Check lead wire and ground wire of compressor clutch for connection. When there is nothing wrong with them, replace compressor clutch.
Light OFF
Connect 12-volt test light to red/black wire of relay. Ground the other end of test light.
Light ON
Replace air conditioner relay.
Light OFF
Ground relay RB lead wire.
Clutch is engaged (ON).
Short GW and R lead wires (of body harness) running to pulser amplifier.
Clutch is not engaged (OFF).
Replace A/C relay.
Clutch is engaged (ON).
Replace pulser or amplifier to determine which is faulty.
Clutch is not engaged (OFF).
Ground RW lead wire running to thermostat.
Clutch is engaged (ON).
Check ground circuit of mode panel switch.
Clutch is not engaged (OFF).
Replace thermostat.

COMPRESSOR CLUTCH DIAGNOSIS LOYALE AND SEDAN WITH PANASONIC SYSTEM

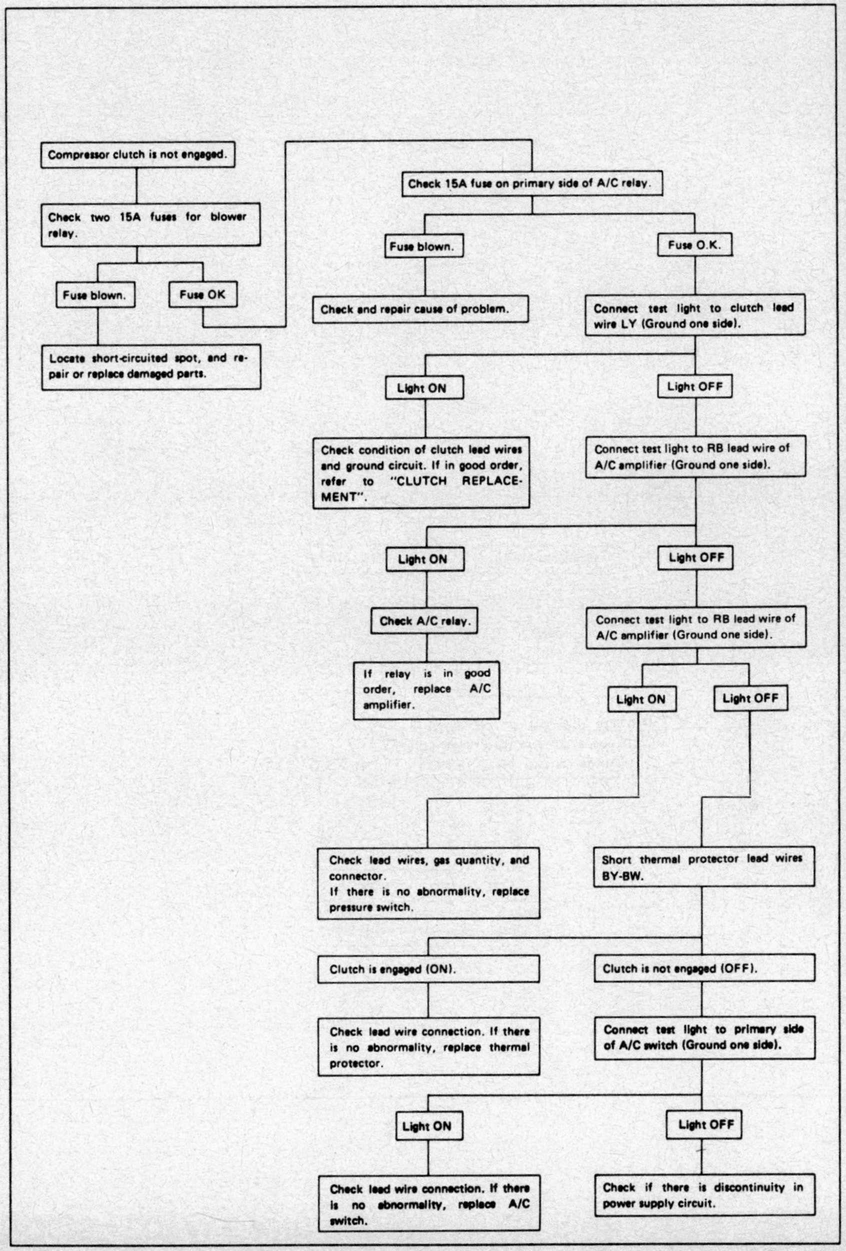
Compressor clutch is not engaged.
Check two 15A fuses for blower relay.
Fuse blown.
Locate short-circuited spot, and repair or replace damaged parts.
Fuse OK
Check 15A fuse on primary side of A/C relay.
Fuse blown.
Check and repair cause of problem.
Fuse O.K.
Connect test light to clutch lead wire LY (Ground one side).
Light ON
Check condition of clutch lead wires and ground circuit. If in good order, refer to "CLUTCH REPLACEMENT".
Light OFF
Connect test light to RB lead wire of A/C amplifier (Ground one side).
Light ON
Check A/C relay.
If relay is in good order, replace A/C amplifier.
Light OFF
Connect test light to RB lead wire of A/C amplifier (Ground one side).
Light ON
Light OFF
Check lead wires, gas quantity, and connector.
If there is no abnormality, replace pressure switch.
Short thermal protector lead wires BY-BW.
Clutch is engaged (ON).
Check lead wire connection. If there is no abnormality, replace thermal protector.
Clutch is not engaged (OFF).
Connect test light to primary side of A/C switch (Ground one side).
Light ON
Check lead wire connection. If there is no abnormality, replace A/C switch.
Light OFF
Check if there is discontinuity in power supply circuit.

RADIATOR MAIN FAN DIAGNOSIS—LOYALE AND SEDAN

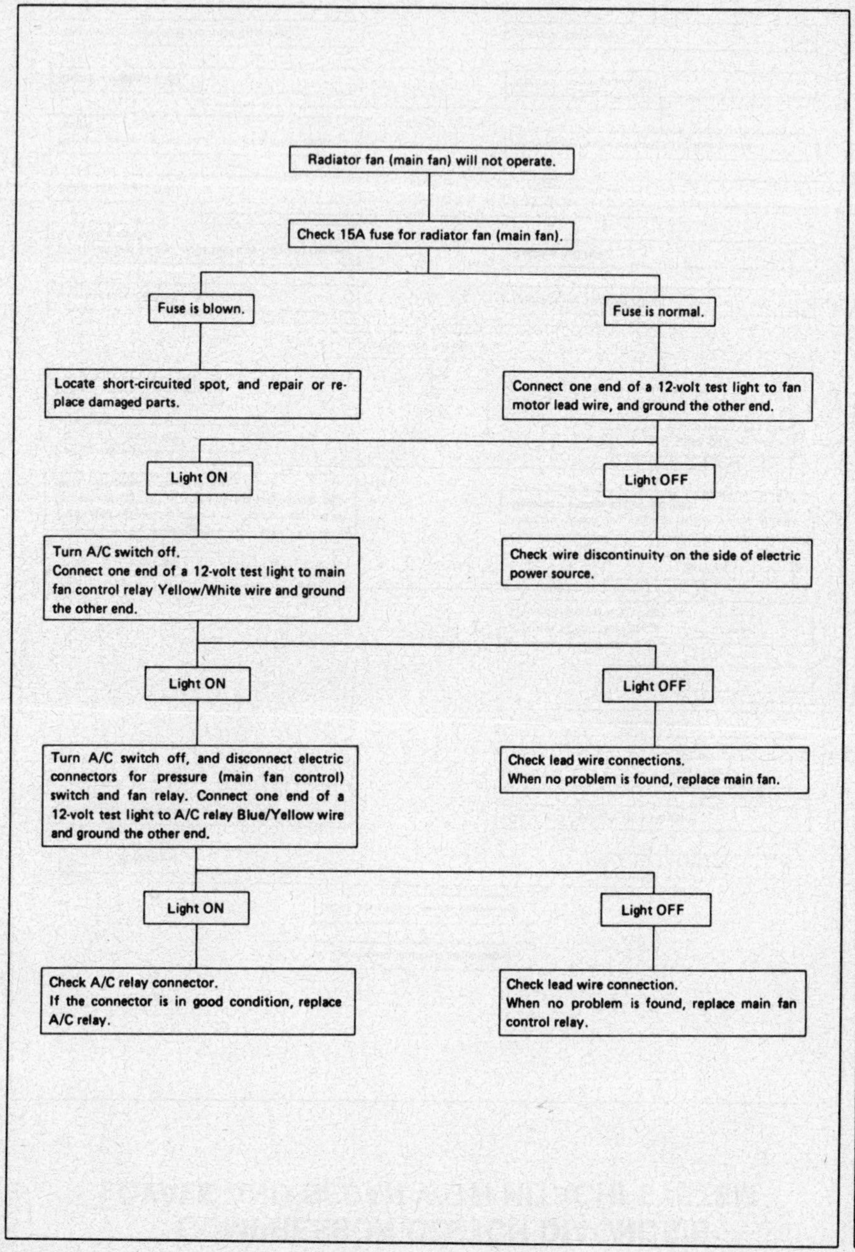
Radiator fan (main fan) will not operate.
Check 15A fuse for radiator fan (main fan).
Fuse is blown.
Fuse is normal.
Locate short-circuited spot, and repair or replace damaged parts.
Connect one end of a 12-volt test light to fan motor lead wire, and ground the other end.
Light ON
Light OFF
Turn A/C switch off.
Connect one end of a 12-volt test light to main fan control relay Yellow/White wire and ground the other end.
Check wire discontinuity on the side of electric power source.
Light ON
Light OFF
Turn A/C switch off, and disconnect electric connectors for pressure (main fan control) switch and fan relay. Connect one end of a 12-volt test light to A/C relay Blue/Yellow wire and ground the other end.
Check lead wire connections.
When no problem is found, replace main fan.
Light ON
Light OFF
Check A/C relay connector.
If the connector is in good condition, replace A/C relay.
Check lead wire connection.
When no problem is found, replace main fan control relay.

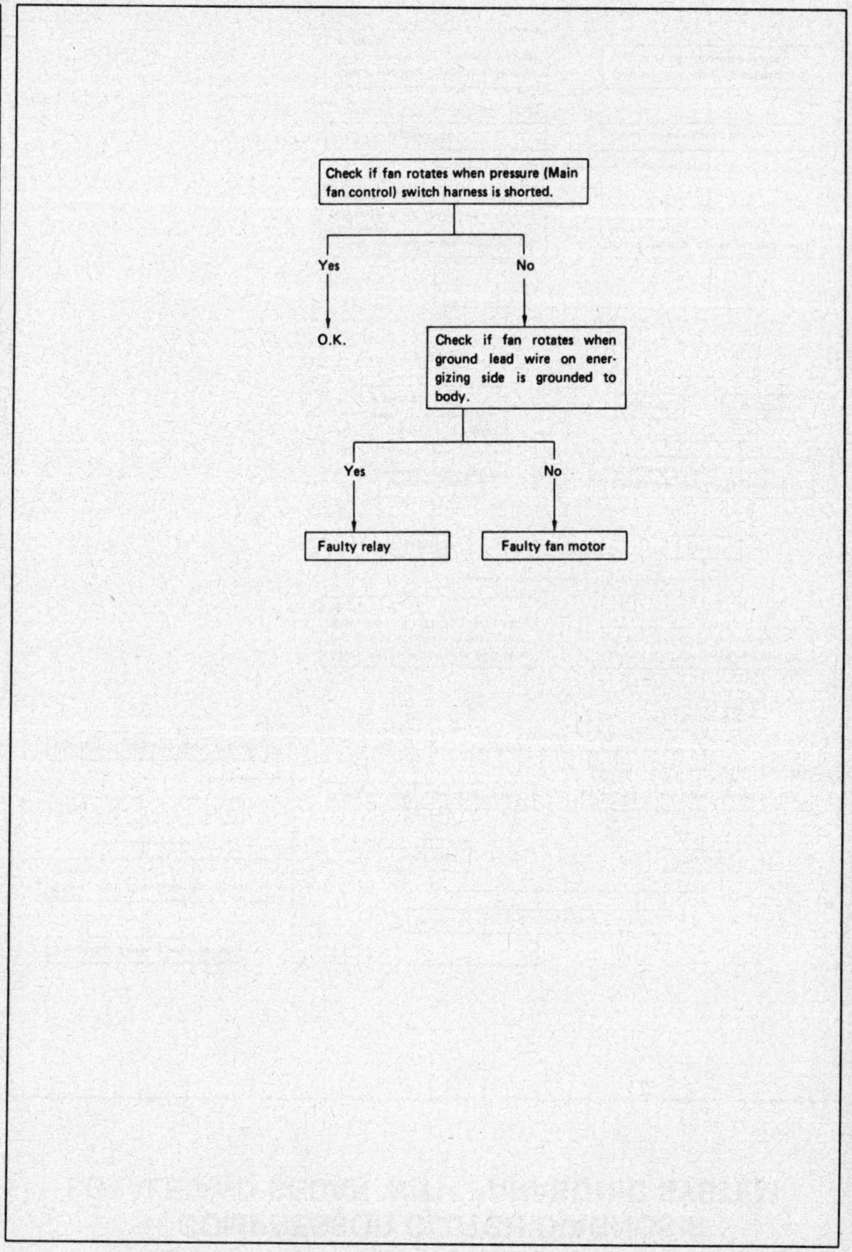
Check if fan rotates when pressure (Main fan control) switch harness is shorted.
Yes
No
O.K.
Check if fan rotates when ground lead wire on energizing side is grounded to body.
Yes
No
Faulty relay
Faulty fan motor

PULSER AMPLIFIER AND RELATED CIRCUIT DIAGNOSIS—LOYALE AND SEDAN WITH HITACHI SYSTEM

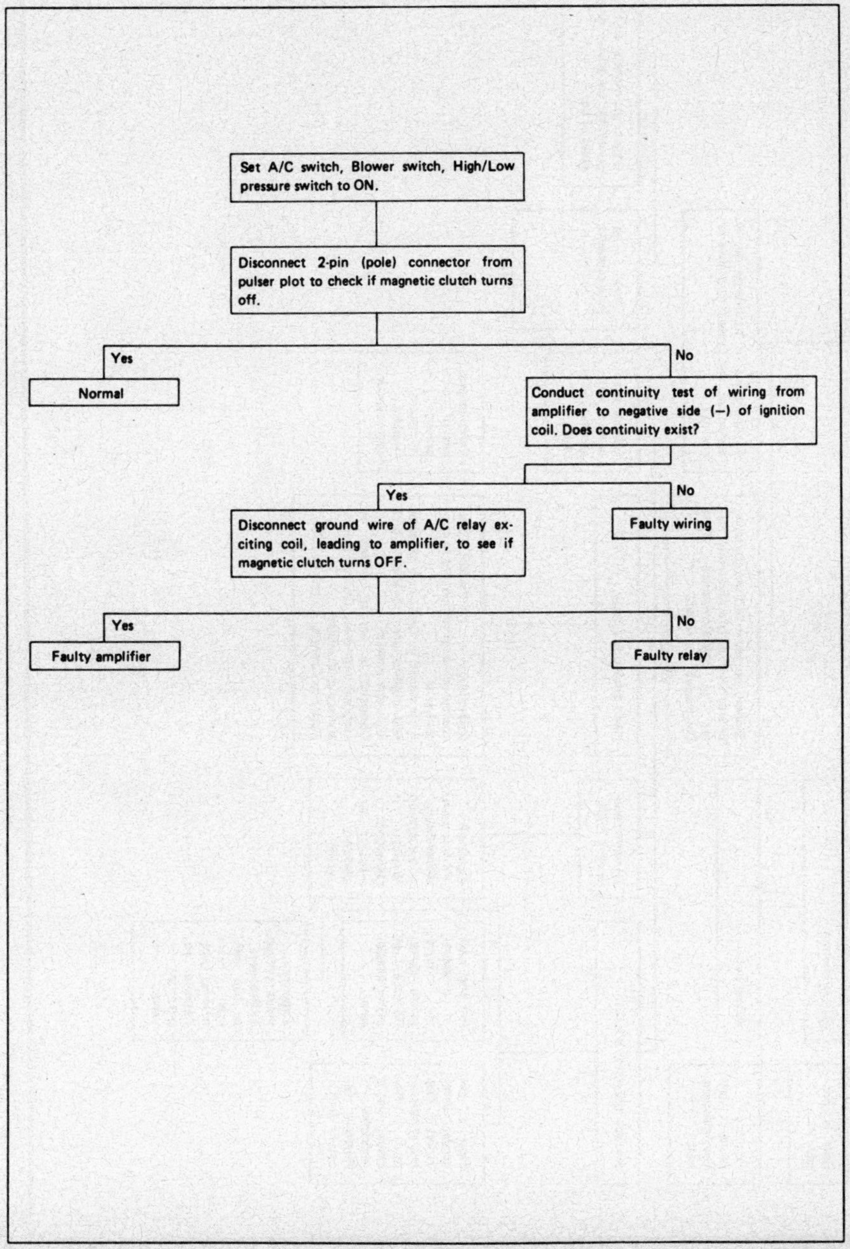
Set A/C switch, Blower switch, High/Low pressure switch to ON.
Disconnect 2-pin (pole) connector from pulser plot to check if magnetic clutch turns off.
Yes
Normal
No
Conduct continuity test of wiring from amplifier to negative side (−) of ignition coil. Does continuity exist?
Yes
Disconnect ground wire of A/C relay exciting coil, leading to amplifier, to see if magnetic clutch turns OFF.
No
Faulty wiring
Yes
Faulty amplifier
No
Faulty relay

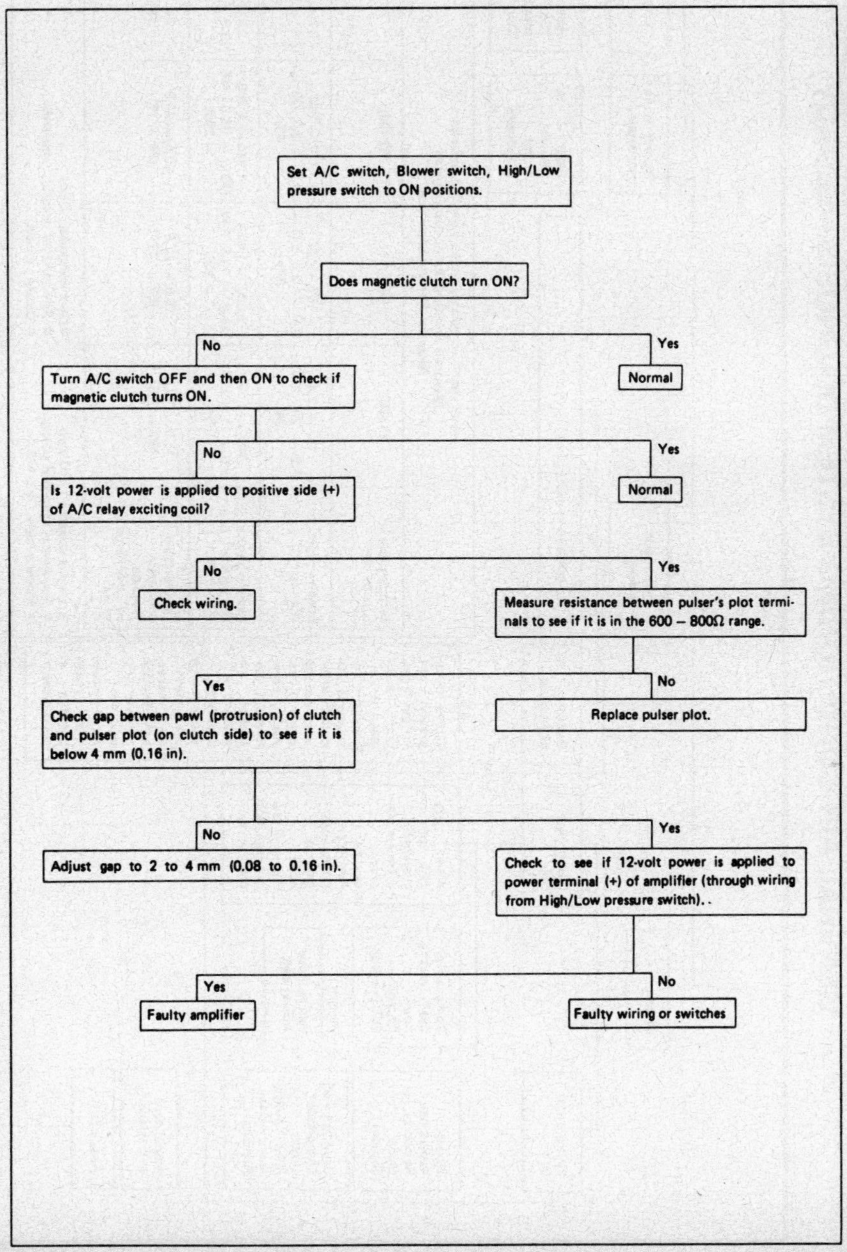
Set A/C switch, Blower switch, High/Low pressure switch to ON positions.
Does magnetic clutch turn ON?
No
Turn A/C switch OFF and then ON to check if magnetic clutch turns ON.
Yes
Normal
No
Is 12-volt power is applied to positive side (+) of A/C relay exciting coil?
Yes
Normal
No
Check wiring.
Yes
Measure resistance between pulser's plot terminals to see if it is in the 600 – 800Ω range.
Yes
Check gap between pawl (protrusion) of clutch and pulser plot (on clutch side) to see if it is below 4 mm (0.16 in).
No
Replace pulser plot.
No
Adjust gap to 2 to 4 mm (0.08 to 0.16 in).
Yes
Check to see if 12-volt power is applied to power terminal (+) of amplifier (through wiring from High/Low pressure switch)..
Yes
Faulty amplifier
No
Faulty wiring or switches

GENERAL AIR CONDITIONING SYSTEM DIAGNOSIS—LEGACY

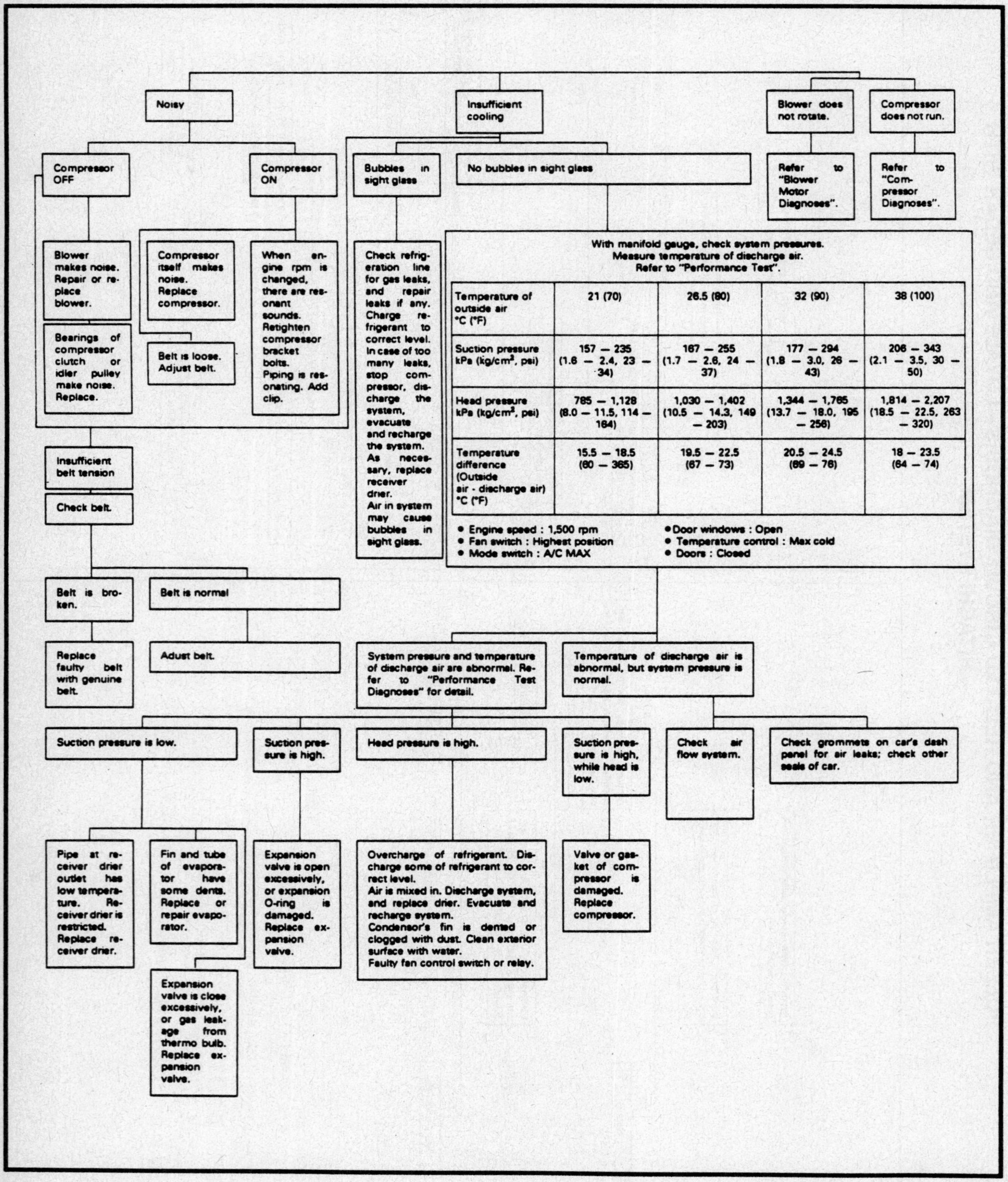
Noisy
Insufficient cooling
Blower does not rotate.
Compressor does not run.
Compressor OFF
Compressor ON
Bubbles in sight glass
No bubbles in sight glass
Refer to "Blower Motor Diagnoses".
Refer to "Compressor Diagnoses".
Blower makes noise. Repair or replace blower.
Compressor itself makes noise. Replace compressor.
When engine rpm is changed, there are resonant sounds. Retighten compressor bracket bolts. Piping is resonating. Add clip.
Check refrigeration line for gas leaks, and repair leaks if any. Charge refrigerant to correct level. In case of too many leaks, stop compressor, discharge the system, evacuate and recharge the system. As necessary, replace receiver drier. Air in system may cause bubbles in sight glass.
With manifold gauge, check system pressures.
Measure temperature of discharge air.
Refer to "Performance Test".
Bearings of compressor clutch or idler pulley make noise. Replace.
Belt is loose. Adjust belt.
Insufficient belt tension
Check belt.
Belt is broken.
Belt is normal
Replace faulty belt with genuine belt.
Adjust belt.
System pressure and temperature of discharge air are abnormal. Refer to "Performance Test Diagnoses" for detail.
Temperature of discharge air is abnormal, but system pressure is normal.
Suction pressure is low.
Suction pressure is high.
Head pressure is high.
Suction pressure is high, while head is low.
Check air flow system.
Check grommets on car's dash panel for air leaks; check other seals of car.
Pipe at receiver drier outlet has low temperature. Receiver drier is restricted. Replace receiver drier.
Fin and tube of evaporator have some dents. Replace or repair evaporator.
Expansion valve is open excessively, or expansion O-ring is damaged. Replace expansion valve.
Overcharge of refrigerant. Discharge some of refrigerant to correct level.
Air is mixed in. Discharge system, and replace drier. Evacuate and recharge system.
Condensor's fin is dented or clogged with dust. Clean exterior surface with water.
Faulty fan control switch or relay.
Valve or gasket of compressor is damaged. Replace compressor.
Expansion valve is close excessively, or gas leakage from thermo bulb. Replace expansion valve.

Temperature of outside air °C (°F)	21 (70)	26.5 (80)	32 (90)	38 (100)
Suction pressure kPa (kg/cm², psi)	157 — 235 (1.6 — 2.4, 23 — 34)	167 — 255 (1.7 — 2.6, 24 — 37)	177 — 294 (1.8 — 3.0, 26 — 43)	206 — 343 (2.1 — 3.5, 30 — 50)
Head pressure kPa (kg/cm², psi)	785 — 1,128 (8.0 — 11.5, 114 — 164)	1,030 — 1,402 (10.5 — 14.3, 149 — 203)	1,344 — 1,765 (13.7 — 18.0, 195 — 256)	1,814 — 2,207 (18.5 — 22.5, 263 — 320)
Temperature difference (Outside air - discharge air) °C (°F)	15.5 — 18.5 (60 — 365)	19.5 — 22.5 (67 — 73)	20.5 — 24.5 (69 — 76)	18 — 23.5 (64 — 74)

- Engine speed : 1,500 rpm
- Fan switch : Highest position
- Mode switch : A/C MAX
- Door windows : Open
- Temperature control : Max cold
- Doors : Closed

Performance Test Diagnoses

Of various conditions caused to othe air conditioning system, the characteristics revealed on manifold gauge reading are shown in the following.
As to the method of a performance test, refer to the item of "Performance Test".
Each shaded area on the following tables indicates a reading of the normal system when the temperature of outside air is 32.5°C (91°F).

Condition		Probable cause	Corrective action
INSUFFICIENT REFRIGERANT CHARGE 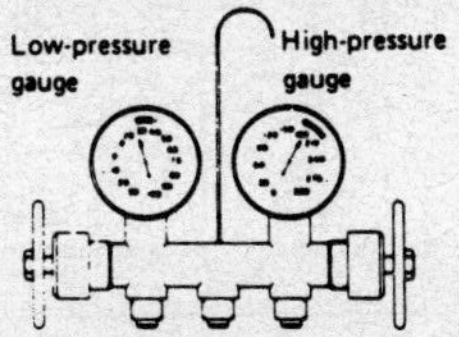 Low-pressure gauge High-pressure gauge	Insufficient cooling. Bubbles appear in sight glass.	Refrigerant is small, or leaking a little.	1. Leak test. 2. Repair leak. 3. Charge system. Evacuate, as necessary, and recharge system.
ALMOST NO REFRIGERANT 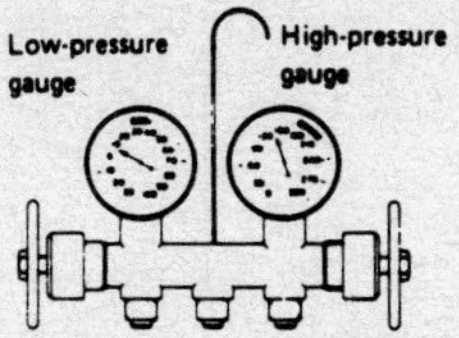 Low-pressure gauge High-pressure gauge	No cooling action. In sight glass appear a lot of bubbles or something like mist.	Serious refrigerant leak.	Stop compressor immediately. 1. Leak test. 2. Discharge system. 3. Repair leak(s). 4. Replace receiver drier if necessary. 5. Check oil level. 6. Evacuate and recharge system.
FAULTY EXPANSION VALVE 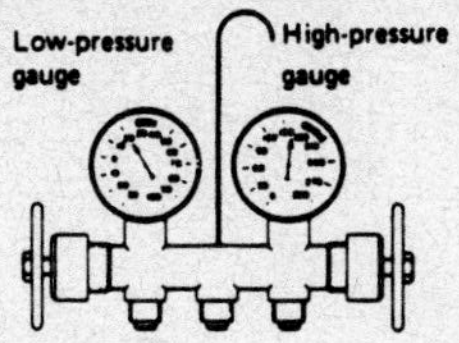 Low-pressure gauge High-pressure gauge	Slight cooling. Sweating or frosted expansion valve inlet.	Expansion valve restricts refrigerant flow. • Expansion valve is clogged. • Expansion valve is inoperative. Valve stuck closed. Thermal bulb has lost charge.	If valve inlet reveals sweat or frost: 1. Discharge system. 2. Remove valve and clean it. Replace it if necessary. 3. Evacuate system. 4. Charge system. If valve does not operate: 1. Discharge system. 2. Replace valve. 3. Evacuate and charge system.

Condition		Probable cause	Corrective action
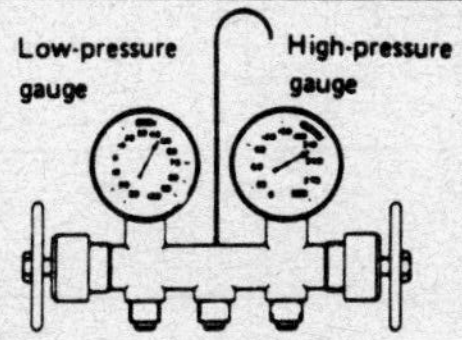 Low-pressure gauge High-pressure gauge 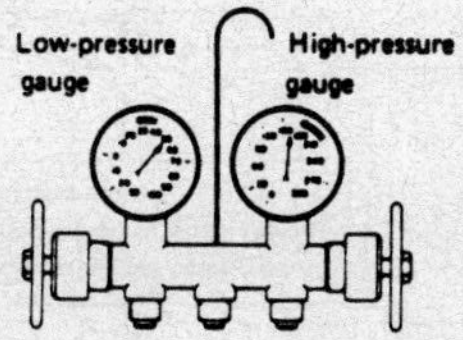 Low-pressure gauge High-pressure gauge	Insufficient cooling. Sweated suction line. No cooling. Sweating or frosted suction line.	Expansion valve allows too much refrigerant through evaporator. Faulty seal of O-ring in expansion valve.	Check valve for operation. If suction side does not show a pressure decrease, replace valve. 1. Discharges system. 2. Remove expansion valve and replace O-ring. 3. Evacuate and replace system.
AIR IN SYSTEM 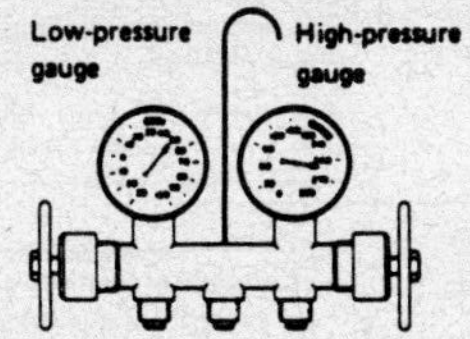 Low-pressure gauge High-pressure gauge	Insufficient cooling. Sight glass shows occasional bubbles.	Air mixed with refrigerant in system.	1. Discharge system. 2. Replace receiver drier. 3. Evacuate and charge system.
MOISTURE IN SYSTEM 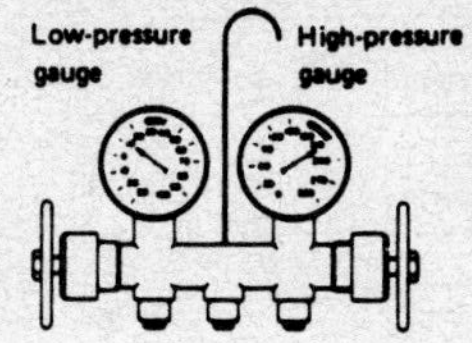 Low-pressure gauge High-pressure gauge	After operation for a while, pressure on suction side may show vacuum pressure reading. During this condition, discharge air will be warm. As warning of this, reading shows 39 kPa (0.4 kg/cm^2, 6 psi) vibration.	Drier is saturated with moisture. Moisture has frozen at expansion valve. Refrigerant flow is restricted.	1. Discharge system. 2. Replace receiver drier (twice if necessary). 3. Evacuate system completely. (Repeat 30-minute evacuating three times.) 4. Recharge system.

PERFORMANCE TEST DIAGNOSIS—LEGACY

Condition		Probable cause	Corrective action
FAULTY CONDENSER 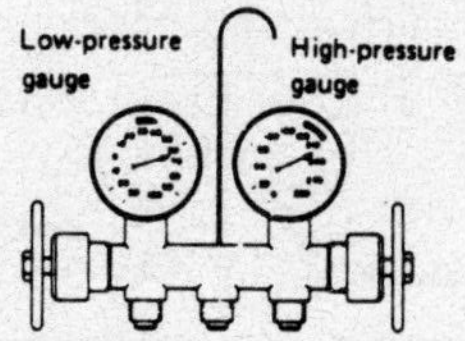 Low-pressure gauge High-pressure gauge	No cooling action: engine may overheat. Bubbles appear in sight glass of drier. Suction line is very hot.	Condenser is often found not functioning well.	• Check condenser cooling fan. • Check condenser for dirt accumulation. • Check engine cooling system for overheat. • Check for refrigerant overcharge. **If pressure remains high in spite of all above actions taken, remove and inspect the condenser for possible oil clogging.**
HIGH PRESSURE LINE BLOCKED 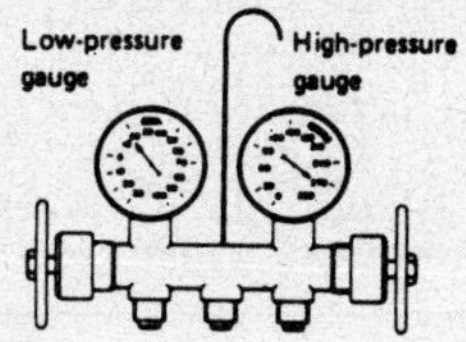 Low-pressure gauge High-pressure gauge	Insufficient cooling. Frosted high pressure liquid line.	Drier clogged, or restriction in high pressure line.	1. Discharge system. 2. Remove receiver drier or strainer and replace it. 3. Evacuate and charge system.
FAULTY COMPRESSOR 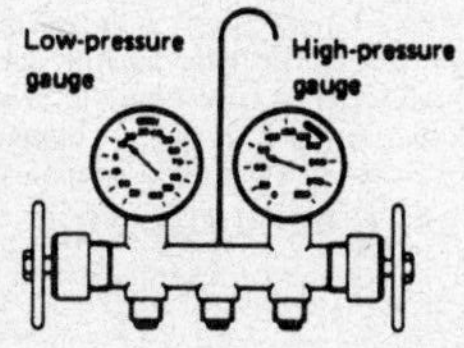 Low-pressure gauge High-pressure gauge	Insufficient cooling.	Internal problem in compressor, or damaged gasket and valve.	1. Discharge system. 2. Remove and check compressor. 3. Repair or replace compressor. 4. Check oil level. 5. Replace receiver drier. 6. Evacuate and charge system

BLOWER MOTOR DIAGNOSIS—LEGACY

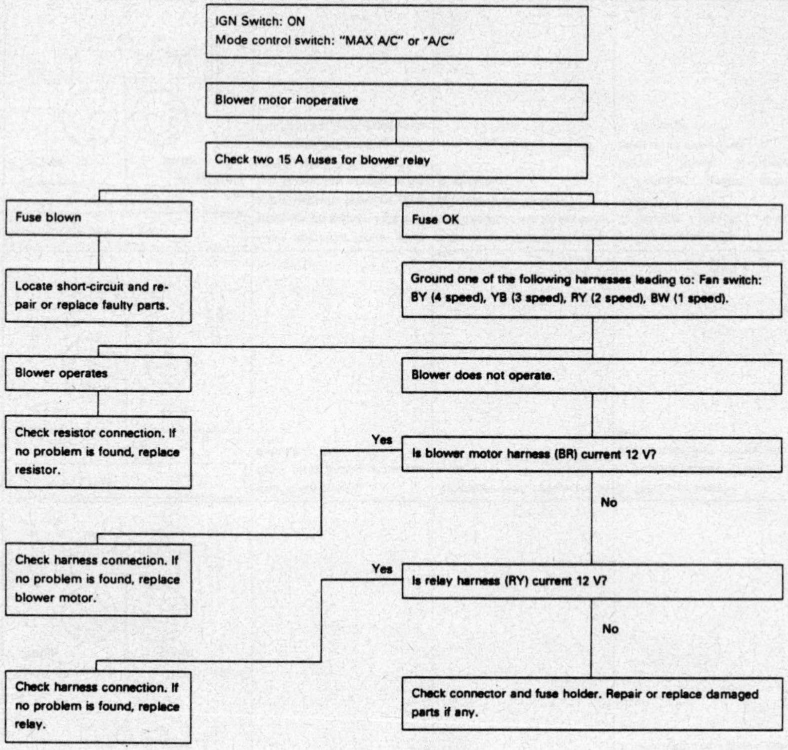
IGN Switch: ON
Mode control switch: "MAX A/C" or "A/C"
Blower motor inoperative
Check two 15 A fuses for blower relay
Fuse blown
Locate short-circuit and repair or replace faulty parts.
Fuse OK
Ground one of the following harnesses leading to: Fan switch: BY (4 speed), YB (3 speed), RY (2 speed), BW (1 speed).
Blower operates
Check resistor connection. If no problem is found, replace resistor.
Blower does not operate.
Is blower motor harness (BR) current 12 V?
Yes
No
Check harness connection. If no problem is found, replace blower motor.
Is relay harness (RY) current 12 V?
Yes
No
Check harness connection. If no problem is found, replace relay.
Check connector and fuse holder. Repair or replace damaged parts if any.

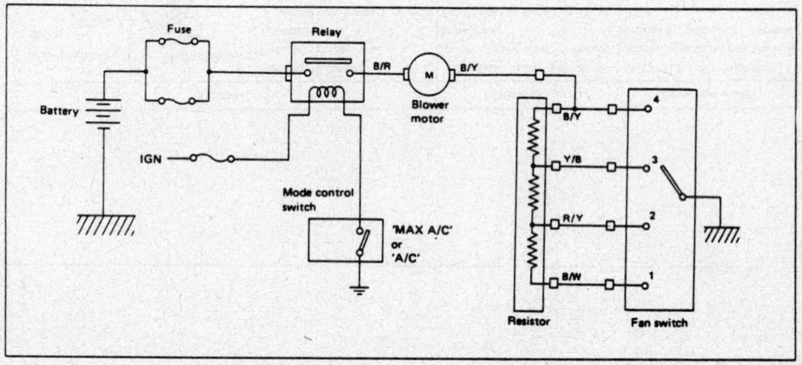
Fuse
Relay
Battery
IGN
B/R
M
B/Y
Blower motor
Mode control switch
'MAX A/C' or 'A/C'
B/Y
Y/B
R/Y
B/W
4
3
2
1
Resistor
Fan switch

COMPRESSOR DIAGNOSIS—LEGACY

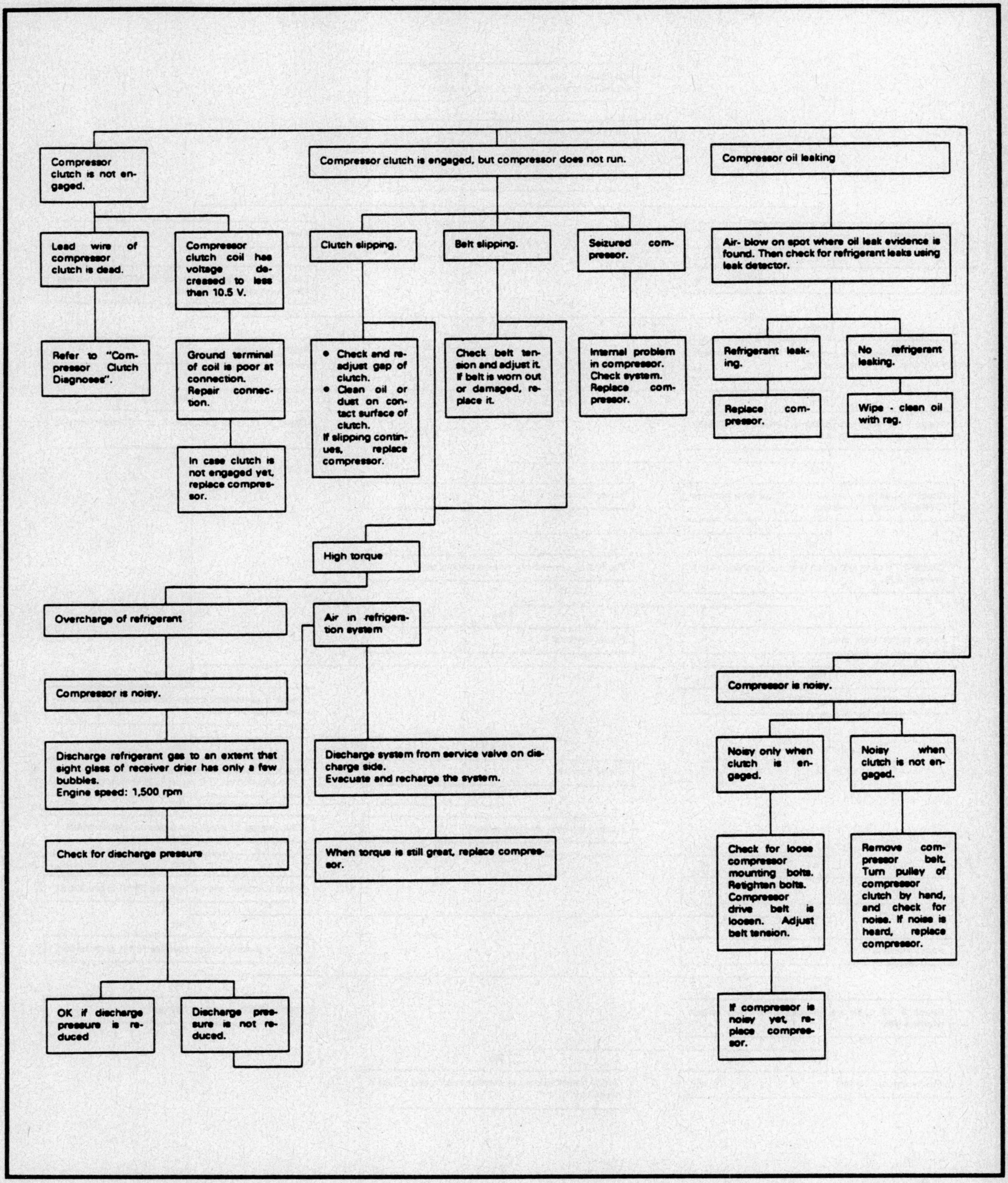
Compressor clutch is not engaged.
Compressor clutch is engaged, but compressor does not run.
Compressor oil leaking
Lead wire of compressor clutch is dead.
Compressor clutch coil has voltage decreased to less than 10.5 V.
Clutch slipping.
Belt slipping.
Seizured compressor.
Air- blow on spot where oil leak evidence is found. Then check for refrigerant leaks using leak detector.
Refer to "Compressor Clutch Diagnoses".
Ground terminal of coil is poor at connection. Repair connection.
In case clutch is not engaged yet, replace compressor.
• Check and readjust gap of clutch.
• Clean oil or dust on contact surface of clutch.
If slipping continues, replace compressor.
Check belt tension and adjust it. If belt is worn out or damaged, replace it.
Internal problem in compressor. Check system. Replace compressor.
Refrigerant leaking.
No refrigerant leaking.
Replace compressor.
Wipe - clean oil with rag.
High torque
Overcharge of refrigerant
Air in refrigeration system
Compressor is noisy.
Discharge refrigerant gas to an extent that sight glass of receiver drier has only a few bubbles.
Engine speed: 1,500 rpm
Discharge system from service valve on discharge side.
Evacuate and recharge the system.
Check for discharge pressure
When torque is still great, replace compressor.
OK if discharge pressure is reduced
Discharge pressure is not reduced.
Compressor is noisy.
Noisy only when clutch is engaged.
Noisy when clutch is not engaged.
Check for loose compressor mounting bolts. Retighten bolts. Compressor drive belt is loosen. Adjust belt tension.
Remove compressor belt. Turn pulley of compressor clutch by hand, and check for noise. If noise is heard, replace compressor.
If compressor is noisy yet, replace compressor.

COMPRESSOR CLUTCH DIAGNOSIS—LEGACY

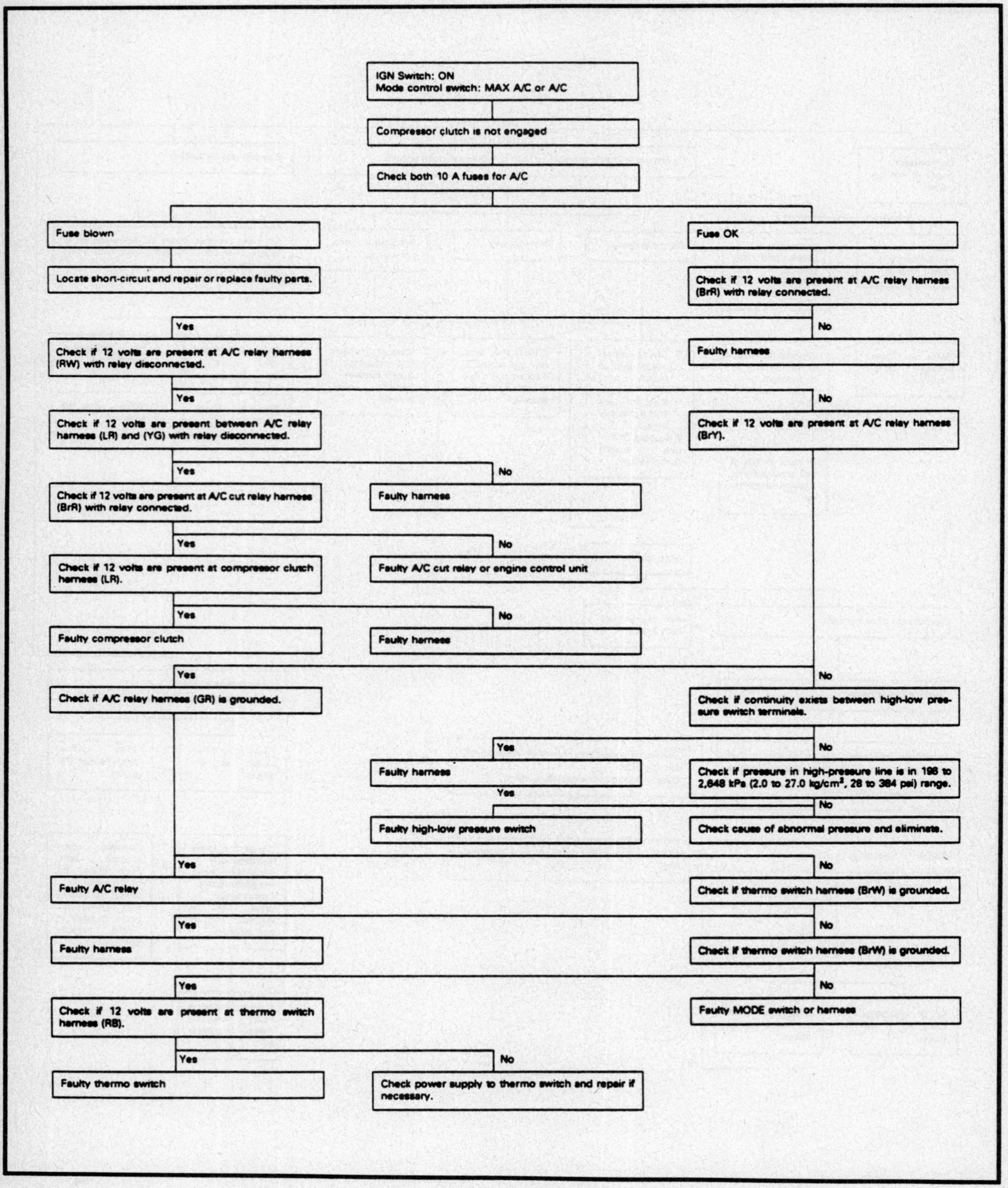
IGN Switch: ON
Mode control switch: MAX A/C or A/C
Compressor clutch is not engaged
Check both 10 A fuses for A/C
Fuse blown
Locate short-circuit and repair or replace faulty parts.
Fuse OK
Check if 12 volts are present at A/C relay harness (BrR) with relay connected.
Yes
Check if 12 volts are present at A/C relay harness (RW) with relay disconnected.
No
Faulty harness
Yes
Check if 12 volts are present between A/C relay harness (LR) and (YG) with relay disconnected.
No
Check if 12 volts are present at A/C relay harness (BrY).
Yes
Check if 12 volts are present at A/C cut relay harness (BrR) with relay connected.
No
Faulty harness
Yes
Check if 12 volts are present at compressor clutch harness (LR).
No
Faulty A/C cut relay or engine control unit
Yes
Faulty compressor clutch
No
Faulty harness
Yes
Check if A/C relay harness (GR) is grounded.
No
Check if continuity exists between high-low pressure switch terminals.
Yes
Faulty harness
No
Check if pressure in high-pressure line is in 196 to 2,648 kPa (2.0 to 27.0 kg/cm², 28 to 384 psi) range.
Yes
Faulty high-low pressure switch
No
Check cause of abnormal pressure and eliminate.
Yes
Faulty A/C relay
No
Check if thermo switch harness (BrW) is grounded.
Yes
Faulty harness
No
Check if thermo switch harness (BrW) is grounded.
Yes
Check if 12 volts are present at thermo switch harness (RB).
No
Faulty MODE switch or harness
Yes
Faulty thermo switch
No
Check power supply to thermo switch and repair if necessary.

RADIATOR MAIN FAN DIAGNOSIS—LEGACY

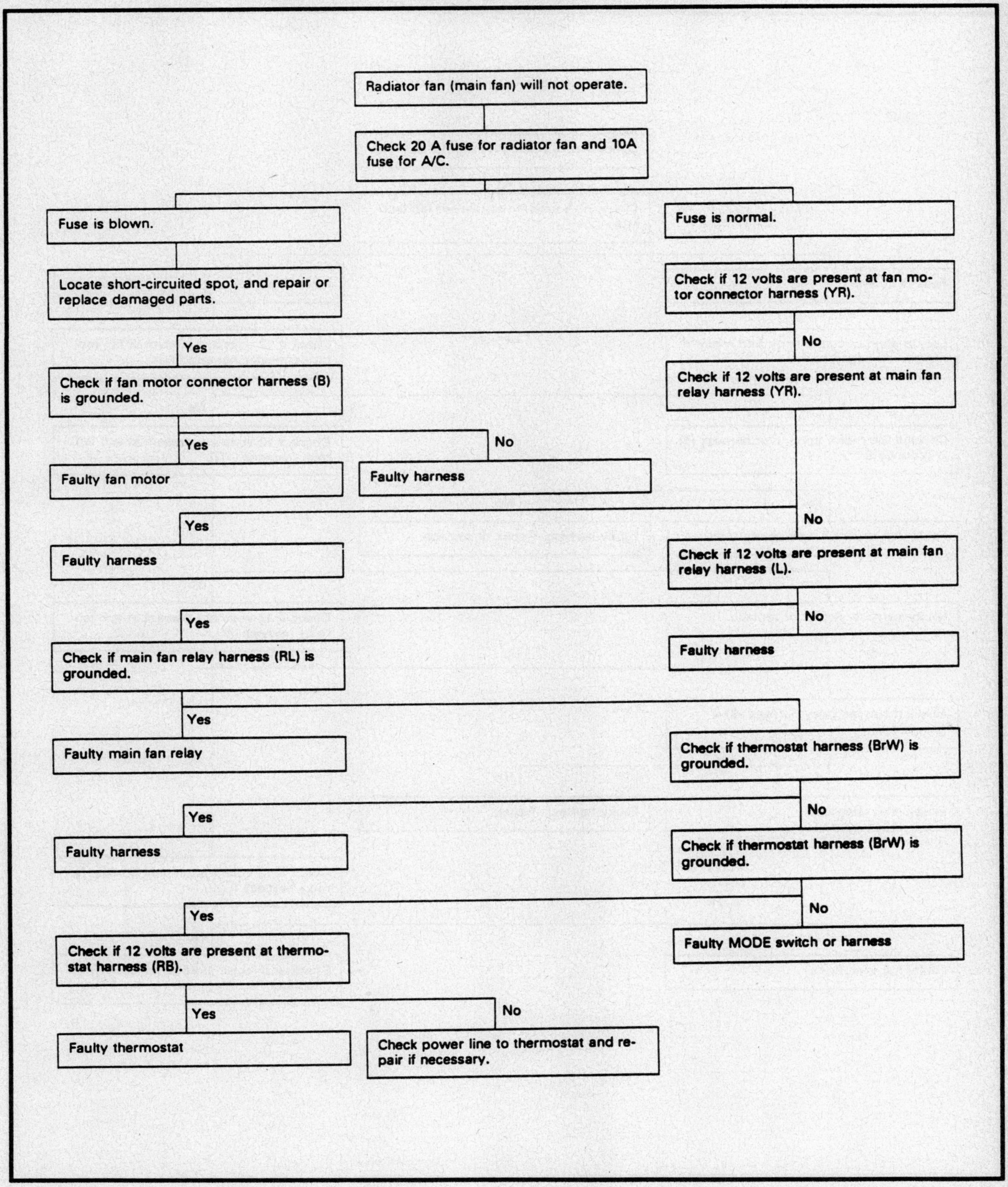
Radiator fan (main fan) will not operate.
Check 20 A fuse for radiator fan and 10A fuse for A/C.
Fuse is blown.
Fuse is normal.
Locate short-circuited spot, and repair or replace damaged parts.
Check if 12 volts are present at fan motor connector harness (YR).
Yes
No
Check if fan motor connector harness (B) is grounded.
Check if 12 volts are present at main fan relay harness (YR).
Yes
No
Faulty fan motor
Faulty harness
Yes
No
Faulty harness
Check if 12 volts are present at main fan relay harness (L).
Yes
No
Check if main fan relay harness (RL) is grounded.
Faulty harness
Yes
Faulty main fan relay
Check if thermostat harness (BrW) is grounded.
Yes
No
Faulty harness
Check if thermostat harness (BrW) is grounded.
Yes
No
Check if 12 volts are present at thermostat harness (RB).
Faulty MODE switch or harness
Yes
No
Faulty thermostat
Check power line to thermostat and repair if necessary.

RADIATOR SUB FAN DIAGNOSIS—LEGACY

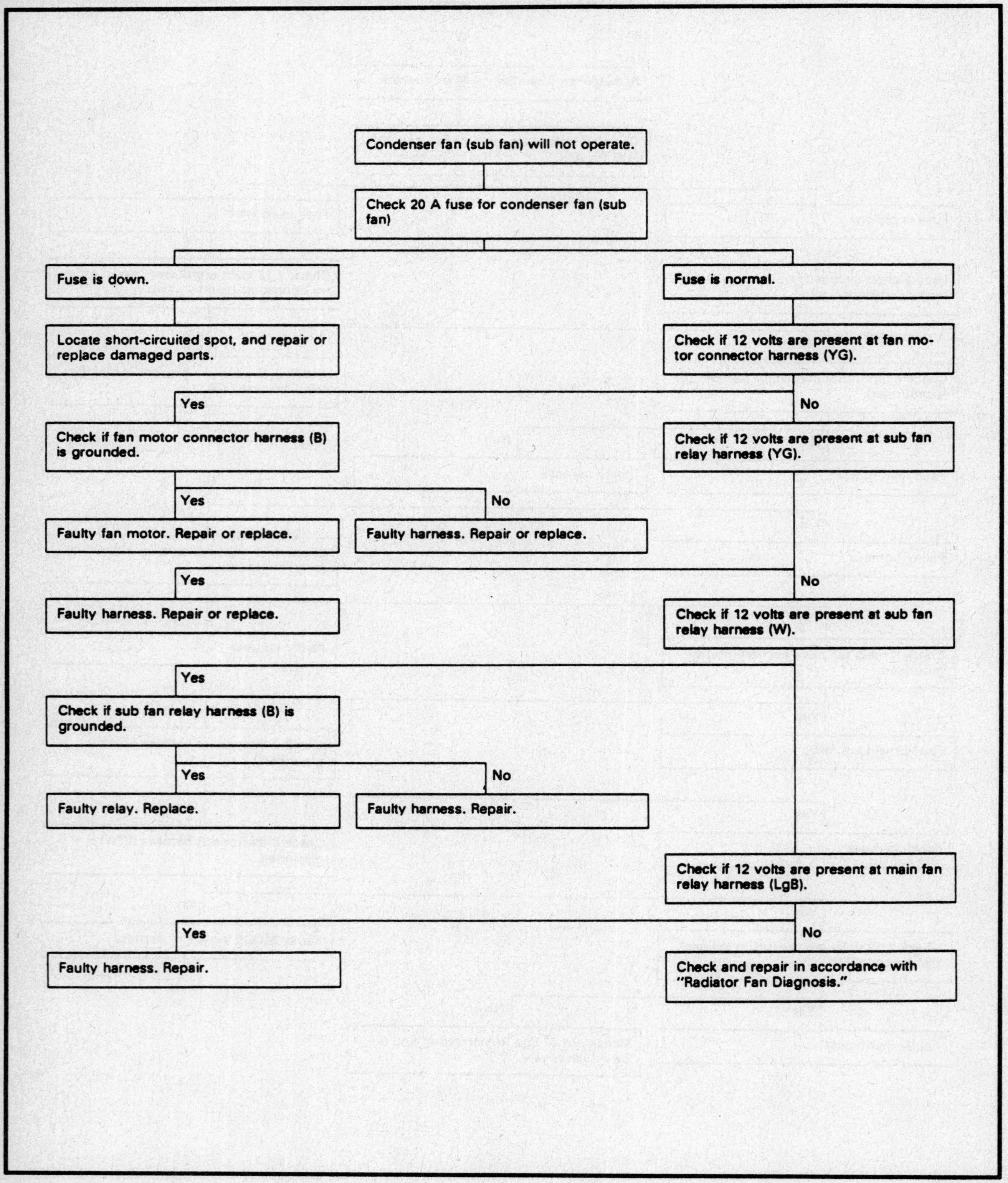
Condenser fan (sub fan) will not operate.
Check 20 A fuse for condenser fan (sub fan)
Fuse is down.
Fuse is normal.
Locate short-circuited spot, and repair or replace damaged parts.
Check if 12 volts are present at fan motor connector harness (YG).
Yes
No
Check if fan motor connector harness (B) is grounded.
Check if 12 volts are present at sub fan relay harness (YG).
Yes
No
Faulty fan motor. Repair or replace.
Faulty harness. Repair or replace.
Yes
No
Faulty harness. Repair or replace.
Check if 12 volts are present at sub fan relay harness (W).
Yes
Check if sub fan relay harness (B) is grounded.
Yes
No
Faulty relay. Replace.
Faulty harness. Repair.
Check if 12 volts are present at main fan relay harness (LgB).
Yes
No
Faulty harness. Repair.
Check and repair in accordance with "Radiator Fan Diagnosis."

RADIATOR SUB FAN DIAGNOSIS—LEGACY

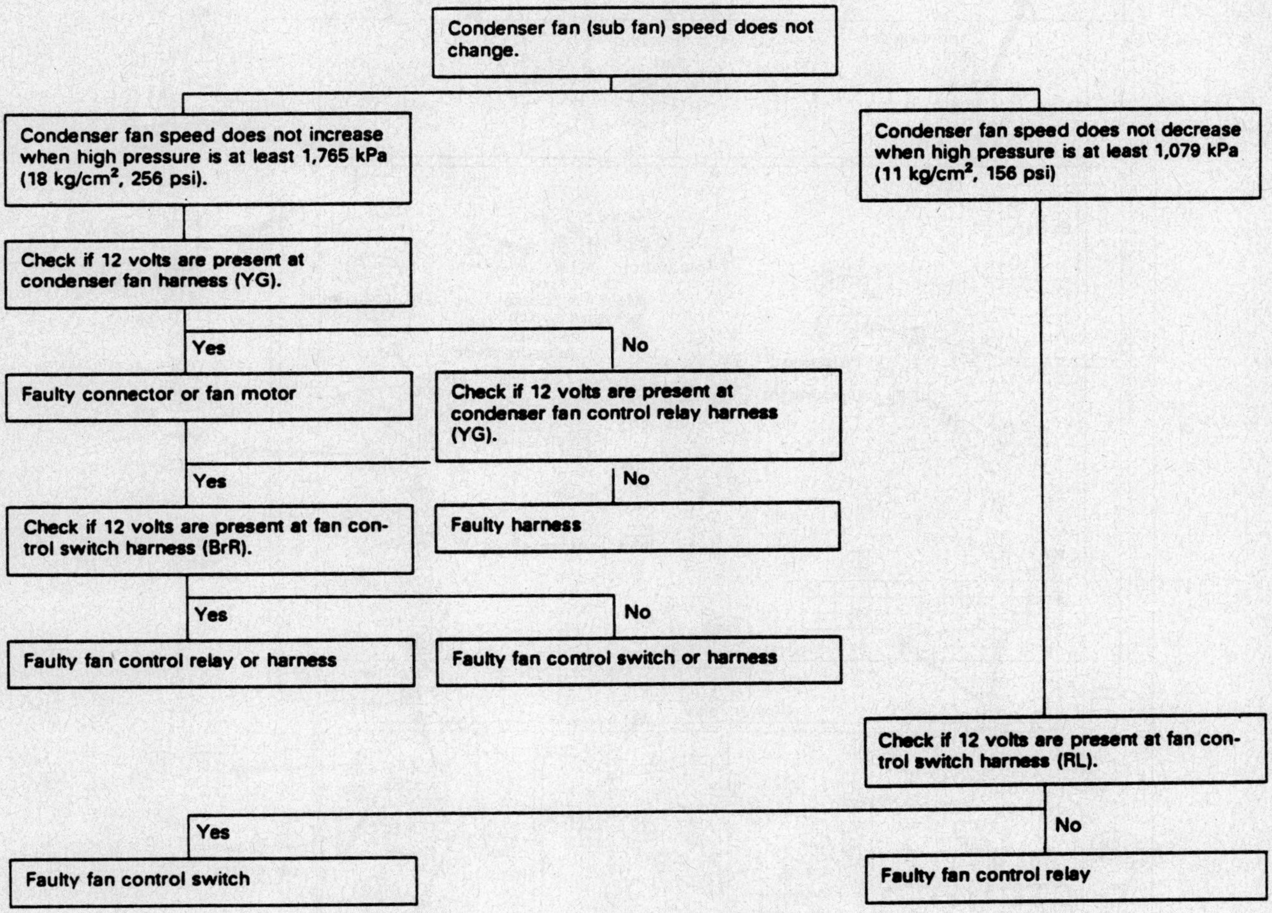
Condenser fan (sub fan) speed does not change.
Condenser fan speed does not increase when high pressure is at least 1,765 kPa (18 kg/cm², 256 psi).
Condenser fan speed does not decrease when high pressure is at least 1,079 kPa (11 kg/cm², 156 psi)
Check if 12 volts are present at condenser fan harness (YG).
Yes
No
Faulty connector or fan motor
Check if 12 volts are present at condenser fan control relay harness (YG).
Yes
No
Check if 12 volts are present at fan control switch harness (BrR).
Faulty harness
Yes
No
Faulty fan control relay or harness
Faulty fan control switch or harness
Check if 12 volts are present at fan control switch harness (RL).
Yes
No
Faulty fan control switch
Faulty fan control relay

WIRING SCHEMATICS

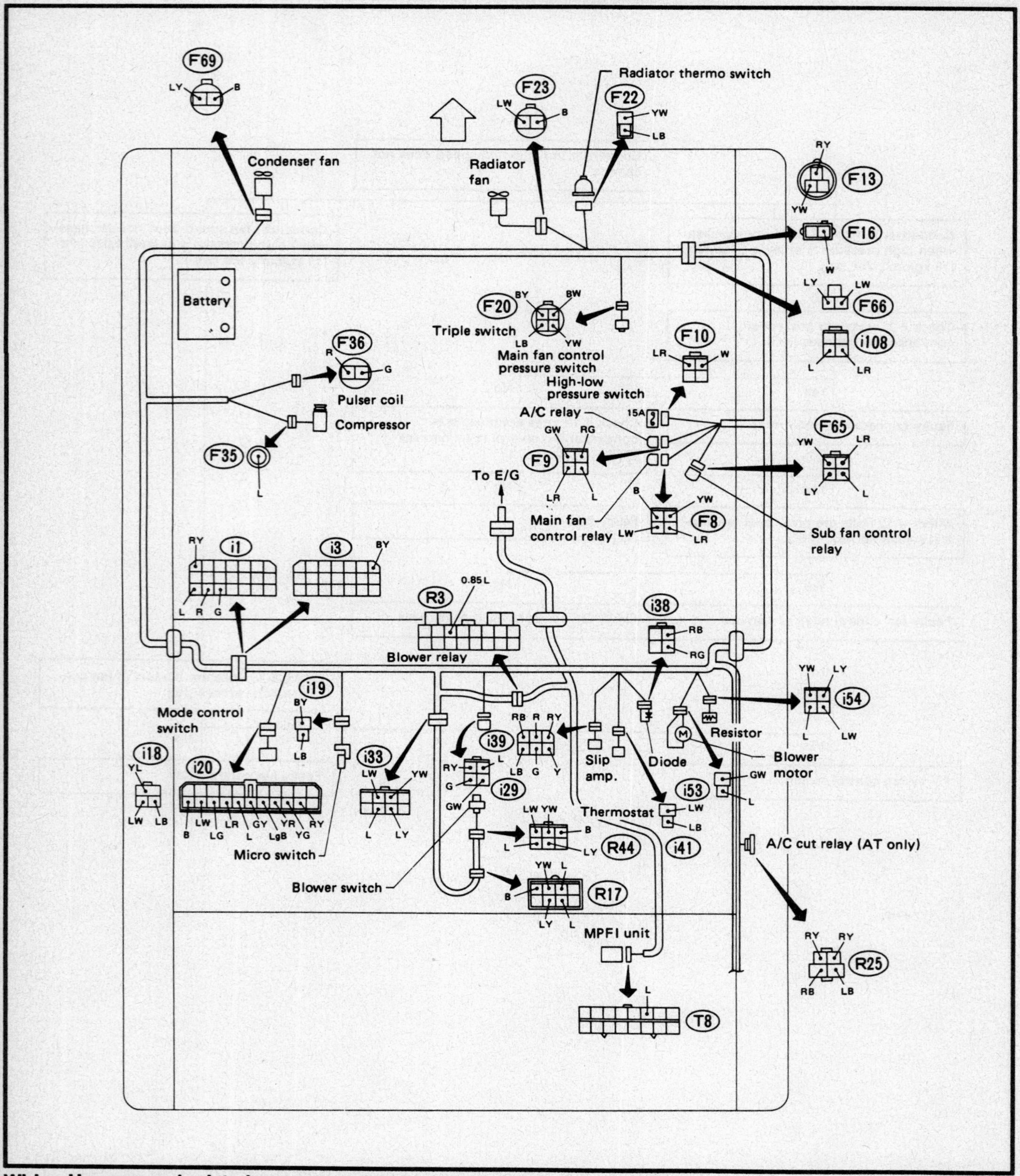
F69
LY
B
Condenser fan
F23
LW
B
Radiator fan
Radiator thermo switch
F22
YW
LB
RY
F13
YW
F16
W
LY
LW
F66
i108
L
LR
Battery
F20
BY
BW
LB
YW
Triple switch
Main fan control pressure switch
High-low pressure switch
F10
LR
W
F36
R
G
Pulser coil
Compressor
F35
L
A/C relay
15A
GW
RG
F9
LR
L
To E/G
F65
YW
LR
LY
L
B
YW
F8
LW
LR
Main fan control relay
Sub fan control relay
RY
i1
L
R
G
i3
BY
0.85 L
R3
Blower relay
i38
RB
RG
i54
YW
LY
L
LW
Resistor
Mode control switch
i19
BY
LB
RB
R
RY
i39
LB
G
Y
Slip amp.
Diode
Blower motor
GW
L
i18
YL
LW
LB
i20
B
LW
LG
LR
L
GY
LgB
YR
YG
RY
Micro switch
i33
LW
YW
L
LY
RY
L
G
GW
i29
LW YW
B
L
LY
R44
Thermostat
i53
LW
LB
i41
A/C cut relay (AT only)
Blower switch
YW
L
B
R17
LY
L
MPFI unit
L
T8
RY
RY
R25
RB
LB

Wiring Harness and related component locations—XT Coupe

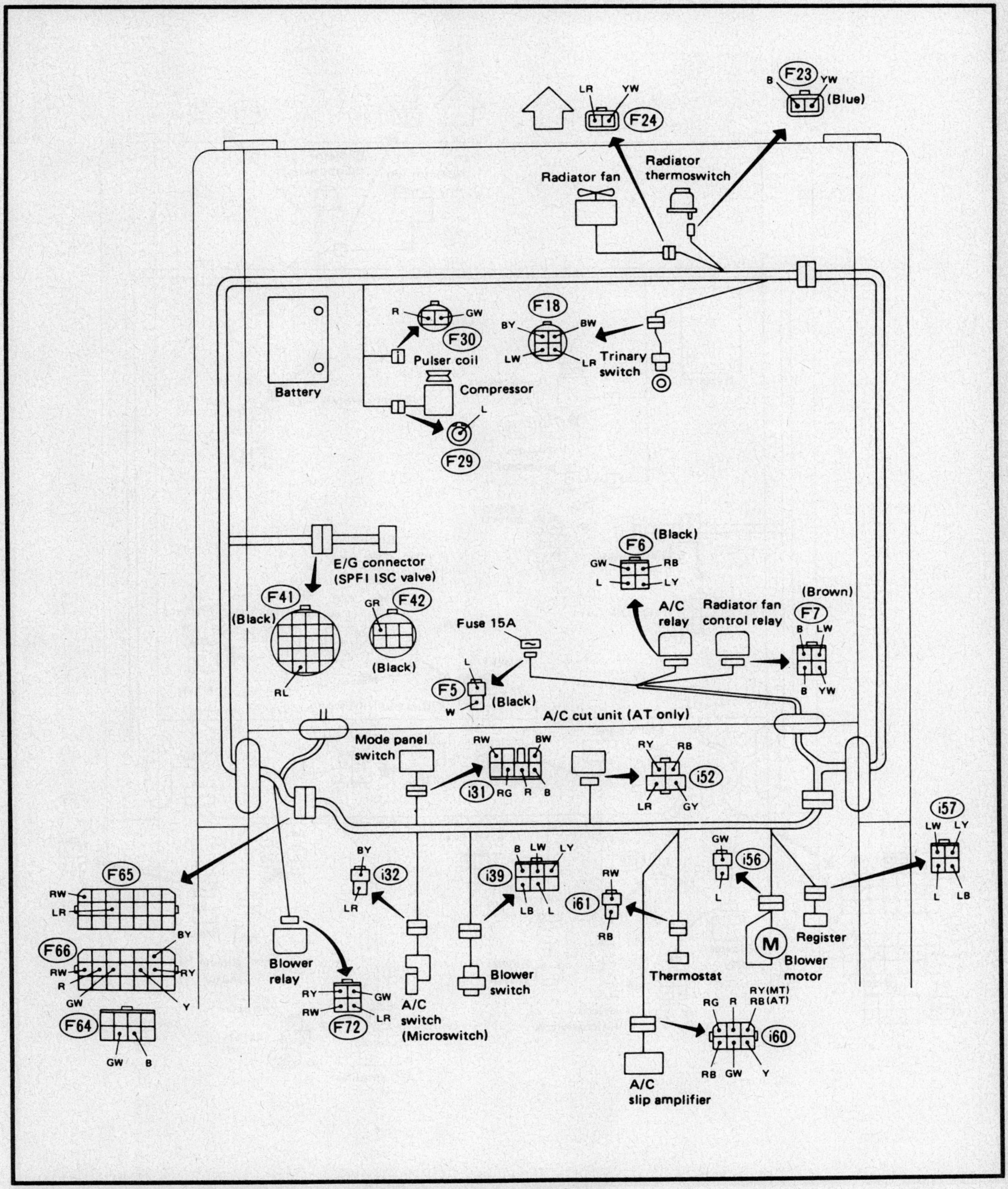
F24
LR
YW
F23
B
YW
(Blue)
Radiator fan
Radiator thermoswitch
Battery
R
GW
F30
Pulser coil
Compressor
L
F29
F18
BY
BW
LW
LR
Trinary switch
E/G connector (SPFI ISC valve)
F41
(Black)
RL
GR
F42
(Black)
F6
(Black)
GW
RB
L
LY
A/C relay
Radiator fan control relay
(Brown)
F7
B
LW
B
YW
Fuse 15A
L
F5
W
(Black)
A/C cut unit (AT only)
Mode panel switch
RW
BW
i31
RG
R
B
RY
RB
i52
LR
GY
i57
LW
LY
L
LB
F65
RW
LR
F66
BY
RW
RY
R
GW
Y
F64
GW
B
Blower relay
RY
GW
RW
LR
F72
BY
i32
LR
A/C switch (Microswitch)
B
LW
LY
i39
LB
L
Blower switch
RW
i61
RB
Thermostat
GW
i56
L
M
Register
Blower motor
RG
R
RY(MT)
RB(AT)
i60
RB
GW
Y
A/C slip amplifier

Wiring Harness and related component locations— Hatachi (USA)

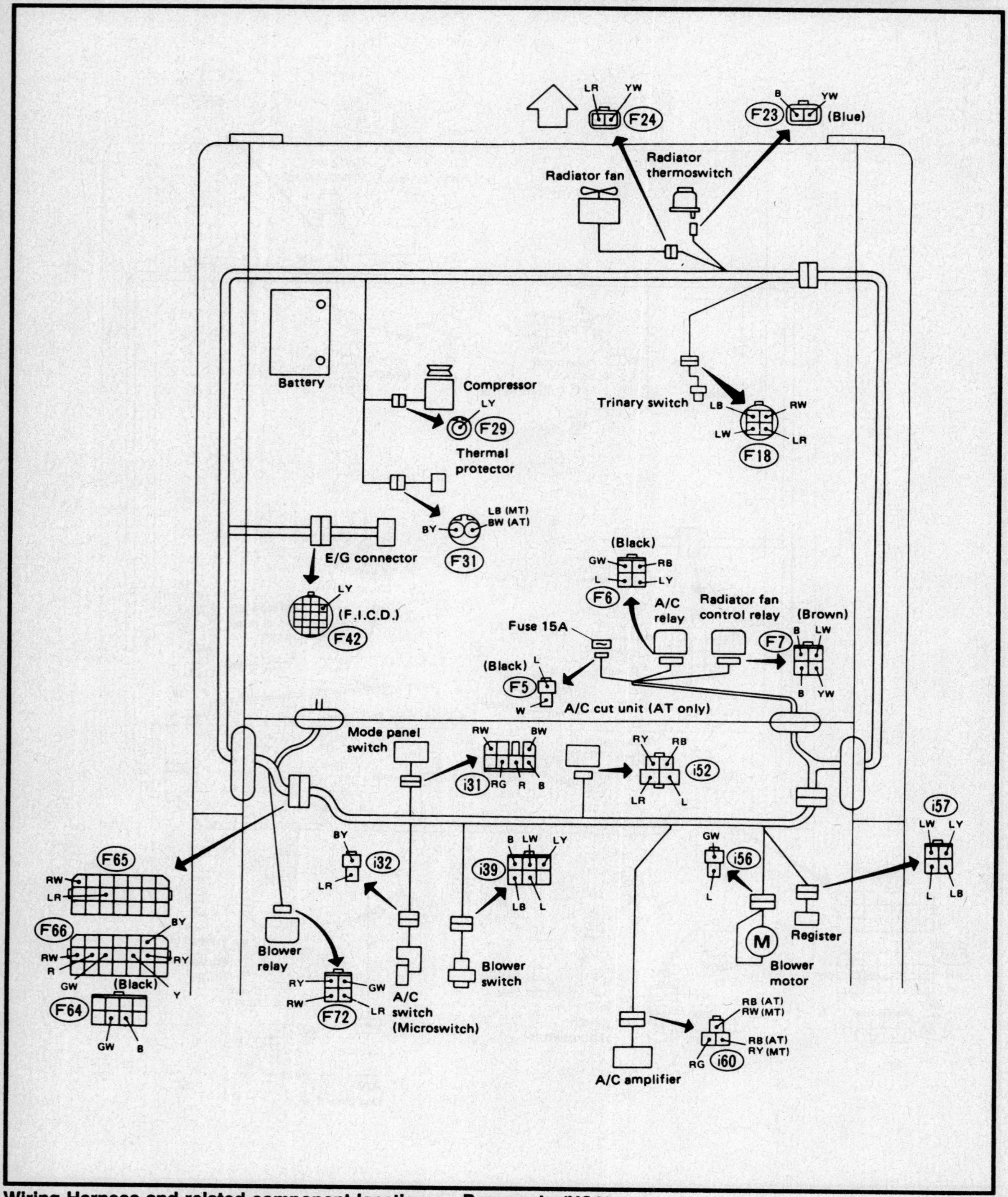
LR
YW
F24
F23
B
YW
(Blue)
Radiator fan
Radiator thermoswitch
Battery
Compressor
LY
F29
Thermal protector
Trinary switch
LB
RW
LW
LR
F18
LB (MT)
BW (AT)
BY
F31
E/G connector
LY
(F.I.C.D.)
F42
(Black)
GW
RB
L
LY
F6
A/C relay
Radiator fan control relay
(Brown)
Fuse 15A
F7
B
LW
B
YW
(Black)
L
F5
W
A/C cut unit (AT only)
Mode panel switch
RW
BW
i31
RG
R
B
RY
RB
i52
LR
L
i57
LW
LY
L
LB
BY
i32
LR
B
LW
LY
i39
LB
L
GW
i56
L
F65
RW
LR
F66
BY
RW
R
RY
GW
(Black)
Y
F64
GW
B
Blower relay
RY
GW
RW
LR
F72
A/C switch (Microswitch)
Blower switch
M
Register
Blower motor
RB (AT)
RW (MT)
RB (AT)
RY (MT)
RG
i60
A/C amplifier

Wiring Harness and related component locations— Panasonic (USA)

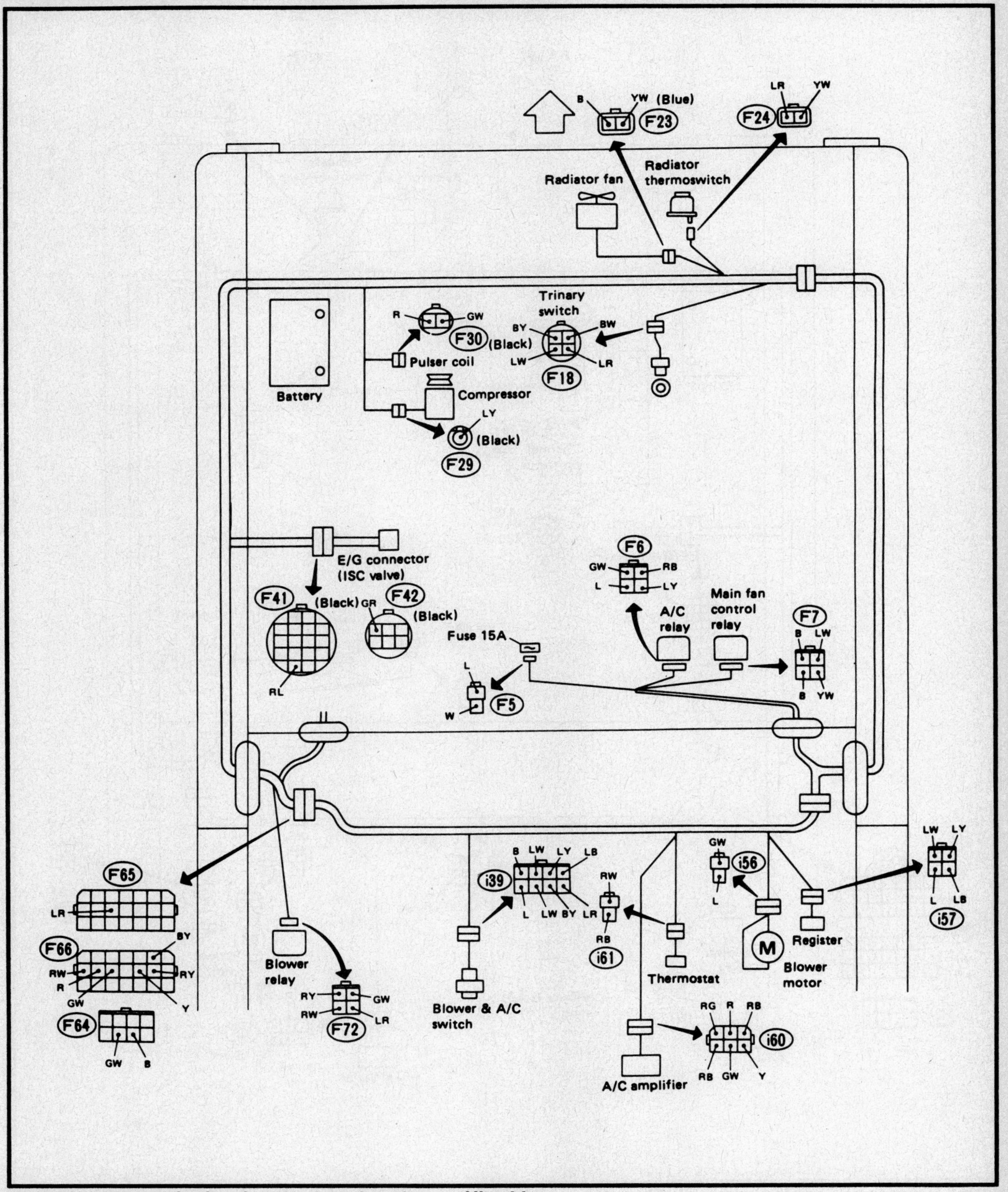
B
YW (Blue)
F23
LR
YW
F24
Radiator fan
Radiator thermoswitch
Trinary switch
R
GW
F30
(Black)
Pulser coil
BY
BW
LW
LR
F18
Battery
Compressor
LY
(Black)
F29
E/G connector (ISC valve)
F41
(Black)
GR
F42
(Black)
RL
F6
GW
RB
L
LY
A/C relay
Main fan control relay
F7
B
LW
B
YW
Fuse 15A
L
W
F5
F65
LR
F66
BY
RW
R
GW
RY
Y
F64
GW
B
Blower relay
RY
GW
RW
LR
F72
B
LW
LY
LB
i39
L
LW
BY
LR
Blower & A/C switch
RW
RB
i61
Thermostat
GW
i56
L
Blower motor
Register
LW
LY
L
LB
i57
RG
R
RB
i60
RB
GW
Y
A/C amplifier

Wiring Harness and related component locations— Hitachi

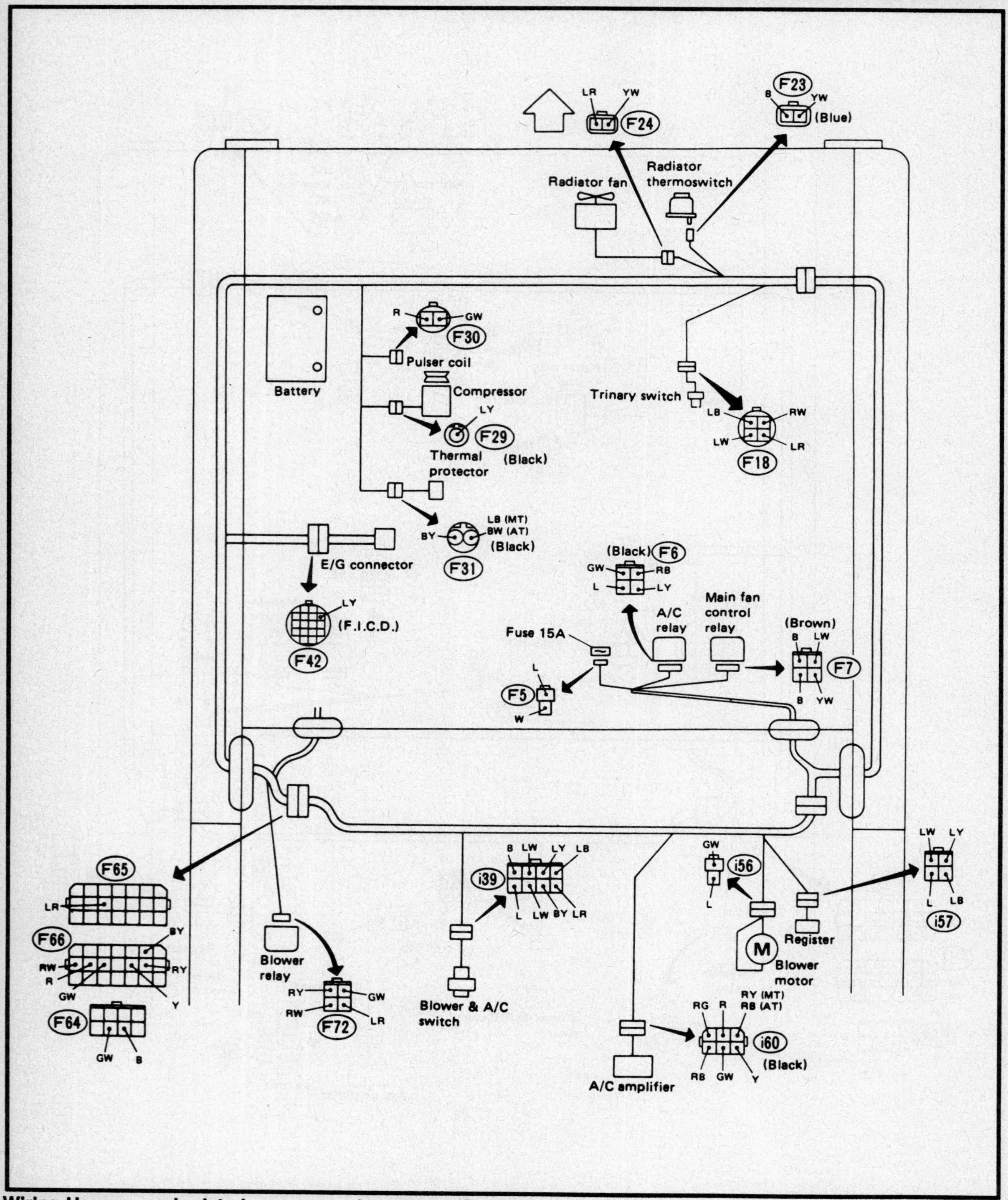
LR
YW
F24
F23
B
YW
(Blue)
Radiator fan
Radiator thermoswitch
R
GW
F30
Pulser coil
Battery
Compressor
LY
F29
Thermal protector
(Black)
Trinary switch
LB
RW
LW
LR
F18
BY
LB (MT)
BW (AT)
(Black)
F31
E/G connector
LY
(F.I.C.D.)
F42
(Black)
F6
GW
RB
L
LY
A/C relay
Main fan control relay
(Brown)
B
LW
F7
B
YW
Fuse 15A
L
F5
W
F65
LR
F66
BY
RW
R
RY
GW
Y
F64
GW
B
Blower relay
RY
GW
RW
LR
F72
B
LW
LY
LB
i39
L
LW
BY
LR
Blower & A/C switch
GW
i56
L
M
Register
Blower motor
LW
LY
L
LB
i57
RG
R
RY (MT)
RB (AT)
i60
(Black)
RB
GW
Y
A/C amplifier

Wiring Harness and related component locations— Panasonic

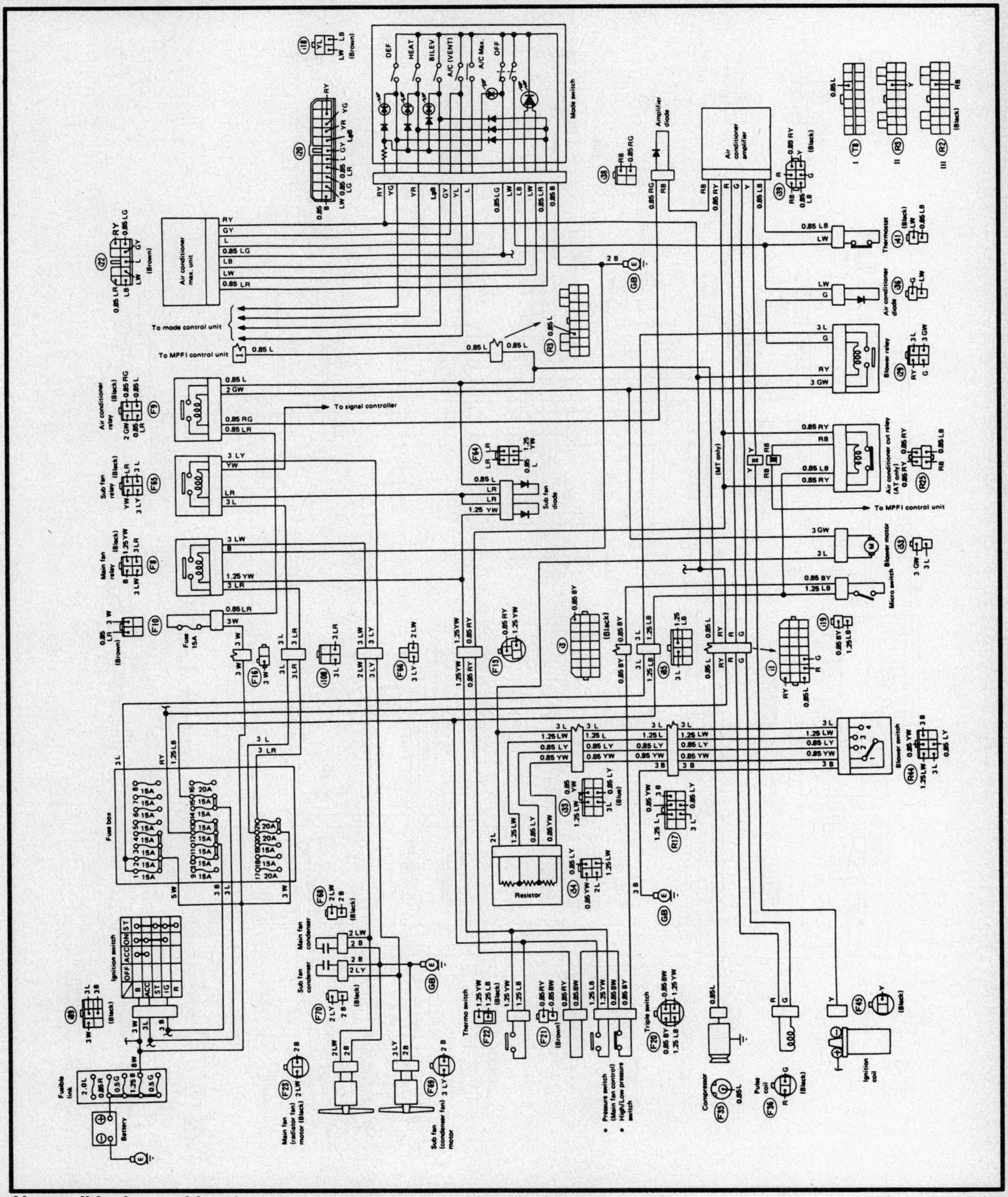
To mode control unit
To MPFI control unit
To signal controller
To MPFI control unit
Fuse box
Resistor

Air conditioning and heating system wiring schematic—XT Coupe

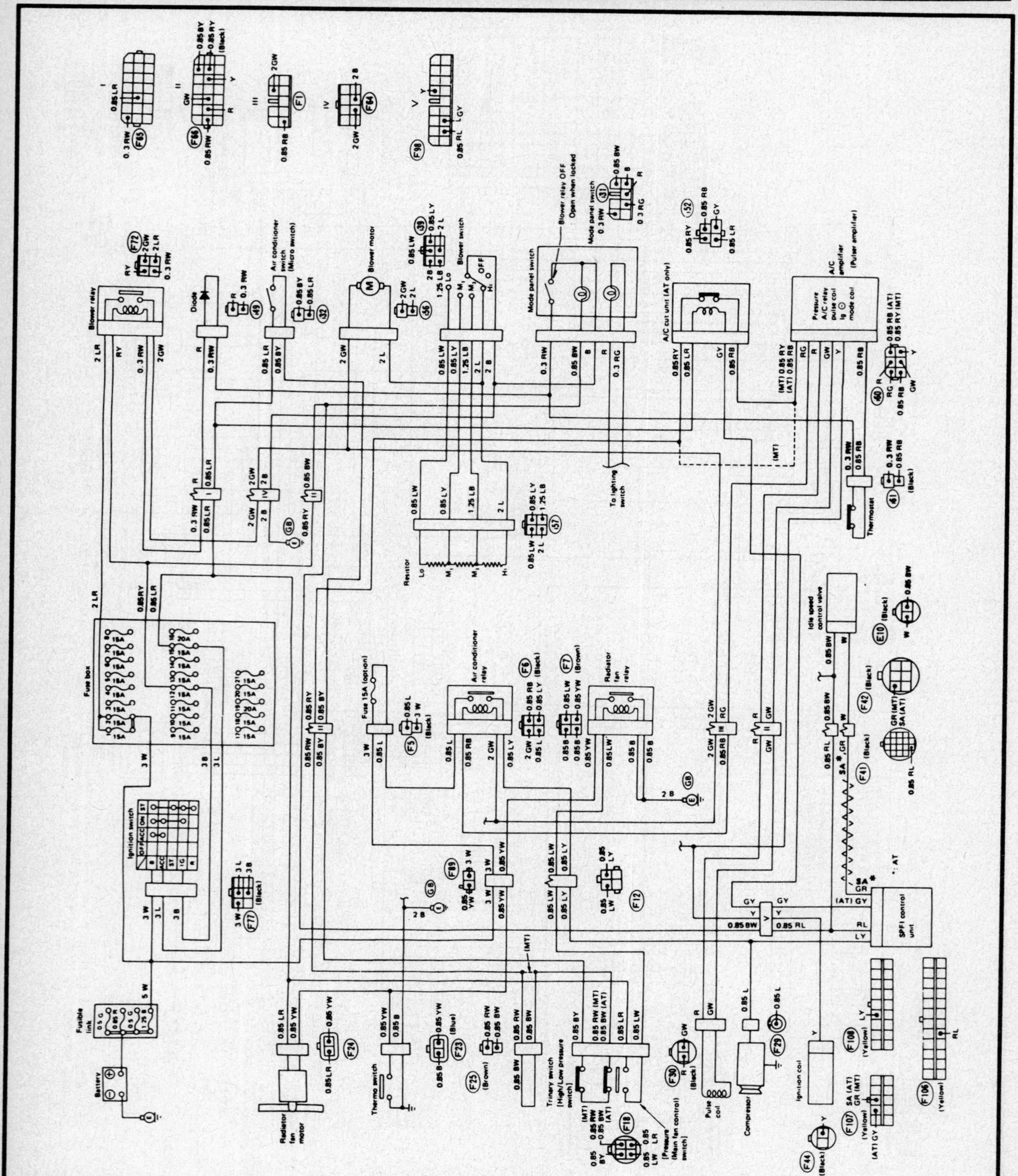
Blower relay
Diode
Air conditioner switch (Micro switch)
Blower motor
Blower switch
Mode panel switch
Blower relay OFF : Open when locked
A/C cut unit (AT only)
A/C amplifier (Pulser amplifier)
Thermostat
To lighting switch
Resistor
Fuse box
Idle speed control valve
Fuse 15A (option)
Air conditioner relay
Radiator fan relay
Ignition switch
SPFI control unit
Fusible link
Battery
Radiator fan motor
Thermo switch
Trinary switch (High/Low pressure switch)
Pressure (Main fan control) switch
Pulse coil
Compressor
Ignition coil

Air conditioning and heating system wiring schematic—Hitachi (USA)

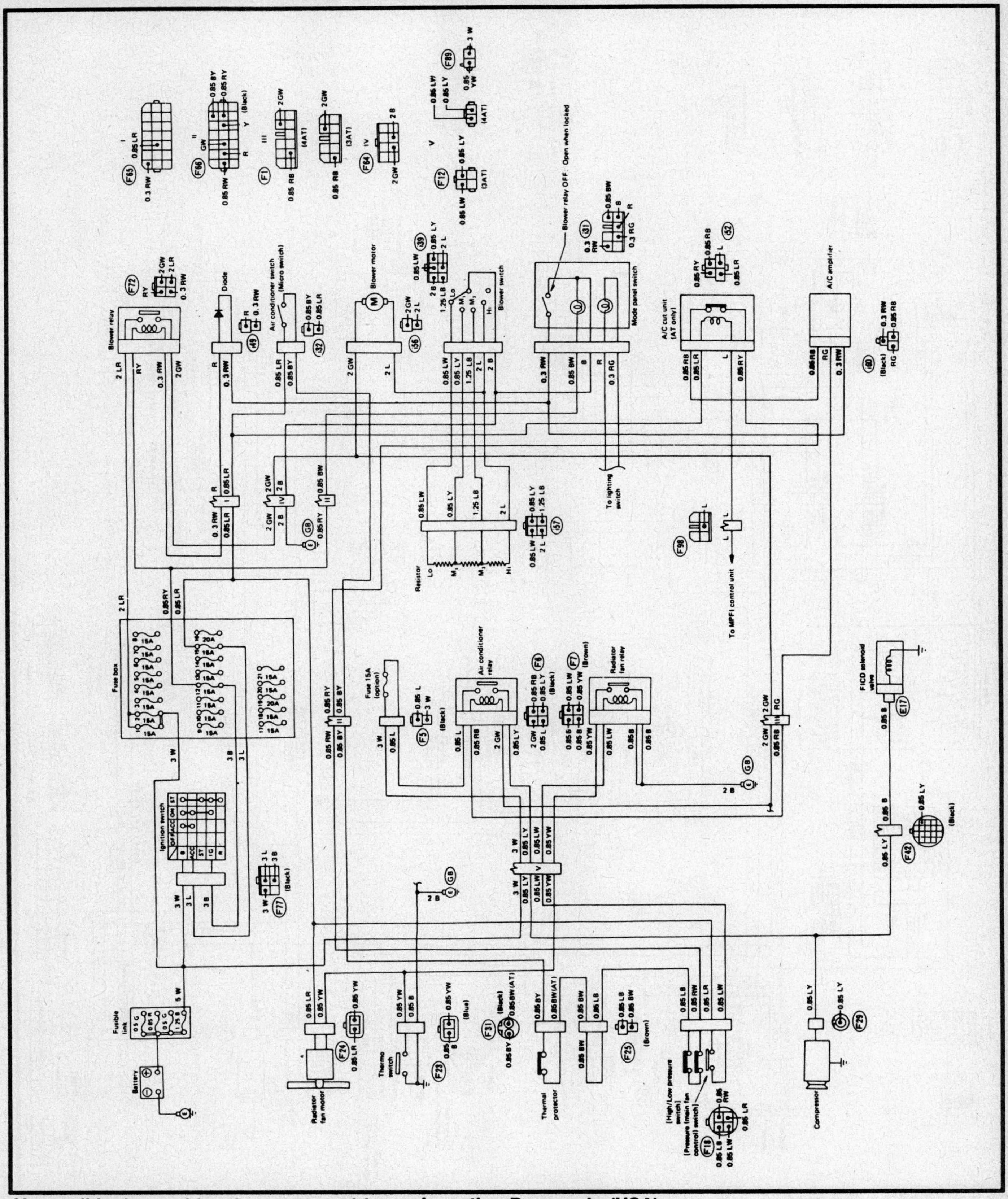
Blower relay
Diode
Air conditioner switch (Micro switch)
Blower motor
Blower switch
Mode panel switch
A/C cut unit (AT only)
A/C amplifier
Resistor
To lighting switch
To MPFI control unit
Fuse box
Fuse 15A (option)
Air conditioner relay
Radiator fan relay
FICD solenoid valve
Ignition switch
Fusible link
Battery
Radiator fan motor
Thermo switch
Thermal protector
Compressor

Air conditioning and heating system wiring schematic—Panasonic (USA)

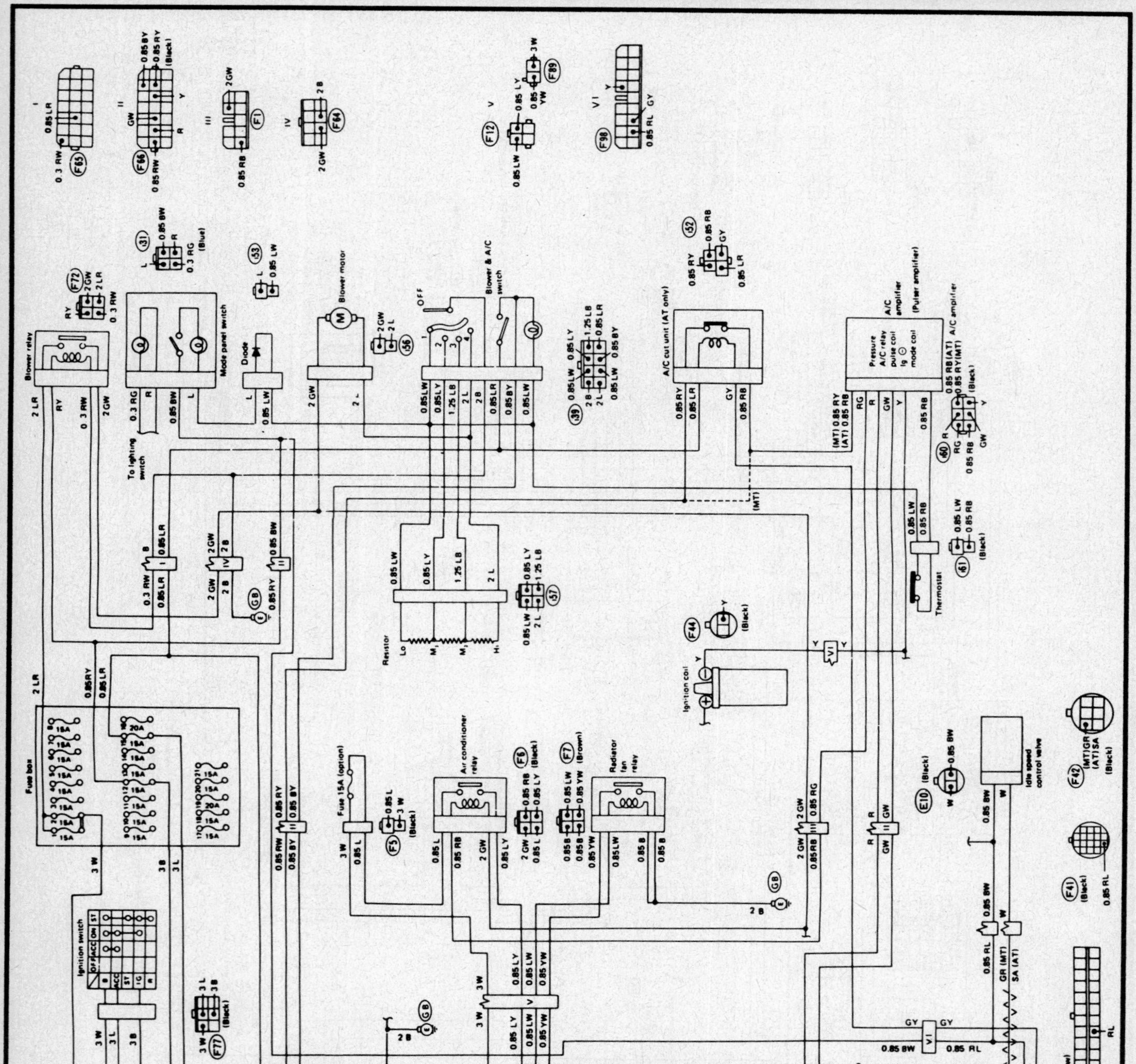
Blower relay
Mode panel switch
Diode
Blower motor
Blower & A/C switch
A/C cut unit (AT only)
A/C amplifier
Thermostat
Resistor
Ignition coil
Fuse box
Ignition switch
Fusible link
Battery
Air conditioner relay
Radiator fan relay
Radiator fan motor
Thermo switch
Trinary switch
Pulse coil
Compressor
SPFI control unit
Idle speed control valve

Air conditioning and heating system wiring schematic—Hitachi

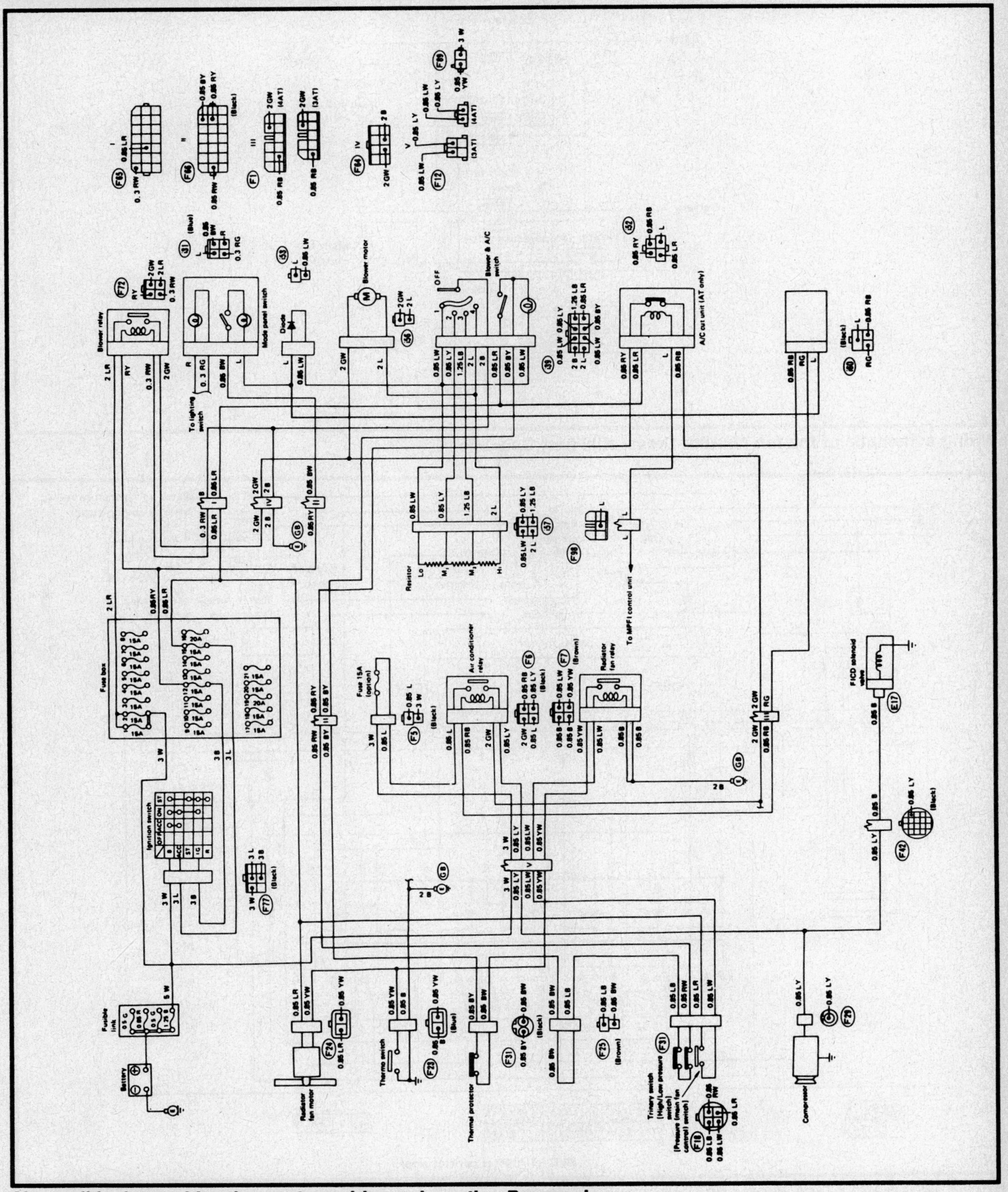

Air conditioning and heating system wiring schematic—Panasonic

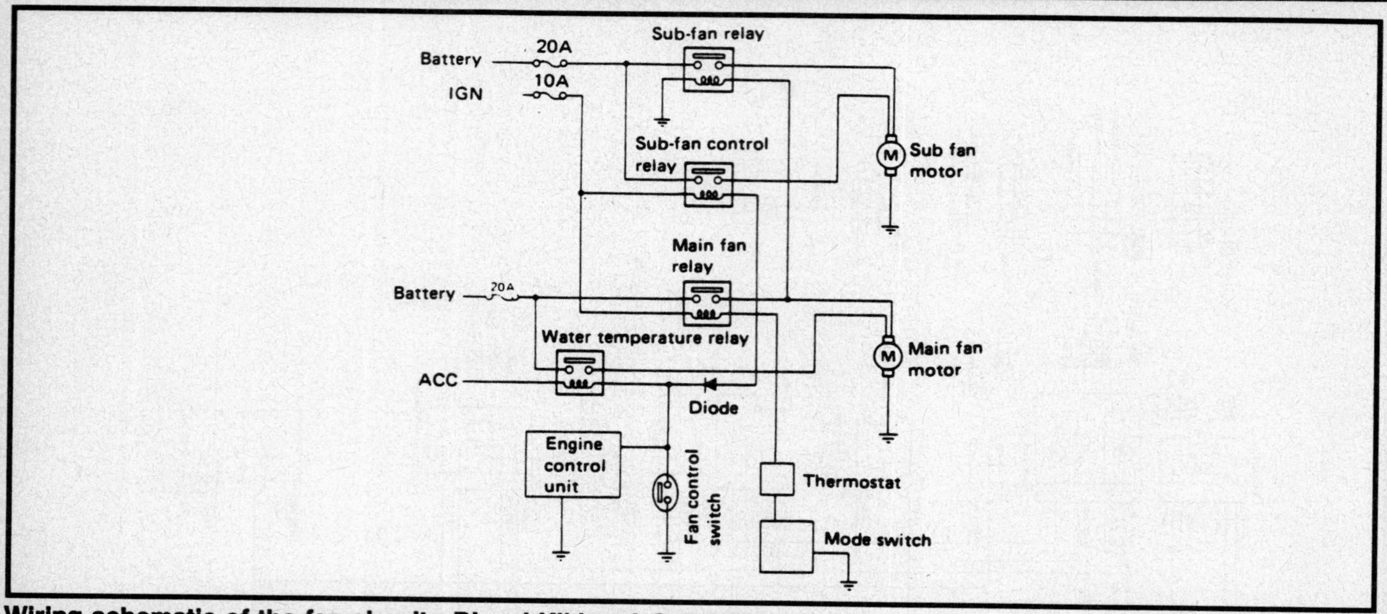
Sub-fan relay
Battery
20A
IGN
10A
Sub fan motor
Sub-fan control relay
Main fan relay
Battery
20A
Water temperature relay
Main fan motor
ACC
Diode
Engine control unit
Fan control switch
Thermostat
Mode switch

Wiring schematic of the fan circuit—Diesel Kiki and Calsonic

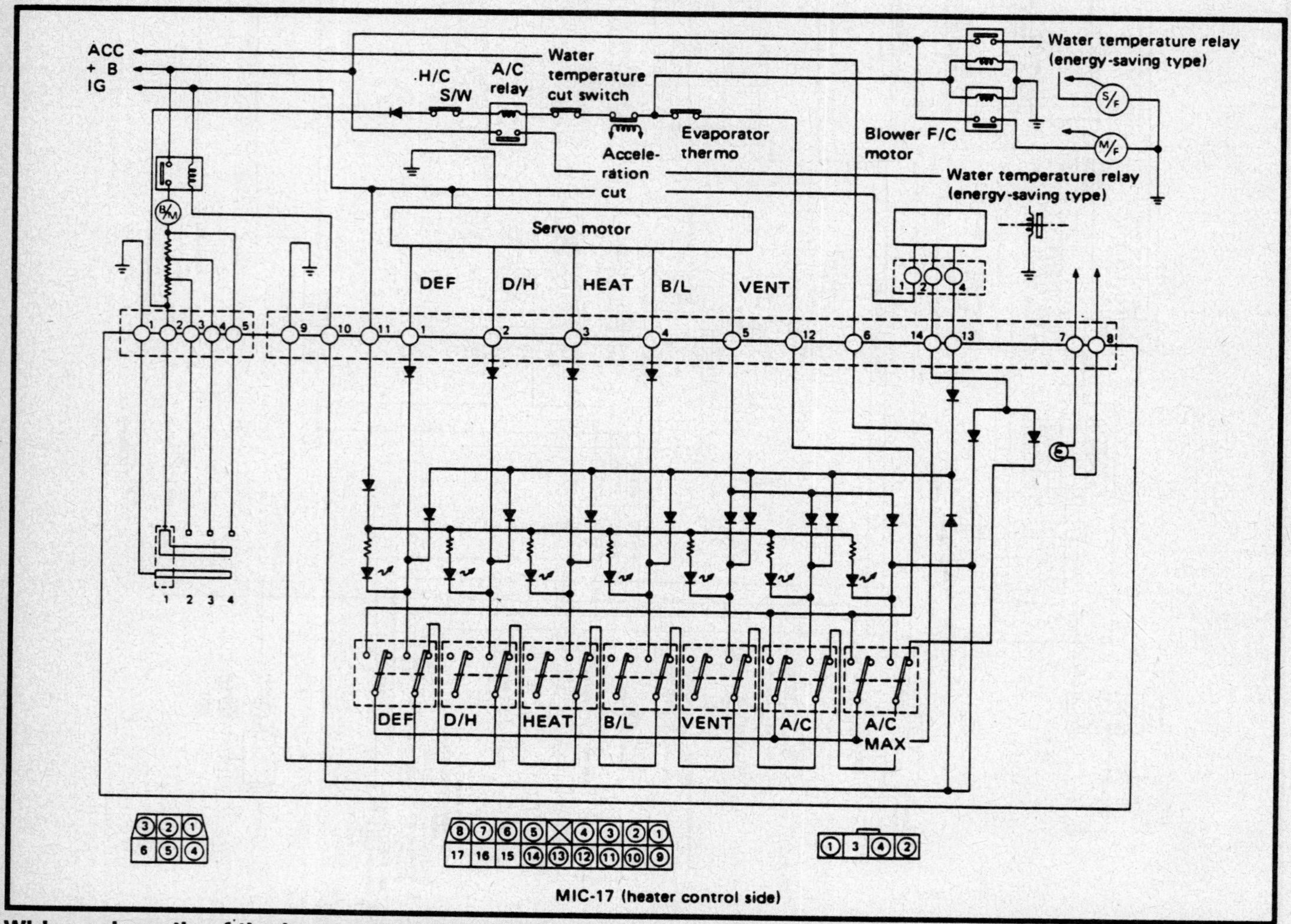
ACC
+ B
IG
H/C S/W
A/C relay
Water temperature cut switch
Acceleration cut
Evaporator thermo
Blower F/C motor
Water temperature relay (energy-saving type)
Water temperature relay (energy-saving type)
Servo motor
DEF
D/H
HEAT
B/L
VENT
DEF
D/H
HEAT
B/L
VENT
A/C
A/C MAX
MIC-17 (heater control side)

Wiring schematic of the heater control circuit— Legacy

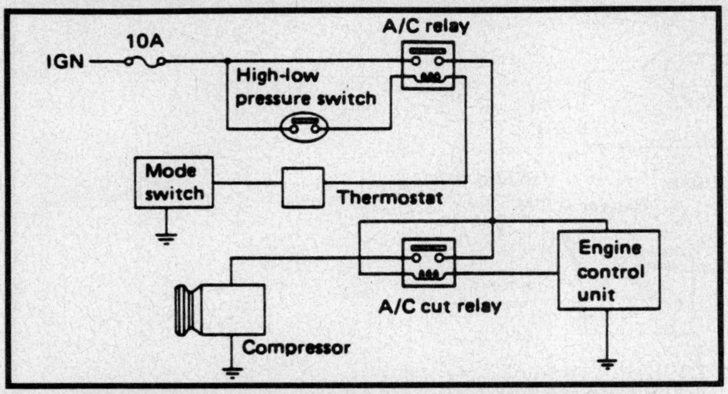
IGN
10A
A/C relay
High-low pressure switch
Mode switch
Thermostat
Engine control unit
A/C cut relay
Compressor

Wiring schematic of the compressor delay circuit—Diesel Kiki and Calsonic

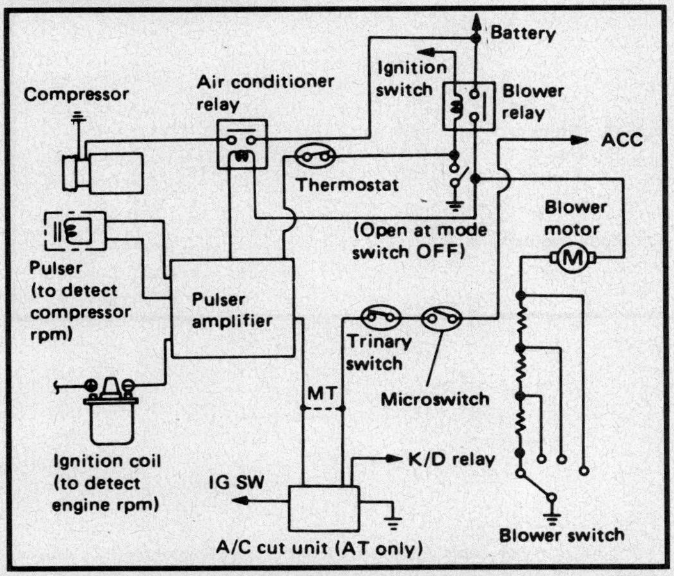
Battery
Compressor
Air conditioner relay
Ignition switch
Blower relay
ACC
Thermostat
(Open at mode switch OFF)
Blower motor
Pulser (to detect compressor rpm)
Pulser amplifier
Trinary switch
Microswitch
MT
Ignition coil (to detect engine rpm)
IG SW
K/D relay
A/C cut unit (AT only)
Blower switch

Wiring schematic of the belt protection system—USA

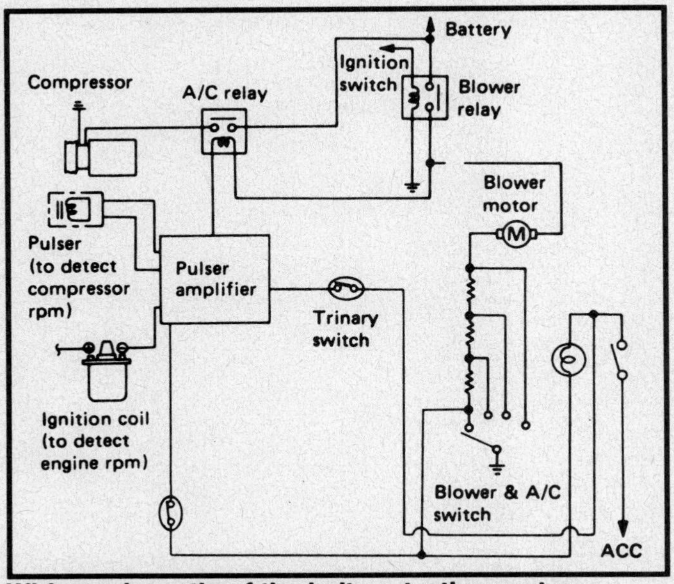
Battery
Compressor
A/C relay
Ignition switch
Blower relay
Blower motor
Pulser (to detect compressor rpm)
Pulser amplifier
Trinary switch
Ignition coil (to detect engine rpm)
Blower & A/C switch
ACC

Wiring schematic of the belt protection system—Canada

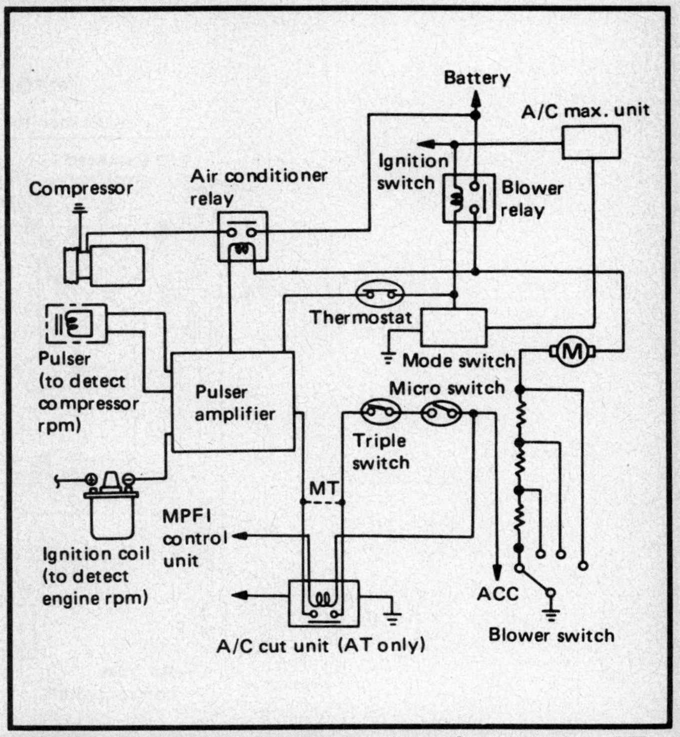
Battery
A/C max. unit
Compressor
Air conditioner relay
Ignition switch
Blower relay
Thermostat
Pulser (to detect compressor rpm)
Pulser amplifier
Mode switch
Micro switch
Triple switch
MT
MPFI control unit
Ignition coil (to detect engine rpm)
ACC
A/C cut unit (AT only)
Blower switch

Wiring schematic of the belt protection system—XT Coupe

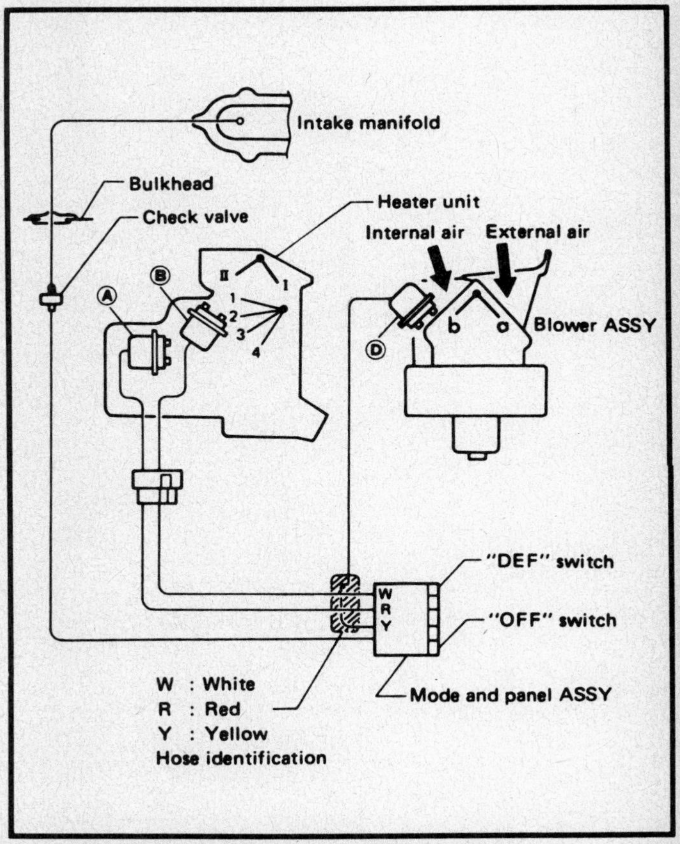
Intake manifold
Bulkhead
Check valve
Heater unit
Internal air
External air
Blower ASSY
"DEF" switch
"OFF" switch
Mode and panel ASSY
W : White
R : Red
Y : Yellow
Hose identification

Vacuum system schematic—USA vehicles

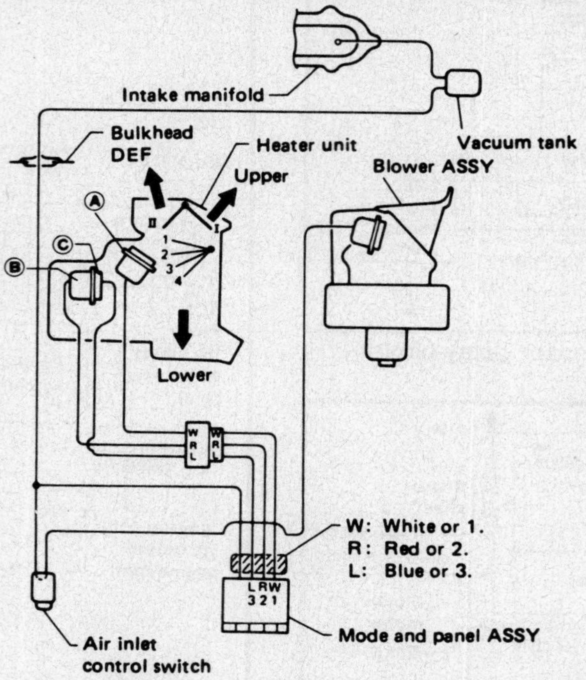
Intake manifold
Vacuum tank
Bulkhead
DEF
Heater unit
Upper
Blower ASSY
A
B
C
II
I
1
2
3
4
Lower
W
R
L
W: White or 1.
R: Red or 2.
L: Blue or 3.
L R W
3 2 1
Mode and panel ASSY
Air inlet
control switch

Vacuum system schematic—Canadian vehicles

26 TOYOTA 26

CAMRY • CELICA • COROLLA • CRESSIDA • MR2 • SUPRA • TERCEL

SPECIFICATIONS

ENGINE IDENTIFICATION

Year	Model	Engine Displacement cu. in. (cc/liter)	Engine Series Identification	No. of Cylinders	Engine Type
1989	Camry	121.9 (1988/2.0)	3S-FE	4	DOHC
		153.0 (2058/2.5)	2VZ-FE	6	DOHC
	Celica	121.9 (1998/2.0)	3S-FE	4	DOHC
		121.9 (1998/2.0)	3S-GE	4	DOHC
		121.9 (1998/2.0)	3S-GTE	4	DOHC, Turbocharged
	Corolla	97.0 (1587/1.6)	4A-F	4	DOHC
		97.0 (1587/1.6)	4A-FE	4	DOHC
		97.0 (1587/1.6)	4A-GE	4	DOHC
	Cressida	180.3 (2954/3.0)	7M-GE	6	DOHC
	MR2	97.0 (1587/1.6)	4A-GE	4	DOHC
		97.0 (1587/1.6)	4A-GZE	4	DOHC, Supercharged
	Supra	180.3 (2954/3.0)	7M-GE	6	DOHC
		180.3 (2954/3.0)	7M-GTE	6	DOHC, Turbocharged
	Tercel	88.9 (1457/1.5)	3E	4	SOHC
1990	Camry	121.9 (1998/2.0)	3S-FE	4	DOHC
		153.0 (2058/2.5)	2VZ-FE	6	DOHC
	Celica	97.0 (1587/1.6)	4A-FE	4	DOHC
		121.9 (1988/2.0)	3S-GTE	4	DOHC, Turbocharged
		132.0 (2164/2.2)	3S-FE	4	DOHC
	Corolla	97.0 (1587/1.6)	4A-FE	4	DOHC
		97.0 (1587/1.6)	4A-GE	4	DOHC
	Cressida	180.3 (2954/3.0)	7M-GE	6	DOHC
	Supra	180.3 (2954/3.0)	7M-GE	6	DOHC
		180.3 (2954/3.0)	7M-GTE	6	DOHC, Turbocharged
	Tercel	88.9 (1457/1.5)	3E	4	SOHC
		88.9 (1457/1.5)	3E-E	4	SOHC
1991	Camry	121.9 (1998/2.0)	3S-FE	4	DOHC
		153.0 (2058/2.5)	2VZ-FE	6	DOHC
	Celica	97.0 (1587/1.6)	4A-FE	4	DOHC
		121.9 (1988/2.0)	3S-GTE	4	DOHC, Turbocharged
		132.0 (2164/2.2)	5S-FE	4	DOHC
	Corolla	97.0 (1587/1.6)	4A-FE	4	DOHC
		97.0 (1587/1.6)	4A-GE	4	DOHC
	Cressida	180.0 (2954/3.0)	7M-GE	6	DOHC
	MR2	121.9 (1988/2.0)	3S-GTE	4	DOHC, Turbocharged
		132.0 (2164/2.2)	5S-FE	4	DOHC
	Supra	180.3 (2954/3.0)	7M-GE	6	DOHC
		180.3 (2954/3.0)	7M-GTE	6	DOHC, Turbocharged
	Tercel	88.9 (1457/1.5)	3E-E	4	SOHC

SOHC—Single overhead cam
DOHC—Dual overhead cam

REFRIGERANT CAPACITIES

Year	Model	Freon (oz.)	Oil (fl. oz.)	Type ①
1989	Camry	19–23	1.4–1.7	Nippondenso
	Celica	19–23	1.4–1.7	Nippondenso
	Corolla	19–23	1.4–1.7	②
	Cressida	23–25	1.4–1.7	Nippondenso
	MR2	24	1.4–1.7	Nippondenso
	Supra	20–23	1.4–1.7	Nippondenso
	Tercel	19–23	1.4–1.7	②
1990	Camry	19–23	1.4–1.7	Nippondenso
	Celica	24–27	1.4–1.7	Nippondenso
	Corolla	19–23	1.4–1.7	②
	Cressida	23–25	1.4–1.7	Nippondenso
	Supra	20–23	1.4–1.7	Nippondenso
	Tercel	19–23	1.4–1.7	②
1991	Camry	19–23	1.4–1.7	Nippondenso
	Celica	24–27	1.4–1.7	Nippondenso
	Corolla	19–23	1.4–1.7	②
	Cressida	23–25	1.4–1.7	Nippondenso
	MR2	28–32	1.4–1.8	Nippondenso
	Supra	20–23	1.4–1.7	Nippondenso
	Tercel	23–27	1.4–1.7	②

① Compressor
② Nippondenso or Rotary

AIR CONDITIONING BELT TENSION CHART

Year	Model	Engine Displacement cu. in. (cc/liter)	Belt Type	New ⑫	Used ⑫
1989	Camry	121.9 (1988/2.0)	V-Belt	170–180	120–140
		153.0 (2058/2.5)	V-Belt	170–180	95–135
	Celica	121.9 (1998/2.0) ①	V-Belt	170–180	120–140
		121.9 (1998/2.0) ②	V-Belt	170–180	95–135
		121.9 (1998/2.0) ③	V-Belt	170–180	95–135
	Corolla	97.0 (1587/1.6) ④	V-Belt	140–180	80–120
		97.0 (1587/1.6) ⑤	V-Belt	140–180	80–120
		97.0 (1587/1.6) ⑥	V-Belt	170–185	95–135
	Cressida	180.3 (2954/3.0)	V-Belt	140–180	95–115
	MR2	97.0 (1587/1.6) ⑦	V-Belt	122–142	78–98
		97.0 (1587/1.6) ⑧	V-Belt	155–175	67–97
	Supra	180.3 (2954/3.0) ⑨	V-Belt	140–180	95–115
		180.3 (2954/3.0) ⑩	V-Belt	140–180	95–115
	Tercel	88.9 (1457/1.5)	V-Belt	150–180	90–130

AIR CONDITIONING BELT TENSION CHART

Year	Model	Engine Displacement cu. in. (cc/liter)	Belt Type	New ⑫	Used ⑫
1990	Camry	121.9 (1998/2.0)	V-Belt	170–180	120–140
		153.0 (2058/2.5)	V-Belt	170–180	95–135
	Celica	97.0 (1587/1.6)	V-Belt	135–185	80–120
		121.9 (1988/2.0) ③	V-Belt	155–175	70–100
		132.0 (2164/2.2)	V-Belt	155–175	100–110
	Corolla	97.0 (1587/1.6) ⑤	V-Belt	140–180	80–120
		97.0 (1587/1.6) ⑥	V-Belt	170–180	95–135
	Cressida	180.3 (2954/3.0)	V-Belt	140–180	95–115
	Supra	180.3 (2954/3.0) ⑨	V-Belt	140–180	95–115
		180.3 (2954/3.0) ⑩	V-Belt	140–180	95–115
	Tercel	88.9 (1457/1.5)	V-Belt	150–180	90–130
		88.9 (1457/1.5) ⑪	V-Belt	150–180	90–130
1991	Camry	121.9 (1998/2.0)	V-Belt	170–180	120–140
		153.0 (2058/2.5)	V-Belt	170–180	95–135
	Celica	97.0 (1587/1.6)	V-Belt	135–185	80–120
		121.9 (1988/2.0) ③	V-Belt	155–175	70–100
		132.0 (2164/2.2)	V-Belt	155–175	100–120
	Corolla	97.0 (1587/1.6) ⑤	V-Belt	140–180	80–120
		97.0 (1587/1.6) ⑥	V-Belt	170–180	95–135
	Cressida	180.0 (2954/3.0)	V-Belt	140–180	95–115
	MR2	121.9 (1988/2.0)	V-Belt	135–185	80–120
		132.0 (2164/2.2)	V-Belt	135–185	80–120
	Supra	180.3 (2954/3.0) ⑨	V-Belt	140–180	95–115
		180.3 (2954/3.0) ⑩	V-Belt	140–180	95–115
	Tercel	88.9 (1457/1.5) ⑪	V-Belt	150–180	90–130

① 3S-FE engine type
② 3S-GE engine type
③ 3S-GTE engine type
④ 4A-F engine type
⑤ 4A-FE engine type
⑥ 4A-GE engine type
⑦ 4A-GE engine type
⑧ 4A-GZE engine type
⑨ 7M-GE engine type
⑩ 7M-GTE engine type
⑪ 3E-E engine type
⑫ Using belt tension gauge—reading in lbs.

SYSTEM DESCRIPTION

General Information

The blend-air type heater system is used on all models. The blend-air method on vehicles without air conditioning uses a controlled flow system with the engine coolant flow controlled through the heater core, with the use of a heater coolant shut-off valve. The temperature of the heated air entering the passenger compartment is controlled by regulating, with the temperature control lever and blend door, the quantity of air which flows through the heater core air passages or fins, then blending the heated air with a controlled amount of cool fresh air which bypasses the heater core. The air flow for the heating system is through the cowl air intake and into the heating system. Defroster operation is controlled by the air control lever and cable or vacuum servo motor, moving the defroster damper to direct heated air to the defroster outlets.

The air conditioning system is designed to cycle a compressor on and off to maintain the desired cooling within the passenger compartment. Passenger compartment comfort is maintained by the temperature lever located on the control head. The system is also designed to prevent the evaporator from freezing.

When an air conditioning mode is selected, electrical current is sent to the compressor clutch coil. The clutch plate and the hub assembly is then drawn rearward which engages the pulley. The clutch plate and the pulley are then locked together and act as a single unit. This in turn drives the compressor shaft which compresses low pressure refrigerant vapor from the evaporator into high pressure. The compressor also circulates refrigerant oil and refrigerant through the air conditioner system. On most models, the compressor is equipped with a cut-off solenoid which will shut the compressor off momentarily under certain conditions. These include wide-open throttle and low idle

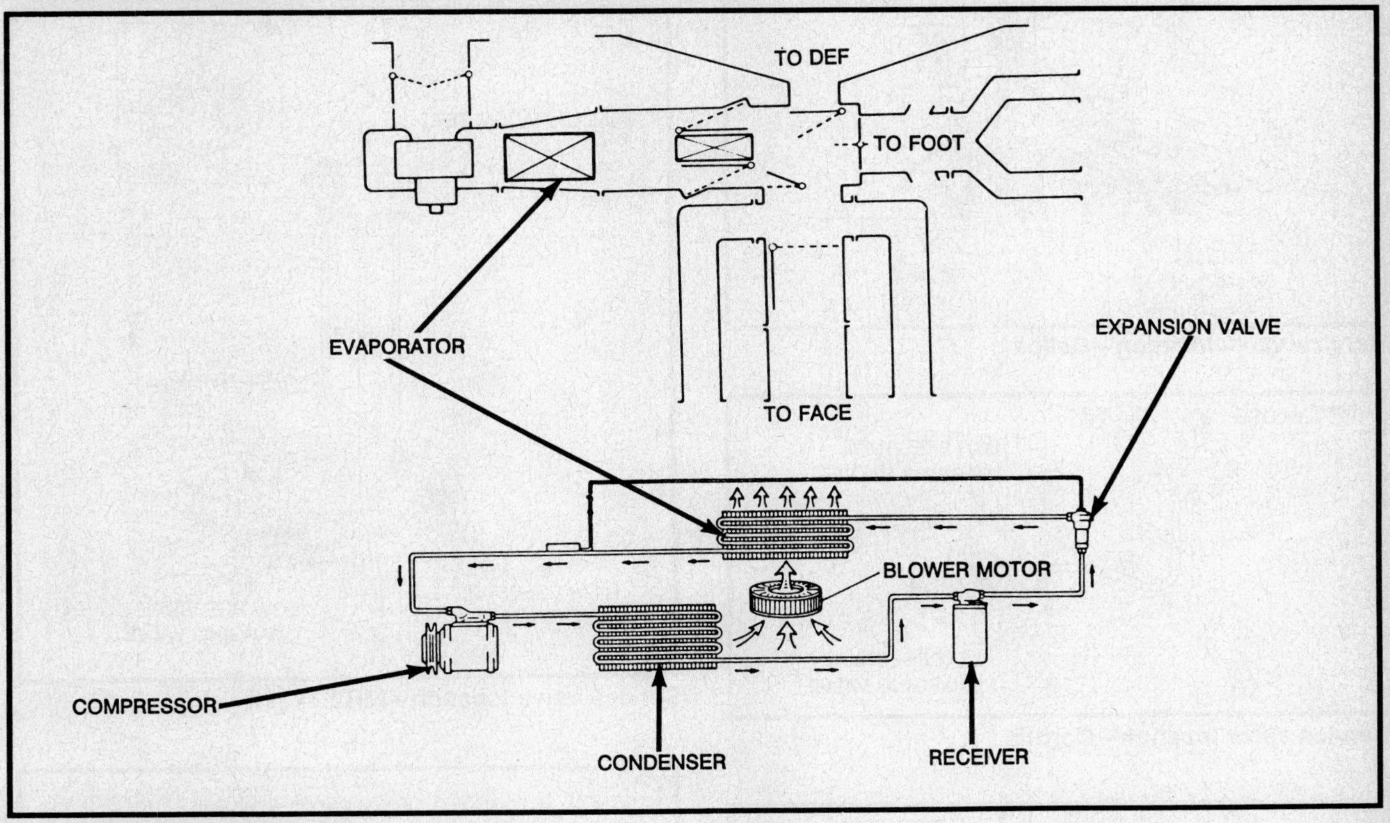
TO DEF
TO FOOT
TO FACE
EVAPORATOR
EXPANSION VALVE
BLOWER MOTOR
COMPRESSOR
CONDENSER
RECEIVER

Typical refrigeration system

speeds. The switches on the control head are used to control the operation of the air conditioning system.

Service Valve Location

There are 2 service access gauge port valves on the system. The high pressure discharge port is located in the discharge line. This port may require the use of a high pressure gauge adapter. The other service port (low pressure side) is located on the low pressure side of the system and is used to measure evaporator pressure.

On most vehicles, the letter **D** (discharge side) marked near the compressor service valve side indicates the high pressure side. The letter **S** (suction side) indicates the low pressure side.

NOTE: To prevent release of refrigerant always use stop valves when installing the manifold gauge set to the service valves.

System Discharging

R-12 refrigerant is a chlorofluorocarbon which, when mishandled, can contribute to the depletion on the ozone layer in the upper atmosphere. Ozone filters out harmful radiation from the sun. In order to protect the ozone layer, an approved R-12 recovery/recycling machine that meets SAE standard J1991 should be employed when discharging the system. Follow the operating instructions provided with the approved equipment exactly to properly discharge the system.

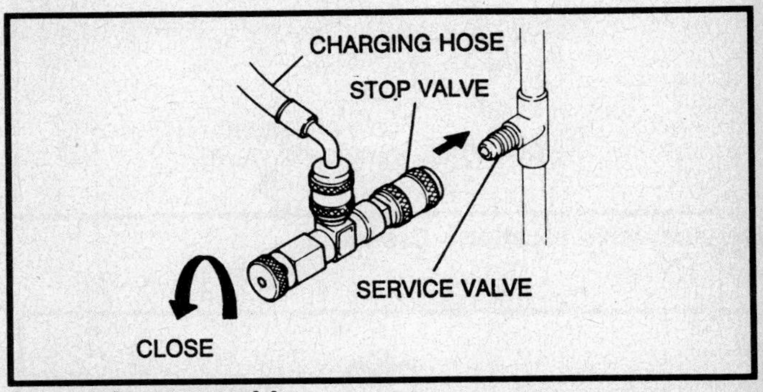
CHARGING HOSE
STOP VALVE
SERVICE VALVE
CLOSE

Stop valve assembly

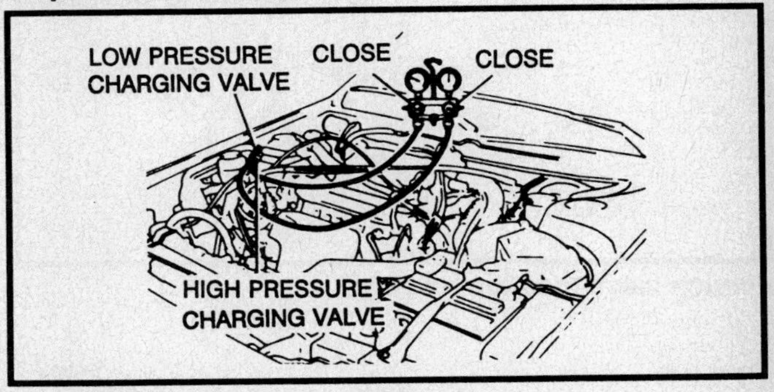
LOW PRESSURE
CHARGING VALVE
CLOSE
CLOSE
HIGH PRESSURE
CHARGING VALVE

Service valve location—Camry

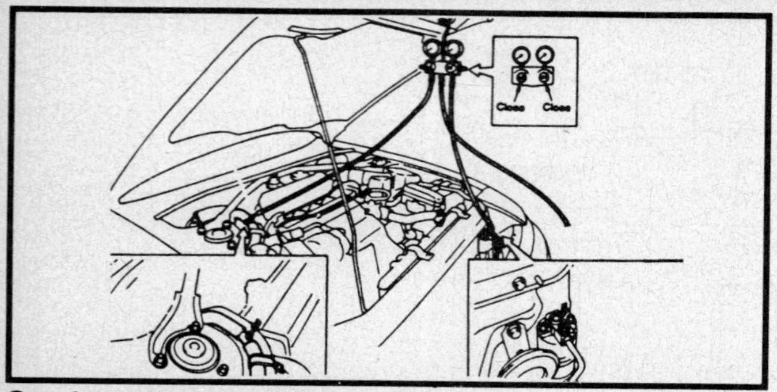

Service valve location—Celica

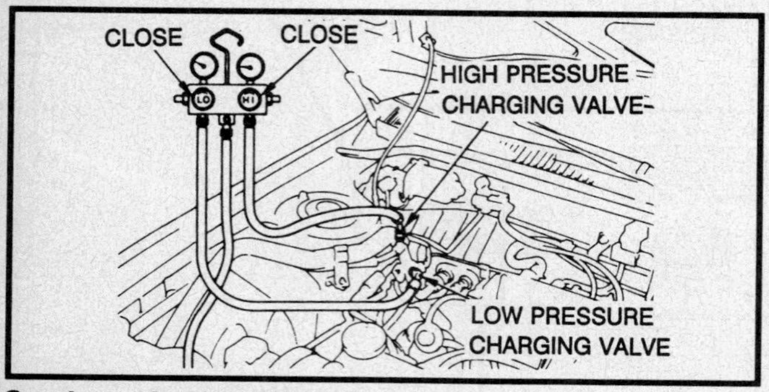
CLOSE
CLOSE
HIGH PRESSURE
CHARGING VALVE
LOW PRESSURE
CHARGING VALVE

Service valve location—Corolla

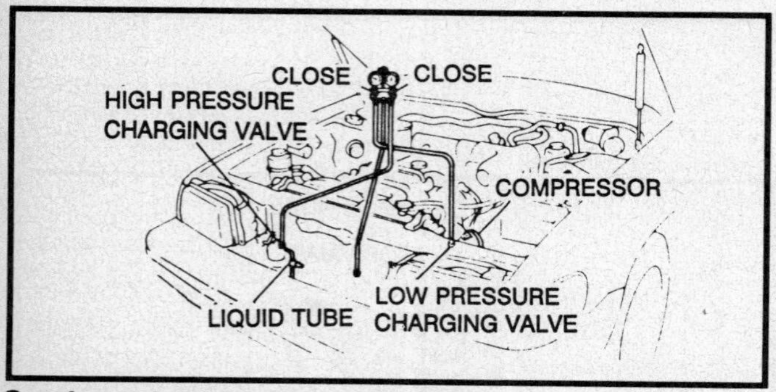
CLOSE
CLOSE
HIGH PRESSURE
CHARGING VALVE
COMPRESSOR
LIQUID TUBE
LOW PRESSURE
CHARGING VALVE

Service valve location—Cressida

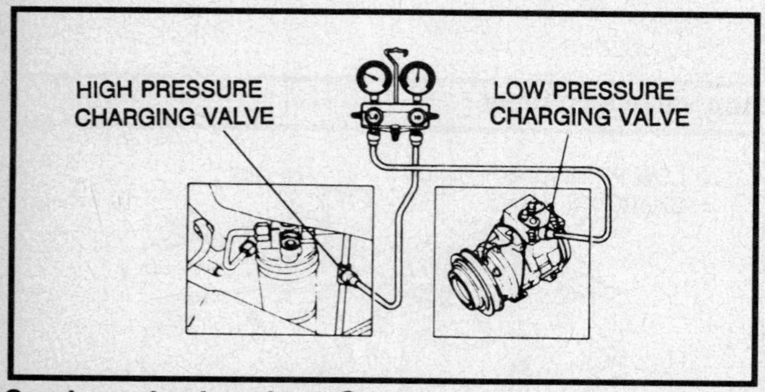
HIGH PRESSURE
CHARGING VALVE
LOW PRESSURE
CHARGING VALVE

Service valve location—Supra

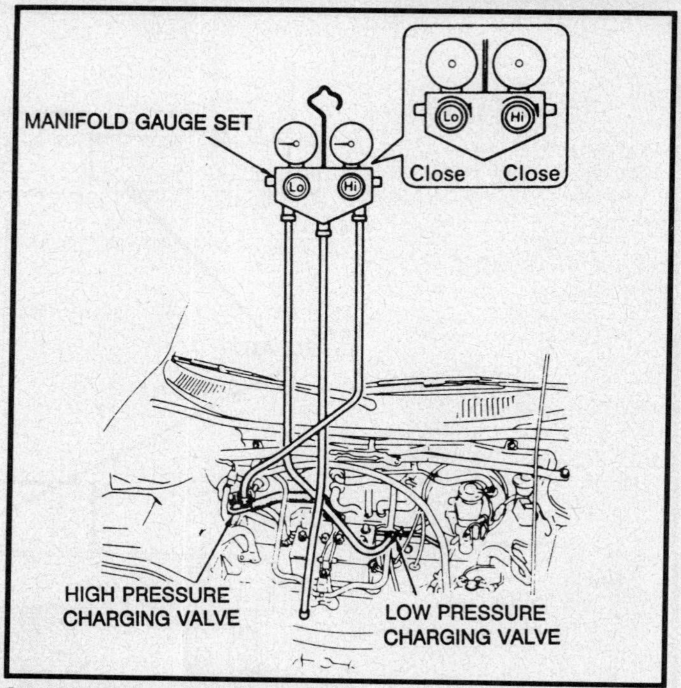
MANIFOLD GAUGE SET
Lo
Hi
Close
Close
HIGH PRESSURE
CHARGING VALVE
LOW PRESSURE
CHARGING VALVE

Service valve location—MR2

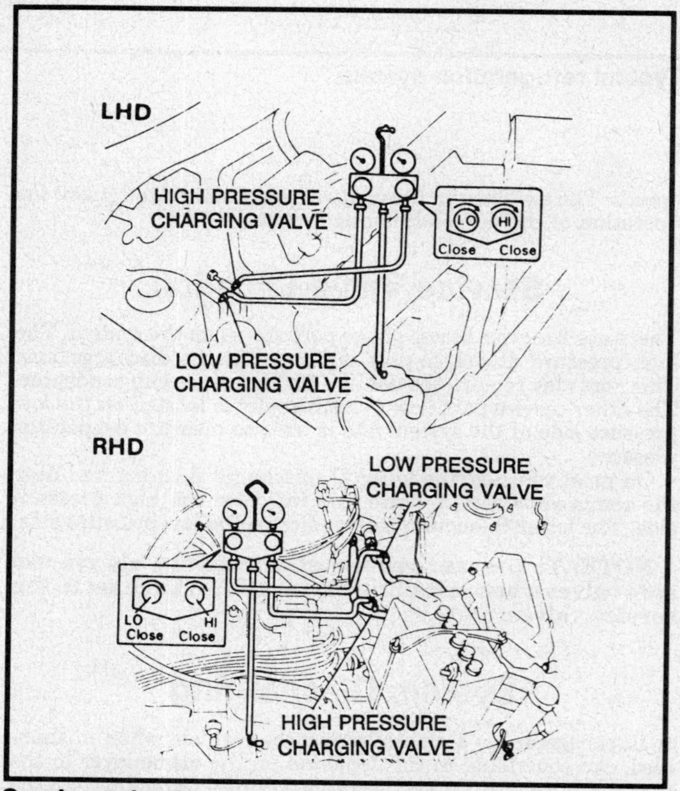
LHD
HIGH PRESSURE
CHARGING VALVE
LO
HI
Close
Close
LOW PRESSURE
CHARGING VALVE
RHD
LOW PRESSURE
CHARGING VALVE
LO
HI
Close
Close
HIGH PRESSURE
CHARGING VALVE

Service valve location—Tercel

System Evacuating

If the air conditioning system has been opened to the atmosphere, it should be air and moisture free before being recharged with refrigerant. Moisture and air mixed with refrigerant will raise the compressor head pressure, possibly damage the system's components and will reduce the performance of the system. To evacuate the system, perform the following procedure:

1. Leak test the system and repair any leaks found.
2. Connect an approved charging station, recovery/recycling machine or manifold gauge set and vacuum pump to the discharge and suction ports. The red hose is normally connected to the discharge (high pressure) line and the blue hose is connected to the suction (low pressure) line.
3. Open the discharge and suction ports and start the vacuum pump. If the pump is not able to pull at least 26 in. Hg of vacuum, there is a leak that must be repaired before evacuation can occur.
4. Once the system has reached at least 26 in. Hg of vacuum, allow the system to evacuate for at least 30 minutes. The longer the system is evacuated, the more contaminants will be removed.
5. Close all valves and turn the pump off. If the system loses more than 2 in. Hg of vacuum after 15 minutes, there is a leak that should be repaired.

System Charging

1. Connect an approved charging station, recovery/recycling machine or manifold gauge set to the discharge and suction ports. The red hose is normally connected to the discharge (high pressure) line and the blue hose is connected to the suction (low pressure) line.
2. Follow the instructions provided with the equipment and charge the system with the specified amount of refrigerant.
3. Perform a leak test.

ADDING REFRIGERANT OIL

It is imperative that the specified type and quantity of refrigerant oil be maintained in a refrigerant system for proper operation. A surplus of oil, the wrong oil viscosity or insufficient oil will cause refrigerant system problems. Insufficient oil or the wrong oil results in poor lubrication and possible compressor damage. A surplus of oil allows too much oil to circulate with the refrigerant, causing the cooling capacity of the system to be reduced. When it is necessary to replace a component in the refrigerant system, certain procedures must be followed to assure that the total oil charge on the system is correct after the new part is installed. During normal air condition operation some refrigerant oil is circulated through the system with the refrigerant and some is retained in the compressor. If certain components of the system are removed for replacement some of the refrigerant oil will go with the component. To maintain the original total oil charge, it is necessary to compensate for the oil loss by adding oil to the system with the replacement part.

SYSTEM COMPONENTS

Radiator

REMOVAL AND INSTALLATION

Camry

1. Disconnect the negative battery cable. Drain engine coolant.
2. Remove the battery. Remove the igniter and bracket assembly and on the 2VZ-FE engine remove the ignition coil.
3. Disconnect the coolant reservoir hose and all radiator hoses.
4. Disconnect the cooling fan motor electrical connections.
5. If equipped with automatic transaxle, disconnect the oil cooler lines. Remove the radiator supports. Remove the radiator assembly with the electrical cooling fans from the vehicle.
6. Remove the electrical cooling fans from the radiator assembly, as necessary.

To install:

7. Install the electrical cooling fans to the radiator assembly. Install the radiator assembly in the vehicle and check that the rubber cushions are in the correct position.
8. If equipped with automatic transaxle, connect the oil cooler lines.
9. Connect the cooling fan motor electrical connections. Connect the radiator hoses and reservoir hose.
10. Install the igniter and bracket assembly on the 2VZ-FE engine and install the ignition coil.
11. Install the battery, reconnect the cables, fill (bleed cooling system) the engine with coolant. Start the engine and check for leaks. Check all fluid levels as necessary.

Celica

1. Disconnect the negative battery cable. Remove the engine undercovers. Drain engine coolant.
2. On the 3S-GTE and 5S-FE engines, disconnect the water temperature switch connector.
3. If equipped with ABS, remove the ABS control relay from the radiator support assembly. On the 3S-GTE engine, remove the air duct as necessary.
4. Remove the engine relay box from the battery as necessary.
5. Remove the upper radiator support seal assembly.
6. Disconnect the coolant reservoir hose and all radiator hoses.
7. Disconnect the cooling fan motor electrical connection.
8. If equipped with automatic transaxle, disconnect the oil cooler lines. Remove the radiator assembly with the electrical cooling fan from the vehicle. Remove the electrical cooling fan from the radiator assembly, as necessary.

To install:

9. Install the electrical cooling fan to the radiator assembly. Install the radiator assembly in the vehicle and check that the rubber cushions are in the correct position.
10. If equipped with automatic transaxle, connect the oil cooler lines.

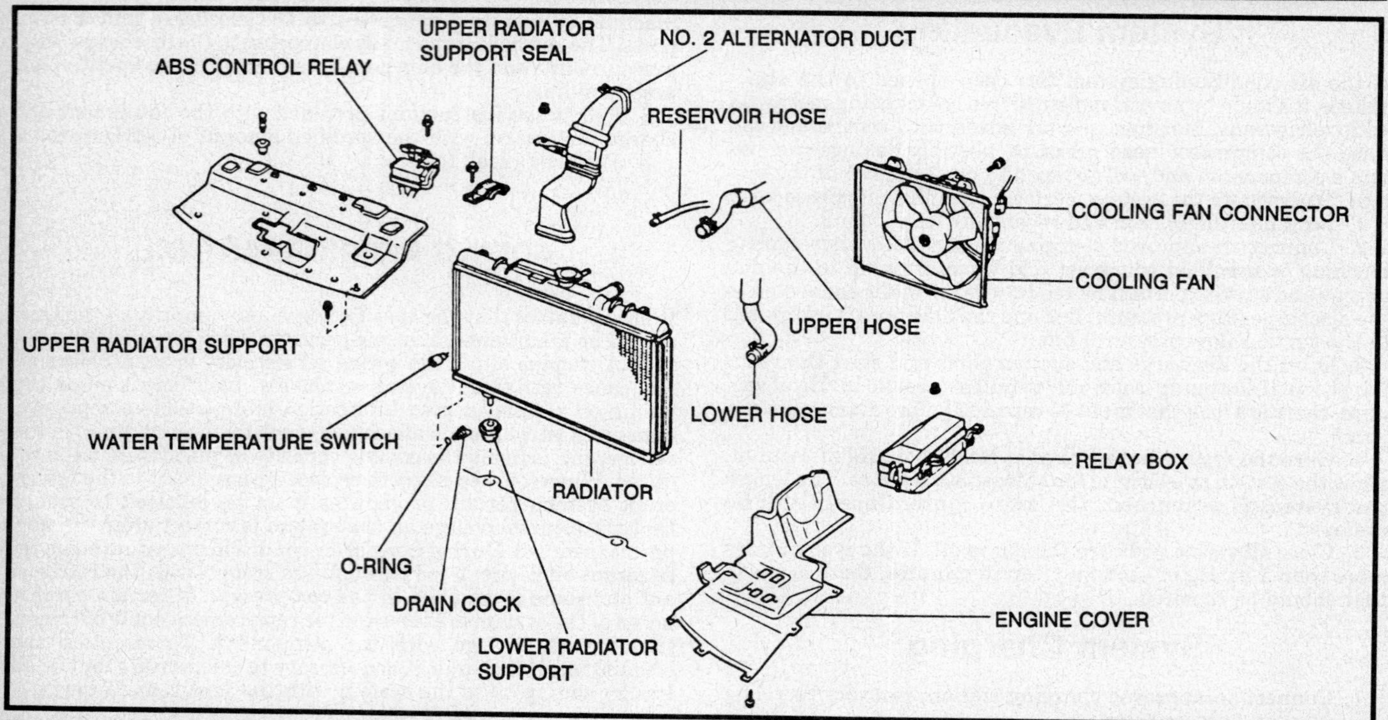
UPPER RADIATOR SUPPORT SEAL
NO. 2 ALTERNATOR DUCT
ABS CONTROL RELAY
RESERVOIR HOSE
COOLING FAN CONNECTOR
COOLING FAN
UPPER HOSE
UPPER RADIATOR SUPPORT
LOWER HOSE
WATER TEMPERATURE SWITCH
RELAY BOX
RADIATOR
O-RING
DRAIN COCK
ENGINE COVER
LOWER RADIATOR SUPPORT

Exploded view radiator assembly—Celica

11. Connect the cooling fan motor electrical connection. Connect the radiator hoses and reservoir hose. Install the the upper radiator support seal assembly.
12. Install the engine relay box to the battery, if necessary. On the 3S-GTE engine install the air duct.
13. If equipped with ABS, install the ABS control relay to the radiator support assembly.
14. On the 3S-GTE and 5S-FE engines, connect the water temperature switch electrical connector.
15. Install the engine undercovers, reconnect the negative battery cable, fill (bleed cooling system) the engine with coolant. Start the engine and check for leaks. Check all fluid levels as necessary.

Corolla

1. Disconnect the negative battery cable.
2. Drain engine coolant.
3. Disconnect the coolant reservoir hose and all radiator hoses.
4. Disconnect the cooling fan motor electrical connection.
5. If equipped with automatic transaxle, disconnect the oil cooler lines. Remove the radiator supports. Remove the radiator assembly with the electrical cooling fan from the vehicle.
6. Remove the electrical cooling fan from the radiator assembly, as necessary.

To install:

7. Install the electrical cooling fan to the radiator assembly. Install the radiator assembly in the vehicle and check that the rubber cushions are in the correct position.
8. If equipped with automatic transaxle, connect the oil cooler lines.
9. Connect the cooling fan motor electrical connection. Connect the radiator hoses and reservoir hose.
10. Reconnect the negative battery cable and fill (bleed cooling system) the engine with coolant. Start the engine and check for leaks. Check all fluid levels, as necessary.

Cressida

1. Disconnect the negative battery cable. Drain engine coolant.
2. Remove the No. 2 fan shroud from the radiator assembly.
3. Disconnect the coolant reservoir hose and all radiator hoses.
4. Disconnect the automatic transmission oil cooler lines. Remove the radiator supports. Remove the radiator assembly with the fan shroud from the vehicle.
5. Remove the fan shroud from the radiator assembly, as necessary.

To install:

6. Install the fan shroud to the radiator assembly. Install the radiator assembly in the vehicle and check that the rubber cushions are in the correct position.
7. Reconnect the automatic transmission oil cooler lines. Connect the radiator hoses and reservoir hose.
8. Install the No. 2 fan shroud.
9. Reconnect the negative battery cable and fill (bleed cooling system) the engine with coolant. Start the engine and check for leaks. Check all fluid levels, as necessary.

MR2

1989

1. Disconnect the negative battery cable. Drain engine coolant.
2. Remove the electrical cooling fan assemblies.
3. Disconnect temperature switch electrical connection.
4. Disconnect the radiator hoses.
5. Remove the radiator supports and remove the radiator from the vehicle.

To install:

6. Install the radiator assembly in the vehicle and check that the rubber cushions are in the correct position.

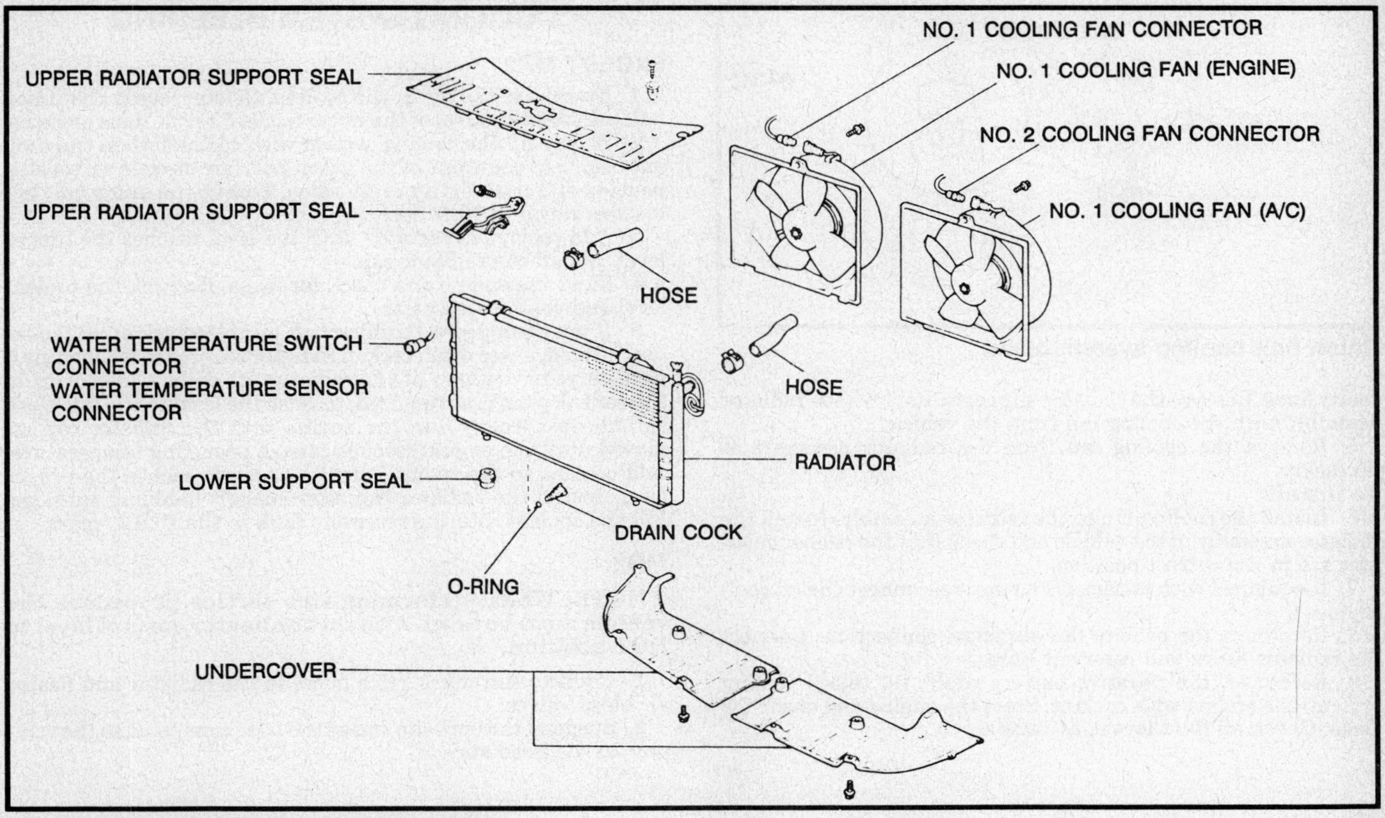
NO. 1 COOLING FAN CONNECTOR
NO. 1 COOLING FAN (ENGINE)
NO. 2 COOLING FAN CONNECTOR
NO. 1 COOLING FAN (A/C)
UPPER RADIATOR SUPPORT SEAL
UPPER RADIATOR SUPPORT SEAL
HOSE
WATER TEMPERATURE SWITCH CONNECTOR
WATER TEMPERATURE SENSOR CONNECTOR
HOSE
RADIATOR
LOWER SUPPORT SEAL
DRAIN COCK
O-RING
UNDERCOVER

Exploded view radiator assembly—MR2

7. Reconnect the radiator hoses. Connect the temperature switch electrical connection.
8. Install the electrical cooling fans.
9. Reconnect the negative battery cable and fill (bleed cooling system) the engine with coolant. Start the engine and check for leaks. Check all fluid levels, as necessary.

1991

1. Disconnect the negative battery cable.
2. Remove the front luggage undercovers. Drain engine coolant.
3. Remove the upper radiator support seal assembly.
4. Disconnet the radiator hoses. Remove the front hood lock assembly.
5. Disconnect the radiator cooling fan electrical connectors.
6. Disconnect water temperature sensor electrical connection.
7. Remove the radiator assembly with the electrical cooling fans from the vehicle.
8. Remove the electrical cooling fans from the radiator assembly, as necessary.

To install:

9. Install the electrical cooling fans to the radiator assembly. Install the radiator assembly in the vehicle and check that the rubber cushions are in the correct position.
10. Reconnect water temperature sensor electrical connection and cooling fans electrical connections.
11. Install the front hood lock assembly.
12. Connect the radiator hoses. Reconnect the negative battery cable and fill (bleed cooling system) the engine with coolant. Start the engine and check for leaks.
13. Install upper radiator support seal and front luggage undercovers.

Supra

1. Disconnect the negative battery cable. Drain engine coolant.
2. Disconnect condenser fan motor electrical connection.
3. Disconnect the coolant reservoir hose and all radiator hoses.
4. If equipped with automatic transmission, disconnect the oil cooler lines. Remove the radiator supports. Remove the radiator assembly with the condenser fan from the vehicle.
5. Remove the condenser fan from the radiator assembly, as necessary.

To install:

6. Install the condenser fan to the radiator assembly. Install the radiator assembly in the vehicle and check that the rubber cushions are in the correct position.
7. If equipped with automatic transmission, connect the oil cooler lines.
8. Connect the condenser fan motor electrical connection. Connect the radiator hoses and reservoir hose.
9. Reconnect the negative battery cable, fill (bleed cooling system) the engine with coolant. Start the engine and check for leaks. Check all fluid levels, as necessary.

Tercel

1. Disconnect the negative battery cable. Remove the engine undercovers. Drain engine coolant.
2. Remove the air intake connector, as necessary. Disconnect electrical cooling fan connection.
3. Disconnect the coolant reservoir hose and all radiator hoses.
4. If equipped with automatic transaxle, disconnect the oil

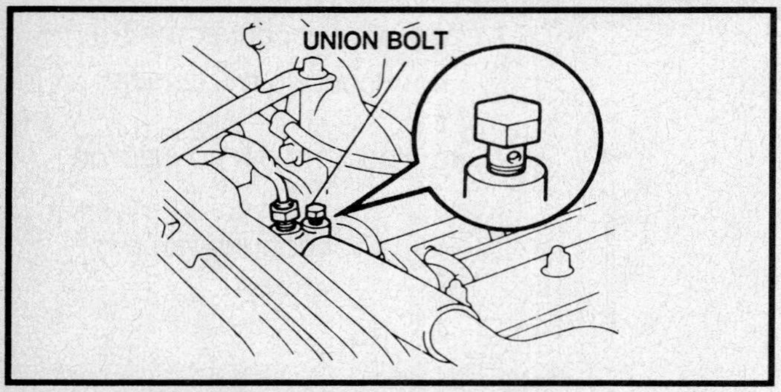
UNION BOLT

Union bolt cooling system bleed

cooler lines. Remove the radiator supports. Remove the radiator assembly with the cooling fan from the vehicle.

5. Remove the cooling fan from the radiator assembly as necessary.

To install:

6. Install the cooling fan to the radiator assembly. Install the radiator assembly in the vehicle and check that the rubber cushions are in the correct position.

7. If equipped with automatic transaxle, connect the oil cooler lines.

8. Reconnect the cooling fan electrical connection. Connect the radiator hoses and reservoir hose.

9. Reconnect the negative battery cable, fill (bleed cooling system) the engine with coolant. Start the engine and check for leaks. Check all fluid levels, as necessary.

COOLING SYSTEM BLEEDING

EXCEPT MR2

1. To release the air in the cooling system, loosen the union bolt (air bleeder valve) of the water outlet 5 revolutions or turns.

2. Slowly fill the cooling system with coolant when the coolant begins to come out of the union bolt (air bleeder valve) stop pouring and close the air drain valve. Torque the union bolt (air bleeder valve) to 13 ft. lbs.

3. Add coolant to radiator until the level reaches the proper level. Install the radiator cap.

4. Start the engine and check for leaks. Recheck the coolant level and refill, as necessary.

5. If not equipped with union bolt (air bleed valve) fill the radiator (open lower drain cock in radiator to remove trapped air if necessary) to the base of the radiator fill neck. Add coolant to the recovery tank, as required, to raise the level to the full mark as indicated (cold). Run the engine with the radiator cap removed until the engine reaches correct operating temperature. Add coolant to the radiator until the level reaches the proper level. Install the radiator cap after coolant bubbling subsides. Fill the coolant into the reservoir tank to the **FULL** mark.

MR2

NOTE: When preforming this service procedure the vehicle must be level. Also set the heater control level to HOT position.

1. Connect suitable service hoses to the radiator and heater air bleed valves.

2. Suspend the opposite end of the hose connected to the radiator to the hood stay.

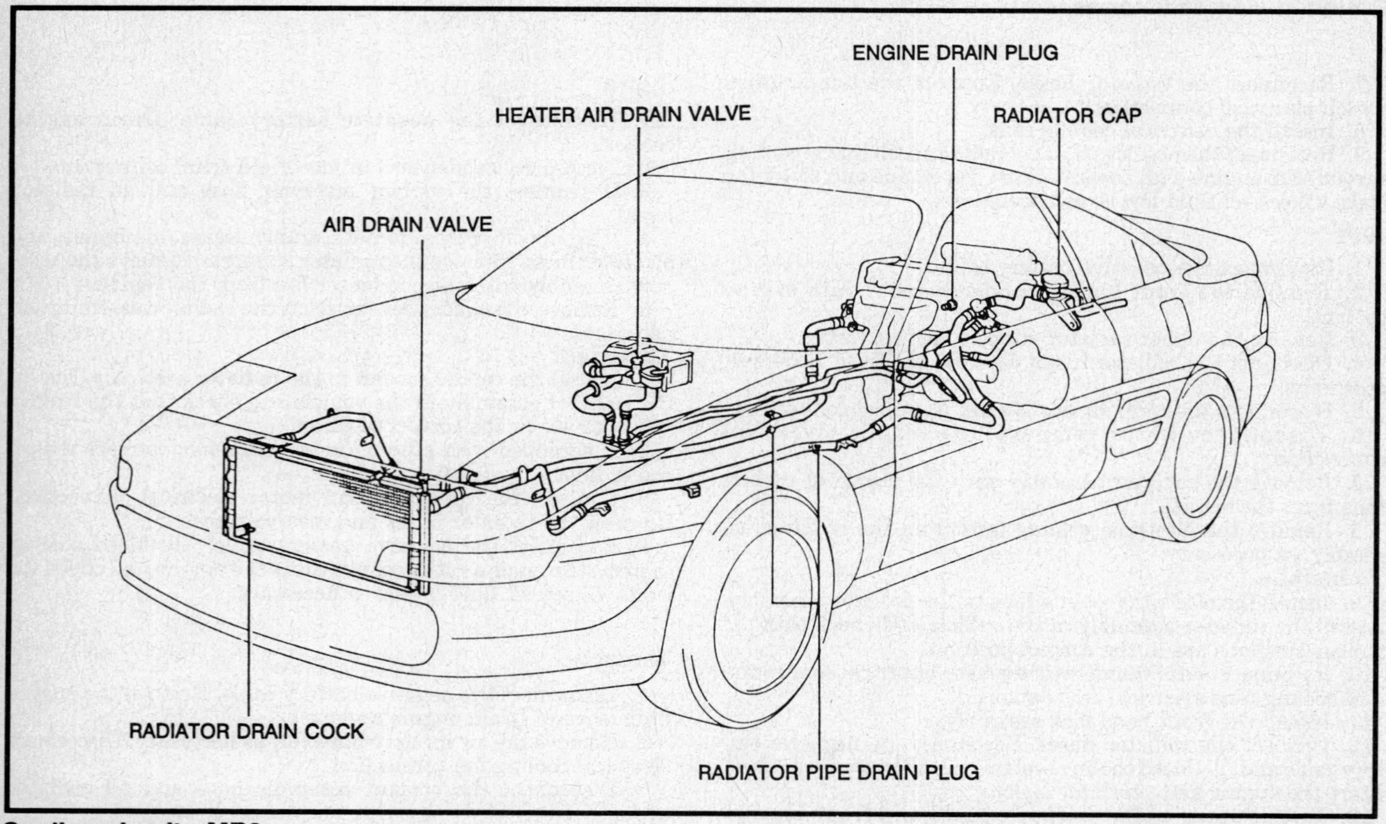
ENGINE DRAIN PLUG
HEATER AIR DRAIN VALVE
RADIATOR CAP
AIR DRAIN VALVE
RADIATOR DRAIN COCK
RADIATOR PIPE DRAIN PLUG

Cooling circuit—MR2

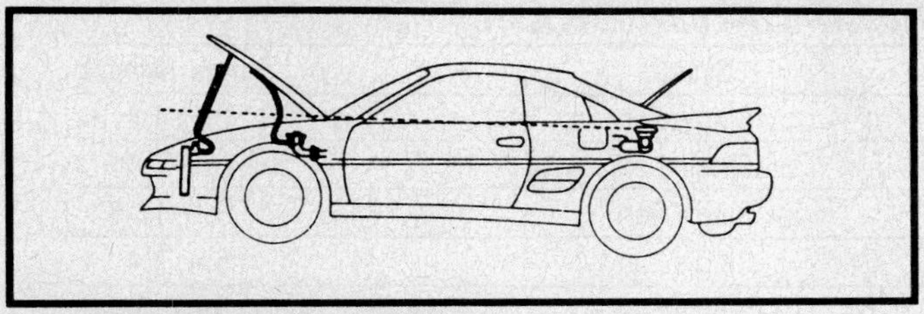
Correct coolant level—MR2

3. Suspend the opposite end of the hose connected to the heater air bleeder valve to the windshield washer tube. Be sure not to close-off or pinch any of the tubes.
4. Open the water inlet, radiator and heater air bleeder valves about 3 turns.
5. Pour the coolant into the water filler. When the coolant begins to come out of the engine air bleeder (water inlet) valve, stop pouring and close the air drain valve.
6. Again pour the coolant in the water filler hole until it is full. Check that the coolant levels in the suspended service hoses (tubes) come up to the level of the water filler nozzle.
7. If the coolant level in either service hose (tube) does not come up to the water filler nozzle level, check the tube for folds or obstructions. Repeat Step 6.
8. Close the radiator and heater air bleeder valves. Disconnect the service hoses.
9. Fasten the radiator cap (water filler cap) to the first stop point. Start the engine and run it at fast idle for approximately 3 minutes and then shut off the engine.
10. If the level of the radiator filler hole falls, add coolant as before. Repeat Step 9.
11. Completely tighten the radiator cap. Fill the coolant into the reservoir tank to the **FULL** mark.

Electric Cooling Fan

TESTING

Single Fan Assembly

LOW TEMPERATURE CONDITION (BELOW 181°F)

1. Turn the ignition switch **ON**. Check that the fan stops. If the fan runs, then check the cooling fan relay and water temperature switch. Check for a separated connector or severed wire between the cooling fan relay and water temperature switch.
2. Disconnect the water temperature switch connector and check to see that the fan rotates.
3. If the fan does not rotate, check the cooling fan relay, fan motor, ignition or engine main relay and fuse. Check for a short circuit between the cooling fan relay and water temperature switch.
4. Reconnect the water temperature switch connector.

HIGH TEMPERATURE CONDITION (ABOVE 199°F)

1. Start the engine and raise the engine coolant temperature to reach above 199°F.
2. Confirm that the fan rotates; if it does not rotate, replace the water temperature switch.

Dual Fan Assembly

LOW TEMPERATURE CONDTION (BELOW 185°F)

1. Turn the ignition switch **ON**. Check that the fans stop. If the fans run, then check the cooling fan relays and water temperature sensor. Check for a separated connector or severed wire between the cooling fan relay and water temperature sensor.
2. Disconnect the water temperature sensor connector, and check to see that the fans rotate.
3. If not, check the cooling fan relays, fan motor, ignition or main relay and fuse. Check for a short circuit between the fan relay and water temperature sensor.
4. Reconnect the water temperature sensor electrical connector.

HIGH TEMPERATURE CONDITION (185–194°F)

1. Start the engine and raise the engine coolant temperature to 185–194°F.
2. Confirm that the fans rotate at low speed; if not, replace the water temperature sensor.

HIGH TEMPERATURE CONDITION (ABOVE 194°F)

1. Start the engine and raise the engine coolant temperature to reach above 194°F.
2. Confirm that the fans rotate at high speed; if not, replace the water temperature sensor.

Fan Motor Load Test

1. Connect the battery and the ammeter to the fan motor connector (complete circuit).
2. Check to see that the motor rotates smoothly. On a single and dual fan assemblies check for the standard amperage specification. Refer to the standard amperage (use these specifications for fan motor load test) specification chart, as required.
3. If any of the above specifications are not as specified, replace the fan motor assembly.

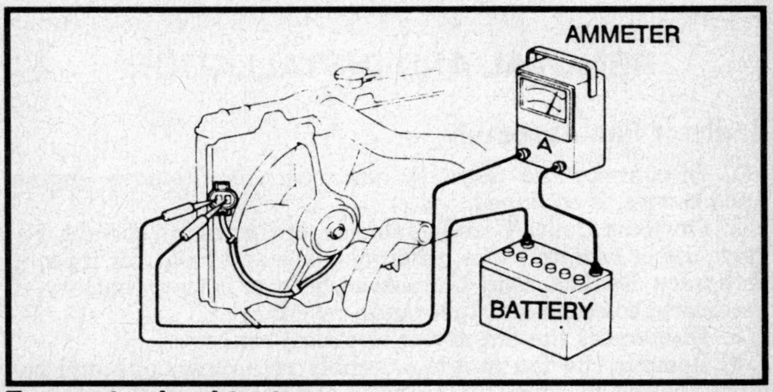
AMMETER
A
BATTERY
Fan motor load test

STANDARD AMPERAGE SPECIFICATION CHART

Year	Vehicle	System	Range (Amps)
1989-91	Camry (2WD M/T)	Single Fan	3.2–4.4
	Camry (2WD A/T and 4WD M/T)	Single Fan	5.8–7.4
	Camry (4WD A/T)	Single Fan	8.8–10.8
	Camry	Dual Fan (No. 1)	12.1–15.1
	Camry	Dual Fan (No. 2)	6.0–7.4

STANDARD AMPERAGE SPECIFICATION CHART

Year	Vehicle	System	Range (Amps)
1989	Celica (3S-FE and 3S-GE M/T)	Single Fan	3.2–4.4
	Celica (3S-FE and 3S-GE A/T)	Single Fan	5.8–7.4
	Celica (3S-GTE)	Single Fan	8.6–11.6
1990–91	Celica	Single Fan	5.4–7.4
	Celica (3S-GTE)	Single Fan	8.8–10.8
1989	Corolla (4A-GE)	Single Fan	3.2–4.4
	Corolla (4A-FE A/T)	Single Fan	8.8–10.8
	Corolla (4A-F)	Single Fan	5.8–7.4
1990–91	Corolla (Canada/Coupe)	Single Fan	8.8–10.8
	Corolla (Others)	Single Fan	5.8–7.4
1989	MR2 (M/T)	Dual Fan (Radiator)	5.8–7.4
	MR2 (A/T)	Dual Fan (Radiator)	8.8–10.8
	MR2	Dual Fan (Engine Compartment)	1.5–2.7
1991	MR2 (M/T with A/C)	Dual Fan	5.8–7.4
	MR2 (A/T with A/C)	Dual Fan	8.8–10.8
	MR2 (M/T without A/C)	Single Fan	5.8–7.4
	MR2 (A/T without A/C)	Single Fan	8.8–10.8
	MR2 (3S-GTE)	Dual Fan (Engine Compartment)	3.1–4.3
1989	Tercel (M/T)	Single Fan	5.7–7.7
	Tercel EZ (A/T)	Single Fan	3.1–4.3
	Tercel (A/T)	Single Fan	8.6–11.6
1990	Tercel (M/T)	Single Fan	3.2–4.4
	Tercel EZ (A/T)	Single Fan	6.0–7.4
	Tercel (A/T)	Single Fan	8.8–10.8
1991	Tercel (USA A/T)	Single Fan	8.8–10.8
	Tercel (Others)	Single Fan	6.0–7.4

REMOVAL AND INSTALLATION

Radiator Fan Assembly

1. Disconnect the negative battery cable. Remove engine undercovers, if equipped.
2. On some Celica/Corolla vehicles, drain engine coolant, remove upper radiator hose, reservoir hose and reservoir tank, if necessary. Remove relay box assembly from battery, battery, if necessary, solenoid and fuel pump resistor.
3. Disconnect the fan motor electrical connector.
4. Remove the fan motor assembly retaining bolts and remove the fan motor assembly from the vehicle.
5. Remove the fan, spacer, if equipped, and nut. Remove the fan motor, bushings and screws from the fan motor assembly.

To install:

6. Install fan to fan motor.
7. Install fan motor to fan motor assembly. Install fan motor assembly in the vehicle.
8. Reconnect the fan motor electrical connection.
9. On Celica/Corolla vehicles install radiator hose, reservoir hose and reservoir tank, if necessary. Install battery, relay box assemble to the battery, solenoid and fuel pump resistor.
10. Install engine undercovers, if equipped. Connect negative battery cable. Refill engine coolant and bleed the cooling system, if necessary.

Engine Compartment Fan Assembly

1. Disconnect the negative battery cable.
2. Remove the right side engine side panel.
3. Remove No. 1 and No. 2 air intake connectors.
4. Disconnect the engine compartment cooling fan electrical connector.
5. Remove the engine compartment cooling fan.
6. Remove the fan, spacer, if equipped, and nut. Remove the fan motor, bushings and screws from the fan motor assembly.

To install:

7. Install fan to fan motor.
8. Install fan motor to fan motor assembly.
9. Install the engine compartment cooling fan assembly in the vehicle. Reconnect the engine compartment cooling fan electrical connector.
10. Install air intake connectors. Install the right side engine side panel. Reconnect the negative battery cable.

Condenser

REMOVAL AND INSTALLATION

Camry

1. Disconnect the negative battery cable.

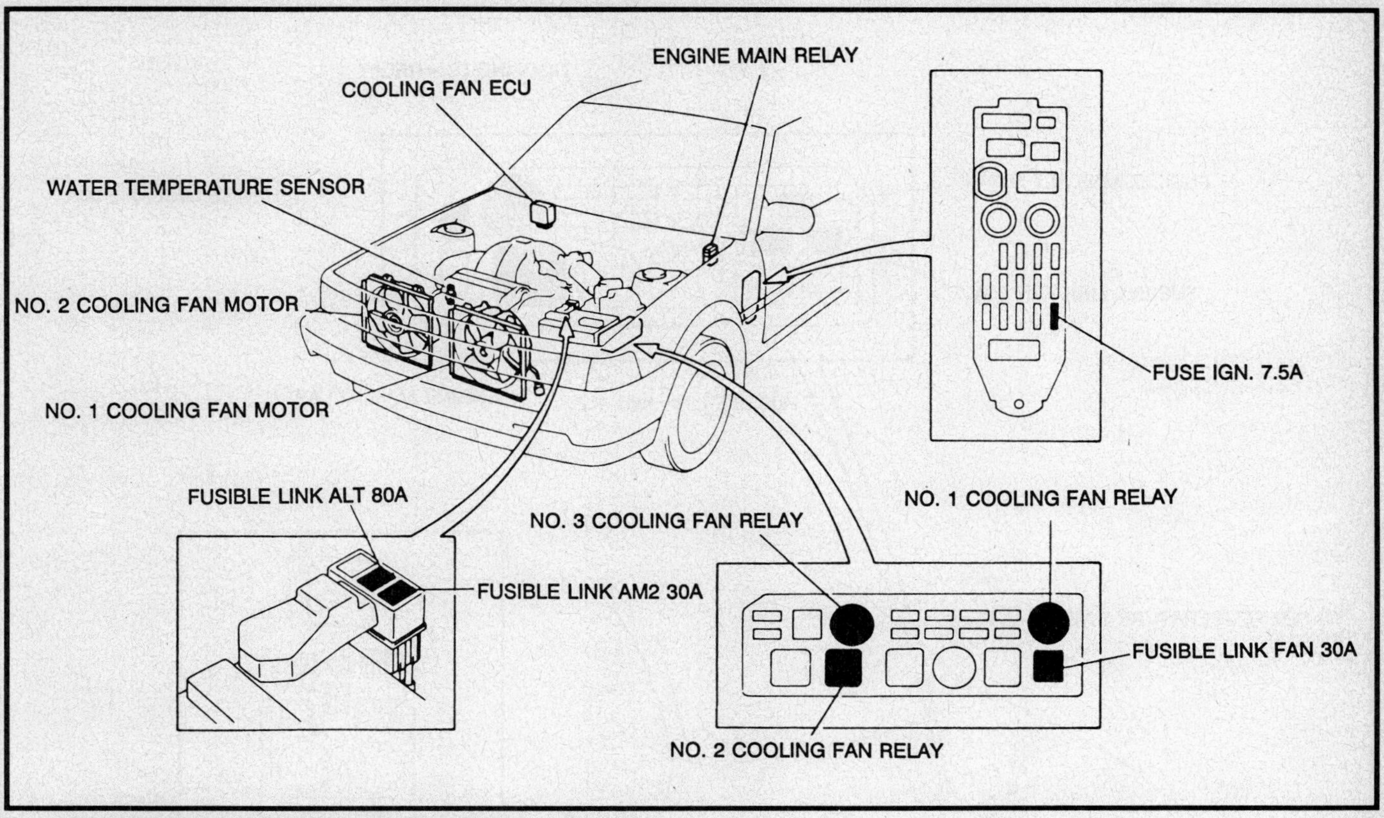
ENGINE MAIN RELAY
COOLING FAN ECU
WATER TEMPERATURE SENSOR
NO. 2 COOLING FAN MOTOR
NO. 1 COOLING FAN MOTOR
FUSE IGN. 7.5A
FUSIBLE LINK ALT 80A
NO. 3 COOLING FAN RELAY
NO. 1 COOLING FAN RELAY
FUSIBLE LINK AM2 30A
FUSIBLE LINK FAN 30A
NO. 2 COOLING FAN RELAY

Location of electric cooling fan components—Camry

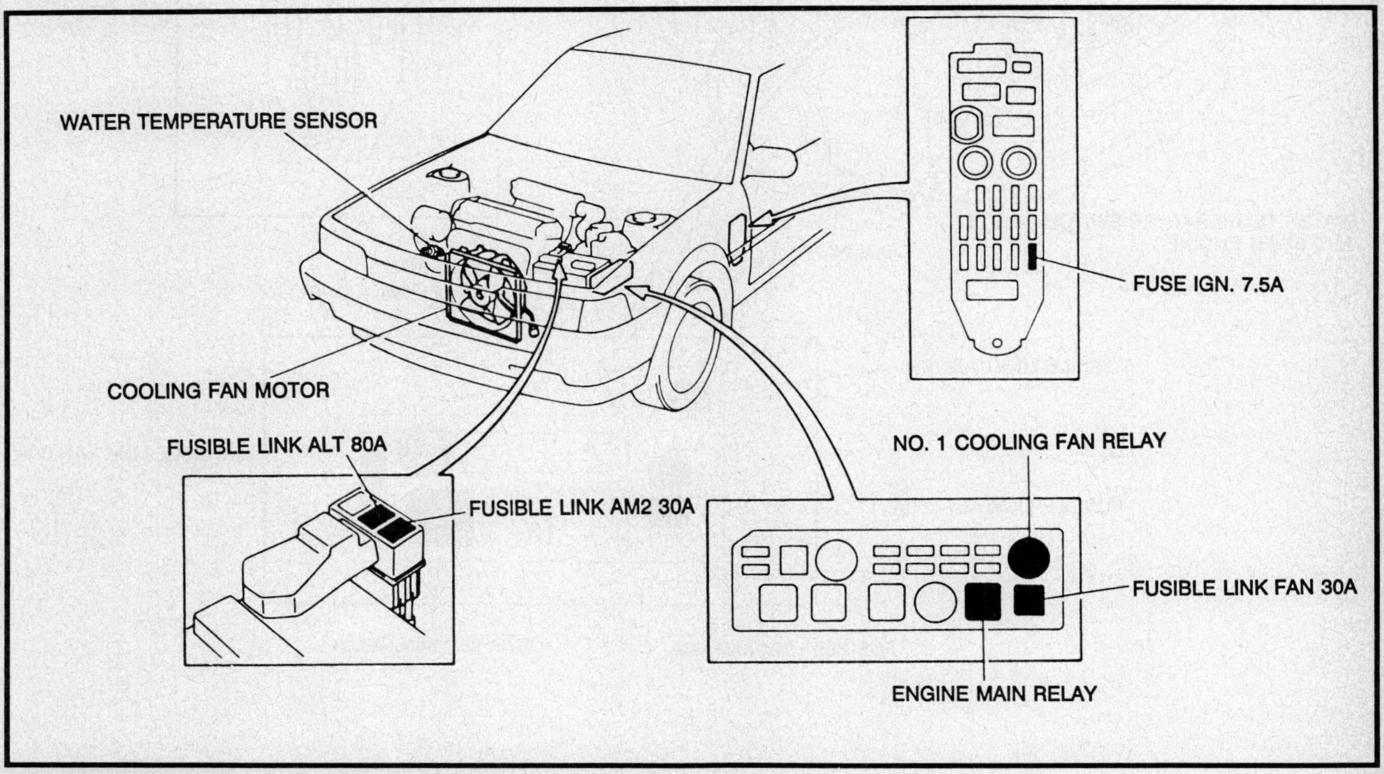
WATER TEMPERATURE SENSOR
FUSE IGN. 7.5A
COOLING FAN MOTOR
FUSIBLE LINK ALT 80A
NO. 1 COOLING FAN RELAY
FUSIBLE LINK AM2 30A
FUSIBLE LINK FAN 30A
ENGINE MAIN RELAY

Location of electric cooling fan components—Camry

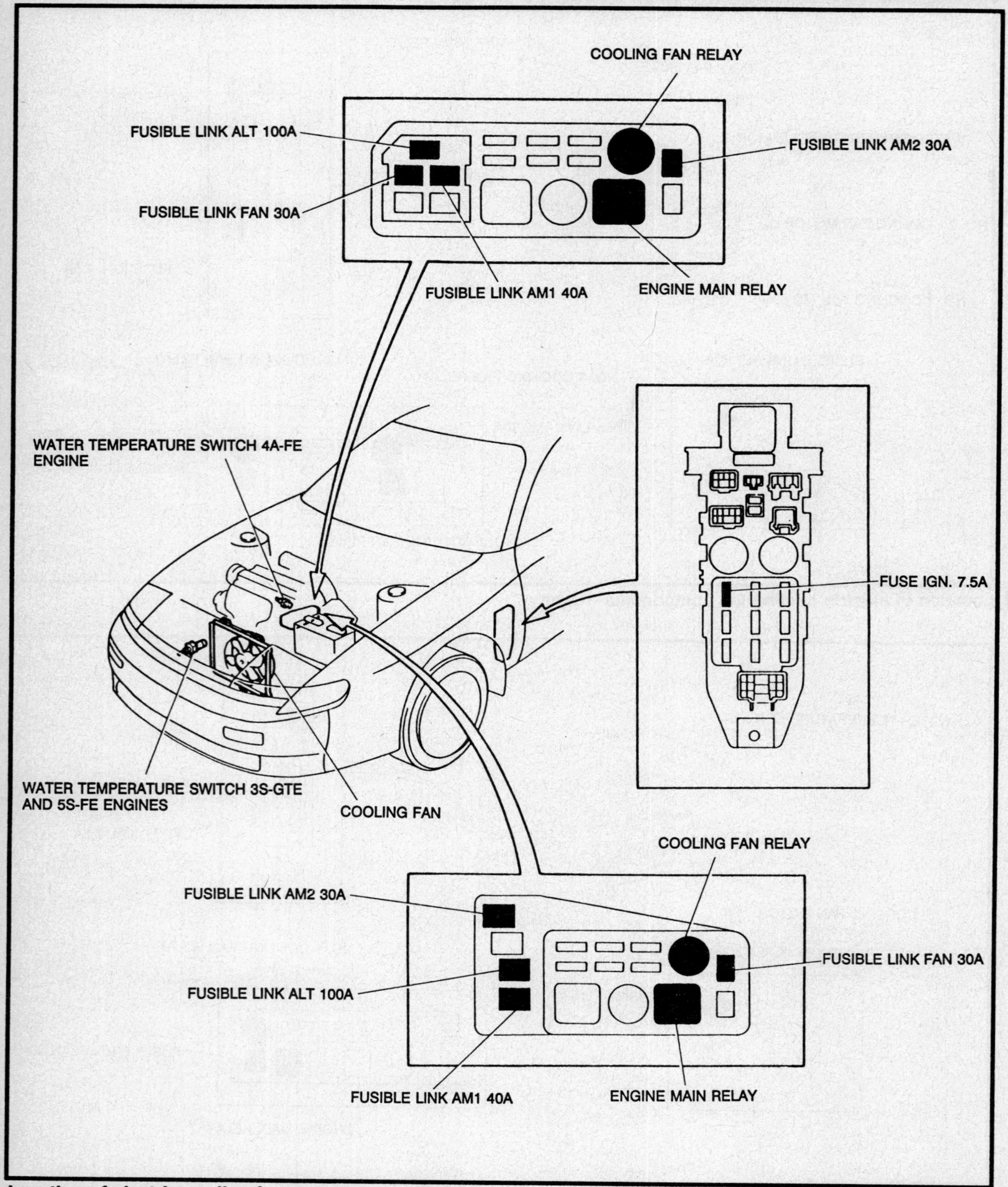
COOLING FAN RELAY
FUSIBLE LINK ALT 100A
FUSIBLE LINK AM2 30A
FUSIBLE LINK FAN 30A
FUSIBLE LINK AM1 40A
ENGINE MAIN RELAY
WATER TEMPERATURE SWITCH 4A-FE ENGINE
FUSE IGN. 7.5A
WATER TEMPERATURE SWITCH 3S-GTE AND 5S-FE ENGINES
COOLING FAN
COOLING FAN RELAY
FUSIBLE LINK AM2 30A
FUSIBLE LINK FAN 30A
FUSIBLE LINK ALT 100A
FUSIBLE LINK AM1 40A
ENGINE MAIN RELAY

Location of electric cooling fan components—Celica

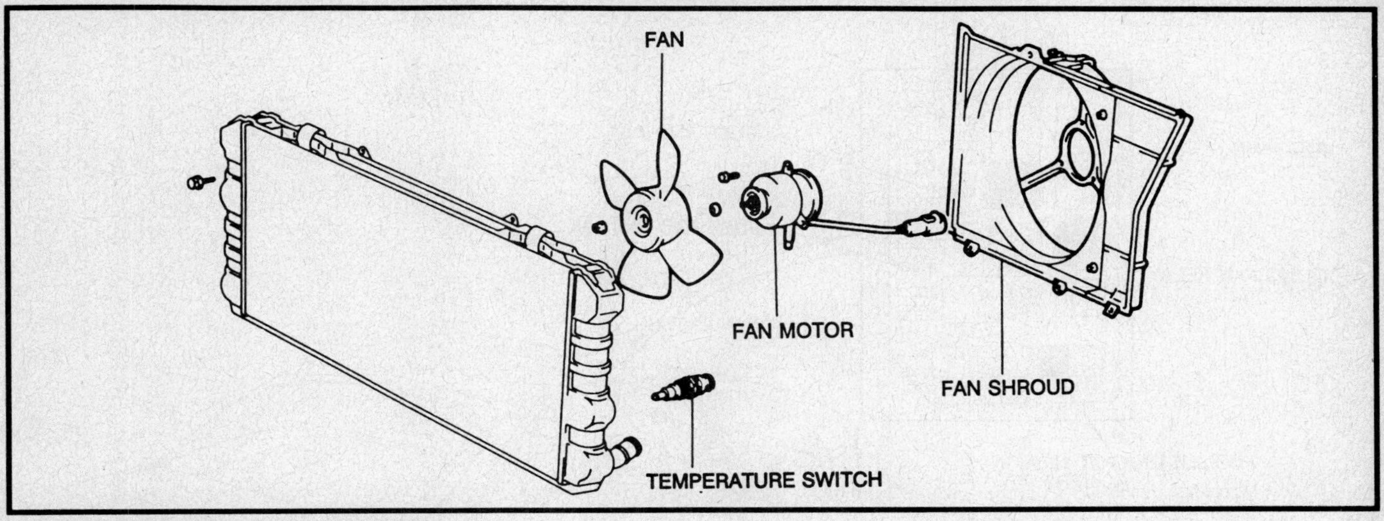
FAN
FAN MOTOR
FAN SHROUD
TEMPERATURE SWITCH

Electric cooling fan radiator—MR2

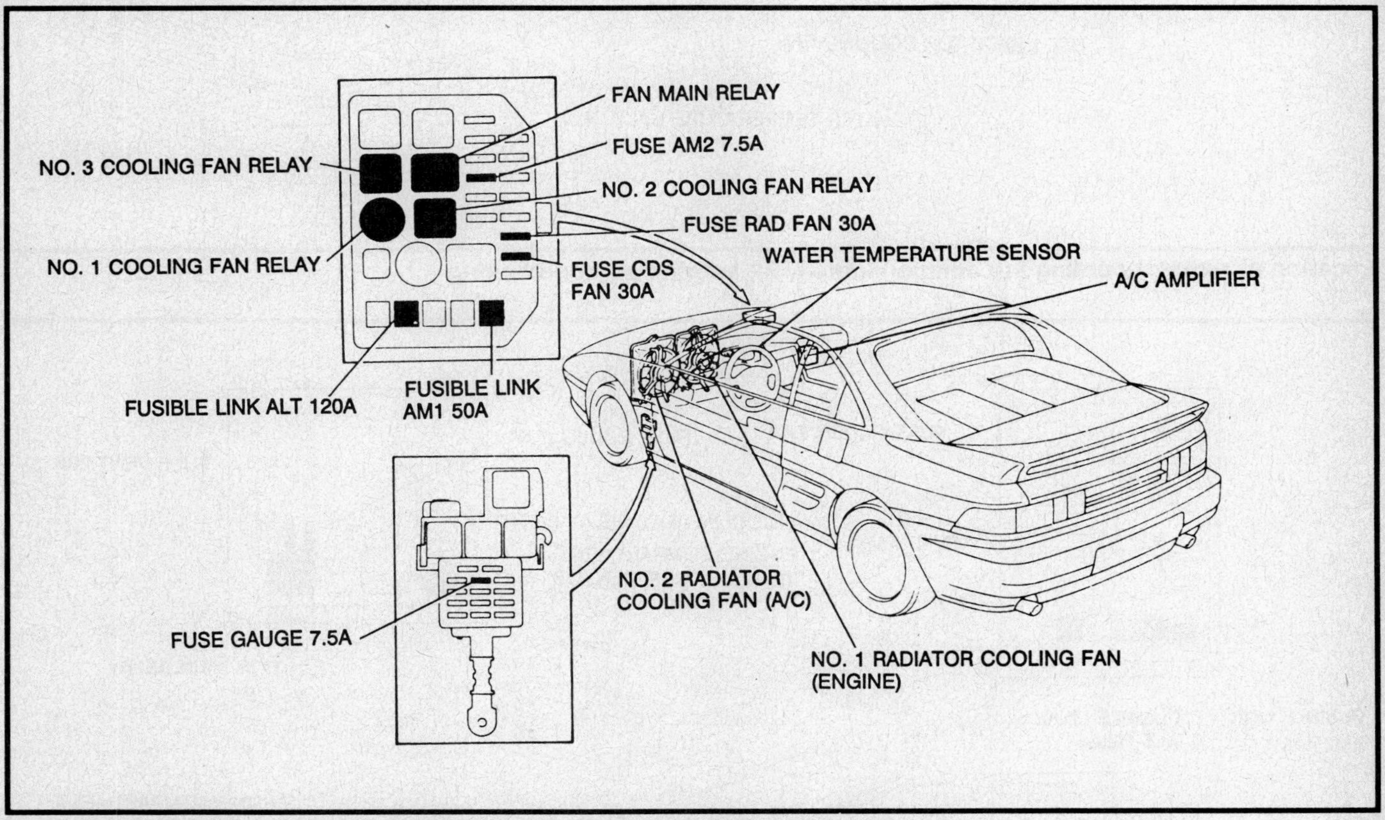
FAN MAIN RELAY
NO. 3 COOLING FAN RELAY
FUSE AM2 7.5A
NO. 2 COOLING FAN RELAY
FUSE RAD FAN 30A
NO. 1 COOLING FAN RELAY
WATER TEMPERATURE SENSOR
FUSE CDS
FAN 30A
A/C AMPLIFIER
FUSIBLE LINK ALT 120A
FUSIBLE LINK
AM1 50A
NO. 2 RADIATOR
COOLING FAN (A/C)
FUSE GAUGE 7.5A
NO. 1 RADIATOR COOLING FAN
(ENGINE)

Location of radiator cooling fan components—MR2 with air conditioning

2. Recover refrigerant (discharge system) from refrigeration system.
3. Remove the battery, ignitor bracket and fan assembly.
4. Remove all refrigerant system connections. Cap open fittings immediately.
5. Remove the condenser.

To install:

6. Install the condenser to the vehicle. Make sure all rubber cushions fit on the mounting flanges correctly.
7. Reconnect all refrigerant system connections. Replace O-rings, if required.
8. Install fan assembly, ignitor bracket and battery.
9. If condenser assembly was replaced, add 1.4–1.7 fl. oz. of compressor oil.
10. Reconnect battery cable. Evacuate, charge and test refrigerant system. Check system for leaks.

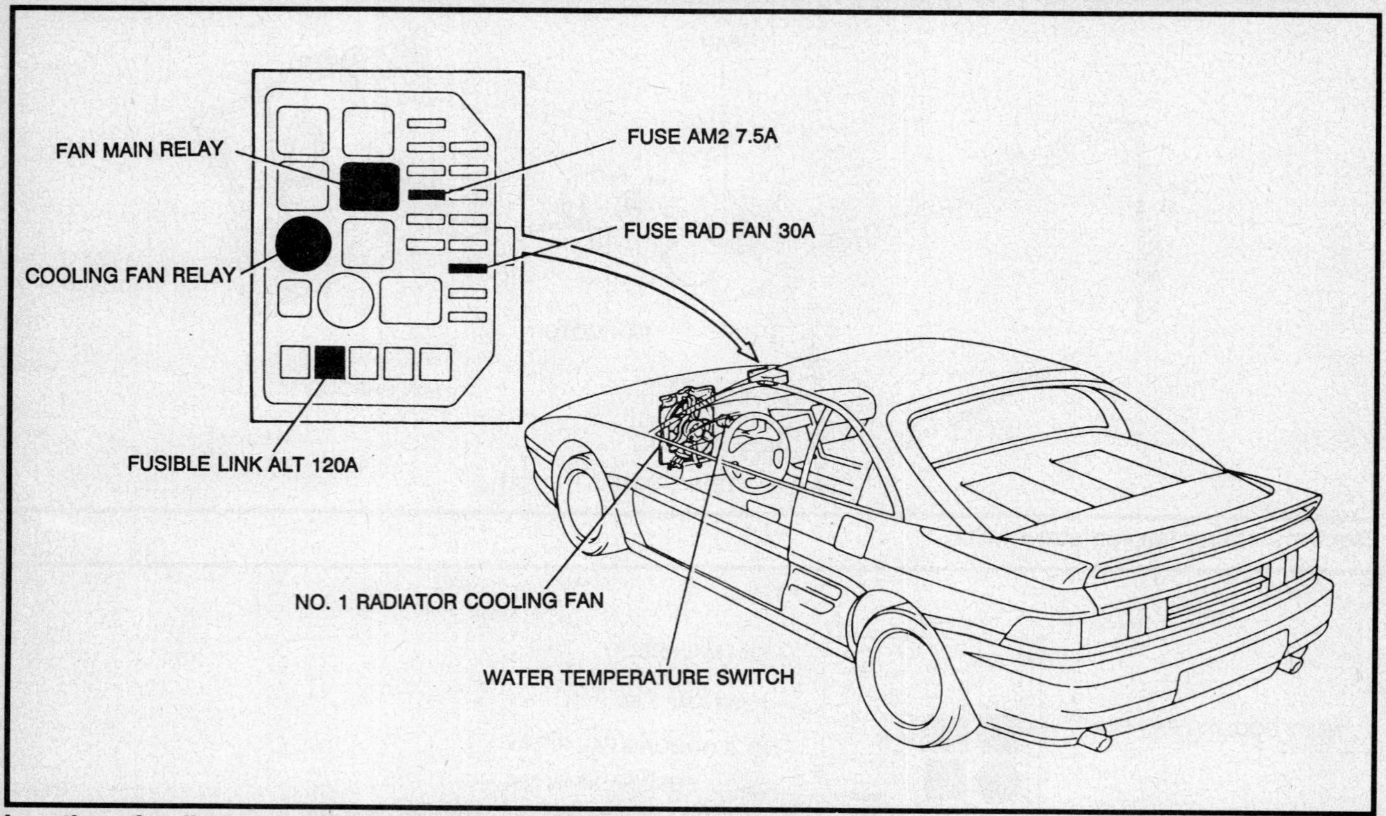
FAN MAIN RELAY
FUSE AM2 7.5A
FUSE RAD FAN 30A
COOLING FAN RELAY
FUSIBLE LINK ALT 120A
NO. 1 RADIATOR COOLING FAN
WATER TEMPERATURE SWITCH

Location of radiator cooling fan components—MR2 without air conditioning

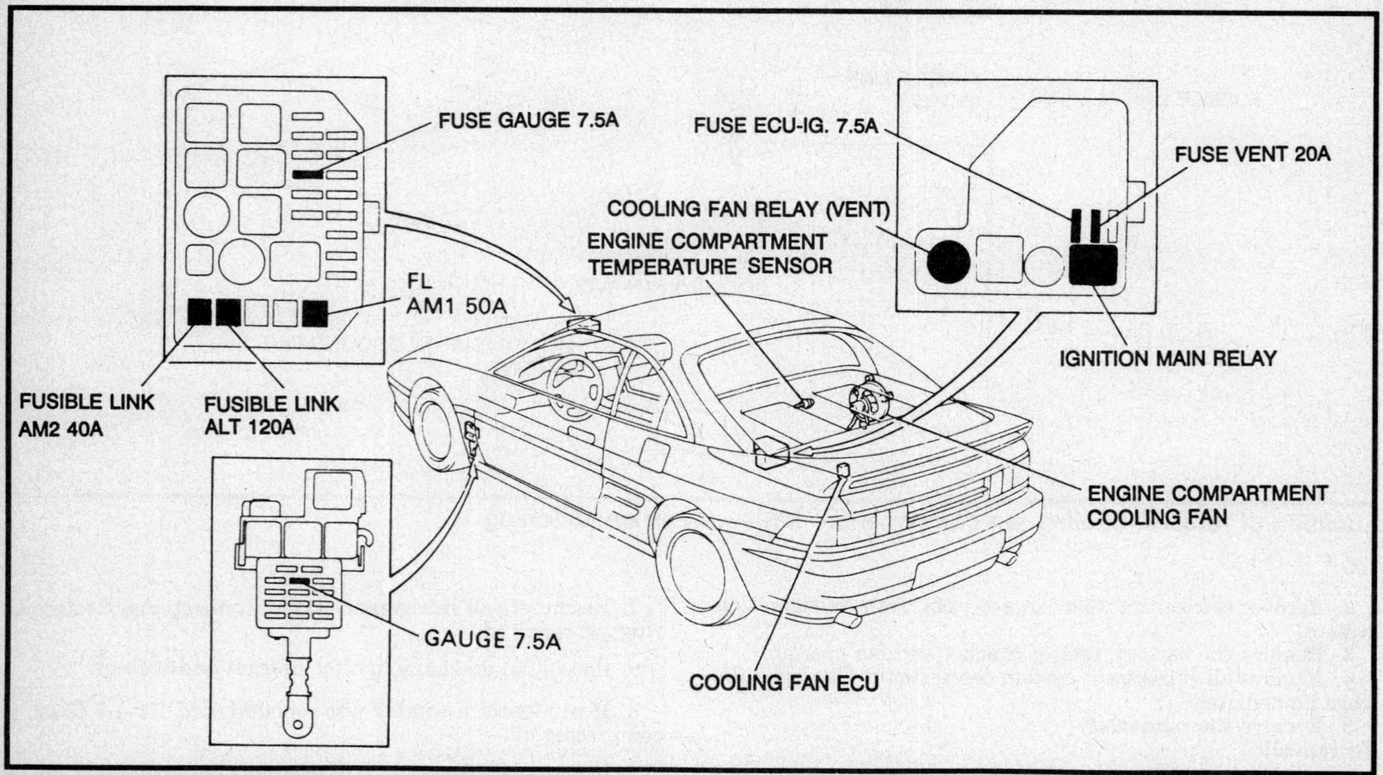
FUSE GAUGE 7.5A
FUSE ECU-IG. 7.5A
FUSE VENT 20A
COOLING FAN RELAY (VENT)
ENGINE COMPARTMENT
TEMPERATURE SENSOR
FL
AM1 50A
IGNITION MAIN RELAY
FUSIBLE LINK
AM2 40A
FUSIBLE LINK
ALT 120A
ENGINE COMPARTMENT
COOLING FAN
GAUGE 7.5A
COOLING FAN ECU

Location of engine compartment cooling fan components—MR2 with 3S-GTE engine

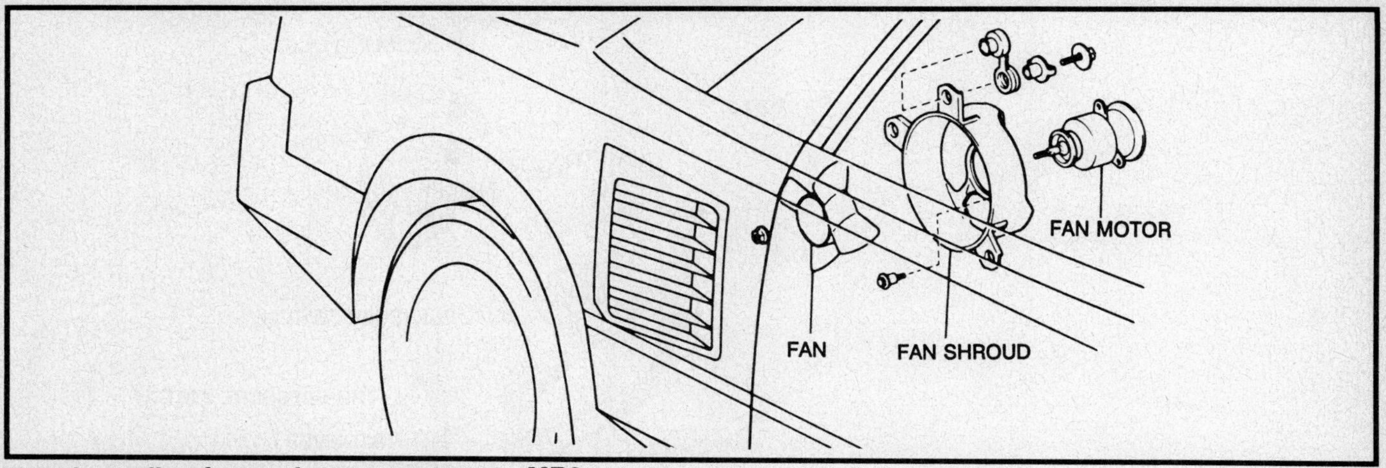
FAN MOTOR
FAN
FAN SHROUD

Electric cooling fan engine compartment—MR2

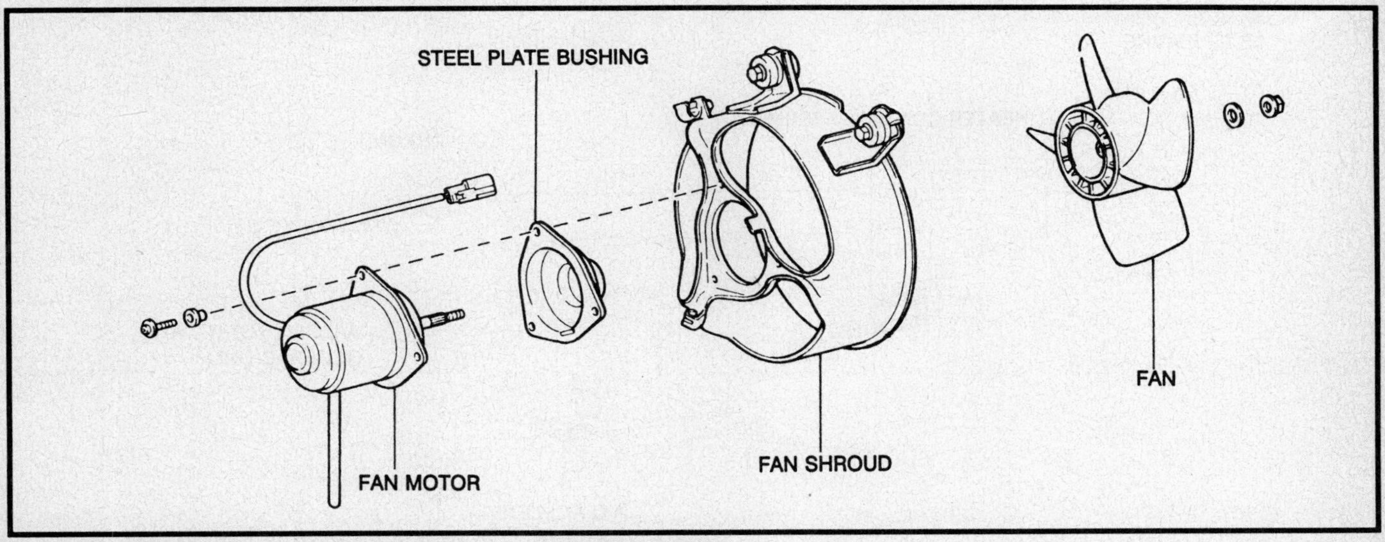
STEEL PLATE BUSHING
FAN
FAN SHROUD
FAN MOTOR

Exploded view of engine compartment cooling fan—MR2

Celica and Corolla

1. Disconnect the negative battery cable.
2. Recover refrigerant (discharge system) from refrigeration system.
3. Remove engine undercover, if equipped. Remove the front grille assembly. Remove the center brace and horns. On Corolla remove front bumper assembly and oil cooler, if equipped.
4. Remove the fan assembly.
5. Remove all refrigerant system connections. Cap open fittings immediately.
6. Remove the condenser.

To install:

7. Install the condenser to the vehicle. Make sure all rubber cushions fit on the mounting flanges correctly.
8. Reconnect all refrigerant system connections. Replace O-rings, if required.
9. Install fan assembly, center brace and horns.
10. On Corolla install oil cooler if so equipped and front bumper assembly. Install front grille and engine undercover.
11. If condenser assembly was replaced, add 1.4–1.7 fl. oz. of compressor oil.
12. Reconnect battery cable. Evacuate, charge and test refrigerant system. Check system for leaks.

Cressida

1. Disconnect the negative battery cable.
2. Recover refrigerant (discharge system) from refrigeration system.
3. Remove the front grille assembly. Remove the hood lock, center brace and horns. Remove the receiver assembly.
4. Remove the front bumper assembly.
5. Remove the fan assembly and oil cooler.
6. Remove all refrigerant system connections. Cap open fittings immediately.
7. Remove the ambient sensor. Remove the condenser.

To install:

8. Install the condenser to the vehicle. Make sure all rubber cushions fit on the mounting flanges correctly. Install ambient sensor.
9. Reconnect all refrigerant system connections. Replace O-rings, if required.
10. Install front grille assembly, hood lock and center brace.
11. Install the horn, receiver, bumper and fan assembly.
12. Install oil cooler.
13. If condenser assembly was replaced, add 1.4–1.7 fl. oz. of compressor oil.

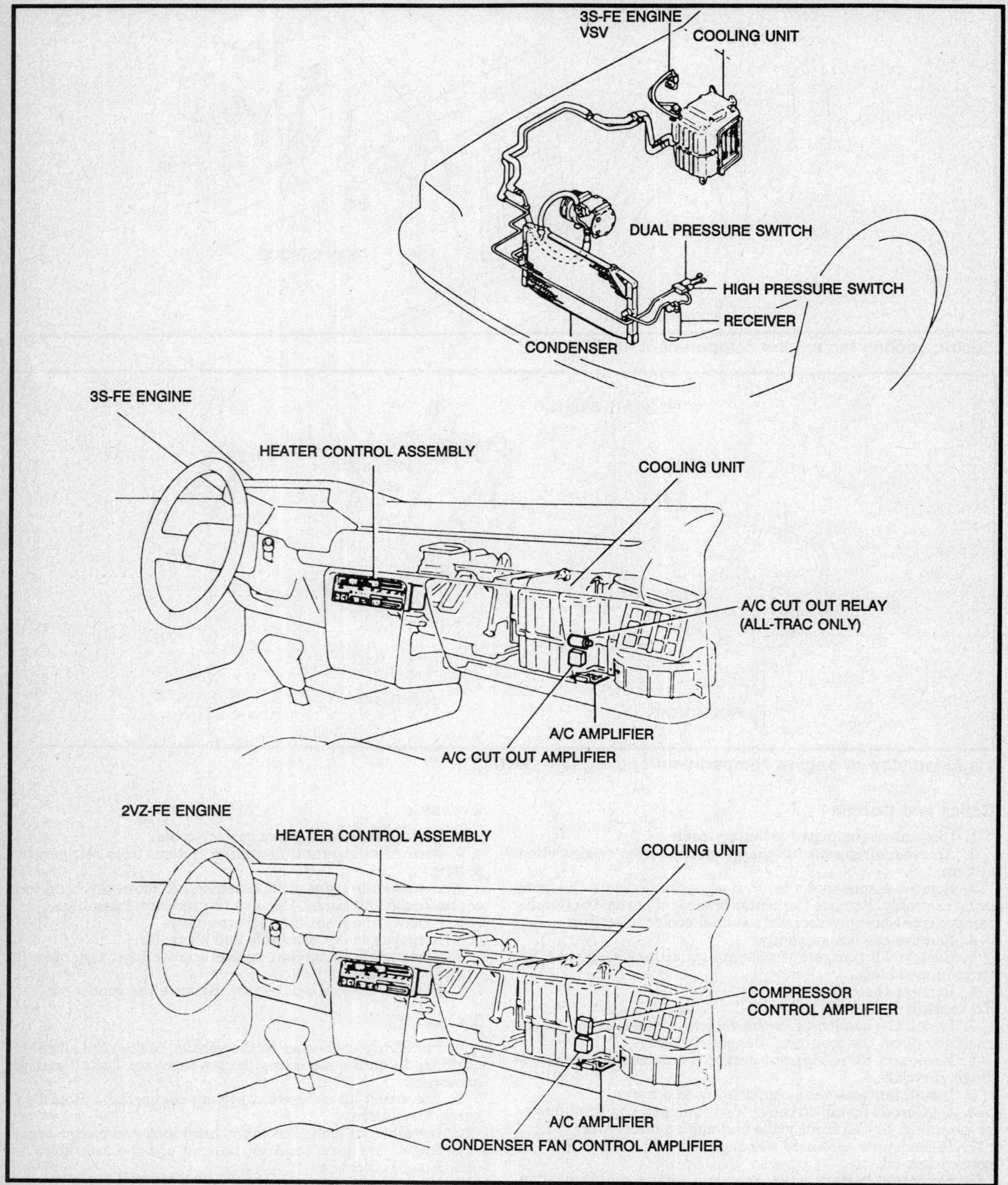
3S-FE ENGINE
VSV
COOLING UNIT
DUAL PRESSURE SWITCH
HIGH PRESSURE SWITCH
RECEIVER
CONDENSER
3S-FE ENGINE
HEATER CONTROL ASSEMBLY
COOLING UNIT
A/C CUT OUT RELAY
(ALL-TRAC ONLY)
A/C AMPLIFIER
A/C CUT OUT AMPLIFIER
2VZ-FE ENGINE
HEATER CONTROL ASSEMBLY
COOLING UNIT
COMPRESSOR
CONTROL AMPLIFIER
A/C AMPLIFIER
CONDENSER FAN CONTROL AMPLIFIER

System components – Camry

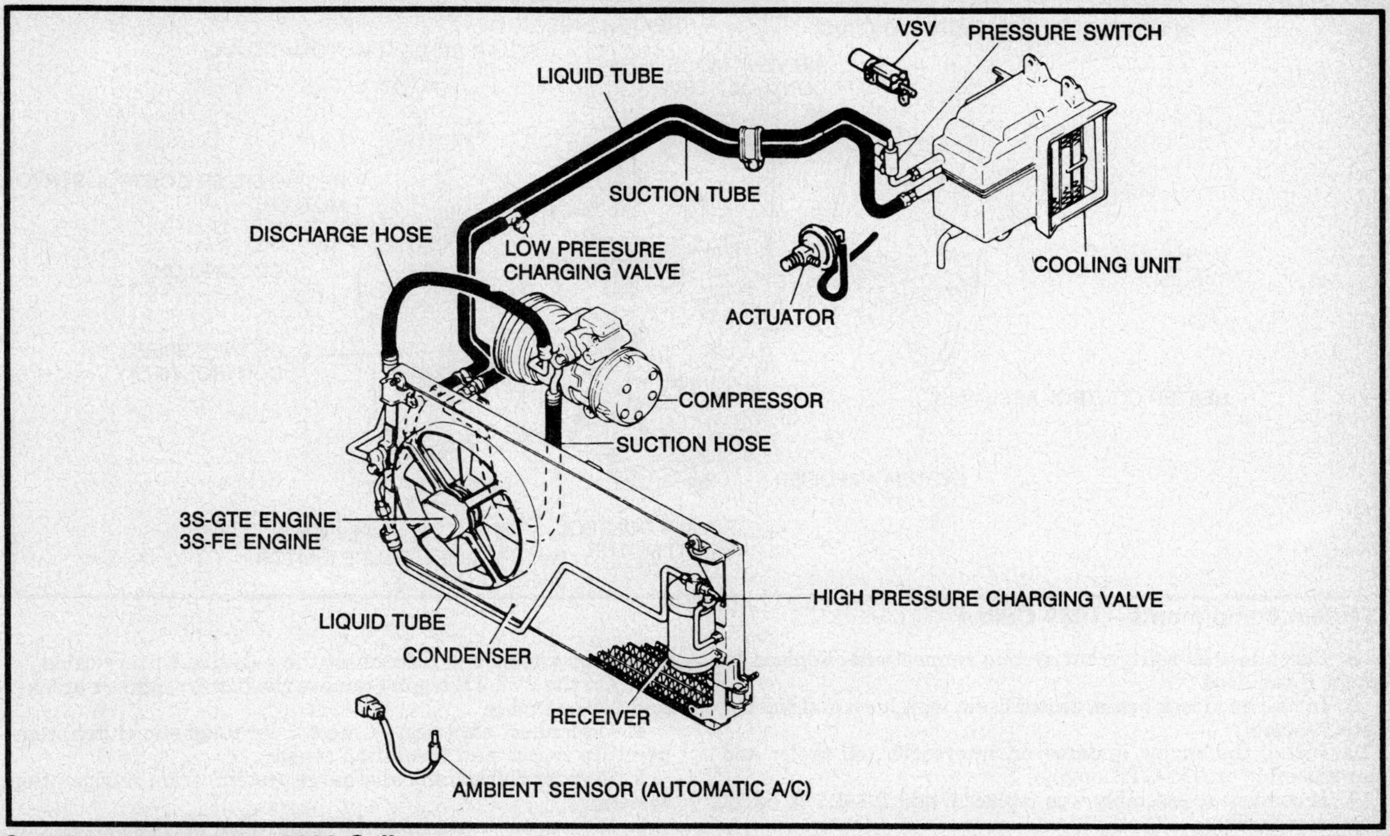
VSV
PRESSURE SWITCH
LIQUID TUBE
SUCTION TUBE
DISCHARGE HOSE
LOW PREESURE CHARGING VALVE
COOLING UNIT
ACTUATOR
COMPRESSOR
SUCTION HOSE
3S-GTE ENGINE
3S-FE ENGINE
HIGH PRESSURE CHARGING VALVE
LIQUID TUBE
CONDENSER
RECEIVER
AMBIENT SENSOR (AUTOMATIC A/C)

System components – 1989 Celica

14. Reconnect the battery cable. Evacuate, charge and test refrigerant system. Check system for leaks.

MR2

1989

1. Disconnect the negative battery cable.
2. Recover refrigerant (discharge system) from refrigeration system.
3. Remove engine undercover and the front grille assembly.
4. Remove the 2 upper condenser retaining bolts. Remove the 2 upper radiator retaining bolts and lean the radiator back.
5. Remove all refrigerant system connections. Cap open fittings immediately.
6. Remove the condenser.

To install:

7. Install the condenser to the vehicle. Make sure all rubber cushions fit on the mounting flanges correctly.
8. Reconnect all refrigerant system connections. Replace O-rings, if required.
9. Install the 2 upper condenser retaining bolts. Install the 2 upper radiator retaining bolts.
10. Install front grille and undercover.
11. If condenser assembly was replaced, add 1.4–1.7 fl. oz. of compressor oil.
12. Reconnect the battery cable. Evacuate, charge and test refrigerant system. Check system for leaks.

1991

1. Disconnect the negative battery cable.
2. Recover refrigerant (discharge system) from refrigeration system.
3. Remove cover and condenser retaining bracket assemblies.
4. Remove all refrigerant system connections. Cap open fittings immediately.
5. Remove the condenser.

To install:

6. Install the condenser to the vehicle. Make sure all rubber cushions fit on the mounting flanges correctly.
7. Reconnect all refrigerant system connections. Replace O-rings, if required.
8. Install condenser retaining bracket assemblies and cover.
9. If condenser assembly was replaced, add 1.4–1.8 fl. oz. of compressor oil.
10. Reconnect the battery cable. Evacuate, charge and test refrigerant system. Check system for leaks.

Supra

1. Disconnect the negative battery cable.
2. Recover refrigerant (discharge system) from refrigeration system.
3. Remove the hood lock, center brace and horns. Remove the washer tank assembly.
4. Remove the engine undercover, intercooler, oil cooler and fan assembly on 7M-GTE engine.
5. Remove all refrigerant system connections. Cap open fittings immediately.
6. Remove the ambient sensor, if equipped. Remove the condenser.

To install:

7. Install the condenser to the vehicle. Make sure all rubber cushions fit on the mounting flanges correctly. Install ambient sensor.

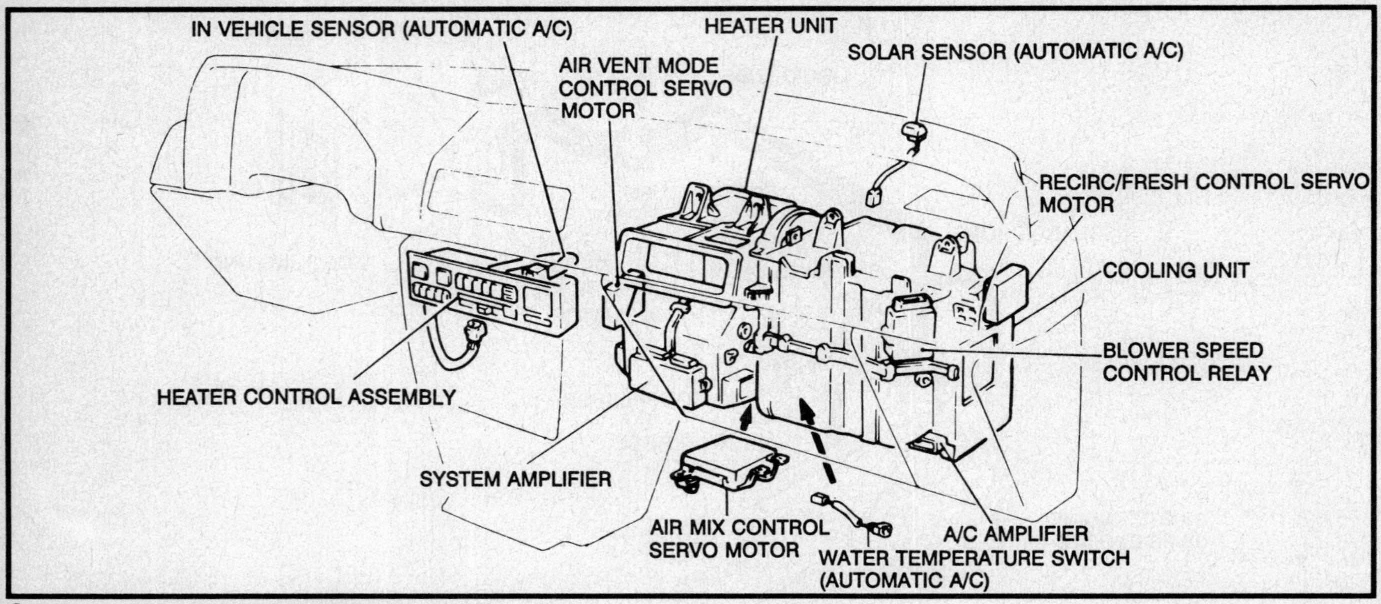
IN VEHICLE SENSOR (AUTOMATIC A/C)
HEATER UNIT
AIR VENT MODE CONTROL SERVO MOTOR
SOLAR SENSOR (AUTOMATIC A/C)
RECIRC/FRESH CONTROL SERVO MOTOR
COOLING UNIT
BLOWER SPEED CONTROL RELAY
HEATER CONTROL ASSEMBLY
SYSTEM AMPLIFIER
AIR MIX CONTROL SERVO MOTOR
A/C AMPLIFIER
WATER TEMPERATURE SWITCH (AUTOMATIC A/C)

System components—1989 Celica

8. Reconnect all refrigerant system connections. Replace O-rings, if required.
9. Install hood lock brace, center brace with horn and washer tank assembly.
10. Install the engine undercover, intercooler, oil cooler and fan assembly on 7M-GTE engine.
11. If condenser assembly was replaced, add 1.4–1.7 fl. oz. of compressor oil.
12. Reconnect battery cable. Evacuate, charge and test refrigerant system. Check system for leaks.

Tercel

1. Disconnect the negative battery cable.
2. Recover refrigerant (discharge system) from refrigeration system.
3. Remove the front grille assembly. Remove the horn, hood lock and center brace.
4. Remove the fan assembly.
5. Remove all refrigerant system connections. Cap open fittings immediately. Remove the receiver with receiver bracket from the condenser.
6. Remove the condenser.

To install:

7. Install the condenser to the vehicle. Make sure all rubber cushions fit on the mounting flanges correctly.
8. Install the receiver with receiver bracket to the condenser assembly.
9. Reconnect all refrigerant system connections. Replace O-rings, if required.
10. Install fan assembly, center brace, hood lock and horn. Install the front grille assembly.
11. If condenser assembly was replaced add, 1.4–1.7 fl. oz. of compressor oil.
12. Reconnect battery cable. Evacuate, charge and test refrigerant system. Check system for leaks.

Compressor

REMOVAL AND INSTALLATION

Camry

1. Run the engine at idle with the air conditioning on for approximately 10 minutes.
2. Stop engine and disconnect the negative battery cable.
3. On the 2VZ-FE engine remove the battery, ignitor bracket and fan assembly.
4. Disconnect electrical connector for magnetic clutch, temperature switch and revolution sensor.
5. Recover refrigerant (discharge system) from refrigeration system.
6. Disconnect hoses from the compressor service valves. Cap open fittings immediately.
7. Loosen the compressor mounting bolts. Remove the compressor drive belt.
8. Remove the compressor mounting bolts. Remove the compressor from the vehicle.

To install:

9. Install compressor with mounting bolts. Install drive belt.
10. Reconnect hoses to the compressor service valves.
11. Connect electrical connector to magnetic clutch, temperature switch and revolution sensor.
12. On the 2VZ-FE engine install the fan assembly, ignitor bracket and battery.
13. Reconnect the battery cables.
14. Evacuate, charge and test refrigerant system. Check system for leaks.

Except Camry

1. Run the engine at idle with the air conditioning on for approximately 10 minutes.
2. Stop engine and disconnect the negative battery cable.
3. Remove the battery.
4. Disconnect all electrical connections.
5. Recover refrigerant (discharge system) from refrigeration system.
6. Disconnect hoses from the compressor service valves. Cap open fittings immediately.
7. Remove engine undercover, if equipped. Loosen the compressor mounting bolts. Remove the compressor drive belt.
8. Remove the compressor mounting bolts. Remove the compressor from the vehicle.

To install:

9. Install compressor with mounting bolts. Install drive belt and engine undercover, if equipped.
10. Reconnect hoses to the compressor service valves.

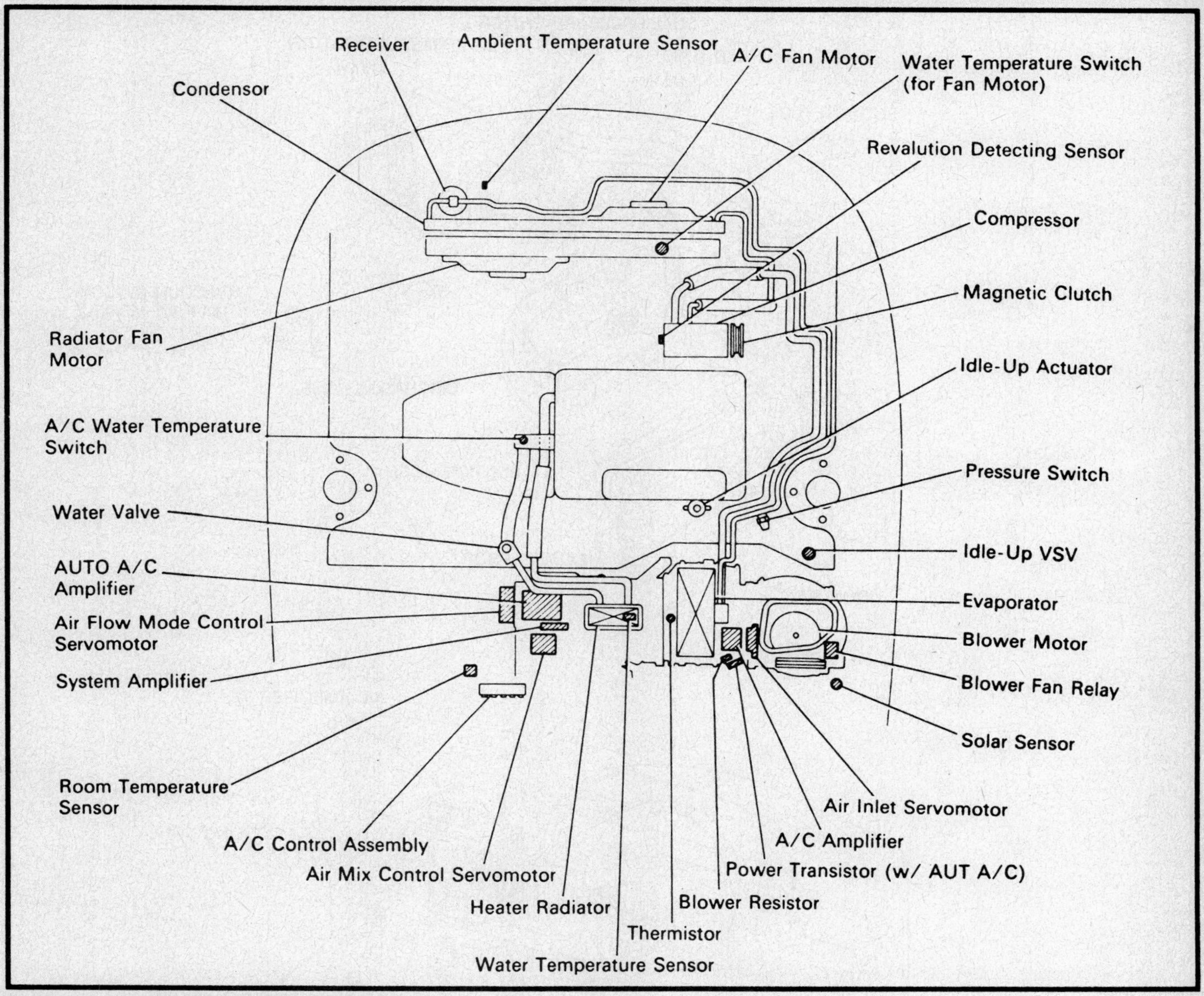
Receiver
Ambient Temperature Sensor
A/C Fan Motor
Water Temperature Switch (for Fan Motor)
Condensor
Revalution Detecting Sensor
Compressor
Magnetic Clutch
Radiator Fan Motor
Idle-Up Actuator
A/C Water Temperature Switch
Pressure Switch
Water Valve
Idle-Up VSV
AUTO A/C Amplifier
Evaporator
Air Flow Mode Control Servomotor
Blower Motor
System Amplifier
Blower Fan Relay
Solar Sensor
Room Temperature Sensor
Air Inlet Servomotor
A/C Amplifier
A/C Control Assembly
Power Transistor (w/ AUT A/C)
Air Mix Control Servomotor
Blower Resistor
Heater Radiator
Thermistor
Water Temperature Sensor

System components—1990–91 Celica

11. Reconnect all electrical connections.
12. Install the battery. Reconnect the battery cables.
13. Evacuate, charge and test refrigerant system. Check system for leaks.

Receiver/Drier

REMOVAL AND INSTALLATION

Camry

1. Disconnect the negative battery cable.
2. Recover refrigerant (discharge system) from refrigeration system.
3. Remove the battery, reserve tank and ignitor bracket.
4. Disconnect lines from the receiver. Cap open fittings immediately. Remove the receiver from the receiver holder assembly.

To install:

5. Install receiver in receiver holder assembly. Reconnect lines to the receiver.
6. Install the ignitor bracket, reserve tank and battery. Reconnect the battery cables.
7. If receiver assembly was replaced, add 0.7 fl. oz. of compressor oil.
8. Evacuate, charge and test refrigerant system. Check system for leaks.

Except Camry

1. Disconnect the negative battery cable.

NOTE: On 1989 MR2 vehicle remove the spare tire and trim cover to gain working access. On the 1991 MR2 vehicle remove the left side front fender liner and undercover to gain working access. On 1991 Tercel remove the front grille assembly to gain working access.

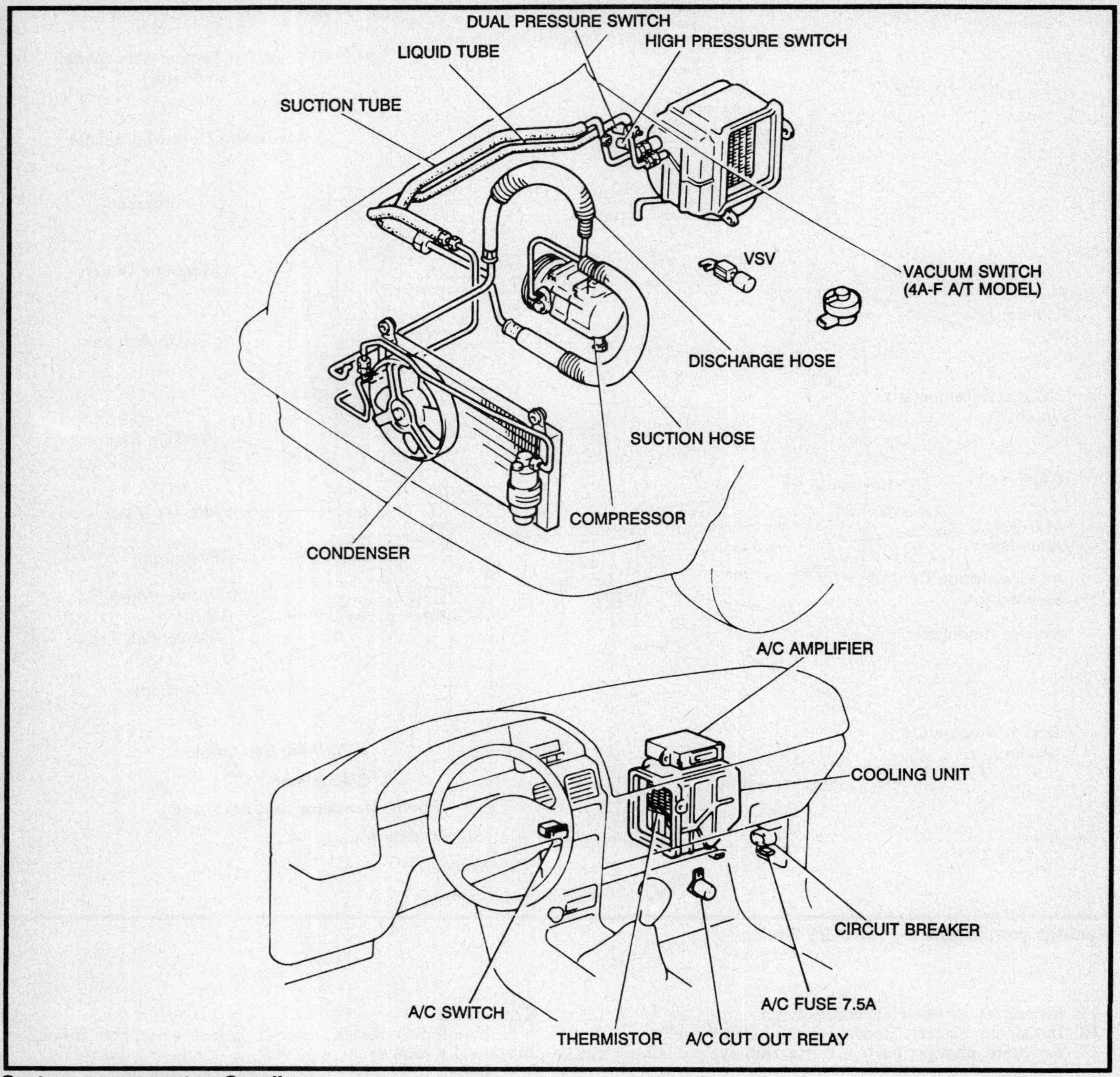
DUAL PRESSURE SWITCH
HIGH PRESSURE SWITCH
LIQUID TUBE
SUCTION TUBE
VSV
VACUUM SWITCH
(4A-F A/T MODEL)
DISCHARGE HOSE
SUCTION HOSE
COMPRESSOR
CONDENSER
A/C AMPLIFIER
COOLING UNIT
CIRCUIT BREAKER
A/C FUSE 7.5A
A/C SWITCH
THERMISTOR
A/C CUT OUT RELAY

System components – Corolla

2. Recover refrigerant (discharge system) from refrigeration system.
3. Disconnect lines from the receiver. Cap open fittings immediately.
4. Remove the receiver from the receiver holder assembly.

To install:

5. Install receiver in receiver holder assembly. Reconnect lines to the receiver. Reconnect the negative battery cable.
6. If receiver assembly was replaced, add 0.7 fl. oz. of compressor oil.
7. Evacuate, charge and test refrigerant system. Check system for leaks.

Expansion Valve

REMOVAL AND INSTALLATION

On all Toyota vehicles the cooling unit or evaporator assembly must be removed before the expansion valve can be replaced. Refer to the the cooling unit or evaporator assembly service procedures.

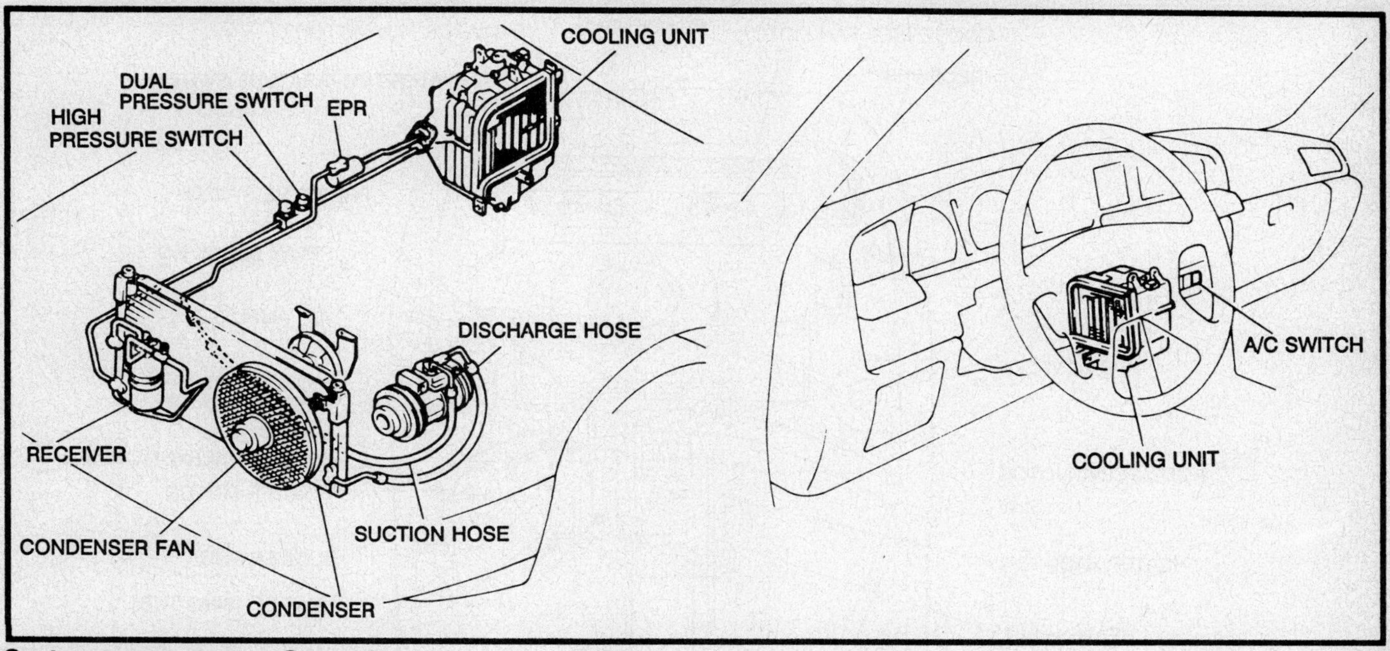
COOLING UNIT
DUAL PRESSURE SWITCH
EPR
HIGH PRESSURE SWITCH
DISCHARGE HOSE
A/C SWITCH
RECEIVER
COOLING UNIT
CONDENSER FAN
SUCTION HOSE
CONDENSER

System components—Cressida

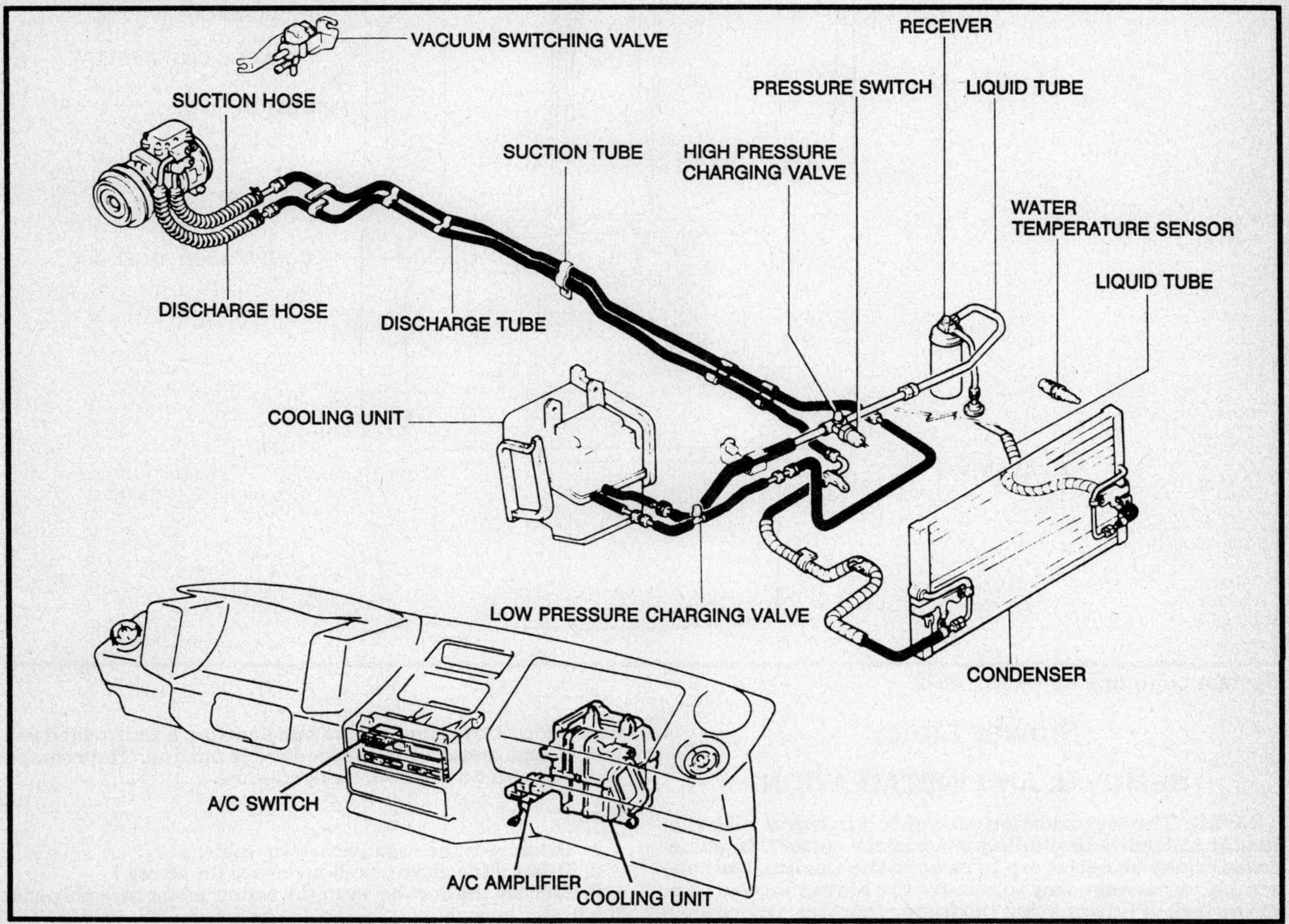
VACUUM SWITCHING VALVE
RECEIVER
PRESSURE SWITCH
LIQUID TUBE
SUCTION HOSE
SUCTION TUBE
HIGH PRESSURE CHARGING VALVE
WATER TEMPERATURE SENSOR
LIQUID TUBE
DISCHARGE HOSE
DISCHARGE TUBE
COOLING UNIT
LOW PRESSURE CHARGING VALVE
CONDENSER
A/C SWITCH
A/C AMPLIFIER
COOLING UNIT

System components—1989 MR2

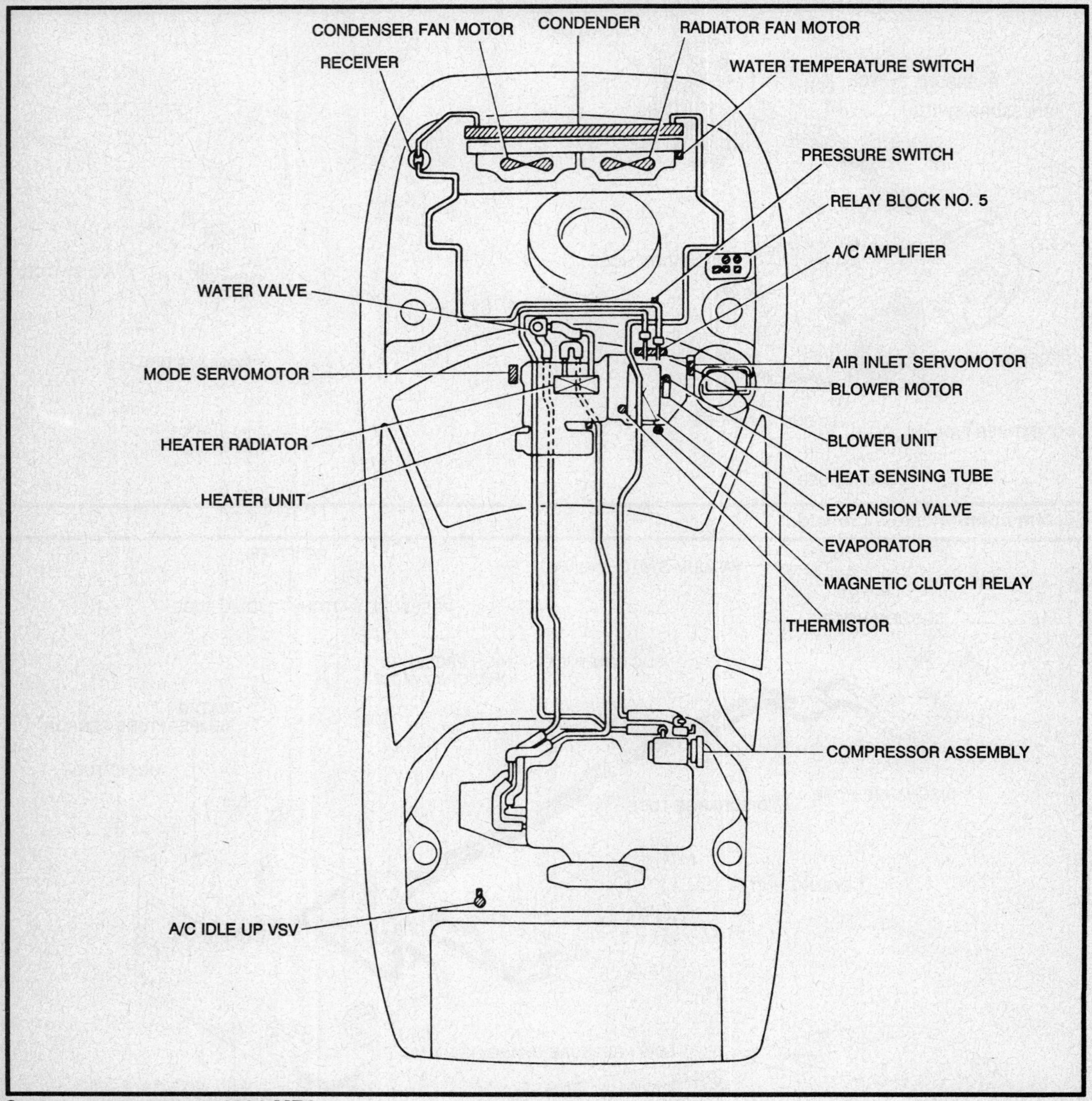
CONDENSER FAN MOTOR
CONDENDER
RADIATOR FAN MOTOR
RECEIVER
WATER TEMPERATURE SWITCH
PRESSURE SWITCH
RELAY BLOCK NO. 5
A/C AMPLIFIER
WATER VALVE
AIR INLET SERVOMOTOR
MODE SERVOMOTOR
BLOWER MOTOR
BLOWER UNIT
HEATER RADIATOR
HEAT SENSING TUBE
HEATER UNIT
EXPANSION VALVE
EVAPORATOR
MAGNETIC CLUTCH RELAY
THERMISTOR
COMPRESSOR ASSEMBLY
A/C IDLE UP VSV

System components—1991 MR2

Blower Motor

REMOVAL AND INSTALLATION

NOTE: The air condition assembly is integral with the heater assembly (including the blower motor). In some cases it may be necessary to remove the Cooling Unit assembly or package tray to remove the blower motor. Due to the lack of information (no factory service procedure) available at the time of this publication, a uniformed removal and installation procedure is outline. The removal steps can be altered, as necessary.

Camry

1. Disconnect the negative battery cable.
2. Remove the glove box, if necessary for access.
3. Remove the duct between the blower motor assembly and the heater assembly.

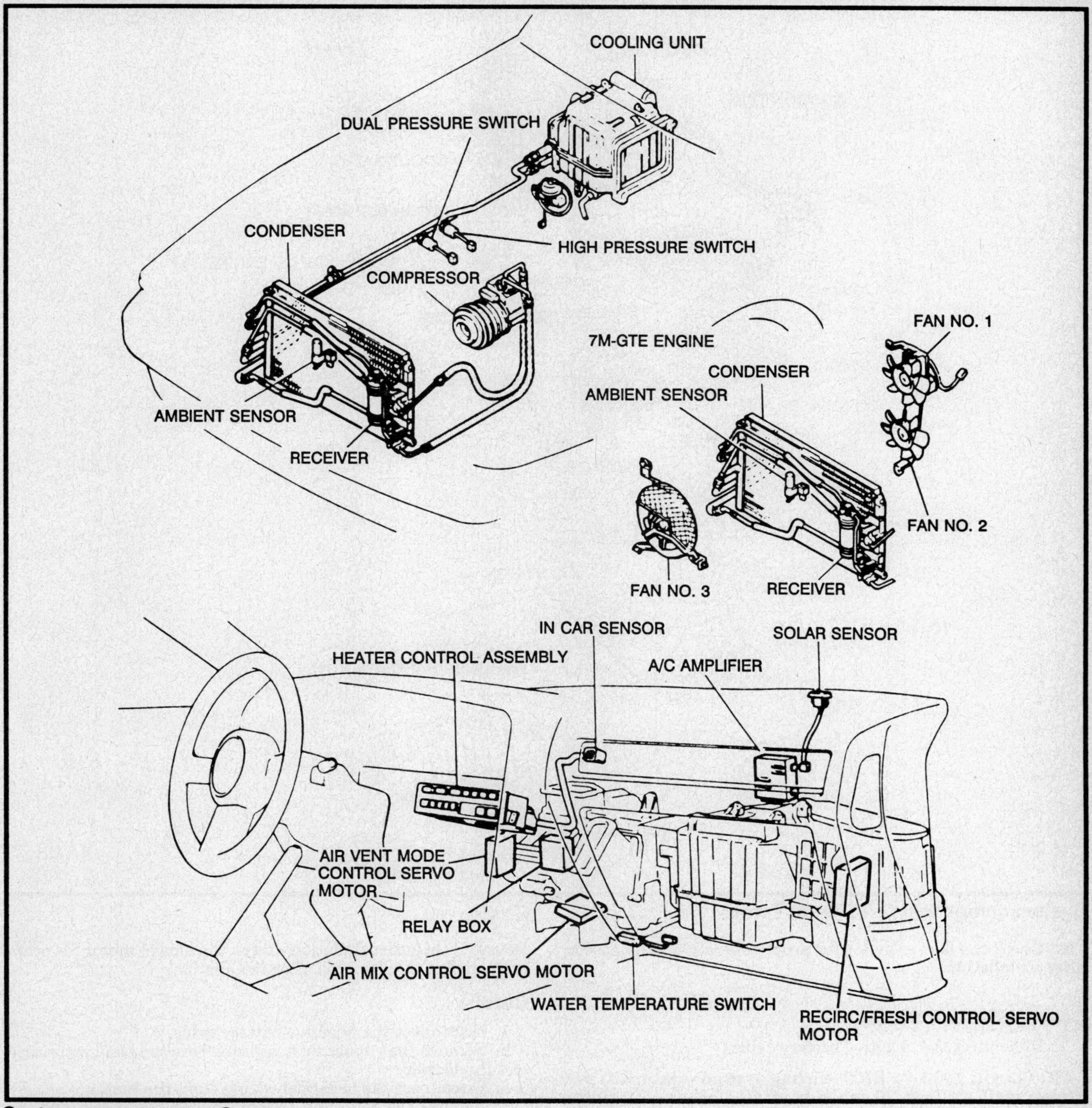
COOLING UNIT
DUAL PRESSURE SWITCH
CONDENSER
HIGH PRESSURE SWITCH
COMPRESSOR
7M-GTE ENGINE
FAN NO. 1
CONDENSER
AMBIENT SENSOR
AMBIENT SENSOR
RECEIVER
FAN NO. 2
FAN NO. 3
RECEIVER
IN CAR SENSOR
SOLAR SENSOR
HEATER CONTROL ASSEMBLY
A/C AMPLIFIER
AIR VENT MODE CONTROL SERVO MOTOR
RELAY BOX
AIR MIX CONTROL SERVO MOTOR
WATER TEMPERATURE SWITCH
RECIRC/FRESH CONTROL SERVO MOTOR

System components—Supra

4. Disconnect the blower motor wire connector at the blower motor case.
5. Disconnect the air source selector control cable at the blower motor assembly or servo control lines.
6. Remove air conditioning amplifier and wiring, if necessary.
7. Remove the mounting screws attaching the blower motor to the blower case, remove the blower motor assembly from the vehicle.

To install:

8. Clean blower motor housing of all dirt, leaves etc. before installation. Install the blower motor assembly in the vehicle.
9. Install air conditioning amplifier and wiring, as necessary. Reconnect all control cables and route servo control lines, as necessary.
10. Reconnet all electrical connections and install duct work.
11. Install glove box and reconnect the negative battery cable.

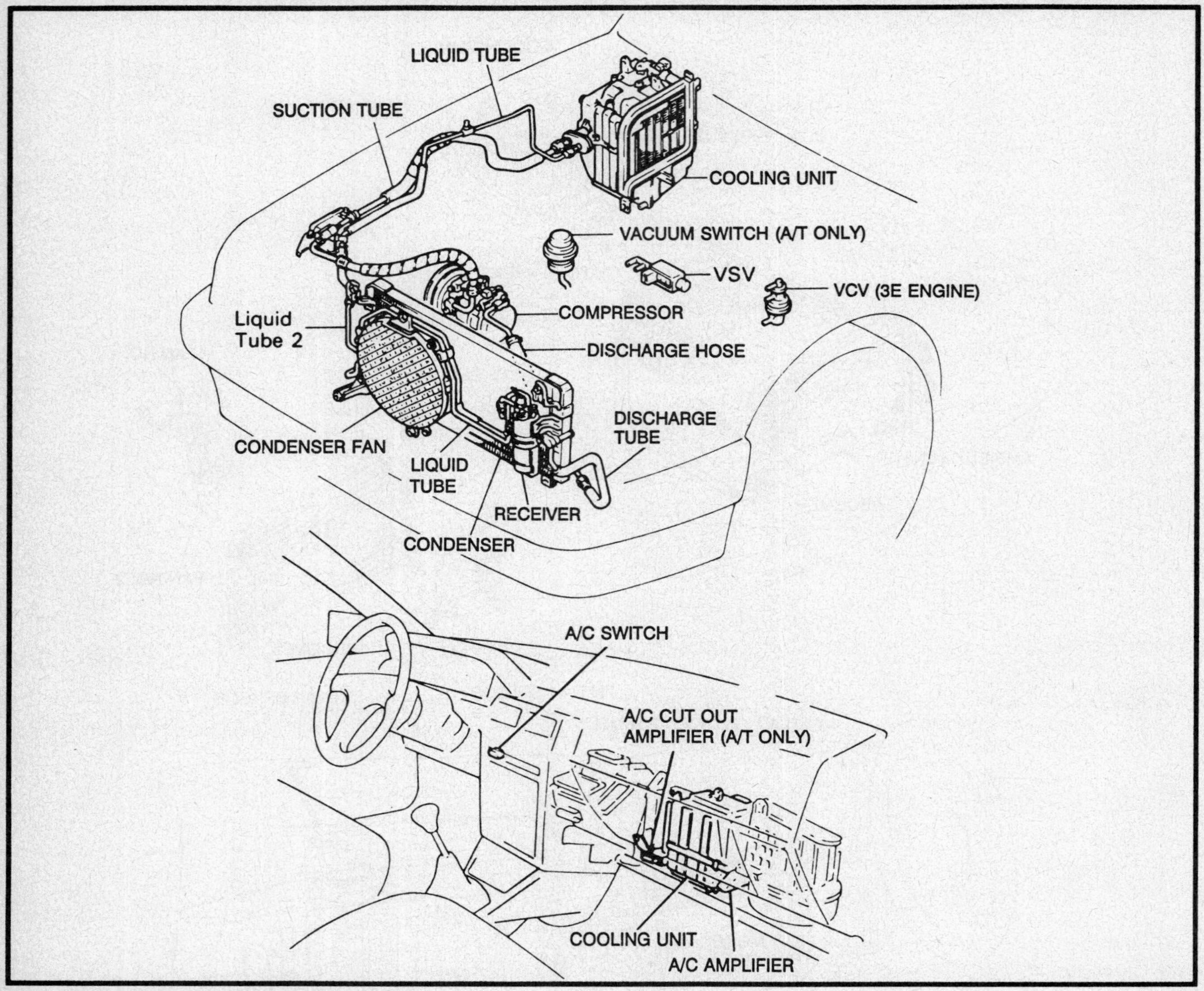
LIQUID TUBE
SUCTION TUBE
COOLING UNIT
VACUUM SWITCH (A/T ONLY)
VSV
VCV (3E ENGINE)
Liquid Tube 2
COMPRESSOR
DISCHARGE HOSE
DISCHARGE TUBE
CONDENSER FAN
LIQUID TUBE
RECEIVER
CONDENSER
A/C SWITCH
A/C CUT OUT AMPLIFIER (A/T ONLY)
COOLING UNIT
A/C AMPLIFIER

System components—1989–90 Tercel

12. Check the blower motor for proper operation at all speeds after installation.

Celica, MR2 and Supra

1. Disconnect the negative battery cable.

NOTE: On 1990–91 SRS (airbag system equipped) vehicles, wait at least 30 seconds after disconnecting the battery before doing any work. The SRS has a built-in backup which will allow the system to remain energized for a period of time after the power is disconnected.

2. Working from under the instrument panel, unfasten the defroster hoses from the heater box, as necessary.
3. Remove all related components, if necessary, to gain access for blower motor assembly. Unplug the multi-connector.
4. Loosen the mounting screws and withdraw the blower assembly.
5. Installation is the reverse order of the service removal procedure. Make sure to clean blower motor housing of all dirt, leaves etc. before installation. Check the blower motor for proper operation at all speeds after installation.

Corolla

1. Disconnect the negative battery cable.
2. Remove the rubber duct running between the heater case and the blower.
3. Disconnect the electrical wiring from the motor.
4. Remove the retaining screws holding the motor and remove the blower motor.
5. Check the case for any debris or signs of fan contact. Inspect the fan for wear spots, cracked blades or hub, loose retaining nut or poor alignment.

To install:

6. Place the blower in position, making sure it is properly aligned within the case. Install the retaining screws.
7. Connect the wiring to the motor.
8. Install the rubber air duct and connect the negative battery cable. Check the blower motor for proper operation at all speeds after installation.

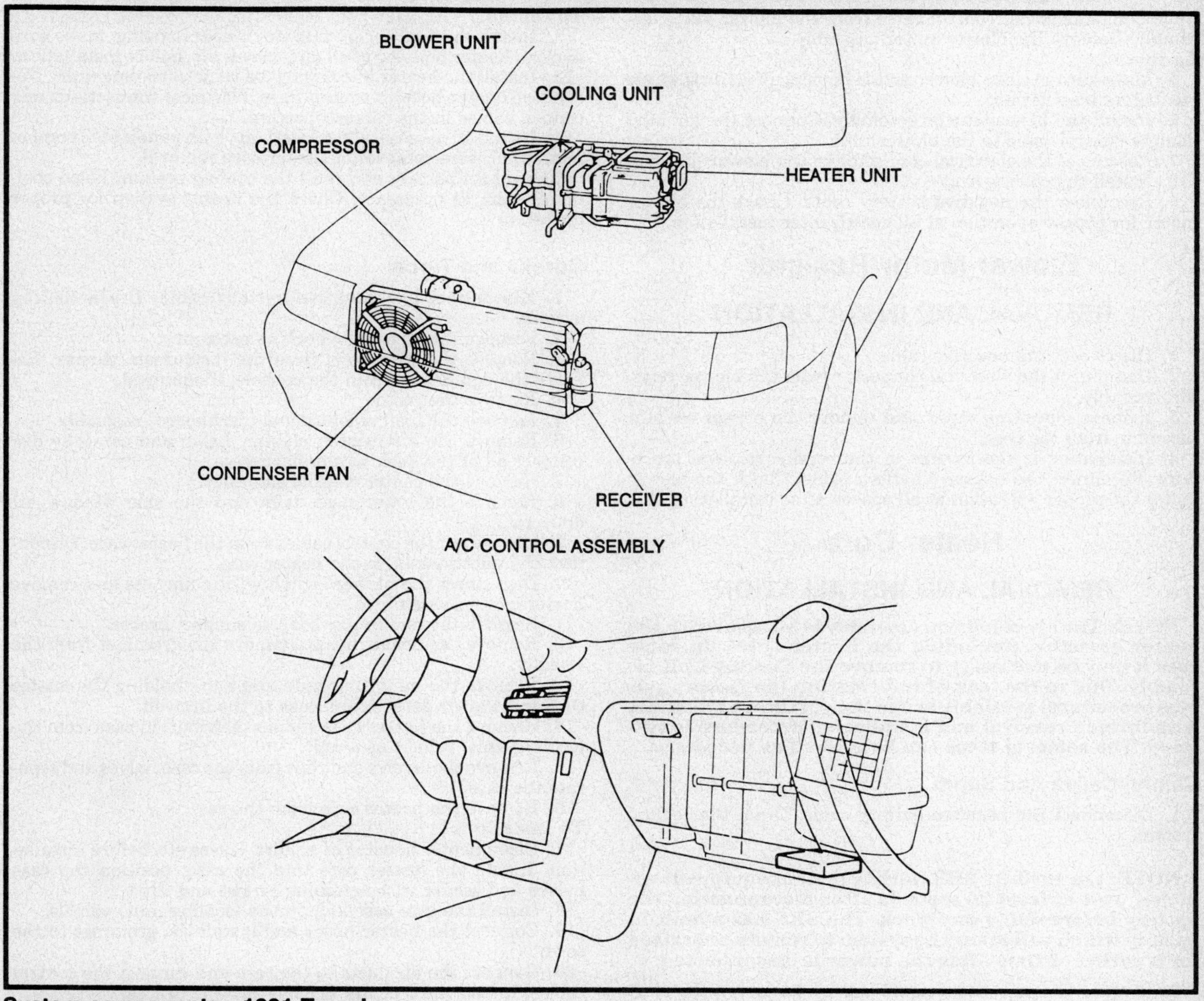
BLOWER UNIT
COOLING UNIT
COMPRESSOR
HEATER UNIT
CONDENSER FAN
RECEIVER
A/C CONTROL ASSEMBLY

System components – 1991 Tercel

Cressida

1. Disconnect the negative battery cable.
2. Remove all electrical connections.
3. Remove the blower motor cooling tube.
4. Remove the retaining screws and the blower motor assembly.

To install:

5. Check the case for any debris or signs of fan contact. Inspect the fan for wear spots, cracked blades or hub, loose retaining nut or poor alignment.
6. Position the blower motor assembly into place and install the retaining screws.
7. Install the blower motor cooling tube. Connect all electrical connections.
8. Connect the negative battery cable. Check the blower motor for proper operation at all speeds after installation.

Tercel

1989–90

1. Disconnect the negative battery cable.
2. Remove all related components, if necessary, to gain access for blower motor assembly. Unplug the multi-connector.
3. Loosen the mounting screws and withdraw the blower assembly.
4. Installation is the reverse order of the service removal procedure. Make sure to clean blower motor housing of all dirt, leaves etc. before installation. Check the blower motor for proper operation at all speeds after installation.

1991

1. Disconnect the negative battery cable.
2. Remove the cooling unit assembly.
3. Disconnect the electrical from the blower motor.
4. Disconnect the air inlet damper (note position of control

cable before removal) control cable from the blower motor assembly. Remove the blower motor assembly.

To install:

5. Make sure to clean blower motor housing of all dirt, leaves etc. before installation.
6. Install the blower motor assembly. Connect the air inlet damper control cable to the blower unit.
7. Reconnect the electrical connector to the blower motor.
8. Install the cooling unit.
9. Reconnect the negative battery cable. Check the blower motor for proper operation at all speeds after installation.

Blower Motor Resistor

REMOVAL AND INSTALLATION

1. Disconnect the negative cable.
2. Disconnect the electrical connector from the blower resistor assembly.
3. Remove mounting screw and remove the blower resistor assembly from the case.
4. Installation is the reverse of the service removal procedure. Reconnect the negative battery cable. Check the blower motor for proper operation at all speeds after installation.

Heater Core

REMOVAL AND INSTALLATION

NOTE: The air condition assembly is integral with the heater assembly (including the heater core). In some case it may be necessary to remove the Cooling Unit assembly. Due to the lack of information (no factory service procedure) available at the time of this publication, a uniformed removal and installation procedure is outlined. The removal steps can be altered as necessary.

Camry, Celica And Supra

1. Disconnect the negative battery cable. Drain the cooling system.

NOTE: On 1990–91 SRS (airbag system equipped) vehicles, wait at least 30 seconds after disconnecting the battery before doing any work. The SRS has a built-in backup which will allow the system to remain energized for a period of time after the power is disconnected.

2. Remove the console, if equipped, by removing the shift knob (manual), wiring connector, and console attaching screws.
3. Remove the package tray, if equipped, and all necessary components.
4. Remove the securing screws and remove the center air outlet.
5. Remove the air conditioning amplifier and wire harness, if necessary.
6. Remove and (mark for correct instalation) all vacuum hoses from heater housing assembly.
7. Remove the blower duct from the the heater housing. Remove all remaining air ducts.
8. Disconnect the 2 heater hoses from the rear of the heater housing assembly.
9. Tag and disconnect all wires and cables leading from the heater housing and position them out of the way.
10. Remove all retaining bolts and then remove the heater housing (split assembly from the cooling unit) carefuly toward the rear of the vehicle.
11. Remove the heater housing assembly from the vehicle. Remove any retaining brackets or hardware that retain the heater core to the heater housing. Grasp the heater core by the end plate and carefully pull it out of the heater housing.

To install:

12. Install the heater core into the heater housing, make sure to clean heater housing of all dirt, leaves etc. before installation.
13. Install the heater housing to the vehicle (cooling unit). Reconnect heater hoses, vacuum lines, electrical connections and control cables in the correct location.
14. Install all necessary (package tray, trim panels etc.) components that were remove for heater core removal.
15. Connect battery and refill the cooling system. Bleed cooling system, as necessary. Check the heater system for proper operation.

Corolla and Tercel

1. Disconnect the negative battery cable. Drain cooling system.
2. Remove the steering wheel, as necessary.
3. Remove the trim bezel from the instrument cluster. Remove the cup holder from the console, if equipped.
4. Remove the radio.
5. Remove the instrument panel (dashboard) assembly.
6. Remove the instrument cluster. Label and carefully disconnect all of the dash wiring harnesses.
7. Remove the center console assembly.
8. Remove the lower dash trim and the side window air deflectors.
9. Disconnect the control cables from the heater case. Disconnect the ductwork from the heater case.
10. Disconnect the blower switch wiring harness and remove heater control assembly.
11. Remove the two center console support braces.
12. Remove the heater hoses. Remove the grommet from the cowling.
13. Remove the mounting nuts and bolts holding the heater core and the air distribution case to the firewall.
14. Remove the heater case and air distribution case from the (cooling unit) vehicle as a unit.
15. Remove the screws and clips from the case halves and separate the case.
16. Remove the heater core from the case.

To install:

17. Clean heater housing of all dirt, leaves etc. before installation. Install the heater core into the case, position the case halves and secure with retaining screws and clips.
18. Install the case assembly in the (cooling unit) vehicle.
19. Connect the heater hoses and install the grommet to the cowl.
20. Connect the air ducts to the case and connect the control cables. Install the 2 center console support braces.
21. Reconnect the blower wiring harness and install the heater control assembly.
22. Install the dashboard assembly in position within the vehicle. Install instrument cluster assembly. Reconnect all wiring harness connectors. Make sure wiring is properly secured.
23. Install the center console assembly, radio, cup holder assembly, if equipped.
24. Install the trim bezel around the instrument cluster. Install the steering wheel.
25. Refill the coolant. Bleed cooling system. Connect the negative battery cable. Start the engine and check heater system for proper operation.

Cressida

1. Disconnect the negative battery cable. Drain the cooling system. Disconnect the heater hoses.
2. Remove the right and left lower hush panel. Remove the upper dash pad.
3. Remove both front speaker assemblies. Remove the front carrier braces and carrier shelf. Remove both side window defrost ducts.

4. Disconnect the electronic control module and position it to the side.
5. Remove the radio trim plate. Remove the upper console trim. Remove the console glove box assembly. Remove the emergency brake handle grip.
6. Remove the screws that secure the console body and position the assembly out of the way.
7. Remove the trim plate from under the steering column. Remove the steering column retaining nuts and lower the column.
8. Remove the instrument panel carrier.
9. Remove the heater core housing cover.
10. Remove the screws that secure the heater core and shroud. Remove the heater core assembly. Remove the heater core from the shroud assembly.

To install:

11. Clean heater housing of all dirt, leaves etc. before installation. Install the heater core assembly. Install the heater core housing cover.
12. Install the instrument panel carrier.
13. Install the steering column and all necessary trim panels.
14. Install the console assembly, brake handle grip, console glove box assembly. Install the upper console trim. Install the radio trim panel.
15. Install the electronic control module assembly. Install the speaker assemblies.
16. Install both side window defrost ducts. Install the front carrier braces and carrier shelf.
17. Install the upper dash pad. Install the right and left lower hush panel.
18. Connect the heater hoses. Connect the negative battery cable. Refill the coolant. Bleed cooling system. Start the engine and check heater system for proper operation.

MR2

NOTE: It may be necessary to remove the heater assembly, to obtain access to the heater core. If the assembly removal is necessary, removing the console and/or passenger seat may facilitate the ease of heater assembly removal. The cooling system must be bleed after this service operation.

1. Disconnect the negative battery cable. Disconnect the heater hose at the engine compartment.
2. Remove the clips retaining the lower part of the heater unit case, then remove the lower part of the case.
3. Using a suitable tool, carefully pry open the lower part of the heater unit case.
4. Remove the heater core assembly from the heater unit case.

To install:

5. Install the heater core into the heater housing, make sure to clean heater housing of all dirt, leaves etc. before installation. Install lower heater unit case.
6. Reconnect the heater hose and refill the coolant system.
7. Connect the negative battery cable. Refill the coolant. Bleed cooling system. Start the engine and check heater system for proper operation.

Evaporator

REMOVAL AND INSTALLATION

Camry, Celica, Corolla, Cressida and MR2

1. Disconnect the negative battery cable. Recover refrigerant (discharge system) from refrigeration system.

NOTE: On Cressida, disconnect the equalizer tube from EPR assembly at this point of the service procedure.

2. Disconnect the suction flexible hose from the cooling unit outlet fitting.
3. Disconnect the liquid line from the cooling unit inlet fitting. Cap the open fittings immediately to keep the moisture out of the system.
4. Remove the grommets from the inlet and outlet fittings.
5. Remove the glove box assembly. Disconnect all necessary connectors and the air conditioning harness.
6. Remove the cooling unit attaching nuts and bolts. Remove the cooling unit from the vehicle.
7. Place the cooling unit on a suitable work bench and remove control amplifier, relay assemblies or power transistor assembly if so equipped.
8. Using suitable tools, remove the upper cooling unit case clamps and retaining screws. Remove thermistor with thermistor holder.
9. Remove the lower cooling unit case from the evaporator. Remove the evaporator from the cooling unit.
10. Remove the heat insulator (heat sensing tube) and the clamp from the outlet tube. Disconnect the liquid line from the inlet fitting of the expansion valve.
11. Disconnect the expansion valve from the inlet fitting of the evaporator. Remove the expansion valve.

NOTE: Before installing the evaporator, check the evaporator fins for blockage. If the fins are clogged, clean them with compressed air. Never use water to clean the evaporator. Check the fittings for cracks and or scratches and replace, as necessary.

To install:

12. Connect the expansion valve to the inlet fitting of the evaporator and torque it to 17 ft. lbs. Be sure the O-ring is positioned on the tube fitting.
13. Connect the liquid line tube to the inlet fitting on the expansion valve. Torque the nut to 10 ft. lbs.
14. Install the clamp and heat insulator (heat sensing tube) to the outlet tube.
15. Install the upper and lower cases on the evaporator. Install the thermistor. Install control amplifier, relay assemblies or power transistor assembly, if equipped.
16. Install the air conditioning wiring harness to the cooling unit and all other necessary components.
17. Install the cooling unit assembly in the vehicle. Be careful not to pinch the wiring harness while installing the cooling unit.
18. Install the glove box assembly and the grommets on the inlet and outlet fittings.
19. Connect the liquid line to the cooling unit inlet fittings and torque to 10 ft. lbs.
20. Connect the suction tube to the cooling unit outlet fitting and torque to 24 ft. lbs.

NOTE: On Cressida, reconnect the equalizer tube to EPR assembly at this point of the service procedure.

21. If the evaporator was replaced, add 1.4–1.7 oz. of compressor oil to the compressor. Connect the negative battery cable.
22. Evacuate, charge and test the refrigeration system.

Supra

1. Disconnect the negative battery cable. Recover refrigerant (discharge system) from refrigeration system.

NOTE: On 1990–91 SRS (airbag system equipped) vehicles, wait at least 30 seconds after disconnecting the battery before doing any work. The SRS has a built-in backup which will allow the system to remain energized for a period of time after the power is disconnected.

2. Remove the charcoal canister with bracket.
3. Disconnect the suction flexible hose from the cooling unit

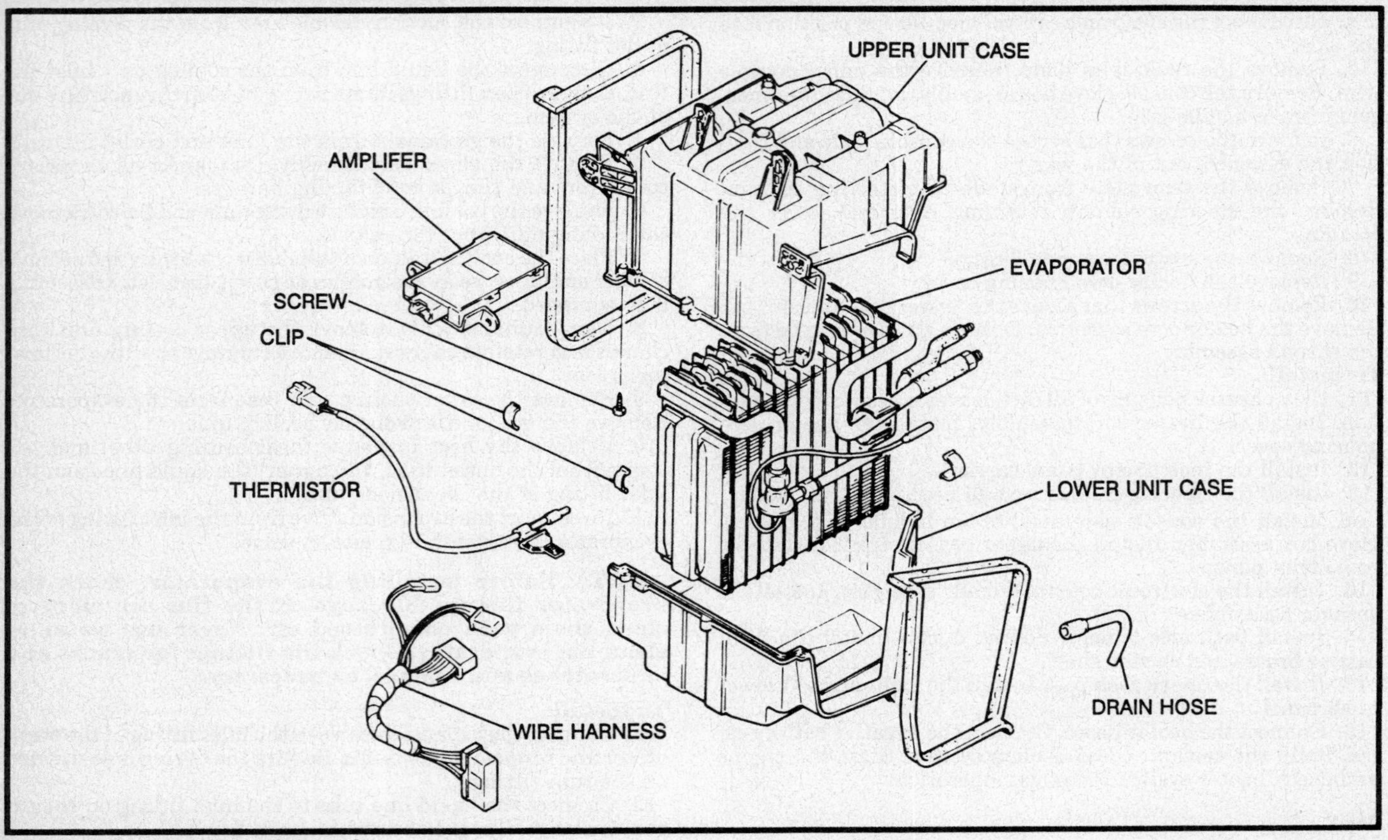
UPPER UNIT CASE
AMPLIFER
EVAPORATOR
SCREW
CLIP
THERMISTOR
LOWER UNIT CASE
DRAIN HOSE
WIRE HARNESS

Exploded view of cooling unit

outlet fitting.

4. Disconnect the liquid line from the cooling unit inlet fitting. Cap the open fittings immediately to keep the moisture out of the system.
5. Remove the grommets from the inlet and outlet fittings.
6. Remove the glove box assembly. Remove the EFI and ABS computer. Disconnect all necessary connectors.
7. Remove the cooling unit attaching nuts and bolts. Remove the cooling unit from the vehicle.
8. Place the cooling unit on a work bench and using suitable tools, remove the upper cooling unit case clamps and retaining screws. Remove thermistor with thermistor holder.
9. Remove the lower cooling unit case from the evaporator. Remove the evaporator from the cooling unit.
10. Remove the heat insulator (heat sensing tube) and the clamp from the outlet tube. Remove the expansion valve from the evaporator assembly.

NOTE: Before installing the evaporator, check the evaporator fins for blockage. If the fins are clogged, clean them with compressed air. Never use water to clean the evaporator. Check the fittings for cracks and or scratches and replace, as necessary.

To install:

11. Connect the expansion valve, suction and liquid tubes to the evaporator. Be sure that O-rings are positioned on the tube fitting.
12. Install the clamp and heat insulator (heat sensing tube).
13. Install the upper and lower cases on the evaporator.
14. Install the thermistor.
15. Install the air conditioning wiring harness to the cooling unit. Install the cooling unit assembly in the vehicle. Be careful not to pinch the wiring harness while installing the cooling unit.
16. Install the EFI and ABS computer. Install the glove box assembly.
17. Install grommets on the inlet and outlet fittings.
18. Connect the liquid line to the cooling unit inlet fittings and torque to 10 ft. lbs.
19. Connect the suction tube to the cooling unit outlet fitting and torque to 24 ft. lbs.
20. If the evaporator was replaced, add 1.4–1.7 oz. of compressor oil to the compressor. Connect the negative battery cable.
21. Install the charcoal cannister assembly.
22. Evacuate, charge and test the refrigeration system.

Tercel

1989–90

1. Disconnect the negative battery cable. Recover refrigerant (discharge system) from refrigeration system.
2. Disconnect the suction flexible hose from the cooling unit outlet fitting.
3. Disconnect the liquid line from the cooling unit inlet fitting. Cap the open fittings immediately to keep the moisture out of the system.
4. Remove the grommets from the inlet and outlet fittings.
5. Remove the glove box assembly. Disconnect all necessary connectors.
6. Remove the cooling unit attaching nuts and bolts. Remove the cooling unit from the vehicle.
7. Place the cooling unit on a suitable work bench and remove control amplifier assembly and wiring harness.
8. Remove the upper cooling unit case clamps and retaining screws. Remove thermistor with thermistor holder.
9. Remove the lower cooling unit case from the evaporator. Remove the evaporator from the cooling unit.

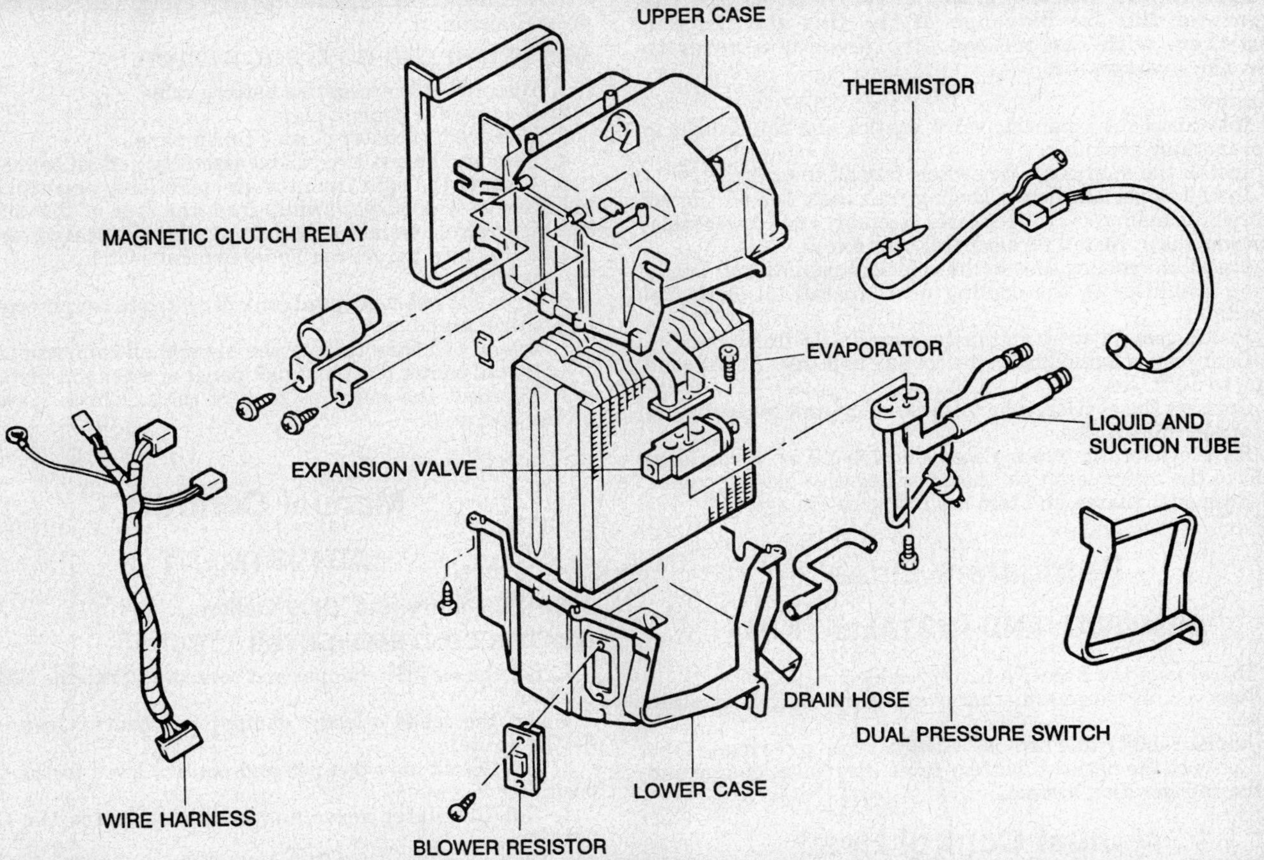
UPPER CASE
THERMISTOR
MAGNETIC CLUTCH RELAY
EVAPORATOR
LIQUID AND SUCTION TUBE
EXPANSION VALVE
DRAIN HOSE
DUAL PRESSURE SWITCH
LOWER CASE
WIRE HARNESS
BLOWER RESISTOR

Exploded view of cooling unit cont'd

10. Remove the heat insulator (heat sensing tube) and the clamp from the outlet tube. Disconnect the liquid line from the inlet fitting of the expansion valve.
11. Disconnect the expansion valve from the inlet fitting of the evaporator. Remove the expansion valve.

NOTE: Before installing the evaporator, check the evaporator fins for blockage. If the fins are clogged, clean them with compressed air. Never use water to clean the evaporator. Check the fittings for cracks and or scratches and replace, as necessary.

To install:
12. Connect the expansion valve to the inlet fitting of the evaporator and torque it to 17 ft. lbs. Be sure that the O-ring is positioned on the tube fitting.
13. Connect the liquid line tube to the inlet fitting on the expansion valve. Torque the nut to 10 ft. lbs.
14. Install the clamp and heat insulator (heat sensing tube) to the outlet tube.
15. Install the upper and lower cases on the evaporator. Install the thermistor. Install control amplifier assembly.
16. Install the air conditioning wiring harness to the cooling unit and all other necessary components.
17. Install the cooling unit assembly in the vehicle. Be careful not to pinch the wiring harness while installing the cooling unit.
18. Install the glove box assembly and the grommets on the inlet and outlet fittings.
19. Connect the liquid line to the cooling unit inlet fittings and torque to 10 ft. lbs.
20. Connect the suction tube to the cooling unit outlet fitting and torque to 24 ft. lbs.
21. If the evaporator was replaced, add 1.4–1.7 oz. of compressor oil to the compressor. Connect the negative battery cable.
22. Evacuate, charge and test the refrigeration system.

1991

1. Disconnect the negative battery cable. Recover refrigerant (discharge system) from refrigeration system.
2. Disconnect the suction flexible hose from the cooling unit outlet fitting.
3. Disconnect the liquid line from the cooling unit inlet fitting. Cap the open fittings immediately to keep the moisture out of the system.
4. Remove the instrument lower finish panel. Disconnect electrical connector from the wiring harness.
5. Remove ground strap. Remove the air conditioning amplifier from the cooling unit.
6. Remove the cooling unit.
7. Place the cooling unit on a suitable work bench and remove the air conditioning main relay assembly (upper case) and blower resistor (lower case).
8. Remove the upper and lower cooling unit case. Remove thermistor and dual pressure switch.
9. Remove the expansion valve, suction and liquid tubes from the evaporator assembly.

NOTE: Before installing the evaporator, check the evaporator fins for blockage. If the fins are clogged, clean them with compressed air. Never use water to clean the evaporator.

To install:

10. Reconnect the expansion valve, suction and liquid tubes to the evaporator assembly.
11. Install the dual pressure switch. Install thermistor.
12. Install upper and lower cooling unit case. Install the air conditioning main relay (upper case) assembly and blower resistor (lower case). Install all electrical connectors.
13. Install the cooling unit in the vehicle. Install the air conditioning amplifier to the cooling unit. Install all electrical connections.
14. Install ground strap and instrument lower finish panel.
15. Connect the liquid line to the cooling unit inlet fittings and torque to 10 ft. lbs.
16. Connect the suction tube to the cooling unit outlet fitting and torque to 24 ft. lbs.
17. If the evaporator was replaced, add 1.4–1.7 oz. of compressor oil to the compressor. Connect the negative battery cable.
18. Evacuate, charge and test the refrigeration system.

Refrigerant Lines

REMOVAL AND INSTALLATION

1. Disconnect the negative battery cable.
2. Recover refrigerant (discharge system) from refrigeration system.
3. Replace faulty line or hose. Always replace O-rings.
4. Connect the negative battery cable. Evacuate, charge and test the refrigeration system.

Manual Control Head

REMOVAL AND INSTALLATION

Camry and MR2

AIR CONDITIONING SWITCH (LEVER TYPE)

1. Disconnect the negative battery cable.
2. Remove the air conditioning switch.
3. Install air conditioning switch. Reconnect negative battery cable.
4. Check system for proper operation.

Celica, Corolla and 1989–90 Tercel

AIR CONDITIONING SWITCH (LEVER TYPE)

1. Disconnect the negative battery cable.
2. Remove the center cluster trim panel. Remove the air conditioning switch.
3. Install air conditioning switch. Install center cluster trim panel.
4. Reconnect negative battery cable.
5. Check system for proper operation.

1991 Tercel

CONTROL PANEL ASSEMBLY

1. Disconnect the negative battery cable.
2. Remove the heater control knobs.
3. Remove the air conditioning switch. Remove the control plate.
4. Remove the control panel assembly.
5. Install control panel assembly. Install control plate and air conditioning switch.
6. Install control knobs.
7. Reconect the negative battery cable. Check system for proper operation.

BLOWER SPEED CONTROL SWITCH

1. Disconnect the negative battery cable.
2. Remove the control plate.
3. Remove the center cluster finish panel.
4. Remove the ash tray, radio assembly and all connections.
5. Remove the light from the air conditioning control assembly. Remove the blower switch from the rear of the air conditioning control assembly. Disconnect the electrical connector to switch. Remove the blower speed control switch.

To install:

6. Install the blower speed control switch to the air conditioning control asembly.
7. Install ash tray, radio assembly and all connections.
8. Install center cluster finish panel and control plate.
9. Reconect the negative battery cable. Check system for proper operation.

Manual Controls

ADJUSTMENT

1989–90 Camry and 1989 Celica

HEATER CONTROL (LEVER TYPE)

1. Set the air inlet damper and control lever to the **RECIRC** position.
2. Set the mode selector damper and control lever to the **FACE** position.
3. Set the air mix damper and control lever to the **COOL** position.
4. Set the water valve and control lever to the **COOL** position.

NOTE: Place the water valve lever on the COOL position and while pushing the outer cable in the direction of COOL position, clamp the outer cable to the water valve bracket.

5. Move the control levers left and right and check for stiffness or binding through the full range of the levers. Test control cable operation.

1991 Camry

HEATER CONTROL (LEVER TYPE)

1. Set the air inlet damper and control lever to the **FRESH** position.
2. Set the mode selector damper and control lever to the **FACE** position.
3. Set the air mix damper and control lever to the **WARM** position.
4. Set the water valve and control lever to the **COOL** position.

NOTE: Place the water valve lever on the COOL position and while pushing the outer cable in the direction of COOL position, clamp the outer cable to the water valve bracket.

5. Move the control levers left and right and check for stiffness or binding through the full range of the levers. Test control cable operation.

Tercel and 1989–90 Corolla

HEATER CONTROL (LEVER TYPE)

1. Set the air inlet damper and control lever to the **FRESH/RECIRC** position.

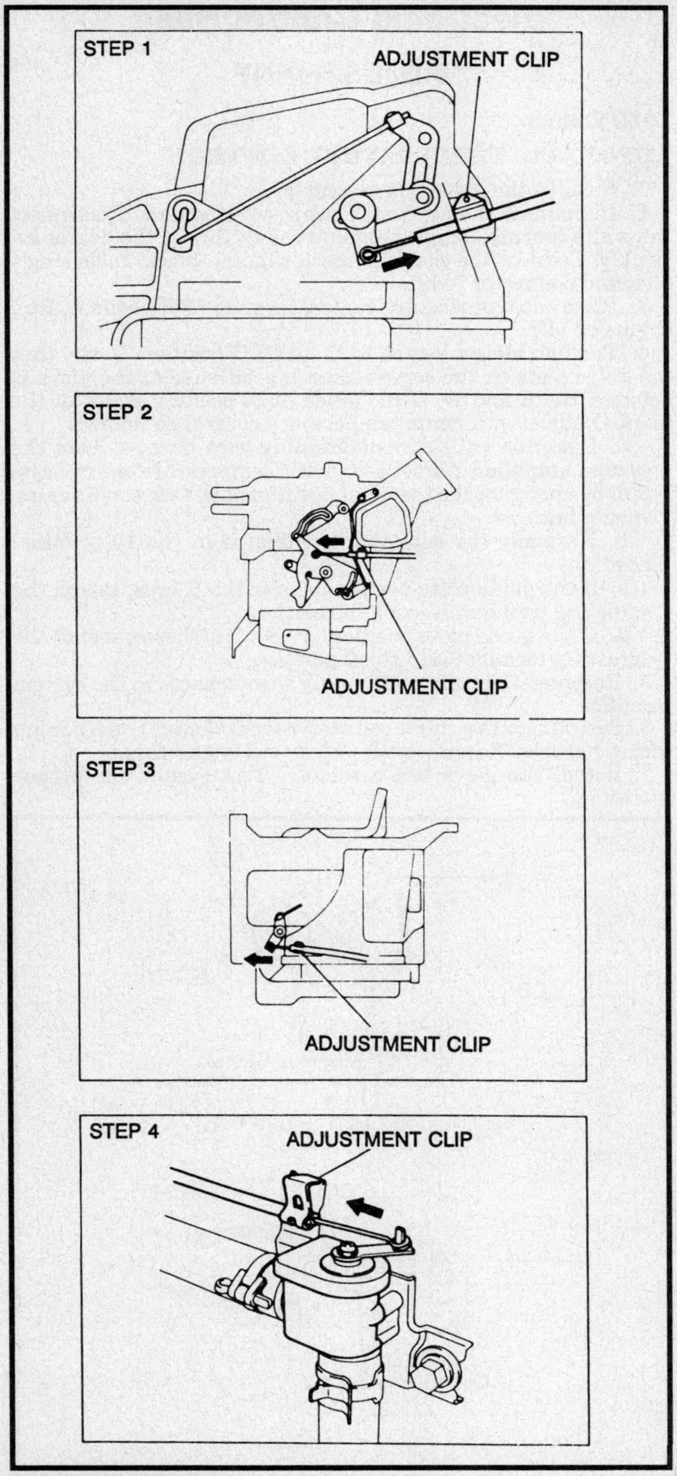
STEP 1
ADJUSTMENT CLIP
STEP 2
ADJUSTMENT CLIP
STEP 3
ADJUSTMENT CLIP
STEP 4
ADJUSTMENT CLIP

Control adjustment

2. Set the mode selector damper and control lever to the **FACE** position.
3. Set the air mix damper and control lever to the **COOL** position.
4. Set the water valve and control lever to the **COOL** position.

NOTE: Place the water valve lever on the COOL position and while pushing the outer cable in the direction of COOL position, clamp the outer cable to the water valve bracket.

5. Move the control levers left and right and check for stiffness or binding through the full range of the levers. Test control cable operation.

1991 Corolla

HEATER CONTROL (LEVER TYPE)

1. Set the air inlet damper and control lever to the **RECIRC** position.
2. Set the mode selector damper and control lever to the **DEF** position.
3. Set the air mix damper and control lever to the **WARM** position.
4. Set the water valve and control lever to the **COOL** position.

NOTE: Place the water valve lever on the COOL position and while pushing the outer cable in the direction of COOL position, clamp the outer cable to the water valve bracket.

5. Move the control levers left and right and check for stiffness or binding through the full range of the levers. Test control cable operation.

Cressida

HEATER CONTROL

1. Adjust the water valve. Position the temperature control knob to counterclockwise (cool side) with the ignition switch **ON**.
2. Set the water valve to the **COOL** side.
3. While pushing the outer cable in the direction of **COOL** position, clamp the outer cable to the water valve bracket. Test control cable operation.

MR2

HEATER CONTROL (TEMPERATURE CONTROL LEVER)

1. Set the air mix damper and control lever to the **COOL** position.
2. Adjust the water valve. Set the water valve and control lever to the **COOL** position.
3. While pushing the outer cable in the direction of **COOL** position, clamp the outer cable to the water valve bracket. Test control cable operation.

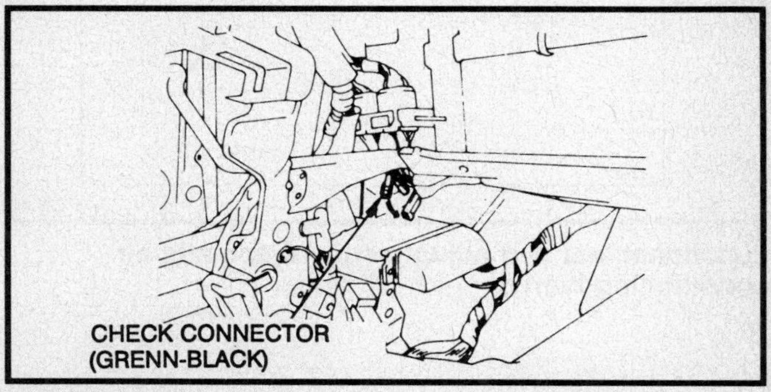
CHECK CONNECTOR
(GRENN-BLACK)

Functional test and adjustment — automatic air conditioning

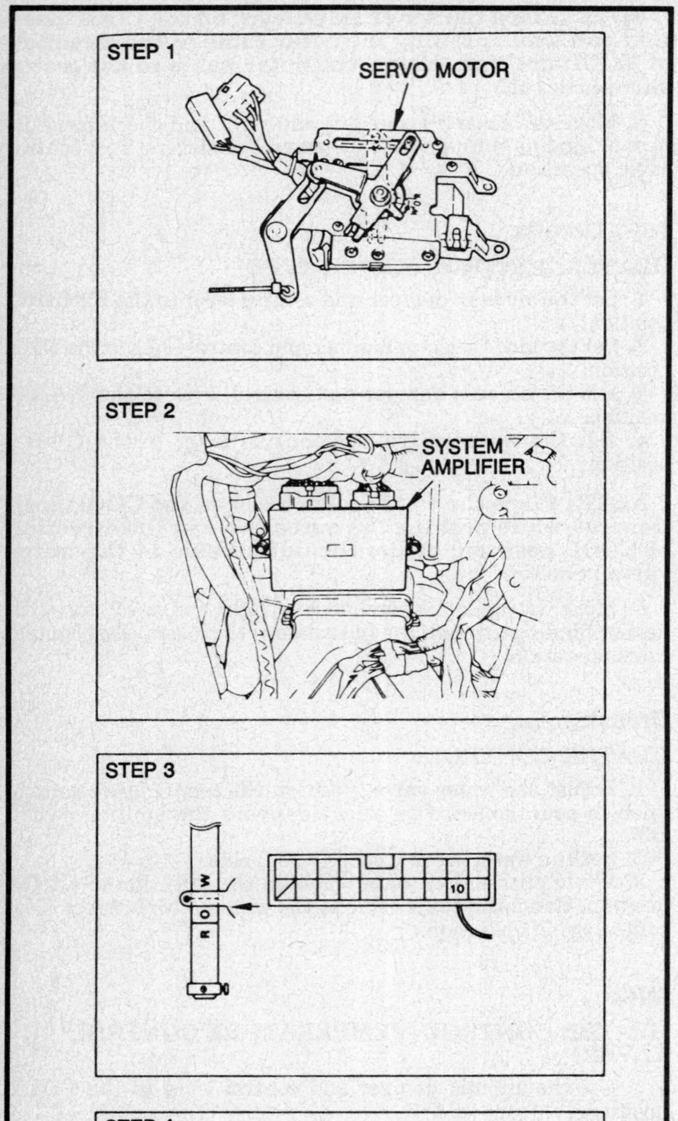
STEP 1
SERVO MOTOR
STEP 2
SYSTEM
AMPLIFIER
STEP 3
W
O
R
10
STEP 4
W
O
R
10
9

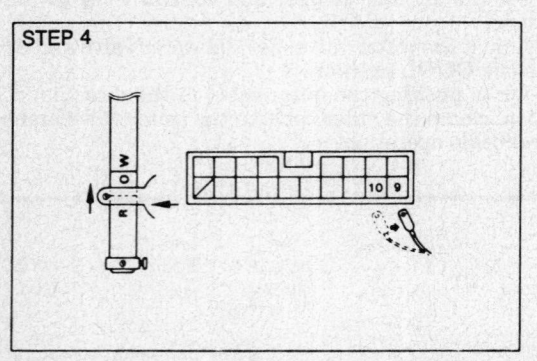

Functional test and adjustment — automatic air conditioning cont'd

Electronic Control Head

ADJUSTMENT

1989 Celica

AUTOMATIC TEMPERATURE CONTROL

1. Remove the glove box assembly.
2. Disconnect the air conditioning wire harness. Disconnect the white (normal) single terminal connectors at the heater assembly. Connect the check connector (green-black) male single terminal connector (white-red).
3. Place the temperature control lever at 77°F position. Run engine at idle.
4. Turn on blower switch to the **AUTO** position. Verify that the guide plate on the servo motor is positioned at the mark **O** between the R and W. If the guide plate position is not at the mark O adjust automatic temperature control as follows:
   a. Disconnect the air conditioning wire harness from the system amplifier. Adjust automatic temperature control system by changing the terminal position at the air conditioning wiring harness.
   b. Normally the adjusting terminal is in the 10 terminal position.
   c. If the guide plate position is over the R area, install the adjusting terminal into the 9 position.
   d. If the guide plate position is over the W area, install the adjusting terminal into the 2 position.
5. Reconnect the air conditioning wire harness to the system amplifier.
6. Disconnect the check connector from the air conditioning wiring harness. Reconnect the white-red connectors.
7. Install the glove box assembly. Test system for proper operation.

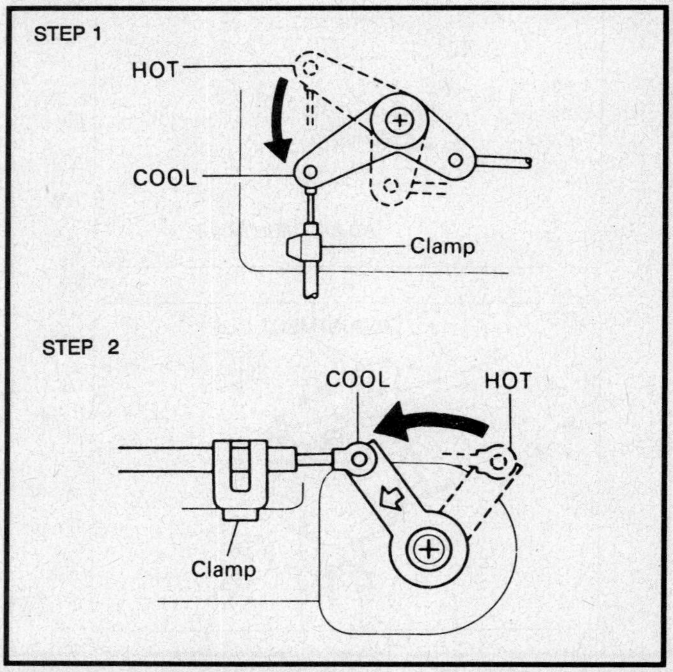
STEP 1
HOT
COOL
Clamp
STEP 2
COOL
HOT
Clamp

Adjustment of control cables

1990–91 Celica

AUTOMATIC TEMPERATURE CONTROL (DIAL TYPE BLOWER CONTROL SWITCH)

1. Adjust the air mix damper control cable. Set the air mix damper and the temperature control switch to **COOL** position. Install the control cable and lock the clamp.
2. Adjust the water valve control cable. Set the water valve to the **COOL** position. Set temperature switch to **COOL** turn ignition to **ON** position with blower motor operating install and lock the clamp.

AUTOMATIC TEMPERATURE CONTROL (PUSH TYPE BLOWER CONTROL SWITCH)

1. Adjust the water valve control cable. Set the water valve to the **COOL** position.
2. Set temperature switch to **COOL** turn ignition to **ON** position with blower motor operating install and lock the clamp.

Supra

AUTOMATIC TEMPERATURE CONTROL

1. Disconnect the short circuit connector. Make short terminals **1** and **3** for test.

2. Place the temperature control lever at 77°F position. Run engine at idle.

3. Turn on blower switch to the **AUTO** position. Verify that the guide plate on the servo motor is positioned at the mark **O** between the R and W. If the guide plate position is not at the mark O adjust automatic temperature control as follows:

   a. If the guide plate position is over the W area connect the red/green and brown/yellow wire harness.
   b. If the guide plate position is over the R area connect the red/green and white/black wire harness.
4. Reconnect the short circuit connector.

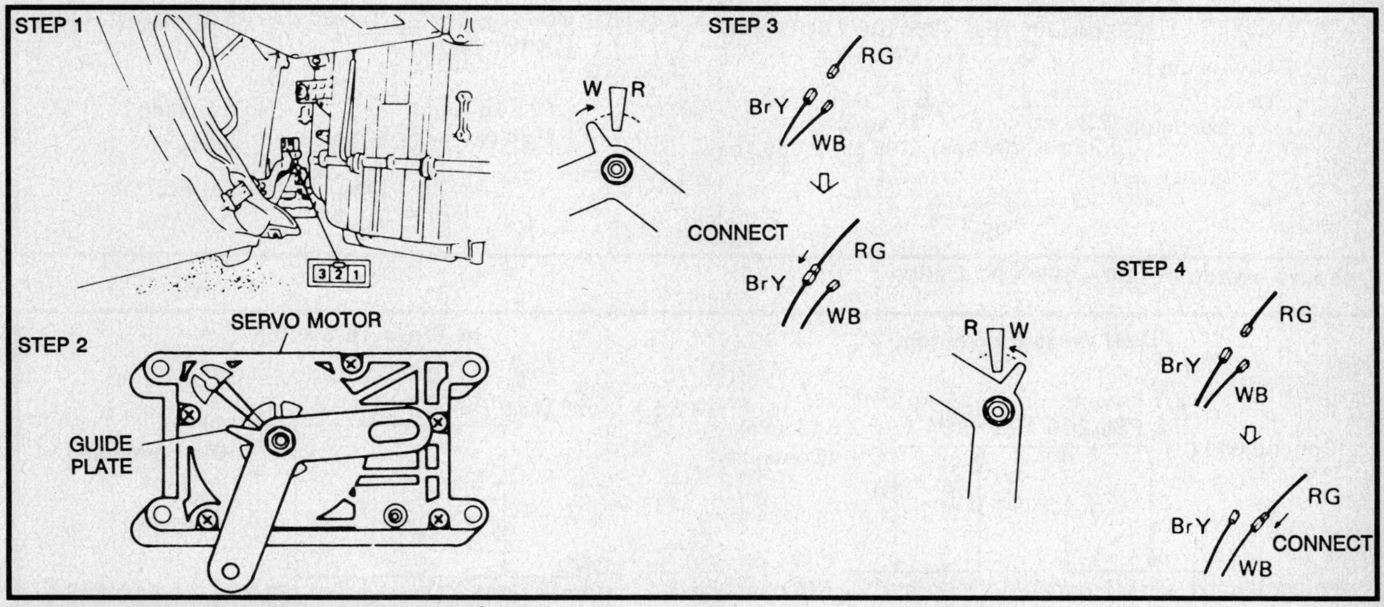
STEP 1
3 2 1
W
R
STEP 3
RG
BrY
WB
CONNECT
RG
BrY
WB
STEP 4
R
W
RG
BrY
WB
RG
BrY
CONNECT
WB
SERVO MOTOR
STEP 2
GUIDE
PLATE
Functional test and adjustment procedure

SENSORS AND SWITCHES

Dual and High Pressure Switch

TESTING

1. Disconnect electrical connector of pressure switch.
2. Install manifold gauge set. Observe gauge reading.
3. Check continuity between the 2 terminals of the pressure switch. Refer to pressure switch diagnosis illustrations.

Water Temperature Switch

TESTING

1. When the water temperature reaches the specified temperature the continuity is broken. Check that the continuity is made again when the temperature of the water falls to the specified temperature.
2. Check continuity of switch. Replace as necessary.
   a. Camry – 234°F OFF (no continuity) 223°F ON (continuity)
   b. Celica, Cressida – (check resistance) 34°F 15–19 kilo-ohms, 104°F 2.5–2.7 kilo-ohms and 158°F 0.8–1.0 kilo-ohms. If resistance valve is not as specified replace.
   c. Corolla (radiator fan) – 194°F OFF (no continuity) 181°F ON (continuity)
   d. Corolla (A/C cutout) – 217°F OFF (no continuity) 208°F ON (continuity)
   e. MR2 – (check resistance) 203°F 1.05 kilo-ohms. If resistance valve is not as specified replace.
   f. Supra (turbocharged engine only) – 234°F OFF (no continuity) 225°F ON (continuity)
   g. Supra – 212°F OFF (no continuity) 203°F ON (continuity)
   h. Tercel – 185°F OFF (no continuity) 172°F ON (continuity)

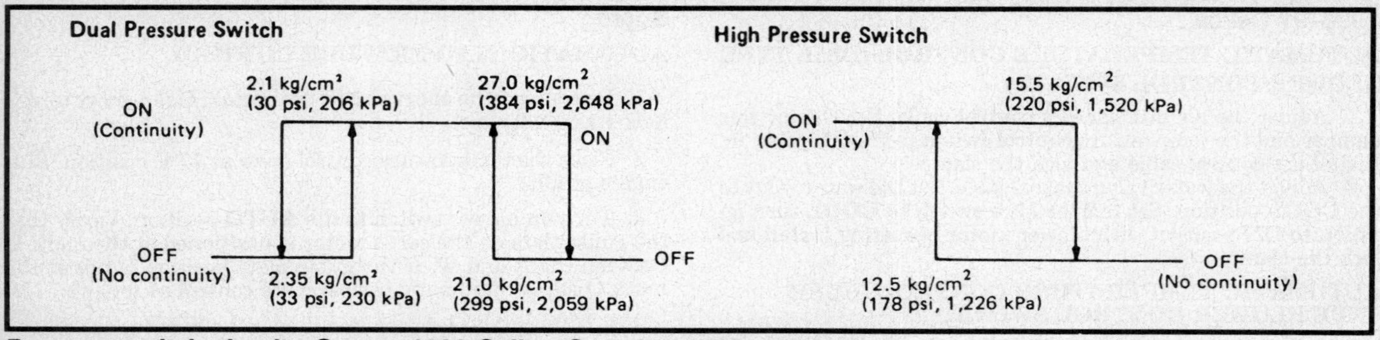
Dual Pressure Switch
High Pressure Switch
ON
(Continuity)
2.1 kg/cm²
(30 psi, 206 kPa)
27.0 kg/cm²
(384 psi, 2,648 kPa)
ON
OFF
(No continuity)
2.35 kg/cm²
(33 psi, 230 kPa)
21.0 kg/cm²
(299 psi, 2,059 kPa)
OFF
15.5 kg/cm²
(220 psi, 1,520 kPa)
ON
(Continuity)
OFF
(No continuity)
12.5 kg/cm²
(178 psi, 1,226 kPa)

Pressure switch circuit—Camry, 1989 Celica, Cressida, MR2 and Supra

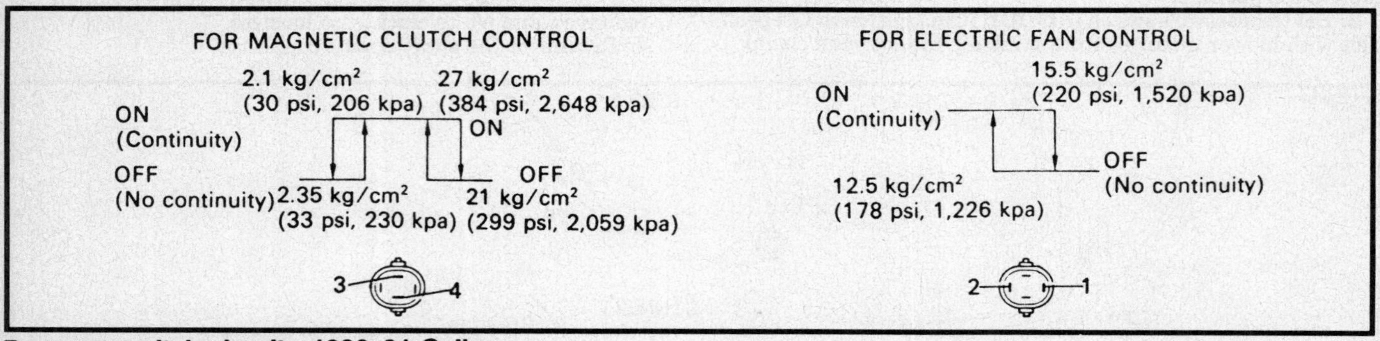
FOR MAGNETIC CLUTCH CONTROL
FOR ELECTRIC FAN CONTROL
2.1 kg/cm²
(30 psi, 206 kpa)
27 kg/cm²
(384 psi, 2,648 kpa)
ON
(Continuity)
ON
OFF
(No continuity)
2.35 kg/cm²
(33 psi, 230 kpa)
OFF
21 kg/cm²
(299 psi, 2,059 kpa)
15.5 kg/cm²
(220 psi, 1,520 kpa)
ON
(Continuity)
OFF
(No continuity)
12.5 kg/cm²
(178 psi, 1,226 kpa)
3
4
2
1

Pressure switch circuit—1990–91 Celica

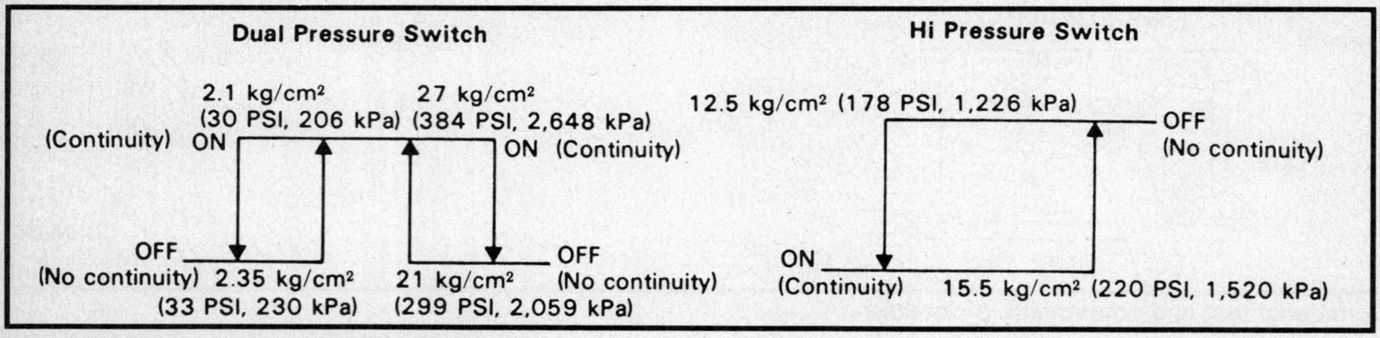
Dual Pressure Switch
Hi Pressure Switch
2.1 kg/cm²
(30 PSI, 206 kPa)
27 kg/cm²
(384 PSI, 2,648 kPa)
(Continuity) ON
ON (Continuity)
OFF
(No continuity)
2.35 kg/cm²
(33 PSI, 230 kPa)
21 kg/cm²
(299 PSI, 2,059 kPa)
OFF
(No continuity)
12.5 kg/cm² (178 PSI, 1,226 kPa)
OFF
(No continuity)
ON
(Continuity)
15.5 kg/cm² (220 PSI, 1,520 kPa)

Pressure switch circuit—Corolla and Tercel

Air Conditioning Relays

TESTING

1. Remove cover of relay box.
2. Remove the relay.
3. Inspect relay continuity. If continuity is not as specified, replace the relay. Refer to wiring schematics, as necessary.

Thermistor

TESTING

1. With the thermistor still install, use an ohmmeter and measure the resistance at the connector (resistance 1500 ohms at 77°F).

2. Place the thermistor in cold water. While varying the temperature of the water measure the resistance at the connector. The colder the water the higher the resistance (MAX. 5500 ohms at 30°F water temperature).

Air Conditioning Switch (Lever Type)

TESTING

1. Using a ohmmeter check continuity between the terminals for each switch position.

NOTE: When checking for continuity in circuits which contain an LED use a tester with a power source of 3 volts or greater to overcome circuit resistance.

2. If continuity is not as specified, replace the switch. Refer to wiring schematics, as necessary.

Air Conditioning (Push Type)

TESTING

1. Using a ohmmeter check continuity between the terminals for each switch position.
2. If continuity is not as specified, replace the switch. Refer to wiring schematics, as necessary.

Air Conditioning Amplifier

TESTING

1. Disconnect the amplifier and inspect the connector on the wire harness side.
2. Constant test conditions are ignition **ON** temperature control lever **MAX. COOL** and blower switch in **HI** position.
3. If the circuit is not as specified, replace the amplifier.

Condenser Fan Amplifier

TESTING

1. Disconnect the amplifier and inspect the connector on the wire harness side.
2. If the circuit is not as specified, replace the amplifier.

Compressor Control Amplifier

TESTING

1. Disconnect the amplifier and inspect the connector on the wire harness side.
2. If the circuit is not as specified, replace the amplifier.

INSPECTION OF AIR CONDITIONING AMPLIFIER CIRCUIT—CAMRY 3S-FE ENGINE

Check for	Tester connection	Condition	Specified value
Continuity	10 — Ground	Constant	Continuity
Voltage	4 — 10	Turn A/C switch on.	Battery voltage
		Turn A/C switch off.	No voltage
	1 — 10	Turn A/C switch on.	Battery voltage
		Turn A/C switch off.	No voltage
Voltage	2 — 10	Turn ignition switch on.	Battery voltage
		Turn ignition switch off.	No voltage
	6 — 10	Turn ignition switch on.	Battery voltage
		Turn ignition switch off.	No voltage
	8 — 10	Start engine.	Approx. 10 to 14 V
		Stop engine.	No voltage
	5 — 10	Turn ignition switch on.	Battery voltage
		Turn ignition switch off.	No voltage
Resistance	3 — 9	Constant	Approx. 1.7 kΩ at 25°C (77°F)
	9 — 13	Constant	Approx. 250 Ω

INSPECTION OF AIR CONDITIONING AMPLIFIER CIRCUIT—CAMRY 2VZ-FE ENGINE

Check for	Tester connection	Condition	Specified value
Continuity	3 — Ground	Constant	Continuity
Voltage	14 — Ground	Turn ignition switch on.	Battery voltage
		Turn ignition switch off.	No voltage
	11 — Ground	Turn ignition switch on.	Battery voltage
		Turn ignition switch off.	No voltage
	2 — Ground	Turn A/C switch on.	Battery voltage
		Turn A/C switch off.	No voltage
	10 — Ground	Turn A/C switch on.	Battery voltage
		Turn A/C switch off.	No voltage
	7 — Ground	Start engine.	Approx. 10 to 14 V
		Stop engine.	No voltage
Resistance	5 — 9	Constant	Approx. 1.5 kΩ at 27°C (77°F)
	8 — 9	Constant	Approx. 250 Ω

INSPECTION OF CONDENSER FAN CONTROL AMPLIFIER CIRCUIT—CAMRY

Check for	Tester connection	Condition	Specified value
Continuity	1 – Ground	Constant	Continuity
	2 – Ground	Constant	Continuity
	5 – Ground	Constant	Continuity
	6 – Ground	Constant	Continuity
Voltage	3 – 6	Turn ignition switch on.	Battery voltage
		Turn ignition switch off.	No voltage
	4 – 6	Turn ignition switch on.	Battery voltage
		Turn ignition switch off.	No voltage

INSPECTION OF COMPRESSOR CONTROL AMPLIFIER CIRCUIT—CAMRY

Check for	Tester connection	Condition	Specified value
Continuity	6 – Ground	Constant	Continuity
Voltage	3 – Ground	Turn ignition switch on.	Battery voltage
		Turn ignition switch off.	No voltage
Resistance	5 – 7	Constant	Approx. 4.4 kΩ 25°C(77°F)

INSPECTION OF AIR CONDITIONING AMPLIFIER CIRCUIT—1989 CELICA

Check for	Tester connection	Condition	Specified value
Continuity	14 – Ground	Constant	Continuity
Voltage	1 – 14	Turn A/C switch on.	Battery voltage
		Turn A/C switch off.	No voltage
	6 – 14	Turn A/C switch on.	Battery voltage
		Turn A/C switch off.	No voltage
	4 – 14	Turn ignition switch on.	Battery voltage
		Turn ignition switch off.	No voltage
	5 – 14	Turn ignition switch on.	Battery voltage
		Turn ignition switch off.	No voltage
	7 – 14	Turn ignition switch on.	Battery voltage
		Turn ignition switch off.	No voltage
	8 – 14	Turn ignition switch on.	Battery voltage
		Turn ignition switch off.	No voltage
	10 – 14	Start the engine.	Approx. 10 to 14 V
		Stop the engine.	No voltage
	13 – 14	Turn ignition switch on.	Battery voltage
		Turn ignition switch off.	No voltage
	18 – 14	Turn ignition switch on.	Battery voltage
		Turn ignition switch off.	No voltage
Resistance	2 – 9	Constant	Approx. 1.5 kΩ at 25°C (77°F)
	16 – 9	Constant	Approx. 115 Ω

<table>
<tr><th>False Signal</th><th>A</th><th>B</th></tr>
<tr><td>Condition</td><td>Interior room temperature is very low.
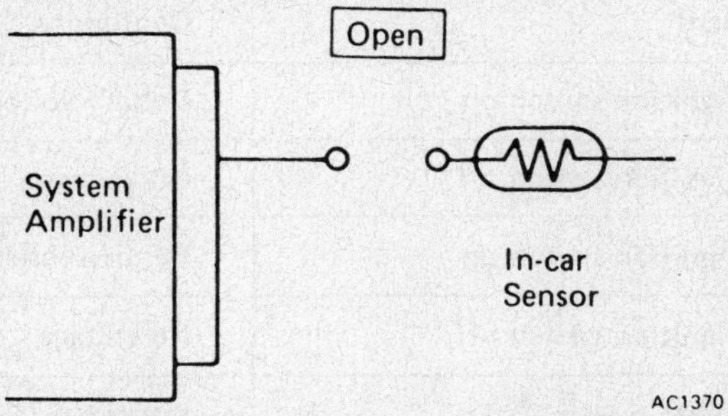
Open
System Amplifier
In-car Sensor
AC1370</td><td>Interior room temperature is very high.
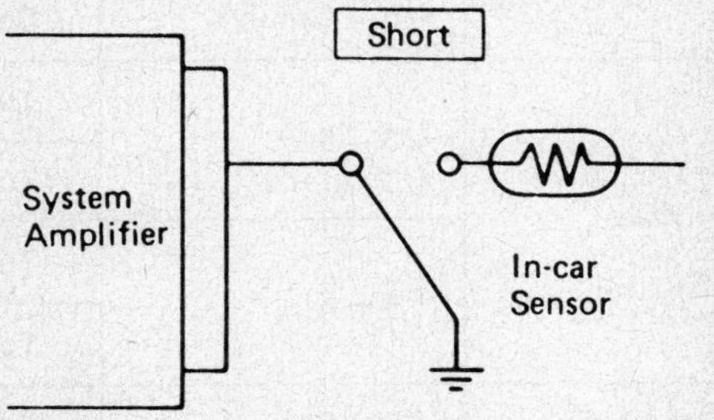
Short
System Amplifier
In-car Sensor</td></tr>
<tr><td>Your Work</td><td>Remove in-car sensor connector.</td><td>Remove in-car sensor, and ground the number 1 pin of in-car sensor female connector.</td></tr>
</table>

INSPECTION OF AIR CONDITIONING AMPLIFIER CIRCUIT—1989 CELICA CONT'D

System Operation when Input False Signal

Condition: Setting Temperature is at 25°C (77°F)

System Main Parts	False Signal	Motion			
Air Mix Control Servo Motor	A	Air mix control servo motor shaft moves towards max-hot side.			
	B	Air mix control servo motor shaft moves towards max-cool side.			
Air Vent Mode Control Servo Motor		Air Vent Mode Damper			
		VENT	BI-LEVEL	HEAT	DEF
	A	Close	Close	Open	Close
	B	Open	Close	Close	Close
Blower Motor	A	Blower motor rotates at high speed.			
	B				
Water Valve	A	OPEN			
	B	CLOSE			
FRE/REC Control Servo Motor	FRE Switch ON	Fresh air is ventilated.			
	REC Switch ON	Recirculation air is ventirated.			

INSPECTION OF CONDENSER FAN CONTROL AMPLIFIER CIRCUIT—1989 CELICA 3S-GTE ENGINE

Check for	Tester connection	Condition	Specified value
Continuity	2 – 6	Constant	Continuity
	6 – Ground	Constant	Continuity
Voltage	3 – 6	Turn ignition switch on	Battery voltage
		Turn ignition switch off	No voltage
	4 – 6	Turn ignition switch on	Battery voltage
		Turn ignition switch off	No voltage
Resistance	7 – 5	Constant	Approx. 570 Ω at 25°C (77°F)

INSPECTION OF AIR CONDITIONING AMPLIFIER CIRCUIT—1990–91 CELICA

Check for	Tester connection	Condition	Specified value
Continuity	*1 2 – ground	Engine coolant less than 95°C (203°F)	Continuity
		Engine coolant more than 100°C (212°F)	No continuity
	15 – ground	Constant	Continuity
Resistance	*1 5 – ground	Constant	Approx. 12 Ω
	9 – 14	Constant	Approx. 115 Ω
	16 – 14	Constant	Approx. 15 kΩ at 25°C (77°F)
Voltage	1 – ground	Turn A/C switch on.	Battery voltage
		Turn A/C switch off.	No voltage
	3 – ground	Turn A/C switch on.	Battery voltage
		Turn A/C switch off.	No voltage
	6 – ground	Turn A/C switch on.	Battery voltage
		Turn A/C switch off.	No voltage
	8 – ground	Constant	Battery voltage
	13 – ground	Turn A/C switch on.	Battery voltage
		Turn A/C switch off.	No voltage
	18 – ground	Start the engine.	Approx. 10 to 14 V
		Stop the engine.	No voltage
*1: with Variable Volume Control Mechanism Compressor			
Continuity	1 – 6	Constant	Continuity
	9 – ground	Constant	Continuity
Resistance*1	5 – 2	Constant	Approx. 3 kΩ
	5 – 10	Constant	Approx. 6 kΩ
	11 – 10	Constant	1.2 – 4.8 kΩ
	12 – 2	Temp switch turned to MAX COOL	Approx. 3 kΩ
Voltage	7 – ground	Constant	Battery voltage
*1: without AUTO A/C models			
Voltage	3 – ground	Temp. control switch turned to MAX HOT	Approx. 0 V*1
		Temp. control switch turned to MAX COOL	Approx. 5 V
	4 – ground	Temp. control switch turned to MAX HOT	Approx. 5 V
		Temp. control switch turned to MAX COOL	Approx. 0 V*1
*1: Voltage becomes 0 V when switch is turned, then soon returns to 5 V.			

INSPECTION OF AIR CONDITIONING AMPLIFIER CIRCUIT—1990–91 CELICA CONT'D

False Signal	A	B
Condition	Interior room temperature is very low. 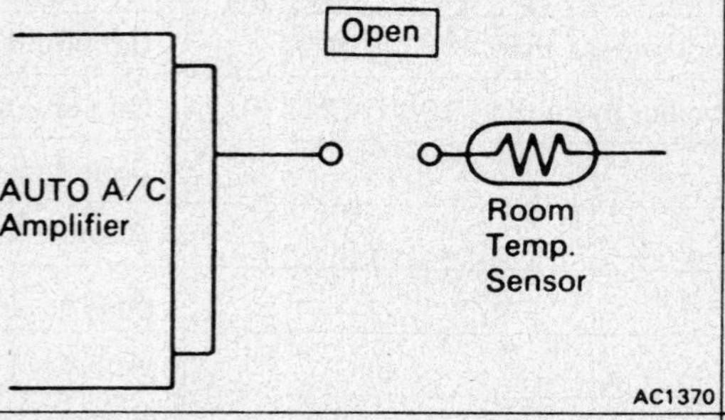 Open AUTO A/C Amplifier Room Temp. Sensor AC1370	Interior room temperature is very high. 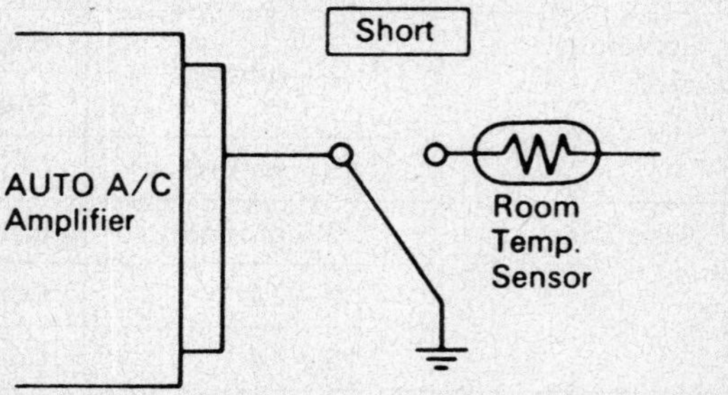 Short AUTO A/C Amplifier Room Temp. Sensor
Your Work	Remove in-car sensor connector.	Remove room temp. sensor, and ground the number 2 pin of room temp. sensor female connector.

Condition: Setting Temperature is at 25°C (77°F)

System Main Parts	False Signal	Motion			
Air Mix Control Servomotor	A	Air mix control servo motor shaft moves towards max-hot side.			
	B	Air mix control servo motor shaft moves towards max-cool side.			
Air Flow Mode Control Servomotor		Air Vent Mode Damper			
		VENT	BI-LEVEL	HEAT	DEF
	A	Close	Close	Open	Close
	B	Open	Close	Close	Close
Blower Motor	A	Blower motor rotates at high speed.			
	B				
Water Valve	A	OPEN			
	B	CLOSE			
FRE/REC Control Servomotor	FRE Switch ON	Fresh air is ventilated.			
	REC Switch ON	Recirculation air is ventilated.			

INSPECTION OF AIR CONDITIONING AMPLIFIER CIRCUIT—COROLLA 4A-GE ENGINE WITH POWER STEERING

Check for	Tester connection	Condition	Specified value
Continuity	2 — 9	Constant	Continuity
	8 — Ground	Constant	Continuity
	13 — Ground	Constant	Continuity
Voltage	1 — Ground	Turn A/C switch on	Battery voltage
		Turn A/C switch off	No voltage
	3 — Ground	Turn blower switch on	Battery voltage
		Turn blower switch off	No voltage
	4 — Ground	Turn blower switch on	Battery voltage
		Turn blower switch off	No voltage
	5 — Ground	Turn blower switch on	Battery voltage
		Turn blower switch off	No voltage
	10 — Ground	Start engine	Approx. 10 to 14 V
		Stop engine	No voltage
	12 — Ground	Turn blower switch on	Battery voltage
		Turn blower switch off	No voltage
	18 — Ground	Turn A/C switch on	Battery voltage
		Turn A/C switch off	No voltage
Resistance	9 — 14	Constant	Approx. 1.7 kΩ at 25°C (77°F)
	11 — Ground	Constant	Approx. 300 Ω
	14 — 17	Constant	Approx. 250 Ω

INSPECTION OF AIR CONDITIONING AMPLIFIER CIRCUIT—COROLLA 4A-FE ENGINE

Check for	Tester connection	Condition	Specified value
Continuity	6 — 12	Constant	Continuity
	10 — Ground	Constant	Continuity
Voltage	1 — Ground	Turn blower switch on	Battery voltage
		Turn blower switch off	No voltage
	2 — Ground	Turn blower switch on	Battery voltage
		Turn blower switch off	No voltage
	3 — Ground	Turn blower switch on	Battery voltage
		Turn blower switch off	No voltage
	4 — Ground	Turn A/C switch on	Battery voltage
		Turn A/C switch off	No voltage
	5 — Ground	Turn blower switch on	Battery voltage
		Turn blower switch off	No voltage
	14 — Ground	Start engine	Approx. 10 to 14 V
		Stop engine	No voltage
Resistance	7 — Ground	Constant	Approx. 40 Ω
	11 — 12	Constant	Approx. 1.7 kΩ at 25°C (77°F)

INSPECTION OF AMPLIFIER CIRCUIT—CRESSIDA

False Signal	A	B
Condition	Interier room temperature is very low. 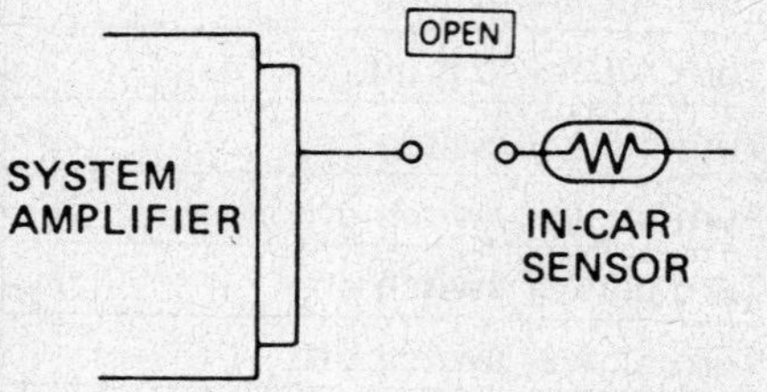OPEN SYSTEM AMPLIFIER IN-CAR SENSOR AC1370	Interior room temperature is very high. 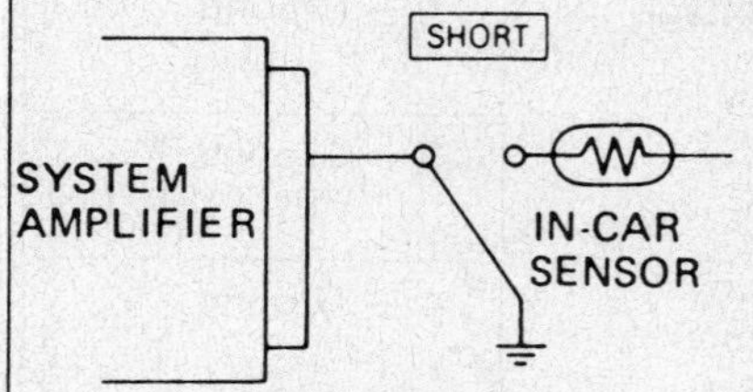SHORT SYSTEM AMPLIFIER IN-CAR SENSOR
Your Work	Remove in-car sensor connector.	Remove in-car sensor, and ground the number 1 pin of in-car sensor female connector.

Condition: Setting Temperature is at 25°C (77°F)

System Main Parts	False Signal	Motion			
Air Mix Control Servo Motor	A	Air mix control servo motor shaft moves towards max-hot side.			
	B	Air mix control servo motor shaft moves towards max-cool side.			
Air Flow Mode Control Servo Motor		Air Flow Mode Damper			
		VENT	BI-LEVEL	HEAT	DEF
	A	Close	Close	Open	Close
	B	Open	Close	Close	Close
Blower Motor	A	Blower motor rotates at high speed			
	B				
Water Valve	A	OPEN			
	B	CLOSE			
Air Inlet Control Servo Motor	FRE Switch ON	Fresh air is ventilated.			
	REC Switch ON	Recirculation air is ventirated.			

INSPECTION OF AIR CONDITIONING AMPLIFIER CIRCUIT—1989 MR2 4A-GE ENGINE

Check for	Tester connection	Condition	Specified value
Continuity	5 – Ground	Constant	Continuity
	7 – Ground	Constant	Continuity
	10 – Ground	Constant	Continuity
Voltage	1 – 10	Turn ignition switch on.	Battery voltage
		Turn ignition switch off.	No voltage
	2 – 10	Turn A/C switch on.	Battery voltage
		Turn A/C switch off.	No voltage
	4 – 10	Turn ignition switch on.	Battery voltage
		Turn ignition switch off.	No voltage
	6 – 10	Turn ignition switch on.	Battery voltage
		Turn ignition switch off.	No voltage
	8 – 10	Turn ignition switch on.	Battery voltage
		Turn ignition switch off.	No voltage
	13 – 10	Start the engine.	Approx. 10 to 14 V
		Stop the engine.	No voltage
	14 – 10	Turn ECONO switch on.	Battery voltage
		Turn ECONO switch off.	No voltage
Resistance	9 – 3	Constant	Approx. 4.5 kΩ
	12 – 11	Constant	Approx. 1.5 kΩ at 25°C (77°F)

INSPECTION OF AIR CONDITIONING AMPLIFIER CIRCUIT—1989 MR2 4A–GZE ENGINE

Continuity	4 – Ground	Constant	Continuity
	10 – Ground	Constant	Continuity
	11 – Ground	Constant	Continuity
	13 – Ground	Constant	Continuity
	15 – Ground	Constant	Continuity
Voltage	2 – 13	Turn ignition switch on.	Battery voltage
		Turn ignition switch off.	No voltage
	3 – 13	Turn A/C switch on.	Battery voltage
		Turn A/C switch off.	No voltage
	3 – 13	Turn ECONO switch on.	Battery voltage
		Turn ECONO switch off.	No voltage
	5 – 13	Turn ignition switch on.	Battery voltage
		Turn ignition switch off.	No voltage
	6 – 13	Start the engine.	Approx. 10 to 14 V
		Stop the engine.	No voltage
	8 – 13	Turn A/C switch on.	Battery voltage
		Turn A/C switch off.	No voltage
	9 – 13	Turn ignition switch on.	Battery voltage
		Turn ignition switch off.	No voltage
	14 – 13	Turn ignition switch on.	Battery voltage
		Turn ignition switch off.	No voltage
	16 – 13	Turn ECONO switch on.	Battery voltage
		Turn ECONO switch off.	No voltage
Resistance	1 – 13	Constant	Approx. 4.5 kΩ
	7 – 17	Constant	Approx. 1.5 kΩ at 25°C (77°F)

INSPECTION OF AIR CONDITIONING AMPLIFIER CIRCUIT—1991 MR2

Check for	Tester connection	Condition		Specified value
Continuity	8 – Engine control ECU terminal A/C	Constant		Continuity
	13 – Ground	Constant		Continuity
Resistance	3 – Ground	Constant		Continuity
	9 – 15	Engine coolant condition	85°C (185°F)	Approx. 1.35 kΩ
			90°C (194°F)	Approx. 1.19 kΩ
			95°C (203°F)	Approx. 1.05 kΩ
	14 – 17	Ambient temperature at 25°C (77°F)		Approx. 1.5 kΩ
Voltage	1 – Ground	Ignition switch position switch ON	LOCK or ACC	No voltage
			ON	Battery voltage
	2 – Ground	Ignition switch position switch ON	LOCK or ACC	No voltage
			ON	Battery voltage
	4 – Ground	Ignition switch position switch ON	LOCK or ACC	No voltage
			ON	Battery voltage
	6 – Ground	A/C switch position with ignition switch ON	OFF	No voltage
			ON	Battery voltage
	7 – Ground (RHD models)	ECON switch position with ignition switch ON	OFF	No voltage
			ON	Battery voltage
	10 – Ground	Ignition switch position switch ON	LOCK or ACC	No voltage
			ON	Battery voltage
	11 – Ground	Ignition switch position switch ON	LOCK or ACC	No voltage
			ON	Battery voltage
	18 – Ground	Engine condition	Running	Approx. 10 to 14 v
			Stopped	No voltage

INSPECTION OF AMPLIFIER CIRCUIT—SUPRA

Check for	Tester connection	Condition	Specified value
Continuity	10 – Ground	Constant	Continuity
Voltage	2 – 10	Turn A/C switch on.	Battery voltage
		Turn A/C switch off.	No voltage
Resistance	6 – 9	Constant	Approx. 1.5 kΩ at 25°C (77°F)

INSPECTION OF AMPLIFIER CIRCUIT—SUPRA CONT'D

False Signal	A	B
Condition	Interior room temperature is very low. 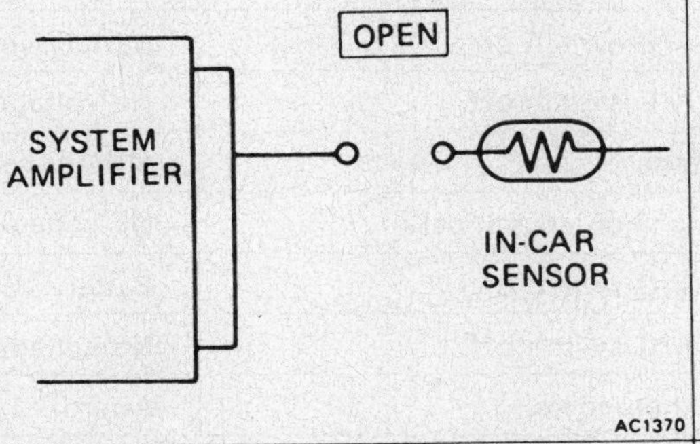 OPEN SYSTEM AMPLIFIER IN-CAR SENSOR AC1370	Interior room temperature is very high. 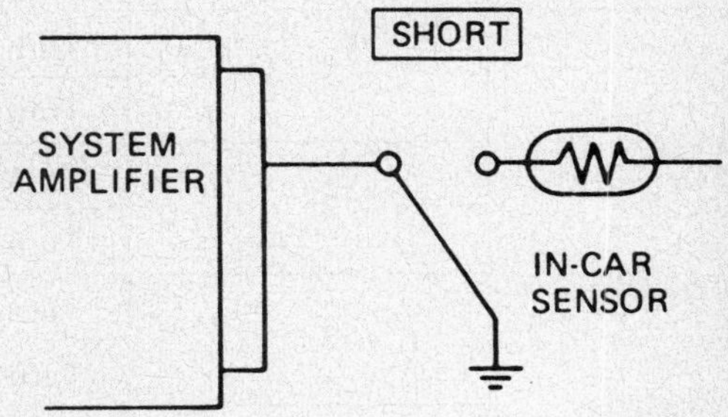 SHORT SYSTEM AMPLIFIER IN-CAR SENSOR
Your Work	Remove in-car sensor connector	Remove in-car sensor and ground the number 1 pin of in-car sensor female connector

Condition: Setting Temperature is at 25°C (77°F)

System Main Parts	False Signal	Motion			
Air Mix Control Servo Motor	A	Air mix control servo motor shaft moves towards max. hot side.			
	B	Air mix control servo motor shaft moves towards max. cool side.			
Air Vent Mode Control Servo Motor		Air Vent Mode Damper			
		VENT	BI-LEVEL	HEAT	DEF
	A	Close	Close	Open	Close
	B	Open	Close	Close	Close
Blower Motor	A	Blower motor rotates at high speed.			
	B				
Water Valve	A	OPEN			
	B	CLOSE			
⋮	⋮	⋮			
FRE/REC Control Servo Motor	FRE Switch ON	Fresh air is ventilated.			
	REC Switch ON	Recirculation air is ventilated.			

INSPECTION OF AIR CONDITIONING AMPLIFIER CIRCUIT—1989–90 TERCEL WITH POWER STEERING

Check for	Tester connection	Condition	Specified value
Continuity	2 – Ground	Constant	Continuity
	4 – 2	Constant	Continuity
	10 – 2	Constant	Continuity
Voltage	1 – 2	Turn A/C switch on.	Battery voltage
		Turn A/C switch off.	No voltage
	3 – 2	Constant	Battery voltage
		Turn ignition switch off.	No voltage
	6 – 2	Turn A/C switch on.	Battery voltage
		Turn A/C switch off.	No voltage
	7 – 2	Start the engine.	Approx. 10 to 14V
		Stop the engine.	No voltage
	8 – 2	Turn A/C switch on.	Battery voltage
		Turn A/C switch off.	No voltage
	11 – 2	Constant	Battery voltage
		Turn ignition switch off.	No voltage
Resistance	5 – 9	Constant	Approx. 1.7 kΩ at 25°C (77°F)
	13 – 9	Constant	Approx. 250 Ω

INSPECTION OF AIR CONDITIONING AMPLIFIER CIRCUIT—1989–90 TERCEL WITHOUT POWER STEERING

Check for	Tester connection	Condition	Specified value
Continuity	7 – Ground	Constant	Continuity
	9 – Ground	Constant	Continuity
Voltage	3 – 7	Turn ignition switch on.	Battery voltage
		Turn ignition switch off.	No voltage
	4 – 7	Turn ignition switch on.	Battery voltage
		Turn ignition switch off.	No voltage
	5 – 7	Start the engine.	Approx. 10 to 14V
		Stop the engine.	No voltage
	8 – 7	Turn A/C switch on.	Battery voltage
		Turn A/C switch off.	No voltage
Resistance	6 – 7		Approx. 1.7 kΩ at 25°C (77°F)

INSPECTION OF ACCELERATION CUT AMPLIFIER CIRCUIT – 1989–90 TERCEL WITH AUTOMATIC TRANSMISSION

Check for	Tester connection	Condition	Specified value
Continuity	6 – Ground	Constant	Continuity
	2 – 6	Constant	Continuity
	1 – Ground	Constant	Continuity
Voltage	3 – 6	Start the engine.	Approx. 10 to 14V
		Stop the engine.	No voltage
	4 – 6	Turn A/C switch on.	Battery voltage
		Turn A/C switch off.	No voltage
	5 – 6	Turn A/C switch on.	No voltage
		Turn A/C switch off.	No voltage
	9 – 5	Turn A/C switch on.	Battery voltage
		Turn A/C switch off.	No voltage

INSPECTION OF AIR CONDITIONING AMPLIFIER CIRCUIT – 1991 TERCEL WITH POWER STEERING

Check for	Tester Connection	Condition	Specified Value
Voltage	1 – Ground	Start the engine	Approx. 10 to 14 V
		Stop the engine	No voltage
	8 – Ground	A/C switch on	Battery voltage
		A/C switch off	No voltage
	7 – Ground	Blower switch on	Battery voltage
		Blower switch off	No voltage
Resistance	2 – 13	Constant	Approx. 1.5 kΩ at 25°C (77°F)
	9 – 13	Constant	Approx. 240 Ω
Continuity	5 – 7	Constant	Continuity
	12 – Ground	Constant	Continuity

INSPECTION OF AIR CONDITIONING AMPLIFIER CIRCUIT – 1991 TERCEL WITHOUT POWER STEERING

Check for	Tester Connection	Condition	Specified Value
Voltage	1 – Ground	Start the engine	Approx. 10 to 14 V
		Stop the engine	No voltage
	8 – Ground	A/C switch on	Battery voltage
		A/C switch off	No voltage
	7 – Ground	Blower switch on	Battery voltage
		Blower switch off	No voltage
Resistance	2 – 12	Constant	Approx. 15 kΩ at 25°C (77°F)
Continuity	5 – 7	Constant	Continuity
	12 – Ground	Constant	Continuity

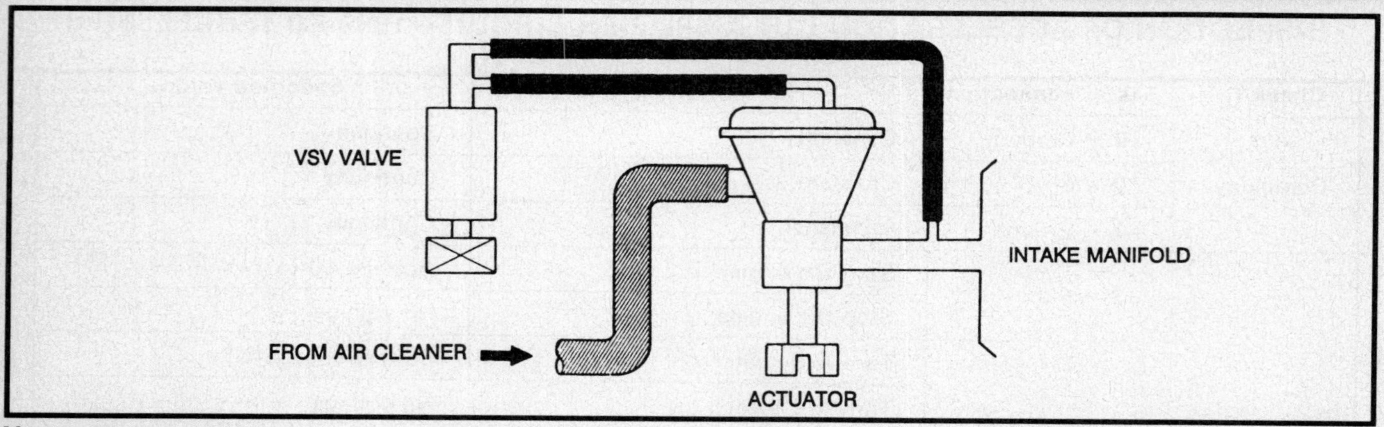
VSV VALVE
INTAKE MANIFOLD
FROM AIR CLEANER
ACTUATOR

Vacuum hose circuit

Vacuum Switching Valve

TESTING

1. Check vacuum circuit continuity in VSV by blowing air into valve. Connect battery voltage to valve blow into pipe A and check that air comes out of pipe B but does not come out C. Disconnect battery voltage blow into pipe A and check that air comes out of filter C but not pipe B.
2. Check valve for short circuit. Check that there is no continuity between each terminal and the body of the valve.
3. Check for open circuit measure resistance between 2 terminals. The specified resistance is 37–44 ohms at 68°F. If resistance valve is not as specified, replace the valve.

In-Vehicle, Ambient and Solar Sensors

TESTING

Check the sensor resistance. If there is a open circuit in the sensor the system will operate at a maximum condition (full hot or cold).

RECIRC/FRESH Control Servo Motor (Push Type)

TESTING

Camry and 1989 Celica

1. With battery voltage applied to terminal **1** and ground at terminal **2** check that the lever moves smoothly from **FRESH** to **RECIRC**.
2. With battery voltage applied to terminal **1** and ground at terminal **3** check that the lever moves smoothly from **RECIRC** to **FRESH**.
3. If operation is not as specified, replace the servo motor. Refer to wiring schematics, as necessary.

Supra

1. With battery voltage applied to terminal **1** and ground at terminal **2** check that the lever moves smoothly. Check for continuity between terminals **3** and **4**.
2. With battery voltage applied to terminal **2** and ground at terminal **1** check that the lever moves smoothly. Check for continuity between terminals **5** and **6**.
3. If operation is not as specified, replace the servo motor. Refer to wiring schematics, as necessary.

Air Mix Control Servo Motor (Push Type)

TESTING

Camry and 1989 Celica

1. With battery voltage applied to terminal **8** and ground at terminal **2** check that the lever moves smoothly from **WARM** to **COOL**.
2. With battery voltage applied to terminal **2** and ground at terminal **8** check that the lever moves smoothly from **COOL** to **WARM**.
3. While operating the servo motor measure the resistance valves at terminals **13** and **15**. The resistance valves from cold to warm will decrease.
4. If operation is not as specified, replace the servo motor. Refer to wiring schematics, as necessary.

Supra

1. With battery voltage applied to terminal **10** and ground at terminal **11** check that the lever moves smoothly from **WARM** to **COOL**.
2. With battery voltage applied to terminal **11** and ground at terminal **10** check that the lever moves smoothly from **COOL** to **WARM**.
3. While operating the servo motor measure the resistance valves at terminals **5** and **6**. The resistance valves from cold to warm will decrease.
4. If operation is not as specified, replace the servo motor. Refer to wiring schematics, as necessary.

Air Vent Mode Control Servo Motor (Push Type)

TESTING

Camry and 1989 Celica

1. With battery voltage applied to terminal **2** and ground at terminal **1** check that the lever moves smoothly from **DEF** to **FACE**.
2. With battery voltage applied to terminal **1** and ground at terminal **2** check that the lever moves smoothly from **FACE** to **DEF**.

3. If operation is not as specified, replace the servo motor. Refer to wiring schematics, as necessary.

Supra

1. With battery voltage applied to terminal **1** and ground at terminal **4** check that the lever moves smoothly.
2. With battery voltage applied to terminal **4** and ground at terminal **1** check that the lever moves smoothly.
3. If operation is not as specified, replace the servo motor. Refer to wiring schematics, as necessary.

Air Inlet Control Servo Motor

TESTING

1990–91 Celica

1. With battery voltage applied to terminal **1** and ground at terminal **3** check that the arm rotates to **FRESH** side.
2. With battery voltage applied to terminal **1** and ground at terminal **2** check that the arm rotates to **RECIRC** side.
3. If operation is not as specified, replace the servo motor. Refer to wiring schematics, as necessary.

Cressida

1. With battery voltage applied to terminal **1** and ground at terminal **3** check that the arm rotates to **FRESH** side.
2. With battery voltage applied to terminal **1** and ground at terminal **2** check that the arm rotates to **RECIRC** side.
3. If operation is not as specified, replace the servo motor. Refer to wiring schematics, as necessary.

Mode Control Servo Motor

TESTING

1990–91 Celica

1. With battery voltage applied to terminal **5** and ground at terminal **6**. Connect a ground lead to each terminal. Check that the arm rotates to each position.
2. If operation is not as specified, replace the servo motor. Refer to wiring schematics, as necessary.

Cressida

1. With battery voltage applied to terminal **1** and ground at terminal **3**. Connect a ground lead to each terminal. Check that the arm rotates to each position.
2. If operation is not as specified, replace the servo motor. Refer to wiring schematics, as necessary.

Air Mix Control Servo Motor

TESTING

1990–91 Celica

1. With battery voltage applied to terminal **2** and ground at terminal **6** check that the lever moves smoothly from **HOT** to **COOL**.
2. With battery voltage applied to terminal **5** and ground at terminal **4** (terminal **2** – 1991 Celica) check that the lever moves smoothly from **COOL** to **HOT**.
3. While operating the servo motor measure the resistance valves at terminals **1** and **3**. The resistance valves from cold to warm will decrease.
4. If operation is not as specified, replace the servo motor. Refer to wiring schematics, as necessary.

Cressida

1. With battery voltage applied to terminal **4** and ground at terminal **5** check that the lever moves smoothly from **HOT** to **COOL**.
2. With battery voltage applied to terminal **5** and ground at terminal **4** check that the lever moves smoothly from **COOL** to **HOT**.
3. If operation is not as specified, replace the servo motor. Refer to wiring schematics, as necessary.

Air Conditioning Control Assembly

TESTING

1990–91 Celica

DIAL TYPE BLOWER SPEED CONTROL SWITCH

1. With battery voltage applied to terminal **A-18** and ground at terminal **A-17** check that the illumination bulb lights. If no light appears check illumination bulb.
2. With battery voltage applied to terminal **A-1** and ground at terminal **A-2** check that the FRESH and RECIRC indicators light alternately each time the air inlet control switch button is pressed. If operation is not as specified, replace the air conditioning control assembly.
3. With battery voltage applied to terminal **A-1** and ground at terminal **A-2** check that each mode buttons lights up when mode buttons are pressed in. If operation is not as specified, replace the air conditioning control assembly.
4. With battery voltage applied to terminal **A-1** and ground at terminal **A-15** push the air conditioning switch button in and check that the indicator lights up. If operation is not as specified, replace the air conditioning control assembly.
5. With battery voltage applied to terminal **A-1** and ground at terminal **A-2** connect a positive lead from the battery to terminal **A-3** and check that the indicators dim. If operation is not as specified, replace the air conditioning control assembly. Refer to wiring schematics, as necessary.

PUSH TYPE BLOWER SPEED CONTROL SWITCH

1. If equipped with automatic air conditioning apply battery voltage to terminal **A-5** and ground at terminal **B-1** or **B-5** check that the FRESH (**B-1**) and RECIRC (**B-5**) indicators light. If operation is not as specified, replace the air conditioning control assembly.
2. If not equipped with automatic air conditioning apply battery voltage to terminal **A-5** and ground at terminal **C-10** check that the FRESH and RECIRC indicators light each time (alternately) the air inlet control switch is pressed. If operation is not as specified, replace the air conditioning control assembly.
3. Apply battery voltage to terminal **A-5** and ground at terminal **C-10** check that each mode buttons lights up when mode buttons (apply ground to these terminals **A-8** FACE, **A-9** B/L, **A-24** FOOT and **B-7** AUTO) are pressed in. If operation is not as specified, replace the air conditioning control assembly.
4. Apply battery voltage to terminal **A-5** and ground at terminal **C-10** check that each blower speed indicators light up when buttons are pressed in. If operation is not as specified, replace the air conditioning control assembly.
5. With battery voltage applied to terminal **A-5** and ground at terminal **C-11** push the air conditioning switch button in and check that the indicator lights up. If operation is not as specified, replace the air conditioning control assembly.
6. With battery voltage applied to terminal **A-5** and ground at terminal **C-10** connect a positive lead from the battery to terminal **A-6** and check that the indicators dim. If operation is not as specified, replace the air conditioning control assembly. Refer to wiring schematics, as necessary.

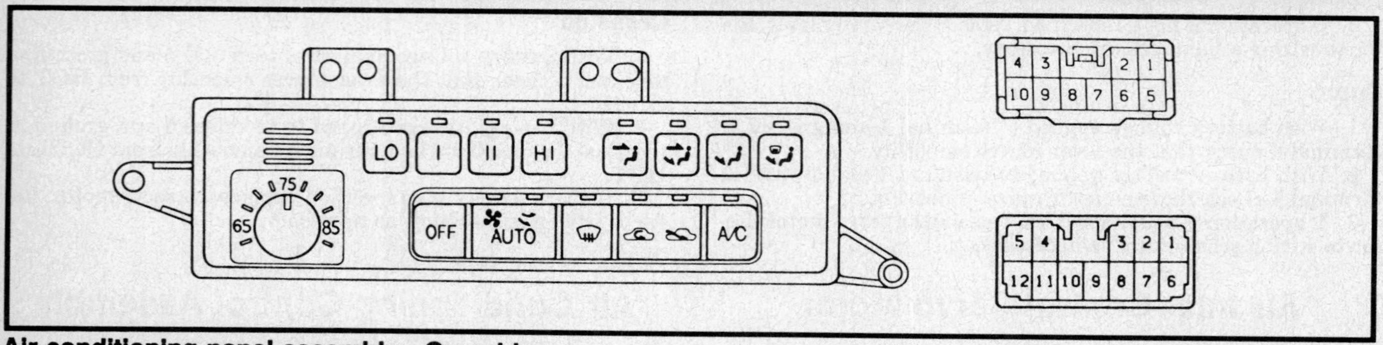
LO
I
II
HI
75
65
85
OFF
AUTO
A/C
4 3 2 1
10 9 8 7 6 5
5 4 3 2 1
12 11 10 9 8 7 6

Air conditioning panel assembly—Cressida

1989–90 Cressida

TEMPERATURE CONTROL KNOB RESISTANCE

1. Check the resistance between terminals **3** and **8** on 10-way connector.
2. If the resistance is not approximately 3000 ohms replace the control panel.
3. Gradually turn the temperature control knob from right side to left side, check.
4. Check that the resistance between terminals **8** and **9** on 10-way connector, increases from 0 to approximately 3000 ohms.
5. If resistance is not within the proper range, replace the control panel.

ILLUMINATION I OPERATION

1. Connect the positive lead from the battery to terminal **12** on 12-way connector.
2. Connect the negative lead from the battery to terminal **11** on 12-way connector.
3. Check that main switch lights.

ILLUMINATION II OPERATION

1. Connect the positive lead from the battery to terminal **1** on the 12-way connector and the negative lead to terminal **1** of the 10-way and terminal **11** of the 12-way connector.
2. Check that the illumination of the sub switch lights up when the blower fan speed control switch or air flow mode control switch is pushed or when the sub switch is opened.
3. If lamp doesn't light check the bulb.

INDICATOR LIGHT OPERATION

1. Connect the positive lead from the battery to terminal **1** of the 12-way connector and negative lead to terminal **1** of the 10-way connector.
2. Check that each indicator light lights when each button is pushed.
3. Check that each bulb is good.
4. If bulbs check good but don't light, replace air conditioning control panel.

BLOWER FAN CONTROLLER

1. Measure the resistance between terminals **4** and **8** on the 10-way connector.
2. Set switch on **LO**, resistance should be approximately 2350 ohms.
3. Set switch on **I**, resistance should be approximately 1880 ohms.
4. Set switch on **II**, resistance should be approximately 1200 ohms.
5. Set switch on **HI**, resistance should be approximately 0 ohms.
6. If resistance is not correct, replace the air conditioning control panel.
7. Check that there is continuity between terminals **1** and **8** of the 10-way connector.
8. With the **FACE** mode switch pushed, check for continuity between terminal **1** of 10-way and terminal **9** of 12-way connectors.
9 With the **BI-LEVEL** mode switch pushed, check for continuity between terminal **1** of 10-way and terminal **3** of 12-way connectors.
10. With the **FOOT** mode switch pushed, check for continuity between terminal **1** and **2** of 10-way connector.
11. With the **FOOT/DEF** mode switch pushed, check for continuity between terminal **1** and **6** of 10-way connectors.
12. With the **AUTO** mode switch pushed, check for continuity between terminal **1** of 10-way and terminal **10** of 12-way connectors.
13. With the blower switch **OFF**, check for no continuity between terminal **4** and **8** of 10-way and terminal.
14. With the blower switch **OFF**, connect the positive lead from battery to terminal **1** of 12-way connector and negative lead to terminal **1** of 10-way connector.
15. Check that the fan speed switch light doesn't light when switch is in **OFF** position.

MODE SWITCH

1. Check that there is no continuity between terminals **1** and **10** of the 10-way connector when the **AUTO** switch is pushed.
2. Connect the positive lead from the battery to terminal **1** of the 12-way connector and negative lead to terminal **1** of the 10-way connector.
3. Check that the 2 indicator lights auto switch light up when the **AUTO** switch is pushed.
4. If operation is not as specified, replace air conditioning control panel.

DEFOGGER MODE SWITCH

1. Check that there is continuity between terminals **1** and **5** of the 10-way connector when the switch is pushed **ON**.
2. Connect the positive lead from the battery to terminal **1** of the 12-way connector and the negative lead to terminal **1** of the 10-way connector.
3. Check that the indicator light of the defogger mode switch lights, when the switch is pushed **ON**.

AIR INLET CONTROL SWITCH

1. Check that there is continuity between terminal **1** of the 10-way connector and terminal **9** of the 12-way connector.
2. Connect the positive lead from the battery to terminal **1** of the 12-way connector and the negative lead to terminal **1** of the 10-way connector.
3. Check that the indicator light glows, when the switch is pushed **ON**.

AIR CONDITIONING SWITCH

1. Check that there is continuity between terminal **1** of the 10-way connector and terminal **2** of the 12-way connector and check that there is continuity between terminal **7** and **8** of the 12-way connector, when the air conditioning switch is pushed **ON**.
2. Connect the positive lead from the battery to terminal **6** of the 12-way connector and negative lead to terminal **1** of the 10-way connector.
3. Check that the indicator light lights, when the air conditioning switch is pushed **ON**.

OPEN/CLOSED SWITCH

1. Connect the positive lead from the battery to terminal **1** of the 12-way and negative to terminal **1** of the 10-way connector.
2. Check the main switch is slid out smoothly when the **OPEN/CLOSED** switch is pushed.
4. If operation is not as specified, replace air conditioning control panel.

1991 Cressida

ILLUMINATIONS

1. Connect the positive lead from the battery to terminal **5** on the 12-way connector and the negative lead to terminal **12** of the 12-way connector.
2. Check that the illuminations light up. If not test bulb.

INDICATOR LIGHTS

1. Connect the positive lead from the battery to terminal **5** of the 10-way connector and negative lead to terminal **1** of the 10-wayconnector.
2. Check that each indicator light glows when each button is pushed.
3. Check that each bulb is good.
4. If bulbs check good but don't light, replace air conditioning control panel.

BLOWER SPEED CONTROL SWITCH

1. Measure the resistance between terminals **4** and **6** on the 12-way connector.
2. Set switch on **LO**, resistance should be approximately 300 ohms.
3. Set switch on **I**, resistance should be approximately 900 ohms.
4. Set switch on **II**, resistance should be approximately 1700 ohms.
5. Set switch on **HI**, resistance should be approximately 3000 ohms.
6. Set switch on **OFF**, resistance should be approximately 0 ohms.
7. If resistance is not correct, replace the air conditioning control panel.
8. Connect the test leads so the current from the ohmmeter can flow from terminal **1** of the 10-way connector to terminal **10** of the 12-way connector. Then check that there is continuity between the terminals when any buttton switch is pushed.

TEMPERATURE CONTROL SWITCH

1. Check the resistance between terminals **6** and **11** on 12-way connector.
2. If the resistance is not approximately 3000 ohms, replace the control panel.
3. Gradually, turn the temperature control knob from right side to left side, check.
4. Check that the resistance between terminals **7** and **11** on 12-way connector, increases from 0 to approximately 3000 ohms.
5. If resistance is not within the proper range, replace the control panel.

AIR FLOW MODE CONTROL SWITCH

1. With the **FACE** mode switch pushed, check for continuity between terminal **1** of 10-way and terminal **8** of 12-way connectors.
2. With the **BI-LEVEL** mode switch pushed, check for continuity between terminal **1** of 10-way and terminal **1** of 12-way connectors.
3. With the **FOOT** mode switch pushed, check for continuity between terminal **1** and **2** of 10-way connector.
4. With the **FOOT/DEF** mode switch pushed, check for continuity between terminal **1** and **7** of 10-way connectors.
5. With the **DEF** mode switch pushed, check for continuity between terminal **1** of 10-way and terminal **8** of 10-way connectors.

AIR INLET CONTROL SWITCH

1. With the switch in the **FRESH** position, check for continuity between terminal **1** of 10-way and terminal **6** of 10-way connectors.
2. With the switch in the **RECIRC** position, check for continuity between terminal **1** of 10-way and terminal **2** of 12-way connectors.
3. If continuity is not as specified replace the air conditioning control panel assembly.

AIR CONDITIONING SWITCH

1. Check that there is continuity between terminal **1** of the 10-way connector and terminal **9** of the 10-way connector.
2. Check that there is continuity between terminal **4** and **10** of the 10-way connector, when the air conditioning switch is pushed **ON**.

1991 MR2

1. With battery voltage applied to terminal **A-18** and ground at terminal **A-8** check that the illumination bulb lights. If no light appears check illumination bulb.
2. With battery voltage applied to terminal **A-10** and ground at terminal **A-15** check that the FRESH and RECIRC indicators light alternately each time the air inlet control switch button is pressed. Then connect a positive lead from the battery to terminal **A-3** and check that the indicator dims. If operation is not as specified, replace the air conditioning control assembly.
3. With battery voltage applied to terminal **A-10** and ground at terminal **A-15** check that each mode buttons lights up when mode buttons are pressed in. Then connect a positive lead from the battery to terminal **A-3** and check that the indicator dims. If operation is not as specified, replace the air conditioning control assembly.
4. With battery voltage applied to terminal **C-1** and ground at terminal **C-4** check that the illumination lights up. If illumination does not light up test bulb.
5. With battery voltage applied to terminal **C-5** and ground at terminal **C-2** push air conditioning switch button in and check that the indicator lights. Then connect battery voltage to terminal **C-3** and check that the indicators dim. If operation is not as specified, replace the air conditioning switch.

Supra

1. Measure output voltage by connecting battery voltage to terminal **1** and **2** and ground to terminal **10**.
2. Connect the negative lead from the voltmeter to terminal **10** and the positive lead to each terminal with the indicated resistance.
3. Check that the output voltage is as shown in the chart. Confirm that each indicator light is operational when the button is pushed.

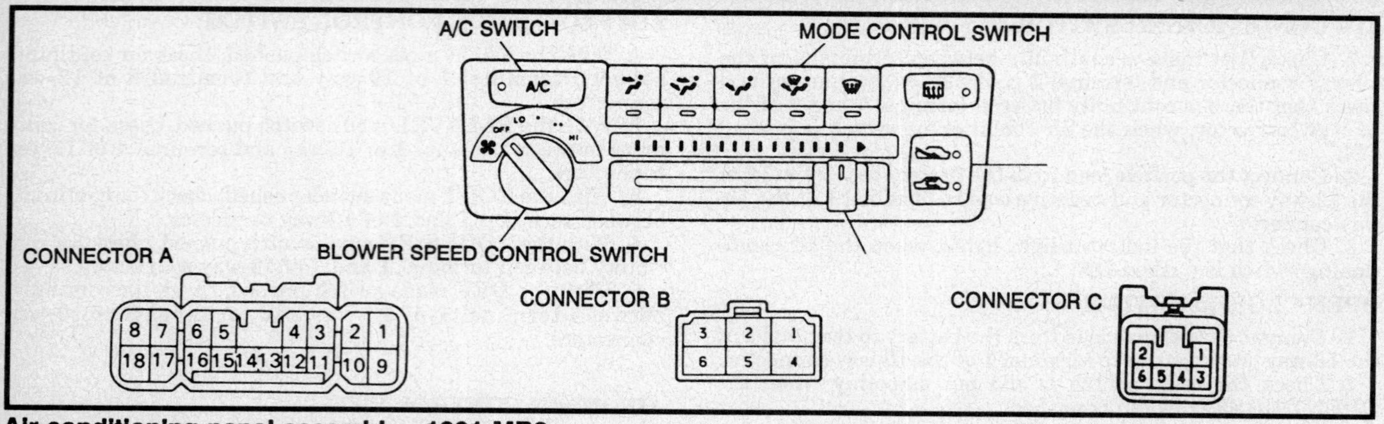
A/C SWITCH
MODE CONTROL SWITCH
A/C
OFF
LO
HI
CONNECTOR A
BLOWER SPEED CONTROL SWITCH
CONNECTOR B
CONNECTOR C
8 7 6 5 4 3 2 1
18 17 16 15 14 13 12 11 10 9
3 2 1
6 5 4
2 1
6 5 4 3

Air conditioning panel assembly—1991 MR2

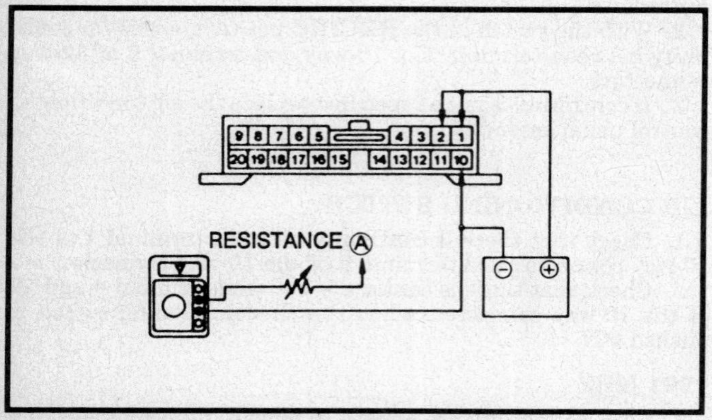
9 8 7 6 5 4 3 2 1
20 19 18 17 16 15 14 13 12 11 10
RESISTANCE Ⓐ

Air conditioning panel assembly—Supra

Heater Blower Switch

TESTING

1. Disconnect electrical connector of switch.
2. Contact the 2 leads of an ohmmeter to each of the check points.
3. Check continuity of switch. Replace as necessary.

Heater Relay

TESTING

Camry, 1989 Celica, 1989 MR2 and 1989–90 Tercel

RELAY CONTINUITY INSPECTION

1. Using a suitable ohmmeter, check that there is continuity between terminals **1** and **3**.
2. Check that there is continuity between terminals **2** and **4**.
3. Check that there is continuity between terminals **4** and **5**.
4. If there is no continuity at the specified terminals, replace the relay. Refer to wiring schematics, as necessary.

RELAY OPERATIONS INSPECTION

1. Apply battery voltage across terminals **1** and **3** of the relay connector.
2. Using a suitable ohmmeter, check that there is continuity between terminals **4** and **5**.
3. Check that there is no continuity (open circuit) between terminals **2** and **4**.
4. If the operation of the relay is not as just described, replace the relay. Refer to wiring schematics, as necessary.

Heater Blower Resistor

TESTING

Camry and 1989 Celica

LEVER TYPE

1. Use an ohmmeter to check that there is continuity between terminals **1** and **3** of of the resistor connector.
2. If there is no continuity, replace the resistor.

PUSH TYPE

1. Use an ohmmeter to check that there is continuity between terminals **5** and **6** of of the resistor connector.
2. If there is no continuity, replace the resistor.

1989 MR2 and 1989–90 Tercel

1. Use an ohmmeter to check that there is continuity between terminals **2** and **3** of the resistor connector.
2. If there is no continuity, replace the resistor.

Blower Speed Control Relay

TESTING

Camry and 1989 Celica

1. Check that there is continuity between terminals **5** and **7**. Check to see there is no continuity between terminals **3** and **4**.
2. With battery voltage applied between terminals **5** and **7**, check that there is continuity between terminals **3** and **4**.
3. Check there is continuity between terminals **5** and **8**. Check to see there is no continuity between terminals **3** and **2**.
4. With battery voltage applied between terminals **5** and **8**, check that there is continuity between terminals **3** and **2**.
5. Check that there is continuity between terminals **5** and **6**. Check to see there is no continuity between terminals **3** and **1**.
6. With battery voltage applied between terminals **5** and **6**, check that there is continuity between terminals **3** and **1**.
7. If any operation is not as specified, replace the relay. Refer to wiring schematics, as necessary.

Control Button				Resistance (Ω)	Terminal Ⓐ	Voltage (V)
A/C	FRS/REC	Mode Control	Blower Speed			
OFF	FRS	AUTO	AUTO	620	14	12 or more
					15	1.5 or less
					17	12 or more
					18	1.0 or less
					8	12 or more
					7	1 or less
					19	12 or more
					16	
					6	
				70	12	1.5 or less
					3	1 or less
					13	12 or more
					4	12 or more
ON				620	14	1 or less
	REC				17	1.5 or less
					15	12 or more
			OFF	70	12	
					3	
			LO		12	1 or less
			M		13	
			HI		4	
					13	12 or more
		DEF		620	6	1 or less
					18	12 or more
					7	
		F/D			16	1 or less
					6	12 or more
		FOOT			19	1 or less
					16	12 or more
		BI-LEVEL			7	1 or less
					19	12 or more
		FACE			8	1 or less
					7	12 or more
		AUTO	AUTO		18	1 or less
					7	1 or less

Air conditioning panel assembly—Supra

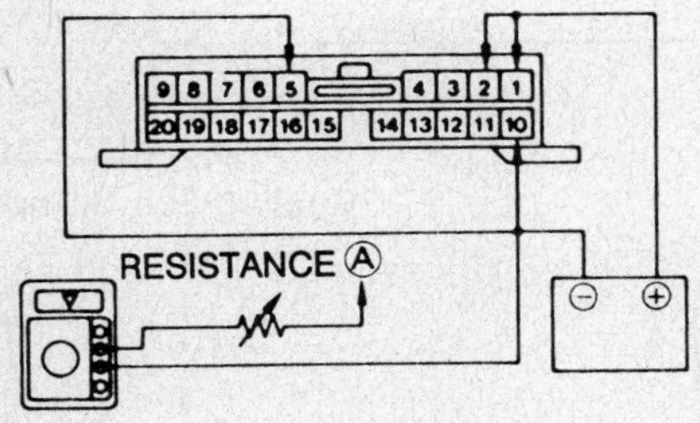
9
8
7
6
5
4
3
2
1
20
19
18
17
16
15
14
13
12
11
10
RESISTANCE Ⓐ
⊖
⊕

Air conditioning panel assembly—Supra cont'd

Control Button				Resistance (Ω)	Terminal Ⓐ	Voltage (V)
A/C	FRS/REC	Mode Control	Blower Speed			
ON	REC	AUTO	AUTO	620	8	1 or less
					7	12 or more
OFF					19	1 or less
					8	12 or more

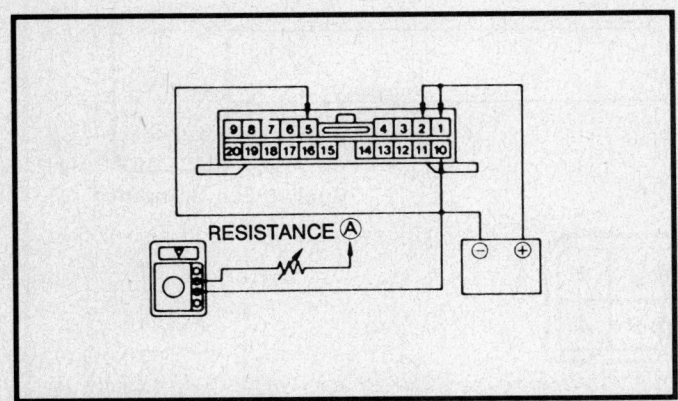

Air conditioning panel assembly—Supra cont'd

WIRING SCHEMATICS

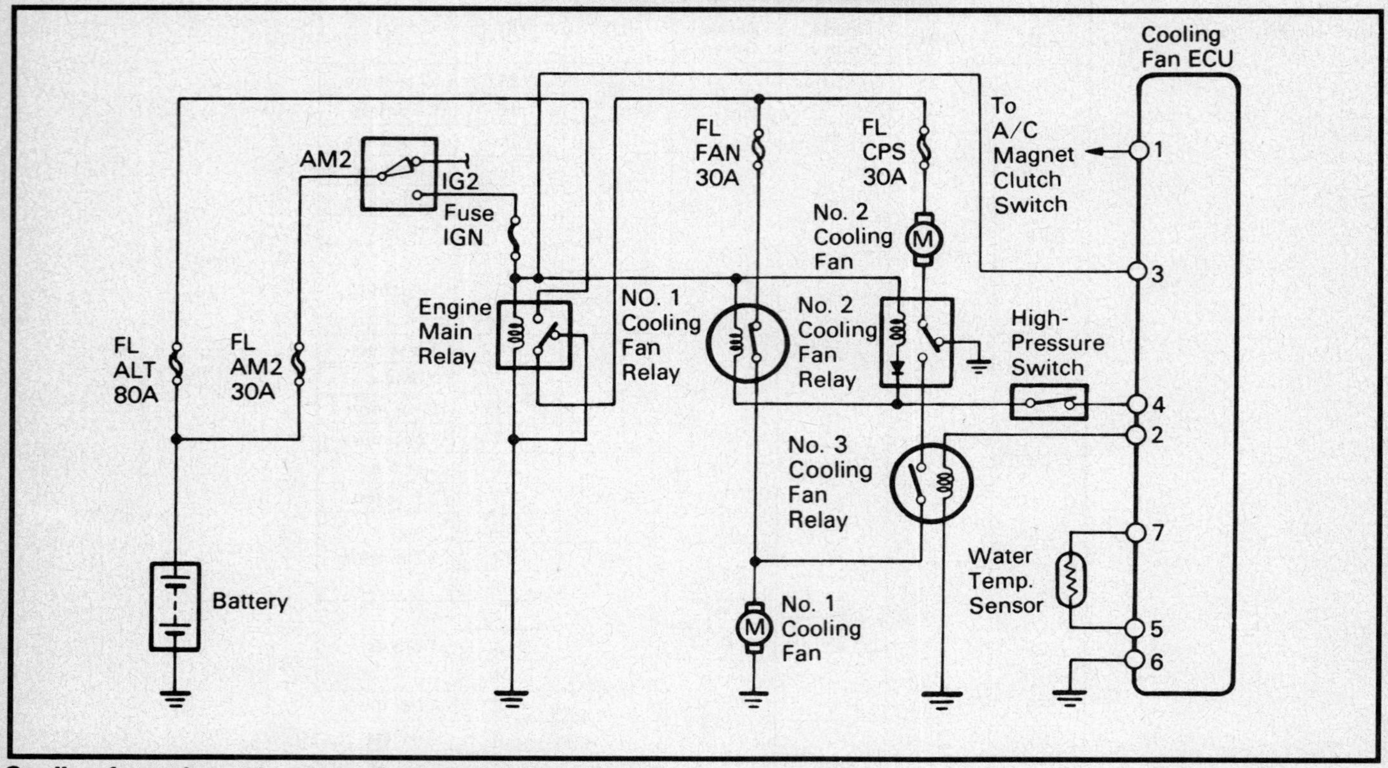
Cooling Fan ECU
To A/C Magnet Clutch Switch
FL FAN 30A
FL CPS 30A
AM2
IG2
Fuse IGN
No. 2 Cooling Fan
Engine Main Relay
NO. 1 Cooling Fan Relay
No. 2 Cooling Fan Relay
High-Pressure Switch
FL ALT 80A
FL AM2 30A
No. 3 Cooling Fan Relay
Water Temp. Sensor
Battery
No. 1 Cooling Fan
1
3
4
2
7
5
6

Cooling fan schematic—1991 Camry 2VZ-FE engine

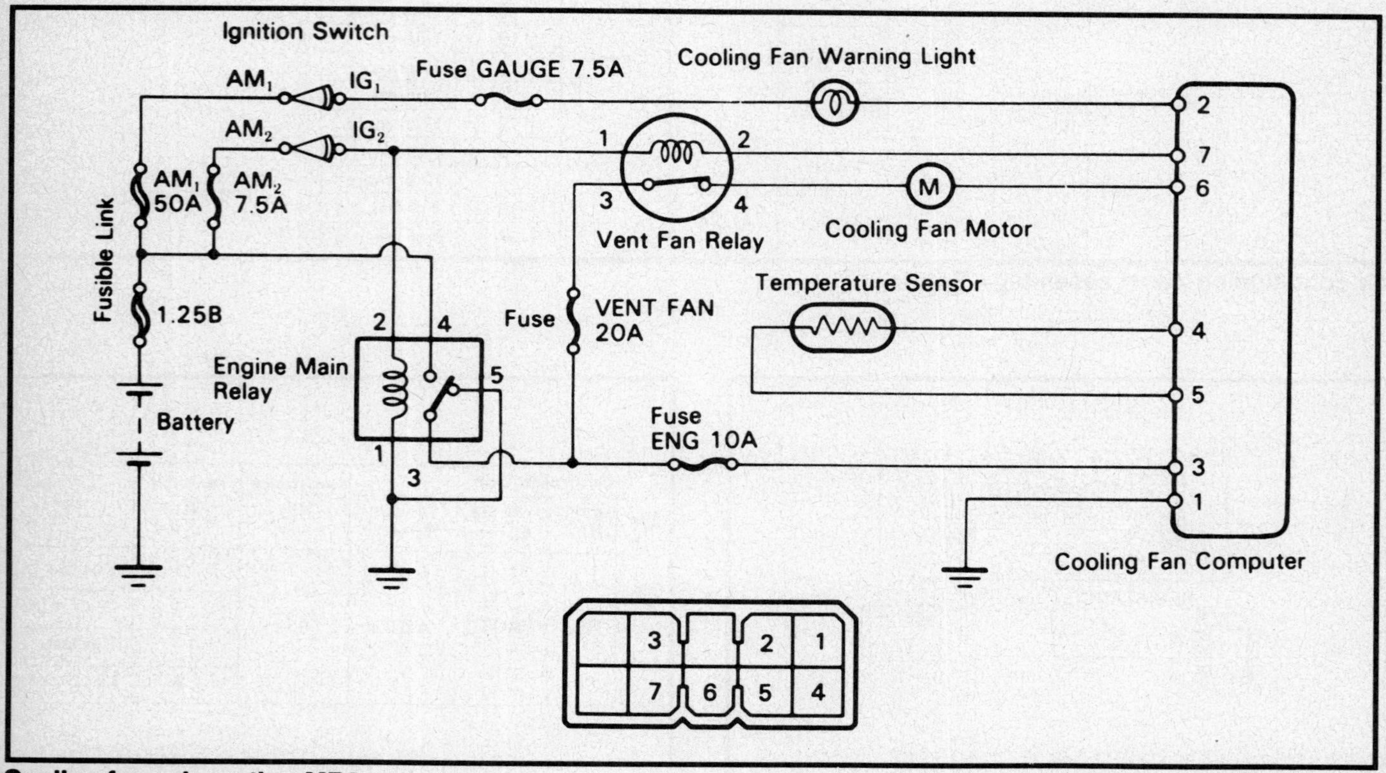
Ignition Switch
AM1
IG1
AM2
IG2
Fuse GAUGE 7.5A
Cooling Fan Warning Light
Fusible Link
AM1 50A
AM2 7.5A
1.25B
Battery
Vent Fan Relay
Cooling Fan Motor
Temperature Sensor
Fuse
VENT FAN 20A
Engine Main Relay
Fuse ENG 10A
Cooling Fan Computer
3
2
1
7
6
5
4

Cooling fan schematic—MR2

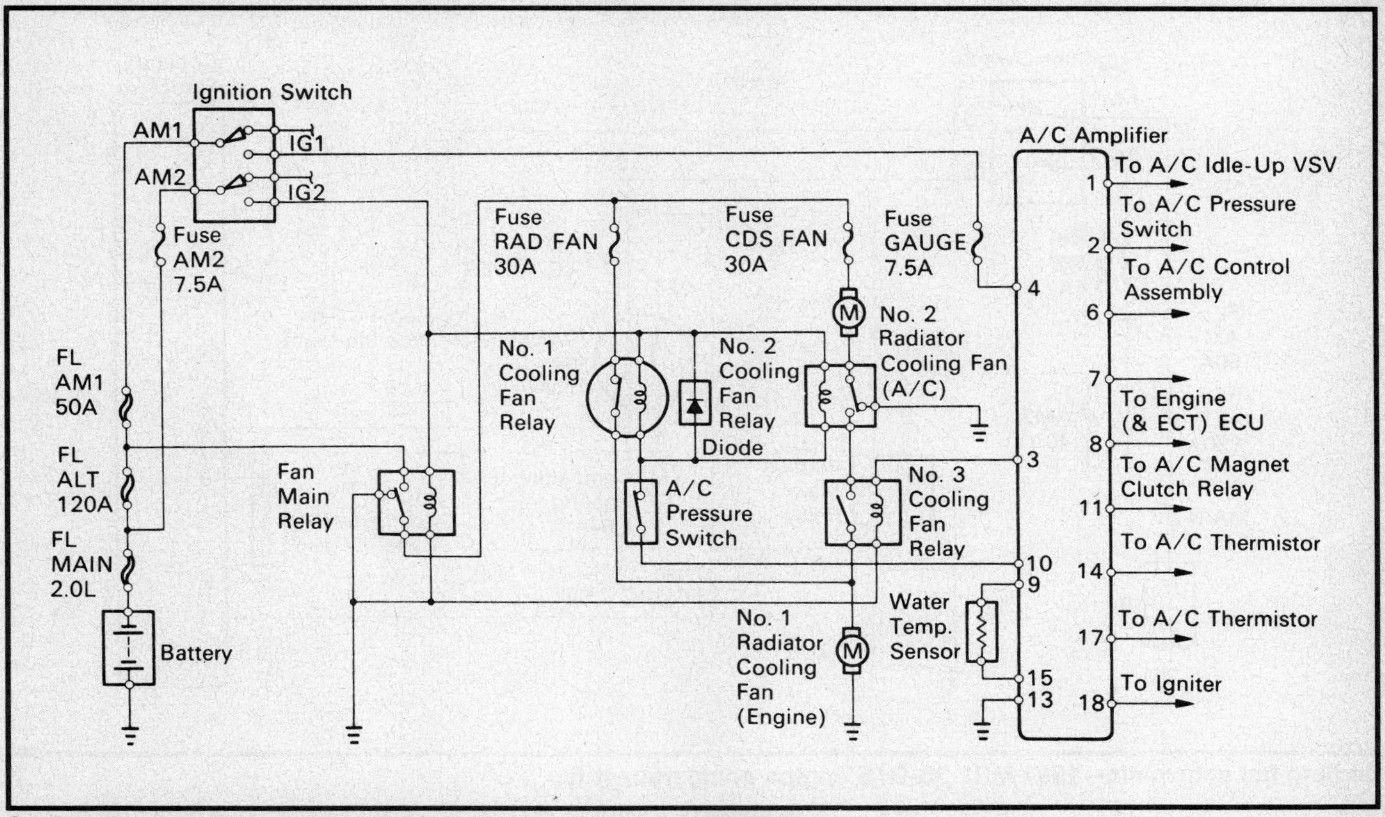
Ignition Switch
AM1
IG1
AM2
IG2
Fuse AM2 7.5A
FL AM1 50A
FL ALT 120A
FL MAIN 2.0L
Battery
Fan Main Relay
Fuse RAD FAN 30A
No. 1 Cooling Fan Relay
Fuse CDS FAN 30A
No. 2 Cooling Fan Relay
Diode
A/C Pressure Switch
Fuse GAUGE 7.5A
No. 2 Radiator Cooling Fan (A/C)
No. 3 Cooling Fan Relay
No. 1 Radiator Cooling Fan (Engine)
Water Temp. Sensor
A/C Amplifier
To A/C Idle-Up VSV
To A/C Pressure Switch
To A/C Control Assembly
To Engine (& ECT) ECU
To A/C Magnet Clutch Relay
To A/C Thermistor
To A/C Thermistor
To Igniter

Cooling fan schematic—1991 MR2 radiator fan with air conditioning

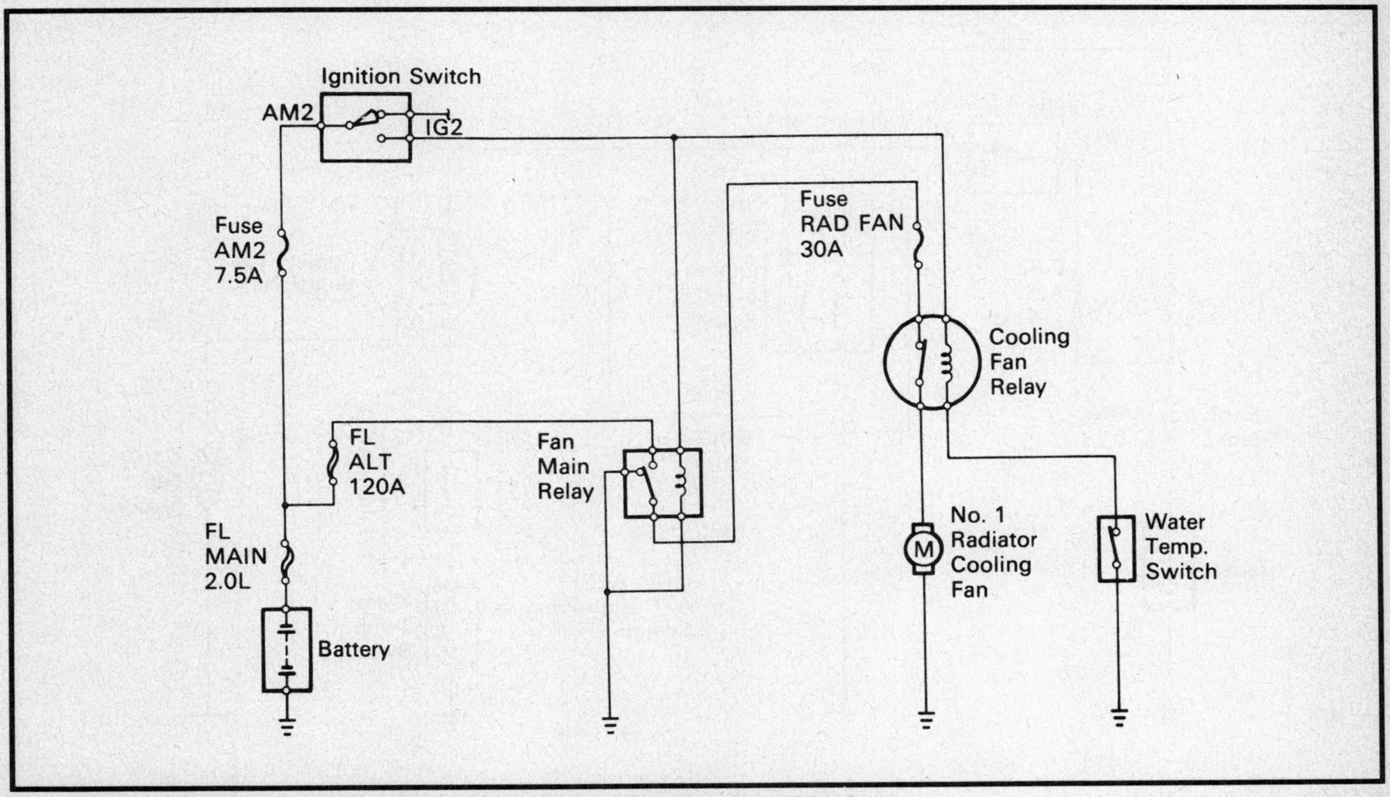
Ignition Switch
AM2
IG2
Fuse AM2 7.5A
FL ALT 120A
FL MAIN 2.0L
Battery
Fan Main Relay
Fuse RAD FAN 30A
Cooling Fan Relay
No. 1 Radiator Cooling Fan
Water Temp. Switch

Cooling fan schematic—1991 MR2 radiator fan without air conditioning

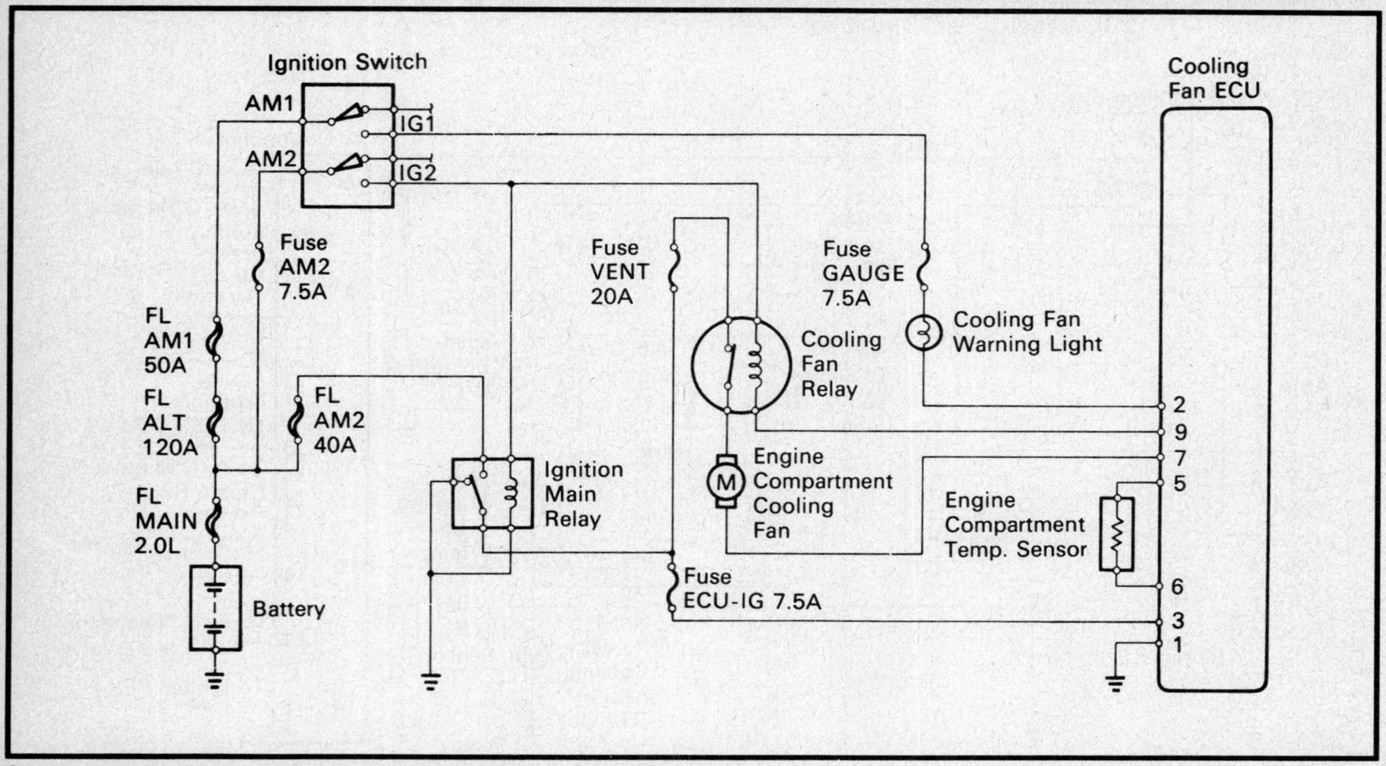
Ignition Switch
AM1
IG1
AM2
IG2
Cooling Fan ECU
Fuse AM2 7.5A
Fuse VENT 20A
Fuse GAUGE 7.5A
FL AM1 50A
Cooling Fan Warning Light
Cooling Fan Relay
FL ALT 120A
FL AM2 40A
2
9
7
5
Ignition Main Relay
Engine Compartment Cooling Fan
FL MAIN 2.0L
Engine Compartment Temp. Sensor
6
Fuse ECU-IG 7.5A
3
1
Battery

Cooling fan schematic—1991 MR2 3S-GTE engine compartment fan

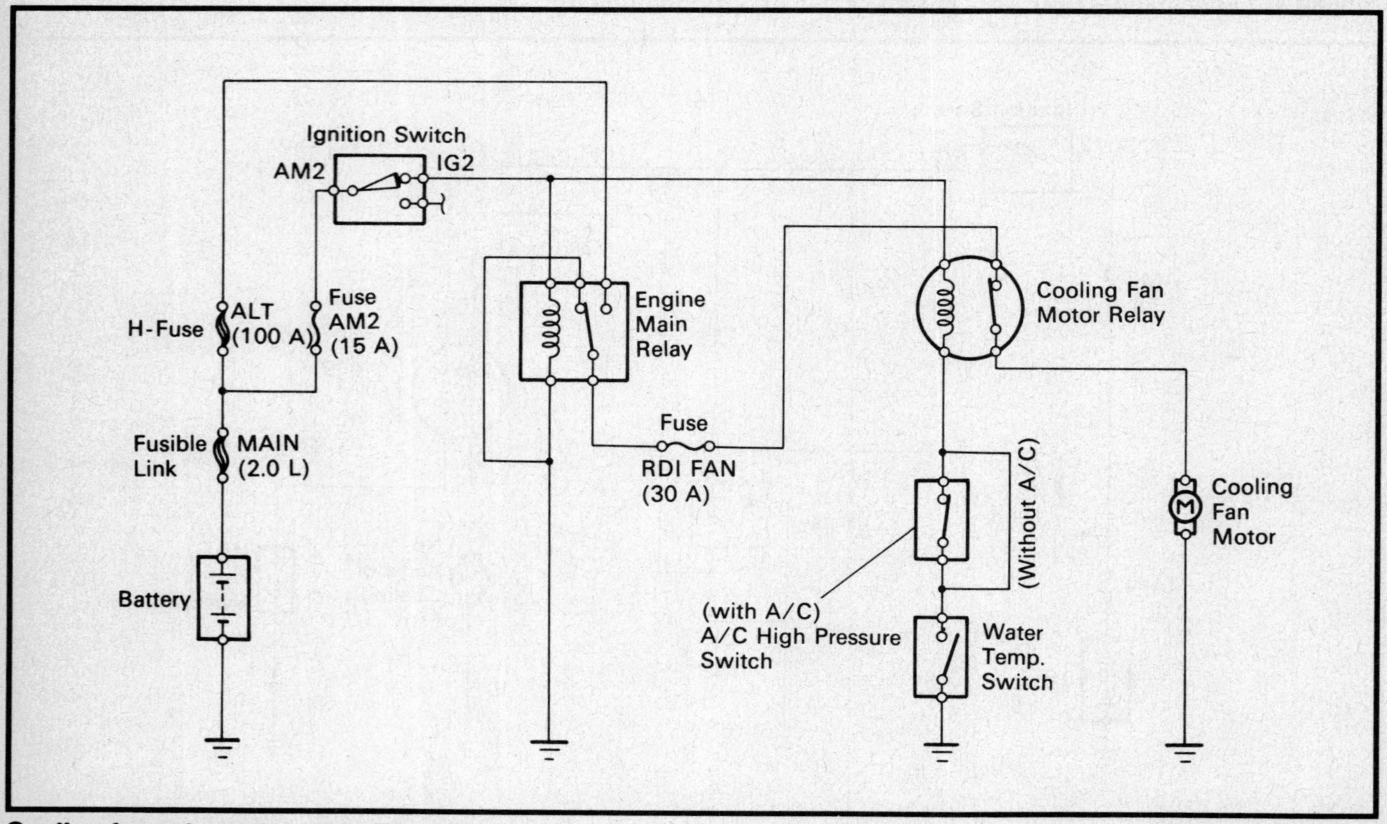
Ignition Switch
AM2
IG2
Engine Main Relay
Cooling Fan Motor Relay
H-Fuse
ALT (100 A)
Fuse AM2 (15 A)
Fuse
RDI FAN (30 A)
Fusible Link
MAIN (2.0 L)
(Without A/C)
Cooling Fan Motor
Battery
(with A/C) A/C High Pressure Switch
Water Temp. Switch

Cooling fan schematic—1991 Tercel

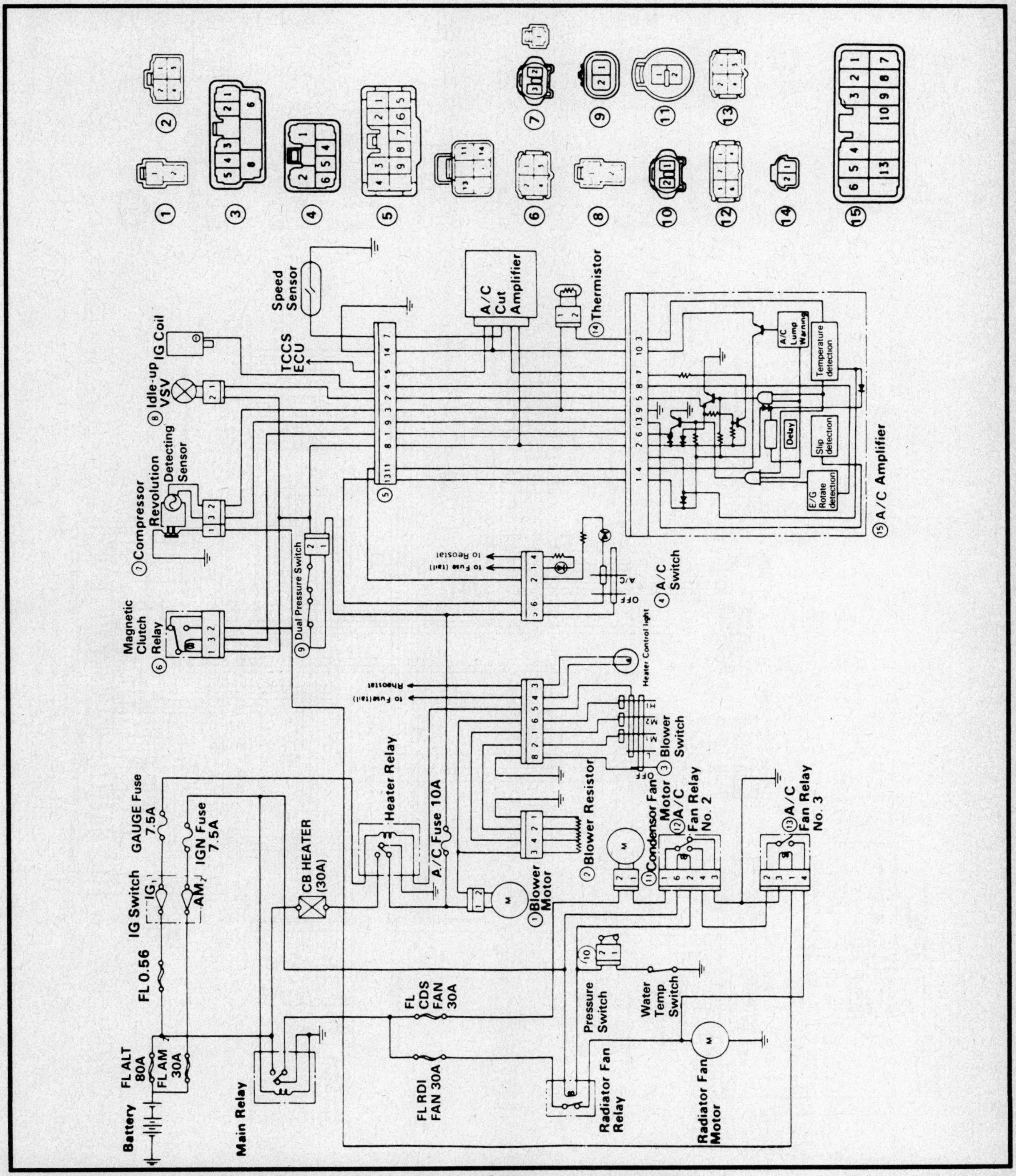
Battery
FL ALT 80A
FL AM 30A
Main Relay
FL 0.56
IG Switch
IG1
AM2
GAUGE Fuse 7.5A
IGN Fuse 7.5A
CB HEATER (30A)
Heater Relay
A/C Fuse 10A
Blower Motor
Blower Resistor
Blower Switch
Heater Control light
to Fuse (tail)
Rheostat
Magnetic Clutch Relay
Dual Pressure Switch
Compressor
Revolution Detecting Sensor
Idle-up VSV
IG Coil
TCCS ECU
Speed Sensor
A/C Cut Amplifier
Thermistor
A/C Switch
A/C Amplifier
A/C Lamp Warning
Temperature detection
Delay
Slip detection
E/G Rotate detection
Condensor Fan Motor
A/C Fan Relay No. 2
A/C Fan Relay No. 3
FL CDS FAN 30A
FL RDI FAN 30A
Pressure Switch
Water Temp Switch
Radiator Fan Relay
Radiator Fan Motor

Air conditioning wiring schematic—1989–90 Camry 3S-FE engine (lever type)

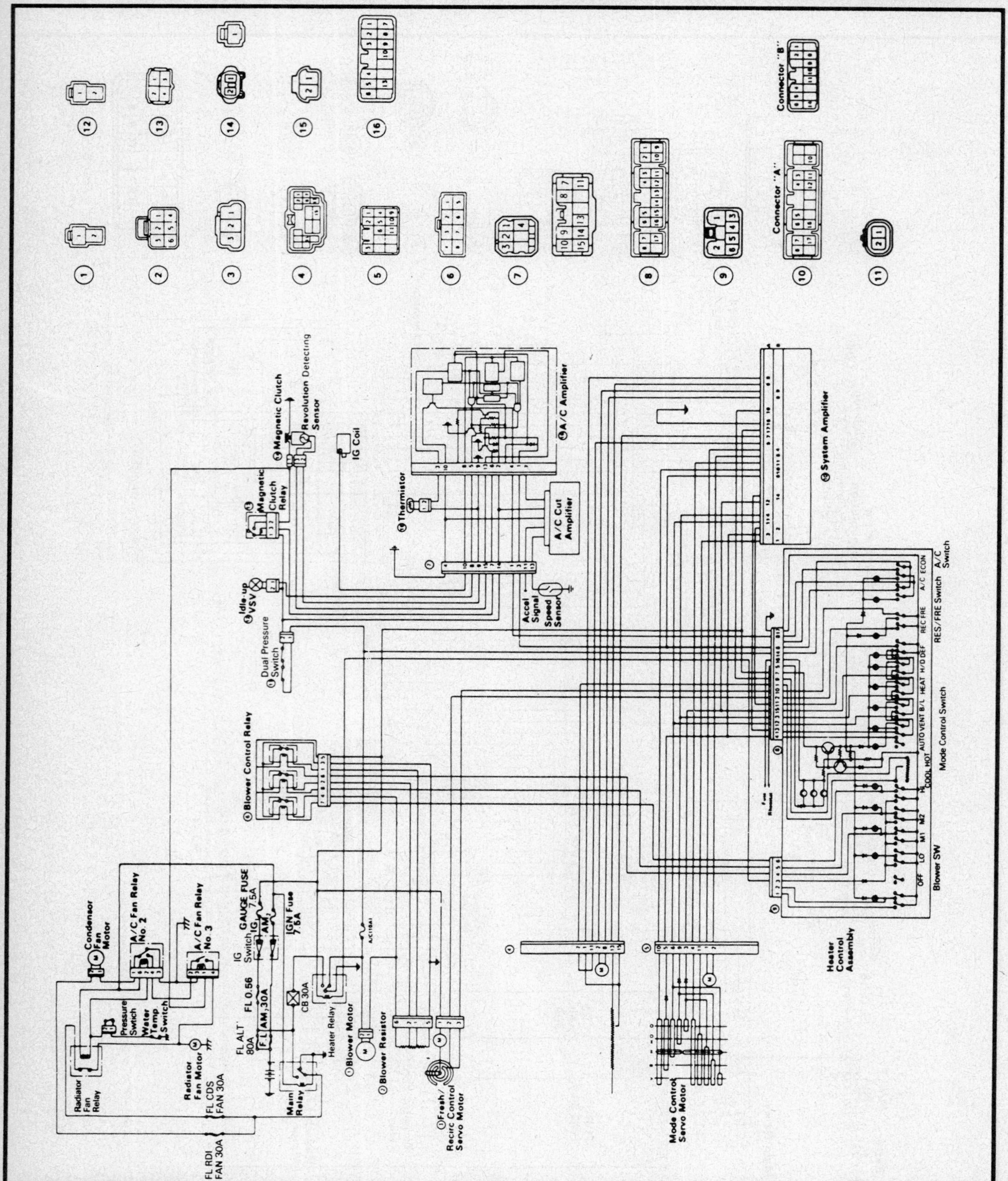
Connector "A"
Connector "B"
Magnetic Clutch
Revolution Detecting Sensor
IG Coil
A/C Amplifier
System Amplifier
Thermistor
Magnetic Clutch Relay
A/C Cut Amplifier
Idle-up VSV
Accel Signal
Speed Sensor
Dual Pressure Switch
Blower Control Relay
Heater Control Assembly
Blower SW
Mode Control Switch
RES/FRE Switch
A/C Switch
Condenser Fan Motor
A/C Fan Relay No. 2
A/C Fan Relay No. 3
GAUGE FUSE 7.5A
IGN Fuse 7.5A
IG Switch
FL 0.56
AM 30A
CB 30A
FL ALT 80A
Pressure Switch
Water Temp Switch
Radiator Fan Relay
Radiator Fan Motor
FL CDS FAN 30A
FL RDI FAN 30A
Main Relay
Heater Relay
Blower Motor
Blower Resistor
Fresh/Recirc Control Servo Motor
Mode Control Servo Motor

Air conditioning wiring schematic—1989–90 Camry 3S-FE engine (push type)

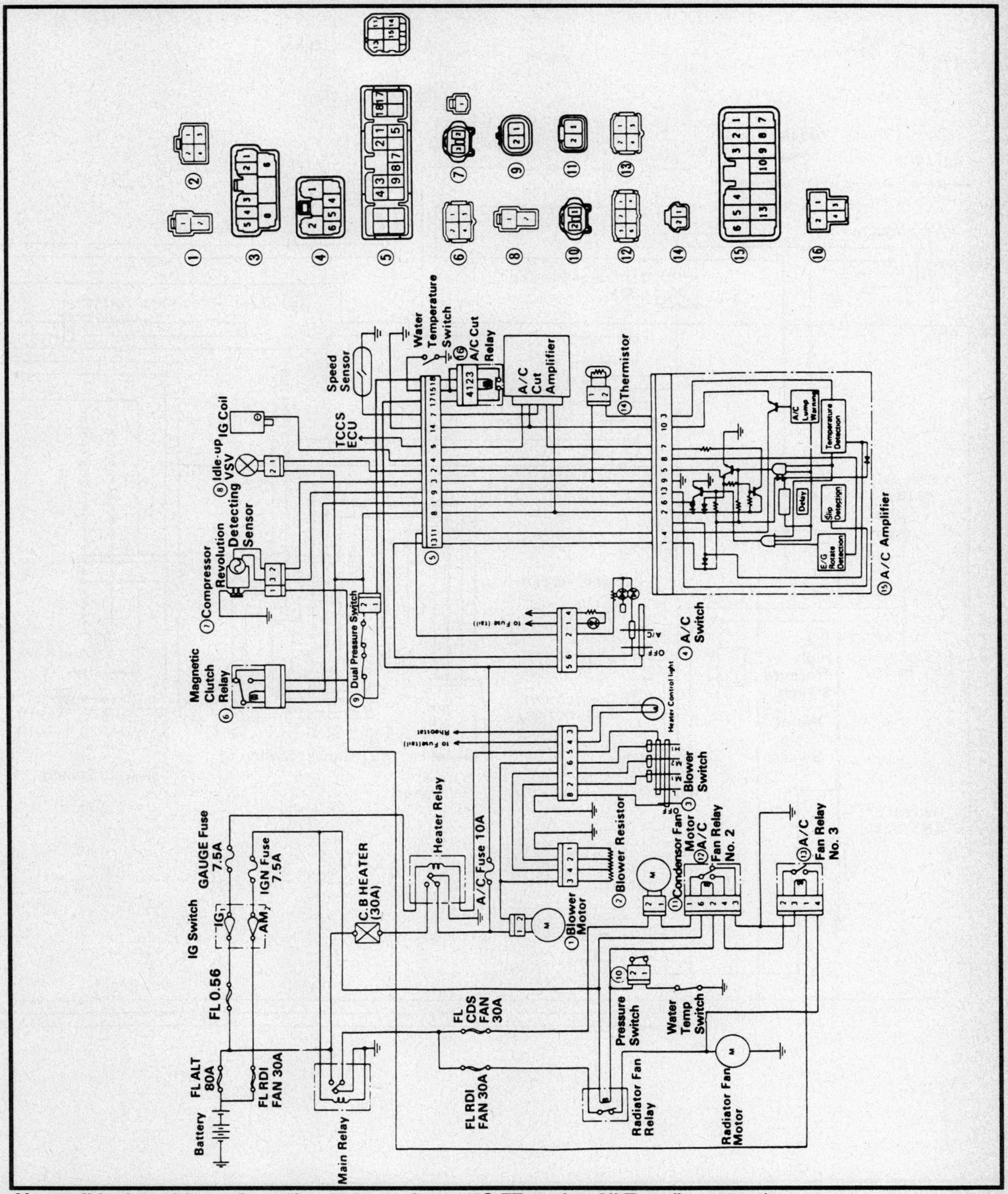
Battery
FL ALT 80A
FL RDI FAN 30A
Main Relay
FL 0.56
IG Switch
GAUGE Fuse 7.5A
IGN Fuse 7.5A
C.B HEATER (30A)
Heater Relay
A/C Fuse 10A
Blower Motor
Blower Resistor
Blower Switch
Condensor Fan Motor
A/C Fan Relay No. 2
A/C Fan Relay No. 3
FL CDS FAN 30A
FL RDI FAN 30A
Radiator Fan Relay
Pressure Switch
Water Temp Switch
Radiator Fan Motor
Magnetic Clutch Relay
Dual Pressure Switch
Compressor
Revolution Detecting Sensor
Idle-up VSV
IG Coil
TCCS ECU
Speed Sensor
Water Temperature Switch
A/C Cut Relay
A/C Cut Amplifier
Thermistor
A/C Switch
A/C Amplifier
Heater Control light
To Fuse (tail)
Rheostat
Delay
Slip Detection
Temperature Detection
E/G Rotate Detection
A/C Lamp Warning

Air conditioning wiring schematic—1989–90 Camry 3S-FE engine All-Trac (lever type)

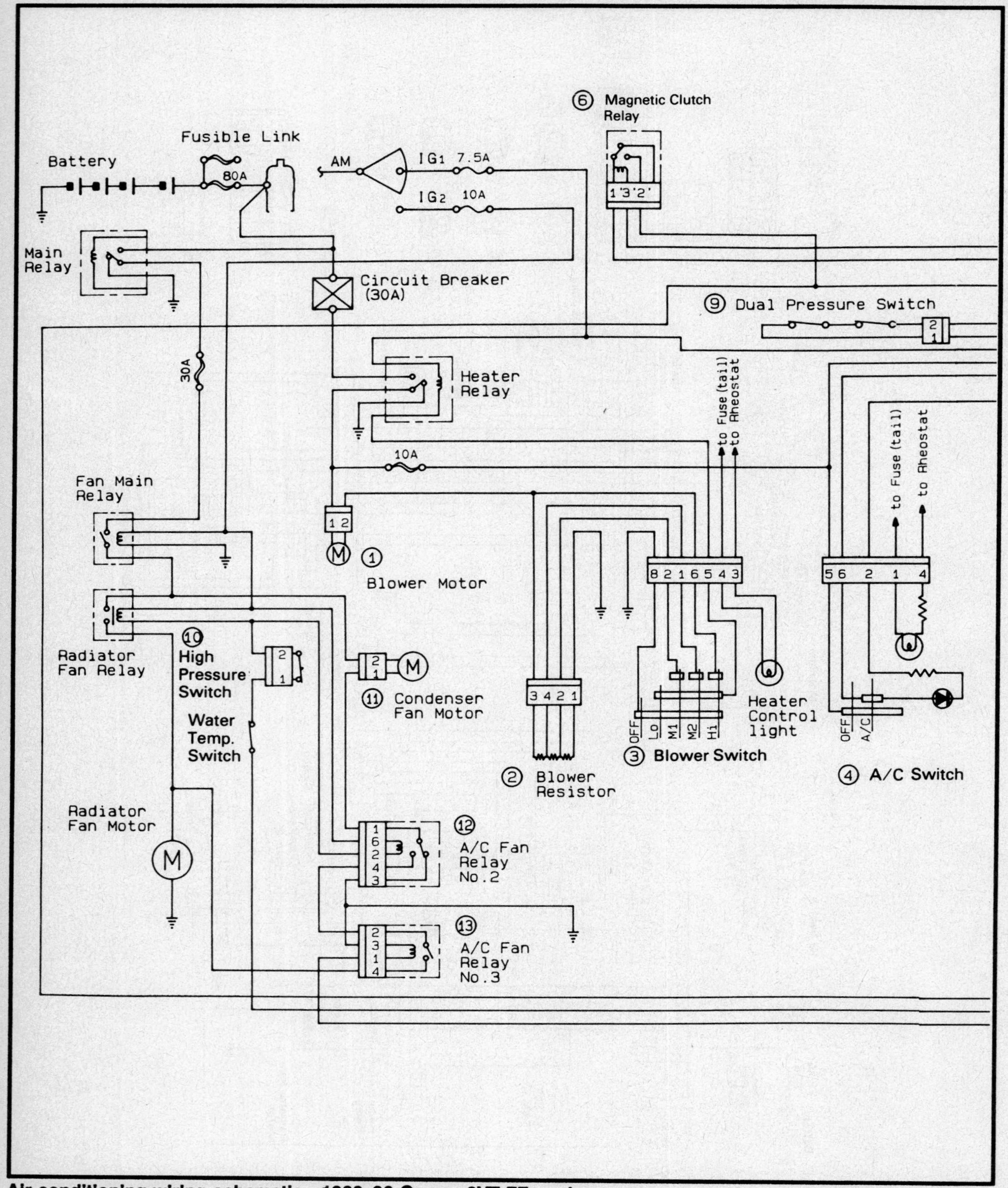
Battery
Fusible Link
80A
AM
IG1 7.5A
IG2 10A
⑥ Magnetic Clutch Relay
Main Relay
Circuit Breaker (30A)
⑨ Dual Pressure Switch
30A
Heater Relay
to Fuse (tail)
to Rheostat
10A
Fan Main Relay
① Blower Motor
Radiator Fan Relay
⑩ High Pressure Switch
⑪ Condenser Fan Motor
Water Temp. Switch
Heater Control light
OFF Lo M1 M2 Hi
③ Blower Switch
OFF A/C
④ A/C Switch
② Blower Resistor
Radiator Fan Motor
⑫ A/C Fan Relay No.2
⑬ A/C Fan Relay No.3

Air conditioning wiring schematic—1989–90 Camry 2VZ-FE engine

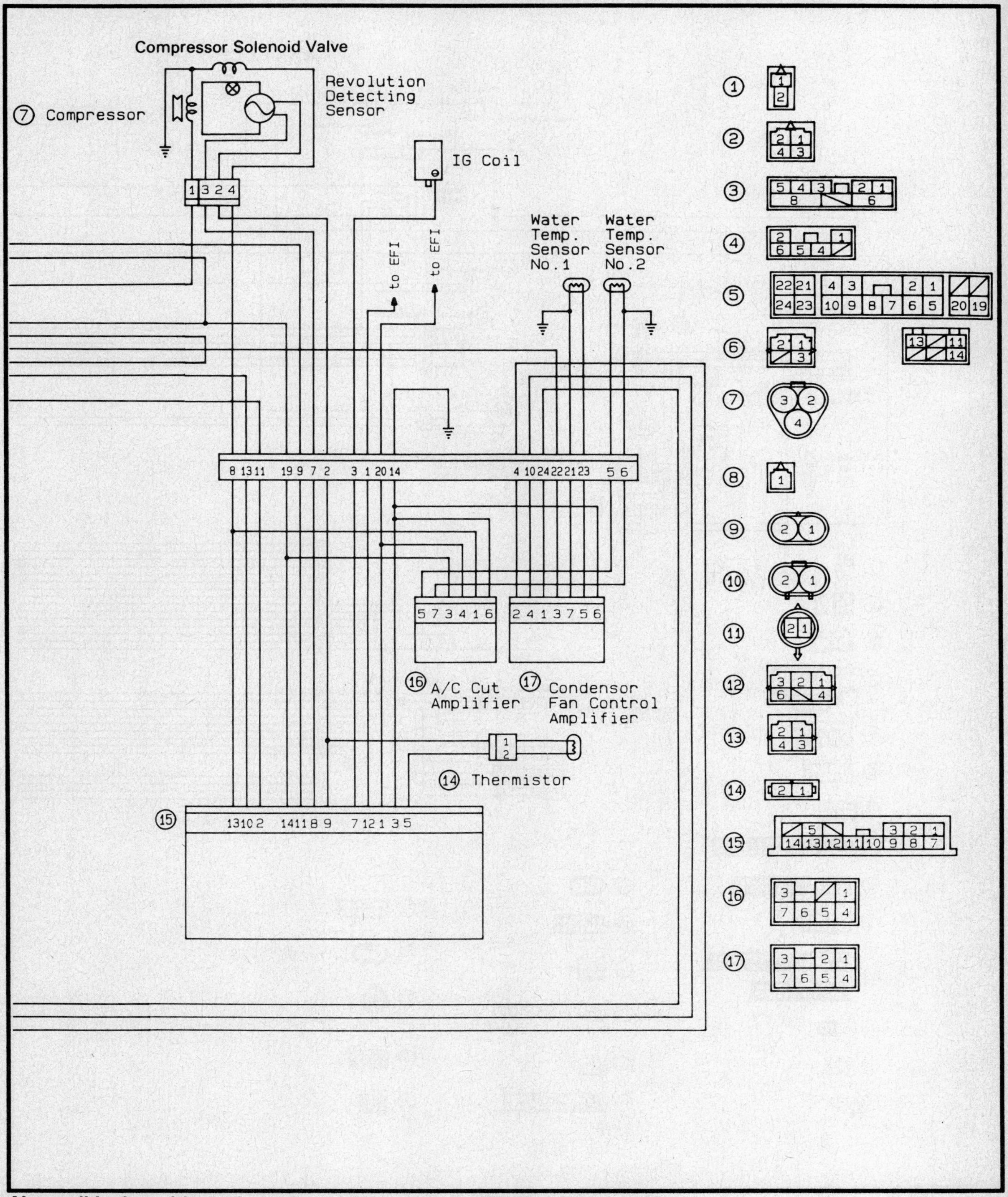
Compressor Solenoid Valve
Revolution Detecting Sensor
⑦ Compressor
IG Coil
to EFI
to EFI
Water Temp. Sensor No.1
Water Temp. Sensor No.2
⑯ A/C Cut Amplifier
⑰ Condensor Fan Control Amplifier
⑭ Thermistor
⑮

Air conditioning wiring schematic—1989–90 Camry 2VZ-FE engine cont'd

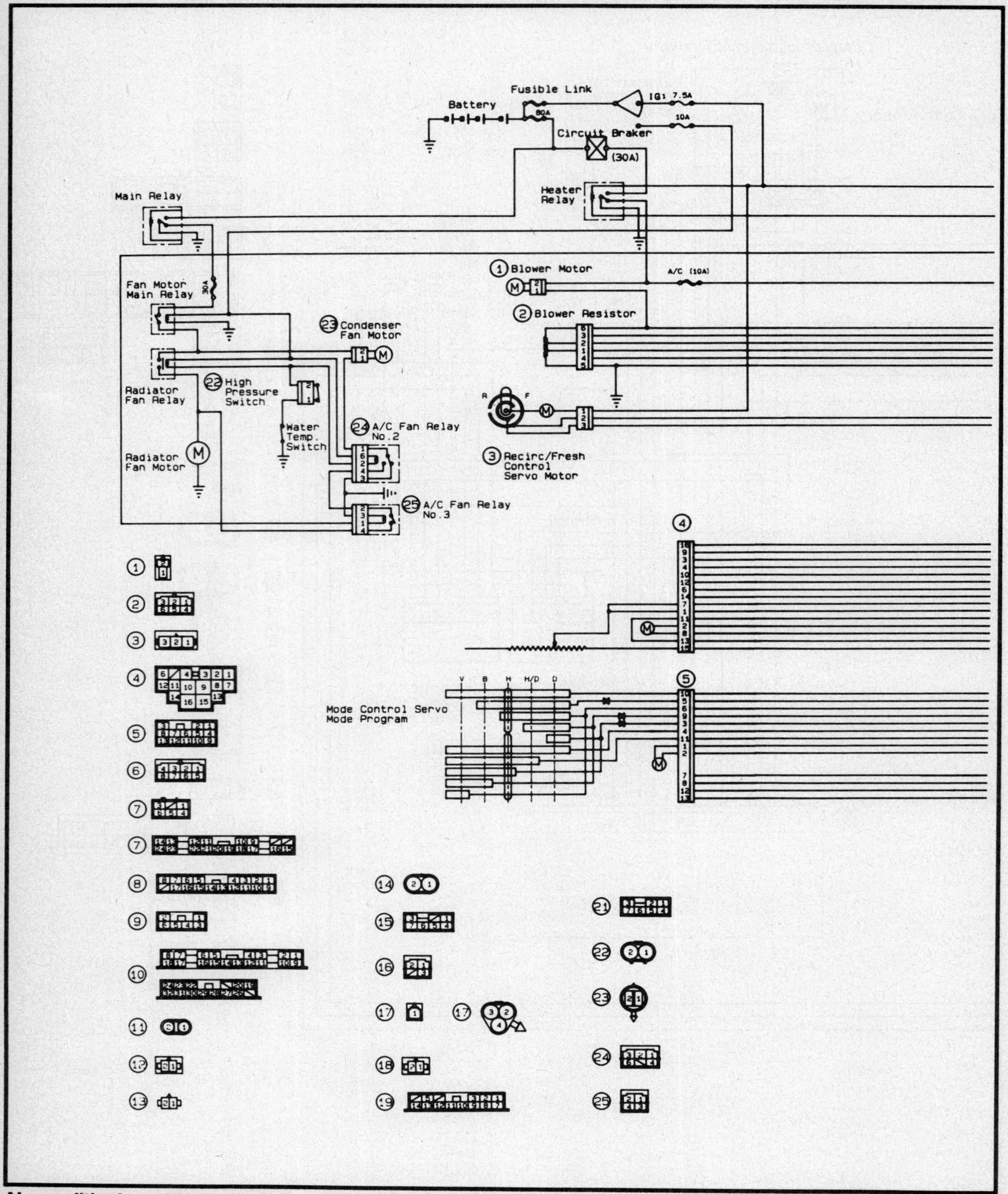
Fusible Link
Battery
IG1 7.5A
80A
10A
Circuit Braker
(30A)
Main Relay
Heater Relay
Fan Motor Main Relay
30A
1 Blower Motor
A/C (10A)
2 Blower Resistor
23 Condenser Fan Motor
Radiator Fan Relay
22 High Pressure Switch
Water Temp. Switch
24 A/C Fan Relay No.2
Radiator Fan Motor
3 Recirc/Fresh Control Servo Motor
25 A/C Fan Relay No.3
Mode Control Servo Mode Program
V B H H/D D

Air conditioning wiring schematic—1989–90 Camry 2VZ-FE engine (push type)

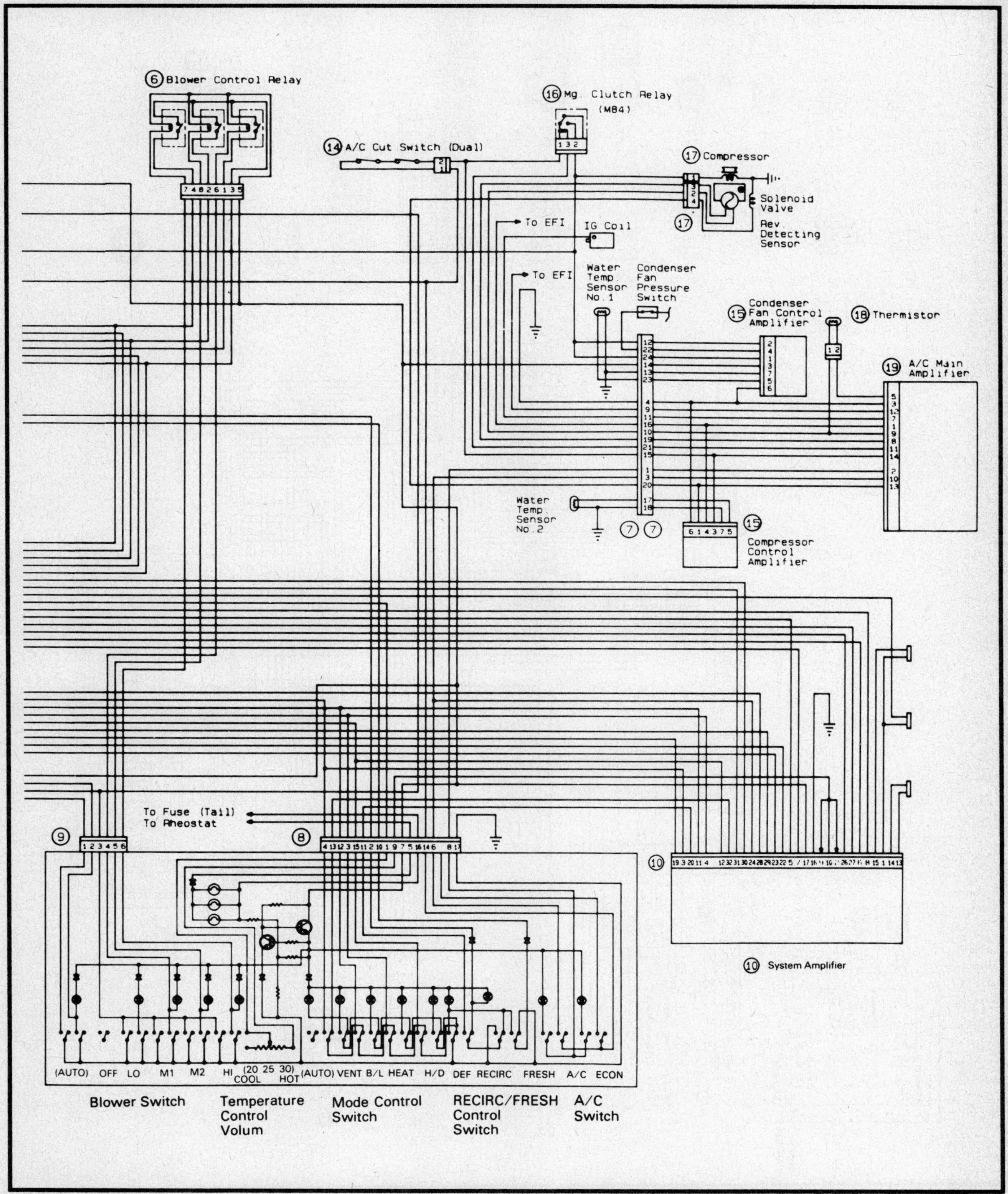
6 Blower Control Relay
16 Mg. Clutch Relay (M84)
14 A/C Cut Switch (Dual)
17 Compressor
Solenoid Valve
Rev. Detecting Sensor
To EFI
IG Coil
To EFI
Water Temp. Sensor No. 1
Condenser Fan Pressure Switch
15 Condenser Fan Control Amplifier
18 Thermistor
19 A/C Main Amplifier
Water Temp. Sensor No. 2
15 Compressor Control Amplifier
To Fuse (Tail)
To Rheostat
10 System Amplifier
(AUTO) OFF LO M1 M2 HI (20 25 30) COOL HOT (AUTO) VENT B/L HEAT H/D DEF RECIRC FRESH A/C ECON
Blower Switch
Temperature Control Volum
Mode Control Switch
RECIRC/FRESH Control Switch
A/C Switch

Air conditioning wiring schematic—1989–90 Camry 2VZ-FE engine (push type) cont'd

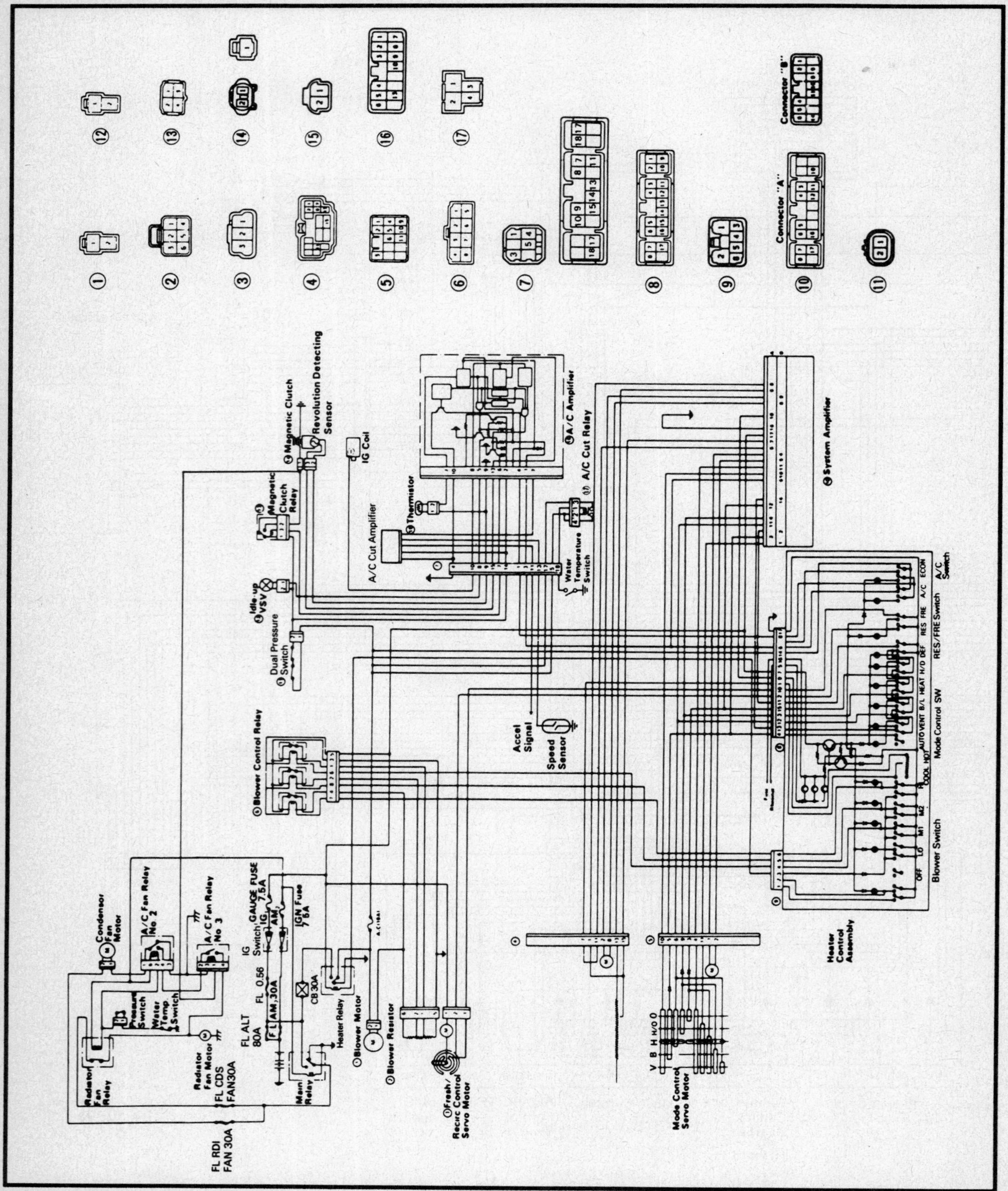
Connector "A"
Connector "B"
Magnetic Clutch
Revolution Detecting Sensor
IG Coil
A/C Amplifier
A/C Cut Relay
System Amplifier
Magnetic Clutch Relay
Thermistor
A/C Cut Amplifier
Water Temperature Switch
Idle-up VSV
Dual Pressure Switch
Blower Control Relay
Accel Signal
Speed Sensor
OFF LO M1 M2 HI
Blower Switch
COOL HOT AUTO VENT B/L HEAT H/D DEF
Mode Control SW
RES FRE
RES/FRE Switch
A/C ECON
A/C Switch
Heater Control Assembly
Condensor Fan Motor
A/C Fan Relay No 2
A/C Fan Relay No 3
Pressure Switch
Water Temp. Switch
Radiator Fan Relay
Radiator Fan Motor
FL CDS FAN30A
FL RDI FAN 30A
FL ALT 80A
FL 0.56 AM 30A
IG Switch
GAUGE FUSE 7.5A
IGN Fuse 7.5A
CB 30A
Heater Relay
Main Relay
Blower Motor
Blower Resistor
Fresh/Recirc Control Servo Motor
Mode Control Servo Motor

Air conditioning wiring schematic—1989–90 Camry 3S-FE engine All-Trac (push type)

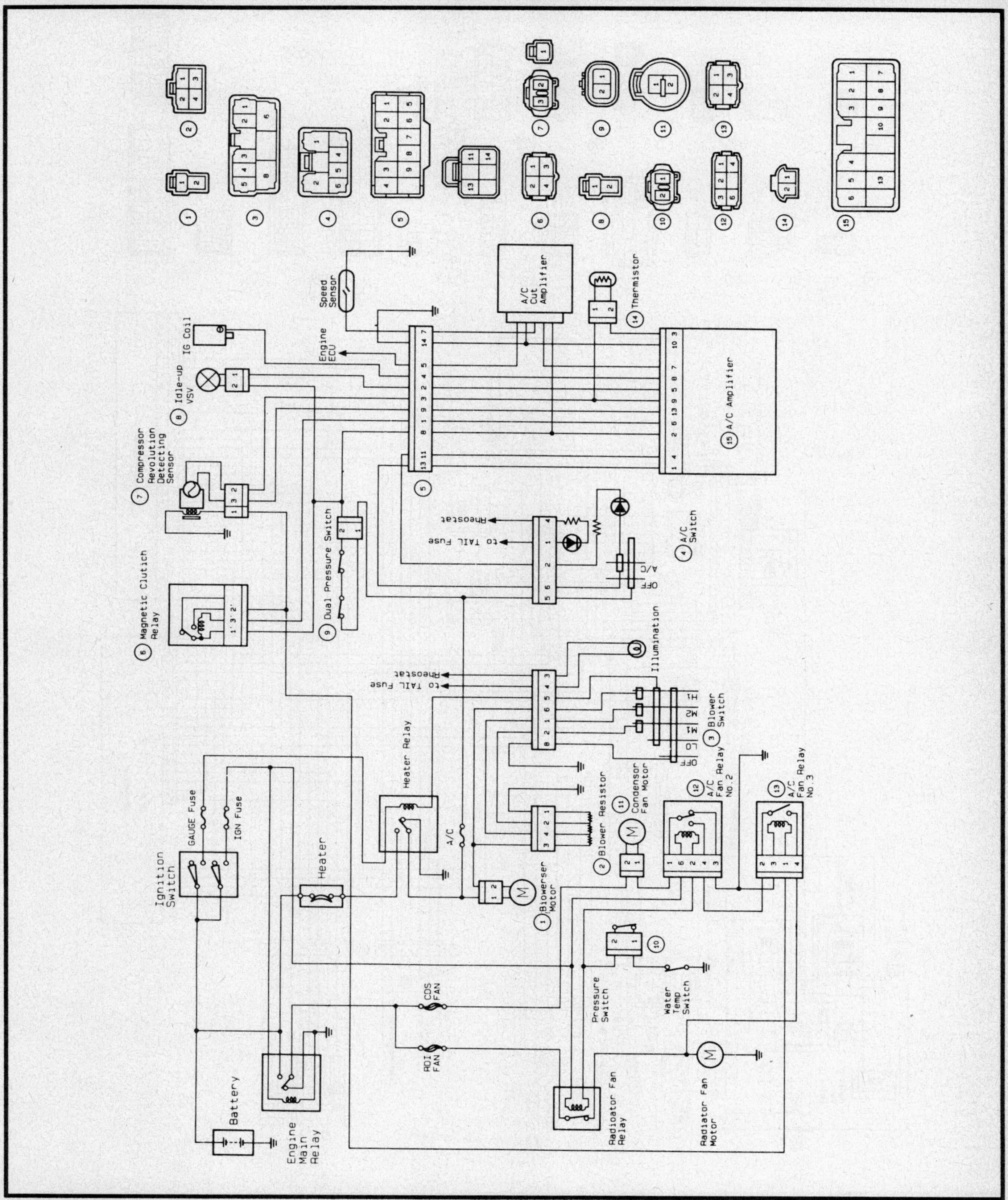
Speed Sensor
A/C Cut Amplifier
Thermistor
IG Coil
Engine ECU
Idle-up VSV
Compressor Revolution Detecting Sensor
A/C Amplifier
Rheostat
to TAIL Fuse
A/C Switch
Magnetic Clutch Relay
Dual Pressure Switch
Illumination
Blower Switch
Heater Relay
A/C Fan Relay No.2
A/C Fan Relay No.3
GAUGE Fuse
IGN Fuse
Ignition Switch
Heater
Blower Resistor
Condensor Fan Motor
Blowerser Motor
Pressure Switch
Water Temp Switch
CDS FAN
RDI FAN
Battery
Engine Main Relay
Radiator Fan Relay
Radiator Fan Motor
Air conditioning wiring schematic—1991 Camry 3S- FE engine (lever type)

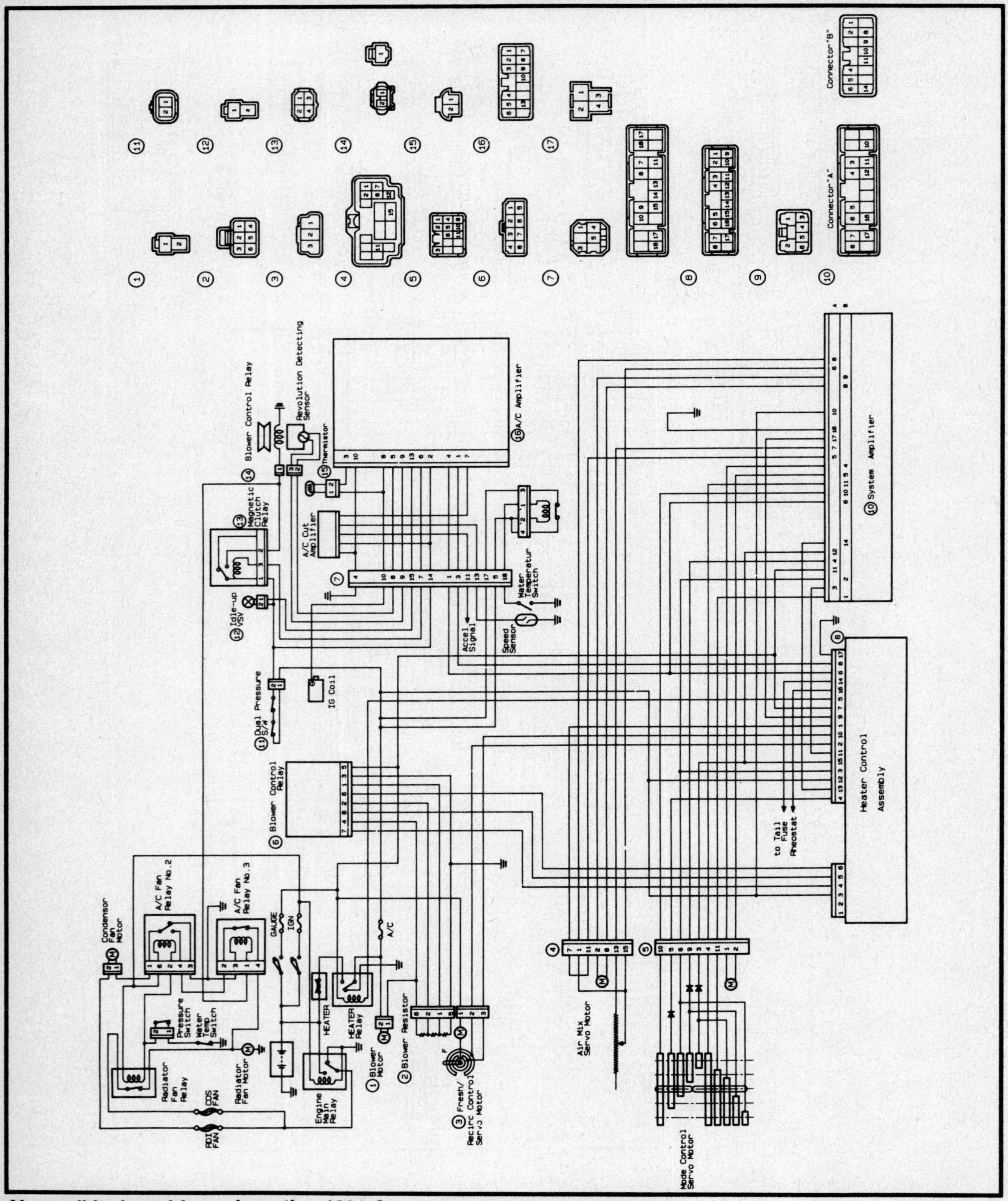
Connector "B"
Connector "A"
Blower Control Relay
Revolution Detecting Sensor
Thermistor
A/C Amplifier
Magnetic Clutch Relay
A/C Cut Amplifier
Water Temperatur Switch
Idle-up VSV
Accel Signal
Speed Sensor
System Amplifier
Dual Pressure S/W
IG Coil
Heater Control Assembly
to Tail Fuse Rheostat
Condensor Fan Motor
A/C Fan Relay No.2
A/C Fan Relay No.3
GAUGE
IGN
A/C
HEATER
HEATER Relay
Pressure Switch
Water Temp Switch
Radiator Fan Relay
Radiator Fan Motor
CDS FAN
RDI FAN
Engine Main Relay
Blower Motor
Blower Resistor
Fresh/ Recirc Control Servo Motor
Air Mix Servo Motor
Mode Control Servo Motor

Air conditioning wiring schematic—1991 Camry 3S- FE engine (push type)

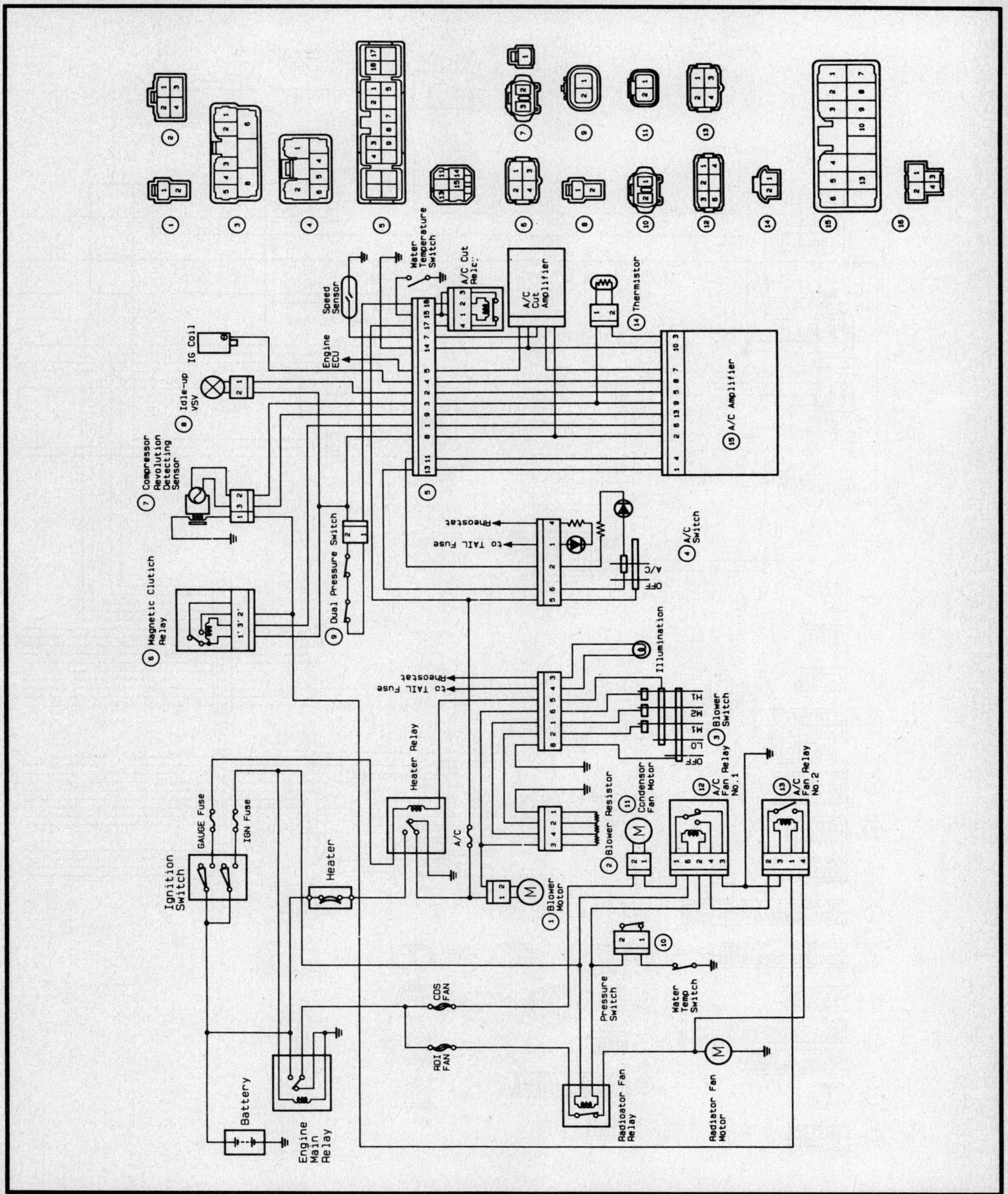
IG Coil
Idle-up VSV
Compressor Revolution Detecting Sensor
Magnetic Clutch Relay
Dual Pressure Switch
Speed Sensor
Engine ECU
Water Temperature Switch
A/C Cut Relay
A/C Cut Amplifier
Thermistor
A/C Amplifier
A/C Switch
to TAIL Fuse
Rheostat
Illumination
Blower Switch
Heater Relay
Blower Resistor
Condensor Fan Motor
A/C Fan Relay No.1
A/C Fan Relay No.2
Ignition Switch
GAUGE Fuse
IGN Fuse
Heater
A/C
Blower Motor
Pressure Switch
Water Temp Switch
CDS FAN
RDI FAN
Battery
Engine Main Relay
Radiator Fan Relay
Radiator Fan Motor

Air conditioning wiring schematic—1991 Camry 3S- FE engine All-Trac (lever type)

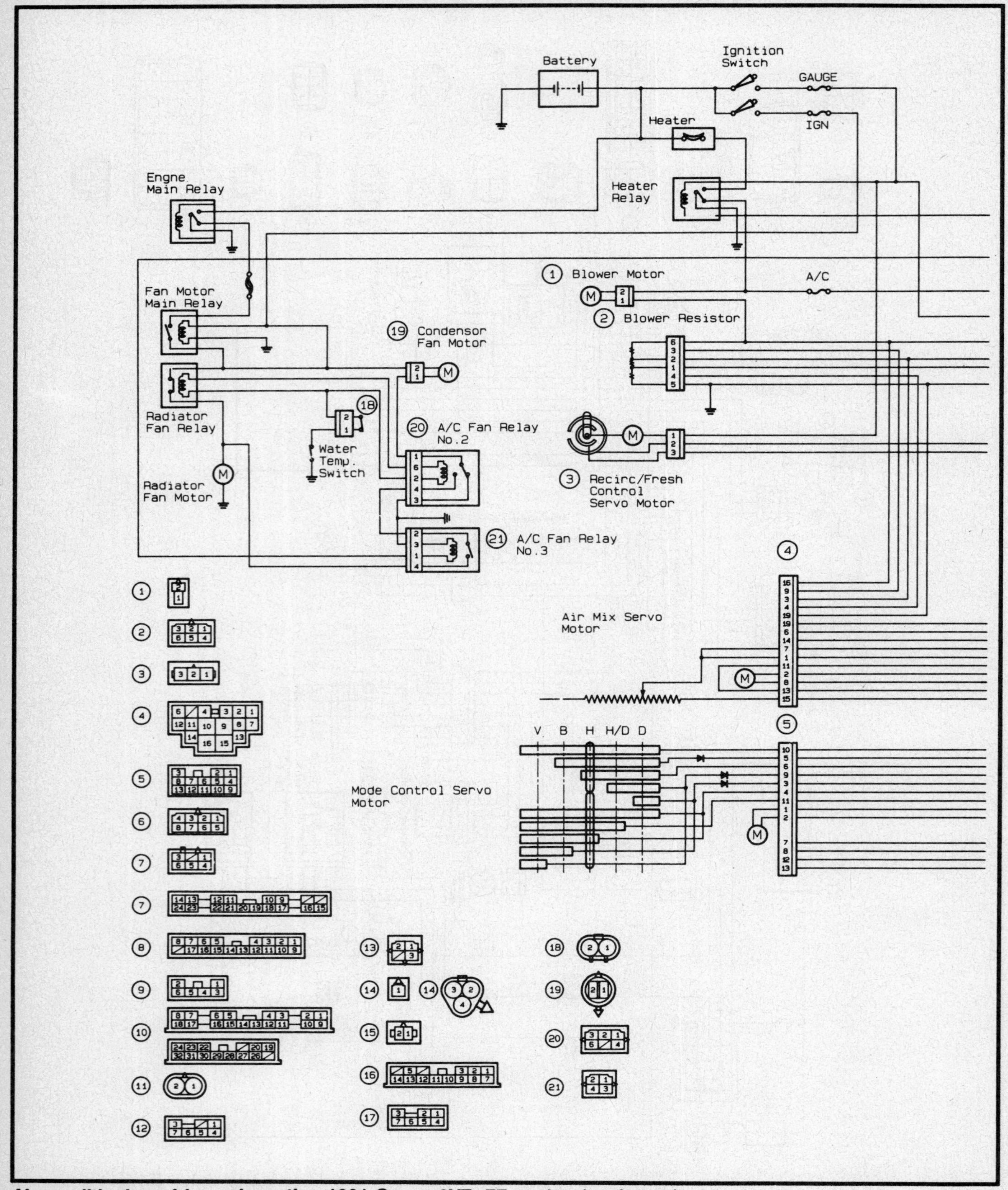
Battery
Ignition Switch
GAUGE
IGN
Heater
Heater Relay
Engne Main Relay
Fan Motor Main Relay
Radiator Fan Relay
Radiator Fan Motor
1 Blower Motor
A/C
2 Blower Resistor
19 Condensor Fan Motor
18
Water Temp. Switch
20 A/C Fan Relay No.2
21 A/C Fan Relay No.3
3 Recirc/Fresh Control Servo Motor
4
Air Mix Servo Motor
5
V B H H/D D
Mode Control Servo Motor

Air conditioning wiring schematic—1991 Camry 2VZ- FE engine (push type)

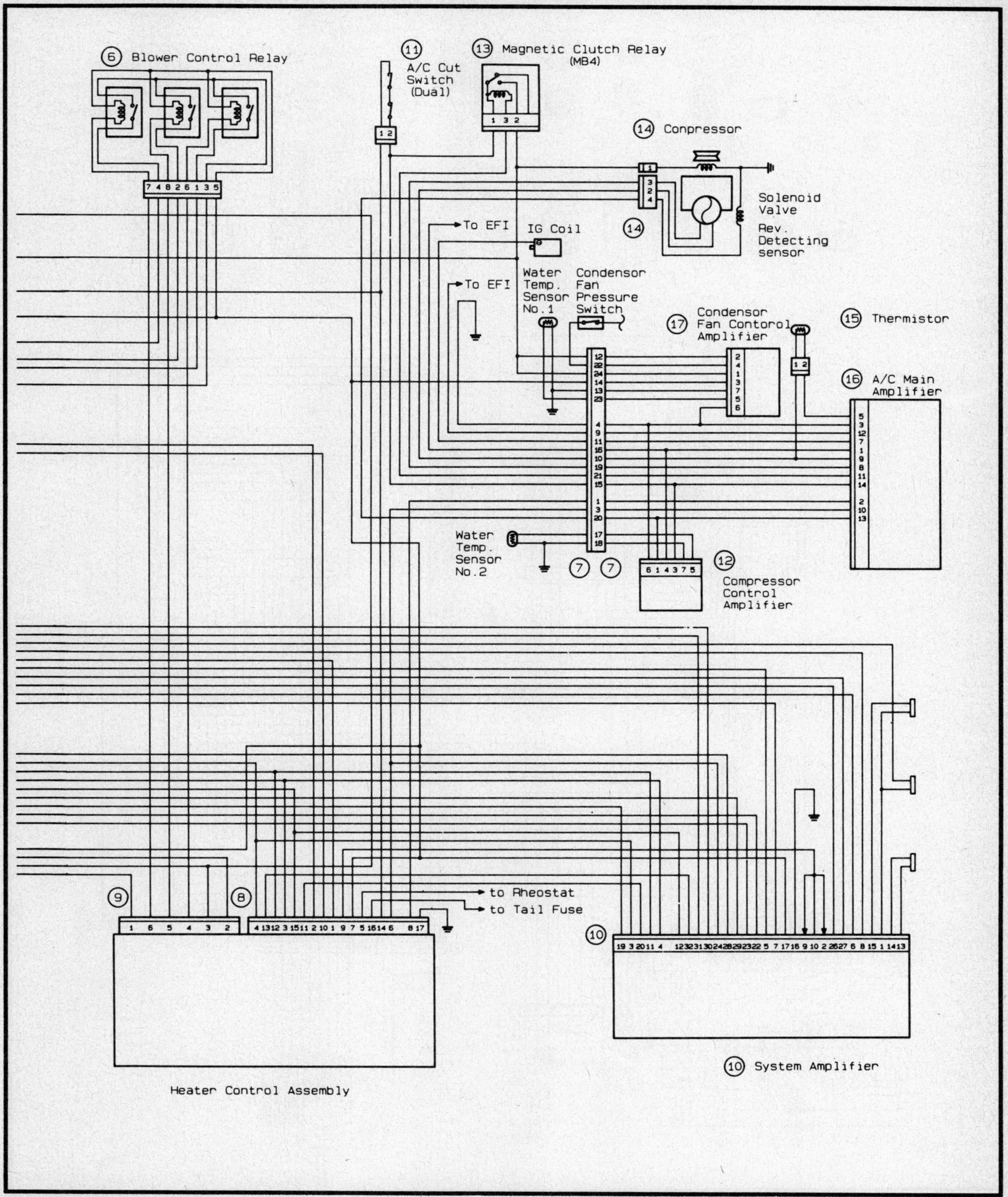
6 Blower Control Relay
11 A/C Cut Switch (Dual)
13 Magnetic Clutch Relay (MB4)
14 Conpressor
Solenoid Valve
14
Rev. Detecting sensor
To EFI
IG Coil
To EFI
Water Temp. Sensor No.1
Condensor Fan Pressure Switch
17 Condensor Fan Contorol Amplifier
15 Thermistor
16 A/C Main Amplifier
Water Temp. Sensor No.2
7 7
12 Compressor Control Amplifier
9
8
to Rheostat
to Tail Fuse
10
Heater Control Assembly
10 System Amplifier

Air conditioning wiring schematic—1991 Camry 2VZ- FE engine (push type) cont'd

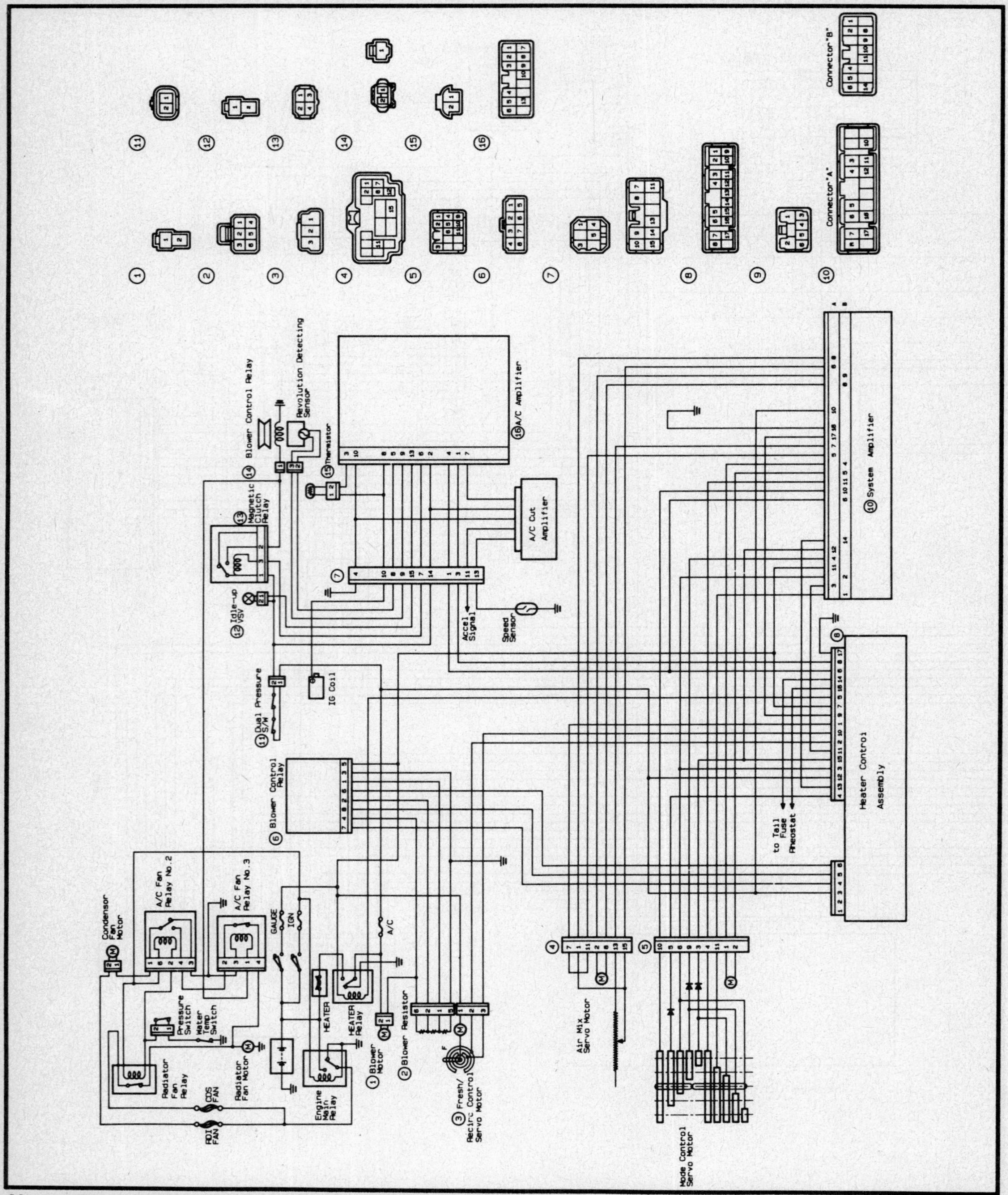
Connector "A"
Connector "B"
Condenser Fan Motor
A/C Fan Relay No.2
A/C Fan Relay No.3
Pressure Switch
Water Temp Switch
Radiator Fan Relay
Radiator Fan Motor
CDS FAN
RDI FAN
Engine Main Relay
GAUGE
IGN
HEATER
HEATER Relay
A/C
1 Blower Motor
2 Blower Resistor
3 Fresh/Recirc Control Servo Motor
4
5
6 Blower Control Relay
7
8
10 System Amplifier
11 Dual Pressure S/W
12 Idle-up VSV
13 Magnetic Clutch Relay
14 Blower Control Relay
15 Thermistor
16 A/C Amplifier
Revolution Detecting Sensor
IG Coil
A/C Cut Amplifier
Accel Signal
Speed Sensor
Heater Control Assembly
to Tail Fuse Rheostat
Air Mix Servo Motor
Mode Control Servo Motor

Air conditioning wiring schematic—1991 Camry 3S- FE engine All-Trac (push type)

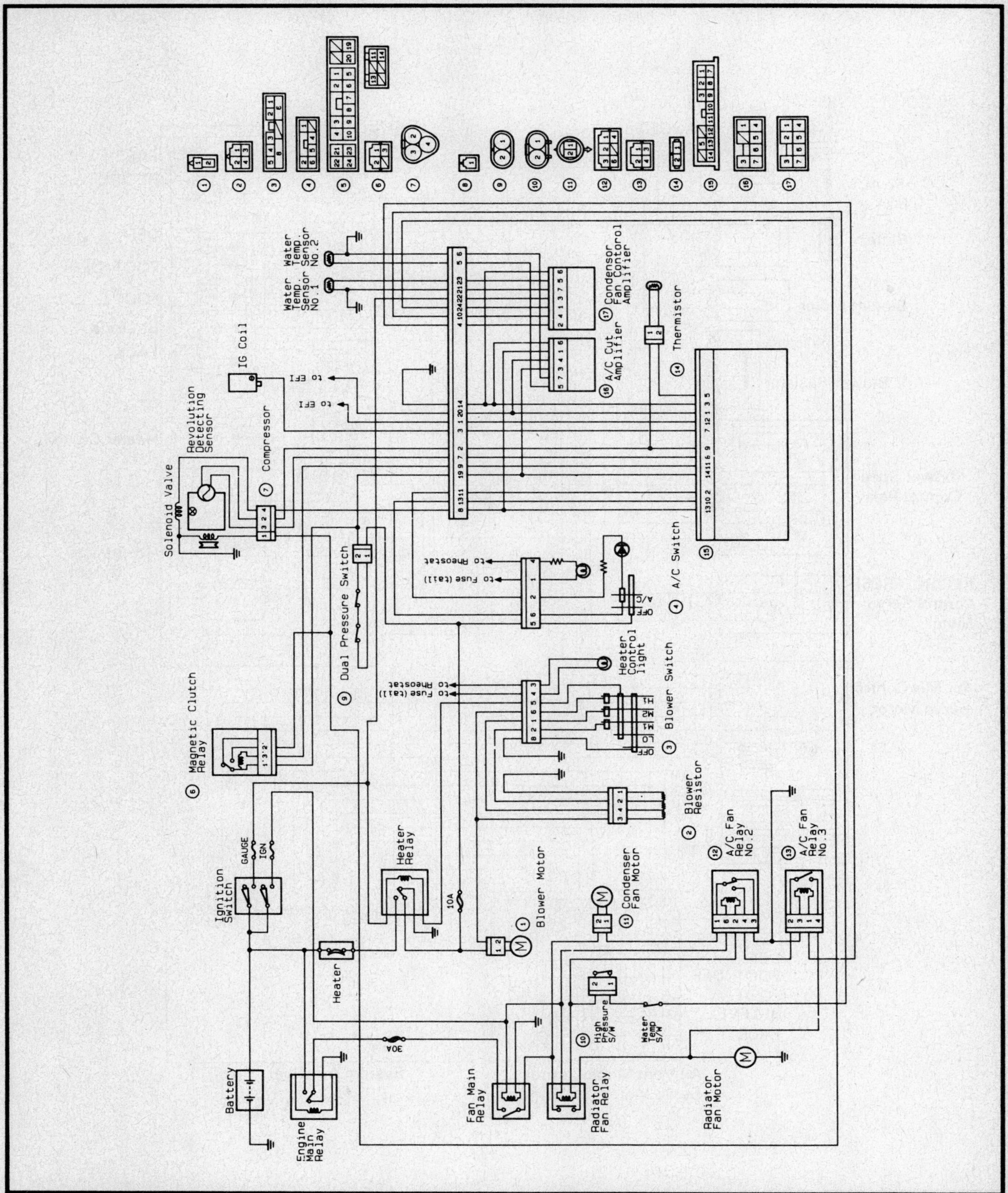
Battery
Engine Main Relay
Ignition Switch
GAUGE
IGN
Heater
Heater Relay
10A
30A
Blower Motor
Fan Main Relay
Radiator Fan Relay
High Pressure S/W
Water Temp S/W
Radiator Fan Motor
Condenser Fan Motor
A/C Fan Relay No.2
A/C Fan Relay No.3
Blower Resistor
Blower Switch
Heater Control light
A/C Switch
to Rheostat
to Fuse (tail)
Magnetic Clutch Relay
Dual Pressure Switch
Solenoid Valve
Compressor
Revolution Detecting Sensor
IG Coil
to EFI
Water Temp. Sensor No.1
Water Temp. Sensor No.2
A/C Cut Amplifier
Condenser Fan Control Amplifier
Thermistor

Air conditioning wiring schematic—1991 Camry 2VZ- FE engine (lever type)

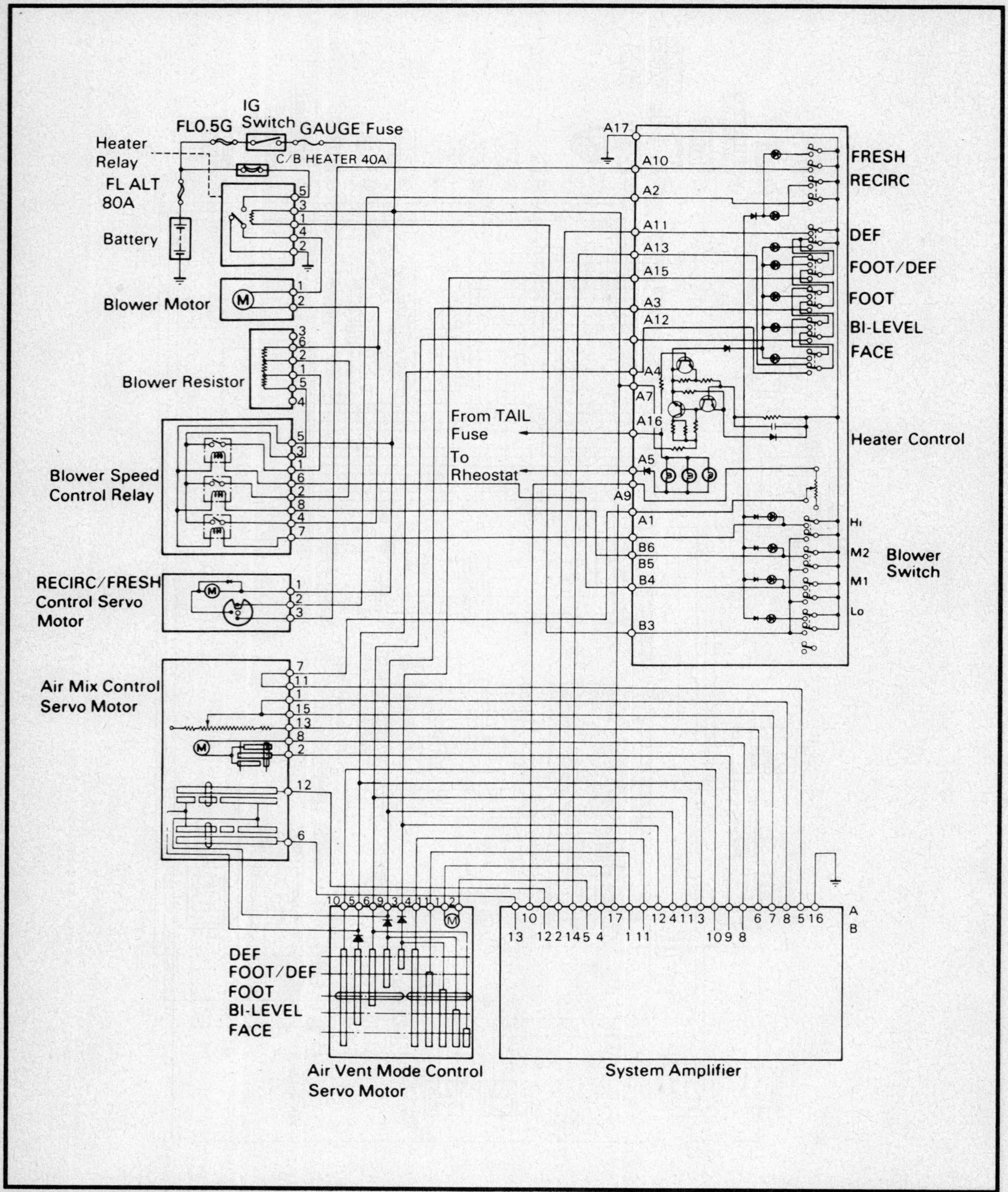
IG Switch
FL0.5G
GAUGE Fuse
Heater Relay
C/B HEATER 40A
FL ALT 80A
Battery
Blower Motor
Blower Resistor
Blower Speed Control Relay
RECIRC/FRESH Control Servo Motor
Air Mix Control Servo Motor
DEF
FOOT/DEF
FOOT
BI-LEVEL
FACE
Air Vent Mode Control Servo Motor
System Amplifier
From TAIL Fuse
To Rheostat
FRESH
RECIRC
DEF
FOOT/DEF
FOOT
BI-LEVEL
FACE
Heater Control
Hı
M2
M1
Lo
Blower Switch

Heater wiring schematic—Camry (push type)

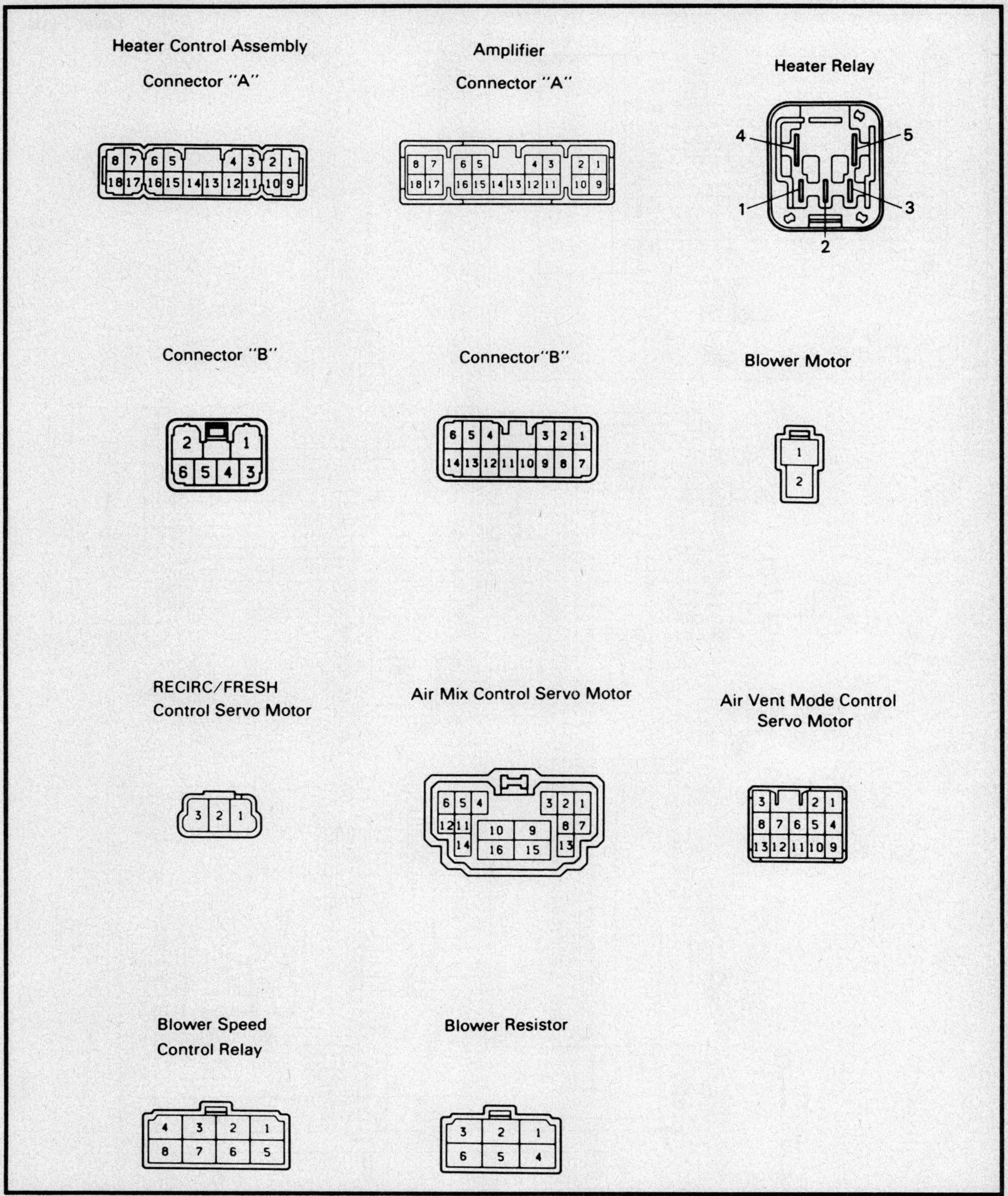
Heater Control Assembly
Connector "A"
Amplifier
Connector "A"
Heater Relay
Connector "B"
Connector "B"
Blower Motor
RECIRC/FRESH
Control Servo Motor
Air Mix Control Servo Motor
Air Vent Mode Control
Servo Motor
Blower Speed
Control Relay
Blower Resistor

Heater wiring schematic—Camry (push type) cont'd

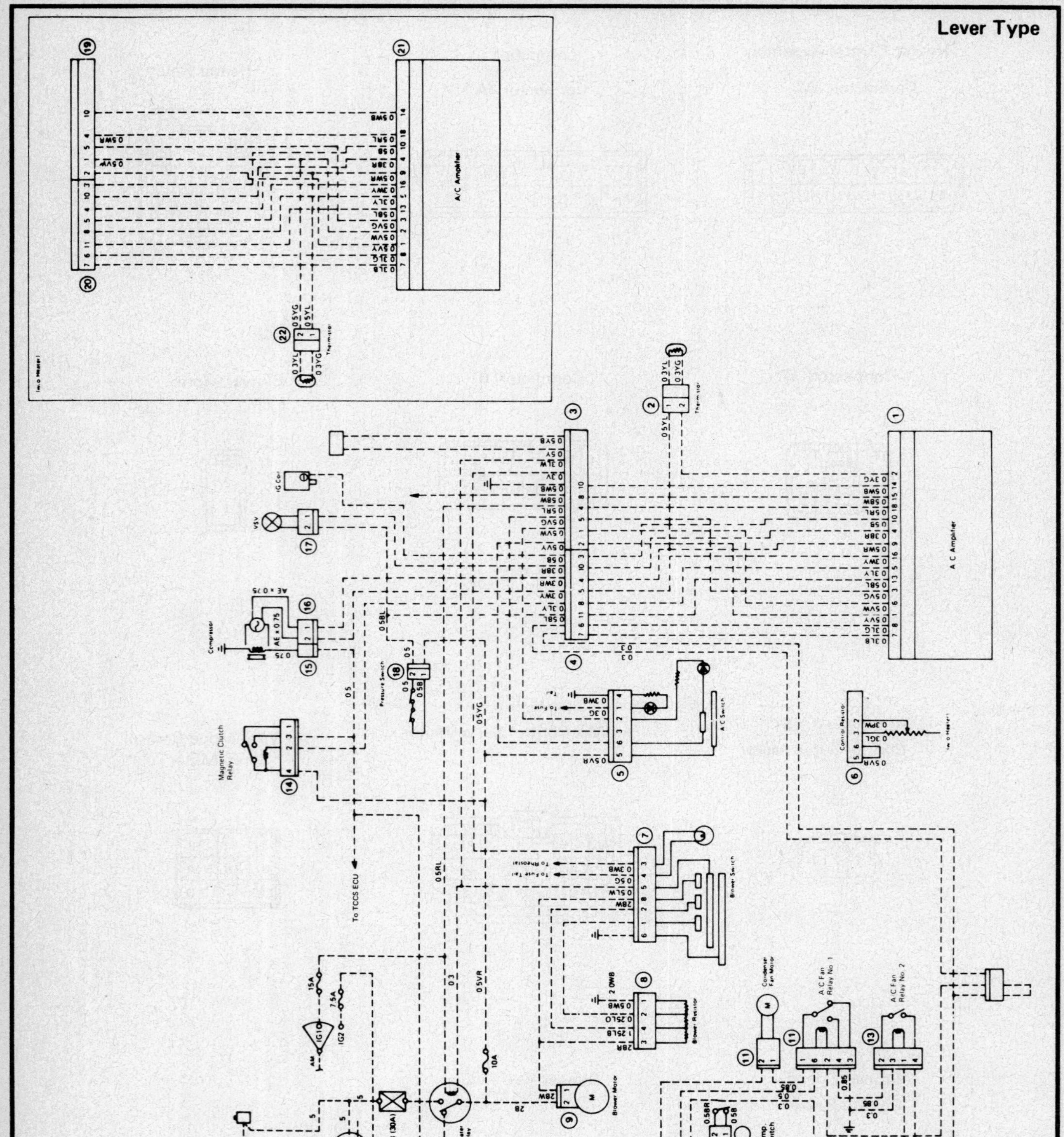
Lever Type
A/C Amplifier
Thermistor
IG Coil
VSV
Compressor
Magnetic Clutch Relay
Pressure Switch
To TCCS ECU
A/C Switch
Control Resistor
Blower Switch
Blower Resistor
Blower Motor
Heater Relay
Main Relay
Battery
Condenser Fan Motor
A/C Fan Relay No. 1
A/C Fan Relay No. 2
Temp. Switch
Fan Main Relay
Radiator Fan Relay
Radiator Fan Motor
To Rheostat
To Fuse Tail

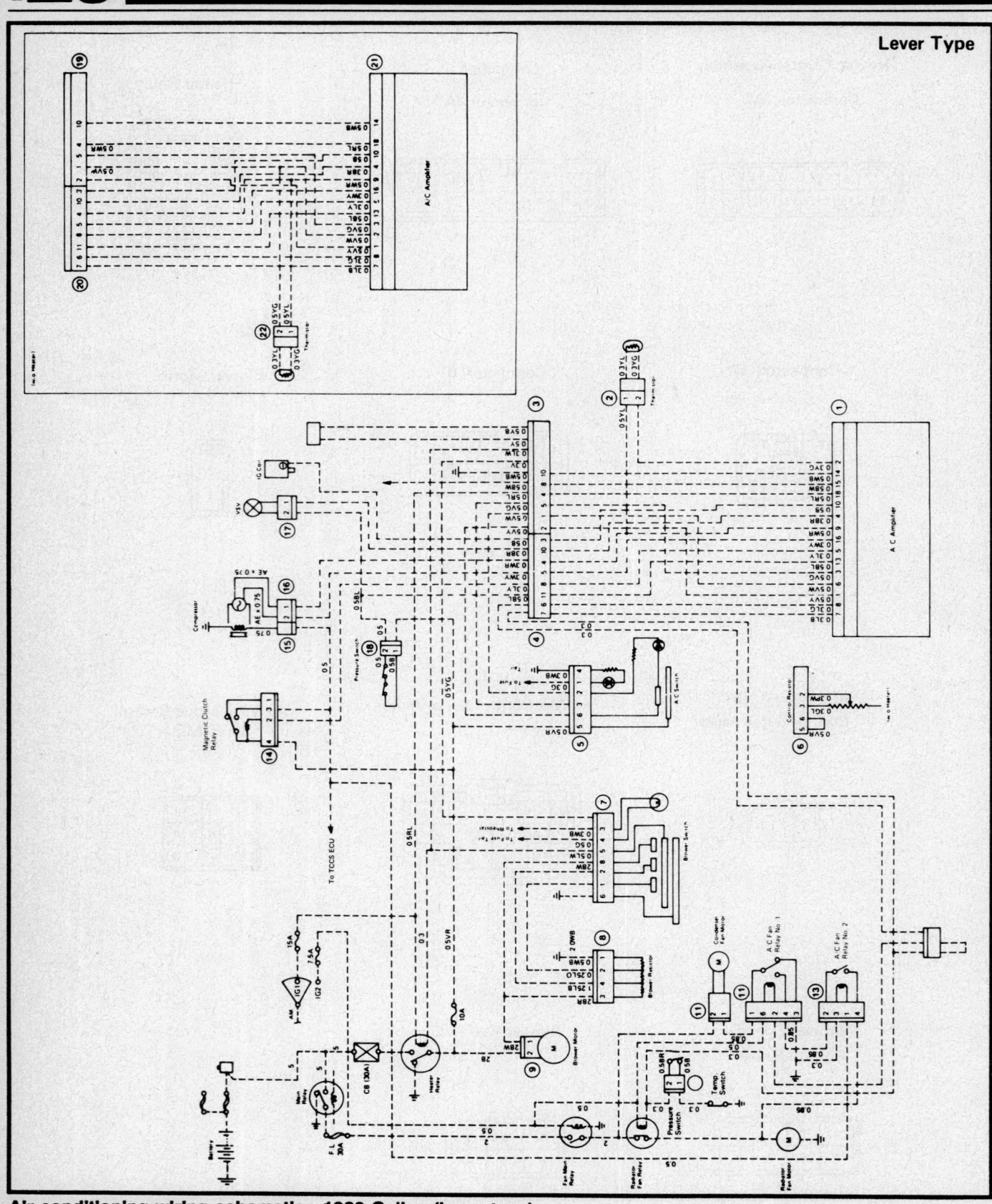

Air conditioning wiring schematic—1989 Celica (lever type)

Lever Type

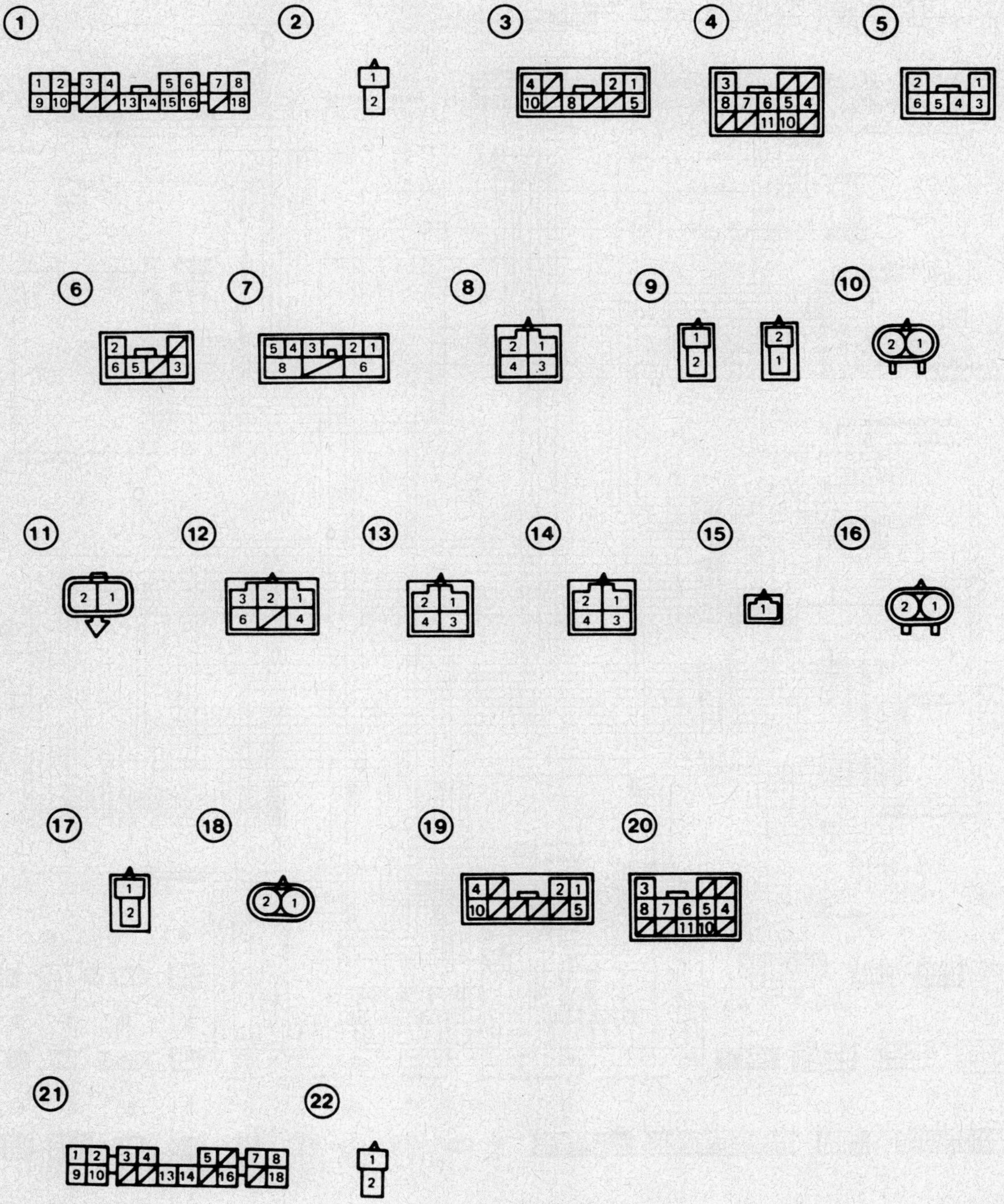
1
2
3
4
5
6
7
8
9
10
11
12
13
14
15
16
17
18
19
20
21
22

Air conditioning wiring schematic—1989 Celica (lever type) cont'd

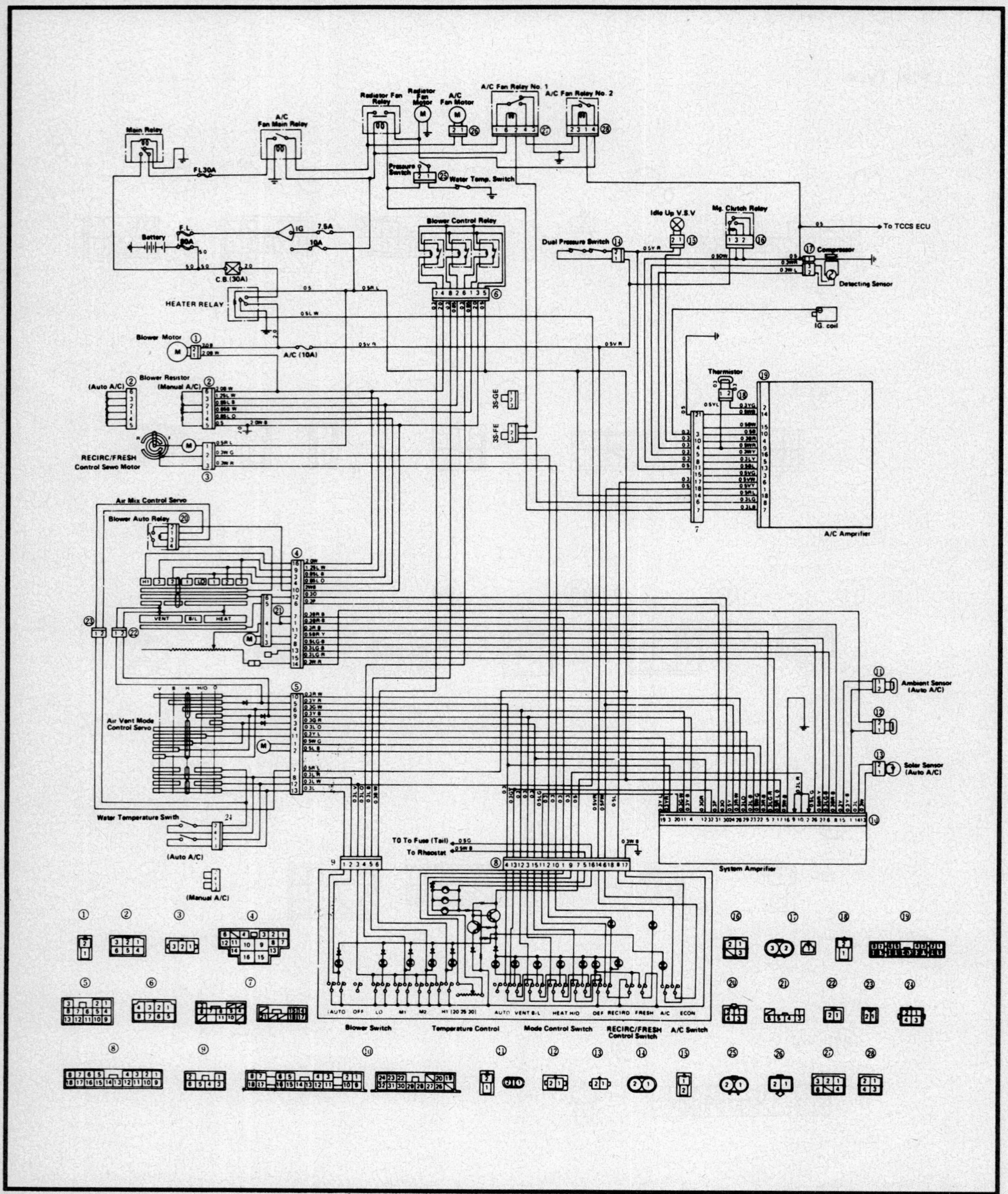
Main Relay
A/C Fan Main Relay
Radiator Fan Relay
Radiator Fan Motor
A/C Fan Motor
A/C Fan Relay No. 1
A/C Fan Relay No. 2
Pressure Switch
Water Temp. Switch
Battery
IG
Blower Control Relay
Idle Up V.S.V
Mg. Clutch Relay
To TCCS ECU
Dual Pressure Switch
Compressor
Detecting Sensor
C.B.(30A)
HEATER RELAY
IG. coil
Blower Motor
A/C (10A)
Thermistor
Blower Resistor
(Auto A/C)
(Manual A/C)
3S-GE
3S-FE
RECIRC/FRESH
Control Sewo Motor
A/C Amprifier
Air Mix Control Servo
Blower Auto Relay
VENT
B/L
HEAT
Ambient Sensor
(Auto A/C)
Air Vent Mode
Control Servo
Solar Sensor
(Auto A/C)
Water Temperature Swith
(Auto A/C)
TO To Fuse (Tail)
To Rheostat
System Amprifier
(Manual A/C)
AUTO
OFF
LO
M1
M2
HI
AUTO
VENT
B/L
HEAT
H/O
DEF
RECIRC
FRESH
A/C
ECON
Blower Switch
Temperature Control
Mode Control Switch
RECIRC/FRESH
Control Switch
A/C Switch

Air conditioning wiring schematic—1989 Celica (push type)

Push Type (All-Track/4WD)

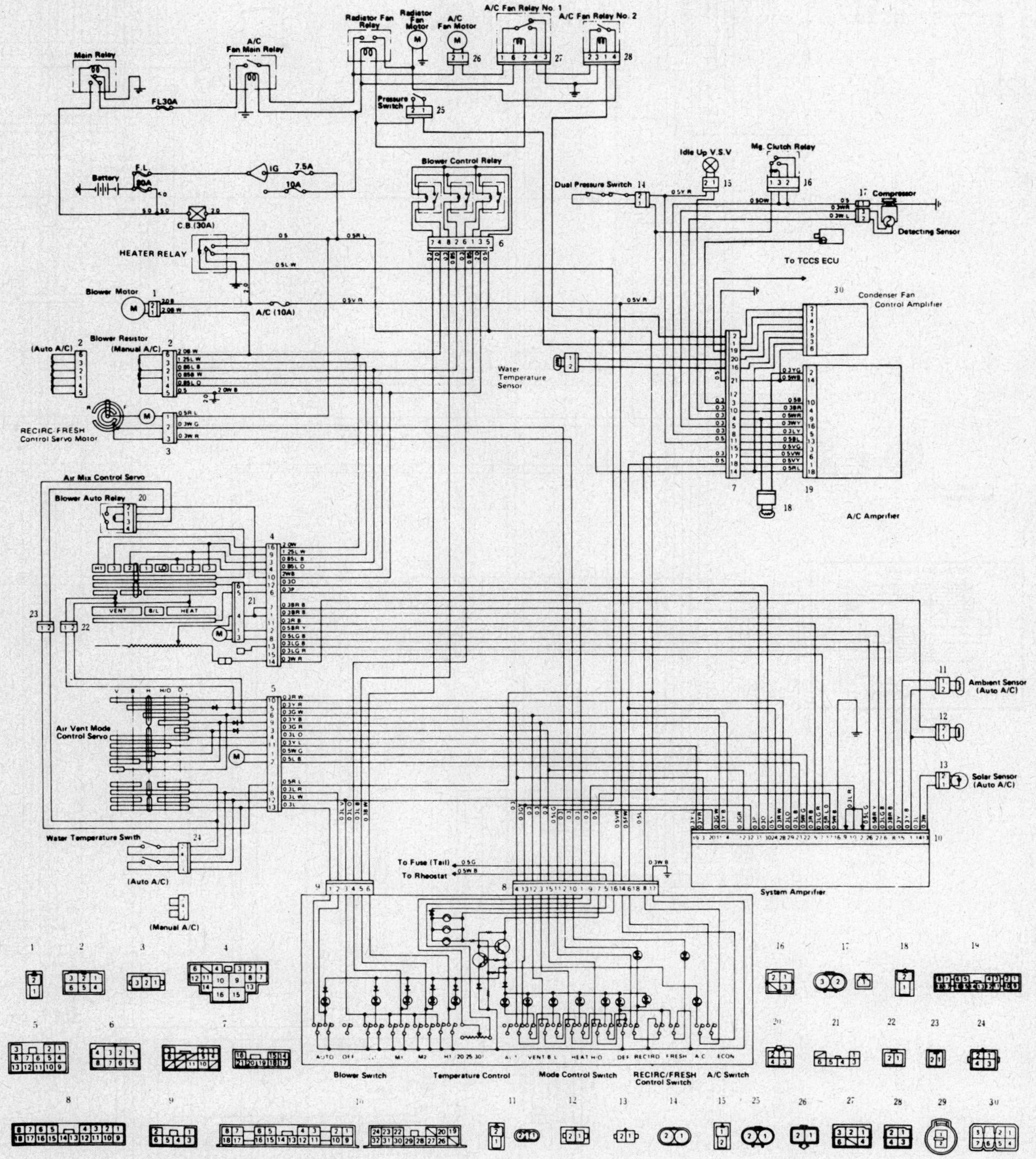
Main Relay
A/C Fan Main Relay
Radiator Fan Relay
Radiator Fan Motor
A/C Fan Motor
A/C Fan Relay No. 1
A/C Fan Relay No. 2
Pressure Switch
FL30A
Battery
F.L. 80A
IG
7.5A
10A
C.B (30A)
HEATER RELAY
Blower Motor
A/C (10A)
Blower Resistor (Manual A/C)
(Auto A/C)
RECIRC FRESH Control Servo Motor
Blower Control Relay
Idle Up V.S.V
Mg. Clutch Relay
Dual Pressure Switch
Compressor
Detecting Sensor
To TCCS ECU
Condenser Fan Control Amplifier
Water Temperature Sensor
A/C Amplifier
Air Mix Control Servo
Blower Auto Relay
VENT
B/L
HEAT
Air Vent Mode Control Servo
Water Temperature Swith
(Auto A/C)
(Manual A/C)
Ambient Sensor (Auto A/C)
Solar Sensor (Auto A/C)
To Fuse (Tail)
To Rheostat
System Amplifier
AUTO
OFF
M1
M2
H1
VENT
HEAT
DEF
RECIRC
FRESH
A/C
ECON
Blower Switch
Temperature Control
Mode Control Switch
RECIRC/FRESH Control Switch
A/C Switch

Air conditioning wiring schematic—1989 Celica (push type All-Trac)

Dial Type Temperature Control Switch (without AUTO A/C)

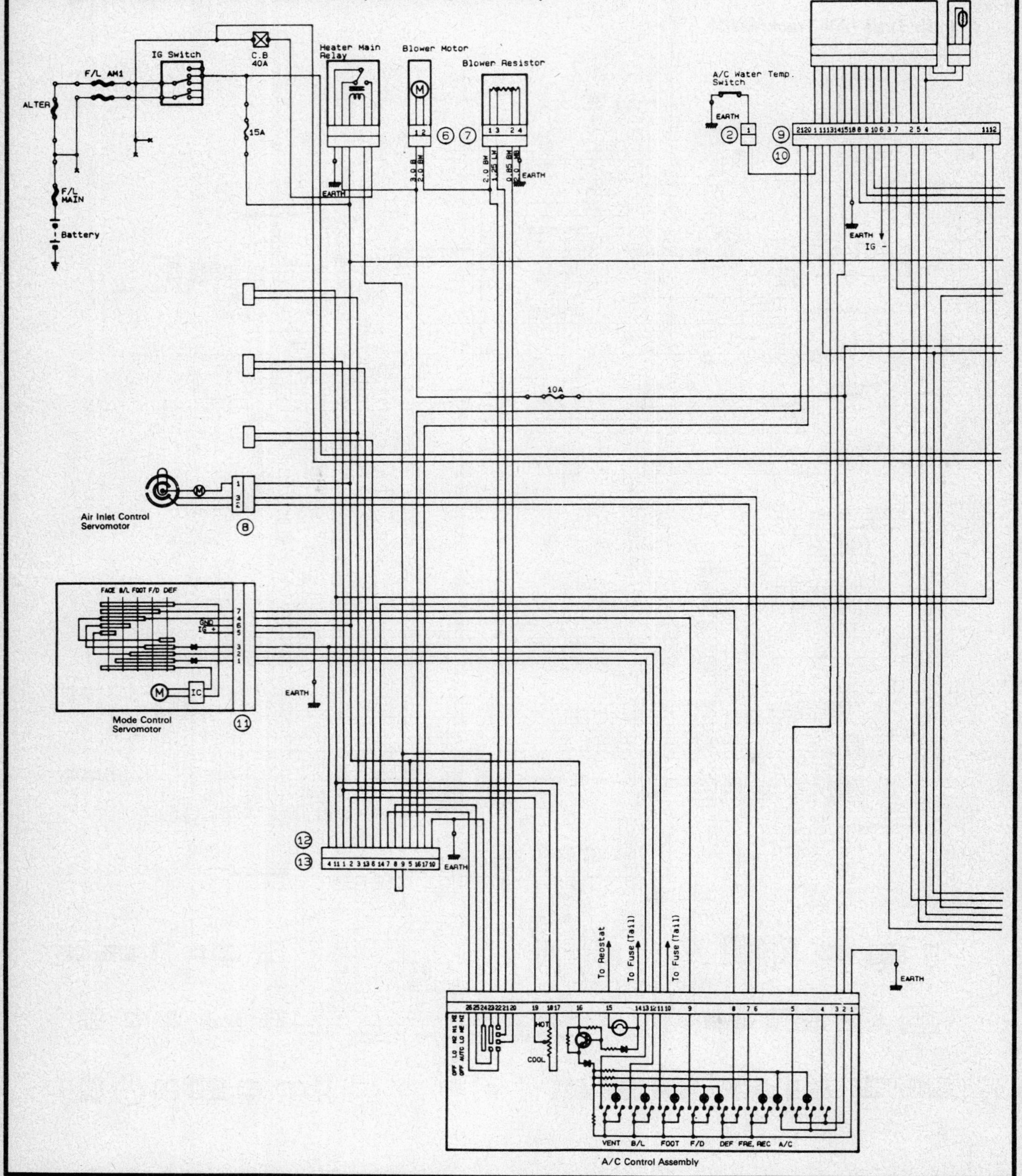
A/C Amplifier
Thermistor
IG Switch
C.B
40A
F/L AM1
ALTER
15A
F/L
MAIN
Battery
Heater Main
Relay
Blower Motor
Blower Resistor
EARTH
A/C Water Temp.
Switch
IG -
10A
Air Inlet Control
Servomotor
FACE B/L FOOT F/D DEF
GND
IG +
Mode Control
Servomotor
To Reostat
To Fuse (Tail)
To Fuse (Tail)
HOT
COOL
VENT
B/L
FOOT
F/D
DEF
FRE. REC
A/C
A/C Control Assembly

Air conditioning wiring schematic—1990–91 Celica

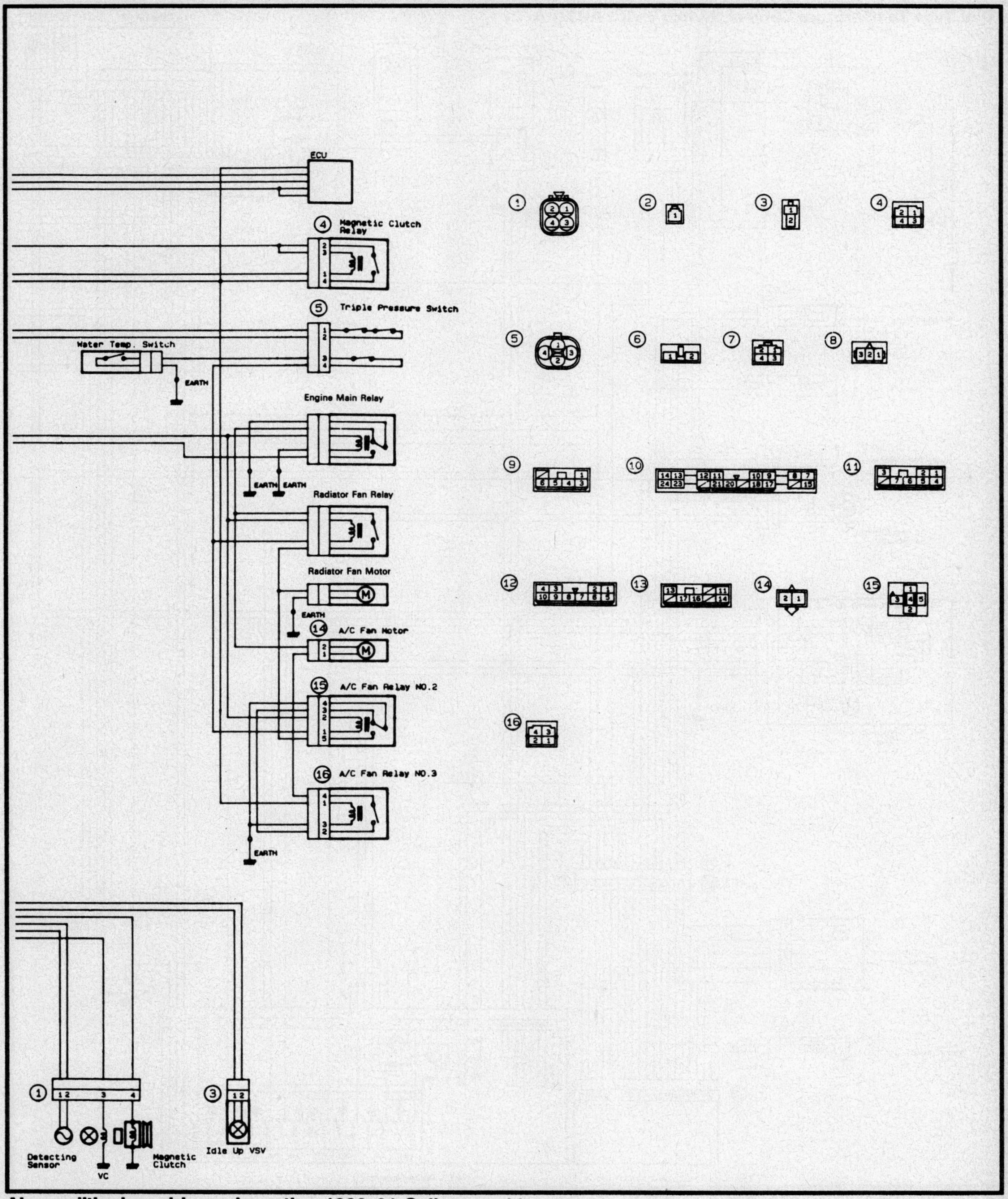
ECU
Magnetic Clutch Relay
Triple Pressure Switch
Water Temp. Switch
EARTH
Engine Main Relay
Radiator Fan Relay
Radiator Fan Motor
A/C Fan Motor
A/C Fan Relay NO.2
A/C Fan Relay NO.3
Detecting Sensor
VC
Magnetic Clutch
Idle Up VSV

Air conditioning wiring schematic—1990–91 Celica cont'd

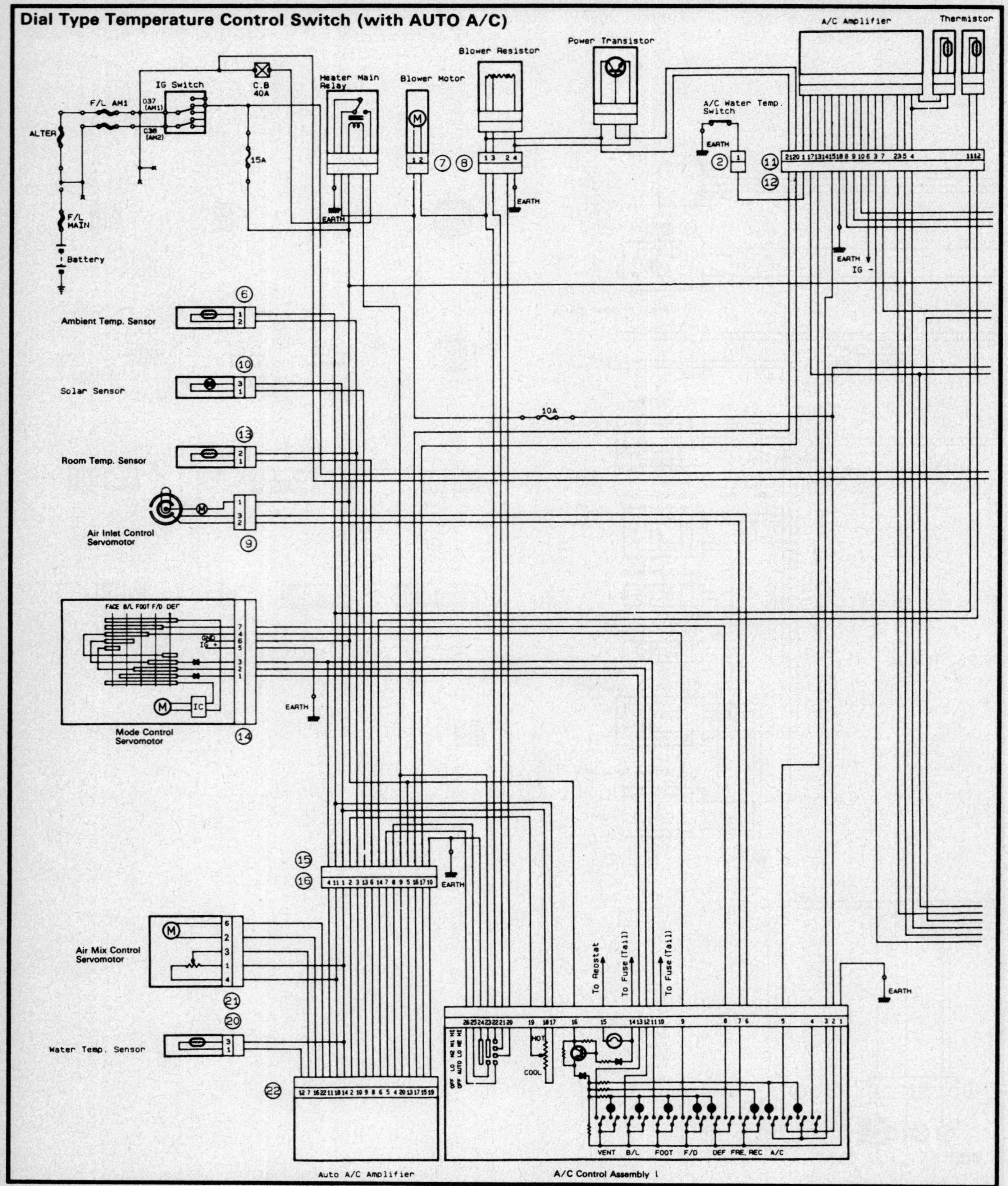
Dial Type Temperature Control Switch (with AUTO A/C)
A/C Amplifier
Thermistor
Power Transistor
Blower Resistor
Heater Main Relay
Blower Motor
IG Switch
C.B 40A
F/L AM1
ALTER
15A
F/L MAIN
Battery
A/C Water Temp. Switch
EARTH
IG -
Ambient Temp. Sensor
Solar Sensor
Room Temp. Sensor
10A
Air Inlet Control Servomotor
FACE B/L FOOT F/D DEF
GND
IG +
Mode Control Servomotor
Air Mix Control Servomotor
Water Temp. Sensor
To Reostat
To Fuse (Tail)
To Fuse (Tail)
HOT
COOL
VENT B/L FOOT F/D DEF FRE. REC A/C
Auto A/C Amplifier
A/C Control Assembly

Air conditioning wiring schematic – 1990–91 Celica

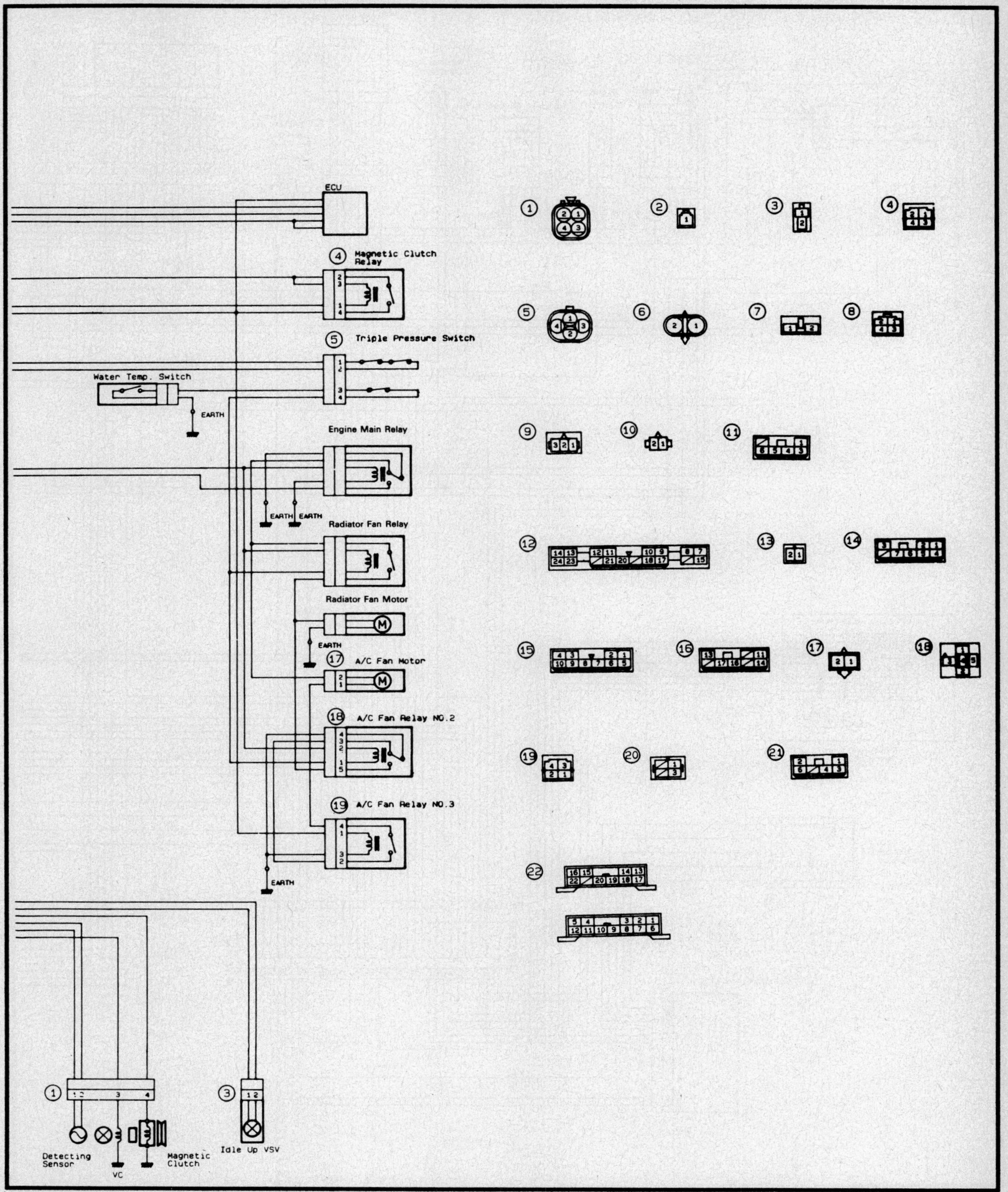
ECU
4 Magnetic Clutch Relay
5 Triple Pressure Switch
Water Temp. Switch
EARTH
Engine Main Relay
Radiator Fan Relay
Radiator Fan Motor
17 A/C Fan Motor
18 A/C Fan Relay NO.2
19 A/C Fan Relay NO.3
Detecting Sensor
VC
Magnetic Clutch
Idle Up VSV

Air conditioning wiring schematic—1990–91 Celica cont'd

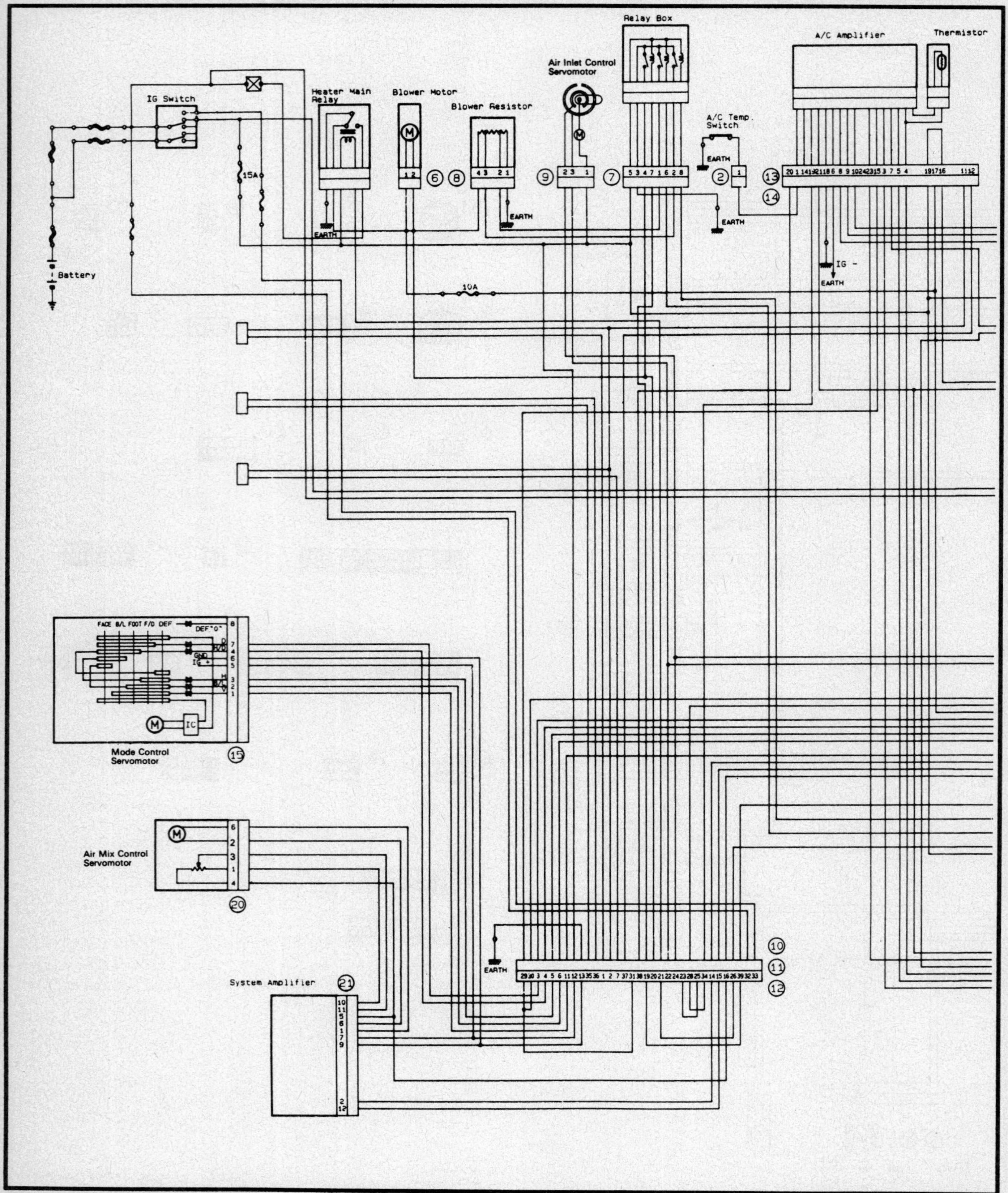
Relay Box
A/C Amplifier
Thermistor
Air Inlet Control Servomotor
IG Switch
Heater Main Relay
Blower Motor
Blower Resistor
A/C Temp. Switch
EARTH
15A
10A
Battery
IG -
FACE B/L FOOT F/D DEF
DEF "0"
Mode Control Servomotor
Air Mix Control Servomotor
System Amplifier

Air conditioning wiring schematic—1990–91 Celica

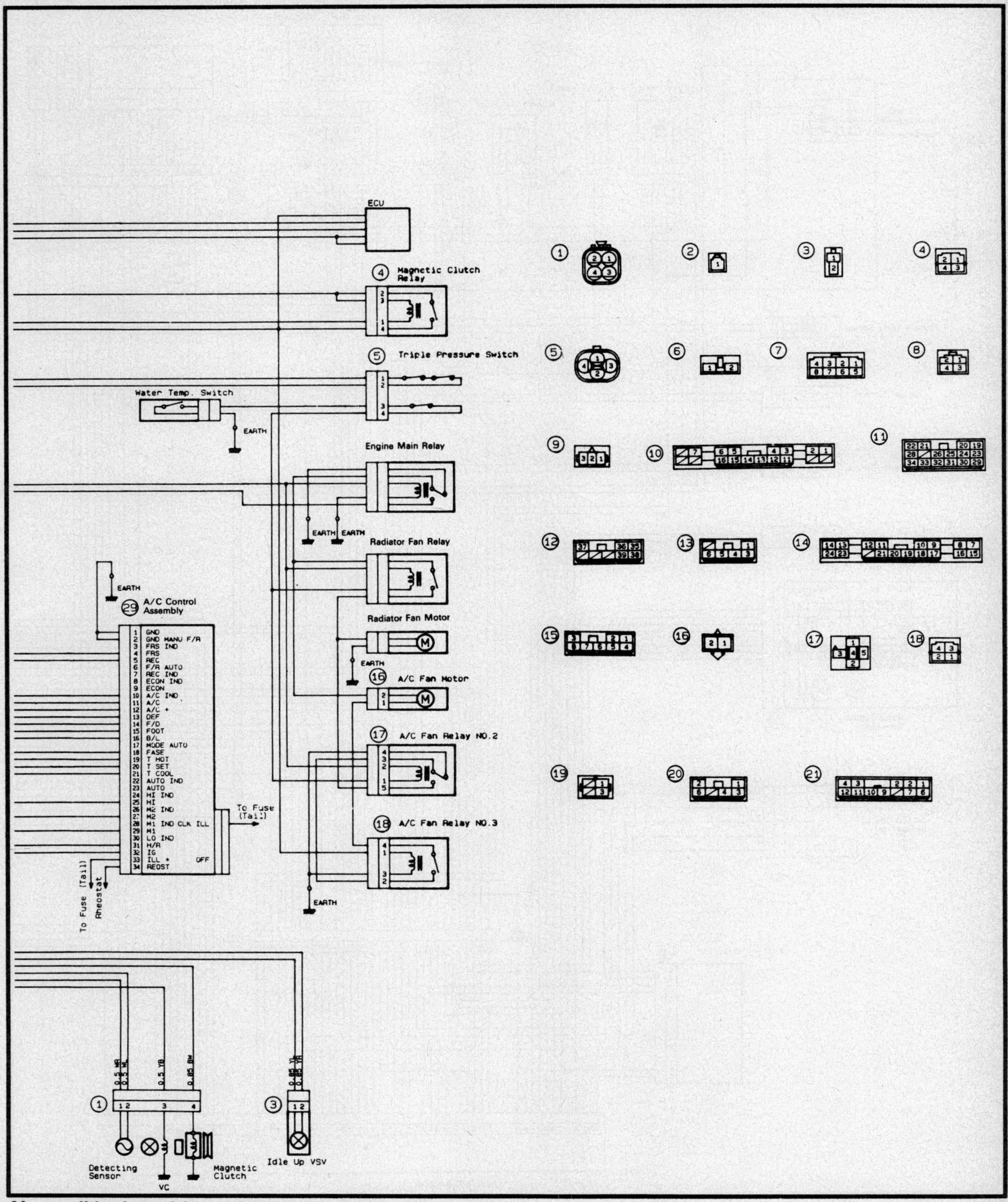
ECU
Magnetic Clutch Relay
Triple Pressure Switch
Water Temp. Switch
EARTH
Engine Main Relay
Radiator Fan Relay
Radiator Fan Motor
A/C Fan Motor
A/C Fan Relay NO.2
A/C Fan Relay NO.3
A/C Control Assembly
1 GND
2 GND MANU F/R
3 FRS IND
4 FRS
5 REC
6 F/R AUTO
7 REC IND
8 ECON IND
9 ECON
10 A/C IND
11 A/C
12 A/C +
13 DEF
14 F/D
15 FOOT
16 B/L
17 MODE AUTO
18 FASE
19 T HOT
20 T SET
21 T COOL
22 AUTO IND
23 AUTO
24 HI IND
25 HI
26 M2 IND
27 M2
28 M1 IND CLK ILL
29 M1
30 LO IND
31 H/R
32 IG
33 ILL + OFF
34 REOST
To Fuse (Tail)
To Fuse (Tail)
Rheostat
Detecting Sensor
Magnetic Clutch
VC
Idle Up VSV

Air conditioning wiring schematic—1990–91 Celica cont'd

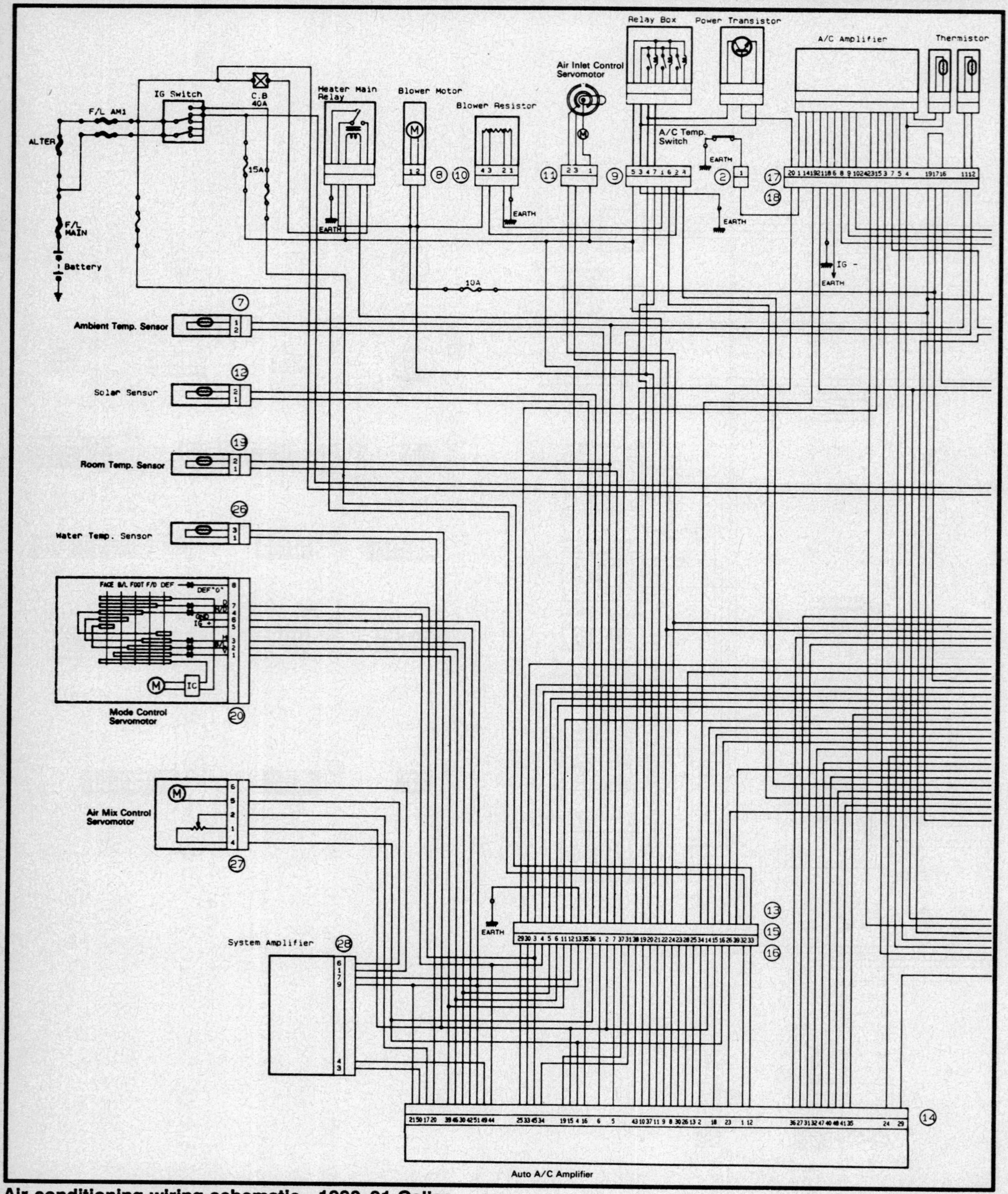
Relay Box
Power Transistor
A/C Amplifier
Thermistor
Air Inlet Control Servomotor
IG Switch
C.B 40A
F/L AM1
ALTER
Heater Main Relay
Blower Motor
Blower Resistor
A/C Temp. Switch
EARTH
15A
F/L MAIN
Battery
10A
IG -
Ambient Temp. Sensor
Solar Sensor
Room Temp. Sensor
Water Temp. Sensor
FACE B/L FOOT F/D DEF
DEF "0"
Mode Control Servomotor
Air Mix Control Servomotor
System Amplifier
Auto A/C Amplifier

Air conditioning wiring schematic – 1990–91 Celica

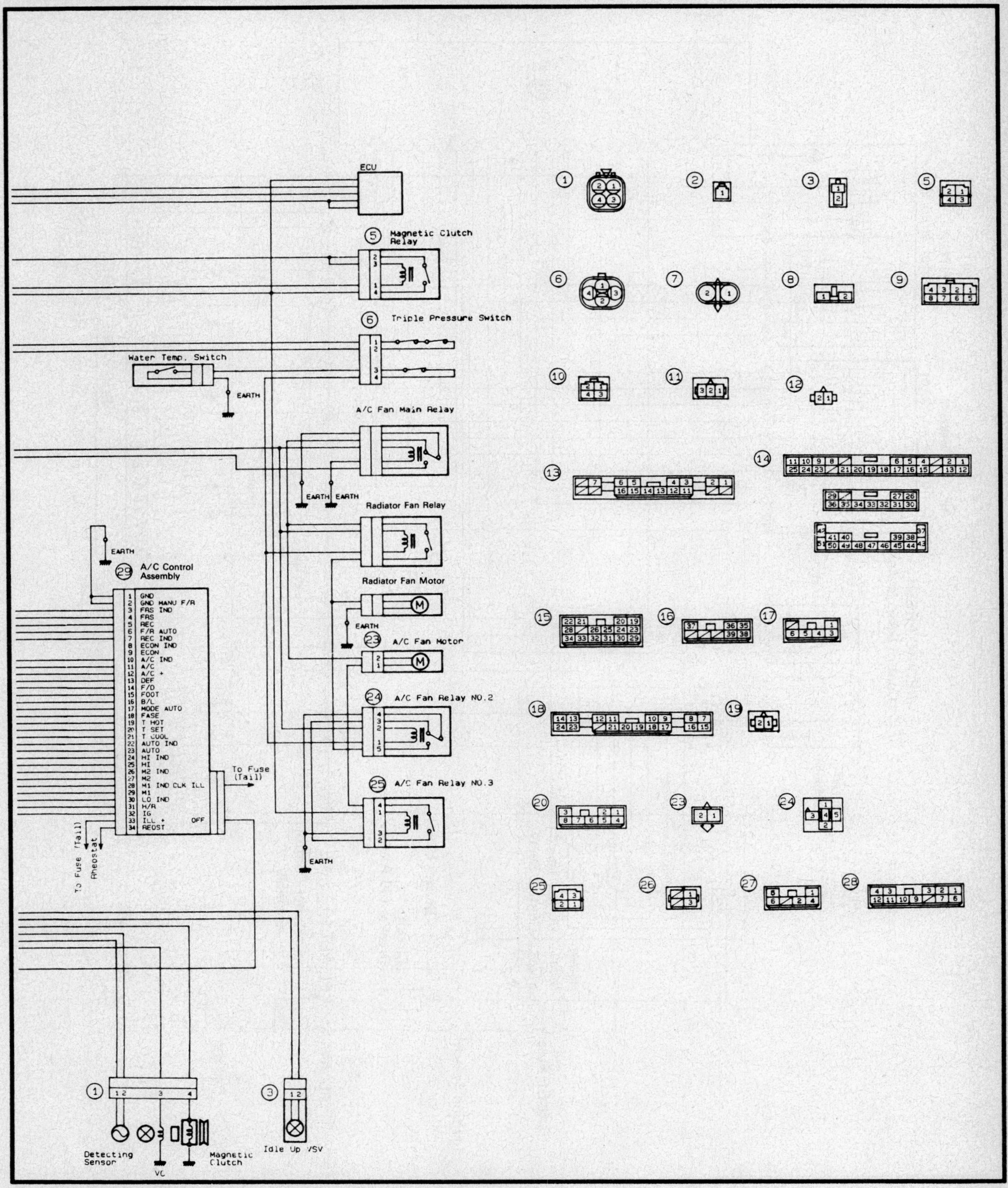
ECU
Magnetic Clutch Relay
Triple Pressure Switch
Water Temp. Switch
EARTH
A/C Fan Main Relay
Radiator Fan Relay
A/C Control Assembly
GND
GND MANU F/R
FRS IND
FRS
REC
F/R AUTO
REC IND
ECON IND
ECON
A/C IND
A/C
A/C +
DEF
F/D
FOOT
B/L
MODE AUTO
FASE
T HOT
T SET
T COOL
AUTO IND
AUTO
HI IND
HI
M2 IND
M2
M1 IND CLK ILL
M1
LO IND
H/R
IG
ILL +
REOST
OFF
To Fuse (Tail)
Rheostat
Radiator Fan Motor
A/C Fan Motor
A/C Fan Relay NO.2
A/C Fan Relay NO.3
Detecting Sensor
VC
Magnetic Clutch
Idle Up VSV

Air conditioning wiring schematic—1990–91 Celica cont'd

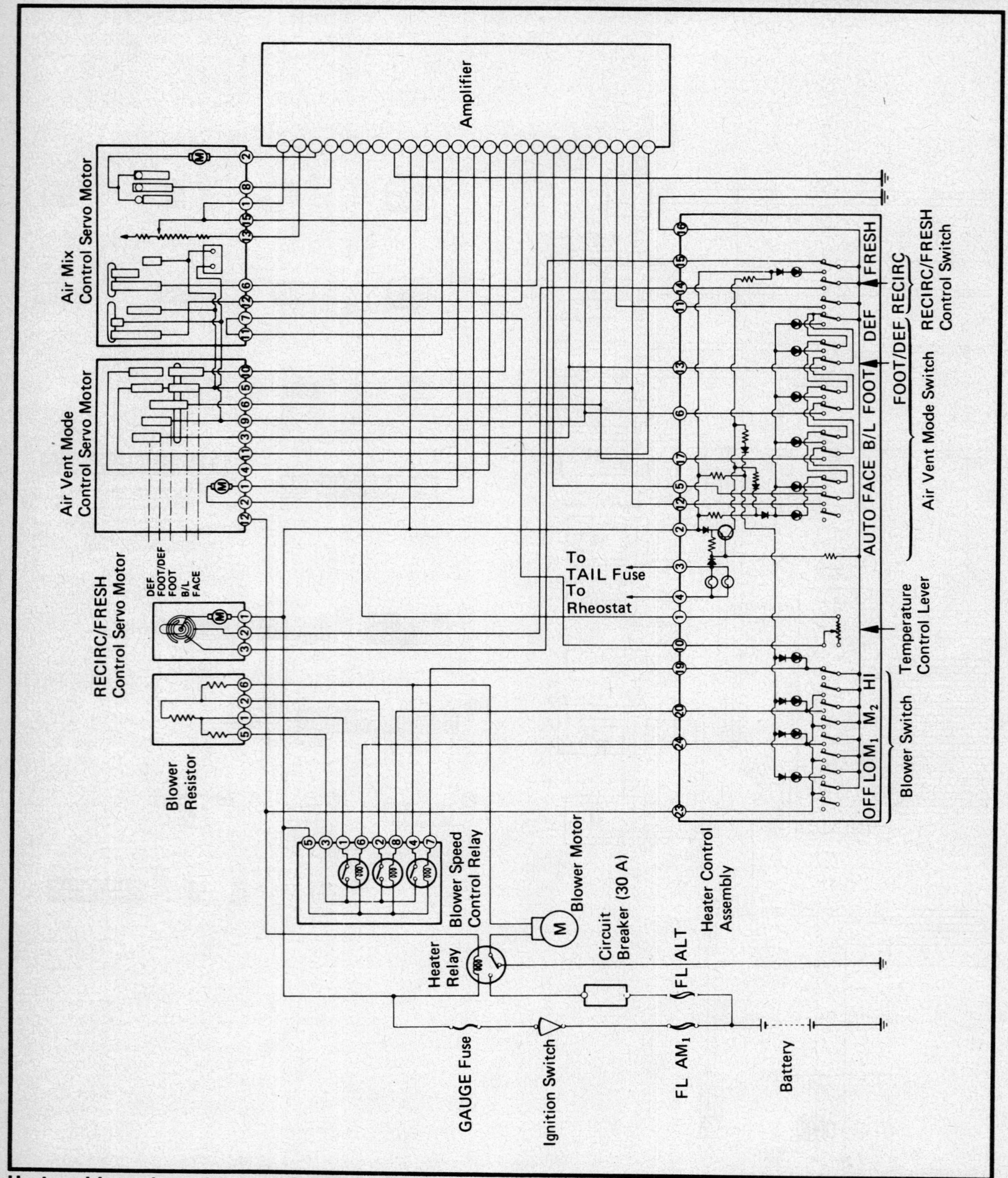
Amplifier
Air Mix Control Servo Motor
Air Vent Mode Control Servo Motor
DEF
FOOT/DEF
FOOT
B/L
FACE
RECIRC/FRESH Control Servo Motor
Blower Resistor
Blower Speed Control Relay
Blower Motor
Heater Relay
Circuit Breaker (30 A)
FL ALT
Heater Control Assembly
GAUGE Fuse
Ignition Switch
FL AM1
Battery
To TAIL Fuse
To Rheostat
FRESH
RECIRC
RECIRC/FRESH Control Switch
DEF
FOOT/DEF
FOOT
B/L
FACE
AUTO
Air Vent Mode Switch
Temperature Control Lever
OFF LO M1 M2 HI
Blower Switch

Heater wiring schematic—1989 Celica (push type)

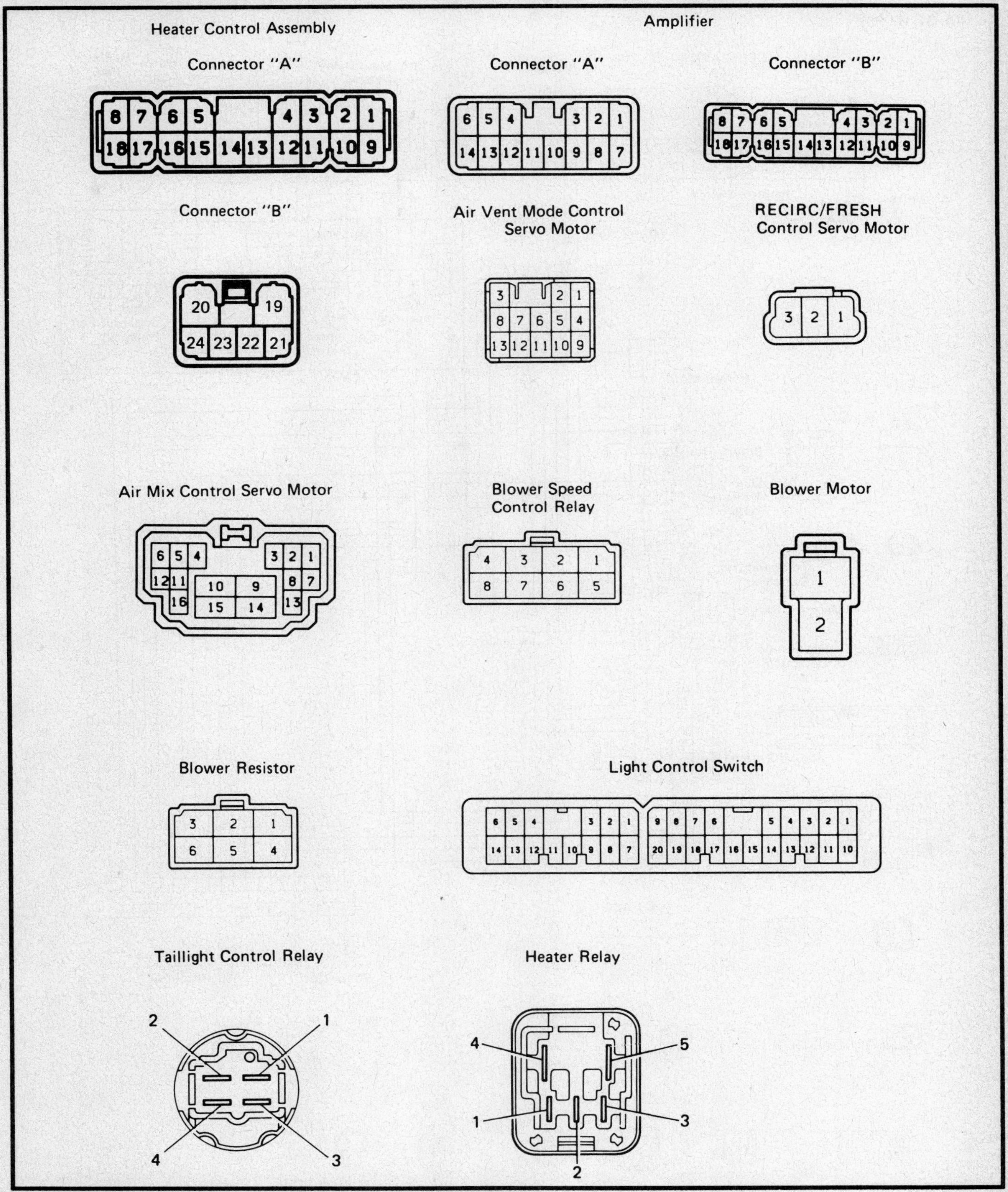
Heater Control Assembly
Connector "A"
Amplifier
Connector "A"
Connector "B"
Connector "B"
Air Vent Mode Control Servo Motor
RECIRC/FRESH Control Servo Motor
Air Mix Control Servo Motor
Blower Speed Control Relay
Blower Motor
Blower Resistor
Light Control Switch
Taillight Control Relay
Heater Relay

Heater wiring schematic—1989 Celica (push type) cont'd

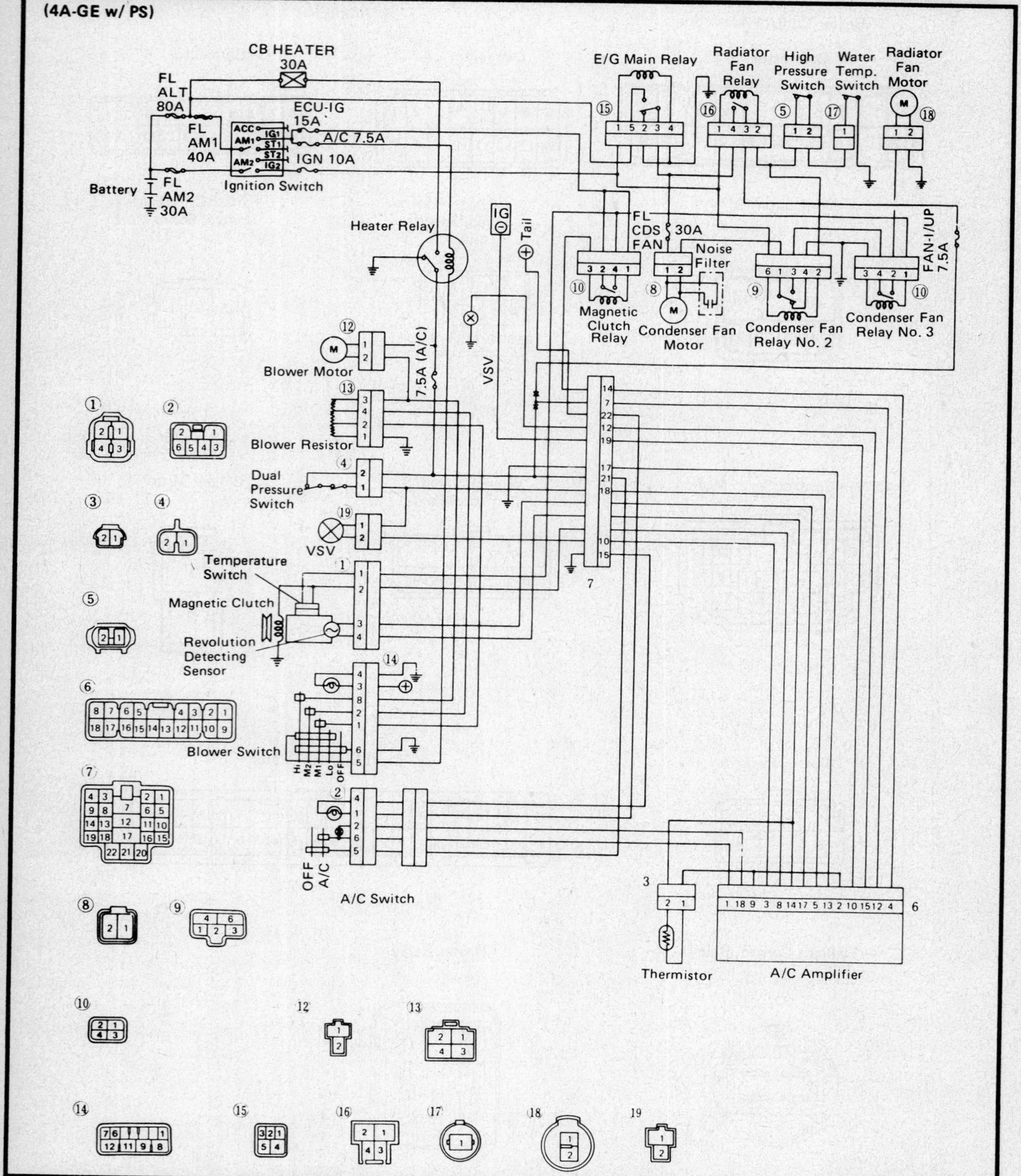
(4A-GE w/ PS)
CB HEATER 30A
FL ALT 80A
FL AM1 40A
Battery
FL AM2 30A
ECU-IG 15A
A/C 7.5A
IGN 10A
ACC
AM1
IG1
ST1
ST2
AM2
IG2
Ignition Switch
E/G Main Relay
Radiator Fan Relay
High Pressure Switch
Water Temp. Switch
Radiator Fan Motor
Heater Relay
IG
Tail
FL CDS FAN 30A
Noise Filter
FAN-I/UP 7.5A
Magnetic Clutch Relay
Condenser Fan Motor
Condenser Fan Relay No. 2
Condenser Fan Relay No. 3
Blower Motor
7.5A (A/C)
VSV
Blower Resistor
Dual Pressure Switch
VSV
Temperature Switch
Magnetic Clutch
Revolution Detecting Sensor
Blower Switch
Hi
M2
M1
Lo
OFF
OFF
A/C
A/C Switch
Thermistor
A/C Amplifier

Air conditioning wiring schematic—Corolla 4A-GE engine

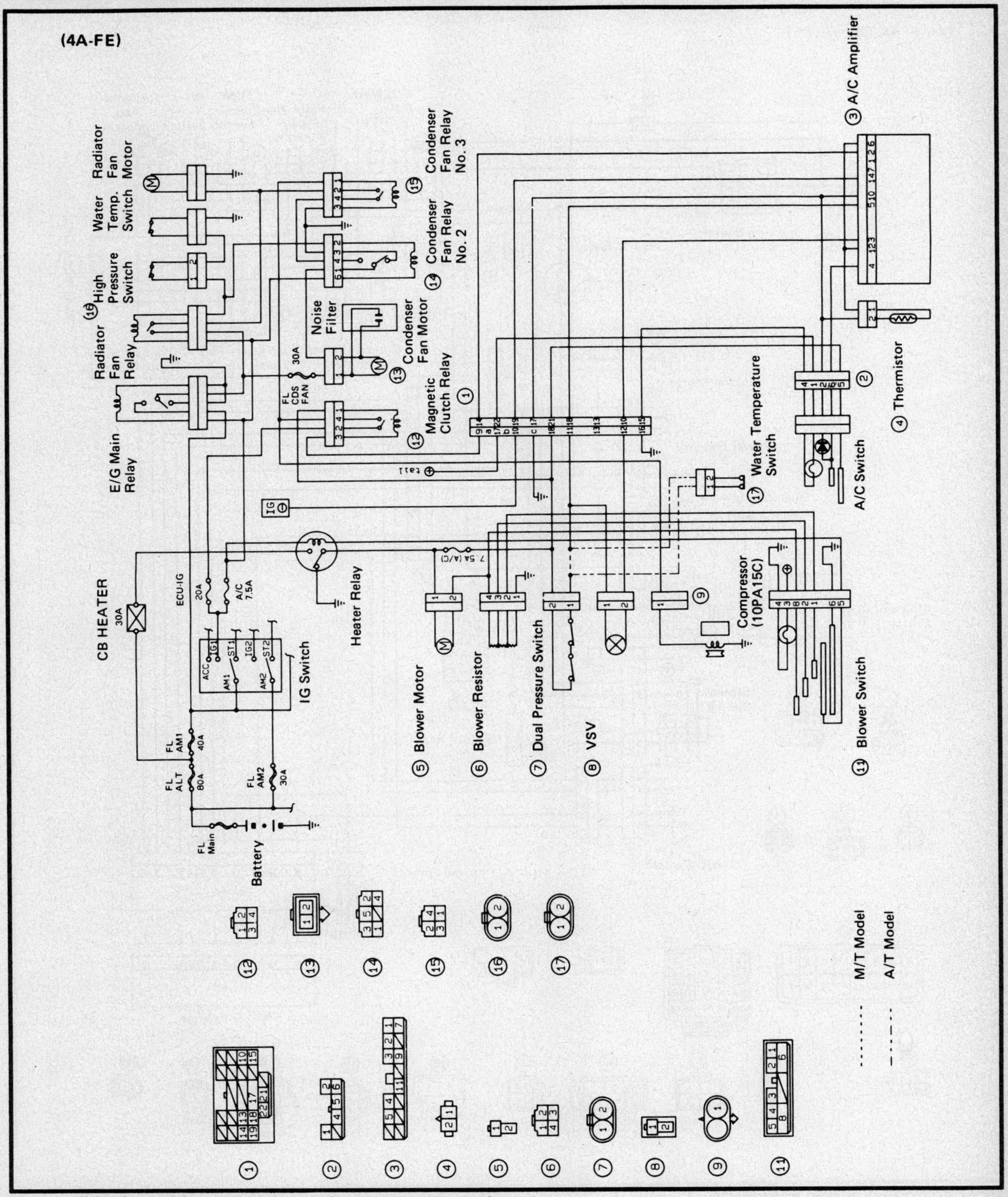
(4A-FE)
Radiator Fan Motor
Water Temp. Switch
High Pressure Switch
Radiator Fan Relay
E/G Main Relay
Noise Filter
Condenser Fan Motor
Condenser Fan Relay No. 2
Condenser Fan Relay No. 3
Magnetic Clutch Relay
A/C Amplifier
Thermistor
Water Temperature Switch
A/C Switch
CB HEATER 30A
ECU-IG 20A
A/C 7.5A
IG Switch
Heater Relay
Blower Motor
Blower Resistor
Dual Pressure Switch
VSV
Compressor (10PA15C)
Blower Switch
Battery
FL Main
FL ALT 80A
FL AM1 40A
FL AM2 30A
FL CDS FAN 30A
7.5A (A/C)
M/T Model
A/T Model

Air conditioning wiring schematic—Corolla 4F-FE engine

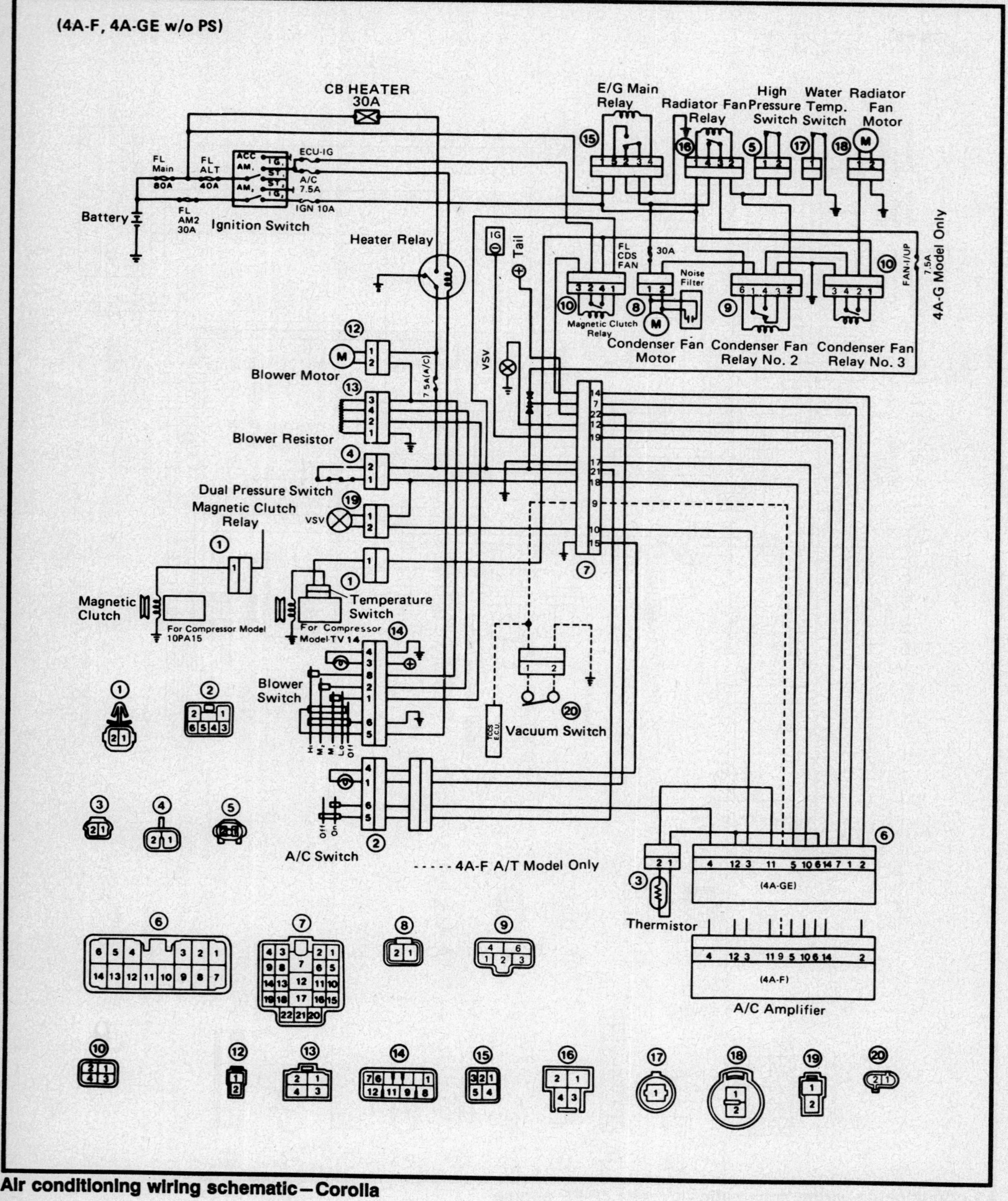
(4A-F, 4A-GE w/o PS)
CB HEATER 30A
E/G Main Relay
Radiator Fan Relay
High Pressure Switch
Water Temp. Switch
Radiator Fan Motor
FL Main 80A
FL ALT 40A
FL AM2 30A
ECU-IG
A/C 7.5A
IGN 10A
Battery
Ignition Switch
Heater Relay
IG
Tail
FL CDS FAN
30A
Noise Filter
7.5A FAN-I/UP
4A-G Model Only
Magnetic Clutch Relay
Condenser Fan Motor
Condenser Fan Relay No. 2
Condenser Fan Relay No. 3
Blower Motor
7.5A(A/C)
VSV
Blower Resistor
Dual Pressure Switch
Magnetic Clutch Relay
Magnetic Clutch
For Compressor Model 10PA15
Temperature Switch
For Compressor Model TV 14
Blower Switch
Hi M2 M1 Lo Off
Vacuum Switch
TCCS E.C.U.
Off On
A/C Switch
----- 4A-F A/T Model Only
Thermistor
(4A-GE)
(4A-F)
A/C Amplifier

Air conditioning wiring schematic—Corolla

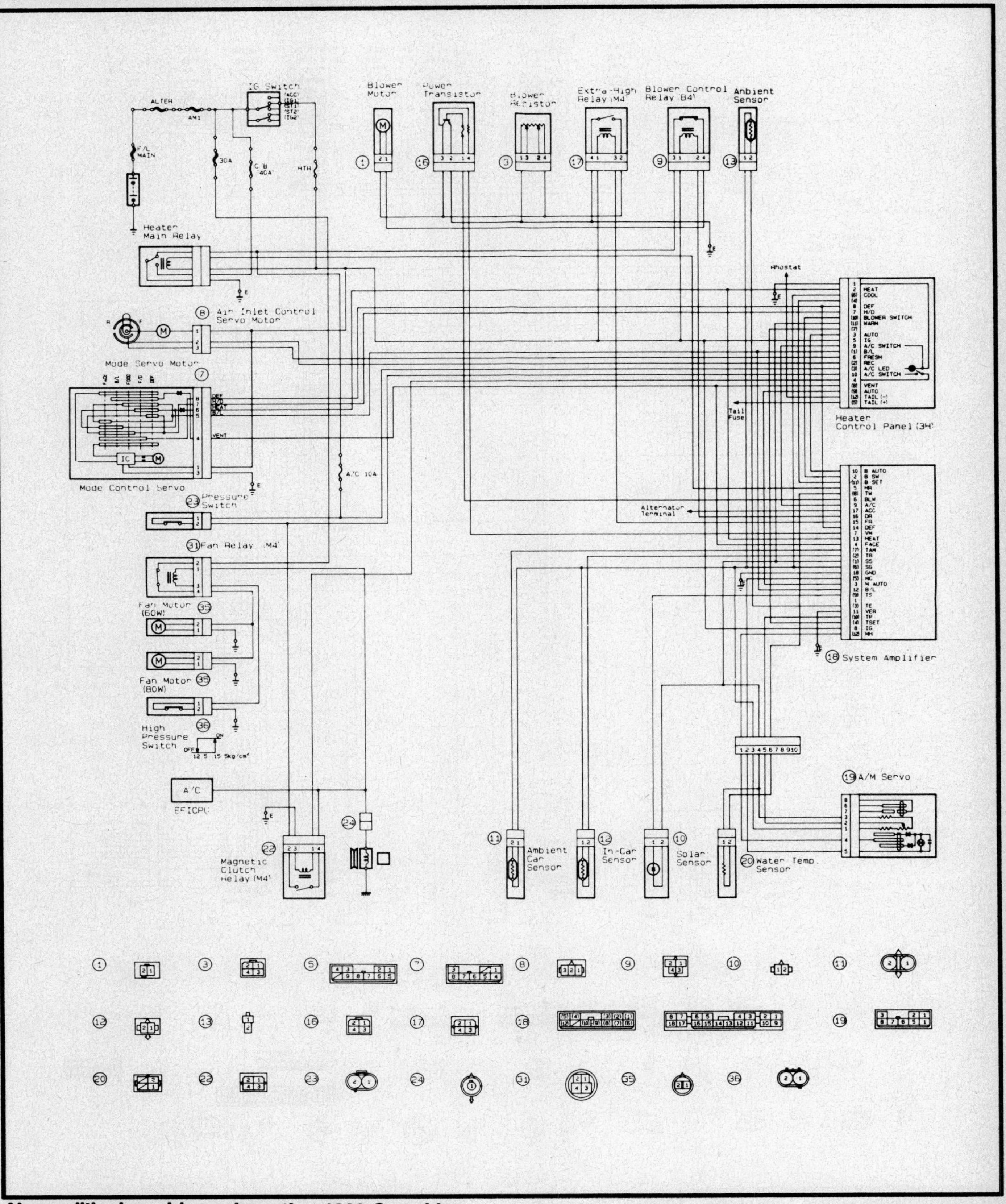

Air conditioning wiring schematic—1989 Cressida

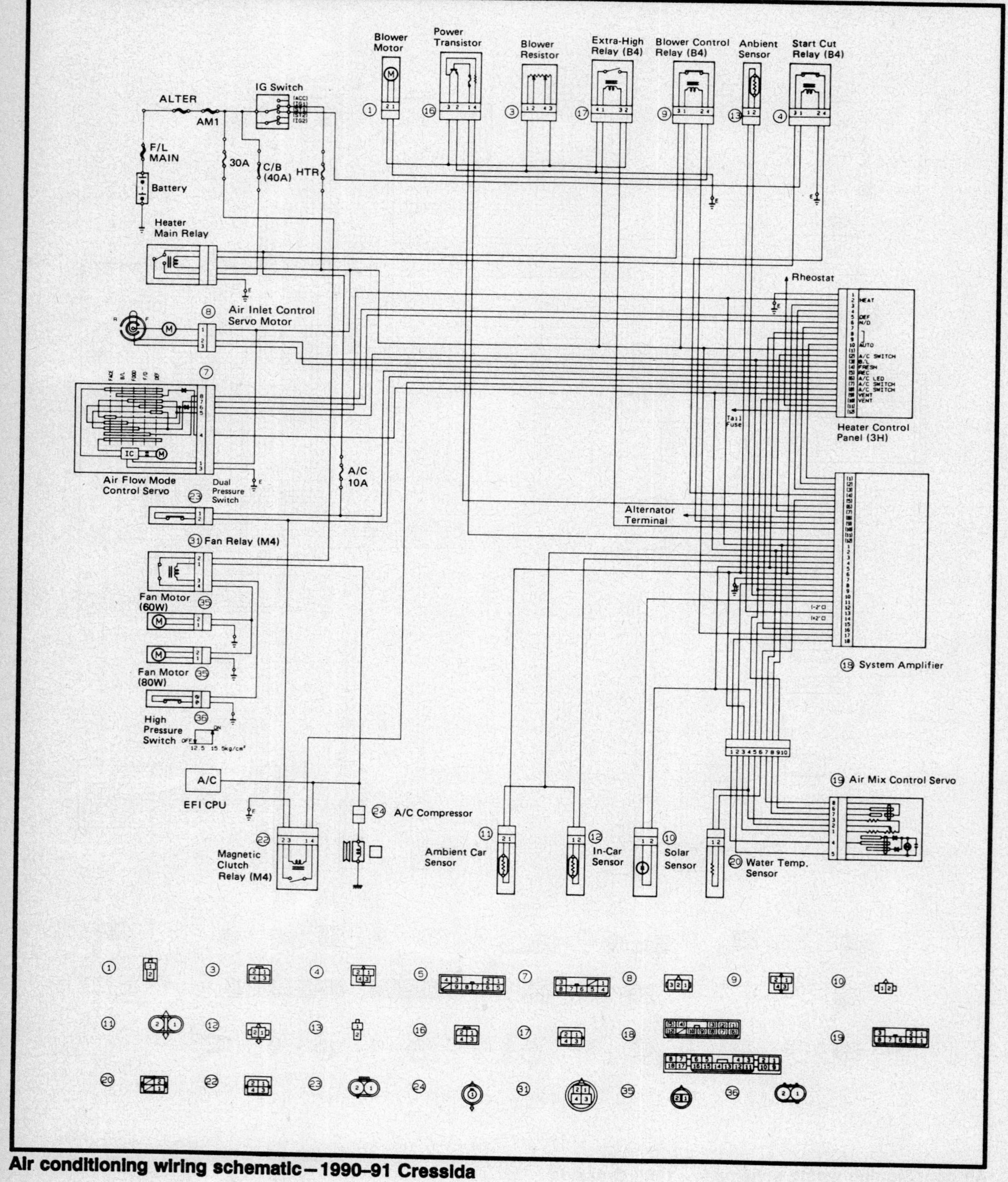
Blower Motor
Power Transistor
Blower Resistor
Extra-High Relay (B4)
Blower Control Relay (B4)
Ambient Sensor
Start Cut Relay (B4)
IG Switch
ALTER
AM1
F/L MAIN
Battery
30A
C/B (40A)
HTR
Heater Main Relay
Rheostat
Air Inlet Control Servo Motor
Heater Control Panel (3H)
Tail Fuse
Air Flow Mode Control Servo
Dual Pressure Switch
A/C 10A
Alternator Terminal
Fan Relay (M4)
Fan Motor (60W)
Fan Motor (80W)
High Pressure Switch
System Amplifier
Air Mix Control Servo
A/C
EFI CPU
A/C Compressor
Magnetic Clutch Relay (M4)
Ambient Car Sensor
In-Car Sensor
Solar Sensor
Water Temp. Sensor

Air conditioning wiring schematic—1990–91 Cressida

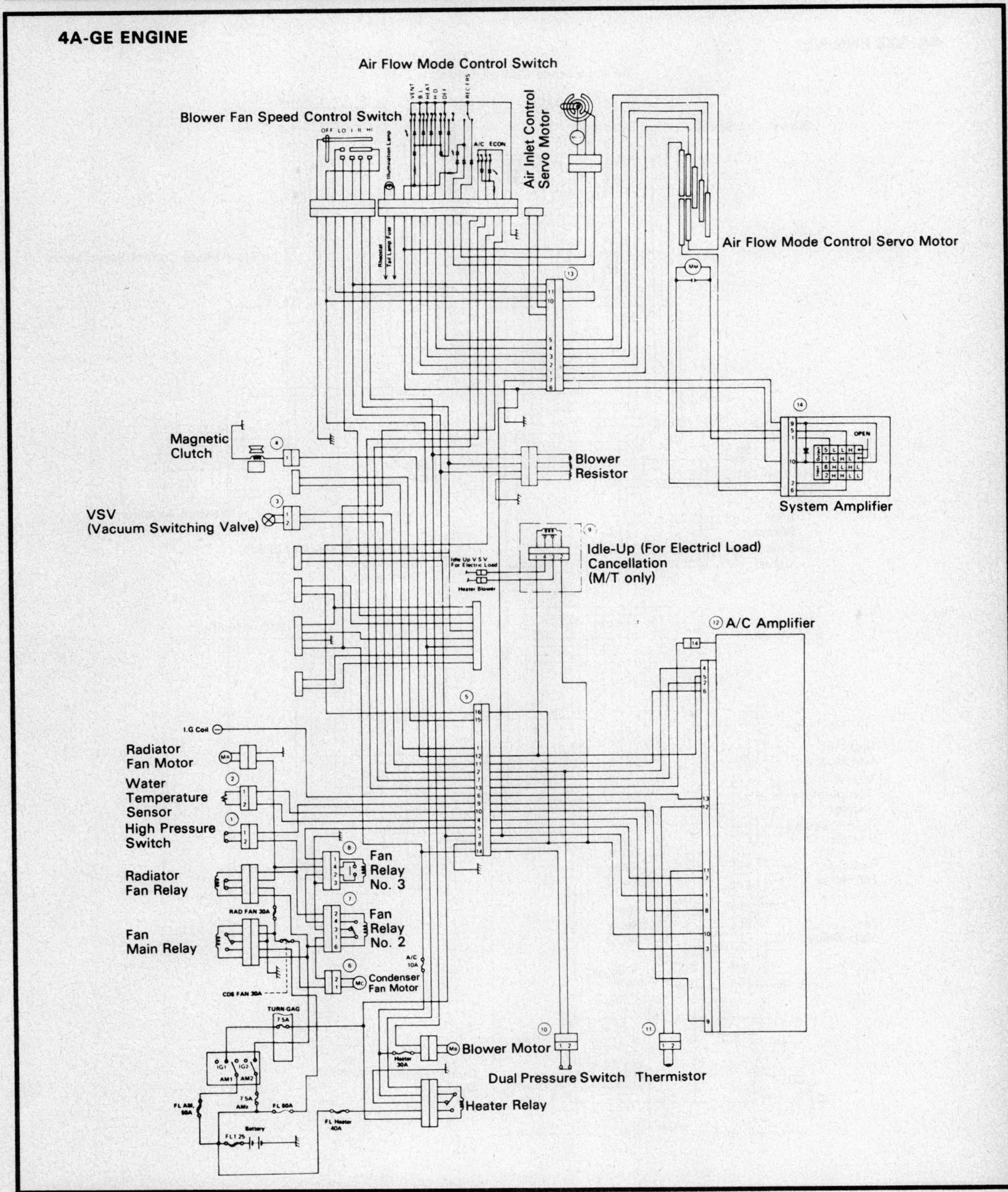
4A-GE ENGINE
Air Flow Mode Control Switch
Blower Fan Speed Control Switch
Air Inlet Control Servo Motor
Air Flow Mode Control Servo Motor
Magnetic Clutch
Blower Resistor
System Amplifier
VSV (Vacuum Switching Valve)
Idle-Up (For Electricl Load) Cancellation (M/T only)
A/C Amplifier
Radiator Fan Motor
Water Temperature Sensor
High Pressure Switch
Radiator Fan Relay
Fan Relay No. 3
Fan Relay No. 2
Fan Main Relay
Condenser Fan Motor
Blower Motor
Dual Pressure Switch
Thermistor
Heater Relay

Air conditioning wiring schematic—1989 MR2 4A-GE engine

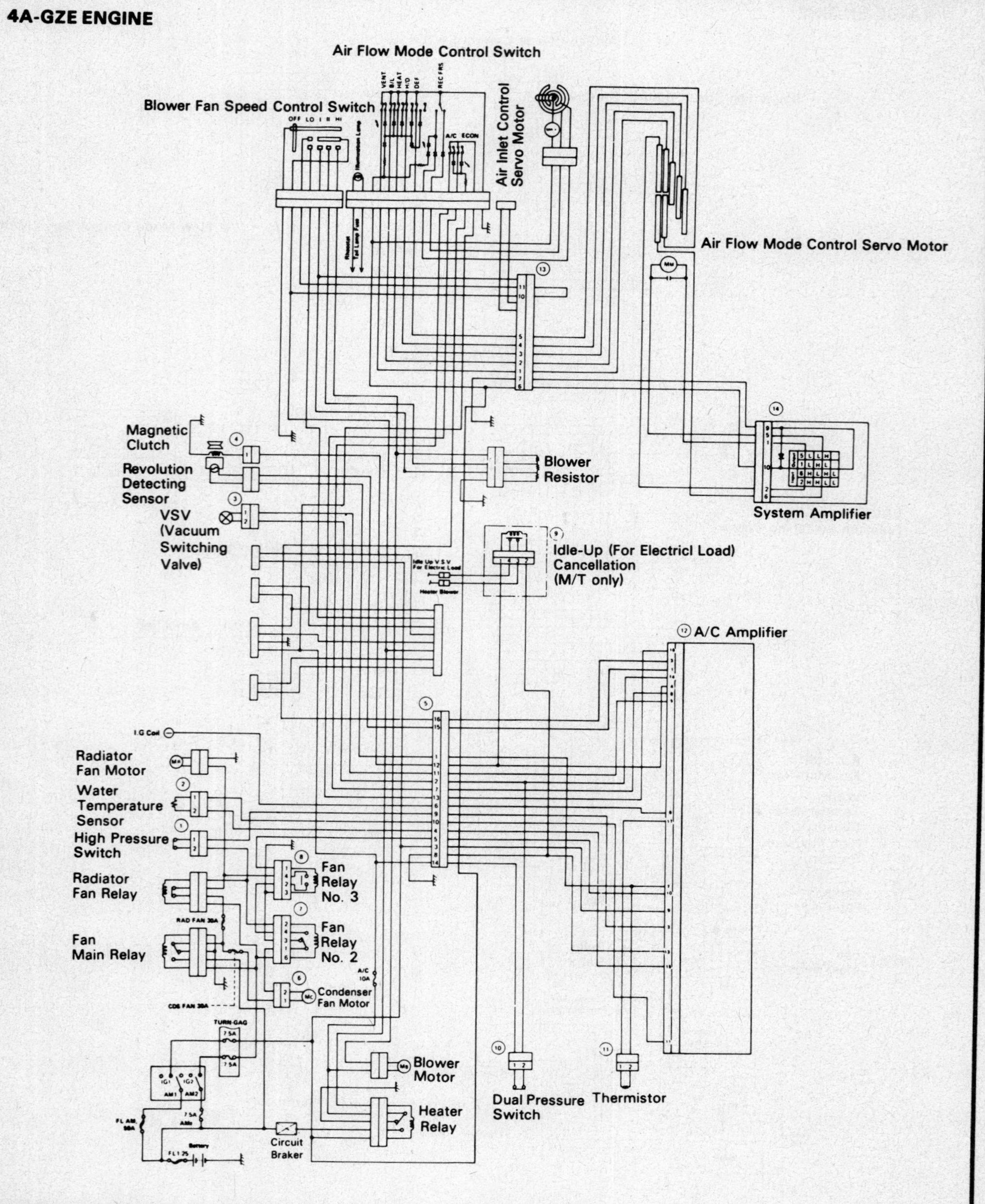
4A-GZE ENGINE
Air Flow Mode Control Switch
Blower Fan Speed Control Switch
Air Inlet Control Servo Motor
Air Flow Mode Control Servo Motor
Magnetic Clutch
Revolution Detecting Sensor
VSV (Vacuum Switching Valve)
Blower Resistor
System Amplifier
Idle-Up (For Electricl Load) Cancellation (M/T only)
A/C Amplifier
Radiator Fan Motor
Water Temperature Sensor
High Pressure Switch
Radiator Fan Relay
Fan Relay No. 3
Fan Relay No. 2
Fan Main Relay
Condenser Fan Motor
Blower Motor
Heater Relay
Circuit Braker
Dual Pressure Switch
Thermistor

Air conditioning wiring schematic—1989 MR2 4A-GZE engine

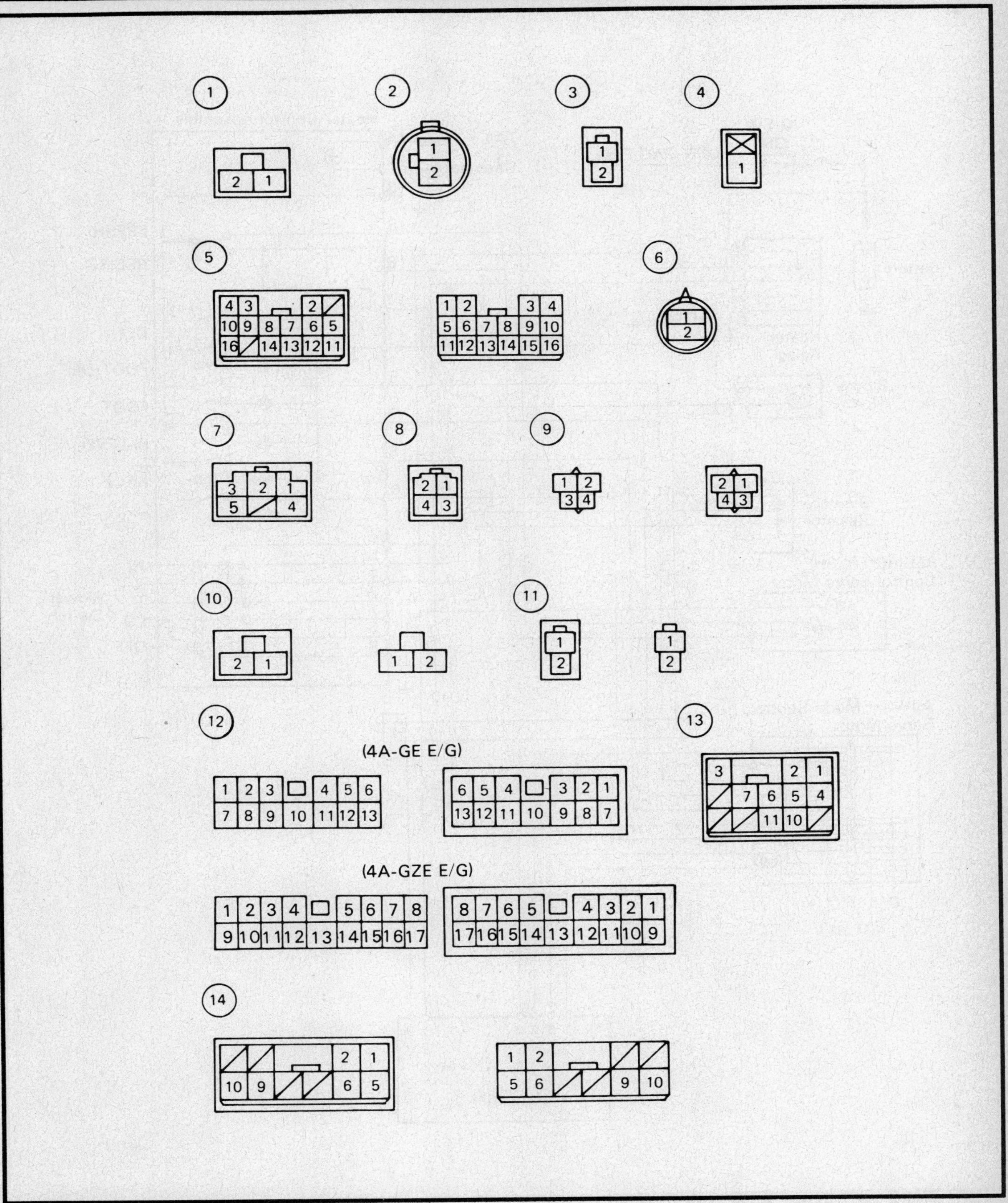
1
2
3
4
5
6
7
8
9
10
11
12
(4A-GE E/G)
(4A-GZE E/G)
13
14

Air conditioning wiring schematic—1989 MR2 cont'd

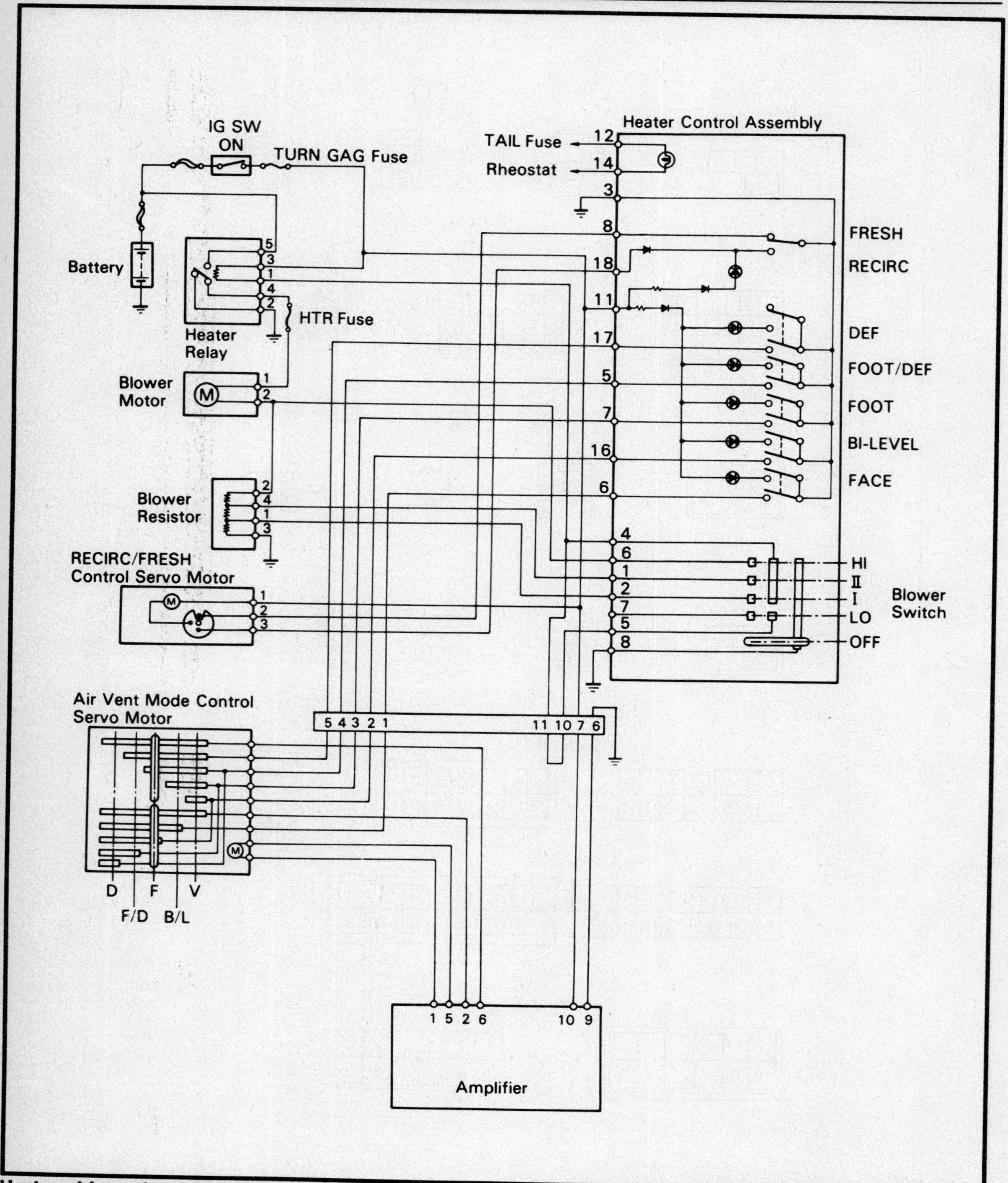
IG SW
ON
TURN GAG Fuse
Battery
Heater
Relay
HTR Fuse
Blower
Motor
Blower
Resistor
RECIRC/FRESH
Control Servo Motor
Air Vent Mode Control
Servo Motor
D
F
V
F/D
B/L
Heater Control Assembly
TAIL Fuse
Rheostat
FRESH
RECIRC
DEF
FOOT/DEF
FOOT
BI-LEVEL
FACE
HI
II
I
LO
OFF
Blower
Switch
Amplifier

Heater wiring schematic—1989 MR2

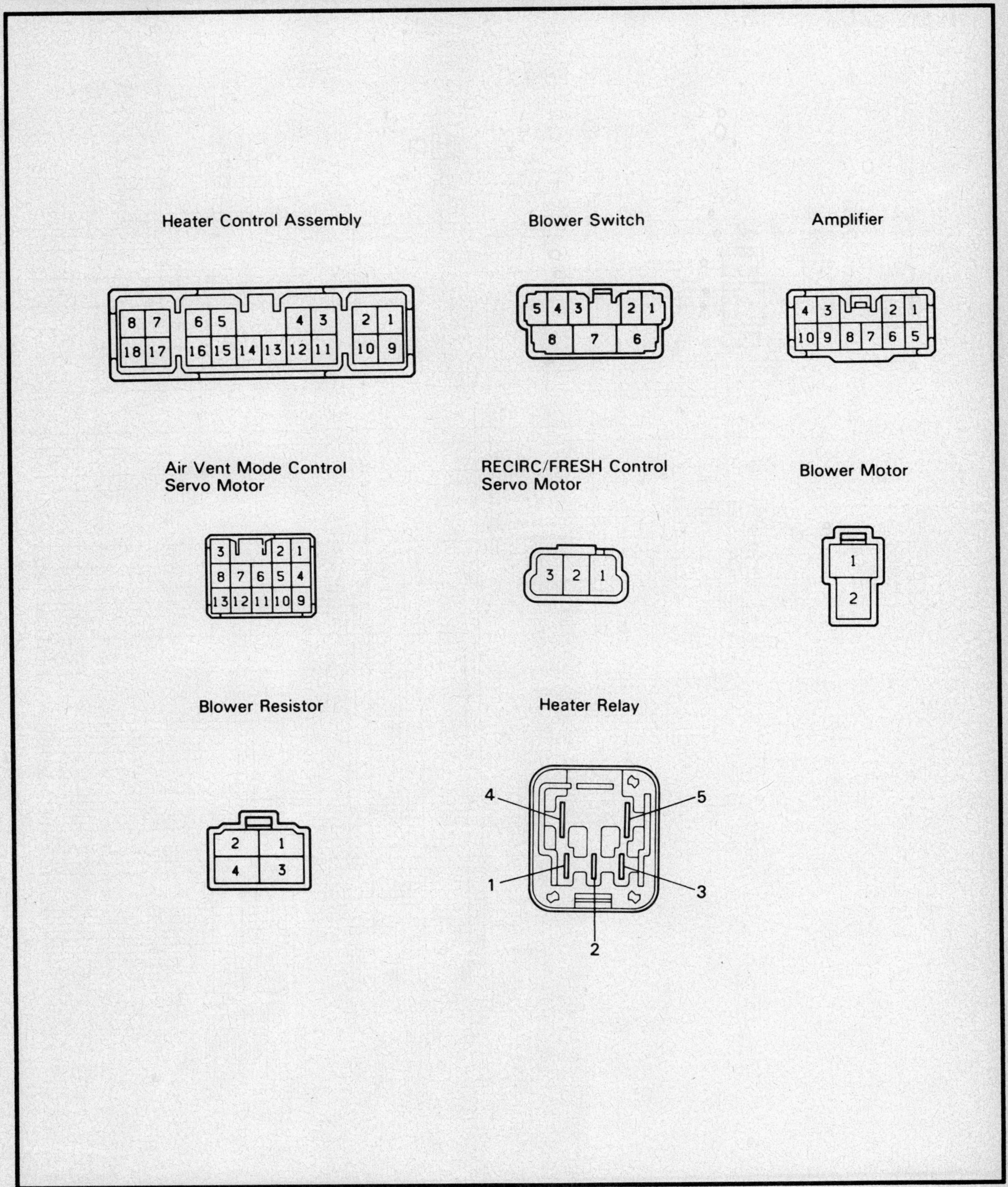
Heater Control Assembly
Blower Switch
Amplifier
Air Vent Mode Control Servo Motor
RECIRC/FRESH Control Servo Motor
Blower Motor
Blower Resistor
Heater Relay

Heater wiring schematic—1989 MR2 cont'd

7M-GTE Engine

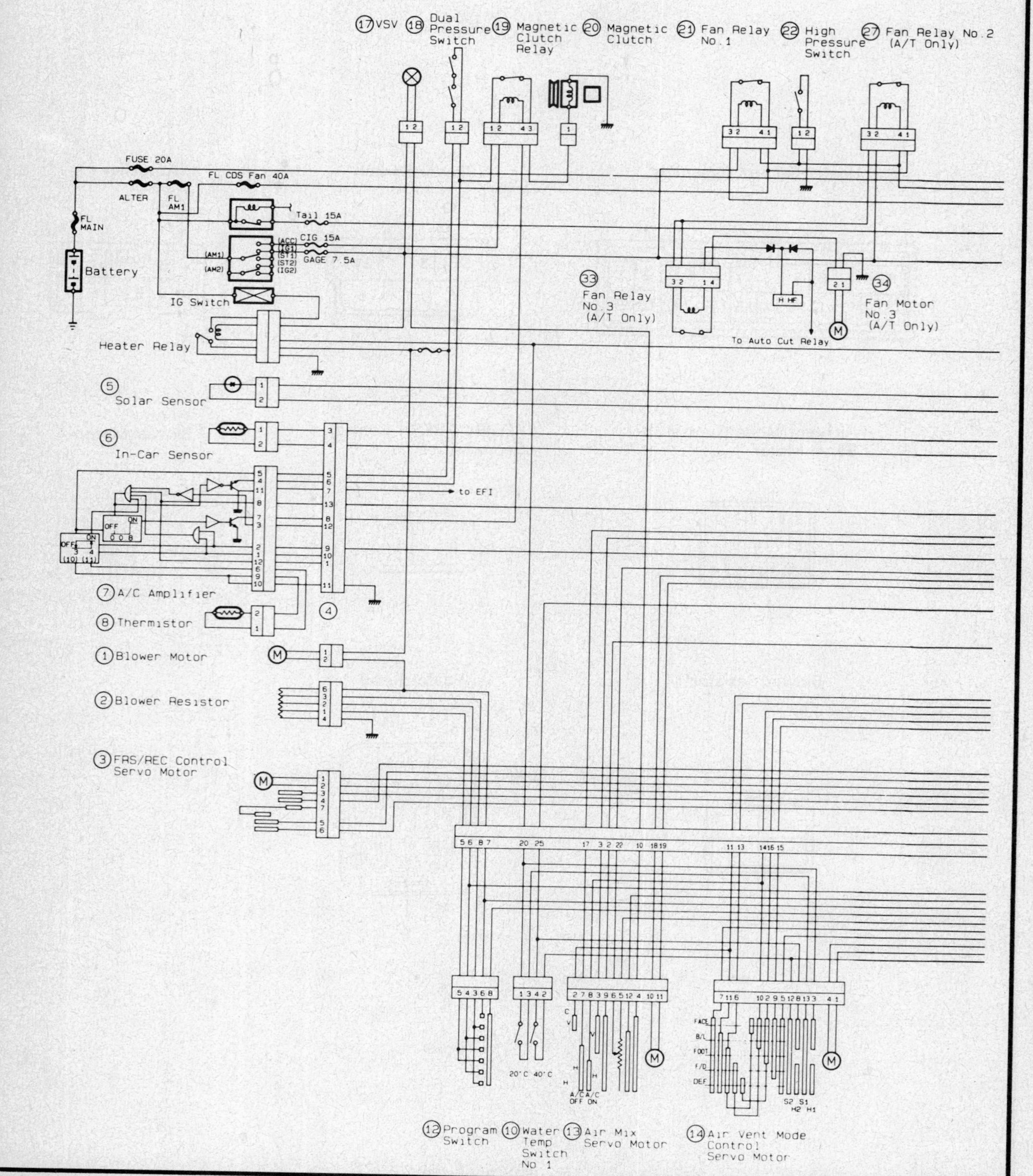
17 VSV
18 Dual Pressure Switch
19 Magnetic Clutch Relay
20 Magnetic Clutch
21 Fan Relay No.1
22 High Pressure Switch
27 Fan Relay No.2 (A/T Only)
FUSE 20A
FL CDS Fan 40A
ALTER
FL AM1
FL MAIN
Battery
Tail 15A
CIG 15A
GAGE 7.5A
(ACC)
(IG1)
(ST1)
(ST2)
(IG2)
(AM1)
(AM2)
IG Switch
Heater Relay
33 Fan Relay No.3 (A/T Only)
34 Fan Motor No.3 (A/T Only)
To Auto Cut Relay
5 Solar Sensor
6 In-Car Sensor
to EFI
7 A/C Amplifier
8 Thermistor
4
1 Blower Motor
2 Blower Resistor
3 FRS/REC Control Servo Motor
20°C 40°C
A/C A/C
OFF ON
FACE
B/L
FOOT
F/D
DEF
S2 S1
H2 H1
12 Program Switch
10 Water Temp Switch No 1
13 Air Mix Servo Motor
14 Air Vent Mode Control Servo Motor

Air conditioning wiring schematic—Supra 7M-GTE engine

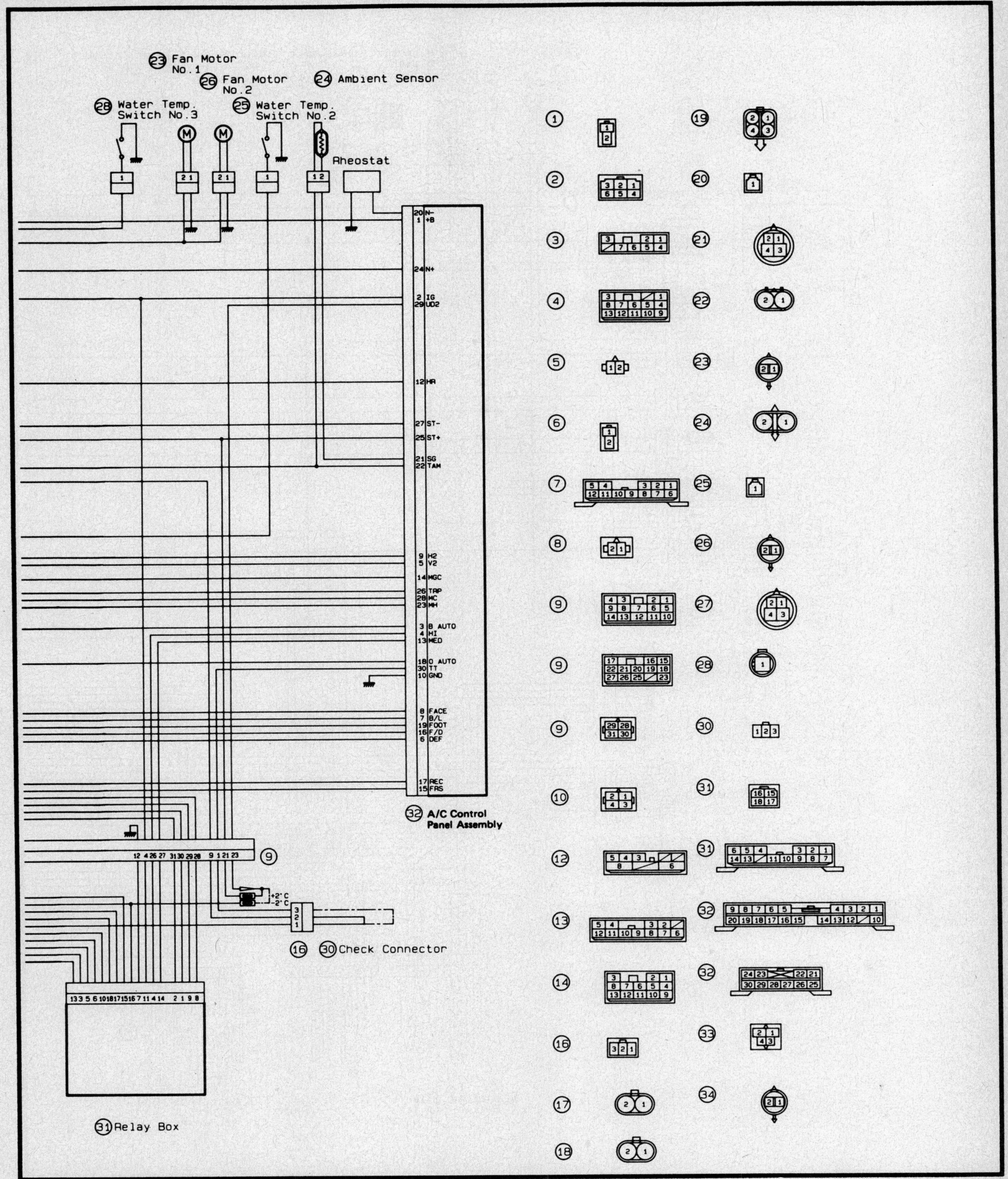
23 Fan Motor No.1
26 Fan Motor No.2
24 Ambient Sensor
28 Water Temp. Switch No.3
25 Water Temp. Switch No.2
Rheostat
20 N-
1 +B
24 N+
2 IG
29 UD2
12 HR
27 ST-
25 ST+
21 SG
22 TAM
9 H2
5 V2
14 MGC
26 TRP
28 MC
23 MH
3 B AUTO
4 HI
13 MED
18 O AUTO
30 TT
10 GND
8 FACE
7 B/L
19 FOOT
16 F/D
6 DEF
17 REC
15 FRS
32 A/C Control Panel Assembly
+2°C
-2°C
16 30 Check Connector
31 Relay Box

Air conditioning wiring schematic—Supra 7M-GTE engine cont'd

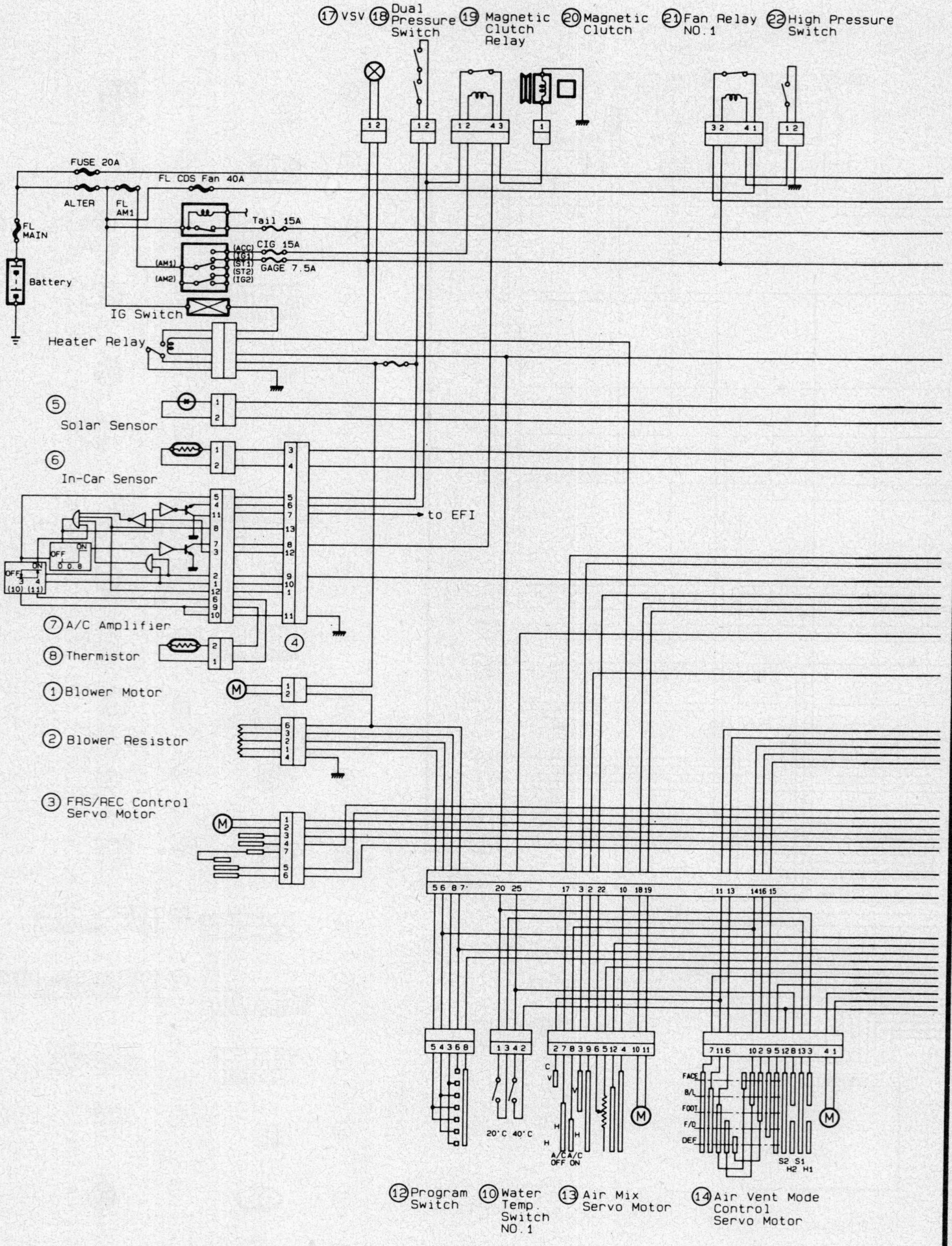
17 VSV
18 Dual Pressure Switch
19 Magnetic Clutch Relay
20 Magnetic Clutch
21 Fan Relay NO.1
22 High Pressure Switch
FUSE 20A
FL CDS Fan 40A
ALTER
FL AM1
FL MAIN
Battery
Tail 15A
CIG 15A
GAGE 7.5A
IG Switch
Heater Relay
5 Solar Sensor
6 In-Car Sensor
to EFI
7 A/C Amplifier
8 Thermistor
1 Blower Motor
2 Blower Resistor
3 FRS/REC Control Servo Motor
12 Program Switch
10 Water Temp. Switch NO.1
13 Air Mix Servo Motor
14 Air Vent Mode Control Servo Motor
20°C 40°C
FACE
B/L
FOOT
F/D
DEF

Air conditioning wiring schematic—Supra 7M-GE engine

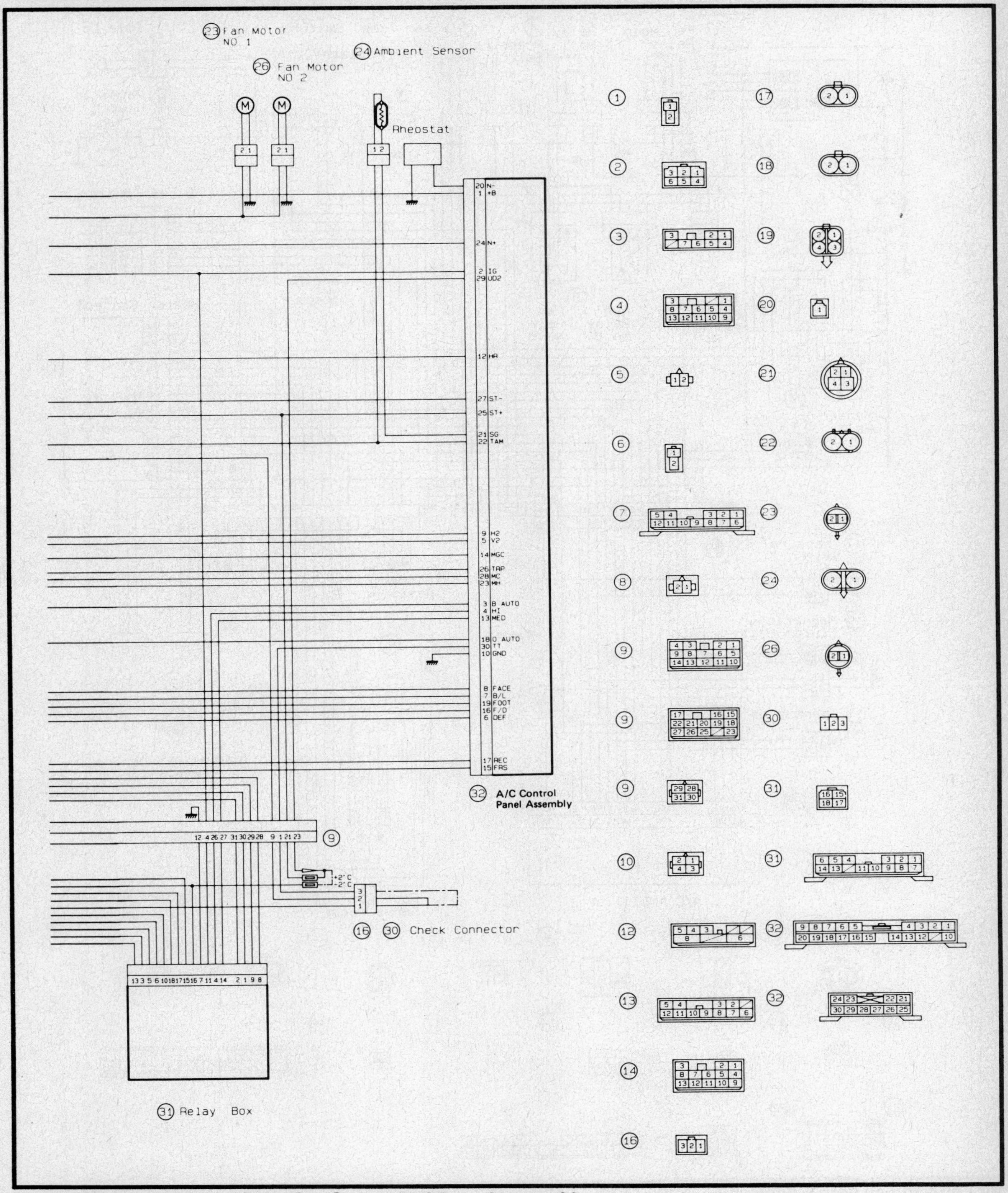
23 Fan Motor NO. 1
24 Ambient Sensor
26 Fan Motor NO. 2
Rheostat
20 N-
1 +B
24 N+
2 IG
29 UD2
12 HR
27 ST-
25 ST+
21 SG
22 TAM
9 H2
5 V2
14 MGC
26 TRP
28 MC
23 MH
3 B AUTO
4 HI
13 MED
18 O AUTO
30 TT
10 GND
8 FACE
7 B/L
19 FOOT
16 F/D
6 DEF
17 REC
15 FRS
32 A/C Control Panel Assembly
+2°C
-2°C
16 30 Check Connector
31 Relay Box

Air conditioning wiring schematic—Supra 7M-GE engine cont'd

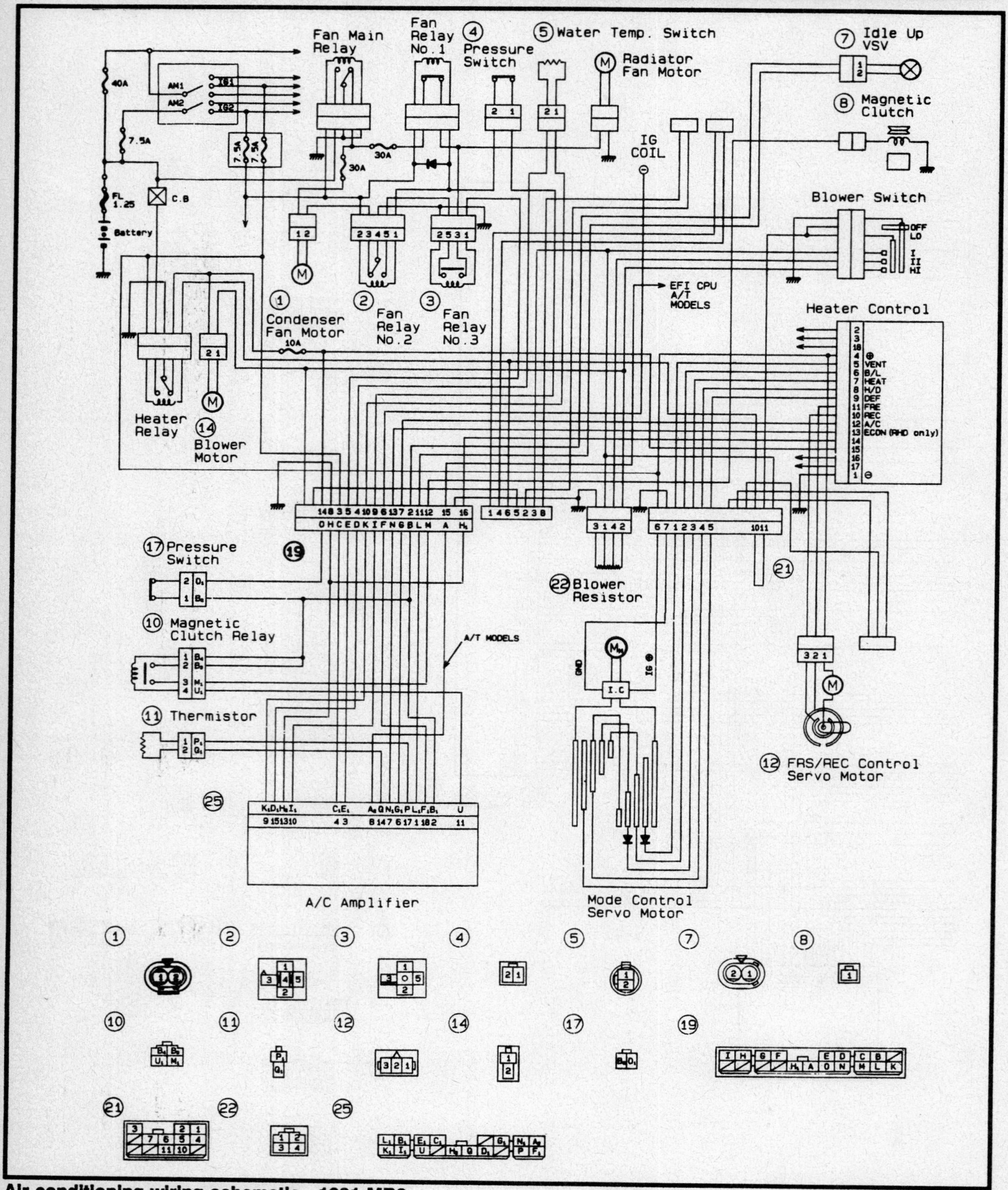
Fan Main Relay
Fan Relay No.1
4 Pressure Switch
5 Water Temp. Switch
Radiator Fan Motor
7 Idle Up VSV
8 Magnetic Clutch
IG COIL
Blower Switch
OFF
LO
I
II
HI
40A
AM1
AM2
IG1
IG2
7.5A
30A
FL 1.25
C.B
Battery
1 Condenser Fan Motor
2 Fan Relay No.2
3 Fan Relay No.3
EFI CPU A/T MODELS
Heater Control
VENT
B/L
HEAT
H/D
DEF
FRE
REC
A/C
ECON (RHD only)
10A
Heater Relay
14 Blower Motor
17 Pressure Switch
19
22 Blower Resistor
21
10 Magnetic Clutch Relay
A/T MODELS
11 Thermistor
12 FRS/REC Control Servo Motor
25
A/C Amplifier
Mode Control Servo Motor

Air conditioning wiring schematic—1991 MR2

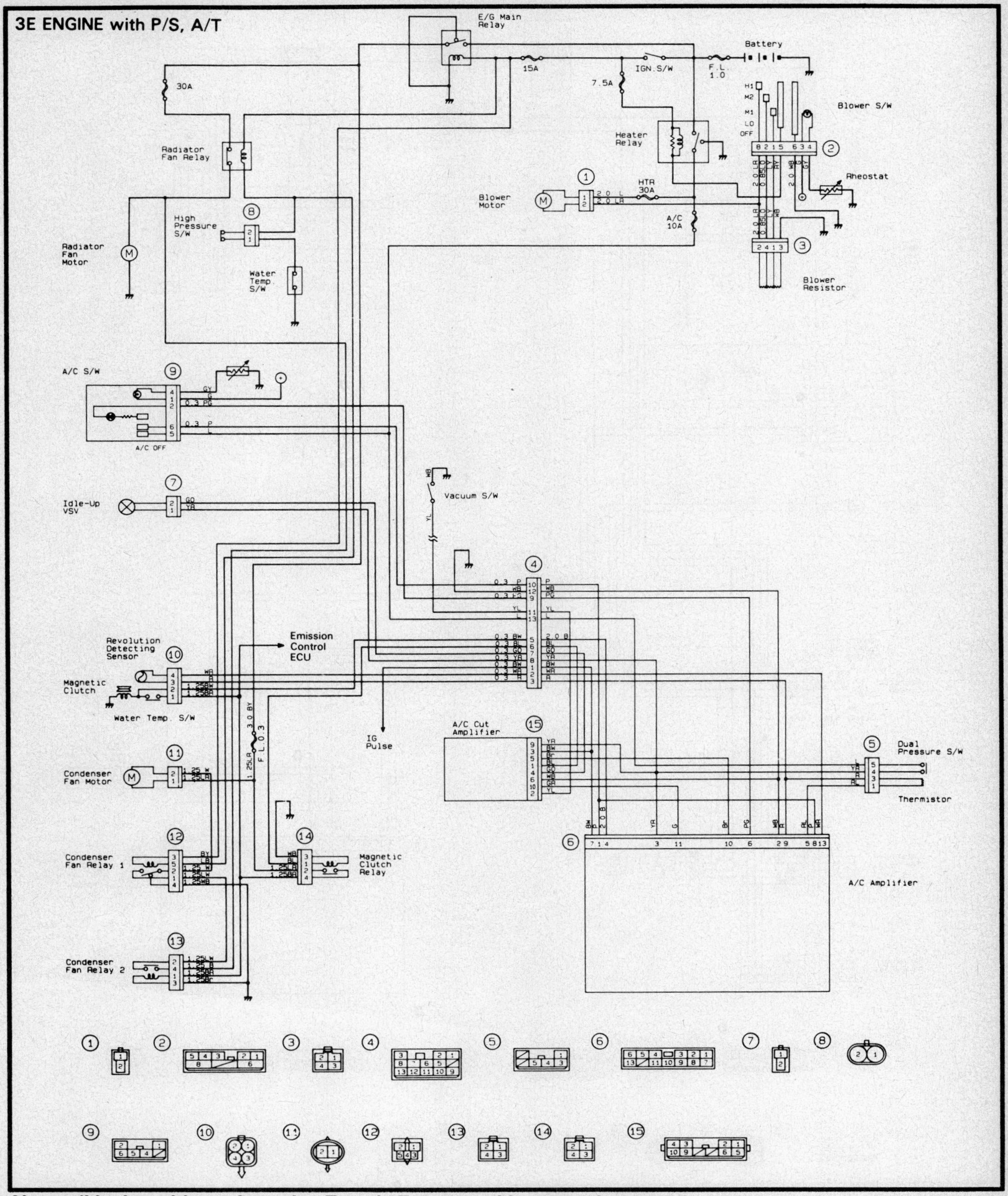
3E ENGINE with P/S, A/T
E/G Main Relay
Battery
15A
IGN.S/W
F.L. 1.0
30A
7.5A
Blower S/W
Heater Relay
Radiator Fan Relay
Rheostat
Blower Motor
HTR 30A
A/C 10A
High Pressure S/W
Radiator Fan Motor
Water Temp. S/W
Blower Resistor
A/C S/W
A/C OFF
Idle-Up VSV
Vacuum S/W
Emission Control ECU
Revolution Detecting Sensor
Magnetic Clutch
Water Temp. S/W
IG Pulse
A/C Cut Amplifier
Dual Pressure S/W
Thermistor
Condenser Fan Motor
Condenser Fan Relay 1
Magnetic Clutch Relay
A/C Amplifier
Condenser Fan Relay 2

Air conditioning wiring schematic—Tercel 3E engine with automatic transaxle

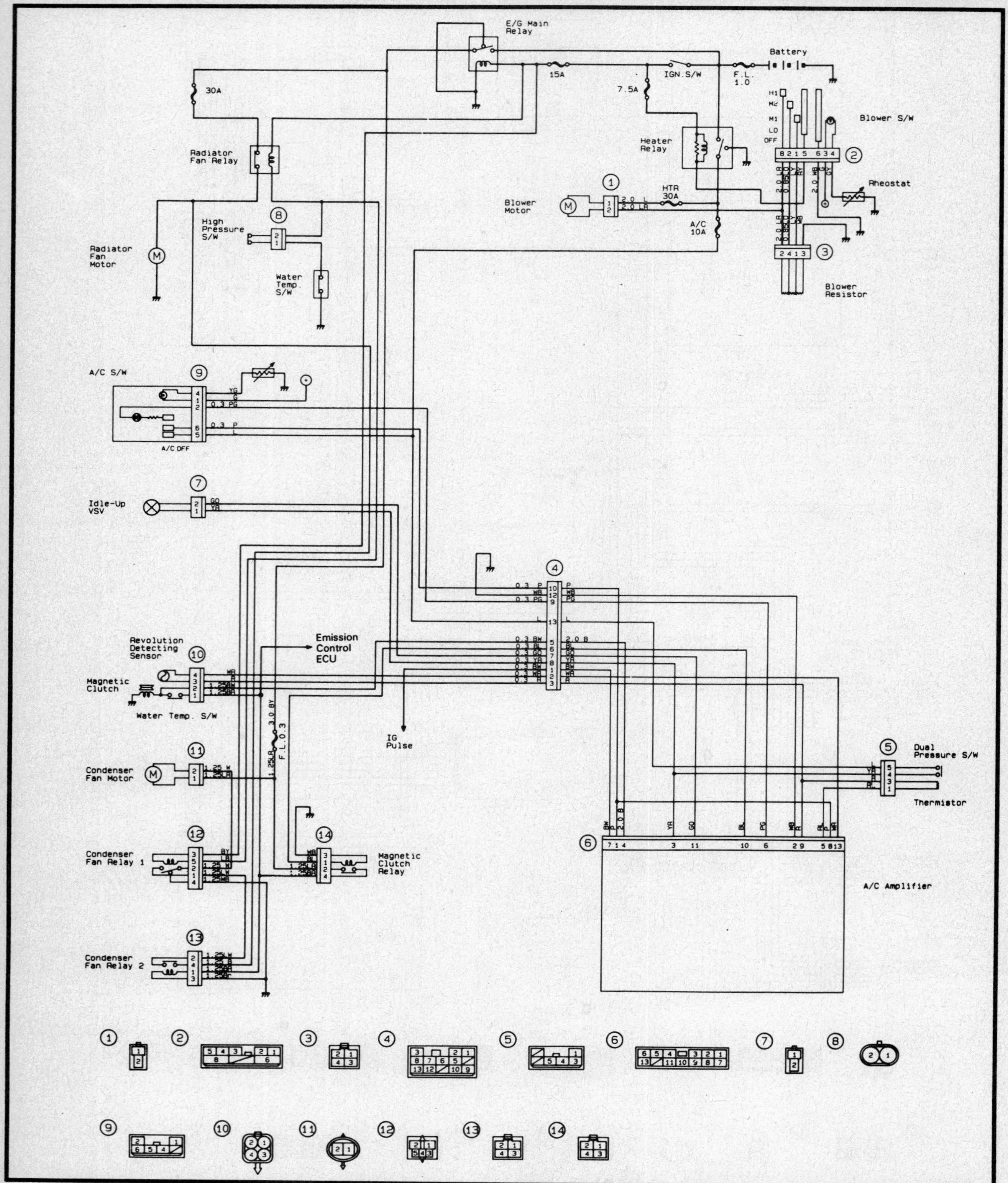
E/G Main Relay
30A
15A
IGN.S/W
F.L. 1.0
Battery
7.5A
Blower S/W
Heater Relay
Radiator Fan Relay
Blower Motor
HTR 30A
Rheostat
A/C 10A
High Pressure S/W
Radiator Fan Motor
Water Temp. S/W
Blower Resistor
A/C S/W
A/C OFF
Idle-Up VSV
Revolution Detecting Sensor
Emission Control ECU
Magnetic Clutch
Water Temp. S/W
IG Pulse
Condenser Fan Motor
Dual Pressure S/W
Thermistor
Condenser Fan Relay 1
Magnetic Clutch Relay
A/C Amplifier
Condenser Fan Relay 2

Air conditioning wiring schematic—Tercel 3E engine with manual transaxle

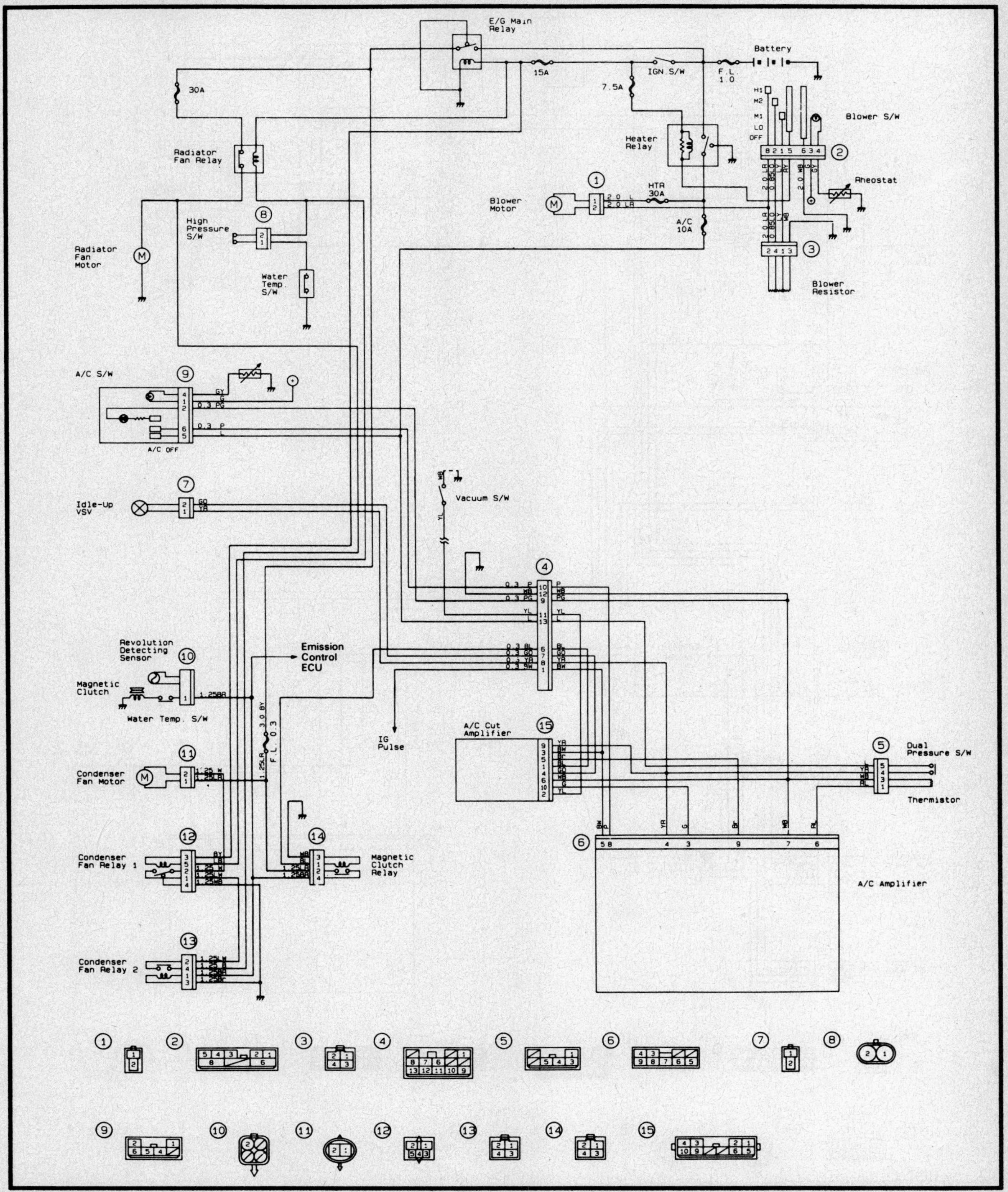
E/G Main Relay
15A
IGN. S/W
F.L. 1.0
Battery
30A
7.5A
Blower S/W
Heater Relay
Rheostat
Radiator Fan Relay
Blower Motor
HTR 30A
A/C 10A
High Pressure S/W
Radiator Fan Motor
Water Temp. S/W
Blower Resistor
A/C S/W
A/C OFF
Idle-Up VSV
Vacuum S/W
Revolution Detecting Sensor
Emission Control ECU
Magnetic Clutch
Water Temp. S/W
IG Pulse
A/C Cut Amplifier
Dual Pressure S/W
Condenser Fan Motor
Thermistor
Condenser Fan Relay 1
Magnetic Clutch Relay
A/C Amplifier
Condenser Fan Relay 2

Air conditioning wiring schematic—Tercel 3E engine without power steering automatic transaxle

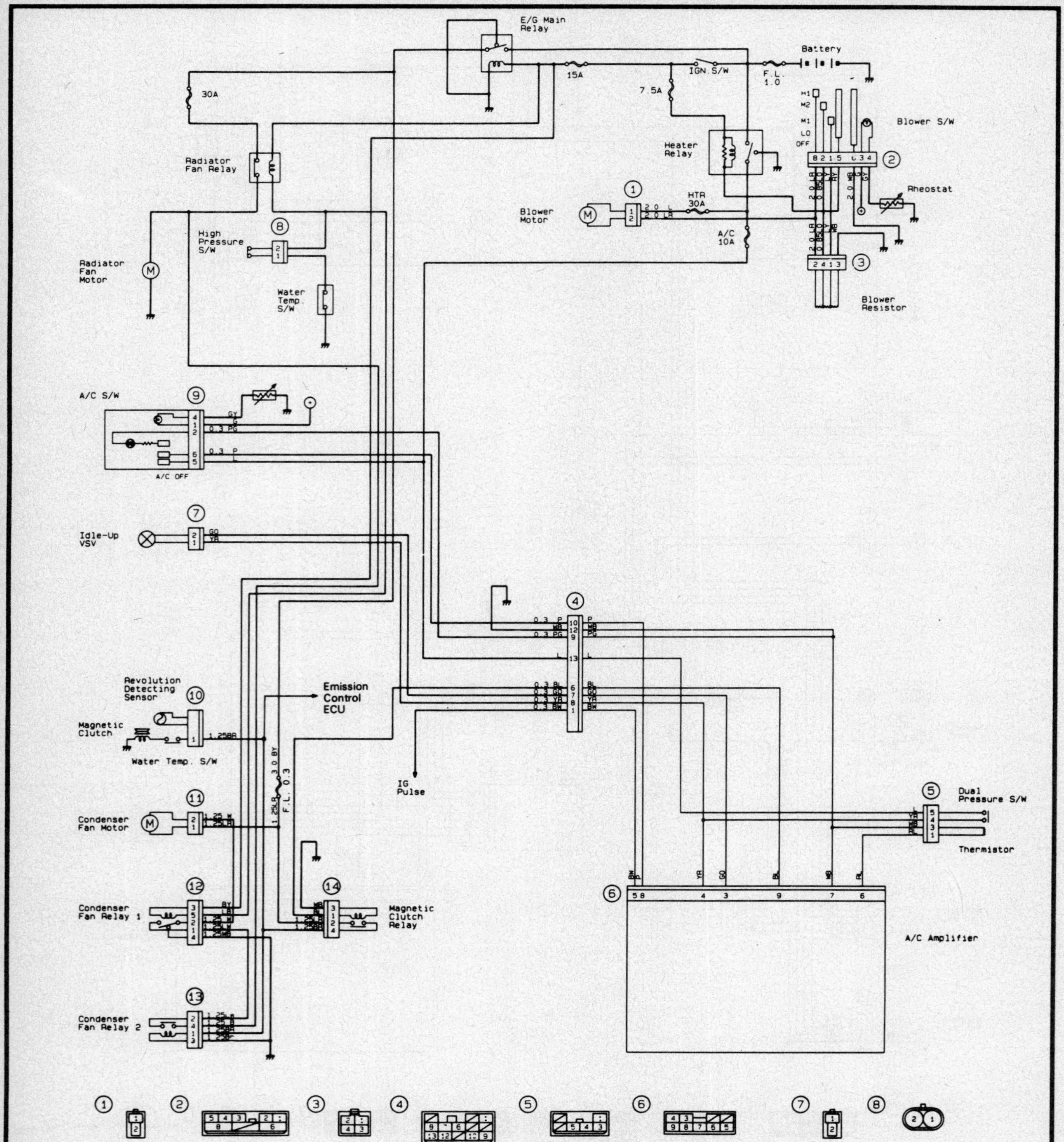
E/G Main Relay
15A
IGN S/W
Battery
F.L. 1.0
30A
7.5A
Blower S/W
HI
M2
M1
LO
OFF
Heater Relay
Radiator Fan Relay
Rheostat
Blower Motor
HTR 30A
A/C 10A
High Pressure S/W
Radiator Fan Motor
Water Temp. S/W
Blower Resistor
A/C S/W
A/C OFF
Idle-Up VSV
Revolution Detecting Sensor
Emission Control ECU
Magnetic Clutch
Water Temp. S/W
IG Pulse
Dual Pressure S/W
Thermistor
Condenser Fan Motor
Condenser Fan Relay 1
Magnetic Clutch Relay
A/C Amplifier
Condenser Fan Relay 2
F.L. 0.3

Air conditioning wiring schematic—Tercel 3E engine without power steering manual transaxle

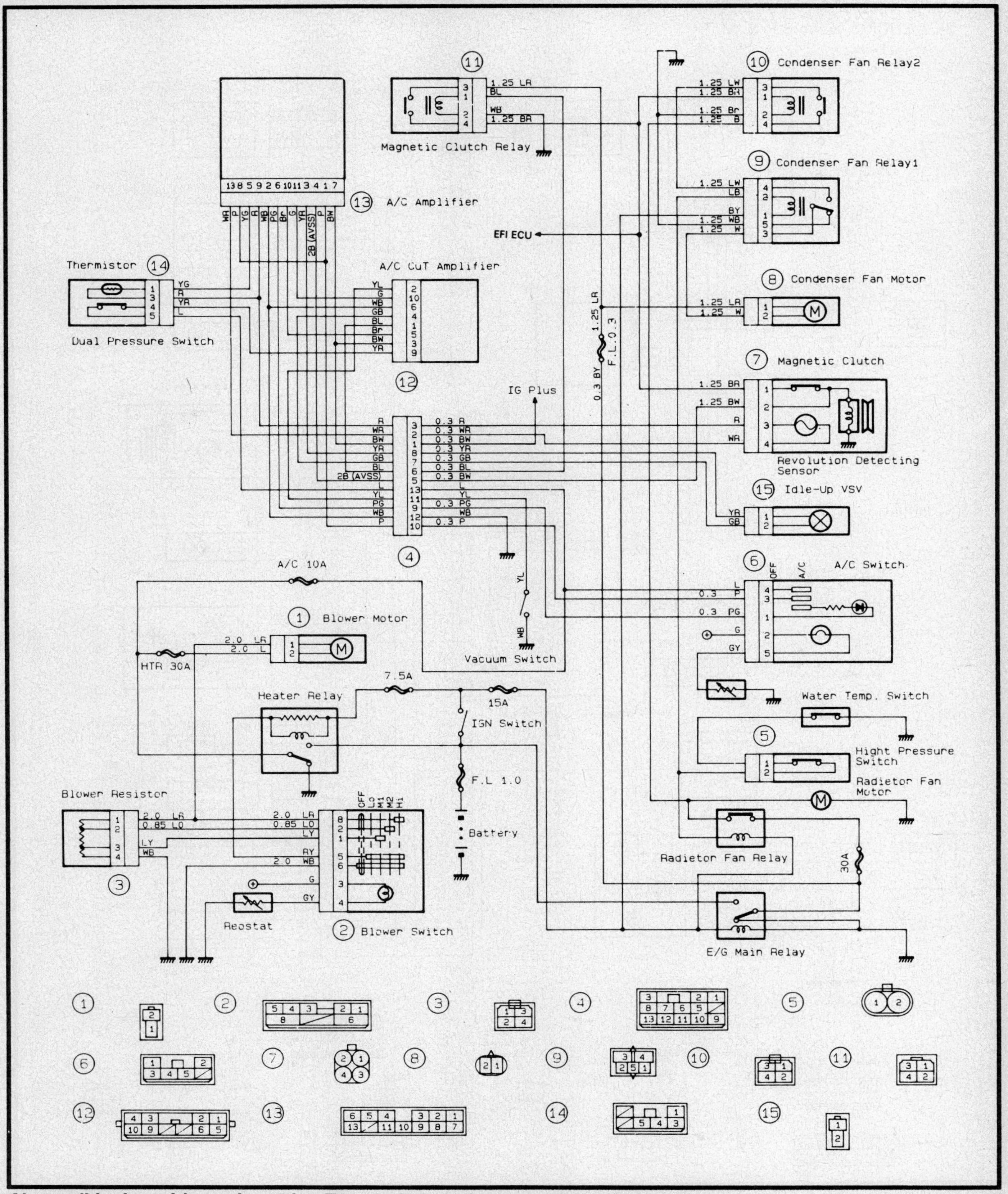
Magnetic Clutch Relay
Condenser Fan Relay2
Condenser Fan Relay1
A/C Amplifier
EFI ECU
Thermistor
A/C CuT Amplifier
Dual Pressure Switch
Condenser Fan Motor
Magnetic Clutch
IG Plus
F.L.0.3
Revolution Detecting Sensor
Idle-Up VSV
A/C Switch
A/C 10A
Blower Motor
Vacuum Switch
HTR 30A
7.5A
Heater Relay
15A
IGN Switch
Water Temp. Switch
Hight Pressure Switch
Radietor Fan Motor
F.L 1.0
Blower Resistor
Battery
Radietor Fan Relay
30A
Reostat
Blower Switch
E/G Main Relay

Air conditioning wiring schematic—Tercel 3E-E engine with automatic transaxle

3E-E ENGINE without P/S, M/T

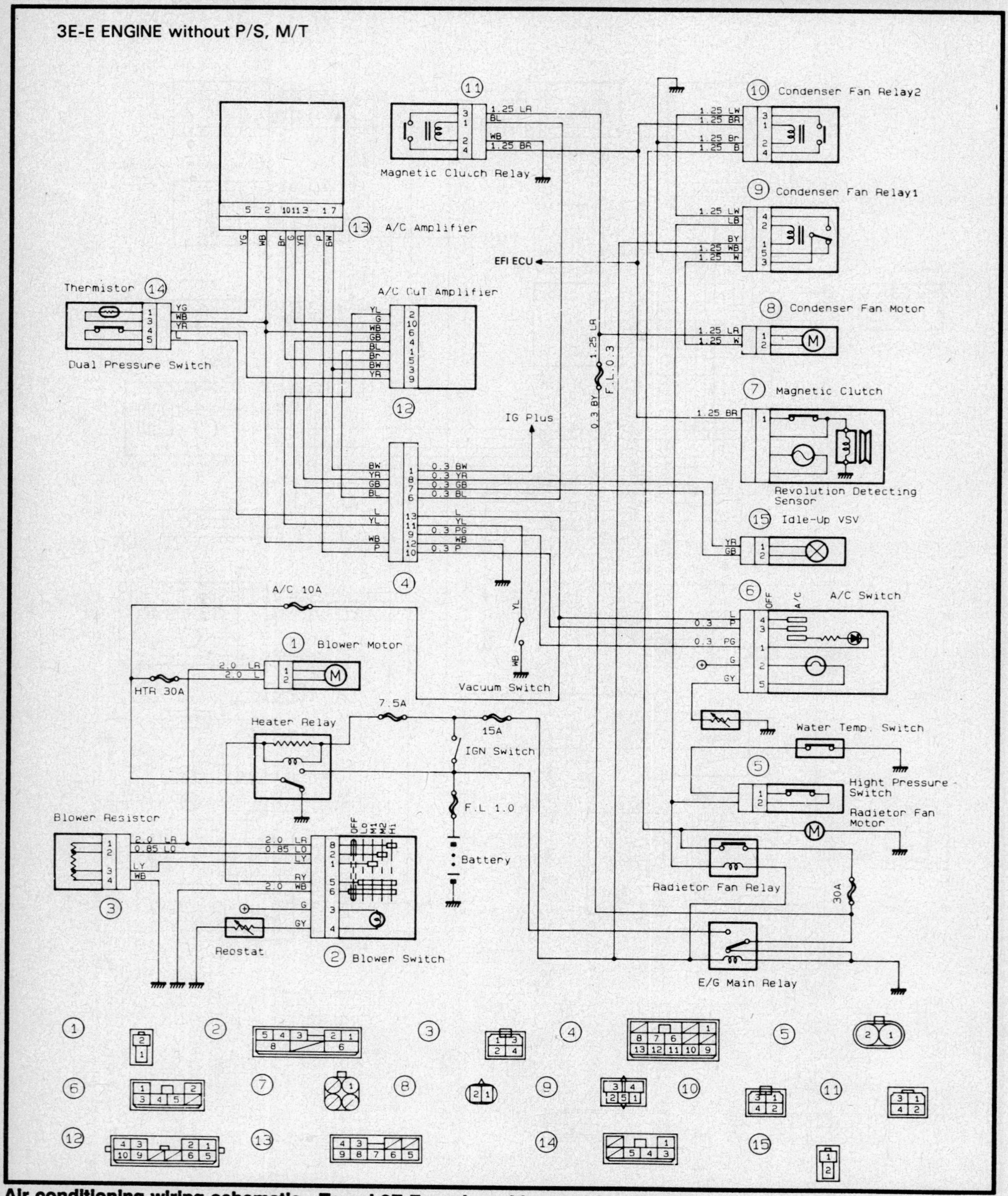
Magnetic Clutch Relay
A/C Amplifier
EFI ECU
Thermistor
A/C Cut Amplifier
Dual Pressure Switch
Condenser Fan Relay2
Condenser Fan Relay1
Condenser Fan Motor
Magnetic Clutch
Revolution Detecting Sensor
IG Plus
Idle-Up VSV
A/C Switch
A/C 10A
Blower Motor
HTR 30A
Vacuum Switch
Heater Relay
7.5A
15A
IGN Switch
Water Temp. Switch
Hight Pressure Switch
Radiator Fan Motor
Blower Resistor
F.L 1.0
Battery
Radiator Fan Relay
30A
Reostat
Blower Switch
E/G Main Relay

Air conditioning wiring schematic—Tercel 3E-E engine with manual transaxle

27 VOLKSWAGEN 27

CABRIOLET • CORRADO • FOX • GOLF • GTI • JETTA • PASSAT
SCIROCCO • VANAGON

SPECIFICATIONS

ENGINE IDENTIFICATION

Year	Model	Engine Displacement cu. in. (cc/liter)	Engine Series Identification	No. of Cylinders	Engine Type
1989	Cabriolet	109 (1780/1.8)	PL	4	SOHC
	Scirocco	109 (1780/1.8)	PL	4	DOHC
	Fox	109 (1780/1.8)	UN	4	SOHC
	Golf	109 (1780/1.8)	PF	4	SOHC
	GTI	109 (1780/1.8)	PF	4	SOHC
	GTI 16V	109 (1780/1.8)	PL	4	DOHC
	Jetta Diesel	97 (1588/1.6)	ME	4	SOHC
	Jetta GL/Carat	109 (1780/1.8)	RV	4	SOHC
	Jetta 16V	109 (1780/1.8)	PL	4	DOHC
	Corrado	109 (1780/1.8)	PG	4	SOHC
	Vanagon	97 (1588/1.6)	CS	4	SOHC
	Vanagon	121 (1984/2.0)	CV	4	①
	Vanagon	129 (2109/2.1)	MV	4	②
1990	Cabriolet	109 (1780/1.8)	PL	4	SOHC
	Fox	109 (1780/1.8)	UN	4	SOHC
	Golf	109 (1780/1.8)	PF	4	SOHC
	GTI	109 (1780/1.8)	PF	4	SOHC
	GTI 16V	121 (1984/2.0)	PL	4	DOHC
	Jetta Diesel	97 (1588/1.6)	ME	4	SOHC
	Jetta GL/Carat	109 (1780/1.8)	RV	4	SOHC
	Jetta 16V	121 (1984/2.0)	PL	4	DOHC
	Corrado	109 (1780/1.8)	PG	4	SOHC
	Passat	121 (1984/2.0)	9A	4	DOHC
	Vanagon	97 (1588/1.6)	CS	4	SOHC
	Vanagon	121 (1984/2.0)	CV	4	①
	Vanagon	129 (2109/2.1)	MV	4	②
1991	Cabriolet	109 (1780/1.8)	PL	4	SOHC
	Fox	109 (1780/1.8)	UN	4	SOHC
	Golf	109 (1780/1.8)	PF	4	SOHC
	GTI	109 (1780/1.8)	PF	4	SOHC
	GTI 16V	121 (1984/2.0)	PL	4	DOHC
	Jetta Diesel	97 (1588/1.6)	ME	4	SOHC
	Jetta GL/Carat	109 (1780/1.8)	PF	4	SOHC
	Jetta 16V	121 (1984/2.0)	PL	4	DOHC
	Corrado	109 (1780/1.8)	PG	4	SOHC
	Passat	121 (1984/2.0)	9A	4	DOHC
	Vanagon	97 (1588/1.6)	CS	4	SOHC
	Vanagon	129 (2109/2.1)	MV	4	①

DOHC—Dual Overhead Cam
SOHC—Single Overhead Cam
① Horizontally opposed—Air cooled
② Horizontally opposed—Water cooled

REFRIGERANT CAPACITIES

Year	Model	Freon (oz.)	Oil (fl. oz.)	Type
1989	Cabriolet	38–42	4.7	R-12
	Scirocco	38–42	4.7	R-12
	Fox	37–40	8.0	R-12
	Golf	37–40	8.0	R-12
	GTI	37–40	8.0	R-12
	Jetta	37–40	8.0	R-12
	Corrado	37–40	4.6	R-12
	Vanagon	50.7	8.0	R-12
1990	Cabriolet	38–42	4.7	R-12
	Fox	37–40	8.0	R-12
	Golf	37–40	8.0	R-12
	GTI	37–40	8.0	R-12
	Jetta	37–40	8.0	R-12
	Corrado	37–40	4.6	R-12
	Passat	40–44	4.6	R-12
	Vanagon	50.7	8.0	R-12
1991	Cabriolet	38–42	4.7	R-12
	Fox	37–40	8.0	R-12
	Golf	37–40	8.0	R-12
	GTI	37–40	8.0	R-12
	Jetta	37–40	4.6	R-12
	Corrado	37–40	4.6	R-12
	Passat	40–44	4.6	R-12
	Vanagon	50.7	8.0	R-12

AIR CONDITIONING BELT TENSION CHART

Year	Model	Engine Displacement cu. in. (cc/liter)	Belt Type	New ①	Used ①
1989	Cabriolet	109 (1780/1.8)	V-Belt	3/16 (5–10 mm)	3/16 (5–10 mm)
	Scirocco	109 (1780/1.8)	V-Belt	3/16 (5–10 mm)	3/16 (5–10 mm)
	Fox	109 (1780/1.8)	V-Belt	3/16 (5–10 mm)	3/16 (5–10 mm)
	Golf	109 (1780/1.8)	V-Belt	3/16 (5–10 mm)	3/16 (5–10 mm)
	GTI	109 (1780/1.8)	V-Belt	3/16 (5–10 mm)	3/16 (5–10 mm)
	GTI 16V	109 (1780/1.8)	V-Belt	3/16 (5–10 mm)	3/16 (5–10 mm)
	Jetta Diesel	97 (1588/1.6)	V-Belt	3/16 (5–10 mm)	3/16 (5–10 mm)
	Jetta GL/Carat	109 (1780/1.8)	V-Belt	3/16 (5–10 mm)	3/16 (5–10 mm)
	Jetta 16V	109 (1780/1.8)	V-Belt	3/16 (5–10 mm)	3/16 (5–10 mm)
	Corrado	109 (1780/1.8)	Serpentine	②	②
	Vanagon Diesel	97 (1588/1.6)	V-Belt	3/8 (10–15 mm)	3/8 (10–15 mm)
	Vanagon	121 (1984/2.0)	V-Belt	3/8 (10–15 mm)	3/8 (10–15 mm)
	Vanagon	129 (2109/2.1)	V-Belt	3/8 (10–15 mm)	3/8 (10–15 mm)

AIR CONDITIONING BELT TENSION CHART

Year	Model	Engine Displacement cu. in. (cc/liter)	Belt Type	New ①	Used ①
1990	Cabriolet	109 (1780/1.8)	V-Belt	3/16 (5–10 mm)	3/16 (5–10 mm)
	Fox	109 (1780/1.8)	V-Belt	3/16 (5–10 mm)	3/16 (5–10 mm)
	Golf	109 (1780/1.8)	V-Belt	3/16 (5–10 mm)	3/16 (5–10 mm)
	GTI	109 (1780/1.8)	V-Belt	3/16 (5–10 mm)	3/16 (5–10 mm)
	GTI 16V	121 (1984/2.0)	V-Belt	3/16 (5–10 mm)	3/16 (5–10 mm)
	Jetta Diesel	97 (1588/1.6)	V-Belt	3/16 (5–10 mm)	3/16 (5–10 mm)
	Jetta GL/Carat	109 (1780/1.8)	V-Belt	3/16 (5–10 mm)	3/16 (5–10 mm)
	Jetta 16V	121 (1984/2.0)	V-Belt	3/16 (5–10 mm)	3/16 (5–10 mm)
	Corrado	109 (1780/1.8)	Serpentine	②	②
	Passat	121 (1984/2.0)	V-Belt	3/16 (5–10 mm)	3/16 (5–10 mm)
	Vanagon Diesel	97 (1588/1.6)	V-Belt	3/8 (10–15 mm)	3/8 (10–15 mm)
	Vanagon	121 (1984/2.0)	V-Belt	3/8 (10–15 mm)	3/8 (10–15 mm)
	Vanagon	129 (2109/2.1)	V-Belt	3/8 (10–15 mm)	3/8 (10–15 mm)
1991	Cabriolet	109 (1780/1.8)	V-Belt	3/16 (5–10 mm)	3/16 (5–10 mm)
	Fox	109 (1780/1.8)	V-Belt	3/16 (5–10 mm)	3/16 (5–10 mm)
	Golf	109 (1780/1.8)	V-Belt	3/16 (5–10 mm)	3/16 (5–10 mm)
	GTI	109 (1780/1.8)	V-Belt	3/16 (5–10 mm)	3/16 (5–10 mm)
	GTI 16V	121 (1984/2.0)	V-Belt	3/16 (5–10 mm)	3/16 (5–10 mm)
	Jetta Diesel	97 (1588/1.6)	V-Belt	3/16 (5–10 mm)	3/16 (5–10 mm)
	Jetta GL/Carat	109 (1780/1.8)	V-Belt	3/16 (5–10 mm)	3/16 (5–10 mm)
	Jetta 16V	121 (1984/2.0)	V-Belt	3/16 (5–10 mm)	3/16 (5–10 mm)
	Corrado	109 (1780/1.8)	Serpentine	②	②
	Passat	121 (1984/2.0)	V-Belt	3/16 (5–10 mm)	3/16 (5–10 mm)
	Vanagon	97 (1588/1.6)	V-Belt	3/8 (10–15 mm)	3/8 (10–15 mm)
	Vanagon	129 (2109/2.1)	V-Belt	3/8 (10–15 mm)	3/8 (10–15 mm)

① Defection under 11 lb. pressure
② Automatic tensioner adjust

SYSTEM DESCRIPTION

General Information

The heater core and blower motor on most vehicles are contained in the heater box fresh air housing, located in the center of the passenger compartment under the dashboard. The blower fan is of a turbine design and is mostly accessible from under the hood, while the heater core is accessible from inside the vehicle.

The air conditioning system is of the conventional expansion valve type with the condenser mounted in front of the radiator, the evaporator mounted within the passenger compartment under the dash on all vehicles, except Vanagon. The evaporator on the Vanagon is located in the rear ceiling. The compressor on all vehicles is mounted to the engine and its electrically controlled clutch pulley driven by a belt from the crankshaft pulley. The air conditioning system is operated by a thermostatic valve to control the cycling of the system, thus, preventing evaporator freeze-up. A receiver/drier is used both as a freon reservoir and a container for the dessicant material. A York, Sankyo or Sanden compressor is used, depending on the year, manufacturing plant and vehicle line.

Add-on or aftermarket, units are available for all vehicles. Should the vehicle be equipped with this type unit, refer to the manufacturer for necessary parts, should the need arise.

Service Valve Location

The service valves are of the schrader type. Locations of the service valves may be in 2 areas depending upon the vehicle. On most vehicles, they are located on the high and low pressure hoses. On others, they may be located on the air conditioning compressor suction and discharge ports.

System Discharging

1. Disconnect the negative battery cable.

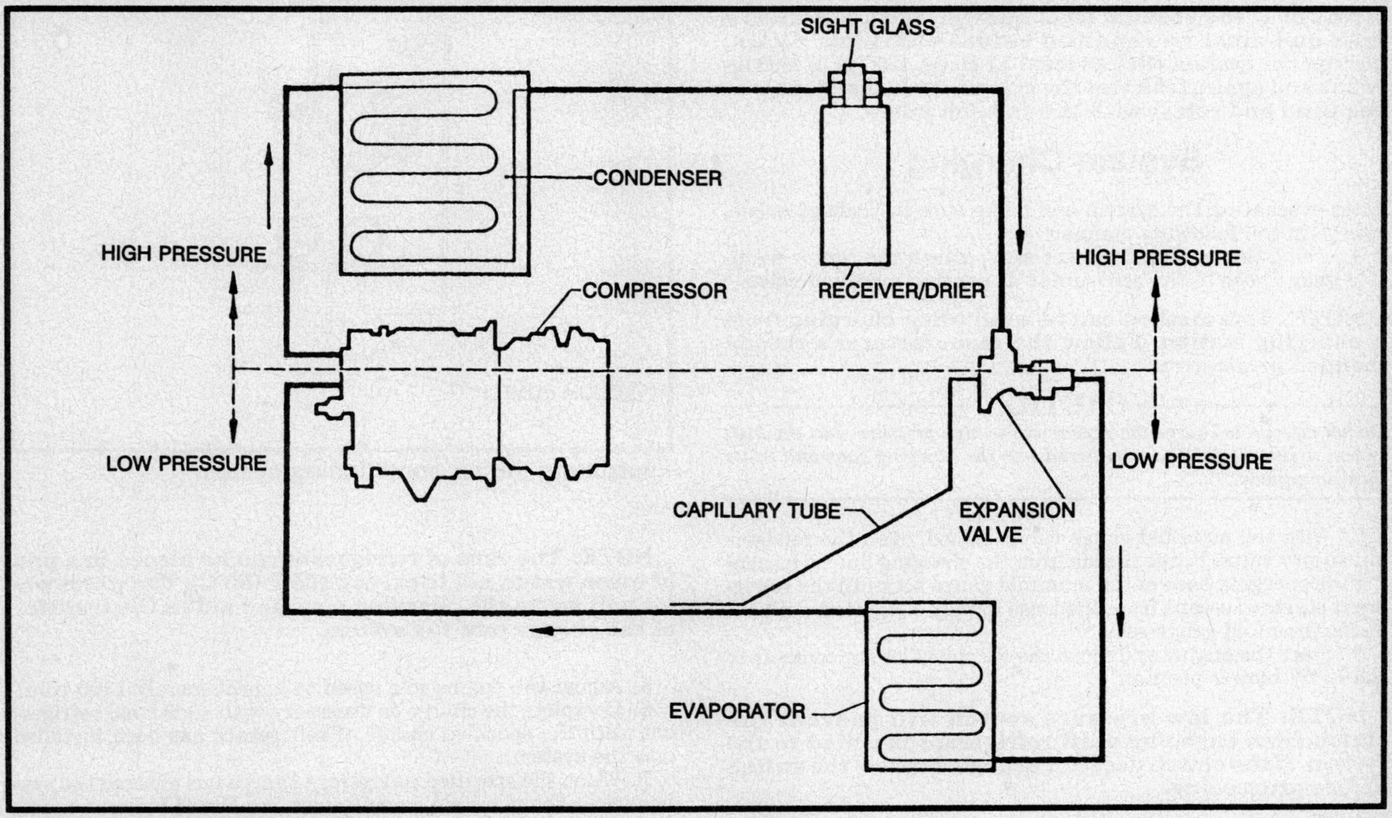
SIGHT GLASS
CONDENSER
HIGH PRESSURE
COMPRESSOR
RECEIVER/DRIER
HIGH PRESSURE
LOW PRESSURE
LOW PRESSURE
CAPILLARY TUBE
EXPANSION VALVE
EVAPORATOR

Typical air conditioning system

2. Connect a manifold gauge set to the service ports of the compressor or the high and low pressure lines.
3. Place the manifold gauge charging hose, into a clean container.
4. Open the compressor discharge and suction pressure valves and allow the refrigerant to discharge slowly into the container.
5. When the air conditioning system has been completely discharged, measure the amount of oil that collected in the can.
6. This measured amount of oil, must be added to the refrigerant system before it is recharged.

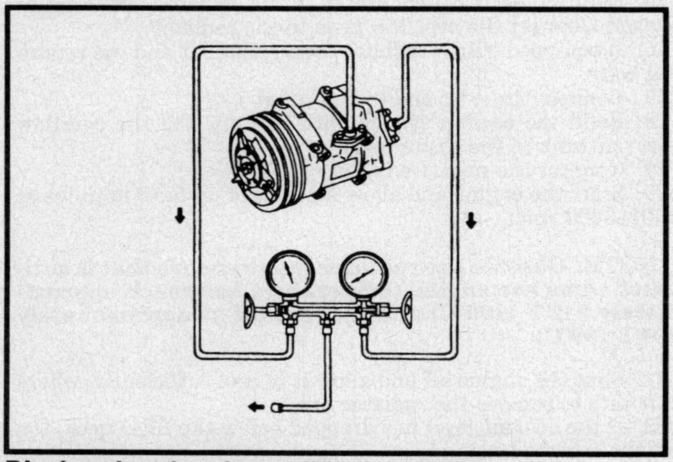

Discharging the air conditioning system

NOTE: Always add new refrigerant oil, never the oil that had been collected from the system.

7. Component replacement or repairs can now be accomplished. Do not allow the system to remain open for any length of time.
8. Connect the negative battery cable.

System Evacuating

Whenever the system has been opened to the atmosphere, the system must be vacuumed or evacuated, to remove all air and moisture that has accumulated in the system.

1. Disconnect the negative battery cable.
2. Connect the manifold gauge set to the compressor and to the discharge service ports. Connect the center (charging) hose to a vacuum pump service port.
3. Open both manifold gauge valves.
4. Start the vacuum pump and operate it until the evaporator suction gauge reads at least 26 in. Hg vacuum.
5. If at least 26 in. Hg of vacuum cannot be reached, either the system has a leak or the vacuum pump is defective.
6. If the vacuum pump proves to be operating, charge the system with at least 14 oz. (397g) of refrigerant, leak test and repair all leaks.
7. Discharge and evacuate the system again. Operate the pump for at least 5 minutes.
8. Turn the manifold gauge valves to their closed position and stop the vacuum pump.
9. Observe the evaporator suction valve for at least 2–5 minutes. The vacuum gauge reading must remain constant.
10. Connect the negative battery cable.

NOTE: If the vacuum level falls off, the system has a leak and must be repaired before charging. Again, charge the system with at least 14 fl. oz. (397g) of refrigerant and again, leak test the system for leaks. Repair as required and retest with the vacuum pump.

System Charging

After evacuating the system and being sure no leakage exists, charge in the following manner:

1. Using the small refrigerant cans, attach the center manifold gauge hose to the refrigerant dispensing manifold valve.

NOTE: This method can be used when charging from a charging station. Follow the manufacturer's recommended procedures.

CAUTION

Do not attempt to charge the system on the high pressure side, the high system pressure could be transferred into the charging cans and cause them to explode.

2. With the manifold gauge valves closed, open the refrigerant supply valve. Purge the air from the charging line by loosening the charging hose at the manifold gauge set until the refrigerant starts to escape from the loose fitting. Retighten the hose at the manifold gauge set.
3. Start the engine and move the air conditioning controls to the **LOW** blower position.

NOTE: The low pressure switch will prevent the clutch from engaging until refrigerant is added to the system. If the clutch does not engage, replace the switch before proceeding.

4. Charge through the suction or low pressure side of the system, by slowly opening the low pressure manifold valve. Adjust the valve as necessary so charging pressure does not exceed 50 psi.

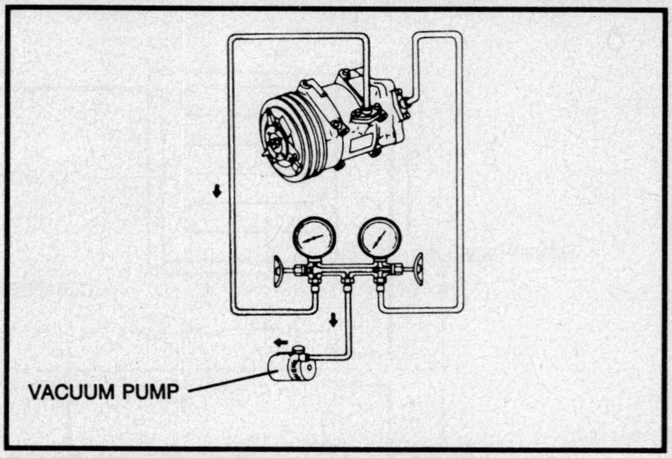
VACUUM PUMP

Evacuating the air conditioning system

NOTE: The cans of refrigerant can be placed in a pan of warm water, not to exceed 125°F (52°C). The warm water will warm the charging cans and aid in the transfer of the charge into the system.

5. Adjust the engine idle speed to approximately 1300 rpm.
6. Complete the charge as necessary with additional refrigerant until the specified charge of refrigerant has been installed into the system.
7. When the specified refrigerant charge has entered the system, close the manifold gauge valves and the refrigerant manifold valves. Reconnect any wiring that may have been disconnected. Disconnect the hoses from the service ports and cap them as required.
8. Operate the system and verify the operation is correct.

SYSTEM COMPONENTS

Radiator

REMOVAL AND INSTALLATION

Except Vanagon

1. Disconnect the negative battery cable and drain the cooling system.
2. Disconnect the inlet and outlet hoses from the engine side.
3. If equipped with a radiator cover, remove the retaining bolts and remove it.
4. Disconnect electrical connector at the radiator temperature sensor. Disconnect the overflow hose from the radiator.
5. Disconnect the fan motor connectors.
6. Remove the fan and shroud assembly retaining bolts and lift the fan shroud assembly out.
7. If equipped with automatic transaxle, disconnect the cooler lines and plug.
8. Remove the radiator upper mounting bracket retaining bolts and remove the mounting brackets.
9. Remove the the radiator from the vehicle.

To install:

10. Lower the radiator into the mounting position and seat the mounting cushions.
11. Install the radiator mounting brackets and secure the radiator in place.
12. If equipped with automatic transaxle, connect the cooler lines to the radiator.
13. Install the fan and shroud assembly and the retaining bolts.
14. Connect the fan motor connectors.
15. Connect electrical connector to the radiator temperature sensor. Connect the overflow hose to the radiator.
16. If equipped with a radiator cover, install it and the retaining bolts.
17. Connect the inlet and outlet hoses.
18. Refill the cooling system with coolant. Fill the overflow resevoir tank to the upper level.
19. Connect the negative battery cable.
20. Start the engine and allow it to warm up 5–10 minutes at 2000–3000 rpm.

NOTE: Observe the radiator fan to ensure that it activates when the engine temperature has reach approximately 212°F (100°C) and will cut off at approximately 194°F (90°C).

21. Shut the engine off and allow it to cool sufficiently, where it is safe to remove the radiator cap.
22. If the coolant level has dropped below the filler neck, top off the coolant level.
23. Install the radiator cap and the vent plug.

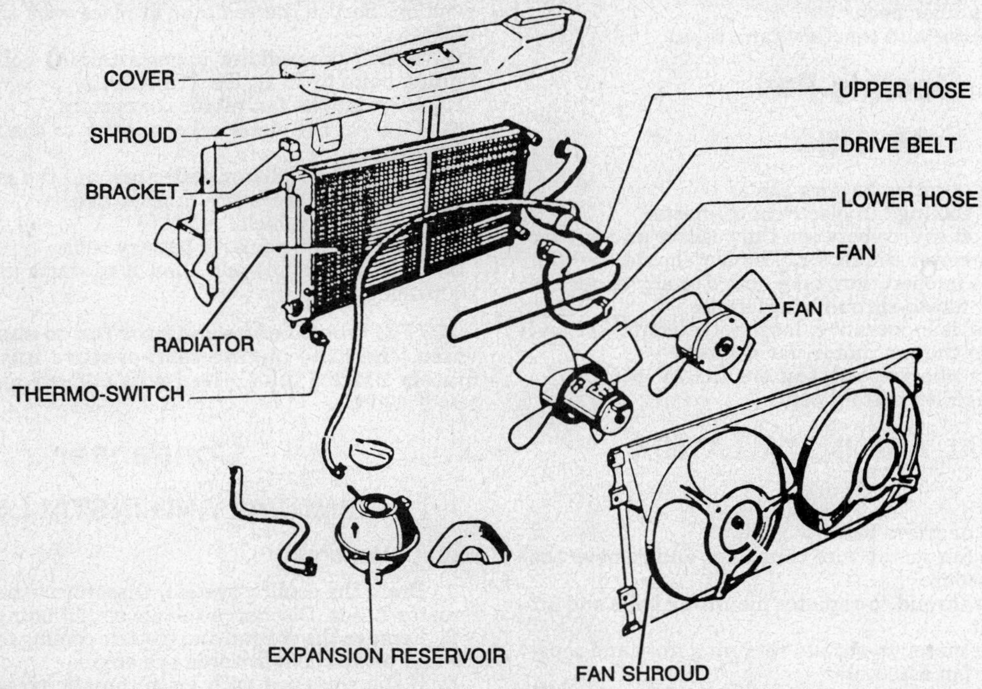
COVER
SHROUD
BRACKET
RADIATOR
THERMO-SWITCH
EXPANSION RESERVOIR
UPPER HOSE
DRIVE BELT
LOWER HOSE
FAN
FAN
FAN SHROUD

Exploded view of the radiator and related components

Vanagon

1. Disconnect the negative battery cable.
2. Drain the cooling system.
3. Raise the vehicle and support it safely.
4. Remove the spare tire and bracket.
5. Remove the radiator grille, the lower air deflector and side defectors.
6. Disconnect the inlet and outlet hoses from the radiator.
7. Disconnect electrical connector at the radiator temperature sensor.
8. Disconnect the fan motor connectors.
9. Remove the radiator upper retaining bolts.
10. Remove the radiator lower retaining bolts. Lower the radiator and fan assembly down and out from under the vehicle.
11. Remove the fan shroud-to-radiator retaining bolts and remove the fan shroud assembly from the radiator.

To install:

12. Position the fan shroud assembly to the radiator and install the retaining bolts. Torque the retaining bolts to 7 ft. lbs. (10 Nm).
13. Install the radiator and fan shroud assembly under the vehicle, in the mounting position. Secure the radiator in place with the lower retaining bolts.
14. Install the radiator upper retaining bolts. Torque the retaining bolts to 11 ft. lbs. (15 Nm).
15. Connect the fan motor connectors.
16. Connect the electrical connector to the radiator temperature sensor.
17. Connect the inlet and outlet hoses to the radiator.
18. Install the radiator deflectors and the grille.
19. Install the spare tire bracket tire.
20. Lower the vehicle.
21. Open the radiator air bleed screw and fill the cooling system with a mixture of anti-freeze and water.
22. When the coolant begins to pour from the air bleed screw opening, close screw.
22. Connect the negative battery cable.
23. Start the engine and allow it to warm up 5–10 minutes at 2000–3000 rpm.

NOTE: Observe the radiator fan to ensure that it activates when the engine temperature has reach approximately 212°F (100°C) and will cut off at approximately 194°F (90°C).

24. Shut the engine off and allow it to cool down, enough to where it is safe to remove the reservoir tank cap.
25. If the coolant level has dropped below the filler neck, top off the coolant level.
26. Install the reservoir cap.

COOLING SYSTEM BLEEDING

After working on the cooling system, even to replace the thermostat, the system must be bled. Air trapped in the system will prevent proper filling and will leave the radiator coolant level low, causing a risk of overheating.

1. To bleed the system, start with the system cool, the radiator cap off and the radiator filled to about 1 inch below the filler neck.
2. Start the engine and run it at slightly above normal idle speed. This will insure adequate circulation. If air bubbles appear and the coolant level drops, fill the system with a mixture of anti-freeze and water to bring the level back to the proper level.
3. Run the engine this way until the thermostat opens. When the happens, the coolant will move abruptly across the top of the radiator and the temperature of the radiator will suddenly rise.
4. At this point, air is often expelled and the level may drop accordingly.
5. Keep refilling the system until the level is near the top of the radiator and remains constant.

6. Fill the radiator overflow tank, to the full mark. Fill the radiator just below the filler neck.
7. Install the radiator and overflow tank caps.

Cooling Fan

TESTING

1. Disconnect the negative battery cable.
2. Disconnect the cooling fan electrical connector.
3. Apply and 12 volt source between the positive an negative terminals of the fan motor connector. The fan should operate.
4. While the fan is in operation, take notice to any abnormal noises, vibrations or fan-to-shroud interference.
5. If the fan motor is inoperative, inspect the connector and harness leading from the fan motor, for damage.
6. If the fan motor checks good, test the thermo-sensor.
7. Connect the negative battery cable.

REMOVAL AND INSTALLATION

Except Vanagon

1. Disconnect the negative battery cable.
2. Disconnect the fan motor wire connector and remove the harness from the shroud.
3. Remove the fan shroud-to-radiator mounting bolts and lift the fan assembly out.
4. Remove the fan motor-to-shroud retaining nuts and separate the shroud and fan assembly.
5. Remove the fan-to-motor retaining nuts and separate the fan from the motor.

To install:

6. Assemble the fan and motor assembly. Prior to installing the retaining nuts, apply a coat of sealant to the threads and install.
7. Assemble the fan to the shroud and install the retaining nuts. Spin the fan and insure that there is no fan-to-shroud interference.
8. Position the fan and shroud assembly to the radiator and install the retaining bolts. Torque the bolts to 7 ft. lbs. (10 Nm).
9. Connect and 12 volt source to the fan lead wire connector and check for noises, vibrations or fan interference.
10. Secure the fan lead wire to the shroud and connect it to the harness connector.
11. Connect the negative battery cable. Start the engine and test fan operation.

Vanagon

1. Disconnect the negative battery cable.
2. Raise the vehicle and support it safely.
3. Remove the spare tire and bracket.
4. Remove the radiator grille, the lower air deflector and side defectors.
5. Disconnect electrical connector at the radiator temperature sensor.
6. Disconnect the fan motor connectors.
7. Remove the radiator upper retaining bolts.
8. Remove the radiator lower retaining bolts. Lower the radiator and fan assembly down.

NOTE: It is not necessary to remove the radiator from the vehicle. The fan shroud assembly is accessible, when the radiator is lowered.

9. Remove the fan shroud-to-radiator retaining bolts and remove the fan shroud assembly from the radiator.

To install:

10. Position the fan shroud assembly to the radiator and install the retaining bolts. Torque the retaining bolts to 7 ft. lbs. (10 Nm).
11. Raise the radiator and fan shroud assembly, in mounting position. Secure the radiator in place with the lower retaining bolts.
12. Install the radiator upper retaining bolts. Torque the retaining bolts to 11 ft. lbs. (15 Nm).
13. Connect the fan motor connectors.
14. Connect the electrical connector to the radiator temperature sensor.
15. Install the radiator deflectors and the grille.
16. Install the spare tire bracket tire.
17. Lower the vehicle.
18. Connect the negative battery cable.
19. Start the engine and allow it to warm up 5–10 minutes at 2000–3000 rpm.

NOTE: Observe the radiator fan to ensure that it activates when the engine temperature has reach approximately 212°F (100°C) and will cut off at approximately 194°F (90°C).

Condenser

REMOVAL AND INSTALLATION

Except Vanagon

1. Drain the cooling system. Disconnect the upper and lower radiator hoses. Discharge the air conditioning system safely.
2. Remove the shroud and electric cooling fan from the radiator and move them towards the engine.
3. If the equipped with an automatic transmission, remove the fluid cooling lines at the radiator.
4. Remove the retaining bolts or nuts from the top and bottom of the radiator and remove the radiator.

NOTE: The battery may be removed to gain additional working clearance.

5. Disconnect the inlet and outlet lines at the condenser. Cap or plug the opening immediately.
6. Remove the retaining bolts or nuts from the condenser and carefully lift the condenser from the front of the vehicle.

To install:

7. Carefully install the condenser into the vehicle.
8. Connect the inlet and outlet lines to the condenser.
9. Install the radiator and secure with the nuts/bolts.
10. If the equipped with an automatic transmission, install the fluid cooling lines to the radiator.
11. Install the shroud and electric cooling fan to the radiator.
12. Install the upper and lower radiator hoses and refill the cooling system.
13. Evacuate and charge the air conditioning system.
14. Add the correct amount of refrigerant oil to the condenser. Evacuate and charge the air conditioning system. Verify the system operates correctly.

Vanagon

1. Disconnect the negative battery cable.
2. Discharge the air conditioning system.
3. Raise the vehicle and support it safely.
4. Drain the cooling system.
5. Remove the spare tire and bracket.
6. Remove the radiator grille, the lower air deflector and side defectors.
7. Disconnect the inlet and outlet hoses from the radiator.
8. Disconnect electrical connector at the radiator temperature sensor.
9. Disconnect the fan motor connectors.

NOTE: The condenser and radiator can be removed from the vehicle as an assembly or the radiator can be removed first and then the condenser.

10. If removing the condenser and radiator together, support the assembly using a hydraulic jack. Remove the condenser-to-support mounting bolts and lower the assembly from the vehicle.
11. Disconnect the inlet and outlet lines at the condenser. Cap or plug the opening immediately.
12. Remove the condenser and radiator assembly.
13. Remove the radiator-to-condenser mounting bolts and detach the radiator and fan shroud assembly, from the condenser.

To install:

14. Assemble the radiator and fan shroud assembly to the condenser. Install the retaining bolts. Torque the retaining bolts to 11 ft. lbs. (15 Nm).
15. Install the radiator and condenser assembly under the vehicle. Connect the inlet and outlet air conditioning lines to the condenser.
16. Using a hydraulic jack, raise the radiator and condenser assembly in mounting position.
17. Secure the assembly in place with the mounting bolts. Torque the bolts to 11 ft. lbs. (15 Nm).
18. Connect the fan motor connectors.
19. Connect the electrical connector to the radiator temperature sensor.
20. Connect the inlet and outlet hoses to the radiator.
21. Install the radiator deflectors and the grille.
22. Install the spare tire bracket tire.
23. Lower the vehicle.
24. Open the radiator air bleed screw and fill the cooling system with a mixture of anti-freeze and water.
25. When the coolant begins to pour from the air bleed screw opening, close screw.
26. Connect the negative battery cable.
27. Start the engine and allow it to warm up 5–10 minutes at 2000–3000 rpm.

NOTE: Observe the radiator fan to ensure that it activates when the engine temperature has reach approximately 212°F (100°C) and will cut off at approximately 194°F (90°C).

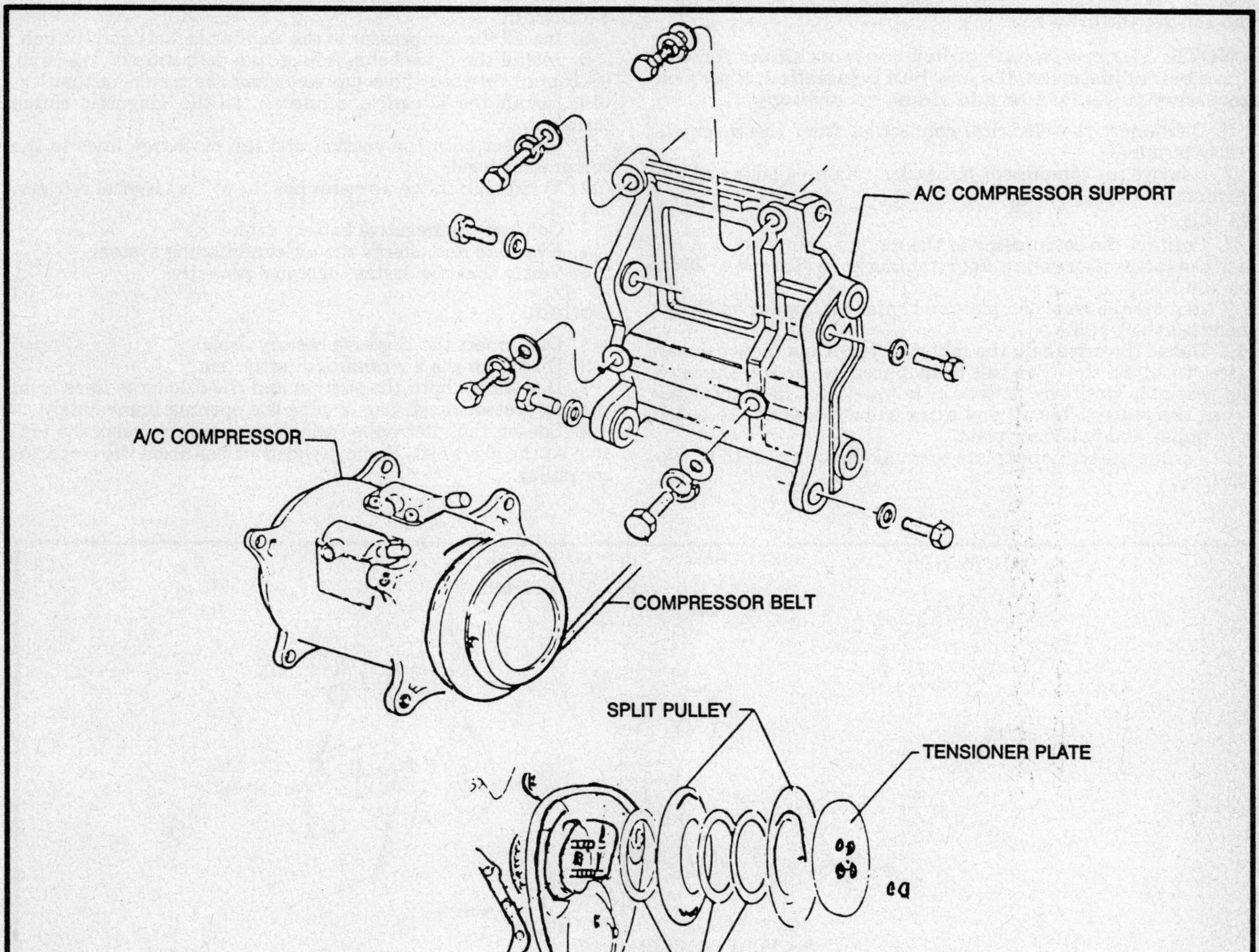
A/C COMPRESSOR SUPPORT
A/C COMPRESSOR
COMPRESSOR BELT
SPLIT PULLEY
TENSIONER PLATE
ADJUSTING SHIMS

Exploded view of compressor and the crankshaft tensioner pulley—Fox

28. Shut the engine off and allow it to cool down, enough to where it is safe to remove the reservoir tank cap.
29. If the coolant level has dropped below the filler neck, top off the coolant level.
30. Install the reservoir cap.
31. When the cooling system is stable, evacuate and charge the air conditioning system.

Compressor

REMOVAL AND INSTALLATION

Fox

The compressor is located under the front of the vehicle.

1. Disconnect the negative battery cable.
2. Discharge the air conditioning system.
3. Raise and safely support the vehicle.
4. Disconnect both the suction and the discharge lines from the compressor head. Cap or plug the opening immediately.
5. At the crankshaft pulley, loosen the tensioner plate nuts and remove the drive belt.

NOTE: The crankshaft pulley contains shims for the drive belt adjustment, if a new belt is installed, it may be necessary to remove or add shims accordingly.

6. Disconnect the electrical connection from the magnetic pulley terminal.
7. Remove the compressor-to-bracket retaining bolts and the compressor from the engine.

To install:

8. Position the compressor to the mounting bracket and install the compressor-to-bracket retaining bolts. Torque to 28 ft. lbs. (38 Nm).
9. Remove the tensioner plate and outer split pulley half from the crankshaft pulley.
10. Install the drive belt, the split pulley half and the tensioner plate. To adjust the drive belt tesnion, remove or add shims to the assembly until the deflection is $^3/_{16}$–$^3/_8$ in. (5–10mm) between the pulleys. Install any extra shims between the outer split pulley and tensioner plate.
11. Torque the tensioner plate-to-crankshaft nuts to 15 ft. lbs. (20 Nm).
12. Connect the electrical connection to the magnetic pulley terminal.
13. Connect both the suction and the discharge lines to the compressor.
14. Connect the negative battery cable.
15. Evacuate and charge the air conditioning system.
16. Verify that the oil level is correct in the compressor and the system is operating correctly.

Scirocco, Cabriolet, Golf, GTI, Jetta and Passat

1. Disconnect the negative battery cable.
2. Discharge the air conditioning system.
3. Remove the electrical connector from the magnetic clutch terminal.
4. Disconnect both the suction and the discharge lines from the compressor head. Cap or plug the opening immediately.
5. Loosen the adjusting bolts on compressor bracket, to provide slack in the drive belt. Remove the drive belt.
6. Remove the alternator drive belt.
7. Remove the compressor retaining bolt from the bracket. Remove the compressor from the engine brackets.

To install:

8. Install the compressor to the engine brackets and the bolt.
9. Install the drive belts. Adjust to a deflection of $^5/_{16}$–$^3/_8$ in. (8–10mm) between the compressor and the crankshaft pulley.
10. Install the electrical connector to the magnetic clutch terminal.
11. Connect both the suction and the discharge lines to the compressor head.
12. Verify that the compressor has the correct level of refrigerant oil.
13. Connect the negative battery cable.
14. Evacuate and charge the air conditioning system.
15. Verify that the system operates properly.

Corrado

1. Disconnect the negative battery cable.
2. Discharge the air conditioning system.
3. Disconnect both the suction and the discharge lines from the compressor head. Cap or plug the opening immediately.
4. Loosen the idler pulley adjustment bolt, to relax the tension on the drive belt. Remove the drive belt from the compressor pulley.

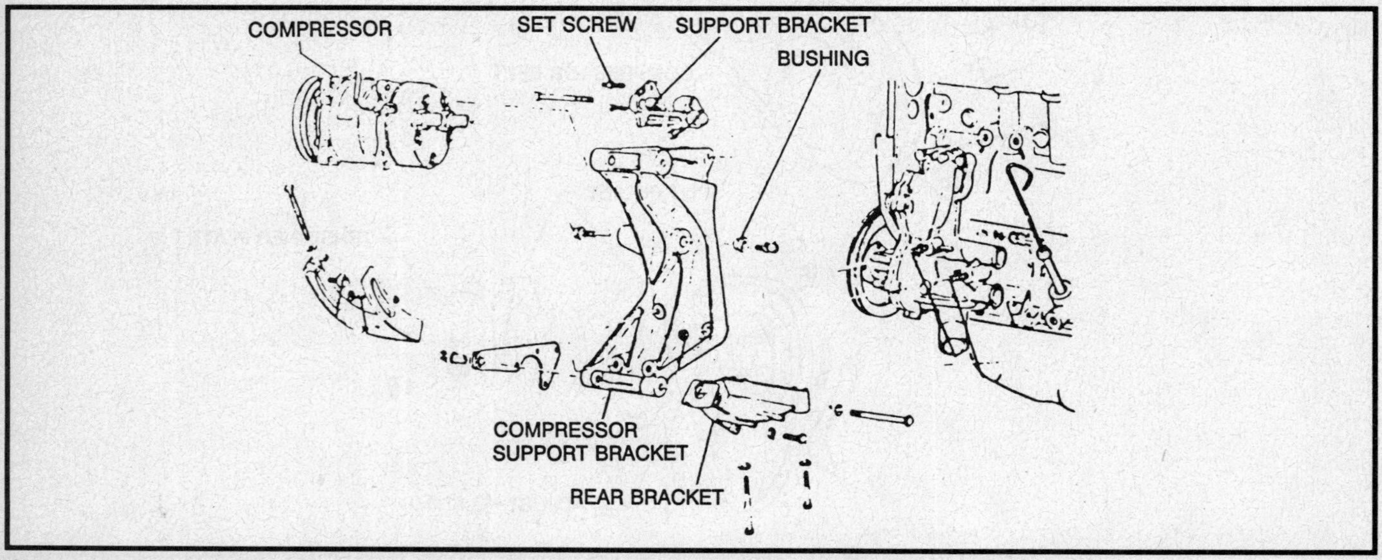
COMPRESSOR
SET SCREW
SUPPORT BRACKET
BUSHING
COMPRESSOR
SUPPORT BRACKET
REAR BRACKET

Compressor removal and installation—Scirocco, Cabriolet, Golf, GTI, Jetta and Passat

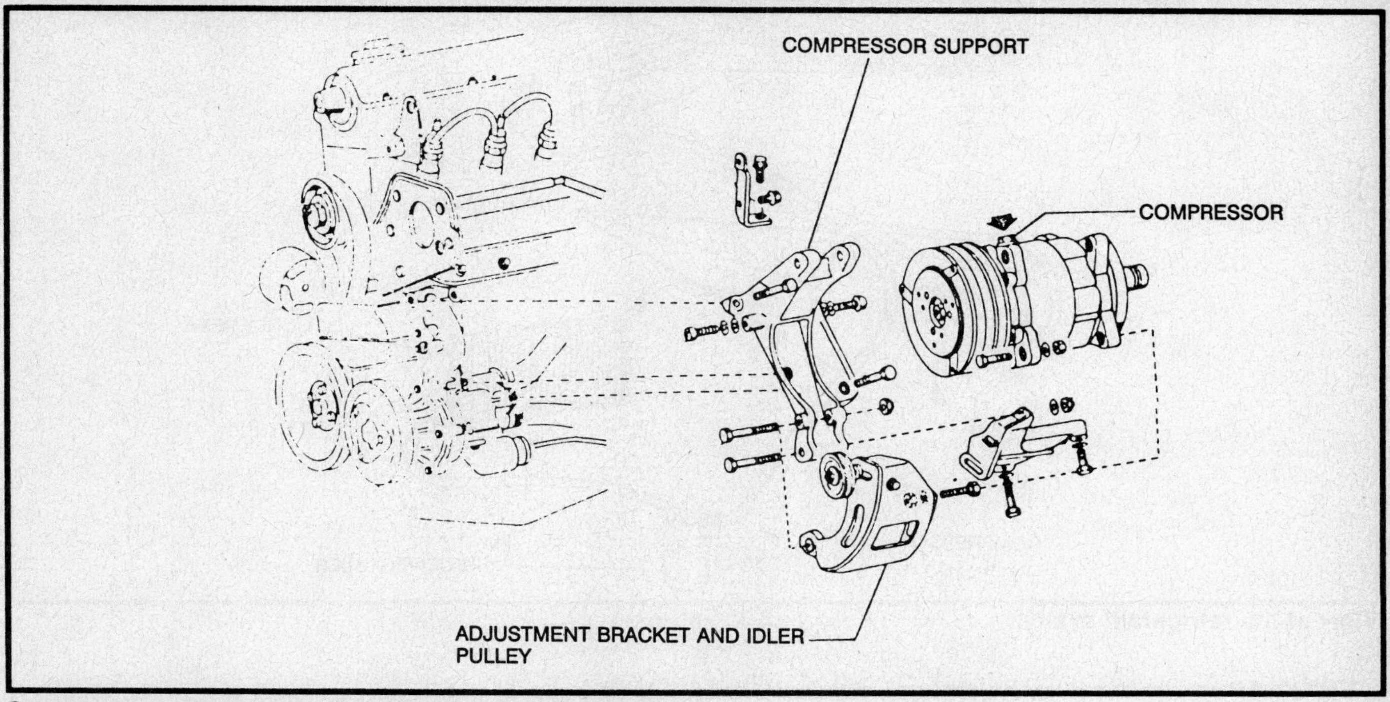
COMPRESSOR SUPPORT
COMPRESSOR
ADJUSTMENT BRACKET AND IDLER PULLEY

Compressor removal and installation with diesel engine

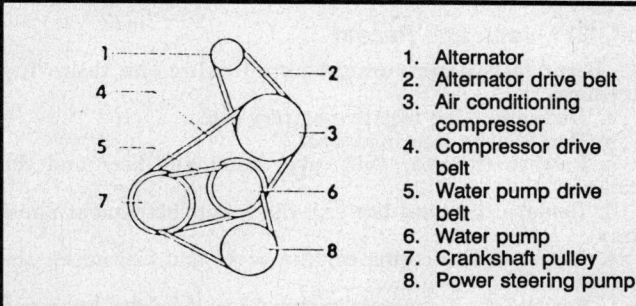

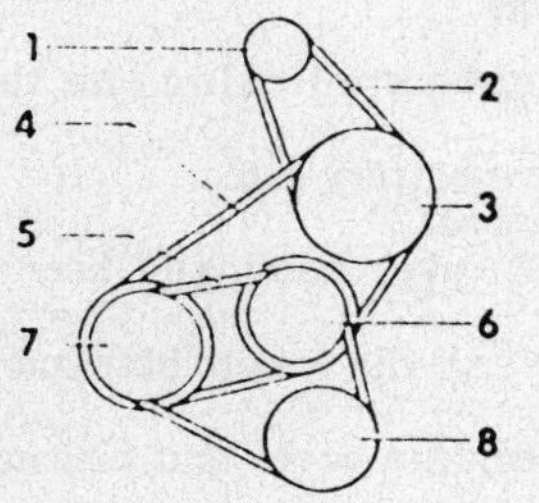
1
2
3
4
5
6
7
8
1. Alternator
2. Alternator drive belt
3. Air conditioning compressor
4. Compressor drive belt
5. Water pump drive belt
6. Water pump
7. Crankshaft pulley
8. Power steering pump

Drive belt arrangement

5. Disconnect the electrical connection from the magnetic pulley terminal.
6. Remove the compressor-to-bracket retaining bolts and remove the compressor from the engine.

NOTE: In some instances, to ease removal and installation, the brackets or part of the brackets can be removed with the compressor or taken from the compressor when on the bench and installed before installation of the compressor.

To install:

7. Install the compressor to the engine and the compressor-to-bracket retaining bolts.
8. Connect the electrical connection to the magnetic pulley terminal.
9. Install the drive belt on the compressor pulley. Adjust the drive belt deflection to $^5/_{16}$–$^3/_8$ in. (8–10mm) between the compressor and the crankshaft pulley. Tighten the idler pulley adjustment bolt.
10. Connect both the suction and the discharge lines to the compressor head.
11. Connect the negative battery cable.
12. Evacuate and charge the air conditioning system.
13. Verify that the oil level is correct in the compressor and the system is operating correctly.

Vanagon

1. Disconnect the negative battery cable.
2. Discharge the air conditioning system.
3. Remove the electrical connector from the magnetic clutch terminal.
4. Disconnect both the suction and the discharge lines from the compressor head. Cap or plug the opening immediately.
5. Loosen the adjusting bolts on compressor bracket, to provide slack in the drive belt. Remove the drive belt.
6. Remove the alternator drive belt.
7. Remove the compressor retaining bolt from the bracket. Remove the compressor from the engine brackets.

To install:

8. Install the compressor to the engine brackets and the bolt.
9. Install the drive belts. Adjust to a deflection of $^5/_{16}$–$^3/_8$ in. (8–10mm) between the compressor and the crankshaft pulley.
10. Install the electrical connector to the magnetic clutch terminal.
11. Connect both the suction and the discharge lines to the compressor head.
12. Verify that the compressor has the correct level of refrigerant oil.
13. Connect the negative battery cable.
14. Evacuate and charge the air conditioning system.
15. Verify that the system operates properly.

Receiver/Drier

REMOVAL AND INSTALLATION

1. Disconnect the negative battery cable.
2. Discharge the refrigerant from the system.

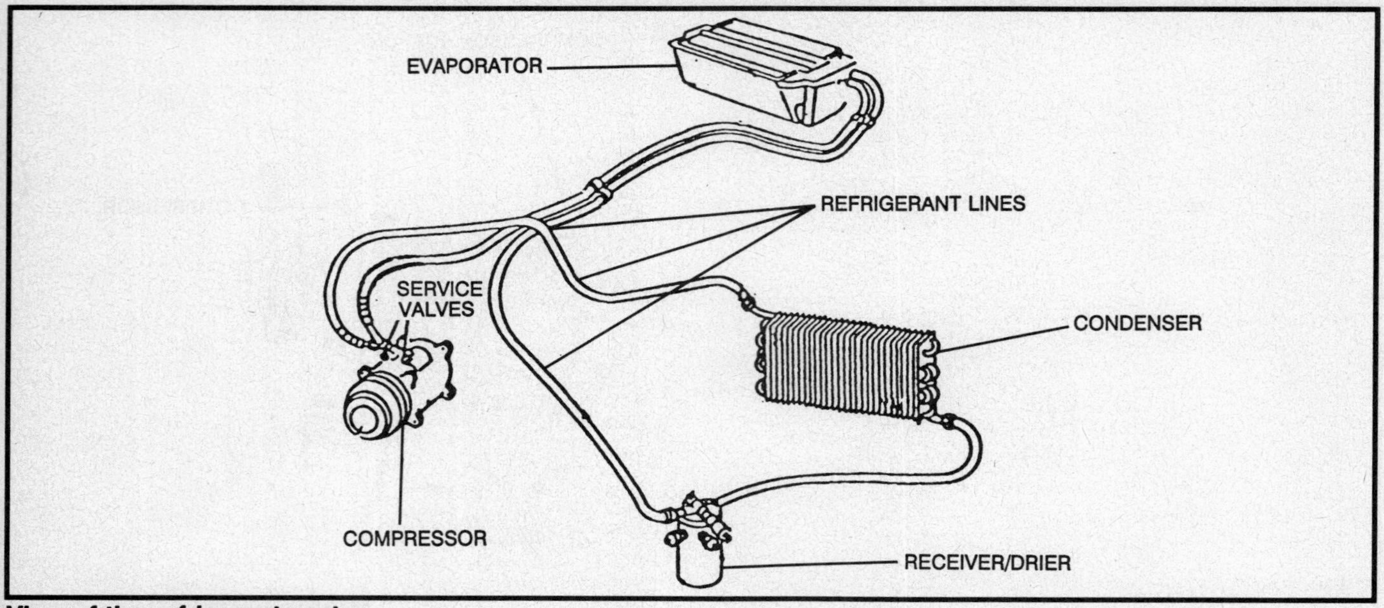
EVAPORATOR
REFRIGERANT LINES
SERVICE VALVES
CONDENSER
COMPRESSOR
RECEIVER/DRIER

View of the refrigerant system

NOTE: After discharging the system, measure the amount of refrigerant oil that was lost with the refrigerant; it must be replaced at the time of reassembly.

3. Disconnect the liquid lines from the receiver/drier inlet and outlet fittings; be sure to plug or cap the openings.
4. Loosen the clamps and remove the receiver/drier from its mounting bracket.
5. Install the receiver/drier into the mounting bracket and secure with the clamps.
6. Connect the liquid line pipes from the receiver/drier inlet and outlet fittings.
7. Evacuate and charge the air conditioning system.
8. Connect the negative battery cable.
9. Verify the air conditioning system operates correctly.

Expansion Valve

REMOVAL AND INSTALLATION

The expansion valve is located within the evaporator housing assembly, with the evaporator core.

Fox

1. Disconnect the negative battery cable.
2. If equipped with a console, remove it.
3. Discharge the air conditioning system.
4. Disconnect the evaporator inlet and outlet pipes and cap or plug the openings immediately.
5. Disconnect the water drain tube from the bottom of the evaporator housing.
6. Separate and lower the evaporator housing from the air conditioning/heater housing, then, remove it from the vehicle.
7. Separate the evaporator from the evaporator housing.
8. Disassemble the expansion valve from the evaporator.

To install:

9. Assemble the expansion valve to the evaporator.
10. Assemble the evaporator and to the evaporator housing and install it in the vehicle.
11. Connect the air conditioning pipes to the evaporator and the water drain tube to the evaporator housing.
12. Evacuate and recharge the air conditioning system.
13. If equipped with a console, install it.
14. Connect the negative battery cable.
15. Verify the air conditioning system is operating correctly.

Golf, GTI, Jetta and Passat

1. Remove the instrument panel using the following procedures:
   a. Disconnect the negative battery cable.
   b. Remove the steering wheel.
   c. Remove the gear shift lever knob, the boot and the console.
   d. Remove the knee bar and the lower instrument panel trays.
   e. Remove the steering column cover and disconnect the steering column switches.
   f. Remove the temperature control unit levers, knob and bezel. Remove the instrument panel face plate and the radio.
   g. Remove the headlight switch and bezel.
   h. From under the rear defogger switch, remove the blank switch cover to expose the instrument cluster retaining screw.
   i. Remove the speedometer cable from the instrument cluster and the instrument cluster.
   j. Remove the temperature control retaining screws and move the control head back.
   k. Remove the relay panel from the bracket and separate the electrical connectors from the left side of the instrument panel.
   l. Remove the glove box and the plenum water drain tray.
   m. Remove the instrument panel-to-chassis fasteners, partially remove the panel and disconnect the electrical connectors from the right side of the panel.
   n. Remove the instrument panel from the vehicle.
2. Drain the cooling system to a level below the heater core and discharge the air conditioning system safely.
3. Disconnect the cables from the evaporator housing. Remove the heater housing wiring, the vacuum hoses, the heater hoses, the evaporator hoses and the cables.
4. Remove the heater/evaporator housing from the vehicle.
5. Separate the halves of the evaporator housing and remove the evaporator.
6. Disassemble the expansion valve from the evaporator.

7. Assemble the expansion valve to the evaporator.
8. Assemble the evaporator housing and install the assembly into the vehicle. Connect the air conditioning hoses to the evaporator.
9. Evacuate and recharge the air conditioning system.
10. Install the heater housing into the vehicle.
11. Connect the cables, the heater hoses, the vacuum hoses and the electrical connectors.
12. Refill the cooling system and check for leaks.

To install:

13. Install the instrument panel using the following procedures:
   a. Install the instrument panel into the vehicle. Connect the electrical connectors to the right side of the panel and secure the instrument panel to the chassis.
   b. Install the glove box and the plenum water drain tray.
   c. Install the electrical connectors to the left side of the instrument panel and the relay panel to the bracket.
   d. Move the control head forward and install the temperature control retaining screws.
   e. Install the instrument cluster and the speedometer cable to the instrument cluster.
   f. Install the headlight switch and bezel.
   g. Install the instrument panel face plate and the radio. Install the temperature control unit levers, knob and bezel.
   h. Install the steering column cover and the steering column switches.
   i. Install the knee bar and the lower instrument panel trays.
   j. Install the gear shift lever knob, the boot and the console.
   k. Install the steering wheel. Connect the battery cable.
14. Verify the cooling system and the air conditioning system is operating correctly.

Scirocco, Cabriolet and Corrado

1. Remove the instrument panel using the following procedures:
   a. Disconnect the battery cable.
   b. Remove the steering wheel. Tilt the shelf downward, remove the screws and remove the shelf.
   c. From the driver's side, remove the instrument panel cover-to-instrument panel screws, pry out the clips and pull the cover downward.
   d. From the passenger's side, remove the shelf-to-instrument panel screws and the shelf. Pry out the lower instrument panel cover-to-instrument panel clips and pull the cover from the guides.
   e. At the console, remove the screws and pull the lower part of the console rearward.
   f. From the heater/fresh air control, remove the knobs and trim.
   g. From the upper part of the console, remove the screws and pull the upper part of the console out slightly. Disconnect the electrical connectors from the console and remove the upper console pan.
   h. At the upper part of the instrument cluster, remove the instrument cluster trim screws and the trim. Remove the instrument cluster (center) screw and tip the cluster forward. Pull off the vacuum hose and multi-point connector from the instrument cluster. Disconnect the speedometer cable from the instrument cluster.
   i. From the instrument panel, push the switch forward (out of the panel), pull the air ducts from the side vents.
   j. Disconnect the electrical connectors from the ashtray housing and the wiring harness from the instrument panel.
   k. Open the glove box and remove the screws from the center, left and right sides.
   l. Pull out the heater/fresh air control, pry off the E-clip and disconnect the flap cable. Remove the control.
   m. Remove the instrument panel-to-chassis screws and clips. Remove the instrument panel from the vehicle.
2. Drain the cooling system to a level below the heater core.
3. From the inside the vehicle, disconnect the heater hoses from the heater core, plug the opening on both the core and hoses and remove the heater core.
4. Discharge the air conditioning system safely.
5. Disconnect the vacuum connectors from the fresh air box.
6. Disconnect the cables as required from the evaporator housing. Remove the retaining bolts, the heater core hoses, the evaporator inlet and outlet hoses and cap or plug the openings immediately.
7. Remove the evaporator housing from the vehicle. Separate the halves of the evaporator housing and remove the evaporator.
8. Disassemble the expansion valve from the evaporator.
9. Assemble the expansion valve to the evaporator.
10. Assemble the evaporator and the housing and install it in the vehicle.
11. Connect the hoses to the heater core and the evaporator. Connect the vacuum hoses and the control cables.
12. Refill the cooling system and check for leaks. Evacuate and recharge the air conditioning system.

To install:

13. Install the instrument panel using the following procedures:
   a. Position the instrument panel into the vehicle and install the screws and clips.
   b. Install the heater/fresh air control, connect the flap control and the E-clip.
   c. Install the glove box and secure with the screws.
   d. Connect the electrical connectors to the ashtray housing and the wiring harness to the instrument panel.
   e. Push the air ducts into the side vents and the switch rearward (into the panel).
   f. Connect the speedometer cable to the instrument cluster. Install the vacuum hose and multi-point connector to the instrument cluster. At the upper part of the instrument cluster, tip the cluster rearward and install the instrument cluster screw, trim and screws.
   g. Install the upper console pan and connect the electrical connectors. At the upper part of the console, install the screws.
   h. At the heater/fresh air control, install the knobs and trim.

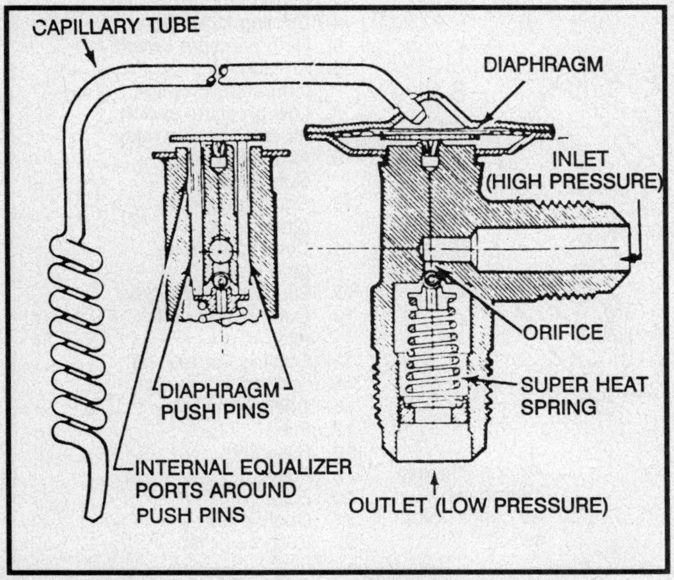
CAPILLARY TUBE
DIAPHRAGM
INLET (HIGH PRESSURE)
ORIFICE
SUPER HEAT SPRING
DIAPHRAGM PUSH PINS
INTERNAL EQUALIZER PORTS AROUND PUSH PINS
OUTLET (LOW PRESSURE)
Cross-section of the typical expansion valve

i. Move the lower part of the console forward and install the screws.
j. At the passenger's side, install the instrument panel cover and the shelf.
k. At the driver's side, install the instrument panel cover.
l. Install the shelf and tilt it upward. Install the steering wheel.
m. Connect the battery cables.
14. Verify the cooling system and the air conditioning system is operating correctly.

Vanagon

NOTE: The evaporator unit is mounted to the roof at the front of the vehicle. It is important to note that factory air conditioning is not available for the Vanagon when it is equipped with the factory installed electric sun roof.

1. Disconnect the negative battery cable.
2. Disconnect the electrical connector from the air conditioning compressor clutch at the air conditioning compressor. Discharge the air conditioning system safely.
3. Remove the sun visors and the retaining clips.
4. Remove the front housing and the front air duct.
5. Disconnect the electrical harness connectors from the air conditioning switches.
6. Remove the center and rear air ducts. Remove the carpet from luggage area, the left rear trim panel and the right rear trim panel.
7. While supporting the evaporator housing, remove the evaporator housing bolts left and right sides and lower the housing.
8. Remove the evaporator housing covers.
9. Remove the inlet and outlet hoses from the expansion valve; cap or plug the opening immediately.
10. Remove the evaporator from the housing and the expansion valve from the evaporator.
11. Disassemble the expansion valve from the evaporator.

To install:

12. Assemble the expansion valve to the evaporator. Install the evaporator into the evaporator housing and the covers. Evacuate and recharge the system.
13. Install the evaporator assembly into the vehicle's roof.
14. Install the carpet from luggage area, the left rear trim panel and the right rear trim panel. Install the center and rear air ducts.
15. Connect the electrical harness connectors to the air conditioning switches.
16. Install the front housing and the front air duct. Install the sun visors and the retaining clips.
17. Connect the electrical connector to the air conditioning compressor clutch at the air conditioning compressor.
18. Install the negative battery cable.
19. Verify that the air conditioning system is operating properly.

Blower Motor

REMOVAL AND INSTALLATION

Fox

1. Disconnect the negative battery cable.
2. Remove the front cover sealing gasket and the water deflector.
3. Loosen the fresh air housing cover retaining clips and remove the front fresh air housing cover.
4. If equipped with air conditioning, remove the lock and disconnect the air distribution flap levers.
5. Remove the rear fresh air housing cover.
6. If equipped with air conditioning, disconnect the vacuum hoses from the vacuum motor and the grommets at the bottom of the fresh air housing.
7. Disconnect the resistor and the thermal circuit breaker from the support.
8. Loosen the blower motor mounting screws and disconnect the electrical terminals, if equipped with air conditioning.
9. Remove the bottom of fresh air housing covers.
10. Remove the fresh air housing cover.
11. Rotate the blower motor towards the front of the vehicle and remove it from the housing.

To install:

12. Position the blower motor in the housing, rotate it rearward and lower it into position.
13. Install the fresh air housing covers.

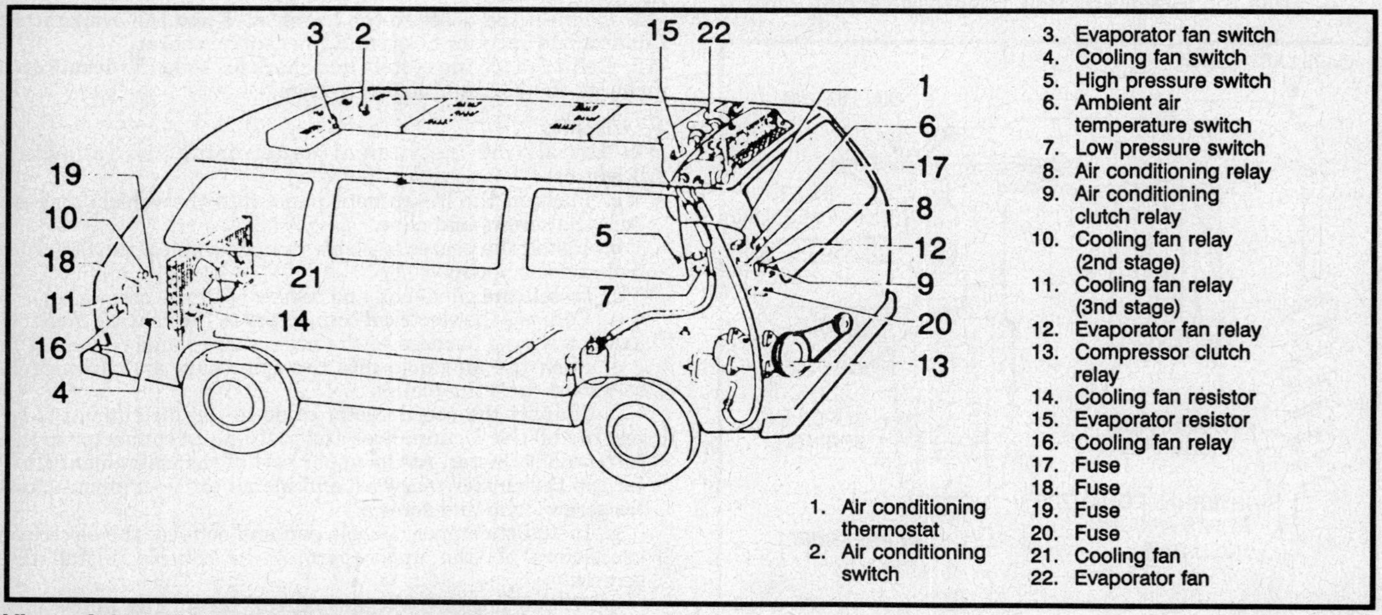
3
2
15
22
1
6
17
8
12
9
20
13
19
10
18
11
16
4
5
7
21
14
1. Air conditioning thermostat
2. Air conditioning switch
3. Evaporator fan switch
4. Cooling fan switch
5. High pressure switch
6. Ambient air temperature switch
7. Low pressure switch
8. Air conditioning relay
9. Air conditioning clutch relay
10. Cooling fan relay (2nd stage)
11. Cooling fan relay (3nd stage)
12. Evaporator fan relay
13. Compressor clutch relay
14. Cooling fan resistor
15. Evaporator resistor
16. Cooling fan relay
17. Fuse
18. Fuse
19. Fuse
20. Fuse
21. Cooling fan
22. Evaporator fan

View of the refrigerant system—Vanagon

14. Install the blower motor mounting screws and connect the electrical terminals, if equipped with air conditioning.
15. Install and connect the thermal circuit breaker and resistor.
16. If equipped with air conditioning, connect the vacuum hoses to the vacuum motor and the grommets at the bottom of the fresh air housing.
17. Install the fresh air housing cover.
18. If equipped with air conditioning, connect the air distribution flap levers and install the lock.
19. Install the front fresh air housing cover and tighten the fresh air housing cover retaining clips.
20. Remove the front cover sealing gasket and the water deflector.
21. Install the negative battery cable and check the operation of the blower motor.

Scirocco, Cabriolet and Corrado

1. Disconnect the negative battery cable.
2. Remove the fresh air recirculation housing and gasket from the heater box, located at the cowl.
3. Disconnect the electrical connector and remove the series resistor holder from the blower motor.
4. Remove the blower motor from the heater box.

To install:

5. Position the blower motor in the heater box.
6. Install the series resistor holder onto the blower motor to secure it.
7. Install the fresh air recirculation housing and gasket.
8. Connect the negative battery cable.
9. Check the blower motor operation.

Golf, GTI, Jetta and Passat

1. Disconnect the negative battery cable.
2. Disconnect the electrical connectors from the blower motor.
3. Disengage the retaining lug.
4. Rotate the blower motor clockwise and lower it from the housing.

To install:

5. Raise the blower motor into position and turn it counterclockwise to lock it into place.
6. Engage the retaining lug.
7. Connect the electrical connectors at the blower motor.
8. Connect the negative battery cable and test the blower motor operation.

Vanagon

1. Disconnect the negative battery cable.
2. Drain the cooling system using the following procedures:
   a. Fully open the heater controls.
   b. Open the expansion tank cap.
   c. Position a catch pan under the water pump.
   d. Disconnect the lower coolant hose from the water pump connection pipe and the center coolant hose from the water pump.
   e. Drain the system to a level below the heater core.
3. Disconnect the electrical, vacuum and cables from the center front heater housing.
4. Remove the center front heater housing from under the instrument panel.
5. Remove the core cover and pull the blower motor from the housing.

To install:

6. Install the blower motor into the housing and install the cover.
7. Under the instrument panel, install the center front heater housing.
8. To the center front heater housing, connect the cables, the vacuum and electrical connections.
9. Connect the negative battery cable.
10. Refill the cooling system using the following procedures:
    a. Set the heater controls to the **WARM** position.
    b. Open the breather valve at the top of the radiator.
    c. Fill the expansion tank to the brim, so it remains full.
    d. Operate the engine at 2500 rpm until the coolant flows at the breather valve with no bubbles.
    e. Close the breather valve.
    f. Check the coolant level and top it off, as necessary.
    g. Close the expansion tank cap.
11. Inspect the blower motor operation.

Heater Core

REMOVAL AND INSTALLATION

Fox

1. Disconnect the negative battery cable.
2. Remove the instrument panel. If equipped with a console, remove it.
3. Drain the cooling system to a level below the heater core.
4. From the inside the vehicle, disconnect the heater hoses from the heater core, plug the opening on both the core and hoses and remove the heater core.
5. Disconnect the cables, as required from the heater housing. Remove the retaining bolts, the heater housing from the vehicle.
6. Separate the halves of the heater housing and remove the heater core.

To install:

7. Assemble the heater core into the heater housing and install it in the vehicle.
8. Connect the hoses to the heater core and the control cables to the housing.
9. Refill the cooling system and check for leaks.
10. Install the instrument panel and the console, if equipped.
11. Verify the cooling system is operating correctly.

Scirocco, Cabriolet and Corrado

1. Remove the instrument panel using the following procedures:
   a. Disconnect the battery cable.
   b. Remove the steering wheel. Tilt the shelf downward, remove the screws and remove the shelf.
   c. From the driver's side, remove the instrument panel cover-to-instrument panel screws, pry out the clips and pull the cover downward.
   d. From the passenger's side, remove the shelf-to-instrument panel screws and the shelf. Pry out the lower instrument panel cover-to-instrument panel clips and pull the cover from the guides.
   e. At the console, remove the screws and pull the lower part of the console rearward.
   f. From the heater/fresh air control, remove the knobs and trim.
   g. From the upper part of the console, remove the screws and pull the upper part of the console out slightly. Disconnect the electrical connectors from the console and remove the upper console pan.
   h. At the upper part of the instrument cluster, remove the instrument cluster trim screws and the trim. Remove the instrument cluster center screw and tip the cluster forward. Pull off the vacuum hose and multi-point connector from the instrument cluster. Disconnect the speedometer cable from the instrument cluster.
   i. From the instrument panel, push the switch forward, out of the panel. Pull the air ducts from the side vents.

j. Disconnect the electrical connectors from the ashtray housing and the wiring harness from the instrument panel.

k. Open the glove box and remove the screws from the center, left and right sides.

l. Pull out the heater/fresh air control, pry off the E-clip and disconnect the flap cable. Remove the control.

m. Remove the instrument panel-to-chassis screws and clips. Remove the instrument panel from the vehicle.

2. Drain the cooling system to a level below the heater core.

3. From the inside the vehicle, disconnect the heater hoses from the heater core, plug the opening on both the core and hoses and remove the heater core.

NOTE: If the unit has a core cover on the side, remove the cover and pull the core from the housing.

To install:

4. Position the heater core into the heater box, connect the heater hoses and install the core cover, if equipped.

5. Refill the cooling system and check for leaks.

6. Install the instrument panel using the following procedures:

a. Position the instrument panel into the vehicle and install the screws and clips.

b. Install the heater/fresh air control, connect the flap control and the E-clip.

c. Install the glove box and secure with the screws.

d. Connect the electrical connectors to the ashtray housing and the wiring harness to the instrument panel.

e. Push the air ducts into the side vents and the switch rearward into the panel.

f. Connect the speedometer cable to the instrument cluster. Install the vacuum hose and multi-point connector to the instrument cluster. At the upper part of the instrument cluster, tip the cluster rearward and install the instrument cluster screw, trim and screws.

g. Install the upper console pan and connect the electrical connectors. At the upper part of the console, install the screws.

h. At the heater/fresh air control, install the knobs and trim.

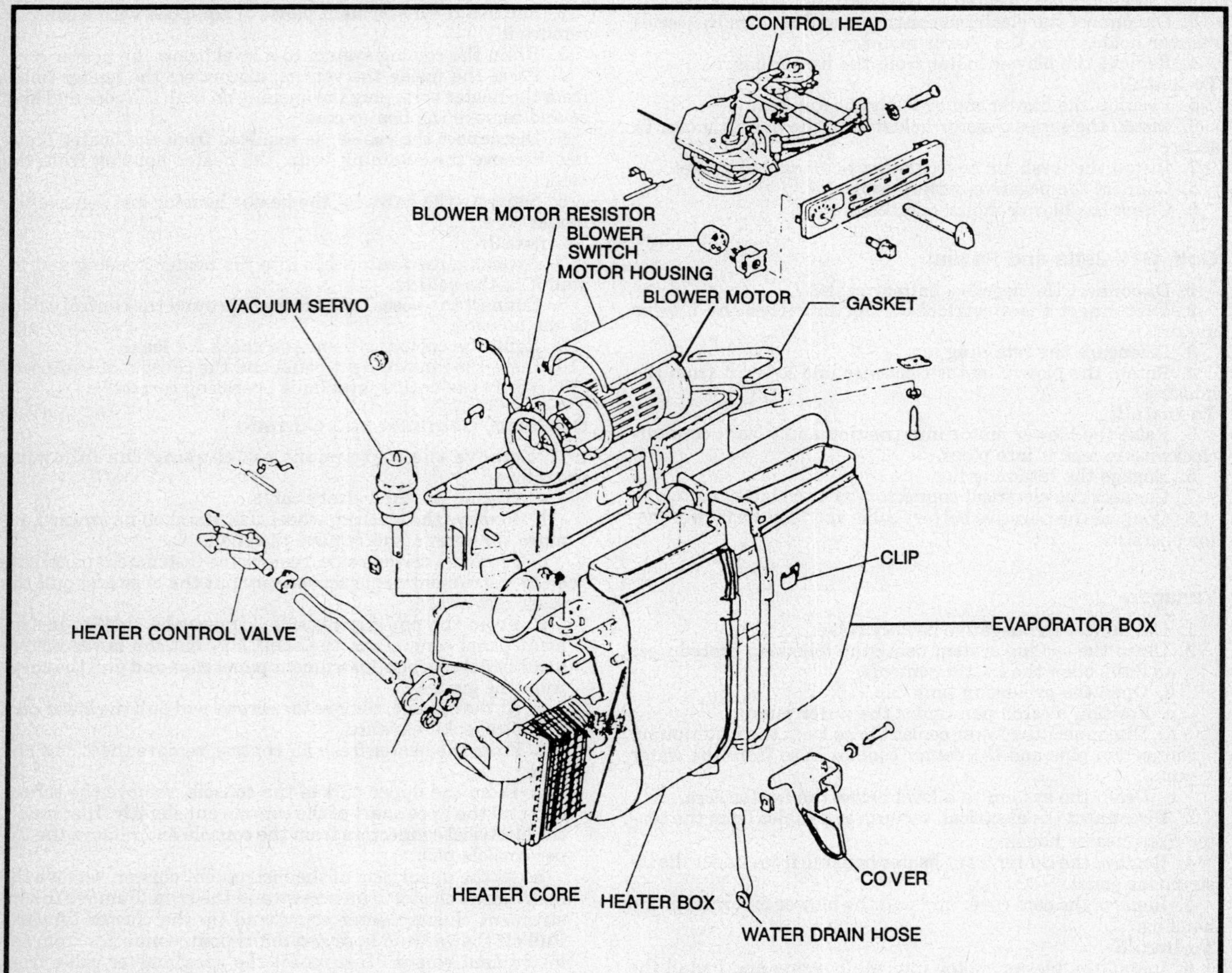
CONTROL HEAD
BLOWER MOTOR RESISTOR
BLOWER SWITCH
MOTOR HOUSING
VACUUM SERVO
BLOWER MOTOR
GASKET
CLIP
EVAPORATOR BOX
HEATER CONTROL VALVE
COVER
HEATER CORE
HEATER BOX
WATER DRAIN HOSE

Exploded view of the heater/evaporator assembly— Scirocco and Cabriolet

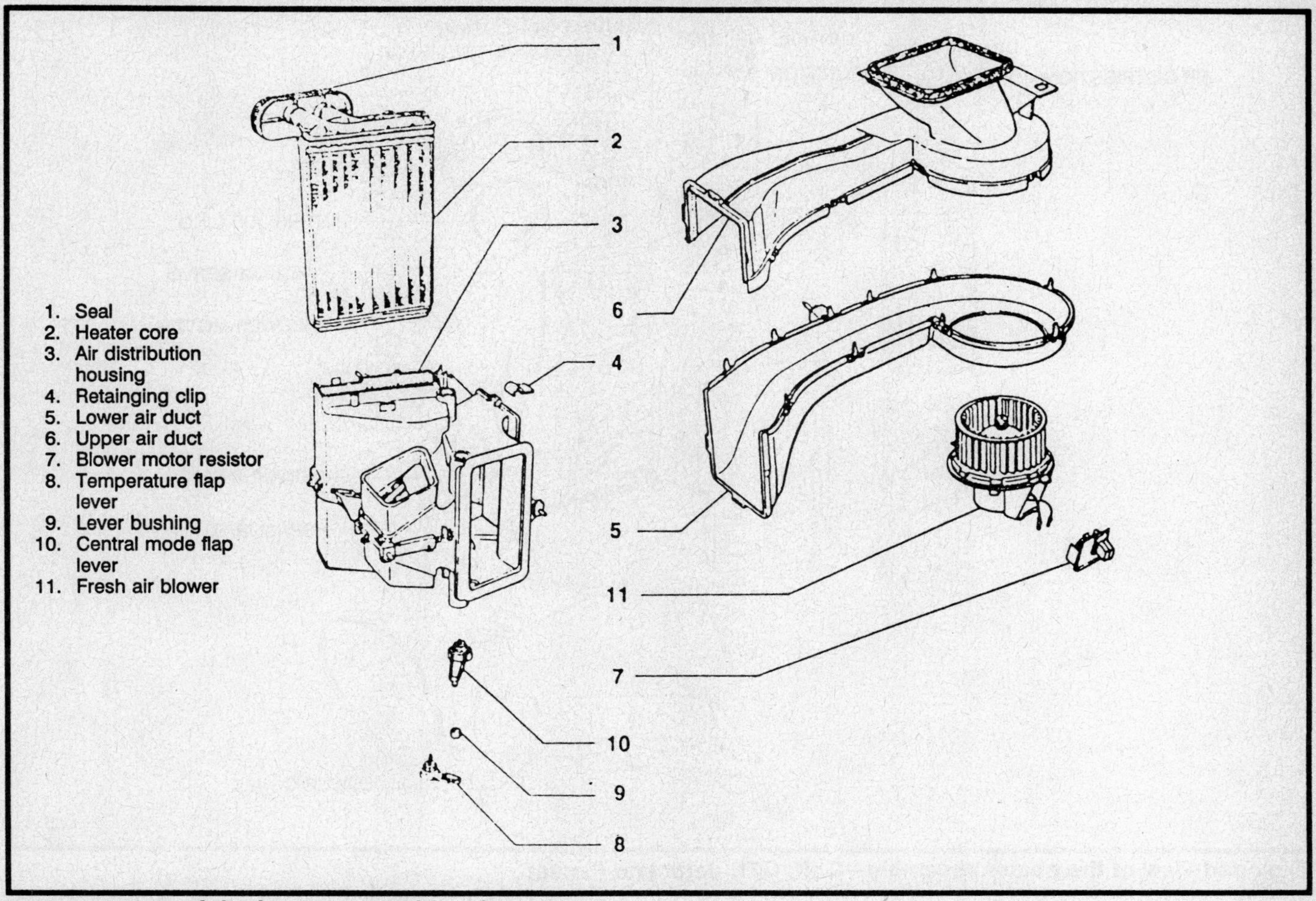
1. Seal
2. Heater core
3. Air distribution housing
4. Retainging clip
5. Lower air duct
6. Upper air duct
7. Blower motor resistor
8. Temperature flap lever
9. Lever bushing
10. Central mode flap lever
11. Fresh air blower
1
2
3
4
5
6
7
8
9
10
11

Exploded view of the heater assembly—Corrado

i. Move the lower part of the console forward and install the screws.

j. At the passenger's side, install the instrument panel cover and the shelf.

k. At the driver's side, install the instrument panel cover.

l. Install the shelf and tilt it upward. Install the steering wheel.

m. Connect the battery cables.

7. Inspect the operation of the heater and the controls.

Golf, GTI, Jetta and Passat

1. Remove the instrument panel using the following procedures:

a. Disconnect the negative battery cable.

b. Remove the steering wheel.

c. Remove the gear shift lever knob, the boot and the console.

d. Remove the knee bar and the lower instrument panel trays.

e. Remove the steering column cover and disconnect the steering column switches.

f. Remove the temperature control unit levers, knob and bezel. Remove the instrument panel face plate and the radio.

g. Remove the headlight switch and bezel.

h. From under the rear defogger switch, remove the blank switch cover to expose the instrument cluster retaining screw.

i. Remove the speedometer cable from the instrument cluster and the instrument cluster.

j. Remove the temperature control retaining screws and move the control head back.

k. Remove the relay panel from the bracket and separate the electrical connectors from the left side of the instrument panel.

l. Remove the glove box and the plenum water drain tray.

m. Remove the instrument panel-to-chassis fasteners, partially remove the panel and disconnect the electrical connectors from the right side of the panel.

n. Remove the instrument panel from the vehicle.

2. Drain the cooling system to a level below the heater core.

3. Remove the heater housing wiring, the vacuum hoses, the heater hoses and the cables.

4. Remove the heater housing from the vehicle. Remove the core cover and pull the core from the housing.

To install:

5. Install the core into the housing and replace the cover. Install the heater housing into the vehicle.

6. Connect the cables, the heater hoses, the vacuum hoses and the electrical connectors.

7. Refill the cooling system and check for leaks.

8. Install the instrument panel using the following procedures:

a. Install the instrument panel into the vehicle. Connect the electrical connectors to the right side of the panel and secure the instrument panel to the chassis.

b. Install the glove box and the plenum water drain tray.

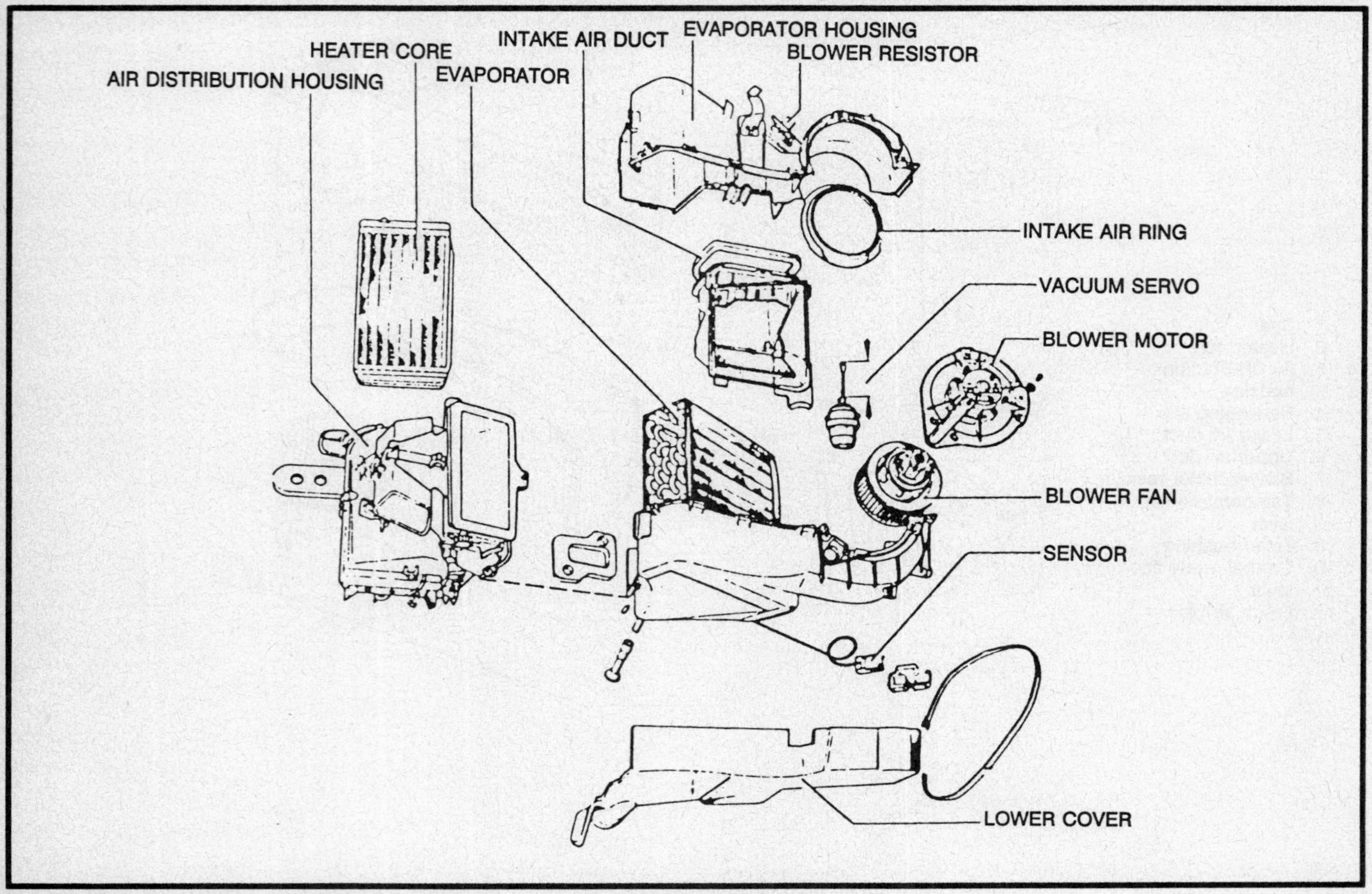
EVAPORATOR HOUSING
HEATER CORE
INTAKE AIR DUCT
BLOWER RESISTOR
AIR DISTRIBUTION HOUSING
EVAPORATOR
INTAKE AIR RING
VACUUM SERVO
BLOWER MOTOR
BLOWER FAN
SENSOR
LOWER COVER

Exploded view of the heater assembly—Golf, GTI, Jetta and Passat

c. Install the electrical connectors to the left side of the instrument panel and the relay panel to the bracket.

d. Move the control head forward and install the temperature control retaining screws.

e. Install the instrument cluster and the speedometer cable to the instrument cluster.

f. Install the headlight switch and bezel.

g. Install the instrument panel face plate and the radio. Install the temperature control unit levers, knob and bezel.

h. Install the steering column cover and the steering column switches.

i. Install the knee bar and the lower instrument panel trays.

j. Install the gear shift lever knob, the boot and the console.

k. Install the steering wheel. Connect the battery cable.

9. Inspect the heating system operation.

Vanagon

1. Disconnect the negative battery cable.
2. Drain the cooling system using the following procedures:

a. Fully open the heater controls.

b. Open the expansion tank cap.

c. Position a catch pan under the water pump.

d. Disconnect the lower coolant hose from the water pump connection pipe and the center coolant hose from the water pump.

e. Drain the system to a level below the heater core.

3. Disconnect the electrical, vacuum and cables from the center front heater housing.
4. Remove the center front heater housing from under the instrument panel.
5. Remove the core cover and pull the heater core from the housing.

To install:

6. Install the heater core into the housing and install the cover.
7. Under the instrument panel, install the center front heater housing.
8. To the center front heater housing, connect the cables, the vacuum and electrical connections.
9. Connect the negative battery cable.
10. Refill the cooling system using the following procedures:

a. Set the heater controls to the **WARM** position.

b. Open the breather valve at the top of the radiator.

c. Fill the expansion tank to the brim, so it remains full.

d. Operate the engine at 2500 rpm until the coolant flows at the breather valve with no bubbles.

e. Close the breather valve.

f. Check the coolant level and top it off as necessary.

g. Close the expansion tank cap.

11. Connect the negative battery cable.
12. Inspect the operation of the heating system.

Evaporator

REMOVAL AND INSTALLATION

Fox

1. If equipped with a console, remove it.
2. Discharge the air conditioning system safely.
3. Disconnect the evaporator inlet and outlet pipes and cap or plug the openings immediately.
4. Disconnect the water drain tube from the bottom of the evaporator housing.
5. Separate and lower the evaporator housing from the air conditioning/heater housing, then, remove it from the vehicle.
6. Separate the evaporator from the evaporator housing.

To install:

7. Assemble the evaporator to the evaporator housing and install it in the vehicle.
8. Connect the air conditioning pipes to the evaporator and the water drain tube to the evaporator housing.
9. Connect the negative battery cable.
10. Evacuate and recharge the air conditioning system.
11. If equipped with a console, install it.
12. Verify the air conditioning system is operating correctly.

Scirco, Cabriolet and Corrado

1. Remove the instrument panel using the following procedures:
   a. Disconnect the battery cable.
   b. Remove the steering wheel. Tilt the shelf downward, remove the screws and remove the shelf.
   c. From the driver's side, remove the instrument panel cover-to-instrument panel screws, pry out the clips and pull the cover downward.
   d. From the passenger's side, remove the shelf-to-instrument panel screws and the shelf. Pry out the lower instrument panel cover-to-instrument panel clips and pull the cover from the guides.
   e. At the console, remove the screws and pull the lower part of the console rearward.
   f. From the heater/fresh air control, remove the knobs and trim.
   g. From the upper part of the console, remove the screws and pull the upper part of the console out slightly. Disconnect the electrical connectors from the console and remove the upper console pan.
   h. At the upper part of the instrument cluster, remove the instrument cluster trim screws and the trim. Remove the instrument cluster (center) screw and tip the cluster forward. Pull off the vacuum hose and multi-point connector from the instrument cluster. Disconnect the speedometer cable from the instrument cluster.
   i. From the instrument panel, push the switch forward out of the panel, pull the air ducts from the side vents.
   j. Disconnect the electrical connectors from the ashtray housing and the wiring harness from the instrument panel.
   k. Open the glove box and remove the screws from the center, left and right sides.
   l. Pull out the heater/fresh air control, pry off the E-clip and disconnect the flap cable. Remove the control.
   m. Remove the instrument panel-to-chassis screws and clips. Remove the instrument panel from the vehicle.
2. Drain the cooling system to a level below the heater core.
3. From the inside the vehicle, disconnect the heater hoses from the heater core, plug the opening on both the core and hoses and remove the heater core.
4. Discharge the air conditioning system safely.
5. Disconnect the vacuum connectors from the fresh air box.
6. Disconnect the cables as required from the evaporator housing. Remove the retaining bolts, the heater core hoses, the evaporator inlet and outlet hoses and cap or plug the openings immediately.
7. Remove the evaporator housing from the vehicle. Separate the halves of the evaporator housing and remove the evaporator.

To install:

8. Assemble the evaporator and the housing and install it in the vehicle.
9. Connect the hoses to the heater core and the evaporator. Connect the vacuum hoses and the control cables.
10. Refill the cooling system and check for leaks. Evacuate and recharge the air conditioning system.
11. Install the instrument panel using the following procedures:
    a. Position the instrument panel into the vehicle and install the screws and clips.
    b. Install the heater/fresh air control, connect the flap control and the E-clip.
    c. Install the glove box and secure with the screws.
    d. Connect the electrical connectors to the ashtray housing and the wiring harness to the instrument panel.
    e. Push the air ducts into the side vents and the switch rearward (into the panel).
    f. Connect the speedometer cable to the instrument cluster. Install the vacuum hose and multi-point connector to the instrument cluster. At the upper part of the instrument cluster, tip the cluster rearward and install the instrument cluster screw, trim and screws.
    g. Install the upper console pan and connect the electrical connectors. At the upper part of the console, install the screws.
    h. At the heater/fresh air control, install the knobs and trim.
    i. Move the lower part of the console forward and install the screws.
    j. At the passenger's side, install the instrument panel cover and the shelf.
    k. At the driver's side, install the instrument panel cover.
    l. Install the shelf and tilt it upward. Install the steering wheel.
    m. Connect the battery cable.
12. Verify the cooling and the air conditioning systems are operating correctly.

Golf, GTI, Jetta and Passat

1. Remove the instrument panel using the following procedures:
   a. Disconnect the negative battery cable.
   b. Remove the steering wheel.
   c. Remove the gear shift lever knob, the boot and the console.
   d. Remove the knee bar and the lower instrument panel trays.
   e. Remove the steering column cover and disconnect the steering column switches.
   f. Remove the temperature control unit levers, knob and bezel. Remove the instrument panel face plate and the radio.
   g. Remove the headlight switch and bezel.
   h. From under the rear defogger switch, remove the blank switch cover to expose the instrument cluster retaining screw.
   i. Remove the speedometer cable from the instrument cluster and the instrument cluster.
   j. Remove the temperature control retaining screws and move the control head back.
   k. Remove the relay panel from the bracket and separate the electrical connectors from the left side of the instrument panel.
   l. Remove the glove box and the plenum water drain tray.
   m. Remove the instrument panel-to-chassis fasteners, par-

tially remove the panel and disconnect the electrical connectors from the right side of the panel.

n. Remove the instrument panel from the vehicle.

2. Drain the cooling system to a level below the heater core and discharge the air conditioning system safely.

3. Disconnect the cables from the evaporator housing. Remove the heater housing wiring, the vacuum hoses, the heater hoses, the evaporator hoses and the cables.

4. Remove the heater/evaporator housing from the vehicle.

5. Separate the halves of the evaporator housing and remove the evaporator.

6. Assemble the evaporator housing and install the assembly into the vehicle. Connect the air conditioning hoses to the evaporator.

7. Evacuate and recharge the air conditioning system.

8. Install the heater housing into the vehicle.

9. Connect the cables, the heater hoses, the vacuum hoses and the electrical connectors.

10. Refill the cooling system and check for leaks.

11. Install the instrument panel using the following procedures:

a. Install the instrument panel into the vehicle. Connect the electrical connectors to the right side of the panel and secure the instrument panel to the chassis.

b. Install the glove box and the plenum water drain tray.

c. Install the electrical connectors to the left side of the instrument panel and the relay panel to the bracket.

d. Move the control head forward and install the temperature control retaining screws.

e. Install the instrument cluster and the speedometer cable to the instrument cluster.

f. Install the headlight switch and bezel.

g. Install the instrument panel face plate and the radio. Install the temperature control unit levers, knob and bezel.

h. Install the steering column cover and the steering column switches.

i. Install the knee bar and the lower instrument panel trays.

j. Install the gear shift lever knob, the boot and the console.

k. Install the steering wheel. Connect the battery cable.

12. Verify the cooling and the air conditioning system are operating correctly.

Vanagon

The evaporator unit is mounted to the roof atthe rear of the vehicle.

1. Disconnect the negative battery cable.

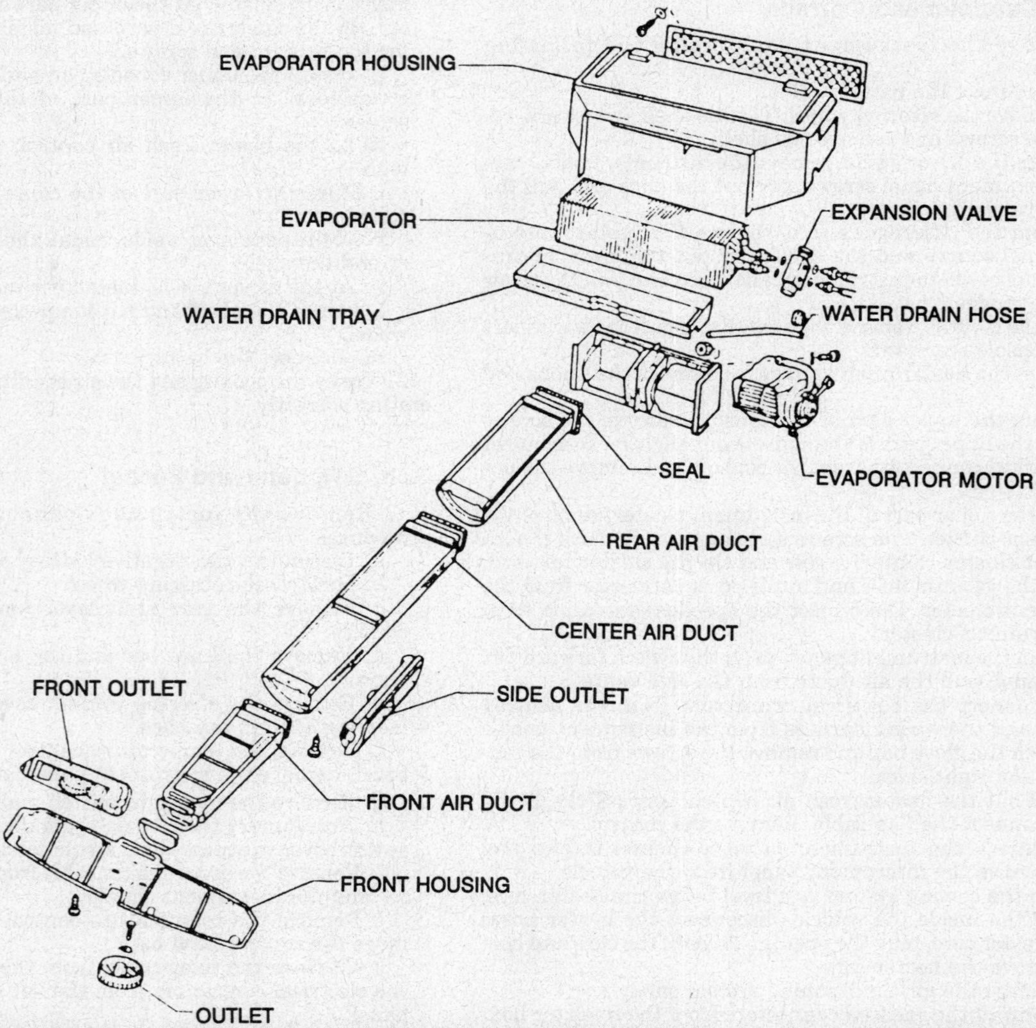
EVAPORATOR HOUSING
EXPANSION VALVE
EVAPORATOR
WATER DRAIN TRAY
WATER DRAIN HOSE
SEAL
EVAPORATOR MOTOR
REAR AIR DUCT
CENTER AIR DUCT
FRONT OUTLET
SIDE OUTLET
FRONT AIR DUCT
FRONT HOUSING
OUTLET

Exploded view of the evaporator and related components—Vanagon

2. Discharge the air conditioning system safely.
3. Remove the center and rear air ducts. Remove the carpet from luggage area, the left rear trim panel and the right rear trim panel.
4. While supporting the evaporator housing, remove the evaporator housing bolts, left and right sides and lower the housing.
5. Remove the evaporator housing covers.
6. Remove the inlet and outlet hoses from the expansion valve; cap or plug the opening immediately.
7. Remove the evaporator from the housing and the expansion valve from the evaporator.

To install:

8. Assemble the expansion valve to the evaporator. Install the evaporator into the evaporator housing.
9. Install the inlet and outlet hoses from the expansion valve
10. Install the evaporator assembly into the vehicle's roof.
11. Install the carpet from luggage area, the left rear trim panel and the right rear trim panel. Install the center and rear air ducts.
12. Install the negative battery cable.
13. Verify that the air conditioning system is operating properly.

Refrigerant Lines

REMOVAL AND INSTALLATION

1. Disconnect the negative battery cable.
2. Properly discharge the air conditioning system.
3. Unscrew the desired line from its adjoining component. If the lines are connected with flare nuts, use a back-up wrench when disassembling. Cover the exposed ends of the lines to minimize contamination.
4. Remove the lines and discard the O-rings.

To install:

5. Coat the O-rings with refrigerant oil and install. Connect the refrigerant lines to the adjoining components and tighten.
6. Evacuate and recharge the air conditioning system.
7. Connect the negative battery cable and check the entire climate control system for proper operation and leaks.

Manual Control Head

REMOVAL AND INSTALLATION

1. Disconnect the negative battery cable.
2. Remove the instrument panel bezel.
3. Remove the radio.
4. Remove the manual control head retaining screws and pull the unit out of the instrument panel.
5. Disconnect all electrical connections, actuating cables and vacuum hoses from the unit and remove from the instrument panel.
6. The installation is the reverse of the removal procedure.
7. Connect the negative battery cable and check the entire climate control system for proper operation.

Manual Control Cables

ADJUSTMENT

1. Disconnect the negative battery cable.
2. Operate the temperature control lever to the **FULL COLD** position.
3. With the control cable attached to the air mix door link, pull the outer cable out and push the inner cable in the opposite direction.
4. Secure the cable in this position with the retaining clamp.
5. Operate the temperature control lever and check freedom of movement at full stroke range.
6. Connect the negative battery cable.

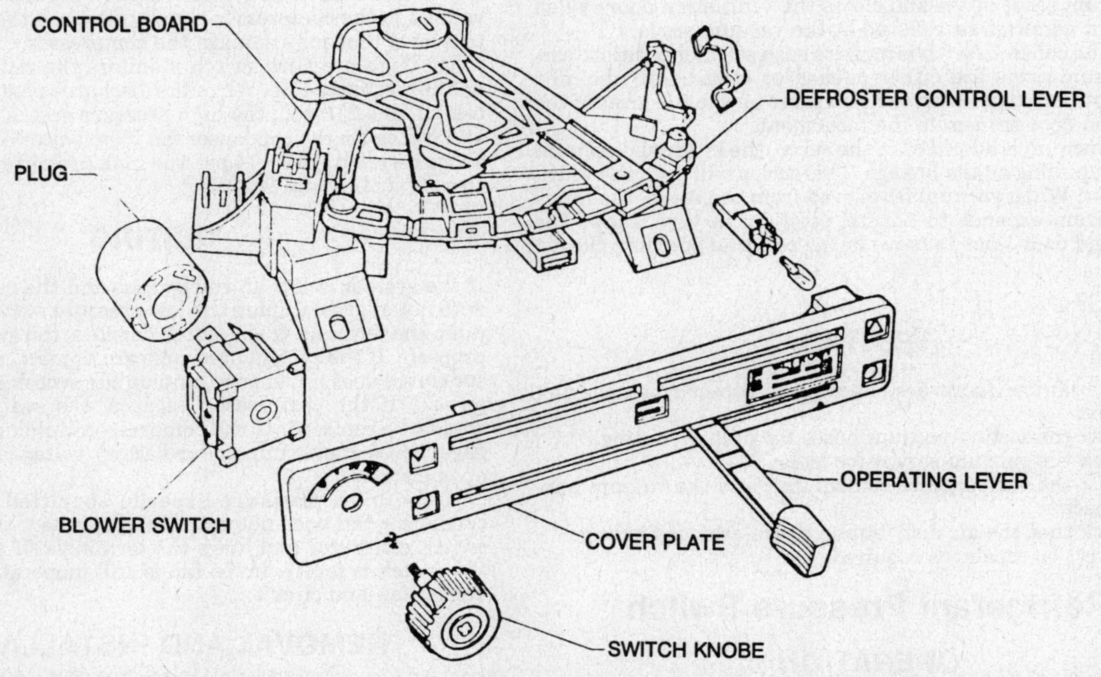
CONTROL BOARD
DEFROSTER CONTROL LEVER
PLUG
OPERATING LEVER
BLOWER SWITCH
COVER PLATE
SWITCH KNOBE

Exploded view of the control head

REMOVAL AND INSTALLATION

1. Disconnect the negative battery cable.
2. Remove the necessary bezel in order to gain access to the control head.
3. Remove the screws that fasten the control head to the instrument panel.
4. Pull the unit out and disconnect the temperature control cable.
5. Disconnect the cable end from the air conditioning housing.
6. Take note of the cable's routing and remove the from the vehicle.

To install:

7. Install the cable by routing it in exactly the same position as it was prior to removal.
8. Connect the self-adjusting clip to the door crank and secure the cable.
9. Connect the upper end of the cable to the control head.
10. Place the temperature lever on the coolest side of its travel. Allowing the self-adjusting clip to slide on the cable, rotate the door counterclockwise by hand until it stops.
11. Cycle the lever back and forth a few times to make sure the cable moves freely.
12. Connect the negative battery cable and check the entire climate control system for proper operation.

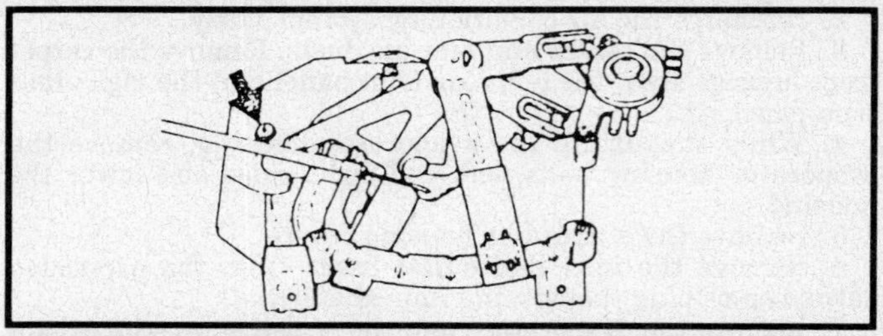

Adjusting the heater control cable at the control head

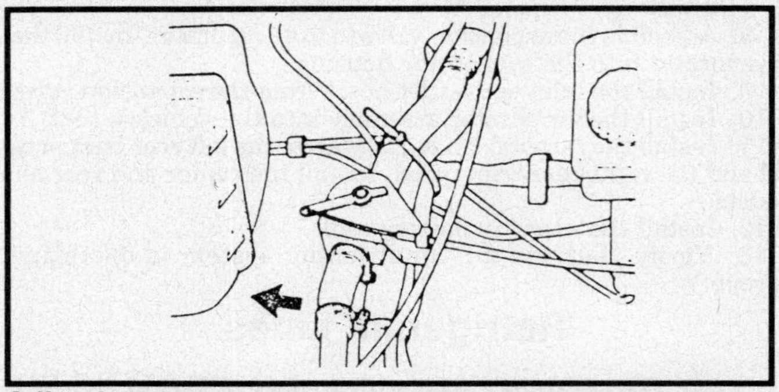

Adjusting the heater control cable at the heat control valve

SENSORS AND SWITCHES

Vacuum Servo

OPERATION

The vacuum servo opens and closes the ventilation doors when vacuum in admitted or relieved at the vacuum servo.

When the control switch is move to each selector position, various vacuum ports are either opened or closed. An adjoining linkage connected between vacuum servo and to the lever of the ventilation door transmits the movement.

When vacuum is admitted to the servo, the internal diaphram contracts, pulling on the linkage. This action will open the ventilation door. When vacuum is relieved from the servo, the internal diaphram expands to normal position, in turn allows the linkage and door lever to move in the opposite position, closing the door.

TESTING

If the ventilation doors are inoperative inpect the following possibilties:

1. Check connecting vacuum hoses for proper routing.
2. Check the vacuum servos for leaks.
3. Check the temperature control unit and the vaccum harness connector.
4. Check that the air distribution doors are not binding.
5. Correct or repair, as required.

Refrigerant Pressure Switch

OPERATION

The air conditioning system incorporates 2 pressure switches; the high pressure switch and the low presssure switch. Essentually, these switches are used to sense the refrigerant pressure of the air conditioning system.

The low pressure switch monitors the refrigerant pressure on the suction side of the system. The low pressure switch turns off voltage to the compressor clutch coil when the presssure drops to a level that may damage the compressor.

The high pressure switch monitors the refrigerant pressure on the discharge side. When the discharge pressure moves in excess of 200–210 psi., the high pressure switch closes the circuit and will cause the condenser fan to activate. When the pressure drops between, 164–174 psi. the high pressure switch opens the circuit, cutting the fan off.

TESTING

If the system is low on refrigerant and the compressor clutch does not engage, unplug the low pressure switch connector and jump the termials. If the clutch engages, the switch is operating properly. If the system pressures are nominal and the compressor clutch does not engage, unplug the switch and jump the terminals. If the compressor engages, the switch is faulty and should be replaced. If the compressor clutch still does not engage, check the terminals for battery voltage and/or a possible open circuit.

If the high pressure exceeds specified limits and the condensor fan does not activate, disconnect the high pressure switch connector and jump the terminals. If the fan operates, the switch is faulty. If the fan is still inoperative, test the condenser fan and circuit.

REMOVAL AND INSTALLATION

The pressure switches are threaded into the refrigerant into the refrigerant lines.

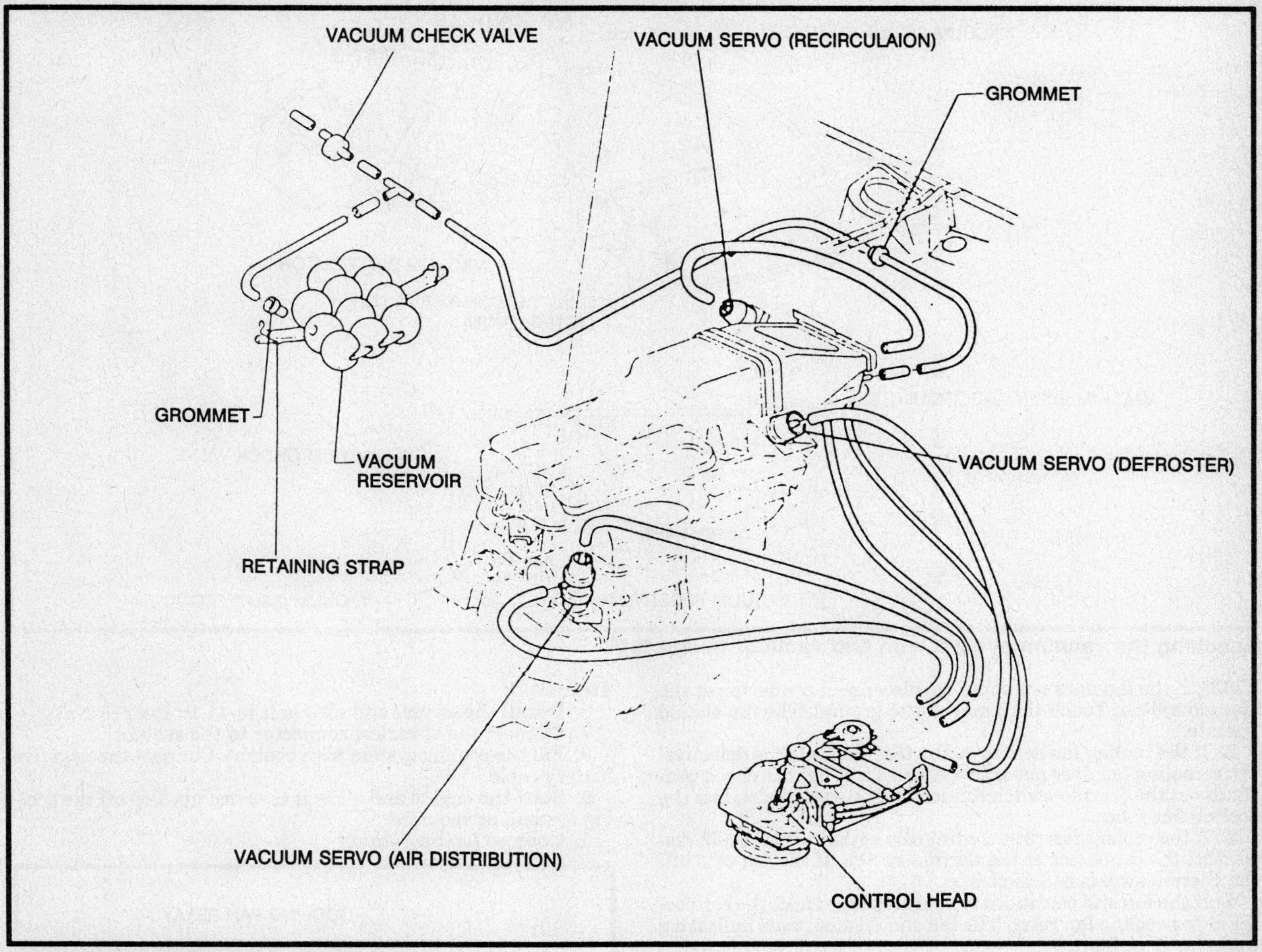
VACUUM CHECK VALVE
VACUUM SERVO (RECIRCULAION)
GROMMET
GROMMET
VACUUM RESERVOIR
VACUUM SERVO (DEFROSTER)
RETAINING STRAP
VACUUM SERVO (AIR DISTRIBUTION)
CONTROL HEAD

View of the vacuum control system

1. Disconnect the negative battery cable.
2. Properly discharge the air conditioning system.
3. Unplug the connector from the switch.
4. Unscrew the switch from the component on which it is mounted.

To install:

5. Seal the threads of the new switch with teflon tape.
6. Install the switch and connect the connector.
7. Evacuate and recharge the system. Check for leaks.
8. Check the switch for proper operation.

Thermo-Switch

OPERATION

The thermo-switch senses the radiator coolant temperature. When the radiator coolant temperature is between 201–226°F, the thermo-switch sends current to the cooling fan relay, in turn the relay activates the cooling fan.

When the coolant temperature drops between 183–206°F, the thermo-switch will cut the current flow to the coolant fan relay, thus causing the fan deactivate.

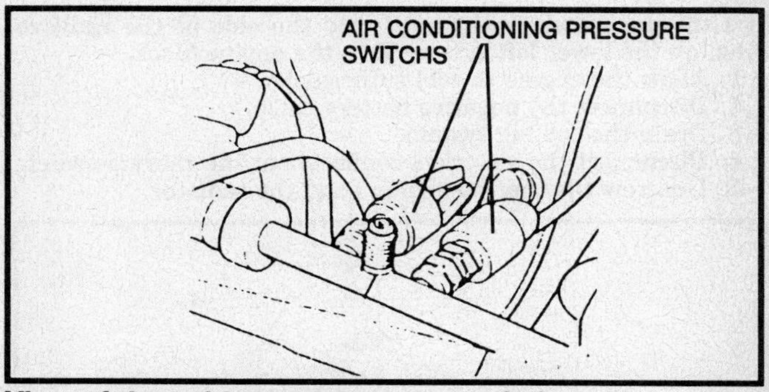
AIR CONDITIONING PRESSURE SWITCHS

View of the refrigerant pressure switches

TESTING

If the coolant fan fails to come on when the radiator temperatures are between 201–226°F or operates continuously, the thermo-switch may be as fault.

1. Start the engine and allow it to warm to approximately

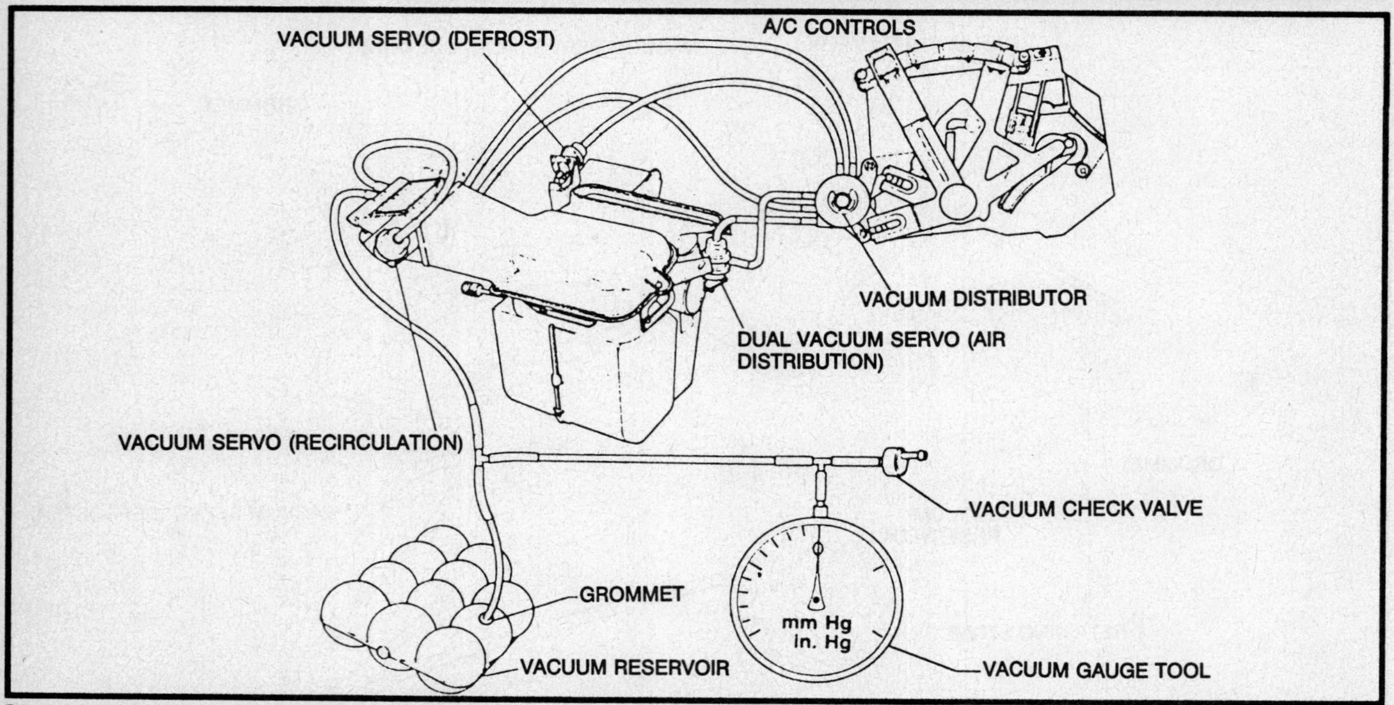
VACUUM SERVO (DEFROST)
A/C CONTROLS
VACUUM DISTRIBUTOR
DUAL VACUUM SERVO (AIR DISTRIBUTION)
VACUUM SERVO (RECIRCULATION)
VACUUM CHECK VALVE
GROMMET
mm Hg
in. Hg
VACUUM RESERVOIR
VACUUM GAUGE TOOL

Checking the vacuum system with and vacuum gauge tool

226°F; if the fan does not come on, disconnect connector at the thermo-switch. Touch the connector to ground. The fan should operate.

2. If the cooling fan activates, the thermo-switch is defective. If the cooling fan does not activate, use a test light to check continuity at the thermo-switch connector. If current exist, test the cooling fan relay.
3. If the coolant fan runs continuosly without cutting off, disconnect the connector at the thermo-switch. If the fan cuts off, the thermo-switch is defective.
4. If the fan still continues to operate; disconnect the connector at the cooling fan relay. The fan should stop, thus indicating the relay is at fault.

REMOVAL AND INSTALLATION

The thermo-switch is threaded into the side of the radiator tank, on the lower left side or in to the engine block.

1. Allow the engine to cool sufficiently.
2. Disconnect the negative battery cable.
3. Drain the cooling system.
4. Disconnect the electrical connector at the thermo-switch.
5. Unscrew the thermo-switch from the radiator.

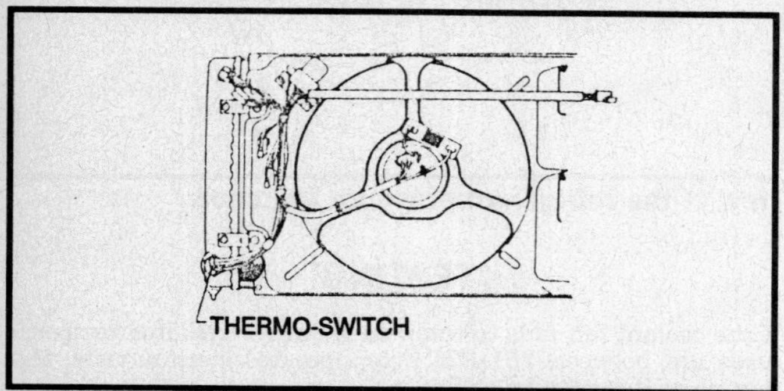
THERMO-SWITCH

Location of the thermo-switch in the radiator

To install:

6. Install the switch and torque it to 11 ft. lbs. (15 Nm).
7. Connect the electrical connector to the switch.
8. Fill the cooling system with coolant. Connect the negative battery cable.
9. Start the engine and allow it to warm up. Top off the cooling system, as required.
10. Observe fan operation.

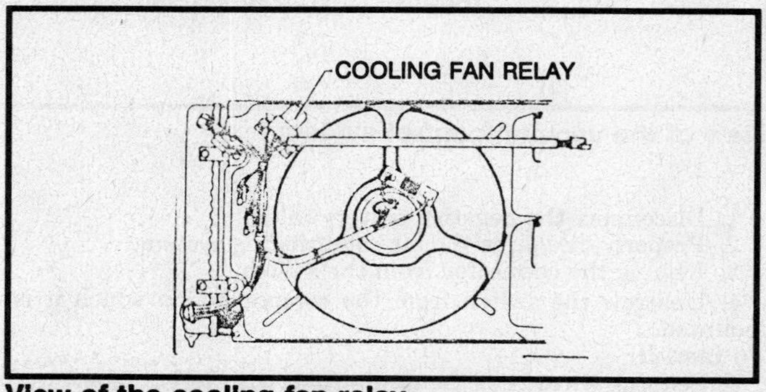
COOLING FAN RELAY

View of the cooling fan relay

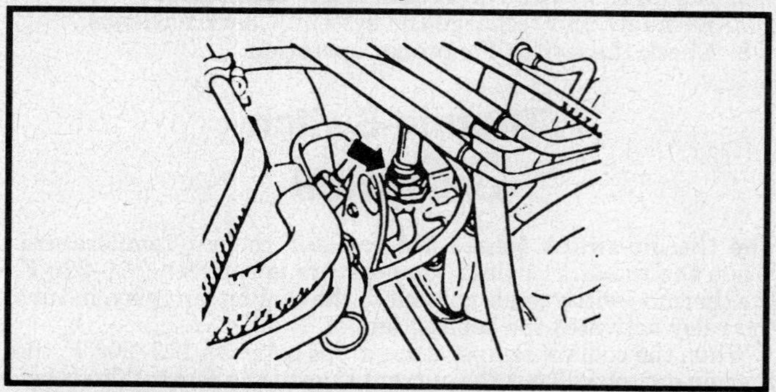

Location of the thermo-switch on the engine

WIRING SCHEMATICS

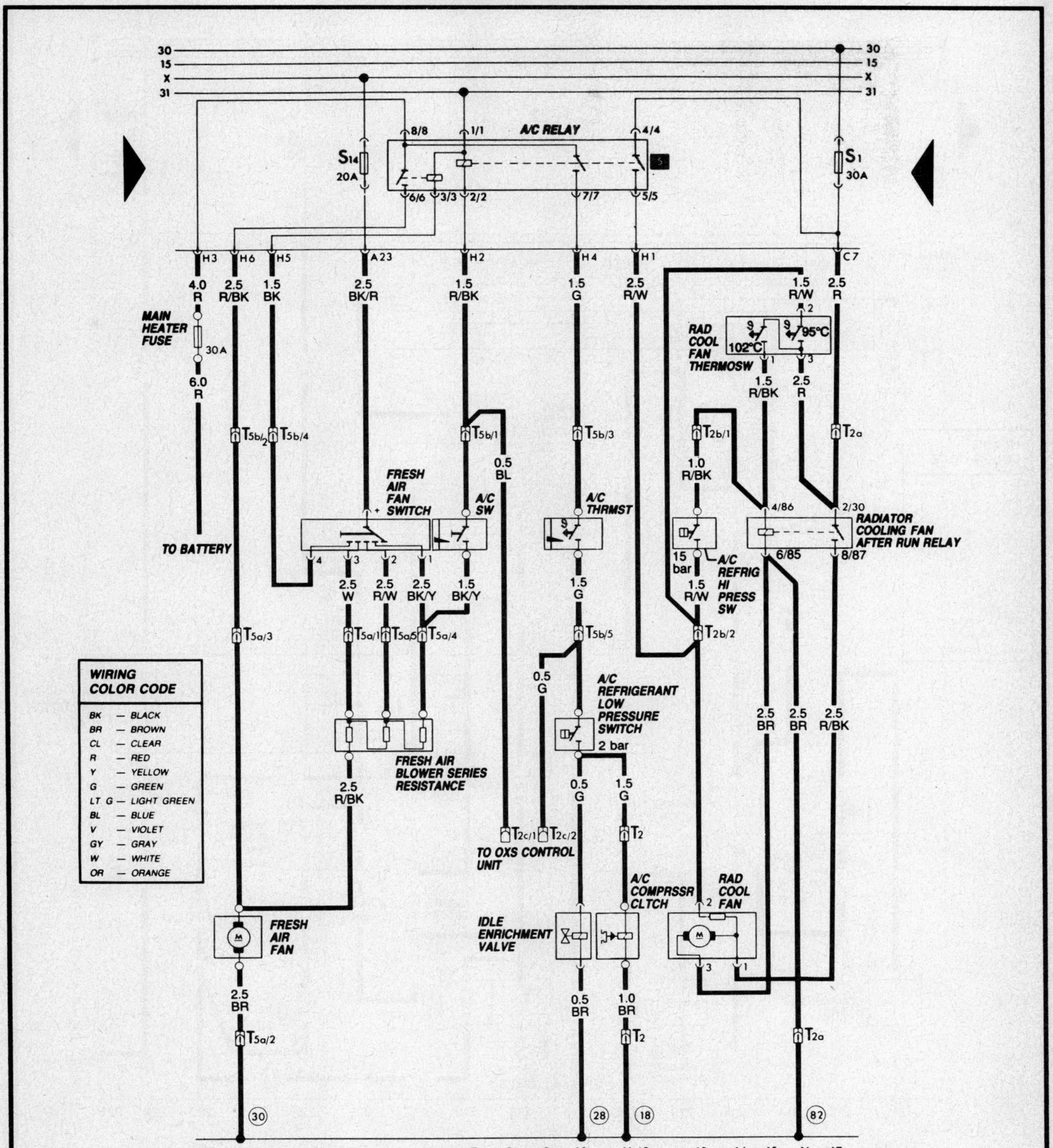
30
15
X
31
A/C RELAY
8/8
1/1
4/4
6/6
3/3
2/2
7/7
5/5
S14
20A
S1
30A
H3
H6
H5
A23
H2
H4
H1
C7
4.0 R
2.5 R/BK
1.5 BK
2.5 BK/R
1.5 R/BK
1.5 G
2.5 R/W
1.5 R/W
2.5 R
MAIN HEATER FUSE
30 A
6.0 R
RAD COOL FAN THERMOSW
102°C
95°C
1.5 R/BK
2.5 R
T5b/2
T5b/4
T5b/1
T5b/3
T2b/1
T2a
0.5 BL
1.0 R/BK
FRESH AIR FAN SWITCH
A/C SW
A/C THRMST
4/86
2/30
RADIATOR COOLING FAN AFTER RUN RELAY
TO BATTERY
15 bar
A/C REFRIG HI PRESS SW
6/85
8/87
2.5 W
2.5 R/W
2.5 BK/Y
1.5 BK/Y
1.5 G
1.5 R/W
T5a/3
T5a/1
T5a/5
T5a/4
T5b/5
T2b/2
0.5 G
A/C REFRIGERANT LOW PRESSURE SWITCH
2 bar
2.5 BR
2.5 BR
2.5 R/BK
FRESH AIR BLOWER SERIES RESISTANCE
2.5 R/BK
0.5 G
1.5 G
T2c/1
T2c/2
T2
TO OXS CONTROL UNIT
A/C COMPRSSR CLTCH
RAD COOL FAN
FRESH AIR FAN
IDLE ENRICHMENT VALVE
2.5 BR
0.5 BR
1.0 BR
T5a/2
T2
T2a
30
28
18
82
1 2 3 4 5 6 7 8 9 10 11 12 13 14 15 16 17
WIRING COLOR CODE
BK — BLACK
BR — BROWN
CL — CLEAR
R — RED
Y — YELLOW
G — GREEN
LT G — LIGHT GREEN
BL — BLUE
V — VIOLET
GY — GRAY
W — WHITE
OR — ORANGE

Air conditioning system wiring schematic—Cabriolet and Scirocco

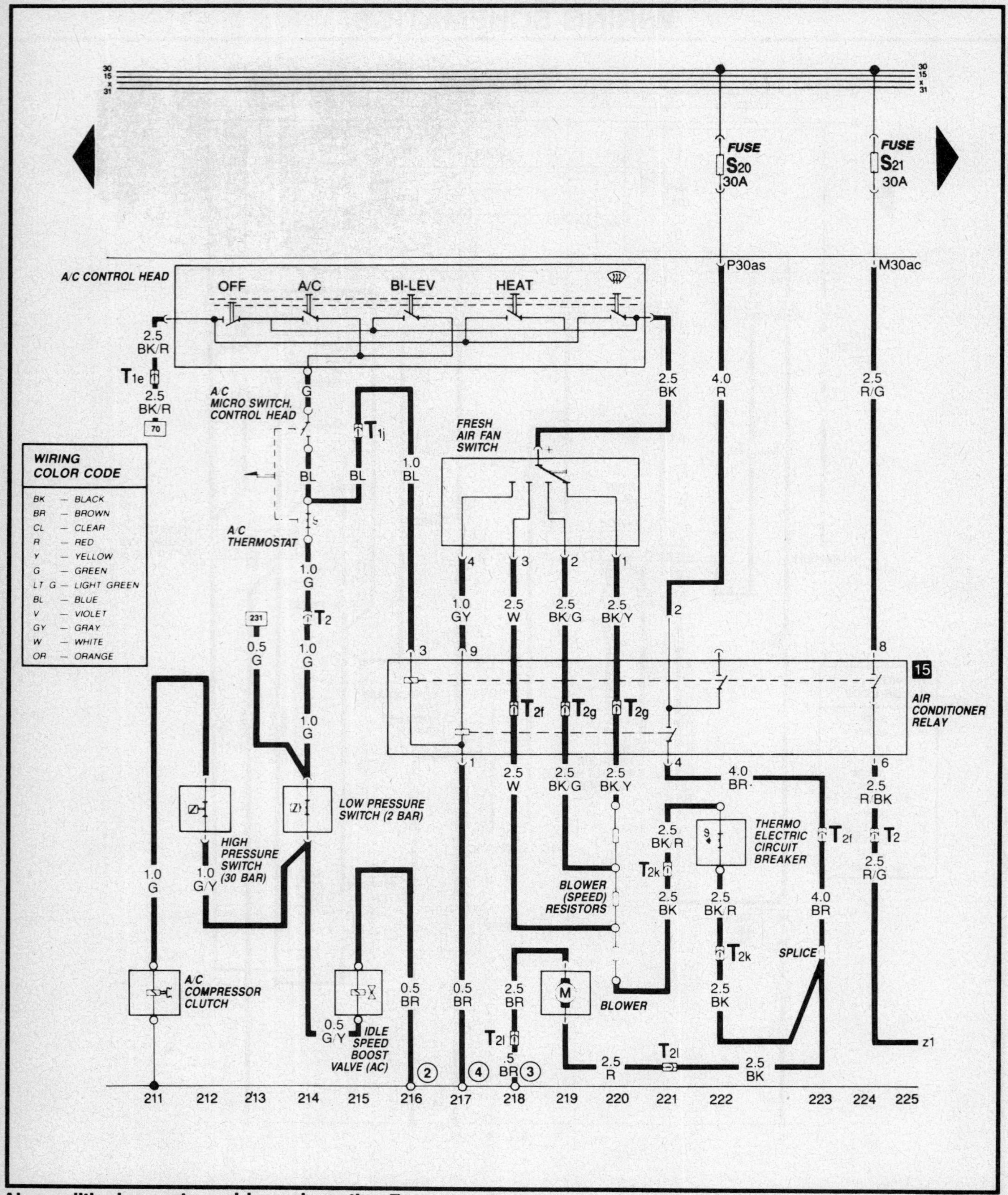
30
15
x
31
FUSE
S20
30A
FUSE
S21
30A
P30as
M30ac
A/C CONTROL HEAD
OFF
A/C
BI-LEV
HEAT
2.5
BK/R
T1e
2.5
BK/R
70
A/C
MICRO SWITCH,
CONTROL HEAD
G
T1j
BL
BL
1.0
BL
2.5
BK
4.0
R
2.5
R/G
FRESH
AIR FAN
SWITCH
WIRING
COLOR CODE
BK — BLACK
BR — BROWN
CL — CLEAR
R — RED
Y — YELLOW
G — GREEN
LT G — LIGHT GREEN
BL — BLUE
V — VIOLET
GY — GRAY
W — WHITE
OR — ORANGE
A/C
THERMOSTAT
1.0
G
231
T2
0.5
G
1.0
G
1.0
G
1.0
GY
2.5
W
2.5
BK/G
2.5
BK/Y
15
AIR
CONDITIONER
RELAY
T2f
T2g
T2g
2.5
W
2.5
BK/G
2.5
BK/Y
4.0
BR
2.5
R/BK
LOW PRESSURE
SWITCH (2 BAR)
HIGH
PRESSURE
SWITCH
(30 BAR)
1.0
G
1.0
G/Y
2.5
BK/R
T2k
THERMO
ELECTRIC
CIRCUIT
BREAKER
T2l
T2
2.5
R/G
BLOWER
(SPEED)
RESISTORS
2.5
BK
2.5
BK/R
4.0
BR
T2k
SPLICE
A/C
COMPRESSOR
CLUTCH
0.5
BR
0.5
BR
2.5
BR
BLOWER
2.5
BK
z1
0.5
G/Y
IDLE
SPEED
BOOST
VALVE (AC)
T2l
.5
BR
T2l
2.5
R
2.5
BK
2
4
3
211
212
213
214
215
216
217
218
219
220
221
222
223
224
225

Air conditioning system wiring schematic—Fox

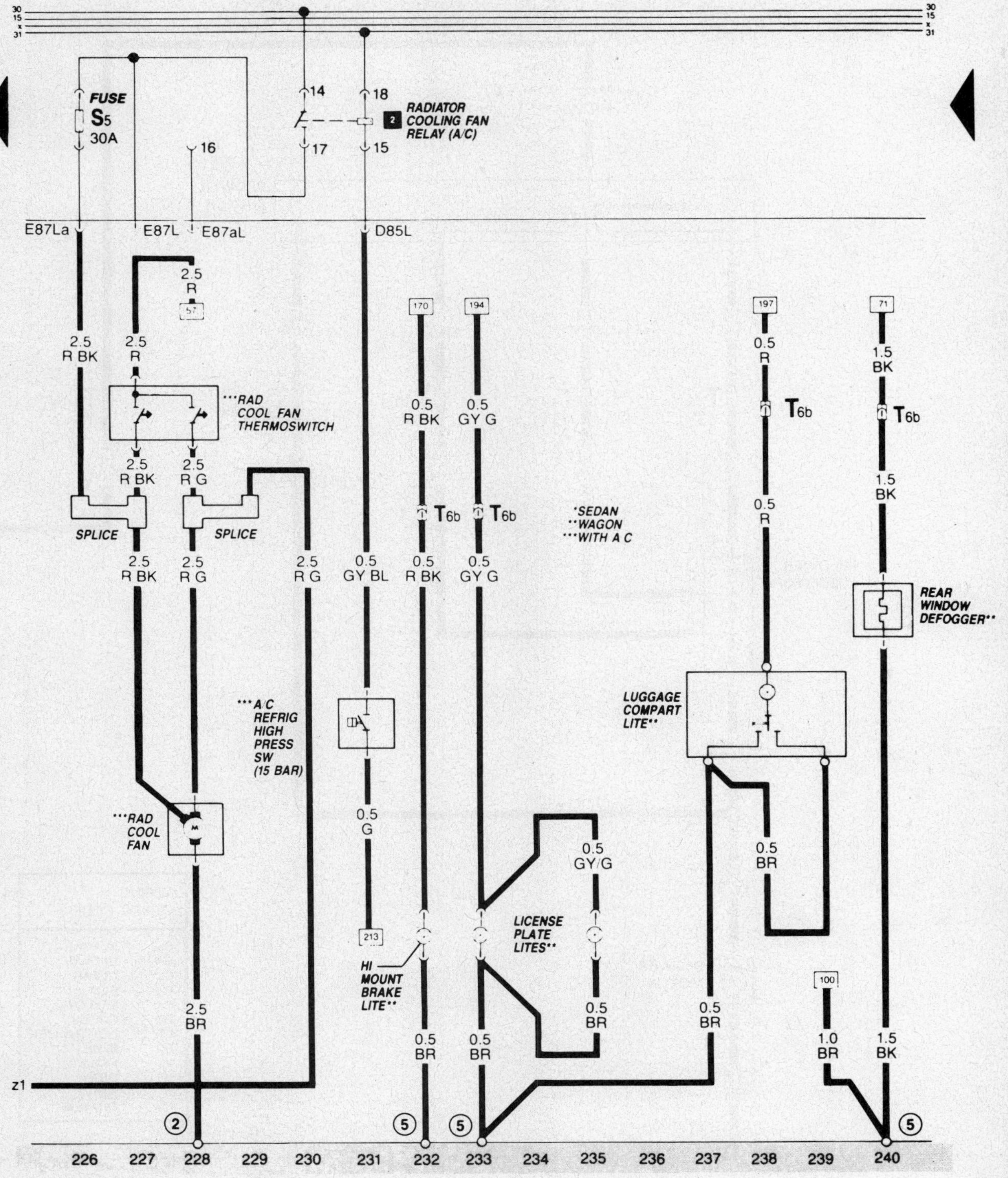
30
15
x
31
FUSE
S5
30A
16
14
17
18
15
2 RADIATOR COOLING FAN RELAY (A/C)
E87La
E87L
E87aL
D85L
2.5 R
57
2.5 R BK
2.5 R
***RAD COOL FAN THERMOSWITCH
2.5 R BK
2.5 R G
SPLICE
SPLICE
2.5 R BK
2.5 R G
2.5 R G
0.5 GY BL
170
194
0.5 R BK
0.5 GY G
T6b
T6b
0.5 R BK
0.5 GY G
*SEDAN
**WAGON
***WITH A C
197
0.5 R
T6b
0.5 R
71
1.5 BK
T6b
1.5 BK
REAR WINDOW DEFOGGER**
LUGGAGE COMPART LITE**
***A/C REFRIG HIGH PRESS SW (15 BAR)
***RAD COOL FAN
0.5 G
213
HI MOUNT BRAKE LITE**
LICENSE PLATE LITES**
0.5 GY/G
0.5 BR
0.5 BR
100
2.5 BR
0.5 BR
0.5 BR
0.5 BR
1.0 BR
1.5 BK
z1
2
5
5
5
226
227
228
229
230
231
232
233
234
235
236
237
238
239
240

Air conditioning system wiring schematic—Fox continued

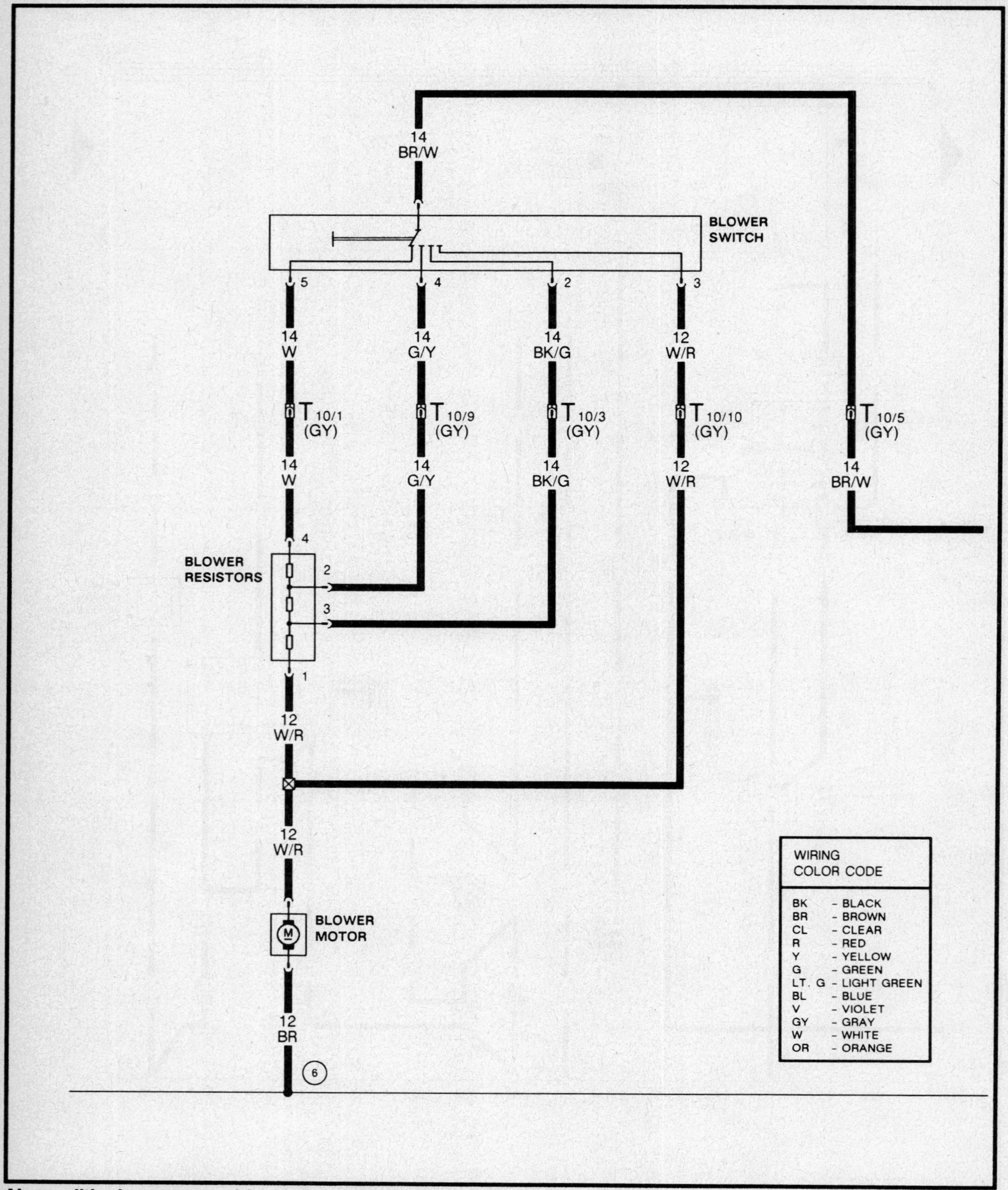
14
BR/W
BLOWER
SWITCH
5
4
2
3
14
W
14
G/Y
14
BK/G
12
W/R
T 10/1
(GY)
T 10/9
(GY)
T 10/3
(GY)
T 10/10
(GY)
T 10/5
(GY)
14
W
14
G/Y
14
BK/G
12
W/R
14
BR/W
4
BLOWER
RESISTORS
2
3
1
12
W/R
12
W/R
M
BLOWER
MOTOR
12
BR
6
WIRING
COLOR CODE
BK - BLACK
BR - BROWN
CL - CLEAR
R - RED
Y - YELLOW
G - GREEN
LT. G - LIGHT GREEN
BL - BLUE
V - VIOLET
GY - GRAY
W - WHITE
OR - ORANGE

Air conditioning system wiring schematic – Golf

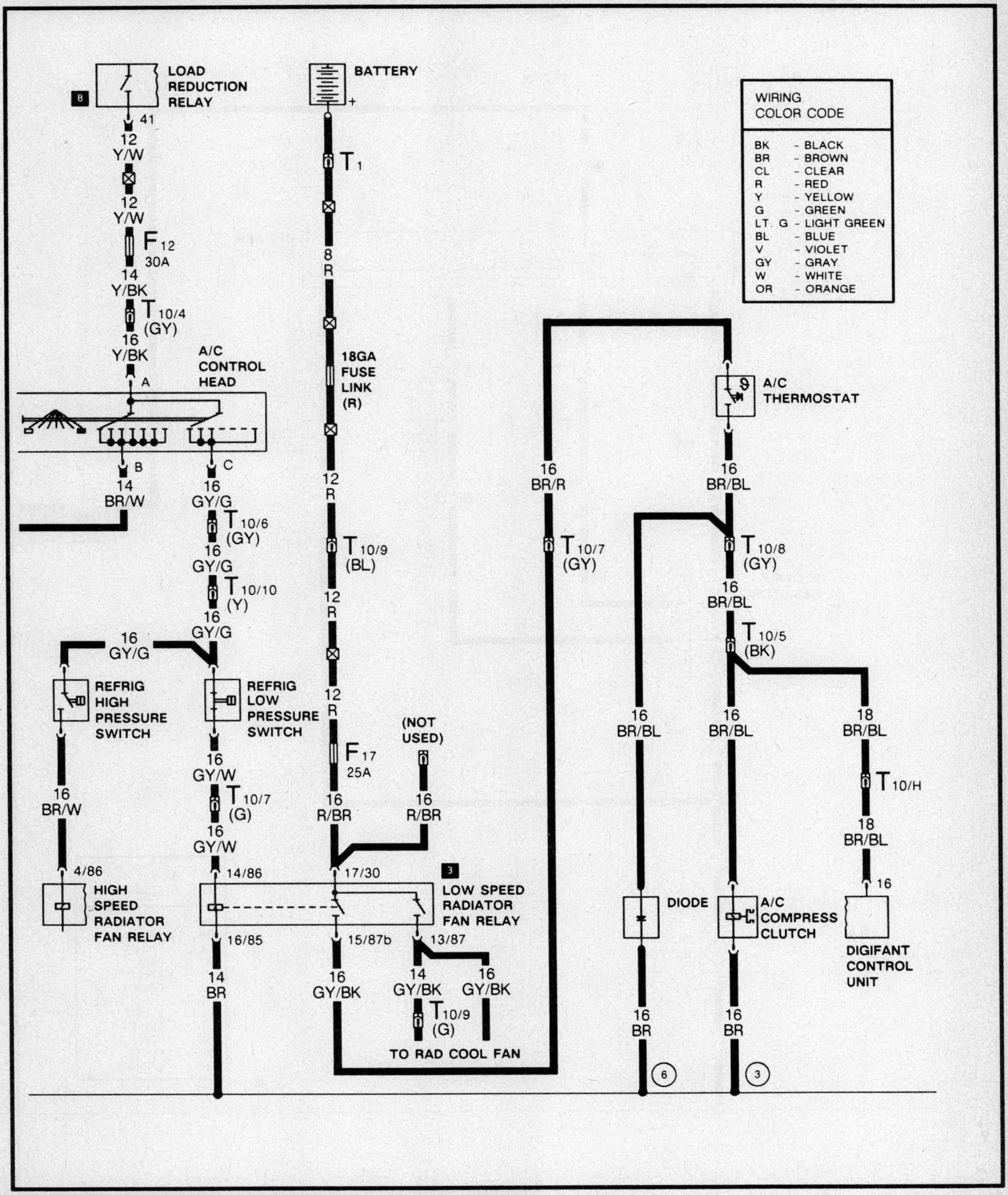
LOAD REDUCTION RELAY
B
41
12 Y/W
12 Y/W
F_{12} 30A
14 Y/BK
$T_{10/4}$ (GY)
16 Y/BK
A/C CONTROL HEAD
A
B
C
14 BR/W
16 GY/G
$T_{10/6}$ (GY)
16 GY/G
$T_{10/10}$ (Y)
16 GY/G
16 GY/G
REFRIG HIGH PRESSURE SWITCH
REFRIG LOW PRESSURE SWITCH
16 BR/W
16 GY/W
$T_{10/7}$ (G)
16 GY/W
4/86
HIGH SPEED RADIATOR FAN RELAY
14/86
16/85
14 BR
BATTERY
+
T_1
8 R
18GA FUSE LINK (R)
12 R
$T_{10/9}$ (BL)
12 R
12 R
F_{17} 25A
(NOT USED)
16 R/BR
16 R/BR
17/30
3
LOW SPEED RADIATOR FAN RELAY
15/87b
13/87
16 GY/BK
14 GY/BK
16 GY/BK
$T_{10/9}$ (G)
TO RAD COOL FAN
16 BR/R
$T_{10/7}$ (GY)
A/C THERMOSTAT
16 BR/BL
$T_{10/8}$ (GY)
16 BR/BL
$T_{10/5}$ (BK)
16 BR/BL
16 BR/BL
18 BR/BL
$T_{10/H}$
18 BR/BL
16
DIODE
A/C COMPRESS CLUTCH
DIGIFANT CONTROL UNIT
16 BR
16 BR
6
3
WIRING COLOR CODE
BK - BLACK
BR - BROWN
CL - CLEAR
R - RED
Y - YELLOW
G - GREEN
LT. G - LIGHT GREEN
BL - BLUE
V - VIOLET
GY - GRAY
W - WHITE
OR - ORANGE

Air conditioning system wiring schematic—Golf continued

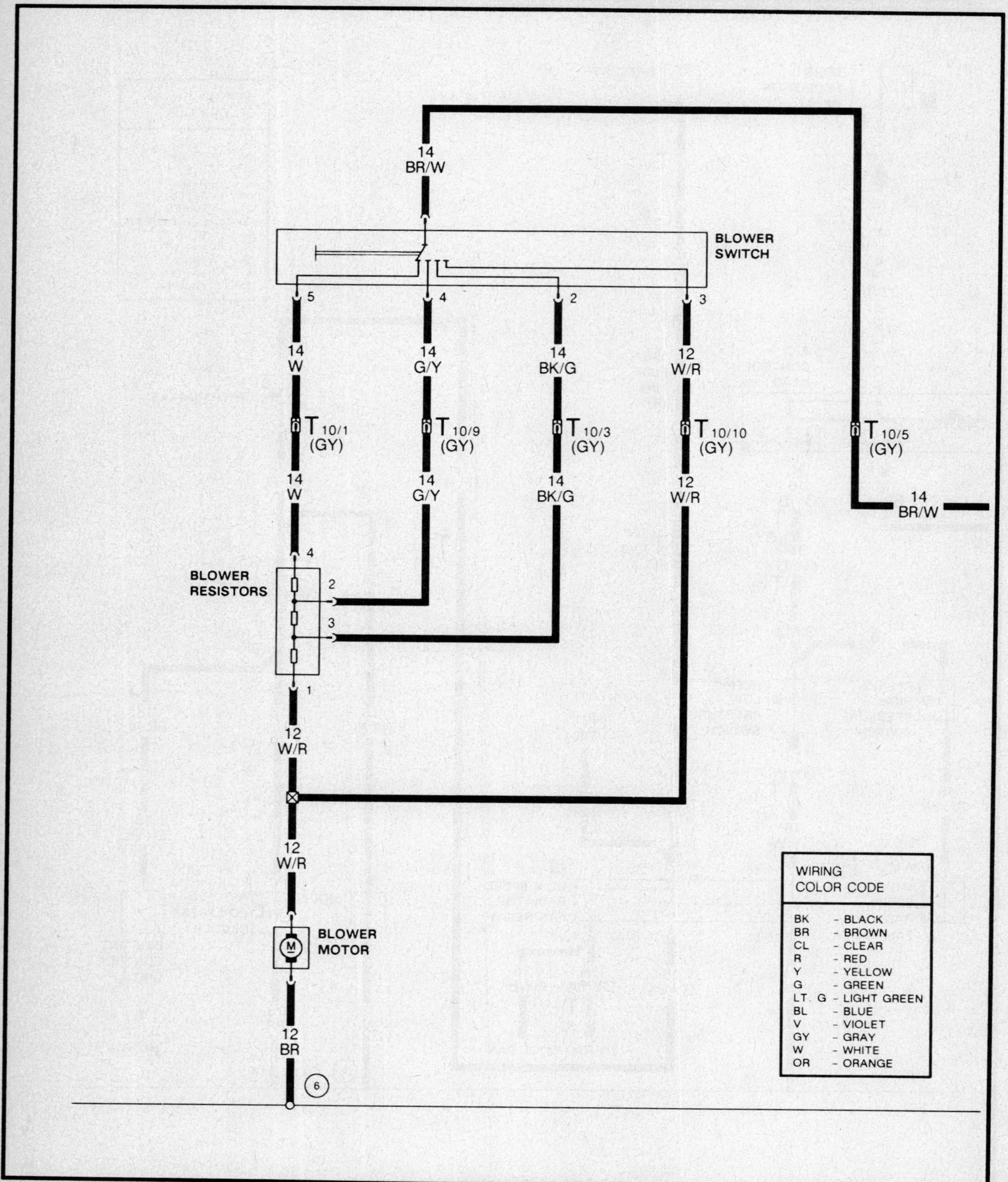
14
BR/W
BLOWER
SWITCH
5
4
2
3
14
W
14
G/Y
14
BK/G
12
W/R
T 10/1
(GY)
T 10/9
(GY)
T 10/3
(GY)
T 10/10
(GY)
T 10/5
(GY)
14
W
14
G/Y
14
BK/G
12
W/R
14
BR/W
4
BLOWER
RESISTORS
2
3
1
12
W/R
12
W/R
BLOWER
MOTOR
12
BR
6
WIRING
COLOR CODE
BK - BLACK
BR - BROWN
CL - CLEAR
R - RED
Y - YELLOW
G - GREEN
LT. G - LIGHT GREEN
BL - BLUE
V - VIOLET
GY - GRAY
W - WHITE
OR - ORANGE

Air conditioning system wiring schematic – Golf with diesel engine

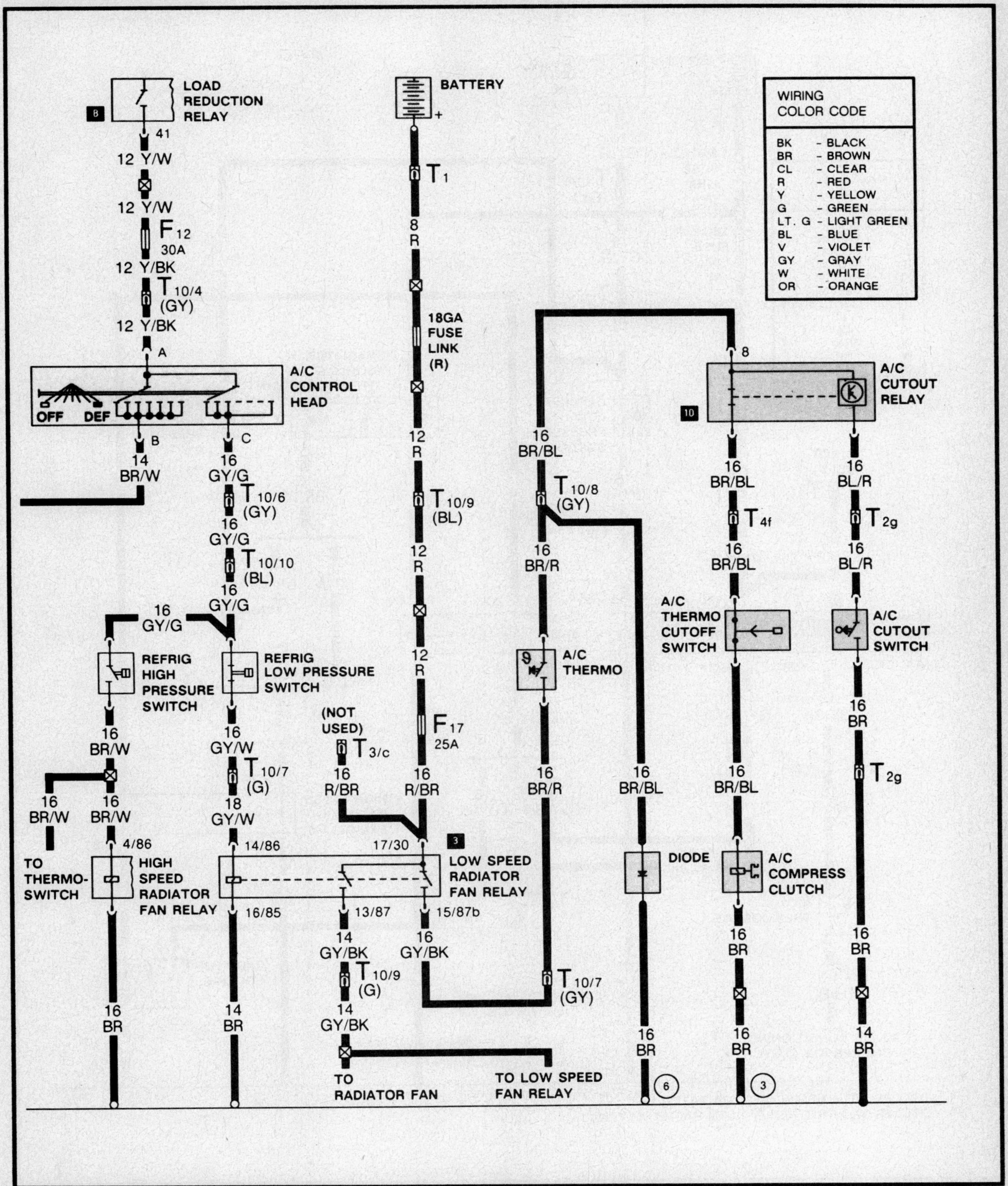
LOAD REDUCTION RELAY
B
41
12 Y/W
12 Y/W
F 12
30A
12 Y/BK
T 10/4 (GY)
12 Y/BK
A
A/C CONTROL HEAD
OFF
DEF
B
C
14 BR/W
16 GY/G
T 10/6 (GY)
16 GY/G
T 10/10 (BL)
16 GY/G
16 GY/G
REFRIG HIGH PRESSURE SWITCH
REFRIG LOW PRESSURE SWITCH
16 BR/W
16 GY/W
T 10/7 (G)
16 BR/W
16 BR/W
18 GY/W
TO THERMO-SWITCH
4/86
HIGH SPEED RADIATOR FAN RELAY
14/86
16/85
16 BR
14 BR
BATTERY
+
T 1
8 R
18GA FUSE LINK (R)
12 R
T 10/9 (BL)
12 R
12 R
F 17
25A
(NOT USED)
T 3/c
16 R/BR
16 R/BR
17/30
3
LOW SPEED RADIATOR FAN RELAY
13/87
15/87b
14 GY/BK
16 GY/BK
T 10/9 (G)
14 GY/BK
TO RADIATOR FAN
TO LOW SPEED FAN RELAY
16 BR/BL
T 10/8 (GY)
16 BR/R
A/C THERMO
16 BR/R
T 10/7 (GY)
16 BR/BL
DIODE
16 BR
6
8
A/C CUTOUT RELAY
10
16 BR/BL
T 4f
16 BR/BL
A/C THERMO CUTOFF SWITCH
16 BR/BL
A/C COMPRESS CLUTCH
16 BR
16 BR
3
16 BL/R
T 2g
16 BL/R
A/C CUTOUT SWITCH
16 BR
T 2g
16 BR
14 BR
WIRING COLOR CODE
BK - BLACK
BR - BROWN
CL - CLEAR
R - RED
Y - YELLOW
G - GREEN
LT. G - LIGHT GREEN
BL - BLUE
V - VIOLET
GY - GRAY
W - WHITE
OR - ORANGE

Air conditioning system wiring schematic—Golf with diesel engine continued

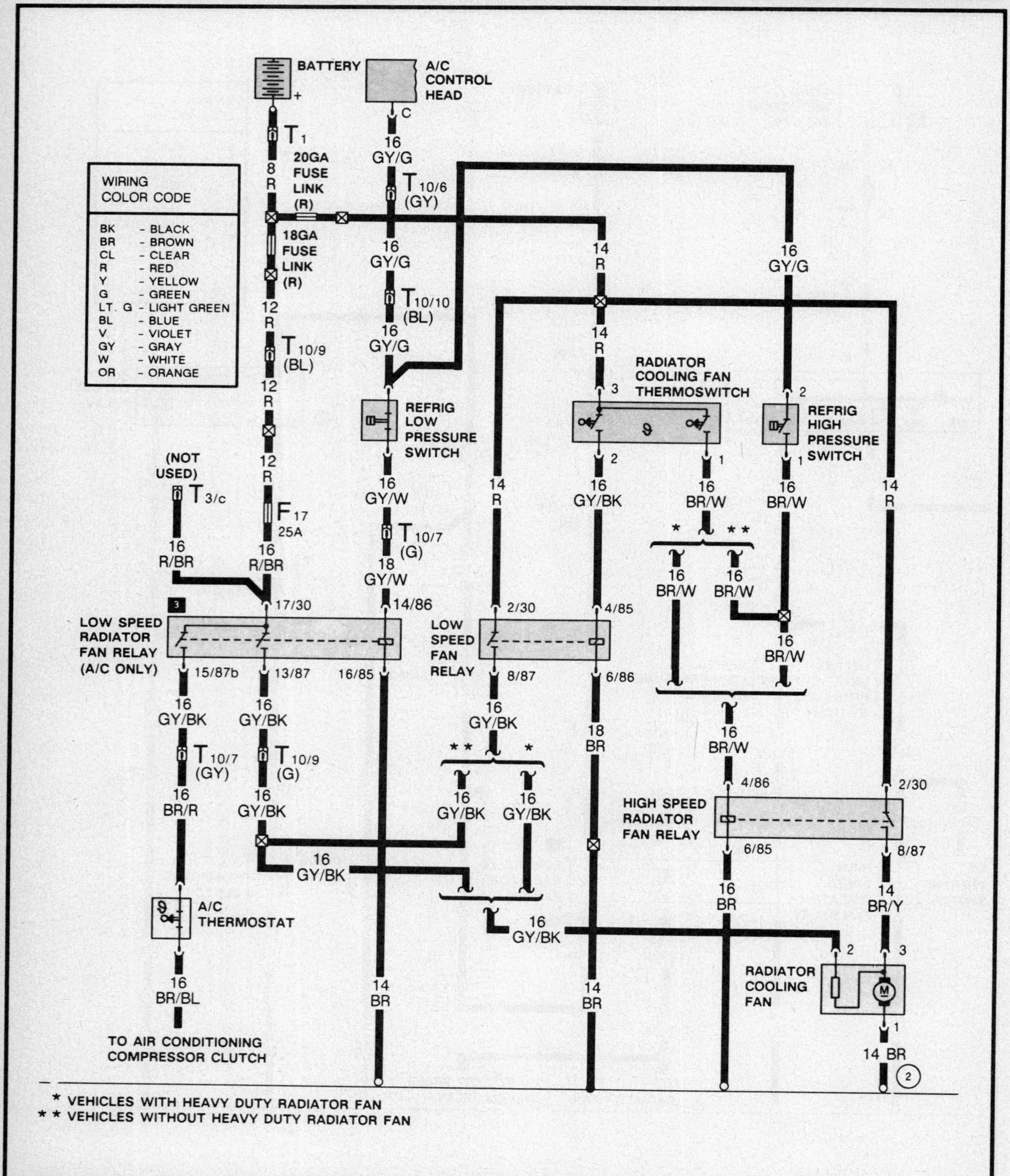
BATTERY
A/C CONTROL HEAD
WIRING COLOR CODE
BK - BLACK
BR - BROWN
CL - CLEAR
R - RED
Y - YELLOW
G - GREEN
LT. G - LIGHT GREEN
BL - BLUE
V - VIOLET
GY - GRAY
W - WHITE
OR - ORANGE
20GA FUSE LINK (R)
18GA FUSE LINK (R)
REFRIG LOW PRESSURE SWITCH
RADIATOR COOLING FAN THERMOSWITCH
REFRIG HIGH PRESSURE SWITCH
(NOT USED)
LOW SPEED RADIATOR FAN RELAY (A/C ONLY)
LOW SPEED FAN RELAY
HIGH SPEED RADIATOR FAN RELAY
A/C THERMOSTAT
RADIATOR COOLING FAN
TO AIR CONDITIONING COMPRESSOR CLUTCH
* VEHICLES WITH HEAVY DUTY RADIATOR FAN
* * VEHICLES WITHOUT HEAVY DUTY RADIATOR FAN

Cooling fan circuit wiring schematic—Golf with diesel engine

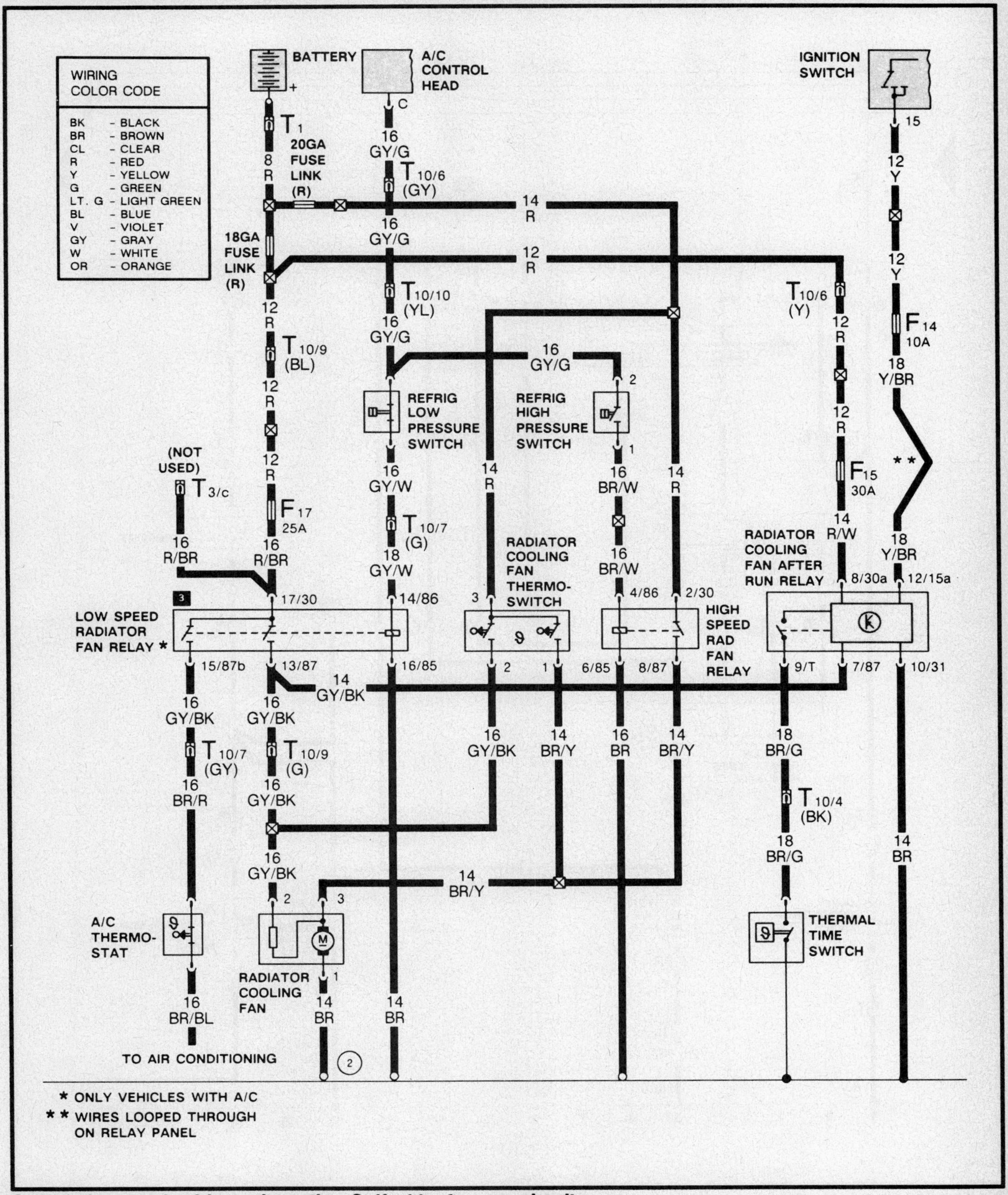
WIRING COLOR CODE
BK - BLACK
BR - BROWN
CL - CLEAR
R - RED
Y - YELLOW
G - GREEN
LT. G - LIGHT GREEN
BL - BLUE
V - VIOLET
GY - GRAY
W - WHITE
OR - ORANGE
BATTERY
A/C CONTROL HEAD
IGNITION SWITCH
20GA FUSE LINK (R)
18GA FUSE LINK (R)
REFRIG LOW PRESSURE SWITCH
REFRIG HIGH PRESSURE SWITCH
(NOT USED)
RADIATOR COOLING FAN THERMO-SWITCH
RADIATOR COOLING FAN AFTER RUN RELAY
LOW SPEED RADIATOR FAN RELAY *
HIGH SPEED RAD FAN RELAY
A/C THERMO-STAT
RADIATOR COOLING FAN
THERMAL TIME SWITCH
TO AIR CONDITIONING
* ONLY VEHICLES WITH A/C
* * WIRES LOOPED THROUGH ON RELAY PANEL

Cooling fan circuit wiring schematic—Golf with after run circuit

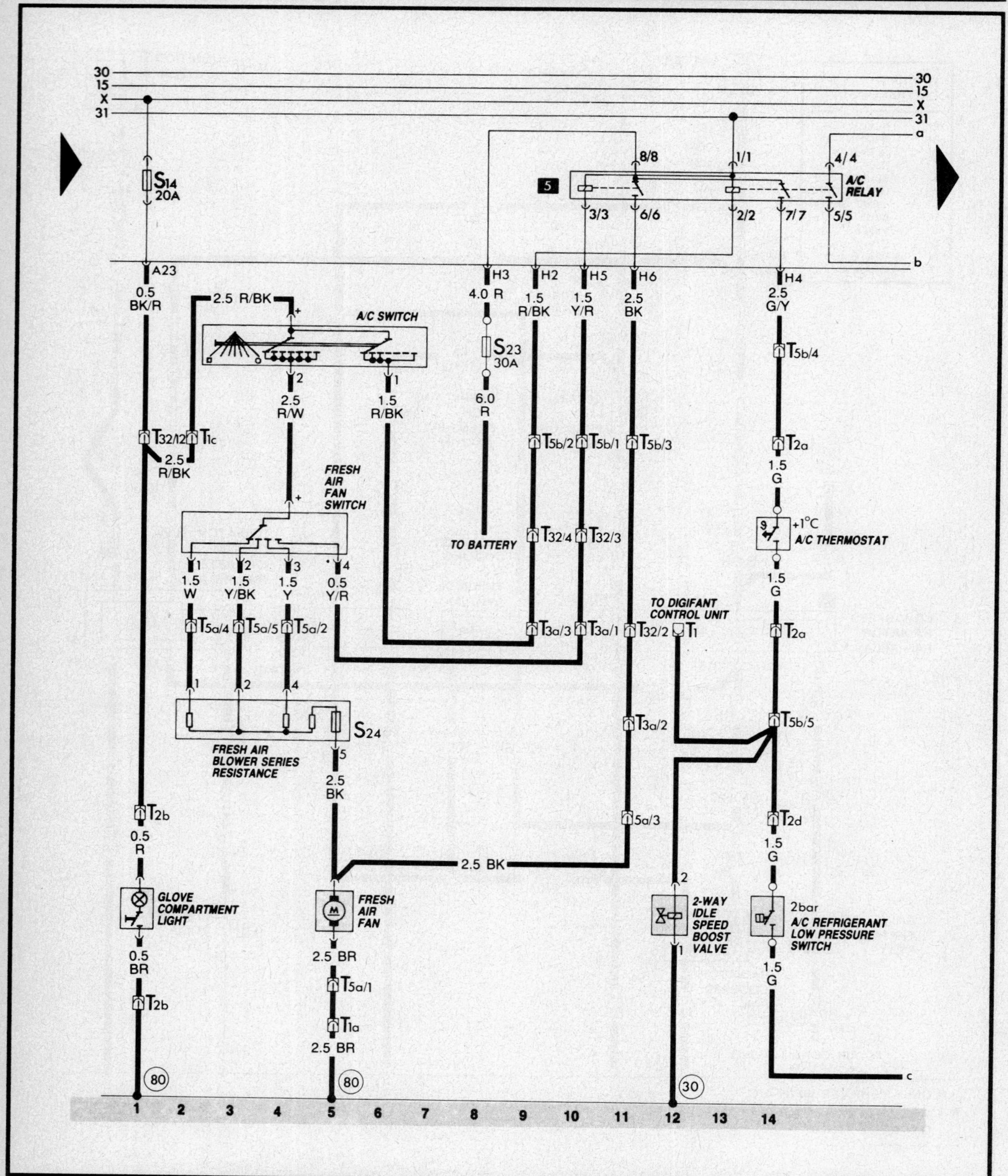
30
15
X
31
a
b
c
S14
20A
A23
0.5
BK/R
2.5 R/BK
A/C SWITCH
2.5
R/W
1.5
R/BK
T32/12
T1c
FRESH
AIR
FAN
SWITCH
1.5
W
1.5
Y/BK
1.5
Y
0.5
Y/R
T5a/4
T5a/5
T5a/2
FRESH AIR
BLOWER SERIES
RESISTANCE
S24
2.5
BK
2.5 BK
T2b
0.5
R
GLOVE
COMPARTMENT
LIGHT
0.5
BR
FRESH
AIR
FAN
2.5 BR
T5a/1
T1a
H3
4.0 R
S23
30A
6.0
R
TO BATTERY
H2
H5
H6
1.5
R/BK
1.5
Y/R
2.5
BK
T5b/2
T5b/1
T5b/3
T32/4
T32/3
T3a/3
T3a/1
T32/2
T1
TO DIGIFANT
CONTROL UNIT
T3a/2
5a/3
2-WAY
IDLE
SPEED
BOOST
VALVE
8/8
1/1
4/4
3/3
6/6
2/2
7/7
5/5
A/C
RELAY
5
H4
2.5
G/Y
T5b/4
T2a
1.5
G
+1°C
A/C THERMOSTAT
T5b/5
T2d
2bar
A/C REFRIGERANT
LOW PRESSURE
SWITCH
80
30
1 2 3 4 5 6 7 8 9 10 11 12 13 14

Air conditioning system wiring schematic—Golf with 16 valve engine

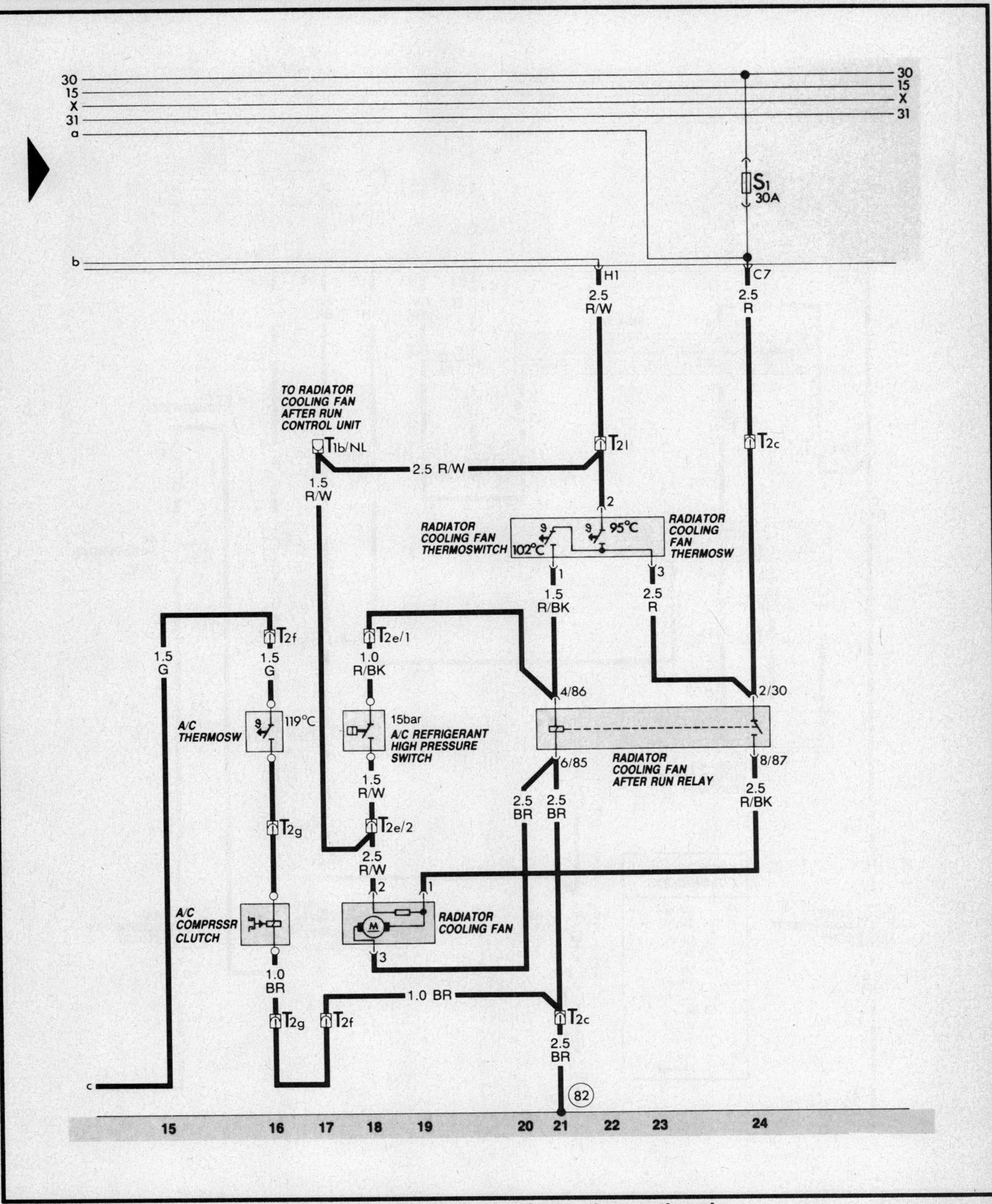
30
15
X
31
a
b
c
S1
30A
H1
2.5
R/W
C7
2.5
R
TO RADIATOR COOLING FAN AFTER RUN CONTROL UNIT
T1b/NL
2.5 R/W
T21
T2c
1.5
R/W
2
RADIATOR COOLING FAN THERMOSWITCH
102°C
95°C
RADIATOR COOLING FAN THERMOSW
1
3
1.5
R/BK
2.5
R
1.5
G
T2f
1.5
G
T2e/1
1.0
R/BK
4/86
2/30
A/C THERMOSW
119°C
15bar
A/C REFRIGERANT HIGH PRESSURE SWITCH
6/85
8/87
RADIATOR COOLING FAN AFTER RUN RELAY
1.5
R/W
2.5
BR
2.5
BR
2.5
R/BK
T2g
T2e/2
2.5
R/W
2
1
A/C COMPRSSR CLUTCH
RADIATOR COOLING FAN
3
1.0
BR
1.0 BR
T2g
T2f
T2c
2.5
BR
82
15
16
17
18
19
20
21
22
23
24

Air conditioning system wiring schematic—Golf with 16 valve engine continued

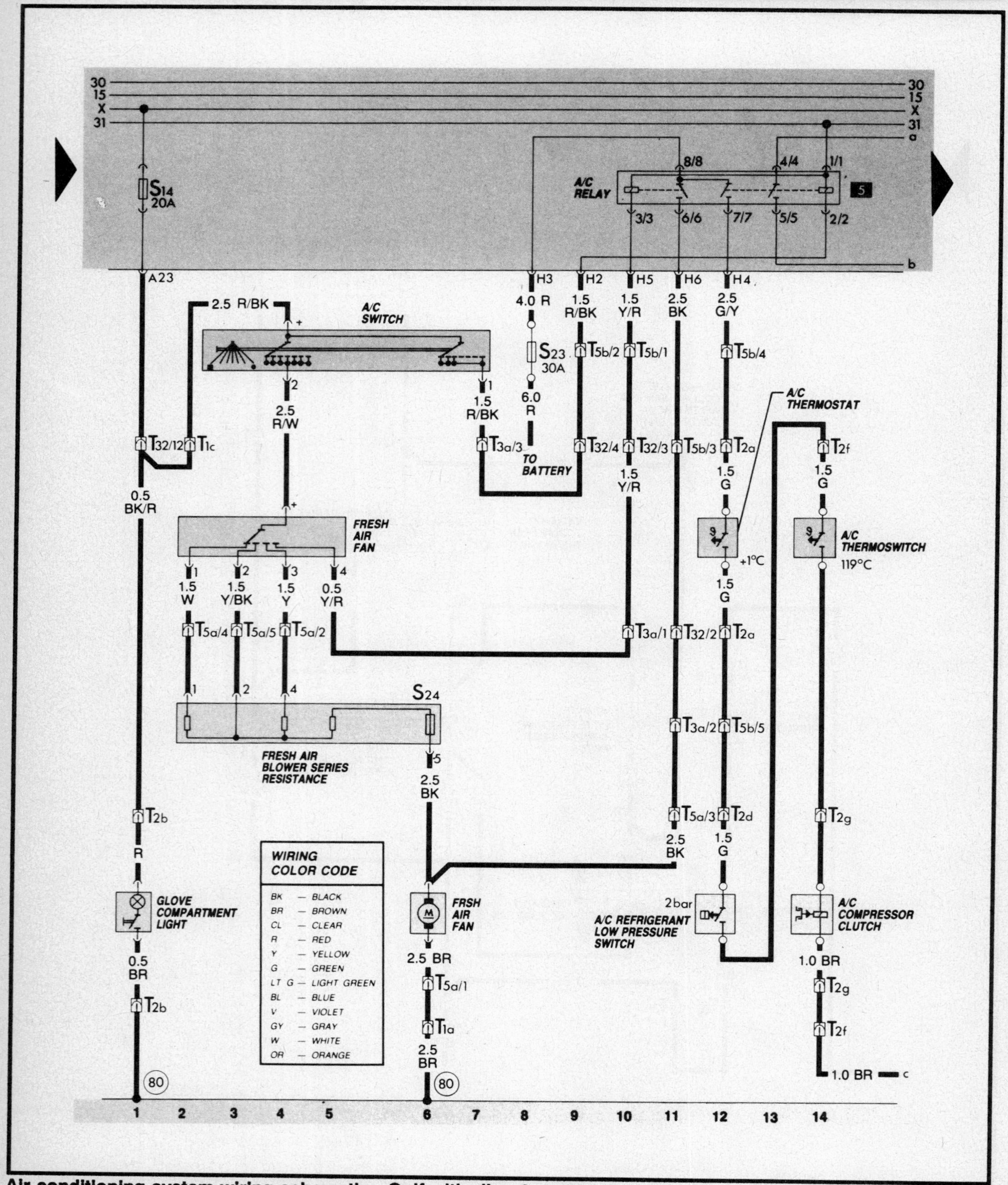
30
15
X
31
S14
20A
A23
A/C RELAY
8/8
4/4
1/1
3/3
6/6
7/7
5/5
2/2
a
b
H3
H2
H5
H6
H4
2.5 R/BK
A/C SWITCH
4.0 R
1.5 R/BK
1.5 Y/R
2.5 BK
2.5 G/Y
S23
30A
T5b/2
T5b/1
T5b/4
2.5 R/W
1.5 R/BK
6.0 R
A/C THERMOSTAT
T32/12
T1c
T3a/3
TO BATTERY
T32/4
T32/3
T5b/3
T2a
T2f
0.5 BK/R
1.5 Y/R
1.5 G
FRESH AIR FAN
A/C THERMOSWITCH
119°C
+1°C
1.5 W
1.5 Y/BK
1.5 Y
0.5 Y/R
T5a/4
T5a/5
T5a/2
T3a/1
T32/2
S24
T3a/2
T5b/5
FRESH AIR BLOWER SERIES RESISTANCE
2.5 BK
T2b
T5a/3
T2d
T2g
R
WIRING COLOR CODE
BK — BLACK
BR — BROWN
CL — CLEAR
R — RED
Y — YELLOW
G — GREEN
LT G — LIGHT GREEN
BL — BLUE
V — VIOLET
GY — GRAY
W — WHITE
OR — ORANGE
GLOVE COMPARTMENT LIGHT
FRSH AIR FAN
2bar
A/C REFRIGERANT LOW PRESSURE SWITCH
A/C COMPRESSOR CLUTCH
0.5 BR
2.5 BR
1.0 BR
T5a/1
T1a
80
c
1
2
3
4
5
6
7
8
9
10
11
12
13
14

Air conditioning system wiring schematic—Golf with diesel engine

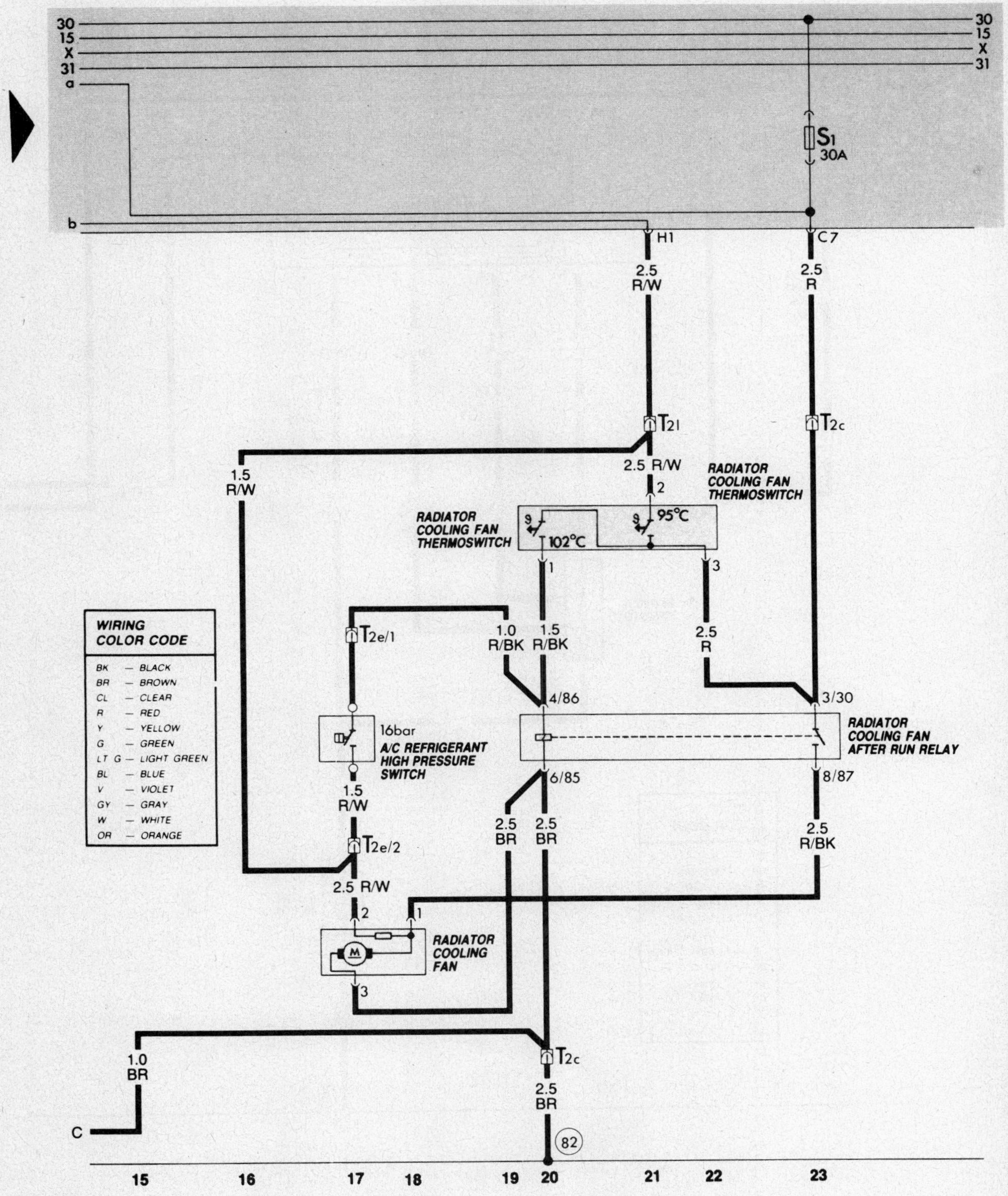
30
15
X
31
a
b
S1
30A
H1
C7
2.5
R/W
2.5
R
T21
T2c
1.5
R/W
2.5 R/W
2
RADIATOR COOLING FAN THERMOSWITCH
RADIATOR COOLING FAN THERMOSWITCH
95°C
102°C
1
3
T2e/1
1.0
R/BK
1.5
R/BK
2.5
R
4/86
3/30
16bar
A/C REFRIGERANT HIGH PRESSURE SWITCH
RADIATOR COOLING FAN AFTER RUN RELAY
6/85
8/87
1.5
R/W
T2e/2
2.5
BR
2.5
BR
2.5
R/BK
2.5 R/W
2
1
M
RADIATOR COOLING FAN
3
1.0
BR
T2c
2.5
BR
C
82
15
16
17
18
19
20
21
22
23
WIRING COLOR CODE
BK — BLACK
BR — BROWN
CL — CLEAR
R — RED
Y — YELLOW
G — GREEN
LT G — LIGHT GREEN
BL — BLUE
V — VIOLET
GY — GRAY
W — WHITE
OR — ORANGE

Air conditioning system wiring schematic—Golf with diesel engine

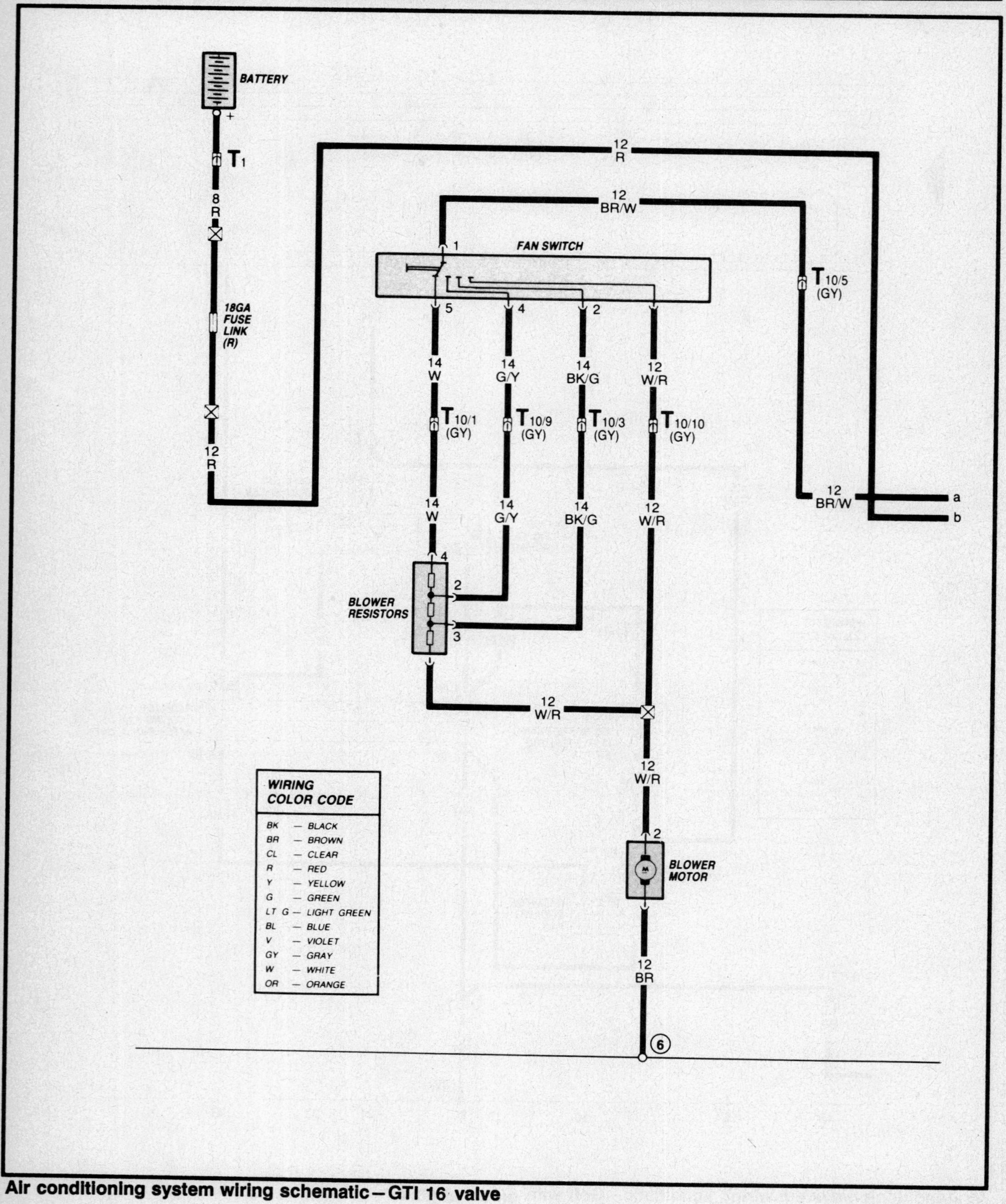
BATTERY
T1
8 R
18GA FUSE LINK (R)
12 R
12 R
12 BR/W
FAN SWITCH
1
5
4
2
14 W
14 G/Y
14 BK/G
12 W/R
T10/1 (GY)
T10/9 (GY)
T10/3 (GY)
T10/10 (GY)
T10/5 (GY)
14 W
14 G/Y
14 BK/G
12 W/R
12 BR/W
a
b
BLOWER RESISTORS
4
2
3
12 W/R
12 W/R
2
BLOWER MOTOR
12 BR
6
WIRING COLOR CODE
BK — BLACK
BR — BROWN
CL — CLEAR
R — RED
Y — YELLOW
G — GREEN
LT G — LIGHT GREEN
BL — BLUE
V — VIOLET
GY — GRAY
W — WHITE
OR — ORANGE

Air conditioning system wiring schematic—GTI 16 valve

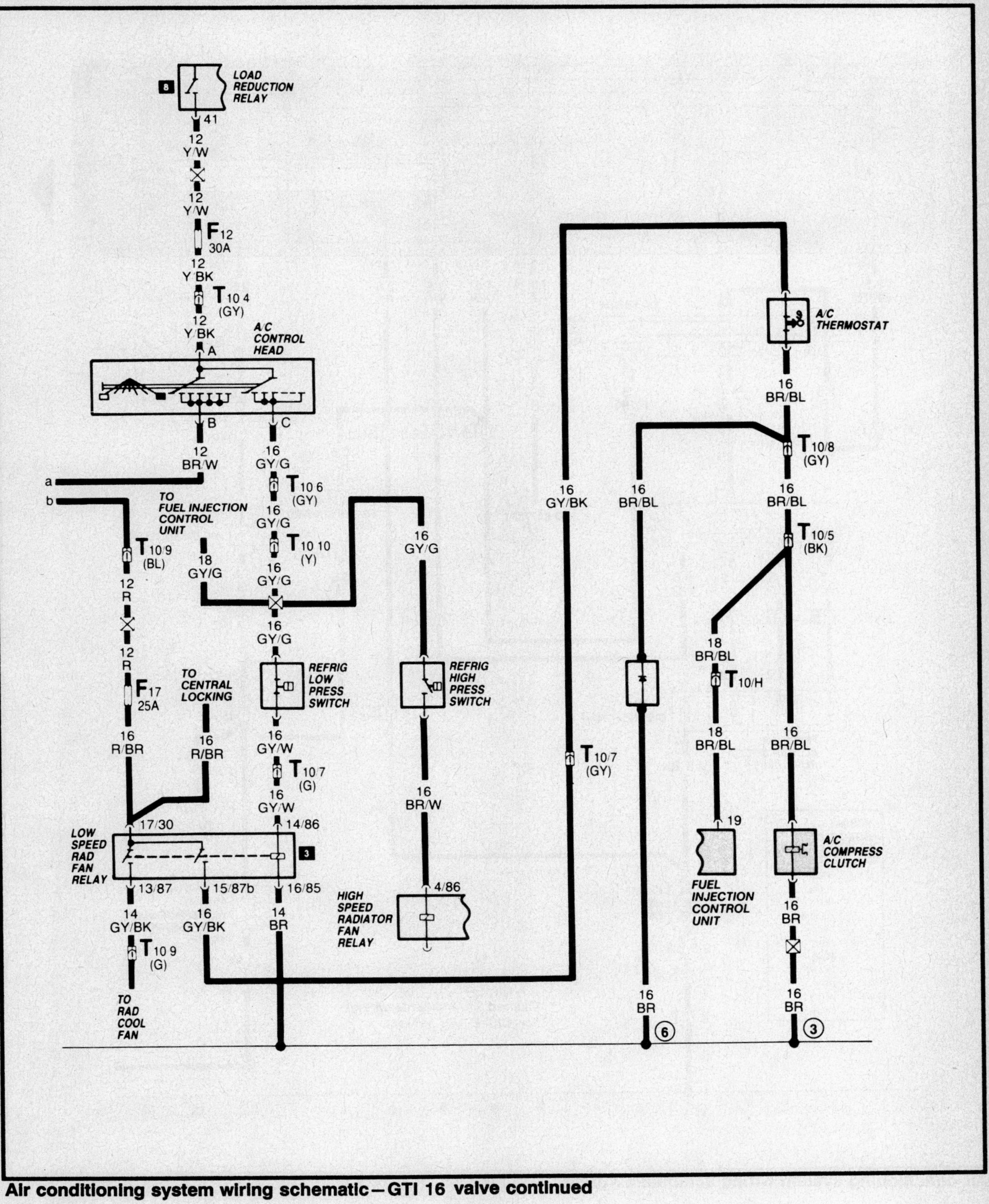
LOAD REDUCTION RELAY
8
41
12 Y/W
12 Y/W
F12 30A
12 Y/BK
T10/4 (GY)
12 Y/BK
A
A/C CONTROL HEAD
B
C
12 BR/W
16 GY/G
a
b
T10/6 (GY)
TO FUEL INJECTION CONTROL UNIT
16 GY/G
T10/10 (Y)
T10/9 (BL)
18 GY/G
16 GY/G
16 GY/G
12 R
12 R
F17 25A
TO CENTRAL LOCKING
REFRIG LOW PRESS SWITCH
REFRIG HIGH PRESS SWITCH
16 R/BR
16 R/BR
16 GY/W
T10/7 (G)
16 GY/W
16 BR/W
17/30
14/86
LOW SPEED RAD FAN RELAY
3
13/87
15/87b
16/85
4/86
14 GY/BK
16 GY/BK
14 BR
HIGH SPEED RADIATOR FAN RELAY
T10/9 (G)
TO RAD COOL FAN
16 GY/BK
T10/7 (GY)
16 BR/BL
A/C THERMOSTAT
16 BR/BL
T10/8 (GY)
16 BR/BL
T10/5 (BK)
18 BR/BL
T10/H
18 BR/BL
16 BR/BL
19
FUEL INJECTION CONTROL UNIT
A/C COMPRESS CLUTCH
16 BR
16 BR
16 BR
6
3

Air conditioning system wiring schematic—GTI 16 valve continued

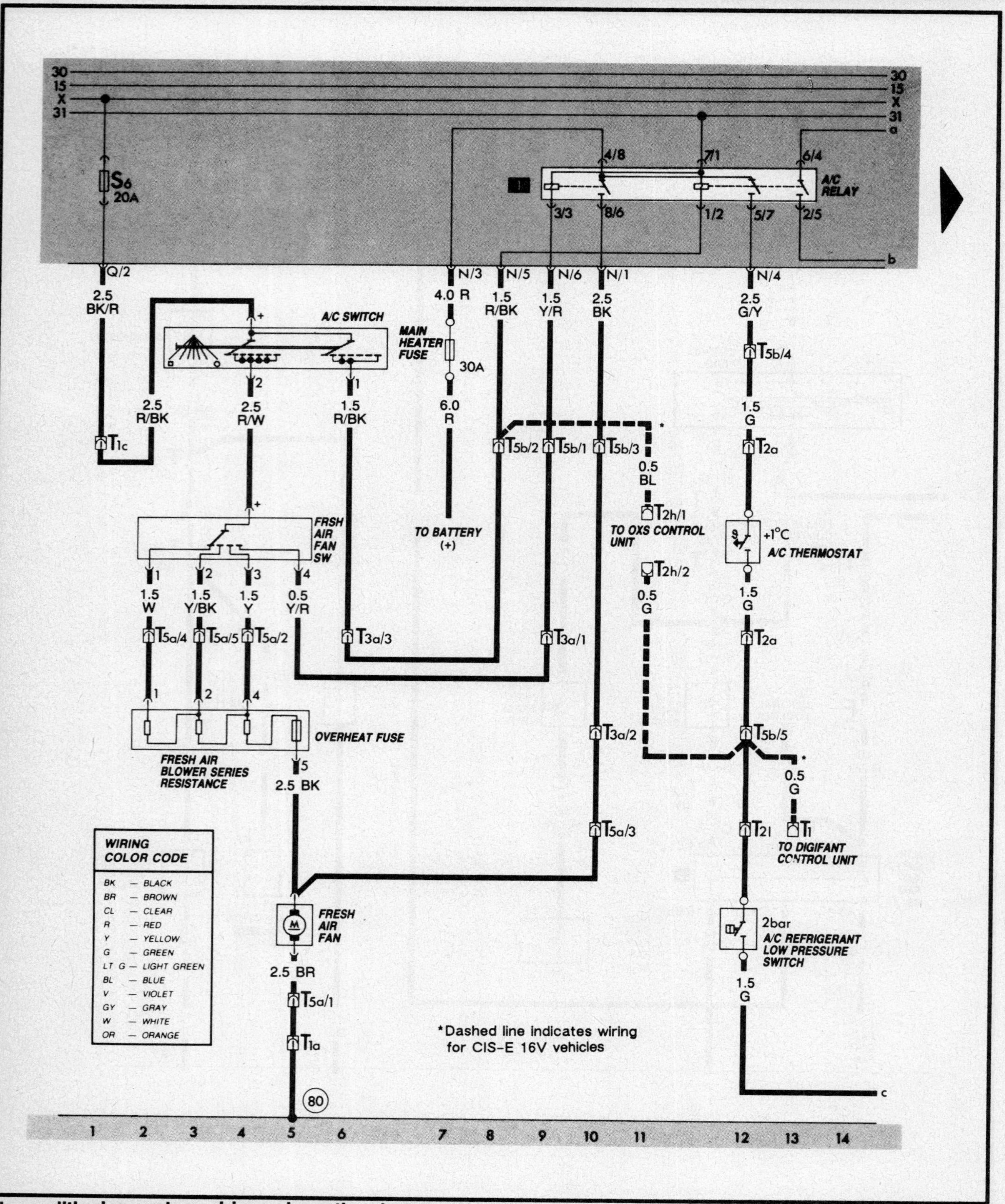
30
15
X
31
a
b
c
S6
20A
A/C RELAY
4/8
7/1
6/4
3/3
8/6
1/2
5/7
2/5
Q/2
N/3
N/5
N/6
N/1
N/4
2.5 BK/R
A/C SWITCH
MAIN HEATER FUSE
30A
4.0 R
6.0 R
TO BATTERY (+)
1.5 R/BK
1.5 Y/R
2.5 BK
2.5 G/Y
T5b/4
1.5 G
T2a
2.5 R/BK
2.5 R/W
1.5 R/BK
T1c
T5b/2
T5b/1
T5b/3
0.5 BL
T2h/1
TO OXS CONTROL UNIT
T2h/2
0.5 G
+1°C
A/C THERMOSTAT
FRSH AIR FAN SW
1.5 W
1.5 Y/BK
1.5 Y
0.5 Y/R
T5a/4
T5a/5
T5a/2
T3a/3
T3a/1
OVERHEAT FUSE
FRESH AIR BLOWER SERIES RESISTANCE
2.5 BK
T3a/2
T5b/5
0.5 G
T5a/3
T21
T1
TO DIGIFANT CONTROL UNIT
WIRING COLOR CODE
BK — BLACK
BR — BROWN
CL — CLEAR
R — RED
Y — YELLOW
G — GREEN
LT G — LIGHT GREEN
BL — BLUE
V — VIOLET
GY — GRAY
W — WHITE
OR — ORANGE
FRESH AIR FAN
2.5 BR
T5a/1
T1a
2bar
A/C REFRIGERANT LOW PRESSURE SWITCH
1.5 G
*Dashed line indicates wiring for CIS-E 16V vehicles
80
1 2 3 4 5 6 7 8 9 10 11 12 13 14

Air conditioning system wiring schematic—Jetta

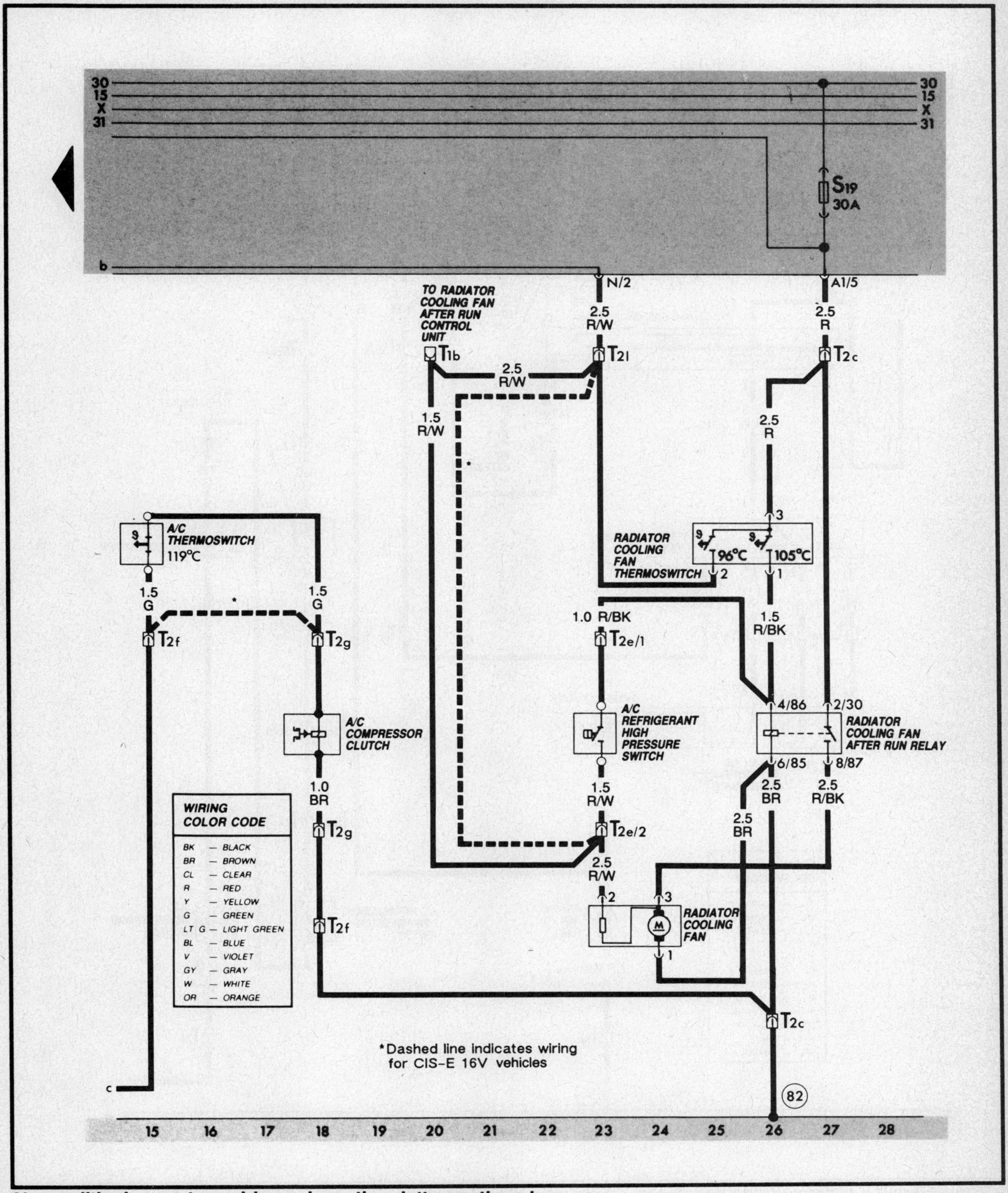
30
15
X
31
b
S19
30A
N/2
A1/5
TO RADIATOR COOLING FAN AFTER RUN CONTROL UNIT
T1b
2.5 R/W
T2l
2.5 R
T2c
1.5 R/W
RADIATOR COOLING FAN THERMOSWITCH
96°C
105°C
A/C THERMOSWITCH 119°C
1.5 G
T2f
T2g
1.0 R/BK
T2e/1
1.5 R/BK
4/86
2/30
A/C COMPRESSOR CLUTCH
A/C REFRIGERANT HIGH PRESSURE SWITCH
RADIATOR COOLING FAN AFTER RUN RELAY
6/85
8/87
1.0 BR
2.5 BR
2.5 R/BK
1.5 R/W
T2e/2
WIRING COLOR CODE
BK — BLACK
BR — BROWN
CL — CLEAR
R — RED
Y — YELLOW
G — GREEN
LT G — LIGHT GREEN
BL — BLUE
V — VIOLET
GY — GRAY
W — WHITE
OR — ORANGE
RADIATOR COOLING FAN
*Dashed line indicates wiring for CIS-E 16V vehicles
c
82
15 16 17 18 19 20 21 22 23 24 25 26 27 28

Air conditioning system wiring schematic—Jetta continued

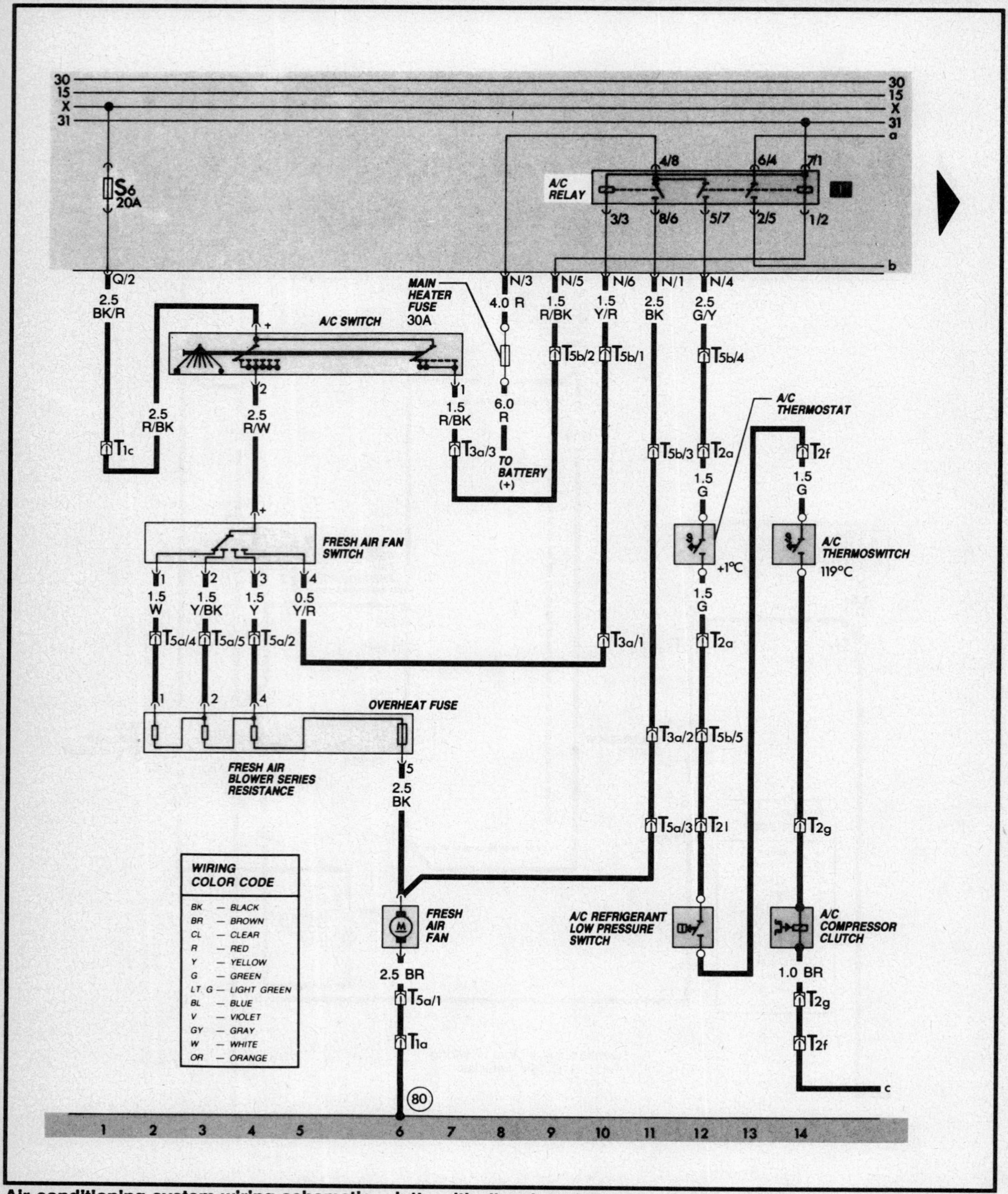
30
15
X
31
a
b
c
S6 20A
Q/2
2.5 BK/R
A/C RELAY
4/8
6/4
7/1
3/3
8/6
5/7
2/5
1/2
N/3
N/5
N/6
N/1
N/4
MAIN HEATER FUSE 30A
4.0 R
1.5 R/BK
1.5 Y/R
2.5 BK
2.5 G/Y
A/C SWITCH
T5b/2
T5b/1
T5b/4
2.5 R/BK
2.5 R/W
1.5 R/BK
6.0 R
T1c
T3a/3
TO BATTERY (+)
A/C THERMOSTAT
T5b/3
T2a
T2f
1.5 G
FRESH AIR FAN SWITCH
A/C THERMOSWITCH
+1°C
119°C
1.5 W
1.5 Y/BK
1.5 Y
0.5 Y/R
T5a/4
T5a/5
T5a/2
T3a/1
OVERHEAT FUSE
FRESH AIR BLOWER SERIES RESISTANCE
T3a/2
T5b/5
2.5 BK
T5a/3
T2l
T2g
WIRING COLOR CODE
BK — BLACK
BR — BROWN
CL — CLEAR
R — RED
Y — YELLOW
G — GREEN
LT. G — LIGHT GREEN
BL — BLUE
V — VIOLET
GY — GRAY
W — WHITE
OR — ORANGE
FRESH AIR FAN
A/C REFRIGERANT LOW PRESSURE SWITCH
A/C COMPRESSOR CLUTCH
2.5 BR
1.0 BR
T5a/1
T1a
80
1 2 3 4 5 6 7 8 9 10 11 12 13 14

Air conditioning system wiring schematic—Jetta with diesel engine

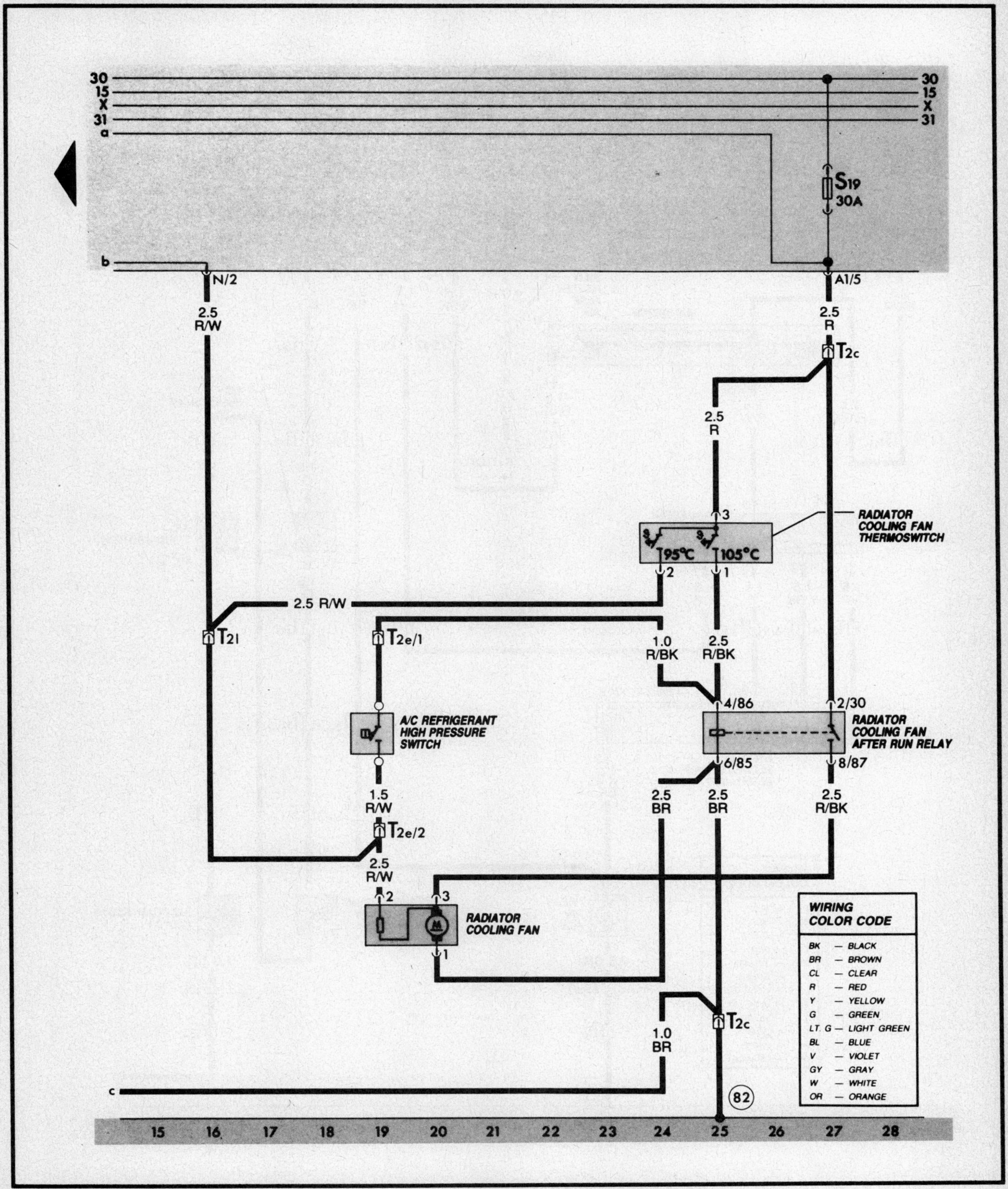
30
15
X
31
a
b
c
S19
30A
N/2
A1/5
2.5
R/W
2.5
R
T2c
RADIATOR
COOLING FAN
THERMOSWITCH
95°C
105°C
2.5 R/W
T21
T2e/1
1.0
R/BK
2.5
R/BK
4/86
2/30
A/C REFRIGERANT
HIGH PRESSURE
SWITCH
RADIATOR
COOLING FAN
AFTER RUN RELAY
6/85
8/87
1.5
R/W
2.5
BR
2.5
R/BK
T2e/2
RADIATOR
COOLING FAN
1.0
BR
82
WIRING
COLOR CODE
BK — BLACK
BR — BROWN
CL — CLEAR
R — RED
Y — YELLOW
G — GREEN
LT. G — LIGHT GREEN
BL — BLUE
V — VIOLET
GY — GRAY
W — WHITE
OR — ORANGE
15 16 17 18 19 20 21 22 23 24 25 26 27 28

Air conditioning system wiring schematic—Jetta with diesel engine continued

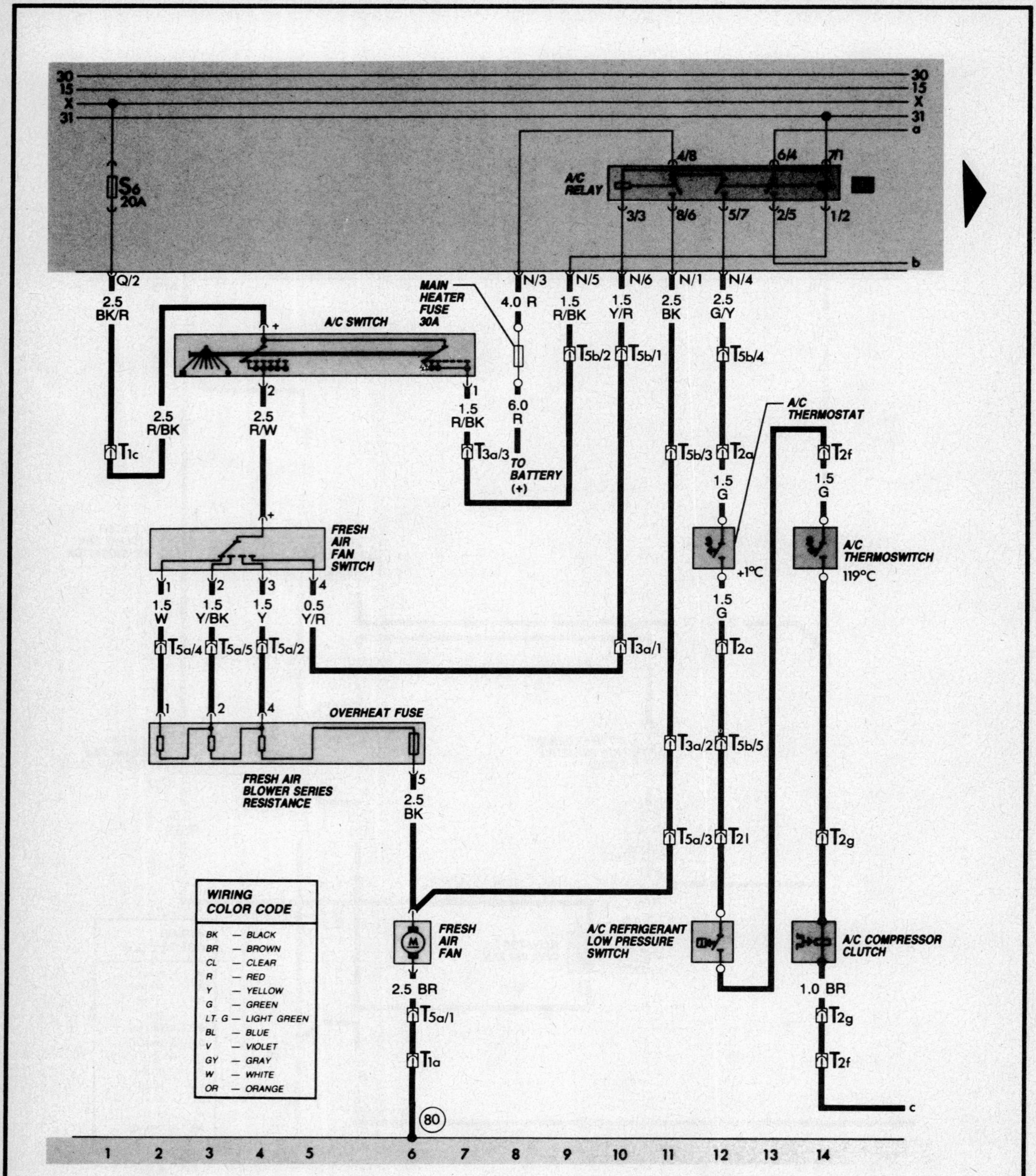
30
15
X
31
S6 20A
Q/2
2.5 BK/R
A/C SWITCH
MAIN HEATER FUSE 30A
A/C RELAY
4/8
6/4
7/1
3/3
8/6
5/7
2/5
1/2
N/3
N/5
N/6
N/1
N/4
4.0 R
1.5 R/BK
1.5 Y/R
2.5 BK
2.5 G/Y
T5b/2
T5b/1
T5b/4
2.5 R/BK
2.5 R/W
1.5 R/BK
6.0 R
T1c
T3a/3
TO BATTERY (+)
A/C THERMOSTAT
T5b/3
T2a
T2f
1.5 G
FRESH AIR FAN SWITCH
A/C THERMOSWITCH
+1°C
119°C
1.5 W
1.5 Y/BK
1.5 Y
0.5 Y/R
T5a/4
T5a/5
T5a/2
T3a/1
OVERHEAT FUSE
T3a/2
T5b/5
FRESH AIR BLOWER SERIES RESISTANCE
2.5 BK
T5a/3
T2l
T2g
WIRING COLOR CODE
BK — BLACK
BR — BROWN
CL — CLEAR
R — RED
Y — YELLOW
G — GREEN
LT. G — LIGHT GREEN
BL — BLUE
V — VIOLET
GY — GRAY
W — WHITE
OR — ORANGE
FRESH AIR FAN
A/C REFRIGERANT LOW PRESSURE SWITCH
A/C COMPRESSOR CLUTCH
2.5 BR
1.0 BR
T5a/1
T1a
80
1 2 3 4 5 6 7 8 9 10 11 12 13 14

Air conditioning system wiring schematic—Jetta with turbocharged diesel engine

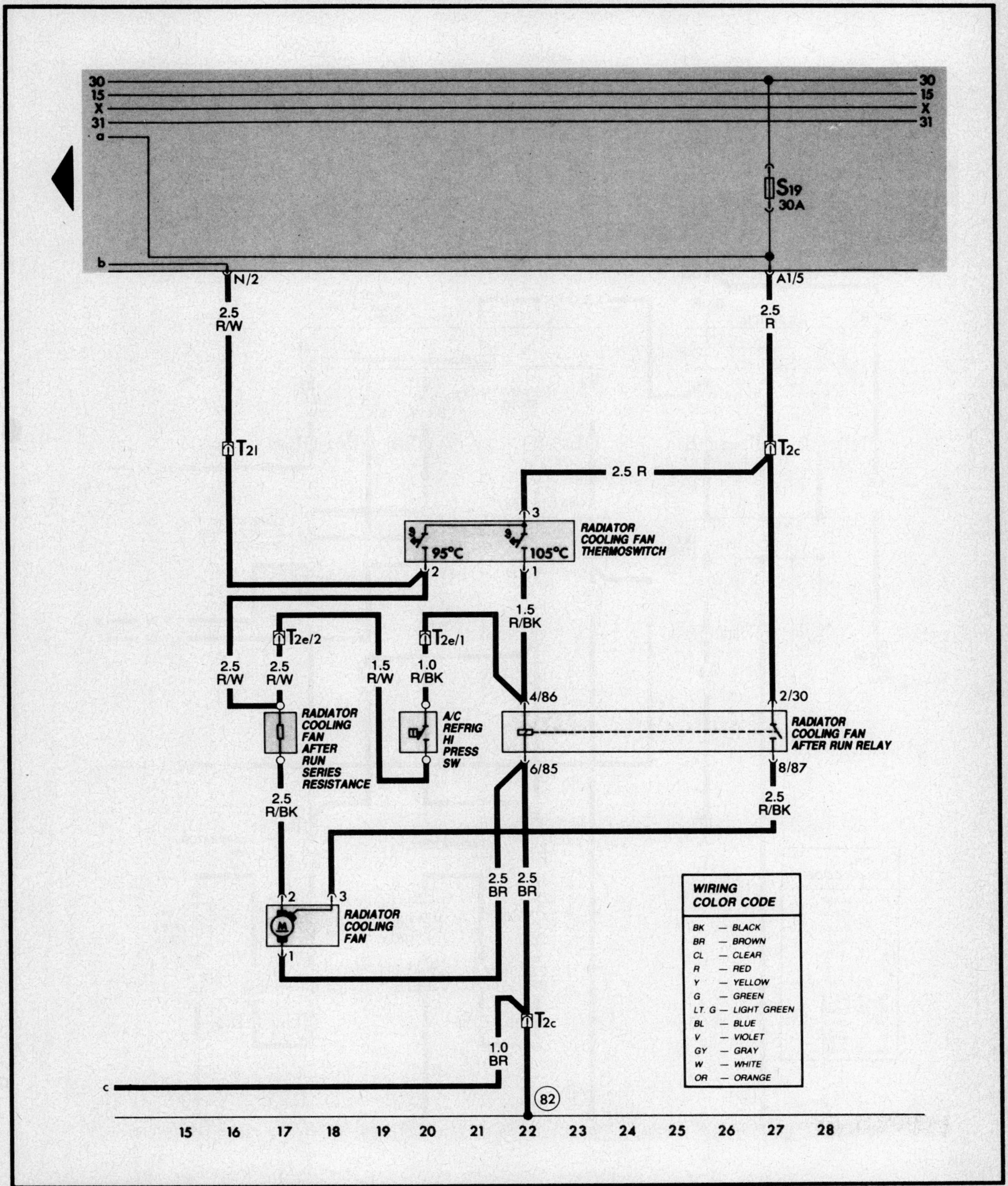
30
15
X
31
a
b
S19
30A
N/2
A1/5
2.5
R/W
2.5
R
T21
T2c
2.5 R
3
RADIATOR
COOLING FAN
THERMOSWITCH
95°C
105°C
2
1
T2e/2
T2e/1
1.5
R/BK
2.5
R/W
1.5
R/W
1.0
R/BK
4/86
2/30
RADIATOR
COOLING
FAN
AFTER
RUN
SERIES
RESISTANCE
A/C
REFRIG
HI
PRESS
SW
RADIATOR
COOLING FAN
AFTER RUN RELAY
6/85
8/87
2.5
R/BK
2.5
BR
RADIATOR
COOLING
FAN
M
1.0
BR
c
82
WIRING
COLOR CODE
BK — BLACK
BR — BROWN
CL — CLEAR
R — RED
Y — YELLOW
G — GREEN
LT. G — LIGHT GREEN
BL — BLUE
V — VIOLET
GY — GRAY
W — WHITE
OR — ORANGE
15
16
17
18
19
20
21
22
23
24
25
26
27
28

Air conditioning system wiring schematic—Jetta with turbocharged diesel engine continued

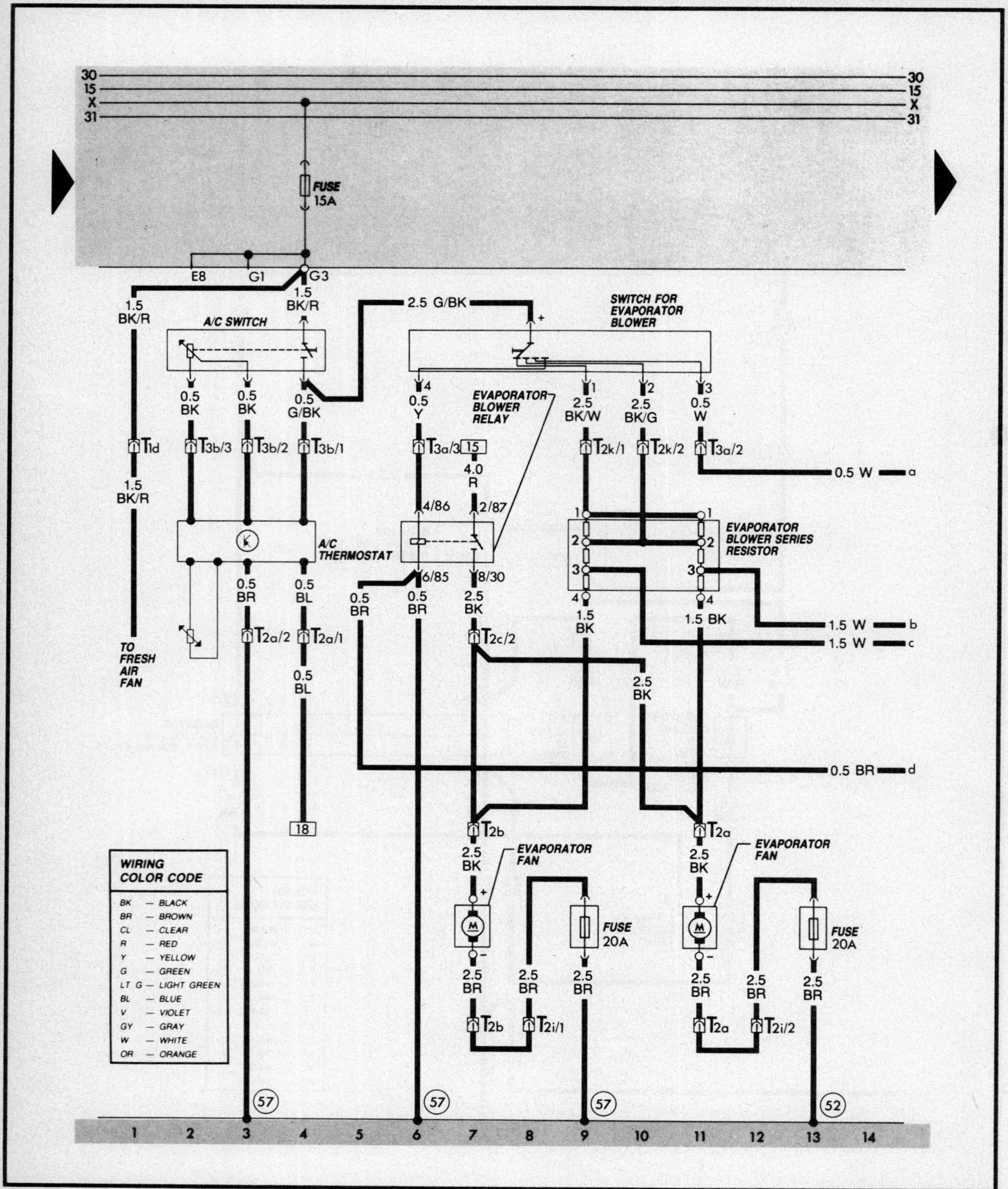
30
15
X
31
FUSE
15A
E8
G1
G3
1.5
BK/R
2.5 G/BK
A/C SWITCH
SWITCH FOR
EVAPORATOR
BLOWER
0.5
BK
0.5
G/BK
0.5
Y
EVAPORATOR
BLOWER
RELAY
2.5
BK/W
2.5
BK/G
0.5
W
T1d
T3b/3
T3b/2
T3b/1
T3a/3
15
T2k/1
T2k/2
T3a/2
0.5 W
4.0
R
4/86
2/87
EVAPORATOR
BLOWER SERIES
RESISTOR
A/C
THERMOSTAT
6/85
8/30
0.5
BR
0.5
BL
2.5
BK
1.5
BK
1.5 BK
1.5 W
T2a/2
T2a/1
T2c/2
TO
FRESH
AIR
FAN
0.5 BR
18
T2b
T2a
EVAPORATOR
FAN
WIRING
COLOR CODE
BK — BLACK
BR — BROWN
CL — CLEAR
R — RED
Y — YELLOW
G — GREEN
LT G — LIGHT GREEN
BL — BLUE
V — VIOLET
GY — GRAY
W — WHITE
OR — ORANGE
FUSE
20A
2.5
BR
T2i/1
T2i/2
57
52
1 2 3 4 5 6 7 8 9 10 11 12 13 14

Air conditioning system wiring schematic—Vanagon

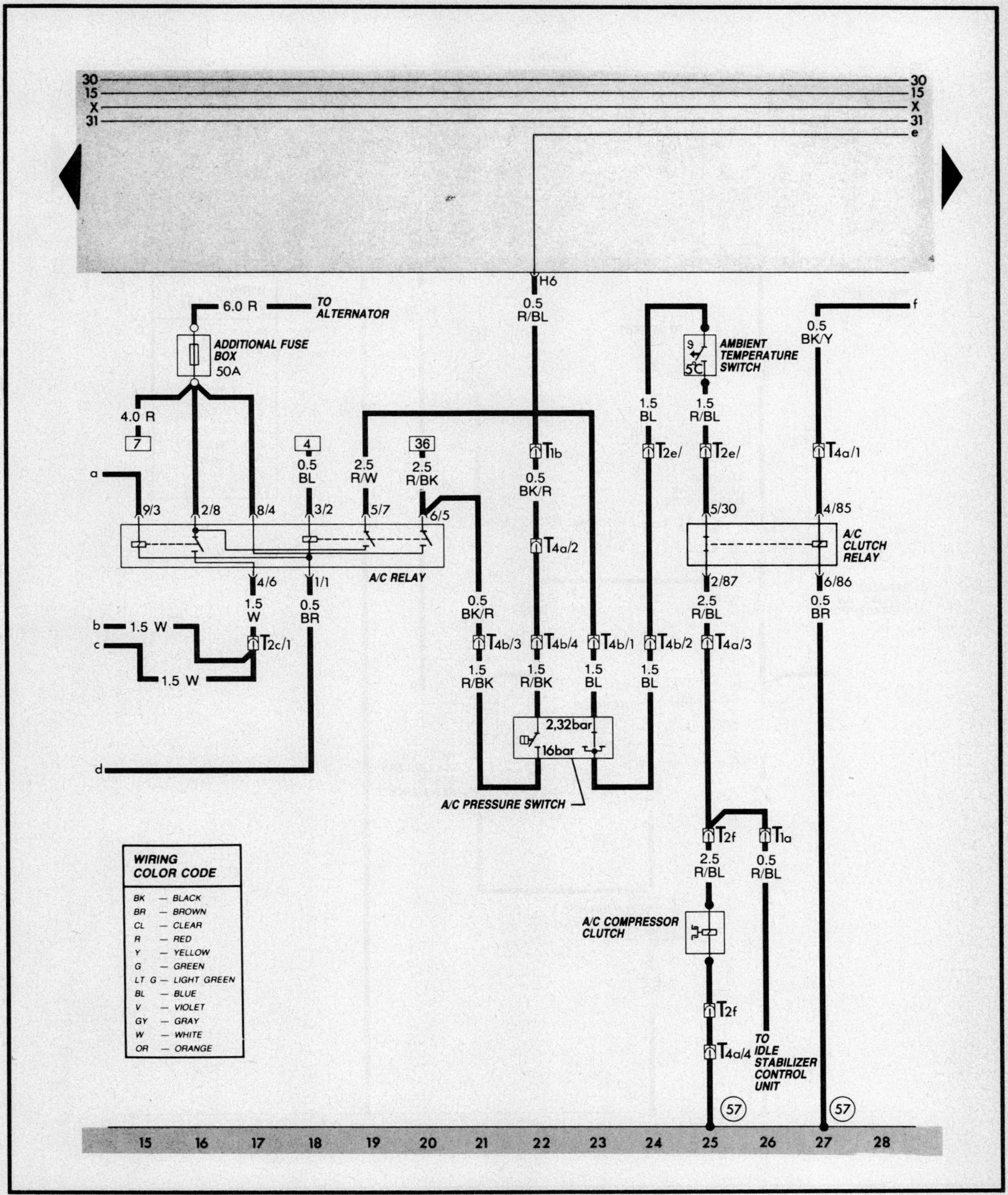
30
15
X
31
e
H6
0.5 R/BL
6.0 R
TO ALTERNATOR
ADDITIONAL FUSE BOX 50A
4.0 R
7
4
36
0.5 BL
2.5 R/W
2.5 R/BK
9/3
2/8
8/4
3/2
5/7
6/5
A/C RELAY
4/6
1/1
1.5 W
0.5 BR
1.5 W
T2c/1
T1b
0.5 BK/R
T4a/2
0.5 BK/R
T4b/3
T4b/4
T4b/1
T4b/2
T4a/3
1.5 R/BK
1.5 R/BK
1.5 BL
1.5 BL
2,32bar
16bar
A/C PRESSURE SWITCH
AMBIENT TEMPERATURE SWITCH
9
5°C
1.5 BL
1.5 R/BL
T2e/
T2e/
5/30
2/87
2.5 R/BL
0.5 BK/Y
T4a/1
4/85
A/C CLUTCH RELAY
6/86
0.5 BR
T2f
T1a
2.5 R/BL
0.5 R/BL
A/C COMPRESSOR CLUTCH
T2f
T4a/4
TO IDLE STABILIZER CONTROL UNIT
57
57
a
b
c
d
f
WIRING COLOR CODE
BK — BLACK
BR — BROWN
CL — CLEAR
R — RED
Y — YELLOW
G — GREEN
LT G — LIGHT GREEN
BL — BLUE
V — VIOLET
GY — GRAY
W — WHITE
OR — ORANGE
15 16 17 18 19 20 21 22 23 24 25 26 27 28

Air conditioning system wiring schematic—Vanagon continued

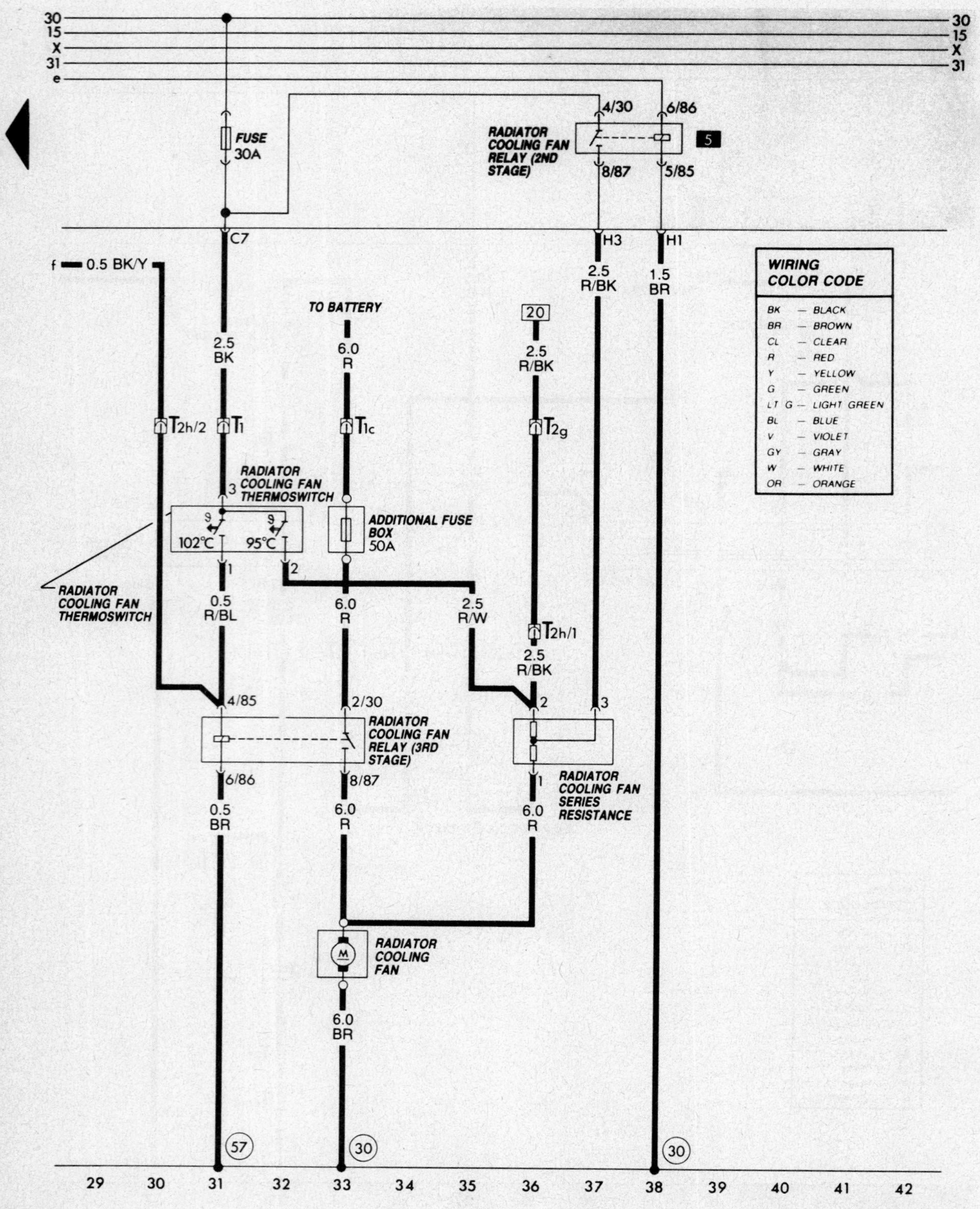
30
15
X
31
e
FUSE
30A
4/30
6/86
RADIATOR COOLING FAN RELAY (2ND STAGE)
5
8/87
5/85
C7
H3
H1
f 0.5 BK/Y
2.5 BK
TO BATTERY
6.0 R
2.5 R/BK
1.5 BR
20
2.5 R/BK
WIRING COLOR CODE
BK — BLACK
BR — BROWN
CL — CLEAR
R — RED
Y — YELLOW
G — GREEN
LT G — LIGHT GREEN
BL — BLUE
V — VIOLET
GY — GRAY
W — WHITE
OR — ORANGE
T2h/2
T1
T1c
T2g
RADIATOR COOLING FAN THERMOSWITCH
3
102°C
95°C
ADDITIONAL FUSE BOX 50A
1
2
RADIATOR COOLING FAN THERMOSWITCH
0.5 R/BL
6.0 R
2.5 R/W
T2h/1
2.5 R/BK
4/85
2/30
RADIATOR COOLING FAN RELAY (3RD STAGE)
2
3
6/86
8/87
1
RADIATOR COOLING FAN SERIES RESISTANCE
0.5 BR
6.0 R
6.0 R
RADIATOR COOLING FAN
M
6.0 BR
57
30
30
29 30 31 32 33 34 35 36 37 38 39 40 41 42

Air conditioning system wiring schematic—Vanagon continued

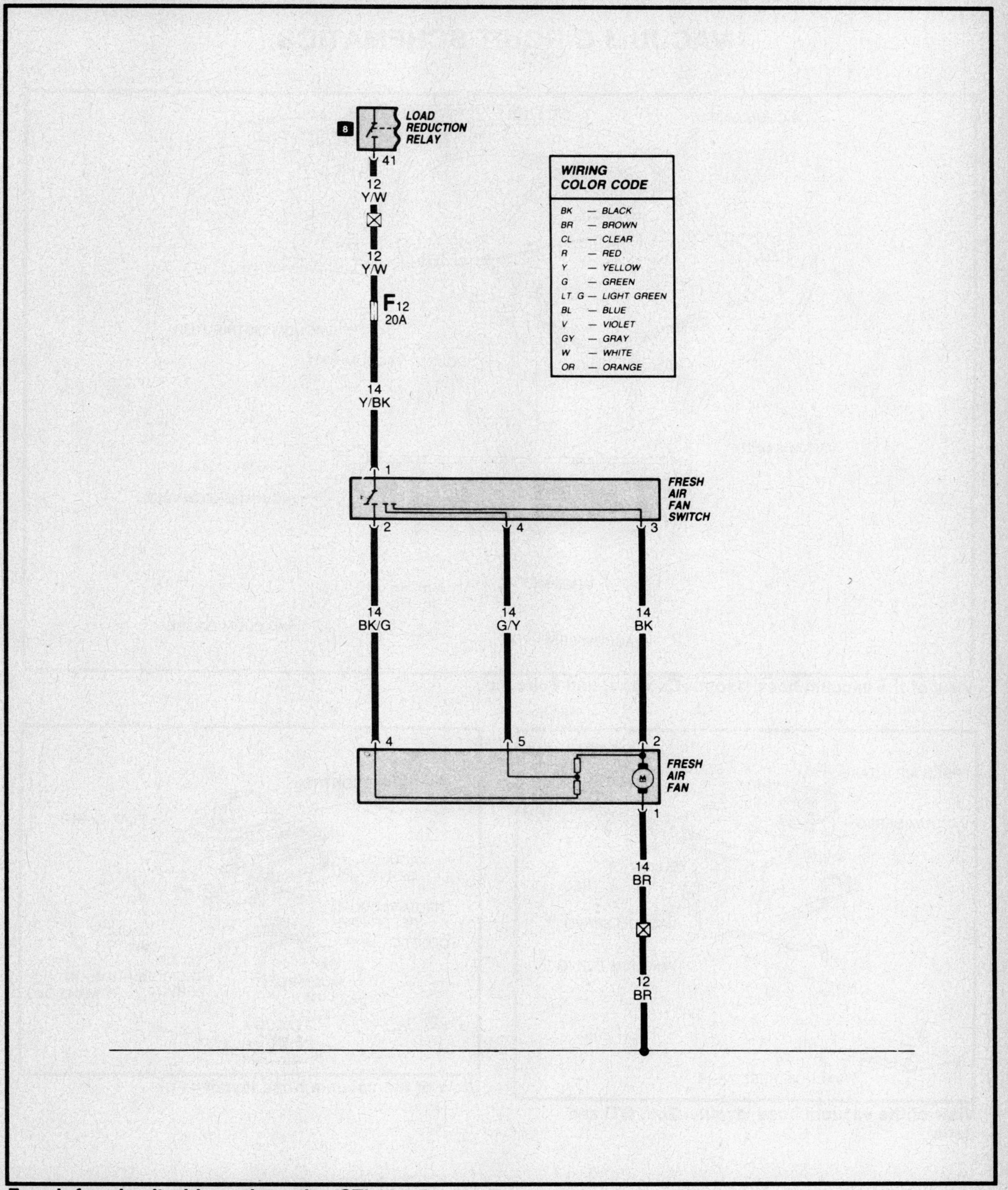
8
LOAD REDUCTION RELAY
41
12 Y/W
12 Y/W
F12 20A
14 Y/BK
1
FRESH AIR FAN SWITCH
2
4
3
14 BK/G
14 G/Y
14 BK
4
5
2
FRESH AIR FAN
1
14 BR
12 BR
WIRING COLOR CODE
BK — BLACK
BR — BROWN
CL — CLEAR
R — RED
Y — YELLOW
G — GREEN
LT G — LIGHT GREEN
BL — BLUE
V — VIOLET
GY — GRAY
W — WHITE
OR — ORANGE

Fan air fan circuit wiring schematic—GTI 16 valve

VACUUM CIRCUIT SCHEMATICS

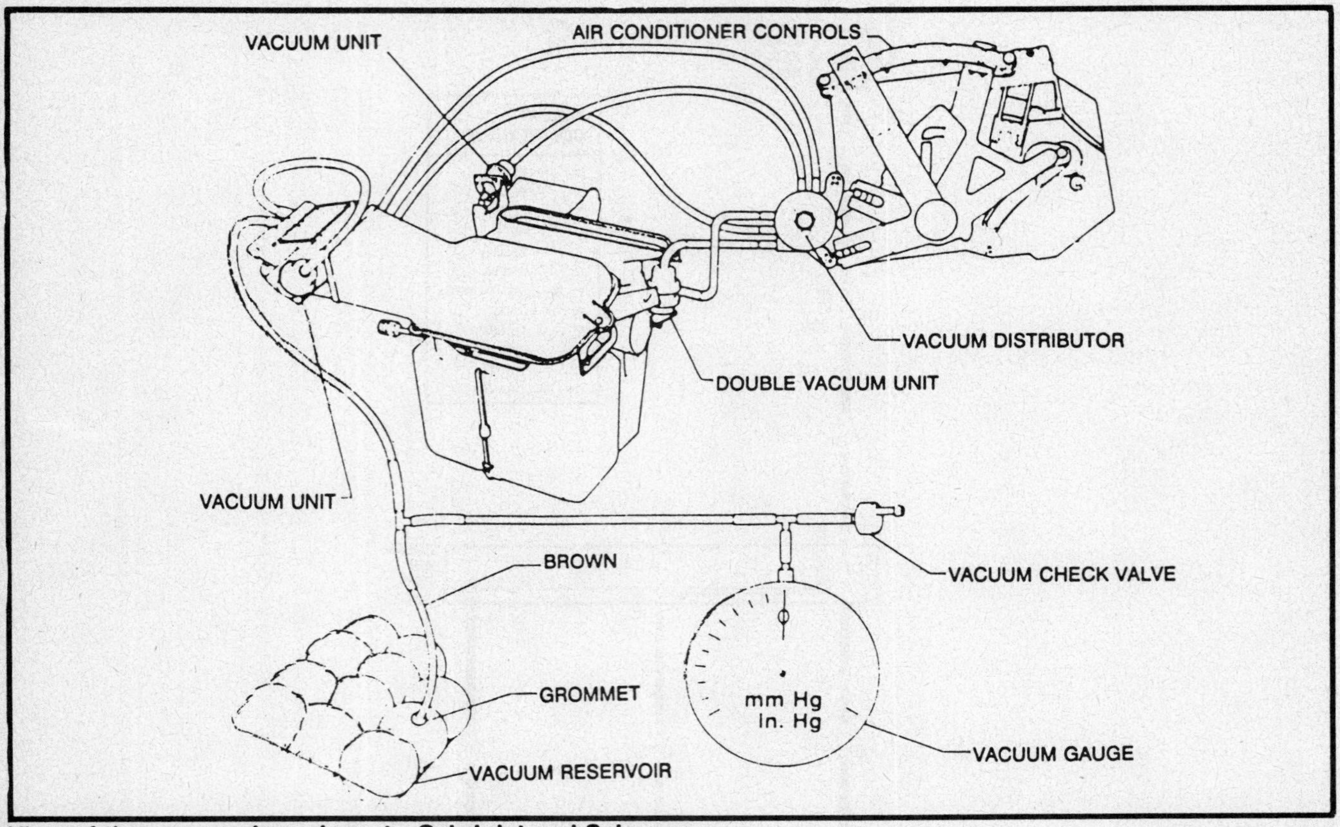
VACUUM UNIT
AIR CONDITIONER CONTROLS
VACUUM DISTRIBUTOR
DOUBLE VACUUM UNIT
VACUUM UNIT
BROWN
VACUUM CHECK VALVE
GROMMET
mm Hg
in. Hg
VACUUM GAUGE
VACUUM RESERVOIR

View of the vacuum hose layout – Cabriolet and Scirocco

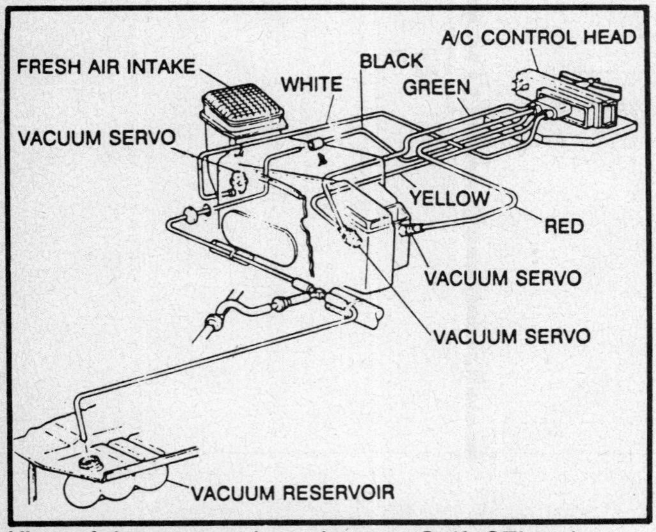
A/C CONTROL HEAD
FRESH AIR INTAKE
BLACK
WHITE
GREEN
VACUUM SERVO
YELLOW
RED
VACUUM SERVO
VACUUM SERVO
VACUUM RESERVOIR

View of the vacuum hose layout – Golf, GTI and Jetta

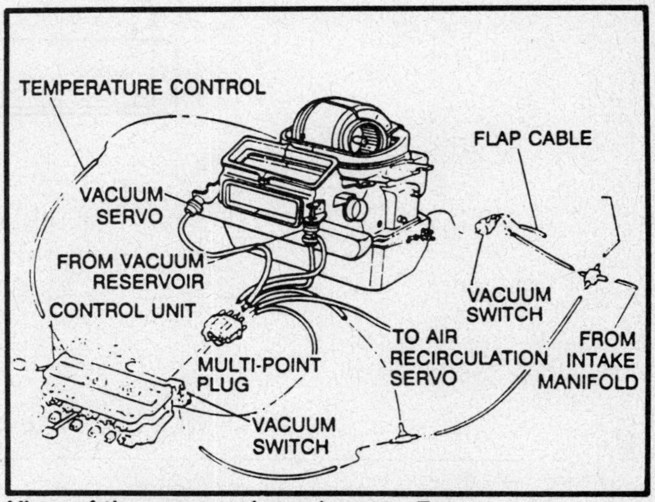
TEMPERATURE CONTROL
FLAP CABLE
VACUUM SERVO
FROM VACUUM RESERVOIR
CONTROL UNIT
VACUUM SWITCH
TO AIR RECIRCULATION SERVO
FROM INTAKE MANIFOLD
MULTI-POINT PLUG
VACUUM SWITCH

View of the vacuum hose layout – Fox

28 VOLVO 28

240 • 740 • 760 • 780 • 940

SPECIFICATIONS

ENGINE IDENTIFICATION

Year	Model	Engine Displacement cu. in. (cc/liter)	Engine Series Identification	No. of Cylinders	Engine Type
1989	240 DL	140 (2320/2.3)	B230F	4	OHC
	240 GL	140 (2320/2.3)	B230F	4	OHC
	740 GL	140 (2320/2.3)	B230F	4	OHC
	740 GLE	140 (2320/2.3)	B234F	4	DOHC
	740 Turbo	140 (2320/2.3)	B230F-Turbo	4	OHC
	760 GLE	174 (2849/2.9)	B280F	6	OHC
	760 Turbo	140 (2320/2.3)	B230F-Turbo	4	OHC
	780	174 (2849/2.9)	B280F	6	OHC
1990	240 DL	140 (2320/2.3)	B230F	4	OHC
	240 GL	140 (2320/2.3)	B230F	4	OHC
	740 GL	140 (2320/2.3)	B230F	4	OHC
	740 GLE	140 (2320/2.3)	B234F	4	DOHC
	740 Turbo	140 (2320/2.3)	B230F-Turbo	4	OHC
	760 GLE	174 (2849/2.9)	B280F	6	OHC
	760 Turbo	140 (2320/2.3)	B230F-Turbo	4	OHC
	780	174 (2849/2.9)	B280F	6	OHC
	780 Turbo	140 (2320/2.3)	B230F-Turbo	4	OHC
1991	240 Series	140 (2320/2.3)	B230F	4	OHC
	740 Series	140 (2320/2.3)	B230F	4	OHC
	740 Turbo	140 (2320/2.3)	B230F-Turbo	4	OHC
	940 GLE	141 (2316/2.3)	B234F	4	DOHC
	940 Turbo	141 (2316/2.3)	B230F-Turbo	4	OHC
	940 SE	141 (2316/2.3)	B230F-Turbo	4	OHC
	940 Coupe	141 (2316/2.3)	B230F-Turbo	4	OHC

OHC—Overhead cam
DOHC—Double overhead cam

REFRIGERANT CAPACITIES

Year	Model	Freon (oz.)	Oil (fl. oz.)	Type ③
1989	200 Series	45.8	6.7	Diesel Kiki
	700 Series	38.0	①	②
1990	200 Series	45.8	6.7	Diesel Kiki
	700 Series	38.0	①	②
1991	200 Series	45.8	6.7	Diesel Kiki
	700 Series	38.0	①	②
	900 Series	38.0	①	②

① Delco R4—6.0
Sankyo SD-510—4.6
York AZ10—10.1
Kiki YA15—6.8
Sanden SD-709—8.1

② Delco R4
Sankyo
York
Diesel Kiki
Sanden

③ Compressor

AIR CONDITIONING BELT TENSION CHART

Year	Model	Engine Displacement cu. in. (cc/liter)	Belt Type	New	Used
1989	240 DL	140 (2320/2.3)	V-Belt	0.2–0.4 in.	0.2–0.4 in.
	240 GL	140 (2320/2.3)	V-Belt	0.2–0.4 in.	0.2–0.4 in.
	740 GL	140 (2320/2.3)	V-Belt	①	①
	740 GLE	140 (2320/2.3)	V-Belt	①	①
	740 Turbo	140 (2320/2.3)	V-Belt	①	①
	760 GLE	174 (2849/2.9)	V-Belt	①	①
	760 Turbo	140 (2320/2.3)	V-Belt	①	①
	780	174 (2849/2.9)	V-Belt	①	①
1990	240 DL	140 (2320/2.3)	V-Belt	0.2–0.4 in.	0.2–0.4 in.
	240 GL	140 (2320/2.3)	V-Belt	0.2–0.4 in.	0.2–0.4 in.
	740 GL	140 (2320/2.3)	V-Belt	①	①
	740 GLE	140 (2320/2.3)	V-Belt	①	①
	740 Turbo	140 (2320/2.3)	V-Belt	①	①
	760 GLE	174 (2849/2.9)	V-Belt	①	①
	760 Turbo	140 (2320/2.3)	V-Belt	①	①
	780	174 (2849/2.9)	V-Belt	①	①
	780 Turbo	140 (2320/2.3)	V-Belt	①	①
1991	240 Series	140 (2320/2.3)	V-Belt	0.2–0.4 in.	0.2–0.4 in.
	740 Series	140 (2320/2.3)	V-Belt	①	①
	740 Turbo	140 (2320/2.3)	V-Belt	①	①
	940 GLE	141 (2316/2.3)	V-Belt	①	①
	940 Turbo	141 (2316/2.3)	V-Belt	①	①
	940 SE	141 (2316/2.3)	V-Belt	①	①
	940 Coupe	141 (2316/2.3)	V-Belt	①	①

① Delco type 0.04–0.08 in. deflection method
Sankyo, Kiki and Sanden types 0.2–0.4 in. deflection method
York type 0.1–0.4 in. deflection method

SYSTEM DESCRIPTION

General Information

HEATING SYSTEM

The heating unit assembly is mostly the same configuration as used in the heating/air conditioning system and the removal and installation procedures are basically the same.

The heater core and blower motor are contained in the heater box (fresh air housing) located in the passenger compartment under the dashboard. The blower fan is of a turbine design and is accessible from under the dash. The heater core is mostly accessible through the removal and disassembly of the heater box.

AIR CONDITIONING SYSTEM

The purpose of the air conditioning unit is to reduce the temperature in the passenger compartment to an acceptable level when ambient temperatures are high. The unit operates on the principle that heat is always transferred from a hot medium to a cold one. In practice, warm air from the passenger compartment is circulated passed an evaporator which contains a cold liquid. Heat is therefore transferred from the air to the liquid and the cooler air is blown into the passenger compartment.

A direct relationship exists between the pressure, temperature and volume of the refrigerant. By allowing the refrigerant to circulate in a closed system and altering the pressure and volume conditions, it is possible to get the refrigerant to boil (evaporate). For this purpose the warm air in the passenger compartment is directed through an evaporator, in which the refrigerant circulates. Heat is absorbed by the refrigerant and in doing so the warm air is cooled down and the refrigerant boils. It is this cold air which is blown into the passenger compartment by the fan. The heat which is absorbed by the refrigerant in the evaporator is transferred to the condenser in the engine compartment, where it is cooled by air flow with the aid of the engine and the electric fans. A compressor is used to circulate the refrigerant within the system.

240 Series

Two climate units (CU) are used and are of common construction, one for the use of a heating system only and the other for the use of both a heating unit and an air conditioning unit combined. The removal and installation of the heating system components and the air conditioning/heating system components are basically the same for both CU units.

740, 760, 780 AND 940 Series

Three types of climate units are used and are of common construction: the Combined Unit (CU), the Automatic Climate Control (ACC) and the Electronic Climate Control (ECC). The difference in the units lie in the equipment used, such as with or without air conditioning and the manner in which the unit is controlled, either manually or automatic.

CLIMATE UNIT WITHOUT AIR CONDITIONING

This is a manually controlled heater and fresh air unit. The unit is prepared for the installation of an air conditioning unit. The panel vents and the water valve are controlled by vacuum and the air mix shutter is controlled by a cable, connected to the temperature control lever. The same control panel is used on vehicles with manually controlled air conditioning systems.

CLIMATE UNIT WITH AIR CONDITIONING

The climate unit is identical to the heater climate unit but with air conditioning included. This unit has 4 control positions, **MAX, NORM, B/L** and **DEFROST**. The positions are controlled manually from the control panel where the mode, fan speed and temperature can be selected. The wiring, vacuum and the air flow schematics are basically the same as the CU unit without air conditioning. If the mode selector is in one of the air conditioning positions and the fan speed is in the **ON** position, the fan will operate automatically in low speed to prevent evaporator ice build-up.

AUTOMATICALLY CONTROLLED CLIMATE UNIT (ACC)

With the ACC unit, the passenger compartment is kept at a preset temperature regardless of the ambient temperature. The unit is set at the control panel but is controlled by a programmer located behind the instrument controlled unit. However, the wiring, vacuum and air flow schematics are different from the other units.

ELECTRONIC CLIMATE CONTROL UNIT (ECC)

The ECC system incorporates a self-diagnosis function; faults are indicated by a series of flashing codes when the **A/C** button is pushed. The control unit is programmed to make the best of the situation if a fault is detected. If a fault is detected, the unit ignores the faulty signal and selects an alternative pre-programmed value. The control unit is also designed to prevent the delivery of faulty outputs. The presence of a fault(s) is indicated by flashing of the **A/C** button. In the workshop, any such fault code may be requested by setting the controls to a specified configuration. The absence of a fault code is not a guarantee that the system is fault-free.

Service Valve Location

YORK COMPRESSOR SYSTEM

The service valve location for high pressure side is at compressor's **DISCH** valve. The service valve location for the low pressure side is at compressor's **SUCTION** valve.

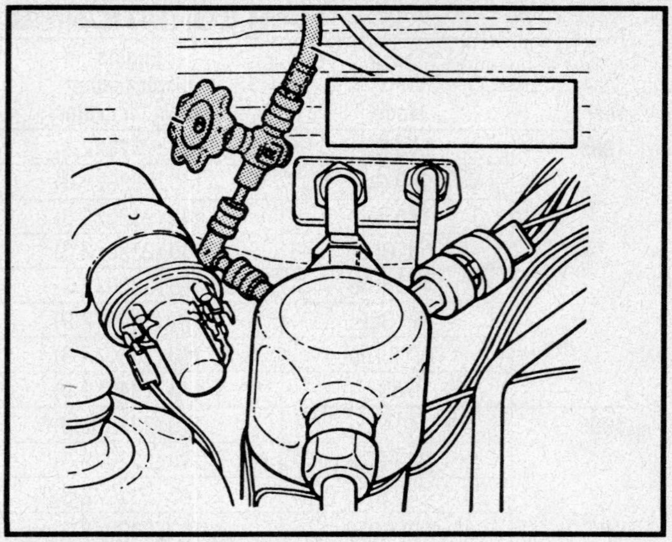

Low side service port location

EXCEPT YORK COMPRESSOR SYSTEM

The high pressure service valve is located on the compressor. The low pressure service valve is located on the receiver/drier assembly.

System Discharging

R-12 refrigerant is a chlorofluorocarbon which, when mishandled, can contribute to the depletion on the ozone layer in the upper atmosphere. Ozone filters out harmful radiation from the sun. In order to protect the ozone layer, an approved R-12 Recovery/Recycling machine that meets SAE standard J1991 should be employed when discharging the system. Follow the operating instructions provided with the approved equipment exactly to properly discharge the system.

System Evacuating

If the air conditioning system has been opened to the atmosphere, it should be air and moisture free before being recharged with refrigerant. Moisture and air mixed with refrigerant will raise the compressor head pressure, possibly damage the system's components and will reduce the performance of the system. To evacuate the system, perform the following procedure:

1. Leak test the system and repair any leaks found.
2. Connect an approved charging station, Recovery/Recycling machine or manifold gauge set and vacuum pump to the discharge and suction ports. The red hose is normally connected to the discharge (high pressure) line and the blue hose is connected to the suction (low pressure) line.
3. Open the discharge and suction ports and start the vacuum pump. If the pump is not able to pull at least 26 in. Hg of vacuum, there is a leak that must be repaired before evacuation can occur.
4. Once the system has reached at least 26 in. Hg of vacuum, allow the system to evacuate for at least 30 minutes. The longer the system is evacuated, the more contaminants will be removed.
5. Close all valves and turn the pump off. If the system loses more than 2 in. Hg of vacuum after 15 minutes, there is a leak that should be repaired.

System Charging

1. Connect an approved charging station, Recovery/Recycling machine or manifold gauge set to the discharge and suction ports. The red hose is normally connected to the discharge (high pressure) line and the blue hose is connected to the suction (low pressure) line.
2. Follow the instructions provided with the equipment and charge the system with the specified amount of refrigerant.
3. Perform a leak test.

SYSTEM COMPONENTS

Radiator

REMOVAL AND INSTALLATION

1. Disconnect the negative battery cable. Drain engine coolant.
2. Remove the expansion tank assembly. Remove upper and lower radiator hoses.
3. Disconnect all electrical connection at radiator assembly.
4. If equipped with automatic transmission disconnect the oil cooler lines. Remove the radiator and fan shroud retaining bolts. Remove the radiator assembly from the vehicle.

To install:

5. Install the radiator and fan shroud assembly in the vehicle. Note the correct placement of the radiator is essential for proper operation check that the rubber cushions if equipped are in the correct position.
6. If equipped, with automatic transmission reconnect the automatic transmission oil cooler lines.
7. Connect all electrical connection at radiator assembly.
8. Install the expansion tank assembly. Reconnect the uppewr and lower radiator hoses.
9. Reconnect the negative battery cable, fill (bleed cooling system) the engine with coolant. Start the engine and check for leaks. Check all fluid levels, as necessary.

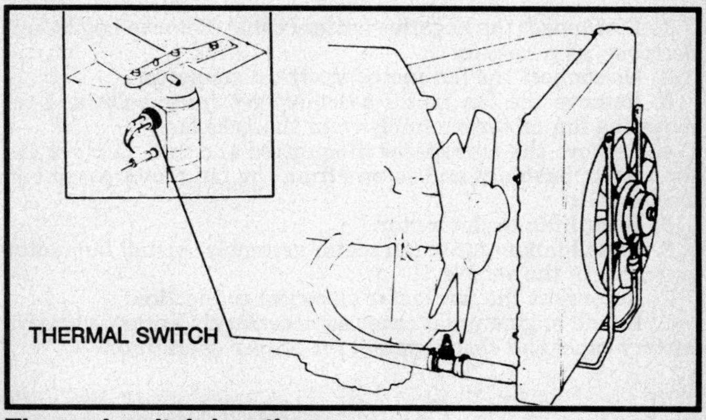
THERMAL SWITCH
Thermal switch locations

COOLING SYSTEM BLEEDING

1. To release the air in the cooling system, loosen the union bolt (air bleeder valve) if equipped.
2. Slowly fill the cooling system with coolant when the coolant begins to come out of the union bolt (air bleeder valve) stop pouring and close the air drain valve. Torque the union bolt (air bleeder valve).
3. Add coolant to radiator until the level reaches the proper level. Install the radiator cap.
4. Start the engine and check for leaks. Recheck the coolant level and refill as necessary.
5. If vehicle, is not equipped with union bolt (air bleed valve) fill the radiator assembly and open cooling system at furthermost point from engine (open lower drain cock in radiator to remove trapped air if necessary). Add coolant to the radiator and recovery tank as required to raise the level to the full mark as indicated (cold). Run the engine with the radiator cap removed until the engine reaches correct operating temperature. Add coolant to the radiator until the level reaches the proper level. Install the radiator cap after coolant bubbling subsides. Fill the coolant into the reservoir tank to the **FULL** mark.

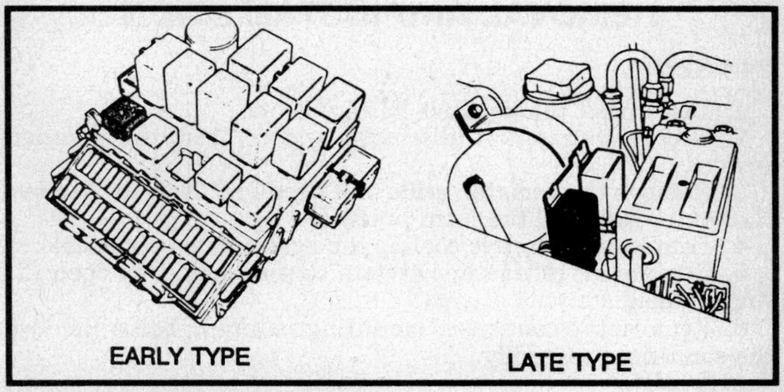
EARLY TYPE
LATE TYPE
Cooling fan relay locations

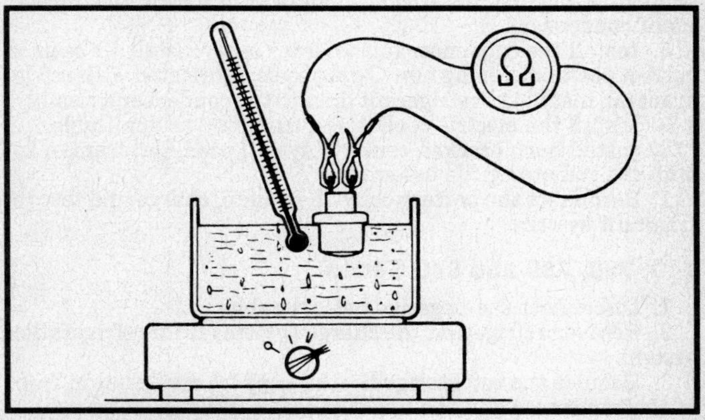
Ω
Testing thermal switch

Cooling Fan

TESTING

System Functional Test

1. Turn ignition to the **ON** position.
2. Connect the two wires at thermal switch to each other-the electric fan should run.
3. If cooling fan does not operate, run direct power source and ground to isolate electric fan operation. If fan operates check wiring and relay for cooling fan circuit.

Checking Radiator Thermal Switch Operation

Check radiator switch operation with ohmmeter across switch terminals. Place switch in water bath contacts should be closed when water temperature is above 190–200°F some applications 207–216° F (complete circuit). Let switch in water bath cool contacts of switch should open when water temperature is 180–188°F some applications 198–207°F (open circuit). The switch operation should turn ON-HOT (complete circuit) and OFF-COLD (open circuit) when temperature range is reached.

REMOVAL AND INSTALLATION

1. Disconnect the negative battery cable. Remove engine undercover, as necessary.
2. Disconnect the fan motor electrical connector.
3. Remove the fan motor assembly retaining bolts and remove the fan motor assembly from the vehicle.
4. Remove the fan, spacer if equipped and nut. Remove the fan motor, bushings and screws from the fan motor assembly.

To install:

5. Install fan to fan motor.
6. Install fan motor to fan motor assembly. Install fan motor assembly in the vehicle.
7. Reconnect the fan motor electrical connection.
8. Install engine undercover as necessary. Connect negative battery cable and check system for proper operation.

Condenser

REMOVAL AND INSTALLATION

240 Series

1. Disconnect the negative battery cable.
2. Recover refrigerant (discharge system) from refrigeration system.
3. Remove the radiator grille and headlight frames. Remove the center stay and the horn bracket.
4. Remove the electric cooling fan assembly as applicable.
5. Remove all refrigerant system connections. Cap open fittings immediately.
6. Remove the condenser mounting retaining bolts. Remove the condenser assembly.

To install:

7. Drain and measure the amount of refrigerant oil from the condenser and install the same amount of new oil in the replacement condenser.
8. Install the condenser (transfer air seals-install air seals in correct position). Using new O-ring seals, lubricated with refrigerant oil, install the refrigerant lines to the condenser assembly.
9. Install the electric cooling fan assembly as applicable.
10. Install horn bracket, center stay and headlight frames. Install the radiator grille assembly.
11. Reconnect the battery cable. Evacuate, charge and test refrigerant system.

740, 760, 780 and 940 Series

1. Disconnect the negative battery cable.
2. Recover refrigerant (discharge system) from refrigeration system.
3. Remove the radiator grille, the support stay from in front of the condenser and the upper radiator member bolts.
4. Remove the hood release cable from the upper radiator member.
5. Remove the air guide panel from the upper radiator member.
6. Remove the upper condenser retaining screws and the upper radiator member. From under the bumper, remove the air guide panel.

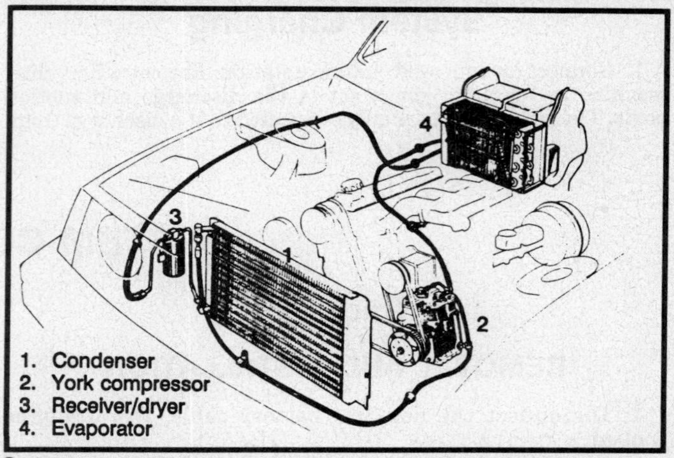
1
2
3
4
1. Condenser
2. York compressor
3. Receiver/dryer
4. Evaporator

System components—York compressor system

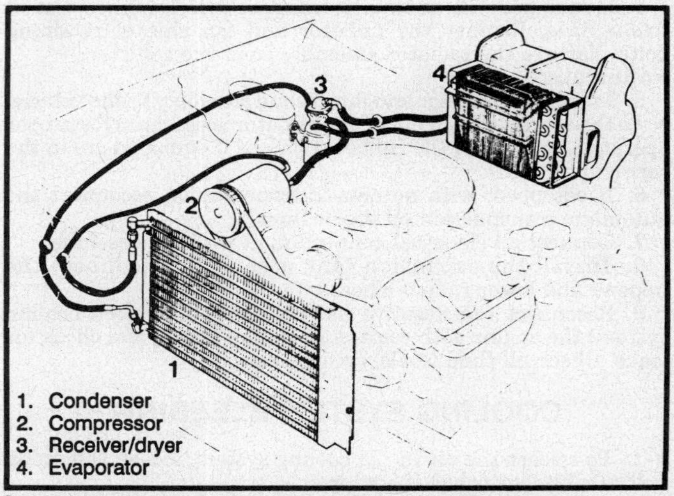
1
2
3
4
1. Condenser
2. Compressor
3. Receiver/dryer
4. Evaporator

System components—except York compressor system

7. Recover refrigerant (discharge system) from refrigeration system.
8. Remove all refrigerant system connections. Cap open fittings immediately.
9. Remove the lower condenser nuts and the condenser assembly from the vehicle.

To install:

10. Drain and measure the amount of refrigerant oil from the condenser and install the same amount of new oil in the replacement condenser.
11. Install the condenser (transfer air seals-install air seals in correct position). Using new O-ring seals, lubricated with refrigerant oil, install the lines to the condenser.
12. Install the lower air guide panel under the bumper and the upper air guide panel to the upper radiator member.
13. Install the hood release cable to the upper radiator member.
14. Install the upper radiator member, the stay support in front of the condenser and the radiator grille.
15. Reconnect the negative battery cable.
16. Evacuate, charge and test refrigerant system. Check system for leaks.

Compressor

REMOVAL AND INSTALLATION

Except York Compressor System

1. Disconnect the negative battery cable.
2. Recover refrigerant (discharge system) from refrigeration system.
3. Remove all refrigerant system connections. Cap open fittings immediately.
4. Loosen the compressor and mounting brackets bolts. Disconnect the electrical connector from the compressor.
5. Remove the drive belt from the compressor, the mounting bolts and the compressor assembly.

To install:

6. Drain the refrigerant oil from the compressor and measure so the same amount can be installed in the compressor, if replacing the unit.
7. Mount the compressor on the mounting brackets and install the mounting bolts. Install compressor assembly.
8. Immediately upon opening the service connection ports, attach the hoses and tighten securely.
9. Install the drive belt. Adjust the drive belt so it not possible to depress it by more than 0.2–0.4 in. for Sankyo and Kiki or 0.04–0.08 in. for Delco at the middle of the longest belt span between pulleys.
10. Connect the negative battery cable.

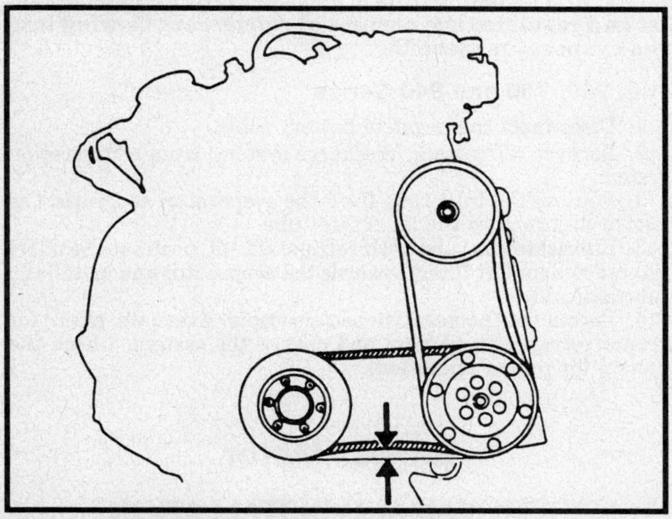

Drive belt tension measurement location

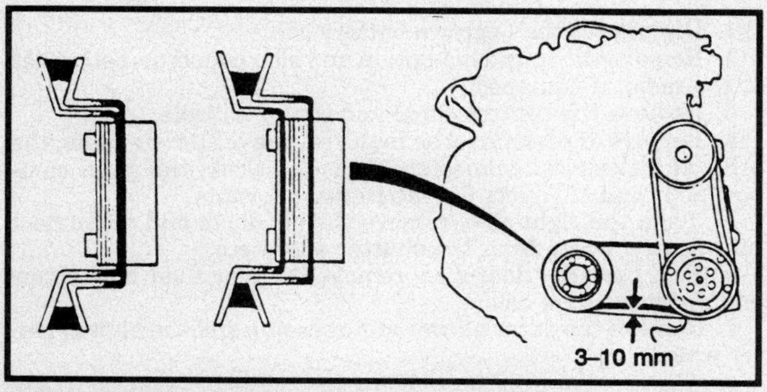
3–10 mm

Adjusting the compressor drive belt—York compressor system

11. Evacuate, check for proper refrigerant oil level and charge the system.
12. Start the engine, allow it to reach normal operating temperatures and the check the system operation.

York Compressor System

1. Disconnect the negative battery cable.
2. Recover refrigerant (discharge system) from refrigeration system.
3. Disconnect both the suction and the discharge service valves from the compressor head. Cap open fittings immediately.
4. At the crankshaft pulley, loosen the tensioner plate nuts and remove the drive belt.
5. Disconnect the electrical connection from compressor assembly.
6. Remove the compressor-to-bracket retaining bolts and the compressor assembly.

To install:

7. Drain the refrigerant oil from the compressor and measure so the same amount can be installed in the compressor, if replacing the unit.
8. Install compressor assembly. Install the compressor-to-bracket retaining bolts and torque to 28 ft. lbs.

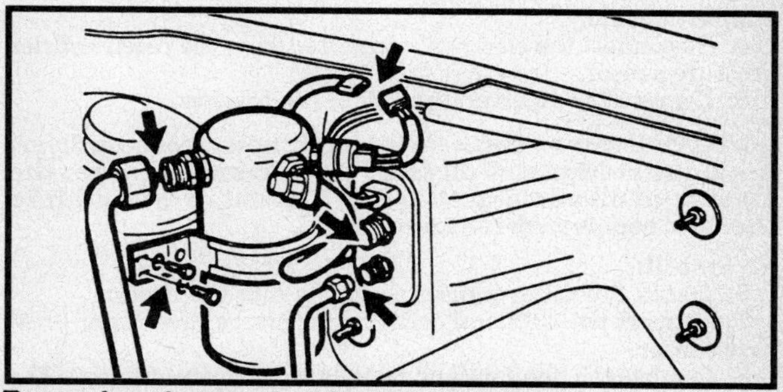

Removing the receiver/dryer assembly

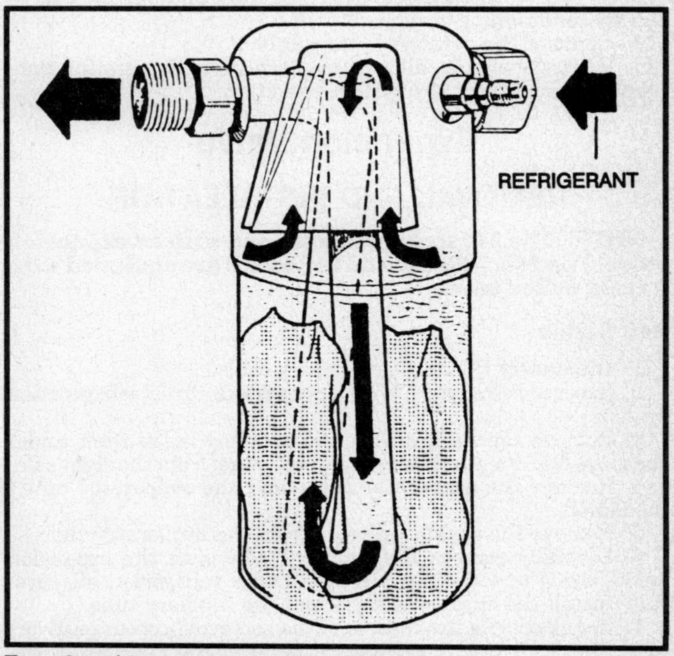
REFRIGERANT

Receiver/dryer assembly operation

9. Remove the tensioner plate and outer split pulley half from the crankshaft pulley.
10. Install the drive belt, the split pulley half and the tensioner plate. To adjust the drive belt tesnion, remove or add shims to the assembly until the deflection is 0.1–0.4 in. between the pulleys. Install any extra shims between the outer split pulley and tensioner plate.
11. Torque the tensioner plate-to-crankshaft nuts to 15 ft. lbs.
12. Reconnect the electrical connection to compressor assembly.
13. Connect both the suction and the discharge service lines to the compressor assembly.
14. Connect the negative battery cable.
15. Evacuate, check for proper refrigerant oil level and charge the system.
16. Start the engine, allow it to reach normal operating temperatures and the check the system operation.

Receiver/Drier

REMOVAL AND INSTALLATION

1. Disconnect the negative battery cable.
2. Recover refrigerant (discharge system) from refrigeration system.
3. Disconnect, cap or plug the refrigerant lines to the receiver/drier assembly.
4. Disconnect the electrical connector from the receiver/drier pressure sensor.
5. Remove the receiver/drier from the bracket.

NOTE: Before replacement of a new receiver/drier, drain the refrigerant oil from the old unit, measure the amount of oil and add the same amount of new oil into the new receiver/drier assembly.

To install:

6. Install the receiver/drier assembly into the bracket.
7. Connect the electrical connector to the receiver/drier pressure sensor.
8. Remove the line caps and install the refrigerant lines to the receiver/drier assembly.
9. Evacuate, check for proper refrigerant oil level and charge the air conditioning system.
10. Connect the negative battery cable.
11. Start the engine, allow it to reach normal operating temperatures and check the system operation.

Expansion Valve

REMOVAL AND INSTALLATION

NOTE: The 240 series are equipped with an expansion valve. The 740, 760, 780 and 940 series are equipped with a fixed orfice tube.

240 Series

1. Disconnect the negative battery cable.
2. Recover refrigerant (discharge system) from refrigeration system.
3. Remove the right side sound proofing panel from under the glove box. Remove the console side panel from the right side.
4. Remove the evaporator cover and the evaporator outlet insulation.
5. Remove the expansion valve from the evaporator tube.
6. Carefully remove the capillary tube with the expansion valve. Using new O-rings lubricated with refrigerant oil, carefully install the expansion valve and the capillary tube.
7. Installation is the reverse of the removal procedure. Evacuate, check for proper refrigerant oil level and charge the system. Check the system for proper operation.

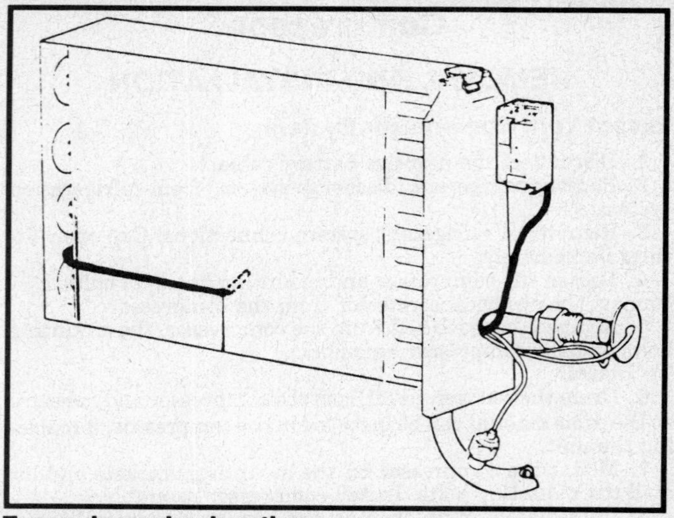

Expansion valve location

Fixed Orifice Tube

REMOVAL AND INSTALLATION

NOTE: The orfice tube is located in the evaporator inlet and regulates the amount of refrigerant flowing into the evaporator assembly.

740, 760, 780 and 940 Series

1. Disconnect the negative battery cable.
2. Recover refrigerant (discharge system) from refrigeration system.
3. Remove the inlet tube from the evaporator, separated the rubber and remove the fix orifice tube.
3. Lubricate the tube with refrigerant oil, position the short filtered end (outlet filter) towards the evaporator and install the tube assembly.
4. Reconnect the negative battery cable. Evacuate, check for proper refrigerant oil level and charge the system. Check the system for proper operation.

Blower Motor

REMOVAL AND INSTALLATION

240 Series

1. Disconnect the negative battery cable.
2. Remove the sound insulation and side panels on both sides of the radio, if equipped.
3. Remove the control panel and center console.
4. Remove or disconnect as required, the center air vents, the cable and electrical connectors from the clock, the glove compartment and air ducts for the center air vents.
5. From the right side, remove the air ducts and disconnect the vacuum hoses from the shutter actuators.
6. Fold back the floor mat, remove the rear floor duct screw and move the duct aside.
7. Remove the outer blower motor casing and the blower motor wheel.

NOTE: It may be necessary to remove the support from under the glove compartment in order to remove the blower motor casing.

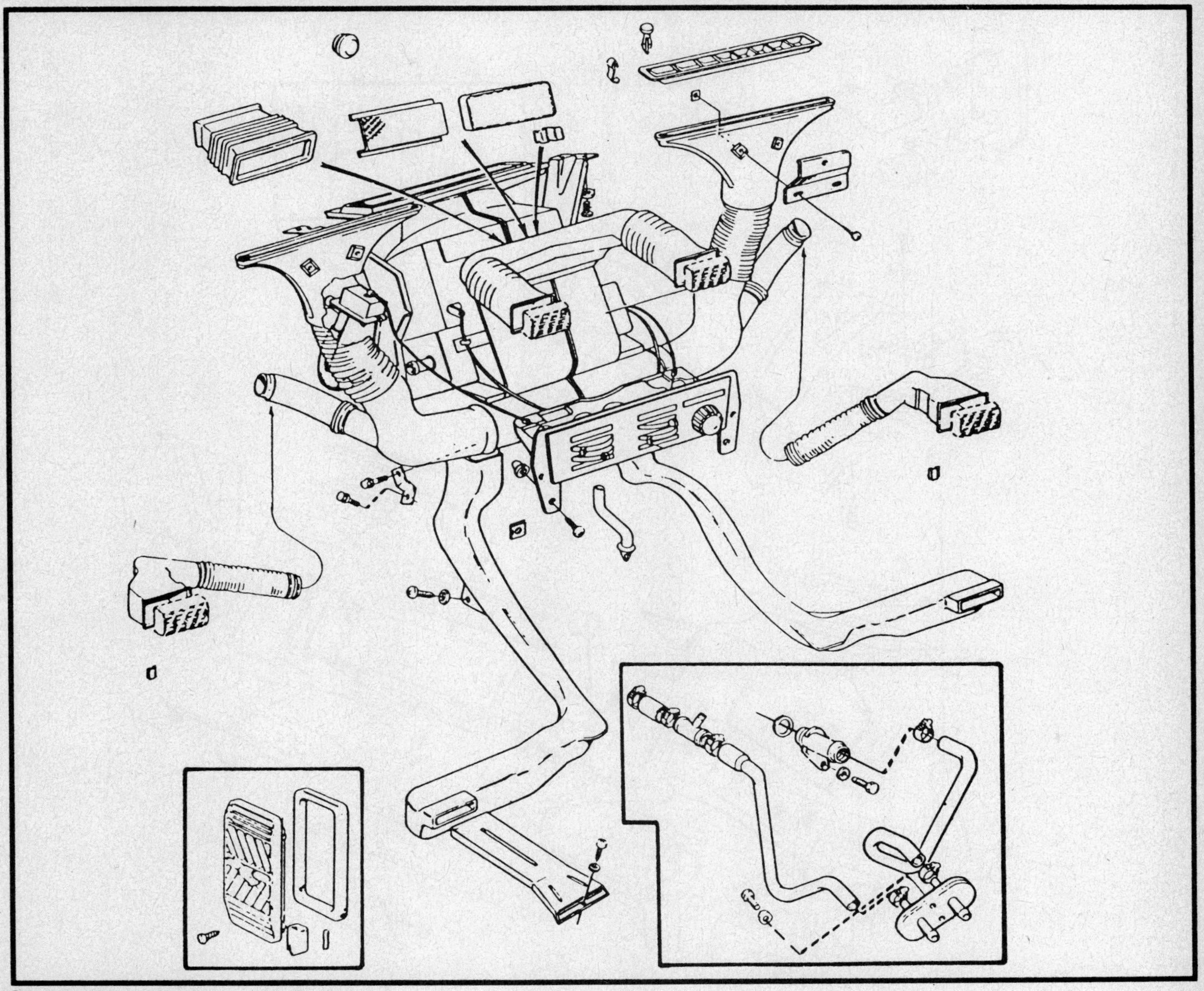

Standard heater unit—200 Series

8. Disconnect the blower motor switch from the center console and the electrical leads from the switch.

9. From the left side, disconnect the air ducts and the vacuum hoses from the shutter actuators.

10. Remove or disconnect the inner blower motor casing, the vacuum hose from the rear floor shutter actuator, the electrical connector and the blower motor.

NOTE: Should the blower motor need to be replaced, a modified replacement unit is available. Certain modifications must be done and instructions are included with the new assembly.

To install:

11. Clean heater housing of all dirt, leaves etc. before installation. Install the blower motor, the electrical connector, the vacuum hose to the rear floor shutter actuator and the inner blower motor casing.

12. Install the blower motor wheel and the outer blower motor casing.

13. Install the rear floor air duct and the floor mat.

14. At the left side, connect the air ducts and the vacuum hoses to the shutter actuators.

15. Connect the electrical leads to the blower motor switch and the switch to the center console.

16. At the right side, install the air ducts and connect the vacuum hoses to the shutter actuators.

17. Install or connect as required the center air vents, the cable and electrical connectors to the clock, the glove compartment and air ducts for the center air vents.

18. Install the control panel and center console.

19. Install the sound insulation and side panels to both sides of the radio.

20. Reconnect the negative battery cable. Check system for proper operation.

740, 760, 780 and 940 Series

NOTE: On some vehicles, a drum type fan is used which can be balanced by fitting steel clips to the outer

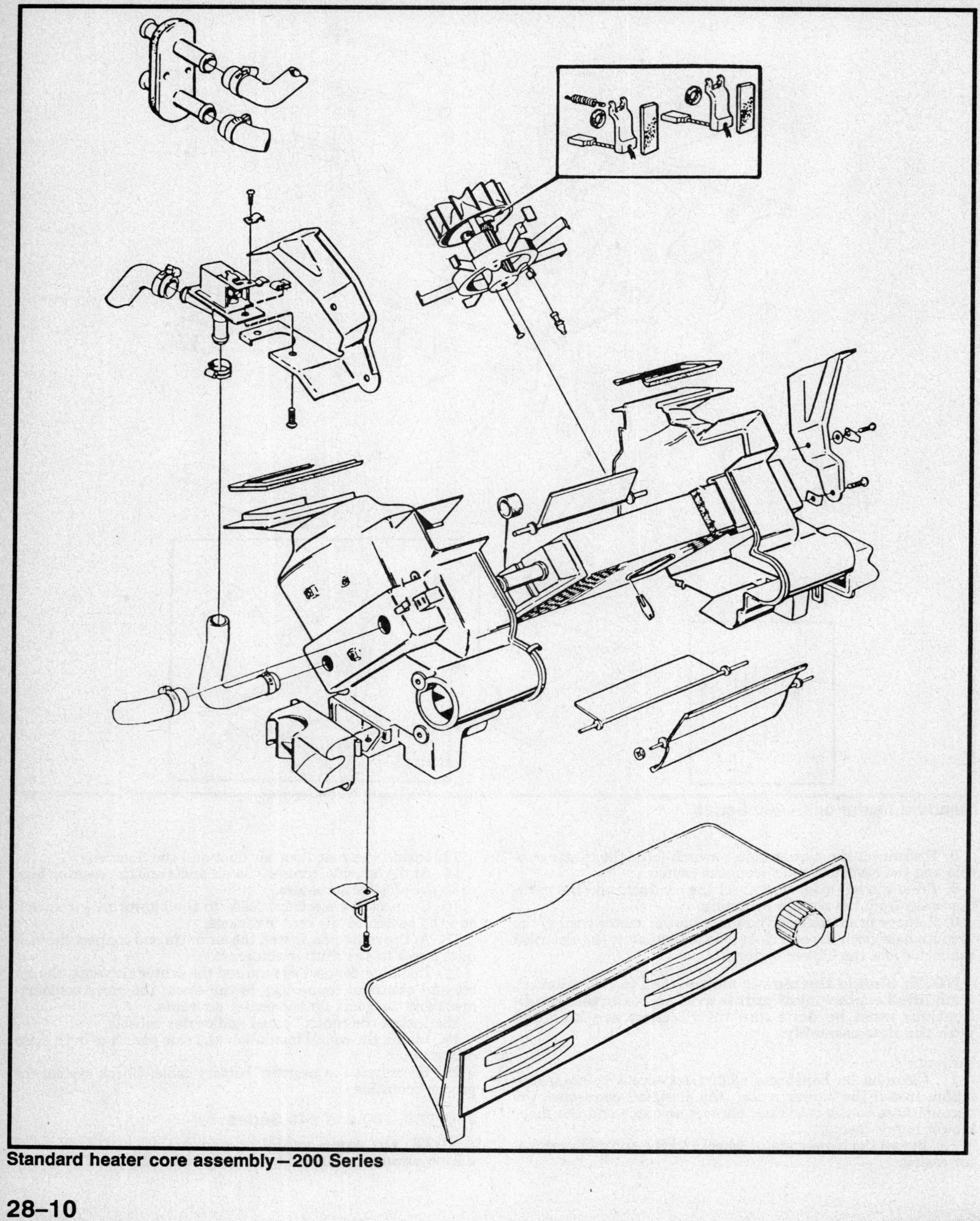

Standard heater core assembly—200 Series

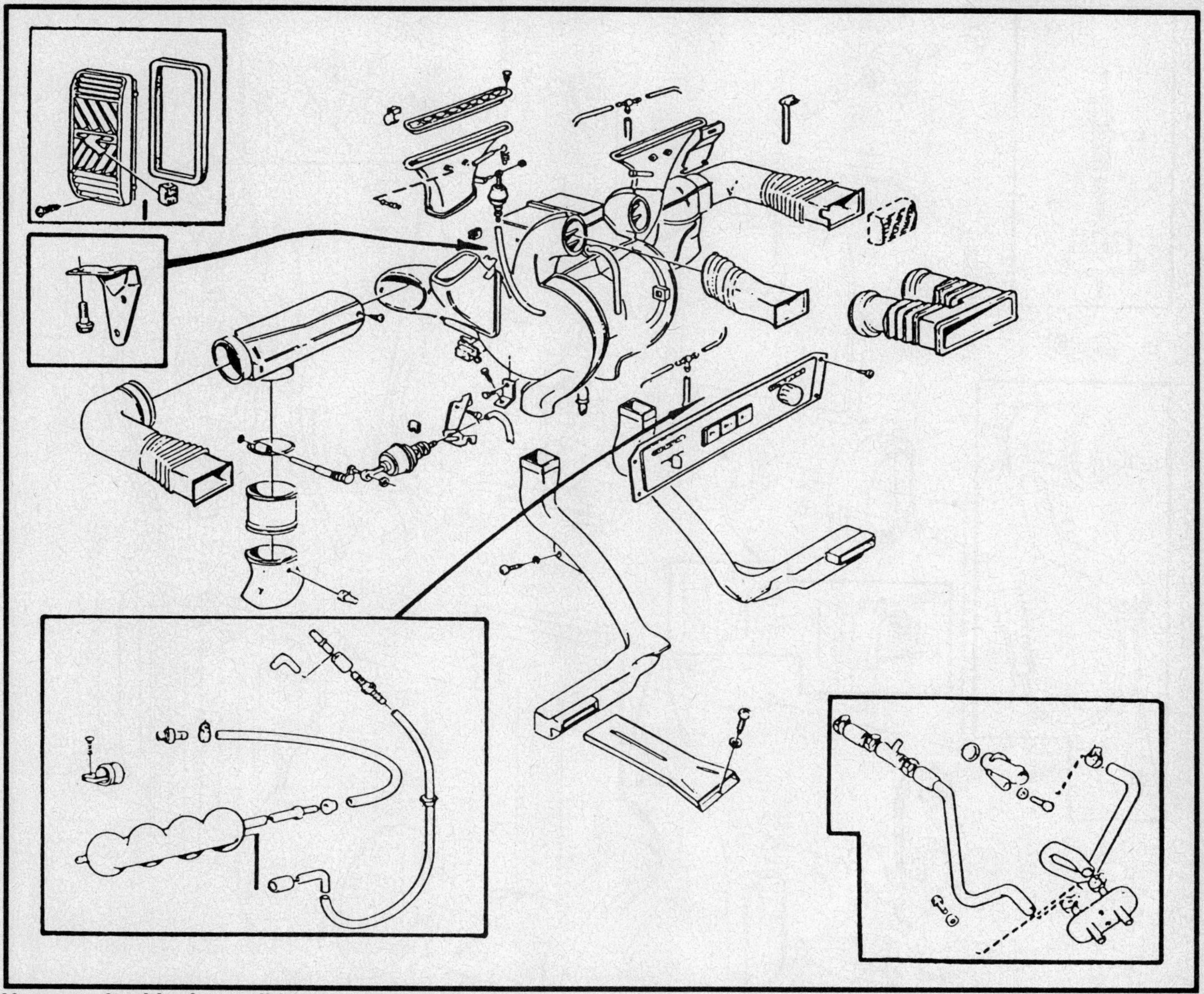

Heater unit with air conditioning—200 Series

edge. On most vehicles a hose is connected to the fan housing to supply cooling air to avoid damage to the fan motor assembly.

740 SERIES

1. Disconnect the negative battery cable.
2. Remove the lower glove box panel and the glove box.
3. Disconnect the electrical connector from the blower motor.
4. Remove the blower motor-to-housing screws and the blower motor assembly.

To install:

5. Clean heater housing of all dirt, leaves etc. before installation. Connect the electrical connector to the blower motor.
6. Install the motor, the screws and the panel beneath the glove compartment.
7. Connect the negative battery cable and check the blower motor operation.

760, 780 AND 940 SERIES/AUTOMATIC CLIMATE CONTROL (ACC)

1. Disconnect the negative battery cable.
2. Remove the lower glove box panel.
3. From the right side, remove the instep moulding.
4. Remove the panel from above the control unit; be careful not damage it upon removal.
5. Disconnect the electrical connector from the control unit.
6. Remove the control unit-to-bracket bolts and the control unit. Remove the bracket-to-chassis bolts and the bracket.
7. Disconnect the electrical connector from the blower motor.
8. Remove the ventilation pipe, the blower motor-to-housing screws and the blower motor.

To install:

9. Clean heater housing of all dirt, leaves etc. before installation. Install the blower motor and the ventilation pipe.
10. Connect the electrical connector to the blower motor.

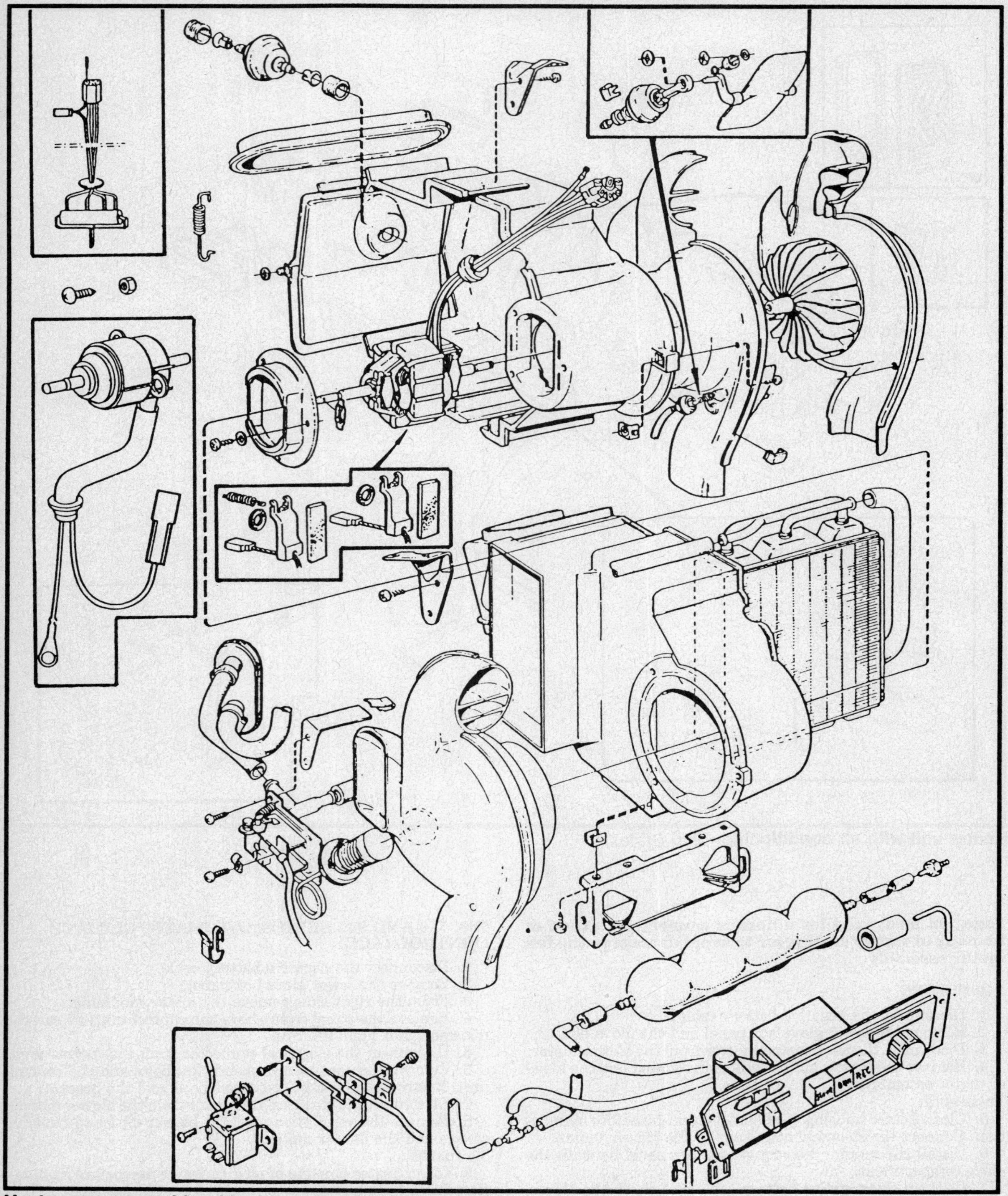

Heater core assembly with air conditioning – 200 Series

11. Install the control unit bracket and the control unit.
12. Connect the electrical connector to the control unit.
13. Install the panel above the control unit, the instep panel and the lower glove box panel.
14. Connect the negative battery cable and check the blower motor operation.

760, 780 AND 940 SERIES/ELECTRONIC CLIMATE CONTROL (ECC)

1. Disconnect the negative battery cable.
2. From the right side, remove the lower glove box panel and the glove box.
3. Disconnect the electrical connector and the mounting bracket from the blower motor housing.
4. Disconnect the electrical connector from the blower motor.
5. Remove the blower motor-to-housing screws and the motor.

To install:

6. Clean heater housing of all dirt, leaves etc. before installation. Install the rubber seal to the blower motor and install assembly.
7. Connect the electrical connector to the blower motor and the positive terminal to the housing.
8. Connect the negative battery cable and check all blower motor speeds.
9. Install the glove box and the lower panel.

Blower Motor Resistor

REMOVAL AND INSTALLATION

1. Disconnect the negative cable.
2. Disconnect the electrical connector from the blower resistor assembly.
3. Remove mounting screw and remove the blower resistor assembly from the case.
4. Installation is the reverse of the service removal procedure. Reconnect the negative battery cable. Check the blower motor for proper operation at all speeds after installation.

NOTE: Some vehicles may be prone to high fan noise in fan speed No. 1. This condition is due to too high a fan speed. Noise level can be lowered by installing an additional resistor in series with the positive lead of the fan switch.

Heater Core

REMOVAL AND INSTALLATION

NOTE: On vehicles equipped with ACC (Automatic Climate Control), a thermal switch is located on the outlet hose from the heater core. It switches on and starts the fan motor only when the water temperature exceeds approximately 95°F. This prevents cold air from being blown into the passenger compartment during winter. The thermal switch is by passed in the defrost position.

240 Series

1. Disconnect the negative battery cable. Drain cooling system.
2. Move the heater controls to the **CLOSED** position.
3. Remove the sound proofing and side panels from both sides of the center dash console.
4. Remove the radio and the center control panel. Disconnect any necessary cables and move the panel aside.
5. Remove the glove box assembly and the strip below the right air vent by carefully prying it off with a small prybar.
6. Remove the steering wheel casing (column cover) and disconnect the choke control with the cover plate.
7. Remove the strip from under the left air vent, the instrument panel lighting intensity and the light switch knobs; do not remove the switch.
8. Remove the speedometer drive cable and any electrical connectors from the instrument panel cover plate and the cover plate.
9. Remove the storage compartment, the center air vents and the instrument panel frame.
10. From the left side, disconnect the windshield wiper connectors.
11. Disconnect the air duct between the heater and the center air vents.
12. Disconnect the electrical connector from the glove box courtesy light and the rubber straps from the defroster vents.
13. Remove the dashboard unit from the dash assembly, as necessary.
14. Remove or disconnect the rear floor air duct screws and lower the duct slightly.
15. Remove or disconnect the following:
    a. The lower heater mount screws
    b. The vacuum hose from the vacuum tank
    c. The cable from the control valve
    d. The upper and lower center console screws
    e. The center support screws located on the console
    f. The fan motor ground electrical connector
    g. The inlet hose from the control valve
16. Disconnect the upper hose from the heater core tube and the vacuum hoses from the shutter actuators.
17. Loosen the upper housing screws.
18. From the right side, disconnect the vacuum hoses from the shutter actuators.
19. Disconnect and remove the air ducts.
20. Disconnect the hoses from the vacuum tank. Remove the rear floor duct screws and lower the duct slightly.
21. Remove the upper and lower console screws and position it aside.
22. Remove the right support screws and the support.
23. Disconnect the electrical connector from the heater fan switch and the positive lead.
24. Disconnect the **REC** shutter vacuum hose from the control panel.
25. Disconnect the input vacuum hose from the T connection-to-floor shutter actuators.
26. Remove the upper heater housing retaining assembly screws and remove the assembly from the vehicle.
27. Place the assembly on a cleared area and remove or disconnect the following:
    a. The upper hose from the heater core.
    b. The air inlet rubber seal from the top of the housing.
    c. The **REC** shutter clips, from the left side.
    d. The rubber seals from both defroster vents.
    e. All outer blower motor casing clips and the casing from the assembly.
28. Remove the blower motor wheel locking clips (from both sides) and the blower motor wheels.
29. Remove the heater core drain hose and the vacuum tank assembly. The vacuum tank bracket screws from the left side. The **REC** shutter spring and heater housing clips.
30. Remove the blower motor screws and the heater control valve capillary tube from the T joint.
31. Pull the heater housing apart from the middle.
32. Remove the blower motor and the heater core assembly.

To install:

33. Install the blower and heater core in the housing assembly. Make sure that the fan motor is correctly positioned in the housing. Install fan motor hose.
34. Using butyl sealant or equivalent coat mating surface of the heater housing and assemble the case.
35. Install the heater control valve capillary tube to the T joint and the blower motor screws.

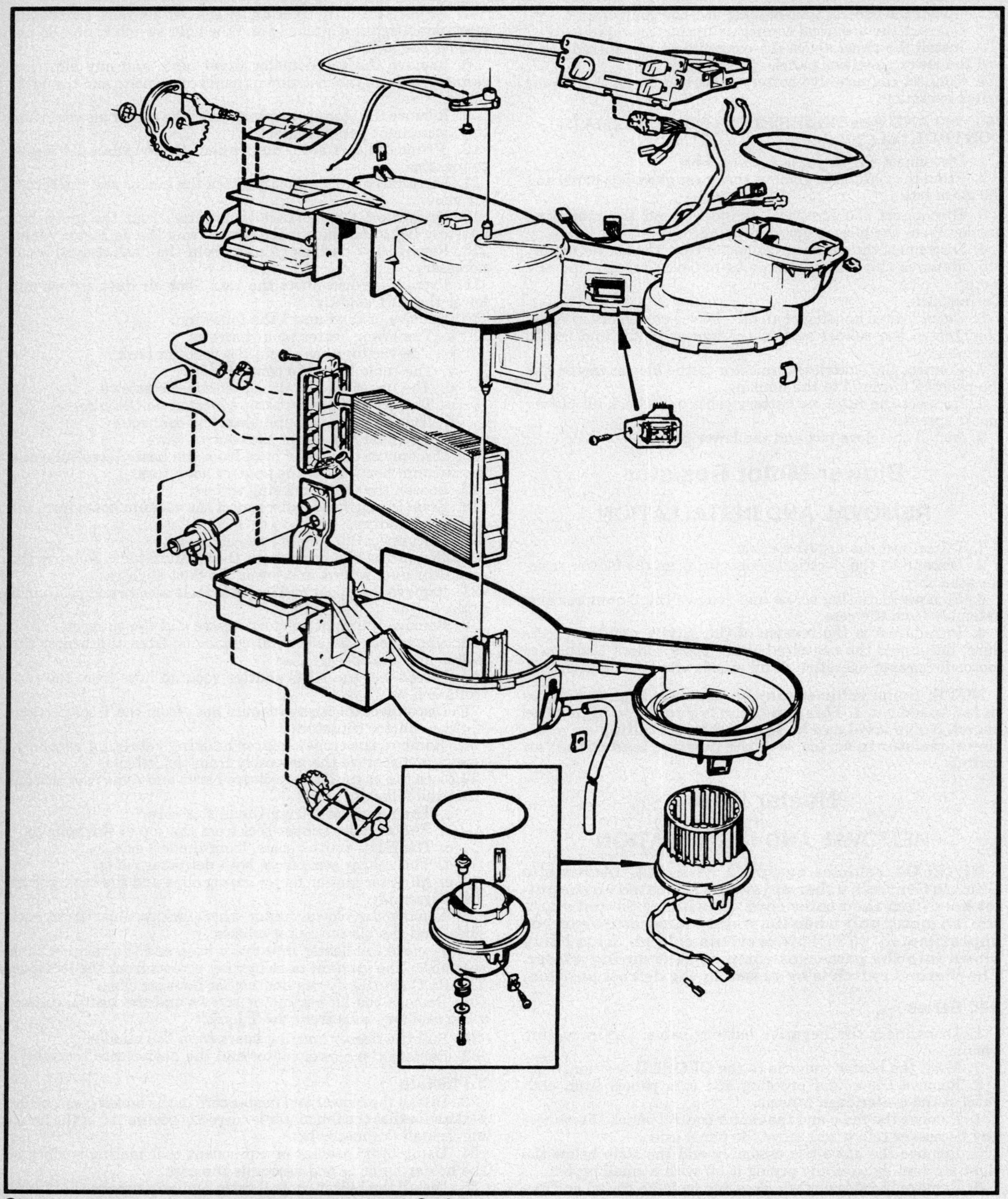

Standard heater core assembly—700 and 900 Series

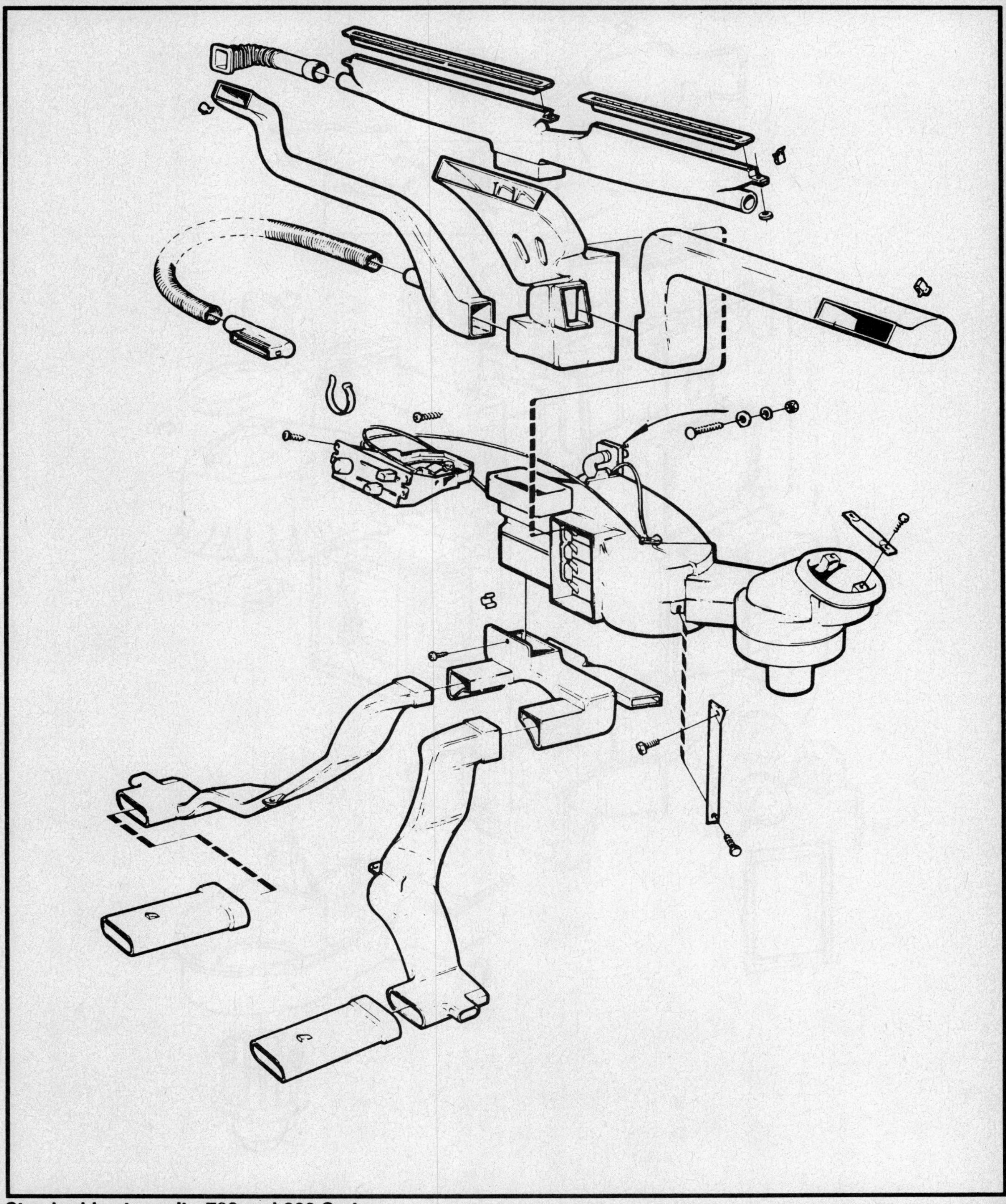

Standard heater unit—700 and 900 Series

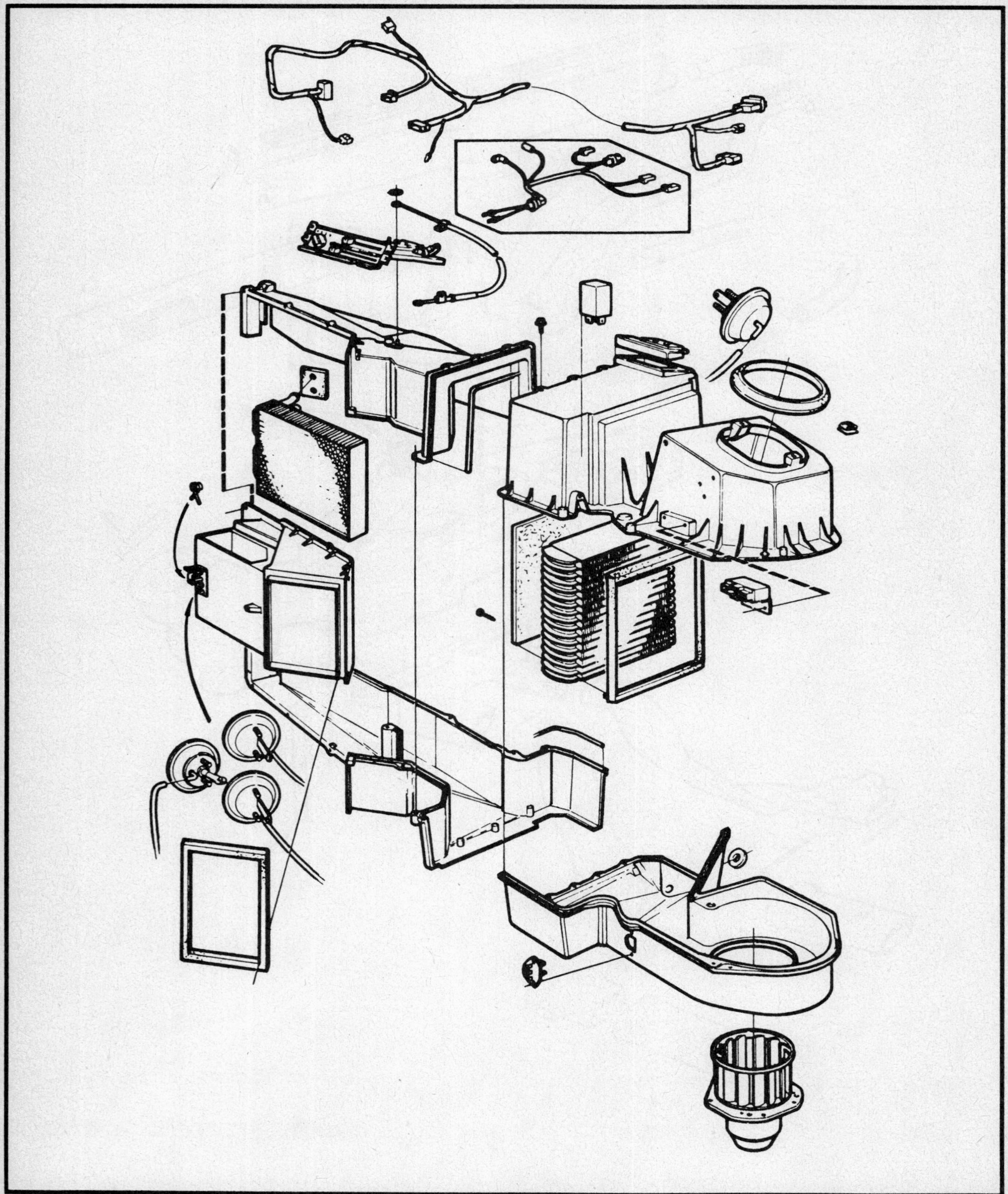

Heater core assembly with air conditioning—700 and 900 Series

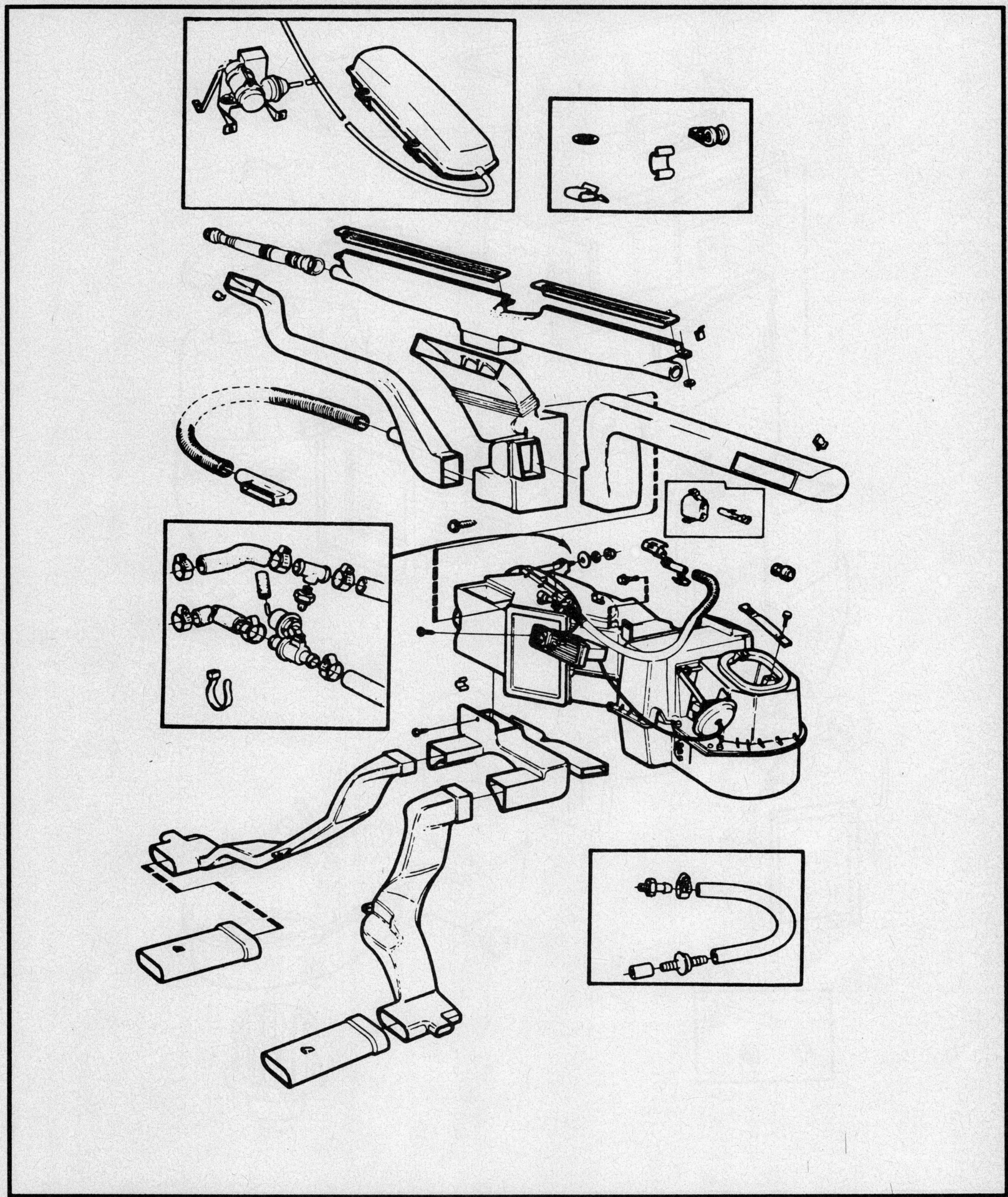

Heater unit with air conditioning—700 and 900 Series

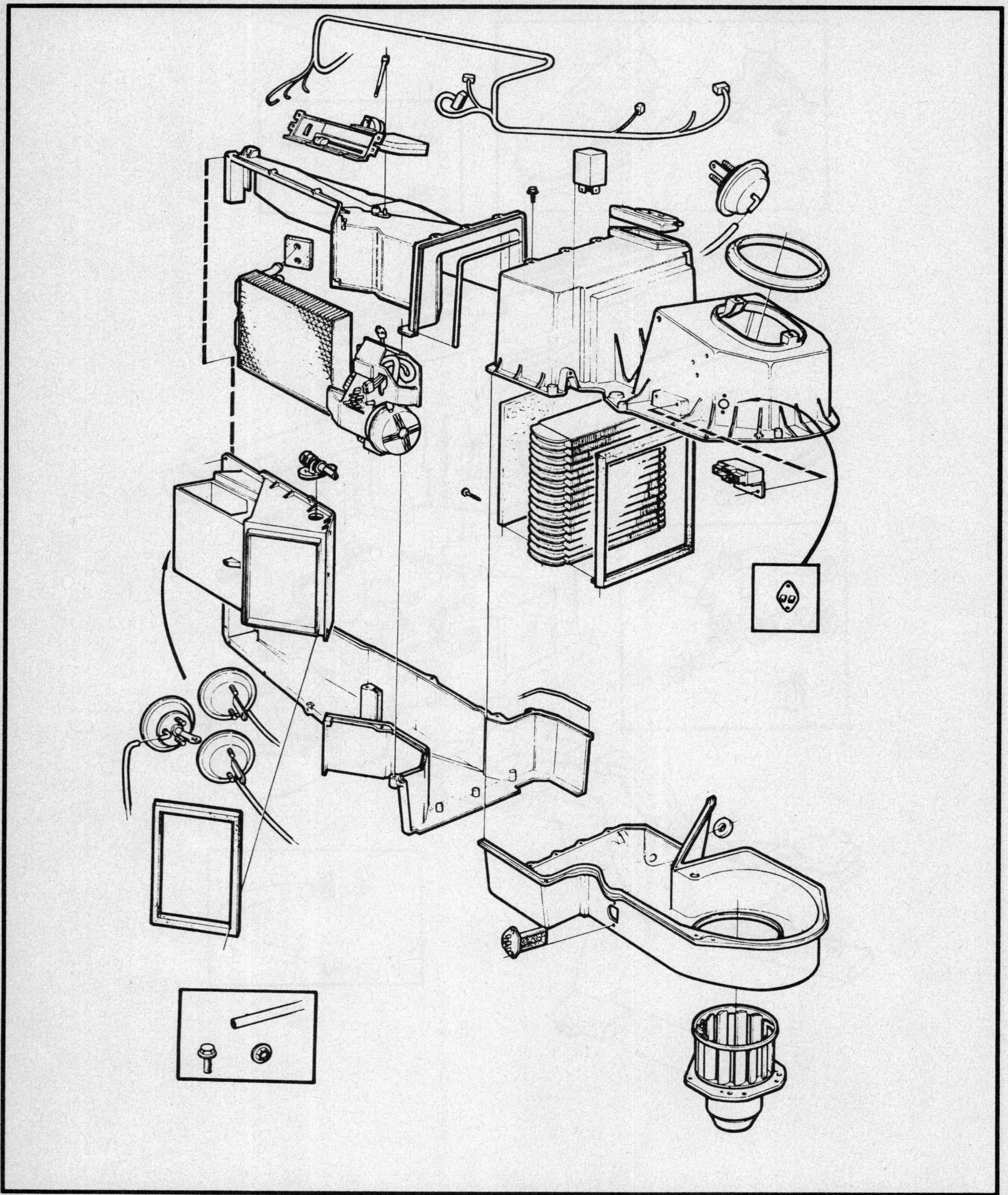

Heater core assembly with automatic air conditioning (ACC)—700 and 900 Series

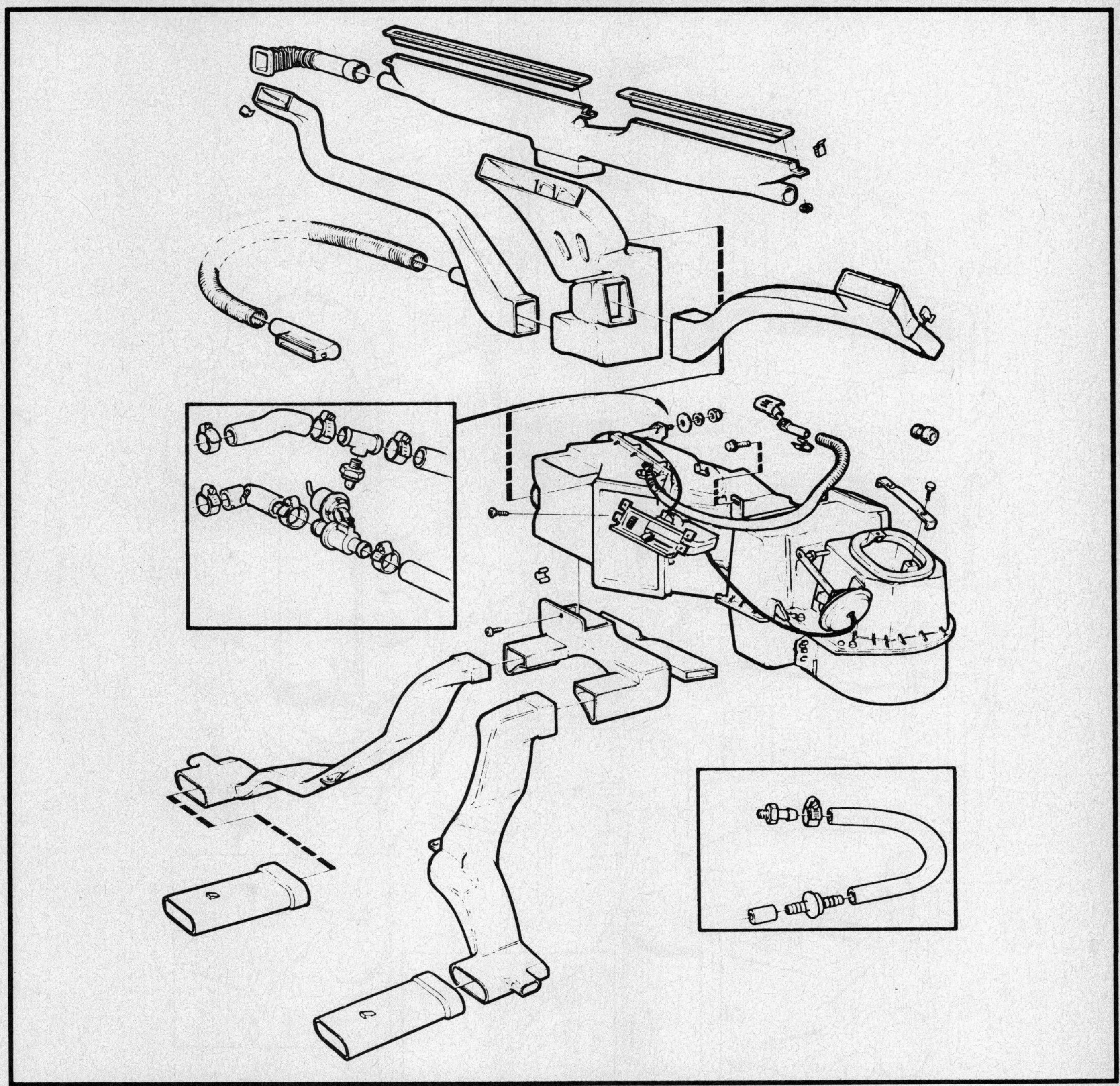

Heater unit with automatic air conditioning (ACC) – 700 and 900 Series

36. Install the heater housing clips and **REC** shutter spring. At the left side, install vacuum tank assembly, the vacuum tank bracket screws and the heater core drain hose.
37. Install the blower motor wheel and the blower motor wheel locking clips to both sides.
38. Install or connect the following items:
   a. The outer blower motor casing clips to the the assembly.
   b. The rubber seals to both defroster vents.
   c. The **REC** shutter clips to the left side.
   d. The air inlet rubber seal to the top of the housing.
   e. The upper hose to the heater core.
39. Install the heater assembly into the vehicle.

NOTE: Before installation, be sure all sealing flanges are correctly sealed to prevent air leakage during the system operation.

40. Install the upper housing retaining screws.
41. Connect the **REC** shutter vacuum hose to the control panel.
42. Connect the electrical connector to the heater fan switch and the positive lead. Install protective cover.
43. Install the right support and console.

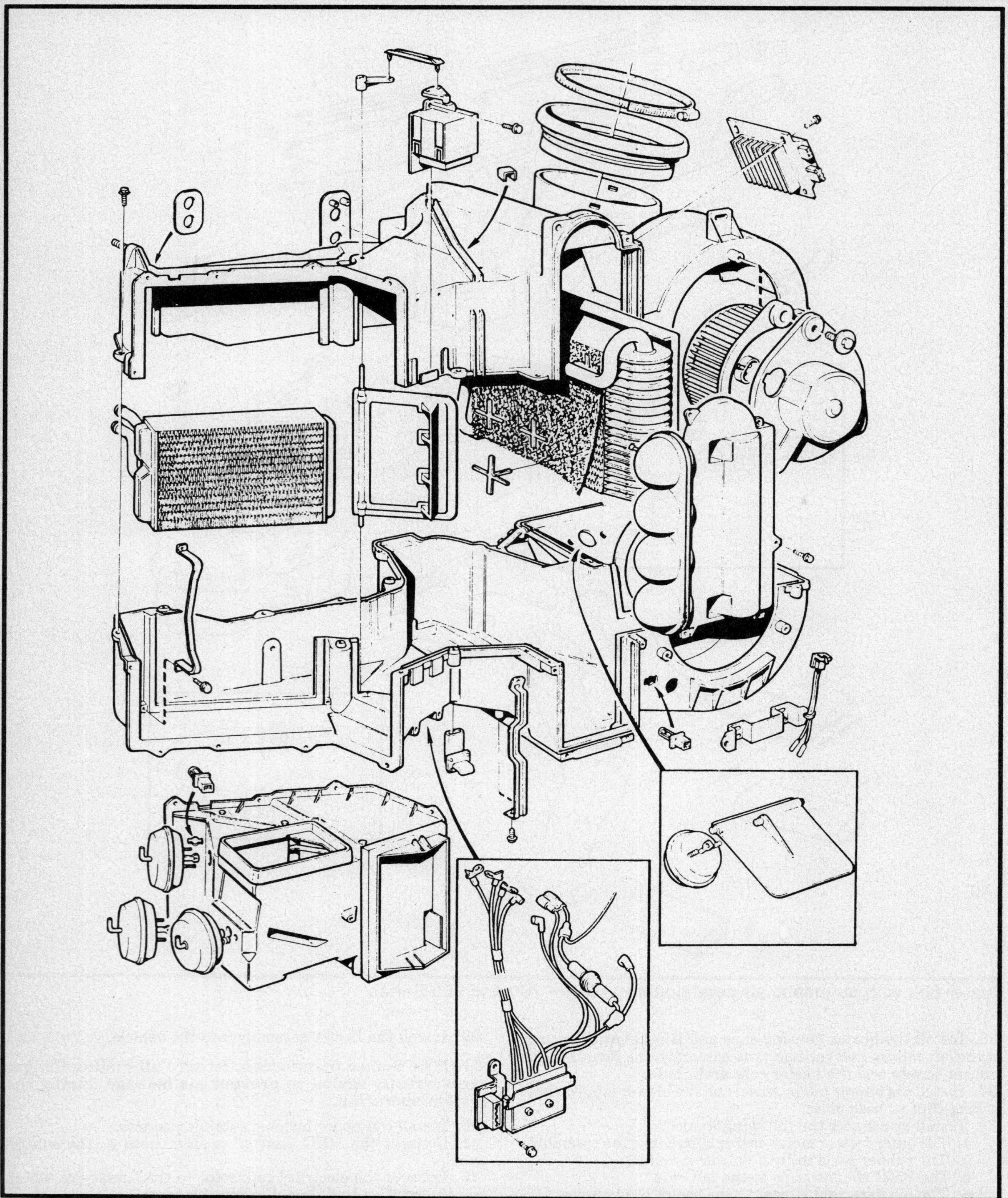

Heater core assembly with electronic air conditioning (ECC)—700 and 900 Series

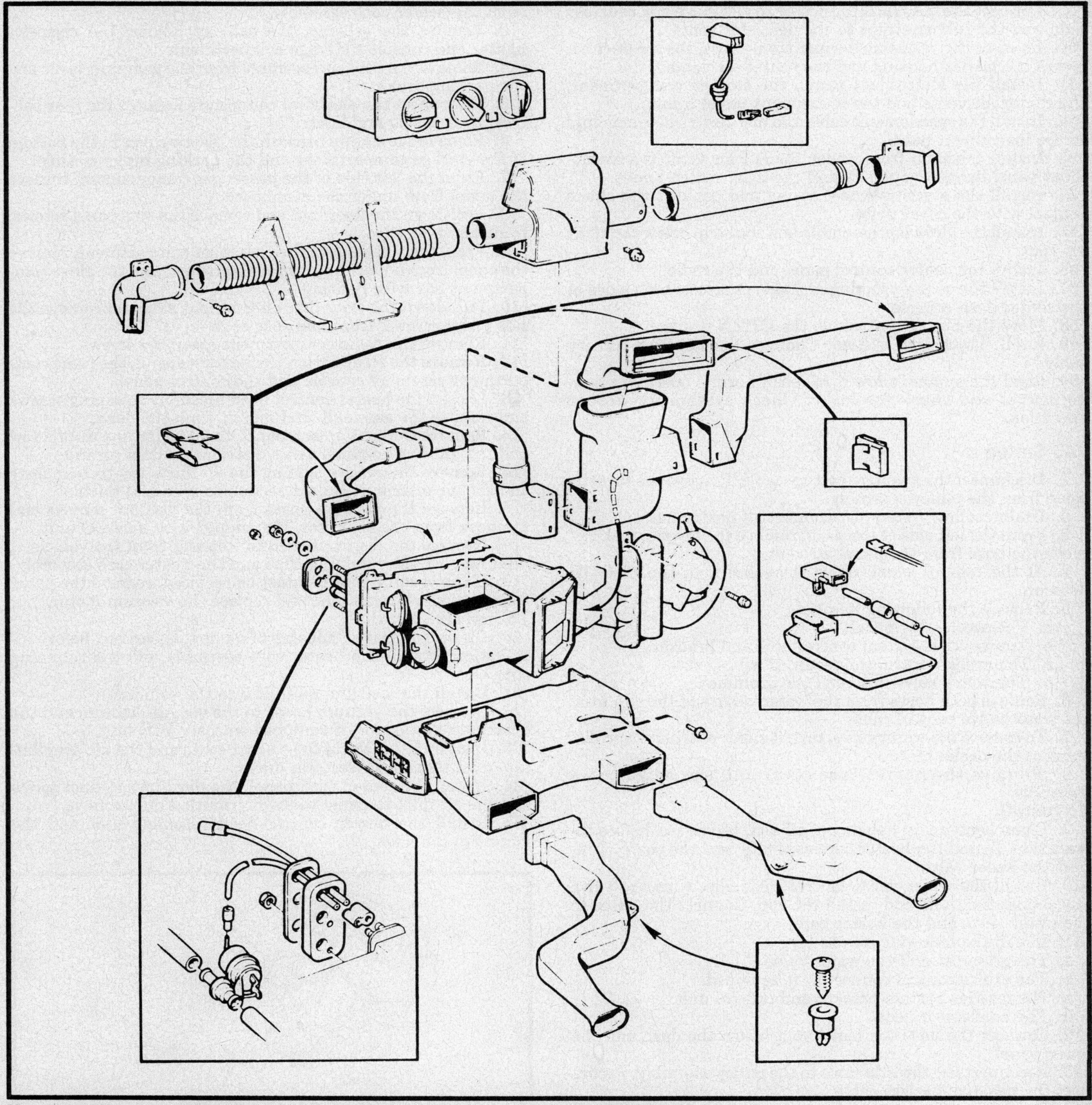

Heater unit with electronic air conditioning (ECC) – 700 and 900 Series

44. Install the heater assembly lower mount and the rear floor duct. Connect the hoses to the vacuum tank.
45. Install the air ducts. At the right side, connect the vacuum hoses to the shutter actuators.
46. Connect the upper hose to the heater core tube and the vacuum hoses to the shutter actuators.
47. Install or connect the following items:
    a. The inlet hose to the control valve
    b. The fan motor ground electrical connector
    c. The console center support and the center console screws
    d. The cable to the control valve
    e. The vacuum hose to the vacuum tank
    f. The lower heater mount screws
48. Install the rear floor air and the dashboard unit to the dash assembly.

49. Connect the electrical connector to the glove box courtesy light and the rubber straps to the defroster vents.
50. Connect the windshield wiper connectors, the air duct between the heater housing and the center air vents.
51. Install the instrument panel, the storage compartment, the center air vents and the instrument panel frame.
52. Install the speedometer cable and any electrical connectors to the instrument panel.
53. Install the strip from under the left air vent, the instrument panel lighting intensity and the light switch knobs.
54. Install the steering wheel casing and connect the choke control with the cover plate.
55. Install the glove box assembly and the strip below the right air vent.
56. Install the center control panel and the radio.
57. Install the sound proofing and side panels to both sides of the center dash console.
58. Move the heater controls to the **OPEN** position.
59. Refill the cooling system. Connect the negative battery cable.
60. Start the engine, allow it to reach normal operating temperatures and check for leaks. Check system for proper operation.

740 Series

1. Disconnect the negative battery cable. Remove the throttle cable from the pulley assembly.
2. Drain cooling system. Disconnect all heater hoses.
3. From the left side of the dash, remove the lower panel. Remove the hose from the panel air vent.
4. At the control panel, move the selector to the **FLOOR** position.
5. Remove the following items:
   a. The accelerator pedal.
   b. The ignition system control unit and bracket.
   c. The cruise control connector, if equipped.
   d. The water valve hose and the grommet.
6. Remove both hoses from the water valve and the clip from the water valve control cable.
7. To remove the water valve, turn it right, pull it out and disconnect the cable.
8. Remove the heater core cover and the heater core assembly.

To install:

9. Clean heater core housing of all dirt, leaves etc. before installation. Install the heater core assembly and the cover. Connect the water valve.
10. Install the water valve control cable clip, turn the valve left, adjust the cable and install the clip. Connect the hoses to the water valve and the heater core.
11. Install the following items:
   a. The grommet and the water valve.
   b. The cruise control connector, if equipped.
   c. The ignition system bracket and control unit.
   d. The accelerator pedal.
12. Connect the hose the panel vent below the dash and the lower panel.
13. Reconnect the throttle cable to the pulley assembly. Reconnect the negative battery cable.
14. Refill the cooling system. Start the vehicle, allow it to reach normal operating temperatures, check for leaks. Check system for proper operation.

760, 780 and 940 Series

NOTE: The following procedure is also for vehicles equipped with Automatic Climate Control (ACC) systems.

1. Disconnect the negative battery cable.
2. Drain the cooling system. Disconnect the heater hoses from the heater core assembly.
3. Remove the ashtray, the ashtray holder, the cigarette lighter and console's storage compartment.
4. Remove the console assembly from the gearshift lever and the parking brake.
5. Disconnect the electrical connector. Remove the rear ashtray, the console and light.
6. Remove the screws beneath the plastic cover in the bottom of the storage compartment and the parking brake console.
7. From the left side of the passenger compartment, remove the panel from under the dashboard.
8. Pull down the floor mat and remove the side panel screws, front and rear edge.
9. From the right side of the passenger compartment, remove the panel from under the glove compartment and the glove compartment box with lighting.
10. Pull down the floor mat on the right side and remove the side panel screws, front and rear edge.
11. Remove the radio compartment assembly screws.
12. Remove the screws from the heater control, the radio compartment assembly console and the control panel.
13. Loosen the heater control head assembly retaining screws and remove the assembly and mount from the dash.
14. Remove the center dash panel, the distribution duct screw and the air duct-to-panel vents/distribution duct screws.
15. Remove the screws holding the air ducts top-to-rear seats and the air distribution duct section-to-rear seat ducts.
16. Remove the vacuum hoses from the vacuum motors and the hose from the aspirator, if equipped with an ACC unit.
17. Remove the distribution unit housing from the vehicle.
18. Remove the retaining clips and the heater core assembly.
19. If the vacuum motors must be replaced, remove the panel from the distribution unit and replace the vacuum motor.

To install:

20. Clean heater core housing of all dirt, leaves etc. before installation. Install the heater core assembly and the retaining clips.
21. Install the distribution unit into the vehicle.
22. Connect the vacuum hoses to the vacuum motors and the hose to the aspirator, if equipped with an ACC unit.
23. Install the air ducts top-to-rear seats and the air distribution duct section-to-rear seat ducts.
24. Install the center dash panel, the distribution duct screw and the air duct-to-panel vents/distribution duct screws.
25. Install the heater control head assembly unit and the mount to the dash.

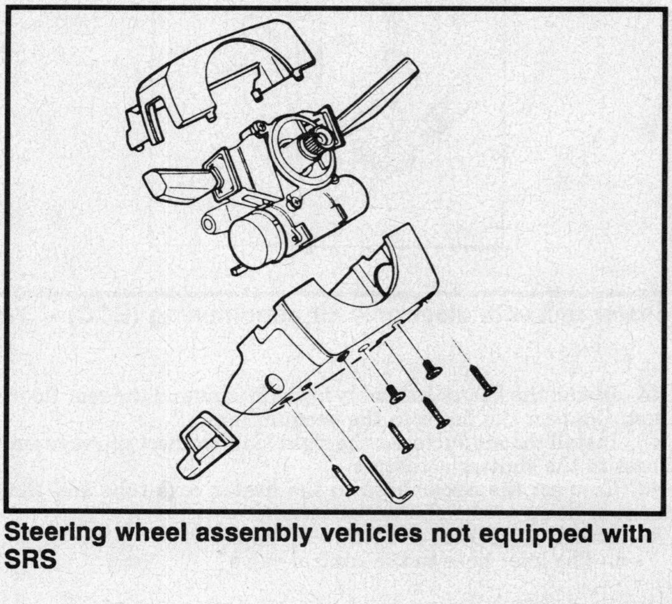

Steering wheel assembly vehicles not equipped with SRS

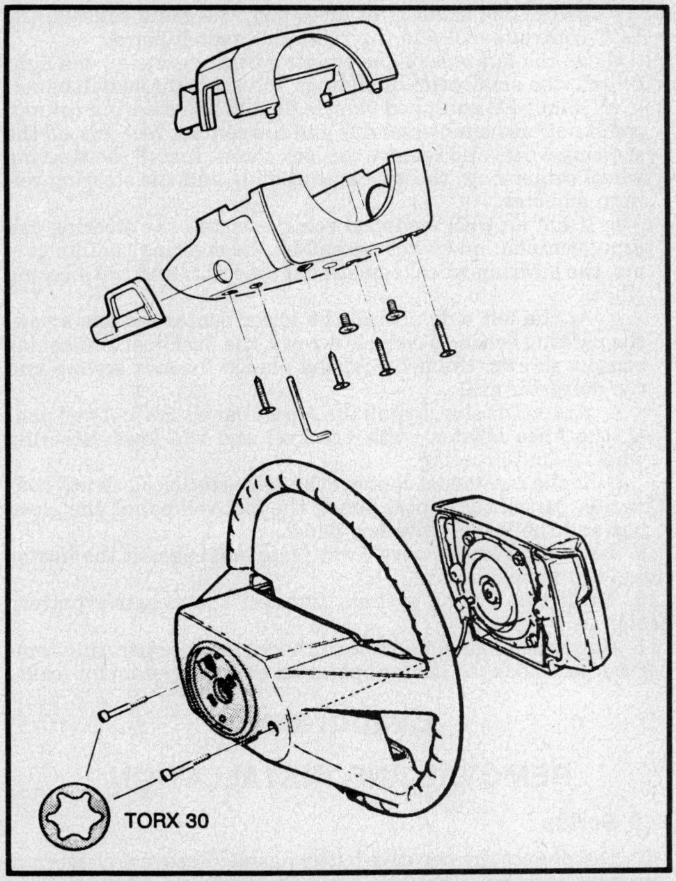
TORX 30

Steering wheel assembly vehicles equipped with SRS

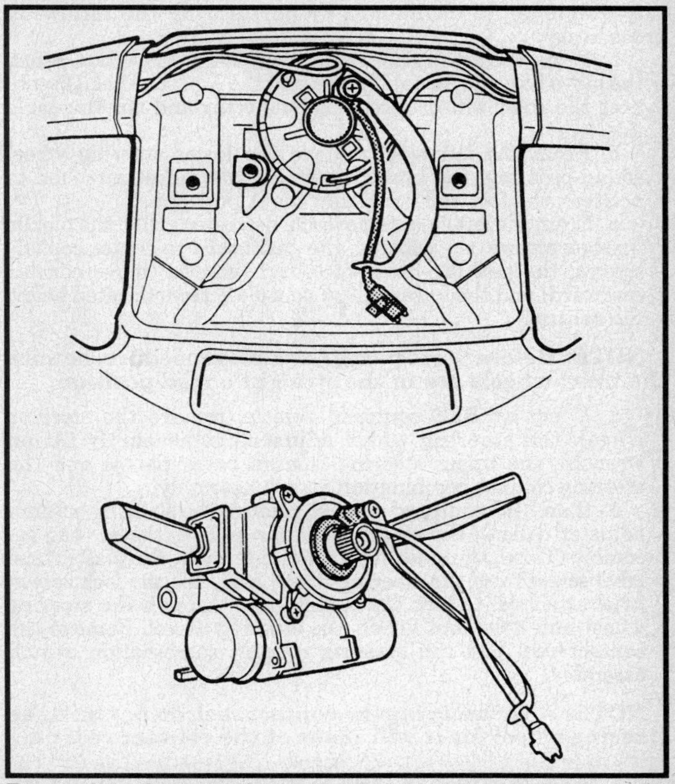

Removing the steering wheel vehicles equipped with SRS—700 and 900 Series

26. Install the heater control, the radio compartment console and the control panel.
27. Install the radio compartment screws.
28. At the right side of the passenger compartment, install the panel under the glove compartment and the glove compartment box with lighting.
29. Install the side panel screws, front and rear edge.
30. At the left side of the passenger compartment, install the panel under the dashboard.
31. Install the plastic cover in the bottom of the storage compartment and the parking brake console.
32. Connect the electrical connector. Instal the rear ashtray, the console and light.
33. Install the console assembly to the gearshift lever and the parking brake.
34. Install the ashtray holder, the ashtray, the cigarette lighter and console's storage compartment.
35. Reconnect the heater core hoses. Refill the cooling system and charge the air conditioning system.
36. Connect the negative battery cable. Start the engine, allow it to reach normal operating temperatures. Check system for proper operation.

760, 780 and 940 Series

NOTE: The following procedure is also for vehicles equipped with the Electronic Climate Control (ECC) system.

1. Disconnect the negative battery cable.
2. Drain cooling system. Disconnect the heater hoses from the heater core assembly. Remove the heater core cover plate.

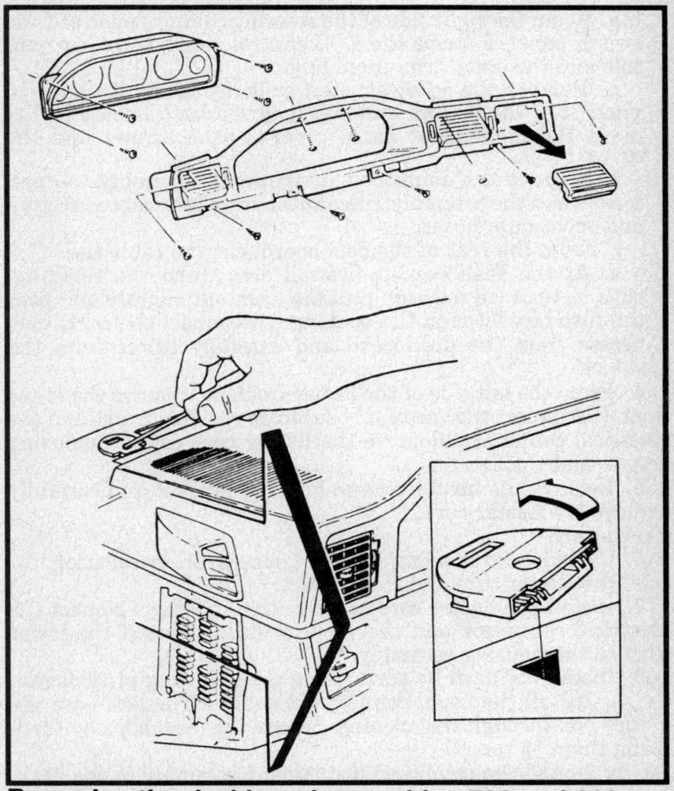

Removing the dashboard assembly—700 and 900 Series

3. Remove the dashboard by performing the following procedures:

a. From the right side, remove the lower glove box panel, the glove box, the footwell panel and the A post panel. Disconnect the solar sensor electrical connector and cut the cable ties.

b. From the left side, remove the lower steering wheel sound-proofing, the knee bolster (leave bracket attached to bolster), the footwell panel and the A post panel.

c. From the left side, remove the defroster grille, the plastic fusebox screws, the ashtray, the dashboard-to-center console screws, the parking brake-to-console screws (move console rearward) and the lower center console screws (located below the ashtray).

NOTE: Before performing the next procedure, be sure the front wheels are in the straight ahead position.

d. If not an SRS equipped vehicle, remove the steering wheel, the steering wheel adjustment assembly (Allen wrench), the upper steering column cover panels and the steering column combination switch assembly.

e. If an SRS equipped vehicle, remove the steering column adjuster (Allen), the steering column covers, the air bag assembly (Torx), the steering wheel center bolt, the plastic tape label screw from the steering wheel hub (use the lock screw, label attached, to lock the contact reel through the steering wheel hub hole) and lift off the steering wheel. Remove the contact reel and the steering column combination switch assembly.

NOTE: After securing the contact reel, do not turn the steering wheel for it will shear of the contact reel pin.

f. From the left side of the steering column, push out the light switch panel. Remove the small trim mouldings and the light switch.

g. From the right side of the steering column, push out the switch panel. Remove the ECC control panel, the radio console and the small trim moulding.

h. Remove the outer air vent grille by lifting it upwards, grasp it at the bottom and pull it upwards to release it. Remove the instrument panel cover-to-dash screws and the cover.

i. Remove the combined instrument assembly-to-dash screws and the assembly; disconnect any electrical connectors and/or vacuum hoses.

j. From the rear of the dashboard, cut the cable ties.

k. At the dashboard-to-firewall area, turn the retaining clips $1/3$ turn (to release), pull the dash out slightly and pass the fuse box through the opening. Disconnect the cable harnesses from the dashboard and carefully lift it from the vehicle.

4. From the left side of the heater housing, remove the lower duct. Disconnect the vacuum hoses from the diaphrams and the electrical connector. Remove the heater core cover-to-housing screws and the cover.

5. Remove the heater core-to-housing bracket and carefully remove the heater core.

To install:

6. Clean heater housing of all dirt, leaves etc. installation. Install the heater core and the bracket.

7. Install the heater core cover to the housing. Connect the electrical connector and the vacuum hoses. Install the lower duct to the housing assembly.

8. Install the dash by performing the following procedures:

a. Install the dash, connect the cable harnesses, pass the fuse box through the opening. Secure the dash clips by turning them $1/3$ turn.

b. Install the combined instrument assembly to the dash. Install the instrument panel cover and the outer air vent grille.

c. Install the small trim moulding, the radio console, the ECC control panel and the right side switch panel.

d. At the left side of the steering column, install the light switch, the small trim mouldings and the light switch panel.

e. If an SRS equipped vehicle, install the steering column combination switch assembly and the contact reel. Install the steering wheel and remove the lock screw. Install the steering wheel center bolt, the air bag assembly and the steering column adjuster.

f. If not an SRS equipped vehicle, install the steering column combination switch assembly, the steering column covers, the steering wheel adjustment assembly and the steering wheel.

g. At the left side, install the lower center console screw, the parking brake-to-console screws, the dashboard-to-center console screws, the ashtray, the plastic fusebox screws and the defroster grille.

h. At the left side, install the A post panel, the footwell panel, the knee bolster (with bracket) and the lower steering wheel sound-proofing.

i. At the right side, connect the solar sensor electrical connector, install the A post panel, the footwell panel, the glove box and the lower glove box panel.

9. Install the heater core cover plate and connect the heater hoses to the heater core.

10. Refill the cooling system. Connect the negative battery cable.

11. Start the engine, allow it to reach normal operating temperatures. Check the heater operation and the system for leaks.

Evaporator

REMOVAL AND INSTALLATION

240 Series

1. Disconnect the negative battery cable. Recover refrigerant (discharge system) from refrigeration system.

2. Remove the glove box, panel below the glove box and side panel next to heater assembly. Remove the right side defroster vent and duct.

3. Remove the expansion valve. Remove the insulation and evaporator cover assembly.

4. Remove all refrigerant system connections. Cap open fittings immediately. Remove the evaporator assembly.

5. Installation is the reverse of the service removal procedure. Install new evaporator seal (insulation) and O-rings at refrigerant system connections. Evacuate, charge and test refrigerant system. Check system for leaks.

740, 760, 780 and 940 Series

MANUAL LEVER AND AUTOMATIC CLIMATE CONTROL TYPE SYSTEMS

1. Disconnect the negative battery cable.

2. Recover refrigerant (discharge system) from refrigeration system.

3. Remove the glove box and panel below the glove box assembly.

4. Remove all refrigerant system connections. Cap open fittings immediately.

5. Remove the right side instep moulding and panel covering the control unit.

6. Remove the control unit and mounting bracket.

7. Remove all electrical connections and 2 lower screws of fan housing. Remove the evaporator housing cover from the assembly. Remove the evaporator assembly.

To install:

8. Transfer rubber seal and filter to evaporator. Apply sealer to lower casing and position the evaporator in the assembly. Install evaporator housing cover.

9. Reconnect all electrical connections. Position wiring harnness to housing cover.
10. Install control unit and bracket. Install panel and right side instep moulding.
11. Install the glove box and panel below the glove box assembly.
12. Reconnect the negative battery cable. Evacuate, charge and test refrigerant system. Check system for leaks.

760, 780 and 940 Series

ELECTRONIC CLIMATE CONTROL TYPE SYSTEM

1. Disconnect the negative battery cable. Recover refrigerant (discharge system) from refrigeration system.
2. Disconnect the electrical connector and unscrew the receiver/drier from the wheel house.
3. Disconnect the electrical connectors from the firewall. Remove the cover plate and the foam rubber seal.
4. From the right side, remove the lower glove box panel and the glove box.
5. Disconnect the vacuum lines from the tank and remove the evaporator cover. Remove the evaporator assembly from the housing.
6. Installation is the reverse of the service removal procedure. Install new evaporator seal (insulation) and O-rings at refrigerant system connections. Evacuate, charge and test refrigerant system. Check system for leaks.

Refrigerant Lines

REMOVAL AND INSTALLATION

1. Disconnect the negative battery cable. Recover refrigerant (discharge system) from refrigeration system.
2. Remove and replace defective line. Install new O-rings, as required.
3. Reconnect the negative battery cable. Evacuate, charge and test refrigerant system. Check system for leaks.

Manual Control Head

REMOVAL AND INSTALLATION

240 Series

1. Disconnect the negative battery cable.
2. Remove the sound proofing and side panels from both sides of the center dash console.
3. Remove the radio assembly. Remove the center control panel. Position the control assembly as far forward as possible.
4. Remove the lever knob, cable from lever and control assembly.
5. Install is the reverse of the service removal procedure. Adjust cable as necessary.

740, 760, 780 and 940 Series

1. Disconnect the negative battery cable.
2. Remove the trim panel. Remove the control assembly from the dashboard.
3. Disconnect control cable clip, vacuum connections and electrical connections.
4. Install is the reverse of the service removal procedure. Adjust cable, as necessary.

Manual Control Cables

ADJUSTMENT

On all vehicles make sure the air mix shutter assembly touches both end stops when the control cable is moved between **COOL** and **WARM** positions on the the manual control head assembly.

REMOVAL AND INSTALLATION

240 Series

1. Disconnect the negative battery cable.
2. Remove the sound proofing and side panels from both sides of the center dash console.
3. Remove the radio assembly. Remove the center control panel. Postion the control assembly as far forward as possible.
4. Remove the (upper end) cable from lever on the control assembly.
5. Disconnect (lower end) from the unit assembly. Note location and position for correct installation. Remove the control cable.
6. Install is the reverse of the service removal procedure. Adjust cable, as necessary.

740, 760, 780 and 940 Series

1. Disconnect the negative battery cable. Remove the glove box and panel below the glove box assembly.
2. Position the heater control to the **WARM** position.
3. Remove the trim panel. Remove the control assembly from the dashboard. Postion the control assembly as far forward as possible.
4. Remove the (upper end) cable from lever on the control assembly.
5. Disconnect (lower end) from the unit assembly. Note location and position for correct installation. Remove the control cable.
6. Install is the reverse of the service removal procedure. Adjust cable, as necessary.

Electronic Control Head

REMOVAL AND INSTALLATION

740, 760, 780 and 940 Series

PROGRAMMER ASSEMBLY

1. Disconnect the negative battery cable. Remove the panel beneath the glove box and the glove box.
2. Remove the outer panel vents and the air ducts.
3. Disconnect the air mix shutter rod from the programmer assembly.
4. Disconnect the electrical connector from the left side of the programmer assembly.
5. Remove the clips for the vacuum hose connections and disconnect the hoses.
6. Remove the programmer assembly.

To install:

7. Install the programmer assembly.
8. Connect the electrical connector to the left side of the programmer and connect the junction.
9. Install the control rod (air mix rod) and adjust as follows:
   a. Start the engine to obtain vacuum, if necessary.
   b. Set the temperature dial to **MAX HEAT** on the thumbwheel. Pull control rod unyil it reaches end position. Secure rod to programmer assembly.
10. Instal the air ducts and panel vents.
11. Install the glove box unit and the lower panels.
12. Reconnect the negative battery cable. Check system for proper operation.

SENSORS AND SWITCHES

Control Panel Temperature Sensor/ Automatic Climate Control

OPERATION

The purpose of the control panel temperature sensor is to energize the fan motor at temperatures above 64°F. At temperatures below 64°F and if engine temperature is below 93°F, the fan motor will not start. This to to prevent cold air from being blown into the passenger compartment.

TESTING

To test the control panel temperature sensor use a volt-amp meter, check that current only flows through the sensor at temperatures above 65°F and the sensor cuts the current off at temperatures below 65°F.

REMOVAL AND INSTALLATION

1. Disconnect the negative battery cable. Remove the control head panel and pull the control head away from the dash.
2. Disconnect the temperature sensor plug electrical connections.
3. Remove the temperature sensor from control head assembly.
4. Installation is the reverse of the service removal procedure.

Thermal Switch/Automatic Climate Control

OPERATION

The purpose of the thermal switch is to switch on the heater fan at coolant temperatures above 93°F. This is done to prevent cold air from being blown into the passenger compartment before the heater assembly has had time to warm up. It is important that the switch is connected at all times. Otherwise, the heater fan will not operate until the temperature of the passenger compartment reaches 64°F.

TESTING

To test the thermal switch use a volt-amp meter, check that current only flows through the switch at temperatures between 86–104°F and the switch cuts the current off at a temperature of 50°F.

REMOVAL AND INSTALLATION

1. Disconnect the negative battery cable. Drain cooling system.
2. Disconnect electrical connection at switch.
3. Remove the thermal switch from the T connection on the water hose.
4. Installation is the reverse of the service removal procedure. Refill cooling system.

In-Vehicle Temperature Sensor/ Automatic Climate Control

OPERATION

The purpose of the in-vehicle temperature sensor is to monitor the vehicle inside compartment air temperature. The in-vehicle temperature sensor is located behind the glovebox.

TESTING

To test the in-vehicle temperature sensor use a volt-amp meter, check that current passes through the sensor. If not, replace sensor.

REMOVAL AND INSTALLATION

1. Disconnect the negative battery cable. Remove the panel from under the glove box assembly.
2. Remove the glove box unit.
3. Disconnect the air hose and electrical connector from the sensor.
4. Remove the retaining clip and remove the sensor.
5. Installation is the reverse of the service removal procedure.

Ambient Temperature Sensor/ Automatic Climate Control

OPERATION

The purpose of the ambient temperature sensor is to monitor the air temperature (outside air) at the heater assembly. The ambient temperature sensor is located on the heater housing assembly near the fan motor.

TESTING

At 68–73°F (room temperature), with the ignition switch turned **ON**, check the resistance across sensor with an ohmmeter. The resistance must be 30–40 ohms. If the reading is 65–100 ohms, the sensor is defective and must be replaced. The higher the room temperature, the lower the resistance value.

REMOVAL AND INSTALLATION

1. Disconnect the negative battery cable. Remove the panel beneath the glove box and the glove box assembly.
2. Disconnect the sensor electrical connector. Remove the screws and the sensor from housing.
3. Installation is the reverse of the service removal procedure.

Self-Diagnostics/Electronic Climate Control

FAULT TRACING

The ECC system incorporates a self-diagnosis function; faults are indicated by a series of flashing codes when the **A/C** button is depressed. The control unit is programmed to make the best of the situation if a fault is detected. If a fault is detected, the unit ignores the faulty signal and selects and alternative pre-programmed value; it is also designed to prevent the delivery of faulty codes.

A fault(s) is indicated by flashing of the **A/C** button; however, the absence of a fault code is not a guarantee the the system is fault free.

Fault Indication To Driver

The driver is warned of a fault when the ignition switch is turned **ON** and the **A/C** button flashes continually.

Further indication of the fault's seriousness is provided when the engine is started:

1. A serious fault will cause the **A/C** button to flash continously, while the engine is running.
2. A less serious fault will cause the **A/C** button to flash for 20 seconds, after the engine has been started.

Fault Indication To Technician

1. Before requesting a fault, the following conditions must be met.
   a. Start and operate the engine.
   b. Set fan control to **AUTO**.
   c. Set the air distribution control to **VENT**.
   d. Set the temperature control to **MAX COOLING**.
   e. Depress the the recirculation switch and release the **A/C** switch.
2. Focus a strong lamp (not fluorescent tube) on the solar sensor (located on the right side of the dash).

NOTE: If a lamp is not used, a fault code will be displayed, even if the system is fault-free. If a lamp is not used, the ignition switch must be turned OFF before the next request; otherwise, the fault code will still be present.

3. To report a fault code, depress and release the **A/C** button within 5 seconds.

NOTE: The first fault code should be requested within the first 5 seconds after starting the engine; this will allow the self-diagnosis function, time to operate and the voltage to stabilize.

4. Since each fault code consists of 3 digits, they will be displayed as follows:
   a. The first digit is indicated by 1 or 2 flashes.
   b. After an interval, the second digit is indicated by 1–6 flashes.
   c. After another interval, the third digit is indicated by 1–9 flashes.
   d. Assemble the flashed digits into the fault code number.

NOTE: Only 3 fault codes can be stored at a time and only 1 fault code will be reported upon request; perform a number of request to be sure that all potential faults are reported.

5. If several fault codes are present, they will be reported in a rolling manner.
6. When the ignition switch is turned **OFF**, the fault codes will be removed from the memory.

Control Unit Response To Faults

If a fault is present, the control unit ignores the signal and selects a pre-programmed value to make the best of the situation.

SYSTEM DIAGNOSIS

MODE DIAGNOSTIC CHART

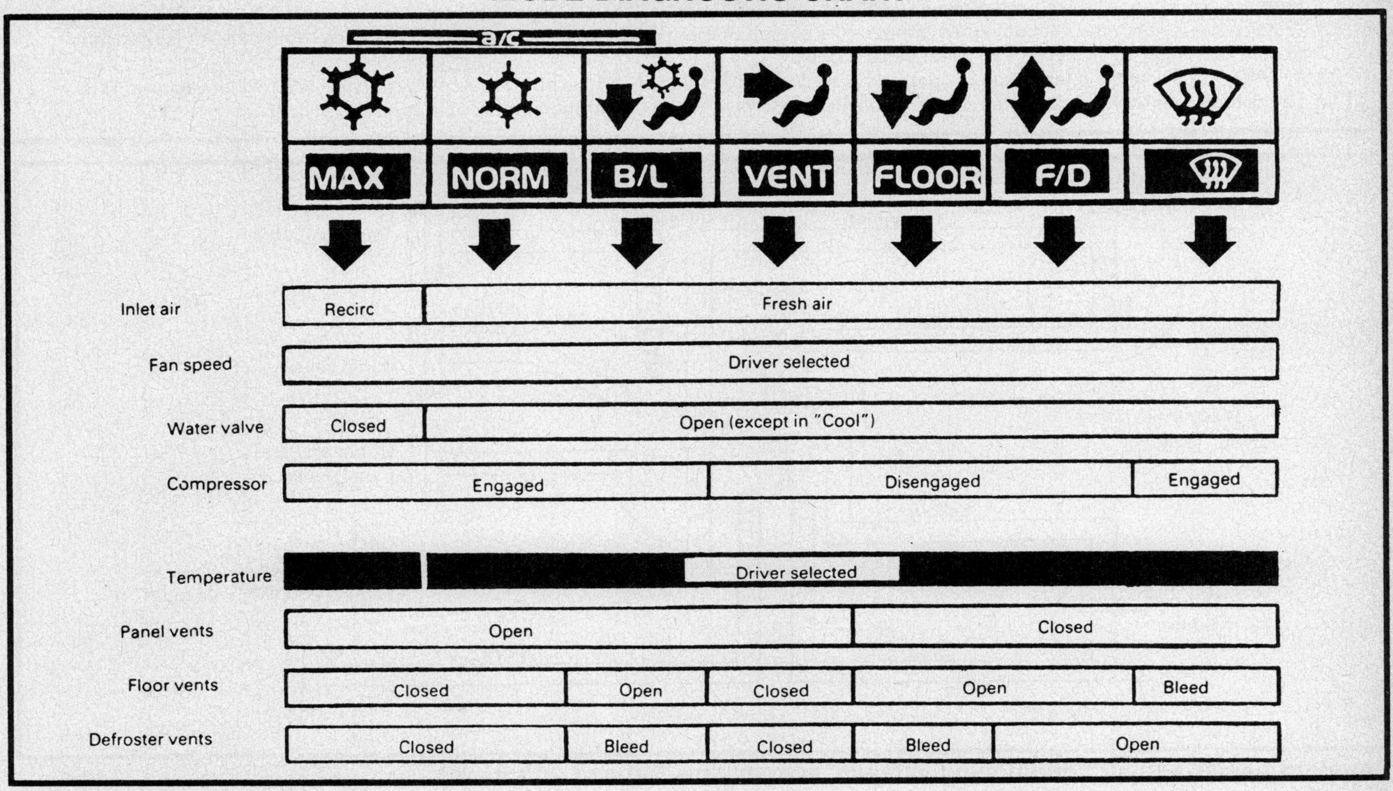
a/c
MAX
NORM
B/L
VENT
FLOOR
F/D
Inlet air
Recirc
Fresh air
Fan speed
Driver selected
Water valve
Closed
Open (except in "Cool")
Compressor
Engaged
Disengaged
Engaged
Temperature
Driver selected
Panel vents
Open
Closed
Floor vents
Closed
Open
Closed
Open
Bleed
Defroster vents
Closed
Bleed
Closed
Bleed
Open

VACUUM FUNCTIONS CHART

Vacuum connection	Connection	MAX	NORM	B/L	VENT	Floor	F/D	DEF
1	Lower shutter for panel vents	Vacuum	Vacuum	Vacuum	Vacuum			
2	Recirculation shutter	Vacuum						
3	Vacuum signal for water valve switch	Closed	Vacuum	Vacuum	Vacuum	Vacuum	Vacuum	Vacuum
5	Floor/defrost[1] shutter supplies air to floor = warm			Vacuum		Vacuum		
6	Floor/defrost shutter supplies air to defroster							Vacuum
7[2]	Water valve	Vacuum[3]						
8[2]	**Source vacuum** supplies vacuum to:	1,2,7,9	1,9	1,5	1,9	5	Closed[1]	6
9	Upper shutter for panel vents	Vacuum	Vacuum		Vacuum			

[1] If shutter is not under vacuum, it is in intermediate position (F/D).
[2] Ports 7 & 8 are connected to each other. The connection is only used in "MAX". Ports 3 to 7 are closed.
[3] Water valve is not under vacuum when temperature control is approx. 10 mm from "Max COOL" or to the right of it. Air is released to port 1 on water valve switch and water valve is open.
If "MAX" is selected and temperature control is at warm, port 3 is closed and the port 7 to 8 connection is placed under vacuum. This closes the water valve and enables cold air to be supplied even though the temperature control is not set at cool.

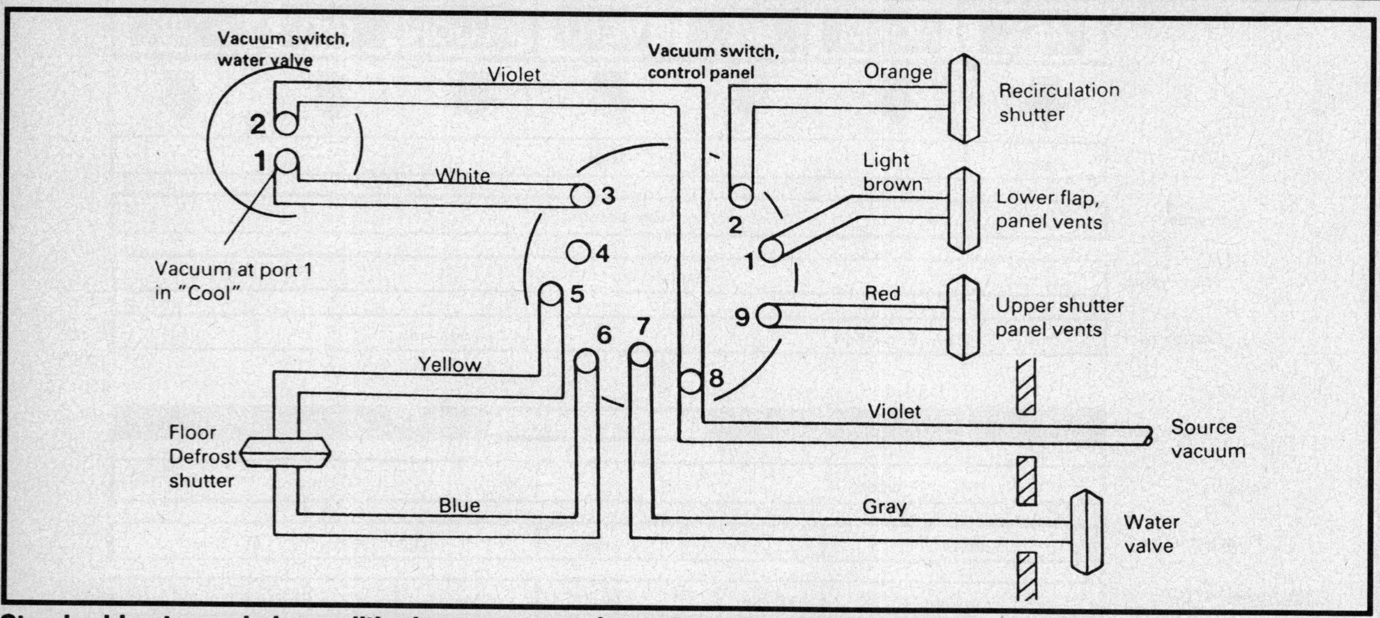
Vacuum switch, water valve
Violet
Vacuum switch, control panel
Orange
Recirculation shutter
2
1
White
3
Light brown
Lower flap, panel vents
4
Vacuum at port 1 in "Cool"
5
Red
9
Upper shutter panel vents
6
7
Yellow
8
Violet
Source vacuum
Floor Defrost shutter
Blue
Gray
Water valve

Standard heater and air conditioning vacuum schematic—700 and 900 Series

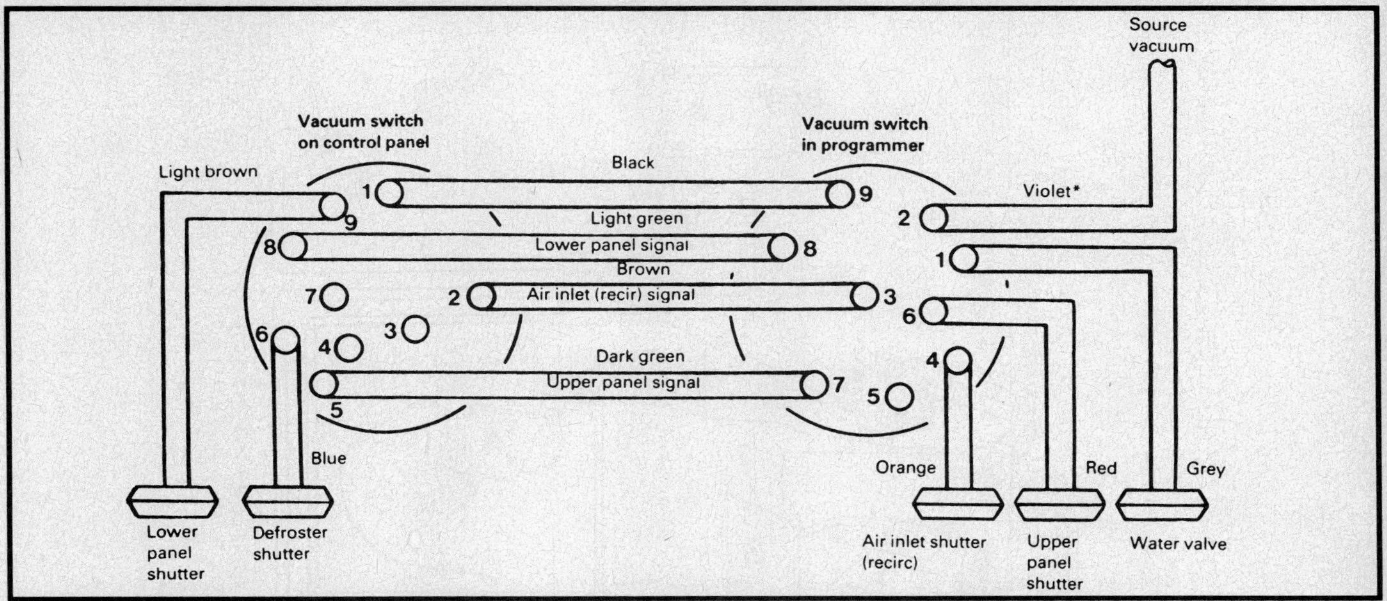
Source vacuum
Vacuum switch on control panel
Vacuum switch in programmer
Light brown
Black
Violet*
Light green
Lower panel signal
Brown
Air inlet (recir) signal
Dark green
Upper panel signal
Blue
Orange
Red
Grey
Lower panel shutter
Defroster shutter
Air inlet shutter (recirc)
Upper panel shutter
Water valve

Automatic climate control heater and air conditioning vacuum schematic—700 and 900 Series

MODE DIAGNOSTIC CHART-AUTOMATIC CLIMATE CONTROL

	0 OFF	ECON	LO	auto aut ●	HI	B/L	
Inlet air	Fresh air			Fresh air of recirc		Fresh air	
Fan speed	Low	Programmed	Low	Programmed	High	Programmed	High
Water valve	Open	Programmed (open or closed)				Open	
Compressor	Disengaged		Engaged				
Temperature	Operator selected						
Panel vents	Closed	Position of vents depends on: – Ambient air temp – In car temp – Temperature dial setting				Open	Closed
Floor vents	Open					Open	Bleed
Defroster vents	Bleed					Bleed	Open
Fan delay	Yes						No

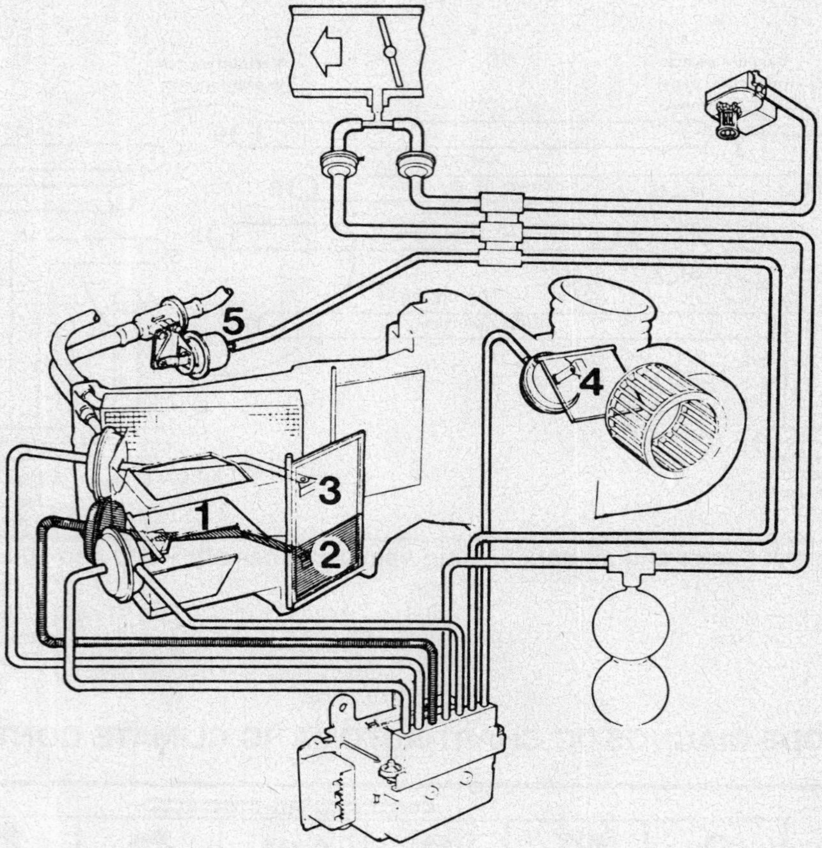
5
4
3
1
2

Vacuum functions

Component	Vacuum hose	Vacuum on	Vacuum off
5 Water valve	Grey	Closed (cold)	Open (warm)
4 Recirculation shutter	Orange	Recirculation	Outside air
3 Vent shutter	Red	Open, also operates bilevel shutter mechanically	Closed
2 Bi-level shutter	Transparent/ beige	Open	Closed
1 Defroster	Blue	Shutter in lower position	Middle* position
1 Floor shutter	Yellow	Shutter in upper position	Middle **

* In upper position if floor duct is under vacuum

** In lower position if defroster duct is under vacuum

Electronic climate control heater and air conditioning vacuum schematic—700 and 900 Series

FAULT CODE DIAGNOSTIC CHART-ELECTRONIC CLIMATE CONTROL

Faults and fault codes

Note: Fault may be caused by defective component or the wiring

Fault	Code	Fault class*
Outside temperature sensor (on fan casing)	121	A
– Short-circuit to ground	121	A
– Open-circuit or short-circuit to +12 V	122	A
Interior temperature sensor (in roof light)		
– Short-circuit to ground	131	A
– Open-circuit or short-circuit to +12 V	132	A
Water temperature sensor (beside heat exchanger)		
– Short-circuit to ground	141	M
– Open-circuit or short-circuit to +12 V	142	M
Alternator		
– D+signal level fault in alternator	151	A
Solar sensor (in loudspeaker grille)	161	I
N.B. Illuminate the device with a lamp, otherwise the fault will be reported even if the sensor is intact.		
Servo motor/potentiometer		
– Open-circuit or short-circuit to ground	211	A
– Short-circuit to +12 V	212	A
Servo motor drive		
– Pin 17 or 18 incorrectly connected to +12 V supply	213	A
Servo motor		
– Failure to operate within 10 s (due to seizure of arm or interruption in electrical supply)	214	A
ECC controls		
– Faulty temperature control	231	A
Fan motor		
– Starting current excessive (motor runs sluggishly or seizes)	233	A
Power unit		
– Incorrect connection of +12 V supply		
Output affected:		
Water valve	241	A
Bi-level (B/L)	242	A
Vent	243	A
Rec	244	A
Defroster	245	A
Floor	246	A
Fan, max. speed relay	247	A
Compressor	248	A
Radiator fan relay	249	A
Fault-free	111	

* Fault class: A = serious fault
M = less serious fault
I = no fault indication to driver

WIRINGS SCHEMATICS

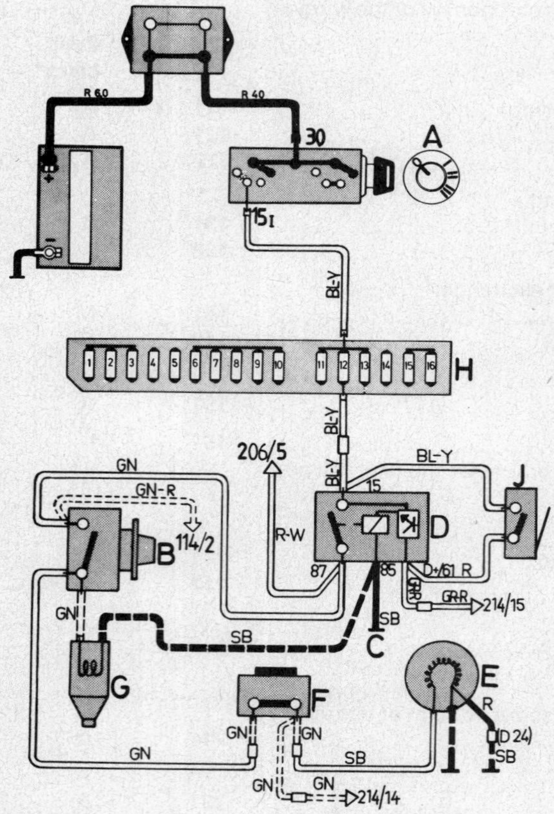
R 60
R 40
30
A
15I
BL-Y
H
BL-Y
206/5
GN
GN-R
114/2
B
R-W
BL-Y
15
BL-Y
D
J
87
85
D+/61 R
GR-R
214/15
SB
C
GN
SB
G
F
E
R
GN
GN
GN
SB
D 24
SB
GN
GN
214/14

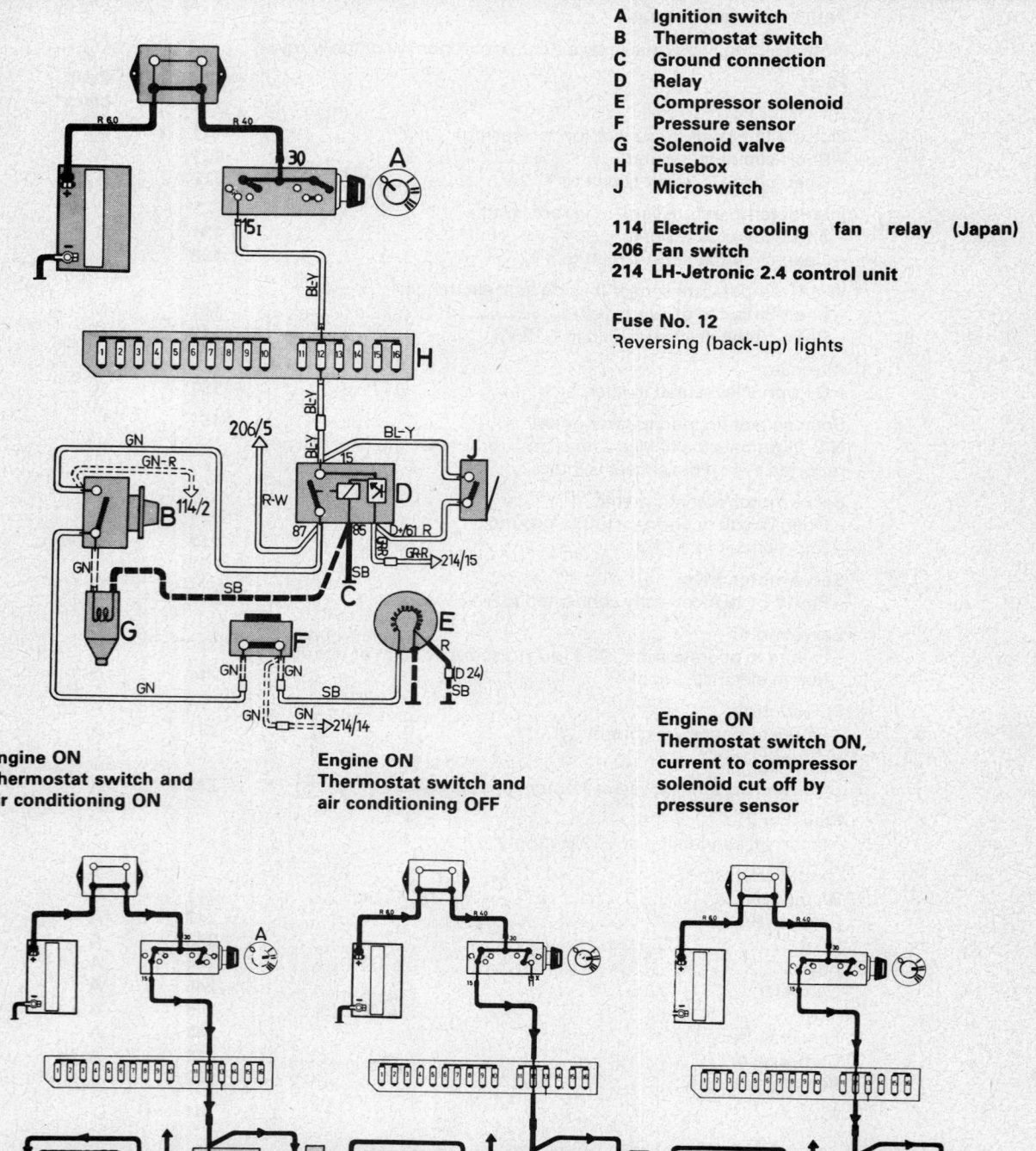

A Ignition switch
B Thermostat switch
C Ground connection
D Relay
E Compressor solenoid
F Pressure sensor
G Solenoid valve
H Fusebox
J Microswitch

114 Electric cooling fan relay (Japan)
206 Fan switch
214 LH-Jetronic 2.4 control unit

Fuse No. 12
Reversing (back-up) lights

Engine ON
Thermostat switch and air conditioning ON

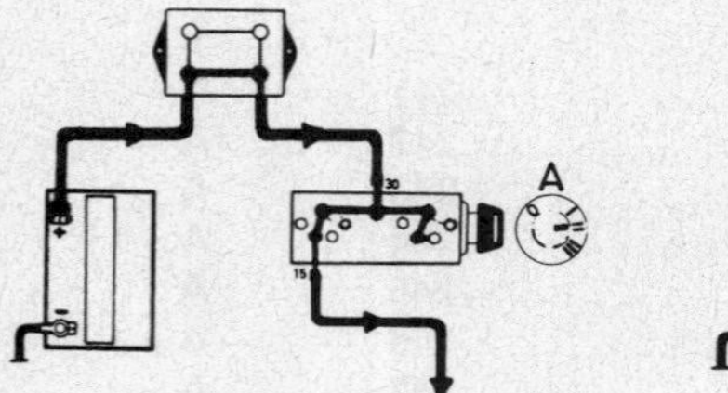

Engine ON
Thermostat switch and air conditioning OFF

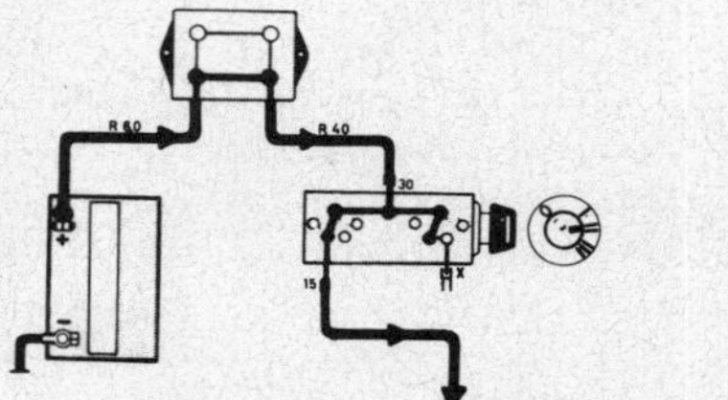

Engine ON
Thermostat switch ON, current to compressor solenoid cut off by pressure sensor

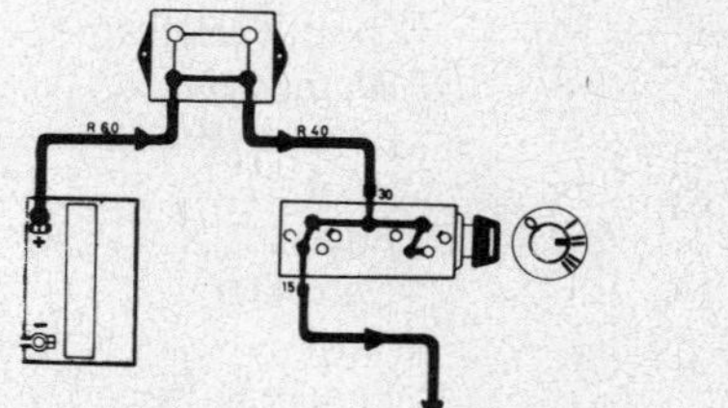

Air conditioning wiring schematic—240 Series

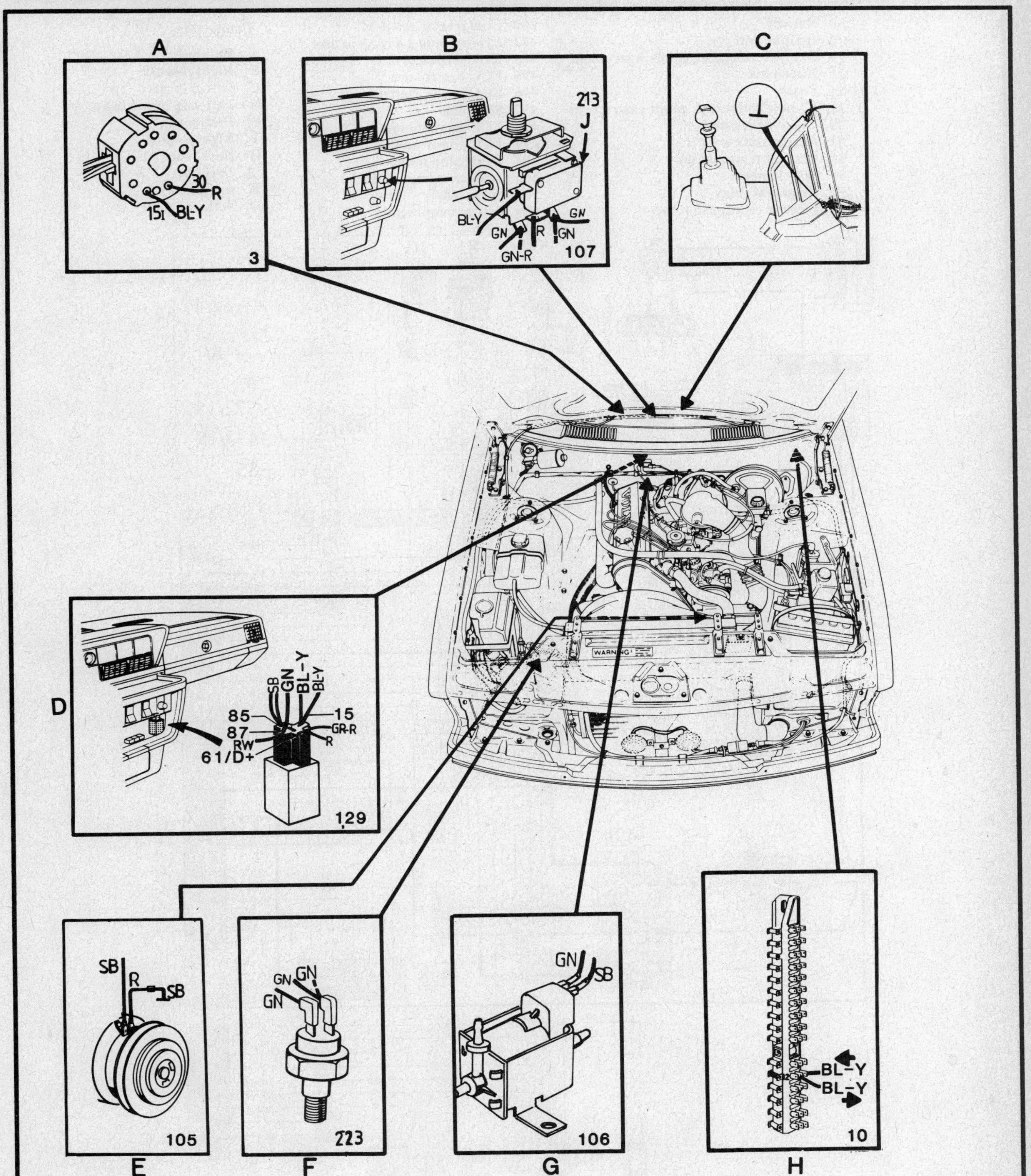
A
30
R
15I
BL-Y
3
B
213
J
BL-Y
GN
GN
R
GN
GN-R
107
C
D
SB
GN
BL-Y
BL-Y
85
15
87
GR-R
RW
R
61/D+
129
SB
R
SB
105
E
GN
GN
GN
223
F
GN
SB
106
G
BL-Y
BL-Y
10
H

Air conditioning component locations—240 Series

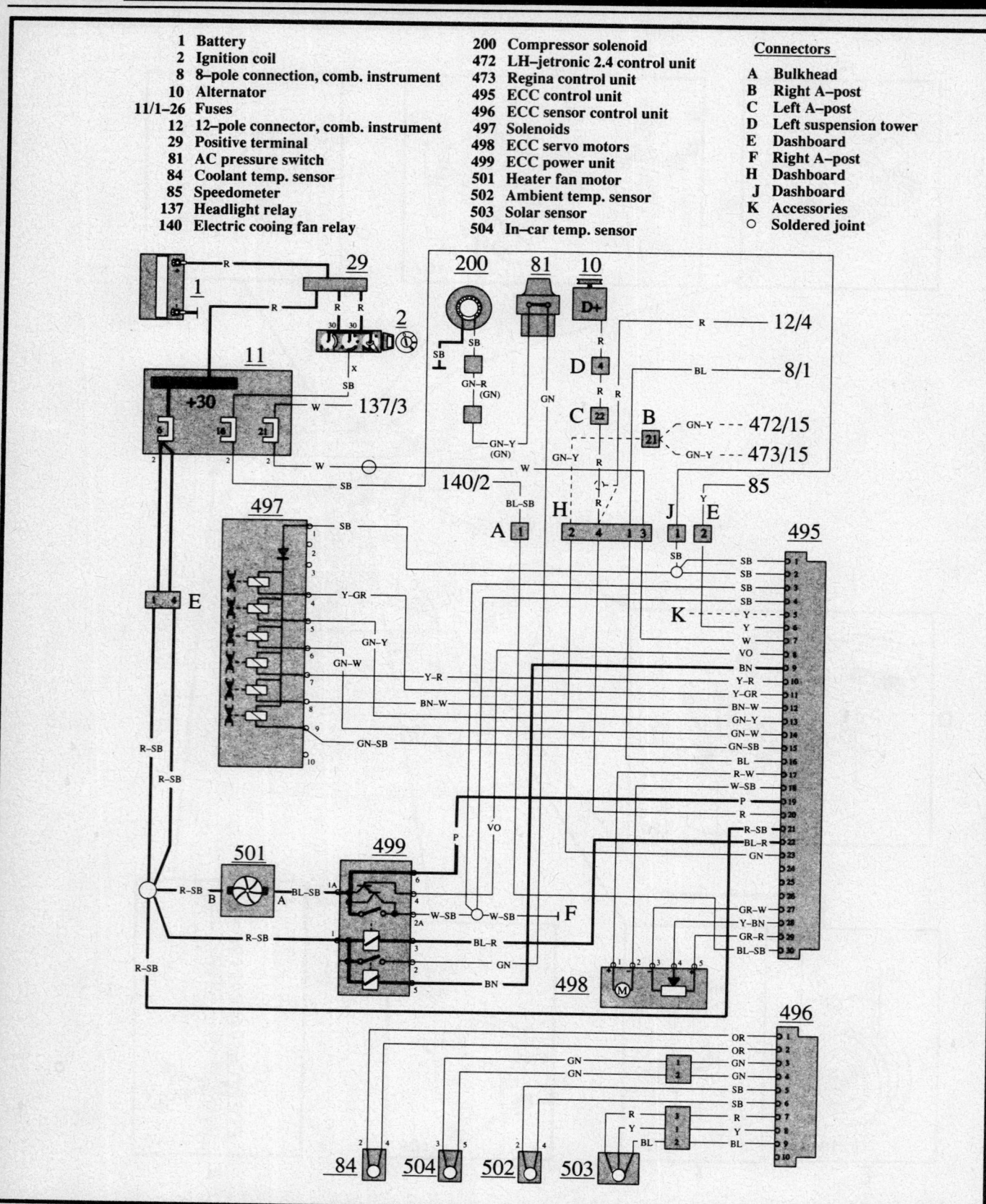

1 Battery
2 Ignition coil
8 8–pole connection, comb. instrument
10 Alternator
11/1–26 Fuses
12 12–pole connector, comb. instrument
29 Positive terminal
81 AC pressure switch
84 Coolant temp. sensor
85 Speedometer
137 Headlight relay
140 Electric cooing fan relay
200 Compressor solenoid
472 LH–jetronic 2.4 control unit
473 Regina control unit
495 ECC control unit
496 ECC sensor control unit
497 Solenoids
498 ECC servo motors
499 ECC power unit
501 Heater fan motor
502 Ambient temp. sensor
503 Solar sensor
504 In–car temp. sensor

Connectors

A Bulkhead
B Right A–post
C Left A–post
D Left suspension tower
E Dashboard
F Right A–post
H Dashboard
J Dashboard
K Accessories
○ Soldered joint

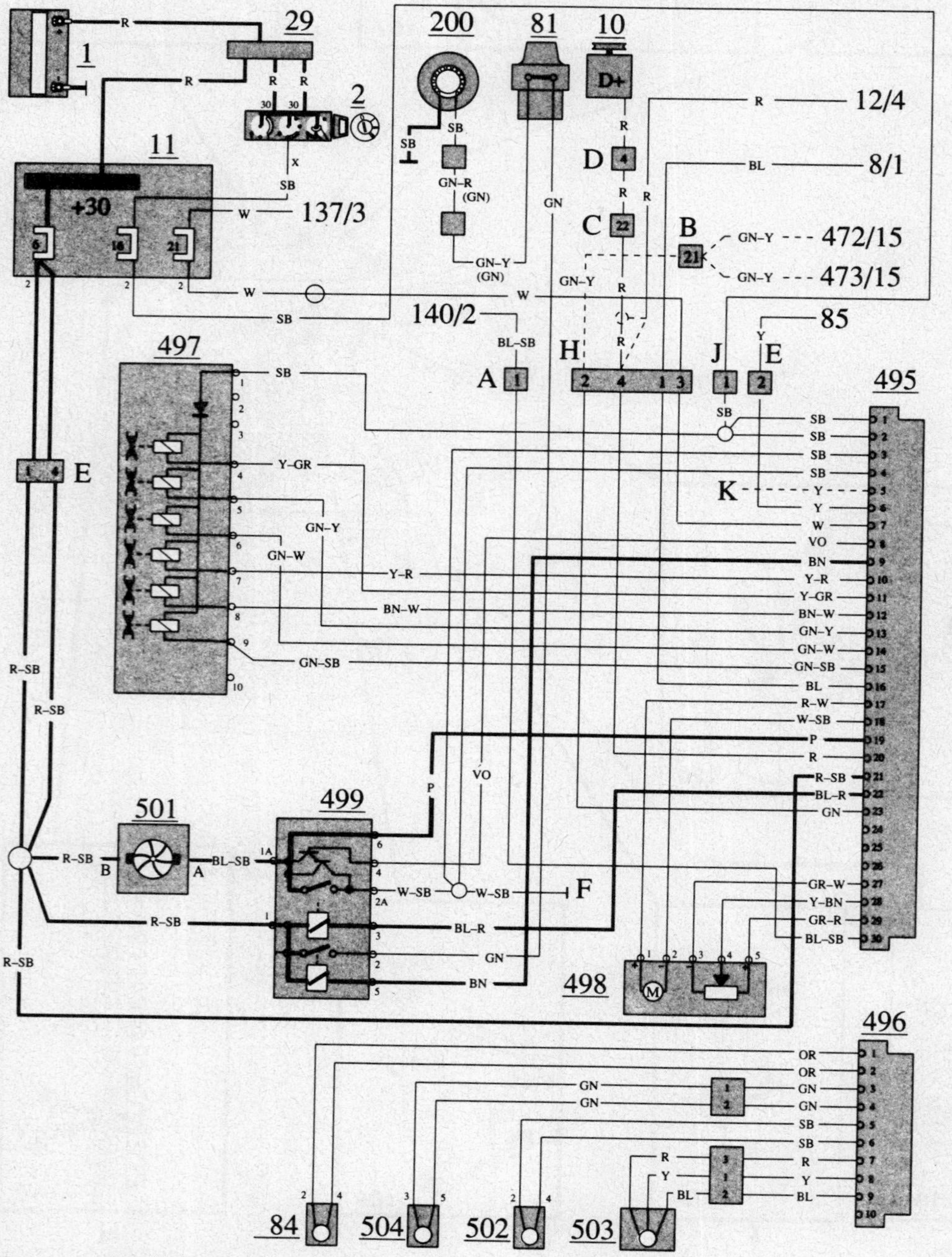
1
29
2
11
+30
137/3
200
81
10
D+
12/4
8/1
472/15
473/15
140/2
85
497
495
496
498
499
501
84
504
502
503
A
B
C
D
E
F
H
J
K
R
SB
W
GN–R
(GN)
GN–Y
GN
BL
BL–SB
Y
Y–GR
GN–W
Y–R
BN–W
GN–SB
R–SB
BL–R
BN
VO
P
W–SB
R–W
GR–W
Y–BN
GR–R
OR

Electronic climate control wiring schematic—740 Series

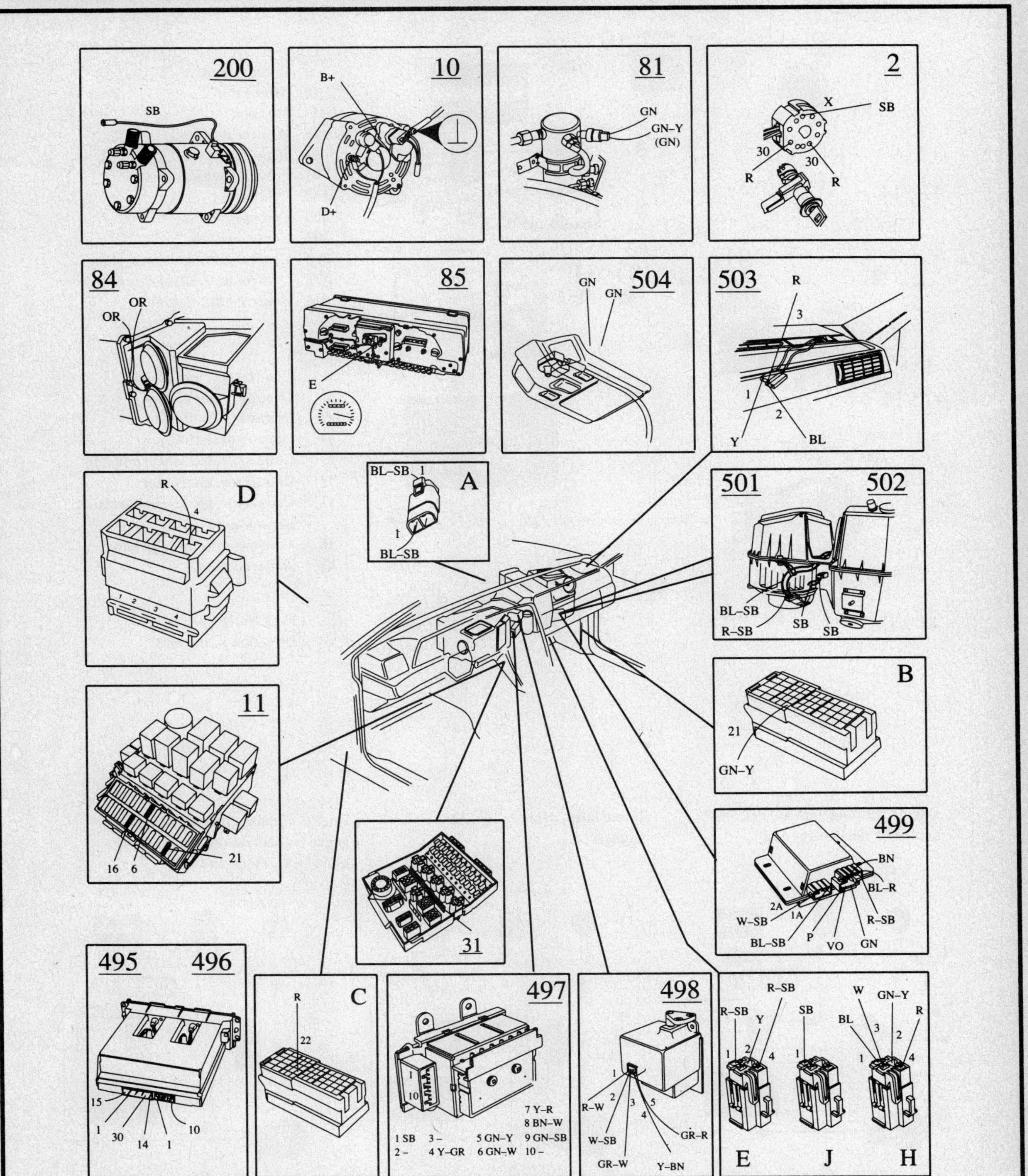
200
SB
10
B+
D+
81
GN
GN–Y
(GN)
2
X
SB
30
R
30
R
84
OR
OR
85
E
504
GN
GN
503
R
3
1
2
Y
BL
D
R
4
1 2 3 4
A
BL–SB 1
1
BL–SB
501
502
BL–SB
R–SB
SB
SB
B
21
GN–Y
11
16 6
21
31
499
BN
BL–R
2A
W–SB
1A
R–SB
BL–SB
P
VO
GN
495
496
15
1
30
14
1
10
C
R
22
497
1
10
7 Y–R
8 BN–W
1 SB
3 –
5 GN–Y
9 GN–SB
2 –
4 Y–GR
6 GN–W
10 –
498
1
R–W
2
3
5
4
W–SB
GR–R
GR–W
Y–BN
R–SB
R–SB
Y
1
2
4
SB
1
W
GN–Y
BL
3
2
R
1
4
E
J
H

Electronic climate control component locations – 740 Series

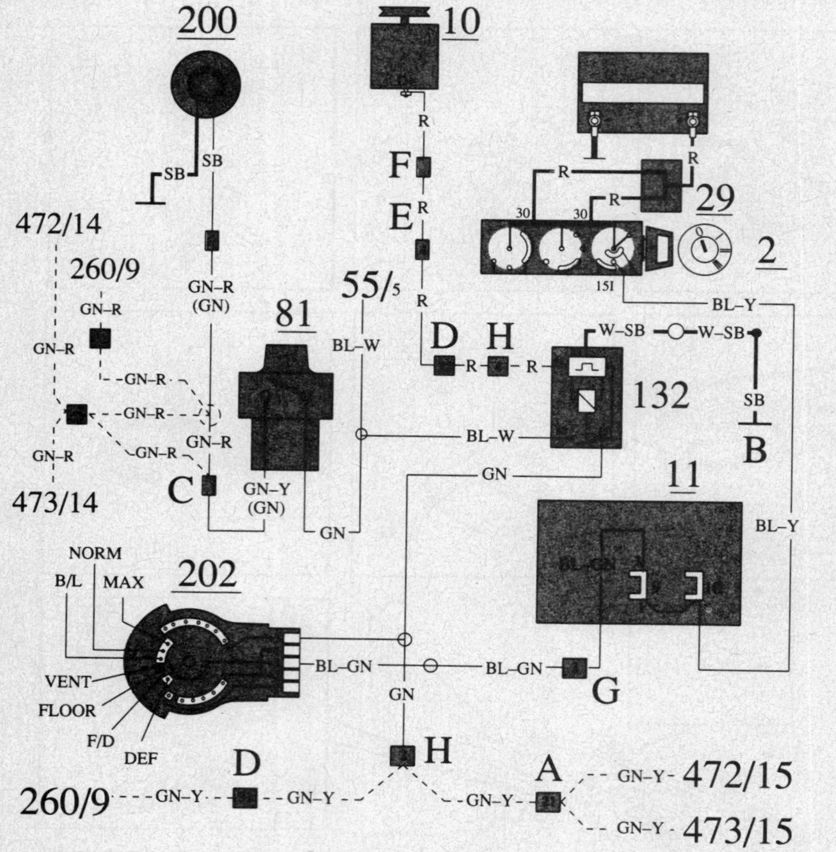
200
10
SB
SB
R
F
R
E
R
30
30
R
R
29
2
472/14
260/9
GN–R
GN–R (GN)
55/5
81
BL–W
D
H
R
R
W–SB
W–SB
132
SB
B
GN–R
GN–R
GN–R
GN–R
GN–R
GN–R
GN–R
BL–W
473/14
C
GN–Y (GN)
GN
GN
11
BL–Y
BL–Y
BL–GN
NORM
B/L
MAX
202
VENT
FLOOR
F/D
DEF
BL–GN
BL–GN
GN
G
H
D
A
260/9
GN–Y
GN–Y
GN–Y
GN–Y
472/15
GN–Y
473/15

2 Ignition switch
10 Alternator
11 Fusebox
29 Positive terminal
55 Heater fan switch
81 Pressure sensor
132 Delay relay
200 Compressor
202 Control panel
260 Control unit, ignition system
472 Control unit, LH–jetronic 2.4
473 Control unit, Regina

A Connector, right A–post
B Ground, right A–post
C Connector, bulkhead
D Connector, left A–post
E Connector, left wheel housing
F Connector, alternator
G Connector, glove compartment, large 4–pole
H 4–pole connector, glovebox
○ Soldered joint

Fuse No. 9
Direction indicators

Engine running, but AC disconnected by delay relay 132

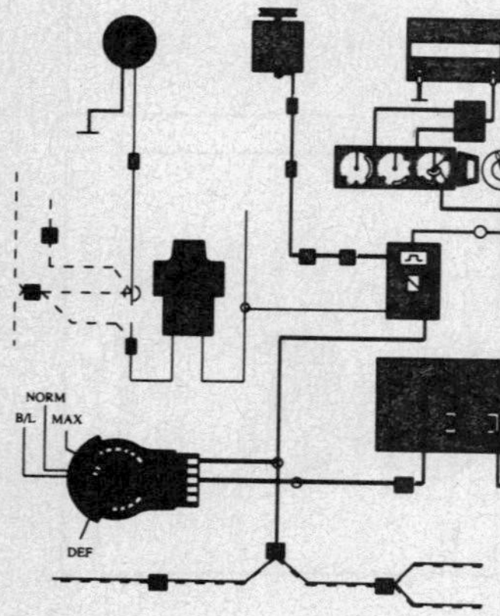
NORM
B/L
MAX
DEF

10 sec later, delay relay 132 engages AC

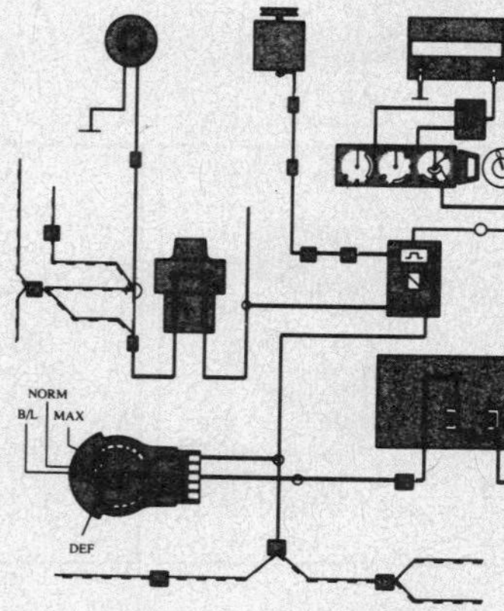
NORM
B/L
MAX
DEF

Engine running, but AC disengaged by control (202) in positions Vent, Floor and F/D

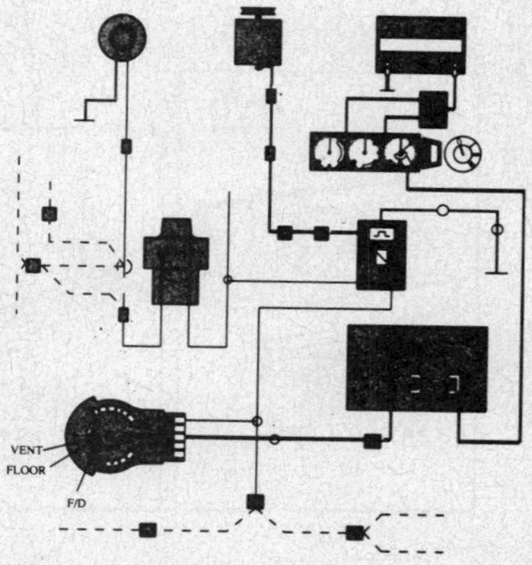
VENT
FLOOR
F/D

Air conditioning wiring schematic—740 Series

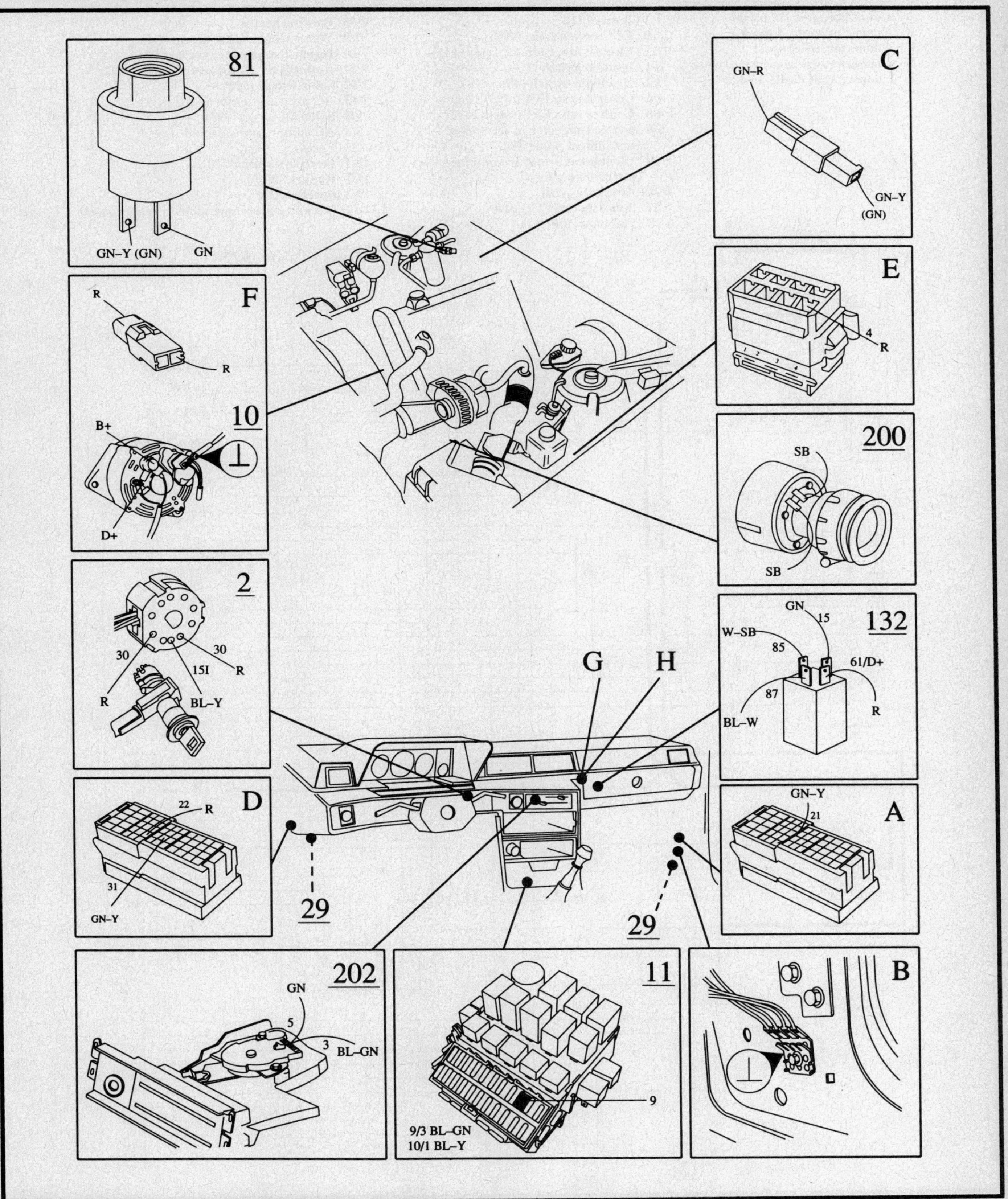
81
GN–Y (GN)
GN
C
GN–R
GN–Y
(GN)
F
R
R
10
B+
D+
E
4
R
200
SB
SB
2
30
30
15I
R
R
BL–Y
132
GN
15
W–SB
85
61/D+
87
R
BL–W
G
H
D
22
R
31
GN–Y
29
29
A
GN–Y
21
202
GN
5
3
BL–GN
11
9
9/3 BL–GN
10/1 BL–Y
B

Air conditioning component locations—740 Series

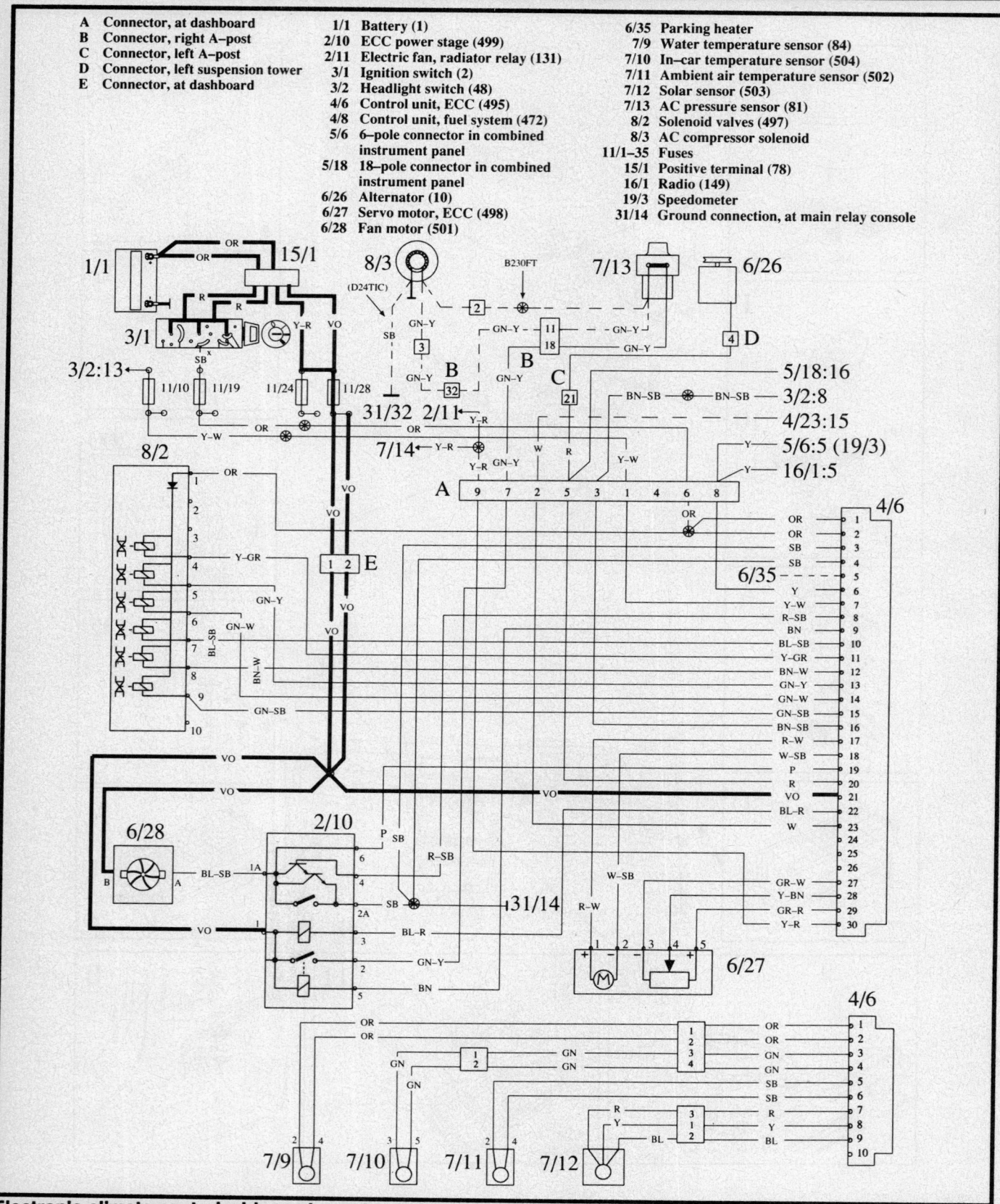

- A Connector, at dashboard
- B Connector, right A–post
- C Connector, left A–post
- D Connector, left suspension tower
- E Connector, at dashboard

- 1/1 Battery (1)
- 2/10 ECC power stage (499)
- 2/11 Electric fan, radiator relay (131)
- 3/1 Ignition switch (2)
- 3/2 Headlight switch (48)
- 4/6 Control unit, ECC (495)
- 4/8 Control unit, fuel system (472)
- 5/6 6–pole connector in combined instrument panel
- 5/18 18–pole connector in combined instrument panel
- 6/26 Alternator (10)
- 6/27 Servo motor, ECC (498)
- 6/28 Fan motor (501)

- 6/35 Parking heater
- 7/9 Water temperature sensor (84)
- 7/10 In–car temperature sensor (504)
- 7/11 Ambient air temperature sensor (502)
- 7/12 Solar sensor (503)
- 7/13 AC pressure sensor (81)
- 8/2 Solenoid valves (497)
- 8/3 AC compressor solenoid
- 11/1–35 Fuses
- 15/1 Positive terminal (78)
- 16/1 Radio (149)
- 19/3 Speedometer
- 31/14 Ground connection, at main relay console

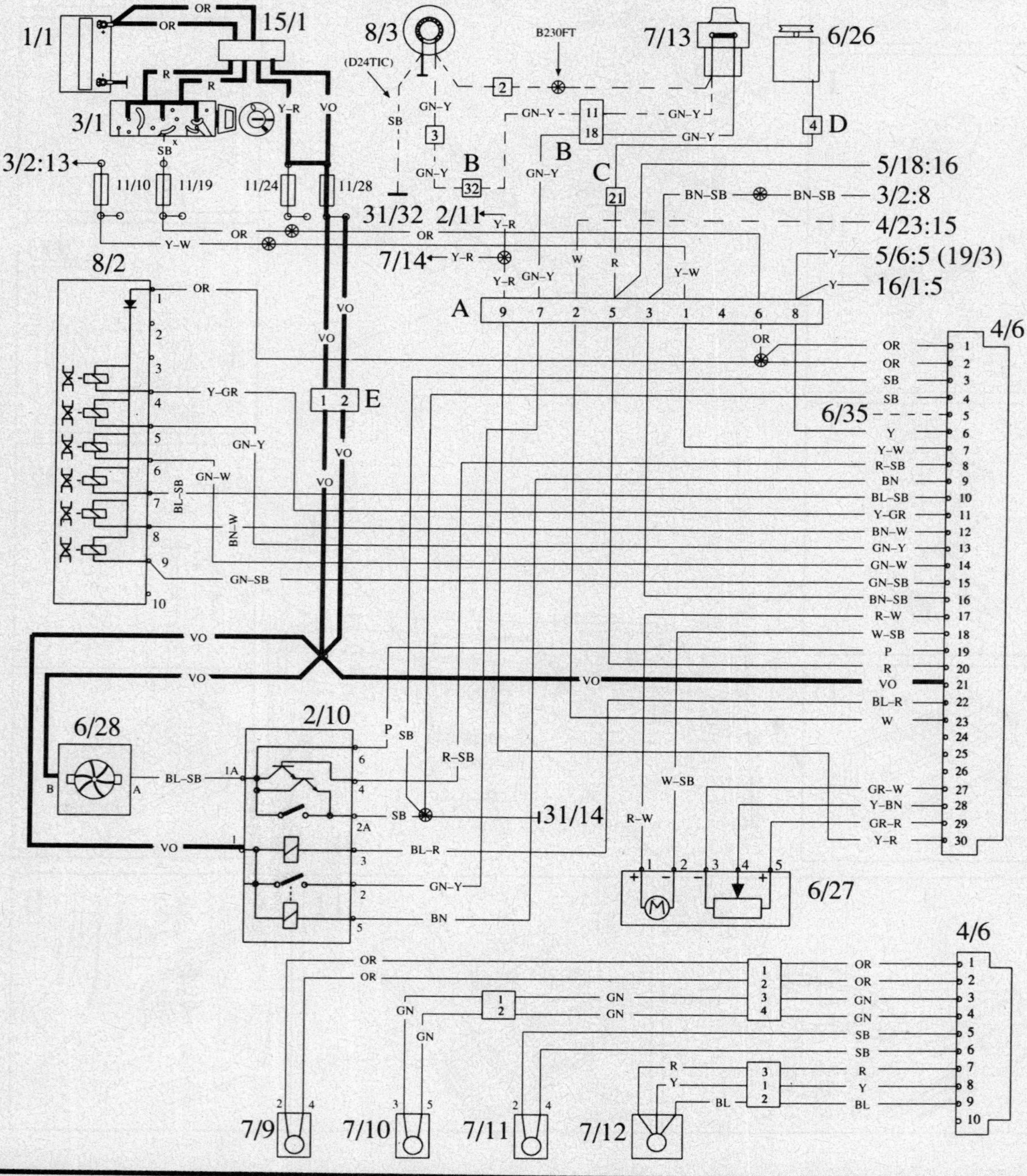
1/1
15/1
3/1
3/2:13
8/3
(D24TIC)
B230FT
7/13
6/26
D
B
C
5/18:16
3/2:8
4/23:15
5/6:5 (19/3)
16/1:5
31/32
2/11
7/14
8/2
A
4/6
E
6/35
6/28
2/10
31/14
6/27
7/9
7/10
7/11
7/12

Electronic climate control wiring schematic—760 Series

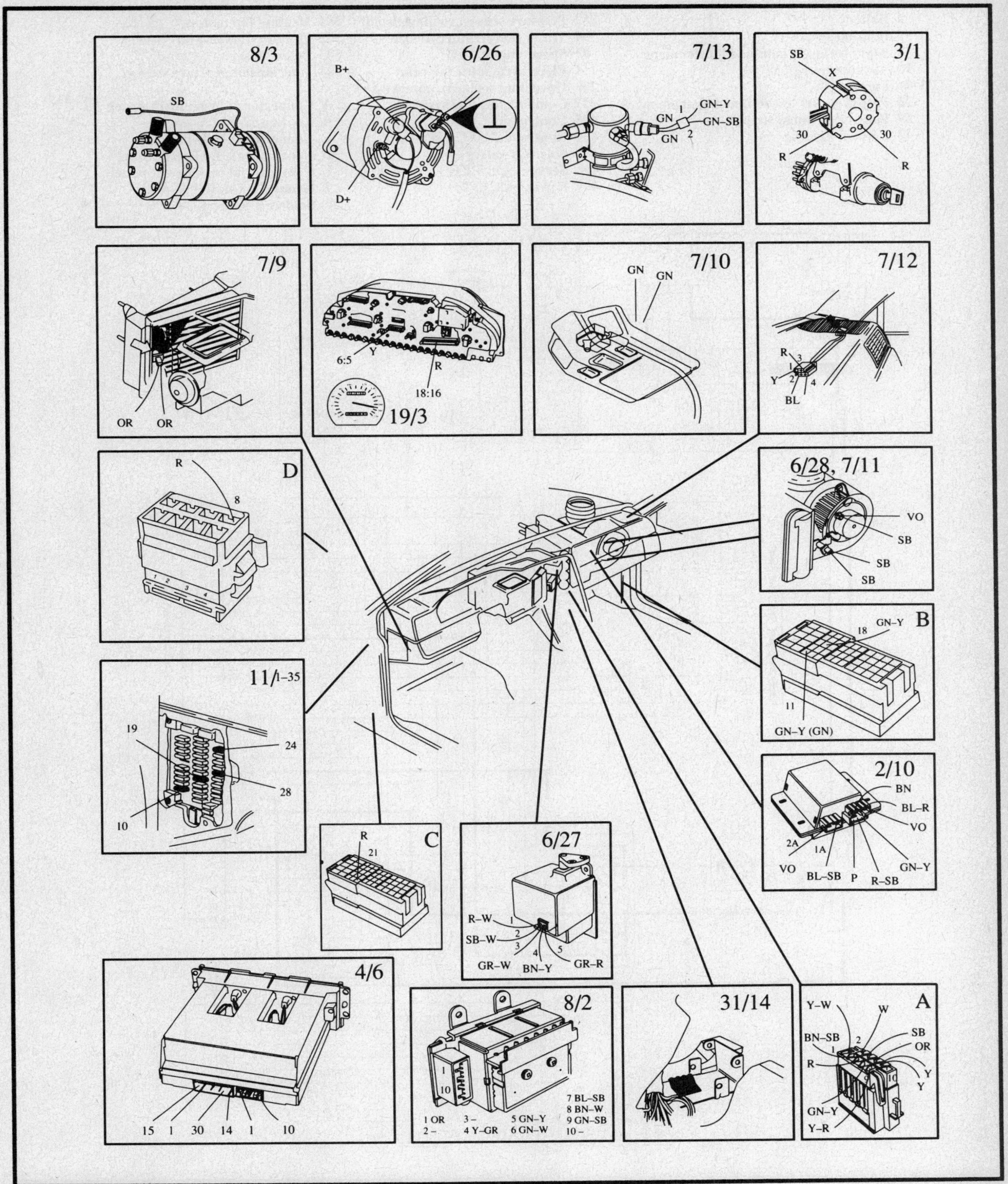
8/3
SB
6/26
B+
D+
7/13
GN–Y
GN
GN–SB
GN
1
2
3/1
SB
X
30
30
R
R
7/9
OR
OR
6:5
Y
R
18:16
19/3
7/10
GN
GN
7/12
R
3
1
Y
2
4
BL
D
R
8
1
2
3
4
6/28, 7/11
VO
SB
SB
SB
B
GN–Y
18
11
GN–Y (GN)
11/1–35
19
24
28
10
2/10
BN
BL–R
VO
2A
1A
VO
BL–SB
P
R–SB
GN–Y
C
R
21
6/27
R–W
1
SB–W
2
3
GR–W
4
BN–Y
5
GR–R
4/6
15
1
30
14
1
10
8/2
1
10
1 OR
2 –
3 –
4 Y–GR
5 GN–Y
6 GN–W
7 BL–SB
8 BN–W
9 GN–SB
10 –
31/14
A
Y–W
W
BN–SB
1
2
SB
OR
R
10
Y
Y
GN–Y
Y–R

Electronic climate control component locations – 760 Series

1 Battery
2 Ignition switch
8 8–pin socket in combined instrument
10 Alternator
11/1–26 Fuses
12 12–pin socket in combined instrument
29 Positive terminal strip
42 Control lighting

81 Pressure sensor, cooling circuit
84 Water temperature sensor
85 Speedometer
131 Electric radiator fan relay
200 Operating solenoid, compressor
217 Control unit, fuel system
495 Control unit, ECC
496 Control unit, ECC sensor
497 Solenoid valves
498 Servomotor, ECC
499 Power unit, ECC

501 Heating fan motor
502 Outdoor temperature sensor
503 Solar sensor
504 Interior temperature sensor

A Connector at instrument panel
B Connector, RH A–post
C Connector, LH A–post
D Connector, LH wheel housing
E Connector at instrument panel
F Ground point, RH A–post
○ Soldered connection

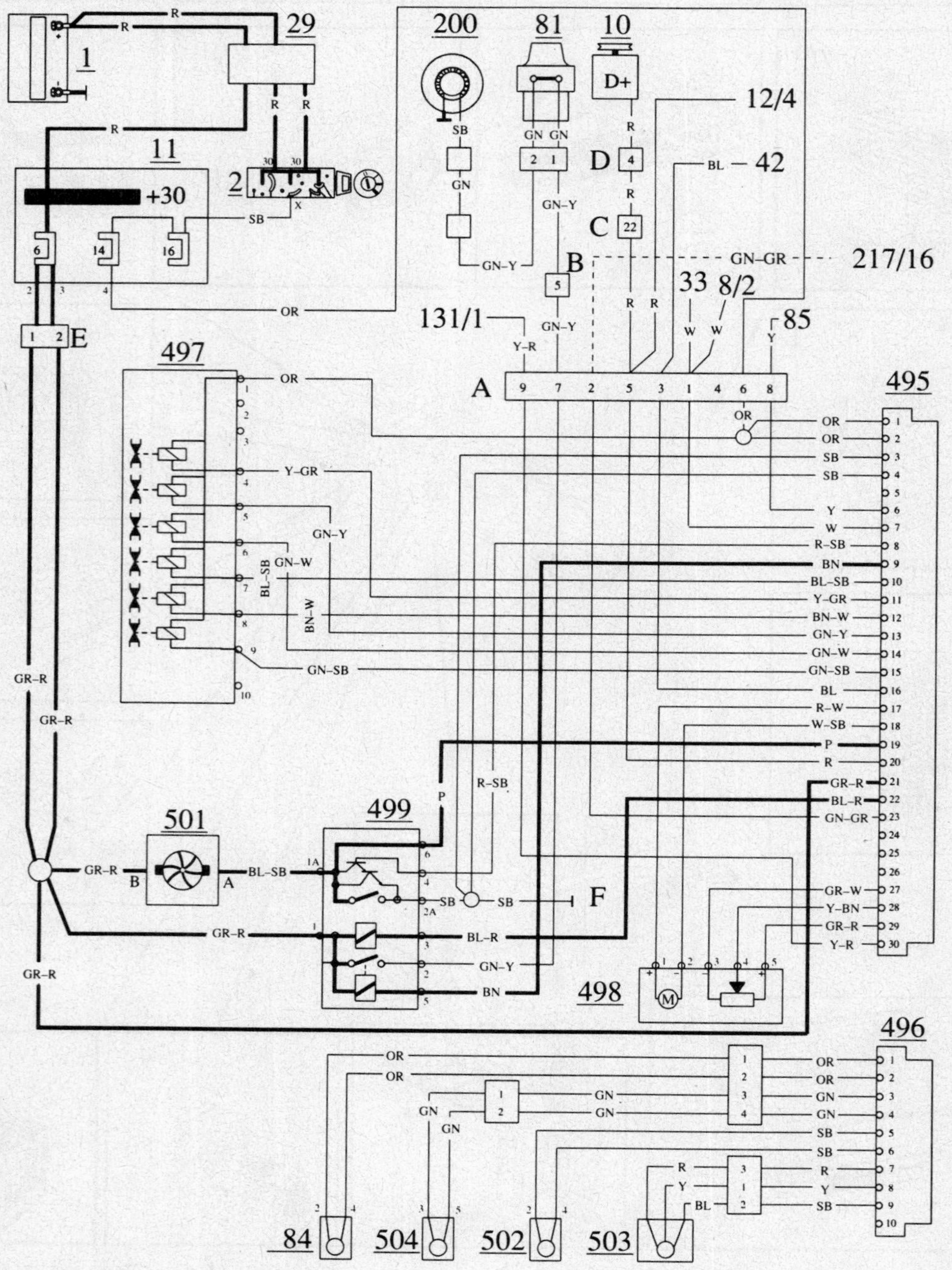
1
29
11
+30
2
200
81
10
D+
12/4
42
217/16
131/1
33
8/2
85
497
495
499
501
498
496
84
504
502
503
A
B
C
D
E
F

Electronic climate control wiring schematic—780 Series

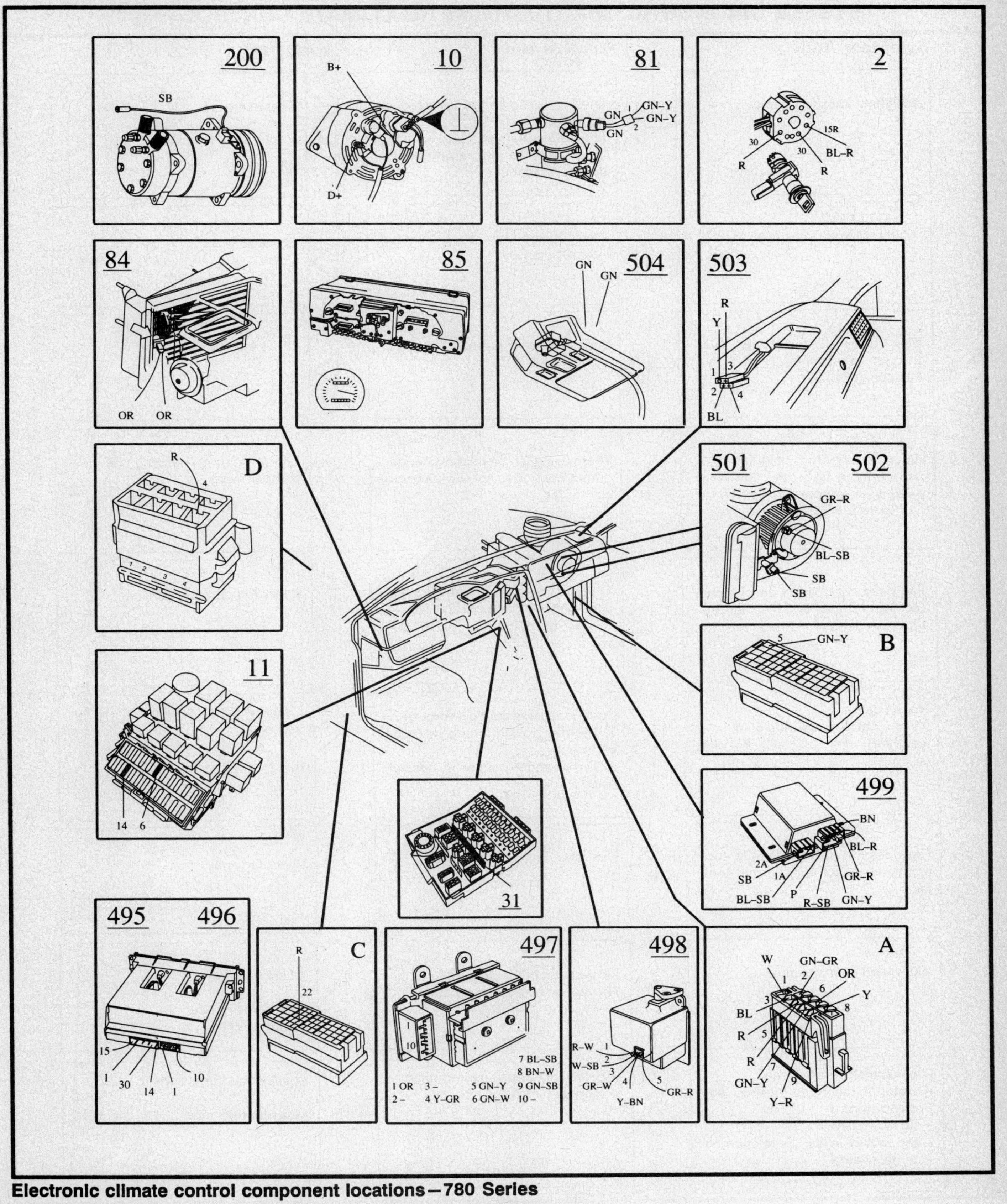
200
SB
10
B+
D+
81
GN
GN-Y
2
84
OR
85
504
503
R
Y
3
4
BL
D
501
502
GR-R
BL-SB
11
14
6
B
5
499
BN
BL-R
2A
SB
1A
BL-SB
P
R-SB
GN-Y
31
495
496
15
30
10
C
22
497
7 BL-SB
8 BN-W
1 OR
3 –
5 GN-Y
9 GN-SB
2 –
4 Y-GR
6 GN-W
10 –
498
R-W
W-SB
GR-W
Y-BN
A
W
GN-GR
OR
BL
Y-R

Electronic climate control component locations—780 Series

SYSTEM DIAGNOSTIC CHART-AUTOMATIC CLIMATE CONTROL

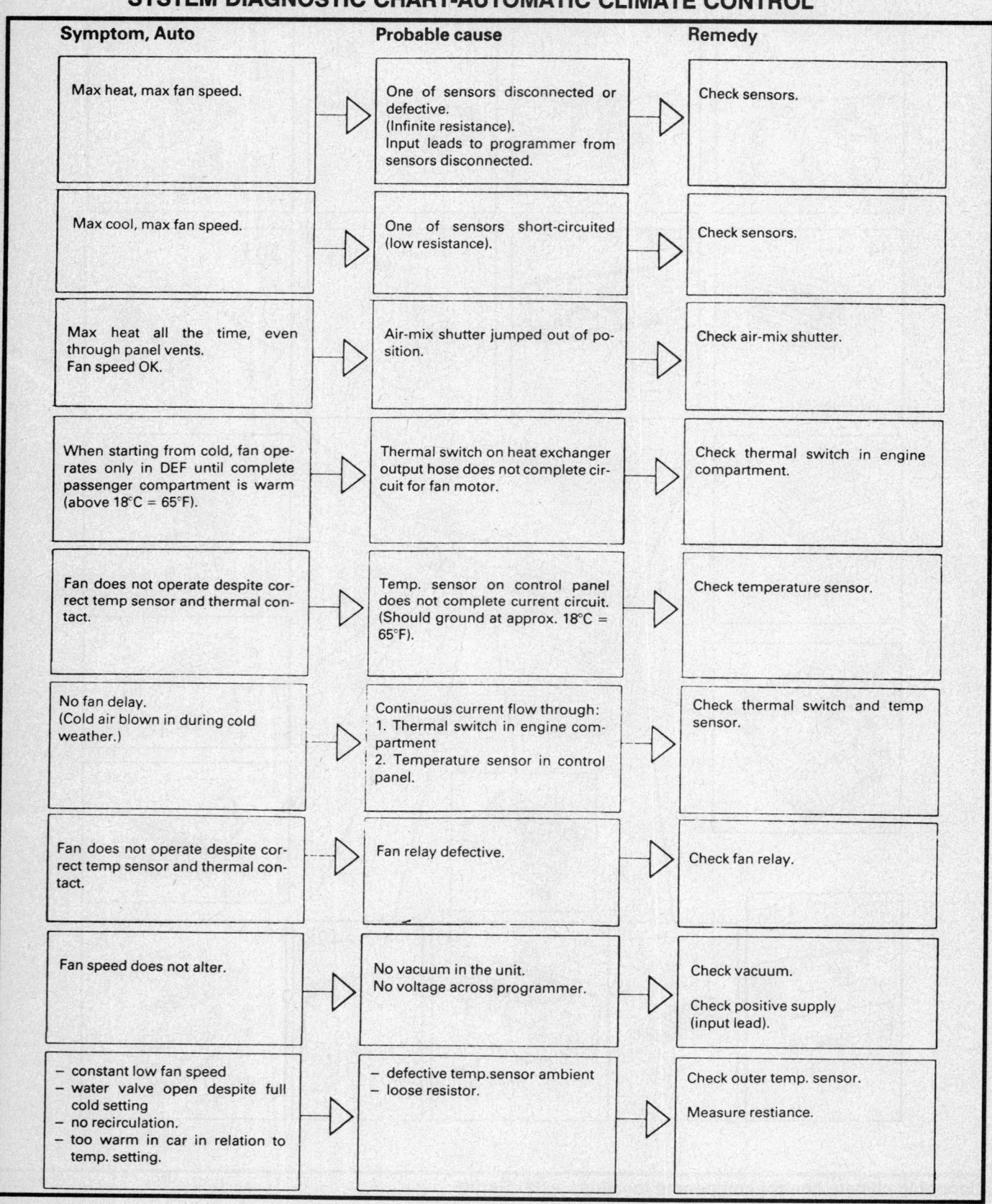

Symptom, Auto	Probable cause	Remedy
Max heat, max fan speed.	One of sensors disconnected or defective. (Infinite resistance). Input leads to programmer from sensors disconnected.	Check sensors.
Max cool, max fan speed.	One of sensors short-circuited (low resistance).	Check sensors.
Max heat all the time, even through panel vents. Fan speed OK.	Air-mix shutter jumped out of position.	Check air-mix shutter.
When starting from cold, fan operates only in DEF until complete passenger compartment is warm (above 18°C = 65°F).	Thermal switch on heat exchanger output hose does not complete circuit for fan motor.	Check thermal switch in engine compartment.
Fan does not operate despite correct temp sensor and thermal contact.	Temp. sensor on control panel does not complete current circuit. (Should ground at approx. 18°C = 65°F).	Check temperature sensor.
No fan delay. (Cold air blown in during cold weather.)	Continuous current flow through: 1. Thermal switch in engine compartment 2. Temperature sensor in control panel.	Check thermal switch and temp sensor.
Fan does not operate despite correct temp sensor and thermal contact.	Fan relay defective.	Check fan relay.
Fan speed does not alter.	No vacuum in the unit. No voltage across programmer.	Check vacuum. Check positive supply (input lead).
– constant low fan speed – water valve open despite full cold setting – no recirculation. – too warm in car in relation to temp. setting.	– defective temp.sensor ambient – loose resistor.	Check outer temp. sensor. Measure restiance.

29 CHRYSLER IMPORT TRUCKS 29

RAM 50 • RAIDER

SPECIFICATIONS

ENGINE IDENTIFICATION

Year	Model	Engine Displacement cu. in. (cc/liter)	Engine Series Identification	No. of Cylinders	Engine Type
1989	Ram 50	122 (1997/2.0)	G63B	4	SOHC
	Ram 50	156 (2555/2.6)	G54B	4	SOHC
	Raider	156 (2555/2.6)	G54B	4	SOHC
	Raider	181 (2972/3.0)	6G72	6	SOHC
1990	Ram 50	143 (2350/2.4)	4G64	4	SOHC
	Ram 50	181 (2972/3.0)	6G72	6	SOHC
1991	Ram 50	143 (2350/2.4)	4G64	4	SOHC
	Ram 50	181 (2972/3.0)	6G72	6	SOHC

REFRIGERANT CAPACITIES

Year	Model	Freon (oz.)	Oil (fl. oz.)	Type ③
1989	Ram 50	32	3.3	DR1013C
	Raider	32	①	②
1990	Ram 50	30	5.5	FX80
1991	Ram 50	30	5.5	FX80

① 2.6L engine—6.7
3.0L engine—4.7
② 2.6L engine—6P148
3.0L engine—10PA15
③ Compressor

AIR CONDITIONING BELT TENSION CHART

Year	Model	Engine cu. in. (cc/liter)	Belt Type	Specification ① New	Specification ① Used
1989	Ram 50	122 (1997/2.0)	V-Belt	0.35	0.35
	Ram 50	156 (2555/2.6)	V-Belt	0.44	0.44
	Raider	156 (2555/2.6)	V-Belt	0.55	0.70
	Raider	181 (2972/3.0)	V-Belt	0.22	0.35
1990	Ram 50	143 (2350/2.4)	V-Belt	0.35	0.35
	Ram 50	181 (2972/3.0)	V-Belt	0.35	0.35
1991	Ram 50	143 (2350/2.4)	V-Belt	0.35	0.35
	Ram 50	181 (2972/3.0)	V-Belt	0.35	0.35

① Inches of deflection at the center of the belt using 22 lbs. force

SYSTEM DESCRIPTION

General Information

The heater unit is located behind the center of the instrument panel with the blower housing and blend-air system. In the blend-air system, hot air and cool air are controlled by blend-air damper to make fine adjustments of temperature. The heater system is also designed as a bi-level heater in which a separator directs warm air to the windshield or to the floor and cool air through the panel outlet.

The temperature inside the vehicle is controlled by means of the temperature control lever, the position of which determines the opening of the blend-air damper and the resulting mixing ratio of cool and hot air is used to control the outlet temperature.

The air conditioning compressor coil will be energized when all of the following conditions are met:

1. The air conditioner switch on the control head is depressed.
2. The blower motor switch is not in the **OFF** position.
3. The low pressure or dual pressure switch is reading at least 30 psi (206 kPa) pressure.
4. The thermistor is sensing at least 37.4°F (3°C).
5. The engine coolant temperature sensor is reading less than 235°F (113°C).
6. On vehicles equipped with a compressor refrigerant temperature sensor, the compressor discharge side refrigerant temperature must be less than 347°F (175°C).

Service Valve Location

The suction valve is located on the compressor. The discharge valve is located either on the compressor or near the compressor on the discharge line.

System Discharging

R-12 refrigerant is a chlorofluorocarbon which, when mishandled, can contribute to the depletion on the ozone layer in the upper atmosphere. Ozone filters out harmful radiation from the sun. In order to protect the ozone layer, an approved R-12 Recovery/Recycling machine that meets SAE standard J1991 should be employed when discharging the system. Follow the operating instructions provided with the approved equipment exactly to properly discharge the system.

System Evacuating

If the air conditioning system has been opened to the atmosphere, it should be air and moisture free before being recharged with refrigerant. Moisture and air mixed with refrigerant will raise the compressor head pressure, possibly damage the system's components and will reduce the performance of the system. Moisture will boil at normal room temperature when exposed to a vacuum. To evacuate the system, perform the following procedure:

1. Leak test the system and repair any leaks found.
2. Connect an approved charging station, Recovery/Recycling machine or manifold gauge set and vacuum pump to the discharge and suction ports. The red hose is normally connected to the discharge (high pressure) line and the blue hose is connected to the suction (low pressure) line.
3. Open the discharge and suction ports and start the vacuum pump. If the pump is not able to pull at least 26 in. Hg of vacuum, there is a leak that must be repaired before evacuation can occur.
4. Once the system has reached at least 26 in. Hg of vacuum, allow the system to evacuate for at least 10 minutes. The longer the system is evacuated, the more contaminants will be removed.
5. Close all valves and turn the pump off. If the system loses more than 2 in. Hg of vacuum after 15 minutes, there is a leak that should be repaired.

System Charging

1. Connect an approved charging station, Recovery/Recycling machine or manifold gauge set to the discharge and suction ports. The red hose is normally connected to the discharge (high pressure) line and the blue hose is connected to the suction (low pressure) line.
2. Follow the instructions provided with the equipment and charge the system with the specified amount of refrigerant.
3. Perform a leak test.

SYSTEM COMPONENTS

Radiator

REMOVAL AND INSTALLATION

1. Disconnect the negative battery cable.
2. Drain the coolant.
3. Remove the upper hose and coolant reserve tank hose from the radiator.
4. Remove the shroud assembly from the radiator.
5. Raise the vehicle and support safely.
6. Remove the lower hose from the radiator.
7. Disconnect and plug the automatic transmission cooler hoses, if equipped. Lower the vehicle.
8. Remove the mounting screws and carefully lift the radiator out of the engine compartment.

To install:

9. Lower the radiator into position and install the mounting screws.
10. Raise the vehicle and support safely. Connect the automatic transmission cooler hoses, if they were removed.
11. Connect the lower hose. Lower the vehicle.
12. Install the shroud assembly.
13. Connect the upper hose and coolant reserve tank hose.
14. Fill the system with coolant.
15. Connect the negative battery cable, run the vehicle until the thermostat opens, fill the radiator completely and check the automatic transmission fluid level, if equipped.
16. Check for leaks. Once the vehicle has cooled, recheck the coolant level.

Electric Cooling Fan

An electric condenser cooling fan is used on Raider. The condenser on Ram 50 is cooled by the belt-driven fan.

TESTING

CAUTION

Make sure the key is in the OFF position when checking the electric cooling fan. If not, the fan could turn ON at any time, causing serious personal injury.

1. Disconnect the negative battery cable.
2. Disconnect the condenser cooling fan connector.
3. Connect the green-with-black-tracer wire to 12 volts and ground the black wire.
4. Make sure the fan runs smoothly, without abnormal noise or vibration.
5. Connect the negative battery cable.

REMOVAL AND INSTALLATION

1. Disconnect the negative battery cable.

2. Open the hood and remove the grille. It is fastened with 3 screws along the top and 3 nuts along the bottom.
3. Disconnect the fan connector.
4. Remove the mounting bolts and remove the fan through the grille opening.
5. The installation is the reverse of the removal procedure.
6. Connect the negative battery cable and check the fan for proper operation.

Condenser

REMOVAL AND INSTALLATION

1. Disconnect the negative battery cable.
2. Properly discharge the air conditioning system.
3. Remove the grille assembly.
4. Remove the condenser cooling fan, if equipped.
5. Using 2 flare nut wrenches, remove the receiver drier and adjoining refrigerant lines.
6. Disconnect any remaining refrigerant lines from the condenser. Cover the exposed ends of the lines to minimize contamination.
7. Remove the condenser mounting bolts and remove the condenser through the grille opening.

To install:

8. Install the condenser and install its mounting bolts.
9. Using new lubricated O-rings, connect the refrigerant lines to the condenser and install the receiver drier.
10. Install the cooling fan if removed.
11. Install the grille assembly.
12. Evacuate and recharge the air conditioning system. If the condenser was replaced, add 1 oz. of refrigerant oil during the recharge.
13. Connect the negative battery cable and check the entire climate control system for proper operation and leaks.

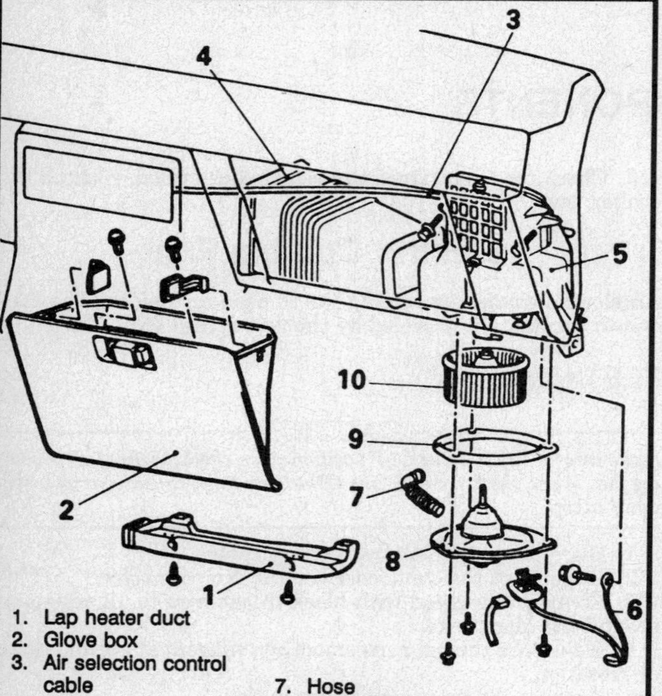
1
2
3
4
5
6
7
8
9
10

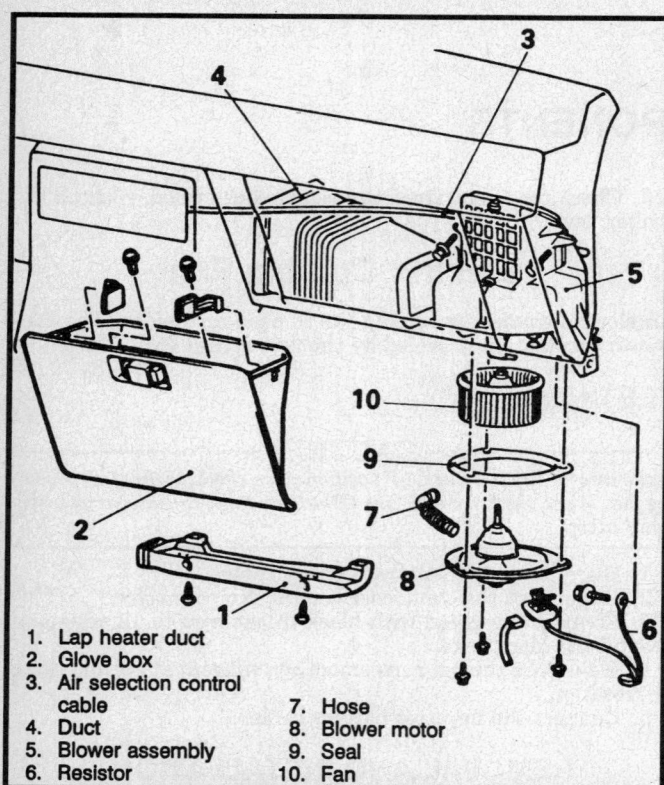

1. Lap heater duct
2. Glove box
3. Air selection control cable
4. Duct
5. Blower assembly
6. Resistor
7. Hose
8. Blower motor
9. Seal
10. Fan

Blower motor and related components—Raider

Compressor

REMOVAL AND INSTALLATION

1. Disconnect the negative battery cable.
2. Properly discharge the air conditioning system.
3. Relieve the tension and remove the compressor drive belt from the clutch pulley. Disconnect the electrical connector.
4. Disconnect the refrigerant lines from the compressor. Cover the exposed ends of the lines to minimize contamination.
5. Remove the retaining bolts and remove the compressor from its mounting bracket.

To install:

6. Install the compressor to its mounting bracket and connect the connector.
7. Using new lubricated O-rings, connect the refrigerant lines to the compressor. Torque the retaining bolts to 17 ft. lbs. (23 Nm).
8. Wrap the drive belt around the pulley and adjust to specification.
9. Evacuate and recharge the air conditioning system.
10. Connect the negative battery cable and check the entire climate control system for proper operation and leaks.

Receiver/Drier

REMOVAL AND INSTALLATION

1. Disconnect the negative battery cable.
2. Properly discharge the air conditioning system.
3. Remove the grille assembly.
4. Disconnect the refrigerant lines from the receiver/drier assembly. Cover the exposed ends of the lines to minimize contamination.
5. Remove the mounting bolts and remove the receiver/drier from the vehicle.
6. The installation is the reverse of the removal procedure.
7. Evacuate and recharge the air conditioning system. If the receiver/drier was replaced, add ¼ oz. of refrigerant oil during the recharge.
8. Connect the negative battery cable and check the entire climate control system for proper operation and leaks.

Expansion Valve

REMOVAL AND INSTALLATION

Except 1989 Ram 50

1. Disconnect the negative battery cable.
2. Properly discharge the air conditioning system.
3. Remove the evaporator housing and separate the upper and lower cases.
4. Remove the expansion valve from the evaporator lines.
5. The installation is the reverse of the removal installation. Use new lubricated O-rings when assembling.
6. Evacuate and recharge the air conditioning system.
7. Connect the negative battery cable and check the entire climate control system for proper operation. Check the system for leaks.

1989 Ram 50

1. Disconnect the negative battery cable.
2. Properly discharge the air conditioning system.
3. Hold the expansion valve stationary and disconnect the refrigerant lines from both sides of the expansion valve.
4. Remove the expansion valve.
5. The installation is the reverse of the removal procedure. Be sure to use new lubricated O-rings when assembling.

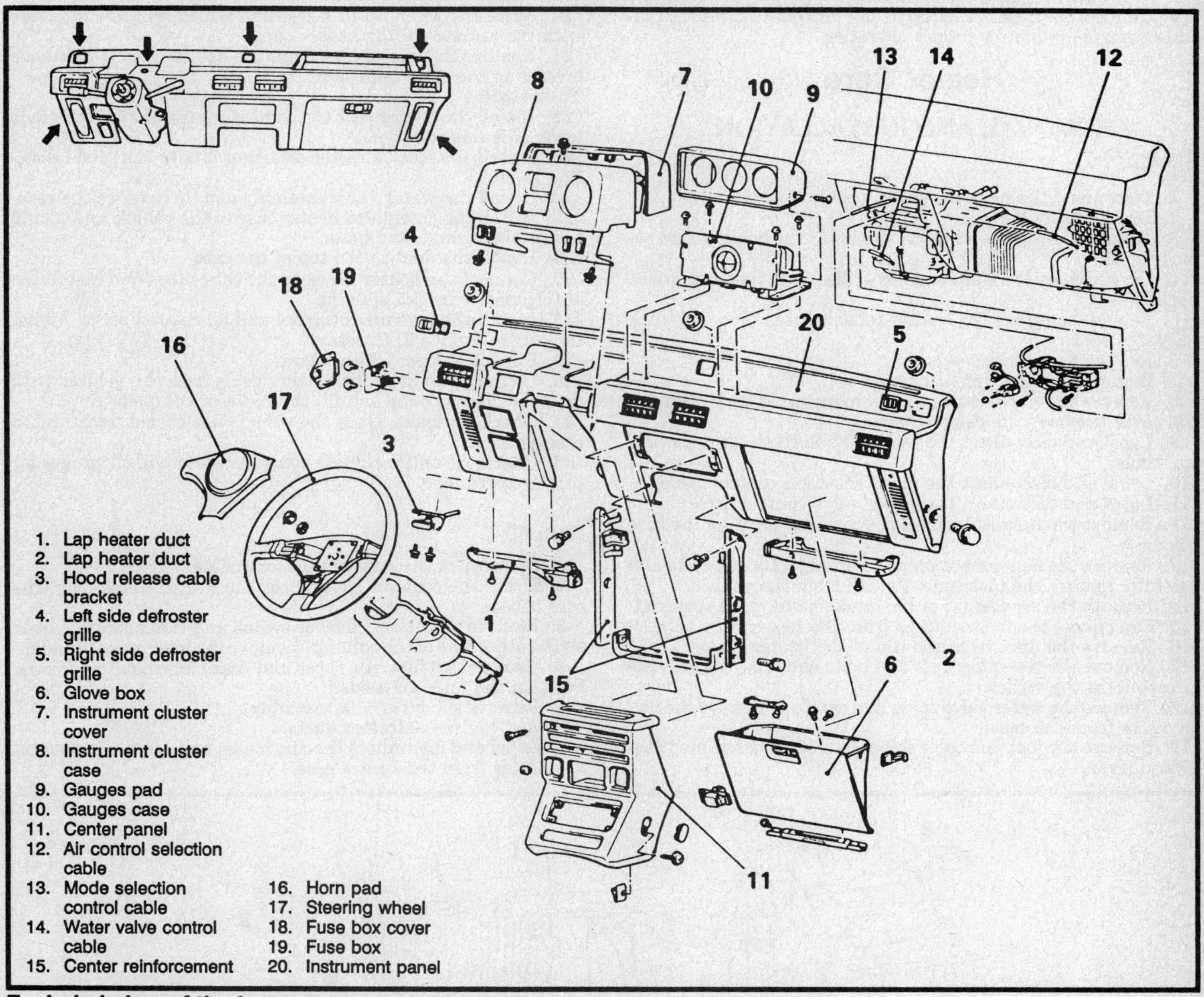
1. Lap heater duct
2. Lap heater duct
3. Hood release cable bracket
4. Left side defroster grille
5. Right side defroster grille
6. Glove box
7. Instrument cluster cover
8. Instrument cluster case
9. Gauges pad
10. Gauges case
11. Center panel
12. Air control selection cable
13. Mode selection control cable
14. Water valve control cable
15. Center reinforcement
16. Horn pad
17. Steering wheel
18. Fuse box cover
19. Fuse box
20. Instrument panel

Exploded view of the instrument panel—Raider

6. Connect the negative battery cable and check the entire climate control system for proper operation and leaks.

Blower Motor

REMOVAL AND INSTALLATION

1. Disconnect the negative battery cable.
2. On Raider, remove the passenger's lap duct.
3. If necessary, remove the glove box assembly.
4. Remove the motor cooling tube.
5. Disconnect the blower motor lead.
6. Remove the blower resistor, as required.
7. Remove the retaining screws and remove the blower from the blower case.
8. Disassemble on a workbench.

To install:

9. Inspect the seal and repair or replace as required. Assemble the fan and motor.
10. Install the motor to the case and install the retaining screws.
11. Install the resistor and connect the blower lead.
12. Install the cooling tube.
13. Install the glove box and lap duct if removed.
14. Connect the negative battery cable and check the blower for proper operation.

Blower Motor Resistor

REMOVAL AND INSTALLATION

1. Disconnect the negative battery cable.
2. Remove the blower motor assembly if it is preventing access to the resistor, located next to the blower.
3. Disconnect the wire harness from the resistor.
4. Remove the mounting screws and remove the resistor.
5. The installation is the reverse of the removal procedure. Make sure the seal is intact when installing.

6. Connect the negative battery cable and check the entire climate control system for proper operation.

Heater Core

REMOVAL AND INSTALLATION

Raider

1. Disconnect the negative battery cable.
2. Drain the coolant.
3. Remove the lap heater ducts and lower the hood release cable bracket.
4. Carefully pry the side demister grilles from the instrument panel.
5. Remove the glove box, center console assembly and center reinforcement.
6. Remove the steering wheel.
7. Remove the instrument cluster.
8. Remove the oil pressure gauge, inclinometer and voltmeter pod cover. Remove the gauge assembly.
9. Label and disconnect the recirculation/fresh air door control cable.
10. Label and disconnect the mode selection control cable.
11. Label and disconnect the water valve control cable.
12. Remove the fuse box retaining screw and position the fuse box aside.
13. Remove the instrument panel retaining nuts and bolts and carefully remove the instrument panel from the vehicle.
14. Remove the air cleaner or air intake plenum, as required.
15. Disconnect the heater hoses from the heater core tubes.
16. Remove the duct from the top of the heater case.
17. Remove the retaining nuts and bolts and remove the heater case from the vehicle.
18. Remove the water valve cover and carefully remove the water valve from the case.
19. Remove the foot/defroster selection link from the mode selection lever.
20. Move the lever up to a position which will not interfere with the removal of the heater core.
21. Remove the heater core from the heater case. If the mode lever is in the way, remove it.

To install:

22. Install the heater core to the heater case. Install the mode lever, if it was removed.
23. Install the foot/defroster selection link to the mode selection lever.
24. Install the water valve assembly and its cover to the case.
25. Install the assembled heater case to the vehicle and install the retaining nuts and bolts.
26. Install the duct to the top of the case.
27. Connect the heater hoses to the core tubes and install the air cleaner or intake plenum.
28. Install the instrument panel and all related parts. Adjust the control cables if necessary.
29. Fill the system with coolant.
30. Connect the negative battery cable, run the vehicle until the thermostat opens and fill the radiator completely.
31. Check for leaks. Once the vehicle has cooled, recheck the coolant level.
32. Check the entire climate control system and all gauges for proper operation.

Ram 50

1. Disconnect the negative battery cable.
2. Drain the coolant. Disconnect the heater hoses from the core tubes.
3. Remove the hazard flasher switch and the matching cover on the other side of the column. Remove the instrument cluster.
4. Remove the fuse box cover and fuse box retaining screws. Position the fuse box aside.
5. Remove the glove box assembly.
6. Remove the defroster ducts.
7. Label and disconnect the air, mode, and temperature control cables from the heater case.

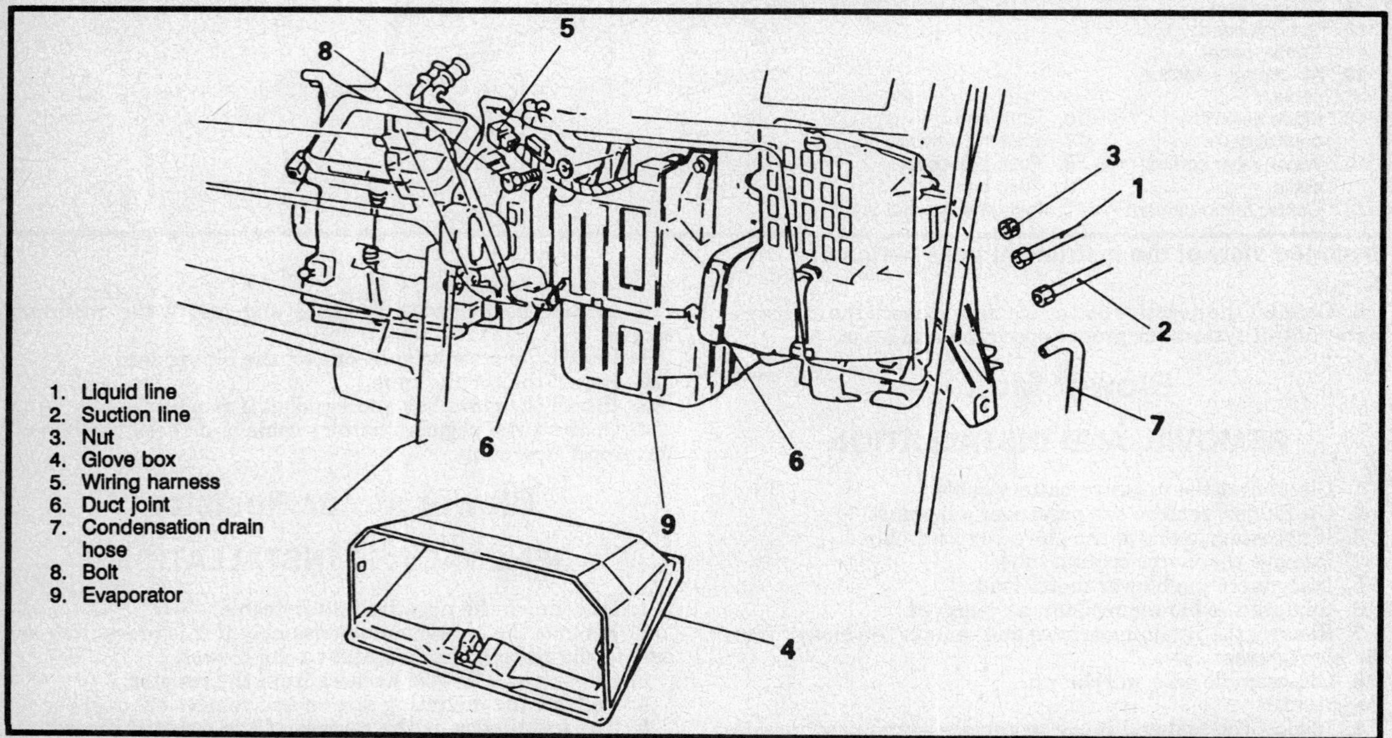
8
5
3
1
2
7
6
6
9
4
1. Liquid line
2. Suction line
3. Nut
4. Glove box
5. Wiring harness
6. Duct joint
7. Condensation drain hose
8. Bolt
9. Evaporator

Evaporator case and related components—Raider

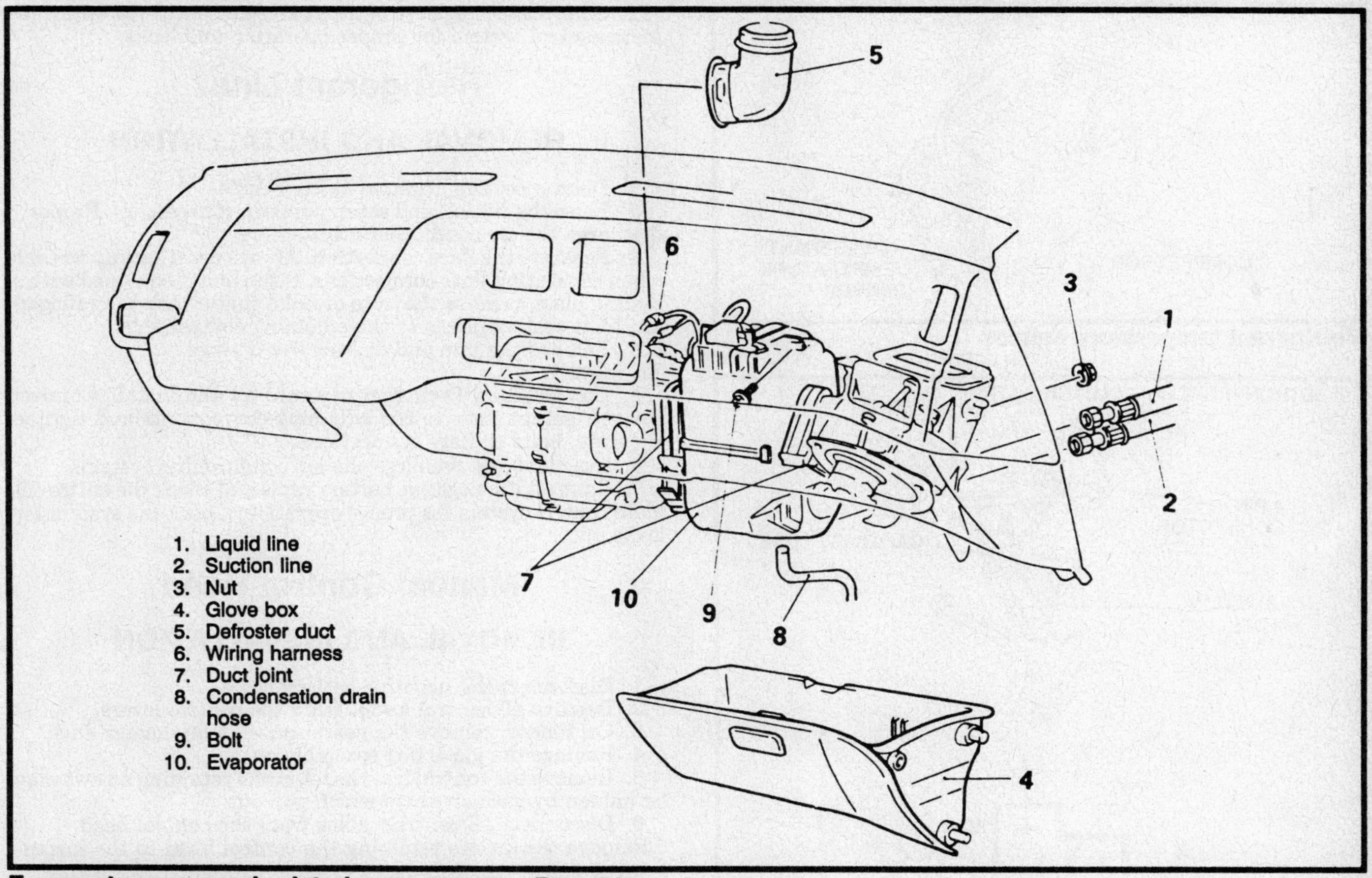
1. Liquid line
2. Suction line
3. Nut
4. Glove box
5. Defroster duct
6. Wiring harness
7. Duct joint
8. Condensation drain hose
9. Bolt
10. Evaporator

Evaporator case and related components—Ram 50

8. Remove the front speaker grilles.
9. Remove the parcel box or clock, as equipped.
10. Remove the nut cover from the top center of the instrument panel.
11. Remove the center cover.
12. Remove the shifter knob and floor console assembly, if equipped.
13. Move the tilt steering column down as far as it will go.
14. Remove the instrument panel retaining nuts and bolts and carefully remove the instrument panel from the vehicle.
15. Remove the duct from the top center of the heater case.
16. Remove the defroster duct from the the left side of the case.
17. Remove the center reinforcement braces.
18. Remove the mounting nuts and remove the heater case from the vehicle.
19. Remove the hose cover, joint hose clamp and the plate from the case.
20. Remove the heater core from the case.

To install:

21. Install the heater core to the heater case.
22. Install the plate, joint hose clamp and hose cover.
23. Install the assembled heater case to the vehicle. Connect the heater hoses to the core tubes.
24. Install the center reinforcement braces.
25. Install the defroster and center ducts to the case.
26. Install the instrument panel and all related parts. Adjust the control cables if necessary.
27. Fill the system with coolant.
28. Connect the negative battery cable, run the vehicle until the thermostat opens and fill the radiator completely.
29. Check for leaks. Once the vehicle has cooled, recheck the coolant level.
30. Check the entire climate control system and all gauges for proper operation.

Evaporator

REMOVAL AND INSTALLATION

1. Disconnect the negative battery cable.
2. Properly discharge the air conditioning system.
3. Use 2 wrenches to disconnect the liquid and suction lines from the evaporator fittings at the firewall.
4. Remove the retaining nut located just above the hoses.
5. Remove the glove box assembly.
6. Remove the defroster duct.
7. Disconnect the electrical harness connector running to the evaporator case.
8. Loosen the duct joint between the evaporator case and the heater case.
9. Remove the condensation drain hose.
10. Remove the retaining bolts and remove the evaporator case from the vehicle.
11. Disassemble the evaporator case and remove the evaporator.

To install:

12. Install the evaporator to the case and assemble. Carefully install the assembled case into the vehicle and tighten the mounting bolts and nuts.
13. Connect the condensation drain hose to the case.
14. Install the duct joints on both sides of the evaporator. Cor-

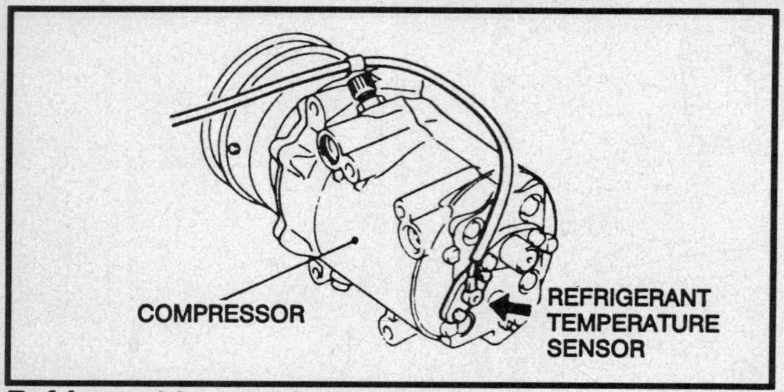
COMPRESSOR
REFRIGERANT
TEMPERATURE
SENSOR

Refrigerant temperature sensor

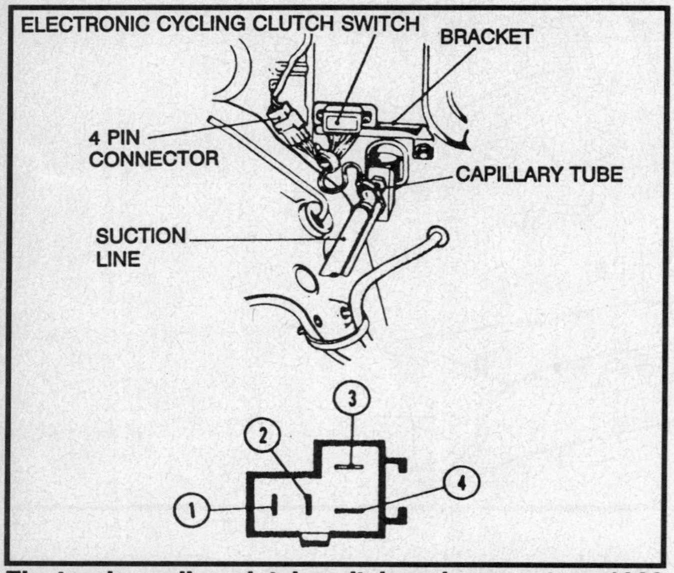
ELECTRONIC CYCLING CLUTCH SWITCH
BRACKET
4 PIN
CONNECTOR
CAPILLARY TUBE
SUCTION
LINE
3
2
4
1

Electronic cycling clutch switch and connector—1989 Ram 50

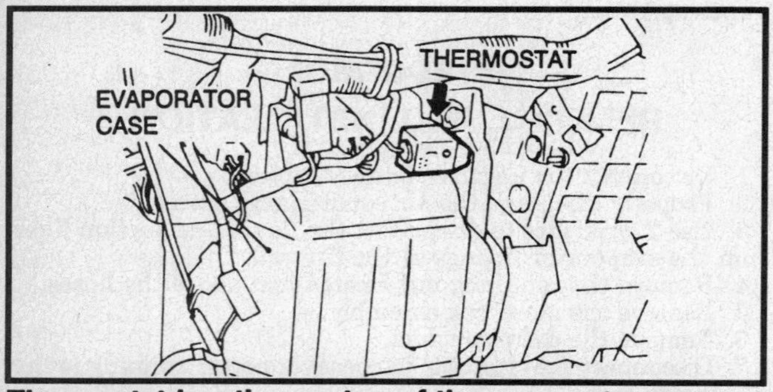
THERMOSTAT
EVAPORATOR
CASE

Thermostat location on top of the evaporator case

rectly installed, the evaporator case should have slight clearance to the joint on each side.

15. Connect the harness electrical connectors.
16. Install the defroster duct.
17. Install the glove box.
18. In the engine compartment, install the retaining nut if not already done during installation.
19. Using new lubricated O-rings, connect the refrigerant lines to the evaporator fittings.
20. Evacuate and recharge the air conditioning system. If the evaporator was replaced, add 1 oz. of refrigerant oil during the recharge.
21. Connect the negative battery cable and check the entire climate control system for proper operation and leaks.

Refrigerant Lines

REMOVAL AND INSTALLATION

1. Disconnect the negative battery cable.
2. Raise the vehicle and safely support, if necessary. Properly discharge the air conditioning system.
3. Separate the flare connection. Always use a backup wrench when separating flare connections. If the line is equipped with a sealing plate, remove the nuts or bolts that attach the refrigerant lines sealing plates to the adjoining components.
4. Remove the line and discard the O-rings.

To install:

5. Coat the new O-rings refrigerant oil and install. Connect the refrigerant lines to the adjoining components and tighten the nuts, bolts or flare connections.
6. Evacuate and recharge the air conditioning system.
7. Connect the negative battery cable and check the entire climate control system for proper operation. Check the system for leaks.

Manual Control Head

REMOVAL AND INSTALLATION

1. Disconnect the negative battery cable.
2. Remove all control knobs from the control levers.
3. On Raider, remove the passenger side lap heater duct.
4. Remove the glove box assembly.
5. Remove the control head bezel. Some retaining screws may be hidden by garnish plugs which pop out.
6. Disconnect all control cables from the control head.
7. Remove the screws retaining the control head to the instrument panel.
8. Pull the control head out and disconnect all wiring connectors.
9. Remove the control head from the vehicle. Disassemble as required.

To install:

10. Connect the wiring and cables and install the control head. Secure with the retaining screws.
11. Connect the cables under the instrument panel.
12. Install the control head bezel.
13. Install the glove box assembly and lap heater duct.
14. Install the control knobs.
15. Connect the negative battery cable and check the entire climate control system for proper operation.

Manual Control Cables

ADJUSTMENT

Mode Selection Control Cable

1. Move the air changeover lever to the far right.
2. Disconnect the mode selection cable from the clamp at the front of the heater case.
3. Move the damper link all the way down and adjust the outer cable tension so the inner cable has no slack.
4. Secure the control cable with the clamp.
5. Check for smooth and proper operation.

Temperature Control Cable

1. Move the temperature control lever to the far left.
2. Disconnect the temperature control cable from the clamp at the front of the heater case.

3. With the blend air damper lever at the front of the heater case pulled up against the stopper, adjust the outer cable tension so the inner cable has no slack.
4. Secure the control cable with the clamp.
5. Check for smooth and proper operation.

Air Selection Control Cable

1. Move the air selection lever to the far right.
2. Disconnect the air selection control cable from the clamp at the air flow box.
3. With the air selection damper lever at the air flow box set all the way to the right, adjust the outer cable tension so the inner cable has no slack.
4. Secure the control cable with the clamp.
5. Check for smooth and proper operation.

REMOVAL AND INSTALLATION

1. Disconnect the negative battery cable.
2. Remove all control knobs from the control levers.
3. On Raider, remove the passenger side lap heater duct.
4. Remove the glove box assembly.
5. Remove the control head bezel. Some retaining screws may be hidden by garnish plugs which pop out.
6. Note the routing and disconnect all control cables from under the instrument panel.
7. Remove the screws retaining the control head to the instrument panel.
8. Pull the control head out and disconnect all wiring connectors.
9. Remove the control head from the vehicle. Disconnect the cables from the control head.

To install:

10. Feed the control cables through instrument panel opening in exactly the same position as before removal. Connect the wiring and install the control head. Secure with its retaining screws.
11. Connect the cables under the instrument panel.
12. Install the control head bezel.
13. Install the glove box assembly and lap heater duct.
14. Install the control knobs.
15. Connect the negative battery cable and check the entire climate control system for proper operation.

SENSORS AND SWITCHES

Dual Pressure Switch

OPERATION

Some vehicles use a dual pressure switch, which is a combination of a low pressure cut off switch and high pressure cut off switch. These functions will stop operation of the compressor in the event of either high of low refrigerant charge, preventing damage to the system. The switch is located on the refrigerant line near the receiver drier.

The dual pressure switch is designed to cut off voltage to the compressor coil when the pressure either drops below 30 psi or rises above 384 psi.

TESTING

1. Check for continuity through the switch. Under all normal conditions, the switch should be continuous.
2. If the switch is open, check for insufficient refrigerant charge or excessive pressures.
3. If neither of the above conditions exist and the switch is open, replace the switch.

REMOVAL AND INSTALLATION

1. Disconnect the negative battery cable.
2. Raise the vehicle and support safely. Properly discharge the air conditioning system.
3. Remove the switch from the refrigerant line.
4. The installation is the reverse of the removal installation.
5. Evacuate and recharge the air conditioning system.
6. Connect the negative battery cable and check the entire climate control system for proper operation. Check the system for leaks.

Low Pressure Cut Off Switch

OPERATION

The low pressure cut off switch monitors the refrigerant gas pressure on the suction side of the system. The switch is connected in series with the compressor and will turn off voltage to the compressor clutch coil when the monitored pressure drops to levels that could damage the compressor. The switch is located to the right of the condenser on Raider and on the refrigerant line near the receiver/drier on Ram 50. It is a sealed unit that must be replaced if faulty.

TESTING

1. Start the engine and allow to idle. Turn the air conditioner ON.
2. Disconnect the switch connector and use a jumper wire to jump between terminals inside the connector boot.
3. If the compressor clutch does not engage, inspect the system for an open circuit.
4. If the clutch engages, connect an air conditioning manifold gauge to the system.
5. Read the low pressure gauge. The low pressure cut off switch should complete the circuit at pressures of at least 30 psi. Check the system for leaks if the pressures are too low.
6. If the pressures are nominal and the system works when the terminals are jumped, the cut off switch is faulty and should be replaced.

REMOVAL AND INSTALLATION

1. Disconnect the negative battery cable.
2. Properly discharge the air conditioning system.
3. Unplug the boot connector from the switch.
4. Using an oil pressure sending unit socket, remove the switch from the receiver/drier.

To install:

5. Seal the threads of the new switch with teflon tape.
6. Install the switch to the receiver/drier and connect the boot connector.
7. Evacuate and recharge the system. Check for leaks.
8. Check the switch for proper operation.

Refrigerant Temperature Sensor

OPERATION

Located on the rear of the compressor, the refrigerant temperature sensor detects the temperature of the refrigerant delivered from the compressor during operation. The switch is designed to cut off the compressor when the temperature of the refrigerant exceeds 347°F (175°C), preventing overheating.

TESTING

1. Measure the resistance across the switch terminals.
2. At 75–80°F, the resistance specification is about 80 kilo ohms.
3. If the reading deviates greatly from the specification, replace the sensor.

REMOVAL AND INSTALLATION

1. Disconnect the negative battery cable.
2. Properly discharge the air conditioning system.
3. Disconnect the connector.
4. Remove the mounting screws and the sensor from the compressor.
5. The installation is the reverse of the removal installation. Use a new lubricated O-ring when installing.
6. Evacuate and recharge the air conditioning system.
7. Connect the negative battery cable and check the entire climate control system for proper operation. Check the system for leaks.

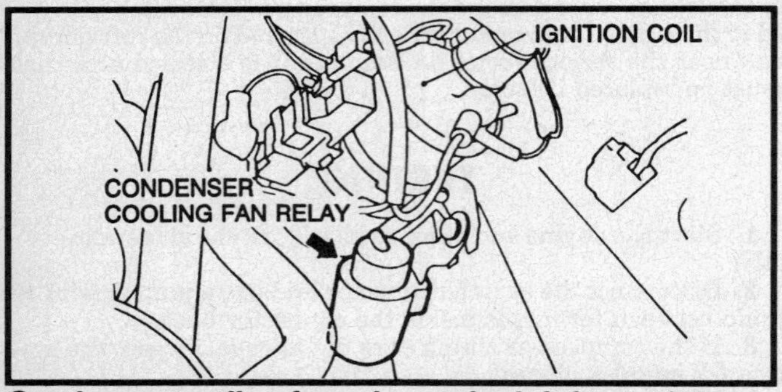
IGNITION COIL
CONDENSER
COOLING FAN RELAY

Condenser cooling fan relay at the left front of the engine compartment—Raider

Engine Coolant Temperature Switch

OPERATION

The engine coolant temperature switch, located on or near the thermostat housing, is connected in series with the compressor clutch relay. The switch is designed to cut off the compressor when the engine coolant temperature rises above 239°F (115°C), preventing engine overheating when the supply of cooling air is not sufficient for both the radiator and condenser.

TESTING

1. If the switch is suspect, unplug and jump across the terminals in the connectors.
2. To test the switch, remove the switch from the engine. The switch should be closed at room temperature.
3. Place the switch in an oil bath and heat to at least 222°F (108°C).
4. The switch should open when it reaches the above temperature.

REMOVAL AND INSTALLATION

1. Disconnect the negative battery cable. Drain out some of the coolant.
2. Unplug the connector.
3. Unscrew the switch from the thermostat housing.
4. The installation is the reverse of the removal installation. Use sealant on the threads when installing.
5. Refill the cooling system.
6. Connect the negative battery cable and check the entire climate control system for proper operation.

Electronic Cycling Clutch Switch

OPERATION

The electronic cycling clutch switch, used on 1989 Ram 50, is mounted on the firewall near the expansion valve. This switch prevents evaporator freeze-up by cycling the compressor clutch coil by monitoring the temperature of the suction line. A thermistor probe in the capillary tube is inserted into a well on the suction line. The well must be filled with special conductive grease to prevent corrosion and allow thermal transfer to the probe. The switch is a sealed unit that should be replaced if defective.

TESTING

1. With the ambient temperature in the test area at 70°F (21°C), supply 12 volts to Pin 3 and ground Pin 2.
2. Check for continuity across Pins 1 and 2.
3. If the test shows continuity, check other parts of the circuit for defects.
4. If continuity is not detected, replace the switch.

REMOVAL AND INSTALLATION

1. Disconnect the negative battery cable.
2. Disconnect the connector.
3. Remove the mounting screws on the firewall.
4. Separate the switch from the firewall and pull the capillary tube out of the capillary tube well on the suction line.

NOTE: The capillary tube well is filled with special temperature conductive grease. If reusing the switch, try to save all the grease. If replacing the switch, new grease will be supplied in the replacement switch package.

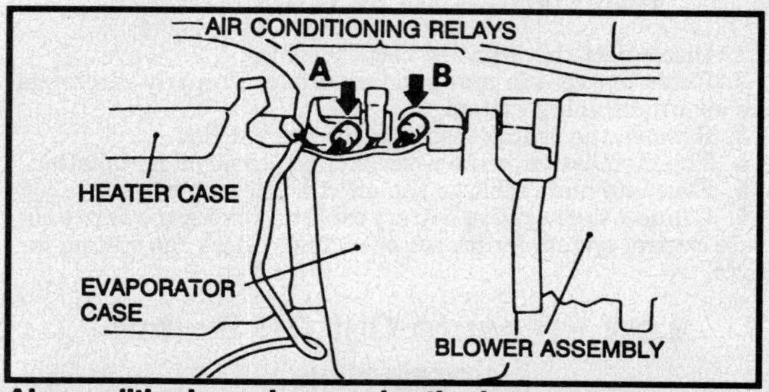
AIR CONDITIONING RELAYS
A
B
HEATER CASE
EVAPORATOR
CASE
BLOWER ASSEMBLY

Air conditioning relays under the instrument panel—Raider

To install:

5. Fill the well with the special grease and insert the capillary tube.
6. Mount the switch to the firewall.
7. Connect the connector.
8. Connect the negative battery cable and check the entire climate control system for proper operation.

Thermistor

OPERATION

Evaporator freeze up is controlled by a thermistor or thermostat. The body of the thermistor assembly is mounted to the evaporator case and the probe is inserted to the evaporator fins. The thermistor is connected in series with the compressor and will cut off voltage when the temperature of the evaporator drops below 37.4°F (3°C).

TESTING

1. If the compressor will not engage, disconnect the thermistor connector and jump across the wires.
2. Depress the air conditioning switch and turn the blower switch on.
3. Momentarily turn the ignition switch **ON**, without cranking, and listen for the click of the clutch engaging.
4. If the clutch engages, the problem is probably the thermistor. If not, inspect other parts of the system for proper operation.

REMOVAL AND INSTALLATION

1. Disconnect the negative battery cable.
2. Properly discharge the air conditioning system.
3. Remove the evaporator case.
4. Disassemble the evaporator case and unclip the thermistor probe from the evaporator fins.
5. Remove the thermistor from the case.

To install:

6. Assemble the evaporator case assembly. Make sure the thermistor probe is securely clipped to the evaporator fin.
7. Apply sealant to the hole in the lower case where the wires pass through.
8. Install the evaporator case to the vehicle.
9. Evacuate and recharge the air conditioning system.
10. Connect the negative battery cable and check the entire climate control system for proper operation and leaks.

Vacuum Solenoid Valve

OPERATION

Vehicles equipped with carbureted engines have this valve. Its function is to raise the idle when the compressor comes on, in order to compensate for the added load on the engine. Typically, the idle should increase about 50 rpm when the compressor cycles on. It is an electrically controlled vacuum device located on the firewall near the windshield wiper motor.

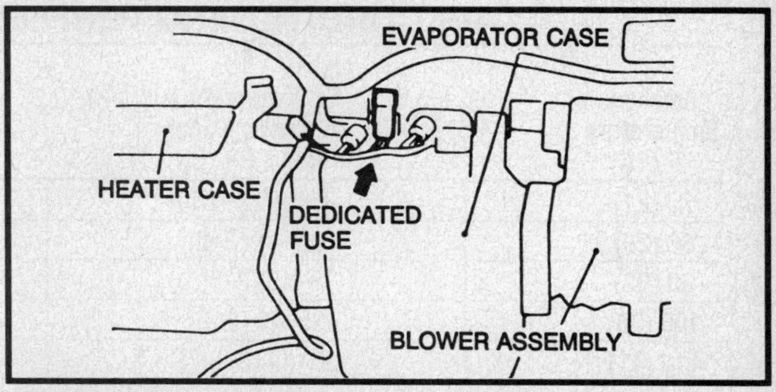
EVAPORATOR CASE
HEATER CASE
DEDICATED
FUSE
BLOWER ASSEMBLY
Air conditioning dedicated fuse behind the glove box—Raider

TESTING

1. With the compressor clutch engaged, check for 12 volts and ground at the solenoid connector.
2. Check for adequate vacuum into and out of the vacuum fittings on the solenoid.
3. Visually check for movement of the link to the throttle plate lever.
4. Repair any problem detected and recheck the system.

REMOVAL AND INSTALLATION

1. Disconnect the negative battery cable.
2. Matchmark and carefully disconnect the vacuum hoses from the fittings on the solenoid by pulling straight out.
3. Disconnect the electrical connector.
4. Remove the mounting screw and remove the solenoid from the firewall.
5. The installation is the reverse of the removal procedure.
6. Connect the negative battery cable and check for proper operation.

System Relays

OPERATION

Many of the systems within the air conditioning systems use relays to send current on its way and energize various components. The relays are positioned throughout the vehicles and many are interchangeable. All are conventional relays with internal contacts and a coil which pulls the contacts closed when energized.

SYSTEM DIAGNOSIS

Air Conditioning Performance

PERFORMANCE TEST

Air temperature in the testing area must be at least 70°F (21°C) to ensure the accuracy of this test.

1. Connect a manifold gauge set the the system.
2. Set the controls to **RECIRC** or **MAX**, the mode lever to the **PANEL** position, temperature control level to the coolest position and the blower on its highest position.
3. Start the engine and adjust the idle speed to 1000 rpm with the compressor clutch engaged.
4. Allow the engine come to normal operating temperature and keep doors and windows closed.
5. Insert a thermometer in the left center panel outlet and operate the engine for 10 minutes. The clutch may cycle depending on the ambient conditions.

AIR CONDITIONING PERFORMANCE CHART—1989 RAM 50

Ambient Temperature °F (°C)	Air Temperature at Center Panel Vent °F (°C)	Compressor Discharge Pressure PSI (kPa)	Compressor Suction Pressure PSI (kPa)
70 (21)	35–40 (2–4.5)	132–188 (930–1322)	18–21 (127–148)
80 (27)	35–41 (2–5)	152–220 (1070–1550)	18–23 (131–162)
90 (32)	35–42 (2–5.5)	172–252 (1210–1772)	19–25 (134–176)
100 (38)	35–43 (2–6)	190–280 (1335–2000)	19–27 (135–188)
110 (41)	35–44 (2–6.5)	200–300 (1400–2110)	19–28 (136–194)

AIR CONDITIONING PERFORMANCE CHART—1990–91 RAM 50

Ambient Temperature °F (°C)	Air Temperature at Center Panel Vent °F (°C)	Compressor Discharge Pressure PSI (kPa)	Compressor Suction Pressure PSI (kPa)
70 (21)	37–40 (3–4.5)	110–190 (758–1310)	19–24 (131–165)
80 (27)	38–41 (3–5)	130–220 (900–1577)	20–26 (138–179)
90 (32)	39–42 (4–6)	160–260 (1100–1800)	21–27 (145–189)
100 (38)	40–45 (4–7)	190–290 (1310–2000)	22–28 (152–193)
110 (41)	40–46 (4–8)	220–320 (1515–2200)	23–29 (159–200)

AIR CONDITIONING PERFORMANCE CHART—RAIDER

Ambient Temperature °F (°C)	Air Temperature at Center Panel Vent °F (°C)	Compressor Discharge Pressure PSI (kPa)	Compressor Suction Pressure PSI (kPa)
70 (21)	35–41 (2–4)	90–121 (620–834)	18–30 (124–205)
80 (27)	35–42 (2–5)	102–142 (700–980)	19–32 (130–221)
90 (32)	36–43 (3–6)	122–165 (840–1140)	20–35 (138–241)
100 (38)	37–45 (3–7)	144–195 (993–1350)	21–37 (145–255)
110 (41)	37–50 (3–10)	164–220 (1130–1515)	22–40 (152–276)

6. With the clutch engaged, compare the discharge air temperature to the performance chart.
7. If the values do not meet specifications, check system components for proper operation.

Air Conditioning Compressor

COMPRESSOR NOISE

Noises that develop during air conditioning operation can be misleading. A noise that sounds like serious compressor damage may only be a loose belt, mounting bolt or clutch assembly. Improper belt tension can also emit a noise that can be mistaken for more serious problems. Check and adjust all possible causes of the noise, including oil level, before replacing the compressor.

COMPRESSOR CLUTCH INOPERATIVE

1. Verify refrigerant charge and charge, as required.
2. Check for 12 volts at the clutch coil connection. If voltage is detected, check the coil.
3. If voltage is not detected at the coil, check the fuse or fusible link. If the fuse is not blown, check for voltage at the clutch relay. If voltage is not detected there, continue working backwards through the system's switches, etc. until an open circuit is detected.
4. Inspect all suspect parts and replace as required.
5. When the repair is complete, perform a complete system performance test.

CLUTCH COIL TESTING

1. Disconnect the negative battery cable.
2. Disconnect the compressor clutch connector.
3. Apply 12 volts to the wire leading to the clutch coil. If the clutch is operating properly, an audible click will occur when the clutch is magnetically pulled into the coil. If a click is not heard, inspect the coil.
4. Check the resistance across the coil lead wire and ground. The specification is 3.4–3.8 ohms at approximately 70°F (20°C).
5. If not within specifications, replace the clutch coil.

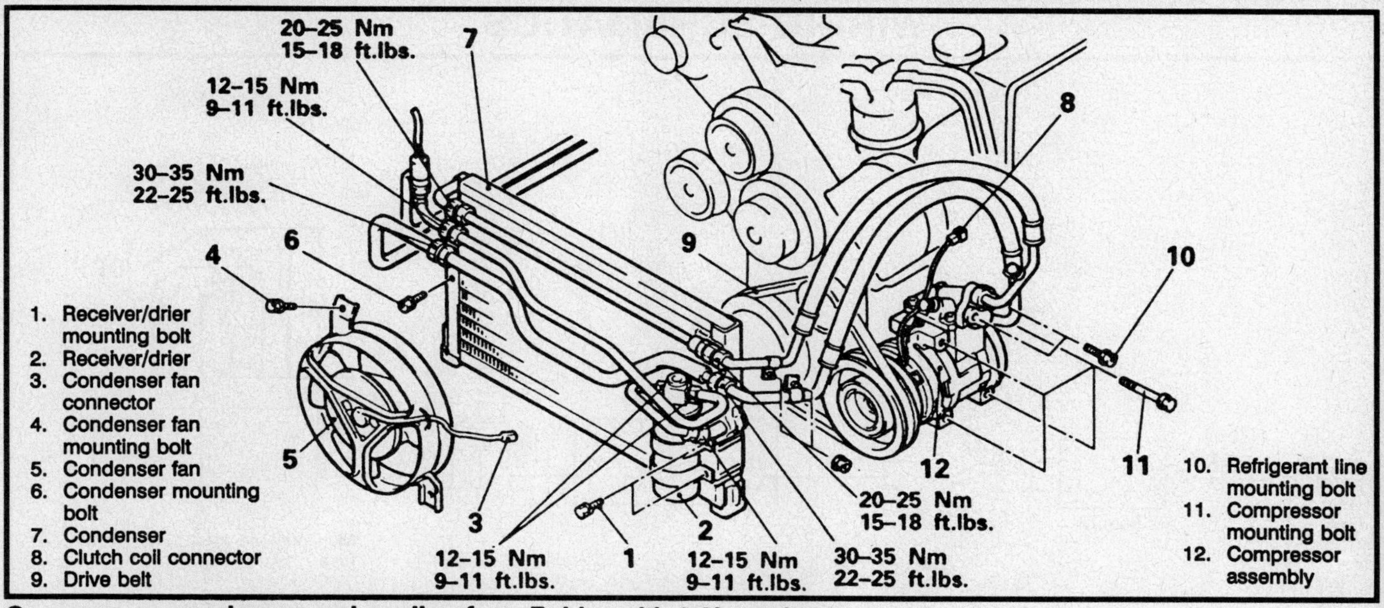
20–25 Nm
15–18 ft.lbs.
12–15 Nm
9–11 ft.lbs.
30–35 Nm
22–25 ft.lbs.
1. Receiver/drier mounting bolt
2. Receiver/drier
3. Condenser fan connector
4. Condenser fan mounting bolt
5. Condenser fan
6. Condenser mounting bolt
7. Condenser
8. Clutch coil connector
9. Drive belt
12–15 Nm
9–11 ft.lbs.
12–15 Nm
9–11 ft.lbs.
20–25 Nm
15–18 ft.lbs.
30–35 Nm
22–25 ft.lbs.
10. Refrigerant line mounting bolt
11. Compressor mounting bolt
12. Compressor assembly

Compressor, condenser and cooling fan—Raider with 3.0L engine

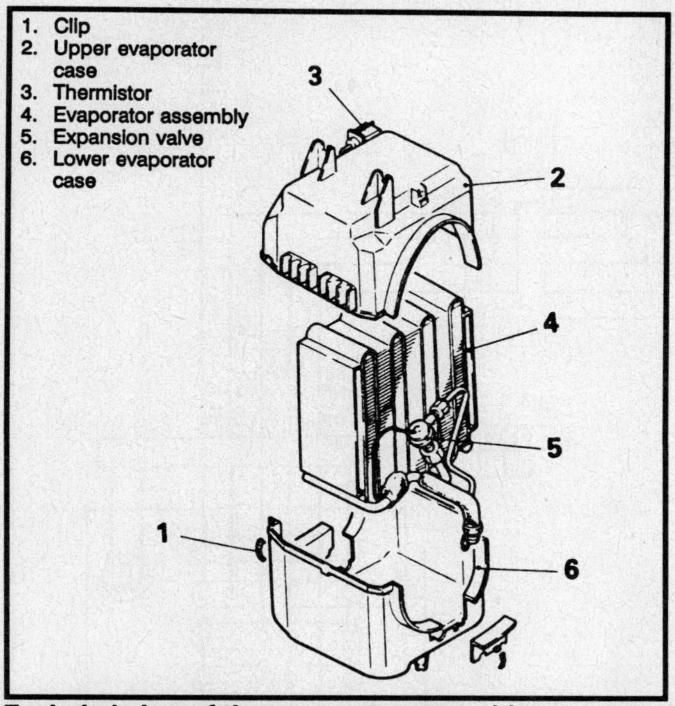
1. Clip
2. Upper evaporator case
3. Thermistor
4. Evaporator assembly
5. Expansion valve
6. Lower evaporator case

Exploded view of the evaporator assembly—except 1989 Ram 50

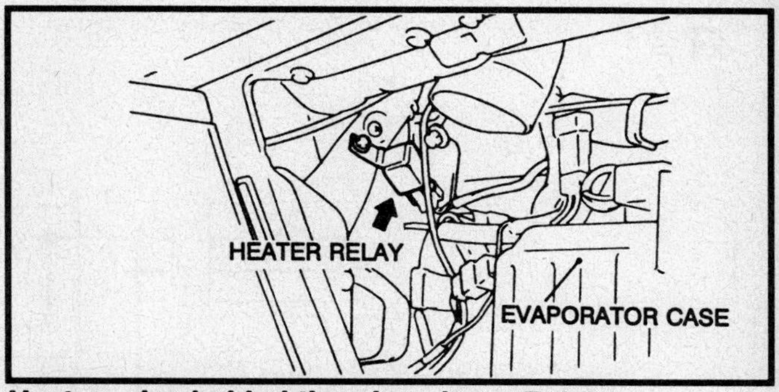
HEATER RELAY
EVAPORATOR CASE

Heater relay behind the glove box—Raider

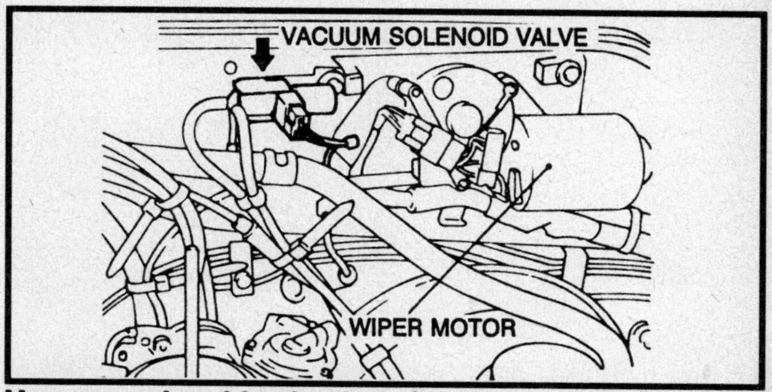
VACUUM SOLENOID VALVE
WIPER MOTOR

Vacuum solenoid valve location on the firewall

WIRING SCHEMATICS

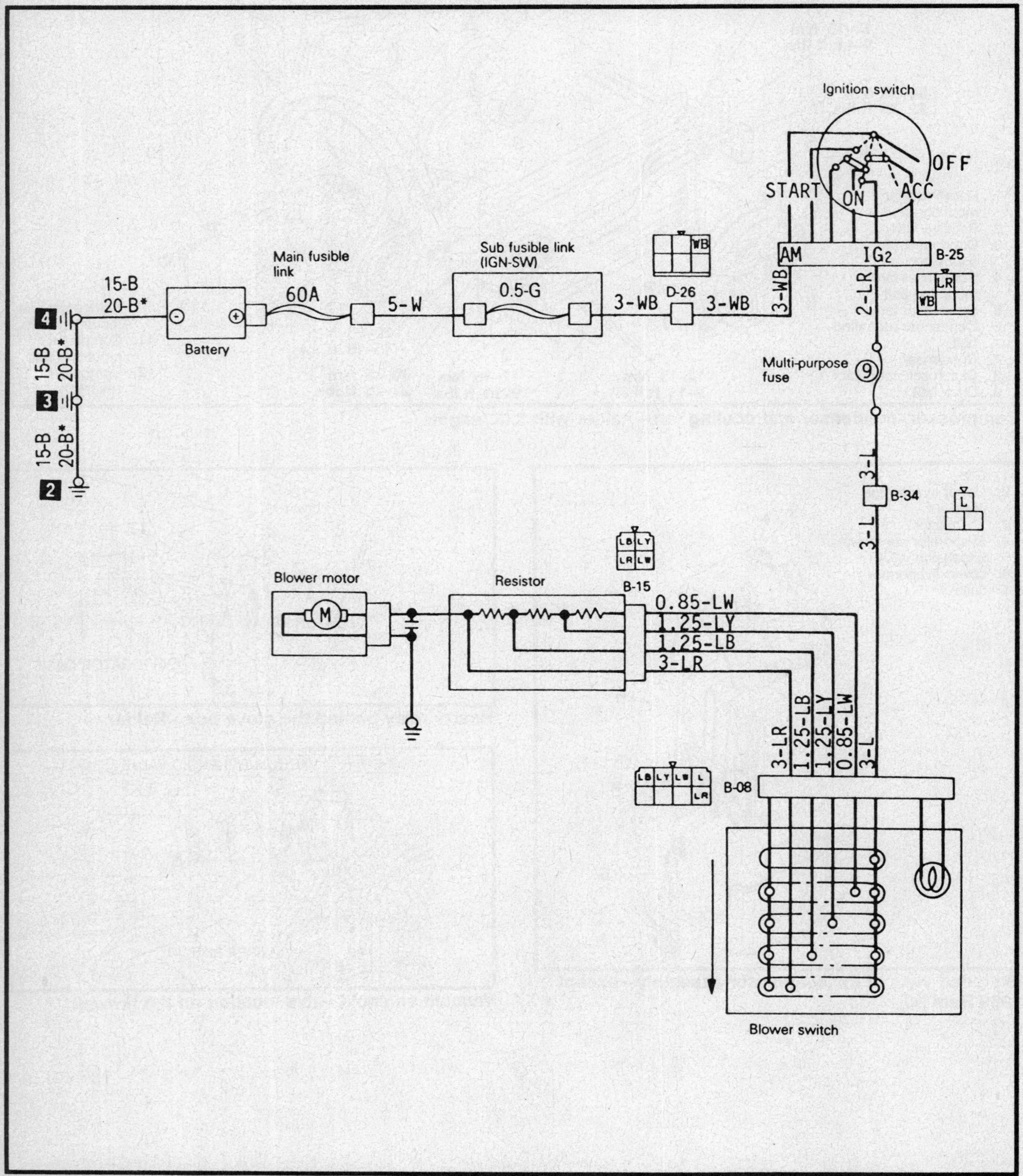
Ignition switch
OFF
START
ON
ACC
AM
IG2
B-25
Main fusible link
60A
Sub fusible link (IGN-SW)
0.5-G
15-B
20-B*
Battery
5-W
3-WB
D-26
3-WB
3-WB
2-LR
Multi-purpose fuse
9
3-L
B-34
3-L
Blower motor
M
Resistor
B-15
0.85-LW
1.25-LY
1.25-LB
3-LR
3-LR
1.25-LB
1.25-LY
0.85-LW
3-L
B-08
Blower switch

Heater system wiring schematic—Ram 50

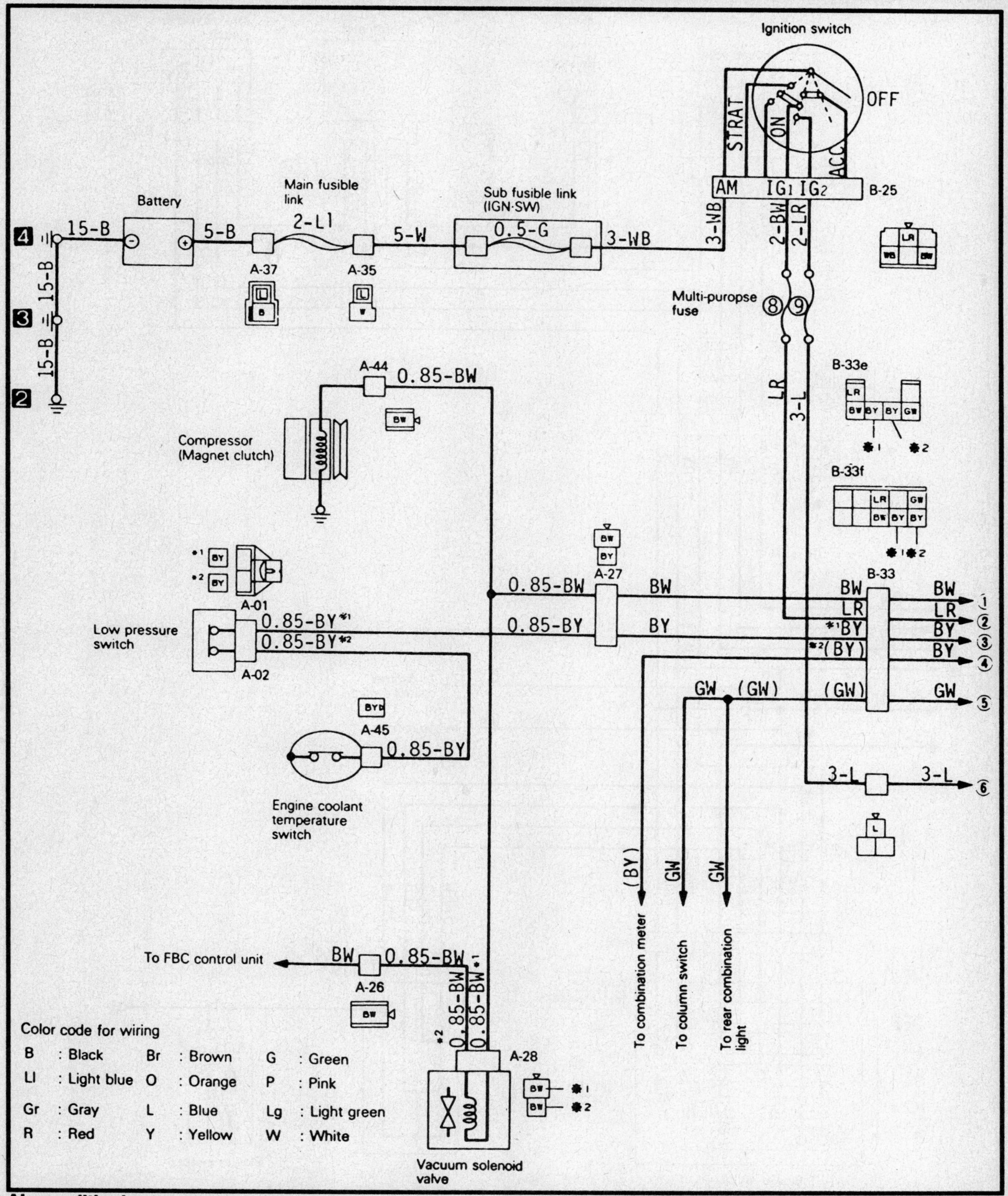
Ignition switch
OFF
STRAT
ON
ACC
AM
IG1
IG2
B-25
Battery
Main fusible link
Sub fusible link (IGN·SW)
15-B
5-B
2-L1
5-W
0.5-G
3-WB
2-BW
2-LR
A-37
A-35
Multi-puropse fuse
LR
3-L
B-33e
B-33f
A-44
0.85-BW
Compressor (Magnet clutch)
A-01
Low pressure switch
0.85-BY*1
0.85-BY*2
A-02
A-27
BW
BY
B-33
(BY)
GW
(GW)
A-45
0.85-BY
Engine coolant temperature switch
To combination meter
To column switch
To rear combination light
To FBC control unit
A-26
0.85-BW*1
0.85-BW*2
A-28
Vacuum solenoid valve
Color code for wiring
B : Black
Br : Brown
G : Green
Ll : Light blue
O : Orange
P : Pink
Gr : Gray
L : Blue
Lg : Light green
R : Red
Y : Yellow
W : White

Air conditioning system schematic—1989 Ram 50

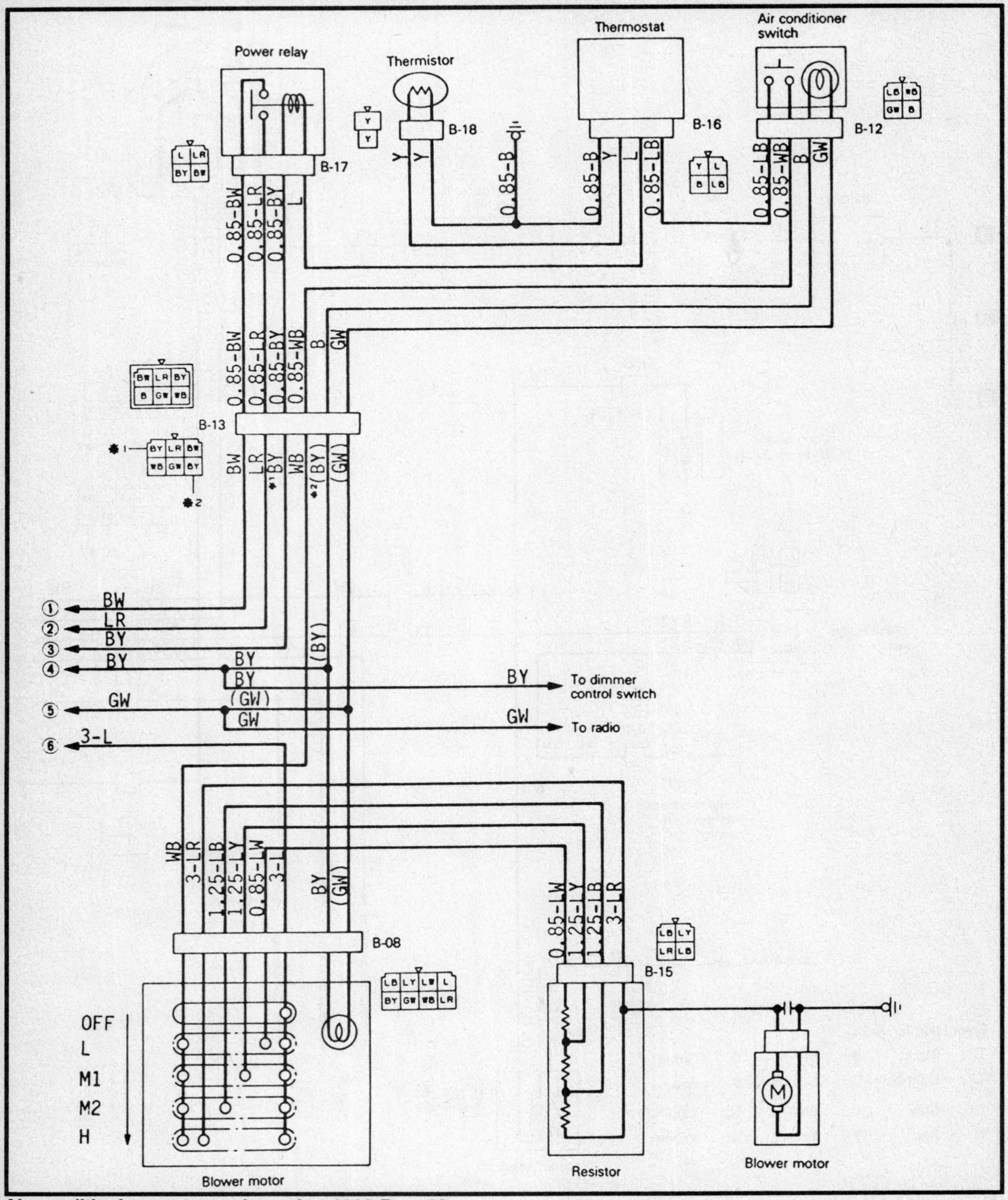
Power relay
Thermistor
Thermostat
Air conditioner switch
B-17
B-18
B-16
B-12
0.85-BW
0.85-LR
0.85-BY
L
Y
0.85-B
0.85-LB
0.85-WB
B
GW
0.85-WB
B-13
BW
LR
*1 BY
WB
*2 (BY)
(GW)
*1
*2
BW
LR
BY
BY
GW
3-L
BY
(GW)
To dimmer control switch
To radio
WB
3-LR
1.25-LB
1.25-LY
0.85-LW
3-L
B-08
B-15
OFF
L
M1
M2
H
Blower motor
Resistor
Blower motor

Air conditioning system schematic—1989 Ram 50

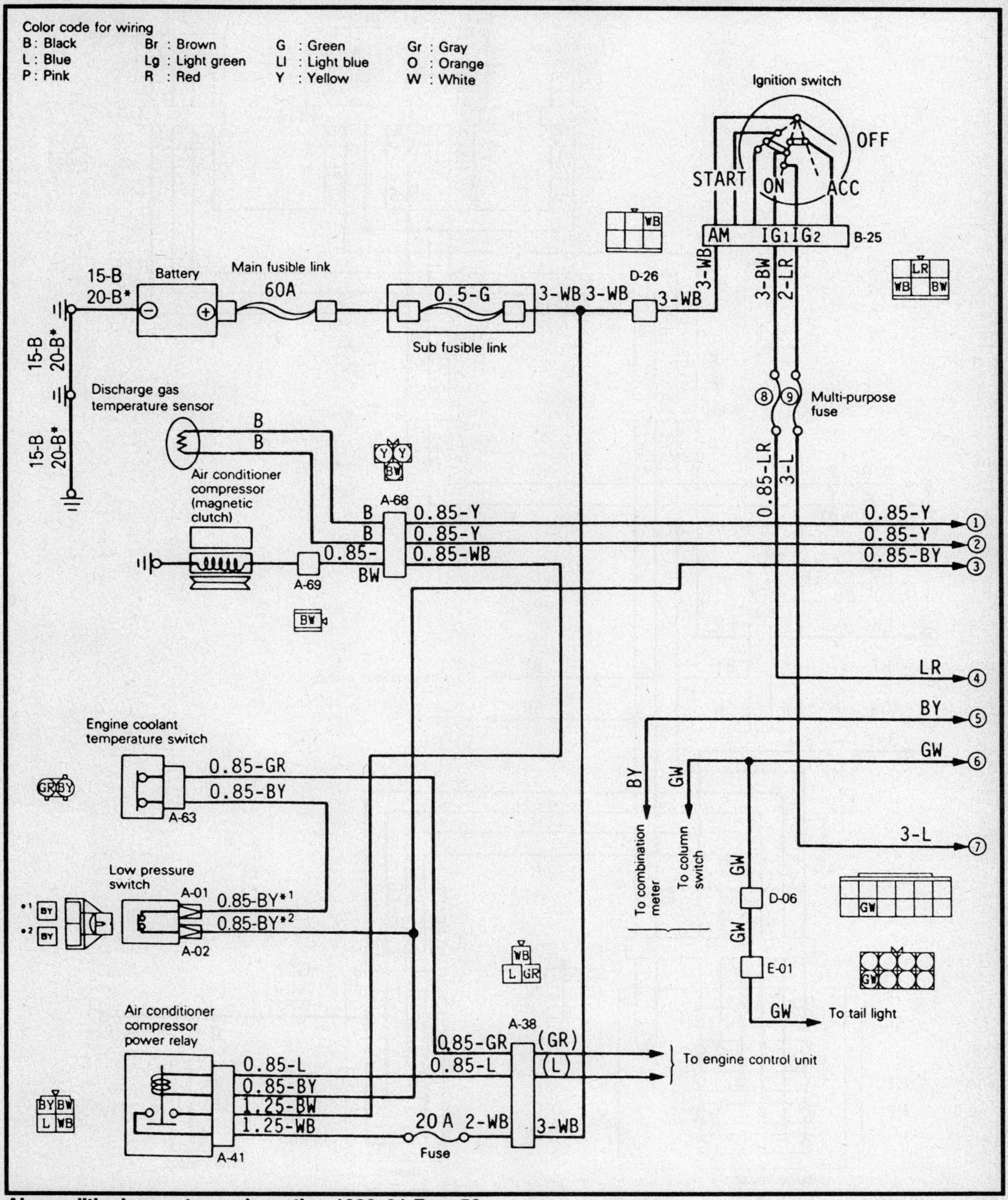
Color code for wiring
B : Black
L : Blue
P : Pink
Br : Brown
Lg : Light green
R : Red
G : Green
Ll : Light blue
Y : Yellow
Gr : Gray
O : Orange
W : White
Ignition switch
OFF
START
ON
ACC
AM
IG1 IG2
B-25
15-B
20-B*
Battery
Main fusible link
60A
0.5-G
3-WB
D-26
Sub fusible link
Discharge gas temperature sensor
Air conditioner compressor (magnetic clutch)
A-68
A-69
0.85-Y
0.85-BY
0.85-BW
0.85-WB
0.85-LR
3-BW
2-LR
3-L
Multi-purpose fuse
LR
BY
GW
To combination meter
To column switch
D-06
E-01
To tail light
Engine coolant temperature switch
0.85-GR
A-63
Low pressure switch
A-01
A-02
0.85-BY*1
0.85-BY*2
Air conditioner compressor power relay
0.85-L
1.25-BW
1.25-WB
A-38
(GR)
(L)
To engine control unit
20 A
2-WB
Fuse
A-41

Air conditioning system schematic—1990–91 Ram 50

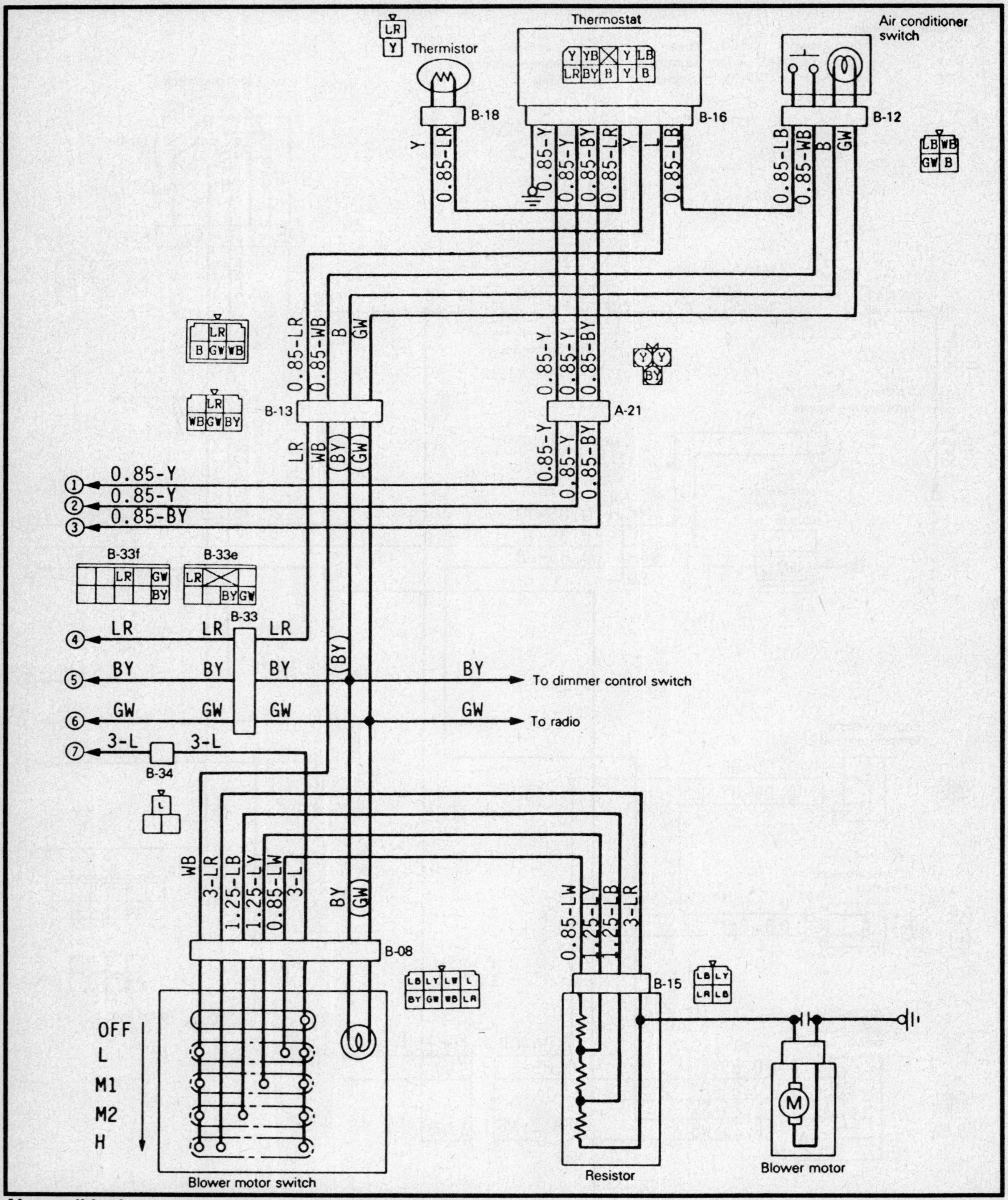
Thermostat
Air conditioner switch
Thermistor
B-18
B-16
B-12
B-13
A-21
B-33f
B-33e
B-33
B-34
B-08
B-15
0.85-Y
0.85-Y
0.85-BY
LR
BY
GW
3-L
To dimmer control switch
To radio
WB
3-LR
1.25-LB
1.25-LY
0.85-LW
0.85-LR
0.85-WB
0.85-LB
OFF
L
M1
M2
H
Blower motor switch
Resistor
Blower motor

Air conditioning system schematic—1990–91 Ram 50

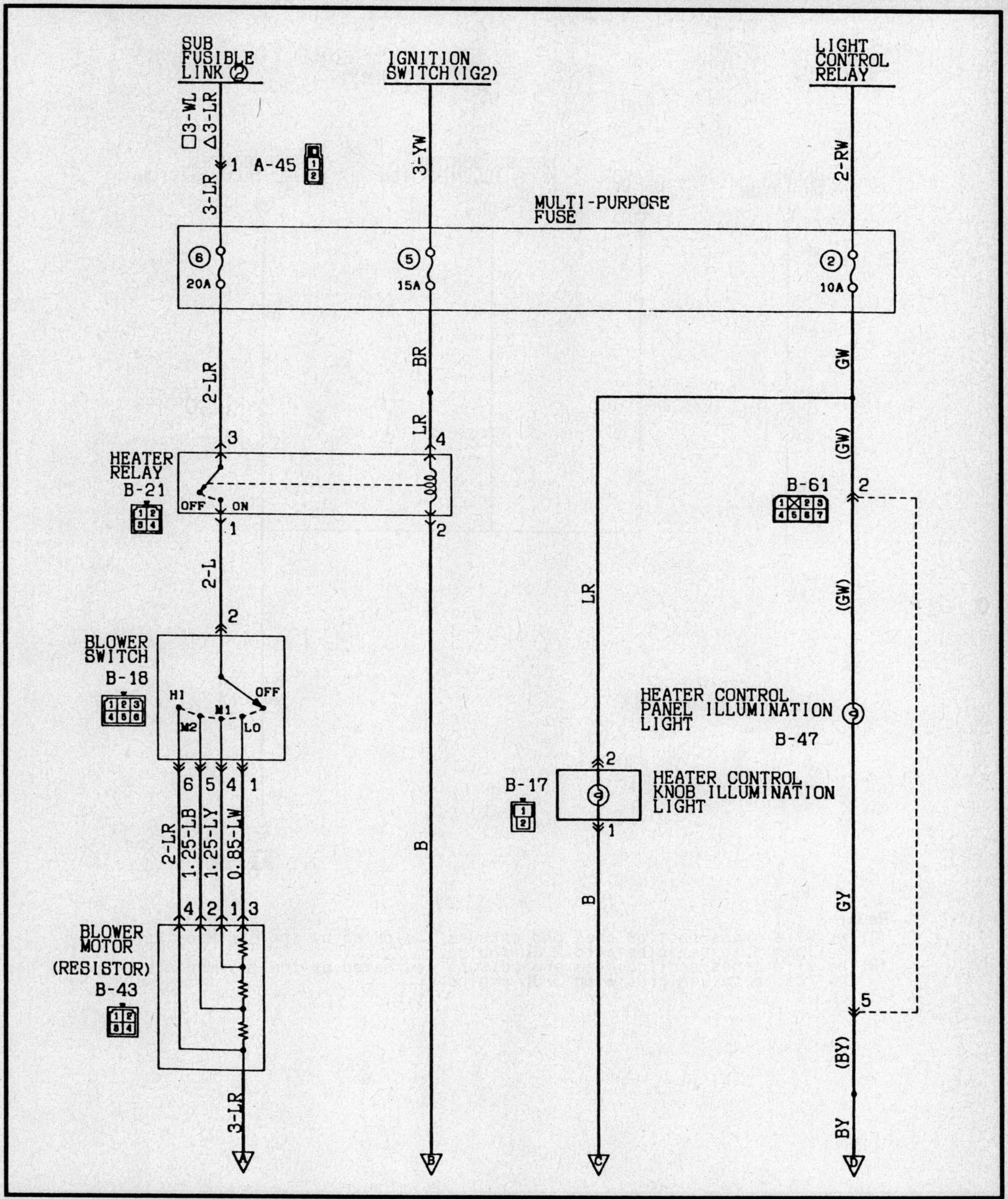
SUB FUSIBLE LINK ②
IGNITION SWITCH (IG2)
LIGHT CONTROL RELAY
□3-WL
Δ3-LR
1 A-45
3-LR
3-YW
2-RW
MULTI-PURPOSE FUSE
⑥ 20A
⑤ 15A
② 10A
2-LR
BR
GW
LR
(GW)
HEATER RELAY B-21
OFF ON
B-61
2-L
BLOWER SWITCH B-18
HI OFF M1 M2 LO
HEATER CONTROL PANEL ILLUMINATION LIGHT
B-47
B-17
HEATER CONTROL KNOB ILLUMINATION LIGHT
2-LR
1.25-LB
1.25-LY
0.85-LW
B
GY
BLOWER MOTOR (RESISTOR) B-43
(BY)
3-LR
BY
A
B
C
D

Heater system wiring schematic—Raider

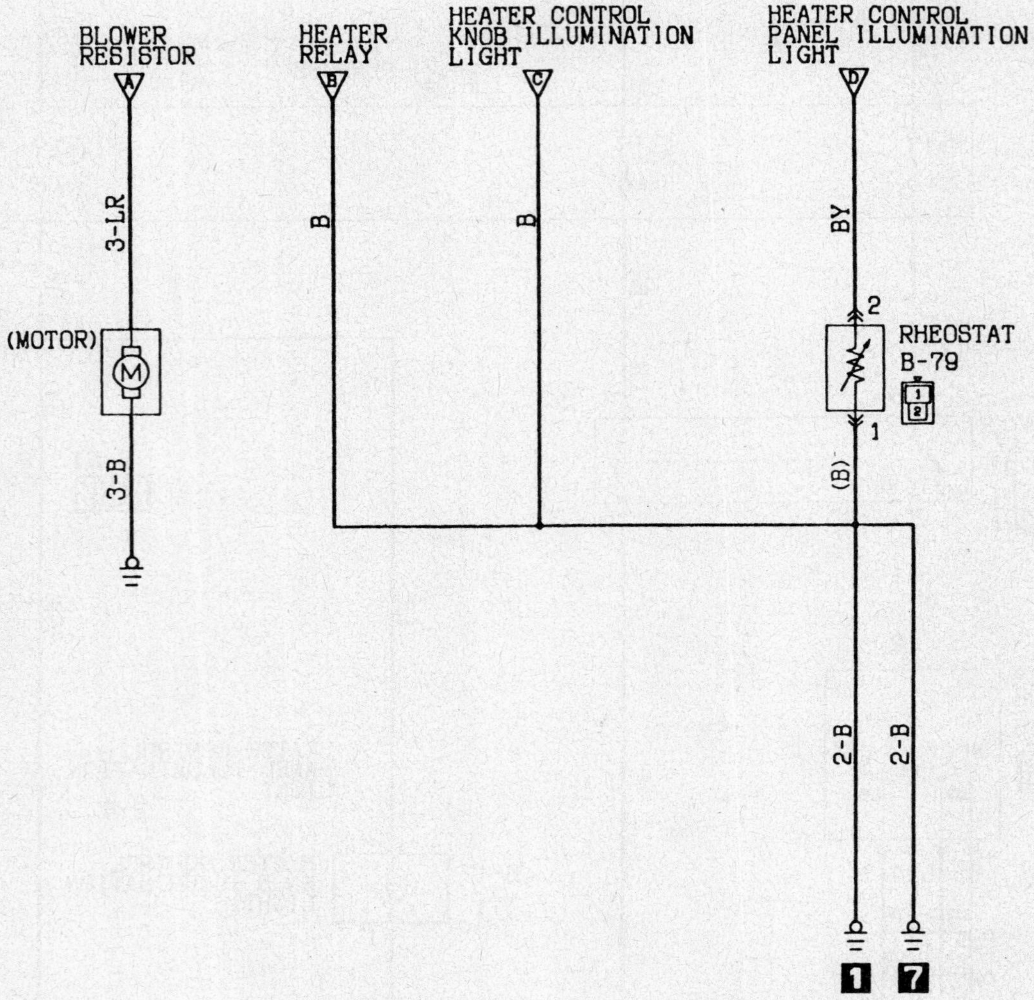
BLOWER RESISTOR
HEATER RELAY
HEATER CONTROL KNOB ILLUMINATION LIGHT
HEATER CONTROL PANEL ILLUMINATION LIGHT
A
B
C
D
3-LR
B
B
BY
(MOTOR)
M
3-B
2
RHEOSTAT
B-79
1
2
1
(B)
2-B
2-B
1
7

Remarks
(1) The wire cross-section area and colours indicated by the □ symbol is applicable to vehicles with 2.6L engine.
(2) The wire cross-section area and colours indicated by the △ symbol is applicable to vehicles with 3.0L engine.

Heater system wiring schematic—Raider

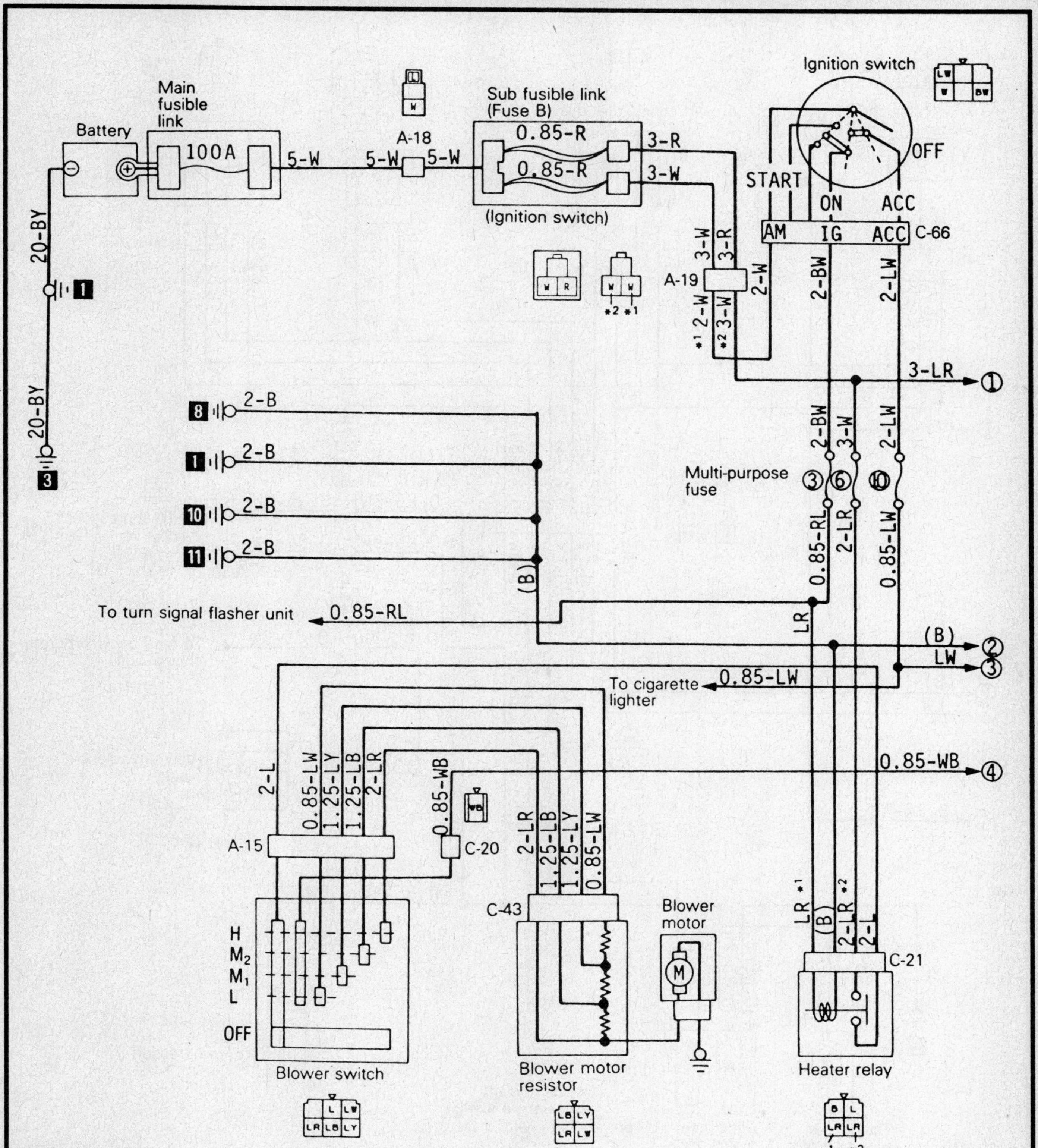
Battery
Main fusible link
100A
5-W
A-18
Sub fusible link (Fuse B)
0.85-R
3-R
3-W
(Ignition switch)
Ignition switch
START
ON
OFF
ACC
AM
IG
ACC
C-66
A-19
20-BY
2-B
(B)
2-BW
2-LW
3-LR
Multi-purpose fuse
0.85-RL
2-LR
0.85-LW
To turn signal flasher unit
LR
LW
To cigarette lighter
0.85-WB
2-L
1.25-LY
1.25-LB
A-15
C-20
C-43
H
OFF
Blower switch
Blower motor resistor
Blower motor
C-21
Heater relay

Wiring color code

B: Black	Br: Brown	G: Green	Gr: Gray	L: Blue	Lg: Light green
Ll: Light blue	O: Orange	P: Pink	R: Red	Y: Yellow	W: White

Air conditioning system schematic—Raider with 2.6L engine

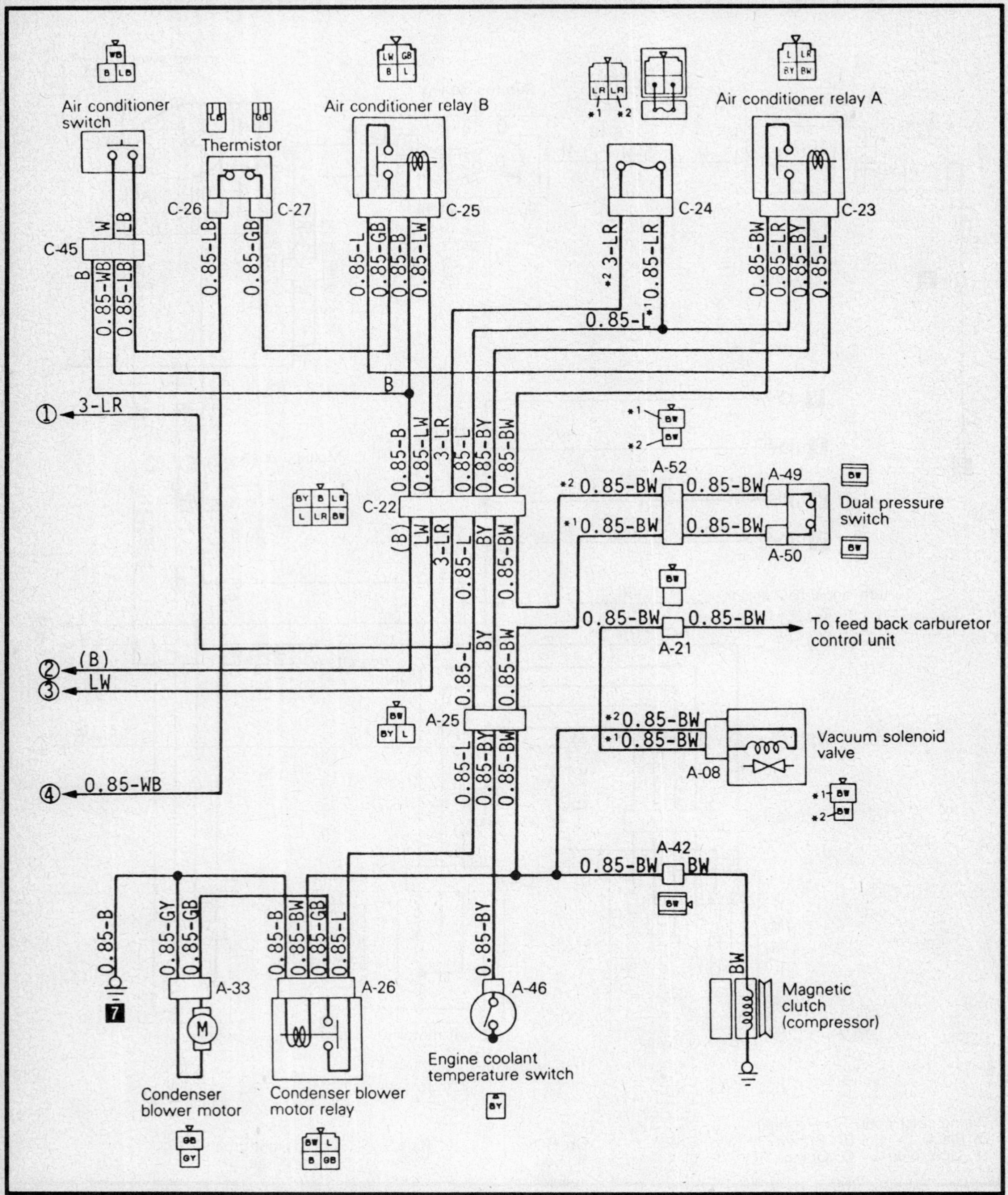
Air conditioner switch
Thermistor
Air conditioner relay B
Air conditioner relay A
C-45
C-26
C-27
C-25
C-24
C-23
C-22
0.85-WB
0.85-LB
0.85-GB
0.85-L
0.85-B
0.85-LW
3-LR
0.85-LR
0.85-BW
0.85-BY
3-LR
(B)
LW
0.85-WB
A-52
A-49
A-50
Dual pressure switch
A-21
To feed back carburetor control unit
A-25
A-08
Vacuum solenoid valve
A-42
0.85-BW
BW
0.85-B
0.85-GY
A-33
A-26
A-46
Condenser blower motor
Condenser blower motor relay
Engine coolant temperature switch
Magnetic clutch (compressor)

Air conditioning system schematic—Raider with 2.6L engine

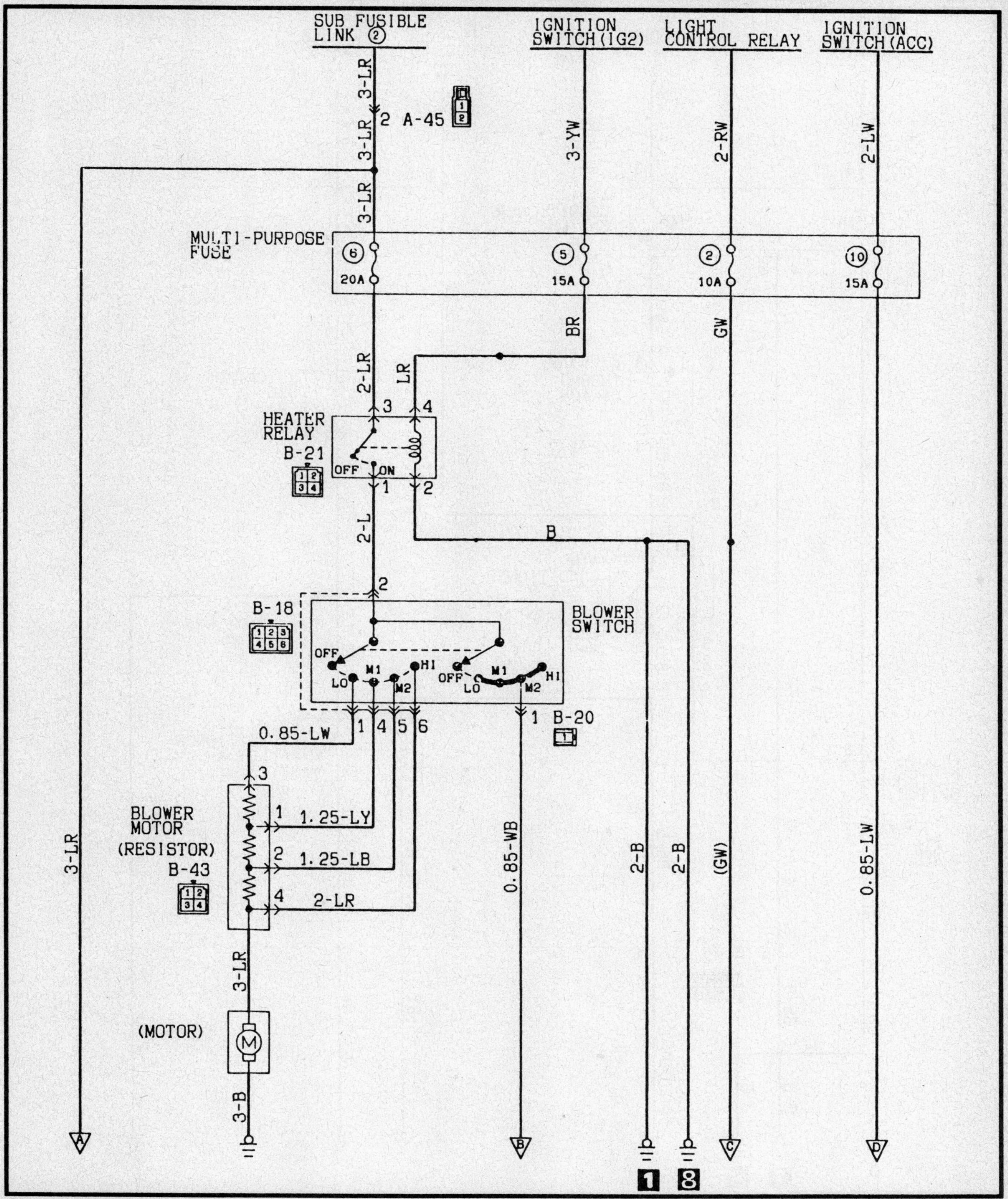
SUB FUSIBLE LINK ②
IGNITION SWITCH (IG2)
LIGHT CONTROL RELAY
IGNITION SWITCH (ACC)
3-LR
2 A-45
3-YW
2-RW
2-LW
MULTI-PURPOSE FUSE
20A
15A
10A
15A
BR
GW
2-LR
LR
HEATER RELAY
B-21
OFF
ON
2-L
B
B-18
BLOWER SWITCH
OFF
LO
M1
M2
HI
0.85-LW
B-20
BLOWER MOTOR (RESISTOR)
B-43
1.25-LY
1.25-LB
2-LR
0.85-WB
2-B
(GW)
0.85-LW
(MOTOR)
3-B
A
B
C
D
1
8

Air conditioning system schematic—Raider with 3.0L engine

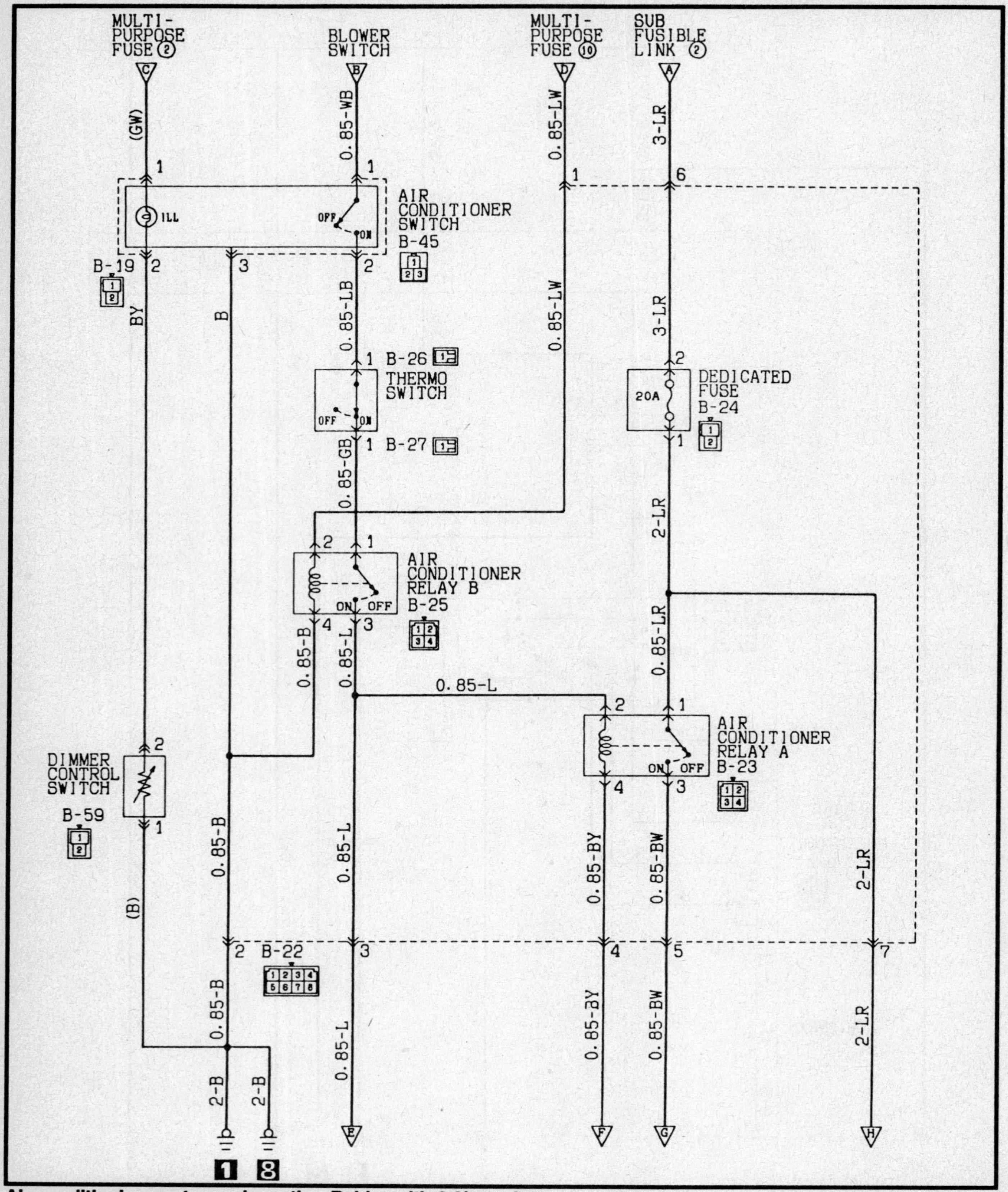
MULTI-PURPOSE FUSE ②
BLOWER SWITCH
MULTI-PURPOSE FUSE ⑩
SUB FUSIBLE LINK ②
C
B
D
A
(GW)
0.85-WB
0.85-LW
3-LR
AIR CONDITIONER SWITCH
B-45
ILL
OFF
ON
B-19
BY
B
0.85-LB
3-LR
B-26
THERMO SWITCH
B-27
DEDICATED FUSE
B-24
20A
0.85-GB
2-LR
AIR CONDITIONER RELAY B
B-25
0.85-B
0.85-L
0.85-LR
AIR CONDITIONER RELAY A
B-23
DIMMER CONTROL SWITCH
B-59
0.85-BY
0.85-BW
2-LR
(B)
B-22
2-B
E
F
G
H
1
8
Air conditioning system schematic—Raider with 3.0L engine

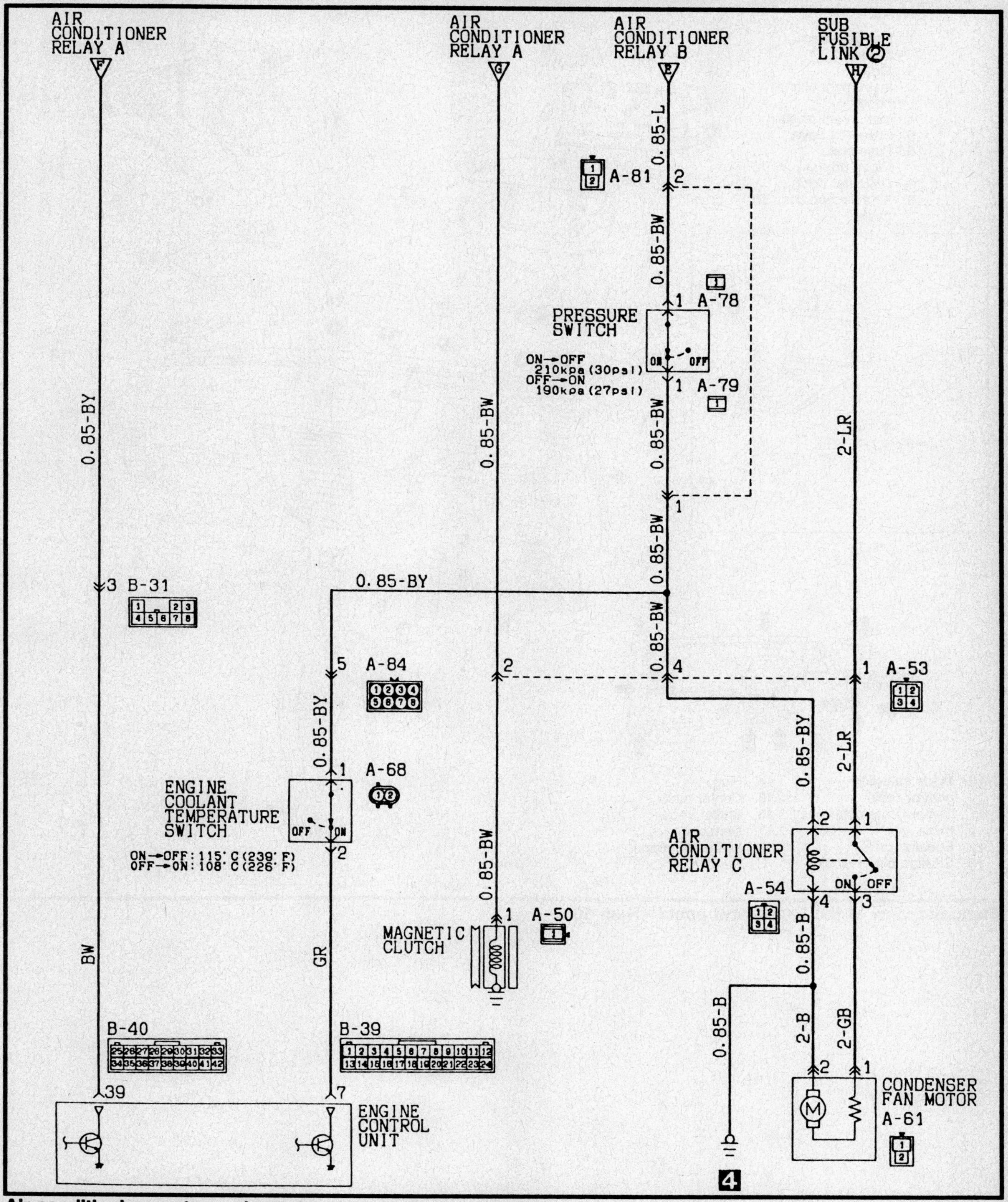
AIR CONDITIONER RELAY A
F
AIR CONDITIONER RELAY A
G
AIR CONDITIONER RELAY B
E
SUB FUSIBLE LINK ②
H
0.85-L
A-81
2
0.85-BW
A-78
1
PRESSURE SWITCH
ON→OFF
210kpa (30psi)
OFF→ON
190kpa (27psi)
ON
OFF
1
A-79
0.85-BY
0.85-BW
0.85-BW
2-LR
1
0.85-BW
0.85-BY
3 B-31
0.85-BW
5
A-84
2
4
1
A-53
0.85-BY
0.85-BY
2-LR
1
A-68
ENGINE COOLANT TEMPERATURE SWITCH
OFF
ON
2
ON→OFF: 115° C (239° F)
OFF→ON: 108° C (226° F)
0.85-BW
2
1
AIR CONDITIONER RELAY C
ON
OFF
A-54
4
3
1
A-50
MAGNETIC CLUTCH
0.85-B
BW
GR
B-40
B-39
0.85-B
2-B
2-GB
39
7
2
1
CONDENSER FAN MOTOR
A-61
ENGINE CONTROL UNIT
4

Air conditioning system schematic—Raider with 3.0L engine

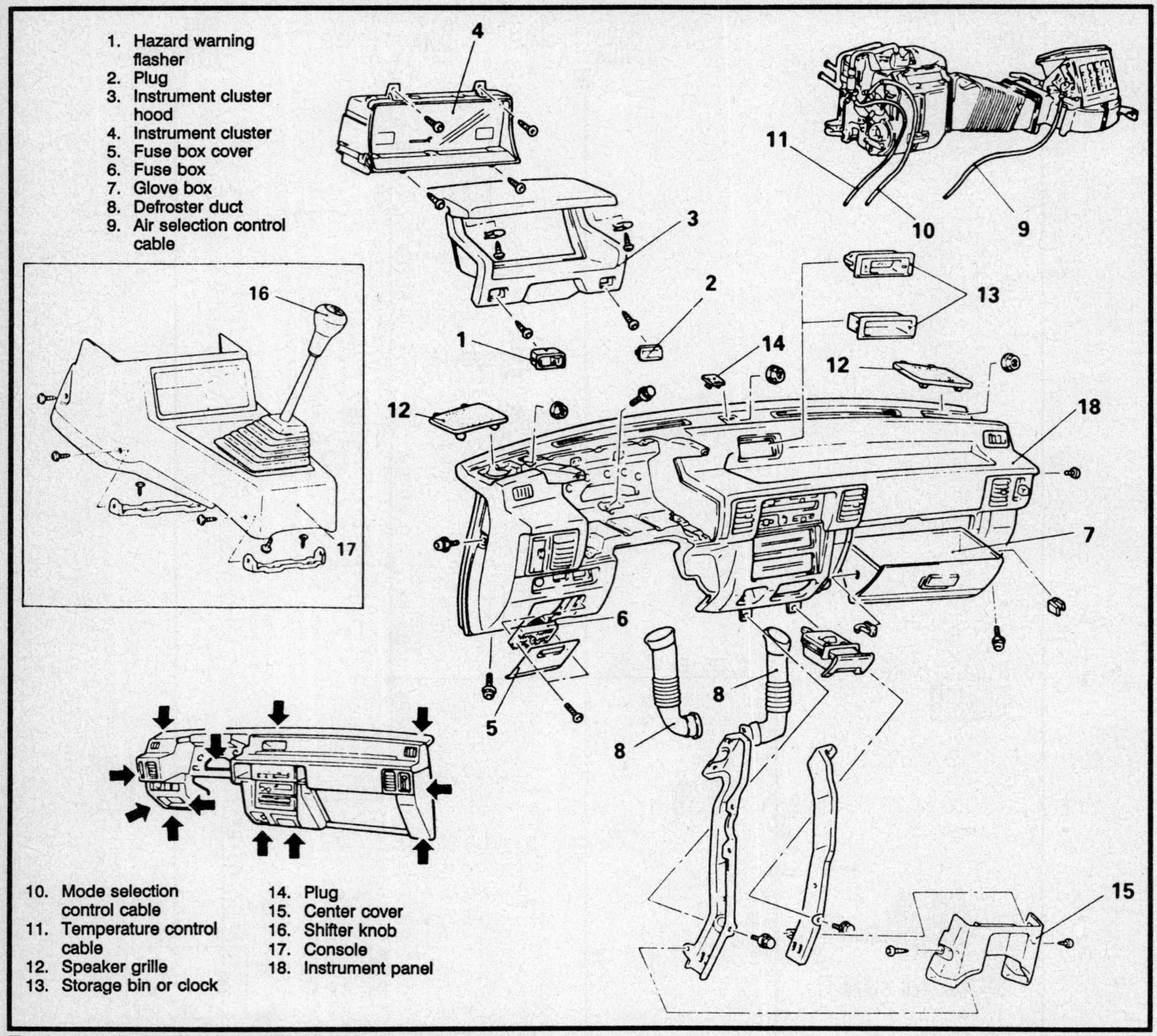
1. Hazard warning flasher
2. Plug
3. Instrument cluster hood
4. Instrument cluster
5. Fuse box cover
6. Fuse box
7. Glove box
8. Defroster duct
9. Air selection control cable
10. Mode selection control cable
11. Temperature control cable
12. Speaker grille
13. Storage bin or clock
14. Plug
15. Center cover
16. Shifter knob
17. Console
18. Instrument panel

Exploded view of the instrument panel—Ram 50

30 ISUZU TRUCKS 30

AMIGO • PICK-UP • RODEO • TROOPER/TROOPER II

SPECIFICATIONS

ENGINE IDENTIFICATION

Year	Model	Engine Displacement cu. in. (cc/liter)	Engine Series Identification	No. of Cylinders	Engine Type
1989	Amigo	138 (2254/2.3)	4ZD1	4	OHC
	Amigo	156 (2559/2.6)	4ZE1	4	OHC
	Pickup	138 (2254/2.3)	4ZD1	4	OHC
	Pickup	156 (2559/2.6)	4ZE1	4	OHC
	Trooper/Trooper II	156 (2559/2.6)	4ZE1	4	OHC
	Trooper/Trooper II	173 (2828/2.8)	CPC	6	OHV
1990	Amigo	138 (2254/2.3)	4ZD1	4	OHC
	Amigo	156 (2559/2.6)	4ZE1	4	OHC
	Pickup	138 (2254/2.3)	4ZD1	4	OHC
	Pickup	156 (2559/2.6)	4ZE1	4	OHC
	Trooper/Trooper II	156 (2559/2.6)	4ZE1	4	OHC
	Trooper/Trooper II	173 (2828/2.8)	CPC	6	OHV
1991	Amigo	138 (2254/2.3)	4ZD1	4	OHC
	Amigo	156 (2559/2.6)	4ZE1	4	OHC
	Pickup	138 (2254/2.3)	4ZD1	4	OHC
	Pickup	156 (2559/2.6)	4ZE1	4	OHC
	Pickup	189 (3137/3.1)	CPC	6	OHV
	Rodeo	156 (2559/2.6)	4ZE1	4	OHC
	Rodeo	189 (3137/3.1)	CPC	6	OHV
	Trooper/Trooper II	156 (2559/2.6)	4ZE1	4	OHC
	Trooper/Trooper II	173 (2828/2.8)	CPC	6	OHV

REFRIGERANT CAPACITIES

Year	Model	Freon (oz.)	Oil (fl. oz.)	Type
1989	Amigo	33.5	5.0	R-12
	Pickup	33.5	5.0 ①	R-12
	Trooper/Trooper II	33.5	5.0 ①	R-12
1990	Amigo	33.5	5.0	R-12
	Pickup	33.5	5.0 ①	R-12
	Trooper/Trooper II	33.5	5.0 ①	R-12
1991	Amigo	33.5	5.0	R-12
	Pickup	33.5	5.0 ①	R-12
	Trooper/Trooper II	33.5	5.0 ①	R-12
	Rodeo	33.5	5.0 ①	R-12

① R-4 Compressor uses 6.0 fl. oz. of Refrigerant Oil

AIR CONDITIONING BELT TENSION CHART

Year	Model	Engine Displacement cu. in. (cc/liter)	Belt Type	New	Used
1989	Amigo	138 ci (2254/2.3)	V-Belt	13/32 ① ②	—
		156 ci (2559/2.6)	V-Belt	13/32 ① ②	—
	Pickup	138 ci (2254/2.3)	V-Belt	13/32 ① ②	—
		156 ci (2559/2.6)	V-Belt	13/32 ① ②	—
	Trooper/Trooper II	156 ci (2559/2.6)	V-Belt	13/32 ① ②	—
		173 ci (2828/2.8)	Serpentine	S/A ③	—
1990	Amigo	138 ci (2554/2.3)	V-Belt	13/32 ① ②	—
		156 ci (2559/2.6)	V-Belt	13/32 ① ②	—
	Pickup	138 ci (2254/2.3)	V-Belt	13/32 ① ②	—
		156 ci (2559/2.6)	V-Belt	13/32 ① ②	—
	Trooper/Trooper II	156 ci (2559/2.6)	V-Belt	13/32 ① ②	—
		173 ci (2828/2.8)	Serpentine	S/A ③	—
1991	Amigo	138 ci (2554/2.3)	V-Belt	13/32 ① ②	—
		156 ci (2559/2.6)	V-Belt	13/32 ① ②	—
	Pickup	138 ci (2254/2.3)	V-Belt	13/32 ① ②	—
		156 ci (2559/2.6)	V-Belt	13/32 ① ②	—
		189 ci (3137/3.1)	Serpentine	S/A ③	—
	Trooper/Trooper II	156 ci (2559/2.6)	V-Belt	13/32 ① ②	—
		173 ci (2828/2.8)	Serpentine	S/A ③	—
	Rodeo	156 ci (2559/2.6)	V-Belt	13/32 ① ②	—
		189 ci (3137/3.1)	Serpentine	S/A ③	—

① Inches of deflection at the midpoint of the belt using 22 lbs. of force
② Metric measurement 10mm
③ Self adjusting

SYSTEM DESCRIPTION

General Information

The heater unit is located in the center of the vehicle along the firewall. The heater system is a bi-level system designed to direct warm air through the vents to either the windshield or the floor and cool air through the panel outlet. The air conditioning system is designed to be activated in combination with a separate air conditioning switch installed in the control assembly and the fan speed switch. The system incorporates a compressor, condenser, evaporator, receiver/drier, pressure switch, expansion valve, thermo switch, refrigerant lines and some models are equipped with a air conditioning cut control unit.

Service Valve Location

Charging valve locations will vary, but most of the time the high or low pressure fitting will be located at the compressor, receiver/drier or along the refrigerant lines. Always discharge, evacuate and recharge at the low side service fitting.

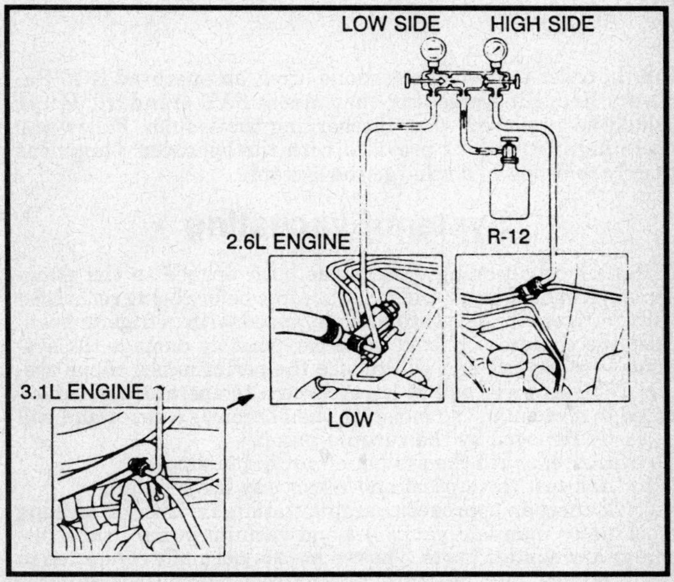
LOW SIDE
HIGH SIDE
R-12
2.6L ENGINE
3.1L ENGINE
LOW
Typical service valve locations

System Discharging

R-12 refrigerant is a chloroflourocarbon which, when mishandled, can contribute to the depletion on the ozone layer in the upper atmosphere. Ozone filters out harmful radiation from the

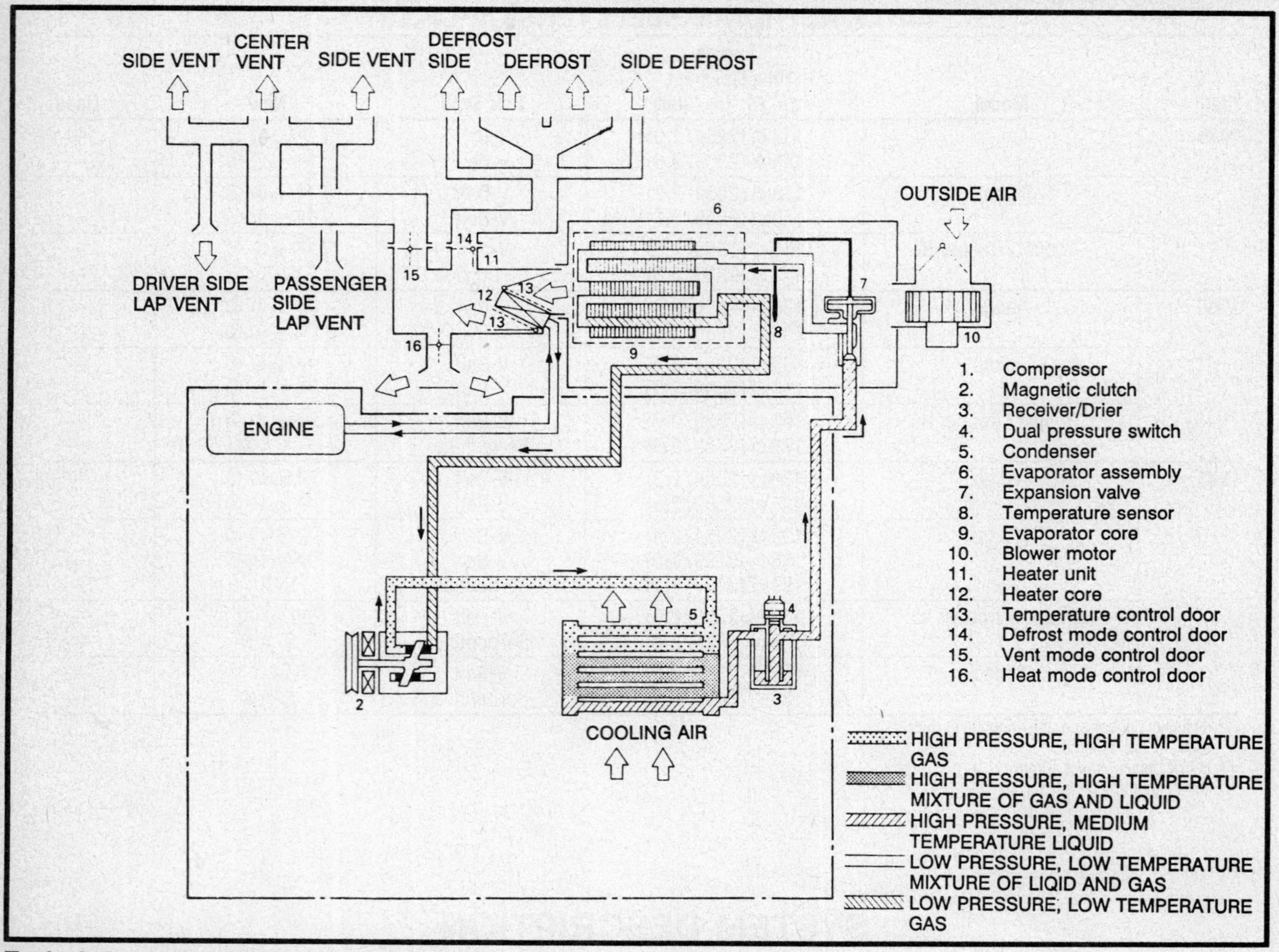
SIDE VENT
CENTER VENT
SIDE VENT
DEFROST SIDE
DEFROST
SIDE DEFROST
OUTSIDE AIR
DRIVER SIDE LAP VENT
PASSENGER SIDE LAP VENT
ENGINE
COOLING AIR
1. Compressor
2. Magnetic clutch
3. Receiver/Drier
4. Dual pressure switch
5. Condenser
6. Evaporator assembly
7. Expansion valve
8. Temperature sensor
9. Evaporator core
10. Blower motor
11. Heater unit
12. Heater core
13. Temperature control door
14. Defrost mode control door
15. Vent mode control door
16. Heat mode control door
HIGH PRESSURE, HIGH TEMPERATURE GAS
HIGH PRESSURE, HIGH TEMPERATURE MIXTURE OF GAS AND LIQUID
HIGH PRESSURE, MEDIUM TEMPERATURE LIQUID
LOW PRESSURE, LOW TEMPERATURE MIXTURE OF LIQID AND GAS
LOW PRESSURE, LOW TEMPERATURE GAS

Typical air conditioning system components

sun. In order to protect the ozone layer, an approved R-12 Recovery/Recycling machine that meets SAE standard J1991 should be employed when discharging the system. Follow the operating instructions provided with the approved equipment exactly to properly discharge the system.

System Evacuating

If the air conditioning system has been opened to the atmosphere, it should be air and moisture free before being recharged with refrigerant. Moisture and air mixed with refrigerant will raise the compressor head pressure, possibly damage the system's components and will reduce the performance of the system. Moisture will boil at normal room temperature when exposed to a vacuum, the moisture then becomes a vapor and will be easily removed by the vacuum pump.

To evacuate, or rid the system of air and moisture:

1. Leak test the system and repair any leaks found.
2. Connect an approved charging station, Recovery/Recycling machine or manifold gauge set and vacuum pump to the discharge and suction ports. The red hose is normally connected to the discharge (high pressure) line, and the blue hose is connected to the suction (low pressure) line.
3. Open the discharge and suction ports and start the vacuum pump. If the pump is not able to pull at least 26 in. Hg vacuum, there is a leak that must be repaired before evacuation can occur.
4. Once the system has reached at least 26 in. Hg vacuum, allow the system to evacuate for at least 10 minutes. The longer the system is evacuated, the more contaminants will be removed.
5. Close all valves and turn the pump off. If the system loses more than 2 in. Hg vacuum after 15 minutes, there is a leak that should be repaired.

System Charging

1. Connect an approved charging station, Recovery/Recycling machine or manifold gauge set to the discharge and suction ports. The red hose is normally connected to the discharge (high pressure) line, and the blue hose is connected to the suction (low pressure) line.
2. Follow the instructions provided with the equipment and charge the system with the specified amount of refrigerant.
3. Perform a leak test.

SYSTEM COMPONENTS

Radiator

REMOVAL AND INSTALLATION

1. Disconnect the negative battery cable.
2. Remove the radiator cap and loosen the drain plug to drain the coolant from the system.
3. Disconnect the radiator and surge tank hoses from the radiator.
4. Remove the fan shroud and the radiator support brackets.

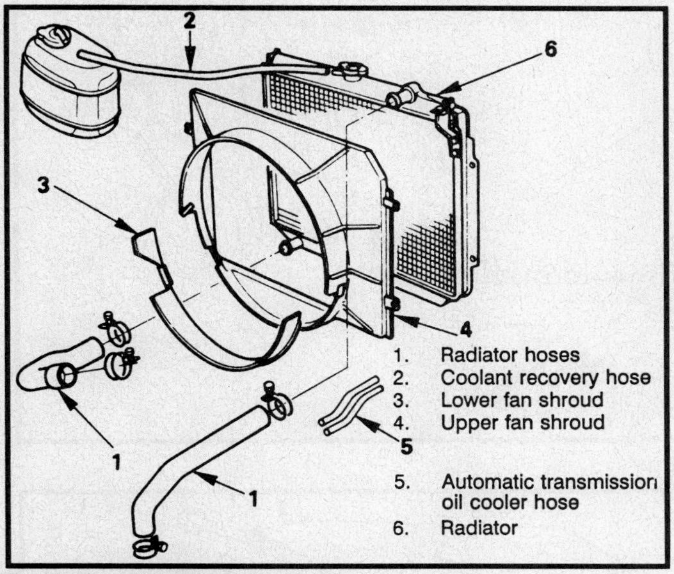
1
2
3
4
5
6
1. Radiator hoses
2. Coolant recovery hose
3. Lower fan shroud
4. Upper fan shroud
5. Automatic transmission oil cooler hose
6. Radiator
Typical radiator assembly

5. Remove the remaining mounting bolts and the radiator.
6. Installation is the reverse of the removal procedure. Fill the radiator with the specified amount of water and anti-freeze.

NOTE: All radiators fins must be free of dirt, grease, oil and must be straight to avoid an overheating condition.

Condenser

REMOVAL AND INSTALLATION

1. Disconnect the negative battery cable.
2. Properly discharge the air conditioner.
3. Remove the radiator grille.
4. Mark and remove radiator grille support bracket.
5. Disconnect pressure switch connector.
6. Using a backup wrench, remove the refrigerant lines.
7. Remove condenser attaching bolts.
8. Remove the condenser assembly.
9. Installation is the reverse of the removal procedure.

Compressor

REMOVAL AND INSTALLATION

2.3L and 2.6L Engines

1. Disconnect the negative battery cable.
2. Properly discharge the air conditioning system.
3. Remove power steering pump and brackets, if required.
4. Disconnect magnetic clutch wire connector.
5. Loosen the center nut of the compressor idler pulley and then loosen the tension adjustment bolt and remove the belt.
6. Remove the compressor refrigerant lines.
7. Remove compressor attaching bolts.

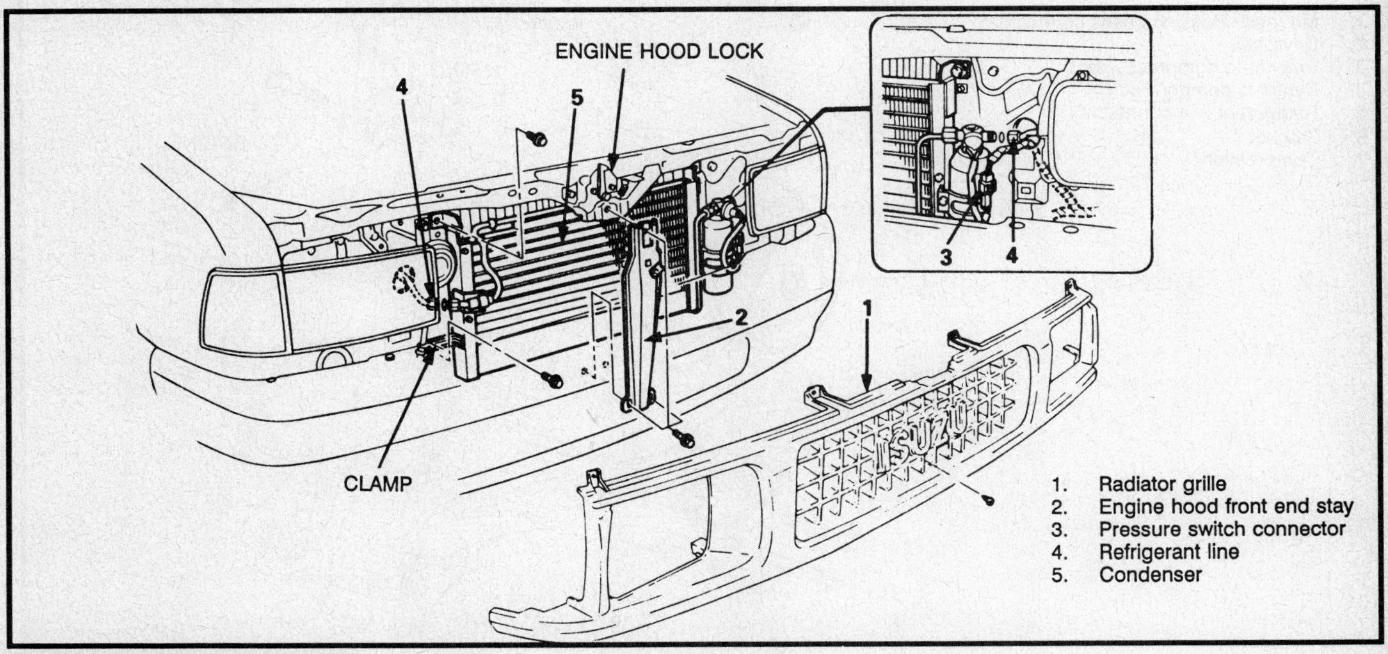
ENGINE HOOD LOCK
4
5
3
4
2
1
CLAMP
1. Radiator grille
2. Engine hood front end stay
3. Pressure switch connector
4. Refrigerant line
5. Condenser
Typical condenser assembly

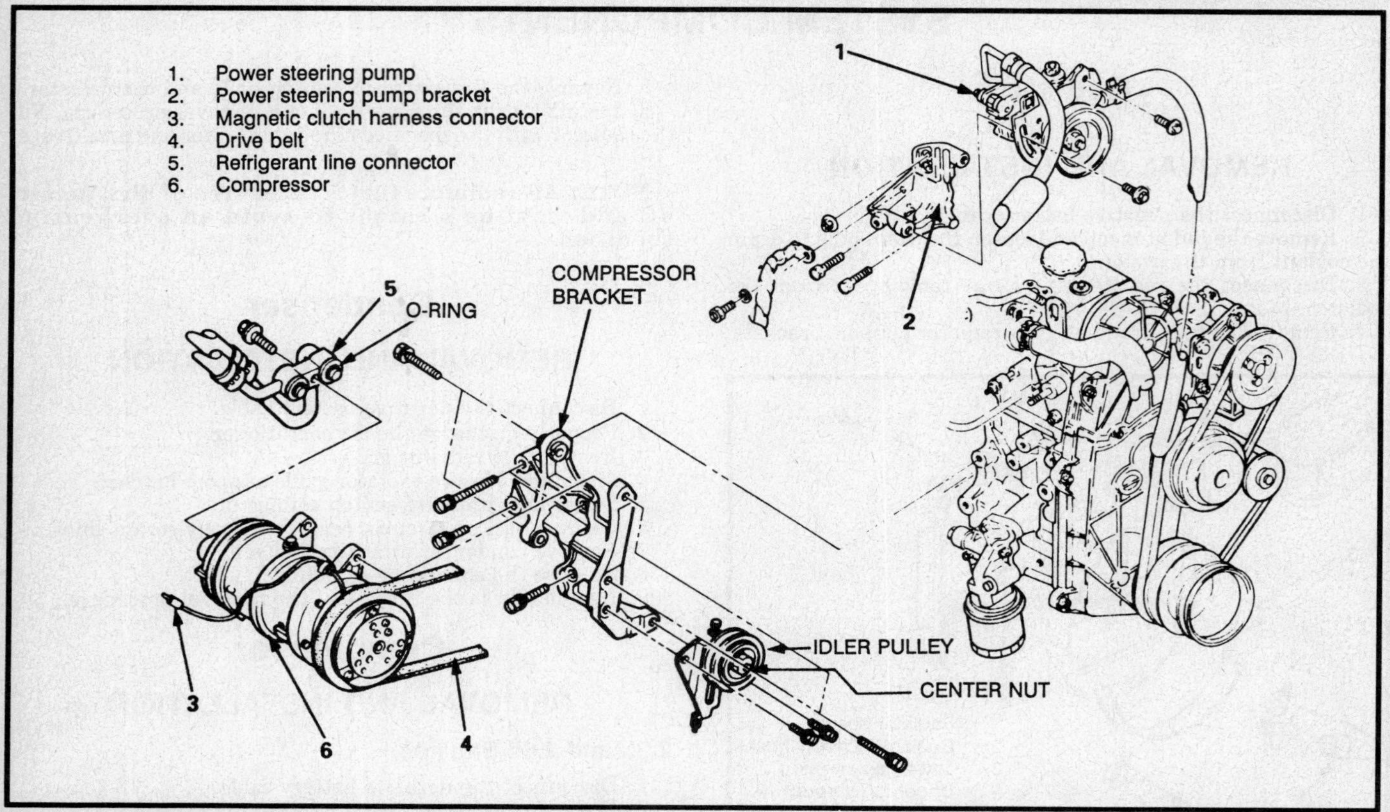
1. Power steering pump
2. Power steering pump bracket
3. Magnetic clutch harness connector
4. Drive belt
5. Refrigerant line connector
6. Compressor
COMPRESSOR BRACKET
O-RING
IDLER PULLEY
CENTER NUT
1
2
3
4
5
6

Typical compressor removal on 2.3L and 2.6L engines

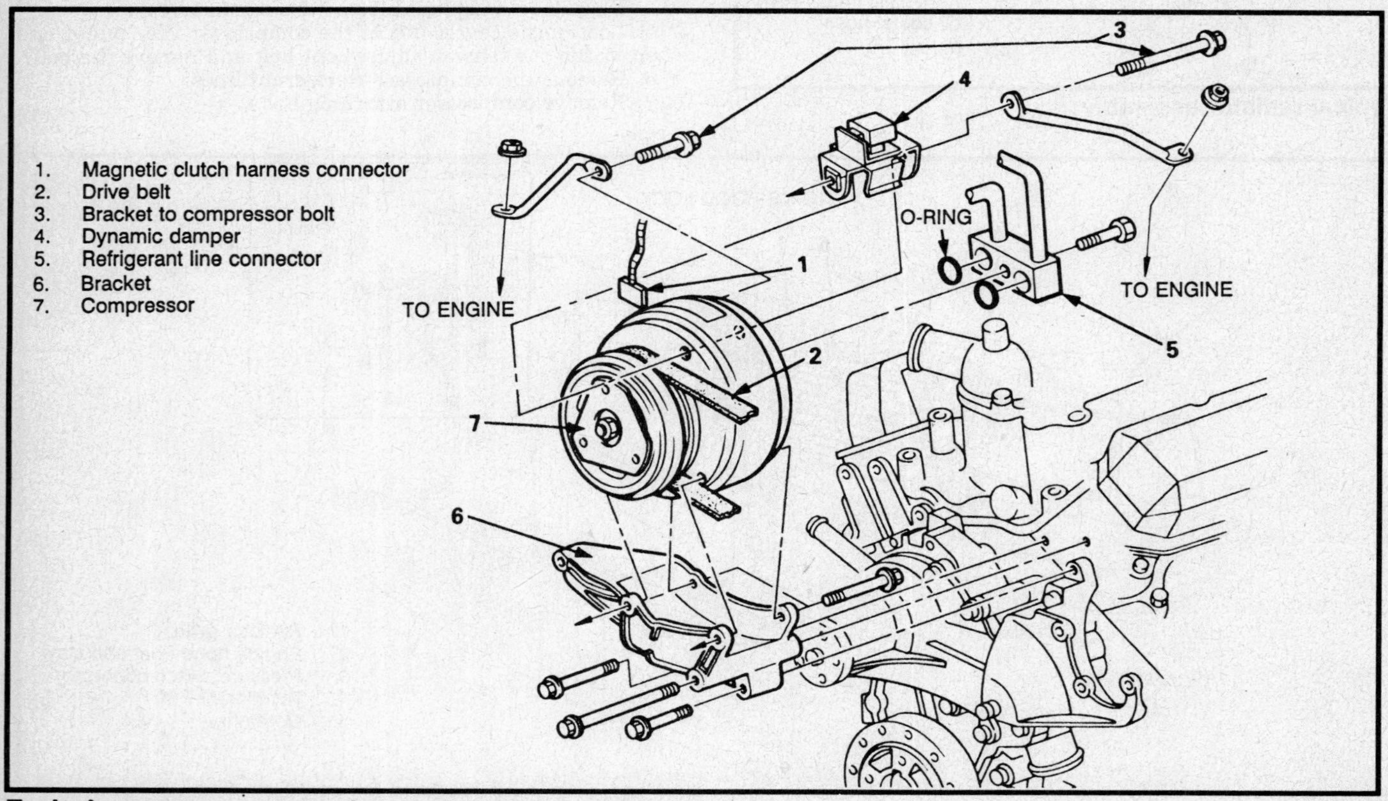
1. Magnetic clutch harness connector
2. Drive belt
3. Bracket to compressor bolt
4. Dynamic damper
5. Refrigerant line connector
6. Bracket
7. Compressor
O-RING
TO ENGINE
TO ENGINE
1
2
3
4
5
6
7

Typical compressor removal on 2.8L and 3.1L engines

8. Remove bolts attaching brackets to compressor, and remove compressor.
9. Installation is the reverse of removal procedure.

2.8L and 3.1L Engines

1. Disconnect the negative battery cable.
2. Properly discharge the air conditioning system.
3. Disconnect the magnetic clutch wire harness.
4. Loosen the idler pulley and remove the drive belt.
5. Remove the brace to compressor bolts.
6. If equipped, remove the compressor dynamic dampner.
7. Remove the refrigerant lines.
8. Remove the compressor bracket to engine bolts and remove the compressor.
9. Installation is the reverse of removal procedure.

NOTE: Immediately plug the compressor and lines to prevent contamination of the system when opened to atmosphere and always use new o-rings with a light coat of refrigerant oil on them.

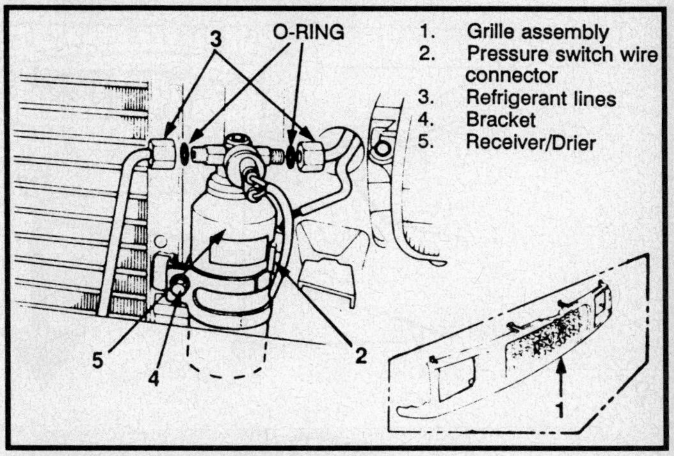
3
O-RING
1. Grille assembly
2. Pressure switch wire connector
3. Refrigerant lines
4. Bracket
5. Receiver/Drier
5
4
2
1

Typical receiver/drier removal

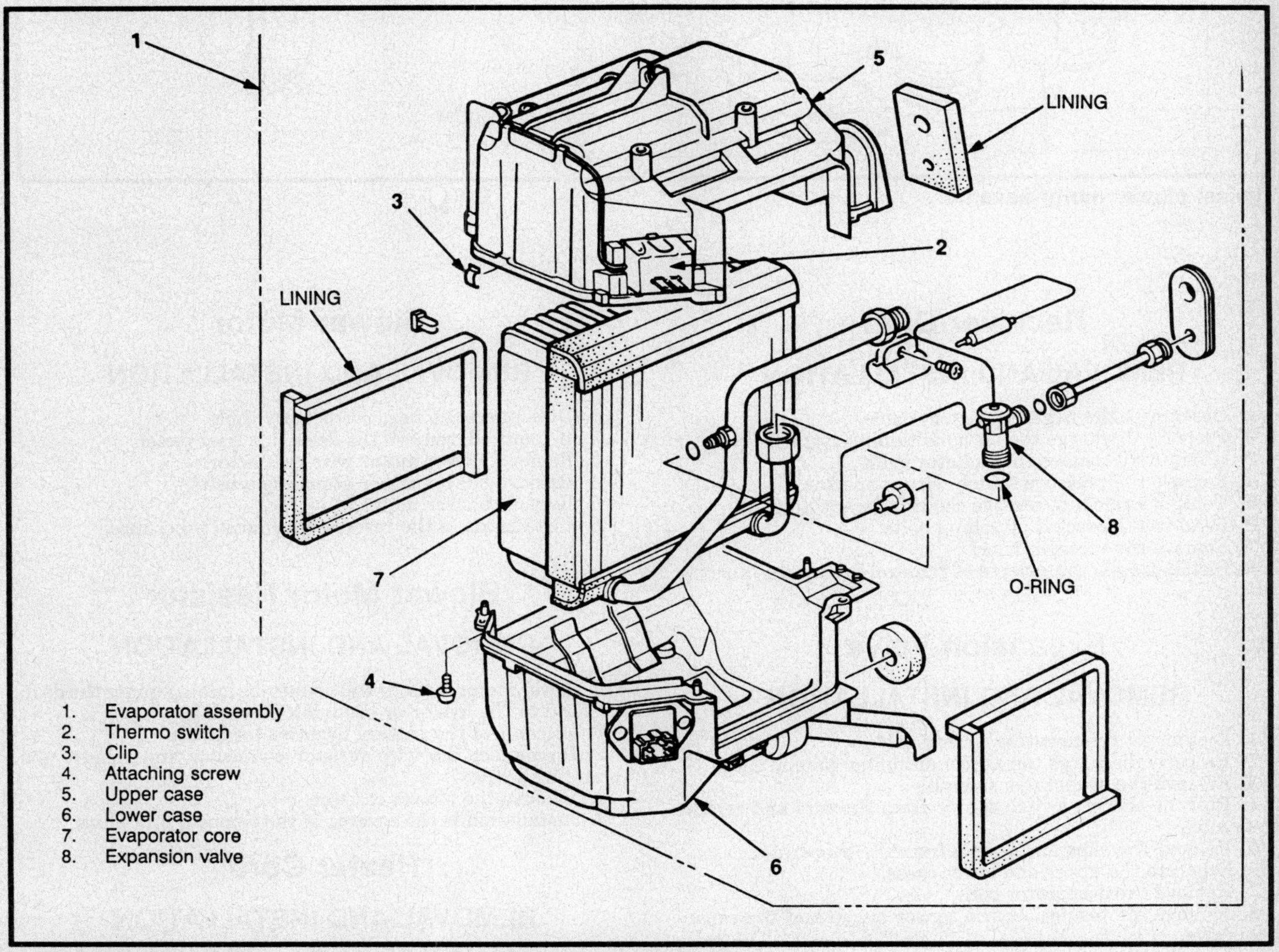
1
5
LINING
3
2
LINING
7
8
O-RING
4
6
1. Evaporator assembly
2. Thermo switch
3. Clip
4. Attaching screw
5. Upper case
6. Lower case
7. Evaporator core
8. Expansion valve

Typical thermo switch, evaporator and expansion valve assembly

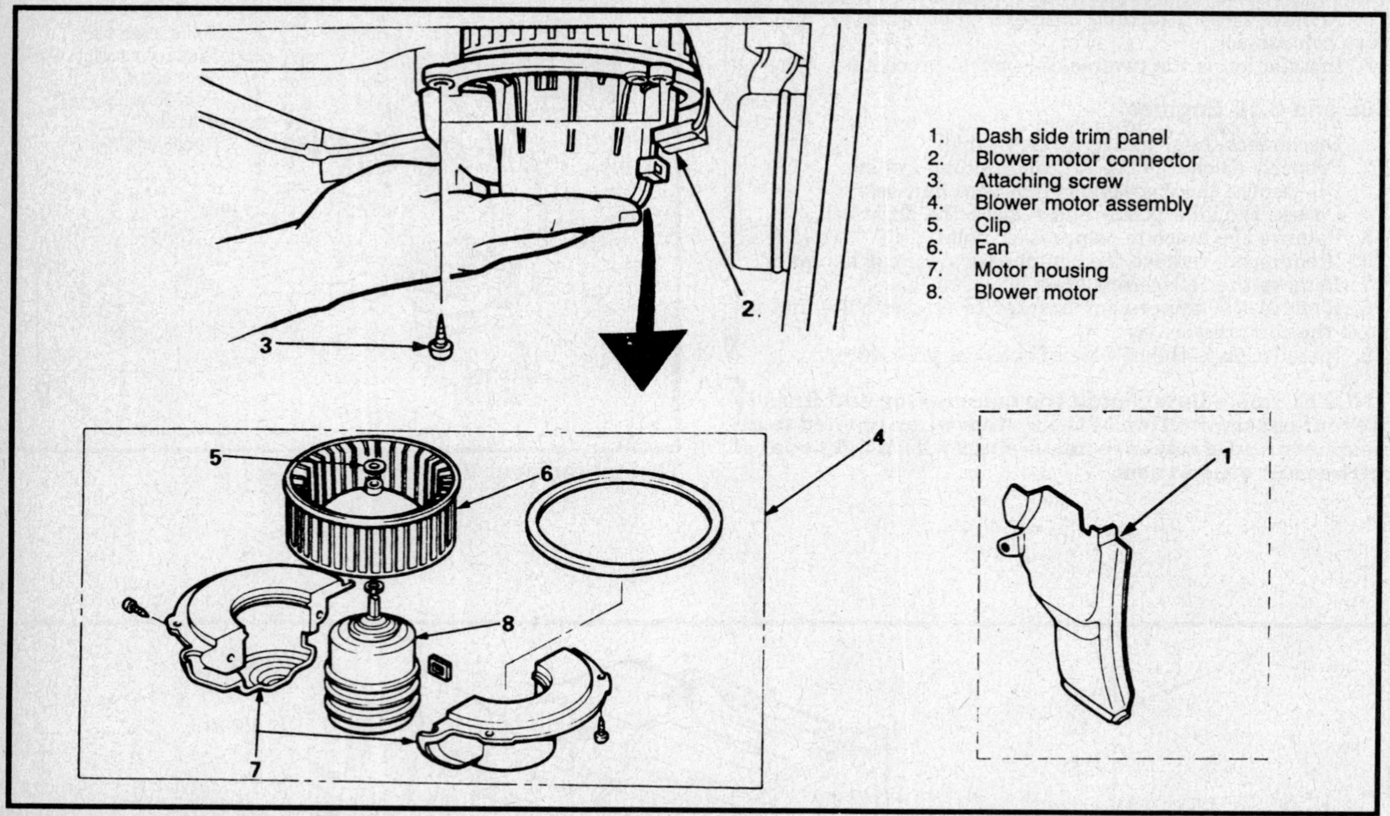
1. Dash side trim panel
2. Blower motor connector
3. Attaching screw
4. Blower motor assembly
5. Clip
6. Fan
7. Motor housing
8. Blower motor
1
2
3
4
5
6
7
8

Typical blower motor assembly

Receiver/Drier

REMOVAL AND INSTALLATION

1. Disconnect the negative battery cable.
2. Properly discharge the air conditioning system.
3. If required, remove the radiator grille.
4. Remove the pressure switch wire connector.
5. Using 2 wrenches, remove the refrigerant lines.
6. Remove the bracket attaching bolts.
7. Remove the receiver/drier.
8. Installation is the reverse of removal procedure.

Expansion Valve

REMOVAL AND INSTALLATION

1. Disconnect the negative battery cable.
2. Properly discharge the air conditioning system.
3. Remove the evaporator assembly.
4. Pull the thermo switch sensor from the core and remove the switch.
5. Remove the clips and screws from the evaporator case.
6. Separate the upper and lower cases.
7. Remove the evaporator core.
8. Remove the insulation, the sensor clamp and the expansion valve.
9. Installation is the reverse of removal procedure.

Blower Motor

REMOVAL AND INSTALLATION

1. Disconnect the negative battery cable.
2. If required, remove the dash side trim panel.
3. Remove blower motor wire connector.
4. Remove blower motor attaching screws.
5. Remove blower motor.
6. Installation is the reverse of removal procedure.

Blower Motor Resistor

REMOVAL AND INSTALLATION

The blower motor resistor will usually be located under the dash attached to the heater or evaporator housing.

1. Disconnect the battery negative terminal.
2. Disconnect the wire resistor connector and remove the mounting screw.
3. Remove the blower resistor.
4. Installation is the reverse of the removal procedure.

Heater Core

REMOVAL AND INSTALLATION

1. Disconnect the negative battery cable.

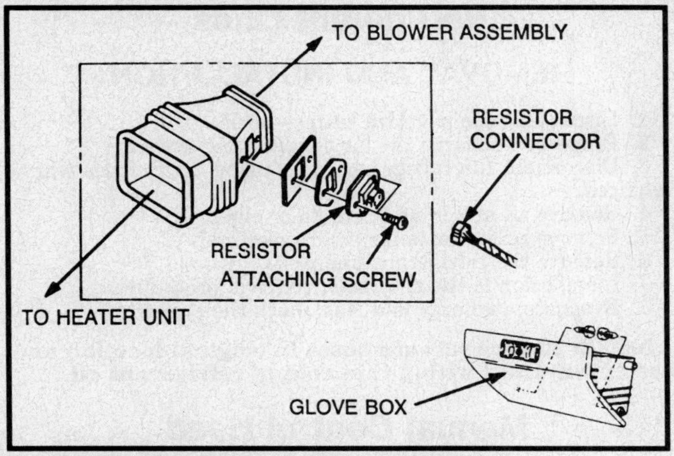
TO BLOWER ASSEMBLY
RESISTOR CONNECTOR
RESISTOR
ATTACHING SCREW
TO HEATER UNIT
GLOVE BOX

Typical blower motor resistor removal

2. Properly discharge the air conditioning system and remove the evaporator lines, if equipped.
3. Properly drain the cooling system and disconnect the heater hoses.
4. Remove the instrument panel.
5. Disconnect the vacuum hose on the heater unit, if equipped.
6. Disconnect the relay wire connectors.
7. Remove the evaporator assembly.
8. Remove the side ventilator duct.
9. Remove the heater unit attaching nuts and remove assembly.

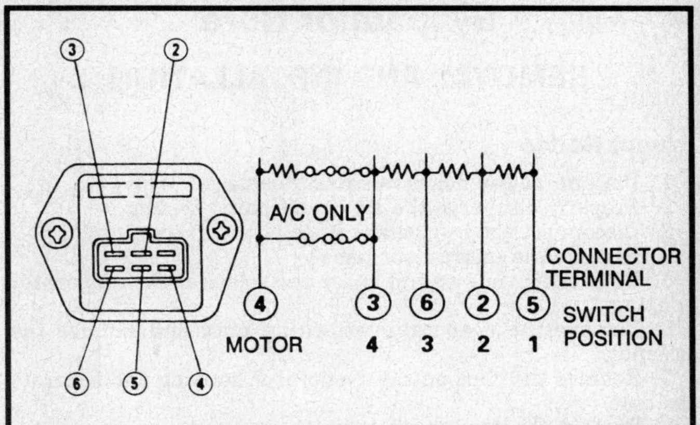
A/C ONLY
CONNECTOR TERMINAL
4 3 6 2 5
MOTOR 4 3 2 1
SWITCH POSITION

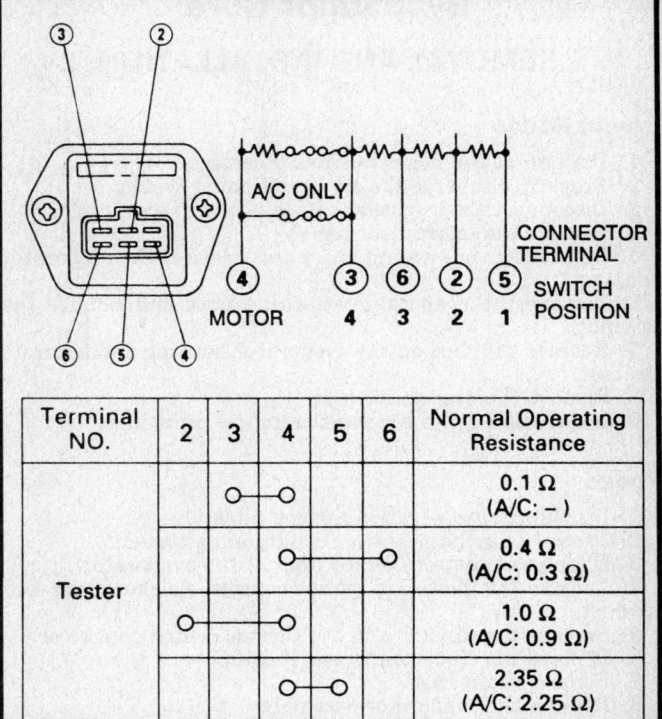

Terminal NO.	2	3	4	5	6	Normal Operating Resistance
Tester		o	o			0.1 Ω (A/C: –)
			o		o	0.4 Ω (A/C: 0.3 Ω)
	o		o			1.0 Ω (A/C: 0.9 Ω)
			o	o		2.35 Ω (A/C: 2.25 Ω)

Rodeo blower resistor testing

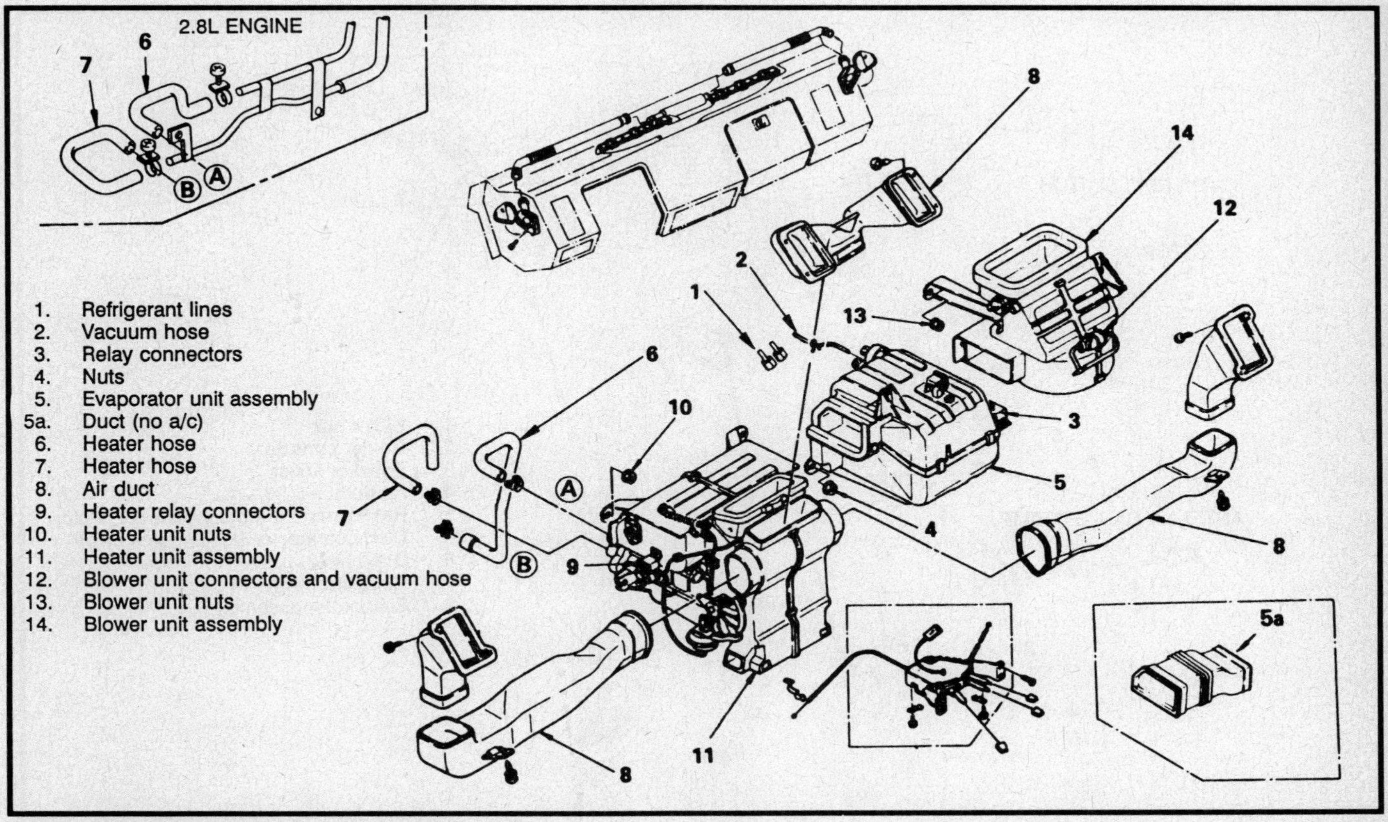
2.8L ENGINE
1. Refrigerant lines
2. Vacuum hose
3. Relay connectors
4. Nuts
5. Evaporator unit assembly
5a. Duct (no a/c)
6. Heater hose
7. Heater hose
8. Air duct
9. Heater relay connectors
10. Heater unit nuts
11. Heater unit assembly
12. Blower unit connectors and vacuum hose
13. Blower unit nuts
14. Blower unit assembly

Typical heater, blower and evaporator unit

Evaporator Core

REMOVAL AND INSTALLATION

Except Rodeo

1. Disconnect the negative battery cable.
2. Properly discharge the air conditioning system.
3. Disconnect the refrigerant lines at the evaporator.
4. Remove the instrument panel.
5. Disconnect the vacuum hoses and relays at the evaporator housing.
6. Remove the evaporator attaching nuts and remove the assembly.
7. Remove the clips on the evaporator housing and separate the case.
8. Remove the evaporator core.
9. Installation is the reverse of removal procedure.

Rodeo

1. Disconnect the negative battery cable.
2. Properly discharge the air conditioning system.
3. Disconnect the refrigerant lines at the evaporator.
4. Remove the glove box, center console, speaker cover and air duct.
5. Remove the resistor and the thermo switch connector.
6. Remove the diode connector, if equipped.
7. Remove drain hose.
8. Remove the evaporator assembly.
9. Installation is the reverse of removal procedure.

Refrigerant Lines

REMOVAL AND INSTALLATION

1. Disconnect the negative battery cable.
2. Properly discharge the air conditioning system.
3. Disconnect the refrigerant lines using 2 wrenches where required.
4. Remove all attaching brackets or clips.
5. Remove reservoir tanks where required.
6. Remove the refrigerant line.
7. Installation is the reverse of removal procedure.
8. Evacuate, recharge and leak check the system.

NOTE: Always reroute hoses in original location and use new O-rings with a thin coat of refrigerant oil.

Manual Control Head

REMOVAL AND INSTALLATION

1. Disconnect the negative battery cable.
2. Remove the glove box assembly.
3. Remove control lever knobs.
4. Remove the heater bezel.
5. Remove the attaching screws and disconnect the control cables at the heater and blower unit.
6. Pull the fan control lever out and disconnect the connectors.
7. Remove the control lever assembly.

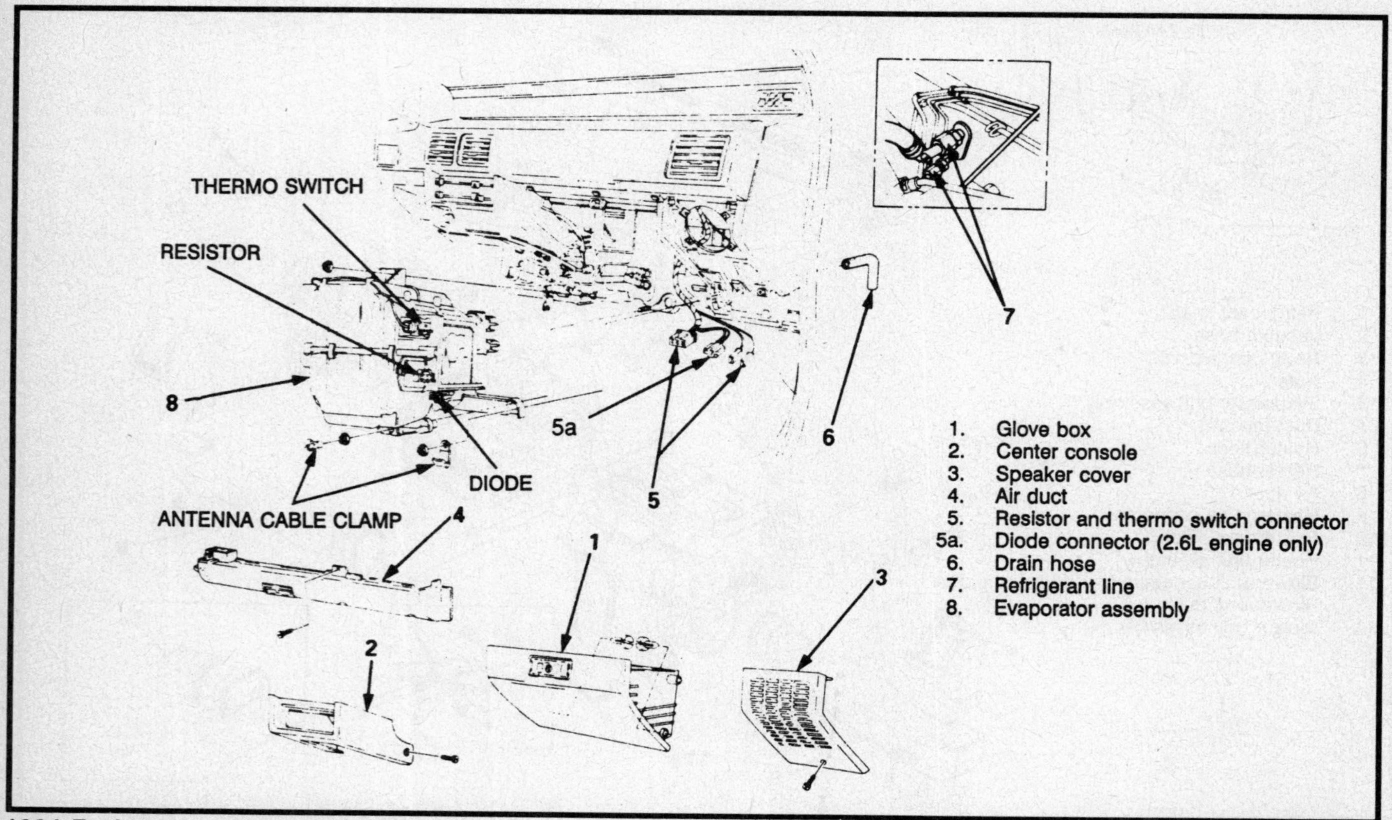
THERMO SWITCH
RESISTOR
8
5a
6
7
DIODE
5
ANTENNA CABLE CLAMP
4
1
2
3
1. Glove box
2. Center console
3. Speaker cover
4. Air duct
5. Resistor and thermo switch connector
5a. Diode connector (2.6L engine only)
6. Drain hose
7. Refrigerant line
8. Evaporator assembly

1991 Rodeo evaporator unit removal

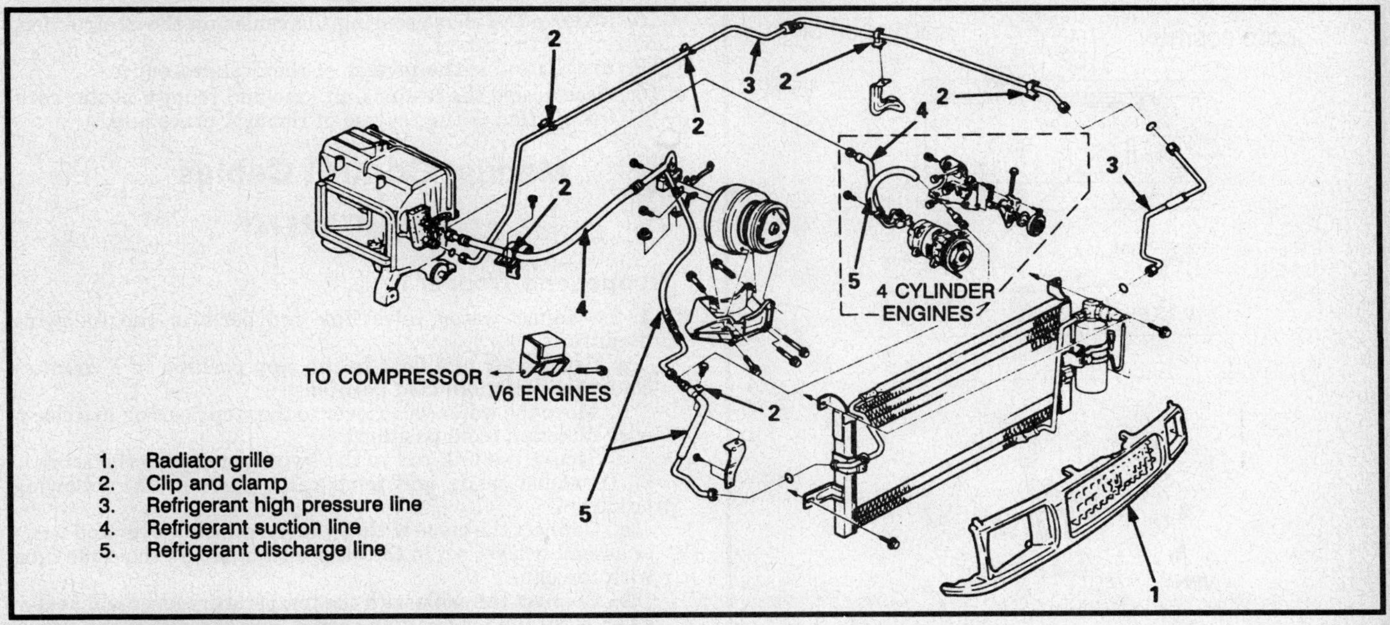
2
3
2
2
4
2
3
2
2
4
5
4 CYLINDER ENGINES
TO COMPRESSOR
V6 ENGINES
2
5
1
1. Radiator grille
2. Clip and clamp
3. Refrigerant high pressure line
4. Refrigerant suction line
5. Refrigerant discharge line

Typical refrigerant line location

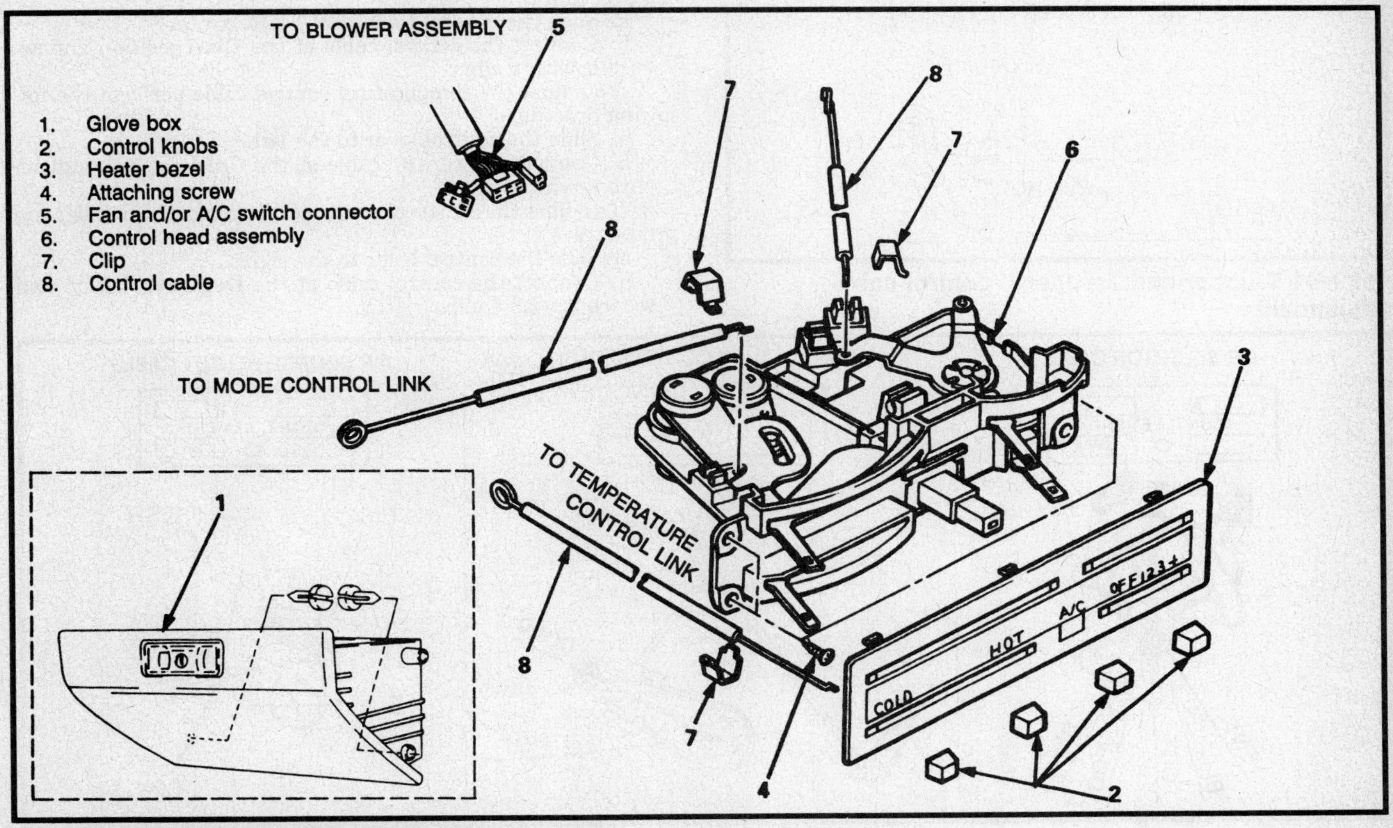
TO BLOWER ASSEMBLY
5
1. Glove box
2. Control knobs
3. Heater bezel
4. Attaching screw
5. Fan and/or A/C switch connector
6. Control head assembly
7. Clip
8. Control cable
8
7
8
7
6
3
TO MODE CONTROL LINK
TO TEMPERATURE CONTROL LINK
1
8
7
4
2
COLD
HOT
A/C
OFF 1 2 3 4

Typical manual control head assembly

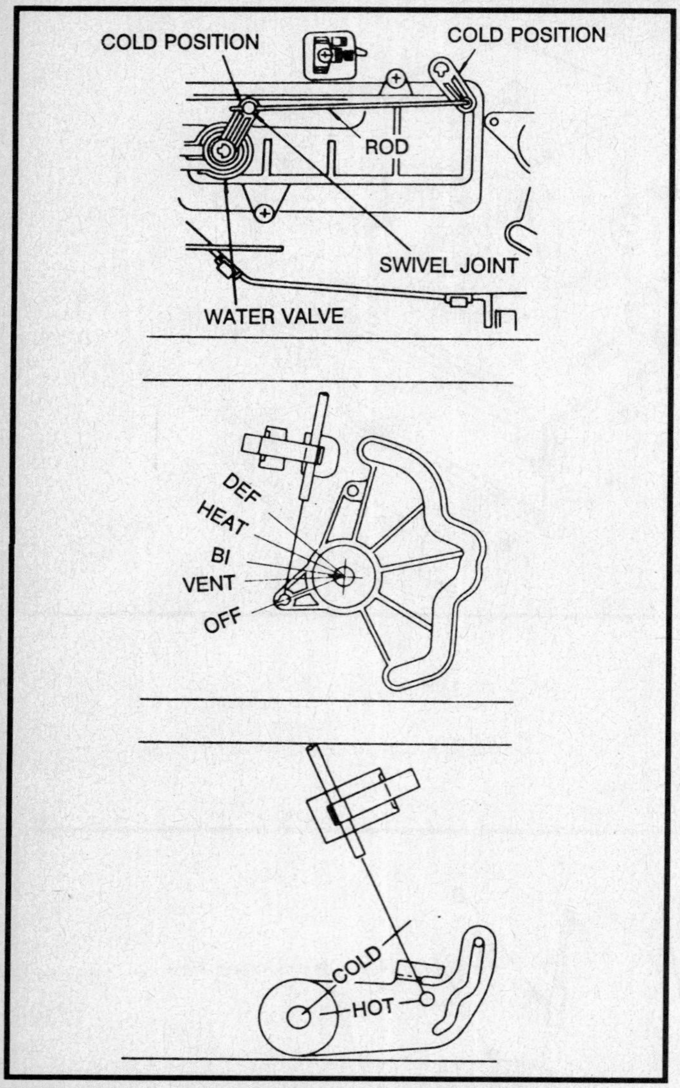
COLD POSITION
COLD POSITION
ROD
SWIVEL JOINT
WATER VALVE
DEF
HEAT
BI
VENT
OFF
COLD
HOT

1989–91 Trooper and Trooper II control cable adjustment

8. Remove the clips securing the cables on the control head and remove the cables.
9. Installation is the reverse of removal procedure.
10. disassemble the heater unit case and remove heater core.
11. Installation is the reverse of removal procedure.

Manual Control Cables

ADJUSTMENT

Trooper and Trooper II

1. To adjust water valve link rod perform the following procedure:
   a. Set the air mix door to the stop position in a counterclockwise direction (cold position).
   b. Move the water valve lever to the stop position in a clockwise direction (cold position).
   c. Secure the link rod to the swivel joint with the screw.
2. To adjust mode and temp cable perform the following procedure:
   a. Connect the cable with the mode selector lever and heater assembly lever set in the off position, secure the cable tube with the clip.
   b. Connect the cable with the temperature lever and heater lever set in the hot position then secure the cable tube with a clip.
   c. Check all mode doors and the water valve, if they are not closing properly, loosen the cable clamp screw at the control and adjust the cable length as required.

Amigo, Pickup and Rodeo

1. To adjust the air source control cable perform the following procedure:
   a. Slide the control lever to the left.
   b. Connect the control cable at the **Circ** position and secure it with a clip.
2. To adjust the temperature control cable perform the following procedure:
   a. Slide the control lever to the left.
   b. Connect the control cable at the **Cold** position and secure it with a clip.
3. To adjust the air select control cable perform the following procedure:
   a. Slide the control lever to the right.
   b. Connect the control cable at the **Defrost** position and secure it with a clip.

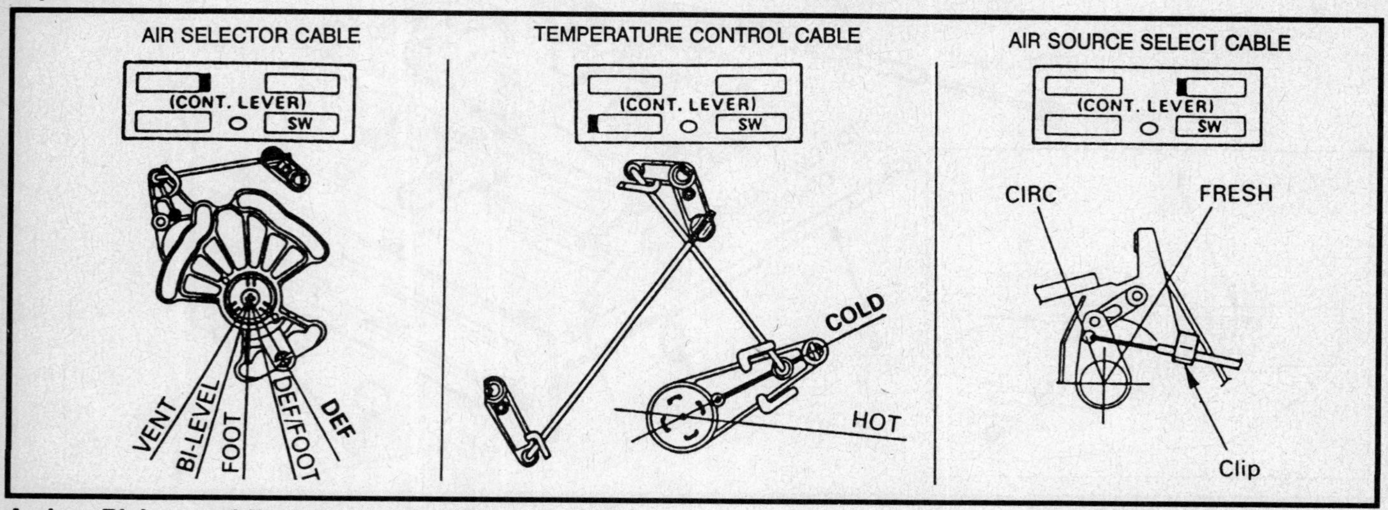
AIR SELECTOR CABLE
(CONT. LEVER)
SW
VENT
BI-LEVEL
FOOT
DEF/FOOT
DEF
TEMPERATURE CONTROL CABLE
(CONT. LEVER)
SW
COLD
HOT
AIR SOURCE SELECT CABLE
(CONT. LEVER)
SW
CIRC
FRESH
Clip

Amigo, Pickup and Rodeo control cable adjustment

SENSORS AND SWITCHES

Dual Pressure Switch

OPERATION

The pressure switch (dual pressure switch) is installed on the upper part of the receiver/drier, it is used to detect excessively high pressure (high pressure switch) and also prevent compressor seizure due to the refrigerant leaking (low pressure switch), by electronically turning the compressor on or off.

TESTING

1. Disconnect the pressure switch wire connector from the receiver/drier.
2. Start vehicle and turn the air conditioner ON.
3. Check for continuity between terminals on switch.
4. Reconnect wire and check for voltage through the switch.
5. At normal high and low pressure readings there should be 12 volts and continuity through the switch.

REMOVAL AND INSTALLATION

1. Disconnect the negative battery cable.
2. Properly discharge the air conditioning system.

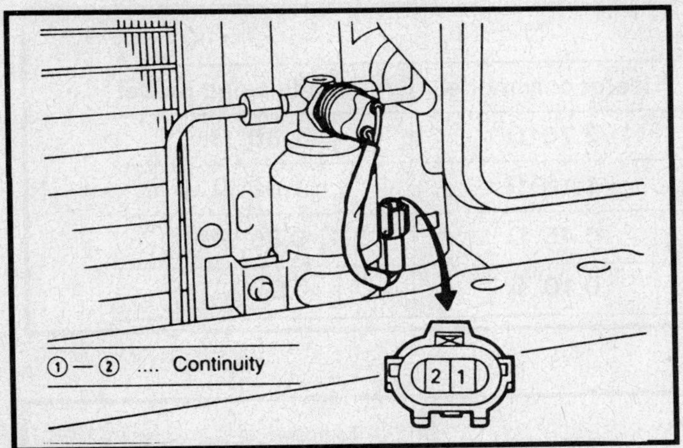
① — ② .... Continuity
2
1
Typical dual pressure switch testing

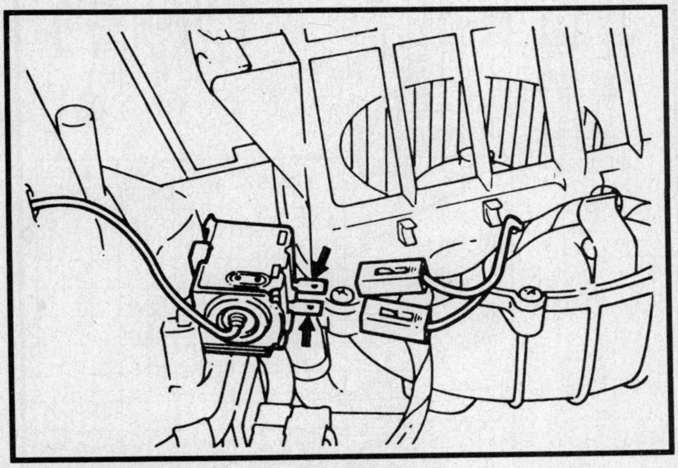
Typical thermo switch testing

3. If required, remove radiator grille.
4. Disconnect the pressure switch wire connector.
5. Use 2 wrenches to remove the pressure switch.
6. Installation is the reverse of removal procedure.

Electro Thermo Sensor

OPERATION

The thermo switch is installed on the evaprator. The switch capillary tube is attached to the core fin of the evaporator in such a way that it senses the temperature of the core fin. This enables the compressor to switch on or off and control the vehicle inside temperature. Also the switching provides protection against evaporator freeze-up.

TESTING

1. Start vehicle and turn the air conditioner ON.
2. Disconnect sensor switch wire connector.
3. Check for continuity between terminals.

REMOVAL AND INSTALLATION

1. Disconnect the negative battery cable.
2. Properly discharge the air conditioning system.
3. Remove the evaporator assembly, if required.
4. Remove the electro thermo sensor.
5. Installation is the reverse of removal procedure.

Relays

OPERATION

Battery and load location may require that a switch be placed some distance from either component. This means a longer wire and a higher voltage drop. The installation of a relay between the battery and the load reduces the voltage drop. Because the switch controls the relay, this means amperage through the switch can be reduced.

TESTING

1. Disconnect the battery negative terminal
2. Disconnect the relays from the fuse and relay box.

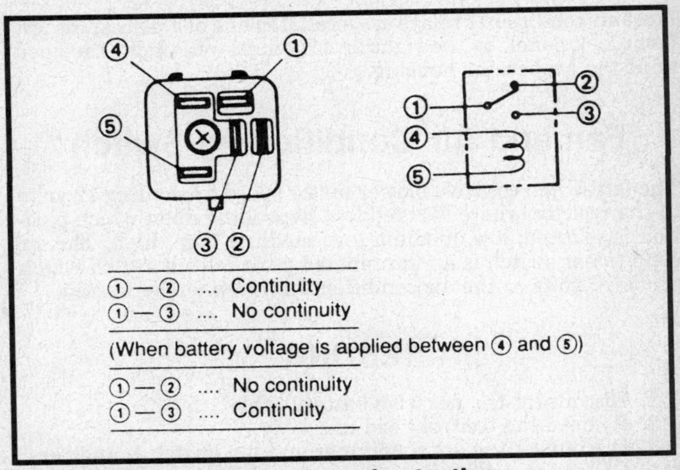
④
①
⑤
③ ②
②
①
③
④
⑤
① — ② .... Continuity
① — ③ .... No continuity
(When battery voltage is applied between ④ and ⑤)
① — ② .... No continuity
① — ③ .... Continuity
Air conditioner and heater relay testing

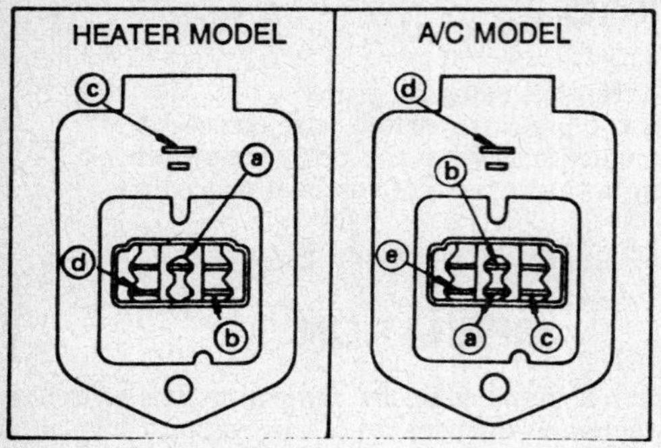
HEATER MODEL
A/C MODEL
c
a
d
b
d
b
e
a
c

Heat mode

Heater only model		Air conditioning model	
d—c	0.39 Ω	e—d	0.38 Ω
d—b	1.23 Ω	e—c	0.71 Ω
d—a	3.19 Ω	e—b	1.25 Ω
	—	e—a	2.20 Ω

Vent mode

Heater only model		Air conditioning model	
c—b	0.84 Ω	d—c	0.33 Ω
c—a	2.80 Ω	d—b	0.87 Ω
		d—a	1.82 Ω

Trooper and Trooper II blower resistor testing

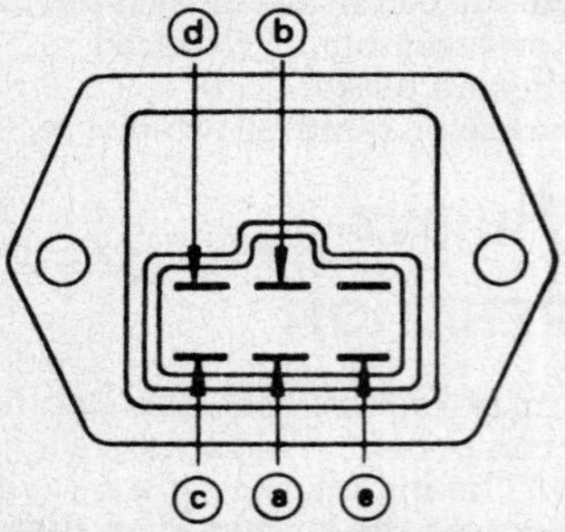
d
b
c
a
e

Heat Mode

	Heater only model	Air conditioning model
e—a	2.70 Ω	2.60 Ω
e—b	1.10 Ω	1.00 Ω
e—c	0.45 Ω	0.35 Ω
e—d	0.10 Ω	0 Ω

Amigo and Pickup blower resistor testing

3. Check for continuity and resistance between terminals of the relays.

REMOVAL AND INSTALLATION

Most air conditioner relays are located in one of 4 places; the left front kick panel, by the right or left fenderwell under the hood or at the evaporator housing.

Fan and Air Conditioning Switch

The fan switch controls blower motor speed by sending 12 volts to the resistor where it is reduced depending upon which position is selected; low, medium low, medium high, high. The air conditioner switch is an illuminated push button switch which sends 12 volts to the air conditioner relay when depressed.

TESTING

1. Disconnect the negative battery cable.
2. Remove the control head assembly.
3. Disconnect the air conditoner and fan switch connectors.
4. Check for continuity between terminals.

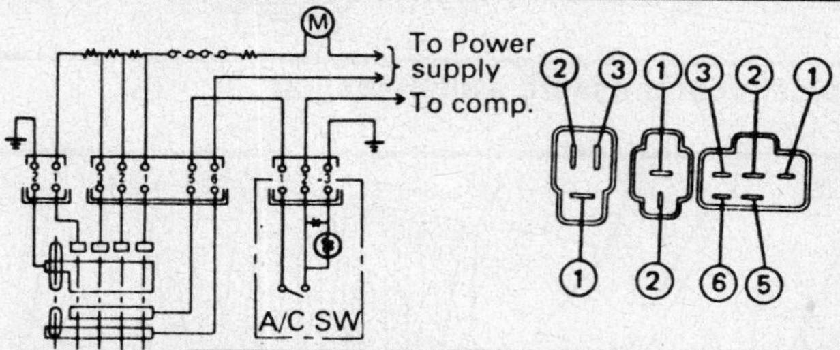
M
To Power supply
To comp.
OFF 1 2 3 4
A/C SW
2
3
1
3
2
1
1
2
6
5

Connector No. / SW Position		FAN SW (A) 1	FAN SW (A) 2	FAN SW (A) 3	FAN SW (A) 4	FAN SW (A) 5	FAN SW (A) 6	FAN SW (B) 1	FAN SW (B) 2	A/C SW 1	A/C SW 2	A/C SW 3
Blower motor	OFF											
	1					o	o	o	o			
	2			o		o	o		o			
	3		o			o	o		o			
	4	o				o	o		o			
A/C	OFF											
	ON									o	o	o

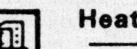

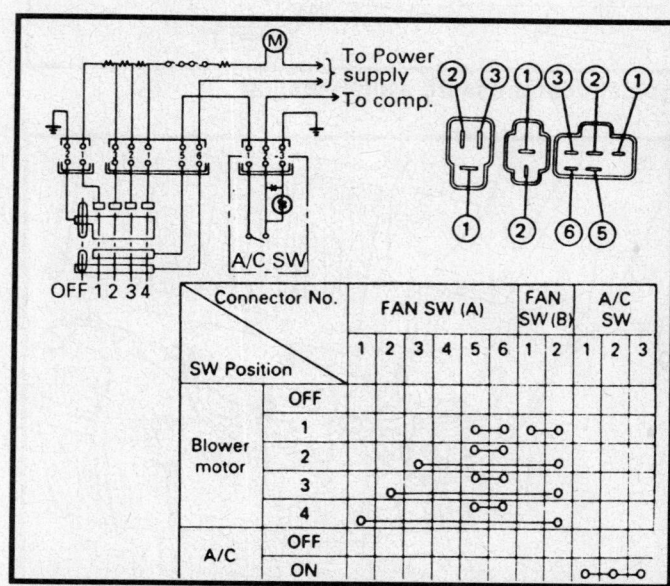

Amigo, Pickup and Rodeo fan and A/C switch testing

REMOVAL AND INSTALLATION

1. Disconnect the negative battery cable.
2. Remove the control head assembly.
3. Disconnect the air conditoner and fan switch connectors.
4. Installation is the reverse of the removal procedure.

REAR AUXILLARY SYSTEM

Blower Motor

REMOVAL AND INSTALLATION

Trooper and Trooper II

1. Disconnect the negative battery cable.
2. Drain the cooling system.
3. Remove rear seat.
4. Disconnect and plug the heater hoses at the heater core.
5. Remove heater unit mounting bolts.
6. Disconnect wire connector.
7. Remove heater unit assembly.
8. Remove securing clips and screws and separate case assembly.
9. Remove heater blower motor.
10. Installation is the reverse of the removal procedure. Fill the cooling system with the proper type and quantity of coolant.

Heater Core

REMOVAL AND INSTALLATION

Trooper and Trooper II

1. Disconnect the negative battery cable.
2. Drain the cooling system.
3. Remove rear seat.
4. Disconnect and plug the heater hoses at the heater core.
5. Remove heater unit mounting bolts.
6. Disconnect wire connector.
7. Remove heater unit assembly.
8. Remove securing clips and screws and separate case assembly.
9. Remove heater core.
10. Installation is the reverse of the removal procedure. Fill the cooling system with the proper type and quantity of coolant.

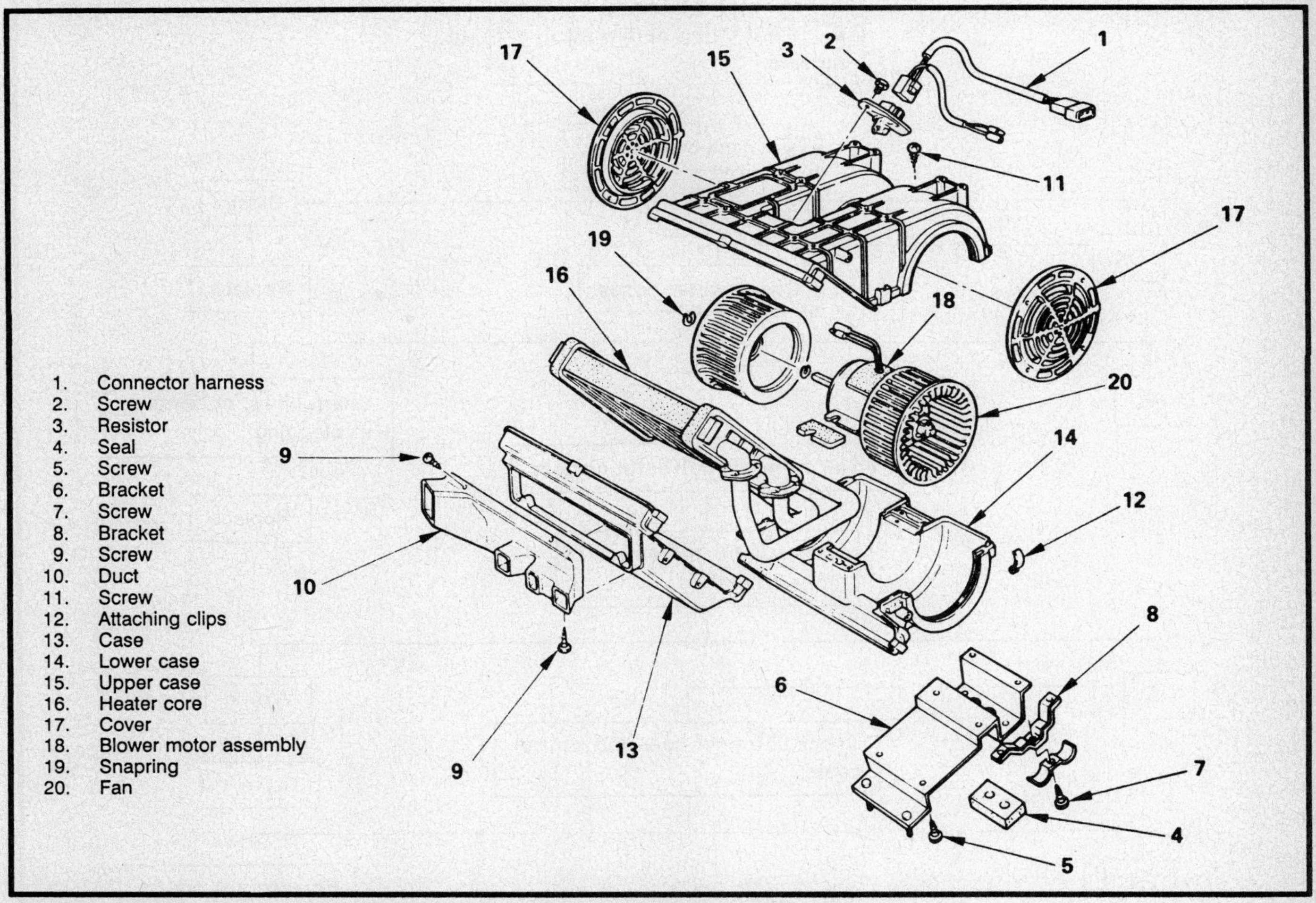
1. Connector harness
2. Screw
3. Resistor
4. Seal
5. Screw
6. Bracket
7. Screw
8. Bracket
9. Screw
10. Duct
11. Screw
12. Attaching clips
13. Case
14. Lower case
15. Upper case
16. Heater core
17. Cover
18. Blower motor assembly
19. Snapring
20. Fan

1989–91 Trooper and Trooper II rear heater and blower motor assembly

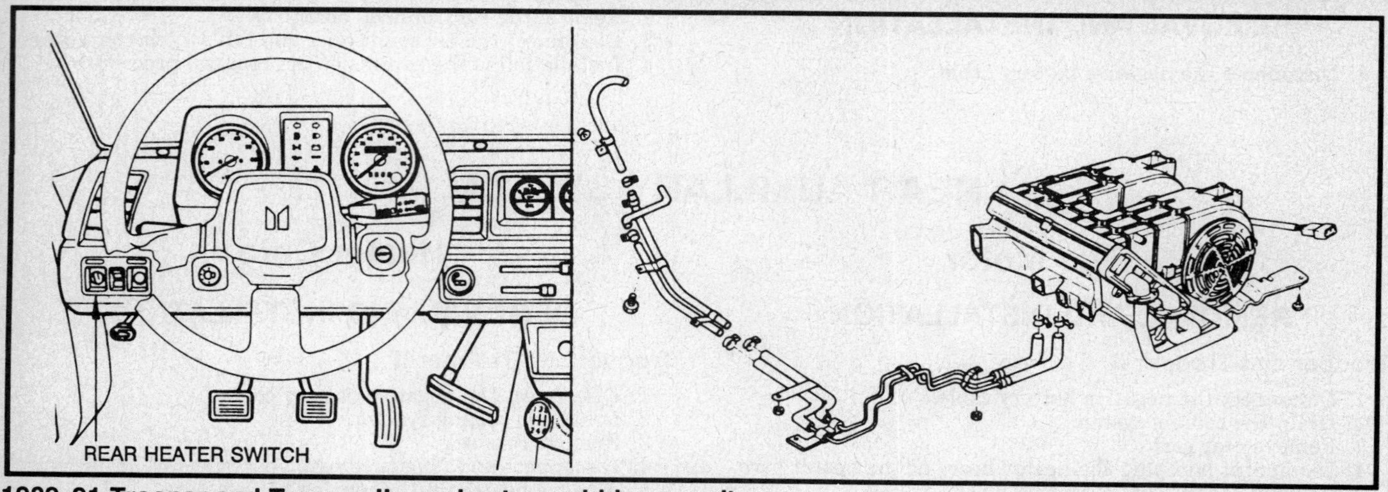
REAR HEATER SWITCH

1989–91 Trooper and Trooper II rear heater and blower unit

SYSTEM DIAGNOSIS

AIR CONDITIONING DIAGNOSTIC CHART

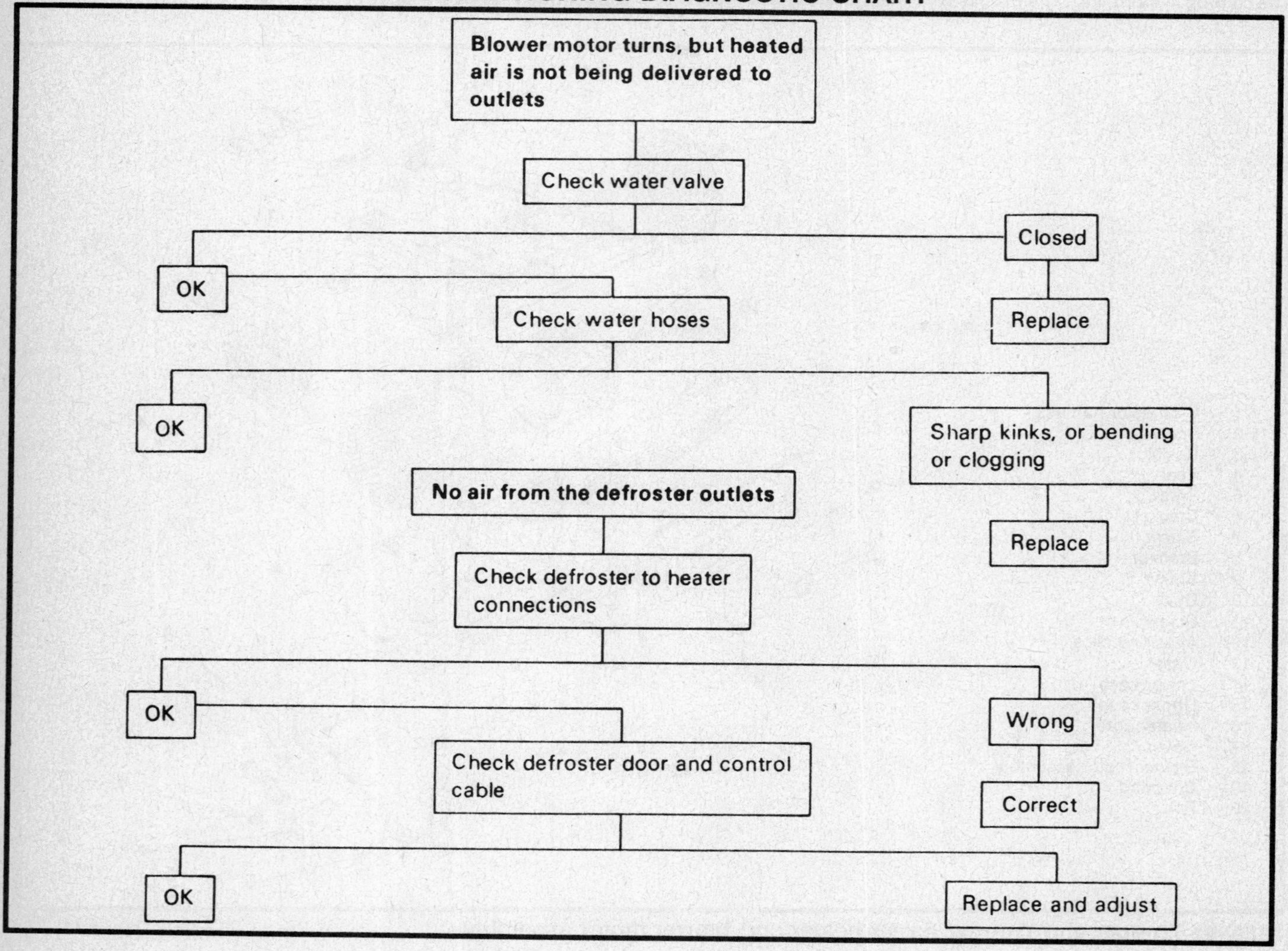
Blower motor turns, but heated air is not being delivered to outlets
Check water valve
OK
Closed
Replace
Check water hoses
OK
Sharp kinks, or bending or clogging
Replace
No air from the defroster outlets
Check defroster to heater connections
OK
Wrong
Correct
Check defroster door and control cable
OK
Replace and adjust

AIR CONDITIONING DIAGNOSTIC CHART—CONTINUED

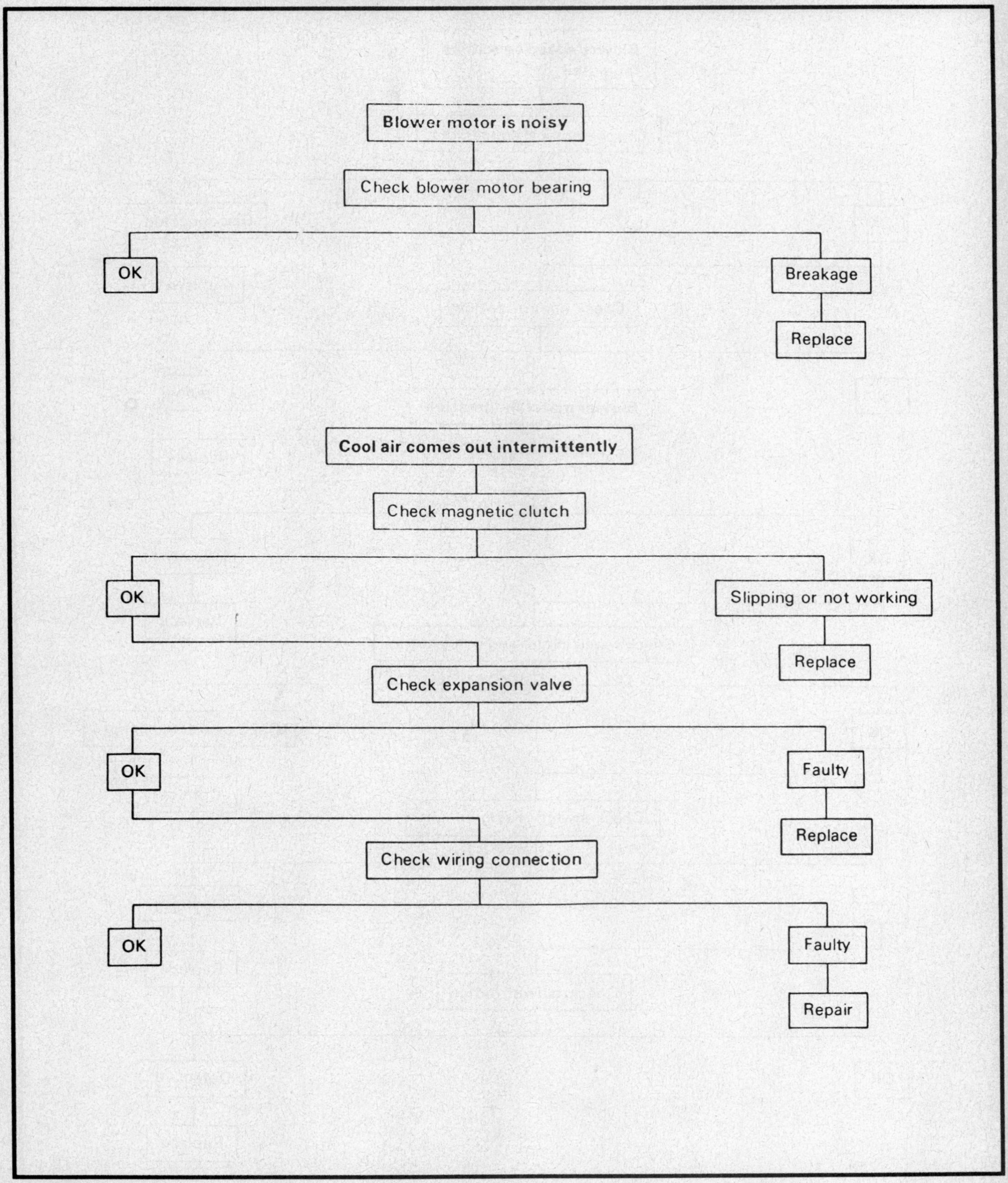
Blower motor is noisy
Check blower motor bearing
OK
Breakage
Replace
Cool air comes out intermittently
Check magnetic clutch
OK
Slipping or not working
Replace
Check expansion valve
OK
Faulty
Replace
Check wiring connection
OK
Faulty
Repair

AIR CONDITIONING DIAGNOSTIC CHART—CONTINUED

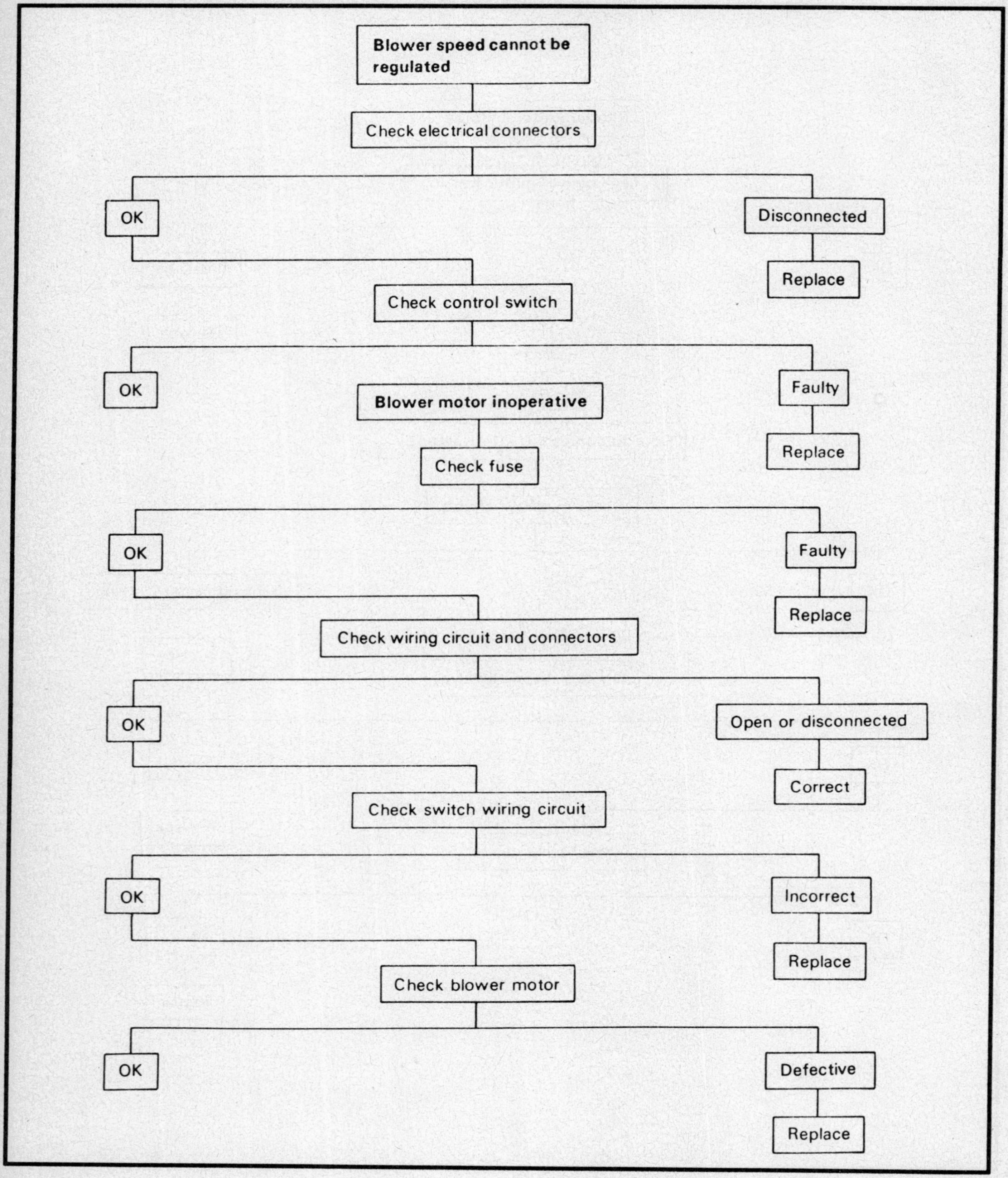
Blower speed cannot be regulated
Check electrical connectors
OK
Disconnected
Replace
Check control switch
OK
Faulty
Replace
Blower motor inoperative
Check fuse
OK
Faulty
Replace
Check wiring circuit and connectors
OK
Open or disconnected
Correct
Check switch wiring circuit
OK
Incorrect
Replace
Check blower motor
OK
Defective
Replace

AIR CONDITIONING DIAGNOSTIC CHART—CONTINUED

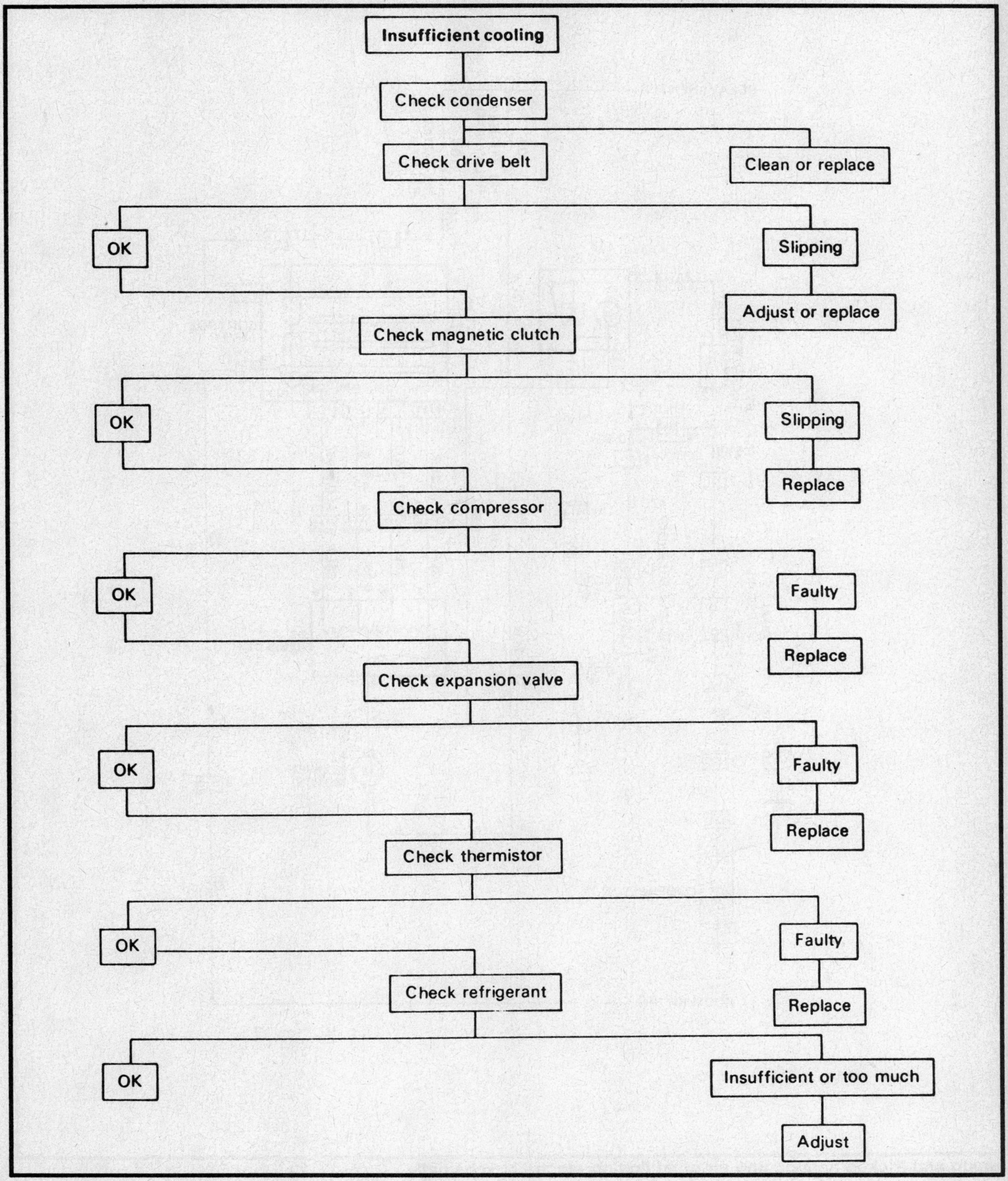
Insufficient cooling
Check condenser
Clean or replace
Check drive belt
OK
Slipping
Adjust or replace
Check magnetic clutch
OK
Slipping
Replace
Check compressor
OK
Faulty
Replace
Check expansion valve
OK
Faulty
Replace
Check thermistor
OK
Faulty
Replace
Check refrigerant
OK
Insufficient or too much
Adjust

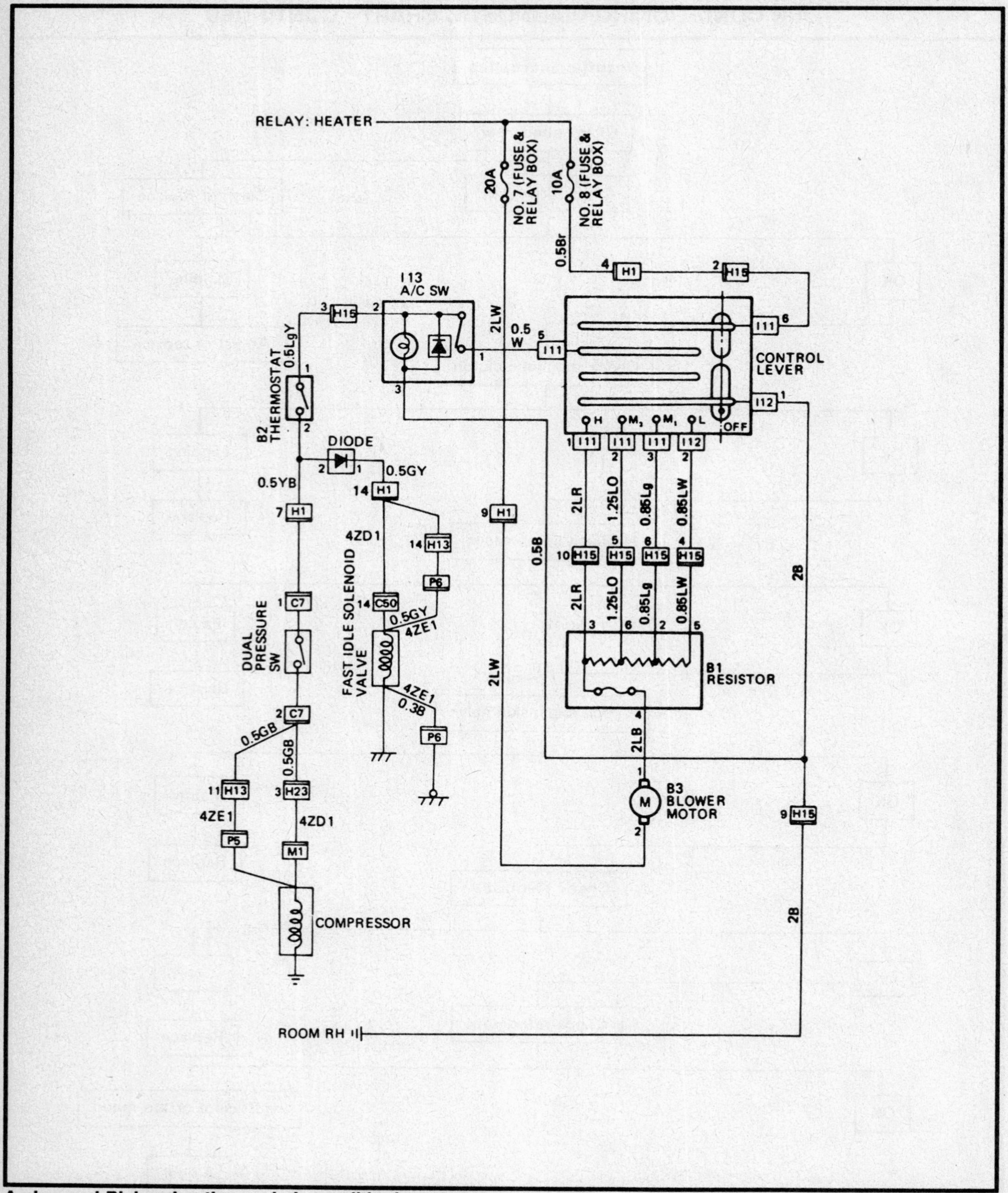
RELAY: HEATER
20A
NO. 7 (FUSE & RELAY BOX)
10A
NO. 8 (FUSE & RELAY BOX)
0.5Br
I13
A/C SW
2LW
0.5 W
CONTROL LEVER
OFF
B2 THERMOSTAT
0.5LgY
DIODE
0.5GY
0.5YB
4ZD1
FAST IDLE SOLENOID VALVE
4ZE1
0.5B
2LR
1.25LO
0.85Lg
0.85LW
2B
DUAL PRESSURE SW
B1 RESISTOR
2LB
0.5GB
0.3B
B3 BLOWER MOTOR
COMPRESSOR
ROOM RH
Amigo and Pickup heating and air conditioning electrical schematic

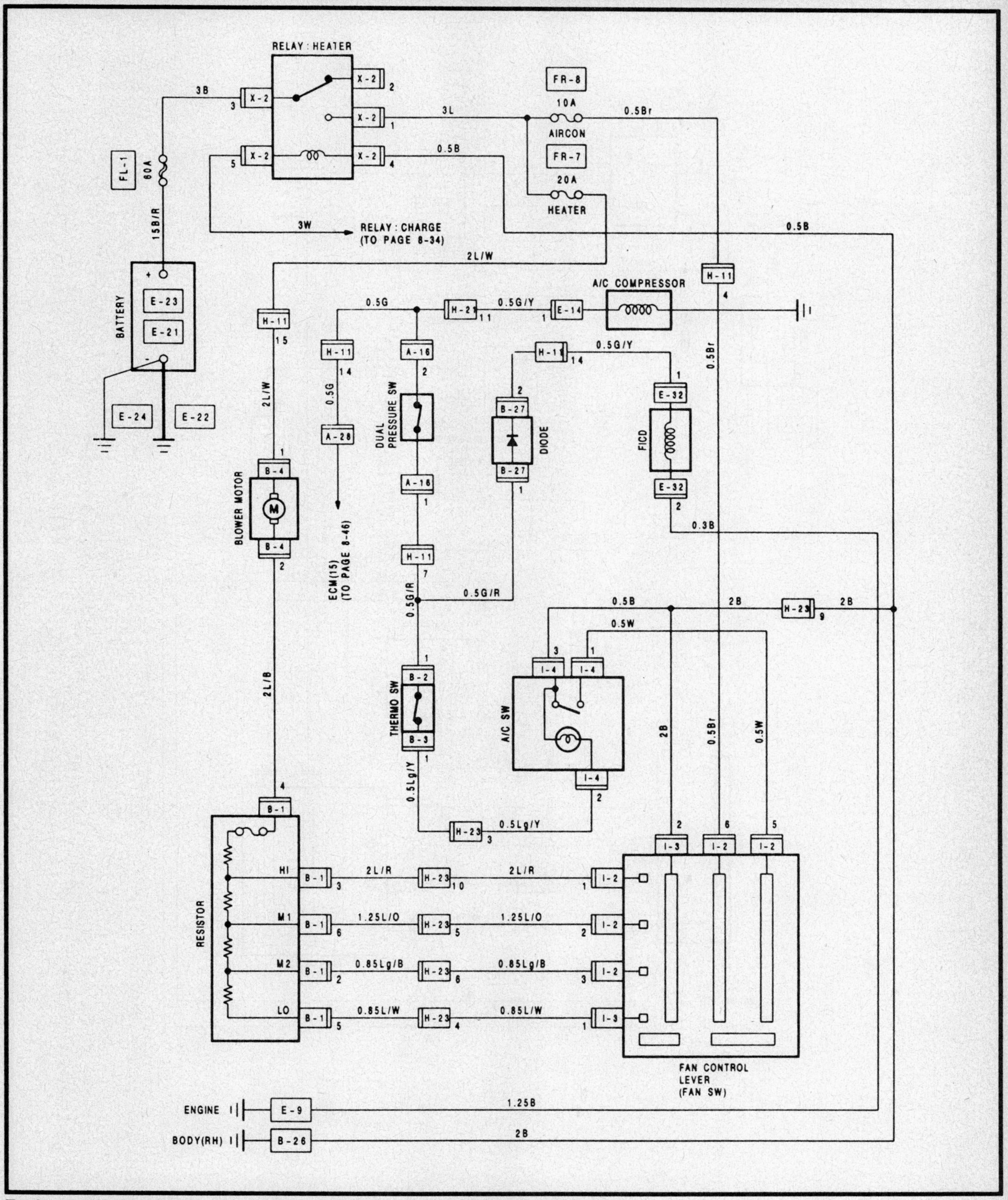
RELAY : HEATER
X-2
3B
FL-1
60A
15B/R
3W
RELAY : CHARGE
(TO PAGE 8-34)
3L
0.5B
FR-8
10A
AIRCON
FR-7
20A
HEATER
0.5Br
2L/W
BATTERY
E-23
E-21
E-24
E-22
H-11
A/C COMPRESSOR
0.5G
0.5G/Y
H-21
E-14
A-16
DUAL PRESSURE SW
A-28
ECM(15)
(TO PAGE 8-46)
DIODE
B-27
FICD
E-32
0.3B
BLOWER MOTOR
B-4
2L/B
0.5G/R
THERMO SW
B-2
B-3
0.5Lg/Y
A/C SW
I-4
0.5W
2B
H-23
RESISTOR
B-1
HI
M1
M2
LO
2L/R
1.25L/O
0.85Lg/B
0.85L/W
I-2
I-3
FAN CONTROL
LEVER
(FAN SW)
ENGINE
E-9
1.25B
BODY(RH)
B-26

Rodeo 2.6L engine heating and air conditioning electrical schematic

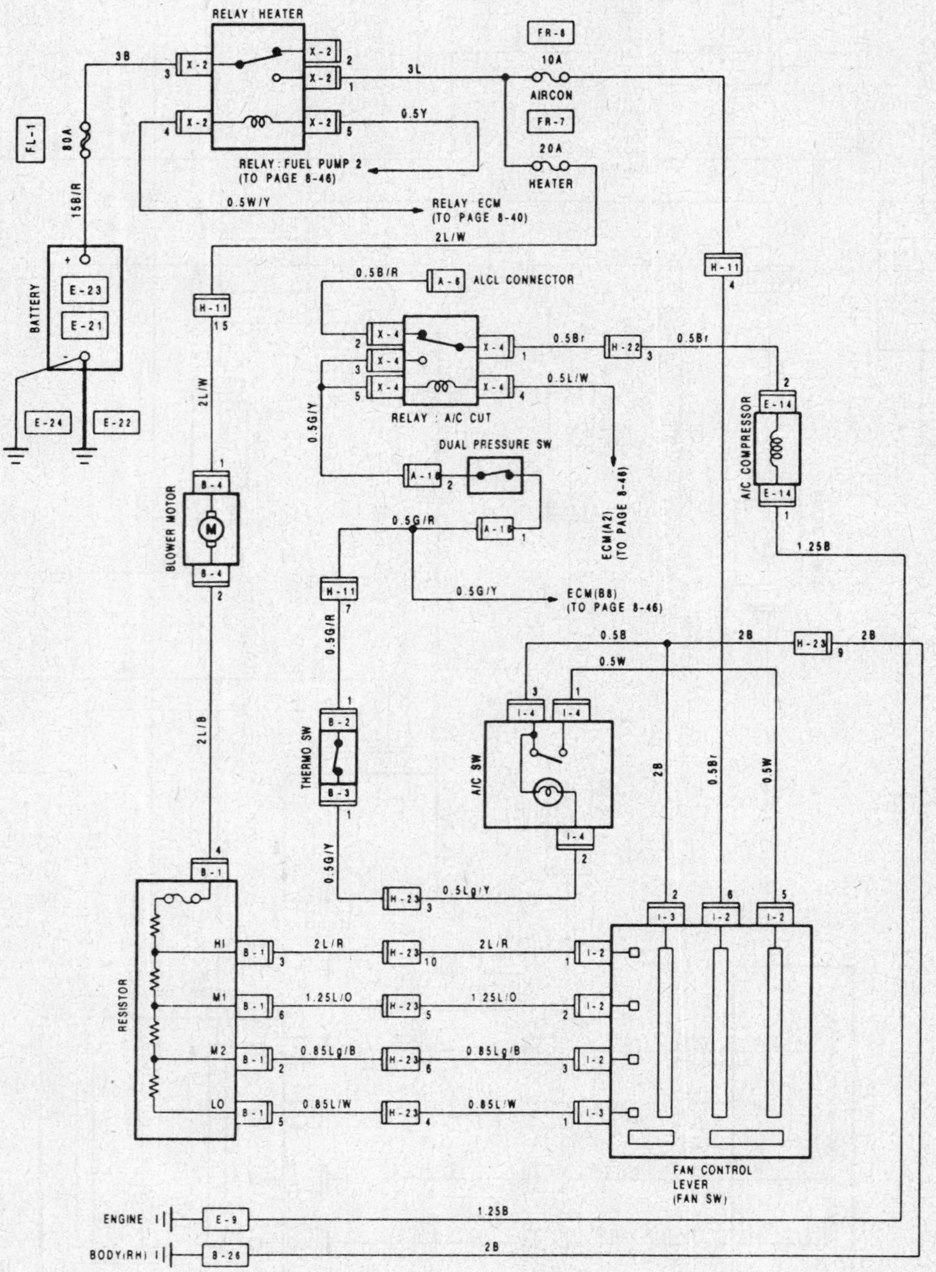
RELAY: HEATER
3B
X-2
3L
0.5Y
FR-8
10A
AIRCON
FR-7
20A
HEATER
FL-1
80A
15B/R
RELAY: FUEL PUMP 2
(TO PAGE 8-46)
0.5W/Y
RELAY ECM
(TO PAGE 8-40)
2L/W
BATTERY
E-23
E-21
E-24
E-22
H-11
0.5B/R
A-6
ALCL CONNECTOR
X-4
0.5Br
H-22
0.5L/W
RELAY : A/C CUT
0.5G/Y
DUAL PRESSURE SW
A-1
E-14
A/C COMPRESSOR
ECM(A2)
(TO PAGE 8-46)
1.25B
0.5G/R
ECM(B8)
(TO PAGE 8-46)
BLOWER MOTOR
B-4
2L/B
THERMO SW
B-2
B-3
0.5B
2B
H-23
0.5W
A/C SW
I-4
0.5Lg/Y
B-1
RESISTOR
HI
M1
M2
LO
2L/R
1.25L/O
0.85Lg/B
0.85L/W
I-2
I-3
FAN CONTROL
LEVER
(FAN SW)
ENGINE
E-9
BODY(RH)
B-26

Rodeo 3.1L engine heating and air conditioning electrical schematic

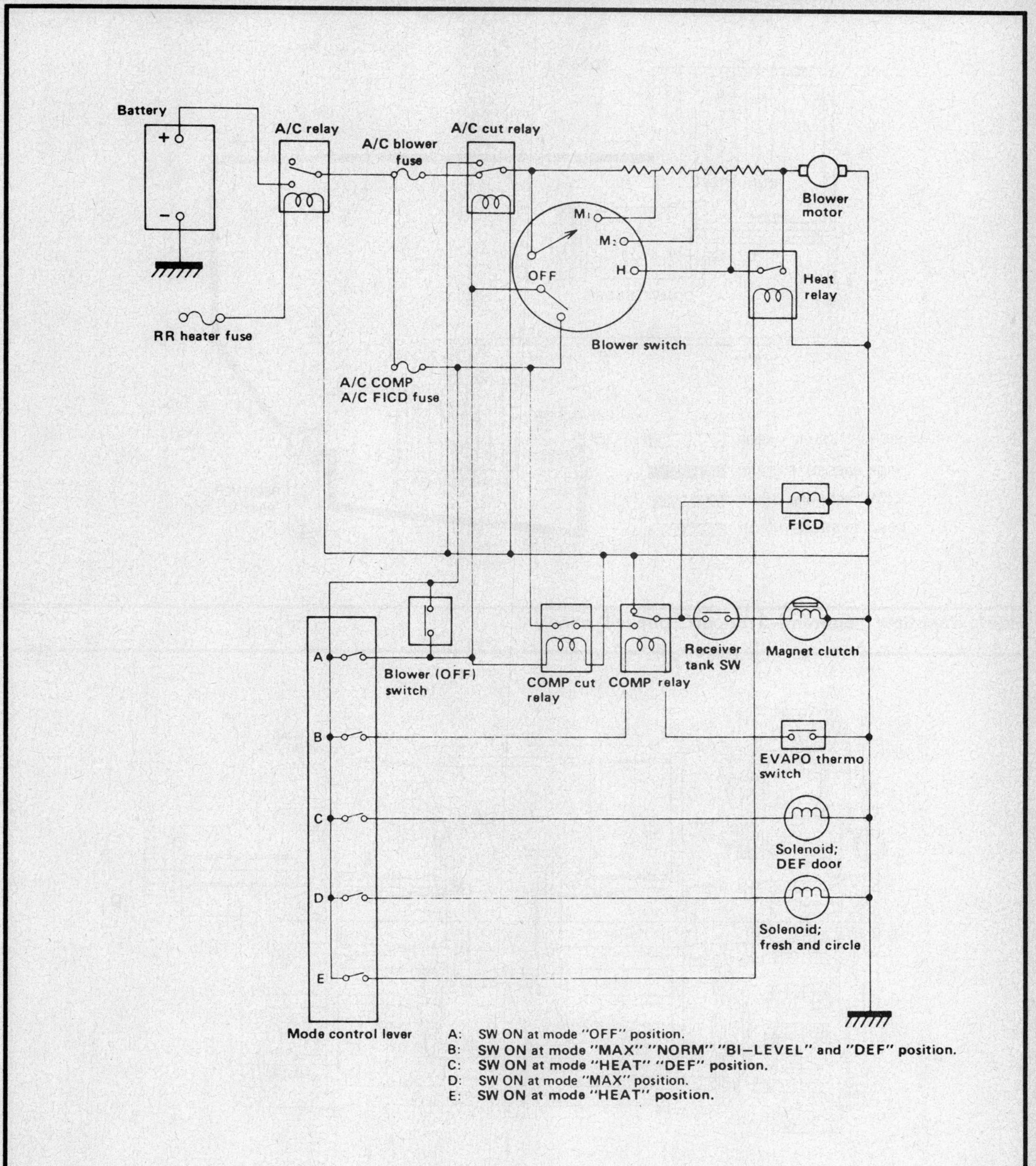
Battery
+
−
A/C relay
A/C blower fuse
A/C cut relay
Blower motor
M1
M2
H
OFF
Heat relay
RR heater fuse
Blower switch
A/C COMP
A/C FICD fuse
FICD
A
B
C
D
E
Blower (OFF) switch
COMP cut relay
COMP relay
Receiver tank SW
Magnet clutch
EVAPO thermo switch
Solenoid; DEF door
Solenoid; fresh and circle
Mode control lever
A: SW ON at mode "OFF" position.
B: SW ON at mode "MAX" "NORM" "BI-LEVEL" and "DEF" position.
C: SW ON at mode "HEAT" "DEF" position.
D: SW ON at mode "MAX" position.
E: SW ON at mode "HEAT" position.

Trooper and Trooper II heating and air conditioning electrical schematic

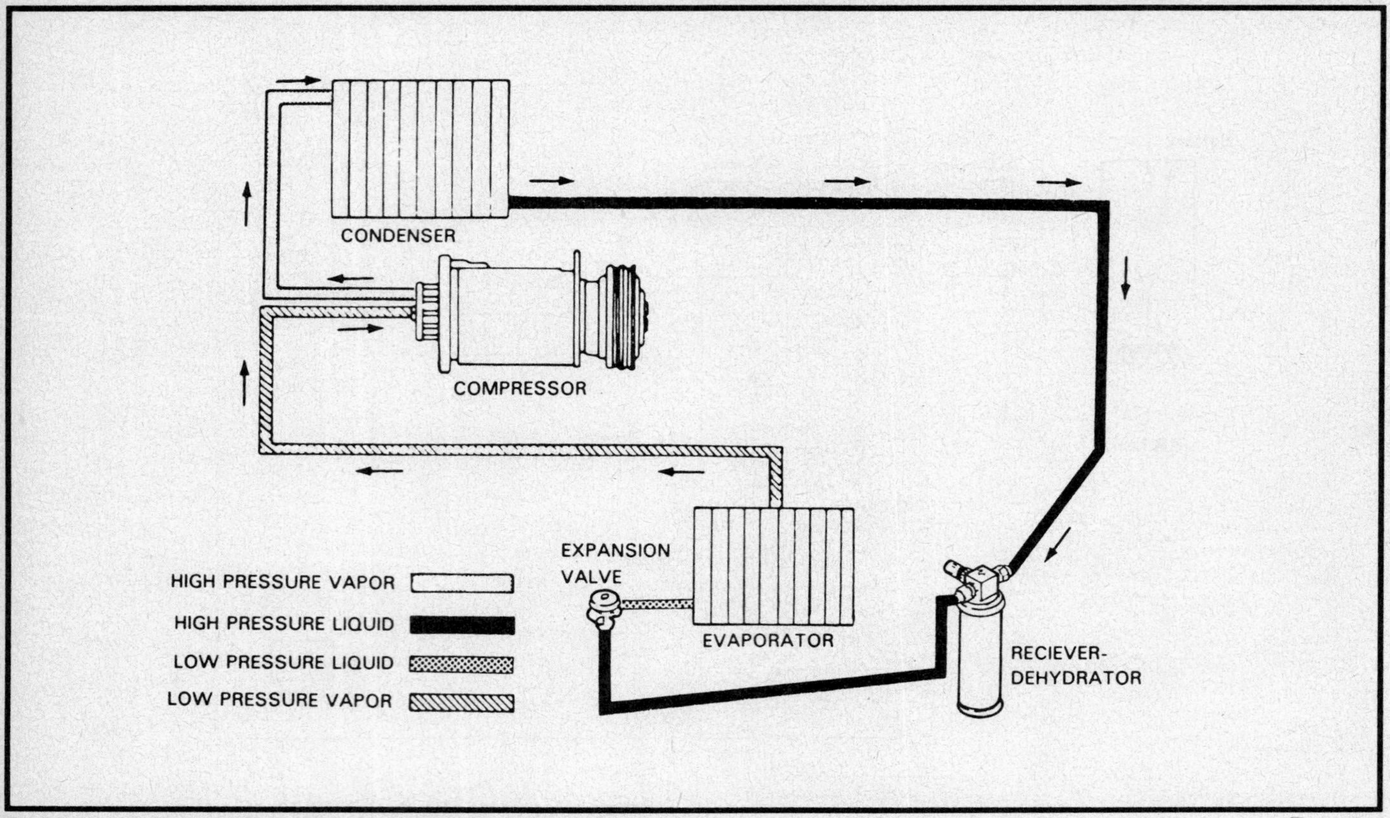
CONDENSER
COMPRESSOR
EXPANSION VALVE
EVAPORATOR
RECIEVER-DEHYDRATOR
HIGH PRESSURE VAPOR
HIGH PRESSURE LIQUID
LOW PRESSURE LIQUID
LOW PRESSURE VAPOR

Refrigerant flow diaghram—Trooper/Trooper II shown

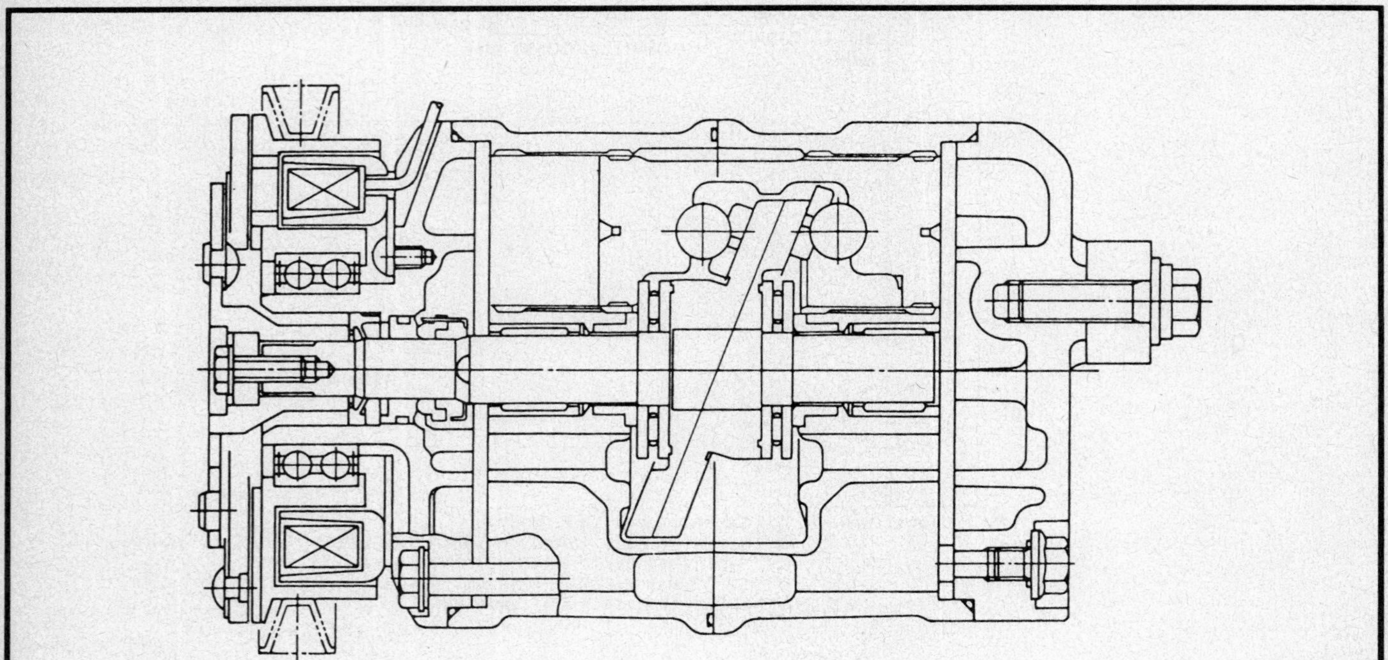

Crossection of typical Isuzu truck compressor

31 MAZDA TRUCKS 31

B2200 • B2600i • NAVAJO • MPV

SPECIFICATIONS

ENGINE IDENTIFICATION

Year	Model	Engine Displacement cu. in. (cc/liter)	Engine Series Identification	No. of Cylinders	Engine Type
1989	B2200	133 (2184/2.2)	F2	4	OHC
	B2600i	159 (2606/2.6)	G6	4	OHC
	MPV	159 (2606/2.6)	G6	4	OHC
	MPV	181 (2954/3.0)	JE	6	DOHC
1990	B2200	133 (2184/2.2)	F2	4	OHC
	B2600i	159 (2606/2.6)	G6	4	OHC
	MPV	159 (2606/2.6)	G6	4	OHC
	MPV	181 (2954/3.0)	JE	6	DOHC
1991	B2200	133 (2184/2.2)	F2	4	OHC
	B2600i	159 (2606/2.6)	G6	4	OHC
	MPV	159 (2606/2.6)	G6	4	OHC
	MPV	181 (2954/3.0)	JE	6	DOHC
	NAVAJO	245 (4016/4.0)	—	6	OHV

REFRIGERANT CAPACITIES

Year	Model	Freon (oz.)	Oil (fl. oz.)	Type
1989	B2200	26.5	4.5	R-12
	B2600i	26.5	4.5	R-12
	MPV	42.4 ①	2.7–3.4	R-12
	MPV	42.4 ①	2.7–3.4	R-12
1990	B2200	26.5	4.5	R-12
	B2600i	26.5	4.5	R-12
	MPV	42.4 ①	2.7–3.4	R-12
	MPV	42.4 ①	2.7–3.4	R-12
1991	B2200	26.5	4.5	R-12
	B2600i	26.5	4.5	R-12
	MPV	42.4 ①	2.7–3.4	R-12
	MPV	42.4 ①	2.7–3.4	R-12
	Navajo	32.0–36.0	7.0	R-12

① Auxiliary air conditioner 49.5

AIR CONDITIONING BELT TENSION CHART

Year	Model	Engine Displacement cu. in. (cc/liter)	Belt Type	New	Used
1989	B2200	133 (2184/2.2)	V-Belt	0.39–0.47 ①	0.47–0.55 ①
	B2600i	159 (2606/2.6)	V-Belt	0.33–0.39 ①	0.39–0.45 ①
	MPV	159 (2606/2.6)	V-Belt	0.33–0.39 ①	0.39–0.45 ①
	MPV	181 (2954/3.0)	V-Belt	0.17–0.20 ①	0.20–0.22 ①

AIR CONDITIONING BELT TENSION CHART

Year	Model	Engine Displacement cu. in. (cc/liter)	Belt Type	New	Used
1990	B2200	133 (2184/2.2)	V-Belt	0.39–0.47 ①	0.47–0.55 ①
	B2600i	159 (2606/2.6)	V-Belt	0.33–0.39 ①	0.39–0.45 ①
	MPV	159 (2606/2.6)	V-Belt	0.33–0.39 ①	0.39–0.45 ①
	MPV	181 (2954/3.0)	V-Belt	0.17–0.20 ①	0.20–0.22 ①
1991	B2200	133 (2184/2.2)	V-Belt	0.39–0.47 ①	0.47–0.55 ①
	B2600i	159 (2606/2.6)	V-Belt	0.33–0.39 ①	0.39–0.45 ①
	MPV	159 (2606/2.6)	V-Belt	0.33–0.39 ①	0.39–0.45 ①
	MPV	181 (2954/3.0)	V-Belt	0.17–0.20 ①	0.20–0.22 ①
	Navajo	245 (4016/4.0)	Serpentine	②	②

① Inches of deflection at midpoint of belt using 22 lbs. of force.
② No adjustment necessary.

SYSTEM DESCRIPTION

General Information

The heater unit is located in the center of the vehicle along the firewall. The heater system is a bi-level system designed to direct warm air through the vents to either the windshield or the floor and cool air through the panel outlet. The air conditioning system is designed to be activated in combination with a separate air conditioning switch installed in the control assembly and the fan speed switch. The system incorporates a compressor, condenser, evaporator, receiver/drier or accumulator, pressure switch, expansion valve or fixed orifice tube, thermo switch or clutch cycling switch, refrigerant lines and some models are equipped with an electronic control head assembly versus the standard cable operated control head.

The MPV model offers an auxiliary rear heater unit which is mounted under the driver's seat, the unit incorporates a heater core, blower motor and water valve. The MPV also offers an auxiliary air conditioning unit which is located at the left rear compartment of the vehicle, the unit incorporates an evaporator, blower motor, expansion valve and thermo switch.

The Navajo uses an electronic engine control system monitors and regulates the air conditioning system by working through the wide open throttle relay disengaging the air conditioning clutch under the following conditions, immediately after start-up, for a brief period during wide open throttle, if engine coolant temperature approaches an overheating condition and when engine rpm is approaching a stall speed. In addition, the electronic engine control senses the output clutch cycling pressure switch and momentarily delays clutch engagement until the engine rpm is raised to an acceptable rate.

Service Valve Location

Charging valve locations will vary, but most of the time the high or low pressure fitting will be located at the compressor, receiver/drier (accumulator) or along the refrigerant lines. Always discharge, evacuate and recharge at the low side service fitting.

System Discharging

R-12 refrigerant is a chlorofluorocarbon which, when mishandled, can contribute to the depletion of the ozone layer in the upper atmosphere. Ozone filters out harmful radiation from the sun. In order to protect the ozone layer, an approved R-12 Recovery/Recycling machine that meets SAE standard J1991 should be employed when discharging the system. Follow the operating instructions provided with the approved equipment exactly to properly discharge the system.

System Evacuating

If the air conditioning system has been opened to the atmosphere, it should be air and moisture free before being recharged with refrigerant. Moisture and air mixed with refrigerant will raise the compressor head pressure, possibly damage the system's components and will reduce the performance of the system. Moisture will boil at normal room temperature when exposed to a vacuum, the moisture then becomes a vapor and will be easily removed by the vacuum pump.

To evacuate or rid the system of air and moisture perform the following procedure:

1. Leak test the system and repair any leaks found.
2. Connect an approved charging station, Recovery/Recycling machine or manifold gauge set and vacuum pump to the discharge and suction ports. The red hose is normally connected to the discharge (high pressure) line, and the blue hose is connected to the suction (low pressure) line.
3. Open the discharge and suction ports and start the vacuum pump. If the pump is not able to pull at least 26 in. Hg vacuum, there is a leak that must be repaired before evacuation can occur.
4. Once the system has reached at least 26 in. Hg vacuum, allow the system to evacuate for at least 10 minutes. The longer the system is evacuated, the more contaminants will be removed.
5. Close all valves and turn the pump off. If the system loses more than 2 in. Hg vacuum after 15 minutes, there is a leak that should be repaired.

System Charging

1. Connect an approved charging station, Recovery/Recycling machine or manifold gauge set to the discharge and suction

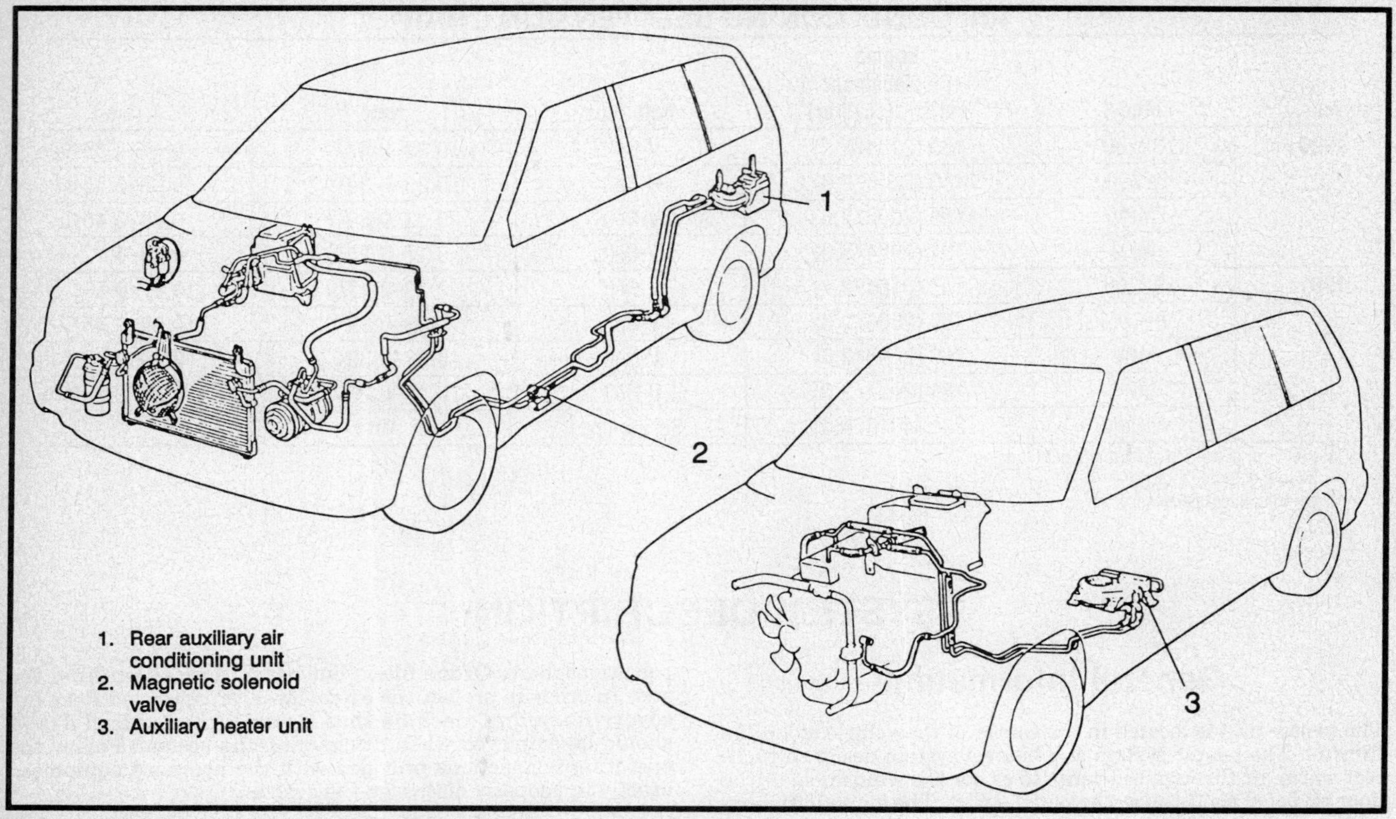
1
2
3
1. Rear auxiliary air conditioning unit
2. Magnetic solenoid valve
3. Auxiliary heater unit

Typical air conditioning and heater component location

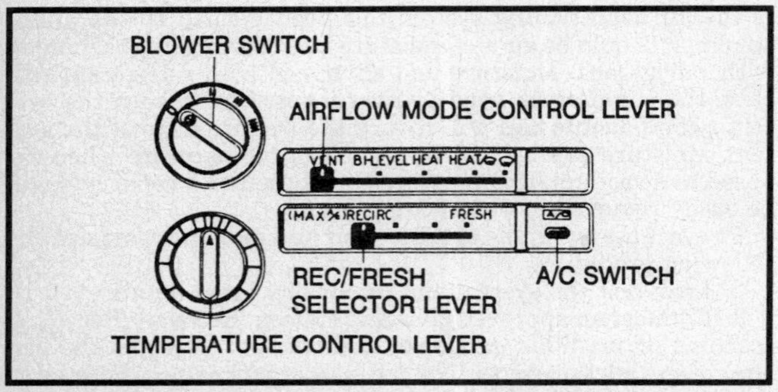
BLOWER SWITCH
AIRFLOW MODE CONTROL LEVER
VENT BI-LEVEL HEAT HEAT
MAX RECIRC FRESH
A/C
REC/FRESH SELECTOR LEVER
A/C SWITCH
TEMPERATURE CONTROL LEVER

Air conditioner and heater control head switches—B2200 and B2600I

ports. The red hose is normally connected to the discharge (high pressure) line, and the blue hose is connected to the suction (low pressure) line.

2. Follow the instructions provided with the equipment and charge the system with the specified amount of refrigerant.

3. Perform a leak test.

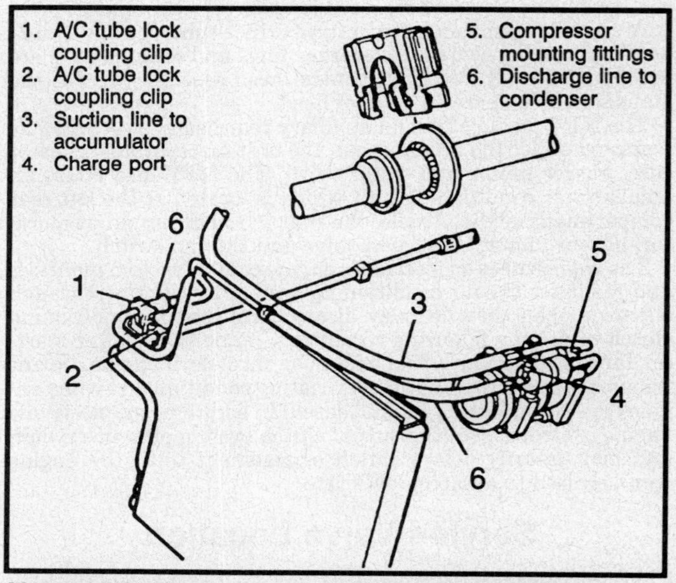
1. A/C tube lock coupling clip
2. A/C tube lock coupling clip
3. Suction line to accumulator
4. Charge port
5. Compressor mounting fittings
6. Discharge line to condenser
1
2
3
4
5
6
6

Air conditioning service valve location—Navajo

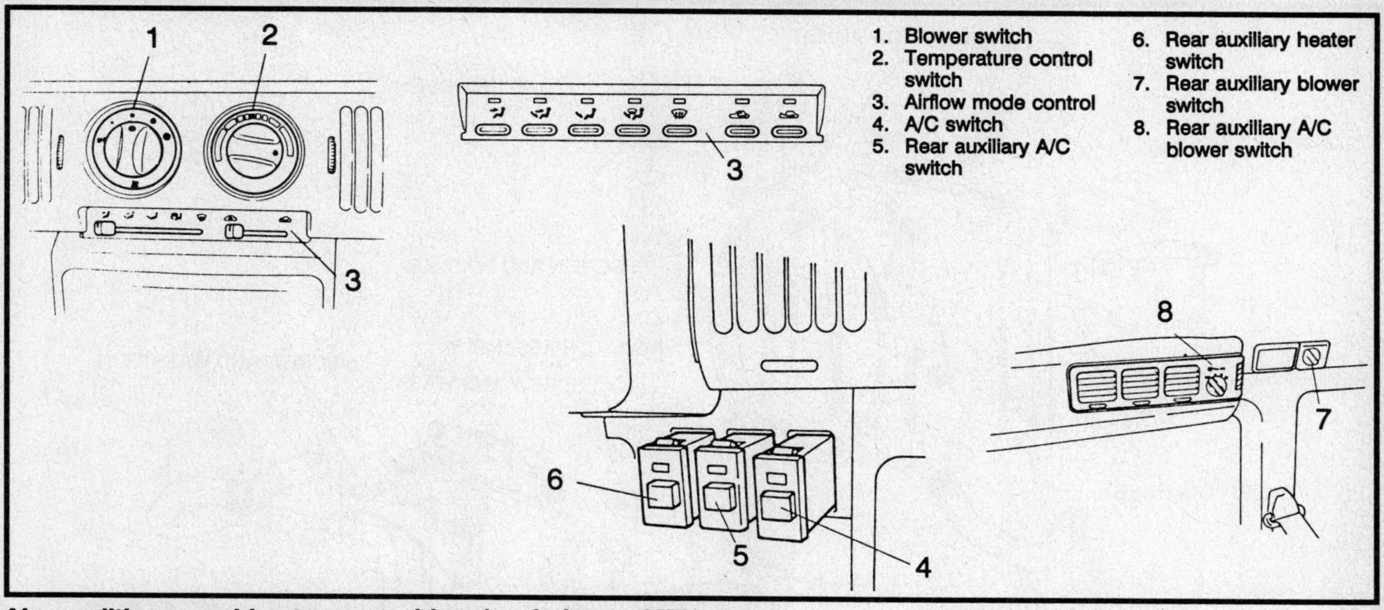
1
2
3
3
8
7
6
5
4
1. Blower switch
2. Temperature control switch
3. Airflow mode control
4. A/C switch
5. Rear auxiliary A/C switch
6. Rear auxiliary heater switch
7. Rear auxiliary blower switch
8. Rear auxiliary A/C blower switch

Air conditioner and heater control head switches— MPV

SYSTEM COMPONENTS

Radiator

REMOVAL AND INSTALLATION

Except Navajo

1. Disconnect the negative terminal at the battery.
2. Drain the cooling system.
3. Disconnect the coolant reservoir hose.
4. Remove the fresh air duct, if equipped.
5. Remove the upper and lower radiator hoses.
6. Disconnect electric fan and thermo switch wire connector, if equipped.
7. Remove electric fan or clutch fan and cowling assembly.
8. Disconnect and plug automatic transaxle cooler lines, if equipped.
9. Remove radiator mounting brackets and bolts.
10. Remove radiator assembly.

To install:

11. Install the radiator assembly.
12. Connect the automatic transaxle cooler lines, if equipped.
13. Install the electric or clutch fan assembly.
14. Install the upper and lower radiator hose.
15. Install teh fresh air duct, if equipped.
16. Connect the coolant reservoir hose.
17. Refill radiator with specified type and quantity of coolant.
18. Check the automatic transaxle fluid level, if equipped.
19. Reconnect the negative batery terminal.
20. Check cooling system for leaks.

Navajo

1. Disconnect the negative battery terminal.
2. Drain the cooling system.

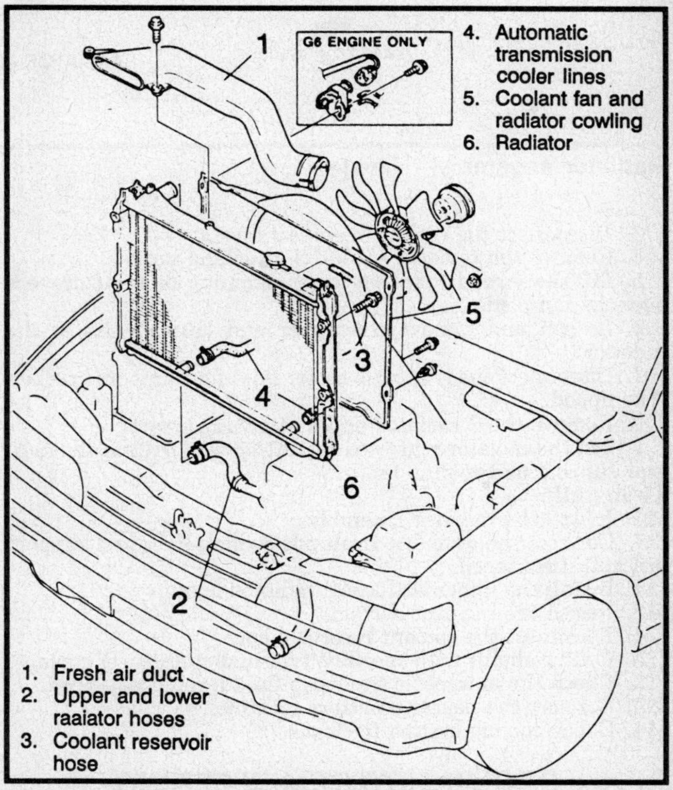
1
G6 ENGINE ONLY
4. Automatic transmission cooler lines
5. Coolant fan and radiator cowling
6. Radiator
5
3
4
6
2
1. Fresh air duct
2. Upper and lower raaiator hoses
3. Coolant reservoir hose

Typical radiator assembly—B2200, B2600I and MPV

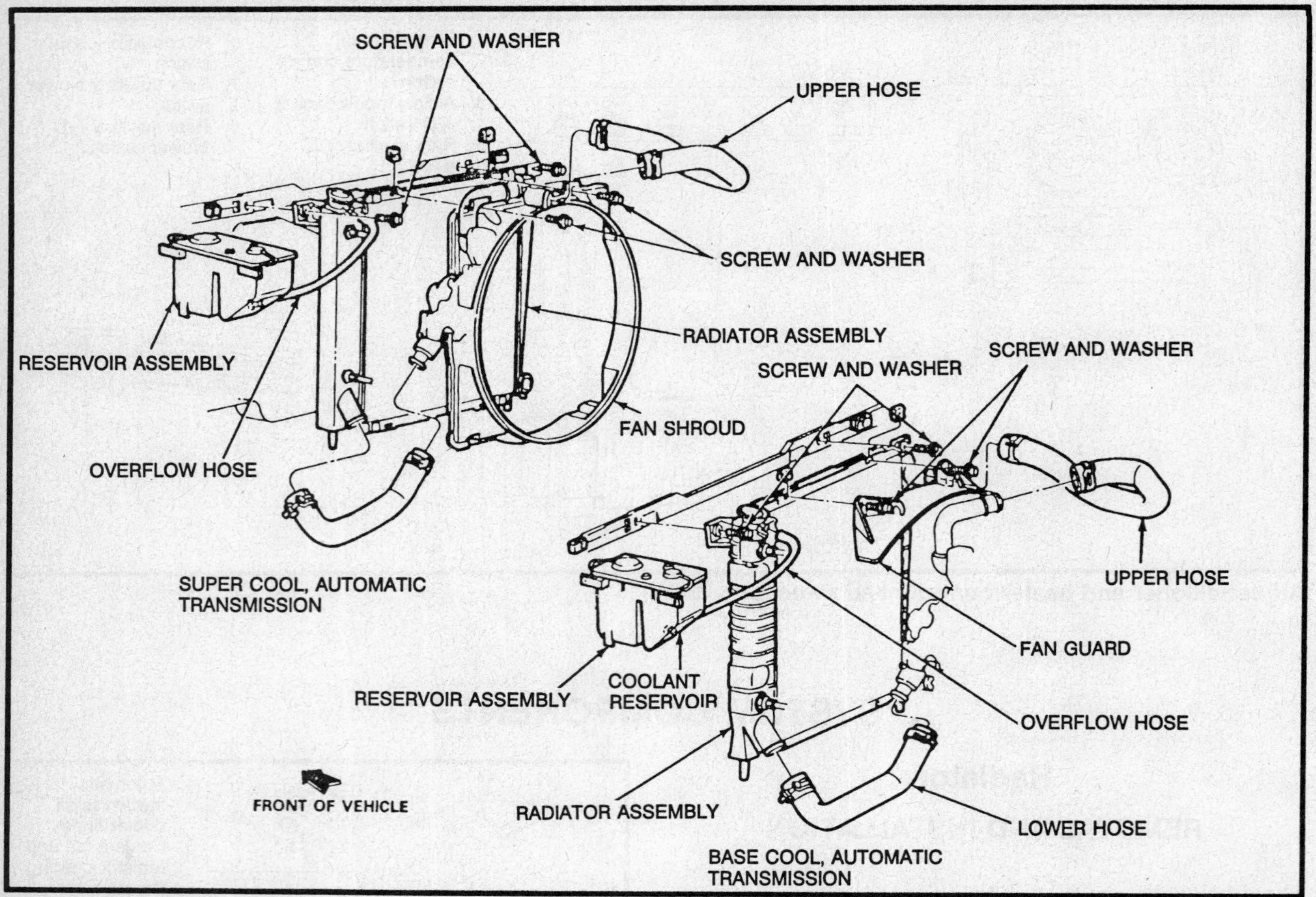
SCREW AND WASHER
UPPER HOSE
SCREW AND WASHER
RADIATOR ASSEMBLY
RESERVOIR ASSEMBLY
SCREW AND WASHER
SCREW AND WASHER
FAN SHROUD
OVERFLOW HOSE
SUPER COOL, AUTOMATIC TRANSMISSION
UPPER HOSE
FAN GUARD
RESERVOIR ASSEMBLY
COOLANT RESERVOIR
OVERFLOW HOSE
FRONT OF VEHICLE
RADIATOR ASSEMBLY
LOWER HOSE
BASE COOL, AUTOMATIC TRANSMISSION

Radiator assembly—Navajo

3. Disconnect the coolant reservoir hose.
4. Remove the radiator shroud 2 attaching screws.
5. Lift the shroud out of the lower retaining clips and drape it over the fan blades.
6. Loosen and remove the upper and lower hoses at the radiator.
7. Disconnect the transaxle cooler lines and support bracket, if equipped.
8. Remove the 2 radiator upper attaching screws.
9. Tilt the radiator rearward and lift upward to clear the radiator support and cooling fan.

To install:

10. Install the radiator assembly..
11. Connect the atomatic transaxle cooling lines and support bracket, if equipped.
12. Install the upper and lower radiator hoses.
13. Install the radiator shroud.
14. Reconnect the coolant reservoir hose.
15. Refill radiator with specified type and quantity of coolant.
12. Check the automatic transaxle fluid level, if equipped.
13. Connect the negative battery terminal.
14. Check cooling system for leaks.

COOLING SYSTEM BLEEDING

Navajo

NOTE: Use the following procedure to remove all trapped air in the cooling system to ensure a complete fill and avoid the possibility of the engine overheating.

1. Ensure that the radiator drain plug is fully closed.
2. Fill the cooling system with a 50/50 mixture of the specified type of coolant.
3. Allow several minutes for coolant to flow through radiator and release any trapped air.
4. Install the radiator cap to the pressure relief position by turning the cap to the fully installed position and then backing off to the first stop to allow for any trapped air to be released.
5. Position the temperature and mode selection lever to the **MAXIMUM HEAT** position.
6. Start the vehicle and set the fast idle at 2000 rpm for approximately 3–4 minutes.
7. Turn the engine **OFF** and carefully remove the radiator cap.
8. Add coolant to bring the level up to the filler neck seat.
9. Install the cap to the pressure relief position.
10. Start the vehicle and run the engine at fast idle until the upper radiator hose is warm.
11. Turn the engine **OFF** and carefully remove the radiator cap.
12. Add coolant to bring the level up to the filler neck seat.
13. Install the cap to the fully installed position.
14. Remove the coolant reservoir cap and fill the reservoir with 1.1 quarts of the specified type of coolant.

Cooling Fan

TESTING

MPV

1. Disconnect the electric cooling fan connector.
2. Apply 12 volts to terminal **a** of fan motor connector and ground terminal **b**.
3. If the fan motor does not operate smoothly, replace the unit.
4. If the fan motor does operate smoothly, turn the ignition switch **ON**.
5. Measure the voltage between the terminals of the wire connector with the air conditioner and blower switch **ON**.
6. If there is not approximately 12 volts at the connector, test the fan relay.

REMOVAL AND INSTALLATION

MPV

1. Disconnect the negative battery terminal.
2. Remove the lower grille and the radiator grille.
3. Remove the hood lock assembly.
4. Disconnect the condenser fan connector.
5. Remove the condenser fan attaching bolts and remove the condenser fan.
6. Installation is the reverse of the removal procedure.

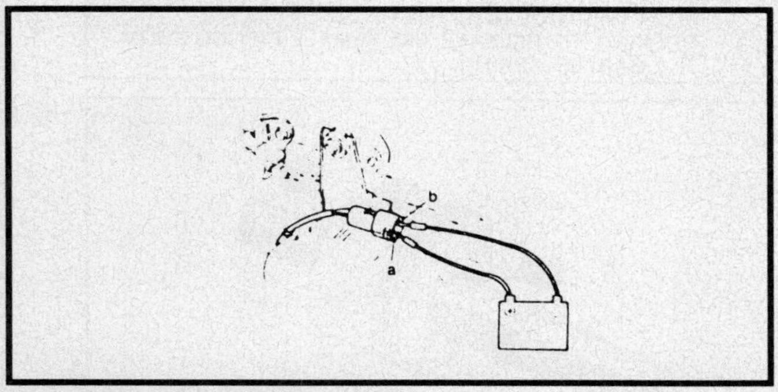
b
a

Condenser fan testing—MPV

Condenser fan removal—MPV

Condenser

REMOVAL AND INSTALLATION

B2200 and B2600i

1. Disconnect the negative battery terminal.
2. Properly discharge the air conditioning system.
3. Remove the radiator grille and the front parking lights.
4. Remove the lower refrigerant line bracket.
5. Disconnect the lower refrigerant line and remove it.
6. Remove the hood lock brace and the center support bracket
7. Disconnect the high and low side refrigerant lines.
8. Remove the condenser attaching nuts and remove the condenser.
9. Installation is the reverse of the removal procedure.

MPV

1. Disconnect the negative battery terminal.
2. Properly discharge the air conditioning system.
3. Remove the lower grille and the radiator grille.
4. Remove the hood lock assembly.
5. Disconnect the condenser fan connector.
6. Remove the condenser fan attaching bolts and remove the condenser fan.

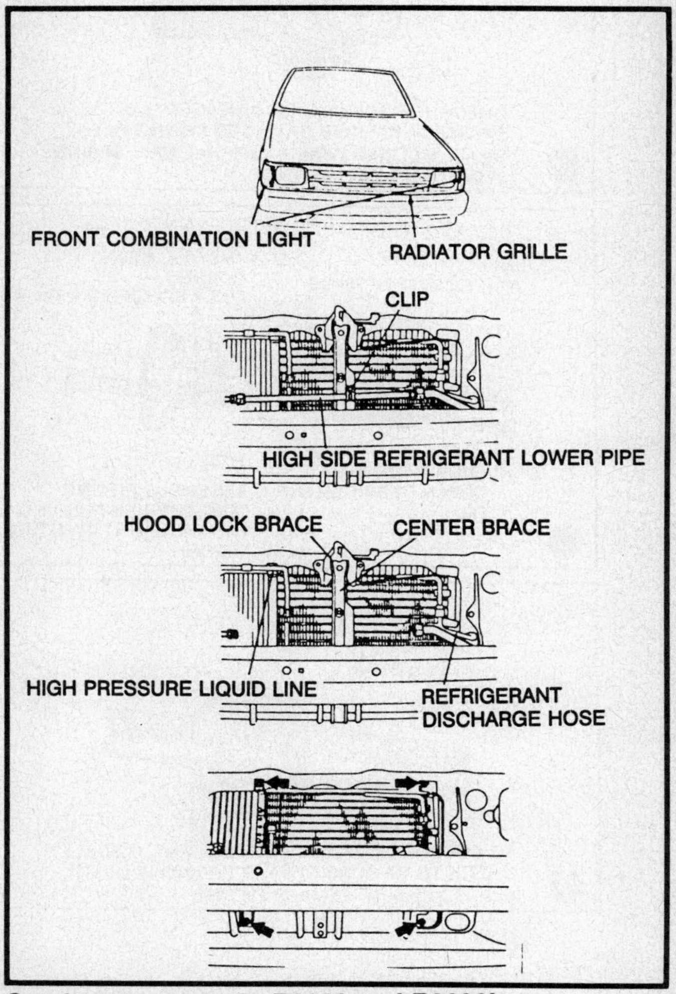
FRONT COMBINATION LIGHT
RADIATOR GRILLE
CLIP
HIGH SIDE REFRIGERANT LOWER PIPE
HOOD LOCK BRACE
CENTER BRACE
HIGH PRESSURE LIQUID LINE
REFRIGERANT DISCHARGE HOSE

Condenser removal—B2200 and B2600i

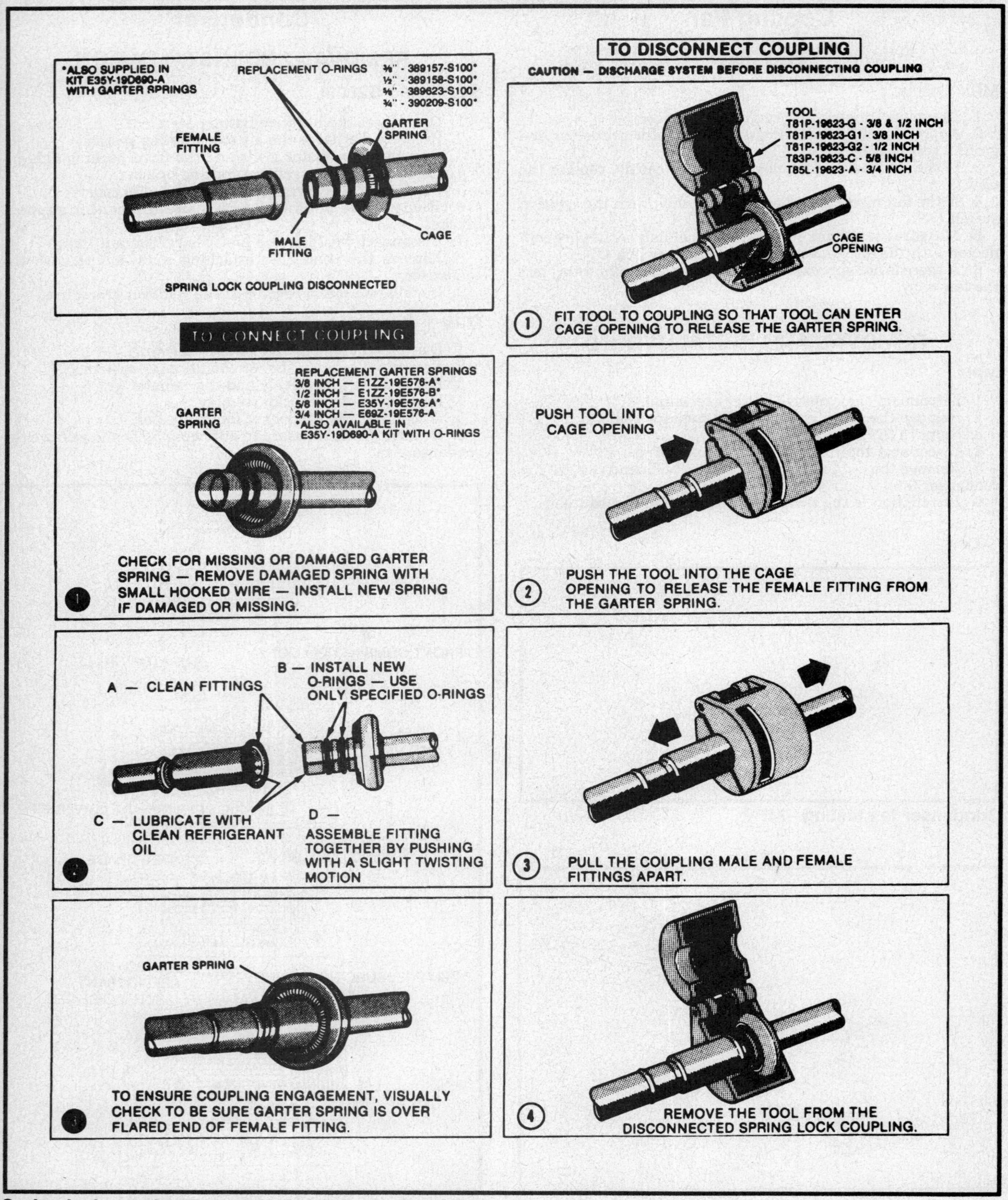
TO DISCONNECT COUPLING
CAUTION — DISCHARGE SYSTEM BEFORE DISCONNECTING COUPLING
*ALSO SUPPLIED IN KIT E35Y-19D690-A WITH GARTER SPRINGS
REPLACEMENT O-RINGS
3/8" - 389157-S100*
1/2" - 389158-S100*
5/8" - 389623-S100*
3/4" - 390209-S100*
GARTER SPRING
FEMALE FITTING
MALE FITTING
CAGE
SPRING LOCK COUPLING DISCONNECTED
TOOL
T81P-19623-G - 3/8 & 1/2 INCH
T81P-19623-G1 - 3/8 INCH
T81P-19623-G2 - 1/2 INCH
T83P-19623-C - 5/8 INCH
T85L-19623-A - 3/4 INCH
CAGE OPENING
1 FIT TOOL TO COUPLING SO THAT TOOL CAN ENTER CAGE OPENING TO RELEASE THE GARTER SPRING.
TO CONNECT COUPLING
REPLACEMENT GARTER SPRINGS
3/8 INCH — E1ZZ-19E576-A*
1/2 INCH — E1ZZ-19E576-B*
5/8 INCH — E35Y-19E576-A*
3/4 INCH — E69Z-19E576-A
*ALSO AVAILABLE IN E35Y-19D690-A KIT WITH O-RINGS
GARTER SPRING
CHECK FOR MISSING OR DAMAGED GARTER SPRING — REMOVE DAMAGED SPRING WITH SMALL HOOKED WIRE — INSTALL NEW SPRING IF DAMAGED OR MISSING.
PUSH TOOL INTO CAGE OPENING
2 PUSH THE TOOL INTO THE CAGE OPENING TO RELEASE THE FEMALE FITTING FROM THE GARTER SPRING.
A — CLEAN FITTINGS
B — INSTALL NEW O-RINGS — USE ONLY SPECIFIED O-RINGS
C — LUBRICATE WITH CLEAN REFRIGERANT OIL
D — ASSEMBLE FITTING TOGETHER BY PUSHING WITH A SLIGHT TWISTING MOTION
3 PULL THE COUPLING MALE AND FEMALE FITTINGS APART.
GARTER SPRING
TO ENSURE COUPLING ENGAGEMENT, VISUALLY CHECK TO BE SURE GARTER SPRING IS OVER FLARED END OF FEMALE FITTING.
4 REMOVE THE TOOL FROM THE DISCONNECTED SPRING LOCK COUPLING.

Spring lock coupler disconnect procedure—Navajo

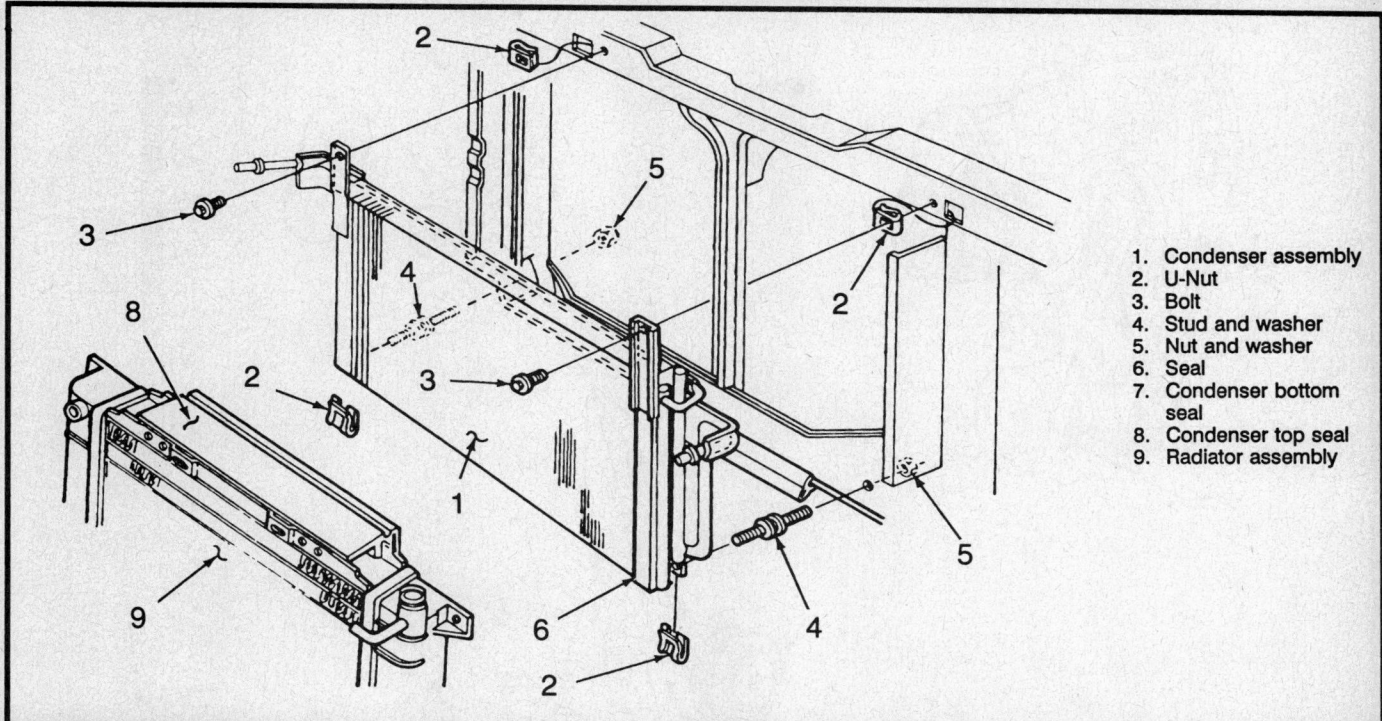

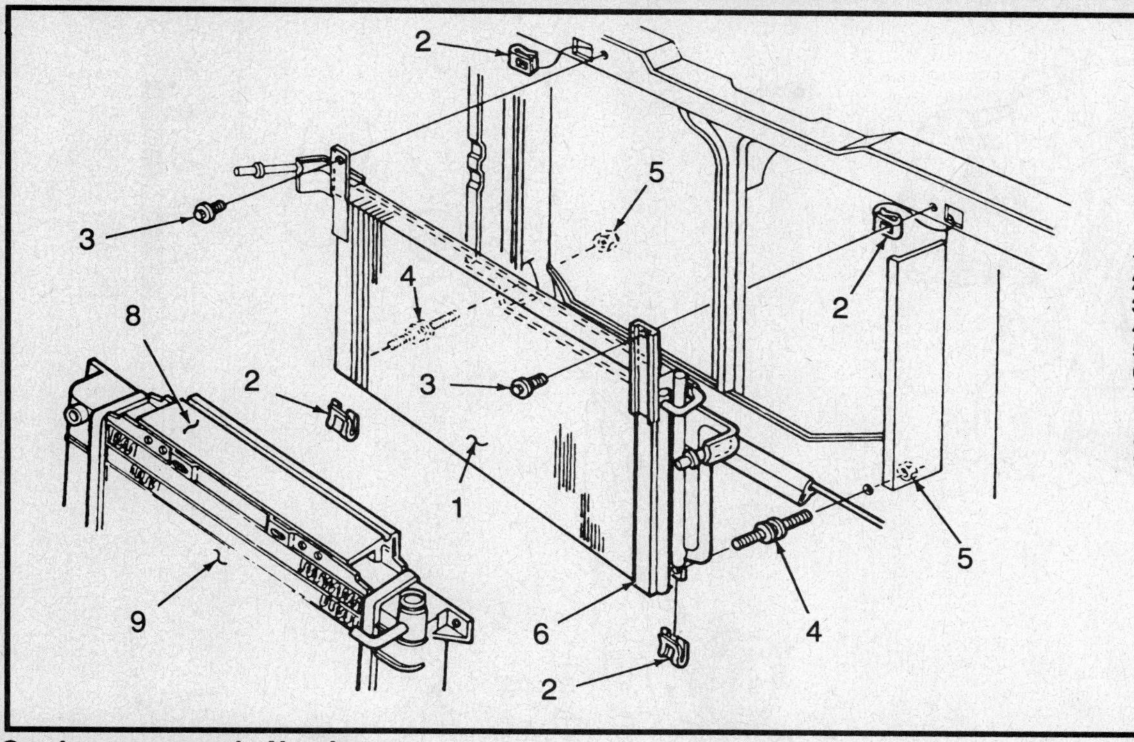
1. Condenser assembly
2. U-Nut
3. Bolt
4. Stud and washer
5. Nut and washer
6. Seal
7. Condenser bottom seal
8. Condenser top seal
9. Radiator assembly

Condenser removal—Navajo

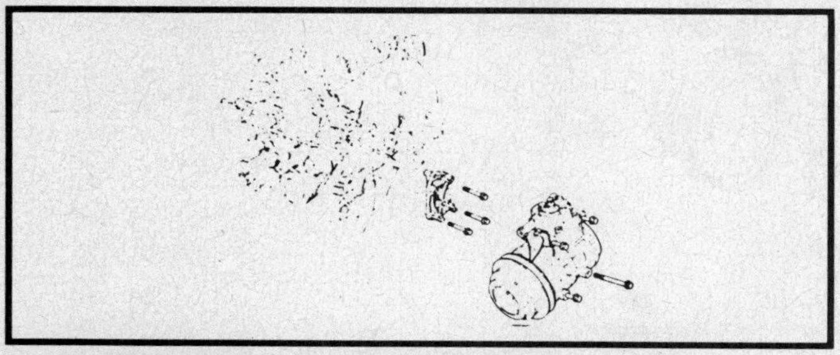

Air conditioner compressor removal—MPV

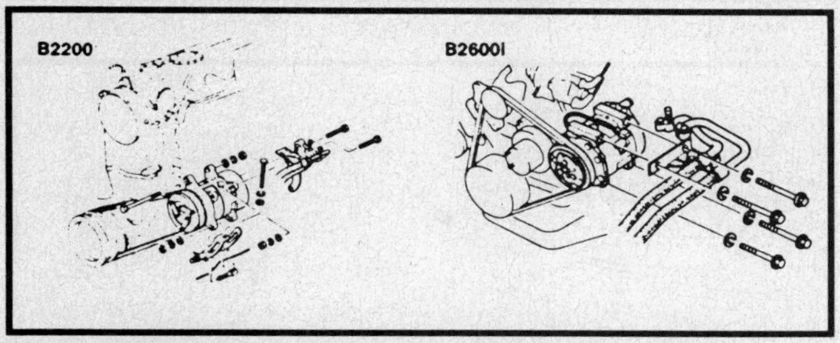
B2200
B2600I

Air conditioner compressor removal—B2200 and B2600I

7. Disconnect the refrigerant high and low side pressure lines.
8. Remove the condenser attaching bolts and remove the condenser.
9. Installation is the reverse of the removal procedure.

Navajo

1. Disconnect the negative battery terminal.
2. Properly discharge the air conditioning system.
3. Disconnect and plug the compressor discharge line at the condenser using the appropriate spring lock coupling tool.
4. Disconnect and plug the condenser liquid line using the appropriate spring lock coupling tool.
5. Raise and support the vehicle safely.
6. Remove the 2 attaching nuts at the lower mounting studs on the condenser.
7. Remove the upper radiator brackets and tilt the radiator rearward being careful not to damage the cooling fan or radiator core.
8. Remove the 2 bolts attaching the condenser to the radiator support.
9. Remove the condenser assembly.
10. Installation is the reverse of the removal procedure.
11. Evacuate, recharge and leak test the system.

Compressor

REMOVAL AND INSTALLATION

1. Disconnect the negative battery terminal.
2. Properly discharge the air conditioning system.
3. Disconnect the magnetic clutch wire connector.
4. Loosen the lock nut and adjusting bolts and remove the compressor belt.
5. Disconnect and plug refrigerant lines at the compressor.
6. Remove compressor mounting bolts and remove compressor.
7. Installation is the reverse of the removal procedure.
8. Evacuate, recharge and test the system.

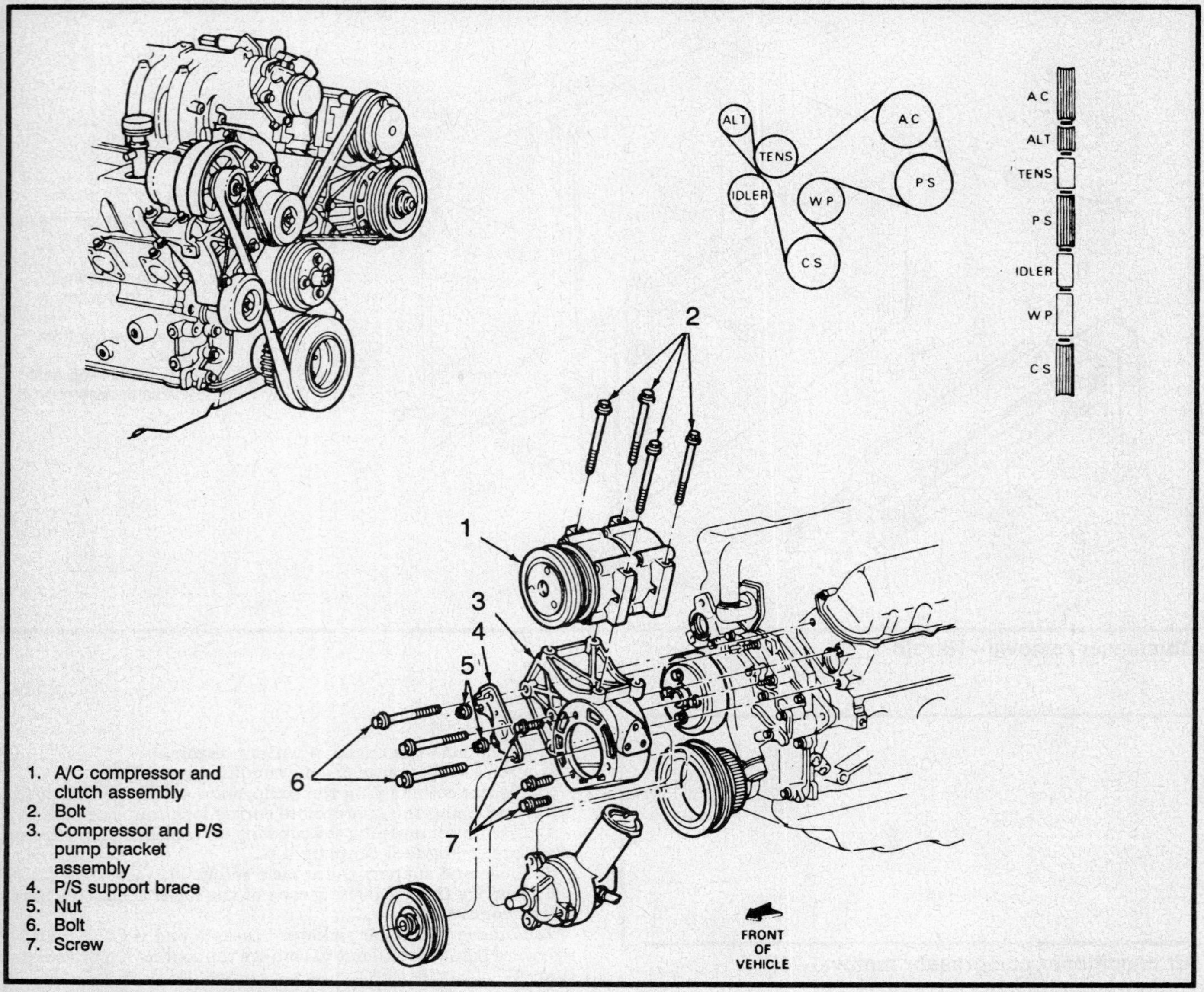
ALT
TENS
IDLER
WP
CS
AC
PS
AC
ALT
TENS
PS
IDLER
WP
CS
1
2
3
4
5
6
7
FRONT
OF
VEHICLE
1. A/C compressor and clutch assembly
2. Bolt
3. Compressor and P/S pump bracket assembly
4. P/S support brace
5. Nut
6. Bolt
7. Screw

Air conditioner compressor removal—Navajo

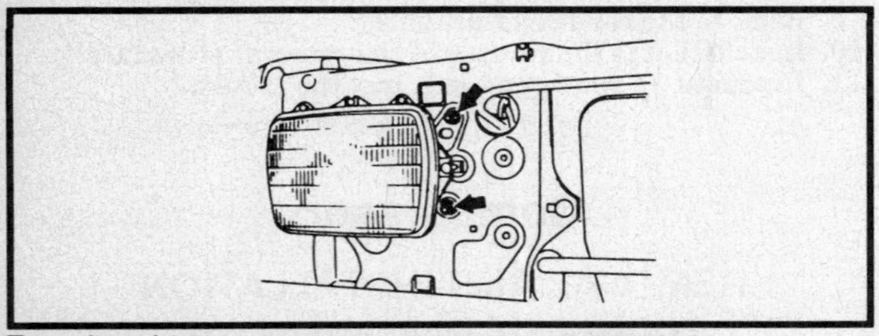

Receiver/drier removal—B2200 and B2600i

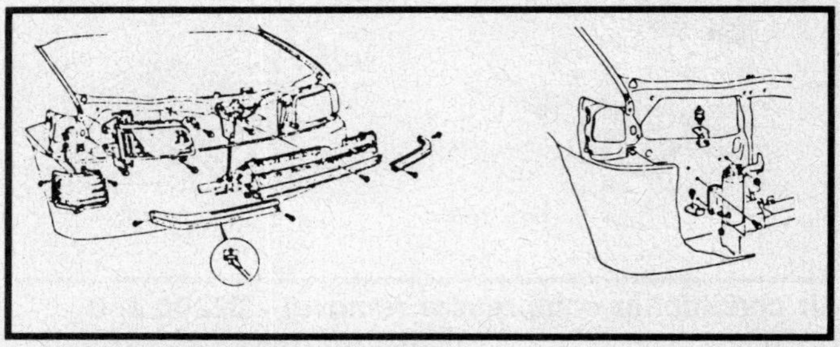

Receiver/drier removal—MPV

Receiver/Drier

REMOVAL AND INSTALLATION

B2200 and B2600I

1. Disconnect the negative battery terminal.
2. Properly discharge the air conditioning system.
3. Remove the radiator grille.
4. Remove the right front parking light and headlight.
5. Disconnect the refrigerant lines at the receiver/drier.
6. Remove the receiver/drier attaching nuts and remove the receiver/drier.
7. Installation is the reverse of the removal procedure.

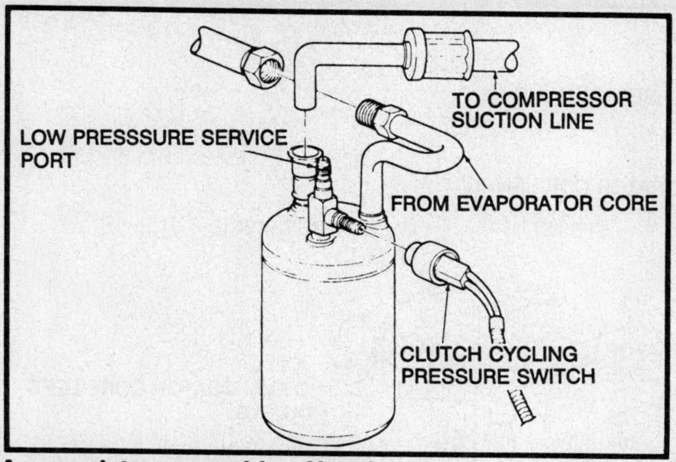
TO COMPRESSOR SUCTION LINE
LOW PRESSSURE SERVICE PORT
FROM EVAPORATOR CORE
CLUTCH CYCLING PRESSURE SWITCH

Accumulator assembly—Navajo

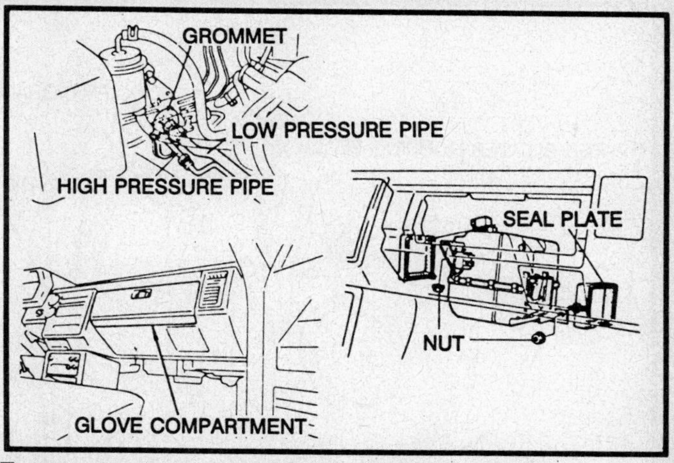
GROMMET
LOW PRESSURE PIPE
HIGH PRESSURE PIPE
SEAL PLATE
NUT
GLOVE COMPARTMENT

Evaporator removal—B2200, B2600I and MPV

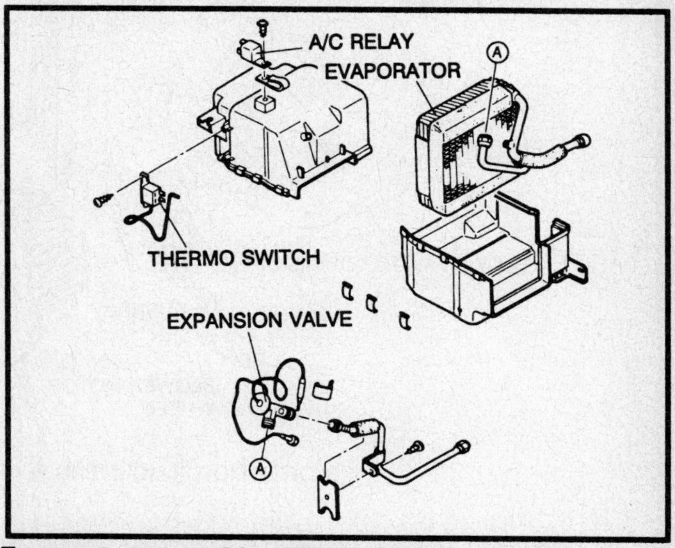
A/C RELAY
A
EVAPORATOR
THERMO SWITCH
EXPANSION VALVE
A

Evaporator assembly—B2200, B2600I and MPV

MPV

1. Disconnect the negative battery terminal.
2. Properly discharge the air conditioning system.
3. Disconnect the right front parking light and headlight.
4. Remove the lower grille and the radiator grille.
5. Remove the right front parking light and headlight.
6. Disconnect the refrigerant lines at the receiver/drier.
7. Remove the receiver/drier attaching bolts and remove the receiver/drier.
8. Installation is the reverse of the removal procedure.

Accumulator

REMOVAL AND INSTALLATION

Navajo

1. Disconnect the negative battery terminal.
2. Properly discharge the air conditioning system.
3. Disconnect the wire connector from the pressure switch at the accumulator.
4. Remove the pressure switch, if required.
5. Disconnect and plug the refrigerant low pressure line using the appropriate spring lock coupling tool.
6. Using a backup wrench, loosen the accumulator to evaporator low pressure line.
7. Loosen the lower attaching screws holding the flanges of the case to the bracket and the evaporator inlet to the accumulator together.
8. Disconnect and plug the accumulator to the evaporator line.
9. Remove the bracket from the accumulator.
10. Installation is the reverse of the removal procedure.

Evaporator

REMOVAL AND INSTALLATION

Except Navajo

1. Disconnect the negative battery terminal.
2. Properly discharge the air conditioning system.
3. Disconnect and plug the refrigerant lines at the evaporator.
4. Remove the grommets at the expansion valve, if equipped.
5. Remove the glove box and lower panel.
6. Remove the air flow ducts.
7. Remove the evaporator unit drain hose.
8. Remove the seal plates from both sides of the evaporator unit.
9. Disconnect the air conditioning wiring harness at the evaporator.
10. Remove the attaching bolts at the evaporator and remove the unit.
11. Installation is the reverse of the removal procedure.

Navajo

1. Disconnect the negative battery terminal.
2. Properly discharge the air conditioning system.
3. Disconnect the wire connector from the pressure switch at the accumulator.
4. Disconnect and plug the low pressure accumulator line using the appropriate spring lock coupling tool.
5. Using a backup wrench, disconnect and plug the evaporator inlet line.
6. Remove the attaching screws holding the vacuum reservoir and evaporator service cover to the evaporator case assembly.
7. Remove the 2 dash panel mounting nuts.
8. Remove the evaporator case service cover from the evaporator case assembly.

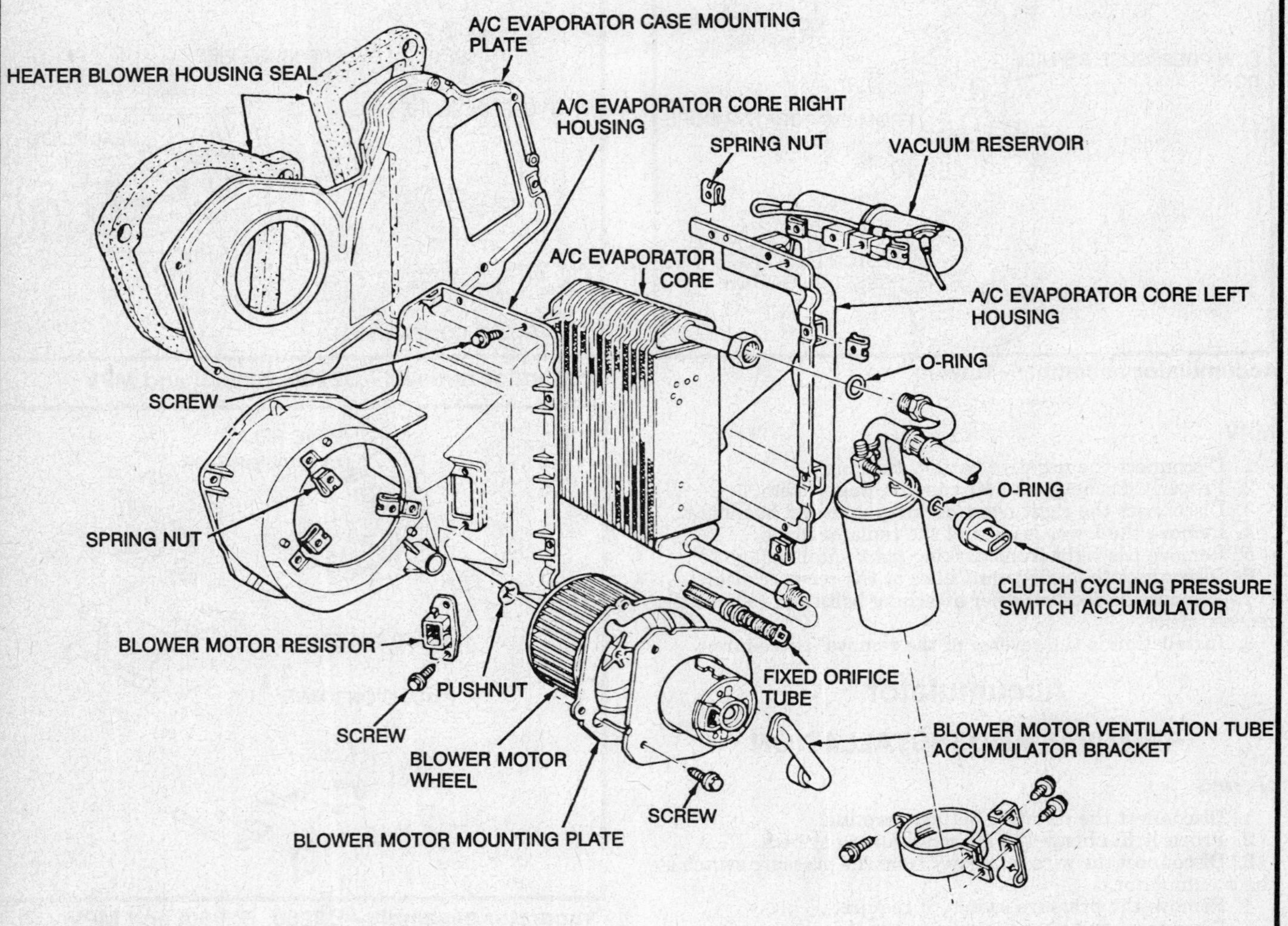
A/C EVAPORATOR CASE MOUNTING PLATE
HEATER BLOWER HOUSING SEAL
A/C EVAPORATOR CORE RIGHT HOUSING
SPRING NUT
VACUUM RESERVOIR
A/C EVAPORATOR CORE
A/C EVAPORATOR CORE LEFT HOUSING
O-RING
SCREW
O-RING
SPRING NUT
CLUTCH CYCLING PRESSURE SWITCH ACCUMULATOR
BLOWER MOTOR RESISTOR
FIXED ORIFICE TUBE
PUSHNUT
SCREW
BLOWER MOTOR VENTILATION TUBE ACCUMULATOR BRACKET
BLOWER MOTOR WHEEL
SCREW
BLOWER MOTOR MOUNTING PLATE

Evaporator assembly—Navajo

9. Remove the evaporator core and accumulator assembly from the vehicle.
10. Separate the evaporator core from the accumulator using 2 wrenches.
11. Installation is the reverse of the removal procedure.

Expansion Valve

REMOVAL AND INSTALLATION

Except Navajo

1. Disconnect the negative battery terminal.
2. Properly discharge the air conditioning system.
3. Disconnect and plug the refrigerant lines at the evaporator.
4. Remove the grommet at the evaporator line connection.
5. Remove the glove box and lower panel.
6. Remove the air flow ducts, if required.
7. Remove the evaporator unit seal plates and remove the unit.
8. Remove evaporator securing clips.
9. Disassemble the unit.
10. Remove the thermo switch.
11. Remove the capillary tube from the outlet pipe.
12. Remove the expansion valve.
13. Installation is the reverse of the removal procedure.

Fixed Orifice Tube

REMOVAL AND INSTALLATION

Navajo

1. Disconnect the negative battery terminal.
2. Properly discharge the air conditioning system.
3. Disconnect and plug the lower evaporator inlet line.

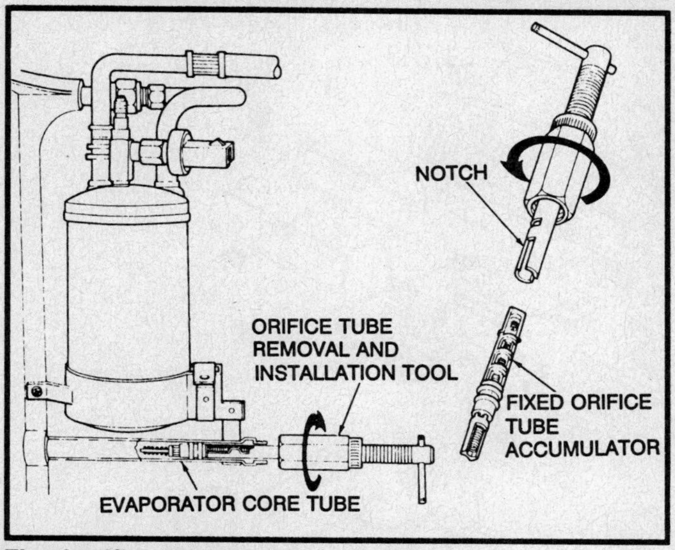
NOTCH
ORIFICE TUBE
REMOVAL AND
INSTALLATION TOOL
FIXED ORIFICE
TUBE
ACCUMULATOR
EVAPORATOR CORE TUBE

Fixed orifice tube removal—Navajo

4. Apply a small amount of refrigerant oil to the evaporator inlet to lubricate the orifice tube during removal.
5. Using a suitable tool, engage the 2 tangs on the orifice tube, being careful not to twist or rotate the tube as this might cause the tube to break off in the evaporator line.
6. Pull the orifice tube directly out.
7. Installation is the reverse of the removal procedure.
8. Apply a thin coat of refrigerant oil on the orifice tube and o-ring.9

Blower Motor

REMOVAL AND INSTALLATION

B2200 and B2600I

1. Disconnect the negative battery terminal.
2. Remove the right side kick panel cover and remove the ECU.
3. Remove the screws and remove the blower motor wire connector.
4. Remove the blower motor cover.
5. Remove the blower motor.
6. Installation is the reverse of the removal procedure.

MPV

1. Disconnect the negative battery terminal.
2. Remove the right side lower panel and undercover.
3. Disconnect the blower motor wire connector.
4. Remove the 3 blower motor attaching screws.
5. Remove the blower motor.
6. Installation is the reverse of the removal procedure.

Navajo

1. Disconnect the negative battery terminal.
2. Remove the air cleaner, if required.
3. Disconnect the wire harness connector from the blower motor.
4. Disconnect the blower motor cooling tube at the blower motor.
5. Remove the blower motor attaching screws.
6. Remove the blower motor from the blower housing.
7. Installation is the reverse of the removal procedure.

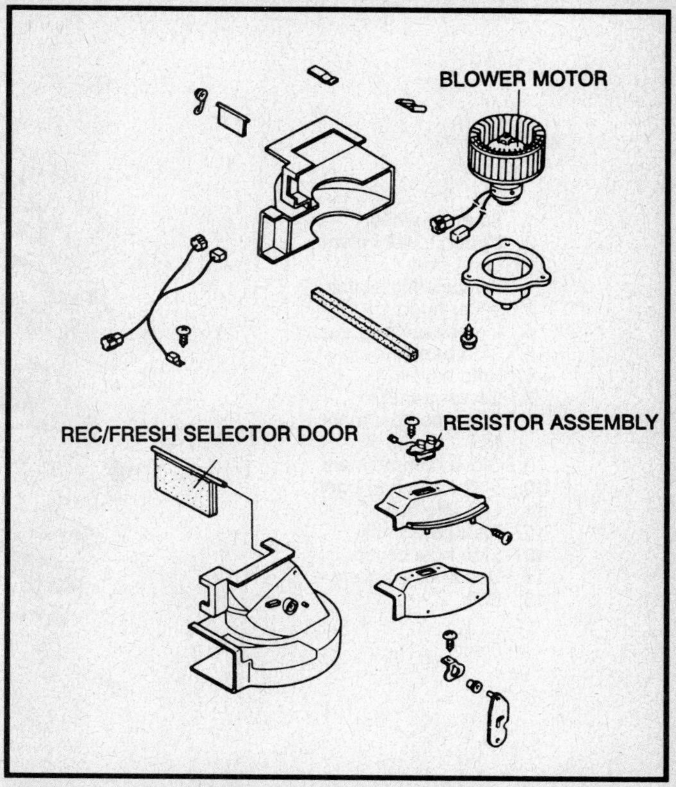
BLOWER MOTOR
REC/FRESH SELECTOR DOOR
RESISTOR ASSEMBLY

Blower motor assembly—B2200, B2600I and MPV

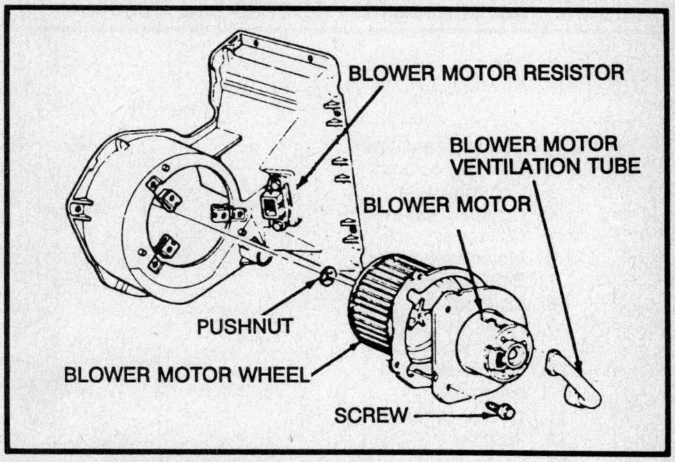
BLOWER MOTOR RESISTOR
BLOWER MOTOR
VENTILATION TUBE
BLOWER MOTOR
PUSHNUT
BLOWER MOTOR WHEEL
SCREW

Blower motor assembly—Navajo

Blower Motor Resistor

REMOVAL AND INSTALLATION

Except Navajo

1. Disconnect the negative battery terminal.
2. Remove the glove box and lower panel, if required.
3. Disconnect the blower motor resistor wire connector.
4. Remove the attaching screw and remove the resistor.
5. Installation is the reverse of the removal procedure.

1. Steering wheel
2. Upper, lower column cover and combination switch
3. Meter hood
4. Meter assembly
5. Side panel
6. Hole cover
7. Center panel
8. Glove compartment lid
9. Glove compartment
10. Shift knob and boot
11. Console box
12. Radio assembly
13. Side hole covers
14. Upper hole covers
15. Bolt

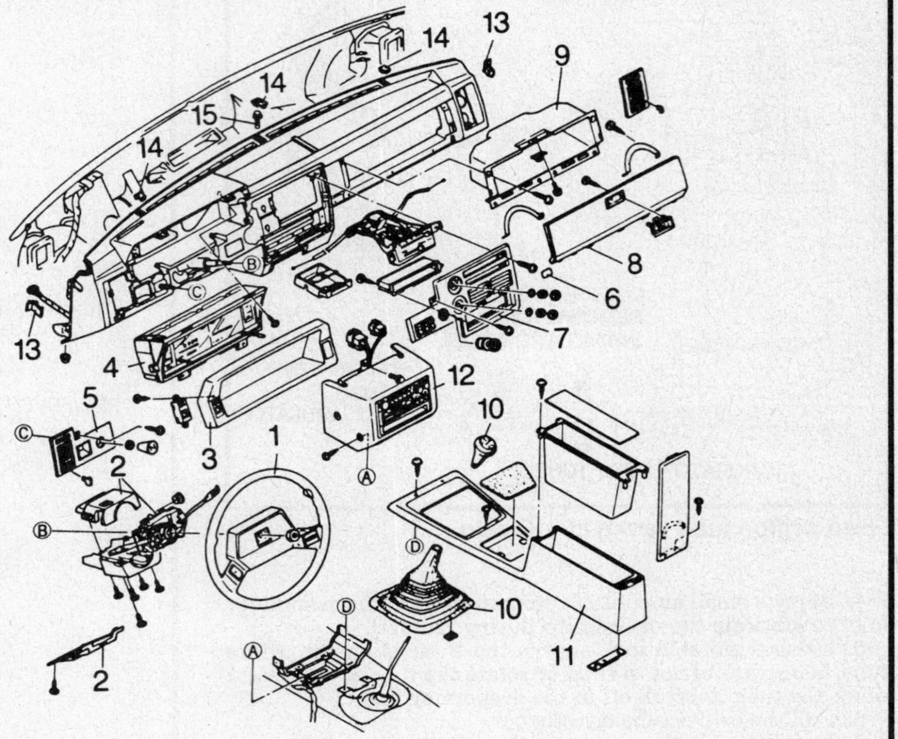

Instrument panel assembly – B2200 and B2600i

1. Hood release knob
2. Steering column
3. Column cover
4. Combination switch
5. Cluster assembly
6. Meter assembly
7. Side cover
8. Undercover
9. R/H lower panel assembly
10. L/H lower panel assembly
11. L/H lower duct
12. Ashtray
13. Audio panel assembly
14. Audio unit
15. Lower panel assembly
16. Knob
17. Switch panel assembly
18. Temperature control switch
19. Blower control switch
20. Airflow mode control
21. Upper garnish
22. Dashpanel

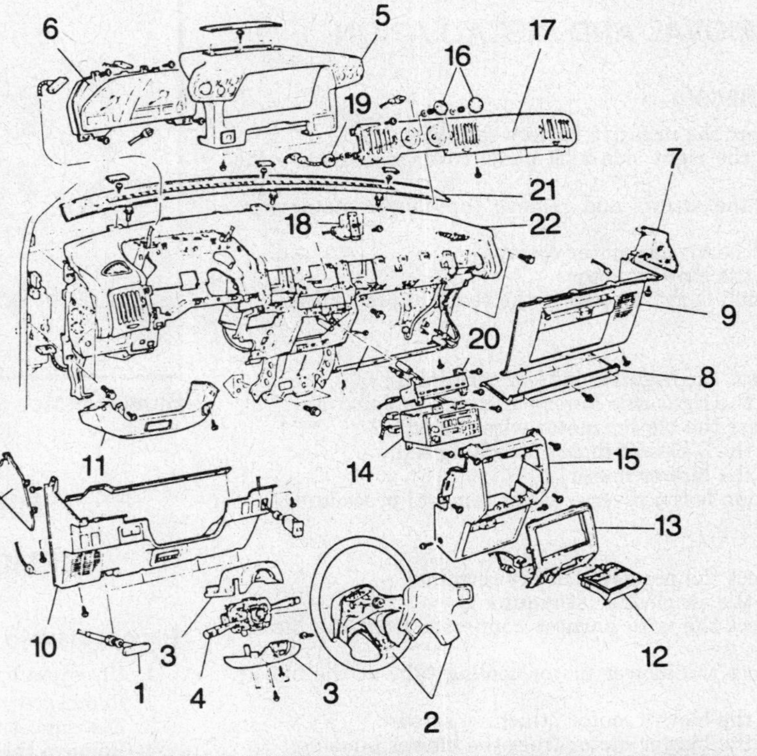

Instrument panel assembly – MPV

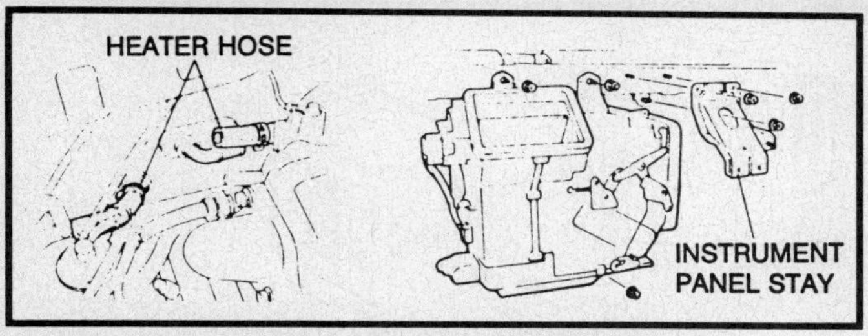
HEATER HOSE
INSTRUMENT PANEL STAY

Heater core removal – B2200, B2600i and MPV

Navajo

1. Disconnect the negative battery terminal.
2. Disconnect the wire connector from the blower motor resistor.
3. Remove the resistor attaching screws.
4. Remove the resistor assembly.
5. Installation is the reverse of the removal procedure.

Heater Core

REMOVAL AND INSTALLATION

Except Navajo

1. Disconnect the negative battery terminal.
2. Drain the engine coolant.
3. Disconnect heater core hoses.
4. Remove instrument panel, as follows:
   a. Remove transmission selector lever or knob.
   b. Remove center console.
   c. Remove the steering wheel.
   d. Remove the upper and lower steering column covers.
   e. Remove the instrument meter hood.
   f. Remove the instrument cluster assembly.
   g. Disconnect speedo cable.
   h. Remove the air ducts.
   i. Remove the instrument hosing lower panels.
   j. Remove the glove box assembly.
   k. Remove the heater control switch and cables, if required.
   l. Remove header and side trim, if required.
   m. Remove the center cap, the side covers and the center bracket bolts on the instrument panel.
   n. Remove the steering shaft bolts.
   o. Disconnect any necessary wire harness connectors.
   p. Remove the instrument panel.
5. Remove the seal plate.
6. Remove the attaching nuts, and the instrument panel attaching bracket.
7. Remove the heater unit.
8. Remove the attaching clips on heater unit and separate assembly.
9. Remove heater core.

To install:

10. Install the heater core.
11. Reattach heater case halves with clips.
12. Install the heater unit.
13. Install the seal plates.
    a. Install the instrument panel.
    b. Reconnect wire harness connectors.
    c. Install the steering shaft securing bolts.
    d. Install the center cap, the side covers and the center bracket bolts on the instrument panel.
    e. Install header and side trim, if removed.
    f. Install the heater control switch and cables.
    g. Install the glove box assembly.
    h. Install the instrument hosing lower panels.
    i. Install the heater ducts.
    j. Reconnect speedo cable.
    k. Install the instrument cluster and meter hood assembly.
    l. Install the upper and lower steering column covers.
    m. Install the steering wheel.
    n. Install the center console and the shift lever or knob.
14. Reconnect heater core hoses.
15. Reconnect the negative battery terminal.
16. Refill cooling system with proper quantity and type of antifreeze.
17. Check the system for leaks.

Navajo

1. Disconnect the negative battery terminal.
2. Drain the engine coolant.
3. Disconnect, remove and the plug the heater core hoses.
4. Remove the 4 screws attaching the heater core access cover to the plenum assembly located in the passenger compartment.
5. Remove the heater core cover.
6. Remove the heater core by pulling rearward and downward.
7. Installation is the reverse of the removal procedure.

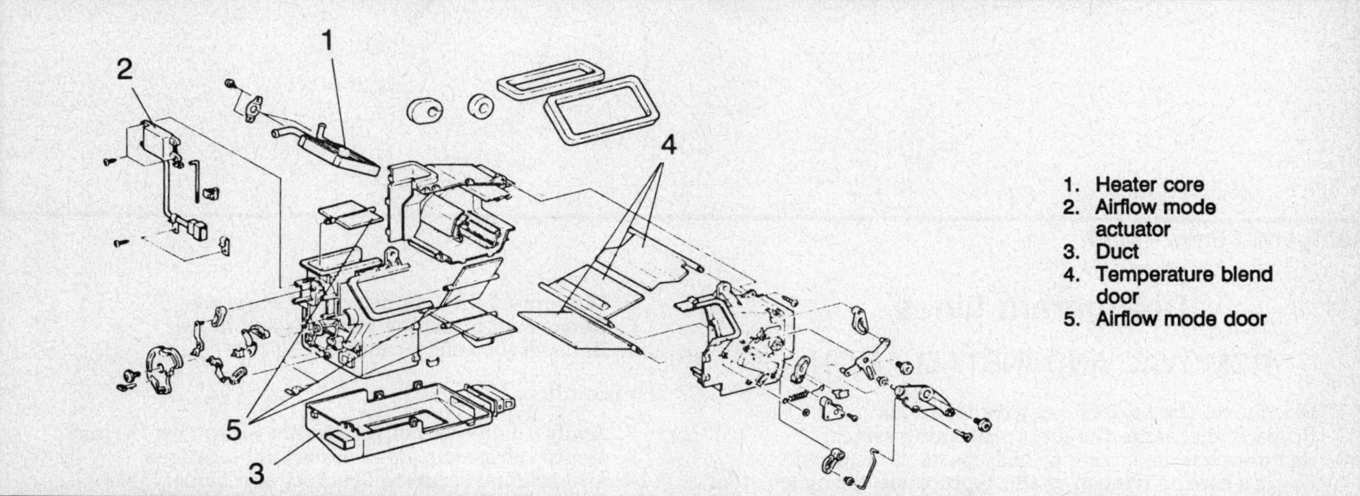
1
2
3
4
5
1. Heater core
2. Airflow mode actuator
3. Duct
4. Temperature blend door
5. Airflow mode door

Heater unit assembly – B2200, B2600i and MPV

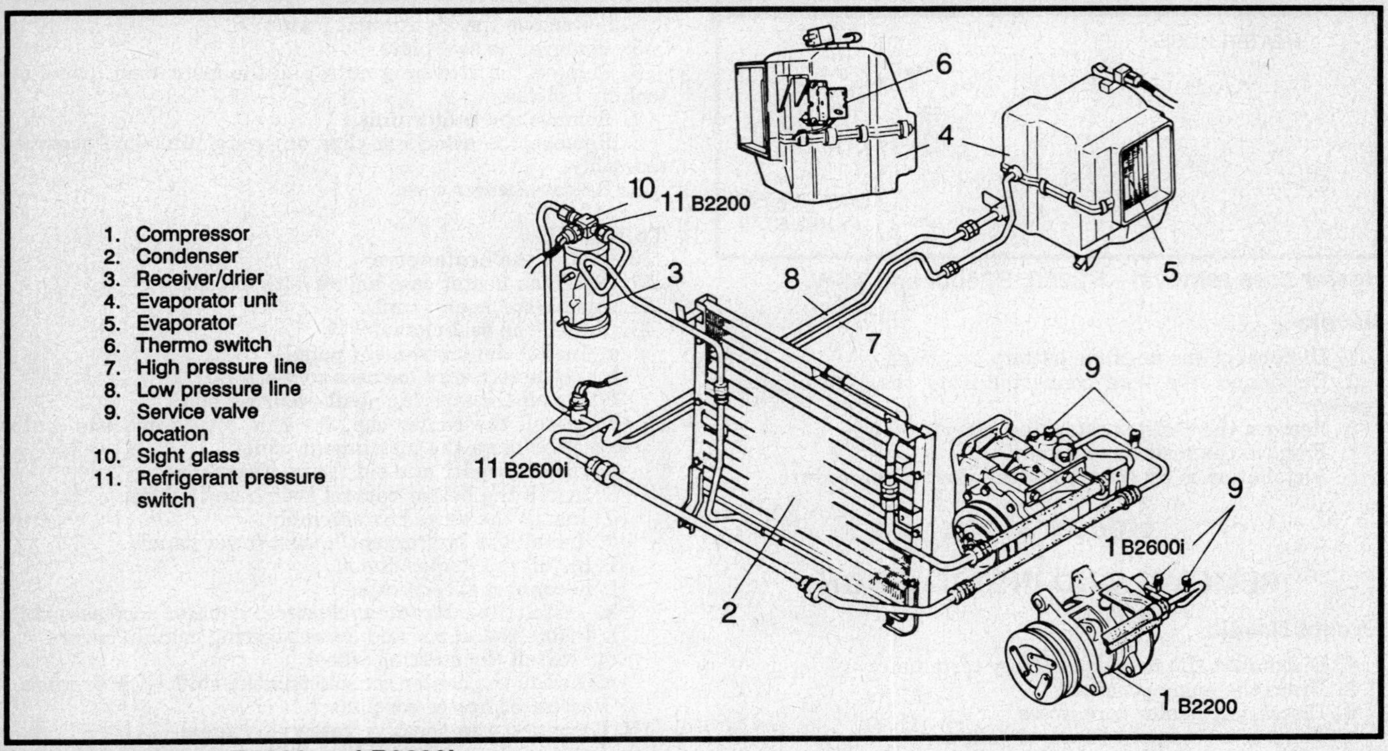
1. Compressor
2. Condenser
3. Receiver/drier
4. Evaporator unit
5. Evaporator
6. Thermo switch
7. High pressure line
8. Low pressure line
9. Service valve location
10. Sight glass
11. Refrigerant pressure switch
10
11 B2200
11 B2600i
1 B2600i
1 B2200

Refrigerant lines—B2200 and B2600i

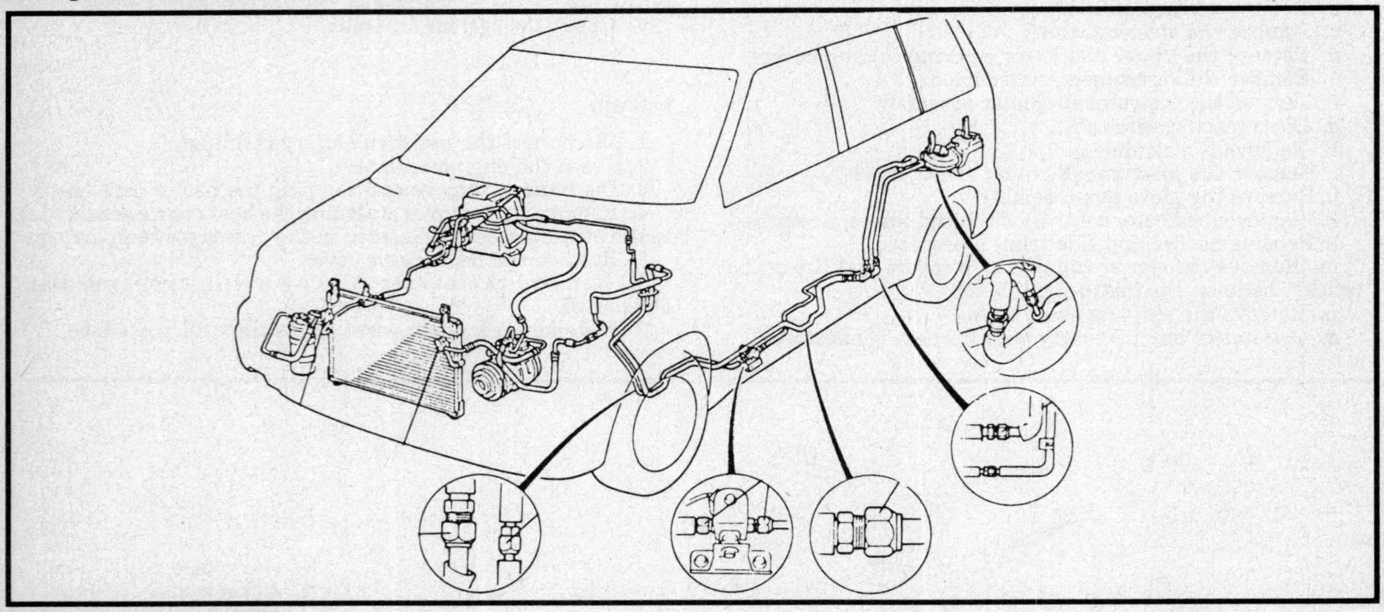

Refrigerant lines—MPV

Refrigerant Lines

REMOVAL AND INSTALLATION

1. Disconnect the battery negative terminal.
2. Properly discharge the air conditioning system.
3. Remove chassis, engine or body parts, if required.
4. Using a backup wrench or the appropriate spring lock tool loosen, disconnect and immediately plug the refrigerant line.
5. Disconnect wire connectors, if required.
6. Remove all attaching brackets and bolts.
7. Remove the refrigerant lines.

To install:

8. Apply a light coat of refrigerant oil to new O-rings.
9. Route refrigerant lines in original locations.
10. Use original securing brackets and bolts.
11. Evacuate, charge and check system for leaks.

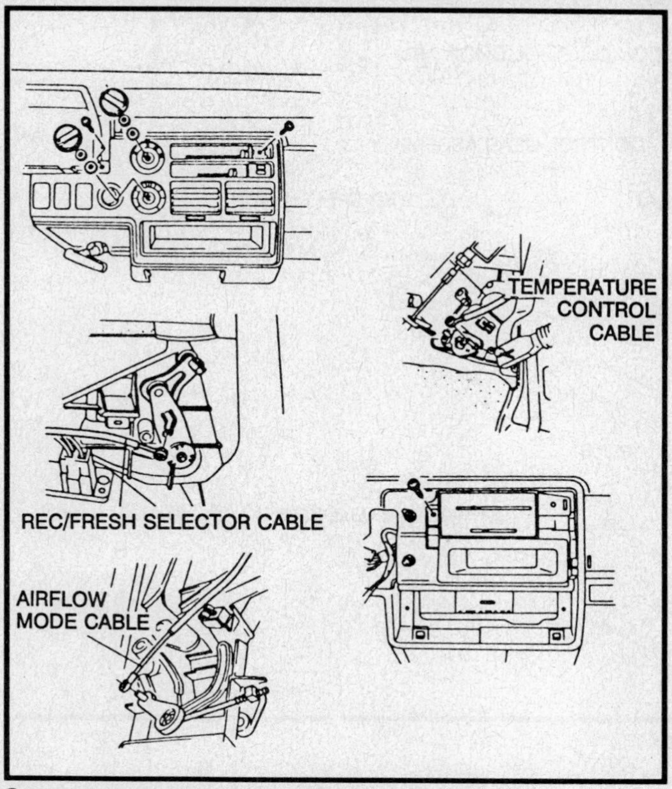
TEMPERATURE CONTROL CABLE
REC/FRESH SELECTOR CABLE
AIRFLOW MODE CABLE
Control head removal—B2200 and B2600i

Manual Control Head

REMOVAL AND INSTALLATION

B2200 and B2600i

1. Disconnect the negative battery terminal.
2. Remove the instrument panel meter hood.
3. Remove the attaching screws, knobs and nuts.
4. Disconnect the air conditioner and cigarette lighter connector.
5. Remove the center panel.
6. Remove the glove compartment.
7. Remove the attaching screws and disconnect the control head wire connectors.
8. Remove the control head assembly.
9. Disconnect the control cables.
10. Installation is the reverse of the removal procedure.

MPV

1. Disconnect the negative battery terminal.
2. Remove the 2 lower side panels and the undercover.
3. Remove the steering column cover, if required.
4. Remove the instrument cluster assembly.
5. Remove the switch panel attaching nuts and washers.
6. Remove the switch panel.
7. Remove the attaching screws and remove the temperature control assembly.
8. Remove the center lower panel.
9. Remove the airflow mode attaching screws.
10. Remove the control assembly and disconnect the wire connectors.
11. Installation is the reverse of the removal procedure.

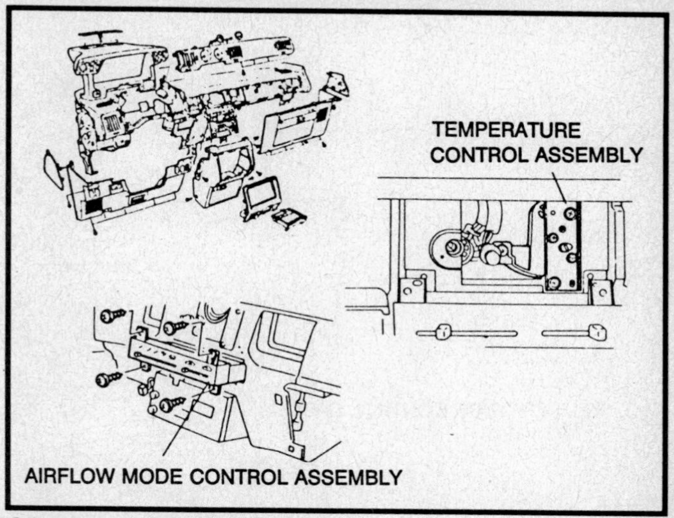
TEMPERATURE CONTROL ASSEMBLY
AIRFLOW MODE CONTROL ASSEMBLY
Control head removal—MPV

Navajo

1. Disconnect the negative battery terminal.
2. Remove the ashtray from its retainer.
3. Disconnect the cigarette lighter wire connector.
4. Remove the 2 screws attaching the ashtray bracket to the instrument panel.
5. Remove the ashtray bracket from the instrument panel.
6. Carefully remove the finish panel from the instrument panel and cluster by pulling the panel straight back then up.
7. Disconnect the 4 × 4 transfer switch, if equipped.
8. Remove the 4 attaching screws at the control head.
9. Pull the control head assembly through the instrument panel opening far enough to allow removal of wire connectors.
10. Disconnect the vacuum hose harness.
11. Disconnect the control head cables.
12. Remove the control head assembly from the vehicle.

To install:

13. Connect the control cables to the control head.
14. Connect the vacuum hoses to the control head.
15. Connect the electrical wire connectors.
16. Install the control head assembly and secure with the 4 attaching screws.
17. Connect the 4 × 4 transfer switch, if equipped.
18. Attach finish panel to the instrument panel.

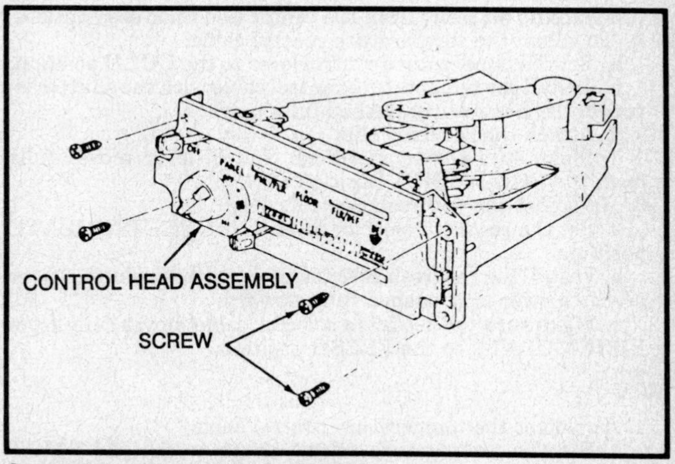
CONTROL HEAD ASSEMBLY
SCREW
Control head removal—Navajo

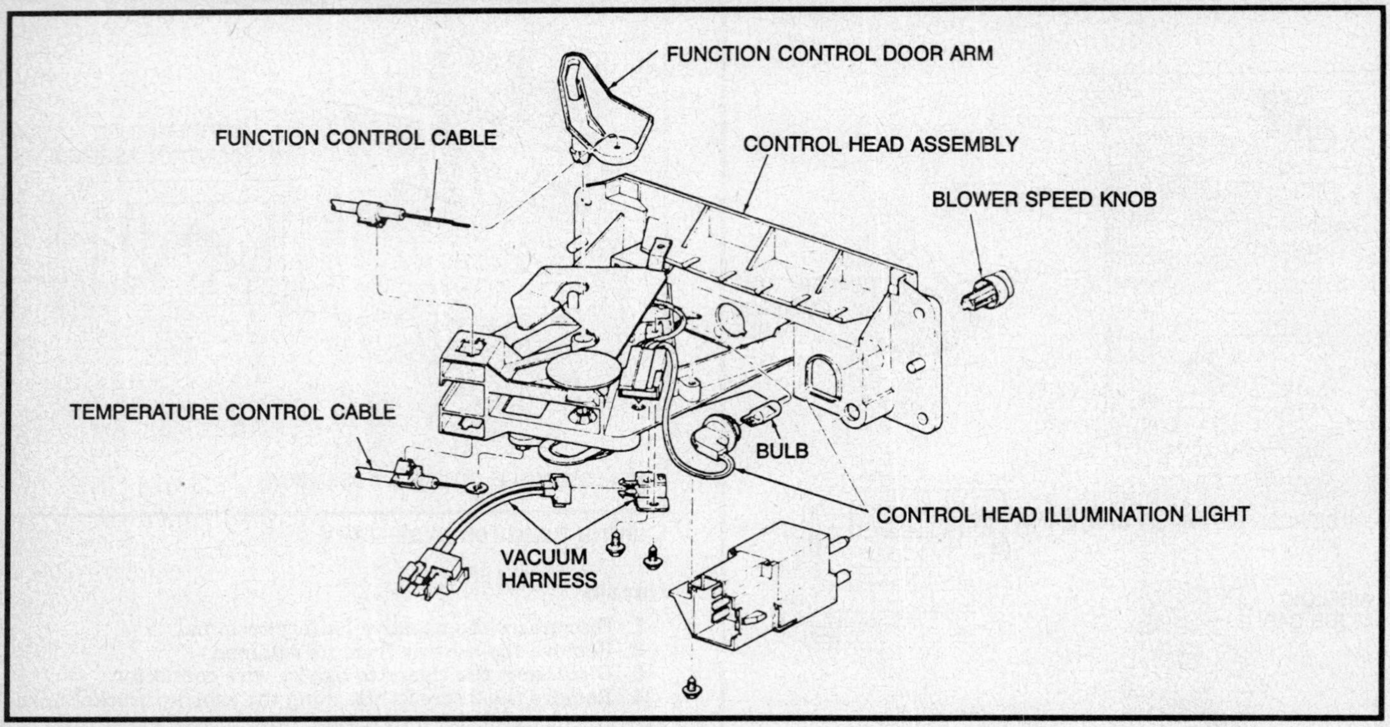
FUNCTION CONTROL DOOR ARM
FUNCTION CONTROL CABLE
CONTROL HEAD ASSEMBLY
BLOWER SPEED KNOB
TEMPERATURE CONTROL CABLE
BULB
CONTROL HEAD ILLUMINATION LIGHT
VACUUM HARNESS

Control head assembly—Navajo

19. Install ashtray, cigarette lighter, wire connector and brackets to the instrument panel.
20. Reconnect the negative battery terminal.

Manual Control Cables

ADJUSTMENT

B2200 and B2600I

1. To adjust airflow mode cable:
   a. Set the airflow mode control lever to the **DEFROST** position.
   b. Install the airflow mode cable with the shutter lever on the heater unit pushed fully downward.
   c. Attach the securing clip.
   d. Turn the blower switch to position **4** and make sure there are no air leaks from the center and floor area outlets.
2. To adjust the temperature control cable:
   a. Set the temperature control lever to the **COLD** position.
   b. Install the temperature control cable with the shutter lever on the heater unit pushed fully upward.
   c. Attach the securing clip.
   d. Make sure the temperature control lever moves fully from the COLD to HOT position.
3. To adjust the rec/fresh control cable:
   a. Set the rec/fresh selector lever to the **RECIRCULATE** position.
   b. Install the rec/fresh selector cable with the shutter lever on the blower unit pushed fully upward.
   c. Make sure the rec/fresh selector cable moves fully from RECIRCULATE to the FRESH position.

MPV

1. To adjust the temperature control cable:
   a. Set the temperature control lever to the **MAX-HOT** position.

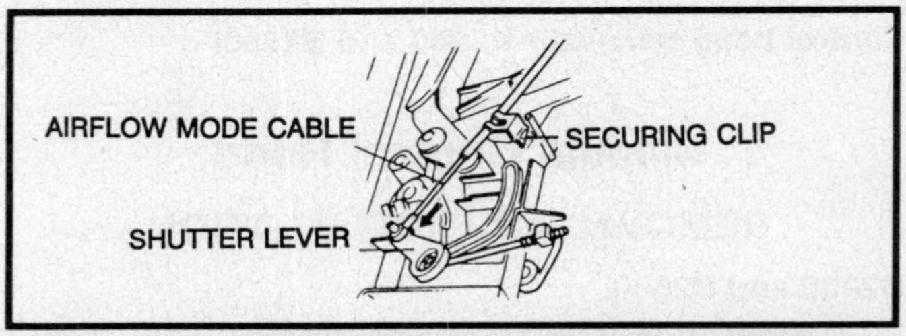
AIRFLOW MODE CABLE
SECURING CLIP
SHUTTER LEVER

Airflow mode cable adjustment—B2200 and B2600I

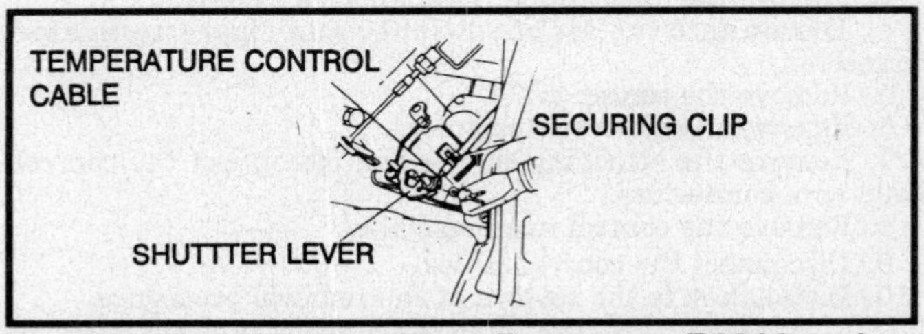
TEMPERATURE CONTROL CABLE
SECURING CLIP
SHUTTTER LEVER

Temperature control cable adjustment—B2200 and B2600I

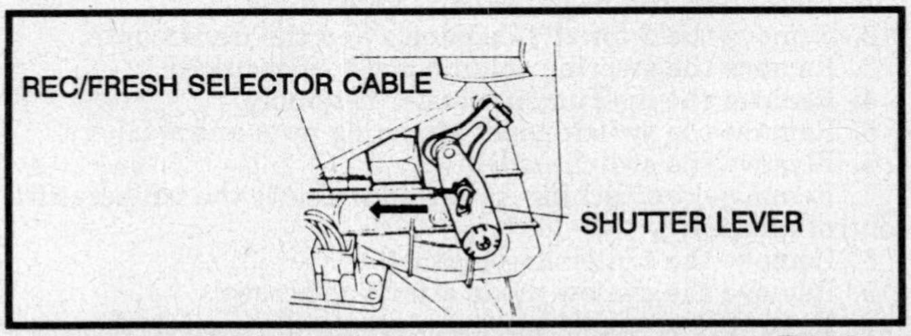
REC/FRESH SELECTOR CABLE
SHUTTER LEVER

Recirculate/Fresh selector cable adjustment—B2200 and B2600I

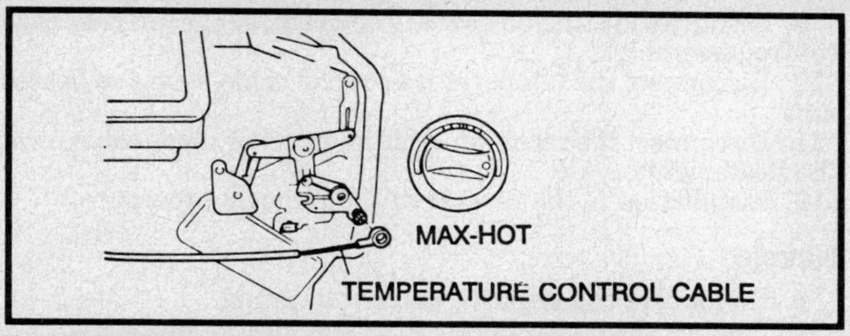
MAX-HOT
TEMPERATURE CONTROL CABLE

Temperature control cable adjustment—MPV

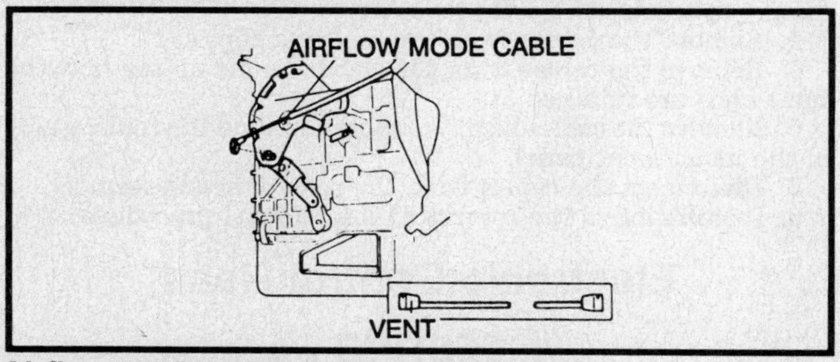
AIRFLOW MODE CABLE
VENT

Airflow mode cable adjustment—MPV

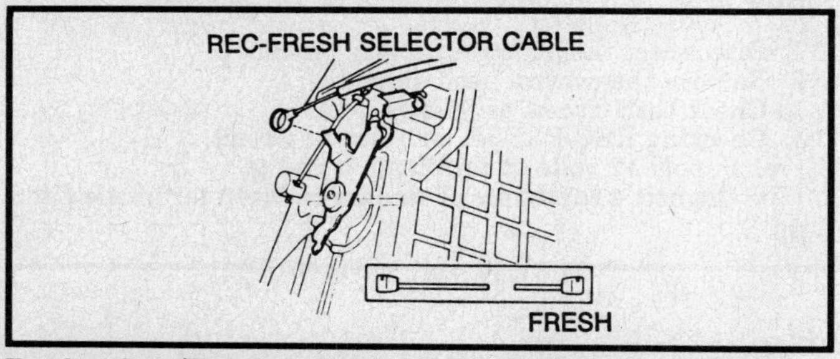
REC-FRESH SELECTOR CABLE
FRESH

Recirculate/Fresh selector cable adjustment—MPV

b. Install the cable and attach the clip with the heater unit shutter lever all the way to the right.

c. Make sure the temperature control lever moves easily from the HOT to COLD position.

2. To adjust airflow mode cable:

a. Set the airflow mode control lever to the **DEFROST** position.

b. Install the cable and attach the clip with the heater unit shutter lever at its closest point.

c. Make sure the temperature control lever moves easily from the DEFROST to the VENT position.

3. To adjust the rec/fresh control cable:

a. Set the rec/fresh selector lever to the **RECIRCULATE** position.

b. Install the cable and attach the clip with the blower unit shutter lever at its closest point.

c. Make sure the temperature control lever moves easily from the RECIRCULATE to the FRESH position.

Navajo

1. Disengage and allow the glove compartment door to hang free by squeezing the sides together.

2. Remove the cable from the securing clip and leave cable attached to the door cams.

3. To adjust the temperature control cables:

a. Set the temperature lever to the **COOL** position and hold.

b. Push gently on the black temperature cable until you feel resistance and the blend door seat.

c. Reattach the cable to the clip.

d. Make sure the temperature control lever moves easily from the **COOL** to the **WARM** position.

4. To adjust the function control cable:

a. Set the function selector lever to the **DEFROST** position and hold.

b. Pull the white function selector cable until there is resistance and the defrost door seats.

c. Reattach the cable to the clip.

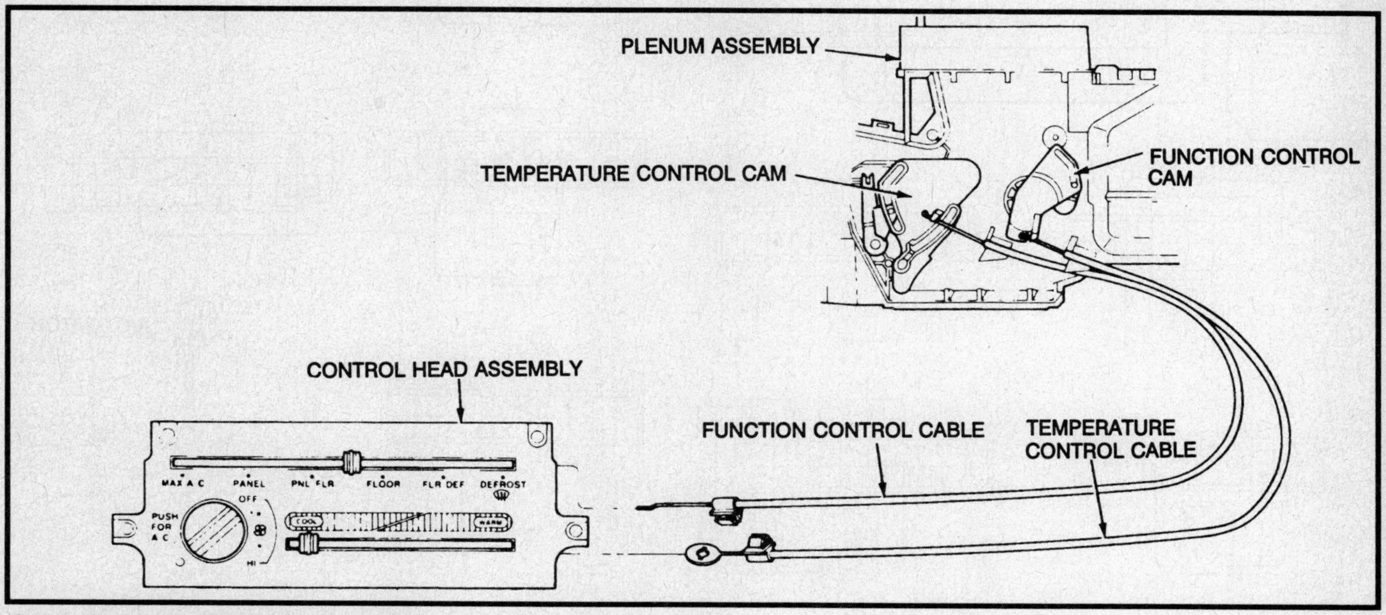
PLENUM ASSEMBLY
TEMPERATURE CONTROL CAM
FUNCTION CONTROL CAM
CONTROL HEAD ASSEMBLY
FUNCTION CONTROL CABLE
TEMPERATURE CONTROL CABLE
MAX A C
PANEL
PNL FLR
FLOOR
FLR DEF
DEFROST
OFF
PUSH FOR A C
COOL
WARM
HI

Control cable adjustment—Navajo

d. Make sure the temperature control lever moves easily from the **DEFROST** to the **PANEL** or **MAX A/C** position.

5. Turn the ignition and blower switch **ON** and actuate the levers, checking that the temperature and function selectors are adjusted properly.

REMOVAL AND INSTALLATION

B2200 and B2600I

1. Disconnect the negative battery terminal.
2. Remove the instrument panel meter hood.
3. Remove the attaching screws, knobs and nuts.
4. Disconnect the air conditioner and cigarette lighter connector.
5. Remove the center panel.
6. Remove the glove compartment.
7. Remove the attaching screws and disconnect the control head wire connectors.
8. Remove the control head assembly.
9. Disconnect the control cables at the control head and the heater unit.
10. Installation is the reverse of the removal procedure.

MPV

1. Disconnect the negative battery terminal.
2. Remove the 2 lower side panels and the undercover.
3. Remove the steering column cover, if required.
4. Remove the instrument cluster assembly.
5. Remove the switch panel attaching nuts.
6. Remove the switch panel.
7. Remove the attaching screws and remove the temperature control assembly.
8. Remove the center lower panel.
9. Remove the attaching screws and remove the airflow mode control assembly.
10. Disconnect the temperature control cable from the heater unit.
11. Disconnect the rec-fresh cable and airflow mode cable from the heater unit.
12. Installation is the reverse of the removal procedure.

Navajo

1. Disconnect the negative battery terminal.
2. Remove the control head from the instrument panel.
3. Disengage and allow the glove compartment door to hang free by squeezing the sides together.
4. Remove the cables from the securing clips.
5. Remove the cables from the control cams noting how the cable ends are retained.
6. Remove the cables from the cable clips and the routing aids in the instrument panel.
7. Disconnect the cables from the control head assembly.
8. Installation is the reverse of the removal procedure.

Electronic Control Head

TESTING

MPV

1. Disconnect the negative battery terminal.
2. Remove the control head assembly.
3. Check each circuit as follows.
4. Checking REC-FRESH air selector circuit:
   a. Supply 12 volts to terminals **h** and **g**.
   b. Connect a resistance of 1k ohm between terminals **f** and **q**.

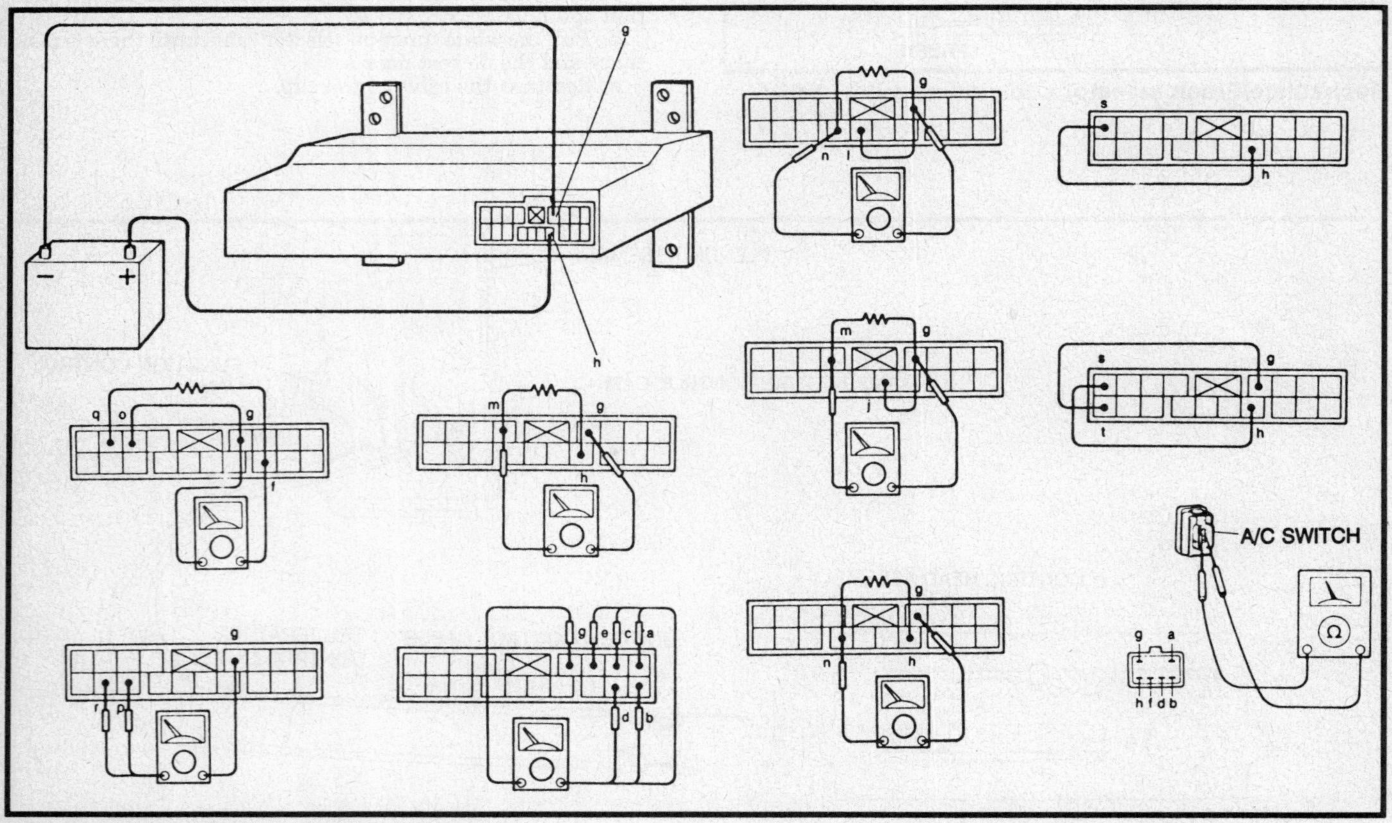
A/C SWITCH

Electronic control head testing—Navajo

c. Ground terminal **o**, then measure the voltage between terminals **g** and **f**.

d. There should be approximately 12 volts at terminals **g** and **f**.

e. If not as specified, replace the electronic control head assembly.

f. Remove the 12 volt supply at terminals **g** and **h**.

g. With the recirculate switch pushed **ON**, there should be continuity between terminals **r** and **g**.

h. With the fresh switch pushed **ON**, there should be continuity between terminals **p** and **g**.

i. If not as specified replace the electronic control head assembly.

5. Checking airflow selector circuit:

a. Supply 12 volts to terminals **h** and **g**.

b. Connect a resistance of 1k ohm between terminals **n** and **g**.

c. Connect a jumper wire between terminals **l** and **g**.

d. There should be approximately 12 volts at terminals **n** and **g**.

e. If not as specified, replace the electronic control head assembly.

f. Connect a resistance of 1k ohm between terminals **m** and **g**.

g. Connect a jumper wire between terminals **j** and **g**.

h. There should be approximately 12 volts at terminals **m** and **g**.

i. If not as specified, replace the electronic control head assembly.

j. Connect a resistance of 1k ohm between terminals **h** and **n**.

k. There should be approximately 12 volts at terminals **n** and **g**.

l. If not as specified, replace the electronic control head assembly.

m. Connect a resistance of 1k ohm between terminals **h** and **m**.

n. There should be approximately 12 volts at terminals **m** and **g**.

o. If not as specified, replace the electronic control head assembly.

p. Remove the 12 volt supply at terminals **g** and **h**.

q. With the vent switch pushed **ON**, there should be continuity between terminals **b** and **g**.

r. With the bi-level switch pushed **ON**, there should be continuity between terminals **a** and **g**.

s. With the heat switch pushed **ON**, there should be continuity between terminals **d** and **g**.

t. With the heat/defrost switch pushed **ON**, there should be continuity between terminals **c** and **g**.

u. With the defrost switch pushed **ON**, there should be continuity between terminals **e** and **g**.

6. Checking indicator lights:

a. Supply 12 volts to terminals **h** and **g**.

b. Check for illumination of the indicator light as each switch is pushed.

c. If any light fails to illuminate, replace the control assembly.

d. Connect a jumper wire between terminals **h** and **s** and verify that the indicator lights dim.

e. If not as specified, replace the control assembly.

AIRFLOW MODE CONTROL ASSEMBLY

Electronic control head removal – Navajo

7. Checking illumination lights:

a. Supply 12 volts to terminals **h** and **g**.

b. Connect a jumper wire between terminals **h** and **s**.

c. Connect a jumper wire between terminals **g** and **t**.

d. Check for illumination of the light, if there is no illumination replace the bulb.

8. Checking the air conditioning switch:

a. With the switch **OFF**, check for continuity between the following terminals.

b. There should be continuity between terminals **b** and **d**.

c. There should be continuity between terminals **f** and **h**.

d. With the switch **ON**, check for continuity between the following terminals.

e. There should be continuity between terminals **d** and **f**.

f. There should be continuity between terminals **c** and **h**.

g. There should be continuity between terminals **c** and **j**.

h. There should be continuity between terminals **h** and **j**.

i. There should be continuity between terminals **h** and **i** in only one direction.

j. If not as specified, replace the switch.

REMOVAL AND INSTALLATION

MPV

1. Disconnect the negative battery terminal.
2. Remove the 2 lower side panels and the undercover.
3. Remove the steering column cover, if required.
4. Remove the instrument cluster assembly.
5. Remove the switch panel attaching nuts and washers.
6. Remove the switch panel.
7. Remove the attaching screws and remove the temperature control assembly.
8. Remove the center lower panel.
9. Remove the airflow mode control assembly attaching screws.
10. Remove the control assembly and disconnect the wire connectors.
11. Installation is the reverse of the removal procedure.

SENSORS AND SWITCHES

Pressure Switches

OPERATION

There are 2 styles of pressure switches being used, the first pressure switch, which switches the magnetic clutch ON or OFF as a result of irregularly high or low pressures of the refrigerant. The second is a pressure switch used on vehicles with automatic transmission to cycle ON and OFF the condenser fan according to system pressure. The pressure switches are located on the high side except the Navajo which has the switch located on the accumulator.

TESTING

Except Navajo

1. Disconnect the pressure switch wire connector from the receiver/drier or from the high pressure line.
2. Start the vehicle and turn the air conditioner **ON**.
3. Hook up the air conditioner gauges or charging station.
4. Check for 12 volts at the pressure switch wire connector.
5. If there is no voltage at either terminal of the wire connector, check the air conditioner relay.
6. Connect a jumper wire between the 2 terminals.
7. Check to see if compressor clutch engages or if condenser fan operates, if equipped.
8. If condenser fan and or compressor magnetic clutch fail to operate, check the unit and the wiring to the unit.
9. Check for continuity through the switch using an ohmmeter.
10. At system normal operating pressures, there should be continuity between the switch wire connector terminals.

Navajo

1. Connect an approved air conditioning charging station.
2. Start the engine and move the function selector lever to the **MAX-A/C**.
3. Set the blower speed switch to **MAX** and the temperature control lever to the extreme **COOL** position.
4. Observe that the compressor magnetic clutch disengages when system operating pressures drops to an approximate 24.5 psi.
5. Observe that the compressor magnetic clutch engages when system operating pressures reach approximately 43.5 psi or above.

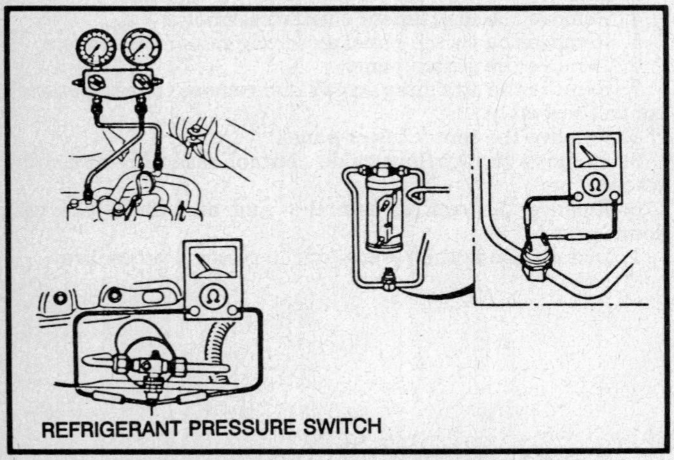
REFRIGERANT PRESSURE SWITCH

Pressure switch testing—B2200, B2600i and MPV

6. If not as specified, replace the pressure switch.

REMOVAL AND INSTALLATION

1. Disconnect the negative battery cable.
2. Properly discharge the air conditioning system, not required on Navajo.
3. Remove radiator grille, if required.
4. Disconnect the pressure switch wire connector.
5. Using a wrench, remove the pressure switch.
6. Installation is the reverse of removal procedure.
7. If the air conditioning system pressure switch has a plastic base, hand tighten only.

Thermo Switch

OPERATION

The thermo switch is mounted at the evaporator core outlet and senses the temperature of the cool air coming through the evaporator via capillary tube. Temperature signals are then input to the thermo switch. The thermo switch then opens or closes the circuit allowing 12 volt to flow to the pressure switch thus turning the magnetic clutch ON and OFF.

TESTING

Except Navajo

1. Disconnect negative battery terminal.
2. Remove the thermo switch.
3. Place thermo switch in ice water.

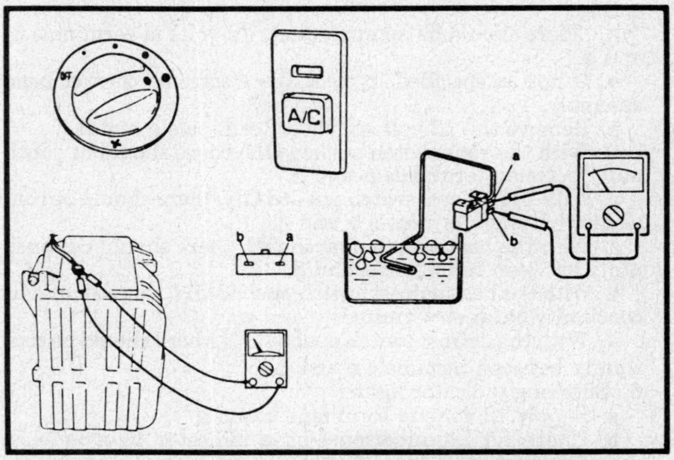
A/C
b
a
a
b

Thermo switch testing—B2200, B2600i and MPV

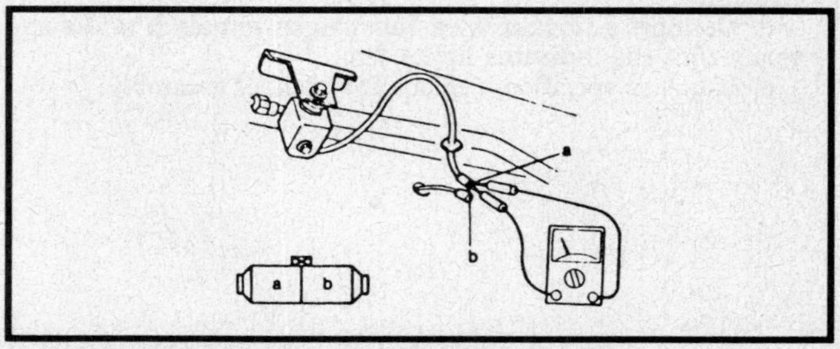
a
b
a
b

Magnetic solenoid valve testing—MPV

4. Check continuity through the switch.
5. There should be no continuity through the switch when it reaches below 32°F (0°C).
6. Replace the thermo switch, if not as specified.

Magnetic Solenoid Valve

OPERATION

The magnetic solenoid valve is mounted on the driver's side undercarriage, the solenoid is routed in the high pressure line. The solenoid is energized only when the rear main air conditioner switch is in the **ON** position, thus allowing the refrigerant to flow to the rear cooling system.

TESTING

MPV

1. Disconnect the negative battery terminal.
2. Remove the grommet and disconnect the magnetic solenoid valve wire connector.
3. Measure the resistance between the wire connector terminals.
4. There should be approximately 20 ohms, if not as specified replace the solenoid valve.

REMOVAL AND INSTALLATION

MPV

1. Disconnect the negative battery terminal.
2. Properly discharge the air conditioning system.
3. Remove the grommet and disconnect the magnetic solenoid valve wire connector.
4. Disconnect the refrigerant lines
5. Remove the attaching nut and remove the magnetic solenoid valve.
6. Installation is the reverse of the removal procedure.

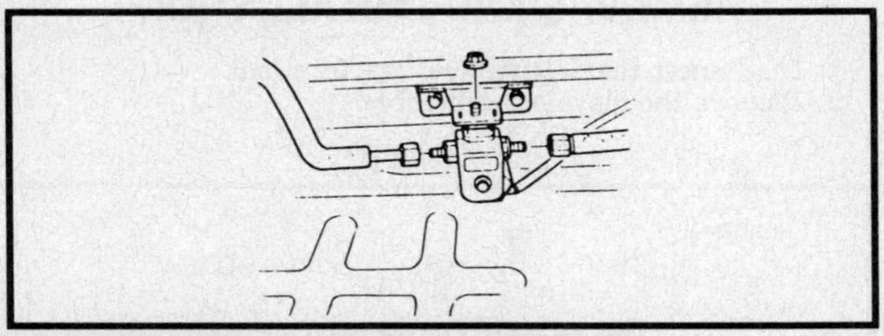

Magnetic solenoid valve removal—MPV

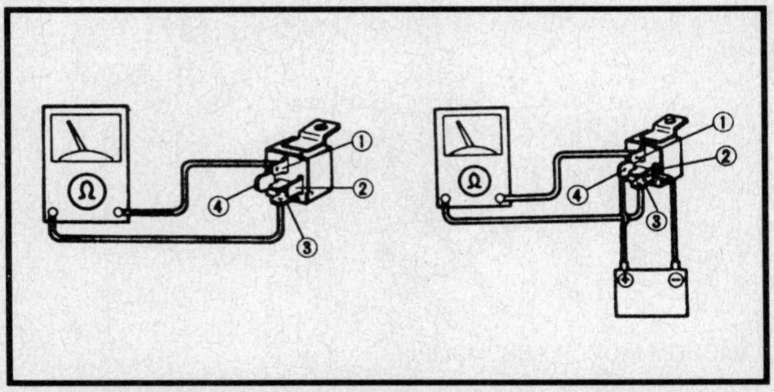
1
2
3
4
1
2
3
4

Air conditioning relay testing—B2200 and B2600i

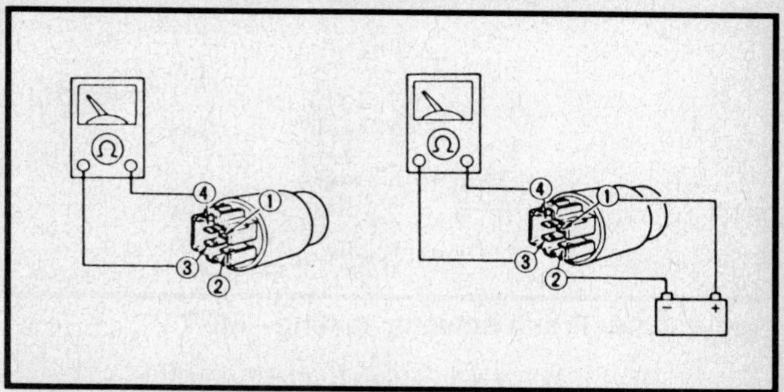
4
1
3
2
4
1
3
2

Air conditioning relay testing—MPV

Relays

OPERATION

Battery and load location may require that a switch be placed some distance from either component. This means a longer wire and a higher voltage drop. The installation of a relay between the battery and the load reduces the voltage drop. Because the switch controls the relay, this means amperage through the switch can be reduced.

TESTING

B2200 and B2600I

1. Disconnect the negative battery terminal.
2. Disconnect the relay wire connector.
3. Check that there is no continuity between terminals **1** and **3** of the relay.
4. If there is continuity, replace the relay.
5. Next apply 12 volts to terminal **4** and ground terminal **2**.
6. Check for continuity between terminals **1** and **3**.
7. If there is no continuity, replace the relay.

MPV

1. Disconnect the negative battery terminal.
2. Disconnect the relay wire connector.
3. Check that there is no continuity between terminals **3** and **4** of the relay.
4. If there is continuity, replace the relay.
5. Next apply 12 volts to terminal **1** and ground terminal **2**.
6. Check for continuity between terminals **3** and **4**.
7. If there is no continuity, replace the relay.

REMOVAL AND INSTALLATION

B2200, B2600I and MPV

1. Disconnect negative battery terminal.
2. Locate relay and disconnect wire connector.
3. If required, remove attaching bolt and remove relay.
4. Installation is the reverse of the removal procedure.

Actuators

When the mode switch on the control head panel is depressed, an output signal corresponding to the depressed switch is issued to the mode actuator. The mode actuator, which then shifts to the selected position, performs opening and closing of the mode door and stops in the specified position.

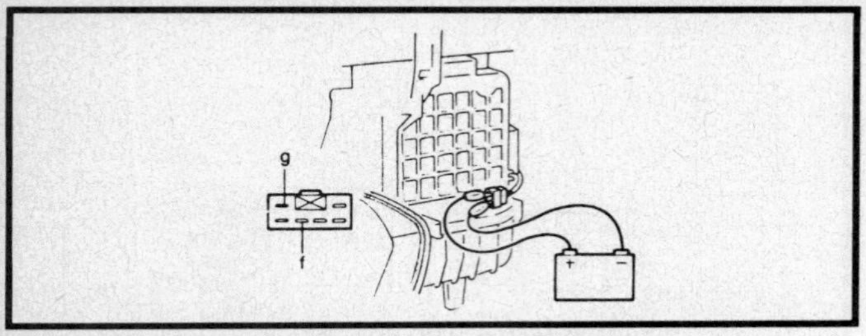
g
f

Recirculate/ Fresh actuator testing – MPV

TESTING

MPV

REC-FRESH SELECTOR DOOR

1. Disconnect the negative battery terminal.
2. Remove the glove box and the undercover.
3. Disconnect the REC-FRESH selector door actuator wire connector.
4. Apply 12 volts, the positive lead to terminal **g** and ground terminal **f** and the actuator motor should operate.
5. If not as specified, replace the actuator.

AIRFLOW MODE ACTUATOR

1. Disconnect the negative battery terminal.
2. Remove the driver's side lower panel.
3. Disconnect the airflow mode actuator wire connector.
4. Apply 12 volts, the positive lead to terminal **k** and ground terminal **i** and the motor should rotate to the **DEF** position.
5. Apply 12 volts, the positive lead to terminal **j** and ground terminal **k** and the motor should rotate to the **VENT** position.
6. If not as specified, replace the actuator.

REMOVAL AND INSTALLATION

1. Disconnect negative battery terminal.
2. Locate the actuator.
3. Remove the passenger or drivers side panel, if required.
4. Disconnect the actuator wire connector.
5. Remove actuator attaching screws.
6. Remove the actuator.
7. Installation is the reverse of the removal procedure.

Outside/Recirculating Air Door Vacuum Motor

OPERATION

On the Navajo the vacuum motor controls the recirculating/

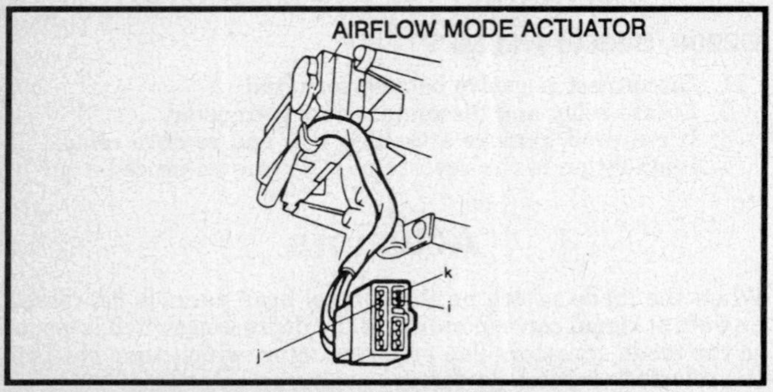
AIRFLOW MODE ACTUATOR
k
i
j

Airflow mode actuator testing – MPV

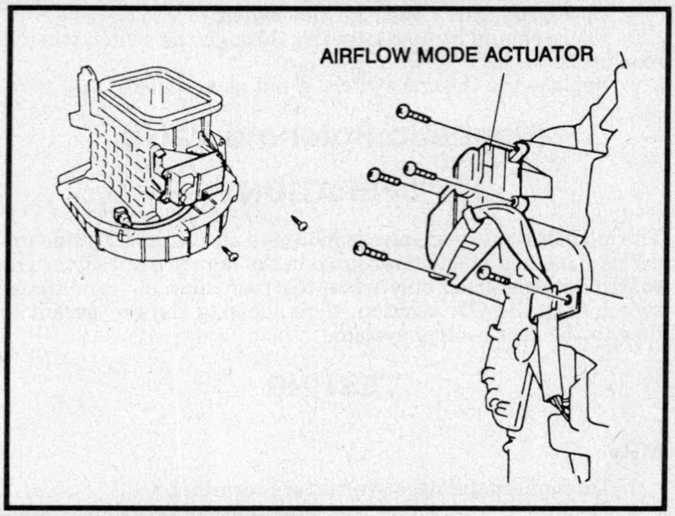
AIRFLOW MODE ACTUATOR

Actuator removal – MPV

fresh air door movement by means of vacuum switch located on the control head. The vacuum motor is located on the right side heater plenum.

TESTING

1. Disconnect the negative battery terminal.
2. Remove the glove box assembly.
3. Disconnect the vacuum connection at the vacuum motor.
4. Using a suitable vacuum pump, apply approximately 12 in. Hg of vacuum to the vacuum motor.
5. The vacuum pump should draw the recirculate/fresh door in and maintain the vacuum reading.
6. If as specified, check for vacuum with control head lever in recirculate or fresh position at vacuum motor.
7. If not as specified, replace the vacuum motor.

REMOVAL AND INSTALLATION

1. Disconnect the negative battery terminal.
2. Remove the glove box assembly.

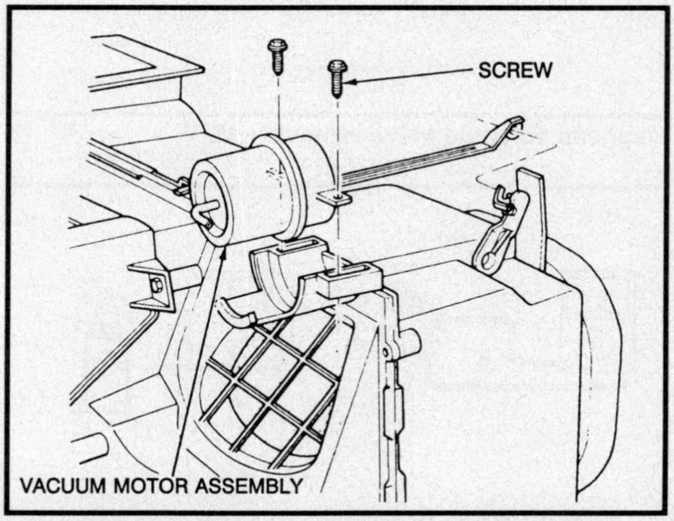
SCREW
VACUUM MOTOR ASSEMBLY

Outside/Recirculate air door vacuum motor – Navajo

3. Disconnect the vacuum connection.
4. Remove the 2 screws attaching the vacuum motor to the plenum.
5. Remove the vacuum motor assembly.
6. Installation is the reverse of the removal procedure.

REAR AUXILIARY SYSTEM

Evaporator

REMOVAL AND INSTALLATION

MPV

1. Disconnect the negative battery terminal.
2. Properly discharge the air conditioning system.
3. Remove the left rear side trim.
4. Disconnect the high and low pressure refrigerant lines.
5. Disconnect the rear cooling unit wire connectors.
6. Remove the rear cooling unit attaching nuts and bolts.
7. Remove the rear cooling unit case.
8. Disassemble the cooling unit.
9. Remove the evaporator core and the expansion valve as a unit.

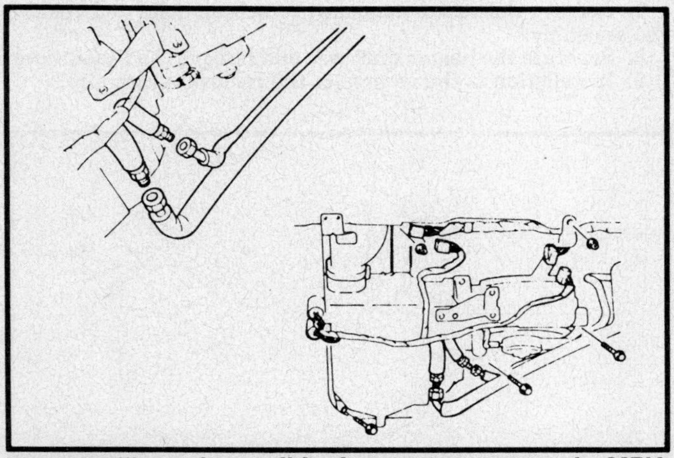

Rear auxiliary air conditioning system removal—MPV

10. Disconnect the inlet and outlet pipes.
11. Remove the capillary tube from the outlet pipe.
12. Remove the expansion valve.

To install:

13. Attach the expansion valve to the evaporator core.
14. Attach the capillary tube from the outlet pipe.
15. Reconnect the inlet and outlet pipes.
16. Install the evaporator core and the expansion valve in the cooler unit.
17. Reassemble the cooling unit.
18. Install the rear cooling unit using the attaching nuts and bolts.
19. Reconnect the rear cooling unit wire connectors.
20. Install the left rear side trim.
21. Reconnect the negative battery terminal.
22. Evacuate, recharge and leak test the rear cooling unit.

Expansion Valve

REMOVAL AND INSTALLATION

MPV

1. Disconnect the negative battery terminal.
2. Properly discharge the air conditioning system.
3. Remove the left rear side trim.
4. Disconnect the high and low pressure refrigerant lines.
5. Disconnect the rear cooling unit wire connectors.
6. Remove the rear cooling unit attaching nuts and bolts.
7. Remove the rear cooling unit case.
8. Disassemble the cooling unit.
9. Remove the evaporator core and the expansion valve as a unit.
10. Disconnect the inlet and outlet pipes.
11. Remove the capillary tube from the outlet pipe.
12. Remove the expansion valve.

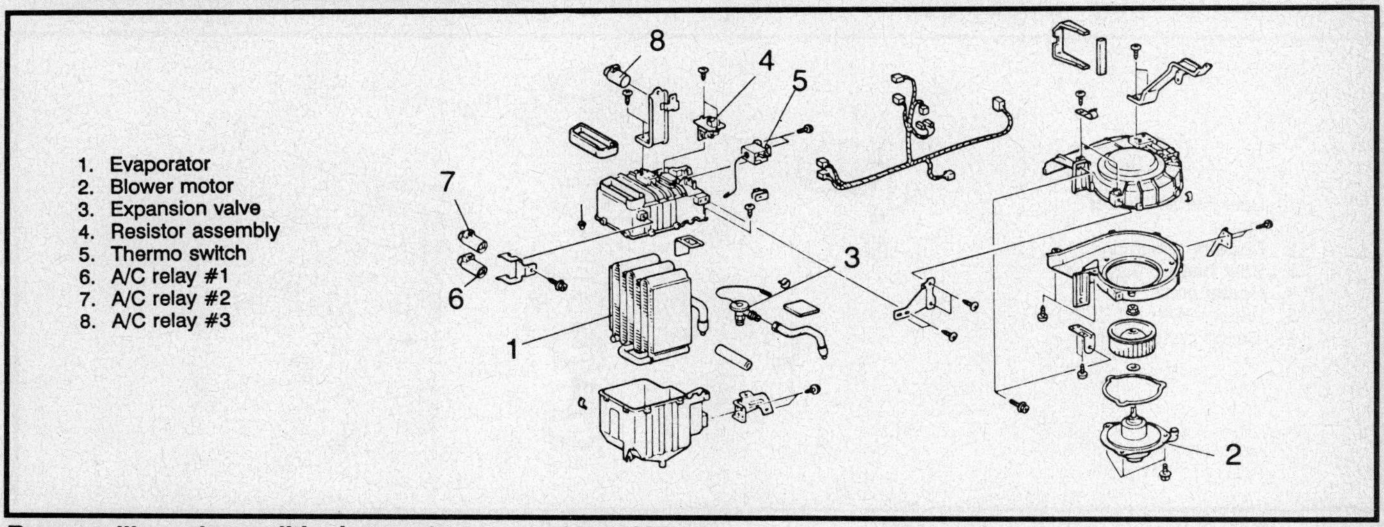
1. Evaporator
2. Blower motor
3. Expansion valve
4. Resistor assembly
5. Thermo switch
6. A/C relay #1
7. A/C relay #2
8. A/C relay #3
8
4
5
7
3
6
1
2

Rear auxiliary air conditioning system assembly— MPV

To install:

13. Attach the expansion valve to the evaporator core.
14. Attach the capillary tube from the outlet pipe.
15. Reconnect the inlet and outlet pipes.
16. Install the evaporator core and the expansion valve in the cooler unit.
17. Reassemble the cooling unit.
18. Install the rear cooling unit using the attaching nuts and bolts.
19. Reconnect the rear cooling unit wire connectors.
20. Install the left rear side trim.
21. Reconnect the negative battery terminal.
22. Evacuate, recharge and leak test the rear cooling unit.

Rear Cooling Unit Blower Motor

REMOVAL AND INSTALLATION

MPV

1. Disconnect the negative battery terminal.
2. Remove the left rear side trim.
3. Disconnect the blower unit wire connector.
4. Remove the blower unit attaching screws.
5. Remove the blower unit.
6. Installation is the reverse of the removal procedure.

Rear Cooling Unit Blower Motor Resistor

REMOVAL AND INSTALLATION

MPV

1. Disconnect the negative battery terminal.
2. Remove the left rear side trim.
3. Disconnect the blower motor resistor wire connector.
4. Remove the resistor attaching screw.
5. Remove the blower motor resistor.
6. Installation is the reverse of the removal procedure.

Refrigerant Lines

REMOVAL AND INSTALLATION

MPV

1. Disconnect the battery negative terminal.
2. Properly discharge the air conditioning system.
3. Remove chassis, engine or body parts, if required.
4. Using a backup wrench loosen, disconnect and immediately plug the refrigerant line.
5. Disconnect wire connectors, if required.
6. Remove all attaching brackets and bolts.
7. Remove the refrigerant lines.

To install:

8. Apply a light coat of refrigerant oil to new O-rings.
9. Route refrigerant lines in original locations.
10. Use original securing brackets and bolts.
11. Evacuate, charge and check the air conditioing system for leaks.

Rear Heater Core

REMOVAL AND INSTALLATION

MPV

1. Disconnect the negative battery terminal.
2. Set the rear heater control knob to the warm position to open the water valve.
3. Drain the cooling system.
4. Remove the driver's seat.
5. Disconnect the heater hoses.
6. Disconnect the rear heater unit wire connector.
7. Remove the rear heater unit attaching bolts and remove the assembly.
8. Separate the heater unit case and remove the heater core.
9. Installation is the reverse of the removal procedure.

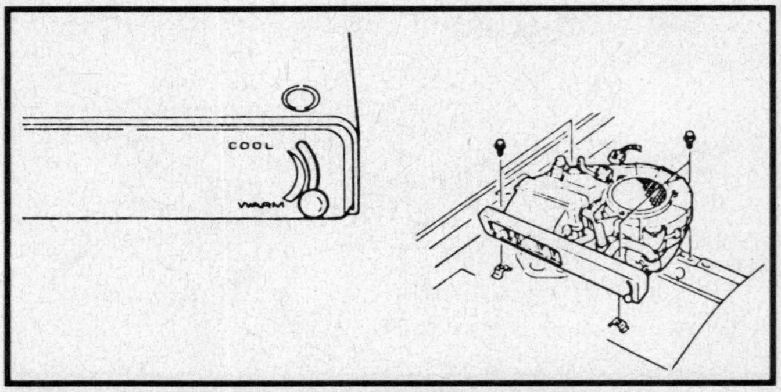
COOL
WARM

Rear auxiliary heater unit removal—MPV

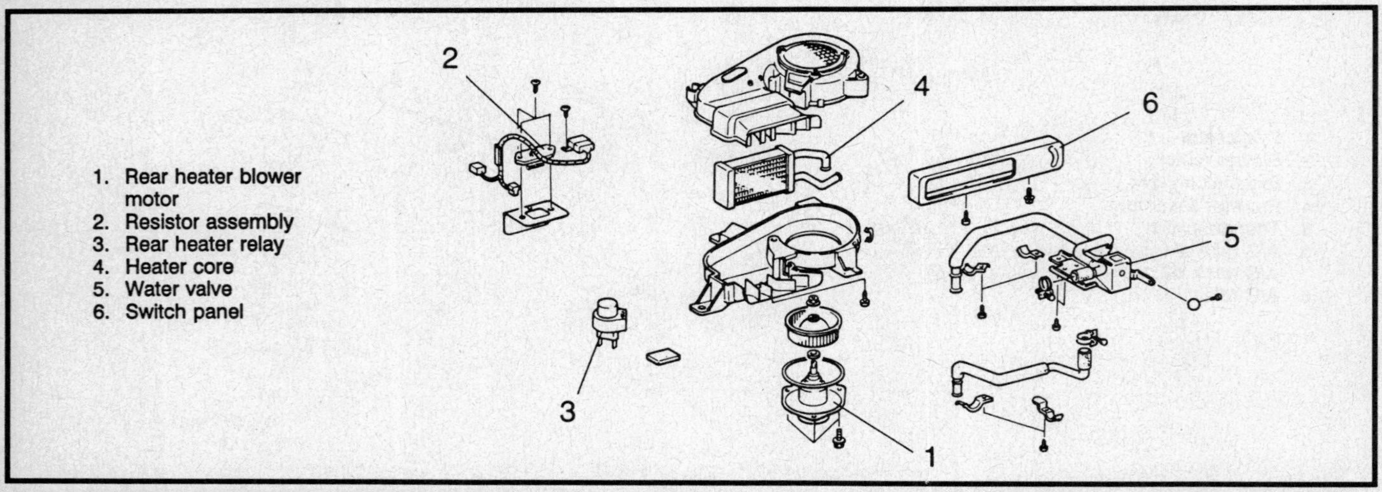
1. Rear heater blower motor
2. Resistor assembly
3. Rear heater relay
4. Heater core
5. Water valve
6. Switch panel
2
4
6
5
3
1

Rear auxiliary heater unit assembly—MPV

Rear Heater Blower Motor

REMOVAL AND INSTALLATION

MPV

1. Disconnect the negative battery terminal.
2. Set the rear heater control knob to the warm position to open the water valve.
3. Drain the cooling system.
4. Remove the drivers seat.
5. Disconnect the heater hoses.
6. Disconnect the rear heater unit wire connector.
7. Remove the rear heater unit attaching bolts and remove the assembly.
8. Remove the blower motor attaching screws and remove the assembly.
9. Installation is the reverse of the removal procedure.

Rear Heater Unit Blower Motor Resistor

REMOVAL AND INSTALLATION

MPV

1. Disconnect the negative battery terminal.
2. Remove the drivers seat.
3. Disconnect the resistor wire connector.
4. Remove the attaching screw and remove the resistor.
5. Installation is the reverse of the removal procedure.

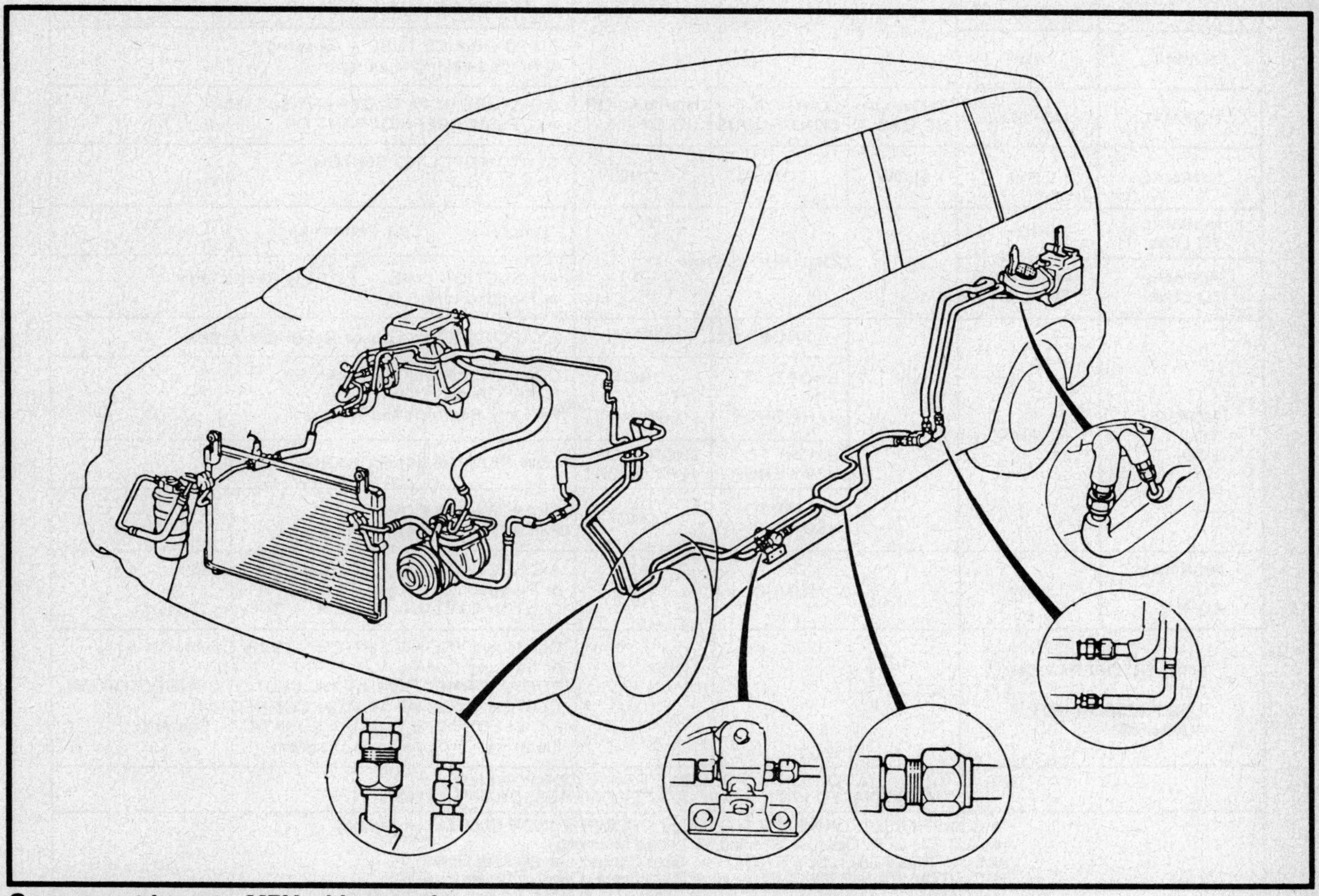

Component layout—MPV with rear air

SYSTEM DIAGNOSIS

AIR CONDITIONING DIAGNOSTIC CHART—NAVAJO

NOTE: System test requirements must be met to obtain accurate test readings for evaluation. Refer to the normal refrigerant system pressure/temperature and the normal clutch cycle rate and times charts.

HIGH (DISCHARGE) PRESSURE	LOW (SUCTION) PRESSURE	CLUTCH CYCLE TIME			COMPONENT — CAUSES
		RATE	ON	OFF	
HIGH	HIGH				CONDENSER — Inadequate Airflow
HIGH	NORMAL TO HIGH				ENGINE OVERHEATING
NORMAL TO HIGH	NORMAL	CONTINUOUS RUN			REFRIGERANT OVERCHARGE (a) AIR IN REFRIGERANT HUMIDITY OR AMBIENT TEMP. VERY HIGH (b)
NORMAL	HIGH				FIXED ORIFICE TUBE — Missing O-Rings Leaking/Missing
NORMAL	NORMAL	SLOW OR NO CYCLE	LONG OR CONTINUOUS	NORMAL OR NO CYCLE	MOISTURE IN REFRIGERANT SYSTEM EXCESSIVE REFRIGERANT OIL
NORMAL	LOW	SLOW	LONG	LONG	CLUTCH CYCLING SWITCH — Low Cut-Out
NORMAL TO LOW	HIGH	CONTINUOUS RUN			Compressor — Low Performance
NORMAL TO LOW	NORMAL TO HIGH				A/C SUCTION LINE — Partially Restricted or Plugged (c)
NORMAL TO LOW	NORMAL	FAST	SHORT	NORMAL	EVAPORATOR - Low or Restricted Airflow
			SHORT TO VERY SHORT	NORMAL TO LONG	CONDENSER, FIXED ORIFICE TUBE, OR A/C LIQUID LINE — Partially Restricted or Plugged
			SHORT TO VERY SHORT	SHORT TO VERY SHORT	LOW REFRIGERANT CHARGE
			SHORT TO VERY SHORT	LONG	EVAPORATOR CORE — Partially Restricted or Plugged
NORMAL TO LOW	LOW	CONTINUOUS RUN			A/C SUCTION LINE — Partially Restricted or Plugged (d) CLUTCH CYCLING SWITCH — Sticking Closed
ERRATIC OPERATION OR COMPRESSOR NOT RUNNING		—	—	—	CLUTCH CYCLING SWITCH — Dirty Contacts or Sticking Open POOR CONNECTION AT A/C CLUTCH CONNECTOR OR CLUTCH CYCLING SWITCH CONNECTOR A/C ELECTRICAL CIRCUIT ERRATIC — See A/C Electrical Circuit Wiring Diagram

ADDITIONAL POSSIBLE CAUSE COMPONENTS ASSOCIATED WITH INADEQUATE COMPRESSOR OPERATION

- COMPRESSOR DRIVE BELT — Loose • COMPRESSOR CLUTCH — Slipping
- CLUTCH COIL Open — Shorted, or Loose Mounting
- CONTROL ASSEMBLY SWITCH — Dirty Contacts or Sticking Open
- CLUTCH WIRING CIRCUIT — High Resistance, Open or Blown Fuse
- COMPRESSOR OPERATION INTERRUPTED BY ENGINE COMPUTER

ADDITIONAL POSSIBLE CAUSE COMPONENTS ASSOCIATED WITH A DAMAGED COMPRESSOR

- CLUTCH CYCLING SWITCH - Sticking Closed or Compressor Clutch Seized
- SUCTION ACCUMULATOR DRIER — Refrigerant Oil Bleed Hole Plugged
- REFRIGERANT LEAKS

(a) Compressor may make noise on initial run. This is slugging condition caused by excessive liquid refrigerant.
(b) Compressor clutch may not cycle in ambient temperatures above 80°F depending on humidity conditions.
(c) Low pressure reading will be normal to high if pressure is taken at accumulator and if restriction is downstream of service access valve.
(d) Low pressure reading will be low if pressure is taken near the compressor and restriction is upstream of service access valve.

AIR CONDITIONING DIAGNOSTIC CHART—NAVAJO, CONT.

INSUFFICIENT A/C COOLING

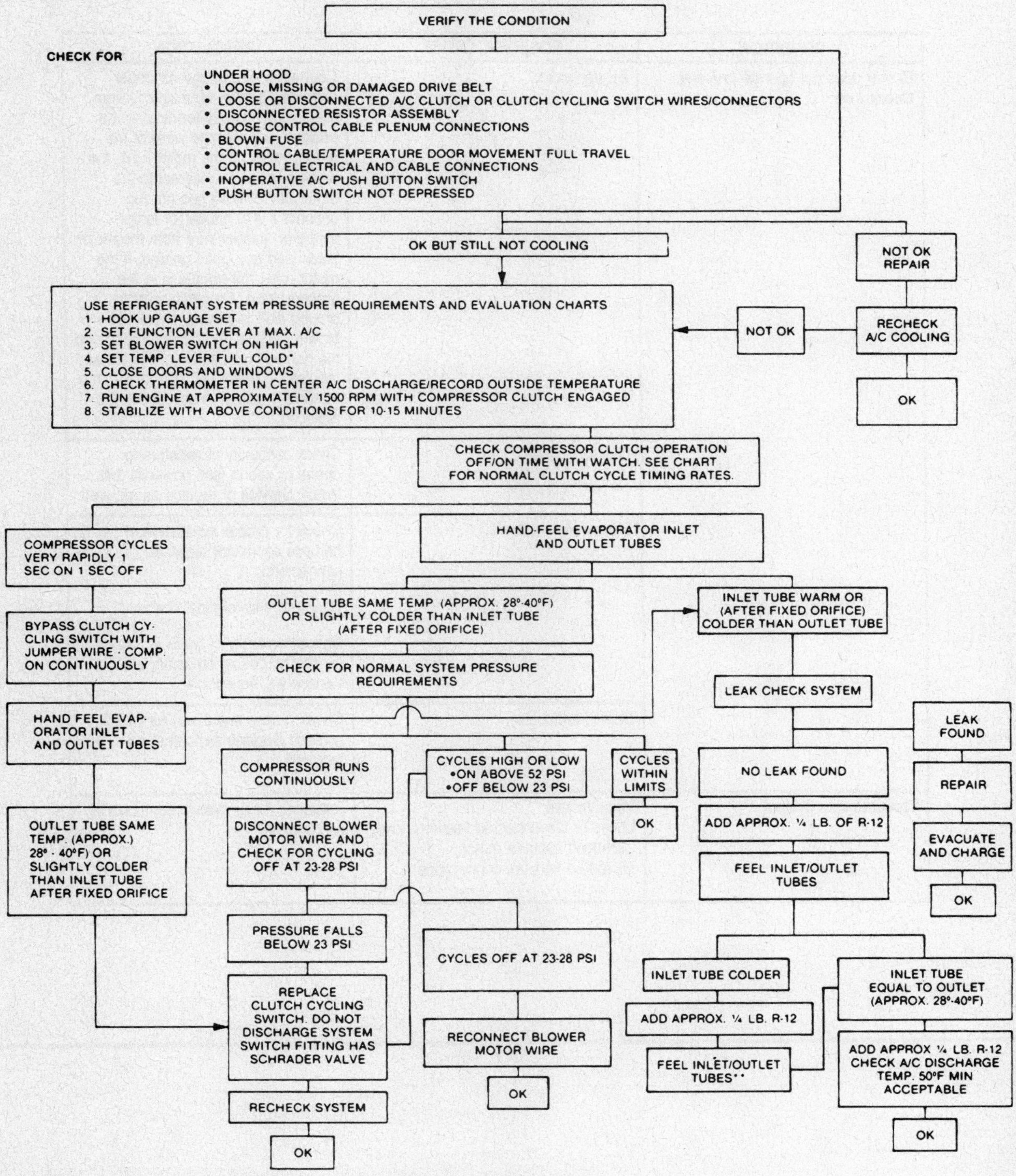
VERIFY THE CONDITION
CHECK FOR
UNDER HOOD
• LOOSE, MISSING OR DAMAGED DRIVE BELT
• LOOSE OR DISCONNECTED A/C CLUTCH OR CLUTCH CYCLING SWITCH WIRES/CONNECTORS
• DISCONNECTED RESISTOR ASSEMBLY
• LOOSE CONTROL CABLE PLENUM CONNECTIONS
• BLOWN FUSE
• CONTROL CABLE/TEMPERATURE DOOR MOVEMENT FULL TRAVEL
• CONTROL ELECTRICAL AND CABLE CONNECTIONS
• INOPERATIVE A/C PUSH BUTTON SWITCH
• PUSH BUTTON SWITCH NOT DEPRESSED
OK BUT STILL NOT COOLING
NOT OK REPAIR
USE REFRIGERANT SYSTEM PRESSURE REQUIREMENTS AND EVALUATION CHARTS
1. HOOK UP GAUGE SET
2. SET FUNCTION LEVER AT MAX. A/C
3. SET BLOWER SWITCH ON HIGH
4. SET TEMP. LEVER FULL COLD*
5. CLOSE DOORS AND WINDOWS
6. CHECK THERMOMETER IN CENTER A/C DISCHARGE/RECORD OUTSIDE TEMPERATURE
7. RUN ENGINE AT APPROXIMATELY 1500 RPM WITH COMPRESSOR CLUTCH ENGAGED
8. STABILIZE WITH ABOVE CONDITIONS FOR 10-15 MINUTES
NOT OK
RECHECK A/C COOLING
OK
CHECK COMPRESSOR CLUTCH OPERATION OFF/ON TIME WITH WATCH. SEE CHART FOR NORMAL CLUTCH CYCLE TIMING RATES.
COMPRESSOR CYCLES VERY RAPIDLY 1 SEC ON 1 SEC OFF
HAND-FEEL EVAPORATOR INLET AND OUTLET TUBES
OUTLET TUBE SAME TEMP. (APPROX. 28°-40°F) OR SLIGHTLY COLDER THAN INLET TUBE (AFTER FIXED ORIFICE)
INLET TUBE WARM OR (AFTER FIXED ORIFICE) COLDER THAN OUTLET TUBE
BYPASS CLUTCH CYCLING SWITCH WITH JUMPER WIRE - COMP. ON CONTINUOUSLY
CHECK FOR NORMAL SYSTEM PRESSURE REQUIREMENTS
LEAK CHECK SYSTEM
HAND FEEL EVAPORATOR INLET AND OUTLET TUBES
LEAK FOUND
COMPRESSOR RUNS CONTINUOUSLY
CYCLES HIGH OR LOW •ON ABOVE 52 PSI •OFF BELOW 23 PSI
CYCLES WITHIN LIMITS
NO LEAK FOUND
REPAIR
OK
ADD APPROX. ¼ LB. OF R-12
OUTLET TUBE SAME TEMP. (APPROX.) 28°-40°F) OR SLIGHTLY COLDER THAN INLET TUBE AFTER FIXED ORIFICE
DISCONNECT BLOWER MOTOR WIRE AND CHECK FOR CYCLING OFF AT 23-28 PSI
EVACUATE AND CHARGE
FEEL INLET/OUTLET TUBES
OK
PRESSURE FALLS BELOW 23 PSI
CYCLES OFF AT 23-28 PSI
INLET TUBE COLDER
INLET TUBE EQUAL TO OUTLET (APPROX. 28°-40°F)
REPLACE CLUTCH CYCLING SWITCH. DO NOT DISCHARGE SYSTEM SWITCH FITTING HAS SCHRADER VALVE
ADD APPROX. ¼ LB. R-12
RECONNECT BLOWER MOTOR WIRE
FEEL INLET/OUTLET TUBES**
ADD APPROX ¼ LB. R-12 CHECK A/C DISCHARGE TEMP. 50°F MIN ACCEPTABLE
OK
RECHECK SYSTEM
OK
OK

*ON ATC SYSTEMS APPLY 15 INCHES VACUUM DIRECTLY TO SERVO VACUUM MOTOR

**CONTINUE TO ADD R-12 IN APPROX. ¼ LB. INCREMENTS UNTIL TUBES FEEL EQUAL IN TEMPERATURE AND APPROX. 28°-40°F

AIR CONDITIONING DIAGNOSTIC CHART—NAVAJO, CONT.

CONDITION	POSSIBLE CAUSE	RESOLUTION
Blower does not operate properly. Check fuse.	Blower motor.	Connect a #10 gauge (or larger diameter) jumper wire directly from the positive battery terminal to the positive lead (orange wire) of the blower motor. If the motor runs, the problem must be external to the motor. If the motor will not run, connect a #10 gauge (or larger diameter) jumper wire from the motor black lead to a good ground. If the motor runs, the trouble is in the ground circuit. On vehicles with ground side switching, check the blower resistor, the blower switch and the harness connections. Service as required. If motor still will not run, the motor is inoperative and should be replaced.
	Blower resistor.	Check continuity of resistors for opens or shorts (self-powered test lamp). Service or replace as required.
	Blower wire harness.	Check for proper installation of harness connector terminal connectors. Check wire-to-terminal continuity. Check continuity of wires in harness for shorts, opens, abrasion, etc. Service as required.
	Blower switch(es).	Check blower switch(es) for proper contact. Replace switch(es) as required.
Vacuum motor system	Vacuum leak. Loose or disconnected vacuum hose. Damaged vacuum motor. Misrouted vacuum connections	Repair or repair system components, as required.

AIR CONDITIONING DIAGNOSTIC CHART—NAVAJO, CONT.

CONDITION	POSSIBLE CAUSE	RESOLUTION
Insufficient, erratic, or no heat or defrost.	Low radiator coolant level due to: Coolant leaks.	Check radiator cap pressure. Replace if below minimum pressure. Fill to specified coolant level. Pressure test for engine cooling system and heater system leaks. Service as required.
	Engine overheating.	Check radiator cap. Replace if below minimum pressure. Remove bugs, leaves, etc. from radiator or condenser fins. Check for: Loose fan belt Sticking thermostat Incorrect ignition timing Water pump impeller damage Restricted cooling system Service as required.
	Loose fan belt.	Replace if cracked or worn and/or adjust belt tension.
	Thermostat.	Check coolant temperature at radiator filler neck. If under 170°F, replace thermostat.
	Plugged or partially plugged heater core.	Clean and backflush engine cooling system and heater core.
	Loose or improperly adjusted control cables.	Adjust to specifications.
	Kinked, clogged, collapsed, soft, swollen, or decomposed engine cooling system or heater system hoses.	Replace damaged hoses and backflush engine cooling system, then heater system, until all particles have been removed.
	Blocked air inlet.	Check cowl air inlet for leaves, foreign material, etc. Remove as required. Check internal blower inlet screen (on vehicles so equipped) for leaves and foreign material.

AIR CONDITIONING DIAGNOSTIC CHART—B2200, B2600i AND MPV

Problem	Possible cause	Remedy
Compressor runs inconsistantly	• Compressor drive belt loose • Clutch face dirty with oil • Excessive gap between the drive plate and pulley	Readjust Clean or replace clutch Readjust gap
Compressor does not run	• Open or loose connection in circuit • Defective A/C relay • Open or short circuit in magnetic clutch • Excessive gap between drive plate and pulley • Defective thermoswitch • Defective refrigerant pressure switch • Defective engine control devices	Repair or reconnect Replace Replace Readjust gap Replace Replace Replace
Insufficient cooling	• Internal malfunction of compressor • Faulty contact of sensing bulb of expansion valve • Faulty insulation of sensing bulb of expansion valve • Expansion valve stuck open • Insufficient refrigerant • Receiver-drier clogged • Expansion valve clogged • Frosted piping • Poor cooling of condenser • Defective condenser fan control circuit • Too much refrigerant • Air in the system	Repair or replace Repair or replace Repair or replace Replace Charge refrigerant Replace Replace Clean or replace Check and clean Refer to above item (Condenser fan does not run) Discharge excess refrigerant Evacuate and charge system

AIR DISTRIBUTION DIAGNOSTIC CHART—B2200, B2600i AND MPV

Problem	Possible cause	Remedy
Insufficient air	• Obstruction in inlet of blower unit • Clogged evaporator • Air leakage	Remove obstruction Clean evaporator Check for leakage at both sides of cooling unit
Outlet air mode cannot be changed	• Mode control wire is loose (wire control) • Open or loose connection (logic control)	Readjust wires Repair or reconnect
Temperature control cannot be done	• Temperature control wire is loose (wire control) • Open or loose connection (logic control) • Trouble in refrigeration system	Readjust wires Repair or reconnect Refer to below items
Blower does not operate	• Open or loose connection in circuit • Main fuse (40 A) is burned out • Defective blower motor relay or IG relay • Defective blower switch in switch panel • Open circuit in blower motor • Open circuit in resistor assembly	Repair or reconnect Check if short circuit is made, then replace fuse Replace Replace Replace Replace

WIRING SCHEMATICS

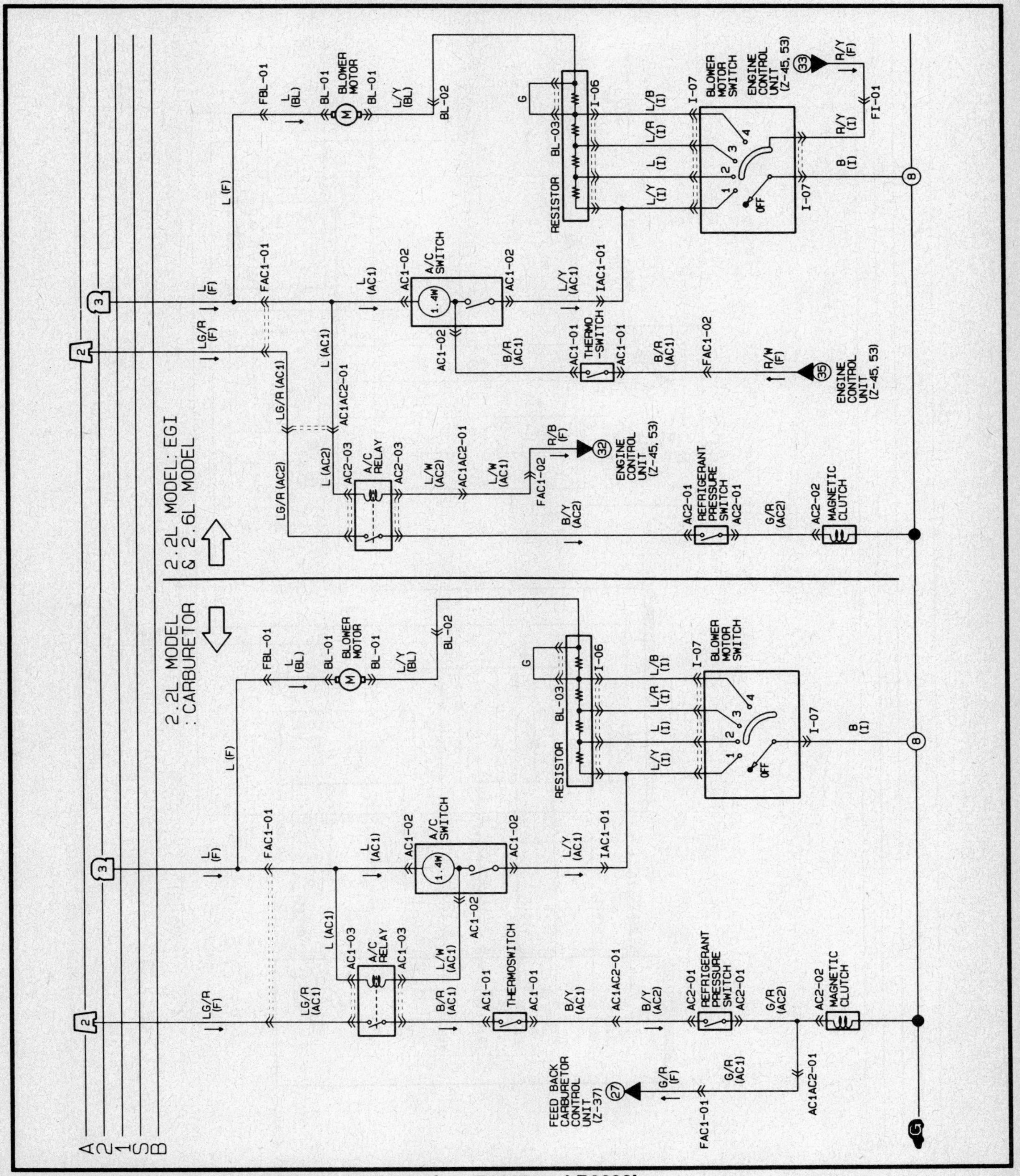
2.2L MODEL: EGI
& 2.6L MODEL
2.2L MODEL
: CARBURETOR
BLOWER MOTOR
RESISTOR
BLOWER MOTOR SWITCH
ENGINE CONTROL UNIT (Z-45, 53)
A/C SWITCH
A/C RELAY
THERMO -SWITCH
THERMOSWITCH
REFRIGERANT PRESSURE SWITCH
MAGNETIC CLUTCH
FEED BACK CARBURETOR CONTROL UNIT (Z-37)
OFF

Heating and air conditioning electrical schematic— B2200 and B2600i

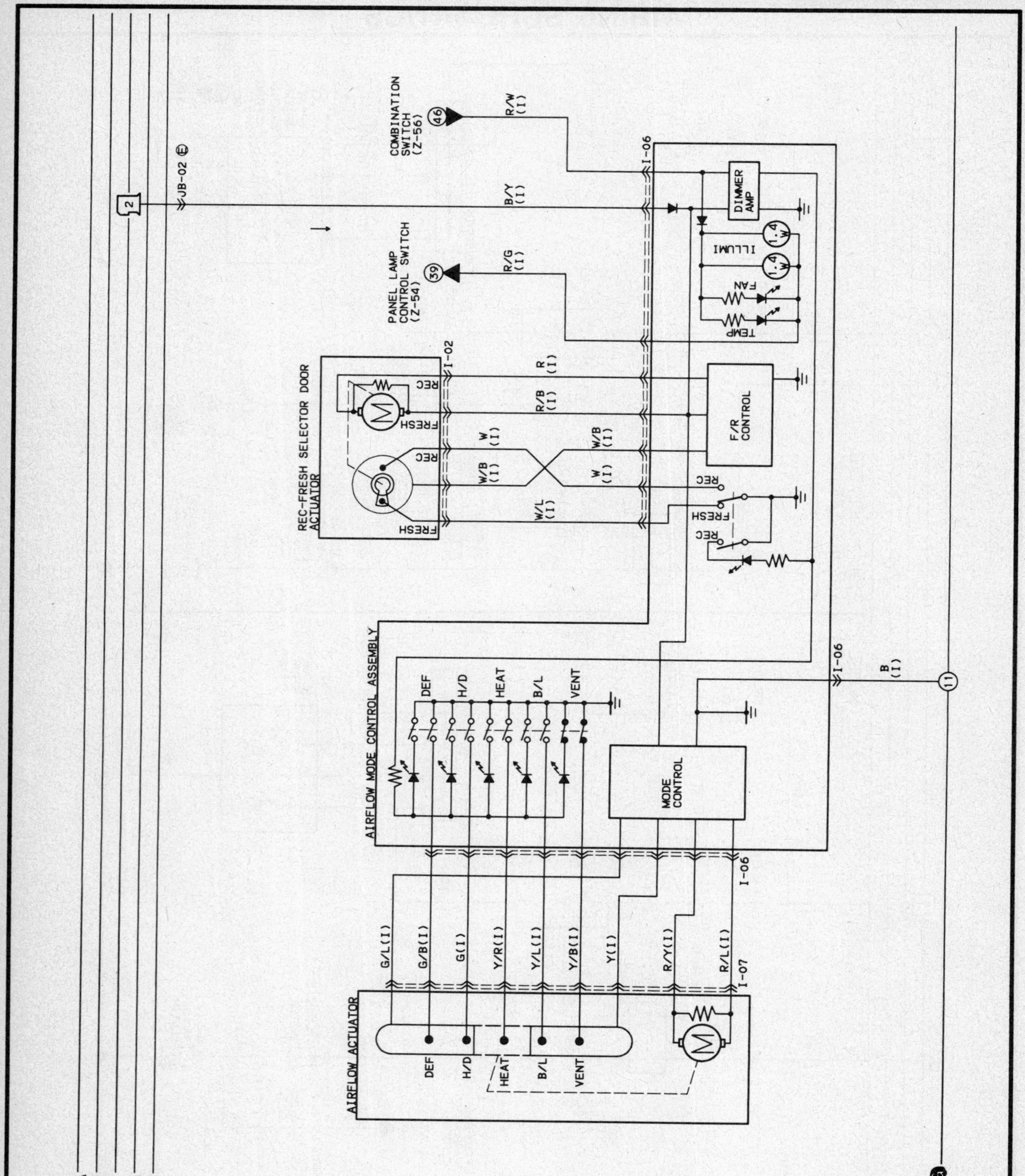
COMBINATION SWITCH (Z-56)
46
R/W (I)
I-06
JB-02
2
B/Y (I)
DIMMER AMP
ILLUMI
1.4 W
1.4 W
FAN
TEMP
PANEL LAMP CONTROL SWITCH (Z-54)
39
R/G (I)
I-02
REC
FRESH
R (I)
R/B (I)
W (I)
W/B (I)
W/L (I)
F/R CONTROL
REC-FRESH SELECTOR DOOR ACTUATOR
AIRFLOW MODE CONTROL ASSEMBLY
DEF
H/D
HEAT
B/L
VENT
MODE CONTROL
B (I)
11
I-07
G/L(I)
G/B(I)
G(I)
Y/R(I)
Y/L(I)
Y/B(I)
Y(I)
R/Y(I)
R/L(I)
AIRFLOW ACTUATOR
A
2
1
S
B
G

Heating and air conditioning electrical schematic with electronic control head—MPV

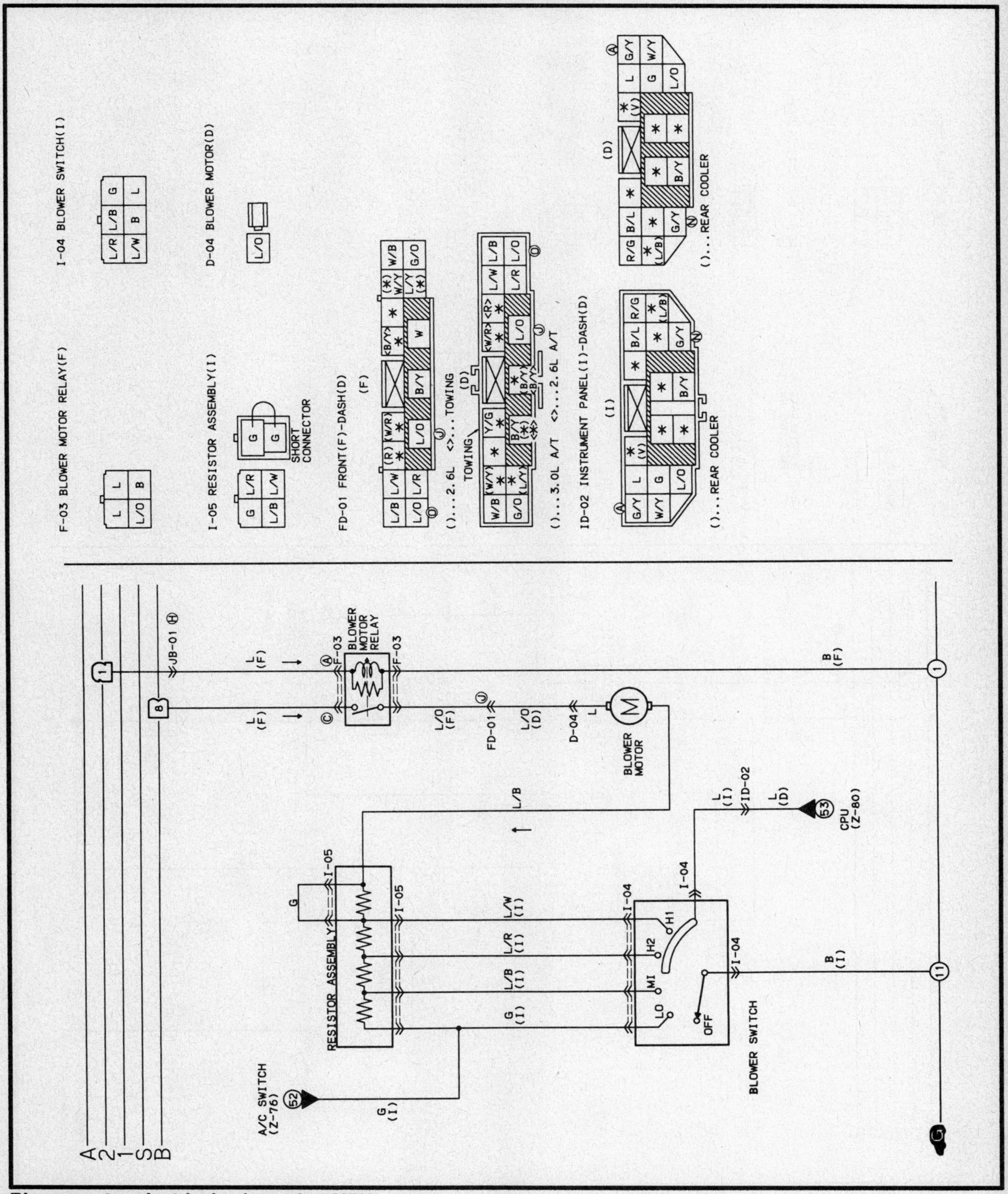
F-03 BLOWER MOTOR RELAY(F)
I-04 BLOWER SWITCH(I)
I-05 RESISTOR ASSEMBLY(I)
SHORT CONNECTOR
D-04 BLOWER MOTOR(D)
FD-01 FRONT(F)-DASH(D)
()...2.6L <>...TOWING
()...3.0L A/T <>...2.6L A/T
ID-02 INSTRUMENT PANEL(I)-DASH(D)
()...REAR COOLER
BLOWER MOTOR RELAY
BLOWER MOTOR
RESISTOR ASSEMBLY
BLOWER SWITCH
A/C SWITCH (Z-76)
CPU (Z-80)
OFF
LO
MI
H2
H1

Blower motor electrical schematic—MPV

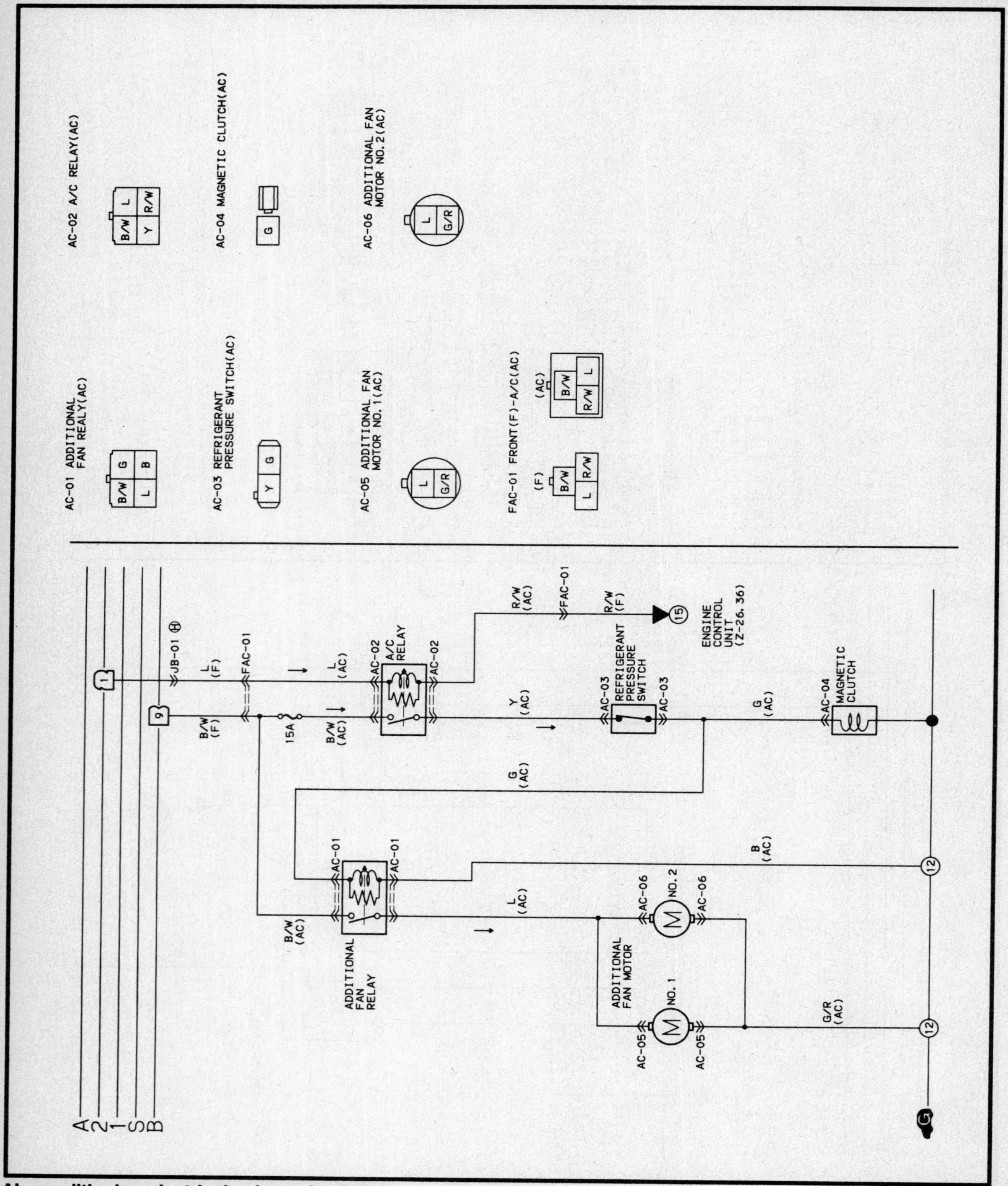
AC-01 ADDITIONAL FAN REALY(AC)
AC-02 A/C RELAY(AC)
AC-03 REFRIGERANT PRESSURE SWITCH(AC)
AC-04 MAGNETIC CLUTCH(AC)
AC-05 ADDITIONAL FAN MOTOR NO.1(AC)
AC-06 ADDITIONAL FAN MOTOR NO.2(AC)
FAC-01 FRONT(F)-A/C(AC)
A/C RELAY
REFRIGERANT PRESSURE SWITCH
ENGINE CONTROL UNIT (Z-26, 36)
MAGNETIC CLUTCH
ADDITIONAL FAN RELAY
ADDITIONAL FAN MOTOR
NO. 1
NO. 2
JB-01
15A

Air conditioning electrical schematic—MPV

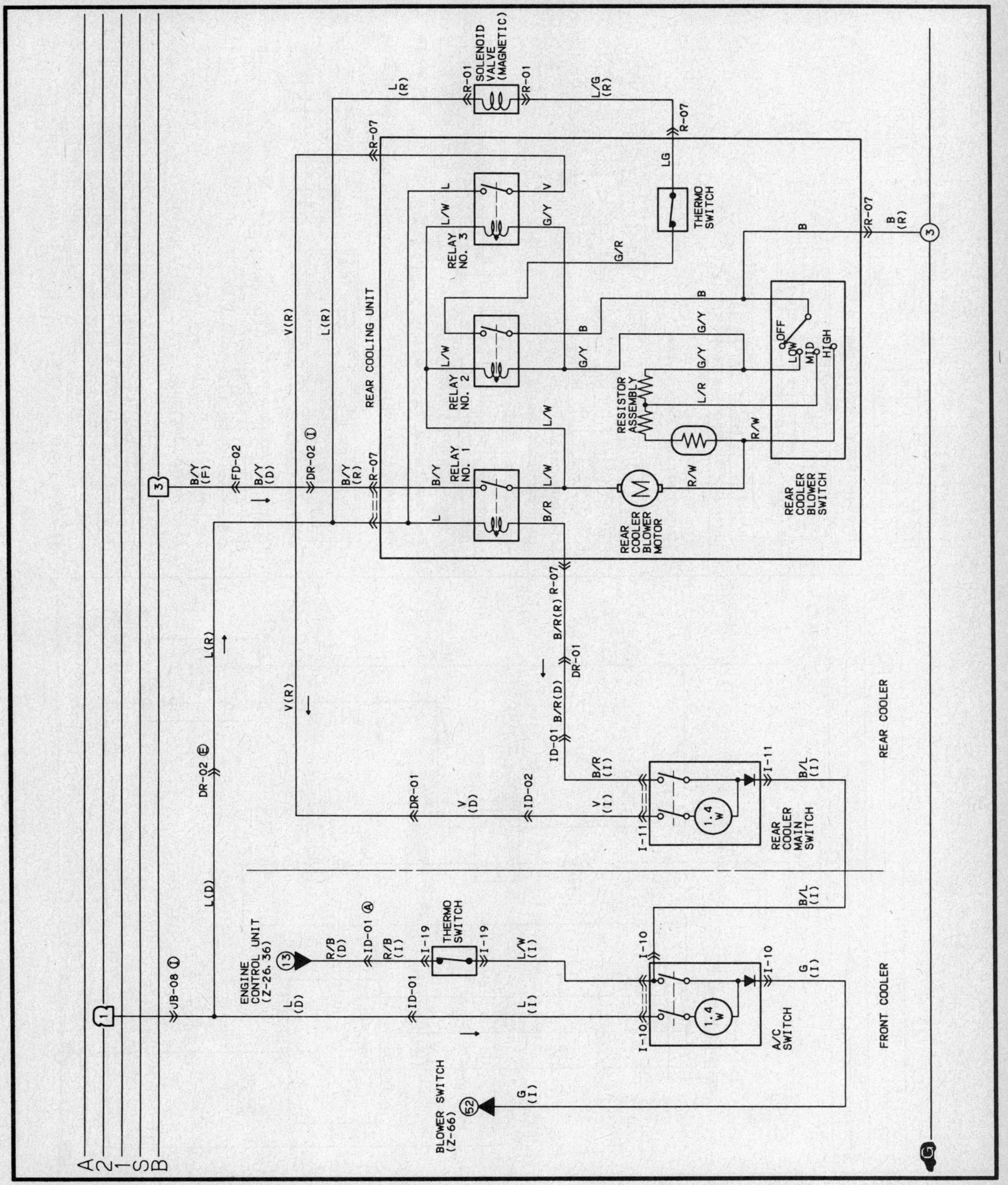
SOLENOID VALVE (MAGNETIC)
RELAY NO. 3
RELAY NO. 2
RELAY NO. 1
THERMO SWITCH
REAR COOLING UNIT
RESISTOR ASSEMBLY
REAR COOLER BLOWER MOTOR
REAR COOLER BLOWER SWITCH
OFF
LOW
MID
HIGH
REAR COOLER MAIN SWITCH
A/C SWITCH
ENGINE CONTROL UNIT (Z-26.36)
BLOWER SWITCH (Z-66)
REAR COOLER
FRONT COOLER

Auxiliary air conditioning electrical schematic—MPV

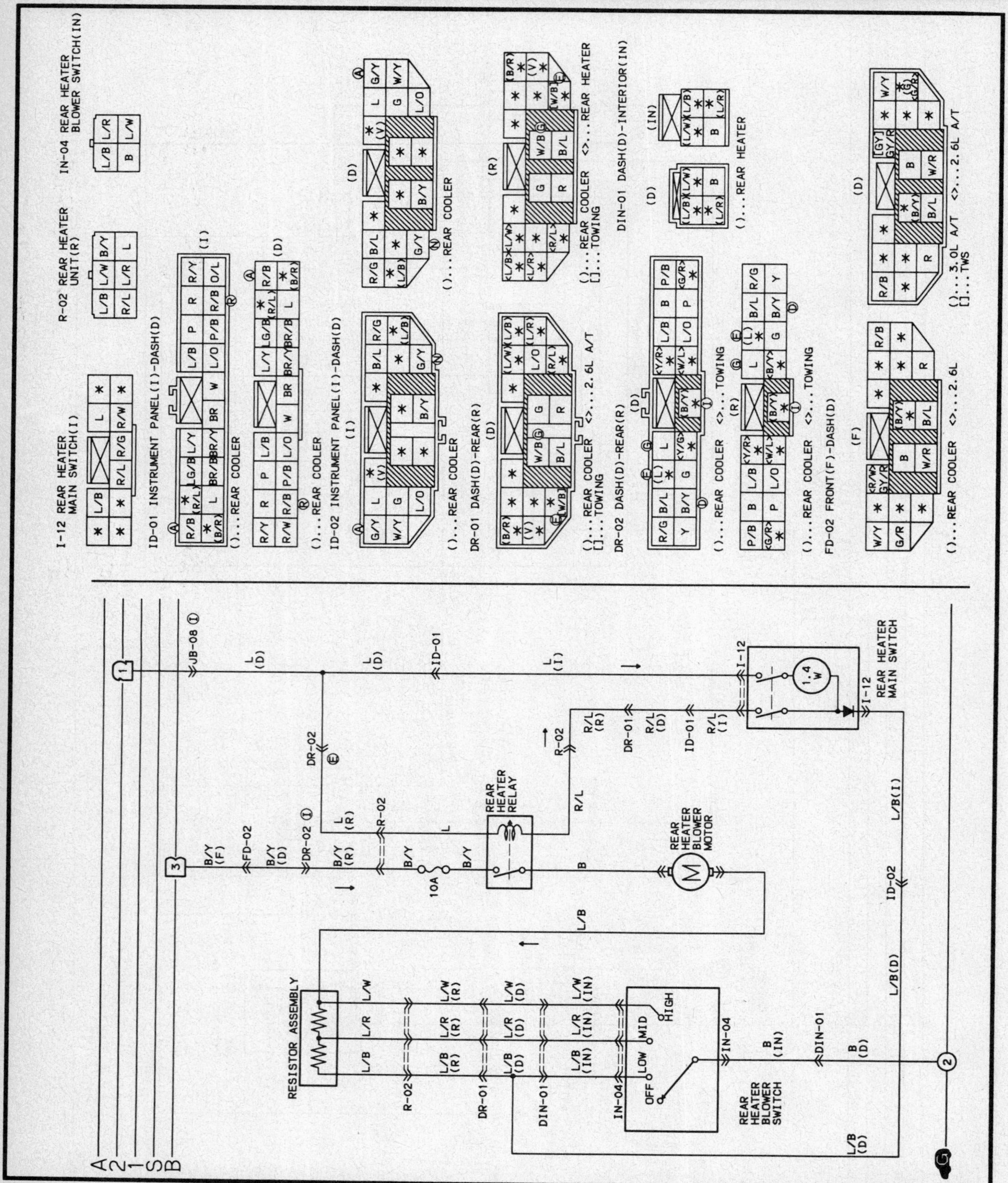
I-12 REAR HEATER MAIN SWITCH(I)
R-02 REAR HEATER UNIT(R)
IN-04 REAR HEATER BLOWER SWITCH(IN)
ID-01 INSTRUMENT PANEL(I)-DASH(D)
ID-02 INSTRUMENT PANEL(I)-DASH(D)
DR-01 DASH(D)-REAR(R)
DR-02 DASH(D)-REAR(R)
DIN-01 DASH(D)-INTERIOR(IN)
FD-02 FRONT(F)-DASH(D)
()...REAR COOLER
()...REAR COOLER <>...2.6L A/T
()...REAR COOLER []...TOWING
()...REAR COOLER <>...TOWING
()...REAR HEATER
()...REAR COOLER <>...REAR HEATER
()...REAR COOLER <>...2.6L
()...3.0L A/T <>...2.6L A/T
[]...TWS
REAR HEATER MAIN SWITCH
REAR HEATER RELAY
REAR HEATER BLOWER MOTOR
RESISTOR ASSEMBLY
REAR HEATER BLOWER SWITCH
10A
OFF
LOW
MID
HIGH

Auxiliary heater unit electrical schematic—MPV

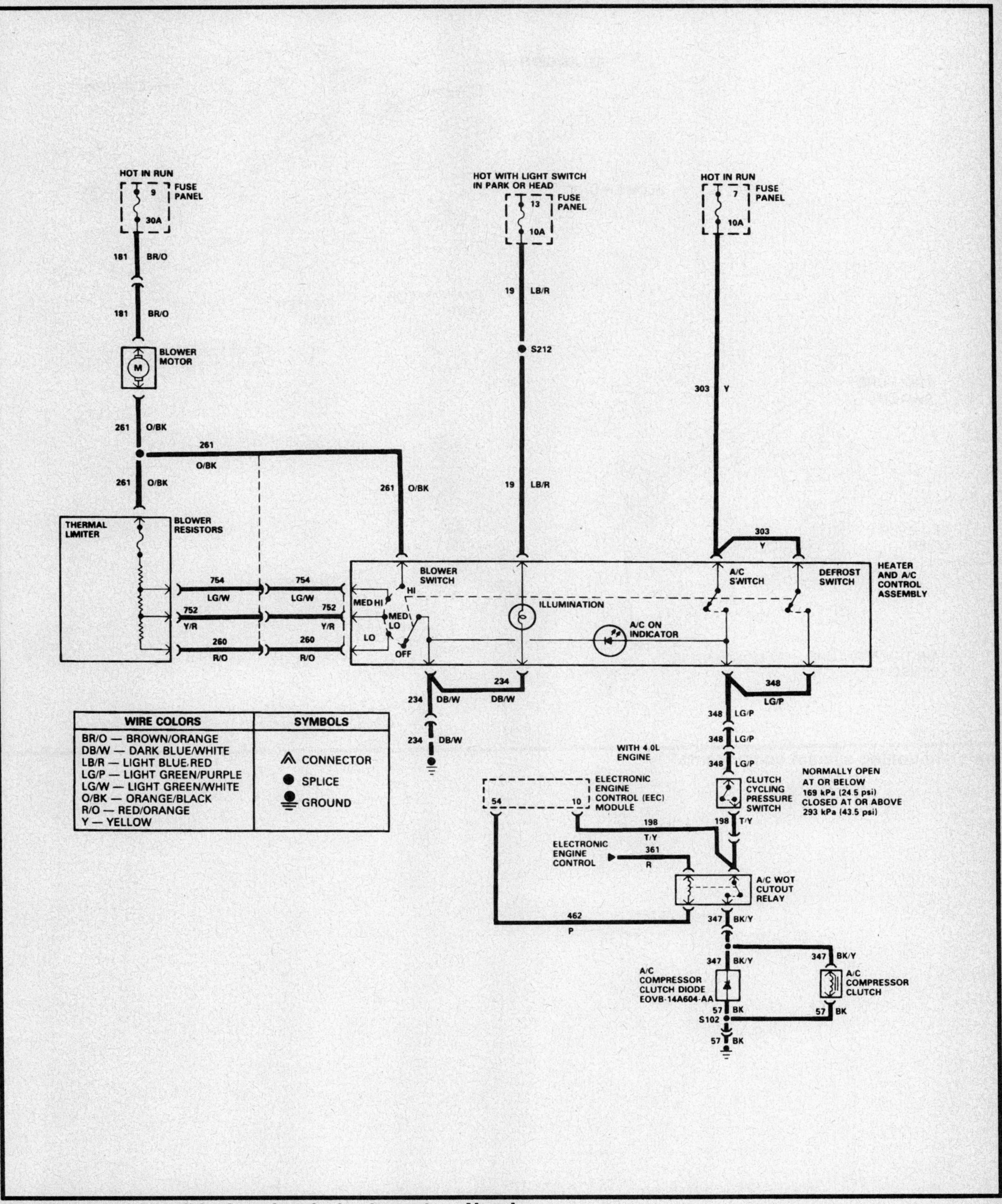
HOT IN RUN
9
FUSE PANEL
30A
181 BR/O
181 BR/O
BLOWER MOTOR
M
261 O/BK
261 O/BK
261 O/BK
THERMAL LIMITER
BLOWER RESISTORS
754 LG/W
752 Y/R
260 R/O
754 LG/W
752 Y/R
260 R/O
261 O/BK
HOT WITH LIGHT SWITCH IN PARK OR HEAD
13
FUSE PANEL
10A
19 LB/R
S212
19 LB/R
HOT IN RUN
7
FUSE PANEL
10A
303 Y
303 Y
BLOWER SWITCH
HI
MED HI
MED
LO
LO
OFF
ILLUMINATION
A/C ON INDICATOR
A/C SWITCH
DEFROST SWITCH
HEATER AND A/C CONTROL ASSEMBLY
234 DB/W
234 DB/W
234 DB/W
348 LG/P
348 LG/P
348 LG/P
348 LG/P
WITH 4.0L ENGINE
54
10
ELECTRONIC ENGINE CONTROL (EEC) MODULE
CLUTCH CYCLING PRESSURE SWITCH
NORMALLY OPEN AT OR BELOW 169 kPa (24.5 psi)
CLOSED AT OR ABOVE 293 kPa (43.5 psi)
198 T/Y
198 T/Y
ELECTRONIC ENGINE CONTROL
361 R
A/C WOT CUTOUT RELAY
462 P
347 BK/Y
347 BK/Y
347 BK/Y
A/C COMPRESSOR CLUTCH DIODE EOVB-14A604-AA
A/C COMPRESSOR CLUTCH
57 BK
S102
57 BK
57 BK
WIRE COLORS
BR/O — BROWN/ORANGE
DB/W — DARK BLUE/WHITE
LB/R — LIGHT BLUE/RED
LG/P — LIGHT GREEN/PURPLE
LG/W — LIGHT GREEN/WHITE
O/BK — ORANGE/BLACK
R/O — RED/ORANGE
Y — YELLOW
SYMBOLS
CONNECTOR
SPLICE
GROUND

Heating and air conditioning electrical schematic— Navajo

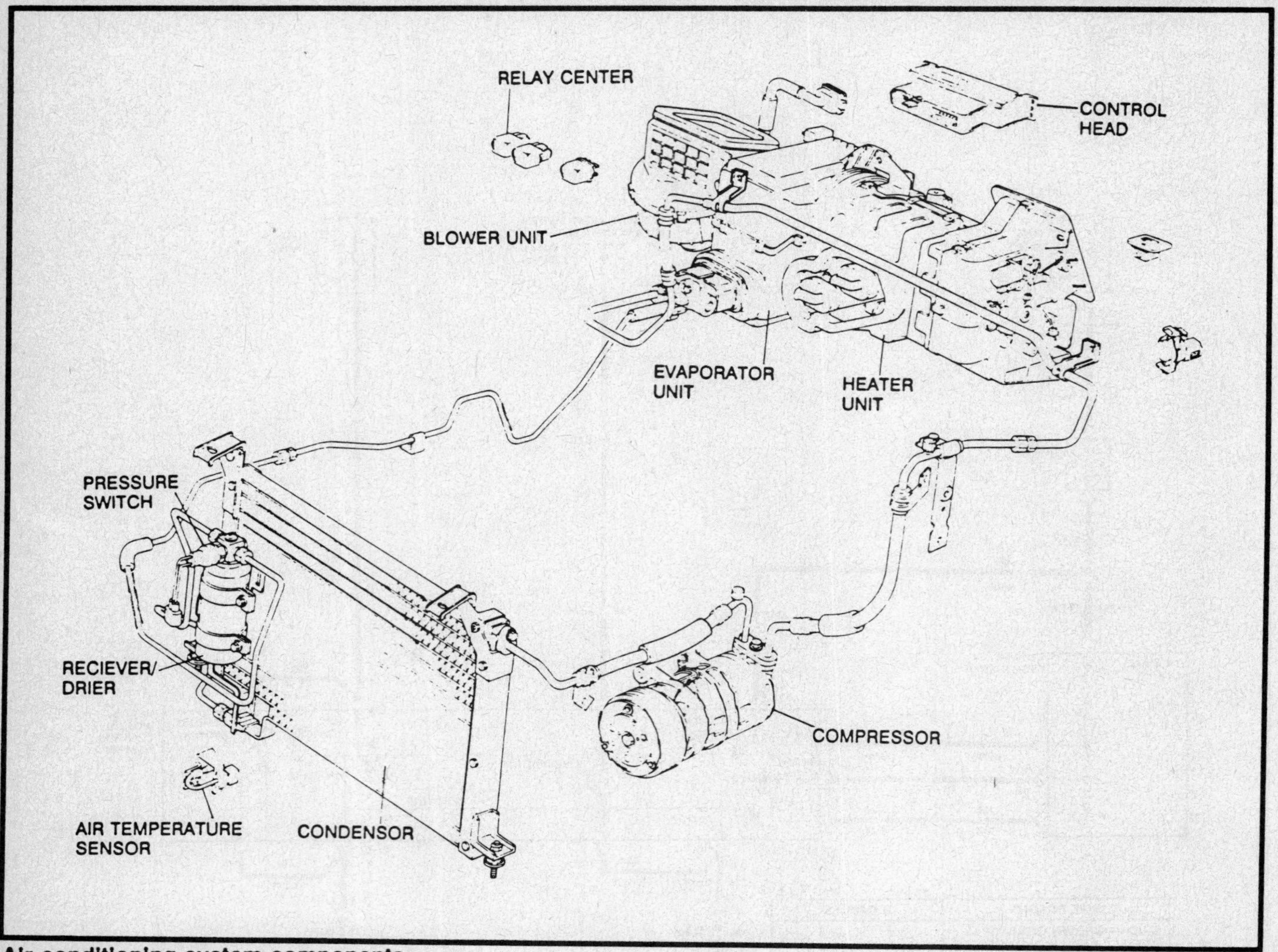
RELAY CENTER
CONTROL HEAD
BLOWER UNIT
EVAPORATOR UNIT
HEATER UNIT
PRESSURE SWITCH
RECIEVER/ DRIER
COMPRESSOR
AIR TEMPERATURE SENSOR
CONDENSOR

Air conditioning system components

32 MITSUBISHI TRUCKS 32

PICK-UP • MONTERO • VAN

SPECIFICATIONS

ENGINE IDENTIFICATION

Year	Model	Engine Displacement cu. in. (cc/liter)	Engine Series Identification	No. of Cylinders	Engine Type
1989	Montero	156 (2555/2.6)	G54B	4	SOHC
	Montero	181 (2972/3.0)	6G72	6	SOHC
	Pick-Up	122 (1997/2.0)	G63B	4	SOHC
	Pick-Up	156 (2555/2.6)	G54B	4	SOHC
	Van	143 (2350/2.4)	4G64	4	SOHC
1990	Montero	181 (2972/3.0)	6G72	6	SOHC
	Pick-Up	143 (2350/2.4)	4G64	4	SOHC
	Pick-Up	181 (2972/3.0)	6G72	6	SOHC
	Van	143 (2350/2.4)	4G64	4	SOHC
1991	Montero	181 (2972/3.0)	6G72	6	SOHC
	Pick-Up	143 (2350/2.4)	4G64	4	SOHC
	Pick-Up	181 (2972/3.0)	6G72	6	SOHC

REFRIGERANT CAPACITIES

Year	Model	Freon (oz.)	Oil (fl. oz.)	Type ⑤
1989	Montero	32	①	②
	Pick-Up	32	3.3	DR1013C
	Van	32 ③	3.3	④
1990	Montero	32	4.7	10PA15
	Pick-Up	30	5.5	FX80
	Van	32 ③	3.3	④
1991	Montero	32	4.7	10PA15
	Pick-Up	30	5.5	FX80

① 2.6L engine—6.7
3.0L engine—4.7
② 2.6L engine—6P148
3.0L engine—10PA15
③ With rear air conditioning—51
④ With single air conditioning—DR1013C
With rear air conditioning—DR1015C
⑤ Compressor

AIR CONDITIONING BELT TENSION CHART

Year	Model	Engine cu. in. (cc/liter)	Belt Type	Specification ① New	Specification ① Used
1989	Montero	156 (2555/2.6)	V-belt	0.55	0.70
	Montero	181 (2972/3.0)	V-belt	0.22	0.35
	Pick-Up	122 (1997/2.0)	V-Belt	0.35	0.35
	Pick-Up	156 (2555/2.6)	V-Belt	0.44	0.44
	Van	143 (2350/2.4)	V-Belt	0.30	0.35
1990	Montero	181 (2972/3.0)	V-belt	0.22	0.35
	Pick-Up	143 (2350/2.4)	V-Belt	0.35	0.35
	Pick-Up	181 (2972/3.0)	V-Belt	0.35	0.35
	Van	143 (2350/2.4)	V-Belt	0.30	0.35
1991	Montero	181 (2972/3.0)	V-belt	0.22	0.35
	Pick-Up	143 (2350/2.4)	V-Belt	0.35	0.35
	Pick-Up	181 (2972/3.0)	V-Belt	0.35	0.35

① Inches of deflection at the center of the belt using 22 lbs. force

SYSTEM DESCRIPTION

General Information

The heater unit is located behind the center of the instrument panel with the blower housing and blend-air system. In the blend-air system, hot air and cool air are controlled by blend-air damper to make fine adjustments of temperature. The heater system is also designed as a bi-level heater in which a separator directs warm air to the windshield or to the floor and cool air through the panel outlet.

The temperature inside the vehicle is controlled by means of the temperature control lever, the position of which determines the opening of the blend-air damper and the resulting mixing ratio of cool and hot air is used to control the outlet temperature.

The air conditioning compressor coil will be energized when all of the following conditions are met:

1. The air conditioner switch on the control head is depressed.
2. The blower motor switch is not in the **OFF** position.
3. The low pressure or dual pressure switch is reading at least 30 psi (206 kPa) pressure.
4. The thermistor is sensing at least 37.4°F (3°C).
5. The engine coolant temperature sensor is reading less than 235°F (113°C).
6. On vehicles equipped with a compressor refrigerant temperature sensor, the compressor discharge side refrigerant temperature must be less than 347°F (175°C).

Service Valve Location

Except Van

The suction valve is located on the compressor on all vehicles. The discharge valve is located either on the compressor or near the compressor on the discharge line.

Van

The valves are located on the refrigerant lines near the reciever/drier and are accessible from underneath the vehicle.

System Discharging

R-12 refrigerant is a chlorofluorocarbon which, when mishandled, can contribute to the depletion on the ozone layer in the upper atmosphere. Ozone filters out harmful radiation from the sun. In order to protect the ozone layer, an approved R-12 Recovery/Recycling machine that meets SAE standard J1991 should be employed when discharging the system. Follow the operating instructions provided with the approved equipment exactly to properly discharge the system.

System Evacuating

If the air conditioning system has been opened to the atmosphere, it should be air and moisture free before being recharged with refrigerant. Moisture and air mixed with refrigerant will raise the compressor head pressure, possibly damage the system's components and will reduce the performance of the system. Moisture will boil at normal room temperature when exposed to a vacuum. To evacuate the system, perform the following procedure:

1. Leak test the system and repair any leaks found.
2. Connect an approved charging station, Recovery/Recycling machine or manifold gauge set and vacuum pump to the discharge and suction ports. The red hose is normally connected to the discharge (high pressure) line and the blue hose is connected to the suction (low pressure) line.
3. Open the discharge and suction ports and start the vacuum pump. If the pump is not able to pull at least 26 in. Hg of vacuum, there is a leak that must be repaired before evacuation can occur.
4. Once the system has reached at least 26 in. Hg of vacuum, allow the system to evacuate for at least 10 minutes. The longer the system is evacuated, the more contaminants will be removed.
5. Close all valves and turn the pump off. If the system loses more than 2 in. Hg of vacuum after 15 minutes, there is a leak that should be repaired.

System Charging

1. Connect an approved charging station, Recovery/Recycling machine or manifold gauge set to the discharge and suction ports. The red hose is normally connected to the discharge (high pressure) line and the blue hose is connected to the suction (low pressure) line.
2. Follow the instructions provided with the equipment and charge the system with the specified amount of refrigerant.
3. Perform a leak test.

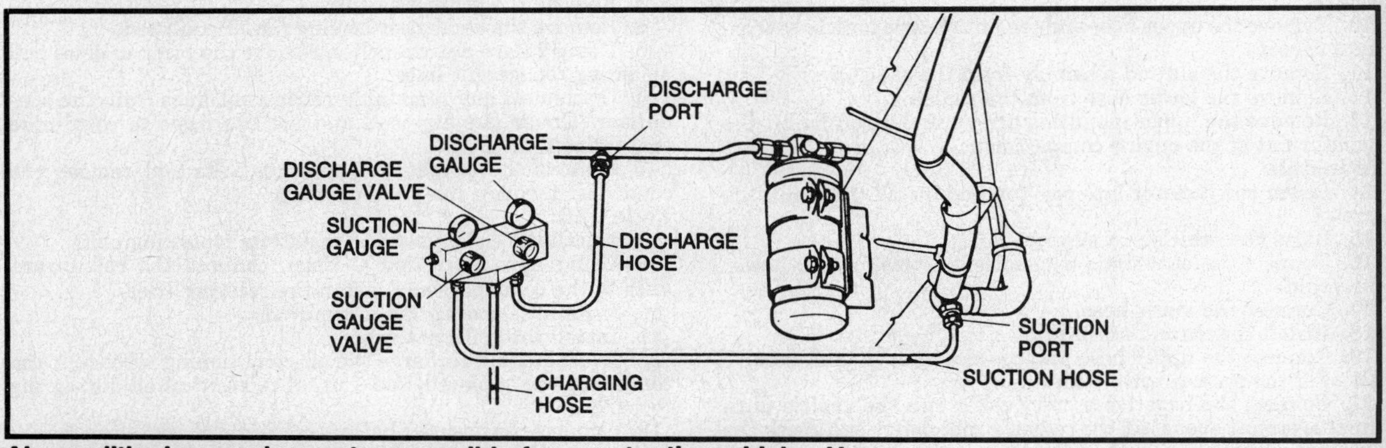
DISCHARGE PORT
DISCHARGE GAUGE
DISCHARGE GAUGE VALVE
SUCTION GAUGE
DISCHARGE HOSE
SUCTION GAUGE VALVE
SUCTION PORT
SUCTION HOSE
CHARGING HOSE

Air conditioning service ports accessible from under the vehicle—Van

SYSTEM COMPONENTS

Radiator

REMOVAL AND INSTALLATION

Except Van

1. Disconnect the negative battery cable.
2. Drain the coolant.
3. Remove the upper hose and coolant reserve tank hose from the radiator.
4. Remove the shroud assembly from the radiator.
5. Raise the vehicle and support safely.
6. Remove the lower hose from the radiator.
7. Disconnect and plug the automatic transmission cooler hoses, if equipped. Lower the vehicle.
8. Remove the mounting screws and carefully lift the radiator out of the engine compartment.

To install:

9. Lower the radiator into position and install the mounting screws.
10. Raise the vehicle and support safely. Connect the automatic transmission cooler hoses, if they were removed.
11. Connect the lower hose. Lower the vehicle.
12. Install the shroud assembly.
13. Connect the upper hose and coolant reserve tank hose.
14. Fill the system with coolant.
15. Connect the negative battery cable, run the vehicle until the thermostat opens, fill the radiator completely and check the automatic transmission fluid level, if equipped.
16. Check for leaks. Once the vehicle has cooled, recheck the coolant level.

Van

1. Remove the battery cover and disconnect the negative battery cable.
2. Release the 2 catches and flip the passenger seat up.
3. Remove the driver's seat.
4. Remove the parking brake lever cover.
5. Remove the parking brake lever and fuel filler fuel release lever retaining screws and remove the levers from the seat under frame.
6. Remove the seat underframe retaining screws and remove the seat underframe from the vehicle.
7. Raise the vehicle and support safely. Drain the radiator.
8. Disconnect and plug the automatic transmission cooler hoses.
9. Remove the lower radiator mounting screws. Lower the vehicle.
10. Remove the upper hose and coolant reserve tank hose from the radiator.
11. Remove the shroud assembly from the radiator.
12. Remove the lower hose from the radiator.
13. Remove the upper mounting screws and carefully lift the radiator out of the engine compartment.

To install:

14. Lower the radiator into position and install the mounting screws.
15. Raise the vehicle and support safely.
16. Connect the automatic transmission cooler hoses. Lower the vehicle.
17. Connect the lower hose.
18. Install the shroud assembly.
19. Connect the upper hose and coolant reserve tank hose.
20. Fill the system with coolant.
21. Connect the negative battery cable, run the vehicle until the thermostat opens, fill the radiator completely and check the automatic transmission fluid level.
22. Check for leaks. Once the vehicle has cooled, recheck the coolant level.
23. Install the seat underframe and all related parts.

Electric Cooling Fan

An electric condenser cooling fan is used on Montero. The condenser on Pick-Up and Van are cooled by the belt-driven fan.

TESTING

CAUTION

Make sure the key is in the OFF position when checking the electric cooling fan. If not, the fan could turn ON at any time, causing serious personal injury.

1. Disconnect the negative battery cable.
2. Disconnect the condenser cooling fan connector.
3. Connect the green-with-black-tracer wire to 12 volts and ground the black wire.
4. Make sure the fan runs smoothly, without abnormal noise or vibration.
5. Connect the negative battery cable.

REMOVAL AND INSTALLATION

1. Disconnect the negative battery cable.
2. Open the hood and remove the grille. It is fastened with 3 screws along the top and 3 nuts along the bottom.
3. Disconnect the fan connector.
4. Remove the mounting bolts and remove the fan through the grille opening.
5. The installation is the reverse of the removal procedure.
6. Connect the negative battery cable and check the fan for proper operation.

Condenser

REMOVAL AND INSTALLATION

Except Van

1. Disconnect the negative battery cable.
2. Properly discharge the air conditioning system.
3. Remove the grille assembly.
4. Remove the condenser cooling fan, if equipped.
5. Using 2 flare nut wrenches, remove the receiver drier and adjoining refrigerant lines.
6. Disconnect any remaining refrigerant lines from the condenser. Cover the exposed ends of the lines to minimize contamination.
7. Remove the condenser mounting bolts and remove the condenser through the grille opening.

To install:

8. Install the condenser and install its mounting bolts.
9. Using new lubricated O-rings, connect the refrigerant lines to the condenser and install the receiver drier.
10. Install the cooling fan if removed.
11. Install the grille assembly.
12. Evacuate and recharge the air conditioning system. If the condenser was replaced, add 1 oz. of refrigerant oil during the recharge.
13. Connect the negative battery cable and check the entire climate control system for proper operation and leaks.

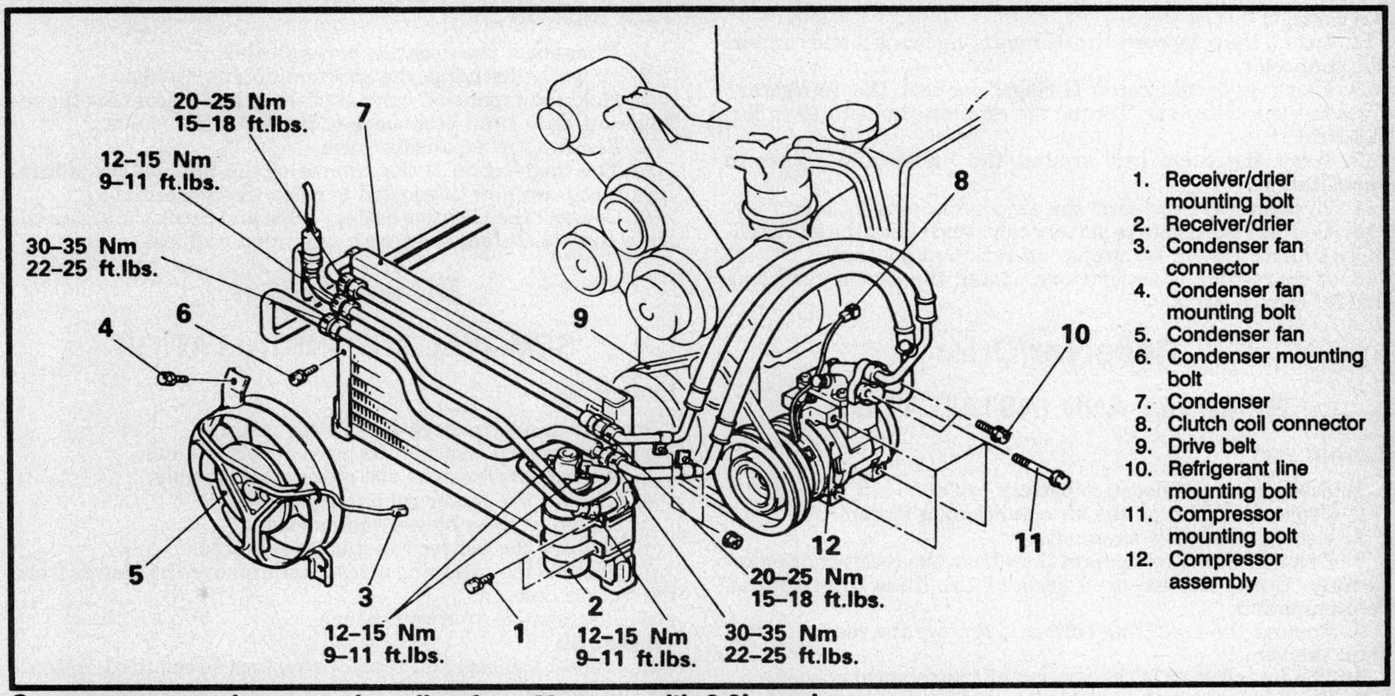
20–25 Nm
15–18 ft.lbs.
7
12–15 Nm
9–11 ft.lbs.
30–35 Nm
22–25 ft.lbs.
4
6
9
8
10
5
3
12–15 Nm
9–11 ft.lbs.
1
2
12–15 Nm
9–11 ft.lbs.
30–35 Nm
22–25 ft.lbs.
20–25 Nm
15–18 ft.lbs.
12
11
1. Receiver/drier mounting bolt
2. Receiver/drier
3. Condenser fan connector
4. Condenser fan mounting bolt
5. Condenser fan
6. Condenser mounting bolt
7. Condenser
8. Clutch coil connector
9. Drive belt
10. Refrigerant line mounting bolt
11. Compressor mounting bolt
12. Compressor assembly

Compressor, condenser and cooling fan—Montero with 3.0L engine

Van

1. Remove the battery cover and disconnect the negative battery cable.
2. Raise the vehicle and safely secure. Properly discharge the air conditioning system. Lower the vehicle.
3. Release the 2 catches and flip the passenger seat up.
4. Remove the driver's seat.
5. Remove the parking brake lever cover.
6. Remove the parking brake lever and fuel filler fuel release lever retaining screws and remove the levers from the seat under frame.
7. Remove the seat underframe retaining screws and remove the seat underframe from the vehicle.
8. Using 2 flare nut wrenches, disconnect the refigerant lines from the condenser. Cover the exposed ends of the lines to minimize contamination.
9. Remove the condenser mounting bolts and remove the condenser.

To install:

10. Install the condenser and secure with its mounting bolts.
11. Using new lubricated O-rings, connect the refrigerant lines to the condenser.
12. Evacuate and recharge the air conditioning system. If the condenser was replaced, add 1 oz. of refrigerant oil during the recharge.
13. Connect the negative battery cable and check the entire climate control system for proper operation and leaks.
14. If everything is satisfactory, install the seat underframe and all related parts.

Compressor

REMOVAL AND INSTALLATION

Except Van

1. Disconnect the negative battery cable.
2. Properly discharge the air conditioning system.
3. Relieve the tension and remove the compressor drive belt from the clutch pulley. Disconnect the electrical connector.
4. Disconnect the refrigerant lines from the compressor. Cover the exposed ends of the lines to minimize contamination.
5. Remove the retaining bolts and remove the compressor from its mounting bracket.

To install:

6. Install the compressor to its mounting bracket and connect the connector.
7. Using new lubricated O-rings, connect the refrigerant lines to the compressor. Torque the retaining bolts to 17 ft. lbs. (23 Nm).
8. Wrap the drive belt around the pulley and adjust to specification.
9. Evacuate and recharge the air conditioning system.
10. Connect the negative battery cable and check the entire climate control system for proper operation and leaks.

Van

1. Remove the battery cover and disconnect the negative battery cable.
2. Raise the vehicle and safely secure. Properly discharge the air conditioning system. Lower the vehicle.
3. Release the 2 catches and flip the passenger seat up.
4. Remove the driver's seat.
5. Remove the parking brake lever cover.
6. Remove the parking brake lever and fuel filler fuel release lever retaining screws and remove the levers from the seat under frame.
7. Remove the seat underframe retaining screws and remove the seat underframe from the vehicle.
8. Relieve the tension and remove the compressor drive belt from the clutch pulley. Disconnect the electrical connector.
9. Disconnect the refrigerant lines from the compressor. Cover the exposed ends of the lines to minimize contamination.
10. Remove the retaining bolts and remove the compressor from its mounting bracket.

To install:

11. Install the compressor to its mounting bracket and connect the connector.
12. Using new lubricated O-rings, connect the refrigerant lines to the compressor. Torque the retaining bolts to 17 ft. lbs. (23 Nm).
13. Wrap the drive belt around the pulley and adjust to specification.
14. Evacuate and recharge the air conditioning system.
15. Connect the negative battery cable and check the entire climate control system for proper operation and leaks.
16. If everything is satisfactory, install the seat underframe and all related parts.

Receiver/Drier

REMOVAL AND INSTALLATION

Except Van

1. Disconnect the negative battery cable.
2. Properly discharge the air conditioning system.
3. Remove the grille assembly.
4. Disconnect the refrigerant lines from the receiver/drier assembly. Cover the exposed ends of the lines to minimize contamination.
5. Remove the mounting bolts and remove the receiver/drier from the vehicle.
6. The installation is the reverse of the removal procedure.
7. Evacuate and recharge the air conditioning system. If the receiver/drier was replaced, add ¼ oz. of refrigerant oil during the recharge.
8. Connect the negative battery cable and check the entire climate control system for proper operation and leaks.

Van

1. Remove the battery cover and disconnect the negative battery cable.
2. Raise the vehicle and safely secure. Properly discharge the air conditioning system.
3. Disconnect the refrigerant lines from the receiver/drier assembly. Cover the exposed ends of the lines to minimize contamination.
4. Remove the mounting bolts and remove the receiver/drier from the vehicle.
5. The installation is the reverse of the removal procedure.
6. Evacuate and recharge the air conditioning system. If the receiver/drier was replaced, add ¼ oz. of refrigerant oil during the recharge.
7. Connect the negative battery cable and check the entire climate control system for proper operation and leaks.

Expansion Valve

REMOVAL AND INSTALLATION

Except 1989 Pick-Up

1. Disconnect the negative battery cable.
2. Properly discharge the air conditioning system.
3. Remove the evaporator housing and separate the upper and lower cases.
4. Remove the expansion valve from the evaporator lines.
5. The installation is the reverse of the removal installation. Use new lubricated O-rings when assembling.
6. Evacuate and recharge the air conditioning system.
7. Connect the negative battery cable and check the entire climate control system for proper operation. Check the system for leaks.

1989 Pick-Up

1. Disconnect the negative battery cable.
2. Properly discharge the air conditioning system.
3. Hold the expansion valve stationary and disconnect the refrigerant lines from both sides of the expansion valve.
4. Remove the expansion valve.
5. The installation is the reverse of the removal procedure. Be sure to use new lubricated O-rings when assembling.
6. Connect the negative battery cable and check the entire climate control system for proper operation and leaks.

Blower Motor

REMOVAL AND INSTALLATION

Except Van

1. Disconnect the negative battery cable.
2. On Montero, remove the passenger's lap duct.
3. If necessary, remove the glove box assembly.
4. Remove the motor cooling tube.
5. Disconnect the blower motor lead.
6. Remove the blower resistor, as required.
7. Remove the retaining screws and remove the blower from the blower case.
8. Disassemble on a workbench.

To install:

9. Inspect the seal and repair or replace as required. Assemble the fan and motor.
10. Install the motor to the case and install the retaining screws.
11. Install the resistor and connect the blower lead.
12. Install the cooling tube.
13. Install the glove box and lap duct if removed.
14. Connect the negative battery cable and check the blower for proper operation.

Van

1. Disconnect the negative battery cable.
2. Remove the lap heater duct and left side defroster duct.
3. Disconnect the resistor block connector and remove the resistor.
4. Remove the blower motor retaining screws and remove from the housing.
5. Remove the fan from the motor.
6. The installation is the reverse of the removal procedure.
7. Connect the negative battery cable and check the blower for proper operation.

Blower Motor Resistor

REMOVAL AND INSTALLATION

1. Disconnect the negative battery cable.
2. Remove the blower motor assembly if it is preventing access to the resistor, located next to the blower.
3. Disconnect the wire harness from the resistor.
4. Remove the mounting screws and remove the resistor.
5. The installation is the reverse of the removal procedure. Make sure the seal is intact when installing.
6. Connect the negative battery cable and check the entire climate control system for proper operation.

Heater Core

REMOVAL AND INSTALLATION

Montero

1. Disconnect the negative battery cable.

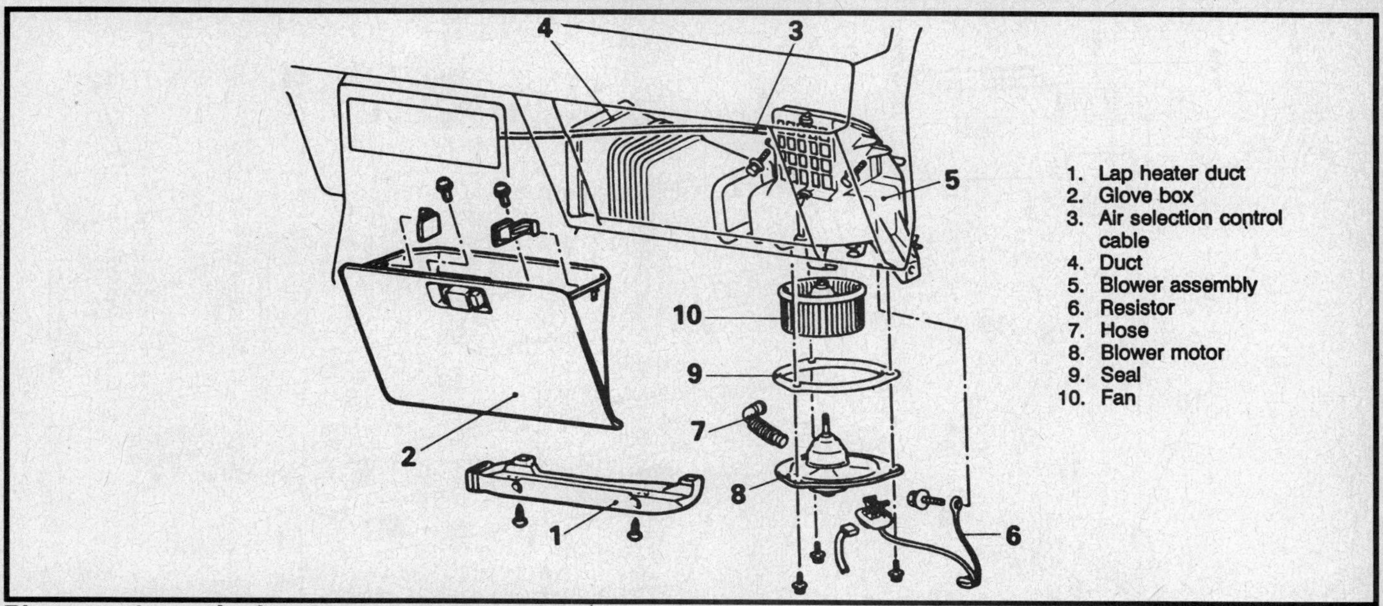
1
2
3
4
5
6
7
8
9
10
1. Lap heater duct
2. Glove box
3. Air selection control cable
4. Duct
5. Blower assembly
6. Resistor
7. Hose
8. Blower motor
9. Seal
10. Fan

Blower motor and related components – Montero

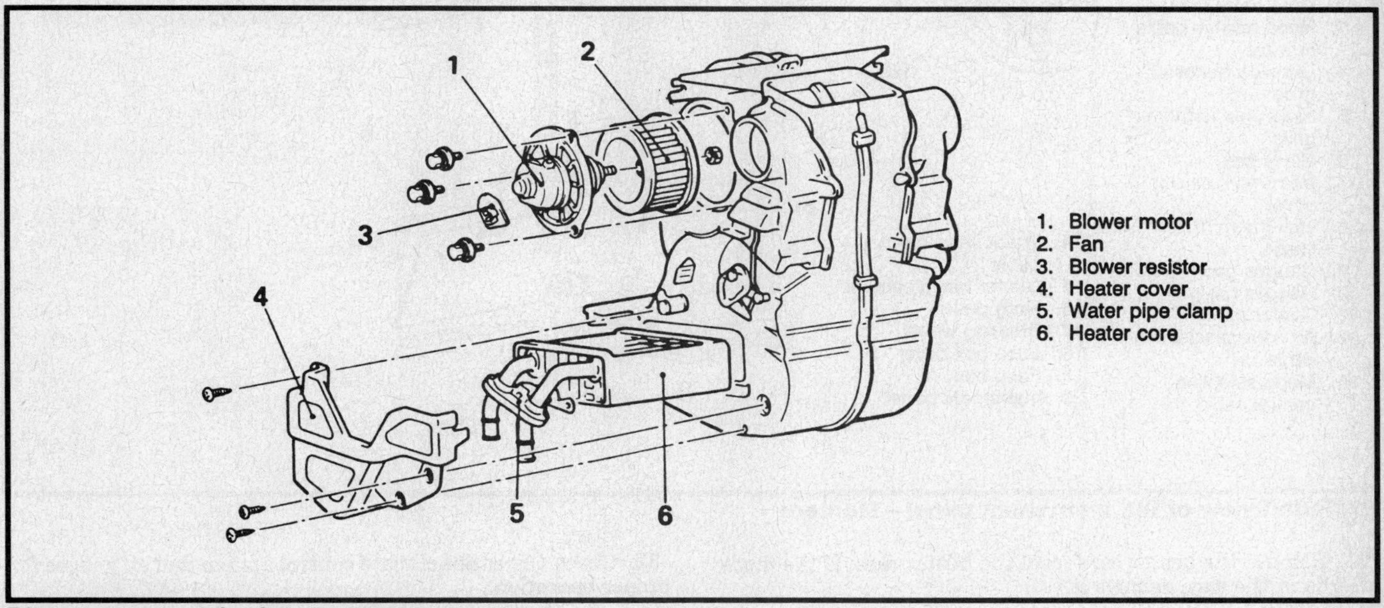
1
2
3
4
5
6
1. Blower motor
2. Fan
3. Blower resistor
4. Heater cover
5. Water pipe clamp
6. Heater core

Blower motor and related components – Van

2. Drain the coolant.
3. Remove the lap heater ducts and lower the hood release cable bracket.
4. Carefully pry the side demister grilles from the instrument panel.
5. Remove the glove box, center console assembly and center reinforcement.
6. Remove the steering wheel.
7. Remove the instrument cluster.
8. Remove the oil pressure gauge, inclinometer and voltmeter pod cover. Remove the gauge assembly.
9. Label and disconnect the recirculation/fresh air door control cable.
10. Label and disconnect the mode selection control cable.
11. Label and disconnect the water valve control cable.
12. Remove the fuse box retaining screw and position the fuse box aside.
13. Remove the instrument panel retaining nuts and bolts and carefully remove the instrument panel from the vehicle.
14. Remove the air cleaner or air intake plenum, as required.
15. Disconnect the heater hoses from the heater core tubes.
16. Remove the duct from the top of the heater case.
17. Remove the retaining nuts and bolts and remove the heater case from the vehicle.
18. Remove the water valve cover and carefully remove the water valve from the case.
19. Remove the foot/defroster selection link from the mode selection lever.
20. Move the lever up to a position which will not interfere with the removal of the heater core.

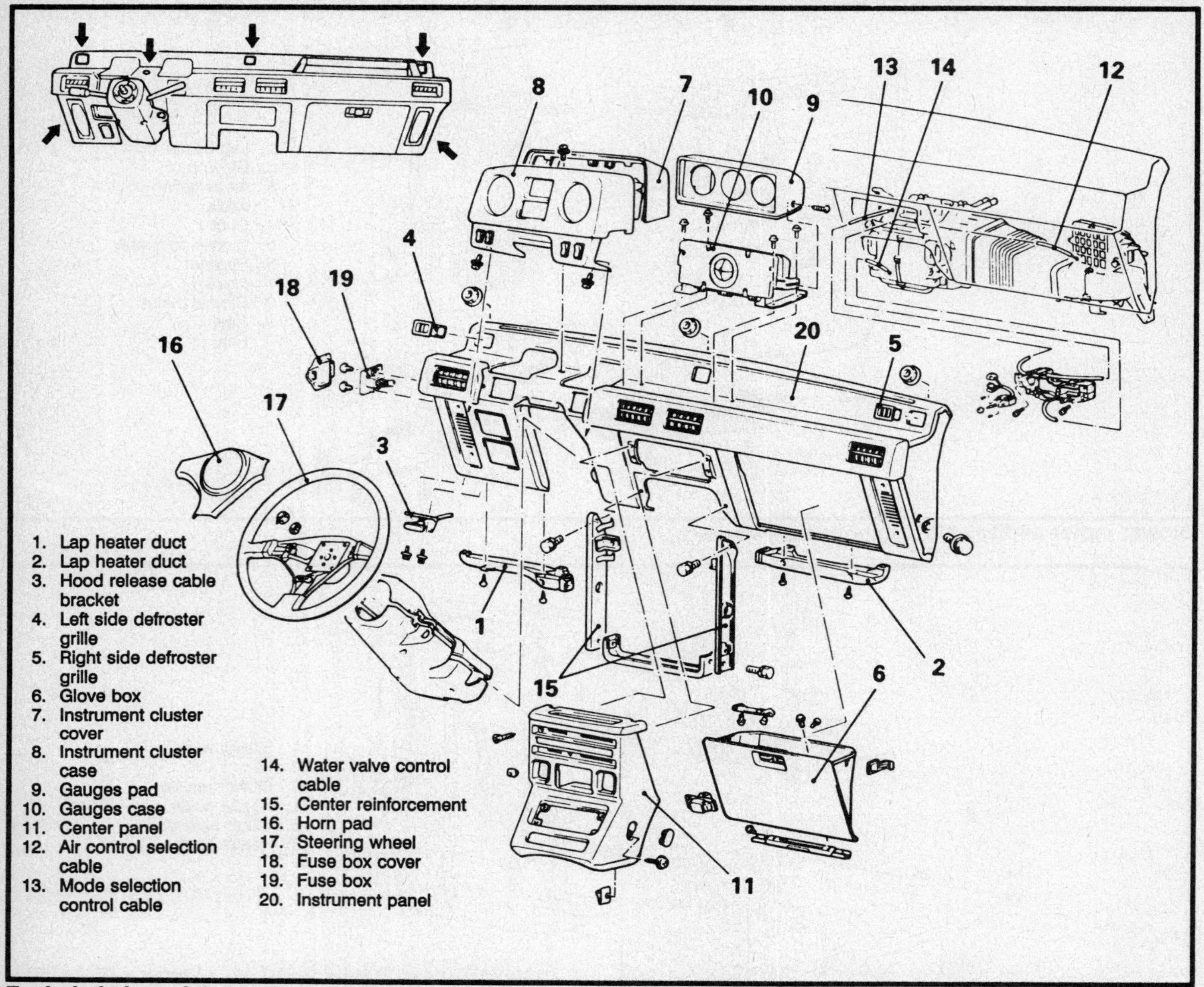
1. Lap heater duct
2. Lap heater duct
3. Hood release cable bracket
4. Left side defroster grille
5. Right side defroster grille
6. Glove box
7. Instrument cluster cover
8. Instrument cluster case
9. Gauges pad
10. Gauges case
11. Center panel
12. Air control selection cable
13. Mode selection control cable
14. Water valve control cable
15. Center reinforcement
16. Horn pad
17. Steering wheel
18. Fuse box cover
19. Fuse box
20. Instrument panel

Exploded view of the instrument panel—Montero

21. Remove the heater core from the heater case. If the mode lever is in the way, remove it.

To install:

22. Install the heater core to the heater case. Install the mode lever, if it was removed.
23. Install the foot/defroster selection link to the mode selection lever.
24. Install the water valve assembly and its cover to the case.
25. Install the assembled heater case to the vehicle and install the retaining nuts and bolts.
26. Install the duct to the top of the case.
27. Connect the heater hoses to the core tubes and install the air cleaner or intake plenum.
28. Install the instrument panel and all related parts. Adjust the control cables if necessary.
29. Fill the system with coolant.
30. Connect the negative battery cable, run the vehicle until the thermostat opens and fill the radiator completely.
31. Check for leaks. Once the vehicle has cooled, recheck the coolant level.
32. Check the entire climate control system and all gauges for proper operation.

Pick-Up

1. Disconnect the negative battery cable.
2. Drain the coolant. Disconnect the heater hoses from the core tubes.
3. Remove the hazard flasher switch and the matching cover on the other side of the column. Remove the instrument cluster.
4. Remove the fuse box cover and fuse box retaining screws. Position the fuse box aside.
5. Remove the glove box assembly.
6. Remove the defroster ducts.
7. Label and disconnect the air, mode, and temperature control cables from the heater case.
8. Remove the front speaker grilles.
9. Remove the parcel box or clock, as equipped.
10. Remove the nut cover from the top center of the instrument panel.
11. Remove the center cover.

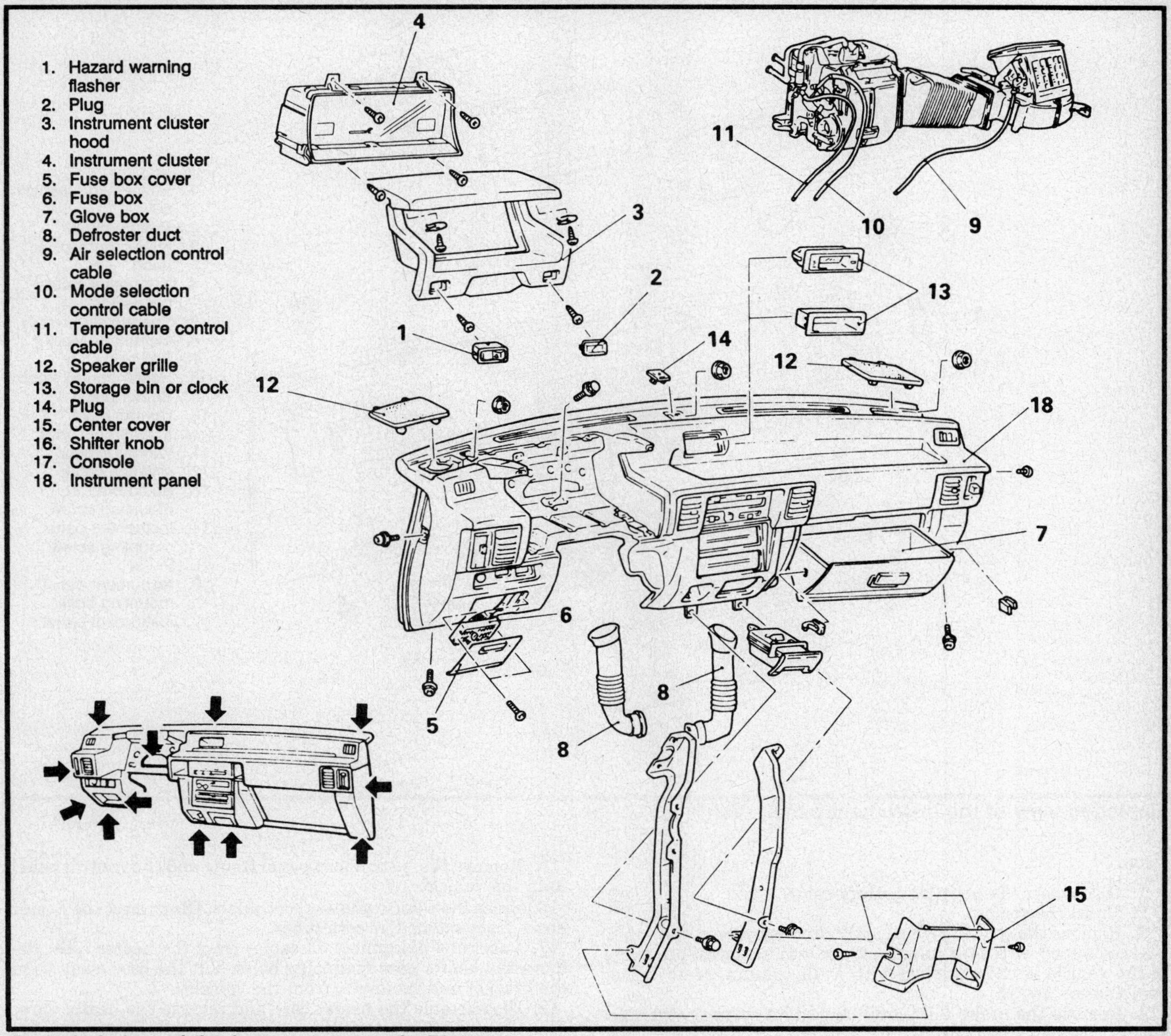
1. Hazard warning flasher
2. Plug
3. Instrument cluster hood
4. Instrument cluster
5. Fuse box cover
6. Fuse box
7. Glove box
8. Defroster duct
9. Air selection control cable
10. Mode selection control cable
11. Temperature control cable
12. Speaker grille
13. Storage bin or clock
14. Plug
15. Center cover
16. Shifter knob
17. Console
18. Instrument panel

Exploded view of the instrument panel—Pick-up

12. Remove the shifter knob and floor console assembly, if equipped.
13. Move the tilt steering column down as far as it will go.
14. Remove the instrument panel retaining nuts and bolts and carefully remove the instrument panel from the vehicle.
15. Remove the duct from the top center of the heater case.
16. Remove the defroster duct from the the left side of the case.
17. Remove the center reinforcement braces.
18. Remove the mounting nuts and remove the heater case from the vehicle.
19. Remove the hose cover, joint hose clamp and the plate from the case.
20. Remove the heater core from the case.

To install:

21. Install the heater core to the heater case.
22. Install the plate, joint hose clamp and hose cover.
23. Install the assembled heater case to the vehicle. Connect the heater hoses to the core tubes.
24. Install the center reinforcement braces.
25. Install the defroster and center ducts to the case.
26. Install the instrument panel and all related parts. Adjust the control cables if necessary.
27. Fill the system with coolant.
28. Connect the negative battery cable, run the vehicle until the thermostat opens and fill the radiator completely.
29. Check for leaks. Once the vehicle has cooled, recheck the coolant level.
30. Check the entire climate control system and all gauges for proper operation.

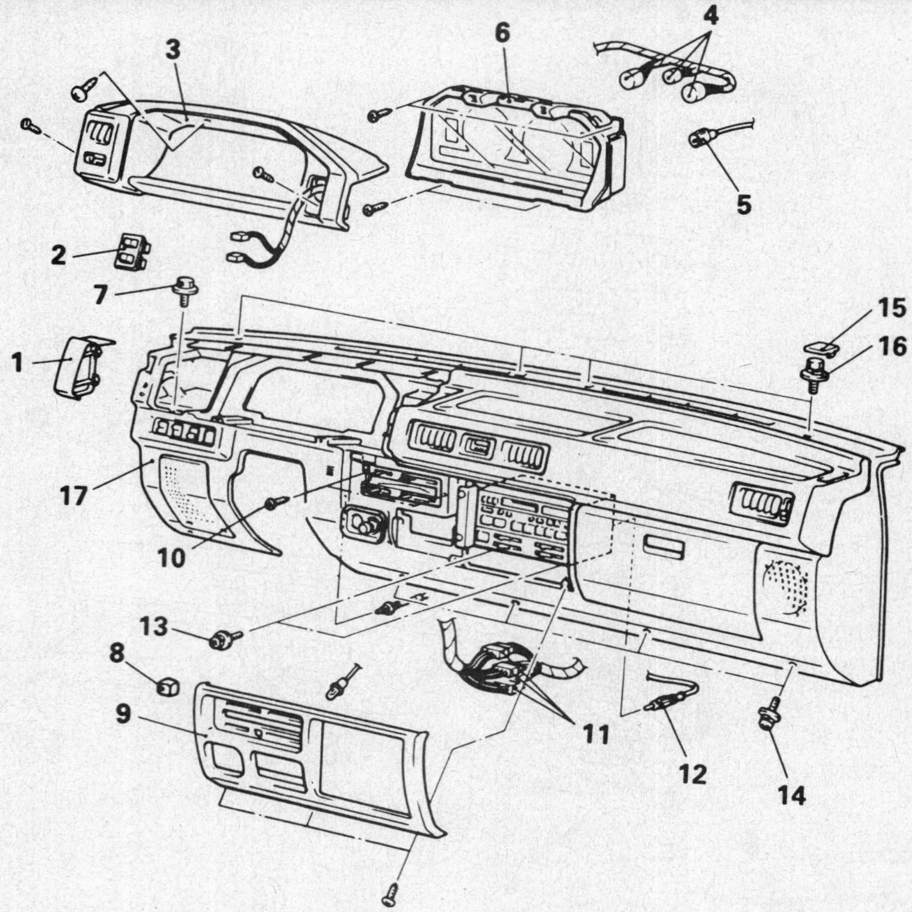
1
2
3
4
5
6
7
8
9
10
11
12
13
14
15
16
17

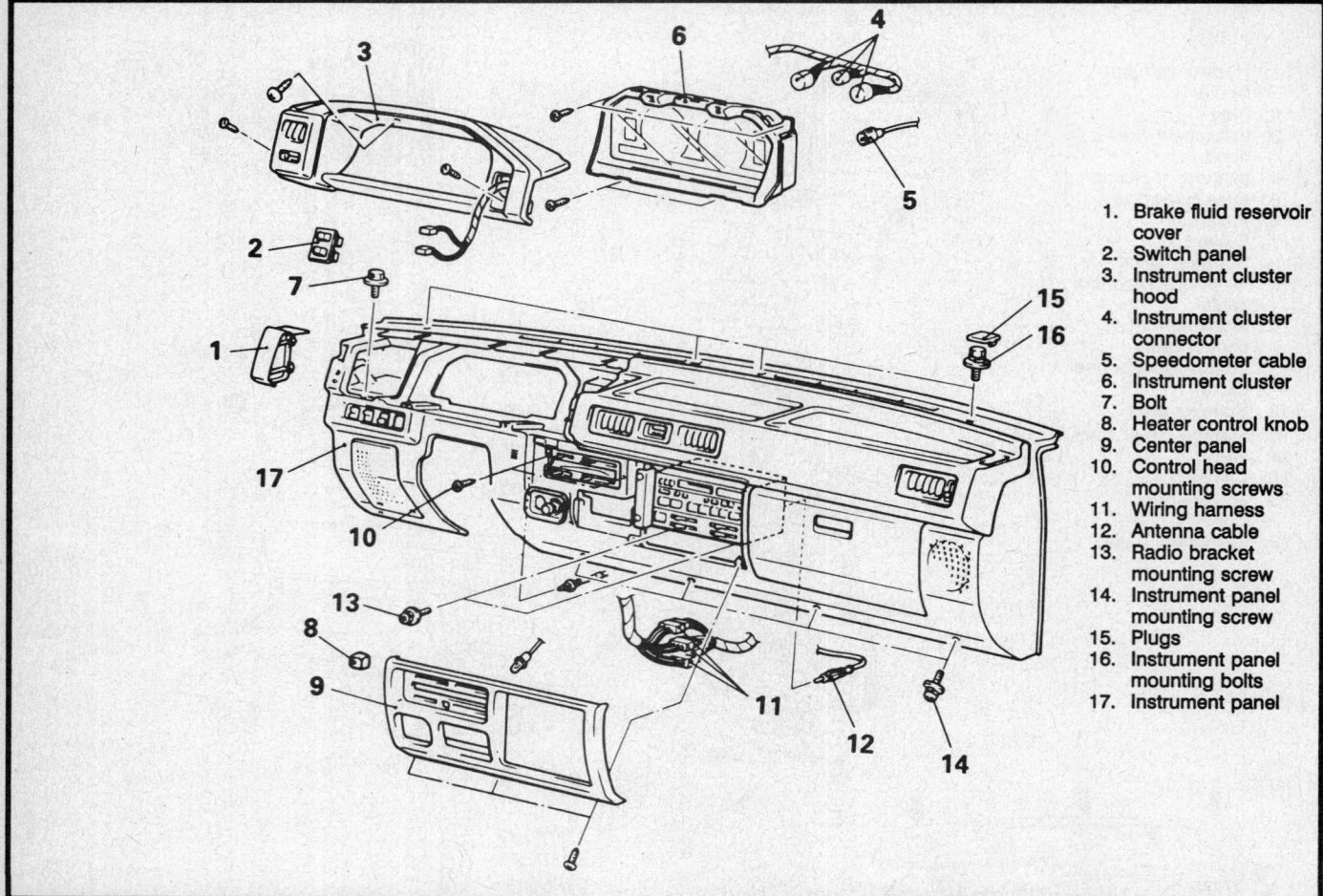

1. Brake fluid reservoir cover
2. Switch panel
3. Instrument cluster hood
4. Instrument cluster connector
5. Speedometer cable
6. Instrument cluster
7. Bolt
8. Heater control knob
9. Center panel
10. Control head mounting screws
11. Wiring harness
12. Antenna cable
13. Radio bracket mounting screw
14. Instrument panel mounting screw
15. Plugs
16. Instrument panel mounting bolts
17. Instrument panel

Exploded view of the instrument panel—Van

Van

1. Disconnect the negative battery cable.
2. Drain the coolant.
3. Remove the steering wheel and column covers. If the vehicle is equipped with a tilt column, lower it to its lowest position. If the vehicle is not equipped with a tilt column, remove the combination switch.
4. Remove the brake fluid level inspection cover on the left side of the instrument panel.
5. Remove the lap heater ducts. Remove the switch panel and remove the instrument cluster assembly.
6. Remove the brake fluid reservoir mounting screws. Do not allow fluid to spill out onto any painted surface; brake fluid will ruin the paint.
7. Remove the heater control knobs and remove the center panel.
8. Remove the heater control mounting screws and push the control panel into the instrument panel.
9. Disconnect the harnesses below the center of the instrument panel.
10. Remove the radio.
11. Remove the mounting screws across the bottom of the instrument panel.
12. Remove the bolt covers across the top of the instrument panel and remove the bolts.
13. Remove the defroster ductwork from the heater unit.
14. Carefully remove the instrument panel from the vehicle.
15. Remove the instrument panel frame and the control panel from the vehicle.
16. Raise the vehicle and support safely. Disconnect the heater hoses from the heater core tubes.
17. Label and disconnect all cables from the heater case. Remove the heater case mounting bolts. Tilt the case away from the bracket and remove it from the vehicle.
18. Disassemble the heater case and remove the heater core.

To install:

19. Install the heater core to the heater case.
20. Install the assembled case to the vehicle, making sure the floor pan seal is seated properly.
21. Connect the heater hoses to the core tubes. Make sure the hoses are not twisted and that the clamps are not touching other parts.
22. Install the instrument panel frame and position the heater control panel.
23. Install the instrument panel and all related parts. Adjust the control cables if necessary.
24. Install the combination switch, if removed. Install the steering wheel and column covers.
25. Fill the system with coolant.
26. Connect the negative battery cable, run the vehicle until the thermostat opens and fill the radiator completely.
27. Check for leaks. Once the vehicle has cooled, recheck the coolant level.

28. Check the entire climate control system and all gauges for proper operation.

Evaporator

REMOVAL AND INSTALLATION

Except Van

1. Disconnect the negative battery cable.
2. Properly discharge the air conditioning system.
3. Use 2 wrenches to disconnect the liquid and suction lines from the evaporator fittings at the firewall.
4. Remove the retaining nut located just above the hoses.
5. Remove the glove box assembly.
6. Remove the defroster duct.
7. Disconnect the electrical harness connector running to the evaporator case.
8. Loosen the duct joint between the evaporator case and the heater case.
9. Remove the condensation drain hose.
10. Remove the retaining bolts and remove the evaporator case from the vehicle.
11. Disassemble the evaporator case and remove the evaporator.

To install:

12. Install the evaporator to the case and assemble. Carefully install the assembled case into the vehicle and tighten the mounting bolts and nuts.
13. Connect the condensation drain hose to the case.
14. Install the duct joints on both sides of the evaporator. Correctly installed, the evaporator case should have slight clearance to the joint on each side.
15. Connect the harness electrical connectors.
16. Install the defroster duct.
17. Install the glove box.
18. In the engine compartment, install the retaining nut if not already done during installation.

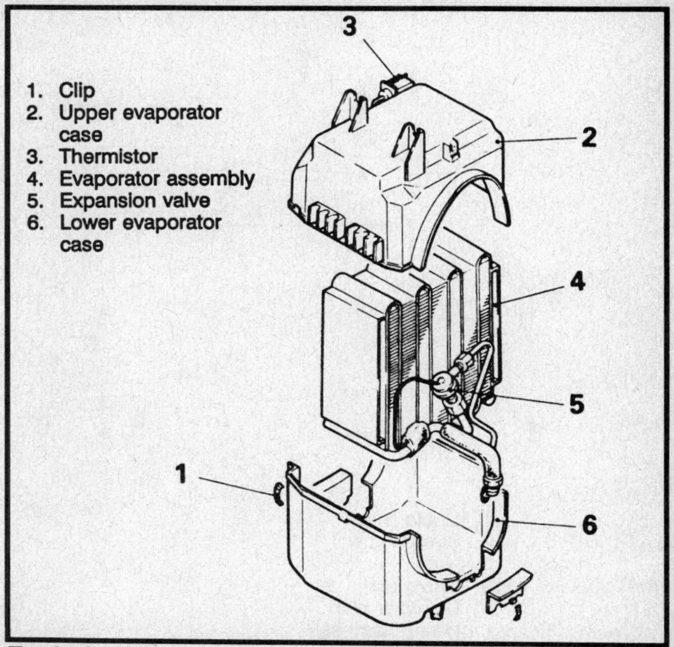
1. Clip
2. Upper evaporator case
3. Thermistor
4. Evaporator assembly
5. Expansion valve
6. Lower evaporator case
1
2
3
4
5
6

Exploded view of the evaporator assembly—except 1989 Pick-Up

19. Using new lubricated O-rings, connect the refrigerant lines to the evaporator fittings.
20. Evacuate and recharge the air conditioning system. If the evaporator was replaced, add 1 oz. of refrigerant oil during the recharge.
21. Connect the negative battery cable and check the entire climate control system for proper operation and leaks.

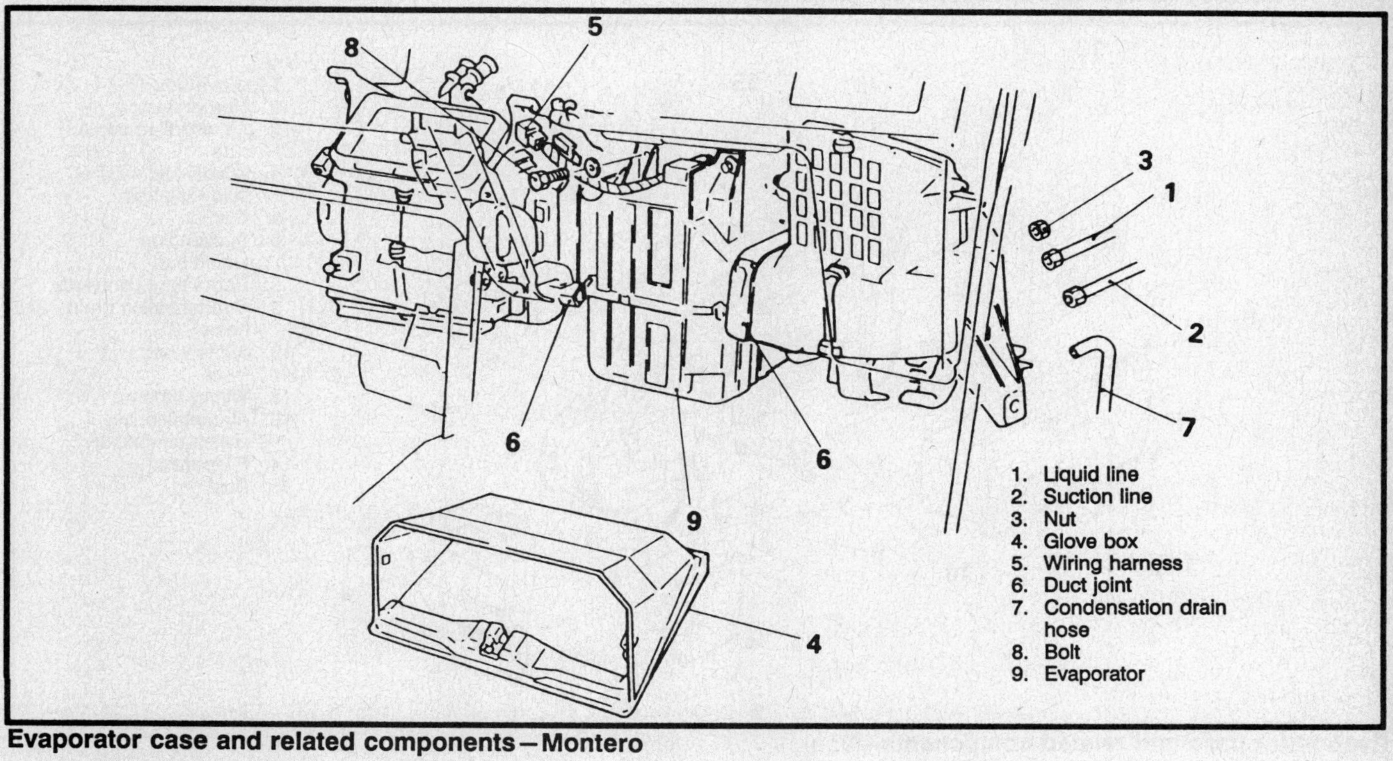
1. Liquid line
2. Suction line
3. Nut
4. Glove box
5. Wiring harness
6. Duct joint
7. Condensation drain hose
8. Bolt
9. Evaporator
1
2
3
4
5
6
6
7
8
9

Evaporator case and related components—Montero

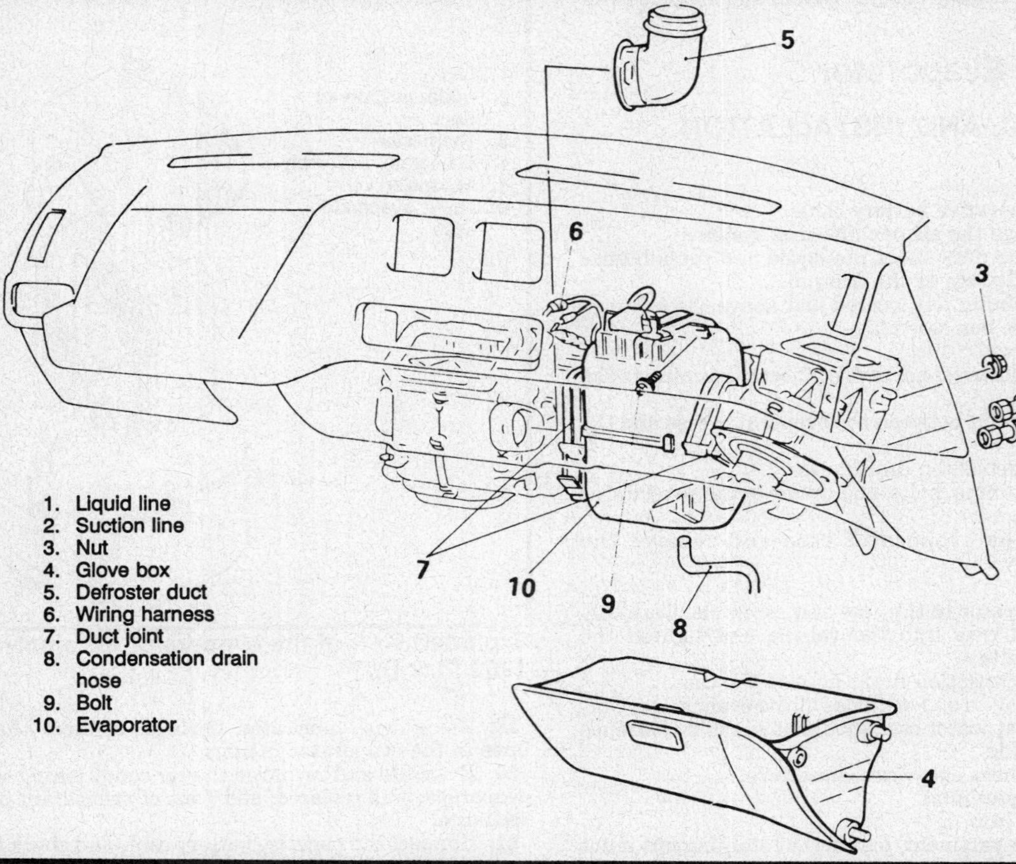
5
6
3
1
2
7
10
9
8
4

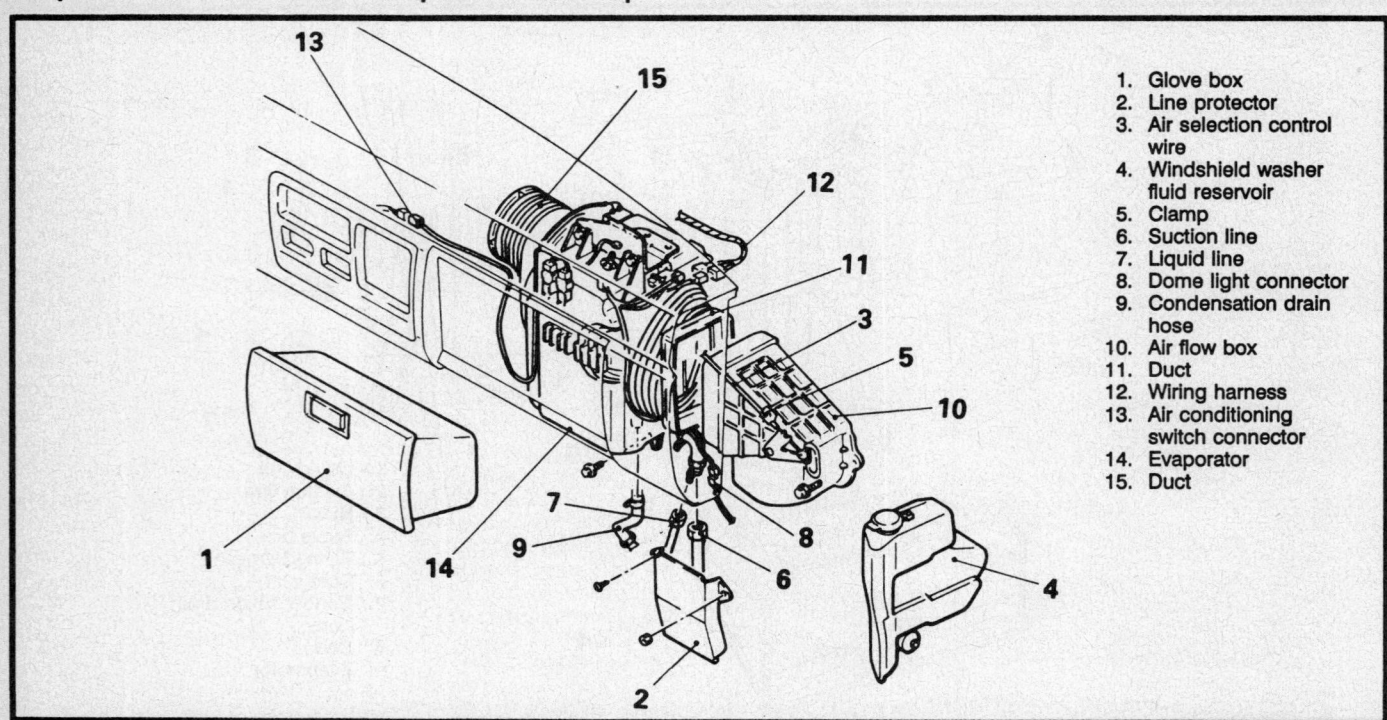

1. Liquid line
2. Suction line
3. Nut
4. Glove box
5. Defroster duct
6. Wiring harness
7. Duct joint
8. Condensation drain hose
9. Bolt
10. Evaporator

Evaporator case and related components—Pick-Up

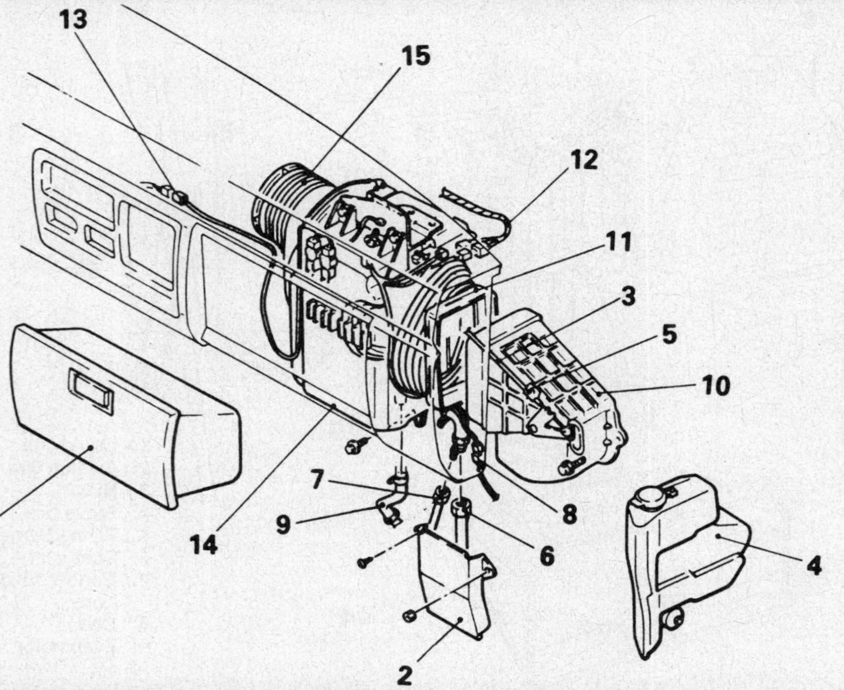
13
15
12
11
3
5
10
7
9
8
6
1
14
4
2

1. Glove box
2. Line protector
3. Air selection control wire
4. Windshield washer fluid reservoir
5. Clamp
6. Suction line
7. Liquid line
8. Dome light connector
9. Condensation drain hose
10. Air flow box
11. Duct
12. Wiring harness
13. Air conditioning switch connector
14. Evaporator
15. Duct

Evaporator case and related components—Van

Van

1. Disconnect the negative battery cable.
2. Raise the vehicle and safely support.
3. Properly discharge the air conditioning system. Disconnect the refrigerant lines from the evaporator fittings. Lower the vehicle.
4. Remove the glove box assembly.
5. Remove the evaporator lines foot protector.
6. Disconnect the air selection control cable.
7. Remove the windshield washer fluid reservoir.
8. Disconnect the engine compartment light connector.
9. Remove the condensation drain hose.
10. Remove the air flow box.
11. Remove the duct between the evaporator and heater cases.
12. Disconnect the thermistor and switch harness connectors.
13. Remove the mounting screws and remove the evaporator case from the vehicle.
14. Disassemble the evaporator case and remove the evaporator.

To install:

15. Install the evaporator to the case and assemble. Carefully install the assembled case into the vehicle and tighten the mounting bolts.
16. Connect the thermistor and switch harness connectors.
17. Install the duct between the evaporator and heater cases.
18. Install the air flow box.
19. Install the condensation drain hose.
20. Connect the engine compartment light connector.
21. Install the windshield washer fluid reservoir.
22. Connect the air selection control cable.
23. Install the evaporator lines foot protector.
23. Install the glove box assembly.
24. Raise the vehicle and safely support.
25. Using new lubricated O-rings, connect the refrigerant lines to the evaporator fitting.
26. Evacuate and recharge the air conditioning system. If the evaporator was replaced, add 1 oz. of refrigerant oil during the recharge.
27. Connect the negative battery cable and check the entire climate control system for proper operation and leaks.

Refrigerant Lines

REMOVAL AND INSTALLATION

1. Disconnect the negative battery cable.
2. Raise the vehicle and safely support, if necessary. Properly discharge the air conditioning system.
3. Separate the flare connection. Always use a backup wrench when separating flare connections. If the line is equipped with a sealing plate, remove the nuts or bolts that attach the refrigerant lines sealing plates to the adjoining components.
4. Remove the line and discard the O-rings.

To install:

5. Coat the new O-rings refrigerant oil and install. Connect the refrigerant lines to the adjoining components and tighten the nuts, bolts or flare connections.
6. Evacuate and recharge the air conditioning system.
7. Connect the negative battery cable and check the entire climate control system for proper operation. Check the system for leaks.

Manual Control Head

REMOVAL AND INSTALLATION

1. Disconnect the negative battery cable.
2. Remove all control knobs from the control levers.
3. On Montero, remove the passenger side lap heater duct.
4. Remove the glove box assembly.
5. Remove the control head bezel. Some retaining screws may be hidden by garnish plugs which pop out.
6. Disconnect all control cables from the control head.
7. Remove the screws retaining the control head to the instrument panel.
8. Pull the control head out and disconnect all wiring connectors.
9. Remove the control head from the vehicle. Disassemble as required.

To install:

10. Connect the wiring and cables and install the control head. Secure with the retaining screws.
11. Connect the cables under the instrument panel.
12. Install the control head bezel.
13. Install the glove box assembly and lap heater duct.
14. Install the control knobs.
15. Connect the negative battery cable and check the entire climate control system for proper operation.

Manual Control Cables

ADJUSTMENT

Mode Selection Control Cable

1. Move the air changeover lever to the far right.
2. Disconnect the mode selection cable from the clamp at the front of the heater case.
3. Move the damper link all the way down and adjust the outer cable tension so the inner cable has no slack.
4. Secure the control cable with the clamp.
5. Check for smooth and proper operation.

Temperature Control Cable

1. Move the temperature control lever to the far left.
2. Disconnect the temperature control cable from the clamp at the front of the heater case.
3. With the blend air damper lever at the front of the heater case pulled up against the stopper, adjust the outer cable tension so the inner cable has no slack.
4. Secure the control cable with the clamp.
5. Check for smooth and proper operation.

Air Selection Control Cable

1. Move the air selection lever to the far right.
2. Disconnect the air selection control cable from the clamp at the air flow box.
3. With the air selection damper lever at the air flow box set all the way to the right, adjust the outer cable tension so the inner cable has no slack.
4. Secure the control cable with the clamp.
5. Check for smooth and proper operation.

REMOVAL AND INSTALLATION

1. Disconnect the negative battery cable.
2. Remove all control knobs from the control levers.
3. On Montero, remove the passenger side lap heater duct.
4. Remove the glove box assembly.
5. Remove the control head bezel. Some retaining screws may be hidden by garnish plugs which pop out.
6. Note the routing and disconnect all control cables from under the instrument panel.
7. Remove the screws retaining the control head to the instrument panel.
8. Pull the control head out and disconnect all wiring connectors.
9. Remove the control head from the vehicle. Disconnect the cables from the control head.

To install:

10. Feed the control cables through instrument panel opening in exactly the same position as before removal. Connect the wiring and install the control head. Secure with its retaining screws.
11. Connect the cables under the instrument panel.
12. Install the control head bezel.
13. Install the glove box assembly and lap heater duct.
14. Install the control knobs.
15. Connect the negative battery cable and check the entire climate control system for proper operation.

SENSORS AND SWITCHES

Dual Pressure Switch

OPERATION

The Van uses a dual pressure switch, which is a combination of a low pressure cut off switch and high pressure cut off switch. These functions will stop operation of the compressor in the event of either high of low refrigerant charge, preventing damage to the system. The switch is located on the refrigerant line near the receiver drier.

The dual pressure switch is designed to cut off voltage to the compressor coil when the pressure either drops below 30 psi or rises above 384 psi.

TESTING

1. Check for continuity through the switch. Under all normal conditions, the switch should be continuous.
2. If the switch is open, check for insufficient refrigerant charge or excessive pressures.
3. If neither of the above conditions exist and the switch is open, replace the switch.

REMOVAL AND INSTALLATION

1. Disconnect the negative battery cable.
2. Raise the vehicle and support safely. Properly discharge the air conditioning system.
3. Remove the switch from the refrigerant line.
4. The installation is the reverse of the removal installation.
5. Evacuate and recharge the air conditioning system.
6. Connect the negative battery cable and check the entire climate control system for proper operation. Check the system for leaks.

Low Pressure Cut Off Switch

OPERATION

On Montero and Pick-Up, the low pressure cut off switch monitors the refrigerant gas pressure on the suction side of the system. The switch is connected in series with the compressor and will turn off voltage to the compressor clutch coil when the monitored pressure drops to levels that could damage the compressor. The switch is located to the right of the condenser on Montero and on the refrigerant line near the receiver/drier on Pick-Up. It is a sealed unit that must be replaced if faulty.

TESTING

1. Start the engine and allow to idle. Turn the air conditioner ON.
2. Disconnect the switch connector and use a jumper wire to jump between terminals inside the connector boot.
3. If the compressor clutch does not engage, inspect the system for an open circuit.
4. If the clutch engages, connect an air conditioning manifold gauge to the system.
5. Read the low pressure gauge. The low pressure cut off switch should complete the circuit at pressures of at least 30 psi. Check the system for leaks if the pressures are too low.
6. If the pressures are nominal and the system works when the terminals are jumped, the cut off switch is faulty and should be replaced.

REMOVAL AND INSTALLATION

1. Disconnect the negative battery cable.
2. Properly discharge the air conditioning system.
3. Unplug the boot connector from the switch.
4. Using an oil pressure sending unit socket, remove the switch from the receiver/drier.

To install:

5. Seal the threads of the new switch with teflon tape.
6. Install the switch to the receiver/drier and connect the boot connector.
7. Evacuate and recharge the system. Check for leaks.
8. Check the switch for proper operation.

Refrigerant Temperature Sensor

OPERATION

Located on the rear of the compressor, the refrigerant temperature sensor detects the temperature of the refrigerant delivered from the compressor during operation. The switch is designed to cut off the compressor when the temperature of the refrigerant exceeds 347°F (175°C), preventing overheating.

TESTING

1. Measure the resistance across the switch terminals.
2. At 75–80°F, the resistance specification is about 80 kilo ohms.
3. If the reading deviates greatly from the specification, replace the sensor.

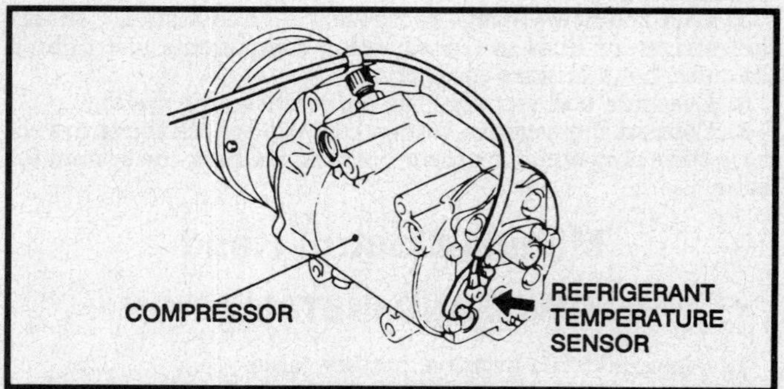
COMPRESSOR
REFRIGERANT
TEMPERATURE
SENSOR

Refrigerant temperature sensor

REMOVAL AND INSTALLATION

1. Disconnect the negative battery cable.
2. Properly discharge the air conditioning system.
3. Disconnect the connector.
4. Remove the mounting screws and the sensor from the compressor.
5. The installation is the reverse of the removal installation. Use a new lubricated O-ring when installing.
6. Evacuate and recharge the air conditioning system.
7. Connect the negative battery cable and check the entire climate control system for proper operation. Check the system for leaks.

Engine Coolant Temperature Switch

OPERATION

The engine coolant temperature switch, located on or near the thermostat housing, is connected in series with the compressor clutch relay. The switch is designed to cut off the compressor when the engine coolant temperature rises above 239°F (115°C), preventing engine overheating when the supply of cooling air is not sufficient for both the radiator and condenser.

TESTING

1. If the switch is suspect, unplug and jump across the terminals in the connectors.
2. To test the switch, remove the switch from the engine. The switch should be closed at room temperature.
3. Place the switch in an oil bath and heat to at least 222°F (108°C).
4. The switch should open when it reaches the above temperature.

REMOVAL AND INSTALLATION

1. Disconnect the negative battery cable. Drain out some of the coolant.
2. Unplug the connector.
3. Unscrew the switch from the thermostat housing.
4. The installation is the reverse of the removal installation. Use sealant on the threads when installing.
5. Refill the cooling system.
6. Connect the negative battery cable and check the entire climate control system for proper operation.

Electronic Cycling Clutch Switch

OPERATION

The electronic cycling clutch switch, used on 1989 Pick-Up, is mounted on the firewall near the expansion valve. This switch prevents evaporator freeze-up by cycling the compressor clutch coil by monitoring the temperature of the suction line. A thermistor probe in the capillary tube is inserted into a well on the suction line. The well must be filled with special conductive grease to prevent corrosion and allow thermal transfer to the probe. The switch is a sealed unit that should be replaced if defective.

TESTING

1. With the ambient temperature in the test area at 70°F (21°C), supply 12 volts to Pin 3 and ground Pin 2.
2. Check for continuity across Pins 1 and 2.
3. If the test shows continuity, check other parts of the circuit for defects.

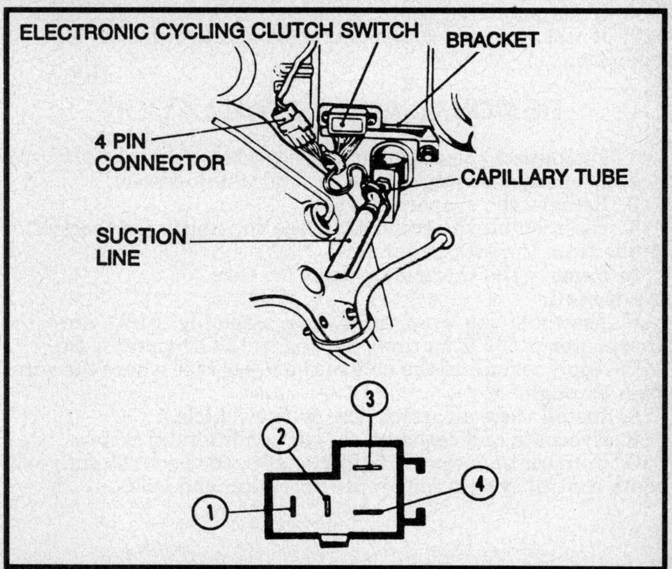
ELECTRONIC CYCLING CLUTCH SWITCH
BRACKET
4 PIN CONNECTOR
CAPILLARY TUBE
SUCTION LINE
1
2
3
4

Electronic cycling clutch switch and connector—1989 Pick-Up

4. If continuity is not detected, replace the switch.

REMOVAL AND INSTALLATION

1. Disconnect the negative battery cable.
2. Disconnect the connector.
3. Remove the mounting screws on the firewall.
4. Separate the switch from the firewall and pull the capillary tube out of the capillary tube well on the suction line.

NOTE: The capillary tube well is filled with special temperature conductive grease. If reusing the switch, try to save all the grease. If replacing the switch, new grease will be supplied in the replacement switch package.

To install:

5. Fill the well with the special grease and insert the capillary tube.
6. Mount the switch to the firewall.
7. Connect the connector.
8. Connect the negative battery cable and check the entire climate control system for proper operation.

Thermistor

OPERATION

Evaporator freeze up is controlled by a thermistor or thermostat. The body of the thermistor assembly is mounted to the evaporator case and the probe is inserted to the evaporator fins. The thermistor is connected in series with the compressor and will cut off voltage when the temperature of the evaporator drops below 37.4°F (3°C).

TESTING

1. If the compressor will not engage, disconnect the thermistor connector and jump across the wires.
2. Depress the air conditioning switch and turn the blower switch on.
3. Momentarily turn the ignition switch **ON**, without cranking, and listen for the click of the clutch engaging.

4. If the clutch engages, the problem is probably the thermistor. If not, inspect other parts of the system for proper operation.

REMOVAL AND INSTALLATION

1. Disconnect the negative battery cable.
2. Properly discharge the air conditioning system.
3. Remove the evaporator case.
4. Disassemble the evaporator case and unclip the thermistor probe from the evaporator fins.
5. Remove the thermistor from the case.

To install:

6. Assemble the evaporator case assembly. Make sure the thermistor probe is securely clipped to the evaporator fin.
7. Apply sealant to the hole in the lower case where the wires pass through.
8. Install the evaporator case to the vehicle.
9. Evacuate and recharge the air conditioning system.
10. Connect the negative battery cable and check the entire climate control system for proper operation and leaks.

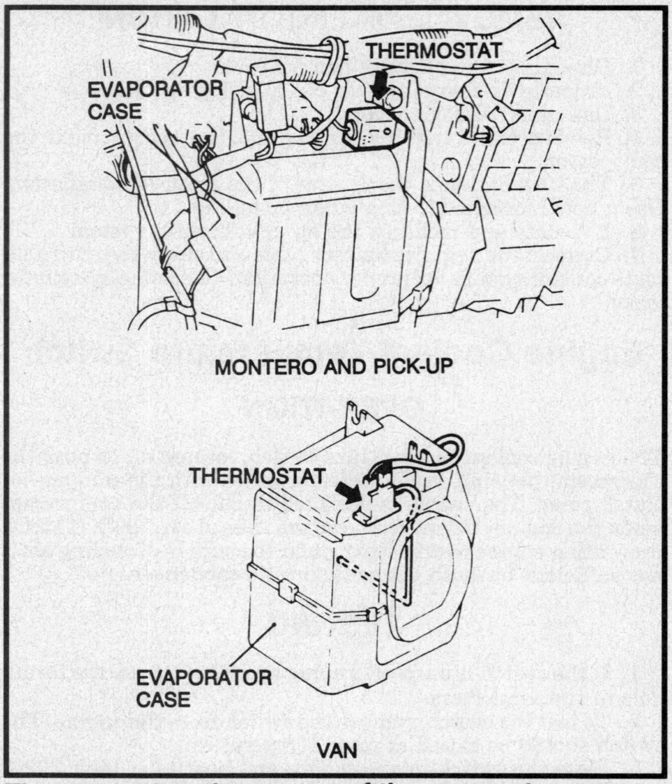
THERMOSTAT
EVAPORATOR CASE
MONTERO AND PICK-UP
THERMOSTAT
EVAPORATOR CASE
VAN
Thermostat location on top of the evaporator case

Vacuum Solenoid Valve

OPERATION

Vehicles equipped with carbureted engines have this valve. Its function is to raise the idle when the compressor comes on, in order to compensate for the added load on the engine. Typically, the idle should increase about 50 rpm when the compressor cycles on. It is an electrically controlled vacuum device located on the firewall near the windshield wiper motor.

TESTING

1. With the compressor clutch engaged, check for 12 volts and ground at the solenoid connector.
2. Check for adequate vacuum into and out of the vacuum fittings on the solenoid.
3. Visually check for movement of the link to the throttle plate lever.
4. Repair any problem detected and recheck the system.

REMOVAL AND INSTALLATION

1. Disconnect the negative battery cable.
2. Matchmark and carefully disconnect the vacuum hoses from the fittings on the solenoid by pulling straight out.
3. Disconnect the electrical connector.
4. Remove the mounting screw and remove the solenoid from the firewall.
5. The installation is the reverse of the removal procedure.
6. Connect the negative battery cable and check for proper operation.

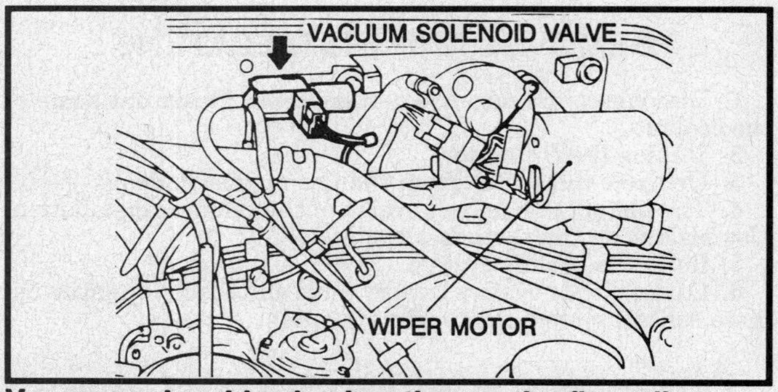
VACUUM SOLENOID VALVE
WIPER MOTOR
Vacuum solenoid valve location on the firewall

System Relays

OPERATION

Many of the systems within the air conditioning systems use relays to send current on its way and energize various components. The relays are positioned throughout the vehicles and many are interchangeable. All are conventional relays with internal contacts and a coil which pulls the contacts closed when energized.

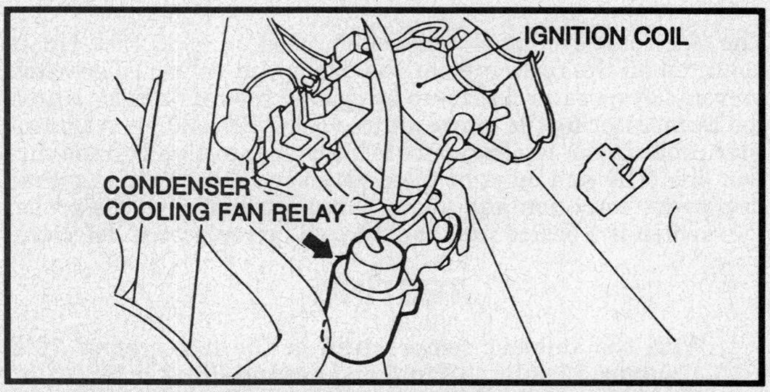
IGNITION COIL
CONDENSER
COOLING FAN RELAY
Condenser cooling fan relay at the left front of the engine compartment—Montero

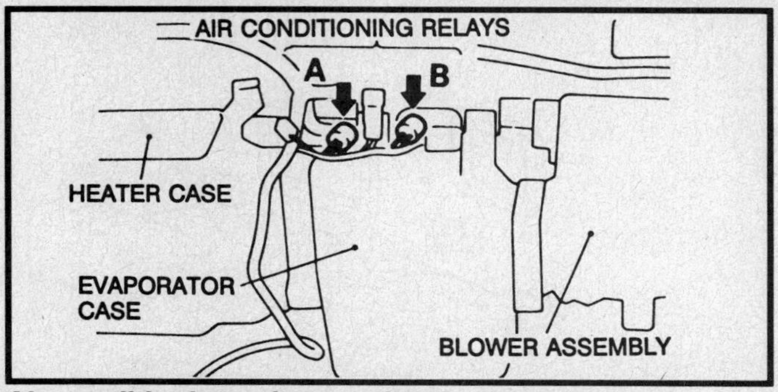
AIR CONDITIONING RELAYS
A
B
HEATER CASE
EVAPORATOR CASE
BLOWER ASSEMBLY

Air conditioning relays under the instrument panel—Montero

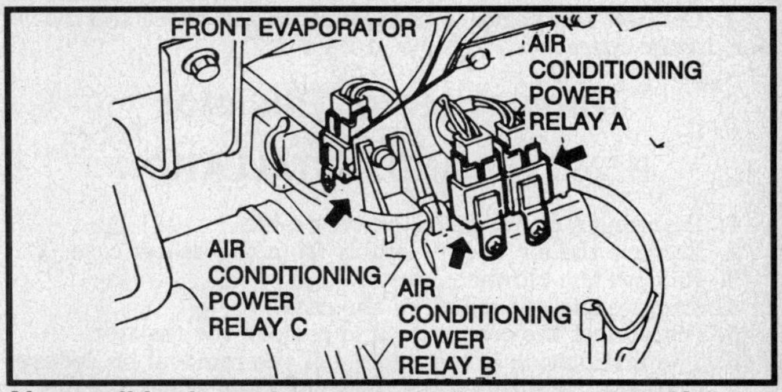
FRONT EVAPORATOR
AIR CONDITIONING POWER RELAY A
AIR CONDITIONING POWER RELAY C
AIR CONDITIONING POWER RELAY B

Air conditioning relays behind the glove box—Van

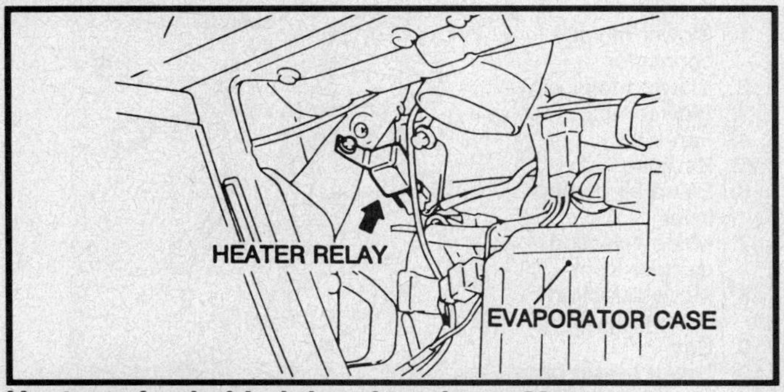
HEATER RELAY
EVAPORATOR CASE

Heater relay behind the glove box—Montero

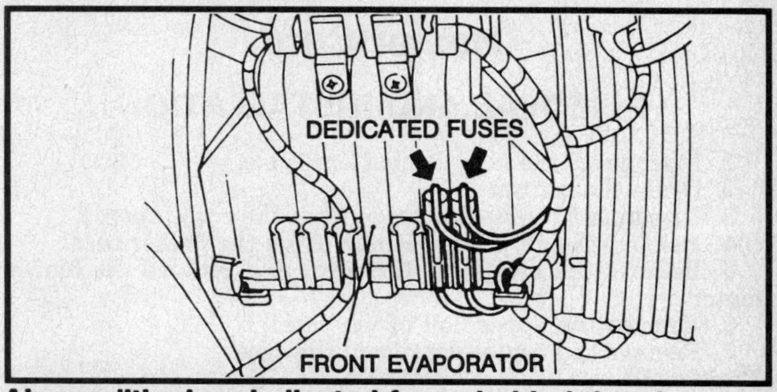
DEDICATED FUSES
FRONT EVAPORATOR

Air conditioning dedicated fuses behind the glove box—Van

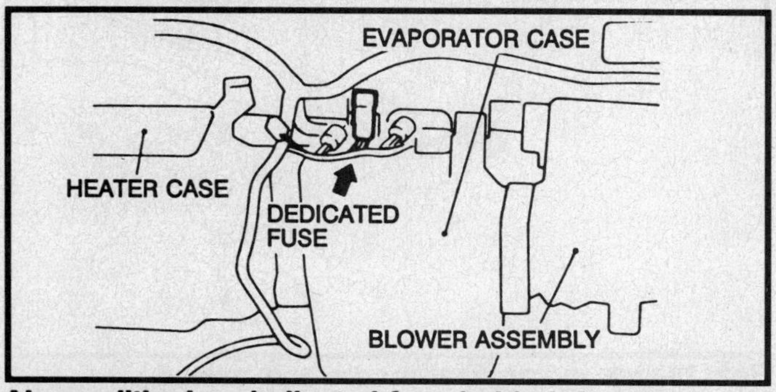
EVAPORATOR CASE
HEATER CASE
DEDICATED FUSE
BLOWER ASSEMBLY

Air conditioning dedicated fuse behind the glove box—Montero

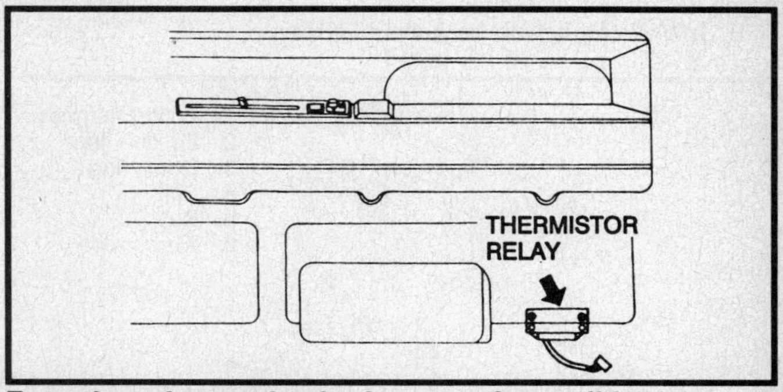
THERMISTOR RELAY

Rear thermistor relay in the rear air conditioning housing—Van

REAR AUXILIARY SYSTEM

Expansion Valve

REMOVAL AND INSTALLATION

1. Disconnect the negative battery cable.
2. Properly discharge the air conditioning system.
3. Remove the evaporator housing and separate the upper and lower cases.
4. Remove the expansion valve from the evaporator lines. Be sure to use 2 wrenches to separate the fittings.
5. The installation is the reverse of the removal installation. Use new lubricated O-rings when assembling.
6. Evacuate and recharge the air conditioning system.
7. Connect the negative battery cable and check the entire climate control system for proper operation. Check the system for leaks.

Blower Motor

REMOVAL AND INSTALLATION

1. Disconnect the negative battery cable.
2. Disconnect the blower motor connector.
3. Remove the blower motor cover.
4. Remove the vent hose.
5. Remove the blower motor retaining screws and remove the assembly from the housing. Remove the fan from the motor.
6. The installation is the reverse of the removal procedure.

7. Connect the negative battery cable and check the blower for proper operation.

Blower Motor Resistor

REMOVAL AND INSTALLATION

1. Disconnect the negative battery cable.
2. Remove the air duct assembly from the heater case.
3. Remove the blower motor.
4. Remove the upper half of the case.
5. Disconnect the connector and remove the resistor.
6. The installation is the reverse of the removal procedure.
7. Connect the negative battery cable and check for proper operation.

Heater Core

REMOVAL AND INSTALLATION

1. Disconnect the negative battery cable.
2. Drain the coolant.
3. Disconnect the heater hoses from the core tubes.
4. Remove the air duct assembly from the heater case.
5. Remove the blower motor cover and remove the blower motor.
6. Remove the upper half of the case.
7. Remove the heater core from the case.

To install:

8. Install the heater core to the case and assemble the cases. When attaching the upper half of the case, make sure the duct seals do not get dislodged.
9. Install the blower motor and cover.

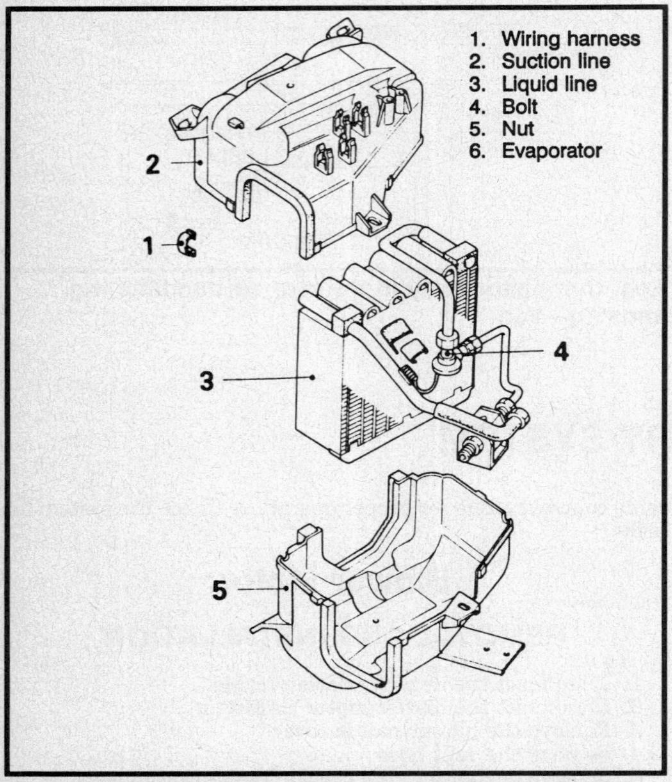
1. Wiring harness
2. Suction line
3. Liquid line
4. Bolt
5. Nut
6. Evaporator
1
2
3
4
5

Rear evaporator assembly and related components—Van

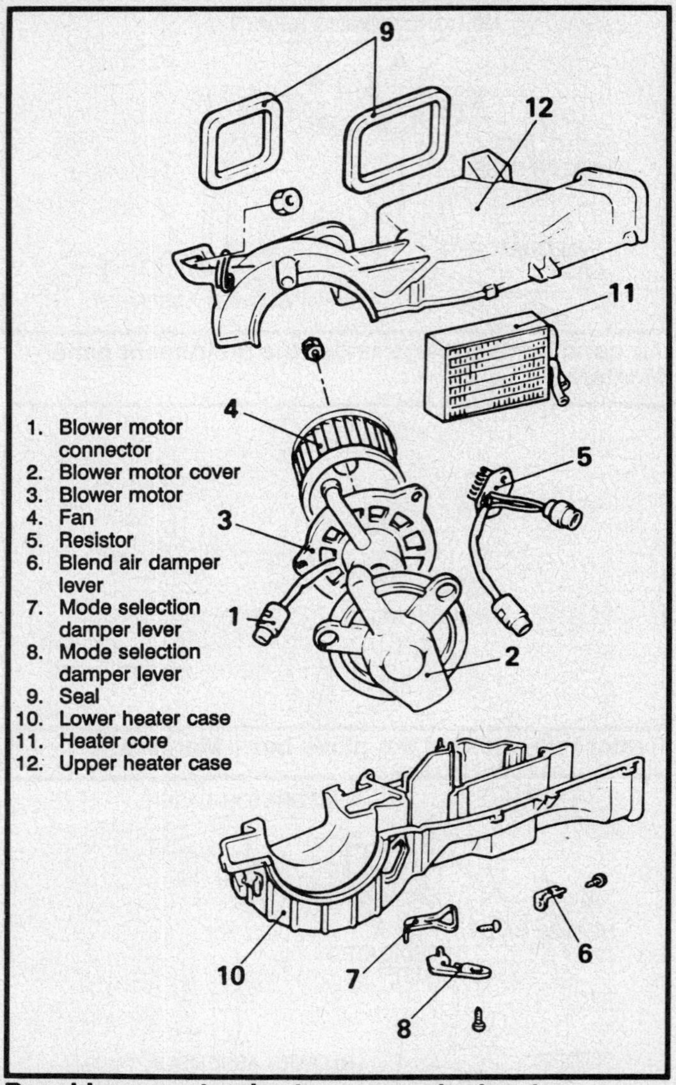
1. Blower motor connector
2. Blower motor cover
3. Blower motor
4. Fan
5. Resistor
6. Blend air damper lever
7. Mode selection damper lever
8. Mode selection damper lever
9. Seal
10. Lower heater case
11. Heater core
12. Upper heater case
1
2
3
4
5
6
7
8
9
10
11
12

Rear blower motor, heater core and related components—Van

10. Install the air duct assembly to the case.
11. Connect the heater hoses to the heater core tubes.
12. Fill the system with coolant.
13. Connect the negative battery cable and check the heater for proper operation.

Evaporator

REMOVAL AND INSTALLATION

1. Disconnect the negative battery cable.
2. Properly discharge the air conditioning system.
3. Disconnect the electrical connector at the case.
4. Disconnect the refrigerant lines from the evaporator. Cover the exposed ends of the lines to minimize contamination.
5. Remove the mounting bolt and nut and remove the evaporator case from the vehicle.
6. Separate the upper evaporator case from the lower.
7. Remove the evaporator from the lower case.

To install:

8. Install the evaporator in its cavity in the lower case.
9. Assemble the cases and install the clip.
10. Install the assembly to the vehicle and secure with the nut and bolt.
11. Using new lubricated O-rings, connect the refrigerant lines to the evaporator.
12. Connect the electrical connector.
13. Evacuate and recharge the air conditioning system. If the evaporator was replaced, add 1 oz. of refrigerant oil during the recharge.
14. Connect the negative battery cable and check the entire climate control system for proper operation and leaks.

SYSTEM DIAGNOSIS

Air Conditioning Performance

PERFORMANCE TEST

Air temperature in the testing area must be at least 70°F (21°C) to ensure the accuracy of this test.

1. Connect a manifold gauge set the the system.
2. Set the controls to **RECIRC** or **MAX**, the mode lever to the **PANEL** position, temperature control level to the coolest position and the blower on its highest position.
3. Start the engine and adjust the idle speed to 1000 rpm with the compressor clutch engaged.
4. Allow the engine come to normal operating temperature and keep doors and windows closed.
5. Insert a thermometer in the left center panel outlet and operate the engine for 10 minutes. The clutch may cycle depending on the ambient conditions.
6. With the clutch engaged, compare the discharge air temperature to the performance chart.
7. If the values do not meet specifications, check system components for proper operation.

AIR CONDITIONING PERFORMANCE CHART—1989 PICK-UP

Ambient Temperature °F (°C)	Air Temperature at Center Panel Vent °F (°C)	Compressor Discharge Pressure PSI (kPa)	Compressor Suction Pressure PSI (kPa)
70 (21)	35–40 (2–4.5)	132–188 (930–1322)	18–21 (127–148)
80 (27)	35–41 (2–5)	152–220 (1070–1550)	18–23 (131–162)
90 (32)	35–42 (2–5.5)	172–252 (1210–1772)	19–25 (134–176)
100 (38)	35–43 (2–6)	190–280 (1335–2000)	19–27 (135–188)
110 (41)	35–44 (2–6.5)	200–300 (1400–2110)	19–28 (136–194)

AIR CONDITIONING PERFORMANCE CHART—1990–91 PICK-UP

Ambient Temperature °F (°C)	Air Temperature at Center Panel Vent °F (°C)	Compressor Discharge Pressure PSI (kPa)	Compressor Suction Pressure PSI (kPa)
70 (21)	37–40 (3–4.5)	110–190 (758–1310)	19–24 (131–165)
80 (27)	38–41 (3–5)	130–220 (900–1577)	20–26 (138–179)
90 (32)	39–42 (4–6)	160–260 (1100–1800)	21–27 (145–189)
100 (38)	40–45 (4–7)	190–290 (1310–2000)	22–28 (152–193)
110 (41)	40–46 (4–8)	220–320 (1515–2200)	23–29 (159–200)

AIR CONDITIONING PERFORMANCE CHART—MONTERO

Ambient Temperature °F (°C)	Air Temperature at Center Panel Vent °F (°C)	Compressor Discharge Pressure PSI (kPa)	Compressor Suction Pressure PSI (kPa)
70 (21)	35–41 (2–4)	90–121 (620–834)	18–30 (124–205)
80 (27)	35–42 (2–5)	102–142 (700–980)	19–32 (130–221)
90 (32)	36–43 (3–6)	122–165 (840–1140)	20–35 (138–241)
100 (38)	37–45 (3–7)	144–195 (993–1350)	21–37 (145–255)
110 (41)	37–50 (3–10)	164–220 (1130–1515)	22–40 (152–276)

AIR CONDITIONING PERFORMANCE CHART—VAN

Ambient Temperature °F (°C)	Air Temperature at Center Panel Vent °F (°C)	Compressor Discharge Pressure PSI (kPa)	Compressor Suction Pressure PSI (kPa)
70 (21)	39–50 (4–10)	108–165 (745–1140)	17–27 (117–186)
80 (27)	39–51 (4–11)	140–200 (960–1355)	18–29 (128–200)
90 (32)	40–52 (4–12)	170–230 (1177–1570)	21–31 (142–210)
100 (38)	41–54 (5–13)	200–260 (1392–1785)	22–32 (150–220)
110 (41)	42–55 (6–14)	235–290 (1618–2010)	24–35 (167–240)

Air Conditioning Compressor

COMPRESSOR NOISE

Noises that develop during air conditioning operation can be misleading. A noise that sounds like serious compressor damage may only be a loose belt, mounting bolt or clutch assembly. Improper belt tension can also emit a noise that can be mistaken for more serious problems. Check and adjust all possible causes of the noise, including oil level, before replacing the compressor.

COMPRESSOR CLUTCH INOPERATIVE

1. Verify refrigerant charge and charge, as required.
2. Check for 12 volts at the clutch coil connection. If voltage is detected, check the coil.
3. If voltage is not detected at the coil, check the fuse or fusible link. If the fuse is not blown, check for voltage at the clutch relay. If voltage is not detected there, continue working backwards through the system's switches, etc. until an open circuit is detected.
4. Inspect all suspect parts and replace as required.
5. When the repair is complete, perform a complete system performance test.

CLUTCH COIL TESTING

1. Disconnect the negative battery cable.
2. Disconnect the compressor clutch connector.
3. Apply 12 volts to the wire leading to the clutch coil. If the clutch is operating properly, an audible click will occur when the clutch is magnetically pulled into the coil. If a click is not heard, inspect the coil.
4. Check the resistance across the coil lead wire and ground. The specification is 3.4–3.8 ohms at approximately 70°F (20°C).
5. If not within specifications, replace the clutch coil.

WIRING SCHEMATICS

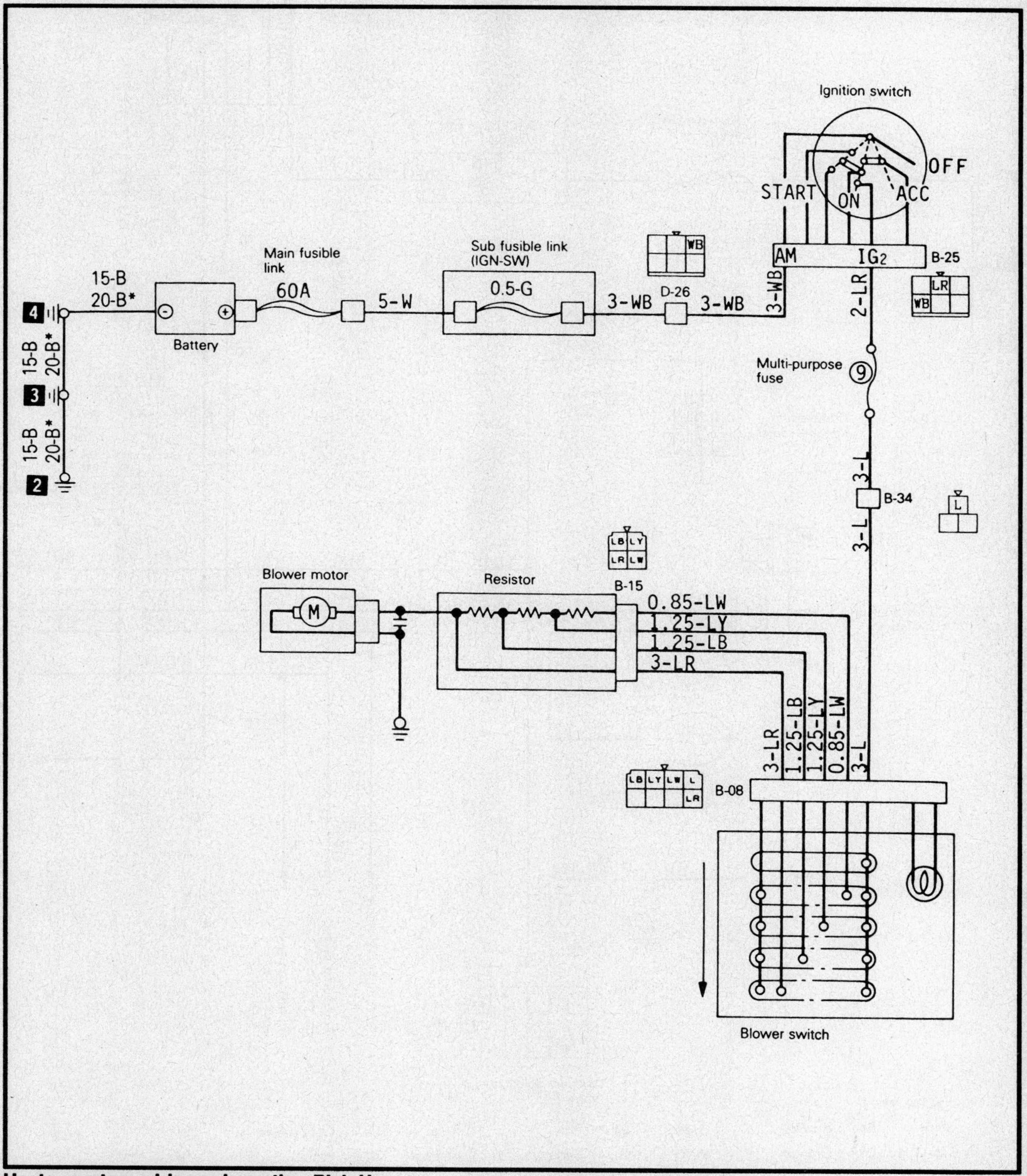
Ignition switch
OFF
START
ON
ACC
AM
IG2
B-25
Main fusible link
60A
Sub fusible link (IGN-SW)
0.5-G
15-B
20-B*
5-W
3-WB
D-26
3-WB
3-WB
2-LR
Battery
Multi-purpose fuse
9
3-L
B-34
3-L
Blower motor
M
Resistor
B-15
0.85-LW
1.25-LY
1.25-LB
3-LR
3-LR
1.25-LB
1.25-LY
0.85-LW
3-L
B-08
Blower switch

Heater system wiring schematic—Pick-Up

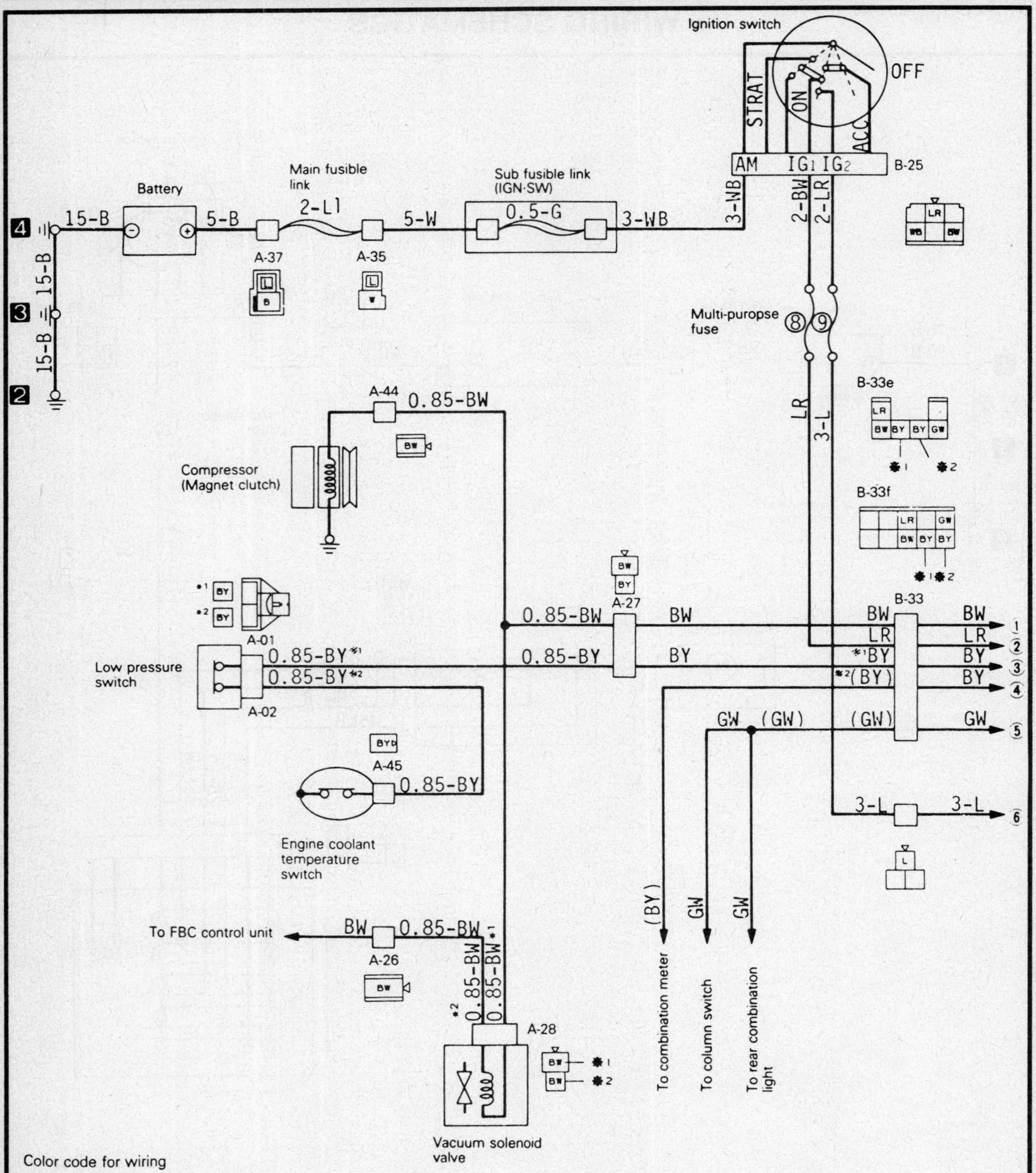
Ignition switch
OFF
STRAT
ON
ACC
AM
IG1
IG2
B-25
Battery
Main fusible link
2-L1
Sub fusible link (IGN·SW)
0.5-G
15-B
5-B
5-W
3-WB
2-BW
2-LR
A-37
A-35
Multi-puropse fuse
8
9
LR
3-L
B-33e
B-33f
A-44
0.85-BW
Compressor (Magnet clutch)
A-27
A-01
Low pressure switch
0.85-BY*1
0.85-BY*2
0.85-BY
A-02
B-33
BW
LR
BY
(BY)
GW
(GW)
A-45
Engine coolant temperature switch
3-L
To FBC control unit
A-26
0.85-BW*1
0.85-BW*2
A-28
Vacuum solenoid valve
To combination meter
To column switch
To rear combination light

Color code for wiring

B	: Black	Br	: Brown	G	: Green	Gr	: Gray	L	: Blue	Lg	: Light green
Ll	: Light blue	O	: Orange	P	: Pink	R	: Red	Y	: Yellow	W	: White

Air conditioning system schematic—1989 Pick-Up

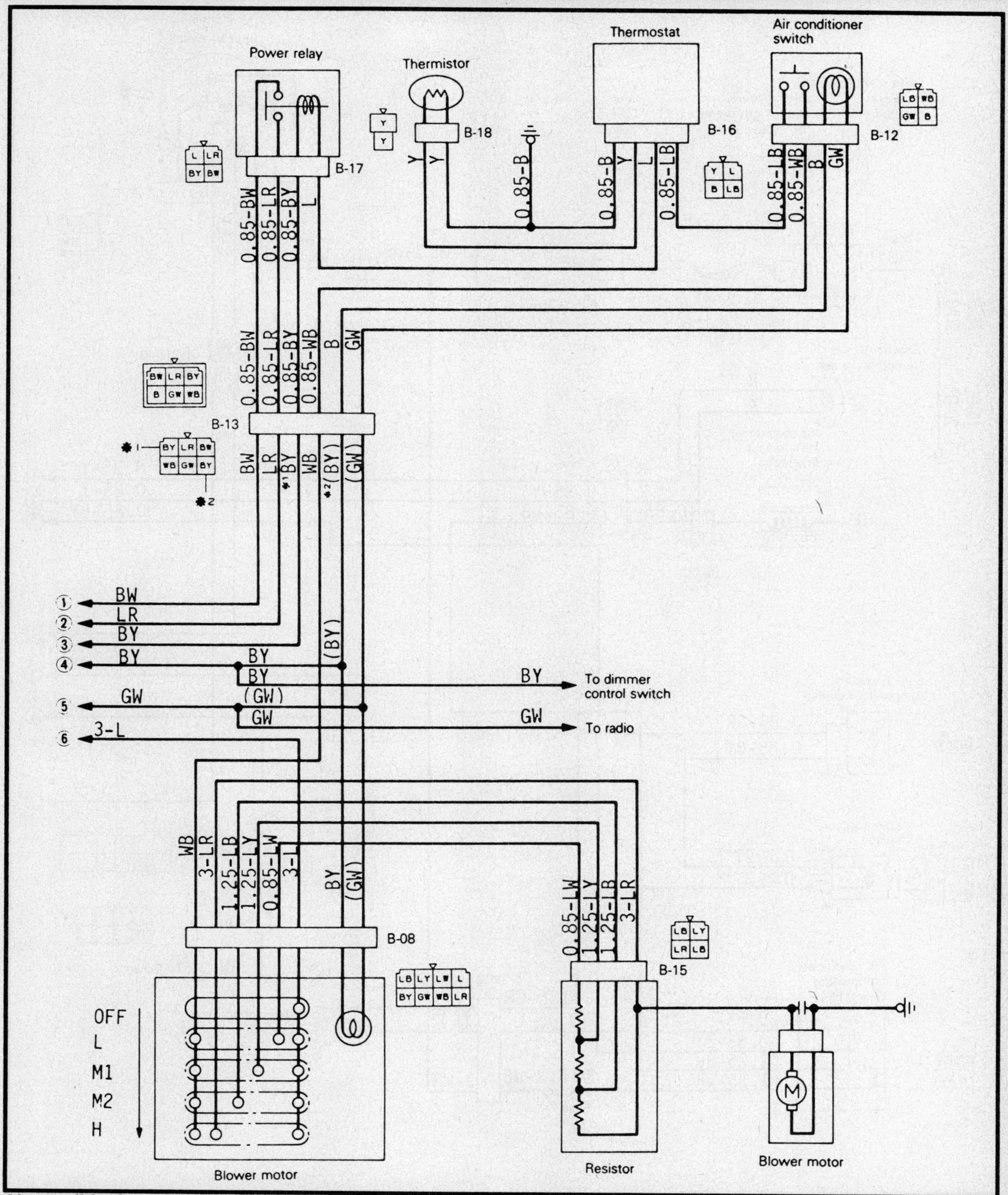
Power relay
Thermistor
Thermostat
Air conditioner switch
B-17
B-18
B-16
B-12
B-13
B-08
B-15
To dimmer control switch
To radio
Blower motor
Resistor
Blower motor
OFF
L
M1
M2
H

Air conditioning system schematic—1989 Pick-Up

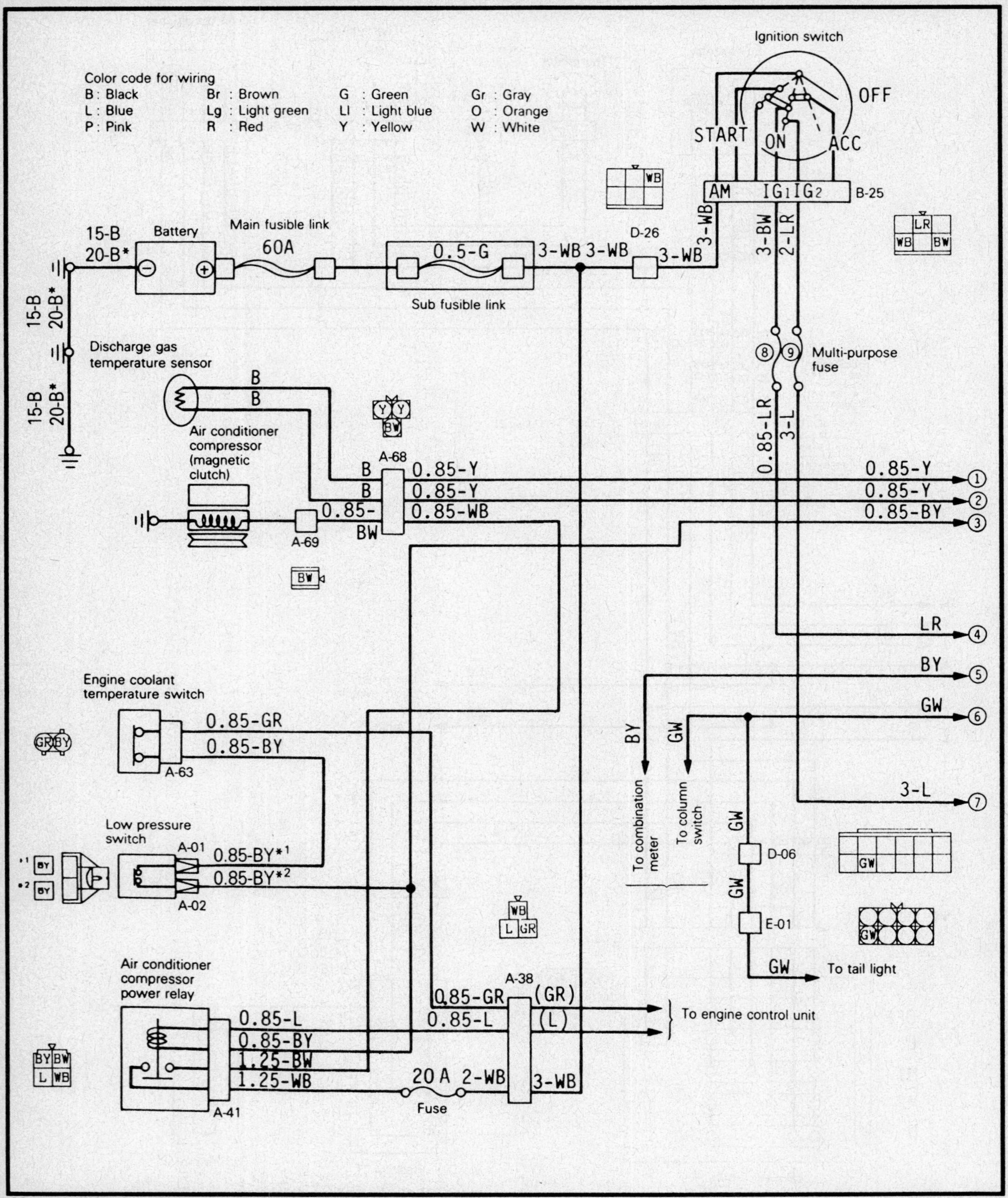
Color code for wiring
B : Black
L : Blue
P : Pink
Br : Brown
Lg : Light green
R : Red
G : Green
Ll : Light blue
Y : Yellow
Gr : Gray
O : Orange
W : White
Ignition switch
OFF
START
ON
ACC
AM
IG1 IG2
B-25
15-B
20-B*
Battery
Main fusible link
60A
0.5-G
Sub fusible link
3-WB
D-26
3-BW
2-LR
Multi-purpose fuse
0.85-LR
3-L
Discharge gas temperature sensor
B
Air conditioner compressor (magnetic clutch)
A-68
0.85-Y
0.85-WB
0.85-BY
0.85-BW
A-69
LR
BY
GW
To combination meter
To column switch
D-06
E-01
To tail light
Engine coolant temperature switch
0.85-GR
A-63
Low pressure switch
A-01
A-02
0.85-BY*1
0.85-BY*2
Air conditioner compressor power relay
A-38
(GR)
(L)
0.85-L
1.25-BW
1.25-WB
20 A
2-WB
Fuse
A-41
To engine control unit

Air conditioning system schematic—1990–91 Pick-Up

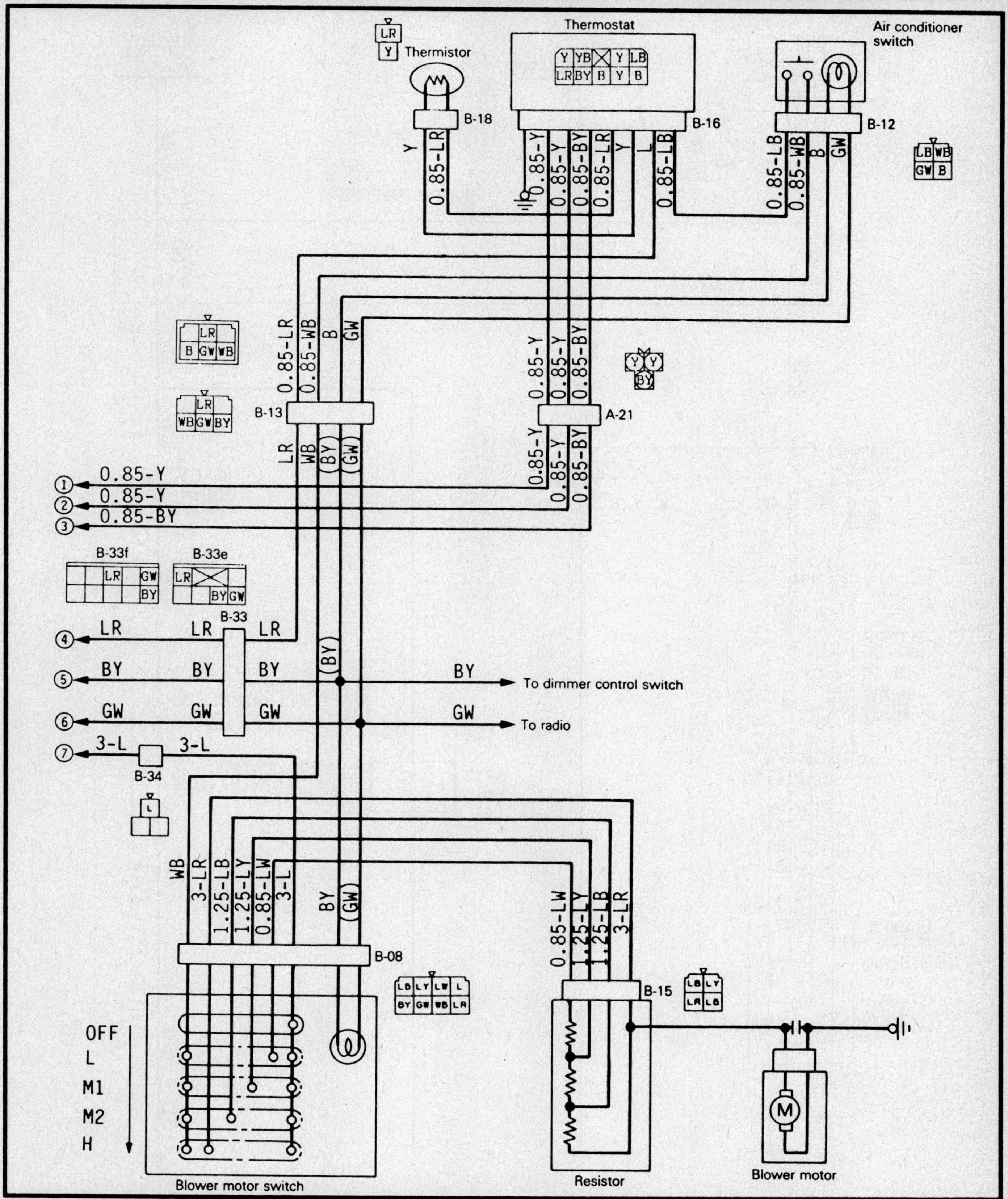
Thermostat
Air conditioner switch
Thermistor
B-18
B-16
B-12
B-13
A-21
B-33f
B-33e
B-33
B-34
B-08
B-15
0.85-Y
0.85-BY
LR
BY
GW
3-L
To dimmer control switch
To radio
OFF
L
M1
M2
H
Blower motor switch
Resistor
Blower motor

Air conditioning system schematic—1990–91 Pick-Up

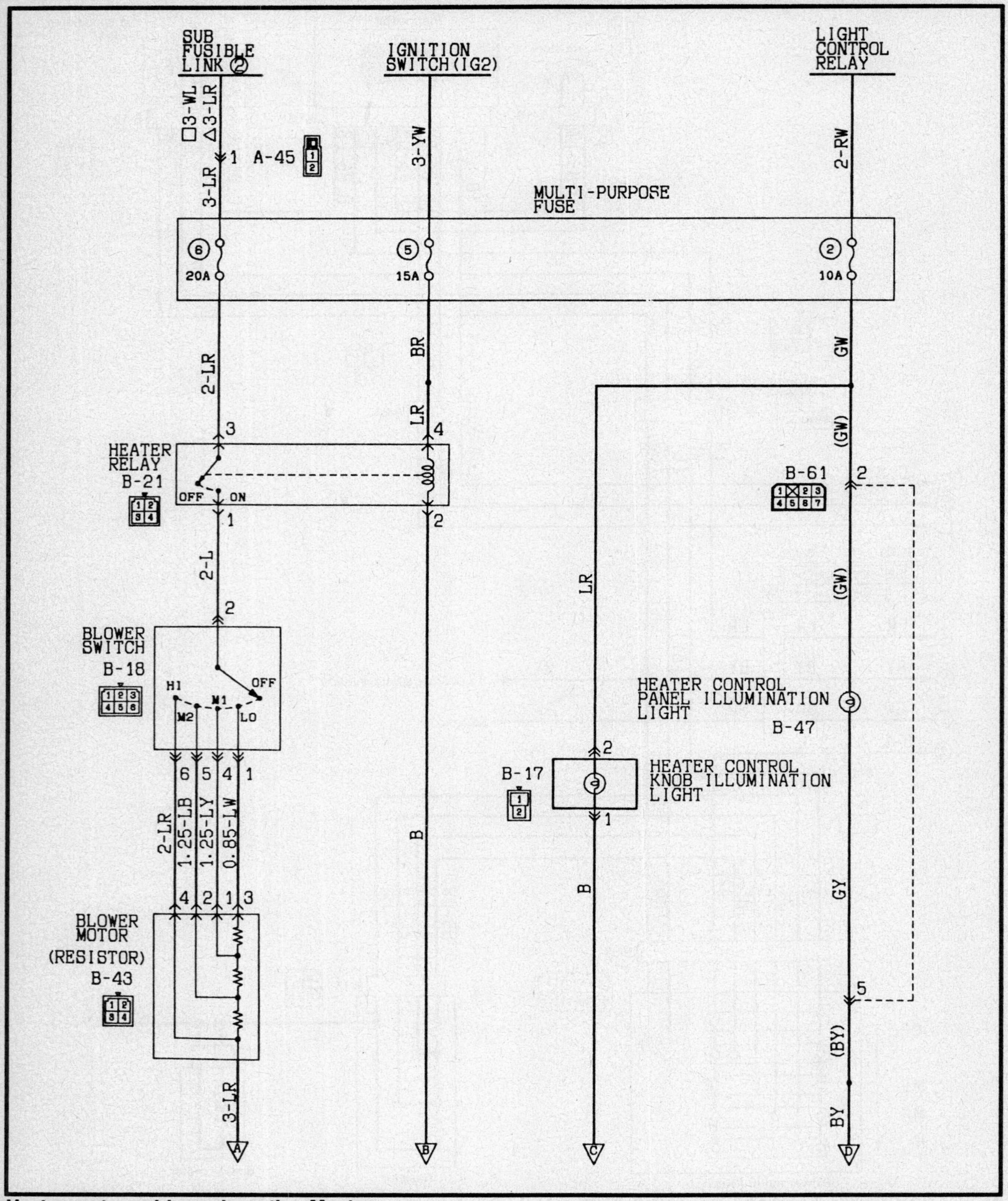
SUB FUSIBLE LINK ②
IGNITION SWITCH (IG2)
LIGHT CONTROL RELAY
□3-WL
△3-LR
A-45
3-LR
3-YW
2-RW
MULTI-PURPOSE FUSE
20A
15A
10A
2-LR
BR
GW
LR
(GW)
HEATER RELAY
B-21
OFF
ON
B-61
2-L
(GW)
LR
BLOWER SWITCH
B-18
HI
OFF
M2
M1
LO
HEATER CONTROL PANEL ILLUMINATION LIGHT
B-47
B-17
HEATER CONTROL KNOB ILLUMINATION LIGHT
2-LR
1.25-LB
1.25-LY
0.85-LW
B
B
GY
BLOWER MOTOR (RESISTOR)
B-43
(BY)
3-LR
BY
A
B
C
D

Heater system wiring schematic—Montero

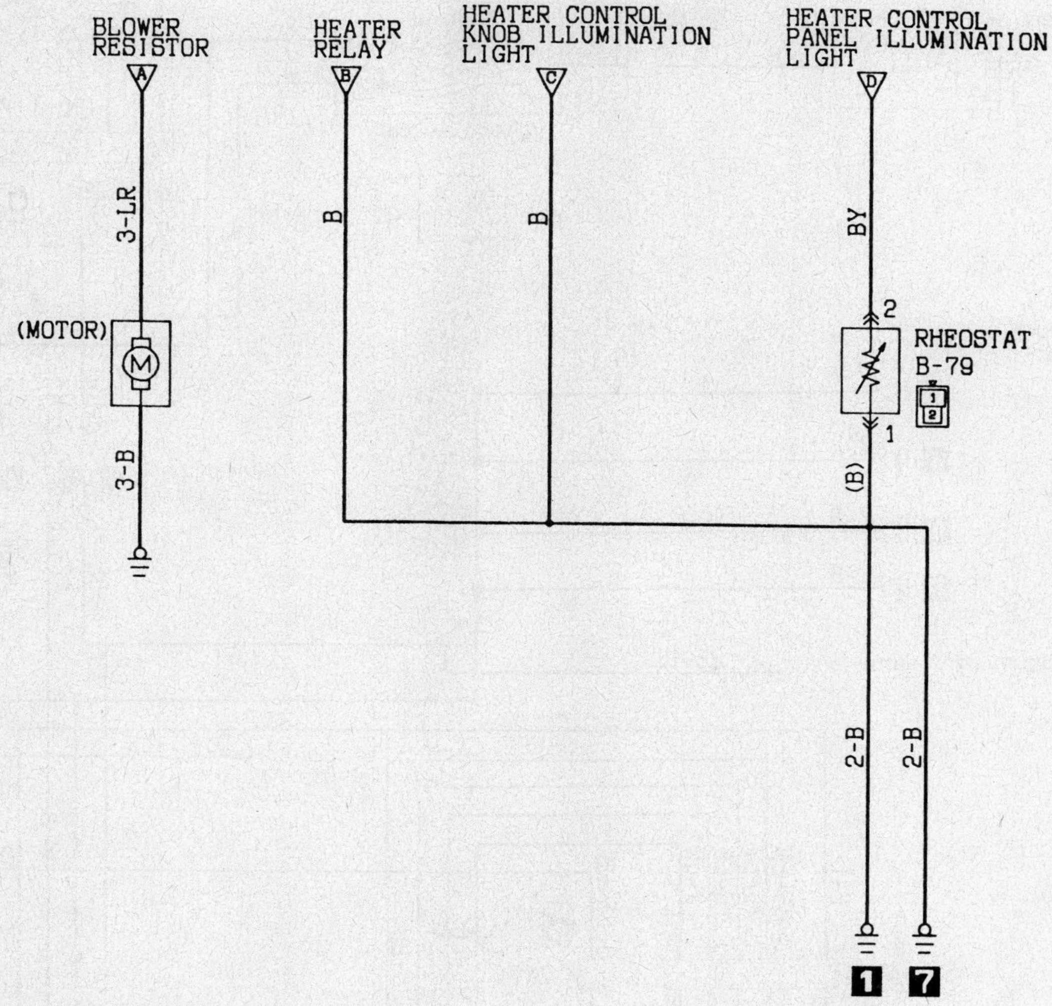
BLOWER RESISTOR
HEATER RELAY
HEATER CONTROL KNOB ILLUMINATION LIGHT
HEATER CONTROL PANEL ILLUMINATION LIGHT
A
B
C
D
3-LR
(MOTOR)
3-B
B
B
BY
2
RHEOSTAT
B-79
1
(B)
2-B
2-B
1
7

Remarks
(1) The wire cross-section area and colours indicated by the □ symbol is applicable to vehicles with 2.6L engine.
(2) The wire cross-section area and colours indicated by the △ symbol is applicable to vehicles with 3.0L engine.

Heater system wiring schematic—Montero

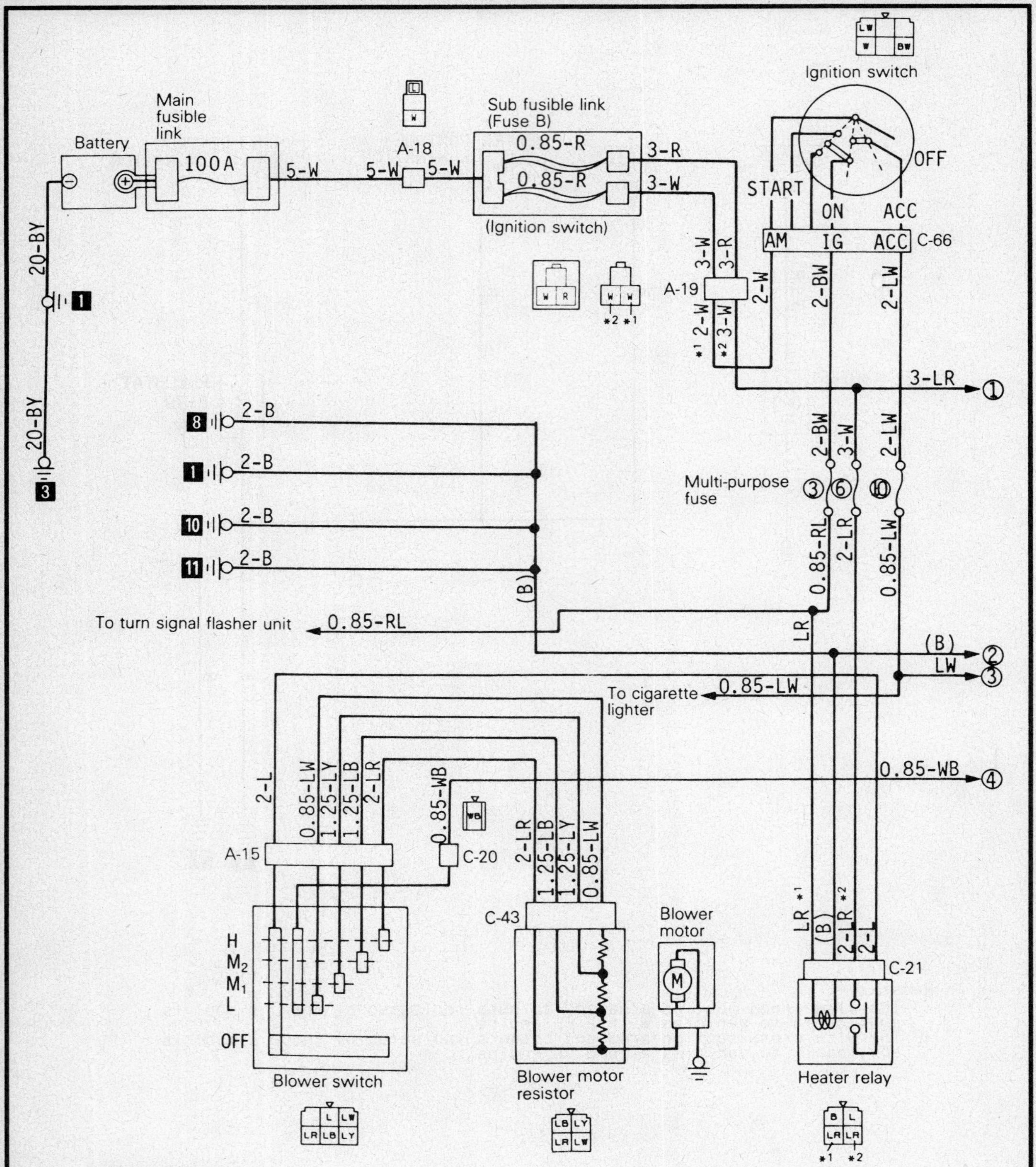
Ignition switch
Main fusible link
Battery
100A
5-W
A-18
Sub fusible link (Fuse B)
0.85-R
3-R
3-W
(Ignition switch)
START
OFF
ON
ACC
AM
IG
C-66
A-19
2-W
2-BW
2-LW
20-BY
3-LR
2-B
(B)
Multi-purpose fuse
0.85-RL
2-LR
0.85-LW
To turn signal flasher unit
LR
LW
To cigarette lighter
0.85-WB
2-L
1.25-LY
1.25-LB
A-15
C-20
C-43
Blower motor
H
M2
M1
L
OFF
Blower switch
Blower motor resistor
C-21
Heater relay

Wiring color code
B: Black Br: Brown G: Green Gr: Gray L: Blue Lg: Light green
Ll: Light blue O: Orange P: Pink R: Red Y: Yellow W: White

Air conditioning system schematic—Montero with 2.6L engine

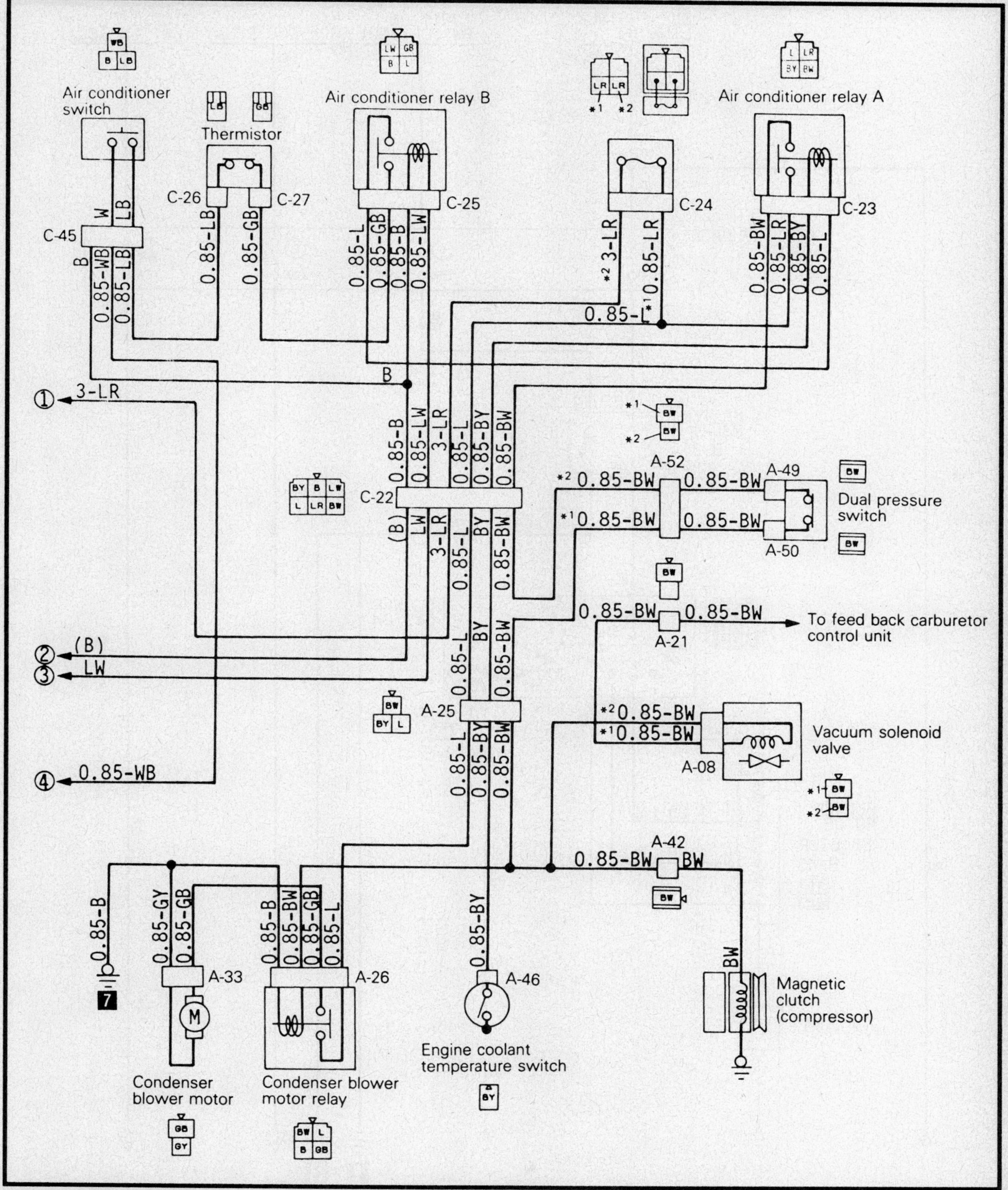
Air conditioner switch
Thermistor
Air conditioner relay B
Air conditioner relay A
C-45
C-26
C-27
C-25
C-24
C-23
C-22
0.85-WB
0.85-LB
0.85-GB
0.85-L
0.85-B
0.85-LW
*2 3-LR
*1 0.85-LR
0.85-BW
0.85-LR
0.85-BY
0.85-L *1
3-LR
(B)
LW
0.85-WB
A-52
A-49
A-50
*2 0.85-BW
*1 0.85-BW
Dual pressure switch
A-21
To feed back carburetor control unit
A-25
A-08
Vacuum solenoid valve
A-42
0.85-GY
A-33
A-26
A-46
Magnetic clutch (compressor)
Engine coolant temperature switch
Condenser blower motor
Condenser blower motor relay
7

Air conditioning system schematic—Montero with 2.6L engine

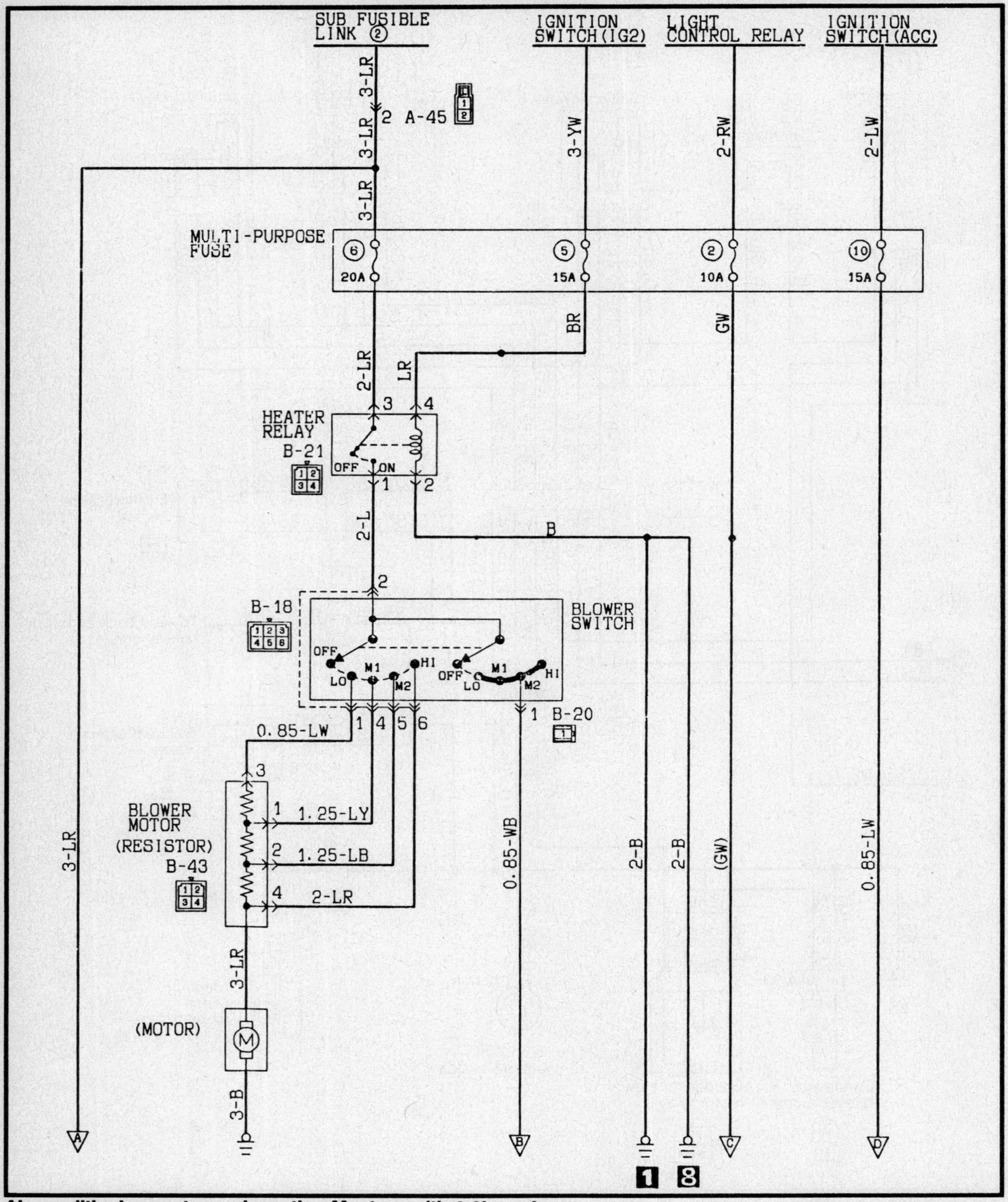
SUB FUSIBLE LINK ②
IGNITION SWITCH (IG2)
LIGHT CONTROL RELAY
IGNITION SWITCH (ACC)
3-LR
2 A-45
3-YW
2-RW
2-LW
MULTI-PURPOSE FUSE
⑥ 20A
⑤ 15A
② 10A
⑩ 15A
BR
GW
2-LR
LR
HEATER RELAY
B-21
OFF
ON
2-L
B
B-18
BLOWER SWITCH
OFF
LO
M1
M2
HI
B-20
0.85-LW
BLOWER MOTOR (RESISTOR)
B-43
1.25-LY
1.25-LB
2-LR
(MOTOR)
3-B
0.85-WB
2-B
(GW)
0.85-LW
A
B
C
D
1
8

Air conditioning system schematic—Montero with 3.0L engine

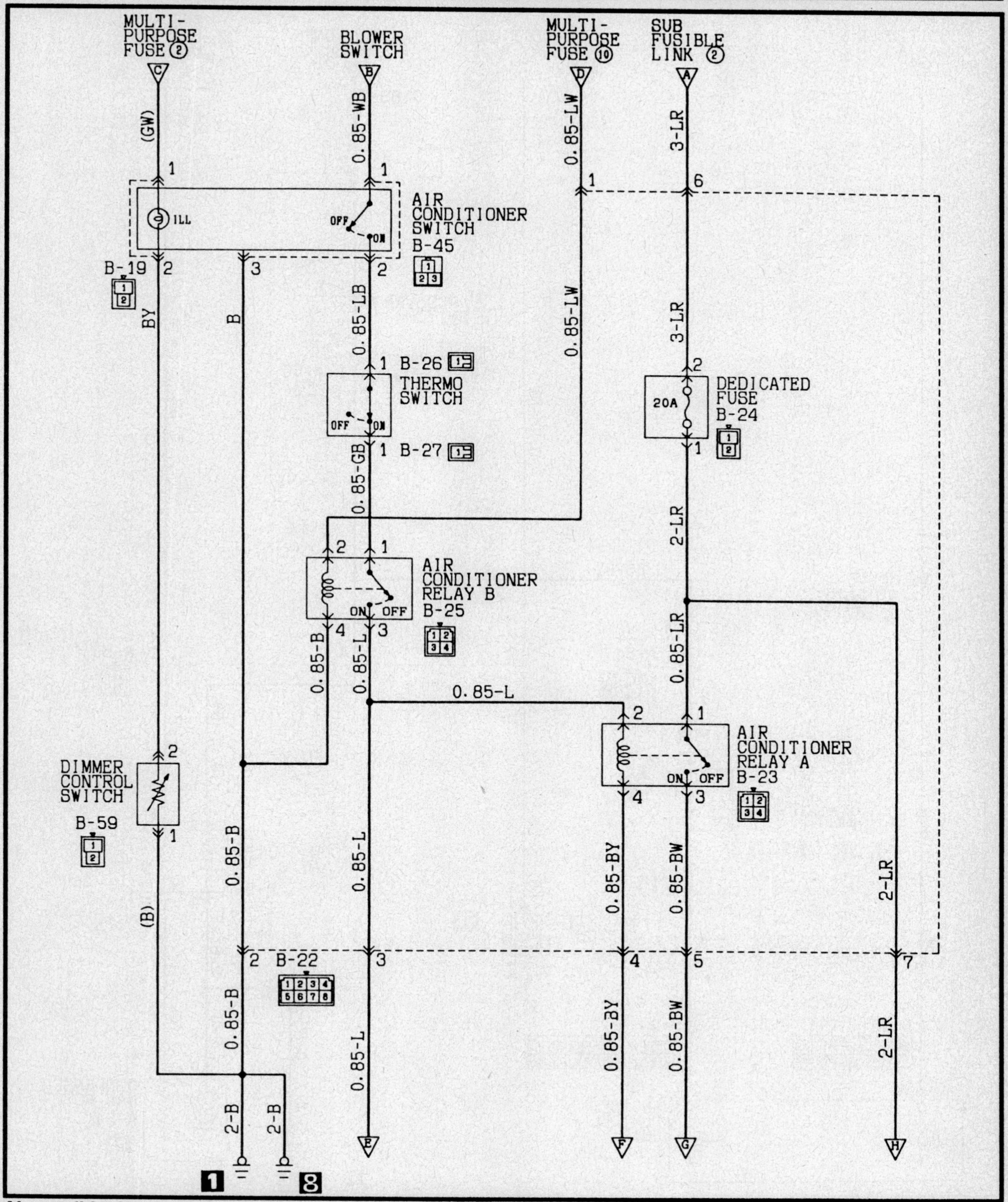
MULTI-PURPOSE FUSE ②
BLOWER SWITCH
MULTI-PURPOSE FUSE ⑩
SUB FUSIBLE LINK ②
C
B
D
A
(GW)
0.85-WB
0.85-LW
3-LR
ILL
OFF
ON
AIR CONDITIONER SWITCH B-45
B-19
BY
B
0.85-LB
B-26
THERMO SWITCH
B-27
0.85-GB
DEDICATED FUSE B-24
20A
2-LR
AIR CONDITIONER RELAY B B-25
0.85-B
0.85-L
0.85-L
0.85-LR
AIR CONDITIONER RELAY A B-23
DIMMER CONTROL SWITCH
B-59
(B)
0.85-B
0.85-BY
0.85-BW
2-LR
B-22
2-B
E
F
G
H
1
8

Air conditioning system schematic—Montero with 3.0L engine

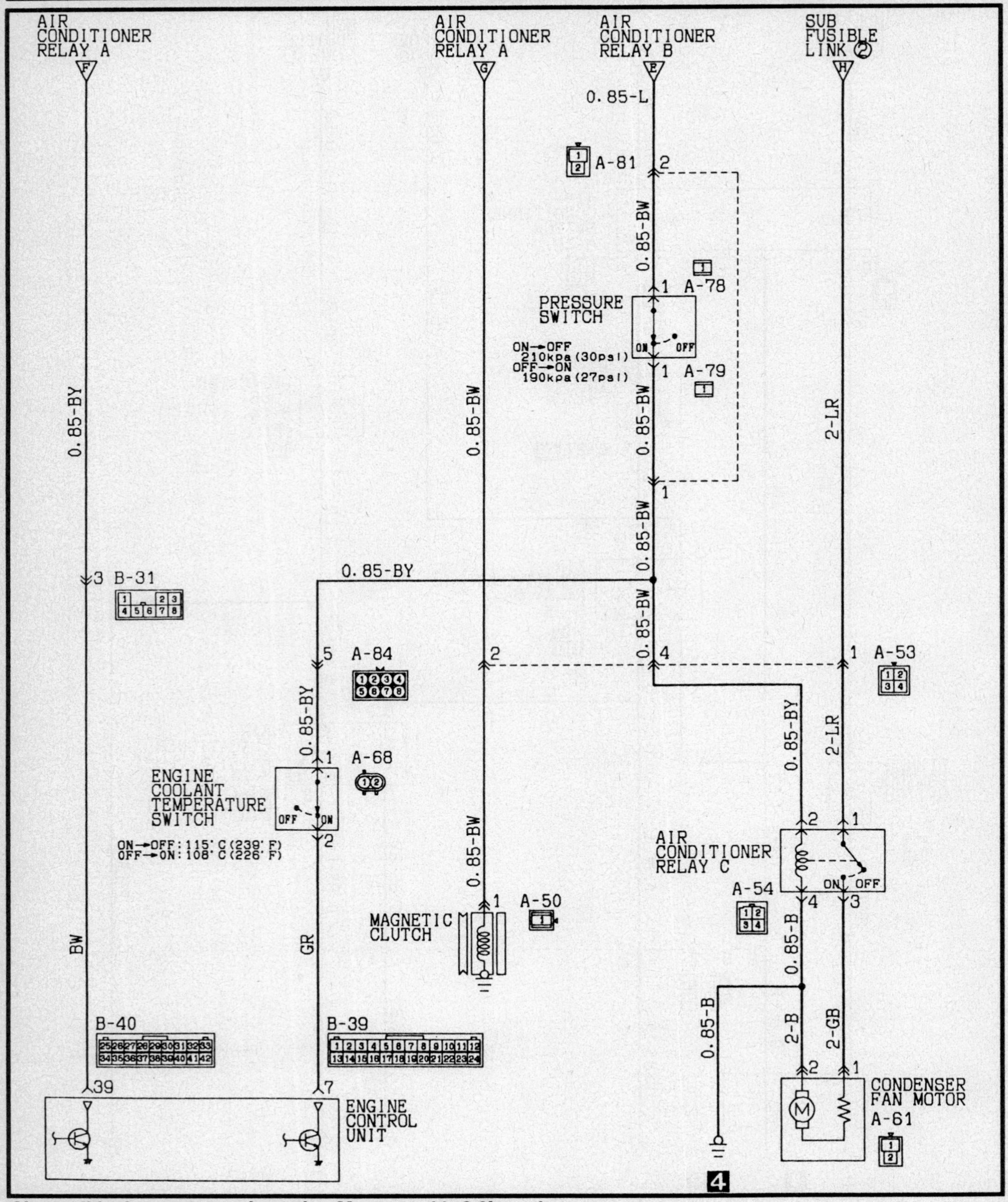
AIR CONDITIONER RELAY A
AIR CONDITIONER RELAY A
AIR CONDITIONER RELAY B
SUB FUSIBLE LINK ②
0.85-L
A-81
0.85-BW
A-78
PRESSURE SWITCH
ON→OFF 210kpa (30psi)
OFF→ON 190kpa (27psi)
A-79
0.85-BY
2-LR
B-31
A-84
A-53
A-68
ENGINE COOLANT TEMPERATURE SWITCH
ON→OFF: 115° C (239° F)
OFF→ON: 108° C (226° F)
AIR CONDITIONER RELAY C
A-54
A-50
MAGNETIC CLUTCH
BW
GR
0.85-B
2-B
2-GB
B-40
B-39
CONDENSER FAN MOTOR
A-61
ENGINE CONTROL UNIT
4

Air conditioning system schematic—Montero with 3.0L engine

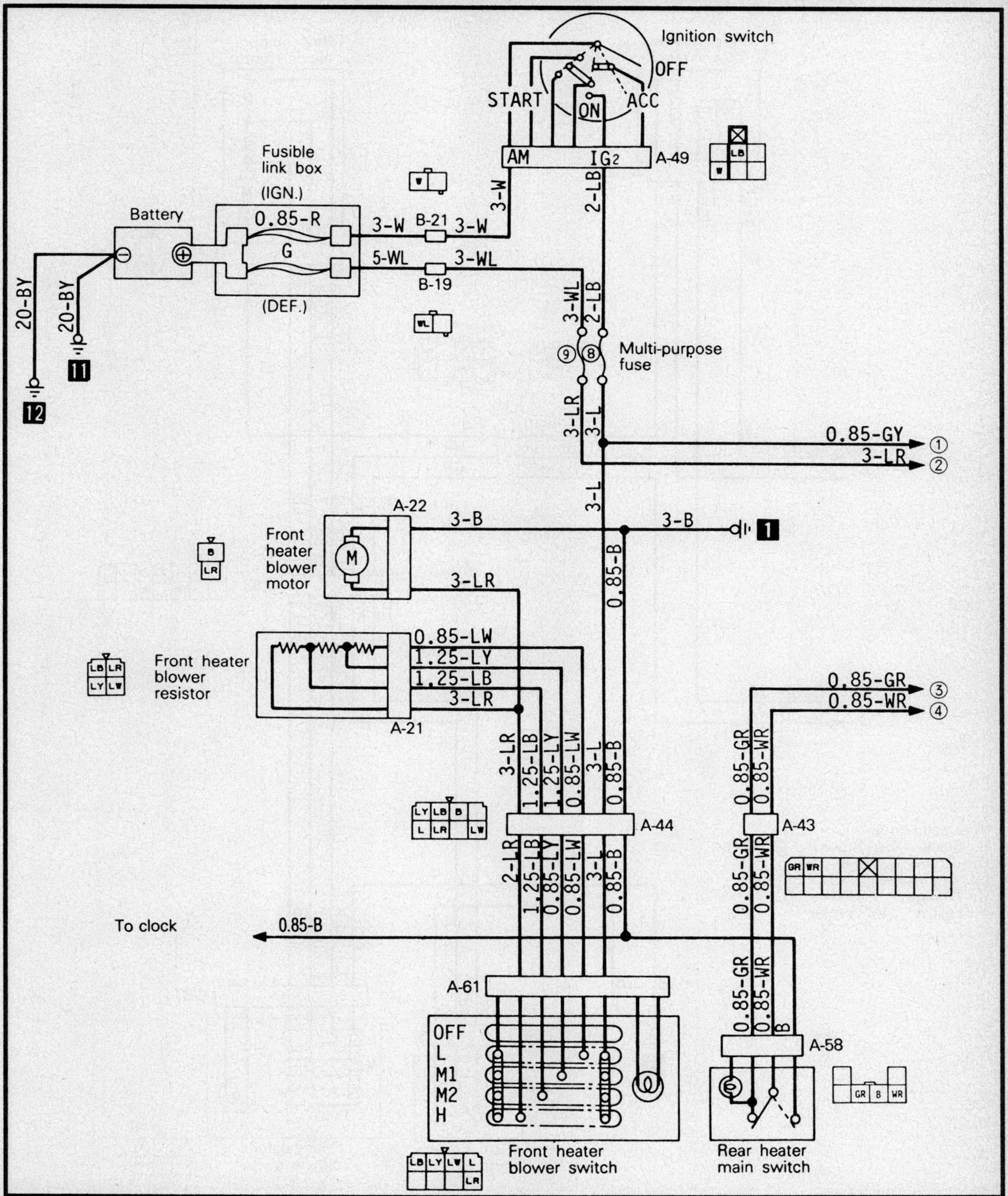
Ignition switch
OFF
START
ON
ACC
AM
IG2
A-49
Fusible link box
(IGN.)
Battery
0.85-R
G
(DEF.)
3-W
B-21
3-W
5-WL
3-WL
B-19
3-W
2-LB
20-BY
20-BY
11
12
3-WL
2-LB
9
8
Multi-purpose fuse
3-LR
3-L
0.85-GY
3-LR
1
2
A-22
3-B
3-B
1
Front heater blower motor
M
3-LR
3-L
0.85-B
Front heater blower resistor
0.85-LW
1.25-LY
1.25-LB
3-LR
A-21
0.85-GR
0.85-WR
3
4
3-LR
1.25-LB
1.25-LY
0.85-LW
3-L
0.85-B
0.85-GR
0.85-WR
A-44
A-43
2-LR
1.25-LB
0.85-LY
0.85-LW
3-L
0.85-B
To clock
0.85-B
A-61
OFF
L
M1
M2
H
Front heater blower switch
A-58
Rear heater main switch

Heater system—Van

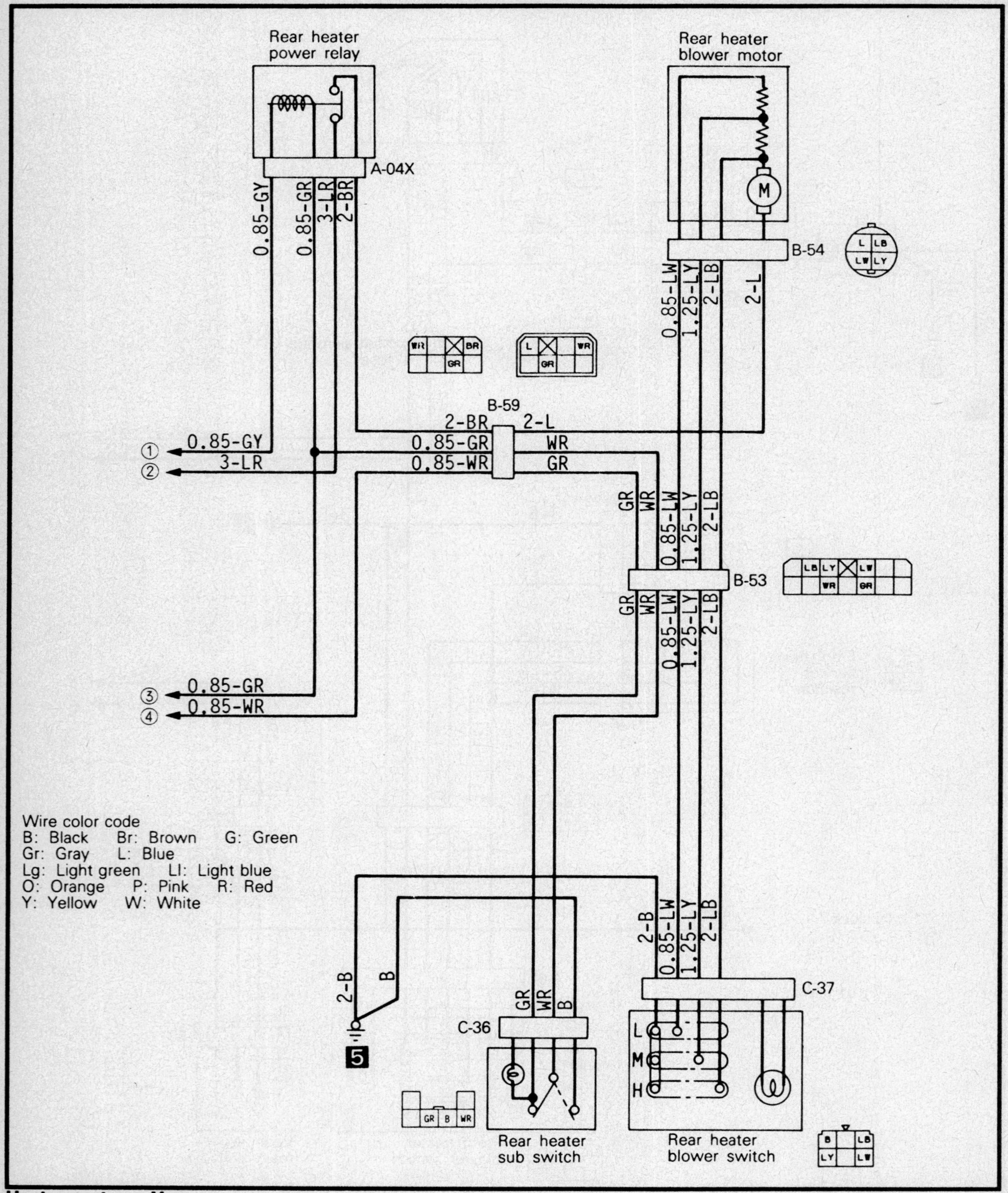
Rear heater power relay
A-04X
0.85-GY
0.85-GR
3-LR
2-BR
Rear heater blower motor
M
B-54
0.85-LW
1.25-LY
2-LB
2-L
B-59
2-BR
2-L
0.85-GR
WR
0.85-WR
GR
① 0.85-GY
② 3-LR
B-53
③ 0.85-GR
④ 0.85-WR
Wire color code
B: Black Br: Brown G: Green
Gr: Gray L: Blue
Lg: Light green Ll: Light blue
O: Orange P: Pink R: Red
Y: Yellow W: White
2-B
B
5
C-36
GR
WR
B
C-37
L
M
H
Rear heater sub switch
Rear heater blower switch

Heater system—Van

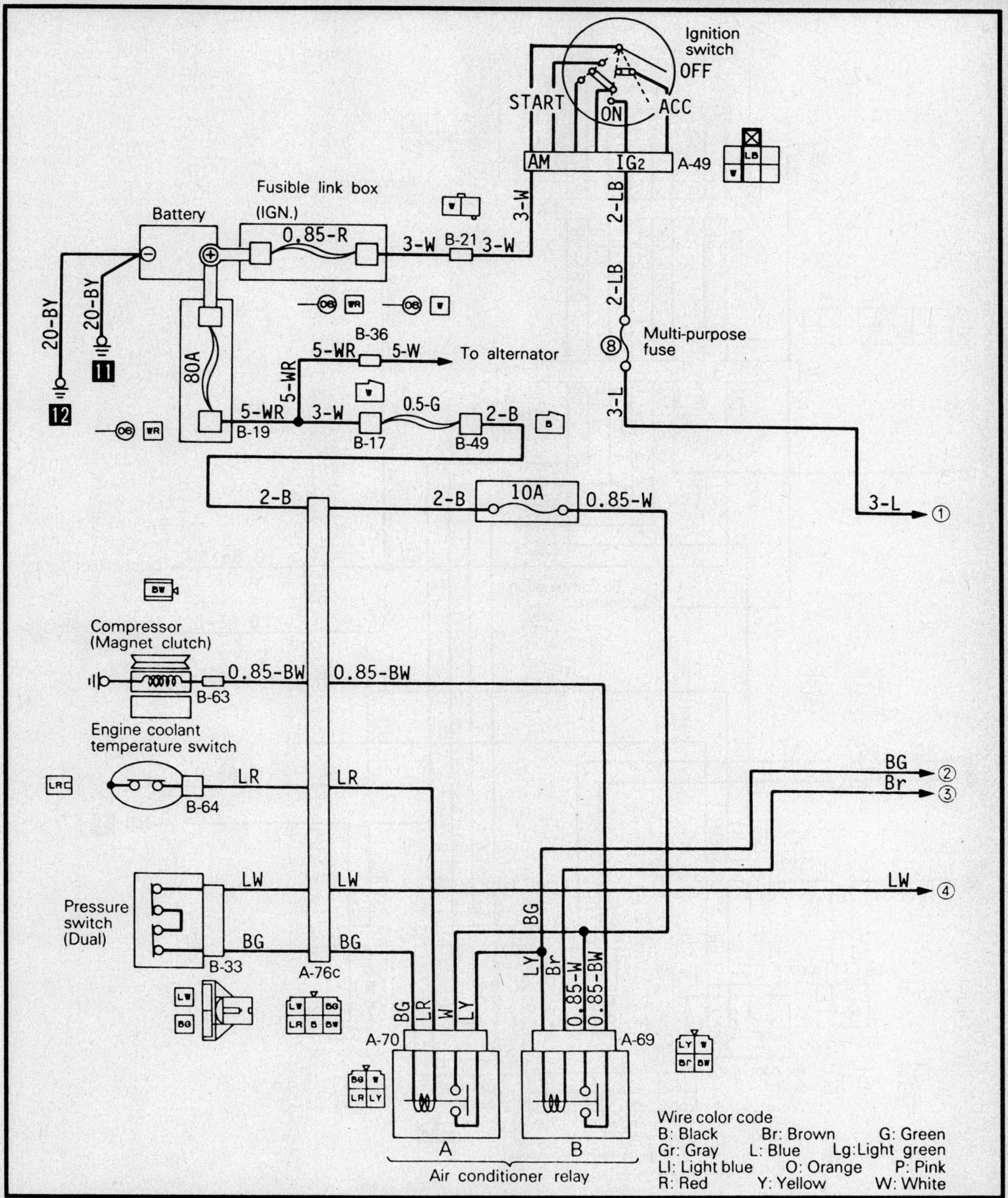
Ignition switch
OFF
START
ON
ACC
AM
IG2
A-49
Fusible link box (IGN.)
Battery
0.85-R
3-W
B-21
3-W
3-W
2-LB
2-LB
20-BY
20-BY
80A
B-36
5-WR
5-W
To alternator
5-WR
5-WR
B-19
3-W
0.5-G
2-B
B-17
B-49
Multi-purpose fuse
3-L
3-L
2-B
2-B
10A
0.85-W
Compressor (Magnet clutch)
0.85-BW
0.85-BW
B-63
Engine coolant temperature switch
LR
LR
B-64
BG
Br
Pressure switch (Dual)
LW
LW
LW
BG
BG
B-33
A-76c
BG
LR
W
LY
LY
Br
0.85-W
0.85-BW
A-70
A-69
A
B
Air conditioner relay
Wire color code
B: Black
Br: Brown
G: Green
Gr: Gray
L: Blue
Lg: Light green
Ll: Light blue
O: Orange
P: Pink
R: Red
Y: Yellow
W: White

Single air conditioning system wiring schematic—Van

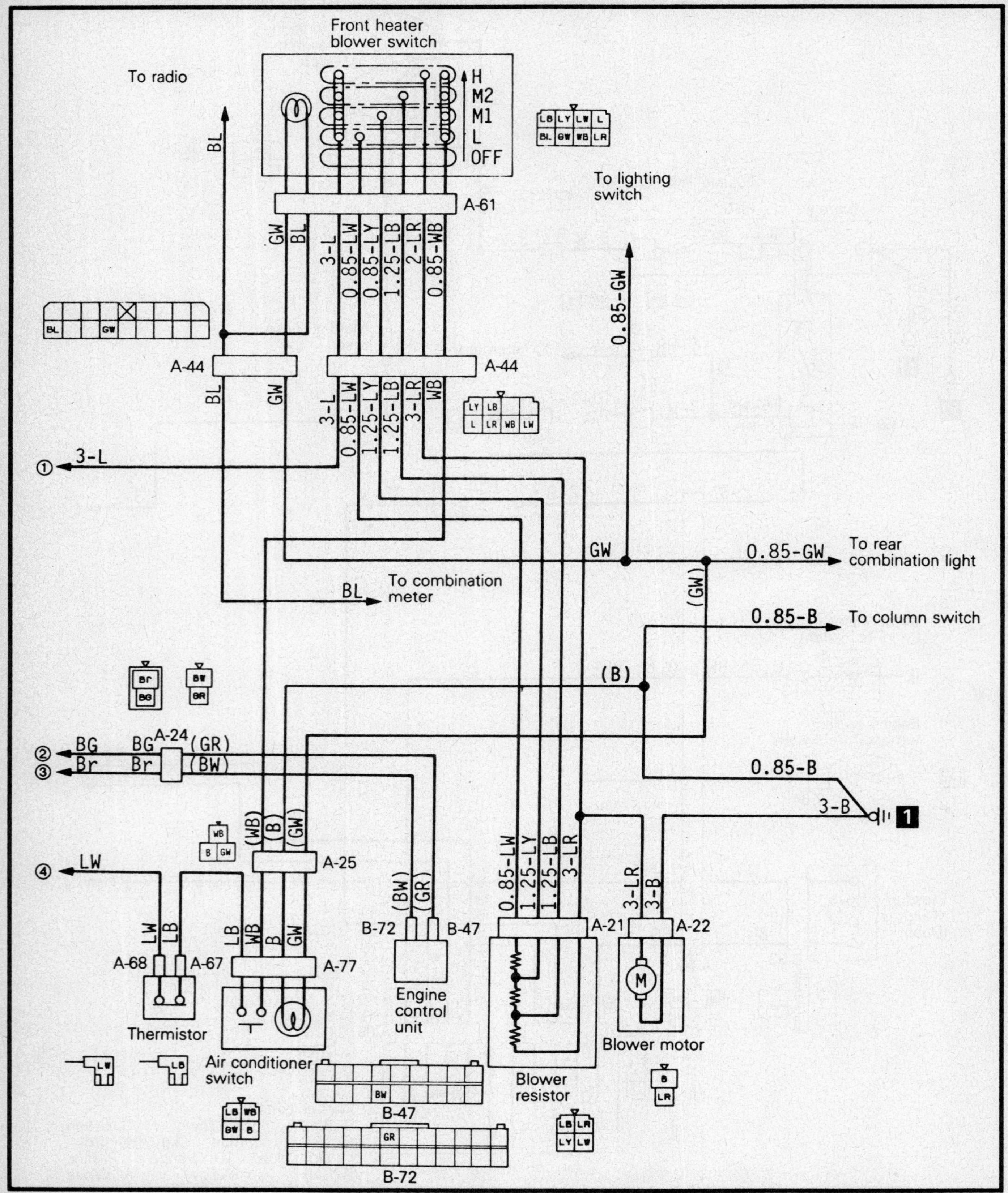
Front heater blower switch
H
M2
M1
L
OFF
To radio
BL
To lighting switch
A-61
GW
BL
3-L
0.85-LW
0.85-LY
1.25-LB
2-LR
0.85-WB
0.85-GW
A-44
A-44
BL
GW
3-L
0.85-LW
1.25-LY
1.25-LB
3-LR
WB
3-L
GW
0.85-GW
To rear combination light
BL
To combination meter
(GW)
0.85-B
To column switch
(B)
BG
BG
A-24
(GR)
Br
Br
(BW)
0.85-B
3-B
1
(WB)
(B)
(GW)
A-25
LW
(BW)
(GR)
B-72
B-47
0.85-LW
1.25-LY
1.25-LB
3-LR
A-21
3-LR
3-B
A-22
LW
LB
A-68
A-67
LB
WB
B
GW
A-77
Engine control unit
Thermistor
Air conditioner switch
Blower motor
Blower resistor
B-47
B-72

Single air conditioning system wiring schematic—Van

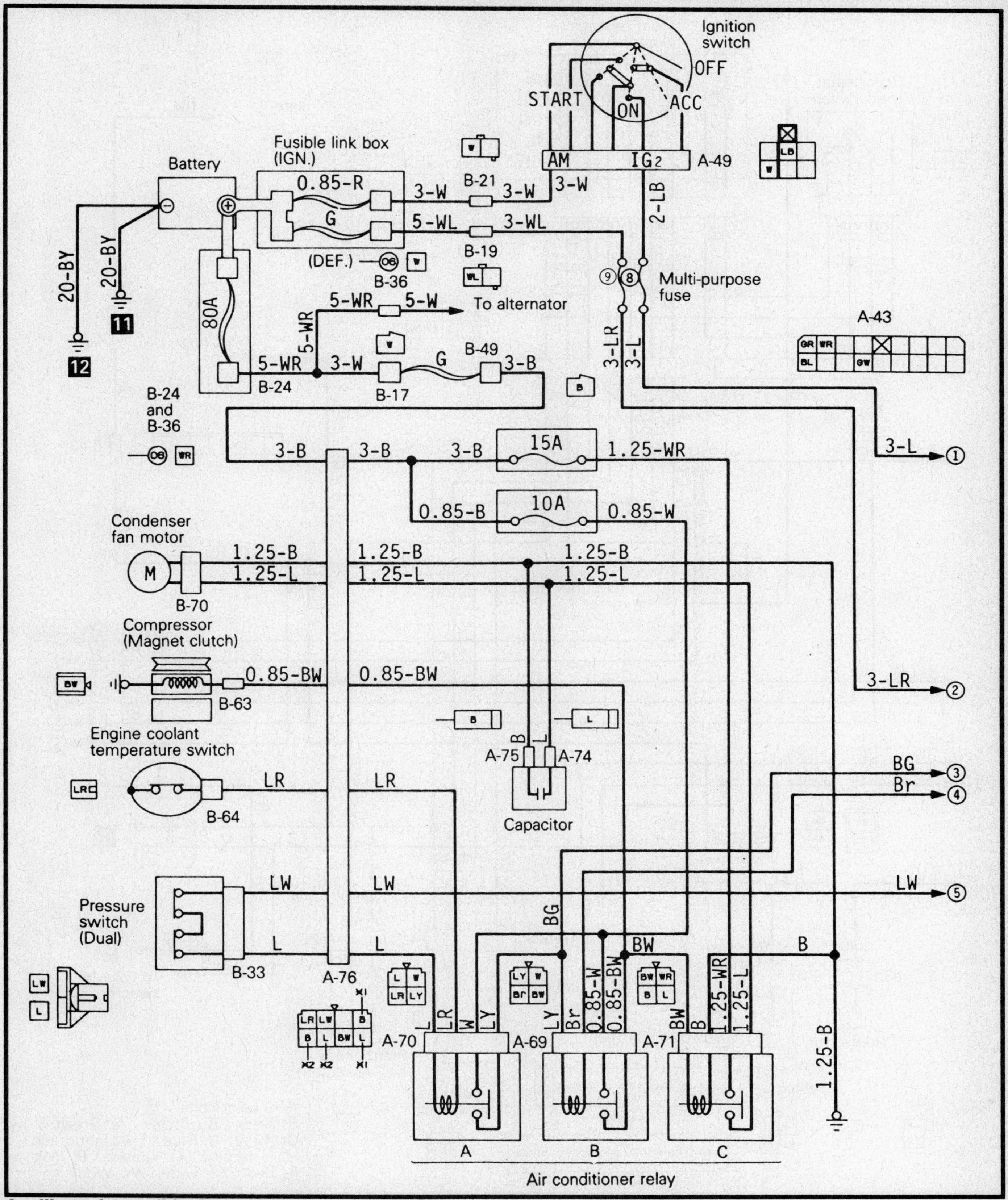
Ignition switch
OFF
START
ON
ACC
AM
IG2
A-49
Fusible link box (IGN.)
Battery
0.85-R
G
3-W
B-21
3-W
3-W
5-WL
3-WL
B-19
2-LB
(DEF.)
B-36
Multi-purpose fuse
9
8
20-BY
20-BY
11
12
80A
5-WR
5-W
To alternator
5-WR
5-WR
3-W
G
B-49
3-B
B-24
B-17
3-LR
3-L
A-43
B-24 and B-36
3-B
3-B
3-B
15A
1.25-WR
3-L
1
10A
0.85-B
0.85-W
Condenser fan motor
M
1.25-B
1.25-L
1.25-B
1.25-L
1.25-B
1.25-L
B-70
Compressor (Magnet clutch)
0.85-BW
0.85-BW
B-63
3-LR
2
Engine coolant temperature switch
A-75
A-74
Capacitor
LR
LR
B-64
BG
3
Br
4
LW
LW
LW
5
Pressure switch (Dual)
L
L
B-33
A-76
BG
BW
B
A-70
A-69
A-71
L LR W LY
LY Br 0.85-W 0.85-BW
BW B 1.25-WR 1.25-L
1.25-B
A
B
C
Air conditioner relay

Auxiliary air conditioning system wiring schematic— Van

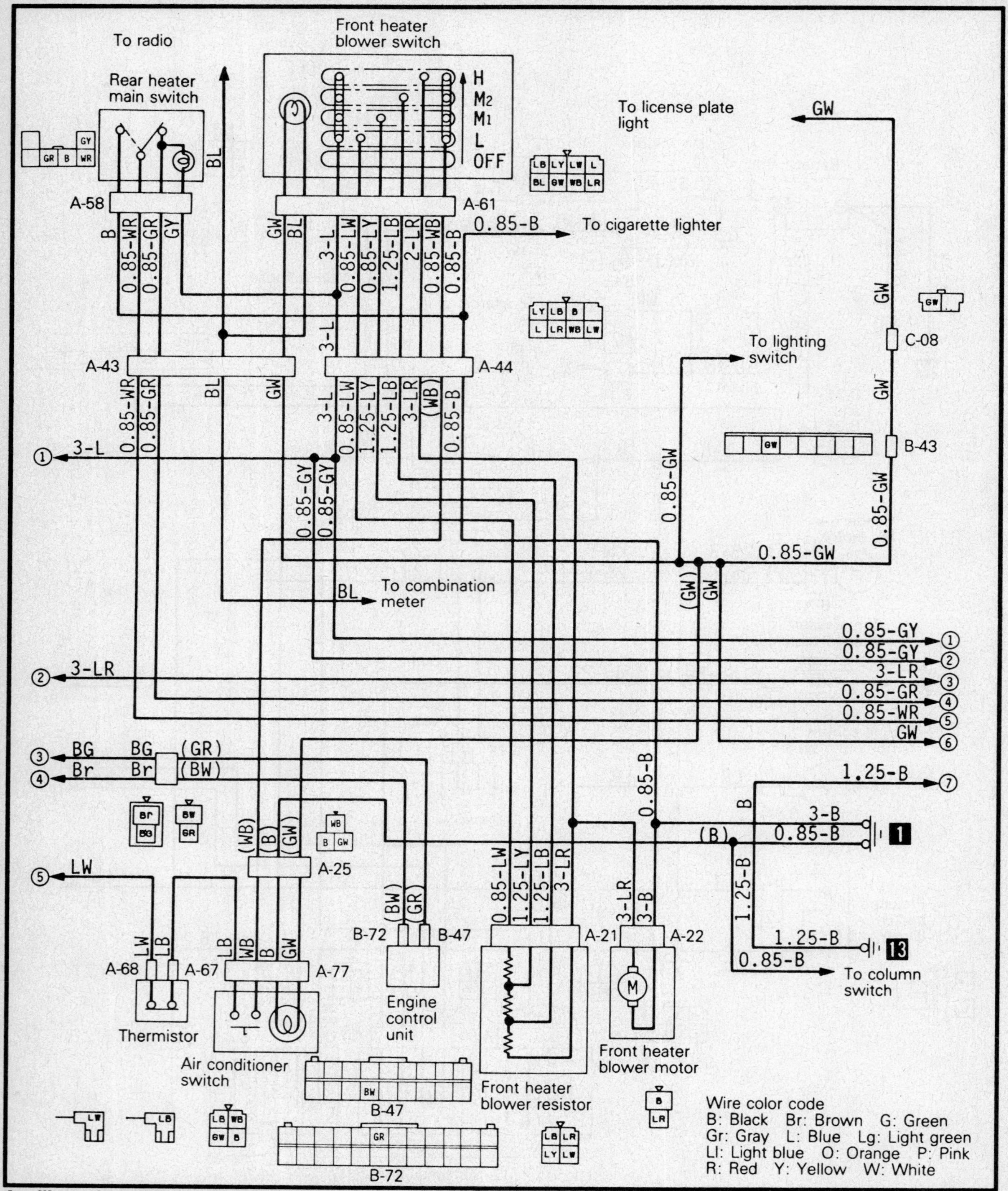
To radio
Rear heater main switch
Front heater blower switch
H
M2
M1
L
OFF
To license plate light
GW
A-58
A-61
0.85-B
To cigarette lighter
B
0.85-WR
0.85-GR
GY
GW
BL
3-L
0.85-LW
0.85-LY
1.25-LB
2-LR
0.85-WB
0.85-B
C-08
To lighting switch
A-43
A-44
B-43
3-L
0.85-GY
0.85-GW
To combination meter
(GW)
0.85-GY
3-LR
0.85-GR
0.85-WR
1.25-B
BG
Br
(GR)
(BW)
0.85-B
3-B
(B)
LW
(WB)
A-25
1.25-B
B-72
B-47
A-21
A-22
To column switch
A-68
A-67
A-77
Thermistor
Air conditioner switch
Engine control unit
Front heater blower motor
Front heater blower resistor
B-47
B-72
Wire color code
B: Black Br: Brown G: Green
Gr: Gray L: Blue Lg: Light green
Ll: Light blue O: Orange P: Pink
R: Red Y: Yellow W: White

Auxiliary air conditioning system wiring schematic— Van

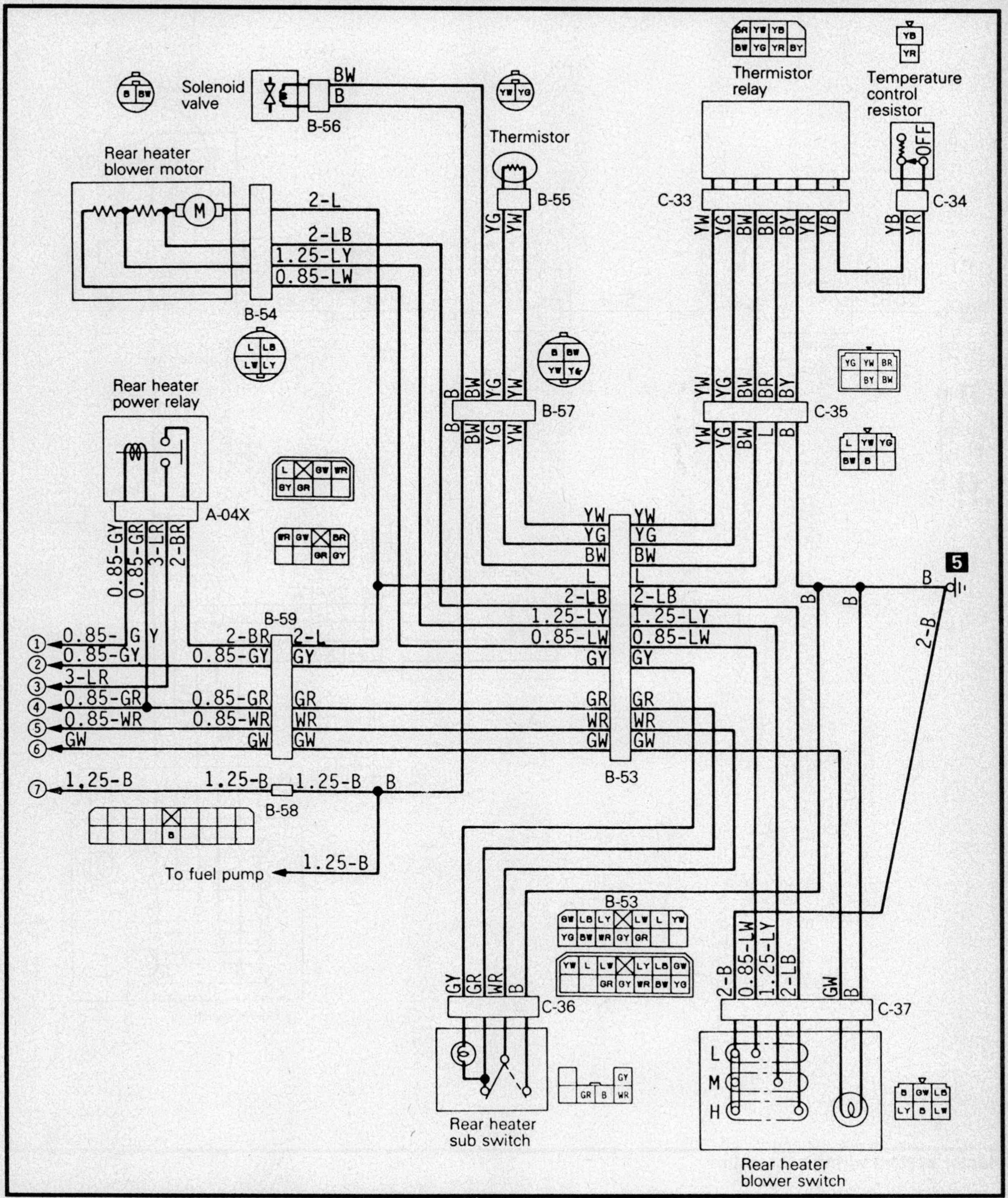
Solenoid valve
B-56
BW
B
Thermistor
B-55
Thermistor relay
Temperature control resistor
OFF
C-33
C-34
Rear heater blower motor
M
2-L
2-LB
1.25-LY
0.85-LW
B-54
B-57
C-35
Rear heater power relay
A-04X
0.85-GY
0.85-GR
3-LR
2-BR
B-59
2-BR
2-L
0.85-GY
GY
0.85-GR
GR
0.85-WR
WR
GW
3-LR
1.25-B
B-58
To fuel pump
YW
YG
BW
L
2-LB
1.25-LY
0.85-LW
GY
GR
WR
GW
B-53
5
B
2-B
C-36
Rear heater sub switch
C-37
L
M
H
Rear heater blower switch

Auxiliary air conditioning system wiring schematic— Van

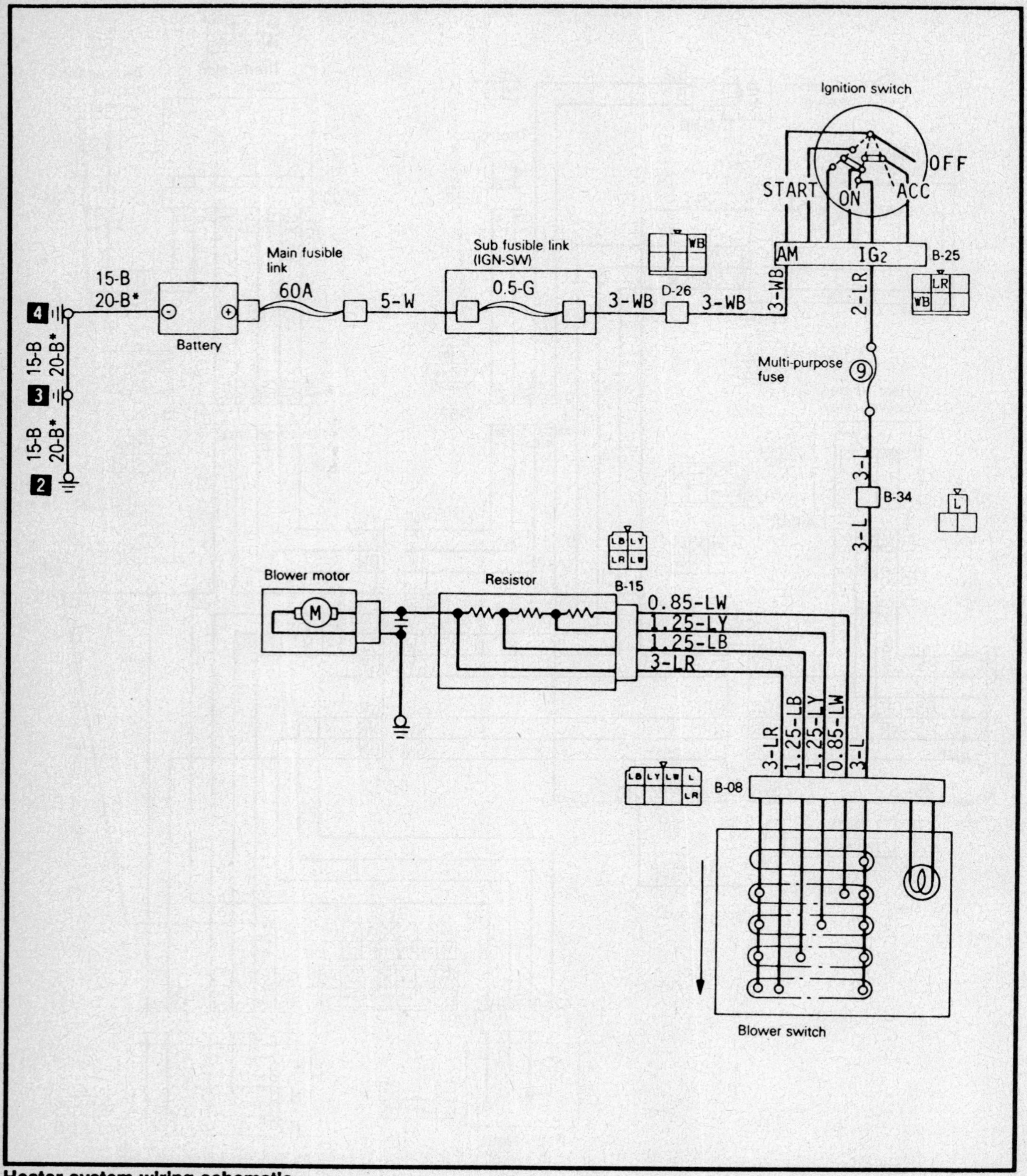
Ignition switch
OFF
START
ON
ACC
AM
IG2
B-25
Main fusible link
60A
Sub fusible link (IGN-SW)
0.5-G
5-W
3-WB
D-26
3-WB
3-WB
2-LR
15-B
20-B*
Battery
Multi-purpose fuse
9
3-L
B-34
3-L
Blower motor
M
Resistor
B-15
0.85-LW
1.25-LY
1.25-LB
3-LR
3-LR
1.25-LB
1.25-LY
0.85-LW
3-L
B-08
Blower switch

Heater system wiring schematic

33 NISSAN TRUCKS 33

AXXESS • PATHFINDER • PICK-UP

SPECIFICATIONS

ENGINE IDENTIFICATION

Year	Model	Engine Displacement cu. in. (cc/liter)	Engine Series Identification	No. of Cylinders	Engine Type
1989	Pick-Up	146 (2389/2.4)	Z24i	4	SOHC
	Pick-Up	181 (2960/3.0)	VG30i	6	DOHC
	Pathfinder	146 (2389/2.4)	Z24i	4	SOHC
	Pathfinder	181 (2960/3.0)	VG30i	6	DOHC
1990	Axxess	146 (2389/2.4)	KA24E	4	SOHC
	Pick-Up	146 (2389/2.4)	KA24E	4	SOHC
	Pick-Up	181 (2960/3.0)	VG30i	6	DOHC
	Pathfinder	146 (2389/2.4)	KA24E	4	SOHC
	Pathfinder	181 (2960/3.0)	VG30i	6	DOHC
1991	Axxess	146 (2389/2.4)	KA24E	4	SOHC
	Pick-Up	146 (2389/2.4)	KA24E	4	SOHC
	Pick-Up	181 (2960/3.0)	VG30i	6	DOHC
	Pathfinder	146 (2389/2.4)	KA24E	4	SOHC
	Pathfinder	181 (2960/3.0)	VG30i	6	DOHC

SOHC—Single Overhead Cam
DOHC—Dual Overhead Cam

REFRIGERANT CAPACITIES

Year	Model	Freon (oz.)	Oil (fl. oz.)	Type
1989	Pick-Up	29–32	6.8 ①	R-12
	Pathfinder	29–32	6.8 ①	R-12
1990	Axxess	32–38.5	6.8 ①	R-12
	Pick-Up	29–32	6.8 ①	R-12
	Pathfinder	29–32	6.8 ①	R-12
1991	Axxess	32–38.5	6.8 ①	R-12
	Pick-Up	29–32	6.8 ①	R-12
	Pathfinder	29–32	6.8 ①	R-12

① Total system capacity

AIR CONDITIONING BELT TENSION CHART

Year	Model	Engine Displacement cu. in. (cc/liter)	Belt Type	New	Used
1989	Pick-Up	146 (2389/2.4)	A-Type	0.24–0.31 ①	0.31–0.51 ①
	Pick-Up	181 (2960/3.0)	A-Type	0.28–0.35 ①	0.35–0.63 ①
	Pathfinder	146 (2389/2.4)	A-Type	0.24–0.31 ①	0.31–0.51 ①
	Pathfinder	181 (2960/3.0)	A-Type	0.28–0.35 ①	0.35–0.63 ①

AIR CONDITIONING BELT TENSION CHART

Year	Model	Engine Displacement cu. in. (cc/liter)	Belt Type	New	Used
1990	Axxess	146 (2389/2.4)	Poly V	0.20–0.24 ①	0.24–0.31 ①
	Pick-Up	146 (2389/2.4)	A-Type	0.31–0.39 ①	0.39–0.63 ①
	Pick-Up	181 (2960/3.0)	A-Type	0.28–0.35 ①	0.35–0.63 ①
	Pathfinder	146 (2389/2.4)	A-Type	0.31–0.39 ①	0.39–0.63 ①
	Pathfinder	181 (2960/3.0)	A-Type	0.28–0.35 ①	0.35–0.63 ①
1991	Axxess	146 (2389/2.4)	Poly V	0.20–0.24 ②	0.24–0.31 ②
	Pick-Up	146 (2389/2.4)	A-Type	0.31–0.39 ①	0.39–0.63 ①
	Pick-Up	181 (2960/3.0)	A-Type	0.28–0.35 ①	0.35–0.63 ①
	Pathfinder	146 (2389/2.4)	A-Type	0.31–0.39 ①	0.39–0.63 ①
	Pathfinder	181 (2960/3.0)	A-Type	0.28–0.35 ①	0.35–0.63 ①

① Inches of deflection using 22 lb. force at upper mid-point of belt

② Inches of deflection using 22 lb. force between adjuster pulley and crankshaft pulley

SYSTEM DESCRIPTION

General Information

The heater in all vehicles is a standard type, circulating engine coolant through a radiator core inside the vehicle. Temperature is controlled with a valve in the core which is operated along with the air mix door in the air distribution system. On automatic systems, there is a temperature sensor touching heater core that sends water temperature information to the control amplifier.

A standard configuration air conditioning system, charged with R-12, is used in all vehicles. The system consists of a compressor pumping the refrigerant to a condenser, a reciever/drier with a dual (high and low) pressure switch, an evaporator in the vehicle, then back to the compressor. The evaporator housing also incorporates the expansion valve. High and low pressure service valves are mounted directly on the lines and a pressure relief valve is mounted in the high pressure line near the compressor. Most vehicles have an over–temperature switch threaded into the compressor which will disengage the clutch to prevent damage from overheating. As a final fail–safe, there is a fusable plug on the reveiver/drier, which melts above about 220° F (105° C) and allows the system to vent rather than explode.

The air distribution system inside the vehicle uses doors to direct the air flow. These doors are either adjusted manually with levers and cables or controlled automatically with electric motors. In both systems the air enters the system from outside or inside the vehicle and passes over the evaporator first, then on to the heater core and/or out through various vents. This allows use of the air conditioner to dry the air for defogging the windshield even if the temperature control is set for heat. All systems include an electric clutch on the compressor, a fan to move air through the condenser and a blower fan to move air through the distribution system. A thermo control amplifier senses the evaporator coil temperature and cycles the compressor on and off to prevent ice fromation.

The Automatic Temperature Control (ATC) system is different from the one used in automobile in that the Potentiometer Temperature Control (PTC) lever adjusts a calibrated resistor, which feeds the control demand to the amplifier. The resulting signal is read by the amplifier which will control blower fan speed and move the air mix door, which has a second adjustable resistor. By keeping these 2 signals mathamatically balanced, the amplifier will maintain the selected temperature. Other information used in the calculation is outside and inside air temperatures, engine coolant temperature, sun load and compressor on signal. There is no on-board diagnostic function with this system but it can be tested with a standard volt/ohm meter.

Except for the special sensors and control amplifier, the manual and automatic systems use the same components.

Service Valve Location

PICK-UP AND PATHFINDER

1. On vehicles with the V6 engine, the high pressure valve is in the high pressure line next to the radiator. The low pressure valve is on the low pressure line near the compressor.
2. On vehicles with the 4 cylinder engine, the high pressure valve is in the high pressure line next to the radiator. The low pressure valve is on the low pressure line at the firewall, near the driver's side.

AXXESS

The high pressure valve is on the high pressure line at the condenser, on the right side of the vehicle. The low pressure valve is on the low pressure line near the steering fluid reservoir.

Special Precautions

1. All refrigerant service work must be done with the proper recycling equipment. Carefully follow the manufacturer's instructions for use of that equipment. Do not allow the freon to discharge to the air.
2. Any amount of water will make the system less effective. When any part of the system has been removed, plug or cap the lines to prevent moisture from the air entering the system.

When installing a new component, do not uncap the fittings until ready to attach the lines.

3. When assembling a fitting, always use a new O-ring and lightly lubricate the fitting with compressor oil.

4. When a compressor is removed, do not leave it on its side or upside down for more than 10 minutes. The oil may leak into the pumping chamber.

5. The proper amount of oil must be maintained in the system to prevent compressor damage and to maintain system efficiency. Be sure to measure and adjust the amount of oil removed or added to the system, especially when replacing the compressor.

System Performance Testing

1. Vehicle must be in a well ventilated area where the engine can be safely run at 1500 rpm, preferably not in direct sunlight. Open the hood to help engine cooling.

2. With windows open, operate the system set for full cooling of recirculated air, blower fan on high speed, air comming from the face vents.

3. Operate the system for more than 10 minutes, then use a thermometer to measure the air outlet temperature at the center dash vent.

4. On Axxess, with a relative humidity of 50–60 percent, the outlet air temperature should be about 30°F cooler than the outside air.

5. On Pick-up and Pathfinder, the difference will be about 20–25°F. The system effectiveness will decrease as the humidity increases.

6. Use the Temperature/Pressure chart for system performance check. The chart is for a relative humidity of 50–70 percent. The compressor discharge and suction pressures will increase with higher outside air temperature and humidity.

System Discharging

1. Install adapter valves to the vehicle service valves and/or connect the refrigerant recycling equipment according to the manufacturer's instructions.

2. Open both the adapter or manifold valves slowly to prevent excess oil loss. Allow the freon to stop flowing before going on to the next step.

System Evacuating

1. Open both the high and low pressure valves and run the vacuum pump for more than 5 minutes. The gauges should stabilize at 29.13–29.92 in. (740–760mm) Hg vacuum.

2. Close the valves and turn the pump off. Check to see that the vacuum gauges remain stable. If the gauge on the low pressure side moves 3.94 in. (100mm) Hg vacuum in about 10 minutes, the system will discharge itself in about 1 month.

3. If the system will not hold vacuum, first check that the service equipment is properly connected and in good working order. If any connections in the vehicle system have been disturbed, make sure they have been properly reconnected. Be sure to use new lightly oiled O-rings and that the fitting is not over torqued.

4. If the system holds vacuum, open the valves and run the pump for more than 20 minutes. Close the valves, then turn the pump off.

System Charging

1. When using recycling equipment, the equipment in use will determine the charging procedure. Carefully follow the manufacturer's instructions and add the correct amount of freon as noted in the specifications chart. Never add freon through the high pressure service valve.

2. If charging directly from the R-12 container, add freon to the low pressure side until it slows or stops flowing. Start the engine, set the controls to maximum cooling and, with the R-12 can upright, continue to flow freon gas, not liqued, into the low pressure side until the specified amount has been added.

3. With the system fully charged and with the correct oil level in the compressor, run the air conditioner at the full cold setting for more than 5 minutes.

4. Stop the engine and immediately check the system for leaks using a suitable leak detector. Be sure to check at every line fitting, the service valves, the pressure switch at the receiver/drier, at the compressor shaft seals, bolt holes and clutch and the pressure and temperature relief valves.

5. To check the evaporator and valves inside the vehicle, insert the leak detector probe into the water drain hose for more than 10 minutes. Leaking freon is heavier than air and will seek the lower exit, so always look for leaks at the lowest point.

Compressor Oil Service

The compressor is lubricated with a special oil that circulates with the freon when the system is operating and drops out of the freon when the system is stopped. Insufficient oil will cause damage to the compressor but too much oil will inhibit the system's cooling ability. When installing new parts or a new compressor, the oil quantity must be adjusted.

1. If a new compressor is being installed, drain the oil out of the old unit and measure the amount.

2. Refer to the specification chart to determine how much oil the system should have.

3. Adjust the quantity of oil in the new compressor as needed. New compressors often come with the full amount of oil, so it will probably be necessary to remove oil. The amount to be removed is the difference between the system specification and the amount drained from the old unit.

4. If installing another major system component, add oil according the the following table:

The evaporator holds about 30% of the total amount.
The condenser holds about 20% of the total amount.
The reciever/drier holds about 10% of the total amount.

5. If a large oil leak is indicated, make the necessary repairs and run the system at idle speed set for full cooling for about 10 minutes. Stop the engine and drain the oil from the compressor to measure how much oil to add.

TEMPERATURE/PRESSURE CHART

Vehicle	Engine	Outside Temperature	High Side Pressure (psi)	Low Side Pressure (psi)
Pick-Up	2.4L	68	137–168	17–24
		77	162–196	20–28
		86	188–228	23–33
		95	213–260	27–37
		104	236–290	31–41
	3.0L	68	145–173	13–20
		77	176–210	17–26
		86	205–247	23–31
		95	235–284	27–37
		104	264–321	33–43
Pathfinder	2.4L	68	137–168	17–24
		77	162–196	20–28
		86	188–228	23–33
		95	213–260	27–37
		104	236–290	31–41
	3.0L	68	145–173	13–20
		77	176–210	17–26
		86	205–247	23–31
		95	235–284	27–37
		104	264–321	33–43
Axxess	2.4L	68	155–188	21–27
		77	188–226	27–33
		86	219–266	33–40
		95	252–303	38–46
		104	283–343	44–53

SYSTEM COMPONENTS

NOTE: When removing any component of the refrigerant system, properly discharge the freon into recovery equipment. Do not vent the freon into the air.

Radiator and Cooling Fan

REMOVAL AND INSTALLATION

1. Disconnect the negative battery cable. On vehicles with theft-protected radios, make sure the owner's reset code is available.
2. Drain the cooling system. On some vehicles, it will be necessary to remove the air cleaner inlet ducting.
3. Disconnect the reservoir tank and upper and lower hoses from the radiator.
4. On vehicles with electric fans, disconnect the temperature switch and fan connectors.
5. On vehicles with automatic transmissions, disconnect and plug the transmission cooling lines.
6. On vehicles with electric fans, it should now be possible to remove the fans and shroud as an assembly. To remove the radiator, remove the upper radiator retaining bolts and lift the unit up and out.
7. On Pick-up and Pathfinder with the fan on the water pump, there may be a bottom section of the shroud which can be removed to lift the shroud out past the fan. If not, remove the fan from the coupling and lay it in the shroud. Remove the shroud retaining screws and lift the fan and shroud out together.

To install:

8. Set the lugs on the bottom of the radiator into the rubber mounts on the body and secure the unit with the upper mounting bolts.
9. Install the fan with the shrouding. On the Pick-up and Pathfinder, if the fan was removed, bolt the fan to the coupling and torque the bolts to 7 ft. lbs. (10 Nm.).
10. Connect the automatic transmission cooling lines and all coolant hoses with the reservoir tank.
11. Fill the cooling system and look for leaks before installing the remaining parts.
12. Plug in all the electrical connectors for the fan and temperature switches.

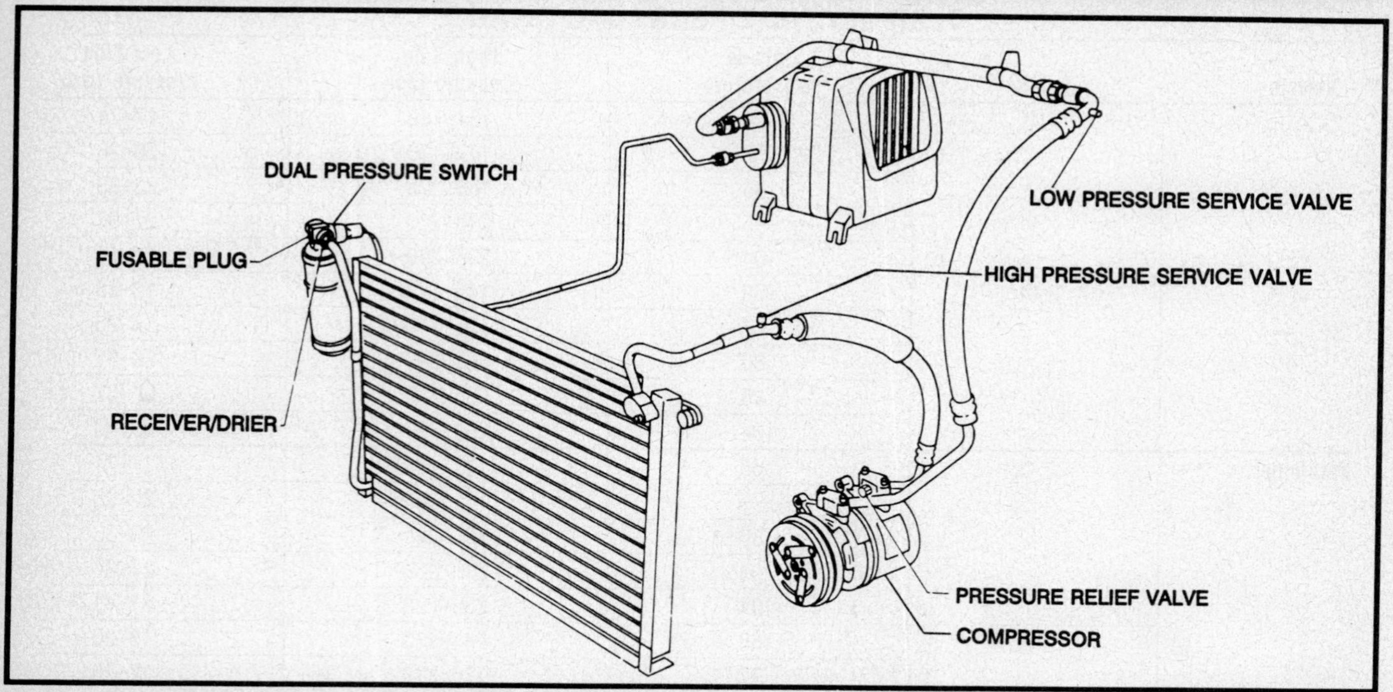
DUAL PRESSURE SWITCH
FUSABLE PLUG
RECEIVER/DRIER
LOW PRESSURE SERVICE VALVE
HIGH PRESSURE SERVICE VALVE
PRESSURE RELIEF VALVE
COMPRESSOR

Typical Nissan refrigerant system components, Pathfinder 4 cylinder system shown

13. Connect the battery and start the engine to bleed the cooling system and check for leaks.

Electric Cooling Fan

TESTING

AXXESS

1. When the air conditioner is running, the electric radiator fan should also run. Turn the ignition switch, air conditioner and blower fan **ON** and check for condenser fan operation.
2. If neither fan runs, check for voltage from the battery to the relays. The engine control computer completes the relay coil circuit to ground. The 2 fan relays are on each end of the right side of the relay panel, to the right of the battery.
3. If there is voltage between relay terminals 1 and 2, check for continuity through the relay coil across terminals 1 and 2. The other terminals are the switched circuits and should have continuity when the relay is activated.
4. If the relays are good and there is voltage to them, test the fan motors. The black wire is ground.

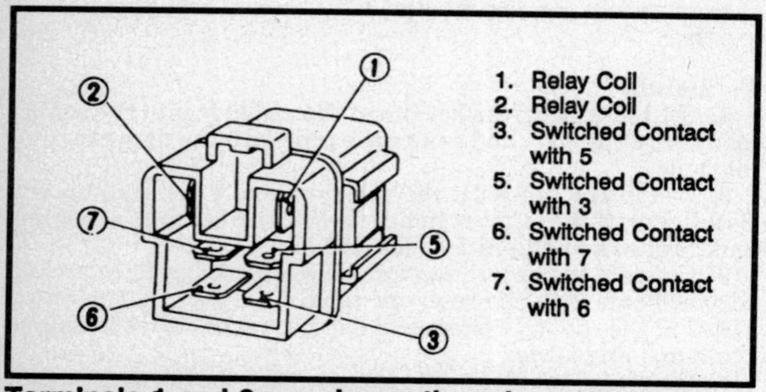
1
2
7
5
6
3
1. Relay Coil
2. Relay Coil
3. Switched Contact with 5
5. Switched Contact with 3
6. Switched Contact with 7
7. Switched Contact with 6

Terminals 1 and 2 are always the relay coil circuit

5. If the motors run, the relays work properly and there is proper voltage to the relays, the engine computer is not turning the fans on. Other malfunctions related to the sensors or computer input/output should be investigated before replacing it.

REMOVAL AND INSTALLATION

AXXESS

1. Remove the apron under the front of the engine, if equipped, and drain about 2 quarts from the cooling system. Remove the air cleaner inlet ducting.
2. Disconnect the reservoir and upper hose from the radiator.
3. Disconnect the temperature switch and electric fan connectors. It should now be possible to remove the fans and shroud as an assembly.
4. Installation is the reverse of removal.

Condenser and Receiver/Drier

REMOVAL AND INSTALLATION

1. Disconnect the negative battery cable. On vehicles with theft-protected radios, make sure the owner's reset code is available.
2. The radiator must be removed first. Remove the apron under the front of the engine, if equipped, and drain the cooling system. Disconnect and plug the oil cooling hoses on automatic transmission models, then remove the fan(s) and radiator.
3. Properly discharge the freon into recovery equipment, disconnect and cap the pressure lines from the condenser. The receiver/drier is attached to the condenser and can be removed along with it. Be sure to disconnect the dual pressure switch wiring first.
4. Installation is the reverse of removal. When installing the condenser, be sure to use new O-ring seals and lightly lubricate them with compressor oil.
5. Do not over torque the fittings or they will be distorted and leak. On Pick-up and Pathfinder, torque the receiver/drier inlet

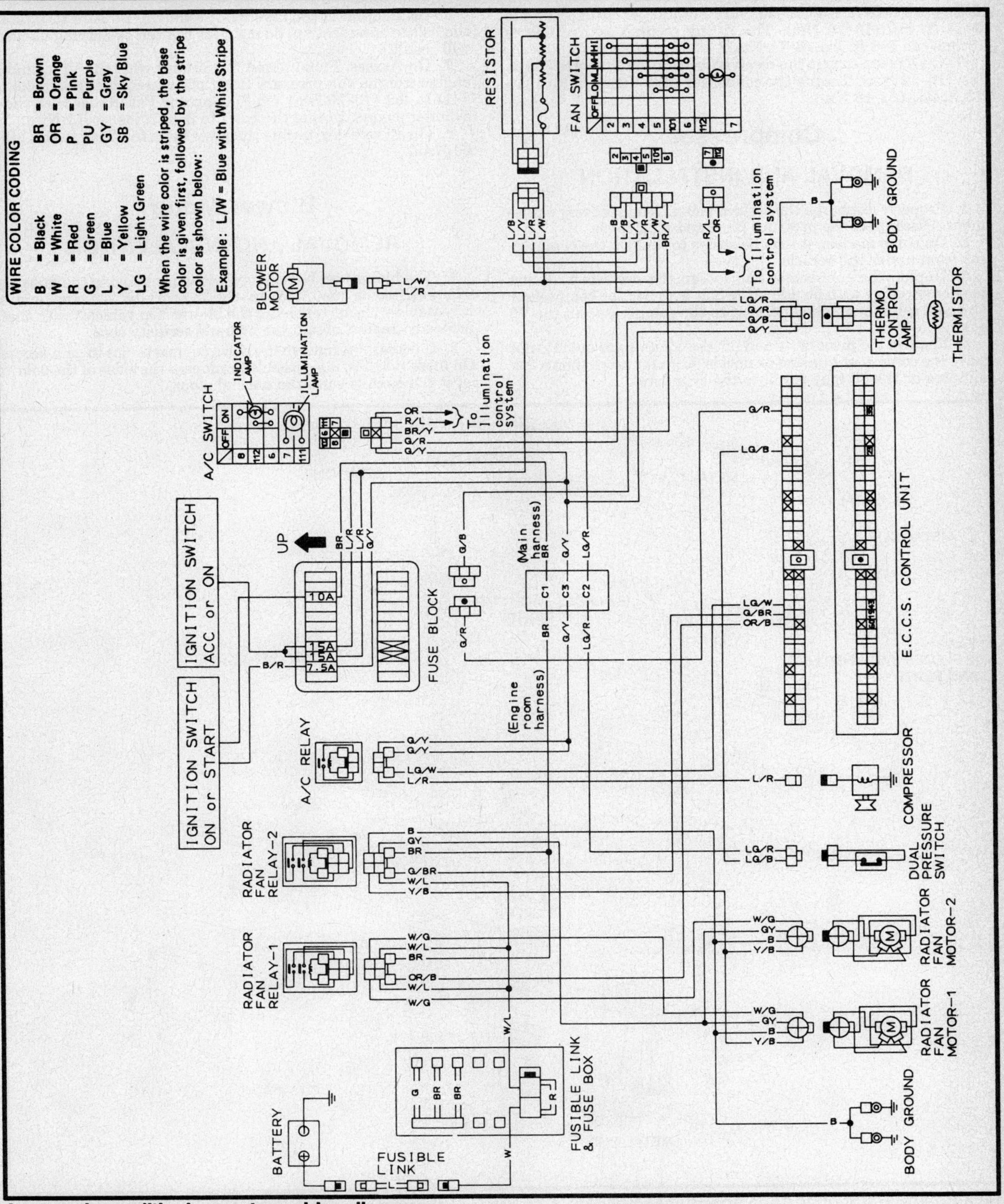
WIRE COLOR CODING
B = Black
W = White
R = Red
G = Green
L = Blue
Y = Yellow
LG = Light Green
BR = Brown
OR = Orange
P = Pink
PU = Purple
GY = Gray
SB = Sky Blue
When the wire color is striped, the base color is given first, followed by the stripe color as shown below:
Example: L/W = Blue with White Stripe
RESISTOR
FAN SWITCH
BLOWER MOTOR
A/C SWITCH
INDICATOR LAMP
ILLUMINATION LAMP
To Illumination control system
BODY GROUND
THERMO CONTROL AMP.
THERMISTOR
IGNITION SWITCH ACC or ON
IGNITION SWITCH ON or START
UP
FUSE BLOCK
(Main harness)
(Engine room harness)
E.C.C.S. CONTROL UNIT
A/C RELAY
COMPRESSOR
RADIATOR FAN RELAY-2
RADIATOR FAN RELAY-1
DUAL PRESSURE SWITCH
RADIATOR FAN MOTOR-2
RADIATOR FAN MOTOR-1
BATTERY
FUSIBLE LINK
FUSIBLE LINK & FUSE BOX

Axxess air conditioning system wiring diagram

fitting to 11–18 ft. lbs. (15–25 Nm). Torque the outlet fitting to 7–14 ft. lbs. (10–20 Nm). The fitting secured with a bolt is torqued to 5–8 ft. lbs. (8–11 Nm).

6. On Axxess, torque the receiver/drier outlet fitting to 7–9 ft. lbs. (10–12 Nm). Torque the condenser inlet fitting bolt to 10–13 ft. lbs. (14–18 Nm).

Compressor

REMOVAL AND INSTALLATION

1. Properly discharge the system using freon recovery equipment. Disconnect the pressure lines and plug them.
2. On some models, it may be easier to remove the compressor from under the vehicle.
4. Unplug the connectors and loosen the drive belt. A belt tensioner pulley with an adjusting bolt is under the compressor on the 4 cylinder engine and next to the compressor on the V6 engine.
5. Remove the pivot bolts and lift the compressor out. Do not leave the compressor on end or upside down for more than a few minutes or the oil may run into the cylinders.
6. Installation is the reverse of removal. Be sure to tighten the belt to specification, do not over tighten or bearing damage will result.
7. On Axxess, Pick-up and Pathfinder with the V6 cylinder engine, torque the pressure line fitting-to-compressor bolts to 7–14 ft. lbs. (10–20 Nm). On Pick-up and Pathfinder with the 4 cylinder engine, torque the bolts to 6–8 ft. lbs. (8–11 Nm).
8. On all vehicles, torque the pivot bolts to 33–44 ft. lbs. (45–60 Nm).

Blower Motor

REMOVAL AND INSTALLATION

1. The blower can be removed without removing the housing. The resistor is mounted on the evaporator housing and is accessable without removing the blower. On vehicles with theft protected radios, obtain the owner's security code.
2. If necessary, remove the glove compartment to gain access. On most vehicles, it is possible to squeeze the sides of the door to let it fall open beyond the normal stops.

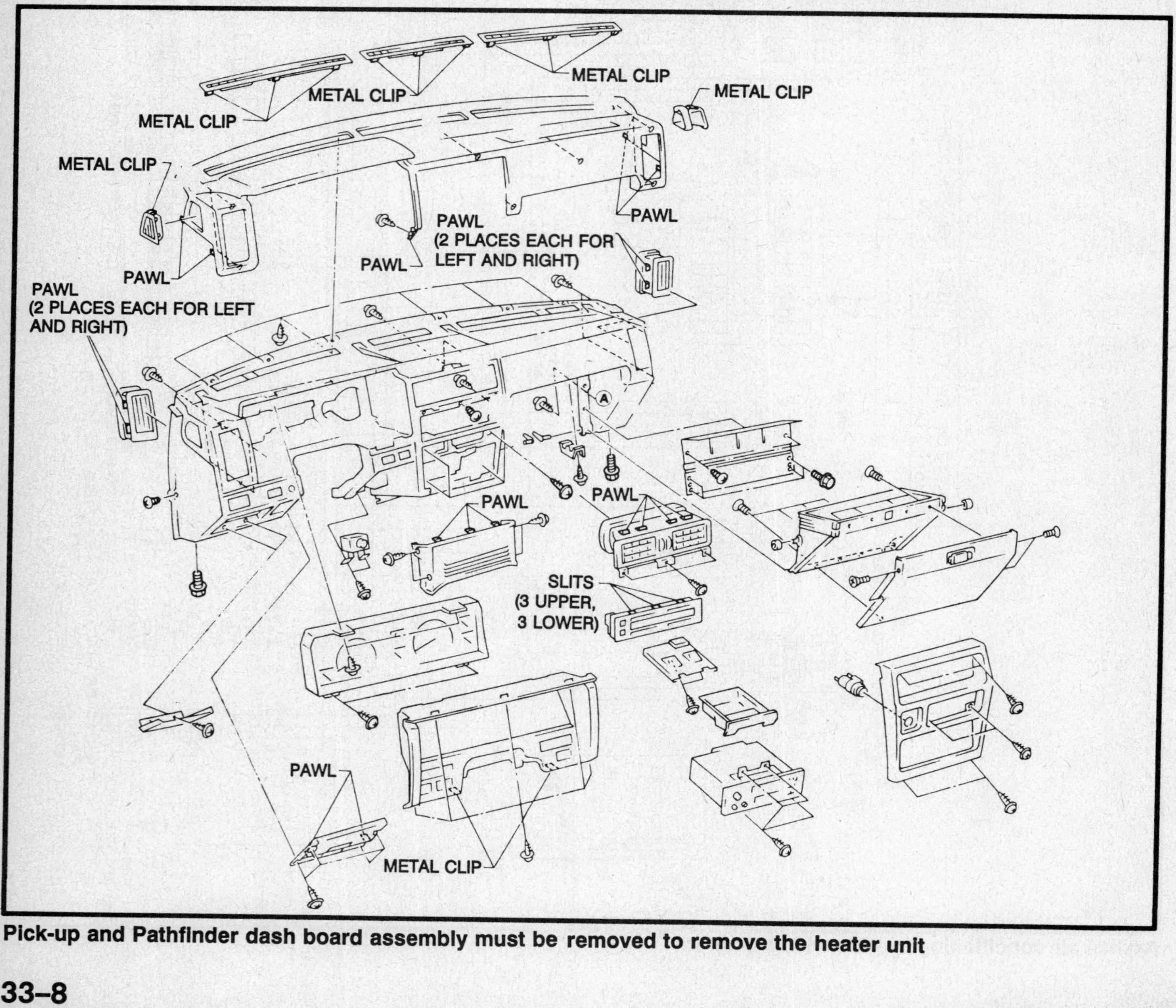
METAL CLIP
METAL CLIP
METAL CLIP
METAL CLIP
METAL CLIP
PAWL
PAWL
(2 PLACES EACH FOR
LEFT AND RIGHT)
PAWL
PAWL
PAWL
(2 PLACES EACH FOR LEFT
AND RIGHT)
A
PAWL
PAWL
SLITS
(3 UPPER,
3 LOWER)
PAWL
METAL CLIP

Pick-up and Pathfinder dash board assembly must be removed to remove the heater unit

3. Disconnect the wiring and remove the mounting bolts to lower the motor out.
4. Installation is the reverse of removal.

Heater Core

REMOVAL AND INSTALLATION

Pick-Up and Pathfinder

1. Disconnect the negative battery cable. On vehicles with theft protected radios, obtain the owner's security code.
2. Set the **TEMP** lever to the maximum **HOT** position and drain the engine coolant.
3. Disconnect the heater hoses at the engine compartment.
4. It is necessary to remove the entire dash board. Start by removing the ash tray and remove the screws holding the center console face cover. Remove the cover, heater controls, radio and center vent.
5. Disconnect the control cables and wiring as needed and remove the dash board.
6. Disconnect the ducts and remove the heater unit. Remove the case clips and split the case to remove the core.

To install:

7. Install the heater core and assemble the heater case halves. Use new gaskets and seals as required. Always check for smooth operation of the air mix door when re-attaching the heater case halves.
8. Install the heater unit and use a new gasket to connect it to the cooling unit.
9. Install the instrument panel.
10. Install the heater control assembly, center vent and radio.
11. Adjust the heater controls and air flow doors as required.
12. Connect the heater hoses and re-fill the cooling system.
13. Connect the negative battery cable and start the engine to test the system.

Axxess

1. Disconnect the negative battery cable. On vehicles with theft protected radios, obtain the owner's security code.
2. Set the **TEMP** lever to the maximum **HOT** position and drain the engine coolant.
3. Disconnect the heater hoses at the engine compartment.
4. The heater unit can be removed without removing the dash board. Remove the glove compartment, ash tray assembly and the radio.
5. Disconnect the heater control cables and wiring as required and remove the control assembly.
6. Disconnect the ducting and remove the heater unit. Split the case to remove the core.

To install:

7. Install the heater core and assemble the heater case halves. Use new gaskets and seals as required. Check for smooth operation of the air mix door when re-attaching the heater case halves.
8. Install the heater unit and use a new gasket to connect it the cooling unit.
9. Install the heater control assembly and radio.
10. Adjust the heater control cables and rods.
11. Connect the heater hoses and re-fill the cooling system.
12. Connect the negative battery cable and start the engine to test the system.

Evaporator and Expansion Valve

REMOVAL AND INSTALLATION

1. The evaporator, which is between the blower and the heater, can be removed without removing the heater core. Properly discharge the system using freon recovery equipment, then disconnect and plug the evaporator and pressure line fittings at the firewall.
2. Remove the glove compartment. On some vehicles the sides of the glove compartment door can be squeezed together to let the door open down past the stops.
3. Disconect the wiring for the blower fan resistor, which is on the evaporator housing. There is also a connector for the thermo control amplifier on the housing, either on the front or the top right.
4. If necessary, remove the blower motor and its housing. On some vehicles, the expansion valve can be accessed once the blower housing is removed.
5. Remove the cooling unit and split the housing to remove the evaporator and expansion valve.

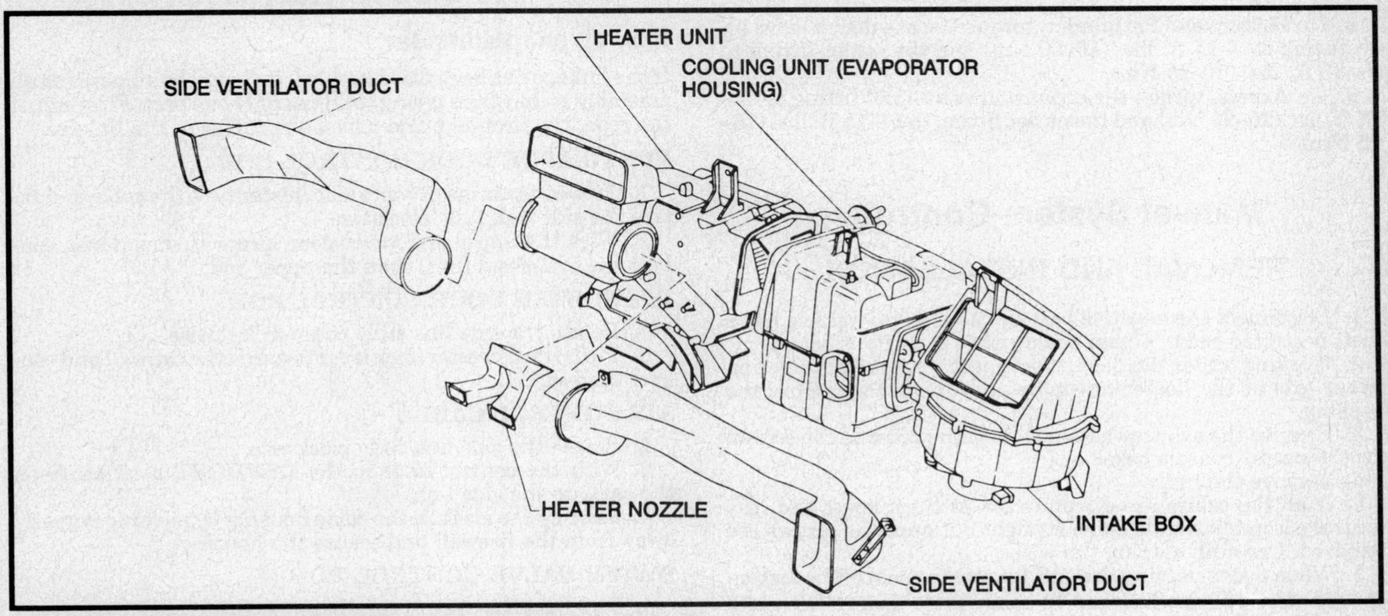
HEATER UNIT
COOLING UNIT (EVAPORATOR HOUSING)
SIDE VENTILATOR DUCT
HEATER NOZZLE
INTAKE BOX
SIDE VENTILATOR DUCT

Pick-up and Pathfinder heater/air conditioner assembly

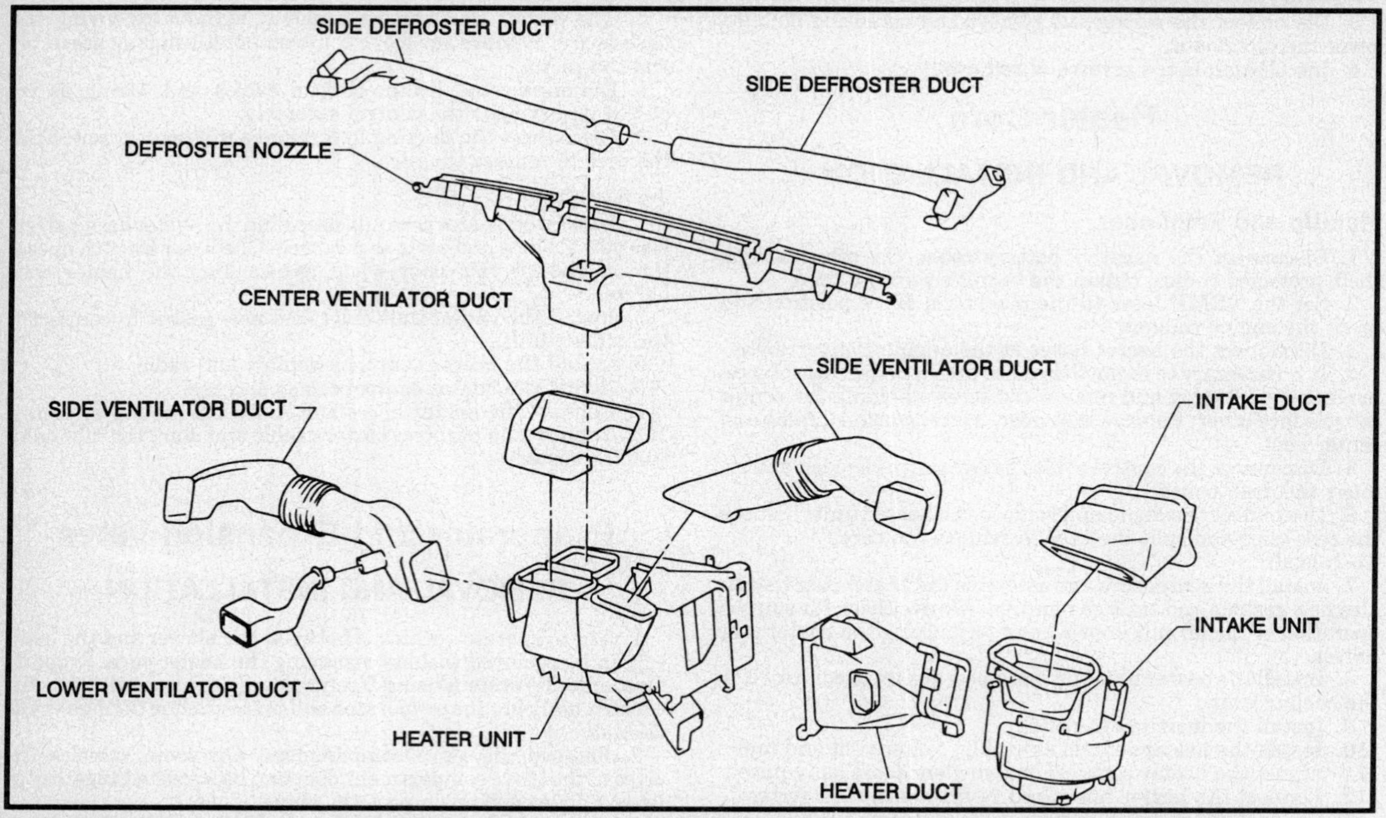
SIDE DEFROSTER DUCT
SIDE DEFROSTER DUCT
DEFROSTER NOZZLE
CENTER VENTILATOR DUCT
SIDE VENTILATOR DUCT
SIDE VENTILATOR DUCT
INTAKE DUCT
INTAKE UNIT
LOWER VENTILATOR DUCT
HEATER UNIT
HEATER DUCT

Axxess heater assembly; units with air conditioning have the evaporator in place of the heater duct

6. Installation is the reverse of removal. Make sure the seals between the housings are in good condition, replace as necessary.
7. When connecting the freon lines, use new O-rings and do not over tighten the fittings. Torque the inlet line fitting to 7–14 ft. lbs. (10–20 Nm) and the outlet line fitting to 14–22 ft. lbs. (20–29 Nm).
8. On Pick-up and Pathfinder, torque the expansion valve inlet fitting to 7–14 ft. lbs. (10–20 Nm) and the outlet fitting to 14–18 ft. lbs. (20–25 Nm).
9. On Axxess, torque the expansion valve inlet fitting to 14–22 ft. lbs. (20–29 Nm) and the outlet fitting to 11–18 ft. lbs. (15–25 Nm).

Manual System Controls

REMOVAL AND INSTALLATION

1. Disconnect the negative battery cable. If the vehicle has a theft protected radio, obtain the owner's security code.
2. Working under the dash, disconnect the control cables on either side of the heater assembly and unclip them from the housing.
3. Remove the ash tray assembly to gain access to the screws for the center console bezel.
4. Remove the radio.
5. If all the cables are disconnected at their lower end, the control assembly should come straight out once the screws are removed. Carefully unplug the wires.
6. When disassembling the unit for repair, most of the fasteners are plastic clips which can be easily pried apart. Be careful not to break the tabs. The knobs on the front can be removed with pliers but wrap a rag around the knob to keep from scratching the finish.
7. Installation is the reverse of removal. Adjust the control cables and connect the battery to test the system.

ADJUSTMENTS

Pick-Up and Pathfinder

If the linkage has been disassembled, it should be adjusted as an assembly rather than trying to adjust only one part. First adjust the rods, then connect and adjust the cables to the linkage.

VENTILATOR DOOR CONTROL ROD

1. Viewed from the driver's side, disconnect the cable and rotate the side link fully clockwise.
2. With the upper and lower door levers pushed down, connect the lower rod first, then the upper rod.

DEFROSTER DOOR CONTROL ROD

1. Rotate the side link fully counterclockwise.
2. Push the defroster door lever towards the firewall and connect the rod.

AIR CONTROL CABLE

1. Rotate the side link fully clockwise.
2. With the control lever in the **DEFROST** position, hook the cable to the side link.
3. Take up the slack in the cable housing by pushing it gently away from the firewall and secure the housing.

WATER VALVE CONTROL ROD

1. To adjust the control rod, disconnect the temperature control cable from the air mix door lever.

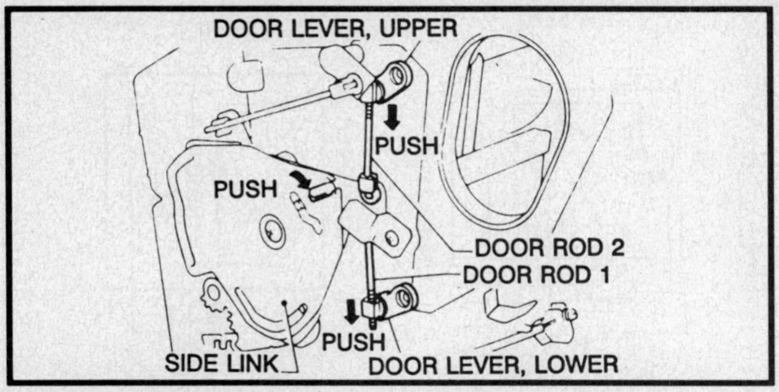
DOOR LEVER, UPPER
PUSH
PUSH
DOOR ROD 2
DOOR ROD 1
PUSH
SIDE LINK
DOOR LEVER, LOWER

Pick-up and Pathfinder ventilator door control rod adjustment

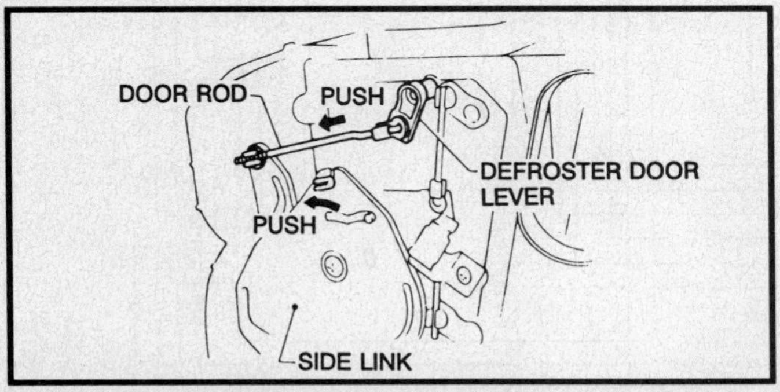
DOOR ROD
PUSH
DEFROSTER DOOR LEVER
PUSH
SIDE LINK

Pick-up and Pathfinder defroster door control rod adjustment

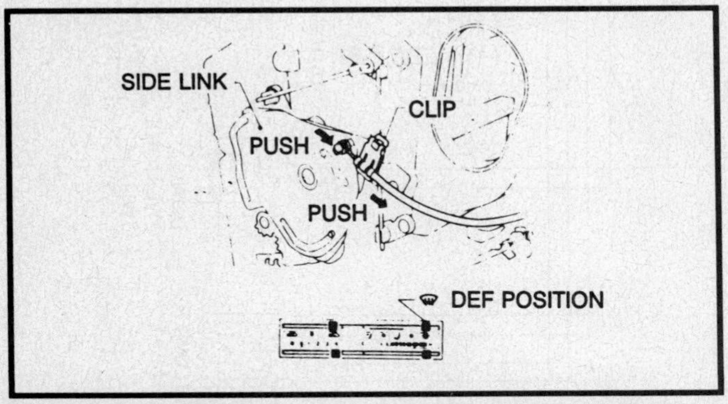
SIDE LINK
CLIP
PUSH
PUSH
DEF POSITION

Pick-up and Pathfinder air control cable adjustment

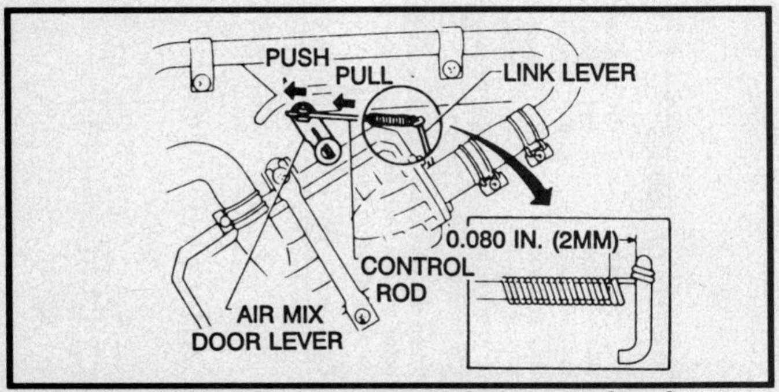
PUSH
PULL
LINK LEVER
0.080 IN. (2MM)
CONTROL ROD
AIR MIX DOOR LEVER

Pick-up and Pathfinder water valve control rod adjustment

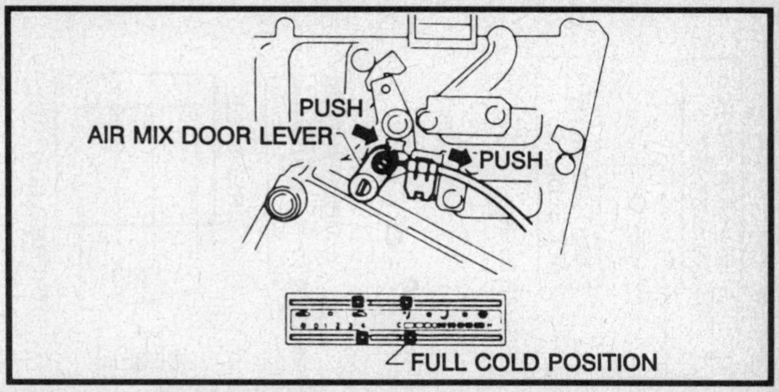
PUSH
AIR MIX DOOR LEVER
PUSH
FULL COLD POSITION

Pick-up and Pathfinder temperature control cable adjustment

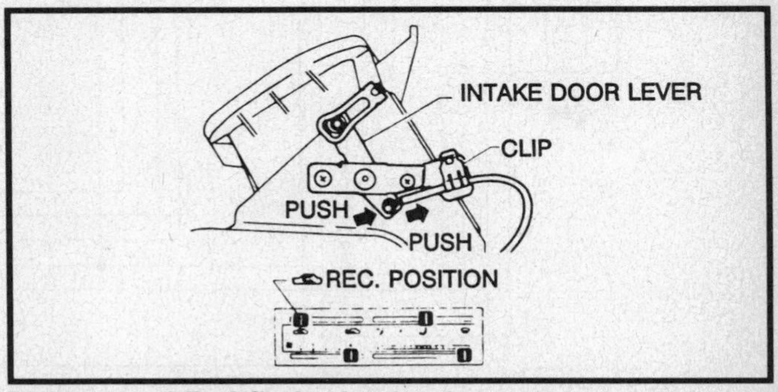
INTAKE DOOR LEVER
CLIP
PUSH
PUSH
REC. POSITION

Pick-up and Pathfinder intake door control cable adjustment

2. The valve end of the rod is attached to the valve link lever with a wire loop. With the rod loose at the air mix door end, move the air mix door lever and the valve link lever all the way in the direction that would pull the rod away from the valve link lever.

3. Gently pull the rod so there is about 0.080 in. (2mm) gap between the rod and valve lever and secure the rod at the door lever.

TEMPERATURE CONTROL CABLE

1. Move the temperature control lever to the full **COLD** position.

2. Rotate the air mix door linkage towards the full hot position.

3. Attach the cable and take up the slack in the cable housing away from the lever.

4. Secure the cable housing with the clip and operate the lever to check for smooth operation.

INTAKE DOOR CONTROL CABLE

1. Move the control lever to the **RECIRCULATE** position.

2. Move the intake door lever all the way towards the cable housing clip.

3. Attach the cable and pull the slack in the housing away from the lever before securing it with the clip.

Axxess

If the linkage has been disassembled, it should be adjusted as an assembly rather than trying to adjust only one part. Adjust the system in the order presented here.

AIR CONTROL CABLE

1. Put the air control lever in the **DEFROST** position.

2. Working from the driver's side, rotate the side link fully clockwise.

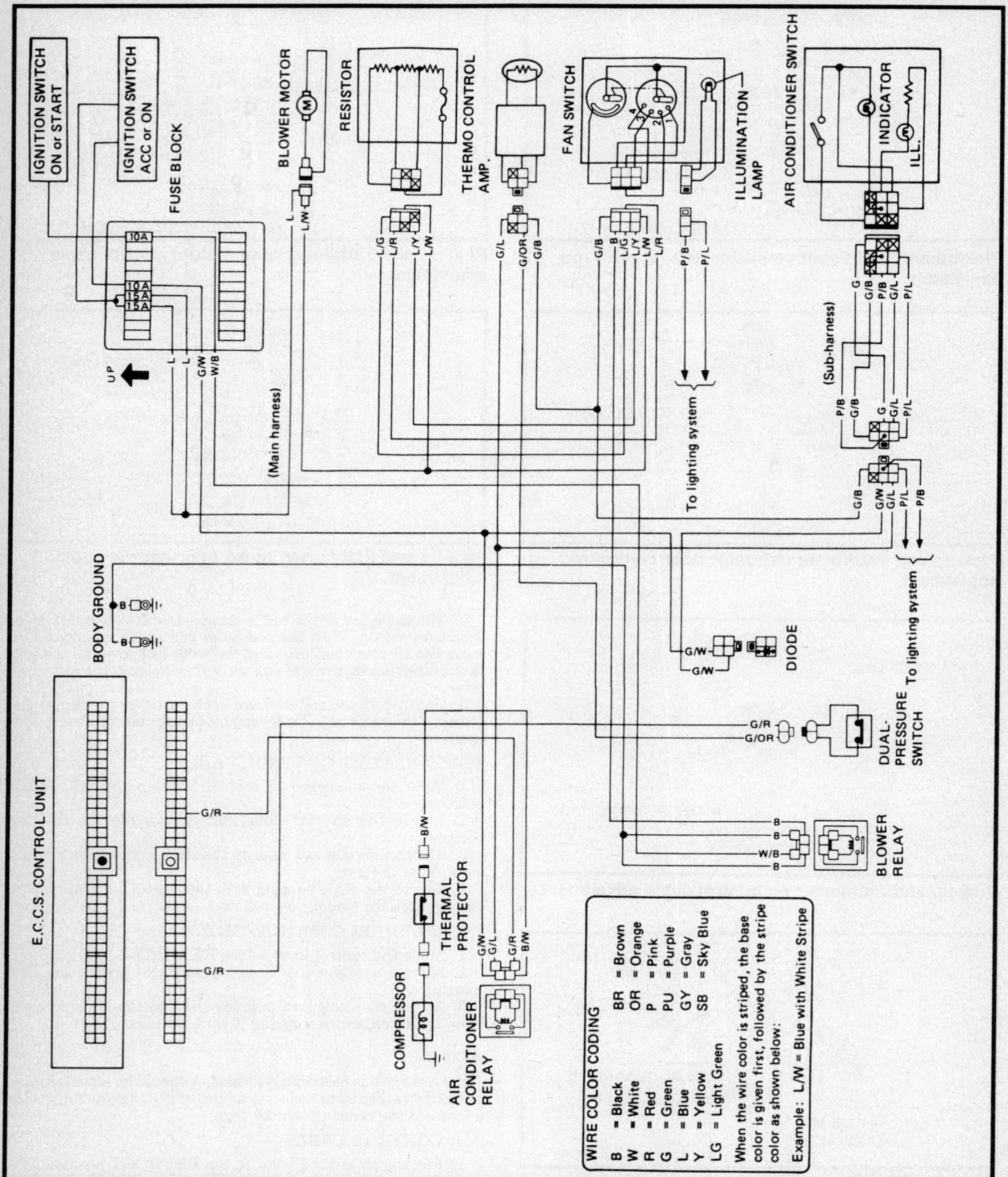
IGNITION SWITCH ON or START
IGNITION SWITCH ACC or ON
FUSE BLOCK
10A
10 A
15 A
15 A
UP
BLOWER MOTOR
RESISTOR
THERMO CONTROL AMP.
FAN SWITCH
ILLUMINATION LAMP
AIR CONDITIONER SWITCH
INDICATOR
ILL.
(Main harness)
(Sub-harness)
To lighting system
BODY GROUND
DIODE
DUAL-PRESSURE SWITCH
BLOWER RELAY
E.C.C.S. CONTROL UNIT
THERMAL PROTECTOR
COMPRESSOR
AIR CONDITIONER RELAY
WIRE COLOR CODING
B = Black
W = White
R = Red
G = Green
L = Blue
Y = Yellow
LG = Light Green
BR = Brown
OR = Orange
P = Pink
PU = Purple
GY = Gray
SB = Sky Blue
When the wire color is striped, the base color is given first, followed by the stripe color as shown below:
Example: L/W = Blue with White Stripe

Pick-up and Pathfinder manual air conditioner wiring diagram

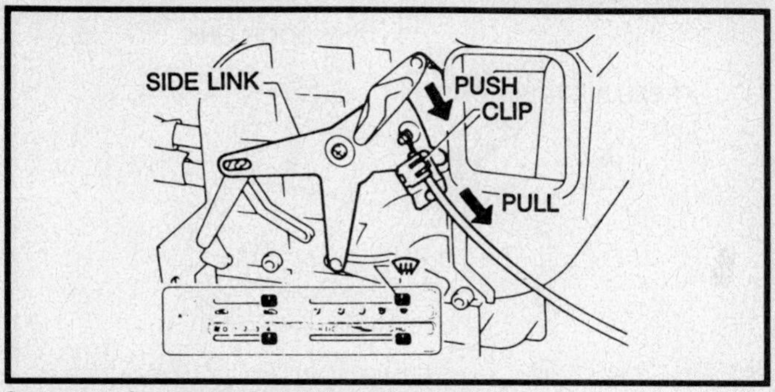
SIDE LINK
PUSH
CLIP
PULL

Axxess air control cable adjustment

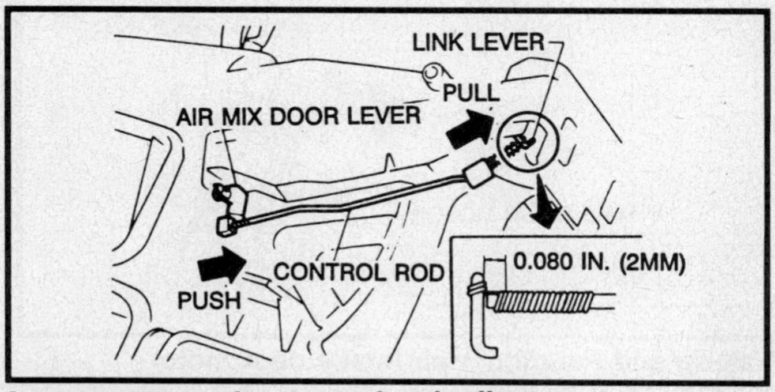
LINK LEVER
PULL
AIR MIX DOOR LEVER
CONTROL ROD
PUSH
0.080 IN. (2MM)

Axxess water valve control rod adjustment

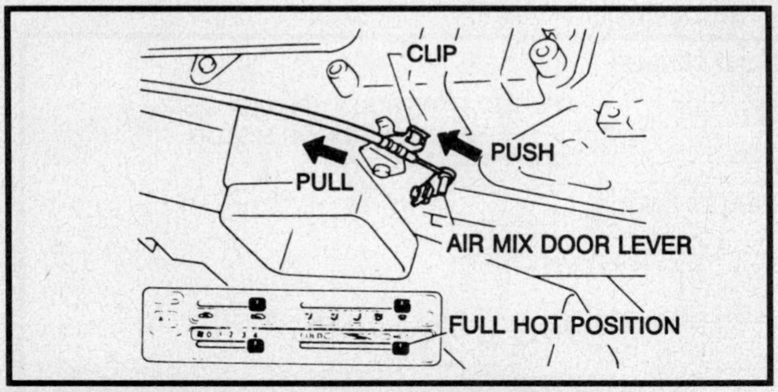
CLIP
PUSH
PULL
AIR MIX DOOR LEVER
FULL HOT POSITION

Axxess temperature control cable adjustment

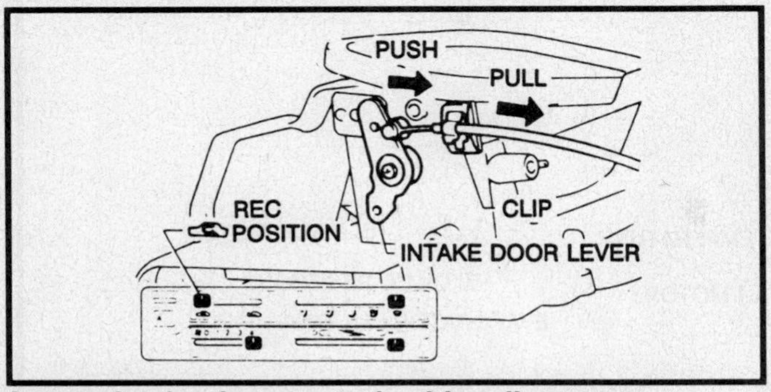
PUSH
PULL
REC
POSITION
CLIP
INTAKE DOOR LEVER

Axxess intake door control cable adjustment

3. Attach the cable to the link and pull the cable housing away from the cable end.
4. Secure the housing and operate the lever to check for smooth operation.

WATER VALVE CONTROL ROD

1. With the temperature control cable disconnected, push the air mix door lever towards the firewall.
2. With the rod loose at the air mix door end, move the valve link lever all the way towards the firewall.
3. The rod is attached to the valve with a wire loop. Gently pull the rod so there is about 0.080 in. (2mm) gap between the rod and valve lever and secure the rod at the door lever. Operate the lever by hand to check for smooth operation.

TEMPERATURE CONTROL CABLE

1. Set the control lever in the full **HOT** position.
2. With the air mix door in the full hot position, attach the cable and take up the slack in the housing away from the door lever.
3. Secure the housing and operate the lever to check for smooth operation.

INTAKE DOOR CONTROL CABLE

1. Set the control lever to the **RECIRCULATE** position.
2. Move the control link towards the cable housing clamp.
3. Attach the cable, take up the slack away from the link and secure the cable housing.

Automatic Temperature Control System

REMOVAL AND INSTALLATION

Pick-up and Pathfinder

1. Disconnect the negative battery cable. If the vehicle has a theft protected radio, obtain the owner's security code.
2. Remove the ash tray assembly to gain access to the screws for the center console bezel.
3. Remove the radio.
4. Remove the screws and carefully slide the control assembly straight out far enough to carefully unplug the wires.
5. When disassembling the unit for repair, most of the fasteners are plastic clips which can be easily pried apart. Be careful not to break the tabs. The knobs on the front can be removed with pliers but wrap a rag around the knob to keep from scratching the finish.
6. Installation is the reverse of removal. Reconnect the battery and test the system before installing the radio and console bezel.

ADJUSTMENTS

Pick-up and Pathfinder

MODE DOOR MOTOR

The mode door determines the air flow through the air distribution system depending on the mode selected (vent, defrost, etc.). The door linkage is located on the left side of the housing and is controled by a motor. The motor has a built–in position sensor and will stop at the position called for by the controls. The adjustment procedure starts with the motor linkage disconnected.

1. Remove the auto amplifier and relay bracket from the side of the heating unit, above the accelerator pedal.
2. Rotate the side link fully counter clockwise into the vent position.
3. If the rods have been disconnect, move the doors to the vent position and secure the rods. Operate the side link by hand to check for smooth operation.
4. With the motor installed on the housing but linkage disconnected, connect the motor wiring and turn the ignition switch **ON**.
5. Set the controls to the **VENT** mode, let the motor stop at its vent position and attach the linkage.

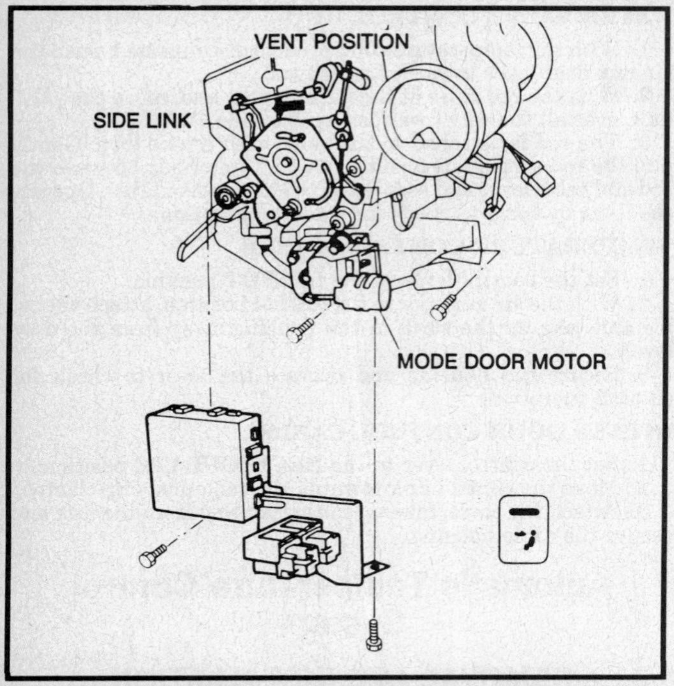
VENT POSITION
SIDE LINK
MODE DOOR MOTOR

Pick-up and Pathfinder mode door motor adjustment

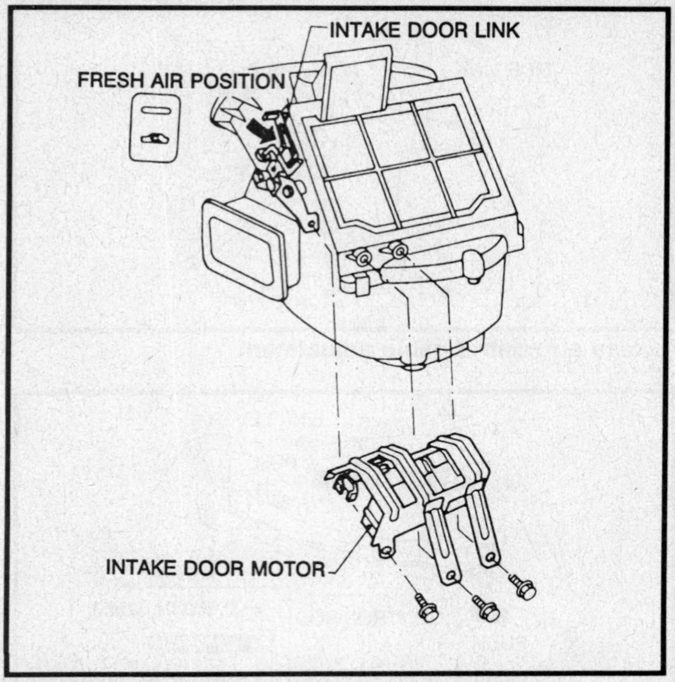
INTAKE DOOR LINK
FRESH AIR POSITION
INTAKE DOOR MOTOR

Pick-up and Pathfinder air intake door motor adjustment

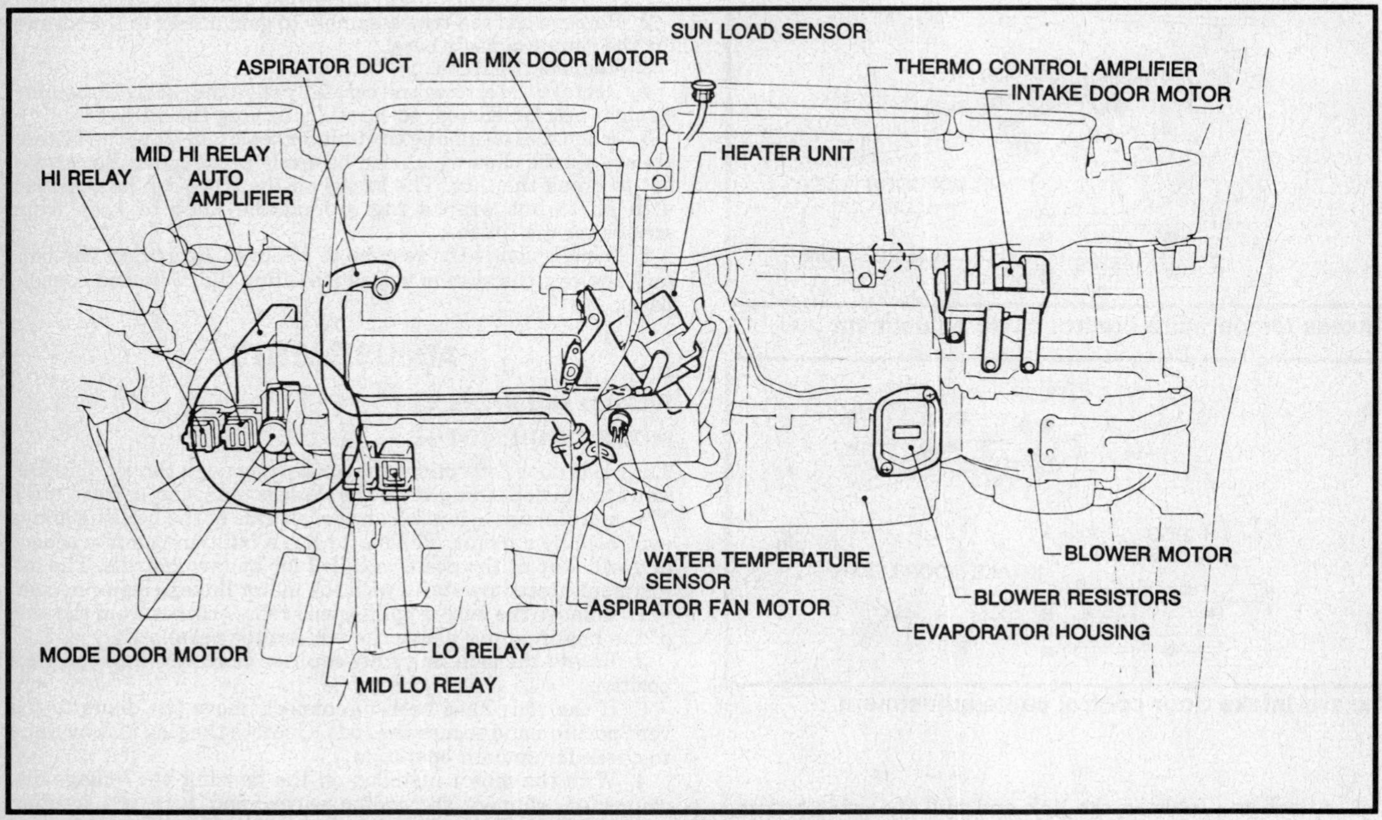
SUN LOAD SENSOR
ASPIRATOR DUCT
AIR MIX DOOR MOTOR
THERMO CONTROL AMPLIFIER
INTAKE DOOR MOTOR
HEATER UNIT
MID HI RELAY
HI RELAY
AUTO AMPLIFIER
WATER TEMPERATURE SENSOR
BLOWER MOTOR
ASPIRATOR FAN MOTOR
BLOWER RESISTORS
EVAPORATOR HOUSING
MODE DOOR MOTOR
LO RELAY
MID LO RELAY

Pick-up and Pathfinder automatic air conditioning system components

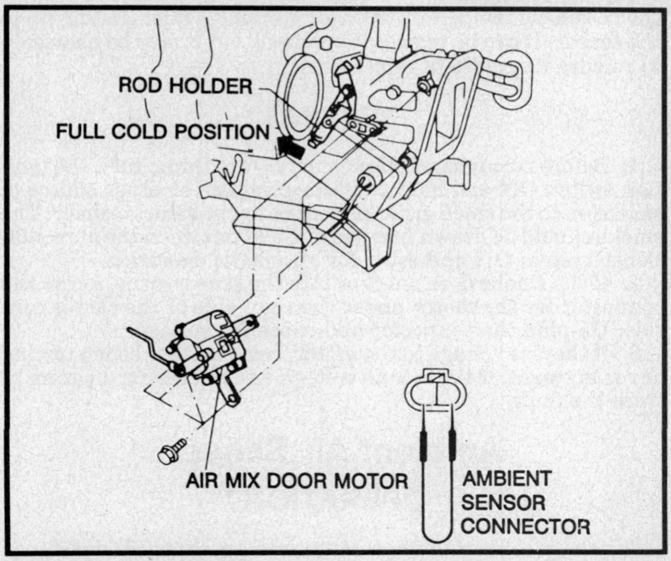
ROD HOLDER
FULL COLD POSITION
AIR MIX DOOR MOTOR
AMBIENT
SENSOR
CONNECTOR

Pick-up and Pathfinder air mix door motor adjustment

6. With the ignition switch **ON**, cycle the system to **DEF** and check the operation of the linkage.

AIR MIX DOOR MOTOR

1. With the motor installed but the rod disconnected, connect the wiring.
2. Near the hood latch in the front of the vehicle, disconnect the ambient temperature sensor and jumper the terminals together.
3. Set the temperature control lever to the full cold position and turn the ignition switch **ON**.
4. The motor will stop at the full cold position. Move the linkage to that position by hand and secure the rod.
5. Move the temperature control lever to full hot position and check the linkage for smooth operation. Remember to reconnect the temperature sensor.

AIR INTAKE DOOR

1. With the door motor removed but wiring connected, turn the ignition switch to **ACC** and make sure the recirculate button is **OFF**.
2. Hold the door in the fresh air position and install the motor.
3. Switch the recirculate button **ON** and **OFF** to check for smooth operation of the door.

SENSORS AND SWITCHES

Potentiometer Temperature Control Resistor

OPERATION

The PTC resistor is adjusted by moving the temperature control lever. Selecting a temperature selects an output value for the resistor that the amplifier will mathematically balance with the values from all the other temperature and position sensors. The resistor is built into the control amplifier and cannot be replaced separately, but it can be tested with an ohmmeter.

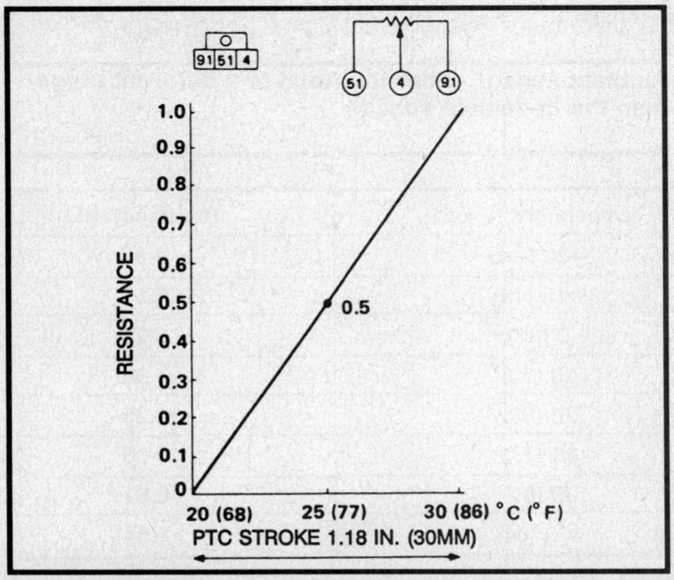
91 51 4
51
4
91
1.0
0.9
0.8
0.7
0.6
0.5
0.4
0.3
0.2
0.1
0
RESISTANCE
0.5
20 (68)
25 (77)
30 (86) °C (°F)
PTC STROKE 1.18 IN. (30MM)

Resistance values over lever position for PTC in the control amplifier, read at terminals 91 and 4

TESTING

1. With the control amplifier removed, touch the probes of an ohmmeter to the connector on the back of the amplifier. Set the meter to the 1000 ohm scale.
2. Move the temperature control lever and compare the resistance reading with the graph.
3. Some slight error may exist but a faulty resistor will produce an obviously bad reading. The resistor cannot be replaced separately.

In-vehicle Temperature Sensor

OPERATION

The sensor converts temperature into a resistance which the amplifier can read. It is in the left side of the control amplifier, behind the small grille and can be tested and replaced separately.

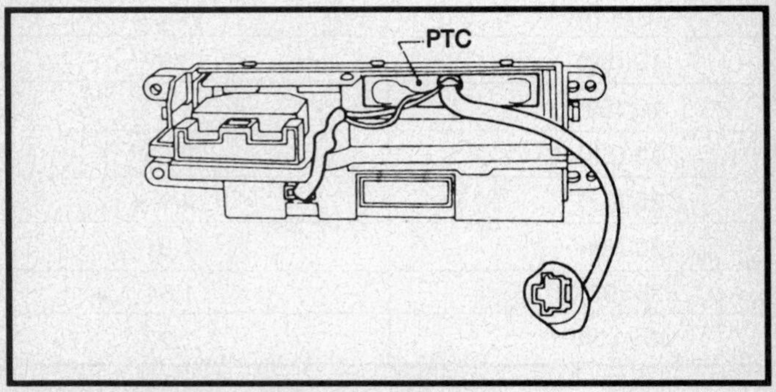
PTC

The PTC has its own wiring harness

TESTING

1. With the control amplifier removed, locate the sensor and its connector. Touch the probes of an ohmmeter to the terminals, with the meter on the 10,000 ohm scale.
2. Measure the resistance and the temperature, using a thermometer.
3. If the reading is greatly different from the specification, remove the sensor and test it at other temperatures before deciding to replace it. Use a cold drink container or a drop light to change the temperature but do not immerse the sensor.
4. If the sensor appears to work correctly, check the voltage supply to the sensor. With the control amplifier connected and the ignition switch **ON**, there should be 5 volts between the yellow/blue wire and ground.
5. If there is no voltage, check for continuity of the wires between the sensor and auto amplifier and for power output at the amplifier. If there is not 5 volts at the amplifier itself, chances are that other sensors are also not working.

Aspirator Motor

OPERATION

There is a small fan mounted in front of the heater unit which runs whenever the ignition is on. This fan draws inside air past the in-vehicle temperature sensor through a duct leading up to the sensor. It can be replaced separately but it may be necessary to remove the radio to gain access.

TESTING

1. Before removing or disconnecting anything, turn the ignition switch **ON** and hold a lighted cigarette or other source of smoke up to the small grille in front of the in-vehicle sensor. The smoke should be drawn into the grille. If not, turn the air conditioner system **ON** and set it for automatic operation.
2. If the smoke does not flow into the sensor grille, locate the connector for the motor under the right side of the center console. Un-plug the connector and check for voltage.
3. If there is voltage to the motor, remove it for bench testing or replacement. If there is no voltage, use the wiring diagram to trace the fault.

Ambient Air Sensor

OPERATION

This sensor converts temperature into an electrical resistance which the auto amplifier can read. It operates in a much different range than the in-vehicle sensor and they are not interchangable. The sensor and connecter are mounted under the hood, near the secondary latch.

TESTING

1. Disconnect the sensor and connect an ohmmeter set on the 10,000 ohm scale.

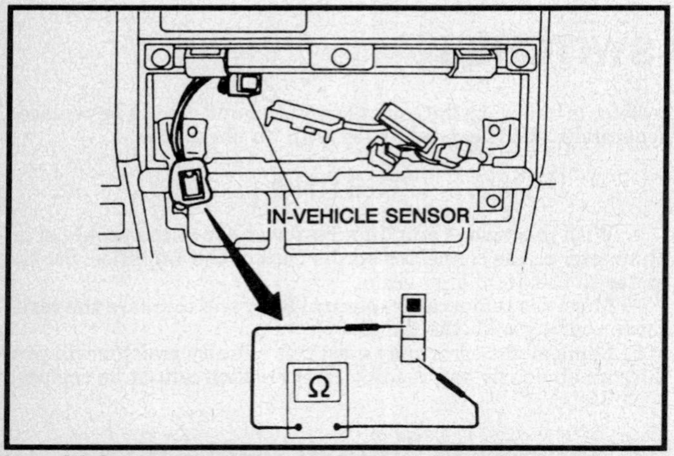
IN-VEHICLE SENSOR
Ω

In-vehicle temperature sensor can be tested with an ohmmeter and a thermometer

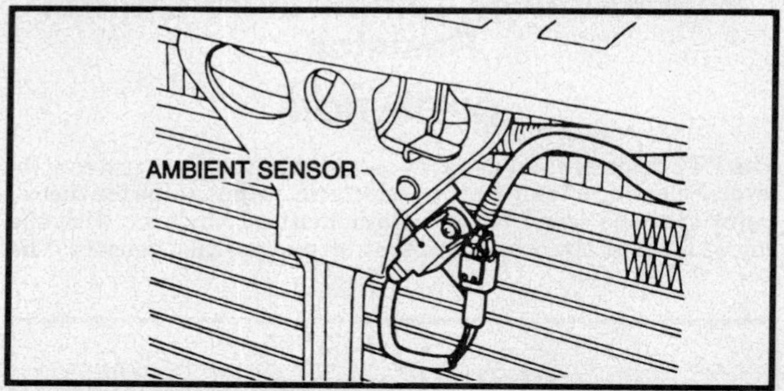
AMBIENT SENSOR

Ambient sensor under the hood is a different range than the in-vehicle sensor

Temperature °C (°F)	Resistance kΩ
0 (32)	6.19
5 (41)	4.95
10 (50)	3.99
15 (59)	3.24
20 (68)	2.65
25 (77)	2.19
30 (86)	1.81
35 (95)	1.51
40 (104)	1.27

Temperature and resistance for in-vehicle sensor

Temperature °C (°F)	Resistance kΩ
−20 (−4)	9.93
−10 (14)	5.57
0 (32)	3.26
10 (50)	1.98
20 (68)	1.25
25 (77)	1.00
30 (86)	0.81
40 (104)	0.54

Temperature and resistance for ambient sensor

2. Measure the resistance and the temperature, using a thermometer.

3. If the reading is greatly different from the specification, test the sensor at other temperatures before deciding to replace it. Use a cold drink container or a drop light to change the temperature but do not immerse the sensor.

4. If the sensor appears to work correctly, check the voltage supply to the sensor. With the control amplifier connected and the ignition switch **ON**, there should be 5 volts between the yellow wire and ground.

5. If there is no voltage, check for continuity of the wires between the sensor and auto amplifier and for power output at the amplifier. If there is not 5 volts at the amplifier itself, chances are that other sensors are also not working.

Sun Load Sensor

OPERATION

The sensor is a diode which converts light to a current that is fed to the auto amplifier. There the current is processed for use by the control amplifier. The sun load sensor is mounted in the defroster outlet vent, held by plastic spring clips on the sensor body.

TESTING

1. Above the accelerator pedal, un-plug the auto amplifier connectors.

2. Measure the voltage between terminal 6 of the large connector and terminal 5 of the smaller connector or between terminal 6 and ground.

3. Changing the light that strikes the sun load sensor should change the voltage and the current it puts out. A very bright light is required to see a change in output.

4. If the sensor appears to work correctly, check the voltage supply to the sensor. With the control amplifier connected and the ignition switch **ON**, there should be 5 volts between the orange wire and ground.

5. If there is no voltage, check for continuity of the wires between the sensor and auto amplifier, and for power output at the amplifier itself. If there is not 5 volts at the amplifier itself, chances are that other sensors are also not working.

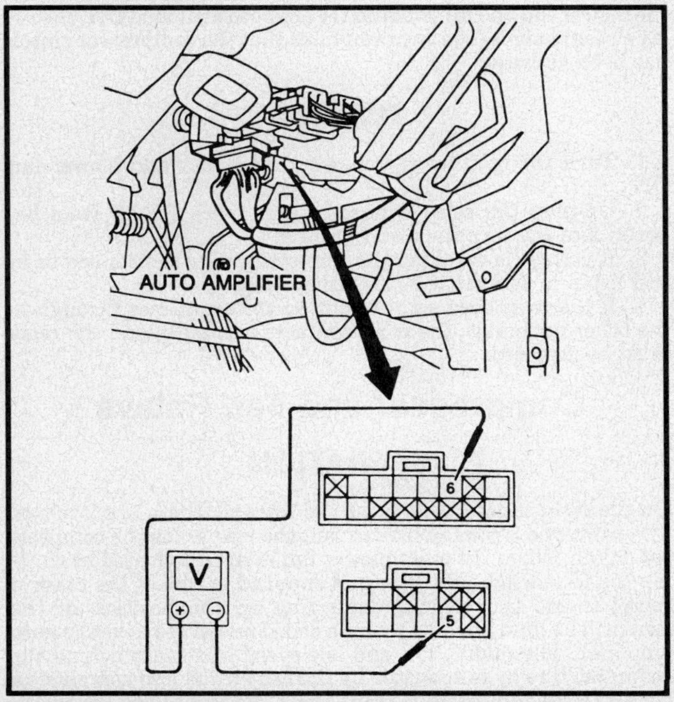
AUTO AMPLIFIER
6
V
5

Measure the voltage at the auto amplifier connectors to test the sun load sensor, compare the readings to the chart

Input current mA	Output voltage V
0	5.00
0.1	4.09
0.2	3.18
0.3	2.27
0.4	1.36
0.5	0.45

Current and voltage output for sun load sensor

Water Temperature Sensor

OPERATION

The sensor is mounted to the right side of the heater core and converts engine coolant temperature into an electrical resistance which the auto amplifier can read. It is dedicated to this system and not connected to any other system. This sensor operates through the micro-switch and is out of the control loop when the system is in **VENT** or **DEF** modes.

TESTING

1. Disconnect the sensor and connect an ohmmeter set on the 10,000 ohm scale.

2. Measure the resistance and the temperature, using a thermometer.

3. If the reading is greatly different from the specification, remove the sensor and test it at other temperatures before deciding to replace it. Use a cold drink container or a drop light to change the temperature but do not immerse the sensor.

4. If the sensor appears to work correctly, check the voltage supply to the sensor. With the control amplifier connected and the ignition switch **ON**, there should be 5 volts between the yellow/red wire and ground.

Ω

The water temperature sensor is on the right side of the heater core

Temperature °C (°F)	Resistance kΩ
0 (32)	3.99
10 (50)	2.54
20 (68)	1.67
30 (86)	1.12
40 (104)	0.78
50 (122)	0.55
60 (140)	0.40
70 (158)	0.29
80 (176)	0.22

Temperature and resistance for water temperature sensor

5. If there is no voltage, check for continuity of the wires between the sensor, the micro switch and the auto amplifier and for power output from the amplifier. If there is not 5 volts at the amplifier itself, chances are that other sensors are also not working.

Micro-Switch

OPERATION

The switch is on the left side of the heater and is activated by the side link. When the controls are set for **VENT** or **DEF**, the micro switch shorts the water temperature sensor circuit and the full 5 volts is returned to the auto amplifier. With the water temperature sensor out of the control loop, temperature control is manual even with the fan switch in the **AUTO** position.

TESTING

1. Turn the ignition switch **ON** and put the system controls in **VENT** mode.
2. Disconnect the micro-switch and check for continutiy between terminals 10 and 93. Make sure there is no continuity between terminals 10 and 52 or between 52 and 93.
3. Put the system controls in **FOOT** mode and check for continuity between terminals 10 and 52. Make sure there is no continuity between 10 and 93.

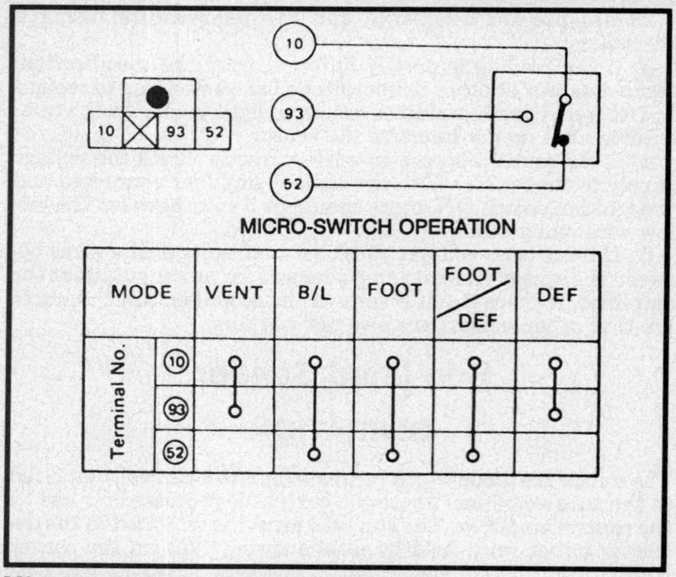
10
93
52
10 93 52
MICRO-SWITCH OPERATION
MODE
VENT
B/L
FOOT
FOOT/DEF
DEF
Terminal No.
10
93
52

Micro-switch testing schematic

Dual Pressure Switch

OPERATION

The switch is mounted in the top of the reciever/drier. Its function is to turn the compressor clutch off if the freon pressure in the high side is too high or too low. It can only be properly tested when gauges are connected to the service valves. Replacing the switch requires discharging the freon from the system into recovery equipment.

TESTING

1. When pressure is decreasing, the switch should open (compressor off) when high side pressure is 26–31 psi. or close (compressor on) when pressure gets down to 270–327 psi.
2. When pressure is increasing, the switch should close (compressor on) when high side pressure is 26–34 psi. or open (compressor off) when pressure is 356–412 psi.
3. If all other tests indicate a faulty dual pressure switch, disconnect the wiring and jumper the terminals to simulate a closed switch. If the compressor clutch operates, make sure the freon pressures are correct before replacing the switch.

Auto Amplifier Relay

OPERATION

The relay is mounted to the inner fender near the battery. When the blower fan and air conditioner are both switched **ON**, the relay closes to signal the auto amplifier that the compressor clutch has been activated.

TESTING

1. Turn the ignition switch, air conditioner and blower fan **ON**.
2. Un-plug the relay connector and check for 12 volts between 2 of the terminals and ground.
3. If voltage is reaching the connector, plug the connector in and listen or feel for the relay activating.
4. If the relay does activate but no voltage passes through to the other terminals, the relay contacts are faulty and the relay must be replaced.

Compressor and Fan Relays

OPERATION

On the right inner fender near the firewall, there are 2 relays. The front one is for the blower fan, the rear is for the compressor clutch. When the main blower fan relay is activated by turning the fan switch **ON**, power is supplied to one of the other 4 relays inside the vehicle, depending on the position of the switch. The high and middle high speed relays are near the auto amplifier. The middle low and low speed relays are behind the radio. Each relay is activated by the fan switch and completes a circuit to the fan resistor mounted on the front of the evaporator housing. The compressor relay is activated by the engine computer through the dual pressure switch and the thremo control amplifier.

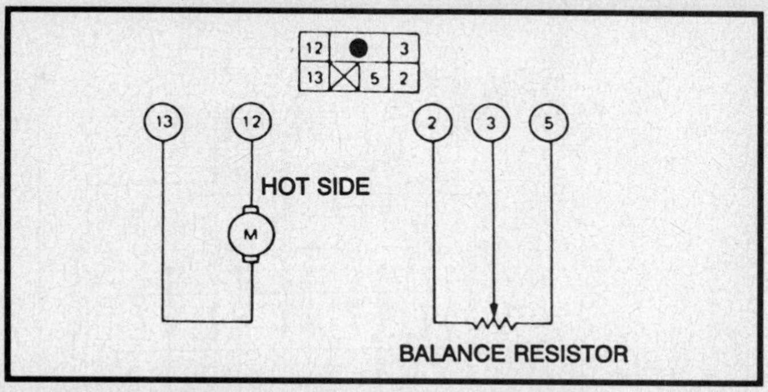
12
3
13
5
2
13
12
2
3
5
HOT SIDE
M
BALANCE RESISTOR

Power balance resistor and motor connections for testing air mix door position sensor

TESTING

1. Turn the ignition switch, air conditioner and blower fan **ON**.
2. Un-plug the relay connector and check for 12 volts between 2 of the terminals and ground.
3. If voltage is reaching the connector, plug the connector in and listen or feel for the relay activating. If no voltage is reaching the connector, make sure the fan switch is in the correct position for the relay being tested.
4. If the relay does activate but no voltage passes through to the other terminals, the relay contacts are faulty and the relay must be replaced.

Air Mix Door Position Sensor

OPERATION

The sensor is a Potentiometer Balance Resistor (PBR) built into the air mix door motor. A voltage is supplied to terminal No. 2 on the motor and a variable resistor returns a portion of the voltage to the amplifier from terminals 3 and 5. The amplifier interprets the return voltage as a door position.

TESTING

1. With all wiring connected and the air mix door in the full cold position, there should be 5 volts between terminal 2 and ground. There should be 12 volts between terminal 12 and ground. If not, check the wiring and power supplies from the auto amplifier.
2. With the air mix door in full cold position, there should be 0 volts between terminals 3 and 5 at the door motor connector.
3. Move the temperature control lever to a warmer position and see that the voltage between terminals 3 and 5 increases to 5 volts as the door position reaches full hot.
4. A faulty resistor unit cannot be repaired, the door motor must be replaced.

Thermo Control Amplifier

OPERATION

This amplifier is mounted on top of the evaporator housing on the blower motor side. Its function is to prevent ice build-up on the evaporator by turning the compressor relay off when the housing air temperature is near freezing. It can be considered a temperature controlled solid state relay, normally closed.

TESTING

1. With the ignition switch and air conditioner **OFF**, un-plug the connector at the dual pressure switch on the receiver/drier. Check for continuity of the green/orange wire between the dual pressure switch and the thermo amplifier.
2. Reconnect the dual pressure switch, turn the air conditioner and ignition **ON** and, at the thermo amplifier connector, check for 8–9 volts between the green/orange wire and ground. With the ignition **OFF**, check for conitinuity between the green/blue wire and ground.
3. If these tests show correct results, the thermo amplifier will allow the compressor to run. If ice builds up in the evaporator housing, the thermo amplifier will not turn the compressor off as required. This amplifier cannot be repaired.

Auto Amplifier

OPERATION

This is literally the brain of the system. The auto amplifier supplies power to all the sensors, reads the return signal and the temperature control lever position and operates the blower fan relays and air mix door motor. The amplifier also sends a signal to the engine control computer when compressor operation is required. The engine computer turns on the air conditioner relay and the Auxiliary Air Control (AAC) valve to increase idle speed. The auto amplifier program includes the ability to average the input from the sun load sensor, so sudden changes like driving in and out of shady areas will not cause sudden oscillations in air conditioner output. If the system is in **AUTO** mode when the engine is started in cold weather, the auto amplifier will run the blower fan at low speed until the heater core temperature is at least 120°F (50°C).

TESTING

1. First check the fuses. With the ignition switch **ON**, make sure power is available to the auto amplifier at terminal No. 1 on the smaller connector. Terminal No. 17 on the same connector is the amplifier ground. Also check for power going to the control unit at terminal No. 34 and a good ground at terminal No. 37.
2. Check that each temperature sensor is getting a steady 5 volts from the amplifier and that each sensor is returning a steady voltage. If supply voltage is not steady, the amplifier is faulty. The return voltage should be less than supply and should also be steady.
3. If the system can be operated in manual mode but not automatic and the voltages to and from the amplifier are correct, this does not necessarily mean the amplifier is faulty. Be sure all other components of the system are correct before replacing the auto amplifier.

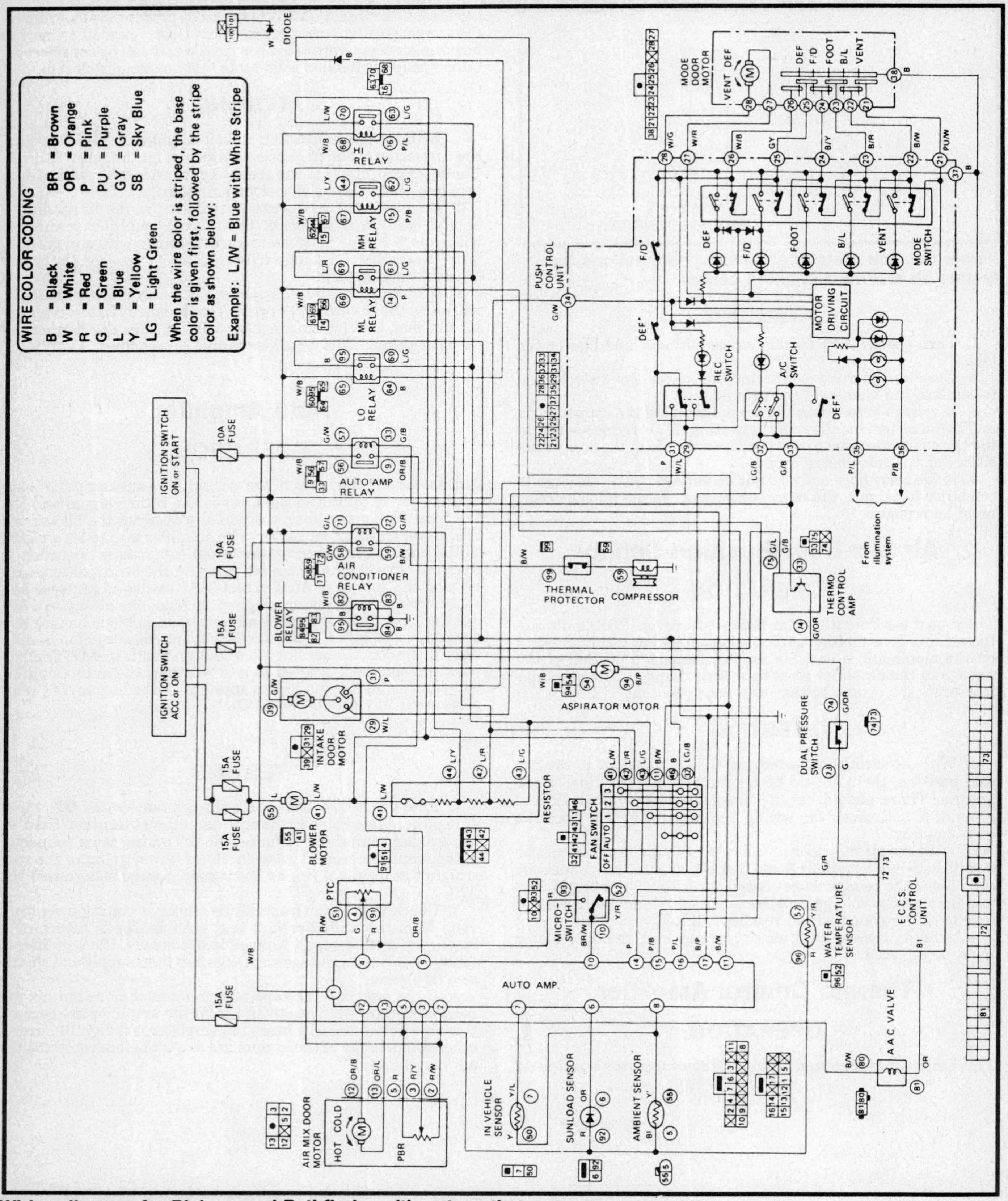
WIRE COLOR CODING
B = Black
W = White
R = Red
G = Green
L = Blue
Y = Yellow
LG = Light Green
BR = Brown
OR = Orange
P = Pink
PU = Purple
GY = Gray
SB = Sky Blue
When the wire color is striped, the base color is given first, followed by the stripe color as shown below:
Example: L/W = Blue with White Stripe
IGNITION SWITCH ON or START
IGNITION SWITCH ACC or ON
10A FUSE
15A FUSE
HI RELAY
MH RELAY
ML RELAY
LO RELAY
AUTO AMP RELAY
AIR CONDITIONER RELAY
BLOWER RELAY
INTAKE DOOR MOTOR
BLOWER MOTOR
RESISTOR
FAN SWITCH
PTC
MICRO-SWITCH
AUTO AMP.
AIR MIX DOOR MOTOR
HOT
COLD
PBR
IN VEHICLE SENSOR
SUNLOAD SENSOR
AMBIENT SENSOR
THERMAL PROTECTOR
COMPRESSOR
ASPIRATOR MOTOR
DUAL PRESSURE SWITCH
THERMO CONTROL AMP
WATER TEMPERATURE SENSOR
ECCS CONTROL UNIT
AAC VALVE
PUSH CONTROL UNIT
MODE DOOR MOTOR
MODE SWITCH
MOTOR DRIVING CIRCUIT
REC SWITCH
A/C SWITCH
From illumination system
DIODE

Wiring diagram for Pick-up and Pathfinder with automatic temperature control

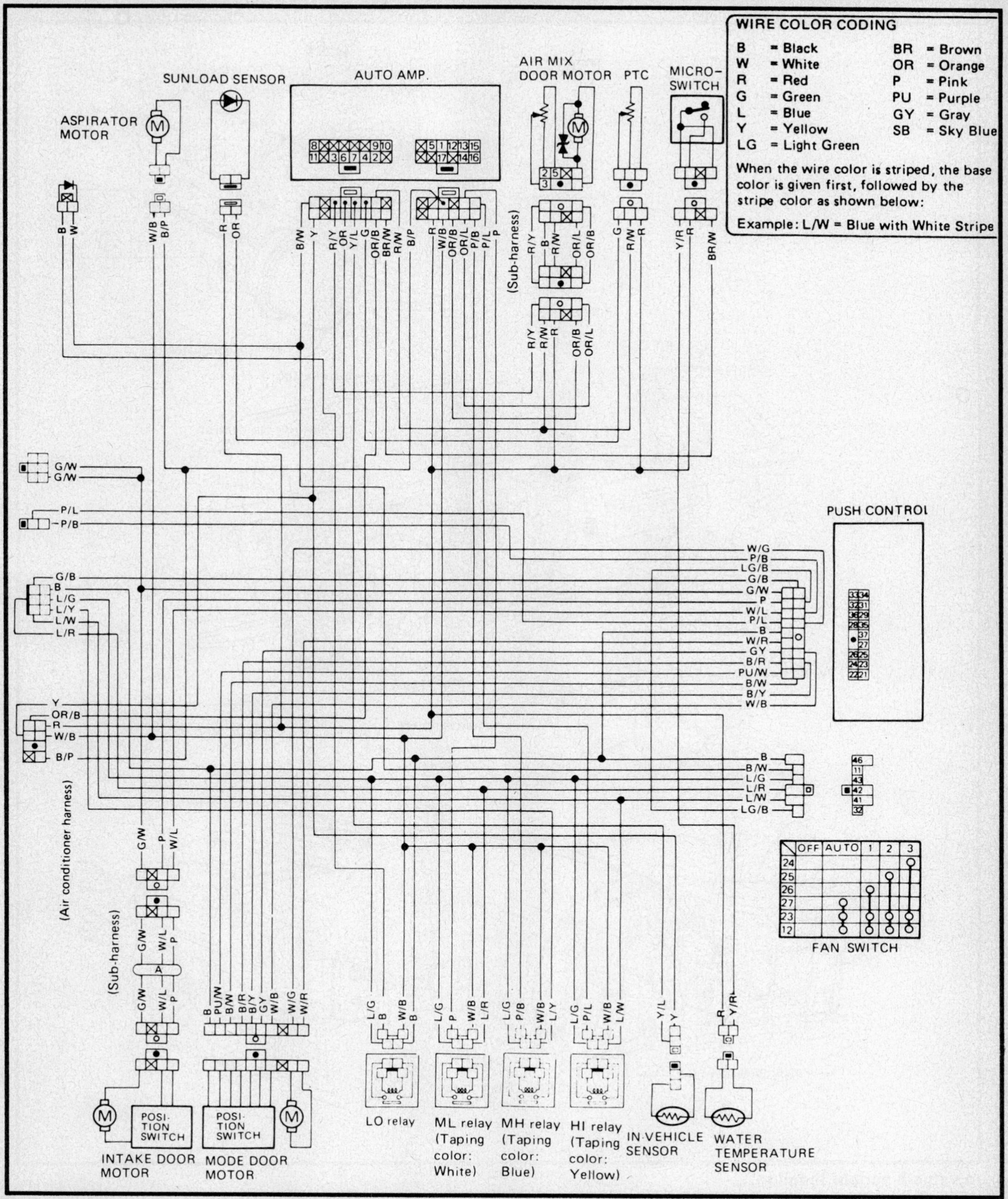
WIRE COLOR CODING
B = Black
W = White
R = Red
G = Green
L = Blue
Y = Yellow
LG = Light Green
BR = Brown
OR = Orange
P = Pink
PU = Purple
GY = Gray
SB = Sky Blue
When the wire color is striped, the base color is given first, followed by the stripe color as shown below:
Example: L/W = Blue with White Stripe
SUNLOAD SENSOR
AUTO AMP.
AIR MIX DOOR MOTOR
PTC
MICRO-SWITCH
ASPIRATOR MOTOR
(Sub-harness)
PUSH CONTROL
(Air conditioner harness)
FAN SWITCH
OFF
AUTO
1
2
3
POSI-TION SWITCH
INTAKE DOOR MOTOR
MODE DOOR MOTOR
LO relay
ML relay (Taping color: White)
MH relay (Taping color: Blue)
HI relay (Taping color: Yellow)
IN-VEHICLE SENSOR
WATER TEMPERATURE SENSOR

Wiring diagram for Pick-up and Pathfinder with automatic temperature control; continued

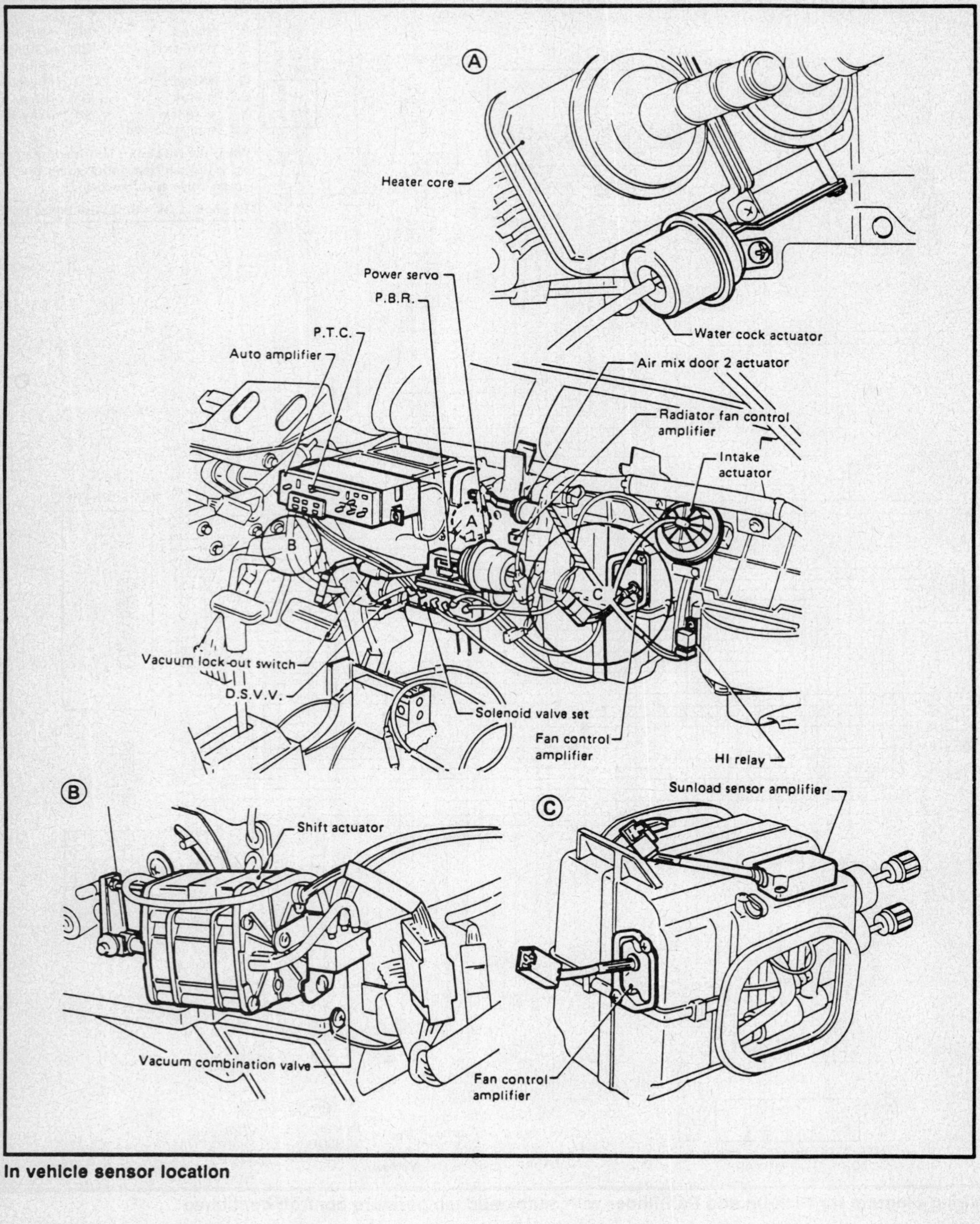
A
Heater core
Water cock actuator
Power servo
P.B.R.
P.T.C.
Auto amplifier
Air mix door 2 actuator
Radiator fan control amplifier
Intake actuator
A
B
C
Vacuum lock-out switch
D.S.V.V.
Solenoid valve set
Fan control amplifier
HI relay
B
Shift actuator
Vacuum combination valve
C
Sunload sensor amplifier
Fan control amplifier

In vehicle sensor location

34 TOYOTA TRUCKS 34

LAND CRUISER • PICK-UP • PREVIA • VAN • 4 RUNNER

SPECIFICATIONS

ENGINE IDENTIFICATION

Year	Model	Engine Displacement cu. in. (cc/liter)	Engine Series Identification	No. of Cylinders	Engine Type
1989	Pick-Up	144.4 (2366/2.4)	22R	4	OHC
	Pick-Up	144.4 (2366/2.4)	22R-E	4	OHC
	Pick-Up	180.5 (2959/3.0)	3VZ-E	6	OHC
	4Runner	144.4 (2366/2.4)	22R-E	4	OHC
	4Runner	180.5 (2959/3.0)	3VZ-E	6	OHC
	Land Cruiser	241.3 (3956/4.0)	3F-E	6	OHV
	Van	136.5 (2237/2.2)	4Y-EC	4	OHC
1990	Pick-Up	144.4 (2366/2.4)	22R	4	OHC
	Pick-Up	144.4 (2366/2.4)	22R-E	4	OHC
	Pick-Up	180.5 (2959/3.0)	3VZ-E	6	OHC
	4Runner	144.4 (2366/2.4)	22R-E	4	OHC
	4Runner	180.5 (2959/3.0)	3VZ-E	6	OHC
	Land Cruiser	241.3 (3956/4.0)	3F-E	6	OHV
	Van	136.5 (2237/2.2)	4Y-EC	4	OHC
1991	Pick-Up	144.4 (2366/2.4)	22R	4	OHC
	Pick-Up	144.4 (2366/2.4)	22R-E	4	OHC
	Pick-Up	180.5 (2959/3.0)	3VZ-E	6	OHC
	4Runner	144.4 (2366/2.4)	22R-E	4	OHC
	4Runner	180.5 (2959/3.0)	3VZ-E	6	OHC
	Land Cruiser	241.3 (3956/4.0)	3F-E	6	OHV
	Previa	148.6 (2438/2.4)	2TZ-FE	4	OHC

REFRIGERANT CAPACITIES

Year	Model	Freon (oz.)	Oil (fl. oz.)	Type
1989	Pick-Up	1.3–1.7	2.0–3.4	R-12
	4Runner	1.7–1.9	2.0–3.4	R-12
	Van	1.3–1.7 ①	2.0–3.4 ②	R-12
	Land Cruiser	1.8–2.0	2.0–3.5	R-12
1990	Pick-Up	1.3–1.7	2.0–3.4	R-12
	4Runner	1.7–1.9	2.0–3.4	R-12
	Van	1.3–1.7 ①	2.0–3.4 ②	R-12
	Land Cruiser	1.8–2.0	2.0–3.5	R-12
1991	Pick-Up	1.3–1.7	2.0–3.4	R-12
	4Runner	1.7–1.9	2.0–3.4	R-12
	Previa	2.0–2.2 ③	2.0–3.4 ④	R-12
	Land Cruiser	1.8–2.0	2.0–3.5	R-12

① Rear Air 3.0–3.2
② Rear Air 4.0–6.5
③ Rear Air 2.7–2.8
④ Rear Air 2.2–3.6

AIR CONDITIONING BELT TENSION CHART

Year	Model	Engine Displacement cu. in. (cc/liter)	Belt Type	New	Used
1989	Pick-Up	144.4 (2366/2.4)	All	100–150	60–100
	Pick-Up	180.5 (2959/3.0)	All	100–150	60–100
	4Runner	144.4 (2366/2.4)	All	100–150	60–100
	4Runner	180.5 (2959/3.0)	All	100–150	60–100
	Land Cruiser	241.3 (3956/4.0)	All	100–150	60–100
	Van	136.5 (2237/2.2)	All	100–150	60–100
1990	Pick-Up	144.4 (2366/2.4)	All	100–150	60–100
	Pick-Up	180.5 (2959/3.0)	All	100–150	60–100
	4Runner	144.4 (2366/2.4)	All	100–150	60–100
	4Runner	180.5 (2959/3.0)	All	100–150	60–100
	Land Cruiser	241.3 (3956/4.0)	All	100–150	60–100
	Van	136.5 (2237/2.2)	All	100–150	60–100
1991	Pick-Up	144.4 (2366/2.4)	All	100–150	60–100
	Pick-Up	180.5 (2959/3.0)	All	100–150	60–100
	4Runner	144.4 (2366/2.4)	All	100–150	60–100
	4Runner	180.5 (2959/3.0)	All	100–150	60–100
	Land Cruiser	241.3 (3956/4.0)	All	100–150	60–100
	Previa	148.6 (2438/2.4)	All	120–160	100–140

SYSTEM DESCRIPTION

General Information

All vehicles use a conventional heating and cooling system. An engine belt driven air conditioning compressor supplies system pressure for the air conditioning. An in-cab mounted cooling unit combines with a radiator mounted condenser and receiver to make up the air conditioning system. Hot water for the heater core is supplied under pressure from the engine cooling system.

A blend-air type fresh air system regulates the temperature of the air in the cab. Control operation is by a combination of manual cable control and electrical switches. On some vehicles, the compressor is equipped with a cut-off solenoid which will momentarily shut off the compressor under certain conditions such as wide-open throttle and low idle speeds.

In order for the compressor clutch to be activated, a series of components must be energized. For example, the ignition switch must be **ON**, the blower switch must be **ON**, also causing the heater relay to switch **ON**. The air conditioning switch must be **ON**, causing the air conditioning amplifier to turn **ON**. The low pressure switch must be **ON**, indicating system pressure is more than 30 psi. The the Vacuum Switching Valve (VSV) must go **ON**, resulting in the idle up signal. After all of these condition have been met, the magnetic clutch should turn ON.

Note that the Van, 4Runner and Previa vehicles may use both a front and rear heating and cooling system.

Service Valve Location

Service valves are located on the compressor. When installing manifold gauges, the fittings for attaching the gauges are also located on the compressor, at the service valves.

System Discharging

Refrigerant containing CFCs for automobile air conditioners is believed to cause harm by depleting the ozone layer which helps protect the earth from the ultraviolet rays of the sun.

For this reason, it is necessary to prevent the release of refrigerant to the atmosphere and to use the minimum amount of new refrigerant when servicing the air conditioner. New equipment is available to recover and recycle used refrigerant. It should be used when discharging the system for service, when moisture or air gets into the system or when excess refrigerant must be removed. To prevent release of refrigerant, use charging hoses with stop valves when installing the manifold gauge set to the service valves.

When handling the recovery machine, always follow the manufacturer's recommended practices. After refrigerant recovery, the amount of compressor oil removed must be measured and the same amount added to the system.

System Evacuating

To prevent release and wasteful use of refrigerant, evacuate air with care from the refrigeration system. Do not evacuate before recovering refrigerant in the system.

The use of a refrigerant recovery machine is recommended. After the refrigerant has been recovered, follow the manufacturer's recommendation to pump down the system to evacuate

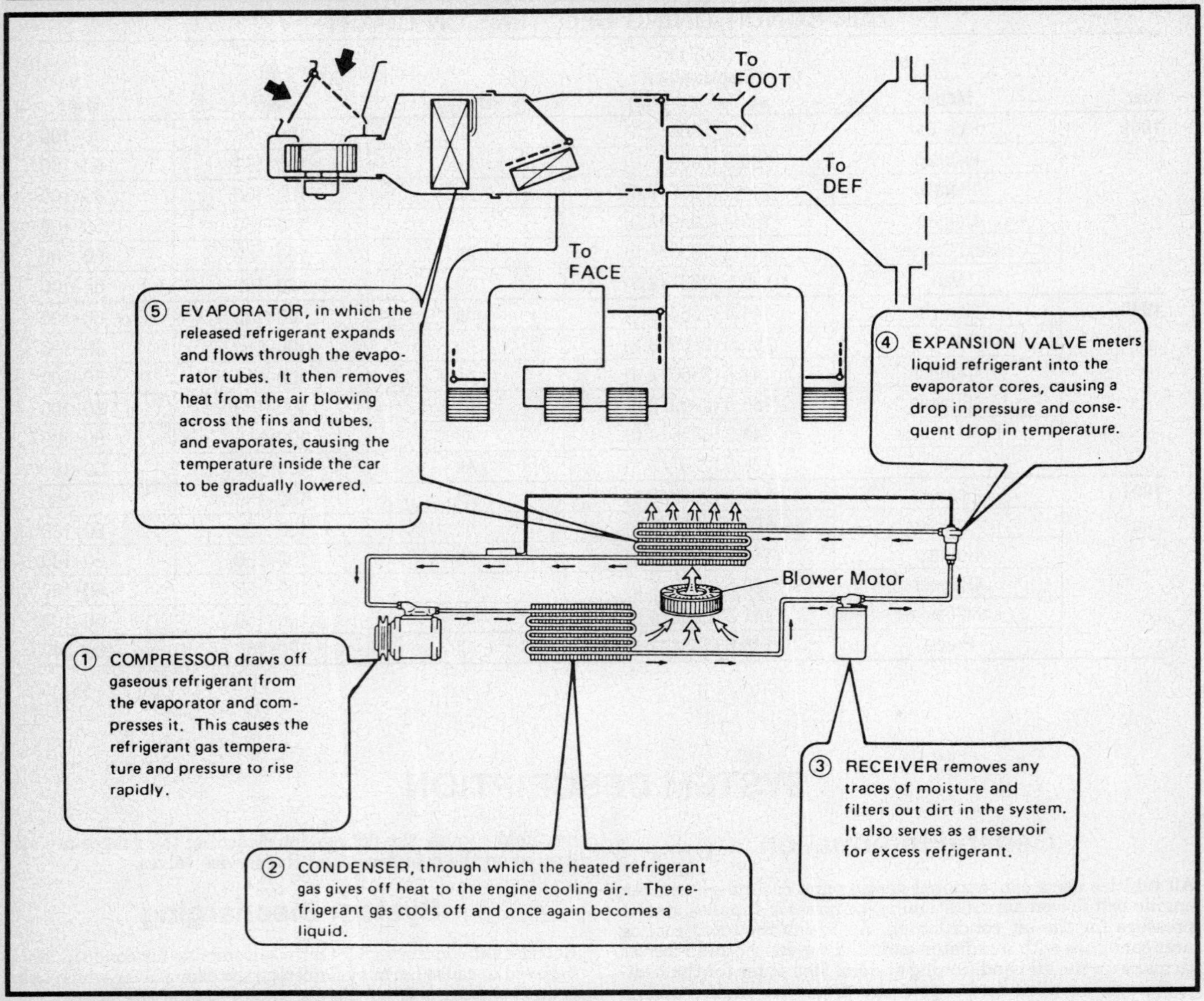
To FOOT
To DEF
To FACE
⑤ EVAPORATOR, in which the released refrigerant expands and flows through the evaporator tubes. It then removes heat from the air blowing across the fins and tubes, and evaporates, causing the temperature inside the car to be gradually lowered.
④ EXPANSION VALVE meters liquid refrigerant into the evaporator cores, causing a drop in pressure and consequent drop in temperature.
Blower Motor
① COMPRESSOR draws off gaseous refrigerant from the evaporator and compresses it. This causes the refrigerant gas temperature and pressure to rise rapidly.
③ RECEIVER removes any traces of moisture and filters out dirt in the system. It also serves as a reservoir for excess refrigerant.
② CONDENSER, through which the heated refrigerant gas gives off heat to the engine cooling air. The refrigerant gas cools off and once again becomes a liquid.

General air conditioning operation and basic components

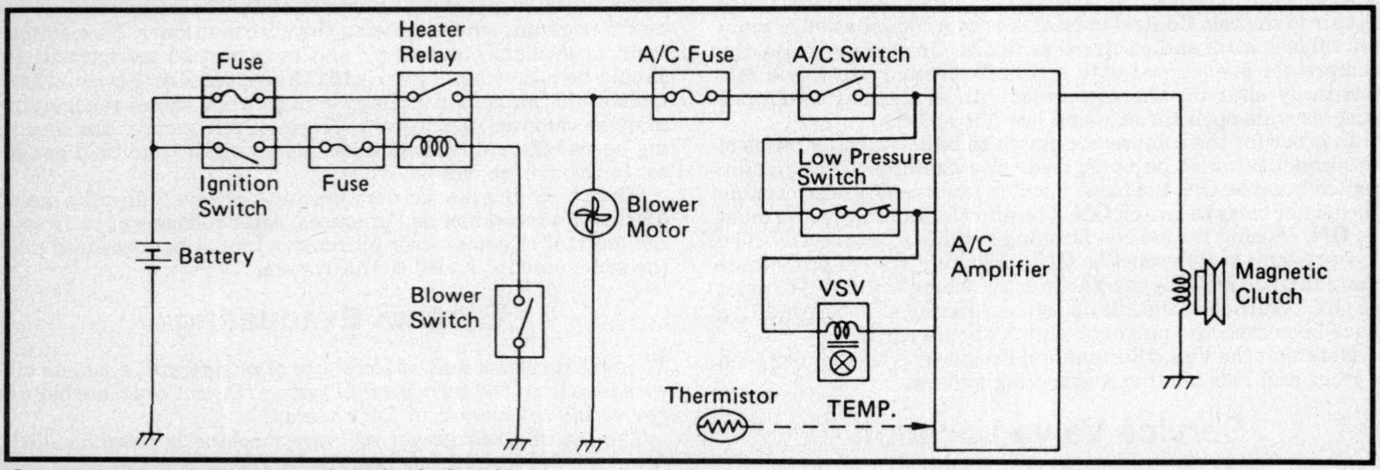
Fuse
Heater Relay
A/C Fuse
A/C Switch
Ignition Switch
Fuse
Low Pressure Switch
Blower Motor
Battery
A/C Amplifier
VSV
Magnetic Clutch
Blower Switch
Thermistor
TEMP.

General air conditioning electrical circuit

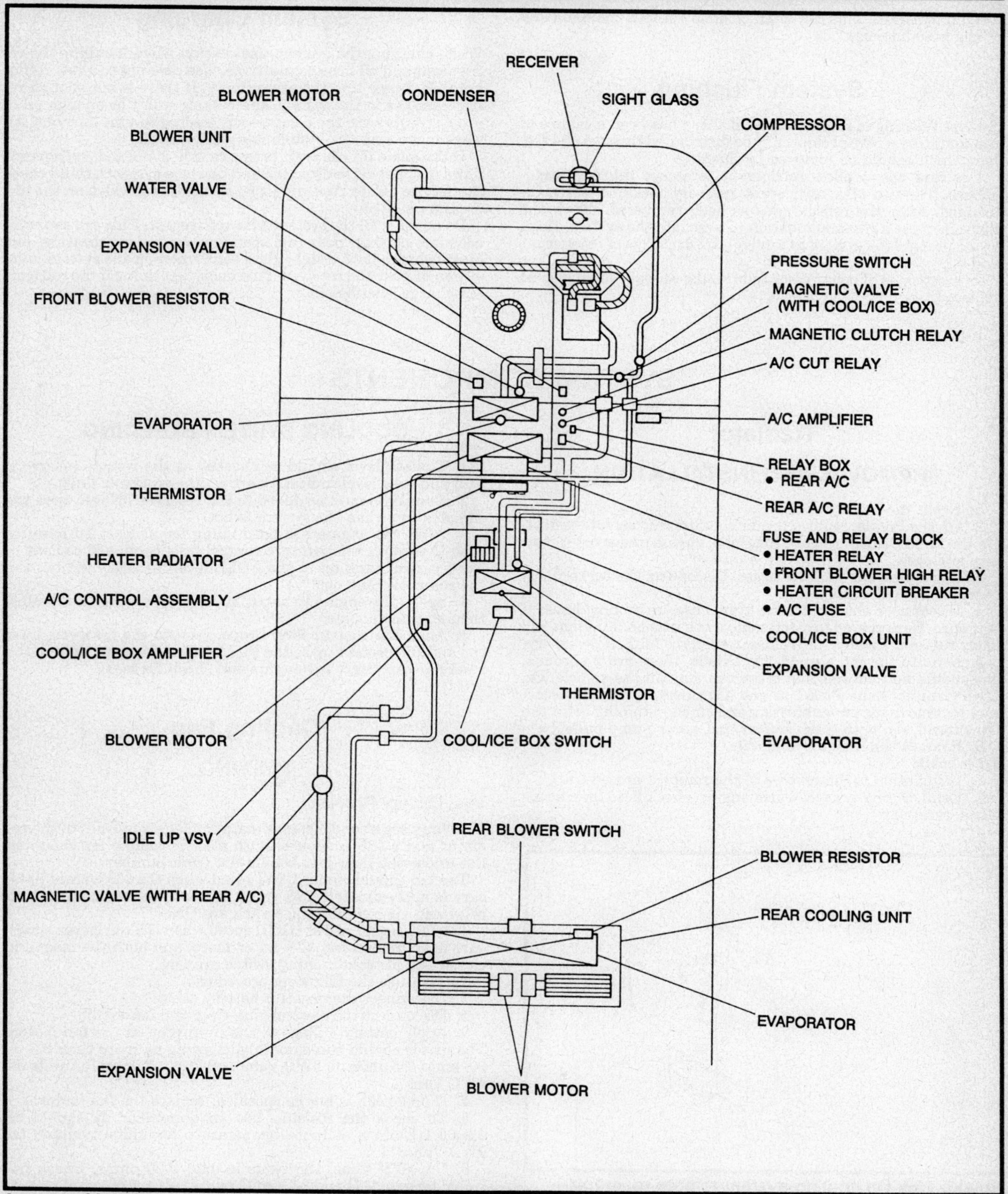
RECEIVER
BLOWER MOTOR
CONDENSER
SIGHT GLASS
COMPRESSOR
BLOWER UNIT
WATER VALVE
EXPANSION VALVE
FRONT BLOWER RESISTOR
PRESSURE SWITCH
MAGNETIC VALVE (WITH COOL/ICE BOX)
MAGNETIC CLUTCH RELAY
A/C CUT RELAY
A/C AMPLIFIER
EVAPORATOR
RELAY BOX
• REAR A/C
THERMISTOR
REAR A/C RELAY
FUSE AND RELAY BLOCK
• HEATER RELAY
• FRONT BLOWER HIGH RELAY
• HEATER CIRCUIT BREAKER
• A/C FUSE
HEATER RADIATOR
A/C CONTROL ASSEMBLY
COOL/ICE BOX UNIT
COOL/ICE BOX AMPLIFIER
EXPANSION VALVE
THERMISTOR
BLOWER MOTOR
COOL/ICE BOX SWITCH
EVAPORATOR
IDLE UP VSV
REAR BLOWER SWITCH
BLOWER RESISTOR
MAGNETIC VALVE (WITH REAR A/C)
REAR COOLING UNIT
EVAPORATOR
EXPANSION VALVE
BLOWER MOTOR

Layout of heating and cooling components—1991 Previa with rear heating

air and moisture. This can often be done without changing any of the hose hookups.

System Flushing

System flushing is recommended if there has been a failure of the compressor. Metal chips may be distributed through the system which should be removed by flushing.

Use care not to allow refrigerant to escape into the atmosphere. The use of a refrigerant recovery machine is recommended. After the refrigerant has been recovered, follow the manufacturer's recommendation to evacuate the system, flush it and prepare the system to receive a fresh charge of refrigerant and oil.

In most cases of compressor failure, the receiver must also be replaced.

System Charging

When charging the system, use caution when handling the refrigerant and all hose connections. Use care not to allow refrigerant to escape into the atmosphere. If there is not enough refrigerant gas in the system, there likely won't be enough oil to properly lubricate the compressor, leading to unit burnout. Always make sure the system has sufficient oil.

If the valve on the high pressure side is opened, refrigerant flows in the reverse direction and on some systems, could cause the service can to rupture. Open and close the valve on the low pressure side only.

Do not overfill the system with refrigerant. This can cause inadequate cooling, poor fuel economy, engine overheating, etc. Most vehicles have a sight glass somewhere in the system, usually on or near the receiver. This helps determine if the refrigerant charge is sufficient.

SYSTEM COMPONENTS

Radiator

REMOVAL AND INSTALLATION

1. Drain the cooling system.
2. On the Previa, remove the air conditioning air intake duct. On the Land Cruiser remove the grille, engine under cover, battery and case.
3. Disconnect the radiator hoses. Disconnect the turbocharger water hose, if equipped.
4. Disconnect the automatic transmission cooling lines, if equipped. Be prepared to catch some transmission fluid that will likely run out. Remove the radiator overflow tank, if necessary.
5. Remove the fan shroud. On Previa, there are 2 shrouds; one should be removed, the other can stay on the vehicle. On Land Cruiser, some Pick-Ups and 4Runners, it may be necessary to remove the power steering and air conditioning belts, the fan shroud, fan with fluid coupler and water pump pulley.
6. Remove the radiator assembly.

To install:

7. Installation is the reverse of the removal procedure.
8. Refill cooling system, warm engine, check fluid level at external reservoir.

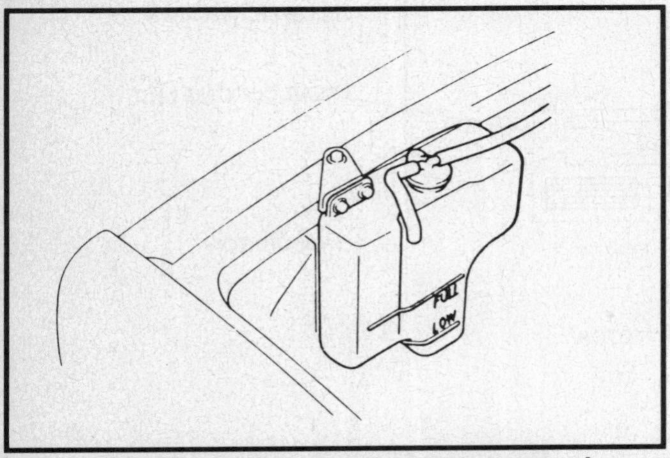
FULL
LOW

Toyota Pick-Up cooling system remote reservoir—others similar

COOLING SYSTEM BLEEDING

1. Coolant level should be checked at the remote reservoir. Full and Low level indicators are on the reservoir tank.
2. Coolant should be added to the reservoir. Never open the radiator cap when the system is hot.
3. After the engine has been idling for at least 10 minutes with the heater temperature control fully open, add coolant to the reservoir tank up to the FULL level. Securely tighten the the reservoir tank cap.
4. Speed the engine to about 2000–3000 rpm for 5 minutes, then stop the engine.
5. After the coolant level drops, remove the reservoir tank cap and add coolant up to the FULL mark. Securely tighten the reservoir cap. Start the engine and check for leaks.

Cooling Fan

TESTING

Van, Except Previa

The Van uses 2 condensers, a main condenser in front of the radiator and a sub condenser with electric cooling fan mounted flat under the floor just behind the front bumper.

The fan should run at LOW speed when the refrigerant pressure is approximately 235 psi or less, and the magnetic clutch relay and air conditioning switch are ON.

The fan should run at HIGH speed when the refrigerant pressure is approximately 235 psi or more, and both the magnetic clutch and air conditioning switch are ON.

To test, use the following procedure:

1. Disconnect the negative battery cable.
2. Disconnect the electric plug from the fan motor.
3. Apply battery voltage to the connector on the fan motor. The motor should run smoothly, drawing no more than 8.3 ± 0.8 amps for units on 2WD Vans or 6.7 ± 0.7 amps for units on 4WD Vans.
4. If operation is not as specified, replace the fan motor.
5. To check the resistor, use an ohmmeter. It should be 0.9 ± 0.1 k ohms at room temperature for units mounted on 2WD Vans.
6. On 4WD Vans, the value is 0.24–0.30 ohms. Check between terminals **B** and **b1** and **D** and **d1**. If out of specification, replace the resistor.

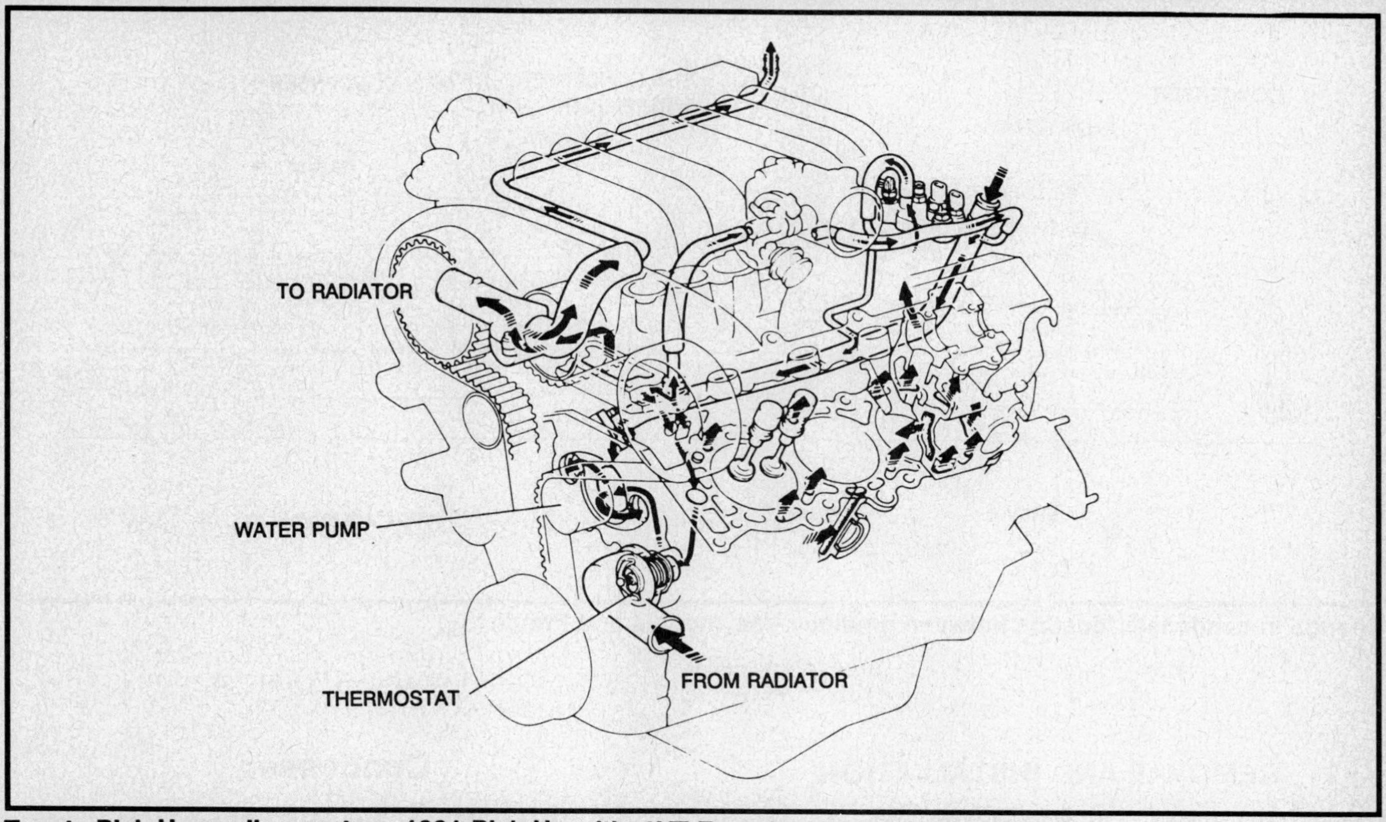
TO RADIATOR
WATER PUMP
THERMOSTAT
FROM RADIATOR

Toyota Pick-Up cooling system. 1991 Pick-Up with 3VZ-E engine shown—others similar

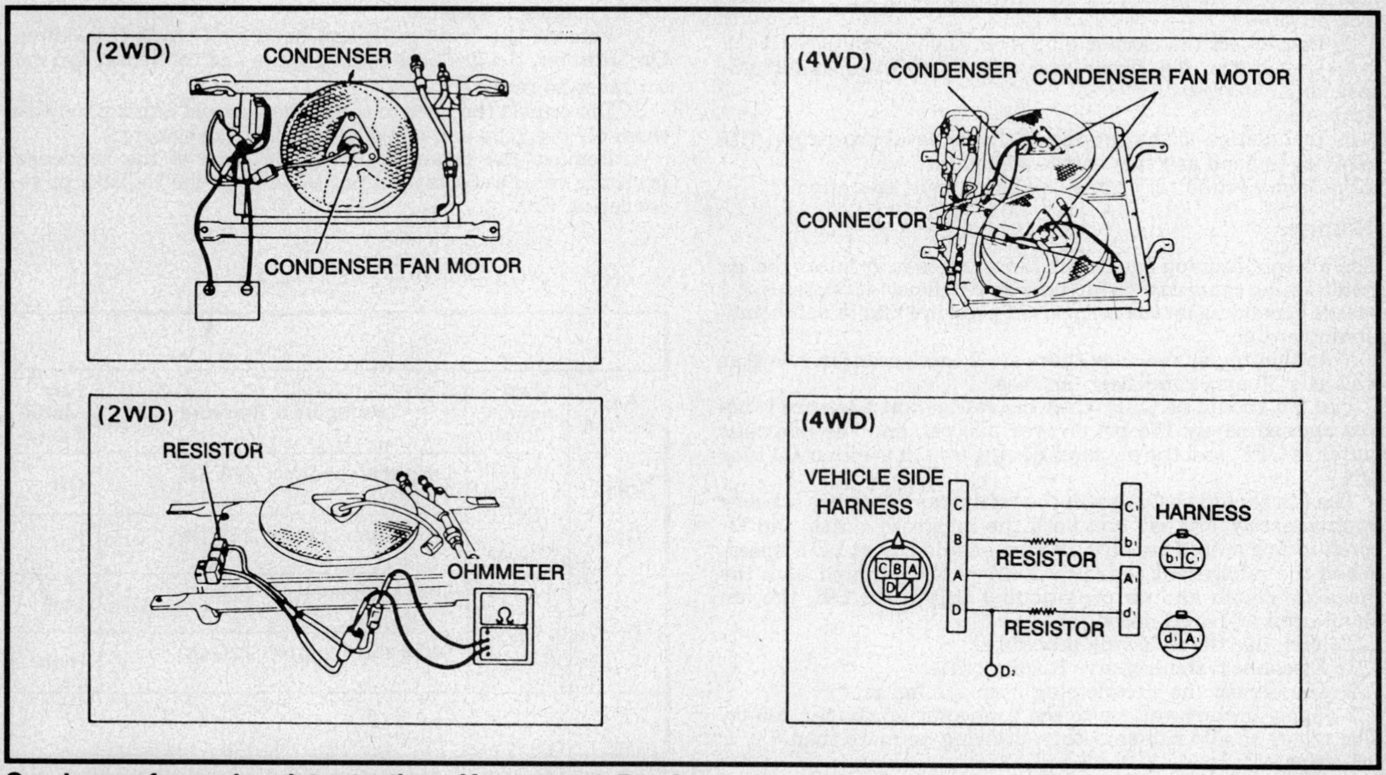
(2WD)
CONDENSER
CONDENSER FAN MOTOR
(4WD)
CONDENSER
CONDENSER FAN MOTOR
CONNECTOR
(2WD)
RESISTOR
OHMMETER
(4WD)
VEHICLE SIDE HARNESS
HARNESS
RESISTOR
RESISTOR

Condenser fan and resistor testing—Van, except Previa

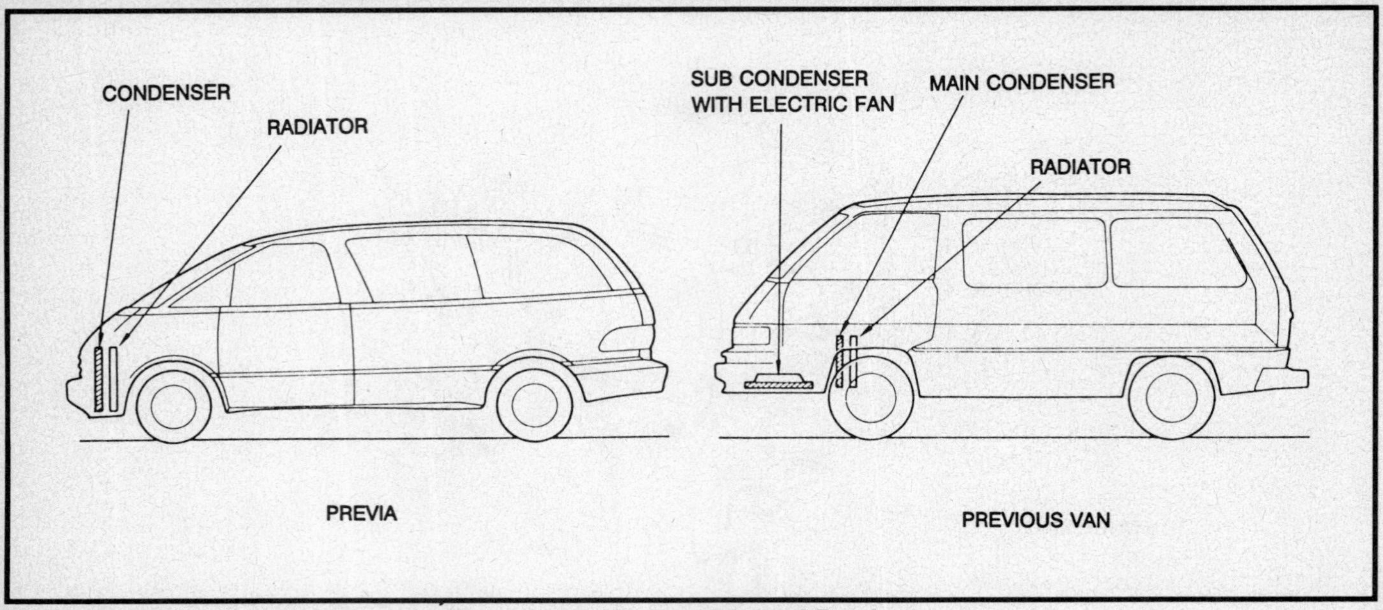
CONDENSER
RADIATOR
PREVIA
SUB CONDENSER
WITH ELECTRIC FAN
MAIN CONDENSER
RADIATOR
PREVIOUS VAN

Change in condenser location between previous Van models and Previa

REMOVAL AND INSTALLATION

Van, Except Previa

1. Disconnect the battery negative cable.
2. Remove the grille and running lights. Remove the hood lock brace.
3. Disconnect the electric plug from the fan motor.
4. Unbolt the fan frame and remove the fan and motor assembly.

To install:

5. Installation is the reverse of the removal procedure. Use care not to bend any fins on the condenser.
6. Reconnect battery cable and check light operation.

4Runner

The air conditioning condenser fan mounts in front of the air conditioning condenser to increase its efficiency. It operates at 2 speeds depending on the refrigerant pressure and the air conditioning switch.

Note that under the hood there are 2 condenser fan relays as well as a 30 amp condenser fan fuse.

The fan should be OFF when the refrigerant pressure is below approximately 178 psi or over 220 psi, and the magnetic clutch is OFF, and the air conditioning switch is either **OFF** or **ON**.

The fan should be ON when the refrigerant pressure is below approximately 178 psi, and both the magnetic clutch and air conditioning switch are **ON**. The fan should run at LOW speed. When the refrigerant pressure is above 220 psi, and both the magnetic clutch and air conditioning switch are **ON**, the fan should run at HIGH speed.

To test, use the following procedure:

1. Disconnect the negative battery cable.
2. Disconnect the electric plug from the fan motor.
3. Apply battery voltage to the connector on the fan motor. The motor should run smoothly, drawing no more than 8.0 ± 0.7 amps.
4. If operation is not as specified, replace the fan motor.

Condenser

REMOVAL AND INSTALLATION

1. Discharge the refrigeration system using a refrigerant recovery system if possible.
2. Remove the front grille and hood lock brace, if required. On 4Runner, the grille, clearance lights and condenser fan motor must be removed.
3. Disconnect the lines to the condenser and immediately cap them off the keep dirt out of the rest of the system.
4. Remove the retaining bolts and remove the condenser from the vehicle. Be careful not to damage the radiator or the condenser fins.

A/C Switch	Magnetic Clutch	Refrigerant Pressure	Fan Motor Speed
OFF or ON	OFF	Less than approx. 178 psi,	Off
		More than approx. 220 psi,	Off
ON	ON	Less than approx. 178 psi	Low
		More than approx. 220 psi	High

4Runner condenser fan switching conditions

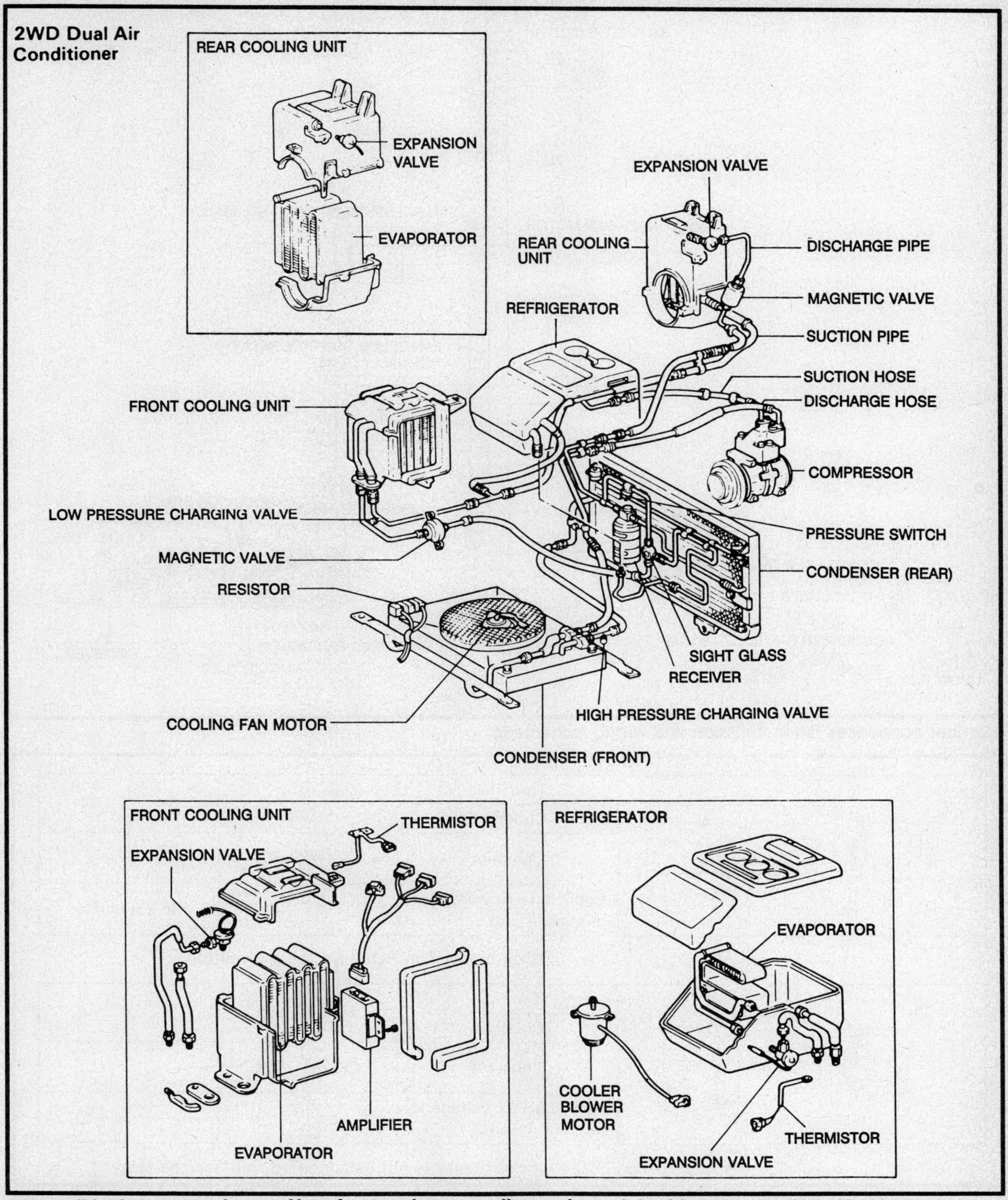
2WD Dual Air Conditioner
REAR COOLING UNIT
EXPANSION VALVE
EVAPORATOR
EXPANSION VALVE
REAR COOLING UNIT
DISCHARGE PIPE
MAGNETIC VALVE
REFRIGERATOR
SUCTION PIPE
SUCTION HOSE
DISCHARGE HOSE
FRONT COOLING UNIT
COMPRESSOR
LOW PRESSURE CHARGING VALVE
PRESSURE SWITCH
MAGNETIC VALVE
CONDENSER (REAR)
RESISTOR
SIGHT GLASS
RECEIVER
HIGH PRESSURE CHARGING VALVE
COOLING FAN MOTOR
CONDENSER (FRONT)
FRONT COOLING UNIT
THERMISTOR
EXPANSION VALVE
AMPLIFIER
EVAPORATOR
REFRIGERATOR
EVAPORATOR
COOLER BLOWER MOTOR
THERMISTOR
EXPANSION VALVE

Air conditioning system layout. Note front and rear cooling and special refrigerator section—Van, except Previa, but similar

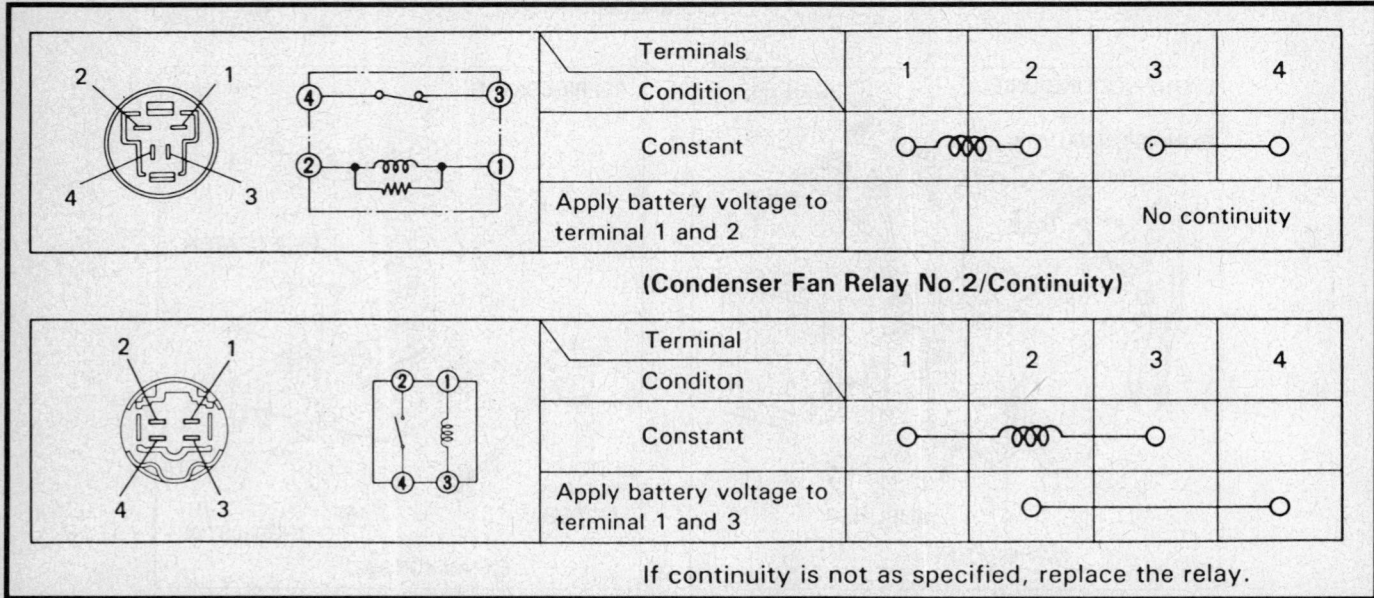

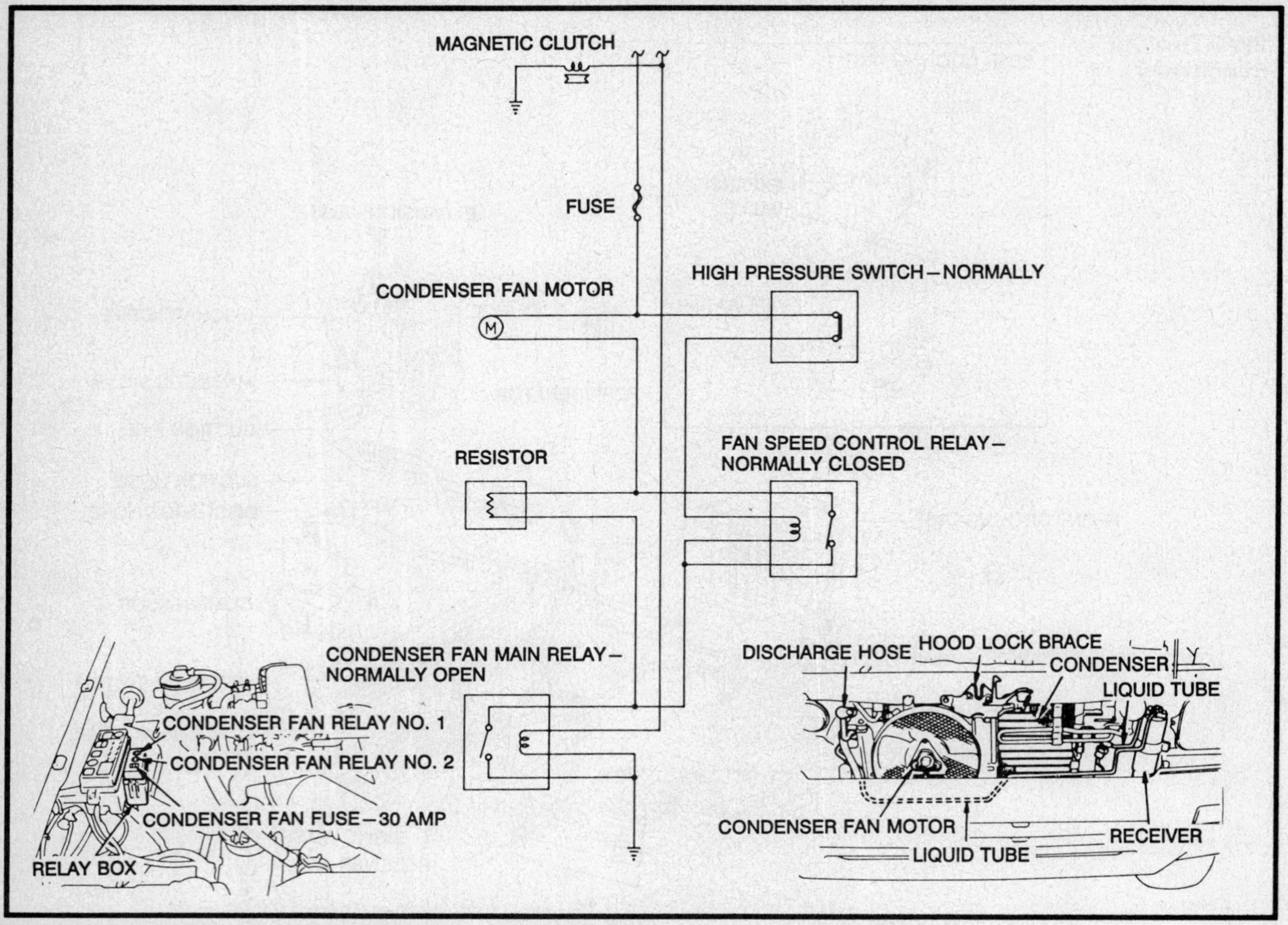
MAGNETIC CLUTCH
FUSE
CONDENSER FAN MOTOR
HIGH PRESSURE SWITCH—NORMALLY
RESISTOR
FAN SPEED CONTROL RELAY—
NORMALLY CLOSED
CONDENSER FAN MAIN RELAY—
NORMALLY OPEN
CONDENSER FAN RELAY NO. 1
CONDENSER FAN RELAY NO. 2
CONDENSER FAN FUSE—30 AMP
RELAY BOX
DISCHARGE HOSE
HOOD LOCK BRACE
CONDENSER
LIQUID TUBE
CONDENSER FAN MOTOR
RECEIVER
LIQUID TUBE

4Runner condenser fan installation and wiring schematic

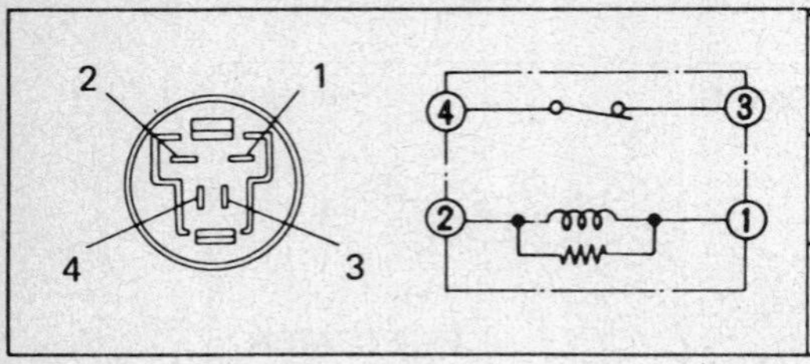
2
1
4
3
4
3
2
1

Terminals / Condition	1	2	3	4
Constant	O—	coil —O	O—	—O
Apply battery voltage to terminal 1 and 2			No continuity	

(Condenser Fan Relay No.2/Continuity)

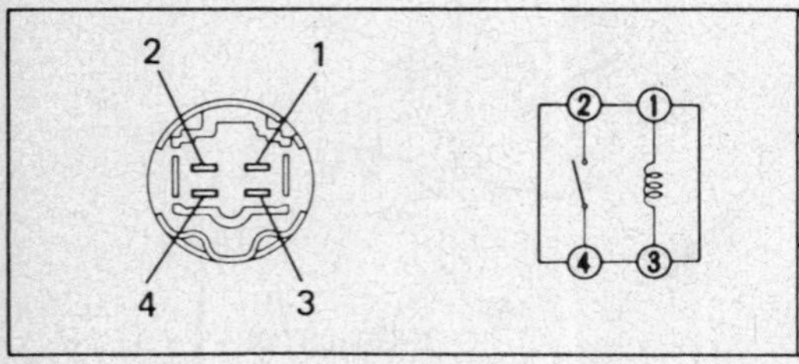
2
1
4
3
2
1
4
3

Terminal / Conditon	1	2	3	4
Constant	O—	— coil —	—O	
Apply battery voltage to terminal 1 and 3		O—	—	—O

If continuity is not as specified, replace the relay.

4Runner condenser fan relay schematic

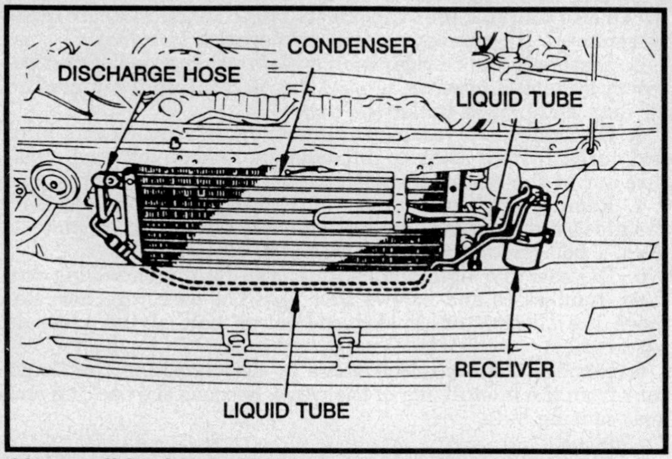
CONDENSER
DISCHARGE HOSE
LIQUID TUBE
RECEIVER
LIQUID TUBE
Air conditioning condenser removal, 1991 Pick-Up shown—others similar

To install:

5. Installation is the reverse of the removal procedure. Evacuate, charge and test the system. If a new condenser has been used, additional refrigerant oil must be added, generally approximately 1 ounce.

Compressor

REMOVAL AND INSTALLATION

1. Run engine at idle with air conditioning on for 10 minutes.
2. Shut off engine. Disconnect battery negative cable.
3. On Pick-Ups with the V6 engine it may be necessary to remove the power steering pump.
4. Disconnect the electrical lead to the compressor clutch.
5. Discharge the refrigeration system using a refrigerant recovery system, if possible.
6. Disconnect the 2 hoses from the compressor service valves and cap immediately to keep dirt and moisture out of the rest of the system.
7. Remove the fan shroud, loosen the drive belt and remove the compressor mounting bolts. Lift the compressor from the vehicle.

To install:

8. Installation is the reverse of the removal procedure. Evacuate, charge and test the system. If a new compressor has been used, additional refrigerant oil must be added, generally approximately 1¾ ounce.

Receiver/Drier

REMOVAL AND INSTALLATION

1. Discharge the refrigeration system using a refrigerant recovery system, if possible.
2. Disconnect the 2 hoses from the receiver and cap immediately to keep dirt and moisture out of the rest of the system.
3. Remove the receiver from the vehicle.

To install:

4. Installation is the reverse of the removal procedure. Evacuate, charge and test the system. If a new receiver has been used, additional refrigerant oil must be added, generally approximately ¾ ounce.

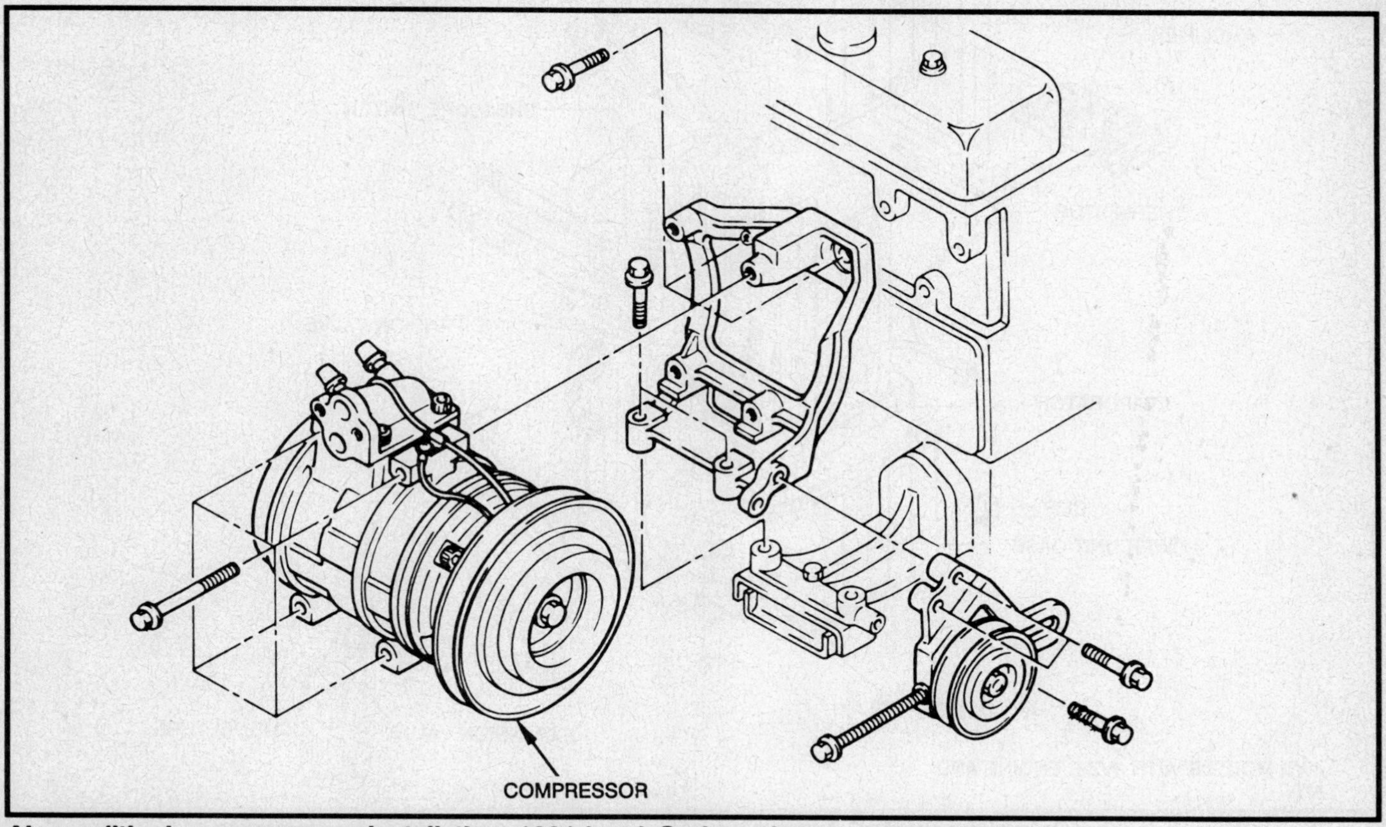
COMPRESSOR
Air conditioning compressor installation, 1991 Land Cruiser shown—others similar

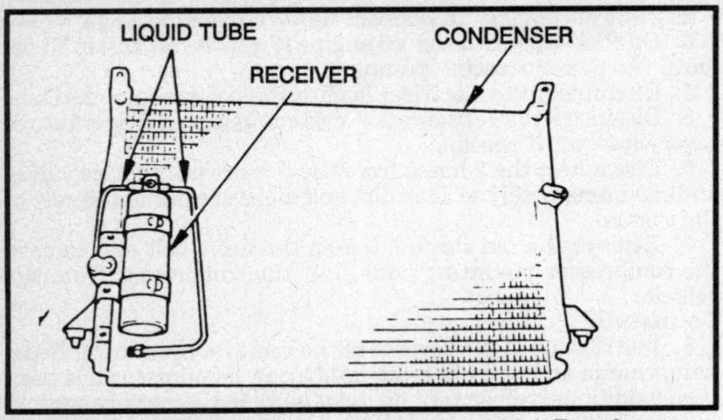
LIQUID TUBE
CONDENSER
RECEIVER

Receiver installation on condenser, 1991 Previa shown—others similar

Expansion Valve

REMOVAL AND INSTALLATION

1. The expansion valve is located inside the cooling unit case which also contains the evaporator. This cooling unit case must be removed. Disconnect the battery negative terminal.
2. Discharge the refrigeration system using a refrigerant recovery system, if possible. On the Previa front unit, remove the air duct and blower under the hood.
3. Disconnect the refrigerant lines from the cooling unit inlet and outlet fittings and cap immediately to keep dirt and moisture out of the rest of the system.
4. Remove the cooling unit. On Pick-Up and Land Cruiser, the glove box may need to be removed. On Previa, remove 2 nuts, 1 bolt and the cover. Remove the cooling unit.
5. Disassemble the cooling unit case by disconnecting the clips, connectors and screws that hold the case together. Remove the thermistor, holder and lower half of the case, as required.
6. Remove the expansion valve by disconnecting the liquid tube from the inlet fitting of the valve. Remove the packing and heat sensing bulb.

To install:

7. Installation is the reverse of the removal procedure. Make sure the expansion valve and thermistor are in the proper places for accurate heat sensing. Check electrical contacts for corrosion.
8. Evacuate, charge and test the system. If a new evaporator has been used, additional refrigerant oil must be added, generally approximately 1¾ ounce.

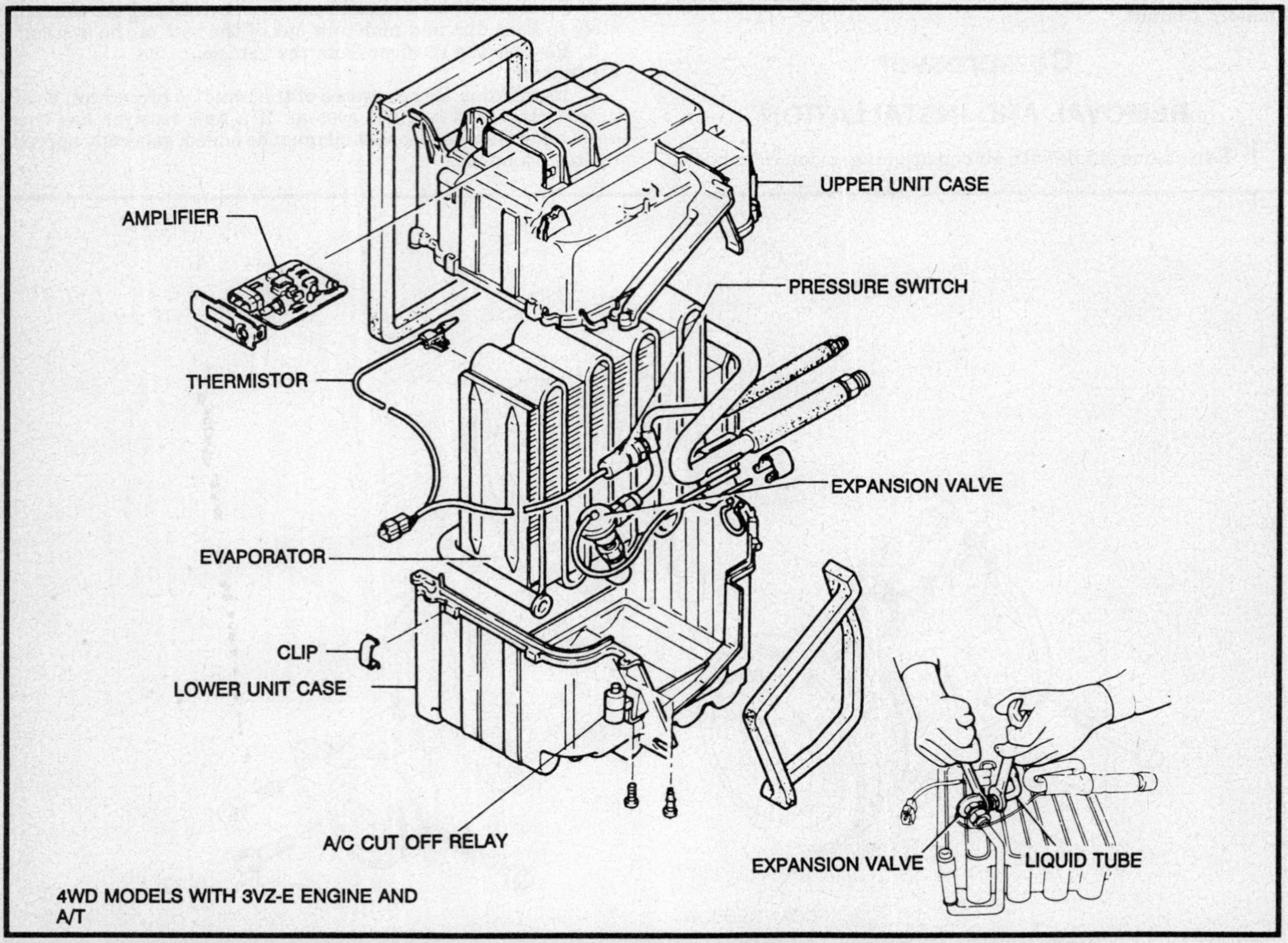
UPPER UNIT CASE
AMPLIFIER
PRESSURE SWITCH
THERMISTOR
EXPANSION VALVE
EVAPORATOR
CLIP
LOWER UNIT CASE
A/C CUT OFF RELAY
EXPANSION VALVE
LIQUID TUBE
4WD MODELS WITH 3VZ-E ENGINE AND A/T

Cooling unit module containing evaporator, expansion valve, thermistor and other components. Pick-Up model shown—others similar

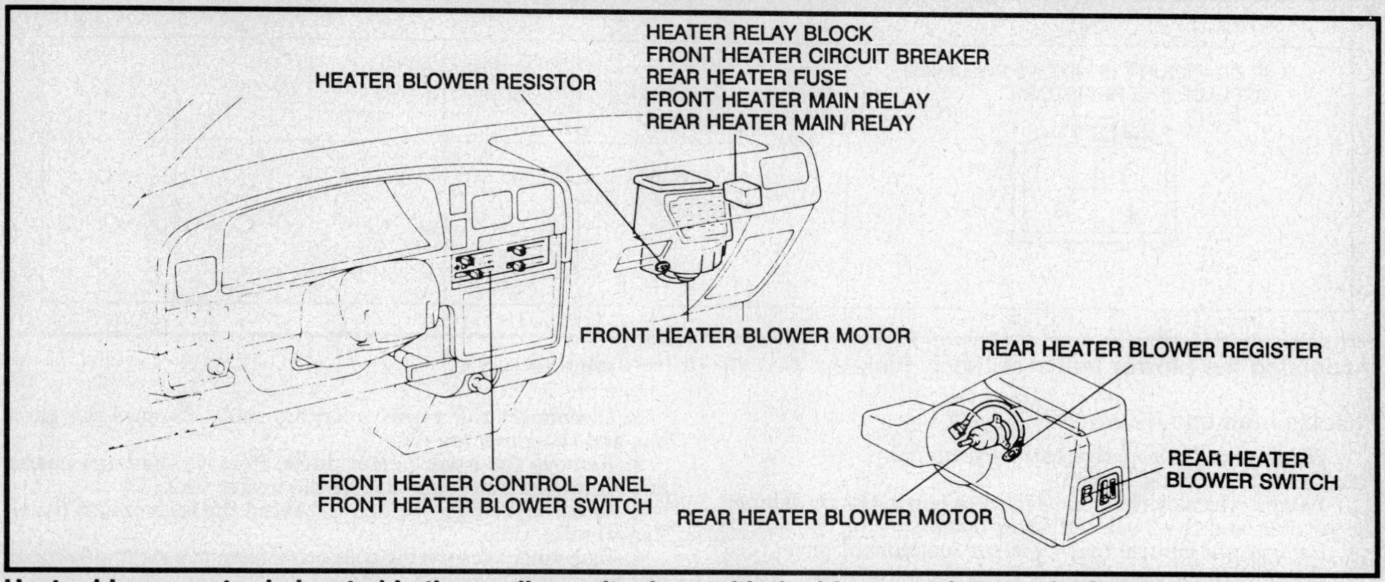
HEATER RELAY BLOCK
FRONT HEATER CIRCUIT BREAKER
REAR HEATER FUSE
FRONT HEATER MAIN RELAY
REAR HEATER MAIN RELAY
HEATER BLOWER RESISTOR
FRONT HEATER BLOWER MOTOR
REAR HEATER BLOWER REGISTER
REAR HEATER
BLOWER SWITCH
FRONT HEATER CONTROL PANEL
FRONT HEATER BLOWER SWITCH
REAR HEATER BLOWER MOTOR

Heater blower motor is located in the cooling unit along with the blower resistor and other components. 4Runner shown—others similar

Blower Motor

REMOVAL AND INSTALLATION

1. In most every case, the blower motor is mounted on the cooling unit case. Examine the installation to see if the cooling case containing the evaporator must be removed to access the blower motor. On Previa, the blower motor is mounted outside the cabin in front of the dash panel.
2. Disconnect the battery negative cable.
3. If the cooling case does not need to be removed, locate and remove the blower motor mounting screws. Disconnect the motor electrical connector. Lift the motor and fan assembly from the cooling case.
4. If the cooling case must be removed to access the blower motor, discharge the refrigeration system using a refrigerant recovery system, if possible.
5. Disconnect the refrigerant lines from the cooling unit inlet and outlet fittings and cap immediately to keep dirt and moisture out of the rest of the system.
6. Remove the cooling unit. On Pick-Up and Land Cruiser, the glove box may need to be removed. On Previa, remove 2 nuts, 1 bolt and the cover. Remove the cooling unit.
7. Disassemble the cooling unit case by disconnecting the clips, connectors and screws that hold the case together. Remove the blower motor assembly.

To install:

8. Installation is the reverse of the removal process. Test the motor before final assembly. Replace any sealing material that may have been disturbed at disassembly.
9. Check electrical contacts for corrosion, especially around the motor resistor.
10. If the system has been opened to remove the cooling unit, evacuate, charge and test the system.

Blower Motor Resistor

REMOVAL AND INSTALLATION

1. The blower motor resistor is mounted near the blower motor usually in the air stream to keep the resistor from burning out. Examine the installation to see if the cooling case containing the evaporator must be removed to access the blower motor resistor.
2. Disconnect the battery negative cable.
3. If the cooling case does not need to be removed, locate and remove the blower motor resistor mounting screws. Disconnect the electrical connector. Remove the resistor from the cooling case.
4. If the cooling case must be removed to access the blower motor, discharge the refrigeration system using a refrigerant recovery system, if possible.
5. Disconnect the refrigerant lines from the cooling unit inlet and outlet fittings and cap immediately to keep dirt and moisture out of the rest of the system.
6. Remove the cooling unit. On Pick-Up and Land Cruiser, the glove box may need to be removed. On Previa, remove 2 nuts, 1 bolt and the cover. Remove the cooling unit.
7. Disassemble the cooling unit case by disconnecting the clips, connectors and screws that hold the case together. Remove the blower motor resistor.

To install:

8. Installation is the reverse of the removal process. Test the motor before final assembly. Replace any sealing material that may have been disturbed at disassembly.
9. Check electrical contacts for corrosion, especially around the motor resistor connector.
10. If the air conditioning system has been opened to remove the cooling unit, evacuate, charge and test the system.

Heater Core

REMOVAL AND INSTALLATION

NOTE: If equipped with air conditioning, the heater and the air conditioning units are separate units. Be certain when working under the dashboard that only the heater hoses are disconnected.

CAUTION

The air conditioning hoses are under pressure. If disconnected, the escaping refrigerant will freeze any surface with which it comes in contact, including skin and eyes.

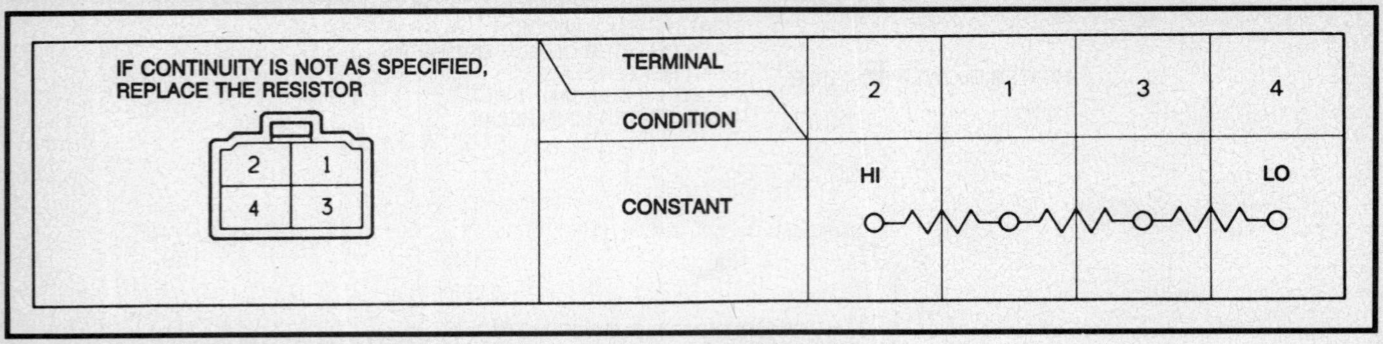
IF CONTINUITY IS NOT AS SPECIFIED, REPLACE THE RESISTOR
2
1
4
3
TERMINAL
CONDITION
2
1
3
4
CONSTANT
HI
LO

Inspecting the blower motor resistor. Pick-Up shown—others similar

Pick-Up, Van and 4Runner

1. Disconnect the negative battery terminal.
2. Drain the cooling system.
3. Remove the glove box, the defroster hoses, the air damper, the air duct and the 2 side defroster ducts.
4. Remove the control unit from the instrument panel.
5. Disconnect the heater hoses from the core tubes.
6. Remove the retaining bolts and lift out the heater unit. At this point, the core may be be pulled from the case.

To install:

7. Installation is the reverse of the removal procedure. Make sure the heater hoses are in good condition, and that all cable controls are in place.
8. Refill cooling system and check for leaks.

Land Cruiser

NOTE: The entire heater unit must be removed to gain access to the heater core. This procedure requires almost complete disassembly of the instrument panel and lowering the steering column.

1. Disconnect the negative battery cable. Remove the glove box and the glove box door.
2. Remove the lower heater ducts. Remove the large heater duct from the passenger side of the heater unit.
3. Remove the ductwork from behind the instrument panel. Remove the radio.
4. Disconnect the wiring connector from the right side inner portion of the glove box opening.
5. Remove the instrument panel pad. Remove the hood release lever. Disconnect the hand throttle cable.
6. Remove the retaining screw from the left side of the fuse block.
7. Remove the steering column-to-instrument panel attaching nuts and carefully lower the steering column. Tag and disconnect the wiring as necessary in order to lower the column assembly.
8. Disconnect the electrical connector from the rheostat located to the left of the steering column opening.
9. Remove the center dual outlet duct which is attached to the upper portion of the heater unit.
10. Remove the lower instrument panel.

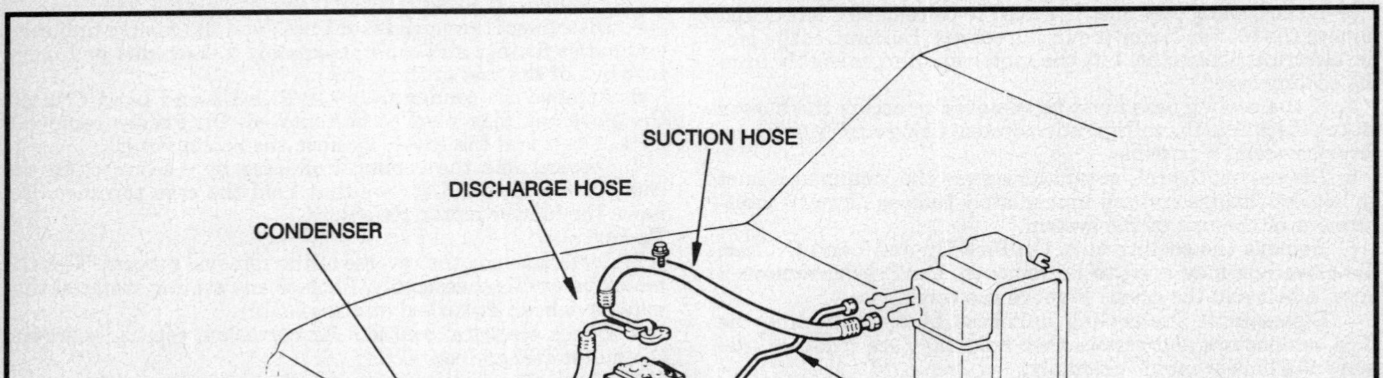
SUCTION HOSE
DISCHARGE HOSE
CONDENSER
COMPRESSOR
LIQUID TUBE
CONDENSER FAN
RECEIVER

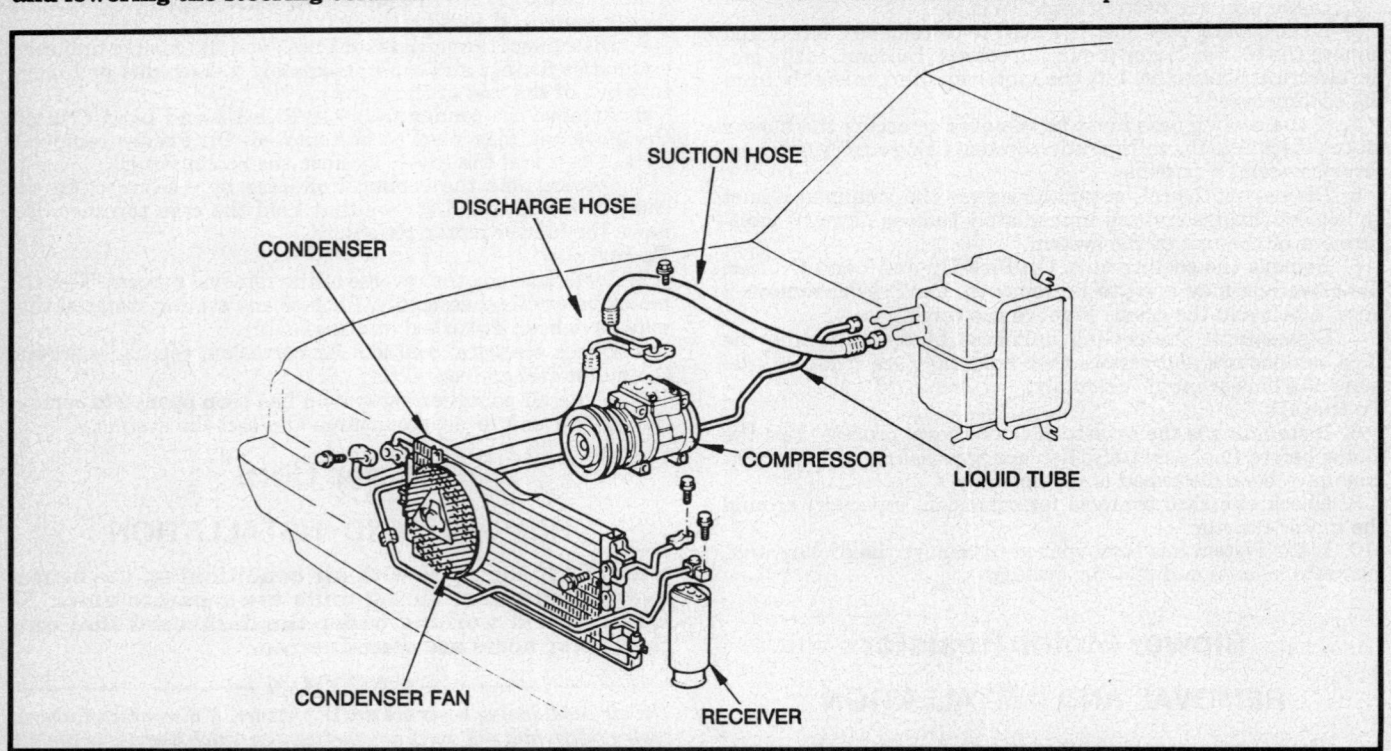

Air conditioning components and refrigerant lines. 4 Runner shown—others similar

11. Tag and disconnect the hoses from the the heater unit. Remove the heater unit-to-firewall fasteners and the heater unit.
12. Remove the heater core-to-heater unit pipe clamps and the heater core retaining clamp. Remove the heater core from the heater unit.

To install:

13. Installation is the reverse of the removal procedure. Take care to reconnect all electrical connectors. Make sure any sealer material that has been removed is replaced.
14. Torque the steering column-to-instrument panel fasteners to 15 ft. lbs.
15. Refill the cooling system.

Evaporator

REMOVAL AND INSTALLATION

1. The evaporator is located inside the cooling unit case. This cooling unit case must be removed. Disconnect the battery negative terminal.
2. Discharge the refrigeration system using a refrigerant recovery system, if possible. On the Previa front unit, remove the air duct and blower under the hood.
3. Disconnect the refrigerant lines from the cooling unit inlet and outlet fittings and cap immediately to keep dirt and moisture out of the rest of the system.
4. Remove the cooling unit. On Van, Pick-Up and Land Cruisers, the glove box may need to be removed. On Previa, remove 2 nuts, 1 bolt and the cover. Remove the cooling unit.
5. Disassemble the cooling unit case by disconnecting the clips, connectors and screws that hold the case together. Remove the thermistor and holder and lower half of the case, as required.
6. Remove the evaporator.

To install:

7. Installation is the reverse of the removal procedure. Make sure the expansion valve and thermistor are in the proper places for accurate heat sensing. Check electrical contacts for corrosion. Replace any sealing material that may have been disturbed at disassembly.
8. Evacuate, charge and test the system. If a new evaporator has been used, additional refrigerant oil must be added, generally approximately 1¾ ounce.

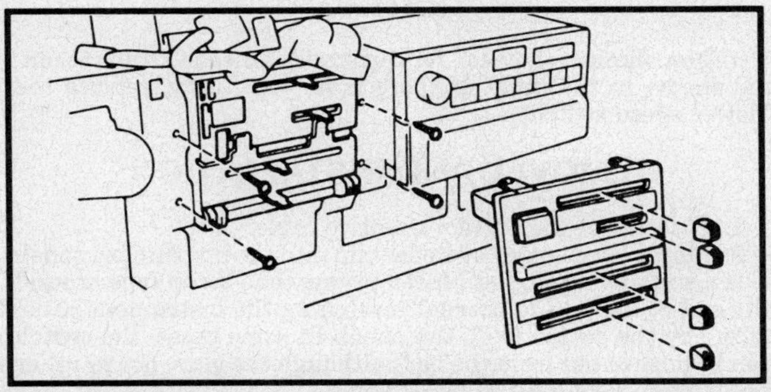

Removing heater control head. Land Cruiser shown—others similar

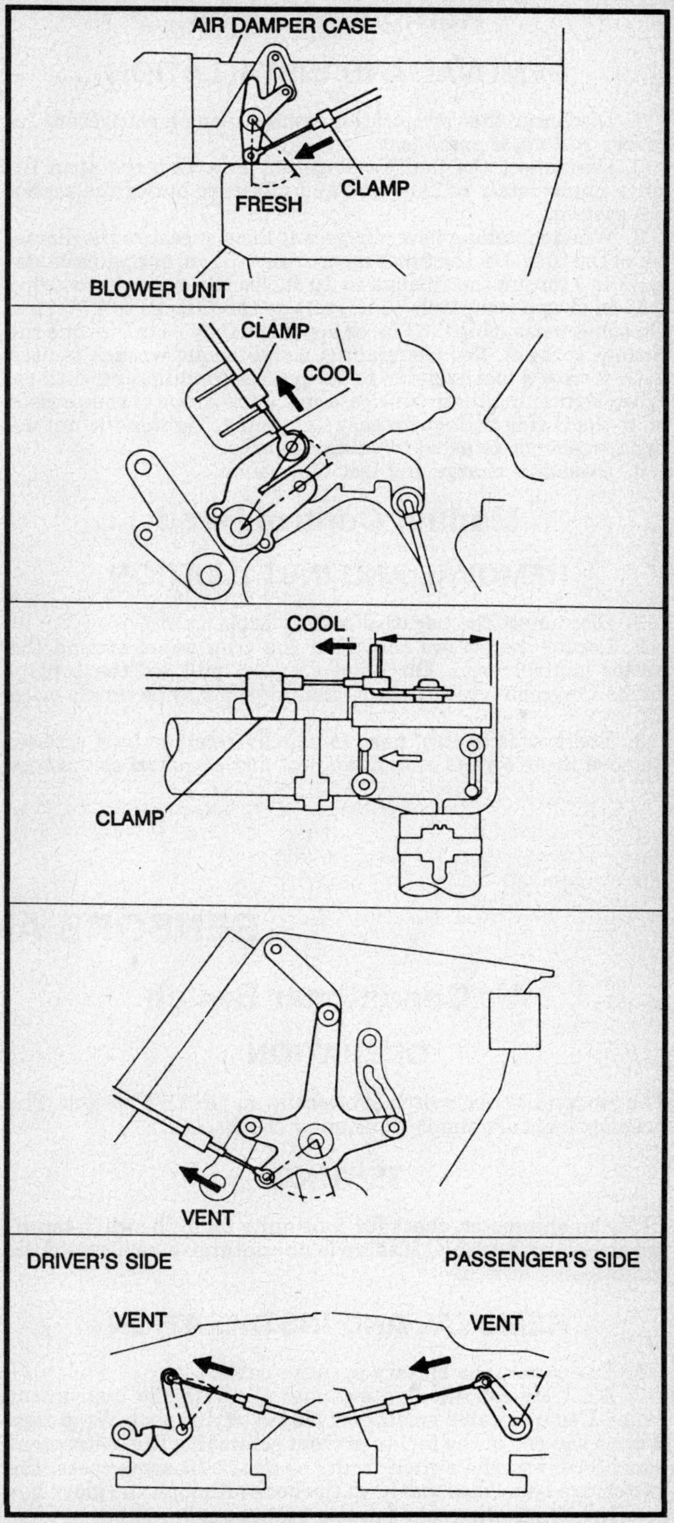
AIR DAMPER CASE
FRESH
CLAMP
BLOWER UNIT
CLAMP
COOL
COOL
CLAMP
VENT
DRIVER'S SIDE
PASSENGER'S SIDE
VENT
VENT

Control cable adjustment points. Previa shown—others similar

Refrigerant Lines

REMOVAL AND INSTALLATION

1. Discharge the refrigeration system using a refrigerant recovery system, if possible.
2. Disconnect the faulty refrigerant line. Cap the open fittings immediately to keep dirt and moisture out of the rest of the system.
3. When installing new refrigerant lines, measure the diameter of the tube. On the tubes measuring 0.31 in. or approximately ⅜ in., torque the fittings to 10 ft. lbs. On tubes measuring 0.50 in or approximately ½ in., torque the fittings to 17 ft. lbs. On tubes measuring 0.62 in. or approximately ⅝ in., torque the fittings to 24 ft. lbs. Generally a small torque wrench is used with a crow's foot adapter to torque air conditioning fittings. When tightening these fittings, apply a few drops of compressor oil to the O-ring fittings for easy tightening. Tighten the nut using 2 wrenches to avoid twisting the tube.
4. Evacuate, charge and test the system.

Manual Control Head

REMOVAL AND INSTALLATION

1. Disconnect the negative battery cable.
2. Locate the screws that hold the trim panel around the heater control head. On Land Cruiser, pull off the control knobs. On some vehicles, the surround trim may be simply pried off.
3. The heater control head is usually retained by 4 screws. Remove these screws and disconnect any electrical connectors as the control head is removed. In some cases, clock and some switch connectors must be removed.

To install:

4. Installation is the reverse of the removal procedure. Securely fasten all control connections. Tighten screws securely to prevent rattles.
5. Reconnect battery cable and test operation.

Manual Control Cables

ADJUSTMENT

1. Move the control levers left and right and check for stiffness and binding through the full range of the levers.
2. To adjust the air inlet damper control cable, remove the cable end from the arm. Set the control lever to the **FRESH** position. Install the control cable and lock the clamp.
3. To adjust the air mix damper control cable, remove the cable end from the arm. Set the control lever to the **COOL** position. Install the control cable and lock the clamp.
4. To adjust the water valve control cable, remove the cable end from the arm. Set the control lever to the **COOL** position. Install the control cable and lock the clamp.
5. To adjust the mode damper control cable, remove the cable end from the arm. Set the control lever to the **VENT** position. Install the control cable and lock the clamp.
6. To adjust the side vent duct control cable on Previa, remove the cable end from the arm. Set the side vent duct and the mode control lever to the **VENT** position. Install the control cable and lock the clamp.

SENSORS AND SWITCHES

Air Conditioner Switch

OPERATION

The air conditioner switch is basically an ON/OFF switch. The primary tests are simply continuity checks.

TESTING

Using an ohmmeter, check for continuity for each switch terminal shown in the table. If there is no continuity, replace the air conditioning switch.

REMOVAL AND INSTALLATION

1. Disconnect the battery negative cable.
2. Most air conditioning switches clip into the instrument panel. Use a suitable small, flat bladed prying tool. Wrap tape around the end of the tool to prevent scratching the instrument panel face. Pry the switch from the panel. In some cases, the switch can be pushed out from the back although the glove box or other obstruction may have to be removed.
3. Disconnect the electrical connector and test the switch terminals for continuity.

To install:

4. Reconnect the electrical connector and push the switch into place until it clicks.
5. Reconnect the negative battery terminal and test switch.

Blower Speed Switch

OPERATION

The blower speed switch feeds power to the blower resistor and the extra-high relay, where equipped.

TESTING

Using an ohmmeter, check for continuity for each switch terminal shown in the table. If there is no continuity, replace the blower speed switch.

REMOVAL AND INSTALLATION

1. Disconnect the battery negative cable.
2. Most blower speed switches clip into the instrument panel. Use a suitable small, flat bladed prying tool. Wrap tape around the end of the tool to prevent scratching the instrument panel face. Pry the switch from the panel. In some cases, the switch can be pushed out from the back although the glove box or other obstruction may have to be removed.
3. Disconnect the electrical connector and test the switch terminals for continuity.

To install:

4. Reconnect the electrical connector and push the switch into place until it clicks.
5. Reconnect the negative battery terminal and test switch.

A/C
LW
G
LR

VAN, EXCEPT PREVIA

Switch position \ Terminal	LW	G	LR
OFF		○	○
ON	○	○	○

SOME RESISTANCE
CONTINUITY
A/C SWITCH

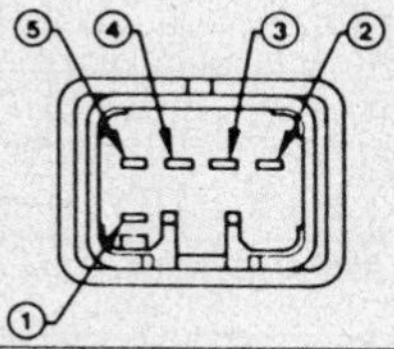
5
4
3
2
1

4RUNNER, PICK-UP

POSITION \ TERMINAL	②	③
OFF		
ON	○	○

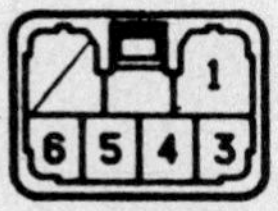
1
6
5
4
3

PREVIA

Switch position \ Terminal	1	3	4	5	6
OFF	○	○		○	
			○	○	
ON	○	○		○	○
			○	○	○

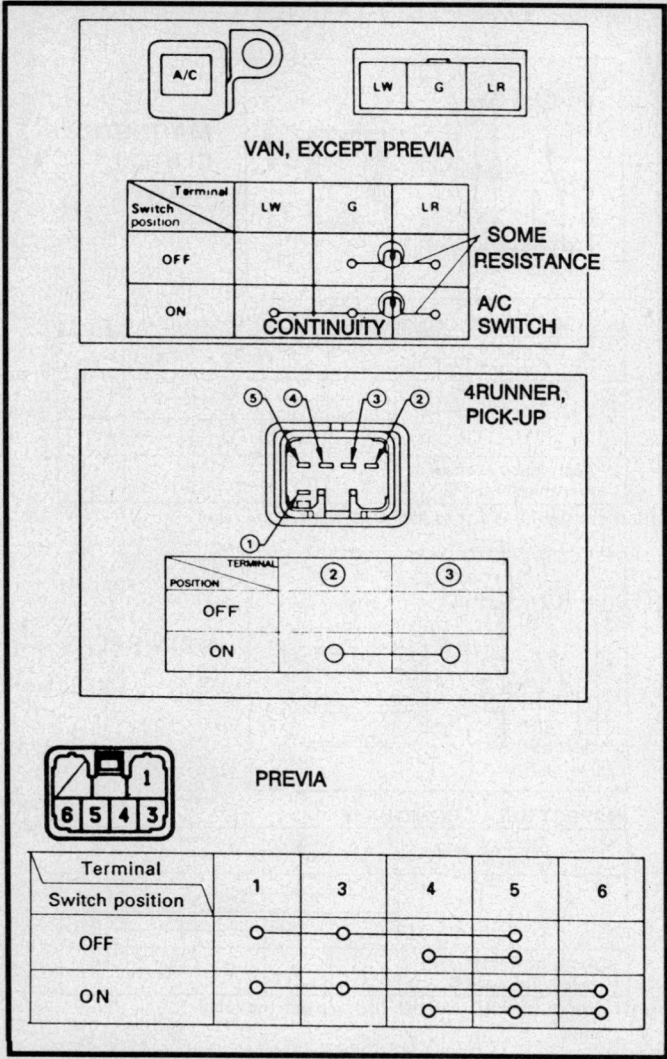

Air conditioning switch check points

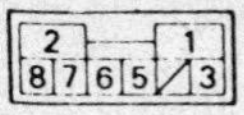
2
1
8
7
6
5
3

VAN, EXCEPT FOR PREVIA

Switch position \ Terminal	2	3	5	6	1
OFF					
LO	○	○			
II	○	○	○		
III	○	○		○	
HI	○	○			○

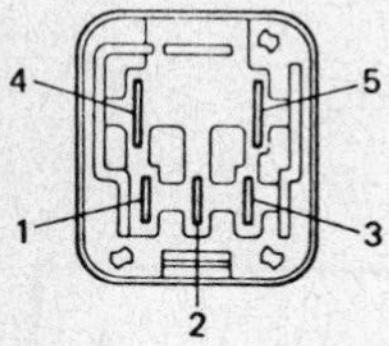
4
5
1
3
2

4RUNNER, PICK-UP

Condition \ Terminal	1	2	3	4	5
Constant	○	(coil)	○		
		○		○	
Apply battery voltage to terminals 1 and 3.				○	○

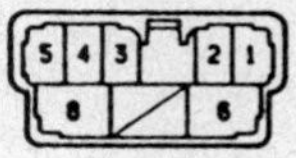
5
4
3
2
1
8
6

PREVIA

Switch position \ Terminal	1	2	5	6	8
OFF					
LO			○	○	
■	○		○	○	
■■		○	○	○	
HI			○	○	○

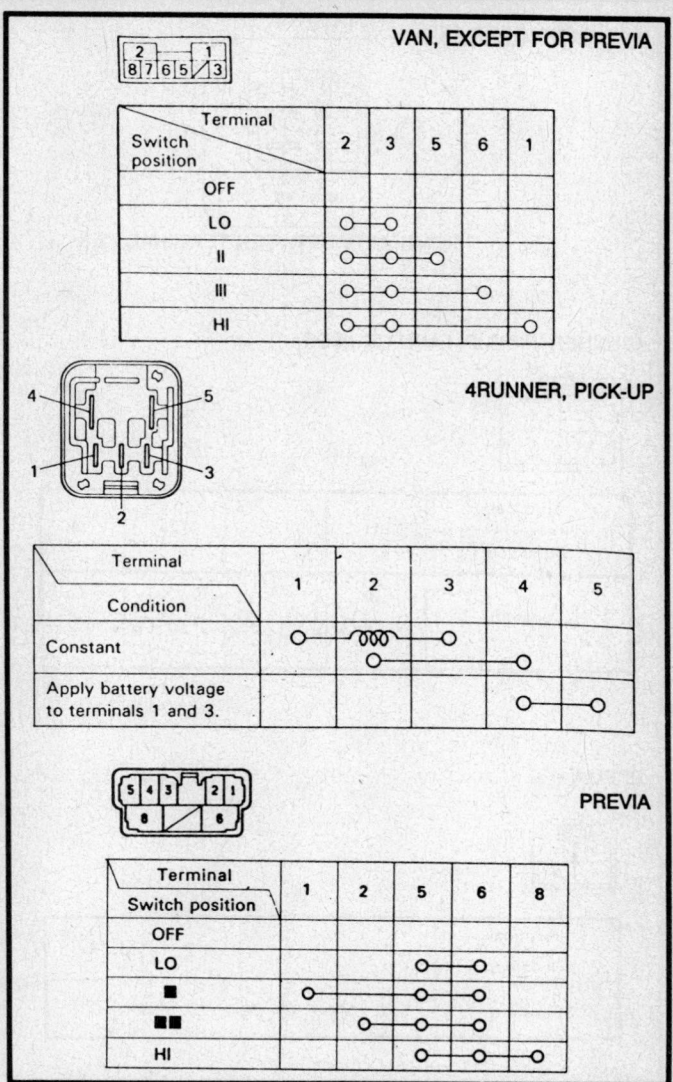

Blower speed control switch check points

Blower Resistor

OPERATION

The blower resistor reduces the amount of power being fed to the blower motor. A group of resistors, often wound metal coils, impedes the flow of current. This heats the resistors. Usually blower motor resistors are mounted in the air duct near the blower motor. The airflow cools the coils to keep them from burning out.

TESTING

1. Disconnect the battery negative cable.
2. Locate the resistor and remove the electrical connector. Some resistors may be tested in place, others may need to be removed to access the terminals. Most blower resistors are secured to their mounting by 1 or 2 screws which can be removed to take out the resistor.
3. Test the resistor terminals for continuity.

To install:

4. Reinstall the resistor, if it was removed and connect the electrical connector.
5. Reconnect the negative battery terminal and test system.

REMOVAL AND INSTALLATION

1. Disconnect the battery negative cable.
2. Locate the resistor and remove the electrical connector. Most blower resistors are secured to their mounting by 1 or 2 screws which are removed to take out the resistor.

To install:

3. Install the resistor and connect the electrical connector.
4. Reconnect the negative battery terminal and test system.

Relays

OPERATION

Toyotas use relays in various locations to control the functions

VAN, EXCEPT PREVIA

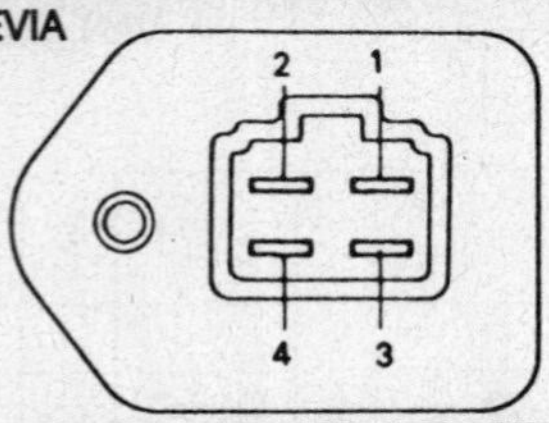
2
1
4
3

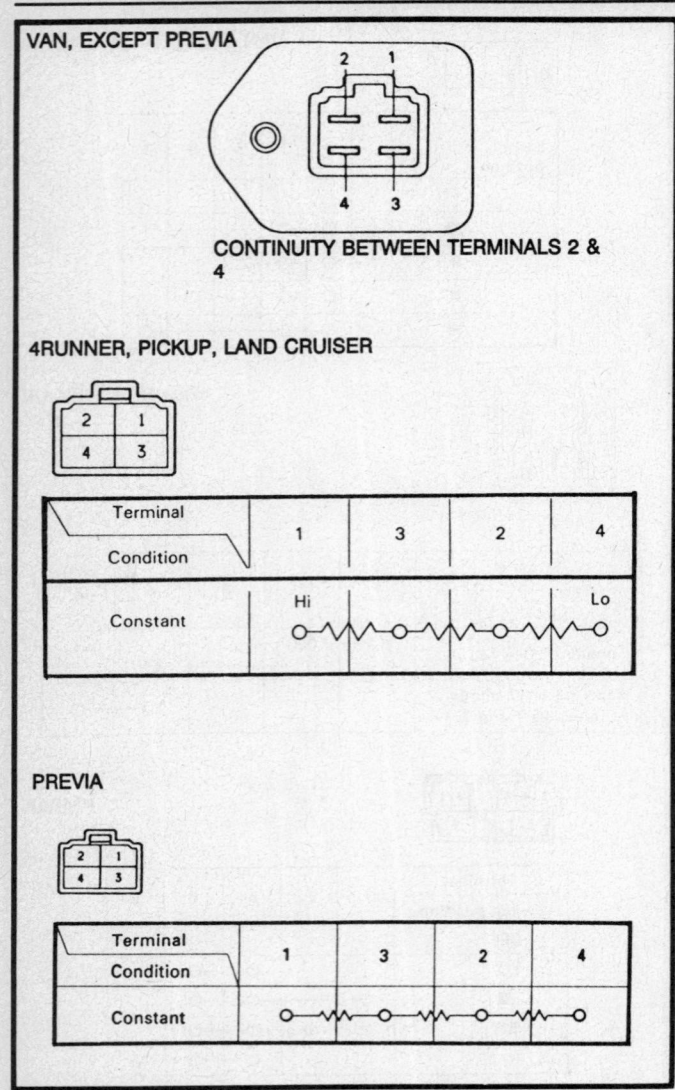

CONTINUITY BETWEEN TERMINALS 2 & 4

4RUNNER, PICKUP, LAND CRUISER

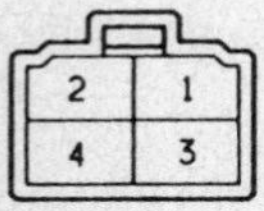
2
1
4
3

Terminal / Condition	1	3	2	4
Constant	Hi ○—resistor—	○—resistor—	○—resistor—	○ Lo

PREVIA

2
1
4
3

Terminal / Condition	1	3	2	4
Constant	○—resistor—	○—resistor—	○—resistor—	○

Blower resistor terminal check points

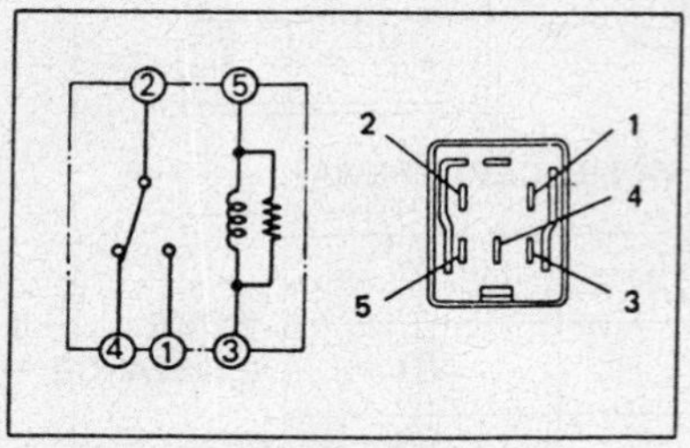
2
5
4
1
3
2
1
4
5
3

MAGNETIC CLUTCH RELAY

INSPECT RELAY CONTINUITY

Terminal / Condition	1	2	3	4	5
–		○	—	○	
			○	—	○
Apply battery voltage to terminal 3 and 5	○	○			

If continuity is not as specified, replace the relay.

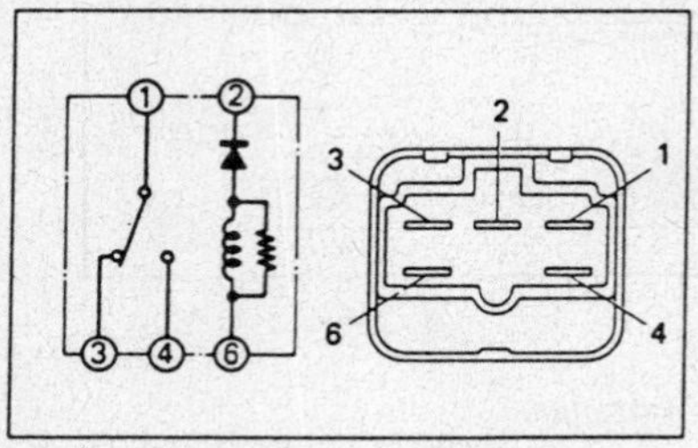
1
2
3
4
6
2
3
1
6
4

MAIN RELAY

INSPECT RELAY CONTNUITY

Terminal / Condition	1	2	3	4	6
–	○	—	○		
		○	—	—	○
Apply battery voltage to terminal 2 and 6	○	—	—	○	

If continuity is not as specified, replace the relay.

Air conditioning clutch and main relay testing—Van, except Previa

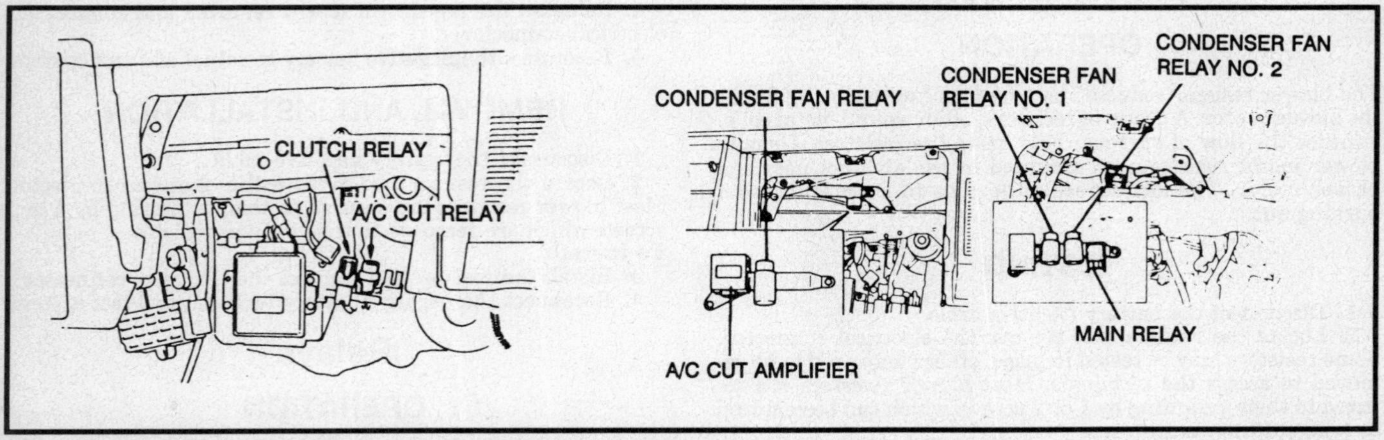
CLUTCH RELAY
A/C CUT RELAY
CONDENSER FAN RELAY
CONDENSER FAN RELAY NO. 1
CONDENSER FAN RELAY NO. 2
MAIN RELAY
A/C CUT AMPLIFIER

Relay locations and identification—Van, except Previa

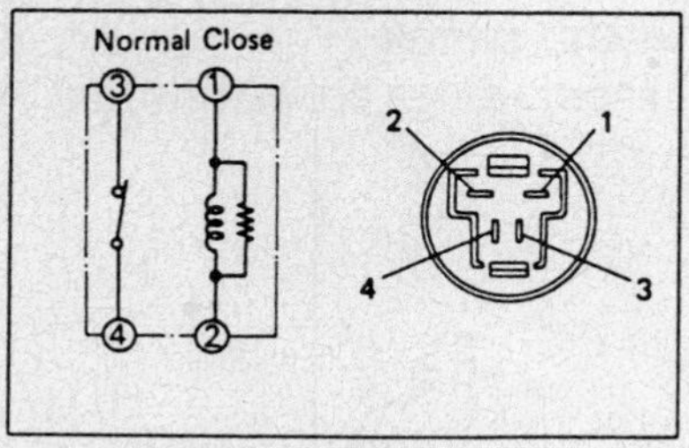
Normal Close
A/C CUT RELAY

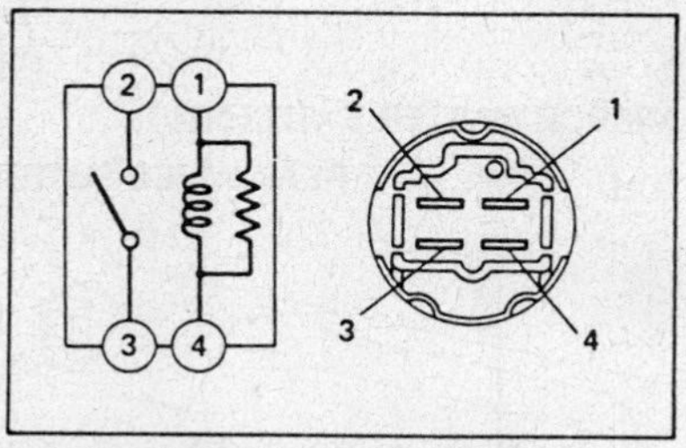
CONDENSER FAN RELAY (2WD)
CONDENSER FAN RELAY NO.2 (4WD)

INSPECT RELAY CONTINUITY

Terminal / Condition	1	2	3	4
–	○—	—○		
			○—	—○
Apply battery voltage to terminal 1 and 2	–			

If continuity is not as specified, replace the relay.

INSPECT RELAY CONTINUITY

Terminal / Condition	1	2	3	4
–	○—	———	———	—○
Apply battery voltage		○—	—○	

If continuity is not as specified, replace the relay.

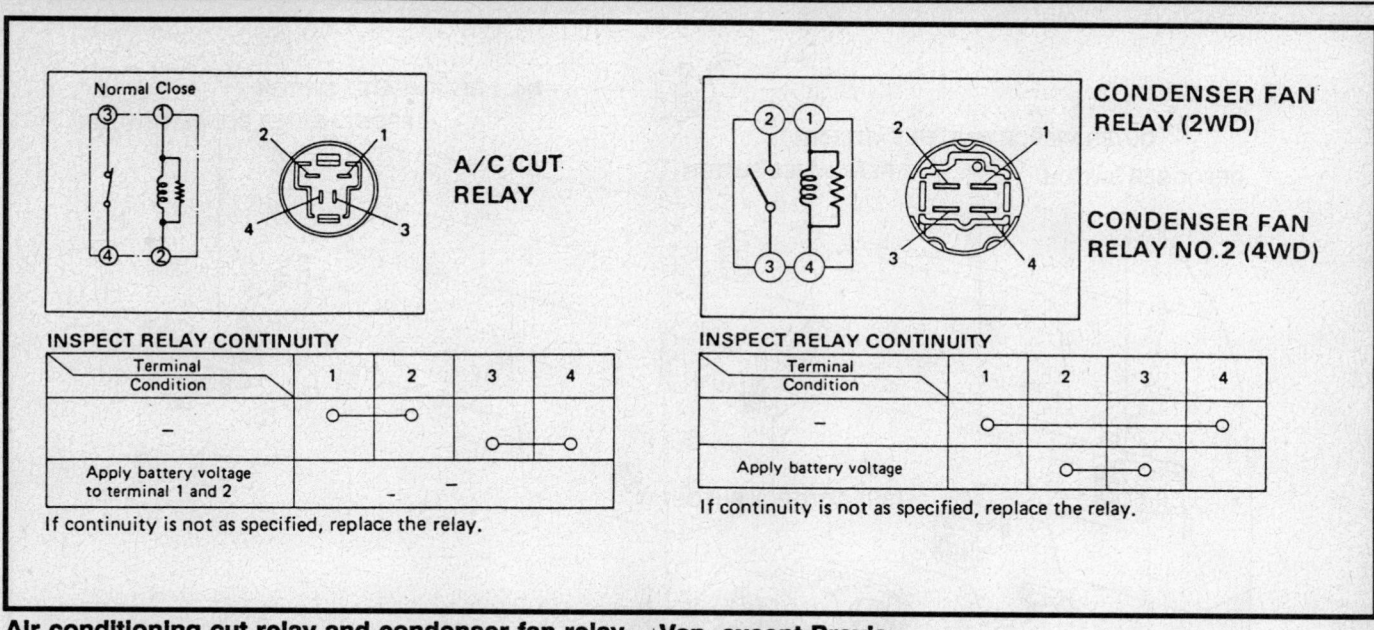

Air conditioning cut relay and condenser fan relay—Van, except Previa

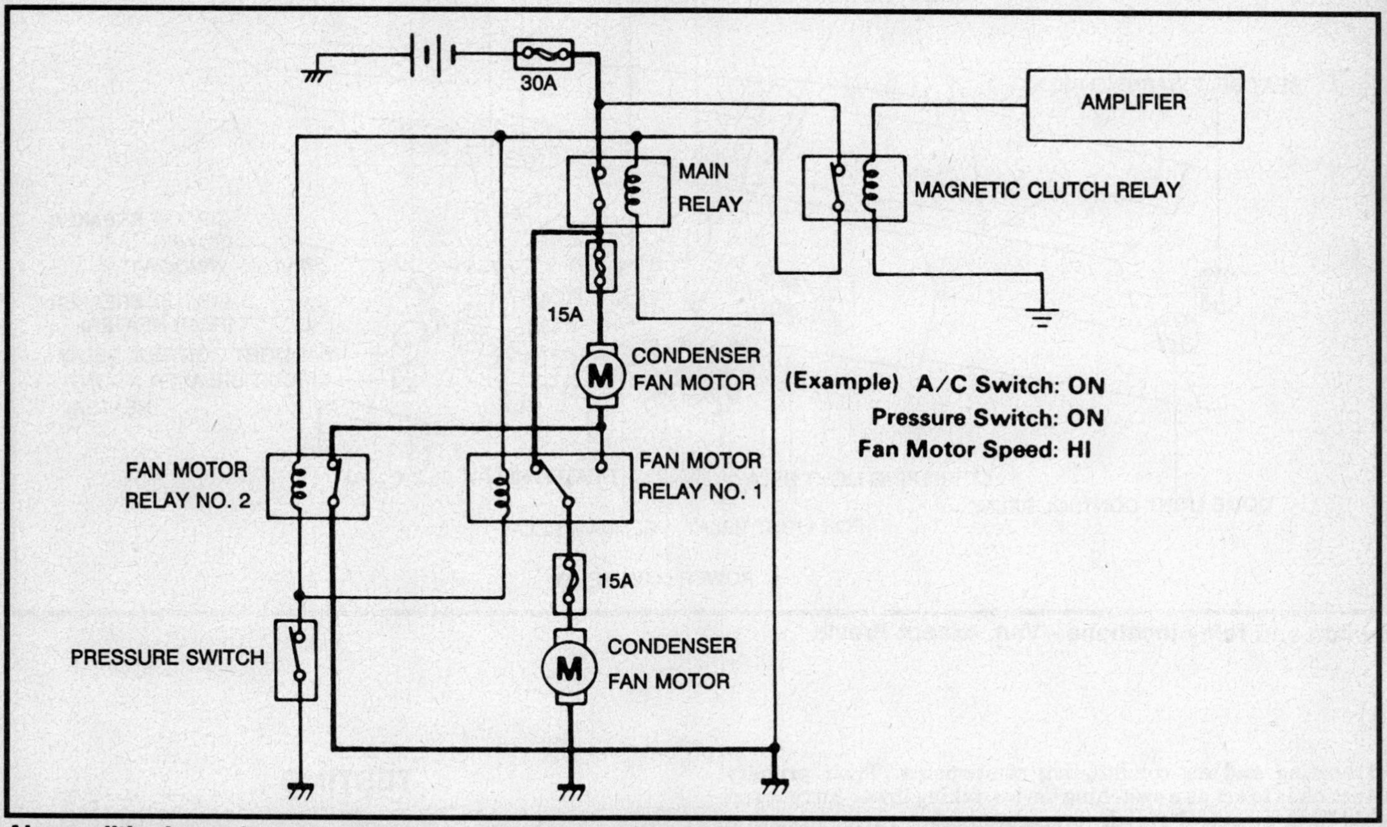
30A
AMPLIFIER
MAIN RELAY
MAGNETIC CLUTCH RELAY
15A
CONDENSER FAN MOTOR
(Example) A/C Switch: ON
Pressure Switch: ON
Fan Motor Speed: HI
FAN MOTOR RELAY NO. 2
FAN MOTOR RELAY NO. 1
15A
PRESSURE SWITCH
CONDENSER FAN MOTOR

Air conditioning schematic showing relay and switch relationship—Van, except Previa

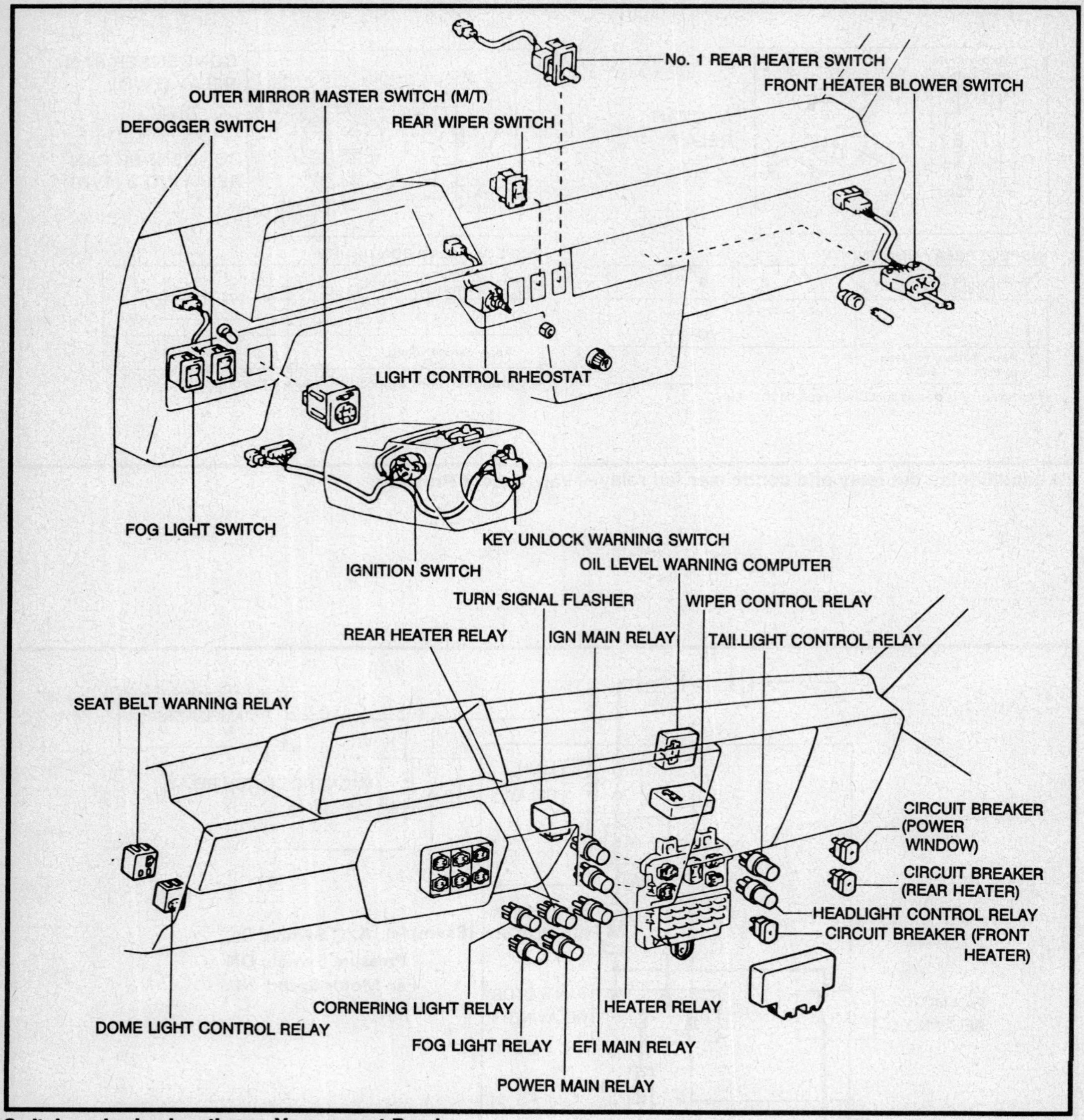
No. 1 REAR HEATER SWITCH
FRONT HEATER BLOWER SWITCH
OUTER MIRROR MASTER SWITCH (M/T)
REAR WIPER SWITCH
DEFOGGER SWITCH
LIGHT CONTROL RHEOSTAT
FOG LIGHT SWITCH
KEY UNLOCK WARNING SWITCH
IGNITION SWITCH
OIL LEVEL WARNING COMPUTER
TURN SIGNAL FLASHER
WIPER CONTROL RELAY
REAR HEATER RELAY
IGN MAIN RELAY
TAILLIGHT CONTROL RELAY
SEAT BELT WARNING RELAY
CIRCUIT BREAKER (POWER WINDOW)
CIRCUIT BREAKER (REAR HEATER)
HEADLIGHT CONTROL RELAY
CIRCUIT BREAKER (FRONT HEATER)
CORNERING LIGHT RELAY
HEATER RELAY
DOME LIGHT CONTROL RELAY
FOG LIGHT RELAY
EFI MAIN RELAY
POWER MAIN RELAY

Switch and relay locations—Van, except Previa

of heating and air conditioning components. Their primary function is to act as a switching device, taking lower current signals from a control switch to operate higher current requirement motors or other components.

TESTING

Tests are confined to continuity checks. Locate the relay, remove from its socket and using an ohmmeter, check for continu-

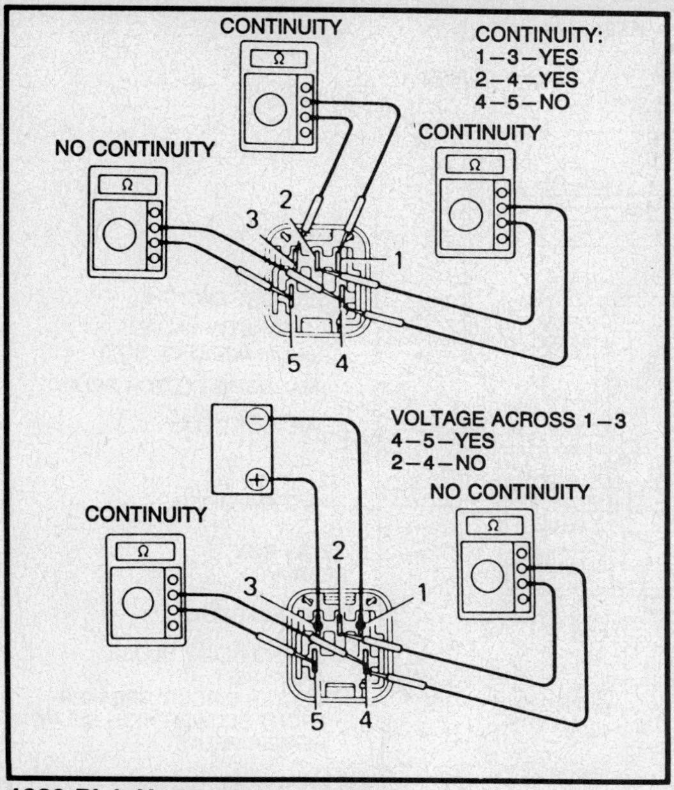
CONTINUITY
CONTINUITY:
1–3–YES
2–4–YES
4–5–NO
CONTINUITY
NO CONTINUITY
VOLTAGE ACROSS 1–3
4–5–YES
2–4–NO
NO CONTINUITY
CONTINUITY

1989 Pick-Up heater relay check

ity at each relay terminal shown in the table. If there is no continuity, replace the relay.

Vacuum Switching Valve (VSV)

OPERATION

The VSV is a load sensing device, monitoring engine vacuum. At times of heavy engine load, in this case, when the air conditioning is turned on, the switch responds to the change in engine vacuum and sends an electric signal to the engine management computer. The computer compares this information with that of other sensors and sends an idle up signal to the engine fuel system.

TESTING

1. Disconnect the vacuum hoses and the electrical connector from the VSV.
2. Check the vacuum circuits inside the valve blowing air into the vacuum connector ports in the following sequence:
   a. Connect the VSV electrical terminals to battery voltage.
   b. Blow into pipe **A** and check that air comes out pipe **B** but does not come out filter **C**.
   c. Disconnect the battery.
   d. Blow into pipe **B** and check that air comes out the filter **C** but does not come out pipe **A**. If a problem is found, replace the VSV.
3. Check for an electrical short circuit or an open circuit using the following procedure:
   a. Using an ohmmeter, check that there is no continuity between each terminal and the VSV body. If there is a problem, replace the VSV.

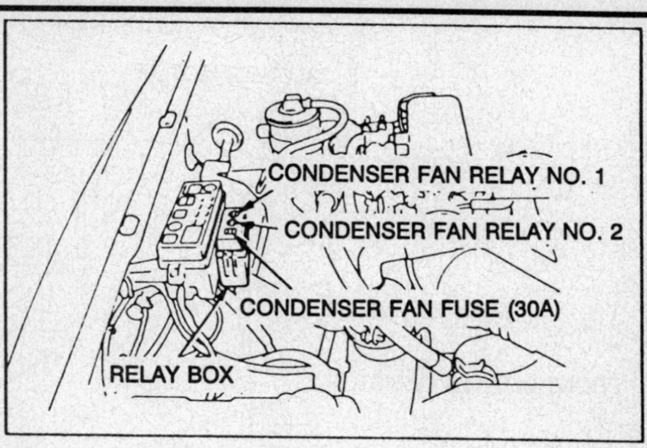
CONDENSER FAN RELAY NO. 1
CONDENSER FAN RELAY NO. 2
CONDENSER FAN FUSE (30A)
RELAY BOX

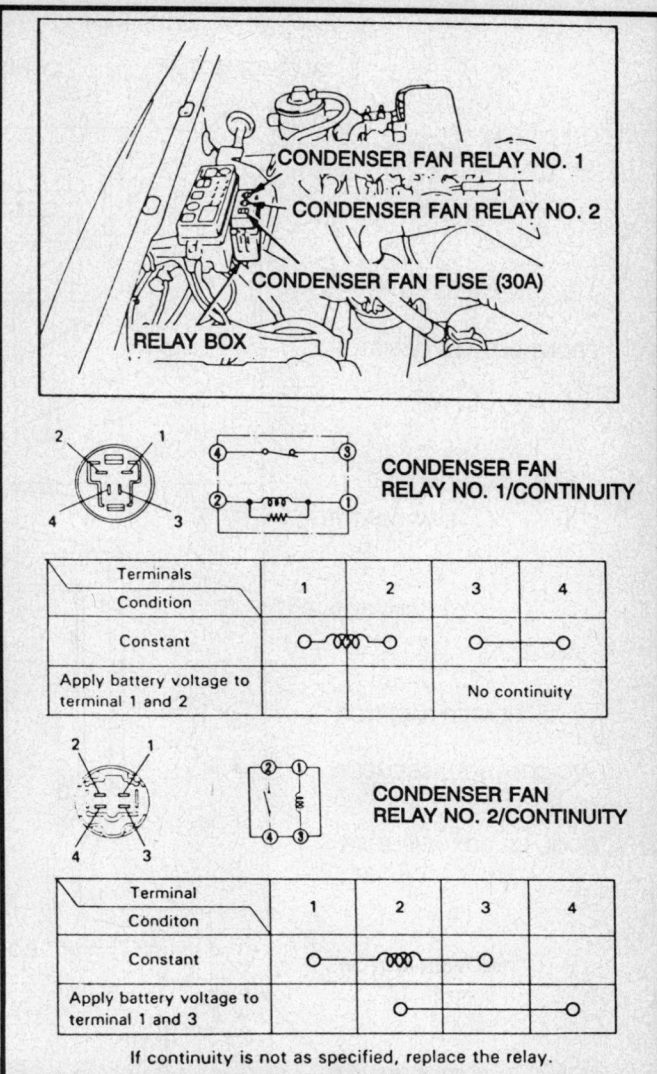

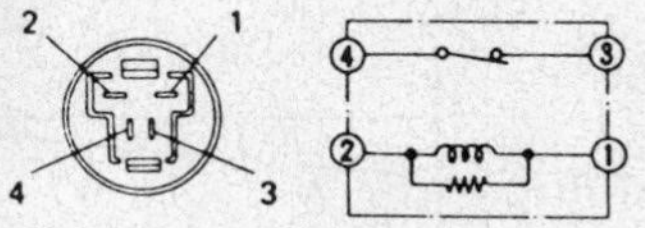
CONDENSER FAN
RELAY NO. 1/CONTINUITY

Terminals / Condition	1	2	3	4
Constant	○—	—○	○—	—○
Apply battery voltage to terminal 1 and 2			No continuity	

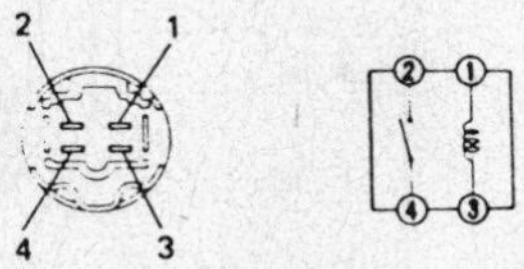
CONDENSER FAN
RELAY NO. 2/CONTINUITY

Terminal / Conditon	1	2	3	4
Constant	○—	—	—○	
Apply battery voltage to terminal 1 and 3		○—	—	—○

If continuity is not as specified, replace the relay.

1990–91 4Runner condenser fan relay checks

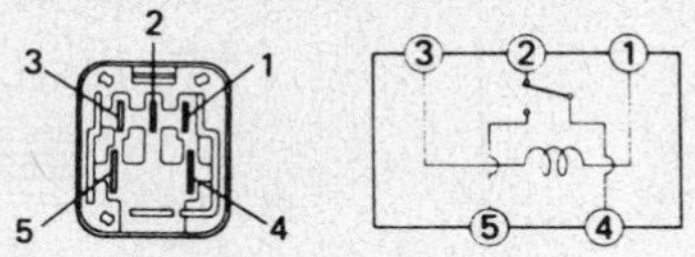
HEATER
RELAY

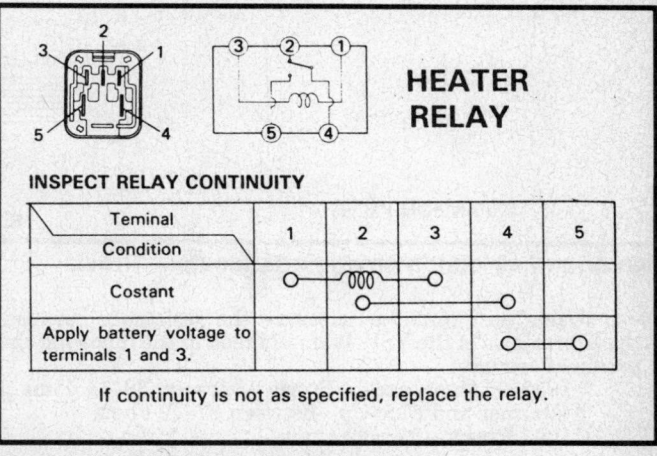

INSPECT RELAY CONTINUITY

Teminal / Condition	1	2	3	4	5
Costant	○—	—	—○		
		○—	—	—○	
Apply battery voltage to terminals 1 and 3.				○—	—○

If continuity is not as specified, replace the relay.

Heater relay testing—Land Cruiser

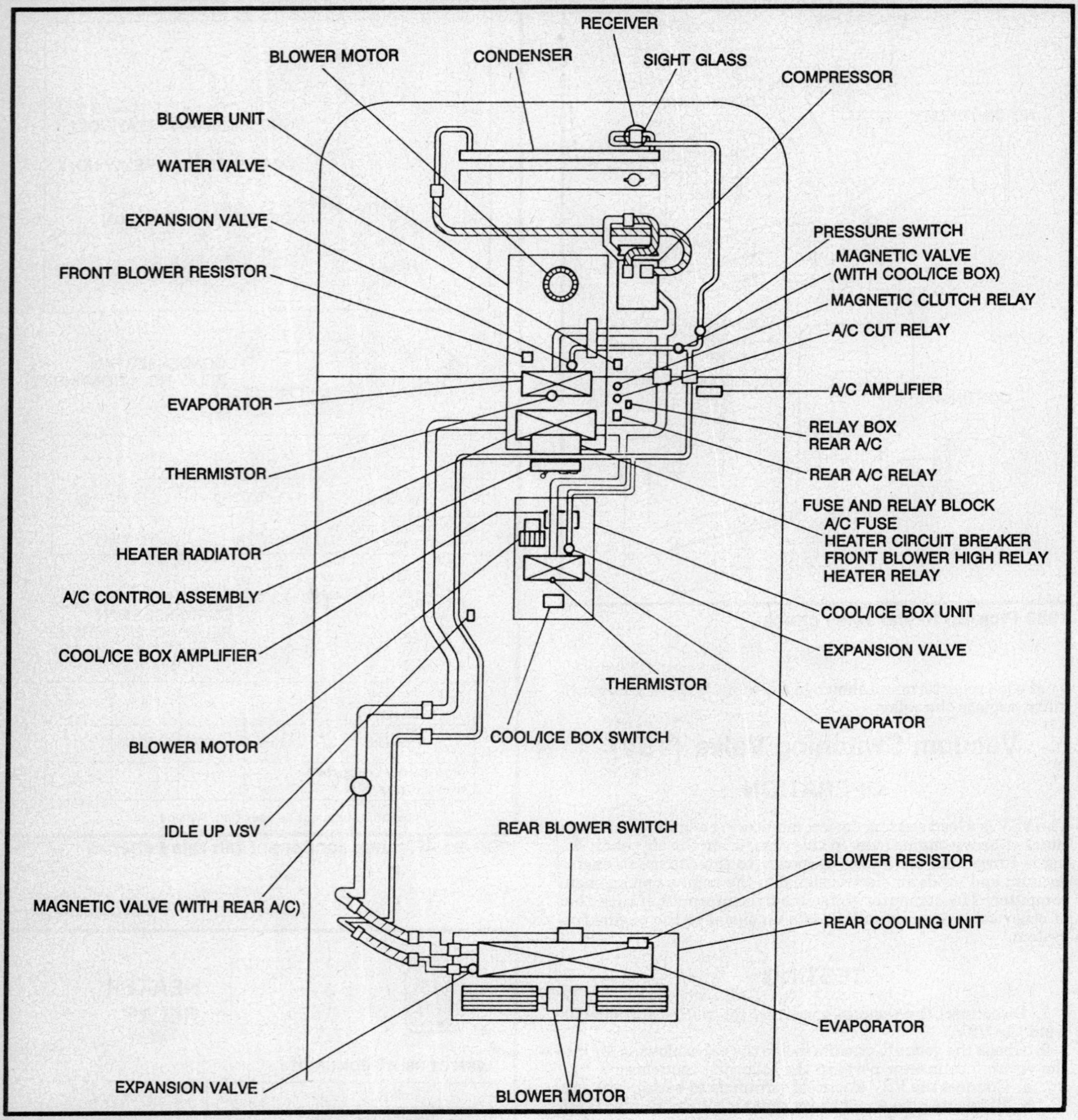
RECEIVER
BLOWER MOTOR
CONDENSER
SIGHT GLASS
COMPRESSOR
BLOWER UNIT
WATER VALVE
EXPANSION VALVE
FRONT BLOWER RESISTOR
PRESSURE SWITCH
MAGNETIC VALVE
(WITH COOL/ICE BOX)
MAGNETIC CLUTCH RELAY
A/C CUT RELAY
A/C AMPLIFIER
EVAPORATOR
RELAY BOX
REAR A/C
THERMISTOR
REAR A/C RELAY
FUSE AND RELAY BLOCK
A/C FUSE
HEATER CIRCUIT BREAKER
FRONT BLOWER HIGH RELAY
HEATER RELAY
HEATER RADIATOR
A/C CONTROL ASSEMBLY
COOL/ICE BOX UNIT
COOL/ICE BOX AMPLIFIER
EXPANSION VALVE
THERMISTOR
EVAPORATOR
BLOWER MOTOR
COOL/ICE BOX SWITCH
IDLE UP VSV
REAR BLOWER SWITCH
BLOWER RESISTOR
MAGNETIC VALVE (WITH REAR A/C)
REAR COOLING UNIT
EVAPORATOR
EXPANSION VALVE
BLOWER MOTOR

Heater and air conditioning parts locator — Previa

b. Using an ohmmeter, measure the resistance between the 2 terminals of the VSV. It should read in the following approximate ranges:

1989–90 Vans, except Previa — between 38–44 ohms
4Runner and Pick-Up — between 37–42 ohms
1991 Previa — 32 ± 2 ohms

4. If resistance is not as specified, replace the VSV.

Air Conditioner Amplifier

OPERATION

An amplifier is used to channel signals from the various air conditioner controls to the proper components that require the signals. In this way, it acts somewhat like a solid-state relay, protecting various components from the high currents required by

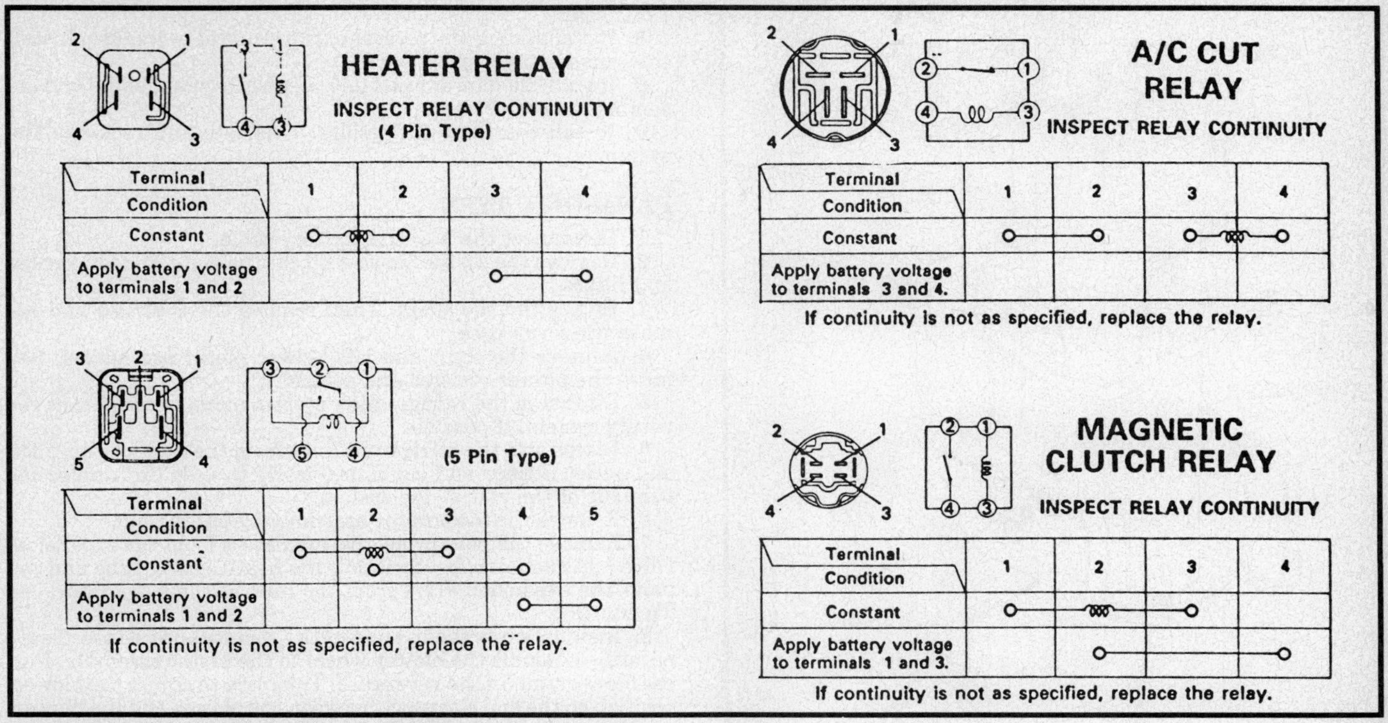
HEATER RELAY
INSPECT RELAY CONTINUITY
(4 Pin Type)
Terminal
Condition
Constant
Apply battery voltage to terminals 1 and 2
(5 Pin Type)
If continuity is not as specified, replace the relay.
A/C CUT RELAY
INSPECT RELAY CONTINUITY
Apply battery voltage to terminals 3 and 4.
If continuity is not as specified, replace the relay.
MAGNETIC CLUTCH RELAY
INSPECT RELAY CONTINUITY
Apply battery voltage to terminals 1 and 3.
If continuity is not as specified, replace the relay.

Heater and air conditioning relay testing—Previa

some other components. For example, signals from the blower switch, low pressure switch, VSV and the thermistor all send information to the amplifier. This information allows the amplifier to decide if the compressor clutch, a high current device, should be energized without exposing the other components to high current rates.

Another example would be the cut amplifier which reads input from various sources to decide if power to the compressor clutch should be cut off. In most cases this would be times of high load on the engine. Some vehicles will use more than one amplifier.

TESTING

Amplifier tests are primarily voltage and continuity checks. Use the following charts to identify both the pin number of the connector and the specified values. Test on the wire harness side. Use care to read the correct chart. In some cases, engine series makes a difference. If all circuits are correct, replace the amplifier.

The amplifier is generally mounted inside the air conditioning cooling unit along with the evaporator.

REAR AUXILIARY SYSTEM

Expansion Valve

REMOVAL AND INSTALLATION

1989–90 Van

1. The rear auxiliary system expansion valve is located inside the rear cooling unit case which also contains an evaporator. This cooling unit case must be removed. Disconnect the battery negative terminal.
2. Discharge the refrigeration system using a refrigerant recovery system, if possible.
3. Disconnect the refrigerant lines from the cooling unit inlet and outlet fittings and cap immediately to keep dirt and moisture out of the rest of the system.
4. Disconnect the electrical connectors.
5. Remove the magnetic valve and rear blower unit.
6. Remove the cooling unit.
7. Remove the expansion valve.

To install:

8. Installation is the reverse of the removal procedure. Make sure the expansion valve and thermistor are in the proper places for accurate heat sensing. Check electrical contacts for corrosion.
9. Evacuate, charge and test the system. If a new evaporator has been used, additional refrigerant oil must be added, generally approximately 1¾ ounce.

Previa

Previa Vans use 2 types of rear cooling system, a Denso type and a Panasonic type. The type of cooling unit can be determined by removing the cover at the side of the cooling unit, slide door side, and looking at the name on the surface of the unit.

Note that some components, such as filters, switches and in some cases, the blowers can be removed without discharging the refrigerant and removing the system.

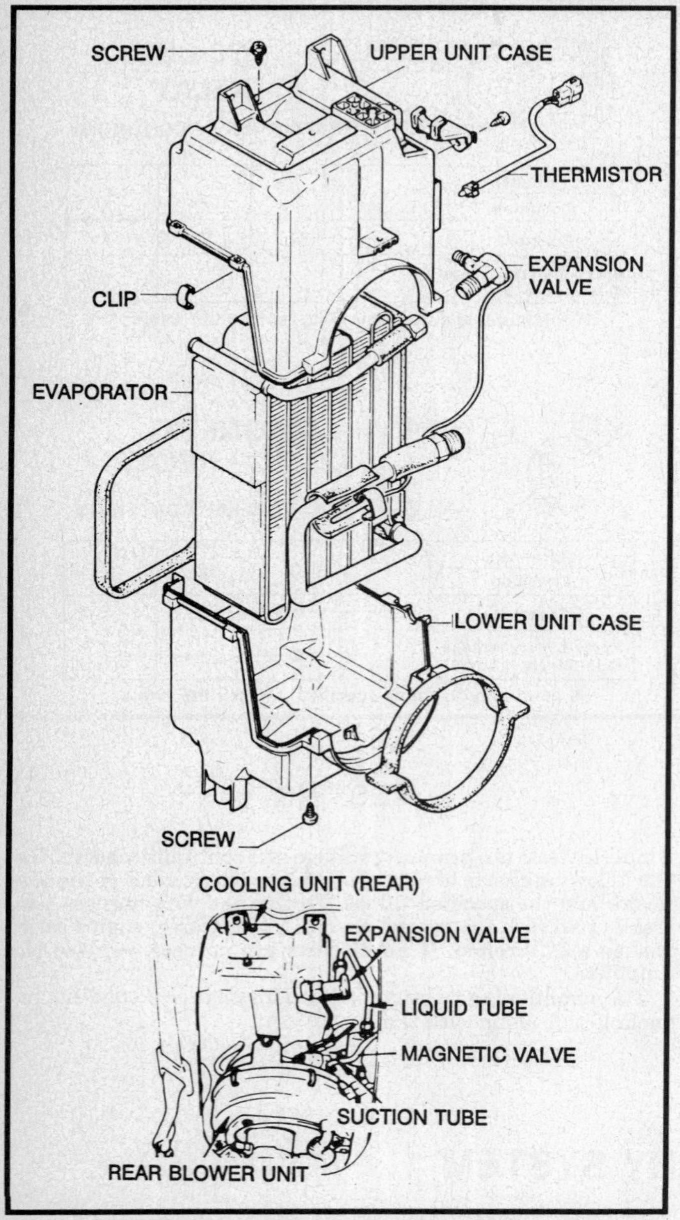
SCREW
UPPER UNIT CASE
THERMISTOR
EXPANSION VALVE
CLIP
EVAPORATOR
LOWER UNIT CASE
SCREW
COOLING UNIT (REAR)
EXPANSION VALVE
LIQUID TUBE
MAGNETIC VALVE
SUCTION TUBE
REAR BLOWER UNIT

Rear auxiliary air conditioning system—Van, except Previa

DENSO TYPE

1. Disconnect the negative battery cable. Remove the right and left air inlet and outlet grilles.
2. Remove the filter and the lower case cover.
3. Remove the rear air conditioning switch.
4. Discharge the refrigeration system using a refrigerant recovery system, if possible.
5. Disconnect the refrigerant lines from the cooling unit inlet and outlet fittings and cap immediately to keep dirt and moisture out of the rest of the system.
6. Remove the evaporator assembly
7. Using an allen wrench, remove 2 bolts and lift off the expansion valve.

To install:

8. Installation is the reverse of the removal procedure. Install the expansion valve.
9. Install the blower assembly, electrical components and assemble the cooler case.
10. Install the filter and grilles. Evacuate and recharge the system.

PANASONIC TYPE

1. Disconnect the negative battery cable.
2. Remove the 12 screws and lift off the right and left grilles and filters.
3. Empty the the drain. Then remove the 9 screws and remove the lower case.
4. Remove the right and left blower motor assemblies. Remove the blower resistor and switch.
5. Discharge the refrigeration system using a refrigerant recovery system, if possible.
6. Disconnect the refrigerant lines from the cooling unit inlet and outlet fittings and cap immediately to keep dirt and moisture out of the rest of the system.
6. Remove the evaporator assembly by pulling out.
7. Remove the heat protective insulators from the expansion valve and suction tube. Separate the heat-sensing tube and remove the expansion valve from the inlet of the evaporator.

To install:

8. Installation is the reverse of the removal procedure. Temporarily assemble the blower wheel to the motor assembly. Put the blower unit on the lower case. Take care to adjust the blower position so the end clearance between the blower and the blower case is equal on both sides. Tighten the screw and make sure the blower wheel turns smoothly. Assemble the blower upper case to the lower case.
9. Connect the liquid line tube to the expansion valve and, using a crow's foot wrench, torque the nut to 10 ft. lbs. Connect the expansion valve to the inlet fitting of the evaporator and torque to 17 ft. lbs. Connect the heat sensing tube to the suction line and reattach the heat insulators around the expansion valve.
10. Install the evaporator to the upper case.
11. Install the switch and the blower motor assemblies to the upper case.
12. Install the lower case, the filters and grilles. Connect the drain hoses. Evacuate and recharge the system.

Blower Motor

REMOVAL AND INSTALLATION

DENSO TYPE

1. Disconnect the negative battery cable. Remove the right and left air inlet and outlet grilles.
2. Remove the filter and the lower case cover.
3. Remove the rear A/C switch.
4. Discharge the refrigeration system using a refrigerant recovery system if at all possible.
5. Remove the evaporator assembly.
6. Remove the left and right blower assemblies.

To install:

7. Installation is the reverse of the removal procedure. Assemble the blower wheels to the motors, if removed. Install the blower resistor, if removed. Install the blower and motor assemblies to the upper case.
8. Install the evaporator assembly to the upper case. Install the rear blower switch.
9. Install the lower case to the upper case. Install the filter and grilles.
10. Evacuate and recharge the system.

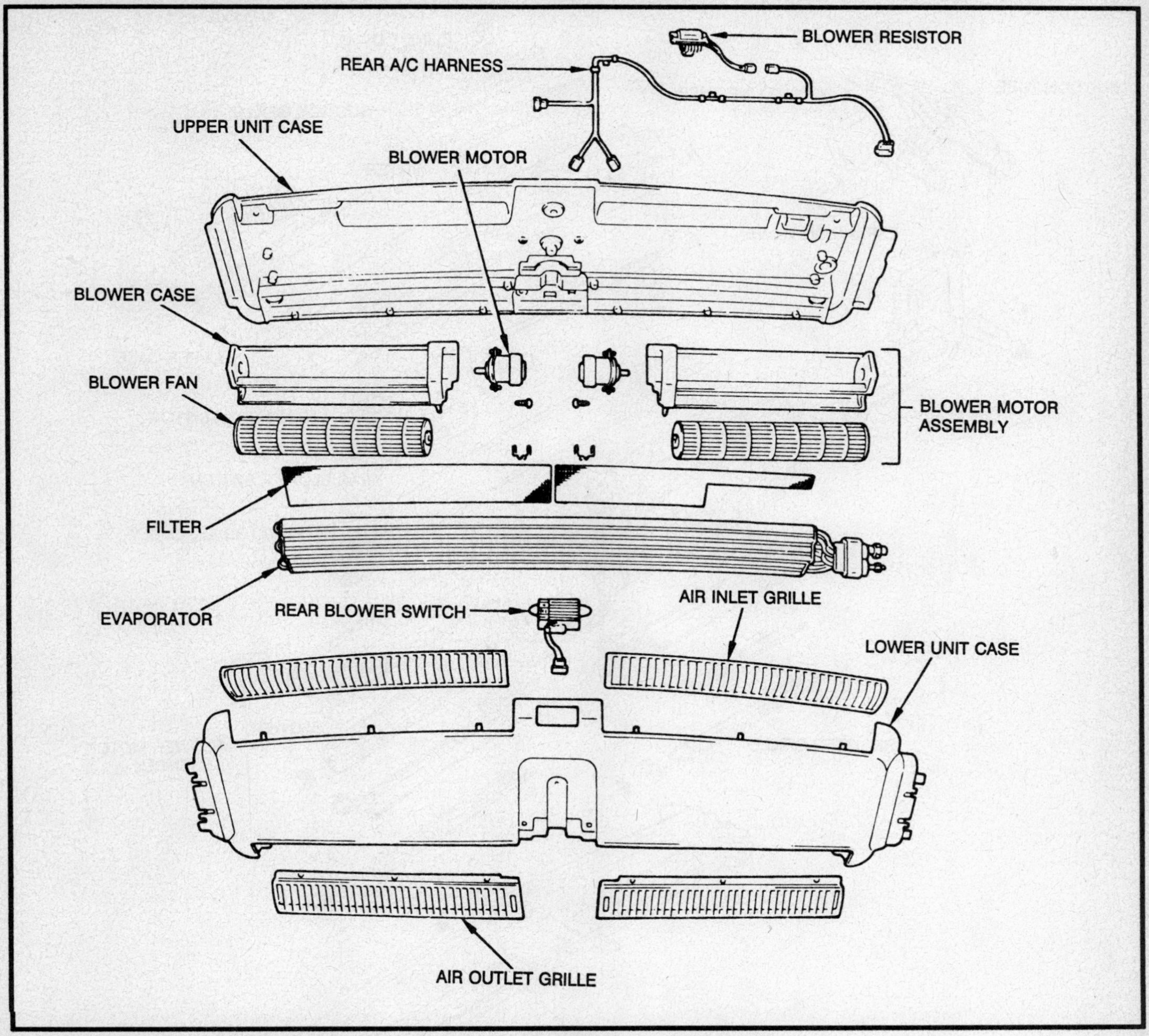
BLOWER RESISTOR
REAR A/C HARNESS
UPPER UNIT CASE
BLOWER MOTOR
BLOWER CASE
BLOWER FAN
BLOWER MOTOR ASSEMBLY
FILTER
EVAPORATOR
REAR BLOWER SWITCH
AIR INLET GRILLE
LOWER UNIT CASE
AIR OUTLET GRILLE

Rear auxiliary air conditioning system—Previa with Denso type cooling unit

PANASONIC TYPE

1. The motor assemblies can be removed without removing the entire cooling system. Remove the 12 screws and lift off the right and left grilles and filters.
2. Empty the the drain. Then remove the 9 screws and remove the lower case.
3. Remove the right and left blower motor assemblies by removing the 3 screws on each assembly and disconnecting the electrical connector. Disengage the 8 retaining pawls and remove the blower assembly.

To install:

4. Installation is the reverse of the removal procedure. Assemble the blower motor assemblies.
5. Install the lower case. Make sure the drains are properly installed.
6. Install the grilles and filters.

Blower Motor Resistor

REMOVAL AND INSTALLATION

DENSO TYPE

1. Disconnect the negative battery cable. Remove the right and left air inlet and outlet grilles.
2. Remove the filter and the lower case cover.
3. Remove the rear air conditioning switch.

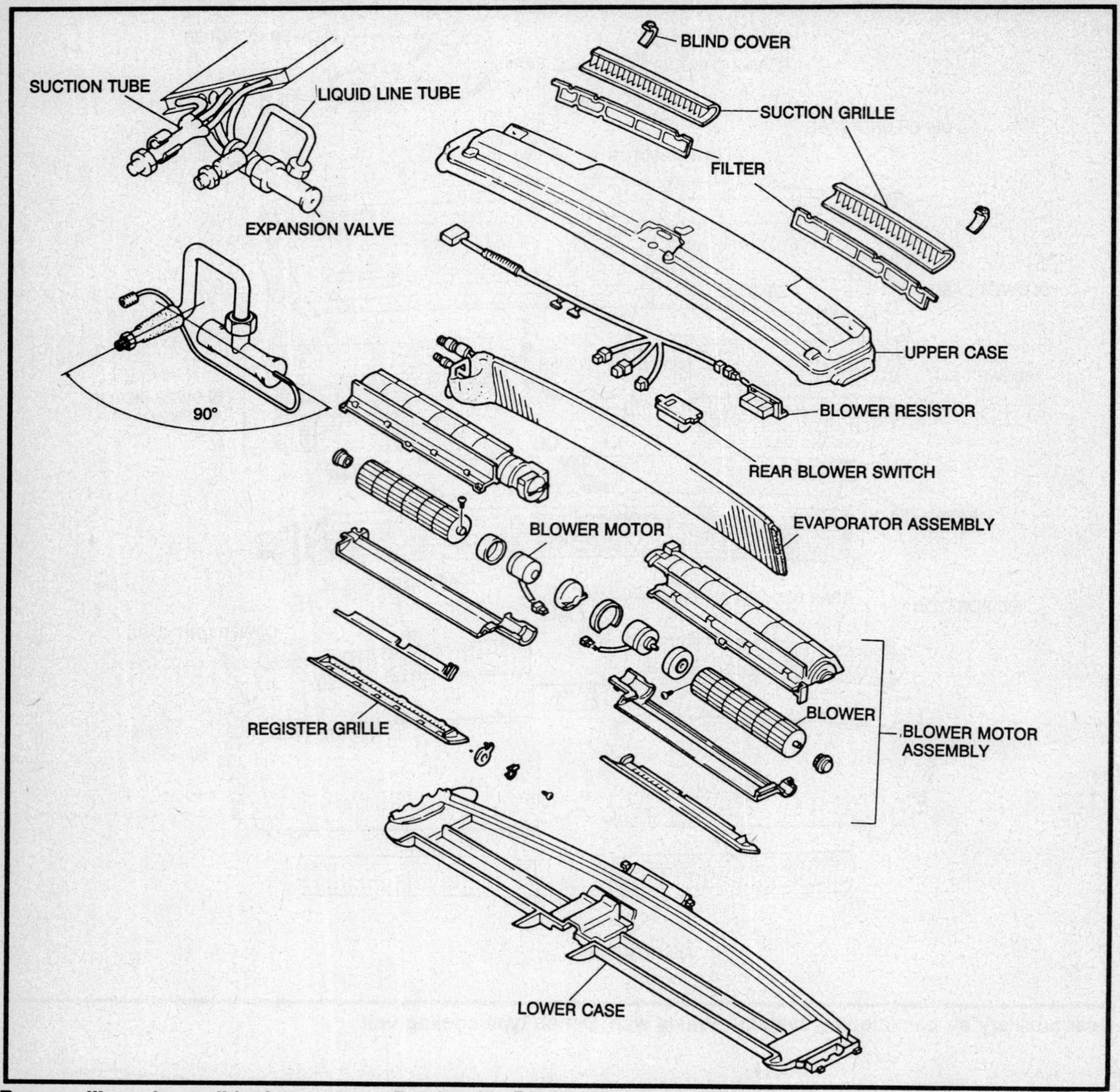
BLIND COVER
SUCTION TUBE
LIQUID LINE TUBE
SUCTION GRILLE
FILTER
EXPANSION VALVE
UPPER CASE
90°
BLOWER RESISTOR
REAR BLOWER SWITCH
EVAPORATOR ASSEMBLY
BLOWER MOTOR
BLOWER
BLOWER MOTOR ASSEMBLY
REGISTER GRILLE
LOWER CASE

Rear auxiliary air conditioning system—Previa with Panasonic type cooling unit

4. Discharge the refrigeration system using a refrigerant recovery system, if possible.
5. Remove the evaporator assembly.
6. Remove the left and right blower assemblies.
7. Remove the blower resistor and disconnect the electrical connection.

To install:

8. Installation is the reverse of the removal procedure. Install the resistor and connect to harness.
9. Install the blower motor assemblies.
10. Install the evaporator assembly and case covers.
11. Evacuate and recharge the system.

Heater Core

REMOVAL AND INSTALLATION

1. Turn off the water valve and disconnect both hoses from the rear heater core.
2. Disconnect the wiring from the rear heater.
3. Remove the mounting bolts and lift out the core.

To install:

4. Installation is the reverse of the removal procedure. Check the heater core for fin damage. When tightening the retaining bolts, tighten smoothly and evenly.
5. Check wiring connectors for corrosion and reconnect.
6. Refill cooling system, as required.

Evaporator

REMOVAL AND INSTALLATION

Previa

DENSO TYPE

1. Disconnect the negative battery cable. Remove the right and left air inlet and outlet grilles.
2. Remove the filter and the lower case cover.
3. Remove the rear air conditioning switch.
4. Discharge the refrigeration system using a refrigerant recovery system, if possible.
5. Disconnect the refrigerant lines from the cooling unit inlet and outlet fittings and cap immediately to keep dirt and moisture out of the rest of the system.
6. Remove the evaporator assembly.

To install:

7. Installation is the reverse of the removal procedure.
8. Install the blower assembly, electrical components and assemble the cooler case.
9. Install the filter and grilles. Evacuate and recharge the system.

PANASONIC TYPE

1. Disconnect the negative battery cable.
2. Remove the 12 screws and lift off the right and left grilles and filters.
3. Empty the the drain. Then remove the 9 screws and remove the lower case.
4. Remove the right and left blower motor assemblies. Remove the blower resistor and switch.
5. Discharge the refrigeration system using a refrigerant recovery system, if possible.
6. Disconnect the refrigerant lines from the cooling unit inlet and outlet fittings and cap immediately to keep dirt and moisture out of the rest of the system.
7. Remove the evaporator assembly by pulling out.

To install:

8. Installation is the reverse of the removal procedure. Temporarily assemble the blower wheel to the motor assembly. Put the blower unit on the lower case. Take care to adjust the blower position so the end clearance between the blower and the blower case is equal on both sides. Tighten the screw and make sure the blower wheel turns smoothly. Assemble the blower upper case to the lower case.
9. Connect the liquid line tube to the expansion valve and, using a crow's foot wrench, torque the nut to 10 ft. lbs. Connect the expansion valve to the inlet fitting of the evaporator and torque to 17 ft. lbs. Connect the heat sensing tube to the suction line and reattach the heat insulators around the expansion valve.
10. Install the evaporator to the upper case.
11. Install the switch and the blower motor assemblies to the upper case.
12. Install the lower case, the filters and grilles. Connect the drain hoses. Evacuate and recharge the system.

Refrigerant Lines

REMOVAL AND INSTALLATION

1. Discharge the refrigeration system using a refrigerant recovery system, if possible.
2. Disconnect the faulty refrigerant line. Cap the open fittings immediately to keep dirt and moisture out of the rest of the system.
4. Some interior trim panels may need to be removed to take out the damaged section of refrigerant line. Due to high pressures used, always replace lines with new ones of equal quality.
5. When installing new refrigerant lines, measure the diameter of the tube. On the tubes measuring 0.31 in. or approximately ⅜ in., torque the fittings to 10 ft. lbs. On tubes measuring 0.50 in. or approximately ½ in., torque the fittings to 17 ft. lbs. On tubes measuring 0.62 in. or approximately ⅝ in., torque the fittings to 24 ft. lbs. Generally a small torque wrench is used with a crow's foot adapter to torque air conditioning fittings. When tightening these fittings, apply a few drops of compressor oil to the O-ring fittings for easy tightening. Tighten the nut using 2 wrenches to avoid twisting the tube.
6. Evacuate, charge and test the system.

SYSTEM DIAGNOSTICS

TROUBLESHOOTING CHART—EXCEPT PREVIA

Problem	Possible cause	Remedy
No cooling or warm air	Magnetic clutch does not engage	
	(a) IGN fuse blown	Replace fuse and check for short
	(b) Magnetic clutch faulty	Check magnetic clutch
	(c) A/C switch faulty	Check switch
	(d) A/C amplifier faulty	Check amplifier
	(e) Wiring or ground faulty	Repair as necessary
	(f) Refrigerant empty	Check refrigerant pressure
	(g) Heater relay faulty	Check heater relay
	(h) Pressure switch faulty	Check pressure switch

TROUBLESHOOTING CHART—EXCEPT PREVIA, CONT.

Problem	Possible cause	Remedy
No cooling or warm air (Cont'd)	Compressor does not rotate properly	Adjust or replace drive belt
	(a) Drive belt loose or broken	Check compressor
	(b) Compressor faulty	Check expansion valve
	Expansion valve faulty	Test system for leaks
	Leak in system	Check receiver
	Fusible plug on receiver blown or clogged screen	
	Blower does not operate	
	(a) HEATER fuse blown	Replace fuse and check for short
	(b) A/C switch faulty	Check A/C switch
	(c) Circuit breaker faulty	Check circuit breaker
	(d) Heater relay faulty	Check heater relay
	(e) Blower motor faulty	Check blower motor
	(f) Wiring faulty	Repair as necessary
Cool air comes out intermittently	Magnetic clutch slipping	Check magnetic clutch
	Expansion valve faulty	Check expansion valve
	Wiring connection faulty	Repair as necessary
	Excessive moisture in system	Evacuate and charge system
	A/C amplifier faulty	Check amplifier
Cool air comes out only at high speed	Condenser clogged	Check condenser
	Drive belt slipping	Check or replace drive belt
	Compressor faulty	Check compressor
	Insufficient or too much refrigerant	Check refrigerant charge
	Air in system	Evacuate and charge system
Insufficient cooling	Condenser clogged	Check condenser
	Drive belt slipping	Check or replace drive belt
	Magnetic clutch faulty	Check magnetic clutch
	Compressor faulty	Check compressor
	Expansion valve faulty	Check expansion valve
	Insufficient or too much refrigerant	Check refrigerant charge
	Air or excessive compressor oil in system	Evacuate and charge system
	Receiver clogged	Check receiver
	Water valve cable faulty	Reset water valve cable
	A/C amplifier faulty	Check amplifier
Insufficient velocity of cool air	Evaporator clogged or frosted	Clean evaporator fins or filters
	Air leakage from cooling unit or air duct	Repair as necessary
	Air inlet blocked	Repair as necessary
	Blower motor faulty	Replace blower motor
	A/C amplifier faulty	Check amplifier

AIR CONDITIONING AMPLIFIER CHECK—PICK-UP

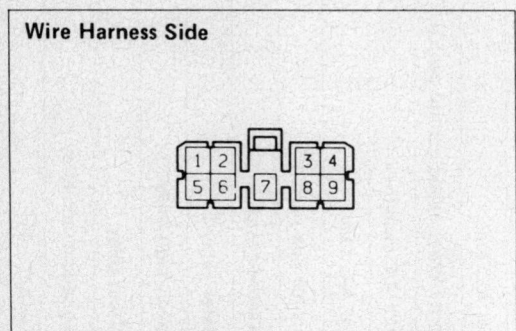

Wire Harness Side

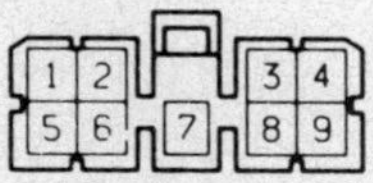
1
2
3
4
5
6
7
8
9

AIR CONDITIONER AMPLIFIER

INSPECTION OF AMPLIFIER

INSPECT AMPLIFIER CIRCUIT

Disconnect the amplifier and inspect the connector on the wire harness side as shown in the chart below.

Test conditions:

(1) Ignition switch: ON

(2) Temperature control lever: MAX COOL

(3) Blower switch: HI

Check for	Tester connection	Condition	Specified value
Continuity	7 – 8	Constant	Continuity
	8 – Ground	Constant	Continuity
Voltage	3 – 8	Turn A/C switch on.	Battery voltage
		Turn A/C switch off.	Battery voltage
	4 – 8	Turn A/C switch on.	Battery voltage
		Turn A/C switch off.	No voltage
	6 – 8	Start the engine.	Approx. 10 to 14 V
		Stop the engine.	No voltage
	8 – 9	Turn A/C switch on.	Battery voltage
		Turn A/C switch off.	Battery voltage
Resistance	5 – 8	Constant	Approx. 1.5 kΩ at 25°C (77°F)
	2 – 5	MAX COOL	Approx. 3 kΩ
		MIN COOL	Approx. 0 Ω

If circuit is correct, replace the amplifier.

TROUBLESHOOTING CHART—PREVIA

Trouble		Inspect volume of refrigerant	Inspect refrigeration system with manifold gauge set	Inspect drive belt tension	Inspect A/C control lever adjustment	Inspect engine coolant volume	Heater CB	A/C fuse	Rear A/C fuse	Front blower speed control switch	Front A/C switch	Rear A/C switch	Cool/Ice box switch	Pressure switch	Heater relay	Blower high relay	A/C cut relay	Magnetic clutch relay	Rear A/C relay
No blower operation	Front						1			3					2				
	Rear								1			3							2
No blower control	Front									2						1			
	Rear											1							
No air flow mode control				1															
No air inlet control				1															
Insufficient flow of air	Front																		
	Rear																		
No cool air comes out	All	1	5	8	10			2						6			3	4	
	Front																		
	Rear																		
	Cool/Ice box																		
Cool air comes out intermittently		1	3	2															
Cool air comes out only at high engine speed		1	3	2															
Insufficient cooling	All	1	3	2	7														
	Front																		
	Rear																		
	Cool/Ice Box																		
No warm air comes out					3	1													
Air temp. control not functioning					2														
No engine idle up when A/C switch on																			

TROUBLESHOOTING CHART—PREVIA, CONT.

	Front blower motor	Rear A/C blower motor	Cool/Ice box blower motor	Front blower resistor	Rear A/C blower resistor	Magnetic valve	Front A/C thermistor	Cool/Ice box thermistor	A/C amplifier	Compressor	Magnetic clutch	Condenser	Receiver	Front A/C evaporator	Rear A/C evaporator	Cool/Ice box evaporator	Front A/C expansion valve	Rear A/C expansion valve	Cool/Ice box expansion valve	Water valve	Heater radiator	Wiring or Wiring connection	Air inlet blocked	Air leakage from heater unit or air duct	A/C VSV	Rear A/C filter
	4			5																		6				
		4																				5				
				3																		4				
					2																	3				
	1			2																	7	3	4	5		
		2			3																	4	5			1
									11	9	5									7		12				
							1							3			2									
						1									3			2								
						1										3			2							
							7		6	5			4													
										5		4														
									8			4	5							6						
														2			1									
															2			1								
																2			1							
																				2	4					
																					1					
									2																1	

TROUBLESHOOTING WITH GAUGES

This is a method in which the trouble is located by using a manifold gauge. Read the manifold gauge pressure when the following conditions are established:

(a) Temperature at the air inlet is 30 – 35°C (86 – 95°F)

(b) Engine running at 1,500 rpm

(c) Blower fan speed switch set at high speed

(d) Temperature control lever set at cool side

HINT: It should be noted that the gauge indications may vary slightly due to ambient temperature conditions.

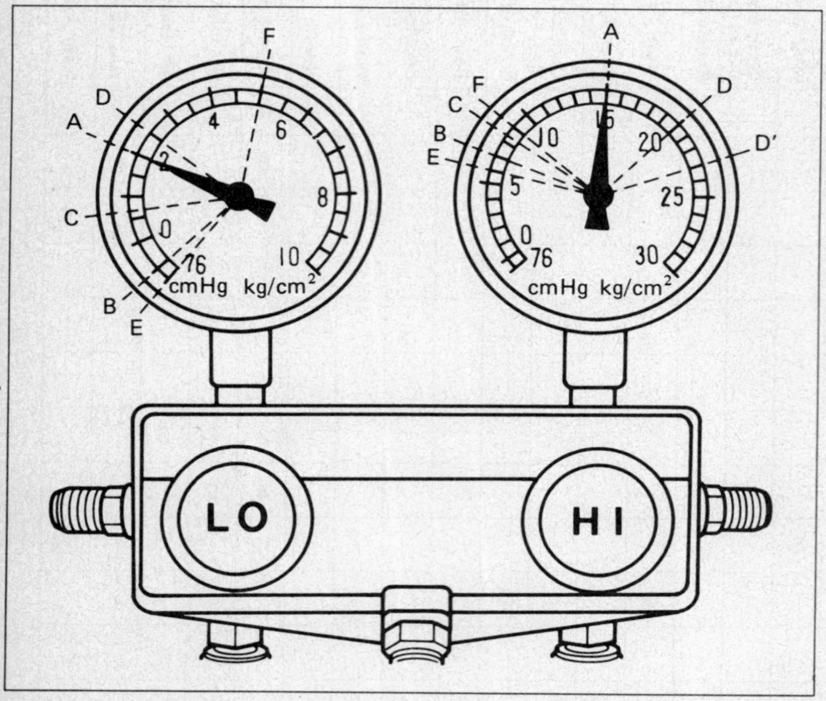
F
D
A
C
B
E
4
6
2
8
0
76
10
cmHg kg/cm²
A
F
C
B
E
D
D'
10
15
20
5
25
0
76
30
cmHg kg/cm²
LO
HI

NORMALLY FUNCTIONING REFRIGERATION SYSTEM

Gauge reading:

Low pressure side
1.5 – 2.0 kg/cm²
(21 – 28 psi, 147 – 196 kPa)

High pressure side
14.5 – 15.0 kg/cm²
(206 – 213 psi, 1,422 – 1,471 kPa)

Each pointer of manifold gauge point to position A.

No.	Trouble	Condition	Position of Pointers
1	Moisture present in refrigeration system	Periodically cools and then fails to cool	Between **A** and **B**
2	Insufficient refrigerant	Insufficient cooling	**C**
3	Poor circulation of refrigerant	Insufficient cooling	**C**
4	Refrigerant overcharge or insufficient cooling of condenser	Does not cool sufficiently	**D**
5	Expansion valve improperly mounted, heat sensing tube defective (Opens too wide)	Insufficient cooling	**D**
6	Air present in refrigeration system	Does not cool sufficiently	Low is **D** High is **D'**
7	Refrigerant does not circulate	Does not cool (Cools from time to time in some cases)	**E**
8	Insufficient compression	Does not cool	**F**

TROUBLESHOOTING WITH GAUGES, CONT.

No.	Symptom seen in refrigeration system	Probable cause	Diagnosis	Remedy
1	During operation, pressure at low pressure side sometimes becomes a vacuum and sometimes normal	Moisture entered in refrigeration system freezes at expansion valve orifice and temporarily stops cycle, but normal state is restored after a time when the ice melts	Drier in oversaturated state ↓ Moisture in refrigeration system freezes at expansion valve orifice and blocks circulation of refrigerant	(1) Replace receiver and drier (2) Remove moisture in cycle through repeated vacuum purging (3) Charge refrigerant to proper amount
2	Pressure low at both low and high pressure sides Bubbles seen in sight glass Insufficient cooling performance	Gas leakage at some place in refrigeration system	Insufficient refrigerant in system ↓ Refrigerant leaking	(1) Check with leak tester and repair (2) Charge refrigerant to proper amount
3	Pressure low at both low and high pressure sides Frost on tubes from receiver to unit	Refrigerant flow obstructed by dirt in receiver	Receiver clogged	Replace receiver
4	Pressure too high at both low and high pressure sides	Unable to develop sufficient performance due to excessive refrigerant in system Condenser cooling insufficient	Excess refrigerant in cycle → refrigerant overcharged Condenser cooling insufficient → condenser fins clogged or fan motor faulty	(1) Clean condenser (2) Check fan motor operation (3) If (1) and (2) are normal, check refrigerant amount HINT: Vent out refrigerant through gauge manifold low pressure side by gradually opening valve.
5	Pressure too high at both low and high pressure sides Frost or large amount of dew on piping at low pressure side	Trouble in expansion valve or heat sensing tube not installed correctly Refrigerant flow out	Excessive refrigerant in low pressure piping ↓ Expansion valve opened too wide	(1) Check heat sensing tube installed condition (2) If (1) is normal, test expansion valve in unit (3) Replace if defective

TROUBLESHOOTING WITH GAUGES, CONT.

No.	Symptom seen in refrigeration system	Probable cause	Diagnosis	Remedy
6	Pressure too high at both low and high pressure sides	Air entered refrigeration system	Air present in refrigeration system ↓ Insufficient vacuum purging	(1) Replace receiver and drier (2) Check compressor oil to see if dirty or insufficient (3) Vacuum purge and charge new refrigerant
7	Vacuum indicated at low pressure side, very low pressure indicated at high pressure side Frost or dew seen on piping before and after receiver and drier or expansion valve	Refrigerant flow obstructed by moisture or dirt in refrigerant freezing or adhering to expansion valve orifice Refrigerant flow obstructed by gas leakage from expansion valve	Expansion valve orifice clogged ↓ Refrigerant does not flow	Allow to stand for some time and then restart operation to determine if trouble is caused by moisture or dirt. If caused by dirt, remove expansion valve and clean off dirt by blowing with air. If unable to remove dirt, replace valve. Vacuum purge and charge new refrigerant to proper amount. For gas leakage from heat sensing tube, replace expansion valve.
8	Pressure too high at low pressure side Pressure too low at high pressure side	Internal leak in compressor	Compression defective ↓ Valve leaking or broken sliding parts (Piston, cylinder, gasket, etc.) broken	Repair or replace compressor

* HINT at No.6
These gauge indications are shown when the refrigeration system has been opened and the refrigerant charged without vacuum purging.

AIR CONDITIONING AMPLIFIER CHECK—4RUNNER

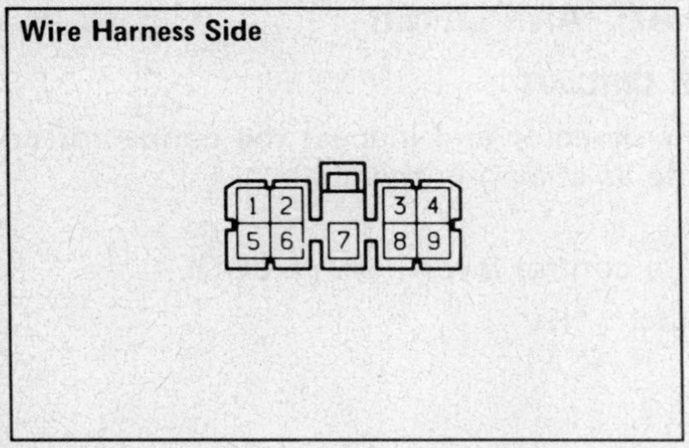
Wire Harness Side
1
2
3
4
5
6
7
8
9

AIR CONDITIONER AMPLIFIER

INSPECTION OF AMPLIFIER

INSPECT AMPLIFIER CIRCUIT

Disconnect the amplifier and inspect the connector on the wire harness side as shown in the chart below.

Test conditions:
(1) Ignition switch: ON
(2) Temperature control lever: MAX COOL
(3) Blower switch: HI

Check for	Tester connection	Condition	Specified value
Continuity	8 – Ground	Constant	Continuity
Voltage	3 – 8	Turn A/C switch on.	Battery voltage
		Turn A/C switch off.	Battery voltage
	4 – 8	Turn A/C switch on.	Battery voltage
		Turn A/C swtich off.	No voltage
	6 – 8	Start the engine.	Approx. 10 to 14 V
		Stop the engine.	No voltage
	8 – 9	Turn A/C switch on.	Battery voltage
		Turn A/C switch off.	Battery voltage
Resistance	5 – 8	Constant	Approx. 1.5 kΩ at 25°C (77°F)
	2 – 5	MAX COOL	Approx. 3 kΩ
		MIN COOL	Approx. 0 Ω
	7 – 8	Constant	Approx. 3.6 Ω

If circuit is as specified, replace the amplifier.

AIR CONDITIONING AMPLIFIER CHECK—PREVIA

Wire Harness Side

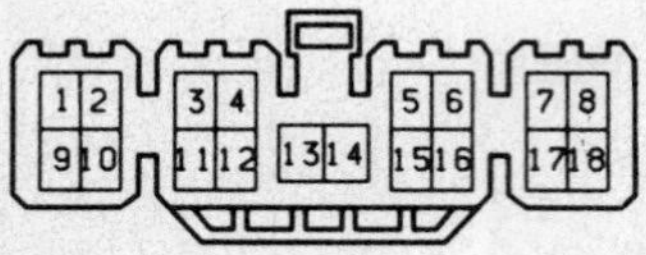
1 2
3 4
5 6
7 8
9 10
11 12
13 14
15 16
17 18

AIR CONDITIONER AMPLIFIER

INSPECTION OF A/C AMPLIFIER

INSPECT AMPLIFIER CIRCUIT

Disconnect the connector and inspect the connector on wire harness side as shown in the chart.
Test conditions:

(1) Temperature control lever: MAX COOL

(2) Blower switch: HI

Check for	Tester connection	Condition		Specified value
Continuity	1 — 2	Constant		Continuity
	11 — Groung	A/C switch position	ON	Continuity
			OFF	No continuity
	12 — Ground	Rear blower switch position	ON	Continuity
			OFF	No continuity
	13 — Ground	Constant		Continuity
	17 — *2	Constant		Continuity
Resistance	1 — 15	Constant		Approx. 1.5 kΩ
	3 — 7	Constant		Approx. 60 Ω
	4 — 8	Constant		Approx. 20 Ω
Voltage	4 — Ground	Ignition switch position	LOCK, ACC or START	No voltage
			ON	Battery voltage
	5 — Ground	Ignition switch position	LOCK, ACC or START	No voltage
			ON	Battery voltage
	6 — Ground	Ignition switch position	LOCK, ACC or START	No voltage
			ON	Battery voltage
	12 — Ground	Engine condition	Running	Battery voltage
			Stopped	No voltage

HINT: "*2" is the terminal of in Cool Box Amplifier.
If circuit is as specified, replace the amplifier.

AIR CONDITIONING AMPLIFIER CHECK—LAND CRUISER

ON-WIRE HARNESS SIDE
A/C Amplifier

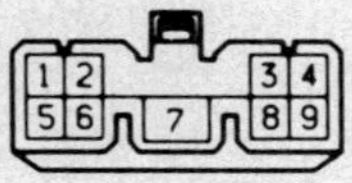
1 2 3 4
5 6 7 8 9

A/C AMPLIFIER

INSPECTION OF AMPLIFIER

INSPECT AMPLIFIER CIRCUIT

Disconnect the amplifier and inspect the connector on the wire harness side as shown in the chart below.

Test conditions:

(1) Ignition switch: ON
(2) Temperature control lever: MAX COOL
(3) Blower switch: HI

Check for	Tester connection	Condition	Specified value
Continuity	6 — Ground	Constant	Continuity
	8 — 9	Constant	Continuity
Voltage	2 — 6	Turn A/C switch on.	Battery voltage
		Turn A/C switch off.	No voltage
	3 — 6	Turn A/C switch on.	Battery voltage
		Turn A/C switch off.	No voltage
	5 — 6	Start the engine.	Approx. 10 to 14 V
		Stop the engine.	No voltage
Resistance	9 — 6	Constant	Approx. 1.5 kΩ at 25°C (77°F)

If circuit is as specified, replace the amplifier.

WIRING SCHEMATICS

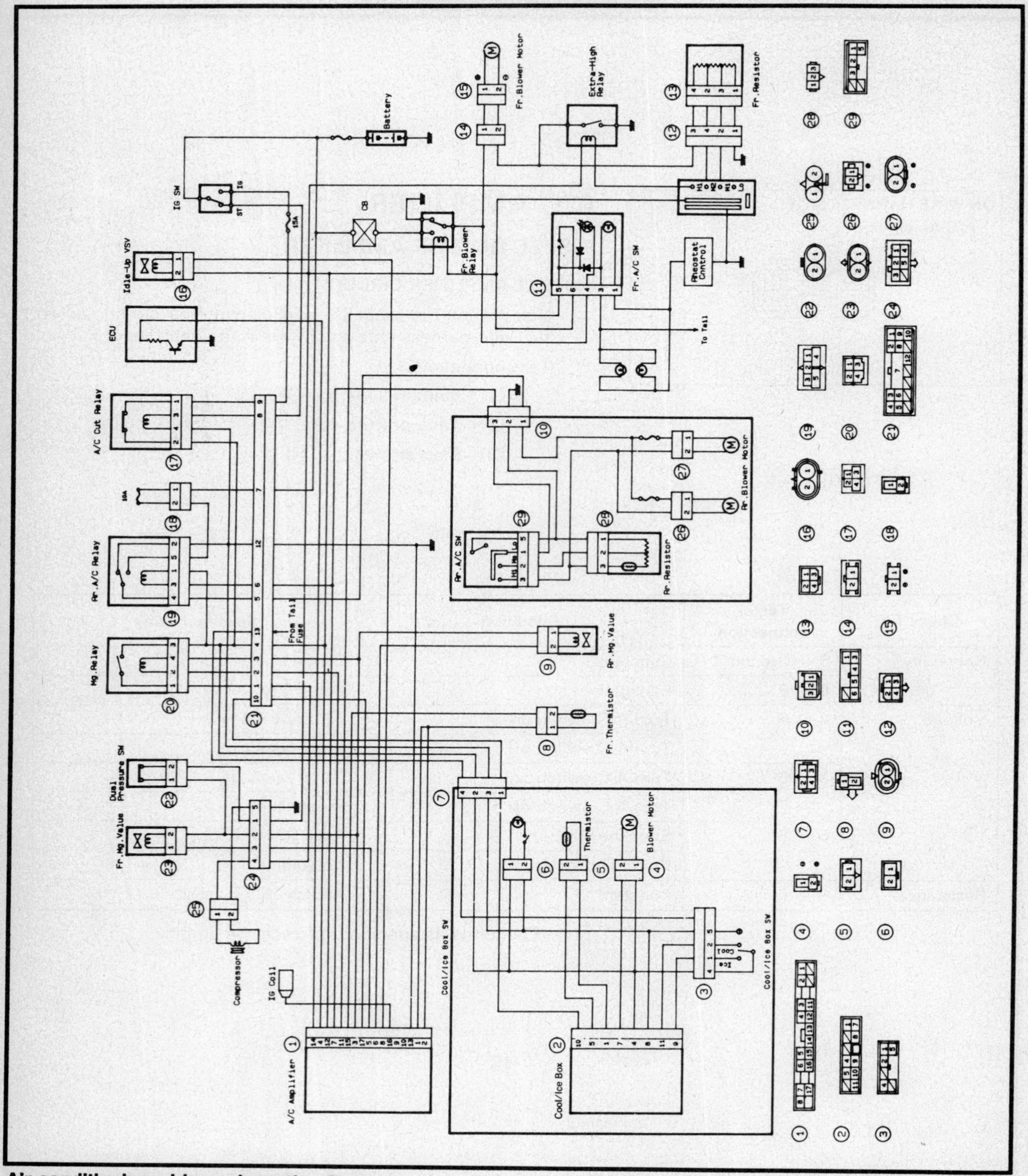
Battery
Fr.Blower Motor
Extra-High Relay
Fr.Resistor
IG SW
CB
Fr.Blower Relay
Fr.A/C SW
Rheostat Control
To Tail
Idle-Up VSV
ECU
A/C Cut Relay
Rr.A/C Relay
Mg.Relay
From Tail Fuse
Rr.Blower Motor
Rr.A/C SW
Rr.Resistor
Rr.Mg.Valve
Fr.Thermistor
Dual Pressure SW
Fr.Mg.Valve
Compressor
IG Coil
Cool/Ice Box SW
Thermistor
Blower Motor
A/C Amplifier
Cool/Ice Box

Air conditioning wiring schematic—Previa

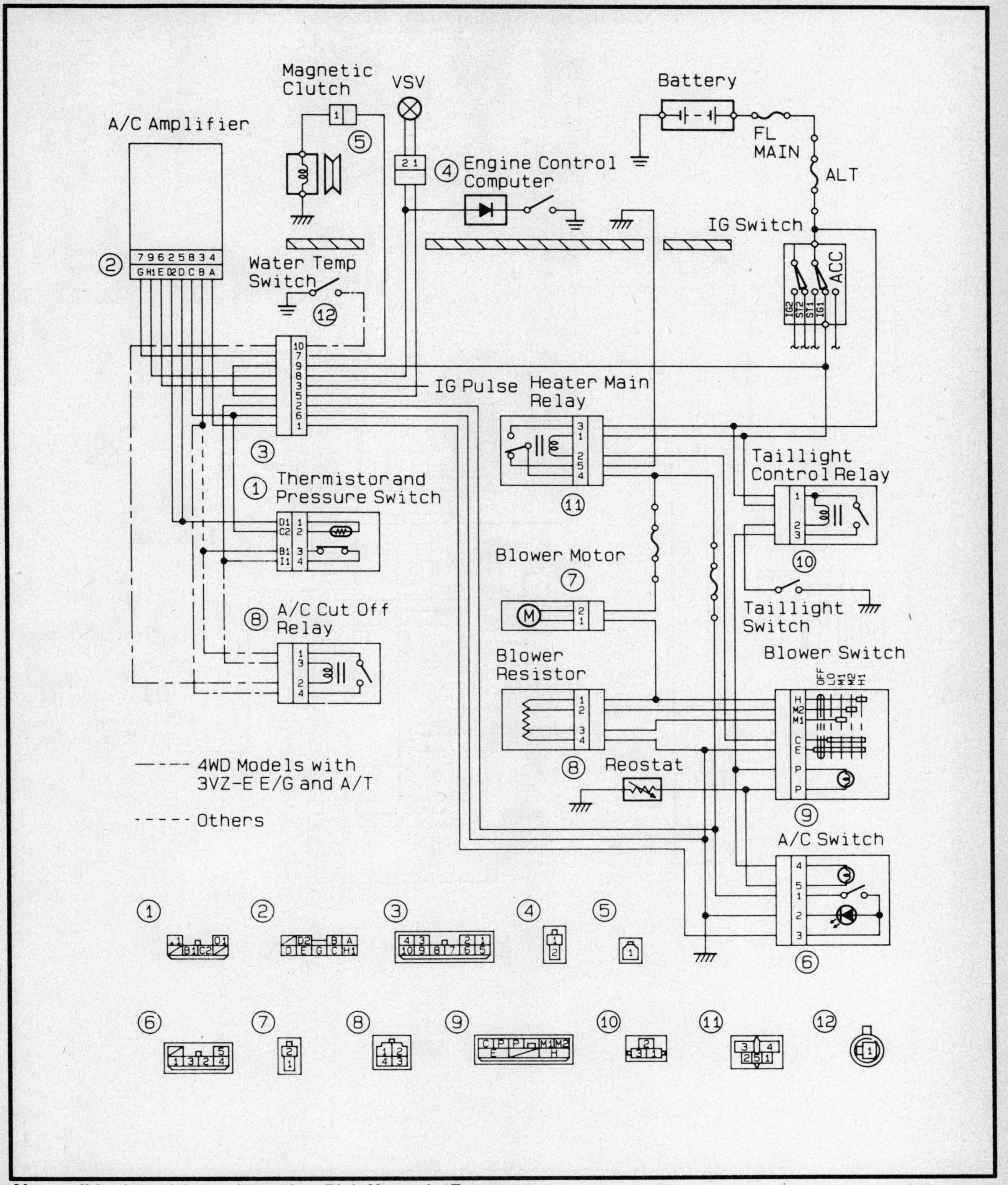
Magnetic Clutch
VSV
Battery
A/C Amplifier
FL MAIN
Engine Control Computer
ALT
IG Switch
ACC
IG2
ST2
ST1
IG1
Water Temp Switch
IG Pulse
Heater Main Relay
Taillight Control Relay
Thermistor and Pressure Switch
Blower Motor
Taillight Switch
A/C Cut Off Relay
Blower Switch
Blower Resistor
OFF
LO
M1
M2
HI
Reostat
4WD Models with 3VZ-E E/G and A/T
Others
A/C Switch

Air conditioning wiring schematic—Pick-Up and 4Runner

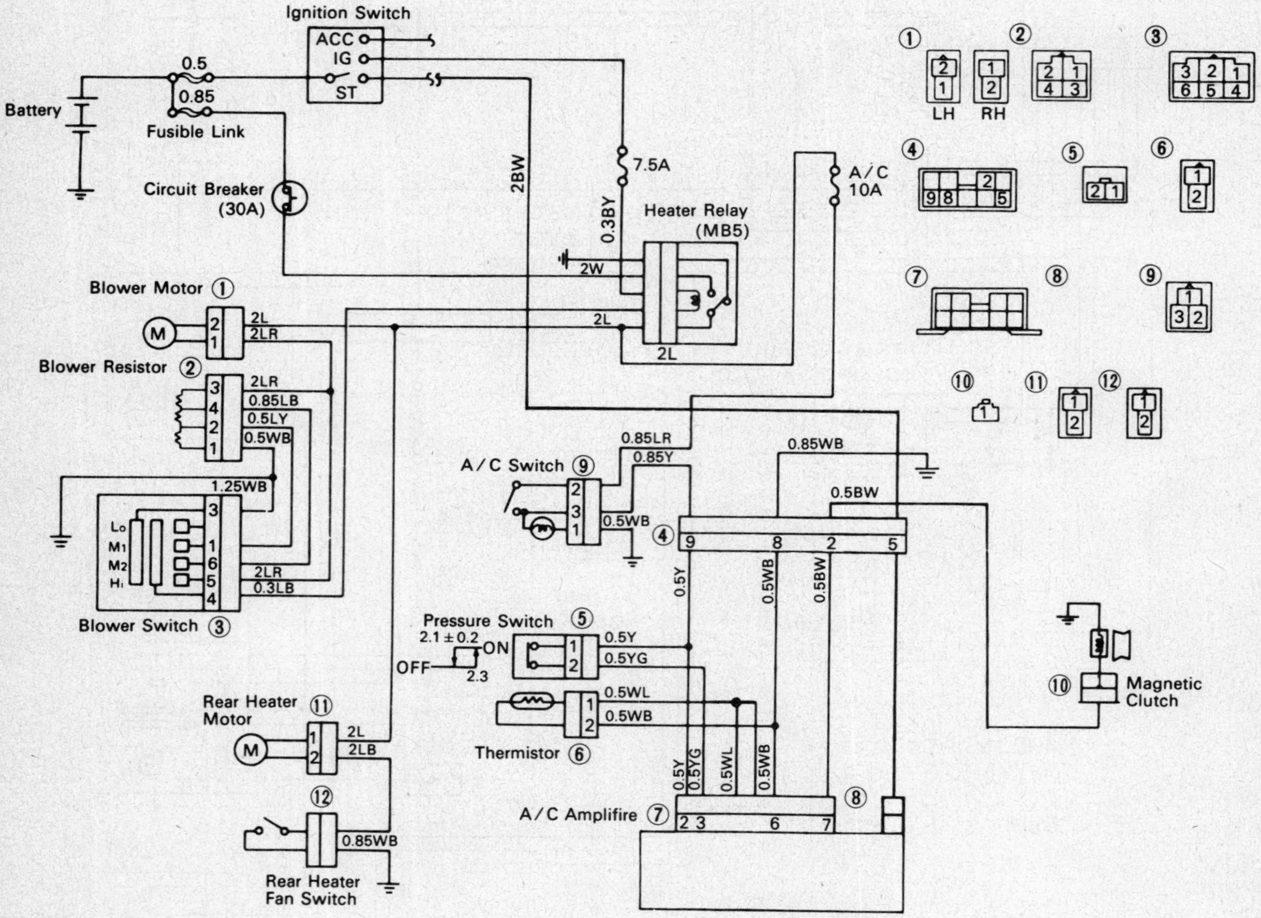
Ignition Switch
ACC
IG
ST
0.5
0.85
Battery
Fusible Link
Circuit Breaker (30A)
2BW
7.5A
0.3BY
A/C 10A
Heater Relay (MB5)
2W
2L
2L
Blower Motor ①
M
2L
2LR
Blower Resistor ②
2LR
0.85LB
0.5LY
0.5WB
1.25WB
Lo
M1
M2
Hi
2LR
0.3LB
Blower Switch ③
0.85LR
0.85Y
A/C Switch ⑨
0.5WB
④
0.85WB
0.5BW
0.5Y
0.5WB
0.5BW
Pressure Switch ⑤
2.1 ± 0.2
ON
OFF
2.3
0.5Y
0.5YG
0.5WL
0.5WB
Thermistor ⑥
Rear Heater Motor ⑪
2L
2LB
⑫
0.85WB
Rear Heater Fan Switch
0.5Y
0.5YG
0.5WL
0.5WB
A/C Amplifire ⑦
⑧
Magnetic Clutch ⑩
LH
RH

Air conditioning wiring schematic—1989–90 Land Cruiser

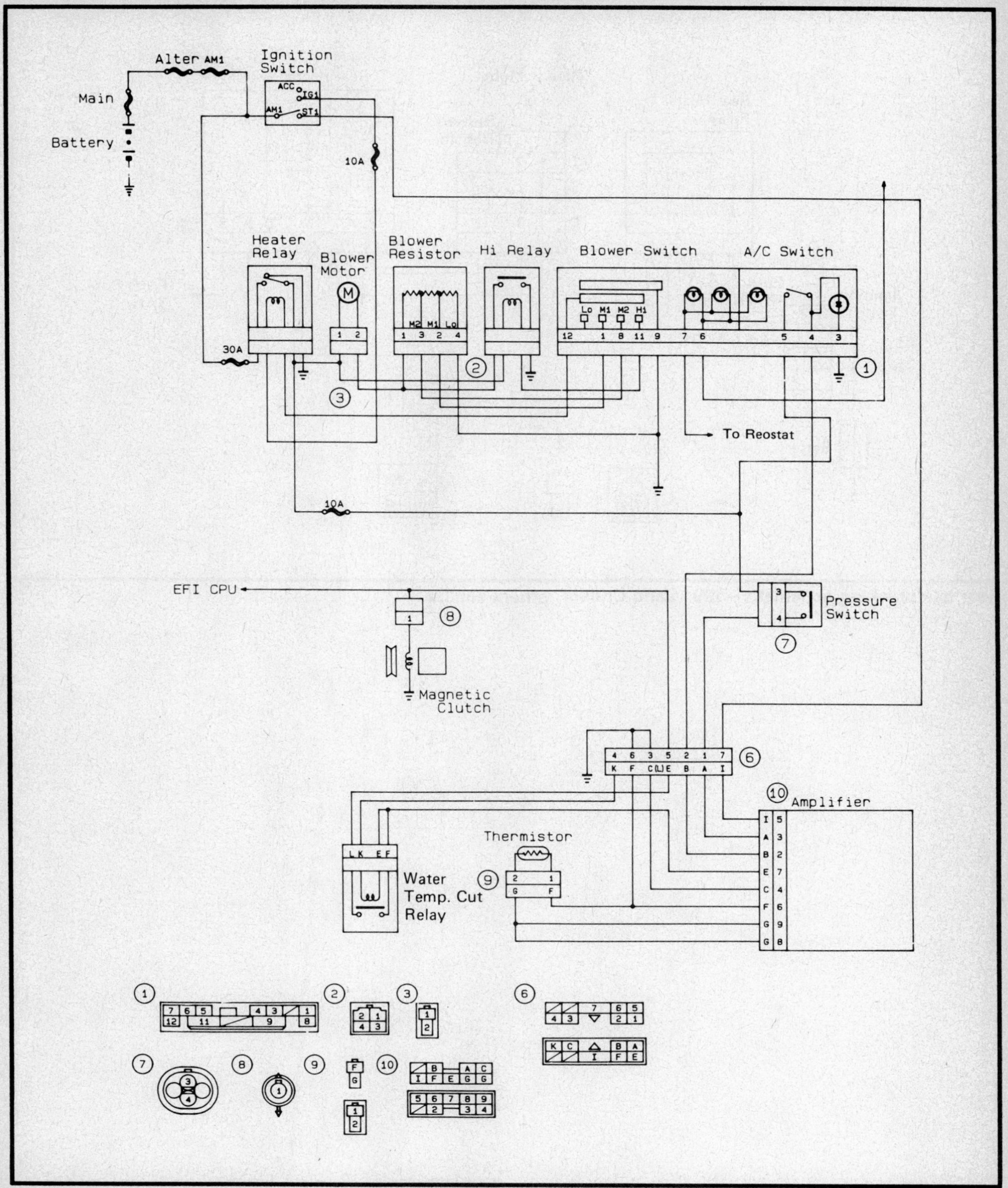
Alter AM1
Ignition Switch
ACC
IG1
AM1
ST1
Main
Battery
10A
Heater Relay
Blower Motor
Blower Resistor
Hi Relay
Blower Switch
A/C Switch
Lo M1 M2 Hi
M2 M1 Lo
30A
To Reostat
10A
EFI CPU
Pressure Switch
Magnetic Clutch
Amplifier
Thermistor
Water Temp. Cut Relay

Air conditioning wiring schematic – 1991 Land Cruiser

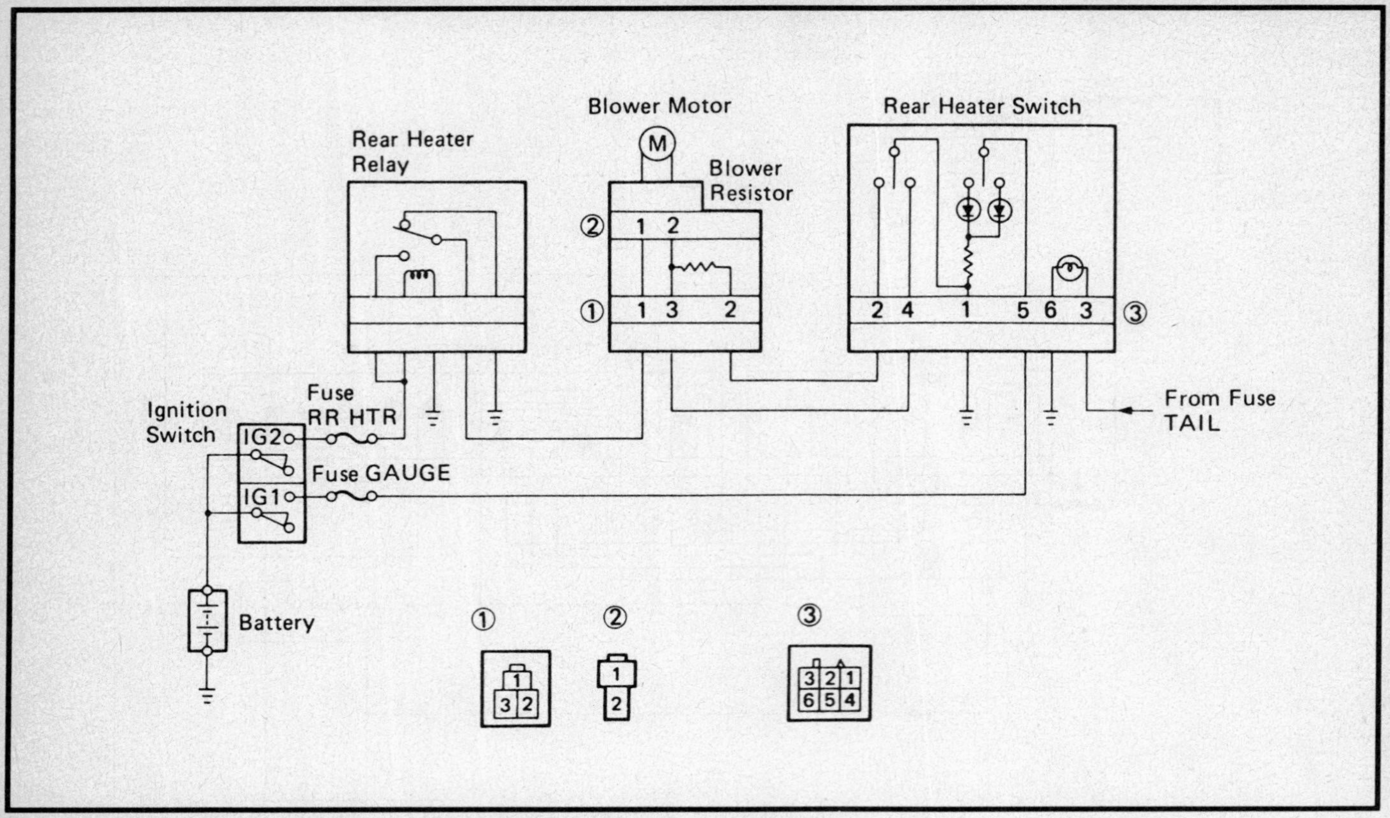
Blower Motor
M
Rear Heater Switch
Rear Heater
Relay
Blower
Resistor
② 1 2
① 1 3 2
2 4 1 5 6 3 ③
Fuse
RR HTR
Ignition
Switch
IG2
Fuse GAUGE
IG1
From Fuse
TAIL
Battery
①
②
③
1
3 2
1
2
3 2 1
6 5 4

Rear heater wiring schematic—1991 Land Cruiser, others similar

35 QUICK REFERENCE SPECIFICATIONS 35

ALFA ROMEO

ENGINE IDENTIFICATION

Year	Model	Engine Displacement cu. in. (cc/liter)	Engine Series Identification	No. of Cylinders	Engine Type
1989	Spider	119.7 (1962/2.0)	AR01544	4	DOHC
	Spider Veloce	119.7 (1962/2.0)	AR01544	4	DOHC
	Graduate	119.7 (1962/2.0)	AR01544	4	DOHC
	Milano	152.1 (2492/2.5)	0.19.11	6	DOHC
	Milano	180.5 (2959/3.0)	061.24	6	DOHC
1990	Spider	119.7 (1962/2.0)	AR01544	4	DOHC
	Spider Veloce	119.7 (1962/2.0)	AR01544	4	DOHC
	Graduate	119.7 (1962/2.0)	AR01544	4	DOHC
1991	Spider	119.7 (1962/2.0)	01588	4	DOHC
	Spider Veloce	119.7 (1962/2.0)	01588	4	DOHC
	164L	180.6 (2959/3.0)	6412T1	6	DOHC
	164S	180.6 (2959/3.0)	6412T2	6	DOHC

REFRIGERANT CAPACITIES

Year	Model	Freon (oz.)	Oil (fl. oz.)	Type
1989	Spider	24.7–28.2	N/A	R-12
	Spider Veloce	24.7–28.2	N/A	R-12
	Graduate	24.7–28.2	N/A	R-12
	Milano	31.7	N/A	R-12
	Milano	31.7	N/A	R-12
1990	Spider	24.7–28.2	N/A	R-12
	Spider Veloce	24.7–28.2	N/A	R-12
	Graduate	24.7–28.2	N/A	R-12
1991	Spider	24.7–28.2	N/A	R-12
	Spider Veloce	24.7–28.2	N/A	R-12
	164L	44.2	4.7	R-12
	164S	44.2	4.7	R-12

AIR CONDITIONING BELT TENSION CHART

Year	Model	Engine Displacement cu. in. (cc/liter)	Belt Type	New	Used
1989	Spider	119.7 (1962/2.0)	V-Belt	0.39–0.59 ①	—
	Spider Veloce	119.7 (1962/2.0)	V-Belt	0.39–0.59 ①	—
	Graduate	119.7 (1962/2.0)	V-Belt	0.39–0.59 ①	—
	Milano	152.1 (2492/2.5)	V-Belt	0.55 ②	—
	Milano	180.5 (2959/3.0)	V-Belt	0.55 ②	—
1990	Spider	119.7 (1962/2.0)	V-Belt	112–123 ③	90-101 ③
	Spider Veloce	119.7 (1962/2.0)	V-Belt	112–123 ③	90-101 ③
	Graduate	119.7 (1962/2.0)	V-Belt	112–123 ③	90-101 ③

AIR CONDITIONING BELT TENSION CHART

Year	Model	Engine Displacement cu. in. (cc/liter)	Belt Type	New	Used
1991	Spider	119.7 (1962/2.0)	V-Belt	112–123③	90–101③
	Spider Veloce	119.7 (1962/2.0)	V-Belt	112–123③	90–101③
	164L	180.6 (2959/3.0)	Serpentine	146–157③	124–135③
	164S	180.6 (2959/3.0)	Serpentine	146–157③	124–135③

① Inches of deflection at midpoint of belt using 17 lbs. of force.
② Inches of deflection at midpoint of belt using 8–14 lbs. of force.
③ Check belt tension with an approved belt tension gauge, measurement in lbs.

AUDI

ENGINE IDENTIFICATION

Year	Model	Engine Displacement cu. in. (cc/liter)	Engine Series Identification	No. of Cylinders	Engine Type
1989	80	121 (1983/2.0)	3A	4	OHC
	80 Quattro	141 (2309/2.3)	NG	5	OHC
	90	121 (1983/2.0)	3A	4	OHC
	90	141 (2309/2.3)	NG	5	OHC
	90 Quattro	141 (2309/2.3)	NG	5	OHC
	100	141 (2309/2.3)	NF	5	OHC
	100 Quattro	141 (2309/2.3)	NF	5	OHC
	200	136 (2226/2.2)	MC	5	OHC
	200 Quattro	136 (2226/2.2)	MC	5	OHC
1990	80	121 (1983/2.0)	3A	4	OHC
	80 Quattro	141 (2309/2.3)	NG	5	OHC
	90	121 (1983/2.0)	3A	4	OHC
	90	141 (2309/2.3)	NG	5	OHC
	90 Quattro	141 (2309/2.3)	NG	5	OHC
	100	141 (2309/2.3)	NF	5	OHC
	100 Quattro	141 (2309/2.3)	NF	5	OHC
	200	136 (2226/2.2)	MC	5	OHC
	200 Quattro	136 (2226/2.2)	MC	5	OHC
	V8 Quattro	220 (3562/3.6)	PT	8	OHC
1991	80	121 (1983/2.0)	3A	4	OHC
	80 Quattro	141 (2309/2.3)	NG	5	OHC
	90	121 (1983/2.0)	3A	4	OHC
	90	141 (2309/2.3)	NG	5	OHC
	90 Quattro	141 (2309/2.3)	NG	5	OHC
	100	141 (2309/2.3)	NF	5	OHC
	100 Quattro	141 (2309/2.3)	NF	5	OHC
	200	136 (2226/2.2)	MC	5	OHC
	200 Quattro	136 (2226/2.2)	MC	5	OHC
	V8 Quattro	220 (3562/3.6)	PT	8	OHC

REFRIGERANT CAPACITIES

Year	Model	Freon (oz.)	Oil (fl. oz.)	Type
1989	80	35.0–35.6	5.2–6.0	Nippodenso
	80 Quattro	35.0–35.6	5.2–6.0	Nippodenso
	90	35.0–35.6	5.2–6.0	Nippodenso
	90	35.0–35.6	5.2–6.0	Nippodenso
	90 Quattro	35.0–35.6	5.2–6.0	Nippodenso
	100	36.5–39.5	5.2–6.0	Nippodenso
	100 Quattro	36.5–39.5	5.2–6.0	Nippodenso
	200	36.5–39.5	5.2–6.0	Nippodenso
	200 Quattro	36.5–39.5	5.2–6.0	Nippodenso
1990	80	35.0–35.6	5.2–6.0	Nippodenso
	80 Quattro	35.0–35.6	5.2–6.0	Nippodenso
	90	35.0–35.6	5.2–6.0	Nippodenso
	90	35.0–35.6	5.2–6.0	Nippodenso
	90 Quattro	35.0–35.6	5.2–6.0	Nippodenso
	100	36.5–39.5	5.2–6.0	Nippodenso
	100 Quattro	36.5–39.5	5.2–6.0	Nippodenso
	200	36.5–39.5	5.2–6.0	Nippodenso
	200 Quattro	36.5–39.5	5.2–6.0	Nippodenso
	V8 Quattro	37.3–40.7	9.1–11.1	Nippodenso
1991	80	35.0–35.6	5.2–6.0	Nippodenso
	80 Quattro	35.0–35.6	5.2–6.0	Nippodenso
	90	35.0–35.6	5.2–6.0	Nippodenso
	90	35.0–35.6	5.2–6.0	Nippodenso
	90 Quattro	35.0–35.6	5.2–6.0	Nippodenso
	100	36.5–39.5	5.2–6.0	Nippodenso
	100 Quattro	36.5–39.5	5.2–6.0	Nippodenso
	200	36.5–39.5	5.2–6.0	Nippodenso
	200 Quattro	36.5–39.5	5.2–6.0	Nippodenso
	V8 Quattro	37.3–40.7	9.1–11.1	Nippodenso

AIR CONDITIONING BELT TENSION CHART

Year	Model	Engine Displacement cu. in (cc/liter)	Belt Type	New ②	Used ②
1989	80	121 (1983/2.0)	V-Belt	5/16	5/16
	80 Quattro	141 (2309/2.3)	V-Belt	5/16	5/16
	90	121 (1983/2.0)	V-Belt	5/16	5/16
	90	141 (2309/2.3)	V-Belt	5/16	5/16
	90 Quattro	141 (2309/2.3)	V-Belt	5/16	5/16
	100	141 (2309/2.3)	V-Belt	13/32	13/32
	100 Quattro	141 (2309/2.3)	V-Belt	13/32	13/32
	200	136 (2226/2.2)	V-Belt	13/32	13/32
	200 Quattro	136 (2226/2.2)	V-Belt	13/32	13/32

AIR CONDITIONING BELT TENSION CHART

Year	Model	Engine Displacement cu. in (cc/liter)	Belt Type	New ②	Used ②
1990	80	121 (1983/2.0)	V-Belt	5/16	5/16
	80 Quattro	141 (2309/2.3)	V-Belt	5/16	5/16
	90	121 (1983/2.0)	V-Belt	5/16	5/16
	90	141 (2309/2.3)	V-Belt	5/16	5/16
	90 Quattro	141 (2309/2.3)	V-Belt	5/16	5/16
	100	141 (2309/2.3)	V-Belt	13/32	13/32
	100 Quattro	141 (2309/2.3)	V-Belt	13/32	13/32
	200	136 (2226/2.2)	V-Belt	13/32	13/32
	200 Quattro	136 (2226/2.2)	V-Belt	13/32	13/32
	V8 Quattro	220 (3562/3.6)	Serpentine	①	①
1991	80	121 (1983/2.0)	V-Belt	5/16	5/16
	80 Quattro	141 (2309/2.3)	V-Belt	5/16	5/16
	90	121 (1983/2.0)	V-Belt	5/16	5/16
	90	141 (2309/2.3)	V-Belt	5/16	5/16
	90 Quattro	141 (2309/2.3)	V-Belt	5/16	5/16
	100	141 (2309/2.3)	V-Belt	13/32	13/32
	100 Quattro	141 (2309/2.3)	V-Belt	13/32	13/32
	200	136 (2226/2.2)	V-Belt	13/32	13/32
	200 Quattro	136 (2226/2.2)	V-Belt	13/32	13/32
	V8 Quattro	220 (3562/3.6)	Serpentine	①	①

① NOT ADJUSTABLE
② Belt deflection measured in inches at center of belt using moderate thumb pressure, except V8 Quattro

DAIHATSU

ENGINE IDENTIFICATION

Year	Model	Engine Displacement cu. in. (cc/liter)	Engine Series Identification	No. of Cylinders	Engine Type
1989	Charade	60.6 (993/1.0)	CB-90	3	OHC
	Rocky	97.0 (1589/1.6)	HD	4	SOHC
1990	Charade G100	60.6 (993/1.0)	CB	3	OHC
	Charade G102	79.0 (1295/1.3)	HC	4	OHC-16V
	Rocky	97.0 (1589/1.6)	HD	4	SOHC-16V
1991	Charade G100	60.6 (993/1.0)	CB	3	OHC
	Charade G102	79.0 (1295/1.3)	HC	4	OHC-16V
	Rocky	97.0 (1589/1.6)	HD	4	SOHC-16V

REFRIGERANT CAPACITIES

Year	Model	Freon (oz.)	Oil (fl. oz.)	Type
1989	Charade	20.0–23.3	4.1–5.0	Nippodenso
	Rocky	N/A	4.1–5.0	Nippodenso
1990	Charade G100	20.0–23.3	4.1–5.0	Nippodenso
	Charade G102	20.0–23.3	4.1–5.0	Nippodenso
	Rocky	N/A	4.1–5.0	Nippodenso

REFRIGERANT CAPACITIES

Year	Model	Freon (oz.)	Oil (fl. oz.)	Type
1991	Charade G100	20.0–23.3	4.1–5.0	Nippodenso
	Charade G102	20.0–23.3	4.1–5.0	Nippodenso
	Rocky	N/A	4.1–5.0	Nippodenso

AIR CONDITIONING BELT TENSION CHART

Year	Model	Engine Displacement cu. in. (cc/liter)	Belt Type	New ①	Used ①
1989	Charade	60.6 (993/1.0)	Ribbed	139–191	88–132
	Rocky	97.0 (1589/1.6)	Ribbed	139–191	110–154
1990	Charade G100	60.6 (993/1.0)	Ribbed	139–191	88–132
	Charade G102	79.0 (1295/1.3)	Ribbed	121–143	99
	Rocky	97.0 (1595/1.6)	Ribbed	139–191	110–154
1991	Charade G100	60.6 (993/1.0)	Ribbed	139–191	88–132
	Charade G102	79.0 (1295/1.3)	Ribbed	121–143	99
	Rocky	97.0 (1595/1.6)	Ribbed	139–191	110–154

① Using appropriate belt tension gauge

JAGUAR

ENGINE IDENTIFICATION

Year	Model	Engine Displacement cu. in. (cc/liter)	Engine Series Identification	No. of Cylinders	Engine Type
1989	XJ6	213 (3590/3.6)	AJ6	6	DOHC
	XJS-6	213 (3590/3.6)	AJ6	6	DOHC
	XJS-12	326 (5345/5.3)	V12	12	DOHC
1990	XJ6	213 (3590/3.6)	AJ6	6	DOHC
	XJS-6	213 (3590/3.6)	AJ6	6	DOHC
	XJS-12	326 (5345/5.3)	V12	12	DOHC
1991	XJ6	213 (3590/3.6)	AJ6	6	DOHC
	XJS-6	213 (3590/3.6)	AJ6	6	DOHC
	XJS-12	326 (5345/5.3)	V12	12	DOHC

REFRIGERANT CAPACITIES

Year	Model	Freon (oz.)	Oil (fl. oz.)	Type
1989	XJ6	N/A	7.0	Sanden
	XJS-6	N/A	7.0	Sanden
	XJS-12	N/A	7.0	Sanden
1990	XJ6	N/A	7.0	Sanden
	XJS-6	N/A	7.0	Sanden
	XJS-12	N/A	7.0	Sanden
1991	XJ6	N/A	7.0	Sanden
	XJS-6	N/A	7.0	Sanden
	XJS-12	N/A	7.0	Sanden

AIR CONDITIONING BELT TENSION CHART

Year	Model	Enginde Displacement cu. in. (cc/liter)	Belt Type	New ①	Used ①
1989	XJ6	213 (3590/3.6)	V-Belt	4.4	4.4
	XJS-6	213 (3590/3.6)	V-Belt	4.4	4.4
	XJS-12	326 (5345/5.3)	V-Belt	4.4	4.4
1990	XJ6	213 (3590/3.6)	V-Belt	4.4	4.4
	XJS-6	213 (3590/3.6)	V-Belt	4.4	4.4
	XJS-12	326 (5345/5.3)	V-Belt	4.4	4.4
1991	XJ6	213 (3590/3.6)	V-Belt	4.4	4.4
	XJS-6	213 (3590/3.6)	V-Belt	4.4	4.4
	XJS-12	326 (5345/5.3)	V-Belt	4.4	4.4

① Millimeters of deflection at midpoint of belt

MERKUR

ENGINE IDENTIFICATION

Year	Model	Engine Displacement cu. in. (cc/liter)	Engine Series Identification	No. of Cylinders	Engine Type
1989	XR4Ti	140 (2300/2.3)	W	4	SOHC
	Scorpio	177 (2900/2.9)	V	6	OHV
1990	Scorpio	177 (2900/2.9)	V	6	OHV

REFRIGERANT CAPACITIES

Year	Model	Freon (oz.)	Oil (fl. oz.)	Type
1989	XR4Ti	27	2.2–2.6	Nippodenso
	Scorpio	27	2.4–3.4	Nippodenso
1990	Scorpio	27	2.4–3.4	Nippodenso

AIR CONDITIONING BELT TENSION CHART

Year	Model	Engine Displacement cu. in. (cc/liter)	Belt Type	New	Used
1989	XR4Ti	140 (2300/2.3)	Cogged	120–160	110–130
	Scorpio	177 (2900/2.9)	V-Belt	101–123	79–101
1990	Scorpio	177 (2900/2.9)	V-Belt	101–123	79–101

PEUGEOT

ENGINE IDENTIFICATION

Year	Model	Engine Displacement cu. in. (cc/liter)	Engine Series Identification	No. of Cylinders	Engine Type
1989	405	116 (1900/1.9)	XU9J2	4	OHC
	405	116 (1900/1.9)	XU9J4	4	DOHC-16V
	505	128 (2100/2.1)	N9TEA	4	OHC-Turbo
	505	134 (2200/2.2)	2DJL	4	OHC
	505	171 (2800/2.8)	2N3J	6	OHC

ENGINE IDENTIFICATION

Year	Model	Engine Displacement cu. in. (cc/liter)	Engine Series Identification	No. of Cylinders	Engine Type
1990	405	116 (1900/1.9)	XU9JZ	4	OHC
	405	116 (1900/1.9)	XU9J4	4	DOHC-16V
	505	128 (2100/2.1)	N9TEA	4	OHC-Turbo
	505	134 (2200/2.2)	2DJL	4	OHC
1991	405	116 (1900/1.9)	XU9J2	4	OHC
	405	116 (1900/1.9)	XU9J4	4	DOHC-16V
	505	128 (2100/2.1)	N9TEA	4	OHC-Turbo
	505	134 (2200/2.2)	2DJL	4	OHC

REFRIGERANT CAPACITIES

Year	Model	Freon (oz.) ④	Oil (fl. oz.)	Type
1989	405	30.0	③	Sanden/Seiko-Seiki
	405	30.0	③	Sanden/Seiko-Seiki
	505	30.0	⑤	N/A
	505 ①	30.0	⑤	N/A
	505 ②	30.0	⑤	N/A
1990	405	30.0	③	Sanden/Seiko-Seiki
	405	30.0	③	Sanden/Seiko-Seiki
	505	30.0	⑤	N/A
	505 ①	30.0	⑤	N/A
1991	405	30.0	③	Sanden/Seiko-Seiki
	405	30.0	③	Sanden/Seiko-Seiki
	505	30.0	⑤	N/A
	505 ①	30.0	⑤	N/A

① Turbocharged
② V6
③ Sanden compressor oil level is to be checked using dipstick P/N 9755.01 & level should reach 4th mark; the Seiko-Seiki compressor oil level is to be checked by draining the compressor & refilling it with 200 cc.
④ Vehicles equipped with diesel engine use 33.3 oz. of R-12
⑤ Oil level is to be checked using dipstick P/N 9766.01 & level should be at the 9th mark

AIR CONDITIONING BELT TENSION CHART

Year	Model	Engine Displacement cu. in. (cc/liter)	Belt Type	New	Used
1989	405 ①	116 (1900/1.9)	Ribbed	44	33
	405 ②	116 (1900/1.9)	Ribbed	52	35–38
	505 ③	128 (2100/2.1)	V-Belt	110	88
	505 ③	134 (2200/2.2)	V-Belt	110	88
	505 ③	171 (2800/2.8)	V-Belt	110	88
1990	405 ①	116 (1900/1.9)	Ribbed	44	33
	405 ②	116 (1900/1.9)	Ribbed	52	35–38
	505 ③	128 (2100/2.1)	V-Belt	110	88
	505 ③	134 (2200/2.2)	V-Belt	110	88

AIR CONDITIONING BELT TENSION CHART

Year	Model	Engine Displacement cu. in. (cc/liter)	Belt Type	New	Used
1991	405 ①	116 (1900/1.9)	Ribbed	44	33
	405 ②	116 (1900/1.9)	Ribbed	52	35–38
	505 ③	128 (2100/2.1)	V-Belt	110	88
	505 ③	134 (2200/2.2)	V-Belt	110	88

① Using a torque wrench apply the specified ft. pound pressure to the idler pulley bracket on the XU9J2 engine
② Make sure the idler pulley bracket is at the end of its slide travel and then tighten the alternator adjusting bolt to the specified ft. pound pressure on the XU9J4 engine
③ Use the appropriate belt tension gauge

PORSCHE

ENGINE IDENTIFICATION

Year	Model	Engine Displacement cu. in. (cc/liter)	Engine Series Identification	No. of Cylinders	Engine Type
1989	911	193 (3164/3.2)	930.25	6	SOHC
	911 Turbo	201 (3299/3.3)	930.68	6	SOHC
	911 Carrera 4	219 (3600/3.6)	M64/01	6	SOHC
	928S4	302 (4957/5.0)	M28/41, 42	8	DOHC
	944	164 (2681/2.7)	M44/11, 12	4	SOHC
	944S2	181 (2969/3.0)	M44/41	4	DOHC
	944 Turbo	151 (2479/2.5)	M44/51	4	SOHC
1990	911 Carrera 2 ①	219 (3600/3.6)	M64/01	6	SOHC
	911 Carrera 4 ②	219 (3600/3.6)	M64/01	6	SOHC
	928S4	302 (4957/5.0)	M28/41, 42	8	DOHC
	944S2	183 (2990/3.0)	M44/41	4	DOHC
1991	911 Carrera 2 ①	219 (3600/3.6)	M64/01	6	SOHC
	922 Carrera 4 ②	219 (3600/3.6)	M64/01	6	SOHC
	928S4	302 (4957/5.0)	M28/41, 42	8	DOHC
	944S2	183 (2990/3.0)	M44/41	4	DOHC

① Includes Carrera 2 Coupe, Targa, Cabriolet
② Includes Carrera 4 Coupe, Targa, Cabriolet

REFRIGERANT CAPACITIES

Year	Model	Freon (oz.)	Oil (fl. oz.) ③	Type
1989	911	47.0	3.3–5.0	R-12
	911 Turbo	47.6	3.3–4.6	R-12
	911 Carrera 4	33.0	3.3–5.0	R-12
	928S4	33.5 ④	12 ⑤	R-12
	944	33.5	2.0–3.3	R-12
	944S2	33.5	2.0–3.3	R-12
	144 Turbo ①	33.5	2.0–3.3	R-12

REFRIGERANT CAPACITIES

Year	Model	Freon (oz.)	Oil (fl. oz.) ③	Type
1990	911 Carrera 2 ①	33.0	3.3–5.0	R-12
	911 Carrera 4 ②	33.0	3.3–5.0	R-12
	928S4	33.5 ④	12 ⑤	R-12
	944S2	33.5	12	R-12
	911 Carrera 2 ①	33.0	3.3–5.0	R-12
	911 Carrera 4 ②	33.0	3.3–5.0	R-12
	928S4	33.5 ④	12 ⑤	R-12
	944S2	33.5	2.0–3.3	R-12

① Includes Carrera 2 Coupe, Targa, Cabriolet
② Includes Carrera 4 Coupe, Targa, Cabriolet
③ Total capacity of oil in compressor
④ Models equipped with auxiliary air conditioner use 35.0–40.0 oz. of R-12
⑤ Models equipped with auxiliary air conditioner use 9.1–10.6 fl. oz. of oil in compressor

AIR CONDITIONING BELT TENSION CHART

Year	Model	Engine Displacement cu. in. (cc/liter)	Belt Type	New ③	Used ③
1989	911	193 (3164/3.2)	V-Belt	5.0	5.0
	911 Turbo	201 (3299/3.3)	V-Belt	5.0	5.0
	911 Carrera 4	219 (3600/3.6)	V-Belt	5.0	5.0
	928S4	302 (4957/5.0)	V-Belt	10.0	10.0
	944	164 (2681/2.7)	Ribbed	9.2–9.8	9.2–9.8
	944S2	181 (2969/3.0)	Ribbed	9.2–9.8	9.2–9.8
	944 Turbo	151 (2479/2.5)	Ribbed	9.2–9.8	9.2–9.8
1990	911 Carrera 2 ①	219 (3600/3.6)	V-Belt	5.0	5.0
	911 Carrera 4 ②	219 (3600/3.6)	V-Belt	5.0	5.0
	928S4	302 (4957/5.0)	V-Belt	10.0	10.0
	944S2	183 (2990/3.0)	Ribbed	9.2–9.8	9.2–9.8
1991	911 Carrera 2 ①	219 (3600/3.6)	V-Belt	5.0	5.0
	911 Carrera 4 ②	219 (3600/3.6)	V-Belt	5.0	5.0
	928S4	302 (4957/5.0)	V-Belt	10.0	10.0
	944S2	183 (2990/3.0)	Ribbed	9.2–9.8	9.2–9.8

① Includes Carrera 2 Coupe, Targa, Cabriolet
② Includes Carrera 4 Coupe, Targa, Cabriolet
③ Millimeters of deflection at center of belt using moderate thumb pressure

SAAB

ENGINE IDENTIFICATION

Year	Model	Engine Displacement cu. in. (cc/liter)	Engine Series Identification	No. of Cylinders	Type
1989	900	121 (1985/2.0)	B202	4	DOHC-16V
	900S	121 (1985/2.0)	B202	4	DOHC-16V
	900 Turbo	121 (1985/2.0)	B202	4	DOHC-16V
	9000	121 (1985/2.0)	B202	4	DOHC-16V
	9000S	121 (1985/2.0)	B202	4	DOHC-16V

ENGINE IDENTIFICATION

Year	Model	Engine Displacement cu. in. (cc/liter)	Engine Series Identification	No. of Cylinders	Type
1990	900	121 (1985/2.0)	B202	4	DOHC-16V
	900S	121 (1985/2.0)	B202	4	DOHC-16V
	900 Turbo	121 (1985/2.0)	B202	4	DOHC-16V
	9000	121 (1985/2.0)	B202	4	DOHC-16V
	9000S	121 (1985/2.0)	B202	4	DOHC-16V
1991	900	129 (2119/2.12)	N/A	4	DOHC-16V
	900S	129 (2119/2.12)	N/A	4	DOHC-16V
	900 Turbo	121 (1985/2.0)	B202	4	DOHC-16V
	900 T-Convertible	121 (1985/2.0)	B202	4	DOHC-16V
	900 T-SPG	121 (1985/2.0)	B202	4	DOHC-16V
	9000	140 (2290/2.0)	N/A	4	DOHC-16V
	9000S	140 (2290/2.3)	N/A	4	DOHC-16V
	9000 Turbo	140 (2290/2.3)	N/A	4	DOHC-16V
	9000 CD	140 (2290/2.3)	N/A	4	DOHC-16V
	9000 CD-Turbo	140 (2290/2.3)	N/A	4	DOHC-16V

REFRIGERANT CAPACITIES

Year	Model	Freon (oz.)	Oil (fl. oz.)	Type
1989	900	35.2–41.6	4.4 ①	Sankyo/Clarion
	900S	35.2–41.6	4.4 ①	Sankyo/Clarion
	900 Turbo	35.2–41.6	4.4 ①	Sankyo/Clarion
	9000	38.5	4.5	Sanden SD510
	9000S	38.5	4.5	Sanden SD510
1990	900	35.2–41.6	4.4 ①	Sankyo/Clarion
	900S	35.2–41.6	4.4 ①	Sankyo/Clarion
	900 Turbo	35.2–41.6	4.4 ①	Sankyo/Clarion
	9000	38.5	4.5	Sanden SD510
	9000S	38.5	4.5	Sanden SD510
1991	900	N/A	N/A	N/A
	900S	N/A	N/A	N/A
	900 Turbo	35.2–41.6	4.4 ①	Sankyo/Clarion
	900 T-Convertible	35.2–41.6	4.4 ①	Sankyo/Clarion
	900 T-SPG	35.2–41.6	4.4 ①	Sankyo/Clarion
	9000	N/A	N/A	N/A
	9000S	N/A	N/A	N/A
	9000 Turbo	N/A	N/A	N/A
	9000 CD	N/A	N/A	N/A
	9000 CD-Turbo	N/A	N/A	N/A

① Clarion compressor system oil capacity is 3.4 fl. oz.

AIR CONDITIONING BELT TENSION CHART

Year	Model	Engine Displacement cu. in. (cc/liter)	Belt Type	New	Used
1989	900	121 (1985/2.0)	V-Belt	3/16 ①	3/16 ①
	900S	121 (1985/2.0)	V-Belt	3/16 ①	3/16 ①
	900 Turbo	121 (1985/2.0)	V-Belt	3/16 ①	3/16 ①
	9000	121 (1985/2.0)	V-Belt	110–130 ②	75–85 ②
	9000S	121 (1985/2.0)	V-Belt	110–130 ②	75–85 ②
1990	900	121 (1985/2.0)	V-Belt	3/16 ①	3/16 ①
	900S	121 (1985/2.0)	V-Belt	3/16 ①	3/16 ①
	900 Turbo	121 (1985/2.0)	V-Belt	3/16 ①	3/16 ①
	9000	121 (1985/2.0)	V-Belt	110–130 ②	75–85 ②
	9000S	121 (1985/2.0)	V-Belt	110–130 ②	75–85 ②
1991	900	129 (2119/2.12)	N/A	N/A	N/A
	900S	129 (2119/2.12)	N/A	N/A	N/A
	900 Turbo	121 (1985/2.0)	V-Belt	3/16 ①	3/16 ①
	900 T-Convertible	121 (1985/2.0)	V-Belt	3/16 ①	3/16 ①
	900 T-SPG	121 (1985/2.0)	V-Belt	3/16 ①	3/16 ①
	9000	140 (2290/2.3)	N/A	N/A	N/A
	9000S	140 (2290/2.3)	N/A	N/A	N/A
	9000 Turbo	140 (2290/2.3)	N/A	N/A	N/A
	9000 CD	140 (2290/2.3)	N/A	N/A	N/A
	9000 CD Turbo	140 (2290/2.3)	N/A	N/A	N/A

① Inches of deflection at midpoint of belt using 10 lbs. of force

② Reading obtained using appropriate belt tension gauge